Food & Beverage Market Place

Volume 2

2021

Twentieth Edition

Food & Beverage Market Place

Volume 2

Equipment, Supplies & Services

Product Categories

Company Profiles

Grey House Publishing

AMENIA, NY 12501

PRESIDENT: Richard Gottlieb
PUBLISHER: Leslie Mackenzie
EDITORIAL DIRECTOR: Laura Mars

PRODUCTION MANAGER: Kristen Hayes
RESEARCH ASSISTANTS: Olivia Parsonson; Sarah Reside
COMPOSITION: David Garoogian

MARKETING DIRECTOR: Jessica Moody

Grey House Publishing, Inc.
4919 Route 22
Amenia, NY 12501
518.789.8700
FAX 845.373.6390
www.greyhouse.com
e-mail: books @greyhouse.com

Copyright © 2020 Grey House Publishing, Inc.
All rights reserved
First edition published 2001
Twentieth edition published 2020
Printed in Canada

Food & beverage market place. — 20th ed. (2021) —
    3 v. ; 27.5 cm. Annual
  Includes index.
  ISSN: 1554-6334

1. Food industry and trade—United States—Directories. 2. Food industry and trade—Canada—Directories. 3. Beverage industry—United States—Directories. 4. Beverage industry—Canada—Directories. I. Grey House Publishing, Inc. II. Title: Food & beverage market place.

HD9003.T48
338-dc21

3-Volume Set   ISBN: 978-1-64265-464-6
Volume 1   ISBN: 978-1-64265-465-3
Volume 2   ISBN: 978-1-64265-466-0
Volume 3   ISBN: 978-1-64265-467-7

Table of Contents

VOLUME 1

Introduction
*Summary of Best Practices for Retail Food Stores, Restaurants, and
    Food Pick-Up/Delivery Services During the COVID-19 Pandemic*
The Impact of COVID-19 on Shopping Behavior

Food & Beverage Manufacturers User Guide
Food & Beverage Product Category List
Food & Beverage Product Categories
Food & Beverage Manufacturer Profiles
Brand Name Index
Ethnic Food Index
Geographic Index
Parent Company Index

VOLUME 2

VOLUME 3

Introduction
Broker Companies User Guide
Broker Company Profiles
Broker Market Index
Brokered Product Index

Importers/Exporters User Guide
Importers/Exporters Company Profiles
Export Region Index
Import Region Index

Transportation Firms User Guide
Transportation Firm Profiles
Transportation Region Index
Transportation Type Index

Warehouse Companies User Guide
Warehouse Company Profiles
Warehouse Region Index
Warehouse Type and Service Index

Wholesalers/Distributors User Guide
Wholesalers/Distributors Company Profiles
Wholesale Product Type Index

ALL BRANDS INDEX
ALL COMPANIES INDEX

Table of Contents

Introduction

This 2021 edition of *Food & Beverage Market Place* represents the largest, most comprehensive resource of food and beverage manufacturers and service suppliers on the market today. These three volumes include over 45,000 company profiles that address all sectors of the industry—finished goods and ingredients manufacturers, equipment manufacturers, and third-party logistics providers, including transportation, warehousing, wholesalers, brokers, importers and exporters.

While the food and beverage industry generally continues to grow, the reality of the COVID-19 pandemic has presented many challenges to this truly essential industry. At the time of this writing, out of home consumption, with its high margin of profit, has been reduced nearly to a standstill for several months. Mandated quarantines have disrupted supply chains. Consumers are shifing to digital shopping and home delivery. The industry is redefining its work force and finding new ways to connect with customers.

One segment has found a silver lining in the cloud of COVID-19, and that is meal-kit companies. As consumers adapt to cooking and eating at home, meal kits, delivered to your door with conveniently packaged food and easy-to-follow recipes, have a huge appeal. Time will tell if they can sustain and build on the momentum created by the current quarantine.

Another interesting consequence of the current environment is the kinds of foods that people are eating. While certain long-standing food trends are well entrenched in our society, especially now, including natural and organic food, like those with antioxidants for healthy aging, and foods with good bacteria that promote digestive health, there is a significant uptick in online searches for cinammon roll and hot cross buns recipes, and a shortage of yeast on supermarket shelves. The growth in plant-based food is significant and, experts say, a trend that is likely to continue. While that would be a good thing, hopefully another trend—quarantine snacking—is temporary, as people start to spend less time around the house. In addition, following this Introduction in Volume 1 are two items that offer more information related to COVID-19 and the food and beverage industry: *Best Practices for Retail Food Stores, Restaurants & Food Pick Up and Delivery Services;* and *The Impact of COVID-19 on Shopping Behavior.*

Other industry trends are likely to continue, as consumers focus on foods that encourage sustainability, foods that are convenient and healthy, foods that are processed in secure and safe environments, and foods with complex world flavors.

As food and beverage consumers' needs evolve, *Food & Beverage Market Place* continues to keep pace. The research for this edition focused on ingredient, nutrition and health food manufacturers. You'll find packaging that is mindful of the environment, and processing systems that are safe and secure. Whatever slice of the market you cater to, you will find your buyers, sellers, and users in this comprehensive, three-volume reference tool containing the complete coverage our subscribers have come to expect. Our extensive indexing makes quick work of locating exactly the company, product or service you are looking for.

Data Statistics

Each of the eight chapters in *Food & Beverage Market Place* reflects a massive update effort. This 2021 edition includes hundreds of new company profiles and thousands of updates throughout the three volumes. You will find 83,214 key executives, 22,668 web sites, and 15,869 e-mails. The volumes break down as follows:

Volume 1   Food, Beverage & Ingredient Manufacturers - 14,086

Volume 2   Equipment, Supply & Service Providers - 13,465

Volume 3   Third Party Logistics
                    Brokers - 1,287
                    Importers & Exporters - 8,818
                    Transportation Firms - 707
                    Warehouse Companies - 1,044
                    Wholesalers & Distributors - 5,904

Arrangement

The product category sections for both food and beverage products in Volume 1 and equipment and supplies in Volume 2 begin with Product Category Lists. These include over 6,000 alphabetical terms for everything from Abalone to Zinc Citrate, from Adhesive Tapes to Zipper Application Systems. Use the detailed cross-references to find the full entry in the Product Category sections that immediately follow. Here you will find up to three levels of detail, for example—*Fish & Seafood: Fish: Abalone* or *Ingredients, Flavors & Additives: Vitamins & Supplements: Zinc Citrate*—with the name, location, phone number and packaging format of companies who manufacturer/process the product you are looking for. Organic and Gluten-Free categories make it easy to locate those manufacturers who focus on these food types.

In addition to company profiles, this edition has 17 indexes, 15 chapter-specific, arranged by geographic region, product or company type, and two—All Brands and All Companies—that comprise all three volumes. See the Table of Contents for a complete list of specific indexes. Plus, chapters include User Guides that help you navigate chapter-specific data.

We are confident that this reference is the foremost research tool in the food and beverage industry. It will prove invaluable to manufacturers, buyers, specifiers, market researchers, consultants, and anyone working in food and beverage—one of the largest industries in the country.

Praise for previous editions:

> *"...This set can be used to find basic information or to track trends in a dynamic industry.... Recommended for large public or academic libraries."*

> *"...Each volume contains helpful user guides and key that describes the field of data that appear in that chapter.... This publication is essential for researchers in the food industry, and large academic and public libraries."*

—American Reference Books Annual

Online Database & Mailing Lists

Food & Beverage Market Place is also available for subscription on https://gold.greyhouse.com for even faster, easier access to this wealth of information. Subscribers can search by product category, state, sales volume, employee size, personnel name, title and much more. Plus, users can print out prospect sheets or download data into their own spreadsheet or database. This database is a must for anyone marketing a product or service to this vast industry. Visit the site, or call 800-562-2139 for a free trial.

EQUIPMENT, SUPPLIES & SERVICES

User Guide
Product Category List
Product Categories
Company Profiles
Brand Name Index
Geographic Index

Equipment User Guide

The **Equipment, Supplies and Services Chapter** of *Food & Beverage Market Place* includes companies that manufacturer equipment and supplies, or offer services, in the food and beverage industry. The chapter begins with a **Category Listing** of equipment, supplies and services that are offered by companies in this chapter. This category list is followed by a **Product Category Index**, organized first by state, then alphabetical by company. Each company listing includes packaging type, city and phone number.

Following the **Product Category Index** are the descriptive listings, which are organized alphabetically. Following the A – Z Equipment, Supplies and Services listings are two indexes: **Brand Name Index**, which lists the brand names of the equipment and supplies in this chapter, and **Geographic Index**, which lists all companies by state. These Indexes refers to listing numbers, not page numbers.

Below is a sample listing illustrating the kind of information that is or might be included in an Equipment, Supplies and Services listing. Each numbered item of information is described in the User Key on the following page.

---

1 → 245600

2 → **(HQ) A.A. A La Carte**

3 → 5600 Bloomingdale Avenue

New Berlin, WI 53151

4 → 062-789-1500

5 → 062-789-1501

6 → 888-789-1501

7 → info@AlaCarte.com

8 → www.AlaCarte.com

9 → Contract packager and exporter of hard candy in decorative tins, jars, and boxes.

10 → President: James Gold
CFO: James Filbert
COO: Gail King
Vice President: Elizabeth Timely
Marketing: Donna Paige

11 → *Estimated Sales*: $1-5 Million

12 → *Number Employees*: 35

13 → *Sq. Footage*: 25000

14 → *Parent Co.*: A.A. Special Lines

15 → *Company is also listed in the following section(s)*: Exporter

16 → Brands: Pierell, Apresa, Cocolot

Equipment Companies User Key

1 ➤ **Record Number:** Entries are listed alphabetically within each category and numbered sequentially. The entry number, rather than the page number, is used in the indexes to refer to listings.

2 ➤ **Company Name:** Formal name of company. HQ indicates headquarter location. If names are completely capitalized, the listing will appear at the beginning of the alphabetized section.

3 ➤ **Address:** Location or permanent address of the company. If the mailing address differs from the street address, it will appear second.

4 ➤ **Phone Number:** The listed phone number is usually for the main office, but may also be for the sales, marketing, or public relations office as provided.

5 ➤ **Fax Number:** This is listed when provided by the company.

6 ➤ **Toll-Free Number:** This is listed when provided by the company.

7 ➤ **E-Mail:** This is listed when provided, and is generally the main office e-mail.

8 ➤ **Web Site:** This is listed when provided by the company and is also referred to as an URL address. These web sites are accessed through the Internet by typing http:// before the URL address.

9 ➤ **Description**: This paragraph contains a brief description of the products or services that are brokered, sometimes including markets served.

10 ➤ **Key Personnel:** Names and titles of company executives.

11 ➤ **Estimated Sales:** This is listed when provided by the company.

12 ➤ **Number of Employees:** Total number of employees within the company.

13 ➤ Indicates what other section in *Food & Beverage Market Place* this company is listed: Volume 1: Manufacturers. Volume 2: Equipment, Supplies & Services; Transportation; Warehouse; Wholesalers/Distributors. Volume 3: Brokers; Importers/Exporters.

14 ➤ **Markets Served:** This further defines the company as serving one or more markers, such as Super Market Chains, Wholesale Distributors, Food Service Operators, etc. Companies are indexed by market.

15 ➤ **Primary Brands Brokered include:** A list of brand names that the company brokers.

16 ➤ **Brokered Products include**: This describes the type of product that the broker handles, such as alcoholic beverages, frozen foods, exports, ingredients, etc. Companies are indexed by product.

A

Adhesive See Packaging Materials & Supplies: Tapes: Adhesive

Advertising Novelties & Specialties See Consultants & Services: Advertising Services: Advertising Novelties & Specialties

Advertising Services See Consultants & Services: Advertising Services

Advertising Signs See Foodservice Equipment & Supplies: Signs: Advertising

Aerosol See Equipment & Machinery: Food Processing: Aerosol

Agglomeration See Consultants & Services: Custom Services: Agglomeration

Agitators See Equipment & Machinery: Food Processing: Agitators

Air Curtain Doors See Building Equipment & Supplies: Doors: Air Curtain

Air Curtains See Building Equipment & Supplies: Air Curtains

Air Filters See Building Equipment & Supplies: Air Filters

Air Knives See Equipment & Machinery: Food Processing: Air Knives

Airport Facilities See Consultants & Services: Foodservice: Airport Facilities

Alarm Systems See Safety & Security Equipment & Supplies: Alarm Systems

Aluminum Bottles See Packaging Materials & Supplies: Bottles: Aluminum

Aluminum Cans See Packaging Materials & Supplies: Cans: Aluminum

Aluminum Foil See Packaging Materials & Supplies: Foil: Aluminum

Aluminum Ware See Food Preparation Equipment, Utensils & Cookware: Aluminum Ware

Amino Acid, Nitrogen Analyzers See Instrumentation & Laboratory Equipment: Analyzers: Amino Acid, Nitrogen

Ammonia See Sanitation Equipment & Supplies: Ammonia

Amusement & Theme Parks See Consultants & Services: Foodservice: Amusement & Theme Parks

Anaerobic & Aerobic See Sanitation Equipment & Supplies: Wastewater Treatment Systems: Anaerobic & Aerobic

Analytical Services See Consultants & Services: Analytical Services

Analyzers See Instrumentation & Laboratory Equipment: Analyzers

Anti-Slip Flooring See Building Equipment & Supplies: Flooring: Anti-Slip

Aprons See Clothing & Protective Apparel: Aprons

Architects See Consultants & Services: Architects

Architectural & Engineering Designers See Consultants & Services: Designers: Architectural & Engineering

Aseptic Packaging See Packaging Materials & Supplies: Packaging: Aseptic

Augers See Equipment & Machinery: Food Processing: Augers

Auto Scrubbing & Burnishing Scrubbers See Equipment & Machinery: Scrubbers: Auto Scrubbing & Burnishing

Automated Guided Vehicles See Transportation & Storage: Automated Guided Vehicles

Automatic/Random Case Sealing Packaging See Equipment & Machinery: Packaging: Automatic/Random Case Sealing

Automation & Controls See Instrumentation & Laboratory Equipment: Controls: Automation & Controls

Automation See Instrumentation & Laboratory Equipment: Automation

Awnings See Building Equipment & Supplies: Awnings

B

Backers Magnetic Label See Foodservice Equipment & Supplies: Magnetic Label: Backers

Bag Closing See Equipment & Machinery: Packaging: Bag Closing

Bag Filling See Equipment & Machinery: Packaging: Bag Filling

Bag Holders See Foodservice Equipment & Supplies: Holders: Bag

Bag Opening See Equipment & Machinery: Packaging: Bag Opening

Bag Ties See Packaging Materials & Supplies: Ties: Bag

Bag, Cellophane & Pliofilm See Equipment & Machinery: Packaging: Bag, Cellophane & Pliofilm

Bag, Paper See Equipment & Machinery: Packaging: Bag, Paper

Bagel Slicer See Food Preparation Equipment, Utensils & Cookware: Slicer: Bagel

Bags See Packaging Materials & Supplies: Bags

Bakers' & Confectioners' Brushes See Food Preparation Equipment, Utensils & Cookware: Brushes: Bakers' & Confectioners'

Bakers' & Confectioners' Molds See Food Preparation Equipment, Utensils & Cookware: Molds: Bakers' & Confectioners'

Bakers' & Confectioners' Utensils See Food Preparation Equipment, Utensils & Cookware: Utensils: Bakers' & Confectioners'

Bakers' Boxes See Packaging Materials & Supplies: Boxes: Bakers'

Bakers' Gloves See Clothing & Protective Apparel: Gloves: Bakers'

Bakers' Mixers See Equipment & Machinery: Food Processing: Mixers: Bakers'

Bakers' Trays & Pans See Food Preparation Equipment, Utensils & Cookware: Trays & Pans: Bakers'

Bakery See Consultants & Services: Contract Manufacturing: Bakery

Bakery Racks See Foodservice Equipment & Supplies: Racks: Bakery

Baking & Roasting Pans See Food Preparation Equipment, Utensils & Cookware: Pans: Baking & Roasting

Baking Industry See Equipment & Machinery: Baking Industry

Balances See Instrumentation & Laboratory Equipment: Balances

Balers or Baling Presses See Equipment & Machinery: Food Processing: Balers or Baling Presses

Ball & Pebble Mills See Equipment & Machinery: Food Processing: Mills: Ball & Pebble

Bamboo Chopsticks See Food Preparation Equipment, Utensils & Cookware: Utensils: Chopsticks: Bamboo

Banquet Carts See Foodservice Equipment & Supplies: Carts: Banquet

Bar Code Devices See Equipment & Machinery: Packaging: Bar Code Devices

Barbecue Equipment & Supplies See Equipment & Machinery: Barbecue Equipment & Supplies

Barley Processing See Equipment & Machinery: Food Processing: Barley Processing

Barrel & Drum Draining Racks See Transportation & Storage: Racks: Barrel & Drum Draining

Barrel & Drum Filling See Equipment & Machinery: Packaging: Barrel & Drum Filling

Barrel Packers See Equipment & Machinery: Packaging: Barrel Packers

Bars & Bar Supplies See Foodservice Equipment & Supplies: Bars & Bar Supplies

Baskets See Food Preparation Equipment, Utensils & Cookware: Baskets; Foodservice Equipment & Supplies: Baskets; Packaging Materials & Supplies: Baskets

Batching, Blending, Weighing See Instrumentation & Laboratory Equipment: Process Controls: Batching, Blending, Weighing

Beam Scales See Equipment & Machinery: Scales: Beam

Bean & Grain Sorters See Equipment & Machinery: Food Processing: Sorters: Bean & Grain

Bean & Pea Hullers See Equipment & Machinery: Food Processing: Hullers: Bean & Pea

Bean, Pea Separators See Equipment & Machinery: Food Processing: Separators: Bean, Pea

Beaters See Food Preparation Equipment, Utensils & Cookware: Beaters

Beer & Ale Cans See Packaging Materials & Supplies: Cans: Beer & Ale

Beer Dispensers See Foodservice Equipment & Supplies: Dispensers: Beer

Beer Keg Movers See Transportation & Storage: Beer Keg Movers

Belt Conveyors See Equipment & Machinery: Conveyors: Belt

Belting See Equipment & Machinery: Belting

Belts See Equipment & Machinery: Belts

Beverage Bins See Packaging Materials & Supplies: Bins: Beverage

Beverage Carts See Foodservice Equipment & Supplies: Carts: Beverage

Beverage Coolers See Refrigeration & Cooling Equipment: Coolers: Beverage

Beverage Dispensers See Foodservice Equipment & Supplies: Dispensers: Beverage

Beverage Hoses See Equipment & Machinery: Hoses: Beverage

Beverage Industry See Equipment & Machinery: Beverage Industry

Beverages, Hot Fill Packaging See Equipment & Machinery: Packaging: Beverages, Hot Fill

Bins See Packaging Materials & Supplies: Bins

Biodegradable, Recyclable Plastic See Packaging Materials & Supplies: Plastic: Biodegradable, Recyclable

Biscuit & Cookie Cutters See Food Preparation Equipment, Utensils & Cookware: Cutters: Biscuit & Cookie

Biscuit Making See Equipment & Machinery: Food Processing: Biscuit Making

Blades See Equipment & Machinery: Food Processing: Blades

Blast Chillers See Refrigeration & Cooling Equipment: Chillers: Blast

Bleaches See Sanitation Equipment & Supplies: Bleaches

Blenders See Equipment & Machinery: Food Processing: Blenders

Blending & Mixing See Consultants & Services: Contract Manufacturing: Blending & Mixing

Blending See Consultants & Services: Custom Services: Blending; Equipment & Machinery: Food Processing: Blending

Blister Packaging See Packaging Materials & Supplies: Packaging: Blister

Blocks See Food Preparation Equipment, Utensils & Cookware: Blocks

Blowers See Equipment & Machinery: Food Processing: Blowers

Boards See Food Preparation Equipment, Utensils & Cookware: Boards

Boiler & Steam Controls See Instrumentation & Laboratory Equipment: Controls: Boiler & Steam

Boilers See Equipment & Machinery: Food Processing: Boilers

Borax See Sanitation Equipment & Supplies: Borax

Bottle & Jar Sealing See Equipment & Machinery: Packaging: Bottle & Jar Sealing; Packaging Materials & Supplies: Seals: Bottle & Jar

Bottle (Compounds) Cleaners See Sanitation Equipment & Supplies: Cleaners: Bottle (Compounds)

Bottle Brushes See Sanitation Equipment & Supplies: Brushes: Bottle

Bottle Cap, Plastic & Metal See Equipment & Machinery: Packaging: Bottle Cap, Plastic & Metal

Bottle Capping & Crowning See Equipment & Machinery: Packaging: Bottle Capping & Crowning

Bottle Cartoning See Equipment & Machinery: Packaging: Bottle Cartoning

Bottle Conveyors See Equipment & Machinery: Conveyors: Bottle

Bottle Corking See Equipment & Machinery: Packaging: Bottle Corking

Bottle Crates See Packaging Materials & Supplies: Crates: Bottle

Bottle Drying See Equipment & Machinery: Packaging: Bottle Drying

Bottle Filling See Equipment & Machinery: Packaging: Bottle Filling

Bottle Openers See Equipment & Machinery: Openers: Bottle

Bottle Racks See Transportation & Storage: Racks: Bottle

Bottle Sleeves See Packaging Materials & Supplies: Sleeves: Bottle

Bottle Sorters *See Equipment & Machinery: Packaging: Sorters: Bottle*

Bottle Washing, Soaking & Rinsing *See Equipment & Machinery: Packaging: Bottle Washing, Soaking & Rinsing*

Bottle, Can & Jar Caps *See Packaging Materials & Supplies: Caps: Bottle, Can & Jar*

Bottled for Cleaning Ammonia *See Sanitation Equipment & Supplies: Ammonia: Bottled for Cleaning*

Bottles *See Packaging Materials & Supplies: Bottles*

Bottling *See Equipment & Machinery: Packaging: Bottling*

Bowls *See Food Preparation Equipment, Utensils & Cookware: Bowls*

Box Closing *See Equipment & Machinery: Packaging: Box Closing*

Box Cutters *See Transportation & Storage: Box Cutters; Equipment & Machinery: Packaging: Box Cutting*

Box Strapping *See Equipment & Machinery: Packaging: Box Strapping; See also Packaging Materials & Supplies: Seals: Box Strapping*

Box, Carton, Case & Crate *See Packaging Materials & Supplies: Linings: Box, Carton, Case & Crate*

Box, Crate, Carton Openers *See Equipment & Machinery: Openers: Box, Crate, Carton*

Box, Paper *See Equipment & Machinery: Packaging: Box, Paper*

Boxes *See Packaging Materials & Supplies: Boxes*

Bread & Cake Slicers *See Equipment & Machinery: Food Processing: Slicers: Bread & Cake*

Bread & Pastry Bags *See Packaging Materials & Supplies: Bags: Bread & Pastry*

Bread Coolers *See Refrigeration & Cooling Equipment: Coolers: Bread*

Bread Knives *See Food Preparation Equipment, Utensils & Cookware: Knives: Bread*

Bread Slicer *See Food Preparation Equipment, Utensils & Cookware: Slicer: Bread*

Bread, Cake & Steak Wood Boards *See Food Preparation Equipment, Utensils & Cookware: Boards: Wood: Bread, Cake & Steak*

Brewery Cookers *See Equipment & Machinery: Food Processing: Cookers: Brewery; Equipment & Machinery: Food Processing: Brewery*

Brine Making Equipment *See Equipment & Machinery: Food Processing: Brine Making Equipment*

Broilers *See Equipment & Machinery: Food Processing: Broilers*

Broom Holders *See Sanitation Equipment & Supplies: Holders: Broom*

Brooms *See Sanitation Equipment & Supplies: Brooms*

Brushes *See Food Preparation Equipment, Utensils & Cookware: Brushes; See also Sanitation Equipment & Supplies: Brushes*

Bulk Bags *See Packaging Materials & Supplies: Bags: Bulk*

Bulk Grinding Grinders *See Equipment & Machinery: Food Processing: Grinders: Bulk Grinding*

Bundle, Package Ties *See Packaging Materials & Supplies: Ties: Bundle, Package*

Bussing Carts *See Foodservice Equipment & Supplies: Carts: Bussing*

Butchers' Blades *See Equipment & Machinery: Food Processing: Saws: Butchers' Blades*

Butchers' Block Scrapers *See Food Preparation Equipment, Utensils & Cookware: Scrapers: Butchers' Block*

Butchers' Blocks *See Food Preparation Equipment, Utensils & Cookware: Blocks: Butchers'*

Butchers' Cleavers *See Food Preparation Equipment, Utensils & Cookware: Cleavers: Butchers'*

Butchers' Coolers *See Refrigeration & Cooling Equipment: Coolers: Butchers'*

Butchers' Knives *See Food Preparation Equipment, Utensils & Cookware: Knives: Butchers'*

Butchers' Scales *See Equipment & Machinery: Scales: Butchers'*

Butchers' Trays *See Foodservice Equipment & Supplies: Trays: Butchers'*

Butter & Cheese Molds *See Food Preparation Equipment, Utensils & Cookware: Molds: Butter & Cheese*

C

Cabinets *See Refrigeration & Cooling Equipment: Cabinets*

Cafeteria Trays *See Foodservice Equipment & Supplies: Trays: Cafeteria*

Cafeteria, Restaurant Counters *See Foodservice Equipment & Supplies: Counters: Cafeteria, Restaurant*

Cafeteria, Restaurant, Foodservice Kitchen Tables *See Foodservice Equipment & Supplies: Tables: Cafeteria, Restaurant, Foodservice Kitchen*

Cake Cutters *See Food Preparation Equipment, Utensils & Cookware: Cutters: Cake*

Cake Knives *See Food Preparation Equipment, Utensils & Cookware: Knives: Cake*

Cake Pan Liners *See Food Preparation Equipment, Utensils & Cookware: Liners: Cake Pan*

Cake Tins *See Food Preparation Equipment, Utensils & Cookware: Tins: Cake*

Cake Turners *See Foodservice Equipment & Supplies: Cake Turners*

Can & Glass Crushers *See Equipment & Machinery: Food Processing: Crushers: Can & Glass*

Can Body Forming *See Equipment & Machinery: Packaging: Can Body Forming*

Can Capping *See Equipment & Machinery: Packaging: Can Capping*

Can Closing *See Equipment & Machinery: Packaging: Can Closing*

Can Drying *See Equipment & Machinery: Packaging: Can Drying*

Can Filling *See Equipment & Machinery: Packaging: Can Filling*

Can Openers *See Equipment & Machinery: Openers: Can*

Can Racks *See Transportation & Storage: Racks: Can*

Can Sealing *See Equipment & Machinery: Packaging: Can Sealing*

Can Seaming *See Equipment & Machinery: Packaging: Can Seaming*

Can Washing *See Equipment & Machinery: Packaging: Can Washing*

Can, Drum & Barrel Linings *See Packaging Materials & Supplies: Linings: Can, Drum & Barrel*

Candles *See Foodservice Equipment & Supplies: Candles*

Candy (Confectioners') Coolers *See Refrigeration & Cooling Equipment: Coolers: Candy (Confectioners')*

Candy Boxes *See Packaging Materials & Supplies: Boxes: Candy*

Candy Sticks *See Packaging Materials & Supplies: Sticks: Candy*

Candy Wrapping Paper *See Packaging Materials & Supplies: Paper: Candy Wrapping*

Cane Shredders *See Equipment & Machinery: Food Processing: Shredders: Cane*

Canners' & Packers' Aprons *See Clothing & Protective Apparel: Aprons: Canners' & Packers'*

Canners' Cookers *See Equipment & Machinery: Food Processing: Cookers: Canners'*

Canners' Coolers *See Refrigeration & Cooling Equipment: Coolers: Canners'*

Canners' Knives *See Food Preparation Equipment, Utensils & Cookware: Knives: Canners'*

Canners *See Consultants & Services: Canners*

Canning & Food Packing *See Equipment & Machinery: Packaging: Canning & Food Packing*

Canning & Preserving Jars *See Packaging Materials & Supplies: Jars: Canning & Preserving*

Canning & Preserving Kettles *See Food Preparation Equipment, Utensils & Cookware: Kettles: Canning & Preserving*

Canning Exhausters *See Equipment & Machinery: Packaging: Exhausters: Canning*

Canning Retorts *See Packaging Materials & Supplies: Retorts: Canning*

Cans *See Packaging Materials & Supplies: Cans*

Cap Torque Test *See Equipment & Machinery: Packaging: Cap Torque Test*

Cappers *See Equipment & Machinery: Packaging: Cappers*

Caps *See Clothing & Protective Apparel: Caps; Packaging Materials & Supplies: Caps*

Carriers *See Packaging Materials & Supplies: Carriers*

Carton *See Equipment & Machinery: Packaging: Carton*

Carton, Case, Box Sealing *See Equipment & Machinery: Packaging: Carton, Case, Box Sealing*

Cartons *See Packaging Materials & Supplies: Cartons*

Carts *See Foodservice Equipment & Supplies: Carts; Sanitation Equipment & Supplies: Carts; See also Transportation & Storage: Carts*

Carving Knives *See Food Preparation Equipment, Utensils & Cookware: Knives: Carving*

Cases *See Foodservice Equipment & Supplies: Cases*

Cash Registers *See Foodservice Equipment & Supplies: Cash Registers*

Cash, Money Drawers *See Foodservice Equipment & Supplies: Drawers: Cash, Money*

Casters *See Transportation & Storage: Casters*

Caustic Soda *See Sanitation Equipment & Supplies: Caustic Soda*

Ceiling Fans *See Building Equipment & Supplies: Fans: Ceiling*

Ceiling Surfaces & Panels *See Building Equipment & Supplies: Ceiling Surfaces & Panels*

Cellophane Bags *See Packaging Materials & Supplies: Bags: Cellophane*

Cellulose & Fiber Tags *See Packaging Materials & Supplies: Tags: Cellulose & Fiber*

Cellulose Acetate Film *See Packaging Materials & Supplies: Film: Cellulose Acetate*

Centrifuge Bags *See Packaging Materials & Supplies: Bags: Centrifuge*

Centrifuges *See Instrumentation & Laboratory Equipment: Centrifuges*

Cereal Contract Manufacturing *See Consultants & Services: Contract Manufacturing: Cereal*

Cereal Cookers *See Equipment & Machinery: Food Processing: Cookers: Cereal*

Cereal Making *See Equipment & Machinery: Food Processing: Cereal Making*

Certification *See Instrumentation & Laboratory Equipment: Certification*

Chafers *See Foodservice Equipment & Supplies: Chafers*

Chain Conveyors *See Equipment & Machinery: Conveyors: Chain*

Chairs *See Foodservice Equipment & Supplies: Chairs*

Chamois Cloths *See Sanitation Equipment & Supplies: Cloths: Chamois*

Changeable Letter Signs *See Foodservice Equipment & Supplies: Signs: Changeable Letter*

Changers *See Foodservice Equipment & Supplies: Changers*

Charcoal Briquette *See Equipment & Machinery: Food Processing: Cooking & Heating Equipment: Charcoal Briquettes*

Charcoal: Mesquite *See Equipment & Machinery: Food Processing: Cooking & Heating Equipment: Charcoal: Mesquite*

Check & Credit Card Verification Systems *See Foodservice Equipment & Supplies: Scanners: Check & Credit Card Verification Systems*

Check Weighing Systems *See Equipment & Machinery: Systems: Check Weighing*

Check, Bill & Voucher Sorters *See Foodservice Equipment & Supplies: Sorters: Check, Bill & Voucher*

Cheese Coating *See Packaging Materials & Supplies: Wax: Cheese Coating*

Cheese Cookers *See Equipment & Machinery: Food Processing: Cookers: Cheese*

Cheese Cutters *See Food Preparation Equipment, Utensils & Cookware: Cutters: Cheese*

Cheese Hoops *See Food Preparation Equipment, Utensils & Cookware: Hoops: Cheese*

Cheese Knives *See Food Preparation Equipment, Utensils & Cookware: Knives: Cheese*

Cheese Making *See Equipment & Machinery: Food Processing: Cheese Making*

Cheese Processing *See Equipment & Machinery: Food Processing: Cheese Processing*

Cheese Shredders *See Equipment & Machinery: Food Processing: Shredders: Cheese*

Cheese Vats *See Equipment & Machinery: Food Processing: Vats: Cheese; See also Transportation & Storage: Vats: Cheese*

Cheesecloth *See Equipment & Machinery: Food Processing: Cheesecloth*

Chemical Dispensing *See Equipment & Machinery: Systems: Chemical Dispensing & Feed*

Chemicals *See Instrumentation & Laboratory Equipment: Chemicals*

Chewing Gum *See Equipment & Machinery: Food Processing: Chewing Gum Processing*

Chicken, Prepared Containers *See Packaging Materials & Supplies: Containers: Chicken, Prepared*

Chillers *See Refrigeration & Cooling Equipment: Chillers*

China *See Foodservice Equipment & Supplies: China*

Chips Clear & Colored Plastic *See Foodservice Equipment & Supplies: Clear & Colored Plastic: Chips*

Chips Wood Grain Plastic *See Foodservice Equipment & Supplies: Wood Grain Plastic: Chips*

Chlorine *See Sanitation Equipment & Supplies: Chlorine*

Chocolate Grinding Mills *See Equipment & Machinery: Food Processing: Mills: Chocolate Grinding*

Chocolate Processing *See Equipment & Machinery: Food Processing: Chocolate Processing*

Chopsticks Utensils *See Food Preparation Equipment, Utensils & Cookware: Utensils: Chopsticks*

Clean Rooms *See Instrumentation & Laboratory Equipment: Clean Rooms*

Clean-In-Place Controls *See Instrumentation & Laboratory Equipment: Controls: Clean-In-Place*

Cleaners & Shellers *See Equipment & Machinery: Food Processing: Peanut Processing: Cleaners & Shellers*

Cleaners *See Sanitation Equipment & Supplies: Cleaners*

Cleaning & Scouring Powder *See Sanitation Equipment & Supplies: Powder: Cleaning & Scouring*

Cleaning Compound Dispensers *See Sanitation Equipment & Supplies: Dispensers: Cleaning Compound*

Cleaning Equipment & Supplies *See Sanitation Equipment & Supplies: Cleaning Equipment & Supplies*

Cleaning Oils *See Sanitation Equipment & Supplies: Oils: Cleaning*

Cleansing Tissue *See Sanitation Equipment & Supplies: Tissue: Cleansing*

Clear & Colored Plastic *See Foodservice Equipment & Supplies: Clear & Colored Plastic*

Clear Plastic *See Foodservice Equipment & Supplies: Clear Plastic*

Cleavers *See Food Preparation Equipment, Utensils & Cookware: Cleavers*

Closures & Closing Devices *See Packaging Materials & Supplies: Closures & Closing Devices*

Cloths *See Sanitation Equipment & Supplies: Cloths*

Clutches & Brakes *See Transportation & Storage: Clutches & Brakes*

Coasters *See Foodservice Equipment & Supplies: Coasters*

Cocktail Forks *See Food Preparation Equipment, Utensils & Cookware: Utensils: Forks: Cocktail*

Cocoa Processing *See Equipment & Machinery: Food Processing: Cocoa Processing*

Coding, Dating & Marking Equipment *See Equipment & Machinery: Packaging: Coding, Dating & Marking Equipment*

Coffee & Tea Urns *See Foodservice Equipment & Supplies: Urns: Coffee & Tea*

Coffee Dispensers *See Foodservice Equipment & Supplies: Dispensers: Coffee*

Coffee Filters *See Equipment & Machinery: Food Processing: Filters: Coffee*

Coffee Hoppers *See Equipment & Machinery: Food Processing: Hoppers: Coffee*

Coffee Industry *See Equipment & Machinery: Coffee Industry*

Coffee Makers *See Equipment & Machinery: Food Processing: Coffee Makers*

Coffee Pot Cleaners *See Sanitation Equipment & Supplies: Cleaners: Coffee Pot*

Coffee Pots *See Equipment & Machinery: Coffee Industry: Stainless Steel: Coffee Pots*

Coffee Processing *See Equipment & Machinery: Food Processing: Coffee Processing*

Coin Counters *See Foodservice Equipment & Supplies: Counters: Coin*

Coin Machinery *See Foodservice Equipment & Supplies: Coin Machinery*

Cold Cream *See Sanitation Equipment & Supplies: Skin Cream & Lotions: Cold Cream*

Cold Storage Doors *See Refrigeration & Cooling Equipment: Doors: Cold Storage*

Cold Storage Room Racks *See Transportation & Storage: Racks: Cold Storage Room*

Colleges & Universities *See Consultants & Services: Foodservice: Colleges & Universities*

Colloid Mills *See Equipment & Machinery: Food Processing: Mills: Colloid*

Color Measuring *See Instrumentation & Laboratory Equipment: Instrumentation: Color Measuring*

Colored Plastic *See Foodservice Equipment & Supplies: Colored Plastic*

Combination Oven/Steamers *See Equipment & Machinery: Food Processing: Combination Oven/Steamers*

Compounds *See Sanitation Equipment & Supplies: Compounds*

Compressors *See Equipment & Machinery: Food Processing: Compressors; Refrigeration & Cooling Equipment: Compressors*

Computer Software, Systems & Services *See Consultants & Services: Computer Software, Systems & Services*

Computing, Weighing *See Equipment & Machinery: Scales: Computing, Weighing*

Concession Supplies & Equipment *See Foodservice Equipment & Supplies: Concession Supplies & Equipment*

Condensed Milk *See Equipment & Machinery: Food Processing: Condensed Milk Processing*

Condensers *See Equipment & Machinery: Food Processing: Condensers*

Condiment Carts *See Foodservice Equipment & Supplies: Carts: Condiment*

Confectioners' Bags *See Packaging Materials & Supplies: Bags: Confectioners'*

Confectioners' Kettles *See Food Preparation Equipment, Utensils & Cookware: Kettles: Confectioners'*

Confectioners', Continuous Cookers *See Equipment & Machinery: Food Processing: Cookers: Confectioners', Continuous*

Confectionery *See Equipment & Machinery: Food Processing: Confectionery*

Confectionery Industry *See Equipment & Machinery: Confectionery Industry*

Construction *See Consultants & Services: Construction*

Consultants *See Consultants & Services: Consultants*

Container *See Equipment & Machinery: Packaging: Container; Packaging Materials & Supplies: Containers*

Containment Systems *See Safety & Security Equipment & Supplies: Containment Systems*

Contract Manufacturing *See Consultants & Services: Contract Manufacturing*

Contract Packaging *See Consultants & Services: Contract Packaging*

Control Panels *See Instrumentation & Laboratory Equipment: Process Controls: Control Panels*

Controls *See Instrumentation & Laboratory Equipment: Controls*

Convection Ovens *See Equipment & Machinery: Food Processing: Convection Ovens*

Convex Mirrors *See Equipment & Machinery: Mirrors: Convex*

Conveyors *See Equipment & Machinery: Conveyors*

Cookers *See Equipment & Machinery: Food Processing: Cookers*

Cookie Sheets *See Food Preparation Equipment, Utensils & Cookware: Sheets: Cookie*

Cooking & Baking Glassware *See Food Preparation Equipment, Utensils & Cookware: Glassware: Cooking & Baking*

Cooking & Heating Equipment *See Equipment & Machinery: Food Processing: Cooking & Heating Equipment*

Cookware *See Food Preparation Equipment, Utensils & Cookware: Cookware*

Coolers *See Equipment & Machinery: Water Treatment: Coolers*

Cooperage *See Equipment & Machinery: Cooperage*

Copper Kettles *See Food Preparation Equipment, Utensils & Cookware: Kettles: Copper*

Copra Grinding & Crushing Mills *See Equipment & Machinery: Food Processing: Mills: Copra Grinding & Crushing*

Cordage, Rope & Twine *See Transportation & Storage: Cordage, Rope & Twine*

Corers *See Equipment & Machinery: Food Processing: Corers*

Corks *See Packaging Materials & Supplies: Corks*

Corkscrews *See Foodservice Equipment & Supplies: Corkscrews*

Corn & Fodder Shredders *See Equipment & Machinery: Food Processing: Shredders: Corn & Fodder*

Corn Chip Processing *See Equipment & Machinery: Food Processing: Corn Chip Processing*

Corn Cob Holders *See Food Preparation Equipment, Utensils & Cookware: Holders: Corn Cob*

Corn Huskers *See Equipment & Machinery: Food Processing: Huskers: Corn*

Corn Meal & Corn Flour Mills *See Equipment & Machinery: Food Processing: Mills: Corn Meal & Corn Flour*

Corn Poppers *See Equipment & Machinery: Food Processing: Corn Poppers*

Corn Processing *See Equipment & Machinery: Food Processing: Co r n Processing*

Correctional Facilities *See Consultants & Services: Foodservice: Correctional Facilities*

Corrosion Resistant Doors *See Building Equipment & Supplies: Doors: Corrosion Resistant*

Corrugated Boxes *See Packaging Materials & Supplies: Boxes: Corrugated*

Corrugated Paper *See Packaging Materials & Supplies: Paper: Corrugated*

Cost Systems *See Equipment & Machinery: Systems: Cost*

Counter Scales *See Equipment & Machinery: Scales: Counter*

Counters *See Foodservice Equipment & Supplies: Counters*

Covers *See Food Preparation Equipment, Utensils & Cookware: Covers*

Crates *See Packaging Materials & Supplies: Crates*

Creamery Cans *See Packaging Materials & Supplies: Cans: Creamery*

Creamery, Dairy Tanks *See Equipment & Machinery: Food Processing: Tanks: Creamery, Dairy*

Crown Corks *See Packaging Materials & Supplies: Corks: Crown*

Cruise Lines *See Consultants & Services: Foodservice: Cruise Lines*

Crumb Belts *See Equipment & Machinery: Belts: Crumb*

Crushers *See Equipment & Machinery: Food Processing: Crushers*

Culinary Knives *See Food Preparation Equipment, Utensils & Cookware: Knives: Culinary*

Culinary Ladles *See Food Preparation Equipment, Utensils & Cookware: Ladles: Culinary*

Culinary, Frying *See Food Preparation Equipment, Utensils & Cookware: Baskets: Culinary, Frying, Etc.*

Cup & Napkin Dispensers *See Foodservice Equipment & Supplies: Dispensers: Cup & Napkin*

Cups *See Packaging Materials & Supplies: Cups*

Curd Knives *See Food Preparation Equipment, Utensils & Cookware: Knives: Curd*

Curd Mills *See Equipment & Machinery: Food Processing: Mills: Curd*

Currency Changers *See Foodservice Equipment & Supplies: Changers: Currency*

Custom Printed Promotional Products *See Consultants & Services: Advertising Services: Custom Printed Promotional Products*

Custom Services *See Consultants & Services: Custom Services*

Cutlery *See Food Preparation Equipment, Utensils & Cookware: Cutlery*

Cutters *See Food Preparation Equipment, Utensils & Cookware: Cutters*

Cutting & Trimming Tables *See Food Preparation Equipment, Utensils & Cookware: Tables: Cutting & Trimming*

Cutting Block *See Food Preparation Equipment, Utensils & Cookware: Boards: Cutting Block*

Cylinders *See Equipment & Machinery: Cylinders*

D

Dairy & Creamery *See Equipment & Machinery: Food Processing: Dairy & Creamery*

Dairy Aprons *See Clothing & Protective Apparel: Aprons: Dairy*

Dairy Cleaners *See Sanitation Equipment & Supplies: Cleaners: Dairy*

EXAMPLE: **Dairy Cooling Vats** *See Equipment & Machinery: Food Processing: Vats: Dairy Cooling*

1. Product or Service you are looking for
2. Main Category, in alphabetical order, located in the page headers starting on page 17
3. Category Description, located in black bars and in page headers
4. Product Category, located in gray bars
5. Product Type, located under gray bars, centered in bold

Dairy Cooling *See Equipment & Machinery: Food Processing: Vats: Dairy Cooling; Refrigeration & Cooling Equipment: Vats: Dairy Cooling*

Dairy Industry *See Equipment & Machinery: Dairy Industry*

Data Loggers *See Instrumentation & Laboratory Equipment: Process Controls: Pressure: Data Loggers*

Dating & Numbering *See Packaging Materials & Supplies: Stamps: Dating & Numbering*

Deaerators *See Equipment & Machinery: Food Processing: Deaerators*

Dealers *See Consultants & Services: Dealers*

Decking *See Building Equipment & Supplies: Decking*

Decorative Items *See Foodservice Equipment & Supplies: Decorative Items*

Deep Fryer Hose *See Equipment & Machinery: Hoses: Deep Fryer*

Deep Fryers *See Equipment & Machinery: Food Processing: Deep Fryers*

Dehydration Equipment *See Equipment & Machinery: Food Processing: Dehydration Equipment*

Delivery Truck Ramps *See Transportation & Storage: Ramps: Delivery Truck*

Depositors *See Equipment & Machinery: Depositors*

Design Consultants *See Consultants & Services: Consultants: Design*

Designers *See Consultants & Services: Designers*

Dessert, Pastry Carts *See Foodservice Equipment & Supplies: Carts: Dessert, Pastry*

Detectors & Alarms *See Safety & Security Equipment & Supplies: Detectors & Alarms*

Detectors *See Equipment & Machinery: Packaging: Detectors; Safety & Security Equipment & Supplies: Detectors*

Detergents *See Sanitation Equipment & Supplies: Detergents*

Dicing Cutters *See Food Preparation Equipment, Utensils & Cookware: Cutters: Dicing*

Dish & Plate Warmers *See Foodservice Equipment & Supplies: Warmers: Dish & Plate*

Dish Cloths *See Sanitation Equipment & Supplies: Cloths: Dish*

Dish Washing Machinery *See Sanitation Equipment & Supplies: Dish Washing Machinery*

Dish, Food Display & Tray Covers *See Food Preparation Equipment, Utensils & Cookware: Covers: Dish, Food Display & Tray*

Dishes *See Foodservice Equipment & Supplies: Dishes*

Dishwasher *See Sanitation Equipment & Supplies: Dishwasher*

Dishwashing Compounds *See Sanitation Equipment & Supplies: Compounds: Dishwashing*

Disinfectants & Germicides *See Sanitation Equipment & Supplies: Disinfectants & Germicides*

Disintegrators *See Equipment & Machinery: Food Processing: Disintegrators*

Dispensers *See Foodservice Equipment & Supplies: Dispensers; Sanitation Equipment & Supplies: Dispensers*

Display Cases *See Foodservice Equipment & Supplies: Cases: Display*

Display Tables *See Foodservice Equipment & Supplies: Tables: Display*

Display, Store Hooks *See Foodservice Equipment & Supplies: Hooks: Display, Store*

Display, Store Racks *See Foodservice Equipment & Supplies: Racks: Display, Store*

Displays *See Foodservice Equipment & Supplies: Displays*

Disposable Gloves *See Clothing & Protective Apparel: Gloves: Disposable*

Disposable Towels *See Foodservice Equipment & Supplies: Towels: Disposable*

Disposable Wipers *See Sanitation Equipment & Supplies: Wipers: Disposable*

Doilies *See Foodservice Equipment & Supplies: Doilies*

Doors *See Building Equipment & Supplies: Doors; Foodservice Equipment & Supplies: Doors; Refrigeration & Cooling Equipment: Doors*

Double Acting Doors *See Building Equipment & Supplies: Doors: Double Acting*

Dough Make-up *See Equipment & Machinery: Food Processing: Dough Make-up*

Dough Sheeter *See Food Preparation Equipment, Utensils & Cookware: Sheeter: Dough*

Drawers *See Foodservice Equipment & Supplies: Drawers*

Drink Mixing *See Equipment & Machinery: Food Processing: Drink Mixing*

Drinking Glasses *See Food Preparation Equipment, Utensils & Cookware: Glasses: Drinking*

Drinking Straws *See Foodservice Equipment & Supplies: Straws: Drinking*

Drive-Thru & Pass-Thru Windows *See Building Equipment & Supplies: Windows: Drive-Thru & Pass-Thru*

Drum Mixers *See Equipment & Machinery: Food Processing: Mixers: Drum*

Drums *See Transportation & Storage: Drums*

Dry Measures *See Equipment & Machinery: Measures: Dry*

Dry Product Contract Packaging *See Consultants & Services: Contract Packaging: Dry Product*

Dry Products Filling *See Equipment & Machinery: Food Processing: Dry Products Filling*

Dryer Systems *See Sanitation Equipment & Supplies: Dryer Systems*

Dryers *See Equipment & Machinery: Food Processing: Dryers*

Drying *See Consultants & Services: Custom Services: Drying*

Drying, Evaporating Tanks *See Equipment & Machinery: Food Processing: Tanks: Drying, Evaporating*

Dumpers *See Equipment & Machinery: Food Processing: Dumpers*

Dust Collectors *See Sanitation Equipment & Supplies: Dust Collectors*

Dust Pans *See Sanitation Equipment & Supplies: Dust Pans*

Dusting Cloths *See Sanitation Equipment & Supplies: Cloths: Dusting*

E

Egg Baskets *See Packaging Materials & Supplies: Baskets: Egg*

Egg Crates *See Packaging Materials & Supplies: Crates: Egg*

Egg Processing *See Equipment & Machinery: Food Processing: Egg Processing & Cleaning*

Egg Slicers *See Equipment & Machinery: Food Processing: Slicers: Egg*

Egg, Cream, Culinary *See Food Preparation Equipment, Utensils & Cookware: Beaters: Egg, Cream, Culinary*

Electric Alarm Mats *See Safety & Security Equipment & Supplies: Mats: Electric Alarm*

Electric Heating *See Building Equipment & Supplies: Heating, Ventilation & Air Conditioning: Heating: Electric*

Electric Lighting *See Building Equipment & Supplies: Lighting Equipment: Lighting Fixtures: Electric*

Electric Signs *See Foodservice Equipment & Supplies: Signs: Electric*

Electric Steam Boilers *See Equipment & Machinery: Food Processing: Boilers: Electric Steam*

Electronic Survey *See Instrumentation & Laboratory Equipment: Process Analysis & Development: Electronic Survey*

Emergency Lighting *See Building Equipment & Supplies: Lighting Equipment: Lighting Fixtures: Emergency*

Employment Agencies *See Consultants & Services: Personnel Services: Employment Agencies*

Envelopes *See Foodservice Equipment & Supplies: Envelopes*

Equipment & Machinery *See Equipment & Machinery*

Equipment & Supplies *See Consultants & Services: Construction: Equipment & Supplies*

Equipment *See Equipment & Machinery: Food Processing: Equipment*

Equipment Packaging *See Equipment & Machinery: Packaging: Equipment*

Espresso & Cappuccino *See Equipment & Machinery: Food Processing: Espresso & Cappuccino Processing*

Ethyl Alcohol *See Instrumentation & Laboratory Equipment: Analyzers: Ethyl Alcohol*

Evaporative Condensers *See Equipment & Machinery: Food Processing: Condensers: Evaporative*

Evaporators *See Equipment & Machinery: Food Processing: Evaporators*

Exhausters *See Equipment & Machinery: Packaging: Exhausters*

Exterminators *See Sanitation Equipment & Supplies: Pest Control: Exterminators*

Extractors *See Equipment & Machinery: Food Processing: Extractors*

Extruders *See Equipment & Machinery: Food Processing: Extruders*

Extrusion *See Consultants & Services: Custom Services: Extrusion*

F

Facility Design *See Consultants & Services: Construction: Facility Design*

Factory, Warehouse, Shop & Industrial Trucks *See Transportation & Storage: Trucks: Factory, Warehouse, Shop & Industrial*

Fancy Boxes *See Packaging Materials & Supplies: Boxes: Fancy*

Fans *See Building Equipment & Supplies: Fans*

Fast Food *See Consultants & Services: Fast Food & Franchises*

Fast Food Restaurants *See Consultants & Services: Foodservice: Fast Food Restaurants*

Fats, Oils Analyzers *See Instrumentation & Laboratory Equipment: Analyzers: Fats, Oils*

Feed Mills *See Equipment & Machinery: Food Processing: Mills: Feed*

Feeders *See Equipment & Machinery: Feeders*

Fiber Boxes *See Packaging Materials & Supplies: Boxes: Fiber*

Fiber, Starch *See Instrumentation & Laboratory Equipment: Analyzers: Fiber, Starch*

Fillers *See Equipment & Machinery: Food Processing: Fillers*

Filling *See Equipment & Machinery: Packaging: Carton: Filling*

Film *See Packaging Materials & Supplies: Film*

Filters *See Equipment & Machinery: Food Processing: Filters*

Filtration and Separation *See Equipment & Machinery: Food Processing: Filtration and Separation*

Filtration Devices & Systems *See Equipment & Machinery: Filtration Devices & Systems*

Fire Alarm Systems *See Safety & Security Equipment & Supplies: Fire Alarm Systems*

Fire Extinguishers *See Safety & Security Equipment & Supplies: Fire Extinguishers*

Fire, Heat & Smoke Detectors & Alarms *See Safety & Security Equipment & Supplies: Detectors & Alarms: Fire, Heat & Smoke*

Fish Cleaning *See Equipment & Machinery: Food Processing: Fish Cleaning*

Fish Cookers *See Equipment & Machinery: Food Processing: Cookers: Fish*

Fish Scalers *See Equipment & Machinery: Food Processing: Scalers: Fish*

Fish Scaling & Slitting Knives *See Food Preparation Equipment, Utensils & Cookware: Knives: Fish Scaling & Slitting*

Fish, Meat & Produce Smokers *See Equipment & Machinery: Food Processing: Smokers: Fish, Meat & Produce*

Fittings *See Equipment & Machinery: Fittings*

Fixtures *See Foodservice Equipment & Supplies: Fixtures*

Flags, Pennants & Banners *See Consultants & Services: Advertising Services: Flags, Pennants & Banners*

Flakers or Flaking Drums *See Equipment & Machinery: Food Processing: Flakers or Flaking Drums*

Flashlights *See Safety & Security Equipment & Supplies: Flashlights*

Flexible Materials *See Packaging Materials & Supplies: Packaging: Flexible Materials*

Floor Cleaning Machinery *See Sanitation Equipment & Supplies: Floor Cleaning Machinery*

Floor Electric Alarm Mats *See Safety & Security Equipment & Supplies: Mats: Electric Alarm: Floor*

Floor Mats *See Building Equipment & Supplies: Flooring: Floor Mats*

Floor Polish *See Sanitation Equipment & Supplies: Polish: Floor*

Floor, Sweeping, Polishing & Waxing Brushes *See Sanitation Equipment & Supplies: Brushes: Floor, Sweeping, Polishing & Waxing*

Flooring *See Building Equipment & Supplies: Flooring*

Flour & Bakers' Sifters *See Food Preparation Equipment, Utensils & Cookware: Sifters: Flour & Bakers'*

Flour & Cereal Mills *See Equipment & Machinery: Food Processing: Mills: Flour & Cereal*

Flour Blending *See Equipment & Machinery: Food Processing: Blending: Flour*

Flour Hoppers *See Equipment & Machinery: Food Processing: Hoppers: Flour*

Flour Mill *See Equipment & Machinery: Food Processing: Flour Mill*

Flour, Meal & Feed Bags *See Packaging Materials & Supplies: Bags: Flour, Meal & Feed*

Flow Measurement *See Instrumentation & Laboratory Equipment: Instrumentation: Flow Measurement, Gas & Liquid*

Flow Meters *See Instrumentation & Laboratory Equipment: Meters: Flow*

Flow Regulators *See Equipment & Machinery: Flow Regulators*

Fluid, Liquid, Weighing Scales *See Equipment & Machinery: Scales: Fluid, Liquid, Weighing*

Fluorescent Lighting *See Building Equipment & Supplies: Lighting Equipment: Fluorescent*

Fluorescent Lighting Fixtures *See Building Equipment & Supplies: Lighting Equipment: Lighting Fixtures: Fluorescent*

Foil *See Packaging Materials & Supplies: Foil*

Folding Tables *See Foodservice Equipment & Supplies: Tables: Folding*

Food & Restaurant Trucks *See Transportation & Storage: Trucks: Food & Restaurant*

Food Bags *See Packaging Materials & Supplies: Bags: Food*

Food Carriers *See Packaging Materials & Supplies: Carriers: Food*

Food Certification *See Instrumentation & Laboratory Equipment: Certification: Food*

Food Closeouts *See Consultants & Services: Food Closeouts, Surplus, Salvage & Liquidators*

Food Deaerators *See Equipment & Machinery: Food Processing: Deaerators: Food*

Food Dispensers *See Foodservice Equipment & Supplies: Dispensers: Food*

Food Dryers *See Equipment & Machinery: Food Processing: Dryers: Food*

Food Filters *See Equipment & Machinery: Food Processing: Filters: Food*

Food Handlers' Protective Apparel *See Clothing & Protective Apparel: Protective Apparel: Food Handlers'*

Food Handling Hoses *See Equipment & Machinery: Hoses: Food Handling*

Food Industry Brushes *See Food Preparation Equipment, Utensils & Cookware: Brushes: Food Industry*

Food Inspection *See Instrumentation & Laboratory Equipment: Testers: Food Inspection*

Food Processing Agitators *See Equipment & Machinery: Food Processing: Agitators: Food Processing*

Food Processing *See Equipment & Machinery: Food Processing: Food Processing: Food*

Food Processing Machine Blades *See Equipment & Machinery: Food Processing: Blades: Food Processing Machine*

Food Processing Machine Knives *See Food Preparation Equipment, Utensils & Cookware: Knives: Food Processing Machine*

Food Processing Mixers *See Equipment & Machinery: Food Processing: Mixers: Food Processing*

Food Processing *See Equipment & Machinery: Food Processing*

Food Protective Packaging *See Packaging Materials & Supplies: Packaging: Food Protective*

Food Pumps *See Equipment & Machinery: Pumps: Food; Instrumentation & Laboratory Equipment: Pumps: Food*

Food Research *See Consultants & Services: Laboratories: Food Research & Development*

Food Storage Supplies *See Transportation & Storage: Food Storage Supplies*

Food Technology Consultants *See Consultants & Services: Consultants: Food Technology*

Food Tongs *See Food Preparation Equipment, Utensils & Cookware: Tongs: Food*

Food Trays *See Foodservice Equipment & Supplies: Trays: Food*

Food Warmers *See Foodservice Equipment & Supplies: Warmers: Food*

Food, Artificial Displays *See Foodservice Equipment & Supplies: Displays: Food, Artificial*

Food, Household, Hotel & Restaurant Mixers *See Equipment & Machinery: Food Processing: Mixers: Food, Household, Hotel & Restaurant*

Foodservice Architects *See Consultants & Services: Architects: Foodservice*

Foodservice Doors *See Foodservice Equipment & Supplies: Doors: Foodservice*

Foodservice Preparation Utensils *See Foodservice Equipment & Supplies: Utensils: Foodservice Preparation*

Foodservice *See Consultants & Services: Foodservice*

Forks *See Food Preparation Equipment, Utensils & Cookware: Utensils: Forks*

Form, Fill & Seal *See Equipment & Machinery: Packaging: Form, Fill & Seal*

Formulations *See Consultants & Services: Custom Services: Formulations*

Freeze Dryers *See Equipment & Machinery: Food Processing: Dryers: Freeze*

Freezer & Frozen Foods *See Refrigeration & Cooling Equipment: Cabinets: Freezer & Frozen Foods*

Freezer Doors *See Refrigeration & Cooling Equipment: Doors: Freezer*

Freezer Tapes *See Packaging Materials & Supplies: Tapes: Freezer*

Freezers *See Refrigeration & Cooling Equipment: Freezers*

Frozen Custard Processing *See Equipment & Machinery: Food Processing: Frozen Custard Processing*

Frozen Food Displays *See Foodservice Equipment & Supplies: Displays: Frozen Food*

Frozen Food Lockers *See Refrigeration & Cooling Equipment: Lockers: Frozen Food*

Frozen Food Wrappers *See Packaging Materials & Supplies: Wrappers: Frozen Food*

Frozen Foods Processing *See Equipment & Machinery: Food Processing: Frozen Foods Processing*

Fruit & Vegetable Bags *See Packaging Materials & Supplies: Bags: Fruit & Vegetable*

Fruit & Vegetable Baskets *See Packaging Materials & Supplies: Baskets: Fruit & Vegetable*

Fruit & Vegetable Boxes *See Packaging Materials & Supplies: Boxes: Fruit & Vegetable*

Fruit & Vegetable Corers *See Equipment & Machinery: Food Processing: Corers: Fruit & Vegetable*

Fruit & Vegetable Juice Extractors *See Equipment & Machinery: Food Processing: Extractors: Fruit & Vegetable Juice*

Fruit & Vegetable Juice Filters *See Equipment & Machinery: Food Processing: Filters: Fruit & Vegetable Juice*

Fruit & Vegetable Parers & Peelers *See Food Preparation Equipment, Utensils & Cookware: Parers & Peelers: Fruit & Vegetable*

Fruit & Vegetable Washers *See Equipment & Machinery: Food Processing: Washers: Fruit & Vegetable*

Fruit & Vegetable Waxers *See Equipment & Machinery: Food Processing: Waxers: Fruit & Vegetable*

Fruit Crushers *See Equipment & Machinery: Food Processing: Crushers: Fruit*

Fruit Dryers *See Equipment & Machinery: Food Processing: Dryers: Fruit*

Fruit Industry *See Equipment & Machinery: Fruit Industry*

Fruit Jar Openers *See Equipment & Machinery: Openers: Fruit Jar*

Fruit Juice Evaporators *See Equipment & Machinery: Food Processing: Evaporators: Fruit Juice*

Fruit Knives *See Food Preparation Equipment, Utensils & Cookware: Knives: Fruit*

Fruit Packers *See Consultants & Services: Packers: Fruit*

Fruit Processing *See Equipment & Machinery: Food Processing: Fruit Processing*

Fruit, Vegetable & Nut Graders *See Equipment & Machinery: Food Processing: Graders: Fruit, Vegetable & Nut*

Frying Pans *See Food Preparation Equipment, Utensils & Cookware: Pans: Frying*

Funnels *See Equipment & Machinery: Funnels*

Furniture Polish *See Sanitation Equipment & Supplies: Polish: Furniture*

G

Garbage & Waste *See Sanitation Equipment & Supplies: Incinerators: Garbage & Waste*

Garbage Bags *See Sanitation Equipment & Supplies: Garbage Bags*

Garbage Compactors *See Sanitation Equipment & Supplies: Garbage Compactors*

Garbage Control Units & Systems *See Sanitation Equipment & Supplies: Garbage Control Units & Systems*

Garbage Disposal Units *See Sanitation Equipment & Supplies: Garbage Disposal Units*

Gas Connectors *See Equipment & Machinery: Gas Connectors*

Gas Fired Boilers *See Equipment & Machinery: Food Processing: Boilers: Gas Fired*

Gas Leak Detectors *See Safety & Security Equipment & Supplies: Detectors: Gas Leak*

Gauges;Sanitary *See Instrumentation & Laboratory Equipment: Process Controls: Pressure: Gauges;Sanitary*

Gesticide Analyses *See Instrumentation & Laboratory Equipment: Gesticide Analyses*

Gift Baskets *See Packaging Materials & Supplies: Baskets: Gift*

Glass Bottles *See Packaging Materials & Supplies: Bottles: Glass*

Glass Dispensers *See Foodservice Equipment & Supplies: Dispensers: Glass*

Glass Jars *See Packaging Materials & Supplies: Jars: Glass*

Glass Trays *See Foodservice Equipment & Supplies: Trays: Glass*

Glasses *See Food Preparation Equipment, Utensils & Cookware: Glasses*

Glassine *See Packaging Materials & Supplies: Paper: Glassine*

Glassware *See Food Preparation Equipment, Utensils & Cookware: Glassware*

Gloves *See Clothing & Protective Apparel: Gloves*

Graders *See Equipment & Machinery: Food Processing: Graders*

Grain & Oat Crushers *See Equipment & Machinery: Food Processing: Crushers: Grain & Oat*

Grain & Seed Cleaners *See Sanitation Equipment & Supplies: Cleaners: Grain & Seed*

Grain Bags *See Packaging Materials & Supplies: Bags: Grain*

Grain Blending *See Equipment & Machinery: Food Processing: Blending: Grain*

Grain Dryers *See Equipment & Machinery: Food Processing: Dryers: Grain*

Grain Elevator *See Equipment & Machinery: Food Processing: Grain Elevator*

Grain, Flour Mill *See Equipment & Machinery: Food Processing: Separators: Grain, Flour Mill*

Grain, Rice & Seed Graders *See Equipment & Machinery: Food Processing: Graders: Grain, Rice & Seed*

Graters *See Equipment & Machinery: Food Processing: Graters*

Grating *See Building Equipment & Supplies: Grating*

Gravimetric, Volumetric, Loss-In-Weight, Etc. Feeders *See Equipment & Machinery: Feeders: Gravimetric, Volumetric, Loss-In-Weight, Etc.*

Grease & Oil Resistant Paper *See Packaging Materials & Supplies: Paper: Grease & Oil Resistant*

Grease Filters *See Equipment & Machinery: Food Processing: Filters: Grease*

Greaseproof Bags *See Packaging Materials & Supplies: Bags: Greaseproof*

Grilles *See Refrigeration & Cooling Equipment: Refrigerators: Grilles*

Grinders *See Equipment & Machinery: Food Processing: Grinders*

Grinding *See Consultants & Services: Custom Services: Grinding*

Grinding Mills *See Equipment & Machinery: Food Processing: Mills: Grinding*

EXAMPLE: **Dairy Cooling Vats** *See Equipment & Machinery: Food Processing: Vats: Dairy Cooling*
(markers 1, 2, 3, 4, 5 above)

1. Product or Service you are looking for
2. Main Category, in alphabetical order, located in the page headers starting on page 17
3. Category Description, located in black bars and in page headers
4. Product Category, located in gray bars
5. Product Type, located under gray bars, centered in bold

H

Gummed Tapes *See Packaging Materials & Supplies: Tapes: Gummed*

Hair Nets *See Clothing & Protective Apparel: Hair Nets*

Hamburger & Meat Patty Processing *See Equipment & Machinery: Food Processing: Hamburger & Meat Patty Processing*

Hammer Mills *See Equipment & Machinery: Food Processing: Mills: Hammer*

Hand Carts *See Transportation & Storage: Carts: Hand*

Hand Cleaners *See Sanitation Equipment & Supplies: Cleaners: Hand*

Hand Trucks *See Transportation & Storage: Trucks: Hand*

Heat Exchangers *See Equipment & Machinery: Food Processing: Heat Exchangers*

Heat Resistant Glassware *See Food Preparation Equipment, Utensils & Cookware: Glassware: Heat Resistant*

Heat Sealed Bags *See Packaging Materials & Supplies: Bags: Heat Sealed*

Heat Sealers *See Equipment & Machinery: Packaging: Sealers: Heat*

Heat Sealing *See Equipment & Machinery: Packaging: Heat Sealing*

Heat Sealing Paper *See Packaging Materials & Supplies: Paper: Heat Sealing*

Heat Sealing Tapes *See Packaging Materials & Supplies: Tapes: Heat Sealing*

Heat Transfer Fluids *See Equipment & Machinery: Food Processing: Heat Transfer Fluids*

Heaters *See Equipment & Machinery: Heaters*

Heating, Ventilation & Air Conditioning *See Building Equipment & Supplies: Heating, Ventilation & Air Conditioning: Heating*

Hoists & Lifting Equipment *See Transportation & Storage: Hoists & Lifting Equipment*

Holders *See Clothing & Protective Apparel: Holders; Food Preparation Equipment, Utensils & Cookware: Holders; Foodservice Equipment & Supplies: Holders; Sanitation Equipment & Supplies: Holders*

Holding & Warming Equipment *See Foodservice Equipment & Supplies: Holding & Warming Equipment*

Holding, Storage Tanks *See Transportation & Storage: Tanks: Holding, Storage*

Hollowware *See Food Preparation Equipment, Utensils & Cookware: Hollowware*

Homogenizers *See Equipment & Machinery: Food Processing: Homogenizers*

Honey Processing *See Equipment & Machinery: Food Processing: Honey Processing*

Hoods *See Building Equipment & Supplies: Hoods*

Hooks *See Food Preparation Equipment, Utensils & Cookware: Hooks; Foodservice Equipment & Supplies: Hooks*

Hoops *See Food Preparation Equipment, Utensils & Cookware: Hoops*

Hoppers *See Equipment & Machinery: Food Processing: Hoppers*

Horizontal Form, Fill & Seal *See Equipment & Machinery: Packaging: Form, Fill & Seal: Horizontal*

Hose Reels *See Equipment & Machinery: Hose Reels*

Hoses *See Equipment & Machinery: Hoses*

Hospitals & Healthcare Foodservice *See Consultants & Services: Foodservice: Hospitals & Healthcare*

Hotel & Restaurant Glassware *See Food Preparation Equipment, Utensils & Cookware: Glassware: Hotel & Restaurant*

Hotel, Bar, Restaurant Interiors *See Foodservice Equipment & Supplies: Interiors: Hotel, Bar, Restaurant*

Household, Consumer Detergents *See Sanitation Equipment & Supplies: Detergents: Household, Consumer*

Household, Kitchen Utensils *See Food Preparation Equipment, Utensils & Cookware: Utensils: Household, Kitchen*

Housekeeping Carts *See Sanitation Equipment & Supplies: Carts: Housekeeping*

Hullers *See Equipment & Machinery: Food Processing: Hullers*

Humidity Loggers *See Instrumentation & Laboratory Equipment: Process Controls: Humidity Loggers*

Huskers *See Equipment & Machinery: Food Processing: Huskers*

I

Ice Breaking, Chipping, Crushing *See Equipment & Machinery: Food Processing: Ice Breaking, Chipping, Crushing*

Ice Carts *See Foodservice Equipment & Supplies: Carts: Ice*

Ice Coolers *See Refrigeration & Cooling Equipment: Coolers: Ice*

Ice Cream & Frozen Yogurt Dispensers *See Foodservice Equipment & Supplies: Dispensers: Ice Cream & Frozen Yogurt*

Ice Cream Cans *See Packaging Materials & Supplies: Cans: Ice Cream*

Ice Cream Cone, Bar, Biscuit Processing *See Equipment & Machinery: Food Processing: Ice Cream Cone, Bar, Biscuit Processing*

Ice Cream Coolers *See Refrigeration & Cooling Equipment: Coolers: Ice Cream*

Ice Cream Freezers *See Refrigeration & Cooling Equipment: Freezers: Ice Cream*

Ice Cream Processing *See Equipment & Machinery: Food Processing: Ice Cream Processing*

Ice Cream Sticks *See Packaging Materials & Supplies: Sticks: Ice Cream*

Ice Cubing *See Equipment & Machinery: Food Processing: Ice Cubing*

Ice Making Plants *See Consultants & Services: Ice Making Plants*

Ice Making, Refrigerating & Cooling *See Equipment & Machinery: Food Processing: Ice Making, Refrigerating & Cooling*

Ice Tongs *See Food Preparation Equipment, Utensils & Cookware: Tongs: Ice*

Incandescent Lighting *See Building Equipment & Supplies: Lighting Equipment: Incandescent*

Incinerators *See Sanitation Equipment & Supplies: Incinerators*

Incubators & Brooders *See Equipment & Machinery: Incubators & Brooders*

Indelible Inks *See Packaging Materials & Supplies: Inks: Indelible*

Indoor Sign Holders *See Foodservice Equipment & Supplies: Clear & Colored Plastic: Indoor Sign Holders*

Industrial Clutches & Brakes *See Transportation & Storage: Clutches & Brakes: Industrial*

Industrial Detergents *See Sanitation Equipment & Supplies: Detergents: Industrial*

Industrial Flooring *See Building Equipment & Supplies: Flooring: Industrial Flooring*

Industrial Lubricants *See Equipment & Machinery: Lubricants: Industrial*

Industrial Plant Serving *See Foodservice Equipment & Supplies: Serving Equipment: Industrial Plant*

Industrial Vacuum Cleaners *See Sanitation Equipment & Supplies: Vacuum Cleaners: Industrial*

Ingredient Water Coolers *See Refrigeration & Cooling Equipment: Coolers: Ingredient Water*

Inks *See Packaging Materials & Supplies: Inks*

Insecticides & Insect Control Systems *See Sanitation Equipment & Supplies: Insecticides & Insect Control Systems*

Inspection & Analysis *See Instrumentation & Laboratory Equipment: Inspection & Analysis Instrumentation & Systems*

Instrumentation *See Instrumentation & Laboratory Equipment: Instrumentation*

Insulated Bins *See Packaging Materials & Supplies: Bins: Insulated*

Insulated Panels *See Building Equipment & Supplies: Panels: Insulated*

Insulated Warehouses *See Transportation & Storage: Warehouses: Insulated*

Insulation *See Refrigeration & Cooling Equipment: Insulation*

Interchangeable Signs *See Foodservice Equipment & Supplies: Signs: Interchangeable*

Interior & Store Fixture Designers *See Consultants & Services: Designers: Interior & Store Fixture*

Interiors *See Foodservice Equipment & Supplies: Interiors*

Irradiation Preservation *See Equipment & Machinery: Food Processing: Preservation: Irradiation*

Irradiation Processing *See Equipment & Machinery: Food Processing: Irradiation Processing*

Isopropyl Alcohol *See Sanitation Equipment & Supplies: Isopropyl Alcohol*

J

Jackets *See Clothing & Protective Apparel: Jackets*

Jar Filling *See Equipment & Machinery: Packaging: Jar Filling*

Jars *See Packaging Materials & Supplies: Jars*

K

Kettles *See Food Preparation Equipment, Utensils & Cookware: Kettles*

Kiosks *See Foodservice Equipment & Supplies: Kiosks*

Kitchen (Commercial, Institutional, Restaurant) Designers *See Consultants & Services: Designers: Kitchen (Commercial, Institutional, Restaurant)*

Kitchen Racks *See Transportation & Storage: Racks: Kitchen*

Knife Sharpeners *See Food Preparation Equipment, Utensils & Cookware: Knife Sharpeners*

Knives *See Food Preparation Equipment, Utensils & Cookware: Knives*

Kosher Food Consultants *See Consultants & Services: Consultants: Kosher Food*

Kraft Paper *See Packaging Materials & Supplies: Paper: Kraft*

Kraut & Slaw Cutters *See Food Preparation Equipment, Utensils & Cookware: Cutters: Kraut & Slaw*

L

Label Holders *See Foodservice Equipment & Supplies: Plastic Back Tag: Label Holders*

Label Paper *See Packaging Materials & Supplies: Paper: Label*

Label Printing *See Equipment & Machinery: Packaging: Label Printing*

Labeling *See Equipment & Machinery: Packaging: Labeling*

Labels *See Packaging Materials & Supplies: Labels*

Laboratories *See Consultants & Services: Laboratories*

Laboratory Balances *See Instrumentation & Laboratory Equipment: Balances: Laboratory*

Laboratory Chemicals *See Instrumentation & Laboratory Equipment: Chemicals: Laboratory*

Laboratory Equipment *See Instrumentation & Laboratory Equipment: Laboratory Equipment*

Laboratory Testers *See Instrumentation & Laboratory Equipment: Testers: Laboratory*

Ladder Covers *See Safety & Security Equipment & Supplies: Ladder Covers*

Ladder Rungs *See Safety & Security Equipment & Supplies: Ladder Rungs*

Ladles *See Food Preparation Equipment, Utensils & Cookware: Ladles*

Laminated Bags *See Packaging Materials & Supplies: Bags: Laminated*

Laminated Paper *See Packaging Materials & Supplies: Paper: Laminated*

Lard Kettles *See Food Preparation Equipment, Utensils & Cookware: Kettles: Lard*

Level, Liquid & Dry Controls *See Instrumentation & Laboratory Equipment: Controls: Level, Liquid & Dry*

Lift Truck Pallets *See Transportation & Storage: Pallets: Lift Truck*

Lighting Equipment *See Building Equipment & Supplies: Lighting Equipment*

Lighting Fixtures *See Building Equipment & Supplies: Lighting Equipment: Lighting Fixtures*

Linen Goods *See Foodservice Equipment & Supplies: Linen Goods*

Liners *See Food Preparation Equipment, Utensils & Cookware: Liners*

Lining Paper *See Packaging Materials & Supplies: Paper: Lining*

Linings *See Packaging Materials & Supplies: Linings*

Liquid Chlorine *See Sanitation Equipment & Supplies: Chlorine: Liquid*

Liquid Product *See Consultants & Services: Contract Packaging: Liquid Product*

Liquid-Solid Separators *See Equipment & Machinery: Food Processing: Separators: Liquid-Solid*

Liquor, Wine Carts *See Foodservice Equipment & Supplies: Carts: Liquor, Wine*

Live Skid Pallets *See Transportation & Storage: Pallets: Live Skid*

Load Cells & Indicators *See Equipment & Machinery: Load Cells & Indicators*

Lockers *See Refrigeration & Cooling Equipment: Lockers*

Loin Knives *See Food Preparation Equipment, Utensils & Cookware: Knives: Loin*

Lotion *See Sanitation Equipment & Supplies: Skin Cream & Lotions: Lotion*

Lubricants *See Equipment & Machinery: Lubricants*

Luminous Tube Signs *See Foodservice Equipment & Supplies: Signs: Luminous Tube*

M

Machine Knives *See Food Preparation Equipment, Utensils & Cookware: Knives: Machine*

Magnetic Chips *See Foodservice Equipment & Supplies: Magnetic Chips*

Magnetic Label *See Foodservice Equipment & Supplies: Magnetic Label*

Magnetic Pocket *See Foodservice Equipment & Supplies: Magnetic Pocket*

Magnets *See Food Preparation Equipment, Utensils & Cookware: Magnets*

Malt Mills *See Equipment & Machinery: Food Processing: Mills: Malt*

Management *See Consultants & Services: Construction: Management*

Manufacturing Screening *See Equipment & Machinery: Screening: Manufacturing*

Markers, Pens & Pencils *See Packaging Materials & Supplies: Markers, Pens & Pencils; Foodservice Equipment & Supplies: Markers*

Marketing & Promotion Consultants *See Consultants & Services: Consultants: Marketing & Promotion*

Marking & Coding Inks *See Packaging Materials & Supplies: Inks: Marking & Coding*

Marking Tapes *See Packaging Materials & Supplies: Tapes: Marking*

Master Planning & Logistics *See Consultants & Services: Master Planning & Logistics*

Matches *See Food Preparation Equipment, Utensils & Cookware: Matches*

Material Handling & Distribution Equipment *See Transportation & Storage: Material Handling & Distribution Equipment*

Material Handling Consultants *See Consultants & Services: Consultants: Material Handling*

Materials *See Equipment & Machinery: Packaging: Equipment: Materials*

Mats & Matting Flooring *See Building Equipment & Supplies: Flooring: Mats & Matting*

Mats *See Safety & Security Equipment & Supplies: Mats*

Measurement Systems *See Instrumentation & Laboratory Equipment: Measurement Systems*

Measures *See Equipment & Machinery: Measures*

Meat Bags *See Packaging Materials & Supplies: Bags: Meat*

Meat Branding *See Packaging Materials & Supplies: Inks: Meat Branding*

Meat Curing *See Equipment & Machinery: Food Processing: Vats: Meat Curing*

Meat Cutters *See Food Preparation Equipment, Utensils & Cookware: Cutters: Meat*

Meat Dealers *See Consultants & Services: Dealers: Meat*

Meat Hooks *See Food Preparation Equipment, Utensils & Cookware: Hooks: Meat*

Meat Micer *See Food Preparation Equipment, Utensils & Cookware: Micer: Meat*

Meat Mincer *See Food Preparation Equipment, Utensils & Cookware: Mincer: Meat*

Meat Packers *See Consultants & Services: Packers: Meat*

Meat Packing Knives *See Food Preparation Equipment, Utensils & Cookware: Knives: Meat Packing*

Meat Preparation Equipment *See Equipment & Machinery: Food Processing: Meat Preparation Equipment*

Meat Slicers *See Equipment & Machinery: Food Processing: Slicers: Meat*

Meat Trucks *See Transportation & Storage: Trucks: Meat*

Menu Boards *See Foodservice Equipment & Supplies: Menu Boards*

Menus *See Foodservice Equipment & Supplies: Menus*

Mercury, High Intensity Lighting Equipment *See Building Equipment & Supplies: Lighting Equipment: Mercury, High Intensity*

Metal & Contamination Detection Systems *See Equipment & Machinery: Systems: Metal & Contamination Detection*

Metal Decking *See Building Equipment & Supplies: Decking: Metal*

Metal Detectors *See Safety & Security Equipment & Supplies: Detectors: Metal; See also Safety & Security Equipment & Supplies: Metal Detectors*

Metal Fabricators *See Consultants & Services: Construction: Metal Fabricators*

Metal Flooring *See Building Equipment & Supplies: Flooring: Metal*

Metal Grating *See Building Equipment & Supplies: Grating: Metal*

Metal Plating *See Building Equipment & Supplies: Plating: Metal*

Meters *See Instrumentation & Laboratory Equipment: Meters*

Micer *See Food Preparation Equipment, Utensils & Cookware: Micer*

Microbiology Instruments & Supplies *See Instrumentation & Laboratory Equipment: Microbiology Instruments & Supplies*

Microprocessor Controls *See Instrumentation & Laboratory Equipment: Controls: Microprocessor*

Microwave Ovens *See Equipment & Machinery: Food Processing: Microwave Ovens*

Milk & Cream Coolers *See Refrigeration & Cooling Equipment: Coolers: Milk & Cream*

Milk & Cream Regenerators *See Equipment & Machinery: Food Processing: Regenerators: Milk & Cream*

Milk & Cream Testers *See Instrumentation & Laboratory Equipment: Testers: Milk & Cream*

Milk Agitators *See Equipment & Machinery: Food Processing: Agitators: Milk*

Milk Bottle Carriers *See Packaging Materials & Supplies: Carriers: Milk Bottle*

Milk Cans *See Packaging Materials & Supplies: Cans: Milk*

Milk Evaporators *See Equipment & Machinery: Food Processing: Evaporators: Milk*

Milking *See Equipment & Machinery: Food Processing: Milking*

Mills *See Equipment & Machinery: Food Processing: Mills*

Mincer *See Food Preparation Equipment, Utensils & Cookware: Mincer*

Mirrors *See Equipment & Machinery: Mirrors*

Mist Collection *See Equipment & Machinery: Systems: Mist Collection*

Mixers *See Equipment & Machinery: Food Processing: Mixers*

Mixing Kettles *See Food Preparation Equipment, Utensils & Cookware: Kettles: Mixing*

Mobile Food Vending Carts *See Foodservice Equipment & Supplies: Carts: Mobile Food Vending*

Modular Tanks *See Transportation & Storage: Tanks: Modular*

Moldings *See Foodservice Equipment & Supplies: Plastic Store Shelf: Moldings*

Molds *See Food Preparation Equipment, Utensils & Cookware: Molds*

Mop Wringers *See Sanitation Equipment & Supplies: Mop Wringers*

Mops *See Sanitation Equipment & Supplies: Mops*

Multi-Wall Bags *See Packaging Materials & Supplies: Bags: Multi-Wall*

Mycotoxins *See Instrumentation & Laboratory Equipment: Analyzers: Mycotoxins*

N

Name Badges *See Clothing & Protective Apparel: Name Badges*

Napery *See Foodservice Equipment & Supplies: Napery*

Napkins *See Foodservice Equipment & Supplies: Napkins*

Netting, Open Mesh Bags *See Packaging Materials & Supplies: Bags: Netting, Open Mesh*

Nitrites, Nitrosamines *See Instrumentation & Laboratory Equipment: Analyzers: Nitrites, Nitrosamines*

Nozzles *See Equipment & Machinery: Nozzles*

Numerical Controls *See Instrumentation & Laboratory Equipment: Controls: Numerical*

Nut Cracking, Shelling & Salting *See Equipment & Machinery: Food Processing: Nut Cracking, Shelling & Salting*

Nut Grinding Mills *See Equipment & Machinery: Food Processing: Mills: Nut Grinding*

Nutritional Analyses & Labeling *See Consultants & Services: Nutritional Analyses & Labeling*

O

Oil Cake Grinding Mills *See Equipment & Machinery: Food Processing: Mills: Oil Cake Grinding*

Oil Extraction *See Equipment & Machinery: Food Processing: Oil Extraction*

Oil, Cottonseed & Linseed Presses *See Equipment & Machinery: Food Processing: Presses: Oil, Cottonseed & Linseed*

Oils *See Sanitation Equipment & Supplies: Oils*

Openers *See Equipment & Machinery: Openers*

Organic Acids *See Instrumentation & Laboratory Equipment: Analyzers: Organic Acids*

Outdoor Lighting *See Building Equipment & Supplies: Lighting Equipment: Outdoor*

Oven Mits *See Clothing & Protective Apparel: Oven Mits*

Ovens *See Equipment & Machinery: Food Processing: Ovens*

Oyster & Clam Knives *See Food Preparation Equipment, Utensils & Cookware: Knives: Oyster & Clam*

P

Package Tying *See Equipment & Machinery: Packaging: Package Tying*

Package, Carton & Display *See Consultants & Services: Designers: Package, Carton & Display*

Packaging & Containerizing *See Packaging Materials & Supplies: Packaging & Containerizing Products*

Packaging Consultants *See Consultants & Services: Consultants: Packaging*

Packaging Line Controls *See Instrumentation & Laboratory Equipment: Controls: Packaging Line*

Packaging Line Detectors *See Equipment & Machinery: Packaging: Detectors: Packaging Line*

Packaging Materials *See Instrumentation & Laboratory Equipment: Testers: Packaging Materials/Containers*

Packaging Services *See Consultants & Services: Packaging Services*

Packaging Systems *See Equipment & Machinery: Systems: Packaging*

Packaging *See Equipment & Machinery: Packaging; Packaging Materials & Supplies: Packaging*

Packers' & Butchers' Processing *See Equipment & Machinery: Food Processing: Packers' & Butchers'*

Packers' Glassware *See Food Preparation Equipment, Utensils & Cookware: Glassware: Packers'*

Packers *See Consultants & Services: Packers*

Packing House Racks *See Transportation & Storage: Racks: Packing House*

Packing House Supplies *See Packaging Materials & Supplies: Packing House Supplies*

Packing House Tables *See Equipment & Machinery: Packaging: Tables: Packing House*

Packing House Trucks *See Transportation & Storage: Trucks: Packing House*

Packing *See Equipment & Machinery: Packaging: Packing*

Paging Systems *See Building Equipment & Supplies: Paging Systems*

Pails *See Equipment & Machinery: Pails*

Pallet Handling Equipment *See Transportation & Storage: Pallet Handling Equipment*

EXAMPLE: **Dairy Cooling Vats** *See Equipment & Machinery: Food Processing: Vats: Dairy Cooling*

1. Product or Service you are looking for
2. Main Category, in alphabetical order, located in the page headers starting on page 17
3. Category Description, located in black bars and in page headers
4. Product Category, located in gray bars
5. Product Type, located under gray bars, centered in bold

Pallet Handling Trucks See Transportation & Storage: Trucks: Pallet Handling

Pallet Racks See Transportation & Storage: Racks: Pallet

Palletizers See Transportation & Storage: Palletizers

Pallets See Transportation & Storage: Pallets; Building Equipment & Supplies: Panels

Panomatic-Flour Collection System See Equipment & Machinery: Food Processing: Panomatic-Flour Collection System

Pans See Food Preparation Equipment, Utensils & Cookware: Pans

Paper Bags See Packaging Materials & Supplies: Bags: Paper

Paper Boxes See Packaging Materials & Supplies: Boxes: Paper

Paper Containers See Packaging Materials & Supplies: Containers: Paper

Paper Cups See Packaging Materials & Supplies: Cups: Paper

Paper Dishes See Foodservice Equipment & Supplies: Dishes: Paper

Paper Filters See Equipment & Machinery: Food Processing: Filters: Paper

Paper Lined Bags See Packaging Materials & Supplies: Bags: Paper Lined

Paper Napkins See Foodservice Equipment & Supplies: Napkins: Paper

Paper Plates See Food Preparation Equipment, Utensils & Cookware: Plates: Paper

Paper Towels See Foodservice Equipment & Supplies: Towels: Paper

Paper Wrappers See Packaging Materials & Supplies: Wrappers: Paper

Paper, Folding Boxes See Packaging Materials & Supplies: Boxes: Paper, Folding

Paper See Foodservice Equipment & Supplies: Paper; Packaging Materials & Supplies: Paper

Paraffin Wax See Packaging Materials & Supplies: Wax: Paraffin

Parers & Peelers See Food Preparation Equipment, Utensils & Cookware: Parers & Peelers

Parts Food Processing See Equipment & Machinery: Food Processing: Food Processing: Parts

Parts See Equipment & Machinery: Parts

Pasta Processing See Equipment & Machinery: Food Processing: Pasta Processing

Paste Products Mixers See Equipment & Machinery: Food Processing: Mixers: Paste Products

Pasteurizers See Equipment & Machinery: Food Processing: Pasteurizers

Peanut Butter Mills See Equipment & Machinery: Food Processing: Mills: Peanut Butter

Peanut Processing See Equipment & Machinery: Food Processing: Peanut Processing

Personnel Services See Consultants & Services: Personnel Services

Pest Control See Sanitation Equipment & Supplies: Pest Control Systems & Devices; Sanitation Equipment & Supplies: Pest Control

Pesticide Residue See Instrumentation & Laboratory Equipment: Analyzers: Pesticide Residue, Antibiotics

pH Loggers See Instrumentation & Laboratory Equipment: Process Controls: pH Loggers

pH Meters See Instrumentation & Laboratory Equipment: Meters: pH

Pharmaceutical Industry See Equipment & Machinery: Pharmaceutical Industry

Pickers See Equipment & Machinery: Food Processing: Pickers

Pickle Cutters See Food Preparation Equipment, Utensils & Cookware: Cutters: Pickle

Pie Pans See Food Preparation Equipment, Utensils & Cookware: Pans: Pie

Pie Plates See Food Preparation Equipment, Utensils & Cookware: Plates: Pie

Pizza & Pizza Products See Equipment & Machinery: Food Processing: Pizza & Pizza Products Processing

Place Mats See Foodservice Equipment & Supplies: Place Mats

Plastic Back Tag See Foodservice Equipment & Supplies: Plastic Back Tag

Plastic Bags See Packaging Materials & Supplies: Bags: Plastic

Plastic Bottles See Packaging Materials & Supplies: Bottles: Plastic

Plastic Boxes See Packaging Materials & Supplies: Boxes: Plastic

Plastic Coated Paper See Packaging Materials & Supplies: Paper: Plastic Coated

Plastic Containers See Packaging Materials & Supplies: Containers: Plastic

Plastic Cups See Packaging Materials & Supplies: Cups: Plastic

Plastic Doors See Building Equipment & Supplies: Doors: Plastic

Plastic Fabricators See Equipment & Machinery: Plastic Fabricators

Plastic Film See Packaging Materials & Supplies: Film: Plastic

Plastic Jars See Packaging Materials & Supplies: Jars: Plastic

Plastic Packaging See Packaging Materials & Supplies: Packaging: Plastic

Plastic Pallets See Transportation & Storage: Pallets: Plastic

Plastic Shelf Covers See Foodservice Equipment & Supplies: Plastic Shelf Covers

Plastic Signs See Foodservice Equipment & Supplies: Signs: Plastic

Plastic Store Shelf See Foodservice Equipment & Supplies: Plastic Store Shelf

Plastic Trays See Foodservice Equipment & Supplies: Trays: Plastic

Plastic Tubing See Equipment & Machinery: Tubing: Plastic

Plastic Utensils See Foodservice Equipment & Supplies: Utensils: Plastic

Plastic, Reusable Plates See Food Preparation Equipment, Utensils & Cookware: Plates: Plastic, Reusable

Plastic, Rubber Gloves See Clothing & Protective Apparel: Gloves: Plastic, Rubber

Plastic See Packaging Materials & Supplies: Plastic

Plastics Printing See Equipment & Machinery: Packaging: Printing: Plastics

Plate & Tray Dispensers See Foodservice Equipment & Supplies: Dispensers: Plate & Tray

Plate/Frame Exchanger See Equipment & Machinery: Plate/Frame Exchanger

Plates See Food Preparation Equipment, Utensils & Cookware: Plates

Platforms See Building Equipment & Supplies: Platforms

Plating See Building Equipment & Supplies: Plating

Platters See Food Preparation Equipment, Utensils & Cookware: Platters

Plumbing & Drainage See Sanitation Equipment & Supplies: Plumbing & Drainage Equipment

Point of Purchase Displays See Foodservice Equipment & Supplies: Displays: Point of Purchase

Point of Purchase Signs See Foodservice Equipment & Supplies: Signs: Point of Purchase

Point of Sale Systems See Foodservice Equipment & Supplies: Point of Sale Systems

Polarimeters See Instrumentation & Laboratory Equipment: Measurement Systems: Polarimeters

Polish See Sanitation Equipment & Supplies: Polish

Polishing, Refinishing, Sanding & Scrubbing See Sanitation Equipment & Supplies: Floor Cleaning Machinery: Polishing, Refinishing, Sanding & Scrubbing

Polyethylene Bags See Packaging Materials & Supplies: Bags: Polyethylene

Polypropylene Bags See Packaging Materials & Supplies: Bags: Polypropylene

Popcorn Bags See Packaging Materials & Supplies: Bags: Popcorn

Portion Control Equipment See Equipment & Machinery: Packaging: Portion Control Equipment

Pot Holders See Clothing & Protective Apparel: Holders: Pot

Potato & Onion Sorters See Equipment & Machinery: Food Processing: Sorters: Potato & Onion

Potato Chip Processing See Equipment & Machinery: Food Processing: Potato Chip Processing

Poultry Pickers See Equipment & Machinery: Food Processing: Pickers: Poultry

Poultry Processing See Equipment & Machinery: Food Processing: Poultry Processing

Poultry Shears See Food Preparation Equipment, Utensils & Cookware: Shears: Poultry

Powder Soap See Sanitation Equipment & Supplies: Soap: Powder

Powder See Sanitation Equipment & Supplies: Powder

Power Meat Cutters See Food Preparation Equipment, Utensils & Cookware: Cutters: Meat: Power

Powered Beer Keg Movers See Transportation & Storage: Beer Keg Movers: Powered

Preservation See Equipment & Machinery: Food Processing: Preservation

Presses See Equipment & Machinery: Food Processing: Presses

Pressure Cookers See Equipment & Machinery: Food Processing: Cookers: Pressure

Pressure Process Controls See Instrumentation & Laboratory Equipment: Process Controls: Pressure

Pressure Sensitive Film See Packaging Materials & Supplies: Film: Pressure Sensitive

Pressure Sensitive Foil See Packaging Materials & Supplies: Foil: Pressure Sensitive

Pressure Sensitive Labels See Packaging Materials & Supplies: Labels: Pressure Sensitive

Pressure Sensitive Paper See Packaging Materials & Supplies: Paper: Pressure Sensitive

Pressure Sensitive Seals See Packaging Materials & Supplies: Seals: Pressure Sensitive

Pressure Sensitive Tags See Packaging Materials & Supplies: Tags: Pressure Sensitive

Pressure Sensitive Tapes See Packaging Materials & Supplies: Tapes: Pressure Sensitive

Pressure Washers See Sanitation Equipment & Supplies: Pressure Washers

Pretzel Processing See Equipment & Machinery: Food Processing: Pretzel Processing

Price & Sign Markers See Foodservice Equipment & Supplies: Markers: Price & Sign

Price Card, Ticket, Etc. Holders See Foodservice Equipment & Supplies: Holders: Price Card, Ticket, Etc.

Price Tag Seals See Packaging Materials & Supplies: Seals: Price Tag

Price Tags See Packaging Materials & Supplies: Tags: Price

Pricer Signs See Foodservice Equipment & Supplies: Pricer Signs

Pricing Systems See Equipment & Machinery: Systems: Pricing

Primary & Secondary Schools Foodservice See Consultants & Services: Foodservice: Primary & Secondary Schools

Printed & Laminated Foil See Packaging Materials & Supplies: Foil: Printed & Laminated

Printing Carton See Equipment & Machinery: Packaging: Carton: Printing

Printing See Equipment & Machinery: Packaging: Printing

Private Label See Packaging Materials & Supplies: Labels: Private Label

Private Label Packaging See Packaging Materials & Supplies: Packaging: Private Label

Process & Production Systems See Equipment & Machinery: Systems: Process & Production

Process Analysis & Development See Instrumentation & Laboratory Equipment: Process Analysis & Development

Process Controls See Instrumentation & Laboratory Equipment: Process Controls

Process Vessels & Tanks See Consultants & Services: Designers: Process Vessels & Tanks

Programmable Process Controls See Instrumentation & Laboratory Equipment: Process Controls: Programmable

Project Management See Consultants & Services: Project Management

Protective Apparel See Clothing & Protective Apparel: Protective Apparel

Protective Gloves See Clothing & Protective Apparel: Gloves: Protective

Pulpers See Equipment & Machinery: Food Processing: Pulpers

Pulverizers See Equipment & Machinery: Food Processing: Pulverizers

Pump feeders See Equipment & Machinery: Pump feeders

Pumps See Equipment & Machinery: Pumps; Foodservice Equipment & Supplies: Pumps; Instrumentation & Laboratory Equipment: Pumps

Purifiers See Equipment & Machinery: Water Treatment: Purifiers

Q

Quality Control *See Consultants & Services: Quality Control*

Quick Freezing *See Refrigeration & Cooling Equipment: Freezers: Quick Freezing*

R

Racks Dishwasher *See Sanitation Equipment & Supplies: Dishwasher: Racks*

Racks Refrigerators *See Refrigeration & Cooling Equipment: Refrigerators: Racks*

Racks *See Foodservice Equipment & Supplies: Racks; Transportation & Storage: Racks*

Radios Paging Systems *See Building Equipment & Supplies: Paging Systems: Radios*

Ramps *See Transportation & Storage: Ramps*

Rat & Mouse Traps *See Sanitation Equipment & Supplies: Pest Control Systems & Devices: Traps: Rat & Mouse*

Rebuilt & Used *See Equipment & Machinery: Food Processing: Food Processing: Rebuilt & Used*

Rebuilt & Used Packaging *See Equipment & Machinery: Packaging: Rebuilt & Used*

Rechargable Flashlights *See Safety & Security Equipment & Supplies: Flashlights: Rechargable*

Recorders *See Instrumentation & Laboratory Equipment: Process Controls: Recorders*

Refinishing *See Consultants & Services: Refinishing & Refurbishing Services*

Refractometers *See Instrumentation & Laboratory Equipment: Measurement Systems: Refractometers*

Refrigerated Display Case Doors *See Refrigeration & Cooling Equipment: Doors: Refrigerated Display Case*

Refrigerated Trailers *See Transportation & Storage: Trailers: Refrigerated*

Refrigerating & Cooling Rooms *See Refrigeration & Cooling Equipment: Refrigerating & Cooling Rooms*

Refrigerating Equipment & Machinery *See Refrigeration & Cooling Equipment: Refrigerating Equipment & Machinery*

Refrigerating Units *See Refrigeration & Cooling Equipment: Refrigerating Units*

Refrigeration & Cold Storage Insulation *See Refrigeration & Cooling Equipment: Insulation: Refrigeration & Cold Storage*

Refrigeration Systems *See Instrumentation & Laboratory Equipment: Controls: Refrigeration Systems*

Refrigeration Valves *See Refrigeration & Cooling Equipment: Valves: Refrigeration*

Refrigerator & Stove Shelves *See Equipment & Machinery: Shelves: Refrigerator & Stove*

Refrigerator Baskets *See Packaging Materials & Supplies: Baskets: Refrigerator*

Refrigerator Doors *See Refrigeration & Cooling Equipment: Doors: Refrigerator*

Refrigerators *See Refrigeration & Cooling Equipment: Refrigerators*

Regenerators *See Equipment & Machinery: Food Processing: Regenerators*

Research & Development *See Consultants & Services: Research & Development*

Resistant Flooring *See Building Equipment & Supplies: Flooring: Thermal Shock: Resistant Flooring*

Restaurant Design *See Consultants & Services: Consultants: Restaurant Design*

Restaurant Supplies & Equipment *See Foodservice Equipment & Supplies: Restaurant Supplies & Equipment*

Retail Architects *See Consultants & Services: Architects: Retail*

Retail Foodservice *See Consultants & Services: Foodservice: Retail*

Retort Pouch *See Equipment & Machinery: Packaging: Retort Pouch Processing*

Retorts *See Packaging Materials & Supplies: Retorts*

Reverse Osmosis *See Equipment & Machinery: Systems: Reverse Osmosis*

Reverse Vending *See Foodservice Equipment & Supplies: Vending Machinery: Reverse*

Rice Grinding Mills *See Equipment & Machinery: Food Processing: Mills: Rice Grinding*

Rice Processing *See Equipment & Machinery: Food Processing: Rice Processing*

Road Plates *See Equipment & Machinery: Road Plates*

Roasters *See Equipment & Machinery: Food Processing: Roasters*

Roasting *See Equipment & Machinery: Food Processing: Roasting*

Rolling Pins *See Food Preparation Equipment, Utensils & Cookware: Rolling Pins*

Room Service *See Foodservice Equipment & Supplies: Tables: Room Service*

Rotisseries *See Equipment & Machinery: Food Processing: Rotisseries*

Routing & Scheduling for Food Industry *See Consultants & Services: Computer Software, Systems & Services: Software: Routing & Scheduling for Food Industry*

Rubber Stamps *See Packaging Materials & Supplies: Stamps: Rubber*

Rubber, Bottle Stoppers *See Instrumentation & Laboratory Equipment: Stoppers: Rubber, Bottle*

S

Safety & Security *See Safety & Security Equipment & Supplies*

Safety Flooring *See Building Equipment & Supplies: Flooring: Safety*

Salad Bars *See Foodservice Equipment & Supplies: Salad Bars*

Salad Carts *See Foodservice Equipment & Supplies: Carts: Salad*

Salt & Pepper Shakers *See Packaging Materials & Supplies: Shakers: Salt & Pepper*

Salt *See Instrumentation & Laboratory Equipment: Analyzers: Salt (Sodium Chloride)*

Salt Processing *See Equipment & Machinery: Food Processing: Salt Processing*

Sampling & Testing *See Instrumentation & Laboratory Equipment: Sampling & Testing Equipment & Instrumentation*

Sandwich Bags *See Packaging Materials & Supplies: Bags: Sandwich*

Sandwich Processing *See Equipment & Machinery: Food Processing: Sandwich Processing*

Sanitary Wall *See Sanitation Equipment & Supplies: Sanitary Wall*

Sanitation Equipment & Supplies *See Sanitation Equipment & Supplies*

Sanitation, Testing & Analysis *See Consultants & Services: Consultants: Sanitation, Testing & Analysis*

Sanitizers *See Sanitation Equipment & Supplies: Sanitizers*

Sauce Pans *See Food Preparation Equipment, Utensils & Cookware: Pans: Sauce*

Sausage Meat Cutters *See Food Preparation Equipment, Utensils & Cookware: Cutters: Meat: Sausage*

Sausage Stuffers *See Equipment & Machinery: Food Processing: Stuffers: Sausage*

Sawdust Smokers *See Equipment & Machinery: Food Processing: Smokers: Sawdust*

Saws *See Equipment & Machinery: Food Processing: Saws*

Scalers *See Equipment & Machinery: Food Processing: Scalers*

Scales *See Instrumentation & Laboratory Equipment: Scales & Weighing Systems; Equipment & Machinery: Scales*

Scanners *See Foodservice Equipment & Supplies: Scanners*

Scoops, Dishers & Spades *See Food Preparation Equipment, Utensils & Cookware: Scoops, Dishers & Spades*

Scouring Pads *See Sanitation Equipment & Supplies: Scouring Pads*

Scrapers *See Food Preparation Equipment, Utensils & Cookware: Scrapers*

Screening *See Equipment & Machinery: Screening*

Scrubbers *See Equipment & Machinery: Scrubbers; See also Sanitation Equipment & Supplies: Scrubbers*

Seafood Preparation *See Equipment & Machinery: Food Processing: Seafood Preparation Equipment*

Sealers *See Equipment & Machinery: Packaging: Sealers*

Sealing Wax *See Packaging Materials & Supplies: Wax: Sealing*

Seals *See Packaging Materials & Supplies: Seals*

Sensors *See Instrumentation & Laboratory Equipment: Sensors*

Separators *See Equipment & Machinery: Food Processing: Separators*

Service Carts *See Foodservice Equipment & Supplies: Carts: Service*

Serving Equipment *See Foodservice Equipment & Supplies: Serving Equipment*

Shakers *See Packaging Materials & Supplies: Shakers*

Shears *See Food Preparation Equipment, Utensils & Cookware: Shears*

Sheeter *See Food Preparation Equipment, Utensils & Cookware: Sheeter*

Sheets *See Food Preparation Equipment, Utensils & Cookware: Sheets*

Shelf Covers *See Foodservice Equipment & Supplies: Wood Grain Plastic: Shelf Covers*

Shelf Strips Clear Plastic *See Foodservice Equipment & Supplies: Clear Plastic: Shelf Strips*

Shelf Strips Colored Plastic *See Foodservice Equipment & Supplies: Colored Plastic: Shelf Strips*

Shelves *See Equipment & Machinery: Shelves*

Shelving *See Foodservice Equipment & Supplies: Shelving; See also Transportation & Storage: Shelving*

Shirts *See Clothing & Protective Apparel: Shirts*

Shish Kebab *See Equipment & Machinery: Food Processing: Shish Kebab Systems*

Shoplifting Detectors *See Safety & Security Equipment & Supplies: Detectors: Shoplifting*

Shopping Bags *See Packaging Materials & Supplies: Bags: Shopping*

Shopping Baskets *See Foodservice Equipment & Supplies: Baskets: Shopping*

Shopping Carts *See Foodservice Equipment & Supplies: Carts: Shopping*

Shredded Paper *See Packaging Materials & Supplies: Paper: Shredded*

Shredders *See Equipment & Machinery: Food Processing: Shredders*

Shrimp Processing *See Equipment & Machinery: Food Processing: Shrimp Processing Equipment*

Shrink Packaging *See Packaging Materials & Supplies: Packaging: Shrink*

Shrinkers: Plastic *See Equipment & Machinery: Packaging: Shrinkers: Plastic Packaging*

Sieves *See Food Preparation Equipment, Utensils & Cookware: Sieves*

Sifters *See Food Preparation Equipment, Utensils & Cookware: Sifters*

Sign & Card Holders *See Foodservice Equipment & Supplies: Magnetic Pocket: Sign & Card Holders*

Signs *See Foodservice Equipment & Supplies: Signs*

Silver Cleaners *See Sanitation Equipment & Supplies: Cleaners: Silver*

Silverware Boxes *See Packaging Materials & Supplies: Boxes: Silverware*

Silverware Cleaning *See Sanitation Equipment & Supplies: Silverware Cleaning Machinery*

Sinks *See Building Equipment & Supplies: Sinks*

Sizers *See Equipment & Machinery: Sizers*

Skewers *See Food Preparation Equipment, Utensils & Cookware: Skewers*

Skids Systems *See Equipment & Machinery: Systems: Skids*

Skids *See Transportation & Storage: Skids*

Skin Cream & Lotions *See Sanitation Equipment & Supplies: Skin Cream & Lotions; Sanitation Equipment & Supplies: Skin Cream & Lotions: Skin Cream*

Skinning *See Equipment & Machinery: Food Processing: Skinning*

Sleeves *See Packaging Materials & Supplies: Sleeves*

Slicer *See Food Preparation Equipment, Utensils & Cookware: Slicer*

Slicers *See Equipment & Machinery: Food Processing: Slicers*

Slicing Knives *See Food Preparation Equipment, Utensils & Cookware: Knives: Slicing*

Smokers *See Equipment & Machinery: Food Processing: Smokers*

EXAMPLE: **Dairy Cooling Vats** *See Equipment & Machinery: Food Processing: Vats: Dairy Cooling*

1. Product or Service you are looking for
2. Main Category, in alphabetical order, located in the page headers starting on page 17
3. Category Description, located in black bars and in page headers
4. Product Category, located in gray bars
5. Product Type, located under gray bars, centered in bold

Snack Food *See Equipment & Machinery: Food Processing: Snack Food Processing*

Sneeze Guards *See Sanitation Equipment & Supplies: Sneeze Guards*

Soap Dispensers *See Sanitation Equipment & Supplies: Dispensers: Soap*

Soap *See Sanitation Equipment & Supplies: Soap*

Soda Fountain, Syrup & Fruit Juice Dispensers *See Foodservice Equipment & Supplies: Dispensers: Soda Fountain, Syrup & Fruit Juice*

Softeners *See Equipment & Machinery: Water Treatment: Softeners*

Software Computer *See Consultants & Services: Computer Software, Systems & Services: Software*

Software Process Controls *See Instrumentation & Laboratory Equipment: Process Controls: Software*

Sorters *See Equipment & Machinery: Food Processing: Sorters; Equipment & Machinery: Packaging: Sorters; Foodservice Equipment & Supplies: Sorters*

Soybean Processing *See Equipment & Machinery: Food Processing: Soybean Processing*

Speed Reducer *See Equipment & Machinery: Feeders: Gravimetric, Volumetric, Loss-In-Weight, Etc.: Speed Reducer*

Spice Grinding *See Equipment & Machinery: Food Processing: Mills: Spice Grinding*

Spice Racks *See Transportation & Storage: Racks: Spice*

Sponges *See Sanitation Equipment & Supplies: Sponges*

Spoons *See Food Preparation Equipment, Utensils & Cookware: Spoons*

Spray Dryers *See Equipment & Machinery: Food Processing: Dryers: Spray*

Spray Drying Services *See Consultants & Services: Spray Drying Services*

Spray Nozzles *See Equipment & Machinery: Nozzles: Spray*

Sprinkling Systems *See Sanitation Equipment & Supplies: Sprinkling Systems*

Squeegees *See Sanitation Equipment & Supplies: Squeegees*

Stacking *See Equipment & Machinery: Stacking*

Stainless Steel *See Food Preparation Equipment, Utensils & Cookware: Pans: Baking & Roasting: Stainless Steel; Equipment & Machinery: Coffee Industry: Stainless Steel*

Stainless Steel Hoods *See Building Equipment & Supplies: Hoods: Stainless Steel*

Stainless Steel Tables *See Food Preparation Equipment, Utensils & Cookware: Tables: Stainless Steel*

Stainless Steel Tanks *See Transportation & Storage: Tanks: Stainless Steel*

Stainless Steel Tubing *See Equipment & Machinery: Tubing: Stainless Steel*

Stamps *See Packaging Materials & Supplies: Stamps*

Stands *See Packaging Materials & Supplies: Stands*

Steak Knives *See Food Preparation Equipment, Utensils & Cookware: Knives: Steak*

Steam Cookers *See Equipment & Machinery: Food Processing: Cookers: Steam*

Steam Generators *See Equipment & Machinery: Steam Generators*

Steam Tables *See Equipment & Machinery: Steam Tables*

Steaming *See Food Preparation Equipment, Utensils & Cookware: Kettles: Steaming*

Steel Shelving *See Transportation & Storage: Shelving: Steel*

Stemmers *See Equipment & Machinery: Food Processing: Stemmers*

Sterilizers *See Sanitation Equipment & Supplies: Sterilizers*

Sticks *See Packaging Materials & Supplies: Sticks*

Stirrers & Picks *See Food Preparation Equipment, Utensils & Cookware: Stirrers & Picks: Cocktail, Hors D'oeuvres*

Stock Racks *See Transportation & Storage: Racks: Stock*

Stoppers *See Instrumentation & Laboratory Equipment: Stoppers*

Storage & Holding Equipment *See Transportation & Storage: Storage & Holding Equipment*

Storage Units *See Transportation & Storage: Storage Units*

Store Fixtures *See Foodservice Equipment & Supplies: Fixtures: Store*

Store Shelving *See Foodservice Equipment & Supplies: Shelving: Store*

Stoves *See Equipment & Machinery: Food Processing: Stoves*

Strainers *See Food Preparation Equipment, Utensils & Cookware: Strainers*

Straws *See Foodservice Equipment & Supplies: Straws*

Strech Sleeve *See Equipment & Machinery: Packaging: Strech Sleeve Application Equipment*

Strip Doors *See Building Equipment & Supplies: Doors: Strip*

Strips Wood Grain *See Foodservice Equipment & Supplies: Wood Grain Plastic: Strips*

Stuffers *See Equipment & Machinery: Food Processing: Stuffers*

Styrofoam Cups *See Packaging Materials & Supplies: Cups: Styrofoam*

Sub-Zero Freezers *See Refrigeration & Cooling Equipment: Freezers: Sub-Zero*

Sugar & Sugar Cane Mills *See Equipment & Machinery: Food Processing: Mills: Sugar & Sugar Cane*

Sugar & Syrup Kettles *See Food Preparation Equipment, Utensils & Cookware: Kettles: Sugar & Syrup*

Sugar & Syrup Processing *See Equipment & Machinery: Food Processing: Sugar & Syrup Processing*

Sugar Pulverizers *See Equipment & Machinery: Food Processing: Pulverizers: Sugar*

Sugars *See Instrumentation & Laboratory Equipment: Analyzers: Sugars (Dextrose, Fructose, Galactose, Lactose, Sucrose)*

Sweeping *See Sanitation Equipment & Supplies: Compounds: Sweeping*

Syrup & Soda Fountain Pumps *See Foodservice Equipment & Supplies: Pumps: Syrup & Soda Fountain*

Systems & Component *See Equipment & Machinery: Conveyors: Systems & Components*

Systems Process Controls *See Instrumentation & Laboratory Equipment: Process Controls: Systems*

Systems *See Equipment & Machinery: Systems*

T

Table Cloths *See Foodservice Equipment & Supplies: Table Cloths*

Tables *See Equipment & Machinery: Packaging: Tables; Food Preparation Equipment, Utensils & Cookware: Tables; Foodservice Equipment & Supplies: Tables*

Tabletop Supplies *See Equipment & Machinery: Tabletop Supplies*

Tags *See Packaging Materials & Supplies: Tags*

Tanks *See Equipment & Machinery: Food Processing:Tanks; Transportation & Storage: Tanks*

Tapes *See Packaging Materials & Supplies: Tapes*

Tea Bag *See Packaging Materials & Supplies: Tags: Tea Bag*

Tea Industry *See Equipment & Machinery: Tea Industry*

Tea Packaging *See Packaging Materials & Supplies: Tea Packaging Materials*

Temperature Controlled *See Transportation & Storage: Storage Units: Temperature Controlled*

Temperature Process Controls *See Instrumentation & Laboratory Equipment: Process Controls: Temperature*

Testers *See Instrumentation & Laboratory Equipment: Testers*

Testing & Sampling Services *See Consultants & Services: Testing & Sampling Services*

Thermal Shock Flooring *See Building Equipment & Supplies: Flooring: Thermal Shock*

Thermometers *See Instrumentation & Laboratory Equipment: Thermometers*

Ties *See Packaging Materials & Supplies: Ties*

Tilt Trucks *See Transportation & Storage: Trucks: Tilt*

Time Process *See Instrumentation & Laboratory Equipment: Process Controls: Time*

Timers *See Equipment & Machinery: Timers*

Tin Cans *See Packaging Materials & Supplies: Cans: Tin*

Tins *See Food Preparation Equipment, Utensils & Cookware: Tins*

Tinware *See Food Preparation Equipment, Utensils & Cookware: Tinware*

Tissue *See Sanitation Equipment & Supplies: Tissue*

Toasters *See Equipment & Machinery: Food Processing: Toasters*

Tongs *See Food Preparation Equipment, Utensils & Cookware: Tongs*

Toothpicks *See Food Preparation Equipment, Utensils & Cookware: Toothpicks*

Tortilla Making *See Equipment & Machinery: Food Processing: Tortilla Making*

Tote Bags *See Foodservice Equipment & Supplies: Tote Bags*

Towels *See Foodservice Equipment & Supplies: Towels*

Trailers *See Transportation & Storage: Trailers*

Transparent Wrappers *See Packaging Materials & Supplies: Wrappers: Transparent*

Transportation Loggers *See Instrumentation & Laboratory Equipment: Process Controls: Transportation Loggers*

Traps *See Sanitation Equipment & Supplies: Pest Control Systems & Devices: Traps*

Tray Sealers *See Equipment & Machinery: Packaging: Sealers: Tray*

Tray Stands *See Packaging Materials & Supplies: Stands: Tray*

Tray, Silverware Carts *See Foodservice Equipment & Supplies: Carts: Tray, Silverware*

Trays & Pans *See Food Preparation Equipment, Utensils & Cookware: Trays & Pans*

Trays Refrigerators *See Refrigeration & Cooling Equipment: Refrigerators: Trays*

Trays *See Foodservice Equipment & Supplies: Trays; Packaging Materials & Supplies: Trays*

Treatment Systems *See Equipment & Machinery: Water Treatment: Treatment Systems*

Truck, Trailer & Refrigerator Car *See Refrigeration & Cooling Equipment: Refrigerating Units: Truck, Trailer & Refrigerator Car*

Trucks *See Transportation & Storage: Trucks*

Tubing *See Equipment & Machinery: Tubing*

Tubularaseptic Processing *See Equipment & Machinery: Systems: Tubularaseptic Processing*

Turn Key *See Consultants & Services: Construction: Turn Key*

U

Ultrasonic Cutters *See Food Preparation Equipment, Utensils & Cookware: Cutters: Ultrasonic*

Uniforms *See Clothing & Protective Apparel: Uniforms & Special Clothing*

Unit, Packaging *See Instrumentation & Laboratory Equipment: Automation: Unit, Packaging, Bulk Handling*

Unscramblers *See Equipment & Machinery: Unscramblers*

Urns *See Foodservice Equipment & Supplies: Urns*

Utensils *See Food Preparation Equipment, Utensils & Cookware: Utensils; See also Foodservice Equipment & Supplies: Utensils*

Utility Carts *See Transportation & Storage: Carts: Utility*

Utility Vault Covers *See Transportation & Storage: Utility Vault Covers*

V

Vaccuum Bags *See Sanitation Equipment & Supplies: Vaccuum Bags*

Vacuum Cleaners *See Sanitation Equipment & Supplies: Vacuum Cleaners*

Vacuum Packing *See Equipment & Machinery: Packaging: Vacuum Packing*

Vacuum Process *See Instrumentation & Laboratory Equipment: Process Controls: Vacuum*

Valve Control *See Equipment & Machinery: Systems: Valve Control*

Valves *See Equipment & Machinery: Valves; Refrigeration & Cooling Equipment: Valves*

Vats *See Equipment & Machinery: Food Processing: Vats; Refrigeration & Cooling Equipment: Vats; Transportation & Storage: Vats*

Vegetable & Fruit Shredders *See Equipment & Machinery: Food Processing: Shredders: Vegetable & Fruit*

Vegetable & Fruit Slicers *See Equipment & Machinery: Food Processing: Slicers: Vegetable & Fruit*

Vegetable Cookers *See Equipment & Machinery: Food Processing: Cookers: Vegetable*

Vegetable Knives *See Food Preparation Equipment, Utensils & Cookware: Knives: Vegetable*

Vegetable Oil *See Sanitation Equipment & Supplies: Soap: Vegetable Oil*

Vegetable Preparation *See Equipment & Machinery: Food Processing: Vegetable Preparation Equipment*

Vegetable Processing *See Equipment & Machinery: Food Processing: Vegetable Processing*

Vender & Visi-Cooler Installation Systems *See Refrigeration & Cooling Equipment: Vender & Visi-Cooler Installation Systems*

Vending Carts *See Foodservice Equipment & Supplies: Vending Carts*

Vending Machinery *See Foodservice Equipment & Supplies: Vending Machinery*

Vertical Form, Fill & Seal *See Equipment & Machinery: Packaging: Form, Fill & Seal: Vertical*

Vibrators *See Equipment & Machinery: Food Processing: Vibrators*

Viscous Products *See Equipment & Machinery: Pumps: Viscous Products*

Vision Verification *See Equipment & Machinery: Systems: Vision Verification*

Vitamin Analyzers *See Instrumentation & Laboratory Equipment: Analyzers: Vitamin*

VOC Control *See Equipment & Machinery: Food Processing: VOC Control*

W

Waffle Irons *See Equipment & Machinery: Food Processing: Waffle Irons*

Walk-In Coolers *See Refrigeration & Cooling Equipment: Coolers: Walk-In*

Walk-In Freezers *See Refrigeration & Cooling Equipment: Freezers: Walk-In*

Warehouses *See Transportation & Storage: Warehouses*

Warmers *See Foodservice Equipment & Supplies: Warmers*

Washers & Fillers *See Equipment & Machinery: Food Processing: Tanks: Washers & Fillers*

Washers *See Equipment & Machinery: Food Processing: Washers*

Washing Compounds *See Sanitation Equipment & Supplies: Compounds: Washing*

Washing Machinery *See Sanitation Equipment & Supplies: Washing Machinery*

Washing, Drying & Polishing *See Sanitation Equipment & Supplies: Silverware Cleaning Machinery: Washing, Drying & Polishing*

Waste Boxes *See Packaging Materials & Supplies: Boxes: Waste*

Waste Handling & Disposal *See Sanitation Equipment & Supplies: Waste Handling & Disposal Equipment*

Wastewater Treatment *See Sanitation Equipment & Supplies: Wastewater Treatment Systems*

Water Activity *See Instrumentation & Laboratory Equipment: Analyzers: Water Activity*

Water Boilers *See Equipment & Machinery: Food Processing: Boilers: Water*

Water Heaters *See Equipment & Machinery: Heaters: Water*

Water Treatment *See Equipment & Machinery: Water Treatment*

Wax *See Packaging Materials & Supplies: Wax*

Waxed Paper *See Packaging Materials & Supplies: Paper: Waxed*

Waxers *See Equipment & Machinery: Food Processing: Waxers*

Waxing *See Equipment & Machinery: Food Processing: Waxing*

Webtension & Torque Controls *See Instrumentation & Laboratory Equipment: Controls: Webtension & Torque*

Weighing *See Equipment & Machinery: Packaging: Weighing*

Wet Strength Paper *See Packaging Materials & Supplies: Paper: Wet Strength*

Windows *See Building Equipment & Supplies: Windows*

Wine Presses *See Equipment & Machinery: Food Processing: Presses: Wine*

Wine Racks *See Transportation & Storage: Racks: Wine*

Wine Storage *See Transportation & Storage: Wine Storage Units*

Wipers *See Sanitation Equipment & Supplies: Wipers*

Wire Cloths *See Sanitation Equipment & Supplies: Cloths: Wire*

Wire Racks *See Transportation & Storage: Racks: Wire*

Wire Shelving *See Transportation & Storage: Shelving: Wire*

Wire Stitching *See Equipment & Machinery: Packaging: Wire Stitching*

Wirebound Boxes *See Packaging Materials & Supplies: Boxes: Wirebound*

Wood Boards *See Food Preparation Equipment, Utensils & Cookware: Boards: Wood*

Wood Grain Plastic *See Foodservice Equipment & Supplies: Wood Grain Plastic*

Wooden Boxes *See Packaging Materials & Supplies: Boxes: Wooden*

Wooden Forks *See Food Preparation Equipment, Utensils & Cookware: Utensils: Forks: Wooden*

Wooden Pallets *See Transportation & Storage: Pallets: Wooden*

Wooden Shipping Crates *See Packaging Materials & Supplies: Crates: Wooden Shipping*

Work Tables *See Food Preparation Equipment, Utensils & Cookware: Tables: Work*

Wrappers *See Packaging Materials & Supplies: Wrappers*

Wrapping *See Equipment & Machinery: Packaging: Wrapping*

Wrapping Paper *See Packaging Materials & Supplies: Paper: Wrapping*

Writing, Forms, Sales & Order Books *See Foodservice Equipment & Supplies: Paper: Writing, Forms, Sales & Order Books*

X

X-ray Contaminant Detection *See Equipment & Machinery: Systems: X-ray Contaminant Detection*

Y

Yeast Processing *See Equipment & Machinery: Food Processing: Yeast Processing*

Z

Zipper Application *See Equipment & Machinery: Systems: Zipper Application*

EXAMPLE: **Dairy Cooling Vats** *See Equipment & Machinery: Food Processing: Vats: Dairy Cooling*

1. Product or Service you are looking for
2. Main Category, in alphabetical order, located in the page headers starting on page 17
3. Category Description, located in black bars and in page headers
4. Product Category, located in gray bars
5. Product Type, located under gray bars, centered in bold

Building Equipment & Supplies

Air Curtains

Apollo Sheet Metal
Kennewick, WA 509-586-1104
Atlas Equipment Company
Kansas City, MO.................800-842-9188
Berner International Corp
New Castle, PA.................800-245-4455
Carnes Company
Verona, WI.................608-845-6411
Chase-Doors
Cincinnati, OH 800-543-4455
Curtainaire
Los Angeles, CA.................323-753-4266
Emco Industrial Plastics
Cedar Grove, NJ.................800-292-9906
Insect-O-Cutor Inc
Stone Mountain, GA.................800-966-8480
Kason
Lewis Center, OH.................740-549-2100
Kason Industries
Newnan, GA.................770-254-0553
King Company
Dallas, TX.................507-451-3770
Lechler Inc
St Charles, IL 800-777-2926
Mankato Tent & Awning Co
North Mankato, MN.................866-747-3524
Mars Air Products
Gardena, CA.................800-421-1266
Plas-Ties Co
Tustin, CA.................800-854-0137
Products A Curtron Div
Pittsburgh, PA.................800-888-9750
QUIKSERV Corp
Houston, TX.................800-388-8307
Ready Access
Chicago, IL 800-621-5045
Stonhard, Inc.
Maple Shade, NJ
Universal Jet Industries
Hialeah, FL 305-887-4378

Air Filters

Air Quality Engineering
Minneapolis, MN 800-328-0787
Airsan Corp
Milwaukee, WI.................800-558-5494
Allergen Air Filter Corp
Houston, TX 800-333-8880
American Ultraviolet Co
Lebanon, IN 800-288-9288
AMSOIL Inc
Superior, WI.................715-392-7101
Beach Filter Products
Hanover, PA 800-232-2485
Blue Tech
Hickory, NC 828-324-5900
CLARCOR Air Filtration Prods
Jeffersonville, IN 866-247-4827
Clyde Bergemann Eec
Halethorpe, MD.................410-712-4280
Dwyer Instruments Inc
Michigan City, IN.................800-872-3141
Eco-Air Products
San Diego, CA 800-284-8111
Elwood Safety Company
Buffalo, NY.................866-326-6060
Falls Filtration Technologies
Stow, OH.................330-928-4100
Flanders Corp
Washington, NC 800-637-2803
Freudenberg Nonwovens
Hopkinsville, KY 270-887-5115
G.W. Dahl Company
Greensboro, NC 800-852-4449
Gaylord Industries
Tualatin, OR 800-547-9696
Halton Company
Scottsville, KY 800-442-5866
Hunter Fan Co
Cordova, TN 901-743-1360
KETCH
Wichita, KS 800-766-3777
King Bag & Mfg Co
Cincinnati, OH 800-444-5464

King Company
Dallas, TX.................507-451-3770
King Engineering - King-Gage
Newell, WV 800-242-8871
Lamports Filter Media
Cleveland, OH 216-881-2050
Mars Air Products
Gardena, CA.................800-421-1266
Monroe Environmental Corp
Monroe, MI.................800-992-7707
Parker-Hannifin Corp
Jeffersonville, IN 866-247-4827
Refractron Technologies Corp
Newark, NY.................315-331-6222
Rolfs @ Boone
Boone, IA 800-265-2010
Ultra Industries Inc
Racine, WI.................800-358-5872
United Air Specialists Inc
Blue Ash, OH 800-992-4422
United States Systems Inc
Kansas City, KS 888-281-2454
Vent Master
Mississauga, ON 800-565-2981
VMC Signs
Victoria, TX.................361-575-0548

Awnings

A A A Awning Co Inc
Houston, TX.................800-281-6193
A&A International
Virginia Beach, VA.................800-252-1446
Academy Awning
Los Angeles, CA.................310-277-8383
Acme Awning
Salinas, CA.................831-424-7134
Acme Awning Co Inc
Bronx, NY.................718-409-1822
Advanced Design Awning & Sign
Cloquet, MN.................800-566-8368
Allied Electric Sign & Awning
Salt Lake City, UT.................801-972-6837
Alpha Canvas & Awning Co
Charlotte, NC.................800-583-9179
Alpha Productions Inc
Los Angeles, CA.................800-223-0883
American Sun Control Awnings
Alpharetta, GA.................800-245-6746
Anchor Industries
Evansville, IN.................812-867-2421
Andgar Corp
Ferndale, WA.................360-366-9900
Arrow Sign & Awning Company
East Bethel, MN.................800-621-9231
Avalon Canvas & Upholstery Inc
Houston, TX.................713-607-9289
Avondale Mills
Monroe, GA.................770-267-2226
Awning Co Inc
Sag Harbor, NY.................631-725-3651
Awning Enterprises
Frederick, MD.................800-735-2453
Awnings by Dee
Little Neck, NY.................516-487-6688
Awnings Plus
Addison, IL 888-627-4770
B & W Awning Co
Lexington, KY 859-252-1619
B H Awning & Tent Co
Benton Harbor, MI.................800-272-2187
Belle Isle Awning
Roseville, MI 586-294-6050
Bower's Awning & Shade
Lebanon, PA 717-273-2351
Brock Awnings LTD
Hampton Bays, NY.................631-728-3367
C.B. Dombach & Son
Lancaster, PA 717-392-0578
Cain Awning Co Inc
Birmingham, AL.................205-323-8379
Camel Canvas Shop
Knoxville, TN.................800-524-2704
Canvas Products
Grand Junction, CO 970-242-1453

Capitol Awning Co Inc
Jamaica, NY 800-241-3539
Charlotte Tent & Awning
Charlotte, NC 704-921-8743
Chattin Awning Company
Edison, NJ.................800-394-3500
Chesterfield Awning Co
Chicago, IL 800-339-6522
Childres Custom Canvas Prods
Duncanville, TX.................972-298-4943
Chilson's Shops Inc
Easthampton, MA.................413-529-8062
City Canvas
San Jose, CA.................408-287-2688
Coastal Canvas Products
Savannah, GA.................800-476-5174
Creative Canopy Design
Hernando Beach, FL.................866-970-5200
Custom Tarpaulin Products Inc
Youngstown, OH.................888-394-5054
Dade Canvas Products Company
Silver Spring, MD.................301-680-2500
Danieli Awnings
Napa, CA.................707-257-6100
Darlington Sign Awning & Neon
Warwick, RI 401-734-5800
Dean Custom Awning
Orangeburg, NY.................845-425-6678
Delta Signs
Haltom City, TX.................866-643-3582
Despro Manufacturing
Cedar Grove, NJ.................800-292-9906
Dize Co
Winston Salem, NC.................800-583-8243
Dualite Sales & Svc Inc
Williamsburg, OH.................513-724-7100
Durasol Awnings
Middletown, NY.................800-444-6131
Ehmke Manufacturing
Philadelphia, PA.................215-324-4200
Eide Industries Inc
Cerritos, CA 800-422-6827
Elegant Awnings
Chino, CA 800-541-9011
Encore Image Inc
Ontario, CA.................800-791-1187
Engineered Textile Products
Mobile, AL 800-222-8277
Evanston Awning Co
Evanston, IL 847-864-4520
F & S Awning & Sign Co
Edison, NJ.................732-738-4110
Fort Wayne Awning
Fort Wayne, IN 800-404-1636
French Awning & Screen Co Inc
Jackson, MS 800-898-1132
Fresno Tent & Awning
Fresno, CA.................559-264-4771
FTL/Happold Tensil Structure Design & Engineering
New York, NY.................212-732-4691
G & J Awning & Canvas Inc
Sauk Rapids, MN 800-467-1744
Geneva Awning & Tent Works Inc
Geneva, NY.................800-789-3151
Georgia Tent & Awning
Atlanta, GA.................800-252-2391
Glawe Manufacturing Company
Fairborn, OH.................800-434-8368
Glen Raven Custom Fabrics LLC
Burlington, NC.................336-227-6211
Global Canvas Products
Philadelphia, PA.................267-634-6207
Goodwin-Cole Co Inc
Sacramento, CA 800-752-4477
Greeley Tent & Awning Co
Greeley, CO.................970-352-0253
Greenville Awning Company
Mauldin, SC 864-288-0063
H.B. Wall & Sons
Ozark, MO.................800-373-1616
Hamilton Awning Co
Beaver, PA.................724-774-7644
Hendee Enterprises Inc
Houston, TX.................800-231-7275
Hogshire Industries
Norfolk, VA.................757-877-2297

J & J Window Sales Inc
Chesterfield, MO 636-532-3320
J W Hulme Co
St Paul, MN.................800-442-8212
Jamestown Awning
Jamestown, NY................716-483-1435
Kohler Awning Inc
Buffalo, NY.................800-875-9091
LA Graphics
Greenville, SC...............864-297-1111
Lafayette Tent & Awning Co
Lafayette, IN................800-458-2955
Laggren's LLC
Monroe Twp, NJ...............609-235-9883
Laurel Awning Co
Apollo, PA..................888-567-5689
Lawrence Fabric Structures
St Louis, MO................800-527-3840
Leavitt & Parris Inc
Portland, ME................800-833-6679
Lincoln Tent Inc
Lincoln, NE.................800-567-4559
Lloyd's of Millville
Millville, NJ................856-825-0345
Macon Awning & Canvas Prod
Macon, GA..................478-743-2684
Maple Leaf Awning & Canvas Co
Sherwood, AR................800-947-4233
Marygrove Awnings-Toledo
Perrysburg, OH...............419-241-9181
Mason City Tent & Awning Co
Mason City, IA...............641-423-0044
Merrillville Awning Co
Merrillville, IN..............800-781-6100
Metal Master Sales Corp
Glendale Heights, IL...........800-488-8729
Miami Awning
Miami, FL..................800-576-0222
Mid-State Awning & Patio Co
Bellefonte, PA...............814-355-8979
Modesto Tent & Awning
Modesto, CA................209-545-6150
Moran Canvas Products Inc
La Mesa, CA................800-515-1130
Mt. Lebanon Awning & Tent Company
Presto, PA.................412-221-2233
Muskegon Awning & Fabrication
Muskegon, MI...............800-968-3686
Neilson Canvas Company
Sandusky, OH...............419-625-0581
New Haven Awnings
New Haven, CT...............800-560-5650
Niantic Awning Company
Windham, NH................978-225-0108
O'Brian Tarping Systems Inc
Wilson, NC.................800-334-8277
Oklahoma Neon
Tulsa, OK..................888-707-6366
Omar Awnings & Signs
Johnson City, TN.............800-274-6627
Ottumwa Tent & Awning Co
Ottumwa, IA................641-682-2257
Palo Alto Awning
San Jose, CA................800-400-4270
Parasol Awnings
Memphis, TN................901-368-4477
Patio Center Inc
Lafayette, LA...............337-233-9896
Pease Awning & Sunroom Co
East Providence, RI...........401-438-2850
Peoria Tent & Awning
Peoria, IL..................309-674-1128
Pike Awning Co
Portland, OR................800-866-9172
Pride Neon Inc
Sioux Falls, SD..............605-336-3561
Quality Aluminum & Hm Imprvmt
Columbus, MS...............662-329-2525
Queen City Awning
Cincinnati, OH...............513-530-9660
R J Mc Cullough Co
Lancaster, PA...............717-735-8772
Reliable Tent & Awning Co
Billings, MT................800-544-1039
RHG Products Company
Castle Rock, CO..............800-553-8131
Rose City Awning Co
Portland, OR................800-446-4104
S L Doery & Son Inc
Lawrence, NY................516-239-8090
San Jose Awnings
San Jose, CA................800-872-9646

Shadetree Canopies
Columbus, OH...............800-894-3801
Shaffer Sports & Events
Houston, TX................713-699-0088
Signtech Electrical Advg Inc
San Diego, CA...............619-527-6100
Sommer Awning Company
Indianapolis, IN.............855-257-4301
South Akron Awning Co
Akron, OH..................330-848-7611
South Jersey Awning
Egg Harbor Township, NJ........609-646-2002
Southern Awning & Sign Company
Woodstock, GA...............770-516-8652
Sundance Architectural Prod
Orlando, FL................800-940-1337
Sunmaster Of Naples Inc
Naples, FL.................239-261-3581
Taylor Made Custom Products
Gloversville, NY.............518-725-0681
TCT&A Industries
Urbana, IL.................800-252-1355
The Canvas Exchange Inc
Cleveland, OH...............216-749-2233
Thermal Bags By Ingrid Inc
Gilberts, IL................800-622-5560
Total Identity Group
Cambridge, ON...............877-551-5529
USA Canvas Shoppe
Dallas, TX.................877-626-8468
Van Nuys Awning Co
Van Nuys, CA...............818-345-4926
Vermont Tent Co
South Burlington, VT..........800-696-8368
Vernon Plastics
Haverhill, MA...............978-373-1551
Walker Engineering Inc
Sun Valley, CA..............818-252-7788
William J. Mills & Company
Greenport, NY...............800-477-1535
Williams Shade & Awning Company
Memphis, TN................901-368-5055
York Tent & Awning
York, PA...................800-864-3510

Ceiling Surfaces & Panels

Arcoplast Wall & Ceiling Systems
St Peters, MO...............888-736-2726

Decking

Metal

Slip Not
Detroit, MI.................800-754-7668

Doors

Air Curtain

Aleco Food Svc Div
Muscle Shoals, AL............800-633-3120
Apple-A-Day Nutritional Labeling Service
San Clemente, CA.............949-855-8954
Atlas Equipment Company
Kansas City, MO..............800-842-9188
Berner International Corp
New Castle, PA...............800-245-4455
Kason Vinyl Products
Newnan, GA.................800-472-7450
Products A Curtron Div
Pittsburgh, PA...............800-888-9750

Corrosion Resistant

Air-Lec Industries, Inc
Madison, WI................608-244-4754
Chem Pruf Door Co LTD
Brownsville, TX..............800-444-6924

Double Acting

Carlson Products
Maize, KS..................800-234-1069
Coldmatic Refrigeration
Concord, ON................905-326-7600
Eliason Corp
Portage, MI................800-828-3655
Products A Curtron Div
Pittsburgh, PA...............800-888-9750
Super Seal ManufacturingLimited
Woodbridge, ON..............800-337-3239

Plastic

Aleco Food Svc Div
Muscle Shoals, AL............800-633-3120
Chase-Doors
Cincinnati, OH...............800-543-4455
Coldmatic Refrigeration
Concord, ON................905-326-7600
FIB-R-DOR
Cincinnati, OH...............800-342-7367
Firl Industries Inc
Fond Du Lac, WI..............800-558-4890
Hormann Flexan Llc
Leetsdale, PA...............800-365-3667
Products A Curtron Div
Pittsburgh, PA...............800-888-9750
Reese Enterprises Inc
Rosemount, MN...............800-328-0953
Seville Display Door
Temecula, CA................800-634-0412
Trimline Corp
Elkhart Lake, WI.............800-555-5895
VT Industries Inc
Holstein, IA................800-827-1615
Western Laminates
Omaha, NE.................402-556-4600

Strip

Aleco Food Svc Div
Muscle Shoals, AL............800-633-3120
Berner International Corp
New Castle, PA...............800-245-4455
Coastal Canvas Products
Savannah, GA...............800-476-5174
Davlynne International
Cudahy, WI.................800-558-5208
Environmental Products Company
North Aurora, IL.............800-677-8479
Firl Industries Inc
Fond Du Lac, WI..............800-558-4890
Flame Gard
Lakewood, NJ...............800-526-3694
Kason Industries
Newnan, GA.................770-254-0553
Kason Vinyl Products
Newnan, GA.................800-472-7450
Kelley Company
Carrollton, TX...............800-558-6960
Manufacturing Warehouse
Miami, FL..................305-635-8886
Products A Curtron Div
Pittsburgh, PA...............800-888-9750
Reese Enterprises Inc
Rosemount, MN...............800-328-0953
Super Seal ManufacturingLimited
Woodbridge, ON..............800-337-3239
Superior Products Company
Saint Paul, MN..............800-328-9800
Tuckahoe Manufacturing Co
Vineland, NJ................800-220-3368
WORC Slitting & Mfg Co
Worcester, MA...............800-356-2961

Fans

Ceiling

Acme Engineering & Mfg Corp
Muskogee, OK...............918-682-7791
Airmaster Fan Co
Jackson, MI................800-255-3084
Canarm, Ltd.
Brockville, ON...............613-342-5424
Carnes Company
Verona, WI.................608-845-6411
Ceilcote Air Pollution Control
Middleburg Hts, OH...........800-554-8673
Con-tech/Conservation Technology
Northbrook, IL..............800-728-0312
Fountainhead
Bensalem, PA...............800-326-8998
Halton Company
Scottsville, KY..............800-442-5866
Hartzell Fan Inc
Piqua, OH..................800-336-3267
Hunter Fan Co
Cordova, TN................901-743-1360
Larkin Industries
Birmingham, AL..............800-322-4036
Main Lamp Corp
Brooklyn, NY................718-436-8500

Nalge Process Technologies Group
  Rochester, NY 585-586-8800
Nu-Con Equipment
  Chanhassen, MN 877-939-0510
Panasonic Commercial Food Service
  Newark, NJ
Penn Barry
  Plano, TX 972-212-4700
SEC
  Plymouth, MI 734-455-4500
Stegall Mechanical INC
  Birmingham, AL 800-633-4373
West Metals
  London, ON 800-300-6667

Flooring

Ahlstrom Filtration LLC
  Madisonville, KY 270-821-0140
Kalman Floor Co Inc
  Evergreen, CO. 866-266-7146
Marazzi USA
  Sunnyvale, TX 972-232-3801
Stonhard
  Maple Shade, NJ 800-257-7953
VibroFloors World
  Fayetteville, GA 770-632-9701

Anti-Slip

Advanced Surfaces Corp
  Villa Rica, GA. 800-963-4632
Slip Not
  Detroit, MI 800-754-7668

Floor Mats

A&A Line & Wire Corporation
  Flushing, NY. 800-886-2657
Airomat Corp
  Fort Wayne, IN 800-348-4905
Atlantic Rubber Products
  East Wareham, MA. 800-695-0446
Boardman Molded Products Inc
  Youngstown, OH. 800-233-4575
Cactus Mat ManufacturingCompany
  El Monte, CA. 626-579-6287
Collins & Aikman
  Canton, OH. 800-321-0244
Corson Rubber Products Inc
  Clover, SC. 803-222-7779
Durable Corp
  Norwalk, OH. 800-537-1603
Golden Star
  N Kansas City, MO. 800-821-2792
JCH International
  Rome, GA. 800-328-9203
John Rohrer Contracting Co
  Kansas City, KS 913-236-5005
Matrix Engineering
  Vero Beach, FL. 800-926-0528
R C Musson Rubber Co
  Akron, OH. 800-321-2381
Reese Enterprises Inc
  Rosemount, MN 800-328-0953
Superior Products Company
  Saint Paul, MN 800-328-9800
Tepromark International
  Osseo, MN 800-645-2622
United Textile Distribution
  Garner, NC 800-262-7624
Wearwell/Tennessee Mat Company
  Nashville, TN 615-254-8381

Industrial Flooring

Corro-Shield International Inc
  Rosemont, IL. 800-298-7637
Dura-Flex
  East Hartford, CT 877-251-5418
Grating Pacific Inc
  Los Alamitos, CA. 800-321-4314
Kagetec
  Montgomery, MN 612-435-7640
Sanicrete
  Farmington Hills, MI 248-893-1000
Tufco International
  Gentry, AR 800-364-0836
VibroFloors World
  Fayetteville, GA 770-632-9701

Mats & Matting

Airomat Corp
  Fort Wayne, IN 800-348-4905
Amco Metals Indl
  City Of Industry, CA. 626-855-2550
Artex International
  Highland, IL 618-654-2113
Atlantic Rubber Products
  East Wareham, MA. 800-695-0446
Atlas Equipment Company
  Kansas City, MO. 800-842-9188
Baker Concrete Construction
  Monroe, OH 800-539-2224
Best Brands Home Products
  New York, NY 212-684-7456
Boardman Molded Products Inc
  Youngstown, OH. 800-233-4575
C R Mfg
  Waverly, NE 877-789-5844
Cactus Mat ManufacturingCompany
  El Monte, CA 626-579-6287
Coast Scientific
  Rancho Santa Fe, CA 800-445-1544
Coburn Company
  Whitewater, WI 800-776-7042
Collins & Aikman
  Canton, OH 800-321-0244
Conimar Corp
  Ocala, FL. 800-874-9735
Continental Identification
  Sparta, MI 800-247-2499
Continental Industrial Supply
  South Pasadena, FL. 727-341-1100
Corson Rubber Products Inc
  Clover, SC. 803-222-7779
Custom Table Pads
  St Paul, MN. 800-325-4643
Dorado Carton Company
  Dorado, PR. 787-796-1670
Drehmann Paving & Flooring Company
  Pennsauken, NJ 800-523-3800
Durable Corp
  Norwalk, OH. 800-537-1603
Golden Star
  N Kansas City, MO. 800-821-2792
Gourmet Table Skirts
  Houston, TX 800-527-0440
Harsco Industrial IKG
  Garrett, IN. 800-467-2345
Have Our Plastic Inc
  Mississauga, ON 800-263-5995
Hoffmaster Group Inc
  Oshkosh, WI 800-327-9774
J. James
  Brooklyn, NY 718-384-6144
J.M. Rogers & Sons
  Moss Point, MS 228-475-7584
J.V. Reed & Company
  Louisville, KY 877-258-7333
Jack the Ripper Table Skirting
  Stafford, TX 800-331-7831
JCH International
  Rome, GA 800-328-9203
John Rohrer Contracting Co
  Kansas City, KS 913-236-5005
Jr Mats
  West Chester, PA. 800-526-7763
K-C Products Company
  Van Nuys, CA 818-267-1600
Larco
  Brainerd, MN 800-523-6996
Matrix Engineering
  Vero Beach, FL 800-926-0528
Millard Manufacturing Corp
  La Vista, NE 800-662-4263
Newell Brands
  Atlanta, GA
Northland Process Piping
  Isle, MN 320-679-2119
Paradise Products
  El Cerrito, CA. 800-227-1092
Proffitt Manufacturing Company
  Dalton, GA 800-241-4682
R C Musson Rubber Co
  Akron, OH. 800-321-2381
Reese Enterprises Inc
  Rosemount, MN 800-328-0953
Royal Paper Products
  Coatesville, PA. 800-666-6655
Saunders Manufacturing Co.
  N Kansas City, MO. 800-821-2792

SCA Tissue
  Philadelphia, PA 866-722-8675
Scranton Lace Company
  Forest City, PA 800-822-1036
Smith-Lee Company
  Oshkosh, WI 800-327-9774
Sultan Linen Inc
  New York, NY 212-689-8900
Summitville Tiles Inc
  Summitville, OH 330-223-1511
Superior Products Company
  Saint Paul, MN 800-328-9800
Tag-Trade Associated Group
  Chicago, IL. 800-621-8350
Tara Linens
  Sanford, NC 800-476-8272
Tennant Co.
  Minneapolis, MN 800-553-8033
Tepromark International
  Osseo, MN 800-645-2622
United Textile Distribution
  Garner, NC 800-262-7624
Wearwell/Tennessee Mat Company
  Nashville, TN 615-254-8381

Metal

Slip Not
  Detroit, MI 800-754-7668

Safety

Slip Not
  Detroit, MI 800-754-7668

Thermal Shock

Resistant Flooring

Dura-Flex
  East Hartford, CT 877-251-5418

Grating

Metal

Slip Not
  Detroit, MI 800-754-7668

Heating, Ventilation & Air Conditioning

A C Horn & Co Sheet Metal
  Dallas, TX. 800-657-6155
A.K. Robins
  Baltimore, MD 800-486-9656
A.O. Smith Water Products Company
  Irving, TX 800-527-1953
Acme Engineering & Mfg Corp
  Muskogee, OK 918-682-7791
ADDCHEK Coils
  Fort Mill, SC. 803-547-7566
Advanced Control Technologies
  Indianapolis, IN 800-886-2281
Aei Corp
  Irvine, CA 949-474-3070
AERCO International Inc
  Blauvelt, NY. 800-526-0288
Aerolator Systems
  Monroe, NC 800-843-8286
Aerovent Co
  Minneapolis, MN 763-551-7500
AFGO Mechanical Svc Inc
  Astoria, NY 800-438-2346
Air Quality Engineering
  Minneapolis, MN 800-328-0787
Airmaster Fan Co
  Jackson, MI. 800-255-3084
Airsan Corp
  Milwaukee, WI 800-558-5494
All State Fabricators Corporation
  Tampa, FL. 800-322-9925
Allergen Air Filter Corp
  Houston, TX 800-333-8880
Allied Engineering
  North Vancouver, BC 877-929-1214
Allstrong Restaurant Eqpt Inc
  South El Monte, CA 800-933-8913
ALPI Food Preparation Equipment
  Bolton, ON 800-928-2574
American Coolair Corp
  Jacksonville, FL 904-389-3646

American Radionic Co Inc
Palm Coast, FL .800-445-6033
American Range
Pacoima, CA 888-753-9898
American Ventilation Company
Grafton, OH 800-854-3267
Andersen 2000
Peachtree City, GA 800-241-5424
Anderson Snow Corp
Schiller Park, IL 800-346-2645
Andgar Corp
Ferndale, WA 360-366-9900
Apollo Sheet Metal
Kennewick, WA 509-586-1104
Ari Industries Inc
Addison, IL 800-237-6725
Armstrong International
Three Rivers, MI 269-273-1415
Ayr King Corp
Louisville, KY 866-266-6290
Babcock & Wilcox Power Generation Group
Barberton, OH 800-222-2625
Baltimore Aircoil Co
Jessup, MD 410-799-1300
Barbeque Wood Flavors Enterprises
Ennis, TX 972-875-8391
Bbc Industries
Pacific, MO 800-654-4205
Becker Brothers Graphite Co
Maywood, IL 708-410-0700
Berner International Corp
New Castle, PA 800-245-4455
Bessamaire Sales Inc
Streetsboro, OH 800-321-5992
Betz Entec
Horsham, PA 800-877-1940
Bioclimatic Air Systems LLC
Delran, NJ 800-962-5594
BKI Worldwide
Simpsonville, SC 800-927-6887
Bryan Boilers
Peru, IN 765-473-6651
Caddy Corporation of America
Bridgeport, NJ 856-467-4222
Canarm, Ltd.
Brockville, ON 613-342-5424
Carnes Company
Verona, WI 608-845-6411
Carroll Manufacturing International
Florham Park, NJ 800-444-9696
Ceilcote Air Pollution Control
Middleburg Hts, OH 800-554-8673
CEM Corporation
Matthews, NC 800-726-3331
Chesmont Engineering Co Inc
Exton, PA 610-594-9200
Chillers Solutions
Pompton Plains, NJ 800-526-5201
Cleaver-Brooks Inc
Thomasville, GA 800-250-5583
Climate Master Inc
Oklahoma City, OK 877-436-0263
CMT
Hamilton, MA 978-768-2555
Commercial Kitchen Co
Los Angeles, CA 323-732-2291
Con-tech/Conservation Technology
Northbrook, IL 800-728-0312
Continental Refrigerator
Bensalem, PA 800-523-7138
Control Pak Intl
Fenton, MI 810-735-2800
Convectronics
Haverhill, MA 800-633-0166
Cook & Beals Inc
Loup City, NE 308-745-0154
Cooling Products Inc
Broken Arrow, OK 918-251-8588
Cooperheat/MQS
Alvin, TX 800-526-4233
Crispy Lite
St. Louis, MO 888-356-5362
Curtainaire
Los Angeles, CA 323-753-4266
Custom Food Machinery
Stockton, CA 209-463-4343
Delfield Co
Mt Pleasant, MI 800-733-8821
Delta Cooling Towers Inc
Rockaway, NJ 800-289-3358
Direct Fire Technical
Benbrook, TX 888-920-2468

Doucette Industries
York, PA 800-445-7511
Dreaco Products
Elyria, OH 800-368-3267
Duke Manufacturing Co
St Louis, MO 800-735-3853
Duo-Aire
Winter Haven, FL 863-294-2272
Dwyer Instruments Inc
Michigan City, IN 800-872-3141
Dynamic Cooking Systems
Huntington Beach, CA 800-433-8466
Eclipse Innovative Thermal Solutions
Toledo, OH 800-662-3966
Economy Paper & Restaurant Co
Clifton, NJ 973-279-5500
Eldorado Miranda Manufacturing Company
Largo, FL 800-330-0708
Elmwood Sensors
Pawtucket, RI 800-356-9663
Energymaster
Walled Lake, MI 248-624-6900
Environmental Products Company
North Aurora, IL 800-677-8479
Epcon Industrial Systems
Conroe, TX 800-447-7872
ET International Technologies
Wheat Ridge, CO 855-412-5726
Exhausto
Atlanta, GA 800-255-2923
F.M. Corporation
Deerfield Beach, FL 954-570-9860
Flame Gard
Lakewood, NJ 800-526-3694
Flanders Corp
Washington, NC 800-637-2803
Floaire
Blue Bell, PA 800-726-5623
Fountainhead
Bensalem, PA 800-326-8998
G W Berkheimer Co
Fort Wayne, IN 800-535-6696
Garland Commercial Ranges
Mississauga, ON 905-624-0260
Gaylord Industries
Tualatin, OR 800-547-9696
Glo-Quartz Electric Heater
Mentor, OH 800-321-3574
Governair Corp
Oklahoma City, OK 405-525-6546
Grease Master
Matthews, NC 704-844-6907
Greenheck Fan Corp
Schofield, WI 715-359-6171
Greitzer
Elizabeth City, NC 252-338-4000
Grillco Inc
Aurora, IL 800-644-0067
Grinnell Fire ProtectionSystems Company
Westminster, MA 800-746-7539
Gustave A Larson Co
Pewaukee, WI 262-542-0200
Hallock Fabricating Corp
Riverhead, NY 631-727-2441
Halton Company
Scottsville, KY 800-442-5866
Hanson Lab Furniture Inc
Newbury Park, CA 805-498-3121
Hartzell Fan Inc
Piqua, OH 800-336-3267
Harvey W Hottel Inc
Gaithersburg, MD 301-921-9599
Heatrex
Meadville, PA 800-394-6589
Hemco Corp
Independence, MO 800-779-4362
Hercules Food Equipment
Weston, ON 416-742-9673
Holman Boiler Works
Dallas, TX 800-331-1956
Hunter Fan Co
Cordova, TN 901-743-1360
Hydro-Thermal Corp
Waukesha, WI 800-952-0121
Ice-Cap
Piermont, NY 888-423-2270
ICM Controls
North Syracuse, NY 800-365-5525
Illinois Range Company
Schiller Park, IL 800-535-7041
J L Becker Co
Plymouth, MI 800-837-4328

Jacob Tubing LP
Memphis, TN 901-566-1110
Jarvis-Cutter Company
Boston, MA 617-567-7532
KEMCO
Wareham, MA 800-231-5955
King Company
Dallas, TX 507-451-3770
Lakewood Engineering & Manufacturing Company
Chicago, IL 800-621-4277
Larkin Industries
Birmingham, AL 800-322-4036
LDI Manufacturing Co
Logansport, IN 800-366-2001
Loren Cook Co
Springfield, MO 800-289-3267
Low Humidity Systems
Covington, GA 770-788-6744
Ludell Manufacturing Co
Milwaukee, WI 800-558-0800
Lumsden Flexx Flow
Lancaster, PA 800-367-3664
Machine Ice Co
Houston, TX 800-423-8822
Mars Air Products
Gardena, CA 800-421-1266
Marshall Air Systems Inc
Charlotte, NC 800-722-3474
Master Air
Lebanon, IN 800-248-8368
MCM Fixture Co
Hazel Park, MI 248-547-9280
Meadows Mills Inc
North Wilkesboro, NC 800-626-2282
Met-Pro Corp
Owosso, MI 989-725-8185
Metal Master Sales Corp
Glendale Heights, IL 800-488-8729
Microtechnologies
Plainville, CT 888-248-7103
Milvan Food Equipment Manufacturing
Rexdale, ON 416-674-3456
Moll-Tron
Lakewood, CO 800-525-9494
Monroe Environmental Corp
Monroe, MI 800-992-7707
Monroe Extinguisher Co Inc
Rochester, NY 585-235-3310
MovinCool/DENSO Products and Services Americas
Long Beach, CA 800-264-9573
Muckler Industries, Inc
Saint Louis, MO 800-444-0283
Muellermist Irrigation Company
Broadview, IL 708-450-9595
Munters Corp
Amesbury, MA 800-843-5360
Nalge Process Technologies Group
Rochester, NY 585-586-8800
National FABCO Manufacturing
St Louis, MO 314-842-4571
Newtech Inc
Randolph, VT 800-210-2361
Noren Products Inc
Menlo Park, CA 866-936-6736
Novar
Cleveland, OH 800-348-1235
Nu-Con Equipment
Chanhassen, MN 877-939-0510
NuTone
Cincinnati, OH 888-336-3948
Omnitemp Refrigeration
Downey, CA 800-423-9660
Pacific Steam Equipment, Inc.
Santa Fe Springs, CA 800-321-4114
Panasonic Commercial Food Service
Newark, NJ
Parkland
Houston, TX 713-926-5055
Partnership Resources
Minneapolis, MN 612-331-2075
Patterson-Kelley   Hars Company
East Stroudsburg, PA 570-421-7500
Peerless of America
Lincolnshire, IL 847-634-7500
Penn Barry
Plano, TX 972-212-4700
Precision Temp Inc
Cincinnati, OH 800-934-9690
Premium Air Systems Inc
Troy, MI 877-430-0333
Process Heating Co
Seattle, WA 866-682-1582

Process Heating Corp
  Shrewsbury, MA 508-842-5200
Products A Curtron Div
  Pittsburgh, PA 800-888-9750
Proheatco Manufacturing
  Pomona, CA 800-423-4195
R K Electric Co Inc
  Mason, OH 800-543-4936
Raypak Inc
  Oxnard, CA. 805-278-5300
Roberts-Gordon LLC
  Buffalo, NY. 800-828-7450
Ron Vallort & Associates
  Oak Brook, IL. 630-734-3821
Royal Prestige Health Moguls
  Westbury, NY .888-802-7433
S&P USA Ventilation Systems, LLC
  Jacksonville, FL 800-961-7370
Scroll Compressors LLC
  Sidney, OH 937-498-3011
Seasons 4 Inc
  Douglasville, GA 770-489-5405
Seattle Boiler Works Inc
  Seattle, WA 206-762-0737
Sellers Engineering Division
  Danville, KY 859-236-3181
South Valley Mfg Inc
  Gilroy, CA. 408-842-5457
Southern Metal Fabricators Inc
  Albertville, AL 800-989-1330
Spencer Turbine Co
  Windsor, CT 800-232-4321
Spiral Manufacturing Co Inc
  Minneapolis, MN 800-426-3643
Stainless International
  Rancho Cordova, CA 888-300-6196
Stainless Steel Fabricators
  Tyler, TX 903-595-6625
Standex International Corp.
  Salem, NH. 603-893-9701
Stegall Mechanical INC
  Birmingham, AL 800-633-4373
Sterling Ball & Jewel
  New Berlin, WI. 800-423-3183
Storm Industrial
  Shawnee Mission, KS. 800-745-7483
Sturdi-Bilt Restaurant Equipment
  Whitmore Lake, MI 800-521-2895
Super Radiator Coils
  N Chesterfield, VA 800-229-2645
Thermalogic Corp
  Hudson, MA 978-562-5974
Toronto Kitchen Equipment
  North York, ON. 416-745-4944
Trane Inc
  Davidson, NC .704-655-4000
Tru Form Plastics
  Gardena, CA 800-510-7999
Ultrafryer Systems Inc
  San Antonio, TX. 800-545-9189
United Fire & Safety Service
  Yonkers, NY 914-968-4459
Universal Jet Industries
  Hialeah, FL 305-887-4378
USECO
  Murfreesboro, TN. 615-893-4820
Vapor Power Intl LLC
  Franklin Park, IL. 888-874-9020
Vent Master
  Mississauga, ON 800-565-2981
Vent-A-Hood Co
  Richardson, TX. 800-331-2492
Vilter Manufacturing Corporation
  Cudahy, WI 414-744-0111
Vulcan Electric Co
  Porter, ME. 800-922-3027
Water Furnace Renewable Energy
  Fort Wayne, IN 260-478-5667
Welbilt Corporation
  Stamford, CT. .203-325-8300
West Metals
  London, ON 800-300-6667
West Star Industries
  Stockton, CA. .800-326-2288
Westfield Sheet Metal Works
  Kenilworth, NJ 908-276-5500
Zmd International
  Long Beach, CA 800-222-9674

Heating

Electric

INDEECO
  St Louis, MO. .800-243-8162

Hoods

Stainless Steel

AGET Manufacturing Co
  Adrian, MI. 517-263-5781

Lighting Equipment

Fluorescent

Eaton Corporation
  Beachwood, OH 800-386-1911
Insect-O-Cutor Inc
  Stone Mountain, GA. 800-966-8480
Lumax Industries
  Altoona, PA. 814-944-2537
Nemco Electric Company
  Seattle, WA 206-622-1551
Oetiker Inc
  Marlette, MI 800-959-0398
Trojan Inc
  Mt Sterling, KY 800-264-0526
UDEC Corp
  Woburn, MA 800-990-8332

Incandescent

Apex Fountain Sales Inc
  Philadelphia, PA 800-523-4586
Boyd Lighting Company
  Sausalito, CA .415-778-4300
Candle Lamp Company
  Corona, CA. 877-526-7748
Command Electronics Inc
  Schoolcraft, MI 269-679-4011
Dura Electric Lamp Company
  Newark, NJ 973-624-0014
G Lighting
  St Louis, MO. .800-331-2425
GE Lighting
  Cleveland, OH 800-435-4448
Holcor
  Riverdale, IL. .708-841-3800
Hubbell Lighting Inc
  Greenville, SC. 864-678-1000
Hybrinetics Inc
  Santa Rosa, CA. 800-247-6900
Indy Lighting
  Fishers, IN. 317-849-1233
Le Jo Enterprises
  Phoenixville, PA 484-924-9187
Luxo Corporation
  Elmsford, NY .800-222-5896
Mason Candlelight Company
  New Albany, MS. 800-556-2766
Nova Industries
  San Leandro, CA. 510-357-0171
Osram Sylvania
  Danvers, MA. .800-544-4828
Philips Lighting Company
  Somerset, NJ 732-563-3000
Prescolite
  Vallejo, CA 707-562-3500
QSR Industrial Supply
  Cherry Hill, NJ 800-257-8282
Renovator's Supply
  Conway, NH 800-659-0203
Sterno
  Lombard, IL 630-792-0080
Strand Lighting
  Dallas, TX. 214-647-7880
Super Vision International
  Orlando, FL. 407-857-9900
Superior-Studio Specialties
  Commerce, CA 800-354-3049
SuppliesForLess
  Hampton, VA .800-235-2201
Trojan Inc
  Mt Sterling, KY 800-264-0526

Lighting Fixtures

Electric

Action Lighting
  Bozeman, MT .800-248-0076
ALP Lighting & Ceiling Products
  Pennsauken, NJ 800-633-7732
Apogee Translite Inc
  Deer Park, NY .631-254-6975
Apollo Acme Lighting Fixture
  Mount Vernon, NY 800-833-9006
Architectural Products
  Highland, NY .845-691-8500
Art Craft Lighting
  Champlain, NY 718-387-8000
Azz/R-A-L
  Houston, TX 713-943-0340
Boyd Lighting Company
  Sausalito, CA .415-778-4300
Brinkmann Corporation
  Dallas, TX. 800-468-5252
C W Cole & Co
  South El Monte, CA 626-443-2473
Capitol Hardware, Inc.,
  Middlebury, IN 800-327-6083
Caselites
  Hialeah, FL 305-819-7766
Casella Lighting
  Sacramento, CA 916-363-2888
Chapman Manufacturing Co Inc
  Avon, MA 508-587-7592
Claude Neon Signs
  Baltimore, MD 410-685-7575
Columbia Jet/JPL
  Houston, TX 800-876-4511
Columbia Lighting
  Greenville, SC. 864-678-1000
Commercial Lighting Design
  Memphis, TN .800-774-5799
Con-tech/Conservation Technology
  Northbrook, IL 800-728-0312
Coronet Chandelier Originals
  Brentwood, NY 631-273-1177
County Neon Sign Corporation
  Plainview, NY .516-349-9550
Custom Lights & Iron
  National City, CA 858-274-7070
Custom Metalcraft, Architectural Lighting
  Boston, MA. 617-242-0868
D'Ac Lighting
  Mamaroneck, NY 914-698-5959
D'Lights
  Glendale, CA .818-956-5656
E-Lite Technologies
  Trumbull, CT .877-520-3951
Eclipse Electric Manufacturing
  St Louis Park, MN 952-929-2500
Econo Frost Night Covers
  Shawnigan Lake, BC 800-519-1222
Edison Price Lighting
  Long Island City, NY 718-685-0700
EGS Electrical Group
  Skokie, IL. 847-679-7800
Electrodex
  Bradenton, FL .800-362-1972
ESD Energy Saving Devices
  St Paul, MN. 651-222-0849
Eximco Manufacturing Company
  Chicago, IL. 773-463-1470
Fenton Art Glass Company
  Williamstown, WV 800-933-6766
Forum Lighting
  Pittsburgh, PA .412-781-5970
Fredrick Ramond Company
  Avon Lake, OH 800-446-5539
G Lighting
  St Louis, MO. .800-331-2425
GE Lighting
  Cleveland, OH 800-435-4448
Gem Electric Manufacturing Company
  Hauppauge, NY 800-275-4361
GERM-O-RAY
  Stone Mountain, GA. 800-966-8480
Glass Industries America LLC
  Wallingford, CT 203-269-6700
Greene Brothers
  Brooklyn, NY .718-388-6800
Guth Lighting
  Saint Louis, MO 314-533-3200
H & H Metal Fabrication Inc
  Belden, MS 662-489-4626

Hanson Brass Rewd Co
Sun Valley, CA 888-841-3773
Hart Designs LLC
Ruston, LA 800-592-3500
Hub Electric Company
Crystal Lake, IL 815-455-4400
Hubbell Lighting Inc
Greenville, SC. 864-678-1000
Hydrel Corporation
Sylmar, CA 818-362-9465
Indy Lighting
Fishers, IN. 317-849-1233
Insect-O-Cutor Inc
Stone Mountain, GA. 800-966-8480
JDO/LNR Lighting
Live Oak, TX 800-597-1570
Jet Lite Products
Highland, IL 618-654-2217
JJI Lighting Group, Inc.
Franklin Park, IL. 847-451-0700
Kensington Lighting Corp
Greensburg, PA 800-434-5005
Kim Lighting
City of Industry, CA 626-968-5666
Kreissle Forge Ornamental
Sarasota, FL 941-355-6795
Le Jo Enterprises
Phoenixville, PA. 484-924-9187
Legion Lighting Co Inc
Brooklyn, NY 800-453-4466
Light Waves Concept
Brooklyn, NY 800-670-8137
Lightolier
Fall River, MA 508-679-8131
Lights On
Yonkers, NY 914-961-0588
Linear Lighting Corp
Long Island City, NY 718-361-7552
Litecontrol
Plympton, MA. 781-294-0164
Lithonia Lighting
Conyers, GA 770-922-9000
Little Giant Pump Company
Fort Wayne, IN 260-824-2900
Louis Baldinger & Sons
New York, NY 718-204-5700
Luminiere Corporation
Bronx, NY. 718-295-5450
Luxo Corporation
Elmsford, NY 800-222-5896
Main Lamp Corp
Brooklyn, NY 718-436-8500
Majestic
Bridgeport, CT 203-367-7900
Manning Lighting Inc
Sheboygan, WI 920-458-2184
Meil Electric Fixture Manufacturing Company
Philadelphia, PA 215-228-8528
Mobern Electric Corporation
Jessup, MD 800-444-9288
Modulightor Inc
New York, NY 212-371-0336
Mulholland-Harper Company
Denton, MD 800-882-3052
Natale Machine & Tool Co Inc
Carlstadt, NJ 800-883-8382
Nemco Electric Company
Seattle, WA 206-622-1551
Neo-Ray Products
Brooklyn, NY 800-221-0946
Newstamp Lighting Factory
North Easton, MA. 508-238-7073
Nova Industries
San Leandro, CA 510-357-0171
Nulco Lighting
Providence, RI 401-728-5200
Osram Sylvania
Danvers, MA. 800-544-4828
Palmer Distributors
St Clair Shores, MI 800-444-1912
Peerless Lighting Corporation
Berkeley, CA. 510-845-2760
Philadelphia Glass Bending Company
Philadelphia, PA 215-726-8468
Prescolite
Vallejo, CA 707-562-3500
Primlite Manufacturing Corporation
Freeport, NY 800-327-7583
Remcraft Lighting Products
Miami, FL. 800-327-6585
Ryther-Purdy
Old Saybrook, CT. 860-388-4405

Sea Gull Lighting Products, LLC
Corona, CA 800-347-5483
Simkar Corp
Philadelphia, PA 215-831-7700
Standex International Corp.
Salem, NH. 603-893-9701
Sterner Lighting Systems
Greenville, SC. 866-898-0131
Strand Lighting
Dallas, TX. 214-647-7880
Super Vision International
Orlando, FL. 407-857-9900
Swivelier Co Inc
Blauvelt, NY 845-353-1455
Tech Lighting LLC
Skokie, IL 800-323-3226
Thomas Lighting Residential
Rosemont, IL. 800-825-5844
Toronto Fabricating & Manufacturing
Mississauga, ON 905-891-2516
Troy Lighting
City Of Industry, CA 800-533-8769
Tru Form Plastics
Gardena, CA 800-510-7999
U L Wholesale Lighting Fixture
Long Island City, NY 718-726-7500
UDEC Corp
Woburn, MA 800-990-8332
V&R Metal Enterprises
Brooklyn, NY 718-768-8142
Versailles Lighting
Delray Beach, FL 888-564-0240
Vimco
King Of Prussia, PA 610-768-0500
Voigt Lighting Industries Inc.
Garfield, NJ 973-928-2252
Western Lighting Inc
Franklin Park, IL. 847-451-7200
Weston Emergency Light Co
Weston, MA 800-649-3756
Yorkraft
York, PA .800-872-2044
Zelco Industries
Mount Vernon, NY 800-431-2486
Zumtobel Staff Lighting
Highland, NY 845-691-6262

Emergency

ALP Lighting & Ceiling Products
Pennsauken, NJ. 800-633-7732
Architectural Products
Highland, NY 845-691-8500
Big Beam Emergency Systems Inc
Crystal Lake, IL 815-459-6100
Brinkmann Corporation
Dallas, TX. 800-468-5252
Carpenter Emergency Lighting
Hamilton, NJ. 888-884-2270
Claude Neon Signs
Baltimore, MD 410-685-7575
Crouse-Hinds
Syracuse, NY 866-764-5454
Eaton Corporation
Beachwood, OH 800-386-1911
Gilbert Insect Light Traps
Jonesboro, AR. 800-643-0400
HD Electric Co
Park City, IL 847-473-4882
Hubbell Lighting Inc
Greenville, SC. 864-678-1000
Natale Machine & Tool Co Inc
Carlstadt, NJ 800-883-8382
Roflan Associates
Tulsa, OK 978-475-0100
UDEC Corp
Woburn, MA 800-990-8332
Weston Emergency Light Co
Weston, MA 800-649-3756

Fluorescent

ALP Lighting & Ceiling Products
Pennsauken, NJ. 800-633-7732
American Louver Co
Skokie, IL 800-772-0355
Apollo Acme Lighting Fixture
Mount Vernon, NY 800-833-9006
C W Cole & Co
South El Monte, CA 626-443-2473
Claude Neon Signs
Baltimore, MD 410-685-7575

Columbia Lighting
Greenville, SC. 864-678-1000
Command Electronics Inc
Schoolcraft, MI 269-679-4011
Crownlite Manufacturing Corporation
Bohemia, NY 631-589-9100
D'Ac Lighting
Mamaroneck, NY 914-698-5959
Day-O-Lite
Warwick, RI 401-467-8232
Diversified Lighting Diffusers Inc
Copiague, NY 800-234-5464
Dura Electric Lamp Company
Newark, NJ 973-624-0014
Edison Price Lighting
Long Island City, NY 718-685-0700
ESD Energy Saving Devices
St Paul, MN. 651-222-0849
Eximco Manufacturing Company
Chicago, IL 773-463-1470
Forum Lighting
Pittsburgh, PA. 412-781-5970
Garvin Industries
Franklin Park, IL. 847-451-6500
GE Lighting
Cleveland, OH 800-435-4448
GENESTA
Rockwall, TX 972-771-1653
GERM-O-RAY
Stone Mountain, GA 800-966-8480
Guth Lighting
Saint Louis, MO 314-533-3200
H & H Metal Fabrication Inc
Belden, MS 662-489-4626
Hasco Electric Corporation
Greenwich, CT 203-531-9400
Hastings Lighting Company
Los Angeles, CA. 213-622-2009
Holcor
Riverdale, IL 708-841-3800
Hybrinetics Inc
Santa Rosa, CA 800-247-6900
Illumination Products Inc
San Juan, PR 787-754-7193
Indy Lighting
Fishers, IN. 317-849-1233
Insect-O-Cutor Inc
Stone Mountain, GA 800-966-8480
Kensington Lighting Corp
Greensburg, PA 800-434-5005
Legion Lighting Co Inc
Brooklyn, NY 800-453-4466
Lightolier
Fall River, MA 508-679-8131
Lithonia Lighting
Conyers, GA 770-922-9000
Louisville Lamp Co
Louisville, KY 502-964-4094
Lumax Industries
Altoona, PA. 814-944-2537
Luxo Corporation
Elmsford, NY 800-222-5896
Meil Electric Fixture Manufacturing Company
Philadelphia, PA 215-228-8528
Nemco Electric Company
Seattle, WA 206-622-1551
Neo-Ray Products
Brooklyn, NY 800-221-0946
Osram Sylvania
Danvers, MA. 800-544-4828
Panasonic Commercial Food Service
Newark, NJ
Paramount Industries
Croswell, MI 800-521-5405
Peerless Lighting Corporation
Berkeley, CA. 510-845-2760
Philips Lighting Company
Somerset, NJ. 732-563-3000
Prudential Lighting
Vernon, CA 800-421-5483
Remcraft Lighting Products
Miami, FL. 800-327-6585
Roflan Associates
Tulsa, OK 978-475-0100
Ryther-Purdy
Old Saybrook, CT. 860-388-4405
Shat R Shield Inc
Salisbury, NC 800-223-0853
Shelden, Dickson, & Steven Company
Omaha, NE 402-571-4848
Simkar Corp
Philadelphia, PA 215-831-7700

Steel Craft Fluorescent Company
Newark, NJ 973-349-1614
Super Vision International
Orlando, FL 407-857-9900
Toronto Fabricating & Manufacturing
Mississauga, ON 905-891-2516
Trojan Inc
Mt Sterling, KY .800-264-0526
UDEC Corp
Woburn, MA 800-990-8332
Varco Products
Chardon, OH 216-481-6895
Versailles Lighting
Delray Beach, FL 888-564-0240
Visual Marketing Assoc
Santee, CA 619-258-0393
Zumtobel Staff Lighting
Highland, NY 845-691-6262

Mercury, High Intensity

GE Lighting
Cleveland, OH .800-435-4448
Grating Pacific Inc
Los Alamitos, CA 800-321-4314
Guth Lighting
Saint Louis, MO 314-533-3200
Holcor
Riverdale, IL 708-841-3800
Hubbell Lighting Inc
Greenville, SC 864-678-1000
J M Canty Inc E1200 Engineers
Lockport, NY 716-625-4227
Prescolite
Vallejo, CA 707-562-3500

Outdoor

Apollo Acme Lighting Fixture
Mount Vernon, NY 800-833-9006
Brinkmann Corporation
Dallas, TX 800-468-5252
Claude Neon Signs
Baltimore, MD 410-685-7575
Crouse-Hinds
Syracuse, NY 866-764-5454
Eaton Corporation
Beachwood, OH 800-386-1911
Faribault Manufacturing Co
Faribault, MN 800-447-6043
GE Lighting
Cleveland, OH .800-435-4448
Hub Electric Company
Crystal Lake, IL .815-455-4400
Hubbell Lighting Inc
Greenville, SC 864-678-1000
Lightolier
Fall River, MA 508-679-8131
Linear Lighting Corp
Long Island City, NY 718-361-7552
Little Giant Pump Company
Fort Wayne, IN .260-824-2900
Natale Machine & Tool Co Inc
Carlstadt, NJ 800-883-8382
Nu-Dell Manufacturing
Des Plaines, IL .847-803-4500
Prescolite
Vallejo, CA 707-562-3500
Primlite Manufacturing Corporation
Freeport, NY 800-327-7583
Progress Lighting
Spartanburg, SC 864-599-6000
QSR Industrial Supply
Cherry Hill, NJ .800-257-8282
Remcraft Lighting Products
Miami, FL 800-327-6585
Sterner Lighting Systems
Greenville, SC 866-898-0131
Thomas Lighting Residential
Rosemont, IL 800-825-5844
Troy Lighting
City of Industry, CA 800-533-8769
Valmont Composite Structures
Newberry, SC 800-800-9008
Zelco Industries
Mount Vernon, NY 800-431-2486

Paging Systems

Command Communications
Centennial, CO .800-288-3491
Instacomm Canada
Oakville, ON 877-426-2783

Long Range Systems
Addison, TX 800-577-8101
NTN Wireless
Norcross, GA 800-637-8639
UAA
Chicago, IL 800-813-1711

Radios

Long Range Systems
Addison, TX 800-577-8101

Panels

Insulated

Advance Energy Technologies
Halfmoon, NY 800-724-0198
Extrutech Plastics Inc
Manitowoc, WI .888-818-0118
Kingspan Insulated Panels, Ltd.
Langley, BC 877-638-3266
Zeroloc
Kirkland, WA 425-823-4888

Platforms

C&R Refrigation Inc,
Center, TX 800-438-6182
Delkor Systems, Inc
Minneapolis, MN 800-328-5558
Slip Not
Detroit, MI 800-754-7668

Plating

Metal

Slip Not
Detroit, MI 800-754-7668

Sinks

Advance Tabco
Edgewood, NY .800-645-3166
Aero Manufacturing Co
Clifton, NJ 800-631-8378
All State Fabricators Corporation
Tampa, FL 800-322-9925
Amtekco
Columbus, OH .800-336-4677
Baker & Co
Norfolk, VA 800-909-4325
Bar Equipment Corporation of America
Downey, CA 888-870-2322
Baxter Manufacturing Inc
Orting, WA 800-777-2828
Best Sanitizers Inc
Penn Valley, CA 888-225-3267
Carts Food Equipment
Brooklyn, NY 718-788-5540
Component Hardware Group Inc
Lakewood, NJ 800-526-3694
Crown Steel Mfg
San Marcos, CA 760-471-1188
D A Berther Inc
Milwaukee, WI .877-357-9622
Den Mar Corp
North Dartmouth, MA 508-999-3295
Duke Manufacturing Co
St Louis, MO 800-735-3853
Duluth Sheet Metal
Duluth, MN 218-722-2613
Dunhill Food Equipment Corporation
Armonk, NY 800-847-4206
Eagle Foodservice   Equipment
Clayton, DE 800-441-8440
Eagle Group
Clayton, DE 800-441-8440
Eldorado Miranda Manufacturing Company
Largo, FL 800-330-0708
Erwin Food Service Equipment
Fort Worth, TX .817-535-0021
Eskay Metal Fabricating
Buffalo, NY 800-836-8015
Fab-X/Metals
Washington, NC 800-677-3229
Fabwright Inc
Garden Grove, CA 800-854-6464
Fisher Manufacturing Company
Tulare, CA 800-421-6162
G K & L Inc
Dickerson, MD .301-948-5538

Griffin Products
Wills Point, TX .800-379-9709
Hercules Food Equipment
Weston, ON 416-742-9673
IMC Teddy Food Service Equipment
Amityville, NY .800-221-5644
Insinger Co
Philadelphia, PA 800-344-4802
John Boos & Co
Effingham, IL 888-431-2667
KEMCO
Wareham, MA .800-231-5955
Kitchen Equipment Fabricating
Houston, TX 713-747-3611
Kitcor Corp
Sun Valley, CA .818-767-4800
Krowne Metal Corp
Wayne, NJ 800-631-0442
La Crosse
Onalaska, WI 800-345-0018
Lambertson Industries Inc
Sparks, NV 800-548-3324
Load King Mfg
Jacksonville, FL 800-531-4975
M-One Specialties
Salt Lake City, UT 800-525-9223
Marlo Manufacturing
Boonton, NJ 800-222-0450
MCM Fixture Co
Hazel Park, MI .248-547-9280
Metal
Columbia, SC 803-776-9252
Metal Kitchen Fabricators Inc
Houston, TX 713-683-8375
Metal Master Sales Corp
Glendale Heights, IL 800-488-8729
Missouri Equipment
St Louis, MO 800-727-6326
Moli-International
Denver, CO 800-525-8468
National Bar Systems
Huntington Beach, CA 714-848-1688
National FABCO Manufacturing
St Louis, MO 314-842-4571
National Scoop & Equipment Company
Spring House, PA 215-646-2040
Polar Ware Company
Sheboygan, WI .800-237-3655
Premium Air Systems Inc
Troy, MI 877-430-0333
Reliable Food Service Equipment
Concord, ON 416-738-6840
Sefi Fabricators Inc
Amityville, NY .631-842-2200
St. Louis Stainless Service
St Louis, MO 800-735-3853
Stainless
La Vergne, TN .800-877-5177
Stainless Equipment Manufacturing
Dallas, TX 800-736-2038
Stainless Fabricating Company
Denver, CO 800-525-8966
Stainless International
Rancho Cordova, CA 888-300-6196
Stainless Steel Fabricators
Tyler, TX 903-595-6625
Starlite Food Service Equipment
Detroit, MI 888-521-6603
Super Sturdy
Weldon, NC 800-253-4833
Superior Products Company
Saint Paul, MN .800-328-9800
Supreme Metal
Alpharetta, GA .800-645-2526
T & S Brass & Bronze Work
Travelers Rest, SC 800-476-4103
Terriss Consolidate
Asbury Park, NJ 800-342-1611
Tru Form Plastics
Gardena, CA 800-510-7999
United Fabricators
Fort Smith, AR .800-235-4101
Universal Stainless
Aurora, CO 800-223-8332
Universal Stainless & Alloy
Titusville, PA 800-295-1909
Weiss Sheet Metal Inc
Avon, MA 508-583-8300
West Metals
London, ON 800-300-6667
West Star Industries
Stockton, CA 800-326-2288

Windows

Drive-Thru & Pass-Thru

Ayr King Corp
Louisville, KY 866-266-6290

Bullet Guard Corporation
West Sacramento, CA 800-233-5632
Creative Industries Inc
Indianapolis, IN 800-776-2068

QUIKSERV Corp
Houston, TX 800-388-8307
Ready Access
Chicago, IL 800-621-5045

Clothing & Protective Apparel

Aprons

A Allred Marketing
Birmingham, AL...................205-251-3700
A.D. Cowdrey Company
Modesto, CA.....................209-538-4677
Adcapitol
Monroe, NC......................800-868-7111
Adex Medical Inc
Riverside, CA...................800-873-4776
Akron Cotton Products
Akron, OH.......................800-899-7173
Alex Delvecchio Enterprises
Troy, MI.......................248-619-9600
American Advertising & Shop Cap Company
Old Tappan, NJ.................800-442-8837
American Apron Inc.
Foxboro, MA....................800-262-7766
American Bag & Linen Co
Cornelia, GA...................706-778-5377
ATD-American Co
Wyncote, PA....................800-523-2300
Atlantic Mills
Lakewood, NJ...................800-242-7374
Bennett's Auto Inc
Neenah, WI.....................800-215-5464
Best Brands Home Products
New York, NY...................212-684-7456
Best Manufacturing
Jersey City, NJ................201-356-3800
Best Value Textiles
North Charleston, SC...........800-858-8589
Boss Manufacturing Co
Kewanee, IL....................800-447-4581
Bragard Professional Uniforms
New York, NY...................800-488-2433
Carson Manufacturing Company
Petaluma, CA...................800-423-2380
Celebrity Promotions
Remsen, IA.....................800-332-6847
Champaign Plastics Company
Champaign, IL..................800-575-0170
Champion America Inc
Branford, CT...................800-521-7000
Charles Craft Inc
Laurinburg, NC.................910-844-3521
Christman Screenprint Inc
Springfield, MI................800-962-9330
Coast Scientific
Rancho Santa Fe, CA............800-445-1544
David Dobbs Enterprise Inc.
St Augustine, FL...............800-889-6368
Dove Screen Printing Co
Royston, GA....................706-245-4975
Elwood Safety Company
Buffalo, NY....................866-326-6060
Erell Manufacturing Co
Elk Grove Vlg, IL..............800-622-6334
Erie Cotton Products
Erie, PA.......................800-289-4737
Fabohio Inc
Uhrichsville, OH...............740-922-4233
Fabriko
Altavista, VA..................888-203-8098
Flavor Wear
Valley Center, CA..............800-647-8372
Foley's Famous Aprons
Wayne, MI......................800-634-3245
Funny Apron Co
Lake Dallas, TX................800-835-5802
Gary Manufacturing Company
National City, CA..............800-775-0804
Gourmet Table Skirts
Houston, TX....................800-527-0440
Gril-Del
Mankato, MN....................800-782-7320
Hall Safety Apparel
Uhrichsville, OH...............800-232-3671
Handgards Inc
El Paso, TX....................800-351-8161
Hank Rivera Associates
Dearborn, MI...................313-581-8300
Hygrade Gloves
Brooklyn, NY...................800-233-8100
Island Poly
Westbury, NY...................800-338-4433

Jomac Products
Niles, IL......................800-566-2289
Kennedy's Specialty Sewing
Erin, ON.......................519-833-9306
Keystone Adjustable Cap Co Inc
Pennsauken, NJ.................800-663-5439
Klever Kuvers
Pasadena, CA...................626-355-8441
LaCrosse Safety and Industrial
Portland, OR...................800-557-7246
Landau Uniforms Inc
Olive Branch, MS...............800-238-7513
Lexidyne of Pennsylvania
Pittsburgh, PA.................800-543-2233
Liberty Ware LLC
Clearfield, UT.................888-500-5885
Locknane
Everett, WA....................800-848-9854
Mell & Co
Niles, IL......................800-262-6355
Midwest Promotional Group
Summit, IL.....................800-305-3388
Milliken & Co
Spartanburg, SC................864-503-2020
National Embroidery Svc Inc
Portsmouth, RI.................800-227-1451
New Chief Fashion
Vernon, CA.....................800-639-2433
New Hatchwear Company
Calgary, AB....................800-661-9249
Omni Apparel
Carrollton, GA.................770-838-1008
Pacific Oasis Enterprise Inc
Santa Fe Springs, CA...........800-424-1475
PolyConversions, Inc.
Rantoul, IL....................888-893-3330
Pop Tops Co Inc
South Easton, MA...............800-647-8677
Rodes Professional Apparel
Louisville, KY.................502-584-3112
Royal Paper Products
Coatesville, PA................800-666-6655
S & H Uniform Corp
White Plains, NY...............800-210-5295
Seven Mile Creek Corp
Eaton, OH......................800-497-6324
Shen Manufacturing Co Inc
Conshohocken, PA...............610-825-2790
ST Restaurant Supplies
Delta, BC......................888-448-4244
Sultan Linen Inc
New York, NY...................212-689-8900
Superior Linen & Work Wear
Kansas City, MO................800-798-7987
Superior Menus
Mankato, MN....................800-464-2182
Superior Uniform Group
Seminole, FL...................800-727-8643
Tara Linens
Sanford, NC....................800-476-8272
Triad Products Company
Springfield, OH................937-323-9422
Tronex Industries
Denville, NJ...................800-833-1181
Tucker Industries
Colorado Springs, CO...........800-786-7287
Universal Overall
Chicago, IL....................800-621-3344
Vicmore Manufacturing Company
Brooklyn, NY...................800-458-8663
Whiting & Davis
Attleboro Falls, MA............800-876-6374
World Pride
St Petersburg, FL..............800-533-2433

Canners' & Packers'

A.D. Cowdrey Company
Modesto, CA....................209-538-4677
Alabama Bag Co Inc
Talladega, AL..................800-888-4921
American Apron Inc.
Foxboro, MA....................800-262-7766
American Bag & Linen Co
Cornelia, GA...................706-778-5377

Bennett's Auto Inc
Neenah, WI.....................800-215-5464
Champaign Plastics Company
Champaign, IL..................800-575-0170
Champion America Inc
Branford, CT...................800-521-7000
Elwood Safety Company
Buffalo, NY....................866-326-6060
Erell Manufacturing Co
Elk Grove Vlg, IL..............800-622-6334
Gary Manufacturing Company
National City, CA..............800-775-0804
Hall Safety Apparel
Uhrichsville, OH...............800-232-3671
Island Poly
Westbury, NY...................800-338-4433
Kennedy's Specialty Sewing
Erin, ON.......................519-833-9306
Locknane
Everett, WA....................800-848-9854
Seven Mile Creek Corp
Eaton, OH......................800-497-6324
Whiting & Davis
Attleboro Falls, MA............800-876-6374

Dairy

American Apron Inc.
Foxboro, MA....................800-262-7766
Champaign Plastics Company
Champaign, IL..................800-575-0170
Champion America Inc
Branford, CT...................800-521-7000
Erell Manufacturing Co
Elk Grove Vlg, IL..............800-622-6334
Seven Mile Creek Corp
Eaton, OH......................800-497-6324

Caps

A Allred Marketing
Birmingham, AL.................205-251-3700

Gloves

Bakers'

Best Value Textiles
North Charleston, SC...........800-858-8589
Champion America Inc
Branford, CT...................800-521-7000
Golden Needles Knitting & Glove Company
Coshocton, OH..................919-667-5102
Great Southern Corp
Memphis, TN....................800-421-7802
Hygrade Gloves
Brooklyn, NY...................800-233-8100
Jomac Products
Niles, IL......................800-566-2289
Panhandler, Inc.
Cordova, TN....................800-654-7237

Disposable

Adex Medical Inc
Riverside, CA..................800-873-4776
AEP Industries Inc
Mankato, MN....................800-999-2374
Afassco
Minden, NV.....................775-783-3555
Alabama Bag Co Inc
Talladega, AL..................800-888-4921
Ansell Healthcare Inc
Iselin, NJ.....................800-800-0444
Bennett's Auto Inc
Neenah, WI.....................800-215-5464
Boss Manufacturing Co
Kewanee, IL....................800-447-4581
Champaign Plastics Company
Champaign, IL..................800-575-0170
Coast Scientific
Rancho Santa Fe, CA............800-445-1544
Erie Cotton Products
Erie, PA.......................800-289-4737
Gann Manufacturing
Baltimore, MD..................800-922-9832

George Glove Company, Inc
Midland Park, NJ 800-631-4292
Goldmax Industries
City Of Industry, CA................626-964-8820
Great Southern Corp
Memphis, TN 800-421-7802
Handgards Inc
El Paso, TX......................800-351-8161
Hygrade Gloves
Brooklyn, NY 800-233-8100
John Plant Co
Ramseur, NC 800-334-2711
Liberty Ware LLC
Clearfield, UT...................888-500-5885
Ontario Glove and Safety Products
Kitchener, ON....................800-265-4554
Pacific Oasis Enterprise Inc
Santa Fe Springs, CA 800-424-1475
Playtex Products, LLC
New Providence, NJ 888-310-4290
Rochester Midland Corp
Rochester, NY 800-387-7174
Royal Paper Products
Coatesville, PA 800-666-6655
Superior Products Company
Saint Paul, MN 800-328-9800
Textile Buff & Wheel
Charlestown, MA 617-241-8100
Triad Scientific
Manasquan, NJ 800-867-6690
Tronex Industries
Denville, NJ 800-833-1181
Wilkens-Anderson Co
Chicago, IL......................800-847-2222
Y-Pers Inc
Philadelphia, PA 800-421-0242

Plastic, Rubber

Allied Glove Corporation
Milwaukee, WI...................800-558-9263
Ansell Healthcare Inc
Iselin, NJ 800-800-0444
Boss Manufacturing Co
Kewanee, IL.....................800-447-4581
Carolina Glove Co
Conover, NC 800-335-1918
Champaign Plastics Company
Champaign, IL...................800-575-0170
Champion America Inc
Branford, CT.....................800-521-7000
Choctaw-Kaul Distribution Company
Detroit, MI......................313-894-9494
Coast Scientific
Rancho Santa Fe, CA 800-445-1544
Comasec Safety, Inc.
Enfield, CT 800-333-0219
Eagle Home Products
Huntington, NY 631-673-3500
Erie Cotton Products
Erie, PA.........................800-289-4737
George Glove Company, Inc
Midland Park, NJ 800-631-4292
Glover Latex
Anaheim, CA 800-243-5110
Goldmax Industries
City Of Industry, CA................626-964-8820
Great Southern Corp
Memphis, TN 800-421-7802
Hall Safety Apparel
Uhrichsville, OH..................800-232-3671
Handgards Inc
El Paso, TX......................800-351-8161
Hygrade Gloves
Brooklyn, NY 800-233-8100
Island Poly
Westbury, NY 800-338-4433
Lambert Company
Chillicothe, MO 800-821-7667
Monte Glove Company
Wilkesboro, NC 662-263-5353
Ontario Glove and Safety Products
Kitchener, ON....................800-265-4554
Pacific Oasis Enterprise Inc
Santa Fe Springs, CA 800-424-1475
Playtex Products, LLC
New Providence, NJ 888-310-4290
Quality Mop & Brush Manufacturers
Needham, MA....................617-884-2999
Rochester Midland Corp
Rochester, NY 800-387-7174

Sterling Rubber
Fergus, ON 519-843-4032
Tronex Industries
Denville, NJ 800-833-1181
Wells Lamont
Niles, IL.........................800-323-2830
Y-Pers Inc
Philadelphia, PA 800-421-0242

Protective

Alabama Bag Co Inc
Talladega, AL 800-888-4921
Allied Glove Corporation
Milwaukee, WI...................800-558-9263
Bennett's Auto Inc
Neenah, WI......................800-215-5464
Carolina Glove Co
Conover, NC 800-335-1918
Century Glove Corp
Summerville, GA 706-857-6444
Champaign Plastics Company
Champaign, IL...................800-575-0170
Champion America Inc
Branford, CT.....................800-521-7000
Coast Scientific
Rancho Santa Fe, CA 800-445-1544
Comasec Safety, Inc.
Enfield, CT 800-333-0219
Fairfield Line Inc
Fairfield, IA 800-247-3383
Gann Manufacturing
Baltimore, MD 800-922-9832
George Glove Company, Inc
Midland Park, NJ 800-631-4292
Glover Latex
Anaheim, CA 800-243-5110
Golden Needles Knitting & Glove Company
Coshocton, OH 919-667-5102
Gril-Del
Mankato, MN 800-782-7320
Healthline Products
Los Angeles, CA..................800-473-4003
Island Poly
Westbury, NY 800-338-4433
Microflex Corp
Reno, NV 800-876-6866
Mid West Quality Gloves Inc
Chillicothe, MO 800-821-3028
Ontario Glove and Safety Products
Kitchener, ON....................800-265-4554
Panhandler, Inc.
Cordova, TN 800-654-7237
Parvin Manufacturing Company
Los Angeles, CA..................800-648-0770
Playtex Products, LLC
New Providence, NJ 888-310-4290
Royal Paper Products
Coatesville, PA 800-666-6655
Samco Freezerwear
St Paul, MN......................651-638-3888
Showa-Best Glove
Menlo, GA 800-241-0323
ST Restaurant Supplies
Delta, BC........................888-448-4244
Star Glove Company
Odon, IN 800-832-7101
Superior Distributing Co
Louisville, KY 800-365-6661
Textile Buff & Wheel
Charlestown, MA 617-241-8100
Triad Scientific
Manasquan, NJ 800-867-6690
Tronex Industries
Denville, NJ 800-833-1181
Wells Lamont
Niles, IL.........................800-247-3295
Wells Lamont
Niles, IL.........................800-323-2830
Whiting & Davis
Attleboro Falls, MA 800-876-6374
Work Well Company
Gahanna, OH.....................614-759-8003
Worksafe Industries
Huntington Station, NY 800-929-9000
Y-Pers Inc
Philadelphia, PA 800-421-0242

Hair Nets

Adex Medical Inc
Riverside, CA 800-873-4776

Cellucap Manufacturing Co
Philadelphia, PA 800-523-3814
Champaign Plastics Company
Champaign, IL...................800-575-0170
Erie Cotton Products
Erie, PA.........................800-289-4737
Hairnet Corporation of America
New York, NY 212-675-5840
Hygrade Gloves
Brooklyn, NY 800-233-8100
Island Poly
Westbury, NY 800-338-4433
Joseph Titone & Sons
Burlington, NJ 800-220-4102
Keystone Adjustable Cap Co Inc
Pennsauken, NJ 800-663-5439
Peekskill Hair Net
Peekskill, NY 914-737-1524
ST Restaurant Supplies
Delta, BC........................888-448-4244
Sta-Rite Ginnie Lou Inc
Shelbyville, IL 800-782-7483
Superior Distributing Co
Louisville, KY 800-365-6661

Holders

Pot

Arden Companies
Southfield, MI....................248-415-8500
Best Brands Home Products
New York, NY 212-684-7456
Best Value Textiles
North Charleston, SC 800-858-8589
Champion America Inc
Branford, CT.....................800-521-7000
Charles Craft Inc
Laurinburg, NC...................910-844-3521
Grayline Housewares Inc
Columbus, OH 800-222-7388
Hank Rivera Associates
Dearborn, MI.....................313-581-8300
Healthline Products
Los Angeles, CA..................800-473-4003
Jomac Products
Niles, IL.........................800-566-2289
Monte Glove Company
Wilkesboro, NC 662-263-5353
Panhandler, Inc.
Cordova, TN 800-654-7237
Shen Manufacturing Co Inc
Conshohocken, PA 610-825-2790
Standard Terry Mills
Souderton, PA....................215-723-8121
Stevens Linen Association
Dudley, MA......................800-772-9269

Jackets

A Allred Marketing
Birmingham, AL..................205-251-3700

Name Badges

Ace Stamp & Engraving
Lakewood, WA...................253-582-3322
Alex Delvecchio Enterprises
Troy, MI 248-619-9600
Artcraft Badge & Sign Company
Olney, MD.......................800-739-0709
ATL-East Tag & Label Inc
West Chester, PA..................866-381-8744
Atlas Labels
Montreal, QC.....................514-852-7000
BAW Plastics Inc
Clairton, PA......................800-783-2229
Berlekamp Plastics Inc
Fremont, OH 419-334-4481
Cawley Co
Manitowoc, WI...................800-822-9539
Central Decal
Burr Ridge, IL....................800-869-7654
Chemi-Graphic Inc
Ludlow, MA 413-589-0151
City Stamp & Seal Co
Austin, TX.......................800-950-6074
Corpus Christi Stamp Works
Corpus Christi, TX 800-322-4515
Crown Marking
Minneapolis, MN 800-305-5249
Cucamonga Sign Shop LLC
Rancho Cucamonga, CA 909-945-5888

Custom ID Systems
Venice, FL.....................800-242-8430
Custom Rubber Stamp Co
Crosby, MN......................888-606-4579
Custom Stamp Company
Anza, CA..........................323-292-0753
Darson Corp
Detroit, MI.....................800-783-7781
Design-Mark Industries
Wareham, MA.................800-451-3275
Dinosaur Plastics
Houston, TX....................713-923-2278
E C Shaw Co
Cincinnati, OH...............866-532-7429
Economy Novelty & Printing Co
New York, NY..................212-481-3022
Ed Smith's Stencil Works LTD
New Orleans, LA.............504-525-2128
Ehrgott Rubber Stamp Company
Indianapolis, IN.............317-353-2222
Elliot Lee
Cedarhurst, NY...............516-569-9595
Emblem & Badge
Providence, RI................800-875-5444
Engraving Services Co.
Woodville South, SA
Engraving Specialists
Royal Oak, MI.................248-542-2244
EPI World Graphics
Midlothian, IL.................708-389-7500
Executive Line
Chatham, NY....................800-333-5761
FORT Hill Sign Products Inc
Hopedale, MA..................781-321-4320
Fox Stamp Sign & Specialty
Menasha, WI.....................920-725-2683
Frost Manufacturing Corp
Worcester, MA..................800-462-0216
George Lauterer Corp
Chicago, IL......................312-913-1881
GM Nameplate
Seattle, WA......................800-366-7668
Granite State Stamps Inc
Manchester, NH................800-937-3736
Graphics Unlimited
San Diego, CA..................858-453-4031
Hartford Stamp Works
Hartford, CT.....................860-249-6205
IdentaBadge
Lafayette, LA...................800-325-8247
Impact Awards & Promotions
Avon Park, FL..................888-203-4225
ITC Systems
Toronto, ON.....................877-482-8326
King Badge & Button Company
Huntingtn Bch, CA...........714-847-3060
Kraus & Sons
New York, NY...................212-620-0408
Label Systems & Solutions
Bohemia, NY....................800-811-2560
Label Systems Inc
Addison, TX.....................800-220-9552
Legible Signs
Loves Park, IL..................800-435-4177
Loria Awards
Yonkers, NY.....................800-540-2927
Martco Engravers
Fremont, NH......................603-895-3561
Mastercraft Manufacturing Co
Long Island City, NY........718-729-5620
Midwest Badge & Novelty Co
Minneapolis, MN..............952-927-9901
Modern Stamp Company
Baltimore, MD..................800-727-3029
MTL Etching Industries
Woodmere, NY..................516-295-9733
My Serenity Pond
Cold Spring, MN...............320-363-0411
N.G. Slater Corporation
New York, NY...................800-848-4621
Nameplate
St Paul, MN......................651-228-1522
Orber Manufacturing Co
Cranston, RI.....................800-761-4059
Paperweights Plus
Medford, NY.....................631-924-3222
Patrick & Co
Dallas, TX........................214-761-0900
Photo Graphics Co
Grandview, MO.................816-761-3333
Plastic Tagtrade Check
Essexville, MI..................989-892-7913

Printsource Group
Wakefield, RI...................401-789-9339
Pro-Ad-Co Inc
Portland, OR....................800-287-5885
Rebel Stamp & Sign Co
Baton Rouge, LA..............800-860-5120
Regal Plastic Supply Co
Kansas City, MO...............800-444-6390
Richardson's Stamp Works
Houston, TX.....................713-973-0314
Royal Label Co
Dorchester, MA.................617-825-6050
Sesame Label System
New York, NY...................800-551-3020
Stoffel Seals Corp
Tallapoosa, GA.................800-422-8247
Sutherland Stamp Company
San Diego, CA..................858-233-7784
Volk Corp
Farmington Hills, MI........800-521-6799
Wind River Environmental
Gloucester, MA.................800-332-6025
Winmark Stamp & Sign
Salt Lake City, UT............800-438-0480
Yeuell Name Plate & Label
Woburn, MA......................781-933-2984

Oven Mits

Abond Plastic Corporation
Lachine, QC.....................800-886-7947
Arden Companies
Southfield, MI..................248-415-8500
Best Brands Home Products
New York, NY...................212-684-7456
Best Value Textiles
North Charleston, SC........800-858-8589
C R Mfg
Waverly, NE.....................877-789-5844
Champion America Inc
Branford, CT....................800-521-7000
Gril-Del
Mankato, MN....................800-782-7320
Jomac Products
Niles, IL...........................800-566-2289
Monte Glove Company
Wilkesboro, NC.................662-263-5353
Parvin Manufacturing Company
Los Angeles, CA...............800-648-0770
Shen Manufacturing Co Inc
Conshohocken, PA.............610-825-2790
Standard Terry Mills
Souderton, PA...................215-723-8121
Tucker Industries
Colorado Springs, CO........800-786-7287
Work Well Company
Gahanna, OH.....................614-759-8003

Protective Apparel

Food Handlers'

Abond Plastic Corporation
Lachine, QC.....................800-886-7947
Adex Medical Inc
Riverside, CA...................800-873-4776
AEP Industries Inc
Mankato, MN....................800-999-2374
Akron Cotton Products
Akron, OH........................800-899-7173
Allied Glove Corporation
Milwaukee, WI..................800-558-9263
American Advertising & Shop Cap Company
Old Tappan, NJ.................800-442-8837
American Apron Inc.
Foxboro, MA.....................800-262-7766
American Bag & Linen Co
Cornelia, GA....................706-778-5377
Best Brands Home Products
New York, NY...................212-684-7456
Best Buy Uniforms
Homestead, PA..................800-345-1924
Best Value Textiles
North Charleston, SC........800-858-8589
Boss Manufacturing Co
Kewanee, IL......................800-447-4581
Bragard Professional Uniforms
New York, NY...................800-488-2433
Carolina Glove Co
Conover, NC.....................800-335-1918
Carry-All Canvas Bag Co.
Brooklyn, NY....................888-425-5224

Century Glove Corp
Summerville, GA...............706-857-6444
Champaign Plastics Company
Champaign, IL..................800-575-0170
Choctaw-Kaul Distribution Company
Detroit, MI......................313-894-9494
Dalloz Safety
Smithfield, RI..................800-977-9177
Eagle Home Products
Huntington, NY.................631-673-3500
Fabohio Inc
Uhrichsville, OH...............740-922-4233
Golden Needles Knitting & Glove Company
Coshocton, OH..................919-667-5102
Gourmet Gear
Los Angeles, CA...............800-682-4635
Gril-Del
Mankato, MN....................800-782-7320
Hall Safety Apparel
Uhrichsville, OH...............800-232-3671
Hygrade Gloves
Brooklyn, NY....................800-233-8100
Island Poly
Westbury, NY....................800-338-4433
John Plant Co
Ramseur, NC.....................800-334-2711
Jomac Products
Niles, IL...........................800-566-2289
Joseph Titone & Sons
Burlington, NJ..................800-220-4102
Kennedy's Specialty Sewing
Erin, ON...........................519-833-9306
Keystone Adjustable Cap Co Inc
Pennsauken, NJ.................800-663-5439
Kimberly-Clark Professional
Roswell, GA.....................800-241-3146
Knapp Shoes
Penn Yan, NY
Koch Equipment LLC
Kansas City, MO................816-931-4557
Lambert Company
Chillicothe, MO.................800-821-7667
Landau Uniforms Inc
Olive Branch, MS..............800-238-7513
Lexidyne of Pennsylvania
Pittsburgh, PA..................800-543-2233
Microflex Corp
Reno, NV..........................800-876-6866
New Chief Fashion
Vernon, CA.......................800-639-2433
New England Overshoe Company
Williston, VT....................888-289-6367
Onguard Industries LLC
Havre De Grace, MD..........800-304-2282
Parvin Manufacturing Company
Los Angeles, CA...............800-648-0770
Playtex Products, LLC
New Providence, NJ...........888-310-4290
PolyConversions, Inc.
Rantoul, IL.......................888-893-3330
Quality Mop & Brush Manufacturers
Needham, MA....................617-884-2999
Refrigiwear Inc
Dahlonega, GA..................800-645-3744
Rodes Professional Apparel
Louisville, KY..................502-584-3112
Samco Freezerwear
St Paul, MN......................651-638-3888
Seven Mile Creek Corp
Eaton, OH.........................800-497-6324
Showa-Best Glove
Menlo, GA........................800-241-0323
Sta-Rite Ginnie Lou Inc
Shelbyville, IL..................800-782-7483
Star Glove Company
Odon, IN...........................800-832-7101
Sultan Linen Inc
New York, NY...................212-689-8900
Superior Distributing Co
Louisville, KY..................800-365-6661
Superior Linen & Work Wear
Kansas City, MO................800-798-7987
Superior Uniform Group
Seminole, FL....................800-727-8643
Triad Scientific
Manasquan, NJ.................800-867-6690
Tronex Industries
Denville, NJ.....................800-833-1181
Tucker Industries
Colorado Springs, CO........800-786-7287
Universal Overall
Chicago, IL......................800-621-3344

Valeo
  Elmsford, Ny. 800-634-2704
Work Well Company
  Gahanna, OH. 614-759-8003
Worksafe Industries
  Huntington Station, NY 800-929-9000
Y-Pers Inc
  Philadelphia, PA 800-421-0242

Shirts

A Allred Marketing
  Birmingham, AL. 205-251-3700

Uniforms & Special Clothing

A Allred Marketing
  Birmingham, AL. 205-251-3700
A T Scafati Inc
  New York, NY 212-695-4944
Abond Plastic Corporation
  Lachine, QC .800-886-7947
Acme Laundry Products Inc
  Chatsworth, CA 818-341-0700
Adcapitol
  Monroe, NC. 800-868-7111
Adex Medical Inc
  Riverside, CA 800-873-4776
Alex Delvecchio Enterprises
  Troy, MI 248-619-9600
Allied Glove Corporation
  Milwaukee, WI. 800-558-9263
American Advertising & Shop Cap Company
  Old Tappan, NJ. 800-442-8837
American Design Studios
  Carlsbad, CA. 800-899-7104
American Identity
  Orange City, IA. 800-369-2277
Ansell Healthcare Inc
  Iselin, NJ. 800-800-0444
Apparel Manufacturing Co Inc
  Lilburn, GA. .800-366-1608
Aramark Uniform Svc
  Burbank, CA. 800-272-6275
ATD-American Co
  Wyncote, PA 800-523-2300
Bennett's Auto Inc
  Neenah, WI. 800-215-5464
Best Brands Home Products
  New York, NY 212-684-7456
Best Buy Uniforms
  Homestead, PA 800-345-1924
Best Manufacturing
  Jersey City, NJ 201-356-3800
Best Value Textiles
  North Charleston, SC 800-858-8589
Big Front Uniforms
  Los Angeles, CA. 800-234-8383
Blue Ridge Converting
  Asheville, NC. 800-438-3893
Boss Manufacturing Co
  Kewanee, IL .800-447-4581
Bragard Professional Uniforms
  New York, NY 800-488-2433
Bunzl Processor Distribution LLC
  Riverside, MO. 816-448-4300
Campus Collection, Inc.
  Tuscaloosa, AL 800-289-8744
Carlisle Food Svc Products Inc
  Oklahoma City, OK 800-654-8210
Carnegie Textile Co
  Cleveland, OH 800-633-4136
Carry-All Canvas Bag Co.
  Brooklyn, NY 888-425-5224
Carson Manufacturing Company
  Petaluma, CA 800-423-2380
CCP Industries, Inc.
  Cleveland, OH 800-321-2840
Celebrity Promotions
  Remsen, IA .800-332-6847
Cellucap Manufacturing Co
  Philadelphia, PA 800-523-3814
Century Glove Corp
  Summerville, GA 706-857-6444
Champaign Plastics Company
  Champaign, IL 800-575-0170
Champion America Inc
  Branford, CT. 800-521-7000
Charles Craft Inc
  Laurinburg, NC. 910-844-3521
Chef Revival
  North Charleston, SC 800-248-9826

Chefwear
  Addison, IL .800-568-2433
Christman Screenprint Inc
  Springfield, MI 800-962-9330
Cintas Corp
  Cincinnati, OH 800-864-3676
Coast Scientific
  Rancho Santa Fe, CA 800-445-1544
Comasec Safety, Inc.
  Enfield, CT. .800-333-0219
Dalloz Safety
  Smithfield, RI 800-977-9177
David Dobbs Enterprise Inc.
  St Augustine, FL 800-889-6368
Dow Cover Co Inc
  New Haven, CT. 800-735-8877
Dunrite Inc
  Fremont, NE 800-782-3061
Elwood Safety Company
  Buffalo, NY. .866-326-6060
Erell Manufacturing Co
  Elk Grove Vlg, IL 800-622-6334
Erie Cotton Products
  Erie, PA. 800-289-4737
F & F and A. Jacobs & Sons, Inc.
  Baltimore, MD 410-727-6397
Fabohio Inc
  Uhrichsville, OH 740-922-4233
Fabriko
  Altavista, VA. 888-203-8098
Fairfield Line Inc
  Fairfield, IA .800-247-3383
Flavor Wear
  Valley Center, CA 800-647-8372
Foley's Famous Aprons
  Wayne, MI. .800-634-3245
Franklin Uniform Corporation
  Baltimore, MD 410-235-8151
Funny Apron Co
  Lake Dallas, TX 800-835-5802
Gann Manufacturing
  Baltimore, MD 800-922-9832
Gary Manufacturing Company
  National City, CA 800-775-0804
George Glove Company, Inc
  Midland Park, NJ 800-631-4292
Glover Latex
  Anaheim, CA 800-243-5110
Golden Needles Knitting & Glove Company
  Coshocton, OH 919-667-5102
Goldmax Industries
  City Of Industry, CA. 626-964-8820
Gourmet Gear
  Los Angeles, CA. 800-682-4635
Gourmet Table Skirts
  Houston, TX 800-527-0440
Graphic Apparel
  Inniasfil, ON 800-757-4867
Great Southern Corp
  Memphis, TN 800-421-7802
Green Seams
  Maple Grove, MN 612-929-3213
Gril-Del
  Mankato, MN 800-782-7320
Haas Tailoring Company
  Baltimore, MD 410-732-3804
Hairnet Corporation of America
  New York, NY 212-675-5840
Hall Safety Apparel
  Uhrichsville, OH 800-232-3671
Handgards Inc
  El Paso, TX. .800-351-8161
Hank Rivera Associates
  Dearborn, MI 313-581-8300
Happy Chef Inc
  Butler, NJ. 800-347-0288
Healthline Products
  Los Angeles, CA. 800-473-4003
Hygrade Gloves
  Brooklyn, NY 800-233-8100
Image Experts Uniforms
  Schenectady, NY. 800-789-2433
Island Poly
  Westbury, NY 800-338-4433
John Plant Co
  Ramseur, NC 800-334-2711
Jomac Products
  Niles, IL 800-566-2289
Kennedy's Specialty Sewing
  Erin, ON 519-833-9306
Key Industries Inc
  Fort Scott, KS 800-835-0365

Keystone Adjustable Cap Co Inc
  Pennsauken, NJ. 800-663-5439
Kingston McKnight
  Redwood City, CA 800-900-0463
Klever Kuvers
  Pasadena, CA 626-355-8441
Knapp Shoes
  Penn Yan, NY
Koch Equipment LLC
  Kansas City, MO. 816-931-4557
LaCrosse Safety and Industrial
  Portland, OR 800-557-7246
Lambert Company
  Chillicothe, MO 800-821-7667
Landau Uniforms Inc
  Olive Branch, MS. 800-238-7513
Lehigh Safety Shoe Co LLC
  Nelsonville, OH 866-442-5429
Lexidyne of Pennsylvania
  Pittsburgh, PA 800-543-2233
Liberty Ware LLC
  Clearfield, UT. 888-500-5885
Lion Apparel Inc
  Dayton, OH .800-548-6614
Locknane
  Everett, WA. 800-848-9854
Marv Holland Industries
  Edmonton, AB 800-661-7269
Metz Premiums
  New York, NY 212-315-4660
Mid West Quality Gloves Inc
  Chillicothe, MO 800-821-3028
Midwest Promotional Group
  Summit, IL 800-305-3388
Monte Glove Company
  Wilkesboro, NC 662-263-5353
National Embroidery Svc Inc
  Portsmouth, RI 800-227-1451
National Scoop & Equipment Company
  Spring House, PA 215-646-2040
New Chief Fashion
  Vernon, CA .800-639-2433
New Hatchwear Company
  Calgary, AB .800-661-9249
Ok Uniform Co Inc
  New York, NY 866-700-5765
Pacific Oasis Enterprise Inc
  Santa Fe Springs, CA 800-424-1475
Panhandler, Inc.
  Cordova, TN 800-654-7237
Parvin Manufacturing Company
  Los Angeles, CA. 800-648-0770
Paul G. Gallin Company
  Yonkers, NY .914-964-5800
Peekskill Hair Net
  Peekskill, NY 914-737-1524
PolyConversions, Inc.
  Rantoul, IL 888-893-3330
Pop Tops Co Inc
  South Easton, MA. 800-647-8677
Print Ons/Express Mark
  Monroe, NC 704-289-8261
Protexall
  Greenville, IL 800-334-8939
Put-Ons USA
  Brooklyn Park, MN. 888-425-1215
Quality Mop & Brush Manufacturers
  Needham, MA. 617-884-2999
R&R Industries
  San Clemente, CA. 800-234-1434
Radio Cap Company
  San Antonio, TX. 210-472-1649
Red Kap Industries
  Nashville, TN 615-565-5000
Refrigiwear Inc
  Dahlonega, GA 800-645-3744
Riverside Manufacturing Company
  Moultrie, GA. 800-841-8677
Rocky Shoes & Boots Inc
  Nelsonville, OH 866-442-4908
Rodes Professional Apparel
  Louisville, KY. 502-584-3112
Royal Paper Products
  Coatesville, PA 800-666-6655
S & H Uniform Corp
  White Plains, NY 800-210-5295
Samco Freezerwear
  St Paul, MN .651-638-3888
Scorpio Apparel
  Northbrook, IL 800-559-3338
Seven Mile Creek Corp
  Eaton, OH 800-497-6324

Shen Manufacturing Co Inc
Conshohocken, PA 610-825-2790
Showa-Best Glove
Menlo, GA 800-241-0323
Signco Stylecraft
Cincinnati, OH 800-733-0045
ST Restaurant Supplies
Delta, BC. 888-448-4244
Standard Terry Mills
Souderton, PA 215-723-8121
Star Glove Company
Odon, IN 800-832-7101
Sterling Rubber
Fergus, ON 519-843-4032
Sultan Linen Inc
New York, NY 212-689-8900
Superior Distributing Co
Louisville, KY 800-365-6661
Superior Linen & Work Wear
Kansas City, MO 800-798-7987
Superior Uniform Group
Seminole, FL. 800-727-8643

Task Footwear
Chippewa Falls, WI 800-962-0166
Terry Manufacturing Company
Birmingham, AL. 205-250-0062
Textile Buff & Wheel
Charlestown, MA 617-241-8100
Todd Uniform
Saint Louis, MO 800-458-3402
Triad Products Company
Springfield, OH. 937-323-9422
Tronex Industries
Denville, NJ 800-833-1181
Tru Form Plastics
Gardena, CA 800-510-7999
Tucker Industries
Colorado Springs, CO. 800-786-7287
Uni First Corp
Wilmington, MA. 800-455-7654
Uniforms To You
Oak Lawn, IL 800-889-6072
Uniforms To You & Co
Chicago, IL 800-864-3676

Universal Overall
Chicago, IL 800-621-3344
Valeo
Elmsford, Ny. 800-634-2704
VCG Uniform
Chicago, IL 800-447-6502
Vicmore Manufacturing Company
Brooklyn, NY 800-458-8663
Weinbrenner Shoe Co
Merrill, WI 800-826-0002
Wells Lamont
Niles, IL 800-323-2830
Whiting & Davis
Attleboro Falls, MA 800-876-6374
Work Well Company
Gahanna, OH. 614-759-8003
Worksafe Industries
Huntington Station, NY 800-929-9000
World Pride
St Petersburg, FL 800-533-2433
Y-Pers Inc
Philadelphia, PA 800-421-0242

Consultants & Services

Advanced Process Solutions
Jeffersonville, IN.................888-294-8118

Advertising Novelties & Specialties

A Allred Marketing
Birmingham, AL.................205-251-3700
AAA Electrical Signs
Donna, TX.......................800-825-5376
Access Solutions
Knoxville, TN...................865-531-0971
Ace Signs
Little Rock, AR.................501-562-0800
Action Signs By Stubblefield
Albuquerque, NM...............505-242-9802
Adams Precision Screen
San Leandro, CA................510-632-8597
Adcapitol
Monroe, NC.....................800-868-7111
Admatch Corporation
New York, NY...................800-777-9909
Alex Delvecchio Enterprises
Troy, MI........................248-619-9600
Alger Creations
Miami, FL.......................954-454-3272
Allen Signs Co
Knoxville, TN...................800-844-3524
Alliance Rubber Co
Hot Springs, AR................800-626-5940
Altrua Marketing & Design
Tallahassee, FL.................800-443-6939
AM Graphics
Edina, MN.......................612-341-2020
American Advertising & Shop Cap Company
Old Tappan, NJ..................800-442-8837
American Identification Industries
West Chicago, IL...............800-255-8890
American Identity
Orange City, IA................800-369-2277
Ameritech Signs & Banners
Santa Monica, CA...............310-829-9359
Amsterdam Printing & Litho Inc
Amsterdam, NY..................800-203-9917
Andersen Sign Company
Woodsville, NH.................603-787-6806
Apparel Manufacturing Co Inc
Lilburn, GA.....................800-366-1608
Art Poly Bag Co
Brooklyn, NY...................800-278-7659
Atlas Match Corporation
Euless, TX......................800-628-2426
Audsam Printing
Marion, OH.....................740-387-6252
B.E. Industries
Stamford, CT....................203-357-8055
Baldwin/Priesmeyer
Saint Louis, MO.................314-535-2800
Bayard Kurth Company
Detroit, MI......................313-891-0800
Betsy Ross Manufacturing Company
Paterson, NJ....................877-238-7976
Bill Carr Signs
Flint, MI........................810-232-1569
BK Graphics
Morristown, TN.................800-581-9159
Black Horse Mfg Co
Chattanooga, TN................423-624-0798
Blue Feather Products Inc
Ashland, OR....................800-472-2487
Brewer-Cantelmo Inc
New York, NY...................212-244-4600
Brown's Sign & Screen Printing
Covington, GA..................800-540-3107
Bynoe Printers
New York, NY...................212-662-5041
C R Mfg
Waverly, NE.....................877-789-5844
California Toytime   Balloons
San Pedro, CA...................310-548-1234
Capital Plastics
Middlefield, OH.................440-632-5800
Caraustar
Franklin, KY....................270-586-9565
Carlton Industries
La Grange, TX...................800-231-5988

Carry-All Canvas Bag Co.
Brooklyn, NY...................888-425-5224
Cawley Co
Manitowoc, WI..................800-822-9539
CCL Label Inc
Cold Spring, KY................800-422-6633
CCS Creative, Inc.
Toronto, ON.....................888-633-2079
Central Decal
Burr Ridge, IL..................800-869-7654
Central Missouri Sheltered Enterprises
Columbia, MO...................573-442-6935
Chain Store Graphics
Decatur, IL......................800-443-7446
Charles E. Roberts Company
Wyckoff, NJ.....................800-237-2684
Chicago Show Inc
Buffalo Grove, IL...............847-955-0200
Christman Screenprint Inc
Springfield, MI.................800-962-9330
Chroma Tone
Saint Clair, PA..................800-878-1552
City Grafx
Eugene, OR.....................800-258-2489
Classy Basket
San Diego, CA...................888-449-4901
Coast Signs & Graphics
Hermosa Beach, CA.............310-379-9921
Comm-Pak
Opelika, AL.....................334-749-6201
Commercial Printing Company
Birmingham, AL.................800-989-9203
Connecticut Laminating Co Inc
New Haven, CT..................800-753-9119
Contemporary Product Inc
Garner, NC.....................919-779-4228
Continental Identification
Sparta, MI......................800-247-2499
Courtesy Signs
Amarillo, TX....................806-373-6609
Creative Enterprises
Kendall Park, NJ................732-422-0300
Creegan Animation Company
Steubenville, OH................740-283-3708
Crown Label Company
Santa Ana, CA...................800-422-3590
Cucamonga Sign Shop LLC
Rancho Cucamonga, CA.........909-945-5888
Curzon Promotional Graphics
Omaha, NE.....................800-769-7446
Cyrk
Monroe, WA.....................800-426-3125
Dave's Imports
Jacksonville, FL.................800-553-2837
David Dobbs Enterprise Inc.
St Augustine, FL.................800-889-6368
Dayton Bag & Burlap Co
Dayton, OH.....................800-543-3400
Deadline Press
Kennesaw, GA..................770-419-2232
Deborah Sales LLC
Newark, NJ.....................973-344-8466
Decal Techniques Inc
West Babylon, NY...............800-735-3322
Design Label Manufacturing
East Lyme, CT...................800-666-1575
Design-Mark Industries
Wareham, MA...................800-451-3275
Designers Plastics
Clearwater, FL..................727-573-1643
Diamond Packaging
Rochester, NY...................800-333-4079
Diamond Sign Co
Costa Mesa, CA.................714-545-1440
Dinosaur Plastics
Houston, TX....................713-923-2278
Distinctive Embedments
Pawtucket, RI...................401-729-0770
DLX Industries
Pomona, NY....................845-517-2200
Dominion Regala
Toronto, ON.....................866-423-4086
Dove Screen Printing Co
Royston, GA....................706-245-4975
Dynamic Packaging
Minneapolis, MN................800-878-9380

E.G. Staats & Company
Mount Pleasant, IA..............800-553-1853
Ebenezer Flag Company
Newport, RI.....................401-846-1891
Eco-Bag Products
Ossining, NY....................800-720-2247
Economy Novelty & Printing Co
New York, NY...................212-481-3022
Einson Freeman
Paramus, NJ....................201-221-2800
EIT
Elmhurst, IL.....................630-279-3400
Elliot Lee
Cedarhurst, NY..................516-569-9595
Emblem & Badge
Providence, RI...................800-875-5444
Emco Industrial Plastics
Cedar Grove, NJ.................800-292-9906
Empire Screen Printing Inc
Onalaska, WI....................608-783-3301
Endurart Inc
New York, NY...................212-779-8522
Engraving Specialists
Royal Oak, MI...................248-542-2244
Erell Manufacturing Co
Elk Grove Vlg, IL................800-622-6334
Executive Line
Chatham, NY....................800-333-5761
Fair Publishing House
Norwalk, OH....................419-668-3746
Flexo Transparent Inc
Buffalo, NY......................877-993-5396
Forbes Products Corp
Rush, NY........................800-316-5235
Forest Manufacturing Co
Twinsburg, OH..................330-425-3805
Forrest Engraving Company
New Rochelle, NY...............914-632-9892
Fox Stamp Sign & Specialty
Menasha, WI....................920-725-2683
Foxfire Marketing Solutions
Newark, DE.....................800-497-0512
Francis & Lusky Company
Nashville, TN....................800-251-3711
FRS Industries
Moorhead, MN..................800-747-4795
Fun-Time International
Philadelphia, PA.................800-776-4386
Gallimore Industries
Lake Villa, IL....................800-927-8020
Gannett Outdoor of New Jersey
Fairfield, NJ.....................973-575-6900
Garland Writing Instruments
Coventry, RI.....................401-828-9582
Gary Plastic Packaging Corporation
Bronx, NY.......................800-227-4279
Geiger Bros
Lewiston, ME....................207-755-2000
General Formulations
Sparta, MI.......................800-253-3664
General Methods Corporation
Peoria, IL........................309-497-3344
George Lauterer Corp
Chicago, IL......................312-913-1881
Globe Ticket & Label Company
Warminster, PA..................800-523-5968
Gold Bond Inc
Hixson, TN......................423-842-5844
Gonterman & Associates
Saint Louis, MO.................314-771-0600
Graphic Calculator Company
Barrington, IL....................847-381-4480
Graphics Unlimited
San Diego, CA...................858-453-4031
Graydon Lettercraft
Great Neck, NY.................516-482-0531
Grays Harbor Stamp Works
Aberdeen, WA...................800-894-3830
Green Mountain Graphics
Long Island City, NY............718-472-3377
Greenfield Packaging
White Plains, NY................914-993-0233
H C Bainbridge Inc
Syracuse, NY....................315-475-5313
Harco Enterprises
Peterborough, ON...............800-361-5361

HMG Worldwide
Morton Grove, IL 847-965-7100
Hughes Manufacturing Company
Giddings, TX 800-414-0765
IdentaBadge
Lafayette, LA 800-325-8247
IDL
Monroeville, PA 724-733-2234
Image Plastics
Houston, TX 800-289-2811
Imperial Plastics Inc
Lakeville, MN 952-469-4951
Inovar Packaging Group
Arlington, TX 800-285-2235
Insignia Systems Inc
Minneapolis, MN 800-874-4648
Jessup Paper Box
Brookston, IN 765-490-9043
Killion Industries Inc
Vista, CA 800-421-5352
King Badge & Button Company
Huntingtn Bch, CA 714-847-3060
Koza's Inc
Pearland, TX 800-594-5555
Kraus & Sons
New York, NY 212-620-0408
Krimstock Enterprises
Pennsauken, NJ 856-665-3676
Kuepper Favor Company, Celebrate Line
Peru, IN 800-321-5823
Label Systems & Solutions
Bohemia, NY 800-811-2560
Label Systems Inc
Addison, TX 800-220-9552
Labelprint America
Newburyport, MA 978-463-4004
Labelquest Inc
Elmhurst, IL 800-999-5301
Lake City Signs
Boulder City, NV 702-293-5805
Lane Award Manufacturing
Phoenix, AZ 800-843-2581
Legible Signs
Loves Park, IL 800-435-4177
Lewisburg Printing
Lewisburg, TN 800-559-1526
Lewtan Industries Corporation
Hartford, CT 860-278-9800
License Ad Plate Co
Cleveland, OH 216-265-4200
Lion/Circle Corp
Chicago, IL 773-284-3666
Logo Specialty Advertising Tems
Tampa, FL 800-704-0094
Lonestar Banners & Flags
Fort Worth, TX 800-288-9625
Loria Awards
Yonkers, NY 800-540-2927
M & M Display
Philadelphia, PA 800-874-7171
Maier Sign Systems
Saddle Brook, NJ 201-845-7555
Mansfield Rubber Stamp
Mansfield, OH 419-524-1442
Mar-Boro Printing & Advertising Specialties
Brooklyn, NY 718-336-4051
Martco Engravers
Fremont, NH 603-895-3561
Mastercraft Manufacturing Co
Long Island City, NY 718-729-5620
MDR International
North Miami, FL 305-944-5019
Memphis Delta Tent & Awning
Memphis, TN 901-522-1238
Merchandising Inventives
Waukegan, IL 800-367-5653
Metz Premiums
New York, NY 212-315-4660
Midwest Badge & Novelty Co
Minneapolis, MN 952-927-9901
Midwest Promotional Group
Summit, IL 800-305-3388
Minges Printing & Advg Specs
Gastonia, NC 704-867-6791
Minnesuing Acres
Lake Nebagamon, WI 715-374-2262
MODAGRAPHICS
Rolling Meadows, IL 847-392-3980
Modern Stamp Company
Baltimore, MD 800-727-3029
Moore Efficient Communication Aids
Denver, CO 303-433-8456

MTL Etching Industries
Woodmere, NY 516-295-9733
N.G. Slater Corporation
New York, NY 800-848-4621
Nameplate
St Paul, MN 651-228-1522
National Emblem
Carson, CA 800-877-5325
National Marking Products Inc
Henrico, VA 800-482-1553
Nationwide Pennant & Flag Mfg
San Antonio, TX 800-383-3524
Norgus Silk Screen Co Inc
Clifton, NJ 973-365-0600
North American Packaging Corp
New York, NY 800-499-3521
Novelty Advertising
Coshocton, OH 800-848-9163
Nutty Bavarian
Sanford, FL 800-382-4788
Orber Manufacturing Co
Cranston, RI 800-761-4059
Pak 2000 Inc
Mirror Lake, NH 603-569-3700
Paperweights Plus
Medford, NY 631-924-3222
Paradise Products
El Cerrito, CA 800-227-1092
Party Yards
Casselberry, FL 877-501-4400
Pelican Products Inc
Bronx, NY 800-552-8820
Photo Graphics Co
Grandview, MO 816-761-3333
Pierrepont Visual Graphics Inc
Rochester, NY 585-235-5620
Pilgrim Plastics
Brockton, MA 800-343-7810
Plastic Fantastics/Buck Signs
Ashland, OR 800-482-1776
Plastic Printing LLC
Dayton, KY 877-581-7748
Pop Tops Co Inc
South Easton, MA 800-647-8677
Print Ons/Express Mark
Monroe, NC 704-289-8261
Printsource Group
Wakefield, RI 401-789-9339
Pro-Ad-Co Inc
Portland, OR 800-287-5885
Process Displays
New Berlin, WI 800-533-1764
Quick Point Inc
Fenton, MO 800-638-1369
R&R Industries
San Clemente, CA 800-234-1434
Radio Cap Company
San Antonio, TX 210-472-1649
Ram Industries
Erwin, TN 800-523-3883
Ray-Craft
Cleveland, OH 216-651-3330
Rex Art Manufacturing Corp.
Lindenhurst, NY 631-884-4600
Riverside Manufacturing Company
Arlington Hts, IL 800-877-3349
Roxanne Signs Inc
Gaithersburg, MD 301-428-4911
Rutler Screen Printing
Easton, PA 610-829-2999
Samsill Corp
Fort Worth, TX 800-255-1100
Sanders Manufacturing Co
Nashville, TN 866-254-6611
Sayco Yo-Yo Molding Company
Cumberland, RI 401-724-5296
Scott Sign Systems
Sarasota, FL 800-237-9447
Screen Print Etc
Anaheim, CA 714-630-1100
Semco Plastic Co
St Louis, MO 314-487-4557
Sesame Label System
New York, NY 800-551-3020
Shild Company
New York, NY 866-435-2949
Sign Factory
Cerritos, CA 562-809-1443
Signs & Shapes Intl
Omaha, NE 800-806-6069
Sillcocks Plastics International
Hudson, MA 800-526-4919

Smyth Co LLC
St Paul, MN 800-473-3464
Source for Packaging
New York, NY 800-223-2527
Southern Tailors Flag & Banner
Atlanta, GA 877-655-2321
Spartan Flag Co
Northport, MI 231-386-5150
Special Events Supply Company
Hauppauge, NY
Steingart Associates Inc
South Fallsburg, NY 845-434-4321
Sterling Novelty Products
Northbrook, IL 847-291-0070
Stoffel Seals Corp
Tallapoosa, GA 800-422-8247
Superior-Studio Specialties
Commerce, CA 800-354-3049
SuppliesForLess
Hampton, VA 800-235-2201
Sutherland Stamp Company
San Diego, CA 858-233-7784
Thermal Bags By Ingrid Inc
Gilberts, IL 800-622-5560
Tin Box Co Of America Inc
Farmingdale, NY 800-888-8467
Token Factory
La Crosse, WI 888-486-5367
Tomsed Corporation
Lillington, NC 800-334-5552
Trevor Owen Limited
Scarborough, ON 866-487-2224
Twenty/Twenty Graphics
Gaithersburg, MD 240-243-0511
Unique Manufacturing
Visalia, CA 888-737-1007
Universal Tag Inc
Dudley, MA 800-332-8247
US Magnetix
Minneapolis, MN 763-540-9497
Variant
Eden Prairie, MN 612-927-8611
Volk Corp
Farmington Hills, MI 800-521-6799
Vonco Products LLC
Lake Villa, IL 800-323-9077
Vynatex
Port Washington, NY 516-944-6130
Wendell August Forge
Grove City, PA 800-923-1390
West Hawk Industries
Ann Arbor, MI 800-678-1286
WGN Flag & Decorating Co
Chicago, IL 773-768-8076
Whirley Industries Inc
Warren, PA 800-825-5575
Willson Industries
Marmora, NJ 800-894-4169
Wishbone Utensil Tableware Line
Wheat Ridge, CO 866-266-5928
World Division
Dallas, TX 800-433-9843
WS Packaging Group Inc
Oak Creek, WI 800-837-3838
WS Packaging Group Inc
Green Bay, WI 877-977-5177

Custom Printed Promotional Products

A Allred Marketing
Birmingham, AL 205-251-3700
Eco-Bag Products
Ossining, NY 800-720-2247
Tangerine Promotion
Northbrook, IL 847-313-6000

Flags, Pennants & Banners

AAA Flag & Banner Manufacturing
Los Angeles, CA 800-266-4222
Ace Signs
Little Rock, AR 501-562-0800
Action Signs By Stubblefield
Albuquerque, NM 505-242-9802
Ad Mart Identity Group
Danville, KY 800-354-2102
Adcapitol
Monroe, NC 800-868-7111
Allen Signs Co
Knoxville, TN 800-844-3524
Altrua Marketing & Design
Tallahassee, FL 800-443-6939

AM Graphics
  Edina, MN...................612-341-2020
American Flag & Banner Co Inc
  Clawson, MI.................800-892-5168
Ameritech Signs & Banners
  Santa Monica, CA............310-829-9359
B H Awning & Tent Co
  Benton Harbor, MI...........800-272-2187
Baldwin/Priesmeyer
  Saint Louis, MO.............314-535-2800
Baltimore Sign Company
  Arnold, MD..................410-276-1500
Banner Idea
  Newport Beach, CA...........949-559-6600
Bannerland
  Santa Fe Springs, CA........800-654-0294
Betsy Ross Manufacturing Company
  Paterson, NJ................877-238-7976
Brown's Sign & Screen Printing
  Covington, GA...............800-540-3107
Capitol Awning Co Inc
  Jamaica, NY.................800-241-3539
Coast Signs & Graphics
  Hermosa Beach, CA...........310-379-9921
Coastal Canvas Products
  Savannah, GA................800-476-5174
Collegeville Flag & Manufacturing Company
  Collegeville, PA............800-523-5630
Courtesy Signs
  Amarillo, TX................806-373-6609
Creative Canopy Design
  Hernando Beach, FL..........866-970-5200
Cucamonga Sign Shop LLC
  Rancho Cucamonga, CA........909-945-5888
Curzon Promotional Graphics
  Omaha, NE...................800-769-7446
Deadline Press
  Kennesaw, GA................770-419-2232
Decal Techniques Inc
  West Babylon, NY............800-735-3322
Diamond Sign Co
  Costa Mesa, CA..............714-545-1440
Dimension Graphics Inc
  Grand Rapids, MI............855-476-1281
Dinosaur Plastics
  Houston, TX.................713-923-2278
Dixie Flag Mfg Co
  San Antonio, TX.............800-356-4085
Dominion Regala
  Toronto, ON.................866-423-4086
Ebenezer Flag Company
  Newport, RI.................401-846-1891
EIT
  Elmhurst, IL................630-279-3400
Emedco
  Williamsville, NY...........877-765-8386
Flexo Transparent Inc
  Buffalo, NY.................877-993-5396
Florart Flock Process
  North Miami, FL.............800-292-3524
Forest Manufacturing Co
  Twinsburg, OH...............330-425-3805
France Personalized Signs
  Cleveland, OH...............216-241-2198
Frost Manufacturing Corp
  Worcester, MA...............800-462-0216
Fuller Flag Company
  Holden, MA..................800-348-6723
George Lauterer Corp
  Chicago, IL.................312-913-1881
Goodwin-Cole Co Inc
  Sacramento, CA..............800-752-4477
Graphics Unlimited
  San Diego, CA...............858-453-4031
Green Mountain Awning Inc
  West Rutland, VT............800-479-2951
H C Bainbridge Inc
  Syracuse, NY................315-475-5313
H. Arnold Wood Turning
  Tarrytown, NY...............888-314-0088
Hammar & Sons
  Pelham, NH..................800-527-7446
Handicap Sign Inc
  Grand Rapids, MI............800-690-4888
Harting Graphics
  Wilmington, DE..............800-848-1373
Hollywood Banners
  Copiague, NY................800-691-5652
Hughes Manufacturing Company
  Giddings, TX................800-414-0765
Industrial Sign Company
  South El Monte, CA..........800-596-3720

Inovar Packaging Group
  Arlington, TX...............800-285-2235
John W Keplinger & Sons
  Norristown, PA..............610-666-6191
KD Kanopy
  Westminster, CO.............800-432-4435
Kennedy's Specialty Sewing
  Erin, ON....................519-833-9306
Kraus & Sons
  New York, NY................212-620-0408
Ladder Works
  Lombard, IL.................800-419-5880
Lake City Signs
  Boulder City, NV............702-293-5805
Lonestar Banners & Flags
  Fort Worth, TX..............800-288-9625
Metropolitan Flag & Banner Co
  Philadelphia, PA............215-426-2775
Nationwide Pennant & Flag Mfg
  San Antonio, TX.............800-383-3524
Norgus Silk Screen Co Inc
  Clifton, NJ.................973-365-0600
Oates Flag Co Inc
  Louisville, KY..............502-267-8200
Paradise Products
  El Cerrito, CA..............800-227-1092
Pierrepont Visual Graphics Inc
  Rochester, NY...............585-235-5620
Plasti-Clip Corp
  Milford, NH.................800-882-2547
Pratt Poster Company
  Indianapolis, IN............800-645-1012
Radio Cap Company
  San Antonio, TX.............210-472-1649
Riverside Manufacturing Company
  Arlington Hts, IL...........800-877-3349
Rose City Awning Co
  Portland, OR................800-446-4104
Roxanne Signs Inc
  Gaithersburg, MD............301-428-4911
Screen Print Etc
  Anaheim, CA.................714-630-1100
Sign Factory
  Cerritos, CA................562-809-1443
Signet Graphic Products
  St Louis, MO................314-426-0200
Signmasters
  Huntington Beach, CA........949-364-9128
Southern Tailors Flag & Banner
  Atlanta, GA.................877-655-2321
Spartan Flag Co
  Northport, MI...............231-386-5150
Special Events Supply Company
  Hauppauge, NY
Sterling Novelty Products
  Northbrook, IL..............847-291-0070
T & M Distributing Co
  Henderson, NV...............702-458-1962
Timely Signs Inc
  Elmont, NY..................800-457-4467
Trevor Owen Limited
  Scarborough, ON.............866-487-2224
Us Flag & Signal
  Portsmouth, VA..............757-497-8947
Volk Corp
  Farmington Hills, MI........800-521-6799
Vomela/Harbor Graphics
  St Paul, MN.................800-645-1012
Walker Co
  Oklahoma City, OK...........800-522-3015
Walker Engineering Inc
  Sun Valley, CA..............818-252-7788
West Hawk Industries
  Ann Arbor, MI...............800-678-1286
WGN Flag & Decorating Co
  Chicago, IL.................773-768-8076
World Division
  Dallas, TX..................800-433-9843

Analytical Services

A&L Western Ag Lab
  Modesto, CA.................209-529-4080
Accra Laboratory
  Cleveland, OH...............800-567-7200
Accu-Labs Research
  Golden, CO..................303-277-9514
Agriculture Consulting Services
  New York City, NY...........347-709-7587
AgriTech
  Columbus, OH................614-488-2772
Agspring
  Leawood, KS.................913-333-3035

Airflow Sciences Corp
  Livonia, MI.................734-525-0300
Altek Co
  Torrington, CT..............860-482-7626
AM Test Laboratories
  Kirkland, WA................425-885-1664
American Technical Services Group
  Norcross, GA................800-893-1944
Analytical Labs
  Boise, ID...................800-574-5773
Anresco Laboratories
  San Francisco, CA...........800-359-0920
Avanti Polar Lipids
  Alabaster, AL...............800-227-0651
Barrow-Agee Laboratories Inc
  Memphis, TN.................901-332-1590
Barry-Wehmiller Design Group
  St Louis, MO................314-862-8000
BCN Research Laboratories
  Rockford, TN................800-236-0505
BluMetric Environmental Inc.
  Ottawa, ON..................613-839-3053
Brown & Caldwell
  Walnut Creek, CA............800-727-2224
Celsis Laboratory Group
  Chicago, IL.................800-222-8260
CERT ID LC
  Fairfield, IA...............641-209-1899
Coffee Enterprises
  Burlington, VT..............800-375-3398
Covance Inc.
  Princeton, NJ...............888-268-2623
CXR Co
  Warsaw, IN..................800-817-5763
Deibel Laboratories Inc
  Madison, WI.................608-241-1177
DFL Laboratories
  Chicago, IL.................312-938-5151
ENSCO Inc
  Springfield, VA.............703-321-9000
Enviro-Test/Perry Laboratories
  Woodridge, IL...............630-324-6685
Environmental Systems
  Culpeper, VA................800-541-2116
Eurofins DQCI
  St Paul, MN.................763-785-0484
Eurofins S-F Analytical Labs
  New Berlin, WI..............800-300-6700
Eurofins Scientific Inc
  Des Moines, IA..............800-841-1110
Eurofins Scientific Inc.
  Dayton, OH..................800-880-1038
Fettig Laboratories
  Grand Rapids, MI............616-245-3000
Food & Agrosystems
  Sunnyvale, CA...............408-245-8450
Food Consulting Company
  Del Mar, CA.................800-793-2844
Food Safety Net Services Ltd
  San Antonio, TX.............888-525-9788
Galbraith Laboratories Inc
  Knoxville, TN...............877-449-8797
Gaynes Labs Inc
  Bridgeview, IL..............708-233-6655
Global Product Development Group
  Northbrook, IL..............847-504-0464
Great Lakes Scientific
  Stevensville, MI............269-429-1000
Hahn Laboratories
  Columbia, SC................803-799-1614
Harold Wainess & Assoc
  Arlington Hts, IL...........847-722-8744
Healthy Dining
  San Diego, CA...............800-266-2049
Howlett Farms
  Avon, NY....................585-226-8340
Industrial Laboratories Co
  Wheat Ridge, CO.............800-456-5288
Ingman Laboratories
  Minneapolis, MN.............612-724-0121
International Approval Services
  Cleveland, OH...............877-235-9791
Irvine Analytical Labs
  Irvine, CA..................877-445-6554
ITS/ETL Testing Laboratories
  Laguna Niguel, CA...........949-448-4100
J Leek Assoc Inc
  Edenton, NC.................252-482-4456
JI Analytical Svc Inc
  Modesto, CA.................209-538-8111
Krueger Food Laboratories
  Chelmsford, MA..............978-256-1220

Lancaster Laboratories
Lancaster, PA 717-656-2300
Laucks' Testing Laboratories
Seattle, WA 206-767-5060
Lebensmittel Consulting
Fostoria, OH 419-435-2774
Libra Technical Center
Metuchen, NJ 732-321-5200
Mccrone Microscopes & Acces
Westmont, IL 630-288-7087
Medallion Laboratories
Minneapolis, MN 800-245-5615
Microbac Laboratories
Pittsburgh, PA 866-515-4668
Microbac-Wilson Devision
Wilson, NC 252-237-4175
Midwest Laboratories
Omaha, NE 402-334-7770
Milligan & Higgins
Johnstown, NY 518-762-4638
Minnesota Valley Testing Lab
New Ulm, MN. 800-782-3557
National Food Laboratories Inc
Livermore, CA 925-828-1440
Northeast Laboratory Svc
Winslow, ME. 866-591-7120
Northland Labs
Northbrook, IL 800-366-3522
Northview Laboratories
Spartanburg, SC 864-574-7728
Northwest Laboratories
Seattle, WA 206-763-6252
Nutrinfo Corporation
Watertown, MA. 800-676-6686
Oklabs
Oklahoma City, OK 405-843-6832
Pearson Research Assoc
Santa Cruz, CA 831-429-9797
Phytopia Inc
Dallas, TX. 888-750-9336
POS Pilot Plant Corporation
Saskatoon, SK 800-230-2751
PSI
Oakbrook Terrace, IL 630-705-9290
Purity Laboratories
Lake Oswego, OR. 800-977-3636
QC
Southampton, PA 215-355-3900
Quest
San Clemente, CA. 949-643-1333
R.C. Keller & Associates
Barnegat, NJ 973-694-8810
Richardson Researches
South San Francisco, CA 510-653-4385
Rtech Laboratories
St Paul, MN. 800-328-9687
RTI Laboratories
Livonia, MI. 734-422-5342
S & J Laboratories Inc
Portage, MI 269-324-7383
Sani-Pure Food Laboratories
Saddle Brook, NJ 201-843-2525
Sensory Spectrum
New Providence, NJ 908-376-7000
Shear/Kershman Laboratories
Chesterfield, MO 636-519-8900
Shuster Laboratories
Canton, MA 800-444-8705
Silliker, Inc
Chicago, IL 312-938-5151
Soyatech Inc
Bar Harbor, ME. 800-424-7692
Spencer Research Inc
Columbus, OH 800-488-3242
Strasburger & Siegel
Hanover, MD 888-726-3753
Suburban Laboratories Inc
Geneva, IL. 800-783-5227
TEI Analytical Svc Inc
Niles, IL 847-647-1345
The Good Food Institute
Washington, DC 866-849-4457
Total Quality Corporation
Branford, CT. 800-453-9729
Truesdail Laboratories
Tustin, CA. 714-730-6239
Underwriters Laboratories Inc
Camas, WA 877-854-3577
VICAM
Milford, MA. 800-338-4381
Warren Analytical Laboratory
Greeley, CO. 800-945-6669

Winston Laboratories Inc
Vernon Hills, IL 800-946-5229
Woodson-Tenent Laboratories
Des Moines, IA. 515-265-1461
Woodson-Tenent Laboratories
Memphis, TN 515-280-8378
Woodson-Tenent Laboratories
Dayton, OH. 937-236-5756
X-R-I Testing Inc
Troy, MI 800-973-4800
YottaMark
Redwood City, CA 866-768-7878

Architects

Foodservice

Barry Wehmiller Design Group
New London, NH 866-526-2585
Excel Engineering
Fond Du Lac, WI 920-926-9800

Retail

Mead & Hunt Inc
Madison, WI 888-364-7272

Canners

Chiquita Brands LLC.
Fort Lauderdale, FL 954-924-5700
Great Lakes Foods
Menominee, MI 800-800-7492
Hormel Foods Corp.
Austin, MN 507-437-5611
LA Monica Fine Foods
Millville, NJ
Poynette Distribution Center
Poynette, WI 608-635-4396
RDM International
North Hollywood, CA 818-985-7654
SOPAKCO Foods
Mullins, SC. 800-276-9678
Sportsmen's Cannery & Smokehouse
Winchester Bay, OR 800-457-8048
Truitt Bros Inc
Salem, OR. 800-547-8712
Washington Frontier
Grandview, WA 509-469-7662
Whitlock Packaging Corp
Fort Gibson, OK 918-478-4300

Computer Software, Systems & Services

AC Label Company
Provo, UT 801-642-3500
Acromag Inc.
Wixom, MI 248-624-1541
Acumen Data Systems Inc
West Springfield, MA. 888-816-0933
Advance Technology Corp
Ramsey, NJ 201-934-7127
Advanced Micro Controls
Terryville, CT 860-585-1254
Advanced Software Designs
Chesterfield, MO 636-532-6021
Agilysys, Inc.
Alpharetta, GA 800-241-8768
Airflow Sciences Corp
Livonia, MI. 734-525-0300
AL Systems
Rockaway, NJ 888-960-8324
Allpax Products
Covington, LA 888-893-9277
American Forms & Labels
Boise, ID 800-388-3554
American Technical Services Group
Norcross, GA 800-893-1944
AMETEK National Controls Corp
West Chicago, IL 800-323-5293
Amplexus Corporation
Novato, CA. 800-423-8268
Ann Arbor Computer
Farmington Hills, MI 800-526-9322
Apigent Solutions
Oklahoma City, OK 800-664-8228
Asap Automation
Addison, IL 800-409-0383
ASI Data Myte
Plymouth, MN. 800-455-4359

ASI/Restaurant Manager
Silver Spring, MD. 800-356-6037
Assembly Technology & Test
Livonia, MI 734-522-1900
At-Your-Svc Software Inc
Bronxville, NY 888-325-6937
Auto Quotes
Jacksonville, FL 904-384-2279
Automation Group
Houston, TX 713-860-5200
Batchmasters Software
Laguna Hills, CA 949-583-1646
Berg Co
Monona, WI 608-221-4281
Broadcom Inc.
San Jose, CA
BSI Instruments
Aliquippa, PA 800-274-9851
Buypass Corporation
Atlanta, GA 770-953-2664
Cache Box
Arlington, VA 800-603-4834
Camstar Systems
San Jose, CA. 800-237-2841
Catalyst International
Lemont, IL 800-236-4600
CaterMate
Ithaca, NY. 800-486-2283
CBORD Group Inc
Ithaca, NY. 607-257-2410
CBORD Group Inc
Ithaca, NY. 800-982-4643
CCR Data Systems
Concord, NH. 800-633-6500
Coconut Code
Lighthouse Point, FL 954-786-0252
Comalex
Van Buren, AR 866-343-2594
Command Line Corporation
Edison, NJ 732-738-6500
Compris Technologies
Duluth, GA 800-615-3301
Computer Aid Inc
Allentown, PA. 800-327-4243
Computer Aided Marketing
Chapel Hill, NC 919-401-0996
Computer Communications Specialists
Marietta, GA 888-231-4227
Computrition
Chatsworth, CA 800-222-4488
Comstar Printing Solutions
Streetsboro, OH 330-528-2800
Comus Restaurant Systems
Frederick, MD. 301-698-6208
Control Module
Enfield, CT 800-722-6654
Crunch Time Information Systems
Boston, MA. 857-202-3000
Custom Business Solutions
Irvine, CA 800-551-7674
Cycle Computer Consultants
Hicksville, NY 516-733-1892
Cyplex
Los Angeles, CA
Data Management
San Angelo, TX 800-749-8463
Data Specialists
Elkhorn, WI. 800-211-1545
Decartes Systems Group
Waterloo, ON 519-746-8110
Digital Dining
Springfield, VA 703-912-3000
Digital Dynamics Inc
Scotts Valley, CA 800-765-1288
Digital Image & Sound Corporation
Rochester, NY. 585-381-0410
Domino Amjet Inc
Gurnee, IL. 800-444-4512
DSA Software
Foxboro, MA 508-543-0400
E2M
Duluth, GA 800-622-4326
Eatec Corporation
Emeryville, CA. 877-374-4783
EBS
Houston, TX 713-939-1000
Ecklund-Harrison Technologies
Fort Myers, FL 239-936-6032
Economic Sciences Corp
Berkeley, CA 510-841-6869
Edgerton Corporation
Strongsville, OH 440-268-0000

Efficient Frontiers
Livermore, CA 888-433-4725

Electro Cam Corp
Roscoe, IL 800-228-5487

Electrol Specialties Co
South Beloit, IL 815-389-2291

Elo Touch Systems
Menlo Park, CA 800-557-1458

Elreha Controls Corporation
St Petersburg, FL 727-327-6236

Emtrol
York, PA 800-634-4927

EPD Technology Corporation
Elmsford, NY 800-892-8926

ERC Parts Inc
Kennesaw, GA 800-241-6880

Esha Research
Salem, OR 800-659-3742

ExecuChef Software
San Anselmo, CA 415-488-9600

First DataBank
San Bruno, CA 800-633-3453

Fred D Pfening Co
Columbus, OH 614-294-5361

GCA
Huntington Beach, CA 714-379-4911

Genesis Total Solutions Inc
Fultondale, AL 205-631-5334

Gerber Innovations
Tolland, CT 800-331-5797

Graphic Technology
New Century, KS 800-767-9920

Great Plains Software
Fargo, ND 800-456-0025

GTCO CalComp
Scottsdale, AZ 800-856-0732

Hampton-Tilley Associates
Chesterfield, MO 813-418-3340

Heart Smart International
Scottsdale, AZ 800-762-7819

Helm Software
Phoenix, AZ 602-522-2999

Hope Industrial Systems
Roswell, GA 877-762-9790

Horizon Software International
Duluth, GA 800-741-7100

HSI
Scottsdale, AZ 480-596-5456

Hudson Control Group Inc
Springfield, NJ 973-376-8265

Iconics Inc
Foxboro, MA 800-946-9679

ID Images
Brunswick, OH 866-516-7300

Illinois Wholesale Cash Rgstr
Elgin, IL 800-544-5493

IMAS Corporation
St. Charles, IL 847-274-9383

Industrious Software Solutions
Inglewood, CA 800-351-4225

InFood Corporation
Evanston, IL 773-338-8485

Infopro Inc
Aurora, IL 630-978-9231

Infor
New York, NY 866-244-5479

Information Access
Cleveland, OH 216-328-0100

Insignia Systems Inc
Minneapolis, MN 800-874-4648

Integrated Distribution
Omaha, NE 937-445-1936

Integrated Restaurant Software/RMS Touch
Timonium, MD 201-461-9096

Intelligent Controls
Saco, ME 800-872-3455

Interactive Sales Solutions
Coppell, TX 800-352-9575

Interlake Mecalux
Chicago, IL 708-344-9999

InterSect Business Systems Inc
Kelowna, BC 250-860-0829

Invictus Systems Corporation
Falls Church, VA

ITC Systems
Toronto, ON 877-482-8326

Junction Solutions
Englewood, CO 877-502-6355

Kaye Instruments
N Billerica, MA 800-343-4624

Kenray Associates
Greenville, IN 812-923-9884

Kochman Consultants LTD
Morton Grove, IL 847-470-1195

Konica Minolta Corp
Ramsey, NJ 888-473-3637

Lablynx Inc
Atlanta, GA 800-585-5969

LDJ Electronics
Troy, MI 248-528-2202

Least Cost Formulations LTD
Virginia Beach, VA 757-467-0954

Lighthouse for the Blindin New Orleans
New Orleans, LA 504-899-4501

LIS Warehouse Systems
Charlotte, NC 888-547-9670

Logility Transportation Group
Des Plaines, IL 847-699-6620

Long Range Systems
Addison, TX 800-577-8101

LPI Information Systems
Overland Park, KS 888-729-2020

Magnetic Technologies LTD
Oxford, MA 508-987-3303

Management Tech of America
Phoenix, AZ 602-381-5800

MAPS Software
Columbus, MS 662-328-6110

Menulink
Huntington Beach, CA 714-934-6368

Microtouch Systems Inc
Methuen, MA 978-659-9000

Microworks Pos Solutions Inc
Webster, GA 800-787-2068

Moisture Register Products
Rancho Cucamonga, CA 800-966-4788

Montalbano Development Inc
Ronkonkoma, NY 800-739-9152

Murata Automated Systems
Charlotte, NC 800-428-8469

National Computer Corporation
Greenville, SC 866-944-5164

Newmarket Corp
Portsmouth, NH 888-829-8871

Norback Ley & Assoc
Middleton, WI. 608-233-3814

Northwest Analytical Inc
Portland, OR 888-692-7638

Novax Group/Point of Sales
New York, NY 212-684-1244

Nutrition & Food Associates
Plymouth, MN. 763-550-9475

OMRON Systems LLC
Schaumburg, IL. 224-520-7650

Oracle Hospitality
Redwood, CA 800-392-2999

Order-Matic Corporation
Oklahoma City, OK 800-767-6733

Parity Corp
Bothell, WA. 425-487-0997

Party Perfect Catering
Houston, TX 800-522-5440

PC/Poll Systems
Dubuque, IA 800-670-1736

PEAK Technologies, Inc.
Columbia, MD 800-926-9212

Preston Scientific
Anaheim, CA 714-632-3700

Prime ProData
North Canton, OH. 877-497-2578

Prism Visual Software Inc
Port Washington, NY 516-944-5920

Progressive Software
Charlotte, NC 704-295-7000

ProVisions Software
Smithfield, RI 800-422-4782

Qualtrax Inc
Christiansburg, VA 800-277-3077

Ramco Systems Corp
Lawrence Twp, NJ 800-472-6461

RDS of Florida
Fort Lauderdale, FL 305-994-7756

Redi-Print
West Babylon, NY 631-491-6373

Reflex International
Norcross, GA 800-642-7640

Remote Equipment Systems
Alpharetta, GA 800-803-9488

Retail Automations Products
New York, NY 800-237-9144

Retalix
Miamisburg, OH 877-794-7237

Rice Lake Weighing Systems
Rice Lake, WI 800-472-6703

Robocom Systems Intl
Farmingdale, NY 631-753-2180

Rockland Technology
Lewisville, TX 972-221-6190

ROI Software, LLC
Knoxville, TN 865-522-2211

Ross Computer Systems
Knoxville, TN 865-690-3008

Round Noon Software
Dallas, TX. 972-789-5191

RTI Inc
Marietta, GA 800-937-1290

Sable Technology Solution
St Paul, MN. 800-722-5390

Sales Partner System
Ormond Beach, FL 800-777-2924

SalesData Software
San Jose, CA 408-281-5811

Sanderson Computers
Worthington, OH 614-781-2525

SBA Software
Doral, FL 800-222-8324

SBS of Financial Industries
Washington, NJ 908-689-5520

Scan Corporation
Brandon, FL 800-881-7226

Schneider Electric
Foxboro, MA 781-534-7535

Schoneman Inc
Ashtabula, OH 800-255-4439

Schreck Software
Woodbury, MN 651-731-6822

SEI Consultants
Slidell, LA 800-738-1000

Shared Data Systems
Charlotte, NC 800-622-2140

SICOM Systems
Doylestown, PA 800-547-4266

Siemens Measurement Systems
Pittsford, NY 800-568-7721

Simply Products
Kunkletown, PA 610-681-6894

Squirrel Systems
Vancouver, BC 800-388-6824

Sterling Scale Co
Southfield, MI. 800-331-9931

Stratix Corp
Peachtree Cor, GA 800-883-8300

Success Systems
Stamford, GA 800-653-3345

Sweetware
Oakland, CA 800-526-7900

Swisslog Logistics Inc
Newport News, VA. 800-777-6862

SYSPRO USA
Costa Mesa, CA 800-369-8649

System Concepts Inc
Scottsdale, AZ. 800-553-2438

Systems Comtrex
Moorestown, NJ 800-220-2669

Tablecheck Technologies, Inc
Austin, TX. 800-522-1347

Tallygenicom
Irvine, CA. 800-665-6210

Tangible Vision
Franklin, TN 800-763-8634

Tek Visions
Temecula, CA 800-466-8005

Televend
Baltimore, MD 410-532-7818

Texture Technologies Corporation
Scarsdale, NY 914-472-0531

Tharo Systems Inc
Brunswick, OH 800-878-6833

Tibersoft
Westborough, MA. 888-888-1969

Tinadre Inc
Tampa, FL. 813-866-0333

TMT Software Company
Mayfield Heights, OH 800-401-6682

Touch Menus
Bellevue, WA 800-688-6368

Tricor Systems Inc
Elgin, IL 800-575-0161

Tricore AEA
Mt Pleasant, WI 262-880-3630

Trola Industries Inc
York, PA 717-848-3700

Unisoft Systems Associates
Dublin, OH 800-448-1574

Universal Dynamics Technologies
Richmond, BC 888-912-7246

Vande Berg SCALES/Vbs Inc
Sioux Center, IA 712-722-1181
Venture Measurement Co LLC
Spartanburg, SC 800-426-9010
Versatile Mobile Systems
Lynnwood, WA 800-262-1633
Vertex Interactive
Clifton, NJ 973-777-3500
W&H Systems
Carlstadt, NJ 201-933-9849
Wallace Computer Services
Chicago, IL 888-925-8324
Weber Packaging Solutions Inc
Arlington Heights, IL 800-843-4242
X-Rite Inc
Grand Rapids, MI 888-800-9580
Xcel Tower Controls
Gilbertsville, NY 800-288-7362
Zebra Technologies Corporation
Lincolnshire, IL 866-230-9494

Software

Routing & Scheduling for Food Industry

Formulator Software, LLC
Clinton, NJ 908-735-2248
Prism Visual Software Inc
Port Washington, NY 516-944-5920

Construction

Facility Design

Amco Mechanical
Spring, TX 281-353-2171
BE&K Building Group
Greenville, SC 864-250-5000
Boldt Co
Appleton, WI 920-739-6321
Dennis Engineering Group
Springfield, MA 413-787-1785
Dennsi Group
Springfield, MA 413-737-1353
Klinger Constructors LLC
Albuquerque, NM 505-822-9990
Shambaugh & Son
Fort Wayne, IN 260-487-7777
Tippmann Group
Fort Wayne, IN 260-490-3000

Management

BE&K Building Group
Greenville, SC 864-250-5000
Dennis Engineering Group
Springfield, MA 413-787-1785
Dennsi Group
Springfield, MA 413-737-1353
Facility Group
Smyrna, GA 770-437-2700
Stellar Group
Jacksonville, FL 800-488-2900

Metal Fabricators

A & B Process Systems Corp
Stratford, WI 888-258-2789
A J Antunes & Co
Carol Stream, IL 800-253-2991
A Legacy Food Svc
Santa Fe Springs, CA 800-848-4440
A-Z Factory Supply
Schiller Park, IL 800-323-4511
Abalon Precision Manufacturing Corporation
Bronx, NY 800-888-2225
ABC Letter Art
Los Angeles, CA 888-261-5367
ABCO Industries Limited
Lunenburg, NS 866-634-8821
Ace Fabrication
Mobile, AL 251-478-0401
Ace Stamp & Engraving
Lakewood, WA 253-582-3322
Acme International
Maplewood, NJ 973-416-0400
ACS Industries, Inc.
Lincoln, RI 866-783-4838
Adam Electric Signs
Massillon, OH 888-886-9911
Adapto Storage Products
Hialeah, FL 305-499-4800

Advance Fittings Corp
Elkhorn, WI. 262-723-6699
Advance Tabco
Edgewood, NY 800-645-3166
Advanced Uniflo Technologies
Wichita, KS 800-688-0400
Aero Manufacturing Co
Clifton, NJ 800-631-8378
AFGO Mechanical Svc Inc
Astoria, NY 800-438-2346
All American Container
Miami, FL 305-887-0797
All Power Inc
Sioux City, IA 712-258-0681
All Southern Fabricators
Clearwater, FL 800-878-2732
All Spun Metal Products
Des Plaines, IL 847-824-4117
All State Fabricators Corporation
Tampa, FL 800-322-9925
All-Clad METALCRAFTERS LLC
Canonsburg, PA 800-255-2523
Allegheny Bradford Corp
Bradford, PA 800-542-0650
Alliance Products LLC
Murfreesboro, TN 800-522-3973
Allied Engineering
North Vancouver, BC 877-929-1214
Alloy Products Corp
Waukesha, WI 800-236-6603
Allstrong Restaurant Eqpt Inc
South El Monte, CA 800-933-8913
ALP Lighting & Ceiling Products
Pennsauken, NJ 800-633-7732
ALPI Food Preparation Equipment
Bolton, ON 800-928-2574
Alumaworks
Sunny Isle Beach, FL 800-277-7267
Amco Metals Indl
City Of Industry, CA 626-855-2550
American Art Stamp
Gardena, CA 310-965-9004
American Lifts
Guthrie, OK. 877-360-6777
American Manufacturing-Engrng
Cleveland, OH 800-822-9402
American Metal Door Company
Richmond, IN 800-428-2737
American Production Co Inc
Redwood City, CA 650-368-5334
Ametco Manufacturing Corp
Willoughby, OH 800-321-7042
Amscor Inc
West Babylon, NY 800-825-9800
Amtekco
Columbus, OH 800-336-4677
Anderson-Crane Company
Minneapolis, MN 800-314-2747
Andgar Corp
Ferndale, WA 360-366-9900
Apache Stainless Equipment
Beaver Dam, WI 800-444-0398
APW Wyott Food Service Equipment Company
Cheyenne, WY 800-527-2100
ARC Specialties
Valencia, CA 661-775-8500
Archer Wire Intl Corp
Chicago, IL 708-563-1700
Architectural Sheet Metals LLC
Cleveland, OH 216-361-9952
Arizona Store Equipment
Phoenix, AZ 800-624-8395
Arkfeld Mfg & Distributing Co
Norfolk, NE. 800-533-0676
Armbrust Paper Tubes Inc
Chicago, IL 773-586-3232
ATD-American Co
Wyncote, PA 800-523-2300
Atlas Tag & Label Inc
Neenah, WI 800-558-6418
Audrey Signs
New York, NY 212-769-4992
Auger Fab
Exton, PA 800-334-1529
Automatic Specialties Inc
Marlborough, MA 800-445-2370
B C Holland Inc
Dousman, WI 262-965-2939
Baldewein Company
Lake Forrest, IL 800-424-5544
Ball Corp
Broomfield, CO 303-469-3131

Ballymore Company
West Chester, PA. 610-696-3250
Baltimore Sign Company
Arnold, MD. 410-276-1500
Barker Wire
Keosauqua, IA 319-293-3176
Barn Furniture Mart
Van Nuys, CA 888-302-2276
Bayhead Products Corp.
Dover, NH 800-229-4323
Beayl Weiner/Pak
Pacific Palisades, CA 310-454-1354
Behlen Manufacturing Co.
Columbus, NE. 402-564-3111
Bennett Manufacturing Company
Alden, NY 800-345-2142
Berloc Manufacturing & Sign Company
Sun Valley, CA 818-503-9823
Berlon Industries
Hustisford, WI 800-899-3580
Berndorf Belt Technology USA
Gilberts, IL 800-393-8450
Bertels Can Company
Belcamp, MD 410-272-0090
BG Industries
Lemont, IL 800-800-5761
BMH
City of Industry, CA 909-349-2530
Boehringer Mfg. Co. Inc.
Felton, CA. 800-630-8665
Bohn & Dawson
St Louis, MO. 800-225-5011
Borroughs Corp
Kalamazoo, MI 800-748-0227
Bowers Process Equipment
Stratford, ON. 800-567-3223
Bradford A Ducon Company
Pewaukee, WI. 800-789-1718
Bremer Manufacturing Co Inc
Elkhart Lake, WI. 920-894-2944
Brenner Tank LLC
Fond Du Lac, WI 800-558-9750
Brute Fabricators
Castroville, TX 800-777-2788
Bulman Products Inc
Grand Rapids, MI 616-363-4416
Burgess Mfg. - Oklahoma
Guthrie, OK. 800-804-1913
Burrows Paper Corp
Little Falls, NY 800-272-7122
C E Rogers Co
Mora, MN 800-279-8081
C Nelson Mfg Co
Oak Harbor, OH 800-922-7339
C R Mfg
Waverly, NE 877-789-5844
C&H Store Equipment Company
Los Angeles, CA. 800-648-4979
Caddy Corporation of America
Bridgeport, NJ 856-467-4222
California Caster & Handtruck
San Francisco, CA 800-950-8750
Canton Sign Co
Canton, OH. 330-456-7151
Caraustar Industries, Inc.
Archdale, NC 800-223-1373
Carbis Inc
Florence, SC 800-948-7750
Carmun International
San Antonio, TX 800-531-7907
Carrier Vibrating Equip Inc
Louisville, KY 502-969-3171
Carter-Hoffmann LLC
Mundelein, IL 800-323-9793
Carton Closing Company
Butler, PA 724-287-7759
Carts Food Equipment
Brooklyn, NY 718-788-5540
Central Fabricators Inc
Cincinnati, OH 800-909-8265
Charlton & Hill
Lethbridge, AB 403-328-3388
Chef Specialties
Smethport, PA 800-440-2433
Chemdet Inc
Sebastian, FL 800-645-1510
Cherry's Industrial Eqpt Corp
Elk Grove Vlg, IL 800-350-0011
Chester-Jensen Co., Inc.
Chester, PA 800-685-3750
Chipmaker Tooling Supply
Whittier, CA 800-659-5840

Claridge Products & Equipment
Harrison, AR
Classico Seating
Peru, IN. 800-968-6655
Clawson Container Company
Clarkston, MI 800-325-8700
Clayton & Lambert Manufacturing
Buckner, KY. 800-626-5819
Cleveland Metal Stamping Company
Berea, OH 440-234-0010
Cleveland Wire Cloth & Mfg Co
Cleveland, OH 800-321-3234
Cobb & Zimmer
Detroit, MI 313-923-0350
Columbian TecTank
Parsons, KS. 800-421-2788
Commercial Kitchen Co
Los Angeles, CA. 323-732-2291
Complex Steel & Wire Corp
Wayne, MI. 734-326-1600
Consolidated Can Co
Paramount, CA 888-793-2199
Consolidated Commercial Controls
Winsted, CT 800-227-1511
Container Supply Co
Garden Grove, CA 562-594-0937
Containment Technology
St Gabriel, LA. 800-388-2467
Continental-Fremont
Tiffin, OH 419-448-4045
Conveyor Components Co
Croswell, MI 800-552-3337
Corby Hall
Randolph, NJ 973-366-8300
Cotter Brothers Corp
Danvers, MA. 978-777-5001
COW Industries Inc
Columbus, OH 800-542-9353
Cramer Inc
Kansas City, MO. 800-366-6700
CRC Inc
Council Bluffs, IA. 712-323-9477
Creative Mobile Systems Inc
Manchester, CT. 800-646-8364
Crown Closures Machinery
Lancaster, OH 740-681-6593
Crown Cork & Seal Co Inc
Philadelphia, PA 215-698-5100
Crown Custom Metal Spinning
Concord, ON 800-750-1924
Crown Manufacturing Corporation
Waterford, CT. 860-442-4325
Crown Metal Mfg Co
Rancho Cucamonga, CA 909-291-8585
Crown Verity
Brantford, ON 888-505-7240
Cucamonga Sign Shop LLC
Rancho Cucamonga, CA 909-945-5888
Custom Diamond Intl.
Laval, QC 800-326-5926
Custom Fabricating & Repair
Marshfield, WI 800-236-8773
D & W Fine Pack
Lake Zurich, IL. 800-323-0422
D A Berther Inc
Milwaukee, WI 877-357-9622
D&D Sign Company
Wichita Falls, TX 940-692-4643
D. Picking & Company
Bucyrus, OH 419-562-6891
Damascus/Bishop Tube Company
Greenville, PA. 724-646-1500
Dansk International Designs
Bristol, PA. 914-697-6400
Davron Technologies Inc
Chattanooga, TN. 423-870-1888
Dayco
Clearwater, FL 727-573-9330
DCI, Inc.
St Cloud, MN 320-252-8200
Den Mar Corp
North Dartmouth, MA 508-999-3295
Despro Manufacturing
Cedar Grove, NJ 800-292-9906
Dimension Graphics Inc
Grand Rapids, MI 855-476-1281
Dinosaur Plastics
Houston, TX 713-923-2278
Doering Co
Clear Lake, MN 320-743-2276
Doran Scales Inc
Batavia, IL. 800-365-0084

Dormont Manufacturing Co
Export, PA. 800-367-6668
Dover Parkersburg
Follansbee, WV
Dreaco Products
Elyria, OH. 800-368-3267
Dubuque Steel Products Co
Dubuque, IA 563-556-6288
Duke Manufacturing Co
St Louis, MO. 800-735-3853
Duluth Sheet Metal
Duluth, MN 218-722-2613
Durham Manufacturing Co
Durham, CT 800-243-3744
E C Shaw Co
Cincinnati, OH 866-532-7429
Eagle Foodservice   Equipment
Clayton, DE. 800-441-8440
Eagle Group
Clayton, DE. 800-441-8440
Eastern Tabletop Mfg
Brooklyn, NY 888-422-4142
Easyup Storage Systems
Tukwila, WA 800-426-9234
EB Metal Industries
Whitehall, NY 518-499-1222
Econofrost Night Covers
Shawnigan Lake, BC 800-519-1222
Economy Paper & Restaurant Co
Clifton, NJ. 973-279-5500
Eldorado Miranda Manufacturing Company
Largo, FL 800-330-0708
Ellett Industries
Port Coquitlam, BC. 604-941-8211
Emc Solutions
Celina, OH 419-586-2388
Emedco
Williamsville, NY 877-765-8386
Enerfab Inc.
Cincinnati, OH 513-641-0500
Engineered Products Group
Madison, WI 800-626-3111
English Manufacturing Inc
Rancho Cordova, CA 800-651-2711
Enterprise Products
Bell Gardens, CA 562-928-1918
Erwin Food Service Equipment
Fort Worth, TX 817-535-0021
Etube & Wire
Shrewsbury, PA 800-618-4720
Eugene Welding Company
Marysville, MI 810-364-7421
Eurodib
Champlain, NY. 888-956-6866
Ex-Cell KAISER LLC
Franklin Park, IL. 847-451-0451
F & A Fabricating Inc
Battle Creek, MI 269-965-8371
F.P. Smith Wire Cloth Company
Northlake, IL. 800-323-6842
Fabricating & Welding Corp
Chicago, IL. 773-928-2050
Fabwright Inc
Garden Grove, CA 800-854-6464
Falcon Fabricators Inc
Nashville, TN 615-832-0027
Fata Automation
Sterling Heights, MI 586-323-9400
Faubion Central States Tank Company
Shawnee Mission, KS 800-450-8265
Federal Heath Sign Co LLC
Oceanside, CA 800-527-9495
FEI Inc
Mansfield, TX. 800-346-5908
Feldmeier Equipment Inc
Syracuse, NY 315-454-8608
Ferrer Corporation
San Juan, PR. 787-761-5151
Fine Woods Manufacturing
Phoenix, AZ 800-279-2871
Finn & Son's Metal Spinning Specialists
South Lebanon, OH 513-494-2898
Fisher Manufacturing Company
Tulare, CA. 800-421-6162
Fishmore
Melbourne, FL 321-723-4751
Fiskars Brands Inc.
Baldwinsville, NY 315-635-9911
Fixtur World
Cookeville, TN 800-634-9887
Flame Gard
Lakewood, NJ 800-526-3694

Flat Plate Inc
York, PA. 888-854-2500
Folding Guard Co
Chicago, IL. 800-622-2214
Food Warming Equipment Co
Crystal Lake, IL 800-222-4393
Forrest Engraving Company
New Rochelle, NY 914-632-9892
Forster & Son
Ada, OK 580-332-6021
Fountainhead
Bensalem, PA 800-326-8998
Frazier Industrial Co
Long Valley, NJ. 800-859-1342
Frazier Signs
Decatur, IL 217-429-2349
FRC Environmental
Gainesville, GA 770-534-3681
Friskem Infinetics
Wilmington, DE 302-658-2471
Fuller Box Co
North Attleboro, MA 508-695-2525
G A Systems Inc
Huntington Beach, CA 714-848-7529
Gasser Chair Co Inc
Youngstown, OH. 800-323-2234
Geerpres Inc
Muskegon, MI. 231-773-3211
General Industries Inc
Goldsboro, NC 888-735-2882
Gillis Associated Industries
Prospect Heights, IL 847-541-6500
Glaro Inc
Hauppauge, NY 631-234-1717
Glo-Quartz Electric Heater
Mentor, OH. 800-321-3574
GM Nameplate
Seattle, WA 800-366-7668
Goergen-Mackwirth Co Inc
Buffalo, NY. 800-728-4446
Gorbel Inc
Victor, NY. 585-924-6262
Graff Tank Erection
Harrisville, PA. 814-385-6671
Great Lakes Brush
Centralia, MO 573-682-2128
Green Brothers
Barrington, RI 401-245-9043
Green Metal Fabricating
West Sacramento, CA. 916-371-2951
Greif Inc
Delaware, OH 740-549-6000
Gribble Stamp & Stencil Co
Houston, TX 713-228-5358
Griffin Products
Wills Point, TX 800-379-9709
H & H Metal Fabrication Inc
Belden, MS 662-489-4626
Hallock Fabricating Corp
Riverhead, NY 631-727-2441
Halton Company
Scottsville, KY 800-442-5866
Hamilton Kettles
Weirton, WV 800-535-1882
Hank Rivera Associates
Dearborn, MI 313-581-8300
Hanset Stainless Inc
Portland, OR 800-360-7030
Hantover Inc
Kansas City, MO. 800-821-7849
Hardware Components Inc
New Matamoras, OH 740-865-2424
Hercules Food Equipment
Weston, ON 416-742-9673
Hewitt Manufacturing Co
Waldron, IN. 765-525-9829
Hillside Metal Ware Company
Union, NJ 908-964-3080
Hines III
Jacksonville, FL 904-398-5110
HMG Worldwide In-Store Marketing
New York, NY 212-736-2300
Hodge Manufacturing Company
Springfield, MA 800-262-4634
Hodges
Vienna, IL. 800-444-0011
Holmco Container Manufacturing, LTD
Baltic, OH 330-897-4503
Holsman Sign Svc
Cleveland, OH 216-761-4433
Hot Food Boxes
Mooresville, IN. 800-733-8073

Houston Wire Works, Inc.
South Houston, TX 800-468-9477
Howard Fabrication
City of Industry, CA 626-961-0114
Howes S Co Inc
Silver Creek, NY 888-255-2611
Hurri-Kleen Corporation
Birmingham, AL 800-455-8265
Ideal of America/Valley Rio Enterprise
Atlanta, GA 770-352-0210
Ideal Wire Works
Alhambra, CA 626-282-0886
Illinois Range Company
Schiller Park, IL 800-535-7041
IMC Teddy Food Service Equipment
Amityville, NY 800-221-5644
IMO Foods
Yarmouth, NS 902-742-3519
Imperial Schrade Corporation
Ellenville, NY 212-210-8600
Independent Can Co
Belcamp, MD 410-272-0090
Indiana Wire Company
Fremont, IN 877-786-6883
Industrial Air Conditioning Systems
Chicago, IL 773-486-4236
Industries Inc Kiefer
Random Lake, WI 920-994-2332
Institutional Equipment Inc
Bolingbrook, IL 630-771-0990
Intrex
Bethel, CT 203-792-7400
Irby
Rocky Mount, NC 252-442-0154
J L Clark Corp
Rockford, IL 815-962-8861
J.V. Reed & Company
Louisville, KY 877-258-7333
Jantec
Traverse City, MI 800-992-3303
Jarke Corporation
Prospect Hts, IL 800-722-5255
Jay-Bee Manufacturing Inc
Tyler, TX 800-445-0610
JEM Wire Products
Middletown, CT 860-347-0447
Jesco Industries
Litchfield, MI 800-455-0019
JH Display & Fixture
Greenwood, IN 317-888-0631
John Boos & Co
Effingham, IL 888-431-2667
Johnson-Rose Corporation
Lockport, NY 800-456-2055
Joyce Engraving Co Inc
Dallas, TX 214-638-1262
Jupiter Mills Corporation
Roslyn, NY 800-853-5121
JW Leser Company
Los Angeles, CA 323-731-4173
K & I Creative Plastics & Wood
Jacksonville, FL 904-387-0438
K C Booth Co
N Kansas City, MO 800-866-5226
Kaines West Michigan Co
Ludington, MI 231-845-1281
Kamflex Corp
Chicago, IL 800-323-2440
Karyall Telday Inc
Cleveland, OH 216-281-4063
Kason Central
Columbus, OH 614-885-1992
KEMCO
Wareham, MA 800-231-5955
Key Material Handling Inc
Simi Valley, CA 800-539-7225
Keystone Adjustable Cap Co Inc
Pennsauken, NJ 800-663-5439
King Sign Company
Akron, OH 330-762-7421
Kitchen Equipment Fabricating
Houston, TX 713-747-3611
Kitcor Corp
Sun Valley, CA 818-767-4800
Klinger Constructors LLC
Albuquerque, NM 505-822-9990
Kloppenberg & Co
Englewood, CO 800-346-3246
Koehler-Gibson Marking
Buffalo, NY 800-875-1562
Kofab
Algona, IA 515-295-7265

Kosempel Manufacturing Company
Philadelphia, PA 800-733-7122
L&H Wood Manufacturing Company
Farmington, MI 248-474-9000
L&L Engraving Company
Gilford, NH 888-524-3032
L&S Products
Coldwater, MI 517-279-9526
L.C. Thompson Company
Kenosha, WI 800-558-4018
La Crosse
Onalaska, WI 800-345-0018
Laidig Inc
Mishawaka, IN 574-256-0204
Lake Shore Industries Inc
Erie, PA 800-458-0463
Lakeside Manufacturing Inc
Milwaukee, WI 888-558-8565
Lakeside-Aris Manufacturing
Milwaukee, WI 800-558-8565
Lambert Material Handling
Syracuse, NY 800-253-5103
Lambertson Industries Inc
Sparks, NV 800-548-3324
Lancaster Colony Corporation
Westerville, OH 614-224-7141
Langer Manufacturing Company
Cedar Rapids, IA 800-728-6445
Lask Seating Company
Chicago, IL 888-573-2846
Laughlin Sales Corp
Fort Worth, TX 817-625-7756
Lavi Industries
Valencia, CA 800-624-6225
Lawrence Metal Products Inc
Bay Shore, NY 800-441-0019
Lazy Man Inc
Belvidere, NJ 800-475-1950
Le Smoker
Salisbury, MD 410-677-3233
Leeds Conveyor Manufacturer Company
Guilford, CT 800-724-1088
Leggett & Platt Storage
Vernon Hills, IL 847-816-6246
Legible Signs
Loves Park, IL 800-435-4177
License Ad Plate Co
Cleveland, OH 216-265-4200
Lincoln Foodservice
Cleveland, OH 800-374-3004
Linvar
Hartford, CT 800-282-5288
Little Rock Crate & Basket Co
Little Rock, AR 800-223-7823
Lloyd Disher Company
Decatur, IL 217-429-0593
Load King Mfg
Jacksonville, FL 800-531-4975
Lodge Manufacturing Company
South Pittsburg, TN 423-837-5919
Lodging By Charter
Liberty, NC 800-327-2548
Lorenz Couplings
Cobourg, ON 800-263-7782
Lorenzen's Cookie Cutters
Wantagh, NY 516-781-7116
Low Temp Industries Inc
Jonesboro, GA 678-674-1317
Loyal Manufacturing
Indianapolis, IN 317-359-3185
LPI Imports
Chicago, IL 877-389-6563
Lyco Wausau
Wausau, WI 715-845-7867
Lyon LLC
Montgomery, IL 630-892-8941
M & E Mfg Co Inc
Kingston, NY 845-331-2110
M O Industries Inc
Whippany, NJ 973-386-9228
Madsen Wire Products Inc
Orland, IN 260-829-6561
Magline Inc
Standish, MI 800-624-5463
Magsys Inc
Milwaukee, WI 414-543-2177
Malco Manufacturing Co
Los Angeles, CA 866-477-7267
Mar-Con Wire Belt
Richmond, BC 877-962-7266
Market Sign Systems
Portland, ME 800-421-1799

Marlin Steel Wire Products
Baltimore, MD 877-762-7546
Marlo Manufacturing
Boonton, NJ 800-222-0450
Marston Manufacturing
Cleveland, OH 216-587-3400
Martin/Baron
Irwindale, CA 626-960-5153
Material Storage Systems
Gadsden, AL 877-543-2467
Mcintyre Metals Inc
Thomasville, NC 800-334-0807
MCM Fixture Co
Hazel Park, MI 248-547-9280
Memphis Delta Tent & Awning
Memphis, TN 901-522-1238
Metal
Columbia, SC 803-776-9252
Metal Container Corporation
St Louis, MO 314-957-9500
Metal Equipment Company
Cleveland, OH 800-700-6326
Metal Kitchen Fabricators Inc
Houston, TX 713-683-8375
Metal Master Sales Corp
Glendale Heights, IL 800-488-8729
Metal Masters Northwest
Lynnwood, WA 425-775-4481
Metcraft
Grandview, MO 800-444-9624
Metko Inc
New Holstein, WI 920-898-4221
Mettler-Toledo, LLC
Columbus, OH 800-638-8537
Metz Premiums
New York, NY 212-315-4660
Micelli Chocolate Mold Company
West Babylon, NY 631-752-2888
Micro Wire Products Inc
Brockton, MA 508-584-0200
Micropure Filtration Inc
Mound, MN 800-654-7873
Mid-State Metal Casting & Mfg
Fresno, CA 559-445-1974
Mid-States Mfg & Engr Co Inc
Milton, IA 800-346-1792
Mid-West Wire Products
Ferndale, MI 800-989-9881
Midwest Metalcraft & Equipment
Windsor, MO 800-647-3167
Midwest Stainless
Menomonie, WI 715-235-5472
Midwest Wire Products LLC
Sturgeon Bay, WI 800-445-0225
MLS Signs Inc
Chesterfield, MI 586-948-0200
Modern Brewing & Design
Santa Rosa, CA 707-542-6620
Modern Metalcraft
Midland, MI 800-948-3182
Modern Metals Industries
El Segundo, CA 800-437-6633
Montebello Packaging
Hawkesbury, ON 613-632-7096
Mouli Manufacturing Corporation
Belleville, NJ 800-789-8285
Mouron & Co Inc
Indianapolis, IN 317-243-7955
Mulholland-Harper Company
Denton, MD 800-882-3052
Multivac
Union Grove, WI 800-640-4213
Music City Metals Inc
Nashville, TN 800-251-2674
Myers Container
Hayward, CA 510-785-8235
National Bar Systems
Huntington Beach, CA 714-848-1688
National Metal Industries
West Springfield, MA 800-628-8850
New Age Industrial
Norton, KS 800-255-0104
New Court
Texarkana, TX 903-838-0521
Nexel Industries Inc
Port Washington, NY 800-245-6682
Northern Metal Products
St Cloud, MN 800-458-5549
Northern Stainless Fabricating
Traverse City, MI 231-947-4580
Northwind Inc
Alpena, AR 877-937-2585

Novelis Foil Products
Atlanta, GA 800-776-8701
Nowakowski
Franklin, WI 800-394-5866
Ohlson Packaging
Taunton, MA 508-977-0004
Old Dominion Wood Products
Lynchburg, VA 800-245-6382
Olde Country Reproductions Inc
York, PA 800-358-3997
Olde Thompson Inc
Oxnard, CA 800-827-1565
Olive Can Company
Elgin, IL 847-468-7474
Omega Industrial Products Inc
Saukville, WI 800-279-6634
Omicron Steel Products Company
Jamaica, NY 718-805-3400
Oneida Food Service
Columbus, OH 800-828-7033
Orber Manufacturing Co
Cranston, RI 800-761-4059
OSF
Toronto, ON 800-465-4000
OTD Corporation
Hinsdale, IL 630-321-9232
Pacific Northwest Wire Works
Dupont, WA 800-222-7699
Pacific Scale Company
Clackamas, OR 800-537-1886
Packaging Aids Corporation
San Rafael, CA 415-454-4868
Padinox
Winsloe, PE. 800-263-9768
Pallet Management Systems
Lawrenceville, VA 800-446-1804
Parisi Inc
Newtown, PA 215-968-6677
Patrick & Co
Dallas, TX 214-761-0900
Paul Mueller Co Inc
Springfield, MO 800-683-5537
Paul O. Abbe
Bensenville, IL 630-350-2200
PBC
Mahwah, NJ 800-514-2739
Penasack Co Inc
Albion, NY 585-589-5873
Penco Products
Skippack, PA. 800-562-1000
Pengo Attachments Inc
Cokato, MN 800-599-0211
Pentwater Wire Products Inc
Pentwater, MI 877-869-6911
Perfect Equipment Inc
Gurnee, IL 800-356-6301
Peter Gray Corporation
Andover, MA 978-470-0990
Peterson Manufacturing Company
Plainfield, IL. 800-547-8995
Petro Moore Manufacturing Corporation
Long Island City, NY 718-784-2516
Pinquist Tool & Die Company
Brooklyn, NY 800-752-0414
Pittsburgh Tank Corp
Monongahela, PA 800-634-0243
Plasti-Line
Knoxville, TN 800-444-7446
Polar Process
Plattsville, ON. 877-896-8077
Polar Ware Company
Sheboygan, WI 800-237-3655
Pollard Brothers
Chicago, IL. 773-763-6868
Polyplastic Forms Inc
Farmingdale, NY 800-428-7659
Precision Printing & Packaging
Clarksville, TN 800-500-4526
Prince Seating Corp
Brooklyn, NY 800-577-4623
Pro-Ad-Co Inc
Portland, OR 800-287-5885
Process Solutions
Riviera Beach, FL. 561-840-0050
Production Equipment Co
Meriden, CT 800-758-5697
Proluxe
Paramount, CA 800-594-5528
Pronto Products Company
Arcadia, CA 800-377-6680
Pulva Corp
Valencia, PA 800-878-5828

Purolator Facet Inc
Greensboro, NC 800-852-4449
Quality Fabrication & Design
Coppell, TX 972-304-3266
Quality Industries Inc
La Vergne, TN. 615-793-3000
Quantum Storage Systems Inc
Miami, FL 800-685-4665
QUIKSERV Corp
Houston, TX 800-388-8307
Quipco Products Inc
Sauget, IL 314-993-1442
R & D Brass
Wappingers Falls, NY. 800-447-6050
R H Saw Corp
Barrington, IL 847-381-8777
R.G. Stephens Engineering
Long Beach, CA 800-499-3001
Randell Manufacturing   Unified Brands
Weidman, MI 888-994-7636
Randware Industries
Prospect Heights, IL 847-299-8884
Rath Manufacturing Company
Janesville, WI 800-367-7284
Redi-Call Inc
Reno, NV 800-648-1849
Reese Enterprises Inc
Rosemount, MN 800-328-0953
Regal Manufacturing Company
Chicago, IL. 773-921-3071
Regal Ware Inc
Kewaskum, WI 262-626-2121
Reinke & Schomann
Milwaukee, WI 414-964-1100
Republic Storage Systems LLC
Canton, OH 800-477-1255
Rex Art Manufacturing Corp.
Lindenhurst, NY 631-884-4600
Richards Industries Systems
West Caldwell, NJ 973-575-7480
Rigidized Metal Corp
Buffalo, NY. 800-836-2580
Rjr Technologies
Oakland, CA 510-638-5901
Robby Vapor Systems
Sunrise, FL 800-888-8711
Robert-James Sales
Buffalo, NY. 800-777-1325
Robertson Furniture Co Inc
Toccoa, GA 800-241-0713
Romatic Manufacturing Co
Southbury, CT. 203-264-3442
Rome Machine & Foundry Co
Rome, GA 800-538-7663
Ross Engineering Inc
Savannah, GA 800-524-7677
Royal Display Corporation
Middletown, CT 800-569-1295
Royal Paper Products
Coatesville, PA 800-666-6655
Royal Welding & Fabricating
Fullerton, CA 714-680-6669
Royce Rolls Ringer Co
Grand Rapids, MI 800-253-9638
RTI Shelving Systems
Elmhurst, NY 800-223-6210
Rubbermaid Commercial Products
Pottsville, PA. 800-233-0314
Rubicon Industries
Brooklyn, NY 800-662-6999
Rytec Corporation
Milwaukee, WI 888-467-9832
S & L Store Fixture
Doral, FL. 800-205-4536
S.S.I. Schaefer System International Limited
Brampton, ON. 905-458-5399
Salem China Company
Salem, OH. 330-337-8771
Samuel Strapping Systems Inc
Woodridge, IL. 800-323-4424
Sani-Fit
Pasadena, CA 626-395-7895
Sarasota Restaurant Equipment
Sarasota, FL 800-434-1410
Savage Brothers Company
Elk Grove Vlg, IL. 800-342-0973
Scherping Systems
Winsted, MN. 320-485-4401
Schwaab, Inc
Milwaukee, WI 800-935-9877
Seating Concepts Inc
Rockdale, IL 800-421-2036

Seattle Boiler Works Inc
Seattle, WA 206-762-0737
Sefi Fabricators Inc
Amityville, NY 631-842-2200
Seneca Environmental Products
Tiffin, OH 419-447-1282
Sfb Plastics Inc
Wichita, KS 800-343-8133
Sharpsville Container Corp
Sharpsville, PA 800-645-1248
Shaw & Slavsky Inc
Detroit, MI 800-521-7527
Sigma Industries
Elkhart, IN. 574-295-9660
Sign Systems, Inc.
Warren, MI 586-758-1600
Signet Marking Devices
Costa Mesa, CA 800-421-5150
Silgan White Cap LLC
Downers Grove, IL 800-515-1565
Sims Machinery Co Inc
Lanett, AL. 334-576-2101
Sirco Systems
Birmingham, AL. 205-731-7800
Solve Needs International
White Lake, MI 800-783-2462
Sossner Steel Stamps
Elizabethton, TN 800-828-9515
South Valley Mfg Inc
Gilroy, CA 408-842-5457
Southern Metal Fabricators Inc
Albertville, AL 800-989-1330
Spanco Crane & Monorail Systems
Morgantown, PA 800-869-2080
Spartanburg Steel Products Inc
Spartanburg, SC 800-974-7500
Specialty Blades
Staunton, VA 540-248-2200
Specific Mechanical Systems
Victoria, BC. 250-652-2111
Speedrack Products Group LTD
Sparta, MI 616-887-0002
Speedways Conveyors
Lancaster, NY 800-800-1022
SPG International
Covington, GA 877-503-4774
Spot Wire Works Company
Philadelphia, PA 215-627-6124
Spring USA Corp
Naperville, IL 800-535-8974
Springfield Metal Products Co
Springfield, NJ 973-379-4600
Springport Steel Wire Products
Elkhart, IN. 574-295-9660
SSW Holding Co Inc
Elizabethtown, KY 270-769-5526
Stainless
La Vergne, TN. 800-877-5177
Stainless Equipment Manufacturing
Dallas, TX 800-736-2038
Stainless Fabricating Company
Denver, CO. 800-525-8966
Stainless Fabrication Inc
Springfield, MO 800-397-8265
Stainless International
Rancho Cordova, CA 888-300-6196
Stainless Products
Somers, WC 800-558-9446
Stainless Specialists Inc
Wausau, WI 800-236-4155
Stainless Steel Fabricator Inc
La Mirada, CA 714-739-9904
Stainless Steel Fabricators
Tyler, TX 903-595-6625
Star Filters
Timmonsville, SC 800-845-5381
Starlite Food Service Equipment
Detroit, MI 888-521-6603
Steel City Corporation
Youngstown, OH. 800-321-0350
Stegall Mechanical INC
Birmingham, AL. 800-633-4373
Stello Products Inc
Spencer, IN 800-878-2246
Sterling Process Engineering
Columbus, OH 800-783-7875
Sterling Scale Co
Southfield, MI. 800-331-9931
Stogsdill Tile Co
Huntley, IL 800-323-7504
Storm Industrial
Shawnee Mission, KS 800-745-7483

Straits Steel & Wire Co
Ludington, MI. 231-843-3416
Streator Dependable Mfg
Streator, IL 800-798-0551
Stryco Wire Products
North York, ON. 416-663-7000
Suburban Signs
College Park, MD 301-474-5051
Super Steel
Milwaukee, WI 414-355-4800
Super Sturdy
Weldon, NC. 800-253-4833
Superior Brush Company
Cleveland, OH 216-941-6987
Supreme Fabricators
Artesia, CA 323-583-8944
Supreme Metal
Alpharetta, GA 800-645-2526
Swanson Wire Works Industries, Inc.
Mesquite, TX 972-288-7465
T & A Metal Products Inc
Deptford, NJ 856-227-1700
T & T Industries Inc
Fort Mohave, AZ 800-437-6246
Table De France: North America
New Brunswick, NJ 888-680-4616
Talbot Industries
Neosho, MO 417-451-5900
Tampa Sheet Metal Co
Tampa, FL 813-251-1845
Tar-Hong MELAMINE USA
City Of Industry, CA. 626-935-1612
Thermo Wisconsin
De Pere, WI. 920-766-7200
Tilly Industries
St Laurent, QC 514-331-4922
Tin Box Co Of America Inc
Farmingdale, NY 800-888-8467
Top Line Process Equipment Company
Bradford, PA 800-458-6095
Tops Manufacturing Co
Darien, CT. 203-655-9367
Traulsen & Co
Fort Worth, TX 800-825-8220
Travelon
Elk Grove Vlg, IL 800-537-5544
Travis Manufacturing Corp
Alliance, OH. 330-875-1661
Tri-Boro Shelving & Partition
Farmville, VA 800-633-3070
Triner Scale & Mfg Co
Olive Branch, MS 800-238-0152
Triple-A Manufacturing Company
Toronto, ON 800-786-2238
Tropic KOOL
Largo, FL .727-581-2824
TWM Manufacturing
Leamington, ON 888-495-4831
Ultratainer
St Jean-Sur-Richelie, QC 514-359-3651
Unifoil Corp
Fairfield, NJ 973-244-9990
United Industries Inc
Beloit, WI .608-365-8891
United Performance Metals
Northbrook, IL 888-922-0040
United Steel Products Company
East Stroudsburg, PA 570-476-1010
UniTrak Corporation
Port Hope, ON 866-883-5749
Universal Stainless
Aurora, CO 800-223-8332
Universal Stainless & Alloy
Titusville, PA 800-295-1909
Uniweb Inc
Corona, CA 800-486-4932
Update International
Vernon, CA 800-747-7124
Upham & Walsh Lumber
Hoffman Estates, IL 847-519-1010
US Can Company
Rosedale, MD. 800-436-8021
US Seating Products
Ocala, FL. .800-999-2589
US Standard Sign
Franklin Park, IL. 800-537-4790
USECO
Murfreesboro, TN 615-893-4820
V&R Metal Enterprises
Brooklyn, NY 718-768-8142
Vacumet Corp
Wayne, NJ. 973-628-1067

Vacuum Depositing Inc
Louisville, KY 502-969-4227
Valley Craft Inc
Lake City, MN 800-328-1480
Valvinox
Iberville, QC 450-346-1981
Vasconia Housewares
San Antonio, TX. 800-377-6723
Venus Corp
Blytheville, AR. 870-763-3830
Versailles Lighting
Delray Beach, FL 888-564-0240
Victone Manufacturing Company
Chicago, IL 312-738-3211
Viking Machine & Design Inc
De Pere, WI. 888-286-2116
Vollrath Co LLC
Sheboygan, WI 800-624-2051
Vulcan Industries
Moody, AL 888-444-4417
W J Egli & Co
Alliance, OH. 330-823-3666
Wahlstrom Manufacturing
Fontana, CA 909-822-4677
Walco
Utica, NY .800-879-2526
Walker Stainless Equipment Co
New Lisbon, WI 608-562-7500
Waukesha Foundry Inc
Waukesha, WI. 800-727-0741
Waukesha Specialty Company
Darien, WI. 262-724-3700
Wayne Industries
Clanton, AL 800-225-3148
Weavewood, Inc.
Golden Valley, MN 800-367-6460
Weiss Sheet Metal Inc
Avon, MA .508-583-8300
Wemas Metal Products
Calgary, AB. 403-276-4451
Wendell August Forge
Grove City, PA 800-923-1390
West Star Industries
Stockton, CA. 800-326-2288
Western Pacific Stge Solutions
San Dimas, CA 800-888-5707
Western Plastics
Calhoun, GA 800-752-4106
Westfield Sheet Metal Works
Kenilworth, NJ 908-276-5500
Wheel Tough Company
Terre Haute, IN 888-765-8833
White Rabbit Dye Inc
St Louis, MO. 800-466-6588
Whiting & Davis
Attleboro Falls, MA 800-876-6374
Wilder Manufacturing Company
Port Jervis, NY 800-832-1319
Williamsburg Metal Spinning
Brooklyn, NY 888-535-5402
Winmark Stamp & Sign
Salt Lake City, UT 800-438-0480
Winston Industries
Louisville, KY 800-234-5286
Wire Belt Co Of America
Londonderry, NH 603-644-2500
Wirefab Inc
Worcester, MA 877-877-4445
Wiremaid Products Div
Coral Springs, FL 800-770-4700
WITT Industries Inc
Mason, OH 800-543-7417
Woerner Wire Works
Omaha, NE 402-451-5414
Woodard
Coppell, TX 800-877-2290
Yargus Manufacturing Inc
Marshall, IL 217-826-8059
Yates Industries Inc
St Clair Shores, MI 586-778-7680
YW Yacht Basin
Easton, MD. 410-822-0414
Zelco Industries
Mount Vernon, NY 800-431-2486
Zol-Mark Industries
Winnipeg, NB 204-943-7393

Turn Key

Barry Wehmiller Design Group
New London, NH 866-526-2585

Consultants

Agriculture Consulting Services
New York City, NY. 347-709-7587
AgriFiber Solutions
Mundelein, IL 847-549-6002
Agworld
Windsor, CO 724-249-6753
AIB International
Manhattan, KS 800-633-5137
Austin Co
Cleveland, OH 440-544-2600
BKI
Oakland, CA 510-444-8707
Boldt Co
Appleton, WI 920-739-6321
Bridgewell Resources LLC
Clackamas, OR 800-481-3557
Burdock Group
Orlando, FL. 407-802-1400
Consulting Nutritional Services
Calabasas, CA. 818-880-6774
Cretel Food Equipment
Holland, MI. 616-786-3980
DuPont
Wilmington, DE 800-441-7515
Excel-A-Tec Inc
Brookfield, WI 262-252-3600
Family Farms Group
Brighton, IL 877-221-3276
FoodLogiQ
Durham, NC 866-492-4468
Fresca Foods Inc.
Louisville, CO. 303-996-8881
Howlett Farms
Avon, NY .585-226-8340
iFoodDecisionSciences
Kenmore, WA 206-219-3703
IMS Food Service™
Shelton, CT. 800-235-7072
In Harvest Inc
Bemidji, MN 800-346-7032
J.S. Ferraro
Toronto, ON 800-278-0018
K-Coe Isom
Loveland, CO 800-461-4702
Maximus Systems
St-Bruno-de-Montarville, QC. 877-445-6556
Murray Runin
Mahwah, NJ 201-512-3885
Outside the Lines, Inc
Sonoma, CA 707-933-0687
Shambaugh & Son
Fort Wayne, IN 260-487-7777
Syngenta
Greensboro, NC 800-334-9481
The Good Food Institute
Washington, DC 866-849-4457
Townsend Research Laboratories, Inc
Indianapolis, IN 317-375-0893
Trimble Agriculture
Westminster, CO
USC Consulting Group
Tampa, FL. 800-888-8872
Virginia Department of Agriculture & Consumer Services
Richmond, VA. 804-786-3520
WineAndHospitalityJobs.com
Sonoma, CA 707-933-0687
Zume
Mountain View, CA

Design

A & B Process Systems Corp
Stratford, WI 888-258-2789
AAMD
Liverpool, NY. 800-887-4167
Accommodation Program
New York, NY 800-929-1414
Agriculture Consulting Services
New York City, NY. 347-709-7587
Aidi International Hotels of America
Washington, DC 202-331-9299
Aldo Locascio
Tucson, AZ 800-488-8729
ALPI Food Preparation Equipment
Bolton, ON 800-928-2574
ALY Group of New York
Pleasantville, NY 603-493-8088
American Agribusiness Assistance
Alexandria, VA 202-429-0500
American Material Handling Inc
N Little Rock, AR. 800-482-5801

American Systems Associates
  Hampton Bays, NY................800-584-3663
Anhydro Inc
  Olympia Fields, IL.............708-747-7000
APA
  Omaha, NE....................402-290-5597
Architectural Products
  Highland, NY.................845-691-8500
Art-Tech Restaurant Design
  Rockville Centre, NY..........516-593-9130
Aseptic Resources
  Overland Park, KS.............913-897-4125
Aspect Engineering
  Westerville, OH...............614-638-7106
Asset Design LLC
  Mooresville, NC...............888-293-1740
Awb Engineers
  Salisbury, MD.................410-742-7299
B T Engineering Inc
  Bala Cynwyd, PA...............610-664-9500
Baker Foodservice Design Inc
  Grand Rapids, MI..............800-968-4011
Bargreen Ellingson
  Tacoma, WA....................800-322-4441
Barry Wehmiller Design
  Alpharetta, GA................800-667-6250
Barry Wehmiller Design Group
  New London, NH................866-526-2585
Barry-Wehmiller Design Group
  St Louis, MO..................314-862-8000
Basic Leasing Corporation
  Kearny, NJ....................973-817-7373
BEC International
  Louisville, KY................877-232-4687
Best Restaurant Equip & Design
  Columbus, OH..................800-837-2378
Big-D Construction Corp
  Salt Lake City, UT............801-415-6000
Bintz Restaurant Supply Company
  Salt Lake City, UT............800-443-4746
Bresco
  Birmingham, AL................205-252-0076
Brevard Restaurant Equipment
  Rockledge, FL.................321-631-0318
Brown/Millunzi & Associates
  Houston, TX...................800-460-3387
Carmona Designs
  Chula Vista, CA...............619-425-2800
Center for Packaging Education
  Somers, NY....................914-276-0425
CHL Systems
  Souderton, PA.................215-723-7284
Chroust Associates International
  Woodland Hills, CA............818-348-1438
CII Food Svc Design
  Lapeer, MI....................810-667-3100
Citra-Tech
  Lefkosia, CY
Clevenger Frable Lavallee
  White Plains, NY..............914-997-9660
Coastal Mechanical Svc Inc
  Stamford, CT..................203-359-3070
Cober Electronics, Inc.
  Norwalk, CT...................800-709-5948
Concepts & Design International, Ltd
  West Nyack, NY................845-358-1558
Container-Quinn Testing Lab
  Wheeling, IL..................847-537-9470
Cooper Decoration Company
  Weston, MA....................315-475-1661
Crepas & Associates
  Elmhurst, IL..................630-833-4880
Curtis Restaurant Equipment
  Springfield, OR...............541-746-7480
D'Addario Design Associates
  New York, NY..................212-302-0059
DCS IPAL Consultants
  Laval, QC.....................450-973-3338
DECI Corporation
  Burgettstown, PA..............724-947-3300
Dembling & Dembling Architects
  Albany, NY....................518-463-8066
Dennsi Group
  Springfield, MA...............413-737-1353
Design Group
  Clearwater, FL................727-441-2825
Diamond & Lappin
  Fair Lawn, NJ.................877-527-7461
Digital Image & Sound Corporation
  Rochester, NY.................585-381-0410
Divercon Inc
  Omaha, NE.....................402-571-5115

Don Walters Company
  Stanton, CA...................714-892-0275
Donalds & Associates
  Long Beach, CA................562-290-8440
Eagle-Concordia Paper Corporation
  Farmingdale, NY...............212-255-3860
Fabricon Products Inc
  River Rouge, MI...............313-841-8200
Fenster Consulting Inc
  Port Washington, NY...........516-944-7108
First Bank of Highland P
  Northbrook, IL................847-272-1300
Fleet Wood Goldco Wyard
  Cockeysville, MD..............410-785-1934
FMB Company
  Broken Bow, OK................580-513-5309
Food & Agrosystems
  Sunnyvale, CA.................408-245-8450
Food Industry ConsultingGroup
  Dunnellon, FL.................800-443-5820
Food Technologies
  Golden Valley, MN.............763-544-8586
Foodpro International
  Stockton, CA..................888-687-5797
Foodservice Design Associates
  Orlando, FL...................407-896-4115
Foster Miller Inc
  Waltham, MA...................781-684-4000
Foth & Van Dyke
  Green Bay, WI.................920-497-2500
Graphic Impressions of Illinois
  River Grove, IL...............708-453-1100
Group One Partners
  Boston, MA....................617-268-7000
H & H Metal Fabrication Inc
  Belden, MS....................662-489-4626
Hampton-Tilley Associates
  Chesterfield, MO..............813-418-3340
Hanson Lab Furniture Inc
  Newbury Park, CA..............805-498-3121
Hunter Graphics
  Umatilla, FL..................407-644-2060
Hy-Ten Plastics Inc
  Milford, NH...................603-673-1611
Industrial Consortium
  Sulphur Springs, TX...........903-885-6610
Inman Foodservices Group LLC
  Nashville, TN.................615-321-5591
Innovations by Design
  Chadds Ford, PA...............610-558-0160
Innovative Space Management
  Woodside, NY..................718-278-4300
Intelplex Designers
  St Louis, MO..................314-983-9996
Interbrand Corporation
  San Francisco, CA.............877-692-7263
IPG International Packaging Group
  Agoura Hills, CA..............818-865-1428
Item Products
  Houston, TX...................800-333-4932
J/W Design Associates
  San Francisco, CA.............415-546-7707
Jacobs Engineering Group
  Dallas, TX....................214-638-0145
Janows Design Associates
  Lincolnwood, IL...............847-763-0620
Jenike & Johanson Inc
  Tyngsboro, MA.................978-649-3300
Joul, Engineering StaffiSolutions
  Edison, NJ....................800-341-0341
Kochman Consultants LTD
  Morton Grove, IL..............847-470-1195
Kohlenberger Associates Consulting Engineering
  Fullerton, CA.................714-738-7733
Landmark Kitchen Design
  Chandler, AZ..................866-621-3192
Laschober & Sovich Inc
  Woodland Hills, CA............818-713-9011
Legge & Associates
  Rockwood, ON..................519-856-0444
Lobsters Alive Company
  Georgetown, ME................207-371-2990
Lockwood Greene Engineers
  Knoxville, TN.................251-476-2400
Lockwood Greene Engineers
  Knoxville, TN.................256-533-9907
Lockwood Greene Engineers
  Brentwood, TN.................615-221-5031
Lockwood Greene Engineers
  Augusta, GA...................706-724-8225
Lockwood Greene Engineers
  Somerset, NJ..................732-560-5700

Lockwood Greene Engineers
  Atlanta, GA...................770-829-6500
Lockwood Greene Engineers
  Guaynabo, PR..................787-781-9050
Lockwood Greene Engineers
  Knoxville, TN.................865-218-5377
Lockwood Greene Engineers
  Dallas, TX....................972-991-5505
Lockwood Greene Technologies
  Augusta, GA...................505-889-3831
Lorrich & Associates
  San Diego, CA.................858-586-0823
Management Insight
  Malborough, MA................508-485-2100
Material Systems Engineering
  Stilesville, IN...............800-634-0904
McNichols Conveyor Company
  Southfield, MI................800-331-1926
Mead & Hunt Inc
  Madison, WI...................888-364-7272
Metcalf & Eddy
  Wakefield, MA.................781-246-5200
Michael Blackman & Assoc
  Santa Monica, CA..............800-889-4925
Moseley Realty LLC
  Franklin, MA..................800-667-3539
Nicosia Creative Expresso
  New York, NY..................212-515-6600
Nimbus Water Systems
  Murrieta, CA..................800-451-9343
Nina Mauritz Design Service
  Libertyville, IL..............847-968-4438
Northeast Box Co
  Ashtabula, OH.................800-362-8100
Nutrinfo Corporation
  Watertown, MA.................800-676-6686
O.B.S. Trading
  Jackson, MO...................573-243-6999
Omega Company
  Stamford, CT..................800-848-4286
Ottenheimer Equipment Company
  Lutherville Timonium, MD......410-597-9700
PacTech Engineering
  Cincinnati, OH................513-792-1090
Patrick E. Panzarello Consulting Services
  Sunland, CA...................818-353-0431
Pharmaceutical & Food Special
  San Jose, CA..................408-275-0161
Phoenix & Eclectic Network
  Elmhurst, IL..................630-530-4373
Premier Restaurant Equipment
  Brooklyn Park, MN.............763-544-8800
Product Solutions
  Wilkes Barre, PA..............888-776-3765
R.C. Keller & Associates
  Barnegat, NJ..................973-694-8810
Raque Food Systems
  Louisville, KY................502-267-9641
Raytheon Co
  Waltham, MA...................781-522-3000
RGN Developers
  New Providence, NJ
RMF Companies
  Grandview, MO.................816-839-9258
Robert C Vncek Design Assoc
  Sussex, NJ....................973-702-8553
Robinett & Assoc
  Richardson, TX................972-234-1945
ROI Software, LLC
  Knoxville, TN.................865-522-2211
Ron Vallort & Associates
  Oak Brook, IL.................630-734-3821
SBS of Financial Industries
  Washington, NJ................908-689-5520
Schroeder Machine
  San Marcos, CA................760-591-9733
Seattle Menu Specialists
  Kent, WA......................800-622-2826
Seiberling Associates Inc
  Beloit, WI....................608-313-1235
Setter, Leach & Lindstrom
  Minneapolis, MN...............612-338-8741
Shook Kelley Design Group
  Charlotte, NC.................704-377-0661
Southern Store Fixtures Inc
  Bessemer, AL..................800-552-6283
Sprinkman Corporation
  Franksville, WI...............800-816-1610
SSOE Group
  Toledo, OH....................419-255-3830
St Onge Ruff & Associates
  Kansas City, MO...............800-800-5261

Stokes Material Handling Systs
Doylestown, PA 215-340-2200
Stratecon International Consultants
Winston Salem, NC.........336-768-6808
Sverdrup Facilities
Saint Louis, MO 800-325-7910
Syngenta
Greensboro, NC 800-334-9481
T E Ibberson Co
Hopkins, MN 952-938-7007
TDF Automation
Cedar Falls, IA 800-553-1777
Tetra Pak
Champlin, MN 763-421-2721
The Good Food Institute
Washington, DC 866-849-4457
Trimble Agriculture
Westminster, CO
Tuchenhagen
Columbia, MD 410-910-6000
Twenty First Century Design
Albany, NY 518-446-0939
UAA
Chicago, IL 800-813-1711
United Industries Group Inc
Lake Forest, CA 949-759-3200
US Magnetix
Minneapolis, MN 763-540-9497
Washington Group International
San Francisco, CA 800-877-0980
Wayne Combustion Systems
Fort Wayne, IN 800-443-4625
Webber Smith Assoc
Lancaster, PA 800-231-0392
Wesley-Kind Associates
Mineola, NY 516-747-3434
Westfield Sheet Metal Works
Kenilworth, NJ 908-276-5500
Wyssmont Co Inc
Fort Lee, NJ 201-947-4600

Food Technology

A&L Western Ag Lab
Modesto, CA. 209-529-4080
ABIC International Consultants
Fairfield, NJ 973-227-7060
ADD Testing & Research
Valley Stream, NY 516-568-9197
Agricultural Research Service
Washington, SW 202-720-3656
AgriTech
Columbus, OH 614-488-2772
AM Test Laboratories
Kirkland, WA 425-885-1664
American Style Foods
Old Hickory, TN 615-847-0410
Ameritech Laboratories
Flushing, NY. 718-461-0475
Anresco Laboratories
San Francisco, CA 800-359-0920
Arthur D Little Inc.
Boston, MA. 617-532-9550
Asi Food Safety Consultants
St Louis, MO. 800-477-0778
Aspect Engineering
Westerville, OH. 614-638-7106
Aspen Research Corporation
White Bear Lake, MN. 651-773-7961
Bedrosian & Assoc
Redwood City, CA 650-367-0259
Bernard Wolnak & Associates
Northbrook, IL 847-480-0427
BFB Consultants
Mississauga, ON 905-819-9856
Bioenergetics Inc
Madison, WI. 608-255-4028
Biovail Technologies
Chantilly, VA 703-995-2400
Brand Specialists
Duncanville, TX 888-323-3708
Broadmoor Baker
Seattle, WA. 206-624-3660
Cardinal Kitchens
London, ON 800-928-0832
Catalent Pharma Solutions Inc
Winchester, KY. 859-745-8679
Chaska Chocolate
Chaska, MN 952-448-5699
Codema
Maple Grove, MN. 763-428-2266

Conatech Consulting Group, Inc
Saint Louis, MO 314-995-9767
Concepts & Design International, Ltd
West Nyack, NY 845-358-1558
Culinar
Montreal, QC 514-255-2811
Cynter Con Technology Adviser
Gaithersburg, MD 800-287-1811
Cyntergy Corporation
Rockville, MD 800-825-5787
Damon Industries
Alliance, OH 800-362-9850
Deibel Laboratories Inc
Madison, WI 608-241-1177
EPL Technologies
Devon, PA 800-637-3743
Eurofins S-F Analytical Labs
New Berlin, WI. 800-300-6700
Food & Agrosystems
Sunnyvale, CA 408-245-8450
Food & Beverage Consultants
Cranston, RI 401-463-5784
Food Consulting Company
Del Mar, CA 800-793-2844
Food Development Centre
Portage La Prairie, NB ...800-870-1044
Food Industry ConsultingGroup
Dunnellon, FL 800-443-5820
Food Science Associates
Crugers, NY 914-739-7541
Food Science Consulting
Walnut Creek, CA 925-947-6785
Food Technologies
Golden Valley, MN 763-544-8586
Food-Tek
Whippany, NJ 800-648-8114
Foods Research Laboratories
Boston, MA. 617-442-3322
Future Foods
Chicago, IL 312-987-9342
George G. Giddings
Randolph, NJ 973-361-4687
George Lapgley Enterprises
Pipersville, PA. 267-221-2426
Healthy Dining
San Diego, CA 800-266-2049
Industrial Laboratories Co
Wheat Ridge, CO 800-456-5288
Ingman Laboratories
Minneapolis, MN 612-724-0121
Innovative Food Solutions LLC
Columbus, OH 800-884-3314
Inter-Access
Etobicoke, ON 514-744-6262
J Leek Assoc Inc
Edenton, NC 252-482-4456
James V. Hurson Associates
Arlington, VA 800-642-6564
Jl Analytical Svc Inc
Modesto, CA. 209-538-8111
Jonessco Enterprises
Plano, TX 972-985-7961
Kashrus Technical Consultants
Lakewood, NJ 732-364-8046
Kelley Advisory Services
Northbrook, IL 847-412-9234
KOF-K Kosher Supervision
Teaneck, NJ 201-837-0500
Landmark Kitchen Design
Chandler, AZ. 866-621-3192
Lawrence-Allen Group
San Mateo, CA 800-609-2909
Lebensmittel Consulting
Fostoria, OH 419-435-2774
Libra Technical Center
Metuchen, NJ 732-321-5200
Line of Snacks Consultants
Dallas, TX. 972-484-1155
M-Tech & Associates
Downers Grove, IL 630-810-9714
Malcolm Stogo Associates
Scarsdale, NY 914-472-7255
Matrix Group Inc.
Bloomfield, NJ 973-338-5638
MC Creation
San Francisco, CA 415-775-1135
Merlin Development Inc
Minneapolis, MN 763-475-0224
Micro-Chem Laboratory
Mississauga, ON 905-795-0490
Microbac-Wilson Devision
Wilson, NC. 252-237-4175

Microwave Research Center
Eagan, MN 651-456-9190
Midwest Laboratories
Omaha, NE 402-334-7770
Miles Willard Technologies
Idaho Falls, ID 208-523-4741
Milligan & Higgins
Johnstown, NY 518-762-4638
Minnesota Valley Testing Lab
New Ulm, MN. 800-782-3557
National Food Laboratories Inc
Livermore, CA 925-828-1440
Natural Marketing Institute
Harleysville, PA 215-513-7300
NorCrest Consulting
Divide, CO 719-687-7635
Northeast Laboratory Svc
Winslow, ME. 866-591-7120
Northland Labs
Northbrook, IL 800-366-3522
Northwest Laboratories
Seattle, WA. 206-763-6252
Nutrinfo Corporation
Watertown, MA. 800-676-6686
Nutrition Network
Irvine, CA 949-753-7998
Nutrition Research
Livingston, MT 406-222-3541
O.B.S. Trading
Jackson, MO 573-243-6999
Oklabs
Oklahoma City, OK 405-843-6832
Omega Company
Stamford, CT. 800-848-4286
Petal
New York, NY 212-947-3662
Peter Kalustian Associates
Boonton, NJ 973-334-3008
Phytopia Inc
Dallas, TX. 888-750-9336
POS Pilot Plant Corporation
Saskatoon, SK. 800-230-2751
Positive Employment Practice
New City, NY 845-638-6442
Power Packaging Inc
Rosendale, WI. 920-872-2181
Protein Research
Livermore, CA 800-948-1991
PSI
Oakbrook Terrace, IL 630-705-9290
Purity Laboratories
Lake Oswego, OR. 800-977-3636
Q Laboratories
Cincinnati, OH 513-471-1300
Quality Bakers of America
Allentown, PA. 973-263-6970
R F Schiffmann Assoc.
New York, NY 212-362-7021
Richardson Researches
South San Francisco, CA ..510-653-4385
Riverview Foods
Warsaw, KY. 859-567-5211
Robin Shepherd Group
Jacksonville, FL 877-896-8774
Schiff & Co
West Caldwell, NJ. 973-227-1830
Schroeder Machine
San Marcos, CA 760-591-9733
Sensory Spectrum
New Providence, NJ 908-376-7000
Sentinel Lubricants Inc
Miami, FL. 800-842-6400
Shear/Kershman Laboratories
Chesterfield, MO 636-519-8900
Simon S. Jackel Plymouth
Tarpon Springs, FL 727-942-3991
Solganik & Associates
Dayton, OH. 800-253-8512
Soyatech Inc
Bar Harbor, ME. 800-424-7692
Soynut Butter Co
Glenview, IL 800-288-1012
Spencer Research Inc
Columbus, OH 800-488-3242
SSOE Group
Toledo, OH 419-255-3830
Stratecon International Consultants
Winston Salem, NC. 336-768-6808
Syngenta
Greensboro, NC 800-334-9481
Thomas J Payne Market Devmnt
San Mateo, CA 650-340-8311

Tiax LLC
Lexington, MA 800-677-3000
Trans-Chemco Inc
Bristol, WI. 800-880-2498
Volumetric Technologies
Cannon Falls, MN. 507-263-0034
Warren Analytical Laboratory
Greeley, CO. 800-945-6669
Wilhelmsen Consulting
Milpitas, CA 408-946-4525
XL Corporate & Research Services
New York, NY 800-221-2972
Zaloom Marketing Corp
South Hackensack, NJ 800-878-7609

Kosher Food

KOF-K Kosher Supervision
Teaneck, NJ. 201-837-0500
Orthodox Union
New York, NY 212-563-4000
Star-K Kosher Certification
Baltimore, MD 410-484-4110

Marketing & Promotion

ABIC International Consultants
Fairfield, NJ 973-227-7060
AgriTech
Columbus, OH 614-488-2772
Aidi International Hotels of America
Washington, DC 202-331-9299
Alpert/Siegel & Associates
Los Angeles, CA. 310-571-0777
American Agribusiness Assistance
Alexandria, VA 202-429-0500
Arthur D Little Inc.
Boston, MA. 617-532-9550
Axces Systems
Westbury, NY 800-355-3534
BFB Consultants
Mississauga, ON. 905-819-9856
BlueKey Inc
Charleston, SC 843-628-6228
BNP Media
2401 W Big Beaver Rd, Su. 248-362-3700
Broadmoor Baker
Seattle, WA 206-624-3660
Calif Canning Peach Assn
Sacramento, CA 916-925-9131
Cannon Equipment Company
Cannon Falls, MN. 800-825-8501
Chain Restaurant Resolutions
Toronto, ON 416-934-4334
Coffee Enterprises
Burlington, VT 800-375-3398
Colonial Marketing Assoc
Freehold, NJ 732-462-2100
Conatech Consulting Group, Inc
Saint Louis, MO 314-995-9767
Concept Hospitality Group
Foster City, CA 650-357-1224
Connecticut Culinary Institute
Farmington, CT. 860-677-7869
Container-Quinn Testing Lab
Wheeling, IL. 847-537-9470
Cooper Decoration Company
Weston, MA 315-475-1661
Cycle Computer Consultants
Hicksville, NY 516-733-1892
Dakota Valley Products, Inc.
Willow Lake, SD. 605-625-2526
Decision Analyst Inc
Arlington, TX 800-262-5974
DMG Financial Inc
Denver, CO 888-331-3882
Dover Hospitality Consulting
Etobicoke, ON 416-622-9294
Edge Resources
Hopedale, MA. 888-849-0998
Engineering & Mgmt Consultants
Franklin Lakes, NJ 201-847-0748
Feedback Plus
Plano, TX .800-882-7467
First Bank of Highland P
Northbrook, IL. 847-272-1300
Food & Beverage Consultants
Cranston, RI 401-463-5784
Food Business Associates
Temple, ME. 207-778-2251
Food Industry ConsultingGroup
Dunnellon, FL. 800-443-5820

Food Insights
Washington, DC 202-296-6540
Food Marketing Servives
Pittsburgh, PA 412-821-8960
Food Science Consulting
Walnut Creek, CA 925-947-6785
Food Technologies
Golden Valley, MN. 763-544-8586
Foodmark, Inc.
Wellesley, MA. 800-535-3447
Francorp
Olympia Fields, IL 800-327-6244
Future Foods
Chicago, IL. 312-987-9342
Graphic Promotions
Topeka, KS 785-234-6684
Grocery Products Distribution
Cedar Knolls, NJ. 973-538-1035
Groth Corp
Stafford, TX 800-354-7684
Harold M. Lincoln Company
Toledo, OH 419-255-1200
HealthFocus
Atlanta, GA. 770-645-1999
Healthy Dining
San Diego, CA 800-266-2049
Heart Smart International
Scottsdale, AZ. 800-762-7819
HMG Worldwide In-Store Marketing
New York, NY 212-736-2300
Innavision Global Marketing Consultants
Racine, WI 262-633-1000
Inter-Access
Etobicoke, ON 514-744-6262
Interbrand Corporation
San Francisco, CA 877-692-7263
Interliance
Santa Ana, CA 800-540-7917
IPG International Packaging Group
Agoura Hills, CA 818-865-1428
J.R. Ralph Marketing Company
Syracuse, NY 315-445-0255
JDG Consulting
Baulkham Hills, NS 800-243-7037
Jonessco Enterprises
Plano, TX .972-985-7961
Kelley Advisory Services
Northbrook, IL. 847-412-9234
Kilcher Company
South Pasadena, FL 727-367-5839
Landmark Kitchen Design
Chandler, AZ. 866-621-3192
Line of Snacks Consultants
Dallas, TX. 972-484-1155
Lorrich & Associates
San Diego, CA 858-586-0823
Main Course Consultants
Skokie, IL .847-869-7633
Malcolm Stogo Associates
Scarsdale, NY 914-472-7255
Management Insight
Malborough, MA 508-485-2100
Marketing Management Inc
Fort Worth, TX 800-433-2004
Mastio & Co
St Joseph, MO. 816-364-6200
Maui Wowi Fresh Hawaiin Blends
Greenwood Village, CO 877-849-6992
MC Creation
San Francisco, CA 415-775-1135
Mic-Ellen Associates
Collegeville, PA 800-872-1252
Michigan Agricultural Cooperative Marketing
Association
Lansing, MI. 800-824-3779
Minnesuing Acres
Lake Nebagamon, WI. 715-374-2262
Monterey Bay Food Group
Aptos, CA. 831-685-8600
Murray Runin
Mahwah, NJ 201-512-3885
National Food Laboratories Inc
Livermore, CA 925-828-1440
National Food Product Research Corporation
West Newbury, MA. 800-363-2144
Natural Marketing Institute
Harleysville, PA 215-513-7300
NCR Counterpoint
Alpharetta, GA. 800-852-5852
Nicholas Marketing Associates
Bogota, NJ 201-343-9414

Nicosia Creative Expresso
New York, NY 212-515-6600
Northland Consultants
Sault Ste. Marie, ON. 705-541-8490
Nutrinfo Corporation
Watertown, MA 800-676-6686
Partners International
Hanover, NH 603-643-8574
Pearson Research Assoc
Santa Cruz, CA 831-429-9797
Peter Kalustian Associates
Boonton, NJ 973-334-3008
Pioneer Marketing International
Los Gatos, CA. 408-356-4990
Positive Employment Practice
New City, NY 845-638-6442
Premier Restaurant Equipment
Brooklyn Park, MN. 763-544-8800
Pro Media Inc
Menomonee Falls, WI. 800-328-0439
Putnam Group
Trumbull, CT 203-452-7270
Quality Bakers of America
Allentown, PA. 973-263-6970
Redwood Vintners
Novato, CA. 415-892-6949
Restaurant Development Svc
Bethesda, MD 301-263-0400
Restaurant Partners
Orlando, FL 407-839-5070
Robert C Vncek Design Assoc
Sussex, NJ. 973-702-8553
Robin Shepherd Group
Jacksonville, FL 877-896-8774
Rqa Product Dynamics
Orland Park, IL 708-364-7055
Rtech Laboratories
St Paul, MN. 800-328-9687
Sales Building Systems
Mentor, OH. 800-435-7576
Selective Foods
Carnegie, PA 412-458-1930
Sensors Quality Management
Toronto, ON 800-866-2624
Simonson Group
Winchester, MA 781-729-8906
SLT Group
Dayton, NJ 732-837-3096
Solganik & Associates
Dayton, OH. 800-253-8512
Sorensen Associates
Troutdale, OR 800-542-4321
Source Distribution Logistics
Batavia, IL. 630-761-1231
Southern United States Trade Association
New Orleans, LA 504-568-5986
Soynut Butter Co
Glenview, IL 800-288-1012
Specialty Cheese Group Limited
New York, NY 212-243-7274
Stewart Marketing Services
Kirkland, WA 425-889-2455
Stratecon
Winston Salem, NC. 336-768-6808
Stratecon International Consultants
Winston Salem, NC. 336-768-6808
Superior Product Pickup Services
Niles, IL 847-647-4720
Supermarket Associates
Durham, NC 919-493-0994
Swander Pace & Company
San Francisco, CA 415-477-8500
Tara Communications
Dunedin, FL 303-417-9602
Technomic Inc
Chicago, IL 312-876-0004
Thomas J Payne Market Devmnt
San Mateo, CA 650-340-8311
Tiax LLC
Lexington, MA 800-677-3000
TLC & Associates
Amarillo, TX. 806-353-1517
Tourtellot & Co
Warwick, RI 401-734-4200
Tragon Corp
Redwood City, CA 800-841-1177
Unity Brands Group
Saint Augustine, FL 904-940-8975
US Magnetix
Minneapolis, MN 763-540-9497
Vine Solutions
Corte Madera, CA 415-927-3308

Virginia Department of Agriculture & Consumer Services
Richmond, VA. 804-786-3520
W.A. Golomski & Associates
Algoma, WI. .920-487-9864
World Trade Center Harrisburg
Harrisburg, PA 717-843-1090
Zaloom Marketing Corp
South Hackensack, NJ 800-878-7609

Material Handling

California Vibratory Feeders
Anaheim, CA .800-354-0972
KLEEN Line Corp
Newburyport, MA. 800-259-5973
Polyair
Toronto, ON .888-765-9847
Trimble Agriculture
Westminster, CO

Packaging

BFB Consultants
Mississauga, ON. 905-819-9856
Conatech Consulting Group, Inc
Saint Louis, MO. 314-995-9767
DCS IPAL Consultants
Laval, QC 450-973-3338
Food Development Centre
Portage La Prairie, NB 800-870-1044
Interbrand Corporation
San Francisco, CA 877-692-7263
Landmark Kitchen Design
Chandler, AZ. 866-621-3192
Pater & Associates
Cincinnati, OH
R F Schiffmann Assoc.
New York, NY 212-362-7021
R.C. Keller & Associates
Barnegat, NJ .973-694-8810
Raque Food Systems
Louisville, KY 502-267-9641
Schroeder Machine
San Marcos, CA 760-591-9733
Stratecon International Consultants
Winston Salem, NC. 336-768-6808

Restaurant Design

Top Source Industries
Addison, IL. 800-362-9625

Sanitation, Testing & Analysis

A & B Process Systems Corp
Stratford, WI. 888-258-2789
A&L Western Ag Lab
Modesto, CA. 209-529-4080
Accra Laboratory
Cleveland, OH 800-567-7200
Accu-Labs Research
Golden, CO. .303-277-9514
Accu-Ray Inspection Services
Elmhurst, IL .800-378-1226
ADD Testing & Research
Valley Stream, NY 516-568-9197
Advanced Ergonomics Inc
Frisco, TX. 800-682-0169
AgriTech
Columbus, OH 614-488-2772
Airflow Sciences Corp
Livonia, MI. .734-525-0300
AM Test Laboratories
Kirkland, WA .425-885-1664
American Glass Research
Maumee, OH. 419-897-9000
American Services Group
Memphis, TN 800-333-6678
Ameritech Laboratories
Flushing, NY. 718-461-0475
Analytical Labs
Boise, ID. 800-574-5773
Anresco Laboratories
San Francisco, CA 415-822-1100
Anresco Laboratories
San Francisco, CA 800-359-0920
Applied Technologies
Brookfield, WI. 262-784-7690
Arthur D Little Inc.
Boston, MA. .617-532-9550
Asi Food Safety Consultants
St Louis, MO. 800-477-0778

Aspect Engineering
Westerville, OH. 614-638-7106
Barrow-Agee Laboratories Inc
Memphis, TN 901-332-1590
BCN Research Laboratories
Rockford, TN 800-236-0505
Betz Entec
Horsham, PA .800-877-1940
Biological Services
Kansas City, MO. 913-236-6868
Brown & Caldwell
Walnut Creek, CA. 800-727-2224
Cal Western Pest Control
Arcadia, CA .800-326-2847
Cardinal Kitchens
London, ON .800-928-0832
Celsis Laboratory Group
Chicago, IL 800-222-8260
Chilton Consulting Group
Rocky Face, GA 706-694-8325
Conam Inspection
Glendale Heights, IL. 630-681-0008
Container Testing Lab
Mamaroneck, NY 800-221-5170
Container-Quinn Testing Lab
Wheeling, IL .847-537-9470
Covance Inc.
Princeton, NJ. 888-268-2623
Cynter Con Technology Adviser
Gaithersburg, MD 800-287-1811
Cyntergy Corporation
Rockville, MD 800-825-5787
Dalare Associates Inc
Philadelphia, PA 215-567-1953
Deibel Laboratories Inc
Madison, WI .608-241-1177
DFL Laboratories
Chicago, IL 312-938-5151
Engineering & Mgmt Consultants
Franklin Lakes, NJ 201-847-0748
Enviro-Test/Perry Laboratories
Woodridge, IL 630-324-6685
Environmental Consultants
Clarksville, IN. 812-282-8481
Environmental Systems
Culpeper, VA. 800-541-2116
Eurofins S-F Analytical Labs
New Berlin, WI. 800-300-6700
Eurofins Scientific Inc
Des Moines, IA 800-841-1110
Fettig Laboratories
Grand Rapids, MI 616-245-3000
Food & Beverage Consultants
Cranston, RI .401-463-5784
Food Consulting Company
Del Mar, CA .800-793-2844
Food Development Centre
Portage La Prairie, NB 800-870-1044
Food Industry ConsultingGroup
Dunnellon, FL. 800-443-5820
Food Sanitation Svc Inc
New York, NY 212-732-9540
Foodpro International
Stockton, CA. 888-687-5797
Foods Research Laboratories
Boston, MA. .617-442-3322
Foodworks
La Grange, KY 502-222-0135
Galbraith Laboratories Inc
Knoxville, TN 877-449-8797
Gaynes Labs Inc
Bridgeview, IL 708-233-6655
Gems Sensors & Controls
Plainville, CT 860-747-3000
Genesis Nutritional Labs
Salt Lake City, UT 801-973-8824
George Lapgley Enterpri ses
Pipersville, PA. 267-221-2426
Gilbert Insect Light Traps
Jonesboro, AR. 800-643-0400
Global Product Development Group
Northbrook, IL 847-504-0464
Great Lakes Scientific
Stevensville, MI 269-429-1000
Hahn Laboratories
Columbia, SC 803-799-1614
Harold Wainess & Assoc
Arlington Hts, IL 847-722-8744
Industrial Laboratories Co
Wheat Ridge, CO 800-456-5288
Ingman Laboratories
Minneapolis, MN 612-724-0121

Innovative Food Solutions LLC
Columbus, OH 800-884-3314
Insect-O-Cutor Inc
Stone Mountain, GA. 800-966-8480
International Approval Services
Cleveland, OH 877-235-9791
ITS/ETL Testing Laboratories
Laguna Niguel, CA. 949-448-4100
J Leek Assoc Inc
Edenton, NC .252-482-4456
Jl Analytical Svc Inc
Modesto, CA .209-538-8111
Krueger Food Laboratories
Chelmsford, MA 978-256-1220
Labelmax Inc
Laredo, TX 956-722-6493
Lancaster Laboratories
Lancaster, PA 717-656-2300
Landmark Kitchen Design
Chandler, AZ. 866-621-3192
Laucks' Testing Laboratories
Seattle, WA 206-767-5060
Lawrence-Allen Group
San Mateo, CA 800-609-2909
Lebensmittel Consulting
Fostoria, OH .419-435-2774
Libra Technical Center
Metuchen, NJ 732-321-5200
M-Tech & Associates
Downers Grove, IL 630-810-9714
Main Course Consultants
Skokie, IL 847-869-7633
Mccrone Microscopes & Acces
Westmont, IL. 630-288-7087
Medallion Laboratories
Minneapolis, MN 800-245-5615
Merieux Nutrisciences
Columbus, OH 614-486-0150
Metcalf & Eddy
Wakefield, MA 781-246-5200
Microbac Laboratories
Pittsburgh, PA 866-515-4668
Microbac-Wilson Devision
Wilson, NC 252-237-4175
Midwest Laboratories
Omaha, NE 402-334-7770
Miles Willard Technologies
Idaho Falls, ID 208-523-4741
Milligan & Higgins
Johnstown, NY 518-762-4638
Minnesota Valley Testing Lab
New Ulm, MN. 800-782-3557
Nimbus Water Systems
Murrieta, CA. 800-451-9343
Northeast Laboratory Svc
Winslow, ME. 866-591-7120
Northland Labs
Northbrook, IL 800-366-3522
Northview Laboratories
Spartanburg, SC 864-574-7728
Northview Pacific Laboratories
Northbrook, IL 847-564-8181
Nutrinfo Corporation
Watertown, MA. 800-676-6686
O.D. Kurtz Associates
Palm Bay, FL. 321-723-0135
Oerlikon Balzers Coating USA
Elgin, IL 847-695-5200
Oklabs
Oklahoma City, OK 405-843-6832
Optipure
Plano, TX 972-422-1212
Orthodox Union
New York, NY 212-563-4000
Pearson Research Assoc
Santa Cruz, CA 831-429-9797
Phytopia Inc
Dallas, TX. 888-750-9336
POS Pilot Plant Corporation
Saskatoon, SK. 800-230-2751
PSI
Oakbrook Terrace, IL 630-705-9290
Purity Laboratories
Lake Oswego, OR. 800-977-3636
Q Laboratories
Cincinnati, OH 513-471-1300
QC
Southampton, PA 215-355-3900
Quest
San Clemente, CA. 949-643-1333
Quick Judith & Assoc
Hancock, MD 301-678-5737

R.C. Keller & Associates
  Barnegat, NJ 973-694-8810
Richardson Researches
  South San Francisco, CA 510-653-4385
Ron Vallort & Associates
  Oak Brook, IL 630-734-3821
Rqa Product Dynamics
  Orland Park, IL 708-364-7055
RTI Laboratories
  Livonia, MI 734-422-5342
San Diego Health & Nutrition
  Bonita, CA 619-470-3345
Sani-Pure Food Laboratories
  Saddle Brook, NJ 201-843-2525
Schiff & Co
  West Caldwell, NJ 973-227-1830
Sensory Spectrum
  New Providence, NJ 908-376-7000
SERCO Laboratories
  St. Anthony, MN 800-388-7173
Sheahan Sanitation Consulting
  Oakley, CA 800-554-4243
Shear/Kershman Laboratories
  Chesterfield, MO 636-519-8900
Shepard Brothers Co
  La Habra, CA 800-645-3594
Shuster Laboratories
  Canton, MA 800-444-8705
Silliker Laboratories Of Ga
  Stone Mountain, GA 770-469-2701
Silliker Laboratories-Pa Inc
  Allentown, PA 610-366-0264
Silliker, Inc
  Chicago, IL 312-938-5151
Simon S. Jackel Plymouth
  Tarpon Springs, FL 727-942-3991
Smith-Emery Co
  Los Angeles, CA............213-745-5333
Soynut Butter Co
  Glenview, IL 800-288-1012
Spencer Research Inc
  Columbus, OH 800-488-3242
Statex
  Montreal, QC 514-527-6039
Stay Tuned Industries
  Clinton, NJ 908-730-8455
Steritech Food Safety & Environmental Hygiene
  Charlotte, NC 800-868-0089
Strasburger & Siegel
  Hanover, MD 888-726-3753
Stratecon International Consultants
  Winston Salem, NC............336-768-6808
Structure Probe
  West Chester, PA............800-242-4774
Suburban Laboratories Inc
  Geneva, IL...........800-783-5227
TEI Analytical Svc Inc
  Niles, IL 847-647-1345
TLC & Associates
  Amarillo, TX...........806-353-1517
Total Quality Corporation
  Branford, CT 800-453-9729
Tragon Corp
  Redwood City, CA 800-841-1177
Trap-Zap Environmental
  Wyckoff, NJ 800-282-8727
Triad Scientific
  Manasquan, NJ 800-867-6690
Truesdail Laboratories
  Tustin, CA...........714-730-6239
Tuchenhagen
  Columbia, MD 410-910-6000
Underwriters Laboratories Inc
  Camas, WA 877-854-3577
Universal Sanitizers & Supplies
  Rockford, TN 888-634-3196
Vivolac Cultures Corp
  Greenfield, IN 800-848-6522
Warren Analytical Laboratory
  Greeley, CO...........800-945-6669
West Agro
  Kansas City, MO...........816-891-7700
Wilhelmsen Consulting
  Milpitas, CA 408-946-4525
Winston Laboratories Inc
  Vernon Hills, IL 800-946-5229
Woodson-Tenent Laboratories
  Des Moines, IA...........515-265-1461
Woodson-Tenent Laboratories
  Memphis, TN 515-280-8378
Woodson-Tenent Laboratories
  Dayton, OH...........937-236-5756

X-R-I Testing Inc
  Troy, MI 800-973-4800

Contract Manufacturing

Agropur MSI, LLC
  La Crosse, WI 800-359-2345
Barrington Nutritionals
  Harrison, NY...........800-684-2436
Bridgewell Resources LLC
  Clackamas, OR 800-481-3557
Haven's Candies
  Westbrook, ME 800-639-6309

Bakery

Pacmoore Products
  Hammond, IN 866-610-2666

Blending & Mixing

D2 Ingredients, LP.
  De Pere, WI...........920-425-8870
Firebird Artisan Mills
  Harvey, ND 701-324-4330
Hermann Laue Spice Company
  Uxbridge, ON 905-852-5100
Pacmoore Products
  Hammond, IN 866-610-2666
Sweeteners Plus Inc
  Lakeville, NY 585-346-3193

Contract Packaging

A La Carte
  Chicago, IL 800-722-2370
Aaron Thomas Co Inc
  Garden Grove, CA 800-394-4776
All American Seasonings
  Denver, CO 303-623-2320
Ameripec
  Buena Park, CA 714-994-2990
AmeriQual Foods
  Evansville, IN 812-867-1444
Athea Laboratories
  Milwaukee, WI 800-743-6417
Baldwin Richardson Foods
  Oakbrook Terrace, IL 866-644-2732
Baron Spices Inc
  St Louis, MO...........314-535-9020
Blendco Inc
  Hattiesburg, MS 888-253-6326
Bridgewell Resources LLC
  Clackamas, OR 800-481-3557
Caraustar
  Austell, GA...........770-948-3101
Carton Service Co
  Shelby, OH 800-533-7744
Century Foods Intl LLC
  Sparta, WI 800-269-1901
Chem Pack Inc
  Cincinnati, OH 800-421-2700
CMS Fine Foods
  Healdsburg, CA 707-473-9561
Cobitco Inc
  Denver, CO...........303-296-8575
Compact Industries Inc
  St Charles, IL 800-513-4262
Conpac
  Warminster, PA 215-322-2755
Contact Industries
  Clackamas, OR 800-345-2232
Contract Comestibles
  East Troy, WI 262-642-9400
Crest Foods Inc
  Ashton, IL...........877-273-7893
Crown Chemical Products
  Mississauga, ON 905-564-0904
Cup Pac Packaging Inc
  South Beloit, IL 877-347-9725
D2 Ingredients, LP.
  De Pere, WI...........920-425-8870
Diamond Packaging
  Rochester, NY 800-333-4079
Do-It Corp
  South Haven, MI...........800-426-4822
Douglas Products
  Liberty, MO...........800-223-3684
EMCO Packaging
  North Chicago, IL...........847-689-2200
General Methods Corporation
  Peoria, IL...........309-497-3344

Ginseng Up Corp
  Worcester, MA 800-446-7364
GKI Foods
  Brighton, MI...........248-486-0055
Hagerty Foods
  Orange, CA 714-628-1230
Hamilton Soap & Oil Products
  Paterson, NJ 973-225-1031
Health Products Corp
  Yonkers, NY 914-423-2900
Hearthside Food Solutions
  Downers Grove, IL 630-967-3600
Hot Mama's Foods
  Springfield, MA 413-737-6572
Hyde & Hyde Inc
  Corona, CA 951-279-5239
Impact Nutrition
  Aurora, CO 720-374-7111
Innovative Food Processors Inc
  Faribault, MN 800-997-4437
Innovative Food Solutions LLC
  Columbus, OH 800-884-3314
Inter-Pack Corporation
  Monroe, MI...........734-242-7755
Jo Mar Laboratories
  Campbell, CA 800-538-4545
Kent Precision Foods Group Inc
  Muscatine, IA 800-442-5242
KETCH
  Wichita, KS 800-766-3777
KIK Custom Products
  Denver, CO 303-728-0871
KIK Custom Products
  Concord, ON...........800-276-8260
LA Monica Fine Foods
  Millville, NJ
Longhorn Packaging Inc
  San Antonio, TX...........800-433-7974
LRM Packaging
  South Hackensack, NJ 201-342-2530
Max Packaging
  Attalla, AL 800-543-5369
Mcclancy Seasonings Co
  Fort Mill, SC 800-843-1968
Mid Atlantic Packaging Co
  Dover, DE...........800-284-1332
Modern Packaging
  Duluth, GA 770-622-1500
Nelipak
  Phoenix, AZ 602-269-7648
New Horizon Foods
  Union City, CA 510-489-8600
Pacific Harvest Products
  Bellevue, WA 425-401-7990
Packaging Associates
  Randolph, NJ 973-252-8890
Packaging Service Co Inc
  Pearland, TX...........800-826-2949
Pacmoore Products
  Hammond, IN 866-610-2666
Pak Technologies
  Milwaukee, WI 414-438-8600
Paket Corporation
  Chicago, IL 773-221-7300
Pepper Source Inc
  Metairie, LA 504-885-3223
Per Pak/Orlandi
  Farmingdale, NY...........631-756-0110
Plaze Inc
  St Clair, MO...........800-986-9509
Pluto Corporation
  French Lick, IN...........812-936-9988
Power Group
  St Charles, IL 630-587-3770
Power Packaging Inc
  Rosendale, WI...........920-872-2181
Proact Inc
  Eagan, MN 877-245-0405
Q & B Foods
  Irwindale, CA 626-334-8090
Rempak Industries
  Fort Lee, NJ 201-585-9007
REX Pure Foods
  New Orleans, LA 800-344-8314
Riverside Industries
  St Helens, OR 503-397-1922
Roberts Packaging Equipment
  Des Plaines, IL 888-221-0700
SOPAKCO Foods
  Mullins, SC 800-276-9678
Specialty Food America Inc
  Hopkinsville, KY 888-881-1633

Specialty Lubricants
  Macedonia, OH 800-238-5823
Stage Coach Sauces
  Palatka, FL 386-328-6330
Techform
  Mount Airy, NC 336-789-2115
Thor Inc
  Ogden, UT 888-846-7462
Threshold Rehabilitation Svc
  Reading, PA 610-777-7691
Todd's
  Des Moines, IA 800-247-5363
Truitt Bros Inc
  Salem, OR 800-547-8712
Unette Corp
  Randolph, NJ 973-328-6800
Vita Key Packaging
  Riverside, CA 909-355-1023
Vitatech Nutritional Sciences
  Tustin, CA 714-832-9700
W H Wildman Company
  New Hampshire, OH 419-568-7531
WePackItAll
  Duarte, CA 626-301-9214
West Penn Oil Co Inc
  Warren, PA 814-723-9000
Westvaco Corporation
  Richmond, VA 804-233-9205
Whitlock Packaging Corp
  Fort Gibson, OK 918-478-4300

Dry Product

All American Seasonings
  Denver, CO 303-623-2320
Magic Seasoning Blends
  New Orleans, LA 800-457-2857

Liquid Product

LA Monica Fine Foods
  Millville, NJ

Custom Services

Blending

A.C. Legg
  Calera, AL 800-422-5344
All American Seasonings
  Denver, CO 303-623-2320
American Pasien Co
  Burlington, NJ 609-387-3130
Arro Corp
  Hodgkins, IL 877-929-2776
Calhoun Bend Mill
  Libuse, LA 800-519-6455
California Blending Co
  El Monte, CA 626-448-1918
Elite Spice Inc
  Jessup, MD 800-232-3531
Invensys APV Products
  Houston, TX 713-329-1600
Popcorn Connection
  North Hollywood, CA 800-852-2676
Shashi Foods
  Toronto, ON 866-748-7441
Texas Spice Co
  Round Rock, TX 800-880-8007
W H Wildman Company
  New Hampshire, OH 419-568-7531
Washington State Juice
  Pacoima, CA 818-899-1195
Watershed Foods
  Gridley, IL 309-747-3000

Drying

American Pasien Co
  Burlington, NJ 609-387-3130

Extrusion

Legacy Plastics
  Henderson, KY 270-827-1318

Formulations

American Pasien Co
  Burlington, NJ 609-387-3130
Apotheca Inc
  Woodbine, IA 800-736-3130

Century Foods Intl LLC
  Sparta, WI 800-269-1901
Clofine Dairy Products Inc
  Linwood, NJ 609-653-1000
Compact Industries Inc
  St Charles, IL 800-513-4262
GKI Foods
  Brighton, MI 248-486-0055
Innovative Food Solutions LLC
  Columbus, OH 800-884-3314
Jimbo's Jumbos Inc
  Edenton, NC 800-334-4771
Kline Process Systems Inc
  Reading, PA 610-371-0300
Magic Seasoning Blends
  New Orleans, LA 800-457-2857
Mancini Packing Co
  Zolfo Springs, FL 800-741-1778
Old Mansion Inc
  Petersburg, VA 800-476-1877
Solo Foods
  Countryside, IL 800-328-7656
SOPAKCO Foods
  Mullins, SC 800-276-9678
Thiel Cheese & Ingredients
  Hilbert, WI 920-989-1440
Thor Inc
  Ogden, UT 888-846-7462
Vita Key Packaging
  Riverside, CA 909-355-1023
W H Wildman Company
  New Hampshire, OH 419-568-7531

Grinding

Shashi Foods
  Toronto, ON 866-748-7441

Dealers

Meat

Becker Foods
  Westminster, CA 714-891-9474
Dicks Packing Plant
  New Lexington, OH 740-342-4150
ELP Inc
  Elizabeth, CO 303-688-2240
Eunice Locker Plant
  Eunice, NM 505-394-2060
Fresh Mark Inc.
  Massillon, OH 330-832-7491
Graham Ice & Locker Plant
  Graham, TX 940-549-1975
Henningsen Foods Inc
  Omaha, NE 800-228-2769
Hormel Foods Corp.
  Austin, MN 507-437-5611
L & L Packing Co
  Chicago, IL 800-628-6328
Marketing Management Inc
  Fort Worth, TX 800-433-2004
Moyer Packing Co.
  Elroy, PA 800-967-8325
Package Concepts & Materials Inc
  Greenville, SC. 800-424-7264
Ritchie's Foods
  Piketon, OH 800-628-1290
Spencer Packing Company
  Washington, NC 252-946-4161
Sugar Creek
  Washington Ct Hs, OH 800-848-8205
Weber-Stephen Products Company
  Palatine, IL 800-446-1071
Welch Brothers
  Bartlett, IL. 847-741-6134

Designers

Architectural & Engineering

Amherst Stainless Fabrication
  Amherst, NY 716-691-7012
Austin Co
  Cleveland, OH 440-544-2600
Boldt Co
  Appleton, WI 920-739-6321
Concepts & Design International, Ltd
  West Nyack, NY 845-358-1558
Facility Group
  Smyrna, GA 770-437-2700

KLEEN Line Corp
  Newburyport, MA 800-259-5973
Select Technologies Inc
  Belmont, MI 616-866-6700
Stellar Group
  Jacksonville, FL 800-488-2900
Tippmann Group
  Fort Wayne, IN 260-490-3000
Webber Smith Assoc
  Lancaster, PA 717-291-2266

Interior & Store Fixture

Accommodation Program
  New York, NY 800-929-1414
Acryline
  North Attleboro, MA 508-695-7124
Air Pak Products & Services
  Winter Park, FL 800-824-7725
Aldo Locascio
  Tucson, AZ 800-488-8729
All About Furniture
  Norcross, GA 800-893-0919
Atlas Restaurant Supply
  Indianapolis, IN 877-528-5275
Bargreen Ellingson
  Tacoma, WA 800-322-4441
Big-D Construction Corp
  Salt Lake City, UT 801-415-6000
Cannon Equipment Company
  Cannon Falls, MN 800-825-8501
Carmona Designs
  Chula Vista, CA 619-425-2800
CDI Service & Mfg Inc
  Largo, FL 727-536-2207
Citra-Tech
  Lefkosia, CY
Design Group
  Clearwater, FL 727-441-2825
Divercon Inc
  Omaha, NE 402-571-5115
Fenster Consulting Inc
  Port Washington, NY 516-944-7108
Group One Partners
  Boston, MA 617-268-7000
Inman Foodservices Group LLC
  Nashville, TN 615-321-5591
Innovations by Design
  Chadds Ford, PA 610-558-0160
Intelplex Designers
  St Louis, MO 314-983-9996
Landmark Kitchen Design
  Chandler, AZ 866-621-3192
Legge & Associates
  Rockwold, ON 519-856-0444
Leotta Designers
  Miami, FL 305-371-4949
Material Systems Engineering
  Stilesville, IN 800-634-0904
Mead & Hunt Inc
  Madison, WI 888-364-7272
Nina Mauritz Design Service
  Libertyville, IL 847-968-4438
Oak Street Manufacturing
  Monticello, IA 877-465-4344
Refrigerated Warehousing
  Jasper, GA 800-873-2008
RGN Developers
  New Providence, NJ
Ridg-U-Rak
  North East, PA 866-479-7225
Shook Kelley Design Group
  Charlotte, NC 704-377-0661
Southern Express
  Saint Louis, MO 800-444-9157
Southern Store Fixtures Inc
  Bessemer, AL 800-552-6283
Spartan Showcase
  Union, MO 800-325-0775
SSOE Group
  Toledo, OH 419-255-3830
TKF Inc
  Cincinnati, OH 513-241-5910
Triad Scientific
  Manasquan, NJ 800-867-6690
TSG Merchandising
  Perkasie, PA 215-453-9220
Twin City Wholesale
  Opelika, AL 800-344-6935
United Insulated Structures
  Berkeley, IL. 800-821-5538

Kitchen (Commercial, Institutional, Restaurant)

Andgar Corp
Ferndale, WA 360-366-9900
Atlas Restaurant Supply
Indianapolis, IN 877-528-5275
Best Restaurant Equip & Design
Columbus, OH 800-837-2378
Carmona Designs
Chula Vista, CA 619-425-2800
G.V. Aikman Company
Indianapolis, IN 800-886-4029
Klinger Constructors LLC
Albuquerque, NM 505-822-9990
Landmark Kitchen Design
Chandler, AZ. 866-621-3192
St Onge Ruff & Associates
Kansas City, MO. 800-800-5261
Tiny Drumsticks
New York, NY 917-526-3263

Package, Carton & Display

Ad Mart Identity Group
Danville, KY. .800-354-2102
Adpro
Solon, OH 440-542-1111
Ball Design Group
Fresno, CA 559-434-6100
C F Napa Brand Design
Napa, CA. 707-265-1891
Center for Packaging Education
Somers, NY. .914-276-0425
D'Addario Design Associates
New York, NY 212-302-0059
Dunn Woodworks
Shrewsbury, PA. 877-835-8592
E2M
Duluth, GA 800-622-4326
Eagle-Concordia Paper Corporation
Farmingdale, NY 212-255-3860
FFR Merchandising Inc
Twinsburg, OH 800-422-2547
Filet Menu
Los Angeles, CA. 310-202-8000
Gary Plastic Packaging Corporation
Bronx, NY. 800-221-8151
Graphic Arts Center
Melbourne, FL 888-345-7436
Graphic Impressions of Illinois
River Grove, IL. 708-453-1100
Greenfield Paper Box Co
Greenfield, MA. 413-773-9414
HMG Worldwide In-Store Marketing
New York, NY 212-736-2300
Hunter Graphics
Umatilla, FL .407-644-2060
IPG International Packaging Group
Agoura Hills, CA 818-865-1428
Krimstock Enterprises
Pennsauken, NJ. 856-665-3676
Landmark Kitchen Design
Chandler, AZ. 866-621-3192
LSI Industries Inc
Blue Ash, OH 513-793-3200
Menu Graphics
Olmsted Falls, OH 216-696-1460
Mold-Rite Plastics LLC
Twinsburg, OH 330-425-4206
Nottingham Spirk
Cleveland, OH 216-231-7830
Omni Craft Inc
Hopkins, MN 952-988-9944
PacTech Engineering
Cincinnati, OH 513-792-1090
Pharmaceutical & Food Special
San Jose, CA. 408-275-0161
Presentations South
Orlando, FL. .407-657-2108
R.C. Keller & Associates
Barnegat, NJ .973-694-8810
Robin Shepherd Group
Jacksonville, FL 877-896-8774
Roxanne Signs Inc
Gaithersburg, MD. 301-428-4911
Seattle Menu Specialists
Kent, WA. 800-622-2826
THE Corporation
Terre Haute, IN 800-783-2151
Thomson-Leeds Company
New York, NY 800-535-9361

TSG Merchandising
Perkasie, PA .215-453-9220
US Magnetix
Minneapolis, MN 763-540-9497
Wishbone Utensil Tableware Line
Wheat Ridge, CO 866-266-5928
WNA Hopple Plastics
Florence, KY. 800-446-4622

Process Vessels & Tanks

Fourinox Inc
Green Bay, WI. 920-336-0621

Food Closeouts, Surplus, Salvage & Liquidators

All About Furniture
Norcross, GA 800-893-0919
CSV Sales
Plymouth, MI 800-886-6866
Mar-Khem Industries
Cinnaminson, NJ
Milton A. Klein Company
New York, NY 800-221-0248

Foodservice

3M
St. Paul, MN .888-364-3577
Mcclancy Seasonings Co
Fort Mill, SC .800-843-1968
Regional Produce
Birmingham, AL 800-726-0711

Amusement & Theme Parks

Alkazone/Better Health Lab
Hackensack, NJ. 800-810-1888

Branded Concepts

Hixson Architecture Engrng
Cincinnati, OH 513-241-1230

Retail

Canon Potato Company
Center, CO 719-754-3445

Supermarkets

99 Ranch Market
Hacienda Heights, CA 626-839-2899
Certified Grocers Midwest
Hodgkins, IL. 708-579-2100
Ingles Markets
Black Mountain, NC. 828-669-2941
Schnuck Markets, Inc.
St. Louis, MO 800-264-4400
Sprouts Farmers Market Inc.
Phoenix, AZ
WEIS Markets Inc.
Sunbury, PA. .866-999-9347

General

Hop Growers Of Washington
Moxee, WA. .509-453-4749

Ice Making Plants

Blast It Clean
Kansas City, MO. 877-379-4233
Boise Cold Storage Co
Boise, ID. 208-344-8477
Buck Ice & Coal Co
Columbus, GA 706-322-5451
Carbonic Reserves
San Antonio, TX 800-880-1911
Four Corners Ice
Farmington, NM 505-325-3813
Girton Manufacturing Co
Millville, PA .570-458-5521
Graham Ice & Locker Plant
Graham, TX .940-549-1975
Home City Ice Co
Cincinnati, OH 800-759-4411
Martin Electric Plants
Ephrata, PA .800-713-7968
Myers Ice Company
Garden City, KS 800-767-5751
Polar Ice
Bloomington, IN 800-733-0423

Turbo Refrigerating Company
Denton, TX .940-387-4301

Laboratories

Food Research & Development

915 Labs
Centennial, CO 855-915-5227
A&L Western Ag Lab
Modesto, CA. 209-529-4080
ABC Laboratories
Columbia, MO 800-538-5227
Accra Laboratory
Cleveland, OH 800-567-7200
ADD Testing & Research
Valley Stream, NY 516-568-9197
Advance Energy Technologies
Halfmoon, NY. 800-724-0198
Agricultural Research Service
Washington, SW 202-720-3656
Analytical Labs
Boise, ID. 800-574-5773
Anresco Laboratories
San Francisco, CA 800-359-0920
Aspen Research Corporation
White Bear Lake, MN. 651-773-7961
BCN Research Laboratories
Rockford, TN 800-236-0505
Blendco Inc
Hattiesburg, MS 888-253-6326
BluMetric Environmental Inc.
Ottawa, ON .613-839-3053
Celsis Laboratory Group
Chicago, IL 800-222-8260
Coffee Enterprises
Burlington, VT 800-375-3398
CPM Roskamp Champion
Waterloo, IA .800-366-2563
Culinar
Montreal, QC 514-255-2811
Deibel Laboratories Inc
Madison, WI. 608-241-1177
ENSCO Inc
Springfield, VA. 703-321-9000
Environmental Express
Charleston, SC 800-343-5319
Eurofins S-F Analytical Labs
New Berlin, WI. 800-300-6700
Eurofins Scientific Inc
Des Moines, IA 800-841-1110
Eurofins Scientific Inc.
Dayton, OH. 800-880-1038
Flow International Corp.
Kent, WA. 800-446-3569
Food Safety Net Services Ltd
San Antonio, TX 888-525-9788
Food-Tek
Whippany, NJ 800-648-8114
Foods Research Laboratories
Boston, MA .617-442-3322
Global Product Development Group
Northbrook, IL 847-504-0464
Hahn Laboratories
Columbia, SC 803-799-1614
Hollander Horizon International
Princeton, NJ. 609-924-7577
Hydro-Thermal Corp
Waukesha, WI. 800-952-0121
Industrial Laboratories Co
Wheat Ridge, CO 800-456-5288
Ingman Laboratories
Minneapolis, MN 612-724-0121
Innovative Food Solutions LLC
Columbus, OH 800-884-3314
Intertek USA
Boxborough, MA 800-967-5352
Irvine Analytical Labs
Irvine, CA. 877-445-6554
ITS/ETL Testing Laboratories
Laguna Niguel, CA. 949-448-4100
J Leek Assoc Inc
Edenton, NC 252-482-4456
Jenike & Johanson Inc
Tyngsboro, MA. 978-649-3300
Krueger Food Laboratories
Chelmsford, MA. 978-256-1220
Lebensmittel Consulting
Fostoria, OH 419-435-2774
Libra Technical Center
Metuchen, NJ 732-321-5200

Medallion Laboratories
    Minneapolis, MN 800-245-5615
Micro-Chem Laboratory
    Mississauga, ON 905-795-0490
Microbac Laboratories
    Pittsburgh, PA 866-515-4668
Microbac-Wilson Devision
    Wilson, NC 252-237-4175
Midwest Laboratories
    Omaha, NE 402-334-7770
Miles Willard Technologies
    Idaho Falls, ID 208-523-4741
National Food Laboratories Inc
    Livermore, CA 925-828-1440
Northeast Laboratory Svc
    Winslow, ME 866-591-7120
Northview Laboratories
    Spartanburg, SC 864-574-7728
Northwest Laboratories
    Seattle, WA 206-763-6252
Nutrition Research
    Livingston, MT 406-222-3541
O.D. Kurtz Associates
    Palm Bay, FL 321-723-0135
Oklabs
    Oklahoma City, OK 405-843-6832
Phytotherapy Research Laboratory
    Lobelville, TN 800-274-3727
POS Pilot Plant Corporation
    Saskatoon, SK 800-230-2751
Protein Research
    Livermore, CA 800-948-1991
Purity Laboratories
    Lake Oswego, OR 800-977-3636
Q Laboratories
    Cincinnati, OH 513-471-1300
Quality Bakers of America
    Allentown, PA 973-263-6970
R F Schiffmann Assoc.
    New York, NY 212-362-7021
Rqa Product Dynamics
    Orland Park, IL 708-364-7055
Rtech Laboratories
    St Paul, MN 800-328-9687
S & J Laboratories Inc
    Portage, MI 269-324-7383
Sani-Pure Food Laboratories
    Saddle Brook, NJ 201-843-2525
Silliker, Inc
    Chicago, IL 312-938-5151
Soyatech Inc
    Bar Harbor, ME 800-424-7692
Strasburger & Siegel
    Hanover, MD 888-726-3753
Structure Probe
    West Chester, PA 800-242-4774
TEI Analytical Svc Inc
    Niles, IL 847-647-1345
Terriss Consolidate
    Asbury Park, NJ 800-342-1611
Trans-Chemco Inc
    Bristol, WI .800-880-2498
Truesdail Laboratories
    Tustin, CA .714-730-6239
USDA-NASS
    Washington, DC 800-727-9540
Valley Lea Laboratories Inc
    Mishawaka, IN 800-822-1283
Vivolac Cultures Corp
    Greenfield, IN 800-848-6522
Warren Analytical Laboratory
    Greeley, CO 800-945-6669
Winston Laboratories Inc
    Vernon Hills, IL 800-946-5229

Master Planning & Logistics

Dennsi Group
    Springfield, MA 413-737-1353

Nutritional Analyses & Labeling

Aibmr Life Sciences
    Puyallup, WA 253-286-2888
BUCHI Corp
    New Castle, DE 877-692-8844
Q Laboratories
    Cincinnati, OH 513-471-1300

Packaging Services

915 Labs
    Centennial, CO 855-915-5227

A La Carte
    Chicago, IL 800-722-2370
Aaron Thomas Co Inc
    Garden Grove, CA 800-394-4776
Baron Spices Inc
    St Louis, MO 314-535-9020
Basic Leasing Corporation
    Kearny, NJ .973-817-7373
Bluegrass Packaging Industries
    Louisville, KY 800-489-3159
Camco Chemicals
    Florence, KY 800-554-1001
Century Foods Intl LLC
    Sparta, WI .800-269-1901
Compact Industries Inc
    St Charles, IL 800-513-4262
David's Goodbatter
    Bausman, PA 717-872-0652
Decko Products Inc
    Sandusky, OH 800-537-6143
Diamond Packaging
    Rochester, NY 800-333-4079
Douglas Products
    Liberty, MO 800-223-3684
Faribault Foods, Inc.
    Fairbault, MN 507-331-1400
Gary Plastic Packaging Corporation
    Bronx, NY .800-221-8151
Ginseng Up Corp
    Worcester, MA 800-446-7364
Grace Tea Co
    Acton, MA .978-635-9500
Griffin Food Co
    Muskogee, OK 800-866-6311
Hamersmith, Inc.
    Miami, FL .305-685-7451
Hearthside Food Solutions
    Downers Grove, IL 630-967-3600
Hogtown Brewing Company
    Mississauga, ON 905-855-9065
iFoodDecisionSciences
    Kenmore, WA 206-219-3703
Impact Nutrition
    Aurora, CO 720-374-7111
Independent Packers Corporation
    Seattle, WA 206-285-6000
Innovative Food Processors Inc
    Faribault, MN 800-997-4437
Jess Jones Vineyard
    Dixon, CA .707-678-3839
K & L Intl
    Ontario, CA 888-598-5588
Kent Precision Foods Group Inc
    Muscatine, IA 800-442-5242
Laundry Aids
    Carlstadt, NJ 201-933-3500
Linker Machines
    Rockaway, NJ 973-983-0001
LRM Packaging
    South Hackensack, NJ 201-342-2530
Luke's Almond Acres
    Reedley, CA 559-638-3483
Nature Most Laboratories
    Middletown, CT 800-234-2112
Pacific Spice Co
    Commerce, CA 323-890-0895
Packaging Associates
    Randolph, NJ 973-252-8890
Packaging Service Co Inc
    Pearland, TX 800-826-2949
Pak Technologies
    Milwaukee, WI 414-438-8600
Pluto Corporation
    French Lick, IN 812-936-9988
Power Group
    St Charles, IL 630-587-3770
Power Packaging Inc
    Rosendale, WI 920-872-2181
Proact Inc
    Eagan, MN 877-245-0405
Q & B Foods
    Irwindale, CA 626-334-8090
Quality Croutons
    Chicago, IL 800-334-2796
Rempak Industries
    Fort Lee, NJ 201-585-9007
REX Pure Foods
    New Orleans, LA 800-344-8314
Ribble Production
    Warminster, PA 215-674-1706
Roberts Packaging Equipment
    Des Plaines, IL 888-221-0700

Robin Shepherd Group
    Jacksonville, FL 877-896-8774
Schroeder Machine
    San Marcos, CA 760-591-9733
Solo Foods
    Countryside, IL 800-328-7656
Sungjae Corporation
    Irvine, CA .949-757-1727
Techform
    Mount Airy, NC 336-789-2115
Thor Inc
    Ogden, UT 888-846-7462
Todd's
    Des Moines, IA 800-247-5363
Twelve Baskets Sales & Market
    Atlanta, GA 800-420-8840
Vita Key Packaging
    Riverside, CA 909-355-1023
Welch Brothers
    Bartlett, IL .847-741-6134
WePackItAll
    Duarte, CA 626-301-9214
Westvaco Corporation
    Richmond, VA 804-233-9205

Packers

Baron Spices Inc
    St Louis, MO 314-535-9020
Bluegrass Packaging Industries
    Louisville, KY 800-489-3159
Compact Industries Inc
    St Charles, IL 800-513-4262
Copper Hills Fruit Sales
    Fresno, CA 559-432-5400
ELP Inc
    Elizabeth, CO 303-688-2240
Family Tree Farms
    Reedley, CA 866-352-8671
Food Pak Corp
    San Mateo, CA 650-341-6559
Ful-Flav-R Foods
    Alamo, CA 925-838-0300
Grace Tea Co
    Acton, MA .978-635-9500
Hamersmith, Inc.
    Miami, FL .305-685-7451
Hogtown Brewing Company
    Mississauga, ON 905-855-9065
Independent Packers Corporation
    Seattle, WA 206-285-6000
Jess Jones Vineyard
    Dixon, CA .707-678-3839
Kent Precision Foods Group Inc
    Muscatine, IA 800-442-5242
Luke's Almond Acres
    Reedley, CA 559-638-3483
Moyer Packing Co.
    Elroy, PA .800-967-8325
Nebraska Bean
    Clearwater, NE 800-253-6502
Pacific Spice Co
    Commerce, CA 323-890-0895
Power Packaging Inc
    Rosendale, WI 920-872-2181
Q & B Foods
    Irwindale, CA 626-334-8090
Quality Croutons
    Chicago, IL 800-334-2796
Rempak Industries
    Fort Lee, NJ 201-585-9007
REX Pure Foods
    New Orleans, LA 800-344-8314
Robin Shepherd Group
    Jacksonville, FL 877-896-8774
Signature Foods
    Pendergrass, DR 706-693-0098
Spencer Packing Company
    Washington, NC 252-946-4161
Twelve Baskets Sales & Market
    Atlanta, GA 800-420-8840
Welch Brothers
    Bartlett, IL .847-741-6134

Fruit

Copper Hills Fruit Sales
    Fresno, CA 559-432-5400
Family Tree Farms
    Reedley, CA 866-352-8671

Meat

ELP Inc
Elizabeth, CO 303-688-2240
Lynden Meat Co
Lynden, WA 360-354-2449
Spencer Packing Company
Washington, NC 252-946-4161
Welch Brothers
Bartlett, IL....................847-741-6134

Personnel Services

Bristol Associates Inc
Los Angeles, CA................310-670-0525
Capitol Recruiting Group
Newport News, VA..............757-812-8677
Clanton & Company
Orange, CA 714-282-7980
Cook Associates
Chicago, IL...................312-329-0900
Dallas Roth Young
Richardson, TX................972-233-5000
David E. Moley & Associates
Wrightsville Beach, NC 910-256-3826
Dixie Search Associates
Dauphin Island, AL 770-675-7300
Executive Referral Services
Chicago, IL...................866-466-3339
Focus
Minneapolis, MN 612-706-4444
Food Executives Network
Milwaukee, WI.................414-962-7684
Fox-Morris Associates
Charlotte, NC 800-777-6503
Futures
Barrington, NH 603-664-5811
Harper Associates
Farmington Hills, MI 248-932-1170
Inter-Access
Etobicoke, ON 514-744-6262
Johnson Associates
Wheaton, IL 630-690-9200
Judge
W Conshohocken, PA............888-228-7162
Kent R Hedman & Assoc
Arlington, TX 817-277-0888
Landsman Foodservice Net
Owing Mills, MD 410-363-7038
Lawless Link
San Antonio, TX................210-342-8899
Lawrence Glaser Associates
Moorestown, NJ 856-778-9500
Management Recruiters
Philadelphia, PA 800-875-4000
McGraw Hill/London House
Park Ridge, IL..................800-221-8378
Metroplex Corporation
Houston, TX...................281-257-8570
Nelson & Associates Recruiting
Kirkland, WA..................425-823-0956
North Company
Waupaca, WI..................715-258-6104
P & A Food Ind Recruiters
Woodbury, NJ.................856-384-4774
Resources in Food & FoodTeam
St Louis, MO..................800-875-1028
Riley Cole Professional Recruitment
Oakland, CA 510-336-2333
Ritt-Ritt & Associates
Rolling Meadows, IL 847-827-7771
Rjo Associates
Bradenton, FL.................941-756-3001
RJR Executive Search
Houston, TX...................281-368-8550
Roth Young Bellevue
Bellevue, WA 425-454-0677
Roth Young Chicago
Mount Prospect, IL..............847-797-9211
Roth Young Farmington Hills
Farmington Hills, MI 248-539-9242
Roth Young Hicksville
Hicksville, NY 516-822-6000
Roth Young Minneapolis
Minneapolis, MN 800-356-6655
Roth Young Murrysville
Murrysville, PA.................724-733-5900
Roth Young New York
New York, NY 212-557-8181
Roth Young of Tampa Bay
Tampa, FL....................800-646-1513
Roth Young Washougal
Washougal, WA.................360-835-3136

S-H-S International of Wilkes
Wilkes Barre, PA..................570-825-3411
SBB & Associates
Norcross, GA 770-449-7610
Search West
Los Angeles, CA................310-203-9797
Tom McCall & Associates
Millsboro, DE..................410-539-0700
Wayne Group LTD
San Francisco, CA...............415-421-2010
William Willis Worldwide
Greenwich, CT 203-532-1919

Employment Agencies

Bristol Associates Inc
Los Angeles, CA................310-670-0525
Capitol Recruiting Group
Newport News, VA..............757-812-8677
Clanton & Company
Orange, CA....................714-282-7980
Cook Associates
Chicago, IL...................312-329-0900
Dallas Roth Young
Richardson, TX................972-233-5000
David E. Moley & Associates
Wrightsville Beach, NC 910-256-3826
Dixie Search Associates
Dauphin Island, AL 770-675-7300
Executive Referral Services
Chicago, IL...................866-466-3339
Focus
Minneapolis, MN 612-706-4444
Food Executives Network
Milwaukee, WI.................414-962-7684
Food Management Search
Springfield, MA 413-732-2666
Fox-Morris Associates
Charlotte, NC 800-777-6503
Futures
Barrington, NH 603-664-5811
Harper Associates
Farmington Hills, MI 248-932-1170
Inter-Access
Etobicoke, ON 514-744-6262
Johnson Associates
Wheaton, IL 630-690-9200
Judge
W Conshohocken, PA............888-228-7162
Kent R Hedman & Assoc
Arlington, TX 817-277-0888
Landsman Foodservice Net
Owing Mills, MD 410-363-7038
Lawless Link
San Antonio, TX................210-342-8899
Lawrence Glaser Associates
Moorestown, NJ 856-778-9500
Management Recruiters
Philadelphia, PA 800-875-4000
McGraw Hill/London House
Park Ridge, IL..................800-221-8378
Metroplex Corporation
Houston, TX...................281-257-8570
Nelson & Associates Recruiting
Kirkland, WA..................425-823-0956
North Company
Waupaca, WI..................715-258-6104
P & A Food Ind Recruiters
Woodbury, NJ.................856-384-4774
Resources in Food & FoodTeam
St Louis, MO..................800-875-1028
Riley Cole Professional Recruitment
Oakland, CA 510-336-2333
Ritt-Ritt & Associates
Rolling Meadows, IL 847-827-7771
Rjo Associates
Bradenton, FL.................941-756-3001
RJR Executive Search
Houston, TX...................281-368-8550
Roth Young Bellevue
Bellevue, WA 425-454-0677
Roth Young Chicago
Mount Prospect, IL..............847-797-9211
Roth Young Farmington Hills
Farmington Hills, MI 248-539-9242
Roth Young Hicksville
Hicksville, NY 516-822-6000
Roth Young Minneapolis
Minneapolis, MN 800-356-6655
Roth Young Murrysville
Murrysville, PA.................724-733-5900

Roth Young New York
New York, NY 212-557-8181
Roth Young of Tampa Bay
Tampa, FL....................800-646-1513
Roth Young Washougal
Washougal, WA.................360-835-3136
S-H-S International of Wilkes
Wilkes Barre, PA...............570-825-3411
SBB & Associates
Norcross, GA 770-449-7610
Search West
Los Angeles, CA................310-203-9797
Tom McCall & Associates
Millsboro, DE..................410-539-0700
Wayne Group LTD
San Francisco, CA...............415-421-2010
William Willis Worldwide
Greenwich, CT 203-532-1919

Project Management

Dennsi Group
Springfield, MA 413-737-1353

Quality Control

AIB International
Manhattan, KS 800-633-5137
Delta Trak
Pleasanton, CA 800-962-6776
FoodLogiQ
Durham, NC 866-492-4468
Haug Quality Equipment
Morgan Hill, CA................408-465-8160
Hollander Horizon International
Princeton, NJ..................609-924-7577
J.M. Swank Company
North Liberty, IA 800-567-9265
Lixi, Inc.
Huntley, IL 847-961-6666
Orthodox Union
New York, NY 212-563-4000
Quality Chekd Dairies Inc
Lisle, IL......................630-717-1110
Raque Food Systems
Louisville, KY 502-267-9641

Refinishing & Refurbishing Services

Ameriglobe LLC
Lafayette, LA 337-234-3211
B&B Neon Sign Company
Austin, TX....................800-791-6366
B.A.G. Corporation
Richardson, TX.................800-331-9200
Big State Spring Companyy
Corpus Christi, TX 800-880-0244
CDI Service & Mfg Inc
Largo, FL.....................727-536-2207
Cutler Brothers Box & Lumber
Fairview, NJ 201-943-2535
General Magnaplate Corp
Linden, NJ....................800-852-3301
Harrison of Texas
Houston, TX..................800-245-5707
Illinois Wholesale Cash Rgstr
Elgin, IL 800-544-5493
J & L Honing
St Francis, WI..................800-747-9501
Refinishing Touch
Alpharetta, GA 800-523-9448
Sonoma Pacific Company
Montebello, CA 323-838-4374

Research & Development

Analyticon Discovery LLC
Rockville, MD 240-406-1256
Blue Diamond Growers
Sacramento, CA 800-987-2329
Dried Ingredients, LLC.
Miami, FL....................786-999-8499
DuPont Nutrition & Biosciences
New Century, KS 913-764-8100
Healthy Grain Foods LLC
Northbrook, IL 847-272-5576
Island Scallops
Qualicum Beach, BC 250-757-9811
J Rettenmaier USA LP
Schoolcraft, MI.................877-895-4099
Jagulana Herbal Products
Badger, CA 888-465-3686

Raque Food Systems
Louisville, KY 502-267-9641
Stratecon International Consultants
Winston Salem, NC.............336-768-6808
Terriss Consolidate
Asbury Park, NJ 800-342-1611
Tiax LLC
Lexington, MA 800-677-3000

Spray Drying Services

APV Americas
Delavan, WI 800-252-5200
Brady Enterprises Inc
East Weymouth, MA..............781-337-5000
Innovative Food Processors Inc
Faribault, MN 800-997-4437
Quality Ingredients
Burnsville, MN 952-898-4002
Vector Corp
Marion, IA...................319-377-8263

Testing & Sampling Services

3M
St. Paul, MN 888-364-3577
A&L Western Ag Lab
Modesto, CA..................209-529-4080
Accra Laboratory
Cleveland, OH 800-567-7200
Accu-Labs Research
Golden, CO...................303-277-9514
Advanced Instruments Inc
Norwood, MA..................800-225-4034
AIB International
Manhattan, KS 800-633-5137
Airflow Sciences Corp
Livonia, MI..................734-525-0300
Altek Co
Torrington, CT 860-482-7626
AM Test Laboratories
Kirkland, WA 425-885-1664
Barrow-Agee Laboratories Inc
Memphis, TN 901-332-1590
Biological Services
Kansas City, MO...............913-236-6868
BluMetric Environmental Inc.
Ottawa, ON...................613-839-3053
Celsis Laboratory Group
Chicago, IL..................800-222-8260

Coffee Enterprises
Burlington, VT 800-375-3398
Covance Inc.
Princeton, NJ.................888-268-2623
Deibel Laboratories Inc
Madison, WI..................608-241-1177
Delta Trak
Pleasanton, CA 800-962-6776
DFL Laboratories
Chicago, IL..................312-938-5151
ENSCO Inc
Springfield, VA...............703-321-9000
Enviro-Test/Perry Laboratories
Woodridge, IL................630-324-6685
Environmental Systems
Culpeper, VA.................800-541-2116
Eurofins DQCI
St Paul, MN..................763-785-0484
Eurofins S-F Analytical Labs
New Berlin, WI................800-300-6700
Eurofins Scientific Inc.
Dayton, OH...................800-880-1038
Gaynes Labs Inc
Bridgeview, IL 708-233-6655
Global Product Development Group
Northbrook, IL................847-504-0464
Healthy Dining
San Diego, CA 800-266-2049
Industrial Laboratories Co
Wheat Ridge, CO...............800-456-5288
Innovative Food Solutions LLC
Columbus, OH 800-884-3314
International Approval Services
Cleveland, OH 877-235-9791
Intertek USA
Boxborough, MA 800-967-5352
ITS/ETL Testing Laboratories
Laguna Niguel, CA.............949-448-4100
JI Analytical Svc Inc
Modesto, CA..................209-538-8111
Krueger Food Laboratories
Chelmsford, MA...............978-256-1220
Libra Technical Center
Metuchen, NJ 732-321-5200
Medallion Laboratories
Minneapolis, MN 800-245-5615
Midwest Laboratories
Omaha, NE 402-334-7770
Milligan & Higgins
Johnstown, NY 518-762-4638

Minnesota Valley Testing Lab
New Ulm, MN..................800-782-3557
Miroil
Allentown, PA.................800-523-9844
Northland Labs
Northbrook, IL................800-366-3522
Northview Laboratories
Spartanburg, SC 864-574-7728
Pearson Research Assoc
Santa Cruz, CA...............831-429-9797
Phytopia Inc
Dallas, TX...................888-750-9336
POS Pilot Plant Corporation
Saskatoon, SK................800-230-2751
PSI
Oakbrook Terrace, IL 630-705-9290
Q Laboratories
Cincinnati, OH 513-471-1300
QC
Southampton, PA 215-355-3900
Richardson Researches
South San Francisco, CA 510-653-4385
Rtech Laboratories
St Paul, MN..................800-328-9687
Sani-Pure Food Laboratories
Saddle Brook, NJ..............201-843-2525
Sensory Spectrum
New Providence, NJ............908-376-7000
Shear/Kershman Laboratories
Chesterfield, MO..............636-519-8900
Soyatech Inc
Bar Harbor, ME................800-424-7692
Suburban Laboratories Inc
Geneva, IL...................800-783-5227
TEI Analytical Svc Inc
Niles, IL....................847-647-1345
Underwriters Laboratories Inc
Camas, WA...................877-854-3577
Valley Lea Laboratories Inc
Mishawaka, IN................800-822-1283
Vivolac Cultures Corp
Greenfield, IN................800-848-6522
Warren Analytical Laboratory
Greeley, CO..................800-945-6669
Woodson-Tenent Laboratories
Des Moines, IA...............515-265-1461
Woodson-Tenent Laboratories
Memphis, TN 515-280-8378
Woodson-Tenent Laboratories
Dayton, OH...................937-236-5756

Equipment & Machinery

Baking Industry

Allied Bakery and Food Service Equipment
Santa Fe Springs, CA 562-945-6506
Andy J. Egan Co.
Grand Rapids, MI 800-594-9244
Blendex Co
Louisville, KY 800-626-6325
C R Mfg
Waverly, NE 877-789-5844
Charles H Baldwin & Sons
West Stockbridge, MA 413-232-7785
Dunbar Co
Lemont, IL 630-257-2900
Ecs Warehouse
Buffalo, NY 716-833-7380
ENJAY Converters Limited
Cobourg, ON 800-427-5517
Exact Mixing Systems Inc
Memphis, TN 901-362-8501
FOODesign from tna
Wilsonville, OR 503-685-5030
Hcs Enterprises
Haryana,
Henry Group
Greenville, TX 903-883-2002
Lucks Food Equipment Company
Kent, WA 811-824-0696
LVO Manufacturing Inc
Rock Rapids, IA 712-472-3734
Marel Food Systems, Inc.
Lenexa, KS 913-888-9110
Nijal USA
Minneapolis, MN 651-353-6702
Oliver Packaging & Equipment Co.
Walker, MI 800-253-3893
Oshikiri Corp Of America
Philadelphia, PA 215-637-8112
Ovention
Milwaukee, WI 855-298-6836
Pro Bake Inc
Twinsburg, OH 800-837-4427
Reiser
Canton, MA 734-821-1290
Render
Buffalo, NY 888-446-1010
Rheon, U.S.A.
Irvine, CA 949-768-1900
Russel T. Bundy Associates, Inc.
Urbana, OH 800-652-2151
Spray Dynamics LTD
St Clair, MO 800-260-7366
Sunset Paper Products
Simi Valley, CA. 800-228-7882
Superior Products Company
Saint Paul, MN 800-328-9800
Twinkle Baker Decor USA
Daly City, CA 707-364-2740
WP Bakery Group
Shelton, CT. 203-929-6530

Barbecue Equipment & Supplies

Amco Metals Indl
City Of Industry, CA. 626-855-2550
Archer Wire Intl Corp
Chicago, IL 708-563-1700
B R Machinery
Wedron, IL 800-310-7057
Bar-B-Q Woods
Newton, KS 800-528-0819
BBQ Pits by Klose
Houston, TX 800-487-7487
Belson Outdoors Inc
North Aurora, IL 800-323-5664
Best Brands Home Products
New York, NY 212-684-7456
Big John Corp
Pleasant Gap, PA 800-326-9575
Blodgett Oven Co
Burlington, VT 800-331-5842
Boehringer Mfg. Co. Inc.
Felton, CA. 800-630-8665
Century Foods Intl LLC
Sparta, WI 800-269-1901
Champion America Inc
Branford, CT. 800-521-7000

Cleveland Metal Stamping Company
Berea, OH 440-234-0010
Cookshack
Ponca City, OK 800-423-0698
Crown Verity
Brantford, ON 888-505-7240
Dar-B-Ques Barbecue Equipment
Minneapolis, MN 612-724-7425
Dynamic Cooking Systems
Huntington Beach, CA 800-433-8466
Esquire Mechanical Corp.
Armonk, NY 800-847-4206
F.P. Smith Wire Cloth Company
Northlake, IL 800-323-6842
GBS Foodservice Equipment, Inc.
Mississauga, ON 888-402-1242
Gril-Del
Mankato, MN 800-782-7320
Grill Greats
Saxonburg, PA 724-352-1511
Grillco Inc
Aurora, IL 800-644-0067
Grills to Go
Fresno, CA 877-869-2253
Hasty Bake Charcoal Grills
Tulsa, OK 800-426-6836
Hercules Food Equipment
Weston, ON 416-742-9673
Hickory Industries
North Bergen, NJ 800-732-9153
Holstein Manufacturing
Holstein, IA 800-368-4342
J & R Mfg Inc
Mesquite, TX 800-527-4831
Jackson Restaurant Supply
Jackson, TN 800-424-8943
Kay Home Products Inc
Antioch, IL 800-600-7009
King Packaging Co
Schenectady, NY. 518-370-5464
Lazy Man Inc
Belvidere, NJ 800-475-1950
Lazzari Fuel Co LLC
Brisbane, CA. 800-242-7265
Lignetics Inc
Sandpoint, ID 800-544-3834
Luhr Jensen & Sons Inc
Hood River, OR 541-386-3811
M.E. Heuck Company
Mason, OH 800-359-3200
Magi Kitch'n
Concord, NH 800-441-1492
Magnum Custom Trailer & BBQ Pits
Austin, TX. 800-662-4686
Mali's All Natural Barbecue Supply Company
East Amherst, NY 800-289-6254
Masterbuilt Manufacturing Inc
Columbus, GA 706-327-5622
Mosshaim Innovations
Jacksonville, FL 888-995-7775
Music City Metals Inc
Nashville, TN 800-251-2674
Napoleon Appliance Corporation
Barrie, ON. 866-820-8686
Nashville Wire Products
Nashville, TN 615-743-2480
Nature's Own
Attleboro, MA. 508-399-8690
Old Mansion Inc
Petersburg, VA 800-476-1877
Ole Hickory Pits
Cape Girardeau, MO. 800-223-9667
Patio King
Cutler Bay, FL 305-316-7508
Porcelain Metals Corporation
Louisville, KY 502-635-7421
Prince Castle Inc
Carol Stream, IL 800-722-7853
Profire Stainless Steel Barbecue
Miami, FL 305-665-5313
Roseville Charcoal & Mfg Co
Zanesville, OH 740-452-5473
Roto-Flex Oven Co
San Antonio, TX. 877-859-1463
Smokaroma
Boley, OK 800-331-5565

Southbend
Fuquay Varina, NC 800-348-2558
Southern Pride Distributing
Alamo, TN 800-851-8180
Standex International Corp.
Salem, NH 603-893-9701
Stryco Wire Products
North York, ON. 416-663-7000
Super Cooker
Lake Park, GA 800-841-7452
Superior Products Company
Saint Paul, MN 800-328-9800
Swanson Wire Works Industries, Inc.
Mesquite, TX 972-288-7465
Thermal Engineering Corp
Columbia, SC 800-331-0097
Toastmaster
Elgin, IL 847-741-3300
Townfood Equipment Corp
Brooklyn, NY 800-221-5032
West Oregon Wood Products Inc
Columbia City, OR 503-397-6707
Wilch Manufacturing
Topeka, KS 785-267-2762
Wood Stone Corp
Bellingham, WA 800-988-8103

Belting

Ace Manufacturing
Cincinnati, OH 800-653-5692
Ammeraal Beltech
Grand Rapids, MI 616-791-0292
Ammeraal Beltech Inc
Skokie, IL 800-323-4170
Andgar Corp
Ferndale, WA 360-366-9900
Asgco Manufacturing Inc
Allentown, PA 800-344-4000
Bamco Belting
Greenville, SC. 800-258-2358
Belt Technologies Inc
Agawam, MA 413-786-9922
BMH
City of Industry, CA 909-349-2530
BNW Industries
Tippecanoe, IN 574-353-7855
Bowman Hollis Mfg Corp
Charlotte, NC 888-269-2358
C R Daniels Inc
Ellicott City, MD. 800-933-2638
California Vibratory Feeders
Anaheim, CA 800-354-0972
Cambridge Intl. Inc.
Cambridge, MD 800-638-9560
Change Parts Inc
Ludington, MI. 231-845-5107
Charles Walker North America
Fort Worth, TX 817-922-9834
Clipper Belt Lacer Company
Grand Rapids, MI 616-459-3196
Dearborn Mid-West Conveyor Co
Overland Park, KS 913-384-9950
Dresco Belting Co Inc
East Weymouth, MA. 781-335-1350
Dyna-Veyor Inc
Newark, NJ 800-326-5009
Elmo Rietschle - A Gardner Denver Product
Qunicy, IL. 217-222-5400
Emco Industrial Plastics
Cedar Grove, NJ 800-292-9906
Fabreeka International
Boise, ID 800-423-4469
Fenner Dunlop Americas Inc
Pittsburgh, PA 412-249-0700
Forbo Siegling LLC
Huntersville, NC 800-255-5581
Furnace Belt Company
Buffalo, NY. 800-354-7213
Georgia Duck & Cordage Mill
Scottdale, GA 404-297-3170
Green Belt Industries Inc
Buffalo, NY. 800-668-1114
Habasit America
Suwanee, GA 800-458-6431

Habasit America Plastic Div
  Reading, PA................................800-445-7898
Habasit Canada Limited
  Oakville, ON..............................905-827-4131
Hoffmeyer Corp
  San Leandro, CA........................888-744-1826
Home Rubber Co
  Trenton, NJ................................800-257-9441
Hudson Belting & Svc Co Inc
  Worcester, MA............................508-756-0090
Intralox LLC
  Harahan, LA..............................800-535-8848
J L Becker Co
  Plymouth, MI..............................800-837-4328
Keystone Rubber Corporation
  Greenbackville, VA......................800-394-5661
Lambeth Band Corporation
  New Bedford, MA........................508-984-4700
LTI Boyd Corp
  Modesto, CA..............................888-244-6931
Lumsden Flexx Flow
  Lancaster, PA............................800-367-3664
M & R Sales & Svc Inc
  Glen Ellyn, IL............................800-736-6431
Mar-Con Wire Belt
  Richmond, BC............................877-962-7266
Maryland Wire Belts
  Cleveland, OH............................800-677-2358
Mell & Co
  Niles, IL....................................800-262-6355
Meriwether Industries
  Bloomfield, NJ............................800-332-2358
Michigan Industrial Belting
  Livonia, MI................................800-778-1650
Midwest Rubber Svc & Supply
  Minneapolis, MN........................800-537-7457
Monarch-McLaren
  Weston, ON................................416-741-9675
Northwind Inc
  Alpena, AR................................877-937-2585
Omni Metalcraft Corporation
  Alpena, MI................................989-358-7000
Our Name is Mud
  New York, NY............................877-683-7867
Rademaker USA
  Hudson, OH................................330-650-2345
Rahmann Belting & Industrial Rubber Products
  Gastonia, NC..............................888-248-8148
Regal Power Transmission Solutions
  Florence, KY..............................859-342-7900
Regina USA
  Oak Creek, WI............................414-571-0032
Shingle Belting
  King Of Prussia, PA....................800-345-6294
Slip-Not Belting Corporation
  Kingsport, TN..............................423-246-8141
Stiles Enterprises Inc
  Rockaway, NJ............................800-325-4232
Tecweigh
  St Paul, MN................................800-536-4880
Universal Die & Stampings
  Prairie Du Sac, WI......................608-643-2477
Vaughn Belting Co-Main Acct
  Spartanburg, SC..........................800-533-9086
Westfield Sheet Metal Works
  Kenilworth, NJ............................908-276-5500
Wire Belt Co Of America
  Londonderry, NH........................603-644-2500

Belts

Crumb

American Conveyor Corporation
  Astoria, NY................................718-386-0480
King Bag & Mfg Co
  Cincinnati, OH............................800-444-5464

Beverage Industry

Alard Equipment Corp
  Williamson, NY..........................315-589-4511
Bottom Line Processing Technologies, Inc.
  Largo, GA..................................888-834-4552
C.F.F. Stainless Steels
  Hamilton, ON..............................800-263-4511
Dacam Machinery
  Madison Heights, VA....................434-369-1259
Distillata
  Cleveland, OH............................800-999-2906
Harrison Electropolishing
  Houston, TX................................832-467-3100

Ipec
  New Castle, PA............................800-377-4732
Jus-Made
  Dallas, TX..................................800-969-3746
Kombucha Brooklyn
  Kingston, NY..............................917-261-3010
Maselli Measurements Inc
  Stockton, CA..............................800-964-9600
Midwest Juice
  Grand Rapids, MI........................877-265-8243
Nidec Minster Corp.
  Minster, OH
Primo Water Corporation
  Winston-Salem, NC......................844-237-7466
Rocheleau Blow Molding Systems
  Fitchburg, MA............................978-345-1723
Severn Trent Svc
  Fort Washington, PA....................215-646-9201
SICK Inc
  Bloomington, MN........................800-325-7425
Spinzer
  Glen Ellyn, IL............................630-469-7184

Coffee Industry

San Marco Coffee, Inc.
  Charlotte, NC..............................800-715-9298
Stratecon International Consultants
  Winston Salem, NC......................336-768-6808
U Roast Em Inc
  Hayward, WI..............................715-634-6255
West Coast Specialty Coffee
  Campbell, CA..............................650-259-9308

Stainless Steel

Coffee Pots

Castella Imports Inc
  Brentwood, NY............................631-231-5500

Confectionery Industry

A & B Process Systems Corp
  Stratford, WI..............................888-258-2789
Aerotech Enterprise Inc
  Chesterland, OH..........................440-729-2616
Aladdin Transparent Packaging
  Hauppauge, NY............................631-273-4747
Andy J. Egan Co.
  Grand Rapids, MI........................800-594-9244
Bakers Choice Products
  Beacon Falls, CT..........................203-720-1000
Braun Brush Co
  Albertson, NY............................800-645-4111
Bryce Corp
  Memphis, TN..............................800-238-7277
C. Cretors & Company
  Chicago, IL................................800-228-1885
Catty Inc
  Harvard, IL................................815-943-2288
Chocolate Concepts
  Hartville, OH..............................330-877-3322
Esterle Mold & Machine Co Inc
  Stow, OH....................................800-411-4086
Hebeler Corp
  Tonawanda, NY..........................800-486-4709
Insect-O-Cutor Inc
  Stone Mountain, GA....................800-966-8480
Kaufman Paper Box Company
  Providence, RI............................401-272-7508
Liberty Engineering Co
  Roscoe, IL..................................877-623-9065
McCarter Corporation
  Norristown, PA............................610-272-3203
Micelli Chocolate Mold Company
  West Babylon, NY........................631-752-2888
Pacquet Oneida
  Charlotte, NC..............................800-631-8388
Precision Brush
  Cleveland, OH............................800-252-4747
Reiser
  Canton, MA................................734-821-1290
Rheo-Tech
  Gurnee, IL..................................847-367-1557
Ribble Production
  Warminster, PA............................215-674-1706
Ritz Packaging Company
  Brooklyn, NY..............................718-366-2300
Saunder Brothers
  Bridgton, ME..............................207-647-3331
Six Hardy Brush Manufacturing
  Suffield, CT................................860-623-8465

Stephan Machinery GmbH
  Mandelein, IL..............................847-247-0182
Taconic
  Petersburg, NY............................800-833-1805
Taylor Precision Products
  Oak Brook, IL..............................866-843-3905
Voorhees Rubber Mfg Co
  Newark, MD................................410-632-1582
West Hawk Industries
  Ann Arbor, MI............................800-678-1286
Wilton Industries CanadaLtd.
  Etobicoke, ON............................800-387-3300

Conveyors

Belt

A T Ferrell Co Inc
  Bluffton, IN................................800-248-8318
A.K. Robins
  Baltimore, MD............................800-486-9656
ABI Limited
  Concord, ON..............................800-297-8666
Advanced Uniflo Technologies
  Wichita, KS................................800-688-0400
All Power Inc
  Sioux City, IA............................712-258-0681
Amark Packaging Systems
  Kansas City, MO..........................816-965-9000
Anderson-Crane Company
  Minneapolis, MN........................800-314-2747
Andgar Corp
  Ferndale, WA..............................360-366-9900
ANDRITZ Inc
  Muncy, PA..................................704-943-4343
Asgco Manufacturing Inc
  Allentown, PA............................800-344-4000
Bamco Belting
  Greenville, SC............................800-258-2358
Berkshire PPM
  Litchfield, CT..............................860-567-3118
Berndorf Belt Technology USA
  Gilberts, IL................................800-393-8450
Bilt-Rite Conveyors
  New London, WI..........................920-982-6600
BMH
  City of Industry, CA....................909-349-2530
Bmh Equipment Inc
  Sacramento, CA..........................800-350-8828
Bowman Hollis Mfg Corp
  Charlotte, NC..............................888-269-2358
BW Container Systems
  Romeoville, IL............................630-759-6800
C R Daniels Inc
  Ellicott City, MD........................800-933-2638
C S Bell Co
  Tiffin, OH..................................888-958-6381
C&R Refrigation Inc,
  Center, TX..................................800-438-6182
California Vibratory Feeders
  Anaheim, CA..............................800-354-0972
Cambelt International Corporation
  Salt Lake City, UT......................801-972-5511
Cambridge Intl. Inc.
  Cambridge, MD..........................800-638-9560
Chantland Company, The
  Humboldt, IA..............................515-332-4040
Cleveland Vibrator Co
  Cleveland, OH............................800-221-3298
Commercial Manufacturing
  Fresno, CA..................................559-237-1855
Conesco Conveyor Corporation
  Clifton, NJ..................................973-365-1440
Conveyor Supply Inc
  Deerfield, IL................................847-945-5670
Cozzini Inc
  Algona, IA..................................888-295-1116
Custom Conveyor & Supply Corp.
  Racine, WI..................................262-634-4920
Davron Technologies Inc
  Chattanooga, TN........................423-870-1888
Dearborn Mid-West Conveyor Co
  Overland Park, KS......................913-384-9950
Descon EDM
  Brocton, NY................................716-792-9300
Design Technology Corporation
  Billerica, MA..............................978-663-7000
Dorner Manufacturing Corp
  Hartland, WI..............................800-397-8664
Duplex Mill & Mfg Co
  Springfield, OH..........................937-325-5555

Dyna-Veyor Inc
Newark, NJ 800-326-5009
Dynamic Storage Systems Inc.
Brooksville, FL 800-974-8211
E-Z Lift Conveyors
Denver, CO 800-821-9966
Eckels Bilt
Fort Worth, TX 800-343-9020
Eisenmann Corp USA
Crystal Lake, IL 815-455-4100
Ermanco
Norton Shores, MI 231-798-4547
F & A Fabricating Inc
Battle Creek, MI 269-965-8371
Filling Equipment Co Inc
Flushing, NY 800-247-7127
FleetwoodGoldcoWyard
Romeoville, IL 630-759-6800
Flodin
Moses Lake, WA 509-766-2996
FreesTech
Sinking Spring, PA 717-560-7560
GEM Equipment Of Oregon Inc
Woodburn, OR 503-982-9902
General Machinery Corp
Sheboygan, WI 888-243-6622
Georgia Duck & Cordage Mill
Scottdale, GA 404-297-3170
Globe Machine
Tacoma, WA 800-523-6575
Goodnature Products
Orchard Park, NY 800-875-3381
Grain Machinery Mfg Corp
Miami, FL 305-620-2525
Graybill Machines Inc
Lititz, PA 717-626-5221
Gulf Arizona Packaging
Humble, TX 800-364-3887
Gulf Systems
Brownsville, TX 800-217-4853
Gulf Systems
Humble, TX 800-364-3887
Gulf Systems
Arlington, TX 817-261-1915
Habasit Canada Limited
Oakville, ON 905-827-4131
Herche Warehouse
Denver, CO 303-371-8186
Hi Roller Enclosed Belt Conveyors
Sioux Falls, SD 800-328-1785
HMC Corp
Hopkinton, NH 603-746-4691
Hurt Conveyor Equipment Company
Los Angeles, CA 323-541-0433
ICB Greenline
Charlotte, NC 800-331-5312
Industrial Design Fab
Sioux City, IA 877-873-5858
Industrial Kinetics
Downers Grove, IL 800-655-0306
Inter-City Welding & Manufacturing
Independence, MO 816-252-1770
Intralox LLC
Harahan, LA 504-733-0463
Jantec
Traverse City, MI 800-992-3303
Kamflex Corp
Chicago, IL 800-323-2440
Kaufman Engineered Systems
Waterville, OH 419-878-9727
Keenline Conveyor Systems
Omro, WI 920-685-0365
Key Material Handling Inc
Simi Valley, CA 800-539-7225
Kinder Morgan Inc
Houston, TX 713-466-0496
Kinergy Corp
Louisville, KY 502-366-5685
Kornylak Corp
Hamilton, OH 800-837-5676
KWS Manufacturing Co LTD
Burleson, TX 800-543-6558
Laros Equipment Co Inc
Portage, MI 269-323-1441
Laughlin Sales Corp
Fort Worth, TX 817-625-7756
Le Fiell Co
Reno, NV 402-592-9993
Leeds Conveyor Manufacturer Company
Guilford, CT 800-724-1088
Lesco Design & Mfg Co
La Grange, KY 502-222-7101

Lewco Inc
Sandusky, OH 419-625-4014
Lewis M Carter Mfg Co Inc
Donalsonville, GA 800-332-8232
Magnetic Products Inc
Highland, MI 800-544-5930
Mar-Con Wire Belt
Richmond, BC 877-962-7266
Marlen International
Astoria, OR 800-862-7536
Martin Engineering
Neponset, IL 800-766-2786
Maryland Wire Belts
Cleveland, OH 800-677-2358
Matthiesen Equipment
San Antonio, TX 800-624-8635
McCormick Enterprises
Arlington Heights, IL 800-323-5201
McNichols Conveyor Company
Southfield, MI 800-331-1926
Mell & Co
Niles, IL 800-262-6355
Meyer Machine & Garroutte Products
San Antonio, TX 210-736-1811
Michigan Industrial Belting
Livonia, MI 800-778-1650
Midwest Metalcraft & Equipment
Windsor, MO 800-647-3167
Millard Manufacturing Corp
La Vista, NE 800-662-4263
Molding Automation Concepts
Woodstock, IL 800-435-6979
Monarch-McLaren
Weston, ON 416-741-9675
National Conveyor Corp
Commerce, CA 323-725-0355
Northwind Inc
Alpena, AR 877-937-2585
Ohio Conveyor & Supply Inc
Findlay, OH 419-422-3825
Omni Metalcraft Corporation
Alpena, MI 989-358-7000
OTP Industrial Solutions
Terre Haute, IN 860-953-7632
Our Name is Mud
New York, NY 877-683-7867
Overhead Conveyor Co
Ferndale, MI 800-396-2554
P & F Machine
Turlock, CA 209-667-2515
Package Conveyor Co
Fort Worth, TX 800-792-1243
Packaging & Processing Equipment
Ayr, ON 519-622-6666
Packaging Systems Intl
Denver, CO 303-244-9000
Parkson Corp
Fort Lauderdale, FL 908-464-0700
Peerless Conveyor & Mfg Corp
Kansas City, KS 913-342-2240
Portec Flowmaster
Canon City, CO 800-777-7471
Power-Pack Conveyor Co
Willoughby, OH 440-975-9955
Priority One Packaging
Waterloo, ON 800-387-9102
Prodo-Pak Corp
Garfield, NJ 973-777-7770
Psc Floturn Inc
Union, NJ 908-687-3225
Quickdraft
Canton, OH 330-477-4574
R.G. Stephens Engineering
Long Beach, CA 800-499-3001
Rapat Corp
Hawley, MN 800-325-6377
Regal Power Transmission Solutions
Florence, KY 859-342-7900
Rexnord Corporation
Milwaukee, WI 866-739-6673
San Fab Conveyor
Sandusky, OH 419-626-4465
Schneider Packaging Eqpt Co
Brewerton, NY 315-676-3035
Screw Conveyor Corp
Hammond, IN 219-931-1450
Simplex Filler Co
Napa, CA 800-796-7539
Smetco
Aurora, OR 800-253-5400
Southern Automatics
Lakeland, FL 800-441-4604

Span Tech LLC
Glasgow, KY 270-651-9166
Specialty Equipment Company
Houston, TX 713-467-1818
Speedways Conveyors
Lancaster, NY 800-800-1022
Sperling Industries
Omaha, NE 800-647-5062
Spurgeon Co
Ferndale, MI 800-396-2554
Stokes Material Handling Systs
Doylestown, PA 215-340-2200
Svedala Industries
Colorado Springs, CO 719-471-3443
Sweet Manufacturing Co
Springfield, OH 800-334-7254
The National Provisioner
Deerfield, IL 847-763-9534
Thomas L. Green & Company
Robenosia, PA 610-693-5816
Transnorm System Inc
Grand Prairie, TX 800-259-2303
Traycon Manufacturing Co
Carlstadt, NJ 201-939-5555
Tri-Pak Machinery Inc
Harlingen, TX 956-423-5140
TWM Manufacturing
Leamington, ON 888-495-4831
UniTrak Corporation
Port Hope, ON 866-883-5749
Universal Die & Stampings
Prairie Du Sac, WI 608-643-2477
Universal Industries Inc
Cedar Falls, IA 800-553-4446
Us Rubber
Brooklyn, NY 718-782-7888
Vande Berg SCALES/Vbs Inc
Sioux Center, IA 712-722-1181
Vaughn Belting Co-Main Acct
Spartanburg, SC 800-533-9086
Versa Conveyor
London, OH 740-852-5609
Viking Machine & Design Inc
De Pere, WI 888-286-2116
Volta Belting Technology, Inc.
Pine Brook, NJ 973-276-7905
Volumetric Technologies
Cannon Falls, MN 507-263-0034
W A Powers Co
Fort Worth, TX 800-792-1243
Wall Conveyor & Manufacturing
Huntington, WV 800-456-1335
Washington Frontier
Grandview, WA 509-469-7662
Yakima Wire Works
Reedley, CA 800-344-8951
Yargus Manufacturing Inc
Marshall, IL 217-826-8059
Ziniz
Louisville, KY 502-955-6573

Bottle

Alliance Industrial Corp
Lynchburg, VA 800-368-3556
Anderson Machine Sales
Fort Lee, NJ
Berkshire PPM
Litchfield, CT 860-567-3118
Bilt-Rite Conveyors
New London, WI 920-982-6600
Bmh Equipment Inc
Sacramento, CA 800-350-8828
California Vibratory Feeders
Anaheim, CA 800-354-0972
Climax Packaging Machinery
Hamilton, OH 513-874-1664
Conveyor Supply Inc
Deerfield, IL 847-945-5670
Ermanco
Norton Shores, MI 231-798-4547
Filling Equipment Co Inc
Flushing, NY 800-247-7127
FleetwoodGoldcoWyard
Romeoville, IL 630-759-6800
Ipec
New Castle, PA 800-377-4732
Kinsley Inc
Doylestown, PA 800-414-6664
Laughlin Sales Corp
Fort Worth, TX 817-625-7756

Lewco Inc
  Sandusky, OH 419-625-4014
Ohio Conveyor & Supply Inc
  Findlay, OH 419-422-3825
OnTrack Automation Inc
  Waterloo, ON 519-886-9090
Priority One Packaging
  Waterloo, ON 800-387-9102
Rexnord Corporation
  Milwaukee, WI 866-739-6673
San Fab Conveyor
  Sandusky, OH 419-626-4465
Simplex Filler Co
  Napa, CA 800-796-7539

Chain

A.K. Robins
  Baltimore, MD 800-486-9656
ABI Limited
  Concord, ON 800-297-8666
Advanced Uniflo Technologies
  Wichita, KS 800-688-0400
Airfloat LLC
  Decatur, IL 800-888-0018
All Power Inc
  Sioux City, IA 712-258-0681
ANDRITZ Inc
  Muncy, PA 704-943-4343
Berkshire PPM
  Litchfield, CT 860-567-3118
BEVCO
  Canada, BC 800-663-0090
Bilt-Rite Conveyors
  New London, WI 920-982-6600
Bmh Equipment Inc
  Sacramento, CA 800-350-8828
BW Container Systems
  Romeoville, IL 630-759-6800
California Vibratory Feeders
  Anaheim, CA 800-354-0972
Cannon Equipment Company
  Cannon Falls, MN 800-825-8501
Conesco Conveyor Corporation
  Clifton, NJ 973-365-1440
Conveyor Supply Inc
  Deerfield, IL 847-945-5670
Custom Conveyor & Supply Corp.
  Racine, WI 262-634-4920
Davron Technologies Inc
  Chattanooga, TN 423-870-1888
Diamond Chain
  Indianapolis, IN 800-872-4246
Donahower & Company
  Olathe, KS 913-829-2650
Dorner Manufacturing Corp
  Hartland, WI 800-397-8664
Duplex Mill & Mfg Co
  Springfield, OH 937-325-5555
Dyna-Veyor Inc
  Newark, NJ 800-326-5009
Eisenmann Corp USA
  Crystal Lake, IL 815-455-4100
Emc Solutions
  Celina, OH 419-586-2388
Filling Equipment Co Inc
  Flushing, NY 800-247-7127
Flodin
  Moses Lake, WA 509-766-2996
FreesTech
  Sinking Spring, PA 717-560-7560
GEM Equipment Of Oregon Inc
  Woodburn, OR 503-982-9902
Graybill Machines Inc
  Lititz, PA 717-626-5221
Hurt Conveyor Equipment Company
  Los Angeles, CA 323-541-0433
ICB Greenline
  Charlotte, NC 800-331-5312
Industrial Kinetics
  Downers Grove, IL 800-655-0306
Laughlin Sales Corp
  Fort Worth, TX 817-625-7756
Le Fiell Co
  Reno, NV 402-592-9993
Lewco Inc
  Sandusky, OH 419-625-4014
Magnetic Products Inc
  Highland, MI 800-544-5930
Martin Cab Div
  Cleveland, OH 216-377-8200

Material Systems Engineering
  Stilesville, IN 800-634-0904
McNichols Conveyor Company
  Southfield, MI 800-331-1926
Mell & Co
  Niles, IL 800-262-6355
Michigan Industrial Belting
  Livonia, MI 800-778-1650
New London Engineering
  New London, WI 800-437-1994
Ohio Conveyor & Supply Inc
  Findlay, OH 419-422-3825
Omni Metalcraft Corporation
  Alpena, MI 989-358-7000
Our Name is Mud
  New York, NY 877-683-7867
Packaging & Processing Equipment
  Ayr, ON 519-622-6666
Priority One Packaging
  Waterloo, ON 800-387-9102
R.G. Stephens Engineering
  Long Beach, CA 800-499-3001
Rexnord Corporation
  Milwaukee, WI 866-739-6673
Richards Industries Systems
  West Caldwell, NJ 973-575-7480
San Fab Conveyor
  Sandusky, OH 419-626-4465
Simplex Filler Co
  Napa, CA 800-796-7539
Specialty Equipment Company
  Houston, TX 713-467-1818
Spurgeon Co
  Ferndale, MI 800-396-2554
Sweet Manufacturing Co
  Springfield, OH 800-334-7254
Tri-Pak Machinery Inc
  Harlingen, TX 956-423-5140
TWM Manufacturing
  Leamington, ON 888-495-4831
Versa Conveyor
  London, OH 740-852-5609
Washington Frontier
  Grandview, WA 509-469-7662
Wilkie Brothers Conveyor Inc
  Marysville, MI 810-364-4820
Yargus Manufacturing Inc
  Marshall, IL 217-826-8059
Ziniz
  Louisville, KY 502-955-6573

Systems & Components

A C Horn & Co Sheet Metal
  Dallas, TX 800-657-6155
A T Ferrell Co Inc
  Bluffton, IN 800-248-8318
A-Z Factory Supply
  Schiller Park, IL 800-323-4511
A.K. Robins
  Baltimore, MD 800-486-9656
ABI Limited
  Concord, ON 800-297-8666
Accutek Packaging Equipment
  Vista, CA 800-989-1828
Adamation
  Commerce, CA 800-383-8800
Advance Weight Systems Inc
  Grafton, WI 440-926-3691
Advanced Detection Systems
  Milwaukee, WI 414-672-0553
Advanced Uniflo Technologies
  Wichita, KS 800-688-0400
Aerocon
  Langhorne, PA 215-860-6056
Aerowerks
  Mississauga, ON 888-774-1616
Airfloat LLC
  Decatur, IL 800-888-0018
All Power Inc
  Sioux City, IA 712-258-0681
Alliance Bakery Systems
  Blythewood, SC 803-691-9227
Alliance Industrial Corp
  Lynchburg, VA 800-368-3556
Alliance Products LLC
  Murfreesboro, TN 800-522-3973
Allied Bakery and Food Service Equipment
  Santa Fe Springs, CA 562-945-6506
Allied Uniking Corp Inc
  Memphis, TN 901-365-7240

Amark Packaging Systems
  Kansas City, MO 816-965-9000
American Auger & Accesories
  West Chester, PA 866-219-9619
American Extrusion Intl
  South Beloit, IL 815-624-6616
American Food Equipment Company
  Hayward, CA 510-783-0255
Ametek Technical & Industrial Products
  Kent, OH 215-256-6601
Ammeraal Beltech
  Grand Rapids, MI 616-791-0292
Anderson Machine Sales
  Fort Lee, NJ
Anderson-Crane Company
  Minneapolis, MN 800-314-2747
Andgar Corp
  Ferndale, WA 360-366-9900
ANDRITZ Inc
  Muncy, PA 704-943-4343
Anver Corporation
  Hudson, MA 800-654-3500
AP Dataweigh Inc
  Cumming, GA 877-409-2562
Apache Inc
  Cedar Rapids, IA 800-553-5455
Apache Stainless Equipment
  Beaver Dam, WI 800-444-0398
Apollo Sheet Metal
  Kennewick, WA 509-586-1104
APV Baker
  Goldsboro, NC 919-736-4309
Asgco Manufacturing Inc
  Allentown, PA 800-344-4000
Ashworth Bros Inc
  Winchester, VA 800-682-4594
Atlas Equipment Company
  Kansas City, MO 800-842-9188
Automated Food Systems
  Waxahachie, TX 469-517-0470
Automated Production Systems Corporation
  New Freedom, PA 888-345-5377
Automatic Handling Int
  Erie, MI 734-847-0633
Automotion Inc
  Oak Lawn, IL 708-229-3700
Baking Machines
  Livermore, CA 925-449-3369
Belco Packaging Systems
  Monrovia, CA 800-833-1833
Belshaw Adamatic Bakery Group
  Auburn, WA 800-578-2547
Belt Technologies Inc
  Agawam, MA 413-786-9922
Berndorf Belt Technology USA
  Gilberts, IL 800-393-8450
Best
  Brunswick, OH 800-827-9237
Best Diversified Products
  Jonesboro, AR 800-327-9209
Bettendorf Stanford Inc
  Salem, IL 800-548-2253
BEVCO
  Canada, BC 800-663-0090
Bilt-Rite Conveyors
  New London, WI 920-982-6600
Biner Ellison Packaging Systs
  Vista, CA 800-733-8162
Blodgett Oven Co
  Burlington, VT 800-331-5842
BMH
  City of Industry, CA 909-349-2530
Bmh Equipment Inc
  Sacramento, CA 800-350-8828
Bowman Hollis Mfg Corp
  Charlotte, NC 888-269-2358
Brothers Metal Products
  Santa Ana, CA 714-972-3008
Brush Research Mfg Co Inc
  Los Angeles, CA 323-261-6162
Bryant Products Inc
  Ixonia, WI 800-825-3874
Buffalo Technologies Corporation
  Buffalo, NY 800-332-2419
Buhler Inc.
  Plymouth, MN 763-847-9900
Bulldog Factory Svc LLC
  Madison Heights, MI 248-541-3500
Bunting Magnetics Co
  Newton, KS 800-835-2526
BW Container Systems
  Romeoville, IL 630-759-6800

C H Babb Co Inc
Raynham, MA 508-977-0600
C R Daniels Inc
Ellicott City, MD. 800-933-2638
C S Bell Co
Tiffin, OH 888-958-6381
C&R Refrigation Inc,
Center, TX. 800-438-6182
C.J. Machine
Fridley, MN 763-767-4630
Caddy Corporation of America
Bridgeport, NJ. 856-467-4222
California Vibratory Feeders
Anaheim, CA 800-354-0972
Caljan America
Denver, CO 303-321-3600
Cambelt International Corporation
Salt Lake City, UT 801-972-5511
Can Lines Engineering Inc
Downey, CA 562-861-2996
Cannon Equipment Company
Cannon Falls, MN 800-825-8501
Capway Conveyor Systems Inc
York, PA 877-222-7929
Carman Industries Inc
Jeffersonville, IN 800-456-7560
Carrier Vibrating Equip Inc
Louisville, KY 502-969-3171
Carron Net Co Inc
Two Rivers, WI. 800-558-7768
Casso-Solar Corporation
Nanuet, NY 800-988-4455
Chantland Company, The
Humboldt, IA 515-332-4040
Charles Walker North America
Fort Worth, TX 817-922-9834
Charlton & Hill
Lethbridge, AB 403-328-3388
Chase-Logeman Corp
Greensboro, NC 336-665-0754
Checker Machine
Minneapolis, MN 888-800-5001
Chicago Conveyor Corporation
Addison, IL 630-543-6300
CHL Systems
Souderton, PA 215-723-7284
Chocolate Concepts
Hartville, OH 330-877-3322
Christianson Systems Inc
Blomkest, MN. 800-328-8896
Christy Machine Co
Fremont, OH 888-332-6451
CIM Bakery Equipment of USA
Arlington Heights, IL 847-818-8121
Cincinnati Industrial Machry
Mason, OH 800-677-0076
Cintex of America
Carol Stream, IL 800-424-6839
Cleveland Vibrator Co
Cleveland, OH 800-221-3298
Climax Packaging Machinery
Hamilton, OH 513-874-1664
Clipper Belt Lacer Company
Grand Rapids, MI 616-459-3196
Coastline Equipment Inc
Bellingham, WA 360-734-8509
Colborne Foodbotics
Lake Forest, IL 847-724-5070
Columbus McKinnon Corporation
Getzville, NY 800-888-0985
Command Belt Cleaning Systems
Hammond, IN 800-433-7627
Commercial Dehydrator Systems
Eugene, OR. 800-369-4283
Commercial Manufacturing
Fresno, CA 559-237-1855
Conesco Conveyor Corporation
Clifton, NJ. 973-365-1440
Conveyance Technologies LLC
Cleveland, OH 800-701-2278
Conveying Industries
Denver, CO 877-600-4874
Conveyor Accessories
Burr Ridge, IL 800-323-7093
Conveyor Components Co
Croswell, MI 800-233-3233
Conveyor Supply Inc
Deerfield, IL 847-945-5670
Corn States Metal Fabricators
West Des Moines, IA 515-225-7961
Coss Engineering Sales Company
Rochester Hills, MI. 800-446-1365

Cozzini Inc
Algona, IA 888-295-1116
Crippen Manufacturing Co
St Louis, MI 800-872-2474
CTC
West Caldwell, NJ. 973-228-2300
Cugar Machine Co
Fort Worth, TX 817-927-0411
Currie Machinery Co
Santa Clara, CA 408-727-0422
Custom Conveyor & Supply Corp.
Racine, WI 262-634-4920
Custom Food Machinery
Stockton, CA. 209-463-4343
Custom Metal Design Inc
Oakland, FL 800-334-1777
Custom Systems Integration Co
Carlsbad, CA. 760-635-1099
Cyclonaire Corp
York, NE 800-445-0730
Davron Technologies Inc
Chattanooga, TN. 423-870-1888
Dearborn Mid-West Conveyor Co
Overland Park, KS 913-384-9950
Delavan Spray Technologies
Bamberg, SC 800-982-6943
Delta/Ducon
Malvern, PA 800-238-2974
Dematic USA
Grand Rapids, MI 877-725-7500
Descon EDM
Brocton, NY 716-792-9300
Design Systems Inc
Farmington Hills, MI 800-660-4374
Design Technology Corporation
Billerica, MA 978-663-7000
Dillin Automation Systems Corp
Perrysburg, OH. 419-666-6789
Diversified Capping Equipment
Perrysburg, OH. 419-666-2566
Diversified Metal Engineering
Charlottetown, PE. 902-628-6900
Donahower & Company
Olathe, KS 913-829-2650
Douglas Machine Inc
Alexandria, MN 320-763-6587
Dresco Belting Co Inc
East Weymouth, MA. 781-335-1350
Duke Manufacturing Co
St Louis, MO. 800-735-3853
Duluth Sheet Metal
Duluth, MN. 218-722-2613
Dunkley International Inc
Kalamazoo, MI 800-666-1264
Dunrite Inc
Fremont, NE 800-782-3061
Duplex Mill & Mfg Co
Springfield, OH. 937-325-5555
Dupps Co
Germantown, OH 937-855-0623
Durand-Wayland Inc
Lagrange, GA 800-241-2308
Dyco
Bloomsburg, PA 800-545-3926
Dyna-Veyor Inc
Newark, NJ 800-326-5009
Dynamet
Kalamazoo, MI 269-385-0006
Dynamic Air Inc
St Paul, MN. 651-484-2900
Dynamic Automation LTD
Simi Valley, CA. 805-584-8476
Dynamic Storage Systems Inc.
Brooksville, FL 800-974-8211
E F Bavis & Assoc Inc
Maineville, OH 513-677-0500
E-Z Lift Conveyors
Denver, CO 800-821-9966
Eckels Bilt
Fort Worth, TX 800-343-9020
Ecs Warehouse
Buffalo, NY. 716-833-7380
Edmeyer
Minneapolis, MN 651-450-1210
Eisenmann Corp USA
Crystal Lake, IL 815-455-4100
Electrical Engineering & Equip
Windsor Heights, IA 800-955-3633
ELF Machinery
La Porte, IN. 800-328-0466
Emc Solutions
Celina, OH 419-586-2388

En-Hanced Products Inc
Westerville, OH. 800-783-7400
Engineered Products Corp
Greenville, SC. 800-868-0145
Equipment Outlet
Meridian, ID 208-887-1472
Eriez Magnetics
Erie, PA 800-346-4946
Ermanco
Norton Shores, MI 231-798-4547
F & A Fabricating Inc
Battle Creek, MI 269-965-8371
F N Smith Corp
Oregon, IL 815-732-2171
F.B. Pease Company
Rochester, NY 585-475-1870
Fabreeka International
Boise, ID 800-423-4469
Fata Automation
Sterling Heights, MI 586-323-9400
FEI Inc
Mansfield, TX 800-346-5908
Fenner Dunlop Americas Inc
Pittsburgh, PA 412-249-0700
Filler Specialties
Zeeland, MI. 616-772-9235
Filling Equipment Co Inc
Flushing, NY 800-247-7127
Fillit
Kirkland, QC 514-694-2390
Fishmore
Melbourne, FL 321-723-4751
Fleet Wood Goldco Wyard
Cockeysville, MD 410-785-1934
Fleetwood Systems
Orlando, FL. 800-432-5433
FleetwoodGoldcoWyard
Romeoville, IL 630-759-6800
Flexco
Downers Grove, IL 800-323-3444
Flexco
Downers Grove, IL 800-541-8028
Flexible Material Handling
Suwanee, GA 800-669-1501
Flexicell Inc
Ashland, VA 804-550-7300
Flexicon
Bethlehem, PA 888-353-9426
Flodin
Moses Lake, WA. 509-766-2996
Fogg Filler Co
Holland, MI. 616-786-3644
Food Engineering Unlimited
Fullerton, CA 714-879-8762
Food Machinery Sales
Bogart, GA 706-549-2207
Food Processing Equipment Co
Santa Fe Springs, CA 562-802-3727
Forbo Siegling LLC
Huntersville, NC 800-255-5581
FPEC Corporation
Santa Fe Springs, CA 562-802-3727
Franz Haas Machinery-America
Henrico, VA 804-222-6022
FreesTech
Sinking Spring, PA 717-560-7560
Frelco
Stephenville, NL 709-643-5668
Frigoscandia Equipment
Northfield, MN 800-426-1283
Frost Food Handling Products
Grand Rapids, MI 800-253-9382
Garvey Corp
Hammonton, NJ 800-257-8581
Gates Manufacturing Company
Saint Louis, MO 800-237-9226
Gbn Machine & Engineering
Woodford, VA 800-446-9871
Gch Internatonal
Louisville, KY 502-636-1374
Gebo Conveyors, Consultants & Systems
Laval, QC 450-973-3337
Gebo Corporation
Bradenton, FL 941-727-1400
GEM Equipment Of Oregon Inc
Woodburn, OR 503-982-9902
Gemini Bakery Equipment
Philadelphia, PA 800-468-9046
General Machinery Corp
Sheboygan, WI 888-243-6622
General Tank
Berwick, PA 800-435-8265

Georgia Duck & Cordage Mill
Scottdale, GA .404-297-3170

Globe Machine
Tacoma, WA .800-523-6575

Goergen-Mackwirth Co Inc
Buffalo, NY. .800-728-4446

Goldco Industries
Loveland, CO 970-663-4770

Gough-Econ Inc
Charlotte, NC 800-204-6844

Graco Inc
Minneapolis, MN 612-623-6000

Grain Machinery Mfg Corp
Miami, FL. 305-620-2525

Graybill Machines Inc
Lititz, PA 717-626-5221

Green Belt Industries Inc
Buffalo, NY. .800-668-1114

Greitzer
Elizabeth City, NC 252-338-4000

Griffin Automation
Buffalo, NY. .716-674-2300

Gulf Arizona Packaging
Humble, TX .800-364-3887

Gulf Systems
Brownsville, TX 800-217-4853

Gulf Systems
Humble, TX .800-364-3887

Gulf Systems
Arlington, TX 817-261-1915

H G Weber & Co
Kiel, WI. 920-894-2221

Habasit America
Suwanee, GA 800-458-6431

Habasit America Plastic Div
Reading, PA .800-445-7898

Habasit Canada Limited
Oakville, ON. 905-827-4131

Halton Packaging Systems
Oakville, ON. 905-847-9141

Hapman Conveyors
Kalamazoo, MI 800-968-7722

Hardy Systems Corporation
Northbrook, IL 800-927-3956

Hart Design & Mfg
Green Bay, WI. 920-468-5927

Hartness International
Greenville, SC. 800-845-8791

Heinzen Sales
Gilroy, CA 408-842-6678

Herche Warehouse
Denver, CO .303-371-8186

Hi Roller Enclosed Belt Conveyors
Sioux Falls, SD 800-328-1785

HMC Corp
Hopkinton, NH 603-746-4691

Hoffmeyer Corp
San Leandro, CA. 888-744-1826

Hoppmann Corporation
Elkwood, VA. 800-368-3582

Howes S Co Inc
Silver Creek, NY. 888-255-2611

Hudson Belting & Svc Co Inc
Worcester, MA 508-756-0090

Hughes Co
Columbus, WI. 866-535-9303

Hurt Conveyor Equipment Company
Los Angeles, CA. 323-541-0433

I J White Corp
Farmingdale, NY. 631-293-2211

ICB Greenline
Charlotte, NC 800-331-5312

Industrial Automation Systems
Santa Clarita, CA. 888-484-4427

Industrial Kinetics
Downers Grove, IL 800-655-0306

Industrial Magnetics
Boyne City, MI 800-662-4638

Inline Filling Systems
Venice, FL. 941-486-8800

Inter-City Welding & Manufacturing
Independence, MO 816-252-1770

Interlake Mecalux
Chicago, IL 708-344-9999

Interroll Corp
Wilmington, NC 800-830-9680

Intralox LLC
Harahan, LA .800-535-8848

Irby
Rocky Mount, NC 252-442-0154

J C Ford Co
La Habra, CA 714-871-7361

J L Becker Co
Plymouth, MI 800-837-4328

J.H. Thornton Company
Olathe, KS. 913-764-6550

Jantec
Traverse City, MI 800-992-3303

Jervis B WEBB Co
Novi, MI 248-553-1000

Jetstream Systems
Wichita, KN .855-861-6916

K-Tron
Salina, KS 785-825-1611

K.F. Logistics
Cincinnati, OH 800-347-9100

Kamflex Corp
Chicago, IL 800-323-2440

KAPS All Packaging
Riverhead, NY 631-727-0300

Kasel Industries Inc
Denver, CO .800-218-4417

Kaufman Engineered Systems
Waterville, OH 419-878-9727

Keenline Conveyor Systems
Omro, WI 920-685-0365

Key Material Handling Inc
Simi Valley, CA. 800-539-7225

Key Technology Inc.
Walla Walla, WA. 509-529-2161

Kinder Morgan Inc
Houston, TX .713-466-0496

Kinergy Corp
Louisville, KY. 502-366-5685

Kinetic Equipment Company
Appleton, WI 806-293-4471

Kinsley Inc
Doylestown, PA 800-414-6664

Kisco Manufacturing
Port Alberni, BC 604-823-7456

KISS Packaging Systems
Vista, CA. 888-522-3538

KLEEN Line Corp
Newburyport, MA. 800-259-5973

Kline Process Systems Inc
Reading, PA .610-371-0300

Klippenstein Corp
Fresno, CA 888-834-4258

Kofab
Algona, IA. 515-295-7265

Kohler Industries Inc
Lincoln, NE. .800-365-6708

Kornylak Corp
Hamilton, OH 800-837-5676

KWS Manufacturing Co LTD
Burleson, TX. 800-543-6558

Laidig Inc
Mishawaka, IN 574-256-0204

Lambert Material Handling
Syracuse, NY 800-253-5103

Laros Equipment Co Inc
Portage, MI .269-323-1441

Laughlin Sales Corp
Fort Worth, TX 817-625-7756

Le Fiell Co
Reno, NV 402-592-9993

Leeds Conveyor Manufacturer Company
Guilford, CT .800-724-1088

Lewco Inc
Sandusky, OH 419-625-4014

Lewis M Carter Mfg Co Inc
Donalsonville, GA 800-332-8232

Lock Inspection Systems
Fitchburg, MA 800-227-5539

Lorenz Couplings
Cobourg, ON. 800-263-7782

Louisville Dryer Company
Louisville, KY 800-735-3613

LPS Technology
Grafton, OH .800-586-1410

LTI Boyd Corp
Modesto, CA. 888-244-6931

Lumsden Flexx Flow
Lancaster, PA 800-367-3664

Lyco Manufacturing
Wausau, WI. .715-845-7867

Lyco Wausau
Wausau, WI. .715-845-7867

MAC Equipment
Kansas City, MO. 800-821-2476

Machine Builders & Design Inc
Shelby, NC 704-482-3456

Magnetic Products Inc
Highland, MI. 800-544-5930

Magsys Inc
Milwaukee, WI 414-543-2177

Mar-Con Wire Belt
Richmond, BC 877-962-7266

Marlen International
Astoria, OR .800-862-7536

Martin Engineering
Neponset, IL .800-766-2786

Martin/Baron
Irwindale, CA 626-960-5153

Maryland Wire Belts
Cleveland, OH 800-677-2358

Material Systems Engineering
Stilesville, IN 800-634-0904

Materials Transportation Co
Temple, TX 800-433-3110

Mathews Conveyor
Danville, KY. 800-628-4397

Matthiesen Equipment
San Antonio, TX. 800-624-8635

McCormick Enterprises
Arlington Heights, IL 800-323-5201

McNichols Conveyor Company
Southfield, MI 800-331-1926

MeGa Industries
Burlington, ON 800-665-6342

Mell & Co
Niles, IL 800-262-6355

Merco/Savory
Mt. Pleasant, MI 800-733-8821

Meriwether Industries
Bloomfield, NJ 800-332-2358

Metko Inc
New Holstein, WI. 920-898-4221

Metzgar Conveyors
Comstock Park, MI. 888-266-8390

Meyer Machine & Garroutte Products
San Antonio, TX. 210-736-1811

Michigan Industrial Belting
Livonia, MI 800-778-1650

Midwest Metalcraft & Equipment
Windsor, MO. 800-647-3167

Midwest Rubber Svc & Supply
Minneapolis, MN. 800-537-7457

Millard Manufacturing Corp
La Vista, NE. 800-662-4263

Miller Hofft Brands
Indianapolis, IN 317-638-6576

Miller Metal Fabrication
Bridgeville, DE 302-337-2291

Molding Automation Concepts
Woodstock, IL. 800-435-6979

Moline Machinery LLC
Duluth, MN. 800-767-5734

Monarch-McLaren
Weston, ON .416-741-9675

Mp Equip. Co.
Buford, GA. .770-614-5355

Mumper Machine Corporation
Butler, WI. 262-781-8908

Murata Automated Systems
Charlotte, NC 800-428-8469

National Conveyor Corp
Commerce, CA 323-725-0355

National Drying Machry Co Inc
Philadelphia, PA 215-464-6070

NECO/Nebraska Engineering
Omaha, NE 800-367-6208

Neos
Elk River, MN. 888-441-6367

Nercon Engineering & Manufacturing
Oshkosh, WI. 920-233-3268

New London Engineering
New London, WI 800-437-1994

Newcastle Co Inc
New Castle, PA 724-658-4516

Niro Inc
Hudson, WI. .715-386-9371

North American Roller Prod Inc
Glen Ellyn, IL 630-858-9161

Northwind Inc
Alpena, AR 877-937-2585

Nothum Food Processing Systems
Springfield, MO 800-435-1297

Nu-Con Equipment
Chanhassen, MN. 877-939-0510

Nutec Manufacturing Inc
New Lenox, IL 815-722-5348

Ohio Magnetics Inc
Maple Heights, OH 800-486-6446

Omega Industrial Products Inc
Saukville, WI 800-279-6634

Omicron Steel Products Company
Jamaica, NY 718-805-3400
Omni Lift Inc
Salt Lake City, UT 801-486-3776
Omni Metalcraft Corporation
Alpena, MI 989-358-7000
OnTrack Automation Inc
Waterloo, ON 519-886-9090
Optek Inc
Galena, OH 800-533-8400
Oshikiri Corp Of America
Philadelphia, PA 215-637-8112
OTP Industrial Solutions
Terre Haute, IN 860-953-7632
Ouellette Machinery Systems
Fenton, MO 800-545-7619
Our Name is Mud
New York, NY 877-683-7867
Oyster Bay Pump Works Inc
Hicksville, NY 516-933-4500
Pa R Systems Inc
St Paul, MN 800-464-1320
Pacific Pneumatics
Rancho Cucamonga, CA 800-221-0961
Package Conveyor Co
Fort Worth, TX 800-792-1243
Packaging Equipment & Conveyors, Inc
Elkhart, IN....................574-266-6995
Packaging Machinery
Montgomery, AL 334-265-9211
Packaging Progressions
Collegeville, PA 610-489-9096
Paget Equipment Co
Marshfield, WI 715-384-3158
Palace Packaging Machines Inc
Downingtown, PA.................610-873-7252
Parkson Corp
Vernon Hills, IL 847-816-3700
Parkson Corp
Fort Lauderdale, FL 908-464-0700
Paxton Products Inc
Blue Ash, OH 800-441-7475
Peerless Conveyor & Mfg Corp
Kansas City, KS 913-342-2240
Peerless Dough Mixing and Make-Up
Sidney, OH 800-999-3327
Peerless Food Equipment
Sidney, OH 937-492-4158
Peerless-Winsmith Inc
Springville, NY.................716-592-9310
Pengo Attachments Inc
Cokato, MN.....................800-599-0211
Peterson Fiberglass Laminates
Shell Lake, WI.................715-468-2306
Piab Vacuum Products
Hingham, MA....................800-321-7422
PlexPack Corp
Toronto, ON 855-635-9238
Pneumatic Conveying Inc
Ontario, CA....................800-655-4481
Polar Process
Plattsville, ON.................877-896-8077
Power-Pack Conveyor Co
Willoughby, OH 440-975-9955
Ppm Technologies LLC
Newberg, OR 800-246-2034
Precision
Miami, FL 800-762-7565
Priority One America
Oshkosh, WI 920-235-5562
Priority One Packaging
Waterloo, ON 800-387-9102
Process Engineering & Fabrication
Afton, VA 800-852-7975
Prodo-Pak Corp
Garfield, NJ...................973-777-7770
Production Systems
Marietta, GA...................800-235-9734
Professional Engineering Assoc
Louisville, KY 502-429-0432
Psc Floturn Inc
Union, NJ 908-687-3225
PTI Packaging
Portage, WI....................800-501-4077
Puritan Manufacturing Inc
Omaha, NE 800-331-0487
Quadrant Epp USA Inc
Fort Wayne, IN 800-628-7264
R.G. Stephens Engineering
Long Beach, CA.................800-499-3001
Rahmann Belting & Industrial Rubber Products
Gastonia, NC...................888-248-8148

Ralphs Pugh Conveyor Rollers
Benicia, CA....................800-486-0021
Rapat Corp
Hawley, MN 800-325-6377
Rapid Industries Inc
Louisville, KY 800-787-4381
Raque Food Systems
Louisville, KY 502-267-9641
Reading Plastic Fabricators
Reading, PA 610-926-3245
Reese Enterprises Inc
Rosemount, MN 800-328-0953
Regal Power Transmission Solutions
Florence, KY 859-342-7900
Regina USA
Oak Creek, WI 414-571-0032
Reinke & Schomann
Milwaukee, WI 414-964-1100
Renold Products
Westfield, NY 800-879-2529
Rexnord Corporation
Milwaukee, WI 866-739-6673
Reyco Systems Inc
Caldwell, ID 208-795-5700
Rhodes Machinery International
Louisville, KY 502-213-3865
Richards Industries Systems
West Caldwell, NJ..............973-575-7480
Rigidized Metal Corp
Buffalo, NY 800-836-2580
Roechling Engineered Plastics
Gastonia, NC...................800-541-4419
Rome Machine & Foundry Co
Rome, GA 800-538-7663
Ruiz Flour Tortillas
Riverside, CA 909-947-7811
Sadler Conveyor Systems
Montreal, QC 888-887-5129
Samuel Pressure Vessel Group
Marinette, WI 715-453-5326
San Fab Conveyor
Sandusky, OH 419-626-4465
Sardee Industries Inc
Orlando, FL....................407-297-6362
Schloss Engineered Equipment
Aurora, CO 303-695-4500
Schlueter Company
Janesville, WI 800-359-1700
Schroeder Machine
San Marcos, CA 760-591-9733
Scientific Process & Research
Kendall Park, NJ...............800-868-4777
Screw Conveyor Corp
Hammond, IN 219-931-1450
Servco Equipment Co
St Louis, MO...................314-781-3189
Shelcon Inc
Ontario, CA....................909-947-4877
Shingle Belting
King Of Prussia, PA 800-345-6294
Shouldice Brothers SheetMetal
Battle Creek, MI 269-962-5579
Shuttleworth North America
Huntington, IN 800-444-7412
SI Systems Inc
Easton, PA 800-523-9464
Sidney Manufacturing Co
Sidney, OH 800-482-3535
Simplex Filler Co
Napa, CA 800-796-7539
Simplimatic Automation
Forest, VA 800-294-2003
Sinco
Red Wing, MN 800-243-6753
Slip-Not Belting Corporation
Kingsport, TN 423-246-8141
Smalley Manufacturing Co Inc
Knoxville, TN 865-966-5866
Smetco
Aurora, OR 800-253-5400
Southern Ag Co Inc
Blakely, GA....................229-723-4262
Southworth Products Corp
Falmouth, ME 800-743-1000
Span Tech LLC
Glasgow, KY 270-651-9166
Spanco Crane & Monorail Systems
Morgantown, PA 800-869-2080
Specialty Equipment Company
Houston, TX 713-467-1818
Speedways Conveyors
Lancaster, NY 800-800-1022

Sperling Industries
Omaha, NE 402-556-4070
Sperling Industries
Omaha, NE 800-647-5062
Spiral Manufacturing Co Inc
Minneapolis, MN 800-426-3643
Springport Steel Wire Products
Elkhart, IN....................574-295-9660
Spudnik Equipment Co
Blackfoot, ID 208-684-4120
Spurgeon Co
Ferndale, MI 800-396-2554
Stainless Specialists Inc
Wausau, WI.....................800-236-4155
Stainless Steel Fabricator Inc
La Mirada, CA 714-739-9904
Steel Storage Systems Inc
Commerce City, CO 800-442-0291
Steinmetz Machine Works Inc
Stamford, CT...................203-327-0118
Sterling Net & Twine Company
Cedar Knolls, NJ 800-342-0316
Stewart Systems Baking LLC
Plano, TX 972-422-5808
Stokes Material Handling Systs
Doylestown, PA 215-340-2200
Superior Industries
Morris, MN 800-321-1558
Svedala Industries
Colorado Springs, CO...........719-471-3443
Temp Air Inc
Burnsville, MN 800-836-7432
The National Provisioner
Deerfield, IL 847-763-9534
Thomas L. Green & Company
Robenosia, PA..................610-693-5816
Titan Industries Inc
New London, WI 800-558-3616
TKF Inc
Cincinnati, OH 513-241-5910
Transnorm System Inc
Grand Prairie, TX 800-259-2303
Traycon Manufacturing Co
Carlstadt, NJ 201-939-5555
Tridyne Process Systems
South Burlington, VT 802-863-6873
Triple S Dynamics Inc
Breckenridge, TX 800-527-2116
True Manufacturing
Mexico, MO 636-240-2400
TWM Manufacturing
Leamington, ON 888-495-4831
Uhrden
Sugarcreek, OH.................800-852-2411
Unex Manufacturing Inc
Lakewood, NJ...................800-334-8639
United Pentek
Indianapolis, IN 800-357-9299
United States Systems Inc
Kansas City, KS 888-281-2454
UniTrak Corporation
Port Hope, ON 866-883-5749
Universal Die & Stampings
Prairie Du Sac, WI 608-643-2477
Universal Industries Inc
Cedar Falls, IA 800-553-4446
Universal Labeling Systems Inc
St Petersburg, FL 877-236-0266
Universal Packaging Inc
Houston, TX 800-324-2610
Us Rubber
Brooklyn, NY 718-782-7888
Vac-U-Max
Belleville, NJ 800-822-8629
Van Der Graaf Corporation
Lithia Springs, GA 770-819-6650
Vertical Systems Intl
Lakeside Park, KY 859-485-9650
Vescom America
Henderson, NC 252-436-9067
W A Powers Co
Fort Worth, TX 800-792-1243
W.G. Durant Corporation
Whittier, CA 562-946-5555
Walker Magnetics Group Inc
Worcester, MA 800-962-4638
Wall Conveyor & Manufacturing
Huntington, WV 800-456-1335
Ward Ironworks
Welland, ON 888-441-9273
Wardcraft Conveyor & Quick Die
Spring Arbor, MI 800-782-2779

Washington Frontier
  Grandview, WA......................509-469-7662
WEBB-Stiles Co
  Valley City, OH....................330-273-9222
Weigh Right Automatic Scale Co
  Joliet, IL...........................800-571-0249
Weiler & Company
  Whitewater, WI.....................800-558-9507
Westfield Sheet Metal Works
  Kenilworth, NJ.....................908-276-5500
Whirl Air Flow
  Big Lake, MN.......................800-373-3461
Wilkie Brothers Conveyor Inc
  Marysville, MI.....................810-364-4820
Wilson Steel Products Company
  Memphis, TN.......................901-527-8742
Win-Holt Equipment Group
  Syosset, NY........................800-444-3595
Wire Belt Co Of America
  Londonderry, NH...................603-644-2500
Witte Co Inc
  Washington, NJ....................908-689-6500
Yakima Wire Works
  Reedley, CA........................800-344-8951
Yargus Manufacturing Inc
  Marshall, IL........................217-826-8059
YW Yacht Basin
  Easton, MD.........................410-822-0414
Ziniz
  Louisville, KY......................502-955-6573

Cooperage

Brooks Barrel Company
  Baltimore, MD......................800-398-2766
EGW Bradbury Enterprises
  Bridgewater, ME....................800-332-6021
Fetzer Vineyards
  Hopland, CA........................800-846-8637
Gibbs Brothers Cooperage
  Hot Springs, AR....................501-623-8881
Oak Barrel Winecraft
  Berkeley, CA.......................510-849-0400
Ramoneda Bros Stave Mill
  Culpeper, VA.......................540-825-9166
Trilla Steel Drum Corporation
  Chicago, IL.........................773-847-7588
Warwick Products
  Cleveland, OH......................800-535-4404

Cylinders

Catalina Cylinders
  Garden Grove, CA..................714-890-0999

Dairy Industry

Cookie Kingdom
  Oglesby, IL.........................815-883-3331
Elmo Rietschle - A Gardner Denver Product
  Quincy, IL..........................217-222-5400
GEA Niro Soavi North America
  Bedford, NH........................603-606-4060
Gea Process Engineering Inc
  Columbia, MD......................410-997-8700
Invensys APV Products
  Houston, TX........................713-329-1600
Marel Food Systems, Inc.
  Lenexa, KS.........................913-888-9110
Reiser
  Canton, MA........................734-821-1290
Schwartz Manufacturing Co
  Two Rivers, WI.....................920-793-1375
Stephan Machinery GmbH
  Mandelein, IL.......................847-247-0182
Stratecon International Consultants
  Winston Salem, NC.................336-768-6808
Tuchenhagen North America
  Portland, ME.......................207-797-9500
Unitherm Food System
  Bristow, OK.........................918-367-0197
Wohlt Cheese Corp
  New London, WI...................920-982-9000

Depositors

Alard Equipment Corp
  Williamson, NY.....................315-589-4511
Bogner Industries
  Ronkonkoma, NY...................631-981-5123
Edhard Corp
  Hackettstown, NJ...................888-334-2731

Polar Process
  Plattsville, ON.....................877-896-8077
Raque Food Systems
  Louisville, KY......................502-267-9641
Reiser
  Canton, MA........................734-821-1290

Feeders

Alard Equipment Corp
  Williamson, NY.....................315-589-4511
All Power Inc
  Sioux City, IA......................712-258-0681
Anderson-Crane Company
  Minneapolis, MN...................800-314-2747
Applied Chemical Technology
  Florence, AL........................800-228-3217
Automated Flexible Conveyors
  Clifton, NJ..........................800-694-7271
Buffalo Technologies Corporation
  Buffalo, NY.........................800-332-2419
California Vibratory Feeders
  Anaheim, CA.......................800-354-0972
Campbell Wrapper Corporation
  De Pere, WI........................920-983-7100
Carman Industries Inc
  Jeffersonville, IN..................800-456-7560
Carrier Vibrating Equip Inc
  Louisville, KY......................502-969-3171
Chicago Conveyor Corporation
  Addison, IL.........................630-543-6300
Cleveland Vibrator Co
  Cleveland, OH......................800-221-3298
Creative Automation
  Passaic, NJ.........................973-778-0061
Custom Systems Integration Co
  Carlsbad, CA.......................760-635-1099
Dema Engineering Co
  St Louis, MO.......................800-325-3362
Eriez Magnetics
  Erie, PA............................800-346-4946
Flow of Solids
  Westford, MA......................978-392-0300
Fuller Weighing Systems
  Columbus, OH......................614-882-8121
Gebo Corporation
  Bradenton, FL......................941-727-1400
Gram Equipment Of America
  Tampa, FL..........................813-248-1978
Graybill Machines Inc
  Lititz, PA...........................717-626-5221
Hart Design & Mfg
  Green Bay, WI.....................920-468-5927
Hoppmann Corporation
  Elkwood, VA........................800-368-3582
Hyer Industries
  Pembroke, MA.....................781-826-8101
Ilapak Inc
  Newtown, PA.......................215-579-2900
Ipec
  New Castle, PA.....................800-377-4732
Key Technology Inc.
  Walla Walla, WA...................509-529-2161
Kinergy Corp
  Louisville, KY......................502-366-5685
KISS Packaging Systems
  Vista, CA...........................888-522-3538
Magnuson
  Pueblo, CO.........................719-948-9500
Martin Vibration Systems
  Marine City, MI....................800-474-4538
MeGa Industries
  Burlington, ON.....................800-665-6342
Mell & Co
  Niles, IL............................800-262-6355
MERRICK Industries Inc
  Lynn Haven, FL....................800-271-7834
Meyer Machine & Garroutte Products
  San Antonio, TX...................210-736-1811
Modular Packaging
  Randolph, NJ.......................973-970-9393
National Drying Machry Co Inc
  Philadelphia, PA...................215-464-6070
Norden Inc
  Branchburg, NJ....................908-252-9483
Norwalt Design Inc
  Randolph, NJ.......................973-927-3200
Nu-Con Equipment
  Chanhassen, MN...................877-939-0510
Omega Design Corp
  Exton, PA..........................800-346-0191
Open Date Systems
  Sunapee, NH.......................877-673-6328

OTP Industrial Solutions
  Terre Haute, IN....................860-953-7632
Our Name is Mud
  New York, NY......................877-683-7867
Pacific Process Technology
  La Jolla, CA........................858-551-3298
Palace Packaging Machines Inc
  Downingtown, PA..................610-873-7252
Paramount Packaging Corp
  Melville, NY........................516-333-8100
Pfankuch Machinery Corporation
  Apple Valley, MN..................952-891-3311
Polar Process
  Plattsville, ON.....................877-896-8077
Presence From Innovation LLC
  St Louis, MO.......................314-423-9777
Professional Engineering Assoc
  Louisville, KY......................502-429-0432
Ram Equipment Co
  Waukesha, WI......................262-513-1114
Schenck Process
  Whitewater, WI.....................888-742-1249
Schneider Packaging Eqpt Co
  Brewerton, NY......................315-676-3035
Shiffer Industries
  Kihei, HI............................800-642-1774
Smalley Manufacturing Co Inc
  Knoxville, TN.......................865-966-5866
Summit Machine Builders Corporation
  Denver, CO.........................800-274-6741
Superior Food Machinery Inc
  Pico Rivera, CA.....................800-944-0396
Tecweigh
  St Paul, MN........................800-536-4880
Universal Labeling Systems Inc
  St Petersburg, FL..................877-236-0266
Vescom America
  Henderson, NC.....................252-436-9067
Ward Ironworks
  Welland, ON........................888-441-9273
Waukesha Cherry-Burrell
  Louisville, KY......................502-491-4310
Weigh Right Automatic Scale Co
  Joliet, IL...........................800-571-0249
Wyssmont Co Inc
  Fort Lee, NJ........................201-947-4600

Gravimetric, Volumetric, Loss-In-Weight, Etc.

Applied Chemical Technology
  Florence, AL........................800-228-3217
Automated Flexible Conveyors
  Clifton, NJ..........................800-694-7271
Chicago Conveyor Corporation
  Addison, IL.........................630-543-6300
Cleveland Vibrator Co
  Cleveland, OH......................800-221-3298
Hyer Industries
  Pembroke, MA.....................781-826-8101
Ilapak Inc
  Newtown, PA.......................215-579-2900
MERRICK Industries Inc
  Lynn Haven, FL....................800-271-7834
Polar Process
  Plattsville, ON.....................877-896-8077
Schenck Process
  Whitewater, WI.....................888-742-1249
Tecweigh
  St Paul, MN........................800-536-4880
Weigh Right Automatic Scale Co
  Joliet, IL...........................800-571-0249

Speed Reducer

Boston Gear
  Boston, MA.........................888-999-9860
F R Drake Co
  Waynesboro, VA....................540-949-6215

Filtration Devices & Systems

A & B Process Systems Corp
  Stratford, WI.......................888-258-2789
ACS Industries, Inc.
  Lincoln, RI..........................866-783-4838
Advance Fittings Corp
  Elkhorn, WI.........................262-723-6699
Air Quality Engineering
  Minneapolis, MN...................800-328-0787
Airsan Corp
  Milwaukee, WI.....................800-558-5494

Alard Equipment Corp
Williamson, NY 315-589-4511
Alexander Machinery
Spartanburg, SC 864-963-3624
Alkazone/Better Health Lab
Hackensack, NJ. 800-810-1888
Allegheny Bradford Corp
Bradford, PA 800-542-0650
Allergen Air Filter Corp
Houston, TX 800-333-8880
American Ultraviolet Co
Lebanon, IN 800-288-9288
Ametek Technical & Industrial Products
Kent, OH. 215-256-6601
Anguil Environmental Systems
Milwaukee, WI 800-488-0230
Applied Chemical Technology
Florence, AL. 800-228-3217
APV Americas
Delavan, WI 800-252-5200
Aqua-Aerobic Systems Inc
Loves Park, IL. 800-940-5008
Aquathin Corporation
Pompano Beach, FL 800-462-7634
Astro Pure Water
Deerfield Beach, FL 954-422-8966
Avery Filter Company
Westwood, NJ 201-666-9664
Avestin
Ottawa, ON 888-283-7846
Baker Hughes
Houston, TX
Beach Filter Products
Hanover, PA 800-232-2485
Berkshire PPM
Litchfield, CT 860-567-3118
Blodgett Oven Co
Burlington, VT 800-331-5842
Bloomfield Industries
St. Louis, MO 888-356-5362
Blue Tech
Hickory, NC 828-324-5900
BluMetric Environmental Inc.
Ottawa, ON 613-839-3053
Bunn-O-Matic Corp
Springfield, IL. 800-352-2866
CE International Trading Corporation
Miami, FL 800-827-1169
CLARCOR Air Filtration Prods
Jeffersonville, IN 866-247-4827
Climate Master Inc
Oklahoma City, OK 877-436-0263
Complete Automation
Lake Orion, MI 248-814-4967
Corrigan Corporation of America
Gurnee, IL 800-462-6478
Crane Environmental
Norristown, PA 800-633-7435
Crispy Lite
St. Louis, MO 888-356-5362
Croll-Reynolds Engineering Company
Trumbull, CT 203-371-1983
Culligan Company
Northbrook, IL. 800-527-8637
Custom Fabricating & Repair
Marshfield, WI 800-236-8773
Dallas Group of America Inc
Whitehouse, NJ. 800-367-4188
Dedert Corporation
Olympia Fields, IL 708-747-7000
Delta Pure Filtration Corp
Ashland, VA 800-785-9450
Diamond Water Conditioning
Hortonville, WI. 800-236-8931
Diebolt & Co
Old Lyme, CT 800-343-2658
Durastill Export Inc
Rockland, MA. 800-449-5260
Dwyer Instruments Inc
Michigan City, IN 800-872-3141
Eaton Filtration, LLC
Tinton Falls, NJ. 800-859-9212
Eco-Air Products
San Diego, CA 800-284-8111
Elwood Safety Company
Buffalo, NY. 866-326-6060
Enting Water Conditioning Inc
Moraine, OH 800-735-5100
Enviro-Clear Co
High Bridge, NJ 908-638-5507
Ertelalsop
Kingston, NY 800-553-7835

Etube & Wire
Shrewsbury, PA. 800-618-4720
Everfilt Corp
Mira Loma, CA. 800-360-8380
Everpure, LLC
Hanover Park, IL. 630-307-3000
F.P. Smith Wire Cloth Company
Northlake, IL. 800-323-6842
Falcon Fabricators Inc
Nashville, TN 615-832-0027
Falls Filtration Technologies
Stow, OH 330-928-4100
Filtercorp
Fresno, CA 800-473-4526
Filtration Systems
Sunrise, FL 954-572-2700
Filtration Systems Prods Inc
Pevely, MO 800-444-4720
Flame Gard
Lakewood, NJ 800-526-3694
Flanders Corp
Washington, NC 800-637-2803
Freudenberg Nonwovens
Hopkinsville, KY 270-887-5115
Frymaster/Dean
Shreveport, LA 800-221-4583
Fuller Ultra Violet Corp
Frankfort, IL 815-469-3301
G.W. Dahl Company
Greensboro, NC 800-852-4449
Gaylord Industries
Tualatin, OR 800-547-9696
Globe Machine
Tacoma, WA 800-523-6575
Goodnature Products
Orchard Park, NY 800-875-3381
Greig Filters Inc
Lafayette, LA 800-456-0177
Gusmer Enterprises Inc
Fresno, CA 866-213-1131
H T I Filtration
Rancho Sta Marg, CA. 877-404-9372
Halton Company
Scottsville, KY 800-442-5866
Hankison International
Canonsburg, PA 724-746-1100
Harborlite Corporation
Lompoc, CA 800-342-8667
Hayes & Stolz Indl Mfg LTD
Fort Worth, TX 800-725-7272
Hayward Industries Inc
Clemmons, NC 336-712-9900
Hemco
Independence, MO 800-779-4362
Hess Machine Intl
Ephrata, PA 800-735-4377
Holland Applied Technologies
Burr Ridge, IL. 630-325-5130
Hungerford & Terry
Clayton, NJ 856-881-3200
Hunter Fan Co
Cordova, TN 901-743-1360
Hydromax Inc
Emmitsburg, MD 800-326-0602
Hydropure Water Treatment Co
Coral Springs, FL 800-753-1547
I.W. Tremont Company
Hawthorne, NJ 973-427-3800
Imperial Manufacturing Co
Corona, IL 800-343-7790
Introdel Products
Itasca, IL 800-323-4772
Kason Central
Columbus, OH 614-885-1992
Kason Industries
Newnan, GA 770-254-0553
Keating Of Chicago Inc
Mc Cook, IL 800-532-8464
Kentwood Spring Water Company
Patterson, LA 985-395-9313
KETCH
Wichita, KS 800-766-3777
Kinetico
Newbury, OH 440-564-9111
King Bag & Mfg Co
Cincinnati, OH 800-444-5464
King Company
Dallas, TX 507-451-3770
King Engineering - King-Gage
Newell, WV 800-242-8871
Kiss International/Di-tech Systems
Vista, CA 800-527-5477

Kraissl Co Inc
Hackensack, NJ. 800-572-4775
L&A Process Systems
Modesto, CA 209-581-0205
L.C. Thompson Company
Kenosha, WI 800-558-4018
Lamports Filter Media
Cleveland, OH 216-881-2050
Lenser Filtration
Lakewood, NJ 732-370-1600
Lewis M Carter Mfg Co Inc
Donalsonville, GA 800-332-8232
Mars Air Products
Gardena, CA 800-421-1266
Melvina Can Machinery Company
Hudson Falls, NY 518-743-0606
Membrane System Specialist Inc
Wisconsin Rapids, WI 715-421-2333
Metlar Us
Riverhead, NY 631-252-5574
Micropure Filtration Inc
Mound, MN 800-654-7873
Mies Products
West Bend, WI 800-480-6437
Miroil
Allentown, PA 800-523-9844
Moll-Tron
Lakewood, CO 800-525-9494
Mountain Safety Research
Seattle, WA 800-877-9677
Muckler Industries, Inc
Saint Louis, MO 800-444-0283
Nederman
Thomasville, NC 800-533-5286
Netzsch Pumps North America
Exton, PA 610-363-8010
Newark Wire Cloth Co
Clifton, NJ. 800-221-0392
Newwaveenviro
Greenwood Vlg, CO 800-592-8371
Niro
Hudson, WI 715-386-9371
Nothum Food Processing Systems
Springfield, MO 800-435-1297
Oc Lugo Co Inc
New City, NY 845-480-5121
Optipure
Plano, TX 972-422-1212
Ozotech Inc
Yreka, CA 530-842-4189
Pacific Process Technology
La Jolla, CA 858-551-3298
Pall Corp
Port Washington, NY 866-905-7255
Pall Filtron
Northborough, MA 800-345-8766
PAR-Kan
Silver Lake, IN 800-291-5487
Parker-Hannifin Corp
Cleveland, OH 800-272-7537
Parker-Hannifin Corp
Jeffersonville, IN 866-247-4827
Parkson Corp
Vernon Hills, IL 847-816-3700
Piab Vacuum Products
Hingham, MA 800-321-7422
Prince Castle Inc
Carol Stream, IL 800-722-7853
Pro-Flo Products
Cedar Grove, NJ 800-325-1057
PURA
Sun Valley, CA 800-292-7872
Purolator Facet Inc
Greensboro, NC 800-852-4449
R F Hunter Co Inc
Dover, NH. 800-332-9565
R R Street & Co
Naperville, IL 630-416-4244
Refractron Technologies Corp
Newark, NY 315-331-6222
Reynold Water Conditioning
Farmington Hills, MI 800-572-9575
Robinson/Kirshbaum Industries
Gardena, CA 800-929-3812
Rolfs @ Boone
Boone, IA 800-265-2010
Sartorius Corp
Edgewood, NY 800-635-2906
Schlueter Company
Janesville, WI 800-359-1700
Scienco Systems
Saint Louis, MO 314-621-2536

Scotsman Ice Systems
Vernon Hills, IL 800-726-8762
Selecto Scientific
Suwanee, GA 800-635-4017
Serfilco
Northbrook, IL 800-323-5431
Sermia International
Blainville, QC 800-567-7483
Severn Trent Svc
Fort Washington, PA 215-646-9201
Shick Esteve
Kansas City, MO 877-744-2587
Sparkler Filters Inc
Conroe, TX 936-756-4471
Spencer Strainer Systems
Jeffersonville, IN 800-801-4977
Stainless Steel Fabricator Inc
La Mirada, CA 714-739-9904
Star Filters
Timmonsville, SC 800-845-5381
Stearns Technical Textiles Company
Cincinnati, OH 800-543-7173
Steri Technologies Inc
Bohemia, NY 800-253-7140
Straight Line Filters
Wilmington, DE 302-654-8805
Tema Systems Inc
Cincinnati, OH 513-792-2840
Therm-Tec Inc
Sherwood, OR 800-292-9163
Thomas Technical Svc
Neillsville, WI 715-743-4666
Trenton Mills Inc
Trenton, TN 731-855-1323
Triad Scientific
Manasquan, NJ 800-867-6690
Ultra Industries Inc
Racine, WI 800-358-5872
Ultrafilter
Norcross, GA 800-543-3634
Ultrapar Inc.
Warren, NJ 908-647-6650
United Air Specialists Inc
Blue Ash, OH 800-992-4422
United Filters Intl
Amarillo, TX 806-373-8386
United Industries Group Inc
Lake Forest, CA 949-759-3200
United States Systems Inc
Kansas City, KS 888-281-2454
US Filter Dewatering Systems
Holland, MI. 800-245-3006
Van Air Systems
Lake City, PA 800-840-9906
Vent Master
Mississauga, ON 800-565-2981
VMC Signs
Victoria, TX 361-575-0548
Washington Frontier
Grandview, WA. 509-469-7662
Water & Power Technologies
Salt Lake City, UT 888-271-3295
Water Sciences Services, Inc.
Jackson, TN 973-584-4131
Water System Group
Santa Clarita, CA 800-350-9283
Waterlink/Sanborn Technologies
Canton, OH. 800-343-3381
Watts Premier Inc
Peoria, AZ 800-752-5582
Whatman
Piscataway, NJ 973-245-8300
Whatman
Haverhill, MA. 978-374-7400
Williams & Mettle Company
Houston, TX 800-526-4954
Womack International Inc
Vallejo, CA 707-647-2370
Yardney Water Management Syst
Riverside, CA 800-854-4788
Zander Insurance Group
Nashville, TN 615-356-1700

Fittings

Accutek Packaging Equipment
Vista, CA. 800-989-1828
Ace Manufacturing
Cincinnati, OH 800-653-5692
Advance Fittings Corp
Elkhorn, WI. 262-723-6699
Anver Corporation
Hudson, MA 800-654-3500

Archon Industries Inc
Suffern, NY. 800-554-1394
Baldewein Company
Lake Forrest, IL 800-424-5544
Bradford A Ducon Company
Pewaukee, WI 800-789-1718
C.F.F. Stainless Steels
Hamilton, ON 800-263-4511
Carmun International
San Antonio, TX 800-531-7907
Crown Industries
East Orange, NJ 877-747-2457
Dormont Manufacturing Co
Export, PA. 800-367-6668
Eischen Enterprises
Fresno, CA 559-834-0013
Ellett Industries
Port Coquitlam, BC. 604-941-8211
Fort, Products
Kansas City, MO 816-741-3000
Gems Sensors & Controls
Plainville, CT 860-747-3000
General Tank
Berwick, PA 800-435-8265
Hoffmeyer Corp
San Leandro, CA. 888-744-1826
Hydra-Flex Inc
Livonia, MI 800-234-0832
Keystone Rubber Corporation
Greenbackville, VA. 800-394-5661
Kuriyama Of America Inc
Schaumburg, IL. 800-800-0320
Lake Process Systems Inc
Lake Barrington, IL 800-331-9260
Magnatech Corp
East Granby, CT 888-393-3602
Nalge Process Technologies Group
Rochester, NY. 585-586-8800
Norgren Inc.
Littleton, CO. 800-514-0129
Parker-Hannifin Corp
Cleveland, OH 800-272-7537
Pure Fit Nutrition Bars
Irvine, CA 866-787-3348
Qosina Corporation
Ronkonkoma, NY 631-242-3000
Qualtech
Quebec, QC. 888-339-3801
Robert-James Sales
Buffalo, NY. 800-777-1325
Rolfs @ Boone
Boone, IA 800-265-2010
Rolland Machining & Fabricating
Moneta, VA 973-827-6911
Rubber Fab Molding & Gasket
Sparta, NJ 866-442-2959
Sanitary Couplers
Springboro, OH. 513-743-0144
Southern Metal Fabricators Inc
Albertville, AL 800-989-1330
Special Products
Springfield, MO 417-881-6114
Spencer Turbine Co
Windsor, CT 800-232-4321
Spraying Systems Company
Wheaton, IL 630-655-5000
Standex International Corp.
Salem, NH. 603-893-9701
T & S Brass & Bronze Work
Travelers Rest, SC 800-476-4103
Tomlinson Industries
Cleveland, OH 800-945-4589
Top Line Process Equipment Company
Bradford, PA 800-458-6095
Tuchenhagen
Columbia, MD 410-910-6000
Unisource Manufacturing Inc
Portland, OR 800-234-2566
Valvinox
Iberville, QC 450-346-1981
Waukesha Cherry-Burrell
Louisville, KY 502-491-4310
Waukesha Specialty Company
Darien, WI. 262-724-3700
WCB Ice Cream
Philadelphia, PA 215-425-4320
Windhorst Blowmold
Euless, TX. 817-540-6639
World Wide Fitting Corp
Vernon Hills, IL 800-393-9894

Flow Regulators

Alard Equipment Corp
Williamson, NY 315-589-4511
American LEWA
Holliston, MA. 888-539-2123
Boston Gear
Boston, MA. 888-999-9860
Carmun International
San Antonio, TX. 800-531-7907
Cashco Inc
Ellsworth, KS 785-472-4461
Linde North America
Murray Hill, NJ. 908-464-8100
Lumenite Control Tech Inc
Franklin Park, IL 800-323-8510
Meltric Corporation
Franklin, WI 800-824-4031
Monitor Technologies LLC
Elburn, IL 800-601-6204
Music City Metals Inc
Nashville, TN 800-251-2674
Norgren Inc.
Littleton, CO. 800-514-0129
Samson Controls
Baytown, TX. 281-383-3677
Spraying Systems Company
Wheaton, IL 630-655-5000
Standard Pump
Auburn, GA. 866-558-8611

Food Processing

Aerosol

John R Nalbach Engineering Co
Countryside, IL. 708-579-9100
Packaging Equipment & Conveyors, Inc
Elkhart, IN. 574-266-6995

Agitators

Food Processing

A & B Process Systems Corp
Stratford, WI 888-258-2789
APV Americas
Delavan, WI 800-252-5200
Berkshire PPM
Litchfield, CT 860-567-3118
Bowers Process Equipment
Stratford, ON. 800-567-3223
Bush Tank Fabricators Inc
Newark, NJ 973-596-1121
Chemineer
Dayton, OH. 937-454-3200
Coastline Equipment Inc
Bellingham, WA 360-734-8509
EKATO Corporation
St Ramsey, NJ 201-825-4684
Et Oakes Corp
Hauppauge, NY 631-232-0002
Expert Industries Inc
Brooklyn, NY 718-434-6060
Falco Technologies
La Prairie, QC 450-444-0566
Fernholtz Engineering
Van Nuys, CA 818-785-5800
Hamilton Kettles
Weirton, WV 800-535-1882
National Oilwell Varco
North Andover, MA 800-643-0641
Norvell Co Inc
Fort Scott, KS 800-653-3147
Patterson Industries
Scarborough, ON 800-336-1110
Process Systems
Barrington, IL. 847-842-8618
Sonic Corp
Stratford, CT 866-493-1378
Washington Frontier
Grandview, WA. 509-469-7662

Milk

Alard Equipment Corp
Williamson, NY 315-589-4511
Bowers Process Equipment
Stratford, ON. 800-567-3223
Falco Technologies
La Prairie, QC. 450-444-0566
Liquid Scale
New Brighton, MN 888-633-2969

National Oilwell Varco
North Andover, MA 800-643-0641
Relco Unisystems Corp
Willmar, MN 320-231-2210
Washington Frontier
Grandview, WA 509-469-7662
Whey Systems
Willmar, MN 320-905-4122

Air Knives

Ametek Technical & Industrial Products
Kent, OH .215-256-6601
Paxton Products Inc
Blue Ash, OH 800-441-7475
Spencer Turbine Co
Windsor, CT 800-232-4321

Augers

A T Ferrell Co Inc
Bluffton, IN. 800-248-8318
Apollo Sheet Metal
Kennewick, WA 509-586-1104
Auger Fab
Exton, PA .800-334-1529
Cal-Coast Manufacturing
Turlock, CA 209-668-9378
Polar Process
Plattsville, ON. 877-896-8077
Relco Unisystems Corp
Willmar, MN 320-231-2210
Spee-Dee Packaging Machinery
Sturtevant, WI 877-375-2121
TWM Manufacturing
Leamington, ON 888-495-4831
Universal Packaging Inc
Houston, TX 800-324-2610
Viking Machine & Design Inc
De Pere, WI. 888-286-2116
Washington Frontier
Grandview, WA 509-469-7662
Whey Systems
Willmar, MN 320-905-4122

Bakers'

A&J Mixing International
Oakville, ON. 800-668-3470
Aaburco Inc
Grass Valley, CA. 800-533-7437
ABI Limited
Concord, ON. 800-297-8666
Adamatic
Auburn, WA 800-578-2547
Allied Bakery and Food Service Equipment
Santa Fe Springs, CA 562-945-6506
American Eagle Food Machinery
Chicago, IL 888-390-0800
AMF Bakery Systems Corp
Richmond, VA. 800-225-3771
AMF CANADA
Sherbrooke, QC 800-255-3869
Andgar Corp
Ferndale, WA 360-366-9900
Arcobaleno Pasta Machines
Lancaster, PA 800-875-7096
Attias Oven Corp
Brooklyn, NY 800-928-8427
Bakery Associates
Setauket, NY 631-751-4156
Baking Machines
Livermore, CA 925-449-3369
Belshaw Adamatic Bakery Group
Auburn, WA 800-578-2547
Bettendorf Stanford Inc
Salem, IL. .800-548-2253
Bevles Company
Dallas, TX. 800-441-1601
Bolling Oven & Machine Company
Avon, OH .440-937-6112
Breddo Likwifier
Kansas City, MO. 800-669-4092
Buss America
Carol Stream, IL. 630-933-9100
C & K Machine Co
Holyoke, MA 413-536-8122
C H Babb Co Inc
Raynham, MA. 508-977-0600
C Palmer Mfg Co Inc
West Newton, PA 724-872-8200
Cannon Equipment Company
Cannon Falls, MN. 800-825-8501

Christy Machine Co
Fremont, OH. 888-332-6451
Cinelli Esperia
Woodbridge, ON 905-856-1820
Clayton Manufacturing Company
Derby, NY 716-549-0392
CMC America Corporation
Joliet, IL 815-726-4337
Cobatco
Peoria, IL. .800-426-2282
Comtec Industries
Woodridge, IL 630-759-9000
Custom Diamond Intl.
Laval, QC .800-326-5926
D.R. McClain & Son
Commerce, CA 800-428-2263
DBE Inc
Concord, ON. 800-461-5313
Delta Machine & Maufacturing
St Rose, LA 504-949-8304
Deluxe Equipment Company
Bradenton, FL 800-367-8931
Don Lee
Philadelphia, PA 760-745-0707
Doyon Equipment
Liniere, QC 800-463-4273
Dutchess Bakers' Machinery Co
Superior, WI 800-777-4498
Edhard Corp
Hackettstown, NJ 888-334-2731
Empire Bakery Equipment
Hicksville, NY 800-878-4070
Epcon Industrial Systems
Conroe, TX 800-447-7872
Et Oakes Corp
Hauppauge, NY 631-232-0002
Everedy Automation
Frederick, PA 610-754-1775
Exact Mixing Systems Inc
Memphis, TN 901-362-8501
Fish Oven & Equipment Co
Wauconda, IL 877-526-8720
Food Engineering Unlimited
Fullerton, CA 714-879-8762
Food Machinery Sales
Bogart, GA 706-549-2207
Food Tools
Santa Barbara, CA 877-836-6386
Franz Haas Machinery-America
Henrico, VA 804-222-6022
Fred D Pfening Co
Columbus, OH 614-294-5361
Friedrich Metal Products
Browns Summit, NC 800-772-0326
Garland Commercial Ranges
Mississauga, ON 905-624-0260
Good Idea
Northampton, MA. 800-462-9237
Goodway Industries Inc
Bohemia, NY 800-943-4501
Graybill Machines Inc
Lititz, PA .717-626-5221
Hayon Manufacturing
Las Vegas, NV 702-562-3377
I J White Corp
Farmingdale, NY. 631-293-2211
Ika-Works Inc
Wilmington, NC 800-733-3037
Imperial Manufacturing Co
Corona, CA 800-343-7790
Indiana Wire Company
Fremont, IN. 877-786-6883
Industrial Air Conditioning Systems
Chicago, IL. 773-486-4236
Industrial Product Corp
Ho Ho Kus, NJ 800-472-5913
JAS Manufacturing Company
Carrollton, TX. 972-380-1150
K B Systems Inc
Bangor, PA 610-588-7788
Knott Slicers
Canton, MA 781-821-0925
Lanly Co
Cleveland, OH. 216-731-1115
Latendorf Corporation
Brielle, NJ .800-526-4057
Lawrence Equipment Inc
South El Monte, CA 800-423-4500
Lematic Inc
Jackson, MI. 517-787-3301
Lil' Orbits
Minneapolis, MN 800-228-8305

LVO Manufacturing Inc
Rock Rapids, IA 712-472-3734
Maddox/Adams International
Miami, FL. 305-592-3337
Magna Machine Co
Cincinnati, OH 800-448-3475
Merco/Savory
Mt. Pleasant, MI 800-733-8821
Mercury Equipment Company
Chino, CA. 800-273-6688
Moffat
San Antonio, TX. 866-589-0664
Moline Machinery LLC
Duluth, MN 800-767-5734
Motom Corporation
Bensenville, IL 630-787-1995
Nemeth Engineering Assoc
Crestwood, KY 502-241-1502
Nothum Food Processing Systems
Springfield, MO 800-435-1297
Oshikiri Corp Of America
Philadelphia, PA 215-637-8112
Pavailler Distribution Company
Northvale, NJ 201-767-0766
Peerless Food Equipment
Sidney, OH 937-492-4158
Peerless Machinery Corporation
Sidney, OH 800-999-3327
PMI Food Equipment Group
Troy, OH .937-332-3000
Radio Frequency Co Inc
Millis, MA 508-376-9555
Ram Equipment Co
Waukesha, WI 262-513-1114
Reading Bakery Systems Inc
Robesonia, PA. 610-693-5816
Reed Oven Co
Kansas City, MO. 816-842-7446
Regal Ware Inc
Kewaskum, WI 262-626-2121
Reiser
Canton, MA 734-821-1290
Revent Inc ,
Piscataway, NJ 732-777-9433
Rheon USA
Irvine, CA .949-768-1900
Rhodes Bakery Equipment
Portland, OR 800-426-3813
Rondo Inc
Moonachie, NJ 800-882-0633
Roto-Flex Oven Co
San Antonio, TX. 877-859-1463
Ruiz Flour Tortillas
Riverside, CA 909-947-7811
Soco System USA
Waukesha, WI. 800-441-6293
Somerset Industries
Billerica, MA 800-772-4404
Southbend
Fuquay Varina, NC 800-348-2558
Stewart Systems Baking LLC
Plano, TX .972-422-5808
T.K. Products
Anaheim, CA. 714-621-0267
Thomas L. Green & Company
Robenosia, PA. 610-693-5816
Thompson Bagel Machine Mfg
Los Angeles, CA. 310-836-0900
TMCo Inc.ÿ
Houston, TX 713-465-3255
Toastmaster
Elgin, IL 847-741-3300
Unifiller Systems
Delta, BC. .888-733-8444
United Bakery Equipment Company
Shawnee Mission, KS 913-541-8700
US Tsubaki Holdings Inc
Wheeling, IL 800-323-7790
Varimixer North America
Charlotte, NC 800-221-1138
Warwick Manufacturing & Equip
North Brunswick, NJ 732-729-0400
Wilder Manufacturing Company
Port Jervis, NY 800-832-1319
Woody Associates Inc
York, PA 717-843-3975
X-Press Manufacturing
New Braunfels, TX. 800-365-9440

Balers or Baling Presses

Advance Lifts Inc
St Charles, IL 800-843-3625
Balemaster
Crown Point, IN 219-663-4525
Consolidated Baling Machine Company
Jacksonville, FL 800-231-9286
Enterprise Company
Santa Ana, CA 714-835-0541
Galbreath LLC
Winamac, IN 574-946-6631
Incinerator International Inc
Houston, TX 713-227-1466
Load King Mfg
Jacksonville, FL 800-531-4975
Logemann Brothers Co
Milwaukee, WI 414-445-3005
Marathon Equipment Co
Vernon, AL 800-269-7237
Maren Engineering Corp
South Holland, IL 800-875-1038
Orwak
Minneapolis, MN 800-747-0449
Ouachita Machine Works
West Monroe, LA 318-396-1468
PTR Baler & Compactor Co
Philadelphia, PA 800-523-3654
Schleicher & Company of America
Sanford, NC 800-775-7570
SP Industries
Hopkins, MI 800-592-5959
Waste Away Systems
Newark, OH 800-223-4741
Wastequip Inc
Charlotte, NC 704-366-7140

Barley Processing

ANDRITZ Inc
Muncy, PA 704-943-4343

Biscuit Making

Exact Mixing Systems Inc
Memphis, TN 901-362-8501
Rademaker USA
Hudson, OH 330-650-2345
Reading Bakery Systems Inc
Robesonia, PA 610-693-5816
Reiser
Canton, MA 734-821-1290
Rheon USA
Irvine, CA 949-768-1900

Blades

Food Processing Machine

Atlanta SharpTech
Peachtree City, GA 800-462-7297
Bettendorf Stanford Inc
Salem, IL 800-548-2253
Boehringer Mfg. Co. Inc.
Felton, CA 800-630-8665
CB Mfg. & Sales Co.
Miamisburg, OH 800-543-6860
Cozzini LLC
Chicago, IL 773-478-9700
E-Z Edge Inc
West New York, NJ 800-232-4470
Garvey Products
Cincinnati, OH 513-771-8710
Good Idea
Northampton, MA 800-462-9237
Hansaloy Corp
Davenport, IA 800-553-4992
Huther Brothers
Rochester, NY 800-334-1115
Industrial Product Corp
Ho Ho Kus, NJ 800-472-5913
Industrial Razorblade
Orange, NJ 973-673-4286
KSW Corp
Des Moines, IA 515-265-5269
Pieco
Manchester, IA 800-334-3929
R H Saw Corp
Barrington, IL 847-381-8777
Ranger Blade Manufacturing Company
Traer, IA 800-377-7860
Save-O-Seal Corporation
Elmsford, NY 800-831-9720

Simmons Engineering Corporation
Wheeling, IL 800-252-3381
Simonds International
Fitchburg, MA 800-343-1616
Specialty Blades
Staunton, VA 540-248-2200
Specialty Saw Inc
Simsbury, CT 800-225-0772
TGW International
Florence, KY 800-407-0173
Thomas Precision, Inc.
Rice Lake, WI 800-657-4808

Blenders

A & B Process Systems Corp
Stratford, WI 888-258-2789
Aaron Equipment Co Div Areco
Bensenville, IL 630-350-2200
Acrison Inc
Moonachie, NJ 800-422-4266
Apache Stainless Equipment
Beaver Dam, WI 800-444-0398
APV Americas
Delavan, WI 800-252-5200
Attias Oven Corp
Brooklyn, NY 800-928-8427
Automated Food Systems
Waxahachie, TX 469-517-0470
Axiflow Technologies, Inc.
Kennesaw, GA 770-795-1195
Bepex International LLC
Minneapolis, MN 800-607-2470
Blue Tech
Hickory, NC 828-324-5900
Bowers Process Equipment
Stratford, ON. 800-567-3223
Breddo Likwifier
Kansas City, MO. 800-669-4092
Bush Tank Fabricators Inc
Newark, NJ 973-596-1121
Century Foods Intl LLC
Sparta, WI 800-269-1901
Charles Ross & Son Co
Hauppauge, NY 800-243-7677
Cleveland-Eastern Mixers
Clinton, CT 800-243-1188
CRC Inc
Council Bluffs, IA 712-323-9477
Dito Dean Food Prep
Charlotte, NC 866-449-4200
Dorton Incorporated
Arlington Hts, IL 800-299-8600
Drum-Mates Inc.
Lumberton, NJ 800-621-3786
Ederback Corporation
Ann Arbor, MI 800-422-2558
Eirich Machines
Gurnee, IL 847-336-2444
Et Oakes Corp
Hauppauge, NY 631-232-0002
Eurodib
Champlain, NY. 888-956-6866
Expert Industries Inc
Brooklyn, NY 718-434-6060
Falco Technologies
La Prairie, QC 450-444-0566
Fernholtz Engineering
Van Nuys, CA 818-785-5800
Ferrell-Ross
Amarillo, TX. 800-299-9051
Fleet Wood Goldco Wyard
Cockeysville, MD. 410-785-1934
Flow of Solids
Westford, MA 978-392-0300
Food Processing Equipment Co
Santa Fe Springs, CA 562-802-3727
FPEC Corporation
Santa Fe Springs, CA 562-802-3727
Glen Mills Inc.
Clifton, NJ. 973-777-0777
Gold Medal Products Co
Cincinnati, OH 800-543-0862
Hamilton Beach Brands
Southern Pines, NC. 800-851-8900
Hayes & Stolz Indl Mfg LTD
Fort Worth, TX 800-725-7272
Hosokawa/Bepex Corporation
Santa Rosa, CA 707-586-6000
International Reserve Equipment Corporation
Clarendon Hills, IL 708-531-0680

Island Oasis Frozen Cocktail
Beloit, WI 800-777-4752
Jenike & Johanson Inc
Tyngsboro, MA 978-649-3300
Karl Schnell
New London, WI 920-982-9974
Kemutec Group Inc
Bristol, PA. 215-788-8013
Kinetic Equipment Company
Appleton, WI 806-293-4471
Krones
Franklin, WI 800-752-3787
M O Industries Inc
Whippany, NJ 973-386-9228
Machanix Fabrication Inc
Chino, CA 800-700-9701
Matcon Americas
Elmhurst, IL 856-256-1330
Materials Transportation Co
Temple, TX 800-433-3110
Midwest Metalcraft & Equipment
Windsor, MO. 800-647-3167
Munson Machinery Co
Utica, NY 800-944-6644
Paget Equipment Co
Marshfield, WI 715-384-3158
Patterson Industries
Scarborough, ON 800-336-1110
Patterson-Kelley   Hars Company
East Stroudsburg, PA 570-421-7500
Paul O. Abbe
Bensenville, IL 630-350-2200
Peerless Machinery Corporation
Sidney, OH 800-999-3327
Polar Process
Plattsville, ON. 877-896-8077
Pro Scientific Inc
Oxford, CT 800-584-3776
Reiser
Canton, MA 734-821-1290
Rubicon Industries
Brooklyn, NY 800-662-6999
Stephan Machinery, Inc.
Mundelein, IL. 800-783-7426
Stricklin Co
Dallas, TX. 214-637-1030
Superior Products Company
Saint Paul, MN 800-328-9800
Swirl Freeze Corp
Salt Lake City, UT 800-262-4275
T D Sawvel Co
Maple Plain, MN. 877-488-1816
TSA Griddle Systems
Kelowna, BC. 250-491-9025
VitaMinder Company
Providence, RI 800-858-8840
Vitamix
Olmsted Twp, OH. 800-437-4654
Waring Products
Torrington, CT 800-492-7464
Wilch Manufacturing
Topeka, KS 785-267-2762
Yargus Manufacturing Inc
Marshall, IL 217-826-8059

Blending

Flour

Automated Food Systems
Waxahachie, TX 469-517-0470
Breddo Likwifier
Kansas City, MO. 800-669-4092
Glen Mills Inc.
Clifton, NJ. 973-777-0777
Hosokawa/Bepex Corporation
Santa Rosa, CA 707-586-6000
Patterson-Kelley   Hars Company
East Stroudsburg, PA 570-421-7500
Peerless Machinery Corporation
Sidney, OH 800-999-3327
Tuchenhagen
Columbia, MD 410-910-6000

Grain

ANDRITZ Inc
Muncy, PA. 704-943-4343
Breddo Likwifier
Kansas City, MO. 800-669-4092
Davron Technologies Inc
Chattanooga, TN 423-870-1888

Glen Mills Inc.
Clifton, NJ 973-777-0777
Hosokawa/Bepex Corporation
Santa Rosa, CA 707-586-6000
M O Industries Inc
Whippany, NJ 973-386-9228
Patterson-Kelley   Hars Company
East Stroudsburg, PA 570-421-7500
Tuchenhagen
Columbia, MD 410-910-6000

Blowers

Aerovent Co
Minneapolis, MN 763-551-7500
Andgar Corp
Ferndale, WA 360-366-9900
Ceilcote Air Pollution Control
Middleburg Hts, OH 800-554-8673
Chicago Conveyor Corporation
Addison, IL 630-543-6300
Gardner Denver Inc.
Milwaukee, WI
Hartzell Fan Inc
Piqua, OH 800-336-3267
Loren Cook Co
Springfield, MO 800-289-3267
Nalge Process Technologies Group
Rochester, NY 585-586-8800
Nu-Con Equipment
Chanhassen, MN 877-939-0510
Palace Packaging Machines Inc
Downingtown, PA 610-873-7252
Paxton Products Inc
Blue Ash, OH 800-441-7475
Ross Cook
Silver Spring, MD 800-233-7339
Spencer Turbine Co
Windsor, CT 800-232-4321
Tuthill Vacuum & Blower Systems
Springfield, MO 800-825-6937
Yakima Wire Works
Reedley, CA 800-344-8951

Boilers

Electric Steam

Sussman Electric Boilers
Long Island City, NY 800-238-3535

Gas Fired

Ecs Warehouse
Buffalo, NY 716-833-7380

Water

A.O. Smith Water Products Company
Irving, TX 800-527-1953
Bryan Boilers
Peru, IN 765-473-6651
Cleaver-Brooks Inc
Thomasville, GA 800-250-5583
Holman Boiler Works
Dallas, TX 800-331-1956
Pacific Steam Equipment, Inc.
Santa Fe Springs, CA 800-321-4114
PVI Industries LLC
Fort Worth, TX 800-784-8326
Quikwater Inc
Sand Springs, OK 918-241-8880
Sellers Engineering Division
Danville, KY 859-236-3181
Sussman Electric Boilers
Long Island City, NY 800-238-3535
Vanguard Technology Inc
Eugene, OR 800-624-4809
Washington Frontier
Grandview, WA 509-469-7662

Brewery

Alfa Laval Inc
Richmond, VA 866-253-2528
ANDRITZ Inc
Muncy, PA 704-943-4343
Anver Corporation
Hudson, MA 800-654-3500
API Heat Transfer Inc
Buffalo, NY 877-274-4328
Berkshire PPM
Litchfield, CT 860-567-3118

BVL Controls
Bois-Des-Filion, QC 866-285-2668
Camerons Brewing Co.
Oakville, ON 905-849-8282
Chester-Jensen Co., Inc.
Chester, PA 800-685-3750
Criveller East
Niagara Falls, ON 888-894-2266
Crown Holdings, Inc.
Yardley, PA 215-698-5100
Crown-Simplimatic
Baltimore, MD 410-563-6700
Diversified Metal Engineering
Charlottetown, PE 902-628-6900
FleetwoodGoldcoWyard
Romeoville, IL 630-759-6800
Globe Machine
Tacoma, WA 800-523-6575
Goodnature Products
Orchard Park, NY 800-875-3381
MacDonald Steel Ltd
Cambridge, ON 800-563-8247
MCNAB Inc
Buena Vista, VA 540-261-1045
Metal Master Sales Corp
Glendale Heights, IL 800-488-8729
Micropub Systems International
Rochester, NY 585-385-3990
Modern Brewing & Design
Santa Rosa, CA 707-542-6620
Newlands Systems
Abbotsford, BC 604-855-4890
Oak Barrel Winecraft
Berkeley, CA 510-849-0400
OI Analytical
College Station, TX 979-690-1711
Rahr Malting Co
Shakopee, MN 952-445-1431
San-Rec-Pak
Tualatin, OR 503-692-5552
Simplex Filler Co
Napa, CA 800-796-7539
The Pub Brewing Company
Santa Rosa, CA
The Pub Brewing Company
Mahwah, NJ 201-512-0387
Vincent Corp
Tampa, FL 813-248-2650
Vineco International Products
St Catharines, ON 905-685-9342

Brine Making Equipment

Berg Chilling Systems
Toronto, ON 416-755-2221
Membrane System Specialist Inc
Wisconsin Rapids, WI 715-421-2333
Northland Process Piping
Isle, MN 320-679-2119
Peterson Fiberglass Laminates
Shell Lake, WI 715-468-2306
Reiser
Canton, MA 734-821-1290
South Valley Mfg Inc
Gilroy, CA 408-842-5457

Broilers

Amber Glo
Chicago, IL 866-705-0515
American Range
Pacoima, CA 888-753-9898
Anetsberger
Concord, NH 603-225-6684
APW Wyott Food Service Equipment Company
Cheyenne, WY 800-527-2100
Bakers Pride Oven Company
New Rochelle, NY 800-431-2745
Broaster Co LLC
Beloit, WI 800-365-8278
Comstock Castle Stove Co
Quincy, IL 800-637-9188
Connerton Co
Santa Ana, CA 714-547-9218
CPM Wolverine Proctor LLC
Horsham, PA 215-443-5200
Dynamic Cooking Systems
Huntington Beach, CA 800-433-8466
Garland Commercial Ranges
Mississauga, ON 905-624-0260
Garland Commercial Ranges Ltd.
Mississauga, ON 905-624-0260

Grande Chef Company
Orangeville, ON 519-942-4470
Holman Cooking Equipment
Saint Louis, MO 888-356-5362
Imperial Manufacturing Co
Corona, CA 800-343-7790
J & R Mfg Inc
Mesquite, TX 800-527-4831
Lang Manufacturing Co
Everett, WA 800-882-6368
Leedal Inc
Northbrook, IL 847-498-0111
Magi Kitch'n
Concord, NH 800-441-1492
Marshall Air Systems Inc
Charlotte, NC 800-722-3474
Merco/Savory
Mt. Pleasant, MI 800-733-8821
Middleby Marshall Inc
Elgin, IL 847-741-3300
Montague Co
Hayward, CA 800-345-1830
Nieco Corporation
Windsor, CA 800-643-2656
Optimal Automatics
Elk Grove Village, IL 847-439-9110
Rankin Delux
Mira Loma, CA 951-685-0081
Renato Specialty Product
Garland, TX 866-575-6316
Southbend
Fuquay Varina, NC 800-348-2558
Stainless Steel Fabricator Inc
La Mirada, CA 714-739-9904
Star Manufacturing Intl Inc
St Louis, MO 800-264-7827
Super-Chef Manufacturing Company
Houston, TX 800-231-3478
Thermal Engineering Corp
Columbia, SC 800-331-0097
Toastmaster
Elgin, IL 847-741-3300
Trimen Foodservice Equipment
North York, ON 877-437-1422
Vulcan Food Equipment Group
Baltimore, MD 800-814-2028
Welbilt Corporation
Stamford, CT 203-325-8300
Wells Manufacturing Company
St. Louis, MO 888-356-5362
Wolf Company
Louisville, KY 800-814-2028
Wood Stone Corp
Bellingham, WA 800-988-8103

Cereal Making

A & B Process Systems Corp
Stratford, WI 888-258-2789
Andgar Corp
Ferndale, WA 360-366-9900
ANDRITZ Inc
Muncy, PA 704-943-4343
Buffalo Technologies Corporation
Buffalo, NY 800-332-2419
Ferrell-Ross
Amarillo, TX 800-299-9051
Lanly Co
Cleveland, OH 216-731-1115
Munson Machinery Co
Utica, NY 800-944-6644
Pavan USA Inc
Emigsville, PA 717-767-4889
Polar Process
Plattsville, ON 877-896-8077
Puritan Manufacturing Inc
Omaha, NE 800-331-0487
UniTrak Corporation
Port Hope, ON 866-883-5749

Cheese Making

A & B Process Systems Corp
Stratford, WI 888-258-2789
Breddo Likwifier
Kansas City, MO 800-669-4092
Custom Fabricating & Repair
Marshfield, WI 800-236-8773
Damrow Company
Fond Du Lac, WI 800-236-1501
Dito Dean Food Prep
Charlotte, NC 866-449-4200

Eischen Enterprises
   Fresno, CA 559-834-0013
Ivarson Inc
   Milwaukee, WI 414-351-0700
Johnson Industries Intl
   Windsor, WI 608-846-4499
Kusel Equipment Company
   Watertown, WI 920-261-4112
Midwest Stainless
   Menomonie, WI 715-235-5472
Pacific Process Technology
   La Jolla, CA 858-551-3298
Peterson Fiberglass Laminates
   Shell Lake, WI 715-468-2306
Polar Process
   Plattsville, ON. 877-896-8077
Rheo-Tech
   Gurnee, IL 847-367-1557
Rosenwach Tank Co LLC
   Long Island City, NY 212-972-4411
Scherping Systems
   Winsted, MN. 320-485-4401
Viking Machine & Design Inc
   De Pere, WI. 888-286-2116
Washington Frontier
   Grandview, WA. 509-469-7662
Whey Systems
   Willmar, MN. 320-905-4122

Cheese Processing

Corenco
   Santa Rosa, CA. 888-267-3626
Loos Machine
   Colby, WI 715-223-2844
Millerbernd Systems
   Winsted, MN. 320-485-2685
Reiser
   Canton, MA 734-821-1290

Cheesecloth

Ace-Tex Enterprises
   Detroit, MI 800-444-3800
Akron Cotton Products
   Akron, OH. 800-899-7173
Armaly Brands
   Commerce Twp, MI 800-772-1222
Cadie Products Corp
   Paterson, NJ 973-278-8300
Canton Sterilized Wiping Cloth
   Canton, OH. 330-455-8157
Clayton L. Hagy & Son
   Philadelphia, PA 215-844-6470
De Royal Textiles
   Camden, SC 800-845-1062
Erie Cotton Products
   Erie, PA 800-289-4737
James Thompson
   New York, NY 212-686-5306
King Bag & Mfg Co
   Cincinnati, OH 800-444-5464
Lexidyne of Pennsylvania
   Pittsburgh, PA 800-543-2233
Mednik Wiping Materials Co
   St Louis, MO. 800-325-7193
Mill Wiping Rags Inc
   Bronx, NY. 718-994-7100
Nu-Tex Styles, Inc.
   Somerset, NJ 732-485-5456
Paley-Lloyd-Donohue
   Elizabeth, NJ. 908-352-5835
Textile Buff & Wheel
   Charlestown, MA 617-241-8100
Textile Products Company
   Anaheim, CA 714-761-0401
Wipe-Tex International Corp
   Bronx, NY. 800-643-9607
Y-Pers Inc
   Philadelphia, PA 800-421-0242

Chewing Gum Processing

A & B Process Systems Corp
   Stratford, WI. 888-258-2789
LIST
   Acton, MA 978-635-9521
UniTrak Corporation
   Port Hope, ON 866-883-5749

Chocolate Processing

A & B Process Systems Corp
   Stratford, WI. 888-258-2789
Buffalo Technologies Corporation
   Buffalo, NY. 800-332-2419
Chocolate Concepts
   Hartville, OH 330-877-3322
Dadant & Sons Inc
   Hamilton, IL 888-922-1293
Glen Mills Inc.
   Clifton, NJ. 973-777-0777
Hillards Chocolate System
   West Bridgewater, MA 800-258-1530
LIST
   Acton, MA 978-635-9521
Savage Brothers Company
   Elk Grove Vlg, IL 800-342-0973
Tricor Systems Inc
   Elgin, IL 800-575-0161
Union Process
   Akron, OH. 330-929-3333
UniTrak Corporation
   Port Hope, ON 866-883-5749
US Tsubaki Holdings Inc
   Wheeling, IL. 800-323-7790
Woody Associates Inc
   York, PA 717-843-3975

Cocoa Processing

A & B Process Systems Corp
   Stratford, WI. 888-258-2789
ANDRITZ Inc
   Muncy, PA. 704-943-4343
Glen Mills Inc.
   Clifton, NJ. 973-777-0777
LIST
   Acton, MA 978-635-9521
Union Process
   Akron, OH. 330-929-3333

Coffee Makers

Acorto
   Bellevue, WA 800-995-9019
Astoria General Espresso
   Greensboro, NC 336-393-0224
Bloomfield Industries
   St. Louis, MO 888-356-5362
Boyd's Coffee Co
   Portland, OR 800-735-2878
Brewmatic Company
   Torrance, CA. 800-421-6860
Bunn-O-Matic Corp
   Springfield, IL. 800-352-2866
Chemex Division/International Housewares Corporation
   Chicopee, MA. 800-243-6399
Formula Espresso
   Brooklyn, NY 718-834-8724
Gabriella Imports
   Cleveland, OH. 800-544-8117
Globex America
   Dallas, TX. 214-353-0328
Grand Silver Company
   Bronx, NY 718-585-1930
Grindmaster-Cecilware Corp
   Louisville, KY 800-695-4500
Lavazza Premium Coffees
   New York, NY 212-725-9196
Melitta USA Inc
   Clearwater, FL 888-635-4880
Newco Enterprises Inc
   St Charles, MO. 800-325-7867
Nuova Distribution Centre
   Ferndale, WA 360-366-2226
Pasquini Espresso Co
   Los Angeles, CA. 800-724-6225
Regal Ware Inc
   Kewaskum, WI 262-626-2121
Rexcraft Fine Chafers
   Long Island City, NY 888-739-2723
Saeco
   Cleveland, OH 440-528-2000
Schaerer USA Corp
   Tustin, CA. 888-989-3004
Sheffield Platers Inc
   San Diego, CA 800-227-9242
Steel Products
   Marion, IA. 800-333-9451
Superior Products Company
   Saint Paul, MN 800-328-9800

Supramatic
   Toronto, ON 877-465-2883
T.J. Topper Company
   Redwood City, CA 650-365-6962
The Carriage Works
   Klamath Falls, OR 541-882-0700
Tops Manufacturing Co
   Darien, CT. 203-655-9367
Wells Manufacturing Company
   St. Louis, MO 888-356-5362
Wilbur Curtis Co
   Montebello, CA 800-421-6150
World Kitchen
   Elmira, NY 800-999-3436
Zelco Industries
   Mount Vernon, NY 800-431-2486

Coffee Processing

Acorto
   Bellevue, WA 800-995-9019
Alfa Laval Inc
   Richmond, VA. 866-253-2528
American Production Co Inc
   Redwood City, CA 650-368-5334
Ascaso
   Bensenville, IL 630-350-0066
Astoria General Espresso
   Greensboro, NC 336-393-0224
Astra Manufacturing Inc
   Canoga Park, CA 877-340-1800
Boyd's Coffee Co
   Portland, OR 800-735-2878
Brewmatic Company
   Torrance, CA. 800-421-6860
Bunn-O-Matic Corp
   Springfield, IL. 800-352-2866
Bunn-O-Matic Corporation
   Aurora, ON 800-263-2256
Chemex Division/International Housewares Corporation
   Chicopee, MA. 800-243-6399
Ditting USA
   Glendale, CA 800-835-5992
Eastern Tabletop Mfg
   Brooklyn, NY 888-422-4142
Eurodib
   Champlain, NY 888-956-6866
Fetco
   Lake Zurich, IL 800-338-2699
Formula Espresso
   Brooklyn, NY 718-834-8724
Gabriella Imports
   Cleveland, OH. 800-544-8117
Gensaco Marketing
   New York, NY 800-506-1935
Grindmaster-Cecilware Corp
   Louisville, KY 800-695-4500
Hamilton Beach Brands
   Southern Pines, NC. 800-851-8900
Kentwood Spring Water Company
   Patterson, LA 985-395-9313
Lavazza Premium Coffees
   New York, NY 212-725-9196
Melitta USA Inc
   Clearwater, FL 888-635-4880
Modern Process Equipment Inc
   Chicago, IL 773-254-3929
Newco Enterprises Inc
   St Charles, MO. 800-325-7867
Pasquini Espresso Co
   Los Angeles, CA. 800-724-6225
PolyMaid Company
   Largo, FL 800-206-9188
Regal Ware Inc
   Kewaskum, WI 262-626-2121
Rexcraft Fine Chafers
   Long Island City, NY 888-739-2723
Saeco
   Cleveland, OH 440-528-2000
Schaerer USA Corp
   Tustin, CA. 888-989-3004
Sivetz Coffee
   Corvallis, OR 541-753-9713
Steel Products
   Marion, IA. 800-333-9451
Supramatic
   Toronto, ON 877-465-2883
The Carriage Works
   Klamath Falls, OR 541-882-0700
Tops Manufacturing Co
   Darien, CT. 203-655-9367

UniTrak Corporation
Port Hope, ON 866-883-5749
Wega USA
Bensenville, IL 630-350-0066
Wells Manufacturing Company
St. Louis, MO 888-356-5362
Wilbur Curtis Co
Montebello, CA 800-421-6150
Zelco Industries
Mount Vernon, NY 800-431-2486

Combination Oven/Steamers

Superior Products Company
Saint Paul, MN 800-328-9800

Compressors

Berkshire PPM
Litchfield, CT 860-567-3118
Blackmer Co
Grand Rapids, MI 616-241-1611
C&R Refrigeration
Center, TX....................800-438-6182
Cameron Intl. Corp.
Houston, TX 281-285-4376
Howe Corp
Chicago, IL 773-235-0200
Ingersoll Rand Inc
Menomonee Falls, WI..........262-232-7275
International Machinery Xchnge
Deerfield, WI 800-279-0191
Kopykake
Torrance, CA..................800-999-5253
Paxton Products Inc
Blue Ash, OH 800-441-7475
Scroll Compressors LLC
Sidney, OH 937-498-3011
Seattle Refrigeration & Manufacturing
Seattle, WA 800-228-8881
Tecumseh Products Co.
Ann Arbor, MI 734-585-9500
Vilter Manufacturing Corporation
Cudahy, WI 414-744-0111
York Refrigeration Marine US
Norman, OK 877-874-7378
Zander Insurance Group
Nashville, TN 615-356-1700

Condensed Milk Processing

A & B Process Systems Corp
Stratford, WI..................888-258-2789
C E Rogers Co
Mora, MN 800-279-8081

Condensers

Evaporative

Baltimore Aircoil Co
Jessup, MD 410-799-1300
Berkshire PPM
Litchfield, CT 860-567-3118
Central Fabricators Inc
Cincinnati, OH 800-909-8265
Chil-Con Products
Brantford, ON.................800-263-0086
Cooling Products Inc
Broken Arrow, OK 918-251-8588
Croll Reynolds Inc
Parsippany, NJ.................908-232-4200
Doucette Industries
York, PA......................800-445-7511
EVAPCO Inc
Taneytown, MD 410-876-3782
Governair Corp
Oklahoma City, OK 405-525-6546
Howe Corp
Chicago, IL 773-235-0200
IMECO Inc
Polo, IL 815-946-2351
Industrial Piping Inc
Pineville, NC..................800-951-0988
Membrane System Specialist Inc
Wisconsin Rapids, WI..........715-421-2333
Niagara Blower Company
Buffalo, NY...................800-426-5169
Paget Equipment Co
Marshfield, WI 715-384-3158
Ron Vallort & Associates
Oak Brook, IL.................630-734-3821

Seattle Refrigeration & Manufacturing
Seattle, WA 800-228-8881
Vilter Manufacturing Corporation
Cudahy, WI 414-744-0111

Confectionery

A & B Process Systems Corp
Stratford, WI..................888-258-2789
A&M Industries
Sioux Falls, SD................800-888-2615
Aerotech Enterprise Inc
Chesterland, OH 440-729-2616
Automated Food Systems
Waxahachie, TX 469-517-0470
C. Cretors & Company
Chicago, IL 800-228-1885
Chocolate Concepts
Hartville, OH..................330-877-3322
Davron Technologies Inc
Chattanooga, TN...............423-870-1888
Design Technology Corporation
Billerica, MA..................978-663-7000
DT Converting Technologies - Stokes
Bristol, PA....................800-635-0036
Et Oakes Corp
Hauppauge, NY 631-232-0002
Gch Internatonal
Louisville, KY..................502-636-1374
Goodway Industries Inc
Bohemia, NY 800-943-4501
Graybill Machines Inc
Lititz, PA.....................717-626-5221
Ideal Wrapping Machine Company
Middletown, NY 845-343-7700
Matiss
St Georges, QC 888-562-8477
Munson Machinery Co
Utica, NY 800-944-6644
Polar Process
Plattsville, ON.................877-896-8077
Production Techniques Limited
Auckland, NZ 649-274-3514
TSA Griddle Systems
Kelowna, BC..................250-491-9025
Unifiller Systems
Delta, BC.....................888-733-8444
Union Process
Akron, OH....................330-929-3333
UniTrak Corporation
Port Hope, ON 866-883-5749
Woody Associates Inc
York, PA......................717-843-3975

Convection Ovens

ALPI Food Preparation Equipment
Bolton, ON 800-928-2574
Anetsberger
Concord, NH..................603-225-6684
Apollo Sheet Metal
Kennewick, WA 509-586-1104
Blodgett Oven Co
Burlington, VT 800-331-5842
Coast Scientific
Rancho Santa Fe, CA 800-445-1544
Cres Cor
Mentor, OH...................877-273-7267
Davron Technologies Inc
Chattanooga, TN...............423-870-1888
Dynamic Cooking Systems
Huntington Beach, CA 800-433-8466
Foster Refrigerator Corporation
Kinderhook, NY 888-828-3311
Garland Commercial Ranges
Mississauga, ON 905-624-0260
Garland Commercial Ranges Ltd.
Mississauga, ON 905-624-0260
Gehnrich Oven Sales Company
East Troy, WI 262-642-3938
Imperial Manufacturing Co
Corona, CA 800-343-7790
Lang Manufacturing Co
Everett, WA...................800-882-6368
Merco/Savory
Mt. Pleasant, MI 800-733-8821
Middleby Corp
Elgin, IL 847-741-3300
Moffat
San Antonio, TX 866-589-0664
Montague Co
Hayward, CA 800-345-1830

Nevo Corporation
Ronkonkoma, NY 631-585-8787
Piper Products Inc
Wausau, WI...................800-544-3057
Roto-Flex Oven Co
San Antonio, TX 877-859-1463
Southbend
Fuquay Varina, NC 800-348-2558
Superior Products Company
Saint Paul, MN 800-328-9800
Welbilt Corporation
Stamford, CT..................203-325-8300

Cookers

Brewery

Custom Food Machinery
Stockton, CA..................209-463-4343
Falco Technologies
La Prairie, QC.................450-444-0566

Canners'

A.K. Robins
Baltimore, MD 800-486-9656
Custom Food Machinery
Stockton, CA..................209-463-4343
Hamilton Kettles
Weirton, WV..................800-535-1882

Cereal

ANDRITZ Inc
Muncy, PA....................704-943-4343
Central Fabricators Inc
Cincinnati, OH 800-909-8265
Hamilton Kettles
Weirton, WV..................800-535-1882
Lauhoff Corporation
Detroit, MI 313-259-0027

Cheese

A & B Process Systems Corp
Stratford, WI..................888-258-2789
Damrow Company
Fond Du Lac, WI 800-236-1501
Hamilton Kettles
Weirton, WV..................800-535-1882
Viking Machine & Design Inc
De Pere, WI...................888-286-2116

Confectioners', Continuous

A & B Process Systems Corp
Stratford, WI..................888-258-2789
Dupps Co
Germantown, OH 937-855-0623
Hamilton Kettles
Weirton, WV..................800-535-1882

Fish

Brinkmann Corporation
Dallas, TX....................800-468-5252
Coastline Equipment Inc
Bellingham, WA 360-734-8509
Diversified Metal Engineering
Charlottetown, PE..............902-628-6900
Hamilton Kettles
Weirton, WV..................800-535-1882

Pressure

A & B Process Systems Corp
Stratford, WI..................888-258-2789
Hamilton Kettles
Weirton, WV..................800-535-1882
Henny Penny, Inc.
Eaton, OH....................800-417-8417
Littleford Day
Florence, KY..................800-365-8555
Vasconia Housewares
San Antonio, TX...............800-377-6723
Winston Industries
Louisville, KY..................800-234-5286

Steam

A.K. Robins
Baltimore, MD 800-486-9656
Accu Temp Products Inc
Fort Wayne, IN 800-210-5907
Alumaworks
Sunny Isle Beach, FL 800-277-7267

Amber Glo
Chicago, IL................................866-705-0515
Aroma Manufacturing Company
San Diego, CA..........................800-276-6286
Blodgett Corp
Burlington, VT..........................800-331-5842
Brinkmann Corporation
Dallas, TX...............................800-468-5252
Cleveland Range
Cleveland, OH..........................800-338-2204
Garland Commercial Ranges
Mississauga, ON........................905-624-0260
Garvis Manufacturing Company
Des Moines, IA.........................515-243-8054
Hamilton Kettles
Weirton, WV............................800-535-1882
Ideas Well Done LLC
Winooski, VT...........................877-877-1224
J C Ford Co
La Habra, CA...........................714-871-7361
Key Technology Inc.
Walla Walla, WA.......................509-529-2161
Komline-Sanderson Engineering
Peapack, NJ............................800-225-5457
Legion Industries Inc
Waynesboro, GA........................800-887-1988
Market Forge Industries Inc
Everett, MA.............................866-698-3188
Middleby Corp
Elgin, IL................................847-741-3300
Sandvik Process Systems
Sweden, NJ.............................973-790-1600
Southbend
Fuquay Varina, NC.....................800-348-2558
Stellar Steam
Winooski, VT...........................802-654-8603
Superior Products Company
Saint Paul, MN.........................800-328-9800
Viatec
Victoria, BC............................800-942-4702
Vulcan Food Equipment Group
Baltimore, MD..........................800-814-2028
Washington Frontier
Grandview, WA.........................509-469-7662
Welbilt Corporation
Stamford, CT...........................203-325-8300

Vegetable

A.K. Robins
Baltimore, MD..........................800-486-9656
Alkar Rapid Pak
Lodi, WI................................608-592-3211
Amco Metals Indl
City Of Industry, CA...................626-855-2550
Brinkmann Corporation
Dallas, TX...............................800-468-5252
Hamilton Kettles
Weirton, WV............................800-535-1882
J C Ford Co
La Habra, CA...........................714-871-7361
Market Forge Industries Inc
Everett, MA.............................866-698-3188
Pick Heaters
West Bend, WI..........................800-233-9030
Washington Frontier
Grandview, WA.........................509-469-7662

Cooking & Heating Equipment

A C Horn & Co Sheet Metal
Dallas, TX...............................800-657-6155
A Legacy Food Svc
Santa Fe Springs, CA...................800-848-4440
Abalon Precision Manufacturing Corporation
Bronx, NY..............................800-888-2225
Abco International
Oneida, NY.............................888-263-7195
Accu Temp Products Inc
Fort Wayne, IN.........................800-210-5907
Acp Inc
Cedar Rapids, IA.......................319-368-8198
Acra Electric Corporation
Tulsa, OK...............................800-223-4328
Adamatic
Auburn, WA.............................800-578-2547
Advance Tabco
Edgewood, NY..........................800-645-3166
All Spun Metal Products
Des Plaines, IL.........................847-824-4117

All State Fabricators Corporation
Tampa, FL...............................800-322-9925
Alliance Products LLC
Murfreesboro, TN.......................800-522-3973
Allied Metal Spinning
Bronx, NY..............................800-615-2266
Alloy Hardfacing & Engineering
Jordan, MN.............................800-328-8408
Allstrong Restaurant Eqpt Inc
South El Monte, CA....................800-933-8913
ALPI Food Preparation Equipment
Bolton, ON..............................800-928-2574
Alto-Shaam
Menomonee Falls, WI...................800-329-8744
Amber Glo
Chicago, IL................................866-705-0515
American Extrusion Intl
South Beloit, IL.........................815-624-6616
American Housewares
Bronx, NY..............................718-665-9500
American Metal Stamping
Brooklyn, NY...........................718-384-1500
American Range
Pacoima, CA............................888-753-9898
American Systems Associates
Hampton Bays, NY.....................800-584-3663
AMF CANADA
Sherbrooke, QC........................800-255-3869
AMI
Richmond, CA..........................800-942-7466
Anchor Hocking Operating Co
Lancaster, OH..........................800-562-7511
Anetsberger
Concord, NH............................603-225-6684
Antrim Manufacturing Inc
Brookfield, WI..........................262-781-6860
Apollo Sheet Metal
Kennewick, WA.........................509-586-1104
APW Wyott Food Service Equipment Company
Cheyenne, WY..........................800-527-2100
Archer Wire Intl Corp
Chicago, IL..............................708-563-1700
Architectural Sheet Metals LLC
Cleveland, OH..........................216-361-9952
Arcobaleno Pasta Machines
Lancaster, PA...........................800-875-7096
Aroma Manufacturing Company
San Diego, CA..........................800-276-6286
Astoria General Espresso
Greensboro, NC........................336-393-0224
Attias Oven Corp
Brooklyn, NY...........................800-928-8427
Autofry
Northborough, MA.....................800-348-2976
Automated Food Systems
Waxahachie, TX........................469-517-0470
Automatic Specialties Inc
Marlborough, MA......................800-445-2370
Avalon Manufacturer
Corona, CA.............................800-676-3040
Awmco Inc
Orland Park, IL........................708-478-6032
Aztec Grill
Dallas, TX...............................800-346-8114
B R Machinery
Wedron, IL.............................800-310-7057
Bakers Pride Oven Company
New Rochelle, NY......................800-431-2745
Bakery Associates
Setauket, NY...........................631-751-4156
Ballantyne Food Service Equipment
Omaha, NE..............................800-424-1215
Bar-B-Q Woods
Newton, KS.............................800-528-0819
Baxter Manufacturing Inc
Orting, WA.............................800-777-2828
Bbc Industries
Pacific, MO.............................800-654-4205
BBQ Pits by Klose
Houston, TX............................800-487-7487
Be & Sco
San Antonio, TX........................800-683-0928
Becker Brothers Graphite Co
Maywood, IL...........................708-410-0700
Belshaw Adamatic Bakery Group
Auburn, WA.............................800-578-2547
Belson Outdoors Inc
North Aurora, IL.......................800-323-5664
Benchmark Thermal
Grass Valley, CA.......................800-748-6189
Benko Products
Sheffield Vlg, OH......................440-934-2180

Bethel Engineering & Equipment Inc
New Hampshire, OH....................800-889-6129
Bevles Company
Dallas, TX...............................800-441-1601
Big John Corp
Pleasant Gap, PA.......................800-326-9575
BKI Worldwide
Simpsonville, SC.......................800-927-6887
Blodgett Corp
Burlington, VT..........................800-331-5842
Blodgett Oven Co
Burlington, VT..........................800-331-5842
Bolling Oven & Machine Company
Avon, OH..............................440-937-6112
Brinkmann Corporation
Dallas, TX...............................800-468-5252
Britt's Barbecue
Birmingham, AL........................205-612-6538
Broaster Co LLC
Beloit, WI..............................800-365-8278
Buhler Inc.
Plymouth, MN..........................763-847-9900
C H Babb Co Inc
Raynham, MA..........................508-977-0600
Carlisle Food Svc Products Inc
Oklahoma City, OK.....................800-654-8210
Casa Herrera
Pomona, CA............................800-624-3916
Casso-Solar Corporation
Nanuet, NY.............................800-988-4455
Cci Industries-Cool Curtain
Costa Mesa, CA........................800-854-5719
Central Fabricators Inc
Cincinnati, OH.........................800-909-8265
Checker Machine
Minneapolis, MN.......................888-800-5001
Chef's Choice Mesquite Charcoal
Carpinteria, CA........................805-684-8284
Chesmont Engineering Co Inc
Exton, PA..............................610-594-9200
Chester-Jensen Co., Inc.
Chester, PA............................800-685-3750
Chromalox Inc
Pittsburgh, PA.........................800-443-2640
Cincinnati Industrial Machry
Mason, OH.............................800-677-0076
Cleveland Range
Cleveland, OH.........................800-338-2204
Coast Scientific
Rancho Santa Fe, CA...................800-445-1544
Cobatco
Peoria, IL...............................800-426-2282
Cober Electronics, Inc.
Norwalk, CT............................800-709-5948
Commercial Dehydrator Systems
Eugene, OR.............................800-369-4283
Comstock Castle Stove Co
Quincy, IL..............................800-637-9188
Connerton Co
Santa Ana, CA..........................714-547-9218
Cooking Systems International
Redwood City, CA......................650-556-6222
Cookshack
Ponca City, OK.........................800-423-0698
CookTek
Chicago, IL..............................888-266-5835
Cove Four
Freeport, NY...........................516-379-4232
CPM Wolverine Proctor LLC
Horsham, PA............................215-443-5200
Craft Industries
Long Island City, NY...................252-753-3152
Cres Cor
Mentor, OH.............................877-273-7267
Crispy Lite
St. Louis, MO...........................888-356-5362
Crown Verity
Brantford, ON..........................888-505-7240
Custom Diamond International
Laval, QC...............................800-363-5926
Custom Diamond Intl.
Laval, QC...............................800-326-5926
Cutler Industries
Morton Grove, IL.......................800-458-5593
D. Picking & Company
Bucyrus, OH............................419-562-6891
Damrow Company
Fond Du Lac, WI........................800-236-1501
Dar-B-Ques Barbecue Equipment
Minneapolis, MN.......................612-724-7425
Davron Technologies Inc
Chattanooga, TN.......................423-870-1888

DBE Inc
  Concord, ON 800-461-5313
Dean Industries
  Gardena, CA 800-995-1210
Defreeze Corporation
  Southborough, MA 508-485-8512
Deluxe Equipment Company
  Bradenton, FL 800-367-8931
Diversified Metal Engineering
  Charlottetown, PE 902-628-6900
Doyon Equipment
  Liniere, QC .800-463-4273
Duke Manufacturing Co
  St Louis, MO 800-735-3853
Dupps Co
  Germantown, OH 937-855-0623
Dura-Ware Company of America
  Oklahoma City, OK 800-664-3872
Duralite Inc
  Riverton, CT 888-432-8797
Dynamic Cooking Systems
  Huntington Beach, CA 800-433-8466
Dynynstyl
  Delray Beach, FL 800-774-7895
Eagle Group
  Clayton, DE. 800-441-8440
Earthstone Wood-Fire Ovens
  Glendale, CA 800-840-4915
Electro-Steam Generator Corp
  Rancocas, NJ 866-617-0764
Emerald City Closets Inc
  Auburn, WA 800-925-1521
Empire Bakery Equipment
  Hicksville, NY 800-878-4070
Epcon Industrial Systems
  Conroe, TX .800-447-7872
Equipex Limited
  Providence, RI 800-649-7885
Erwin Food Service Equipment
  Fort Worth, TX 817-535-0021
Esquire Mechanical Corp.
  Armonk, NY 800-847-4206
Eurodib
  Champlain, NY 888-956-6866
Fab-X/Metals
  Washington, NC 800-677-3229
Filtercorp
  Fresno, CA .800-473-4526
Fish Oven & Equipment Co
  Wauconda, IL 877-526-8720
FlashBake Ovens Food Service
  Fremont, CA 800-843-6836
FleetwoodGoldcoWyard
  Romeoville, IL 630-759-6800
Flodin
  Moses Lake, WA 509-766-2996
Food Engineering Unlimited
  Fullerton, CA 714-879-8762
FOODesign from tna
  Wilsonville, OR 503-685-5030
Foster Refrigerator Corporation
  Kinderhook, NY 888-828-3311
Franrica Systems
  Stockton, CA. 209-948-2811
Franz Haas Machinery-America
  Henrico, VA 804-222-6022
Friedrich Metal Products
  Browns Summit, NC. 800-772-0326
Fry Tech Corporation
  Dubuque, IA 319-583-1559
Frymaster/Dean
  Shreveport, LA 800-221-4583
Garland Commercial Ranges
  Mississauga, ON 905-624-0260
Garland Commercial Ranges Ltd.
  Mississauga, ON 905-624-0260
Garvis Manufacturing Company
  Des Moines, IA. 515-243-8054
GBS Foodservice Equipment, Inc.
  Mississauga, ON. 888-402-1242
Gehnrich Oven Sales Company
  East Troy, WI 262-642-3938
GEM Equipment Of Oregon Inc
  Woodburn, OR 503-982-9902
General Cage
  Elwood, IN .800-428-6403
Giles Enterprises Inc
  Montgomery, AL. 800-288-1555
Glenro Inc
  Paterson, NJ 888-453-6761
Glowmaster Corporation
  Clifton, NJ. .800-272-7008

Gold Medal Products Co
  Cincinnati, OH 800-543-0862
Gralab Instruments
  Centerville, OH. 800-876-8353
Grand Silver Company
  Bronx, NY. .718-585-1930
Grande Chef Company
  Orangeville, ON 519-942-4470
Grill Greats
  Saxonburg, PA. 724-352-1511
Grillco Inc
  Aurora, IL 800-644-0067
Grills to Go
  Fresno, CA .877-869-2253
GSW Jackes-Evans Manufacturing Company
  Saint Louis, MO 800-325-6173
H.F. Coors China Company
  New Albany, MS. 800-782-6677
Hamilton Kettles
  Weirton, WV 800-535-1882
Hardt Equipment Manufacturing
  Lachine, QC 888-848-4408
Hasty Bake Charcoal Grills
  Tulsa, OK 800-426-6836
Hatco Corp
  Milwaukee, WI 800-558-0607
Heat-It Manufacturing
  San Antonio, TX. 800-323-9336
Henny Penny, Inc.
  Eaton, OH .800-417-8417
Hercules Food Equipment
  Weston, ON 416-742-9673
HH Controls Company
  Arilington, MA 781-646-2626
Hickory Industries
  North Bergen, NJ 800-732-9153
Holman Boiler Works
  Dallas, TX. .800-331-1956
Holman Cooking Equipment
  Saint Louis, MO 888-356-5362
Holstein Manufacturing
  Holstein, IA. 800-368-4342
Hughes Co
  Columbus, WI. 866-535-9303
Hydro-Thermal Corp
  Waukesha, WI 800-952-0121
Idaho Steel Products Inc
  Idaho Falls, ID 208-522-1275
Ideas Well Done LLC
  Winooski, VT 877-877-1224
Illinois Range Company
  Schiller Park, IL 800-535-7041
Illinois Tool Works
  Glenview, IL 224-661-8870
Imperial Manufacturing Co
  Corona, CA 800-343-7790
Industrial Ceramic Products
  Marysville, OH. 800-427-2278
Intedge Manufacturing
  Woodruff, SC 866-969-9605
IR Systems
  Jupiter, FL .800-893-7540
Iwatani International Corporation of America
  Houston, TX 800-775-5506
J & R Mfg Inc
  Mesquite, TX 800-527-4831
J C Ford Co
  La Habra, CA 714-871-7361
Jackson Msc LLC
  Gray, KY 888-800-5672
Jackson Restaurant Supply
  Jackson, TN 800-424-8943
Jade Products Co
  Brea, CA 800-884-5233
Kady International
  Scarborough, ME 800-367-5239
Karl Schnell
  New London, WI 920-982-9974
Kay Home Products Inc
  Antioch, IL .800-600-7009
Keating Of Chicago Inc
  Mc Cook, IL 800-532-8464
Kelmin Products
  Plymouth, FL 407-886-6079
Key Technology Inc.
  Walla Walla, WA. 509-529-2161
King Packaging Co
  Schenectady, NY. 518-370-5464
KNOX Stove Works Inc
  Knoxville, TN 865-524-4113
Komline-Sanderson Engineering
  Peapack, NJ. 800-225-5457

Krispy Kist Company
  Chicago, IL .312-733-0900
Lancaster Colony Corporation
  Westerville, OH. 614-224-7141
Lang Manufacturing Co
  Everett, WA 800-882-6368
Lanly Co
  Cleveland, OH. 216-731-1115
Lauhoff Corporation
  Detroit, MI .313-259-0027
Lazy Man Inc
  Belvidere, NJ 800-475-1950
Le Smoker
  Salisbury, MD 410-677-3233
Leedal Inc
  Northbrook, IL 847-498-0111
Legion Industries Inc
  Waynesboro, GA. 800-887-1988
Liberty Ware LLC
  Clearfield, UT 888-500-5885
Lignetics Inc
  Sandpoint, ID 800-544-3834
Lil' Orbits
  Minneapolis, MN 800-228-8305
Lincoln Foodservice
  Cleveland, OH 800-374-3004
Littleford Day
  Florence, KY. 800-365-8555
LPS Technology
  Grafton, OH 800-586-1410
Magi Kitch'n
  Concord, NH. 800-441-1492
Market Forge Industries Inc
  Everett, MA. 866-698-3188
Marshall Air Systems Inc
  Charlotte, NC 800-722-3474
Martin/Baron
  Irwindale, CA 626-960-5153
Masterbuilt Manufacturing Inc
  Columbus, GA 706-327-5622
Mastex Industries
  Petersburg, VA 804-732-8300
Maytag Corporation
  Benton Harbor, MI 800-344-1274
Merco/Savory
  Mt. Pleasant, MI 800-733-8821
Metal Masters Northwest
  Lynnwood, WA 425-775-4481
Metro Corporation
  Wilkes Barre, PA. 800-992-1776
Microdry
  Crestwood, KY 502-241-8933
Middleby Corp
  Elgin, IL 847-741-3300
Middleby Marshall Inc
  Elgin, IL 847-741-3300
Midwest Aircraft Products Co
  Lexington, OH 419-884-2164
Midwest Wire Products LLC
  Sturgeon Bay, WI 800-445-0225
Mies Products
  West Bend, WI 800-480-6437
Miracle Exclusives
  Danbury, CT 203-796-5493
Mirro Company
  Lancaster, OH 800-848-7200
Moffat
  San Antonio, TX. 866-589-0664
Moli-International
  Denver, CO 800-525-8468
Moline Machinery LLC
  Duluth, MN. 800-767-5734
Montague Co
  Hayward, CA 800-345-1830
Mosshaim Innovations
  Jacksonville, FL 888-995-7775
Motion Technologies
  Northborough, MA 800-468-2976
Motom Corporation
  Bensenville, IL 630-787-1995
Mouli Manufacturing Corporation
  Belleville, NJ 800-789-8285
Mountain Safety Research
  Seattle, WA 800-877-9677
Mr. Bar-B-Q
  Winston-Salem, NC 800-333-2124
Music City Metals Inc
  Nashville, TN 800-251-2674
Napoleon Appliance Corporation
  Barrie, ON. .866-820-8686
National Drying Machry Co Inc
  Philadelphia, PA 215-464-6070

National Hotpack
Stone Ridge, NY 800-431-8232
Nature's Own
Attleboro, MA. 508-399-8690
Nemeth Engineering Assoc
Crestwood, KY 502-241-1502
Nevo Corporation
Ronkonkoma, NY 631-585-8787
Nieco Corporation
Windsor, CA 800-643-2656
Normandie Metal Fabricators
Port Washington, NY 800-221-2398
Northern Stainless Fabricating
Traverse City, MI 231-947-4580
Nothum Food Processing Systems
Springfield, MO 800-435-1297
NuTone
Cincinnati, OH 888-336-3948
Ogden Manufacturing Company
Pittsburgh, PA 412-967-3906
Olde Country Reproductions Inc
York, PA 800-358-3997
Ole Hickory Pits
Cape Girardeau, MO. 800-223-9667
Otto Braun Bakery Equipment
Buffalo, NY .716-824-1252
Padinox
Winsloe, PE 800-263-9768
Panasonic Commercial Food Service
Newark, NJ
Paragon International
Nevada, IA .800-433-0333
Patio King
Cutler Bay, FL. 305-316-7508
Peerless Ovens
Sandusky, OH 800-548-4514
Peerless-Premier Appliance Co
Belleville, IL 618-233-0475
Perfect Fry Company
Calgary, AB. 800-265-7711
Peter Gray Corporation
Andover, MA 978-470-0990
Pick Heaters
West Bend, WI 800-233-9030
Pier 1 Imports
Woodcliff Lake, NJ 800-448-9993
Pino's Pasta Veloce
Staten Island, NY 718-273-6660
Piper Products Inc
Wausau, WI. 800-544-3057
Pitco Frialator Inc
Bow, NH 800-258-3708
PMI Food Equipment Group
Troy, OH 937-332-3000
Polar Ware Company
Sheboygan, WI 800-237-3655
Porcelain Metals Corporation
Louisville, KY 502-635-7421
Power Flame Inc
Parsons, KS 800-862-4256
Precision
Miami, FL 800-762-7565
Prince Castle Inc
Carol Stream, IL 800-722-7853
Process Heating Corp
Shrewsbury, MA 508-842-5200
Process Systems
Barrington, IL 847-842-8618
Profire Stainless Steel Barbecue
Miami, FL 305-665-5313
Proheatco Manufacturing
Pomona, CA 800-423-4195
Proluxe
Paramount, CA 800-594-5528
Q-Matic Technologies
Carol Stream, IL 800-880-6836
QNC Inc
Dallas, TX. .888-668-3687
Quadra-Tech
Columbus, OH 800-443-2766
Quality Fabrication & Design
Coppell, TX 972-304-3266
Quantem Corp
Ewing, NJ 609-883-9879
Quasar Industries
Rochester Hills, MI. 248-852-0300
Randell Manufacturing   Unified Brands
Weidman, MI 888-994-7636
Rankin Delux
Mira Loma, CA. 951-685-0081
Rational Cooking Systems
Schaumburg, IL. 888-320-7274

Reading Bakery Systems Inc
Robesonia, PA. 610-693-5816
Reed Oven Co
Kansas City, MO. 816-842-7446
Regal Ware Inc
Kewaskum, WI 262-626-2121
Reliable Food Service Equipment
Concord, ON 416-738-6840
Remco Industries International
Fort Lauderdale, FL 800-987-3626
Renato Specialty Product
Garland, TX 866-575-6316
Revent Inc
Piscataway, NJ 732-777-9433
Ricoh Technologies
Grand Prairie, TX 800-585-9367
Rival Manufacturing Company
Kansas City, MO. 816-943-4100
Rotisol France Inc
Inglewood, CA 800-651-5969
Roto-Flex Oven Co
San Antonio, TX. 877-859-1463
Roundup Food Equip
Carol Stream, IL 800-253-2991
Royal Oak Enterprises
Roswell, GA 678-461-3200
Royalton Foodservice Equip Co
North Royalton, OH 800-662-8765
Sandvik Process Systems
Sweden, NJ 973-790-1600
Saunder Brothers
Bridgton, ME 207-647-3331
Savage Brothers Company
Elk Grove Vlg, IL. 800-342-0973
SCK Direct Inc
Stratford, CT. 800-327-8766
Seidman Brothers
Chelsea, MA 800-437-7770
Server Products Inc
Richfield, WI 800-558-8722
Sharp Electronics Corporation
Mahwah, NJ 800-237-4277
Sharpsville Container Corp
Sharpsville, PA 800-645-1248
Shat R Shield Inc
Salisbury, NC 800-223-0853
Shelcon Inc
Ontario, CA. 909-947-4877
Shouldice Brothers SheetMetal
Battle Creek, MI 269-962-5579
Silesia Grill Machines Inc
St Petersburg, FL 800-237-4766
Silesia Grill Machines Inc
St Petersburg, FL 800-267-4766
Silver Weibull
Aurora, CO .303-373-2311
Smokaroma
Boley, OK 800-331-5565
South Valley Mfg Inc
Gilroy, CA. .408-842-5457
Southbend
Fuquay Varina, NC 800-348-2558
Southern Pride Distributing
Alamo, TN .800-851-8180
Spring USA Corp
Naperville, IL 800-535-8974
Stainless Steel Fabricator Inc
La Mirada, CA 714-739-9904
Standex International Corp.
Salem, NH .603-893-9701
Star Manufacturing Intl Inc
St Louis, MO. 800-264-7827
Starkey Chemical Process Company
La Grange, IL 800-323-3040
State Products
Long Beach, CA 800-730-5150
Stewart Systems Baking LLC
Plano, TX 972-422-5808
Stricklin Co
Dallas, TX. .214-637-1030
Stryco Wire Products
North York, ON. 416-663-7000
Super Cooker
Lake Park, GA 800-841-7452
Super-Chef Manufacturing Company
Houston, TX 800-231-3478
Superior Food Machinery Inc
Pico Rivera, CA 800-944-0396
Superior Products Company
Saint Paul, MN 800-328-9800
Svedala Industries
Colorado Springs, CO. 719-471-3443

Swanson Wire Works Industries, Inc.
Mesquite, TX 972-288-7465
Tablecraft Products Co Inc
Gurnee, IL. .800-323-8321
TEMP-TECH Company
Springfield, MA 800-343-5579
Tempco Electric Heater Corporation
Wood Dale, IL 888-268-6396
Texas Corn Roasters
Granbury, TX 800-772-4345
Thermal Engineering Corp
Columbia, SC 800-331-0097
Thermo King Corp
Bloomington, MN. 888-887-2202
Thermodyne Foodservice Prods
Fort Wayne, IN 800-526-9182
Thermoquest
Riviera Beach, FL 888-383-2025
Thermos Company
Schaumburg, IL. 800-243-0745
Thomas L. Green & Company
Robenosia, PA. 610-693-5816
Toastmaster
Elgin, IL 847-741-3300
Tolan Machinery Company
Rockaway, NJ 973-983-7212
Tomlinson Industries
Cleveland, OH 800-945-4589
Toronto Kitchen Equipment
North York, ON 416-745-4944
Townfood Equipment Corp
Brooklyn, NY 800-221-5032
Traeger Industries
Portland, OR 800-872-3437
Trak-Air/Rair
Denver, CO .800-688-8725
Tramontina USA
Sugar Land, TX. 800-221-7809
Trimen Foodservice Equipment
North York, ON. 877-437-1422
TruHeat Corporation
Allegan, MI. 800-879-6199
Tupperware Brands Corporation
Orlando, FL. 800-366-3800
TURBOCHEF Technologies
Carrollton, TX. 800-908-8726
Ultrafryer Systems Inc
San Antonio, TX. 800-545-9189
Utility Refrigerator Company
Los Angeles, CA. 800-884-5233
Valad Electric Heating Corporation
Tarrytown, NY 914-631-4927
Vasconia Housewares
San Antonio, TX. 800-377-6723
Vimco
King Of Prussia, PA 610-768-0500
Vortron Smokehouse/Ovens
Iron Ridge, WI 800-874-1949
Vulcan Food Equipment Group
Baltimore, MD 800-814-2028
Wayne Combustion Systems
Fort Wayne, IN 800-443-4625
Welbilt Corporation
Stamford, CT. 203-325-8300
Wells Manufacturing Company
St. Louis, MO 888-356-5362
West Oregon Wood Products Inc
Columbia City, OR 503-397-6707
Western Combustion Engineering
Carson, CA .310-834-9389
Wheel Tough Company
Terre Haute, IN 888-765-8833
Whitford Corporation
Frazer, PA 610-296-3200
Wilch Manufacturing
Topeka, KS .785-267-2762
Wilder Manufacturing Company
Port Jervis, NY 800-832-1319
Wilton Brands LLC
Woodridge, IL 630-963-7100
Win-Holt Equipment Group
Syosset, NY. 800-444-3595
Winston Industries
Louisville, KY 800-234-5286
Wisco Industries Assembly
Oregon, WI .800-999-4726
Wittco Foodservice Equipment
Milwaukee, WI 800-367-8413
Wittco Foodservice Equipment
Milwaukee, WI 800-821-3912
Wolf Company
Louisville, KY 800-814-2028

Wood Stone Corp
Bellingham, WA 800-988-8103
World Kitchen
Elmira, NY .800-999-3436
X-Press Manufacturing
New Braunfels, TX 800-365-9440

Charcoal Briquettes

Grill Greats
Saxonburg, PA 724-352-1511
King Packaging Co
Schenectady, NY 518-370-5464
Lazzari Fuel Co LLC
Brisbane, CA 800-242-7265
Le Smoker
Salisbury, MD 410-677-3233
Mali's All Natural Barbecue Supply Company
East Amherst, NY 800-289-6254
Mex-Char
Douglas, AZ 520-364-2138
Music City Metals Inc
Nashville, TN 800-251-2674
Nature's Own
Attleboro, MA 508-399-8690
Roseville Charcoal & Mfg Co
Zanesville, OH 740-452-5473
Royal Oak Enterprises
Roswell, GA 678-461-3200

Charcoal: Mesquite

Chef's Choice Mesquite Charcoal
Carpinteria, CA 805-684-8284
Lazzari Fuel Co LLC
Brisbane, CA 800-242-7265
Le Smoker
Salisbury, MD 410-677-3233
Lignetics Inc
Sandpoint, ID 800-544-3834
Mali's All Natural Barbecue Supply Company
East Amherst, NY 800-289-6254
Mex-Char
Douglas, AZ 520-364-2138
Music City Metals Inc
Nashville, TN 800-251-2674

Corers

Fruit & Vegetable

A.D. Cowdrey Company
Modesto, CA 209-538-4677
Amco Metals Indl
City Of Industry, CA 626-855-2550
F.B. Pease Company
Rochester, NY 585-475-1870
Globe Machine
Tacoma, WA 800-523-6575
Goodnature Products
Orchard Park, NY 800-875-3381

Corn Chip Processing

A C Horn & Co Sheet Metal
Dallas, TX .800-657-6155
Casa Herrera
Pomona, CA 800-624-3916
Graybill Machines Inc
Lititz, PA 717-626-5221
J C Ford Co
La Habra, CA 714-871-7361
Krispy Kist Company
Chicago, IL 312-733-0900
Maddox/Adams International
Miami, FL .305-592-3337
Pavan USA Inc
Emigsville, PA 717-767-4889
Polar Process
Plattsville, ON 877-896-8077

Corn Poppers

A C Horn & Co Sheet Metal
Dallas, TX .800-657-6155
C. Cretors & Company
Chicago, IL 800-228-1885
Dunbar Manufacturing Co
South Elgin, IL 847-741-6394
Fun City Popcorn
Las Vegas, NV 800-423-1710
Gold Medal Products Co
Cincinnati, OH 800-543-0862

Great Western Co LLC
Hollywood, AL 256-259-3578
Maddox/Adams International
Miami, FL .305-592-3337
Paragon International
Nevada, IA .800-433-0333
Server Products Inc
Richfield, WI 800-558-8722
Star Manufacturing Intl Inc
St Louis, MO 800-264-7827
Treier Popcorn Farms
Bloomdale, OH 419-454-2811

Corn Processing

ANDRITZ Inc
Muncy, PA .704-943-4343
Automated Food Systems
Waxahachie, TX 469-517-0470
Custom Millers Supply Co
Monmouth, IL 309-734-6312
Hughes Co
Columbus, WI 866-535-9303
J C Ford Co
La Habra, CA 714-871-7361
Lee Financial Corporation
Dallas, TX .972-960-1001
Oxbo International Corp
Clear Lake, WI 800-628-6196
Texas Corn Roasters
Granbury, TX 800-772-4345

Crushers

Can & Glass

A T Ferrell Co Inc
Bluffton, IN 800-248-8318
Berkshire PPM
Litchfield, CT 860-567-3118
C S Bell Co
Tiffin, OH .888-958-6381
Compactors Inc
Hilton Head Isle, SC 800-423-4003
Consolidated Baling Machine Company
Jacksonville, FL 800-231-9286
Ertelalsop
Kingston, NY 800-553-7835
Glen Mills Inc.
Clifton, NJ .973-777-0777
Langsenkamp Manufacturing
Indianapolis, IN 877-585-1950
Maren Engineering Corp
South Holland, IL 800-875-1038
Waring Products
Torrington, CT 800-492-7464

Fruit

A.K. Robins
Baltimore, MD 800-486-9656
Globe Machine
Tacoma, WA 800-523-6575
Goodnature Products
Orchard Park, NY 800-875-3381
Healdsburg Machine Company
Santa Rosa, CA 707-433-3348
Oak Barrel Winecraft
Berkeley, CA 510-849-0400

Grain & Oat

C S Bell Co
Tiffin, OH .888-958-6381
CPM Roskamp Champion
Waterloo, IA 800-366-2563
Glen Mills Inc.
Clifton, NJ .973-777-0777
M O Industries Inc
Whippany, NJ 973-386-9228
Schutte Buffalo Hammermill
Buffalo, NY 800-447-4634

Dairy & Creamery

A & B Process Systems Corp
Stratford, WI 888-258-2789
Advance Energy Technologies
Halfmoon, NY 800-724-0198
Apex Packing & Rubber Co
Farmingdale, NY 800-645-9110
Aw Sheepscot Holding Co Inc
Franksville, WI 800-850-6110

B T Engineering Inc
Bala Cynwyd, PA 610-664-9500
Ben H. Anderson Manufacturers
Morrisonville, WI 608-846-5474
Berlon Industries
Hustisford, WI 800-899-3580
Bowers Process Equipment
Stratford, ON 800-567-3223
C E Rogers Co
Mora, MN .800-279-8081
C&R Refrigation Inc,
Center, TX .800-438-6182
Cal-Coast Manufacturing
Turlock, CA 209-668-9378
Cannon Equipment Company
Cannon Falls, MN 800-825-8501
Chester-Jensen Co., Inc.
Chester, PA 800-685-3750
Coburn Company
Whitewater, WI 800-776-7042
Custom Fabricating & Repair
Marshfield, WI 800-236-8773
Custom Food Machinery
Stockton, CA 209-463-4343
Damrow Company
Fond Du Lac, WI 800-236-1501
Dipwell Co
Northampton, MA 413-587-4673
Diversified Metal Engineering
Charlottetown, PE 902-628-6900
Doering Machines Inc
San Francisco, CA 415-526-2131
Dyna-Veyor Inc
Newark, NJ 800-326-5009
Dynamic Automation LTD
Simi Valley, CA. 805-584-8476
Eischen Enterprises
Fresno, CA .559-834-0013
Equipment Specialists Inc
Manassas, VA 703-361-2227
Food Resources International
Concord, ON. 905-482-8967
GEA North America
Naperville, IL 630-369-8100
Gea Us
Galesville, WI 608-582-3081
General Machinery Corp
Sheboygan, WI 888-243-6622
Girton Manufacturing Co
Millville, PA 570-458-5521
Globe Food Equipment Co
Moraine, OH 800-347-5423
Gruenewald ManufacturingCompany
Danvers, MA 800-229-9447
Ika-Works Inc
Wilmington, NC 800-733-3037
Ivarson Inc
Milwaukee, WI 414-351-0700
Johnson Industries Intl
Windsor, WI 608-846-4499
Kusel Equipment Company
Watertown, WI 920-261-4112
Leland Limited Inc
South Plainfield, NJ 800-984-9793
Lyco Manufacturing
Wausau, WI 715-845-7867
Lyco Wausau
Wausau, WI. 715-845-7867
Master-Bilt
New Albany, MS. 800-647-1284
Membrane System Specialist Inc
Wisconsin Rapids, WI 715-421-2333
Millebernd Systems
Winsted, MN. 320-485-2685
Nicholas Machine and Grinding
Houston, TX 800-747-1256
Omni International
Kennesaw, GA 800-776-4431
Opal Manufacturing Ltd
Toronto, ON 416-646-5232
Pacific Process Technology
La Jolla, CA 858-551-3298
Papertech
North Vancouver, BC 877-787-2737
Paradigm Technologies
Eugene, OR 541-345-5543
Peterson Fiberglass Laminates
Shell Lake, WI 715-468-2306
Polar Process
Plattsville, ON. 877-896-8077
Pro Scientific Inc
Oxford, CT .800-584-3776

Reiser
Canton, MA 734-821-1290
Relco Unisystems Corp
Willmar, MN. 320-231-2210
Rheo-Tech
Gurnee, IL. 847-367-1557
Sanchelima International
Miami, FL. 305-591-4343
Scherping Systems
Winsted, MN. 320-485-4401
Schlueter Company
Janesville, WI. 800-359-1700
Sepragen Corp
Hayward, CA 510-475-0650
Sonic Corp
Stratford, CT. 866-493-1378
Stanfos
Edmonton, AB 800-661-5648
Superflex Limited
Brooklyn, NY 800-394-3665
Swirl Freeze Corp
Salt Lake City, UT 800-262-4275
T D Sawvel Co
Maple Plain, MN. 877-488-1816
Tetra Pak
Denton, TX 940-380-4630
Tindall Packaging
Vicksburg, MI 269-649-1163
Tuchenhagen North America
Portland, ME. 207-797-9500
WCB Ice Cream
Philadelphia, PA 215-425-4320
Whey Systems
Willmar, MN 320-905-4122

Deaerators

Food

B.A.G. Corporation
Richardson, TX. 800-331-9200
Bryan Boilers
Peru, IN 765-473-6651
Cornell Machine Co
Springfield, NJ 973-379-6860
Hebeler Corp
Tonawanda, NY 800-486-4709
Sellers Engineering Division
Danville, KY. 859-236-3181
South Valley Mfg Inc
Gilroy, CA. 408-842-5457

Deep Fryers

Abalon Precision Manufacturing Corporation
Bronx, NY. 800-888-2225
All State Fabricators Corporation
Tampa, FL. 800-322-9925
Alumaworks
Sunny Isle Beach, FL 800-277-7267
American Extrusion Intl
South Beloit, IL 815-624-6616
Autofry
Northborough, MA. 800-348-2976
Automated Food Systems
Waxahachie, TX 469-517-0470
Ballantyne Food Service Equipment
Omaha, NE 800-424-1215
Baxter Manufacturing Inc
Orting, WA 800-777-2828
Belshaw Adamatic Bakery Group
Auburn, WA 800-578-2547
Blodgett Oven Co
Burlington, VT 800-331-5842
Broaster Co LLC
Beloit, WI .800-365-8278
Comstock Castle Stove Co
Quincy, IL. 800-637-9188
Crispy Lite
St. Louis, MO 888-356-5362
Davron Technologies Inc
Chattanooga, TN. 423-870-1888
Dean Industries
Gardena, CA 800-995-1210
FOODesign from tna
Wilsonville, OR 503-685-5030
Fry Tech Corporation
Dubuque, IA 319-583-1559
Frymaster/Dean
Shreveport, LA 800-221-4583

Garland Commercial Ranges
Mississauga, ON 905-624-0260
GEM Equipment Of Oregon Inc
Woodburn, OR 503-982-9902
Giles Enterprises Inc
Montgomery, AL. 800-288-1555
Gold Medal Products Co
Cincinnati, OH 800-543-0862
Imperial Manufacturing Co
Corona, CA 800-343-7790
Keating Of Chicago Inc
Mc Cook, IL 800-532-8464
Krispy Kist Company
Chicago, IL. 312-733-0900
Lang Manufacturing Co
Everett, WA. 800-882-6368
Lucks Food Equipment Company
Kent, WA. .811-824-0696
Market Forge Industries Inc
Everett, MA. 866-698-3188
Masterbuilt Manufacturing Inc
Columbus, GA 706-327-5622
Meyer Machine & Garroutte Products
San Antonio, TX 210-736-1811
Middleby Corp
Elgin, IL 847-741-3300
Mies Products
West Bend, WI 800-480-6437
Moline Machinery LLC
Duluth, MN. 800-767-5734
Motion Technologies
Northborough, MA. 800-468-2976
Nothum Food Processing Systems
Springfield, MO 800-435-1297
Otto Braun Bakery Equipment
Buffalo, NY. 716-824-1252
Perfect Fry Company
Calgary, AB. 800-265-7711
Pitco Frialator Inc
Bow, NH 800-258-3708
Ricoh Technologies
Grand Prairie, TX 800-585-9367
Southbend
Fuquay Varina, NC 800-348-2558
Stafford-Smith Inc
Kalamazoo, MI 800-968-2442
Stainless Steel Fabricator Inc
La Mirada, CA 714-739-9904
Star Manufacturing Intl Inc
St Louis, MO. 800-264-7827
Super-Chef Manufacturing Company
Houston, TX 800-231-3478
Superior Products Company
Saint Paul, MN. 800-328-9800
Toastmaster
Elgin, IL 847-741-3300
Trak-Air/Rair
Denver, CO 800-688-8725
TWM Manufacturing
Leamington, ON 888-495-4831
Ultrafryer Systems Inc
San Antonio, TX 800-545-9189
Vulcan Food Equipment Group
Baltimore, MD 800-814-2028
Welbilt Corporation
Stamford, CT. 203-325-8300
Wells Manufacturing Company
St. Louis, MO 888-356-5362
Western Combustion Engineering
Carson, CA 310-834-9389
Wheel Tough Company
Terre Haute, IN 888-765-8833
Wolf Company
Louisville, KY 800-814-2028

Dehydration Equipment

A&J Mixing International
Oakville, ON 800-668-3470
ANDRITZ Inc
Muncy, PA. 704-943-4343
B.A.G. Corporation
Richardson, TX. 800-331-9200
BNW Industries
Tippecanoe, IN 574-353-7855
Brothers Metal Products
Santa Ana, CA 714-972-3008
Brown International Corp LLC
Winter Haven, FL 863-299-2111
Buhler Inc
Plymouth, MN. 763-847-9900

C E Rogers Co
Mora, MN .800-279-8081
Commercial Dehydrator Systems
Eugene, OR 800-369-4283
Davenport Machine
Rock Island, IL 309-786-1500
Davron Technologies Inc
Chattanooga, TN. 423-870-1888
Dito Dean Food Prep
Charlotte, NC 866-449-4200
EnWave Corporation
Vancouver, BC 604-806-6110
Evaporator Dryer Technologies
Hammond, WI. 715-796-2313
Flodin
Moses Lake, WA 509-766-2996
Fluid Air Inc
Aurora, IL .630-665-5001
Fluid Energy Processing & Eqpt
Hatfield, PA 215-368-2510
French Oil Mill Machinery Co
Piqua, OH .937-773-3420
Globe Machine
Tacoma, WA 800-523-6575
Goodnature Products
Orchard Park, NY 800-875-3381
H. Gartenberg & Company
Buffalo Grove, IL 847-821-7590
Joneca Corp
Anaheim, CA 714-993-5997
Lanly Co
Cleveland, OH 216-731-1115
Littleford Day
Florence, KY. 800-365-8555
Low Humidity Systems
Covington, GA 770-788-6744
M-E-C Co
Neodesha, KS 620-325-2673
Muth Associates
Springfield, MA 800-388-0157
National Drying Machry Co Inc
Philadelphia, PA 215-464-6070
P & F Machine
Turlock, CA 209-667-2515
Patterson Industries
Scarborough, ON 800-336-1110
Raytheon Co
Waltham, MA 781-522-3000
SP Industries Inc
Warminster, PA 800-523-2327
Thermex Thermatron
Louisville, KY 502-493-1299
Thoreson Mc Cosh Inc
Troy, MI 800-959-0805
United Mc Gill Corp
Groveport, OH 614-829-1200
Van Air Systems
Lake City, PA 800-840-9906
Wittemann Company
Palm Coast, FL 386-445-4200

Disintegrators

Schutte Buffalo Hammermill
Buffalo, NY. 800-447-4634

Dough Make-up

Benier
Lithia Springs, GA 770-745-2200
La Poblana Food Machines
Mesa, AZ. .480-258-2091
Rheon, U.S.A.
Irvine, CA. .949-768-1900

Drink Mixing

A & B Process Systems Corp
Stratford, WI. 888-258-2789
Component Hardware Group Inc
Lakewood, NJ. 800-526-3694
Nuova Distribution Centre
Ferndale, WA 360-366-2226
Polar Beer Systems
Sun City, CA 951-928-8174
Vitamix
Olmsted Twp, OH 800-437-4654

Dry Products Filling

Inspired Automation Inc
Agoura Hills, CA 818-991-4598

Tuchenhagen North America
Portland, ME.........................207-797-9500

Dryers

Gea Processing
Hudson, WI........................800-376-6476
Relco Unisystems Corp
Willmar, MN.......................320-231-2210
Spiral Systems
Fair Oaks, CA.....................800-998-6111

Food

A & B Process Systems Corp
Stratford, WI.....................888-258-2789
Ametek Technical & Industrial Products
Kent, OH..........................215-256-6601
Anhydro Inc
Olympia Fields, IL................708-747-7000
Apollo Sheet Metal
Kennewick, WA.....................509-586-1104
Applied Chemical Technology
Florence, AL......................800-228-3217
APV Americas
Delavan, WI.......................800-252-5200
Berg Chilling Systems
Toronto, ON, ON...................416-755-2221
BNW Industries
Tippecanoe, IN....................574-353-7855
Brothers Metal Products
Santa Ana, CA.....................714-972-3008
Buffalo Technologies Corporation
Buffalo, NY.......................800-332-2419
Buhler Inc.
Plymouth, MN......................763-847-9900
C E Rogers Co
Mora, MN..........................800-279-8081
Carrier Vibrating Equip Inc
Louisville, KY....................502-969-3171
Casso-Solar Corporation
Nanuet, NY........................800-988-4455
Columbus Instruments
Columbus, OH......................800-669-5011
Commercial Dehydrator Systems
Eugene, OR........................800-369-4283
Davron Technologies Inc
Chattanooga, TN...................423-870-1888
Delux Manufacturing Co
Kearney, NE.......................800-658-3240
Dito Dean Food Prep
Charlotte, NC.....................866-449-4200
Dupps Co
Germantown, OH....................937-855-0623
Fernholtz Engineering
Van Nuys, CA......................818-785-5800
FFI Corporation
Assumption, IL....................217-226-5100
Fitzpatrick Co
Elmhurst, IL......................630-592-4425
Fluid Air Inc
Aurora, IL........................630-665-5001
Fluid Energy Processing & Eqpt
Hatfield, PA......................215-368-2510
French Oil Mill Machinery Co
Piqua, OH.........................937-773-3420
Gaston County Dyeing Mach Co
Mt Holly, NC......................704-822-5000
Glatt Air Techniques Inc
Ramsey, NJ........................201-825-8700
Hebeler Corp
Tonawanda, NY.....................800-486-4709
Heinzen Sales
Gilroy, CA........................408-842-6678
Idaho Steel Products Inc
Idaho Falls, ID...................208-522-1275
International Reserve Equipment Corporation
Clarendon Hills, IL...............708-531-0680
K & L Intl
Ontario, CA.......................888-598-5588
Komline-Sanderson Engineering
Peapack, NJ.......................800-225-5457
Lanly Co
Cleveland, OH.....................216-731-1115
LIST
Acton, MA.........................978-635-9521
Littleford Day
Florence, KY......................800-365-8555
M-E-C Co
Neodesha, KS......................620-325-2673
Mannhart
Fort Worth, TX....................817-421-0100

Marriott Walker Corporation
Bingham Farms, MI.................248-644-6868
MCD Technologies
Tacoma, WA........................253-476-0968
National Drying Machry Co Inc
Philadelphia, PA..................215-464-6070
Nemeth Engineering Assoc
Crestwood, KY.....................502-241-1502
Paget Equipment Co
Marshfield, WI....................715-384-3158
Patterson Industries
Scarborough, ON...................800-336-1110
Patterson-Kelley   Hars Company
East Stroudsburg, PA...............570-421-7500
Paul O. Abbe
Bensenville, IL...................630-350-2200
Paxton Products Inc
Blue Ash, OH......................800-441-7475
Plainview Milk Products
Plainview, MN.....................800-356-5606
Procedyne Corp
New Brunswick, NJ.................732-249-8347
Radio Frequency Co Inc
Millis, MA........................508-376-9555
Raytheon Co
Waltham, MA.......................781-522-3000
Sandvik Process Systems
Sweden, NJ........................973-790-1600
Shanzer Grain Dryer
Sioux Falls, SD...................800-843-9887
Shivvers
Corydon, IA.......................641-872-1007
SP Industries Inc
Warminster, PA....................800-523-2327
Spray Drying
Sykesville, MD....................410-549-8090
Steri Technologies Inc
Bohemia, NY.......................800-253-7140
Thermex Thermatron
Louisville, KY....................502-493-1299
Ultrafilter
Norcross, GA......................800-543-3634
United Mc Gill Corp
Groveport, OH.....................614-829-1200
Van Air Systems
Lake City, PA.....................800-840-9906
Vector Corp
Marion, IA........................319-377-8263
Vortron Smokehouse/Ovens
Iron Ridge, WI....................800-874-1949
Witte Co Inc
Washington, NJ....................908-689-6500
Wittemann Company
Palm Coast, FL....................386-445-4200
Wyssmont Co Inc
Fort Lee, NJ......................201-947-4600
Zeeco Inc
Broken Arrow, OK..................918-258-8551

Freeze

Apollo Sheet Metal
Kennewick, WA.....................509-586-1104
Berg Chilling Systems
Toronto, ON, ON...................416-755-2221
Berndorf Belt Technology USA
Gilberts, IL......................800-393-8450
SP Industries Inc
Warminster, PA....................800-523-2327

Fruit

Ametek Technical & Industrial Products
Kent, OH..........................215-256-6601
Apollo Sheet Metal
Kennewick, WA.....................509-586-1104
BNW Industries
Tippecanoe, IN....................574-353-7855
Davron Technologies Inc
Chattanooga, TN...................423-870-1888
Globe Machine
Tacoma, WA........................800-523-6575
Goodnature Products
Orchard Park, NY..................800-875-3381
Paxton Products Inc
Blue Ash, OH......................800-441-7475
Sandvik Process Systems
Sweden, NJ........................973-790-1600

Grain

Apollo Sheet Metal
Kennewick, WA.....................509-586-1104

Chief Industries
Kearney, NE.......................800-359-8833
Davenport Machine
Rock Island, IL...................309-786-1500
Davron Technologies Inc
Chattanooga, TN...................423-870-1888
Delux Manufacturing Co
Kearney, NE.......................800-658-3240
DMC-David Manufacturing Company
Mason City, IA....................641-424-7010
Driall Inc
Attica, IN........................765-295-2255
FFI Corporation
Assumption, IL....................217-226-5100
Forster & Son
Ada, OK...........................580-332-6021
Grain Machinery Mfg Corp
Miami, FL.........................305-620-2525
NECO/Nebraska Engineering
Omaha, NE.........................800-367-6208
Patterson-Kelley   Hars Company
East Stroudsburg, PA...............570-421-7500
Sandvik Process Systems
Sweden, NJ........................973-790-1600
Shanzer Grain Dryer
Sioux Falls, SD...................800-843-9887
Shivvers
Corydon, IA.......................641-872-1007

Spray

A & B Process Systems Corp
Stratford, WI.....................888-258-2789
Davron Technologies Inc
Chattanooga, TN...................423-870-1888
Evaporator Dryer Technologies
Hammond, WI.......................715-796-2313
Food Resources International
Concord, ON.......................905-482-8967
Gardner Denver Inc.
Milwaukee, WI
Marriott Walker Corporation
Bingham Farms, MI.................248-644-6868
Niro
Hudson, WI........................715-386-9371
Paget Equipment Co
Marshfield, WI....................715-384-3158
Spray Drying
Sykesville, MD....................410-549-8090
Spraying Systems Company
Wheaton, IL.......................630-655-5000
Stainless Fabrication Inc
Springfield, MO...................800-397-8265

Dumpers

American Food Equipment Company
Hayward, CA.......................510-783-0255
Andgar Corp
Ferndale, WA......................360-366-9900
Apache Stainless Equipment
Beaver Dam, WI....................800-444-0398
Automated Flexible Conveyors
Clifton, NJ.......................800-694-7271
Bridge Machine Company
Palmyra, NJ.......................877-754-1800
Cecor
Verona, WI........................800-356-9042
Cleasby Manufacturing Co
San Francisco, CA.................800-253-2729
Coastline Equipment Inc
Bellingham, WA....................360-734-8509
Cozzini Inc
Algona, IA........................888-295-1116
Cugar Machine Co
Fort Worth, TX....................817-927-0411
Custom Food Machinery
Stockton, CA......................209-463-4343
Dynamet
Kalamazoo, MI.....................269-385-0006
Flodin
Moses Lake, WA....................509-766-2996
Food Processing Equipment Co
Santa Fe Springs, CA..............562-802-3727
GEM Equipment Of Oregon Inc
Woodburn, OR......................503-982-9902
Heinzen Sales
Gilroy, CA........................408-842-6678
Jesco Industries
Litchfield, MI....................800-455-0019
Kinetic Equipment Company
Appleton, WI......................806-293-4471

MAF Industries Inc
Traver, CA.................559-897-2905
Materials Transportation Co
Temple, TX.................800-433-3110
Midwest Metalcraft & Equipment
Windsor, MO.................800-647-3167
Palace Packaging Machines Inc
Downingtown, PA.................610-873-7252
Phelps Industries
Little Rock, AR.................501-568-5550
Pucel Enterprises Inc
Cleveland, OH.................800-336-4986
Reiser
Canton, MA.................734-821-1290
Screw Conveyor Corp
Hammond, IN.................219-931-1450
SP Industries
Hopkins, MI.................800-592-5959
TWM Manufacturing
Leamington, ON.................888-495-4831
Uhrden
Sugarcreek, OH.................800-852-2411
Vanmark Equipment
Creston, IA.................800-523-6261
Vertical Systems Intl
Lakeside Park, KY.................859-485-9650

Egg Processing & Cleaning

A & B Process Systems Corp
Stratford, WI.................888-258-2789
ADSI Inc
Durant, OK.................580-924-4461
Behrens Manufacturing LLC
Winona, MN.................507-454-4664
Brush Research Mfg Co Inc
Los Angeles, CA.................323-261-6162
Davidson's Safest Choice Eggs
Lansing, IL.................800-410-7619
Diamond Automation
Farmington Hills, MI.................248-426-9394
Eggboxes Inc
Deerfield Beach, FL.................800-326-6667
H. Gartenberg & Company
Buffalo Grove, IL.................847-821-7590
Hayon Manufacturing
Las Vegas, NV.................702-562-3377
KL Products, Ltd.
London, ON.................800-388-5744
Kuhl Corporation
Flemington, NJ.................908-782-5696

Equipment

Advance Energy Technologies
Halfmoon, NY.................800-724-0198
Ashcroft Inc
Stratford, CT.................800-328-8258
Eirich Machines
Gurnee, IL.................847-336-2444
Ever Extruder Co
Festus, MO.................636-937-8830
Famco Automatic Sausage Linkers
Pittsburgh, PA.................412-241-6410
Gea Process Engineering Inc
Columbia, MD.................410-997-8700
Graybill Machines Inc
Lititz, PA.................717-626-5221
Gridpath
Stony Creek, ON.................905-643-0955
I. Fm Usa Inc.
Franklin Park, IL.................866-643-6872
Lyco Manufacturing
Wausau, WI.................715-845-7867
Lyco Manufacturing Inc
Columbus, WI.................920-623-4152
M-Vac Systems Inc
Bluffdale, UT.................801-523-3962
Marlen Research Corporation
Shawnee Mission, KS.................913-888-3333
MPS North America, Inc.
Lenexa, KS.................913-310-0055
Murzan Inc
Peachtree Cor, GA.................770-448-0583
Paramount Packaging Corp
Melville, NY.................516-333-8100
Reiser
Canton, MA.................734-821-1290
Rheon, U.S.A.
Irvine, CA.................949-768-1900
Risco USA Corp
South Easton, MA.................888-474-7267

Ross Industries Inc
Midland, VA.................540-439-3271
Ryowa Company America
Elk Grove Village, IL.................800-700-9692
Stephan Machinery GmbH
Mandelein, IL.................847-247-0182
Sympak, Inc.
Mundelein, IL.................847-247-0182
Terlet USA
Swedesboro, NJ.................856-241-9970

Espresso & Cappuccino Processing

Acorto
Bellevue, WA.................800-995-9019
Ascaso
Bensenville, IL.................630-350-0066
Astoria General Espresso
Greensboro, NC.................336-393-0224
Boston's Best Coffee Roasters
South Easton, MA.................800-898-8393
Espresso Roma
Emeryville, CA.................800-437-1668
Formula Espresso
Brooklyn, NY.................718-834-8724
Gabriella Imports
Cleveland, OH.................800-544-8117
Gensaco Marketing
New York, NY.................800-506-1935
Grindmaster-Cecilware Corp
Louisville, KY.................800-695-4500
Lavazza Premium Coffees
New York, NY.................212-725-9196
Michaelo Espresso
Seattle, WA.................800-545-2883
Nuova Distribution Centre
Ferndale, WA.................360-366-2226
Pasquini Espresso Co
Los Angeles, CA.................800-724-6225
Pier 1 Imports
Woodcliff Lake, NJ.................800-448-9993
Saeco
Cleveland, OH.................440-528-2000
Schaerer USA Corp
Tustin, CA.................888-989-3004
Steel Products
Marion, IA.................800-333-9451
Supramatic
Toronto, ON.................877-465-2883
The Carriage Works
Klamath Falls, OR.................541-882-0700
Wega USA
Bensenville, IL.................630-350-0066
Wells Manufacturing Company
St. Louis, MO.................888-356-5362

Evaporators

Fruit Juice

A & B Process Systems Corp
Stratford, WI.................888-258-2789
Berkshire PPM
Litchfield, CT.................860-567-3118
Central Fabricators Inc
Cincinnati, OH.................800-909-8265
Custom Food Machinery
Stockton, CA.................209-463-4343
Dedert Corporation
Olympia Fields, IL.................708-747-7000
Globe Machine
Tacoma, WA.................800-523-6575
Goodnature Products
Orchard Park, NY.................800-875-3381
L&A Process Systems
Modesto, CA.................209-581-0205
South Valley Mfg Inc
Gilroy, CA.................408-842-5457
Washington Frontier
Grandview, WA.................509-469-7662

Milk

A & B Process Systems Corp
Stratford, WI.................888-258-2789
Central Fabricators Inc
Cincinnati, OH.................800-909-8265
LIST
Acton, MA.................978-635-9521
Marriott Walker Corporation
Bingham Farms, MI.................248-644-6868
Membrane System Specialist Inc
Wisconsin Rapids, WI.................715-421-2333

Niro
Hudson, WI.................715-386-9371

Extractors

Fruit & Vegetable Juice

A.K. Robins
Baltimore, MD.................800-486-9656
Berkshire PPM
Litchfield, CT.................860-567-3118
Brown International Corp LLC
Winter Haven, FL.................863-299-2111
Chop-Rite Two Inc
Harleysville, PA.................800-683-5858
Custom Food Machinery
Stockton, CA.................209-463-4343
Dorton Incorporated
Arlington Hts, IL.................800-299-8600
Eurodib
Champlain, NY.................888-956-6866
French Oil Mill Machinery Co
Piqua, OH.................937-773-3420
Globe Machine
Tacoma, WA.................800-523-6575
Goodnature Products
Orchard Park, NY.................800-875-3381
Hollymatic Corp
Countryside, IL.................708-579-3700
JBT Food Tech
Lakeland, FL.................863-683-5411
Juice Tree
Omaha, NE.................714-891-4425
Mandeville Company
Minneapolis, MN.................800-328-8490
Mulligan Associates
Mequon, WI.................800-627-2886
Nutrifaster Inc
Seattle, WA.................800-800-2641
Omega Products Inc
Harrisburg, PA.................800-633-3401
Ruby Manufacturing & Sales
South El Monte, CA.................626-443-1171
Technium
Medford, NJ.................609-702-5910
Waring Products
Torrington, CT.................800-492-7464
Washington Frontier
Grandview, WA.................509-469-7662

Extruders

Bogner Industries
Ronkonkoma, NY.................631-981-5123
Polar Process
Plattsville, ON.................877-896-8077
Reiser
Canton, MA.................734-821-1290

Fillers

Bogner Industries
Ronkonkoma, NY.................631-981-5123
Edhard Corp
Hackettstown, NJ.................888-334-2731
Fogg Filler Co
Holland, MI.................616-786-3644
G & F Mfg
Oak Lawn, IL.................800-282-1574
HAMBA USA, Inc
Saint Peters, MO
Handtmann Inc
Lake Forest, IL.................800-477-3585
Innovative Foods, Inc.
South San Francisco, CA.................650-871-8912
Niro Inc
Hudson, WI.................715-386-9371
Raque Food Systems
Louisville, KY.................502-267-9641
Reiser
Canton, MA.................734-821-1290
Risco USA Corp
South Easton, MA.................888-474-7267
SeamTech
Acampo, CA.................209-464-4610
Statco Engineering
Huntington Beach, CA.................800-421-0362
T D Sawvel Co
Maple Plain, MN.................877-488-1816
Terlet USA
Swedesboro, NJ.................856-241-9970

Filters

Coffee

Andex Corp
Rochester, NY 585-328-3790
Boston's Best Coffee Roasters
South Easton, MA 800-898-8393
Bunn-O-Matic Corp
Springfield, IL 800-352-2866
Chemex Division/International Housewares Corporation
Chicopee, MA 800-243-6399
Coffee Sock Company
Eugene, OR 541-344-7698
Kennedy's Specialty Sewing
Erin, ON 519-833-9306
Keurig Dr Pepper
Plano, TX 800-696-5891
Lamports Filter Media
Cleveland, OH 216-881-2050
Melitta Canada
Vaughan, ON 800-565-4882
Melitta USA Inc
Clearwater, FL 888-635-4880
Rockline Industries
Sheboygan, WI 800-558-7790
Superior Products Company
Saint Paul, MN 800-328-9800
Tops Manufacturing Co
Darien, CT 203-655-9367
UniPro Foodservice, Inc.
Atlanta, GA 770-952-0871

Food

Alexander Machinery
Spartanburg, SC 864-963-3624
Avalon Manufacturer
Corona, CA 800-676-3040
Baker Hughes
Houston, TX
Cambridge Intl. Inc.
Cambridge, MD 800-638-9560
Crispy Lite
St. Louis, MO 888-356-5362
Eaton Filtration, LLC
Tinton Falls, NJ 800-859-9212
Ertelalsop
Kingston, NY 800-553-7835
Falcon Fabricators Inc
Nashville, TN 615-832-0027
Filtercorp
Fresno, CA 800-473-4526
Globe Machine
Tacoma, WA 800-523-6575
Goodnature Products
Orchard Park, NY 800-875-3381
Greig Filters Inc
Lafayette, LA 800-456-0177
Gusmer Enterprises Inc
Fresno, CA 866-213-1131
International Reserve Equipment Corporation
Clarendon Hills, IL 708-531-0680
Komline-Sanderson Engineering
Peapack, NJ 800-225-5457
L.C. Thompson Company
Kenosha, WI 800-558-4018
Micropure Filtration Inc
Mound, MN 800-654-7873
Mies Products
West Bend, WI 800-480-6437
Pall Filtron
Northborough, MA 800-345-8766
Piab Vacuum Products
Hingham, MA 800-321-7422
Prince Castle Inc
Carol Stream, IL 800-722-7853
Purolator Facet Inc
Greensboro, NC 800-852-4449
Refractron Technologies Corp
Newark, NY 315-331-6222
Sparkler Filters Inc
Conroe, TX 936-756-4471
Steri Technologies Inc
Bohemia, NY 800-253-7140
Ultrafilter
Norcross, GA 800-543-3634
Ultrafryer Systems Inc
San Antonio, TX 800-545-9189
Williams & Mettle Company
Houston, TX 800-526-4954
Womack International Inc
Vallejo, CA 707-647-2370

Fruit & Vegetable Juice

Berkshire PPM
Litchfield, CT 860-567-3118
Conwed Global Netting Sltns
Roanoke, VA 800-368-3610
Delta Pure Filtration Corp
Ashland, VA 800-785-9450
F.P. Smith Wire Cloth Company
Northlake, IL 800-323-6842
Filtration Systems
Sunrise, FL 954-572-2700
Globe Machine
Tacoma, WA 800-523-6575
Goodnature Products
Orchard Park, NY 800-875-3381
Komline-Sanderson Engineering
Peapack, NJ 800-225-5457
Lenser Filtration
Lakewood, NJ 732-370-1600
Metlar Us
Riverhead, NY 631-252-5574
Refractron Technologies Corp
Newark, NY 315-331-6222
Washington Frontier
Grandview, WA 509-469-7662

Grease

Component Hardware Group Inc
Lakewood, NJ 800-526-3694
Flame Gard
Lakewood, NJ 800-526-3694
Trine Rolled Moulding Corp
Bronx, NY 800-223-8075

Paper

Andex Corp
Rochester, NY 585-328-3790
Avery Filter Company
Westwood, NJ 201-666-9664

Filtration and Separation

Wes Tech Engineering Inc
Salt Lake City, UT 801-265-1000

Fish Cleaning

Coastline Equipment Inc
Bellingham, WA 360-734-8509
Crane Research & Engineering
Hampton, VA 757-826-1707
Design Technology Corporation
Billerica, MA 978-663-7000
Diversified Metal Engineering
Charlottetown, PE 902-628-6900
Fishmore
Melbourne, FL 321-723-4751
Skrmetta Machinery Corporation
New Orleans, LA 504-488-4413
Steamway Corporation
Scottsburg, IN 800-259-8171
TWM Manufacturing
Leamington, ON 888-495-4831

Flakers or Flaking Drums

Biro Manufacturing Co
Lakeside Marblhd, OH 419-798-4451
Buffalo Technologies Corporation
Buffalo, NY 800-332-2419
CPM Roskamp Champion
Waterloo, IA 800-366-2563
Ferrell-Ross
Amarillo, TX 800-299-9051
General Machinery Corp
Sheboygan, WI 888-243-6622
Hoshizaki America Inc
Peachtree City, GA 800-438-6087
Lauhoff Corporation
Detroit, MI 313-259-0027

Flour Mill

Buffalo Technologies Corporation
Buffalo, NY 800-332-2419
Commodity Traders International
Trilla, IL 217-235-4322
Forster & Son
Ada, OK 580-332-6021

Food Processing

915 Labs
Centennial, CO 855-915-5227
Advance Energy Technologies
Halfmoon, NY 800-724-0198
Alard Equipment Corp
Williamson, NY 315-589-4511
Amfec Inc
Hayward, CA 510-780-0134
Anderson Chemical Co
Litchfield, MN 320-693-2477
Anritsu Industrial Solutions
Elk Grove Vlg, IL 847-419-9729
Axiflow Technologies, Inc.
Kennesaw, GA 770-795-1195
Bizerba USA
Piscataway, NJ 732-565-6000
Bogner Industries
Ronkonkoma, NY 631-981-5123
CPM Century Extrusion
Traverse City, MI 231-947-6400
CPM Roskamp Champion
Waterloo, IA 800-366-2563
CPM Wolverine Proctor LLC
Horsham, PA 215-443-5200
Cresco Food Technologies
Cresco, IA 563-547-4241
Eischen Enterprises
Fresno, CA 559-834-0013
Ennio International
Aurora, IL 630-851-5808
Evonik Corporation   North America
Parsippany, NJ 973-929-8000
F R Drake Co
Waynesboro, VA 540-949-6215
Fourinox Inc
Green Bay, WI 920-336-0621
Frost ET Inc
Grand Rapids, MI 800-253-9382
Gea Process Engineering Inc
Columbia, MD 410-997-8700
Gridpath, Inc.
Stony Creek, ON 905-643-0955
Hughes Co
Columbus, WI 920-623-2000
Incomec-Cerex Industries
Fairfield, CT 203-335-1050
Insect-O-Cutor Inc
Stone Mountain, GA 800-966-8480
JCS Controls, Inc.
Rochester, NY 585-227-5910
Kasel Engineering
Dayton, OH 937-854-8875
KL Products, Ltd.
London, ON 800-388-5744
Lechler Inc
St Charles, IL 800-777-2926
Libra Technical Center
Metuchen, NJ 732-321-5200
Loeb Equipment
Chicago, IL 773-496-5720
Loos Machine
Colby, WI 715-223-2844
Lyco Manufacturing
Wausau, WI 715-845-7867
Marel Food Systems, Inc.
Lenexa, KS 913-888-9110
Marlen
Riverside, MO 913-888-3333
Microthermics
Raleigh, NC 919-878-8045
Mtc Food Equipment
Poulsbo, WA 360-697-6319
Qualtech
Quebec, QC 888-339-3801
Raque Food Systems
Louisville, KY 502-267-9641
Reiser
Canton, MA 734-821-1290
Ripon Manufacturing Co Inc
Ripon, CA 800-800-1232
Risco USA Corp
South Easton, MA 888-474-7267
Scott Process Equipment & Controls
Guelph, ON 888-343-5421
SICK Inc
Bloomington, MN 800-325-7425
Simply Manufacturing
Prairie Du Sac, WI 608-643-6656
Sperling Boss
Sperling, MB 877-626-3401

Statco Engineering
Huntington Beach, CA 800-421-0362
Stone Enterprises Inc.
Omaha, NE 877-653-0500
Superior Products Company
Saint Paul, MN 800-328-9800
Thunderbird Food Machinery
Blaine, WA 866-875-6868
Ultra Process Systems
Oak Ridge, TN 865-483-2772
Warren Rupp Inc
Mansfield, OH 419-524-8388
Washington Frontier
Grandview, WA 509-469-7662
Weiler Equipment
Whitewater, WI 800-558-9507
Young & Associates
Kenosha, WI 262-657-6394

Food

A & B Process Systems Corp
Stratford, WI 888-258-2789
A C Horn & Co Sheet Metal
Dallas, TX .800-657-6155
A C Tool & Machine Co
Louisville, KY 502-447-5505
A T Ferrell Co Inc
Bluffton, IN 800-248-8318
A&J Mixing International
Oakville, ON 800-668-3470
A&M Industries
Sioux Falls, SD 800-888-2615
A&M Process Equipment
Ajax, ON 905-619-8001
A.K. Robins
Baltimore, MD 800-486-9656
Aaburco Inc
Grass Valley, CA 800-533-7437
Aaron Equipment Co Div Areco
Bensenville, IL 630-350-2200
ABCO Industries Limited
Lunenburg, NS 866-634-8821
Abel Pumps
Sewickley, PA 412-741-3222
ABI Limited
Concord, ON 800-297-8666
ABO Industries
San Diego, CA 858-566-9750
Acra Electric Corporation
Tulsa, OK .800-223-4328
Acraloc Corp
Oak Ridge, TN 865-483-1368
Acrison Inc
Moonachie, NJ 800-422-4266
ADMIX
Manchester, NH 800-466-2369
ADSI Inc
Durant, OK 580-924-4461
Aerotech Enterprise Inc
Chesterland, OH 440-729-2616
AEW Thurne
Lake Zurich, IL 800-239-7297
Agricultural Data Systems
Laguna Niguel, CA 800-328-2246
Albion Machine & Tool Co
Albion, MI .517-629-9135
Alfa Laval Ashbrook Simon-Hartley
Houston, TX 713-934-3160
Alfa Laval Inc
Richmond, VA 866-253-2528
Alkar Rapid Pak
Lodi, WI 608-592-3211
Allegheny Bradford Corp
Bradford, PA 800-542-0650
Allen Gauge & Tool Co
Pittsburgh, PA 412-241-6410
Alloy Hardfacing & Engineering
Jordan, MN 800-328-8408
Allpax Products
Covington, LA 888-893-9277
Alpha Omega Technology
Cedar Knolls, NJ 800-442-1969
ALPI Food Preparation Equipment
Bolton, ON 800-928-2574
Altman Industries
Gray, GA 478-986-3116
AM-Mac
Fairfield, NJ 800-829-2018
American Extrusion Intl
South Beloit, IL 815-624-6616
American Food Equipment Company
Hayward, CA 510-783-0255

American Housewares
Bronx, NY 718-665-9500
American Manufacturing-Engrng
Cleveland, OH 800-822-9402
American Metal Stamping
Brooklyn, NY 718-384-1500
Ametek Technical & Industrial Products
Kent, OH .215-256-6601
AMF Bakery Systems Corp
Richmond, VA 800-225-3771
AMF CANADA
Sherbrooke, QC 800-255-3869
Anderson International Corp
Stow, OH .800-336-4730
Andgar Corp
Ferndale, WA 360-366-9900
ANDRITZ Inc
Muncy, PA 704-943-4343
Anhydro Inc
Olympia Fields, IL 708-747-7000
Apache Stainless Equipment
Beaver Dam, WI 800-444-0398
APEC
Lake Odessa, MI 616-374-1000
API Heat Transfer Inc
Buffalo, NY 877-274-4328
Apollo Sheet Metal
Kennewick, WA 509-586-1104
Applied Chemical Technology
Florence, AL 800-228-3217
APV Americas
Delavan, WI 800-252-5200
Architectural Sheet Metals LLC
Cleveland, OH 216-361-9952
Arcobaleno Pasta Machines
Lancaster, PA 800-875-7096
Arde Inc
Carlstadt, NJ 800-909-6070
Arrow Tank Co
Buffalo, NY 716-893-7200
Artisan Controls Corp
Randolph, NJ 800-457-4950
Artisan Industries
Waltham, MA 781-893-6800
Ashlock Co
San Leandro, CA 510-351-0560
Astoria General Espresso
Greensboro, NC 336-393-0224
Atlanta SharpTech
Peachtree City, GA 800-462-7297
Atlas Minerals & Chemicals Inc
Mertztown, PA 800-523-8269
Atlas Pacific Engineering
Pueblo, CO 719-948-3040
Auger Fab
Exton, PA .800-334-1529
Automated Food Systems
Waxahachie, TX 469-517-0470
Avestin
Ottawa, ON 888-283-7846
Ay Machine Company
Ephrata, PA 717-733-0335
Ayr King Corp
Louisville, KY 866-266-6290
B & P Process Equipment
Saginaw, MI 989-757-1300
B C Holland Inc
Dousman, WI 262-965-2939
B T Engineering Inc
Bala Cynwyd, PA 610-664-9500
B.A.G. Corporation
Richardson, TX 800-331-9200
Backwoods Smoker Inc
Shreveport, LA 318-220-0380
Bake Star
Somerset, WI 763-427-7611
Baker Hughes
Houston, TX
Bakery Machinery Dealers
Holbrook, NY 631-567-6666
Baking Machines
Livermore, CA 925-449-3369
Baldewein Company
Lake Forrest, IL 800-424-5544
Be & Sco
San Antonio, TX 800-683-0928
Bean Machines
Sonoma, CA 707-996-0706
BEI
South Haven, MI 800-364-7425
Belshaw Adamatic Bakery Group
Auburn, WA 800-578-2547

Bematek Systems Inc
Salem, MA 877-236-2835
Ben H. Anderson Manufacturers
Morrisonville, WI 608-846-5474
Bepex International LLC
Minneapolis, MN 800-607-2470
Berg Chilling Systems
Toronto, ON 416-755-2221
Berkshire PPM
Litchfield, CT 860-567-3118
Bermar America
Malvern, PA 888-289-5838
Best & Donovan
Blue Ash, OH 800-553-2378
Bete Fog Nozzle Inc
Greenfield, MA 800-235-0049
Bettcher Industries Inc
Wakeman, OH 800-321-8763
Bettendorf Stanford Inc
Salem, IL .800-548-2253
BFM Equipment Sales
Fall River, WI 920-484-3341
Bijur Lubricating Corporation
Morrisville, NC 800-631-0168
Billington Welding & Mfg Inc
Modesto, CA 800-932-9312
Biomerieux Inc
Durham, NC 800-682-2666
Biro Manufacturing Co
Lakeside Marblhd, OH 419-798-4451
Blackmer Co
Grand Rapids, MI 616-241-1611
Blakeslee, Inc.
Addison, IL 630-532-5021
Bloomfield Industries
St. Louis, MO 888-356-5362
Blue Tech
Hickory, NC 828-324-5900
BluMetric Environmental Inc.
Ottawa, ON 613-839-3053
Bmh Equipment Inc
Sacramento, CA 800-350-8828
Boehringer Mfg. Co. Inc.
Felton, CA 800-630-8665
Bonnot Co
Akron, OH 330-896-6544
Bowers Process Equipment
Stratford, ON 800-567-3223
Branson Ultrasonics Corp
Danbury, CT 203-796-0400
Breddo Likwifier
Kansas City, MO 800-669-4092
Bridge Machine Company
Palmyra, NJ 877-754-1800
Brothers Metal Products
Santa Ana, CA 714-972-3008
Brower
Houghton, IA 800-553-1791
Brown International Corp LLC
Winter Haven, FL 863-299-2111
Buffalo Technologies Corporation
Buffalo, NY 800-332-2419
Buhler Inc.
Plymouth, MN 763-847-9900
Bulldog Factory Svc LLC
Madison Heights, MI 248-541-3500
Bunting Magnetics Co
Newton, KS 800-835-2526
Buss America
Carol Stream, IL 630-933-9100
BVL Controls
Bois-Des-Filion, QC 866-285-2668
C E Rogers Co
Mora, MN .800-279-8081
C H Babb Co Inc
Raynham, MA 508-977-0600
C S Bell Co
Tiffin, OH .888-958-6381
C. Cretors & Company
Chicago, IL 800-228-1885
Cal-Coast Manufacturing
Turlock, CA 209-668-9378
Cameron Intl. Corp.
Houston, TX 281-285-4376
Camerons Brewing Co.
Oakville, ON 905-849-8282
Capway Conveyor Systems Inc
York, PA 877-222-7929
Carolina Knife
Asheville, NC 800-520-5030
Carrier Vibrating Equip Inc
Louisville, KY 502-969-3171

Carter-Day International Inc
Minneapolis, MN 763-571-1000
Casa Herrera
Pomona, CA 800-624-3916
Casso-Solar Corporation
Nanuet, NY 800-988-4455
Champion Trading Corporation
Marlboro, NJ 732-780-4200
Charles Ross & Son Co
Hauppauge, NY 800-243-7677
Chart Inc
New Prague, MN 800-428-3777
Chemicolloid Laboratories, Inc.
New Hyde Park, NY 516-747-2666
Chester-Jensen Co., Inc.
Chester, PA 800-685-3750
Chicago Stainless Eqpt Inc
Palm City, FL 800-927-8575
Chil-Con Products
Brantford, ON 800-263-0086
Chocolate Concepts
Hartville, OH 330-877-3322
Chop-Rite Two Inc
Harleysville, PA 800-683-5858
Cleveland-Eastern Mixers
Clinton, CT 800-243-1188
Clextral USA
Tampa, FL 813-854-4434
CMC America Corporation
Joliet, IL 815-726-4337
Coastline Equipment Inc
Bellingham, WA 360-734-8509
Cobatco
Peoria, IL. 800-426-2282
Coburn Company
Whitewater, WI. 800-776-7042
Codema
Maple Grove, MN. 763-428-2266
Columbus Instruments
Columbus, OH 800-669-5011
Commercial Dehydrator Systems
Eugene, OR. 800-369-4283
Commercial Manufacturing
Fresno, CA 559-237-1855
Commodity Traders International
Trilla, IL 217-235-4322
Computer Controlled Machines
Pueblo, CO 719-948-9500
Convay Systems
Minnetonka, MN. 800-334-1099
Cook & Beals Inc
Loup City, NE 308-745-0154
Corenco
Santa Rosa, CA. 888-267-3626
Cornell Machine Co
Springfield, NJ 973-379-6860
Cornell Pump Company
Portland, OR 503-653-0330
Cozzini Inc
Algona, IA. 888-295-1116
Cozzini LLC
Chicago, IL 773-478-9700
CPM Roskamp Champion
Waterloo, IA 800-366-2563
Crane Pumps & Systems
Piqua, OH 937-778-8947
Crane Research & Engineering
Hampton, VA 757-826-1707
CRC Inc
Council Bluffs, IA. 712-323-9477
Croll Reynolds Inc
Parsippany, NJ. 908-232-4200
Crown Controls Inc.
Charlotte, NC 800-541-7874
Crown Iron Works Company
Roseville, MN. 888-703-7500
Cugar Machine Co
Fort Worth, TX 817-927-0411
Custom Fabricating & Repair
Marshfield, WI. 800-236-8773
Custom Food Machinery
Stockton, CA. 209-463-4343
Custom Metal Crafts
Springfield, MO 417-862-9324
Custom Pools Inc
Portsmouth, NH 800-323-9509
Cutrite Company
Fremont, OH 800-928-8748
D & S Mfg
Auburn, MA 508-799-7812
D A Berther Inc
Milwaukee, WI. 877-357-9622

D.R. McClain & Son
Commerce, CA 800-428-2263
Dadant & Sons Inc
Hamilton, IL 888-922-1293
Daily Printing Inc
Plymouth, MN. 800-622-6596
Daleco
West Chester, PA. 610-429-0181
Damrow Company
Fond Du Lac, WI 800-236-1501
Davenport Machine
Rock Island, IL 309-786-1500
Davron Technologies Inc
Chattanooga, TN. 423-870-1888
DBE Inc
Concord, ON 800-461-5313
DCI, Inc.
St Cloud, MN 320-252-8200
Dedert Corporation
Olympia Fields, IL 708-747-7000
Defreeze Corporation
Southborough, MA 508-485-8512
Dehyco Company
Memphis, TN 901-774-3322
Delta Machine & Maufacturing
St Rose, LA. 504-949-8304
Delux Manufacturing Co
Kearney, NE 800-658-3240
Demaco
Ridgewood, NY
Design Technology Corporation
Billerica, MA 978-663-7000
Designpro Engineering
Clearwater, MN. 800-221-4144
Diamond Automation
Farmington Hills, MI 248-426-9394
Dipwell Co
Northampton, MA. 413-587-4673
Direct South
Macon, GA 478-746-3518
Dito Dean Food Prep
Charlotte, NC 866-449-4200
Diversified Metal Engineering
Charlottetown, PE. 902-628-6900
Dixie Canner Machine Shop
Athens, GA 706-549-0592
Doering Co
Clear Lake, MN 320-743-2276
Doering Machines Inc
San Francisco, CA 415-526-2131
Dole Refrigerating Co
Lewisburg, TN 800-251-8990
Dorton Incorporated
Arlington Hts, IL 800-299-8600
Driall Inc
Attica, IN. 765-295-2255
Drum-Mates Inc.
Lumberton, NJ 800-621-3786
DSW Converting Knives
Birmingham, AL 205-322-2021
DT Converting Technologies - Stokes
Bristol, PA. 800-635-0036
Dunbar Manufacturing Co
South Elgin, IL 847-741-6394
Dunkley International Inc
Kalamazoo, MI 800-666-1264
Duplex Mill & Mfg Co
Springfield, OH. 937-325-5555
Dupps Co
Germantown, OH 937-855-0623
Duralite Inc
Riverton, CT 888-432-8797
Dutchess Bakers' Machinery Co
Superior, WI. 800-777-4498
Dynamic Automation LTD
Simi Valley, CA. 805-584-8476
Eaton Sales & Service
Denver, CO 800-208-2657
Ecklund-Harrison Technologies
Fort Myers, FL 239-936-6032
Eclipse Systems Inc
Milpitas, CA 408-263-2201
Edhard Corp
Hackettstown, NJ 888-334-2731
Edlund Co
Burlington, VT 800-772-2126
Eirich Machines
Gurnee, IL. 847-336-2444
EKATO Corporation
St Ramsey, NJ. 201-825-4684
Electro Cam Corp
Roscoe, IL. 800-228-5487

Elliott Manufacturing Co Inc
Fresno, CA 559-233-6235
Emerald City Closets Inc
Auburn, WA 800-925-1521
Emery Thompson Machine &Supply Company
Brooksville, FL 718-588-7300
Empire Bakery Equipment
Hicksville, NY 800-878-4070
Engineered Products Group
Madison, WI. 800-626-3111
Equipment Specialists Inc
Manassas, VA 703-361-2227
Ertelalsop
Kingston, NY 800-553-7835
Esco Products Inc
Houston, TX 800-966-5514
Et Oakes Corp
Hauppauge, NY 631-232-0002
Eurodib
Champlain, NY 888-956-6866
Evaporator Dryer Technologies
Hammond, WI. 715-796-2313
Eveready Automation
Frederick, PA 610-754-1775
Exact Mixing Systems Inc
Memphis, TN 901-362-8501
Expert Industries Inc
Brooklyn, NY 718-434-6060
F N Smith Corp
Oregon, IL. 815-732-2171
F.B. Pease Company
Rochester, NY 585-475-1870
Falcon Fabricators Inc
Nashville, TN 615-832-0027
Feldmeier Equipment Inc
Syracuse, NY 315-454-8608
Fernholtz Engineering
Van Nuys, CA 818-785-5800
Fish Oven & Equipment Co
Wauconda, IL 877-526-8720
Fishmore
Melbourne, FL 321-723-4751
Fitzpatrick Co
Elmhurst, IL 630-592-4425
Fleet Wood Goldco Wyard
Cockeysville, MD. 410-785-1934
FleetwoodGoldcoWyard
Romeoville, IL 630-759-6800
Flex-Hose Co Inc
East Syracuse, NY. 315-437-1611
Flodin
Moses Lake, WA. 509-766-2996
Flow Aerospace
Jeffersonville, IN 812-283-7888
Flow International Corp.
Kent, WA. 800-446-3569
Flow of Solids
Westford, MA 978-392-0300
Fluid Air Inc
Aurora, IL 630-665-5001
Fluid Energy Processing & Eqpt
Hatfield, PA. 215-368-2510
Fluid Metering Inc
Syosset, NY. 800-223-3388
Flux Pumps Corporation
Atlanta, GA. 800-367-3589
Food Engineering Unlimited
Fullerton, CA 714-879-8762
Food Processing Equipment Co
Santa Fe Springs, CA 562-802-3727
Food Resources International
Concord, ON. 905-482-8967
Food Service Equipment Corporation
Cape Coral, FL 941-574-7767
Food Tools
Santa Barbara, CA 877-836-6386
Forster & Son
Ada, OK 580-332-6021
Foster Miller Inc
Waltham, MA 781-684-4000
FPEC Corporation
Santa Fe Springs, CA 562-802-3727
Franrica Systems
Stockton, CA. 209-948-2811
Frelco
Stephenville, NL 709-643-5668
French Oil Mill Machinery Co
Piqua, OH 937-773-3420
Friedr Dick Corp
Farmingdale, NY 800-554-3425
Frosty Factory Of America Inc
Ruston, LA 800-544-4071

Gabriella Imports
Cleveland, OH 800-544-8117
Garroutte
San Antonio, TX 888-457-4997
Gch Internatonal
Louisville, KY 502-636-1374
GEA North America
Naperville, IL 630-369-8100
Gea Us
Galesville, WI 608-582-3081
GEM Equipment Of Oregon Inc
Woodburn, OR 503-982-9902
General Machinery Corp
Sheboygan, WI 888-243-6622
General, Inc
Weston, FL 954-202-7419
Giles Enterprises Inc
Montgomery, AL 800-288-1555
Gilson Co Inc
Lewis Center, OH 800-444-1508
Glatt Air Techniques Inc
Ramsey, NJ 201-825-8700
Global Manufacturing
Little Rock, AR 800-551-3569
Globe Food Equipment Co
Moraine, OH 800-347-5423
Goodnature Products
Orchard Park, NY 800-875-3381
Goodway Industries Inc
Bohemia, NY 800-943-4501
Grain Machinery Mfg Corp
Miami, FL 305-620-2525
Gram Equipment Of America
Tampa, FL 813-248-1978
Granco Manufacturing Inc
San Ramon, CA 510-652-8847
Grant-Letchworth
Tonawanda, NY 716-692-1000
Graybill Machines Inc
Lititz, PA 717-626-5221
Great Western Manufacturing Company
Leavenworth, KS 800-682-3121
Green Belt Industries Inc
Buffalo, NY 800-668-1114
Gregor Jonsson Inc
Lake Forest, IL 847-247-4200
Grote Co
Columbus, OH 888-534-7683
H. Gartenberg & Company
Buffalo Grove, IL 847-821-7590
Hamilton Beach Brands
Southern Pines, NC 800-851-8900
Hamilton Kettles
Weirton, WV 800-535-1882
Hayes & Stolz Indl Mfg LTD
Fort Worth, TX 800-725-7272
HBD Industries
Salisbury, NC 800-438-2312
Healdsburg Machine Company
Santa Rosa, CA 707-433-3348
Health Star
Randolph, MA 800-545-3639
Helken Equipment Co
Crystal Lake, IL 847-697-3690
Hinds-Bock Corp
Bothell, WA 425-885-1183
Hollymatic Corp
Countryside, IL 708-579-3700
Hosokawa/Bepex Corporation
Santa Rosa, CA 707-586-6000
Howard Fabrication
City of Industry, CA 626-961-0114
Hughes Co
Columbus, WI 866-535-9303
Hydro-Miser
San Marcos, CA 800-736-5083
Hydro-Thermal Corp
Waukesha, WI 800-952-0121
Hyer Industries
Pembroke, MA 781-826-8101
IBA Food Safety
Memphis, TN 800-777-9012
Idaho Steel Products Inc
Idaho Falls, ID 208-522-1275
Ika-Works Inc
Wilmington, NC 800-733-3037
Indiana Wire Company
Fremont, IN 877-786-6883
Industrial Automation Systems
Santa Clarita, CA 888-484-4427
Industrial Piping Inc
Pineville, NC 800-951-0988

Insta-Pro International
Urbandale, IA 800-383-4524
International Knife & Saw
Florence, SC 800-354-9872
International Machinery Xchnge
Deerfield, WI 800-279-0191
International Reserve Equipment Corporation
Clarendon Hills, IL 708-531-0680
Ivarson Inc
Milwaukee, WI 414-351-0700
J C Ford Co
La Habra, CA 714-871-7361
Jarvis Products Corp
Middletown, CT 860-347-7271
Jay-Bee Manufacturing Inc
Tyler, TX 800-445-0610
Jayhawk Manufacturing Co Inc
Hutchinson, KS 866-886-8269
JBT Food Tech
Lakeland, FL 863-683-5411
Jenike & Johanson Inc
Tyngsboro, MA 978-649-3300
Jescorp
Des Plaines, IL 847-299-7800
Johnson Food Equipment Inc
Kansas City, KS 800-288-3434
Johnson Industries Intl
Windsor, WI 608-846-4499
Johnson Pump Of America
Hanover Park, IL 847-671-7867
Juice Tree
Omaha, NE 714-891-4425
JW Leser Company
Los Angeles, CA 323-731-4173
Kady International
Scarborough, ME 800-367-5239
Karl Schnell
New London, WI 920-982-9974
Kasel Industries Inc
Denver, CO 800-218-4417
Kemutec Group Inc
Bristol, PA 215-788-8013
Kerian Machines Inc
Grafton, ND 701-352-0480
Key Technology Inc.
Walla Walla, WA 509-529-2161
Kinetic Equipment Company
Appleton, WI 806-293-4471
King Company
Dallas, TX 507-451-3770
Kirkco Corp
Monroe, NC 704-289-7090
Kitcor Corp
Sun Valley, CA 818-767-4800
Knott Slicers
Canton, MA 781-821-0925
Koch Equipment LLC
Kansas City, MO 816-931-4557
Kofab
Algona, IA 515-295-7265
Kohler Industries Inc
Lincoln, NE 800-365-6708
Krispy Kist Company
Chicago, IL 312-733-0900
Krogh Pump Co
Benicia, CA 800-225-7644
Krones
Franklin, WI 800-752-3787
Kuest Enterprise
Filer, ID 208-326-4084
Kusel Equipment Company
Watertown, WI 920-261-4112
L&A Process Systems
Modesto, CA 209-581-0205
Laciny Brothers Inc
St Louis, MO 314-862-8330
Langsenkamp Manufacturing
Indianapolis, IN 877-585-1950
Latendorf Corporation
Brielle, NJ 800-526-4057
Lauhoff Corporation
Detroit, MI 313-259-0027
Le Jo Enterprises
Phoenixville, PA 484-924-9187
Lee Financial Corporation
Dallas, TX 972-960-1001
Leland Limited Inc
South Plainfield, NJ 800-984-9793
Leland Limited Inc
South Plainfield, NJ 908-561-2000
Lematic Inc
Jackson, MI 517-787-3301

Letrah International Corp
Fort Atkinson, WI 920-563-6597
Lewis M Carter Mfg Co Inc
Donalsonville, GA 800-332-8232
Liberty Engineering Co
Roscoe, IL 877-623-9065
Lil' Orbits
Minneapolis, MN 800-228-8305
Lima Sheet Metal
Lima, OH 419-229-1161
LineSource
Springfield, MA 413-747-9488
Linker Machines
Rockaway, NJ 973-983-0001
Liquid Controls LLC
Lake Bluff, IL 800-458-5262
Liquid Scale
New Brighton, MN 888-633-2969
LIST
Acton, MA 978-635-9521
Littleford Day
Florence, KY 800-365-8555
Louisville Dryer Company
Louisville, KY 800-735-3613
Luhr Jensen & Sons Inc
Hood River, OR 541-386-3811
Lumenite Control Tech Inc
Franklin Park, IL 800-323-8510
Luthi Machinery Company, Inc.
Pueblo, CO 719-948-1110
Lyco Wausau
Wausau, WI 715-845-7867
M O Industries Inc
Whippany, NJ 973-386-9228
M-One Specialties
Salt Lake City, UT 800-525-9223
Machanix Fabrication Inc
Chino, CA 800-700-9701
Maddox/Adams International
Miami, FL 305-592-3337
Magna Machine Co
Cincinnati, OH 800-448-3475
Magnetool Inc
Troy, MI 248-588-5400
Magnuson
Pueblo, CO 719-948-9500
Maja Equipment Company
Omaha, NE 402-346-6252
Mandeville Company
Minneapolis, MN 800-328-8490
Mar-Con Wire Belt
Richmond, BC 877-962-7266
Marel Stork Poultry Processing
Gainesville, GA 770-532-7041
Market Forge Industries Inc
Everett, MA 866-698-3188
Marlen International
Astoria, OR 800-862-7536
Marlo Manufacturing
Boonton, NJ 800-222-0450
Marriott Walker Corporation
Bingham Farms, MI 248-644-6868
Martin Engineering
Neponset, IL 800-766-2786
Martin/Baron
Irwindale, CA 626-960-5153
Matcon Americas
Elmhurst, IL 856-256-1330
Materials Transportation Co
Temple, TX 800-433-3110
Matfer Inc
Van Nuys, CA 800-766-0333
Matiss
St Georges, QC 888-562-8477
Maurer North America
Kansas City, MO 816-914-3518
May-Wes Manufacturing Inc
Hutchinson, MN 800-788-6483
MBC Food Machinery Corp
Hackensack, NJ 201-489-7000
McCarter Corporation
Norristown, PA 610-272-3203
McCormick Enterprises
Arlington Heights, IL 800-323-5201
MCD Technologies
Tacoma, WA 253-476-0968
MDS Nordion
Ottawa, ON 800-465-3666
Meadows Mills Inc
North Wilkesboro, NC 800-626-2282
Membrane System Specialist Inc
Wisconsin Rapids, WI 715-421-2333

Mepsco
 Batavia, IL 800-323-8535
Mercury Equipment Company
 Chino, CA 800-273-6688
Merlin Process Equipment
 Houston, TX 713-221-1651
Mesa Laboratories Inc
 Lakewood, CO 800-525-1215
Met-Pro Corp
 Owosso, MI 800-392-7621
Metal Master Sales Corp
 Glendale Heights, IL 800-488-8729
Metcraft
 Grandview, MO 800-444-9624
Meyer & Garroutte Systems
 San Antonio, TX 210-736-1811
Microdry
 Crestwood, KY 502-241-8933
Microfluidics International
 Westwood, MA 800-370-5452
Micropub Systems International
 Rochester, NY 585-385-3990
MicroThermics, Inc.
 Raleigh, NC 919-878-8045
Middleby Corp
 Elgin, IL 847-741-3300
Midwest Metalcraft & Equipment
 Windsor, MO 800-647-3167
Midwest Stainless
 Menomonie, WI 715-235-5472
Millard Manufacturing Corp
 La Vista, NE 800-662-4263
Miller Technical Svc
 Plymouth, MI 734-414-1769
Modern Electronics Inc
 Grand Cane, LA 318-872-4764
Modern Process Equipment Inc
 Chicago, IL 773-254-3929
Moline Machinery LLC
 Duluth, MN 800-767-5734
Monroe Environmental Corp
 Monroe, MI 800-992-7707
Morris & Associates
 Garner, NC 919-582-9200
Motom Corporation
 Bensenville, IL 630-787-1995
Mouli Manufacturing Corporation
 Belleville, NJ 800-789-8285
Moyno
 Springfield, OH 937-327-3111
Mulligan Associates
 Mequon, WI 800-627-2886
Mumper Machine Corporation
 Butler, WI 262-781-8908
Munson Machinery Co
 Utica, NY 800-944-6644
Murotech
 St Marys, OH 800-565-6876
National Band Saw Co
 Santa Clarita, CA 800-851-5050
National Drying Machry Co Inc
 Philadelphia, PA 215-464-6070
National Equipment Corporation
 Bronx, NY 800-237-8873
National Oilwell Varco
 North Andover, MA 800-643-0641
NECO/Nebraska Engineering
 Omaha, NE 800-367-6208
Nederman
 Thomasville, NC 800-533-5286
Nemeth Engineering Assoc
 Crestwood, KY 502-241-1502
Netzsch Pumps North America
 Exton, PA 610-363-8010
Newlands Systems
 Abbotsford, BC 604-855-4890
Niro
 Hudson, WI 715-386-9371
Northwind Inc
 Alpena, AR 877-937-2585
Norvell Co Inc
 Fort Scott, KS 800-653-3147
Nothum Food Processing Systems
 Springfield, MO 800-435-1297
Nowakowski
 Franklin, WI 800-394-5866
NST Metals
 Louisville, KY 502-584-5846
Nu CO2 LLC
 Stuart, FL 800-472-2855
Nutec Manufacturing Inc
 New Lenox, IL 815-722-5348

Nutrifaster Inc
 Seattle, WA 800-800-2641
Nydree Flooring
 Forest, VA 800-682-5698
Oak Barrel Winecraft
 Berkeley, CA 510-849-0400
Oden Machinery
 Tonawanda, NY 800-658-3622
Odenberg Engineering
 West Sacramento, CA 800-688-8396
Omcan Inc.
 Mississauga, ON 800-465-0234
Omega Products Inc
 Harrisburg, PA 800-633-3401
Omni International
 Kennesaw, GA 800-776-4431
Oxbo International Corp
 Clear Lake, WI 800-628-6196
P & F Machine
 Turlock, CA 209-667-2515
Pacific Process Technology
 La Jolla, CA 858-551-3298
Pacific Tank
 Adelanto, CA 800-449-5838
Packaging & Processing Equipment
 Ayr, ON 519-622-6666
Packaging Progressions
 Collegeville, PA 610-489-9096
Paget Equipment Co
 Marshfield, WI 715-384-3158
Paoli Properties
 Rockford, IL 815-965-0621
Paradigm Technologies
 Eugene, OR 541-345-5543
Paragon Group USA
 St Petersburg, FL 800-835-6962
Parkson Corporation
 Fort Lauderdale, FL 954-974-6610
Patterson Industries
 Scarborough, ON 800-336-1110
Patterson-Kelley Hars Company
 East Stroudsburg, PA 570-421-7500
Paul O. Abbe
 Bensenville, IL 630-350-2200
Pavailler Distribution Company
 Northvale, NJ 201-767-0766
Pavan USA Inc
 Emigsville, PA 717-767-4889
Paxton Corp
 Bristol, RI 401-396-9062
Peerless Food Equipment
 Sidney, OH 937-492-4158
Peerless Machinery Corporation
 Sidney, OH 800-999-3327
Peerless-Winsmith Inc
 Springville, NY 716-592-9310
Peterson Fiberglass Laminates
 Shell Lake, WI 715-468-2306
Phase II Pasta Machine Inc
 Farmingdale, NY 800-457-5070
Piab Vacuum Products
 Hingham, MA 800-321-7422
Pickwick Manufacturing Svc
 Cedar Rapids, IA 800-397-9797
Pier 1 Imports
 Woodcliff Lake, NJ 800-448-9993
Planet Products Corp
 Blue Ash, OH 513-984-5544
Polar Process
 Plattsville, ON 877-896-8077
PolyMaid Company
 Largo, FL 800-206-9188
Prawnto Systems
 Caddo Mills, TX 800-426-7254
Preferred Machining Corporation
 Englewood, CO 303-761-1535
Pressure Pack
 Williamsburg, VA 757-220-3693
Prince Castle Inc
 Carol Stream, IL 800-722-7853
Prince Industries Inc
 Murrayville, GA 800-441-3303
Pro Scientific Inc
 Oxford, CT 800-584-3776
Procedyne Corp
 New Brunswick, NJ 732-249-8347
Process Engineering & Fabrication
 Afton, VA 800-852-7975
Process Systems
 Barrington, IL 847-842-8618

Production Packaging & Processing Equipment
 Company
 Savannah, GA 912-856-4281
Professional Engineering Assoc
 Louisville, KY 502-429-0432
Pulva Corp
 Valencia, PA 800-878-5828
Puritan Manufacturing Inc
 Omaha, NE 800-331-0487
Putsch & Co Inc
 Fletcher, NC 800-847-8427
Quality Fabrication & Design
 Coppell, TX 972-304-3266
Quality Industries
 Cleveland, OH 216-961-5566
Quantum Topping Systems Quantum Technical Services
 Inc
 Frankfort, IL 888-464-1540
R Murphy Co Inc
 Ayer, MA 888-772-3481
R.G. Stephens Engineering
 Long Beach, CA 800-499-3001
Ram Equipment Co
 Waukesha, WI 262-513-1114
Ranger Blade Manufacturing Company
 Traer, IA 800-377-7860
Raque Food Systems
 Louisville, KY 502-267-9641
RAS Process Equipment Inc
 Trenton, NJ 609-371-1220
Raytheon Co
 Waltham, MA 781-522-3000
RBS Fab Inc
 Hummelstown, PA 717-566-9513
Readco Kurimoto LLC
 York, PA 800-395-4959
Reading Bakery Systems Inc
 Robesonia, PA 610-693-5816
Regal Ware Inc
 Kewaskum, WI 262-626-2121
Renard Machine Company
 Green Bay, WI 920-432-8412
Respirometry Plus, LLC
 Fond Du Lac, WI 800-328-7518
Rheo-Tech
 Gurnee, IL 847-367-1557
Rheon USA
 Irvine, CA 949-768-1900
Rhodes Bakery Equipment
 Portland, OR 800-426-3813
RMF Companies
 Grandview, MO 816-839-9258
Robot Coupe
 Ridgeland, MS 800-824-1646
Rome Machine & Foundry Co
 Rome, GA 800-538-7663
Rondo Inc
 Moonachie, NJ 800-882-0633
Rosenwach Tank Co LLC
 Long Island City, NY 212-972-4411
Ross Cook
 Silver Spring, MD 800-233-7339
Ross Engineering Inc
 Savannah, GA 800-524-7677
Ruiz Flour Tortillas
 Riverside, CA 909-947-7811
S J Controls Inc
 Signal Hill, CA 562-494-1400
Samson Controls
 Baytown, TX 281-383-3677
Samuel Pressure Vessel Group
 Marinette, WI 715-453-5326
Samuel Underberg Food Store
 Brooklyn, NY 718-363-0787
San-Rec-Pak
 Tualatin, OR 503-692-5552
Sanchelima International
 Miami, FL 305-591-4343
Sandvik Process Systems
 Sweden, NJ 973-790-1600
Sanford Redmond Company
 Stamford, CT 203-351-9800
SaniServ
 Mooresville, IN 800-733-8073
Sasib Beverage & Food North America
 Plano, TX 800-558-3814
Satake USA
 Stafford, TX 281-276-3600
Savage Brothers Company
 Elk Grove Vlg, IL 800-342-0973
Scherping Systems
 Winsted, MN 320-485-4401

Schlagel Inc
  Cambridge, MN 800-328-8002
Schlueter Company
  Janesville, WI 800-359-1700
Schutte Buffalo Hammermill
  Buffalo, NY .800-447-4634
Scientific Process & Research
  Kendall Park, NJ 800-868-4777
Scott Turbon Mixer
  Adelanto, CA 800-285-8512
Seepex Inc
  Enon, OH 800-695-3659
Sellers Engineering Division
  Danville, KY 859-236-3181
Semi-Bulk Systems Inc
  Fenton, MO .800-732-8769
Separators Inc
  Indianapolis, IN 800-233-9022
Sepragen Corp
  Hayward, CA 510-475-0650
Shanzer Grain Dryer
  Sioux Falls, SD 800-843-9887
Sharp Brothers
  Bayonne, NJ 201-339-0404
Sharpsville Container Corp
  Sharpsville, PA 800-645-1248
Silver Weibull
  Aurora, CO .303-373-2311
Silverson Machines Inc
  East Longmeadow, MA 800-204-6400
Simmons Engineering Corporation
  Wheeling, IL 800-252-3381
Simplimatic Automation
  Forest, VA 800-294-2003
Sine Pump
  Arvada, CO .888-504-8301
Smico Manufacturing Co Inc
  Oklahoma City, OK 800-351-9088
Smith-Berger Marine
  Seattle, WA .206-764-4650
Solbern Corp
  Fairfield, NJ 973-227-3030
Somerset Industries
  Billerica, MA 800-772-4404
Sonic Corp
  Stratford, CT 866-493-1378
Sonics & Materials Inc
  Newtown, CT 800-745-1105
Sortex
  Fremont, CA 510-797-5000
South River Machine
  Hackensack, NJ 201-487-1736
South Shore Controls Inc
  Perry, OH 440-259-2500
Southern Ag Co Inc
  Blakely, GA 229-723-4262
SP Industries Inc
  Warminster, PA 800-523-2327
Sperling Industries
  Omaha, NE .402-556-4070
Sperling Industries
  Omaha, NE .800-647-5062
Spray Dynamics LTD
  St Clair, MO 800-260-7366
SPX Flow Inc
  Charlotte, NC 800-252-5200
Stainless Fabrication Inc
  Springfield, MO 800-397-8265
Stainless Specialists Inc
  Wausau, WI 800-236-4155
Stainless Steel Fabricator Inc
  La Mirada, CA 714-739-9904
Standard Casing Company
  Lyndhurst, NJ 800-847-4141
Stanfos
  Edmonton, AB 800-661-5648
STARMIX srl
  Marano, VI 044- 57- 659
Stephan Machinery, Inc.
  Mundelein, IL 800-783-7426
Steri Technologies Inc
  Bohemia, NY 800-253-7140
Stock America Inc
  Grafton, WI 262-375-4100
Stork Townsend Inc.
  Des Moines, IA 800-247-8609
Straight Line Filters
  Wilmington, DE 302-654-8805
Strategic Equipment & Supply
  Scottsdale, AZ 480-905-5530
Straub Designs Co
  St Louis Park, MN 952-546-6686

Stricklin Co
  Dallas, TX .214-637-1030
Sturdi-Bilt Restaurant Equipment
  Whitmore Lake, MI 800-521-2895
Stutz Products Corp
  Hartford City, IN 765-348-2510
Superior Food Machinery Inc
  Pico Rivera, CA 800-944-0396
Sweco Inc
  Florence, KY 800-807-9326
Swirl Freeze Corp
  Salt Lake City, UT 800-262-4275
T & S Perfection Chain Prods
  Cullman, AL 888-856-4864
T D Sawvel Co
  Maple Plain, MN 877-488-1816
T.K. Products
  Anaheim, CA 714-621-0267
Taylor Manufacturing Co
  Moultrie, GA 229-985-5445
TDH
  Sand Springs, OK 888-251-7961
Techno-Design
  Union, KY .800-641-1822
Tema Systems Inc
  Cincinnati, OH 513-792-2840
Tetra Pak
  Vernon Hills, IL 847-955-6000
Tetra Pak
  Denton, TX 940-380-4630
TGW International
  Florence, KY 800-407-0173
Thomas L. Green & Company
  Robenosia, PA 610-693-5816
Thoreson Mc Cosh Inc
  Troy, MI 800-959-0805
Tindall Packaging
  Vicksburg, MI 269-649-1163
Todd's
  Des Moines, IA 800-247-5363
Tolan Machinery Company
  Rockaway, NJ 973-983-7212
Torpac Capsules
  Fairfield, NJ 973-244-1125
Tranter INC
  Wichita Falls, TX 940-723-7125
Tri-Pak Machinery Inc
  Harlingen, TX 956-423-5140
Triple S Dynamics Inc
  Breckenridge, TX 800-527-2116
Tru Form Plastics
  Gardena, CA 800-510-7999
TSA Griddle Systems
  Kelowna, BC 250-491-9025
Tuthill Vacuum & Blower Systems
  Springfield, MO 800-825-6937
TWM Manufacturing
  Leamington, ON 888-495-4831
Unifiller Systems
  Delta, BC 888-733-8444
Union Process
  Akron, OH 330-929-3333
United Mc Gill Corp
  Groveport, OH 614-829-1200
United Performance Metals
  Northbrook, IL 888-922-0040
UniTrak Corporation
  Port Hope, ON 866-883-5749
Univex Corp
  Salem, NH 800-258-6358
Vacuum Barrier Corp
  Woburn, MA 781-933-3570
Van Air Systems
  Lake City, PA 800-840-9906
Vanmark Equipment
  Creston, IA 800-523-6261
Varimixer North America
  Charlotte, NC 800-221-1138
Vector Corp
  Marion, IA 319-377-8263
Viatec
  Victoria, BC 800-942-4702
Viking Machine & Design Inc
  De Pere, WI 888-286-2116
Vincent Corp
  Tampa, FL 813-248-2650
Vineco International Products
  St Catharines, ON 905-685-9342
Virginia Industrial Services
  Waynesboro, VA 800-825-3050
VitaMinder Company
  Providence, RI 800-858-8840

Vitamix
  Olmsted Twp, OH 800-437-4654
Vortron Smokehouse/Ovens
  Iron Ridge, WI 800-874-1949
Vulcan Food Equipment Group
  Baltimore, MD 800-814-2028
Walton's Inc
  Wichita, KS 800-835-2832
Waring Products
  Torrington, CT 800-492-7464
Warwick Manufacturing & Equip
  North Brunswick, NJ 732-729-0400
Washington Frontier
  Grandview, WA 509-469-7662
Waukesha Cherry-Burrell
  Louisville, KY 502-491-4310
Waukesha Cherry-Burrell
  Louisville, KY 800-252-5200
WCB Ice Cream
  Philadelphia, PA 215-425-4320
Webb's Machine Design
  Clearwater, FL 727-799-1768
Weiler & Company
  Whitewater, WI 800-558-9507
Welbilt Corporation
  Stamford, CT 203-325-8300
Welliver Metal Products Corporation
  Salem, OR 503-362-1568
Wemas Metal Products
  Calgary, AB 403-276-4451
Western Polymer Corp
  Moses Lake, WA 800-362-6845
Westfalia Separator
  Northvale, NJ 800-722-6622
White Mountain Freezer
  Kansas City, MO 816-943-4100
Wilch Manufacturing
  Topeka, KS 785-267-2762
Wilevco Inc
  Billerica, MA 978-667-0400
Wyssmont Co Inc
  Fort Lee, NJ 201-947-4600
X-Press Manufacturing
  New Braunfels, TX 800-365-9440
Yargus Manufacturing Inc
  Marshall, IL 217-826-8059
York Saw & Knife
  York, PA 800-233-1969
Zenith Cutter
  Loves Park, IL 800-223-5202
Zitropack Limited
  Addison, IL 630-543-1016

Parts

A C Tool & Machine Co
  Louisville, KY 502-447-5505
A-L-L Magnetics Inc
  Anaheim, CA 800-262-4638
ABB
  Cary, NC 800-435-7365
Accuflex Industrial Hose LTD
  Romulus, MI 734-713-4100
Action Technology
  Prussia, PA 217-935-8311
AFT Advanced Fiber Technologies
  Sherbrooke, QC 800-668-7273
AGC
  Bristow, VA 800-825-8820
Alard Equipment Corp
  Williamson, NY 315-589-4511
All Weather Energy Systems
  Plymouth, MI 888-636-8324
American Extrusion Intl
  South Beloit, IL 815-624-6616
American Manufacturing-Engrng
  Cleveland, OH 800-822-9402
Andgar Corp
  Ferndale, WA 360-366-9900
Apex Packing & Rubber Co
  Farmingdale, NY 800-645-9110
APV Americas
  Delavan, WI 800-252-5200
Artisan Controls Corp
  Randolph, NJ 800-457-4950
Automatic Specialties Inc
  Marlborough, MA 800-445-2370
Ay Machine Company
  Ephrata, PA 717-733-0335
Baader-Linco
  Kansas City, KS 800-288-3434
Baker Hughes
  Houston, TX

Baldewein Company
Lake Forrest, IL 800-424-5544
Baldor Electric Co
Fort Smith, AR 479-646-4711
Bardo Abrasives
Ridgewood, NY 718-456-6400
Beacon Specialties
New York, NY 800-221-9405
Becker Brothers Graphite Co
Maywood, IL 708-410-0700
Bert Manufacturing
Gardnerville, NV 775-265-3900
Bodine Electric Co
Northfield, IL 773-478-3515
Boston Gear
Boston, MA 888-999-9860
Bradford A Ducon Company
Pewaukee, WI 800-789-1718
Cal Controls
Gurnee, IL 800-866-6659
Candy Manufacturing Co
Niles, IL 847-588-2639
Chicago Stainless Eqpt Inc
Palm City, FL 800-927-8575
Chipmaker Tooling Supply
Whittier, CA 800-659-5840
Continental Disc Corp
Liberty, MO 816-792-1500
Conxall Corporation
Villa Park, IL 630-834-7504
Corenco
Santa Rosa, CA 888-267-3626
Cornell Pump Company
Portland, OR 503-653-0330
Crouzet Corporation
Carrollton, TX 800-677-5311
Debbie Wright Sales
Fort Worth, TX 800-935-7883
Duralite Inc
Riverton, CT 888-432-8797
Dyna-Veyor Inc
Newark, NJ 800-326-5009
Electro Cam Corp
Roscoe, IL 800-228-5487
Esco Products Inc
Houston, TX 800-966-5514
Fabreeka International
Boise, ID 800-423-4469
Falcon Fabricators Inc
Nashville, TN 615-832-0027
Florida Knife Co
Sarasota, FL 800-966-5643
Gary W. Pritchard Engineer
Huntington Beach, CA 714-893-5441
GED, LLC
Laurel, DE 302-856-1756
General Grinding Inc
Oakland, CA 800-806-6037
Glo-Quartz Electric Heater
Mentor, OH 800-321-3574
Good Idea
Northampton, MA 800-462-9237
Granco Manufacturing Inc
San Ramon, CA 510-652-8847
Graphite Metalizing Corp
Yonkers, NY 914-968-8400
Green Belt Industries Inc
Buffalo, NY 800-668-1114
Gridpath, Inc.
Stony Creek, ON 905-643-0955
H. Yamamoto
Port Washington, NY 718-821-7700
Habasit Canada Limited
Oakville, ON 905-827-4131
Hansaloy Corp
Davenport, IA 800-553-4992
Harrington's Equipment Co
Fairfield, PA 800-468-8467
Hayes & Stolz Indl Mfg LTD
Fort Worth, TX 800-725-7272
Hi-Temp Inc
Tuscumbia, AL 800-239-5066
Home Rubber Co
Trenton, NJ 800-257-9441
Hydra-Flex Inc
Livonia, MI 800-234-0832
Industrial Product Corp
Ho Ho Kus, NJ 800-472-5913
Infitec Inc
East Syracuse, NY 800-334-0837
International Tank & Pipe Co
Clackamas, OR 888-988-0011

Introdel Products
Itasca, IL 800-323-4772
Ivarson Inc
Milwaukee, WI 414-351-0700
Jokamsco Group
Waterford,, NY 518-237-6416
Keystone Rubber Corporation
Greenbackville, VA 800-394-5661
Kinetic Equipment Company
Appleton, WI 806-293-4471
King Company
Dallas, TX 507-451-3770
Knobs Unlimited
Bowling Green, OH 419-353-8215
L.C. Thompson Company
Kenosha, WI 800-558-4018
Lako Tool & Mfg Inc
Perrysburg, OH 800-228-2982
Lambeth Band Corporation
New Bedford, MA 508-984-4700
LEESON Electric Corp
Grafton, WI 262-377-8810
Lil' Orbits
Minneapolis, MN 800-228-8305
Lucas Industrial
Cedar Hill, TX 800-877-1720
M-One Specialties
Salt Lake City, UT 800-525-9223
Master Magnetics
Castle Rock, CO 800-525-3536
Mckey Perforating Co Inc
New Berlin, WI 800-345-7373
Meadows Mills Inc
North Wilkesboro, NC 800-626-2282
Metal Master Sales Corp
Glendale Heights, IL 800-488-8729
Miller Technical Svc
Plymouth, MI 734-414-1769
Modern Process Equipment Inc
Chicago, IL 773-254-3929
Moyno
Springfield, OH 937-327-3111
Nalge Process Technologies Group
Rochester, NY 585-586-8800
National Band Saw Co
Santa Clarita, CA 800-851-5050
National Metal Industries
West Springfield, MA 800-628-8850
Newman Sanitary Gasket Co
Lebanon, OH 513-932-7379
Northland Process Piping
Isle, MN 320-679-2119
Oerlikon Leybold Vacuum
Export, PA 724-327-5700
Pacer Pumps
Lancaster, PA 800-233-3861
Paramount Packing & Rubber Inc
Baltimore, MD 866-727-7225
Paul Mueller Co Inc
Springfield, MO 800-683-5537
Payne Controls Co
Scott Depot, WV 800-331-1345
Piab Vacuum Products
Hingham, MA 800-321-7422
Polychem Corp
Mentor, OH 440-357-1500
Pres-Air-Trol Corporation
Altoona, WI 800-431-2625
Pure Fit Nutrition Bars
Irvine, CA 866-787-3348
Qosina Corporation
Ronkonkoma, NY 631-242-3000
Quadrant Epp USA Inc
Fort Wayne, IN 800-628-7264
Quality Industries
Cleveland, OH 216-961-5566
Rath Manufacturing Company
Janesville, WI 800-367-7284
Rigidized Metal Corp
Buffalo, NY 800-836-2580
Robert-James Sales
Buffalo, NY 800-777-1325
Salem-Republic Rubber Co
Sebring, OH 800-425-5079
Sanchelima International
Miami, FL 305-591-4343
Sani-Fit
Pasadena, CA 626-395-7895
Sanitary Couplers
Springfield, OH 513-743-0144
Schwartz Manufacturing Co
Two Rivers, WI 920-793-1375

Sellers Engineering Division
Danville, KY 859-236-3181
Senior Flexonics
Bartlett, IL 800-473-0474
Sew-Eurodrive Inc
Lyman, SC 864-439-8792
Sharon Manufacturing Inc
Deer Park, NY 800-424-6455
Simolex Rubber Corp
Plymouth, MI 734-453-4500
Simply Manufacturing
Prairie Du Sac, WI 608-643-6656
Sine Pump
Arvada, CO 888-504-8301
Specialty Blades
Staunton, VA 540-248-2200
STD Precision Gear
West Bridgewater, MA 888-783-4327
Strahman Valves Inc
Bethlehem, PA 877-787-2462
Stutz Products Corp
Hartford City, IN 765-348-2510
Thomas Precision, Inc.
Rice Lake, WI 800-657-4808
Top Line Process Equipment Company
Bradford, PA 800-458-6095
TWM Manufacturing
Leamington, ON 888-495-4831
Union Cord Products Company
Schaumburg, IL 847-240-1500
United Performance Metals
Northbrook, IL 888-922-0040
US Tsubaki Holdings Inc
Wheeling, IL 800-323-7790
Valvinox
Iberville, QC 450-346-1981
Vaughn Belting Co-Main Acct
Spartanburg, SC 800-533-9086
Viking Machine & Design Inc
De Pere, WI 888-286-2116
Warner Electric Inc
South Beloit, IL 800-234-3369
Washington Frontier
Grandview, WA 509-469-7662
Waukesha Cherry-Burrell
Louisville, KY 800-252-5200
Wilden Pump & Engineering LLC
Grand Terrace, CA 909-422-1700
Wire Belt Co Of America
Londonderry, NH 603-644-2500
Womack International Inc
Vallejo, CA 707-647-2370
World Wide Fitting Corp
Vernon Hills, IL 800-393-9894
Yates Industries Inc
St Clair Shores, MI 586-778-7680
Zenith Cutter
Loves Park, IL 800-223-5202

Rebuilt & Used

A C Tool & Machine Co
Louisville, KY 502-447-5505
A&M Industries
Sioux Falls, SD 800-888-2615
Alard Equipment Corp
Williamson, NY 315-589-4511
Albion Machine & Tool Co
Albion, MI 517-629-9135
Alpha Resources Inc
Stevensville, MI 800-833-3083
Ay Machine Company
Ephrata, PA 717-733-0335
Berkshire PPM
Litchfield, CT 860-567-3118
Big State Spring Companyy
Corpus Christi, TX 800-880-0244
Buffalo Wire Works Co Inc
Buffalo, NY 800-828-7028
Champion Trading Corporation
Marlboro, NJ 732-780-4200
Commodity Traders International
Trilla, IL 217-235-4322
Custom Food Machinery
Stockton, CA 209-463-4343
Delphi Food Machinery
Tempe, AZ 480-483-8361
Denman Equipment
Memphis, TN 901-755-7135
Equipment Specialists Inc
Manassas, VA 703-361-2227
Esco Products Inc
Houston, TX 800-966-5514

Food Resources International
Concord, ON 905-482-8967
GED, LLC
Laurel, DE 302-856-1756
Hallmark Equipment Inc
Morgan Hill, CA 408-782-2600
Harrington's Equipment Co
Fairfield, PA 800-468-8467
Health Star
Randolph, MA 800-545-3639
Helken Equipment Co
Crystal Lake, IL 847-697-3690
International Machinery Xchnge
Deerfield, WI 800-279-0191
Jarboe Equipment
Georgetown, DE 800-699-7988
Lehman Sales Associates
Sun Prairie, WI 608-575-7712
Machinery Corporation ofAmerica
Capitola, CA 831-479-9901
Mandeville Company
Minneapolis, MN 800-328-8490
Mba Suppliers Inc.
Bellevue, NE 800-467-1201
McNeil Food Machinery
Stockton, CA 209-463-4343
Miller Technical Svc
Plymouth, MI 734-414-1769
National Equipment Corporation
Bronx, NY 800-237-8873
Naughton Equipment Sales
Fort Calhoun, NE 866-858-4682
Pacific Process Machinery
Santa Rosa, CA 707-523-4122
Packaging & Processing Equipment
Ayr, ON 519-622-6666
Paxton Corp
Bristol, RI 401-396-9062
Peerless Machinery Corporation
Sidney, OH 800-999-3327
Polar Process
Plattsville, ON 877-896-8077
Regal Equipment Inc
Ravenna, OH 330-325-9000
Separators Inc
Indianapolis, IN 800-233-9022
Stone Enterprises Inc.
Omaha, NE 877-653-0500
Thomas Precision, Inc.
Rice Lake, WI 800-657-4808
Warwick Manufacturing & Equip
North Brunswick, NJ 732-729-0400
Wohl Associates Inc
Bohemia, NY 631-244-7979
Zitropack Limited
Addison, IL 630-543-1016

Frozen Custard Processing

Emery Thompson Machine &Supply Company
Brooksville, FL 718-588-7300

Frozen Foods Processing

Automated Food Systems
Waxahachie, TX 469-517-0470
Chart Inc
New Prague, MN 800-428-3777
Design Technology Corporation
Billerica, MA 978-663-7000
Dipwell Co
Northampton, MA 413-587-4673
Dole Refrigerating Co
Lewisburg, TN 800-251-8990
Emery Thompson Machine &Supply Company
Brooksville, FL 718-588-7300
Flodin
Moses Lake, WA 509-766-2996
Food Engineering Unlimited
Fullerton, CA 714-879-8762
Frazier & Son
Conroe, TX 800-365-5438
Gabriella Imports
Cleveland, OH 800-544-8117
MBC Food Machinery Corp
Hackensack, NJ 201-489-7000
Millard Manufacturing Corp
La Vista, NE 800-662-4263
Multi-Fill Inc
West Jordan, UT 801-280-1570
Raque Food Systems
Louisville, KY 502-267-9641

Techno-Design
Union, KY 800-641-1822
TWM Manufacturing
Leamington, ON 888-495-4831
UniTrak Corporation
Port Hope, ON 866-883-5749

Fruit Processing

A.K. Robins
Baltimore, MD 800-486-9656
ABCO Industries Limited
Lunenburg, NS 866-634-8821
Advance Energy Technologies
Halfmoon, NY 800-724-0198
Altman Industries
Gray, GA 478-986-3116
Ametek Technical & Industrial Products
Kent, OH 215-256-6601
Andgar Corp
Ferndale, WA 360-366-9900
Ashlock Co
San Leandro, CA 510-351-0560
Atlas Pacific Engineering
Pueblo, CO 719-948-3040
Autoline
Reedley, CA 559-638-5432
Automated Food Systems
Waxahachie, TX 469-517-0470
Bake Star
Somerset, WI 763-427-7611
BEI
South Haven, MI 800-364-7425
Bmh Equipment Inc
Sacramento, CA 800-350-8828
BNW Industries
Tippecanoe, IN 574-353-7855
Branson Ultrasonics Corp
Danbury, CT 203-796-0400
Brown International Corp LLC
Winter Haven, FL 863-299-2111
Chop-Rite Two Inc
Harleysville, PA 800-683-5858
Citra-Tech
Lefkosia, CY
Coastline Equipment Inc
Bellingham, WA 360-734-8509
Commercial Dehydrator Systems
Eugene, OR 800-369-4283
Corenco
Santa Rosa, CA 888-267-3626
Custom Food Machinery
Stockton, CA 209-463-4343
Dixie Canner Machine Shop
Athens, GA 706-549-0592
Dunkley International Inc
Kalamazoo, MI 800-666-1264
Durand-Wayland Inc
Lagrange, GA 800-241-2308
Elliott Manufacturing Co Inc
Fresno, CA 559-233-6235
Everedy Automation
Frederick, PA 610-754-1775
F.B. Pease Company
Rochester, NY 585-475-1870
Globe Machine
Tacoma, WA 800-523-6575
Goodnature Products
Orchard Park, NY 800-875-3381
Healdsburg Machine Company
Santa Rosa, CA 707-433-3348
JBT Food Tech
Lakeland, FL 863-683-5411
Juice Tree
Omaha, NE 714-891-4425
Kerian Machines Inc
Grafton, ND 701-352-0480
Key Technology Inc.
Walla Walla, WA 509-529-2161
Lyco Wausau
Wausau, WI 715-845-7867
Mulligan Associates
Mequon, WI 800-627-2886
Murotech
St Marys, OH 800-565-6876
Odenberg Engineering
West Sacramento, CA 800-688-8396
Paxton Corp
Bristol, RI 401-396-9062
Paxton Products Inc
Blue Ash, OH 800-441-7475

Pick Heaters
West Bend, WI 800-233-9030
Tew Manufacturing Corp
Penfield, NY 800-380-5839
Tri-Pak Machinery Inc
Harlingen, TX 956-423-5140
TWM Manufacturing
Leamington, ON 888-495-4831
UniTrak Corporation
Port Hope, ON 866-883-5749
Vanmark Equipment
Creston, IA 800-523-6261
Vincent Corp
Tampa, FL 813-248-2650
Webb's Machine Design
Clearwater, FL 727-799-1768
White Mountain Freezer
Kansas City, MO 816-943-4100

Graders

Fruit, Vegetable & Nut

A.K. Robins
Baltimore, MD 800-486-9656
Berkshire PPM
Litchfield, CT 860-567-3118
Commercial Manufacturing
Fresno, CA 559-237-1855
Descon EDM
Brocton, NY 716-792-9300
Durand-Wayland Inc
Lagrange, GA 800-241-2308
Hughes Co
Columbus, WI 866-535-9303
Kerian Machines Inc
Grafton, ND 701-352-0480
Key Technology Inc.
Walla Walla, WA 509-529-2161
Sortex
Fremont, CA 510-797-5000
Tri-Pak Machinery Inc
Harlingen, TX 956-423-5140
Welliver Metal Products Corporation
Salem, OR 503-362-1568

Grain, Rice & Seed

ANDRITZ Inc
Muncy, PA 704-943-4343
Commercial Manufacturing
Fresno, CA 559-237-1855
Commodity Traders International
Trilla, IL 217-235-4322
Crippen Manufacturing Co
St Louis, MI 800-872-2474
Grain Machinery Mfg Corp
Miami, FL 305-620-2525
Sortex
Fremont, CA 510-797-5000
Welliver Metal Products Corporation
Salem, OR 503-362-1568

Grain Elevator

ANDRITZ Inc
Muncy, PA 704-943-4343
Chief Industries
Kearney, NE 800-359-8833
Dunrite Inc
Fremont, NE 800-782-3061
NECO/Nebraska Engineering
Omaha, NE 800-367-6208
Schlagel Inc
Cambridge, MN 800-328-8002
Screw Conveyor Corp
Hammond, IN 219-931-1450
Universal Industries Inc
Cedar Falls, IA 800-553-4446
Yargus Manufacturing Inc
Marshall, IL 217-826-8059

Graters

Acme International
Maplewood, NJ 973-416-0400
Amco Metals Indl
City Of Industry, CA 626-855-2550
Browne & Company
Markham, ON 905-475-6104
Corenco
Santa Rosa, CA 888-267-3626

Giunta Brothers
Philadelphia, PA 215-389-9670
Leggett & Platt Storage
Vernon Hills, IL 847-816-6246
Polar Process
Plattsville, ON. 877-896-8077
Samuel Underberg Food Store
Brooklyn, NY 718-363-0787

Grinders

Bulk Grinding

Ditting USA
Glendale, CA 800-835-5992
La Poblana Food Machines
Mesa, AZ. 480-258-2091
Marlen Research Corporation
Shawnee Mission, KS. 913-888-3333
Reiser
Canton, MA 734-821-1290
Risco USA Inc
South Easton, MA. 888-474-7267
Weiler Equipment
Whitewater, WI. 800-558-9507

Hamburger & Meat Patty Processing

Bridge Machine Company
Palmyra, NJ. 877-754-1800
Daleco
West Chester, PA. 610-429-0181
Design Technology Corporation
Billerica, MA 978-663-7000
Hollymatic Corp
Countryside, IL 708-579-3700
Nieco Corporation
Windsor, CA 800-643-2656
Nutec Manufacturing Inc
New Lenox, IL 815-722-5348
Reiser
Canton, MA 734-821-1290

Heat Exchangers

A & B Process Systems Corp
Stratford, WI. 888-258-2789
AFGO Mechanical Svc Inc
Astoria, NY. 800-438-2346
AGC
Bristow, VA. 800-825-8820
Allegheny Bradford Corp
Bradford, PA. 800-542-0650
Allied Engineering
North Vancouver, BC 877-929-1214
Alloy Hardfacing & Engineering
Jordan, MN. 800-328-8408
Andgar Corp
Ferndale, WA. 360-366-9900
API Heat Transfer Inc
Buffalo, NY. 877-274-4328
Apollo Sheet Metal
Kennewick, WA. 509-586-1104
APV Americas
Delavan, WI 800-252-5200
Baltimore Aircoil Co
Jessup, MD. 410-799-1300
Bimetalix
Sullivan, WI. 262-593-8066
Buffalo Technologies Corporation
Buffalo, NY. 800-332-2419
Carmel Engineering
Kirklin, IN. 888-427-0497
Carnes Company
Verona, WI 608-845-6411
Central Fabricators Inc
Cincinnati, OH 800-909-8265
Chester-Jensen Co., Inc.
Chester, PA. 800-685-3750
Chil-Con Products
Brantford, ON 800-263-0086
Cooling Products Inc
Broken Arrow, OK 918-251-8588
Doucette Industries
York, PA 800-445-7511
E.L. Nickell Company
Constantine, MI 269-435-2475
Eclipse Innovative Ther mal Solutions
Toledo, OH 800-662-3966
Eischen Enterprises
Fresno, CA. 559-834-0013
Ellett Industries
Port Coquitlam, BC. 604-941-8211

Enerquip Inc
Medford, WI. 715-748-5888
EVAPCO Inc
Taneytown, MD 410-876-3782
Feldmeier Equipment Inc
Syracuse, NY 315-454-8608
Flat Plate Inc
York, PA. 888-854-2500
Franrica Systems
Stockton, CA. 209-948-2811
Gaston County Dyeing Mach Co
Mt Holly, NC 704-822-5000
GEA Refrigeration North America
York, PA. 800-888-4337
Gram Equipment Of America
Tampa, FL. 813-248-1978
Harris Equipment Corp
Melrose Park, IL 800-365-0315
Hebeler Corp
Tonawanda, NY 800-486-4709
International Machinery Xchnge
Deerfield, IL 800-279-0191
Lake Process Systems Inc
Lake Barrington, IL 800-331-9260
Louisville Dryer Company
Louisville, KY 800-735-3613
Ludell Manufacturing Co
Milwaukee, WI 800-558-0800
M G Newell Corp
Greensboro, NC 800-334-0231
MadgeTech, Inc.
Contoocook, NH 603-456-2011
Midwest Stainless
Menomonie, WI 715-235-5472
National Oilwell Varco
North Andover, MA 800-643-0641
Noren Products Inc
Menlo Park, CA. 866-936-6736
Patterson Industries
Scarborough, ON 800-336-1110
Pick Heaters
West Bend, WI 800-233-9030
RAS Process Equipment Inc
Trenton, NJ. 609-371-1220
Samuel Pressure Vessel Group
Marinette, WI 715-453-5326
Seattle Boiler Works Inc
Seattle, WA. 206-762-0737
Seattle Refrigeration & Manufacturing
Seattle, WA. 800-228-8881
Standard Refrigeration Co
Wood Dale, IL 708-345-5400
Statco Engineering
Huntington Beach, CA 800-421-0362
Svedala Industries
Colorado Springs, CO. 719-471-3443
Tolan Machinery Company
Rockaway, NJ. 973-983-7212
Tranter INC
Wichita Falls, TX 940-723-7125
Ultra Process Systems
Oak Ridge, TN 865-483-2772
Vilter Manufacturing Corporation
Cudahy, WI 414-744-0111
Washington Frontier
Grandview, WA. 509-469-7662
Waukesha Cherry-Burrell
Louisville, KY 800-252-5200
Wilevco Inc
Billerica, MA 978-667-0400

Heat Transfer Fluids

Brown Fired Heater
Elyria, OH. 440-323-3291
Paratherm Corporation
Conshohocken, PA 800-222-3611
Quikwater Inc
Sand Springs, OK 918-241-8880
Washington Frontier
Grandview, WA. 509-469-7662

Homogenizers

APV Americas
Delavan, WI 800-252-5200
Avestin
Ottawa, ON. 888-283-7846
Bematek Systems Inc
Salem, MA 877-236-2835
Berkshire PPM
Litchfield, CT 860-567-3118

Cornell Machine Co
Springfield, NJ 973-379-6860
Ederback Corporation
Ann Arbor, MI 800-422-2558
Eischen Enterprises
Fresno, CA. 559-834-0013
Et Oakes Corp
Hauppauge, NY 631-232-0002
GEA Niro Soavi North America
Bedford, NH 603-606-4060
Glen Mills Inc.
Clifton, NJ. 973-777-0777
Goodway Industries Inc
Bohemia, NY 800-943-4501
Ika-Works Inc
Wilmington, NC 800-733-3037
JW Leser Company
Los Angeles, CA. 323-731-4173
National Oilwell Varco
North Andover, MA 800-643-0641
Omni International
Kennesaw, GA 800-776-4431
Pro Scientific Inc
Oxford, CT. 800-584-3776
Sanchelima International
Miami, FL. 305-591-4343
Silverson Machines Inc
East Longmeadow, MA 800-204-6400
Sonic Corp
Stratford, CT. 866-493-1378
Special Products
Springfield, MO 417-881-6114
Statco Engineering
Huntington Beach, CA 800-421-0362
Stephan Machinery, Inc.
Mundelein, IL. 800-783-7426
WCB Ice Cream
Philadelphia, PA. 215-425-4320

Honey Processing

Cook & Beals Inc
Loup City, NE. 308-745-0154
Dadant & Sons Inc
Hamilton, IL. 888-922-1293

Hoppers

Anderson-Crane Company
Minneapolis, MN 800-314-2747
Andgar Corp
Ferndale, WA. 360-366-9900
ANDRITZ Inc
Muncy, PA. 704-943-4343
Bonar Plastics
West Chicago, IL 800-295-3725
COW Industries Inc
Columbus, OH 800-542-9353
Food Processing Equipment Co
Santa Fe Springs, CA. 562-802-3727
Galbreath LLC
Winamac, IN. 574-946-6631
Jesco Industries
Litchfield, MI 800-455-0019
Midwest Metalcraft & Equipment
Windsor, MO. 800-647-3167
Our Name is Mud
New York, NY 877-683-7867
Palace Packaging Machines Inc
Downingtown, PA. 610-873-7252
Pittsburgh Tank Corp
Monongahela, PA 800-634-0243
Puritan Manufacturing Inc
Omaha, NE. 800-331-0487
Schlueter Company
Janesville, WI 800-359-1700
Sharpsville Container Corp
Sharpsville, PA. 800-645-1248
Shick Esteve
Kansas City, MO. 877-744-2587
TWM Manufacturing
Leamington, ON 888-495-4831
UniTrak Corporation
Port Hope, ON 866-883-5749
Wilson Steel Products Company
Memphis, TN 901-527-8742

Coffee

Bonar Plastics
West Chicago, IL 800-295-3725
Pittsburgh Tank Corp
Monongahela, PA 800-634-0243

Sharpsville Container Corp
  Sharpsville, PA 800-645-1248
Shick Esteve
  Kansas City, MO 877-744-2587
TWM Manufacturing
  Leamington, ON 888-495-4831
UniTrak Corporation
  Port Hope, ON 866-883-5749

Flour

Anderson-Crane Company
  Minneapolis, MN 800-314-2747
ANDRITZ Inc
  Muncy, PA 704-943-4343
Bonar Plastics
  West Chicago, IL 800-295-3725
COW Industries Inc
  Columbus, OH 800-542-9353
Food Processing Equipment Co
  Santa Fe Springs, CA 562-802-3727
Galbreath LLC
  Winamac, IN 574-946-6631
Midwest Metalcraft & Equipment
  Windsor, MO 800-647-3167
Pittsburgh Tank Corp
  Monongahela, PA 800-634-0243
Puritan Manufacturing Inc
  Omaha, NE 800-331-0487
Schlueter Company
  Janesville, WI 800-359-1700
Sharpsville Container Corp
  Sharpsville, PA 800-645-1248
Shick Esteve
  Kansas City, MO 877-744-2587
TWM Manufacturing
  Leamington, ON 888-495-4831
Wilson Steel Products Company
  Memphis, TN 901-527-8742

Hullers

Bean & Pea

A C Horn & Co Sheet Metal
  Dallas, TX 800-657-6155
A.K. Robins
  Baltimore, MD 800-486-9656
Grain Machinery Mfg Corp
  Miami, FL 305-620-2525
Lee Financial Corporation
  Dallas, TX 972-960-1001

Huskers

Corn

Berkshire PPM
  Litchfield, CT 860-567-3118
Hughes Co
  Columbus, WI 866-535-9303

Ice Breaking, Chipping, Crushing

Clawson Machine Co Inc
  Franklin, NJ 800-828-4088
Flodin
  Moses Lake, WA 509-766-2996
Hoshizaki America Inc
  Peachtree City, GA 800-438-6087
Howe Corp
  Chicago, IL 773-235-0200
International Cooling Systems
  Richmond Hill, ON 888-213-5566
Island Oasis Frozen Cocktail
  Beloit, WI 800-777-4752
Machine Ice Co
  Houston, TX 800-423-8822
Swing-A-Way Manufacturing Company
  St Louis, MO 314-773-1488
Vitamix
  Olmsted Twp, OH 800-437-4654
Vogt Tube Ice
  Louisville, KY 800-853-8648
Waring Products
  Torrington, CT 800-492-7464
Welbilt Corporation
  Stamford, CT 203-325-8300

Ice Cream Cone, Bar, Biscuit Processing

Darfill
  Westerville, OH 614-890-3274

Eischen Enterprises
  Fresno, CA 559-834-0013
Norse Dairy Systems
  Columbus, OH 800-338-7465
Schroeder Machine
  San Marcos, CA 760-591-9733

Ice Cream Processing

A & B Process Systems Corp
  Stratford, WI 888-258-2789
Advance Energy Technologies
  Halfmoon, NY 800-724-0198
Carpigiani Corporation of America
  Winston Salem, NC 800-648-4389
Dipwell Co
  Northampton, MA 413-587-4673
Emery Thompson Machine &Supply Company
  Brooksville, FL 718-588-7300
Frosty Factory Of America Inc
  Ruston, LA 800-544-4071
Gram Equipment Of America
  Tampa, FL 813-248-1978
H C Duke & Son Inc
  East Moline, IL 309-755-4553
Master-Bilt
  New Albany, MS 800-647-1284
Norse Dairy Systems
  Columbus, OH 800-338-7465
Swirl Freeze Corp
  Salt Lake City, UT 800-262-4275
Tetra Pak
  Vernon Hills, IL 847-955-6000
Tindall Packaging
  Vicksburg, MI 269-649-1163
Vitamix
  Olmsted Twp, OH 800-437-4654
White Mountain Freezer
  Kansas City, MO 816-943-4100

Ice Cubing

Hoshizaki America Inc
  Peachtree City, GA 800-438-6087
Iceomatic
  Denver, CO 800-423-3367
Machine Ice Co
  Houston, TX 800-423-8822
Morris & Associates
  Garner, NC 919-582-9200
Scotsman Ice Systems
  Vernon Hills, IL 800-726-8762
SerVend International
  Sellersburg, IN 800-367-4233
Vogt Tube Ice
  Louisville, KY 800-853-8648
Water Sciences Services, Inc.
  Jackson, TN 973-584-4131
Welbilt Corporation
  Stamford, CT 203-325-8300

Ice Making, Refrigerating & Cooling

A-1 Refrigeration Co
  Ontario, CA 800-669-4423
Advance Energy Technologies
  Halfmoon, NY 800-724-0198
American Food Equipment
  Miami, FL 305-377-8991
Applied Chemical Technology
  Florence, AL 800-228-3217
Arctic Glacier Premium Ice
  Winnepeg, MB 888-783-9857
Attias Oven Corp
  Brooklyn, NY 800-928-8427
Berg Chilling Systems
  Toronto, ON, ON 416-755-2221
BVL Controls
  Bois-Des-Filion, QC 866-285-2668
C&R Refrigeration
  Center, TX 800-438-6182
Carbonic Machines Inc
  Minneapolis, MN 612-824-0745
Cooling Technology Inc
  Charlotte, NC 800-872-1448
Cornelius
  Mason City, IA 800-238-3600
Cornelius Inc.
  Osseo, MN 800-238-3600
Cornelius Wilshire Corporation
  Schaumburg, IL 847-397-4600
Delta Cooling Towers Inc
  Rockaway, NJ 800-289-3358

Dole Refrigerating Co
  Lewisburg, TN 800-251-8990
Flakice Corporation
  Everett, WA 800-654-4630
Follett Corp
  Easton, PA 800-523-9361
Hoshizaki America Inc
  Peachtree City, GA 800-438-6087
Howe Corp
  Chicago, IL 773-235-0200
Iceomatic
  Denver, CO 800-423-3367
IMI Cornelius
  Schaumburg, IL 800-323-4789
International Cooling Systems
  Richmond Hill, ON 888-213-5566
Kloppenberg & Co
  Englewood, CO 800-346-3246
Leer Inc
  New Lisbon, WI 800-237-8350
Louisville Dryer Company
  Louisville, KY 800-735-3613
Machine Ice Co
  Houston, TX 800-423-8822
Maja Equipment Company
  Omaha, NE 402-346-6252
Mannhardt Inc
  Sheboygan Falls, WI 800-423-2327
Master-Bilt
  New Albany, MS 800-647-1284
Matthiesen Equipment
  San Antonio, TX 800-624-8635
Maximicer
  Georgetown, TX 800-289-9098
McCormack Manufacturing Company
  Lake Oswego, OR 800-395-1593
Morris & Associates
  Garner, NC 919-582-9200
North Star Ice EquipmentCorporation
  Seattle, WA 800-321-1381
Scotsman Ice Systems
  Vernon Hills, IL 800-726-8762
Seattle Refrigeration & Manufacturing
  Seattle, WA 800-228-8881
Semco Manufacturing Company
  Pharr, TX 956-787-4203
SerVend International
  Sellersburg, IN 800-367-4233
Superior Products Company
  Saint Paul, MN 800-328-9800
Tom Lockerbie
  Edmeston, NY 315-737-5612
Turbo Refrigerating Company
  Denton, TX 940-387-4301
U-Line Corporation
  Milwaukee, WI 800-779-2547
Vilter Manufacturing Corporation
  Cudahy, WI 414-744-0111
Welbilt Corporation
  Stamford, CT 203-325-8300
Welbilt Inc.
  New Port Richey, FL 877-375-9300
Wittemann Company
  Palm Coast, FL 386-445-4200

Irradiation Processing

Alpha Omega Technology
  Cedar Knolls, NJ 800-442-1969
IBA Food Safety
  Memphis, TN 800-777-9012
Insect-O-Cutor Inc
  Stone Mountain, GA 800-966-8480
MDS Nordion
  Ottawa, ON 800-465-3666
New Horizon Technologies
  Richland, WA 509-372-4868

Meat Preparation Equipment

A C Tool & Machine Co
  Louisville, KY 502-447-5505
AEW Thurne
  Lake Zurich, IL 800-239-7297
Alfa Laval Inc
  Richmond, VA 866-253-2528
Allen Gauge & Tool Co
  Pittsburgh, PA 412-241-6410
AM-Mac
  Fairfield, NJ 800-829-2018
Andgar Corp
  Ferndale, WA 360-366-9900

ANKOM Technology
Macedon, NY 315-986-8090
Ashcroft Inc
Stratford, CT 800-328-8258
Atlanta SharpTech
Peachtree City, GA 800-462-7297
Automated Food Systems
Waxahachie, TX 469-517-0470
B H Bunn Co
Lakeland, FL 800-222-2866
Beacon Inc
Chicago, IL 800-445-4203
Biro Manufacturing Co
Lakeside Marblhd, OH 419-798-4451
Blakeslee, Inc.
Addison, IL 630-532-5021
Boehringer Mfg. Co. Inc.
Felton, CA 800-630-8665
Bridge Machine Company
Palmyra, NJ 877-754-1800
Chop-Rite Two Inc
Harleysville, PA 800-683-5858
Cozzini Inc
Algona, IA 888-295-1116
Cozzini LLC
Chicago, IL 773-478-9700
Cutrite Company
Fremont, OH 800-928-8748
Daleco
West Chester, PA 610-429-0181
Dc Tech
Kansas City, MO 877-742-9090
Design Technology Corporation
Billerica, MA 978-663-7000
E-Z Edge Inc
West New York, NJ 800-232-4470
EZE-Lap Diamond Products
Carson City, NV 800-843-4815
Friedr Dick Corp
Farmingdale, NY 800-554-3425
Friedrich Metal Products
Browns Summit, NC 800-772-0326
G.F. Frank & Sons
Fairfield, OH 513-870-9075
General Machinery Corp
Sheboygan, WI 888-243-6622
General, Inc
Weston, FL 954-202-7419
Globe Food Equipment Co
Moraine, OH 800-347-5423
Haban Saw Company
St.Louis, MO 314-968-3991
Handtmann Inc
Lake Forest, IL 800-477-3585
Hansaloy Corp
Davenport, IA 800-553-4992
Hoegger Food Technology
Minneapolis, MN 877-789-5400
Hollingsworth Custom Wood Products
Sault Ste. Marie, ON 705-759-1756
Hollymatic Corp
Countryside, IL 708-579-3700
I. Fm Usa Inc.
Franklin Park, IL 866-643-6872
ICB Greenline
Charlotte, NC 800-331-5312
Indeco Products Inc
San Marcos, TX 888-246-3326
Jarvis Products Corp
Middletown, CT 860-347-7271
Kasel Industries Inc
Denver, CO 800-218-4417
Kentmaster Manufacturing Co
Monrovia, CA 800-421-1477
Key Technology Inc.
Walla Walla, WA 509-529-2161
Koch Equipment LLC
Kansas City, MO 816-931-4557
Le Fiell Co
Reno, NV 402-592-9993
Linker Machines
Rockaway, NJ 973-983-0001
Loos Machine
Colby, WI 715-223-2844
Luthi Machinery Company, Inc.
Pueblo, CO 719-948-1110
M-One Specialties
Salt Lake City, UT 800-525-9223
Maja Equipment Company
Omaha, NE 402-346-6252
Mandeville Company
Minneapolis, MN 800-328-8490

Marlen
Riverside, MO 913-888-3333
Marlen International
Astoria, OR 800-862-7536
Mba Suppliers Inc.
Bellevue, NE 800-467-1201
Mepsco
Batavia, IL 800-323-8535
Michigan Maple Block Co
Petoskey, MI 800-447-7975
Mp Equip. Co.
Buford, GA 770-614-5355
MPS North America, Inc.
Lenexa, KS 913-310-0055
National Band Saw Co
Santa Clarita, CA 800-851-5050
Nieco Corporation
Windsor, CA 800-643-2656
Nutec Manufacturing Inc
New Lenox, IL 815-722-5348
Packaging Progressions
Collegeville, PA 610-489-9096
Paoli Properties
Rockford, IL 815-965-0621
Paragon Group USA
St Petersburg, FL 800-835-6962
Patty O Matic Machinery
Farmingdale, NJ 877-938-5244
Pemberton & Associates
Brooklyn, NY 800-736-2664
Planet Products Corp
Blue Ash, OH 513-984-5544
Prince Castle Inc
Carol Stream, IL 800-722-7853
Prince Industries Inc
Murrayville, GA 800-441-3303
Quickdraft
Canton, OH 330-477-4574
R Murphy Co Inc
Ayer, MA 888-772-3481
Ranger Tool Co Inc
Memphis, TN 800-737-9999
Reiser
Canton, MA 734-821-1290
Rheo-Tech
Gurnee, IL 847-367-1557
Rollstock Inc
Kansas City, MO 800-954-6020
SFK Danfotech, Inc.
Kansas City, MO 816-891-7357
Simmons Engineering Corporation
Wheeling, IL 800-252-3381
Simonds International
Fitchburg, MA 978-345-7521
Sperling Industries
Omaha, NE 402-556-4070
Sperling Industries
Omaha, NE 800-647-5062
Standard Casing Company
Lyndhurst, NJ 800-847-4141
Stanfos
Edmonton, AB 800-661-5648
Stephan Machinery GmbH
Mandelein, IL 847-247-0182
Stone Enterprises Inc.
Omaha, NE 877-653-0500
Stork Townsend Inc.
Des Moines, IA 800-247-8609
Superior Distributing Co
Louisville, KY 800-365-6661
Tech-Roll Inc
Blaine, WA 888-946-3929
TGW International
Florence, KY 800-407-0173
Tni Packaging Inc
West Chicago, IL 800-383-0990
Trenton Mills Inc
Trenton, TN 731-855-1323
Unitherm Food System
Bristow, OK 918-367-0197
Univex Corp
Salem, NH 800-258-6358
Walton's Inc
Wichita, KS 800-835-2832
Weber Inc
Kansas City, MO 816-891-8397

Microwave Ovens

Accu Temp Products Inc
Fort Wayne, IN 800-210-5907

Acp Inc
Cedar Rapids, IA 319-368-8198
Cober Electronics, Inc.
Norwalk, CT 800-709-5948
Defreeze Corporation
Southborough, MA 508-485-8512
Hickory Industries
North Bergen, NJ 800-732-9153
Kreative Koncepts
Marquette, MI 800-638-2019
Microdry
Crestwood, KY 502-241-8933
Panasonic Commercial Food Service
Newark, NJ
Quasar Industries
Rochester Hills, MI. 248-852-0300
R F Schiffmann Assoc.
New York, NY 212-362-7021
Sharp Electronics Corporation
Mahwah, NJ 800-237-4277

Milking

Ben H. Anderson Manufacturers
Morrisonville, WI 608-846-5474
Coburn Company
Whitewater, WI 800-776-7042
Lyco Wausau
Wausau, WI 715-845-7867
Schlueter Company
Janesville, WI 800-359-1700

Mills

Ball & Pebble

Fernholtz Engineering
Van Nuys, CA 818-785-5800
Glen Mills Inc.
Clifton, NJ 973-777-0777
NaraKom
Peapack, NJ 908-234-1776
Paul O. Abbe
Bensenville, IL 630-350-2200
Union Process
Akron, OH 330-929-3333

Chocolate Grinding

Glen Mills Inc.
Clifton, NJ 973-777-0777
Union Process
Akron, OH 330-929-3333

Colloid

Bematek Systems Inc
Salem, MA 877-236-2835
Berkshire PPM
Litchfield, CT 860-567-3118
Chemicolloid Laboratories, Inc.
New Hyde Park, NY 516-747-2666
Glen Mills Inc.
Clifton, NJ 973-777-0777
National Oilwell Varco
North Andover, MA 800-643-0641
Silverson Machines Inc
East Longmeadow, MA 800-204-6400
Sonic Corp
Stratford, CT 866-493-1378
Waukesha Cherry-Burrell
Louisville, KY 502-491-4310

Copra Grinding & Crushing

ANDRITZ Inc
Muncy, PA 704-943-4343
Corenco
Santa Rosa, CA 888-267-3626

Corn Meal & Corn Flour

C S Bell Co
Tiffin, OH 888-958-6381
Glen Mills Inc.
Clifton, NJ 973-777-0777
International Reserve Equipment Corporation
Clarendon Hills, IL 708-531-0680
La Poblana Food Machines
Mesa, AZ 480-258-2091
M O Industries Inc
Whippany, NJ 973-386-9228

Curd

Damrow Company
Fond Du Lac, WI 800-236-1501

Feed

A T Ferrell Co Inc
Bluffton, IN. 800-248-8318
Amherst Milling Co
Amherst, VA 434-946-7601
ANDRITZ Inc
Muncy, PA. 704-943-4343
C S Bell Co
Tiffin, OH 888-958-6381
Custom Millers Supply Co
Monmouth, IL 309-734-6312
Forster & Son
Ada, OK 580-332-6021
Germantown Milling Company
Germantown, KY 606-728-5857
Meadows Mills Inc
North Wilkesboro, NC 800-626-2282
Summit Machine Builders Corporation
Denver, CO 800-274-6741

Flour & Cereal

CHS Inc.
Inver Grove Hts., MN 800-328-6539
Fernholtz Engineering
Van Nuys, CA 818-785-5800
Ferrell-Ross
Amarillo, TX. 800-299-9051
Germantown Milling Company
Germantown, KY 606-728-5857
International Reserve Equipment Corporation
Clarendon Hills, IL 708-531-0680
Lauhoff Corporation
Detroit, MI 313-259-0027
Lehi Mills
Lehi, UT 877-311-3566
Meadows Mills Inc
North Wilkesboro, NC 800-626-2282
Mill Engineering & Machinery Company
Oakland, CA 510-562-1832
Norvell Co Inc
Fort Scott, KS 800-653-3147
Satake USA
Stafford, TX 281-276-3600

Grinding

A C Horn & Co Sheet Metal
Dallas, TX. 800-657-6155
ANDRITZ Inc
Muncy, PA. 704-943-4343
Autio Co
Astoria, OR. 800-483-8884
C S Bell Co
Tiffin, OH 888-958-6381
Corenco
Santa Rosa, CA. 888-267-3626
Daily Printing Inc
Plymouth, MN. 800-622-6596
Ferrell-Ross
Amarillo, TX. 800-299-9051
Fitzpatrick Co
Elmhurst, IL 630-592-4425
Fluid Air Inc
Aurora, IL 630-665-5001
Fluid Energy Processing & Eqpt
Hatfield, PA. 215-368-2510
Gilson Co Inc
Lewis Center, OH 800-444-1508
Glen Mills Inc.
Clifton, NJ. 973-777-0777
Globe Machine
Tacoma, WA 800-523-6575
Goodnature Products
Orchard Park, NY 800-875-3381
Jayhawk Manufacturing Co Inc
Hutchinson, KS. 866-886-8269
Kemutec Group Inc
Bristol, PA. 215-788-8013
Lasermation Inc
Philadelphia, PA 800-523-2759
M O Industries Inc
Whippany, NJ 973-386-9228
Modern Process Equipment Inc
Chicago, IL 773-254-3929
NaraKom
Peapack, NJ. 908-234-1776

Nederman
Thomasville, NC. 800-533-5286
Netzsch Pumps North America
Exton, PA 610-363-8010
Straub Designs Co
St Louis Park, MN 952-546-6686
Union Process
Akron, OH. 330-929-3333

Hammer

A C Horn & Co Sheet Metal
Dallas, TX. 800-657-6155
A T Ferrell Co Inc
Bluffton, IN. 800-248-8318
ANDRITZ Inc
Muncy, PA. 704-943-4343
Berkshire PPM
Litchfield, CT 860-567-3118
C S Bell Co
Tiffin, OH 888-958-6381
Corenco
Santa Rosa, CA. 888-267-3626
CPM Roskamp Champion
Waterloo, IA 800-366-2563
Dehyco Company
Memphis, TN 901-774-3322
Duplex Mill & Mfg Co
Springfield, OH. 937-325-5555
Fernholtz Engineering
Van Nuys, CA 818-785-5800
Fitzpatrick Co
Elmhurst, IL 630-592-4425
Forster & Son
Ada, OK 580-332-6021
Glen Mills Inc.
Clifton, NJ. 973-777-0777
Globe Machine
Tacoma, WA 800-523-6575
Goodnature Products
Orchard Park, NY 800-875-3381
Jay-Bee Manufacturing Inc
Tyler, TX. 800-445-0610
Meadows Mills Inc
North Wilkesboro, NC 800-626-2282
NaraKom
Peapack, NJ. 908-234-1776
Schutte Buffalo Hammermill
Buffalo, NY. 800-447-4634

Malt

ANDRITZ Inc
Muncy, PA. 704-943-4343

Nut Grinding

A C Horn & Co Sheet Metal
Dallas, TX. 800-657-6155
ANDRITZ Inc
Muncy, PA. 704-943-4343
Corenco
Santa Rosa, CA. 888-267-3626
Straub Designs Co
St Louis Park, MN 952-546-6686

Oil Cake Grinding

ANDRITZ Inc
Muncy, PA. 704-943-4343
Corenco
Santa Rosa, CA. 888-267-3626

Peanut Butter

A C Horn & Co Sheet Metal
Dallas, TX. 800-657-6155
Berkshire PPM
Litchfield, CT 860-567-3118
Glen Mills Inc.
Clifton, NJ. 973-777-0777

Rice Grinding

ANDRITZ Inc
Muncy, PA. 704-943-4343
Satake USA
Stafford, TX 281-276-3600

Spice Grinding

ANDRITZ Inc
Muncy, PA. 704-943-4343
Berkshire PPM
Litchfield, CT 860-567-3118

Browne & Company
Markham, ON. 905-475-6104
C S Bell Co
Tiffin, OH 888-958-6381
Chef Specialties
Smethport, PA 800-440-2433
Corenco
Santa Rosa, CA. 888-267-3626
Ferrell-Ross
Amarillo, TX. 800-299-9051
Glen Mills Inc.
Clifton, NJ. 973-777-0777

Sugar & Sugar Cane

Silver Weibull
Aurora, CO 303-373-2311

Mixers

Eirich Machines
Gurnee, IL 847-336-2444
G & F Mfg
Oak Lawn, IL 800-282-1574
Hamilton Beach Brands
Southern Pines, NC. 800-851-8900
Quadro Engineering
Waterloo, ON 519-884-9660
Reiser
Canton, MA 734-821-1290
Thunderbird Food Machinery
Blaine, WA 866-875-6868

Bakers'

A&J Mixing International
Oakville, ON 800-668-3470
ABI Limited
Concord, ON 800-297-8666
Adamatic
Auburn, WA 800-578-2547
Alliance Bakery Systems
Blythewood, SC 803-691-9227
American Eagle Food Machinery
Chicago, IL 888-390-0800
AMF CANADA
Sherbrooke, QC 800-255-3869
Arcobaleno Pasta Machines
Lancaster, PA 800-875-7096
Arde Inc
Carlstadt, NJ 800-909-6070
Benier USA
Lithia Springs, GA 770-745-2200
Blakeslee, Inc.
Addison, IL 630-532-5021
Breddo Likwifier
Kansas City, MO. 800-669-4092
CMC America Corporation
Joliet, IL 815-726-4337
DBE Inc
Concord, ON. 800-461-5313
Empire Bakery Equipment
Hicksville, NY 800-878-4070
Exact Mixing Systems Inc
Memphis, TN 901-362-8501
Excellent Bakery Equipment Co
Fairfield, NJ 973-244-1664
Food Engineering Unlimited
Fullerton, CA 714-879-8762
Gemini Bakery Equipment
Philadelphia, PA 800-468-9046
Goodway Industries Inc
Bohemia, NY 800-943-4501
Hayes & Stolz Indl Mfg LTD
Fort Worth, TX 800-725-7272
Hebeler Corp
Tonawanda, NY 800-486-4709
International Reserve Equipment Corporation
Clarendon Hills, IL 708-531-0680
Kemper Bakery Systems
Rockaway, NJ 973-625-1566
Leland Limited Inc
South Plainfield, NJ 908-561-2000
Magna Machine Co
Cincinnati, OH 800-448-3475
Moline Machinery LLC
Duluth, MN. 800-767-5734
Packaging & Processing Equipment
Ayr, ON 519-622-6666
Pavailler Distribution Company
Northvale, NJ 201-767-0766
Peerless Dough Mixing and Make-Up
Sidney, OH 800-999-3327

Peerless Food Equipment
Sidney, OH 937-492-4158
Peerless Machinery Corporation
Sidney, OH 800-999-3327
Pro Bake Inc
Twinsburg, OH 800-837-4427
Rondo Inc
Moonachie, NJ 800-882-0633
T.K. Products
Anaheim, CA 714-621-0267
Thomas L. Green & Company
Robenosia, PA 610-693-5816
TMCo Inc.ÿ
Houston, TX 713-465-3255
Varimixer North America
Charlotte, NC 800-221-1138

Drum

Arde Inc
Carlstadt, NJ 800-909-6070
Custom Food Machinery
Stockton, CA 209-463-4343
Drum-Mates Inc.
Lumberton, NJ 800-621-3786
Eclipse Systems Inc
Milpitas, CA 408-263-2201
Glen Mills Inc.
Clifton, NJ 973-777-0777
Munson Machinery Co
Utica, NY 800-944-6644
National Oilwell Varco
North Andover, MA 800-643-0641
Packaging & Processing Equipment
Ayr, ON 519-622-6666
Scott Turbon Mixer
Adelanto, CA 800-285-8512

Food Processing

A & B Process Systems Corp
Stratford, WI 888-258-2789
A&J Mixing International
Oakville, ON 800-668-3470
A&M Process Equipment
Ajax, ON 905-619-8001
ADMIX
Manchester, NH 800-466-2369
AM-Mac
Fairfield, NJ 800-829-2018
American Extrusion Intl
South Beloit, IL 815-624-6616
American Food Equipment Company
Hayward, CA 510-783-0255
American Manufacturing-Engrng
Cleveland, OH 800-822-9402
AMF CANADA
Sherbrooke, QC 800-255-3869
Apache Stainless Equipment
Beaver Dam, WI 800-444-0398
APEC
Lake Odessa, MI 616-374-1000
APV Americas
Delavan, WI 800-252-5200
Arcobaleno Pasta Machines
Lancaster, PA 800-875-7096
Arde Inc
Carlstadt, NJ 800-909-6070
Automated Food Systems
Waxahachie, TX 469-517-0470
AZO Food
Memphis, TN 901-794-9480
B C Holland Inc
Dousman, WI 262-965-2939
Baldewein Company
Lake Forrest, IL 800-424-5544
Bematek Systems Inc
Salem, MA 877-236-2835
Bepex International LLC
Minneapolis, MN 800-607-2470
Berkshire PPM
Litchfield, CT 860-567-3118
Biro Manufacturing Co
Lakeside Marblhd, OH 419-798-4451
Blakeslee, Inc.
Addison, IL 630-532-5021
Blue Tech
Hickory, NC 828-324-5900
Bowers Process Equipment
Stratford, ON 800-567-3223
Breddo Likwifier
Kansas City, MO 800-669-4092

Bulldog Factory Svc LLC
Madison Heights, MI 248-541-3500
Bush Tank Fabricators Inc
Newark, NJ 973-596-1121
California Vibratory Feeders
Anaheim, CA 800-354-0972
Carlisle Food Svc Products Inc
Oklahoma City, OK 800-654-8210
Charles Ross & Son Co
Hauppauge, NY 800-243-7677
Cinelli Esperia
Woodbridge, ON 905-856-1820
Cleveland-Eastern Mixers
Clinton, CT 800-243-1188
CMC America Corporation
Joliet, IL 815-726-4337
Coastline Equipment Inc
Bellingham, WA 360-734-8509
Columbus Instruments
Columbus, OH 800-669-5011
Cornell Machine Co
Springfield, NJ 973-379-6860
CRC Inc
Council Bluffs, IA 712-323-9477
Custom Food Machinery
Stockton, CA 209-463-4343
Davron Technologies Inc
Chattanooga, TN 423-870-1888
Dito Dean Food Prep
Charlotte, NC 866-449-4200
Dorton Incorporated
Arlington Hts, IL 800-299-8600
Drum-Mates Inc.
Lumberton, NJ 800-621-3786
Duplex Mill & Mfg Co
Springfield, OH 937-325-5555
Eclipse Systems Inc
Milpitas, CA 408-263-2201
Eirich Machines
Gurnee, IL 847-336-2444
EKATO Corporation
St Ramsey, NJ 201-825-4684
Empire Bakery Equipment
Hicksville, NY 800-878-4070
Ertelalsop
Kingston, NY 800-553-7835
Et Oakes Corp
Hauppauge, NY 631-232-0002
Exact Mixing Systems Inc
Memphis, TN 901-362-8501
Expert Industries Inc
Brooklyn, NY 718-434-6060
Falco Technologies
La Prairie, QC 450-444-0566
Fernholtz Engineering
Van Nuys, CA 818-785-5800
Fish Oven & Equipment Co
Wauconda, IL 877-526-8720
Fitzpatrick Co
Elmhurst, IL 630-592-4425
Food Engineering Unlimited
Fullerton, CA 714-879-8762
Food Processing Equipment Co
Santa Fe Springs, CA 562-802-3727
GEM Equipment Of Oregon Inc
Woodburn, OR 503-982-9902
General, Inc
Weston, FL 954-202-7419
Glen Mills Inc.
Clifton, NJ 973-777-0777
Goodway Industries Inc
Bohemia, NY 800-943-4501
Grant-Letchworth
Tonawanda, NY 716-692-1000
Hamilton Beach Brands
Southern Pines, NC 800-851-8900
Hayes & Stolz Indl Mfg LTD
Fort Worth, TX 800-725-7272
Hebeler Corp
Tonawanda, NY 800-486-4709
Hollymatic Corp
Countryside, IL 708-579-3700
Hosokawa/Bepex Corporation
Santa Rosa, CA 707-586-6000
Howard Fabrication
City of Industry, CA 626-961-0114
Howes S Co Inc
Silver Creek, NY 888-255-2611
International Reserve Equipment Corporation
Clarendon Hills, IL 708-531-0680
JW Leser Company
Los Angeles, CA 323-731-4173

Kady International
Scarborough, ME 800-367-5239
Karl Schnell
New London, WI 920-982-9974
Kelmin Products
Plymouth, FL 407-886-6079
Kemutec Group Inc
Bristol, PA 215-788-8013
Kinetic Equipment Company
Appleton, WI 806-293-4471
KOFLO Corp
Cary, IL 800-782-8427
Leland Limited Inc
South Plainfield, NJ 908-561-2000
LIST
Acton, MA 978-635-9521
Littleford Day
Florence, KY 800-365-8555
Machanix Fabrication Inc
Chino, CA 800-700-9701
Mandeville Company
Minneapolis, MN 800-328-8490
Marel Food Systems, Inc.
Lenexa, KS 913-888-9110
Matcon Americas
Elmhurst, IL 856-256-1330
Matfer Inc
Van Nuys, CA 800-766-0333
McCarter Corporation
Norristown, PA 610-272-3203
Merlin Process Equipment
Houston, TX 713-221-1651
Microfluidics International
Westwood, MA 800-370-5452
Midwest Metalcraft & Equipment
Windsor, MO. 800-647-3167
Modern Process Equipment Inc
Chicago, IL 773-254-3929
Munson Machinery Co
Utica, NY 800-944-6644
Nalge Process Technologies Group
Rochester, NY 585-586-8800
National Oilwell Varco
North Andover, MA 800-643-0641
Pacific Process Technology
La Jolla, CA 858-551-3298
Package Concepts & Materials Inc
Greenville, SC. 800-424-7264
Packaging & Processing Equipment
Ayr, ON 519-622-6666
Patterson-Kelley   Hars Company
East Stroudsburg, PA 570-421-7500
Paul Mueller Co Inc
Springfield, MO 800-683-5537
Paul O. Abbe
Bensenville, IL 630-350-2200
Paxton Corp
Bristol, RI 401-396-9062
Peerless Machinery Corporation
Sidney, OH 800-999-3327
Polar Process
Plattsville, ON 877-896-8077
PolyMaid Company
Largo, FL 800-206-9188
Prince Castle Inc
Carol Stream, IL 800-722-7853
Process Systems
Barrington, IL 847-842-8618
Production Packaging & Processing Equipment Company
Savannah, GA 912-856-4281
Provisur Technologies, Inc.
Mokena, IL 708-479-3500
Puritan Manufacturing Inc
Omaha, NE 800-331-0487
Readco Kurimoto LLC
York, PA 800-395-4959
Reading Bakery Systems Inc
Robesonia, PA. 610-693-5816
Reiser
Canton, MA 734-821-1290
Ross Engineering Inc
Savannah, GA 800-524-7677
Savage Brothers Company
Elk Grove Vlg, IL 800-342-0973
Scott Turbon Mixer
Adelanto, CA 800-285-8512
Semi-Bulk Systems Inc
Fenton, MO. 800-732-8769
Silverson Machines Inc
East Longmeadow, MA 800-204-6400

Sonic Corp
Stratford, CT................866-493-1378
South River Machine
Hackensack, NJ.............201-487-1736
Specific Mechanical Systems
Victoria, BC...............250-652-2111
Stainless Fabrication Inc
Springfield, MO 800-397-8265
Stephan Machinery, Inc.
Mundelein, IL 800-783-7426
Stricklin Co
Dallas, TX................214-637-1030
Superior Products Company
Saint Paul, MN 800-328-9800
T.K. Products
Anaheim, CA 714-621-0267
TDH
Sand Springs, OK.........888-251-7961
Thomas L. Green & Company
Robenosia, PA.............610-693-5816
TSA Griddle Systems
Kelowna, BC..............250-491-9025
Varimixer North America
Charlotte, NC.............800-221-1138
Viatec
Victoria, BC..............800-942-4702
Vitamix
Olmsted Twp, OH.........800-437-4654
Waring Products
Torrington, CT............800-492-7464
Washington Frontier
Grandview, WA............509-469-7662
Weiler & Company
Whitewater, WI............800-558-9507
Welbilt Corporation
Stamford, CT..............203-325-8300
Wilevco Inc
Billerica, MA 978-667-0400

Food, Household, Hotel & Restaurant

Arcobaleno Pasta Machines
Lancaster, PA 800-875-7096
Attias Oven Corp
Brooklyn, NY 800-928-8427
Blakeslee, Inc.
Addison, IL 630-532-5021
CRC Inc
Council Bluffs, IA..........712-323-9477
Custom Food Machinery
Stockton, CA..............209-463-4343
Dorton Incorporated
Arlington Hts, IL 800-299-8600
General, Inc
Weston, FL 954-202-7419
Island Oasis Frozen Cocktail
Beloit, WI 800-777-4752
Jiffy Mixer Co Inc
Corona, CA 800-560-2903
Leland Limited Inc
South Plainfield, NJ 908-561-2000
Mandeville Company
Minneapolis, MN 800-328-8490
Matfer Inc
Van Nuys, CA.............800-766-0333
Nalge Process Technologies Group
Rochester, NY.............585-586-8800
Packaging & Processing Equipment
Ayr, ON..................519-622-6666
Paul Mueller Co Inc
Springfield, MO 800-683-5537
Paxton Corp
Bristol, RI................401-396-9062
Prince Castle Inc
Carol Stream, IL...........800-722-7853
Puritan Manufacturing Inc
Omaha, NE 800-331-0487
Superior Products Company
Saint Paul, MN 800-328-9800
T.K. Products
Anaheim, CA 714-621-0267
Toronto Kitchen Equipment
North York, ON............416-745-4944
Univex Corp
Salem, NH. 800-258-6358
Varimixer North America
Charlotte, NC.............800-221-1138
VitaMinder Company
Providence, RI 800-858-8840
Welbilt Corporation
Stamford, CT..............203-325-8300

Paste Products

A & B Process Systems Corp
Stratford, WI..............888-258-2789
Breddo Likwifier
Kansas City, MO...........800-669-4092
Kelmin Products
Plymouth, FL 407-886-6079
McCarter Corporation
Norristown, PA 610-272-3203
National Oilwell Varco
North Andover, MA 800-643-0641
Packaging & Processing Equipment
Ayr, ON..................519-622-6666
Paxton Corp
Bristol, RI................401-396-9062
Polar Process
Plattsville, ON.............877-896-8077
Reiser
Canton, MA 734-821-1290

Nut Cracking, Shelling & Salting

A C Horn & Co Sheet Metal
Dallas, TX................800-657-6155
Carolina Cracker
Garner, NC 919-779-6899
Design Technology Corporation
Billerica, MA 978-663-7000
Key Technology Inc.
Walla Walla, WA...........509-529-2161
Krispy Kist Company
Chicago, IL 312-733-0900
Lewis M Carter Mfg Co Inc
Donalsonville, GA 800-332-8232
Maddox/Adams International
Miami, FL 305-592-3337
Modern Electronics Inc
Grand Cane, LA 318-872-4764
Nutty Bavarian
Sanford, FL 800-382-4788
Satake USA
Stafford, TX..............281-276-3600

Oil Extraction

Abanaki Corp
Chagrin Falls, OH..........800-358-7546
Alfa Laval Inc
Richmond, VA.............866-253-2528
Anderson International Corp
Stow, OH.................800-336-4730
Caron Products & Svc Inc
Marietta, OH..............800-648-3042
Crown Iron Works Company
Roseville, MN..............888-703-7500
French Oil Mill Machinery Co
Piqua, OH................937-773-3420

Ovens

A C Horn & Co Sheet Metal
Dallas, TX................800-657-6155
ABI Limited
Concord, ON..............800-297-8666
Accu Temp Products Inc
Fort Wayne, IN 800-210-5907
Acp Inc
Cedar Rapids, IA...........319-368-8198
Adamatic
Auburn, WA..............800-578-2547
Allied Bakery and Food Service Equipment
Santa Fe Springs, CA 562-945-6506
ALPI Food Preparation Equipment
Bolton, ON...............800-928-2574
Alto-Shaam
Menomonee Falls, WI.......800-329-8744
American Extrusion Intl
South Beloit, IL 815-624-6616
American Range
Pacoima, CA..............888-753-9898
AMF CANADA
Sherbrooke, QC 800-255-3869
Anetsberger
Concord, NH..............603-225-6684
Antrim Manufacturing Inc
Brookfield, WI 262-781-6860
Apollo Sheet Metal
Kennewick, WA............509-586-1104
Attias Oven Corp
Brooklyn, NY 800-928-8427
Bakers Pride Oven Company
New Rochelle, NY 800-431-2745

Bakery Associates
Setauket, NY..............631-751-4156
Ballantyne Food Service Equipment
Omaha, NE 800-424-1215
Baxter Manufacturing Inc
Orting, WA 800-777-2828
Bbc Industries
Pacific, MO...............800-654-4205
Benier USA
Lithia Springs, GA 770-745-2200
Benko Products
Sheffield Vlg, OH..........440-934-2180
Bethel Engineering & Equipment Inc
New Hampshire, OH........800-889-6129
Bevles Company
Dallas, TX................800-441-1601
BKI Worldwide
Simpsonville, SC 800-927-6887
Blodgett Inc
Burlington, VT 800-331-5842
Blodgett Oven Co
Burlington, VT 800-331-5842
Bolling Oven & Machine Company
Avon, OH 440-937-6112
C H Babb Co Inc
Raynham, MA.............508-977-0600
Casso-Solar Corporation
Nanuet, NY...............800-988-4455
Chase Industries Inc
West Chester, OH..........800-543-4455
Checker Machine
Minneapolis, MN 888-800-5001
Chesmont Engineering Co Inc
Exton, PA 610-594-9200
Cincinnati Industrial Machry
Mason, OH...............800-677-0076
Cinelli Esperia
Woodbridge, ON...........905-856-1820
Cleveland Range
Cleveland, OH.............800-338-2204
Coast Scientific
Rancho Santa Fe, CA 800-445-1544
Cober Electronics, Inc.
Norwalk, CT..............800-709-5948
Comstock Castle Stove Co
Quincy, IL 800-637-9188
Cookshack
Ponca City, OK............800-423-0698
Custom Diamond International
Laval, QC 800-363-5926
Cutler Industries
Morton Grove, IL 800-458-5593
Davron Technologies Inc
Chattanooga, TN...........423-870-1888
DBE Inc
Concord, ON..............800-461-5313
Defreeze Corporation
Southborough, MA.........508-485-8512
Deluxe Equipment Company
Bradenton, FL.............800-367-8931
Doyon Equipment
Liniere, QC 800-463-4273
Duke Manufacturing Co
St Louis, MO..............800-735-3853
Dynamic Cooking Systems
Huntington Beach, CA 800-433-8466
Earthstone Wood-Fire Ovens
Glendale, CA 800-840-4915
Empire Bakery Equipment
Hicksville, NY 800-878-4070
Ensign Ribbon Burners LLC
Pelham, NY...............914-813-0815
Epcon Industrial Systems
Conroe, TX...............800-447-7872
Equipex Limited
Providence, RI 800-649-7885
Excellent Bakery Equipment Co
Fairfield, NJ 973-244-1664
Fab-X/Metals
Washington, NC 800-677-3229
FBM/Baking Machines Inc
Cranbury, NJ 800-449-0433
FECO/MOCO
Warren, OH..............800-547-1527
Fish Oven & Equipment Co
Wauconda, IL 877-526-8720
FlashBake Ovens Food Service
Fremont, CA..............800-843-6836
Food Engineering Unlimited
Fullerton, CA 714-879-8762
FOODesign from tna
Wilsonville, OR 503-685-5030

Foster Refrigerator Corporation
Kinderhook, NY 888-828-3311
Franz Haas Machinery-America
Henrico, VA 804-222-6022
Friedrich Metal Products
Browns Summit, NC 800-772-0326
Garland Commercial Ranges
Mississauga, ON 905-624-0260
Garland Commercial Ranges Ltd.
Mississauga, ON 905-624-0260
Gehnrich Oven Sales Company
East Troy, WI 262-642-3938
Gemini Bakery Equipment
Philadelphia, PA 800-468-9046
Glenro Inc
Paterson, NJ 888-453-6761
Grande Chef Company
Orangeville, ON 519-942-4470
Hardt Equipment Manufacturing
Lachine, QC 888-848-4408
Hasty Bake Charcoal Grills
Tulsa, OK .800-426-6836
Hatco Corp
Milwaukee, WI 800-558-0607
Henry Group
Greenville, TX 903-883-2002
Hercules Food Equipment
Weston, ON 416-742-9673
Hickory Industries
North Bergen, NJ 800-732-9153
Holman Cooking Equipment
Saint Louis, MO 888-356-5362
Illinois Range Company
Schiller Park, IL 800-535-7041
Imperial Manufacturing Co
Corona, CA 800-343-7790
Industronics Service Co
South Windsor, CT 800-878-1551
IR Systems
Jupiter, FL 800-893-7540
J C Ford Co
La Habra, CA 714-871-7361
Jackson Msc LLC
Gray, KY .888-800-5672
K B Systems Inc
Bangor, PA 610-588-7788
Kemper Bakery Systems
Rockaway, NJ 973-625-1566
La Poblana Food Machines
Mesa, AZ .480-258-2091
Laboratory Devices
Holliston, MA 508-429-1716
Lang Manufacturing Co
Everett, WA 800-882-6368
Lanly Co
Cleveland, OH 216-731-1115
Legion Industries Inc
Waynesboro, GA 800-887-1988
LPS Technology
Grafton, OH 800-586-1410
Ltg Inc
Spartanburg, SC 864-599-6340
Lucks Food Equipment Company
Kent, WA .811-824-0696
M F & B Restaurant Systems Inc
Dunbar, PA 724-628-3050
Market Forge Industries Inc
Everett, MA 866-698-3188
Martin/Baron
Irwindale, CA 626-960-5153
Mayekawa USA, Inc.
Chicago, IL 773-516-5070
Merco/Savory
Mt. Pleasant, MI 800-733-8821
Meyer Machine & Garroutte Products
San Antonio, TX 210-736-1811
Microdry
Crestwood, KY 502-241-8933
Middleby Corp
Elgin, IL 847-741-3300
Middleby Marshall Inc
Elgin, IL 847-741-3300
Moffat
San Antonio, TX 866-589-0664
Montague Co
Hayward, CA 800-345-1830
Mosshaim Innovations
Jacksonville, FL 888-995-7775
Motom Corporation
Bensenville, IL 630-787-1995
Mugnaini Imports
Watsonville, CA 888-887-7206

National Drying Machry Co Inc
Philadelphia, PA 215-464-6070
National Hotpack
Stone Ridge, NY 800-431-8232
Nevo Corporation
Ronkonkoma, NY 631-585-8787
Normandie Metal Fabricators
Port Washington, NY 800-221-2398
Nothum Food Processing Systems
Springfield, MO 800-435-1297
Nu-Vu Food Service Systems
Menominee, MI 800-338-9886
Packotronics
Glenview, IL 947-487-1281
Panasonic Commercial Food Service
Newark, NJ
Pavailler Distribution Company
Northvale, NJ 201-767-0766
Peerless Gouet LLC
Lafayette, CO 720-890-7306
Peerless Ovens
Sandusky, OH 800-548-4514
Peerless-Premier Appliance Co
Belleville, IL 618-233-0475
Pier 1 Imports
Woodcliff Lake, NJ 800-448-9993
Piper Products Inc
Wausau, WI 800-544-3057
PMI Food Equipment Group
Troy, OH .937-332-3000
Pro Scientific Inc
Oxford, CT 800-584-3776
Process Heating Corp
Shrewsbury, MA 508-842-5200
Proheatco Manufacturing
Pomona, CA 800-423-4195
Proluxe
Paramount, CA 800-594-5528
Q-Matic Technologies
Carol Stream, IL 800-880-6836
QNC Inc
Dallas, TX 888-668-3687
Quasar Industries
Rochester Hills, MI 248-852-0300
Randell Manufacturing   Unified Brands
Weidman, MI 888-994-7636
Rankin Delux
Mira Loma, CA 951-685-0081
Rational Cooking Systems
Schaumburg, IL 888-320-7274
Reading Bakery Systems Inc
Robesonia, PA 610-693-5816
Reed Oven Co
Kansas City, MO 816-842-7446
Reliable Food Service Equipment
Concord, ON 416-738-6840
Remco Industries International
Fort Lauderdale, FL 800-987-3626
Renato Specialty Product
Garland, TX 866-575-6316
Revent Inc
Piscataway, NJ 732-777-9433
Rotisol France Inc
Inglewood, CA 800-651-5969
Roto-Flex Oven Co
San Antonio, TX 877-859-1463
Royalton Foodservice Equip Co
North Royalton, OH 800-662-8765
Ruiz Flour Tortillas
Riverside, CA 909-947-7811
Server Products Inc
Richfield, WI 800-558-8722
Sharp Electronics Corporation
Mahwah, NJ 800-237-4277
Shouldice Brothers SheetMetal
Battle Creek, MI 269-962-5579
Solbern Corp
Fairfield, NJ 973-227-3030
Southbend
Fuquay Varina, NC 800-348-2558
Southern Pride Distributing
Alamo, TN 800-851-8180
Stafford-Smith Inc
Kalamazoo, MI 800-968-2442
Stainless Steel Fabricator Inc
La Mirada, CA 714-739-9904
Standex International Corp.
Salem, NH 603-893-9701
Stewart Systems Baking LLC
Plano, TX .972-422-5808
Super-Chef Manufacturing Company
Houston, TX 800-231-3478

Superior Products Company
Saint Paul, MN 800-328-9800
Thermodyne Foodservice Prods
Fort Wayne, IN 800-526-9182
Thomas L. Green & Company
Robenosia, PA 610-693-5816
Toastmaster
Elgin, IL 847-741-3300
Toronto Kitchen Equipment
North York, ON 416-745-4944
Townfood Equipment Corp
Brooklyn, NY 800-221-5032
Trak-Air/Rair
Denver, CO 800-688-8725
Triad Scientific
Manasquan, NJ 800-867-6690
Trimen Foodservice Equipment
North York, ON 877-437-1422
TURBOCHEF Technologies
Carrollton, TX 800-908-8726
Valad Electric Heating Corporation
Tarrytown, NY 914-631-4927
Vortron Smokehouse/Ovens
Iron Ridge, WI 800-874-1949
Vulcan Food Equipment Group
Baltimore, MD 800-814-2028
Welbilt Corporation
Stamford, CT 203-325-8300
Western Combustion Engineering
Carson, CA 310-834-9389
Win-Holt Equipment Group
Syosset, NY 800-444-3595
Winston Industries
Louisville, KY 800-234-5286
Wisco Industries Assembly
Oregon, WI 800-999-4726
Wittco Foodservice Equipment
Milwaukee, WI 800-367-8413
Wolf Company
Louisville, KY 800-814-2028
Wood Stone Corp
Bellingham, WA 800-988-8103

Packers' & Butchers'

Aaron Equipment Co Div Areco
Bensenville, IL 630-350-2200
Allen Gauge & Tool Co
Pittsburgh, PA 412-241-6410
AM-Mac
Fairfield, NJ 800-829-2018
Architecture Plus Intl Inc
Rocky Point, FL 813-281-9299
Automated Food Systems
Waxahachie, TX 469-517-0470
B H Bunn Co
Lakeland, FL 800-222-2866
Best & Donovan
Blue Ash, OH 800-553-2378
Biro Manufacturing Co
Lakeside Marblhd, OH 419-798-4451
Chop-Rite Two Inc
Harleysville, PA 800-683-5858
CMC America Corporation
Joliet, IL 815-726-4337
Compacker Systems LLC
Davenport, IA 563-391-2751
Customized Equipment SE
Tucker, GA 770-934-9300
Dc Tech
Kansas City, MO 877-742-9090
Doering Co
Clear Lake, MN 320-743-2276
Durable Packaging Corporation
Countryside, IL 800-700-5677
Ennio International
Aurora, IL .630-851-5808
Friedr Dick Corp
Farmingdale, NY 800-554-3425
Globe Food Equipment Co
Moraine, OH 800-347-5423
Grant-Letchworth
Tonawanda, NY 716-692-1000
Hollymatic Corp
Countryside, IL 708-579-3700
Indeco Products Inc
San Marcos, TX 888-246-3326
Kasel Industries Inc
Denver, CO 800-218-4417
Kohler Industries Inc
Lincoln, NE 800-365-6708

Linker Machines
   Rockaway, NJ 973-983-0001
Marlen International
   Astoria, OR .800-862-7536
Molins/Sandiacre Richmond
   Richmond, VA 864-486-4000
Pemberton & Associates
   Brooklyn, NY 800-736-2664
Pickwick Manufacturing Svc
   Cedar Rapids, IA 800-397-9797
Preferred Machining Corporation
   Englewood, CO 303-761-1535
Pressure Pack
   Williamsburg, VA 757-220-3693
Professional Marketing Group
   Seattle, WA .800-227-3769
Ranger Tool Co Inc
   Memphis, TN 800-737-9999
Schroeder Machine
   San Marcos, CA 760-591-9733
Sperling Industries
   Omaha, NE 402-556-4070
Stork Townsend Inc.
   Des Moines, IA 800-247-8609
Walsroder Packaging
   Willowbrook, IL 800-882-9987

Panomatic-Flour Collection System

AGET Manufacturing Co
   Adrian, MI 517-263-5781

Pasta Processing

A.K. Robins
   Baltimore, MD 800-486-9656
ALPI Food Preparation Equipment
   Bolton, ON 800-928-2574
APV Baker
   Goldsboro, NC 919-736-4309
Arcobaleno Pasta Machines
   Lancaster, PA 800-875-7096
Demaco
   Ridgewood, NY
Design Technology Corporation
   Billerica, MA 978-663-7000
Exact Mixing Systems Inc
   Memphis, TN 901-362-8501
Gemini Bakery Equipment
   Philadelphia, PA 800-468-9046
I J White Corp
   Farmingdale, NY 631-293-2211
Industrial Product Corp
   Ho Ho Kus, NJ 800-472-5913
Kemper Bakery Systems
   Rockaway, NJ 973-625-1566
Lawrence Equipment Inc
   South El Monte, CA 800-423-4500
Lyco Manufacturing
   Wausau, WI. .715-845-7867
MBC Food Machinery Corp
   Hackensack, NJ. 201-489-7000
Molded Fiber Glass Tray Company
   Linesville, PA 800-458-6050
Mouli Manufacturing Corporation
   Belleville, NJ 800-789-8285
Multi-Fill Inc
   West Jordan, UT 801-280-1570
Oshikiri Corp Of America
   Philadelphia, PA 215-637-8112
Pavan USA Inc
   Emigsville, PA 717-767-4889
Peerless Dough Mixing and Make-Up
   Sidney, OH 800-999-3327
Phase II Pasta Machine Inc
   Farmingdale, NY 800-457-5070
Pier 1 Imports
   Woodcliff Lake, NJ 800-448-9993
Pro Bake Inc
   Twinsburg, OH 800-837-4427
Rademaker USA
   Hudson, OH .330-650-2345
Reiser
   Canton, MA .734-821-1290
Rheon USA
   Irvine, CA 949-768-1900
Shick Esteve
   Kansas City, MO. 877-744-2587
South River Machine
   Hackensack, NJ. 201-487-1736
Spraying Systems Company
   Wheaton, IL .630-655-5000

Stephan Machinery, Inc.
   Mundelein, IL 800-783-7426
Techno-Design
   Union, KY 800-641-1822
TWM Manufacturing
   Leamington, ON 888-495-4831
UniTrak Corporation
   Port Hope, ON 866-883-5749
US Tsubaki Holdings Inc
   Wheeling, IL .800-323-7790
Wohl Associates Inc
   Bohemia, NY 631-244-7979

Pasteurizers

AGC
   Bristow, VA. .800-825-8820
API Heat Transfer Inc
   Buffalo, NY .877-274-4328
Arcobaleno Pasta Machines
   Lancaster, PA 800-875-7096
B T Engineering Inc
   Bala Cynwyd, PA 610-664-9500
Chad Co Inc
   Olathe, KS. 800-444-8360
Chester-Jensen Co., Inc.
   Chester, PA 800-685-3750
Convay Systems
   Minnetonka, MN 800-334-1099
Eischen Enterprises
   Fresno, CA 559-834-0013
Feldmeier Equipment Inc
   Syracuse, NY 315-454-8608
FleetwoodGoldcoWyard
   Romeoville, IL 630-759-6800
Frigoscandia
   Redmond, WA. 800-423-1743
Globe Machine
   Tacoma, WA .800-523-6575
Goodnature Products
   Orchard Park, NY 800-875-3381
Krones
   Franklin, WI .800-752-3787
MicroThermics, Inc.
   Raleigh, NC .919-878-8045
Pacific Process Technology
   La Jolla, CA .858-551-3298
Packaging & Processing Equipment
   Ayr, ON 519-622-6666
Pneumatic Scale Angelus
   Cuyahoga Falls, OH 330-923-0491
Relco Unisystems Corp
   Willmar, MN 320-231-2210
Sanchelima International
   Miami, FL 305-591-4343
Schlueter Company
   Janesville, WI 800-359-1700
South Valley Mfg Inc
   Gilroy, CA 408-842-5457
Stanfos
   Edmonton, AB 800-661-5648
Stephan Machinery, Inc.
   Mundelein, IL 800-783-7426
Unitherm Food System
   Bristow, OK .918-367-0197
Whey Systems
   Willmar, MN 320-905-4122

Peanut Processing

A C Horn & Co Sheet Metal
   Dallas, TX. 800-657-6155
ANDRITZ Inc
   Muncy, PA. 704-943-4343
Krispy Kist Company
   Chicago, IL 312-733-0900
Lewis M Carter Mfg Co Inc
   Donalsonville, GA 800-332-8232
Star Manufacturing Intl Inc
   St Louis, MO. 800-264-7827
Straub Designs Co
   St Louis Park, MN 952-546-6686
Suffolk Iron Works Inc
   Suffolk, VA 757-539-2353
UniTrak Corporation
   Port Hope, ON 866-883-5749

Cleaners & Shellers

Southern Ag Co Inc
   Blakely, GA. .229-723-4262

Pickers

Poultry

Brower
   Houghton, IA 800-553-1791
M & M Poultry Equipment Inc
   Hollister, MO 800-872-9687
MSSH
   Greensburg, IN 812-663-2180
Pickwick Manufacturing Svc
   Cedar Rapids, IA. 800-397-9797

Pizza & Pizza Products Processing

ABI Limited
   Concord, ON. 800-297-8666
AC Dispensing Equipment
   Lower Sackville, NS 888-777-9990
ALPI Food Preparation Equipment
   Bolton, ON 800-928-2574
APV Baker
   Goldsboro, NC 919-736-4309
Bakers Pride Oven Company
   New Rochelle, NY 800-431-2745
Benier USA
   Lithia Springs, GA 770-745-2200
C H Babb Co Inc
   Raynham, MA. 508-977-0600
Christy Machine Co
   Fremont, OH 888-332-6451
CIM Bakery Equipment of USA
   Arlington Heights, IL 847-818-8121
Comtec Industries
   Woodridge, IL 630-759-9000
DBE Inc
   Concord, ON. 800-461-5313
Doughpro
   Perris, CA 800-594-5528
DoughXpress
   Pittsburg, KS 800-835-0606
Doyon Equipment
   Liniere, QC 800-463-4273
Dutchess Bakers' Machinery Co
   Superior, WI .800-777-4498
Exact Mixing Systems Inc
   Memphis, TN 901-362-8501
Fritsch USA
   San Antonio, TX. 210-491-9309
Garland Commercial Ranges
   Mississauga, ON 905-624-0260
Garland Commercial Ranges Ltd.
   Mississauga, ON 905-624-0260
Gemini Bakery Equipment
   Philadelphia, PA 800-468-9046
Grote Co
   Columbus, OH 888-534-7683
I J White Corp
   Farmingdale, NY. 631-293-2211
Industrial Ceramic Products
   Marysville, OH 800-427-2278
Kemper Bakery Systems
   Rockaway, NJ 973-625-1566
Lanly Co
   Cleveland, OH 216-731-1115
Lawrence Equipment Inc
   South El Monte, CA 800-423-4500
Martin/Baron
   Irwindale, CA 626-960-5153
Matiss
   St Georges, QC 888-562-8477
Merco/Savory
   Mt. Pleasant, MI 800-733-8821
Molded Fiber Glass Tray Company
   Linesville, PA 800-458-6050
Normandie Metal Fabricators
   Port Washington, NY 800-221-2398
Oshikiri Corp Of America
   Philadelphia, PA 215-637-8112
Paxton Corp
   Bristol, RI 401-396-9062
Peerless Dough Mixing and Make-Up
   Sidney, OH 800-999-3327
Peerless Food Equipment
   Sidney, OH 937-492-4158
Peerless Ovens
   Sandusky, OH 800-548-4514
Piper Products Inc
   Wausau, WI. .800-544-3057
Pizzamatic USA
   South Holland, IL 888-749-9279
Pro Bake Inc
   Twinsburg, OH 800-837-4427

Proluxe
Paramount, CA 800-594-5528
Rademaker USA
Hudson, OH 330-650-2345
Raque Food Systems
Louisville, KY 502-267-9641
Reiser
Canton, MA 734-821-1290
Remco Industries International
Fort Lauderdale, FL 800-987-3626
Renato Specialty Product
Garland, TX 866-575-6316
Rheon USA
Irvine, CA 949-768-1900
Roto-Flex Oven Co
San Antonio, TX 877-859-1463
Server Products Inc
Richfield, WI 800-558-8722
Shick Esteve
Kansas City, MO 877-744-2587
Southbend
Fuquay Varina, NC 800-348-2558
Stephan Machinery, Inc.
Mundelein, IL 800-783-7426
Trak-Air/Rair
Denver, CO 800-688-8725
US Tsubaki Holdings Inc
Wheeling, IL 800-323-7790
Vulcan Food Equipment Group
Baltimore, MD 800-814-2028
Wood Stone Corp
Bellingham, WA 800-988-8103

Potato Chip Processing

Graybill Machines Inc
Lititz, PA 717-626-5221
Krispy Kist Company
Chicago, IL 312-733-0900
Pavan USA Inc
Emigsville, PA 717-767-4889
Paxton Corp
Bristol, RI 401-396-9062
Polar Process
Plattsville, ON 877-896-8077

Poultry Processing

Advance Energy Technologies
Halfmoon, NY 800-724-0198
Automated Food Systems
Waxahachie, TX 469-517-0470
Bluffton Motor Works
Bluffton, IN 800-579-8527
Brower
Houghton, IA 800-553-1791
Designpro Engineering
Clearwater, MN 800-221-4144
Doering Co
Clear Lake, MN 320-743-2276
Ennio International
Aurora, IL 630-851-5808
Falcon Fabricators Inc
Nashville, TN 615-832-0027
Gainco Inc
Gainesville, GA 800-467-2828
ICB Greenline
Charlotte, NC 800-331-5312
Johnson Food Equipment Inc
Kansas City, KS 800-288-3434
Kent Co
North Miami, FL 800-521-4886
Lyco Wausau
Wausau, WI 715-845-7867
Maja Equipment Company
Omaha, NE 402-346-6252
Marel Stork Poultry Processing
Gainesville, GA 770-532-7041
Marlen International
Astoria, OR 800-862-7536
Mepsco
Batavia, IL 800-323-8535
Millard Manufacturing Corp
La Vista, NE 800-662-4263
Miller Metal Fabrication
Bridgeville, DE 302-337-2291
Morris & Associates
Garner, NC 919-582-9200
Mp Equip. Co.
Buford, GA 770-614-5355
MSSH
Greensburg, IN 812-663-2180

P & F Machine
Turlock, CA 209-667-2515
Paoli Properties
Rockford, IL 815-965-0621
Pemberton & Associates
Brooklyn, NY 800-736-2664
Pickwick Manufacturing Svc
Cedar Rapids, IA 800-397-9797
Polar Process
Plattsville, ON 877-896-8077
Preferred Machining Corporation
Englewood, CO 303-761-1535
Prince Industries Inc
Murrayville, GA 800-441-3303
Reiser
Canton, MA 734-821-1290
Stork Townsend Inc.
Des Moines, IA 800-247-8609
Tech-Roll Inc
Blaine, WA 888-946-3929

Preservation

Irradiation

Nydree Flooring
Forest, VA 800-682-5698
Paragon Group USA
St Petersburg, FL 800-835-6962

Presses

Oil, Cottonseed & Linseed

Alfa Laval Ashbrook Simon-Hartley
Houston, TX 713-934-3160
Anderson International Corp
Stow, OH 800-336-4730
Davenport Machine
Rock Island, IL 309-786-1500
French Oil Mill Machinery Co
Piqua, OH 937-773-3420
Packaging & Processing Equipment
Ayr, ON 519-622-6666

Wine

Alfa Laval Ashbrook Simon-Hartley
Houston, TX 713-934-3160
Globe Machine
Tacoma, WA 800-523-6575
Goodnature Products
Orchard Park, NY 800-875-3381
Oak Barrel Winecraft
Berkeley, CA 510-849-0400
P & F Machine
Turlock, CA 209-667-2515

Pretzel Processing

Design Technology Corporation
Billerica, MA 978-663-7000
Exact Mixing Systems Inc
Memphis, TN 901-362-8501
Graybill Machines Inc
Lititz, PA 717-626-5221
I J White Corp
Farmingdale, NY 631-293-2211
Industrial Product Corp
Ho Ho Kus, NJ 800-472-5913
Krispy Kist Company
Chicago, IL 312-733-0900
Lanly Co
Cleveland, OH 216-731-1115
Peerless Dough Mixing and Make-Up
Sidney, OH 800-999-3327
Rademaker USA
Hudson, OH 330-650-2345
Rheon USA
Irvine, CA 949-768-1900
Shick Esteve
Kansas City, MO 877-744-2587
Stephan Machinery, Inc.
Mundelein, IL 800-783-7426
UniTrak Corporation
Port Hope, ON 866-883-5749
US Tsubaki Holdings Inc
Wheeling, IL 800-323-7790

Pulpers

Brown International Corp LLC
Winter Haven, FL 863-299-2111

Corenco
Santa Rosa, CA 888-267-3626
Corp Somat
Lancaster, PA 800-237-6628
Custom Food Machinery
Stockton, CA 209-463-4343
Dixie Canner Machine Shop
Athens, GA 706-549-0592

Pulverizers

Sugar

Glen Mills Inc.
Clifton, NJ 973-777-0777
Pro Scientific Inc
Oxford, CT 800-584-3776

Regenerators

Milk & Cream

Chester-Jensen Co., Inc.
Chester, PA 800-685-3750

Rice Processing

ANDRITZ Inc
Muncy, PA 704-943-4343
Grain Machinery Mfg Corp
Miami, FL 305-620-2525
Multi-Fill Inc
West Jordan, UT 801-280-1570

Roasters

A C Horn & Co Sheet Metal
Dallas, TX 800-657-6155
Alumaworks
Sunny Isle Beach, FL 800-277-7267
Amco Metals Indl
City Of Industry, CA 626-855-2550
Browne & Company
Markham, ON 905-475-6104
Commercial Dehydrator Systems
Eugene, OR 800-369-4283
Davron Technologies Inc
Chattanooga, TN 423-870-1888
Gourmet COFFEE Roasters
Wixom, MI 866-933-6300
Imperial Manufacturing Co
Corona, CA 800-343-7790
Krispy Kist Company
Chicago, IL 312-733-0900
National Drying Machry Co Inc
Philadelphia, PA 215-464-6070
Star Manufacturing Intl Inc
St Louis, MO 800-264-7827
Superior Products Company
Saint Paul, MN 800-328-9800
Sweet Manufacturing Co
Springfield, OH 800-334-7254
Texas Corn Roasters
Granbury, TX 800-772-4345
Unitherm Food System
Bristow, OK 918-367-0197

Roasting

A C Horn & Co Sheet Metal
Dallas, TX 800-657-6155
Gourmet COFFEE Roasters
Wixom, MI 866-933-6300
Imperial Manufacturing Co
Corona, CA 800-343-7790
Krispy Kist Company
Chicago, IL 312-733-0900
Renato Specialty Product
Garland, TX 866-575-6316
Sivetz Coffee
Corvallis, OR 541-753-9713

Rotisseries

American Range
Pacoima, CA 888-753-9898
Attias Oven Corp
Brooklyn, NY 800-928-8427
Aztec Grill
Dallas, TX 800-346-8114
Ballantyne Food Service Equipment
Omaha, NE 800-424-1215

Belson Outdoors Inc
North Aurora, IL 800-323-5664
BKI Worldwide
Simpsonville, SC 800-927-6887
Broaster Co LLC
Beloit, WI 800-365-8278
Esquire Mechanical Corp.
Armonk, NY 800-847-4206
Friedrich Metal Products
Browns Summit, NC 800-772-0326
Grillco Inc
Aurora, IL 800-644-0067
Hardt Equipment Manufacturing
Lachine, QC 888-848-4408
Henny Penny, Inc.
Eaton, OH 800-417-8417
Hickory Industries
North Bergen, NJ 800-732-9153
J & R Mfg Inc
Mesquite, TX 800-527-4831
Merco/Savory
Mt. Pleasant, MI 800-733-8821
Music City Metals Inc
Nashville, TN 800-251-2674
Remco Industries International
Fort Lauderdale, FL 800-987-3626
Renato Specialty Product
Garland, TX 866-575-6316
Roto-Flex Oven Co
San Antonio, TX 877-859-1463
Shelcon Inc
Ontario, CA 909-947-4877
Southern Pride Distributing
Alamo, TN 800-851-8180
Superior Products Company
Saint Paul, MN 800-328-9800
Toastmaster
Elgin, IL 847-741-3300
Welbilt Corporation
Stamford, CT 203-325-8300
Win-Holt Equipment Group
Syosset, NY 800-444-3595
Wood Stone Corp
Bellingham, WA 800-988-8103

Salt Processing

A C Horn & Co Sheet Metal
Dallas, TX 800-657-6155
Viking Machine & Design Inc
De Pere, WI 888-286-2116

Sandwich Processing

APV Baker
Goldsboro, NC 919-736-4309
Design Technology Corporation
Billerica, MA 978-663-7000
Machine Builders & Design Inc
Shelby, NC 704-482-3456
Nuova Distribution Centre
Ferndale, WA 360-366-2226
Peerless Food Equipment
Sidney, OH 937-492-4158
Polar Process
Plattsville, ON 877-896-8077

Saws

Butchers' Blades

Acraloc Corp
Oak Ridge, TN 865-483-1368
AEW Thurne
Lake Zurich, IL 800-239-7297
Atlanta SharpTech
Peachtree City, GA 800-462-7297
Best & Donovan
Blue Ash, OH 800-553-2378
Biro Manufacturing Co
Lakeside Marblhd, OH 419-798-4451
California Saw & Knife Works
San Francisco, CA 888-729-6533
Carter Products
Grand Rapids, MI 888-622-7837
Cass Saw & Tool   Sharpening
Westmont, IL 630-968-1617
EZE-Lap Diamond Products
Carson City, NV 800-843-4815
Haban Saw Company
St.Louis, MO. 314-968-3991
Hollymatic Corp
Countryside, IL 708-579-3700

Jarvis Products Corp
Middletown, CT 860-347-7271
Kentmaster Manufacturing Co
Monrovia, CA 800-421-1477
Mandeville Company
Minneapolis, MN 800-328-8490
Pieco
Manchester, IA 800-334-3929
Simmons Engineering Corporation
Wheeling, IL 800-252-3381
Simonds International
Fitchburg, MA 800-343-1616
Specialty Saw Inc
Simsbury, CT 800-225-0772

Scalers

Fish

Cretel Food Equipment
Holland, MI. 616-786-3980
Fishmore
Melbourne, FL 321-723-4751
Samuel Underberg Food Store
Brooklyn, NY 718-363-0787

Seafood Preparation Equipment

Alfa Laval Inc
Richmond, VA. 866-253-2528
Buck Knives
Post Falls, ID. 800-326-2825
Crane Research & Engineering
Hampton, VA 757-826-1707
Defreeze Corporation
Southborough, MA 508-485-8512
Design Technology Corporation
Billerica, MA 978-663-7000
E-Z Edge Inc
West New York, NJ 800-232-4470
Fishmore
Melbourne, FL 321-723-4751
Gregor Jonsson Inc
Lake Forest, IL 847-247-4200
Key Technology Inc.
Walla Walla, WA 509-529-2161
Mp Equip. Co.
Buford, GA 770-614-5355
Nieco Corporation
Windsor, CA 800-643-2656
Paoli Properties
Rockford, IL 815-965-0621
Patty O Matic Machinery
Farmingdale, NJ 877-938-5244
Prawnto Systems
Caddo Mills, TX 800-426-7254
R Murphy Co Inc
Ayer, MA 888-772-3481
Simmons Engineering Corporation
Wheeling, IL 800-252-3381
Skrmetta Machinery Corporation
New Orleans, LA 504-488-4413
Smith-Berger Marine
Seattle, WA 206-764-4650
Steamway Corporation
Scottsburg, IN 800-259-8171
Stork Townsend Inc.
Des Moines, IA 800-247-8609
Superior Products Company
Saint Paul, MN 800-328-9800
Universal Stainless
Aurora, CO 800-223-8332
Universal Stainless & Alloy
Titusville, PA 800-295-1909

Separators

Bean, Pea

A C Horn & Co Sheet Metal
Dallas, TX. 800-657-6155
A.K. Robins
Baltimore, MD 800-486-9656
ANDRITZ Inc
Muncy, PA. 704-943-4343
Crippen Manufacturing Co
St Louis, MI 800-872-2474
Hebeler Corp
Tonawanda, NY 800-486-4709
Lewis M Carter Mfg Co Inc
Donalsonville, GA 800-332-8232
Lyco Manufacturing Inc
Columbus, WI. 920-623-4152

Magnetool Inc
Troy, MI 248-588-5400
Pro Scientific Inc
Oxford, CT 800-584-3776
Thomas Precision, Inc.
Rice Lake, WI. 800-657-4808
TWM Manufacturing
Leamington, ON 888-495-4831

Grain, Flour Mill

A T Ferrell Co Inc
Bluffton, IN. 800-248-8318
Alfa Laval Inc
Richmond, VA. 866-253-2528
ANDRITZ Inc
Muncy, PA. 704-943-4343
Cleland Manufacturing Company
Columbia Heights, MN 763-571-4606
Crippen Manufacturing Co
St Louis, MI 800-872-2474
Dehyco Company
Memphis, TN 901-774-3322
Eischen Enterprises
Fresno, CA 559-834-0013
Hebeler Corp
Tonawanda, NY 800-486-4709
International Reserve Equipment Corporation
Clarendon Hills, IL 708-531-0680
Magnetic Products Inc
Highland, MI. 800-544-5930
Magnetool Inc
Troy, MI 248-588-5400
Meadows Mills Inc
North Wilkesboro, NC 800-626-2282
Pro Scientific Inc
Oxford, CT 800-584-3776
Southern Ag Co Inc
Blakely, GA 229-723-4262
TWM Manufacturing
Leamington, ON 888-495-4831

Liquid-Solid

Abanaki Corp
Chagrin Falls, OH 800-358-7546
AFL Industries
West Palm Beach, FL 800-807-2709
Alfa Laval Inc
Richmond, VA. 866-253-2528
Alkota Cleaning Systems Inc
Alcester, SD 800-255-6823
Baker Hughes
Houston, TX
Bunting Magnetics Co
Newton, KS. 800-835-2526
Chil-Con Products
Brantford, ON. 800-263-0086
Compatible Components Corporation
Houston, TX 713-688-2008
Cook & Beals Inc
Loup City, NE. 308-745-0154
Dedert Corporation
Olympia Fields, IL 708-747-7000
Dings Co Magnetic Group
Milwaukee, WI. 414-672-7830
Enviro-Clear Co
High Bridge, NJ 908-638-5507
Everfilt Corp
Mira Loma, CA. 800-360-8380
Fernholtz Engineering
Van Nuys, CA 818-785-5800
Filtration Systems
Sunrise, FL 954-572-2700
French Oil Mill Machinery Co
Piqua, OH 937-773-3420
General Industries Inc
Goldsboro, NC 888-735-2882
Globe Machine
Tacoma, WA 800-523-6575
Goodnature Products
Orchard Park, NY 800-875-3381
Hebeler Corp
Tonawanda, NY 800-486-4709
Hosokawa/Bepex Corporation
Santa Rosa, CA. 707-586-6000
Jay R Smith Mfg Co
Montgomery, AL. 334-277-8520
Lyco Manufacturing Inc
Columbus, WI. 920-623-4152
Membrane Process & Controls
Edgar, WI 715-352-3206

Membrane System Specialist Inc
Wisconsin Rapids, WI 715-421-2333
Monroe Environmental Corp
Monroe, MI. 800-992-7707
Pacific Process Technology
La Jolla, CA 858-551-3298
Pall Filtron
Northborough, MA 800-345-8766
Pro Scientific Inc
Oxford, CT 800-584-3776
Provisur Technologies, Inc.
Mokena, IL 708-479-3500
Relco Unisystems Corp
Willmar, MN 320-231-2210
Scienco Systems
Saint Louis, MO 314-621-2536
Sermia International
Blainville, QC. 800-567-7483
Statco Engineering
Huntington Beach, CA 800-421-0362
Sweco Inc
Florence, KY. 800-807-9326
Tema Systems Inc
Cincinnati, OH 513-792-2840
TWM Manufacturing
Leamington, ON 888-495-4831
Ultrafilter
Norcross, GA 800-543-3634
Van Air Systems
Lake City, PA 800-840-9906
Vincent Corp
Tampa, FL 813-248-2650
Waterlink/Sanborn Technologies
Canton, OH 800-343-3381
Welliver Metal Products Corporation
Salem, OR 503-362-1568
Westfalia Separator
Northvale, NJ 800-722-6622

Shish Kebab Systems

Automated Food Systems
Waxahachie, TX 469-517-0470
Wishbone Utensil Tableware Line
Wheat Ridge, CO 866-266-5928

Shredders

Cane

Silver Weibull
Aurora, CO 303-373-2311

Cheese

Corenco
Santa Rosa, CA 888-267-3626
Deville Technologies
St Laurent, QC 866-404-4545
Reiser
Canton, MA 734-821-1290

Corn & Fodder

Dito Dean Food Prep
Charlotte, NC 866-449-4200
Grote Co
Columbus, OH 888-534-7683

Vegetable & Fruit

Corenco
Santa Rosa, CA 888-267-3626
Globe Machine
Tacoma, WA 800-523-6575
Goodnature Products
Orchard Park, NY 800-875-3381
Paxton Corp
Bristol, RI 401-396-9062
Reiser
Canton, MA 734-821-1290
Rival Manufacturing Company
Kansas City, MO. 816-943-4100
Superior Products Company
Saint Paul, MN 800-328-9800
Univex Corp
Salem, NH 800-258-6358

Shrimp Processing Equipment

Steamway Corporation
Scottsburg, IN. 800-259-8171
Tri-Pak Machinery Inc
Harlingen, TX 956-423-5140

Skinning

Cretel Food Equipment
Holland, MI. 616-786-3980
Mtc Food Equipment
Poulsbo, WA 360-697-6319

Slicers

Bread & Cake

ABI Limited
Concord, ON. 800-297-8666
AM-Mac
Fairfield, NJ 800-829-2018
American Eagle Food Machinery
Chicago, IL 888-390-0800
AMF CANADA
Sherbrooke, QC 800-255-3869
Bettendorf Stanford Inc
Salem, IL. 800-548-2253
C & K Machine Co
Holyoke, MA 413-536-8122
Chicago Scale & Slicer Company
Franklin Park, IL. 847-455-3400
Clayton Manufacturing Company
Derby, NY. 716-549-0392
Deluxe Equipment Company
Bradenton, FL. 800-367-8931
DoughXpress
Pittsburg, KS. 800-835-0606
Empire Bakery Equipment
Hicksville, NY 800-878-4070
Food Tools
Santa Barbara, CA 877-836-6386
Good Idea
Northampton, MA. 800-462-9237
Grote Co
Columbus, OH 888-534-7683
Hansaloy Corp
Davenport, IA 800-553-4992
Knott Slicers
Canton, MA 781-821-0925
Lematic Inc
Jackson, MI. 517-787-3301
Soco System USA
Waukesha, WI. 800-441-6293
Solbern Corp
Fairfield, NJ 973-227-3030
Steinmetz Machine Works Inc
Stamford, CT. 203-327-0118
Toronto Kitchen Equipment
North York, ON. 416-745-4944
United Bakery Equipment Company
Shawnee Mission, KS. 913-541-8700
Waring Products
Torrington, CT 800-492-7464

Egg

Acme International
Maplewood, NJ 973-416-0400
Amco Metals Indl
City Of Industry, CA. 626-855-2550
Grote Co
Columbus, OH 888-534-7683
Polar Process
Plattsville, ON. 877-896-8077
Superior Products Company
Saint Paul, MN 800-328-9800

Meat

AEW Thurne
Lake Zurich, IL 800-239-7297
AM-Mac
Fairfield, NJ 800-829-2018
Automated Food Systems
Waxahachie, TX 469-517-0470
Bettcher Industries Inc
Wakeman, OH. 800-321-8763
Biro Manufacturing Co
Lakeside Marblhd, OH 419-798-4451
Bizerba USA
Piscataway, NJ 732-565-6000
Blakeslee, Inc.
Addison, IL. 630-532-5021
Bridge Machine Company
Palmyra, NJ 877-754-1800
Browne & Company
Markham, ON 905-475-6104
Chicago Scale & Slicer Company
Franklin Park, IL. 847-455-3400

Edlund Co
Burlington, VT 800-772-2126
General Machinery Corp
Sheboygan, WI 888-243-6622
General, Inc
Weston, FL 954-202-7419
Globe Food Equipment Co
Moraine, OH 800-347-5423
Grote Co
Columbus, OH 888-534-7683
Handtmann Inc
Lake Forest, IL 800-477-3585
I. Fm Usa Inc.
Franklin Park, IL. 866-643-6872
Kasel Industries Inc
Denver, CO 800-218-4417
Machanix Fabrication Inc
Chino, CA .800-700-9701
Mandeville Company
Minneapolis, MN 800-328-8490
Marlen International
Astoria, OR 800-862-7536
Mtc Food Equipment
Poulsbo, WA 360-697-6319
Planet Products Corp
Blue Ash, OH 513-984-5544
Prince Castle Inc
Carol Stream, IL 800-722-7853
Quantum Topping Systems Quantum Technical Services
Inc
Frankfort, IL 888-464-1540
Reiser
Canton, MA 734-821-1290
Ross Industries Inc
Midland, VA 540-439-3271
Spiral Slices Ham Market
Detroit, MI 313-259-6262
Spiro-Cut Equipment Co
Fort Worth, TX 888-887-4267
Standex International Corp.
Salem, NH. 603-893-9701
STARMIX srl
Marano, VI 044- 57- 659
Superior Products Company
Saint Paul, MN 800-328-9800
Toronto Kitchen Equipment
North York, ON 416-745-4944
TWM Manufacturing
Leamington, ON 888-495-4831
Univex Corp
Salem, NH. 800-258-6358
Waring Products
Torrington, CT 800-492-7464
Weber Inc
Kansas City, MO. 800-505-9591
Weber Inc
Kansas City, MO. 816-891-8397

Vegetable & Fruit

A.K. Robins
Baltimore, MD 800-486-9656
AM-Mac
Fairfield, NJ 800-829-2018
Ashlock Co
San Leandro, CA. 510-351-0560
Atlas Pacific Engineering
Pueblo, CO 719-948-3040
Automated Food Systems
Waxahachie, TX 469-517-0470
Blakeslee, Inc.
Addison, IL. 630-532-5021
Bluffton Slaw Cutter Company
Bluffton, OH 419-358-9840
Brothers Metal Products
Santa Ana, CA 714-972-3008
Chicago Scale & Slicer Company
Franklin Park, IL. 847-455-3400
Dito Dean Food Prep
Charlotte, NC 866-449-4200
Edlund Co
Burlington, VT 800-772-2126
F.B. Pease Company
Rochester, NY. 585-475-1870
General, Inc
Weston, FL 954-202-7419
Goodnature Products
Orchard Park, NY 800-875-3381
Grote Co
Columbus, OH 888-534-7683
Insinger Co
Philadelphia, PA 800-344-4802

International Knife & Saw
Florence, SC 800-354-9872

Keen Kutter
Torrance, CA. 310-370-6941

Knott Slicers
Canton, MA 781-821-0925

Lincoln Foodservice
Cleveland, OH 800-374-3004

Machanix Fabrication Inc
Chino, CA 800-700-9701

Mandeville Company
Minneapolis, MN 800-328-8490

Mannhart
Fort Worth, TX 817-421-0100

Matfer Inc
Van Nuys, CA 800-766-0333

Nemco Food Equipment
Hicksville, OH 800-782-6761

Paxton Corp
Bristol, RI 401-396-9062

Prince Castle Inc
Carol Stream, IL 800-722-7853

Reiser
Canton, MA 734-821-1290

Rival Manufacturing Company
Kansas City, MO. 816-943-4100

Slicechief Co
Toledo, OH 419-241-7647

South Valley Mfg Inc
Gilroy, CA. 408-842-5457

Stafford-Smith Inc
Kalamazoo, MI 800-968-2442

Superior Products Company
Saint Paul, MN 800-328-9800

Toronto Kitchen Equipment
North York, ON. 416-745-4944

TWM Manufacturing
Leamington, ON 888-495-4831

Univex Corp
Salem, NH 800-258-6358

Urschel Laboratories
Valparaiso, IN 219-464-4811

Waring Products
Torrington, CT 800-492-7464

Smokers

Fish, Meat & Produce

Alto-Shaam
Menomonee Falls, WI. 800-329-8744

Backwoods Smoker Inc
Shreveport, LA 318-220-0380

Ballantyne Food Service Equipment
Omaha, NE 800-424-1215

BBQ Pits by Klose
Houston, TX 800-487-7487

Brinkmann Corporation
Dallas, TX. 800-468-5252

Britt's Barbecue
Birmingham, AL. 205-612-6538

Cookshack
Ponca City, OK 800-423-0698

Custom Diamond Intl.
Laval, QC 800-326-5926

Friedrich Metal Products
Browns Summit, NC. 800-772-0326

Gregg Industries Inc
Waunakee, WI. 608-846-5143

Le Smoker
Salisbury, MD. 410-677-3233

Luhr Jensen & Sons Inc
Hood River, OR 541-386-3811

Masterbuilt Manufacturing Inc
Columbus, GA 706-327-5622

Reiser
Canton, MA 734-821-1290

Roto-Flex Oven Co
San Antonio, TX. 877-859-1463

Seven B Plus
Sandy, OR 503-668-5079

Smokaroma
Boley, OK 800-331-5565

Southern Pride Distributing
Alamo, TN 800-851-8180

Super Cooker
Lake Park, GA 800-841-7452

Superior Products Company
Saint Paul, MN 800-328-9800

Townfood Equipment Corp
Brooklyn, NY 800-221-5032

Traeger Industries
Portland, OR 800-872-3437

Unitherm Food System
Bristow, OK 918-367-0197

Vortron Smokehouse/Ovens
Iron Ridge, WI. 800-874-1949

Win-Holt Equipment Group
Syosset, NY. 800-444-3595

Sawdust

American Wood Fibers
Columbia, MD 800-624-9663

Northeastern Products Corp
Warrensburg, NY 800-873-8233

West Oregon Wood Products Inc
Columbia City, OR 503-397-6707

Snack Food Processing

A & B Process Systems Corp
Stratford, WI. 888-258-2789

A C Horn & Co Sheet Metal
Dallas, TX. 800-657-6155

Automated Food Systems
Waxahachie, TX 469-517-0470

Berkshire PPM
Litchfield, CT 860-567-3118

Design Technology Corporation
Billerica, MA 978-663-7000

Et Oakes Corp
Hauppauge, NY 631-232-0002

Exact Mixing Systems Inc
Memphis, TN 901-362-8501

Food Machinery Sales
Bogart, GA 706-549-2207

Formost Packaging Machines
Woodinville, WA. 425-483-9090

Fritsch USA
San Antonio, TX. 210-491-9309

Graybill Machines Inc
Lititz, PA 717-626-5221

Industrial Product Corp
Ho Ho Kus, NJ 800-472-5913

J C Ford Co
La Habra, CA 714-871-7361

Krispy Kist Company
Chicago, IL. 312-733-0900

Lanly Co
Cleveland, OH 216-731-1115

Oshikiri Corp Of America
Philadelphia, PA. 215-637-8112

Pavan USA Inc
Emigsville, PA 717-767-4889

Peerless Dough Mixing and Make-Up
Sidney, OH 800-999-3327

Polar Process
Plattsville, ON 877-896-8077

Pro Bake Inc
Twinsburg, OH 800-837-4427

Reading Bakery Systems Inc
Robesonia, PA. 610-693-5816

Reiser
Canton, MA 734-821-1290

Stephan Machinery, Inc.
Mundelein, IL 800-783-7426

Superior Food Machinery Inc
Pico Rivera, CA. 800-944-0396

UniTrak Corporation
Port Hope, ON 866-883-5749

US Tsubaki Holdings Inc
Wheeling, IL. 800-323-7790

Woody Associates Inc
York, PA. 717-843-3975

Sorters

Bean & Grain

A.K. Robins
Baltimore, MD 800-486-9656

Oxbo International Corp
Clear Lake, WI 800-628-6196

Sortex
Fremont, CA 510-797-5000

Welliver Metal Products Corporation
Salem, OR. 503-362-1568

Potato & Onion

A.K. Robins
Baltimore, MD 800-486-9656

Andgar Corp
Ferndale, WA 360-366-9900

Atlas Pacific Engineering
Pueblo, CO 719-948-3040

Odenberg Engineering
West Sacramento, CA 800-688-8396

Southern Automatics
Lakeland, FL 800-441-4604

Welliver Metal Products Corporation
Salem, OR. 503-362-1568

Soybean Processing

A.K. Robins
Baltimore, MD 800-486-9656

ANDRITZ Inc
Muncy, PA. 704-943-4343

Bean Machines
Sonoma, CA 707-996-0706

Corenco
Santa Rosa, CA 888-267-3626

Insta-Pro International
Urbandale, IA 800-383-4524

Stemmers

Healdsburg Machine Company
Santa Rosa, CA 707-433-3348

Stoves

American Range
Pacoima, CA. 888-753-9898

Connerton Co
Santa Ana, CA 714-547-9218

Dynamic Cooking Systems
Huntington Beach, CA 800-433-8466

Gold Star Products
Oak Park, MI. 800-800-0205

Imperial Manufacturing Co
Corona, CA 800-343-7790

Iwatani International Corporation of America
Houston, TX 800-775-5506

Krispy Kist Company
Chicago, IL 312-733-0900

Maytag Corporation
Benton Harbor, MI 800-344-1274

Mosshaim Innovations
Jacksonville, FL 888-995-7775

Mountain Safety Research
Seattle, WA 800-877-9677

Mr. Bar-B-Q
Winston-Salem, NC 800-333-2124

Savage Brothers Company
Elk Grove Vlg, IL. 800-342-0973

Seidman Brothers
Chelsea, MA 800-437-7770

Superior Products Company
Saint Paul, MN 800-328-9800

Toronto Kitchen Equipment
North York, ON. 416-745-4944

Townfood Equipment Corp
Brooklyn, NY 800-221-5032

Stuffers

Sausage

Biro Manufacturing Co
Lakeside Marblhd, OH 419-798-4451

Famco Automatic Sausage Linkers
Pittsburgh, PA. 412-241-6410

Friedr Dick Corp
Farmingdale, NY 800-554-3425

Handtmann Inc
Lake Forest, IL 800-477-3585

Hitec Food Equipment
Wood Dale, IL. 630-521-9460

Marlen
Riverside, MO. 913-888-3333

Polar Process
Plattsville, ON. 877-896-8077

Reiser
Canton, MA 734-821-1290

Stork Townsend Inc.
Des Moines, IA. 800-247-8609

Sugar & Syrup Processing

Alfa Laval Inc
Richmond, VA. 866-253-2528

Custom Food Machinery
Stockton, CA. 209-463-4343

Honiron Corp
Jeanerette, LA 337-276-6314

Mulligan Associates
   Mequon, WI 800-627-2886
Progressive Tractor & Implement Co.
   Parks, LA 337-845-5080
Putsch & Co Inc
   Fletcher, NC 800-847-8427
Raytheon Co
   Waltham, MA 781-522-3000
Silver Weibull
   Aurora, CO 303-373-2311
Vendome Copper & Brass Works
   Louisville, KY 888-384-5161

Tanks

Creamery, Dairy

A & B Process Systems Corp
   Stratford, WI 888-258-2789
Bowers Process Equipment
   Stratford, ON 800-567-3223
C E Rogers Co
   Mora, MN 800-279-8081
Chester-Jensen Co., Inc.
   Chester, PA 800-685-3750
DCI, Inc.
   St Cloud, MN 320-252-8200
Diversified Metal Engineering
   Charlottetown, PE 902-628-6900
Eischen Enterprises
   Fresno, CA 559-834-0013
Electrol Specialties Co
   South Beloit, IL 815-389-2291
Enerfab Inc.
   Cincinnati, OH 513-641-0500
Falco Technologies
   La Prairie, QC 450-444-0566
Feldmeier Equipment Inc
   Syracuse, NY 315-454-8608
Howard Fabrication
   City of Industry, CA 626-961-0114
Midwest Stainless
   Menomonie, WI 715-235-5472
Northland Process Piping
   Isle, MN 320-679-2119
Packaging & Processing Equipment
   Ayr, ON 519-622-6666
Paul Mueller Co Inc
   Springfield, MO 800-683-5537
Puritan Manufacturing Inc
   Omaha, NE 800-331-0487
Rosenwach Tank Co LLC
   Long Island City, NY 212-972-4411
Sanchelima International
   Miami, FL 305-591-4343
Scherping Systems
   Winsted, MN 320-485-4401
Schlueter Company
   Janesville, WI 800-359-1700
Sharpsville Container Corp
   Sharpsville, PA 800-645-1248
Stainless Fabrication Inc
   Springfield, MO 800-397-8265
Viatec
   Victoria, BC 800-942-4702
Walker Stainless Equipment Co
   New Lisbon, WI 608-562-7500

Drying, Evaporating

A & B Process Systems Corp
   Stratford, WI 888-258-2789
Behlen Manufacturing Co.
   Columbus, NE 402-564-3111
DCI, Inc.
   St Cloud, MN 320-252-8200
Electrol Specialties Co
   South Beloit, IL 815-389-2291
Ellett Industries
   Port Coquitlam, BC 604-941-8211
Falco Technologies
   La Prairie, QC 450-444-0566
Gaston County Dyeing Mach Co
   Mt Holly, NC 704-822-5000
Northland Process Piping
   Isle, MN 320-679-2119
Packaging & Processing Equipment
   Ayr, ON 519-622-6666
Paget Equipment Co
   Marshfield, WI 715-384-3158
Pittsburgh Tank Corp
   Monongahela, PA 800-634-0243

Sharpsville Container Corp
   Sharpsville, PA 800-645-1248
Stainless Fabrication Inc
   Springfield, MO 800-397-8265

Washers & Fillers

Abco Automation
   Browns Summit, NC 336-375-6400

Toasters

APW Wyott Food Service Equipment Company
   Cheyenne, WY 800-527-2100
Attias Oven Corp
   Brooklyn, NY 800-928-8427
Hatco Corp
   Milwaukee, WI 800-558-0607
Holman Cooking Equipment
   Saint Louis, MO 888-356-5362
Machanix Fabrication Inc
   Chino, CA 800-700-9701
Merco/Savory
   Mt. Pleasant, MI 800-733-8821
Middleby Corp
   Elgin, IL 847-741-3300
Middleby Marshall Inc
   Elgin, IL 847-741-3300
Prince Castle Inc
   Carol Stream, IL 800-722-7853
Roundup Food Equip
   Carol Stream, IL 800-253-2991
Superior Products Company
   Saint Paul, MN 800-328-9800
Toastmaster
   Elgin, IL 847-741-3300
Welbilt Corporation
   Stamford, CT 203-325-8300

Tortilla Making

Alliance Bakery Systems
   Blythewood, SC 803-691-9227
Baking Machines
   Livermore, CA 925-449-3369
Be & Sco
   San Antonio, TX 800-683-0928
Bettendorf Stanford Inc
   Salem, IL 800-548-2253
Burford Corp
   Maysville, OK 877-287-3673
Casa Herrera
   Pomona, CA 800-624-3916
Christy Machine Co
   Fremont, OH 888-332-6451
Design Technology Corporation
   Billerica, MA 978-663-7000
Dutchess Bakers' Machinery Co
   Superior, WI 800-777-4498
Exact Mixing Systems Inc
   Memphis, TN 901-362-8501
Food Tools
   Santa Barbara, CA 877-836-6386
Formost Packaging Machines
   Woodinville, WA 425-483-9090
Fritsch USA
   San Antonio, TX 210-491-9309
Gemini Bakery Equipment
   Philadelphia, PA 800-468-9046
I J White Corp
   Farmingdale, NY 631-293-2211
J C Ford Co
   La Habra, CA 714-871-7361
K B Systems Inc
   Bangor, PA 610-588-7788
Lanly Co
   Cleveland, OH 216-731-1115
Lawrence Equipment Inc
   South El Monte, CA 800-423-4500
Maddox/Adams International
   Miami, FL 305-592-3337
Peerless Dough Mixing and Make-Up
   Sidney, OH 800-999-3327
Peerless Food Equipment
   Sidney, OH 937-492-4158
Pinckney Molded Plastics
   Howell, MI 800-854-2920
Proluxe
   Paramount, CA 800-594-5528
Rademaker USA
   Hudson, OH 330-650-2345
Rheon USA
   Irvine, CA 949-768-1900

Shick Esteve
   Kansas City, MO 877-744-2587
Soco System USA
   Waukesha, WI 800-441-6293
Stephan Machinery, Inc.
   Mundelein, IL 800-783-7426
Superior Food Machinery Inc
   Pico Rivera, CA 800-944-0396
X-Press Manufacturing
   New Braunfels, TX 800-365-9440

VOC Control

Anguil Environmental Systems
   Milwaukee, WI 800-488-0230
Dennsi Group
   Springfield, MA 413-737-1353
Lyco Manufacturing
   Wausau, WI 715-845-7867

Vats

Cheese

Relco Unisystems Corp
   Willmar, MN 320-231-2210

Dairy Cooling

Relco Unisystems Corp
   Willmar, MN 320-231-2210

Meat Curing

Dc Tech
   Kansas City, MO 877-742-9090
Dubuque Steel Products Co
   Dubuque, IA 563-556-6288

Vegetable Preparation Equipment

A.K. Robins
   Baltimore, MD 800-486-9656
Altman Industries
   Gray, GA 478-986-3116
Berkshire PPM
   Litchfield, CT 860-567-3118
Bluffton Slaw Cutter Company
   Bluffton, OH 419-358-9840
Brothers Metal Products
   Santa Ana, CA 714-972-3008
Brown International Corp LLC
   Winter Haven, FL 863-299-2111
Computer Controlled Machines
   Pueblo, CO 719-948-9500
Design Technology Corporation
   Billerica, MA 978-663-7000
Diversified Metal Engineering
   Charlottetown, PE 902-628-6900
Eurodib
   Champlain, NY 888-956-6866
French Oil Mill Machinery Co
   Piqua, OH 937-773-3420
General, Inc
   Weston, FL 954-202-7419
Globe Machine
   Tacoma, WA 800-523-6575
Goodnature Products
   Orchard Park, NY 800-875-3381
Harold F Haines Manufacturing Inc
   Presque Isle, ME 207-762-1411
Hughes Co
   Columbus, WI 866-535-9303
Keen Kutter
   Torrance, CA 310-370-6941
Kerian Machines Inc
   Grafton, ND 701-352-0480
Key Technology Inc.
   Walla Walla, WA 509-529-2161
Knott Slicers
   Canton, MA 781-821-0925
Kusel Equipment Company
   Watertown, WI 920-261-4112
Lee Financial Corporation
   Dallas, TX 972-960-1001
Mannhart
   Fort Worth, TX 817-421-0100
Matfer Inc
   Van Nuys, CA 800-766-0333
Mumper Machine Corporation
   Butler, WI 262-781-8908
Murotech
   St Marys, OH 800-565-6876

Nemco Food Equipment
  Hicksville, OH 800-782-6761
Odenberg Engineering
  West Sacramento, CA. 800-688-8396
OXO International
  New York, NY 212-242-3333
Patty O Matic Machinery
  Farmingdale, NJ 877-938-5244
Paxton Corp
  Bristol, RI 401-396-9062
Pick Heaters
  West Bend, WI 800-233-9030
Power Brushes
  Toledo, OH 800-968-9600
Prince Castle Inc
  Carol Stream, IL 800-722-7853
Reiser
  Canton, MA 734-821-1290
Simmons Engineering Corporation
  Wheeling, IL 800-252-3381
South Valley Mfg Inc
  Gilroy, CA. .408-842-5457
Superior Products Company
  Saint Paul, MN 800-328-9800
Taylor Manufacturing Co
  Moultrie, GA. 229-985-5445
Univex Corp
  Salem, NH. .800-258-6358
Urschel Laboratories
  Valparaiso, IN. 219-464-4811
Vanmark Equipment
  Creston, IA .800-523-6261

Vegetable Processing

A.K. Robins
  Baltimore, MD 800-486-9656
ABCO Industries Limited
  Lunenburg, NS 866-634-8821
Altman Industries
  Gray, GA. 478-986-3116
AM-Mac
  Fairfield, NJ 800-829-2018
Ametek Technical & Industrial Products
  Kent, NJ 215-256-6601
Andgar Corp
  Ferndale, WA 360-366-9900
Berkshire PPM
  Litchfield, CT 860-567-3118
Brown International Corp LLC
  Winter Haven, FL 863-299-2111
Computer Controlled Machines
  Pueblo, CO .719-948-9500
Corenco
  Santa Rosa, CA. 888-267-3626
Custom Food Machinery
  Stockton, CA. 209-463-4343
Dipwell Co
  Northampton, MA. 413-587-4673
Dito Dean Food Prep
  Charlotte, NC 866-449-4200
Diversified Metal Engineering
  Charlottetown, PE. 902-628-6900
Dixie Canner Machine Shop
  Athens, GA .706-549-0592
F.B. Pease Company
  Rochester, NY 585-475-1870
Franrica Systems
  Stockton, CA. 209-948-2811
Globe Machine
  Tacoma, WA 800-523-6575
Goodnature Products
  Orchard Park, NY 800-875-3381
Harold F Haines Manufacturing Inc
  Presque Isle, ME. 207-762-1411
Hughes Co
  Columbus, WI. 866-535-9303
Kerian Machines Inc
  Grafton, ND 701-352-0480
Key Technology Inc.
  Walla Walla, WA. 509-529-2161
Kusel Equipment Company
  Watertown, WI 920-261-4112
Lyco Wausau
  Wausau, WI. 715-845-7867
Mannhart
  Fort Worth, TX 817-421-0100
Mouli Manufacturing Corporation
  Belleville, NJ 800-789-8285
Multi-Fill Inc
  West Jordan, UT 801-280-1570

Mumper Machine Corporation
  Butler, WI 262-781-8908
Murotech
  St Marys, OH 800-565-6876
Nemco Food Equipment
  Hicksville, OH 800-782-6761
Paxton Corp
  Bristol, RI 401-396-9062
Paxton Products Inc
  Blue Ash, OH 800-441-7475
Reiser
  Canton, MA 734-821-1290
Semco Manufacturing Company
  Pharr, TX. 956-787-4203
Slicechief Co
  Toledo, OH 419-241-7647
Taylor Manufacturing Co
  Moultrie, GA. 229-985-5445
Tew Manufacturing Corp
  Penfield, NY 800-380-5839
UniTrak Corporation
  Port Hope, ON 866-883-5749
Urschel Laboratories
  Valparaiso, IN. 219-464-4811
Vanmark Equipment
  Creston, IA .800-523-6261

Vibrators

MeGa Industries
  Burlington, ON 800-665-6342

Waffle Irons

Superior Products Company
  Saint Paul, MN 800-328-9800

Washers

Fruit & Vegetable

A.K. Robins
  Baltimore, MD 800-486-9656
Atlas Pacific Engineering
  Pueblo, CO 719-948-3040
Berkshire PPM
  Litchfield, CT 860-567-3118
Brogdex Company
  Pomona, CA 909-622-1021
Davron Technologies Inc
  Chattanooga, TN. 423-870-1888
Globe Machine
  Tacoma, WA 800-523-6575
Goodnature Products
  Orchard Park, NY 800-875-3381
Harold F Haines Manufacturing Inc
  Presque Isle, ME. 207-762-1411
Hughes Co
  Columbus, WI. 866-535-9303
Key Technology Inc.
  Walla Walla, WA. 509-529-2161
Leon C. Osborn Company
  Houston, TX 281-488-0755
N & A Mfg
  Mallard, IA .712-425-3512
Tew Manufacturing Corp
  Penfield, NY 800-380-5839
Tri-Pak Machinery Inc
  Harlingen, TX. 956-423-5140
Vanmark Equipment
  Creston, IA .800-523-6261

Waxers

International Wax Refining Company
  Warren, NJ .908-561-2500
Sandvik Process Systems
  Sweden, NJ 973-790-1600

Waxing

Kent Co
  North Miami, FL. 800-521-4886
MAF Industries Inc
  Traver, CA. .559-897-2905
Tri-Pak Machinery Inc
  Harlingen, TX. 956-423-5140

Yeast Processing

Alfa Laval Inc
  Richmond, VA. 866-253-2528

Sharp Brothers
  Bayonne, NJ 201-339-0404
Tuchenhagen
  Columbia, MD 410-910-6000
Vendome Copper & Brass Works
  Louisville, KY 888-384-5161

Fruit Industry

Alard Equipment Corp
  Williamson, NY 315-589-4511
Ocs Checkweighers, Inc.
  Snellville, GA 678-344-8030

Funnels

American Metalcraft Inc
  Franklin Park, IL 708-345-1177
Behrens Manufacturing LLC
  Winona, MN 507-454-4664
Jacob Tubing LP
  Memphis, TN 901-566-1110
Kosempel Manufacturing Company
  Philadelphia, PA 800-733-7122
M O Industries Inc
  Whippany, NJ 973-386-9228
Southern Metal Fabricators Inc
  Albertville, AL 800-989-1330
Superior Products Company
  Saint Paul, MN 800-328-9800
Tolco Corp
  Toledo, OH 800-537-4786
Wilks Precision Instr Co Inc
  Union Bridge, MD 410-775-7917
World Kitchen
  Elmira, NY .800-999-3436
Zeier Plastic & Mfg Inc
  Madison, WI 608-244-5782

Gas Connectors

Dormont Manufacturing Co
  Export, PA. .800-367-6668
Hose Master Inc
  Euclid, OH .216-481-2020
Linde North America
  Murray Hill, NJ. 908-464-8100
Spraying Systems Company
  Wheaton, IL 630-655-5000
Superior Products Company
  Saint Paul, MN 800-328-9800

General

915 Labs
  Centennial, CO 855-915-5227
AgroFresh
  Philadelphia, PA 866-850-6846
Alard Equipment Corp
  Williamson, NY 315-589-4511
ALLCAMS Machine Company
  Folsom, PA .610-534-9004
Allied Purchasing Co
  Mason City, IA 800-247-5956
Altra Industrial Motion Corp
  Braintree, MA 781-917-0600
American Conveyor Corporation
  Astoria, NY 718-386-0480
Amerivap Systems Inc
  Dawsonville, GA 800-763-7687
Amsler Equipment Inc
  Richmond Hill, ON, ON. 877-738-2569
Annie's Frozen Yogurt
  Minneapolis, MN 800-969-9648
Automation Ideas Inc
  Rockford, MI 877-254-3327
Baldor Electric Co
  Fort Smith, AR 479-646-4711
Bison Gear & Engineering Corp.
  St. Charles, IL 800-282-4766
Blentech Corp
  Santa Rosa, CA. 707-523-5949
Boston Gear
  Boston, MA. 888-999-9860
Bunzl Processor Distribution LLC
  Riverside, MO. 816-448-4300
Butler Winery
  Bloomington, IN 812-332-6660
Carmel Engineering
  Kirklin, IN. .888-427-0497
Cipriani
  Rancho Sta Marg, CA. 949-589-3978

Cold Jet, LLC
Loveland, OH 800-337-9423
Control Concepts, Inc.
Putnam, CT.................860-928-6551
Control Techniques
Eden Prairie, MN 800-893-2321
Coperion Corp
Sewell, NJ.................854-253-3265
Culinary Depot
Monsey, NY.................888-845-8200
Ecolab Inc
St. Paul, MN 800-352-5326
Emerson Industrial Automation
Eden Prairie, MN 800-893-2321
Euchner-USA
East Syracuse, NY 315-701-0315
Gates Mectrol Inc
Salem, NH.................800-394-4844
Ickler Co Inc
St Cloud, MN 800-243-8382
Illinois Tool Works
Glenview, IL 224-661-8870
Kastalon, Inc.
Alsip, IL 800-527-8566
KION North America
Summerville, SC.................843-875-8000
La Poblana Food Machines
Mesa, AZ.................480-258-2091
Lenze Americas
Uxbridge, MA.................800-217-9100
Lepel Corp
Waukesha, WI 800-231-6008
Liburdi Group of Companies
Mooresville, NC.................800-533-9353
Lumaco Inc
Hackensack, NJ.................800-735-8258
Material Handling Technology, Inc
Morrisville, NC.................800-779-2475
Meltric Corporation
Franklin, WI 800-824-4031
Motoman
West Carrollton, OH 937-847-6200
Mountain States Processing
Fort Lupton, CO 303-857-0380
Nigrelli Systems Purchasing
Kiel, WI.................800-693-3144
Nijal USA
Minneapolis, MN 651-353-6702
PCM Delasco Inc
Houston, TX.................713-896-4888
Plymouth Tube Company
East Troy, WI 262-642-8201
Precision Plus
Sanborn, NY.................800-526-2707
Quadro Engineering
Waterloo, ON 519-884-9660
Reiser
Canton, MA 734-821-1290
Rocheleau Blow Molding Systems
Fitchburg, MA.................978-345-1723
Rockwell Automation Inc
Milwaukee, WI.................414-382-2000
Ryowa Company America
Elk Grove Village, IL 800-700-9692
Schneider Packaging Eqpt Co
Brewerton, NY.................315-676-3035
Scrivner Equipment Co Inc
Carthage, MS 601-267-7614
Septimatech Group
Waterloo, ON 888-777-6775
Serac Inc
Carol Stream, IL 630-510-9343
SICK Inc
Bloomington, MN.................800-325-7425
Specialty Food America Inc
Hopkinsville, KY.................888-881-1633
Spencer Strainer Systems
Jeffersonville, IN 800-801-4977
Stainless Motors Inc
Rio Rancho, NM 505-867-0224
Standard Pump
Auburn, GA.................866-558-8611
Sterling Electric Inc
Indianapolis, IN 800-654-6220
Strongarm
Horsham, PA.................215-443-3400
Sundyne Corp
Arvada, CO.................303-425-0800
Superior Menus
Mankato, MN 800-464-2182
T-Drill Industries Inc
Norcross, GA.................800-554-2730

Technical Tool Solutions Inc.
Lake Forest, IL 847-235-5551
Tente Casters Inc
Hebron, KY.................800-783-2470
Uhrden
Sugarcreek, OH.................800-852-2411
Ultra Process Systems
Oak Ridge, TN 865-483-2772
Unisource Manufacturing Inc
Portland, OR.................800-234-2566
Volumetric Technologies
Cannon Falls, MN.................507-263-0034
W.Y. International
Los Angeles, CA.................323-726-8733
World Water Works
Elmsford, NY 800-607-7873
Young & Associates
Kenosha, WI 262-657-6394

Heaters

Water

Alard Equipment Corp
Williamson, NY 315-589-4511
Andgar Corp
Ferndale, WA 360-366-9900
Hatco Corp
Milwaukee, WI.................800-558-0607
Hubbell Electric Heater Co
Stratford, CT.................800-647-3165
PVI Industries LLC
Fort Worth, TX.................800-784-8326
Quikwater Inc
Sand Springs, OK 918-241-8880
ScanTech Sciences
Norcross, GA 470-359-3660
Vanguard Technology Inc
Eugene, OR.................800-624-4809

Hose Reels

Hannay Reels
Westerlo, NY.................877-467-3357
Kuriyama Of America Inc
Schaumburg, IL.................800-800-0320
Reelcraft Industries Inc
Columbia City, IN.................800-444-3134
Unisource Manufacturing Inc
Portland, OR.................800-234-2566

Hoses

Beverage

Accuflex Industrial Hose LTD
Romulus, MI.................734-713-4100
Action Technology
Prussia, PA.................217-935-8311
Alard Equipment Corp
Williamson, NY 315-589-4511
Associated Industrial Rubber
Magna, UT.................800-526-6288
Cardinal Rubber & Seal Inc
Roanoke, VA.................800-542-5737
Emco Industrial Plastics
Cedar Grove, NJ.................800-292-9906
Nalge Process Technologies Group
Rochester, NY.................585-586-8800
Parker-Hannifin Corp
Wickliffe, OH 440-943-5700
Simolex Rubber Corp
Plymouth, MI 734-453-4500
Superflex Limited
Brooklyn, NY 800-394-3665
Superior Products Company
Saint Paul, MN 800-328-9800
Union Plastics Co
Marshville, NC.................704-624-2112

Deep Fryer

Diebolt & Co
Old Lyme, CT.................800-343-2658

Food Handling

Accuflex Industrial Hose LTD
Romulus, MI.................734-713-4100
Action Technology
Prussia, PA.................217-935-8311
Baldewein Company
Lake Forrest, IL 800-424-5544

Cardinal Rubber & Seal Inc
Roanoke, VA.................800-542-5737
Emco Industrial Plastics
Cedar Grove, NJ.................800-292-9906
Fabwright Inc
Garden Grove, CA.................800-854-6464
Flex-Hose Co Inc
East Syracuse, NY.................315-437-1611
HBD Industries
Salisbury, NC 800-438-2312
Hoffmeyer Corp
San Leandro, CA.................888-744-1826
Home Rubber Co
Trenton, NJ.................800-257-9441
Hydra-Flex Inc
Livonia, MI.................800-234-0832
Keystone Rubber Corporation
Greenbackville, VA.................800-394-5661
L.C. Thompson Company
Kenosha, WI.................800-558-4018
Marlow Watson Inc
Wilmington, MA.................800-282-8823
Nalge Process Technologies Group
Rochester, NY.................585-586-8800
Parker-Hannifin Corp
Wickliffe, OH.................440-943-5700
Pure Fit Nutrition Bars
Irvine, CA.................866-787-3348
Salem-Republic Rubber Co
Sebring, OH.................800-425-5079
Sanitary Couplers
Springboro, OH.................513-743-0144
Strahman Valves Inc
Bethlehem, PA.................877-787-2462
Superflex Limited
Brooklyn, NY.................800-394-3665
Union Plastics Co
Marshville, NC.................704-624-2112
Us Rubber
Brooklyn, NY.................718-782-7888
Vaughn Belting Co-Main Acct
Spartanburg, SC 800-533-9086

Incubators & Brooders

Kuhl Corporation
Flemington, NJ.................908-782-5696
National Hotpack
Stone Ridge, NY.................800-431-8232
Pro Scientific Inc
Oxford, CT.................800-584-3776
Triad Scientific
Manasquan, NJ.................800-867-6690

Load Cells & Indicators

Tedea-Huntliegh
Chatsworth, CA 800-423-5483

Lubricants

Industrial

Alex E Fergusson Co Inc
Chambersburg, PA 800-345-1329
AMSOIL Inc
Superior, WI 715-392-7101
Bel-Ray Co LLC
Wall Township, NJ 732-938-2421
Boyer Corporation
La Grange, IL 800-323-3040
Cantol
Markham, ON.................800-387-9773
Cellier Corporation
Taunton, MA.................508-655-5906
Crc Industries Inc
Warminster, PA.................800-556-5074
DT Industrials
Holland, OH.................567-703-8550
Graco Inc
Minneapolis, MN 612-623-6000
Haynes Manufacturing Co
Westlake, OH.................800-992-2166
Huskey Specialty Lubricants
Norco, CA.................888-448-7539
Kluber Lubrication N America
Londonderry, NH.................800-447-2238
Kurtz Oil Company
Winston Salem, NC.................336-768-1515
LANXESS Corp.
Pittsburgh, PA.................800-526-9377
Linker Machines
Rockaway, NJ.................973-983-0001

Lubriplate Lubricants
   Newark, NJ 800-733-4755
Lubriquip
   Minneapolis, MN 612-623-6000
Moly-XL Company
   Westville, NJ....................856-848-2880
Momar
   Atlanta, GA.....................800-556-3967
National Purity LLC
   Brooklyn Center, MN 612-672-0022
Orelube Corp
   Bellport, NY 800-645-9124
Rock Valley Oil & Chemical Co
   Loves Park, IL...................815-654-2401
Sentinel Lubricants Inc
   Miami, FL 800-842-6400
Specialty Lubricants
   Macedonia, OH..................800-238-5823
Stoner
   Quarryville, PA 800-227-5538
Thermoil Corporation
   Brooklyn, NY 718-855-0544
Tribology Tech Lube
   Yaphank, NY.....................800-569-1757
US Industrial Lubricants
   Cincinnati, OH 800-562-5454

Measures

Dry

Alard Equipment Corp
   Williamson, NY 315-589-4511
Frye's Measure Mill
   Wilton, NH 603-654-6581
Optek-Danulat
   Germantown, WI. 888-551-4288

Mirrors

Convex

American Louver Co
   Skokie, IL 800-772-0355
American Store Fixtures
   Skokie, IL
Emco Industrial Plastics
   Cedar Grove, NJ 800-292-9906
Emedco
   Williamsville, NY 877-765-8386
Mirror Tech Mfg Co Inc
   Yonkers, NY 914-423-1600
Rosco Inc
   Jamaica, NY 800-227-2095
Se Kure Controls Inc
   Franklin Park, IL................800-250-9260

Nozzles

Spray

Arthur Products Co
   Medina, OH. 800-322-0510
Bete Fog Nozzle Inc
   Greenfield, MA..................800-235-0049
California Vibratory Feeders
   Anaheim, CA....................800-354-0972
Delavan Spray Technologies
   Charlotte, NC 704-423-7000
Greenfield Packaging
   White Plains, NY 914-993-0233
Lechler Inc
   St Charles, IL 800-777-2926
Sani-Matic
   Madison, WI....................800-356-3300
Spraying Systems Company
   Wheaton, IL 630-655-5000
Superior Products Company
   Saint Paul, MN 800-328-9800
Viking Corp
   Hastings, MI 800-968-9501

Openers

Bottle

Amco Metals Indl
   City Of Industry, CA. 626-855-2550
Brown Manufacturing Company
   Decatur, GA 404-378-8311
Browne & Company
   Markham, ON 905-475-6104

C R Mfg
   Waverly, NE 877-789-5844
Cleveland Metal Stamping Company
   Berea, OH 440-234-0010
G.G. Greene Enterprises
   West Warren, PA 814-723-5700
Superior Products Company
   Saint Paul, MN 800-328-9800

Box, Crate, Carton

Climax Packaging Machinery
   Hamilton, OH 513-874-1664
Edson Packaging Machinery
   Hamilton, ON 800-493-3766
Gulf Arizona Packaging
   Humble, TX 800-364-3887
Innovative Marketing
   Riverside, CA 800-438-4627
Listo Pencil Corp
   Alameda, CA. 800-547-8648
Samuel Underberg Food Store
   Brooklyn, NY 718-363-0787
Seal-O-Matic Corp
   Jacksonville, OR 800-631-2072
Thiele Technologies-Reedley
   Reedley, CA 800-344-8951

Can

Berkshire PPM
   Litchfield, CT 860-567-3118
C R Mfg
   Waverly, NE 877-789-5844
CanPacific Engineering
   Delta, BC. 604-946-1680
Dorton Incorporated
   Arlington Hts, IL 800-299-8600
Edlund Co
   Burlington, VT 800-772-2126
G.G. Greene Enterprises
   West Warren, PA 814-723-5700
Langsenkamp Manufacturing
   Indianapolis, IN 877-585-1950
Lincoln Foodservice
   Cleveland, OH 800-374-3004
Morrison Timing Screw Co
   Glenwood, IL 708-331-6600
Rival Manufacturing Company
   Kansas City, MO. 816-943-4100
Swing-A-Way Manufacturing Company
   St Louis, MO. 314-773-1488
T & S Perfection Chain Prods
   Cullman, AL 888-856-4864

Fruit Jar

Swing-A-Way Manufacturing Company
   St Louis, MO...................314-773-1488

Packaging

A M S Filling Systems
   Glenmoore, PA 800-647-5390
A Snow Craft Co Inc
   New Hyde Park, NY 516-739-1399
A&M Industries
   Sioux Falls, SD. 800-888-2615
A-A1 Aaction Bag
   Denver, CO. 800-783-1224
A-B-C Packaging Machine Corp
   Tarpon Springs, FL. 800-237-5975
A.B. Sealer, Inc.
   Beaver Dam, WI................877-885-9299
A.K. Robins
   Baltimore, MD 800-486-9656
Aabbitt Adhesives
   Chicago, IL.....................800-222-2488
AAMD
   Liverpool, NY..................800-887-4167
Aaron Equipment Co Div Areco
   Bensenville, IL.................630-350-2200
About Packaging Robotics
   Thornton, CO 303-449-2559
Accu-Pak
   Akron, OH
Accurate Paper Box Co Inc
   Knoxville, TN..................865-690-0311
Accutek Packaging Equipment
   Vista, CA.......................800-989-1828
Ace Technical Plastics Inc
   East Hartford, CT 860-278-2444

Achilles USA
   Everett, WA. 425-353-7000
ACMA/GD
   Richmond, VA. 800-525-2735
Acraloc Corp
   Oak Ridge, TN 865-483-1368
Actionpac Scales Automation
   Oxnard, CA 800-394-0154
ADCO Manufacturing Inc
   Sanger, CA 559-875-5563
Adhesive Products Inc
   Vernon, CA 800-669-5516
Adhesive Technologies Inc
   Hampton, NH 800-458-3486
Adpro
   Solon, OH 440-542-1111
Advance Engineering Co
   Canton, MI 800-497-6388
Advance Weight Systems Inc
   Grafton, OH 440-926-3691
Advanced Poly-Packaging Inc
   Akron, OH. 800-754-4403
AEP Industries
   South Hackensack, NJ 800-999-2374
Ag-Pak
   Gasport, NY 716-772-2651
Air Products & Chemicals Inc
   Allentown, PA. 800-224-2724
Air Technical Industries
   Mentor, OH 888-857-6265
Aladdin Transparent Packaging
   Hauppauge, NY 631-273-4747
Alard Equipment Corp
   Williamson, NY 315-589-4511
Alcoa - Lake Charles Carbon Plant
   Lake Charles, LA 337-480-7600
Alcoa - Massena Operations
   Massena, NY
Alcoa - Warrick Operations
   Newburgh, IN 812-853-6111
Alcon Packaging
   Weston, ON. 416-742-8910
Alfa Systems Inc
   Westfield, NJ. 908-654-0255
Aline Heat Seal Corporation
   Los Angeles, CA. 888-285-3917
All American Poly
   Piscataway, NJ 800-526-3551
All Fill Inc
   Exton, PA 866-255-4455
All Packaging Machinery Corp
   Ronkonkoma, NY 800-637-8808
All Sorts Premium Packaging
   Buffalo, NY. 888-565-9727
Alliance Rubber Co
   Hot Springs, AR 800-626-5940
ALLIED Graphics Inc
   St Michael, MN. 800-490-9931
Alloyd Brands
   Dekalb, IL. 800-756-7639
Allpac
   Dallas, TX. 214-630-8804
Amark Packaging Systems
   Kansas City, MO. 816-965-9000
Amco Products Co
   Fort Smith, AR 479-646-8949
Amcor
   Oshkosh, WI. 800-544-4672
American Bag & Burlap Company
   Chelsea, MA 617-884-7600
American Excelsior Co
   Arlington, TX 800-777-7645
American Glass Research
   Butler, PA 724-482-2163
American Labelmark Co
   Chicago, IL. 800-621-5808
American Manufacturing-Engrng
   Cleveland, OH 800-822-9402
American Printpak Inc
   Sussex, WI 800-441-8003
American Renolit Corp LA
   Commerce, CA 323-721-2720
Ameripak Packaging Equipment
   Warrington, PA 215-343-1530
Amerivacs
   San Diego, CA 619-498-8227
AMF Bakery Systems Corp
   Richmond, VA. 800-225-3771
AMF CANADA
   Sherbrooke, QC 800-255-3869
Ampak
   Cleveland, OH 800-342-6329

Anderson Machine Sales
Fort Lee, NJ
Anderson Tool & Engineering Company
Anderson, IN......765-643-6691
Andy Printed Products
Lagrangeville, NY......845-223-5101
Anver Corporation
Hudson, MA......800-654-3500
Applied Product Sales
Lilburn, GA......650-218-3104
APS Packaging Systems
San Jose, CA......800-526-2276
Archer Daniels Midland Company
Chicago, IL......312-634-8100
Architecture Plus Intl Inc
Rocky Point, FL......813-281-9299
Arthur G Russell Co Inc
Bristol, CT......860-583-4109
Artistic Packaging Concepts
Massapequa Pk, NY......516-797-4020
ARY
Kansas City, MO......800-821-7849
ASCENT Technics Corporation
Brick, NJ......800-774-7077
Associated Packaging Equipment Corporation
Markham, ON......905-475-6647
Astoria Laminations
St Clair Shores, MI......800-526-7325
Atlantic Foam & Packaging Company
Sanford, FL......407-328-9444
Atlas Packaging Inc
Opa Locka, FL......800-662-0630
Atlas Tag & Label Inc
Neenah, WI......800-558-6418
Audion Automation
Carrollton, TX......972-389-0777
Auger Fab
Exton, PA......800-334-1529
Automated Packaging Systems
Streetsboro, OH......800-527-0733
Automated Production Systems Corporation
New Freedom, PA......888-345-5377
Autoprod
Davenport, IA......563-391-1100
Avon Tape
Chestnut Hill, MA......508-584-8273
B H Bunn Co
Lakeland, FL......800-222-2866
B T Engineering Inc
Bala Cynwyd, PA......610-664-9500
B.A.G. Corporation
Richardson, TX......800-331-9200
Bagcraft Papercon
Chicago, IL......800-621-8468
Balemaster
Crown Point, IN......219-663-4525
Barnes Machine Company
Saint Petersburg, FL......727-327-9452
Barrette Outdoor Living
Cleveland, OH......800-336-2383
Batching Systems
Prince Frederick, MD......800-311-0851
Baur Tape & Label Co
San Antonio, TX......877-738-3222
Bedford Industries
Worthington, MN......800-533-5314
BEI
Goleta, GA......800-350-2727
BEI
South Haven, MI......800-364-7425
Berlin Foundry & Mach Co
Berlin, NH......603-752-4550
Bernal Technology
Rochester Hills, MI......800-237-6251
Berry Global
Evansville, IN......800-343-1295
Bertek Systems Inc
Fairfax, VT......800-367-0210
Bettendorf Stanford Inc
Salem, IL......800-548-2253
Better Packages
Ansonia, CT......800-237-9151
Biner Ellison Packaging Systs
Vista, CA......800-733-8162
Bivac Enterprise
Brick, NJ......732-920-0080
Black Brothers
Mendota, IL......800-252-2568
Blako Industries
Dunbridge, OH......419-833-4491
Blodgett Co
Houston, TX......281-933-6195

Blue Print Automation
S Chesterfield, VA......804-520-5400
Bosch Packaging Technology
New Richmond, WI......715-246-6511
BP
Houston, TX......281-366-2000
Bradman Lake Inc
Rock Hill, SC......803-366-3688
Branson Ultrasonics Corp
Danbury, CT......203-796-0400
Brechteen
Chesterfield, MI......586-949-2240
Brenton Engineering Co
Alexandria, MN......800-535-2730
Brentwood Plastics In
St Louis, MO......314-968-1135
Brothers Metal Products
Santa Ana, CA......714-972-3008
Brown Machine LLC
Beaverton, MI......877-702-4142
Bulman Products Inc
Grand Rapids, MI......616-363-4416
Burghof Engineering & Mfg Co
Prairie View, IL......847-634-0737
BW Container Systems
Romeoville, IL......630-759-6800
C & K Machine Co
Holyoke, MA......413-536-8122
C.J. Machine
Fridley, MN......763-767-4630
California Vibratory Feeders
Anaheim, CA......800-354-0972
Campbell Wrapper Corporation
De Pere, WI......920-983-7100
Can Creations
Pembroke Pines, FL......954-581-3312
Cannon Equipment Company
Cannon Falls, MN......800-825-8501
Cantech Industries Inc
Johnson City, TN......800-654-3947
Capmatic, Ltd.
Monreal North, QC......514-332-0062
Carando Technologies Inc
Stockton, CA......209-948-6500
Care Controls, Inc.
Mill Creek, WA......800-593-6050
Carlisle Plastics
Minneapolis, MN......952-884-1309
Carpenter-Hayes Paper Box Company
East Hampton, CT......203-267-4436
Carroll Co
Garland, TX......800-527-5722
Carroll Packaging
Dearborn, MI......313-584-0400
Carton Closing Company
Butler, PA......724-287-7759
Cartpac Inc
Carol Stream, IL......630-510-1100
Catty Inc
Harvard, IL......815-943-2288
Cellotape, Inc.
Newark, CA......510-651-5551
Central Coated Products Inc
Alliance, OH......330-821-9830
Central Fine Pack Inc
Fort Wayne, IN......260-432-3027
Central Ohio Bag & Burlap
Columbus, OH......800-798-9405
Chaffee Co
Rocklin, CA......916-630-3980
Chambers Container Company
Gastonia, NC......704-377-6317
Champion Trading Corporation
Marlboro, NJ......732-780-4200
Change Parts Inc
Ludington, MI......231-845-5107
Charles Beck Machine Corporation
King of Prussia, PA......610-265-0500
Chase Industries Inc
West Chester, OH......800-543-4455
Chase-Logeman Corp
Greensboro, NC......336-665-0754
Circle Packaging Machinery Inc
De Pere, WI......920-983-3420
City Box Company
Aurora, IL......773-277-5500
CL&D Graphics
Oconomowoc, WI......800-777-1114
Clamco Corporation
Berea, OH......216-267-1911
Clayton Corp.
Fenton, MO......800-729-8220

Clearwater Packaging Inc
Clearwater, FL......800-299-2596
Cleveland Plastic Films
Elyria, OH......800-832-6799
Cleveland Wire Cloth & Mfg Co
Cleveland, OH......800-321-3234
Climax Packaging Machinery
Hamilton, OH......513-874-1664
CMD Corp
Appleton, WI......920-730-6888
Collectors Gallery
St Charles, IL......800-346-3063
Colonial Transparent Products Company
Hicksville, NY......516-822-4430
Colter & Peterson
Paterson, NJ......973-684-0901
Columbia Labeling Machinery
Benton City, WA......888-791-9590
Combi Packaging Systems LLC
Canton, OH......866-472-5236
Compacker Systems LLC
Davenport, IA......563-391-2751
Conflex, Inc.
Germantown, WI......800-225-4296
Constantia Colmar
Colmar, PA......215-997-6222
Continental Packaging Corporation
Elgin, IL......847-289-6400
Contour Products
Kansas City, KS......800-638-3626
Control & Metering
Mississauga, ON......800-736-5739
CoolBrands International
Ronkonkoma, NY......631-737-9700
Corfab
Chicago, IL......708-458-8750
Corrugated Inner-Pak Corporation
Conshohocken, PA......610-825-0200
Corrugated Packaging
Sarasota, FL......941-371-0000
Cortec Aero
St Paul, MN......800-426-7832
Cozzoli Machine Co
Somerset, NJ......732-564-0400
Crandall Filling Machinery
Buffalo, NY......800-280-8551
Crayex Corp
Piqua, OH......800-837-1747
Creative Automation
Passaic, NJ......973-778-0061
Creative Coatings Corporation
Nashua, NH......800-229-1957
Creative Foam Corp
Fenton, MI......810-629-4149
Crystal Creative Products
Middletown, OH......800-776-6762
Crystal-Flex Packaging Corporation
Rockville Centre, NY......888-246-7325
Crystal-Vision Packaging Systems
Torrance, CA......800-331-3240
CSS International Corp
Philadelphia, PA......800-278-8107
CTK Plastics
Moose Jaw, SK......800-667-8847
Cup Pac Packaging Inc
South Beloit, IL......877-347-9725
Custom Card & Label Corporation
Lincoln Park, NJ......973-492-0022
Custom Foam Molders
Foristell, MO......636-441-2307
Custom Food Machinery
Stockton, CA......209-463-4343
Custom Metal Design Inc
Oakland, FL......800-334-1777
Customized Equipment SE
Tucker, GA......770-934-9300
CVP Systems Inc
Downers Grove, IL......800-422-4720
Cyro Industries/Degussa
Parsippany, NJ......800-631-5384
D & L Manufacturing
Milwaukee, WI......414-256-8160
Dacam Corporation
Madison Heights, VA......434-929-4001
Dacam Machinery
Madison Heights, VA......434-369-1259
Dalemark Industries
Lakewood, NJ......732-367-3100
Danafilms Inc
Westborough, MA......508-366-8884
Data Scale
Fremont, CA......800-651-7350

Davis Core & Pa
Cave Spring, GA 800-235-7483
Decker Plastics
Council Bluffs, IA 866-869-6293
Decko Products Inc
Sandusky, OH 800-537-6143
Dehyco Company
Memphis, TN 901-774-3322
Delta Cyklop Orga Pac
Charlotte, NC 800-446-4347
Delta Engineering Corporation
Walpole, MA 781-729-8650
Desert Box & Supply Corporation
Thermal, CA 760-399-5161
Design Packaging Company
Glencoe, IL 800-321-7659
Design Plastics Inc
Omaha, NE 800-491-0786
Design Technology Corporation
Billerica, MA 978-663-7000
Design-Mark Industries
Wareham, MA 800-451-3275
Developak Corporation
Vista, CA 760-598-7404
Diamond Automation
Farmington Hills, MI 248-426-9394
Diversified Capping Equipment
Perrysburg, OH 419-666-2566
Diversified Metal Engineering
Charlottetown, PE 902-628-6900
Dixie Canner Machine Shop
Athens, GA 706-549-0592
Dolco Packaging Co
Decatur, IN 260-728-2161
DomainMarket
Potomac, MD 888-694-6735
Donahower & Company
Olathe, KS 913-829-2650
Dorell Equipment Inc
Somerset, NJ 732-247-5400
Douglas Machine Inc
Alexandria, MN 320-763-6587
DT Converting Technologies - Stokes
Bristol, PA 800-635-0036
Durable Engravers
Franklin Park, IL 800-869-9565
Durable Packaging Corporation
Countryside, IL 800-700-5677
Durand-Wayland Inc
Lagrange, GA 800-241-2308
Durango-Georgia Paper
Tampa, FL 813-286-2718
Dyco
Bloomsburg, PA 800-545-3926
Dynaclear Packaging
Wyckoff, NJ 201-337-1001
Dynamic Packaging
Minneapolis, MN 800-878-9380
Dynamic Pak LLC
Syracuse, NY 315-474-8593
Dynaric Inc
Virginia Beach, VA 800-526-0827
East Coast Group New York
Springfield Gardens, NY 718-527-8464
Eastern Machine
Middlebury, CT 203-598-0066
Ebel Tape & Label
Cincinnati, OH 513-471-1067
Econocorp Inc
Randolph, MA 781-986-7500
Edl Packaging Engineers
Green Bay, WI 920-336-7744
Edmeyer
Minneapolis, MN 651-450-1210
Edson Packaging Machinery
Hamilton, ON 800-493-3766
Electro Cam Corp
Roscoe, IL 800-228-5487
ELF Machinery
La Porte, IN 800-328-0466
Ellehammer Industries
Langley, BC 604-882-9326
Elliott Manufacturing Co Inc
Fresno, CA 559-233-6235
Elmar Worldwide
Depew, NY 800-433-3562
Elmark Packaging Inc
West Chester, PA 800-670-9688
Elopak Americas
Wixom, MI 248-486-4600
Emerald Packaging Inc
Union City, CA 510-429-5700

Energy Sciences Inc
Wilmington, MA 978-658-3731
Engineered Automation
Biddeford, MI 207-200-8301
Enhance Packaging Technologies
Whitby, ON 905-668-5811
Ensinger Inc
Washington, PA 800-243-3221
Enviropak Corp
Earth City, MO 314-739-1202
Equipment Outlet
Meridian, ID 208-887-1472
Esselte Meto
Morris Plains, NJ 800-645-3290
Evergreen Packaging
Memphis, TN 901-821-5350
Exact Equipment Corporation
Morrisville, PA 215-295-2000
Excelsior Transparent Bag Manufacturing
Yonkers, NY 914-968-1300
F N Smith Corp
Oregon, IL 815-732-2171
Fabricon Products Inc
River Rouge, MI 313-841-8200
Fairchild Industrial Products
Winston Salem, NC 800-334-8422
Fallas Automation Inc.
Waco, TX 254-772-9524
Farnell Packaging
Dartmouth, NS 800-565-9378
Fawema Packaging Machinery
Palmetto, FL 941-351-9597
Federal Label Systems
Elmhurst, NY 800-238-0015
Fehlig Brothers Box & Lbr Co
St Louis, MO 314-241-6900
Felco Packaging Specialist
Baltimore, MD 800-673-8488
Felins USA Inc
Milwaukee, WI 800-343-5667
Fibre Converters Inc
Constantine, MI 269-279-1700
Fibre Leather Manufacturing Company
New Bedford, MA 800-358-6012
Fiedler Technology
Maple, ON 905-832-0493
Filler Specialties
Zeeland, MI 616-772-9235
Filling Equipment Co Inc
Flushing, NY 800-247-7127
Film-Pak Inc
Crowley, TX 800-526-1838
Filmco Inc
Aurora, OH 800-545-8457
Fischbein LLC
Statesville, NC 704-838-4600
Fitec International Inc
Memphis, TN 800-332-6387
Flexicell Inc
Ashland, VA 804-550-7300
Flojet
Foothill Ranch, CA 800-235-6538
Florida Knife Co
Sarasota, FL 800-966-5643
Foam Concepts Inc
Uxbridge, MA 508-278-7255
Foam Pack Industries
Springfield, NJ 973-376-3700
Fogg Filler Co
Holland, MI 616-786-3644
Folding Carton/Flexible Packaging
North Hollywood, CA 818-896-3449
Food Equipment Manufacturing Company
Bedford Heights, OH 216-672-5859
Food Pak Corp
San Mateo, CA 650-341-6559
Formflex
Bloomingdale, IN 800-255-7659
Formost Packaging Machines
Woodinville, WA 425-483-9090
Four M Manufacturing Group
San Jose, CA 408-998-1141
Fowler Products Co LLC
Athens, GA 877-549-3301
Framarx Corp
S Chicago Hts, IL 800-336-3936
Frazier & Son
Conroe, TX 800-365-5438
Free Flow Packaging Corporation
Redwood City, CA 800-888-3725
Fremont Die Cut Products
Fremont, OH 800-223-3177

Friendly City Box Co Inc
Johnstown, PA 814-266-6287
Frontier Bag
Kansas City, MO 816-765-4811
Fuller Weighing Systems
Columbus, OH 614-882-8121
Fulton-Denver Co
Denver, CO 800-521-1414
Future Commodities Intl Inc
Rancho Cucamonga, CA 888-588-2378
Gallo
Racine, WI 262-752-9950
Ganz Brothers
Paramus, NJ 201-845-6010
Garvey Products
Cincinnati, OH 513-771-8710
Gbs
North Canton, OH 800-552-2427
GCA
Huntington Beach, CA 714-379-4911
GE Appliances
Louisville, KY 877-959-8688
GEI Autowrappers
Exton, PA 610-321-1115
GEI Turbo
Exton, PA 800-345-1308
Gemini Plastic Films Corporation
Garfield, NJ 800-789-4732
General Bag Corporation
Cleveland, OH 800-837-9396
General Corrugated Machinery Company
Palisades Park, NJ 201-944-0644
General Formulations
Sparta, MI 800-253-3664
General Methods Corporation
Peoria, IL 309-497-3344
General Packaging Equipment Co
Houston, TX 713-686-4331
General Processing Systems
Holland, MI 800-547-9370
Genpak
Peterborough, ON 800-461-1995
GHM Industries Inc
Charlton, MA 800-793-7013
Giltron Inc
Norwood, MA 781-762-4310
Gleason Industries
Roseville, CA 916-784-1302
Glenmarc Manufacturing
Chicago, IL 800-323-5350
Glopak
St Leonard, QC 800-361-6994
Goex Corporation
Janesville, WI 608-754-3303
Goldco Industries
Loveland, CO 970-663-4770
Goodwrappers Inc
Halethorpe, MD 800-638-1127
Gram Equipment Of America
Tampa, FL 813-248-1978
Grand Valley Labels
Grand Rapids, MI
Graphic Impressions of Illinois
River Grove, IL 708-453-1100
Graybill Machines Inc
Lititz, PA 717-626-5221
Great Southern Corp
Memphis, TN 800-421-7802
Green Tek
Janesville, WI 800-747-6440
Greenbush Tape & Label Inc
Albany, NY 518-465-2389
Greenfield Packaging
White Plains, NY 914-993-0233
Greif Inc
Delaware, OH 740-549-6000
GTI
Arvada, CO 303-420-6699
Gulf Arizona Packaging
Humble, TX 800-364-3887
Gulf Packaging Company
Safety Harbor, FL 800-749-3466
Gulf Systems
Brownsville, TX 800-217-4853
Gulf Systems
Humble, TX 800-364-3887
Gulf Systems
Arlington, TX 817-261-1915
H B Fuller Co
St. Paul, MN 651-236-5900
H G Weber & Co
Kiel, WI 920-894-2221

H&H Lumber Company
　Amarillo, TX 806-335-1813
Halpak Plastics
　Deer Park, NY 800-442-5725
Halton Packaging Systems
　Oakville, ON 905-847-9141
Hampden Papers Inc
　Holyoke, MA 413-536-1000
Hamrick Manufacturing & Svc
　Mogadore, OH 800-321-9590
Handy Wacks Corp
　Sparta, MI 800-445-4434
Hannan Products
　Corona, CA 800-954-4266
Hantover Inc
　Kansas City, MO 800-821-7849
Harbro Packaging Co
　Chicago, IL 877-428-5812
Harpak-ULMA Packaging LLC
　Ball Ground, GA 770-345-5300
Hart Design & Mfg
　Green Bay, WI 920-468-5927
Hartford Containers
　Terryville, CT 860-584-1194
Hartness International
　Greenville, SC 800-845-8791
Harwil Corp
　Oxnard, CA 800-562-2447
Haumiller Engineering Co
　Elgin, IL 847-695-9111
Hayes Machine Co Inc
　Des Moines, IA 800-860-6224
Hayssen Flexible Systems
　Duncan, SC 864-486-4000
Health Star
　Randolph, MA 800-545-3639
Heisler Machine & Tool Co
　Fairfield, NJ 973-227-6300
Henkel Consumer Adhesive
　Avon, OH 800-321-0253
Henley Paper Company
　Greensboro, NC 336-668-0081
Henschel Coating & Laminating
　New Berlin, WI 800-866-5683
Herche Warehouse
　Denver, CO 303-371-8186
Highland Plastics Inc
　Mira Loma, CA 800-368-0491
Highland Supply Corp
　Highland, IL 800-472-3645
Highlight Industries
　Wyoming, MI 800-531-2465
Hinchcliff Products Company
　Strongsville, OH 440-238-5200
Holland Applied Technologies
　Burr Ridge, IL 630-325-5130
Hollymatic Corp
　Countryside, IL 708-579-3700
Hoppmann Corporation
　Elkwood, VA 800-368-3582
Hudson Control Group Inc
　Springfield, NJ 973-376-8265
Hudson Poly Bag Inc
　Hudson, MA 800-229-7566
Hudson-Sharp Machine Co
　Green Bay, WI 800-950-4362
Hudson-Sharp Machine Company
　Green Bay, WI 920-494-4571
Huhtamaki Food Service Plastics
　Lake Forest, IL 800-244-6382
Huntsman Packaging
　South Deerfield, MA 413-665-2145
Hurst Corp
　Wayne, PA 610-687-2404
IBC Shell Packaging
　New Hyde Park, NY 516-352-5138
ID Images
　Brunswick, OH 866-516-7300
Ideal of America
　Charlotte, NC 704-523-1604
Ideal of America/Valley Rio Enterprise
　Atlanta, GA 770-352-0210
Ideal Wrapping Machine Company
　Middletown, NY 845-343-7700
Ilapak Inc
　Newtown, PA 215-579-2900
Iman Pack
　Westland, MI 800-810-4626
Imar
　Miami Beach, FL 305-531-5757
In-Line Corporation
　Hopkins, MN 952-938-0046

Indeco Products Inc
　San Marcos, TX 888-246-3326
Indiana Carton Co Inc
　Bremen, IN 800-348-2390
Industrial Automation Systems
　Santa Clarita, CA 888-484-4427
Industrial Devices Corporation
　Petaluma, CA 707-789-1000
Industrial Machine Manufacturing
　Richmond, VA 804-271-6979
Industrial Magnetics
　Boyne City, MI 800-662-4638
Inland Paperboard & Packaging
　Rock Hill, SC 803-366-4103
Inline Filling Systems
　Venice, FL 941-486-8800
Innovative Packaging Solution
　Martin, MI 616-656-2100
Inspired Automation Inc
　Agoura Hills, CA 818-991-4598
Instabox
　Calgary, AB 800-482-6173
Inter-Pack Corporation
　Monroe, MI 734-242-7755
International Adhesive Coating
　Windham, NH 800-253-4450
International Omni-Pac Corporation
　La Verne, CA 909-593-2833
International Packaging Machinery
　Naples, FL 800-237-6496
International Paper Box Machine Company
　Nashua, NH 603-889-6651
Interstate Packaging
　White Bluff, TN 800-251-1072
Intertape Polymer Group
　Menasha, WI 800-558-5006
ITW United Silicone
　Lancaster, NY 716-681-8222
Ivarson Inc
　Milwaukee, WI 414-351-0700
Ives-Way Products
　Round Lake Beach, IL 847-740-0658
Jagenberg
　Enfield, CT 860-741-2501
January & Wood Company
　Maysville, KY 606-564-3301
Jarisch Paper Box Company
　North Adams, MA 413-663-5396
Jay Packaging Group Inc
　Warwick, RI 401-244-1300
Jeb Plastics
　Wilmington, DE 800-556-2247
Jescorp
　Des Plaines, IL 847-299-7800
Jetstream Systems
　Wichita, KN 855-861-6916
Jif-Pak Manufacturing
　Vista, CA 800-777-6613
Jilson Group
　Lodi, NJ 800-969-5400
JMC Packaging Equipment
　Burlington, ON 800-263-5252
John E. Ruggles & Company
　New Bedford, MA 508-992-9766
John R Nalbach Engineering Co
　Countryside, IL 708-579-9100
Johnson Corrugated Products Corporation
　Thompson, CT 860-923-9563
Jones Packaging Machinery
　Ooltewah, TN 423-238-4558
JW Aluminum
　Mt Holly, SC 800-568-1100
JW Leser Company
　Los Angeles, CA 323-731-4173
K & L Intl
　Ontario, CA 888-598-5588
Kammann Machine
　Portsmouth, NH 978-463-0050
Kapak Corporation
　Minneapolis, MN 952-541-0730
KAPCO
　Kent, OH 800-843-5368
KAPS All Packaging
　Riverhead, NY 631-727-0300
Karolina Polymers
　Hickory, NC 828-328-2247
Kaufman Engineered Systems
　Waterville, OH 419-878-9727
Kennedy Group
　Willoughby, OH 440-951-7660
Key Automation
　Eagan, MN 651-455-0547

Keystone Packaging Svc Inc
　Phillipsburg, NJ 800-473-8567
KHL Engineered Packaging
　Montebello, CA 323-721-5300
Khs USA Inc
　Sarasota, FL 877-227-8358
Kinsley Inc
　Doylestown, PA 800-414-6664
Kirkco Corp
　Monroe, NC 704-289-7090
Kisters Kayat
　Sarasota, FL 386-424-0101
Kliklok-Woodman
　Decatur, GA 770-981-5200
Klippenstein Corp
　Fresno, CA 888-834-4258
Klockner Pentaplast of America
　Gordonsville, VA 540-832-3600
Kloppenberg & Co
　Englewood, CO 800-346-3246
KM International Corp
　Kenton, TN 731-749-8700
Knapp Container
　Beacon Falls, CT 203-888-0511
Koch Equipment LLC
　Kansas City, MO 816-931-4557
Kohler Industries Inc
　Lincoln, NE 800-365-6708
Korab Engineering Company
　Los Angeles, CA 310-670-7710
Kord Products Inc.
　Brantford, ON 800-452-9070
Krones
　Franklin, WI 800-752-3787
KWIK Lok Corp
　Yakima, WA 800-688-5945
L&H Wood Manufacturing Company
　Farmington, MI 248-474-9000
LAB Equipment
　Skaneateles, NY 800-522-5781
Label Makers
　Pleasant Prairie, WI 800-208-3331
Label Technology Inc
　Merced, CA 800-388-1990
Lako Tool & Mfg Inc
　Perrysburg, OH 800-228-2982
Lamcraft Inc
　Lees Summit, MO 800-821-1333
Langen Packaging
　Mississauga, ON 905-670-7200
Laub-Hunt Packaging Systems
　Norwalk, CA 888-671-9338
Lawrence Schiff Silk Mills
　New York, NY 800-272-4433
Leader Engineering-Fab Inc
　Napoleon, OH 419-592-0008
Leal True Form Corporation
　Freeport, NY 516-379-2008
Leco Plastic Inc
　Hackensack, NJ 201-343-3330
Lematic Inc
　Jackson, MI 517-787-3301
Lenkay Sani Products Corporation
　Brooklyn, NY 718-927-9260
Lester Box & Mfg Div
　Long Beach, CA 562-437-5123
Letrah International Corp
　Fort Atkinson, WI 920-563-6597
Levin Brothers Paper
　Cicero, IL 800-545-6200
Liqui-Box Corp
　Richmond, VA 804-325-1400
Livingston-Wilbor Corporation
　Edison, NJ 908-322-8403
Lockwood Packaging
　Woburn, MA 800-641-3100
Loeb Equipment
　Chicago, IL 773-496-5720
Longford Equipment US
　Glastonbury, CT 416-298-6622
Longhorn Packaging Inc
　San Antonio, TX 800-433-7974
Longview Fibre Co
　Longview, WA 800-929-8111
Los Angeles Paper Box & Board Mills
　Los Angeles, CA 323-685-8900
Loveshaw Corp
　South Canaan, PA 800-572-3434
Luetzow Industries
　South Milwaukee, WI 800-558-6055
Lunn Industries
　Glen Cove, NY 516-671-9000

Lyco Wausau
  Wausau, WI 715-845-7867
Lydall
  Doswell, VA 804-266-9611
Lynch Corp
  Greenwich, CT 203-340-2590
M & G Packaging Corp
  Floral Park, NY 800-240-5288
M & Q Packaging Corp
  North Wales, PA 267-498-4000
M S Plastics & Packaging Inc
  Butler, NJ 800-593-1802
M S Willett Inc
  Cockeysville, MD 410-771-0460
M&R Flexible Packaging
  Springboro, OH 800-543-3380
MAC Tac LLC
  Stow, OH 866-262-2822
Machine Electronics Company
  Brooklyn, NY 718-384-3211
Madison County Wood Products
  St Louis, MO 314-772-1722
MAF Industries Inc
  Traver, CA 559-897-2905
Magnuson
  Pueblo, CO 719-948-9500
Mail-Well Label
  Sparks, NV 775-359-1703
Malnove Of Nebraska
  Omaha, NE 800-228-9877
Malo Inc
  Tulsa, OK 918-583-2743
Manchester Tool & Die Inc
  North Manchester, IN 260-982-8524
Maren Engineering Corp
  South Holland, IL 800-875-1038
Mark Products Company
  Denville, NJ 973-983-8818
Markwell Manufacturing Company
  Norwood, MA 800-666-1123
Marlen International
  Astoria, OR 800-862-7536
Maro Paper Products Company
  Bellwood, IL 708-649-9982
Marq Packaging Systems Inc
  Yakima, WA 800-998-4301
Marshall Paper Products
  East Norwich, NY
Marshall Plastic Film Inc
  Martin, MI 269-672-5511
Maryland Packaging Corporation
  Elkridge, MD 410-540-9700
Massachusetts Container Corporation
  North Haven, CT 203-248-2161
Mastercraft International
  Charlotte, NC 704-392-7436
Material Handling Technology, Inc
  Morrisville, NC 800-779-2475
Matiss
  St Georges, QC 888-562-8477
Matrix Packaging Machinery
  Saukville, WI 888-628-7491
Matthiesen Equipment
  San Antonio, TX 800-624-8635
Maull-Baker Box Company
  Brookfield, WI 414-463-1290
Maxco Supply
  Parlier, CA 559-646-6700
Maypak Inc
  Wayne, NJ 973-696-0780
Measurex/S&L Plastics
  Nazareth, PA 800-752-0650
Medical Packaging Corporation
  Camarillo, CA 805-388-2383
Merix Chemical Company
  Chicago, IL 312-573-1400
Merryweather Foam Inc
  Sylacauga, AL 256-249-8546
Micro Solutions Ent Tech & Dev
  Van Nuys, CA 800-673-4968
Mid Cities Paper Box Company
  Downey, CA 877-277-6272
Miller Technical Svc
  Plymouth, MI 734-414-1769
Milprint
  Oshkosh, WI 920-303-8600
Milwaukee Tool & MachineCompany
  Okauchee, WI 262-821-0160
Minipack
  Orange, CA 714-283-4200
Mitsubishi Polyester Film, Inc.
  Greer, SC 864-879-5000

Modern Packaging Inc
  Deer Park, NY 631-595-2437
Modular Packaging
  Randolph, NJ 973-970-9393
Moen Industries
  Santa Fe Springs, CA 800-732-7766
Mold-Rite Plastics LLC
  Twinsburg, OH 330-425-4206
Molins/Sandiacre Richmond
  Richmond, VA 864-486-4000
Monument Industries Inc
  Bennington, VT 802-442-8187
Moore Production Tool Spec Inc
  Farmington Hills, MI 248-476-1200
Morphy Container Company
  Brantford, ON 519-752-5428
Mount Hope Machinery Company
  Westborough, MA 508-616-9458
Mount Vernon Plastics
  Mamaroneck, NY 914-698-1122
Multi-Plastics Extrusions Inc
  Hazleton, PA 570-455-2021
Multisorb Technologies Inc
  Buffalo, NY 800-445-9890
Muth Associates
  Springfield, MA 800-388-0157
Namco Controls Corporation
  Cleveland, OH 800-626-8324
NAP Industries
  Brooklyn, NY 877-635-4948
Nashua Corporation
  Nashua, NH 603-661-2004
National Equipment Corporation
  Bronx, NY 800-237-8873
National Instruments
  Baltimore, MD 866-258-1914
National Package SealingCompany
  Santa Ana, CA 714-630-1505
National Packaging
  Rumford, RI 401-434-1070
National Poly Bag Manufacturing Corporation
  Brooklyn, NY 718-629-9800
National Velour Corp
  Warwick, RI 800-556-6523
Neos
  Elk River, MN 888-441-6367
New England Machinery Inc
  Bradenton, FL 941-755-5550
New Jersey Wire Stitching Machine Company
  Cherry Hill, NJ 856-428-2572
Nichols Specialty Products
  Southborough, MA 508-481-4367
Nigrelli Systems Purchasing
  Kiel, WI 800-693-3144
Niro
  Hudson, WI 715-386-9371
Nitech
  Columbus, NE 800-237-6496
NJM/CLI
  Pointe Claire, QC 514-630-6990
Norden Inc
  Branchburg, NJ 908-252-9483
Nordson Corp
  Duluth, GA 800-683-2314
Nordson Sealant Equipment
  Plymouth, MI 734-459-8600
Norpak Corp
  Newark, NJ 800-631-6970
North American Container Corp
  Marietta, GA 800-929-0610
Northeast Packaging Materials
  Monsey, NY 845-426-2900
Norwalt Design Inc
  Randolph, NJ 973-927-3200
Norwood Paper Inc
  Chicago, IL 773-788-1528
Novelis Foil Products
  Atlanta, GA 800-776-8701
Now Plastics Inc
  East Longmeadow, MA 413-525-1010
Nu-Con Equipment
  Chanhassen, MN 877-939-0510
Nu-Trend Plastics Thermoformer
  Jacksonville, FL 904-353-5936
NYP
  Leola, PA 800-541-0961
Ocme America Corporation
  York, PA .717-843-6263
OCS Checkweighers Inc
  Snellville, GA 678-344-8300
Oden Machinery
  Tonawanda, NY 800-658-3622

Oerlikon Leybold Vacuum
  Export, PA 724-327-5700
Old Dominion Box Company
  Burlington, NC 336-226-4491
Oliver Packaging & Equipment Co.
  Walker, MI 800-253-3893
Olney Machinery
  Westernville, NY 315-827-4208
Omega Design Corp
  Exton, PA 800-346-0191
Omnitech International
  Midland, MI 989-631-3377
OMNOVA Solutions
  Fairlawn, OH 330-869-4200
OnTrack Automation Inc
  Waterloo, ON 519-886-9090
Orange Plastics
  Compton, CA 310-609-2121
Orics Industries
  Farmingdale, NY 718-461-8613
Orion Packaging Systems Inc
  Alexandria, MN 800-333-6556
Osgood Industries
  Oldsmar, FL 813-855-7337
Ossid Corp
  Battleboro, NC 800-334-8369
Ouachita Machine Works
  West Monroe, LA 318-396-1468
Outlook Packaging
  Neenah, WI 920-722-1666
Oystar North America
  Edison, NJ 732-343-7600
Pa R Systems Inc
  St Paul, MN 800-464-1320
Pacemaker Packaging Corp
  Woodside, NY 718-458-1188
Pack Line Corporation
  Racine, WI 800-248-6868
Pack Rite Machine Mettler
  Mt Pleasant, WI 800-248-6868
Pack West Machinery
  Baldwin Park, CA 626-814-4766
Package Machinery Co Inc
  Holyoke, MA 413-315-3801
Package Service Company of Colorado
  Northmoor, MO 800-748-7799
Package Systems Corporation
  Danielson, CT 800-522-3548
Packaging & Processing Equipment
  Ayr, ON 519-622-6666
Packaging Aids Corporation
  San Rafael, CA 415-454-4868
Packaging Associates
  Randolph, NJ 973-252-8890
Packaging By Design Of Il
  Elgin, IL 847-741-5600
Packaging Dynamics
  Walnut Creek, CA 925-938-2711
Packaging Dynamics Corp
  Chicago, IL 773-843-8000
Packaging Dynamics International
  Caldwell, OH 740-732-5665
Packaging Enterprises
  Rockledge, PA 800-453-6213
Packaging Equipment & Conveyors, Inc
  Elkhart, IN 574-266-6995
Packaging Machinery & Equipment
  West Orange, NJ 973-325-2418
Packaging Machinery International
  Elk Grove Village, IL 800-871-4764
Packaging Materials Inc
  Cambridge, OH 800-565-8550
Packaging Products Corp
  Mission, KS 913-262-3033
Packaging Progressions
  Collegeville, PA 610-489-9096
Packing Material Company
  Southfield, MI 248-489-7000
Packotronics
  Glenview, IL 947-487-1281
Packrite Packaging
  Archdale, NC 336-431-1111
Packworld USA
  Nazareth, PA 610-746-2765
Paco Manufacturing
  Clarksville, IN 812-283-7963
Pacur
  Oshkosh, WI 920-236-2888
Page Slotting Saw Co Inc
  Toledo, OH 419-476-7475
Pak-Rapid
  Conshohocken, PA 610-828-3511

Pakmark
Chesterfield, MO 800-423-1379
Palmetto Canning
Palmetto, FL 941-722-1100
Paper Box & Specialty Co
Sheboygan, WI 888-240-3756
Paper Converting MachineCompany
Green Bay, WI. 920-494-5601
Paper Machinery Corp
Milwaukee, WI. 414-354-8050
Paper Pak Industries
La Verne, CA 909-392-1750
Paper Service
Hinsdale, NH 603-239-6344
Paragon Films Inc
Broken Arrow, OK 800-274-9727
PASCO
St Louis, MO. 800-489-3300
Pater & Associates
Cincinnati, OH
PDC International
Austin, TX. 512-302-0194
PDMP
Leesburg, VA 703-777-8400
Pearson Packaging Systems
Spokane, WA. 800-732-7766
Peco Controls Corporation
Modesto, CA..................... 800-732-6285
Peerless Food Equipment
Sidney, OH 937-492-4158
Peerless-Winsmith Inc
Springville, NY. 716-592-9310
Penny Plate
Haddonfield, NJ 856-429-7583
Pepperell Paper Company
Lawrence, MA 978-433-6951
Per-Fil Industries Inc
Riverside, NJ. 856-461-5700
Performance Packaging
Trail Creek, IN 219-874-6226
Perl Packaging Systems
Middlebury, CT. 800-864-2853
Pfankuch Machinery Corporation
Apple Valley, MN 952-891-3311
PFM Packaging Machinery Corporation
Newmarket, ON 905-836-6709
Phase Fire Systems
Vista, CA. 888-741-2341
Phoenix Closures Inc
Naperville, IL 630-544-3475
Plastech Corp
Atlanta, GA. 404-355-9682
Plasti-Mach Corporation
Valley Cottage, NY. 800-394-1128
Plastic Suppliers Inc
Columbus, OH 800-722-5577
Plastics Color Corp
Chicago, IL 800-922-9936
PlexPack Corp
Toronto, ON 855-635-9238
Pneumatic Scale Angelus
Cuyahoga Falls, OH 330-923-0491
Polar Tech Industries Inc
Genoa, IL 800-423-2749
Poly Plastic Products Inc
Delano, PA 570-467-3000
Poly Shapes Corporation
Elyria, OH 800-605-9359
Polypack Inc
Pinellas Park, FL 727-578-5000
Polyplastics
Austin, TX. 800-753-7659
Portco Corporation
Vancouver, WA 800-426-1794
Powertex Inc
Rouses Point, NY 800-769-3783
Praxair Inc
Danbury, CT 800-772-9247
Preferred Packaging Systems
San Dimas, CA 800-378-4777
Premier Plastics Inc
Omaha, NE 866-446-2998
Premium Foil Products Company
Louisville, KY 502-459-2820
Pres-On Products
Addison, IL 800-323-7467
Pressure Pack
Williamsburg, VA 757-220-3693
Prestige Label Company
Burgaw, NC. 800-969-4449
Print & Peel
New York, NY 800-451-0807

Printpack Inc.
Atlanta, GA. 404-460-7000
Priority One America
Oshkosh, WI 920-235-5562
Priority One Packaging
Waterloo, ON 800-387-9102
Prodo-Pak Corp
Garfield, NJ. 973-777-7770
Production Packaging & Processing Equipment
Company
Savannah, GA.................... 912-856-4281
Production Systems
Marietta, GA 800-235-9734
Professional Marketing Group
Seattle, WA 800-227-3769
Progressive Packaging Inc
Minneapolis, MN 800-844-7889
Propac Marketing Inc
Addison, TX. 972-733-3199
Prototype Equipment Corporation
Libertyville, IL 847-680-4433
PTI Packaging
Portage, WI. 800-501-4077
Pure & Secure LLC-Cust Svc
Lincoln, NE. 800-875-5915
Quality Films
Three Rivers, MI. 269-679-5263
Quality Industries
Cleveland, OH 216-961-5566
Quantum Performance Films
Streamwood, IL 800-323-6963
R R Donnelley
Chicago, IL 800-742-4455
Racine Paper Box Manufacturing
Chicago, IL 773-227-3900
RAM Center
Red Wing, MN 800-309-5431
Ramoneda Bros Stave Mill
Culpeper, VA..................... 540-825-9166
Ranger Blade Manufacturing Company
Traer, IA 800-377-7860
Raque Food Systems
Louisville, KY 502-267-9641
Ray C. Sprosty Bag Company
Wooster, OH 330-264-8559
Refrigiwear Inc
Dahlonega, GA................... 800-645-3744
Reggie Balls Cajun Foods
Lake Charles, LA 337-436-0291
Reilly Foam Corporation
Conshohocken, PA 610-834-1900
Reiser
Canton, MA 734-821-1290
Remcon Plastics Inc
Reading, PA 800-360-3636
Renard Machine Company
Green Bay, WI. 920-432-8412
Rennco LLC
Homer, MI. 800-409-5225
Republic Foil
Danbury, CT 800-722-3645
Rer Services
Northridge, CA 818-993-1826
Resina
Temecula, CA 800-207-4804
Restaurant Data
Irvington, NY 800-346-9390
Rexford Paper Company
Racine, WI 262-886-9100
Rico Packaging Company
Chicago, IL 773-523-9190
Rigidized Metal Corp
Buffalo, NY. 800-836-2580
Riverwood International
Atlanta, GA..................... 770-984-5477
Robert Bosch LLC
Farmington, MI. 917-421-7209
Roberts Packaging Equipment
Des Plaines, IL 888-221-0700
Roberts Poly Pro Inc
Charlotte, NC 800-269-7409
Rockford-Midland Corporation
Rockford, IL 800-327-7908
Rohrer Corp.
Wadsworth, OH. 800-243-6640
Rollprint Packaging Prods Inc
Addison, IL. 800-276-7629
Romanow Container
Westwood, MA 781-320-9200
Rondo of America
Naugatuck, CT 203-723-7474

Ropak Manufacturing Co Inc
Decatur, AL. 256-350-4241
Roplast Industries Inc
Oroville, CA 800-767-5278
Rose City Awning Co
Portland, OR 800-446-4104
Rose Forgrove
Saint Charles, IL 630-443-1317
Ross Industries Inc
Midland, VA 540-439-3271
Rowland Technologies
Wallingford, CT 203-269-9500
Royal Label Co
Dorchester, MA. 617-825-6050
RTS Packaging
Scarborough, ME 207-883-8921
RTS Packaging
Hillside, IL 708-338-2800
Rudd Container Corp
Chicago, IL 773-847-7600
Ruffino Paper Box Co
Hackensack, NJ. 201-487-1260
Rutan Poly Industries Inc
Mahwah, NJ 800-872-1474
Rutherford Engineering
Rockford, IL 815-623-2141
S L Sanderson & Co
Berry Creek, CA 800-763-7845
S.V. Dice Designers
Rowland Heights, CA 888-478-3423
Sabel Engineering Corporation
Villard, MN 320-554-3611
Salinas Valley Wax Paper Co
Salinas, CA. 831-424-2747
Samuel P. Harris
Rumford, RI 401-438-4020
Samuel Strapping Systems Inc
Woodridge, IL 800-323-4424
San Fab Conveyor
Sandusky, OH 419-626-4465
Sanchelima International
Miami, FL 305-591-4343
Sanford Redmond Company
Stamford, CT. 203-351-9800
Sasib Beverage & Food North America
Plano, TX. 800-558-3814
Scandia Packaging Machinery Co
Fairfield, NJ 973-473-6100
Schaefer Machine Co Inc
Deep River, CT 800-243-5143
Schneider Packaging Eqpt Co
Brewerton, NY 315-676-3035
Schroeder Machine
San Marcos, CA 760-591-9733
Seal-O-Matic Corp
Jacksonville, OR 800-631-2072
Sealstrip Corporation
Boyertown, PA 610-367-6282
Seepex Inc
Enon, OH 800-695-3659
Seiler Plastics
St Louis, MO. 888-673-4537
Sekisui TA Industries
Brea, CA. 800-258-8273
Serac Inc
Carol Stream, IL 630-510-9343
Serpa Packaging Solutions
Visalia, CA 800-348-5453
Sertapak Packaging Corporation
Woodstock, ON................... 800-265-1162
Servpak Corp
Hollywood, FL 800-782-0840
Seville Flexpack Corp
Oak Creek, WI 414-761-2751
Shamrock Paper Company
Saint Louis, MO 314-241-2370
Shawano Specialty Papers
Shawano, WI. 800-543-5554
Sherwood Tool
Owings Mills, MD 860-828-4161
Shields Bag & Printing Co
Yakima, WA 800-541-8630
Shields Products Inc
West Pittston, PA. 570-655-4596
Shippers Supply
Saskatoon, SK 800-661-5639
Shippers Supply, Labelgraphic
Calgary, AB. 800-661-5639
ShockWatch
Dallas, TX. 800-393-7920
Shrinkfast Marketing
Newport, NH.................... 800-867-4746

Sierra Dawn Products
Santa Rosa, CA 707-535-0172
SIG Combibloc USA, Inc.
Chester, PA 610-546-4200
Sig Pack
Oakland, CA 800-824-3245
Signature Packaging
West Orange, NJ 800-376-2299
Signode Industrial Group LLC
Glenview, IL 800-323-2464
Silgan Plastic Closure Sltns
Downers Grove, IL 800-727-8652
Silgan Plastic Closure Sltns
Downers Grove, IL 800-767-8652
Silgan White Cap LLC
Downers Grove, IL 800-515-1565
Silver Spur Corp
Cerritos, CA 562-921-6880
Simolex Rubber Corp
Plymouth, MI 734-453-4500
Simplex Filler Co
Napa, CA. 800-796-7539
Simplimatic Automation
Forest, VA 800-294-2003
Sitma USA
Spilamberto, MO 800-728-1254
SKW Gelatin & Specialties
Waukesha, WI. 800-654-2396
Slautterback Corporation
Duluth, GA 800-827-3308
Snapware
Fullerton, CA 800-334-3062
Sohn Manufacturing
Elkhart Lake, WI. 920-876-3361
Somerville Packaging
Toronto, ON 416-754-7228
Somerville Packaging
Mississauga, ON 905-678-8211
Soudal Accumetric
Elizabethtown, KY 800-928-2677
Southern Automatics
Lakeland, FL. 800-441-4604
Southern Container Corporation
Deer Park, NY. 631-586-6006
Southern Film Extruders
High Point, NC 800-334-6101
Southern Packaging Machinery
Athens, GA 706-208-0814
Southern Pallet
Christchurch, NZ 901-942-4603
Southern Tool
West Monroe, LA 800-458-3687
Spartec Plastics
Conneaut, OH 800-325-5176
Spartech Plastics
Wichita, KS 316-722-8621
Spartech Plastics
Portage, WI. 800-998-7123
Spartech Poly Com
Clayton, MI 888-721-4242
Specialty Films & Associates
Hebron, KY 800-984-3346
Specialty Packaging Inc
Fort Worth, TX 800-284-7722
Spee-Dee Packaging Machinery
Sturtevant, WI. 877-375-2121
St. Clair Pakwell
Bellwood, IL. 800-323-1922
St. Pierre Box & Lumber Company
Canton, CT 860-693-2089
Stainless Specialists Inc
Wausau, WI. 800-236-4155
Standard-Knapp Inc
Portland, CT 800-628-9565
Staplex Co Inc
Brooklyn, NY 800-221-0822
Star Poly Bag Inc
Brooklyn, NY 718-384-7034
Starview Packaging Machinery
Dorval, QC 888-278-5555
Stewart Mechanical Seals
Bakersfield, CA 661-391-9332
Stiles Enterprises Inc
Rockaway, NJ 800-325-4232
Stock America Inc
Grafton, WI. 262-375-4100
Stone Container
Chicago, IL 312-346-6600
Stormax International
Concord, NH 800-874-7629
Straub Designs Co
St Louis Park, MN 800-959-3708

Stretch-Vent Packaging System
Ontario, CA. 800-822-8368
Sungjae Corporation
Irvine, CA 949-757-1727
Superior Distributing Co
Louisville, KY 800-365-6661
Superior Packaging Equipment Corporation
Fairfield, NJ 973-575-8818
Surekap Inc
Winder, GA. 770-867-5793
SWF Co
Reedley, CA 800-344-8951
SWF McDowell
Orlando, FL. 800-877-7971
Sycamore Containers
Sycamore, IL. 815-895-2343
Systems Technology Inc
San Bernardino, CA 909-799-9950
T & T Industries Inc
Fort Mohave, AZ 800-437-6246
T D Sawvel Co
Maple Plain, MN. 877-488-1816
T.O. Plastics
Minneapolis, MN 952-854-2131
Taconic
Petersburg, NY 800-833-1805
Target Industries
North Salt Lake, UT 866-617-2253
Taylor Products Co
Parsons, KS 888-882-9567
TDF Automation
Cedar Falls, IA 800-553-1777
Technistar Corporation
Denver, CO 303-651-0188
Tecweigh
St Paul, MN. 800-536-4880
Telesonic Packaging
Wilmington, DE 302-658-6945
Temco
Oakland, CA 707-746-5966
Templock Corporation
Santa Barbara, CA 800-777-1715
TEQ
Huntley, IL 800-874-7113
Terkelsen Machine Company
Hyannis, MA. 508-775-6229
Terphane Inc
Bloomfield, NY 800-724-3456
THARCO
San Lorenzo, CA. 800-772-2332
Tharo Systems Inc
Brunswick, OH 800-878-6833
Thiele Engineering Company
Fergus Falls, MN 218-739-3321
Thiele Technologies Inc
Minneapolis, MN 612-782-1200
Thiele Technologies-Reedley
Reedley, CA 800-344-8951
Thomas Tape & Supply Co Inc
Springfield, OH 937-325-6414
Tieco-Unadilla Corporation
Unadilla, NY. 877-889-6540
Tilly Industries
St Laurent, QC 514-331-4922
Tisma Machinery Corporation
Elk Grove Village, IL 847-427-9525
TMT Vacuum Filters
Danville, IL. 217-446-0742
TNA Packaging Solutions
Coppell, TX 972-462-6500
Tolas Health Care Packaging
Feasterville Trevose, PA. 215-322-7900
Tomac Packaging
Woburn, MA 800-641-3100
Trans World Services
Melrose, MA 800-882-2105
Trenton Mills Inc
Trenton, TN. 731-855-1323
Tri-Sterling
Altamonte Spgs, FL 407-260-0330
Triangle Package Machinery Co
Chicago, IL. 800-621-4170
Trico Converting Inc
Fullerton, CA 714-563-0701
Tridyne Process Systems
South Burlington, VT 802-863-6873
Trinity Packaging
Cheektowaga, NY 800-778-3111
True Pac
New Castle, DE 800-825-7890
Tucson Container Corp
Tucson, AZ 520-746-3171

Tyco Plastics
Lakeville, MN. 800-328-4080
UCB Inc
Smyrna, GA 770-970-8338
Ultrapak
Dunkirk, NY 800-228-6030
Unifoil Corp
Fairfield, NJ 973-244-9990
Unique Boxes
Chicago, IL 800-281-1670
United Desiccants
Reno, NE. 888-659-1377
United Flexible
Westbury, NY 516-222-2150
United Systems Inc
Kansas City, KS 888-281-2454
UniTrak Corporation
Port Hope, ON 866-883-5749
Universal Labeling Systems Inc
St Petersburg, FL 877-236-0266
Universal Packaging Inc
Houston, TX 800-324-2610
Universal Paper Box
Seattle, WA 800-228-1045
UPACO Adhesives
Richmond, VA 800-446-9984
US Label Corporation
Greensboro, NC 336-332-7000
US Line Company
Westfield, MA. 413-562-3629
V C 999 Packaging Systems
Kansas City, MO 800-728-2999
Vacumet Corp
Wayne, NJ 973-628-1067
Vacumet Corporation
Austell, GA 800-776-0865
Vacuum Depositing Inc
Louisville, KY 502-969-4227
Valco Melton
West Chester, OH 513-874-6550
VIFAN Canada
Lanoraie, QC 800-557-0192
Viking Industries
New Smyrna Beach, FL 888-605-5560
Viking Packaging & Display
San Jose, CA 408-998-1000
Virginia Plastics Co
Roanoke, VA. 800-777-8541
Vista Internatlonal Packaging
Kenosha, WI 800-558-4058
Volk Corp
Farmington Hills, MI 800-521-6799
Volumetric Technologies
Cannon Falls, MN. 507-263-0034
W.G. Durant Corporation
Whittier, CA 562-946-5555
Warwick Manufacturing & Equip
North Brunswick, NJ 732-729-0400
Washington Frontier
Grandview, WA 509-469-7662
Wasserman Bag Company
Center Moriches, NY 631-909-8656
Water Sciences Services, Inc.
Jackson, TN 973-584-4131
Waukesha Cherry-Burrell
Louisville, KY 502-491-4310
Wayne Automation Corp
Eagleville, PA 610-630-8900
WCB Ice Cream
Philadelphia, PA 215-425-4320
WE Killam Enterprises
Waterford, ON. 519-443-7421
Weber Display & Packaging Inc
Philadelphia, PA 215-426-3500
Weigh Right Automatic Scale Co
Joliet, IL 800-571-0249
WeighPack Systems/Paxiom Group
Montreal, QC 888-934-4472
Welliver Metal Products Corporation
Salem, OR. 503-362-1568
Wepackit
Orangeville, ON 519-942-1700
West-Pak
Dallas, TX 214-337-8984
Western Plastics
Portland, TN 615-325-7331
Western Plastics
Calhoun, GA 800-752-4106
Westervelt Co Inc
Tuscaloosa, AL 205-562-5000
Wexxar Corporation
Chicago, IL 630-983-6666

Wexxar Packaging Inc
  Richmond, BC 888-565-3219
Whirley Industries Inc
  Warren, PA 800-825-5575
Wick's Packaging Service
  Cutler, IN 574-967-3104
Wilks Precision Instr Co Inc
  Union Bridge, MD 410-775-7917
Williamson & Co
  Greer, SC 800-849-3263
Winpak Portion Packaging
  San Bernardino, CA 800-804-4224
Winpak Technologies
  Toronto, ON 416-421-1700
Winzen Film
  Taylor, TX 800-779-7595
Wisconsin Film & Bag Inc
  Shawano, WI 800-765-9224
Witt Plastics
  Greenville, OH 800-227-9181
Woodstock Line Co
  Putnam, CT 860-928-6557
Woodward Manufacturing
  Paramus, NJ 201-262-6700
Wrap Pack
  Yakima, WA 800-879-9727
Wrapade Packaging Systems
  Fairfield, NJ 888-815-8564
Wraps
  East Orange, NJ 973-673-7873
WS Packaging Group Inc
  Green Bay, WI 877-977-5177
Y-Z Sponge & Foam Products
  Delta, BC 604-525-1665
Yakima Wire Works
  Reedley, CA 800-344-8951
Yohay Baking Co
  Lindenhurst, NY 631-225-0300
Zed Industries
  Vandalia, OH 937-667-8407
Zepf Technologies
  Clearwater, FL 727-535-4100
Zerand Corp
  New Berlin, WI 262-827-3800
Zimmer Custom-Made Packaging
  Indianapolis, IN 317-263-3436
Zitropack Limited
  Addison, IL 630-543-1016
Zume Manufacturing
  Mountain View, CA

Automatic/Random Case Sealing

Alard Equipment Corp
  Williamson, NY 315-589-4511
Reiser
  Canton, MA 734-821-1290
S&R Machinery
  Olyphant, PA 800-229-4896
Tetra Pak
  Champlin, MN 763-421-2721

Bag Closing

About Packaging Robotics
  Thornton, CO 303-449-2559
Alard Equipment Corp
  Williamson, NY 315-589-4511
Aline Heat Seal Corporation
  Los Angeles, CA.........................888-285-3917
Amark Packaging Systems
  Kansas City, MO.........................816-965-9000
American Bag & Burlap Company
  Chelsea, MA..............................617-884-7600
Andgar Corp
  Ferndale, WA 360-366-9900
Automated Packaging Systems
  Streetsboro, OH 800-527-0733
Bosch Packaging Technology
  New Richmond, WI 715-246-6511
Branson Ultrasonics Corp
  Danbury, CT 203-796-0400
Chaffee Co
  Rocklin, CA 916-630-3980
Clamco Corporation
  Berea, OH 216-267-1911
Crystal-Vision Packaging Systems
  Torrance, CA.............................800-331-3240
Custom Food Machinery
  Stockton, CA.............................209-463-4343
Customized Equipment SE
  Tucker, GA 770-934-9300

Dynamic Automation LTD
  Simi Valley, CA..........................805-584-8476
Fawema Packaging Machinery
  Palmetto, FL 941-351-9597
Fischbein LLC
  Statesville, NC 704-838-4600
Gulf Arizona Packaging
  Humble, TX 800-364-3887
Gulf Systems
  Brownsville, TX 800-217-4853
Gulf Systems
  Humble, TX 800-364-3887
Gulf Systems
  Arlington, TX 817-261-1915
Harwil Corp
  Oxnard, CA 800-562-2447
Herche Warehouse
  Denver, CO 303-371-8186
Herrmann Ultrasonics
  Bartlett, IL 630-626-1626
ID Images
  Brunswick, OH 866-516-7300
Iman Pack
  Westland, MI.............................800-810-4626
Industrial Automation Systems
  Santa Clarita, CA 888-484-4427
JMC Packaging Equipment
  Burlington, ON 800-263-5252
KWIK Lok Corp
  Yakima, WA 800-688-5945
Lockwood Packaging
  Woburn, MA 800-641-3100
Matthiesen Equipment
  San Antonio, TX 800-624-8635
New Jersey Wire Stitching Machine Company
  Cherry Hill, NJ 856-428-2572
Pacemaker Packaging Corp
  Woodside, NY............................718-458-1188
Pack Rite Machine Mettler
  Mt Pleasant, WI 800-248-6868
Packaging Systems Intl
  Denver, CO 303-244-9000
Pacmac Inc
  Fayetteville, AR 800-834-1544
PlexPack Corp
  Toronto, ON 855-635-9238
Prodo-Pak Corp
  Garfield, NJ..............................973-777-7770
Save-O-Seal Corporation
  Elmsford, NY 800-831-9720
Staplex Co Inc
  Brooklyn, NY 800-221-0822
Tomac Packaging
  Woburn, MA 800-641-3100
Triangle Package Machinery Co
  Chicago, IL 800-621-4170
Weigh Right Automatic Scale Co
  Joliet, IL 800-571-0249

Bag Filling

About Packaging Robotics
  Thornton, CO 303-449-2559
Actionpac Scales Automation
  Oxnard, CA...............................800-394-0154
Ag-Pak
  Gasport, NY 716-772-2651
Alard Equipment Corp
  Williamson, NY 315-589-4511
Amark Packaging Systems
  Kansas City, MO.........................816-965-9000
American Bag & Burlap Company
  Chelsea, MA..............................617-884-7600
Ameriglobe LLC
  Lafayette, LA 337-234-3211
Andgar Corp
  Ferndale, WA 360-366-9900
Audion Automation
  Carrollton, TX............................972-389-0777
Automated Packaging Systems
  Streetsboro, OH 800-527-0733
Batching Systems
  Prince Frederick, MD 800-311-0851
Bettendorf Stanford Inc
  Salem, IL 800-548-2253
California Vibratory Feeders
  Anaheim, CA 800-354-0972
Chantland Company, The
  Humboldt, IA 515-332-4040
Circle Packaging Machinery Inc
  De Pere, WI...............................920-983-3420

Control & Metering
  Mississauga, ON 800-736-5739
Crystal-Vision Packaging Systems
  Torrance, CA.............................800-331-3240
Custom Food Machinery
  Stockton, CA.............................209-463-4343
Custom Metal Design Inc
  Oakland, FL 800-334-1777
Customized Equipment SE
  Tucker, GA 770-934-9300
Enhance Packaging Technologies
  Whitby, ON 905-668-5811
Fawema Packaging Machinery
  Palmetto, FL 941-351-9597
Franrica Systems
  Stockton, CA.............................209-948-2811
Glopak
  St Leonard, QC 800-361-6994
Hudson-Sharp Machine Co
  Green Bay, WI............................800-950-4362
ID Images
  Brunswick, OH 866-516-7300
Ideal of America
  Charlotte, NC 704-523-1604
Iman Pack
  Westland, MI.............................800-810-4626
JMC Packaging Equipment
  Burlington, ON 800-263-5252
Khs USA Inc
  Sarasota, FL 877-227-8358
Kloppenberg & Co
  Englewood, CO...........................800-346-3246
Liqui-Box
  Richmond, VA............................804-325-1400
Liqui-Box Corp
  Richmond, VA............................804-325-1400
Lockwood Packaging
  Woburn, MA 800-641-3100
Machine Electronics Company
  Brooklyn, NY 718-384-3211
Multi-Fill Inc
  West Jordan, UT 801-280-1570
Oden Machinery
  Tonawanda, NY 800-658-3622
Pacemaker Packaging Corp
  Woodside, NY............................718-458-1188
Packaging Enterprises
  Rockledge, PA............................800-453-6213
Packaging Systems Intl
  Denver, CO 303-244-9000
Pacmac Inc
  Fayetteville, AR 800-834-1544
Palace Packaging Machines Inc
  Downingtown, PA........................610-873-7252
PlexPack Corp
  Toronto, ON 855-635-9238
Pneumatic Scale Angelus
  Cuyahoga Falls, OH 330-923-0491
Prodo-Pak Corp
  Garfield, NJ..............................973-777-7770
Prototype Equipment Corporation
  Libertyville, IL 847-680-4433
Reiser
  Canton, MA 734-821-1290
Save-O-Seal Corporation
  Elmsford, NY 800-831-9720
Simplex Filler Co
  Napa, CA..................................800-796-7539
Summit Machine Builders Corporation
  Denver, CO 800-274-6741
Taylor Products Co
  Parsons, KS...............................888-882-9567
Telesonic Packaging
  Wilmington, DE 302-658-6945
Temco
  Oakland, CA..............................707-746-5966
TMT Vacuum Filters
  Danville, IL...............................217-446-0742
Triangle Package Machinery Co
  Chicago, IL 800-621-4170
Tridyne Process Systems
  South Burlington, VT 802-863-6873
United States Systems Inc
  Kansas City, KS 888-281-2454
UniTrak Corporation
  Port Hope, ON 866-883-5749
V C 999 Packaging Systems
  Kansas City, MO.........................800-728-2999
Water Sciences Services, Inc.
  Jackson, TN 973-584-4131
WCB Ice Cream
  Philadelphia, PA 215-425-4320

Weigh Right Automatic Scale Co
Joliet, IL 800-571-0249

Bag Opening

About Packaging Robotics
Thornton, CO 303-449-2559
Alard Equipment Corp
Williamson, NY 315-589-4511
Audion Automation
Carrollton, TX. 972-389-0777
Automated Packaging Systems
Streetsboro, OH 800-527-0733
General Processing Systems
Holland, MI. 800-547-9370
Gulf Arizona Packaging
Humble, TX 800-364-3887
Gulf Systems
Brownsville, TX 800-217-4853
Gulf Systems
Humble, TX 800-364-3887
Gulf Systems
Arlington, TX 817-261-1915
Herche Warehouse
Denver, CO 303-371-8186
Lockwood Packaging
Woburn, MA. 800-641-3100
Our Name is Mud
New York, NY 877-683-7867
Packaging Systems Intl
Denver, CO 303-244-9000
Pacmac Inc
Fayetteville, AR 800-834-1544
Temco
Oakland, CA 707-746-5966

Bag, Cellophane & Pliofilm

Alard Equipment Corp
Williamson, NY 315-589-4511
Automated Packaging Systems
Streetsboro, OH 800-527-0733
Batching Systems
Prince Frederick, MD 800-311-0851
Dynaclear Packaging
Wyckoff, NJ 201-337-1001
Fawema Packaging Machinery
Palmetto, FL 941-351-9597
Hudson-Sharp Machine Co
Green Bay, WI. 800-950-4362
Hudson-Sharp Machine Company
Green Bay, WI. 920-494-4571
Liqui-Box Corp
Richmond, VA. 804-325-1400
M & Q Packaging Corp
North Wales, PA 267-498-4000

Bag, Paper

About Packaging Robotics
Thornton, CO 303-449-2559
Alard Equipment Corp
Williamson, NY 315-589-4511
H G Weber & Co
Kiel, WI. 920-894-2221
New Jersey Wire Stitching Machine Company
Cherry Hill, NJ 856-428-2572
PlexPack Corp
Toronto, ON 855-635-9238
V C 999 Packaging Systems
Kansas City, MO. 800-728-2999

Bar Code Devices

Accu-Sort Systems
Telford, PA 800-227-2633
Alard Equipment Corp
Williamson, NY 315-589-4511
Alfa Systems Inc
Westfield, NJ. 908-654-0255
American Forms & Labels
Boise, ID 800-388-3554
Baublys Control Laser
Orlando, FL. 866-612-8619
Cognitive
Golden, CO 800-765-6600
Columbia Labeling Machinery
Benton City, WA. 888-791-9590
Command Line Corporation
Edison, NJ. 732-738-6500
Computype Inc
St Paul, MN. 800-328-0852

Comstar Printing Solutions
Streetsboro, OH 330-528-2800
Control Module
Enfield, CT 800-722-6654
Creative Automation
Passaic, NJ 973-778-0061
CRS Marking Systems
Portland, OR 800-547-7158
Durable Engravers
Franklin Park, IL 800-869-9565
Esselte Meto
Morris Plains, NJ 800-645-3290
Exact Equipment Corporation
Morrisville, PA 215-295-2000
Fairbanks Scales
Kansas City, MO. 800-451-4107
Fernqvist Labeling Solutions
Mountain View, CA 800-426-8215
Formulator Software, LLC
Clinton, NJ 908-735-2248
Fotel
Lombard, IL 800-834-4920
GCA
Huntington Beach, CA 714-379-4911
Graphic Technology
New Century, KS 800-767-9920
Herche Warehouse
Denver, CO 303-371-8186
ID Images
Brunswick, OH 866-516-7300
Imaging Technologies
Cookeville, TN 800-488-2804
Imaje
Kennesaw, GA 678-594-7153
InterSect Business Systems Inc
Kelowna, BC. 250-860-0829
ITW Diagraph
St Charles, MO. 800-722-1125
L G I Intl Inc
Portland, OR 800-345-0534
Label Products Inc
Burnsville, MN 877-370-0688
Los Angeles Label Company
Commerce, CA 800-606-5223
Marsh Company
Belleville, IL 800-527-6275
Microscan Systems Inc
Renton, WA. 800-762-1149
Qsx Labels
Everett, MA. 800-225-3496
Sato America
Charlotte, NC 888-871-8741
Southern Atlantic Label Co
Chesapeake, VA 800-456-5999
Stratix Corp
Peachtree Cor, GA 800-883-8300
Tallygenicom
Irvine, CA. 800-665-6210
Tharo Systems Inc
Brunswick, OH 800-878-6833
Trident
Brookfield, CT 203-740-9333
Vertex Interactive
Clifton, NJ. 973-777-3500
Videx Inc
Corvallis, OR 541-738-5500
Wallace Computer Services
Chicago, IL. 888-925-8324
Zebra Technologies Corporation
Lincolnshire, IL 866-230-9494

Barrel & Drum Filling

Alard Equipment Corp
Williamson, NY 315-589-4511
Custom Food Machinery
Stockton, CA. 209-463-4343
Data Scale
Fremont, CA 800-651-7350
J.G. Machine Works
Holmdel, NJ 732-203-2077
Washington Frontier
Grandview, WA. 509-469-7662

Barrel Packers

Alard Equipment Corp
Williamson, NY 315-589-4511
Buffalo Technologies Corporation
Buffalo, NY. 800-332-2419
Centennial Moldings
Hastings, NE 888-883-2189

Beverages, Hot Fill

Alard Equipment Corp
Williamson, NY 315-589-4511
Innovative Food Solutions LLC
Columbus, OH 800-884-3314
Power Packaging Inc
Rosendale, WI. 920-872-2181
Promens
St. John, NB 800-295-3725
Washington Frontier
Grandview, WA. 509-469-7662

Bottle & Jar Sealing

AAMD
Liverpool, NY. 800-887-4167
Alard Equipment Corp
Williamson, NY 315-589-4511
Anderson Machine Sales
Fort Lee, NJ
Arkansas Poly
N Little Rock, AR. 800-342-7659
Crown Closures Machinery
Lancaster, OH 740-681-6593
Custom Food Machinery
Stockton, CA. 209-463-4343
Giltron Inc
Norwood, MA. 781-762-4310
Herrmann Ultrasonics
Bartlett, IL 630-626-1626
Lyco Wausau
Wausau, WI. 715-845-7867
New England Machinery Inc
Bradenton, FL. 941-755-5550
Pack Line Corporation
Racine, WI 800-248-6868
Packaging & Processing Equipment
Ayr, ON 519-622-6666
Promens
St. John, NB 800-295-3725
Resina
Temecula, CA 800-207-4804
Sanchelima International
Miami, FL. 305-591-4343

Bottle Cap, Plastic & Metal

AAMD
Liverpool, NY. 800-887-4167
Alard Equipment Corp
Williamson, NY 315-589-4511
Anderson Machine Sales
Fort Lee, NJ
Auto-Mate Technologies
Riverhead, NY 631-727-8886
Berkshire PPM
Litchfield, CT 860-567-3118
California Vibratory Feeders
Anaheim, CA 800-354-0972
Crown Closures Machinery
Lancaster, OH 740-681-6593
Custom Food Machinery
Stockton, CA. 209-463-4343
Maverick Enterprises Inc
Ukiah, CA. 707-463-5591
Silgan Plastic Closure Sltns
New Castle, PA 724-658-3004
Silgan Plastic Closure Sltns
Downers Grove, IL 800-727-8652
Surekap Inc
Winder, GA 770-867-5793

Bottle Capping & Crowning

AAMD
Liverpool, NY. 800-887-4167
Accutek Packaging Equipment
Vista, CA. 800-989-1828
Alard Equipment Corp
Williamson, NY 315-589-4511
Alcoa - Massena Operations
Massena, NY
Anderson Machine Sales
Fort Lee, NJ
Automated Production Systems Corporation
New Freedom, PA 888-345-5377
Berkshire PPM
Litchfield, CT 860-567-3118
Biner Ellison Packaging Systs
Vista, CA. 800-733-8162
California Vibratory Feeders
Anaheim, CA 800-354-0972

Chase-Logeman Corp
Greensboro, NC 336-665-0754
Closure Systems Intl Inc
Indianapolis, IN 800-311-2740
Cozzoli Machine Co
Somerset, NJ 732-564-0400
Crown Closures Machinery
Lancaster, OH 740-681-6593
Custom Food Machinery
Stockton, CA 209-463-4343
Diversified Capping Equipment
Perrysburg, OH 419-666-2566
Donahower & Company
Olathe, KS 913-829-2650
Dynamic Automation LTD
Simi Valley, CA................805-584-8476
Eastern Machine
Middlebury, CT.................203-598-0066
ELF Machinery
La Porte, IN...................800-328-0466
Elmar Worldwide
Depew, NY 800-433-3562
Filler Specialties
Zeeland, MI....................616-772-9235
Filling Equipment Co Inc
Flushing, NY...................800-247-7127
Fillit
Kirkland, QC...................514-694-2390
Fogg Filler Co
Holland, MI....................616-786-3644
Fowler Products Co LLC
Athens, GA 877-549-3301
Giltron Inc
Norwood, MA...................781-762-4310
Haumiller Engineering Co
Elgin, IL......................847-695-9111
Horix Manufacturing Co
Mc Kees Rocks, PA..............412-771-1111
Inline Filling Systems
Venice, FL.....................941-486-8800
KAPS All Packaging
Riverhead, NY..................631-727-0300
Kinsley Inc
Doylestown, PA 800-414-6664
KISS Packaging Systems
Vista, CA......................888-522-3538
Lake Eyelet Manufacturing Company
Weatogue, CT...................860-628-5543
National Instruments
Baltimore, MD..................866-258-1914
New England Machinery Inc
Bradenton, FL..................941-755-5550
Nichols Specialty Products
Southborough, MA...............508-481-4367
NJM/CLI
Pointe Claire, QC..............514-630-6990
Norwalt Design Inc
Randolph, NJ...................973-927-3200
Packaging & Processing Equipment
Ayr, ON........................519-622-6666
Palace Packaging Machines Inc
Downingtown, PA................610-873-7252
Perl Packaging Systems
Middlebury, CT.................800-864-2853
Production Packaging & Processing Equipment
Company
Savannah, GA...................912-856-4281
Resina
Temecula, CA...................800-207-4804
Silgan Containers LLC
Woodland Hills, CA.............818-710-3700
Silgan Plastic Closure Sltns
New Castle, PA.................724-658-3004
Silgan Plastic Closure Sltns
Downers Grove, IL..............800-767-8652
Silgan White Cap LLC
Downers Grove, IL..............800-515-1565
Simplex Filler Co
Napa, CA.......................800-796-7539
Surekap Inc
Winder, GA.....................770-867-5793
Universal Labeling Systems Inc
St Petersburg, FL..............877-236-0266
Us Bottlers Machinery Co Inc
Charlotte, NC..................704-588-4750

Bottle Cartoning

Alard Equipment Corp
Williamson, NY.................315-589-4511
Berkshire PPM
Litchfield, CT.................860-567-3118

Cannon Equipment Company
Cannon Falls, MN...............800-825-8501
Packaging & Processing Equipment
Ayr, ON........................519-622-6666
Sasib Beverage & Food North America
Plano, TX......................800-558-3814

Bottle Corking

Alard Equipment Corp
Williamson, NY.................315-589-4511
Power Packaging Inc
Rosendale, WI..................920-872-2181

Bottle Drying

Alard Equipment Corp
Williamson, NY.................315-589-4511
Ametek Technical & Industrial Products
Kent, OH.......................215-256-6601
Custom Food Machinery
Stockton, CA...................209-463-4343
Gardner Denver Inc.
Milwaukee, WI
Paxton Products Inc
Blue Ash, OH...................800-441-7475

Bottle Filling

A.K. Robins
Baltimore, MD..................800-486-9656
Accutek Packaging Equipment
Vista, CA......................800-989-1828
Alard Equipment Corp
Williamson, NY.................315-589-4511
B T Engineering Inc
Bala Cynwyd, PA................610-664-9500
Berkshire PPM
Litchfield, CT.................860-567-3118
Biner Ellison Packaging Systs
Vista, CA......................800-733-8162
California Vibratory Feeders
Anaheim, CA....................800-354-0972
Chase-Logeman Corp
Greensboro, NC.................336-665-0754
Cozzoli Machine Co
Somerset, NJ...................732-564-0400
Custom Food Machinery
Stockton, CA...................209-463-4343
E2M
Duluth, GA.....................800-622-4326
Eischen Enterprises
Fresno, CA.....................559-834-0013
Elmar Worldwide
Depew, NY......................800-433-3562
Federal Mfg Co
Milwaukee, WI..................414-384-3200
Filler Specialties
Zeeland, MI....................616-772-9235
Fogg Filler Co
Holland, MI....................616-786-3644
Globe Machine
Tacoma, WA.....................800-523-6575
Goodnature Products
Orchard Park, NY...............800-875-3381
Horix Manufacturing Co
Mc Kees Rocks, PA..............412-771-1111
J.G. Machine Works
Holmdel, NJ....................732-203-2077
Jetstream Systems
Wichita, KN....................855-861-6916
John R Nalbach Engineering Co
Countryside, IL................708-579-9100
KAPS All Packaging
Riverhead, NY..................631-727-0300
Kinsley Inc
Doylestown, PA.................800-414-6664
KISS Packaging Systems
Vista, CA......................888-522-3538
Liqui-Box
Richmond, VA...................804-325-1400
Lyco Wausau
Wausau, WI.....................715-845-7867
Morrison Timing Screw Co
Glenwood, IL...................708-331-6600
Multi-Fill Inc
West Jordan, UT................801-280-1570
National Instruments
Baltimore, MD..................866-258-1914
Oden Machinery
Tonawanda, NY..................800-658-3622
Packaging & Processing Equipment
Ayr, ON........................519-622-6666

Packaging Dynamics
Walnut Creek, CA...............925-938-2711
Packaging Enterprises
Rockledge, PA..................800-453-6213
Per-Fil Industries Inc
Riverside, NJ..................856-461-5700
Perl Packaging Systems
Middlebury, CT.................800-864-2853
Pneumatic Scale Angelus
Cuyahoga Falls, OH.............330-923-0491
Power Packaging Inc
Rosendale, WI..................920-872-2181
Sanchelima International
Miami, FL......................305-591-4343
Sasib Beverage & Food North America
Plano, TX......................800-558-3814
Simplex Filler Co
Napa, CA.......................800-796-7539
Tindall Packaging
Vicksburg, MI..................269-649-1163
Universal Labeling Systems Inc
St Petersburg, FL..............877-236-0266
Us Bottlers Machinery Co Inc
Charlotte, NC..................704-588-4750
Volckening Inc
Brooklyn, NY...................800-221-0276

Bottle Washing, Soaking & Rinsing

Alard Equipment Corp
Williamson, NY.................315-589-4511
Alliance Industrial Corp
Lynchburg, VA..................800-368-3556
Berkshire PPM
Litchfield, CT.................860-567-3118
BEVCO
Canada, BC.....................800-663-0090
Custom Food Machinery
Stockton, CA...................209-463-4343
Davron Technologies Inc
Chattanooga, TN................423-870-1888
Horix Manufacturing Co
Mc Kees Rocks, PA..............412-771-1111
Jetstream Systems
Wichita, KN....................855-861-6916
Krones
Franklin, WI...................800-752-3787
Mcbrady Engineering Co
Rockdale, IL...................815-744-8900
Metal Equipment Company
Cleveland, OH..................800-700-6326
Namco Machinery
Maspeth, NY
National Hotpack
Stone Ridge, NY................800-431-8232
Palace Packaging Machines Inc
Downingtown, PA................610-873-7252
Priority One Packaging
Waterloo, ON...................800-387-9102
Sasib Beverage & Food North America
Plano, TX......................800-558-3814
Us Bottlers Machinery Co Inc
Charlotte, NC..................704-588-4750

Bottling

AC Label Company
Provo, UT......................801-642-3500
Alard Equipment Corp
Williamson, NY.................315-589-4511
Amco Products Co
Fort Smith, AR.................479-646-8949
Ametek Technical & Industrial Products
Kent, OH.......................215-256-6601
Anver Corporation
Hudson, MA.....................800-654-3500
Berkshire PPM
Litchfield, CT.................860-567-3118
Capmatic, Ltd.
Monreal North, QC..............514-332-0062
Crown Holdings, Inc.
Yardley, PA....................215-698-5100
Custom Food Machinery
Stockton, CA...................209-463-4343
Filling Equipment Co Inc
Flushing, NY...................800-247-7127
Fowler Products Co LLC
Athens, GA.....................877-549-3301
Horix Manufacturing Co
Mc Kees Rocks, PA..............412-771-1111
Improved Blow Molding
Hollis, NH.....................800-256-1766

KAPS All Packaging
Riverhead, NY 631-727-0300
Kinsley Inc
Doylestown, PA 800-414-6664
Krones
Franklin, WI 800-752-3787
New England Machinery Inc
Bradenton, FL 941-755-5550
Oak Barrel Winecraft
Berkeley, CA. 510-849-0400
OnTrack Automation Inc
Waterloo, ON 519-886-9090
Pace Packaging Corp
Fairfield, NJ 800-867-2726
Packaging & Processing Equipment
Ayr, ON 519-622-6666
Packaging Dynamics
Walnut Creek, CA. 925-938-2711
Palace Packaging Machines Inc
Downingtown, PA. 610-873-7252
Paxton Products Inc
Blue Ash, OH 800-441-7475
Pearson Packaging Systems
Spokane, WA. 800-732-7766
Peerless-Winsmith Inc
Springville, NY 716-592-9310
Pneumatic Scale Angelus
Cuyahoga Falls, OH 330-923-0491
Pure & Secure LLC-Cust Svc
Lincoln, NE. 800-875-5915
Rocheleau Blow Molding Systems
Fitchburg, MA 978-345-1723
Silver Spur Corp
Cerritos, CA. 562-921-6880
Simplex Filler Co
Napa, CA. 800-796-7539
Universal Aqua Technologies
Torrance, CA. 800-777-6939

Box Closing

Berkshire PPM
Litchfield, CT 860-567-3118
Charles Beck Machine Corporation
King of Prussia, PA. 610-265-0500
Custom Food Machinery
Stockton, CA. 209-463-4343
Gulf Arizona Packaging
Humble, TX 800-364-3887
Gulf Systems
Brownsville, TX 800-217-4853
Gulf Systems
Humble, TX 800-364-3887
Gulf Systems
Arlington, TX 817-261-1915
Herche Warehouse
Denver, CO 303-371-8186
Iman Pack
Westland, MI. 800-810-4626
Moen Industries
Santa Fe Springs, CA 800-732-7766
Nordson Sealant Equipment
Plymouth, MI 734-459-8600
Thiele Technologies-Reedley
Reedley, CA 800-344-8951
WE Killam Enterprises
Waterford, ON. 519-443-7421
Weigh Right Automatic Scale Co
Joliet, IL 800-571-0249

Box Cutting

Accurate Paper Box Co Inc
Knoxville, TN. 865-690-0311
Charles Beck Machine Corporation
King of Prussia, PA. 610-265-0500
D & L Manufacturing
Milwaukee, WI. 414-256-8160
Premier Packages
Saint Louis, MO 800-466-6588

Box Strapping

Delta Cyklop Orga Pac
Charlotte, NC 800-446-4347
Dynaric Inc
Virginia Beach, VA. 800-526-0827
Gulf Arizona Packaging
Humble, TX 800-364-3887
Gulf Systems
Brownsville, TX 800-217-4853
Gulf Systems
Humble, TX 800-364-3887

Gulf Systems
Arlington, TX 817-261-1915
Herche Warehouse
Denver, CO 303-371-8186

Box, Paper

Accurate Paper Box Co Inc
Knoxville, TN. 865-690-0311
Ameripak Packaging Equipment
Warrington, PA 215-343-1530
Barnes Machine Company
Saint Petersburg, FL 727-327-9452
Colter & Peterson
Paterson, NJ 973-684-0901
D & L Manufacturing
Milwaukee, WI. 414-256-8160
Fuller Box Co
North Attleboro, MA 508-695-2525
General Corrugated Machinery Company
Palisades Park, NJ. 201-944-0644
Gram Equipment Of America
Tampa, FL 813-248-1978
International Paper Box Machine Company
Nashua, NH 603-889-6651
Marquip Ward United
Phillips, WI 715-339-2191
Moen Industries
Santa Fe Springs, CA 800-732-7766
New Jersey Wire Stitching Machine Company
Cherry Hill, NJ 856-428-2572
Standard Paper Box Mach Co Inc
Bronx, NY 800-367-8755
Superior Packaging Equipment Corporation
Fairfield, NJ 973-575-8818
Thiele Technologies-Reedley
Reedley, CA 800-344-8951

Can Body Forming

Custom Food Machinery
Stockton, CA. 209-463-4343
Dietzco
Hudson, MA 508-481-4000
M S Willett Inc
Cockeysville, MD 410-771-0460
Melvina Can Machinery Company
Hudson Falls, NY 518-743-0606
Omnitech International
Midland, MI 989-631-3377
Precision Component Industries
Canton, OH 330-477-6287

Can Capping

Accutek Packaging Equipment
Vista, CA. 800-989-1828
Alcoa - Massena Operations
Massena, NY
Anderson Machine Sales
Fort Lee, NJ
Berkshire PPM
Litchfield, CT 860-567-3118
BW Container Systems
Romeoville, IL 630-759-6800
Custom Food Machinery
Stockton, CA. 209-463-4343
Filling Equipment Co Inc
Flushing, NY. 800-247-7127
Nichols Specialty Products
Southborough, MA. 508-481-4367
Pack Line Corporation
Racine, WI 800-248-6868
Pneumatic Scale Angelus
Cuyahoga Falls, OH 330-923-0491
Production Packaging & Processing Equipment
Company
Savannah, GA 912-856-4281
Resina
Temecula, CA 800-207-4804
Silgan Containers LLC
Woodland Hills, CA 818-710-3700

Can Closing

Berkshire PPM
Litchfield, CT 860-567-3118
Custom Food Machinery
Stockton, CA. 209-463-4343
Dixie Canner Machine Shop
Athens, GA 706-549-0592
Heisler Machine & Tool Co
Fairfield, NJ 973-227-6300

Herrmann Ultrasonics
Bartlett, IL. 630-626-1626
Schroeder Machine
San Marcos, CA 760-591-9733

Can Drying

Ametek Technical & Industrial Products
Kent, OH. 215-256-6601
BFM Equipment Sales
Fall River, WI 920-484-3341
Custom Food Machinery
Stockton, CA. 209-463-4343
Gardner Denver Inc.
Milwaukee, WI
Mountaingate Engineering
Campbell, CA. 408-866-5100
Paxton Products Inc
Blue Ash, OH 800-441-7475

Can Filling

A.K. Robins
Baltimore, MD 800-486-9656
Berkshire PPM
Litchfield, CT 860-567-3118
Custom Food Machinery
Stockton, CA. 209-463-4343
E2M
Duluth, GA 800-622-4326
Elmar Worldwide
Depew, NY 800-433-3562
Horix Manufacturing Co
Mc Kees Rocks, PA. 412-771-1111
J.G. Machine Works
Holmdel, NJ 732-203-2077
Jetstream Systems
Wichita, KN 855-861-6916
John R Nalbach Engineering Co
Countryside, IL 708-579-9100
KISS Packaging Systems
Vista, CA. 888-522-3538
Luthi Machinery Company, Inc.
Pueblo, CO 719-948-1110
Marlen International
Astoria, OR 800-862-7536
Multi-Fill Inc
West Jordan, UT 801-280-1570
Nu-Con Equipment
Chanhassen, MN 877-939-0510
Oden Machinery
Tonawanda, NY 800-658-3622
Per-Fil Industries Inc
Riverside, NJ. 856-461-5700
Pneumatic Scale Angelus
Cuyahoga Falls, OH 330-923-0491
Pressure Pack
Williamsburg, VA 757-220-3693
Rutherford Engineering
Rockford, IL 815-623-2141
Sasib Beverage & Food North America
Plano, TX 800-558-3814
SeamTech
Acampo, CA 209-464-4610
SICK Inc
Bloomington, MN. 800-325-7425
Simplex Filler Co
Napa, CA. 800-796-7539
Temco
Oakland, CA 707-746-5966
Tindall Packaging
Vicksburg, MI 269-649-1163
Weigh Right Automatic Scale Co
Joliet, IL 800-571-0249

Can Sealing

AAMD
Liverpool, NY. 800-887-4167
Alcoa - Massena Operations
Massena, NY
Anderson Machine Sales
Fort Lee, NJ
Berkshire PPM
Litchfield, CT 860-567-3118
BW Container Systems
Romeoville, IL 630-759-6800
Custom Food Machinery
Stockton, CA. 209-463-4343
Herrmann Ultrasonics
Bartlett, IL. 630-626-1626
Ives-Way Products
Round Lake Beach, IL 847-740-0658

Nu-Con Equipment
Chanhassen, MN............877-939-0510

Can Seaming

Berkshire PPM
Litchfield, CT.................860-567-3118
BW Container Systems
Romeoville, IL................630-759-6800
Custom Food Machinery
Stockton, CA.................209-463-4343
Jescorp
Des Plaines, IL...............847-299-7800
Melvina Can Machinery Company
Hudson Falls, NY.............518-743-0606
Pneumatic Scale Angelus
Cuyahoga Falls, OH 330-923-0491
SeamTech
Acampo, CA.................209-464-4610

Can Washing

A.K. Robins
Baltimore, MD 800-486-9656
BFM Equipment Sales
Fall River, WI................920-484-3341
Cincinnati Industrial Machry
Mason, OH 800-677-0076
Custom Food Machinery
Stockton, CA.................209-463-4343
Davron Technologies Inc
Chattanooga, TN.............423-870-1888
IMC Teddy Food Service Equipment
Amityville, NY................800-221-5644

Canning & Food Packing

A.K. Robins
Baltimore, MD................800-486-9656
ABCO Industries Limited
Lunenburg, NS 866-634-8821
Acraloc Corp
Oak Ridge, TN................865-483-1368
Ametek Technical & Industrial Products
Kent, OH 215-256-6601
Apollo Sheet Metal
Kennewick, WA 509-586-1104
Berkshire PPM
Litchfield, CT.................860-567-3118
Blue Print Automation
S Chesterfield, VA 804-520-5400
BW Container Systems
Romeoville, IL................630-759-6800
Custom Food Machinery
Stockton, CA.................209-463-4343
Dixie Canner Machine Shop
Athens, GA...................706-549-0592
Douglas Machine Inc
Alexandria, MN...............320-763-6587
E2M
Duluth, GA...................800-622-4326
Et Oakes Corp
Hauppauge, NY...............631-232-0002
Horix Manufacturing Co
Mc Kees Rocks, PA............412-771-1111
Hughes Co
Columbus, WI................866-535-9303
JBT Food Tech
Lakeland, FL.................863-683-5411
Krones
Franklin, WI.................800-752-3787
Langsenkamp Manufacturing
Indianapolis, IN 877-585-1950
Leader Engineering-Fab Inc
Napoleon, OH................419-592-0008
Lima Sheet Metal
Lima, OH....................419-229-1161
M S Willett Inc
Cockeysville, MD..............410-771-0460
Magnuson
Pueblo, CO..................719-948-9500
Melco Steel Inc
Azusa, CA...................626-334-7875
Millard Manufacturing Corp
La Vista, NE.................800-662-4263
Muskogee Rubber Stamp & Seal Company
Fort Gibson, OK..............918-478-3046
Olney Machinery
Westernville, NY..............315-827-4208
Paxton Products Inc
Blue Ash, OH.................800-441-7475
Reid Boiler Works
Bellingham, WA...............360-714-6157

Riverwood International
Atlanta, GA..................770-984-5477
T D Sawvel Co
Maple Plain, MN..............877-488-1816
Techno-Design
Union, KY....................800-641-1822
Welliver Metal Products Corporation
Salem, OR...................503-362-1568

Cap Torque Test

Vibrac LLC-Fax
Amherst, NH.................603-886-3857

Cappers

G & F Mfg
Oak Lawn, IL.................800-282-1574

Carton

ADCO Manufacturing Inc
Sanger, CA...................559-875-5563
Berkshire PPM
Litchfield, CT.................860-567-3118
Bradman Lake Inc
Rock Hill, SC.................803-366-3688
C & K Machine Co
Holyoke, MA.................413-536-8122
Combi Packaging Systems LLC
Canton, OH 866-472-5236
Custom Food Machinery
Stockton, CA.................209-463-4343
D & L Manufacturing
Milwaukee, WI................414-256-8160
Delkor Systems, Inc
Minneapolis, MN 800-328-5558
Douglas Machine Inc
Alexandria, MN...............320-763-6587
Econocorp Inc
Randolph, MA 781-986-7500
F N Smith Corp
Oregon, IL...................815-732-2171
Future Commodities Intl Inc
Rancho Cucamonga, CA.......888-588-2378
Gram Equipment Of America
Tampa, FL...................813-248-1978
Hayes Machine Co Inc
Des Moines, IA...............800-860-6224
Heisler Machine & Tool Co
Fairfield, NJ.................973-227-6300
International Paper Box Machine Company
Nashua, NH..................603-889-6651
Micro Solutions Ent Tech & Dev
Van Nuys, CA................800-673-4968
Packaging Machinery & Equipment
West Orange, NJ..............973-325-2418
Prototype Equipment Corporation
Libertyville, IL................847-680-4433
San Fab Conveyor
Sandusky, OH................419-626-4465
Scandia Packaging Machinery Co
Fairfield, NJ.................973-473-6100
Serpa Packaging Solutions
Visalia, CA...................800-348-5453
TDF Automation
Cedar Falls, IA...............800-553-1777
Thiele Technologies-Reedley
Reedley, CA..................800-344-8951
Tisma Machinery Corporation
Elk Grove Village, IL...........847-427-9525

Filling

ADCO Manufacturing Inc
Sanger, CA...................559-875-5563
Bradman Lake Inc
Rock Hill, SC.................803-366-3688
C & K Machine Co
Holyoke, MA.................413-536-8122
Cannon Equipment Company
Cannon Falls, MN.............800-825-8501
Crystal-Vision Packaging Systems
Torrance, CA.................800-331-3240
Custom Food Machinery
Stockton, CA.................209-463-4343
Design Technology Corporation
Billerica, MA.................978-663-7000
Doering Machines Inc
San Francisco, CA.............415-526-2131
Eischen Enterprises
Fresno, CA...................559-834-0013

Elliott Manufacturing Co Inc
Fresno, CA...................559-233-6235
Iman Pack
Westland, MI.................800-810-4626
Key Automation
Eagan, MN...................651-455-0547
Khs USA Inc
Sarasota, FL 877-227-8358
MAF Industries Inc
Traver, CA...................559-897-2905
Multi-Fill Inc
West Jordan, UT..............801-280-1570
Optek Inc
Galena, OH 800-533-8400
Packaging Dynamics
Walnut Creek, CA.............925-938-2711
Pomona Service & Pkgng Co LA
Yakima, WA..................509-452-7121
R A Jones & Co Inc
Ft Mitchell, KY................859-341-1807
Simplex Filler Co
Napa, CA....................800-796-7539
Summit Machine Builders Corporation
Denver, CO..................800-274-6741
TDF Automation
Cedar Falls, IA...............800-553-1777
Temco
Oakland, CA.................707-746-5966
Thiele Engineering Company
Fergus Falls, MN..............218-739-3321
Tindall Packaging
Vicksburg, MI.................269-649-1163
Tisma Machinery Corporation
Elk Grove Village, IL...........847-427-9525
Tridyne Process Systems
South Burlington, VT..........802-863-6873
Universal Labeling Systems Inc
St Petersburg, FL 877-236-0266
Weigh Right Automatic Scale Co
Joliet, IL....................800-571-0249

Printing

Algene Marking Equipment Company
Garfield, NJ..................973-478-9041
Custom Food Machinery
Stockton, CA.................209-463-4343
Matthews Marking Systems Div
Pittsburgh, PA................412-665-2500
Trident
Brookfield, CT................203-740-9333
WE Killam Enterprises
Waterford, ON................519-443-7421

Carton, Case, Box Sealing

A.B. Sealer, Inc.
Beaver Dam, WI...............877-885-9299
Accutek Packaging Equipment
Vista, CA....................800-989-1828
ADCO Manufacturing Inc
Sanger, CA...................559-875-5563
Barnes Machine Company
Saint Petersburg, FL...........727-327-9452
Belco Packaging Systems
Monrovia, CA.................800-833-1833
Berkshire PPM
Litchfield, CT.................860-567-3118
Better Packages
Ansonia, CT 800-237-9151
Bradman Lake Inc
Rock Hill, SC.................803-366-3688
Brenton Engineering Co
Alexandria, MN...............800-535-2730
C.J. Machine
Fridley, MN..................763-767-4630
Charles Beck Machine Corporation
King of Prussia, PA............610-265-0500
Combi Packaging Systems LLC
Canton, OH 866-472-5236
Compacker Systems LLC
Davenport, IA................563-391-2751
Custom Food Machinery
Stockton, CA.................209-463-4343
Customized Equipment SE
Tucker, GA...................770-934-9300
Douglas Machine Inc
Alexandria, MN...............320-763-6587
Durable Packaging Corporation
Countryside, IL...............800-700-5677
Econocorp Inc
Randolph, MA 781-986-7500

Elliott Manufacturing Co Inc
Fresno, CA 559-233-6235
Future Commodities Intl Inc
Rancho Cucamonga, CA 888-588-2378
General Corrugated Machinery Company
Palisades Park, NJ 201-944-0644
Gulf Arizona Packaging
Humble, TX 800-364-3887
Gulf Systems
Brownsville, TX 800-217-4853
Gulf Systems
Humble, TX 800-364-3887
Gulf Systems
Arlington, TX 817-261-1915
Hayes Machine Co Inc
Des Moines, IA 800-860-6224
Heisler Machine & Tool Co
Fairfield, NJ 973-227-6300
Herche Warehouse
Denver, CO 303-371-8186
Herrmann Ultrasonics
Bartlett, IL 630-626-1626
Iman Pack
Westland, MI 800-810-4626
Intertape Polymer Group
Menasha, WI................... 800-558-5006
Kirkco Corp
Monroe, NC 704-289-7090
Kisters Kayat
Sarasota, FL 386-424-0101
Klippenstein Corp
Fresno, CA 888-834-4258
Liqui-Box
Richmond, VA.................. 804-325-1400
Loveshaw Corp
South Canaan, PA 800-572-3434
Markwell Manufacturing Company
Norwood, MA................... 800-666-1123
Marq Packaging Systems Inc
Yakima, WA 800-998-4301
Mastercraft International
Charlotte, NC 704-392-7436
Moen Industries
Santa Fe Springs, CA 800-732-7766
On-Hand Adhesives
Lake Zurich, IL................ 800-323-5158
Packaging & Processing Equipment
Ayr, ON 519-622-6666
Peace Industries
Rolling Meadows, IL 800-873-2239
Pearson Packaging Systems
Spokane, WA.................. 800-732-7766
Prototype Equipment Corporation
Libertyville, IL 847-680-4433
Rockford-Midland Corporation
Rockford, IL 800-327-7908
S.V. Dice Designers
Rowland Heights, CA............ 888-478-3423
Sabel Engineering Corporation
Villard, MN................... 320-554-3611
Samuel Strapping Systems Inc
Woodridge, IL................. 800-323-4424
San Fab Conveyor
Sandusky, OH 419-626-4465
Scandia Packaging Machinery Co
Fairfield, NJ 973-473-6100
Sekisui TA Industries
Brea, CA 800-258-8273
Staplex Co Inc
Brooklyn, NY 800-221-0822
Superior Packaging Equipment Corporation
Fairfield, NJ 973-575-8818
SWF McDowell
Orlando, FL................... 800-877-7971
TDF Automation
Cedar Falls, IA 800-553-1777
Technistar Corporation
Denver, CO................... 303-651-0188
Temco
Oakland, CA.................. 707-746-5966
Thiele Engineering Company
Fergus Falls, MN 218-739-3321
Thiele Technologies-Reedley
Reedley, CA 800-344-8951
Triangle Package Machinery Co
Chicago, IL 800-621-4170
WE Killam Enterprises
Waterford, ON................. 519-443-7421
Weigh Right Automatic Scale Co
Joliet, IL 800-571-0249
Wepackit
Orangeville, ON 519-942-1700

Wexxar Corporation
Chicago, IL 630-983-6666
Wexxar Packaging Inc
Richmond, BC 888-565-3219
Zed Industries
Vandalia, OH.................. 937-667-8407

Coding, Dating & Marking Equipment

A.D. Johnson Engraving Company
Kalamazoo, MI 269-342-5500
A.D. Joslin Manufacturing Company
Manistee, MI 231-723-2908
ABC Stamp Signs & Awards
Boise, ID..................... 208-375-4470
ABM Marking
Belleville, IL 800-626-9012
Accent Mark
Palmdale, CA 661-274-8191
Accu-Sort Systems
Telford, PA 800-227-2633
Ace Stamp & Engraving
Lakewood, WA 253-582-3322
Allmark Impressions LTD
Fort Worth, TX 817-834-0080
American Art Stamp
Gardena, CA 310-965-9004
American Forms & Labels
Boise, ID..................... 800-388-3554
Ameristamp/Sign-A-Rama
Evansville, IN 800-543-6693
Applied Products Co
El Segundo, CA 888-551-0447
Astoria Laminations
St Clair Shores, MI 800-526-7325
Atlas Rubber Stamp & Printing
York, PA 717-751-0459
Authentic Biocode Corp
Addison, IL 866-434-1402
Axiohm USA
Myrtle Beach, SC 843-443-3155
Baublys Control Laser
Orlando, FL................... 866-612-8619
Bell-Mark Corporation
Pine Brook, NJ 973-882-0202
Bishop Machine Shop
Zanesville, OH 740-453-8818
Bren Instruments
Franklin, TN.................. 615-794-6825
Chattanooga Rubber Stamp & Stencil Works
Sale Creek, TN 800-894-1164
City Stamp & Seal Co
Austin, TX.................... 800-950-6074
Cognitive
Golden, CO 800-765-6600
Columbia Labeling Machinery
Benton City, WA 888-791-9590
Computype Inc
St Paul, MN................... 800-328-0852
Comstar Printing Solutions
Streetsboro, OH 330-528-2800
Control Module
Enfield, CT 800-722-6654
Corpus Christi Stamp Works
Corpus Christi, TX 800-322-4515
Crown Marking
Minneapolis, MN 800-305-5249
CRS Marking Systems
Portland, OR.................. 800-547-7158
Cup Pac Packaging Inc
South Beloit, IL 877-347-9725
Custom Food Machinery
Stockton, CA.................. 209-463-4343
Custom Rubber Stamp Co
Crosby, MN................... 888-606-4579
Custom Stamp Company
Anza, CA..................... 323-292-0753
Custom Stamping & Manufacturing
Portland, OR.................. 503-238-3700
D & L Manufacturing
Milwaukee, WI................ 414-256-8160
Dalemark Industries
Lakewood, NJ 732-367-3100
Daymark Safety Systems
Bowling Green, OH 419-353-2458
Dayton Marking Devices Company
Dayton, OH................... 937-432-0285
Design Technology Corporation
Billerica, MA 978-663-7000
Detroit Marking Products
Detroit, MI 800-833-8222

Dixie Rubber Stamp & Seal Company
Atlanta, GA................... 404-875-8883
Domino Amjet Inc
Gurnee, IL.................... 800-444-4512
Dorell Equipment Inc
Somerset, NJ 732-247-5400
Drs Designs
Bethel, CT.................... 888-792-3740
Durable Engravers
Franklin Park, IL............... 800-869-9565
E C Shaw Co
Cincinnati, OH 866-532-7429
E2M
Duluth, GA 800-622-4326
East Memphis Rubber Stamp Company
Bartlett, TN................... 901-384-0887
Easterday Fluid Technologies
Saint Francis, WI 414-482-4488
Ed Smith's Stencil Works LTD
New Orleans, LA 504-525-2128
Ehrgott Rubber Stamp Company
Indianapolis, IN............... 317-353-2222
ELF Machinery
La Porte, IN................... 800-328-0466
Elmark Packaging Inc
West Chester, PA............... 800-670-9688
EMCO
Miamisburg, OH............... 800-722-3626
Everett Rubber Stamp
Everett, WA................... 425-258-6747
Fairbanks Scales
Kansas City, MO............... 800-451-4107
Fas-Co Coders
Lithia Springs, GA............. 800-478-0685
Federal Stamp & Seal Manufacturing Company
Atlanta, GA................... 800-333-7726
Fleming Packaging Corporation
Peoria, IL.................... 309-676-7657
Flint Rubber Stamp Works
Flint, MI 810-235-2341
Fox Stamp Sign & Specialty
Menasha, WI.................. 920-725-2683
Franklin Rubber Stamp Co
Wilmington, DE 302-654-8841
Fraser Stamp & Seal
Chicago, IL................... 800-540-8565
Frost Manufacturing Corp
Worcester, MA 800-462-0216
Fuller Box Co
North Attleboro, MA 508-695-2525
G&R Graphics
West Orange, NJ 813-503-8592
Garvey Products
Cincinnati, OH 513-771-8710
Garvey Products
West Chester, OH 800-543-1908
GCA
Huntington Beach, CA 714-379-4911
Glover Rubber Stamp & Crafts
Wills Point, TX 214-824-6900
Gotham Pen Co Inc
Bronx, NY.................... 800-334-7970
Granite State Stamps Inc
Manchester, NH 800-937-3736
Graphic Impressions of Illinois
River Grove, IL................ 708-453-1100
Graphic Technology
New Century, KS 800-767-9920
Grays Harbor Stamp Works
Aberdeen, WA................. 800-894-3830
Gribble Stamp & Stencil Co
Houston, TX 713-228-5358
Grueny's Rubber Stamps
Little Rock, AR................ 501-376-0393
Gulf Systems
Humble, TX 800-364-3887
Gulf Systems
Arlington, TX 817-261-1915
H G Weber & Co
Kiel, WI..................... 920-894-2221
Hartford Stamp Works
Hartford, CT 860-249-6205
Hathaway Stamps
Cincinnati, OH 513-621-1052
Herche Warehouse
Denver, CO................... 303-371-8186
House Stamp Works
Chicago, IL................... 312-939-7177
Houston Label
Pasadena, TX 800-477-6995
Houston Stamp & Stencil Company
Houston, TX 713-869-4337

Howard Imprinting Machine Company
Houston, TX 800-334-6943
Hub Pen Company
Quincy, MA. 617-471-9900
Huntington Park Rbr Stamp Co
Huntington Park, CA 800-882-0029
ID Images
Brunswick, OH 866-516-7300
Ideal Stencil Machine & Tape Company
Marion, IL 800-388-0162
Imaging Technologies
Cookeville, TN 800-488-2804
Imaje
Kennesaw, GA 678-594-7153
Independent Ink
Gardena, CA 800-446-5538
Innovative Ceramic Corp
East Liverpool, OH. 330-385-6515
Irby
Rocky Mount, NC 252-442-0154
ITW Diagraph
St Charles, MO 800-722-1125
Jim Lake Companies
Dallas, TX. 214-741-5018
Joyce Engraving Co Inc
Dallas, TX. 214-638-1262
Justrite Rubber Stamp & Seal
Kansas City, MO. 800-229-5010
Kirkco Corp
Monroe, NC 704-289-7090
Koehler-Gibson Marking
Buffalo, NY 800-875-1562
Kwikprint Manufacturing Inc
Jacksonville, FL 800-940-5945
L&L Engraving Company
Gilford, NH 888-524-3032
Label Art
Tucker, GA 800-652-1072
Label-Aire Inc
Fullerton, CA 714-441-0700
Labelprint America
Newburyport, MA. 978-463-4004
Lake Eyelet Manufacturing Company
Weatogue, CT 860-628-5543
Lakeland Rubber Stamp Company
Lakeland, FL. 863-682-5111
Lakeview Rubber Stamp Co
Chicago, IL. 773-539-1525
Larry B Newman Printing
Knoxville, TN 888-835-4566
Lasertechnics Marking Corporation
Nepean, ON. 613-749-4895
Listo Pencil Corp
Alameda, CA 800-547-8648
Long Island Stamp Corporation
Flushing, NY. 800-547-8267
Lord Label Machine Systems
Charlotte, NC 704-644-1650
Loveshaw Corp
South Canaan, PA 800-572-3434
Mankuta Bros Rubber Stamp Co
Bohemia, NY 800-223-4481
Mansfield Rubber Stamp
Mansfield, OH 419-524-1442
Mark-It Rubber Stamp & Label Company
Stamford, CT. 203-348-3204
Marking Devices Inc
Cleveland, OH 216-861-4498
Marking Methods Inc
Alhambra, CA. 626-308-5800
Marsh Company
Belleville, IL. 800-527-6275
Mastermark
Kent, WA. 206-762-9610
Matthews Marking Systems Div
Pittsburgh, PA 412-665-2500
Mecco Marking & Traceability
Cranberry Township, PA. 888-369-9190
Menke Marking Devices
Santa Fe Springs, CA 800-231-6023
Mettler-Toledo, LLC
Columbus, OH 800-638-8537
Modern Stamp Company
Baltimore, MD 800-727-3029
Moore Efficient Communication Aids
Denver, CO 303-433-8456
Muskogee Rubber Stamp & Seal Company
Fort Gibson, OK 918-478-3046
My Serenity Pond
Cold Spring, MN. 320-363-0411
National Metal Industries
West Springfield, MA. 800-628-8850

National Pen Co
San Diego, CA 858-675-3000
NCR Corp
Atlanta, GA 800-225-5627
Newstamp Lighting Factory
North Easton, MA. 508-238-7073
Northern Berkshire Tourist
North Adams, MA 413-663-9204
Norwood Marking Systems
Downers Grove, IL 800-626-3464
O.K. Marking Devices
Regina, SK 306-522-2856
Oak International
Sturgis, MI 269-651-9790
OK Stamp & Seal Company
Oklahoma City, OK 405-235-7853
Open Date Systems
Sunapee, NH 877-673-6328
Oration Rubber Stamp Company
Columbus, NJ 908-496-4161
Organic Products Co
Irving, TX 972-438-7321
Oshikiri Corp Of America
Philadelphia, PA 215-637-8112
Packaging & Processing Equipment
Ayr, ON 519-622-6666
Packaging Machinery & Equipment
West Orange, NJ 973-325-2418
Plastimatic Arts Corporation
Mishawaka, IN 800-442-3593
Printcraft Marking Devices Inc
Buffalo, NY. 716-873-8181
Pulse Systems
Los Alamos, NM. 505-662-7599
Qsx Labels
Everett, MA. 800-225-3496
Quick Stamp & Sign Mfg
Lafayette, LA 337-232-2171
R R Donnelley
Chicago, IL 800-742-4455
R.P. Childs Stamp Company
Ludlow, MA 413-733-1211
Rebel Stamp & Sign Co
Baton Rouge, LA 800-860-5120
Richardson's Stamp Works
Houston, TX 713-973-0314
Rubber Stamp Shop
Accokeek, MD 800-835-0839
Sancoa International
Lumberton, NJ 609-953-5050
Sato America
Charlotte, NC 888-871-8741
Schwaab, Inc
Milwaukee, WI 800-935-9877
Signet Marking Devices
Costa Mesa, CA 800-421-5150
Sioux Falls Rbr Stamp Works
Sioux Falls, SD 855-334-5990
Smyth Co LLC
St Paul, MN. 800-473-3464
Sossner Steel Stamps
Elizabethton, TN. 800-828-9515
Southern Rubber Stamp
Tulsa, OK 888-826-4304
Spectrum Enterprises
Evansville, IN 812-425-1771
Spencer Business Form Company
Spencer, WV. 304-372-8877
Sprinter Marking Inc
Zanesville, OH 740-453-1000
Stratix Corp
Peachtree Cor, GA 800-883-8300
Sutherland Stamp Company
San Diego, CA 858-233-7784
Tallygenicom
Irvine, CA 800-665-6210
Tharo Systems Inc
Brunswick, OH 800-878-6833
TNA Packaging Solutions
Coppell, TX 972-462-6500
Trident
Brookfield, CT 203-740-9333
United Ribtype Co
Fort Wayne, IN 800-473-4039
Universal Die & Stampings
Prairie Du Sac, WI 608-643-2477
Universal Packaging Inc
Houston, TX 800-324-2610
Vande Berg SCALES/Vbs Inc
Sioux Center, IA 712-722-1181
Varitronic Systems
Brooklyn Park, MN. 763-536-6400

Videojet Technologies Inc
Wood Dale, IL. 800-843-3610
Videx Inc
Corvallis, OR 541-738-5500
Volk Corp
Farmington Hills, MI 800-521-6799
Walker Co
Oklahoma City, OK 800-522-3015
Wallace Computer Services
Chicago, IL. 888-925-8324
WE Killam Enterprises
Waterford, ON. 519-443-7421
Weber Packaging Solutions Inc
Arlington Heights, IL 800-843-4242
Wichita Stamp & Seal Inc
Wichita, KS. 316-263-4223
Wildes Printing Co Inc
White Plains, MD 301-870-4141
Willett America
Wood Dale, IL. 800-259-2600
Winmark Stamp & Sign
Salt Lake City, UT 800-438-0480
Zanasi USA
Brooklyn Park, MN. 800-627-2633
Zerand Corp
New Berlin, WI. 262-827-3800

Coding, Marking, Dating

A.D. Johnson Engraving Company
Kalamazoo, MI 269-342-5500
A.D. Joslin Manufacturing Company
Manistee, MI. 231-723-2908
Algene Marking Equipment Company
Garfield, NJ. 973-478-9041
American Art Stamp
Gardena, CA 310-965-9004
American Forms & Labels
Boise, ID 800-388-3554
Ameristamp/Sign-A-Rama
Evansville, IN 800-543-6693
Astoria Laminations
St Clair Shores, MI 800-526-7325
Baublys Control Laser
Orlando, FL. 866-612-8619
Bell-Mark Corporation
Pine Brook, NJ 973-882-0202
Berkshire PPM
Litchfield, CT 860-567-3118
Bishop Machine Shop
Zanesville, OH 740-453-8818
Bren Instruments
Franklin, TN 615-794-6825
Century Rubber Stamp Company
New York, NY 212-962-6165
Cognitive
Golden, CO 800-765-6600
Columbia Labeling Machinery
Benton City, WA 888-791-9590
Computype Inc
St Paul, MN. 800-328-0852
Crown Marking
Minneapolis, MN 800-305-5249
Cup Pac Packaging Inc
South Beloit, IL 877-347-9725
Custom Food Machinery
Stockton, CA 209-463-4343
D & L Manufacturing
Milwaukee, WI 414-256-8160
Dalemark Industries
Lakewood, NJ. 732-367-3100
Daymark Safety Systems
Bowling Green, OH 419-353-2458
Dayton Marking Devices Company
Dayton, OH. 937-432-0285
Dorell Equipment Inc
Somerset, NJ 732-247-5400
E C Shaw Co
Cincinnati, OH 866-532-7429
E2M
Duluth, GA 800-622-4326
Easterday Fluid Technologies
Saint Francis, WI 414-482-4488
Ed Smith's Stencil Works LTD
New Orleans, LA 504-525-2128
ELF Machinery
La Porte, IN. 800-328-0466
Elmark Packaging Inc
West Chester, PA. 800-670-9688
Esselte Meto
Morris Plains, NJ 800-645-3290

Everett Rubber Stamp
Everett, WA.........................425-258-6747
Fairbanks Scales
Kansas City, MO..................800-451-4107
Fas-Co Coders
Lithia Springs, GA...............800-478-0685
Federal Stamp & Seal Manufacturing Company
Atlanta, GA.......................800-333-7726
Franklin Rubber Stamp Co
Wilmington, DE 302-654-8841
Fsi Technologies
Lombard, IL.......................800-468-6009
Fuller Box Co
North Attleboro, MA 508-695-2525
Garvey Products
Cincinnati, OH...................513-771-8710
GCA
Huntington Beach, CA 714-379-4911
Glover Rubber Stamp & Crafts
Wills Point, TX...................214-824-6900
Granite State Stamps Inc
Manchester, NH..................800-937-3736
Graphic Technology
New Century, KS.................800-767-9920
Gulf Arizona Packaging
Humble, TX.......................800-364-3887
Gulf Systems
Brownsville, TX...................800-217-4853
Gulf Systems
Humble, TX.......................800-364-3887
Gulf Systems
Arlington, TX......................817-261-1915
H G Weber & Co
Kiel, WI...........................920-894-2221
Herche Warehouse
Denver, CO.......................303-371-8186
Howard Imprinting Machine Company
Houston, TX......................800-334-6943
Huntington Park Rbr Stamp Co
Huntington Park, CA 800-882-0029
ID Images
Brunswick, OH...................866-516-7300
Ideal Stencil Machine & Tape Company
Marion, IL.........................800-388-0162
Imaje
Kennesaw, GA....................678-594-7153
Independent Ink
Gardena, CA......................800-446-5538
Irby
Rocky Mount, NC.................252-442-0154
ITW Diagraph
St Charles, MO...................800-722-1125
Joyce Engraving Co Inc
Dallas, TX.........................214-638-1262
Kirkco Corp
Monroe, NC 704-289-7090
Koehler-Gibson Marking
Buffalo, NY.......................800-875-1562
Kwikprint Manufacturing Inc
Jacksonville, FL...................800-940-5945
Labelprint America
Newburyport, MA.................978-463-4004
Lake Eyelet Manufacturing Company
Weatogue, CT....................860-628-5543
Lasertechnics Marking Corporation
Nepean, ON.......................613-749-4895
Loveshaw Corp
South Canaan, PA.................800-572-3434
Marking Methods Inc
Alhambra, CA.....................626-308-5800
Marsh Company
Belleville, IL.......................800-527-6275
Matthews Marking Systems Div
Pittsburgh, PA.....................412-665-2500
Mecco Marking & Traceability
Cranberry Township, PA...........888-369-9190
Menke Marking Devices
Santa Fe Springs, CA 800-231-6023
Moore Efficient Communication Aids
Denver, CO.......................303-433-8456
Muskogee Rubber Stamp & Seal Company
Fort Gibson, OK...................918-478-3046
National Metal Industries
West Springfield, MA..............800-628-8850
Newstamp Lighting Factory
North Easton, MA.................508-238-7073
Norwood Marking Systems
Downers Grove, IL.................800-626-3464
Oration Rubber Stamp Company
Columbus, NJ 908-496-4161
Packaging & Processing Equipment
Ayr, ON 519-622-6666

Precision Component Industries
Canton, OH........................330-477-6287
Pulse Systems
Los Alamos, NM..................505-662-7599
R.P. Childs Stamp Company
Ludlow, MA.......................413-733-1211
Rebel Stamp & Sign Co
Baton Rouge, LA 800-860-5120
Rubber Stamp Shop
Accokeek, MD....................800-835-0839
Schwaab, Inc
Milwaukee, WI...................800-935-9877
Shiffer Industries
Kihei, HI..........................800-642-1774
Signet Marking Devices
Costa Mesa, CA...................800-421-5150
Sossner Steel Stamps
Elizabethton, TN..................800-828-9515
Southern Rubber Stamp
Tulsa, OK.........................888-826-4304
Sprinter Marking Inc
Zanesville, OH....................740-453-1000
Tallygenicom
Irvine, CA.........................800-665-6210
Tharo Systems Inc
Brunswick, OH...................800-878-6833
Trident
Brookfield, CT....................203-740-9333
Universal Die & Stampings
Prairie Du Sac, WI................608-643-2477
Vande Berg SCALES/Vbs Inc
Sioux Center, IA...................712-722-1181
Varitronic Systems
Brooklyn Park, MN................763-536-6400
Videojet Technologies Inc
Wood Dale, IL.....................800-843-3610
Videx Inc
Corvallis, OR.....................541-738-5500
Volk Corp
Farmington Hills, MI..............800-521-6799
WE Killam Enterprises
Waterford, ON....................519-443-7421
Weber Packaging Solutions Inc
Arlington Heights, IL..............800-843-4242
Wichita Stamp & Seal Inc
Wichita, KS.......................316-263-4223
Willett America
Wood Dale, IL.....................800-259-2600
Zanasi USA
Brooklyn Park, MN................800-627-2633
Zerand Corp
New Berlin, WI....................262-827-3800

Container

About Packaging Robotics
Thornton, CO 303-449-2559
Barnes Machine Company
Saint Petersburg, FL...............727-327-9452
Berry Global
Evansville, IN.....................800-343-1295
Burd & Fletcher
Independence, MO 800-821-2776
Carando Technologies Inc
Stockton, CA......................209-948-6500
Carleton Helical Technologies
Doylestown, PA 215-230-8900
Dietzco
Hudson, MA.......................508-481-4000
Heisler Machine & Tool Co
Fairfield, NJ.......................973-227-6300
Heuft USA Inc
Downers Grove, IL.................630-968-9011
Hoegger Food Technology
Minneapolis, MN 877-789-5400
Marquip Ward United
Phillips, WI........................715-339-2191
Neos
Elk River, MN.....................888-441-6367
Osgood Industries
Oldsmar, FL.......................813-855-7337
Paradise Inc
Plant City, FL......................813-752-1155
Peco Controls Corporation
Modesto, CA......................800-732-6285
Plastic Ingenuity
Cross Plains, WI...................608-798-3071
Plastipak Industries
La Prairie, QC.....................800-387-7452
Promens
St. John, NB 800-295-3725

Quick Label Systems
West Warwick, RI 877-757-7978
Rotonics Manufacturing
Gardena, CA......................310-327-5401
Silver Spur Corp
Cerritos, CA.......................562-921-6880
Solbern Corp
Fairfield, NJ.......................973-227-3030
Southworth Products Corp
Falmouth, ME.....................800-743-1000
Stormax International
Concord, NH......................800-874-7629
Tindall Packaging
Vicksburg, MI.....................269-649-1163
V C 999 Packaging Systems
Kansas City, MO..................800-728-2999

Detectors

Packaging Line

Aw Sheepscot Holding Co Inc
Franksville, WI....................800-850-6110
Axelrod, Norman N
New York, NY.....................212-369-2885
Binks Industries Inc
Montgomery, IL...................630-801-1100
Care Controls, Inc.
Mill Creek, WA....................800-593-6050
Carter Products
Grand Rapids, MI.................888-622-7837
Daystar
Glen Arm, MD.....................800-494-6537
Eriez Magnetics
Erie, PA............................800-346-4946
F I L T E C-Inspection Systems
Torrance, CA.......................888-434-5832
LDJ Electronics
Troy, MI...........................248-528-2202
Lixi Inc
Carpentersville, IL.................847-961-6666
Lock Inspection Systems
Fitchburg, MA.....................800-227-5539
Mettler-Toledo Safeline Inc
Lutz, FL............................800-638-8537
Mocon Inc
Minneapolis, MN 763-493-7229
Nikka Densok
Lakewood, CO....................800-806-4587
Ohio Magnetics Inc
Maple Heights, OH................800-486-6446
Peco Controls Corporation
Modesto, CA......................800-732-6285
ShockWatch
Dallas, TX.........................800-393-7920
Tec5USA
Plainview, NY.....................516-653-2000
Vande Berg SCALES/Vbs Inc
Sioux Center, IA...................712-722-1181

Equipment

Materials

Loeb Equipment
Chicago, IL........................773-496-5720
Lyco Manufacturing
Wausau, WI.......................715-845-7867
Priority One Packaging
Waterloo, ON 800-387-9102

Exhausters

Canning

A.K. Robins
Baltimore, MD 800-486-9656
Dixie Canner Machine Shop
Athens, GA........................706-549-0592
Ross Cook
Silver Spring, MD.................800-233-7339

Form, Fill & Seal

Horizontal

ACMA/GD
Richmond, VA.....................800-525-2735
Bradman Lake Inc
Rock Hill, SC......................803-366-3688
Campbell Wrapper Corporation
De Pere, WI.......................920-983-7100

Circle Packaging Machinery Inc
  De Pere, WI....................920-983-3420
Elopak Americas
  Wixom, MI......................248-486-4600
Enhance Packaging Technologies
  Whitby, ON.....................905-668-5811
Equipment Outlet
  Meridian, ID...................208-887-1472
Formost Packaging Machines
  Woodinville, WA................425-483-9090
Herrmann Ultrasonics
  Bartlett, IL...................630-626-1626
Ilapak Inc
  Newtown, PA....................215-579-2900
Iman Pack
  Westland, MI...................800-810-4626
Maryland Packaging Corporation
  Elkridge, MD...................410-540-9700
Ossid Corp
  Battleboro, NC.................800-334-8369
Packaging Dynamics
  Walnut Creek, CA...............925-938-2711
Prodo-Pak Corp
  Garfield, NJ...................973-777-7770
Reiser
  Canton, MA.....................734-821-1290
Sitma USA
  Spilamberto, MO................800-728-1254
Southern Packaging Machinery
  Athens, GA.....................706-208-0814
Zed Industries
  Vandalia, OH...................937-667-8407

Vertical

Accu-Pak
  Akron, OH
ACMA/GD
  Richmond, VA...................800-525-2735
Amark Packaging Systems
  Kansas City, MO................816-965-9000
Blodgett Co
  Houston, TX....................281-933-6195
Bradman Lake Inc
  Rock Hill, SC..................803-366-3688
Circle Packaging Machinery Inc
  De Pere, WI....................920-983-3420
Elopak Americas
  Wixom, MI......................248-486-4600
Enhance Packaging Technologies
  Whitby, ON.....................905-668-5811
Equipment Outlet
  Meridian, ID...................208-887-1472
Formost Packaging Machines
  Woodinville, WA................425-483-9090
General Packaging Equipment Co
  Houston, TX....................713-686-4331
Hayssen Flexible Systems
  Duncan, SC.....................864-486-4000
Herrmann Ultrasonics
  Bartlett, IL...................630-626-1626
Ilapak Inc
  Newtown, PA....................215-579-2900
Iman Pack
  Westland, MI...................800-810-4626
Key-Pak Machines
  Lebanon, NJ....................908-236-2111
Korab Engineering Company
  Los Angeles, CA................310-670-7710
Longhorn Packaging Inc
  San Antonio, TX................800-433-7974
Matrix Packaging Machinery
  Saukville, WI..................888-628-7491
Ossid Corp
  Battleboro, NC.................800-334-8369
Packaging Dynamics
  Walnut Creek, CA...............925-938-2711
Pacmac Inc
  Fayetteville, AR...............800-834-1544
PFM Packaging Machinery Corporation
  Newmarket, ON..................905-836-6709
Prodo-Pak Corp
  Garfield, NJ...................973-777-7770
TNA Packaging Solutions
  Coppell, TX....................972-462-6500
Universal Packaging Inc
  Houston, TX....................800-324-2610
Wick's Packaging Service
  Cutler, IN.....................574-967-3104
Zed Industries
  Vandalia, OH...................937-667-8407

Heat Sealing

AAMD
  Liverpool, NY..................800-887-4167
Audion Automation
  Carrollton, TX.................972-389-0777
Bosch Packaging Technology
  New Richmond, WI...............715-246-6511
Branson Ultrasonics Corp
  Danbury, CT....................203-796-0400
Chaffee Co
  Rocklin, CA....................916-630-3980
Chase Industries Inc
  West Chester, OH...............800-543-4455
Circle Packaging Machinery Inc
  De Pere, WI....................920-983-3420
Custom Food Machinery
  Stockton, CA...................209-463-4343
Design Technology Corporation
  Billerica, MA..................978-663-7000
Edson Packaging Machinery
  Hamilton, ON...................800-493-3766
Food Equipment Manufacturing Company
  Bedford Heights, OH............216-672-5859
Giltron Inc
  Norwood, MA....................781-762-4310
Green Tek
  Janesville, WI.................800-747-6440
Harwil Corp
  Oxnard, CA.....................800-562-2447
Key-Pak Machines
  Lebanon, NJ....................908-236-2111
Kliklok-Woodman
  Decatur, GA....................770-981-5200
On-Hand Adhesives
  Lake Zurich, IL................800-323-5158
PlexPack Corp
  Toronto, ON....................855-635-9238
Pressure Pack
  Williamsburg, VA...............757-220-3693
Reiser
  Canton, MA.....................734-821-1290
Rockford-Midland Corporation
  Rockford, IL...................800-327-7908
Save-O-Seal Corporation
  Elmsford, NY...................800-831-9720
Servpak Corp
  Hollywood, FL..................800-782-0840
Stock America Inc
  Grafton, WI....................262-375-4100
Wraps
  East Orange, NJ................973-673-7873
Zed Industries
  Vandalia, OH...................937-667-8407

Jar Filling

A.K. Robins
  Baltimore, MD..................800-486-9656
Berkshire PPM
  Litchfield, CT.................860-567-3118
Custom Food Machinery
  Stockton, CA...................209-463-4343
Dana Labels
  Beaverton, OR..................800-255-1492
Delta Plastics
  Hot Springs, AR................501-760-3000
Elmar Worldwide
  Depew, NY......................800-433-3562
J.G. Machine Works
  Holmdel, NJ....................732-203-2077
Morrison Timing Screw Co
  Glenwood, IL...................708-331-6600
Multi-Fill Inc
  West Jordan, UT................801-280-1570
Oden Machinery
  Tonawanda, NY..................800-658-3622
Packaging Enterprises
  Rockledge, PA..................800-453-6213
SICK Inc
  Bloomington, MN................800-325-7425
Simplex Filler Co
  Napa, CA.......................800-796-7539
Tindall Packaging
  Vicksburg, MI..................269-649-1163
Weigh Right Automatic Scale Co
  Joliet, IL.....................800-571-0249

Label Printing

Advent Machine Co
  Commerce, CA...................800-846-7716

Apex Machine Company
  Oakland Park, FL...............954-566-1572
Auto Labe
  Fort Pierce, FL................800-634-5376
Cam Tron Systems
  Addison, IL....................630-543-2884
Comstar Printing Solutions
  Streetsboro, OH................330-528-2800
Dana Labels
  Beaverton, OR..................800-255-1492
Dorell Equipment Inc
  Somerset, NJ...................732-247-5400
Dynic USA Corp
  Hillsboro, OR..................800-326-1249
Fairbanks Scales
  Kansas City, MO................800-451-4107
Fernqvist Labeling Solutions
  Mountain View, CA..............800-426-8215
Grand Valley Labels
  Grand Rapids, MI
ID Images
  Brunswick, OH..................866-516-7300
Labelprint America
  Newburyport, MA................978-463-4004
Lord Label Group
  Charlotte, NC..................800-341-5225
Mateer Burt
  Exton, PA......................800-345-1308
Matthews Marking Systems Div
  Pittsburgh, PA.................412-665-2500
MPI Label Systems
  Sebring, OH....................800-837-2134
Paper Converting Machine Company
  Green Bay, WI..................920-494-5601
PEAK Technologies, Inc.
  Columbia, MD...................800-926-9212
Reliable Label
  Downers Grove, IL..............800-323-7265
Robbie Manufacturing Inc
  Lenexa, KS.....................800-255-6328
Sohn Manufacturing
  Elkhart Lake, WI...............920-876-3361
Start International
  Addison, TX....................800-259-1986
StickerYou
  Toronto, ON....................416-532-7373
Tharo Systems Inc
  Brunswick, OH..................800-878-6833
Virginia Artesian Bottling Company
  Mechanicsville, VA.............804-779-7500
Wishbone Utensil Tableware Line
  Wheat Ridge, CO................866-266-5928
WS Packaging Group Inc
  Rochester, NY..................800-836-8186
Wt Nickell Co
  Batavia, OH....................888-899-1991

Labeling

A.D. Joslin Manufacturing Company
  Manistee, MI...................231-723-2908
About Packaging Robotics
  Thornton, CO...................303-449-2559
AC Label Company
  Provo, UT......................801-642-3500
Accraply/Trine
  Burlington Ontario, ON.........800-387-6742
Accu Place
  Plantation, FL.................954-791-1500
Accutek Packaging Equipment
  Vista, CA......................800-989-1828
ASCENT Technics Corporation
  Brick, NJ......................800-774-7077
Associated Packaging Equipment Corporation
  Markham, ON....................905-475-6647
Auto Labe
  Fort Pierce, FL................800-634-5376
Automated Packaging Systems
  Streetsboro, OH................800-527-0733
Bell & Howell Company
  Lincolnwood, IL................800-647-2290
Berkshire PPM
  Litchfield, CT.................860-567-3118
C-P Flexible Packaging
  Newtown, PA....................800-448-8183
Cam Tron Systems
  Addison, IL....................630-543-2884
Cognitive
  Golden, CO.....................800-765-6600
Columbia Labeling Machinery
  Benton City, WA................888-791-9590

Convergent Label Technology
Tampa, FL .800-252-6111
CRS Marking Systems
Portland, OR 800-547-7158
Custom Food Machinery
Stockton, CA. 209-463-4343
CVP Systems Inc
Downers Grove, IL 800-422-4720
D & L Manufacturing
Milwaukee, WI 414-256-8160
Dalemark Industries
Lakewood, NJ. 732-367-3100
Daymark Safety Systems
Bowling Green, OH 419-353-2458
Dispensa-Matic Label Dispense
Rocky Mount, MO 800-325-7303
Dorell Equipment Inc
Somerset, NJ 732-247-5400
Dow Industries
Wilmington, MA 800-776-1201
ELF Machinery
La Porte, IN. 800-328-0466
Elmark Packaging Inc
West Chester, PA. 800-670-9688
EMCO
Miamisburg, OH 800-722-3626
EPI Labelers
New Freedom, PA. 800-755-8344
Esselte Meto
Morris Plains, NJ 800-645-3290
Exact Equipment Corporation
Morrisville, PA 215-295-2000
Fairbanks Scales
Kansas City, MO. 800-451-4107
Fast Industries
Fort Lauderdale, FL 800-775-5345
Fernqvist Labeling Solutions
Mountain View, CA 800-426-8215
Garvey Products
West Chester, OH 800-543-1908
GCA
Huntington Beach, CA 714-379-4911
GEI PPM
Exton, PA .800-345-1308
Glen Mills Inc.
Clifton, NJ. 973-777-0777
Gluemaster
Kenosha, WI 262-857-7212
Gulf Arizona Packaging
Humble, TX 800-364-3887
Gulf Systems
Brownsville, TX 800-217-4853
Gulf Systems
Humble, TX 800-364-3887
Gulf Systems
Arlington, TX 817-261-1915
Heisler Machine & Tool Co
Fairfield, NJ 973-227-6300
Herche Warehouse
Denver, CO 303-371-8186
Horix Manufacturing Co
Mc Kees Rocks, PA. 412-771-1111
Houston Label
Pasadena, TX 800-477-6995
Hurst Corp
Wayne, PA. 610-687-2404
Hurst Labeling Systems
Chatsworth, CA 800-969-1705
Industrial Automation Systems
Santa Clarita, CA 888-484-4427
Innovative Packaging Solution
Martin, MI. 616-656-2100
ITW Diagraph
St Charles, MO 800-722-1125
KISS Packaging Systems
Vista, CA. .888-522-3538
Krones
Franklin, WI 800-752-3787
Label Technology Inc
Merced, CA. 800-388-1990
Label-Aire Inc
Fullerton, CA 714-441-0700
Labelette Company
Forest Park, IL 708-366-2010
Labelprint America
Newburyport, MA 978-463-4004
Livingston-Wilbor Corporation
Edison, NJ. 908-322-8403
Lord Label Group
Charlotte, NC 800-341-5225
Lord Label Machine Systems
Charlotte, NC 704-644-1650

Loveshaw Corp
South Canaan, PA. 800-572-3434
Marking Methods Inc
Alhambra, CA. 626-308-5800
Master Magnetics
Castle Rock, CO 800-525-3536
Mateer Burt
Exton, PA .800-345-1308
Matthews Marking Systems Div
Pittsburgh, PA. 412-665-2500
Miken Cosmpanies
Buffalo, NY. 716-668-6311
Modular Packaging
Randolph, NJ 973-970-9393
MPI Label Systems
Sebring, OH 800-837-2134
National Label Co
Lafayette Hill, PA 610-825-3250
National Package SealingCompany
Santa Ana, CA 714-630-1505
Nercon Engineering & Manufacturing
Oshkosh, WI 920-233-3268
New Way Packaging Machinery
Hanover, PA 800-522-3537
NJM/CLI
Pointe Claire, QC 514-630-6990
Nordson Corp
Duluth, GA 800-683-2314
OnTrack Automation Inc
Waterloo, ON 519-886-9090
Package Systems Corporation
Danielson, CT. 800-522-3548
Packaging & Processing Equipment
Ayr, ON 519-622-6666
Paragon Labeling
St Paul, MN. 800-429-7722
PDC International
Austin, TX. 512-302-0194
PEAK Technologies, Inc.
Columbia, MD 800-926-9212
Perl Packaging Systems
Middlebury, CT. 800-864-2853
PMI Food Equipment Group
Troy, OH .937-332-3000
Priority One Packaging
Waterloo, ON 800-387-9102
Production Packaging & Processing Equipment
Company
Savannah, GA 912-856-4281
Qsx Labels
Everett, MA. 800-225-3496
Quadrel Labeling Systems
Mentor, OH 800-321-8509
Renard Machine Company
Green Bay, WI. 920-432-8412
Roberts Poly Pro Inc
Charlotte, NC 800-269-7409
Sasib Beverage & Food North America
Plano, TX. 800-558-3814
Schaefer Machine Co Inc
Deep River, CT. 800-243-5143
Seal-O-Matic Corp
Jacksonville, OR 800-631-2072
Smyth Co LLC
St Paul, MN. 800-473-3464
Tamarack Products Inc
Wauconda, IL 847-526-9333
Tharo Systems Inc
Brunswick, OH 800-878-6833
Universal Labeling Systems Inc
St Petersburg, FL 877-236-0266
Vande Berg SCALES/Vbs Inc
Sioux Center, IA 712-722-1181
Varitronic Systems
Brooklyn Park, MN. 763-536-6400
Wallace Computer Services
Chicago, IL 888-925-8324
WE Killam Enterprises
Waterford, ON. 519-443-7421
Weber Packaging Solutions Inc
Arlington Heights, IL 800-843-4242
WS Packaging Group Inc
Rochester, NY 800-836-8186
Zebra Technologies Corporation
Lincolnshire, IL 866-230-9494

Package Tying

B H Bunn Co
Lakeland, FL 800-222-2866
Delta Cyklop Orga Pac
Charlotte, NC 800-446-4347

Felins USA Inc
Milwaukee, WI 800-343-5667
Gulf Arizona Packaging
Humble, TX 800-364-3887
Gulf Systems
Brownsville, TX 800-217-4853
Gulf Systems
Humble, TX 800-364-3887
Gulf Systems
Arlington, TX 817-261-1915
Herche Warehouse
Denver, CO 303-371-8186
KWIK Lok Corp
Yakima, WA 800-688-5945
Machine Electronics Company
Brooklyn, NY 718-384-3211
Steinmetz Machine Works Inc
Stamford, CT. 203-327-0118

Packing

A.K. Robins
Baltimore, MD 800-486-9656
Aaron Equipment Co Div Areco
Bensenville, IL 630-350-2200
About Packaging Robotics
Thornton, CO 303-449-2559
ADCO Manufacturing Inc
Sanger, CA 559-875-5563
Amark Packaging Systems
Kansas City, MO 816-965-9000
Architecture Plus Intl Inc
Rocky Point, FL 813-281-9299
Arthur G Russell Co Inc
Bristol, CT 860-583-4109
Automated Production Systems Corporation
New Freedom, PA 888-345-5377
B H Bunn Co
Lakeland, FL 800-222-2866
B T Engineering Inc
Bala Cynwyd, PA 610-664-9500
BEI
South Haven, MI. 800-364-7425
Belco Packaging Systems
Monrovia, CA 800-833-1833
Blue Print Automation
S Chesterfield, VA 804-520-5400
Bradman Lake Inc
Rock Hill, SC 803-366-3688
Branson Ultrasonics Corp
Danbury, CT. 203-796-0400
Brechteen
Chesterfield, MI 586-949-2240
BW Container Systems
Romeoville, IL 630-759-6800
C.J. Machine
Fridley, MN. 763-767-4630
Clamco Corporation
Berea, OH 216-267-1911
Cleveland Vibrator Co
Cleveland, OH 800-221-3298
Climax Packaging Machinery
Hamilton, OH 513-874-1664
Coastline Equipment Inc
Bellingham, WA 360-734-8509
Combi Packaging Systems LLC
Canton, OH 866-472-5236
Compacker Systems LLC
Davenport, IA 563-391-2751
Custom Food Machinery
Stockton, CA. 209-463-4343
CVP Systems Inc
Downers Grove, IL 800-422-4720
Data Scale
Fremont, CA 800-651-7350
Design Technology Corporation
Billerica, MA 978-663-7000
Diversified Metal Engineering
Charlottetown, PE. 902-628-6900
Dorell Equipment Inc
Somerset, NJ 732-247-5400
Douglas Machine Inc
Alexandria, MN 320-763-6587
Durable Packaging Corporation
Countryside, IL 800-700-5677
Durand-Wayland Inc
Lagrange, GA 800-241-2308
Eastern Machine
Middlebury, CT. 203-598-0066
Edl Packaging Engineers
Green Bay, WI. 920-336-7744

Edmeyer
Minneapolis, MN 651-450-1210
Edson Packaging Machinery
Hamilton, ON 800-493-3766
Elliott Manufacturing Co Inc
Fresno, CA 559-233-6235
Fillit
Kirkland, QC 514-694-2390
Fogg Filler Co
Holland, MI 616-786-3644
Fox Iv Technologies
Export, PA 877-436-2434
Gainco Inc
Gainesville, GA 800-467-2828
GEI Autowrappers
Exton, PA 610-321-1115
General Bag Corporation
Cleveland, OH 800-837-9396
General Processing Systems
Holland, MI 800-547-9370
Gram Equipment Of America
Tampa, FL 813-248-1978
Grigg Box Company
Detroit, MI 313-273-9000
GTI
Arvada, CO 303-420-6699
Halton Packaging Systems
Oakville, ON 905-847-9141
Hamrick Manufacturing & Svc
Mogadore, OH 800-321-9590
Harpak-ULMA Packaging LLC
Taunton, MA 508-238-8884
Hart Design & Mfg
Green Bay, WI 920-468-5927
Hartness International
Greenville, SC 800-845-8791
Herrmann Ultrasonics
Bartlett, IL 630-626-1626
Hoegger Food Technology
Minneapolis, MN 877-789-5400
Hudson Control Group Inc
Springfield, NJ 973-376-8265
ID Images
Brunswick, OH 866-516-7300
Ideal of America
Charlotte, NC 704-523-1604
Ilapak Inc
Newtown, PA 215-579-2900
Iman Pack
Westland, MI 800-810-4626
Industrial Magnetics
Boyne City, MI 800-662-4638
International Omni-Pac Corporation
La Verne, CA 909-593-2833
Jagenberg
Enfield, CT 860-741-2501
Jeb Plastics
Wilmington, DE 800-556-2247
Jetstream Systems
Wichita, KN 855-861-6916
Kisters Kayat
Sarasota, FL 386-424-0101
Kohler Industries Inc
Lincoln, NE 800-365-6708
Krones
Franklin, WI 800-752-3787
L&H Wood Manufacturing Company
Farmington, MI 248-474-9000
Lako Tool & Mfg Inc
Perrysburg, OH 800-228-2982
Langen Packaging
Mississauga, ON 905-670-7200
Longford Equipment US
Glastonbury, CT 416-298-6622
Machine Builders & Design Inc
Shelby, NC 704-482-3456
Malo Inc
Tulsa, OK 918-583-2743
Maren Engineering Corp
South Holland, IL 800-875-1038
Marq Packaging Systems Inc
Yakima, WA 800-998-4301
Mateer Burt
Exton, PA 800-345-1308
Matthiesen Equipment
San Antonio, TX 800-624-8635
Melco Steel Inc
Azusa, CA 626-334-7875
Molins/Sandiacre Richmond
Richmond, VA 864-486-4000
Newcastle Co Inc
New Castle, PA 724-658-4516

Nigrelli Systems Purchasing
Kiel, WI .800-693-3144
Nu-Con Equipment
Chanhassen, MN 877-939-0510
Olney Machinery
Westernville, NY 315-827-4208
Pacemaker Packaging Corp
Woodside, NY 718-458-1188
Package Systems Corporation
Danielson, CT 800-522-3548
Peco Controls Corporation
Modesto, CA 800-732-6285
Per-Fil Industries Inc
Riverside, NJ 856-461-5700
Pneumatic Scale Angelus
Cuyahoga Falls, OH 330-923-0491
Pressure Pack
Williamsburg, VA 757-220-3693
Priority One America
Oshkosh, WI 920-235-5562
Professional Marketing Group
Seattle, WA 800-227-3769
Promarks
Ontario, CA 909-923-3888
Prototype Equipment Corporation
Libertyville, IL 847-680-4433
PTI Packaging
Portage, WI 800-501-4077
RAM Center
Red Wing, MN 800-309-5431
Reiser
Canton, MA 734-821-1290
Remcon Plastics Inc
Reading, PA 800-360-3636
Rennco LLC
Homer, MI 800-409-5225
Riverwood International
Atlanta, GA 770-984-5477
Rockford-Midland Corporation
Rockford, IL 800-327-7908
Ropak Manufacturing Co Inc
Decatur, AL 256-350-4241
Rose Forgrove
Saint Charles, IL 630-443-1317
Sabel Engineering Corporation
Villard, MN 320-554-3611
Schroeder Machine
San Marcos, CA 760-591-9733
Semco Manufacturing Company
Pharr, TX 956-787-4203
Serpa Packaging Solutions
Visalia, CA 800-348-5453
Southern Automatics
Lakeland, FL 800-441-4604
Standard-Knapp Inc
Portland, CT 800-628-9565
T D Sawvel Co
Maple Plain, MN 877-488-1816
TDF Automation
Cedar Falls, IA 800-553-1777
Thiele Engineering Company
Fergus Falls, MN 218-739-3321
Thiele Technologies-Reedley
Reedley, CA 800-344-8951
Trio Packaging Corp
Ronkonkoma, NY 800-331-0492
Universal Packaging Inc
Houston, TX 800-324-2610
W.G. Durant Corporation
Whittier, CA 562-946-5555
Wayne Automation Corp
Eagleville, PA 610-630-8900
WE Killam Enterprises
Waterford, ON 519-443-7421
WeighPack Systems/Paxiom Group
Montreal, QC 888-934-4472
Wick's Packaging Service
Cutler, IN 574-967-3104
Wrapade Packaging Systems
Fairfield, NJ 888-815-8564
Zepf Technologies
Clearwater, FL 727-535-4100

Portion Control Equipment

AC Dispensing Equipment
Lower Sackville, NS 888-777-9990
Acme Scale Co
San Leandro, CA 888-638-5040
AEW Thurne
Lake Zurich, IL 800-239-7297

AM-Mac
Fairfield, NJ 800-829-2018
Avery Weigh-Tronix LLC
Fairmont, MN 800-368-2039
Beer Magic Devices
Hamilton, ON 905-522-3081
BVL Controls
Bois-Des-Filion, QC 866-285-2668
CCi Scale Company
Clovis, CA 800-900-0224
Crestware
North Salt Lake, UT 800-345-0513
Daleco
West Chester, PA 610-429-0181
Design Technology Corporation
Billerica, MA 978-663-7000
Detecto Scale Co
Webb City, MO 800-641-2008
Diversified Metal Engineering
Charlottetown, PE 902-628-6900
Doering Machines Inc
San Francisco, CA 415-526-2131
Edlund Co
Burlington, VT 800-772-2126
Genpak
Peterborough, ON 800-461-1995
Hoegger Food Technology
Minneapolis, MN 877-789-5400
Hollymatic Corp
Countryside, IL 708-579-3700
Industrial Laboratory Eqpt Co
Charlotte, NC 704-357-3930
Label Makers
Pleasant Prairie, WI 800-208-3331
Liberty Ware LLC
Clearfield, UT 888-500-5885
Little Squirt
Toronto, ON 416-665-6605
Magnuson Industries
Rockford, IL 800-435-2816
Opal Manufacturing Ltd
Toronto, ON 416-646-5232
Packaging Progressions
Collegeville, PA 610-489-9096
Patty O Matic Machinery
Farmingdale, NJ 877-938-5244
Pelouze Scale Company
Bridgeview, IL 800-323-8363
Pino's Pasta Veloce
Staten Island, NY 718-273-6660
Plastic Fantastics/Buck Signs
Ashland, OR 800-482-1776
Proluxe
Paramount, CA 800-594-5528
Quantum Topping Systems Quantum Technical Services Inc
Frankfort, IL 888-464-1540
Reiser
Canton, MA 734-821-1290
Superior Products Company
Saint Paul, MN 800-328-9800
Traex
Dane, WI 800-356-8006
TWM Manufacturing
Leamington, ON 888-495-4831
Unifiller Systems
Delta, BC 888-733-8444
Weiler & Company
Whitewater, WI 800-558-9507
Zeroll Company
Fort Pierce, FL 800-872-5000

Printing

ABM Marking
Belleville, IL 800-626-9012
Accurate Paper Box Co Inc
Knoxville, TN 865-690-0311
Advanced Poly-Packaging Inc
Akron, OH 800-754-4403
Algene Marking Equipment Company
Garfield, NJ 973-478-9041
Apex Machine Company
Oakland Park, FL 954-566-1572
Axiohm USA
Myrtle Beach, SC 843-443-3155
Bell-Mark Corporation
Pine Brook, NJ 973-882-0202
Bren Instruments
Franklin, TN 615-794-6825
Carl Strutz & Company
Mars, PA 724-625-1501

Cognitive
  Golden, CO 800-765-6600
Columbia Labeling Machinery
  Benton City, WA 888-791-9590
Computype Inc
  St Paul, MN. 800-328-0852
Comstar Printing Solutions
  Streetsboro, OH 330-528-2800
D & L Manufacturing
  Milwaukee, WI 414-256-8160
Dana Labels
  Beaverton, OR 800-255-1492
Dependable Machine, Inc.
  d'Alene, ID 866-967-0146
Desco Equipment Corporation
  Twinsburg, OH 330-405-1581
Domino Amjet Inc
  Gurnee, IL 800-444-4512
Donnick Label Systems
  Jacksonville, FL 800-334-7849
Dorell Equipment Inc
  Somerset, NJ 732-247-5400
Durable Engravers
  Franklin Park, IL. 800-869-9565
EMCO
  Miamisburg, OH 800-722-3626
Esselte Meto
  Morris Plains, NJ 800-645-3290
Exact Equipment Corporation
  Morrisville, PA 215-295-2000
Fernqvist Labeling Solutions
  Mountain View, CA 800-426-8215
GCA
  Huntington Beach, CA 714-379-4911
GM Nameplate
  Seattle, WA 800-366-7668
GTCO CalComp
  Scottsdale, AZ. 800-856-0732
H G Weber & Co
  Kiel, WI. 920-894-2221
Howard Imprinting Machine Company
  Houston, TX 800-334-6943
ID Images
  Brunswick, OH 866-516-7300
Imaging Technologies
  Cookeville, TN 800-488-2804
Kammann Machine
  Portsmouth, NH 978-463-0050
KASE Equipment
  Cleveland, OH 216-642-9040
Kurz Transfer Products LP
  Charlotte, NC 800-333-2306
Kwikprint Manufacturing Inc
  Jacksonville, FL 800-940-5945
Label Systems & Solutions
  Bohemia, NY 800-811-2560
Labelmart
  Maple Grove, MN. 888-577-0141
Loveshaw Corp
  South Canaan, PA 800-572-3434
Marsh Company
  Belleville, IL. 800-527-6275
Mettler-Toledo, LLC
  Columbus, OH 800-638-8537
MPI Label Systems
  Sebring, OH 800-837-2134
Norwood Marking Systems
  Downers Grove, IL. 800-626-3464
Packaging Machinery & Equipment
  West Orange, NJ 973-325-2418
Paper Converting Machine Company
  Green Bay, WI. 920-494-5601
Paper Converting MachineCompany
  Green Bay, WI. 920-494-5601
Paragon Labeling
  St Paul, MN. 800-429-7722
Reflex International
  Norcross, GA 800-642-7640
Service Stamp Works
  Chicago, IL 312-666-8839
Sohn Manufacturing
  Elkhart Lake, WI. 920-876-3361
Star Micronics
  Edison, NJ 800-782-7636
Stratix Corp
  Peachtree Cor, GA 800-883-8300
Tallygenicom
  Irvine, CA 800-665-6210
Tamarack Products Inc
  Wauconda, IL 847-526-9333
TEC America
  Atlanta, GA. 770-453-0868

Tharo Systems Inc
  Brunswick, OH 800-878-6833
Trident
  Brookfield, CT 203-740-9333
Varitronic Systems
  Brooklyn Park, MN. 763-536-6400
Videojet Technologies Inc
  Wood Dale, IL. 800-843-3610
Wallace Computer Services
  Chicago, IL 888-925-8324
Wichita Stamp & Seal Inc
  Wichita, KS. 316-263-4223
Wt Nickell Co
  Batavia, OH. 888-899-1991
Yamato Corporation
  Colorado Springs, CO. 800-538-1762
Zebra Technologies Corporation
  Lincolnshire, IL 866-230-9494
Zerand Corp
  New Berlin, WI. 262-827-3800

Plastics

Carl Strutz & Company
  Mars, PA 724-625-1501
Desco Equipment Corporation
  Twinsburg, OH 330-405-1581
Trident
  Brookfield, CT 203-740-9333
Uniloy Milacron
  Tecumseh, MI 517-424-8900
WE Killam Enterprises
  Waterford, ON. 519-443-7421

Rebuilt & Used

A&M Industries
  Sioux Falls, SD 800-888-2615
American Equipment Co
  Aberdeen, MD 410-272-2626
Ameripak Packaging Equipment
  Warrington, PA 215-343-1530
Automated Packaging Systems
  Streetsboro, OH 800-527-0733
Berkshire PPM
  Litchfield, CT 860-567-3118
Cartpac Inc
  Carol Stream, IL 630-510-1100
Champion Trading Corporation
  Marlboro, NJ 732-780-4200
Change Parts Inc
  Ludington, MI 231-845-5107
Circle Packaging Machinery Inc
  De Pere, WI. 920-983-3420
Colter & Peterson
  Paterson, NJ 973-684-0901
Custom Food Machinery
  Stockton, CA. 209-463-4343
Eischen Enterprises
  Fresno, CA 559-834-0013
Equipment Specialists Inc
  Manassas, VA 703-361-2227
Gulf Systems
  Humble, TX 800-364-3887
Gulf Systems
  Arlington, TX 817-261-1915
Hallmark Equipment Inc
  Morgan Hill, CA 408-782-2600
Health Star
  Randolph, MA 800-545-3639
Ilapak Inc
  Newtown, PA 215-579-2900
Lehman Sales Associates
  Sun Prairie, WI 608-575-7712
Madison County Wood Products
  St Louis, MO. 314-772-1722
McNeil Food Machinery
  Stockton, CA. 209-463-4343
Miller Technical Svc
  Plymouth, MI 734-414-1769
National Equipment Corporation
  Bronx, NY. 800-237-8873
Package Machinery Co Inc
  Holyoke, MA 413-315-3801
Packaging & Processing Equipment
  Ayr, ON. 519-622-6666
Packaging Machinery & Equipment
  West Orange, NJ 973-325-2418
Palace Packaging Machines Inc
  Downingtown, PA. 610-873-7252
Plasti-Mach Corporation
  Valley Cottage, NY 800-394-1128

Production Packaging & Processing Equipment
Company
  Savannah, GA 912-856-4281
Professional Marketing Group
  Seattle, WA 800-227-3769
QMS International, Inc.
  Mississauga, Ontario, ON. 905-820-7225
Schroeder Machine
  San Marcos, CA 760-591-9733
Warwick Manufacturing & Equip
  North Brunswick, NJ 732-729-0400
Wick's Packaging Service
  Cutler, IN 574-967-3104

Retort Pouch Processing

AmeriQual Foods
  Evansville, IN 812-867-1444
SOPAKCO Foods
  Mullins, SC 800-276-9678
Stock America Inc
  Grafton, WI 262-375-4100
Sungjae Corporation
  Irvine, CA 949-757-1727

Sealers

Heat

AAMD
  Liverpool, NY 800-887-4167
Audion Automation
  Carrollton, TX. 972-389-0777
Branson Ultrasonics Corp
  Danbury, CT 203-796-0400
Carson Manufacturing Company
  Petaluma, CA 800-423-2380
Chaffee Co
  Rocklin, CA 916-630-3980
Chase Industries Inc
  West Chester, OH 800-543-4455
Durable Packaging Corporation
  Countryside, IL 800-700-5677
Giltron Inc
  Norwood, MA. 781-762-4310
Gulf Arizona Packaging
  Humble, TX 800-364-3887
Herche Warehouse
  Denver, CO 303-371-8186
ITW United Silicone
  Lancaster, NY 716-681-8222
Jeb Plastics
  Wilmington, DE 800-556-2247
Korab Engineering Company
  Los Angeles, CA. 310-670-7710
Lako Tool & Mfg Inc
  Perrysburg, OH. 800-228-2982
Matthiesen Equipment
  San Antonio, TX 800-624-8635
Moen Industries
  Santa Fe Springs, CA 800-732-7766
Nordson Corporation
  Duluth, GA 800-683-2314
Osgood Industries
  Oldsmar, FL 813-855-7337
Pack Rite Machine Mettler
  Mt Pleasant, WI 800-248-6868
Packaging & Processing Equipment
  Ayr, ON 519-622-6666
Packaging Aids Corporation
  San Rafael, CA 415-454-4868
Packworld USA
  Nazareth, PA 610-746-2765
Plasti-Mach Corporation
  Valley Cottage, NY 800-394-1128
PlexPack Corp
  Toronto, ON 855-635-9238
Pressure Pack
  Williamsburg, VA 757-220-3693
Reiser
  Canton, MA 734-821-1290
Rockford-Midland Corporation
  Rockford, IL 800-327-7908
Seal-O-Matic Corp
  Jacksonville, OR 800-631-2072
Servpak Corp
  Hollywood, FL 800-782-0840
Wraps
  East Orange, NJ 973-673-7873
Zed Industries
  Vandalia, OH. 937-667-8407

Tray

K & L Intl
Ontario, CA.....................888-598-5588
Reiser
Canton, MA 734-821-1290

Shrinkers: Plastic Packaging

Adex Medical Inc
Riverside, CA....................800-873-4776
AEP Industries Inc
Mankato, MN 800-999-2374
Alfa Systems Inc
Westfield, NJ....................908-654-0255
Aline Heat Seal Corporation
Los Angeles, CA.................888-285-3917
Architecture Plus Intl Inc
Rocky Point, FL..................813-281-9299
Arkansas Poly
N Little Rock, AR................800-342-7659
Audion Automation
Carrollton, TX...................972-389-0777
Bollore Inc
Dayville, CT.....................860-774-2930
Brenton Engineering Co
Alexandria, MN 800-535-2730
Chase Industries Inc
West Chester, OH................800-543-4455
CiMa-Pak Corp.
Dorval, QC......................877-631-2462
Clamco Corporation
Berea, OH.......................216-267-1911
Conflex, Inc.
Germantown, WI..................800-225-4296
Douglas Machine Inc
Alexandria, MN 320-763-6587
Ideal of America
Charlotte, NC....................704-523-1604
Ideal of America/Valley Rio Enterprise
Atlanta, GA......................770-352-0210
Iman Pack
Westland, MI.....................800-810-4626
L&H Wood Manufacturing Company
Farmington, MI...................248-474-9000
M & Q Packaging Corp
North Wales, PA..................267-498-4000
M S Plastics & Packaging Inc
Butler, NJ.......................800-593-1802
Packaging Machinery International
Elk Grove Village, IL..............800-871-4764
Phase Fire Systems
Vista, CA.......................888-741-2341
Polypack Inc
Pinellas Park, FL.................727-578-5000
Reiser
Canton, MA 734-821-1290
Rennco LLC
Homer, MI.......................800-409-5225
Robbie Manufacturing Inc
Lenexa, KS......................800-255-6328
Triune Enterprises
Gardena, CA.....................310-719-1600
V C 999 Packaging Systems
Kansas City, MO..................800-728-2999
Vector Packaging
Oak Brook, IL....................800-435-9100
Zepf Technologies
Clearwater, FL...................727-535-4100

Sorters

Bottle

California Vibratory Feeders
Anaheim, CA 800-354-0972
Heuft USA Inc
Downers Grove, IL................630-968-9011
Kinsley Inc
Doylestown, PA 800-414-6664
Packaging & Processing Equipment
Ayr, ON.........................519-622-6666
Palace Packaging Machines Inc
Downingtown, PA.................610-873-7252

Tables

Packing House

A.K. Robins
Baltimore, MD 800-486-9656
Atlas Equipment Company
Kansas City, MO..................800-842-9188

Belco Packaging Systems
Monrovia, CA....................800-833-1833
Brothers Metal Products
Santa Ana, CA 714-972-3008
Cleveland Vibrator Co
Cleveland, OH...................800-221-3298
Columbus McKinnon Corporation
Getzville, NY 800-888-0985
Cozzini Inc
Algona, IA......................888-295-1116
Dc Tech
Kansas City, MO.................877-742-9090
Key Material Handling Inc
Simi Valley, CA..................800-539-7225
MeGa Industries
Burlington, ON 800-665-6342
MSSH
Greensburg, IN 812-663-2180
Packaging & Processing Equipment
Ayr, ON.........................519-622-6666
Sperling Industries
Omaha, NE 800-647-5062

Vacuum Packing

Cretel Food Equipment
Holland, MI - A Gardner Denver Product...616-786-3980
Elmo Rietschle - A Gardner Denver Product
Qunicy, IL......................217-222-5400
Market Sales Company
Newton, MA 617-232-0239
Promarks
Ontario, CA.....................909-923-3888
Reiser
Canton, MA 734-821-1290
RMF Companies
Grandview, MO...................816-839-9258
Rollstock Inc
Kansas City, MO..................800-954-6020

Weighing

A&D Weighing
San Jose, CA....................800-726-3364
Abel Manufacturing Co
Appleton, WI....................920-734-4443
Accu-Pak
Akron, OH
Acme Scale Co
San Leandro, CA.................888-638-5040
Action Packaging Automation
Roosevelt, NJ....................800-241-2724
Actionpac Scales Automation
Oxnard, CA......................800-394-0154
Ag-Pak
Gasport, NY 716-772-2651
All Fill Inc
Exton, PA........................866-255-4455
Amark Packaging Systems
Kansas City, MO..................816-965-9000
American Bag & Burlap Company
Chelsea, MA 617-884-7600
Ameriglobe LLC
Lafayette, LA 337-234-3211
Andgar Corp
Ferndale, WA 360-366-9900
AP Dataweigh Inc
Cumming, GA....................877-409-2562
APEC
Lake Odessa, MI..................616-374-1000
Arkfeld Mfg & Distributing Co
Norfolk, NE......................800-533-0676
Avery Weigh-Tronix
Fairmont, MN....................877-368-2039
Bell & Howell Company
Lincolnwood, IL..................800-647-2290
BLH Electronics
Canton, MA 781-821-2000
Blodgett Co
Houston, TX.....................281-933-6195
Cardinal Scale Mfg Co
Webb City, MO...................800-441-4237
Care Controls, Inc.
Mill Creek, WA...................800-593-6050
CCi Scale Company
Clovis, CA.......................800-900-0224
Chemi-Graphic Inc
Ludlow, MA 413-589-0151
Chlorinators Inc
Stuart, FL.......................800-327-9761
Cintex of America
Carol Stream, IL.................800-424-6839

Convergent Label Technology
Tampa, FL.......................800-252-6111
Crestware
North Salt Lake, UT 800-345-0513
Crystal-Vision Packaging Systems
Torrance, CA.....................800-331-3240
Delta Engineering Corporation
Walpole, MA.....................781-729-8650
Detecto Scale Co
Webb City, MO...................800-641-2008
Doran Scales Inc
Batavia, IL.......................800-365-0084
Edlund Co
Burlington, VT....................800-772-2126
Emery Winslow Scale Co
Seymour, CT.....................203-881-9333
Equipment Outlet
Meridian, ID 208-887-1472
Exact Equipment Corporation
Morrisville, PA...................215-295-2000
Fairbanks Scales
Kansas City, MO..................800-451-4107
Fawema Packaging Machinery
Palmetto, FL.....................941-351-9597
Fuller Weighing Systems
Columbus, OH...................614-882-8121
Gainco Inc
Gainesville, GA...................800-467-2828
General Packaging Equipment Co
Houston, TX.....................713-686-4331
Grain Machinery Mfg Corp
Miami, FL.......................305-620-2525
Hardy Systems Corporation
Northbrook, IL...................800-927-3956
Howes S Co Inc
Silver Creek, NY..................888-255-2611
Hyer Industries
Pembroke, MA...................781-826-8101
IEW
Niles, OH 330-652-0113
Ilapak Inc
Newtown, PA....................215-579-2900
Iman Pack
Westland, MI.....................800-810-4626
Industrial Laboratory Eqpt Co
Charlotte, NC....................704-357-3930
Inspired Automation Inc
Agoura Hills, CA..................818-991-4598
IWS Scales
San Diego, CA....................800-881-9755
Key Material Handling Inc
Simi Valley, CA...................800-539-7225
Kliklok-Woodman
Decatur, GA......................770-981-5200
Lock Inspection Systems
Fitchburg, MA 800-227-5539
Lockwood Packaging
Woburn, MA.....................800-641-3100
Loma International
Carol Stream, IL..................800-872-5662
Mandeville Company
Minneapolis, MN.................800-328-8490
MERRICK Industries Inc
Lynn Haven, FL..................800-271-7834
Mettler-Toledo, LLC
Columbus, OH...................800-638-8537
Micro-Strain
Spring City, PA...................610-948-4550
Mortec Industries Inc
Brush, CO.......................800-541-9983
National Scoop & Equipment Company
Spring House, PA.................215-646-2040
Newton OA & Son Co
Bridgeville, DE...................800-726-5745
Ocs Checkweighers, Inc.
Snellville, GA....................678-344-8030
Ohaus Corp
Parsippany, NJ...................800-672-7722
Ohlson Packaging
Taunton, MA.....................508-977-0004
Pacific Scale Company
Clackamas, OR...................800-537-1886
Peco Controls Corporation
Modesto, CA.....................800-732-6285
Pelouze Scale Company
Bridgeview, IL....................800-323-8363
PMI Food Equipment Group
Troy, OH........................937-332-3000
Pomona Service & Pkgng Co LA
Yakima, WA......................509-452-7121
Quest Corp
North Royalton, OH 440-230-9400

Renard Machine Company
  Green Bay, WI. 920-432-8412
Rice Lake Weighing Systems
  Rice Lake, WI. 800-472-6703
Sartorius Corp
  Edgewood, NY 800-635-2906
Schaffer Poidometer Company
  Pittsburgh, PA 412-281-9031
Scientech, Inc
  Boulder, CO .800-525-0522
Si-Lodec
  Tukwila, WA .800-255-8274
Sig Pack
  Oakland, CA .800-824-3245
Sterling Scale Co
  Southfield, MI 800-331-9931
Sterling Systems & Controls
  Sterling, IL 800-257-7214
Taylor Precision Products
  Oak Brook, IL 866-843-3905
Taylor Products Co
  Parsons, KS .888-882-9567
TEC America
  Atlanta, GA .770-453-0868
Tecweigh
  St Paul, MN. .800-536-4880
Temco
  Oakland, CA .707-746-5966
Tomac Packaging
  Woburn, MA .800-641-3100
Toroid Corp
  Huntsville, AL 256-837-7510
Triangle Package Machinery Co
  Chicago, IL 800-621-4170
Tridyne Process Systems
  South Burlington, VT 802-863-6873
Triner Scale & Mfg Co
  Olive Branch, MS 800-238-0152
Vande Berg SCALES/Vbs Inc
  Sioux Center, IA 712-722-1181
Venture Measurement Co LLC
  Spartanburg, SC 800-426-9010
VitaMinder Company
  Providence, RI 800-858-8840
Water Sciences Services, Inc.
  Jackson, TN .973-584-4131
Weigh Right Automatic Scale Co
  Joliet, IL 800-571-0249
WeighPack Systems/Paxiom Group
  Montreal, QC 888-934-4472
Yakima Wire Works
  Reedley, CA .800-344-8951
Yargus Manufacturing Inc
  Marshall, IL .217-826-8059

Wire Stitching

New Jersey Wire Stitching Machine Company
  Cherry Hill, NJ 856-428-2572

Wrapping

Air Technical Industries
  Mentor, OH. .888-857-6265
Aline Heat Seal Corporation
  Los Angeles, CA. 888-285-3917
Allpac
  Dallas, TX. 214-630-8804
Ampak
  Cleveland, OH 800-342-6329
APS Packaging Systems
  San Jose, CA .800-526-2276
Architecture Plus Intl Inc
  Rocky Point, FL 813-281-9299
Audion Automation
  Carrollton, TX. 972-389-0777
Automatic Electronic Machines Company
  Brooklyn, NY 718-384-3211
B W Cooney & Associates
  Bolton, Ontario, ON 905-857-7880
Berkshire PPM
  Litchfield, CT. 860-567-3118
Berlin Foundry & Mach Co
  Berlin, NH. 603-752-4550
Brenton Engineering Co
  Alexandria, MN 800-535-2730
C & K Machine Co
  Holyoke, MA 413-536-8122
Campbell Wrapper Corporation
  De Pere, WI. .920-983-7100
Charles Beseler Company
  Stroudsburg, PA 800-237-3537

Chase Industries Inc
  West Chester, OH 800-543-4455
Circle Packaging Machinery Inc
  De Pere, WI. .920-983-3420
Conflex, Inc.
  Germantown, WI. 800-225-4296
Crystal-Vision Packaging Systems
  Torrance, CA. 800-331-3240
Delkor Systems, Inc
  Minneapolis, MN 800-328-5558
Design Technology Corporation
  Billerica, MA 978-663-7000
Doering Machines Inc
  San Francisco, CA 415-526-2131
Dorell Equipment Inc
  Somerset, NJ 732-247-5400
Edl Packaging Engineers
  Green Bay, WI. 920-336-7744
Exact Equipment Corporation
  Morrisville, PA 215-295-2000
Felins USA Inc
  Milwaukee, WI. 800-343-5667
Formost Packaging Machines
  Woodinville, WA. 425-483-9090
Ganz Brothers
  Paramus, NJ .201-845-6010
GEI Autowrappers
  Exton, PA. 610-321-1115
Goodwrappers Inc
  Halethorpe, MD 800-638-1127
Halton Packaging Systems
  Oakville, ON 905-847-9141
Hart Design & Mfg
  Green Bay, WI. 920-468-5927
Hayssen Flexible Systems
  Duncan, SC .864-486-4000
Highlight Industries
  Wyoming, MI 800-531-2465
Ideal of America
  Charlotte, NC 704-523-1604
Ideal of America/Valley Rio Enterprise
  Atlanta, GA .770-352-0210
Ideal Wrapping Machine Company
  Middletown, NY 845-343-7700
Ilapak Inc
  Newtown, PA 215-579-2900
Illinois Tool Works
  Glenview, IL .224-661-8870
International Packaging Machinery
  Naples, FL 800-237-6496
Kisters Kayat
  Sarasota, FL .386-424-0101
Machine Electronics Company
  Brooklyn, NY 718-384-3211
Mark Products Company
  Denville, NJ .973-983-8818
Marquip Ward United
  Phillips, WI .715-339-2191
Maryland Packaging Corporation
  Elkridge, MD 410-540-9700
Nitech
  Columbus, NE. 800-237-6496
Orion Packaging Systems Inc
  Alexandria, MN 800-333-6556
Ossid Corp
  Battleboro, NC 800-334-8369
Pack Line Corporation
  Racine, WI 800-248-6868
Packaging & Processing Equipment
  Ayr, ON 519-622-6666
Packaging Dynamics
  Walnut Creek, CA. 925-938-2711
Peerless Food Equipment
  Sidney, OH 937-492-4158
Pfankuch Machinery Corporation
  Apple Valley, MN 952-891-3311
PMI Food Equipment Group
  Troy, OH 937-332-3000
Polypack Inc
  Pinellas Park, FL. 727-578-5000
Renard Machine Company
  Green Bay, WI. 920-432-8412
Rose Forgrove
  Saint Charles, IL. 630-443-1317
Sanford Redmond Company
  Stamford, CT. 203-351-9800
Scan Coin
  Ashburn, VA 800-336-3311
Scandia Packaging Machinery Co
  Fairfield, NJ .973-473-6100
Seal-O-Matic Corp
  Jacksonville, OR 800-631-2072

Shrinkfast Marketing
  Newport, NH. 800-867-4746
Sitma USA
  Spilamberto, MO 800-728-1254
Telesonic Packaging
  Wilmington, DE 302-658-6945

Pails

Acra Electric Corporation
  Tulsa, OK 800-223-4328
All American Container
  Miami, FL 305-887-0797
Container Supply Co
  Garden Grove, CA 562-594-0937
Greenfield Packaging
  White Plains, NY 914-993-0233
Hedwin Division
  Baltimore, MD 800-638-1012
Indianapolis Container Company
  Indianapolis, IN 800-760-3318
IPL Inc
  Saint-Damien, QC 800-463-4755
Landis Plastics
  Alsip, IL 708-396-1470
Louisville Container Company
  Indianapolis, IN 888-539-7225
National Scoop & Equipment Company
  Spring House, PA 215-646-2040
Poly One Corp
  Avon Lake, OH. 866-765-9663
Prolon
  Port Gibson, MS 888-480-9828
Reliance Product
  Winnipeg, MB. 800-665-0258

Parts

A C Tool & Machine Co
  Louisville, KY 502-447-5505
ABB
  Cary, NC 800-435-7365
Accuflex Industrial Hose LTD
  Romulus, MI. 734-713-4100
Acromag Inc.
  Wixom, MI 248-624-1541
Action Technology
  Prussia, PA 217-935-8311
Advance Fittings Corp
  Elkhorn, WI. .262-723-6699
Advanced Control Technologies
  Indianapolis, IN 800-886-2281
AFT Advanced Fiber Technologies
  Sherbrooke, QC 800-668-7273
AGC
  Bristow, VA. 800-825-8820
Air Quality Engineering
  Minneapolis, MN 800-328-0787
Alkota Cleaning Systems Inc
  Alcester, SD .800-255-6823
All Packaging Machinery Corp
  Ronkonkoma, NY 800-637-8808
AllPoints Foodservice
  Mt. Prospect, IL
American Extrusion Intl
  South Beloit, IL 815-624-6616
American Radionic Co Inc
  Palm Coast, FL 800-445-6033
Ampco Pumps Co Inc
  Milwaukee, WI. 800-737-8671
Andantex USA Inc
  Ocean, NJ 800-713-6170
ANVER Corporation
  Hudson, MA 800-654-3500
Apex Packing & Rubber Co
  Farmingdale, NY. 800-645-9110
APV Americas
  Delavan, WI .800-252-5200
Arc Machines Inc
  Pacoima, CA. 818-896-9556
Architecture Plus Intl Inc
  Rocky Point, FL 813-281-9299
Arctic Seal & Gasket
  Palm City, FL 800-881-4663
Armstrong Hot Water
  Three Rivers, MI. 269-279-3602
Arthur Products Co
  Medina, OH. 800-322-0510
Artisan Controls Corp
  Randolph, NJ 800-457-4950
Automatic Specialties Inc
  Marlborough, MA 800-445-2370

Bal Seal Engineering Inc
Foothill Ranch, CA.............800-366-1006
Baldewein Company
Lake Forrest, IL 800-424-5544
Banner Equipment Co
Morris, IL 800-621-4625
Bardo Abrasives
Ridgewood, NY 718-456-6400
Basiloid Products Corp
Elnora, IN 866-692-5511
Bayside Motion Group
Port Washington, NY 800-305-4555
Beacon Specialties
New York, NY 800-221-9405
Beam Industries
Webster City, IA 800-369-2326
Becker Brothers Graphite Co
Maywood, IL...................708-410-0700
Benchmark Thermal
Grass Valley, CA 800-748-6189
Bert Manufacturing
Gardnerville, NV 775-265-3900
Bettendorf Stanford Inc
Salem, IL 800-548-2253
BFM Equipment Sales
Fall River, WI 920-484-3341
Bodine Electric Co
Northfield, IL 773-478-3515
Bohn & Dawson
St Louis, MO 800-225-5011
Bolzoni Auramo
Homewood, IL 800-358-5438
Boston Gear
Boston, MA...................888-999-9860
Bradford A Ducon Company
Pewaukee, WI 800-789-1718
C & D Valve Mfg Co
Oklahoma City, OK 800-654-9233
Cal Controls
Gurnee, IL 800-866-6659
Caldwell Group
Rockford, IL 800-628-4263
Caloritech
Greensburg, IN 800-473-2403
Carmun International
San Antonio, TX 800-531-7907
Carter Products
Grand Rapids, MI 888-622-7837
Cashco Inc
Ellsworth, KS 785-472-4461
Cat Pumps
Minneapolis, MN 763-780-5440
Change Parts Inc
Ludington, MI.................231-845-5107
Chicago Stainless Eqpt Inc
Palm City, FL 800-927-8575
Chipmaker Tooling Supply
Whittier, CA 800-659-5840
Chromalox Inc
Pittsburgh, PA 800-443-2640
Clark-Cooper Division   Magnatrol Valve Corporation
Cinnaminson, NJ...............856-829-4580
Clean Water Systems
Klamath Falls, OR 866-273-9993
Consolidated Commercial Controls
Winsted, CT 800-227-1511
Continental Disc Corp
Liberty, MO...................816-792-1500
Conveyor Accessories
Burr Ridge, IL 800-323-7093
Conxall Corporation
Villa Park, IL..................630-834-7504
Cornell Pump Company
Portland, OR 503-653-0330
Cramer Company
South Windsor, CT 877-684-6464
Crown Battery Mfg
Fremont, OH 800-487-2879
CSS International Corp
Philadelphia, PA 800-278-8107
Delavan Spray Technologies
Charlotte, NC 704-423-7000
Doering Co
Clear Lake, MN 320-743-2276
Dormont Manufacturing Co
Export, PA....................800-367-6668
Dyna-Veyor Inc
Newark, NJ 800-326-5009
Electro Cam Corp
Roscoe, IL....................800-228-5487
Elite Forming Design Solutions
Rome, GA 706-232-3021

Ellett Industries
Port Coquitlam, BC.............604-941-8211
Ernst Timing Screw Co
Bensalem, PA 215-639-1438
Esco Products Inc
Houston, TX 800-966-5514
Fabreeka International
Boise, ID 800-423-4469
Falcon Fabricators Inc
Nashville, TN 615-832-0027
Faribault Manufacturing Co
Faribault, MN 800-447-6043
Federal Machine Corp
Clive, IA 800-247-2446
FEI Inc
Mansfield, TX 800-346-5908
Fleetwood Systems
Orlando, FL...................800-432-5433
Flomatic International
Sellersburg, IN 800-367-4233
Florida Knife Co
Sarasota, FL 800-966-5643
Fluid Metering Inc
Syosset, NY...................800-223-3388
Frost Food Handling Products
Grand Rapids, MI..............800-253-9382
Furnace Belt Company
Buffalo, NY...................800-354-7213
G.W. Dahl Company
Greensboro, NC 800-852-4449
Garvey Products
West Chester, OH 800-543-1908
GE Interlogix Industrial
Tualatin, OR 800-247-9447
Gems Sensors & Controls
Plainville, CT 860-747-3000
Glo-Quartz Electric Heater
Mentor, OH 800-321-3574
Globe Fire Sprinkler Corp
Standish, MI 800-248-0278
Good Idea
Northampton, MA 800-462-9237
Granco Manufacturing Inc
San Ramon, CA 510-652-8847
Graphite Metalizing Corp
Yonkers, NY 914-968-8400
Green Belt Industries Inc
Buffalo, NY...................800-668-1114
H & H Metal Fabrication Inc
Belden, MS 662-489-4626
H A Phillips & Co
Dekalb, IL 630-377-0050
Habasit Canada Limited
Oakville, ON 905-827-4131
Hansaloy Corp
Davenport, IA 800-553-4992
Haumiller Engineering Co
Elgin, IL 847-695-9111
Hayes & Stolz Indl Mfg LTD
Fort Worth, TX 800-725-7272
Hi-Temp Inc
Tuscumbia, AL 800-239-5066
Hoffmeyer Corp
San Leandro, CA...............888-744-1826
Home Rubber Co
Trenton, NJ 800-257-9441
Hose Master Inc
Euclid, OH 216-481-2020
Ika-Works Inc
Wilmington, NC 800-733-3037
IMI Precision Engineering
Brookville, OH 937-833-4033
Indemax Inc
Vernon, NJ 800-345-7185
Industrial Product Corp
Ho Ho Kus, NJ 800-472-5913
Infitec Inc
East Syracuse, NY 800-334-0837
International Tank & Pipe Co
Clackamas, OR 888-988-0011
Introdel Products
Itasca, IL 800-323-4772
Irby
Rocky Mount, NC 252-442-0154
Ivarson Inc
Milwaukee, WI 414-351-0700
J & J Industries Inc
Bensenville, IL 630-595-8878
Jilson Group
Lodi, NJ 800-969-5400
Jokamsco Group
Waterford,, NY 518-237-6416

Kason Central
Columbus, OH 614-885-1992
Kinetic Equipment Company
Appleton, WI 806-293-4471
King Company
Dallas, TX....................507-451-3770
Kinsley Inc
Doylestown, PA 800-414-6664
Knobs Unlimited
Bowling Green, OH 419-353-8215
Kraissl Co Inc
Hackensack, NJ................800-572-4775
KWS Manufacturing Co LTD
Burleson, TX..................800-543-6558
L.C. Thompson Company
Kenosha, WI 800-558-4018
Lake Process Systems Inc
Lake Barrington, IL 800-331-9260
Lakeside Manufacturing Inc
Milwaukee, WI 888-558-8565
Lako Tool & Mfg Inc
Perrysburg, OH 800-228-2982
Lambeth Band Corporation
New Bedford, MA 508-984-4700
Liburdi Group of Companies
Mooresville, NC 800-533-9353
Lil' Orbits
Minneapolis, MN 800-228-8305
Livingston-Wilbor Corporation
Edison, NJ 908-322-8403
Lorenz Couplings
Cobourg, ON. 800-263-7782
Lucas Industrial
Cedar Hill, TX 800-877-1720
Lumsden Flexx Flow
Lancaster, PA 800-367-3664
M & R Sales & Svc Inc
Glen Ellyn, IL 800-736-6431
M O Industries Inc
Whippany, NJ 973-386-9228
M.H. Rhodes Cramer
South Windsor, CT 877-684-6464
Master Magnetics
Castle Rock, CO 800-525-3536
Mastercraft Industries Inc
Newburgh, NY 800-835-7812
McCormack Manufacturing Company
Lake Oswego, OR..............800-395-1593
Mckey Perforating Co Inc
New Berlin, WI................800-345-7373
Meadows Mills Inc
North Wilkesboro, NC 800-626-2282
Membrane Process & Controls
Edgar, WI 715-352-3206
Metal Master Sales Corp
Glendale Heights, IL............800-488-8729
Micro Solutions Ent Tech & Dev
Van Nuys, CA.................800-673-4968
Midwest Rubber Svc & Supply
Minneapolis, MN 800-537-7457
Midwest Stainless
Menomonie, WI 715-235-5472
Miller Metal Fabrication
Bridgeville, DE 302-337-2291
Miller Technical Svc
Plymouth, MI 734-414-1769
Mollenberg-Betz Inc
Buffalo, NY...................716-614-7473
Monarch-McLaren
Weston, ON 416-741-9675
Morse Manufacturing Co Inc
East Syracuse, NY 315-437-8475
Motion Industries Inc
Birmingham, AL 877-609-7975
Moyno
Springfield, OH 937-327-3111
Murtech Manufacturing
Kenilworth, NJ 908-245-1556
Nalge Process Technologies Group
Rochester, NY.................585-586-8800
National Band Saw Co
Santa Clarita, CA 800-851-5050
National Metal Industries
West Springfield, MA 800-628-8850
Nelles Automation
Houston, TX..................713-939-9399
Newman Sanitary Gasket Co
Lebanon, OH.................513-932-7379
Norgren Inc.
Littleton, CO 800-514-0129
Northland Process Piping
Isle, MN 320-679-2119

Ogden Manufacturing Company
Pittsburgh, PA 412-967-3906
Pacer Pumps
Lancaster, PA 800-233-3861
Package Machinery Co Inc
Holyoke, MA 413-315-3801
Parker-Hannifin Corp
Cleveland, OH 800-272-7537
Partex Corporation
Flint, MI 810-736-5656
Pengo Attachments Inc
Cokato, MN 800-599-0211
Piab Vacuum Products
Hingham, MA 800-321-7422
Plasti-Clip Corp
Milford, NH 800-882-2547
Polychem Corp
Mentor, OH 440-357-1500
Pres-Air-Trol Corporation
Altoona, WI. 800-431-2625
Pure Fit Nutrition Bars
Irvine, CA 866-787-3348
Pyromation Inc
Fort Wayne, IN 260-484-2580
Qosina Corporation
Ronkonkoma, NY 631-242-3000
Quadrant Epp USA Inc
Fort Wayne, IN 800-628-7264
Quality Industries
Cleveland, OH 216-961-5566
R K Electric Co Inc
Mason, OH 800-543-4936
R.H. Chandler Company
Saint Louis, MO 314-962-9353
Ralphs Pugh Conveyor Rollers
Benicia, CA. 800-486-0021
Ranger Blade Manufacturing Company
Traer, IA 800-377-7860
Rath Manufacturing Company
Janesville, WI 800-367-7284
Reading Plastic Fabricators
Reading, PA 610-926-3245
Rees Inc
Fremont, IN. 260-495-9811
Refrigeration Research
Brighton, MI 810-227-1151
Reid Boiler Works
Bellingham, WA 360-714-6157
Rigidized Metal Corp
Buffalo, NY. 800-836-2580
RM Waite Inc
Clintonville, WI 715-823-4327
Robert-James Sales
Buffalo, NY. 800-777-1325
Rolland Machining & Fabricating
Moneta, VA 973-827-6911
Salem-Republic Rubber Co
Sebring, OH 800-425-5079
Sanchelima International
Miami, FL 305-591-4343
Sani-Fit
Pasadena, CA 626-395-7895
Sanitary Couplers
Springboro, OH 513-743-0144
Seattle Refrigeration & Manufacturing
Seattle, WA 800-228-8881
Sellers Engineering Division
Danville, KY. 859-236-3181
Senior Flexonics
Bartlett, IL. 800-473-0474
Sew-Eurodrive Inc
Lyman, SC. 864-439-8792
Sharon Manufacturing Inc
Deer Park, NY 800-424-6455
Shingle Belting
King Of Prussia, PA 800-345-6294
Shivvers
Corydon, IA 641-872-1007
Simolex Rubber Corp
Plymouth, MI 734-453-4500
Sine Pump
Arvada, CO 888-504-8301
Smokehouse Limited
Franklinville, NC 800-554-8385
Southern Metal Fabricators Inc
Albertville, AL 800-989-1330
Special Products
Springfield, MO 417-881-6114
Specialty Blades
Staunton, VA 540-248-2200
Spot Wire Works Company
Philadelphia, PA 215-627-6124

Stainless Products
Somers, WC 800-558-9446
Standex International Corp.
Salem, NH. 603-893-9701
STD Precision Gear
West Bridgewater, MA 888-783-4327
Step Products
Round Rock, TX. 800-777-7837
Storm Industrial
Shawnee Mission, KS. 800-745-7483
Strahman Valves Inc
Bethlehem, PA 877-787-2462
Stroter Inc
Freeport, IL. 815-616-2506
Stutz Products Corp
Hartford City, IN. 765-348-2510
Super Radiator Coils
N Chesterfield, VA 800-229-2645
Super Steel
Milwaukee, WI 414-355-4800
Svedala Industries
Colorado Springs, CO. 719-471-3443
T & S Brass & Bronze Work
Travelers Rest, SC 800-476-4103
Tema Systems Inc
Cincinnati, OH 513-792-2840
Tente Casters Inc
Hebron, KY. 800-783-2470
Top Line Process Equipment Company
Bradford, PA 800-458-6095
Travis Manufacturing Corp
Alliance, OH 330-875-1661
Tropic KOOL
Largo, FL 727-581-2824
TruHeat Corporation
Allegan, MI. 800-879-6199
Tuchenhagen
Columbia, MD 410-910-6000
Unifiller Systems
Delta, BC. 888-733-8444
United Performance Metals
Northbrook, IL 888-922-0040
US Tsubaki Holdings Inc
Wheeling, IL. 800-323-7790
Valvinox
Iberville, QC 450-346-1981
Vaughn Belting Co-Main Acct
Spartanburg, SC 800-533-9086
Vilter Manufacturing Corporation
Cudahy, WI 414-744-0111
Wade Manufacturing Company
Tigard, OR 800-222-7246
Warner Electric Inc
South Beloit, IL. 800-234-3369
Waukesha Cherry-Burrell
Louisville, KY 502-491-4310
Waukesha Cherry-Burrell
Louisville, KY 800-252-5200
Waukesha Foundry Inc
Waukesha, WI. 800-727-0741
Waukesha Specialty Company
Darien, WI. 262-724-3700
Wico Corporation
Niles, IL. 800-367-9426
Wiegmann & Rose Thermxchanger
Oakland, CA 510-632-8828
Wilden Pump & Engineering LLC
Grand Terrace, CA 909-422-1700
Windhorst Blowmold
Euless, TX. 817-540-6639
Wire Belt Co Of America
Londonderry, NH 603-644-2500
Womack International Inc
Vallejo, CA 707-647-2370
World Wide Fitting Corp
Vernon Hills, IL 800-393-9894
Wright Metal Products Crates
Greenville, SC. 864-297-6610
Wt Nickell Co
Batavia, OH. 888-899-1991
Yates Industries Inc
St Clair Shores, MI 586-778-7680

Pharmaceutical Industry

Arro Corp
Hodgkins, IL. 877-929-2776
Decagon Devices Inc
Pullman, WA. 800-755-2751
Medical Packaging Corporation
Camarillo, CA. 805-388-2383

Plastic Fabricators

A Allred Marketing
Birmingham, AL. 205-251-3700
A La Carte
Chicago, IL 800-722-2370
A-A1 Aaction Bag
Denver, CO 800-783-1224
Abbott Industries
Paterson, NJ
ABC Letter Art
Los Angeles, CA. 888-261-5367
ABI Limited
Concord, ON. 800-297-8666
Abond Plastic Corporation
Lachine, QC 800-886-7947
Ace Stamp & Engraving
Lakewood, WA 253-582-3322
Ace Technical Plastics Inc
East Hartford, CT 860-278-2444
Achilles USA
Everett, WA 425-353-7000
Acme Bag Co
Chula Vista, CA 800-275-2263
Aco Container Systems
Pickering, ON 800-542-9942
Adam Electric Signs
Massillon, OH 888-886-9911
Advance Engineering Co
Canton, MI 800-497-6388
Advantage Puck Technologies
Corry, PA. 814-664-4810
AEP Industries
South Hackensack, NJ 800-999-2374
AEP Industries Inc
Mankato, MN 800-999-2374
Aero Housewares
Fayetteville, GA 770-914-4240
Aero Manufacturing Co
Clifton, NJ. 800-631-8378
Aeromat Plastics Inc
Burnsville, MN 888-286-8729
Alger Creations
Miami, FL 954-454-3272
All American Container
Miami, FL 305-887-0797
All American Poly
Piscataway, NJ 800-526-3551
Alouf Plastics
Orangeburg, NY 800-394-2247
ALP Lighting & Ceiling Products
Pennsauken, NJ. 800-633-7732
Alpack
Centerville, NA. 774-994-8086
Altira Inc
Miami, FL. 305-687-8074
Amcel
Watertown, MA. 800-225-7992
Amco Metals Indl
City Of Industry, CA. 626-855-2550
American Bag & Burlap Company
Chelsea, MA 617-884-7600
American Identification Industries
West Chicago, IL 800-255-8890
American Renolit Corp LA
Commerce, CA 323-721-2720
Ameriglobe LLC
Lafayette, LA 337-234-3211
Ametco Manufacturing Corp
Willoughby, OH 800-321-7042
Archer Daniels Midland Company
Chicago, IL. 312-634-8100
Arena Products
Rochester, NY. 844-762-0127
Art Poly Bag Co
Brooklyn, NY 800-278-7659
Artcraft Badge & Sign Company
Olney, MD. 800-739-0709
Artistic Packaging Concepts
Massapequa Pk, NY 516-797-4020
Atlantis Industries Inc
Milton, DE 302-684-8542
Audrey Signs
New York, NY 212-769-4992
B&B Neon Sign Company
Austin, TX. 800-791-6366
Bag Company
Kennesaw, GA 800-533-1931
Bag Masters
St Petersburg, FL 800-330-2247
Bagcraft Papercon
Chicago, IL. 800-621-8468

117

Baltimore Sign Company
Arnold, MD..............410-276-1500
Bardes Plastics Inc
Milwaukee, WI..............800-558-5161
Barrette Outdoor Living
Cleveland, OH..............800-336-2383
BAW Plastics Inc
Clairton, PA..............800-783-2229
Bayhead Products Corp.
Dover, NH..............800-229-4323
Beayl Weiner/Pak
Pacific Palisades, CA..............310-454-1354
Bel-Art Products
Wayne, NJ..............800-423-5278
Belleview
Brookline, NH..............603-878-1583
Bergen Barrel & Drum Company
Kearny, NJ..............201-998-3500
Berloc Manufacturing & Sign Company
Sun Valley, CA..............818-503-9823
Berry Global
Evansville, IN..............800-343-1295
BG Industries
Lemont, IL..............800-800-5761
Blako Industries
Dunbridge, OH..............419-833-4491
Bloomfield Industries
St. Louis, MO..............888-356-5362
BOC Plastics Inc
Winston Salem, NC..............800-334-8687
Bonar Plastics
West Chicago, IL..............800-295-3725
Boss Manufacturing Co
Kewanee, IL..............800-447-4581
Brechteen
Chesterfield, MI..............586-949-2240
Brentwood Plastics In
St Louis, MO..............314-968-1135
Brown International Corp LLC
Winter Haven, FL..............863-299-2111
Brown Paper Goods Co
Waukegan, IL..............847-688-1450
Buckhorn Inc
Milford, OH..............800-543-4454
Budget Blinds Inc
Orange, CA..............800-800-9250
Bulk Lift International, LLC
Carpentersville, IL..............800-879-2247
Burgess Mfg. - Oklahoma
Guthrie, OK..............800-804-1913
C R Daniels Inc
Ellicott City, MD..............800-933-2638
C R Mfg
Waverly, NE..............877-789-5844
C-P Flexible Packaging
Newtown, PA..............800-448-8183
Canton Sign Co
Canton, OH..............330-456-7151
Caraustar
Franklin, KY..............270-586-9565
Caraustar Industries, Inc.
Archdale, NC..............800-223-1373
Cardinal Packaging
Evansville, IN..............800-343-1295
Cardinal Rubber & Seal Inc
Roanoke, VA..............800-542-5737
Carlisle Food Svc Products Inc
Oklahoma City, OK..............800-654-8210
Carlisle Plastics
Minneapolis, MN..............952-884-1309
Carolina Glove Co
Conover, NC..............800-335-1918
Carroll Co
Garland, TX..............800-527-5722
Carson Industries
Pomona, CA..............800-735-5566
Cash Caddy
Palm Desert, CA..............888-522-2221
Castle Bag Co.
Wilmington, DE..............302-656-1001
Cayne Industrial Sales Corp
Bronx, NY..............718-993-5800
Ccw Products
Arvada, CO..............303-427-9663
CDF Corp
Plymouth, MA..............800-443-1920
Cell-O-Core Company
Sharon Center, OH..............800-239-4370
Cello Bag Company
Bowling Green, KY..............800-347-0338
Central Bag Company
Leavenworth, KS..............913-250-0325

Central Fine Pack Inc
Fort Wayne, IN..............260-432-3027
Central Package & Display
Minneapolis, MN..............763-425-7444
Chalmur Bag Company, LLC
Philadelphia, PA..............800-349-2247
Champion Plastics
Clifton, NJ..............800-526-1230
Chase-Doors
Cincinnati, OH..............800-543-4455
Checker Bag Co
St Louis, MO..............800-489-3130
Chem-Tainer Industries Inc
West Babylon, NY..............800-275-2436
Chem-Tainer Industries Inc
West Babylon, NY..............800-938-8896
Chester Plastics
Chester, NS..............902-275-3522
Chili Plastics
Rochester, NY..............585-889-4680
Chinet Company
Laguna Niguel, CA..............949-348-1711
Chipmaker Tooling Supply
Whittier, CA..............800-659-5840
Chocolate Concepts
Hartville, OH..............330-877-3322
Choctaw-Kaul Distribution Company
Detroit, MI..............313-894-9494
Choklit Molds LTD
Lincoln, RI..............800-777-6653
City Signs LLC
Jackson, TN..............877-248-9744
CKS Packaging
Atlanta, GA..............800-800-4257
Clawson Container Company
Clarkston, MI..............800-325-8700
Clear View Bag Co Inc Of Nc
Albany, NY..............800-458-7153
Clear View Bag Company
Thomasville, NC..............336-885-8131
Cleveland Plastic Films
Elyria, OH..............800-832-6799
Cleveland Specialties Co
Loveland, OH..............513-677-9787
CMD Corporation
Appleton, WI..............920-730-6888
Coast Scientific
Rancho Santa Fe, CA..............800-445-1544
Collins & Aikman
Canton, OH..............800-321-0244
Colonial Transparent Products Company
Hicksville, NY..............516-822-4430
Conn Container Corp
North Haven, CT..............203-248-0241
Connecticut Laminating Co Inc
New Haven, CT..............800-753-9119
Consolidated Container Co LLC
Atlanta, GA..............888-831-2184
Consolidated Plastics Co Inc
Stow, OH..............800-858-5001
Container Specialties
Melrose Park, IL..............800-548-7513
Container Supply Co
Garden Grove, CA..............562-594-0937
Contico Container
Norwalk, CA..............562-921-9967
Continental Commercial Products
Bridgeton, MO..............800-325-1051
Continental Packaging Corporation
Elgin, IL..............847-289-6400
Continental Products
Mexico, MO..............800-325-0216
Contour Packaging
Philadelphia, PA..............215-457-1600
Convoy
Canton, OH..............800-899-1583
Cope Plastics Inc
Alton, IL..............800-851-5510
Cork Specialties
Miami, FL..............305-477-1506
Covestro LLC
Sheffield, MA..............800-628-5084
Crayex Corp
Piqua, OH..............800-837-1747
Creative Essentials
Ronkonkoma, NY..............800-355-5891
Creative Forming
Ripon, WI..............920-748-7285
Creative Packaging
Hayward, CA..............510-785-6500
Crespac Incorporated
Tucker, GA..............800-438-1900

Crystal-Flex Packaging Corporation
Rockville Centre, NY..............888-246-7325
CTK Plastics
Moose Jaw, SK..............800-667-8847
Custom Bottle of Connecticut
Naugatuck, CT..............203-723-6661
Custom Foam Molders
Foristell, MO..............636-441-2307
Custom ID Systems
Venice, FL..............800-242-8430
Custom Molders
Rocky Mount, NC..............919-688-8061
Custom Plastics Inc
Decatur, GA..............404-373-1691
Custom Poly Packaging
Fort Wayne, IN..............800-548-6603
Dadant & Sons Inc
Hamilton, IL..............888-922-1293
Danafilms Inc
Westborough, MA..............508-366-8884
Danbury Plastics
Cumming, GA..............678-455-7391
Dansk International Designs
Bristol, PA..............914-697-6400
Dart Canada Inc.
Toronto, ON..............800-465-9696
Dart Container Corp.
Mason, MI..............800-248-5960
Dashco
Gloucester, ON..............613-834-6825
Davron Technologies Inc
Chattanooga, TN..............423-870-1888
Dayton Bag & Burlap Co
Dayton, OH..............800-543-3400
De Ster Corporation
Atlanta, GA..............800-237-8270
Decker Plastics
Council Bluffs, IA..............866-869-6293
DEFCO
Landenberg, PA..............215-274-8245
DEL-Tec Packaging Inc
Greer, SC..............800-747-8683
Delfin Design & Mfg
Rancho Sta Marg, CA..............800-354-7919
Delta Cooling Towers Inc
Rockaway, NJ..............800-289-3358
Den Ray Sign Company
Jackson, TN..............800-530-7291
Design Packaging Company
Glencoe, IL..............800-321-7659
Design Plastics Inc
Omaha, NE..............800-491-0786
Design Specialties Inc
Hamden, CT..............800-999-1584
Designers Plastics
Clearwater, FL..............727-573-1643
Detroit Forming
Southfield, MI..............248-440-1317
Development Workshop Inc
Idaho Falls, ID..............800-657-5597
Dimension Graphics Inc
Grand Rapids, MI..............855-476-1281
Dinosaur Plastics
Houston, TX..............713-923-2278
Display Tray
Mont-Royal, QC..............800-782-8861
Dispoz-O Plastics
Fountain Inn, SC..............864-862-4004
Diversified Lighting Diffusers Inc
Copiague, NY..............800-234-5464
Dixie Poly Packaging
Greenville, SC..............864-268-3751
Do-It Corp
South Haven, MI..............800-426-4822
Donoco Industries
Huntington Beach, CA..............888-822-8763
Dordan Manufacturing Co
Woodstock, IL..............800-663-5460
Douglas Stephen Plastics Inc
Paterson, NJ..............973-523-3030
Dow Packaging
Midland, MI..............800-331-6451
Dowling Signs Inc
Fredericksburg, VA..............800-572-2100
Dub Harris Corporation
Pomona, CA..............909-596-6300
Dwinell's Central Neon
Yakima, WA..............800-932-8832
Dyna-Veyor Inc
Newark, NJ..............800-326-5009
East Coast Group New York
Springfield Gardens, NY..............718-527-8464

Eastern Poly Packaging Company
Brooklyn, NY 800-421-6006
Eaton Manufacturing Co
Houston, TX 800-328-6610
Eaton Quade Plastics & Sign Co
Oklahoma City, OK 405-236-4475
Economy Label Sales Company
Daytona Beach, FL 386-253-4741
Ed Smith's Stencil Works LTD
New Orleans, LA 504-525-2128
Edco Industries
Bridgeport, CT 203-333-8982
Ellehammer Industries
Langley, BC 604-882-9326
Elliot Lee
Cedarhurst, NY 516-569-9595
Elopak Americas
Wixom, MI 248-486-4600
Elrene Home Fashions
New York, NY 212-213-0425
Emco Industrial Plastics
Cedar Grove, NJ 800-292-9906
Emedco
Williamsville, NY 877-765-8386
Encore Plastics
Huntington Beach, CA 888-822-8763
Engineered Plastics Inc
Gibsonville, NC 800-711-1740
Engraving Services Co.
Woodville South, SA
Erell Manufacturing Co
Elk Grove Vlg, IL 800-622-6334
ES Robbins Corp
Muscle Shoals, AL 800-633-3325
Esterle Mold & Machine Co Inc
Stow, OH 800-411-4086
Everett Rubber Stamp
Everett, WA 425-258-6747
Exhibitron Co
Grants Pass, OR 800-437-4571
Fabohio Inc
Uhrichsville, OH 740-922-4233
Fabreeka International
Boise, ID 800-423-4469
Fabri-Kal Corp
Kalamazoo, MI 800-888-5054
Fan Bag Company
Chicago, IL 773-342-2752
Faribault Manufacturing Co
Faribault, MN 800-447-6043
Farnell Packaging
Dartmouth, NS 800-565-9378
Fast Bags
Fort Worth, TX 800-321-3687
Fato Industries
Kankakee, IL 815-932-3015
Federal Heath Sign Co LLC
Oceanside, CA 800-527-9495
Ferrer Corporation
San Juan, PR 787-761-5151
Field Manufacturing Corporation
Torrance, CA. 310-781-9292
Film X
Dayville, CT 800-628-6128
Film-Pak Inc
Crowley, TX 800-526-1838
Filmco Inc
Aurora, OH 800-545-8457
Filmpack Plastic Corporation
Dayton, NJ 732-329-6523
Finn Industries
Ontario, CA 909-930-1500
Firl Industries Inc
Fond Du Lac, WI 800-558-4890
First Plastics Co Inc
Leominster, MA 978-840-6908
Five-M Plastics Company
Allentown, PA. 610-628-4291
Flex Products
Carlstadt, NJ 800-526-6273
FLEXcon Company
Spencer, MA. 508-885-8200
Flexible Foam Products
Elkhart, IN. 800-678-3626
FMI Display
Elkins Park, PA. 215-663-1998
Foamex
Cornelius, NC 704-892-8081
Formflex
Bloomingdale, IN 800-255-7659
Forrest Engraving Company
New Rochelle, NY 914-632-9892

FORT Hill Sign Products Inc
Hopedale, MA. 781-321-4320
Fort James Canada
Toronto, ON 416-784-1621
Fortune Plastics, Inc
Old Saybrook, CT 800-243-0306
France Personalized Signs
Cleveland, OH 216-241-2198
Franklin Rubber Stamp Co
Wilmington, DE 302-654-8841
Frankston Paper Box Company of Texas
Frankston, TX 903-876-2550
Fredman Bag Co
Milwaukee, WI 800-945-5686
Freeman Electric Co Inc
Panama City, FL 850-785-7448
Fremont Die Cut Products
Fremont, OH 800-223-3177
Fresno Pallet, Inc.
Sultana, CA 559-591-4111
Frontier Bag
Kansas City, MO 816-765-4811
Fuller Industries LLC
Great Bend, KS. 800-522-0499
Fulton-Denver Co
Denver, CO. 800-521-1414
Gary Manufacturing Company
National City, CA 800-775-0804
Gary Plastic Packaging Corporation
Bronx, NY 800-221-8151
Gary Plastic Packaging Corporation
Bronx, NY 800-227-4279
Gastro-Gnomes
West Hartford, CT. 800-747-4666
GE Appliances
Louisville, KY 877-959-8688
Geerpres Inc
Muskegon, MI. 231-773-3211
Gelberg Signs
Washington, DC 800-443-5237
Gemini Plastic Films Corporation
Garfield, NJ. 800-789-4732
General Films Inc
Covington, OH 888-436-3456
General Neon Sign Co
San Antonio, TX 210-227-1203
GENESTA
Rockwall, TX 972-771-1653
Genpak
Peterborough, ON 800-461-1995
Genpak LLC
Lakeville, MN 800-328-4556
Genpak LLC
Charlotte, NC 800-626-6695
Gessner Products
Ambler, PA. 800-874-7808
Gibraltar Packaging Group Inc
Hastings, NE. 402-463-1366
Glover Latex
Anaheim, CA. 800-243-5110
GM Nameplate
Seattle, WA. 800-366-7668
Goebel Fixture Co
Hutchinson, MN 888-339-0509
Goex Corporation
Janesville, WI 608-754-3303
Golden West Packaging Concept
Lake Forest, CA 949-855-9646
Goldmax Industries
City Of Industry, CA. 626-964-8820
Graham Engineering Corp
York, PA 717-848-3755
Gralab Instruments
Centerville, OH. 800-876-8353
Grande Ronde Sign Company
La Grande, OR 541-963-5841
Great Northern Corp.
Appleton, WI 800-236-3671
Great Southern Corp
Memphis, TN 800-421-7802
Green Tek
Janesville, WI 800-747-6440
Greif Inc
Delaware, OH 740-549-6000
Gulf Arizona Packaging
Humble, TX 800-364-3887
Gulf Coast Plastics
Tampa, FL 800-277-7491
Gulf Packaging Company
Safety Harbor, FL 800-749-3466
H P Mfg Co
Cleveland, OH 216-361-6500

H&H Lumber Company
Amarillo, TX. 806-335-1813
Habasit America Plastic Div
Reading, PA 800-445-7898
Hal-One Plastics
Olathe, KS. 800-626-5784
Hall Manufacturing Co
Ringwood, NJ 973-962-6022
Hall Safety Apparel
Uhrichsville, OH. 800-232-3671
Handgards Inc
El Paso, TX 800-351-8161
Handy Wacks Corp
Sparta, MI. 800-445-4434
Hank Rivera Associates
Dearborn, MI 313-581-8300
Harbor Pallet Company
Anaheim, CA 714-871-0932
Harco Enterprises
Peterborough, ON 800-361-5361
Hardin Signs Inc
Peoria, IL 309-688-4111
Have Our Plastic Inc
Mississauga, ON. 800-263-5995
Hayward Industries Inc
Clemmons, NC 336-712-9900
Heath & Company
Roswell, GA 770-650-2724
Hedwin Division
Baltimore, MD 800-638-1012
Herche Warehouse
Denver, CO 303-371-8186
Heritage Bag Co
Roanoke, TX. 800-527-2247
Highland Plastics Inc
Mira Loma, CA. 800-368-0491
Himolene
Carrollton, TX 800-777-4411
HMG Worldwide In-Store Marketing
New York, NY 212-736-2300
Hoarel Sign Co
Amarillo, TX. 806-373-2175
Hoffmaster Group Inc
Oshkosh, WI 800-367-2877
Hoffmaster Group Inc.
Oshkosh, WI 800-558-9300
Hollywood Banners
Copiague, NY 800-691-5652
Holsman Sign Svc
Cleveland, OH 216-761-4433
Home Plastics Inc
Des Moines, IA 515-265-2562
Hood Packaging
Burlington, ON 877-462-6627
HPI North America/   Plastics
Eagan, MN 800-752-7462
HPI North America/Plastics
Chicago, IL. 800-327-3534
Hubco Inc
Hutchinson, KS. 800-563-1867
Hudson Poly Bag Inc
Hudson, MA 800-229-7566
Hughes Manufacturing Company
Giddings, TX 800-414-0765
Huntsman Packaging
South Deerfield, MA 413-665-2145
Huntsman Packaging Corporation
Birmingham, Bi. 205-328-4720
Ideal Office Supply & Rubber Stamp Company
Kingsport, TN 423-246-7371
Image Plastics
Houston, TX 800-289-2811
Indeco Products Inc
San Marcos, TX 888-246-3326
Indian Valley Industries
Johnson City, NY 800-659-5111
Indiana Bottle Co
Scottsburg, IN. 800-752-8702
Indiana Vac Form Inc
Warsaw, IN 574-269-1725
Indianapolis Container Company
Indianapolis, IN 800-760-3318
Industrial Nameplate Inc
Warminster, PA. 800-878-6263
Inland Showcase & Fixture Company
Fresno, CA 559-237-4158
Inline Plastic Corp
McDonough, GA 678-466-3467
Innovative Molding
Sebastopol, CA. 707-829-2666
Innovative Plastics Corp
Orangeburg, NY 845-359-7500

119

Insulair
Vernalis, CA 800-343-3402
Inteplast Bags & Films Corporation
Delta, BC 604-946-5431
Intermold Corporation
Greenville, SC 864-627-0300
International Polymers Corp
Allentown, PA 800-526-0953
Interplast
Troy, OH 937-332-1110
Interstate Packaging
White Bluff, TN 800-251-1072
Intralox LLC
Harahan, LA 800-535-8848
Intrex
Bethel, CT 203-792-7400
IPL Plastics
Edmundston, NB 800-739-9595
Island Poly
Westbury, NY 800-338-4433
J A Heilferty & Co
Teaneck, NJ 201-836-5060
J L Clark Corp
Rockford, IL 815-962-8861
J.E. Roy
St Claire, QC 418-883-2711
James River Canada
North York, ON 416-789-5151
Jamison Plastic Corporation
Allentown, PA 610-391-1400
Jarden Home Brands
Cloquet, MN 218-879-6700
Jarden Home Brands
Daleville, IN 800-392-2575
Jarisch Paper Box Company
North Adams, MA 413-663-5396
Jeb Plastics
Wilmington, DE 800-556-2247
Jeffcoat Signs
Gainesville, FL 877-377-4248
Jescorp
Des Plaines, IL 847-299-7800
Jet Plastica Industries
Hatfield, PA
Jewell Bag Company
Dallas, TX 214-749-1223
JH Display & Fixture
Greenwood, IN 317-888-0631
Jilson Group
Lodi, NJ 800-969-5400
Jim Scharf Holdings
Perdue, SK 800-667-9727
Johnson Refrigerated Truck
Rice Lake, WI 800-922-8360
Johnstown Manufacturing
Columbus, OH 614-236-8853
Jomar Corp
Egg Harbor Twp, NJ 609-646-8000
Jomar Plastics Industry
Nanty Glo, PA 800-681-4039
Jones-Zylon Co
West Lafayette, OH 800-848-8160
Joseph Struhl Co Inc
New Hyde Park, NY 800-552-0023
Juice Merchandising Corp
Kansas City, MO 800-950-1998
Juice Tree
Omaha, NE 714-891-4425
Jupiter Mills Corporation
Roslyn, NY 800-853-5121
Just Plastics Inc
New York, NY 212-569-8500
K & I Creative Plastics & Wood
Jacksonville, FL 904-387-0438
K-C Products Company
Van Nuys, CA 818-267-1600
Kadon Corporation
Milford, OH 937-299-0088
Kal Pac Corp
Montgomery, NY 800-852-5722
Keena Corporation
Newton, MA 617-244-9800
Kendrick Johnson & Assoc Inc
Minneapolis, MN 800-826-1271
Kenro
Fredonia, WI 262-692-2411
Key Packaging Co
Sarasota, FL 941-355-2728
KHM Plastics Inc
Gurnee, IL 847-249-4910
Kimball Companies
East Longmeadow, MA 413-525-1881

King Plastic Corp
North Port, FL 800-780-5502
Kitchener Plastics
Kitchener, ON 800-429-5633
Klever Kuvers
Pasadena, CA 626-355-8441
Klockner Pentaplast of America
Gordonsville, VA 540-832-3600
KM International Corp
Kenton, TN 731-749-8700
Knobs Unlimited
Bowling Green, OH 419-353-8215
Kord Products Inc.
Brantford, ON 800-452-9070
Kornylak Corp
Hamilton, OH 800-837-5676
Kuriyama Of America Inc
Schaumburg, IL 800-800-0320
L & C Plastic Bags
Covington, OH 937-473-2968
L T Hampel Corp
Germantown, WI 800-681-6979
L&H Wood Manufacturing Company
Farmington, MI 248-474-9000
L&L Engraving Company
Gilford, NH 888-524-3032
Lafayette Sign Company
Little Falls, NJ 800-343-5366
Lakeside Manufacturing Inc
Milwaukee, WI 888-558-8565
Lakeside-Aris Manufacturing
Milwaukee, WI 800-558-8565
Lamb Sign
Manassas, VA 703-791-7960
Lambert Company
Chillicothe, MO 800-821-7667
Lamcraft Inc
Lees Summit, MO 800-821-1333
Landis Plastics
Alsip, IL 708-396-1470
Laughlin Sales Corp
Fort Worth, TX 817-625-7756
Laydon Company
Brown City, MI 810-346-2952
Leathertone
Findlay, OH 419-429-0188
Leeds Conveyor Manufacturer Company
Guilford, CT 800-724-1088
Legible Signs
Loves Park, IL 800-435-4177
Letica Corp
Rochester Hills, MI 800-538-4221
Lexington Logistics LLC
Portage, WI 800-356-8150
Linvar
Hartford, CT 800-282-5288
Liqui-Box Corp
Richmond, VA 804-325-1400
Liquitane
Berwick, PA 570-759-6200
LMK Containers
Centerville, UT 626-821-9984
Locknane
Everett, WA 800-848-9854
Long Island Stamp Corporation
Flushing, NY 800-547-8267
Longhorn Packaging Inc
San Antonio, TX 800-433-7974
LoTech Industries
Lakewood, CO 800-295-0199
LPI Imports
Chicago, IL 877-389-6563
Luetzow Industries
South Milwaukee, WI 800-558-6055
Lynn Sign Inc
Andover, OH 800-225-5764
M & E Mfg Co Inc
Kingston, NY 845-331-2110
M & G Packaging Corp
Floral Park, NY 800-240-5288
M S Plastics & Packaging Inc
Butler, NJ 800-593-1802
M&R Flexible Packaging
Springboro, OH 800-543-3380
Maco Bag Corp
Newark, NY 315-226-1000
Majestic
Bridgeport, CT 203-367-7900
Malpack Polybag
Ajax, ON 905-428-3751
Marco Products
Adrian, MI 517-265-3333

Marpac Industries
Philmont, NY 888-462-7722
Marshall Plastic Film Inc
Martin, MI 269-672-5511
Martin/Baron
Irwindale, CA 626-960-5153
Mason Transparent Package Company
Armonk, NY 718-792-6000
Max Packaging
Attalla, AL 800-543-5369
May-Wes Manufacturing Inc
Hutchinson, MN 800-788-6483
Maypak Inc
Wayne, NJ 973-696-0780
MBX Packaging Specialists
Wausau, WI 715-845-1171
Mcbride Sign Co
Madison Heights, VA 434-847-4151
McQueen Sign & Lighting
Canton, OH 330-452-5769
MDR International
North Miami, FL 305-944-5019
Measurex/S&L Plastics
Nazareth, PA 800-752-0650
Melmat Inc
Huntington Beach, CA 800-635-6289
Merchandising Inventives
Waukegan, IL 800-367-5653
Merryweather Foam Inc
Sylacauga, AL 256-249-8546
Micelli Chocolate Mold Company
West Babylon, NY 631-752-2888
Micro Qwik
Cross Plains, WI 608-798-3071
Microplas Industries
Dunwoody, GA 800-952-4528
Midco Plastics
Enterprise, KS 800-235-2729
Midland Manufacturing Co
Monroe, IA 800-394-2625
Millhiser
Richmond, VA 800-446-2247
Mimi et Cie
Seattle, WA 206-545-1850
Mini-Bag Company
Farmingdale, NY 631-694-3325
MIT Poly-Cart Corp
New York, NY 800-234-7659
Mohawk Northern Plastics
Auburn, WA 800-426-1100
Mold-Rite Plastics LLC
Twinsburg, OH 330-425-4206
Molded Container Corporation
Portland, OR 503-233-8601
Monument Industries Inc
Bennington, VT 802-442-8187
Moser Bag & Paper Company
Cleveland, OH 800-433-6638
Mount Vernon Plastics
Mamaroneck, NY 914-698-1122
Mr Ice Bucket
New Brunswick, NJ 732-545-0420
Mulholland-Harper Company
Denton, MD 800-882-3052
Mullnix Packages Inc
Fort Wayne, IN 260-747-3149
Multi-Plastics Extrusions Inc
Hazleton, PA 570-455-2021
Naltex
Austin, TX 800-531-5112
NAP Industries
Brooklyn, NY 877-635-4948
National Marker Co Inc
North Smithfield, RI 800-453-2727
National Poly Bag Manufacturing Corporation
Brooklyn, NY 718-629-9800
National Sign Corporation
Seattle, WA 206-282-0700
NCC
Groveland, FL 800-429-9037
Neokraft Signs Inc
Lewiston, ME 800-339-2258
Net Pack Systems
Oakland, ME 207-465-4531
Newell Brands
Atlanta, GA
Newman Sanitary Gasket Co
Lebanon, OH 513-932-7379
Nolon Industries
Mantua, OH 330-274-2283
Norgus Silk Screen Co Inc
Clifton, NJ 973-365-0600

North American Packaging Corp
New York, NY.....................800-499-3521
North American Plastic Manufacturing Company
Bethel, CT........................800-934-7752
Northeast Packaging Materials
Monsey, NY......................845-426-2900
Northwind Inc
Alpena, AR.......................877-937-2585
Noteworthy Company
Amsterdam, NY...................800-696-7849
Novelty Crystal
Long Island City, NY.............800-622-0250
Now Plastics Inc
East Longmeadow, MA..........413-525-1010
Nu-Trend Plastics Thermoformer
Jacksonville, FL..................904-353-5936
Nucon Corporation
Deerfield, IL......................877-545-0070
Nutty Bavarian
Sanford, FL.......................800-382-4788
Nyman Manufacturing Company
Rumford, RI......................401-438-3410
NYP
Leola, PA.........................800-541-0961
Occidental Chemical Corporation
Dallas, TX........................800-733-3665
Ockerlund Industries
Addison, IL.......................708-771-7707
Oklahoma Neon
Tulsa, OK........................888-707-6366
Olcott Plastics
St Charles, IL.....................888-313-5277
Olde Thompson Inc
Oxnard, CA.......................800-827-1565
OMNOVA Solutions
Fairlawn, OH.....................330-869-4200
Ontario Glove and Safety Products
Kitchener, ON....................800-265-4554
ORBIS
Oconomowoc, WI................262-560-5000
ORBIS
Oconomowoc, WI................800-890-7292
Orbis Corp.
Rexdale, ON......................800-890-7292
OWD
Tupper Lake, NY.................800-836-1693
Owens-Illinois Inc
Perrysburg, OH...................567-336-5000
P M Plastics
Pewaukee, WI....................262-691-1700
Pace Packaging Corp
Fairfield, NJ......................800-867-2726
Pacific Oasis Enterprise Inc
Santa Fe Springs, CA.............800-424-1475
Pacific Paper Box Co
Cudahy, CA.......................323-771-7733
Packaging Associates
Randolph, NJ.....................973-252-8890
Packing Material Company
Southfield, MI....................248-489-7000
Pactiv LLC
Lake Forest, IL...................800-476-4300
Pak 2000 Inc
Mirror Lake, NH..................603-569-3700
Pak-Sak Industries I
Sparta, MI........................800-748-0431
Pallet Management Systems
Lawrenceville, VA................800-446-1804
Palmer Snyder
Brookfield, WI....................800-762-0415
Pan Pacific Plastics Inc
Hayward, CA.....................888-475-6888
Papelera Puertorriquena
Utuado, PR.......................787-894-2098
Par-Pak
Houston, TX......................713-686-6700
Par-Pak
Houston, TX......................888-727-7252
Parade Packaging
Mundelein, IL.....................847-566-6264
Paradigm Packaging Inc
Upland, CA.......................909-985-2750
Paragon Packaging
Ferndale, CA......................888-615-0065
Parisian Novelty Company
Homewood, IL....................773-847-1212
Park Custom Molding
Linden, NJ........................908-486-8882
Parkway Plastic Inc
Piscataway, NJ...................800-881-4996
Parsons Manufacturing Corp.
Menlo Park, CA..................650-324-4726

Parta
Kent, OH.........................800-543-5781
Party Yards
Casselberry, FL...................877-501-4400
Peerless Packages
Cleveland, OH....................216-464-3620
Pelco Packaging Corporation
Stirling, NJ.......................908-647-3500
Pelican Displays
Homer, IL.........................800-627-1517
Pelican Products Inc
Bronx, NY........................800-552-8820
Penda Form Corp
New Concord, OH................800-837-2574
Penley Corporation
West Paris, ME....................800-368-6449
Penn Bottle & Supply Company
Philadelphia, PA..................215-365-5700
Penn Products
Portland, CT......................800-490-7366
Perfex Corporation
Poland, NY.......................800-848-8483
Peter Gray Corporation
Andover, MA.....................978-470-0990
Pexco Packaging Corporation
Toledo, OH.......................800-227-9950
Pfeil & Holding Inc
Woodside, NY....................800-247-7955
Phoenix Sign Company
Aberdeen, WA....................360-532-1111
Pilant Corp
Bloomington, IN..................800-366-3525
Pilgrim Plastics
Brockton, MA.....................800-343-7810
Pioneer Plastics Inc
Dixon, KY........................800-951-1551
Plascal Corp
Farmingdale, NY.................800-899-7527
Plastech Corp
Atlanta, GA.......................404-355-9682
Plasti Print Inc
Burlingame, CA...................650-652-4950
Plasti-Clip Corp
Milford, NH.......................800-882-2547
Plasti-Line
Knoxville, TN.....................800-444-7446
Plastic Assembly Corporation
Ayer, MA
Plastic Craft Products Corp
West Nyack, NY..................800-627-3010
Plastic Fantastics/Buck Signs
Ashland, OR......................800-482-1776
Plastic Suppliers Inc
Columbus, OH....................800-722-5577
Plastic Tagtrade Check
Essexville, MI.....................989-892-7913
Plastic Turning Company
Leominster, MA...................978-534-8326
Plastican Corporation
Fairfield, NJ......................973-227-7817
Plastics Industries
Athens, TN........................800-894-4876
Plastipak Packaging
Plymouth, MI.....................734-354-3510
Plastipro
Los Angeles, CA..................800-779-0561
Plastiques Cascades Group
Montreal, QC.....................888-703-6515
Plaxall Inc
Long Island City, NY.............800-876-5706
Podnar Plastics Inc
Kent, OH.........................800-673-5277
Polar Plastics
St Laurent, QC....................514-331-0207
Poliplastic
Granby, QC.......................450-378-8417
Poly Processing Co
French Camp, CA.................877-325-3142
Poly Shapes Corporation
Elyria, OH........................800-605-9359
Polybottle Group
Surrey, BC........................604-594-4999
PolyConversions, Inc.
Rantoul, IL........................888-893-3330
Polyplastic Forms Inc
Farmingdale, NY.................800-428-7659
Port Erie Plastics Inc
Harborcreek, PA..................814-899-7602
Portco Corporation
Vancouver, WA...................800-426-1794
Prairie Packaging Inc
Mooresville, NC...................704-660-6600

Pretium Packaging
Chesterfield, MO..................314-727-8673
Pretium Packaging
Hazle Twp, PA....................570-459-1800
Printpack Inc.
Atlanta, GA.......................404-460-7000
Priority Plastics Inc
Grinnell, IA.......................800-798-3512
Pro-Gram Plastics Inc
Geneva, OH.......................440-466-8080
Progressive Plastics
Cleveland, OH....................800-252-0053
Prolon
Port Gibson, MS..................888-480-9828
Quality Container Company
Ypsilanti, MI......................734-481-1373
Quality Films
Three Rivers, MI..................269-679-5263
Quality Plastic Bag Corporation
Flushing, NY......................800-532-2247
Quantum Performance Films
Streamwood, IL...................800-323-6963
Quantum Storage Systems Inc
Miami, FL.........................800-685-4665
Quintex Corp
Nampa, ID........................208-467-1113
Qyk Syn Industries
Miami, FL.........................800-354-5640
R C Molding Inc
Greer, SC.........................864-879-7279
R H Saw Corp
Barrington, IL.....................847-381-8777
Rainbow Neon Sign Company
Houston, TX......................713-923-2759
Ram Industries
Erwin, TN........................800-523-3883
Rand-Whitney Group LLC
Worcester, MA....................508-791-2301
RAPAC Inc
Oakland, TN......................800-280-6333
Ray C. Sprosty Bag Company
Wooster, OH......................330-264-8559
Rayne Sign Co
Rayne, LA.........................337-334-4276
Reading Plastic Fabricators
Reading, PA.......................610-926-3245
Redi-Call Inc
Reno, NV.........................800-648-1849
Reese Enterprises Inc
Rosemount, MN..................800-328-0953
Regal Plastic Company
Mission, KS.......................800-852-1556
Regal Plastic Supply Co
Kansas City, MO..................800-444-6390
Regina USA
Oak Creek, WI....................414-571-0032
Reidler Decal Corporation
Saint Clair, PA....................800-628-7770
Reilly Foam Corporation
Conshohocken, PA................610-834-1900
Reliance Product
Winnipeg, MB.....................800-665-0258
Rez-Tech Corp
Kent, OH.........................800-673-5277
Richard Read Construction Company
Arcadia, CA.......................888-450-7343
Richards Packaging
Memphis, TN.....................800-583-0327
Riverside Manufacturing Company
Arlington Hts, IL..................800-877-3349
Rjr Technologies
Oakland, CA......................510-638-5901
RMI-C/Rotonics Manaufacturing
Bensenville, IL....................630-773-9510
Roberts Poly Pro Inc
Charlotte, NC.....................800-269-7409
Robinson Industries Inc
Coleman, MI......................989-465-6111
Rochester Midland Corp
Rochester, NY....................800-387-7174
Roechling Engineered Plastics
Gastonia, NC.....................800-541-4419
Roll-O-Sheets Canada
Barrie, ON........................888-767-3456
Rolland Machining & Fabricating
Moneta, VA.......................973-827-6911
Ropak
Oak Brook, IL.....................800-527-2267
Roplast Industries Inc
Oroville, CA.......................800-767-5278
Ross & Wallace Inc
Hammond, LA....................800-854-2300

Rosson Sign Co
Macon, GA 478-788-3905
Roth Sign Systems
Petaluma, CA 800-585-7446
Rowland Technologies
Wallingford, CT 203-269-9500
Royal Ecoproducts
Vaughan, ON 800-465-7670
RubaTex Polymer
Middlefield, OH 440-632-1691
Rutan Poly Industries Inc
Mahwah, NJ 800-872-1474
RXI Silgan Specialty Plastics
Triadelphia, WV 304-547-9100
Rytec Corporation
Milwaukee, WI 888-467-9832
Sabert Corp
Sayreville, NJ 800-722-3781
Sacramento Bag Manufacturing
Woodland, CA 530-662-6130
Saeplast Canada
St John, NB 800-567-3966
Samuel P. Harris
Rumford, RI 401-438-4020
Samuel Strapping Systems Inc
Woodridge, IL 800-323-4424
San Miguel Label Manufacturing
Ciales, PR 787-871-3120
Sani-Top Products
De Leon Springs, FL 800-874-6094
Schlueter Company
Janesville, WI 800-359-1700
Schoeneck Containers Inc
New Berlin, WI 262-786-9360
Scott Sign Systems
Sarasota, FL 800-237-9447
Sealed Air Corp
Charlotte, NC 800-391-5645
Seiler Plastics
St Louis, MO 888-673-4537
Selby Sign Co Inc
Pocomoke City, MD 410-742-0095
Semco Plastic Co
St Louis, MO 314-487-4557
Senior Housing Options Inc
Denver, CO 800-659-2656
Sertapak Packaging Corporation
Woodstock, ON 800-265-1162
Service Neon Signs
Springfield, VA 703-354-3000
Setco
Monroe Twp, NJ 609-655-4600
Setco
Anaheim, CA 714-777-5200
Seton Indentification Products
Branford, CT 800-571-2596
Seville Display Door
Temecula, CA 800-634-0412
Sfb Plastics Inc
Wichita, KS 800-343-8133
Shamrock Plastics
Mt Vernon, OH 800-765-1611
Sharpsville Container Corp
Sharpsville, PA 800-645-1248
Shaw-Clayton Corporation
San Rafael, CA 800-537-6712
Sheboygan Paper Box Co
Sheboygan, WI 800-458-8373
Shields Bag & Printing Co
Yakima, WA 800-541-8630
Shingle Belting
King Of Prussia, PA 800-345-6294
Ship Rite Packaging
Bergenfield, NJ 800-721-7447
Shippers Supply
Saskatoon, SK 800-661-5639
Sign Graphics
Evansville, IN 812-476-9151
Sign Systems, Inc.
Warren, MI 586-758-1600
SignArt Advertising
Van Buren, AR 479-474-8581
Signature Packaging
West Orange, NJ 800-376-2299
Silgan Plastics Canada
Chesterfield, MO 800-274-5426
Silgan Plastics LLC
Chesterfield, MO 800-274-5426
Silgan White Cap LLC
Downers Grove, IL 800-515-1565
Skd Distribution Corp
Jamaica, NY 800-458-8753

Snapware
Fullerton, CA 800-334-3062
Snyder Crown
Marked Tree, AR 870-358-3400
Snyder Industries Inc.
Lincoln, NE 800-351-1363
Sommers Plastic Product Co Inc
Clifton, NJ 800-225-7677
Soodhalter Plastics
Los Angeles, CA 213-747-0231
Southern Film Extruders
High Point, NC 800-334-6101
Spartanburg Steel Products Inc
Spartanburg, SC 800-974-7500
Spartec Plastics
Conneaut, OH 800-325-5176
Spartech Plastics
Portage, WI 800-998-7123
Spartech Poly Com
Clayton, MI 888-721-4242
Specialty Films & Associates
Hebron, KY 800-984-3346
Spectrum Plastics
Las Vegas, NV 702-876-8650
Spir-It/Zoo Piks
Andover, MA 800-343-0996
Spirit Foodservice, Inc.
Andover, MA 800-343-0996
SQP
Schenectady, NY 800-724-1129
Star Container Company
Phoenix, AZ 480-281-4200
Star Filters
Timmonsville, SC 800-845-5381
Steel City Corporation
Youngstown, OH 800-321-0350
Stelray Plastic Products Inc
Ansonia, CT 800-735-2331
Step Products
Round Rock, TX 800-777-7837
Sterling Net & Twine Company
Cedar Knolls, NJ 800-342-0316
Sterling Novelty Products
Northbrook, IL 847-291-0070
Stoffel Seals Corp
Tallapoosa, GA 800-422-8247
Storm Industrial
Shawnee Mission, KS 800-745-7483
Stratis Plastic Pallets
Indianapolis, IN 800-725-5387
Straubel Company
De Pere, WI 888-336-1412
Stripper Bags
Henderson, NV 800-354-2247
Suburban Sign Company
Anoka, MN 763-753-8849
Suburban Signs
College Park, MD 301-474-5051
Sun Plastics
Clearwater, MN 800-862-1673
Sunland Manufacturing Company
Minneapolis, MN 800-790-1905
Superfos Packaging Inc
Cumberland, MD 800-537-9242
Sutherland Stamp Company
San Diego, CA 858-233-7784
T & T Industries Inc
Fort Mohave, AZ 800-437-6246
T&S Blow Molding
Scarborough, ON 416-752-8330
T.O. Plastics
Minneapolis, MN 952-854-2131
Tablet & Ticket Co
West Chicago, IL 800-438-4959
Tar-Hong MELAMINE USA
City Of Industry, CA 626-935-1612
Target Industries
North Salt Lake, UT 866-617-2253
Taymar Industries
Palm Desert, CA 800-624-1972
Techform
Mount Airy, NC 336-789-2115
TEMP-TECH Company
Springfield, MA 800-343-5579
Templock Corporation
Santa Barbara, CA 800-777-1715
TEQ
Huntley, IL 800-874-7113
Terphane Inc
Bloomfield, NY 800-724-3456
Thermo Service
Dallas, TX 800-635-5559

Thermodynamics
Commerce City, CO 800-627-9037
Thermodyne International LTD
Ontario, CA 909-923-9945
Thombert
Newton, IA 800-433-3572
Thornton Plastics
Salt Lake City, UT 800-248-3434
Three P
Salt Lake City, UT 801-486-7407
Tolas Health Care Packaging
Feasterville Trevose, PA 215-322-7900
Tolco Corp
Toledo, OH 800-537-4786
Toledo Sign Co Inc
Toledo, OH 419-244-4444
Toscarora
Sandusky, OH 419-625-7343
Total Identity Group
Cambridge, ON 877-551-5529
Trans Flex Packagers Inc
Unionville, CT 860-673-2531
Tray-Pak Corp
Reading, PA 610-926-5800
Trevor Industries
Eden, NY 716-992-4775
Tri-State Plastics
Henderson, KY 270-826-8361
Tri-State Plastics
Glenwillard, PA 724-457-6900
Triad Scientific
Manasquan, NJ 800-867-6690
Trident Plastics
Ivyland, PA 800-222-2318
Trinity Packaging
Cheektowaga, NY 800-778-3111
Triple Dot Corp
Santa Ana, CA 714-241-0888
Triple-A Manufacturing Company
Toronto, ON 800-786-2238
Tru Form Plastics
Gardena, CA 800-510-7999
Tuckahoe Manufacturing Co
Vineland, NJ 800-220-3368
Tulsa Plastics Co
Tulsa, OK 888-273-5303
Tupperware Brands Corporation
Orlando, FL 800-366-3800
Tyco Plastics
Lakeville, MN 800-328-4080
UCB Inc
Smyrna, GA 770-970-8338
Uniloy Milacron
Tecumseh, MI 517-424-8900
Union Industries
Providence, RI 800-556-6454
Uniplast Films
Palmer, MA 800-343-1295
Unique Manufacturing
Visalia, CA 888-737-1007
Unique Plastics
Rio Rico, AZ 800-658-5946
United Bags Inc
St Louis, MO 800-550-2247
United Commercial Corporation
Shrewsbury, NJ 800-498-7147
United Flexible
Westbury, NY 516-222-2150
United Seal & Tag Corporation
Port Charlotte, FL 800-211-9552
Universal Container Corporation
Odessa, FL 800-582-7477
Universal Paper Box
Seattle, WA 800-228-1045
Universal Sign Company and Manufacturing Company
Lafayette, LA 337-234-1466
Upham & Walsh Lumber
Hoffman Estates, IL 847-519-1010
Vacumet Corporation
Austell, GA 800-776-0865
Valley City Sign Co
Comstock Park, MI 616-784-5711
Valley Packaging Supply Co
Green Bay, WI 920-336-9012
Vermont Bag & Film
Bennington, VT 802-442-3166
Vicmore Manufacturing Company
Brooklyn, NY 800-458-8663
VIFAN Canada
Lanoraie, QC 800-557-0192
Virginia Plastics Co
Roanoke, VA 800-777-8541

Visual Packaging Corp
Haskell, NJ 973-835-7055
Volk Corp
Farmington Hills, MI 800-521-6799
Vollrath Co LLC
Sheboygan, WI 800-624-2051
Vonco Products LLC
Lake Villa, IL 800-323-9077
VPI Manufacturing
Draper, UT .801-495-2310
Vulcan Industries
Moody, AL .888-444-4417
Waddington North America
Chelmsford, MA 888-962-2877
Wasserman Bag Company
Center Moriches, NY 631-909-8656
Wedlock Paper ConvertersLtd.
Mississauga, ON 800-388-0447
Wells Lamont
Niles, IL 800-323-2830
West Rock
Atlanta, GA 770-448-2193
Western Plastics
Portland, TN 615-325-7331
Western Plastics
Calhoun, GA 800-752-4106
Wilks Precision Instr Co Inc
Union Bridge, MD 410-775-7917
Winmark Stamp & Sign
Salt Lake City, UT 800-438-0480
Winnebago Sign Company
Fond Du Lac, WI 920-922-5930
Winpak Portion Packaging
San Bernardino, CA 800-804-4224
Winzen Film
Taylor, TX .800-779-7595
Wisconsin Film & Bag Inc
Shawano, WI. 800-765-9224
Witt Plastics
Greenville, OH 800-227-9181
WNA
Lancaster, TX 800-334-2877
WNA
Chattanooga, TN. 800-404-9318
Wna Comet West Inc
City Of Industry, CA. 800-225-0939
Wolens Company
Dallas, TX .214-634-0800
Woodstock Plastics Co Inc
Marengo, IL 815-568-5281
WORC Slitting & Mfg Co
Worcester, MA 800-356-2961
Wright Plastics Company
Prattville, AL 800-874-7659
Zeier Plastic & Mfg Inc
Madison, WI 608-244-5782
Zimmer Custom-Made Packaging
Indianapolis, IN 317-263-3436
Zip-Pak
Manteno, IL 800-488-6973

Plate/Frame Exchanger

Harris Equipment Corp
Melrose Park, IL. 800-365-0315

Pump Feeders

John Crane Mechanical Sealing Devices
Chicago, IL
Polar Process
Plattsville, ON. 877-896-0077
Warren Rupp Inc
Mansfield, OH 419-524-8388

Pumps

Food

A.K. Robins
Baltimore, MD 800-486-9656
Abel Pumps
Sewickley, PA 412-741-3222
ABO Industries
San Diego, CA 858-566-9750
Alloy Hardfacing & Engineering
Jordan, MN 800-328-8408
American LEWA
Holliston, MA 888-539-2123
APV Americas
Delavan, WI 800-252-5200
Arcobaleno Pasta Machines
Lancaster, PA 800-875-7096

Autio Co
Astoria, OR. 800-483-8884
Automated Food Systems
Waxahachie, TX 469-517-0470
Axiflow Technologies, Inc.
Kennesaw, GA 770-795-1195
Baldewein Company
Lake Forrest, IL 800-424-5544
Blackmer Co
Grand Rapids, MI 616-241-1611
Bran & Luebbe
Schaumburg, IL. 847-882-8116
Calmar
Richmond, VA. 804-444-1000
Chocolate Concepts
Hartville, OH 330-877-3322
Commercial Manufacturing
Fresno, CA 559-237-1855
Cook & Beals Inc
Loup City, NE 308-745-0154
Cornell Pump Company
Portland, OR 503-653-0330
Crane Pumps & Systems
Piqua, OH .937-778-8947
Custom Food Machinery
Stockton, CA 209-463-4343
Doering Machines Inc
San Francisco, CA 415-526-2131
Dupps Co
Germantown, OH 937-855-0623
Eirich Machines
Gurnee, IL .847-336-2444
Eischen Enterprises
Fresno, CA 559-834-0013
Esco Products Inc
Houston, TX 800-966-5514
Flojet
Foothill Ranch, CA. 800-235-6538
Flow of Solids
Westford, MA 978-392-0300
Flux Pumps Corporation
Atlanta, GA 800-367-3589
Franrica Systems
Stockton, CA 209-948-2811
Fristam Pumps USA LLP
Middleton, WI. 608-831-5001
Fristam Pumps USA LLP
Middleton, WI. 800-841-5001
GEA Niro Soavi North America
Bedford, NH 603-606-4060
General Tank
Berwick, PA 800-435-8265
Granco Manufacturing Inc
San Ramon, CA 510-652-8847
Greenfield Packaging
White Plains, NY 914-993-0233
Handtmann Inc
Lake Forest, IL 800-477-3585
Healdsburg Machine Company
Santa Rosa, CA 707-433-3348
Hinds-Bock Corp
Bothell, WA. 425-885-1183
John Crane Mechanical Sealing Devices
Chicago, IL
Johnson Pump Of America
Hanover Park, IL 847-671-7867
Karl Schnell
New London, WI 920-982-9974
Kelmin Products
Plymouth, FL 407-886-6079
Key Technology Inc.
Walla Walla, WA. 509-529-2161
Kinetic Equipment Company
Appleton, WI 806-293-4471
Krogh Pump Co
Benicia, CA. 800-225-7644
L.C. Thompson Company
Kenosha, WI. 800-558-4018
Langsenkamp Manufacturing
Indianapolis, IN 877-585-1950
Lear Romec
Elyria, OH. 440-323-3211
Liberty Engineering Co
Roscoe, IL .877-623-9065
Lyco Manufacturing
Wausau, WI. 715-845-7867
Lyco Wausau
Wausau, WI. 715-845-7867
Marlen
Riverside, MO. 913-888-3333
Marlow Watson Inc
Wilmington, MA. 800-282-8823

MBC Food Machinery Corp
Hackensack, NJ. 201-489-7000
Met-Pro Corp
Owosso, MI. 800-392-7621
Midwest Stainless
Menomonie, WI 715-235-5472
Moyno
Springfield, OH. 937-327-3111
Murzan Inc
Peachtree Cor, GA 770-448-0583
Oerlikon Leybold Vacuum
Export, PA 724-327-5700
Pacer Pumps
Lancaster, PA 800-233-3861
Pacific Pneumatics
Rancho Cucamonga, CA 800-221-0961
Pacific Process Technology
La Jolla, CA 858-551-3298
Piab Vacuum Products
Hingham, MA 800-321-7422
Polar Process
Plattsville, ON. 877-896-8077
Preferred Machining Corporation
Englewood, CO. 303-761-1535
Prince Industries Inc
Murrayville, GA 800-441-3303
Raque Food Systems
Louisville, KY 502-267-9641
Redi-Call Inc
Reno, NV .800-648-1849
Reiser
Canton, MA 734-821-1290
Rheo-Tech
Gurnee, IL .847-367-1557
Rieke Packaging Systems
Auburn, IN 260-925-3700
Roto-Jet Pump
Salt Lake City, UT 801-359-8731
Seepex
Enon, OH .800-695-3659
Server Products Inc
Richfield, WI 800-558-8722
SHURflo
Costa Mesa, CA 800-854-3218
Sine Pump
Arvada, CO 888-504-8301
Special Products
Springfield, MO 417-881-6114
Stainless Products
Somers, WC 800-558-9446
TDH
Sand Springs, OK 888-251-7961
Top Line Process Equipment Company
Bradford, PA 800-458-6095
Tuchenhagen North America
Portland, ME. 207-797-9500
Valvinox
Iberville, QC 450-346-1981
Walton's Inc
Wichita, KS 800-835-2832
Waukesha Cherry-Burrell
Louisville, KY 502-491-4310
Waukesha Cherry-Burrell
Louisville, KY 800-252-5200
WCB Ice Cream
Philadelphia, PA 215-425-4320
Wilden Pump & Engineering LLC
Grand Terrace, CA 909-422-1700

Viscous Products

Invensys APV Products
Houston, TX 713-329-1600
John Crane Mechanical Sealing Devices
Chicago, IL
Murzan Inc
Peachtree Cor, GA 770-448-0583
PCM Delasco Inc
Houston, TX 713-896-4888
Polar Process
Plattsville, ON. 877-896-8077
Precision Plus
Sanborn, NY 800-526-2707
Qualtech
Quebec, QC. 888-339-3801
Raque Food Systems
Louisville, KY 502-267-9641
Reiser
Canton, MA 734-821-1290
Standard Pump
Auburn, GA 866-558-8611

Sundyne Corp
Arvada, CO 303-425-0800
Warren Rupp Inc
Mansfield, OH 419-524-8388

Road Plates

Slip Not
Detroit, MI 800-754-7668

Scales

Beam

Fairbanks Scales
Kansas City, MO 800-451-4107
Q A Supplies LLC
Norfolk, VA 800-472-7205
Vande Berg SCALES/Vbs Inc
Sioux Center, IA 712-722-1181

Butchers'

Acme Scale Co
San Leandro, CA 888-638-5040
Arkfeld Mfg & Distributing Co
Norfolk, NE 800-533-0676
Exact Equipment Corporation
Morrisville, PA 215-295-2000
Fairbanks Scales
Kansas City, MO 800-451-4107
Mandeville Company
Minneapolis, MN 800-328-8490
Marel Food Systems, Inc.
Lenexa, KS 913-888-9110
Q A Supplies LLC
Norfolk, VA 800-472-7205
Vande Berg SCALES/Vbs Inc
Sioux Center, IA 712-722-1181

Computing, Weighing

Acme Scale Co
San Leandro, CA 888-638-5040
Automated Packaging Systems
Streetsboro, OH 800-527-0733
Avery Weigh-Tronix
Fairmont, MN 877-368-2039
Avery Weigh-Tronix LLC
Fairmont, MN 800-368-2039
Bizerba USA
Piscataway, NJ 732-565-6000
Brechbuhler Scales
Canton, OH 330-453-2424
Browne & Company
Markham, ON 905-475-6104
Bunzl Processor Distribution LLC
Riverside, MO 816-448-4300
Cardinal Scale Mfg Co
Webb City, MO 800-441-4237
Detecto Scale Co
Webb City, MO 800-641-2008
Emery Winslow Scale Co
Seymour, CT 203-881-9333
Exact Equipment Corporation
Morrisville, PA 215-295-2000
Fairbanks Scales
Kansas City, MO 800-451-4107
Gainco Inc
Gainesville, GA 800-467-2828
Ilapak Inc
Newtown, PA 215-579-2900
Iman Pack
Westland, MI 800-810-4626
Industrial Laboratory Eqpt Co
Charlotte, NC 704-357-3930
Intercomp
Hamel, MN 800-328-3336
IWS Scales
San Diego, CA 800-881-9755
Key-Pak Machines
Lebanon, NJ 908-236-2111
Kisco Manufacturing
Port Alberni, BC 604-823-7456
Mandeville Company
Minneapolis, MN 800-328-8490
Mettler-Toledo, LLC
Columbus, OH 800-638-8537
Q A Supplies LLC
Norfolk, VA 800-472-7205
Si-Lodec
Tukwila, WA 800-255-8274

Sig Pack
Oakland, CA 800-824-3245
Sterling Scale Co
Southfield, MI 800-331-9931
Taylor Precision Products
Oak Brook, IL 866-843-3905
Thermo BLH
Canton, MA 781-821-2000
Tridyne Process Systems
South Burlington, VT 802-863-6873
Vande Berg SCALES/Vbs Inc
Sioux Center, IA 712-722-1181
Weigh Right Automatic Scale Co
Joliet, IL 800-571-0249
Yamato Corporation
Colorado Springs, CO 800-538-1762

Counter

Acme Scale Co
San Leandro, CA 888-638-5040
Action Packaging Automation
Roosevelt, NJ 800-241-2724
Automated Packaging Systems
Streetsboro, OH 800-527-0733
Detecto Scale Co
Webb City, MO 800-641-2008
Fairbanks Scales
Kansas City, MO 800-451-4107
Iman Pack
Westland, MI 800-810-4626
Industrial Laboratory Eqpt Co
Charlotte, NC 704-357-3930
Mettler-Toledo, LLC
Columbus, OH 800-638-8537
NJM/CLI
Pointe Claire, QC 514-630-6990
Q A Supplies LLC
Norfolk, VA 800-472-7205
Vande Berg SCALES/Vbs Inc
Sioux Center, IA 712-722-1181
Yamato Corporation
Colorado Springs, CO 800-538-1762

Fluid, Liquid, Weighing

APEC
Lake Odessa, MI 616-374-1000
Fairbanks Scales
Kansas City, MO 800-451-4107
Fuller Weighing Systems
Columbus, OH 614-882-8121
Industrial Laboratory Eqpt Co
Charlotte, NC 704-357-3930
Magnetic Products Inc
Highland, MI 800-544-5930
Sartorius Corp
Edgewood, NY 800-635-2906
Thermo BLH
Canton, MA 781-821-2000
Vande Berg SCALES/Vbs Inc
Sioux Center, IA 712-722-1181
Yamato Corporation
Colorado Springs, CO 800-538-1762

Screening

Manufacturing

ANKOM Technology
Macedon, NY 315-986-8090
Buffalo Wire Works Co Inc
Buffalo, NY 800-828-7028

Scrubbers

Auto Scrubbing & Burnishing

Surtec Inc
Tracy, CA 800-877-6330

Shelves

Refrigerator & Stove

Bmh Equipment Inc
Sacramento, CA 800-350-8828
E-Z Shelving Systems Inc
Shawnee, KS 800-353-1331
FFR Merchandising Inc
Twinsburg, OH 800-422-2547

G.F. Frank & Sons
Fairfield, OH 513-870-9075
Grillco Inc
Aurora, IL 800-644-0067
Kaines West Michigan Co
Ludington, MI 231-845-1281
Kason Industries
Newnan, GA 770-254-0553
Marlin Steel Wire Products
Baltimore, MD 877-762-7546
Metro Corporation
Wilkes Barre, PA 800-992-1776
Midwest Wire Specialties
Chicago, IL 800-238-0228
Olson Wire Products Co
Baltimore, MD 410-242-7900
Pacific Northwest Wire Works
Dupont, WA 800-222-7699
Princeton Shelving
Cedar Rapids, IA 319-369-0355
SSW Holding Co Inc
Elizabethtown, KY 270-769-5526
Straits Steel & Wire Co
Ludington, MI 231-843-3416
Superior Products Company
Saint Paul, MN 800-328-9800
Triple-A Manufacturing Company
Toronto, ON 800-786-2238
Wald Wire & Mfg Co
Oshkosh, WI 800-236-0053

Sizers

Andgar Corp
Ferndale, WA 360-366-9900
Bepex International LLC
Minneapolis, MN 800-607-2470
Brown International Corp LLC
Winter Haven, FL 863-299-2111
Carter-Day International Inc
Minneapolis, MN 763-571-1000
Durand-Wayland Inc
Lagrange, GA 800-241-2308
Glen Mills Inc.
Clifton, NJ 973-777-0777
Harold F Haines Manufacturing Inc
Presque Isle, ME 207-762-1411
Hosokawa/Bepex Corporation
Santa Rosa, CA 707-586-6000
Kerian Machines Inc
Grafton, ND 701-352-0480
Lewis M Carter Mfg Co Inc
Donalsonville, GA 800-332-8232
MAF Industries Inc
Traver, CA 559-897-2905
Southern Ag Co Inc
Blakely, GA 229-723-4262
Southern Automatics
Lakeland, FL 800-441-4604
Suffolk Iron Works Inc
Suffolk, VA 757-539-2353
Tri-Pak Machinery Inc
Harlingen, TX 956-423-5140

Stacking

Anver Corporation
Hudson, MA 800-654-3500
Architecture Plus Intl Inc
Rocky Point, FL 813-281-9299
Bmh Equipment Inc
Sacramento, CA 800-350-8828
C.J. Machine
Fridley, MN 763-767-4630
Food Equipment Manufacturing Company
Bedford Heights, OH 216-672-5859
Gbn Machine & Engineering
Woodford, VA 800-446-9871
Graybill Machines Inc
Lititz, PA 717-626-5221
Kisters Kayat
Sarasota, FL 386-424-0101
Lift Rite
Mississauga, ON 905-456-2603
Marquip Ward United
Phillips, WI 715-339-2191
Packaging Systems Intl
Denver, CO 303-244-9000
Peerless Food Equipment
Sidney, OH 937-492-4158
Planet Products Corp
Blue Ash, OH 513-984-5544

Roberts Poly Pro Inc
  Charlotte, NC 800-269-7409
Vertical Systems Intl
  Lakeside Park, KY 859-485-9650

Steam Generators

AERCO International Inc
  Blauvelt, NY 800-526-0288
Direct Fire Technical
  Benbrook, TX 888-920-2468
Electro-Steam Generator Corp
  Rancocas, NJ 866-617-0764
PVI Industries LLC
  Fort Worth, TX 800-784-8326
Vapor Power Intl LLC
  Franklin Park, IL 888-874-9020

Steam Tables

Allstrong Restaurant Eqpt Inc
  South El Monte, CA 800-933-8913
Caselites
  Hialeah, FL 305-819-7766
Craig Manufacturing
  Irvington, NJ 800-631-7936
Custom Diamond Intl.
  Laval, QC 800-326-5926
Delfield Co
  Mt Pleasant, MI 800-733-8821
Den Mar Corp
  North Dartmouth, MA 508-999-3295
Duke Manufacturing Co
  St Louis, MO 800-735-3853
Dunhill Food Equipment Corporation
  Armonk, NY 800-847-4206
Habco
  Concord, CA 925-682-6203
Hot Food Boxes
  Mooresville, IN 800-733-8073
Institutional Equipment Inc
  Bolingbrook, IL 630-771-0990
LA Rosa Refrigeration & Equip
  Detroit, MI 800-527-6723
Lambertson Industries Inc
  Sparks, NV 800-548-3324
Lazy Man Inc
  Belvidere, NJ 800-475-1950
Leedal Inc
  Northbrook, IL 847-498-0111
M&S Manufacturing
  Arnold, MO 636-464-2739
Mayekawa USA, Inc.
  Chicago, IL 773-516-5070
Newell Brands
  Atlanta, GA
Professional Bakeware Company
  Willis, TX 800-440-9547
Randell Manufacturing   Unified Brands
  Weidman, MI 888-994-7636
Reliable Food Service Equipment
  Concord, ON 416-738-6840
Rexcraft Fine Chafers
  Long Island City, NY 888-739-2723
Superior Products Company
  Saint Paul, MN 800-328-9800
Supreme Metal
  Alpharetta, GA 800-645-2526
Update International
  Vernon, CA 800-747-7124
West Metals
  London, ON 800-300-6667

Systems

Check Weighing

Cintex of America
  Carol Stream, IL 800-424-6839
Gainco Inc
  Gainesville, GA 800-467-2828
New-Ma Co. Llc
  Grand Rapids, MI 616-942-5500
SICK Inc
  Bloomington, MN 800-325-7425
Thompson Scale Co
  Houston, TX 713-932-9071

Chemical Dispensing & Feed

Solvox Manufacturing Company
  Milwaukee, WI 414-774-5664

Cost

Berg Co
  Monona, WI 608-221-4281
InFood Corporation
  Evanston, IL 773-338-8485

Metal & Contamination Detection

Cintex of America
  Carol Stream, IL 800-424-6839
Loma Systems
  Carol Stream, IL 800-872-5662

Mist Collection

AGET Manufacturing Co
  Adrian, MI. 517-263-5781

Packaging

Advance Weight Systems Inc
  Grafton, OH 440-926-3691
AGA Gas
  Cleveland, OH 216-642-6600
Alfa Systems Inc
  Westfield, NJ 908-654-0255
Bradman Lake Inc
  Rock Hill, SC 803-366-3688
California Vibratory Feeders
  Anaheim, CA 800-354-0972
Campbell Wrapper Corporation
  De Pere, WI. 920-983-7100
Creative Foam Corp
  Fenton, MI 810-629-4149
Indeco Products Inc
  San Marcos, TX 888-246-3326
New-Ma Co. Llc
  Grand Rapids, MI 616-942-5500
Niro
  Hudson, WI. 715-386-9371
Pa R Systems Inc
  St Paul, MN. 800-464-1320
Palace Packaging Machines Inc
  Downingtown, PA. 610-873-7252
Parish Manufacturing Inc
  Indianapolis, IN 800-592-2268
Promarks
  Ontario, CA. 909-923-3888
Raque Food Systems
  Louisville, KY 502-267-9641
Reiser
  Canton, MA 734-821-1290
Schroeder Machine
  San Marcos, CA 760-591-9733
Sertapak Packaging Corporation
  Woodstock, ON. 800-265-1162
SIG Combibloc USA, Inc.
  Chester, PA. 610-546-4200
Simplimatic Automation
  Forest, VA 800-294-2003
Somerville Packaging
  Toronto, ON 416-754-7228
Stock America Inc
  Grafton, WI. 262-375-4100
TNA Packaging Solutions
  Coppell, TX 972-462-6500

Pricing

Astoria Laminations
  St Clair Shores, MI 800-526-7325
Garvey Products
  West Chester, OH 800-543-1908
L.A. Darling Co., LLC
  Paragould, AR. 800-682-5730
Stratecon International Consultants
  Winston Salem, NC. 336-768-6808

Process & Production

Ace Manufacturing
  Cincinnati, OH 800-653-5692
All Fill Inc
  Exton, PA 800-334-1529
ANKOM Technology
  Macedon, NY 315-986-8090
Cog-Veyor Systems, Inc.
  Woodbridge, Ontario, ON. 888-337-2358
Dennsi Group
  Springfield, MA 413-737-1353
F R Drake Co
  Waynesboro, VA 540-949-6215

Gainco Inc
  Gainesville, GA 800-467-2828
Newtech Inc
  Randolph, VT. 800-210-2361
Reiser
  Canton, MA 734-821-1290
Spray Dynamics LTD
  St Clair, MO. 800-260-7366
Strongarm
  Horsham, PA. 215-443-3400

Reverse Osmosis

Aquathin Corporation
  Pompano Beach, FL 800-462-7634
Culligan Company
  Northbrook, IL 800-527-8637
Ecodyne Water Treatment, LLC
  Naperville, IL 800-228-9326
Enting Water Conditioning Inc
  Moraine, OH. 800-735-5100
Hungerford & Terry
  Clayton, NJ 856-881-3200
Hydropure Water Treatment Co
  Coral Springs, FL 800-753-1547
Kiss International/Di-tech Systems
  Vista, CA. 800-527-5477
Multiplex Co Inc
  Sellersburg, IN 800-787-8880
Pacific Process Technology
  La Jolla, CA 858-551-3298
Thomas Technical Svc
  Neillsville, WI. 715-743-4666
Water & Power Technologies
  Salt Lake City, UT 888-271-3295
Waterlink/Sanborn Technologies
  Canton, OH. 800-343-3381

Skids

Relco Unisystems Corp
  Willmar, MN. 320-231-2210

Tubularaseptic Processing

Excel-A-Tec Inc
  Brookfield, WI 262-252-3600

Valve Control

Andersen 2000
  Peachtree City, GA 800-241-5424

Vision Verification

Cintex of America
  Carol Stream, IL 800-424-6839
Cotton Goods Mfg Co
  Chicago, IL 773-265-0088
SICK Inc
  Bloomington, MN 800-325-7425

X-ray Contaminant Detection

Cintex of America
  Carol Stream, IL 800-424-6839

Zipper Application

Com-Pac International Inc
  Carbondale, IL 888-297-2824
Zip-Pak
  Manteno, IL 815-468-6500

Tabletop Supplies

A1 Tablecloth Co
  South Hackensack, NJ 800-727-8987
Abco International
  Melville, NY 866-240-2226
Adcapitol
  Monroe, NC. 800-868-7111
AJM Packaging Corporation
  Bloomfield Hills, MI 248-901-0040
Amcel
  Watertown, MA. 800-225-7992
Anchor Hocking Operating Co
  Lancaster, OH. 800-562-7511
Artex International
  Highland, IL 618-654-2113
Arthur Corporation
  Huron, OH. 419-433-7202
Atlantis Industries Inc
  Milton, DE 302-684-8542

AWP Butcher Block Inc
Horse Cave, KY 800-764-7840
Babco International, Inc
Tucson, AZ 520-628-7596
Benner China & Glassware Inc
Jacksonville, FL 904-733-4620
Best Buy Uniforms
Homestead, PA 800-345-1924
Bib Pak
Racine, WI 262-633-5803
Bright of America
Summersville, WV 304-872-3000
Brooklace
Oshkosh, WI 800-572-4552
Browne & Company
Markham, ON 905-475-6104
Buffalo China
Buffalo, NY 716-824-8515
C R Mfg
Waverly, NE 877-789-5844
Carnegie Textile Co
Cleveland, OH 800-633-4136
Carthage Cup Company
Longview, TX 903-238-9833
Ceramica De Espana
Doral, FL 305-597-9161
Chef Specialties
Smethport, PA 800-440-2433
China Lenox Incorporated
Bristol, PA 267-525-7800
Chinet Company
Winter Springs, FL 800-539-3726
Chinet Company
Laguna Niguel, CA 949-348-1711
City Grafx
Eugene, OR 800-258-2489
Colonial Paper Company
Silver Springs, FL 352-622-4171
Creative Converting Inc
Clintonville, WI 800-826-0418
Custom Table Pads
St Paul, MN 800-325-4643
Cyclamen Collection
Oakland, CA 510-434-7620
Dansk International Designs
Bristol, PA 914-697-6400
Dart Canada Inc.
Toronto, ON 800-465-9696
Dart Container Corp.
Mason, MI. 800-248-5960
De Ster Corporation
Atlanta, GA 800-237-8270
Delco Tableware
Port Washington, NY 800-221-9557
Delfin Design & Mfg
Rancho Sta Marg, CA 800-354-7919
Design Specialties Inc
Hamden, CT 800-999-1584
Dorado Carton Company
Dorado, PR 787-796-1670
Drapes 4 Show
Sylmar, CA 800-525-7469
Durango-Georgia Paper
Tampa, FL. 813-286-2718
Dynynstyl
Delray Beach, FL 800-774-7895
Eastern Tabletop Mfg
Brooklyn, NY 888-422-4142
Eide Industries Inc
Cerritos, CA 800-422-6827
Elrene Home Fashions
New York, NY 212-213-0425
Erving Industries
Erving, MA. 413-422-2700
Fabri-Kal Corp
Kalamazoo, MI. 800-888-5054
Fenton Art Glass Company
Williamstown, WV 800-933-6766
Filet Menu
Los Angeles, CA. 310-202-8000
Filmpack Plastic Corporation
Dayton, NJ 732-329-6523
Flamingo Food Service Products
Hialeah, FL 800-432-8269
Fonda Group
Goshen, IN 574-534-2515
Fort James Canada
Toronto, ON 416-784-1621
Four M Manufacturing Group
San Jose, CA 408-998-1141
Gaetano America
El Monte, CA 626-442-2858

Genpak
Peterborough, ON 800-461-1995
Genpak LLC
Charlotte, NC 800-626-6695
Georgia Pacific
Green Bay, WI. 920-435-8821
Gourmet Table Skirts
Houston, TX 800-527-0440
Grand Silver Company
Bronx, NY .718-585-1930
H.F. Coors China Company
New Albany, MS 800-782-6677
Hal-One Plastics
Olathe, KS .800-626-5784
Hall China Co
East Liverpool, OH 800-445-4255
Hartstone Pottery Inc
Zanesville, OH 740-452-9999
Have Our Plastic Inc
Mississauga, ON 800-263-5995
Hilden Halifax
South Boston, VA 800-431-2514
Hoffman & Levy Inc Tasseldepot
Deerfield Beach, FL 954-698-0001
Hoffmaster Group Inc
Oshkosh, WI 800-327-9774
Hoffmaster Group Inc
Oshkosh, WI 800-367-2877
Hoffmaster Group Inc.
Oshkosh, WI 800-558-9300
Hollowick Inc
Manlius, NY 800-367-3015
Homer Laughlin China Co
Newell, WV 800-452-4462
HPI North America/   Plastics
Eagan, MN 800-752-7462
HPI North America/Plastics
Chicago, IL. 800-327-3534
Image Plastics
Houston, TX 800-289-2811
International Paper Co.
Memphis, TN
J. James
Brooklyn, NY 718-384-6144
Jack the Ripper Table Skirting
Stafford, TX 800-331-7831
Jarden Home Brands
Cloquet, MN 218-879-6700
JBC Plastics
St Louis, MO. 877-834-5526
Jet Plastica Industries
Hatfield, PA
Jones-Zylon Co
West Lafayette, OH. 800-848-8160
K-C Products Company
Van Nuys, CA 818-267-1600
Kenro
Fredonia, WI 262-692-2411
Klever Kuvers
Pasadena, CA 626-355-8441
Kuepper Favor Company, Celebrate Line
Peru, IN. 800-321-5823
Libbey Inc.
Toledo, OH 419-325-2100
Libby Canada
Mississauga, ON 905-607-8280
Liberty Ware LLC
Clearfield, UT. 888-500-5885
Louis Jacobs & Son
Brooklyn, NY 718-782-3500
Mack-Chicago Corporation
Chicago, IL. 800-992-6225
Majestic
Bridgeport, CT 203-367-7900
Marston Manufacturing
Cleveland, OH 216-587-3400
Mason Candlelight Company
New Albany, MS. 800-556-2766
Mastercraft
Appleton, WI 800-242-6602
Masterpiece Crystal
Jane Lew, WV. 304-884-7841
Metal Master Sales Corp
Glendale Heights, IL. 800-488-8729
Michael Leson Dinnerware
Youngstown, OH. 800-821-3541
Milliken & Co
Spartanburg, SC 864-503-2020
Mr Ice Bucket
New Brunswick, NJ 732-545-0420
Novelty Crystal
Long Island City, NY 800-622-0250

Olde Country Reproductions Inc
York, PA 800-358-3997
Oneida Food Service
Columbus, OH 800-828-7033
Oneida LTD Silversmiths
Oneida, NY 888-263-7195
OWD
Tupper Lake, NY 800-836-1693
Palmland Paper Company
Fort Lauderdale, FL 800-266-9067
Paradise Products
El Cerrito, CA. 800-227-1092
Party Linens
Chicago, IL 800-281-0003
Party Yards
Casselberry, FL 877-501-4400
Penley Corporation
West Paris, ME 800-368-6449
Philmont Manufacturing Co.
Englewood, NJ 888-379-6483
Placemat Printers
Fogelsville, PA 800-628-7746
Plastiques Cascades Group
Montreal, QC 888-703-6515
Potlatch Corp
Spokane, WA. 509-835-1500
Prairie Packaging Inc
Mooresville, NC 704-660-6600
Premier
Cincinnati, OH 800-354-9817
Premier Skirting Products
Lawrence, NY 800-544-2516
Prestige Skirting & Tablecloths
Orangeburg, NY 800-635-3313
Racket Group
Kansas City, MO. 816-283-0490
Reed & Barton Food Service
Taunton, MA 800-797-9675
Resource One/Resource Two
Reseda, CA 818-343-3451
Rixie Paper Products Inc
Pottstown, PA 800-377-2692
Ronnie's Ceramic Company
San Francisco, CA 800-888-8218
Royal Paper Products
Coatesville, PA 800-666-6655
Royal Prestige Health Moguls
Westbury, NY 888-802-7433
Rubbermaid Canada
Oakville, ON 905-279-1010
Sabert Corp
Sayreville, NJ 800-722-3781
Salem China Company
Salem, OH. 330-337-8771
Sani-Top Products
De Leon Springs, FL. 800-874-6094
SCA Tissue
Philadelphia, PA 866-722-8675
Scan Group
Appleton, WI 920-730-9150
Sims Superior Seating
Locust Grove, GA 800-729-9178
Smith-Lee Company
Oshkosh, WI 800-327-9774
Snap Drape Inc
Carrollton, TX. 800-527-5147
Solo Cup Company
Lake Forest, IL
Something Different Linen
Clifton, NJ 800-422-2180
Spir-It/Zoo Piks
Andover, MA 800-343-0996
Spirit Foodservice, Inc.
Andover, MA 800-343-0996
Stanley Roberts
Piscataway, NJ 973-778-5900
Sterling Paper Company
Ohio, PA 800-282-1124
Stevens Linen Association
Dudley, MA. 800-772-9269
Straubel Company
De Pere, WI. 888-336-1412
Superior Linen & Work Wear
Kansas City, MO. 800-798-7987
Superior Products Company
Saint Paul, MN 800-328-9800
Table De France: North America
New Brunswick, NJ 888-680-4616
Tag-Trade Associated Group
Chicago, IL. 800-621-8350
Tango Shatterproof Drinkware
Walpole, MA. 888-898-2646

Tar-Hong MELAMINE USA
City Of Industry, CA 626-935-1612
TEMP-TECH Company
Springfield, MA 800-343-5579
Townfood Equipment Corp
Brooklyn, NY 800-221-5032
Tradeco International Corp
Addison, IL 800-628-3738
Traex
Dane, WI 800-356-8006
Uhtamaki Foods Services
Waterville, ME 207-873-3351
Ullman, Shapiro & UllmanLLP
New York, NY 212-755-0299
Ultimate Textile
Paterson, NJ 973-523-5866
Vertex China
Pomona, CA 800-483-7839
Vicmore Manufacturing Company
Brooklyn, NY 800-458-8663
Victoria Porcelain
Miami, FL 888-593-2353
Waddington North America
Chelmsford, MA 888-962-2877
Wiltec
Leominster, MA 978-537-1497
Wilton Armetale
Mt Joy, PA 800-779-4586
Wishbone Utensil Tableware Line
Wheat Ridge, CO 866-266-5928
WNA
Chattanooga, TN 800-404-9318
Wna Comet West Inc
City Of Industry, CA 800-225-0939
Xtreme Beverages, LLC
Dana Point, CA 949-495-7929

Tea Industry

Washington Frontier
Grandview, WA 509-469-7662

Timers

Alarm Controls Corp
Deer Park, NY 800-645-5538
Amco Metals Indl
City Of Industry, CA 626-855-2550
American Time & Signal Co
Dassel, MN 800-328-8996
AMETEK National Controls Corp
West Chicago, IL 800-323-5293
Automatic Timing & Controls
Newell, WV 800-727-5646
Chaney Instrument Co
Lake Geneva, WI 800-777-0565
Coley Industries
Wayland, NY 716-728-2390
Control Products Inc
Chanhassen, MN 800-947-9098
Cramer Company
South Windsor, CT 877-684-6464
Dayton Marking Devices Company
Dayton, OH 937-432-0285
Elreha Controls Corporation
St Petersburg, FL 727-327-6236
ERC Parts Inc
Kennesaw, GA 800-241-6880
Gralab Instruments
Centerville, OH 800-876-8353
M.H. Rhodes Cramer
South Windsor, CT 877-684-6464
National Time Recording Eqpt
New York, NY 212-227-3310
Pelouze Scale Company
Bridgeview, IL 800-323-8363
Prince Castle Inc
Carol Stream, IL 800-722-7853
R.P. Childs Stamp Company
Ludlow, MA 413-733-1211
SCK Direct Inc
Stratford, CT 800-327-8766
Superior Products Company
Saint Paul, MN 800-328-9800
Wilkens-Anderson Co
Chicago, IL 800-847-2222

Tubing

Plastic

Arbee Transparent Inc
Elk Grove Vlg, IL 800-642-2247

Emco Industrial Plastics
Cedar Grove, NJ 800-292-9906
Flexo Transparent Inc
Buffalo, NY 877-993-5396
Hall Manufacturing Co
Ringwood, NJ 973-962-6022
Home Plastics Inc
Des Moines, IA 515-265-2562
Legacy Plastics
Henderson, KY 270-827-1318
M S Plastics & Packaging Inc
Butler, NJ 800-593-1802
Roechling Engineered Plastics
Gastonia, NC 800-541-4419
Rubber Fab Molding & Gasket
Sparta, NJ 866-442-2959
Target Industries
North Salt Lake, UT 866-617-2253
Trident Plastics
Ivyland, PA 800-222-2318
Wilkens-Anderson Co
Chicago, IL 800-847-2222

Stainless Steel

Accutek Packaging Equipment
Vista, CA 800-989-1828
Arc Machines Inc
Pacoima, CA 818-896-9556
Baldewein Company
Lake Forrest, IL 800-424-5544
Damascus/Bishop Tube Company
Greenville, PA 724-646-1500
J & L Honing
St Francis, WI 800-747-9501
Jacob Tubing LP
Memphis, TN 901-566-1110
L&S Products
Coldwater, MI 517-279-9526
L.C. Thompson Company
Kenosha, WI 800-558-4018
Liburdi Group of Companies
Mooresville, NC 800-533-9353
Melrose Displays
Passaic, NJ 973-471-7700
Northland Process Piping
Isle, MN 320-679-2119
Pinquist Tool & Die Company
Brooklyn, NY 800-752-0414
Plymouth Tube Company
East Troy, WI 262-642-8201
Rath Manufacturing Company
Janesville, WI 800-367-7284
Robert-James Sales
Buffalo, NY 800-777-1325
Spencer Turbine Co
Windsor, CT 800-232-4321
Sterling Process Engineering
Columbus, OH 800-783-7875
Sudmo North America, Inc
Machesney Park, IL 800-218-3915
T-Drill Industries Inc
Norcross, GA 800-554-2730
Top Line Process Equipment Company
Bradford, PA 800-458-6095
United Industries Inc
Beloit, WI 608-365-8891
Valvinox
Iberville, QC 450-346-1981

Unscramblers

A.K. Robins
Baltimore, MD 800-486-9656
BEVCO
Canada, BC 800-663-0090
Chase-Logeman Corp
Greensboro, NC 336-665-0754
ELF Machinery
La Porte, IN 800-328-0466
Fogg Filler Co
Holland, MI 616-786-3644
Inline Filling Systems
Venice, FL 941-486-8800
John R Nalbach Engineering Co
Countryside, IL 708-579-9100
JW Leser Company
Los Angeles, CA 323-731-4173
KAPS All Packaging
Riverhead, NY 631-727-0300
Kinsley Inc
Doylestown, PA 800-414-6664

Leader Engineering-Fab Inc
Napoleon, OH 419-592-0008
Leeds Conveyor Manufacturer Company
Guilford, CT 800-724-1088
Mcbrady Engineering Co
Rockdale, IL 815-744-8900
New England Machinery Inc
Bradenton, FL 941-755-5550
Norwalt Design Inc
Randolph, NJ 973-927-3200
Omega Design Corp
Exton, PA 800-346-0191
Pace Packaging Corp
Fairfield, NJ 800-867-2726
Palace Packaging Machines Inc
Downingtown, PA 610-873-7252
Pearson Packaging Systems
Spokane, WA 800-732-7766
Perl Packaging Systems
Middlebury, CT 800-864-2853
Simplex Filler Co
Napa, CA 800-796-7539
Spurgeon Co
Ferndale, MI 800-396-2554
Stiles Enterprises Inc
Rockaway, NJ 800-325-4232
Weigh Right Automatic Scale Co
Joliet, IL 800-571-0249

Valves

Advance Fittings Corp
Elkhorn, WI 262-723-6699
Anver Corporation
Hudson, MA 800-654-3500
APV Americas
Delavan, WI 800-252-5200
Archon Industries Inc
Suffern, NY 800-554-1394
Armstrong Hot Water
Three Rivers, MI 269-279-3602
Baldewein Company
Lake Forrest, IL 800-424-5544
Boston Gear
Boston, MA 888-999-9860
Bradford A Ducon Company
Pewaukee, WI 800-789-1718
C & D Valve Mfg Co
Oklahoma City, OK 800-654-9233
C&R Refrigeration Inc,
Center, TX 800-438-6182
C.F.F. Stainless Steels
Hamilton, ON 800-263-4511
Cashco Inc
Ellsworth, KS 785-472-4461
Chlorinators Inc
Stuart, FL 800-327-9761
Cincinnati Industrial Machry
Mason, OH 800-677-0076
Cipriani
Rancho Sta Marg, CA 949-589-3978
Clark-Cooper Division   Magnatrol Valve Corporation
Cinnaminson, NJ 856-829-4580
Conbraco Industries Inc
Matthews, NC 704-841-6000
Delavan Spray Technologies
Bamberg, SC 800-982-6943
Doering Co
Clear Lake, MN 320-743-2276
Dormont Manufacturing Co
Export, PA 800-367-6668
Duplex Mill & Mfg Co
Springfield, OH 937-325-5555
EVAPCO Inc
Taneytown, MD 410-876-3782
Firematic Sprinkler Devices
Shrewsbury, MA 800-225-7288
Flomatic International
Sellersburg, IN 800-367-4233
Flynn Burner Corporation
New Rochelle, NY 800-643-8910
General Tank
Berwick, PA 800-435-8265
Globe Fire Sprinkler Corp
Standish, MI 800-248-0278
Harris Equipment Corp
Melrose Park, IL 800-365-0315
Hayes & Stolz Indl Mfg LTD
Fort Worth, TX 800-725-7272
Hayward Industries Inc
Clemmons, NC 336-712-9900
Heuft USA Inc
Downers Grove, IL 630-968-9011

Hi-Temp Inc
Tuscumbia, AL 800-239-5066
Hilliard Corp
Elmira, NY 607-733-7121
Holland Applied Technologies
Burr Ridge, IL 630-325-5130
Hydra-Flex Inc
Livonia, MI 800-234-0832
IMI Precision Engineering
Brookville, OH 937-833-4033
Invensys APV Products
Houston, TX 713-329-1600
Josam Co
Michigan City, IN 800-365-6726
K-Tron
Salina, KS 785-825-1611
Kemutec Group Inc
Bristol, PA....................... 215-788-8013
Kraissl Co Inc
Hackensack, NJ................... 800-572-4775
L.C. Thompson Company
Kenosha, WI 800-558-4018
Lumaco Inc
Hackensack, NJ................... 800-735-8258
M O Industries Inc
Whippany, NJ 973-386-9228
M-One Specialties
Salt Lake City, UT 800-525-9223
Matcon Americas
Elmhurst, IL 856-256-1330
Midwest Stainless
Menomonie, WI 715-235-5472
Moyno
Springfield, OH.................. 937-327-3111
Norgren Inc.
Littleton, CO..................... 800-514-0129
Northland Process Piping
Isle, MN 320-679-2119
Numatics Inc
Novi, MI 248-596-3200
Parker-Hannifin Corp
Cleveland, OH 800-272-7537
Paxton Corp
Bristol, RI 401-396-9062
PBM Inc
Irwin, PA........................ 800-967-4PBM
Plast-O-Matic Valves Inc
Cedar Grove, NJ 973-256-9344
Qosina Corporation
Ronkonkoma, NY 631-242-3000
Qualtech
Quebec, QC 888-339-3801
Robert-James Sales
Buffalo, NY...................... 800-777-1325
Rubber Fab Molding & Gasket
Sparta, NJ 866-442-2959
Rutherford Engineering
Rockford, IL 815-623-2141
Samson Controls
Baytown, TX..................... 281-383-3677
Sanchelima International
Miami, FL 305-591-4343
SerVend International
Sellersburg, IN 800-367-4233
Shick Esteve
Kansas City, MO.................. 877-744-2587
Special Products
Springfield, MO 417-881-6114
Spraying Systems Company
Wheaton, IL 630-655-5000
Stainless Products
Somers, WC 800-558-9446
Storm Industrial
Shawnee Mission, KS 800-745-7483
Strahman Valves Inc
Bethlehem, PA.................... 877-787-2462
Sudmo North America, Inc
Machesney Park, IL 800-218-3915
TechnipFMC
Houston, TX 218-591-4000
Top Line Process Equipment Company
Bradford, PA..................... 800-458-6095
Tuchenhagen
Columbia, MD 410-910-6000
Tuchenhagen North America
Portland, ME..................... 207-797-9500
Valvinox
Iberville, QC 450-346-1981
Van Air Systems
Lake City, PA..................... 800-840-9906
Viatec
Victoria, BC 800-942-4702

Viking Corp
Hastings, MI 800-968-9501
Vilter Manufacturing Corporation
Cudahy, WI 414-744-0111
Watts Regulator Co
North Andover, MA 978-688-1811
Waukesha Cherry-Burrell
Louisville, KY 800-252-5200
Waukesha Specialty Company
Darien, WI. 262-724-3700

Water Treatment

Alar Engineering Corp
Mokena, IL 708-479-6100
Alkazone/Better Health Lab
Hackensack, NJ................... 800-810-1888
American Ultraviolet Co
Lebanon, IN 800-288-9288
AMSOIL Inc
Superior, WI 715-392-7101
Anderson Chemical Co
Litchfield, MN 320-693-2477
Astro Pure Water
Deerfield Beach, FL 954-422-8966
Babcock & Wilcox MEGTEC
De Pere, WI...................... 920-336-5715
Bloomfield Industries
St. Louis, MO 888-356-5362
Crane Environmental
Norristown, PA 800-633-7435
Croll-Reynolds Engineering Company
Trumbull, CT 203-371-1983
Culligan Company
Northbrook, IL 800-527-8637
Delta Pure Filtration Corp
Ashland, VA 800-785-9450
Diamond Water Conditioning
Hortonville, WI................... 800-236-8931
Eaton Filtration, LLC
Tinton Falls, NJ 800-859-9212
Enting Water Conditioning Inc
Moraine, OH 800-735-5100
Everpure, LLC
Hanover Park, IL 630-307-3000
Filtrine Manufacturing
Keene, NH........................ 800-930-3367
Freudenberg Nonwovens
Hopkinsville, KY 270-887-5115
G.W. Dahl Company
Greensboro, NC 800-852-4449
Gusmer Enterprises Inc
Fresno, CA....................... 866-213-1131
Hess Machine Intl
Ephrata, PA 800-735-4377
Holland Applied Technologies
Burr Ridge, IL.................... 630-325-5130
Hungerford & Terry
Clayton, NJ 856-881-3200
Hydromax Inc
Emmitsburg, MD 800-326-0602
Hydropure Water Treatment Co
Coral Springs, FL 800-753-1547
Introdel Products
Itasca, IL 800-323-4772
Jamieson Laboratories
Windsor, ON 800-265-5088
Kinetico
Newbury, OH 440-564-9111
King Bag & Mfg Co
Cincinnati, OH 800-444-5464
Lamports Filter Media
Cleveland, OH 216-881-2050
Miura Boilers
Atlanta, GA...................... 770-916-1695
Moll-Tron
Lakewood, CO 800-525-9494
Optipure
Plano, TX 972-422-1212
Our Name is Mud
New York, NY 877-683-7867
Parkson Corp
Vernon Hills, IL 847-816-3700
PURA
Sun Valley, CA 800-292-7872
RainSoft Water Treatment System
Elk Grove Vlg, IL 847-437-9400
Refractron Technologies Corp
Newark, NY 315-331-6222
Reynold Water Conditioning
Farmington Hills, MI 800-572-9575
Selecto Scientific
Suwanee, GA 800-635-4017

Sermia International
Blainville, QC.................... 800-567-7483
Star Filters
Timmonsville, SC................. 800-845-5381
Trisep Corporation
Goleta, CA 805-964-8003
VMC Signs
Victoria, TX 361-575-0548
Water Management Resources
Overton, NV 800-552-5797
Water Sciences Services, Inc.
Jackson, TN 973-584-4131
Watts Premier Inc
Peoria, AZ....................... 800-752-5582

Coolers

Allied Bakery and Food Service Equipment
Santa Fe Springs, CA 562-945-6506
Baxter Manufacturing Inc
Orting, WA 800-777-2828
DBE Inc
Concord, ON..................... 800-461-5313
Distillata
Cleveland, OH 800-999-2906
Fred D Pfening Co
Columbus, OH 614-294-5361
Girard Spring Water
North Providence, RI 800-477-9287
Hoshizaki
Worthington, OH................. 800-642-1140
Lucks Food Equipment Company
Kent, WA........................ 811-824-0696
Moli-International
Denver, CO 800-525-8468
Oshikiri Corp Of America
Philadelphia, PA 215-637-8112
Pavailler Distribution Company
Northvale, NJ 201-767-0766
Perfect Equipment Inc
Gurnee, IL 800-356-6301
Pro Bake Inc
Twinsburg, OH 800-837-4427
Pro-Flo Products
Cedar Grove, NJ 800-325-1057
Sunroc Corporation
Columbus, OH 800-478-6762

Purifiers

Aquathin Corporation
Pompano Beach, FL 800-462-7634
Astro Pure Water
Deerfield Beach, FL 954-422-8966
Bestech Inc
Pompano Beach, FL 800-977-2378
Diamond Water Conditioning
Hortonville, WI................... 800-236-8931
Distillata
Cleveland, OH 800-999-2906
Durastill Export Inc
Rockland, MA.................... 800-449-5260
Enting Water Conditioning Inc
Moraine, OH 800-735-5100
Fuller Ultra Violet Corp
Frankfort, IL 815-469-3301
Hydromax Inc
Emmitsburg, MD 800-326-0602
Hydropure Water Treatment Co
Coral Springs, FL 800-753-1547
Joneca Corp
Anaheim, CA 714-993-5997
Kinetico
Newbury, OH 440-564-9111
Kiss International/Di-tech Systems
Vista, CA........................ 800-527-5477
Manhattan Truck Lines
Paterson, NJ 800-370-7627
RainSoft Water Treatment System
Elk Grove Vlg, IL 847-437-9400
Reynold Water Conditioning
Farmington Hills, MI 800-572-9575
Royal Prestige Health Moguls
Westbury, NY 888-802-7433
Ulcra Dynamics
Colmar, PA 800-727-6931
United Industries Group Inc
Lake Forest, CA 949-759-3200
Water & Power Technologies
Salt Lake City, UT 888-271-3295
Watts Premier Inc
Peoria, AZ....................... 800-752-5582

Softeners

Aquathin Corporation
Pompano Beach, FL 800-462-7634
Culligan Company
Northbrook, IL 800-527-8637
Diamond Water Conditioning
Hortonville, WI. 800-236-8931
Ecodyne Water Treatment, LLC
Naperville, IL 800-228-9326
Enting Water Conditioning Inc
Moraine, OH. 800-735-5100
Hungerford & Terry
Clayton, NJ. 856-881-3200
Reynold Water Conditioning
Farmington Hills, MI 800-572-9575

Treatment Systems

A-L-L Magnetics Inc
Anaheim, CA 800-262-4638
ABJ/Sanitaire Corporation
Milwaukee, WI. 414-365-2200
Action Engineering
Liburn, GA 800-228-4668
ADI Systems Inc
Fredericton, NB 800-561-2831
Aeration Industries Intl LLC
Chaska, MN 800-328-8287
Aeromix Systems
Minneapolis, MN 800-879-3677
AERTEC
North Andover, MA 978-475-6385
AFL Industries
West Palm Beach, FL 800-807-2709
Alar Engineering Corp
Mokena, IL 708-479-6100
ALCO Designs
Gardena, CA 800-228-2346
Alkazone/Better Health Lab
Hackensack, NJ. 800-810-1888
Alkota Cleaning Systems Inc
Alcester, SD 800-255-6823
Alloy Hardfacing & Engineering
Jordan, MN 800-328-8408
American Ultraviolet Co
Lebanon, IN 800-288-9288
Andco Environmental Processes
Amherst, NY 716-691-2100
API Industries
Tulsa, OK 918-664-4010
Applied Membranes
Vista, CA. 800-321-9321
Aqua-Aerobic Systems Inc
Loves Park, IL 800-940-5008
Aquathin Corporation
Pompano Beach, FL 800-462-7634
Astro Pure Water
Deerfield Beach, FL 954-422-8966
Atlantic Ultraviolet Corp
Hauppauge, NY 866-958-9085
Ayer Sales Inc
Woburn, MA 800-225-5736
Bestech Inc
Pompano Beach, FL 800-977-2378
Betz Entec
Horsham, PA. 800-877-1940
Bio Cide Intl Inc
Norman, OK 800-323-1398
Bioionix Inc
Mc Farland, WI. 608-838-0300
Biothane Corporation
Camden, NJ. 856-541-3500
BluMetric Environmental Inc.
Ottawa, ON 613-839-3053
Centrisys
Kenosha, WI 262-654-6006
ChemTreat, Inc.
Glen Allen, VA 800-648-4579
Chicago Conveyor Corporation
Addison, IL. 630-543-6300
Chlorinators Inc
Stuart, FL 800-327-9761
Clean Water Systems
Klamath Falls, OR 866-273-9993
Clean Water Technology
Los Angeles, CA. 310-380-4658
Conquest International LLC
Plainville, KS 785-434-2483
Continental Industrial Supply
South Pasadena, FL. 727-341-1100
Corp Somat
Lancaster, PA 800-237-6628

Crane Environmental
Norristown, PA 800-633-7435
Culligan Company
Northbrook, IL 800-527-8637
Diamond Water Conditioning
Hortonville, WI. 800-236-8931
Discovery Chemical
Marietta, GA. 800-973-9881
Durastill Export Inc
Rockland, MA. 800-449-5260
Eaton Filtration, LLC
Tinton Falls, NJ. 800-859-9212
Ecodyne Water Treatment, LLC
Naperville, IL 800-228-9326
Enting Water Conditioning Inc
Moraine, OH. 800-735-5100
Equipment Enterprises
Charlotte, NC 800-221-3681
ESD Waste2water Inc
Ocala, FL. 800-277-3279
Eutek Systems
Hillsboro, OR 503-601-0843
Everfilt Corp
Mira Loma, CA. 800-360-8380
Evoqua Water Technologies
Thomasville, GA. 800-841-1550
Filtrine Manufacturing
Keene, NH. 800-930-3367
FRC Environmental
Gainesville, GA 770-534-3681
Global Water Group Inc
Dallas, TX. 214-678-9866
Hess Machine Intl
Ephrata, PA. 800-735-4377
Hibrett Puratex
Pennsauken, NJ. 800-260-5124
Hoshizaki
Worthington, OH. 800-642-1140
Hubbell Electric Heater Co
Stratford, CT. 800-647-3165
Hungerford & Terry
Clayton, NJ. 856-881-3200
Hydrite Chemical Co
Brookfield, WI. 262-792-1450
HydroCal
Laguna Hills, CA. 800-877-0765
Hydromax Inc
Emmitsburg, MD 800-326-0602
Hydropure Water Treatment Co
Coral Springs, FL 800-753-1547
Innova-Tech
Paoli, PA. 800-523-7299
Interlab
The Woodlands, TX 888-876-2844
International Reserve Equipment Corporation
Clarendon Hills, IL. 708-531-0680
Introdel Products
Itasca, IL 800-323-4772
Jamieson Laboratories
Windsor, ON 800-265-5088
Jemolo Enterprises
Porterville, CA 559-784-5566
Kinetico
Newbury, OH 440-564-9111
Kiss International/Di-tech Systems
Vista, CA. 800-527-5477
KMT Aqua-Dyne Inc
Baxter Springs, KS 800-826-9274
Komline-Sanderson Engineering
Peapack, NJ. 800-225-5457
Lechler Inc
St Charles, IL 800-777-2926
Little Giant Pump Company
Fort Wayne, IN 260-824-2900
Loprest Co
Rodeo, CA. 888-228-5982
Ludell Manufacturing Co
Milwaukee, WI. 800-558-0800
Manhattan Truck Lines
Paterson, NJ. 800-370-7627
Membrane System Specialist Inc
Wisconsin Rapids, WI 715-421-2333
Midbrook Inc
Jackson, MI. 800-966-9274
Moll-Tron
Lakewood, CO 800-525-9494
Momar
Atlanta, GA. 800-556-3967
Mountain Safety Research
Seattle, WA 800-877-9677
Multiplex Co Inc
Sellersburg, IN 800-787-8880

Navy Brand
St Louis, MO. 800-325-3312
Newco Enterprises Inc
St Charles, MO. 800-325-7867
Newtech Inc
Randolph, VT 800-210-2361
Nijhuis Water Technology
Chicago, IL 312-466-9900
Nimbus Water Systems
Murrieta, CA 800-451-9343
Otterbine Barebo Inc
Emmaus, PA 800-237-8837
Ozotech Inc
Yreka, CA. 530-842-4189
Parkson Corp
Vernon Hills, IL 847-816-3700
Parkson Corporation
Fort Lauderdale, FL 954-974-6610
Polychem Corp
Mentor, OH. 440-357-1500
Pro-Flo Products
Cedar Grove, NJ. 800-325-1057
PURA
Sun Valley, CA 800-292-7872
Pure & Secure LLC-Cust Svc
Lincoln, NE. 800-875-5915
Puronics Water Systems Inc
Livermore, CA 925-456-7000
Quality Control Equipment Co
Des Moines, IA 515-266-2268
RainSoft Water Treatment System
Elk Grove Vlg, IL. 847-437-9400
Reynold Water Conditioning
Farmington Hills, MI 800-572-9575
Rochester Midland Corp
Rochester, NY. 800-836-1627
Ryter Corporation
Saint James, MN. 800-643-2184
Scaltrol Inc
Suwanee, GA 800-868-0629
Scienco Systems
Saint Louis, MO 314-621-2536
Sermia International
Blainville, QC 800-567-7483
Severn Trent Svc
Fort Washington, PA. 215-646-9201
Severn Trent Svc
Colmar, PA. 215-822-2901
Shepard Brothers Co
La Habra, CA. 800-645-3594
Southeastern Filtration Systs
Canton, GA. 800-935-8500
Star Filters
Timmonsville, SC 800-845-5381
SUEZ Water Technologies & Solutions
Trevose, PA. 866-439-2837
Systems IV
Chandler, AZ. 800-852-4221
Telechem Corp
Atlanta, GA. 800-637-0495
TLB Corporation
Ellicott, MD 410-773-9443
TRITEN Corporation
Houston, TX 832-214-5000
Ulcra Dynamics
Colmar, PA. 800-727-6931
United Industries Group Inc
Lake Forest, CA 949-759-3200
US Filter
Palm Desert, CA 760-340-0098
US Filter/Continental Water
San Antonio, TX. 800-426-3426
Vulcan Materials Co
Vestavia, AL 205-298-3000
Wade Manufacturing Company
Tigard, OR 800-222-7246
Water & Power Technologies
Salt Lake City, UT 888-271-3295
Water System Group
Santa Clarita, CA 800-350-9283
Waterlink/Sanborn Technologies
Canton, OH. 800-343-3381
Watts Premier Inc
Peoria, AZ. 800-752-5582
World Water Works
Elmsford, NY 800-607-7873
Yardney Water Management Syst
Riverside, CA. 800-854-4788

Food Preparation Equipment, Utensils & Cookware

Aluminum Ware

A Legacy Food Svc
  Santa Fe Springs, CA 800-848-4440
Advance Tabco
  Edgewood, NY 800-645-3166
Alumaworks
  Sunny Isle Beach, FL 800-277-7267
C R Mfg
  Waverly, NE 877-789-5844
Culinary Depot
  Monsey, NY 888-845-8200
Dur-Able Aluminum Corporation
  Hoffman Estates, IL 847-843-1100
Econofrost Night Covers
  Shawnigan Lake, BC 800-519-1222
H. Yamamoto
  Port Washington, NY 718-821-7700
Handi-Foil Corp
  Wheeling, IL 847-520-8347
Hillside Metal Ware Company
  Union, NJ 908-964-3080
Johnson-Rose Corporation
  Lockport, NY 800-456-2055
Lloyd Disher Company
  Decatur, IL 217-429-0593
Montebello Packaging
  Hawkesbury, ON. 613-632-7096
Regal Ware Inc
  Kewaskum, WI. 262-626-2121
Vasconia Housewares
  San Antonio, TX 800-377-6723
Weavewood, Inc.
  Golden Valley, MN 800-367-6460
Wilkinson Manufacturing Company
  Fort Calhoun, NE 402-468-5511
Williamsburg Metal Spinning
  Brooklyn, NY 888-535-5402

Baskets

Culinary, Frying, Etc.

Archer Wire Intl Corp
  Chicago, IL. 708-563-1700
Atlanta Burning Bush
  Newnan, GA 800-665-5611
Automatic Specialties Inc
  Marlborough, MA. 800-445-2370
Barker Wire
  Keosauqua, IA 319-293-3176
Bluebird Manufacturing
  Montreal, QC 800-406-2505
Dean Industries
  Gardena, CA 800-995-1210
Etube & Wire
  Shrewsbury, PA. 800-618-4720
F.P. Smith Wire Cloth Company
  Northlake, IL. 800-323-6842
J.C. Products Inc.
  Haddam, CT 860-267-5516
Jesco Industries
  Litchfield, MI 800-455-0019
Keating Of Chicago Inc
  Mc Cook, IL 800-532-8464
Madsen Wire Products Inc
  Orland, IN 260-829-6561
Mid-West Wire Products
  Ferndale, MI 800-989-9881
Midwest Wire Products LLC
  Sturgeon Bay, WI 800-445-0225
Mouli Manufacturing Corporation
  Belleville, NJ 800-789-8285
Music City Metals Inc
  Nashville, TN 800-251-2674
Pitco Frialator Inc
  Bow, NH 800-258-3708
Prince Castle Inc
  Carol Stream, IL 800-722-7853
Pronto Products Company
  Arcadia, CA 800-377-6680
Quadra-Tech
  Columbus, OH 800-443-2766
SSW Holding Co Inc
  Elizabethtown, KY 270-769-5526
Stryco Wire Products
  North York, ON. 416-663-7000

Technibilt/Cari-All
  Newton, NC 800-233-3972
Wirefab Inc
  Worcester, MA 877-877-4445

Blocks

Butchers'

Anderson Wood Products
  Louisville, KY 502-778-5591
Bally Block Co
  Bally, PA 610-845-7511
Canada Goose Wood Produc
  Gloucester, ON 888-890-6506
Emco Industrial Plastics
  Cedar Grove, NJ 800-292-9906
Greensburg Manufacturing Company
  Greensburg, KY 270-932-5511
Hollingsworth Custom Wood Products
  Sault Ste. Marie, ON 705-759-1756
John Boos & Co
  Effingham, IL 888-431-2667
M & E Mfg Co Inc
  Kingston, NY 845-331-2110
Michigan Maple Block Co
  Petoskey, MI 800-447-7975
Perfect Plank Co
  Oroville, CA 800-327-1961

Boards

Cutting Block

Arrow Plastic Mfg Co
  Elk Grove Vlg, IL. 847-595-9000
Bally Block Co
  Bally, PA 610-845-7511
Browne & Company
  Markham, ON. 905-475-6104
C R Mfg
  Waverly, NE 877-789-5844
Canada Goose Wood Produc
  Gloucester, ON 888-890-6506
Capital Plastics
  Middlefield, OH 440-632-5800
Catskill Craftsmen Inc
  Stamford, NY 607-652-7321
Chef Specialties
  Smethport, PA. 800-440-2433
Ellingers Agatized Wood Inc
  Sheboygan, WI 888-287-8906
Emco Industrial Plastics
  Cedar Grove, NJ 800-292-9906
Goebel Fixture Co
  Hutchinson, MN 888-339-0509
Greensburg Manufacturing Company
  Greensburg, KY 270-932-5511
Hollingsworth Custom Wood Products
  Sault Ste. Marie, ON. 705-759-1756
John Boos & Co
  Effingham, IL 888-431-2667
KTG
  Cincinnati, OH 888-533-6900
M & E Mfg Co Inc
  Kingston, NY 845-331-2110
Michigan Maple Block Co
  Petoskey, MI 800-447-7975
Newell Brands
  Atlanta, GA
Read Products Inc
  Seattle, WA 800-445-3416
Spartec Plastics
  Conneaut, OH 800-325-5176
Superior Products Company
  Saint Paul, MN 800-328-9800
Vermillion Flooring
  Springfield, MO 417-862-3785
Wolf Works
  Arroyo Grande, CA. 800-549-3806
Wooster Novelty Company
  Brooklyn, NY 718-852-8934

Wood

Bread, Cake & Steak

Enjay Converters Ltd.
  Cobourg, ON. 800-427-5517
H A Stiles
  Westbrook, ME. 800-447-8537
Lady Mary
  Rockingham, NC 910-997-7321
Lillsun Manufacturing Co
  Huntington, IN 260-356-6514
Marston Manufacturing
  Cleveland, OH 216-587-3400
Michigan Maple Block Co
  Petoskey, MI 800-447-7975
Sunset Paper Products
  Simi Valley, CA. 800-228-7882
Wooster Novelty Company
  Brooklyn, NY 718-852-8934

Bowls

AJM Packaging Corporation
  Bloomfield Hills, MI 248-901-0040
Amco Metals Indl
  City Of Industry, CA. 626-855-2550
Apex Fountain Sales Inc
  Philadelphia, PA 800-523-4586
Atlantis Industries Inc
  Milton, DE 302-684-8542
BG Industries
  Lemont, IL 800-800-5761
C R Mfg
  Waverly, NE 877-789-5844
Cal-Mil Plastic Products Inc
  Oceanside, CA 800-321-9069
Carlisle Food Svc Products Inc
  Oklahoma City, OK 800-654-8210
Carthage Cup Company
  Longview, TX. 903-238-9833
Chef Specialties
  Smethport, PA 800-440-2433
Cleveland Metal Stamping Company
  Berea, OH 440-234-0010
Coley Industries
  Wayland, NY. 716-728-2390
Cyclamen Collection
  Oakland, CA 510-434-7620
Delfin Design & Mfg
  Rancho Sta Marg, CA 800-354-7919
Design Specialties Inc
  Hamden, CT 800-999-1584
Dover Parkersburg
  Follansbee, WV
Eastern Tabletop Mfg
  Brooklyn, NY 888-422-4142
Ellingers Agatized Wood Inc
  Sheboygan, WI 888-287-8906
Engineered Plastics Inc
  Gibsonville, NC 800-711-1740
Finn & Son's Metal Spinning Specialists
  South Lebanon, OH 513-494-2898
Gaetano America
  El Monte, CA 626-442-2858
Genpak LLC
  Charlotte, NC 800-626-6695
Grand Silver Company
  Bronx, NY. 718-585-1930
Granville Manufacturing Co
  Granville, VT 800-828-1005
Hoffmaster Group Inc.
  Oshkosh, WI. 800-558-9300
HPI North America/Plastics
  Chicago, IL. 800-327-3534
Jones-Zylon Co
  West Lafayette, OH. 800-848-8160
Kendrick Johnson & Assoc Inc
  Minneapolis, MN 800-826-1271
Kosempel Manufacturing Company
  Philadelphia, PA 800-733-7122
Leggett & Platt Storage
  Vernon Hills, IL 847-816-6246
Majestic
  Bridgeport, CT 203-367-7900
NCC
  Groveland, FL. 800-429-9037

Novelty Crystal
Long Island City, NY 800-622-0250
Olde Country Reproductions Inc
York, PA 800-358-3997
Palmer Distributors
St Clair Shores, MI 800-444-1912
Polar Ware Company
Sheboygan, WI 800-237-3655
Prairie Packaging Inc
Mooresville, NC 704-660-6600
Prolon
Port Gibson, MS 888-480-9828
Sani-Top Products
De Leon Springs, FL.............. 800-874-6094
Savage Brothers Company
Elk Grove Vlg, IL 800-342-0973
Service Ideas
Woodbury, MN 800-328-4493
Superior Products Company
Saint Paul, MN 800-328-9800
Tablecraft Products Co Inc
Gurnee, IL 800-323-8321
Techform
Mount Airy, NC 336-789-2115
Ullman, Shapiro & UllmanLLP
New York, NY 212-755-0299
Vertex China
Pomona, CA 800-483-7839
Victoria Porcelain
Miami, FL 888-593-2353
Weavewood, Inc.
Golden Valley, MN 800-367-6460
Western Stoneware
Monmouth, IL.................... 309-734-2161
Wiltec
Leominster, MA 978-537-1497
WNA
Chattanooga, TN................. 800-404-9318
Wna Comet West Inc
City Of Industry, CA.............. 800-225-0939

Brushes

Bakers' & Confectioners'

Amco Metals Indl
City Of Industry, CA.............. 626-855-2550
Braun Brush Co
Albertson, NY.................... 800-645-4111
Carlisle Food Svc Products Inc
Oklahoma City, OK 800-654-8210
Kiefer Brushes, Inc
Franklin, NJ 800-526-2905
Kopykake
Torrance, CA..................... 800-999-5253
Linzer Products Corp
West Babylon, NY 800-423-3254
Music City Metals Inc
Nashville, TN..................... 800-251-2674
Opie Brush Company
Independence, MO 800-877-6743
Precision Brush
Cleveland, OH 800-252-4747
Six Hardy Brush Manufacturing
Suffield, CT...................... 860-623-8465
Tucel Industries, Inc.
Forestdale, VT 800-558-8235

Food Industry

Abco Products
Miami, FL....................... 888-694-2226
Akron Cotton Products
Akron, OH....................... 800-899-7173
All Weather Energy Systems
Plymouth, MI.................... 888-636-8324
Amco Metals Indl
City Of Industry, CA.............. 626-855-2550
American Brush Company
Portland, OR 800-826-8492
Anderson Products
Cresco, PA....................... 800-729-4694
Baldewein Company
Lake Forrest, IL 800-424-5544
Bouras Mop Manufacturing Company
Saint Louis, MO 800-634-9153
Braun Brush Co
Albertson, NY.................... 800-645-4111
Brush Research Mfg Co Inc
Los Angeles, CA.................. 323-261-6162
Carlisle Food Svc Products Inc
Oklahoma City, OK 800-654-8210

Carlisle Sanitary Mntnc Prods
Oklahoma City, OK 800-654-8210
Cosgrove Enterprises Inc
Miami Lakes, FL................. 800-888-3396
Detroit Quality Brush Mfg Co
Livonia, MI...................... 800-722-3037
Furgale Industries Ltd.
Winnipeg, NB 800-665-0506
Great Lakes Brush
Centralia, MO 573-682-2128
Greenwood Mop & Broom Inc
Greenwood, SC................... 800-635-6849
Harper Brush Works Inc
Fairfield, IA 800-223-7894
Hoge Brush Company
New Knoxville, OH 800-494-4643
Hub City Brush Co
Petal, MS........................ 800-278-7452
Ideal Stencil Machine & Tape Company
Marion, IL....................... 800-388-0162
Industries For The Blind
Milwaukee, WI................... 800-642-8778
Justman Brush Co
Omaha, NE 800-800-6940
Keating Of Chicago Inc
Mc Cook, IL 800-532-8464
Kiefer Brushes, Inc
Franklin, NJ 800-526-2905
Labpride Chemicals
Bronx, NY....................... 800-467-1255
Libman Co
Arcola, IL........................ 877-818-3380
Messina Brothers Manufacturing Company
Brooklyn, NY 800-924-6454
Mill-Rose Co
Mentor, OH...................... 800-321-3598
Murk Brush Company
New Britain, CT 860-249-2550
Music City Metals Inc
Nashville, TN..................... 800-251-2674
Nation/Ruskin
Montgomeryville, PA 800-523-2489
National Novelty Brush Co
Lancaster, PA 717-299-5681
Nationwide Wire & Brush Manufacturing
Lodi, CA......................... 209-334-9660
Newell Brands
Atlanta, GA
Newton Broom Co
Newton, IL 618-783-4424
O'Dell Corp
Ware Shoals, SC 800-342-2843
O-Cedar
Aurora, IL........................ 800-543-8105
Opie Brush Company
Independence, MO 800-877-6743
Pepper Mill
Mobile, AL....................... 800-669-5175
Power Brushes
Toledo, OH 800-968-9600
Precision Brush
Cleveland, OH 800-252-4747
Quality Mop & Brush Manufacturers
Needham, MA.................... 617-884-2999
Quickie Manufacturing Corp
Cinnaminson, NJ 856-829-7900
Remco Products Corp
Zionsville, IN 800-585-8619
RidgeView Products LLC
La Crosse, WI 888-782-1221
Six Hardy Brush Manufacturing
Suffield, CT...................... 860-623-8465
Special Products
Springfield, MO 417-881-6114
Superior Products Company
Saint Paul, MN 800-328-9800
TRC
Middlefield, OH 440-834-0078
Tucel Industries, Inc.
Forestdale, VT 800-558-8235
Urnex Brands Inc
Elmsford, NY 800-222-2826
Volckening Inc
Brooklyn, NY 800-221-0276
Walker Brush Inc
Webster, NY 585-545-4748
Warren E. Conley Corporation
Carmel, IN....................... 800-367-7875
Wilen Professional Cleaning Products
Atlanta, GA...................... 800-241-7371
Young & Swartz Inc
Buffalo, NY...................... 800-466-7682

Zephyr Manufacturing Co
Sedalia, MO 660-827-0352
Zoia Banquetier Co
Cleveland, OH 216-631-6414

Cleavers

Butchers'

Lamson & Goodnow
Shelburne Falls, MA............... 800-872-6564

Cookware

A Legacy Food Svc
Santa Fe Springs, CA.............. 800-848-4440
Alegacy
Santa Fe Springs, CA.............. 800-848-4440
All-Clad METALCRAFTERS LLC
Canonsburg, PA.................. 800-255-2523
Alumaworks
Sunny Isle Beach, FL 800-277-7267
Amber Glo
Chicago, IL 866-705-0515
American Griddle Corp.
Fort Wayne, IN 800-428-6550
APW Wyott Food Service Equipment Company
Cheyenne, WY 800-527-2100
Baking Machines
Livermore, CA 925-449-3369
Bluebird Manufacturing
Montreal, QC 800-406-2505
Browne & Company
Markham, ON 905-475-6104
CookTek
Chicago, IL 888-266-5835
Crown Custom Metal Spinning
Concord, ON..................... 800-750-1924
Cyclamen Collection
Oakland, CA 510-434-7620
Danger Men Cooking
Highland, NY 845-691-7029
Dover Parkersburg
Follansbee, WV
Dura-Ware Company of America
Oklahoma City, OK 800-664-3872
Eagleware Manufacturing
Compton, CA 310-604-0404
Esterle Mold & Machine Co Inc
Stow, OH 800-411-4086
Eurodib
Champlain, NY 888-956-6866
Finn & Son's Metal Spinning Specialists
South Lebanon, OH 513-494-2898
Floaire
Blue Bell, PA..................... 800-726-5623
H.F. Coors China Company
New Albany, MS.................. 800-782-6677
Harold Leonard Southwest Corporation
Houston, TX 800-245-8105
Hartstone Pottery Inc
Zanesville, OH 740-452-9999
Hillside Metal Ware Company
Union, NJ 908-964-3080
Johnson-Rose Corporation
Lockport, NY 800-456-2055
Lancaster Colony Corporation
Westerville, OH................... 614-224-7141
Legion Industries Inc
Waynesboro, GA.................. 800-887-1988
Liberty Ware LLC
Clearfield, UT.................... 888-500-5885
Lincoln Foodservice
Cleveland, OH 800-374-3004
Lodge Manufacturing Company
South Pittsburg, TN 423-837-5919
Marston Manufacturing
Cleveland, OH 216-587-3400
Mirro Company
Lancaster, OH 800-848-7200
Padinox
Winsloe, PE...................... 800-263-9768
Professional Bakeware Company
Willis, TX........................ 800-440-9547
Regal Ware Inc
Kewaskum, WI 262-626-2121
Ricoh Technologies
Grand Prairie, TX 800-585-9367
Royal Prestige Health Moguls
Westbury, NY 888-802-7433
Spring USA Corp
Naperville, IL 800-535-8974

131

Superior Products Company
Saint Paul, MN 800-328-9800
Thermoquest
Riviera Beach, FL 888-383-2025
Thermos Company
Schaumburg, IL 800-243-0745
Tomlinson Industries
Cleveland, OH 800-945-4589
Tramontina USA
Sugar Land, TX 800-221-7809
Tufty Ceramics Inc
Andover, NY 607-478-5150
Tupperware Brands Corporation
Orlando, FL .800-366-3800
United Performance Metals
Northbrook, IL 888-922-0040
Vasconia Housewares
San Antonio, TX 800-377-6723
Vorwerk
Thousand Oaks, CA 888-867-9375
WaffleWaffle
Nutley, NJ 201-559-1286
World Kitchen
Elmira, NY 800-999-3436
Xtreme Beverages, LLC
Dana Point, CA 949-495-7929

Covers

Dish, Food Display & Tray

A1 Tablecloth Co
South Hackensack, NJ 800-727-8987
Acryline
North Attleboro, MA 508-695-7124
Amco Metals Indl
City Of Industry, CA 626-855-2550
American Metalcraft Inc
Franklin Park, IL 708-345-1177
Apple-A-Day Nutritional Labeling Service
San Clemente, CA 949-855-8954
Arden Companies
Southfield, MI 248-415-8500
Bardes Plastics Inc
Milwaukee, WI 800-558-5161
Brooklace
Oshkosh, WI 800-572-4552
C-Through Covers
San Diego, CA 619-286-0671
Carlisle Food Svc Products Inc
Oklahoma City, OK 800-654-8210
Davlynne International
Cudahy, WI 800-558-5208
Delfin Design & Mfg
Rancho Sta Marg, CA 800-354-7919
Delta Plastics
Hot Springs, AR 501-760-3000
Dilley Manufacturing Co
Des Moines, IA 800-247-5087
Dow Cover Co Inc
New Haven, CT 800-735-8877
Dynynstyl
Delray Beach, FL 800-774-7895
Eaton Quade Plastics & Sign Co
Oklahoma City, OK 405-236-4475
Econofrost Night Covers
Shawnigan Lake, BC 800-519-1222
Eide Industries Inc
Cerritos, CA 800-422-6827
Eliason Corp
Portage, MI 800-828-3655
Erving Industries
Erving, MA .413-422-2700
Fato Industries
Kankakee, IL 815-932-3015
Goldenwest Sales
Cerritos, CA 800-827-6175
Highland Supply Corp
Highland, IL 800-472-3645
Hoffmaster Group Inc
Oshkosh, WI 800-327-9774
J. James
Brooklyn, NY 718-384-6144
J.V. Reed & Company
Louisville, KY 877-258-7333
Jordan Specialty Company
Brooklyn, NY 877-567-3265
K & L Intl
Ontario, CA 888-598-5588
K-C Products Company
Van Nuys, CA 818-267-1600

Kendrick Johnson & Assoc Inc
Minneapolis, MN 800-826-1271
Lakeside Manufacturing Inc
Milwaukee, WI 888-558-8565
Michael Leson Dinnerware
Youngstown, OH 800-821-3541
Midco Plastics
Enterprise, KS 800-235-2729
Morris Transparent Box Co
East Providence, RI 401-438-6116
MultiFab Plastics
Boston, MA 888-293-5754
Nyman Manufacturing Company
Rumford, RI 401-438-3410
Palmer Distributors
St Clair Shores, MI 800-444-1912
Penda Form Corp
New Concord, OH 800-837-2574
Polar Plastics
St Laurent, QC 514-331-0207
Polar Ware Company
Sheboygan, WI 800-237-3655
Products A Curtron Div
Pittsburgh, PA 800-888-9750
Reading Plastic Fabricators
Reading, PA 610-926-3245
Samsill Corp
Fort Worth, TX 800-255-1100
Sani-Top Products
De Leon Springs, FL 800-874-6094
Sims Superior Seating
Locust Grove, GA 800-729-9178
Springprint Medallion
Augusta, GA 800-543-5990
Standard Terry Mills
Souderton, PA 215-723-8121
Steril-Sil Company
Bowmansville, PA 800-784-5537
Superior Linen & Work Wear
Kansas City, MO 800-798-7987
Superior Products Company
Saint Paul, MN 800-328-9800
Tara Linens
Sanford, NC 800-476-8272
TEMP-TECH Company
Springfield, MA 800-343-5579
Thermal Bags By Ingrid Inc
Gilberts, IL .800-622-5560
Tri-State Plastics
Glenwillard, PA 724-457-6900
WORC Slitting & Mfg Co
Worcester, MA 800-356-2961
Zoia Banquetier Co
Cleveland, OH 216-631-6414

Cutlery

A G Russell Knives
Rogers, AR 800-255-9034
Ace Co Precision Mfg
Boise, ID 800-359-7012
Acme International
Maplewood, NJ 973-416-0400
Amcel
Watertown, MA 800-225-7992
American Housewares
Bronx, NY .718-665-9500
Babco International, Inc
Tucson, AZ 520-628-7596
Bettendorf Stanford Inc
Salem, IL 800-548-2253
BOC Plastics Inc
Winston Salem, NC 800-334-8687
Boehringer Mfg. Co. Inc.
Felton, CA .800-630-8665
Brooklyn Boys Pizza & Pasta
Boca Raton, FL 561-477-3663
Browne & Company
Markham, ON 905-475-6104
Buck Knives
Post Falls, ID 800-326-2825
Burrell Cutlery Company
Ellicottville, NY 716-699-2343
C R Mfg
Waverly, NE 877-789-5844
CB Mfg. & Sales Co.
Miamisburg, OH 800-543-6860
Chef Revival
North Charleston, SC 800-248-9826
Chicago Scale & Slicer Company
Franklin Park, IL 847-455-3400
Chuppa Knife Manufacturing
Jackson, TN 731-424-1212

Conimar Corp
Ocala, FL 800-874-9735
CUTCO Corp
Olean, NY .716-372-3111
Cutrite Company
Fremont, OH 800-928-8748
Dart Container Corp.
Mason, MI .800-248-5960
De Ster Corporation
Atlanta, GA 800-237-8270
Delco Tableware
Port Washington, NY 800-221-9557
Dexter Russell Inc
Southbridge, MA 800-343-6042
Dispoz-O Plastics
Fountain Inn, SC 864-862-4004
E K Lay Co
Philadelphia, PA 800-523-3220
E-Z Edge Inc
West New York, NJ 800-232-4470
Edge Resources
Hopedale, MA 888-849-0998
Edgecraft Corp
Avondale, PA 800-342-3255
F N Smith Corp
Oregon, IL .815-732-2171
Fioriware
Zanesville, OH 740-454-7400
Florida Knife Co
Sarasota, FL 800-966-5643
Friedr Dick Corp
Farmingdale, NY 800-554-3425
General Cutlery Co
Fremont, OH 419-332-2316
Gerber Legendary Blades
Portland, OR 800-950-6161
Gril-Del
Mankato, MN 800-782-7320
Hansaloy Corp
Davenport, IA 800-553-4992
Hantover Inc
Kansas City, MO 800-821-7849
Hoffmaster Group Inc
Oshkosh, WI 800-367-2877
Hollymatic Corp
Countryside, IL 708-579-3700
Imperial Schrade Corporation
Ellenville, NY 212-210-8600
Izabel Lam International
Brooklyn, NY 718-797-3983
James River Canada
North York, ON. 416-789-5151
Jarden Home Brands
Cloquet, MN 218-879-6700
Jet Plastica Industries
Hatfield, PA
Jim Scharf Holdings
Perdue, SK 800-667-9727
John J. Adams Die Corporation
Worcester, MA 508-757-3894
Kinetic Co
Greendale, WI 414-425-8221
KSW Corp
Des Moines, IA 515-265-5269
Lamson & Goodnow
Shelburne Falls, MA 800-872-6564
Les Industries Touch Inc
Sherbrooke, QC 800-267-4140
Lifetime Brands Inc
Garden City, NY 516-683-6000
Mandeville Company
Minneapolis, MN 800-328-8490
Max Packaging
Attalla, AL .800-543-5369
Mundial
Norwood, MA 800-487-2224
Omcan Manufacturing & Distributing Company
Mississauga, ON 800-465-0234
Oneida Food Service
Columbus, OH 800-828-7033
Penley Corporation
West Paris, ME 800-368-6449
Polar Plastics
St Laurent, QC 514-331-0207
Prairie Packaging Inc
Mooresville, NC 704-660-6600
R H Saw Corp
Barrington, IL 847-381-8777
R Murphy Co Inc
Ayer, MA 888-772-3481
Ranger Blade Manufacturing Company
Traer, IA 800-377-7860

132

Replacements LTD
Mc Leansville, NC 800-737-5223
Rhineland Cutlery
Melbourne, FL 321-725-2101
Royal Prestige Health Moguls
Westbury, NY 888-802-7433
Royal Silver Mfg Co Inc
Norfolk, VA. 757-855-6004
Safe-T-Cut Inc
Monson, MA. 413-267-9984
Salem China Company
Salem, OH. 330-337-8771
Simmons Engineering Corporation
Wheeling, IL 800-252-3381
Spir-It/Zoo Piks
Andover, MA 800-343-0996
Superior Products Company
Saint Paul, MN 800-328-9800
Tramontina USA
Sugar Land, TX. 800-221-7809
Utica Cutlery Co
Utica, NY 800-879-2526
Waddington North America
Chelmsford, MA. 888-962-2877
Walco
Utica, NY 800-879-2526
Warther Museum
Dover, OH. 330-343-7513
Wishbone Utensil Tableware Line
Wheat Ridge, CO 866-266-5928
Wna Comet West Inc
City Of Industry, CA. 800-225-0939
Zelco Industries
Mount Vernon, NY 800-431-2486

Cutters

Biscuit & Cookie

Amco Metals Indl
City Of Industry, CA. 626-855-2550
Ann Clark, LTD
Rutland, VT 800-252-6798
Arcobaleno Pasta Machines
Lancaster, PA 800-875-7096
Boehringer Mfg. Co. Inc.
Felton, CA. 800-630-8665
Browne & Company
Markham, ON 905-475-6104
Dito Dean Food Prep
Charlotte, NC 866-449-4200
Don Lee
Philadelphia, PA 760-745-0707
Educational Products Company
Hope, NJ 800-272-3822
Irresistible Cookie Jar
Hayden Lake, ID. 208-664-1261
Lee Financial Corporation
Dallas, TX. 972-960-1001
Lorenzen's Cookie Cutters
Wantagh, NY. 516-781-7116
LoTech Industries
Lakewood, CO 800-295-0199
Moline Machinery LLC
Duluth, MN. 800-767-5734
Parrish's Cake Decorating
Gardena, CA 800-736-8443
Polar Process
Plattsville, ON. 877-896-8077
Pro Bake Inc
Twinsburg, OH 800-837-4427
Rademaker USA
Hudson, OH 330-650-2345
Reading Bakery Systems Inc
Robesonia, PA. 610-693-5816
Rhodes Bakery Equipment
Portland, OR. 800-426-3813
Soco System USA
Waukesha, WI. 800-441-6293
Superior Products Company
Saint Paul, MN 800-328-9800

Cake

Belshaw Adamatic Bakery Group
Auburn, WA 800-578-2547
Colborne Foodbotics
Lake Forest, IL 847-724-5070
Hinds-Bock Corp
Bothell, WA. 425-885-1183
Matiss
St Georges, QC 888-562-8477

Polar Process
Plattsville, ON. 877-896-8077

Cheese

Amco Metals Indl
City Of Industry, CA. 626-855-2550
Berkshire PPM
Litchfield, CT 860-567-3118
Bluffton Slaw Cutter Company
Bluffton, OH 419-358-9840
C&R Refrigation Inc,
Center, TX. 800-438-6182
General Machinery Corp
Sheboygan, WI 888-243-6622
Globe Food Equipment Co
Moraine, OH 800-347-5423
Hart Design & Mfg
Green Bay, WI. 920-468-5927
Lincoln Foodservice
Cleveland, OH 800-374-3004
Mouli Manufacturing Corporation
Belleville, NJ 800-789-8285
Polar Process
Plattsville, ON. 877-896-8077
Samuel Underberg Food Store
Brooklyn, NY 718-363-0787
Superior Products Company
Saint Paul, MN 800-328-9800
TGW International
Florence, KY. 800-407-0173

Dicing

Berkshire PPM
Litchfield, CT 860-567-3118
Custom Food Machinery
Stockton, CA. 209-463-4343
D & S Mfg
Auburn, MA 508-799-7812
General Machinery Corp
Sheboygan, WI 888-243-6622
Insinger Co
Philadelphia, PA 800-344-4802
Luthi Machinery Company, Inc.
Pueblo, CO 719-948-1110
Paxton Corp
Bristol, RI 401-396-9062
Slicechief Co
Toledo, OH 419-241-7647
Superior Products Company
Saint Paul, MN 800-328-9800
Urschel Laboratories
Valparaiso, IN 219-464-4811

Kraut & Slaw

A.K. Robins
Baltimore, MD 800-486-9656
Bluffton Slaw Cutter Company
Bluffton, OH 419-358-9840
Clawson Machine Co Inc
Franklin, NJ 800-828-4088
Paxton Corp
Bristol, RI 401-396-9062

Meat

Power

AEW Thurne
Lake Zurich, IL 800-239-7297
Berkshire PPM
Litchfield, CT 860-567-3118
Biro Manufacturing Co
Lakeside Marblhd, OH 419-798-4451
Globe Food Equipment Co
Moraine, OH 800-347-5423
Jarvis Products Corp
Middletown, CT 860-347-7271
Prince Castle Inc
Carol Stream, IL 800-722-7853
Superior Products Company
Saint Paul, MN 800-328-9800
TGW International
Florence, KY. 800-407-0173
Urschel Laboratories
Valparaiso, IN 219-464-4811

Sausage

Automated Food Systems
Waxahachie, TX 469-517-0470

Cozzini LLC
Chicago, IL 773-478-9700
General Machinery Corp
Sheboygan, WI 888-243-6622
Handtmann Inc
Lake Forest, IL 800-477-3585
Linker Machines
Rockaway, NJ 973-983-0001
Marlen International
Astoria, OR. 800-862-7536
Sperling Industries
Omaha, NE 402-556-4070
TGW International
Florence, KY. 800-407-0173

Pickle

A.K. Robins
Baltimore, MD 800-486-9656
Berkshire PPM
Litchfield, CT 860-567-3118
Custom Food Machinery
Stockton, CA. 209-463-4343

Ultrasonic

Polar Process
Plattsville, ON. 877-896-8077

Glasses

Drinking

Anchor Hocking Operating Co
Lancaster, OH 800-562-7511
ATAGO USA Inc
Bellevue, WA 877-282-4687
Atlantis Industries Inc
Milton, DE 302-684-8542
Babco International, Inc
Tucson, AZ. 520-628-7596
Benner China & Glassware Inc
Jacksonville, FL 904-733-4620
Browne & Company
Markham, ON 905-475-6104
Carlisle Food Svc Products Inc
Oklahoma City, OK 800-654-8210
Design Specialties Inc
Hamden, CT 800-999-1584
Donoco Industries
Huntington Beach, CA 888-822-8763
Edco Industries
Bridgeport, CT 203-333-8982
Encore Plastics
Huntington Beach, CA 888-822-8763
Epic Products
Santa Ana, CA 800-548-9791
HPI North America/Plastics
Chicago, IL 800-327-3534
Ideas Etc Inc
Louisville, KY 800-733-0337
Image Plastics
Houston, TX 800-289-2811
Indiana Glass Company
Columbus, OH 800-543-0357
Izabel Lam International
Brooklyn, NY 718-797-3983
Jet Plastica Industries
Hatfield, PA
Jones-Zylon Co
West Lafayette, OH 800-848-8160
Judel Products
Elmsford, NY 800-583-3526
Libby Canada
Mississauga, ON 905-607-8280
Loria Awards
Yonkers, NY 800-540-2927
Majestic
Bridgeport, CT 203-367-7900
MDR International
North Miami, FL. 305-944-5019
Michael Leson Dinnerware
Youngstown, OH. 800-821-3541
Mikasa Hotelware
Secaucus, NJ 866-645-2721
Novelty Crystal
Long Island City, NY 800-622-0250
Prairie Packaging Inc
Mooresville, NC 704-660-6600
Prolon
Port Gibson, MS 888-480-9828
Royal Prestige Health Moguls
Westbury, NY 888-802-7433

Spirit Foodservice, Inc.
Andover, MA .800-343-0996
Superior Products Company
Saint Paul, MN 800-328-9800
Tango Shatterproof Drinkware
Walpole, MA 888-898-2646
Tar-Hong MELAMINE USA
City Of Industry, CA. 626-935-1612
Ullman, Shapiro & UllmanLLP
New York, NY 212-755-0299
Wiltec
Leominster, MA 978-537-1497
Xtreme Beverages, LLC
Dana Point, CA 949-495-7929

Glassware

Cooking & Baking

Anchor Hocking Operating Co
Lancaster, OH 800-562-7511
Judel Products
Elmsford, NY 800-583-3526
Oneida LTD Silversmiths
Oneida, NY .888-263-7195
World Kitchen
Elmira, NY 800-999-3436

Heat Resistant

Automated Packaging Systems
Streetsboro, OH 800-527-0733
Corning Life Sciences
Tewksbury, MA. 800-492-1110
Hartstone Pottery Inc
Zanesville, OH 740-452-9999
Judel Products
Elmsford, NY 800-583-3526
Triad Scientific
Manasquan, NJ 800-867-6690
World Kitchen
Elmira, NY 800-999-3436

Hotel & Restaurant

Abco International
Oneida, NY .888-263-7195
Anchor Hocking Operating Co
Lancaster, OH 800-562-7511
ATAGO USA Inc
Bellevue, WA 877-282-4687
Browne & Company
Markham, ON 905-475-6104
Epic Products
Santa Ana, CA 800-548-9791
Fenton Art Glass Company
Williamstown, WV 800-933-6766
Judel Products
Elmsford, NY 800-583-3526
Lancaster Colony Corporation
Westerville, OH. 614-224-7141
Libbey Inc.
Toledo, OH .419-325-2100
Libby Canada
Mississauga, ON 905-607-8280
Masterpiece Crystal
Jane Lew, WV 304-884-7841
Mikasa Hotelware
Secaucus, NJ 866-645-2721
Minners Designs   Inc.
New York, NY 212-688-7441
Mr Ice Bucket
New Brunswick, NJ 732-545-0420
Novelty Crystal
Long Island City, NY 800-622-0250
Oneida Food Service
Columbus, OH 800-828-7033
Royal Prestige Health Moguls
Westbury, NY 888-802-7433
Superior Products Company
Saint Paul, MN 800-328-9800
Tango Shatterproof Drinkware
Walpole, MA 888-898-2646
Variety Glass Inc
Cambridge, OH 740-432-3643
World Kitchen
Elmira, NY 800-999-3436
Xtreme Beverages, LLC
Dana Point, CA. 949-495-7929

Packers'

All American Container
Miami, FL 305-887-0797
Indianapolis Container Company
Indianapolis, IN 800-760-3318
Kelman Bottles LLC
Glenshaw, PA 412-486-9100

Holders

Corn Cob

Jarden Home Brands
Daleville, IN 800-392-2575

Hollowware

Abco International
Oneida, NY .888-263-7195
Americana Marketing
Newbury Park, CA 800-742-7520
Browne & Company
Markham, ON 905-475-6104
Corby Hall
Randolph, NJ 973-366-8300
Delco Tableware
Port Washington, NY 800-221-9557
Dynynstyl
Delray Beach, FL 800-774-7895
Grand Silver Company
Bronx, NY. .718-585-1930
Lenox Corp
Bristol, PA 800-223-4311
Libby Canada
Mississauga, ON 905-607-8280
Oneida Food Service
Columbus, OH 800-828-7033
Oneida LTD Silversmiths
Oneida, NY. 888-263-7195
Reed & Barton Food Service
Taunton, MA. 800-797-9675
Rexcraft Fine Chafers
Long Island City, NY 888-739-2723
Superior Products Company
Saint Paul, MN 800-328-9800
Tradeco International Corp
Addison, IL .800-628-3738
Walco
Utica, NY 800-879-2526
Xtreme Beverages, LLC
Dana Point, CA 949-495-7929

Hooks

Meat

Boehringer Mfg. Co. Inc.
Felton, CA 800-630-8665
G.F. Frank & Sons
Fairfield, OH 513-870-9075
Le Fiell Co
Reno, NV 402-592-9993
Samuel Underberg Food Store
Brooklyn, NY 718-363-0787

Hoops

Cheese

Damrow Company
Fond Du Lac, WI 800-236-1501
Viking Machine & Design Inc
De Pere, WI. 888-286-2116

Kettles

G & F Mfg
Oak Lawn, IL 800-282-1574

Canning & Preserving

A.K. Robins
Baltimore, MD 800-486-9656
Berkshire PPM
Litchfield, CT 860-567-3118
Central Fabricators Inc
Cincinnati, OH 800-909-8265
Custom Food Machinery
Stockton, CA 209-463-4343
El Cerrito Steel
El Cerrito, CA 510-230-4709

Hamilton Kettles
Weirton, WV 800-535-1882
Packaging & Processing Equipment
Ayr, ON 519-622-6666
Production Packaging & Processing Equipment
Company
Savannah, GA 912-856-4281

Confectioners'

A & B Process Systems Corp
Stratford, WI 888-258-2789
Berkshire PPM
Litchfield, CT 860-567-3118
Chocolate Concepts
Hartville, OH 330-877-3322
D. Picking & Company
Bucyrus, OH 419-562-6891
Hamilton Kettles
Weirton, WV 800-535-1882
Packaging & Processing Equipment
Ayr, ON 519-622-6666
Vendome Copper & Brass Works
Louisville, KY 888-384-5161

Copper

All Spun Metal Products
Des Plaines, IL 847-824-4117
D. Picking & Company
Bucyrus, OH 419-562-6891
Packaging & Processing Equipment
Ayr, ON 519-622-6666
Savage Brothers Company
Elk Grove Vlg, IL 800-342-0973
Vendome Copper & Brass Works
Louisville, KY 888-384-5161

Lard

A & B Process Systems Corp
Stratford, WI 888-258-2789
Hamilton Kettles
Weirton, WV 800-535-1882
Packaging & Processing Equipment
Ayr, ON 519-622-6666

Mixing

A & B Process Systems Corp
Stratford, WI 888-258-2789
Berkshire PPM
Litchfield, CT 860-567-3118
Bowers Process Equipment
Stratford, ON. 800-567-3223
Chocolate Concepts
Hartville, OH 330-877-3322
Custom Food Machinery
Stockton, CA 209-463-4343
DCI, Inc.
St Cloud, MN 320-252-8200
Eischen Enterprises
Fresno, CA 559-834-0013
Hamilton Kettles
Weirton, WV 800-535-1882
Packaging & Processing Equipment
Ayr, ON 519-622-6666
Savage Brothers Company
Elk Grove Vlg, IL 800-342-0973
Sharpsville Container Corp
Sharpsville, PA 800-645-1248
South Valley Mfg Inc
Gilroy, CA. .408-842-5457
Stainless Fabrication Inc
Springfield, MO 800-397-8265

Steaming

Berkshire PPM
Litchfield, CT 860-567-3118
Chester-Jensen Co., Inc.
Chester, PA .800-685-3750
Cleasby Manufacturing Co
San Francisco, CA 800-253-2729
Cleveland Range
Cleveland, OH 800-338-2204
Eischen Enterprises
Fresno, CA 559-834-0013
Electro-Steam Generator Corp
Rancocas, NJ. 866-617-0764
Hamilton Kettles
Weirton, WV 800-535-1882

Legion Industries Inc
  Waynesboro, GA 800-887-1988
Packaging & Processing Equipment
  Ayr, ON 519-622-6666
Process Systems
  Barrington, IL 847-842-8618
Sharpsville Container Corp
  Sharpsville, PA 800-645-1248
South Valley Mfg Inc
  Gilroy, CA 408-842-5457
Southbend
  Fuquay Varina, NC 800-348-2558
Welbilt Corporation
  Stamford, CT .203-325-8300
Welliver Metal Products Corporation
  Salem, OR 503-362-1568

Sugar & Syrup

A & B Process Systems Corp
  Stratford, WI .888-258-2789
Hamilton Kettles
  Weirton, WV .800-535-1882
Packaging & Processing Equipment
  Ayr, ON 519-622-6666

Knife Sharpeners

Browne & Company
  Markham, ON 905-475-6104
Cass Saw & Tool   Sharpening
  Westmont, IL .630-968-1617
Diamond Machining Technology
  Marlborough, MA 800-666-4368
Edgecraft Corp
  Avondale, PA .800-342-3255
EZE-Lap Diamond Products
  Carson City, NV 800-843-4815
Fortune Products Inc
  Cedar Park, TX 512-249-0334
Friedr Dick Corp
  Farmingdale, NY 800-554-3425
General Grinding Inc
  Oakland, CA 800-806-6037
Imperial Schrade Corporation
  Ellenville, NY 212-210-8600
R X Honing Machine Corp
  Mishawaka, IN 800-346-6464
Serr-Edge Machine Company
  Cleveland, CI .800-443-8097
Superior Products Company
  Saint Paul, MN 800-328-9800
Tru Hone Corp
  Ocala, FL 800-237-4663

Knives

Bread

Brooklyn Boys Pizza & Pasta
  Boca Raton, FL 561-477-3663
Lamson & Goodnow
  Shelburne Falls, MA 800-872-6564
Mundial
  Norwood, MA 800-487-2224
Simmons Engineering Corporation
  Wheeling, IL .800-252-3381
Superior Products Company
  Saint Paul, MN 800-328-9800

Butchers'

Atlanta SharpTech
  Peachtree City, GA 800-462-7297
Boehringer Mfg. Co. Inc.
  Felton, CA 800-630-8665
Chicago Scale & Slicer Company
  Franklin Park, IL 847-455-3400
General Cutlery Co
  Fremont, OH .419-332-2316
Jarvis Products Corp
  Middletown, CT 860-347-7271
Lamson & Goodnow
  Shelburne Falls, MA 800-872-6564
Mandeville Company
  Minneapolis, MN 800-328-8490
Mundial
  Norwood, MA 800-487-2224
R Murphy Co Inc
  Ayer, MA 888-772-3481
Simmons Engineering Corporation
  Wheeling, IL .800-252-3381

Superior Products Company
  Saint Paul, MN 800-328-9800

Cake

C R Mfg
  Waverly, NE .877-789-5844
Mundial
  Norwood, MA 800-487-2224
Polar Process
  Plattsville, ON 877-896-8077
Simmons Engineering Corporation
  Wheeling, IL .800-252-3381

Canners'

A.D. Cowdrey Company
  Modesto, CA .209-538-4677
A.K. Robins
  Baltimore, MD 800-486-9656
General Cutlery Co
  Fremont, OH .419-332-2316

Carving

Browne & Company
  Markham, ON 905-475-6104
Burrell Cutlery Company
  Ellicottville, NY 716-699-2343
CUTCO Corp
  Olean, NY 716-372-3111
Dexter Russell Inc
  Southbridge, MA 800-343-6042
General Cutlery Co
  Fremont, OH .419-332-2316
Gerber Legendary Blades
  Portland, OR .800-950-6161
Imperial Schrade Corporation
  Ellenville, NY 212-210-8600
Mandeville Company
  Minneapolis, MN 800-328-8490
Mundial
  Norwood, MA 800-487-2224
R Murphy Co Inc
  Ayer, MA 888-772-3481
Superior Products Company
  Saint Paul, MN 800-328-9800

Cheese

Browne & Company
  Markham, ON 905-475-6104
General Cutlery Co
  Fremont, OH .419-332-2316
Lamson & Goodnow
  Shelburne Falls, MA 800-872-6564
Mundial
  Norwood, MA 800-487-2224
Polar Process
  Plattsville, ON 877-896-8077
TGW International
  Florence, KY .800-407-0173

Culinary

Browne & Company
  Markham, ON 905-475-6104
Buck Knives
  Post Falls, ID .800-326-2825
Burrell Cutlery Company
  Ellicottville, NY 716-699-2343
Dexter Russell Inc
  Southbridge, MA 800-343-6042
Gerber Legendary Blades
  Portland, OR .800-950-6161
Gunter Wilhelm Cutlery
  Fair Lawn, NJ 201-569-6866
Imperial Schrade Corporation
  Ellenville, NY 212-210-8600
John J. Adams Die Corporation
  Worcester, MA 508-757-3894
Lamson & Goodnow
  Shelburne Falls, MA 800-872-6564
Lifetime Brands Inc
  Garden City, NY 516-683-6000
Mundial
  Norwood, MA 800-487-2224
OWD
  Tupper Lake, NY 800-836-1693
Superior Products Company
  Saint Paul, MN 800-328-9800

Curd

Damrow Company
  Fond Du Lac, WI 800-236-1501
Engineered Products Corp
  Greenville, SC 800-868-0145

Fish Scaling & Slitting

Buck Knives
  Post Falls, ID .800-326-2825
Dexter Russell Inc
  Southbridge, MA 800-343-6042
E-Z Edge Inc
  West New York, NJ 800-232-4470
General Cutlery Co
  Fremont, OH .419-332-2316
Imperial Schrade Corporation
  Ellenville, NY 212-210-8600
R Murphy Co Inc
  Ayer, MA 888-772-3481
Simmons Engineering Corporation
  Wheeling, IL .800-252-3381
Steamway Corporation
  Scottsburg, IN 800-259-8171
TGW International
  Florence, KY .800-407-0173

Food Processing Machine

Ace Co Precision Mfg
  Boise, ID 800-359-7012
AM-Mac
  Fairfield, NJ .800-829-2018
Branson Ultrasonics Corp
  Danbury, CT .203-796-0400
Brooklyn Boys Pizza & Pasta
  Boca Raton, FL 561-477-3663
California Saw & Knife Works
  San Francisco, CA 888-729-6533
Carolina Knife
  Asheville, NC 800-520-5030
Chapman Corp
  St Louis, MO .800-843-1404
Dexter Russell Inc
  Southbridge, MA 800-343-6042
DSW Converting Knives
  Birmingham, AL 205-322-2021
Florida Knife Co
  Sarasota, FL .800-966-5643
Huther Brothers
  Rochester, NY 800-334-1115
International Knife & Saw
  Florence, SC .800-354-9872
KSW Corp
  Des Moines, IA 515-265-5269
Lako Tool & Mfg Inc
  Perrysburg, OH 800-228-2982
Pappas Inc.
  Detroit, MI 800-521-0888
R H Saw Corp
  Barrington, IL 847-381-8777
Simmons Engineering Corporation
  Wheeling, IL .800-252-3381
Simonds International
  Fitchburg, MA 800-343-1616
Simonds International
  Fitchburg, MA 978-345-7521
Specialty Blades
  Staunton, VA .540-248-2200
Stutz Products Corp
  Hartford City, IN 765-348-2510
TGW International
  Florence, KY .800-407-0173
York Saw & Knife
  York, PA 800-233-1969
Zenith Cutter
  Loves Park, IL 800-223-5202

Fruit

Amco Metals Indl
  City Of Industry, CA 626-855-2550
Burrell Cutlery Company
  Ellicottville, NY 716-699-2343
Globe Machine
  Tacoma, WA .800-523-6575
Goodnature Products
  Orchard Park, NY 800-875-3381
International Knife & Saw
  Florence, SC .800-354-9872
Mundial
  Norwood, MA 800-487-2224

Q A Supplies LLC
  Norfolk, VA.......................800-472-7205
Simmons Engineering Corporation
  Wheeling, IL......................800-252-3381
TGW International
  Florence, KY.....................800-407-0173

Loin

Mound Tool Co
  St Louis, MO.....................314-968-3991

Machine

Ace Co Precision Mfg
  Boise, ID........................800-359-7012
Bettendorf Stanford Inc
  Salem, IL........................800-548-2253
California Saw & Knife Works
  San Francisco, CA................888-729-6533
Carolina Knife
  Asheville, NC....................800-520-5030
D & S Mfg
  Auburn, MA.......................508-799-7812
DSW Converting Knives
  Birmingham, AL...................205-322-2021
Florida Knife Co
  Sarasota, FL.....................800-966-5643
Greenfield Disston
  Greensboro, NC...................336-855-4200
Huther Brothers
  Rochester, NY....................800-334-1115
International Knife & Saw
  Florence, SC.....................800-354-9872
Kinetic Co
  Greendale, WI....................414-425-8221
KSW Corp
  Des Moines, IA...................515-265-5269
Lako Tool & Mfg Inc
  Perrysburg, OH...................800-228-2982
Moore Production Tool Spec Inc
  Farmington Hills, MI.............248-476-1200
Nitsch Tool Co Inc
  Syracuse, NY.....................315-472-4044
Page Slotting Saw Co Inc
  Toledo, OH.......................419-476-7475
Polar Process
  Plattsville, ON..................877-896-8077
Rudolph Industries
  Mississauga, ON..................905-564-6160
Simonds International
  Fitchburg, MA....................800-343-1616
Simonds International
  Fitchburg, MA....................978-345-7521
Specialty Blades
  Staunton, VA.....................540-248-2200
Stutz Products Corp
  Hartford City, IN................765-348-2510
TGW International
  Florence, KY.....................800-407-0173
York Saw & Knife
  York, PA.........................800-233-1969
Zenith Cutter
  Loves Park, IL...................800-223-5202

Meat Packing

Cutrite Company
  Fremont, OH......................800-928-8748
E-Z Edge Inc
  West New York, NJ................800-232-4470
General Cutlery Co
  Fremont, OH......................419-332-2316
Lamson & Goodnow
  Shelburne Falls, MA..............800-872-6564
Mandeville Company
  Minneapolis, MN..................800-328-8490
Omcan Manufacturing & Distributing Company
  Mississauga, ON..................800-465-0234
Specialty Blades
  Staunton, VA.....................540-248-2200
TGW International
  Florence, KY.....................800-407-0173

Oyster & Clam

Mundial
  Norwood, MA......................800-487-2224
Superior Products Company
  Saint Paul, MN...................800-328-9800
TGW International
  Florence, KY.....................800-407-0173

Slicing

Bettendorf Stanford Inc
  Salem, IL........................800-548-2253
Browne & Company
  Markham, ON......................905-475-6104
Burrell Cutlery Company
  Ellicottville, NY................716-699-2343
Dexter Russell Inc
  Southbridge, MA..................800-343-6042
Friedr Dick Corp
  Farmingdale, NY..................800-554-3425
Gerber Legendary Blades
  Portland, OR.....................800-950-6161
Gril-Del
  Mankato, MN......................800-782-7320
Huther Brothers
  Rochester, NY....................800-334-1115
Industrial Razorblade
  Orange, NJ.......................973-673-4286
International Knife & Saw
  Florence, SC.....................800-354-9872
Lamson & Goodnow
  Shelburne Falls, MA..............800-872-6564
Mundial
  Norwood, MA......................800-487-2224
Pappas Inc.
  Detroit, MI......................800-521-0888
R H Saw Corp
  Barrington, IL...................847-381-8777
Rudolph Industries
  Mississauga, ON..................905-564-6160
Simmons Engineering Corporation
  Wheeling, IL.....................800-252-3381
Stutz Products Corp
  Hartford City, IN................765-348-2510
TGW International
  Florence, KY.....................800-407-0173

Steak

Browne & Company
  Markham, ON......................905-475-6104
Burrell Cutlery Company
  Ellicottville, NY................716-699-2343
Delco Tableware
  Port Washington, NY..............800-221-9557
General Cutlery Co
  Fremont, OH......................419-332-2316
Gerber Legendary Blades
  Portland, OR.....................800-950-6161
Lamson & Goodnow
  Shelburne Falls, MA..............800-872-6564
Mundial
  Norwood, MA......................800-487-2224
Superior Products Company
  Saint Paul, MN...................800-328-9800
Walco
  Utica, NY........................800-879-2526

Vegetable

AM-Mac
  Fairfield, NJ....................800-829-2018
Brooklyn Boys Pizza & Pasta
  Boca Raton, FL...................561-477-3663
Browne & Company
  Markham, ON......................905-475-6104
International Knife & Saw
  Florence, SC.....................800-354-9872
Jim Scharf Holdings
  Perdue, SK.......................800-667-9727
Mundial
  Norwood, MA......................800-487-2224
Simmons Engineering Corporation
  Wheeling, IL.....................800-252-3381
Superior Products Company
  Saint Paul, MN...................800-328-9800
TGW International
  Florence, KY.....................800-407-0173

Ladles

Culinary

Amco Metals Indl
  City Of Industry, CA.............626-855-2550
Browne & Company
  Markham, ON......................905-475-6104
Carlisle Food Svc Products Inc
  Oklahoma City, OK................800-654-8210
Eastern Tabletop Mfg
  Brooklyn, NY.....................888-422-4142

Leggett & Platt Storage
  Vernon Hills, IL.................847-816-6246
Liberty Ware LLC
  Clearfield, UT...................888-500-5885
Olde Country Reproductions Inc
  York, PA.........................800-358-3997
Superior Products Company
  Saint Paul, MN...................800-328-9800
Vollrath Co LLC
  Sheboygan, WI....................800-624-2051
Wiltec
  Leominster, MA...................978-537-1497

Liners

Cake Pan

Brown Paper Goods Co
  Waukegan, IL.....................847-688-1450
M S Plastics & Packaging Inc
  Butler, NJ.......................800-593-1802
Norpak Corp
  Newark, NJ.......................800-631-6970
State Products
  Long Beach, CA...................800-730-5150
Taconic
  Petersburg, NY...................800-833-1805
Zenith Specialty Bag Co
  City Of Industry, CA.............800-962-2247

Magnets

Industrial Magnetics
  Boyne City, MI...................800-662-4638

Matches

Admatch Corporation
  New York, NY.....................800-777-9909
Atlas Match Company
  Toronto, ON......................888-285-2783
Atlas Match Corporation
  Euless, TX.......................800-628-2426
Bradley Industries
  Westchester, IL..................815-469-2314
D D Bean & Sons Co
  Jaffrey, NH......................800-326-8311
Jarden Home Brands
  Cloquet, MN......................218-879-6700
K & L Intl
  Ontario, CA......................888-598-5588
Palmland Paper Company
  Fort Lauderdale, FL..............800-266-9067
Penley Corporation
  West Paris, ME...................800-368-6449

Micer

Meat

Thunderbird Food Machinery
  Blaine, WA.......................866-875-6868

Mincer

Thunderbird Food Machinery
  Blaine, WA.......................866-875-6868

Molds

Bakers' & Confectioners'

Amco Metals Indl
  City Of Industry, CA.............626-855-2550
Carnegie Manufacturing Company
  Fairfield, NJ....................973-575-3449
Chocolate Concepts
  Hartville, OH....................330-877-3322
Choklit Molds LTD
  Lincoln, RI......................800-777-6653
D.R. McClain & Son
  Commerce, CA.....................800-428-2263
Edhard Corp
  Hackettstown, NJ.................888-334-2731
Hartstone Pottery Inc
  Zanesville, OH...................740-452-9999
Hillside Metal Ware Company
  Union, NJ........................908-964-3080
Intermold Corporation
  Greenville, SC...................864-627-0300
Liberty Engineering Co
  Roscoe, IL.......................877-623-9065

Matfer Inc
Van Nuys, CA 800-766-0333
Micelli Chocolate Mold Company
West Babylon, NY 631-752-2888
Moline Machinery LLC
Duluth, MN 800-767-5734
Parrish's Cake Decorating
Gardena, CA 800-736-8443
Somerset Industries
Billerica, MA 800-772-4404
Voorhees Rubber Mfg Co
Newark, MD 410-632-1582

Butter & Cheese

Carnegie Manufacturing Company
Fairfield, NJ 973-575-3449
Lancaster Colony Corporation
Westerville, OH. 614-224-7141
Roaring Brook Dairy
Chappaqua, NY. 646-559-9330
Sanchelima International
Miami, FL 305-591-4343
Viking Machine & Design Inc
De Pere, WI. 888-286-2116

Pans

Baking & Roasting

ABI Limited
Concord, ON. 800-297-8666
Advance Tabco
Edgewood, NY 800-645-3166
Allied Metal Spinning
Bronx, NY. 800-615-2266
Alumaworks
Sunny Isle Beach, FL 800-277-7267
American Metal Stamping
Brooklyn, NY. 718-384-1500
APW Wyott Food Service Equipment Company
Cheyenne, WY 800-527-2100
Baking Machines
Livermore, CA 925-449-3369
Bluebird Manufacturing
Montreal, QC 800-406-2505
Browne & Company
Markham, ON. 905-475-6104
Cambro Manufacturing Co
Huntington Beach, CA 800-833-3003
Carlson Products
Maize, KS 800-234-1069
Crestware
North Salt Lake, UT 800-345-0513
Crown Custom Metal Spinning
Concord, ON. 800-750-1924
D & W Fine Pack
Lake Zurich, IL. 800-323-0422
Dur-Able Aluminum Corporation
Hoffman Estates, IL 847-843-1100
Dura-Ware Company of America
Oklahoma City, OK 800-664-3872
G & S Metal Products Co Inc
Cleveland, OH 216-441-0700
Hillside Metal Ware Company
Union, NJ 908-964-3080
Kosempel Manufacturing Company
Philadelphia, PA 800-733-7122
Legion Industries Inc
Waynesboro, GA. 800-887-1988
Lincoln Foodservice
Cleveland, OH 800-374-3004
Magna Industries Inc
Lakewood, NJ 800-510-9856
Matfer Inc
Van Nuys, CA 800-766-0333
Mouli Manufacturing Corporation
Belleville, NJ 800-789-8285
National Cart Co
St Charles, MO 636-947-3800
Parrish's Cake Decorating
Gardena, CA 800-736-8443
Pfeil & Holding Inc
Woodside, NY. 800-247-7955
Piper Products Inc
Wausau, WI. 800-544-3057
Southbend
Fuquay Varina, NC 800-348-2558
State Products
Long Beach, CA 800-730-5150
Superior Products Company
Saint Paul, MN 800-328-9800

Vollrath Co LLC
Sheboygan, WI. 800-624-2051
Williamsburg Metal Spinning
Brooklyn, NY. 888-535-5402
World Kitchen
Elmira, NY 800-999-3436

Stainless Steel

Castella Imports Inc
Brentwood, NY. 631-231-5500

Frying

Adcraft
Hicksville, NY 800-223-7750
Alumaworks
Sunny Isle Beach, FL 800-277-7267
Bluebird Manufacturing
Montreal, QC 800-406-2505
Browne & Company
Markham, ON. 905-475-6104
Crown Custom Metal Spinning
Concord, ON. 800-750-1924
Dura-Ware Company of America
Oklahoma City, OK 800-664-3872
Imperial Manufacturing Co
Corona, CA 800-343-7790
Liberty Ware LLC
Clearfield, UT. 888-500-5885
Market Forge Industries Inc
Everett, MA 866-698-3188
Matfer Inc
Van Nuys, CA 800-766-0333
Olde Country Reproductions Inc
York, PA 800-358-3997
Regal Ware Inc
Kewaskum, WI. 262-626-2121
Superior Products Company
Saint Paul, MN 800-328-9800
Vollrath Co LLC
Sheboygan, WI. 800-624-2051

Pie

ABI Limited
Concord, ON. 800-297-8666
Allied Metal Spinning
Bronx, NY. 800-615-2266
Browne & Company
Markham, ON. 905-475-6104
Carlson Products
Maize, KS 800-234-1069
Crown Custom Metal Spinning
Concord, ON. 800-750-1924
D & W Fine Pack
Lake Zurich, IL. 800-323-0422
Lincoln Foodservice
Cleveland, OH 800-374-3004
Malco Manufacturing Co
Los Angeles, CA. 866-477-7267
Revere Packaging
Shelbyville, KY 800-626-2668
Superior Products Company
Saint Paul, MN 800-328-9800
V&R Metal Enterprises
Brooklyn, NY. 718-768-8142

Sauce

Alumaworks
Sunny Isle Beach, FL 800-277-7267
Bluebird Manufacturing
Montreal, QC 800-406-2505
Dover Parkersburg
Follansbee, WV
Dura-Ware Company of America
Oklahoma City, OK 800-664-3872
Lincoln Foodservice
Cleveland, OH 800-374-3004
Regal Ware Inc
Kewaskum, WI. 262-626-2121
Superior Products Company
Saint Paul, MN 800-328-9800

Parers & Peelers

Fruit & Vegetable

A.K. Robins
Baltimore, MD 800-486-9656
Amco Metals Indl
City Of Industry, CA. 626-855-2550

Atlas Pacific Engineering
Pueblo, CO 719-948-3040
Blakeslee, Inc.
Addison, IL 630-532-5021
Browne & Company
Markham, ON. 905-475-6104
Conimar Corp
Ocala, FL. 800-874-9735
F.B. Pease Company
Rochester, NY. 585-475-1870
Insinger Co
Philadelphia, PA 800-344-4802
Juice Tree
Omaha, NE 714-891-4425
Magnuson
Pueblo, CO 719-948-9500
Mouli Manufacturing Corporation
Belleville, NJ 800-789-8285
Murotech
St Marys, OH 800-565-6876
Odenberg Engineering
West Sacramento, CA 800-688-8396
Superior Products Company
Saint Paul, MN 800-328-9800
Univex Corp
Salem, NH 800-258-6358
Vanmark Equipment
Creston, IA 800-523-6261
White Mountain Freezer
Kansas City, MO. 816-943-4100

Plates

Paper

AJM Packaging Corporation
Bloomfield Hills, MI 248-901-0040
Bergschrond
Seattle, WA 206-763-3502
Carthage Cup Company
Longview, TX. 903-238-9833
Chinet Company
Laguna Niguel, CA 949-348-1711
Creative Converting Inc
Clintonville, WI 800-826-0418
Dart Canada Inc.
Toronto, ON 800-465-9696
Durango-Georgia Paper
Tampa, FL 813-286-2718
E K Lay Co
Philadelphia, PA 800-523-3220
Enviro-Ware
Pittsburgh, PA 888-233-7857
Fonda Group
Goshen, IN 574-534-2515
Four M Manufacturing Group
San Jose, CA 408-998-1141
Genpak LLC
Charlotte, NC 800-626-6695
Hoffmaster Group Inc.
Oshkosh, WI. 800-558-9300
James River Canada
North York, ON. 416-789-5151
Jones-Zylon Co
West Lafayette, OH. 800-848-8160
Premier
Cincinnati, OH 800-354-9817
Primary Liquidation
Bohemia, NY 631-244-1410
Scan Group
Appleton, WI. 920-730-9150
Smith-Lee Company
Oshkosh, WI. 800-327-9774
Solo Cup Company
Lake Forest, IL
Sterling Paper Company
Ohio, PA 800-282-1124
Westervelt Co Inc
Tuscaloosa, AL. 205-562-5000

Pie

Carlisle Food Svc Products Inc
Oklahoma City, OK 800-654-8210
Norandal
Franklin, TX 615-771-5700

Plastic, Reusable

Dart Canada Inc.
Toronto, ON 800-465-9696
De Ster Corporation
Atlanta, GA 800-237-8270

Hoffmaster Group Inc
Oshkosh, WI............................800-367-2877
HPI North America/Plastics
Chicago, IL............................800-327-3534
K & L Intl
Ontario, CA............................888-598-5588
Kendrick Johnson & Assoc Inc
Minneapolis, MN.....................800-826-1271
OWD
Tupper Lake, NY....................800-836-1693
Plastiques Cascades Group
Montreal, QC.........................888-703-6515
Wiltec
Leominster, MA......................978-537-1497

Platters

Bon Chef
Lafayette, NJ.........................800-331-0177
Browne & Company
Markham, ON.........................905-475-6104
Cal-Mil Plastic Products Inc
Oceanside, CA........................800-321-9069
Carlisle Food Svc Products Inc
Oklahoma City, OK..................800-654-8210
Cyclamen Collection
Oakland, CA...........................510-434-7620
Delfin Design & Mfg
Rancho Sta Marg, CA..............800-354-7919
First Plastics Co Inc
Leominster, MA......................978-840-6908
Gaetano America
El Monte, CA..........................626-442-2858
Gril-Del
Mankato, MN.........................800-782-7320
M & E Mfg Co Inc
Kingston, NY.........................845-331-2110
Michael Leson Dinnerware
Youngstown, OH....................800-821-3541
Olde Country Reproductions Inc
York, PA...............................800-358-3997
Olde Thompson Inc
Oxnard, CA............................800-827-1565
Prolon
Port Gibson, MS.....................888-480-9828
Ronnie's Ceramic Company
San Francisco, CA..................800-888-8218
Sabert Corp
Sayreville, NJ........................800-722-3781
Sims Superior Seating
Locust Grove, GA...................800-729-9178
Superior Products Company
Saint Paul, MN.......................800-328-9800
Tomlinson Industries
Cleveland, OH........................800-945-4589
Ullman, Shapiro & UllmanLLP
New York, NY........................212-755-0299
Vertex China
Pomona, CA...........................800-483-7839
Weavewood, Inc.
Golden Valley, MN..................800-367-6460
WNA
Chattanooga, TN....................800-404-9318

Rolling Pins

H. Arnold Wood Turning
Tarrytown, NY.......................888-314-0088
Read Products Inc
Seattle, WA...........................800-445-3416
Superior Products Company
Saint Paul, MN.......................800-328-9800
Thorpe Rolling Pin Co
Hamden, CT...........................800-344-6966

Scoops, Dishers & Spades

Amco Metals Indl
City Of Industry, CA................626-855-2550
Bremer Manufacturing Co Inc
Elkhart Lake, WI....................920-894-2944
C R Mfg
Waverly, NE..........................877-789-5844
Carlisle Food Svc Products Inc
Oklahoma City, OK..................800-654-8210
E-Z Dip
Frankfort, IN.........................866-347-3279
Landis Plastics
Alsip, IL................................708-396-1470
Lloyd Disher Company
Decatur, IL............................217-429-0593
Measurex/S&L Plastics
Nazareth, PA.........................800-752-0650

National Scoop & Equipment Company
Spring House, PA....................215-646-2040
Penn Scale ManufacturingCompany
Philadelphia, PA.....................215-739-9644
Prolon
Port Gibson, MS.....................888-480-9828
Superior Products Company
Saint Paul, MN.......................800-328-9800
Tolco Corp
Toledo, OH............................800-537-4786
Zeroll Company
Fort Pierce, FL.......................800-872-5000

Scrapers

Butchers' Block

Boehringer Mfg. Co. Inc.
Felton, CA.............................800-630-8665
C R Mfg
Waverly, NE..........................877-789-5844
Goodell Tools
New Hope, MN.......................800-542-3906

Shears

Poultry

Amco Metals Indl
City Of Industry, CA................626-855-2550
Cutrite Company
Fremont, OH..........................800-928-8748
E-Z Edge Inc
West New York, NJ.................800-232-4470
Imperial Schrade Corporation
Ellenville, NY.........................212-210-8600
Mundial
Norwood, MA.........................800-487-2224
Superior Products Company
Saint Paul, MN.......................800-328-9800

Sheeter

Dough

Thunderbird Food Machinery
Blaine, WA............................866-875-6868

Sheets

Cookie

Browne & Company
Markham, ON.........................905-475-6104
Dover Parkersburg
Follansbee, WV
Lincoln Foodservice
Cleveland, OH........................800-374-3004
Matfer Inc
Van Nuys, CA........................800-766-0333
State Products
Long Beach, CA......................800-730-5150
Superior Products Company
Saint Paul, MN.......................800-328-9800

Sieves

ANDRITZ Inc
Muncy, PA.............................704-943-4343
ATM Corporation
New Berlin, WI.......................800-511-2096
Browne & Company
Markham, ON.........................905-475-6104
Cleveland Vibrator Co
Cleveland, OH........................800-221-3298
CSC Scientific Co Inc
Fairfax, VA............................800-621-4778
Gilson Co Inc
Lewis Center, OH...................800-444-1508
Glen Mills Inc.
Clifton, NJ............................973-777-0777
Great Western Manufacturing Company
Leavenworth, KS....................800-682-3121
Newark Wire Cloth Co
Clifton, NJ............................800-221-0392
Norvell Co Inc
Fort Scott, KS.......................800-653-3147
Vorti-Siv
Salem, OH.............................800-227-7487

Sifters

Flour & Bakers'

Amco Metals Indl
City Of Industry, CA................626-855-2550
Ayr King Corp
Louisville, KY........................866-266-6290
B & P Process Equipment
Saginaw, MI...........................989-757-1300
Browne & Company
Markham, ON.........................905-475-6104
Buffalo Technologies Corporation
Buffalo, NY...........................800-332-2419
F.P. Smith Wire Cloth Company
Northlake, IL..........................800-323-6842
Fred D Pfening Co
Columbus, OH........................614-294-5361
Great Western Manufacturing Company
Leavenworth, KS....................800-682-3121
Howes S Co Inc
Silver Creek, NY....................888-255-2611
K B Systems Inc
Bangor, PA............................610-588-7788
Kemutec Group Inc
Bristol, PA............................215-788-8013
Meadows Mills Inc
North Wilkesboro, NC..............800-626-2282
Norvell Co Inc
Fort Scott, KS.......................800-653-3147
Shick Esteve
Kansas City, MO.....................877-744-2587
Sifter Parts & Svc
Wesley Chapel, FL..................800-367-3591
Smico Manufacturing Co Inc
Oklahoma City, OK..................800-351-9088
Stewart Systems Baking LLC
Plano, TX..............................972-422-5808

Skewers

Amco Metals Indl
City Of Industry, CA................626-855-2550
Automated Food Systems
Waxahachie, TX......................469-517-0470
C R Mfg
Waverly, NE..........................877-789-5844
Chicago Dowel Co Inc
Chicago, IL............................800-333-6935
Coastline Equipment Inc
Bellingham, WA......................360-734-8509
G.F. Frank & Sons
Fairfield, OH..........................513-870-9075
H. Arnold Wood Turning
Tarrytown, NY.......................888-314-0088
Hardwood Products Co LP
Guilford, ME..........................800-289-3340
Jarden Home Brands
Daleville, IN...........................800-392-2575
K & L Intl
Ontario, CA............................888-598-5588
Les Industries Touch Inc
Sherbrooke, QC......................800-267-4140
Lynch-Jamentz Company
Lakewood, CA........................800-828-6217
Royal Paper Products
Coatesville, PA.......................800-666-6655
Saunder Brothers
Bridgton, ME.........................207-647-3331
Trepte's Wire & Metal Works
Bellflower, CA........................800-828-6217

Slicer

Bagel

Larien Products
Northampton, MA...................800-462-9237

Bread

Paramount Packaging Corp
Melville, NY...........................516-333-8100
Thunderbird Food Machinery
Blaine, WA............................866-875-6868

Spoons

Abco International
Oneida, NY............................888-263-7195
Amco Metals Indl
City Of Industry, CA................626-855-2550

American Housewares
Bronx, NY 718-665-9500
C R Mfg
Waverly, NE 877-789-5844
Carlisle Food Svc Products Inc
Oklahoma City, OK 800-654-8210
CUTCO Corp
Olean, NY 716-372-3111
Dart Canada Inc.
Toronto, ON 800-465-9696
Design Specialties Inc
Hamden, CT 800-999-1584
Fab-X/Metals
Washington, NC 800-677-3229
Fioriware
Zanesville, OH 740-454-7400
Hal-One Plastics
Olathe, KS 800-626-5784
Harco Enterprises
Peterborough, ON 800-361-5361
Hardwood Products Co LP
Guilford, ME. 800-289-3340
Imperial Schrade Corporation
Ellenville, NY 212-210-8600
Jarden Home Brands
Daleville, IN 800-392-2575
Jones-Zylon Co
West Lafayette, OH. 800-848-8160
Lifetime Brands Inc
Garden City, NY 516-683-6000
LoTech Industries
Lakewood, CO 800-295-0199
Lynch-Jamentz Company
Lakewood, CA 800-828-6217
OWD
Tupper Lake, NY 800-836-1693
Polar Plastics
St Laurent, QC 514-331-0207
Polar Ware Company
Sheboygan, WI 800-237-3655
Solon Manufacturing Company
North Haven, CT. 800-341-6640
Superior Products Company
Saint Paul, MN 800-328-9800
Tops Manufacturing Co
Darien, CT. 203-655-9367
Trepte's Wire & Metal Works
Bellflower, CA 800-828-6217
Vollrath Co LLC
Sheboygan, WI 800-624-2051
Weavewood, Inc.
Golden Valley, MN 800-367-6460
Wiltec
Leominster, MA 978-537-1497

Stirrers & Picks: Cocktail, Hors D'oeuvres

C R Mfg
Waverly, NE 877-789-5844
Cell-O-Core Company
Sharon Center, OH 800-239-4370
Epic Products
Santa Ana, CA 800-548-9791
Goldmax Industries
City Of Industry, CA. 626-964-8820
Harco Enterprises
Peterborough, ON 800-361-5361
Hardwood Products Co LP
Guilford, ME. 800-289-3340
Jarden Home Brands
Daleville, IN 800-392-2575
Johnstown Manufacturing
Columbus, OH 614-236-8853
Pelican Products Inc
Bronx, NY. 800-552-8820
Royal Paper Products
Coatesville, PA 800-666-6655
Soodhalter Plastics
Los Angeles, CA. 213-747-0231
Spinzer
Glen Ellyn, IL 630-469-7184
Spir-It/Zoo Piks
Andover, MA 800-343-0996
Spirit Foodservice, Inc.
Andover, MA 800-343-0996
SQP
Schenectady, NY 800-724-1129
Superior Products Company
Saint Paul, MN 800-328-9800
Token Factory
La Crosse, WI 888-486-5367

Tops Manufacturing Co
Darien, CT. 203-655-9367
Trevor Industries
Eden, NY 716-992-4775
Ursini Plastics
Bracebridge, ON 705-646-2701
Waddington North America
Chelmsford, MA 888-962-2877

Strainers

Amco Metals Indl
City Of Industry, CA. 626-855-2550
American Metal Stamping
Brooklyn, NY 718-384-1500
C R Mfg
Waverly, NE 877-789-5844
Eaton Filtration, LLC
Tinton Falls, NJ. 800-859-9212
Feldmeier Equipment Inc
Syracuse, NY 315-454-8608
Giunta Brothers
Philadelphia, PA 215-389-9670
Globe Machine
Tacoma, WA 800-523-6575
Goodnature Products
Orchard Park, NY 800-875-3381
L.C. Thompson Company
Kenosha, WI 800-558-4018
Lincoln Foodservice
Cleveland, OH 800-374-3004
Mouli Manufacturing Corporation
Belleville, NJ 800-789-8285
Schlueter Company
Janesville, WI 800-359-1700
South Valley Mfg Inc
Gilroy, CA. 408-842-5457
Superior Products Company
Saint Paul, MN 800-328-9800

Tables

Cutting & Trimming

Bally Block Co
Bally, PA 610-845-7511
Bmh Equipment Inc
Sacramento, CA 800-350-8828
Catskill Craftsmen Inc
Stamford, NY 607-652-7321
Dunhill Food Equipment Corporation
Armonk, NY. 800-847-4206
Fishmore
Melbourne, FL 321-723-4751
Frelco
Stephenville, NL 709-643-5668
Michigan Maple Block Co
Petoskey, MI 800-447-7975
MSSH
Greensburg, IN 812-663-2180
Rheon USA
Irvine, CA 949-768-1900
Triple-A Manufacturing Company
Toronto, ON 800-786-2238
Ultrafryer Systems Inc
San Antonio, TX. 800-545-9189

Stainless Steel

A J Antunes & Co
Carol Stream, IL 800-253-2991
A-1 Booth Manufacturing
Burley, ID 800-820-3285
Advance Tabco
Edgewood, NY 800-645-3166
All State Fabricators Corporation
Tampa, FL 800-322-9925
Allstrong Restaurant Eqpt Inc
South El Monte, CA 800-933-8913
Amtekco
Columbus, OH 800-336-4677
Andgar Corp
Ferndale, WA 360-366-9900
ARC Specialties
Valencia, CA. 661-775-8500
Atlas Equipment Company
Kansas City, MO. 800-842-9188
Avalon Manufacturer
Corona, CA 800-676-3040
California Vibratory Feeders
Anaheim, CA 800-354-0972
Carts Food Equipment
Brooklyn, NY 718-788-5540

Cobb & Zimmer
Detroit, MI 313-923-0350
Commercial Kitchen Co
Los Angeles, CA 323-732-2291
Custom Diamond Intl.
Laval, QC 800-326-5926
D A Berther Inc
Milwaukee, WI 877-357-9622
Dayco
Clearwater, FL 727-573-9330
Den Mar Corp
North Dartmouth, MA 508-999-3295
Duluth Sheet Metal
Duluth, MN. 218-722-2613
Eagle Group
Clayton, DE. 800-441-8440
Eldorado Miranda Manufacturing Company
Largo, FL 800-330-0708
Erwin Food Service Equipment
Fort Worth, TX 817-535-0021
Fabwright Inc
Garden Grove, CA 800-854-6464
Falcon Fabricators Inc
Nashville, TN 615-832-0027
Fixtur World
Cookeville, TN 800-634-9887
Gasser Chair Co Inc
Youngstown, OH. 800-323-2234
Griffin Products
Wills Point, TX 800-379-9709
Hot Food Boxes
Mooresville, IN. 800-733-8073
IMC Teddy Food Service Equipment
Amityville, NY 800-221-5644
Industries Inc Kiefer
Random Lake, WI. 920-994-2332
Institutional Equipment Inc
Bolingbrook, IL 630-771-0990
John Boos & Co
Effingham, IL 888-431-2667
KEMCO
Wareham, MA 800-231-5955
Kitchen Equipment Fabricating
Houston, TX 713-747-3611
Lakeside Manufacturing Inc
Milwaukee, WI 888-558-8565
Load King Mfg
Jacksonville, FL 800-531-4975
M & E Mfg Co Inc
Kingston, NY 845-331-2110
Marlo Manufacturing
Boonton, NJ 800-222-0450
MCM Fixture Co
Hazel Park, MI 248-547-9280
Metal
Columbia, SC 803-776-9252
Metal Master Sales Corp
Glendale Heights, IL. 800-488-8729
Miami Metal
Miami, FL. 305-576-3600
Midwest Folding Products
Chicago, IL 800-344-2864
Mouron & Co Inc
Indianapolis, IN 317-243-7955
New Age Industrial
Norton, KS 800-255-0104
Northern Stainless Fabricating
Traverse City, MI 231-947-4580
Omicron Steel Products Company
Jamaica, NY 718-805-3400
Pollard Brothers
Chicago, IL. 773-763-6868
Premium Air Systems Inc
Troy, MI. 877-430-0333
Quipco Products Inc
Sauget, IL 314-993-1442
Randell Manufacturing   Unified Brands
Weidman, MI 888-994-7636
Sarasota Restaurant Equipment
Sarasota, FL 800-434-1410
Savage Brothers Company
Elk Grove Vlg, IL. 800-342-0973
Schlueter Company
Janesville, WI 800-359-1700
Sefi Fabricators Inc
Amityville, NY 631-842-2200
South Valley Mfg Inc
Gilroy, CA. 408-842-5457
Southwestern Porcelain Steel
Sand Springs, OK 918-245-1375
Stainless
La Vergne, TN. 800-877-5177

Stainless Fabricating Company
Denver, CO 800-525-8966
Stainless International
Rancho Cordova, CA 888-300-6196
Stainless Steel Fabricators
Tyler, TX .903-595-6625
Starlite Food Service Equipment
Detroit, MI 888-521-6603
Super Sturdy
Weldon, NC. 800-253-4833
Superior Products Company
Saint Paul, MN 800-328-9800
Supreme Metal
Alpharetta, GA 800-645-2526
Travis Manufacturing Corp
Alliance, OH 330-875-1661
Unarco Industries LLC
Wagoner, OK. 800-654-4100
Universal Stainless
Aurora, CO 800-223-8332
Universal Stainless & Alloy
Titusville, PA 800-295-1909
Vande Berg SCALES/Vbs Inc
Sioux Center, IA 712-722-1181
Weiss Sheet Metal Inc
Avon, MA 508-583-8300
West Star Industries
Stockton, CA. 800-326-2288
Wilder Manufacturing Company
Port Jervis, NY 800-832-1319
Zol-Mark Industries
Winnipeg, NB 204-943-7393

Work

Advance Tabco
Edgewood, NY 800-645-3166
Allstrong Restaurant Eqpt Inc
South El Monte, CA 800-933-8913
Bmh Equipment Inc
Sacramento, CA 800-350-8828
Carts Food Equipment
Brooklyn, NY 718-788-5540
Eldorado Miranda Manufacturing Company
Largo, FL 800-330-0708
Falcon Fabricators Inc
Nashville, TN 615-832-0027
John Boos & Co
Effingham, IL 888-431-2667
Lakeside Manufacturing Inc
Milwaukee, WI. 888-558-8565
MCM Fixture Co
Hazel Park, MI 248-547-9280
Metro Corporation
Wilkes Barre, PA. 800-992-1776
National Bar Systems
Huntington Beach, CA 714-848-1688
Stainless Equipment Manufacturing
Dallas, TX. 800-736-2038
Superior Products Company
Saint Paul, MN 800-328-9800
Weiss Sheet Metal Inc
Avon, MA 508-583-8300

Tins

Cake

Browne & Company
Markham, ON. 905-475-6104
Dover Parkersburg
Follansbee, WV
Independent Can Co
Belcamp, MD 410-272-0090
Olive Can Company
Elgin, IL .847-468-7474

Tinware

Dover Parkersburg
Follansbee, WV
Greenfield Packaging
White Plains, NY 914-993-0233
Independent Can Co
Belcamp, MD 410-272-0090
Xtreme Beverages, LLC
Dana Point, CA. 949-495-7929

Tongs

Food

Amco Metals Indl
City Of Industry, CA. 626-855-2550
Atlanta Burning Bush
Newnan, GA 800-665-5611
Browne & Company
Markham, ON. 905-475-6104
C R Mfg
Waverly, NE 877-789-5844
Carlisle Food Svc Products Inc
Oklahoma City, OK 800-654-8210
First Plastics Co Inc
Leominster, MA 978-840-6908
Gril-Del
Mankato, MN 800-782-7320
Liberty Ware LLC
Clearfield, UT 888-500-5885
LoTech Industries
Lakewood, CO 800-295-0199
Music City Metals Inc
Nashville, TN 800-251-2674
Superior Products Company
Saint Paul, MN 800-328-9800
Vollrath Co LLC
Sheboygan, WI 800-624-2051
Weavewood, Inc.
Golden Valley, MN 800-367-6460
Wiltec
Leominster, MA 978-537-1497
Wishbone Utensil Tableware Line
Wheat Ridge, CO 866-266-5928

Ice

Browne & Company
Markham, ON. 905-475-6104
C R Mfg
Waverly, NE 877-789-5844
Superior Products Company
Saint Paul, MN 800-328-9800
Weavewood, Inc.
Golden Valley, MN 800-367-6460
Wiltec
Leominster, MA 978-537-1497

Toothpicks

Admatch Corporation
New York, NY 800-777-9909
Atlas Match Company
Toronto, ON 888-285-2783
C R Mfg
Waverly, NE 877-789-5844
Cell-O-Core Company
Sharon Center, OH 800-239-4370
Goldmax Industries
City Of Industry, CA. 626-964-8820
H A Stiles
Westbrook, ME 800-447-8537
Jarden Home Brands
Cloquet, MN 218-879-6700
Jarden Home Brands
Daleville, IN 800-392-2575
K & L Intl
Ontario, CA. 888-598-5588
Les Industries Touch Inc
Sherbrooke, QC 800-267-4140
Penley Corporation
West Paris, ME 800-368-6449
Royal Paper Products
Coatesville, PA 800-666-6655
Unique Manufacturing
Visalia, CA 888-737-1007
Z 2000 The Pick of the Millenium
Bartlesville, OK 800-654-7311

Trays & Pans

Bakers'

Aeromat Plastics Inc
Burnsville, MN. 888-286-8729
Allied Bakery and Food Service Equipment
Santa Fe Springs, CA 562-945-6506
Allied Metal Spinning
Bronx, NY. 800-615-2266
American Metal Stamping
Brooklyn, NY. 718-384-1500

American Metalcraft Inc
Franklin Park, IL. 708-345-1177
Browne & Company
Markham, ON. 905-475-6104
Buckhorn Inc
Milford, OH 800-543-4454
COW Industries Inc
Columbus, OH 800-542-9353
D & W Fine Pack
Lake Zurich, IL 800-323-0422
Dur-Able Aluminum Corporation
Hoffman Estates, IL 847-843-1100
Green Tek
Janesville, WI 800-747-6440
Music City Metals Inc
Nashville, TN 800-251-2674
National Cart Co
St Charles, MO 636-947-3800
Omega Industries
St Louis, MO. 314-961-1668
Paper Products Company
Cincinnati, OH 513-921-4717
Polar Ware Company
Sheboygan, WI 800-237-3655
Superior Products Company
Saint Paul, MN 800-328-9800
Toscarora
Sandusky, OH 419-625-7343
Unique Plastics
Rio Rico, AZ. 800-658-5946

Utensils

Bakers' & Confectioners'

Allied Metal Spinning
Bronx, NY. 800-615-2266
Amco Metals Indl
City Of Industry, CA. 626-855-2550
August Thomsen Corp
Glen Cove, NY 800-645-7170
Automated Food Systems
Waxahachie, TX 469-517-0470
Belshaw Adamatic Bakery Group
Auburn, WA 800-578-2547
Browne & Company
Markham, ON. 905-475-6104
Dur-Able Aluminum Corporation
Hoffman Estates, IL 847-843-1100
Esterle Mold & Machine Co Inc
Stow, OH. 800-411-4086
Florida Knife Co
Sarasota, FL 800-966-5643
H. Arnold Wood Turning
Tarrytown, NY 888-314-0088
Hodges
Vienna, IL 800-444-0011
Johnson Corrugated Products Corporation
Thompson, CT 860-923-9563
Kosempel Manufacturing Company
Philadelphia, PA 800-733-7122
Lady Mary
Rockingham, NC 910-997-7321
Leggett & Platt Storage
Vernon Hills, IL 847-816-6246
Leon Bush Manufacturer
Glenview, IL 847-657-8888
Measurex/S&L Plastics
Nazareth, PA 800-752-0650
Parrish's Cake Decorating
Gardena, CA 800-736-8443
Pfeil & Holding Inc
Woodside, NY. 800-247-7955
Saunder Brothers
Bridgton, ME 207-647-3331
State Products
Long Beach, CA 800-730-5150
T & S Perfection Chain Prods
Cullman, AL. 888-856-4864
Unifiller Systems
Delta, BC. 888-733-8444
Wishbone Utensil Tableware Line
Wheat Ridge, CO 866-266-5928
Zeier Plastic & Mfg Inc
Madison, WI. 608-244-5782

Chopsticks

Bamboo

K & L Intl
Ontario, CA. 888-598-5588

Forks

Cocktail

Amco Metals Indl
  City Of Industry, CA.................626-855-2550
C R Mfg
  Waverly, NE.....................877-789-5844
Jarden Home Brands
  Daleville, IN....................800-392-2575
Pelican Products Inc
  Bronx, NY......................800-552-8820
Soodhalter Plastics
  Los Angeles, CA.................213-747-0231
Wishbone Utensil Tableware Line
  Wheat Ridge, CO................866-266-5928

Wooden

Coley Industries
  Wayland, NY....................716-728-2390
Jarden Home Brands
  Daleville, IN....................800-392-2575
Weavewood, Inc.
  Golden Valley, MN...............800-367-6460

Household, Kitchen

A G Russell Knives
  Rogers, AR.....................800-255-9034
Abco International
  Oneida, NY.....................888-263-7195
Abond Plastic Corporation
  Lachine, QC....................800-886-7947
Ace Fabrication
  Mobile, AL.....................251-478-0401
Acme International
  Maplewood, NJ..................973-416-0400
All-Clad METALCRAFTERS LLC
  Canonsburg, PA.................800-255-2523
Amco Metals Indl
  City Of Industry, CA.............626-855-2550
American Housewares
  Bronx, NY......................718-665-9500
American Time & Signal Co
  Dassel, MN.....................800-328-8996
Bally Block Co
  Bally, PA.......................610-845-7511
Best Manufacturers
  Portland, OR....................800-500-1528
Bluffton Slaw Cutter Company
  Bluffton, OH....................419-358-9840
Bremer Manufacturing Co Inc
  Elkhart Lake, WI................920-894-2944
Brown Manufacturing Company
  Decatur, GA....................404-378-8311
Browne & Company
  Markham, ON....................905-475-6104
Buck Knives
  Post Falls, ID...................800-326-2825
Burrell Cutlery Company
  Ellicottville, NY.................716-699-2343
C R Mfg
  Waverly, NE.....................877-789-5844
Carlisle Food Svc Products Inc
  Oklahoma City, OK..............800-654-8210
Carolina Cracker
  Garner, NC.....................919-779-6899
Chef Revival
  North Charleston, SC............800-248-9826
Chef Specialties
  Smethport, PA..................800-440-2433
Chicago Scale & Slicer Company
  Franklin Park, IL................847-455-3400
Cleveland Metal Stamping Company
  Berea, OH......................440-234-0010
Coley Industries
  Wayland, NY....................716-728-2390
Conimar Corp
  Ocala, FL.......................800-874-9735
Corby Hall
  Randolph, NJ....................973-366-8300
CUTCO Corp
  Olean, NY......................716-372-3111
Cyclamen Collection
  Oakland, CA....................510-434-7620
Dart Container Corp.
  Mason, MI......................800-248-5960
Dexter Russell Inc
  Southbridge, MA................800-343-6042
Diamond Machining Technology
  Marlborough, MA................800-666-4368

Dorton Incorporated
  Arlington Hts, IL................800-299-8600
Dynynstyl
  Delray Beach, FL................800-774-7895
E K Lay Co
  Philadelphia, PA................800-523-3220
Edco Industries
  Bridgeport, CT..................203-333-8982
Educational Products Company
  Hope, NJ.......................800-272-3822
Fab-X/Metals
  Washington, NC.................800-677-3229
Fioriware
  Zanesville, OH..................740-454-7400
Fortune Products Inc
  Cedar Park, TX..................512-249-0334
Fun-Time International
  Philadelphia, PA................800-776-4386
G & S Metal Products Co Inc
  Cleveland, OH..................216-441-0700
G.G. Greene Enterprises
  West Warren, PA................814-723-5700
Giunta Brothers
  Philadelphia, PA................215-389-9670
Goebel Fixture Co
  Hutchinson, MN.................888-339-0509
Gold Star Products
  Oak Park, MI....................800-800-0205
Good Idea
  Northampton, MA................800-462-9237
Goodell Tools
  New Hope, MN...................800-542-3906
Grand Silver Company
  Bronx, NY......................718-585-1930
Gril-Del
  Mankato, MN...................800-782-7320
H A Stiles
  Westbrook, ME..................800-447-8537
H. Arnold Wood Turning
  Tarrytown, NY..................888-314-0088
Hardwood Products Co LP
  Guilford, ME....................800-289-3340
Harold Leonard Southwest Corporation
  Houston, TX....................800-245-8105
Hillside Metal Ware Company
  Union, NJ.......................908-964-3080
Insinger Co
  Philadelphia, PA................800-344-4802
James River Canada
  North York, ON.................416-789-5151
Jim Scharf Holdings
  Perdue, SK.....................800-667-9727
Kosempel Manufacturing Company
  Philadelphia, PA................800-733-7122
Lady Mary
  Rockingham, NC.................910-997-7321
Lamson & Goodnow
  Shelburne Falls, MA.............800-872-6564
Lancaster Colony Corporation
  Westerville, OH.................614-224-7141
Leggett & Platt Storage
  Vernon Hills, IL.................847-816-6246
Lenox Corp
  Bristol, PA......................800-223-4311
Libby Canada
  Mississauga, ON................905-607-8280
Liberty Ware LLC
  Clearfield, UT...................888-500-5885
Lifetime Brands Inc
  Garden City, NY.................516-683-6000
Lincoln Foodservice
  Cleveland, OH..................800-374-3004
Lloyd Disher Company
  Decatur, IL.....................217-429-0593
Lodge Manufacturing Company
  South Pittsburg, TN.............423-837-5919
Lorenzen's Cookie Cutters
  Wantagh, NY...................516-781-7116
Luce Corp
  Hamden, CT....................800-344-6966
Lynch-Jamentz Company
  Lakewood, CA..................800-828-6217
M & E Mfg Co Inc
  Kingston, NY...................845-331-2110
M.E. Heuck Company
  Mason, OH.....................800-359-3200
Majestic
  Bridgeport, CT..................203-367-7900
Mastex Industries
  Petersburg, VA.................804-732-8300
Measurex/S&L Plastics
  Nazareth, PA...................800-752-0650

Michael Leson Dinnerware
  Youngstown, OH................800-821-3541
Michigan Maple Block Co
  Petoskey, MI....................800-447-7975
Mid-West Wire Products
  Ferndale, MI....................800-989-9881
Mundial
  Norwood, MA...................800-487-2224
Music City Metals Inc
  Nashville, TN...................800-251-2674
National Novelty Brush Co
  Lancaster, PA...................717-299-5681
New Age Industrial
  Norton, KS.....................800-255-0104
Novelty Crystal
  Long Island City, NY............800-622-0250
Olde Country Reproductions Inc
  York, PA.......................800-358-3997
Olde Thompson Inc
  Oxnard, CA.....................800-827-1565
Oneida Food Service
  Columbus, OH..................800-828-7033
Oneida LTD Silversmiths
  Oneida, NY.....................888-263-7195
OWD
  Tupper Lake, NY................800-836-1693
OXO International
  New York, NY...................212-242-3333
Penley Corporation
  West Paris, ME..................800-368-6449
Pinn Pack Packaging LLC
  Oxnard, CA.....................805-385-4100
Polar Ware Company
  Sheboygan, WI.................800-237-3655
Prairie Packaging Inc
  Mooresville, NC.................704-660-6600
Ranger Blade Manufacturing Company
  Traer, IA.......................800-377-7860
Regal Ware Inc
  Kewaskum, WI..................262-626-2121
Reiner Products
  Waterbury, CT..................800-345-6775
Replacements LTD
  Mc Leansville, NC...............800-737-5223
Rival Manufacturing Company
  Kansas City, MO................816-943-4100
RubaTex Polymer
  Middlefield, OH.................440-632-1691
Samuel Underberg Food Store
  Brooklyn, NY...................718-363-0787
Saunder Brothers
  Bridgton, ME...................207-647-3331
Serr-Edge Machine Company
  Cleveland, CI...................800-443-8097
Slicechief Co
  Toledo, OH.....................419-241-7647
Spir-It/Zoo Piks
  Andover, MA...................800-343-0996
ST Restaurant Supplies
  Delta, BC......................888-448-4244
Stanley Roberts
  Piscataway, NJ.................973-778-5900
Sturdi-Bilt Restaurant Equipment
  Whitmore Lake, MI..............800-521-2895
Swing-A-Way Manufacturing Company
  St Louis, MO....................314-773-1488
T & A Metal Products Inc
  Deptford, NJ....................856-227-1700
T & S Perfection Chain Prods
  Cullman, AL....................888-856-4864
Table De France: North America
  New Brunswick, NJ..............888-680-4616
Tar-Hong MELAMINE USA
  City Of Industry, CA.............626-935-1612
Techform
  Mount Airy, NC.................336-789-2115
Thorpe Rolling Pin Co
  Hamden, CT....................800-344-6966
Tops Manufacturing Co
  Darien, CT......................203-655-9367
Traeger Industries
  Portland, OR....................800-872-3437
TRC
  Middlefield, OH.................440-834-0078
Trepte's Wire & Metal Works
  Bellflower, CA...................800-828-6217
Tru Hone Corp
  Ocala, FL.......................800-237-4663
Ultrafryer Systems Inc
  San Antonio, TX.................800-545-9189
Unique Manufacturing
  Visalia, CA.....................888-737-1007

United Performance Metals
Northbrook, IL 888-922-0040
United Showcase Company
Wood Ridge, NJ 800-526-6382
Utica Cutlery Co
Utica, NY 800-879-2526
Vermillion Flooring
Springfield, MO 417-862-3785
Vita Craft Corp
Shawnee, KS 800-359-3444
Vollrath Co LLC
Sheboygan, WI 800-624-2051
Waddington North America
Chelmsford, MA 888-962-2877

Walco
Utica, NY 800-879-2526
Warren E. Conley Corporation
Carmel, IN 800-367-7875
Warther Museum
Dover, OH 330-343-7513
Waukesha Cherry-Burrell
Louisville, KY 502-491-4310
Weavewood, Inc.
Golden Valley, MN 800-367-6460
Western Stoneware
Monmouth, IL 309-734-2161
Wiltec
Leominster, MA 978-537-1497

Wilton Brands LLC
Woodridge, IL 630-963-7100
Wishbone Utensil Tableware Line
Wheat Ridge, CO 866-266-5928
World Kitchen
Elmira, NY 800-999-3436
York Saw & Knife
York, PA 800-233-1969
Zelco Industries
Mount Vernon, NY 800-431-2486
Zeroll Company
Fort Pierce, FL 800-872-5000

Foodservice Equipment & Supplies

Bars & Bar Supplies

Admatch Corporation
New York, NY 800-777-9909

Advanced Design Mfg
Concord, CA 800-690-0002

Alegacy
Santa Fe Springs, CA 800-848-4440

Alluserv
West Milwaukee, WI 800-558-8565

Alpine Store Equipment Corporation
Long Island City, NY 718-361-1213

Alvarado Manufacturing Co Inc
Chino, CA 800-423-4143

AMC Industries
Palmetto, FL 941-479-7834

Amco Metals Indl
City Of Industry, CA. 626-855-2550

American Coaster Company
Sanborn, NY 888-423-8628

American Metalcraft Inc
Franklin Park, IL 708-345-1177

AMI
Richmond, CA 800-942-7466

Amtekco
Columbus, OH 800-336-4677

Anchor Hocking Operating Co
Lancaster, OH 800-562-7511

Atlas Match Company
Toronto, ON 888-285-2783

Atlas Match Corporation
Euless, TX 800-628-2426

Automatic Bar Controls Inc
Vacaville, CA 800-722-6738

Ballantyne Food Service Equipment
Omaha, NE 800-424-1215

Bar Equipment Corporation of America
Downey, CA 888-870-2322

Bar-Maid Corp
Garfield, NJ 800-227-6243

Berg Co
Monona, WI 608-221-4281

Best Brands Home Products
New York, NY 212-684-7456

Best Buy Uniforms
Homestead, PA 800-345-1924

Booth
Dallas, TX 800-497-2958

Bradley Industries
Westchester, IL 815-469-2314

Brass Smith
Denver, CO 800-662-9595

Brown Manufacturing Company
Decatur, GA 404-378-8311

Browne & Company
Markham, ON 905-475-6104

C R Mfg
Waverly, NE 877-789-5844

Carlisle Food Svc Products Inc
Oklahoma City, OK 800-654-8210

Carnegie Textile Co
Cleveland, OH 800-633-4136

Carpigiani Corporation of America
Winston Salem, NC. 800-648-4389

Carroll Chair Company
Onalaska, WI. 800-331-4704

Carts Food Equipment
Brooklyn, NY 718-788-5540

CCS Stone, Inc.
Moonachie, NJ 800-227-7785

CDI Service & Mfg Inc
Largo, FL 727-536-2207

Cell-O-Core Company
Sharon Center, OH 800-239-4370

Chaircraft
Hickory, NC 828-326-8458

Classico Seating
Peru, IN. 800-968-6655

Co-Rect Products Inc
Golden Valley, MN 800-328-5702

Coastal Canvas Products
Savannah, GA. 800-476-5174

Cobb & Zimmer
Detroit, MI 313-923-0350

Commercial Seating Specialists
Santa Clara, CA 408-453-8983

Conimar Corp
Ocala, FL. 800-874-9735

Control Beverage
Adelanto, CA 330-549-5376

Cork Specialties
Miami, FL. 305-477-1506

Cove Woodworking
Gloucester, MA. 800-273-0037

Craig Manufacturing
Irvington, NJ 800-631-7936

Cruvinet Winebar Co LLC
Sparks, NV 800-278-8463

Culinary Depot
Monsey, NY 888-845-8200

D D Bean & Sons Co
Jaffrey, NH 800-326-8311

De Felsco Corp
Ogdensburg, NY 800-448-3835

Dometic Mini Bar
Elkhart, IN. 800-301-8118

Dorado Carton Company
Dorado, PR 787-796-1670

Eagle Group
Clayton, DE. 800-441-8440

Eagle Products Company
Houston, TX 713-690-1161

Edco Industries
Bridgeport, CT 203-333-8982

Electric Contract Furniture
New York, NY. 888-311-6272

Ellingers Agatized Wood Inc
Sheboygan, WI 888-287-8906

English Manufacturing Inc
Rancho Cordova, CA 800-651-2711

Epic Products
Santa Ana, CA 800-548-9791

Erie Cotton Products
Erie, PA. 800-289-4737

Ex-Cell KAISER LLC
Franklin Park, IL. 847-451-0451

Felix Storch Inc
Bronx, NY. 800-932-4267

Flojet
Foothill Ranch, CA. 800-235-6538

Fun-Time International
Philadelphia, PA 800-776-4386

Gar Products
Lakewood, NJ 800-424-2477

Gasser Chair Co Inc
Youngstown, OH. 800-323-2234

Gensaco Marketing
New York, NY 800-506-1935

Glastender
Saginaw, MI 800-748-0423

Goldmax Industries
City Of Industry, CA. 626-964-8820

GSW Jackes-Evans Manufacturing Company
Saint Louis, MO 800-325-6173

H A Stiles
Westbrook, ME. 800-447-8537

Harbour House Bar Crafting
Stamford, CT. 800-755-1227

Harco Enterprises
Peterborough, ON 800-361-5361

Hardwood Products Co LP
Guilford, ME. 800-289-3340

Hines III
Jacksonville, FL. 904-398-5110

Hoshizaki America Inc
Peachtree City, GA 800-438-6087

Ideas Etc Inc
Louisville, KY 800-733-0337

Ilc Dover
Frederica, DE 800-631-9567

IMI Cornelius
Schaumburg, IL. 800-323-4789

Infra Corp
Waterford, MI 888-434-6372

J.H. Carr & Sons
Seattle, WA 800-523-8842

Jarden Home Brands
Cloquet, MN 218-879-6700

Jarden Home Brands
Daleville, IN. 800-392-2575

Jarlan Manufacturing
Los Angeles, CA. 323-752-1211

Johnstown Manufacturing
Columbus, OH 614-236-8853

K & I Creative Plastics & Wood
Jacksonville, FL 904-387-0438

K-Way Products
Mount Carroll, IL 800-622-9163

Karma
Watertown, WI 800-558-9565

Kings River Casting
Sanger, CA 888-545-5157

Krowne Metal Corp
Wayne, NJ. 800-631-0442

La Crosse
Onalaska, WI. 800-345-0018

Lakeside Manufacturing Inc
Milwaukee, WI 888-558-8565

Lask Seating Company
Chicago, IL. 888-573-2846

Lauritzen Makin Inc
Fort Worth, TX 817-921-0218

Lavi Industries
Valencia, CA. 800-624-6225

Lawrence Metal Products Inc
Bay Shore, NY 800-441-0019

Leggett & Platt Storage
Vernon Hills, IL 847-816-6246

Les Industries Touch Inc
Sherbrooke, QC 800-267-4140

Lodging By Charter
Liberty, NC 800-327-2548

Long Range Systems
Addison, TX 800-577-8101

Magnuson Industries
Rockford, IL 800-435-2816

Majestic
Bridgeport, CT 203-367-7900

Manitowoc Foodservice
Sellersburg, IN 800-367-4233

Marcal Paper Mills
Elmwood Park, NJ 800-631-8451

Mars Systems
Dallas, TX. 214-634-7441

Metal Master Sales Corp
Glendale Heights, IL. 800-488-8729

Milvan Food Equipment Manufacturing
Rexdale, ON 416-674-3456

Mts Seating
Temperance, MI 734-847-3875

National Bar Systems
Huntington Beach, CA 714-848-1688

National Plastics Co
Santa Fe Springs, CA 800-221-9149

Newell Brands
Atlanta, GA

Northwest Art Glass
Redmond, WA. 800-888-9444

Omicron Steel Products Company
Jamaica, NY 718-805-3400

OWD
Tupper Lake, NY 800-836-1693

Palmland Paper Company
Fort Lauderdale, FL 800-266-9067

Parisi Inc
Newtown, PA 215-968-6677

Pelican Products Inc
Bronx, NY. 800-552-8820

Penley Corporation
West Paris, ME 800-368-6449

Perfect Equipment Inc
Gurnee, IL. 800-356-6301

Perlick Corp
Milwaukee, WI 800-558-5592

Peter Gray Corporation
Andover, MA 978-470-0990

Placemat Printers
Fogelsville, PA 800-628-7746

Polar Hospitality Products
Philadelphia, PA 800-831-7823

Polar Ware Company
Sheboygan, WI 800-237-3655

Precision Pours
Minneapolis, MN 800-549-4491

Prince Seating Corp
Brooklyn, NY 800-577-4623

ProBar Systems Inc.
Barrie, ON. 800-521-7294

Redi-Call Inc
Reno, NV 800-648-1849
Regal Manufacturing Company
Chicago, IL 773-921-3071
Richardson Seating Corp
Chicago, IL 800-522-1883
Rixie Paper Products Inc
Pottstown, PA 800-377-2692
Rodo Industries
London, ON 519-668-3711
Royal Oak Enterprises
Roswell, GA 678-461-3200
Royal Paper Products
Coatesville, PA 800-666-6655
S & R Products
Bronson, MI 800-328-3887
Salem China Company
Salem, OH 330-337-8771
San Jamar
Elkhorn, WI 800-248-9826
SaniServ
Mooresville, IN 800-733-8073
Scheb International
North Barrington, IL 847-381-2573
Semco Plastic Co
St Louis, MO 314-487-4557
Sentry/Bevcon North America
Adelanto, CA 800-661-3003
Servco Equipment Co
St Louis, MO 314-781-3189
Server Products Inc
Richfield, WI 800-558-8722
Sipco Products
Peoria Heights, IL 309-682-5400
Smith-Lee Company
Oshkosh, WI 800-327-9774
Smoke Right
Chicago, IL 888-375-8885
Sneezeguard Solutions
Columbia, MO 800-569-2056
Soodhalter Plastics
Los Angeles, CA 213-747-0231
Spir-It/Zoo Piks
Andover, MA 800-343-0996
Spirit Foodservice, Inc.
Andover, MA 800-343-0996
Springprint Medallion
Augusta, GA 800-543-5990
SQP
Schenectady, NY 800-724-1129
Stainless International
Rancho Cordova, CA 888-300-6196
Summit Commercial
Bronx, NY 800-932-4267
Superior Menus
Mankato, MN 800-464-2182
Supreme Metal
Alpharetta, GA 800-645-2526
Token Factory
La Crosse, WI 888-486-5367
Tops Manufacturing Co
Darien, CT. 203-655-9367
Toronto Fabricating & Manufacturing
Mississauga, ON 905-891-2516
Trevor Industries
Eden, NY 716-992-4775
True Food Service Equipment, Inc.
O Fallon, MO 800-325-6152
U B KLEM Furniture Co Inc
St Anthony, IN 800-264-1995
United Showcase Company
Wood Ridge, NJ 800-526-6382
Ursini Plastics
Bracebridge, ON 705-646-2701
Valley Fixtures
Sparks, NV 775-331-1050
Vintage
Jasper, IN 800-992-3491
Vitro Seating Products
St Louis, MO 800-325-7093
Vynatex
Port Washington, NY 516-944-6130
Waddington North America
Chelmsford, MA 888-962-2877
Wag Industries
Skokie, IL 800-621-3305
Wallace & Hinz
Blue Lake, CA 800-831-8282
Walsh & Simmons Seating
Saint Louis, MO 800-727-0364
Weavewood, Inc.
Golden Valley, MN 800-367-6460

West Metals
London, ON 800-300-6667
Wind River Environmental
Gloucester, MA. 800-332-6025
Wood & Laminates
Lodi, NJ. 973-773-7475
Wylie Systems
Mississauga, ON 800-525-6609
Yorkraft
York, PA 800-872-2044
Z 2000 The Pick of the Millenium
Bartlesville, OK 800-654-7311
Zol-Mark Industries
Winnipeg, NB 204-943-7393

Baskets

Shopping

American Louver Co
Skokie, IL 800-772-0355
American Store Fixtures
Skokie, IL
Clamp Swing Pricing Co Inc
Oakland, CA 800-227-7615
Day Basket Factory
North East, MD. 410-398-5150
Pentwater Wire Products Inc
Pentwater, MI 877-869-6911
Peterboro Basket Co
Peterborough, NH. 603-924-3861
Southern Imperial Inc
Rockford, IL 800-747-4665

Cake Turners

American Housewares
Bronx, NY. 718-665-9500
Dexter Russell Inc
Southbridge, MA 800-343-6042

Candles

Amco Metals Indl
City Of Industry, CA. 626-855-2550
Culinart Inc
Cincinnati, OH 800-333-5678
Empire Candle Mfg LLC
Kansas City, KS 800-231-9398
General Wax & Candle Co
North Hollywood, CA 800-929-7867
Hollowick Inc
Manlius, NY 800-367-3015
Jarden Home Brands
Cloquet, MN 218-879-6700
Mason Candlelight Company
New Albany, MS. 800-556-2766
Neo-Image Candle Light
Mississauga, ON 800-375-8023
Spin-Tech Corporation
Hoboken, NJ 800-977-4692
Sterno
Lombard, IL 630-792-0080
Will & Baumer
Syracuse, NY 315-451-1000
Xtreme Beverages, LLC
Dana Point, CA 949-495-7929

Carts

Banquet

Amco Metals Indl
City Of Industry, CA. 626-855-2550
Bmh Equipment Inc
Sacramento, CA 800-350-8828
Carter-Hoffmann LLC
Mundelein, IL 800-323-9793
Duke Manufacturing Co
St Louis, MO. 800-735-3853
EPCO
Murfreesboro, TN 800-251-3398
Forbes Industries
Ontario, CA. 909-923-4549
Hot Food Boxes
Mooresville, IN. 800-733-8073
Lakeside Manufacturing Inc
Milwaukee, WI 888-558-8565
Leggett & Platt Storage
Vernon Hills, IL 847-816-6246
Shammi Industries
Corona, CA 800-417-9260

Superior Products Company
Saint Paul, MN 800-328-9800
Wilder Manufacturing Company
Port Jervis, NY 800-832-1319

Beverage

ARC Specialties
Valencia, CA. 661-775-8500
Bmh Equipment Inc
Sacramento, CA 800-350-8828
Cannon Equipment Company
Cannon Falls, MN. 800-825-8501
Carlisle Food Svc Products Inc
Oklahoma City, OK 800-654-8210
Custom Sales & Svc Inc
Hammonton, NJ 800-257-7855
Duke Manufacturing Co
St Louis, MO. 800-735-3853
Espresso Carts and Supplies
Lindenwold, NJ. 856-782-1775
Hot Food Boxes
Mooresville, IN. 800-733-8073
Lakeside Manufacturing Inc
Milwaukee, WI 888-558-8565
Midwest Aircraft Products Co
Lexington, OH 419-884-2164
Prestige Metal Products Inc
Antioch, IL 847-395-0775
Superior Products Company
Saint Paul, MN 800-328-9800
The Carriage Works
Klamath Falls, OR 541-882-0700

Bussing

Amco Metals Indl
City Of Industry, CA. 626-855-2550
Bmh Equipment Inc
Sacramento, CA 800-350-8828
Forbes Industries
Ontario, CA. 909-923-4549
Lakeside Manufacturing Inc
Milwaukee, WI 888-558-8565
Leggett & Platt Storage
Vernon Hills, IL 847-816-6246
Paxton Corp
Bristol, RI 401-396-9062
Shammi Industries
Corona, CA 800-417-9260
Sneezeguard Solutions
Columbia, MO 800-569-2056
Superior Products Company
Saint Paul, MN 800-328-9800

Condiment

Bmh Equipment Inc
Sacramento, CA 800-350-8828
Lakeside Manufacturing Inc
Milwaukee, WI 888-558-8565

Dessert, Pastry

ARC Specialties
Valencia, CA. 661-775-8500
Bmh Equipment Inc
Sacramento, CA 800-350-8828
Lakeside Manufacturing Inc
Milwaukee, WI 888-558-8565
Merchandising Frontiers Inc
Winterset, IA. 800-421-2278
Superior Products Company
Saint Paul, MN 800-328-9800

Ice

Bmh Equipment Inc
Sacramento, CA 800-350-8828
Cannon Equipment Company
Cannon Falls, MN. 800-825-8501
Kloppenberg & Co
Englewood, CO. 800-346-3246
Lakeside Manufacturing Inc
Milwaukee, WI 888-558-8565
Tooterville Trolley Company
Newburgh, IN 812-858-8585

Liquor, Wine

Amco Metals Indl
City Of Industry, CA. 626-855-2550

Bmh Equipment Inc
Sacramento, CA 800-350-8828
Cannon Equipment Company
Cannon Falls, MN. 800-825-8501
La Crosse
Onalaska, WI. 800-345-0018
Lakeside Manufacturing Inc
Milwaukee, WI. 888-558-8565
Leggett & Platt Storage
Vernon Hills, IL 847-816-6246

Mobile Food Vending

All A Cart Custom Mfg
Columbus, OH 800-695-2278
All Star Carts & Vehicles
Bay Shore, NY 800-831-3166
All State Fabricators Corporation
Tampa, FL .800-322-9925
Alliance Products LLC
Murfreesboro, TN. 800-522-3973
Alto-Shaam
Menomonee Falls, WI. 800-329-8744
Amco Metals Indl
City Of Industry, CA. 626-855-2550
AMI
Richmond, CA 800-942-7466
ARC Specialties
Valencia, CA. 661-775-8500
Automated Food Systems
Waxahachie, TX 469-517-0470
B R Machinery
Wedron, IL .800-310-7057
Barrette Outdoor Living
Cleveland, OH 800-336-2383
BBQ Pits by Klose
Houston, TX 800-487-7487
Blodgett Oven Co
Burlington, VT 800-331-5842
Boyd's Coffee Co
Portland, OR 800-735-2878
Burgess Enterprises, Inc
Renton, WA. 800-927-3286
C Nelson Mfg Co
Oak Harbor, OH 800-922-7339
Caddy Corporation of America
Bridgeport, NJ. 856-467-4222
Carlin Manufacturing
Fresno, CA .888-212-0801
Carlisle Food Svc Products Inc
Oklahoma City, OK 800-654-8210
Carts Of Colorado Inc
Greenwood Vlg, CO 800-227-8634
Continental Cart by Kullman Industries
Lebanon, NJ 888-882-2278
Corsair Display Systems
Canandalgua, NY 800-347-5245
Creative Mobile Systems Inc
Manchester, CT. 800-646-8364
Custom Diamond Intl.
Laval, QC .800-326-5926
Custom Sales & Svc Inc
Hammonton, NJ 800-257-7855
Delfield Co
Mt Pleasant, MI. 800-733-8821
Dometic Mini Bar
Elkhart, IN. 800-301-8118
Duke Manufacturing Co
St Louis, MO. 800-735-3853
Embee Sunshade Co
Brooklyn, NY 718-387-8566
EPCO
Murfreesboro, TN. 800-251-3398
Eskay Metal Fabricating
Buffalo, NY. 800-836-8015
Ex-Cell KAISER LLC
Franklin Park, IL. 847-451-0451
Fetco
Lake Zurich, IL. 800-338-2699
Gensaco Marketing
New York, NY 800-506-1935
Global Carts and Equipment
Jackson, NJ 800-653-0881
Gold Medal Products Co
Cincinnati, OH 800-543-0862
Hot Food Boxes
Mooresville, IN. 800-733-8073
Hotshot Delivery System
Bloomingdale, IL 630-924-8817
InterMetro Industries
Wilkes-Barre, PA 570-825-2741

International Thermal Dispensers
Boston, MA. 617-239-3600
King Arthur
Statesville, NC 800-257-7244
Lakeside Manufacturing Inc
Milwaukee, WI. 888-558-8565
Lakeside-Aris Manufacturing
Milwaukee, WI. 800-558-8565
Leggett & Platt Storage
Vernon Hills, IL 847-816-6246
Lil' Orbits
Minneapolis, MN 800-228-8305
Magnum Custom Trailer & BBQ Pits
Austin, TX. 800-662-4686
Merchandising Frontiers Inc
Winterset, IA 800-421-2278
Metal Master Sales Corp
Glendale Heights, IL. 800-488-8729
Metro Corporation
Wilkes Barre, PA. 800-992-1776
Michaelo Espresso
Seattle, WA. 800-545-2883
Midwest Aircraft Products Co
Lexington, OH 419-884-2164
National FABCO Manufacturing
St Louis, MO. 314-842-4571
New Age Industrial
Norton, KS 800-255-0104
Palmer Snyder
Brookfield, WI. 800-762-0415
Paragon International
Nevada, IA 800-433-0333
Plastocon
Oconomowoc, WI. 800-966-0103
Precision
Miami, FL .800-762-7565
Prestige Metal Products Inc
Antioch, IL .847-395-0775
Proluxe
Paramount, CA 800-594-5528
Quantum Storage Systems Inc
Miami, FL .800-685-4665
Sico Inc
Minneapolis, MN 800-328-6138
Sopralco
Plantation, FL 954-584-2225
Sould Manufacturing
Winnepeg, NB. 204-339-3499
Southern Express
Saint Louis, MO. 800-444-9157
SPG International
Covington, GA 877-503-4774
Star Manufacturing Intl Inc
St Louis, MO. 800-264-7827
Steamway Corporation
Scottsburg, IN. 800-259-8171
Super Sturdy
Weldon, NC. 800-253-4833
Super-Chef Manufacturing Company
Houston, TX 800-231-3478
Supreme Products
Waco, TX .254-799-4941
Technibilt/Cari-All
Newton, NC 800-233-3972
The Carriage Works
Klamath Falls, OR 541-882-0700
Tooterville Trolley Company
Newburgh, IN 812-858-8585
USECO
Murfreesboro, TN. 615-893-4820
Vollrath Co LLC
Sheboygan, WI. 800-624-2051
Wag Industries
Skokie, IL .800-621-3305
Wittco Foodservice Equipment
Milwaukee, WI. 800-821-3912
Worksman 800 Buy Cart
Ozone Park, NY 800-289-2278
WR Key
Scarborough, ON 416-291-6246
Yorkraft
York, PA 800-872-2044

Salad

Bmh Equipment Inc
Sacramento, CA 800-350-8828
Lakeside Manufacturing Inc
Milwaukee, WI. 888-558-8565
Steamway Corporation
Scottsburg, IN. 800-259-8171

Tooterville Trolley Company
Newburgh, IN 812-858-8585

Service

Amco Metals Indl
City Of Industry, CA. 626-855-2550
ARC Specialties
Valencia, CA. 661-775-8500
Blodgett Oven Co
Burlington, VT 800-331-5842
Bmh Equipment Inc
Sacramento, CA 800-350-8828
Cannon Equipment Company
Cannon Falls, MN. 800-825-8501
Duke Manufacturing Co
St Louis, MO. 800-735-3853
Gillis Associated Industries
Prospect Heights, IL 847-541-6500
Glowmaster Corporation
Clifton, NJ. 800-272-7008
Hanson Brass Rewd Co
Sun Valley, CA 888-841-3773
Hot Food Boxes
Mooresville, IN. 800-733-8073
Infanti International
Staten Island, NY 800-874-8590
King Arthur
Statesville, NC 800-257-7244
Lakeside Manufacturing Inc
Milwaukee, WI. 888-558-8565
Leggett & Platt Storage
Vernon Hills, IL 847-816-6246
Marlen
Riverside, MO. 913-888-3333
Moli-International
Denver, CO 800-525-8468
Paxton Corp
Bristol, RI .401-396-9062
Princeton Shelving
Cedar Rapids, IA. 319-369-0355
Shammi Industries
Corona, CA 800-417-9260
Sico Inc
Minneapolis, MN 800-328-6138
Superior Products Company
Saint Paul, MN 800-328-9800
Tri-Boro Shelving & Partition
Farmville, VA 800-633-3070
USECO
Murfreesboro, TN. 615-893-4820

Shopping

Assembled Products Corp
Rogers, AR 800-548-3373
Seymour Housewares
Seymour, IN 800-457-9881
Technibilt/Cari-All
Newton, NC 800-233-3972
Unarco Industries LLC
Wagoner, OK. 800-654-4100

Tray, Silverware

Alliance Products LLC
Murfreesboro, TN. 800-522-3973
Duke Manufacturing Co
St Louis, MO. 800-735-3853
EPCO
Murfreesboro, TN. 800-251-3398
Hot Food Boxes
Mooresville, IN. 800-733-8073
Lakeside Manufacturing Inc
Milwaukee, WI. 888-558-8565
National Cart Co
St Charles, MO. 636-947-3800
Paramount Packaging Corp
Melville, NY 516-333-8100
Traycon Manufacturing Co
Carlstadt, NJ 201-939-5555
Wilder Manufacturing Company
Port Jervis, NY 800-832-1319

Cases

Display

Accent Store Fixtures
Kenosha, WI 800-545-1144
Acme Display Fixture Company
Los Angeles, CA. 800-959-5657

ALCO Designs
Gardena, CA 800-228-2346
All State Fabricators Corporation
Tampa, FL 800-322-9925
Allstate Manufacturing Company
Manchester, OH 800-262-2340
Alto-Shaam
Menomonee Falls, WI. 800-329-8744
Arctica Showcase Company
Cayuga, ON. 800-839-5536
Arizona Store Equipment
Phoenix, AZ 800-624-8395
Arneg LLC
Lexington, NC 800-276-3487
Bailly Showcase & Fixture Company
Las Vegas, NV 702-947-6885
Barker Company
Keosauqua, IA 319-293-3777
BKI Worldwide
Simpsonville, SC 800-927-6887
Bon Chef
Lafayette, NJ. 800-331-0177
Brass Smith
Denver, CO 800-662-9595
C&H Store Equipment Company
Los Angeles, CA. 800-648-4979
Carman And Company
Burlington, MA. 781-221-3500
Caselites
Hialeah, FL 305-819-7766
Claridge Products & Equipment
Harrison, AR . . . .
Coldstream Products Corporation
Crossfield, AB 888-946-4097
Corsair Display Systems
Canandalgua, NY 800-347-5245
Craig Manufacturing
Irvington, NJ. 800-631-7936
Crispy Lite
St. Louis, MO 888-356-5362
Crown Metal Manufacturing Company
Elmhurst, IL 630-279-9800
Cruvinet Winebar Co LLC
Sparks, NV 800-278-8463
CSC Worldwide
Columbus, OH 800-848-3573
Delfield Co
Mt Pleasant, MI. 800-733-8821
Display Creations
Brooklyn, NY 718-257-2300
Dunhill Food Equipment Corporation
Armonk, NY 800-847-4206
Dunn Woodworks
Shrewsbury, PA. 877-835-8592
Empire Bakery Equipment
Hicksville, NY 800-878-4070
Esquire Mechanical Corp.
Armonk, NY 800-847-4206
Federal Industries
Belleville, WI 800-356-4206
Fogel Jordon Commercial Refrigeration Company
Philadelphia, PA 800-523-0171
Forbes Industries
Ontario, CA. 909-923-4549
Greene Industries
East Greenwich, RI. 401-884-7530
Handy Manufacturing Co Inc
Newark, NJ. 800-631-4280
Hardt Equipment Manufacturing
Lachine, QC 888-848-4408
Hercules Food Equipment
Weston, ON. 416-742-9673
Hoshizaki America Inc
Peachtree City, GA 800-438-6087
Interstate Showcase & Fixture Company
West Orange, NJ 973-483-5555
Jordan Specialty Company
Brooklyn, NY 877-567-3265
Kedco Wine Storage Systems
Farmingdale, NY 800-654-9988
Langer Manufacturing Company
Cedar Rapids, IA. 800-728-6445
Leggett & Platt Inc
Carthage, MO 417-358-8131
Lynn Sign Inc
Andover, MA 800-225-5764
Madix
Goodwater, AL 256-839-6354
Mayworth Showcase Works Inc
Tampa, FL. 813-251-1558
Merco/Savory
Mt. Pleasant, MI 800-733-8821

Mercury Equipment Company
Chino, CA 800-273-6688
Merix Chemical Company
Chicago, IL. 312-573-1400
Modar
Benton Harbor, MI 800-253-6186
Modern Store Fixtures Company
Dallas, TX. 800-634-7777
Moli-International
Denver, CO 800-525-8468
MultiFab Plastics
Boston, MA. 888-293-5754
Nor-Lake
Salem, NH. 603-893-9701
Northwestern
Van Nuys, CA 818-786-1581
Omega Industries
St Louis, MO. 314-961-1668
Omnitemp Refrigeration
Downey, CA. 800-423-9660
Oscartek
Burlingame, CA 855-885-2400
OSF
Toronto, ON 800-465-4000
Palmer Distributors
St Clair Shores, MI 800-444-1912
Parisi Inc
Newtown, PA 215-968-6677
Plastic Supply Inc
Londonderry, NH 800-752-7759
Poblocki Sign Co
Milwaukee, WI 414-453-4010
Premier Brass
Atlanta, GA 800-251-5800
Process Displays
New Berlin, WI. 800-533-1764
QBD Modular Systems
Santa Clara, CA 800-663-3005
Rathe Productions
New York, NY 212-242-9000
Refcon
Medford, NJ. 609-714-2330
Refrigeration Engineering
Grand Rapids, MI 800-968-3227
Regal Custom Fixture Company
Westampton, NJ 800-525-3092
Retail Decor
Ironton, OH 800-726-3402
Robelan Displays Inc
Hempstead, NY. 865-564-8600
RW Products
Edgewood, NY 800-345-1022
Sani-Top Products
De Leon Springs, FL. 800-874-6094
Seattle Plastics
Seattle, WA 800-441-0679
Silver King Refrigeration Inc
Minneapolis, MN 800-328-3329
Sitka Store Fixtures
Kansas City, MO. 800-821-7558
Southern Store Fixtures Inc
Bessemer, AL 800-552-6283
Spartan Showcase
Union, MO 800-325-0775
Standex International Corp.
Salem, NH. 603-893-9701
Taymar Industries
Palm Desert, CA 800-624-1972
Top Source Industries
Addison, IL 800-362-9625
True Food Service Equipment, Inc.
O Fallon, MO 800-325-6152
United Showcase Company
Wood Ridge, NJ 800-526-6382
Universal Folding Box
East Orange, NJ 973-482-4300
West Metals
London, ON 800-300-6667
William Hecht
Philadelphia, PA 215-925-6223

Cash Registers

Data Visible Corporation
Charlottesville, VA 800-368-3494
Kelmin Products
Plymouth, FL 407-886-6079
OMRON Systems LLC
Schaumburg, IL. 224-520-7650
PAR Tech Inc
New Hartford, NY 800-448-6505
Superior Products Company
Saint Paul, MN 800-328-9800

TEC America
Atlanta, GA 770-453-0868

Chafers

Apex Fountain Sales Inc
Philadelphia, PA 800-523-4586
ARC Specialties
Valencia, CA 661-775-8500
Bon Chef
Lafayette, NJ 800-331-0177
Browne & Company
Markham, ON 905-475-6104
Candle Lamp Company
Corona, CA 877-526-7748
Crestware
North Salt Lake, UT 800-345-0513
Dura-Ware Company of America
Oklahoma City, OK 800-664-3872
Dynynstyl
Delray Beach, FL 800-774-7895
Eastern Tabletop Mfg
Brooklyn, NY 888-422-4142
Glowmaster Corporation
Clifton, NJ. 800-272-7008
Kelmin Products
Plymouth, FL 407-886-6079
King Arthur
Statesville, NC 800-257-7244
Mack-Chicago Corporation
Chicago, IL 800-992-6225
Mosshaim Innovations
Jacksonville, FL 888-995-7775
Polar Ware Company
Sheboygan, WI 800-237-3655
Randware Industries
Prospect Heights, IL 847-299-8884
Rexcraft Fine Chafers
Long Island City, NY 888-739-2723
Superior Products Company
Saint Paul, MN 800-328-9800

Chairs

A-1 Booth Manufacturing
Burley, ID 800-820-3285
AMC Industries
Palmetto, FL 941-479-7834
Barn Furniture Mart
Van Nuys, CA 888-302-2276
Beaufurn
Advance, NC 888-766-7706
Beka Furniture
Concord, ON. 905-669-4255
Bennington Furniture Corporation
Bennington, PA 802-447-3212
Brill Manufacturing Co
Ludington, MI. 866-896-6420
Carroll Chair Company
Onalaska, WI. 800-331-4704
CCS Stone, Inc.
Moonachie, NJ. 800-227-7785
Chaircraft
Hickory, NC 828-326-8458
Classico Seating
Peru, IN 800-968-6655
Commercial Furniture Group Inc
Newport, TN 800-873-3252
Commercial Seating Specialists
Santa Clara, CA 408-453-8983
Cosco Home & Office Products
Columbus, IN 800-628-8321
Cramer Inc
Kansas City, MO. 800-366-6700
Eagle Products Company
Houston, TX 713-690-1161
Electric Contract Furniture
New York, NY. 888-311-6272
Fab-X/Metals
Washington, NC 800-677-3229
FDL/Flair Designs
Kokomo, IN 765-452-6000
Fiskars Brands Inc.
Baldwinsville, NY 315-635-9911
Fixtur World
Cookeville, TN 800-634-9887
Fixtures Furniture
Florence, AL 855-321-4999
Fred Beesley's Booth & Upholstery
Centerville, UT 801-364-8189
Furniturelab
Carrboro, NC 800-449-8677

Gar Products
Lakewood, NJ 800-424-2477
Gasser Chair Co Inc
Youngstown, OH. 800-323-2234
Gaychrome Division of CSL
Crystal Lake, IL 800-873-4370
Hines III
Jacksonville, FL 904-398-5110
Imperial
Carlstadt, NJ 800-526-6261
Infanti International
Staten Island, NY 800-874-8590
International Patterns, Inc.
Bay Shore, NY 631-952-2000
J.A. Thurston Company
Rumford, ME 207-364-7921
J.H. Carr & Sons
Seattle, WA 800-523-8842
John Boos & Co
Effingham, IL 888-431-2667
K C Booth Co
N Kansas City, MO. 800-866-5226
Ken Coat
Bardstown, KY 888-536-2628
Kings River Casting
Sanger, CA 888-545-5157
Krueger International Holding
Green Bay, WI. 800-424-2432
Lask Seating Company
Chicago, IL 888-573-2846
Lauritzen Makin Inc
Fort Worth, TX 817-921-0218
LB Furniture Industries
Hudson, NY 800-221-8752
Line-Master Products
Cocolalla, ID. 208-265-4743
Lodging By Charter
Liberty, NC 800-327-2548
Marston Manufacturing
Cleveland, OH 216-587-3400
Merric
Bridgeton, MO 314-770-9944
Miami Metal
Miami, FL 305-576-3600
Mity Lite Inc
Orem, UT 800-909-8034
Mlp Seating
Elk Grove Vlg, IL 800-723-3030
Mts Seating
Temperance, MI 734-847-3875
Old Dominion Wood Products
Lynchburg, VA 800-245-6382
Omicron Steel Products Company
Jamaica, NY 718-805-3400
Palmer Snyder
Brookfield, WI 800-762-0415
Pinnacle Furnishing
Aberdeen, NC 866-229-5704
Plymold
Kenyon, MN 800-759-6653
Prince Castle Inc
Carol Stream, IL 800-722-7853
Prince Seating Corp
Brooklyn, NY 800-577-4623
Quality Highchairs
Pacoima, CA 800-969-9635
Quality Seating Co
Youngstown, OH. 800-323-2234
Regal Manufacturing Company
Chicago, IL 773-921-3071
Richardson Seating Corp
Chicago, IL 800-522-1883
Robertson Furniture Co Inc
Toccoa, GA 800-241-0713
Rodo Industries
London, ON 519-668-3711
Rollhaus Seating Products Inc
Long Island City, NY 800-822-6684
Rosenwach Tank Co LLC
Long Island City, NY 212-972-4411
Sandler Seating
Atlanta, GA. 404-982-9000
Sauvagnat Inc
Huntersville, NC 800-258-5619
Seating Concepts Inc
Rockdale, IL 800-421-2036
Shafer Commercial Seating
Denver, CO 303-322-7792
Shelby Williams Industries Inc
Newport, TN 800-873-3252
Sims Superior Seating
Locust Grove, GA. 800-729-9178

Superior Products Company
Saint Paul, MN 800-328-9800
Thorpe & Associates
Siler City, NC 919-742-5516
Toronto Fabricating & Manufacturing
Mississauga, ON 905-891-2516
Trojan Commercial Furni ture Inc.
Montereal, QC 877-271-3878
U B KLEM Furniture Co Inc
St Anthony, IN 800-264-1995
US Seating Products
Ocala, FL. 800-999-2589
Vintage
Jasper, IN 800-992-3491
Vitro Seating Products
St Louis, MO. 800-325-7093
Walsh & Simmons Seating
Saint Louis, MO 800-727-0364
Waymar Industries
Burnsville, MN 888-474-1112
Wheel Tough Company
Terre Haute, IN 888-765-8833
Woodard
Coppell, TX 800-877-2290
World Wide Hospitality Furn
Paramount, CA 800-728-8262
Xiaoping Design
New York, NY 800-891-9896
Zol-Mark Industries
Winnipeg, NB 204-943-7393

Changers

Currency

Advantus Corp.
Jacksonville, FL 904-482-0091
Automated Business Products
Hackensack, NJ. 800-334-1440
Giesecke & Devrient America
Dulles, VA. 800-856-7712
Hamilton Manufacturing Corp
Holland, OH 888-723-4858
Rowe International
Grand Rapids, MI 616-246-0483

China

Abco International
Oneida, NY 888-263-7195
Americana Art China Company
Sebring, OH 800-233-6133
Babco International, Inc
Tucson, AZ 520-628-7596
Bel-Terr China
Warren, OH. 800-900-2371
Benner China & Glassware Inc
Jacksonville, FL 904-733-4620
Brooklyn Boys Pizza & Pasta
Boca Raton, FL. 561-477-3663
Buffalo China
Buffalo, NY. 716-824-8515
China Lenox Incorporated
Bristol, PA 267-525-7800
Crestware
North Salt Lake, UT 800-345-0513
Dansk International Designs
Bristol, PA. 914-697-6400
Delco Tableware
Port Washington, NY 800-221-9557
Dynynstyl
Delray Beach, FL 800-774-7895
H.F. Coors China Company
New Albany, MS. 800-782-6677
Hall China Co
East Liverpool, OH. 800-445-4255
Hartstone Pottery Inc
Zanesville, OH 740-452-9999
Homer Laughlin China Co
Newell, WV 800-452-4462
Izabel Lam International
Brooklyn, NY 718-797-3983
Lenox Corp
Bristol, PA 800-223-4311
Libby Canada
Mississauga, ON 905-607-8280
Michael Leson Dinnerware
Youngstown, OH. 800-821-3541
Mikasa Hotelware
Secaucus, NJ 866-645-2721
Minners Designs   Inc.
New York, NY 212-688-7441

Oneida Food Service
Columbus, OH 800-828-7033
Oneida LTD Silversmiths
Oneida, NY 888-263-7195
Pickard China
Antioch, IL 847-395-3800
Prolon
Port Gibson, MS 888-480-9828
Rego China Corporation
Melville, NY 800-221-1707
Rexcraft Fine Chafers
Long Island City, NY 888-739-2723
Royal Prestige Health Moguls
Westbury, NY 888-802-7433
Salem China Company
Salem, OH 330-337-8771
Sterling China Company
Wellsville, OH. 800-682-7628
Superior Products Company
Saint Paul, MN 800-328-9800
Syracuse China Company
Syracuse, NY 800-448-5711
Townfood Equipment Corp
Brooklyn, NY 800-221-5032
Tradeco International Corp
Addison, IL 800-628-3738
Vertex China
Pomona, CA 800-483-7839
Victoria Porcelain
Miami, FL 888-593-2353
Wedgwood USA
Wall Township, NJ 800-999-9936
Xtreme Beverages, LLC
Dana Point, CA 949-495-7929

Clear & Colored Plastic

Chips

Hopp Co Inc
New Hyde Park, NY. 800-889-8425

Indoor Sign Holders

Hopp Co Inc
New Hyde Park, NY. 800-889-8425

Clear Plastic

Shelf Strips

Hopp Co Inc
New Hyde Park, NY. 800-889-8425

Coasters

Admatch Corporation
New York, NY 800-777-9909
Amco Metals Indl
City Of Industry, CA. 626-855-2550
American Coaster Company
Sanborn, NY 888-423-8628
Atlas Match Company
Toronto, ON 888-285-2783
Best Brands Home Products
New York, NY 212-684-7456
Conimar Corp
Ocala, FL. 800-874-9735
Edco Industries
Bridgeport, CT 203-333-8982
Gessner Products
Ambler, PA 800-874-7808
Harco Enterprises
Peterborough, ON 800-361-5361
IB Concepts
Elizabeth, NJ 888-671-0800
Majestic
Bridgeport, CT 203-367-7900
Pelican Products Inc
Bronx, NY. 800-552-8820
Polar Hospitality Products
Philadelphia, PA 800-831-7823
Rixie Paper Products Inc
Pottstown, PA 800-377-2692
Royal Paper Products
Coatesville, PA 800-666-6655
Springprint Medallion
Augusta, GA 800-543-5990
Tops Manufacturing Co
Darien, CT. 203-655-9367
Unique Manufacturing
Visalia, CA 888-737-1007

Weavewood, Inc.
Golden Valley, MN 800-367-6460

Coin Machinery

Giesecke & Devrient America
Dulles, VA 800-856-7712
Scan Coin
Ashburn, VA 800-336-3311
Wico Corporation
Niles, IL 800-367-9426

Colored Plastic

Shelf Strips

Hopp Co Inc
New Hyde Park, NY 800-889-8425

Concession Supplies & Equipment

All Star Carts & Vehicles
Bay Shore, NY 800-831-3166
Alliance Products LLC
Murfreesboro, TN 800-522-3973
Automated Food Systems
Waxahachie, TX 469-517-0470
Carlin Manufacturing
Fresno, CA 888-212-0801
Century Industries Inc
Sellersburg, IN 800-248-3371
Creative Mobile Systems Inc
Manchester, CT 800-646-8364
Delfield Co
Mt Pleasant, MI. 800-733-8821
Fun City Popcorn
Las Vegas, NV 800-423-1710
Gold Medal Products Co
Cincinnati, OH 800-543-0862
Great Western Co LLC
Hollywood, AL 256-259-3578
Holstein Manufacturing
Holstein, IA 800-368-4342
International Thermal Dispensers
Boston, MA. 617-239-3600
Karma
Watertown, WI 800-558-9565
Kloss Manufacturing Co Inc
Allentown, PA 800-445-7100
Lazy Man Inc
Belvidere, NJ 800-475-1950
Magnum Custom Trailer & BBQ Pits
Austin, TX. 800-662-4686
Marston Manufacturing
Cleveland, OH 216-587-3400
New Centennial
Columbus, GA 800-241-7541
Rio Syrup Co
St Louis, MO. 800-325-7666
Server Products Inc
Richfield, WI 800-558-8722
Steamway Corporation
Scottsburg, IN 800-259-8171
Supreme Products
Waco, TX 254-799-4941
Texas Corn Roasters
Granbury, TX 800-772-4345
The Carriage Works
Klamath Falls, OR 541-882-0700
Thermal Bags By Ingrid Inc
Gilberts, IL 800-622-5560
Yorkraft
York, PA 800-872-2044

Corkscrews

Amco Metals Indl
City Of Industry, CA. 626-855-2550
C R Mfg
Waverly, NE 877-789-5844
Cove Four
Freeport, NY 516-379-4232
Pelican Products Inc
Bronx, NY. 800-552-8820
Superior Products Company
Saint Paul, MN 800-328-9800
Swing-A-Way Manufacturing Company
St Louis, MO. 314-773-1488

Counters

Cafeteria, Restaurant

Accent Store Fixtures
Kenosha, WI 800-545-1144
Ace Fabrication
Mobile, AL 251-478-0401
All State Fabricators Corporation
Tampa, FL 800-322-9925
Alpine Store Equipment Corporation
Long Island City, NY 718-361-1213
American Creative Solutions
Matthews, NC 877-925-4406
Atlas Metal Industries
Miami, FL 800-762-7565
Baker & Co
Norfolk, VA. 800-909-4325
Barn Furniture Mart
Van Nuys, CA 888-302-2276
Borroughs Corp
Kalamazoo, MI 800-748-0227
Cara Products Company
Jonesboro, GA 770-478-9802
Carman And Company
Burlington, MA. 781-221-3500
Catskill Craftsmen Inc
Stamford, NY 607-652-7321
Cobb & Zimmer
Detroit, MI 313-923-0350
Custom Diamond Intl.
Laval, QC 800-326-5926
Delfield Co
Mt Pleasant, MI. 800-733-8821
Duke Manufacturing Co
St Louis, MO. 800-735-3853
Duluth Sheet Metal
Duluth, MN. 218-722-2613
Dunhill Food Equipment Corporation
Armonk, NY. 800-847-4206
Economy Paper & Restaurant Co
Clifton, NJ. 973-279-5500
Erwin Food Service Equipment
Fort Worth, TX 817-535-0021
Eskay Metal Fabricating
Buffalo, NY. 800-836-8015
Fixtur World
Cookeville, TN 800-634-9887
Fred Beesley's Booth & Upholstery
Centerville, UT 801-364-8189
Gervasi Wood Products
Madison, WI 608-274-6752
Habco
Concord, CA 925-682-6203
Hallock Fabricating Corp
Riverhead, NY 631-727-2441
Hercules Food Equipment
Weston, ON. 416-742-9673
IGS Store Fixtures
Peabody, MA. 978-532-0010
Inland Showcase & Fixture Company
Fresno, CA 559-237-4158
Institutional Equipment Inc
Bolingbrook, IL 630-771-0990
Kitchen Equipment Fabricating
Houston, TX 713-747-3611
Kitcor Corp
Sun Valley, CA 818-767-4800
Lauritzen Makin Inc
Fort Worth, TX 817-921-0218
Load King Mfg
Jacksonville, FL 800-531-4975
Low Temp Industries Inc
Jonesboro, GA 678-674-1317
Marlo Manufacturing
Boonton, NJ 800-222-0450
MCM Fixture Co
Hazel Park, MI 248-547-9280
Mcroyal Industries Inc
Youngstown, OH. 800-785-2556
Merric
Bridgeton, MO 314-770-9944
Metal Kitchen Fabricators Inc
Houston, TX 713-683-8375
Metal Master Sales Corp
Glendale Heights, IL. 800-488-8729
Missouri Equipment
St Louis, MO. 800-727-6326
Monroe Extinguisher Co Inc
Rochester, NY. 585-235-3310
Mouron & Co Inc
Indianapolis, IN 317-243-7955

National FABCO Manufacturing
St Louis, MO. 314-842-4571
Omicron Steel Products Company
Jamaica, NY 718-805-3400
Oscartek
Burlingame, CA 855-885-2400
Paramount Manufacturing Company
Wilmington, MA 978-657-4300
Parisi Inc
Newtown, PA 215-968-6677
Perfect Plank Co
Oroville, CA 800-327-1961
Pierce Laminated Products Inc
Rockford, IL 815-968-9651
PMI Food Equipment Group
Troy, OH 937-332-3000
Quipco Products Inc
Sauget, IL 314-993-1442
Sarasota Restaurant Equipment
Sarasota, FL 800-434-1410
Seating Concepts Inc
Rockdale, IL 800-421-2036
Sefi Fabricators Inc
Amityville, NY 631-842-2200
Shelley Cabinet Company
Shelley, ID. 208-357-3700
Solid Surface Acrylics
North Tonawanda, NY 888-595-4114
Southwestern Porcelain Steel
Sand Springs, OK 918-245-1375
Spartan Showcase
Union, MO 800-325-0775
St. Louis Stainless Service
St Louis, MO. 800-735-3853
Stainless Equipment Manufacturing
Dallas, TX. 800-736-2038
Stainless Fabricating Company
Denver, CO. 800-525-8966
Stainless International
Rancho Cordova, CA 888-300-6196
Stainless Steel Fabricators
Tyler, TX. 903-595-6625
Top Source Industries
Addison, IL 800-362-9625
Trojan Commercial Furni ture Inc.
Montreal, QC 877-271-3878
United Fabricators
Fort Smith, AR 800-235-4101
Universal Stainless
Aurora, CO 800-223-8332
Universal Stainless & Alloy
Titusville, PA 800-295-1909
Walsh & Simmons Seating
Saint Louis, MO 800-727-0364
Weiss Sheet Metal Inc
Avon, MA 508-583-8300
West Coast Industries Inc
San Francisco, CA 800-243-3150
Western Laminates
Omaha, NE 402-556-4600

Coin

Automated Business Products
Hackensack, NJ. 800-334-1440
Giesecke & Devrient America
Dulles, VA 800-856-7712
Scan Coin
Ashburn, VA 800-336-3311

Decorative Items

Hollowick Inc
Manlius, NY 800-367-3015
Irresistible Cookie Jar
Hayden Lake, ID 208-664-1261
Stanpac, Inc.
Smithville, ON 905-957-3326
Xtreme Beverages, LLC
Dana Point, CA. 949-495-7929

Dishes

Paper

Design Specialties Inc
Hamden, CT 800-999-1584
Hoffmaster Group Inc.
Oshkosh, WI 800-558-9300
Primary Liquidation
Bohemia, NY 631-244-1410

Dispensers

Beer

Autobar Systems
Asbury Park, NJ 732-922-3355
Automatic Bar Controls Inc
Vacaville, CA 800-722-6738
Banner Equipment Co
Morris, IL 800-621-4625
Beer Magic Devices
Hamilton, ON 905-522-3081
Berg Co
Monona, WI 608-221-4281
Bijur Lubricating Corporation
Morrisville, NC. 800-631-0168
Carbonic Machines Inc
Minneapolis, MN 612-824-0745
Carmun International
San Antonio, TX 800-531-7907
Custom Diamond International
Laval, QC 800-363-5926
Easybar Corp
Tualatin, OR 888-294-7405
Felix Storch Inc
Bronx, NY. 800-932-4267
Flojet
Foothill Ranch, CA. 800-235-6538
IMI Cornelius
Schaumburg, IL. 800-323-4789
K-Way Products
Mount Carroll, IL 800-622-9163
Multiplex Co Inc
Sellersburg, IN 800-787-8880
Perlick Corp
Milwaukee, WI 800-558-5592
Sentry/Bevcon North America
Adelanto, CA 800-661-3003
Stainless One DispensingSystem
Vacaville, CA 888-723-3827
Summit Commercial
Bronx, NY. 800-932-4267
Superior Products Company
Saint Paul, MN 800-328-9800
True Food Service Equipment, Inc.
O Fallon, MO 800-325-6152

Beverage

Action Technology
Prussia, PA 217-935-8311
American Manufacturing-Engrng
Cleveland, OH 800-822-9402
Apex Fountain Sales Inc
Philadelphia, PA 800-523-4586
Autobar Systems
Asbury Park, NJ 732-922-3355
Automatic Bar Controls Inc
Vacaville, CA 800-722-6738
Automatic Products
Williston, SC. 800-523-8363
Azbar Plus
Qu,bec, QC 418-687-3672
Banner Equipment Co
Morris, IL 800-621-4625
Beer Magic Devices
Hamilton, ON 905-522-3081
Berg Co
Monona, WI 608-221-4281
Bevistar
Oswego, IL 877-238-7827
BG Industries
Lemont, IL 800-800-5761
Bijur Lubricating Corporation
Morrisville, NC. 800-631-0168
Booth
Dallas, TX 800-497-2958
C R Mfg
Waverly, NE 877-789-5844
Carbonic Machines Inc
Minneapolis, MN 612-824-0745
Carlisle Food Svc Products Inc
Oklahoma City, OK 800-654-8210
Carmun International
San Antonio, TX. 800-531-7907
Carpigiani Corporation of America
Winston Salem, NC. 800-648-4389
Chill Rite Mfg
Slidell, LA. 800-256-2190
Cleland Sales Corp
Los Alamitos, CA 562-598-6616

Commercial Refrigeration Service, Inc.
Phoenix, AZ 623-869-8881
Control Beverage
Adelanto, CA 330-549-5376
Cornelius Inc.
Osseo, MN 800-238-3600
Cornelius Wilshire Corporation
Schaumburg, IL. 847-397-4600
Cruvinet Winebar Co LLC
Sparks, NV 800-278-8463
Custom Diamond International
Laval, QC 800-363-5926
Delfield Co
Mt Pleasant, MI. 800-733-8821
Easybar Corp
Tualatin, OR 888-294-7405
Elmeco SRL
Bartlett, TN 901-385-0490
Eurodib
Champlain, NY 888-956-6866
Federal Machine Corp
Clive, IA 800-247-2446
Felix Storch Inc
Bronx, NY 800-932-4267
Fetco
Lake Zurich, IL 800-338-2699
Flojet
Foothill Ranch, CA 800-235-6538
Fountainhead
Bensalem, PA 800-326-8998
Grindmaster-Cecilware Corp
Louisville, KY 800-695-4500
Hedwin Division
Baltimore, MD 800-638-1012
Hoshizaki America Inc
Peachtree City, GA 800-438-6087
Icee-USA Corporation
Ontario, CA. 800-426-4233
Igloo Products Corp
Katy, TX 866-509-3503
IMI Cornelius
Schaumburg, IL. 800-323-4789
In Sink Erator
Racine, WI 800-558-5700
Juicy Whip Inc
La Verne, CA 909-392-7500
K-Way Products
Mount Carroll, IL 800-622-9163
Karma
Watertown, WI 800-558-9565
Lancaster Colony Corporation
Westerville, OH. 614-224-7141
Lancer Corp
Roselle, IL. 877-814-2271
Lancer Corp
San Antonio, TX. 888-676-5196
Leland Limited Inc
South Plainfield, NJ 800-984-9793
Little Squirt
Toronto, ON 416-665-6605
Magnuson Industries
Rockford, IL 800-435-2816
Manitowoc Foodservice
Sellersburg, IN 800-367-4233
Moli-International
Denver, CO 800-525-8468
Mulligan Associates
Mequon, WI 800-627-2886
Multiplex Co Inc
Sellersburg, IN 800-787-8880
Perfect Equipment Inc
Gurnee, IL. 800-356-6301
Perlick Corp
Milwaukee, WI 800-558-5592
Polar Beer Systems
Sun City, CA 951-928-8174
Precision Pours
Minneapolis, MN 800-549-4491
Pro-Flo Products
Cedar Grove, NJ 800-325-1057
ProBar Systems Inc.
Barrie, ON. 800-521-7294
PROCON Products
Smyrna, TN. 615-355-8000
Prolon
Port Gibson, MS 888-480-9828
Regal Ware Inc
Kewaskum, WI 262-626-2121
Remco Products Corp
Zionsville, IN 800-585-8619
Rieke Packaging Systems
Auburn, IN 260-925-3700

Robinson/Kirshbaum Industries
Gardena, CA 800-929-3812
Rocket Man
Louisville, KY 800-365-6661
S & R Products
Bronson, MI 800-328-3887
SaniServ
Mooresville, IN. 800-733-8073
Scotsman Ice Systems
Vernon Hills, IL 800-726-8762
Sea Breeze Fruit Flavors
Towaco, NJ 800-732-2733
Sentry/Bevcon North America
Adelanto, CA 800-661-3003
SerVend International
Sellersburg, IN 800-367-4233
Server Products Inc
Richfield, WI 800-558-8722
Silver King Refrigeration Inc
Minneapolis, MN 800-328-3329
Sopralco
Plantation, FL 954-584-2225
Spin-Tech Corporation
Hoboken, NJ 800-977-4692
Spinco Metal Products Inc
Newark, NY 315-331-6285
Stainless One DispensingSystem
Vacaville, CA 888-723-3827
Star Manufacturing Intl Inc
St Louis, MO. 800-264-7827
Steel Products
Marion, IA. 800-333-9451
Summit Commercial
Bronx, NY. 800-932-4267
Sunroc Corporation
Columbus, OH 800-478-6762
Superflex Limited
Brooklyn, NY 800-394-3665
Superior Products Company
Saint Paul, MN 800-328-9800
Tablecraft Products Co Inc
Gurnee, IL 800-323-8321
Technium
Medford, NJ 609-702-5910
Thermos Company
Schaumburg, IL. 800-243-0745
Tops Manufacturing Co
Darien, CT. 203-655-9367
True Food Service Equipment, Inc.
O Fallon, MO 800-325-6152
Wells Manufacturing Company
St. Louis, MO 888-356-5362
Wilch Manufacturing
Topeka, KS 785-267-2762
Wine Chillers of California
Santa Ana, CA 800-331-4274
Winekeeper
Santa Barbara, CA 805-963-3451

Coffee

American Production Co Inc
Redwood City, CA 650-368-5334
Bevistar
Oswego, IL 877-238-7827
Custom Diamond International
Laval, QC 800-363-5926
Fetco
Lake Zurich, IL 800-338-2699
Franke Americas
Hatfield, PA. 215-822-6590
K-Way Products
Mount Carroll, IL 800-622-9163
Karma
Watertown, WI 800-558-9565
Midwest Juice
Grand Rapids, MI 877-265-8243
Red Diamond Coffee & Tea
Moody, AL 800-292-4651
Regal Ware Inc
Kewaskum, WI 262-626-2121
Sopralco
Plantation, FL 954-584-2225
Steel Products
Marion, IA. 800-333-9451
Superior Products Company
Saint Paul, MN 800-328-9800
Thermos Company
Schaumburg, IL. 800-243-0745
Tops Manufacturing Co
Darien, CT. 203-655-9367

Wells Manufacturing Company
St. Louis, MO .888-356-5362

Cup & Napkin

Atlas Metal Industries
Miami, FL. 800-762-7565
Browne & Company
Markham, ON 905-475-6104
C R Mfg
Waverly, NE 877-789-5844
Component Hardware Group Inc
Lakewood, NJ 800-526-3694
Custom Diamond International
Laval, QC .800-363-5926
Dispense Rite
Northbrook, IL 800-772-2877
Diversified Metal Products Inc
Northbrook, IL 800-772-2877
Georgia Pacific
Green Bay, WI. 920-435-8821
Igloo Products Corp
Katy, TX 866-509-3503
K & L Intl
Ontario, CA. 888-598-5588
Levelmatic
Miami, FL .800-762-7565
M-One Specialties
Salt Lake City, UT 800-525-9223
Palmer Fixture Company
Green Bay, WI. 800-558-8678
Plastic Fantastics/Buck Signs
Ashland, OR 800-482-1776
Pronto Products Company
Arcadia, CA 800-377-6680
Redi-Call Inc
Reno, NV .800-648-1849
San Jamar
Elkhorn, WI. 800-248-9826
Sanitor Manufacturing Co
Portage, MI 800-379-5314
SerVend International
Sellersburg, IN 800-367-4233
Superior Products Company
Saint Paul, MN 800-328-9800
Tomlinson Industries
Cleveland, OH 800-945-4589
Tops Manufacturing Co
Darien, CT. 203-655-9367
Traex
Dane, WI. .800-356-8006

Food

AC Dispensing Equipment
Lower Sackville, NS. 888-777-9990
Action Technology
Prussia, PA 217-935-8311
American Production Co Inc
Redwood City, CA 650-368-5334
Automatic Bar Controls Inc
Vacaville, CA 800-722-6738
Belshaw Adamatic Bakery Group
Auburn, WA 800-578-2547
Bijur Lubricating Corporation
Morrisville, NC 800-631-0168
Calmar
Richmond, VA. 804-444-1000
Carlisle Food Svc Products Inc
Oklahoma City, OK 800-654-8210
Carpigiani Corporation of America
Winston Salem, NC. 800-648-4389
Cornelius Wilshire Corporation
Schaumburg, IL. 847-397-4600
Creamery Plastics Products, Ltd
Chilliwack, BC 604-792-0232
Custom Diamond International
Laval, QC .800-363-5926
Design Technology Corporation
Billerica, MA 978-663-7000
Dispense Rite
Northbrook, IL 800-772-2877
Diversified Metal Products Inc
Northbrook, IL 800-772-2877
Drum-Mates Inc.
Lumberton, NJ 800-621-3786
Dunkin' Brands Inc.
Canton, MA 800-859-5339
Eurodispenser
Decatur, IL 217-864-4061
Federal Machine Corp
Clive, IA 800-247-2446

Gruenewald ManufacturingCompany
Danvers, MA. 800-229-9447
Hoshizaki America Inc
Peachtree City, GA 800-438-6087
K & L Intl
Ontario, CA. 888-598-5588
Karma
Watertown, WI 800-558-9565
Lakeside Manufacturing Inc
Milwaukee, WI 888-558-8565
LBP Manufacturing LLC
Cicero, IL .708-652-5600
Lincoln Foodservice
Cleveland, OH 800-374-3004
Mid-Southwest Marketing
Edmond, OK 405-341-3962
National Scoop & Equipment Company
Spring House, PA 215-646-2040
Neos
Elk River, MN. 888-441-6367
Nuova Distribution Centre
Ferndale, WA 360-366-2226
Opal Manufacturing Ltd
Toronto, ON 416-646-5232
Perfect Equipment Inc
Gurnee, IL. 800-356-6301
Pez Candy Inc
Orange, CT 203-795-0531
Plastic Fantastics/Buck Signs
Ashland, OR 800-482-1776
Precision Pours
Minneapolis, MN 800-549-4491
Prestige Metal Products Inc
Antioch, IL 847-395-0775
Prince Castle Inc
Carol Stream, IL 800-722-7853
Pro-Flo Products
Cedar Grove, NJ 800-325-1057
Ragtime
Ceres, CA .209-667-5525
Rieke Packaging Systems
Auburn, IN 260-925-3700
San Jamar
Elkhorn, WI. 800-248-9826
SaniServ
Mooresville, IN. 800-733-8073
Server Products Inc
Richfield, WI 800-558-8722
Silver King Refrigeration Inc
Minneapolis, MN 800-328-3329
Steril-Sil Company
Bowmansville, PA. 800-784-5537
Summit Machine Builders Corporation
Denver, CO 800-274-6741
Tablecraft Products Co Inc
Gurnee, IL. 800-323-8321
Texican Specialty Products
Houston, TX 800-869-5918
Thermos Company
Schaumburg, IL. 800-243-0745
Tomlinson Industries
Cleveland, OH 800-945-4589
Traex
Dane, WI. .800-356-8006
Viking Industries
New Smyma Beach, FL 888-605-5560
Wells Manufacturing Company
St. Louis, MO 888-356-5362
Wilch Manufacturing
Topeka, KS 785-267-2762

Glass

Lakeside Manufacturing Inc
Milwaukee, WI. 888-558-8565

Ice Cream & Frozen Yogurt

Carpigiani Corporation of America
Winston Salem, NC. 800-648-4389
Custom Diamond International
Laval, QC .800-363-5926
Delfield Co
Mt Pleasant, MI. 800-733-8821
Dispense Rite
Northbrook, IL 800-772-2877
Diversified Metal Products Inc
Northbrook, IL 800-772-2877
Dunkin' Brands Inc.
Canton, MA 800-859-5339
Federal Machine Corp
Clive, IA 800-247-2446

Flavor Burst
Danville, IN 800-264-3528
Frosty Factory Of America Inc
Ruston, LA 800-544-4071
Gruenewald ManufacturingCompany
Danvers, MA. 800-229-9447
H C Duke & Son Inc
East Moline, IL 309-755-4553
Oceanpower America
Leesburg, VA 305-721-7823
SaniServ
Mooresville, IN. 800-733-8073
Superior Products Company
Saint Paul, MN 800-328-9800
Wilch Manufacturing
Topeka, KS 785-267-2762

Plate & Tray

APW Wyott Food Service Equipment Company
Cheyenne, WY 800-527-2100
Atlas Metal Industries
Miami, FL. 800-762-7565
Custom Diamond International
Laval, QC .800-363-5926
Delfield Co
Mt Pleasant, MI. 800-733-8821
K & L Intl
Ontario, CA. 888-598-5588
Lakeside Manufacturing Inc
Milwaukee, WI. 888-558-8565

Soda Fountain, Syrup & Fruit Juice

Automatic Bar Controls Inc
Vacaville, CA 800-722-6738
Bevistar
Oswego, IL 877-238-7827
Carbonic Machines Inc
Minneapolis, MN 612-824-0745
Commercial Refrigeration Service, Inc.
Phoenix, AZ 623-869-8881
Control Beverage
Adelanto, CA 330-549-5376
Custom Diamond International
Laval, QC .800-363-5926
Easybar Corp
Tualatin, OR 888-294-7405
Eurodispenser
Decatur, IL 217-864-4061
Follett Corp
Easton, PA 800-523-9361
IMI Cornelius
Schaumburg, IL. 800-323-4789
K-Way Products
Mount Carroll, IL 800-622-9163
Karma
Watertown, WI 800-558-9565
Leland Limited Inc
South Plainfield, NJ 800-984-9793
Manitowoc Foodservice
Sellersburg, IN 800-367-4233
Sentry/Bevcon North America
Adelanto, CA 800-661-3003
Server Products Inc
Richfield, WI 800-558-8722

Displays

Food, Artificial

Accent Store Fixtures
Kenosha, WI 800-545-1144
Buffet Enhancements Intl
Point Clear, AL 251-990-6119
Cal-Mil Plastic Products Inc
Oceanside, CA 800-321-9069
Consolidated Display Co Inc
Oswego, IL 888-851-7669
Despro Manufacturing
Cedar Grove, NJ 800-292-9906
Display Studios Inc
Kansas City, KS 800-648-8479
Dufeck Manufacturing Co
Denmark, WI. 888-603-9663
Fax Foods
Vista, CA. .760-599-6030
GCJ Mattei Company
Louisville, KY 502-583-4774
Hiclay Studios
St Louis, MO. 314-533-8393
Madix
Goodwater, AL 256-839-6354

Marineland Commercial Aquariums
  Blacksburg, VA....................800-322-1266
Merchandising Frontiers Inc
  Winterset, IA......................800-421-2278
Rathe Productions
  New York, NY.....................212-242-9000
Schmidt Progressive
  Lebanon, OH......................800-272-3706
Trade Fixtures
  Little Rock, AR....................800-872-3490
Vomela/Harbor Graphics
  St Paul, MN.......................800-645-1012

Frozen Food

Arneg LLC
  Lexington, NC....................800-276-3487
Coldstream Products Corporation
  Crossfield, AB....................888-946-4097
Display Studios Inc
  Kansas City, KS..................800-648-8479
G A Systems Inc
  Huntington Beach, CA..........714-848-7529
GCJ Mattei Company
  Louisville, KY....................502-583-4774
Hercules Food Equipment
  Weston, ON......................416-742-9673
Hiclay Studios
  St Louis, MO.....................314-533-8393
Novelty Baskets
  Hurst, TX.........................817-268-5426
Oscartek
  Burlingame, CA..................855-885-2400
Oscartielle Equipment Company
  Burlingame, CA..................800-672-2784
Refcon
  Medford, NJ......................609-714-2330
Retail Decor
  Ironton, OH......................800-726-3402
Vomela/Harbor Graphics
  St Paul, MN.......................800-645-1012

Point of Purchase

ABC Letter Art
  Los Angeles, CA..................888-261-5367
Accent Store Fixtures
  Kenosha, WI......................800-545-1144
ALCO Designs
  Gardena, CA......................800-228-2346
Alger Creations
  Miami, FL.........................954-454-3272
Alphabet Signs
  Gap, PA...........................800-582-6366
American Led-Gible
  Columbus, OH...................614-851-1100
AMI
  Richmond, CA....................800-942-7466
Archer Wire Intl Corp
  Chicago, IL.......................708-563-1700
Arlington Display Industries
  Detroit, MI.......................313-837-1212
Art Wire Works Co
  Chicago, IL.......................708-458-3993
Art-Phyl Creations
  Hialeah, FL.......................800-327-8318
Atlas Packaging Inc
  Opa Locka, FL....................800-662-0630
B S C Signs
  Broomfield, CO..................866-223-0101
B&B Neon Sign Company
  Austin, TX........................800-791-6366
Baltimore Sign Company
  Arnold, MD.......................410-276-1500
Barrette Outdoor Living
  Cleveland, OH...................800-336-2383
Beemak-IDL Display
  La Mirada, CA....................800-421-4393
Better Bilt Products
  Addison, IL.......................800-544-4550
Bill Carr Signs
  Flint, MI..........................810-232-1569
Blue Ridge Signs
  Weatherford, TX.................800-659-5645
Boston Retail
  Medford, MA.....................800-225-1633
Boxes.com
  Livingston, NJ....................201-646-9050
Cannon Equipment Company
  Cannon Falls, MN................800-825-8501
Canton Sign Co
  Canton, OH.......................330-456-7151

Capitol Hardware, Inc.,
  Middlebury, IN...................800-327-6083
Ccw Products
  Arvada, CO.......................303-427-9663
Cellox Corp
  Reedsburg, WI...................608-524-2316
Chicago Show Inc
  Buffalo Grove, IL.................847-955-0200
Chroma Tone
  Saint Clair, PA...................800-878-1552
Clearr Corporation
  Minneapolis, MN.................800-548-3269
Collegeville Flag & Manufacturing Company
  Collegeville, PA..................800-523-5630
Comm-Pak
  Opelika, AL.......................334-749-6201
Commercial Corrugated Co Inc
  Baltimore, MD...................800-242-8861
Conn Container Corp
  North Haven, CT.................203-248-0241
Containair Packaging Corporation
  Paterson, NJ......................888-276-6500
Corfab
  Chicago, IL.......................708-458-8750
Corman & Assoc Inc
  Lexington, KY....................859-233-0544
Corr Pak Corp
  Mc Cook, IL......................708-442-7806
Courtesy Signs
  Amarillo, TX......................806-373-6609
Creative Enterprises
  Kendall Park, NJ.................732-422-0300
Cucamonga Sign Shop LLC
  Rancho Cucamonga, CA........909-945-5888
Curry Enterprises
  Atlanta, GA.......................800-241-7308
Curzon Promotional Graphics
  Omaha, NE.......................800-769-7446
Custom ID Systems
  Venice, FL........................800-242-8430
Custom Packaging Inc
  Richmond, VA....................804-232-3299
Daytech Limited
  Toronto, ON......................877-329-1907
Derse Inc
  Milwaukee, WI...................800-562-2300
Designers Plastics
  Clearwater, FL...................727-573-1643
Despro Manufacturing
  Cedar Grove, NJ.................800-292-9906
Diamond Packaging
  Rochester, NY....................800-333-4079
Dinosaur Plastics
  Houston, TX......................713-923-2278
Display Concepts
  Trenton, ME......................800-446-0033
Display Studios Inc
  Kansas City, KS..................800-648-8479
Drake Co
  Houston, TX......................800-299-5644
Dunn Woodworks
  Shrewsbury, PA..................877-835-8592
Eastern Container Corporation
  Mansfield, MA....................508-337-0400
Eastern Plastics
  Pawtucket, RI....................800-442-8585
Eaton Quade Plastics & Sign Co
  Oklahoma City, OK..............405-236-4475
EGW Bradbury Enterprises
  Bridgewater, ME.................800-332-6021
Einson Freeman
  Paramus, NJ......................201-221-2800
Embro Manufacturing Company
  East Canton, OH.................330-489-3500
Emco Industrial Plastics
  Cedar Grove, NJ.................800-292-9906
Enterprise Products
  Bell Gardens, CA.................562-928-1918
ERC Parts Inc
  Kennesaw, GA...................800-241-6880
ERS International
  Norwalk, CT......................800-377-4685
Esco Manufacturing Inc
  Watertown, SD...................800-843-3726
Everbrite LLC
  Greenfield, WI....................800-558-3888
Exhibitron Co
  Grants Pass, OR.................800-437-4571
Expo Displays
  Birmingham, AL..................800-367-3976
FFR Merchandising Inc
  Twinsburg, OH...................800-422-2547

Filet Menu
  Los Angeles, CA..................310-202-8000
First Bank of Highland P
  Northbrook, IL....................847-272-1300
Fitzpatrick Container Company
  North Wales, PA..................215-699-3515
Five-M Plastics Company
  Allentown, PA....................610-628-4291
Fleetwood International Paper
  Vernon, CA.......................323-588-7121
Florida Plastics Intl
  Evergreen Park, IL...............800-499-0400
FMI Display
  Elkins Park, PA...................215-663-1998
Foxfire Marketing Solutions
  Newark, DE.......................800-497-0512
France Personalized Signs
  Cleveland, OH...................216-241-2198
Freely Display
  Cleveland, OH...................216-721-6056
Fresno Neon Sign Co Inc
  Fresno, CA........................559-292-2944
Fuller Packaging Inc
  Central Falls, RI..................401-725-4300
Garvin Industries
  Franklin Park, IL..................847-451-6500
GCJ Mattei Company
  Louisville, KY....................502-583-4774
Gelberg Signs
  Washington, DC..................800-443-5237
GENESTA
  Rockwall, TX.....................972-771-1653
Great Northern Corp
  Chippewa Falls, WI..............800-472-1800
Greif Inc
  Delaware, OH....................800-476-1635
Hager Containers Inc
  Carrollton, TX....................972-416-7660
Handicap Sign Inc
  Grand Rapids, MI................800-690-4888
Hanley Sign Company
  Latham, NY.......................518-783-6183
Harmar
  Sarasota, FL......................800-833-0478
Harting Graphics
  Wilmington, DE..................800-848-1373
Hiclay Studios
  St Louis, MO.....................314-533-8393
HMG Worldwide
  Morton Grove, IL.................847-965-7100
HMG Worldwide In-Store Marketing
  New York, NY.....................212-736-2300
Hoarel Sign Co
  Amarillo, TX......................806-373-2175
Hunter Packaging Corporation
  South Elgin, IL....................800-428-4747
IBC Shell Packaging
  New Hyde Park, NY..............516-352-5138
Icee-USA Corporation
  Ontario, CA.......................800-426-4233
Illuma Display
  Brookfield, WI....................800-501-0128
Industrial Nameplate Inc
  Warminster, PA..................800-878-6263
Industrial Sign Company
  South El Monte, CA..............800-596-3720
Innovative Space Management
  Woodside, NY....................718-278-4300
International Patterns, Inc.
  Bay Shore, NY....................631-952-2000
J.C. Products Inc.
  Haddam, CT......................860-267-5516
Jay Packaging Group Inc
  Warwick, RI.......................401-244-1300
JBC Plastics
  St Louis, MO.....................877-834-5526
JEM Wire Products
  Middletown, CT..................860-347-0447
Jesse Jones Box Corporation
  Philadelphia, PA.................215-425-6600
Just Plastics Inc
  New York, NY.....................212-569-8500
K & I Creative Plastics & Wood
  Jacksonville, FL..................904-387-0438
Kehr-Buffalo Wire Frame Co Inc
  Buffalo, NY.......................800-875-4212
King Products
  Mississauga, ON.................866-454-6757
Koch Container
  Victor, NY.........................585-924-1600
Krimstock Enterprises
  Pennsauken, NJ..................856-665-3676

151

L.A. Darling Co., LLC
Paragould, AR..................800-682-5730
LBP Manufacturing LLC
Cicero, IL....................708-652-5600
Lil' Orbits
Minneapolis, MN...............800-228-8305
Lorac Union Tool Co
Providence, RI................888-680-3236
Loy Lange Box Co
St Louis, MO..................800-886-4712
LSI Industries Inc
Blue Ash, OH..................513-793-3200
M & M Display
Philadelphia, PA..............800-874-7171
Mack-Chicago Corporation
Chicago, IL...................800-992-6225
Madsen Wire Products Inc
Orland, IN....................260-829-6561
Mainstreet Menu Systems
Brookfield, WI................800-782-6222
Mall City Containers Inc
Kalamazoo, MI.................800-643-6721
Mannkraft Corporation
Newark, NJ....................973-589-7400
Mark Slade ManufacturingCompany
Seymour, WI...................920-833-6557
Market Sign Systems
Portland, ME..................800-421-1799
Mcintyre Metals Inc
Thomasville, NC...............800-334-0807
Mcroyal Industries Inc
Youngstown, OH................800-785-2556
MDI Worldwide
Farmington Hills, MI..........800-228-8925
Meilahn Manufacturing Co
Chicago, IL...................773-581-5204
Melrose Displays
Passaic, NJ...................973-471-7700
Merchandising Inventives
Waukegan, IL..................800-367-5653
Merric
Bridgeton, MO.................314-770-9944
Metaline Products Co Inc
South Amboy, NJ...............732-721-1373
Michigan Box Co
Detroit, MI...................888-642-4269
Micro Wire Products Inc
Brockton, MA..................508-584-0200
Mid Cities Paper Box Company
Downey, CA....................877-277-6272
Mid-West Wire Products
Ferndale, MI..................800-989-9881
Midwest Wire Specialties
Chicago, IL...................800-238-0228
Miller Group Multiplex
Dupo, IL......................800-325-3350
Mirro Products Company
High Point, NC................336-885-4166
Modar
Benton Harbor, MI.............800-253-6186
Modern Metalcraft
Midland, MI...................800-948-3182
Morrissey Displays & Models
Port Washington, NY...........516-883-6944
Moseley Realty LLC
Franklin, CA..................800-667-3539
Multi-Panel Display Corporation
Brooklyn, NY..................800-439-0879
MultiFab Plastics
Boston, MA....................888-293-5754
Nashville Display Manufacturing Company
Lebanon, TN...................888-743-2572
Neal Walters Poster Corporation
Bentonville, AR...............501-273-2489
Nelipak
Phoenix, AZ...................602-269-7648
North American Plastic Manufacturing Company
Bethel, CT....................800-934-7752
Northeast Box Co
Ashtabula, OH.................800-362-8100
Northern Metal Products
St Cloud, MN..................800-458-5549
Northwestern
Van Nuys, CA..................818-786-1581
Nu-Dell Manufacturing
Des Plaines, IL...............847-803-4500
Omega Industries
St Louis, MO..................314-961-1668
Omni Craft Inc
Hopkins, MN...................952-988-9944
OSF
Toronto, ON...................800-465-4000

P M Plastics
Pewaukee, WI..................262-691-1700
Pacific Store Designs Inc
Garden Grove, CA..............800-772-5661
Pentwater Wire Products Inc
Pentwater, MI.................877-869-6911
Peter Pepper Products Inc
Compton, CA...................310-639-0390
PFI Displays Inc
Rittman, OH...................800-925-9075
Philipp Lithographing Co
Grafton, WI...................800-657-0871
Pilgrim Plastics
Brockton, MA..................800-343-7810
Plastech
Monrovia, CA..................626-358-9306
Plasti-Clip Corp
Milford, NH...................800-882-2547
Plasti-Line
Knoxville, TN.................800-444-7446
Plastic Fantastics/Buck Signs
Ashland, OR...................800-482-1776
PMI Food Equipment Group
Troy, OH......................937-332-3000
Prengler Products
Sherman, TX...................903-892-9791
Presentations South
Orlando, FL...................407-657-2108
Prestige Plastics Corporation
Delta, BC.....................604-930-2931
Princeton Shelving
Cedar Rapids, IA..............319-369-0355
Pro-Ad-Co Inc
Portland, OR..................800-287-5885
Process Displays
New Berlin, WI................800-533-1764
Propak
Burlington, ON................800-263-4872
R R Donnelley
Chicago, IL...................800-742-4455
R T C
Rolling Meadows, IL...........847-640-2400
R Wireworks Inc
Elmira, NY....................800-550-4009
Racks
San Diego, CA.................619-661-0987
Rairdon Dodge Chrysler Jeep
Kirkland, WA..................425-821-1777
Rand-Whitney Group LLC
Worcester, MA.................508-791-2301
Randware Industries
Prospect Heights, IL..........847-299-8884
Rapid Displays Inc
Chicago, IL...................800-356-5775
Rathe Productions
New York, NY..................212-242-9000
Reading Plastic Fabricators
Reading, PA...................610-926-3245
Reeve Store Equipment Co
Pico Rivera, CA...............800-927-3383
Refcon
Medford, NJ...................609-714-2330
Reflex International
Norcross, GA..................800-642-7640
Render
Buffalo, NY...................888-446-1010
Retail Decor
Ironton, OH...................800-726-3402
Rex Art Manufacturing Corp.
Lindenhurst, NY...............631-884-4600
Rice Packaging Inc
Ellington, CT.................800-367-6725
Robelan Displays Inc
Hempstead, NY.................865-564-8600
Royal Display Corporation
Middletown, CT................800-569-1295
Royce Corp
Glendale, AZ..................602-256-0006
RPA Process Technologies
Marblehead, MA................800-631-9707
Rudd Container Corp
Chicago, IL...................773-847-7600
Russell-William
Odenton, MD...................410-551-3602
Rutler Screen Printing
Easton, PA....................610-829-2999
Sam Pievac Company
Santa Fe Springs, CA..........800-742-8585
San Juan Signs Inc
Farmington, NM................505-326-5511
Schiffenhaus Industries
Newark, NJ....................973-484-5000

SEMCO
Ocala, FL.....................800-749-6894
Smurfit Kappa
Carson, CA....................310-537-8190
Smurfit Stone
Norcross, GA..................314-656-5300
Smurfit-Stone Container Corp
Santa Fe Springs, CA..........714-523-3550
Smyth Co LLC
St Paul, MN...................800-473-3464
Source Packaging Inc
Mahwah, NJ....................888-665-9768
Southern Container Corporation
Deer Park, NY.................631-586-6006
Southern Imperial Inc
Rockford, IL..................800-747-4665
Special Events Supply Company
Hauppauge, NY.................
St Joseph Packaging Inc
St Joseph, MO.................800-383-3000
St. Elizabeth Street Display Corporation
Hackensack, NJ................201-883-0333
Standex International Corp.
Salem, NH.....................603-893-9701
Steel City Corporation
Youngstown, OH................800-321-0350
Stoffel Seals Corp
Tallapoosa, GA................800-422-8247
Stout Sign Company
Saint Louis, MO...............800-325-8530
Stricker & Co
La Plata, MD..................301-934-8346
Stylmark Inc
Minneapolis, MN...............800-328-2495
Sutton Designs
Ithaca, NY....................800-326-8119
Talbot Industries
Neosho, MO....................417-451-5900
THARCO
San Lorenzo, CA...............800-772-2332
Thomson-Leeds Company
New York, NY..................800-535-9361
TMCo Inc.ÿ
Houston, TX...................713-465-3255
Top Source Industries
Addison, IL...................800-362-9625
Traitech Industries
Vaughan, ON...................877-872-4835
Traub Container Corporation
Cleveland, OH.................216-475-5100
Travelon
Elk Grove Vlg, IL.............800-537-5544
Trinkle Sign & Display
Youngstown, OH................330-747-9712
Tru Form Plastics
Gardena, CA...................800-510-7999
Twenty/Twenty Graphics
Gaithersburg, MD..............240-243-0511
Universal Folding Box
East Orange, NJ...............973-482-4300
Uniweb Inc
Corona, CA....................800-486-4932
US Magnetix
Minneapolis, MN...............763-540-9497
Vacuform Inc.
Sebring, OH...................330-938-9674
Vega Mfg Ltd.
Port Coquitlam, BC............800-224-8342
Viking Packaging & Display
San Jose, CA..................408-998-1000
VIP Real Estate LTD
Chicago, IL...................773-376-5000
Visual Marketing Assoc
Santee, CA....................619-258-0393
Vomela/Harbor Graphics
St Paul, MN...................800-645-1012
VPC Gordon Sign
Denver, CO....................303-629-6121
Vulcan Industries
Moody, AL.....................888-444-4417
Wahlstrom Manufacturing
Fontana, CA...................909-822-4677
Warwick Products
Cleveland, OH.................800-535-4404
Wayne Industries
Clanton, AL...................800-225-3148
Webster Packaging Corporation
Loveland, OH..................513-683-5666
Welbilt Corporation
Stamford, CT..................203-325-8300
West Rock
Atlanta, GA...................770-448-2193

White Way Sign & Maintenance
Mt Prospect, IL 800-621-4122
Willamette Industries
Beaverton, OR. 503-641-1131
Willson Industries
Marmora, NJ. 800-894-4169
Wiremaid Products Div
Coral Springs, FL 800-770-4700
Woodstock Plastics Co Inc
Marengo, IL 815-568-5281
WS Packaging Group Inc
Neenah, WI. 888-532-3334

Doilies

American Pan Co
Urbana, OH. 800-652-2151
Brooklace
Oshkosh, WI 800-572-4552
Cannon Equipment Company
Cannon Falls, MN. 800-825-8501
Dorado Carton Company
Dorado, PR 787-796-1670
Frost ET Inc
Grand Rapids, MI 800-253-9382
Hoffmaster Group Inc
Oshkosh, WI 800-327-9774
IB Concepts
Elizabeth, NJ. 888-671-0800
Pinckney Molded Plastics
Howell, MI 800-854-2920
Pro Bake Inc
Twinsburg, OH 800-837-4427
Smith-Lee Company
Oshkosh, WI 800-327-9774
Stein-DSI
Northfield, MN 507-645-9546
Sunset Paper Products
Simi Valley, CA. 800-228-7882

Doors

Foodservice

Aleco Food Svc Div
Muscle Shoals, AL 800-633-3120
American Metal Door Company
Richmond, IN 800-428-2737
Andgar Corp
Ferndale, WA 360-366-9900
Beta Screen Corp
Carlstadt, NJ 800-272-7336
Eliason Corp
Portage, MI 800-828-3655
FIB-R-DOR
Cincinnati, OH 800-342-7367
Hoffman Co
Corpus Christi, TX 361-882-9281
Hormann Flexan Llc
Leetsdale, PA 800-365-3667
Kedco Wine Storage Systems
Farmingdale, NY 800-654-9988
Marlite
Dover, OH 800-377-1221
Plas-Ties Co
Tustin, CA 800-854-0137
Products A Curtron Div
Pittsburgh, PA 800-888-9750
Rasco Industries
Hamel, MN 800-537-3802
Stanley Access Technologies
Farmington, CT. 800-722-2377
Super Seal ManufacturingLimited
Woodbridge, ON 800-337-3239
Trimline Corp
Elkhart Lake, WI. 800-555-5895
Woodfold-Marco Manufacturing
Forest Grove, OR 503-357-7181

Drawers

Cash, Money

APG Cash Drawer
Fridley, MN 763-571-5000
E F Bavis & Assoc Inc
Maineville, OH 513-677-0500
Leggett & Platt Inc
Carthage, MO 417-358-8131
Loyal Manufacturing
Indianapolis, IN 317-359-3185

Superior Products Company
Saint Paul, MN 800-328-9800

Envelopes

Appleson Press
Syosset, NY. 800-888-2775
Archer Daniels Midland Company
Chicago, IL 312-634-8100
Artistic Packaging Concepts
Massapequa Pk, NY 516-797-4020
Barkley Filing Supplies
Hattiesburg, MS 800-647-3070
BAW Plastics Inc
Clairton, PA. 800-783-2229
Cenveo Inc
Chicago, IL 800-388-8406
Check Savers Inc
Garland, TX 800-276-8315
Coleman Resources
Greensboro, NC 336-852-4006
Commercial Envelope Manufacturing Company
Hauppauge, NY
Continental Envelope
Geneva, IL 800-621-8155
Dagher Printing
Jacksonville, FL 904-998-0921
Double Envelope Corp
Roanoke, VA. 540-362-3311
Eastern Envelope
Flanders, NJ 973-584-3311
Eaton Manufacturing Co
Houston, TX 800-328-6610
Enterprise Box Company
Montclair, NJ 973-509-2200
Enterprise Envelope Inc
Grand Rapids, MI 800-422-4255
Excelsior Transparent Bag Manufacturing
Yonkers, NY 914-968-1300
Flexo Transparent Inc
Buffalo, NY. 877-993-5396
Forbes Products Corp
Rush, NY. 800-316-5235
Grand Valley Labels
Grand Rapids, MI
Heinrich Envelope Corp
Minneapolis, MN 800-346-7957
Innova Envelopes
La Salle, QC 514-595-0555
International Envelope Company
Exton, PA 610-363-0900
Mac Papers Inc
Jacksonville, FL 800-334-7026
Miami Systems Corporation
Blue Ash, OH 800-543-4540
Murray Envelope Corporation
Hattiesburg, MS 601-583-8292
North American Packaging Corp
New York, NY. 800-499-3521
Oles De Puerto Rico Inc
Bayamon, PR 787-786-1700
Poser Envelope
Oakland, CA. 800-208-6100
Steingart Associates Inc
South Fallsburg, NY 845-434-4321
Stone Container
Chicago, IL 312-346-6600
Volk Corp
Farmington Hills, MI 800-521-6799
Westrick Paper Co
Jacksonville, FL 904-737-2122
Worcester Envelope Co
Auburn, MA 508-832-5397

Fixtures

Store

A.T. Foote Woodworking Company
Hartford, CT 860-249-6821
AAA Mill
Austin, TX. 512-385-2215
Acme Display Fixture Company
Los Angeles, CA. 800-959-5657
Acme Fixture Company
Los Angeles, CA. 888-379-9566
Acraloc Corporation
Oak Ridge, TN 865-483-1368
ALCO Designs
Gardena, CA 800-228-2346
Amscor Inc
West Babylon, NY 800-825-9800

Amtekco
Columbus, OH 800-336-4677
Andrew's Fixture Co
Tacoma, WA 253-627-8388
Architectural Sheet Metals LLC
Cleveland, OH 216-361-9952
Arizona Store Equipment
Phoenix, AZ 800-624-8395
Art-Phyl Creations
Hialeah, FL 800-327-8318
B J Wood Products Inc
Ladysmith, WI 715-532-6626
Bailly Showcase & Fixture Company
Las Vegas, NV 702-947-6885
Baker Cabinet Co
Costa Mesa, CA 714-540-5515
Blue Ridge Signs
Weatherford, TX 800-659-5645
Boston Retail
Medford, MA 800-225-1633
C&H Store Equipment Company
Los Angeles, CA. 800-648-4979
Cannon Equipment Company
Cannon Falls, MN 800-825-8501
Capitol Hardware, Inc.,
Middlebury, IN 800-327-6083
Chicago Show Inc
Buffalo Grove, IL 847-955-0200
Clearr Corporation
Minneapolis, MN 800-548-3269
Corman & Assoc Inc
Lexington, KY 859-233-0544
Crown Metal Manufacturing Company
Elmhurst, IL 630-279-9800
Crown Metal Mfg Co
Rancho Cucamonga, CA 909-291-8585
CSC Worldwide
Columbus, OH 800-848-3573
Custom Business Interiors
Henderson, NV 702-564-6661
Custom Craft Laminates
Tampa, FL 800-486-4367
Display Craft Mfg Co
Halethorpe, MD 410-242-0400
Display Creations
Brooklyn, NY 718-257-2300
Dunn Woodworks
Shrewsbury, PA. 877-835-8592
East Bay Fixture Co
Emeryville, CA 800-995-4521
EGW Bradbury Enterprises
Bridgewater, ME. 800-332-6021
Emco Industrial Plastics
Cedar Grove, NJ 800-292-9906
Enterprise Products
Bell Gardens, CA 562-928-1918
Exhibits & More Shopworks
Liverpool, NY 888-326-9100
Fab-X/Metals
Washington, NC 800-677-3229
FFR Merchandising Inc
Twinsburg, OH 800-422-2547
Field Manufacturing Corporation
Torrance, CA. 310-781-9292
Fine Woods Manufacturing
Phoenix, AZ 800-279-2871
Freely Display
Cleveland, OH 216-721-6056
Garvey Products
West Chester, OH 800-543-1908
GDM Concepts
Paramount, CA 562-633-0195
General Cage
Elwood, IN 800-428-6403
Handy Manufacturing Co Inc
Newark, NJ 800-631-4280
Heartwood
Montclair, CA 909-626-8104
Henry Hanger & Fixture Corporation of America
New York City, NY. 877-279-0852
Hoffman Co
Corpus Christi, TX 361-882-9281
Huck Store Fixture Company
Quincy, IL 800-680-4823
Hurlingham Company
San Pedro, CA. 310-538-0236
IGS Store Fixtures
Peabody, MA. 978-532-0010
Inland Showcase & Fixture Company
Fresno, CA 559-237-4158
Interior Systems Inc
Milwaukee, WI 800-837-8373

Interstate Showcase & Fixture Company
West Orange, NJ 973-483-5555
Ironwood Displays
Niles, MI 231-683-8500
J.K. Harman, Inc.
Hamden, CT 800-248-1627
Kedco Wine Storage Systems
Farmingdale, NY 800-654-9988
Kehr-Buffalo Wire Frame Co Inc
Buffalo, NY 800-875-4212
Kent Corp
Birmingham, AL 800-252-5368
Killion Industries Inc
Vista, CA 800-421-5352
L A Cabinet & Finishing Co
Los Angeles, CA 323-233-7245
L&S Products
Coldwater, MI .517-279-9526
L.A. Darling Co., LLC
Paragould, AR .800-682-5730
Lauritzen Makin Inc
Fort Worth, TX 817-921-0218
Leggett & Platt Inc
Carthage, MO .417-358-8131
Lozier Corp
Omaha, NE 800-228-9882
Madix
Goodwater, AL 256-839-6354
Madix Inc
Terrell, TX 800-776-2349
Mark Slade ManufacturingCompany
Seymour, WI 920-833-6557
Melrose Displays
Passaic, NJ 973-471-7700
Merchandising Systems Manufacturing
Union City, CA 800-523-1468
Metal Master Sales Corp
Glendale Heights, IL 800-488-8729
Micro Wire Products Inc
Brockton, MA .508-584-0200
Modar
Benton Harbor, MI 800-253-6186
Modern Store Fixtures Company
Dallas, TX 800-634-7777
New Court
Texarkana, TX 903-838-0521
Northern Metal Products
St Cloud, MN .800-458-5549
Northwestern
Van Nuys, CA .818-786-1581
Omaha Fixture Mfg
Omaha, NE 800-637-2257
Omicron Steel Products Company
Jamaica, NY 718-805-3400
Omni Craft Inc
Hopkins, MN .952-988-9944
Oscartek
Burlingame, CA 855-885-2400
OSF
Toronto, ON .800-465-4000
Pacific Store Designs Inc
Garden Grove, CA 800-772-5661
Paramount Manufacturing Company
Wilmington, MA 978-657-4300
Peacock Crate Factory
Jacksonville, TX 800-657-2200
Pentwater Wire Products Inc
Pentwater, MI 877-869-6911
Peter Pepper Products Inc
Compton, CA .310-639-0390
PFI Displays Inc
Rittman, OH .800-925-9075
Pierce Laminated Products Inc
Rockford, IL 815-968-9651
Premier Brass
Atlanta, GA 800-251-5800
Primlite Manufacturing Corporation
Freeport, NY .800-327-7583
Quality Cabinet & Fixture Co
San Diego, CA 619-266-1011
R C Smith Co
Burnsville, MN 800-747-7648
R Wireworks Inc
Elmira, NY 800-550-4009
Rairdon Dodge Chrysler Jeep
Kirkland, WA .425-821-1777
Reeve Store Equipment Co
Pico Rivera, CA 800-927-3383
Reeves Enterprises
La Verne, CA .909-392-9999
Regal Plastic Supply Co
Kansas City, MO 800-444-6390

Russell-William
Odenton, MD .410-551-3602
RW Products
Edgewood, NY 800-345-1022
S & L Store Fixture
Doral, FL 800-205-4536
Sam Pievac Company
Santa Fe Springs, CA 800-742-8585
SEMCO
Ocala, FL 800-749-6894
Shelley Cabinet Company
Shelley, ID. 208-357-3700
Sinicrope & Sons Inc
Alhambra, CA .323-283-5131
Sitka Store Fixtures
Kansas City, MO 800-821-7558
Southern Store Fixtures Inc
Bessemer, AL .800-552-6283
Spartan Showcase
Union, MO 800-325-0775
Specialty Wood Products
Clanton, AL 800-322-5343
Stanly Fixtures Co Inc
Norwood, NC .704-474-3184
Streater Inc
Albert Lea, MN 800-527-4197
Tables Cubed
Chesterfield, MO 800-878-3001
Talbert Display
Fort Worth, TX 817-429-4504
Thomson-Leeds Company
New York, NY 800-535-9361
Thorco Industries LLC
Lamar, MO 800-445-3375
Tulsa Plastics Co
Tulsa, OK 888-273-5303
Unarco Industries LLC
Wagoner, OK. .800-654-4100
Uniweb Inc
Corona, CA 800-486-4932
Valley Fixtures
Sparks, NV 775-331-1050
Van Dereems Mfg Co
Hawthorne, NJ 973-427-2355
View-Rite Manufacturing
Daly City, CA .415-468-3856
Vulcan Industries
Moody, AL 888-444-4417
Warwick Products
Cleveland, OH 800-535-4404
William Hecht
Philadelphia, PA 215-925-6223

Holders

Bag

Eastern Plastics
Pawtucket, RI .800-442-8585
Grayline Housewares Inc
Columbus, OH 800-222-7388
Seattle Plastics
Seattle, WA 800-441-0679
Sipco Products
Peoria Heights, IL 309-682-5400
Thorco Industries LLC
Lamar, MO 800-445-3375
UniTrak Corporation
Port Hope, ON 866-883-5749

Price Card, Ticket, Etc.

Amco Metals Indl
City Of Industry, CA. 626-855-2550
BAW Plastics Inc
Clairton, PA. 800-783-2229
Beemak-IDL Display
La Mirada, CA .800-421-4393
C R Mfg
Waverly, NE 877-789-5844
Cannon Equipment Company
Cannon Falls, MN. 800-825-8501
Clamp Swing Pricing Co Inc
Oakland, CA 800-227-7615
Cleveland Menu Printing
Cleveland, OH 800-356-6368
Creative Essentials
Ronkonkoma, NY 800-355-5891
Crown Metal Mfg Co
Rancho Cucamonga, CA 909-291-8585
Fast Industries
Fort Lauderdale, FL 800-775-5345

FFR Merchandising Inc
Twinsburg, OH 800-422-2547
Forbes Industries
Ontario, CA 909-923-4549
Gastro-Gnomes
West Hartford, CT 800-747-4666
Illuma Display
Brookfield, WI 800-501-0128
JBC Plastics
St Louis, MO. .877-834-5526
Jordan Specialty Company
Brooklyn, NY .877-567-3265
Just Plastics Inc
New York, NY 212-569-8500
Lorac Union Tool Co
Providence, RI 888-680-3236
Lynn Sign Inc
Andover, MA .800-225-5764
Market Sign Systems
Portland, ME. .800-421-1799
Menu Men
Palm Harbor, FL 727-934-7191
MultiFab Plastics
Boston, MA. 888-293-5754
National Plastics Co
Santa Fe Springs, CA 800-221-9149
Plasti-Clip Corp
Milford, NH 800-882-2547
Ram Industries
Erwin, TN 800-523-3883
Redi-Call Inc
Reno, NV 800-648-1849
Reeve Store Equipment Co
Pico Rivera, CA 800-927-3383
RPA Process Technologies
Marblehead, MA. 800-631-9707
Spirit Foodservice, Inc.
Andover, MA .800-343-0996
Sutton Designs
Ithaca, NY 800-326-8119
US Magnetix
Minneapolis, MN 763-540-9497

Holding & Warming Equipment

Acra Electric Corporation
Tulsa, OK 800-223-4328
Aladdin Temp-Rite, LLC
Hendersonville, TN. 800-888-8018
Alliance Products LLC
Murfreesboro, TN. 800-522-3973
Alto-Shaam
Menomonee Falls, WI. 800-329-8744
American Creative Solutions
Matthews, NC 877-925-4406
American Metalcraft Inc
Franklin Park, IL 708-345-1177
American Production Co Inc
Redwood City, CA 650-368-5334
Antrim Manufacturing Inc
Brookfield, WI 262-781-6860
Apex Fountain Sales Inc
Philadelphia, PA 800-523-4586
APW Wyott Food Service Equipment Company
Cheyenne, WY 800-527-2100
ARC Specialties
Valencia, CA. .661-775-8500
Arctica Showcase Company
Cayuga, ON. .800-839-5536
Aroma Manufacturing Company
San Diego, CA 800-276-6286
Ballantyne Food Service Equipment
Omaha, NE 800-424-1215
BEVCO
Canada, BC 800-663-0090
Bevles Company
Dallas, TX 800-441-1601
BG Industries
Lemont, IL 800-800-5761
BKI Worldwide
Simpsonville, SC 800-927-6887
Bon Chef
Lafayette, NJ .800-331-0177
Brass Smith
Denver, CO 800-662-9595
Brewmatic Company
Torrance, CA. 800-421-6860
Broaster Co LLC
Beloit, WI 800-365-8278
Canadian Display Systems
Concord, ON. 800-895-5862
Candle Lamp Company
Corona, CA 877-526-7748

Carlisle Food Svc Products Inc
Oklahoma City, OK 800-654-8210
Carter-Hoffmann LLC
Mundelein, IL 800-323-9793
Caselites
Hialeah, FL 305-819-7766
Convay Systems
Minnetonka, MN 800-334-1099
Craig Manufacturing
Irvington, NJ 800-631-7936
Creative Mobile Systems Inc
Manchester, CT 800-646-8364
Cres Cor
Mentor, OH 877-273-7267
Crispy Lite
St. Louis, MO 888-356-5362
Custom Diamond Intl.
Laval, QC .800-326-5926
D'Lights
Glendale, CA 818-956-5656
Delfield Co
Mt Pleasant, MI. 800-733-8821
Deluxe Equipment Company
Bradenton, FL 800-367-8931
Duke Manufacturing Co
St Louis, MO. 800-735-3853
Dynynstyl
Delray Beach, FL 800-774-7895
Eagle Foodservice   Equipment
Clayton, DE 800-441-8440
Eagle Group
Clayton, DE 800-441-8440
EPCO
Murfreesboro, TN 800-251-3398
Esquire Mechanical Corp.
Armonk, NY 800-847-4206
Faubion Central States Tank Company
Shawnee Mission, KS 800-450-8265
Fixtur World
Cookeville, TN 800-634-9887
FleetwoodGoldcoWyard
Romeoville, IL 630-759-6800
Food Warming Equipment Co
Crystal Lake, IL 800-222-4393
Fred D Pfening Co
Columbus, OH 614-294-5361
Galley
Jupiter, FL .800-537-2772
Garland Commercial Ranges
Mississauga, ON 905-624-0260
Gold Medal Products Co
Cincinnati, OH 800-543-0862
Habco
Concord, CA 925-682-6203
Hatco Corp
Milwaukee, WI 800-558-0607
Heat-It Manufacturing
San Antonio, TX 800-323-9336
Henny Penny, Inc.
Eaton, OH .800-417-8417
Hickory Industries
North Bergen, NJ 800-732-9153
Hot Food Boxes
Mooresville, IN. 800-733-8073
InfraTech Corporation
Azusa, CA .800-955-2476
Intedge Manufacturing
Woodruff, SC 866-969-9605
J.V. Reed & Company
Louisville, KY 877-258-7333
Karma
Watertown, WI 800-558-9565
Keating of Chicago Inc
Mc Cook, IL 800-532-8464
Kelmin Products
Plymouth, FL 407-886-6079
King Arthur
Statesville, NC 800-257-7244
LA Rosa Refrigeration & Equip
Detroit, MI 800-527-6723
Lakeside Manufacturing Inc
Milwaukee, WI 888-558-8565
Lambertson Industries Inc
Sparks, NV 800-548-3324
Lazy Man Inc
Belvidere, NJ 800-475-1950
Leedal Inc
Northbrook, IL 847-498-0111
Lewco Inc
Sandusky, OH 419-625-4014
Lincoln Foodservice
Cleveland, OH 800-374-3004

Low Temp Industries Inc
Jonesboro, GA 678-674-1317
M&S Manufacturing
Arnold, MO. 636-464-2739
Marshall Air Systems Inc
Charlotte, NC 800-722-3474
Mastex Industries
Petersburg, VA 804-732-8300
Merco/Savory
Mt. Pleasant, MI 800-733-8821
Metal Masters Northwest
Lynnwood, WA 425-775-4481
Metro Corporation
Wilkes Barre, PA 800-992-1776
Mies Products
West Bend, WI 800-480-6437
Moffat
San Antonio, TX 866-589-0664
Monroe Extinguisher Co Inc
Rochester, NY 585-235-3310
Mosshaim Innovations
Jacksonville, FL 888-995-7775
Mr. Bar-B-Q
Winston-Salem, NC 800-333-2124
Nutty Bavarian
Sanford, FL 800-382-4788
Parvin Manufacturing Company
Los Angeles, CA 800-648-0770
Piper Products Inc
Wausau, WI 800-544-3057
Plastocon
Oconomowoc, WI 800-966-0103
Prince Castle Inc
Carol Stream, IL 800-722-7853
Products A Curtron Div
Pittsburgh, PA 800-888-9750
Proluxe
Paramount, CA 800-594-5528
Randell Manufacturing   Unified Brands
Weidman, MI 888-994-7636
Randware Industries
Prospect Heights, IL 847-299-8884
Reliable Food Service Equipment
Concord, ON 416-738-6840
Remco Industries International
Fort Lauderdale, FL 800-987-3626
Rexcraft Fine Chafers
Long Island City, NY 888-739-2723
Royalton Foodservice Equip Co
North Royalton, OH 800-662-8765
Server Products Inc
Richfield, WI 800-558-8722
Sheffield Platers Inc
San Diego, CA 800-227-9242
Sico Inc
Minneapolis, MN 800-328-6138
Sould Manufacturing
Winnipeg, NB. 204-339-3499
Southern Pride Distributing
Alamo, TN 800-851-8180
Super-Chef Manufacturing Company
Houston, TX 800-231-3478
Superior Products Company
Saint Paul, MN 800-328-9800
Tempco Electric Heater Corporation
Wood Dale, IL. 888-268-6396
Texican Specialty Products
Houston, TX 800-869-5918
Thermal Bags By Ingrid Inc
Gilberts, IL 800-622-5560
Tomlinson Industries
Cleveland, OH 800-945-4589
Tranter INC
Wichita Falls, TX 940-723-7125
Ultrafryer Systems Inc
San Antonio, TX 800-545-9189
Update International
Vernon, CA 800-747-7124
Valad Electric Heating Corporation
Tarrytown, NY 914-631-4927
Vimco
King Of Prussia, PA 610-768-0500
Vollrath Co LLC
Sheboygan, WI 800-624-2051
Vulcan Food Equipment Group
Baltimore, MD 800-814-2028
Welbilt Corporation
Stamford, CT 203-325-8300
Wells Manufacturing Company
St. Louis, MO 888-356-5362
West Metals
London, ON 800-300-6667

Wilder Manufacturing Company
Port Jervis, NY 800-832-1319
Will & Baumer
Syracuse, NY 315-451-1000
Williamsburg Metal Spinning
Brooklyn, NY 888-535-5402
Win-Holt Equipment Group
Syosset, NY. 800-444-3595
Wisco Industries Assembly
Oregon, WI 800-999-4726
Wittco Foodservice Equipment
Milwaukee, WI 800-367-8413
Wittco Foodservice Equipment
Milwaukee, WI 800-821-3912
Zoia Banquetier Co
Cleveland, OH 216-631-6414

Hooks

Display, Store

Cannon Equipment Company
Cannon Falls, MN. 800-825-8501
Clamp Swing Pricing Co Inc
Oakland, CA 800-227-7615
Etube & Wire
Shrewsbury, PA. 800-618-4720
FFR Merchandising Inc
Twinsburg, OH 800-422-2547
Mark Slade ManufacturingCompany
Seymour, WI 920-833-6557
Merchandising Inventives
Waukegan, IL 800-367-5653
SEMCO
Ocala, FL. .800-749-6894
Southern Imperial Inc
Rockford, IL 800-747-4665

Interiors

Hotel, Bar, Restaurant

American Creative Solutions
Matthews, NC. 877-925-4406
Commercial Furniture Group Inc
Newport, TN 800-873-3252
Original Wood Seating
Atlanta, GA 678-966-0406

Kiosks

All A Cart Custom Mfg
Columbus, OH 800-695-2278
Burgess Enterprises, Inc
Renton, WA. 800-927-3286
Carts Of Colorado Inc
Greenwood Vlg, CO 800-227-8634
Corsair Display Systems
Canandaigua, NY 800-347-5245
Daytech Limited
Toronto, ON 877-329-1907
Lakeside Manufacturing Inc
Milwaukee, WI 888-558-8565
Landmark Kitchen Design
Chandler, AZ. 866-621-3192
Mcroyal Industries Inc
Youngstown, OH. 800-785-2556
Merchandising Frontiers Inc
Winterset, IA. 800-421-2278
Michaelo Espresso
Seattle, WA 800-545-2883
Moseley Realty LLC
Franklin, MA 800-667-3539
Reflex International
Norcross, GA 800-642-7640
Southern Express
Saint Louis, MO 800-444-9157
Steamway Corporation
Scottsburg, IN. 800-259-8171
The Carriage Works
Klamath Falls, OR 541-882-0700

Linen Goods

A1 Tablecloth Co
South Hackensack, NJ 800-727-8987
Artex International
Highland, IL 618-654-2113
ATD-American Co
Wyncote, PA 800-523-2300
Babco International, Inc
Tucson, AZ 520-628-7596

Best Brands Home Products
New York, NY 212-684-7456
Best Buy Uniforms
Homestead, PA 800-345-1924
Bragard Professional Uniforms
New York, NY 800-488-2433
Champion America Inc
Branford, CT..................800-521-7000
Cotton Goods Mfg Co
Chicago, IL 773-265-0088
Drapes 4 Show
Sylmar, CA 800-525-7469
Fashion Industries
Griffin, GA 770-412-9214
Gary Manufacturing Company
National City, CA 800-775-0804
Gourmet Table Skirts
Houston, TX 800-527-0440
Happy Chef Inc
Butler, NJ 800-347-0288
Hilden Halifax
South Boston, VA 800-431-2514
Jack the Ripper Table Skirting
Stafford, TX 800-331-7831
Jones-Zylon Co
West Lafayette, OH 800-848-8160
K Katen & Company
Rahway, NJ..................732-381-0220
Marko Inc
Spartanburg, SC 866-466-2756
Party Linens
Chicago, IL 800-281-0003
Philmont Manufacturing Co.
Englewood, NJ 888-379-6483
Premier Skirting Products
Lawrence, NY..................800-544-2516
Prestige Skirting & Tablecloths
Orangeburg, NY 800-635-3313
Radius Display Products
Dallas, TX 888-322-7429
Stevens Linen Association
Dudley, MA..................800-772-9269
Sultan Linen Inc
New York, NY 212-689-8900
Tara Linens
Sanford, NC 800-476-8272

Magnetic Chips

Hopp Co Inc
New Hyde Park, NY..................800-889-8425

Magnetic Label

Backers

Hopp Co Inc
New Hyde Park, NY..................800-889-8425

Magnetic Pocket

Sign & Card Holders

Hopp Co Inc
New Hyde Park, NY..................800-889-8425

Markers

Price & Sign

Atlas Rubber Stamp & Printing
York, PA 717-751-0459
Century Rubber Stamp Company
New York, NY..................212-962-6165
Courtesy Signs
Amarillo, TX..................806-373-6609
Display Concepts
Trenton, ME 800-446-0033
Ed Smith's Stencil Works LTD
New Orleans, LA 504-525-2128
FFR Merchandising Inc
Twinsburg, OH 800-422-2547
Garvey Products
Cincinnati, OH 513-771-8710
Grueny's Rubber Stamps
Little Rock, AR..................501-376-0393
Lamb Sign
Manassas, VA 703-791-7960
Muskogee Rubber Stamp & Seal Company
Fort Gibson, OK 918-478-3046
Neal Walters Poster Corporation
Bentonville, AR 501-273-2489

Plastimatic Arts Corporation
Mishawaka, IN 800-442-3593
Quick Stamp & Sign Mfg
Lafayette, LA 337-232-2171
US Magnetix
Minneapolis, MN 763-540-9497
Wildes Printing Co Inc
White Plains, MD 301-870-4141

Menu Boards

Qyk Syn Industries
Miami, FL..................800-354-5640

Menus

A Allred Marketing
Birmingham, AL..................205-251-3700
Ad Art Litho.
Cleveland, OH 800-875-6368
Beaverite Corporation
Croghan, NY 800-424-6337
Brass Smith
Denver, CO 800-662-9595
Charles Mayer Studios
Akron, OH..................330-535-6121
City Grafx
Eugene, OR..................800-258-2489
Cleveland Menu Printing
Cleveland, OH 800-356-6368
Corsair Display Systems
Canandalgua, NY 800-347-5245
Creative Essentials
Ronkonkoma, NY 800-355-5891
Creative Impressions
Buena Park, CA 800-524-5278
Creative Printing Co
Burr Ridge, IL..................630-734-3244
Custom Color Corp
Lenexa, KS 888-605-4050
David Dobbs Enterprise Inc.
St Augustine, FL..................800-889-6368
Dilley Manufacturing Co
Des Moines, IA..................800-247-5087
Encore Image Inc
Ontario, CA 800-791-1187
Ennis Inc.
Midlothian, TX..................800-972-1069
Everbrite LLC
Greenfield, WI 800-558-3888
Filet Menu
Los Angeles, CA..................310-202-8000
Florida Plastics Intl
Evergreen Park, IL..................800-499-0400
Forbes Industries
Ontario, CA..................909-923-4549
Frost Manufacturing Corp
Worcester, MA 800-462-0216
Futura 2000 Corporation
Miami, FL..................305-256-5877
GA Design Menu Company
Wixom, MI 313-561-2530
Gastro-Gnomes
West Hartford, CT..................800-747-4666
Have Our Plastic Inc
Mississauga, ON 800-263-5995
Impulse Signs
Toronto, ON 866-636-8273
International Patterns, Inc.
Bay Shore, NY 631-952-2000
Jordan Specialty Company
Brooklyn, NY 877-567-3265
Kenyon Press
Signal Hill, CA..................800-752-9395
Landmark Kitchen Design
Chandler, AZ..................866-621-3192
Legible Signs
Loves Park, IL..................800-435-4177
Lynn Sign Inc
Andover, MA 800-225-5764
Maier Sign Systems
Saddle Brook, NJ 201-845-7555
Mainstreet Menu Systems
Brookfield, WI 800-782-6222
Mastercraft
Appleton, WI 800-242-6602
MDI Worldwide
Farmington Hills, MI 800-228-8925
Menu Graphics
Olmsted Falls, OH 216-696-1460
Menu Men
Palm Harbor, FL 727-934-7191

Menu Promotions
Bronx, NY..................718-324-3800
Milwaukee Sign Company
Grafton, WI 262-375-5740
National Menuboard
Auburn, WA 800-800-5237
National Plastics Co
Santa Fe Springs, CA 800-221-9149
National Sign Systems
Hilliard, OH 800-544-6726
Placemat Printers
Fogelsville, PA 800-628-7746
Polar Hospitality Products
Philadelphia, PA 800-831-7823
Posterloid Corporation
Long Island City, NY 800-651-5000
Ram Industries
Erwin, TN 800-523-3883
RAO Contract Sales Inc
Paterson, NJ 888-324-0020
Redi-Print
West Babylon, NY 631-491-6373
Retail Decor
Ironton, OH 800-726-3402
Roxanne Signs Inc
Gaithersburg, MD 301-428-4911
Samsill Corp
Fort Worth, TX 800-255-1100
School Marketing Partners
San Juan Cpstrno, CA 800-565-7778
Seattle Menu Specialists
Kent, WA..................800-622-2826
Signets/Menu-Quik
Mentor, OH 800-775-6368
Spokane House of Hose Inc
Spokane Valley, WA 800-541-6351
Sutton Designs
Ithaca, NY..................800-326-8119
Tablet & Ticket Co
West Chicago, IL 800-438-4959
Unique Manufacturing
Visalia, CA 888-737-1007
Vacuform Inc.
Sebring, OH 330-938-9674
VC Menus
Eastland, TX 800-826-3687
Visual Marketing Assoc
Santee, CA 619-258-0393
Visual Planning Corp
Champlain, NY 800-361-1192
VMC Signs
Victoria, TX 361-575-0548
Vynatex
Port Washington, NY 516-944-6130
Wayne Industries
Clanton, AL 800-225-3148
Western Textile & Manufacturing Inc.
Sausalito, CA 800-734-8683
Wind River Environmental
Gloucester, MA..................800-332-6025
Your Place Menu Systems
Carson City, NV 800-321-8105

Napery

A1 Tablecloth Co
South Hackensack, NJ 800-727-8987
Adcapitol
Monroe, NC..................800-868-7111
Americo
West Memphis, AR..................800-626-2350
Artex International
Highland, IL 618-654-2113
Best Brands Home Products
New York, NY 212-684-7456
Best Buy Uniforms
Homestead, PA 800-345-1924
Carnegie Textile Co
Cleveland, OH 800-633-4136
Champion America Inc
Branford, CT..................800-521-7000
Connecticut Laminating Co Inc
New Haven, CT..................800-753-9119
Cotton Goods Mfg Co
Chicago, IL 773-265-0088
Drapes 4 Show
Sylmar, CA 800-525-7469
Erving Industries
Erving, MA 413-422-2700
Fashion Industries
Griffin, GA 770-412-9214
Filet Menu
Los Angeles, CA..................310-202-8000

Gary Manufacturing Company
National City, CA 800-775-0804
Gourmet Table Skirts
Houston, TX 800-527-0440
Happy Chef Inc
Butler, NJ 800-347-0288
Hilden Halifax
South Boston, VA 800-431-2514
Jack the Ripper Table Skirting
Stafford, TX 800-331-7831
Jones-Zylon Co
West Lafayette, OH 800-848-8160
K Katen & Company
Rahway, NJ 732-381-0220
K-C Products Company
Van Nuys, CA 818-267-1600
Marcal Paper Mills
Elmwood Park, NJ 800-631-8451
Marko Inc
Spartanburg, SC 866-466-2756
Palmland Paper Company
Fort Lauderdale, FL 800-266-9067
Paper Service
Hinsdale, NH 603-239-6344
Party Linens
Chicago, IL 800-281-0003
Premier Skirting Products
Lawrence, NY 800-544-2516
Prestige Skirting & Tablecloths
Orangeburg, NY 800-635-3313
Resource One/Resource Two
Reseda, CA 818-343-3451
Scan Group
Appleton, WI 920-730-9150
Scranton Lace Company
Forest City, PA 800-822-1036
Shen Manufacturing Co Inc
Conshohocken, PA 610-825-2790
Showeray Corporation
Brooklyn, NY 718-965-3633
Smith-Lee Company
Oshkosh, WI 800-327-9774
Something Different Linen
Clifton, NJ 800-422-2180
Springprint Medallion
Augusta, GA 800-543-5990
Sultan Linen Inc
New York, NY 212-689-8900
Tag-Trade Associated Group
Chicago, IL 800-621-8350
Tara Linens
Sanford, NC 800-476-8272
Ultimate Textile
Paterson, NJ 973-523-5866

Napkins

Paper

Admatch Corporation
New York, NY 800-777-9909
Alex Delvecchio Enterprises
Troy, MI 248-619-9600
Atlas Match Company
Toronto, ON 888-285-2783
Chinet Company
Laguna Niguel, CA 949-348-1711
Creative Converting Inc
Clintonville, WI 800-826-0418
Erving Industries
Erving, MA 413-422-2700
Flamingo Food Service Products
Hialeah, FL 800-432-8269
Georgia Pacific
Green Bay, WI 920-435-8821
Gold Star Products
Oak Park, MI 800-800-0205
Hoffmaster Group Inc
Oshkosh, WI 800-367-2877
Hoffmaster Group Inc.
Oshkosh, WI 800-558-9300
K & L Intl
Ontario, CA 888-598-5588
Kentfield's
Greenbrae, CA 888-461-7454
Kimberly-Clark Professional
Roswell, GA 800-241-3146
Lasermation Inc
Philadelphia, PA 800-523-2759
Marcal Paper Mills
Elmwood Park, NJ 800-631-8451

Palmland Paper Company
Fort Lauderdale, FL 800-266-9067
Paper Service
Hinsdale, NH 603-239-6344
Paradise Products
El Cerrito, CA 800-227-1092
Potlatch Corp
Spokane, WA 509-835-1500
Primary Liquidation
Bohemia, NY 631-244-1410
SCA Tissue
Philadelphia, PA 866-722-8675
SCA Tissue North America
S Glens Falls, NY 518-743-0240
Scan Group
Appleton, WI 920-730-9150
Schroeder Machine
San Marcos, CA 760-591-9733
Sorg Paper Company
Middletown, OH 513-420-5300
Spirit Foodservice, Inc.
Andover, MA 800-343-0996
Springprint Medallion
Augusta, GA 800-543-5990
SQP
Schenectady, NY 800-724-1129

Paper

Writing, Forms, Sales & Order Books

Access Solutions
Knoxville, TN 865-531-0971
Appleson Press
Syosset, NY 800-888-2775
Atlas Match Corporation
Euless, TX 800-628-2426
Conimar Corp
Ocala, FL 800-874-9735
Dagher Printing
Jacksonville, FL 904-998-0921
Double Envelope Corp
Roanoke, VA 540-362-3311
Durango-Georgia Paper
Tampa, FL 813-286-2718
Ennis Inc.
Midlothian, TX 800-972-1069
Fay Paper Products
Foxboro, MA 800-765-4620
Graydon Lettercraft
Great Neck, NY 516-482-0531
Hazen Paper Co
Holyoke, MA 413-538-8204
Holden Graphic Services
Minneapolis, MN 612-339-0241
Larry B Newman Printing
Knoxville, TN 888-835-4566
Miami Systems Corporation
Blue Ash, OH 800-543-4540
Mohawk Paper Mills
Clifton Park, NY 518-371-6700
Monadnock Paper Mills Inc
Bennington, NH 603-588-3311
Neal Walters Poster Corporation
Bentonville, AR 501-273-2489
North American Packaging Corp
New York, NY 800-499-3521
Old English Printing & Label Company
Delray Beach, FL 561-997-9990
Pan American Papers Inc
Miami, FL 305-635-2534
Patrick & Co
Dallas, TX 214-761-0900
Randall Printing
Brockton, MA 508-588-3830
Salinas Valley Wax Paper Co
Salinas, CA 831-424-2747
Steingart Associates Inc
South Fallsburg, NY 845-434-4321
Tops Business Forms
Covington, TN 800-762-7283
Visual Planning Corp
Champlain, NY 800-361-1192
Westrick Paper Co
Jacksonville, FL 904-737-2122

Place Mats

Abond Plastic Corporation
Lachine, QC 800-886-7947
Admatch Corporation
New York, NY 800-777-9909

Artex International
Highland, IL 618-654-2113
Bright of America
Summersville, WV 304-872-3000
Brooklace
Oshkosh, WI 800-572-4552
Conimar Corp
Ocala, FL 800-874-9735
Connecticut Laminating Co Inc
New Haven, CT 800-753-9119
Creative Essentials
Ronkonkoma, NY 800-355-5891
Custom Table Pads
St Paul, MN 800-325-4643
Decolin
Montreal, QC 514-384-2910
Dorado Carton Company
Dorado, PR 787-796-1670
Elrene Home Fashions
New York, NY 212-213-0425
Ennis Inc.
Midlothian, TX 800-972-1069
Erving Industries
Erving, MA 413-422-2700
Filet Menu
Los Angeles, CA 310-202-8000
Gourmet Table Skirts
Houston, TX 800-527-0440
Have Our Plastic Inc
Mississauga, ON 800-263-5995
Hoffmaster Group Inc
Oshkosh, WI 800-327-9774
Hoffmaster Group Inc
Oshkosh, WI 800-367-2877
J. James
Brooklyn, NY 718-384-6144
Jack the Ripper Table Skirting
Stafford, TX 800-331-7831
K-C Products Company
Van Nuys, CA 818-267-1600
Louisville Bedding Co Inc.
Louisville, KY 502-813-8059
Marko Inc
Spartanburg, SC 866-466-2756
Mastercraft
Appleton, WI 800-242-6602
Milliken & Co
Spartanburg, SC 864-503-2020
Palmland Paper Company
Fort Lauderdale, FL 800-266-9067
Paradise Products
El Cerrito, CA 800-227-1092
Placemat Printers
Fogelsville, PA 800-628-7746
Premier Skirting Products
Lawrence, NY 800-544-2516
Process Displays
New Berlin, WI 800-533-1764
Rixie Paper Products Inc
Pottstown, PA 800-377-2692
Royal Paper Products
Coatesville, PA 800-666-6655
SCA Tissue
Philadelphia, PA 866-722-8675
Scranton Lace Company
Forest City, PA 800-822-1036
Seattle Menu Specialists
Kent, WA 800-622-2826
Shen Manufacturing Co Inc
Conshohocken, PA 610-825-2790
Smith-Lee Company
Oshkosh, WI 800-327-9774
Springprint Medallion
Augusta, GA 800-543-5990
Stevens Linen Association
Dudley, MA 800-772-9269
Sultan Linen Inc
New York, NY 212-689-8900
Tag-Trade Associated Group
Chicago, IL 800-621-8350
Tara Linens
Sanford, NC 800-476-8272

Plastic Back Tag

Label Holders

Hopp Co Inc
New Hyde Park, NY 800-889-8425

Plastic Shelf Covers

Hopp Co Inc
New Hyde Park, NY 800-889-8425

Plastic Store Shelf

Moldings

Hopp Co Inc
New Hyde Park, NY 800-889-8425

Point of Sale Systems

APG Cash Drawer
Fridley, MN 763-571-5000
ASI/Restaurant Manager
Silver Spring, MD 800-356-6037
Astoria Laminations
St Clair Shores, MI 800-526-7325
Business Control Systems
Iselin, NJ 800-233-5876
Cache Box
Arlington, VA 800-603-4834
CDI Service & Mfg Inc
Largo, FL 727-536-2207
Compris Technologies
Duluth, GA 800-615-3301
Comtek Systems
San Antonio, TX 210-340-8253
Comus Restaurant Systems
Frederick, MD 301-698-6208
Custom Business Solutions
Irvine, CA 800-551-7674
Cyplex
Los Angeles, CA
Data Management
San Angelo, TX 800-749-8463
Digital Dining
Springfield, VA 703-912-3000
Elo Touch Systems
Menlo Park, CA 800-557-1458
FFR Merchandising Inc
Twinsburg, OH 800-422-2547
Illinois Wholesale Cash Rgstr
Elgin, IL 800-544-5493
ITC Systems
Toronto, ON 877-482-8326
Lowen Color Graphics
Hutchinson, KS 800-545-5505
Loyal Manufacturing
Indianapolis, IN 317-359-3185
Madix Inc
Terrell, TX 800-776-2349
MAPS Software
Columbus, MS 662-328-6110
Metro Corporation
Wilkes Barre, PA 800-992-1776
Microcheck Solutions
Humble, TX 800-647-4524
Microtouch Systems Inc
Methuen, MA 978-659-9000
National Computer Corporation
Greenville, SC 866-944-5164
Novax Group/Point of Sales
New York, NY 212-684-1244
OMRON Systems LLC
Schaumburg, IL 224-520-7650
Order-Matic Corporation
Oklahoma City, OK 800-767-6733
PAR Tech Inc
New Hartford, NY 800-448-6505
PC/Poll Systems
Dubuque, IA 800-670-1736
RDS of Florida
Fort Lauderdale, FL 305-994-7756
Reflex International
Norcross, GA 800-642-7640
Retail Automations Products
New York, NY 800-237-9144
Retail Decor
Ironton, OH 800-726-3402
Retalix
Miamisburg, OH 877-794-7237
Sable Technology Solution
St Paul, MN 800-722-5390
SalesData Software
San Jose, CA 408-281-5811
Scan Corporation
Brandon, FL 800-881-7226
SICOM Systems
Doylestown, PA 800-547-4266

Simply Products
Kunkletown, PA 610-681-6894
Southern Atlantic Label Co
Chesapeake, VA 800-456-5999
Squirrel Systems
Vancouver, BC 800-388-6824
Star Micronics
Edison, NJ 800-782-7636
Stoffel Seals Corp
Tallapoosa, GA 800-422-8247
Systems Comtrex
Moorestown, NJ 800-220-2669
TEC America
Atlanta, GA 770-453-0868
Tinadre Inc
Tampa, FL 813-866-0333
Touch Menus
Bellevue, WA 800-688-6368
US Magnetix
Minneapolis, MN 763-540-9497
Veri Fone Inc
Alpharetta, GA 770-663-0196

Pricer Signs

Dualite Sales & Svc Inc
Williamsburg, OH 513-724-7100

Pumps

Syrup & Soda Fountain

Fristam Pumps USA LLP
Middleton, WI 800-841-5001
John Crane Mechanical Sealing Devices
Chicago, IL
Manitowoc Foodservice
Sellersburg, IN 800-367-4233
PROCON Products
Smyrna, TN 615-355-8000
Rio Syrup Co
St Louis, MO 800-325-7666
Server Products Inc
Richfield, WI 800-558-8722
SHURflo
Costa Mesa, CA 800-854-3218
Standex International Corp.
Salem, NH 603-893-9701
Superflex Limited
Brooklyn, NY 800-394-3665

Racks

Bakery

AFCO Manufacturing
Cincinnati, OH 800-747-7332
Allied Bakery and Food Service Equipment
Santa Fe Springs, CA 562-945-6506
Amco Metals Indl
City Of Industry, CA 626-855-2550
ARC Specialties
Valencia, CA 661-775-8500
Better Bilt Products
Addison, IL 800-544-4550
Bmh Equipment Inc
Sacramento, CA 800-350-8828
California Caster & Handtruck
San Francisco, CA 800-950-8750
Cannon Equipment Company
Cannon Falls, MN 800-825-8501
Crown Custom Metal Spinning
Concord, ON 800-750-1924
DBE Inc
Concord, ON 800-461-5313
Dubuque Steel Products Co
Dubuque, IA 563-556-6288
EPCO
Murfreesboro, TN 800-251-3398
Esterle Mold & Machine Co Inc
Stow, OH 800-411-4086
Hodges
Vienna, IL 800-444-0011
Lakeside Manufacturing Inc
Milwaukee, WI 888-558-8565
Langer Manufacturing Company
Cedar Rapids, IA 800-728-6445
Leggett & Platt Storage
Vernon Hills, IL 847-816-6246
Lynch-Jamentz Company
Lakewood, CA 800-828-6217

M & E Mfg Co Inc
Kingston, NY 845-331-2110
Magna Industries Inc
Lakewood, NJ 800-510-9856
Malco Manufacturing Co
Los Angeles, CA 866-477-7267
Market Forge Industries Inc
Everett, MA 866-698-3188
Marlin Steel Wire Products
Baltimore, MD 877-762-7546
Metro Corporation
Wilkes Barre, PA 800-992-1776
Micro Wire Products Inc
Brockton, MA 508-584-0200
National Cart Co
St Charles, MO 636-947-3800
Olson Wire Products Co
Baltimore, MD 410-242-7900
Omega Industries
St Louis, MO 314-961-1668
Otto Braun Bakery Equipment
Buffalo, NY 716-824-1252
Piper Products Inc
Wausau, WI 800-544-3057
Products A Curtron Div
Pittsburgh, PA 800-888-9750
Proluxe
Paramount, CA 800-594-5528
Sitka Store Fixtures
Kansas City, MO 800-821-7558
SPG International
Covington, GA 877-503-4774
Stein-DSI
Northfield, MN 507-645-9546
Storage Unlimited
Nixa, MO 800-478-6642
Straits Steel & Wire Co
Ludington, MI 231-843-3416
Superior Products Company
Saint Paul, MN 800-328-9800
Trepte's Wire & Metal Works
Bellflower, CA 800-828-6217
Wirefab Inc
Worcester, MA 877-877-4445

Display, Store

Abalon Precision Manufacturing Corporation
Bronx, NY 800-888-2225
Acryline
North Attleboro, MA 508-695-7124
ARC Specialties
Valencia, CA 661-775-8500
Arlington Display Industries
Detroit, MI 313-837-1212
Art Wire Works Co
Chicago, IL 708-458-3993
Art-Phyl Creations
Hialeah, FL 800-327-8318
Beemak-IDL Display
La Mirada, CA 800-421-4393
Best Brands Home Products
New York, NY 212-684-7456
Better Bilt Products
Addison, IL 800-544-4550
Bmh Equipment Inc
Sacramento, CA 800-350-8828
Cannon Equipment Company
Cannon Falls, MN 800-825-8501
Chroma Tone
Saint Clair, PA 800-878-1552
Dayton Wire Products
Dayton, OH 888-265-1711
Despro Manufacturing
Cedar Grove, NJ 800-292-9906
Display Creations
Brooklyn, NY 718-257-2300
Dubuque Steel Products Co
Dubuque, IA 563-556-6288
Dunn Woodworks
Shrewsbury, PA 877-835-8592
E-Z Shelving Systems Inc
Shawnee, KS 800-353-1331
Eastern Plastics
Pawtucket, RI 800-442-8585
Emco Industrial Plastics
Cedar Grove, NJ 800-292-9906
Enterprise Products
Bell Gardens, CA 562-928-1918
Fab-X/Metals
Washington, NC 800-677-3229

General Cage
Elwood, IN ... 800-428-6403
Harmar
Sarasota, FL ... 800-833-0478
Hewitt Manufacturing Co
Waldron, IN ... 765-525-9829
HMG Worldwide In-Store Marketing
New York, NY ... 212-736-2300
Hodges
Vienna, IL ... 800-444-0011
Houston Wire Works, Inc.
South Houston, TX ... 800-468-9477
Ideal Wire Works
Alhambra, CA ... 626-282-0886
InterMetro Industries
Wilkes-Barre, PA ... 570-825-2741
Ironwood Displays
Niles, MI ... 231-683-8500
JEM Wire Products
Middletown, CT ... 860-347-0447
Kaines West Michigan Co
Ludington, MI ... 231-845-1281
Key Material Handling Inc
Simi Valley, CA ... 800-539-7225
L&S Products
Coldwater, MI ... 517-279-9526
L.A. Darling Co., LLC
Paragould, AR ... 800-682-5730
Langer Manufacturing Company
Cedar Rapids, IA ... 800-728-6445
Load King Mfg
Jacksonville, FL ... 800-531-4975
Loyal Manufacturing
Indianapolis, IN ... 317-359-3185
Marlin Steel Wire Products
Baltimore, MD ... 877-762-7546
McMillin Manufacturing Corporation
Los Angeles, CA ... 323-268-1900
Melrose Displays
Passaic, NJ ... 973-471-7700
Merchandising Systems Manufacturing
Union City, CA ... 800-523-1468
Metaline Products Co Inc
South Amboy, NJ ... 732-721-1373
Metro Corporation
Wilkes Barre, PA ... 800-992-1776
Midwest Wire Products LLC
Sturgeon Bay, WI ... 800-445-0225
Mirro Products Company
High Point, NC ... 336-885-4166
Multi-Panel Display Corporation
Brooklyn, NY ... 800-439-0879
Olson Wire Products Co
Baltimore, MD ... 410-242-7900
Omega Industries
St Louis, MO ... 314-961-1668
Peterson Manufacturing Company
Plainfield, IL ... 800-547-8995
Pinquist Tool & Die Company
Brooklyn, NY ... 800-752-0414
Piper Products Inc
Wausau, WI ... 800-544-3057
Princeton Shelving
Cedar Rapids, IA ... 319-369-0355
Quality Industries Inc
La Vergne, TN ... 615-793-3000
R & D Brass
Wappingers Falls, NY ... 800-447-6050
R.I. Enterprises
Hernando, MS ... 662-429-7863
Racks
San Diego, CA ... 619-661-0987
Rex Art Manufacturing Corp.
Lindenhurst, NY ... 631-884-4600
Ridg-U-Rak
North East, PA ... 866-479-7225
Riverside Wire & Metal Co.
Ionia, MI ... 616-527-3500
Royal Display Corporation
Middletown, CT ... 800-569-1295
Royce Corp
Glendale, AZ ... 602-256-0006
Selma Wire Products Company
Selma, IN ... 765-282-3532
SEMCO
Ocala, FL ... 800-749-6894
Southern Imperial Inc
Rockford, IL ... 800-747-4665
Southwest Fixture
Dallas, TX ... 214-634-2800
Spot Wire Works Company
Philadelphia, PA ... 215-627-6124
Steel City Corporation
Youngstown, OH ... 800-321-0350
Straits Steel & Wire Co
Ludington, MI ... 231-843-3416
Superior Products Company
Saint Paul, MN ... 800-328-9800
Swanson Wire Works Industries, Inc.
Mesquite, TX ... 972-288-7465
Technibilt/Cari-All
Newton, NC ... 800-233-3972
Thorco Industries LLC
Lamar, MO ... 800-445-3375
Toledo Wire Products
Toledo, OH ... 888-430-7445
Vomela/Harbor Graphics
St Paul, MN ... 800-645-1012
Vulcan Industries
Moody, AL ... 888-444-4417
W J Egli & Co
Alliance, OH ... 330-823-3666
Wahlstrom Manufacturing
Fontana, CA ... 909-822-4677
Wald Wire & Mfg Co
Oshkosh, WI ... 800-236-0053
Wire Products Mfg
Merrill, WI ... 715-536-7884
Wiremaid Products Div
Coral Springs, FL ... 800-770-4700
Woerner Wire Works
Omaha, NE ... 402-451-5414
Xtreme Beverages, LLC
Dana Point, CA ... 949-495-7929
Yeager Wire Works
Berwick, PA ... 570-752-2769

Restaurant Supplies & Equipment

A Legacy Food Svc
Santa Fe Springs, CA ... 800-848-4440
Action Lighting
Bozeman, MT ... 800-248-0076
Advance Energy Technologies
Halfmoon, NY ... 800-724-0198
AMC Industries
Palmetto, FL ... 941-479-7834
Anderson Wood Products
Louisville, KY ... 502-778-5591
Architectural Sheet Metals LLC
Cleveland, OH ... 216-361-9952
ASI/Restaurant Manager
Silver Spring, MD ... 800-356-6037
Bargreen Ellingson
Tacoma, WA ... 800-322-4441
Bargreen Ellingson
Fife, WA ... 866-722-2665
Best Buy Uniforms
Homestead, PA ... 800-345-1924
Blue Line Foodservice Distr
Farmington Hills, MI ... 800-892-8272
Browne & Company
Markham, ON ... 905-475-6104
Carroll Chair Company
Onalaska, WI ... 800-331-4704
Champion America Inc
Branford, CT ... 800-521-7000
Charles Mayer Studios
Akron, OH ... 330-535-6121
Co-Rect Products Inc
Golden Valley, MN ... 800-328-5702
Coastal Canvas Products
Savannah, GA ... 800-476-5174
Cove Woodworking
Gloucester, MA ... 800-273-0037
Daga Restaurant Ware
Honolulu, HI ... 808-847-3100
Dorado Carton Company
Dorado, PR ... 787-796-1670
Electro-Steam Generator Corp
Rancocas, NJ ... 866-617-0764
Ex-Cell KAISER LLC
Franklin Park, IL ... 847-451-0451
Green Metal Fabricating
West Sacramento, CA ... 916-371-2951
H A Sparke Co
Shreveport, LA ... 318-222-0927
Inland Showcase & Fixture Company
Fresno, CA ... 559-237-4158
Instacomm Canada
Oakville, ON ... 877-426-2783
K & L Intl
Ontario, CA ... 888-598-5588
Kessenich's Limited
Madison, WI ... 800-248-0555
Lauritzen Makin Inc
Fort Worth, TX ... 817-921-0218
Libra Technical Center
Metuchen, NJ ... 732-321-5200
Lockwood Manufacturing
Livonia, MI ... 800-521-0238
Menu Graphics
Olmsted Falls, OH ... 216-696-1460
Metal Masters Northwest
Lynnwood, WA ... 425-775-4481
Metro Corporation
Wilkes Barre, PA ... 800-992-1776
Mosshaim Innovations
Jacksonville, FL ... 888-995-7775
NTN Wireless
Norcross, GA ... 800-637-8639
Order-Matic Corporation
Oklahoma City, OK ... 800-767-6733
Original Wood Seating
Atlanta, GA ... 678-966-0406
Pinnacle Furnishing
Aberdeen, NC ... 866-229-5704
Products A Curtron Div
Pittsburgh, PA ... 800-888-9750
R X Honing Machine Corp
Mishawaka, IN ... 800-346-6464
RDS of Florida
Fort Lauderdale, FL ... 305-994-7756
Sable Technology Solution
St Paul, MN ... 800-722-5390
Sandler Seating
Atlanta, GA ... 404-982-9000
Sarasota Restaurant Equipment
Sarasota, FL ... 800-434-1410
Shanker Industries
Deer Park, NY ... 877-742-6561
Sign Classics
San Jose, CA ... 408-298-1600
Sign Products
Sheridan, WY ... 800-532-4753
Sims Superior Seating
Locust Grove, GA ... 800-729-9178
Standex International Corp.
Salem, NH ... 603-893-9701
Sturdi-Bilt Restaurant Equipment
Whitmore Lake, MI ... 800-521-2895
Superior Products Company
Saint Paul, MN ... 800-328-9800
Superior Uniform Group
Seminole, FL ... 800-727-8643
Tango Shatterproof Drinkware
Walpole, MA ... 888-898-2646
TEC America
Atlanta, GA ... 770-453-0868
Tec Art Industries Inc
Wixom, MI ... 800-886-6615
Trojan Commercial Furni ture Inc.
Montereal, QC ... 877-271-3878
Valley Fixtures
Sparks, NV ... 775-331-1050
Waymar Industries
Burnsville, MN ... 888-474-1112
Wheel Tough Company
Terre Haute, IN ... 888-765-8833
Woodard
Coppell, TX ... 800-877-2290

Salad Bars

Advanced Design Mfg
Concord, CA ... 800-690-0002
Atlas Metal Industries
Miami, FL ... 800-762-7565
Brass Smith
Denver, CO ... 800-662-9595
Craig Manufacturing
Irvington, NJ ... 800-631-7936
Custom Plastics Inc
Decatur, GA ... 404-373-1691
Delfield Co
Mt Pleasant, MI ... 800-733-8821
Duke Manufacturing Co
St Louis, MO ... 800-735-3853
Forbes Industries
Ontario, CA ... 909-923-4549
Galley
Jupiter, FL ... 800-537-2772
Just Plastics Inc
New York, NY ... 212-569-8500
LA Rosa Refrigeration & Equip
Detroit, MI ... 800-527-6723
Lavi Industries
Valencia, CA ... 800-624-6225

Load King Mfg
Jacksonville, FL 800-531-4975
Northern Stainless Fabricating
Traverse City, MI 231-947-4580
Northwest Art Glass
Redmond, WA.................800-888-9444
Plymold
Kenyon, MN 800-759-6653
PMI Food Equipment Group
Troy, OH 937-332-3000
R & D Brass
Wappingers Falls, NY 800-447-6050
Steamway Corporation
Scottsburg, IN 800-259-8171
Stryco Wire Products
North York, ON...............416-663-7000
Superior Products Company
Saint Paul, MN 800-328-9800
Tables Cubed
Chesterfield, MO 800-878-3001
United Showcase Company
Wood Ridge, NJ 800-526-6382
Wylie Systems
Mississauga, ON..............800-525-6609
Yorkraft
York, PA 800-872-2044

Scanners

Check & Credit Card Verification Systems

Axiohm USA
Myrtle Beach, SC 843-443-3155
Bruins Instruments
Salem, NH......................603-898-6527
CSPI
Billerica, MA 978-663-7598
Intercard Inc
St Louis, MO...................314-275-8066
NCR Corp
Atlanta, GA....................800-225-5627
Reflex International
Norcross, GA 800-642-7640
Retalix
Miamisburg, OH................877-794-7237
Scan Corporation
Brandon, FL 800-881-7226
TEC America
Atlanta, GA....................770-453-0868

Serving Equipment

A J Antunes & Co
Carol Stream, IL 800-253-2991
Ace Fabrication
Mobile, AL 251-478-0401
Advance Engineering Co
Canton, MI 800-497-6388
Advanced Plastic Coating Svc
Parsons, KS 620-421-1660
Aero Manufacturing Co
Clifton, NJ 800-631-8378
Aladdin Temp-Rite, LLC
Hendersonville, TN.............800-888-8018
All State Fabricators Corporation
Tampa, FL.....................800-322-9925
Amco Metals Indl
City Of Industry, CA............626-855-2550
AMI
Richmond, CA 800-942-7466
Apex Fountain Sales Inc
Philadelphia, PA 800-523-4586
ARC Specialties
Valencia, CA 661-775-8500
Art Wire Works Co
Chicago, IL....................708-458-3993
Aurora Design Associates, Inc.
Salt Lake City, UT..............801-588-0111
Automatic Specialties Inc
Marlborough, MA...............800-445-2370
Bakers Choice Products
Beacon Falls, CT...............203-720-1000
Bardes Plastics Inc
Milwaukee, WI.................800-558-5161
Bloomfield Industries
St. Louis, MO..................888-356-5362
Bon Chef
Lafayette, NJ..................800-331-0177
Boyd's Coffee Co
Portland, OR..................800-735-2878

Brooklace
Oshkosh, WI..................800-572-4552
C R Mfg
Waverly, NE 877-789-5844
Cal-Mil Plastic Products Inc
Oceanside, CA 800-321-9069
California Vibratory Feeders
Anaheim, CA 800-354-0972
Carlisle Food Svc Products Inc
Oklahoma City, OK.............800-654-8210
Carter-Hoffmann LLC
Mundelein, IL 800-323-9793
Component Hardware Group Inc
Lakewood, NJ 800-526-3694
Creative Forming
Ripon, WI 920-748-7285
Crespac Incorporated
Tucker, GA 800-438-1900
Crestware
North Salt Lake, UT.............800-345-0513
Custom Diamond International
Laval, QC 800-363-5926
Custom Molders
Rocky Mount, NC...............919-688-8061
Cyclamen Collection
Oakland, CA 510-434-7620
Dart Container Corp.
Mason, MI.....................800-248-5960
De Ster Corporation
Atlanta, GA....................800-237-8270
Delco Tableware
Port Washington, NY 800-221-9557
Delfin Design & Mfg
Rancho Sta Marg, CA 800-354-7919
Detroit Forming
Southfield, MI..................248-440-1317
Douglas Stephen Plastics Inc
Paterson, NJ 973-523-3030
Duke Manufacturing Co
St Louis, MO...................800-735-3853
Dura-Ware Company of America
Oklahoma City, OK.............800-664-3872
Dynynstyl
Delray Beach, FL 800-774-7895
Eastern Tabletop Mfg
Brooklyn, NY 888-422-4142
Edco Industries
Bridgeport, CT 203-333-8982
Ellingers Agatized Wood Inc
Sheboygan, WI.................888-287-8906
Engineered Plastics Inc
Gibsonville, NC 800-711-1740
EPCO
Murfreesboro, TN..............800-251-3398
Epic Products
Santa Ana, CA 800-548-9791
Eskay Metal Fabricating
Buffalo, NY....................800-836-8015
Fetco
Lake Zurich, IL.................800-338-2699
Fold-Pak South
Columbus, GA 706-689-2924
Food Warming Equipment Co
Crystal Lake, IL 800-222-4393
Gaetano America
El Monte, CA 626-442-2858
Galley
Jupiter, FL 800-537-2772
Gaychrome Division of CSL
Crystal Lake, IL 800-873-4370
Gessner Products
Ambler, PA 800-874-7808
Glaro Inc
Hauppauge, NY 631-234-1717
Gourmet Display
Kent, WA 800-767-4711
Grand Silver Company
Bronx, NY.....................718-585-1930
Gril-Del
Mankato, MN 800-782-7320
Hal-One Plastics
Olathe, KS.....................800-626-5784
Hot Food Boxes
Mooresville, IN.................800-733-8073
HPI North America/ Plastics
Eagan, MN 800-752-7462
HPI North America/Plastics
Chicago, IL....................800-327-3534
Infanti International
Staten Island, NY 800-874-8590
Innovative Plastics Corp
Orangeburg, NY 845-359-7500

Institutional & Supermarket
Plantation, FL 954-584-3100
International Patterns, Inc.
Bay Shore, NY 631-952-2000
Jack Stack
Inwood, NY....................800-999-9840
Jones-Zylon Co
West Lafayette, OH.............800-848-8160
K & I Creative Plastics & Wood
Jacksonville, FL 904-387-0438
K & L Intl
Ontario, CA....................888-598-5588
Keating Of Chicago Inc
Mc Cook, IL 800-532-8464
Kelmin Products
Plymouth, FL 407-886-6079
Key Packaging Co
Sarasota, FL 941-355-2728
King Arthur
Statesville, NC 800-257-7244
Lakeside Manufacturing Inc
Milwaukee, WI.................888-558-8565
Lambertson Industries Inc
Sparks, NV 800-548-3324
Lancaster Colony Corporation
Westerville, OH.................614-224-7141
Leggett & Platt Storage
Vernon Hills, IL 847-816-6246
Leon Bush Manufacturer
Glenview, IL 847-657-8888
Lincoln Foodservice
Cleveland, OH 800-374-3004
Lodge Manufacturing Company
South Pittsburg, TN 423-837-5919
LoTech Industries
Lakewood, CO 800-295-0199
Low Temp Industries Inc
Jonesboro, GA 678-674-1317
M & E Mfg Co Inc
Kingston, NY 845-331-2110
Mack-Chicago Corporation
Chicago, IL....................800-992-6225
Madsen Wire Products Inc
Orland, IN.....................260-829-6561
Majestic
Bridgeport, CT 203-367-7900
Metal Master Sales Corp
Glendale Heights, IL.............800-488-8729
Metal Masters Northwest
Lynnwood, WA 425-775-4481
Mid-West Wire Products
Ferndale, MI 800-989-9881
Moli-International
Denver, CO 800-525-8468
Mosshaim Innovations
Jacksonville, FL 888-995-7775
Mr Ice Bucket
New Brunswick, NJ 732-545-0420
National Scoop & Equipment Company
Spring House, PA 215-646-2040
NCC
Groveland, FL..................800-429-9037
Normandie Metal Fabricators
Port Washington, NY 800-221-2398
Novelty Crystal
Long Island City, NY 800-622-0250
Olde Country Reproductions Inc
York, PA 800-358-3997
Olde Thompson Inc
Oxnard, CA....................800-827-1565
Olive Can Company
Elgin, IL 847-468-7474
Orbis Corp.
Rexdale, ON 800-890-7292
PacknWood
New York, NY 201-604-3840
Palmer Distributors
St Clair Shores, MI 800-444-1912
Par-Pak
Houston, TX 888-727-7252
Plastocon
Oconomowoc, WI..............800-966-0103
PMC Global Inc.
Sun Valley, CA 818-896-1101
Polar Beer Systems
Sun City, CA 951-928-8174
Polar Ware Company
Sheboygan, WI.................800-237-3655
Precision
Miami, FL 800-762-7565
Process Displays
New Berlin, WI.................800-533-1764

Prolon
Port Gibson, MS 888-480-9828
Quipco Products Inc
Sauget, IL 314-993-1442
Rexcraft Fine Chafers
Long Island City, NY 888-739-2723
Robinson Industries Inc
Coleman, MI 989-465-6111
Rolland Machining & Fabricating
Moneta, VA 973-827-6911
Ronnie's Ceramic Company
San Francisco, CA 800-888-8218
Sani-Top Products
De Leon Springs, FL 800-874-6094
Server Products Inc
Richfield, WI 800-558-8722
Service Ideas
Woodbury, MN 800-328-4493
Shammi Industries
Corona, CA 800-417-9260
Sheffield Platers Inc
San Diego, CA 800-227-9242
Sico Inc
Minneapolis, MN 800-328-6138
Sonofresco
Burlington, WA 360-757-2800
Spin-Tech Corporation
Hoboken, NJ 800-977-4692
Superior Products Company
Saint Paul, MN 800-328-9800
Techform
Mount Airy, NC 336-789-2115
TEMP-TECH Company
Springfield, MA 800-343-5579
Thermo Service
Dallas, TX 800-635-5559
Thermodynamics
Commerce City, CO 800-627-9037
Thermos Company
Schaumburg, IL 800-243-0745
Tomlinson Industries
Cleveland, OH 800-945-4589
Tops Manufacturing Co
Darien, CT 203-655-9367
Toscarora
Sandusky, OH 419-625-7343
Toska Foodservice Systems
Lannon, WI 262-253-4782
Tramontina USA
Sugar Land, TX 800-221-7809
Tray-Pak Corp
Reading, PA 610-926-5800
Tri-State Plastics
Glenwillard, PA 724-457-6900
Ullman, Shapiro & UllmanLLP
New York, NY 212-755-0299
Unique Plastics
Rio Rico, AZ 800-658-5946
Update International
Vernon, CA 800-747-7124
Vermillion Flooring
Springfield, MO 417-862-3785
Vollrath Co LLC
Sheboygan, WI 800-624-2051
Waddington North America
Chelmsford, MA 888-962-2877
Weavewood, Inc.
Golden Valley, MN 800-367-6460
Wells Manufacturing Company
St. Louis, MO 888-356-5362
Wilton Armetale
Mt Joy, PA 800-779-4586
WR Key
Scarborough, ON 416-291-6246
Yorkraft
York, PA 800-872-2044
Zeier Plastic & Mfg Inc
Madison, WI 608-244-5782
Zeroll Company
Fort Pierce, FL 800-872-5000
Zoia Banquetier Co
Cleveland, OH 216-631-6414

Industrial Plant

Andgar Corp
Ferndale, WA 360-366-9900
Ashcroft Inc
Stratford, CT 800-328-8258
Bmh Equipment Inc
Sacramento, CA 800-350-8828

Institutional & Supermarket
Plantation, FL 954-584-3100
National Scoop & Equipment Company
Spring House, PA 215-646-2040
Quipco Products Inc
Sauget, IL 314-993-1442
Standex International Corp.
Salem, NH 603-893-9701

Shelving

Store

Accent Store Fixtures
Kenosha, WI 800-545-1144
Amscor Inc
West Babylon, NY 800-825-9800
Arizona Store Equipment
Phoenix, AZ 800-624-8395
Bmh Equipment Inc
Sacramento, CA 800-350-8828
Borroughs Corp
Kalamazoo, MI 800-748-0227
Cannon Equipment Company
Cannon Falls, MN 800-825-8501
Continental Commercial Products
Bridgeton, MO 800-325-1051
Despro Manufacturing
Cedar Grove, NJ 800-292-9906
E-Z Shelving Systems Inc
Shawnee, KS 800-353-1331
Easyup Storage Systems
Tukwila, WA 800-426-9234
Handy Manufacturing Co Inc
Newark, NJ 800-631-4280
Hodge Manufacturing Company
Springfield, MA 800-262-4634
Hodges
Vienna, IL 800-444-0011
InterMetro Industries
Wilkes-Barre, PA 570-825-2741
Kent Corp
Birmingham, AL 800-252-5368
L.A. Darling Co., LLC
Paragould, AR 800-682-5730
Leggett & Platt Inc
Carthage, MO 417-358-8131
LPI Imports
Chicago, IL 877-389-6563
Lyon LLC
Montgomery, IL 630-892-8941
Madix Inc
Terrell, TX 800-776-2349
Madsen Wire Products Inc
Orland, IN 260-829-6561
Metro Corporation
Wilkes Barre, PA 800-992-1776
Modar
Benton Harbor, MI 800-253-6186
Newcourt, Inc.
Madison, IN 800-933-0006
Pacific Store Designs Inc
Garden Grove, CA 800-772-5661
Princeton Shelving
Cedar Rapids, IA 319-369-0355
Quantum Storage Systems Inc
Miami, FL 800-685-4665
RTI Shelving Systems
Elmhurst, NY 800-223-6210
S & L Store Fixture
Doral, FL 800-205-4536
Sefi Fabricators Inc
Amityville, NY 631-842-2200
SPG International
Covington, GA 877-503-4774
Strong Hold Products
Louisville, KY 800-880-2625
Teilhaber Manufacturing Corp
Broomfield, CO 800-358-7225
Tennsco Corp
Dickson, TN 800-251-8184
Triple-A Manufacturing Company
Toronto, ON 800-786-2238
Western Pacific Stge Solutions
San Dimas, CA 800-888-5707

Signs

Advertising

A Allred Marketing
Birmingham, AL 205-251-3700

AAA Electrical Signs
Donna, TX 800-825-5376
AAA Flag & Banner Manufacturing
Los Angeles, CA 800-266-4222
ABC Letter Art
Los Angeles, CA 888-261-5367
Ace Signs
Little Rock, AR 501-562-0800
Ace Stamp & Engraving
Lakewood, WA 253-582-3322
ACME Sign Corp
Peabody, MA 978-535-6600
Ad Mart Identity Group
Danville, KY 800-354-2102
Adam Electric Signs
Massillon, OH 888-886-9911
Affiliated Resource Inc
Chicago, IL 800-366-9336
Alex Delvecchio Enterprises
Troy, MI 248-619-9600
Allen Industries Inc
Greensboro, NC 800-967-2553
Allen Signs Co
Knoxville, TN 800-844-3524
Altrua Marketing & Design
Tallahassee, FL 800-443-6939
AM Graphics
Edina, MN 612-341-2020
American Art Stamp
Gardena, CA 310-965-9004
American Labelmark Co
Chicago, IL 800-621-5808
American Led-Gible
Columbus, OH 614-851-1100
American Menu Displays
Long Island City, NY 877-544-8046
Ameritech Signs & Banners
Santa Monica, CA 310-829-9359
Andersen Sign Company
Woodsville, NH 603-787-6806
Andrew H Lawson Co
Philadelphia, PA 800-411-6628
Andrew W Nissly Inc
Lancaster, PA 717-393-3841
Arrow Sign & Awning Company
East Bethel, MN 800-621-9231
Artcraft Badge & Sign Company
Olney, MD 800-739-0709
Artkraft Strauss LLC
New York, NY 212-265-5156
Audrey Signs
New York, NY 212-769-4992
B S C Signs
Broomfield, CO 866-223-0101
B&B Neon Sign Company
Austin, TX 800-791-6366
Baltimore Sign Company
Arnold, MD 410-276-1500
Banner Idea
Newport Beach, CA 949-559-6600
Barlo Signs
Hudson, NH 800-227-5674
Berloc Manufacturing & Sign Company
Sun Valley, CA 818-503-9823
Blue Ridge Signs
Weatherford, TX 800-659-5645
Brown's Sign & Screen Printing
Covington, GA 800-540-3107
Cal-Mil Plastic Products Inc
Oceanside, CA 800-321-9069
Canton Sign Co
Canton, OH 330-456-7151
Capital City Signs
Monona, WI 608-222-1881
Cascade Signs & Neon
Salem, OR 503-378-0012
Century Sign Company
Fargo, ND 701-235-5323
Chain Store Graphics
Decatur, IL 800-443-7446
Chapman Sign
Warren, MI 586-758-1600
Charles Mayer Studios
Akron, OH 330-535-6121
Chatelain Plastics
Findlay, OH 866-421-4323
Chicago Show Inc
Buffalo Grove, IL 847-955-0200
Christman Screenprint Inc
Springfield, MI 800-962-9330
Chroma Tone
Saint Clair, PA 800-878-1552

City Grafx
Eugene, OR. 800-258-2489
City Neon Sign Company
Spokane, WA 509-483-5171
City Sign Svc Inc
Dallas, TX. .214-826-4475
City Signs LLC
Jackson, TN 877-248-9744
City Stamp & Seal Co
Austin, TX. .800-950-6074
Classic Signs Inc
Amherst, NH. 800-734-7446
Clearr Corporation
Minneapolis, MN 800-548-3269
Coleman Rubber Stamps
Daytona Beach, FL. 386-252-8597
Color Ad Tech Signs
Amarillo, TX. 806-374-8117
Comco Signs
Charlotte, NC 704-375-2338
Comet Signs
San Antonio, TX. 210-341-7244
Command Packaging
Vernon, CA .800-996-2247
Connecticut Laminating Co Inc
New Haven, CT. 800-753-9119
Cook Neon Signs
Tullahoma, TN 800-488-0944
Corsair Display Systems
Canandaigua, NY 800-347-5245
Couch & Philippi
Stanton, CA. 800-854-3360
Courtesy Signs
Amarillo, TX. 806-373-6609
Creative Signage System,
College Park, MD 800-220-7446
Crown Marking
Minneapolis, MN 800-305-5249
Cucamonga Sign Shop LLC
Rancho Cucamonga, CA 909-945-5888
Cuerden Sign Co
Conway, AR 501-375-7705
Cummings
Nashville, TN 615-673-8999
Curzon Promotional Graphics
Omaha, NE .800-769-7446
Custom Color Corp
Lenexa, KS .888-605-4050
Custom ID Systems
Venice, FL 800-242-8430
D&D Sign Company
Wichita Falls, TX 940-692-4643
Darlington Sign Awning & Neon
Warwick, RI 401-734-5800
Day Nite Neon Signs
Dartmouth, NS 902-469-7095
Daytech Limited
Toronto, ON 877-329-1907
Delta Signs
Haltom City, TX 866-643-3582
Derse Inc
Milwaukee, WI 800-562-2300
Dewey & Wilson Displays
Lincoln, NE. 402-489-0868
Diamond Sign Co
Costa Mesa, CA 714-545-1440
Dimension Graphics Inc
Grand Rapids, MI 855-476-1281
Dinosaur Plastics
Houston, TX. 713-923-2278
Display Concepts
Trenton, ME 800-446-0033
Dixie Neon Company
Tampa, FL 813-248-2531
Dixie Signs Inc
Lakeland, FL. 863-644-3521
Dove Screen Printing Co
Royston, GA 706-245-4975
Dowling Signs Inc
Fredericksburg, VA. 800-572-2100
Doyle Signs Inc
Addison, IL .630-543-9490
Drs Designs
Bethel, CT. .888-792-3740
Dualite Sales & Svc Inc
Williamsburg, OH 513-724-7100
Dwinell's Central Neon
Yakima, WA 800-932-8832
Dynamic Packaging
Minneapolis, MN 800-878-9380
Ehrgott Rubber Stamp Company
Indianapolis, IN 317-353-2222

Electric City Signs & Neon Inc.
Anderson, SC 800-270-5851
Elro Signs
Gardena, CA 800-927-4555
Empire Screen Printing Inc
Onalaska, WI. 608-783-3301
Encore Image Inc
Ontario, CA. 800-791-1187
Engraving Specialists
Royal Oak, MI 248-542-2244
Esco Manufacturing Inc
Watertown, SD 800-843-3726
Everett Rubber Stamp
Everett, WA 425-258-6747
Exhibitron Co
Grants Pass, OR 800-437-4571
Fair Publishing House
Norwalk, OH 419-668-3746
Federal Heath Sign Co LLC
Oceanside, CA 800-527-9495
Federal Sign
Providence, RI 401-421-9643
Ferrer Corporation
San Juan, PR 787-761-5151
Fiber Does
San Jose, CA 408-453-5533
First Choice Sign & Lighting
Escondido, CA 800-659-0629
Flexlume Sign Corp
Buffalo, NY .716-884-2020
FMI Display
Elkins Park, PA 215-663-1998
Foley Sign Co
Seattle, WA .206-324-3040
Formflex
Bloomingdale, IN 800-255-7659
FORT Hill Sign Products Inc
Hopedale, MA. 781-321-4320
Fox Stamp Sign & Specialty
Menasha, WI. 920-725-2683
France Personalized Signs
Cleveland, OH 216-241-2198
Frank O Carlson & Co
Chicago, IL .773-847-6900
Franklin Rubber Stamp Co
Wilmington, DE 302-654-8841
Frazier Signs
Decatur, IL .217-429-2349
Frost Manufacturing Corp
Worcester, MA 800-462-0216
Futura 2000 Corporation
Miami, FL 305-256-5877
Gannett Outdoor of New Jersey
Fairfield, NJ 973-575-6900
Gardenville Signs
Baltimore, MD 410-485-4800
Gary Sign Co
Merrillville, IN 219-942-3191
Gelberg Signs
Washington, DC 800-443-5237
General Neon Sign Co
San Antonio, TX. 210-227-1203
General Sign Co
Sheffield, AL. 256-383-3176
Gessner Products
Ambler, PA .800-874-7808
Glaro Inc
Hauppauge, NY 631-234-1717
Glover Rubber Stamp & Crafts
Wills Point, TX 214-824-6900
Grays Harbor Stamp Works
Aberdeen, WA. 800-894-3830
Green Mountain Graphics
Long Island City, NY 718-472-3377
Gribble Stamp & Stencil Co
Houston, TX. 713-228-5358
Gulf Coast Sign Company
Pensacola, FL. 800-768-3549
Haden Signs of Texas
Lubbock, TX. 806-744-4404
Hammar & Sons
Pelham, NH. 800-527-7446
Handicap Sign Inc
Grand Rapids, MI 800-690-4888
Hanley Sign Company
Latham, NY. 518-783-6183
Hardin Signs Inc
Peoria, IL. 309-688-4111
Harlan Laws Corp
Durham, NC 800-596-7602
Harting Graphics
Wilmington, DE 800-848-1373

Heath & Company
Roswell, GA 770-650-2724
Hiclay Studios
St Louis, MO. 314-533-8393
HMG Worldwide In-Store Marketing
New York, NY 212-736-2300
Hoarel Sign Co
Amarillo, TX. 806-373-2175
Holsman Sign Svc
Cleveland, OH 216-761-4433
Horn & Todak
Fairfax, VA .703-352-7330
Hutz Sign & Awning
Youngstown, OH. 330-743-5168
IdentaBadge
Lafayette, LA 800-325-8247
Image National Inc
Nampa, ID. .208-345-4020
Imperial Plastics Inc
Lakeville, MN 952-469-4951
Imperial Signs & Manufacturing
Rapid City, SD 605-348-2511
Industrial Sign Company
South El Monte, CA 800-596-3720
Industrial Signs
Elmwood, LA 504-736-0600
Inovar Packaging Group
Arlington, TX 800-285-2235
Insignia Systems Inc
Minneapolis, MN 800-874-4648
Interior Systems Inc
Milwaukee, WI 800-837-8373
International Patterns, Inc.
Bay Shore, NY 631-952-2000
J.V. Reed & Company
Louisville, KY 877-258-7333
Jack Stone Lighting & Electrical
Landover, MD. 301-322-3323
Janedy Sign Company
Everett, MA 617-776-5700
JBC Plastics
St Louis, MO. 877-834-5526
Jeffcoat Signs
Gainesville, FL 877-377-4248
Johnson Brothers Sign Co Inc
South Whitley, IN 800-477-7516
Joseph Struhl Co Inc
New Hyde Park, NY 800-552-0023
Jutras Signs & Flags
Manchester, NH 800-924-3524
K & I Creative Plastics & Wood
Jacksonville, FL 904-387-0438
K & M Intl Inc
Twinsburg, OH. 330-425-2550
Kessler Sign Co
Zanesville, OH 800-686-1870
King Electric Sign Co
Nampa, ID. .208-466-2000
King Sign Company
Akron, OH. .330-762-7421
Krimstock Enterprises
Pennsauken, NJ. 856-665-3676
Krusoe Sign Co
Cleveland, OH. 216-447-1177
L&L Engraving Company
Gilford, NH .888-524-3032
La Crosse Sign Co.
Eau Claire, WI 715-835-6189
Lake Shore Industries Inc
Erie, PA 800-458-0463
Lamar Advertising Co
Baton Rouge, LA 225-926-1000
Lamar Advertising Co
Pearl, MS. 800-893-2560
Lasermation Inc
Philadelphia, PA 800-523-2759
Lawrence Sign
St Paul, MN. 800-998-8901
Leathertone
Findlay, OH. 419-429-0188
License Ad Plate Co
Cleveland, OH 216-265-4200
Lion Labels Inc
South Easton, MA 800-875-5300
Little Rock Sign
Conway, AR 501-372-7403
Lonestar Banners & Flags
Fort Worth, TX 800-288-9625
Long Island Stamp Corporation
Flushing, NY 800-547-8267
LSI Industries Inc
Blue Ash, OH 513-793-3200

Lynn Sign Inc
Andover, MA 800-225-5764

M & M Display
Philadelphia, PA 800-874-7171

Macdonald Signs & Advertising
Edinburg, TX 956-787-0016

Maier Sign Systems
Saddle Brook, NJ 201-845-7555

Maltese Signs
Norcross, GA 770-368-0911

Mankuta Bros Rubber Stamp Co
Bohemia, NY 800-223-4481

Mansfield Rubber Stamp
Mansfield, OH .419-524-1442

Master Printers
Canon City, CO. 719-275-8608

Master Signs-Div Of Masterco
Dallas, TX. 214-381-6207

Mastermark
Kent, WA. 206-762-9610

Mcbride Sign Co
Madison Heights, VA 434-847-4151

Mcneill Signs Inc
Pompano Beach, FL 954-946-3474

MDI Worldwide
Farmington Hills, MI 800-228-8925

Metro Signs
N Las Vegas, NV. 702-649-9333

Milwaukee Sign Company
Grafton, WI. 262-375-5740

Mirro Products Company
High Point, NC .336-885-4166

MLS Signs Inc
Chesterfield, MI 586-948-0200

MODAGRAPHICS
Rolling Meadows, IL 847-392-3980

Modern Stamp Company
Baltimore, MD .800-727-3029

Morrow Technologies Corporation
St Petersburg, FL. 877-526-8711

Mulholland-Harper Company
Denton, MD 800-882-3052

Muskogee Rubber Stamp & Seal Company
Fort Gibson, OK 918-478-3046

Nameplate
St Paul, MN. 651-228-1522

National Sign Corporation
Seattle, WA 206-282-0700

National Sign Systems
Hilliard, OH 800-544-6726

National Stock Sign Co
Santa Cruz, CA 800-462-7726

Neal Walters Poster Corporation
Bentonville, AR 501-273-2489

Nebraska Neon Sign Co
Lincoln, NE. 402-476-6563

Nelson Custom Signs
Plymouth, MI 734-455-0500

Neon Design-a-Sign
Laguna Niguel, CA. 888-636-6327

Norgus Silk Screen Co Inc
Clifton, NJ. 973-365-0600

North American Signs
South Bend, IN 800-348-5000

Nu-Dell Manufacturing
Des Plaines, IL 847-803-4500

O.K. Marking Devices
Regina, SK 306-522-2856

Parisian Novelty Company
Homewood, IL .773-847-1212

Patrick & Co
Dallas, TX. 214-761-0900

Patrick Signs
Rockville, MD .301-770-6200

Pearson Signs Service
Hampstead, MD 410-239-3838

Perfect Plank Co
Oroville, CA 800-327-1961

Peterson Sign Co
Honolulu, HI 808-521-6785

Phoenix Sign Company
Aberdeen, WA. 360-532-1111

Pierrepont Visual Graphics Inc
Rochester, NY. 585-235-5620

Pioneer Sign Company
Lewiston, ID 208-743-1275

Plasti-Line
Knoxville, TN. .800-444-7446

Plastic Craft Products Corp
West Nyack, NY 800-627-3010

Plastic Fantastics/Buck Signs
Ashland, OR 800-482-1776

Plastic Turning Company
Leominster, MA 978-534-8326

Poblocki Sign Co
Milwaukee, WI 414-453-4010

Polyplastic Forms Inc
Farmingdale, NY 800-428-7659

Posterloid Corporation
Long Island City, NY 800-651-5000

Pratt Poster Company
Indianapolis, IN 800-645-1012

Pride Neon Inc
Sioux Falls, SD 605-336-3561

Printsource Group
Wakefield, RI .401-789-9339

Pro-Ad-Co Inc
Portland, OR 800-287-5885

Process Displays
New Berlin, WI. 800-533-1764

Qyk Syn Industries
Miami, FL 800-354-5640

R R Donnelley
Chicago, IL 800-742-4455

R T C
Rolling Meadows, IL 847-640-2400

R Wireworks Inc
Elmira, NY 800-550-4009

Radding Signs
Springfield, MA 413-736-5400

Rainbow Neon Sign Company
Houston, TX 713-923-2759

Ramsay Signs Inc
Portland, OR. 206-623-3100

Rapid Displays Inc
Chicago, IL 800-356-5775

Rayne Sign Co
Rayne, LA. 337-334-4276

Reading Plastic Fabricators
Reading, PA 610-926-3245

Regal Plastic Supply Co
Kansas City, MO. 800-444-6390

Reinhold Sign Svc Inc
Green Bay, WI. .920-494-7161

Retail Decor
Ironton, OH 800-726-3402

Rex Art Manufacturing Corp.
Lindenhurst, NY 631-884-4600

Rosson Sign Co
Macon, GA 478-788-3905

Roth Sign Systems
Petaluma, CA .800-585-7446

Roxanne Signs Inc
Gaithersburg, MD 301-428-4911

RPA Process Technologies
Marblehead, MA. 800-631-9707

Rueff Sign Co Inc
Louisville, KY .502-582-1714

Rutler Screen Printing
Easton, PA 610-829-2999

S & S Metal & Plastics Inc
Jacksonville, FL 904-730-4655

San Juan Signs Inc
Farmington, NM 505-326-5511

Scott Sign Systems
Sarasota, FL 800-237-9447

Screen Print Etc
Anaheim, CA 714-630-1100

Seiz Sign Co Inc
Hot Spgs Natl Pk, AR 501-623-3181

Selby Sign Co Inc
Pocomoke City, MD 410-742-0095

Service Neon Signs
Springfield, VA 703-354-3000

Seton Indentification Products
Branford, CT 800-571-2596

Sexton Sign
Anderson, SC .864-226-6071

Shaw & Slavsky Inc
Detroit, MI 800-521-7527

Shelby Co
Westlake, OH .800-842-1650

Sheridan Sign Company
Salisbury, MD .410-749-7441

Sign Classics
San Jose, CA 408-298-1600

Sign Expert
Pacific, MO. 800-874-9942

Sign Factory
Cerritos, CA 562-809-1443

Sign Graphics
Evansville, IN .812-476-9151

Sign Products
Sheridan, WY .800-532-4753

Sign Systems, Inc.
Warren, MI 586-758-1600

Sign Warehouse
Denison, TX 800-699-5512

SignArt Advertising
Van Buren, AR 479-474-8581

Signco Inc
Kansas City, KS 913-722-1377

Signet Graphic Products
St Louis, MO. 314-426-0200

Signmasters
Huntington Beach, CA 949-364-9128

Signs & Designs
Palmdale, CA .888-480-7446

Signs & Shapes Intl
Omaha, NE 800-806-6069

Signs O' Life
Avon, MA 800-750-1475

Southwest Neon Signs
San Antonio, TX 800-927-3221

Southwestern Porcelain Steel
Sand Springs, OK 918-245-1375

Steel Art Co
Norwood, MA. .800-322-2828

Steingart Associates Inc
South Fallsburg, NY 845-434-4321

Stello Products Inc
Spencer, IN 800-878-2246

Stoffel Seals Corp
Tallapoosa, GA 800-422-8247

Stout Sign Company
Saint Louis, MO 800-325-8530

Stricker & Co
La Plata, MD 301-934-8346

Stylmark Inc
Minneapolis, MN 800-328-2495

Suburban Sign Company
Anoka, MN 763-753-8849

Suburban Signs
College Park, MD 301-474-5051

Sun Ray Sign Group Inc
Holland, MI 616-392-2824

Super Vision International
Orlando, FL. 407-857-9900

Superior Neon Signs Inc
Oklahoma City, OK 405-528-5515

SuppliesForLess
Hampton, VA .800-235-2201

Sutherland Stamp Company
San Diego, CA 858-233-7784

Symmetry Products Group
Lincoln, RI 401-365-6272

Tec Art Industries Inc
Wixom, MI 800-886-6615

Timely Signs Inc
Elmont, NY 800-457-4467

Toledo Sign Co Inc
Toledo, OH 419-244-4444

Total Identity Group
Cambridge, ON. 877-551-5529

Triangle Sign & Svc
Halethorpe, MD 410-247-5300

Trident Plastics
Ivyland, PA 800-222-2318

Trinkle Sign & Display
Youngstown, OH. 330-747-9712

Trumbull Nameplates
New Smyrna Beach, FL 386-423-1105

Twenty/Twenty Graphics
Gaithersburg, MD 240-243-0511

Twin State Signs
Essex Junction, VT 802-872-8949

Universal Sign Company and Manufacturing Company
Lafayette, LA .337-234-1466

University-Brink
Foxboro, MA 617-926-4400

US Magnetix
Minneapolis, MN 763-540-9497

US Standard Sign
Franklin Park, IL. 800-537-4790

Vacuform Inc.
Sebring, OH 330-938-9674

Valley City Sign Co
Comstock Park, MI 616-784-5711

Varco Products
Chardon, OH .216-481-6895

Visual Marketing Assoc
Santee, CA 619-258-0393

VMC Signs
Victoria, TX 361-575-0548

Volk Corp
Farmington Hills, MI 800-521-6799

Vomela/Harbor Graphics
St Paul, MN..........................800-645-1012
VPC Gordon Sign
Denver, CO.....................303-629-6121
Walker Co
Oklahoma City, OK 800-522-3015
Walker Engineering Inc
Sun Valley, CA...................818-252-7788
Wayne Industries
Clanton, AL......................800-225-3148
Webster Packaging Corporation
Loveland, OH.....................513-683-5666
Wedlock Paper ConvertersLtd.
Mississauga, ON..................800-388-0447
Welch Stencil Company
Scarborough, ME..................800-635-3506
West Hawk Industries
Ann Arbor, MI 800-678-1286
Western Lighting Inc
Franklin Park, IL................847-451-7200
WGN Flag & Decorating Co
Chicago, IL......................773-768-8076
Winmark Stamp & Sign
Salt Lake City, UT...............800-438-0480
Winnebago Sign Company
Fond Du Lac, WI..................920-922-5930
World Division
Dallas, TX.......................800-433-9843
YESCO
Salt Lake City, UT...............800-444-3847

Changeable Letter

AAA Electrical Signs
Donna, TX........................800-825-5376
ABC Letter Art
Los Angeles, CA..................888-261-5367
ACME Sign Corp
Peabody, MA......................978-535-6600
Ad Mart Identity Group
Danville, KY.....................800-354-2102
Alex Delvecchio Enterprises
Troy, MI.........................248-619-9600
Arrow Sign & Awning Company
East Bethel, MN 800-621-9231
Audrey Signs
New York, NY 212-769-4992
Charles Mayer Studios
Akron, OH........................330-535-6121
Claridge Products & Equipment
Harrison, AR
Classic Signs Inc
Amherst, NH......................800-734-7446
Comco Signs
Charlotte, NC....................704-375-2338
Exhibitron Co
Grants Pass, OR 800-437-4571
FFR Merchandising Inc
Twinsburg, OH....................800-422-2547
Gelberg Signs
Washington, DC 800-443-5237
Hardin Signs Inc
Peoria, IL.......................309-688-4111
Heath & Company
Roswell, GA......................770-650-2724
Hiclay Studios
St Louis, MO.....................314-533-8393
Hoarel Sign Co
Amarillo, TX.....................806-373-2175
International Patterns, Inc.
Bay Shore, NY....................631-952-2000
Lamb Sign
Manassas, VA.....................703-791-7960
Lynn Sign Inc
Andover, MA......................800-225-5764
Mcbride Sign Co
Madison Heights, VA..............434-847-4151
MDI Worldwide
Farmington Hills, MI.............800-228-8925
Neon Design-a-Sign
Laguna Niguel, CA................888-636-6327
Nu-Dell Manufacturing
Des Plaines, IL..................847-803-4500
Omaha Neon Sign Co
Omaha, NE........................800-786-6366
Poblocki Sign Co
Milwaukee, WI....................414-453-4010
Roth Sign Systems
Petaluma, CA.....................800-585-7446
Selby Sign Co Inc
Pocomoke City, MD 410-742-0095

Seton Indentification Products
Branford, CT.....................800-571-2596
Signets/Menu-Quik
Mentor, OH.......................800-775-6368
Signs O' Life
Avon, MA.........................800-750-1475
Super Vision International
Orlando, FL......................407-857-9900
Tablet & Ticket Co
West Chicago, IL.................800-438-4959
Toledo Sign Co Inc
Toledo, OH.......................419-244-4444
Total Identity Group
Cambridge, ON....................877-551-5529
Vomela/Harbor Graphics
St Paul, MN......................800-645-1012

Electric

A Allred Marketing
Birmingham, AL...................205-251-3700
AAA Electrical Signs
Donna, TX........................800-825-5376
ACME Sign Corp
Peabody, MA......................978-535-6600
Ad Mart Identity Group
Danville, KY.....................800-354-2102
Adam Electric Signs
Massillon, OH....................888-886-9911
Affiliated Resource Inc
Chicago, IL......................800-366-9336
Allen Industries Inc
Greensboro, NC...................800-967-2553
Allen Signs Co
Knoxville, TN....................800-844-3524
Alphabet Signs
Gap, PA..........................800-582-6366
American Led-Gible
Columbus, OH.....................614-851-1100
Attracta Sign
Rogers, MN.......................763-428-6377
B S C Signs
Broomfield, CO...................866-223-0101
Barlo Signs
Hudson, NH.......................800-227-5674
Big Beam Emergency Systems Inc
Crystal Lake, IL.................815-459-6100
Canton Sign Co
Canton, OH.......................330-456-7151
Cascade Signs & Neon
Salem, OR........................503-378-0012
Chapman Sign
Warren, MI.......................586-758-1600
City Neon Sign Company
Spokane, WA......................509-483-5171
City Sign Svc Inc
Dallas, TX.......................214-826-4475
City Signs LLC
Jackson, TN......................877-248-9744
Classic Signs Inc
Amherst, NH......................800-734-7446
Claude Neon Signs
Baltimore, MD....................410-685-7575
Clearr Corporation
Minneapolis, MN 800-548-3269
Comco Signs
Charlotte, NC 704-375-2338
Comet Signs
San Antonio, TX..................210-341-7244
Cook Neon Signs
Tullahoma, TN 800-488-0944
Corsair Display Systems
Canandalgua, NY..................800-347-5245
County Neon Sign Corporation
Plainview, NY....................516-349-9550
Cuerden Sign Co
Conway, AR.......................501-375-7705
Cummings
Nashville, TN....................615-673-8999
Custom ID Systems
Venice, FL.......................800-242-8430
Darlington Sign Awning & Neon
Warwick, RI......................401-734-5800
Day Nite Neon Signs
Dartmouth, NS....................902-469-7095
Delta Signs
Haltom City, TX..................866-643-3582
Den Ray Sign Company
Jackson, TN......................800-530-7291
Dixie Neon Company
Tampa, FL........................813-248-2531

Dowling Signs Inc
Fredericksburg, VA...............800-572-2100
Doyle Signs Inc
Addison, IL......................630-543-9490
Dualite Sales & Svc Inc
Williamsburg, OH.................513-724-7100
Dwinell's Central Neon
Yakima, WA.......................800-932-8832
Electric City Signs & Neon Inc.
Anderson, SC.....................800-270-5851
Electro-Lite Signs
Rancho Cucamonga, CA.............909-945-3555
Elro Signs
Gardena, CA......................800-927-4555
Encore Image Inc
Ontario, CA......................800-791-1187
Engraving Services Co.
Woodville South, SA
Esco Manufacturing Inc
Watertown, SD....................800-843-3726
Everbrite LLC
Greenfield, WI...................800-558-3888
Federal Sign
Providence, RI...................401-421-9643
Ferrer Corporation
San Juan, PR.....................787-761-5151
Fiber Does
San Jose, CA.....................408-453-5533
First Choice Sign & Lighting
Escondido, CA....................800-659-0629
Frank Torrone & Sons
Staten Island, NY................718-273-7600
Frazier Signs
Decatur, IL......................217-429-2349
Freeman Electric Co Inc
Panama City, FL..................850-785-7448
Fresno Neon Sign Co Inc
Fresno, CA 559-292-2944
Frohling Sign Co
Nanuet, NY.......................845-623-2258
Gainesville Neon & Signs
Gainesville, FL..................800-852-1407
Gelberg Signs
Washington, DC...................800-443-5237
General Neon Sign Co
San Antonio, TX..................210-227-1203
General Sign Co
Sheffield, AL....................256-383-3176
Gilbert Insect Light Traps
Jonesboro, AR....................800-643-0400
Grande Ronde Sign Company
La Grande, OR 541-963-5841
Gulf Coast Sign Company
Pensacola, FL 800-768-3549
Haden Signs of Texas
Lubbock, TX......................806-744-4404
Hammar & Sons
Pelham, NH.......................800-527-7446
Harlan Laws Corp
Durham, NC.......................800-596-7602
Heath & Company
Roswell, GA......................770-650-2724
Heath Signs
Reno, NV.........................775-359-9007
Hiclay Studios
St Louis, MO.....................314-533-8393
Hoarel Sign Co
Amarillo, TX.....................806-373-2175
Holsman Sign Svc
Cleveland, OH....................216-761-4433
Houser Neon Sign Company
Houston, TX......................713-691-5765
Image National Inc
Nampa, ID........................208-345-4020
Industrial Neon Sign Corp
Houston, TX......................713-748-6600
Industrial Sign Company
South El Monte, CA...............800-596-3720
Industrial Signs
Elmwood, LA......................504-736-0600
International Patterns, Inc.
Bay Shore, NY 631-952-2000
Jack Stone Lighting & Electrical
Landover, MD.....................301-322-3323
Johnson Brothers Sign Co Inc
South Whitley, IN................800-477-7516
Jutras Signs & Flags
Manchester, NH 800-924-3524
K & M Intl Inc
Twinsburg, OH....................330-425-2550
King Electric Sign Co
Nampa, ID........................208-466-2000

La Crosse Sign Co.
  Eau Claire, WI 715-835-6189
Lafayette Sign Company
  Little Falls, NJ. 800-343-5366
Lake City Signs
  Boulder City, NV 702-293-5805
Leroy Signs, Inc.
  Brooklyn Park, MN. 763-535-0080
Little Rock Sign
  Conway, AR 501-372-7403
Master Signs-Div Of Masterco
  Dallas, TX. 214-381-6207
Mcbride Sign Co
  Madison Heights, VA 434-847-4151
Mcneill Signs Inc
  Pompano Beach, FL 954-946-3474
McQueen Sign & Lighting
  Canton, OH 330-452-5769
MDI Worldwide
  Farmington Hills, MI 800-228-8925
Milwaukee Sign Company
  Grafton, WI. 262-375-5740
Mirro Products Company
  High Point, NC 336-885-4166
MLS Signs Inc
  Chesterfield, MI 586-948-0200
Mt Vernon Neon Inc
  Mt Vernon, IL 618-242-0645
Mulholland-Harper Company
  Denton, MD 800-882-3052
MultiMedia Electronic Displays
  Rancho Cordova, CA 800-888-3007
National Menuboard
  Auburn, WA 800-800-5237
National Sign Corporation
  Seattle, WA 206-282-0700
National Sign Systems
  Hilliard, OH 800-544-6726
Nelson Custom Signs
  Plymouth, MI 734-455-0500
Neon Design-a-Sign
  Laguna Niguel, CA. 888-636-6327
North American Signs
  South Bend, IN 800-348-5000
Nu-Dell Manufacturing
  Des Plaines, IL 847-803-4500
Oklahoma Neon
  Tulsa, OK 888-707-6366
Omaha Neon Sign Co
  Omaha, NE 800-786-6366
Pearson Signs Service
  Hampstead, MD 410-239-3838
Phoenix Sign Company
  Aberdeen, WA 360-532-1111
Plastic Art Signs
  Pensacola, FL 866-662-7060
Poblocki Sign Co
  Milwaukee, WI 414-453-4010
Pride Neon Inc
  Sioux Falls, SD 605-336-3561
Radding Signs
  Springfield, MA 413-736-5400
Rainbow Neon Sign Company
  Houston, TX 713-923-2759
Ramsay Signs Inc
  Portland, OR 206-623-3100
Rosson Sign Co
  Macon, GA 478-788-3905
Roth Sign Systems
  Petaluma, CA 800-585-7446
Roxanne Signs Inc
  Gaithersburg, MD. 301-428-4911
Rueff Sign Co Inc
  Louisville, KY 502-582-1714
Sasser Signs
  Danville, VA 800-752-6091
Selby Sign Co Inc
  Pocomoke City, MD 410-742-0095
Service Neon Signs
  Springfield, VA 703-354-3000
Sexton Sign
  Anderson, SC 864-226-6071
Sheridan Sign Company
  Salisbury, MD 410-749-7441
Sign Art
  Charlotte, NC 800-929-3521
SignArt Advertising
  Van Buren, AR 479-474-8581
Signs & Designs
  Palmdale, CA 888-480-7446
Signs O' Life
  Avon, MA 800-750-1475

Southwest Neon Signs
  San Antonio, TX. 800-927-3221
Spann Sign Company
  Kenosha, WI. 262-658-1288
Steel Art Signs
  Markham, ON 800-771-6971
Stylmark Inc
  Minneapolis, MN 800-328-2495
Super Vision International
  Orlando, FL. 407-857-9900
Superior Neon Signs Inc
  Oklahoma City, OK 405-528-5515
Superior Products Company
  Saint Paul, MN 800-328-9800
Tec Art Industries Inc
  Wixom, MI 800-886-6615
Texas Neon Advertising Inc
  San Antonio, TX. 210-734-6694
Thomson-Leeds Company
  New York, NY 800-535-9361
Toledo Sign Co Inc
  Toledo, OH 419-244-4444
Total Identity Group
  Cambridge, ON. 877-551-5529
Triple A Neon Company
  Valley Village, CA 323-877-5381
Twin State Signs
  Essex Junction, VT 802-872-8949
United Sign Corp
  Kansas City, MO. 816-923-9512
Universal Sign Company and Manufacturing Company
  Lafayette, LA 337-234-1466
University-Brink
  Foxboro, MA 617-926-4400
Valley City Sign Co
  Comstock Park, MI 616-784-5711
Varco Products
  Chardon, OH. 216-481-6895
Visual Marketing Assoc
  Santee, CA 619-258-0393
VMC Signs
  Victoria, TX 361-575-0548
VPC Gordon Sign
  Denver, CO 303-629-6121
Western Lighting Inc
  Franklin Park, IL. 847-451-7200
Weston Emergency Light Co
  Weston, MA 800-649-3756
White Way Sign & Maintenance
  Mt Prospect, IL 800-621-4122
Wilhite Sign Company
  Joplin, MO 417-623-1411
Winnebago Sign Company
  Fond Du Lac, WI 920-922-5930
YESCO
  Salt Lake City, UT 800-444-3847

Interchangeable

ACME Sign Corp
  Peabody, MA. 978-535-6600
Ad Mart Identity Group
  Danville, KY. 800-354-2102
Allen Industries Inc
  Greensboro, NC 800-967-2553
American Menu Displays
  Long Island City, NY 877-544-8046
Audrey Signs
  New York, NY 212-769-4992
Claridge Products & Equipment
  Harrison, AR
Comco Signs
  Charlotte, NC 704-375-2338
Diskey Architectural Signs
  Fort Wayne, IN 260-424-0233
Display Concepts
  Trenton, ME 800-446-0033
Everbrite LLC
  Greenfield, WI 800-558-3888
Exhibitron Co
  Grants Pass, OR 800-437-4571
Forbes Industries
  Ontario, CA 909-923-4549
Frost Manufacturing Corp
  Worcester, MA 800-462-0216
Gelberg Signs
  Washington, DC 800-443-5237
Heath & Company
  Roswell, GA 770-650-2724
Hoarel Sign Co
  Amarillo, TX. 806-373-2175

Impulse Signs
  Toronto, ON 866-636-8273
Lynn Sign Inc
  Andover, MA 800-225-5764
Maier Sign Systems
  Saddle Brook, NJ 201-845-7555
Mainstreet Menu Systems
  Brookfield, WI 800-782-6222
Mcbride Sign Co
  Madison Heights, VA 434-847-4151
McQueen Sign & Lighting
  Canton, OH. 330-452-5769
MDI Worldwide
  Farmington Hills, MI 800-228-8925
Menu Men
  Palm Harbor, FL 727-934-7191
Norgus Silk Screen Co Inc
  Clifton, NJ. 973-365-0600
Plasti-Line
  Knoxville, TN 800-444-7446
Roth Sign Systems
  Petaluma, CA 800-585-7446
Screen Print Etc
  Anaheim, CA 714-630-1100
Tablet & Ticket Co
  West Chicago, IL 800-438-4959
Toledo Sign Co Inc
  Toledo, OH 419-244-4444
Total Identity Group
  Cambridge, ON 877-551-5529
US Magnetix
  Minneapolis, MN 763-540-9497
Vomela/Harbor Graphics
  St Paul, MN. 800-645-1012
VPC Gordon Sign
  Denver, CO 303-629-6121
Wayne Industries
  Clanton, AL 800-225-3148
Your Place Menu Systems
  Carson City, NV 800-321-8105

Luminous Tube

A Allred Marketing
  Birmingham, AL. 205-251-3700
AAA Electrical Signs
  Donna, TX. 800-825-5376
ACME Sign Corp
  Peabody, MA. 978-535-6600
Adam Electric Signs
  Massillon, OH. 888-886-9911
Alphabet Signs
  Gap, PA. 800-582-6366
Arrow Sign & Awning Company
  East Bethel, MN 800-621-9231
Audrey Signs
  New York, NY 212-769-4992
B S C Signs
  Broomfield, CO 866-223-0101
B&B Neon Sign Company
  Austin, TX. 800-791-6366
Capital City Signs
  Monona, WI 608-222-1881
Cascade Signs & Neon
  Salem, OR 503-378-0012
Century Sign Company
  Fargo, ND 701-235-5323
Cheshire Signs
  Keene, NH. 603-352-5985
City Neon Sign Company
  Spokane, WA. 509-483-5171
City Signs LLC
  Jackson, TN 877-248-9744
Claude Neon Signs
  Baltimore, MD 410-685-7575
Cobb Sign Co Inc
  Burlington, NC 336-227-0181
Comco Signs
  Charlotte, NC 704-375-2338
Cook Neon Signs
  Tullahoma, TN 800-488-0944
County Neon Sign Corporation
  Plainview, NY. 516-349-9550
Custom ID Systems
  Venice, FL. 800-242-8430
D&D Sign Company
  Wichita Falls, TX 940-692-4643
Darlington Sign Awning & Neon
  Warwick, RI 401-734-5800
Day Nite Neon Signs
  Dartmouth, NS 902-469-7095

Den Ray Sign Company
Jackson, TN 800-530-7291
Display Concepts
Trenton, ME 800-446-0033
Dowling Signs Inc
Fredericksburg, VA..............800-572-2100
Dualite Sales & Svc Inc
Williamsburg, OH................513-724-7100
Dwinell's Central Neon
Yakima, WA 800-932-8832
Electric City Signs & Neon Inc.
Anderson, SC 800-270-5851
Elro Signs
Gardena, CA 800-927-4555
Encore Image Inc
Ontario, CA.....................800-791-1187
Esco Manufacturing Inc
Watertown, SD 800-843-3726
Everbrite LLC
Greenfield, WI 800-558-3888
Federal Sign
Providence, RI 401-421-9643
Ferrer Corporation
San Juan, PR 787-761-5151
Frazier Signs
Decatur, IL 217-429-2349
Freeman Electric Co Inc
Panama City, FL 850-785-7448
Fresno Neon Sign Co Inc
Fresno, CA 559-292-2944
Frohling Sign Co
Nanuet, NY 845-623-2258
Gainesville Neon & Signs
Gainesville, FL 800-852-1407
General Neon Sign Co
San Antonio, TX 210-227-1203
Grande Ronde Sign Company
La Grande, OR 541-963-5841
Gulf Coast Sign Company
Pensacola, FL 800-768-3549
Haden Signs of Texas
Lubbock, TX.....................806-744-4404
Hammar & Sons
Pelham, NH 800-527-7446
Hardin Signs Inc
Peoria, IL 309-688-4111
Harlan Laws Corp
Durham, NC 800-596-7602
Heath & Company
Roswell, GA 770-650-2724
Heath Signs
Reno, NV 775-359-9007
Hedges Neon Sales
Salina, KS 785-827-9341
Hoarel Sign Co
Amarillo, TX 806-373-2175
Holsman Sign Svc
Cleveland, OH 216-761-4433
Houser Neon Sign Company
Houston, TX.....................713-691-5765
Imperial Signs & Manufacturing
Rapid City, SD 605-348-2511
Industrial Signs
Elmwood, LA 504-736-0600
Jeffcoat Signs
Gainesville, FL 877-377-4248
Jenkins Sign Co
Youngstown, OH..................330-799-3205
Jet Lite Products
Highland, IL 618-654-2217
Jim Did It Sign Company
Allston, MA 617-782-2410
Johnson Brothers Sign Co Inc
South Whitley, IN...............800-477-7516
Jutras Signs & Flags
Manchester, NH 800-924-3524
K & M Intl Inc
Twinsburg, OH...................330-425-2550
King Electric Sign Co
Nampa, ID.......................208-466-2000
La Crosse Sign Co.
Eau Claire, WI 715-835-6189
Lafayette Sign Company
Little Falls, NJ................800-343-5366
Leroy Signs, Inc.
Brooklyn Park, MN...............763-535-0080
Maier Sign Systems
Saddle Brook, NJ 201-845-7555
Master Signs-Div Of Masterco
Dallas, TX......................214-381-6207
Mcbride Sign Co
Madison Heights, VA.............434-847-4151

Mcneill Signs Inc
Pompano Beach, FL 954-946-3474
McQueen Sign & Lighting
Canton, OH......................330-452-5769
MDI Worldwide
Farmington Hills, MI............800-228-8925
Mt Vernon Neon Inc
Mt Vernon, IL 618-242-0645
National Sign Corporation
Seattle, WA 206-282-0700
National Sign Systems
Hilliard, OH 800-544-6726
Nebraska Neon Sign Co
Lincoln, NE 402-476-6563
Neokraft Signs Inc
Lewiston, ME 800-339-2258
Neonetics Inc
Hampstead, MD 410-374-8057
North American Signs
South Bend, IN 800-348-5000
Oklahoma Neon
Tulsa, OK 888-707-6366
Omaha Neon Sign Co
Omaha, NE 800-786-6366
Pacific Sign Construction
Poway, CA 858-486-8006
Pearson Signs Service
Hampstead, MD 410-239-3838
Peskin Sign Co
Youngstown, OH..................330-783-2470
Phoenix Sign Company
Aberdeen, WA 360-532-1111
Plastic Art Signs
Pensacola, FL 866-662-7060
Poblocki Sign Co
Milwaukee, WI 414-453-4010
Porter Bowers Signs
Des Moines, IA 515-253-9622
Pride Neon Inc
Sioux Falls, SD 605-336-3561
Qyk Syn Industries
Miami, FL 800-354-5640
R R Donnelley
Chicago, IL 800-742-4455
Rainbow Neon Sign Company
Houston, TX.....................713-923-2759
Rainbow Sign Co
Salt Lake City, UT 801-466-7856
Ramsay Signs Inc
Portland, OR 206-623-3100
Rosson Sign Co
Macon, GA 478-788-3905
Roth Sign Systems
Petaluma, CA 800-585-7446
Roxanne Signs Inc
Gaithersburg, MD 301-428-4911
Ruggles Sign Company
Versailles, KY 859-879-1199
Safety Light Corporation
Bloomsburg, PA 570-784-4344
Sasser Signs
Danville, VA 800-752-6091
Selby Sign Co Inc
Pocomoke City, MD 410-742-0095
Service Neon Signs
Springfield, VA 703-354-3000
Sheridan Sign Company
Salisbury, MD...................410-749-7441
Sign Products
Sheridan, WY 800-532-4753
SignArt Advertising
Van Buren, AR 479-474-8581
Signs & Designs
Palmdale, CA 888-480-7446
Signs O' Life
Avon, MA 800-750-1475
Spann Sign Company
Kenosha, WI 262-658-1288
Stylmark Inc
Minneapolis, MN 800-328-2495
Super Vision International
Orlando, FL.....................407-857-9900
SuppliesForLess
Hampton, VA 800-235-2201
Tablet & Ticket Co
West Chicago, IL 800-438-4959
Tec Art Industries Inc
Wixom, MI 800-886-6615
Texas Neon Advertising Inc
San Antonio, TX 210-734-6694
Toledo Sign Co Inc
Toledo, OH 419-244-4444

Total Identity Group
Cambridge, ON...................877-551-5529
Triangle Sign & Svc
Halethorpe, MD 410-247-5300
Twin State Signs
Essex Junction, VT 802-872-8949
United Sign Corp
Kansas City, MO.................816-923-9512
Universal Sign Company and Manufacturing Company
Lafayette, LA 337-234-1466
University-Brink
Foxboro, MA 617-926-4400
VMC Signs
Victoria, TX 361-575-0548
Western Lighting Inc
Franklin Park, IL 847-451-7200
Wilhite Sign Company
Joplin, MO 417-623-1411
Winnebago Sign Company
Fond Du Lac, WI 920-922-5930
Your Place Menu Systems
Carson City, NV 800-321-8105

Plastic

A Allred Marketing
Birmingham, AL 205-251-3700
ABC Letter Art
Los Angeles, CA 888-261-5367
Ace Stamp & Engraving
Lakewood, WA 253-582-3322
Ad Mart Identity Group
Danville, KY 800-354-2102
Adam Electric Signs
Massillon, OH 888-886-9911
Andrew W Nissly Inc
Lancaster, PA 717-393-3841
Audrey Signs
New York, NY 212-769-4992
B&B Neon Sign Company
Austin, TX......................800-791-6366
Baltimore Sign Company
Arnold, MD 410-276-1500
Berlekamp Plastics Inc
Fremont, OH 419-334-4481
Berryhill Signs
Memphis, TN 901-324-1730
Canton Sign Co
Canton, OH 330-456-7151
Capital City Signs
Monona, WI 608-222-1881
Century Sign Company
Fargo, ND 701-235-5323
Chain Store Graphics
Decatur, IL 800-443-7446
Chatelain Plastics
Findlay, OH.....................866-421-4323
Cheshire Signs
Keene, NH 603-352-5985
Chroma Tone
Saint Clair, PA.................800-878-1552
City Neon Sign Company
Spokane, WA.....................509-483-5171
City Signs LLC
Jackson, TN 877-248-9744
City Stamp & Seal Co
Austin, TX......................800-950-6074
Clearr Corporation
Minneapolis, MN 800-548-3269
Cobb Sign Co Inc
Burlington, NC 336-227-0181
Comco Signs
Charlotte, NC 704-375-2338
Continental Commercial Products
Bridgeton, MO 800-325-1051
Creative Signage System,
College Park, MD 800-220-7446
Custom ID Systems
Venice, FL 800-242-8430
Custom Plastics Inc
Decatur, GA 404-373-1691
Custom Rubber Stamp Co
Crosby, MN......................888-606-4579
Den Ray Sign Company
Jackson, TN 800-530-7291
Dimension Graphics Inc
Grand Rapids, MI 855-476-1281
Dinosaur Plastics
Houston, TX.....................713-923-2278
Diskey Architectural Signs
Fort Wayne, IN..................260-424-0233

Dixie Neon Company
Tampa, FL 813-248-2531
Dowling Signs Inc
Fredericksburg, VA 800-572-2100
Dwinell's Central Neon
Yakima, WA 800-932-8832
Eaton Quade Plastics & Sign Co
Oklahoma City, OK 405-236-4475
Ed Smith's Stencil Works LTD
New Orleans, LA 504-525-2128
Electric City Signs & Neon Inc.
Anderson, SC 800-270-5851
Elro Signs
Gardena, CA 800-927-4555
Emco Industrial Plastics
Cedar Grove, NJ 800-292-9906
Emedco
Williamsville, NY 877-765-8386
Engraving Services Co.
Woodville South, SA
Engraving Specialists
Royal Oak, MI 248-542-2244
Everett Rubber Stamp
Everett, WA 425-258-6747
Exhibitron Co
Grants Pass, OR 800-437-4571
Federal Heath Sign Co LLC
Oceanside, CA 800-527-9495
Ferrer Corporation
San Juan, PR 787-761-5151
Five-M Plastics Company
Allentown, PA 610-628-4291
Forrest Engraving Company
New Rochelle, NY 914-632-9892
FORT Hill Sign Products Inc
Hopedale, MA 781-321-4320
France Personalized Signs
Cleveland, OH 216-241-2198
Franklin Rubber Stamp Co
Wilmington, DE 302-654-8841
Frazier Signs
Decatur, IL 217-429-2349
Freeman Electric Co Inc
Panama City, FL 850-785-7448
Fresno Neon Sign Co Inc
Fresno, CA 559-292-2944
Frohling Sign Co
Nanuet, NY 845-623-2258
Gelberg Signs
Washington, DC 800-443-5237
General Neon Sign Co
San Antonio, TX 210-227-1203
Grande Ronde Sign Company
La Grande, OR 541-963-5841
Gulf Coast Sign Company
Pensacola, FL 800-768-3549
Hardin Signs Inc
Peoria, IL 309-688-4111
Heath & Company
Roswell, GA 770-650-2724
HMG Worldwide In-Store Marketing
New York, NY 212-736-2300
Hoarel Sign Co
Amarillo, TX 806-373-2175
Holsman Sign Svc
Cleveland, OH 216-761-4433
Houser Neon Sign Company
Houston, TX 713-691-5765
Houston Stamp & Stencil Company
Houston, TX 713-869-4337
Ideal Office Supply & Rubber Stamp Company
Kingsport, TN 423-246-7371
Impact Awards & Promotions
Avon Park, FL 888-203-4225
Imperial Plastics Inc
Lakeville, MN 952-469-4951
Imperial Signs & Manufacturing
Rapid City, SD 605-348-2511
Industrial Neon Sign Corp
Houston, TX 713-748-6600
Jeffcoat Signs
Gainesville, FL 877-377-4248
Jenkins Sign Co
Youngstown, OH 330-799-3205
Jim Did It Sign Company
Allston, MA 617-782-2410
Johnson Brothers Sign Co Inc
South Whitley, IN 800-477-7516
Joseph Struhl Co Inc
New Hyde Park, NY 800-552-0023
Just Plastics Inc
New York, NY 212-569-8500

K & I Creative Plastics & Wood
Jacksonville, FL 904-387-0438
King Electric Sign Co
Nampa, ID 208-466-2000
King Products
Mississauga, ON 866-454-6757
King Sign Company
Akron, OH 330-762-7421
Kitchener Plastics
Kitchener, ON 800-429-5633
Krusoe Sign Co
Cleveland, OH 216-447-1177
L&L Engraving Company
Gilford, NH 888-524-3032
La Crosse Sign Co.
Eau Claire, WI 715-835-6189
Lafayette Sign Company
Little Falls, NJ 800-343-5366
Lamb Sign
Manassas, VA 703-791-7960
Leathertone
Findlay, OH 419-429-0188
Legacy Plastics
Henderson, KY 270-827-1318
Legible Signs
Loves Park, IL 800-435-4177
Leroy Signs, Inc.
Brooklyn Park, MN 763-535-0080
License Ad Plate Co
Cleveland, OH 216-265-4200
Little Rock Sign
Conway, AR 501-372-7403
Lynn Sign Inc
Andover, MA 800-225-5764
Maier Sign Systems
Saddle Brook, NJ 201-845-7555
Mansfield Rubber Stamp
Mansfield, OH 419-524-1442
Master Signs-Div Of Masterco
Dallas, TX 214-381-6207
Mcbride Sign Co
Madison Heights, VA 434-847-4151
Mcneill Signs Inc
Pompano Beach, FL 954-946-3474
McQueen Sign & Lighting
Canton, OH 330-452-5769
MDI Worldwide
Farmington Hills, MI 800-228-8925
Mirro Products Company
High Point, NC 336-885-4166
Mulholland Co
Fort Worth, TX 817-624-1153
Mulholland-Harper Company
Denton, MD 800-882-3052
National Marker Co Inc
North Smithfield, RI 800-453-2727
National Marking Products Inc
Henrico, VA 800-482-1553
National Sign Corporation
Seattle, WA 206-282-0700
National Stock Sign Co
Santa Cruz, CA 800-462-7726
Neokraft Signs Inc
Lewiston, ME 800-339-2258
Norgus Silk Screen Co Inc
Clifton, NJ 973-365-0600
Oklahoma Neon
Tulsa, OK 888-707-6366
Omaha Neon Sign Co
Omaha, NE 800-786-6366
P M Plastics
Pewaukee, WI 262-691-1700
Parisian Novelty Company
Homewood, IL 773-847-1212
Pearson Signs Service
Hampstead, MD 410-239-3838
Peskin Sign Co
Youngstown, OH 330-783-2470
Phoenix Sign Company
Aberdeen, WA 360-532-1111
Plastech Corp
Atlanta, GA 404-355-9682
Plasti-Line
Knoxville, TN 800-444-7446
Plastic Art Signs
Pensacola, FL 866-662-7060
Plastic Craft Products Corp
West Nyack, NY 800-627-3010
Plastic Turning Company
Leominster, MA 978-534-8326
Plastimatic Arts Corporation
Mishawaka, IN 800-442-3593

Printsource Group
Wakefield, RI 401-789-9339
Qyk Syn Industries
Miami, FL 800-354-5640
R R Donnelley
Chicago, IL 800-742-4455
Rainbow Neon Sign Company
Houston, TX 713-923-2759
Rayne Sign Co
Rayne, LA 337-334-4276
Regal Plastic Supply Co
Kansas City, MO 800-444-6390
Reidler Decal Corporation
Saint Clair, PA 800-628-7770
Reinhold Sign Svc Inc
Green Bay, WI 920-494-7161
Richardson's Stamp Works
Houston, TX 713-973-0314
Rosson Sign Co
Macon, GA 478-788-3905
Roth Sign Systems
Petaluma, CA 800-585-7446
Rueff Sign Co Inc
Louisville, KY 502-582-1714
Ruggles Sign Company
Versailles, KY 859-879-1199
S & S Metal & Plastics Inc
Jacksonville, FL 904-730-4655
Scott Sign Systems
Sarasota, FL 800-237-9447
Service Neon Signs
Springfield, VA 703-354-3000
Seton Indentification Products
Branford, CT 800-571-2596
Sign Graphics
Evansville, IN 812-476-9151
Sign Systems, Inc.
Warren, MI 586-758-1600
SignArt Advertising
Van Buren, AR 479-474-8581
Signet Graphic Products
St Louis, MO 314-426-0200
Signs & Designs
Palmdale, CA 888-480-7446
Spann Sign Company
Kenosha, WI 262-658-1288
Stoffel Seals Corp
Tallapoosa, GA 800-422-8247
Suburban Sign Company
Anoka, MN 763-753-8849
Suburban Signs
College Park, MD 301-474-5051
Superior Neon Signs Inc
Oklahoma City, OK 405-528-5515
Sutherland Stamp Company
San Diego, CA 858-233-7784
Tablet & Ticket Co
West Chicago, IL 800-438-4959
Three P
Salt Lake City, UT 801-486-7407
Toledo Sign Co Inc
Toledo, OH 419-244-4444
Total Identity Group
Cambridge, ON 877-551-5529
Triangle Sign & Svc
Halethorpe, MD 410-247-5300
Trident Plastics
Ivyland, PA 800-222-2318
Tulsa Plastics Co
Tulsa, OK 888-273-5303
United Sign Corp
Kansas City, MO 816-923-9512
Universal Sign Company and Manufacturing Company
Lafayette, LA 337-234-1466
University-Brink
Foxboro, MA 617-926-4400
Valley City Sign Co
Comstock Park, MI 616-784-5711
Volk Corp
Farmington Hills, MI 800-521-6799
Vomela/Harbor Graphics
St Paul, MN 800-645-1012
Wilhite Sign Company
Joplin, MO 417-623-1411
Winnebago Sign Company
Fond Du Lac, WI 920-922-5930
Wolens Company
Dallas, TX 214-634-0800

Point of Purchase

A Allred Marketing
Birmingham, AL.....................205-251-3700
ACME Sign Corp
Peabody, MA......................978-535-6600
Arlington Display Industries
Detroit, MI.......................313-837-1212
B&B Neon Sign Company
Austin, TX.......................800-791-6366
Barlo Signs
Hudson, NH......................800-227-5674
Blanc Industries
Dover, NJ.......................888-332-5262
Carlton Industries
La Grange, TX....................800-231-5988
Chicago Show Inc
Buffalo Grove, IL.................847-955-0200
City Signs LLC
Jackson, TN......................877-248-9744
Clearr Corporation
Minneapolis, MN..................800-548-3269
Comco Signs
Charlotte, NC....................704-375-2338
Curzon Promotional Graphics
Omaha, NE.......................800-769-7446
Daytech Limited
Toronto, ON......................877-329-1907
Dimension Graphics Inc
Grand Rapids, MI.................855-476-1281
Dunn Woodworks
Shrewsbury, PA...................877-835-8592
Emco Industrial Plastics
Cedar Grove, NJ..................800-292-9906
Empire Screen Printing Inc
Onalaska, WI.....................608-783-3301
Federal Stamp & Seal Manufacturing Company
Atlanta, GA......................800-333-7726
FFR Merchandising Inc
Twinsburg, OH....................800-422-2547
Florida Plastics Intl
Evergreen Park, IL................800-499-0400
FMI Display
Elkins Park, PA...................215-663-1998
Futura 2000 Corporation
Miami, FL.......................305-256-5877
Gelberg Signs
Washington, DC...................800-443-5237
Greif Inc
Delaware, OH.....................800-476-1635
Hammar & Sons
Pelham, NH.......................800-527-7446
Harting Graphics
Wilmington, DE...................800-848-1373
Heath & Company
Roswell, GA......................770-650-2724
Hoarel Sign Co
Amarillo, TX.....................806-373-2175
Impulse Signs
Toronto, ON......................866-636-8273
Insignia Systems Inc
Minneapolis, MN..................800-874-4648
JBC Plastics
St Louis, MO.....................877-834-5526
Mcbride Sign Co
Madison Heights, VA..............434-847-4151
MDI Worldwide
Farmington Hills, MI..............800-228-8925
National Sign Systems
Hilliard, OH.....................800-544-6726
Neal Walters Poster Corporation
Bentonville, AR...................501-273-2489
Norgus Silk Screen Co Inc
Clifton, NJ......................973-365-0600
Pilgrim Plastics
Brockton, MA.....................800-343-7810
Plasti-Line
Knoxville, TN....................800-444-7446
Pratt Poster Company
Indianapolis, IN..................800-645-1012
Prestige Plastics Corporation
Delta, BC.......................604-930-2931
Rex Art Manufacturing Corp.
Lindenhurst, NY..................631-884-4600
Royal Display Corporation
Middletown, CT...................800-569-1295
RPA Process Technologies
Marblehead, MA...................800-631-9707
Shelby Co
Westlake, OH.....................800-842-1650
Stoffel Seals Corp
Tallapoosa, GA...................800-422-8247

Toledo Sign Co Inc
Toledo, OH.......................419-244-4444
Total Identity Group
Cambridge, ON....................877-551-5529
Trident Plastics
Ivyland, PA......................800-222-2318
Twin State Signs
Essex Junction, VT................802-872-8949
US Magnetix
Minneapolis, MN..................763-540-9497
Vomela/Harbor Graphics
St Paul, MN......................800-645-1012
Wayne Industries
Clanton, AL......................800-225-3148
Welch Stencil Company
Scarborough, ME..................800-635-3506
Wichita Stamp & Seal Inc
Wichita, KS......................316-263-4223
Willson Industries
Marmora, NJ......................800-894-4169

Sorters

Check, Bill & Voucher

Automated Business Products
Hackensack, NJ...................800-334-1440
Bell & Howell Company
Lincolnwood, IL..................800-647-2290
C R Mfg
Waverly, NE......................877-789-5844
Savasort Inc
Riviera Beach, FL.................800-255-8744
Scan Coin
Ashburn, VA......................800-336-3311
Sortie/Kohlhaas
Monee, IL.......................708-534-3940

Straws

Drinking

C R Mfg
Waverly, NE......................877-789-5844
Cell-O-Core Company
Sharon Center, OH................800-239-4370
Fun-Time International
Philadelphia, PA..................800-776-4386
Goldmax Industries
City Of Industry, CA..............626-964-8820
Jet Plastica Industries
Hatfield, PA
Johnstown Manufacturing
Columbus, OH.....................614-236-8853
K & L Intl
Ontario, CA......................888-598-5588
OWD
Tupper Lake, NY..................800-836-1693
Penley Corporation
West Paris, ME...................800-368-6449
RubaTex Polymer
Middlefield, OH..................440-632-1691
Semco Plastic Co
St Louis, MO.....................314-487-4557
Spinzer
Glen Ellyn, IL...................630-469-7184
Spir-It/Zoo Piks
Andover, MA......................800-343-0996
Spirit Foodservice, Inc.
Andover, MA......................800-343-0996
SQP
Schenectady, NY..................800-724-1129
Superior Products Company
Saint Paul, MN...................800-328-9800
Trevor Industries
Eden, NY........................716-992-4775
Waddington North America
Chelmsford, MA...................888-962-2877

Table Cloths

A1 Tablecloth Co
South Hackensack, NJ.............800-727-8987
Abond Plastic Corporation
Lachine, QC......................800-886-7947
Adcapitol
Monroe, NC.......................800-868-7111
AEP Industries Inc
Mankato, MN......................800-999-2374
Americo
West Memphis, AR.................800-626-2350

Artex International
Highland, IL.....................618-654-2113
Best Brands Home Products
New York, NY.....................212-684-7456
Best Buy Uniforms
Homestead, PA....................800-345-1924
Best Value Textiles
North Charleston, SC..............800-858-8589
Carnegie Textile Co
Cleveland, OH....................800-633-4136
Champion America Inc
Branford, CT.....................800-521-7000
Cotton Goods Mfg Co
Chicago, IL......................773-265-0088
Creative Converting Inc
Clintonville, WI..................800-826-0418
Custom Table Pads
St Paul, MN......................800-325-4643
Decolin
Montreal, QC.....................514-384-2910
Drapes 4 Show
Sylmar, CA.......................800-525-7469
Elrene Home Fashions
New York, NY.....................212-213-0425
Erving Industries
Erving, MA.......................413-422-2700
Fashion Industries
Griffin, GA......................770-412-9214
Gary Manufacturing Company
National City, CA.................800-775-0804
Gourmet Table Skirts
Houston, TX......................800-527-0440
Hilden Halifax
South Boston, VA.................800-431-2514
Hoffmaster Group Inc.
Oshkosh, WI......................800-558-9300
Jack the Ripper Table Skirting
Stafford, TX.....................800-331-7831
K Katen & Company
Rahway, NJ.......................732-381-0220
K-C Products Company
Van Nuys, CA.....................818-267-1600
Klever Kuvers
Pasadena, CA.....................626-355-8441
Louis Jacobs & Son
Brooklyn, NY.....................718-782-3500
Louisville Bedding Co Inc.
Louisville, KY....................502-813-8059
Marko Inc
Spartanburg, SC..................866-466-2756
Milliken & Co
Spartanburg, SC..................864-503-2020
Party Linens
Chicago, IL......................800-281-0003
Philmont Manufacturing Co.
Englewood, NJ....................888-379-6483
Premier Skirting Products
Lawrence, NY.....................800-544-2516
Radius Display Products
Dallas, TX.......................888-322-7429
Resource One/Resource Two
Reseda, CA.......................818-343-3451
SCA Tissue
Philadelphia, PA..................866-722-8675
Showeray Corporation
Brooklyn, NY.....................718-965-3633
Something Different Linen
Clifton, NJ......................800-422-2180
Straubel Company
De Pere, WI......................888-336-1412
Sultan Linen Inc
New York, NY.....................212-689-8900
Superior Products Company
Saint Paul, MN...................800-328-9800
Tag-Trade Associated Group
Chicago, IL......................800-621-8350
Tara Linens
Sanford, NC......................800-476-8272
Ultimate Textile
Paterson, NJ.....................973-523-5866
Vicmore Manufacturing Company
Brooklyn, NY.....................800-458-8663

Tables

Cafeteria, Restaurant, Foodservice Kitchen

A J Antunes & Co
Carol Stream, IL..................800-253-2991
A-1 Booth Manufacturing
Burley, ID.......................800-820-3285

Advance Tabco
Edgewood, NY 800-645-3166
Aero Manufacturing Co
Clifton, NJ 800-631-8378
All State Fabricators Corporation
Tampa, FL 800-322-9925
Allstrong Restaurant Eqpt Inc
South El Monte, CA 800-933-8913
AMC Industries
Palmetto, FL 941-479-7834
AMI
Richmond, CA .800-942-7466
Amtab Manufacturing Corp
Aurora, IL 800-878-2257
Anderson Wood Products
Louisville, KY .502-778-5591
ARC Specialties
Valencia, CA 661-775-8500
ATD-American Co
Wyncote, PA 800-523-2300
Atlas Metal Industries
Miami, FL 800-762-7565
AWP Butcher Block Inc
Horse Cave, KY 800-764-7840
Barn Furniture Mart
Van Nuys, CA .888-302-2276
Barrette Outdoor Living
Cleveland, OH .800-336-2383
Beaufurn
Advance, NC 888-766-7706
Beka Furniture
Concord, ON 905-669-4255
Berco
St Louis, MO 888-772-4788
Bessco Tube Bending & Pipe Fabricating
Thornton, IL 800-337-3977
Brill Manufacturing Co
Ludington, MI .866-896-6420
Carts Food Equipment
Brooklyn, NY .718-788-5540
Catskill Craftsmen Inc
Stamford, NY .607-652-7321
CCS Stone, Inc.
Moonachie, NJ .800-227-7785
CDI Service & Mfg Inc
Largo, FL 727-536-2207
Charter House
Zeeland, MI 800-314-7659
Chocolate Concepts
Hartville, OH 330-877-3322
Classico Seating
Peru, IN 800-968-6655
Cobb & Zimmer
Detroit, MI 313-923-0350
Colecraft Commercial Furnishings
Jamestown, NY 800-622-2777
Commercial Furniture Group Inc
Newport, TN 800-873-3252
Commercial Seating Specialists
Santa Clara, CA 408-453-8983
Component Hardware Group Inc
Lakewood, NJ .800-526-3694
Cove Woodworking
Gloucester, MA 800-273-0037
Crown Industries
East Orange, NJ 877-747-2457
Crown Steel Mfg
San Marcos, CA 760-471-1188
Custom Diamond International
Laval, QC 800-363-5926
Custom Diamond Intl.
Laval, QC 800-326-5926
Dayco
Clearwater, FL .727-573-9330
Delfield Co
Mt Pleasant, MI 800-733-8821
Den Mar Corp
North Dartmouth, MA 508-999-3295
Duke Manufacturing Co
St Louis, MO 800-735-3853
Duluth Sheet Metal
Duluth, MN 218-722-2613
Dunhill Food Equipment Corporation
Armonk, NY 800-847-4206
Eagle Foodservice   Equipment
Clayton, DE 800-441-8440
Eagle Group
Clayton, DE 800-441-8440
Eagle Products Company
Houston, TX 713-690-1161
Eash Industries
Elkhart, IN 574-295-4450

Economy Paper & Restaurant Co
Clifton, NJ 973-279-5500
Edgemold Products
Oconomowoc, WI 800-450-0051
Eldorado Miranda Manufacturing Company
Largo, FL 800-330-0708
Electric Contract Furniture
New York, NY .888-311-6272
Empire Bakery Equipment
Hicksville, NY .800-878-4070
Erwin Food Service Equipment
Fort Worth, TX 817-535-0021
Eskay Metal Fabricating
Buffalo, NY 800-836-8015
Fab-X/Metals
Washington, NC 800-677-3229
FCD Tabletops
Brooklyn, NY .800-822-5399
Fiskars Brands Inc.
Baldwinsville, NY 315-635-9911
Fixtur World
Cookeville, TN .800-634-9887
Fixtures Furniture
Florence, AL 855-321-4999
Forbes Industries
Ontario, CA 909-923-4549
Fred Beesley's Booth & Upholstery
Centerville, UT .801-364-8189
Furniturelab
Carrboro, NC 800-449-8677
Gar Products
Lakewood, NJ .800-424-2477
Gasser Chair Co Inc
Youngstown, OH 800-323-2234
Gates Manufacturing Company
Saint Louis, MO 800-237-9226
Harbour House Bar Crafting
Stamford, CT 800-755-1227
Hines III
Jacksonville, FL 904-398-5110
Hot Food Boxes
Mooresville, IN .800-733-8073
Industrial Plastics Company
Fort Smith, AR .800-850-0916
Industries Inc Kiefer
Random Lake, WI 920-994-2332
J.H. Carr & Sons
Seattle, WA 800-523-8842
John Boos & Co
Effingham, IL 888-431-2667
K C Booth Co
N Kansas City, MO 800-866-5226
KaiRak
Anaheim, CA 714-870-8661
Kamran & Co
Santa Barbara, CA 800-480-9418
Kay Home Products Inc
Antioch, IL 800-600-7009
Ken Coat
Bardstown, KY .888-536-2628
Kings River Casting
Sanger, CA 888-545-5157
Krueger International Holding
Green Bay, WI .800-424-2432
Lakeside Manufacturing Inc
Milwaukee, WI .888-558-8565
Lambertson Industries Inc
Sparks, NV 800-548-3324
Lask Seating Company
Chicago, IL 888-573-2846
LB Furniture Industries
Hudson, NY 800-221-8752
Load King Mfg
Jacksonville, FL 800-531-4975
Lodging By Charter
Liberty, NC 800-327-2548
Lumacurve Airfield Signs
Macedonia, OH 800-258-1997
M & E Mfg Co Inc
Kingston, NY 845-331-2110
M&S Manufacturing
Arnold, MO 636-464-2739
MCM Fixture Co
Hazel Park, MI .248-547-9280
Mcroyal Industries Inc
Youngstown, OH 800-785-2556
Merric
Bridgeton, MO .314-770-9944
Metal
Columbia, SC 803-776-9252
Metal Master Sales Corp
Glendale Heights, IL 800-488-8729

Metro Corporation
Wilkes Barre, PA 800-992-1776
Miami Metal
Miami, FL 305-576-3600
Michigan Maple Block Co
Petoskey, MI 800-447-7975
Midwest Folding Products
Chicago, IL 800-344-2864
Migali Industries
Camden, NJ 800-852-5292
Milvan Food Equipment Manufacturing
Rexdale, ON 416-674-3456
Missouri Equipment
St Louis, MO 800-727-6326
Mity Lite Inc
Orem, UT 800-909-8034
Mlp Seating
Elk Grove Vlg, IL 800-723-3030
Monroe Extinguisher Co Inc
Rochester, NY .585-235-3310
Mosshaim Innovations
Jacksonville, FL 888-995-7775
Mouron & Co Inc
Indianapolis, IN 317-243-7955
Mts Seating
Temperance, MI 734-847-3875
National Bar Systems
Huntington Beach, CA 714-848-1688
National FABCO Manufacturing
St Louis, MO 314-842-4571
Nor-Lake
Salem, NH 603-893-9701
Normandie Metal Fabricators
Port Washington, NY 800-221-2398
Northern Stainless Fabricating
Traverse City, MI 231-947-4580
Old Dominion Wood Products
Lynchburg, VA .800-245-6382
Palmer Snyder
Brookfield, WI .800-762-0415
Paramount Manufacturing Company
Wilmington, MA 978-657-4300
Parisi Inc
Newtown, PA 215-968-6677
Peter Pepper Products Inc
Compton, CA 310-639-0390
Petro Moore Manufacturing Corporation
Long Island City, NY 718-784-2516
Pinnacle Furnishing
Aberdeen, NC 866-229-5704
Plymold
Kenyon, MN 800-759-6653
PMI Food Equipment Group
Troy, OH 937-332-3000
Pollard Brothers
Chicago, IL 773-763-6868
Prince Seating Corp
Brooklyn, NY .800-577-4623
Quadra-Tech
Columbus, OH .800-443-2766
Quality Seating Co
Youngstown, OH 800-323-2234
Quipco Products Inc
Sauget, IL 314-993-1442
R.R. Scheibe Company
Newton Center, MA 508-584-4900
Robertson Furniture Co Inc
Toccoa, GA 800-241-0713
Rodo Industries
London, ON 519-668-3711
Rollhaus Seating Products Inc
Long Island City, NY 800-822-6684
Sandler Seating
Atlanta, GA 404-982-9000
Sarasota Restaurant Equipment
Sarasota, FL 800-434-1410
Sauvagnat Inc
Huntersville, NC 800-258-5619
Seating Concepts Inc
Rockdale, NY 800-421-2036
Sefi Fabricators Inc
Amityville, NY .631-842-2200
Shafer Commercial Seating
Denver, CO 303-322-7792
Shammi Industries
Corona, CA 800-417-9260
Sico Inc
Minneapolis, MN 800-328-6138
Silver King Refrigeration Inc
Minneapolis, MN 800-328-3329
Solid Surface Acrylics
North Tonawanda, NY 888-595-4114

St. Louis Stainless Service
St Louis, MO 800-735-3853
Stainless
La Vergne, TN 800-877-5177
Stainless Equipment Manufacturing
Dallas, TX 800-736-2038
Stainless Steel Fabricators
Tyler, TX 903-595-6625
Starlite Food Service Equipment
Detroit, MI 888-521-6603
Straubel Company
De Pere, WI 888-336-1412
Super Sturdy
Weldon, NC 800-253-4833
Superior Products Company
Saint Paul, MN 800-328-9800
Supreme Metal
Alpharetta, GA 800-645-2526
Thorpe & Associates
Siler City, NC 919-742-5516
Toronto Fabricating & Manufacturing
Mississauga, ON 905-891-2516
Trimen Foodservice Equipment
North York, ON 877-437-1422
Trojan Commercial Furni ture Inc.
Montereal, QC 877-271-3878
True Food Service Equipment, Inc.
O Fallon, MO 800-325-6152
U B KLEM Furniture Co Inc
St Anthony, IN 800-264-1995
United Fabricators
Fort Smith, AR 800-235-4101
Universal Stainless
Aurora, CO 800-223-8332
Universal Stainless & Alloy
Titusville, PA 800-295-1909
US Seating Products
Ocala, FL 800-999-2589
Versailles Lighting
Delray Beach, FL 888-564-0240
Vintage
Jasper, IN 800-992-3491
Vitro Seating Products
St Louis, MO 800-325-7093
Walsh & Simmons Seating
Saint Louis, MO 800-727-0364
Waymar Industries
Burnsville, MN 888-474-1112
Weiss Sheet Metal Inc
Avon, MA 508-583-8300
West Coast Industries Inc
San Francisco, CA 800-243-3150
West Metals
London, ON 800-300-6667
Wheel Tough Company
Terre Haute, IN 888-765-8833
Wilder Manufacturing Company
Port Jervis, NY 800-832-1319
Wood Goods Industries
Luck, WI 715-472-2226
Woodard
Coppell, TX 800-877-2290
World Wide Hospitality Furn
Paramount, CA 800-728-8262
Xiaoping Design
New York, NY 800-891-9896
Zol-Mark Industries
Winnipeg, NB 204-943-7393

Display

Altrua Marketing & Design
Tallahassee, FL 800-443-6939
Bmh Equipment Inc
Sacramento, CA 800-350-8828
Cal-Mil Plastic Products Inc
Oceanside, CA 800-321-9069
Dunn Woodworks
Shrewsbury, PA 877-835-8592
Eskay Metal Fabricating
Buffalo, NY 800-836-8015
Juice Tree
Omaha, NE 714-891-4425
Kehr-Buffalo Wire Frame Co Inc
Buffalo, NY 800-875-4212
Schmidt Progressive
Lebanon, OH 800-272-3706
Southern Store Fixtures Inc
Bessemer, AL 800-552-6283

Folding

Amtab Manufacturing Corp
Aurora, IL 800-878-2257
Mity Lite Inc
Orem, UT 800-909-8034
Palmer Snyder
Brookfield, WI 800-762-0415
Rheon USA
Irvine, CA 949-768-1900
Rollhaus Seating Products Inc
Long Island City, NY 800-822-6684
Superior Products Company
Saint Paul, MN 800-328-9800

Room Service

Forbes Industries
Ontario, CA 909-923-4549
Lakeside Manufacturing Inc
Milwaukee, WI 888-558-8565

Tote Bags

Eco-Bag Products
Ossining, NY 800-720-2247

Towels

Disposable

Adex Medical Inc
Riverside, CA 800-873-4776
Akron Cotton Products
Akron, OH. 800-899-7173
American Textile Mills Inc
Kansas City, MO 816-842-2909
Atlantic Mills
Lakewood, NJ 800-242-7374
Best Brands Home Products
New York, NY 212-684-7456
Blue Ridge Converting
Asheville, NC 800-438-3893
Browne & Company
Markham, ON 905-475-6104
C R Mfg
Waverly, NE 877-789-5844
Diamond Wipes Intl Inc
Chino, CA 800-454-1077
Erie Cotton Products
Erie, PA 800-289-4737
Georgia Pacific
Green Bay, WI. 920-435-8821
Healthline Products
Los Angeles, CA. 800-473-4003
IFC Disposables Inc
Brownsville, TN 800-432-9473
Kimberly-Clark Professional
Roswell, GA 800-241-3146
Lexidyne of Pennsylvania
Pittsburgh, PA 800-543-2233
Mainline Industries Inc
Springfield, MA 800-527-7917
Mednik Wiping Materials Co
St Louis, MO. 800-325-7193
National Towelette
Bensalem, PA 215-245-7300
Nosaj Disposables
Paterson, NJ 800-631-3809
Nu-Towel Co
Kansas City, MO. 800-800-7247
Rockline Industries
Sheboygan, WI 800-558-7790
SCA Tissue
Philadelphia, PA 866-722-8675
Superior Linen & Work Wear
Kansas City, MO. 800-798-7987
Wipeco Inc
Hillside, IL 708-544-7247

Paper

Bro-Tex Inc
St Paul, MN. 800-328-2282
Diamond Wipes Intl Inc
Chino, CA 800-454-1077
Erie Cotton Products
Erie, PA 800-289-4737
Georgia Pacific
Green Bay, WI. 920-435-8821
Goodman Wiper & Paper Co
Auburn, ME 207-784-5779

K & L Intl
Ontario, CA 888-598-5588
Kentfield's
Greenbrae, CA 888-461-7454
Kimberly-Clark Corporation
Irving, TX 972-281-1200
Marcal Paper Mills
Elmwood Park, NJ 800-631-8451
Mednik Wiping Materials Co
St Louis, MO. 800-325-7193
Nice-Pak Products Inc
Orangeburg, NY 800-444-6725
Nosaj Disposables
Paterson, NJ 800-631-3809
Potlatch Corp
Spokane, WA. 509-835-1500
SCA Hygiene Paper
San Ramon, CA 800-992-8675
SCA Tissue
Philadelphia, PA 866-722-8675
SCA Tissue North America
S Glens Falls, NY 518-743-0240
Sorg Paper Company
Middletown, OH 513-420-5300
United Textile Distribution
Garner, NC 800-262-7624
Wipeco Inc
Hillside, IL 708-544-7247

Trays

Butchers'

Buckhorn Inc
Milford, OH 800-543-4454
COW Industries Inc
Columbus, OH 800-542-9353
Quality Industries Inc
La Vergne, TN. 615-793-3000
Tenneco Specialty Packaging
Smyrna, GA 800-241-4402

Cafeteria

Browne & Company
Markham, ON 905-475-6104
Carlisle Food Svc Products Inc
Oklahoma City, OK 800-654-8210
Central Fine Pack Inc
Fort Wayne, IN 260-432-3027
Hoffmaster Group Inc.
Oshkosh, WI 800-558-9300
Innovative Plastics Corp
Orangeburg, NY 845-359-7500
Kendrick Johnson & Assoc Inc
Minneapolis, MN 800-826-1271
Lincoln Foodservice
Cleveland, OH 800-374-3004
Polar Ware Company
Sheboygan, WI 800-237-3655
Prolon
Port Gibson, MS 888-480-9828
Superior Products Company
Saint Paul, MN 800-328-9800
Traex
Dane, WI 800-356-8006
Wiltec
Leominster, MA 978-537-1497
Xtreme Beverages, LLC
Dana Point, CA. 949-495-7929

Food

Advance Engineering Co
Canton, MI 800-497-6388
Advanced Plastic Coating Svc
Parsons, KS 620-421-1660
ALCO Designs
Gardena, CA 800-228-2346
Allied Metal Spinning
Bronx, NY 800-615-2266
Ample Industries
Franklin, OH 888-818-9700
Art Wire Works Co
Chicago, IL 708-458-3993
Automatic Specialties Inc
Marlborough, MA 800-445-2370
Bakers Choice Products
Beacon Falls, CT 203-720-1000
Bardes Plastics Inc
Milwaukee, WI 800-558-5161
Brooklace
Oshkosh, WI 800-572-4552

Browne & Company
Markham, ON 905-475-6104
Buckhorn Inc
Milford, OH 800-543-4454
Cal-Mil Plastic Products Inc
Oceanside, CA 800-321-9069
Canada Goose Wood Produc
Gloucester, ON 888-890-6506
Carlisle Food Svc Products Inc
Oklahoma City, OK 800-654-8210
Delfin Design & Mfg
Rancho Sta Marg, CA 800-354-7919
Designers Folding Box Corp
Buffalo, NY 716-853-5141
Detroit Forming
Southfield, MI 248-440-1317
Display Tray
Mont-Royal, QC 800-782-8861
Dynynstyl
Delray Beach, FL 800-774-7895
Eastern Tabletop Mfg
Brooklyn, NY 888-422-4142
Ellingers Agatized Wood Inc
Sheboygan, WI 888-287-8906
Engineered Plastics Inc
Gibsonville, NC 800-711-1740
Esterle Mold & Machine Co Inc
Stow, OH 800-411-4086
Ex-Cell KAISER LLC
Franklin Park, IL 847-451-0451
Foam Packaging Inc
Vicksburg, MS 800-962-2655
Fold-Pak South
Columbus, GA 706-689-2924
Handy Wacks Corp
Sparta, MI .800-445-4434
Hoffmaster Group Inc.
Oshkosh, WI 800-558-9300
K & I Creative Plastics & Wood
Jacksonville, FL 904-387-0438
K & L Intl
Ontario, CA 888-598-5588
Kay Home Products Inc
Antioch, IL 800-600-7009
Kendrick Johnson & Assoc Inc
Minneapolis, MN 800-826-1271
Key Packaging Co
Sarasota, FL 941-355-2728
Lakeside Manufacturing Inc
Milwaukee, WI 888-558-8565
Lancaster Colony Corporation
Westerville, OH. 614-224-7141
Lin Pac Plastics
Roswell, GA 770-751-6006
Newell Brands
Atlanta, GA
Olive Can Company
Elgin, IL 847-468-7474
Par-Pak
Houston, TX 888-727-7252
Pinn Pack Packaging LLC
Oxnard, CA. 805-385-4100
Plastiques Cascades Group
Montreal, QC 888-703-6515
Plastocon
Oconomowoc, WI. 800-966-0103
Polar Ware Company
Sheboygan, WI 800-237-3655
Premier
Cincinnati, OH 800-354-9817
Process Displays
New Berlin, WI 800-533-1764
Promens
St. John, NB 800-295-3725
R.R. Scheibe Company
Newton Center, MA 508-584-4900
Sani-Top Products
De Leon Springs, FL. 800-874-6094
Spin-Tech Corporation
Hoboken, NJ 800-977-4692
SQP
Schenectady, NY 800-724-1129
Sterling Paper Company
Ohio, PA 800-282-1124
Stock America Inc
Grafton, WI 262-375-4100
Superior Products Company
Saint Paul, MN 800-328-9800
Tenneco Inc
Lake Forest, IL 800-403-3393
Tenneco Specialty Packaging
Smyrna, GA 800-241-4402

Toscarora
Sandusky, OH 419-625-7343
Traex
Dane, WI. 800-356-8006
Traitech Industries
Vaughan, ON 877-872-4835
Unique Plastics
Rio Rico, AZ. 800-658-5946
Vermillion Flooring
Springfield, MO 417-862-3785
Westervelt Co Inc
Tuscaloosa, AL 205-562-5000
Wiltec
Leominster, MA 978-537-1497
WNA Hopple Plastics
Florence, KY. 800-446-4622
Xtreme Beverages, LLC
Dana Point, CA 949-495-7929

Glass

Browne & Company
Markham, ON 905-475-6104
Superior Products Company
Saint Paul, MN 800-328-9800
World Kitchen
Elmira, NY .800-999-3436

Plastic

ACO
Moore, OK .405-794-7662
Advance Engineering Co
Canton, MI 800-497-6388
Aeromat Plastics Inc
Burnsville, MN 888-286-8729
Anchor Packaging
Ballwin, MO 800-467-3900
Arthur Corporation
Huron, OH. 419-433-7202
Bardes Plastics Inc
Milwaukee, WI 800-558-5161
Barrette Outdoor Living
Cleveland, OH 800-336-2383
Buckhorn Inc
Milford, OH 800-543-4454
C R Mfg
Waverly, NE 877-789-5844
Cambro Manufacturing Co
Huntington Beach, CA 800-833-3003
Carlisle Food Svc Products Inc
Oklahoma City, OK 800-654-8210
Cash Caddy
Palm Desert, CA 888-522-2221
Central Fine Pack Inc
Fort Wayne, IN 260-432-3027
Creative Forming
Ripon, WI .920-748-7285
Crespac Incorporated
Tucker, GA 800-438-1900
Custom Molders
Rocky Mount, NC 919-688-8061
Dart Container Corp.
Mason, MI. 800-248-5960
De Ster Corporation
Atlanta, GA 800-237-8270
DEL-Tec Packaging Inc
Greer, SC. .800-747-8683
Delfin Design & Mfg
Rancho Sta Marg, CA. 800-354-7919
Design Specialties Inc
Hamden, CT 800-999-1584
Detroit Forming
Southfield, MI. 248-440-1317
Display Tray
Mont-Royal, QC 800-782-8861
Douglas Stephen Plastics Inc
Paterson, NJ 973-523-3030
Edco Industries
Bridgeport, CT 203-333-8982
Engineered Plastics Inc
Gibsonville, NC 800-711-1740
Esterle Mold & Machine Co Inc
Stow, OH 800-411-4086
Fato Industries
Kankakee, IL. 815-932-3015
Gateway Plastics Inc
Mequon, WI. 262-242-2020
Gessner Products
Ambler, PA 800-874-7808
Hal-One Plastics
Olathe, KS .800-626-5784

Hoffmaster Group Inc.
Oshkosh, WI 800-558-9300
HPI North America/   Plastics
Eagan, MN 800-752-7462
Imperial Plastics Inc
Lakeville, MN 952-469-4951
Inline Plastic Corp
McDonough, GA 678-466-3467
Innovative Plastics Corp
Orangeburg, NY 845-359-7500
IVEX Packaging Corporation
Longueuil, QC 450-651-8887
Kendrick Johnson & Assoc Inc
Minneapolis, MN 800-826-1271
Kenro
Fredonia, WI. 262-692-2411
Key Packaging Co
Sarasota, FL 941-355-2728
Majestic
Bridgeport, CT 203-367-7900
Mr Ice Bucket
New Brunswick, NJ 732-545-0420
Novelty Crystal
Long Island City, NY 800-622-0250
Nu-Trend Plastics Thermoformer
Jacksonville, FL 904-353-5936
Orbis Corp.
Rexdale, ON 800-890-7292
Penda Form Corp
New Concord, OH 800-837-2574
Plastech Corp
Atlanta, GA 404-355-9682
Plaxall Inc
Long Island City, NY 800-876-5706
Prolon
Port Gibson, MS 888-480-9828
Promens
St. John, NB 800-295-3725
Robinson Industries Inc
Coleman, MI 989-465-6111
Rolland Machining & Fabricating
Moneta, VA. 973-827-6911
Sani-Top Products
De Leon Springs, FL 800-874-6094
Snapware
Fullerton, CA 800-334-3062
Spirit Foodservice, Inc.
Andover, MA 800-343-0996
Stock America Inc
Grafton, WI 262-375-4100
Techform
Mount Airy, NC 336-789-2115
TEMP-TECH Company
Springfield, MA 800-343-5579
Thermodynamics
Commerce City, CO 800-627-9037
Toscarora
Sandusky, OH 419-625-7343
Tray-Pak Corp
Reading, PA 610-926-5800
Tri-State Plastics
Glenwillard, PA. 724-457-6900
Tulip Molded Plastics Corp
Milwaukee, WI 414-963-3120
Unique Plastics
Rio Rico, AZ 800-658-5946
Wilks Precision Instr Co Inc
Union Bridge, MD 410-775-7917
Wiltec
Leominster, MA 978-537-1497
WNA Hopple Plastics
Florence, KY. 800-446-4622
Zeier Plastic & Mfg Inc
Madison, WI 608-244-5782

Urns

Coffee & Tea

BG Industries
Lemont, IL .800-800-5761
Bon Chef
Lafayette, NJ. 800-331-0177
Bunn-O-Matic Corp
Springfield, IL 800-352-2866
Eastern Tabletop Mfg
Brooklyn, NY 888-422-4142
Grindmaster-Cecilware Corp
Louisville, KY 800-695-4500
Kelmin Products
Plymouth, FL 407-886-6079

Lancaster Colony Corporation
Westerville, OH. 614-224-7141
Lazy Man Inc
Belvidere, NJ 800-475-1950
Red Diamond Coffee & Tea
Moody, AL 800-292-4651
Regal Ware Inc
Kewaskum, WI 262-626-2121
Rexcraft Fine Chafers
Long Island City, NY 888-739-2723
Sheffield Platers Inc
San Diego, CA 800-227-9242
T.J. Topper Company
Redwood City, CA 650-365-6962
Wells Manufacturing Company
St. Louis, MO 888-356-5362
World Kitchen
Elmira, NY 800-999-3436
Xtreme Beverages, LLC
Dana Point, CA 949-495-7929

Utensils

Foodservice Preparation

Abond Plastic Corporation
Lachine, QC 800-886-7947
Ace Fabrication
Mobile, AL 251-478-0401
All Southern Fabricators
Clearwater, FL 800-878-2732
Amco Metals Indl
City Of Industry, CA 626-855-2550
American Metal Stamping
Brooklyn, NY 718-384-1500
Browne & Company
Markham, ON 905-475-6104
C R Mfg
Waverly, NE 877-789-5844
Carlisle Food Svc Products Inc
Oklahoma City, OK 800-654-8210
Chef Revival
North Charleston, SC 800-248-9826
Chef Specialties
Smethport, PA 800-440-2433
Chuppa Knife Manufacturing
Jackson, TN 731-424-1212
Crestware
North Salt Lake, UT 800-345-0513
Cugar Machine Co
Fort Worth, TX 817-927-0411
Cutrite Company
Fremont, OH 800-928-8748
Cyclamen Collection
Oakland, CA 510-434-7620
Delco Tableware
Port Washington, NY 800-221-9557
Dur-Able Aluminum Corporation
Hoffman Estates, IL 847-843-1100
E-Z Dip
Frankfort, IN 866-347-3279
E-Z Edge Inc
West New York, NJ 800-232-4470
Eagleware Manufacturing
Compton, CA 310-604-0404
Edge Resources
Hopedale, MA 888-849-0998
Edgecraft Corp
Avondale, PA 800-342-3255
Ellingers Agatized Wood Inc
Sheboygan, WI 888-287-8906
Fab-X/Metals
Washington, NC 800-677-3229
Fioriware
Zanesville, OH 740-454-7400
Fortune Products Inc
Cedar Park, TX 512-249-0334
Franke Americas
Hatfield, PA 215-822-6590
Gerber Legendary Blades
Portland, OR 800-950-6161
Goebel Fixture Co
Hutchinson, MN 888-339-0509
Good Idea
Northampton, MA 800-462-9237
Goodell Tools
New Hope, MN 800-542-3906
Grand Silver Company
Bronx, NY 718-585-1930
Greensburg Manufacturing Company
Greensburg, KY 270-932-5511

H. Arnold Wood Turning
Tarrytown, NY 888-314-0088
Hank Rivera Associates
Dearborn, MI 313-581-8300
Hantover Inc
Kansas City, MO 800-821-7849
Hodges
Vienna, IL 800-444-0011
Hollingsworth Custom Wood Products
Sault Ste. Marie, ON 705-759-1756
Imperial Schrade Corporation
Ellenville, NY 212-210-8600
Industrial Razorblade
Orange, NJ 973-673-4286
John Boos & Co
Effingham, IL 888-431-2667
John J. Adams Die Corporation
Worcester, MA 508-757-3894
Keen Kutter
Torrance, CA. 310-370-6941
Kosempel Manufacturing Company
Philadelphia, PA 800-733-7122
KTG
Cincinnati, OH 888-533-6900
Lady Mary
Rockingham, NC 910-997-7321
Lamson & Goodnow
Shelburne Falls, MA. 800-872-6564
Leggett & Platt Storage
Vernon Hills, IL 847-816-6246
Leon Bush Manufacturer
Glenview, IL 847-657-8888
Lillsun Manufacturing Co
Huntington, IN 260-356-6514
Lodge Manufacturing Company
South Pittsburg, TN 423-837-5919
LoTech Industries
Lakewood, CO 800-295-0199
M & E Mfg Co Inc
Kingston, NY 845-331-2110
Matfer Inc
Van Nuys, CA 800-766-0333
Mill-Rose Co
Mentor, OH 800-321-3598
Mosshaim Innovations
Jacksonville, FL 888-995-7775
Mouli Manufacturing Corporation
Belleville, NJ 800-789-8285
Mulligan Associates
Mequon, WI 800-627-2886
Mundial
Norwood, MA 800-487-2224
National Novelty Brush Co
Lancaster, PA 717-299-5681
Nemco Food Equipment
Hicksville, OH 800-782-6761
Novelty Crystal
Long Island City, NY 800-622-0250
Olde Thompson Inc
Oxnard, CA. 800-827-1565
Pepper Mill
Mobile, AL 800-669-5175
Polar Ware Company
Sheboygan, WI 800-237-3655
Proluxe
Paramount, CA 800-594-5528
R H Saw Corp
Barrington, IL. 847-381-8777
R Murphy Co Inc
Ayer, MA. 888-772-3481
R X Honing Machine Corp
Mishawaka, IN 800-346-6464
Read Products Inc
Seattle, WA 800-445-3416
Royal Paper Products
Coatesville, PA 800-666-6655
Samuel Underberg Food Store
Brooklyn, NY 718-363-0787
Slicechief Co
Toledo, OH 419-241-7647
Spartec Plastics
Conneaut, OH 800-325-5176
Sturdi-Bilt Restaurant Equipment
Whitmore Lake, MI 800-521-2895
Superior Products Company
Saint Paul, MN 800-328-9800
T & A Metal Products Inc
Deptford, NJ 856-227-1700
T & S Perfection Chain Prods
Cullman, AL 888-856-4864
Tablecraft Products Co Inc
Gurnee, IL. 800-323-8321

Thorpe Rolling Pin Co
Hamden, CT 800-344-6966
Toronto Kitchen Equipment
North York, ON. 416-745-4944
Townfood Equipment Corp
Brooklyn, NY 800-221-5032
Update International
Vernon, CA 800-747-7124
Varimixer North America
Charlotte, NC 800-221-1138
Vermillion Flooring
Springfield, MO 417-862-3785
Vita Craft Corp
Shawnee, KS 800-359-3444
Vollrath Co LLC
Sheboygan, WI 800-624-2051
Wilton Armetale
Mt Joy, PA 800-779-4586
Wishbone Utensil Tableware Line
Wheat Ridge, CO 866-266-5928
Zeroll Company
Fort Pierce, FL 800-872-5000

Plastic

Action Technology
Prussia, PA 217-935-8311
BOC Plastics Inc
Winston Salem, NC. 800-334-8687
C R Mfg
Waverly, NE 877-789-5844
Carlisle Food Svc Products Inc
Oklahoma City, OK 800-654-8210
Chinet Company
Laguna Niguel, CA 949-348-1711
Dart Canada Inc.
Toronto, ON 800-465-9696
Design Specialties Inc
Hamden, CT 800-999-1584
Dispoz-O Plastics
Fountain Inn, SC 864-862-4004
First Plastics Co Inc
Leominster, MA 978-840-6908
Hal-One Plastics
Olathe, KS. 800-626-5784
Harold Leonard Southwest Corporation
Houston, TX 800-245-8105
Hoffmaster Group Inc
Oshkosh, WI 800-367-2877
HPI North America/Plastics
Chicago, IL 800-327-3534
James River Canada
North York, ON. 416-789-5151
Jarden Home Brands
Daleville, IN 800-392-2575
Jet Plastica Industries
Hatfield, PA
Jones-Zylon Co
West Lafayette, OH 800-848-8160
LoTech Industries
Lakewood, CO 800-295-0199
Max Packaging
Attalla, AL 800-543-5369
Measurex/S&L Plastics
Nazareth, PA 800-752-0650
Novelty Crystal
Long Island City, NY 800-622-0250
Nyman Manufacturing Company
Rumford, RI 401-438-3410
Olde Thompson Inc
Oxnard, CA. 800-827-1565
OWD
Tupper Lake, NY 800-836-1693
Penley Corporation
West Paris, ME 800-368-6449
Polar Plastics
St Laurent, QC 514-331-0207
Prairie Packaging Inc
Mooresville, NC 704-660-6600
R H Saw Corp
Barrington, IL. 847-381-8777
Spir-It/Zoo Piks
Andover, MA 800-343-0996
Tenneco Specialty Packaging
Smyrna, GA 800-241-4402
Waddington North America
Chelmsford, MA. 888-962-2877
Wiltec
Leominster, MA 978-537-1497
Wishbone Utensil Tableware Line
Wheat Ridge, CO 866-266-5928

WNA
Chattanooga, TN 800-404-9318

Vending Carts

All Star Carts & Vehicles
Bay Shore, NY 800-831-3166
All State Fabricators Corporation
Tampa, FL 800-322-9925
Alliance Products LLC
Murfreesboro, TN 800-522-3973
Alto-Shaam
Menomonee Falls, WI 800-329-8744
Amco Metals Indl
City Of Industry, CA 626-855-2550
ARC Specialties
Valencia, CA 661-775-8500
Automated Food Systems
Waxahachie, TX 469-517-0470
BBQ Pits by Klose
Houston, TX 800-487-7487
Corsair Display Systems
Canandaigua, NY 800-347-5245
Custom Sales & Svc Inc
Hammonton, NJ 800-257-7855
Eskay Metal Fabricating
Buffalo, NY 800-836-8015
Hackney Brothers
Washington, NC 800-763-0700
Hot Food Boxes
Mooresville, IN 800-733-8073
Hotshot Delivery System
Bloomingdale, IL 630-924-8817
International Thermal Dispensers
Boston, MA 617-239-3600
Lakeside Manufacturing Inc
Milwaukee, WI 888-558-8565
Leggett & Platt Storage
Vernon Hills, IL 847-816-6246
Magnum Custom Trailer & BBQ Pits
Austin, TX 800-662-4686
Merchandising Frontiers Inc
Winterset, IA 800-421-2278
Metal Master Sales Corp
Glendale Heights, IL 800-488-8729
Michaelo Espresso
Seattle, WA 800-545-2883
Moseley Realty LLC
Franklin, MA 800-667-3539
Paragon International
Nevada, IA 800-433-0333
Prestige Metal Products Inc
Antioch, IL 847-395-0775
Proluxe
Paramount, CA 800-594-5528
Southern Express
Saint Louis, MO 800-444-9157
Steamway Corporation
Scottsburg, IN 800-259-8171
Super Sturdy
Weldon, NC 800-253-4833
Super-Chef Manufacturing Company
Houston, TX 800-231-3478
Supreme Products
Waco, TX 254-799-4941
The Carriage Works
Klamath Falls, OR 541-882-0700
Tooterville Trolley Company
Newburgh, IN 812-858-8585
Vollrath Co LLC
Sheboygan, WI 800-624-2051
Wag Industries
Skokie, IL 800-621-3305
Worksman 800 Buy Cart
Ozone Park, NY 800-289-2278

Vending Machinery

Reverse

Can & Bottle Systems, Inc.
Milwaukie, OR 866-302-2636
Environmental Products Corp
Naugatuck, CT 800-275-3861

Warmers

Dish & Plate

Bloomfield Industries
St. Louis, MO 888-356-5362
Convay Systems
Minnetonka, MN 800-334-1099
Cyclamen Collection
Oakland, CA 510-434-7620
Kelmin Products
Plymouth, FL 407-886-6079
Mastex Industries
Petersburg, VA 804-732-8300
Metro Corporation
Wilkes Barre, PA 800-992-1776
Monroe Extinguisher Co Inc
Rochester, NY 585-235-3310
Super-Chef Manufacturing Company
Houston, TX 800-231-3478
Wells Manufacturing Company
St. Louis, MO 888-356-5362

Food

Aroma Manufacturing Company
San Diego, CA 800-276-6286
BG Industries
Lemont, IL 800-800-5761
BKI Worldwide
Simpsonville, SC 800-927-6887
Bon Chef
Lafayette, NJ 800-331-0177
Broaster Co LLC
Beloit, WI 800-365-8278
Canadian Display Systems
Concord, ON 800-895-5862
Cres Cor
Mentor, OH 877-273-7267
Crispy Lite
St. Louis, MO 888-356-5362
D'Lights
Glendale, CA 818-956-5656
Deluxe Equipment Company
Bradenton, FL 800-367-8931
Duke Manufacturing Co
St Louis, MO 800-735-3853
Dynynstyl
Delray Beach, FL 800-774-7895
Eagle Foodservice   Equipment
Clayton, DE 800-441-8440
Eagle Group
Clayton, DE 800-441-8440
Esquire Mechanical Corp.
Armonk, NY 800-847-4206
Garland Commercial Ranges
Mississauga, ON 905-624-0260
Gold Medal Products Co
Cincinnati, OH 800-543-0862
Hatco Corp
Milwaukee, WI 800-558-0607
Henny Penny, Inc.
Eaton, OH 800-417-8417
Hot Food Boxes
Mooresville, IN 800-733-8073

InfraTech Corporation
Azusa, CA 800-955-2476
Keating Of Chicago Inc
Mc Cook, IL 800-532-8464
Lincoln Foodservice
Cleveland, OH 800-374-3004
Merco/Savory
Mt. Pleasant, MI 800-733-8821
Metro Corporation
Wilkes Barre, PA 800-992-1776
Middleby Marshall Inc
Elgin, IL 847-741-3300
Mies Products
West Bend, WI 800-480-6437
Monroe Extinguisher Co Inc
Rochester, NY 585-235-3310
Mosshaim Innovations
Jacksonville, FL 888-995-7775
Prince Castle Inc
Carol Stream, IL 800-722-7853
Remco Industries International
Fort Lauderdale, FL 800-987-3626
Rexcraft Fine Chafers
Long Island City, NY 888-739-2723
Server Products Inc
Richfield, WI 800-558-8722
Sico Inc
Minneapolis, MN 800-328-6138
Southern Pride Distributing
Alamo, TN 800-851-8180
Star Manufacturing Intl Inc
St Louis, MO 800-264-7827
Super-Chef Manufacturing Company
Houston, TX 800-231-3478
Tomlinson Industries
Cleveland, OH 800-945-4589
Ultrafryer Systems Inc
San Antonio, TX 800-545-9189
Vulcan Food Equipment Group
Baltimore, MD 800-814-2028
Welbilt Corporation
Stamford, CT 203-325-8300
Wells Manufacturing Company
St. Louis, MO 888-356-5362
Wilder Manufacturing Company
Port Jervis, NY 800-832-1319
Win-Holt Equipment Group
Syosset, NY 800-444-3595
Wisco Industries Assembly
Oregon, WI 800-999-4726
Zoia Banquetier Co
Cleveland, OH 216-631-6414

Wood Grain Plastic

Chips

Hopp Co Inc
New Hyde Park, NY 800-889-8425

Shelf Covers

Hopp Co Inc
New Hyde Park, NY 800-889-8425

Strips

Hopp Co Inc
New Hyde Park, NY 800-889-8425

Instrumentation & Laboratory Equipment

Analyzers

Entech Instruments Inc.
Simi Valley, CA. 805-527-5939

Amino Acid, Nitrogen

Bran & Luebbe
Schaumburg, IL. 847-882-8116
Petroleum Analyzer Co LP
Houston, TX 800-444-8378

Ethyl Alcohol

Greer's Ferry Glass Work
Dubuque, IA 501-589-2947
NDC Infrared EngineeringInc
Irwindale, CA 626-960-3300
YSI Inc
Yellow Springs, OH 800-765-4974

Fats, Oils

Ashcroft Inc
Stratford, CT. 800-328-8258
Bran & Luebbe
Schaumburg, IL. 847-882-8116
CEM Corporation
Matthews, NC 800-726-3331
Columbus Instruments
Columbus, OH 800-669-5011
Foss Nirsystems
Silver Spring, MD. 301-755-5200
Industrial Laboratories Co
Wheat Ridge, CO 800-456-5288
Libra Technical Center
Metuchen, NJ 732-321-5200
NDC Infrared EngineeringInc
Irwindale, CA 626-960-3300
Univex Corp
Salem, NH. 800-258-6358

Fiber, Starch

Supelco Inc
Bellefonte, PA. 800-247-6628
Texture Technologies Corporation
Scarsdale, NY 914-472-0531

Mycotoxins

R-Biopharm Inc
Washington, MO. 269-789-3033
Supelco Inc
Bellefonte, PA. 800-247-6628
VICAM
Milford, MA 800-338-4381

Nitrites, Nitrosamines

Supelco Inc
Bellefonte, PA. 800-247-6628

Organic Acids

YSI Inc
Yellow Springs, OH 800-765-4974

Pesticide Residue, Antibiotics

Charm Sciences Inc
Lawrence, MA 978-687-9200
R-Biopharm Inc
Washington, MO. 269-789-3033
Supelco Inc
Bellefonte, PA. 800-247-6628

Salt (Sodium Chloride)

Ashcroft Inc
Stratford, CT. 800-328-8258
Greer's Ferry Glass Work
Dubuque, IA 501-589-2947
Hanna Instruments
Woonsocket, RI. 800-426-6287
Newport Electronics Inc
Santa Ana, CA 800-639-7678
Q A Supplies LLC
Norfolk, VA. 800-472-7205

Sugars (Dextrose, Fructose, Galactose, Lactose, Su

Foss Nirsystems
Silver Spring, MD. 301-755-5200
Greer's Ferry Glass Work
Dubuque, IA 501-589-2947
MISCO Refractometer
Cleveland, OH 866-831-1999
YSI Inc
Yellow Springs, OH 800-765-4974

Vitamin

Industrial Laboratories Co
Wheat Ridge, CO 800-456-5288

Water Activity

Arizona Instrument LLC
Chandler, AZ. 800-528-7411
Astro/Polymetron Zellweger
League City, TX 281-332-2484
Biopath
West Palm Beach, FL 800-645-2302
Burkert Fluid Control
Irvine, CA 800-325-1405
CEM Corporation
Matthews, NC 800-726-3331
Chemetrics Inc
Midland, VA 800-356-3072
CSC Scientific Co Inc
Fairfax, VA 800-621-4778
Forte Technology
South Easton, MA. 508-297-2363
Foss Nirsystems
Silver Spring, MD. 301-755-5200
Machine Applications Corp
Sandusky, OH 419-621-2322
Mocon Inc
Minneapolis, MN 763-493-7229
NDC Infrared EngineeringInc
Irwindale, CA 626-960-3300
Onset Computer Corp
Bourne, MA 800-564-4377
Orion Research
Beverly, MA 978-232-6000
Precision Systems Inc
Natick, MA 508-655-7010
Rosemount Analytical Inc
Irvine, CA 800-543-8257
Rotronic Instrument Corp Inc
Hauppauge, NY 800-628-7101
Severn Trent Svc
Colmar, PA 215-822-2901
Suburban Laboratories Inc
Geneva, IL. 800-783-5227
Thermo Detection
Franklin, MA 866-269-0070
Troxler Electronic Lab Inc
Durham, NC 877-876-9537

Automation

Unit, Packaging, Bulk Handling

Andgar Corp
Ferndale, WA 360-366-9900
Barclay & Assoc PC
Ames, IA. 515-292-3023
California Vibratory Feeders
Anaheim, CA 800-354-0972
Falco Technologies
La Prairie, QC 450-444-0566
Hampton-Tilley Associates
Chesterfield, MO 813-418-3340
Jacobs Engineering Group
Dallas, TX. 214-638-0145
Lockwood Greene Engineers
Knoxville, TN 251-476-2400
Lockwood Greene Engineers
Knoxville, TN 256-533-9907
Lockwood Greene Engineers
Brentwood, TN 615-221-5031
Lockwood Greene Engineers
Augusta, GA 706-724-8225

Lockwood Greene Engineers
Somerset, NJ 732-560-5700
Lockwood Greene Engineers
Atlanta, GA 770-829-6500
Lockwood Greene Engineers
Guaynabo, PR 787-781-9050
Lockwood Greene Engineers
Knoxville, TN 865-218-5377
Lockwood Greene Engineers
Dallas, TX. 972-991-5505
Lockwood Greene Technologies
Augusta, GA 505-889-3831
Priority One Packaging
Waterloo, ON 800-387-9102
Schroeder Machine
San Marcos, CA 760-591-9733
Stock America Inc
Grafton, WI. 262-375-4100
Vande Berg SCALES/Vbs Inc
Sioux Center, IA 712-722-1181
Washington Frontier
Grandview, WA. 509-469-7662

Balances

Laboratory

A&D Weighing
San Jose, CA. 800-726-3364
Denver Instrument Company
Bohemia, NY 800-321-1135
Fairbanks Scales
Kansas City, MO. 800-451-4107
Precision Solutions Inc
Quakertown, PA 215-536-4400
Q A Supplies LLC
Norfolk, VA. 800-472-7205
Sartorius Corp
Edgewood, NY 800-635-2906
Vande Berg SCALES/Vbs Inc
Sioux Center, IA 712-722-1181
Vertex Interactive
Clifton, NJ. 973-777-3500
Wilkens-Anderson Co
Chicago, IL. 800-847-2222

Centrifuges

Alfa Laval Inc
Richmond, VA. 866-253-2528
Ampco Pumps Co Inc
Milwaukee, WI 800-737-8671
Baker Hughes
Houston, TX
C&R Refrigation Inc,
Center, TX. 800-438-6182
Cameron Intl. Corp.
Houston, TX 281-285-4376
Centrisys
Kenosha, WI 262-654-6006
Commercial Manufacturing
Fresno, CA 559-237-1855
Dedert Corporation
Olympia Fields, IL 708-747-7000
International Machinery Xchnge
Deerfield, WI 800-279-0191
International Reserve Equipment Corporation
Clarendon Hills, IL 708-531-0680
Pacer Pumps
Lancaster, PA 800-233-3861
Pacific Process Technology
La Jolla, CA 858-551-3298
Pro Scientific Inc
Oxford, CT 800-584-3776
Ross Cook
Silver Spring, MD. 800-233-7339
Separators Inc
Indianapolis, IN 800-233-9022
Silver Weibull
Aurora, CO 303-373-2311
Tecumseh Products Co.
Ann Arbor, MI 734-585-9500
Tema Systems Inc
Cincinnati, OH 513-792-2840

Certification

Food

International Kosher Supervision
  Keller, TX 817-337-4700
KOF-K Kosher Supervision
  Teaneck, NJ. 201-837-0500
Lloyd's Register QualityAssurance
  Houston, TX 888-877-8001
Ok Kosher Certification
  Brooklyn, NY 718-756-7500
Orthodox Union
  New York, NY 212-563-4000
Star-K Kosher Certification
  Baltimore, MD 410-484-4110

Chemicals

Laboratory

Advance Energy Technologies
  Halfmoon, NY. 800-724-0198
CFS North America
  Urbandale, IA 844-808-2063
Exaxol Chemical Corp
  Clearwater, FL 800-739-2965
Fisher Scientific Company
  Pittsburgh, PA. 412-490-8300
Ricca Chemical Co
  Batesville, IN 888-467-4222
S & J Laboratories Inc
  Portage, MI 269-324-7383
Solvox Manufacturing Company
  Milwaukee, WI 414-774-5664
Wilkens-Anderson Co
  Chicago, IL 800-847-2222

Controls

Automation & Controls

Dennsi Group
  Springfield, MA 413-737-1353
Eaton Electrical Sector
  Moon Township, PA 877-386-2273
M G Newell Corp
  Greensboro, NC 800-334-0231
Red Lion Controls Inc
  York, PA 717-767-6511
SICK Inc
  Bloomington, MN. 800-325-7425
Sterling Electric Inc
  Indianapolis, IN 800-654-6220

Boiler & Steam

Acme Control Svc Inc
  Chicago, IL 800-621-6427
Heatrex
  Meadville, PA 800-394-6589
Paxton Corp
  Bristol, RI .401-396-9062
Sellers Engineering Division
  Danville, KY. 859-236-3181
Vega Americas Inc
  Cincinnati, OH 800-367-5383
Washington Frontier
  Grandview, WA. 509-469-7662

Clean-In-Place

A & B Process Systems Corp
  Stratford, WI. 888-258-2789
Ashcroft Inc
  Stratford, CT. 800-328-8258
Debelak Technical Systems
  Greenville, WI 800-888-4207
Electrol Specialties Co
  South Beloit, IL 815-389-2291
Lake Process Systems Inc
  Lake Barrington, IL 800-331-9260
Letrah International Corp
  Fort Atkinson, WI. 920-563-6597
Northland Process Piping
  Isle, MN 320-679-2119
Papertech
  North Vancouver, BC 877-787-2737
Scherping Systems
  Winsted, MN. 320-485-4401
Stainless Products
  Somers, WC 800-558-9446

Sterling Process Engineering
  Columbus, OH 800-783-7875
West Agro
  Kansas City, MO. 816-891-7700

Level, Liquid & Dry

A & B Process Systems Corp
  Stratford, WI. 888-258-2789
Anderson-Negele
  Fultonville, NY 800-833-0081
ASI Electronics Inc
  Cypress, TX 800-231-6066
Azbar Plus
  Qu‚bec, QC 418-687-3672
Banner Engineering Corp
  Minneapolis, MN 888-373-6767
Berthold Technologies
  Oak Ridge, TN 865-483-1488
Clean Water Systems
  Klamath Falls, OR 866-273-9993
Conveyor Components Co
  Croswell, MI 800-233-3233
Crown Controls Inc.
  Charlotte, NC 800-541-7874
Distaview Corp
  Bowling Green, OH 800-795-9970
Gems Sensors & Controls
  Plainville, CT 860-747-3000
Heuft USA Inc
  Downers Grove, IL 630-968-9011
Honeywell Sensing & Internet of Things
  DE 800-537-6945
Infitec Inc
  East Syracuse, NY 800-334-0837
Innovative Components
  Southington, CT 800-789-2851
Intelligent Controls
  Saco, ME. .800-872-3455
King Engineering - King-Gage
  Newell, WV 800-242-8871
Knight Equipment International
  Lake Forest, CA 800-854-3764
Letrah International Corp
  Fort Atkinson, WI. 920-563-6597
Liquid Scale
  New Brighton, MN 888-633-2969
Lumenite Control Tech Inc
  Franklin Park, IL. 800-323-8510
Peco Controls Corporation
  Modesto, CA. 800-732-6285
SICK Inc
  Bloomington, MN. 800-325-7425
Tokheim Co
  Marion, IA. .800-747-3442
Vega Americas Inc
  Cincinnati, OH 800-367-5383
Washington Frontier
  Grandview, WA. 509-469-7662

Microprocessor

GEA Refrigeration North America
  York, PA 800-888-4337

Numerical

American Autogard Corporation
  Rockford, IL 815-229-3190
Candy Manufacturing Co
  Niles, IL 847-588-2639
ENM Co
  Chicago, IL 773-775-8400

Packaging Line

Alfa Systems Inc
  Westfield, NJ. 908-654-0255
Andantex USA Inc
  Ocean, NJ .800-713-6170
ASI Electronics Inc
  Cypress, TX 800-231-6066
Aw Sheepscot Holding Co Inc
  Franksville, WI 800-850-6110
Banner Engineering Corp
  Minneapolis, MN 888-373-6767
Blodgett Co
  Houston, TX 281-933-6195
Cal Controls
  Gurnee, IL. .800-866-6659
Candy Manufacturing Co
  Niles, IL 847-588-2639

Centent Co
  Santa Ana, CA 714-979-6491
Container Machinery Corporation
  Albany, NY .518-694-3310
Contrex Inc
  Maple Grove, MN. 763-424-7800
Control & Metering
  Mississauga, ON. 800-736-5739
Conveyor Components Co
  Croswell, MI 800-233-3233
Electro Cam Corp
  Roscoe, IL .800-228-5487
Fairchild Industrial Products
  Winston Salem, NC. 800-334-8422
Gebo Conveyors, Consultants & Systems
  Laval, QC .450-973-3337
Harland Simon Control Systems USA
  Oakbrook, IL. 630-572-7650
Honeywell Sensing & Internet of Things
  DE 800-537-6945
Hoppmann Corporation
  Elkwood, VA. 800-368-3582
Hudson Control Group Inc
  Springfield, NJ 973-376-8265
Industrial Devices Corporation
  Petaluma, CA 707-789-1000
Industrial Magnetics
  Boyne City, MI 800-662-4638
Kinematics & Controls Corporation
  Brooksville, FL 800-833-8103
Letrah International Corp
  Fort Atkinson, WI. 920-563-6597
Moeller Electric
  Houston, TX 800-394-5687
Namco Controls Corporation
  Cleveland, OH 800-626-8324
OMRON Systems LLC
  Schaumburg, IL. 800-556-6766
Optek Inc
  Galena, OH 800-533-8400
Payne Controls Co
  Scott Depot, WV. 800-331-1345
Peco Controls Corporation
  Modesto, CA. 800-732-6285
Rexroth Corporation
  Hoffman Estates, IL 847-645-3600
Schroeder Machine
  San Marcos, CA 760-591-9733
Sure Torque
  Lakewood, CO 800-387-6572
Tri-Tronics
  Tampa, FL .800-237-0946
W.G. Durant Corporation
  Whittier, CA 562-946-5555
Washington Frontier
  Grandview, WA. 509-469-7662

Refrigeration Systems

Andgar Corp
  Ferndale, WA 360-366-9900
Apollo Sheet Metal
  Kennewick, WA 509-586-1104
Chillers Solutions
  Pompton Plains, NJ. 800-526-5201
Cooling Technology Inc
  Charlotte, NC 800-872-1448
Frigoscandia
  Redmond, WA. 800-423-1743
H A Phillips & Co
  Dekalb, IL. .630-377-0050
Hansen Technologies Corporation
  Bolingbrook, IL 800-426-7368
Johnson Controls Inc
  Milwaukee, WI 414-524-1200
Letrah International Corp
  Fort Atkinson, WI. 920-563-6597
Novar
  Cleveland, OH 800-348-1235
Paragon Electric Company
  Two Rivers, WI. 920-793-1161
Quantem Corp
  Ewing, NJ .609-883-9879
Ron Vallort & Associates
  Oak Brook, IL. 630-734-3821
Selco Products Company
  Anaheim, CA 800-257-3526
WA Brown & Son
  Salisbury, NC 704-636-5131

Webtension & Torque

Magpowr
Fenton, MO 800-624-7697

General

Alpha MOS America
Hanover, MD 800-257-4249
Bio-Rad Laboratories Inc.
Hercules, CA 510-724-7000
EMD Performance Materials
Philadelphia, PA 888-367-3275
FactoryTalk
Milwaukee, WI 414-382-2000
Shimadzu Scientific Instrs
Columbia, MD 800-477-1227

Inspection & Analysis Instrumentation & Systems

Abbeon Cal Inc
Santa Barbara, CA 800-922-0977
Accu-Ray Inspection Services
Elmhurst, IL 800-378-1226
ACR Systems
Surrey, BC 800-663-7845
Acrison Inc
Moonachie, NJ 800-422-4266
Advanced Detection Systems
Milwaukee, WI 414-672-0553
Advanced Instruments Inc
Norwood, MA 800-225-4034
Agricultural Data Systems
Laguna Niguel, CA 800-328-2246
Agtron Inc
Reno, NV 775-850-4600
Air Logic Power Systems
Milwaukee, WI 800-325-8717
Altek Co
Torrington, CT 860-482-7626
American Gas & Chemical Co LTD
Northvale, NJ 800-288-3647
American Glass Research
Butler, PA 724-482-2163
AMETEK Brookfield
Middleboro, MA 800-628-8139
Analytical Development
Dahlonega, GA 770-237-2330
Analytical Measurements
Chester, NJ 800-635-5580
Aqua Measure
Rancho Cucamonga, CA 800-966-4788
Arizona Instrument LLC
Chandler, AZ 800-528-7411
Aromascan PLC
Hollis, NH 603-598-2922
Arthur G Russell Co Inc
Bristol, CT 860-583-4109
Ashcroft Inc
Stratford, CT 800-328-8258
Astro/Polymetron Zellweger
League City, TX 281-332-2484
Atkins Technical
Gainesville, FL 800-284-2842
ATS Rheosystems
Bordentown, NJ 609-298-2522
Automation Service
Earth City, MO 800-325-4808
Baltimore Aircoil Co
Jessup, MD 410-799-1300
Banner Engineering Corp
Minneapolis, MN 888-373-6767
Barco Inc
Duluth, GA 678-475-8000
Becton Dickinson & Co.
Franklin Lakes, NJ 201-847-6800
Bel-Art Products
Wayne, NJ 800-423-5278
Bentley Instruments Inc
Chaska, MN 952-448-7600
Berthold Technologies
Oak Ridge, TN 865-483-1488
Bia Diagnostics
Colchester, VT 802-540-0148
Binks Industries Inc
Montgomery, IL 630-801-1100
Biocontrol Systems Inc
Bellevue, WA 800-245-0113
Biolog Inc
Hayward, CA 800-284-4949
Biological Services
Kansas City, MO 913-236-6868

Biomerieux Inc
Durham, NC 800-682-2666
Bioscience International Inc
Rockville, MD 301-231-7400
Biotest Diagnostics Corporation
Rockaway, NJ 800-522-0090
Bran & Luebbe
Schaumburg, IL 847-882-8116
Brooks Instrument LLC
Hatfield, PA 888-554-3569
C.W. Brabender Instruments
South Hackensack, NJ 201-343-8425
CanPacific Engineering
Delta, BC 604-946-1680
Care Controls, Inc.
Mill Creek, WA 800-593-6050
Carleton Technologies Inc
Orchard Park, NY 716-662-0006
Caron Products & Svc Inc
Marietta, OH 800-648-3042
Carter Products
Grand Rapids, MI 888-622-7837
CEA Instrument Inc
Westwood, NJ 888-893-9640
CEM Corporation
Matthews, NC 800-726-3331
Charm Sciences Inc
Lawrence, MA 978-687-9200
Chicago Stainless Eqpt Inc
Palm City, FL 800-927-8575
Chord Engineering
Niwot, CO 303-449-5812
Cintex of America
Carol Stream, IL 800-424-6839
Clean Water Systems
Klamath Falls, OR 866-273-9993
Columbus Instruments
Columbus, OH 800-669-5011
Comark Instruments
Everett, WA 800-555-6658
Container Machinery Corporation
Albany, NY 518-694-3310
Control Instruments Corp
Fairfield, NJ 973-575-9114
Cooperheat/MQS
Alvin, TX 800-526-4233
Crown Controls Inc.
Charlotte, NC 800-541-7874
Crystal Chem Inc.
Downers Grove, IL 630-889-9003
CSC Scientific Co Inc
Fairfax, VA 800-621-4778
CSPI
Billerica, MA 978-663-7598
Custom Pools Inc
Portsmouth, NH 800-323-9509
CXR Co
Warsaw, IN 800-817-5763
Datapaq
Wilmington, MA 800-326-5270
Debelak Technical Systems
Greenville, WI 800-888-4207
Delavan-Delta
Naugatuck, CT 203-720-5610
Delta F Corporation
Woburn, MA 781-935-4600
Design Technology Corporation
Billerica, MA 978-663-7000
Devar Inc
Bridgeport, CT 800-566-6822
Dipix Technologies
Ottawa, ON 613-596-4942
Dunkley International Inc
Kalamazoo, MI 800-666-1264
Dupps Co
Germantown, OH 937-855-0623
Ecklund-Harrison Technologies
Fort Myers, FL 239-936-6032
Endress & Hauser
Greenwood, IN 800-428-4344
ENSCO Inc
Springfield, VA 703-321-9000
EPD Technology Corporation
Elmsford, NY 800-892-8926
Eurotherm
Ashburn, VA 703-726-0138
F I L T E C-Inspection Systems
Torrance, CA 888-434-5832
Food Instrument Corp
Federalsburg, MD 800-542-5688
Food Technology Corporation
Sterling, VA 703-444-1870

Forte Technology
South Easton, MA 508-297-2363
Foss Nirsystems
Silver Spring, MD 301-755-5200
Fsi Technologies
Lombard, IL 800-468-6009
Garver Manufacturing Inc
Union City, IN 765-964-5828
Gems Sensors & Controls
Plainville, CT 860-747-3000
Geo. Olcott Company
Scottsboro, AL 800-634-2769
Gerstel Inc
Linthicum Hts, MD 800-413-8160
Grace Instrument Co
Houston, TX 800-304-5859
Gralab Instruments
Centerville, OH 800-876-8353
Greer's Ferry Glass Work
Dubuque, IA 501-589-2947
Haake
Paramus, NJ 800-631-1369
Hanna Instruments
Woonsocket, RI 800-426-6287
Heuft USA Inc
Downers Grove, IL 630-968-9011
High-Purity Standards
North Charleston, SC 866-767-4771
Hoffer Flow Controls Inc
Elizabeth City, NC 800-628-4584
Hygiena LLC
Camarillo, CA 805-388-8007
I.W. Tremont Company
Hawthorne, NJ 973-427-3800
Idexx Laboratories Inc
Westbrook, ME 800-548-6733
IMC Instruments
Menomonee Falls, WI 262-252-4620
Innovative Components
Southington, CT 800-789-2851
International Equipment Trading
Vernon Hills, IL 800-438-4522
International Tank & Pipe Co
Clackamas, OR 888-988-0011
Interstate Monroe Machinery
Seattle, WA 206-682-4870
IQ Scientific Instruments
Loveland, CO 800-227-4224
J M Canty Inc E1200 Engineers
Lockport, NY 716-625-4227
Kodex Inc
Nutley, NJ 800-325-6339
Koehler Instrument Co Inc
Bohemia, NY 800-878-9070
Konica Minolta Corp
Ramsey, NJ 888-473-3637
Labconco Corp
Kansas City, MO 800-821-5525
Labvantage Solutions Inc
Somerset, NJ 888-346-5467
Leeman Labs Inc
Hudson, NH 800-634-9942
Leica Microsystems
Depew, NY 800-346-4560
Light Technology Ind
Gaithersburg, MD 301-990-4050
Lixi Inc
Carpentersville, IL 847-961-6666
Lock Inspection Systems
Fitchburg, MA 800-227-5539
Loma International
Carol Stream, IL 800-872-5662
Lumenite Control Tech Inc
Franklin Park, IL 800-323-8510
Machine Applications Corp
Sandusky, OH 419-621-2322
Malthus Diagnostics
North Ridgeville, OH 800-346-7202
MAP Tech Packaging Inc
Hilton Head Isle, SC 843-342-5900
Maselli Measurements Inc
Stockton, CA 800-964-9600
MDS-Vet Inc
Valrico, FL 813-653-1180
Mesa Laboratories Inc
Lakewood, CO 800-525-1215
Mettler-Toledo Process Analytics, Inc
Billerica, MA 800-352-8763
Mettler-Toledo Safeline Inc
Lutz, FL 800-638-8537
Miroil
Allentown, PA 800-523-9844

MISCO Refractometer
Cleveland, OH 866-831-1999
Mocon Inc
Minneapolis, MN 763-493-7229
Moisture Register Products
Rancho Cucamonga, CA 800-966-4788
Namco Controls Corporation
Cleveland, OH 800-626-8324
National Hotpack
Stone Ridge, NY 800-431-8232
NDC Infrared EngineeringInc
Irwindale, CA 626-960-3300
Neogen Corp
Lansing, MI 800-234-5333
New Brunswick Scientific Co
Enfield, CT 800-645-3050
Noral
Natick, MA 800-348-2345
Ohio Magnetics Inc
Maple Heights, OH 800-486-6446
Omni Controls Inc
Tampa, FL 800-783-6664
Omnion
Rockland, MA 781-878-7200
OMRON Systems LLC
Schaumburg, IL 800-556-6766
Onevision Corp
Westerville, OH 614-794-1144
Optel Vision
Quebec, QC 866-688-0334
Orion Research
Beverly, MA 978-232-6000
Pacific Scientific Instrument
Grants Pass, OR 800-866-7889
Paktronics Controls
Southfield, MI 248-356-1400
Peco Controls Corporation
Modesto, CA 800-732-6285
Perten Instruments
Springfield, IL 888-773-7836
Petroleum Analyzer Co LP
Houston, TX 800-444-8378
Polyscience
Niles, IL 800-229-7569
Process Sensors Corp
Milford, MA 508-473-9901
Promega
Madison, WI 800-356-9526
Pyrometer Instrument Co Inc
Windsor, NJ 800-468-7976
Q A Supplies LLC
Norfolk, VA 800-472-7205
QMI
St Paul, MN 651-501-2337
Quality Control Equipment Co
Des Moines, IA 515-266-2268
Quest Corp
North Royalton, OH 440-230-9400
Reotemp Instrument Corp
San Diego, CA 800-648-7737
Rexroth Corporation
Hoffman Estates, IL 847-645-3600
Rheometric Scientific
New Castle, DE 732-560-8550
Rosemount Analytical Inc
Irvine, CA 800-543-8257
Rotronic Instrument Corp Inc
Hauppauge, NY 800-628-7101
SDIX
Newark, DE 800-544-8881
Sensidyne
St. Petersburg, FL 800-451-9444
Sensitech Inc
Beverly, MA 800-843-8367
Sensitech Inc
Redmond, WA 800-999-7926
Sensor Systems
Chatsworth, CA 818-341-5366
Sentry Equipment Corp
Oconomowoc, WI 262-567-7256
ShockWatch
Dallas, TX 800-393-7920
SIGHTech Vision Systems
Santa Clara, CA 408-282-3770
Spectro
Marble Falls, TX 800-580-6608
Spiral Biotech Inc
Norwood, MA 800-554-1620
Sure Torque
Lakewood, CO 800-387-6572
Tangent Systems
Charlotte, NC 800-992-7577

Technistar Corporation
Denver, CO 303-651-0188
Teledyne Benthos Inc
North Falmouth, MA 508-563-1000
Teledyne TEKMAR
Mason, OH 800-874-2004
Testing Machines Inc
New Castle, DE 800-678-3221
Texture Technologies Corporation
Scarsdale, NY 914-472-0531
Thermedics Detection
Chelmsford, MA 888-846-7226
Thermo Detection
Franklin, MA 866-269-0070
Thermo Fisher Scientific
Waltham, MA 800-678-5599
Theta Sciences
San Diego, CA 760-745-3311
Thorn Smith Laboratories
Beulah, MI 231-882-4672
Tricor Systems Inc
Elgin, IL 800-575-0161
Troxler Electronic Lab Inc
Durham, NC 877-876-9537
TVC Systems
Portsmouth, NH 888-431-5251
Tyco Fire Protection Products
Marinette, WI 800-862-6785
Univex Corp
Salem, NH 800-258-6358
Vee Gee Scientific Inc
Kirkland, WA 800-423-8842
Venture Measurement Co LLC
Spartanburg, SC 864-574-8960
VICAM
Milford, MA 800-338-4381
Washington Frontier
Grandview, WA 509-469-7662
Whatman
Haverhill, MA 978-374-7400
Wilkens-Anderson Co
Chicago, IL 800-847-2222
X-R-I Testing Inc
Troy, MI 800-973-4800
Xylem Inc
Rye Brook, NY 914-323-5700
YSI Inc
Yellow Springs, OH 800-765-4974
Zeltex
Hagerstown, MD 800-732-1950

Instrumentation

Color Measuring

BYK Gardner Inc
Columbia, MD 301-483-6500
Hunter Lab
Reston, VA 703-471-6870
Konica Minolta Corp
Ramsey, NJ 888-473-3637
SICK Inc
Bloomington, MN 800-325-7425
Wilkens-Anderson Co
Chicago, IL 800-847-2222

Flow Measurement, Gas & Liquid

ACR Systems
Surrey, BC 800-663-7845
Auburn Systems LLC
Danvers, MA 800-255-5008
Berthold Technologies
Oak Ridge, TN 865-483-1488
Brooks Instrument LLC
Hatfield, PA 888-554-3569
CEA Instrument Inc
Westwood, NJ 888-893-9640
CEM Corporation
Matthews, NC 800-726-3331
Columbus Instruments
Columbus, OH 800-669-5011
Endress & Hauser
Greenwood, IN 800-428-4344
Hardy Systems Corporation
Northbrook, IL 800-927-3956
Hoffer Flow Controls Inc
Elizabeth City, NC 800-628-4584
IMC Instruments
Menomonee Falls, WI 262-252-4620
Interstate Monroe Machinery
Seattle, WA 206-682-4870

Labconco Corp
Kansas City, MO 800-821-5525
MAP Tech Packaging Inc
Hilton Head Isle, SC 843-342-5900
Mocon Inc
Minneapolis, MN 763-493-7229
Omni Controls Inc
Tampa, FL 800-783-6664
Optek Inc
Galena, OH 800-533-8400
Rotronic Instrument Corp Inc
Hauppauge, NY 800-628-7101
Tuchenhagen
Columbia, MD 410-910-6000
Washington Frontier
Grandview, WA 509-469-7662

Laboratory Equipment

Acme Scale Co
San Leandro, CA 888-638-5040
Advance Energy Technologies
Halfmoon, NY 800-724-0198
Advance Technology Corp
Ramsey, NJ 201-934-7127
Agri-Equipment International
Longs, SC 877-550-4709
AMETEK Brookfield
Middleboro, MA 800-628-8139
Analytical Measurements
Chester, NJ 800-635-5580
Arizona Instrument LLC
Chandler, AZ 800-528-7411
Ashcroft Inc
Stratford, CT 800-328-8258
Atkins Technical
Gainesville, FL 800-284-2842
Bahnson Environmental Specs
Raleigh, NC 800-688-5859
Barnant Company
Lake Barrington, IL 800-637-3739
Becton Dickinson & Co.
Franklin Lakes, NJ 201-847-6800
Bel-Art Products
Wayne, NJ 800-423-5278
Bematek Systems Inc
Salem, MA 877-236-2835
Bentley Instruments Inc
Chaska, MN 952-448-7600
Biocontrol Systems Inc
Bellevue, WA 800-245-0113
Bioscience International Inc
Rockville, MD 301-231-7400
Bran & Luebbe
Schaumburg, IL 847-882-8116
Brimrose Corporation of America
Sparks Glencoe, MD 410-472-7070
C.W. Brabender Instruments
South Hackensack, NJ 201-343-8425
Caron Products & Svc Inc
Marietta, OH 800-648-3042
Charm Sciences Inc
Lawrence, MA 978-687-9200
Chemindustrial Systems Inc
Cedarburg, WI 262-375-8570
Clark-Cooper Division   Magnatrol Valve Corporation
Cinnaminson, NJ 856-829-4580
Cleveland Vibrator Co
Cleveland, OH 800-221-3298
Corning Life Sciences
Tewksbury, MA 800-492-1110
Crown Controls Inc.
Charlotte, NC 800-541-7874
Custom Poly Packaging
Fort Wayne, IN 800-548-6603
E & E Process Instrumentation
Concord, Ontario, ON 905-669-4857
Ederback Corporation
Ann Arbor, MI 800-422-2558
ENSCO Inc
Springfield, VA 703-321-9000
Fluid Imaging Technologies Inc
Scarborough, ME 207-846-6100
Food Technology Corporation
Sterling, VA 703-444-1870
Foss Nirsystems
Silver Spring, MD 301-755-5200
Gerstel Inc
Linthicum Hts, MD 800-413-8160
Glen Mills Inc
Clifton, NJ 973-777-0777
Grace Instrument Co
Houston, TX 800-304-5859

Gralab Instruments
Centerville, OH 800-876-8353
Greer's Ferry Glass Work
Dubuque, IA 501-589-2947
Haake
Paramus, NJ 800-631-1369
Hanna Instruments
Woonsocket, RI 800-426-6287
Hanson Lab Furniture Inc
Newbury Park, CA 805-498-3121
Hemco Corp
Independence, MO 800-779-4362
Henry Troemner LLC
West Deptford, NJ 856-686-1600
Hunter Lab
Reston, VA 703-471-6870
Idexx Laboratories Inc
Westbrook, ME 800-548-6733
Ika-Works Inc
Wilmington, NC 800-733-3037
IMC Instruments
Menomonee Falls, WI 262-252-4620
IQ Scientific Instruments
Loveland, CO 800-227-4224
Labconco Corp
Kansas City, MO 800-821-5525
Laboratory Devices
Holliston, MA 508-429-1716
Labvantage Solutions Inc
Somerset, NJ 888-346-5467
Lauhoff Corporation
Detroit, MI 313-259-0027
Leeman Labs Inc
Hudson, NH 800-634-9942
Leica Microsystems
Depew, NY 800-346-4560
Libra Technical Center
Metuchen, NJ 732-321-5200
Maselli Measurements Inc
Stockton, CA 800-964-9600
MicroThermics, Inc.
Raleigh, NC 919-878-8045
National Hotpack
Stone Ridge, NY 800-431-8232
National Oilwell Varco
North Andover, MA 800-643-0641
NDC Infrared EngineeringInc
Irwindale, CA 626-960-3300
Netzsch Pumps North America
Exton, PA 610-363-8010
New Brunswick Scientific Co
Enfield, CT 800-645-3050
Noral
Natick, MA 800-348-2345
Omnion
Rockland, MA 781-878-7200
Pa R Systems Inc
St Paul, MN 800-464-1320
Pacific Scientific Instrument
Grants Pass, OR 800-866-7889
Patterson-Kelley   Hars Company
East Stroudsburg, PA 570-421-7500
Perten Instruments
Springfield, IL 888-773-7836
Polyscience
Niles, IL 800-229-7569
Pro Line Co
Haverhill, MA 978-521-2600
Pro Scientific Inc
Oxford, CT 800-584-3776
Q A Supplies LLC
Norfolk, VA 800-472-7205
Radiation Processing Division
Parsippany, NJ 800-442-1969
Rosemount Analytical Inc
Irvine, CA 800-543-8257
Schlueter Company
Janesville, WI 800-359-1700
Scott Turbon Mixer
Adelanto, CA 800-285-8512
Sefi Fabricators Inc
Amityville, NY 631-842-2200
Silverson Machines Inc
East Longmeadow, MA 800-204-6400
Spiral Biotech Inc
Norwood, MA 800-554-1620
Stewart Laboratories
Strattanville, PA 800-640-7869
Straub Designs Co
St Louis Park, MN 952-546-6686
Texture Technologies Corporation
Scarsdale, NY 914-472-0531

Thermex Thermatron
Louisville, KY 502-493-1299
TMCo Inc.ÿ
Houston, TX 713-465-3255
Triad Scientific
Manasquan, NJ 800-867-6690
Tricor Systems Inc
Elgin, IL 800-575-0161
Variety Glass Inc
Cambridge, OH 740-432-3643
Vee Gee Scientific Inc
Kirkland, WA 800-423-8842
VICAM
Milford, MA 800-338-4381
Weber Scientific Inc
Trenton, NJ 800-328-8378
Whatman
Piscataway, NJ 973-245-8300
Whatman
Haverhill, MA 978-374-7400
Wilkens-Anderson Co
Chicago, IL 800-847-2222
X-R-I Testing Inc
Troy, MI 800-973-4800
X-Rite Inc
Grand Rapids, MI 888-800-9580
YSI Inc
Yellow Springs, OH 800-765-4974

Clean Rooms

Advance Energy Technologies
Halfmoon, NY 800-724-0198

Laboratory Sample Testing

Great Lakes Scientific
Stevensville, MI 269-429-1000
Kerry, Inc
Beloit, WI 608-363-1200
Promega
Madison, WI 800-356-9526

Measurement Systems

A&D Weighing
San Jose, CA 800-726-3364
A&M Thermometer Corporation
Asheville, NC 800-685-9211
Abbeon Cal Inc
Santa Barbara, CA 800-922-0977
Abel Manufacturing Co
Appleton, WI 920-734-4443
Acme Scale Co
San Leandro, CA 888-638-5040
Acrison Inc
Moonachie, NJ 800-422-4266
Action Packaging Automation
Roosevelt, NJ 800-241-2724
Advanced Instruments Inc
Norwood, MA 800-225-4034
Agri-Equipment International
Longs, SC 877-550-4709
Agtron Inc
Reno, NV 775-850-4600
Alnor Instrument Company
Skokie, IL 800-424-7427
Ametek
Sellersville, PA 215-257-6531
AMETEK Brookfield
Middleboro, MA 800-628-8139
Analytical Measurements
Chester, NJ 800-635-5580
Anderson-Negele
Fultonville, NY 800-833-0081
Aqua Measure
Rancho Cucamonga, CA 800-966-4788
Arkfeld Mfg & Distributing Co
Norfolk, NE 800-533-0676
ASI Electronics Inc
Cypress, TX 800-231-6066
Athena Controls Inc
Plymouth Meeting, PA 800-782-6776
Atkins Technical
Gainesville, FL 800-284-2842
ATM Corporation
New Berlin, WI 800-511-2096
ATS Rheosystems
Bordentown, NJ 609-298-2522
Aw Sheepscot Holding Co Inc
Franksville, WI 800-850-6110
Badger Meter Inc
Milwaukee, WI 800-876-3837

Banner Engineering Corp
Minneapolis, MN 888-373-6767
Barnant Company
Lake Barrington, IL 800-637-3739
Berthold Technologies
Oak Ridge, TN 865-483-1488
Blancett
Racine, WI 800-235-1638
BLH Electronics
Canton, MA 781-821-2000
Blodgett Co
Houston, TX 281-933-6195
Bowtemp
Mont-Royal, QC 514-735-5551
Brooks Instrument LLC
Hatfield, PA 888-554-3569
Brown Fired Heater
Elyria, OH 440-323-3291
Bry-Air Inc
Sunbury, OH 877-379-2479
BYK Gardner Inc
Columbia, MD 301-483-6500
Cambridge Viscosity, Inc.
Medford, MA 800-554-4639
CEA Instrument Inc
Westwood, NJ 888-893-9640
Chaney Instrument Co
Lake Geneva, WI 800-777-0565
Chemindustrial Systems Inc
Cedarburg, WI 262-375-8570
Chocolate Concepts
Hartville, OH 330-877-3322
Clark-Cooper Division   Magnatrol Valve Corporation
Cinnaminson, NJ 856-829-4580
Clayton Industries
City Of Industry, CA 800-423-4585
CMT
Hamilton, MA 978-768-2555
Columbus Instruments
Columbus, OH 800-669-5011
Comark Instruments
Everett, WA 800-555-6658
Conax Buffalo Technologies
Buffalo, NY 800-223-2389
Control Products Inc
Chanhassen, MN 800-947-9098
Crystal-Vision Packaging Systems
Torrance, CA 800-331-3240
Cyvex Nutrition
Irvine, CA 888-992-9839
Datapaq
Wilmington, MA 800-326-5270
Debelak Technical Systems
Greenville, WI 800-888-4207
Delavan-Delta
Naugatuck, CT 203-720-5610
Devar Inc
Bridgeport, CT 800-566-6822
Dwyer Instruments Inc
Michigan City, IN 800-872-3141
E & E Process Instrumentation
Concord, Ontario, ON 905-669-4857
Electronic Weighing Systems
Opa Locka, FL 305-685-8067
ELISA Technologies, Inc.
Gainesville, FL 352-337-3929
Endress & Hauser
Greenwood, IN 800-428-4344
ENM Co
Chicago, IL 773-775-8400
EPD Technology Corporation
Elmsford, NY 800-892-8926
Esco Products Inc
Houston, TX 800-966-5514
Exact Mixing Systems Inc
Memphis, TN 901-362-8501
Flow Technology Inc
Tempe, AZ 800-833-2448
Food Technology Corporation
Sterling, VA 703-444-1870
Forte Technology
South Easton, MA 508-297-2363
Frazier Precision Instr Co
Hagerstown, MD 301-790-2585
Frye's Measure Mill
Wilton, NH 603-654-6581
Gea Us
Galesville, WI 608-582-3081
Grace Instrument Co
Houston, TX 800-304-5859
Greer's Ferry Glass Work
Dubuque, IA 501-589-2947

Haake
    Paramus, NJ 800-631-1369
Hanna Instruments
    Woonsocket, RI. 800-426-6287
HD Electric Co
    Park City, IL 847-473-4882
Hoffer Flow Controls Inc
    Elizabeth City, NC 800-628-4584
Hunter Lab
    Reston, VA .703-471-6870
Hyer Industries
    Pembroke, MA 781-826-8101
IMC Instruments
    Menomonee Falls, WI. 262-252-4620
Industrial Automation Specs
    Hampton, VA 800-916-4272
Industrial Laboratory Eqpt Co
    Charlotte, NC 704-357-3930
Inspired Automation Inc
    Agoura Hills, CA 818-991-4598
Intelligent Controls
    Saco, ME. 800-872-3455
IQ Scientific Instruments
    Loveland, CO 800-227-4224
IVEK Corp
    N Springfield, VT 800-356-4746
Kason Central
    Columbus, OH 614-885-1992
Kason Industries
    Newnan, GA 770-254-0553
King Engineering - King-Gage
    Newell, WV 800-242-8871
Konica Minolta Corp
    Ramsey, NJ 888-473-3637
L.C. Thompson Company
    Kenosha, WI. 800-558-4018
Leica Microsystems
    Depew, NY .800-346-4560
Liquid Controls LLC
    Lake Bluff, IL 800-458-5262
Liquid Scale
    New Brighton, MN. 888-633-2969
Liquid Solids Control Inc
    Upton, MA .508-529-3377
Lockwood Packaging
    Woburn, MA 800-641-3100
Loma International
    Carol Stream, IL 800-872-5662
Loma Systems
    Carol Stream, IL 800-872-5662
Love Controls Division
    Michigan City, IN 800-828-4588
Lumenite Control Tech Inc
    Franklin Park, IL 800-323-8510
M.H. Rhodes Cramer
    South Windsor, CT 877-684-6464
Machine Applications Corp
    Sandusky, OH 419-621-2322
Maselli Measurements Inc
    Stockton, CA. 800-964-9600
Mesa Laboratories Inc
    Lakewood, CO 800-525-1215
Micro-Strain
    Spring City, PA 610-948-4550
Miljoco Corp
    Mt Clemens, MI 888-888-1498
Moisture Register Products
    Rancho Cucamonga, CA 800-966-4788
Monitor Company
    Modesto, CA. 800-537-3201
Monitor Technologies LLC
    Elburn, IL .800-601-6204
MTL Etching Industries
    Woodmere, NY 516-295-9733
Munters Corp
    Amesbury, MA 800-843-5360
Music City Metals Inc
    Nashville, TN 800-251-2674
National Time Recording Eqpt
    New York, NY 212-227-3310
NDC Infrared EngineeringInc
    Irwindale, CA. 626-960-3300
Nicol Scales & Measurement LP
    Dallas, TX. .800-225-8181
Noral
    Natick, MA 800-348-2345
Ogden Manufacturing Company
    Pittsburgh, PA 412-967-3906
Optek-Danulat
    Germantown, WI. 888-551-4288
Orion Research
    Beverly, MA 978-232-6000

Oyster Bay Pump Works Inc
    Hicksville, NY 516-933-4500
Pacific Scale Company
    Clackamas, OR 800-537-1886
Pacific Scientific Instrument
    Grants Pass, OR 800-866-7889
Paktronics Controls
    Southfield, MI. 248-356-1400
Paratherm Corporation
    Conshohocken, PA 800-222-3611
Peco Controls Corporation
    Modesto, CA. 800-732-6285
Pelouze Scale Company
    Bridgeview, IL 800-323-8363
Perten Instruments
    Springfield, IL. 888-773-7836
Prince Castle Inc
    Carol Stream, IL 800-722-7853
Process Sensors Corp
    Milford, MA 508-473-9901
Reotemp Instrument Corp
    San Diego, CA 800-648-7737
Rheometric Scientific
    New Castle, DE. 732-560-8550
Rosemount Analytical Inc
    Irvine, CA .800-543-8257
Rotronic Instrument Corp Inc
    Hauppauge, NY 800-628-7101
S J Controls Inc
    Signal Hill, CA 562-494-1400
Samson Controls
    Baytown, TX. 281-383-3677
Scientech, Inc
    Boulder, CO 800-525-0522
Sensitech Inc
    Beverly, MA 800-843-8367
Sensor Systems
    Chatsworth, CA 818-341-5366
Sentron
    Gig Harbor, WA 800-472-4361
Siko Products Inc
    Dexter, MI. 800-447-7456
Spinco Metal Products Inc
    Newark, NY 315-331-6285
Sure Torque
    Lakewood, CO 800-387-6572
Tangent Systems
    Charlotte, NC 800-992-7577
Taylor Precision Products
    Oak Brook, IL 866-843-3905
TechnipFMC
    Houston, TX 218-591-4000
Tel-Tru Manufacturing Co
    Rochester, NY 800-232-5335
Testing Machines Inc
    New Castle, DE. 800-678-3221
Texture Technologies Corporation
    Scarsdale, NY 914-472-0531
Thermalogic Corp
    Hudson, MA 978-562-5974
Thermo Detection
    Franklin, MA 866-269-0070
Thermo Instruments
    Yaphank, NY 631-924-0880
Thermo King Corp
    Bloomington, MN. 888-887-2202
Triad Scientific
    Manasquan, NJ 800-867-6690
Tuchenhagen
    Columbia, MD 410-910-6000
Venture Measurement Co LLC
    Spartanburg, SC 800-426-9010
Venture Measurement Co LLC
    Spartanburg, SC 864-574-8960
VitaMinder Company
    Providence, RI 800-858-8840
Water Sciences Services, Inc.
    Jackson, TN 973-584-4131
Weiss Instruments Inc
    Holtsville, NY 631-207-1200
Wescor
    Logan, UT. 800-453-2725
Whatman
    Haverhill, MA 978-374-7400
Wika Instrument LP
    Lawrenceville, GA 800-645-0606
X-Rite Inc
    Grand Rapids, MI 888-800-9580
YSI Inc
    Yellow Springs, OH 800-765-4974

Polarimeters

Bellingham + Stanley
    Suwanee, GA 800-678-8573
Cyvex Nutrition
    Irvine, CA .888-992-9839

Refractometers

Bellingham + Stanley
    Suwanee, GA 800-678-8573
Cyvex Nutrition
    Irvine, CA .888-992-9839

Meters

Flow

Ametek
    Sellersville, PA 215-257-6531
Anderson-Negele
    Fultonville, NY. 800-833-0081
Auburn Systems LLC
    Danvers, MA. 800-255-5008
Aw Sheepscot Holding Co Inc
    Franksville, WI 800-850-6110
Badger Meter Inc
    Milwaukee, WI. 800-876-3837
Barnant Company
    Lake Barrington, IL 800-637-3739
Blancett
    Racine, WI 800-235-1638
Chemindustrial Systems Inc
    Cedarburg, WI. 262-375-8570
Conflow Technologies, Inc.
    Brampton, ON. 800-275-9887
Crown Controls Inc.
    Charlotte, NC 800-541-7874
DMC-David Manufacturing Company
    Mason City, IA 641-424-7010
Flow Technology Inc
    Tempe, AZ 800-833-2448
Hayward Industries Inc
    Clemmons, NC 336-712-9900
Hoffer Flow Controls Inc
    Elizabeth City, NC. 800-628-4584
Kisco Manufacturing
    Port Alberni, BC 604-823-7456
Liquid Controls LLC
    Lake Bluff, IL 800-458-5262
Lumenite Control Tech Inc
    Franklin Park, IL. 800-323-8510
Machine Applications Corp
    Sandusky, OH 419-621-2322
Mesa Laboratories Inc
    Lakewood, CO 800-525-1215
Monitor Technologies LLC
    Elburn, IL 800-601-6204
Music City Metals Inc
    Nashville, TN 800-251-2674
Quality Control Equipment Co
    Des Moines, IA 515-266-2268
S J Controls Inc
    Signal Hill, CA 562-494-1400
Samson Controls
    Baytown, TX 281-383-3677
Schenck Process
    Whitewater, WI. 888-742-1249
Special Products
    Springfield, MO 417-881-6114
Spinco Metal Products Inc
    Newark, NY 315-331-6285
TechnipFMC
    Houston, TX 218-591-4000
TWM Manufacturing
    Leamington, ON 888-495-4831

pH

Analytical Measurements
    Chester, NJ 800-635-5580
Ashcroft Inc
    Stratford, CT. 800-328-8258
BYK Gardner Inc
    Columbia, MD 301-483-6500
Chemindustrial Systems Inc
    Cedarburg, WI. 262-375-8570
Cyvex Nutrition
    Irvine, CA 888-992-9839
DeltaTrak
    Pleasanton, CA 800-962-6776
Devar Inc
    Bridgeport, CT 800-566-6822

E & E Process Instrumentation
Concord, Ontario, ON 905-669-4857
Hanna Instruments
Woonsocket, RI 800-426-6287
IQ Scientific Instruments
Loveland, CO 800-227-4224
Q A Supplies LLC
Norfolk, VA 800-472-7205
Tricor Systems Inc
Elgin, IL .800-575-0161
Wilkens-Anderson Co
Chicago, IL 800-847-2222
X-Rite Inc
Grand Rapids, MI 888-800-9580
YSI Inc
Yellow Springs, OH 800-765-4974

Microbiology Instruments & Supplies

Baltimore Aircoil Co
Jessup, MD 410-799-1300
Becton Dickinson & Co.
Franklin Lakes, NJ 201-847-6800
Biolog Inc
Hayward, CA 800-284-4949
Biomerieux Inc
Durham, NC 800-682-2666
Malthus Diagnostics
North Ridgeville, OH 800-346-7202
Microbiologics Inc
St Cloud, MN 800-599-2847
Neutec Group
Farmingdale, NY 888-810-5179
New Brunswick Scientific Co
Enfield, CT 800-645-3050
Q A Supplies LLC
Norfolk, VA 800-472-7205
VICAM
Milford, MA 800-338-4381
Whatman
Piscataway, NJ 973-245-8300
Wilkens-Anderson Co
Chicago, IL 800-847-2222

Process Analysis & Development

A & B Process Systems Corp
Stratford, WI 888-258-2789
Asset Design Inc
Mooresville, NC 888-293-1740
Datapaq
Wilmington, MA 800-326-5270
Emerson Process Management
Boulder, CO 800-522-6277
Food & Agrosystems
Sunnyvale, CA 408-245-8450
J M Canty Inc E1200 Engineers
Lockport, NY 716-625-4227
Vee Gee Scientific Inc
Kirkland, WA 800-423-8842

Electronic Survey

Innovative Food Solutions LLC
Columbus, OH 800-884-3314
Libra Technical Center
Metuchen, NJ 732-321-5200
Long Range Systems
Addison, TX 800-577-8101

Process Controls

Batching, Blending, Weighing

A & B Process Systems Corp
Stratford, WI 888-258-2789
Abel Manufacturing Co
Appleton, WI 920-734-4443
APEC
Lake Odessa, MI 616-374-1000
ASI Electronics Inc
Cypress, TX 800-231-6066
Autocon Mixing Systems
St Helena, CA 800-225-6192
AZO Food
Memphis, TN 901-794-9480
Batching Systems
Prince Frederick, MD 800-311-0851
BLH Electronics
Canton, MA 781-821-2000
Chicago Conveyor Corporation
Addison, IL 630-543-6300

Coastline Equipment Inc
Bellingham, WA 360-734-8509
Conflow Technologies, Inc.
Brampton, ON 800-275-9887
Digital Dynamics Inc
Scotts Valley, CA 800-765-1288
Hoffer Flow Controls Inc
Elizabeth City, NC 800-628-4584
JCS Controls, Inc.
Rochester, NY 585-227-5910
Letrah International Corp
Fort Atkinson, WI 920-563-6597
Liquid Solids Control Inc
Upton, MA 508-529-3377
Matiss
St Georges, QC 888-562-8477
MERRICK Industries Inc
Lynn Haven, FL 800-271-7834
Nu-Con Equipment
Chanhassen, MN 877-939-0510
Pickwick Manufacturing Svc
Cedar Rapids, IA 800-397-9797
Pro Scientific Inc
Oxford, CT 800-584-3776
Quest Corp
North Royalton, OH 440-230-9400
Schaffer Poidometer Company
Pittsburgh, PA 412-281-9031
Schenck Process
Whitewater, WI 888-742-1249
Silverson Machines Inc
East Longmeadow, MA 800-204-6400
Sterling Systems & Controls
Sterling, IL 800-257-7214
T D Sawvel Co
Maple Plain, MN 877-488-1816
Tecweigh
St Paul, MN 800-536-4880
Thermedics Detection
Chelmsford, MA 888-846-7226
Trola Industries Inc
York, PA .717-848-3700

Control Panels

A & B Process Systems Corp
Stratford, WI 888-258-2789
Asap Automation
Addison, IL 800-409-0383
Digital Dynamics Inc
Scotts Valley, CA 800-765-1288
Letrah International Corp
Fort Atkinson, WI 920-563-6597
Novar
Cleveland, OH 800-348-1235
Our Name is Mud
New York, NY 877-683-7867
Pro Controls Inc
Yakima, WA 800-488-3386
Process Solutions
Riviera Beach, FL 561-840-0050
Red Lion Controls Inc
York, PA .717-767-6511
South Shore Controls Inc
Perry, OH .440-259-2500
Trola Industries Inc
York, PA .717-848-3700
Viatran Corporation
North Tonawanda, NY 800-688-0030
Washington Frontier
Grandview, WA 509-469-7662

Humidity Loggers

Ashcroft Inc
Stratford, CT 800-328-8258

Pressure

ACR Systems
Surrey, BC 800-663-7845
Acromag Inc.
Wixom, MI 248-624-1541
Alnor Instrument Company
Skokie, IL .800-424-7427
Ashcroft Inc
Stratford, CT 800-328-8258
Chicago Stainless Eqpt Inc
Palm City, FL 800-927-8575
Control Products Inc
Chanhassen, MN 800-947-9098
Endress & Hauser
Greenwood, IN 800-428-4344

IMC Instruments
Menomonee Falls, WI 262-252-4620
Omni Controls Inc
Tampa, FL 800-783-6664
Peco Controls Corporation
Modesto, CA 800-732-6285
Samson Controls
Baytown, TX 281-383-3677
United Electric Controls Co
Watertown, MA 617-926-1000
Washington Frontier
Grandview, WA 509-469-7662
Weiss Instruments Inc
Holtsville, NY 631-207-1200

Data Loggers

Ashcroft Inc
Stratford, CT 800-328-8258
JUMO Process Control Inc
East Syracuse, NY 800-554-5866

Gauges; Sanitary

Ashcroft Inc
Stratford, CT 800-328-8258

Programmable

ACR Systems
Surrey, BC 800-663-7845
Allpax Products
Covington, LA 888-893-9277
American Autogard Corporation
Rockford, IL 815-229-3190
Ashcroft Inc
Stratford, CT 800-328-8258
Boston Gear
Boston, MA 888-999-9860
Chicago Conveyor Corporation
Addison, IL 630-543-6300
Intelligent Controls
Saco, ME .800-872-3455
Pro Scientific Inc
Oxford, CT 800-584-3776
Selco Products Company
Anaheim, CA 800-257-3526
Sterling Systems & Controls
Sterling, IL 800-257-7214
Thermex Thermatron
Louisville, KY 502-493-1299
Theta Sciences
San Diego, CA 760-745-3311

Recorders

Ashcroft Inc
Stratford, CT 800-328-8258
Datapaq
Wilmington, MA 800-326-5270
Delta Trak
Pleasanton, CA 800-962-6776
Devar Inc
Bridgeport, CT 800-566-6822
Hanna Instruments
Woonsocket, RI 800-426-6287
Industrial Automation Specs
Hampton, VA 800-916-4272
Mesa Laboratories Inc
Lakewood, CO 800-525-1215
Pyrometer Instrument Co Inc
Windsor, NJ 800-468-7976
Sensitech Inc
Redmond, WA 800-999-7926
Simplex Time Recorder Company
Santa Ana, CA 949-724-5000

Software

Iconics Inc
Foxboro, MA 800-946-9679
Loma Systems
Carol Stream, IL 800-872-5662

Systems

A & B Process Systems Corp
Stratford, WI 888-258-2789
Abel Manufacturing Co
Appleton, WI 920-734-4443
Ace Specialty Mfg Co Inc
Rosemead, CA 626-444-3867
Acrison Inc
Moonachie, NJ 800-422-4266

Acromag Inc.
Wixom, MI 248-624-1541
Advanced Instruments Inc
Norwood, MA 800-225-4034
AL Systems
Rockaway, NJ 888-960-8324
Allegheny Bradford Corp
Bradford, PA 800-542-0650
Allpax Products
Covington, LA 888-893-9277
Alnor Instrument Company
Skokie, IL 800-424-7427
American Autogard Corporation
Rockford, IL 815-229-3190
American LEWA
Holliston, MA 888-539-2123
American Metal Door Company
Richmond, IN 800-428-2737
Analite
Plainview, NY 800-229-3357
Andantex USA Inc
Ocean, NJ 800-713-6170
Anderson-Negele
Fultonville, NY 800-833-0081
Applexion
Chicago, IL 773-243-0454
APV Americas
Delavan, WI 800-252-5200
Artisan Controls Corp
Randolph, NJ 800-457-4950
Asap Automation
Addison, IL 800-409-0383
ASI Electronics Inc
Cypress, TX 800-231-6066
Athena Controls Inc
Plymouth Meeting, PA 800-782-6776
Auburn Systems LLC
Danvers, MA 800-255-5008
Autocon Mixing Systems
St Helena, CA 800-225-6192
Automation Service
Earth City, MO 800-325-4808
Autotron
Oak Creek, WI 800-527-7500
Axelrod, Norman N
New York, NY 212-369-2885
AZO Food
Memphis, TN 901-794-9480
B T Engineering Inc
Bala Cynwyd, PA 610-664-9500
Batching Systems
Prince Frederick, MD 800-311-0851
Bentley Instruments Inc
Chaska, MN 952-448-7600
BLH Electronics
Canton, MA 781-821-2000
Blue Tech
Hickory, NC 828-324-5900
Brown Fired Heater
Elyria, OH 440-323-3291
Bry-Air Inc
Sunbury, OH 877-379-2479
BSI Instruments
Aliquippa, PA 800-274-9851
Burling Instrument Inc
Chatham, NJ 800-635-2526
Burns Engineering Inc
Hopkins, MN 800-328-3871
Cal Controls
Gurnee, IL 800-866-6659
Cashco Inc
Ellsworth, KS 785-472-4461
Centent Co
Santa Ana, CA 714-979-6491
Chil-Con Products
Brantford, ON 800-263-0086
Chillers Solutions
Pompton Plains, NJ 800-526-5201
Cleveland Motion Controls
Cleveland, OH 800-321-8072
Coastline Equipment Inc
Bellingham, WA 360-734-8509
Conflow Technologies, Inc.
Brampton, ON. 800-275-9887
Contrex Inc
Maple Grove, MN 763-424-7800
Control Concepts Inc.
Chanhassen, MN. 800-765-2799
Control Pak Intl
Fenton, MI 810-735-2800
Control Products Inc
Chanhassen, MN. 800-947-9098

Control Systems Design
Forest Hill, MD. 410-296-0466
Control Technology Corp
Hopkinton, MA 800-282-5008
Conveyor Components Co
Croswell, MI 800-233-3233
Cotter Brothers Corp
Danvers, MA 978-777-5001
Cramer Company
South Windsor, CT 877-684-6464
Crouzet Corporation
Carrollton, TX 800-677-5311
Damrow Company
Fond Du Lac, WI 800-236-1501
Debelak Technical Systems
Greenville, WI 800-888-4207
DEFCO
Landenberg, PA 215-274-8245
Delavan-Delta
Naugatuck, CT 203-720-5610
Design Technology Corporation
Lexington, MA 800-597-7063
Devar Inc
Bridgeport, CT 800-566-6822
Diamond Automation
Farmington Hills, MI 248-426-9394
Dickson
Addison, IL 800-757-3747
Digital Dynamics Inc
Scotts Valley, CA 800-765-1288
Dipix Technologies
Ottawa, ON 613-596-4942
Distaview Corp
Bowling Green, OH 800-795-9970
Dwyer Instruments Inc
Michigan City, IN 800-872-3141
Ecklund-Harrison Technologies
Fort Myers, FL 239-936-6032
Electro Cam Corp
Roscoe, IL 800-228-5487
Electrol Specialties Co
South Beloit, IL 815-389-2291
Endress & Hauser
Greenwood, IN 800-428-4344
ESE, Inc
Marshfield, WI 800-236-4778
Eurotherm
Ashburn, VA 703-726-0138
Fata Automation
Sterling Heights, MI 586-323-9400
Flow Aerospace
Jeffersonville, IN 812-283-7888
Forte Technology
South Easton, MA. 508-297-2363
Foxboro Company
Houston, TX 888-369-2676
Gems Sensors & Controls
Plainville, CT 860-747-3000
Glatt Air Techniques Inc
Ramsey, NJ 201-825-8700
Gralab Instruments
Centerville, OH 800-876-8353
Hanna Instruments
Woonsocket, RI 800-426-6287
Harland Simon Control Systems USA
Oakbrook, IL 630-572-7650
Hectronic
Oklahoma City, OK 405-946-3574
Hoffer Flow Controls Inc
Elizabeth City, NC 800-628-4584
Hudson Control Group Inc
Springfield, NJ 973-376-8265
Innovative Components
Southington, CT 800-789-2851
Intelligent Controls
Saco, ME. 800-872-3455
Interstate Monroe Machinery
Seattle, WA 206-682-4870
ITW Engineered Polymers
Oxford, MI 248-628-2587
Kinematics & Controls Corporation
Brooksville, FL 800-833-8103
L.C. Thompson Company
Kenosha, WI 800-558-4018
Lake Process Systems Inc
Lake Barrington, IL 800-331-9260
LDJ Electronics
Troy, MI 248-528-2202
Letrah International Corp
Fort Atkinson, WI. 920-563-6597
Light Technology Ind
Gaithersburg, MD. 301-990-4050

Liquid Controls LLC
Lake Bluff, IL 800-458-5262
Liquid Solids Control Inc
Upton, MA 508-529-3377
Love Controls Division
Michigan City, IN 800-828-4588
Lumenite Control Tech Inc
Franklin Park, IL. 800-323-8510
Maselli Measurements Inc
Stockton, CA 800-964-9600
MeGa Industries
Burlington, ON 800-665-6342
Membrane Process & Controls
Edgar, WI 715-352-3206
MERRICK Industries Inc
Lynn Haven, FL 800-271-7834
Micromeritics
Norcross, GA 770-638-7569
Midwest Stainless
Menomonie, WI 715-235-5472
Monitor Technologies LLC
Elburn, IL 800-601-6204
Murata Automated Systems
Charlotte, NC 800-428-8469
Murzan Inc
Peachtree Cor, GA 770-448-0583
Namco Controls Corporation
Cleveland, OH 800-626-8324
Napco Security Systems Inc
Amityville, NY 631-842-0253
Nelles Automation
Houston, TX 713-939-9399
Novar
Cleveland, OH 800-348-1235
Nu-Con Equipment
Chanhassen, MN. 877-939-0510
Omni Controls Inc
Tampa, FL 800-783-6664
OMRON Systems LLC
Schaumburg, IL. 800-556-6766
Onset Computer Corp
Bourne, MA 800-564-4377
Optek Inc
Galena, OH 800-533-8400
Paktronics Controls
Southfield, MI 248-356-1400
Papertech
North Vancouver, BC 877-787-2737
Partnership Resources
Minneapolis, MN 612-331-2075
Payne Controls Co
Scott Depot, WV. 800-331-1345
Peco Controls Corporation
Modesto, CA 800-732-6285
Pro Controls Inc
Yakima, WA 800-488-3386
Process Automation
Hurst, TX 800-460-9546
Process Solutions
Riviera Beach, FL. 561-840-0050
Process Systems
Barrington, IL 847-842-8618
Production Systems
Marietta, GA 800-235-9734
Professional Engineering Assoc
Louisville, KY 502-429-0432
Pyrometer Instrument Co Inc
Windsor, NJ. 800-468-7976
Quest Corp
North Royalton, OH 440-230-9400
R.G. Stephens Engineering
Long Beach, CA 800-499-3001
Ram Equipment Co
Waukesha, WI 262-513-1114
Relco Unisystems Corp
Willmar, MN 320-231-2210
Rexroth Corporation
Hoffman Estates, IL 847-645-3600
Rheometric Scientific
New Castle, DE. 732-560-8550
Roberts-Gordon LLC
Buffalo, NY. 800-828-7450
S J Controls Inc
Signal Hill, CA 562-494-1400
Samson Controls
Baytown, TX. 281-383-3677
Schneider Electric
Foxboro, MA 781-534-7535
Scientech, Inc
Boulder, CO 800-525-0522
SCK Direct Inc
Stratford, CT 800-327-8766

Seneca Environmental Products
Tiffin, OH 419-447-1282
Sepragen Corp
Hayward, CA 510-475-0650
Simpson Electric
Elgin, IL 847-697-2260
South Shore Controls Inc
Perry, OH 440-259-2500
Spinco Metal Products Inc
Newark, NY 315-331-6285
Stainless Products
Somers, WC 800-558-9446
Sterling Ball & Jewel
New Berlin, WI 800-423-3183
Sterling Systems & Controls
Sterling, IL 800-257-7214
T D Sawvel Co
Maple Plain, MN 877-488-1816
Tecweigh
St Paul, MN 800-536-4880
Thermedics Detection
Chelmsford, MA 888-846-7226
Thermo Detection
Franklin, MA 866-269-0070
Thermo King Corp
Bloomington, MN 888-887-2202
Theta Sciences
San Diego, CA 760-745-3311
Transbotics Corp
Charlotte, NC 704-362-1115
Trola Industries Inc
York, PA 717-848-3700
Tuchenhagen
Columbia, MD 410-910-6000
TVC Systems
Portsmouth, NH 888-431-5251
TWM Manufacturing
Leamington, ON 888-495-4831
Vee Gee Scientific Inc
Kirkland, WA 800-423-8842
Videx Inc
Corvallis, OR 541-738-5500
Vulcan Electric Co
Porter, ME 800-922-3027
W.G. Durant Corporation
Whittier, CA 562-946-5555
Watlow Electric
San Jose, CA
Watlow Electric
St Louis, MO 314-878-4600
Waukesha Cherry-Burrell
Louisville, KY 800-252-5200
Webb-Triax Company
Farmington Hills, MI 248-553-1000
WeighPack Systems/Paxiom Group
Montreal, QC 888-934-4472
Williamson & Co
Greer, SC 800-849-3263
Xcel Tower Controls
Gilbertsville, NY 800-288-7362

Temperature

ACR Systems
Surrey, BC 800-663-7845
Acromag Inc.
Wixom, MI 248-624-1541
Advance Energy Technologies
Halfmoon, NY 800-724-0198
Alnor Instrument Company
Skokie, IL 800-424-7427
Analite
Plainview, NY 800-229-3357
Ari Industries Inc
Addison, IL 800-237-6725
Artisan Controls Corp
Randolph, NJ 800-457-4950
Athena Controls Inc
Plymouth Meeting, PA 800-782-6776
Automatic Timing & Controls
Newell, WV 800-727-5646
Brown Fired Heater
Elyria, OH 440-323-3291
Bry-Air Inc
Sunbury, OH 877-379-2479
Burling Instrument Inc
Chatham, NJ 800-635-2526
Burns Engineering Inc
Hopkins, MN 800-328-3871
Chicago Stainless Eqpt Inc
Palm City, FL 800-927-8575

CMT
Hamilton, MA 978-768-2555
Control Concepts Inc.
Chanhassen, MN 800-765-2799
Control Pak Intl
Fenton, MI 810-735-2800
Control Products Inc
Chanhassen, MN 800-947-9098
Cooling Technology Inc
Charlotte, NC 800-872-1448
Crouzet Corporation
Carrollton, TX 800-677-5311
Debelak Technical Systems
Greenville, WI 800-888-4207
Dwyer Instruments Inc
Michigan City, IN 800-872-3141
Eurotherm
Ashburn, VA 703-726-0138
Glo-Quartz Electric Heater
Mentor, OH 800-321-3574
Hanna Instruments
Woonsocket, RI 800-426-6287
Heatrex
Meadville, PA 800-394-6589
IMC Instruments
Menomonee Falls, WI. 262-252-4620
Kaye Instruments
N Billerica, MA 800-343-4624
L.C. Thompson Company
Kenosha, WI 800-558-4018
Laboratory Devices
Holliston, MA 508-429-1716
Love Controls Division
Michigan City, IN 800-828-4588
Lumenite Control Tech Inc
Franklin Park, IL 800-323-8510
Munters Corp
Amesbury, MA 800-843-5360
Novar
Cleveland, OH 800-348-1235
Ogden Manufacturing Company
Pittsburgh, PA 412-967-3906
Omni Controls Inc
Tampa, FL 800-783-6664
OMRON Systems LLC
Schaumburg, IL. 800-556-6766
Paktronics Controls
Southfield, MI 248-356-1400
Paratherm Corporation
Conshohocken, PA 800-222-3611
Payne Controls Co
Scott Depot, WV 800-331-1345
Polyscience
Niles, IL 800-229-7569
Pyrometer Instrument Co Inc
Windsor, NJ 800-468-7976
Quantem Corp
Ewing, NJ 609-883-9879
Selco Products Company
Anaheim, CA 800-257-3526
Sterling Ball & Jewel
New Berlin, WI 800-423-3183
Thermalogic Corp
Hudson, MA 978-562-5974
Thermo King Corp
Bloomington, MN 888-887-2202
United Electric Controls Co
Watertown, MA 617-926-1000
Vulcan Electric Co
Porter, ME 800-922-3027
Weiss Instruments Inc
Holtsville, NY 631-207-1200

Data Loggers

Ashcroft Inc
Stratford, CT 800-328-8258

Time

Artisan Controls Corp
Randolph, NJ 800-457-4950
Ashcroft Inc
Stratford, CT 800-328-8258
Automatic Timing & Controls
Newell, WV 800-727-5646
Control Products Inc
Chanhassen, MN 800-947-9098
Dayton Marking Devices Company
Dayton, OH 937-432-0285
M.H. Rhodes Cramer
South Windsor, CT 877-684-6464

Pro Scientific Inc
Oxford, CT 800-584-3776

Transportation Loggers

Ashcroft Inc
Stratford, CT 800-328-8258

Vacuum

Ashcroft Inc
Stratford, CT 800-328-8258
BUCHI Corp
New Castle, DE. 877-692-8244
Lyco Wausau
Wausau, WI 715-845-7867

pH Loggers

Ashcroft Inc
Stratford, CT 800-328-8258

Pumps

Food

Barnant Company
Lake Barrington, IL 800-637-3739
Clark-Cooper Division   Magnatrol Valve Corporation
Cinnaminson, NJ. 856-829-4580
Fluid Metering Inc
Syosset, NY. 800-223-3388
Glen Mills Inc.
Clifton, NJ. 973-777-0777
Kelmin Products
Plymouth, FL 407-886-6079
Lyco Wausau
Wausau, WI. 715-845-7867
Marlow Watson Inc
Wilmington, MA 800-282-8823
Netzsch Pumps North America
Exton, PA 610-363-8010
Northland Process Piping
Isle, MN 320-679-2119
Pump Solutions Group
Oakbrook Terrace, IL 630-487-2240
Roto-Jet Pump
Salt Lake City, UT 801-359-8731
Savage Brothers Company
Elk Grove Vlg, IL. 800-342-0973
Waukesha Cherry-Burrell
Louisville, KY 800-252-5200

Sampling & Testing Equipment & Instrumentation

ACR Systems
Surrey, BC. 800-663-7845
Advance Fittings Corp
Elkhorn, WI. 262-723-6699
Advanced Instruments Inc
Norwood, MA 800-225-4034
Air Logic Power Systems
Milwaukee, WI 800-325-8717
Atkins Technical
Gainesville, FL 800-284-2842
Barco Inc
Duluth, GA 678-475-8000
Binks Industries Inc
Montgomery, IL 630-801-1100
Biocontrol Systems Inc
Bellevue, WA 800-245-0113
Bioscience International Inc
Rockville, MD 301-231-7400
Biotest Diagnostics Corporation
Rockaway, NJ 800-522-0090
Bran & Luebbe
Schaumburg, IL. 847-882-8116
Charm Sciences Inc
Lawrence, MA 978-687-9200
Comark Instruments
Everett, WA. 800-555-6658
DeltaTrak
Pleasanton, CA 800-962-6776
Elwood Safety Company
Buffalo, NY. 866-326-6060
ENSCO Inc
Springfield, VA 703-321-9000
F I L T E C-Inspection Systems
Torrance, CA. 888-434-5832
Gerstel Inc
Linthicum Hts, MD 800-413-8160

Glen Mills Inc.
Clifton, NJ....................973-777-0777
Grace Instrument Co
Houston, TX...................800-304-5859
HD Electric Co
Park City, IL.................847-473-4882
I.W. Tremont Company
Hawthorne, NJ.................973-427-3800
Idexx Laboratories Inc
Westbrook, ME.................800-548-6733
IQ Scientific Instruments
Loveland, CO..................800-227-4224
Kodex Inc
Nutley, NJ....................800-325-6339
Konica Minolta Corp
Ramsey, NJ....................888-473-3637
Labvantage Solutions Inc
Somerset, NJ..................888-346-5467
Light Technology Ind
Gaithersburg, MD..............301-990-4050
Machine Applications Corp
Sandusky, OH..................419-621-2322
Maselli Measurements Inc
Stockton, CA..................800-964-9600
Mosshaim Innovations
Jacksonville, FL..............888-995-7775
National Hotpack
Stone Ridge, NY...............800-431-8232
Neogen Corp
Lansing, MI...................800-234-5333
Noral
Natick, MA....................800-348-2345
Ohio Magnetics Inc
Maple Heights, OH.............800-486-6446
Orion Research
Beverly, MA...................978-232-6000
Paul N. Gardner Company
Pompano Beach, FL.............800-762-2478
Peco Controls Corporation
Modesto, CA...................800-732-6285
Perten Instruments
Springfield, IL...............888-773-7836
Polyscience
Niles, IL.....................800-229-7569
Promega
Madison, WI...................800-356-9526
QMI
St Paul, MN...................651-501-2337
Quality Control Equipment Co
Des Moines, IA................515-266-2268
Remel
Lenexa, KS....................800-255-6730
SDIX
Newark, DE....................800-544-8881
Sensidyne
St. Petersburg, FL............800-451-9444
Sentry Equipment Corp
Oconomowoc, WI................262-567-7256
Spiral Biotech Inc
Norwood, MA...................800-554-1620
Staplex Co Inc
Brooklyn, NY..................800-221-0822
Tricor Systems Inc
Elgin, IL.....................800-575-0161
Troxler Electronic Lab Inc
Durham, NC....................877-876-9537
Univex Corp
Salem, NH.....................800-258-6358
Vee Gee Scientific Inc
Kirkland, WA..................800-423-8842
Weber Scientific Inc
Trenton, NJ...................800-328-8378
Whatman
Haverhill, MA.................978-374-7400

Scales & Weighing Systems

A&D Weighing
San Jose, CA..................800-726-3364
Abel Manufacturing Co
Appleton, WI..................920-734-4443
Accu-Pak
Akron, OH
Acme Scale Co
San Leandro, CA...............888-638-5040
Action Packaging Automation
Roosevelt, NJ.................800-241-2724
Actionpac Scales Automation
Oxnard, CA....................800-394-0154
Adamatic
Auburn, WA....................800-578-2547
Advance Weight Systems Inc
Grafton, OH...................440-926-3691

Ag-Pak
Gasport, NY...................716-772-2651
All Fill Inc
Exton, PA.....................866-255-4455
Amark Packaging Systems
Kansas City, MO...............816-965-9000
American Bag & Burlap Company
Chelsea, MA...................617-884-7600
Andgar Corp
Ferndale, WA..................360-366-9900
AP Dataweigh Inc
Cumming, GA...................877-409-2562
APEC
Lake Odessa, MI...............616-374-1000
Arkfeld Mfg & Distributing Co
Norfolk, NE...................800-533-0676
ASI Electronics Inc
Cypress, TX...................800-231-6066
Atlas Equipment Company
Kansas City, MO...............800-842-9188
Automated Packaging Systems
Streetsboro, OH...............800-527-0733
Avery Weigh-Tronix
Fairmont, MN..................877-368-2039
Avery Weigh-Tronix LLC
Fairmont, MN..................800-368-2039
AZO Food
Memphis, TN...................901-794-9480
B & P Process Equipment
Saginaw, MI...................989-757-1300
BLH Electronics
Canton, MA....................781-821-2000
Blodgett Co
Houston, TX...................281-933-6195
Brechbuhler Scales
Canton, OH....................330-453-2424
Cardinal Scale Mfg Co
Webb City, MO.................800-441-4237
CCi Scale Company
Clovis, CA....................800-900-0224
Chemi-Graphic Inc
Ludlow, MA....................413-589-0151
Chlorinators Inc
Stuart, FL....................800-327-9761
Cintex of America
Carol Stream, IL..............800-424-6839
Circuits & Systems Inc
East Rockaway, NY.............800-645-4301
Crestware
North Salt Lake, UT...........800-345-0513
Crystal-Vision Packaging Systems
Torrance, CA..................800-331-3240
DBE Inc
Concord, ON...................800-461-5313
Delavan Spray Technologies
Bamberg, SC...................800-982-6943
Detecto Scale Co
Webb City, MO.................800-641-2008
Dipix Technologies
Ottawa, ON....................613-596-4942
Doran Scales Inc
Batavia, IL...................800-365-0084
Edlund Co
Burlington, VT................800-772-2126
Electronic Weighing Systems
Opa Locka, FL.................305-685-8067
Emery Winslow Scale Co
Seymour, CT...................203-881-9333
Equipment Outlet
Meridian, ID..................208-887-1472
Exact Equipment Corporation
Morrisville, PA...............215-295-2000
Fairbanks Scales
Kansas City, MO...............800-451-4107
Fawema Packaging Machinery
Palmetto, FL..................941-351-9597
Frazier Precision Instr Co
Hagerstown, MD................301-790-2585
Fred D Pfening Co
Columbus, OH..................614-294-5361
Fuller Weighing Systems
Columbus, OH..................614-882-8121
General Bag Corporation
Cleveland, OH.................800-837-9396
General Packaging Equipment Co
Houston, TX...................713-686-4331
Grain Machinery Mfg Corp
Miami, FL.....................305-620-2525
Hardy Systems Corporation
Northbrook, IL................800-927-3956
Howes S Co Inc
Silver Creek, NY..............888-255-2611

Hyer Industries
Pembroke, MA..................781-826-8101
IEW
Niles, OH.....................330-652-0113
Ilapak Inc
Newtown, PA...................215-579-2900
Iman Pack
Westland, MI..................800-810-4626
Industrial Laboratory Eqpt Co
Charlotte, NC.................704-357-3930
Inspired Automation Inc
Agoura Hills, CA..............818-991-4598
Intercomp
Hamel, MN.....................800-328-3336
IWS Scales
San Diego, CA.................800-881-9755
Key Material Handling Inc
Simi Valley, CA...............800-539-7225
Key-Pak Machines
Lebanon, NJ...................908-236-2111
Kisco Manufacturing
Port Alberni, BC..............604-823-7456
Kliklok-Woodman
Decatur, GA...................770-981-5200
Lock Inspection Systems
Fitchburg, MA.................800-227-5539
Lockwood Packaging
Woburn, MA....................800-641-3100
MAC Equipment
Kansas City, MO...............800-821-2476
Mandeville Company
Minneapolis, MN...............800-328-8490
Measurement Systems Intl
Tukwila, WA...................800-874-4320
MERRICK Industries Inc
Lynn Haven, FL................800-271-7834
Micro-Strain
Spring City, PA...............610-948-4550
MTL Etching Industries
Woodmere, NY..................516-295-9733
National Scoop & Equipment Company
Spring House, PA..............215-646-2040
Nicol Scales & Measurement LP
Dallas, TX....................800-225-8181
Ohaus Corp
Parsippany, NJ................800-672-7722
Pacific Scale Company
Clackamas, OR.................800-537-1886
Peco Controls Corporation
Modesto, CA...................800-732-6285
Pelouze Scale Company
Bridgeview, IL................800-323-8363
Penn Scale ManufacturingCompany
Philadelphia, PA..............215-739-9644
Precision Solutions Inc
Quakertown, PA................215-536-4400
Q A Supplies LLC
Norfolk, VA...................800-472-7205
Quest Corp
North Royalton, OH............440-230-9400
Renard Machine Company
Green Bay, WI.................920-432-8412
Renold Products
Westfield, NY.................800-879-2529
Rice Lake Weighing Systems
Rice Lake, WI.................800-472-6703
Sartorius Corp
Edgewood, NY..................800-635-2906
Schaffer Poidometer Company
Pittsburgh, PA................412-281-9031
Scientech, Inc
Boulder, CO...................800-525-0522
Si-Lodec
Tukwila, WA...................800-255-8274
Sig Pack
Oakland, CA...................800-824-3245
Sterling Scale Co
Southfield, MI................800-331-9931
Sterling Systems & Controls
Sterling, IL..................800-257-7214
Summit Machine Builders Corporation
Denver, CO....................800-274-6741
Superior Products Company
Saint Paul, MN................800-328-9800
Taylor Products Co
Parsons, KS...................888-882-9567
TEC America
Atlanta, GA...................770-453-0868
Tecweigh
St Paul, MN...................800-536-4880
Temco
Oakland, CA...................707-746-5966

Thermo BLH
Canton, MA 781-821-2000
Thurman Scale
Groveport, OH 800-688-9741
Tomac Packaging
Woburn, MA 800-641-3100
Toroid Corp
Huntsville, AL 256-837-7510
Triangle Package Machinery Co
Chicago, IL 800-621-4170
Tridyne Process Systems
South Burlington, VT 802-863-6873
Triner Scale & Mfg Co
Olive Branch, MS 800-238-0152
Vande Berg SCALES/Vbs Inc
Sioux Center, IA 712-722-1181
Vega Americas Inc
Cincinnati, OH 800-367-5383
Vertex Interactive
Clifton, NJ 973-777-3500
VitaMinder Company
Providence, RI 800-858-8840
Weigh Right Automatic Scale Co
Joliet, IL 800-571-0249
WeighPack Systems/Paxiom Group
Montreal, QC 888-934-4472
Yakima Wire Works
Reedley, CA 800-344-8951
Yamato Corporation
Colorado Springs, CO. 800-538-1762
Yargus Manufacturing Inc
Marshall, IL 217-826-8059

Sensors

Applied Robotics Inc
Schenectady, NY 800-309-3475
Ari Industries Inc
Addison, IL 800-237-6725
Ashcroft Inc
Stratford, CT 800-328-8258
Automatic Timing & Controls
Newell, WV 800-727-5646
Aw Sheepscot Holding Co Inc
Franksville, WI 800-850-6110
Axelrod, Norman N
New York, NY 212-369-2885
Banner Engineering Corp
Minneapolis, MN 888-373-6767
Burns Engineering Inc
Hopkins, MN 800-328-3871
Clean Water Systems
Klamath Falls, OR 866-273-9993
Conax Buffalo Technologies
Buffalo, NY 800-223-2389
Eurotherm
Ashburn, VA 703-726-0138
Fsi Technologies
Lombard, IL 800-468-6009
GE Interlogix Industrial
Tualatin, OR 800-247-9447
Honeywell Sensing & Internet of Things
DE 800-537-6945
Industrial Devices Corporation
Petaluma, CA 707-789-1000
Infitec Inc
East Syracuse, NY 800-334-0837
Kinematics & Controls Corporation
Brooksville, FL 800-833-8103
Light Technology Ind
Gaithersburg, MD. 301-990-4050
Love Controls Division
Michigan City, IN. 800-828-4588
Magpowr
Fenton, MO. 800-624-7697
Mesa Laboratories Inc
Lakewood, CO 800-525-1215
Migatron Corp
Woodstock, IL. 888-644-2876
Monitor Technologies LLC
Elburn, IL 800-601-6204
Namco Controls Corporation
Cleveland, OH 800-626-8324
OMRON Systems LLC
Schaumburg, IL. 800-556-6766
Ozotech Inc
Yreka, CA. 530-842-4189
Prominent Fluid Controls Inc
Pittsburgh, PA. 412-787-2484
Pyrometer Instrument Co Inc
Windsor, NJ. 800-468-7976
Quantem Corp
Ewing, NJ 609-883-9879

Raytek Corporation
Santa Cruz, CA 800-866-5478
Reflectronics
Lexington, KY 888-415-0441
SICK Inc
Bloomington, MN 800-325-7425
Tri-Tronics
Tampa, FL. 800-237-0946
United Electric Controls Co
Watertown, MA 617-926-1000
Vega Americas Inc
Cincinnati, OH 800-367-5383
Venture Measurement Co LLC
Spartanburg, SC 864-574-8960
Viatran Corporation
North Tonawanda, NY 800-688-0030
Vulcan Electric Co
Porter, ME................800-922-3027
Watlow Electric
Richmond, IL

Stoppers

Rubber, Bottle

Crown Holdings, Inc.
Yardley, PA 215-698-5100
Imperial Plastics Inc
Lakeville, MN.............952-469-4951
Oak Barrel Winecraft
Berkeley, CA..............510-849-0400
Qualiform, Inc
Wadsworth, OH...........330-336-6777
RubaTex Polymer
Middlefield, OH 440-632-1691
Simolex Rubber Corp
Plymouth, MI 734-453-4500
Wilkens-Anderson Co
Chicago, IL 800-847-2222

Testers

Food Inspection

Advanced Instruments Inc
Norwood, MA.............800-225-4034
Ameritech Laboratories
Flushing, NY.............718-461-0475
Ashcroft Inc
Stratford, CT 800-328-8258
Biotek Instruments Inc
Winooski, VT 802-655-4040
Charm Sciences Inc
Lawrence, MA 978-687-9200
DeltaTrak
Pleasanton, CA 800-962-6776
Eurofins Scientific Inc.
Dayton, OH...............800-880-1038
Fettig Laboratories
Grand Rapids, MI 616-245-3000
Industrial Laboratories Co
Wheat Ridge, CO 800-456-5288
Kodex Inc
Nutley, NJ 800-325-6339
Libra Technical Center
Metuchen, NJ 732-321-5200
Loma Systems
Carol Stream, IL 800-872-5662
Marshfield Food Safety
Marshfield, WI 888-780-9897
MISCO Refractometer
Cleveland, OH 866-831-1999
Neogen Corp
Lansing, MI. 800-234-5333
Northwest Laboratories
Seattle, WA 206-763-6252
Pacific Scientific Instrument
Grants Pass, OR 800-866-7889
Q A Supplies LLC
Norfolk, VA. 800-472-7205
Radiation Processing Division
Parsippany, NJ. 800-442-1969
Raytek Corporation
Santa Cruz, CA 800-866-5478
Reichert Analytical Instruments
Depew, NY 716-686-4500
SDIX
Newark, DE. 800-544-8881
Supelco Inc
Bellefonte, PA. 800-247-6628
Total Quality Corporation
Branford, CT. 800-453-9729

Woodson-Tenent Laboratories
Des Moines, IA 515-265-1461
Woodson-Tenent Laboratories
Memphis, TN 515-280-8378
Woodson-Tenent Laboratories
Dayton, OH...............937-236-5756

Laboratory

Aerotech Laboratories
Phoenix, AZ 800-651-4802
Analytical Measurements
Chester, NJ 800-635-5580
Ashcroft Inc
Stratford, CT 800-328-8258
Beckman Coulter Inc.
Brea, CA. 800-526-3821
Biocontrol Systems Inc
Bellevue, WA 800-245-0113
BluMetric Environmental Inc.
Ottawa, ON 613-839-3053
C.W. Brabender Instruments
South Hackensack, NJ 201-343-8425
Charm Sciences Inc
Lawrence, MA 978-687-9200
Chestnut Labs
Springfield, MO 417-829-3788
CSC Scientific Co Inc
Fairfax, VA 800-621-4778
Enviro-Test/Perry Laboratories
Woodridge, IL.............630-324-6685
Eurofins Scientific Inc
Des Moines, IA 800-841-1110
Eurofins Scientific Inc.
Dayton, OH...............800-880-1038
Industrial Laboratories Co
Wheat Ridge, CO 800-456-5288
Libra Technical Center
Metuchen, NJ 732-321-5200
Northwest Laboratories
Seattle, WA 206-763-6252
Oxoid
Nepean, ON. 800-567-8378
Perten Instruments
Springfield, IL. 888-773-7836
Radiation Processing Division
Parsippany, NJ. 800-442-1969
Remel
Lenexa, KS 800-255-6730
Spiral Biotech Inc
Norwood, MA.............800-554-1620
Teledyne TEKMAR
Mason, OH 800-874-2004
Texture Technologies Corporation
Scarsdale, NY 914-472-0531
Troxler Electronic Lab Inc
Durham, NC 877-876-9537
Vee Gee Scientific Inc
Kirkland, WA 800-423-8842
VICAM
Milford, MA 800-338-4381
Wilkens-Anderson Co
Chicago, IL 800-847-2222
Woodson-Tenent Laboratories
Des Moines, IA 515-265-1461
Woodson-Tenent Laboratories
Memphis, TN 515-280-8378
Woodson-Tenent Laboratories
Dayton, OH...............937-236-5756

Milk & Cream

Advanced Instruments Inc
Norwood, MA.............800-225-4034

Packaging Materials/Containers

Air Logic Power Systems
Milwaukee, WI 800-325-8717
Altek Co
Torrington, CT 860-482-7626
Carleton Technologies Inc
Orchard Park, NY 716-662-0006
Daystar
Glen Arm, MD 800-494-6537
Food Instrument Corp
Federalsburg, MD. 800-542-5688
Kodex Inc
Nutley, NJ 800-325-6339
Libra Technical Center
Metuchen, NJ 732-321-5200
Mocon Inc
Minneapolis, MN 763-493-7229

NDC Infrared EngineeringInc
Irwindale, CA 626-960-3300
United Desiccants
Reno, NE 888-659-1377

Thermometers

A&M Thermometer Corporation
Asheville, NC 800-685-9211
Agri-Equipment International
Longs, SC 877-550-4709
Alnor Instrument Company
Skokie, IL 800-424-7427
Ametek
Sellersville, PA 215-257-6531
AMETEK National Controls Corp
West Chicago, IL 800-323-5293
Ashcroft Inc
Stratford, CT 800-328-8258
Atkins Technical
Gainesville, FL 800-284-2842
Barnant Company
Lake Barrington, IL 800-637-3739
Bowtemp
Mont-Royal, QC 514-735-5551
Browne & Company
Markham, ON 905-475-6104
Chaney Instrument Co
Lake Geneva, WI 800-777-0565
Chicago Stainless Eqpt Inc
Palm City, FL 800-927-8575
Comark Instruments
Everett, WA 800-555-6658
Crestware
North Salt Lake, UT 800-345-0513
Datapaq
Wilmington, MA 800-326-5270
Delta Trak
Pleasanton, CA 800-962-6776
DeltaTrak
Pleasanton, CA 800-962-6776
Dynasys Technologies
Clearwater, FL 800-867-5968

E & E Process Instrumentation
Concord, Ontario, ON 905-669-4857
Elreha Controls Corporation
St Petersburg, FL 727-327-6236
EPD Technology Corporation
Elmsford, NY 800-892-8926
Esco Products Inc
Houston, TX 800-966-5514
Eurotherm
Ashburn, VA 703-726-0138
Grace Instrument Co
Houston, TX 800-304-5859
Greer's Ferry Glass Work
Dubuque, IA 501-589-2947
Hanna Instruments
Woonsocket, RI 800-426-6287
Kason Central
Columbus, OH 614-885-1992
Kason Industries
Newnan, GA 770-254-0553
L.C. Thompson Company
Kenosha, WI 800-558-4018
Liberty Ware LLC
Clearfield, UT 888-500-5885
Love Controls Division
Michigan City, IN 800-828-4588
Luma Sense Technologies Inc
Santa Clara, CA 800-631-0176
Marshall Instruments Inc
Anaheim, CA 800-222-8476
Matfer Inc
Van Nuys, CA 800-766-0333
Mesa Laboratories Inc
Lakewood, CO 800-525-1215
Miljoco Corp
Mt Clemens, MI 888-888-1498
Music City Metals Inc
Nashville, TN 800-251-2674
National Time Recording Eqpt
New York, NY 212-227-3310
Noral
Natick, MA 800-348-2345

Pelouze Scale Company
Bridgeview, IL 800-323-8363
Q A Supplies LLC
Norfolk, VA 800-472-7205
Raytek Corporation
Santa Cruz, CA 800-866-5478
Reotemp Instrument Corp
San Diego, CA 800-648-7737
Sensitech Inc
Beverly, MA 800-843-8367
Sensitech Inc
Redmond, WA 800-999-7926
Special Products
Springfield, MO 417-881-6114
Superior Products Company
Saint Paul, MN 800-328-9800
Taylor Precision Products
Las Cruces, NM 575-526-0945
Taylor Precision Products
Oak Brook, IL 866-843-3905
Tel-Tru Manufacturing Co
Rochester, NY 800-232-5335
TESTO
Sparta, NJ 800-227-0729
Thermo Instruments
Yaphank, NY 631-924-0880
Trans World Services
Melrose, MA 800-882-2105
United Electric Controls Co
Watertown, MA 617-926-1000
Weiss Instruments Inc
Holtsville, NY 631-207-1200
Wescor
Logan, UT 800-453-2725
Wika Instrument LP
Lawrenceville, GA 800-645-0606
Wilkens-Anderson Co
Chicago, IL 800-847-2222

Packaging Materials & Supplies

Bags

Ampac Packaging, LLC
Cincinnati, OH 800-543-7030
Bella Vita
Phoenix, AZ 877-827-3638
Can Creations
Pembroke Pines, FL 800-272-0235
Clear Lam Packaging
Elk Grove Village, IL 847-439-8570
Clorox Company
Oakland, CA 510-271-7000
Dura-Pack Inc.
Taylor, MI 313-299-9600
Grayling Industries
Alpharetta, GA 800-635-1551
Libra Technical Center
Metuchen, NJ 732-321-5200
Nashville Wraps LLC
Hendersonville, TN 800-547-9727
Novolex
Hartsville, SC 800-845-6051
Polytarp Products
Toronto, ON 800-606-2231
Revere Group
Seattle, WA 206-545-1850
S Walter Packaging Corp
Philadelphia, PA 888-429-5673
Temkin International
Payson, UT 800-235-5263
Tenka Flexible Packaging
Chino, CA 888-836-5255
Vista Internatlonal Packaging
Kenosha, WI 800-558-4058

Bread & Pastry

Aladdin Transparent Packaging
Hauppauge, NY 631-273-4747
All American Poly
Piscataway, NJ 800-526-3551
Arbee Transparent Inc
Elk Grove Vlg, IL 800-642-2247
Checker Bag Co
St Louis, MO 800-489-3130
Flexo Transparent Inc
Buffalo, NY 877-993-5396
Jomar Plastics Industry
Nanty Glo, PA 800-681-4039
Malpack Polybag
Ajax, ON 905-428-3751
Mini-Bag Company
Farmingdale, NY 631-694-3325
Moser Bag & Paper Company
Cleveland, OH 800-433-6638
Pactiv LLC
Lake Forest, IL 800-476-4300
Pak-Sher
Kilgore, TX 903-984-8596
Pater & Associates
Cincinnati, OH
Pexco Packaging Corporation
Toledo, OH 800-227-9950
Pfeil & Holding Inc
Woodside, NY 800-247-7955
Seal-Tite Bag Company
Philadelphia, PA 717-917-1949
Specialty Paper Bag Company
City of Industry, CA 800-962-2247
Star Poly Bag Inc
Brooklyn, NY 718-384-7034
Stewart Sutherland Inc
Vicksburg, MI 269-649-0530

Bulk

King Bag & Mfg Co
Cincinnati, OH 800-444-5464

Cellophane

Arbee Transparent Inc
Elk Grove Vlg, IL 800-642-2247
Beayl Weiner/Pak
Pacific Palisades, CA 310-454-1354
Chalmur Bag Company, LLC
Philadelphia, PA 800-349-2247

Checker Bag Co
St Louis, MO 800-489-3130
Collectors Gallery
St Charles, IL 800-346-3063
Formel Industries
Franklin Park, IL 800-373-3300
Milprint
Oshkosh, WI 920-303-8600
Pater & Associates
Cincinnati, OH
Ultrapak
Dunkirk, NY 800-228-6030

Centrifuge

King Bag & Mfg Co
Cincinnati, OH 800-444-5464

Confectioners'

Accurate Flannel Bag Company
Paterson, NJ 800-234-9200
Arbee Transparent Inc
Elk Grove Vlg, IL 800-642-2247
August Thomsen Corp
Glen Cove, NY 800-645-7170
Checker Bag Co
St Louis, MO 800-489-3130
Collectors Gallery
St Charles, IL 800-346-3063
Colonial Transparent Products Company
Hicksville, NY 516-822-4430
Flexo Transparent Inc
Buffalo, NY 877-993-5396
Milprint
Oshkosh, WI 920-303-8600
Mimi et Cie
Seattle, WA 206-545-1850
Star Poly Bag Inc
Brooklyn, NY 718-384-7034
Stewart Sutherland Inc
Vicksburg, MI 269-649-0530
Wisconsin Converting Inc
Green Bay, WI 800-544-1935

Flour, Meal & Feed

Accurate Flannel Bag Company
Paterson, NJ 800-234-9200
Chatfield & Woods Sack Company
Harrison, OH 513-202-9700
Coveris
Excelsior Springs, MO
Dayton Bag & Burlap Co
Dayton, OH 800-543-3400
Flexo Transparent Inc
Buffalo, NY 877-993-5396
Frontier Bag Co Inc
Omaha, NE 800-278-2247
Fulton-Denver Co
Denver, CO 800-521-1414
Hubco Inc
Hutchinson, KS 800-563-1867
Indian Valley Industries
Johnson City, NY 800-659-5111
Set Point Paper Company
Mansfield, MA 800-225-0501
Star Poly Bag Inc
Brooklyn, NY 718-384-7034
Werthan Packaging
White House, TN 615-672-3336

Food

Accurate Flannel Bag Company
Paterson, NJ 800-234-9200
Aladdin Transparent Packaging
Hauppauge, NY 631-273-4747
All American Poly
Piscataway, NJ 800-526-3551
Arbee Transparent Inc
Elk Grove Vlg, IL 800-642-2247
Automated Packaging Systems
Streetsboro, OH 800-527-0733
Bag Masters
St Petersburg, FL 800-330-2247

Bagcraft Papercon
Chicago, IL 800-621-8468
Brown Paper Goods Co
Waukegan, IL 847-688-1450
Bryce Corp
Memphis, TN 800-238-7277
Cadie Products Corp
Paterson, NJ 973-278-8300
Castle Bag Co.
Wilmington, DE 302-656-1001
Checker Bag Co
St Louis, MO 800-489-3130
Cincinnati Convertors Inc
Cincinnati, OH 513-731-6600
Cleveland Plastic Films
Elyria, OH 800-832-6799
Collectors Gallery
St Charles, IL 800-346-3063
Conwed Global Netting Sltns
Roanoke, VA 800-368-3610
COVERIS
Tomah, WI 608-372-2153
David Dobbs Enterprise Inc.
St Augustine, FL 800-889-6368
Development Workshop Inc
Idaho Falls, ID 800-657-5597
Dixie Poly Packaging
Greenville, SC 864-268-3751
Eco-Bag Products
Ossining, NY 800-720-2247
Emoshun
Rancho Cucamonga, CA 909-484-9559
Fabriko
Altavista, VA 888-203-8098
Fischer Paper Products Inc
Antioch, IL 800-323-9093
Flexo Transparent Inc
Buffalo, NY 877-993-5396
Food Pak Corp
San Mateo, CA 650-341-6559
Fulton-Denver Co
Denver, CO 800-521-1414
Glopak
St Leonard, QC 800-361-6994
GP Plastics Corporation
Medley, FL 305-888-3555
Gulf Arizona Packaging
Humble, TX 800-364-3887
Gulf Systems
Brownsville, TX 800-217-4853
Gulf Systems
Humble, TX 800-364-3887
Gulf Systems
Arlington, TX 817-261-1915
Hank Rivera Associates
Dearborn, MI 313-581-8300
Herche Warehouse
Denver, CO 303-371-8186
Hubco Inc
Hutchinson, KS 800-563-1867
Jomar Plastics Industry
Nanty Glo, PA 800-681-4039
K & L Intl
Ontario, CA. 888-598-5588
Keeper Thermal Bag Co
Bartlett, IL 800-765-9244
Liqui-Box
Richmond, VA 804-325-1400
Masternet, Ltd
Mississauga, ON 800-216-2536
McDowell Industries
Memphis, TN 800-622-3695
Millhiser
Richmond, VA 800-446-2247
Mimi et Cie
Seattle, WA 206-545-1850
Mini-Bag Company
Farmingdale, NY 631-694-3325
Morgan Brothers Bag Company
Richmond, VA 804-355-9107
Moser Bag & Paper Company
Cleveland, OH 800-433-6638
Naltex
Austin, TX 800-531-5112
Net Pack Systems
Oakland, ME 207-465-4531

Noteworthy Company
Amsterdam, NY 800-696-7849
NOVOLEX
Glendale, AZ 800-243-0306
Orange Plastics
Compton, CA 310-609-2121
Pactiv LLC
Lake Forest, IL 800-476-4300
Pak-Sher
Kilgore, TX 903-984-8596
Pan Pacific Plastics Inc
Hayward, CA 888-475-6888
Parvin Manufacturing Company
Los Angeles, CA 800-648-0770
Pater & Associates
Cincinnati, OH
Petoskey Plastics
Morristown, TN 423-586-8917
Pexco Packaging Corporation
Toledo, OH 800-227-9950
Poly Plastic Products Inc
Delano, PA 570-467-3000
Portco Corporation
Vancouver, WA 800-426-1794
Rapak
Romeoville, IL 815-372-3670
Ray C. Sprosty Bag Company
Wooster, OH 330-264-8559
Roplast Industries Inc
Oroville, CA 800-767-5278
Ross & Wallace Inc
Hammond, LA 800-854-2300
Rutan Poly Industries Inc
Mahwah, NJ 800-872-1474
Scholle IPN
Merced, CA 209-384-3100
Service Manufacturing
Aurora, IL 888-325-2788
Sheboygan Paper Box Co
Sheboygan, WI 800-458-8373
Signature Packaging
West Orange, NJ 800-376-2299
Specialty Paper Bag Company
City of Industry, CA 800-962-2247
Star Poly Bag Inc
Brooklyn, NY 718-384-7034
Sterling Net & Twine Company
Cedar Knolls, NJ 800-342-0316
Sterling Novelty Products
Northbrook, IL 847-291-0070
Stewart Sutherland Inc
Vicksburg, MI 269-649-0530
Storsack Inc
Houston, TX 800-841-4982
Stretch-Vent Packaging System
Ontario, CA 800-822-8368
TEMP-TECH Company
Springfield, MA 800-343-5579
Tenka Flexible Packaging
Chino, CA 888-836-5255
Thermal Bags By Ingrid Inc
Gilberts, IL 800-622-5560
Trevor Owen Limited
Scarborough, ON 866-487-2224
Urnex Brands Inc
Elmsford, NY 800-222-2826
Valley Packaging Supply Co
Green Bay, WI 920-336-9012
Vonco Products LLC
Lake Villa, IL 800-323-9077
Walnut Packaging Inc
Farmingdale, NY 631-293-3836
Wins Paper Products
Springtown, TX 800-733-2420
Wisconsin Converting Inc
Green Bay, WI 800-544-1935

Fruit & Vegetable

Accurate Flannel Bag Company
Paterson, NJ 800-234-9200
Arbee Transparent Inc
Elk Grove Vlg, IL 800-642-2247
Conwed Global Netting Sltns
Roanoke, VA 800-368-3610
Eco-Bag Products
Ossining, NY 800-720-2247
Flexo Transparent Inc
Buffalo, NY 877-993-5396
Frontier Bag Co Inc
Omaha, NE 800-278-2247

Fulton-Denver Co
Denver, CO 800-521-1414
Gulf Arizona Packaging
Humble, TX 800-364-3887
Gulf Systems
Brownsville, TX 800-217-4853
Gulf Systems
Humble, TX 800-364-3887
Gulf Systems
Arlington, TX 817-261-1915
Herche Warehouse
Denver, CO 303-371-8186
Indian Valley Industries
Johnson City, NY 800-659-5111
Inteplast Bags & Films Corporation
Delta, BC. 604-946-5431
Langston Co Inc
Memphis, TN 901-774-4440
Masternet, Ltd
Mississauga, ON 800-216-2536
McDowell Industries
Memphis, TN 800-622-3695
Mini-Bag Company
Farmingdale, NY 631-694-3325
Morgan Brothers Bag Company
Richmond, VA. 804-355-9107
Naltex
Austin, TX. 800-531-5112
Net Pack Systems
Oakland, ME. 207-465-4531
Orange Plastics
Compton, CA 310-609-2121
Pan Pacific Plastics Inc
Hayward, CA 888-475-6888
Pater & Associates
Cincinnati, OH
Portco Corporation
Vancouver, WA 800-426-1794
Roplast Industries Inc
Oroville, CA 800-767-5278
Signature Packaging
West Orange, NJ 800-376-2299
Sterling Net & Twine Company
Cedar Knolls, NJ 800-342-0316
Urnex Brands Inc
Elmsford, NY 800-222-2826
Werthan Packaging
White House, TN 615-672-3336

Grain

Coveris
Excelsior Springs, MO
Dayton Bag & Burlap Co
Dayton, OH. 800-543-3400
Development Workshop Inc
Idaho Falls, ID 800-657-5597
Flexo Transparent Inc
Buffalo, NY. 877-993-5396
Indian Valley Industries
Johnson City, NY 800-659-5111
McDowell Industries
Memphis, TN 800-622-3695
Portco Corporation
Vancouver, WA 800-426-1794
Storsack Inc
Houston, TX 800-841-4982

Greaseproof

Arbee Transparent Inc
Elk Grove Vlg, IL 800-642-2247
Brown Paper Goods Co
Waukegan, IL 847-688-1450
Cincinnati Convertors Inc
Cincinnati, OH 513-731-6600
COVERIS
Tomah, WI 608-372-2153
Coveris
Excelsior Springs, MO
Dayton Bag & Burlap Co
Dayton, OH. 800-543-3400
Mini-Bag Company
Farmingdale, NY 631-694-3325

Heat Sealed

Aladdin Transparent Packaging
Hauppauge, NY 631-273-4747
Arbee Transparent Inc
Elk Grove Vlg, IL 800-642-2247
Atlas Tag & Label Inc
Neenah, WI 800-558-6418

Automated Packaging Systems
Streetsboro, OH 800-527-0733
Beayl Weiner/Pak
Pacific Palisades, CA 310-454-1354
Chalmur Bag Company, LLC
Philadelphia, PA 800-349-2247
Cincinnati Convertors Inc
Cincinnati, OH 513-731-6600
COVERIS
Tomah, WI 608-372-2153
Coveris
Excelsior Springs, MO
Flexo Transparent Inc
Buffalo, NY. 877-993-5396
Gulf Arizona Packaging
Humble, TX 800-364-3887
Gulf Systems
Humble, TX 800-364-3887
Gulf Systems
Arlington, TX 817-261-1915
Herche Warehouse
Denver, CO 303-371-8186
Home Plastics Inc
Des Moines, IA 515-265-2562
Keystone Packaging Svc Inc
Phillipsburg, NJ 800-473-8567
Liqui-Box
Richmond, VA. 804-325-1400
Mini-Bag Company
Farmingdale, NY 631-694-3325
NAP Industries
Brooklyn, NY 877-635-4948
Net Pack Systems
Oakland, ME. 207-465-4531
Pater & Associates
Cincinnati, OH
Ram Industries
Erwin, TN 800-523-3883
Seal-Tite Bag Company
Philadelphia, PA 717-917-1949
Servin Company
New Baltimore, MI 800-824-0962
Set Point Paper Company
Mansfield, MA 800-225-0501
Star Poly Bag Inc
Brooklyn, NY 718-384-7034
Thermal Bags By Ingrid Inc
Gilberts, IL 800-622-5560
Ultrapak
Dunkirk, NY 800-228-6030
Urnex Brands Inc
Elmsford, NY 800-222-2826

Laminated

Arbee Transparent Inc
Elk Grove Vlg, IL 800-642-2247
BAW Plastics Inc
Clairton, PA. 800-783-2229
Cincinnati Convertors Inc
Cincinnati, OH 513-731-6600
Coveris
Excelsior Springs, MO
Gulf Arizona Packaging
Humble, TX 800-364-3887
Gulf Systems
Humble, TX 800-364-3887
Gulf Systems
Arlington, TX 817-261-1915
Herche Warehouse
Denver, CO. 303-371-8186
Pater & Associates
Cincinnati, OH
Sheboygan Paper Box Co
Sheboygan, WI 800-458-8373
Sungjae Corporation
Irvine, CA 949-757-1727
Vonco Products LLC
Lake Villa, IL 800-323-9077
Workman Packaging Inc.
Saint-Laurent, QC. 800-252-5208

Meat

Accurate Flannel Bag Company
Paterson, NJ 800-234-9200
All American Poly
Piscataway, NJ 800-526-3551
Arbee Transparent Inc
Elk Grove Vlg, IL 800-642-2247
Flexo Transparent Inc
Buffalo, NY. 877-993-5396

187

Frontier Bag
Kansas City, MO 816-765-4811
Jomar Plastics Industry
Nanty Glo, PA 800-681-4039
Morgan Brothers Bag Company
Richmond, VA. 804-355-9107
NAP Industries
Brooklyn, NY 877-635-4948
Net Pack Systems
Oakland, ME. 207-465-4531
Pan Pacific Plastics Inc
Hayward, CA. 888-475-6888
VPI Manufacturing
Draper, UT 801-495-2310

Multi-Wall

Central Bag Co
Leavenworth, KS 913-250-0325
Colonial Transparent Products Company
Hicksville, NY 516-822-4430
Coveris
Excelsior Springs, MO
Durango-Georgia Paper
Tampa, FL. 813-286-2718
First Midwest of Iowa Corporation
Des Moines, IA 800-247-8411
Flexo Transparent Inc
Buffalo, NY. 877-993-5396
Hood Packaging
Madison, MS. 800-321-8115
Indian Valley Industries
Johnson City, NY 800-659-5111
Langston Co Inc
Memphis, TN 901-774-4440
Northeast Packaging Co
Presque Isle, ME. 207-764-6271
NYP
Leola, PA. 800-541-0961
Ray C. Sprosty Bag Company
Wooster, OH 330-264-8559
Santa Fe Bag Company
Vernon, CA. 323-585-7225
Stone Container
Chicago, IL. 312-346-6600
United Bags Inc
St Louis, MO. 800-550-2247
Werthan Packaging
White House, TN 615-672-3336

Netting, Open Mesh

Alabama Bag Co Inc
Talladega, AL 800-888-4921
Conwed Global Netting Sltns
Roanoke, VA. 800-368-3610
Fitec International Inc
Memphis, TN 800-332-6387
Friedman Bag Company
Manhattan Beach, CA. 213-628-2341
Fulton-Denver Co
Denver, CO. 800-521-1414
General Bag Corporation
Cleveland, OH 800-837-9396
Indian Valley Industries
Johnson City, NY 800-659-5111
Jif-Pak Manufacturing
Vista, CA. 800-777-6613
Langston Co Inc
Memphis, TN 901-774-4440
Masternet, Ltd
Mississauga, ON 800-216-2536
Naltex
Austin, TX. 800-531-5112
Net Pack Systems
Oakland, ME. 207-465-4531
NYP
Leola, PA. 800-541-0961
Sterling Net & Twine Company
Cedar Knolls, NJ. 800-342-0316
Tni Packaging Inc
West Chicago, IL 800-383-0990
Tree Saver
Englewood, CO. 800-676-7741
United Bags Inc
St Louis, MO. 800-550-2247
Wasserman Bag Company
Center Moriches, NY 631-909-8656

Paper

A-A1 Aaction Bag
Denver, CO. 800-783-1224

Acme Bag Co
Chula Vista, CA 800-275-2263
AJM Packaging Corporation
Bloomfield Hills, MI 248-901-0040
American Bag & Burlap Company
Chelsea, MA 617-884-7600
Bancroft Bag Inc
West Monroe, LA 318-387-2550
Brown Paper Goods Co
Waukegan, IL 847-688-1450
Burrows Paper Corp
Little Falls, NY 800-272-7122
Clearwater Paper Corporation
Spokane, WA. 877-847-7831
Coveris
Excelsior Springs, MO
Custom Poly Packaging
Fort Wayne, IN 800-548-6603
Dayton Bag & Burlap Co
Dayton, OH 800-543-3400
El Dorado Packaging Inc
El Dorado, AR 870-862-4977
F&G Packaging
Yulee, FL. 904-225-5121
Fabricon Products Inc
River Rouge, MI 313-841-8200
Fast Bags
Fort Worth, TX 800-321-3687
Felco Packaging Specialist
Baltimore, MD 800-673-8488
First Midwest of Iowa Corporation
Des Moines, IA 800-247-8411
Fischer Paper Products Inc
Antioch, IL 800-323-9093
Fortifiber Building Systs Grp
Fernley, NV. 800-773-4777
Fulton-Denver Co
Denver, CO. 800-521-1414
Gateway Packaging Co ·
Kansas City, MO. 816-483-9800
General Bag Corporation
Cleveland, OH 800-837-9396
Gilchrist Bag Co Inc
Camden, AR 800-643-1513
Hood Packaging
Madison, MS. 800-321-8115
Indian Valley Industries
Johnson City, NY 800-659-5111
Keystone Packaging Svc Inc
Phillipsburg, NJ 800-473-8567
Langston Co Inc
Memphis, TN 901-774-4440
Milprint
Oshkosh, WI 920-303-8600
Mimi et Cie
Seattle, WA 206-545-1850
Moser Bag & Paper Company
Cleveland, OH 800-433-6638
North American Packaging Corp
New York, NY 800-499-3521
Northeast Packaging Co
Presque Isle, ME. 207-764-6271
NYP
Leola, PA. 800-541-0961
Package Containers Inc
Canby, OR. 800-266-5806
Pak 2000 Inc
Mirror Lake, NH 603-569-3700
Pak-Sher
Kilgore, TX. 903-984-8596
Papelera Puertorriquena
Utuado, PR 787-894-2098
Peerless Packages
Cleveland, OH 216-464-3620
Portco Corporation
Vancouver, WA 800-426-1794
Ray C. Sprosty Bag Company
Wooster, OH 330-264-8559
Ross & Wallace Inc
Hammond, LA 800-854-2300
Samuels Products Inc
Blue Ash, OH 800-543-7155
Santa Fe Bag Company
Vernon, CA. 323-585-7225
Seaboard Bag Corporation
Richmond, VA
Shippers Paper Products Co
Sheridan, AR. 800-468-1230
Solo Cup Company
Lake Forest, IL
Specialty Packaging Inc
Fort Worth, TX 800-284-7722

Specialty Paper Bag Company
City of Industry, CA. 800-962-2247
Stone Container
Chicago, IL. 312-346-6600
Surfine Central Corporation
Pine Bluff, AR 870-247-2387
TULSACK
Tulsa, OK 800-228-1936
United Bags Inc
St Louis, MO. 800-550-2247
Walker Bag Mfg Co
Louisville, KY 800-642-4949
Wasserman Bag Company
Center Moriches, NY 631-909-8656
Wedlock Paper ConvertersLtd.
Mississauga, ON 800-388-0447
Wins Paper Products
Springtown, TX 800-733-2420
Wisconsin Converting Inc
Green Bay, WI. 800-544-1935
Zenith Specialty Bag Co
City Of Industry, CA. 800-962-2247

Paper Lined

Coveris
Excelsior Springs, MO
Dayton Bag & Burlap Co
Dayton, OH. 800-543-3400

Plastic

A La Carte
Chicago, IL. 800-722-2370
A-A1 Aaction Bag
Denver, CO. 800-783-1224
Abond Plastic Corporation
Lachine, QC 800-886-7947
Acme Bag Co
Chula Vista, CA 800-275-2263
Alabama Bag Co Inc
Talladega, AL 800-888-4921
Alger Creations
Miami, FL. 954-454-3272
All American Poly
Piscataway, NJ 800-526-3551
Alouf Plastics
Orangeburg, NY 800-394-2247
Amcel
Watertown, MA. 800-225-7992
American Bag & Burlap Company
Chelsea, MA 617-884-7600
Ameriglobe LLC
Lafayette, LA 337-234-3211
Arbee Transparent Inc
Elk Grove Vlg, IL. 800-642-2247
Archer Daniels Midland Company
Chicago, IL. 312-634-8100
Art Poly Bag Co
Brooklyn, NY. 800-278-7659
Artistic Packaging Concepts
Massapequa Pk, NY 516-797-4020
Automated Packaging Systems
Streetsboro, OH 800-527-0733
Avantage Group Inc
Redondo Beach, CA. 310-379-3933
Bag Company
Kennesaw, GA 800-533-1931
Bag Masters
St Petersburg, FL 800-330-2247
Beayl Weiner/Pak
Pacific Palisades, CA. 310-454-1354
Bennett's Auto Inc
Neenah, WI. 800-215-5464
Blako Industries
Dunbridge, OH 419-833-4491
Brown Paper Goods Co
Waukegan, IL 847-688-1450
Bulk Lift International, LLC
Carpentersville, IL 800-879-2247
C-P Flexible Packaging
Newtown, PA. 800-448-8183
Carlisle Plastics
Minneapolis, MN 952-884-1309
Carroll Co
Garland, TX. 800-527-5722
Castle Bag Co.
Wilmington, DE 302-656-1001
Cello Bag Company
Bowling Green, KY 800-347-0338
Central Bag Co
Leavenworth, KS 913-250-0325

Central Package & Display
   Minneapolis, MN 763-425-7444
Chalmur Bag Company, LLC
   Philadelphia, PA 800-349-2247
Champion Plastics
   Clifton, NJ 800-526-1230
Checker Bag Co
   St Louis, MO........................800-489-3130
Clear View Bag Co Inc Of Nc
   Albany, NY..........................800-458-7153
Clear View Bag Company
   Thomasville, NC.....................336-885-8131
Cleveland Plastic Films
   Elyria, OH..........................800-832-6799
Coast Scientific
   Rancho Santa Fe, CA 800-445-1544
Colonial Transparent Products Company
   Hicksville, NY 516-822-4430
Command Packaging
   Vernon, CA 800-996-2247
Continental Extrusion Corporation
   Cedar Grove, NJ 800-822-4748
Continental Packaging Corporation
   Elgin, IL 847-289-6400
Continental Products
   Mexico, MO 800-325-0216
Conwed Global Netting Sltns
   Roanoke, VA 800-368-3610
Cortec Aero
   St Paul, MN 800-426-7832
COVERIS
   Tomah, WI 608-372-2153
Coveris
   Excelsior Springs, MO
Crayex Corp
   Piqua, OH 800-837-1747
Crystal-Flex Packaging Corporation
   Rockville Centre, NY 888-246-7325
Custom Poly Packaging
   Fort Wayne, IN 800-548-6603
Dairyland Plastics Company
   Colfax, WI..........................715-962-3425
Dashco
   Gloucester, ON 613-834-6825
Dayton Bag & Burlap Co
   Dayton, OH..........................800-543-3400
Decker Plastics
   Council Bluffs, IA..................866-869-6293
Design Packaging Company
   Glencoe, IL 800-321-7659
Development Workshop Inc
   Idaho Falls, ID 800-657-5597
Dixie Poly Packaging
   Greenville, SC......................864-268-3751
Dub Harris Corporation
   Pomona, CA 909-596-6300
Dynamic Packaging
   Minneapolis, MN 800-878-9380
East Coast Group New York
   Springfield Gardens, NY 718-527-8464
Eastern Poly Packaging   Company
   Brooklyn, NY........................800-421-6006
Eaton Manufacturing Co
   Houston, TX 800-328-6610
Ellehammer Industries
   Langley, BC 604-882-9326
Elliot Lee
   Cedarhurst, NY 516-569-9595
Fabohio Inc
   Uhrichsville, OH....................740-922-4233
Fan Bag Company
   Chicago, IL.........................773-342-2752
Fast Bags
   Fort Worth, TX 800-321-3687
Flexo Transparent Inc
   Buffalo, NY 877-993-5396
Fortune Plastics, Inc
   Old Saybrook, CT....................800-243-0306
Fredman Bag Co
   Milwaukee, WI.......................800-945-5686
Friedman Bag Company
   Manhattan Beach, CA.................213-628-2341
Frontier
   Kansas City, MO.....................816-765-4811
Fulton-Denver Co
   Denver, CO..........................800-521-1414
Garvey Products
   West Chester, OH 800-543-1908
Gemini Plastic Films Corporation
   Garfield, NJ........................800-789-4732
General Bag Corporation
   Cleveland, OH 800-837-9396

General Films Inc
   Covington, OH 888-436-3456
Genpak LLC
   Lakeville, MN.......................800-328-4556
Gibraltar Packaging Group Inc
   Hastings, NE........................402-463-1366
Goldmax Industries
   City Of Industry, CA................626-964-8820
GP Plastics Corporation
   Medley, FL 305-888-3555
Gulf Arizona Packaging
   Humble, TX 800-364-3887
Gulf Coast Plastics
   Tampa, FL 800-277-7491
Gulf Systems
   Brownsville, TX 800-217-4853
Gulf Systems
   Humble, TX 800-364-3887
Gulf Systems
   Arlington, TX 817-261-1915
Handgards Inc
   El Paso, TX.........................800-351-8161
Hedwin Division
   Baltimore, MD 800-638-1012
Herche Warehouse
   Denver, CO..........................303-371-8186
Heritage Bag Co
   Roanoke, TX.........................800-527-2247
Himolene
   Carrollton, TX 800-777-4411
Hubco Inc
   Hutchinson, KS......................800-563-1867
Hudson Poly Bag Inc
   Hudson, MA 800-229-7566
INA Co
   San Carlos, CA 650-631-7066
Indian Valley Industries
   Johnson City, NY 800-659-5111
Interstate Packaging
   White Bluff, TN 800-251-1072
J A Heilferty & Co
   Teaneck, NJ.........................201-836-5060
Jeb Plastics
   Wilmington, DE 800-556-2247
Jomar Plastics Industry
   Nanty Glo, PA.......................800-681-4039
Jupiter Mills Corporation
   Roslyn, NY..........................800-853-5121
K & L Intl
   Ontario, CA.........................888-598-5588
K-C Products Company
   Van Nuys, CA........................818-267-1600
Kal Pac Corp
   Montgomery, NY......................800-852-5722
KANE Bag Supply Co
   Baltimore, MD 410-732-5800
KM International Corp
   Kenton, TN..........................731-749-8700
L & C Plastic Bags
   Covington, OH 937-473-2968
Luetzow Industries
   South Milwaukee, WI.................800-558-6055
M & G Packaging Corp
   Floral Park, NY.....................800-240-5288
M S Plastics & Packaging Inc
   Butler, PA..........................800-593-1802
M&R Flexible Packaging
   Springboro, OH......................800-543-3380
Maco Bag Corp
   Newark, NY 315-226-1000
Malpack Polybag
   Ajax, ON............................905-428-3751
Marshall Plastic Film Inc
   Martin, MI..........................269-672-5511
Mason Transparent Package Company
   Armonk, NY..........................718-792-6000
Mercury Plastic Bag Company
   Passaic, NJ 973-778-7200
Microplas Industries
   Dunwoody, GA........................800-952-4528
Midco Plastics
   Enterprise, KS......................800-235-2729
Millhiser
   Richmond, VA........................800-446-2247
Mini-Bag Company
   Farmingdale, NY.....................631-694-3325
Mohawk Northern Plastics
   Auburn, WA..........................800-426-1100
Mohawk Western Plastics Inc
   La Verne, CA........................909-593-7547
Mount Vernon Plastics
   Mamaroneck, NY......................914-698-1122

Naltex
   Austin, TX..........................800-531-5112
NAP Industries
   Brooklyn, NY........................877-635-4948
National Poly Bag Manufacturing Corporation
   Brooklyn, NY........................718-629-9800
Net Pack Systems
   Oakland, ME.........................207-465-4531
North American Packaging Corp
   New York, NY........................800-499-3521
Noteworthy Company
   Amsterdam, NY 800-696-7849
NOVOLEX
   Glendale, AZ........................800-243-0306
Now Plastics Inc
   East Longmeadow, MA 413-525-1010
NYP
   Leola, PA...........................800-541-0961
Osterneck Company
   Lumberton, NC.......................800-682-2416
Packaging Enterprises
   Rockledge, PA.......................800-453-6213
Packaging Materials Inc
   Cambridge, OH.......................800-565-8550
Pactiv LLC
   Lake Forest, IL 800-476-4300
Pak 2000 Inc
   Mirror Lake, NH.....................603-569-3700
Pak-Sak Industries I
   Sparta, MI..........................800-748-0431
Pak-Sher
   Kilgore, TX.........................903-984-8596
Pan Pacific Plastics Inc
   Hayward, CA 888-475-6888
Papelera Puertorriquena
   Utuado, PR..........................787-894-2098
Parade Packaging
   Mundelein, IL 847-566-6264
Paradise Plastics
   Brooklyn, NY........................718-788-3733
Pater & Associates
   Cincinnati, OH
Peerless Packages
   Cleveland, OH 216-464-3620
Pexco Packaging Corporation
   Toledo, OH 800-227-9950
Pilant Corp
   Bloomington, IN.....................800-366-3525
Poliplastic
   Granby, QC 450-378-8417
Poly Plastic Products Inc
   Delano, PA..........................570-467-3000
Poly Shapes Corporation
   Elyria, OH..........................800-605-9359
Portco Corporation
   Vancouver, WA 800-426-1794
ProAmpac
   Cincinnati, OH 800-543-7030
Quality Plastic Bag Corporation
   Flushing, NY........................800-532-2247
Quality Transparent Bag Co
   Bay City, MI........................989-893-3561
Ram Industries
   Erwin, TN 800-523-3883
Ray C. Sprosty Bag Company
   Wooster, OH 330-264-8559
Roplast Industries Inc
   Oroville, CA........................800-767-5278
Ross & Wallace Inc
   Hammond, LA 800-854-2300
Rutan Poly Industries Inc
   Mahwah, NJ 800-872-1474
Sacramento Bag Manufacturing
   Woodland, CA........................530-662-6130
San Miguel Label Manufacturing
   Ciales, PR..........................787-871-3120
Seal-Tite Bag Company
   Philadelphia, PA....................717-917-1949
Seattle-Tacoma Box Co
   Kent, WA............................253-854-9700
Senior Housing Options Inc
   Denver, CO..........................800-659-2656
Servin Company
   New Baltimore, MI 800-824-0962
Shamrock Plastics
   Mt Vernon, OH 800-765-1611
Sheboygan Paper Box Co
   Sheboygan, WI.......................800-458-8373
Shields Bag & Printing Co
   Yakima, WA..........................800-541-8630
Ship Rite Packaging
   Bergenfield, NJ.....................800-721-7447

Shippers Paper Products Co
  Sheridan, AR. 800-468-1230
Signature Packaging
  West Orange, NJ 800-376-2299
Silver State Plastics Inc
  Greeley, CO. 970-346-8667
Specialty Films & Associates
  Hebron, KY. 800-984-3346
Specialty Paper Bag Company
  City of Industry, CA 800-962-2247
Spectrum Plastics
  Las Vegas, NV 702-876-8650
Star Poly Bag Inc
  Brooklyn, NY 718-384-7034
Steel City Corporation
  Youngstown, OH. 800-321-0350
Sterling Net & Twine Company
  Cedar Knolls, NJ. 800-342-0316
Sterling Novelty Products
  Northbrook, IL. 847-291-0070
Stone Container
  Chicago, IL 312-346-6600
Stretch-Vent Packaging System
  Ontario, CA. 800-822-8368
Stripper Bags
  Henderson, NV 800-354-2247
Sungjae Corporation
  Irvine, CA .949-757-1727
Sunland Manufacturing Company
  Minneapolis, MN 800-790-1905
Target Industries
  North Salt Lake, UT 866-617-2253
Thermal Bags By Ingrid Inc
  Gilberts, IL 800-622-5560
Trans Flex Packagers Inc
  Unionville, CT 860-673-2531
Trinity Packaging
  Cheektowaga, NY 800-778-3111
Tyco Plastics
  Lakeville, MN 800-328-4080
United Bags Inc
  St Louis, MO. 800-550-2247
United Flexible
  Westbury, NY 516-222-2150
Universal Plastics
  Holyoke, MA 800-553-0120
US Plastic Corporation
  Swampscott, MA 781-595-1030
Valley Packaging Supply Co
  Green Bay, WI. 920-336-9012
Vermont Bag & Film
  Bennington, VT 802-442-3166
Vonco Products LLC
  Lake Villa, IL 800-323-9077
VPI Manufacturing
  Draper, UT 801-495-2310
Walker Bag Mfg Co
  Louisville, KY 800-642-4949
Walnut Packaging Inc
  Farmingdale, NY 631-293-3836
Wasserman Bag Company
  Center Moriches, NY 631-909-8656
Wisconsin Film & Bag Inc
  Shawano, WI. 800-765-9224
Wright Plastics Company
  Prattville, AL 800-874-7659
Zip-Pak
  Manteno, IL 800-488-6973

Polyethylene

AEP Industries
  South Hackensack, NJ 800-999-2374
Alabama Bag Co Inc
  Talladega, AL 800-888-4921
All American Poly
  Piscataway, NJ 800-526-3551
Alouf Plastics
  Orangeburg, NY 800-394-2247
Arbee Transparent Inc
  Elk Grove Vlg, IL 800-642-2247
Art Poly Bag Co
  Brooklyn, NY 800-278-7659
Automated Packaging Systems
  Streetsboro, OH 800-527-0733
Bag Company
  Kennesaw, GA 800-533-1931
Bag Masters
  St Petersburg, FL 800-330-2247
Beayl Weiner/Pak
  Pacific Palisades, CA 310-454-1354

Bennett's Auto Inc
  Neenah, WI. 800-215-5464
Blako Industries
  Dunbridge, OH 419-833-4491
C-P Flexible Packaging
  Newtown, PA 800-448-8183
Carlisle Plastics
  Minneapolis, MN 952-884-1309
Castle Bag Co.
  Wilmington, DE 302-656-1001
Central Package & Display
  Minneapolis, MN 763-425-7444
Chalmur Bag Company, LLC
  Philadelphia, PA 800-349-2247
Champion Plastics
  Clifton, NJ. 800-526-1230
Checker Bag Co
  St Louis, MO. 800-489-3130
Cleveland Plastic Films
  Elyria, OH. 800-832-6799
Coast Scientific
  Rancho Santa Fe, CA 800-445-1544
Collectors Gallery
  St Charles, IL 800-346-3063
Command Packaging
  Vernon, CA. 800-996-2247
Continental Packaging Corporation
  Elgin, IL .847-289-6400
Cortec Aero
  St Paul, MN. 800-426-7832
Coveris
  Excelsior Springs, MO
Crayex Corp
  Piqua, OH. 800-837-1747
Crystal-Flex Packaging Corporation
  Rockville Centre, NY 888-246-7325
Custom Poly Packaging
  Fort Wayne, IN 800-548-6603
Decker Plastics
  Council Bluffs, IA. 866-869-6293
Dixie Poly Packaging
  Greenville, SC. 864-268-3751
Dynamic Packaging
  Minneapolis, MN 800-878-9380
Eastern Poly Packaging   Company
  Brooklyn, NY 800-421-6006
Eaton Manufacturing Co
  Houston, TX 800-328-6610
Emerald Packaging Inc
  Union City, CA 510-429-5700
Film-Pak Inc
  Crowley, TX 800-526-1838
Flexo Transparent Inc
  Buffalo, NY. 877-993-5396
Fortune Plastics, Inc
  Old Saybrook, CT. 800-243-0306
Fredman Bag Co
  Milwaukee, WI 800-945-5686
Friedman Bag Company
  Manhattan Beach, CA. 213-628-2341
Frontier Bag
  Kansas City, MO. 816-765-4811
Fulton-Denver Co
  Denver, CO. 800-521-1414
Gemini Plastic Films Corporation
  Garfield, NJ. 800-789-4732
Genpak LLC
  Lakeville, MN. 800-328-4556
Gibraltar Packaging Group Inc
  Hastings, NE. 402-463-1366
GP Plastics Corporation
  Medley, FL 305-888-3555
Gulf Arizona Packaging
  Humble, TX 800-364-3887
Gulf Systems
  Brownsville, TX 800-217-4853
Gulf Systems
  Humble, TX 800-364-3887
Gulf Systems
  Arlington, TX 817-261-1915
Herche Warehouse
  Denver, CO. 303-371-8186
Home Plastics Inc
  Des Moines, IA. 515-265-2562
Hudson Poly Bag Inc
  Hudson, MA 800-229-7566
Indian Valley Industries
  Johnson City, NY 800-659-5111
Inteplast Bags & Films Corporation
  Delta, BC. 604-946-5431
Interstate Packaging
  White Bluff, TN 800-251-1072

J A Heilferty & Co
  Teaneck, NJ. 201-836-5060
Jewell Bag Company
  Dallas, TX. 214-749-1223
King Bag & Mfg Co
  Cincinnati, OH 800-444-5464
KM International Corp
  Kenton, TN 731-749-8700
L & C Plastic Bags
  Covington, OH 937-473-2968
Luetzow Industries
  South Milwaukee, WI 800-558-6055
M S Plastics & Packaging Inc
  Butler, NJ 800-593-1802
Malpack Polybag
  Ajax, ON. 905-428-3751
Mason Transparent Package Company
  Armonk, NY 718-792-6000
Microplas Industries
  Dunwoody, GA. 800-952-4528
Millhiser
  Richmond, VA. 800-446-2247
Mini-Bag Company
  Farmingdale, NY 631-694-3325
Mohawk Northern Plastics
  Auburn, WA 800-426-1100
Mohawk Western Plastics Inc
  La Verne, CA 909-593-7547
Monument Industries Inc
  Bennington, VT 802-442-8187
NAP Industries
  Brooklyn, NY 877-635-4948
Net Pack Systems
  Oakland, ME. 207-465-4531
Noteworthy Company
  Amsterdam, NY 800-696-7849
NOVOLEX
  Glendale, AZ. 800-243-0306
NYP
  Leola, PA. 800-541-0961
Packaging Materials Inc
  Cambridge, OH 800-565-8550
Pactiv LLC
  Lake Forest, IL 800-476-4300
Pak-Sak Industries I
  Sparta, MI 800-748-0431
Pater & Associates
  Cincinnati, OH
Pexco Packaging Corporation
  Toledo, OH 800-227-9950
Pilant Corp
  Bloomington, IN. 800-366-3525
Portco Corporation
  Vancouver, WA 800-426-1794
ProAmpac
  Cincinnati, OH 800-543-7030
Quality Transparent Bag Co
  Bay City, MI 989-893-3561
Rutan Poly Industries Inc
  Mahwah, NJ 800-872-1474
Sacramento Bag Manufacturing
  Woodland, CA. 530-662-6130
Shields Bag & Printing Co
  Yakima, WA 800-541-8630
Ship Rite Packaging
  Bergenfield, NJ 800-721-7447
Signature Packaging
  West Orange, NJ 800-376-2299
Silver State Plastics Inc
  Greeley, CO. 970-346-8667
Sungjae Corporation
  Irvine, CA 949-757-1727
Sunland Manufacturing Company
  Minneapolis, MN 800-790-1905
Superior Distributing Co
  Louisville, KY 800-365-6661
Target Industries
  North Salt Lake, UT 866-617-2253
Trans Flex Packagers Inc
  Unionville, CT 860-673-2531
Trinity Packaging
  Cheektowaga, NY 800-778-3111
United Flexible
  Westbury, NY 516-222-2150
US Plastic Corporation
  Swampscott, MA 781-595-1030
VPI Manufacturing
  Draper, UT 801-495-2310
Walnut Packaging Inc
  Farmingdale, NY 631-293-3836
Wasserman Bag Company
  Center Moriches, NY 631-909-8656

Workman Packaging Inc.
Saint-Laurent, QC 800-252-5208
Wright Plastics Company
Prattville, AL 800-874-7659
Zip-Pak
Manteno, IL 800-488-6973

Polypropylene

Arbee Transparent Inc
Elk Grove Vlg, IL 800-642-2247
Astro Plastics
Oakland, NJ 201-337-8170
Automated Packaging Systems
Streetsboro, OH 800-527-0733
Bag Company
Kennesaw, GA 800-533-1931
Bag Masters
St Petersburg, FL 800-330-2247
Beayl Weiner/Pak
Pacific Palisades, CA 310-454-1354
Bulk Lift International, LLC
Carpentersville, IL 800-879-2247
Central Bag Co
Leavenworth, KS 913-250-0325
Checker Bag Co
St Louis, MO 800-489-3130
Custom Poly Packaging
Fort Wayne, IN 800-548-6603
Dayton Bag & Burlap Co
Dayton, OH 800-543-3400
Design Packaging Company
Glencoe, IL 800-321-7659
Eastern Poly Packaging Company
Brooklyn, NY 800-421-6006
Eaton Manufacturing Co
Houston, TX 800-328-6610
Flexo Transparent Inc
Buffalo, NY 877-993-5396
Gibraltar Packaging Group Inc
Hastings, NE 402-463-1366
Gulf Arizona Packaging
Humble, TX 800-364-3887
Gulf Systems
Brownsville, TX 800-217-4853
Gulf Systems
Humble, TX 800-364-3887
Gulf Systems
Arlington, TX 817-261-1915
Herche Warehouse
Denver, CO 303-371-8186
Hubco Inc
Hutchinson, KS 800-563-1867
Indian Valley Industries
Johnson City, NY 800-659-5111
Mason Transparent Package Company
Armonk, NY 718-792-6000
Masternet, Ltd
Mississauga, ON 800-216-2536
Mercury Plastic Bag Company
Passaic, NJ 973-778-7200
Millhiser
Richmond, VA 800-446-2247
Mimi et Cie
Seattle, WA 206-545-1850
NYP
Leola, PA 800-541-0961
Pater & Associates
Cincinnati, OH
Pexco Packaging Corporation
Toledo, OH 800-227-9950
Ray C. Sprosty Bag Company
Wooster, OH 330-264-8559
Sacramento Bag Manufacturing
Woodland, CA 530-662-6130
Shields Bag & Printing Co
Yakima, WA 800-541-8630
Sterling Net & Twine Company
Cedar Knolls, NJ 800-342-0316
Storsack Inc
Houston, TX 800-841-4982
Target Industries
North Salt Lake, UT 866-617-2253
Trans Flex Packagers Inc
Unionville, CT 860-673-2531
United Bags Inc
St Louis, MO 800-550-2247
Walker Bag Mfg Co
Louisville, KY 800-642-4949
Wasserman Bag Company
Center Moriches, NY 631-909-8656

Workman Packaging Inc.
Saint-Laurent, QC 800-252-5208

Popcorn

Arbee Transparent Inc
Elk Grove Vlg, IL 800-642-2247
Coveris
Excelsior Springs, MO
Flexo Transparent Inc
Buffalo, NY 877-993-5396
Hubco Inc
Hutchinson, KS 800-563-1867
Stewart Sutherland Inc
Vicksburg, MI 269-649-0530

Sandwich

Aladdin Transparent Packaging
Hauppauge, NY 631-273-4747
Arbee Transparent Inc
Elk Grove Vlg, IL 800-642-2247
Brown Paper Goods Co
Waukegan, IL 847-688-1450
Castle Bag Co.
Wilmington, DE 302-656-1001
Colonial Transparent Products Company
Hicksville, NY 516-822-4430
Food Pak Corp
San Mateo, CA 650-341-6559
Pater & Associates
Cincinnati, OH
Stewart Sutherland Inc
Vicksburg, MI 269-649-0530
Vermont Bag & Film
Bennington, VT 802-442-3166

Shopping

All American Poly
Piscataway, NJ 800-526-3551
American Advertising & Shop Cap Company
Old Tappan, NJ 800-442-8837
Arbee Transparent Inc
Elk Grove Vlg, IL 800-642-2247
Celebrity Promotions
Remsen, IA 800-332-6847
Colonial Transparent Products Company
Hicksville, NY 516-822-4430
Continental Extrusion Corporation
Cedar Grove, NJ 800-822-4748
Continental Products
Mexico, MO 800-325-0216
Custom Poly Packaging
Fort Wayne, IN 800-548-6603
David Dobbs Enterprise Inc.
St Augustine, FL 800-889-6368
Eco-Bag Products
Ossining, NY 800-720-2247
Excelsior Transparent Bag Manufacturing
Yonkers, NY 914-968-1300
Fabriko
Altavista, VA 888-203-8098
Fischer Paper Products Inc
Antioch, IL 800-323-9093
Fitec International Inc
Memphis, TN 800-332-6387
Genpak LLC
Lakeville, MN 800-328-4556
Green Seams
Maple Grove, MN 612-929-3213
Hall Manufacturing Company
Henderson, TX 903-657-4501
J A Heilferty & Co
Teaneck, NJ 201-836-5060
Memphis Delta Tent & Awning
Memphis, TN 901-522-1238
Millhiser
Richmond, VA 800-446-2247
Moser Bag & Paper Company
Cleveland, OH 800-433-6638
NAP Industries
Brooklyn, NY 877-635-4948
North American Packaging Corp
New York, NY 800-499-3521
Pater & Associates
Cincinnati, OH
Pexco Packaging Corporation
Toledo, OH 800-227-9950
Poliplastic
Granby, QC 450-378-8417
Save-A-Tree
Berkeley, CA 510-843-5233

Shamrock Plastics
Mt Vernon, OH 800-765-1611
Sheboygan Paper Box Co
Sheboygan, WI 800-458-8373
Source for Packaging
New York, NY 800-223-2527
Star Poly Bag Inc
Brooklyn, NY 718-384-7034
Tree Saver
Englewood, CO.................... 800-676-7741
Vermont Bag & Film
Bennington, VT 802-442-3166
Walker Bag Mfg Co
Louisville, KY 800-642-4949
Wisconsin Converting Inc
Green Bay, WI. 800-544-1935

Baskets

Egg

Langer Manufacturing Company
Cedar Rapids, IA. 800-728-6445
Xtreme Beverages, LLC
Dana Point, CA.................... 949-495-7929

Fruit & Vegetable

Berlin Fruit Box Company
Berlin Heights, OH 800-877-7721
Classy Basket
San Diego, CA 888-449-4901
Collectors Gallery
St Charles, IL 800-346-3063
Day Basket Factory
North East, MD. 410-398-5150
Farmer's Co-Op Elevator Co
Hudsonville, MI 800-439-9859
Frobisher Industries
Waterborough, NB 506-362-2198
Fruit Growers Package Company
Grandville, MI 616-724-1400
Harvey's Indian River Groves
Rockledge, FL. 800-327-9312
Langer Manufacturing Company
Cedar Rapids, IA. 800-728-6445
Little Rock Crate & Basket Co
Little Rock, AR. 800-223-7823
Longaberger Basket Company
Dresden, OH 740-518-8018
Peacock Crate Factory
Jacksonville, TX 800-657-2200
Peterboro Basket Co
Peterborough, NH 603-924-3861
Shipley Basket Mfg Co
Dayton, TN. 800-251-0806
Smalley Package Company
Berryville, VA. 540-955-2550
Specialty Wood Products
Clanton, AL 800-322-5343
Straits Steel & Wire Co
Ludington, MI. 231-843-3416
Thorco Industries LLC
Lamar, MO 800-445-3375
Traitech Industries
Vaughan, ON. 877-872-4835
Xtreme Beverages, LLC
Dana Point, CA.................... 949-495-7929

Gift

All Sorts Premium Packaging
Buffalo, NY....................... 888-565-9727
Andrea Basket
Bohemia, NY 888-272-8826
Baskets Extraordinaires
Westbury, NY 800-666-1685
Classy Basket
San Diego, CA 888-449-4901
Coe & Dru Inc
San Dimas, CA 800-722-7538
Collectors Gallery
St Charles, IL 800-346-3063
Dufeck Manufacturing Co
Denmark, WI. 888-603-9663
Gril-Del
Mankato, MN 800-782-7320
Harvey's Indian River Groves
Rockledge, FL. 800-327-9312
Houdini Inc
Fullerton, CA 714-525-0325
Mar-Boro Printing & Advertising Specialties
Brooklyn, NY 718-336-4051

Metrovock Snacks
Maywood, CA 800-428-0522
Peacock Crate Factory
Jacksonville, TX 800-657-2200
Roofian
Sun Valley, CA 800-431-3886
Seymour Woodenware Company
Seymour, WI 920-833-6551
United Basket Co Inc
Maspeth, NY 718-894-5454
Xtreme Beverages, LLC
Dana Point, CA 949-495-7929

Refrigerator

Coastline Equipment Inc
Bellingham, WA 360-734-8509
Langer Manufacturing Company
Cedar Rapids, IA. 800-728-6445
Straits Steel & Wire Co
Ludington, MI 231-843-3416

Bins

A-Z Factory Supply
Schiller Park, IL 800-323-4511
ABI Limited
Concord, ON 800-297-8666
American Pallet Inc
Oakdale, CA 209-847-6122
Anderson-Crane Company
Minneapolis, MN 800-314-2747
Andgar Corp
Ferndale, WA 360-366-9900
Atlas Equipment Company
Kansas City, MO 800-842-9188
AZO Food
Memphis, TN 901-794-9480
BestBins Corporation
Chaska, MN 866-448-3114
Bonar Plastics
West Chicago, IL 800-295-3725
Bonar Plastics
Ridgefield, WA 800-972-5252
Bowers Process Equipment
Stratford, ON. 800-567-3223
Buhler Inc.
Plymouth, MN. 763-847-9900
Cecor
Verona, WI 800-356-9042
Centennial Moldings
Hastings, NE 888-883-2189
Chief Industries
Kearney, NE 800-359-8833
Clayton & Lambert Manufacturing
Buckner, KY 800-626-5819
Containair Packaging Corporation
Paterson, NJ 888-276-6500
Continental-Fremont
Tiffin, OH 419-448-4045
Corbox-Meyers Inc
Cleveland, OH 800-321-7286
Davron Technologies Inc
Chattanooga, TN. 423-870-1888
DBE Inc
Concord, ON 800-461-5313
DEL-Tec Packaging Inc
Greer, SC. 800-747-8683
Despro Manufacturing
Cedar Grove, NJ 800-292-9906
Duke Manufacturing Co
St Louis, MO. 800-735-3853
Earl Soesbe Company
Romeoville, IL 219-866-4191
Eastern Plastics
Pawtucket, RI 800-442-8585
Electrical Engineering & Equip
Windsor Heights, IA 800-955-3633
Emco Industrial Plastics
Cedar Grove, NJ 800-292-9906
Expert Industries Inc
Brooklyn, NY 718-434-6060
F N Smith Corp
Oregon, IL. 815-732-2171
F.E. Wood & Sons
West Baldwin, ME 207-286-5003
Falco Technologies
La Prairie, QC. 450-444-0566
Faribault Manufacturing Co
Faribault, MN 800-447-6043
Flow of Solids
Westford, MA 978-392-0300

Follett Corp
Easton, PA 800-523-9361
Forbes Industries
Ontario, CA 909-923-4549
Fred D Pfening Co
Columbus, OH 614-294-5361
Frem Corporation
Worcester, MA 508-791-3152
Fresno Pallet, Inc.
Sultana, CA 559-591-4111
Gates Manufacturing Company
Saint Louis, MO 800-237-9226
Gch Internatonal
Louisville, KY 502-636-1374
Goergen-Mackwirth Co Inc
Buffalo, NY. 800-728-4446
Goldenwest Sales
Cerritos, CA 800-827-6175
Graff Tank Erection
Harrisville, PA. 814-385-6671
Hardy Systems Corporation
Northbrook, IL 800-927-3956
Hedstrom Corporation
Ashland, OH 700-765-9665
Hodge Manufacturing Company
Springfield, MA 800-262-4634
Hoshizaki America Inc
Peachtree City, GA 800-438-6087
Imperial Industries Inc
Rothschild, WI 800-558-2945
International Wood Industries
Snohomish, WA 800-922-6141
Jacksonville Box & Woodwork Co
Jacksonville, FL 800-683-2699
Jarlan Manufacturing
Los Angeles, CA. 323-752-1211
Jenike & Johanson Inc
Tyngsboro, MA. 978-649-3300
K & I Creative Plastics & Wood
Jacksonville, FL 904-387-0438
K-Tron
Salina, KS 785-825-1611
Kason
Lewis Center, OH 740-549-2100
KHM Plastics Inc
Gurnee, IL. 847-249-4910
Kimball Companies
East Longmeadow, MA 413-525-1881
Lakeside Manufacturing Inc
Milwaukee, WI 888-558-8565
Longview Fibre Company
Beaverton, OR 503-350-1600
Machine Ice Co
Houston, TX 800-423-8822
Mannhardt Inc
Sheboygan Falls, WI. 800-423-2327
Material Storage Systems
Gadsden, AL. 877-543-2467
Matthiesen Equipment
San Antonio, TX. 800-624-8635
MeGa Industries
Burlington, ON 800-665-6342
Mell & Co
Niles, IL 800-262-6355
Melmat Inc
Huntington Beach, CA 800-635-6289
Michiana Box & Crate
Niles, MI 800-677-6372
Miller Hofft Brands
Indianapolis, IN 317-638-6576
Moli-International
Denver, CO 800-525-8468
Mt Valley Farms & Lumber Prods
Biglerville, PA. 717-677-6166
MultiFab Plastics
Boston, MA. 888-293-5754
NEPA Pallet & Container Co
Snohomish, WA 360-568-3185
Newell Brands
Atlanta, GA
NST Metals
Louisville, KY 502-584-5846
Omega Industries
St Louis, MO. 314-961-1668
Our Name is Mud
New York, NY 877-683-7867
Pallet One Inc
Bartow, FL. 800-771-1148
Pelican Displays
Homer, IL 800-627-1517
Pittsburgh Tank Corp
Monongahela, PA 800-634-0243

Precision Plastics Inc
Beltsville, MD. 800-922-1317
Prestige Plastics Corporation
Delta, BC. 604-930-2931
Prince Castle Inc
Carol Stream, IL 800-722-7853
Pro Bake Inc
Twinsburg, OH 800-837-4427
Process Solutions
Riviera Beach, FL. 561-840-0050
Pruitt's Packaging Services
Grand Rapids, MI 800-878-0553
Quantum Storage Systems Inc
Miami, FL 800-685-4665
Ram Equipment Co
Waukesha, WI 262-513-1114
Remcon Plastics Inc
Reading, PA 800-360-3636
Render
Buffalo, NY 888-446-1010
RMI-C/Rotonics Manufacturing
Bensenville, IL 630-773-9510
Rotonics Manufacturing
Gardena, CA 310-327-5401
Schenck Process
Whitewater, WI 888-742-1249
Scotsman Ice Systems
Vernon Hills, IL 800-726-8762
Seattle Plastics
Seattle, WA 800-441-0679
SEMCO
Ocala, FL. 800-749-6894
SerVend International
Sellersburg, IN 800-367-4233
Shouldice Brothers SheetMetal
Battle Creek, MI 269-962-5579
Snyder Crown
Marked Tree, AR 870-358-3400
Solve Needs International
White Lake, MI 800-783-2462
Southern Ag Co Inc
Blakely, GA. 229-723-4262
Spudnik Equipment Co
Blackfoot, ID 208-684-4120
Stainless Fabrication Inc
Springfield, MO 800-397-8265
Stearnswood Inc
Hutchinson, MN 800-657-0144
Supreme Metal
Alpharetta, GA 800-645-2526
Thermodynamics
Commerce City, CO 800-627-9037
Tolan Machinery Company
Rockaway, NJ 973-983-7212
Trade Fixtures
Little Rock, AR. 800-872-3490
Tri-Boro Shelving & Partition
Farmville, VA 800-633-3070
Triple-A Manufacturing Company
Toronto, ON 800-786-2238
Tulip Molded Plastics Corp
Milwaukee, WI 414-963-3120
Upham & Walsh Lumber
Hoffman Estates, IL 847-519-1010
Vande Berg SCALES/Vbs Inc
Sioux Center, IA 712-722-1181
Vanmark Equipment
Creston, IA 800-523-6261
Warwick Products
Cleveland, OH 800-535-4404
Welbilt Inc.
New Port Richey, FL. 877-375-9300
Westeel
Saskatoon, SK. 306-931-2855
Westfield Sheet Metal Works
Kenilworth, NJ 908-276-5500
Wilder Manufacturing Company
Port Jervis, NY 800-832-1319
Wilson Steel Products Company
Memphis, TN 901-527-8742
Woodstock Plastics Co Inc
Marengo, IL 815-568-5281

Beverage

Crown Plastics Inc
Minneapolis, MN 800-423-2769
Falco Technologies
La Prairie, QC. 450-444-0566
Lakeside Manufacturing Inc
Milwaukee, WI 888-558-8565

Insulated

ABI Limited
  Concord, ON 800-297-8666
Falco Technologies
  La Prairie, QC 450-444-0566
Lakeside Manufacturing Inc
  Milwaukee, WI 888-558-8565
Melmat Inc
  Huntington Beach, CA 800-635-6289
Promens
  St. John, NB 800-295-3725

Bottles

Aluminum

California Vibratory Feeders
  Anaheim, CA 800-354-0972
Elemental Containers
  Union, NJ 800-577-7624
Mountain Safety Research
  Seattle, WA 800-877-9677

Glass

Ameripec
  Buena Park, CA 714-994-2990
Arkansas Glass Container Corp
  Jonesboro, AR 800-527-4527
Bal/Foster Glass Container Company
  Port Allegany, PA 814-642-2521
Ball Foster Glass
  Fairfield, CA 707-863-4061
Ball Foster Glass Container Company
  Sapulpa, OK 918-224-1440
Ball Glass Container Corporation
  El Monte, CA 626-448-9831
California Vibratory Feeders
  Anaheim, CA 800-354-0972
Foster-Forbes Glass Company
  Vernon, CA 800-767-4527
Greenfield Packaging
  White Plains, NY 914-993-0233
Indiana Glass Company
  Columbus, OH 800-543-0357
Indianapolis Container Company
  Indianapolis, IN 800-760-3318
Kelman Bottles LLC
  Glenshaw, PA 412-486-9100
LMK Containers
  Centerville, UT 626-821-9984
Louisville Container Company
  Indianapolis, IN 888-539-7225
Oak Barrel Winecraft
  Berkeley, CA 510-849-0400
Palmer Distributors
  St Clair Shores, MI 800-444-1912
Penn Bottle & Supply Company
  Philadelphia, PA 215-365-5700
Richards Packaging
  Memphis, TN 800-583-0327
Stanpac, Inc.
  Smithville, ON 905-957-3326
World Kitchen
  Elmira, NY 800-999-3436
Xtreme Beverages, LLC
  Dana Point, CA 949-495-7929

Plastic

Abbott Industries
  Paterson, NJ
Alpack
  Centerville, NA 774-994-8086
Altira Inc
  Miami, FL 305-687-8074
Brown International Corp LLC
  Winter Haven, FL 863-299-2111
California Vibratory Feeders
  Anaheim, CA 800-354-0972
CapSnap Equipment
  Jackson, MI 517-787-3481
Chester Plastics
  Chester, NS 902-275-3522
CMD Corporation
  Appleton, WI 920-730-6888
Consolidated Container Co LLC
  Atlanta, GA 888-831-2184
Consolidated Plastics Co Inc
  Stow, OH 800-858-5001
Constar International
  Plymouth, MI 734-455-3600

Container Specialties
  Melrose Park, IL 800-548-7513
Continental Plastic Container
  Dallas, TX 972-303-1825
Contour Packaging
  Philadelphia, PA 215-457-1600
CTK Plastics
  Moose Jaw, SK 800-667-8847
Custom Bottle of Connecticut
  Naugatuck, CT 203-723-6661
Flexo Transparent Inc
  Buffalo, NY 877-993-5396
Fuller Industries LLC
  Great Bend, KS 800-522-0499
Graham Engineering Corp
  York, PA 717-848-3755
Greenfield Packaging
  White Plains, NY 914-993-0233
Hartford Plastics
  Omaha, NE
Hedwin Division
  Baltimore, MD 800-638-1012
Indiana Bottle Co
  Scottsburg, IN 800-752-8702
Indianapolis Container Company
  Indianapolis, IN 800-760-3318
Intertech Corp
  Greensboro, NC 800-364-2255
J.E. Roy
  St Claire, QC 418-883-2711
Juice Merchandising Corp
  Kansas City, MO 800-950-1998
Jupiter Mills Corporation
  Roslyn, NY 800-853-5121
Liqui-Box
  Richmond, VA 804-325-1400
Liquitane
  Berwick, PA 570-759-6200
LMK Containers
  Centerville, UT 626-821-9984
Louisville Container Company
  Indianapolis, IN 888-539-7225
Marpac Industries
  Philmont, NY 888-462-7722
Owens-Illinois Inc
  Perrysburg, OH 567-336-5000
Packaging Associates
  Randolph, NJ 973-252-8890
Parkway Plastic Inc
  Piscataway, NJ 800-881-4996
Penn Bottle & Supply Company
  Philadelphia, PA 215-365-5700
Plastics Industries
  Athens, TN 800-894-4876
Plastipak Packaging
  Plymouth, MI 734-354-3510
Podnar Plastics Inc
  Kent, OH 800-673-5277
Polycon Industries
  Chicago, IL 773-374-5500
Pretium Packaging
  Chesterfield, MO 314-727-8673
Pretium Packaging
  Hazle Twp, PA 570-459-1800
Pretium Packaging
  Hermann, MO 573-486-2811
Pretium Packaging, LLC.
  Chesterfield, MO 314-727-8200
Priority Plastics Inc
  Grinnell, IA 800-798-3512
Pro-Gram Plastics Inc
  Geneva, OH 440-466-8080
Progressive Plastics
  Cleveland, OH 800-252-0053
Q Pak Inc
  Newark, NJ 973-483-4404
Quintex Corp
  Nampa, ID 208-467-1113
RAPAC Inc
  Oakland, TN 800-280-6333
Redi-Call Inc
  Reno, NV 800-648-1849
Reliance Product
  Winnipeg, MB 800-665-0258
Richard Read Construction Company
  Arcadia, IN 888-450-7343
Richards Packaging
  Memphis, TN 800-583-0327
RXI Silgan Specialty Plastics
  Triadelphia, WV 304-547-9100
Sailor Plastics
  Adrian, MN 800-380-7429

Schoeneck Containers Inc
  New Berlin, WI 262-786-9360
Setco
  Monroe Twp, NJ 609-655-4600
Setco
  Anaheim, CA 714-777-5200
Silgan Plastics Canada
  Chesterfield, MO 800-274-5426
Silgan Plastics LLC
  Chesterfield, MO 800-274-5426
Snapware
  Fullerton, CA 800-334-3062
T&S Blow Molding
  Scarborough, ON 416-752-8330
Thornton Plastics
  Salt Lake City, UT 800-248-3434
Tolco Corp
  Toledo, OH 800-537-4786
Wheaton Plastic Containers
  Millville, NJ 856-825-1400

Boxes

Bakers'

International Paper Co.
  Memphis, TN
Morris Transparent Box Co
  East Providence, RI 401-438-6116
Pater & Associates
  Cincinnati, OH
Piper Products Inc
  Wausau, WI 800-544-3057
Premier Packages
  Saint Louis, MO 800-466-6588
Reliable Container Corporation
  Downey, CA 562-745-0200
Ritz Packaging Company
  Brooklyn, NY 718-366-2300
Schiefer Packaging Corporation
  Syracuse, NY 315-422-0615
Schroeder Machine
  San Marcos, CA 760-591-9733
Smyrna Container Co
  Atlanta, GA 800-868-4305
Xtreme Beverages, LLC
  Dana Point, CA 949-495-7929

Candy

A La Carte
  Chicago, IL 800-722-2370
Cardinal Packaging Prod LLC
  Crystal Lake, IL 866-216-4942
Central Paper Box
  Kansas City, MO 816-753-3126
Collectors Gallery
  St Charles, IL 800-346-3063
Creative Cookie
  Easton, MD 800-451-4005
Elegant Packaging
  Cicero, IL 800-367-5493
Friend Box Co
  Danvers, MA 978-774-0240
Gary Plastic Packaging Corporation
  Bronx, NY 800-227-4279
H.P. Neun
  Fairport, NY 585-388-1360
Impress Industries
  Emmaus, PA 610-967-6027
Kaufman Paper Box Company
  Providence, RI 401-272-7508
Lengsfield Brothers
  New Orleans, LA 504-529-2235
Nashville Wraps LLC
  Hendersonville, TN. 800-547-9727
Pater & Associates
  Cincinnati, OH
Ritz Packaging Company
  Brooklyn, NY 718-366-2300
Schiefer Packaging Corporation
  Syracuse, NY 315-422-0615
Taylor Box Co
  Warren, RI 800-304-6361
Visual Packaging Corp
  Haskell, NJ 973-835-7055
Xtreme Beverages, LLC
  Dana Point, CA 949-495-7929

Corrugated

Adpro
  Solon, OH 440-542-1111

American Containers Inc
Plymouth, IN 574-936-4068
Atlas Packaging Inc
Opa Locka, FL 800-662-0630
Bell Container
Newark, NJ 973-344-6997
Bell Packaging Corporation
Marion, IN 800-382-0153
Boxes.com
Livingston, NJ 201-646-9050
Cantwell-Cleary Co Inc
Elkridge, MD 301-773-9800
Cantwell-Cleary Co Inc
Richmond, VA 804-329-9800
Capital City Container Corporation
Buda, TX 512-312-1222
Capitol Carton Company
Sacramento, CA 916-388-7848
Capitol City Container Corp
Indianapolis, IN 800-233-5145
Cardinal Container Corp
Indianapolis, IN 800-899-2715
Cardinal Packaging Prod LLC
Crystal Lake, IL 866-216-4942
Carolina Container
High Point, NC 800-627-0825
Carpet City Paper Box Company
Amsterdam, NY 518-842-5430
Cedar Box Co
Minneapolis, MN 612-332-4287
Central Package & Display
Minneapolis, MN 763-425-7444
Chambers Container Company
Gastonia, NC 704-377-6317
Champlin Co
Hartford, CT 800-458-5261
City Box Company
Aurora, IL 773-277-5500
Color Carton Corp
Bronx, NY 718-665-0840
Columbus Paperbox Company
Columbus, OH 800-968-0797
Commencement Bay Corrugated
Orting, WA 253-845-3100
Commercial Corrugated Co Inc
Baltimore, MD 800-242-8861
Complete Packaging & Shipping
Freeport, NY 877-269-3236
Conn Container Corp
North Haven, CT 203-248-0241
Corbox-Meyers Inc
Cleveland, OH 800-321-7286
Corfab
Chicago, IL 708-458-8750
Corr Pak Corp
Mc Cook, IL 708-442-7806
Corrugated Packaging
Sarasota, FL 941-371-0000
Corrugated Specialties
Plainwell, MI 269-685-9821
Craft Corrugated Box Inc
New Bedford, MA 508-998-2115
Creative Packaging
Hayward, CA 510-785-6500
Cush-Pak Container Corporation
Henderson, TX 903-657-0555
Custom Packaging Inc
Richmond, VA 804-232-3299
Dakota Corrugated Box
Sioux Falls, SD 605-332-3501
Deline Box Co
Denver, CO 303-376-1283
Desert Box & Supply Corporation
Thermal, CA 760-399-5161
Diamond Packaging
Rochester, NY 800-333-4079
Die Cut Specialties Inc
Savage, MN 952-890-7590
Display One
Hartford, WI 262-673-5880
Dixie Printing & Packaging
Glen Burnie, MD 800-433-4943
Dorado Carton Company
Dorado, PR 787-796-1670
Drake Co
Houston, TX 800-299-5644
Drescher Paper Box Inc
Buffalo, NY 716-854-0288
Dusobox Company
Haverhill, MA 978-372-7192
Duval Container Co
Jacksonville, FL 800-342-8194

Dzignpak LLC Englander
Waco, TX 888-314-5259
E-Cooler
Chicago, IL 866-955-3266
Eagle Box Company
Farmingdale, NY 212-255-3860
EB Box Company
Richmond Hill, ON 800-513-2269
Felco Packaging Specialist
Baltimore, MD 800-673-8488
Ferguson Containers
Phillipsburg, NJ 908-454-9755
Fitzpatrick Container Company
North Wales, PA 215-699-3515
Fleetwood International Paper
Vernon, CA 323-588-7121
Flint Boxmakers Inc
Flint, MI 810-743-0400
Four M Manufacturing Group
San Jose, CA 408-998-1141
Frankston Paper Box Company of Texas
Frankston, TX 903-876-2550
Fuller Box Co
North Attleboro, MA 508-695-2525
Gateway Packaging Corp
Export, PA 888-289-2693
Gaylord Container Corporation
Tampa, FL 813-621-3591
General Bag Corporation
Cleveland, OH 800-837-9396
Genesee Corrugated
Flint, MI 810-228-3702
Georgia-Pacific LLC
Atlanta, GA 800-283-5547
Goldman Manufacturing Company
Detroit, MI 313-834-5535
Graphic Packaging Intl
Elk Grove Vlg, IL 847-437-1700
Great Lakes-Triad Package Corporation
Grand Rapids, MI 616-241-6441
Great Northern Corp
Chippewa Falls, WI 800-472-1800
Great Northern Corp
Racine, WI 800-558-4711
Green Bay Packaging Inc.
Tulsa, OK 918-446-3341
Green Bay Packaging Inc.
Green Bay, WI 920-433-5111
Greenfield Packaging
White Plains, NY 914-993-0233
Greif Inc
Delaware, OH 740-549-6000
Gulf Arizona Packaging
Humble, TX 800-364-3887
Gulf Systems
Brownsville, TX 800-217-4853
Gulf Systems
Humble, TX 800-364-3887
Gulf Systems
Arlington, TX 817-261-1915
H.P. Neun
Fairport, NY 585-388-1360
Hager Containers Inc
Carrollton, TX 972-416-7660
Hawkeye Corrugated Box
Cedar Falls, IA 319-268-0407
Herche Warehouse
Denver, CO 303-371-8186
Hinkle Manufacturing
Perrysburg, OH 419-666-5367
Hope Paper Box Company
Pawtucket, RI 401-724-5700
Hunter Packaging Corporation
South Elgin, IL 800-428-4747
Il Valley Container Inc
Peru, IL 815-223-7200
Imperial Containers
City of Industry, CA 626-333-6363
Imperial Packaging Corporation
Pawtucket, RI 401-753-7778
Impress Industries
Emmaus, PA 610-967-6027
Industrial Container Corp
High Point, NC 336-886-7031
Industrial Crating & Packing
Tukwila, WA 800-942-0499
Inland Consumer Packaging
Harrington, DE 302-398-4211
Inland Paper Company
Ontario, CA 909-923-4505
Inland Paperboard & Packaging
Rock Hill, SC 803-366-4103

Instabox
Calgary, AB 800-482-6173
Ivarson Inc
Milwaukee, WI 414-351-0700
J&J Corrugated Box Corporation
Franklin, MA 508-528-6200
J&J Mid-South Container Corporation
Augusta, GA 800-395-1025
Jamestown Container Corporation
Buffalo, NY 855-234-4054
Jayhawk Boxes
Fremont, NE 800-642-8363
Jesse Jones Box Corporation
Philadelphia, PA 215-425-6600
Jessup Paper Box
Brookston, IN 765-490-9043
Jet Box Co
Troy, MI 248-362-1260
Johnson Corrugated Products Corporation
Thompson, CT 860-923-9563
Jupiter Mills Corporation
Roslyn, NY 800-853-5121
K & H Corrugated Corp
Walden, NY 845-778-3555
K&H Container
Wallingford, CT 203-265-1547
Kelly Box & Packaging Corp
Fort Wayne, IN 260-432-4570
Kendel
Countryside, IL 800-323-1100
Kerrigan Paper Products Inc
Haverhill, MA 978-374-4797
Kimball Companies
East Longmeadow, MA 413-525-1881
Knapp Container
Beacon Falls, CT 203-888-0511
Koch Container
Victor, NY 585-924-1600
Kole Industries
Miami, FL 305-633-2556
Lakeside Container Corp
Plattsburgh, NY 518-561-6150
Lansing Corrugated Products
Lansing, MI 517-323-2752
Laval Paper Box
Pointe Claire, QC 450-669-3551
Lawrence Paper Co
Lawrence, KS 785-843-8111
Leaman Container
Fort Worth, TX 817-429-2660
Levin Brothers Paper
Cicero, IL 800-545-6200
Liberty Carton Co.
Golden Valley, MN 800-328-1784
LinPac
San Angelo, TX 800-453-7393
Lone Star Container Corp
Irving, TX 800-552-6937
Loy Lange Box Co
St Louis, MO 800-886-4712
Mack-Chicago Corporation
Chicago, IL 800-992-6225
MacMillan Bloedel Packaging
Montgomery, AL 800-239-4464
Mall City Containers Inc
Kalamazoo, MI 800-643-6721
Mannkraft Corporation
Newark, NJ 973-589-7400
Manufacturers Corrugate Box
Flushing, NY 718-894-7200
Marfred Industries
Sun Valley, CA 800-529-5156
Mark Container Corporation
San Leandro, CA 510-483-4440
Maro Paper Products Company
Bellwood, IL 708-649-9982
Massachusetts Container Corporation
North Haven, CT 203-248-2161
Menasha Corp
Neenah, WI 800-558-5073
Michiana Corrugate Products
Sturgis, MI 269-651-5225
Michigan Box Co
Detroit, MI 888-642-4269
Midwest Box Co
Cleveland, OH 216-281-3980
Midwest Fibre Products Inc
Viola, IL 309-596-2955
Midwest Paper Products Company
Louisville, KY 502-636-2741
Morphy Container Company
Brantford, ON 519-752-5428

Muth Associates
Springfield, MA 800-388-0157
Neff Packaging
Simpsonville, KY 800-445-4383
Nelson Container Corp
Germantown, WI. 262-250-5000
New England Wooden Ware
Gardner, MA .800-252-9214
New York Corrugated Box Co
Paterson, NJ .973-742-5000
Northeast Box Co
Ashtabula, OH 800-362-8100
Northeast Container Corporation
Dumont, NJ. .201-385-6200
Northern Box Co Inc
Elkhart, IN. 574-264-2161
Northern Package Corporation
Minneapolis, MN 952-881-5861
Ockerlund Industries
Addison, IL 708-771-7707
Old Dominion Box Co Inc
Madison Heights, VA 434-929-6701
Packaging Design Corp
Burr Ridge, IL. 630-323-1354
Palmetto Packaging
Florence, SC .843-662-5800
Parlor City Paper Box Co Inc
Binghamton, NY 607-772-0600
Pel-Pak Container
Pell City, AL .800-239-2699
Performance Packaging
Trail Creek, IN 219-874-6226
Phoenix Industries Corp
Madison, WI .888-241-7482
Pratt Industries
Conyers, GA .800-428-9269
Pratt Industries
Raleigh, NC .919-334-7400
Premier Packages
Saint Louis, MO 800-466-6588
President Container Inc
Moonachie, NJ 212-244-0345
Propak
Burlington, ON 800-263-4872
Providence Packaging
Mooresville, NC 866-779-4945
Quality Packaging Inc
Fond Du Lac, WI 800-923-3633
R&R Corrugated Container
Terryville, CT 860-584-1194
Rand-Whitney Group LLC
Worcester, MA 508-791-2301
Rand-Whitney Packaging Corp
Portsmouth, NH 508-791-2301
RDA Container Corp
Gates, NY 585-247-2323
Regal Box Corp
Milwaukee, WI 414-562-5890
Reliable Container Corporation
Downey, CA .562-745-0200
Reliance-Paragon
Philadelphia, PA 215-743-1231
Rex Carton Co Inc
Chicago, IL 773-581-4115
Richmond Corrugated Box Company
Richmond, VA 804-222-1300
Romanow Container
Westwood, MA. 781-320-9200
Royal Group
Cicero, IL 708-656-2020
Rudd Container Corp
Chicago, IL 773-847-7600
Ruffino Paper Box Co
Hackensack, NJ. 201-487-1260
Rusken Packaging
Cullman, AL .256-775-0014
Schermerhorn Inc
Chicopee, MA. 413-598-8348
Schiffenhaus Industries
Newark, NJ 973-484-5000
Scope Packaging
Orange, CA 714-998-4411
Seattle-Tacoma Box Co
Kent, WA. 253-854-9700
Sebring Container Corporation
Salem, OH. 330-332-1533
Security Packaging
North Bergen, NJ 201-854-1955
Sheboygan Paper Box Co
Sheboygan, WI. 800-458-8373
Shillington Box Co LLC
St Louis, MO. 636-825-6471

Shippers Supply
Saskatoon, SK 800-661-5639
Shippers Supply, Labelgraphic
Calgary, AB. .800-661-5639
Simkins Industries Inc
East Haven, CT. 203-787-7171
Smith Packaging
Mississauga, ON 905-564-6640
Smurfit Stone
Norcross, GA 314-656-5300
Smurfit-Stone Container Corp
Santa Fe Springs, CA 714-523-3550
Solve Needs International
White Lake, MI. 800-783-2462
Somerville Packaging
Toronto, ON .416-754-7228
Southern Missouri Containers
Springfield, MO 800-999-7666
Southern Packaging Machinery
Athens, GA 706-208-0814
Spring Cove Container Div
Roaring Spring, PA 814-224-5141
SQP
Schenectady, NY. 800-724-1129
St Joseph Packaging Inc
St Joseph, MO. 800-383-3000
Stand Fast Pkgng Prods Inc
Addison, IL 630-543-6390
Star Container Corporation
Leominster, MA 978-537-1676
State Container Corp
Moonachie, NJ 201-933-5200
Stearnswood Inc
Hutchinson, MN 800-657-0144
Stone Container
Moss Point, MS 502-491-4870
Stronghaven Containers Co
Matthews, NC. 800-222-7919
Suburban Corrugated Box Company
Indianhead Park, IL 630-920-1230
Supply One Inc
Tulsa, OK
Tampa Corrugated Carton Company
Tampa, FL 813-623-5115
Taylor Box Co
Warren, RI 800-304-6361
Tenneco Packaging
Westmont, IL. 630-850-7034
Tennessee Packaging
Loudon, TN 800-968-6894
THARCO
San Lorenzo, CA. 800-772-2332
Traub Container Corporation
Cleveland, OH 216-475-5100
Trent Corp
Trenton, NJ 609-587-7515
Triple A Containers
Buena Park, CA 714-521-2820
Tucson Container Corp
Tucson, AZ 520-746-3171
Union Camp Corporation
Denver, CO. .303-371-0760
Unique Boxes
Chicago, IL 800-281-1670
Universal Folding Box
East Orange, NJ 973-482-4300
Valley Container Corporation
Saint Louis, MO 314-652-8050
Valley Container Inc
Bridgeport, CT 203-368-6546
Vermont Container Corp
Bennington, VT 802-442-5455
Victory Box Corp
Roselle, NJ 908-245-5100
Victory Packaging, Inc.
Houston, TX .800-486-5606
Volk Packaging Corp
Biddeford, ME 207-282-6151
Wagner Brothers Containers
Baltimore, MD 410-354-0044
Wasserman Bag Company
Center Moriches, NY 631-909-8656
Weber Display & Packaging Inc
Philadelphia, PA 215-426-3500
Webster Packaging Corporation
Loveland, OH 513-683-5666
Welch Packaging Group Inc
Elkhart, IN. 574-295-2460
Westvaco Corporation
Newark, DE. .302-453-7200
Weyerhaeuser Co
Seattle, WA. .800-525-5440

Willamette Industries
Beaverton, OR. 503-641-1131
Willard Packaging Co
Gaithersburg, MD. 301-948-7700
Woodson Pallet Co
Anmoore, WV. 304-623-2858
Xtreme Beverages, LLC
Dana Point, CA. 949-495-7929
York Container Co
York, PA. 717-757-7611

Fancy

Can Creations
Pembroke Pines, FL 954-581-3312
Central Paper Box
Kansas City, MO. 816-753-3126
Colbert Packaging Corp
Lake Forest, IL 847-367-5990
Collectors Gallery
St Charles, IL 800-346-3063
Elegant Packaging
Cicero, IL 800-367-5493
Gates
West Peterborough, NH 888-543-6316
Godshall Paper Box Company
Oshkosh, WI. 920-235-4040
H.P. Neun
Fairport, NY .585-388-1360
McGraw Box Company
Mc Graw, NY 607-836-6465
Nordic Printing & Packaging
New Hope, MN. 763-535-6440
North American Packaging Corp
New York, NY 800-499-3521
Paragon Packaging
Ferndale, CA .888-615-0065
Pater & Associates
Cincinnati, OH
Paul T. Freund Corporation
Palmyra, NY .800-333-0091
Racine Paper Box Manufacturing
Chicago, IL 773-227-3900
Smurfit Stone
Norcross, GA 314-656-5300
Xtreme Beverages, LLC
Dana Point, CA. 949-495-7929

Fiber

Goldman Manufacturing Company
Detroit, MI 313-834-5535
Greenfield Packaging
White Plains, NY 914-993-0233
Jupiter Mills Corporation
Roslyn, NY. .800-853-5121
Lansing Corrugated Products
Lansing, MI. .517-323-2752
North American Container Corp
Marietta, GA .800-929-0610
Palmetto Packaging
Florence, SC .843-662-5800
Romanow Container
Westwood, MA. 781-320-9200
Round Paper Packages Inc
Erlanger, KY .859-331-7200
Smith Packaging
Mississauga, ON 905-564-6640
Solve Needs International
White Lake, MI. 800-783-2462
State Container Corp
Moonachie, NJ 201-933-5200
Tucson Container Corp
Tucson, AZ 520-746-3171
Union Camp Corporation
Denver, CO. .303-371-0760
Volk Packaging Corp
Biddeford, ME 207-282-6151

Fruit & Vegetable

Franklin Crates
Micanopy, FL 352-466-3141
Frobisher Industries
Waterborough, NB 506-362-2198
Jacksonville Box & Woodwork Co
Jacksonville, FL 800-683-2699
Luke's Almond Acres
Reedley, CA .559-638-3483
Remmey Wood Products
Southampton, PA 215-355-3335
Schiefer Packaging Corporation
Syracuse, NY 315-422-0615

Supply One Inc
Tulsa, OK
Upham & Walsh Lumber
Hoffman Estates, IL 847-519-1010
Wnc Pallet & Forest Pdts Co
Candler, NC 828-667-5426
Xtreme Beverages, LLC
Dana Point, CA. 949-495-7929

Paper

Accurate Paper Box Co Inc
Knoxville, TN 865-690-0311
Adpro
Solon, OH 440-542-1111
Alcan Packaging
Baie D'Urfe, QC. 514-457-4555
Ample Industries
Franklin, OH 888-818-9700
Artistic Carton
Auburn, IN 800-735-7225
Artistic Carton Co
Elgin, IL 847-741-0247
Bancroft Bag Inc
West Monroe, LA 318-387-2550
Bell Packaging Corporation
Marion, IN. 800-382-0153
Boxes.com
Livingson, NJ. 201-646-9050
Brewer-Cantelmo Inc
New York, NY 212-244-4600
Burrows Paper Corp
Little Falls, NY 800-272-7122
Capitol Carton Company
Sacramento, CA 916-388-7848
Cardinal Packaging Prod LLC
Crystal Lake, IL 866-216-4942
Carpenter-Hayes Paper Box Company
East Hampton, CT. 203-267-4436
Carpet City Paper Box Company
Amsterdam, NY 518-842-5430
Cedar Box Co
Minneapolis, MN 612-332-4287
Central Paper Box
Kansas City, MO. 816-753-3126
Chambers Container Company
Gastonia, NC 704-377-6317
Cleveland Specialties Co
Loveland, OH 513-677-9787
Coast Paper Box Company
San Bernardino, CA 909-382-3475
Colbert Packaging Corp
Lake Forest, IL 847-367-5990
Color Box
Richmond, IN 765-966-7588
Color Carton Corp
Bronx, NY. 718-665-0840
Columbus Paperbox Company
Columbus, OH 800-968-0797
Commencement Bay Corrugated
Orting, WA 253-845-3100
Commercial Corrugated Co Inc
Baltimore, MD 800-242-8861
Complete Packaging & Shipping
Freeport, NY. 877-269-3236
Conn Container Corp
North Haven, CT. 203-248-0241
Corbox-Meyers Inc
Cleveland, OH 800-321-7286
Corfab
Chicago, IL. 708-458-8750
Corpak
San Juan, PR. 787-787-9085
Corr Pak Corp
Mc Cook, IL 708-442-7806
Corrobilt Container Company
Livermore, CA 925-373-0880
Corrugated Packaging
Sarasota, FL 941-371-0000
Corson Manufacturing Company
Lockport, NY 716-434-8871
Crane Carton Corporation
Chicago, IL. 773-722-0555
Creative Packaging
Hayward, CA 510-785-6500
Curtis Packaging
Sandy Hook, CT 203-426-5861
Custom Packaging Inc
Richmond, VA. 804-232-3299
Day Manufacturing Company
Sherman, TX. 903-893-1138

Designers Folding Box Corp
Buffalo, NY. 716-853-5141
Diamond Packaging
Rochester, NY. 800-333-4079
Dixie Printing & Packaging
Glen Burnie, MD 800-433-4943
Dorado Carton Company
Dorado, PR 787-796-1670
Drescher Paper Box Inc
Buffalo, NY. 716-854-0288
Dusobox Company
Haverhill, MA. 978-372-7192
Duval Container Co
Jacksonville, FL 800-342-8194
Eagle Box Company
Farmingdale, NY 212-255-3860
EB Box Company
Richmond Hill, ON. 800-513-2269
Economy Folding Box Corporation
Chicago, IL 800-771-1053
Elegant Packaging
Cicero, IL 800-367-5493
Enterprise Box Company
Montclair, NJ 973-509-2200
Eureka Paper Box Company
Williamsport, PA. 570-326-9147
F C MEYER Packaging LLC
Jeannette, PA. 724-523-5565
Felco Packaging Specialist
Baltimore, MD 800-673-8488
Finn Industries
Ontario, CA. 909-930-1500
Fitzpatrick Container Company
North Wales, PA 215-699-3515
Flashfold Carton Inc
Fort Wayne, IN 260-423-9431
Flour City Press-Pack Company
Minneapolis, MN 952-831-1265
Folding Carton/Flexible Packaging
North Hollywood, CA 818-896-3449
Food Pak Corp
San Mateo, CA 650-341-6559
Four M Manufacturing Group
San Jose, CA 408-998-1141
Frankston Paper Box Company of Texas
Frankston, TX 903-876-2550
Friend Box Co
Danvers, MA. 978-774-0240
Friendly City Box Co Inc
Johnstown, PA. 814-266-6287
Fuller Box Co
North Attleboro, MA 508-695-2525
Fuller Packaging Inc
Central Falls, RI 401-725-4300
Gateway Packaging Corp
Export, PA. 888-289-2693
Godshall Paper Box Company
Oshkosh, WI 920-235-4040
Goldman Manufacturing Company
Detroit, MI 313-834-5535
Graphic Packaging Intl
Elk Grove Vlg, IL. 847-437-1700
Great Northern Corp
Chippewa Falls, WI 800-472-1800
Green Bay Packaging Inc.
Tulsa, OK 918-446-3341
Green Bay Packaging Inc.
Green Bay, WI. 920-433-5111
Green Brothers
Barrington, RI 401-245-9043
Greenfield Paper Box Co
Greenfield, MA. 413-773-9414
Greif Inc
Delaware, OH 740-549-6000
Grigsby Brothers Paper Box Manufacturers
Portland, OR 866-233-4690
Gulf Packaging Company
Safety Harbor, FL 800-749-3466
H.P. Neun
Fairport, NY 585-388-1360
Hager Containers Inc
Carrollton, TX. 972-416-7660
Harvard Folding Box Company
Lynn, MA 781-598-1600
Henry Ira L Co
Watertown, WI 920-261-0648
Hope Paper Box Company
Pawtucket, RI 401-724-5700
Hub Folding Box Co
Mansfield, MA 508-339-0102
Hunter Packaging Corporation
South Elgin, IL 800-428-4747

Imperial Packaging Corporation
Pawtucket, RI 401-753-7778
Impress Industries
Emmaus, PA 610-967-6027
Industrial Nameplate Inc
Warminster, PA 800-878-6263
Inland Consumer Packaging
Harrington, DE 302-398-4211
Inland Paper Company
Ontario, CA. 909-923-4505
Inland Paperboard & Packaging
Rock Hill, SC 803-366-4103
Ivarson Inc
Milwaukee, WI 414-351-0700
Jamestown Container Corporation
Buffalo, NY. 855-234-4054
Jarisch Paper Box Company
North Adams, MA 413-663-5396
Jesse Jones Box Corporation
Philadelphia, PA 215-425-6600
Jessup Paper Box
Brookston, IN 765-490-9043
Johnson Corrugated Products Corporation
Thompson, CT 860-923-9563
Jordan Box Co
Syracuse, NY 315-422-3419
Jordan Paper Box Co
Chicago, IL. 773-287-5362
Jupiter Mills Corporation
Roslyn, NY 800-853-5121
K & H Corrugated Corp
Walden, NY. 845-778-3555
K & L Intl
Ontario, CA. 888-598-5588
K&H Container
Wallingford, CT. 203-265-1547
Kaufman Paper Box Company
Providence, RI 401-272-7508
Kendel
Countryside, IL 800-323-1100
Knight Paper Box Company
Chicago, IL. 773-585-2035
Koch Container
Victor, NY 585-924-1600
Lakeside Container Corp
Plattsburgh, NY 518-561-6150
Levin Brothers Paper
Cicero, IL 800-545-6200
Liberty Carton Co.
Golden Valley, MN. 800-328-1784
LinPac
San Angelo, TX 800-453-7393
Lone Star Container Corp
Irving, TX 800-552-6937
Los Angeles Paper Box & Board Mills
Los Angeles, CA. 323-685-8900
Lowell Paper Box Company
Nashua, NH. 603-595-0700
Loy Lange Box Co
St Louis, MO. 800-886-4712
Mack-Chicago Corporation
Chicago, IL. 800-992-6225
MacMillan Bloedel Packaging
Montgomery, AL. 800-239-4464
Mall City Containers Inc
Kalamazoo, MI 800-643-6721
Malnove Of Nebraska
Omaha, NE 800-228-9877
Marcus Carton Company
Melville, NY 631-752-4200
Marfred Industries
Sun Valley, CA 800-529-5156
Marion Paper Box Co
Marion, IN. 765-664-6435
Maro Paper Products Company
Bellwood, IL 708-649-9982
Master Paper Box Co
Chicago, IL. 877-927-0252
Maypak Inc
Wayne, NJ. 973-696-0780
Menasha Corp
Neenah, WI. 800-558-5073
Merchants Publishing Company
Kalamazoo, MI 269-345-1175
Meyer Packaging
Palmyra, PA. 717-838-6300
Michiana Corrugate Products
Sturgis, MI 269-651-5225
Michigan Box Co
Detroit, MI 888-642-4269
Mid Cities Paper Box Company
Downey, CA 877-277-6272

Midwest Fibre Products Inc
Viola, IL 309-596-2955
Modern Paper Box Company
Providence, RI 401-861-7357
Moore Paper Boxes Inc
Dayton, OH 937-278-7327
Morphy Container Company
Brantford, ON 519-752-5428
Mt Vernon Packaging Inc
Mt Vernon, OH 888-397-3221
Muth Associates
Springfield, MA 800-388-0157
Nagel Paper & Box Company
Saginaw, MI 800-292-3654
Neff Packaging
Simpsonville, KY 800-445-4383
New England Wooden Ware
Gardner, MA 800-252-9214
New York Corugated Box Co
Paterson, NJ 973-742-5000
New York Folding Box Co Inc
Stanhope, NJ 973-347-6932
Norristown Box Company
Norristown, PA 610-275-5540
Northeast Box Co
Ashtabula, OH 800-362-8100
Northeast Container Corporation
Dumont, NJ 201-385-6200
Northern Package Corporation
Minneapolis, MN 952-881-5861
Oakes Carton Co
Kalamazoo, MI 269-381-6022
Ockerlund Industries
Addison, IL 708-771-7707
Old Dominion Box Co Inc
Madison Heights, VA 434-929-6701
Old Dominion Box Company
Burlington, NC 336-226-4491
Oracle Packaging
Winston Salem, NC. 800-952-9536
Original Packaging & Display Company
Saint Louis, MO 314-772-7797
Ott Packagings
Selinsgrove, PA. 570-374-2811
Pacific Paper Box Co
Cudahy, CA. 323-771-7733
Packaging Corporation of America
Lake Forest, IL 800-456-4725
Packaging Design Corp
Burr Ridge, IL. 630-323-1354
Packrite Packaging
Archdale, NC. 336-431-1111
Paddington Corporation
Fort Lee, NJ 201-461-7800
Paper Box & Specialty Co
Sheboygan, WI 888-240-3756
Paper Works Industries Inc
Baldwinsville, NY 800-847-5677
Paragon Packaging
Ferndale, CA. 888-615-0065
Parlor City Paper Box Co Inc
Binghamton, NY 607-772-0600
Parta
Kent, OH. .800-543-5781
Pater & Associates
Cincinnati, OH
Paul T. Freund Corporation
Palmyra, NY 800-333-0091
Peerless Packages
Cleveland, OH 216-464-3620
Pell Paper Box Company
Elizabeth City, NC 252-335-4361
Performance Packaging
Trail Creek, IN 219-874-6226
Pioneer Packaging
Chicopee, MA 413-378-6930
Pioneer Packaging & Printing
Anoka, MN 800-708-1705
Piqua Paper Box Co
Piqua, OH .800-536-2136
Pohlig Brothers
N Chesterfield, VA 804-275-9000
Portland Paper Box Company
Portland, OR 800-547-2571
Premier Packages
Saint Louis, MO 800-466-6588
Quality Packaging Inc
Fond Du Lac, WI 800-923-3633
Rand-Whitney Group LLC
Worcester, MA 508-791-2301
Rand-Whitney Packaging Corp
Portsmouth, NH 508-791-2301

RDA Container Corp
Gates, NY .585-247-2323
Reliable Container Corporation
Downey, CA 562-745-0200
Reliance-Paragon
Philadelphia, PA 215-743-1231
Rhoades Paper Box Corporation
Springfield, OH. 800-441-6494
Rice Paper Box Company
Colorado Springs, CO. 303-733-1000
Ritz Packaging Company
Brooklyn, NY 718-366-2300
Rock-Tenn Company
Norcross, GA 608-223-6272
Romanow Container
Westwood, MA 781-320-9200
Round Paper Packages Inc
Erlanger, KY. 859-331-7200
Roy's Folding Box
Cleveland, OH. 216-464-1191
Royal Paper Box Co
Montebello, CA 323-728-7041
Ruffino Paper Box Co
Hackensack, NJ. 201-487-1260
Rusken Packaging
Cullman, AL. 256-775-0014
Schermerhorn Inc
Chicopee, MA. 413-598-8348
Schwarz Supply Source
Morton Grove, IL 800-323-4903
Scope Packaging
Orange, CA. 714-998-4411
Seaboard Carton Company
Downers Grove, IL 708-344-0575
Seaboard Folding Box Corp
Fitchburg, MA 800-255-6313
Seattle-Tacoma Box Co
Kent, WA. .253-854-9700
Sebring Container Corporation
Salem, OH. 330-332-1533
Security Packaging
North Bergen, NJ 201-854-1955
Sheboygan Paper Box Co
Sheboygan, WI 800-458-8373
Shillington Box Co LLC
St Louis, MO. 636-825-6471
Shippers Supply
Saskatoon, SK. 800-661-5639
Shippers Supply, Labelgraphic
Calgary, AB. 800-661-5639
Shore Paper Box Co
Mardela Springs, MD 410-749-7125
Shorewood Packaging
Carlstadt, NJ 201-933-3203
Simkins Industries Inc
East Haven, CT. 203-787-7171
Smith-Lustig Paper Box Manufacturing
Cleveland, OH. 216-621-0454
Smurfit Stone
Norcross, GA. 314-656-5300
Smurfit-Stone Container Corp
Santa Fe Springs, CA 714-523-3550
Smyrna Container Co
Atlanta, GA. 800-868-4305
Solve Needs International
White Lake, MI. 800-783-2462
Somerville Packaging
Toronto, ON 416-754-7228
Sonderen Packaging
Spokane, WA. 800-727-9139
Southern Champion Tray LP
Chattanooga, TN. 800-468-2222
Southern Missouri Containers
Springfield, MO. 800-999-7666
Southern Packaging Machinery
Athens, GA. 706-208-0814
Specialized Packaging London
London, ON 519-659-7011
Spring Cove Container Div
Roaring Spring, PA. 814-224-5141
SQP
Schenectady, NY. 800-724-1129
St Joseph Packaging Inc
St Joseph, MO. 800-383-3000
St. Louis Carton Company
Saint Louis, MO 314-241-0990
Stand Fast Pkgng Prods Inc
Addison, IL. 630-543-6390
Stearnswood Inc
Hutchinson, MN. 800-657-0144
Sterling Paper Company
Ohio, PA. .800-282-1124

Stone Container
Moss Point, MS 502-491-4870
Stronghaven Containers Co
Matthews, NC. 800-222-7919
Suburban Corrugated Box Company
Indianhead Park, IL 630-920-1230
T J Smith Box Co
Fort Smith, AR 877-540-7933
Tampa Corrugated Carton Company
Tampa, FL. 813-623-5115
Taylor Box Co
Warren, RI. 800-304-6361
THARCO
San Lorenzo, CA. 800-772-2332
Traub Container Corporation
Cleveland, OH 216-475-5100
Trent Corp
Trenton, NJ 609-587-7515
Unipak Inc
West Chester, PA 610-436-6600
Unique Boxes
Chicago, IL 800-281-1670
Universal Folding Box
East Orange, NJ 973-482-4300
Universal Folding Box Company
Hoboken, NJ. 201-659-7373
Universal Paper Box
Seattle, WA. 800-228-1045
Utah PaperBox Company
Salt Lake City, UT 801-363-0093
Victory Box Corp
Roselle, NJ 908-245-5100
Victory Packaging, Inc.
Houston, TX 800-486-5606
VIP Real Estate LTD
Chicago, IL 773-376-5000
Volk Packaging Corp
Biddeford, ME 207-282-6151
Wasserman Bag Company
Center Moriches, NY 631-909-8656
West Rock
Atlanta, GA 770-448-2193
Western Container Company
Kansas City, MO. 816-924-5700
Westvaco Corporation
Newark, DE. 302-453-7200
Willamette Industries
Beaverton, OR. 503-641-1131
Winchester Carton
Eutaw, AL. 205-372-3337
Woodson Pallet Co
Anmoore, WV. 304-623-2858
Wright Brothers Paper Box Company
Fond Du Lac, WI 920-921-8270
Xtreme Beverages, LLC
Dana Point, CA. 949-495-7929
York Container Co
York, PA. 717-757-7611

Paper, Folding

Adpro
Solon, OH .440-542-1111
Alcan Packaging
Baie D'Urfe, QC 514-457-4555
Ample Industries
Franklin, OH. 888-818-9700
Artistic Carton
Auburn, IN 800-735-7225
Artistic Carton Co
Elgin, IL 847-741-0247
Bell Packaging Corporation
Marion, IN. 800-382-0153
Boxes.com
Livingston, NJ. 201-646-9050
Brewer-Cantelmo Inc
New York, NY 212-244-4600
Burrows Paper Corp
Little Falls, NY 800-272-7122
Capitol Carton Company
Sacramento, CA 916-388-7848
Cardinal Packaging Prod LLC
Crystal Lake, IL 866-216-4942
Carpet City Paper Box Company
Amsterdam, NY 518-842-5430
Carton Service Co
Shelby, OH. 800-533-7744
Cedar Box Co
Minneapolis, MN 612-332-4287
Central Paper Box
Kansas City, MO. 816-753-3126

Chambers Container Company
Gastonia, NC 704-377-6317
Cleveland Specialties Co
Loveland, OH 513-677-9787
Coast Paper Box Company
San Bernardino, CA 909-382-3475
Collectors Gallery
St Charles, IL 800-346-3063
Color Carton Corp
Bronx, NY 718-665-0840
Columbus Paperbox Company
Columbus, OH 800-968-0797
Commencement Bay Corrugated
Orting, WA 253-845-3100
Commercial Corrugated Co Inc
Baltimore, MD 800-242-8861
Complete Packaging & Shipping
Freeport, NY 877-269-3236
Conn Container Corp
North Haven, CT 203-248-0241
Corbox-Meyers Inc
Cleveland, OH 800-321-7286
Corfab
Chicago, IL 708-458-8750
Corr Pak Corp
Mc Cook, IL 708-442-7806
Corrobilt Container Company
Livermore, CA 925-373-0880
Corrugated Packaging
Sarasota, FL 941-371-0000
Corson Manufacturing Company
Lockport, NY 716-434-8871
Crane Carton Corporation
Chicago, IL 773-722-0555
Creative Packaging
Hayward, CA 510-785-6500
Curtis Packaging
Sandy Hook, CT 203-426-5861
Day Manufacturing Company
Sherman, TX 903-893-1138
Designers Folding Box Corp
Buffalo, NY 716-853-5141
Diamond Packaging
Rochester, NY 800-333-4079
Dixie Printing & Packaging
Glen Burnie, MD 800-433-4943
Dorado Carton Company
Dorado, PR 787-796-1670
Drescher Paper Box Inc
Buffalo, NY 716-854-0288
Dusobox Company
Haverhill, MA 978-372-7192
Duval Container Co
Jacksonville, FL 800-342-8194
Eagle Box Company
Farmingdale, NY 212-255-3860
EB Box Company
Richmond Hill, ON 800-513-2269
Eureka Paper Box Company
Williamsport, PA 570-326-9147
F C MEYER Packaging LLC
Jeannette, PA 724-523-5565
Felco Packaging Specialist
Baltimore, MD 800-673-8488
Finn Industries
Ontario, CA 909-930-1500
Fitzpatrick Container Company
North Wales, PA 215-699-3515
Flashfold Carton Inc
Fort Wayne, IN 260-423-9431
Flour City Press-Pack Company
Minneapolis, MN 952-831-1265
Folding Carton/Flexible Packaging
North Hollywood, CA 818-896-3449
Food Pak Corp
San Mateo, CA 650-341-6559
Four M Manufacturing Group
San Jose, CA 408-998-1141
Frankston Paper Box Company of Texas
Frankston, TX 903-876-2550
Friendly City Box Co Inc
Johnstown, PA 814-266-6287
Goldman Manufacturing Company
Detroit, MI 313-834-5535
Graphic Packaging Intl
Elk Grove Vlg, IL 847-437-1700
Great Northern Corp
Chippewa Falls, WI 800-472-1800
Green Bay Packaging Inc.
Tulsa, OK 918-446-3341
Green Bay Packaging Inc.
Green Bay, WI 920-433-5111

Greenfield Packaging
White Plains, NY 914-993-0233
Greenfield Paper Box Co
Greenfield, MA 413-773-9414
Greif Inc
Delaware, OH 740-549-6000
Grigsby Brothers Paper Box Manufacturers
Portland, OR 866-233-4690
Gulf Packaging Company
Safety Harbor, FL 800-749-3466
H.P. Neun
Fairport, NY 585-388-1360
Hager Containers Inc
Carrollton, TX 972-416-7660
Harvard Folding Box Company
Lynn, MA 781-598-1600
Heritage Corrugated Box Corporation
Brooklyn, NY 718-495-1500
Hope Paper Box Company
Pawtucket, RI 401-724-5700
Hub Folding Box Co
Mansfield, MA 508-339-0102
Hunter Packaging Corporation
South Elgin, IL 800-428-4747
Imperial Packaging Corporation
Pawtucket, RI 401-753-7778
Impress Industries
Emmaus, PA 610-967-6027
Indiana Carton Co Inc
Bremen, IN 800-348-2390
Industrial Nameplate Inc
Warminster, PA 800-878-6263
Inland Consumer Packaging
Harrington, DE 302-398-4211
Inland Paper Company
Ontario, CA 909-923-4505
Inland Paperboard & Packaging
Rock Hill, SC 803-366-4103
International Paper Co.
Memphis, TN
Ivarson Inc
Milwaukee, WI 414-351-0700
Jamestown Container Corporation
Buffalo, NY 855-234-4054
Jarisch Paper Box Company
North Adams, MA 413-663-5396
Jesse Jones Box Corporation
Philadelphia, PA 215-425-6600
Jessup Paper Box
Brookston, IN 765-490-9043
Jupiter Mills Corporation
Roslyn, NY 800-853-5121
Kendel
Countryside, IL 800-323-1100
Knight Paper Box Company
Chicago, IL 773-585-2035
Koch Container
Victor, NY 585-924-1600
Lakeside Container Corp
Plattsburgh, NY 518-561-6150
Levin Brothers Paper
Cicero, IL 800-545-6200
Lone Star Container Corp
Irving, TX 800-552-6937
Los Angeles Paper Box & Board Mills
Los Angeles, CA 323-685-8900
Lowell Paper Box Company
Nashua, NH 603-595-0700
Loy Lange Box Co
St Louis, MO 800-886-4712
MacMillan Bloedel Packaging
Montgomery, AL 800-239-4464
Malnove Of Nebraska
Omaha, NE 800-228-9877
Marcus Carton Company
Melville, NY 631-752-4200
Marfred Industries
Sun Valley, CA 800-529-5156
Marion Paper Box Co
Marion, IN 765-664-6435
Maro Paper Products Company
Bellwood, IL 708-649-9982
Master Paper Box Co
Chicago, IL 877-927-0252
Menasha Corp
Neenah, WI 800-558-5073
Merchants Publishing Company
Kalamazoo, MI 269-345-1175
Meyer Packaging
Palmyra, PA 717-838-6300
Michigan Box Co
Detroit, MI 888-642-4269

Mid Cities Paper Box Company
Downey, CA 877-277-6272
Midvale Paper Box
Wilkes Barre, PA 570-824-3577
Midwest Fibre Products Inc
Viola, IL 309-596-2955
Nagel Paper & Box Company
Saginaw, MI 800-292-3654
Neff Packaging
Simpsonville, KY 800-445-4383
New England Wooden Ware
Gardner, MA 800-252-9214
New York Corugated Box Co
Paterson, NJ 973-742-5000
New York Folding Box Co Inc
Stanhope, NJ 973-347-6932
Norristown Box Company
Norristown, PA 610-275-5540
Northeast Box Co
Ashtabula, OH 800-362-8100
Northeast Container Corporation
Dumont, NJ 201-385-6200
Oakes Carton Co
Kalamazoo, MI 269-381-6022
Ockerlund Industries
Addison, IL 708-771-7707
Old Dominion Box Co Inc
Madison Heights, VA 434-929-6701
Old Dominion Box Company
Burlington, NC 336-226-4491
Oracle Packaging
Winston Salem, NC 800-952-9536
Original Packaging & Display Company
Saint Louis, MO 314-772-7797
Ott Packagings
Selinsgrove, PA 570-374-2811
Packaging Design Corp
Burr Ridge, IL 630-323-1354
Packrite Packaging
Archdale, NC 336-431-1111
Paper Works Industries Inc
Baldwinsville, NY 800-847-5677
Paragon Packaging
Ferndale, CA 888-615-0065
Parlor City Paper Box Co Inc
Binghamton, NY 607-772-0600
Parta
Kent, OH 800-543-5781
Pater & Associates
Cincinnati, OH
Peerless Cartons
Bartlett, IL 312-226-7952
Peerless Packages
Cleveland, OH 216-464-3620
Pell Paper Box Company
Elizabeth City, NC 252-335-4361
Performance Packaging
Trail Creek, IN 219-874-6226
Pioneer Packaging
Chicopee, MA 413-378-6930
Pioneer Packaging & Printing
Anoka, MN 800-708-1705
Piqua Paper Box Co
Piqua, OH 800-536-2136
Pohlig Brothers
N Chesterfield, VA 804-275-9000
Portland Paper Box Company
Portland, OR 800-547-2571
Premier Packages
Saint Louis, MO 800-466-6588
Prystup Packaging Products
Livingston, AL 205-652-9583
Quality Packaging Inc
Fond Du Lac, WI 800-923-3633
Racine Paper Box Manufacturing
Chicago, IL 773-227-3900
Rand-Whitney Group LLC
Worcester, MA 508-791-2301
Rand-Whitney Packaging Corp
Portsmouth, NH 508-791-2301
RDA Container Corp
Gates, NY 585-247-2323
Reliable Container Corporation
Downey, CA 562-745-0200
Reliance-Paragon
Philadelphia, PA 215-743-1231
Rhoades Paper Box Corporation
Springfield, OH 800-441-6494
Rice Paper Box Company
Colorado Springs, CO 303-733-1000
Ritz Packaging Company
Brooklyn, NY 718-366-2300

Rock-Tenn Company
Norcross, GA 608-223-6272
Romanow Container
Westwood, MA 781-320-9200
Rondo of America
Naugatuck, CT 203-723-7474
Roy's Folding Box
Cleveland, OH. 216-464-1191
Royal Paper Box Co
Montebello, CA 323-728-7041
Ruffino Paper Box Co
Hackensack, NJ 201-487-1260
Rusken Packaging
Cullman, AL 256-775-0014
San Diego Paper Box Company
Spring Valley, CA 619-660-9566
Schermerhorn Inc
Chicopee, MA 413-598-8348
Schiefer Packaging Corporation
Syracuse, NY 315-422-0615
Schwarz Supply Source
Morton Grove, IL 800-323-4903
Scope Packaging
Orange, CA 714-998-4411
Scott & Daniells
Portland, CT 860-342-1932
Seaboard Carton Company
Downers Grove, IL 708-344-0575
Seaboard Folding Box Corp
Fitchburg, MA 800-255-6313
Seattle-Tacoma Box Co
Kent, WA 253-854-9700
Sebring Container Corporation
Salem, OH. 330-332-1533
Security Packaging
North Bergen, NJ 201-854-1955
SFBC, LLC dba Seaboard Folding Box
Fitchburg, MA 800-225-6313
Sheboygan Paper Box Co
Sheboygan, WI 800-458-8373
Shelby Co
Westlake, OH 800-842-1650
Shillington Box Co LLC
St Louis, MO. 636-825-6471
Shippers Supply
Saskatoon, SK. 800-661-5639
Shippers Supply, Labelgraphic
Calgary, AB. 800-661-5639
Shore Paper Box Co
Mardela Springs, MD 410-749-7125
Shorewood Packaging
Carlstadt, NJ 201-933-3203
Simkins Industries Inc
East Haven, CT. 203-787-7171
Smurfit-Stone Container Corp
Santa Fe Springs, CA 714-523-3550
Smyrna Container Co
Atlanta, GA. 800-868-4305
Somerville Packaging
Toronto, ON 416-754-7228
Sonderen Packaging
Spokane, WA. 800-727-9139
SoOPAK
Mississauga, ON 905-677-9666
Southern Champion Tray LP
Chattanooga, TN. 800-468-2222
Southern Missouri Containers
Springfield, MO 800-999-7666
Southern Packaging Machinery
Athens, GA 706-208-0814
Spring Cove Container Div
Roaring Spring, PA. 814-224-5141
SQP
Schenectady, NY. 800-724-1129
St Joseph Packaging Inc
St Joseph, MO. 800-383-3000
St. Louis Carton Company
Saint Louis, MO 314-241-0990
Stand Fast Pkgng Prods Inc
Addison, IL. 630-543-6390
Stearnswood Inc
Hutchinson, MN 800-657-0144
Stone Container
Moss Point, MS 502-491-4870
Stoneway Carton Company
Mercer Island, WA 800-498-2185
Suburban Corrugated Box Company
Indianhead Park, IL 630-920-1230
T J Smith Box Co
Fort Smith, AR 877-540-7933
Tampa Corrugated Carton Company
Tampa, FL. 813-623-5115

Taylor Box Co
Warren, RI. 800-304-6361
THARCO
San Lorenzo, CA. 800-772-2332
Traub Container Corporation
Cleveland, OH 216-475-5100
Trent Corp
Trenton, NJ 609-587-7515
Unique Boxes
Chicago, IL 800-281-1670
Universal Folding Box
East Orange, NJ 973-482-4300
Universal Folding Box Company
Hoboken, NJ 201-659-7373
Utah PaperBox Company
Salt Lake City, UT 801-363-0093
Victory Box Corp
Roselle, NJ 908-245-5100
Victory Packaging, Inc.
Houston, TX 800-486-5606
VIP Real Estate LTD
Chicago, IL 773-376-5000
Volk Packaging Corp
Biddeford, ME 207-282-6151
Warren Packaging
San Bernardino, CA 909-888-7008
West Rock
Atlanta, GA. 770-448-2193
Western Container Company
Kansas City, MO. 816-924-5700
Westvaco Corporation
Newark, DE. 302-453-7200
Willamette Industries
Beaverton, OR. 503-641-1131
Woodson Pallet Co
Anmoore, WV. 304-623-2858
Wright Brothers Paper Box Company
Fond Du Lac, WI 920-921-8270
Xtreme Beverages, LLC
Dana Point, CA. 949-495-7929
York Container Co
York, PA 717-757-7611

Plastic

ACO
Moore, OK 405-794-7662
Alpack
Centerville, NA. 774-994-8086
Bardes Plastics Inc
Milwaukee, WI. 800-558-5161
Billie-Ann Plastics Packaging
Brooklyn, NY. 888-245-5432
Buckhorn Canada
Brampton, ON. 800-461-7579
Buckhorn Inc
Milford, OH 800-543-4454
Cambro Manufacturing Co
Huntington Beach, CA 800-833-3003
CKS Packaging
Atlanta, GA. 800-800-4257
Convoy
Canton, OH. 800-899-1583
DEL-Tec Packaging Inc
Greer, SC. 800-747-8683
Emco Industrial Plastics
Cedar Grove, NJ 800-292-9906
Finn Industries
Ontario, CA. 909-930-1500
Frankston Paper Box Company of Texas
Frankston, TX. 903-876-2550
Fremont Die Cut Products
Fremont, OH. 800-223-3177
Gary Plastic Packaging Corporation
Bronx, NY. 800-221-8151
Georg Fischer Central Plastics
Shawnee, OK. 800-654-3872
Great Northern Corp.
Appleton, WI 800-236-3671
Gulf Packaging Company
Safety Harbor, FL 800-749-3466
Imperial Plastics Inc
Lakeville, MN. 952-469-4951
Jarisch Paper Box Company
North Adams, MA 413-663-5396
Jupiter Mills Corporation
Roslyn, NY. 800-853-5121
K & L Intl
Ontario, CA. 888-598-5588
Kimball Companies
East Longmeadow, MA 413-525-1881

Midland Manufacturing Co
Monroe, IA. 800-394-2625
Morris Transparent Box Co
East Providence, RI. 401-438-6116
Nolon Industries
Mantua, OH. 330-274-2283
Ockerlund Industries
Addison, IL. 708-771-7707
Pacific Paper Box Co
Cudahy, CA. 323-771-7733
Paragon Packaging
Ferndale, CA. 888-615-0065
Parkway Plastic Inc
Piscataway, NJ 800-881-4996
Parsons Manufacturing Corp.
Menlo Park, CA 650-324-4726
Peerless Packages
Cleveland, OH 216-464-3620
Pelco Packaging Corporation
Stirling, NJ 908-647-3500
Penn Products
Portland, CT 800-490-7366
Piqua Paper Box Co
Piqua, OH. 800-536-2136
Prestige Plastics Corporation
Delta, BC. 604-930-2931
Prolon
Port Gibson, MS 888-480-9828
Quantum Storage Systems Inc
Miami, FL. 800-685-4665
R C Molding Inc
Greer, SC. 864-879-7279
Regal Plastic Company
Mission, KS 800-852-1556
Reliance-Paragon
Philadelphia, PA 215-743-1231
Ropak
Oak Brook, IL. 800-527-2267
Saeplast Canada
St John, NB 800-567-3966
Semco Plastic Co
St Louis, MO. 314-487-4557
Sharpsville Container Corp
Sharpsville, PA. 800-645-1248
Snyder Industries Inc.
Lincoln, NE. 800-351-1363
Spartech Plastics
Portage, WI. 800-998-7123
Tectonics
Westmoreland, NH 603-352-8894
Thermodynamics
Commerce City, CO 800-627-9037
Thermodyne International LTD
Ontario, CA. 909-923-9945
Tri-State Plastics
Henderson, KY 270-826-8361
Tulip Molded Plastics Corp
Milwaukee, WI. 414-963-3120
Visual Packaging Corp
Haskell, NJ 973-835-7055
WES Plastics
Richmond Hill, ON. 905-508-1546
Wilks Precision Instr Co Inc
Union Bridge, MD 410-775-7917
Wiltec
Leominster, MA 978-537-1497
Zero Manufacturing Inc
North Salt Lake, UT 800-959-5050

Silverware

Gates Manufacturing Company
Saint Louis, MO. 800-237-9226
Lakeside Manufacturing Inc
Milwaukee, WI. 888-558-8565
McGraw Box Company
Mc Graw, NY 607-836-6465
Newell Brands
Atlanta, GA. . . . .
Supreme Metal
Alpharetta, GA 800-645-2526

Waste

Anova
St Louis, MO. 800-231-1327
Bennett Manufacturing Company
Alden, NY. 800-345-2142
Continental Commercial Products
Bridgeton, MO 800-325-1051
Erwyn Products Inc
Morganville, NJ 800-331-9208

Ex-Cell KAISER LLC
Franklin Park, IL 847-451-0451
Frem Corporation
Worcester, MA 508-791-3152
Glaro Inc
Hauppauge, NY 631-234-1717
Hodge Manufacturing Company
Springfield, MA 800-262-4634
Intrex
Bethel, CT 203-792-7400
J.V. Reed & Company
Louisville, KY 877-258-7333
Lakeside Manufacturing Inc
Milwaukee, WI 888-558-8565
Rubbermaid Commercial Products
Pottsville, PA 800-233-0314

Wirebound

Corbett Timber Co
Wilmington, NC 800-334-0684
Elberta Crate & Box Company
Carpentersville, IL 888-672-9260
Franklin Crates
Micanopy, FL 352-466-3141
Gulf Arizona Packaging
Humble, TX 800-364-3887
Gulf Systems
Brownsville, TX 800-217-4853
Gulf Systems
Humble, TX 800-364-3887
Gulf Systems
Arlington, TX 817-261-1915
Herche Warehouse
Denver, CO 303-371-8186
L&H Wood Manufacturing Company
Farmington, MI 248-474-9000
Milan Box Corporation
Milan, TN 800-225-8057
Wisconsin Box Co
Wausau, WI 800-876-6658

Wooden

A.M. Loveman Lumber & Box Company
Nashville, TN 615-297-1397
American Box Corporation
Lisbon, OH 330-424-8055
Auto Pallets-Boxes
Lathrup Village, MI 800-875-2699
Babcock Co
Bath, NY 607-776-3341
Buckeye Group
South Charleston, OH 937-462-8361
Burgess Mfg. - Oklahoma
Guthrie, OK 800-804-1913
Caravan Packaging Inc
Brookpark, OH 440-243-4100
Cassel Box & Lumber Co Inc
Grafton, WI 262-377-9503
Cedar Box Co
Minneapolis, MN 612-332-4287
Century Box Company
Chicago, IL 773-847-7070
Champlin Co
Hartford, CT 800-458-5261
Coastal Pallet Corp
Bridgeport, CT 203-333-6222
Corinth Products
Corinth, ME 207-285-3387
Corrugated Inner-Pak Corporation
Conshohocken, PA 610-825-0200
Cush-Pak Container Corporation
Henderson, TX 903-657-0555
D&M Pallet Company
Neshkoro, WI 920-293-4616
Davis Brothers Produce Boxes
Evergreen, NC 910-654-4913
Denver Reel & Pallet Company
Denver, CO 303-321-1920
Desert Box & Supply Corporation
Thermal, CA 760-399-5161
Die Cut Specialties Inc
Savage, MN 952-890-7590
Donnelly Industries, Inc
Wayne, NJ 973-672-1800
Dufeck Manufacturing Co
Denmark, WI 888-603-9663
Eichler Wood Products
Laurys Station, PA 610-262-6749
Farmer's Co-Op Elevator Co
Hudsonville, MI 800-439-9859

Fehlig Brothers Box & Lbr Co
St Louis, MO. 314-241-6900
Fox Valley Wood Products Inc
Kaukauna, WI 920-766-4069
Frobisher Industries
Waterborough, NB 506-362-2198
Frye's Measure Mill
Wilton, NH 603-654-6581
Gates
West Peterborough, NH 888-543-6316
Gatewood Products LLC
Parkersburg, WV 800-827-5461
H. Arnold Wood Turning
Tarrytown, NY 888-314-0088
Hampton Roads Box Company
Suffolk, VA 757-934-2355
Hanson Box & Lumber Company
Wakefield, MA 617-245-0358
Harbor Pallet Company
Anaheim, CA 714-871-0932
Heritage Packaging
Victor, NY 585-742-3310
Herkimer Pallet & Wood Products Company
Herkimer, NY 315-866-4591
Hinchcliff Products Company
Strongsville, OH 440-238-5200
Hunter Woodworks
Carson, CA 800-966-4751
Industrial Contracting & Rggng
Mahwah, NJ 888-427-7444
Industrial Hardwood
Perrysburg, OH 419-666-2503
Industrial Lumber & Packaging
Spring Lake, MI 616-842-1457
Industrial Woodfab & Packaging
Riverview, MI 734-284-4808
Jacksonville Box & Woodwork Co
Jacksonville, FL 800-683-2699
Jupiter Mills Corporation
Roslyn, NY 800-853-5121
Kelley Wood Products
Fitchburg, MA 978-345-7531
Kelly Box & Packaging Corp
Fort Wayne, IN 260-432-4570
KETCH
Wichita, KS. 800-766-3777
Killington Wood ProductsCompany
Rutland, VT. 802-773-9111
Kimball Companies
East Longmeadow, MA 413-525-1881
Kontane
Charleston, SC 843-352-0011
L&H Wood Manufacturing Company
Farmington, MI. 248-474-9000
Lester Box & Mfg Div
Long Beach, CA 562-437-5123
Longhorn Imports Inc
Irving, TX. 800-641-8348
Luke's Almond Acres
Reedley, CA 559-638-3483
Lumber & Things
Keyser, WV 800-296-5656
Manufacturers Wood Supply Company
Cleveland, OH 216-771-7848
Marshall Boxes Inc
Rochester, NY 585-458-7432
Maull-Baker Box Company
Brookfield, WI 414-463-1290
Maypak Inc
Wayne, NJ 973-696-0780
McGraw Box Company
Mc Graw, NY 607-836-6465
Mcintosh Box & Pallet Co
East Syracuse, NY 800-219-9552
Meriden Box Company
Southington, CT 860-621-7141
Michiana Box & Crate
Niles, MI 800-677-6372
Michigan Pallet Inc
St Charles, MI 989-865-9915
Milan Box Corporation
Milan, TN 800-225-8057
Moorecraft Box & Crate
Tarboro, NC 252-823-2510
Nefab Packaging, Inc.
Coppell, TX 800-322-4425
New Mexico Products Inc
Albuquerque, NM 877-345-7864
Oak Creek Pallet Company
Milwaukee, WI 414-762-7170
Ockerlund Industries
Addison, IL 708-771-7707

Original Lincoln Logs
Chestertown, NY 800-833-2461
Pack-Rite
Newington, CT 860-953-0120
Packing Material Company
Southfield, MI 248-489-7000
Pallox Incorporated
Onsted, MI 517-456-4101
PPC Perfect Packaging Co
Perrysburg, OH 419-874-3167
Precision Wood of Hawaii
Vancouver, WA 808-682-2055
Pruitt's Packaging Services
Grand Rapids, MI 800-878-0553
Rand-Whitney Group LLC
Worcester, MA 508-791-2301
Reading Box Co Inc
Reading, PA 610-372-7411
Red River Lumber Company
Saint Helena, CA 707-963-1251
Remmey Wood Products
Southampton, PA 215-355-3335
Roddy Products Pkgng Co Inc
Aldan, PA 610-623-7040
Romanow Container
Westwood, MA 781-320-9200
Seattle-Tacoma Box Co
Kent, WA. 253-854-9700
Seymour Woodenware Company
Seymour, WI 920-833-6551
Smalley Package Company
Berryville, VA 540-955-2550
Smith Packaging
Mississauga, ON 905-564-6640
Smith Pallet Co Inc
Hatfield, AR 870-389-6184
Southern Pallet
Christchurch, NZ 901-942-4603
Spring Wood Products
Geneva, OH 440-466-1135
St. Pierre Box & Lumber Company
Canton, CT 860-693-2089
Stearnswood Inc
Hutchinson, MN 800-657-0144
Tampa Pallet Co
Tampa, FL. 813-626-5700
Technipac
Le Sueur, MN 507-665-6658
Thunder Pallet Inc
Theresa, WI. 800-354-0643
Treen Box & Pallet Inc
Bensalem, PA 215-639-5100
Van Dereems Mfg Co
Hawthorne, NJ 973-427-2355
Volk Packaging Corp
Biddeford, ME 207-282-6151
Wisconsin Box Co
Wausau, WI. 800-876-6658
Wnc Pallet & Forest Pdts Co
Candler, NC 828-667-5426
Xtreme Beverages, LLC
Dana Point, CA. 949-495-7929

Cans

Aluminum

Ball Corp
Broomfield, CO 303-469-3131
Can Corp Of America Inc
Blandon, PA 610-926-3044
CCL Container
Toronto, ON 416-756-8500
IMO Foods
Yarmouth, NS 902-742-3519
Impress USA Inc
San Pedro, CA. 310-519-2400
Metal Container Corporation
St Louis, MO. 314-957-9500
Montebello Packaging
Hawkesbury, ON 613-632-7096
Schroeder Machine
San Marcos, CA 760-591-9733
US Can Company
Rosedale, MD 800-436-8021

Beer & Ale

Crown Holdings, Inc.
Yardley, PA 215-698-5100
Metal Container Corporation
St Louis, MO. 314-957-9500

Creamery

Schroeder Machine
San Marcos, CA 760-591-9733

Ice Cream

Armbrust Paper Tubes Inc
Chicago, IL 773-586-3232
Independent Can Co
Belcamp, MD 410-272-0090
Phoenix Industries Corp
Madison, WI 888-241-7482

Milk

Schroeder Machine
San Marcos, CA 760-591-9733

Tin

Bertels Can Company
Belcamp, MD 410-272-0090
Consolidated Can Co
Paramount, CA 888-793-2199
Container Supply Co
Garden Grove, CA 562-594-0937
Crown Cork & Seal Co Inc
Philadelphia, PA 215-698-5100
Crown Holdings, Inc.
Yardley, PA 215-698-5100
GED, LLC
Laurel, DE 302-856-1756
Independent Can Co
Belcamp, MD 410-272-0090
J L Clark Corp
Rockford, IL 815-962-8861
Jupiter Mills Corporation
Roslyn, NY 800-853-5121
Quality Containers
Weston, ON 416-749-6247
Schroeder Machine
San Marcos, CA 760-591-9733
US Can Company
Rosedale, MD 800-436-8021
Xtreme Beverages, LLC
Dana Point, CA 949-495-7929

Caps

Bottle, Can & Jar

All American Container
Miami, FL 305-887-0797
Alpha Packaging
St Louis, MO 800-421-4772
California Vibratory Feeders
Anaheim, CA 800-354-0972
Clayton Corp.
Fenton, MO 800-729-8220
Consolidated Can Co
Paramount, CA 888-793-2199
Crown Closures Machinery
Lancaster, OH 740-681-6593
Crown Holdings, Inc.
Yardley, PA 215-698-5100
Danbury Packaging
Cumming, GA 678-455-7391
Eastern Cap & Closure Company
Baltimore, MD 410-327-5640
ES Robbins Corp
Muscle Shoals, AL 800-633-3325
Greenfield Packaging
White Plains, NY 914-993-0233
Ideal Wire Works
Alhambra, CA 626-282-0886
Innovative Molding
Sebastopol, CA 707-829-2666
Keystone Adjustable Cap Co Inc
Pennsauken, NJ 800-663-5439
Label Makers
Pleasant Prairie, WI 800-208-3331
Landis Plastics
Alsip, IL 708-396-1470
LMK Containers
Centerville, UT 626-821-9984
Metal Container Corporation
St Louis, MO 314-957-9500
Nagel Paper & Box Company
Saginaw, MI 800-292-3654
National Novelty Brush Co
Lancaster, PA 717-299-5681

Nyman Manufacturing Company
Rumford, RI 401-438-3410
Olcott Plastics
St Charles, IL 888-313-5277
Orca Inc
New Britain, CT 860-223-4180
Parkway Plastic Inc
Piscataway, NJ 800-881-4996
Phoenix Closures Inc
Naperville, IL 630-544-3475
Romatic Manufacturing Co
Southbury, CT 203-264-3442
RXI Silgan Specialty Plastics
Triadelphia, WV 304-547-9100
Silgan Containers LLC
Woodland Hills, CA 818-710-3700
Silgan Plastic Closure Sltns
Downers Grove, IL 800-727-8652
Silgan Plastics Canada
Chesterfield, MO 800-274-5426
Smith-Lee Company
Oshkosh, WI 800-327-9774
Snapware
Fullerton, CA 800-334-3062
Sonoco Paperboard Specialties
Norcross, GA 800-264-7494
Tecnocap
Glen Dale, WV 800-999-2567
Van Blarcom Closures Inc
Brooklyn, NY 718-855-3810
Wheaton Plastic Containers
Millville, NJ 856-825-1400

Carriers

Food

B&H Labeling Systems
Ceres, CA 209-537-5785
Cambro Manufacturing Co
Huntington Beach, CA 800-833-3003
Carlisle Food Svc Products Inc
Oklahoma City, OK 800-654-8210
Champion America Inc
Branford, CT 800-521-7000
Fold-Pak Corporation
Newark, NY 315-331-3159
Hank Rivera Associates
Dearborn, MI 313-581-8300
Igloo Products Corp
Katy, TX 866-509-3503
ITW Hi-Cone
Itasca, IL 630-438-5300
K & L Intl
Ontario, CA 888-598-5588
Keeper Thermal Bag Co
Bartlett, IL 800-765-9244
Naltex
Austin, TX 800-531-5112
Newell Brands
Atlanta, GA
Owens-Illinois Inc
Perrysburg, OH 567-336-5000
Paper Works Industries Inc
Baldwinsville, NY 800-847-5677
Plastocon
Oconomowoc, WI 800-966-0103
Service Manufacturing
Aurora, IL 888-325-2788
Sterling Paper Company
Ohio, PA 800-282-1124
Thermal Bags By Ingrid Inc
Gilberts, IL 800-622-5560
Vollrath Co LLC
Sheboygan, WI 800-624-2051

Milk Bottle

B&H Labeling Systems
Ceres, CA 209-537-5785
Graphic Packaging Corporation
Golden, CO 800-677-2886
Paper Works Industries Inc
Baldwinsville, NY 800-847-5677

Cartons

A La Carte
Chicago, IL 800-722-2370
Accurate Paper Box Co Inc
Knoxville, TN 865-690-0311
Adpro
Solon, OH 440-542-1111

Alcan Packaging
Baie D'Urfe, QC 514-457-4555
Americraft Carton Inc
St Paul, MN 651-227-6655
Americraft Carton Inc
Prairie Village, KS 913-387-3700
Artistic Carton
Auburn, IN 800-735-7225
Artistic Carton Co
Elgin, IL 847-741-0247
Atlas Packaging Inc
Opa Locka, FL 800-662-0630
B F Nelson Cartons Inc
Savage, MN 800-328-2380
Boelter Industries
Winona, MN 507-452-2315
Cardinal Container Corp
Indianapolis, IN 800-899-2715
Cardinal Packaging Prod LLC
Crystal Lake, IL 866-216-4942
Carpenter-Hayes Paper Box Company
East Hampton, CT 203-267-4436
Carton Service Co
Shelby, OH 800-533-7744
Central Paper Box
Kansas City, MO 816-753-3126
City Box Company
Aurora, IL 773-277-5500
CKS Packaging
Atlanta, GA 800-800-4257
Cleveland Specialties Co
Loveland, OH 513-677-9787
Coast Paper Box Company
San Bernardino, CA 909-382-3475
Color Box
Richmond, IN 765-966-7588
Columbus Paperbox Company
Columbus, OH 800-968-0797
Commencement Bay Corrugated
Orting, WA 253-845-3100
Commercial Corrugated Co Inc
Baltimore, MD 800-242-8861
Complete Packaging & Shipping
Freeport, NY 877-269-3236
Conn Container Corp
North Haven, CT 203-248-0241
Containair Packaging Corporation
Paterson, NJ 888-276-6500
Corrobilt Container Company
Livermore, CA 925-373-0880
Corson Manufacturing Company
Lockport, NY 716-434-8871
Curtis Packaging
Sandy Hook, CT 203-426-5861
Cush-Pak Container Corporation
Henderson, TX 903-657-0555
Day Manufacturing Company
Sherman, TX 903-893-1138
Diamond Packaging
Rochester, NY 800-333-4079
Donnelly Industries, Inc
Wayne, NJ 973-672-1800
Dorado Carton Company
Dorado, PR 787-796-1670
Eagle Box Company
Farmingdale, NY 212-255-3860
EB Box Company
Richmond Hill, ON 800-513-2269
Elopak Americas
Wixom, MI 248-486-4600
Eureka Paper Box Company
Williamsport, PA 570-326-9147
Farmer's Co-Op Elevator Co
Hudsonville, MI 800-439-9859
Finn Industries
Ontario, CA 909-930-1500
Flashfold Carton Inc
Fort Wayne, IN 260-423-9431
Flour City Press-Pack Company
Minneapolis, MN 952-831-1265
Foam Packaging Inc
Vicksburg, MS 800-962-2655
Fold-Pak Corporation
Newark, NY 315-331-3159
Folding Carton/Flexible Packaging
North Hollywood, CA 818-896-3449
Food Pak Corp
San Mateo, CA 650-341-6559
Four M Manufacturing Group
San Jose, CA 408-998-1141
Friendly City Box Co Inc
Johnstown, PA 814-266-6287

Fulton-Denver Co
Denver, CO 800-521-1414
Gaylord Container Corporation
Tampa, FL 813-621-3591
Georg Fischer Central Plastics
Shawnee, OK 800-654-3872
Gibraltar Packaging Group Inc
Hastings, NE 402-463-1366
Goldman Manufacturing Company
Detroit, MI 313-834-5535
Graphic Packaging Corporation
Golden, CO 800-677-2886
Graphic Packaging Intl
Elk Grove Vlg, IL 847-437-1700
Green Bay Packaging Inc.
Green Bay, WI. 920-433-5111
Greenfield Packaging
White Plains, NY 914-993-0233
Greif Brothers Corporation
Cleveland, OH 800-424-0342
Grigsby Brothers Paper Box Manufacturers
Portland, OR 866-233-4690
Gulf Arizona Packaging
Humble, TX 800-364-3887
Gulf Systems
Brownsville, TX 800-217-4853
Gulf Systems
Humble, TX 800-364-3887
Gulf Systems
Arlington, TX 817-261-1915
H.J. Jones & Sons
London, ON 800-667-0476
Hager Containers Inc
Carrollton, TX 972-416-7660
Herche Warehouse
Denver, CO 303-371-8186
Hope Paper Box Company
Pawtucket, RI 401-724-5700
Hunter Packaging Corporation
South Elgin, IL 800-428-4747
Impress Industries
Emmaus, PA 610-967-6027
Indiana Carton Co Inc
Bremen, IN 800-348-2390
Inland Consumer Packaging
Harrington, DE 302-398-4211
Innovative Folding Carton Company
South Plainfield, NJ 908-757-0205
Instabox
Calgary, AB. 800-482-6173
International Paper Co.
Memphis, TN
Jamestown Container Corporation
Buffalo, NY. 855-234-4054
Jarisch Paper Box Company
North Adams, MA 413-663-5396
Jordan Paper Box Co
Chicago, IL 773-287-5362
Jupiter Mills Corporation
Roslyn, NY 800-853-5121
Kelly Box & Packaging Corp
Fort Wayne, IN 260-432-4570
Kendel
Countryside, IL 800-323-1100
Laminated Paper Products
San Jose, CA 408-888-0880
Lawrence Paper Co
Lawrence, KS 785-843-8111
Lexel
Fort Worth, TX 817-332-4061
Liberty Carton Co.
Golden Valley, MN 800-328-1784
Lin Pac Plastics
Roswell, GA 770-751-6006
Lowell Paper Box Company
Nashua, NH 603-595-0700
Loy Lange Box Co
St Louis, MO. 800-886-4712
LTI Printing Inc
Sturgis, MI 269-651-7574
M & G Packaging Corp
Floral Park, NY. 800-240-5288
Malnove Of Nebraska
Omaha, NE 800-228-9877
Mannkraft Corporation
Newark, NJ. 973-589-7400
Marcus Carton Company
Melville, NY. 631-752-4200
Marfred Industries
Sun Valley, CA 800-529-5156
Marion Paper Box Co
Marion, IN. 765-664-6435

Maro Paper Products Company
Bellwood, IL. 708-649-9982
Massachusetts Container Corporation
North Haven, CT. 203-248-2161
Maull-Baker Box Company
Brookfield, WI 414-463-1290
Maypak Inc
Wayne, NJ 973-696-0780
Melville Plastics
Haw River, NC 336-578-5800
Merchants Publishing Company
Kalamazoo, MI 269-345-1175
Mid Cities Paper Box Company
Downey, CA 877-277-6272
Midlands Packaging Corp
Lincoln, NE. 402-464-9124
Muth Associates
Springfield, MA 800-388-0157
Neff Packaging
Simpsonville, KY 800-445-4383
New York Corrugated Box Co
Paterson, NJ 973-742-5000
Northeast Container Corporation
Dumont, NJ 201-385-6200
Nosco
Waukegan, IL 847-360-4806
Oakes Carton Co
Kalamazoo, MI 269-381-6022
Old Dominion Box Co Inc
Madison Heights, VA 434-929-6701
Old Dominion Box Company
Burlington, NC 336-226-4491
Oracle Packaging
Winston Salem, NC. 800-952-9536
Packaging Solutions
Los Altos Hills, CA 650-917-1022
Packrite Packaging
Archdale, NC. 336-431-1111
Pactiv LLC
Lake Forest, IL 800-476-4300
Paper Products Company
Cincinnati, OH 513-921-4717
Paper Works Industries Inc
Baldwinsville, NY 800-847-5677
Parta
Kent, OH 800-543-5781
Pater & Associates
Cincinnati, OH
Peerless Cartons
Bartlett, IL. 312-226-7952
Piqua Paper Box Co
Piqua, OH 800-536-2136
Premier Packages
Saint Louis, MO 800-466-6588
Prestige Plastics Corporation
Delta, BC. 604-930-2931
Quantum Storage Systems Inc
Miami, FL. 800-685-4665
Rand-Whitney Group LLC
Worcester, MA 508-791-2301
Reliance-Paragon
Philadelphia, PA 215-743-1231
Rex Carton Co Inc
Chicago, IL 773-581-4115
Rice Packaging Inc
Ellington, CT 800-367-6725
Rjr Technologies
Oakland, CA 510-638-5901
Rock-Tenn Company
Norcross, GA 608-223-6272
Rose City Printing & Packaging
Vancouver, WA 800-704-8693
Rudd Container Corp
Chicago, IL 773-847-7600
Rusken Packaging
Cullman, AL 256-775-0014
San Diego Paper Box Company
Spring Valley, CA 619-660-9566
Schroeder Machine
San Marcos, CA 760-591-9733
Scott & Daniells
Portland, CT 860-342-1932
Seaboard Carton Company
Downers Grove, IL 708-344-0575
Security Packaging
North Bergen, NJ 201-854-1955
Set Point Paper Company
Mansfield, MA 800-225-0501
Sheboygan Paper Box Co
Sheboygan, WI. 800-458-8373
Shelby Co
Westlake, OH 800-842-1650

Shippers Supply
Winnipeg, NB 800-661-5639
Shore Paper Box Co
Mardela Springs, MD 410-749-7125
Smith Packaging
Mississauga, ON 905-564-6640
Smurfit Stone Container
St Louis, MO. 314-679-2300
Smurfit-Stone Container Corp
Santa Fe Springs, CA 714-523-3550
Somerville Packaging
Toronto, ON 416-754-7228
Somerville Packaging
Mississauga, ON 905-678-8211
SoOPAK
Mississauga, ON 905-677-9666
Southern Champion Tray LP
Chattanooga, TN. 800-468-2222
Southern Missouri Containers
Springfield, MO 800-999-7666
Southern Packaging Machinery
Athens, GA 706-208-0814
Specialized Packaging London
London, ON 519-659-7011
Spring Cove Container Div
Roaring Spring, PA 814-224-5141
SQP
Schenectady, NY. 800-724-1129
St Joseph Packaging Inc
St Joseph, MO. 800-383-3000
St. Louis Carton Company
Saint Louis, MO 314-241-0990
St. Pierre Box & Lumber Company
Canton, CT 860-693-2089
Standard Folding Cartons Inc
Flushing, NY. 718-396-4522
Stearnswood Inc
Hutchinson, MN 800-657-0144
Sterling Paper Company
Ohio, PA 800-282-1124
Stoneway Carton Company
Mercer Island, WA 800-498-2185
Suburban Corrugated Box Company
Indianhead Park, IL 630-920-1230
Tampa Corrugated Carton Company
Tampa, FL. 813-623-5115
Thermodyne International LTD
Ontario, CA. 909-923-9945
Traub Container Corporation
Cleveland, OH 216-475-5100
Unipak Inc
West Chester, PA. 610-436-6600
Unique Boxes
Chicago, IL 800-281-1670
Universal Folding Box
East Orange, NJ 973-482-4300
Universal Folding Box Company
Hoboken, NJ. 201-659-7373
Utah PaperBox Company
Salt Lake City, UT 801-363-0093
Victory Packaging, Inc.
Houston, TX 800-486-5606
VIP Real Estate LTD
Chicago, IL 773-376-5000
Volk Packaging Corp
Biddeford, ME 207-282-6151
Warren Packaging
San Bernardino, CA 909-888-7008
Weber Display & Packaging Inc
Philadelphia, PA 215-426-3500
Welch Packaging Group Inc
Elkhart, IN. 574-295-2460
West Rock
Atlanta, GA. 770-448-2193
Western Container Company
Kansas City, MO 816-924-5700
Westervelt Co Inc
Tuscaloosa, AL 205-562-5000
Westvaco Corporation
Newark, DE. 302-453-7200
Willamette Industries
Beaverton, OR. 503-641-1131
Willard Packaging Co
Gaithersburg, MD 301-948-7700
Winchester Carton
Eutaw, AL 205-372-3337
Woodson Pallet Co
Anmoore, WV. 304-623-2858
Wright Brothers Paper Box Company
Fond Du Lac, WI. 920-921-8270
WS Packaging Group Inc
Green Bay, WI. 877-977-5177

York Container Co
    York, PA 717-757-7611

Closures & Closing Devices

AAMD
    Liverpool, NY 800-887-4167
All American Container
    Miami, FL 305-887-0797
Allendale Cork Company
    Rye, NY 800-816-2675
Alliance Rubber Co
    Hot Springs, AR 800-626-5940
Alpha Packaging
    St Louis, MO. 800-421-4772
American National Rubber
    Ceredo, WV 304-453-1311
American Printpak Inc
    Sussex, WI 800-441-8003
American Star Cork Company
    Woodside, NY 800-338-3581
Autoprod
    Davenport, IA 563-391-1100
Bal Seal Engineering Inc
    Foothill Ranch, CA. 800-366-1006
Ball Corp
    Broomfield, CO 303-469-3131
Bedford Industries
    Worthington, MN 800-533-5314
Bericap North America, Inc.
    CDN-Burlington, ON 905-634-2248
Berry Global
    Evansville, IN. 800-343-1295
Bettag & Associates
    O Fallon, MO 800-325-0959
Blackhawk Molding Co Inc
    Addison, IL. 630-458-2100
Brown International Corp LLC
    Winter Haven, FL 863-299-2111
Cameo Metal Products Inc
    Brooklyn, NY 718-788-1106
Caraustar
    Franklin, KY 270-586-9565
Carton Closing Company
    Butler, PA 724-287-7759
Chaffee Co
    Rocklin, CA 916-630-3980
Chase-Logeman Corp
    Greensboro, NC 336-665-0754
Clayton Corp.
    Fenton, MO. 800-729-8220
Cleveland Specialties Co
    Loveland, OH 513-677-9787
Conax Buffalo Technologies
    Buffalo, NY 800-223-2389
Consolidated Can Co
    Paramount, CA 888-793-2199
Constantia Colmar
    Colmar, PA 215-997-6222
Cork Specialties
    Miami, FL 305-477-1506
Crandall Filling Machinery
    Buffalo, NY. 800-280-8551
Creative Packaging Corporation
    Buffalo Grove, IL 847-459-1001
Cresthill Industries
    Yonkers, NY 914-965-9510
Crown Closures Machinery
    Lancaster, OH. 740-681-6593
Crown Holdings, Inc.
    Yardley, PA 215-698-5100
Cup Pac Packaging Inc
    South Beloit, IL 877-347-9725
Danbury Plastics
    Cumming, GA. 678-455-7391
Dickey Manufacturing Company
    St Charles, IL 630-584-2918
Diversified Capping Equipment
    Perrysburg, OH 419-666-2566
Eastern Cap & Closure Company
    Baltimore, MD 410-327-5640
Et Oakes Corp
    Hauppauge, NY 631-232-0002
Filler Specialties
    Zeeland, MI. 616-772-9235
Flex Products
    Carlstadt, NJ 800-526-6273
Gallo
    Racine, WI 262-752-9950
Gateway Plastics Inc
    Mequon, WI 262-242-2020
Gemini Plastic Films Corporation
    Garfield, NJ 800-789-4732

General Press Corp
    Natrona Heights, PA 724-224-3500
Genpak
    Peterborough, ON 800-461-1995
Greenfield Packaging
    White Plains, NY 914-993-0233
Gulf Arizona Packaging
    Humble, TX 800-364-3887
Gulf Systems
    Brownsville, TX 800-217-4853
Gulf Systems
    Humble, TX 800-364-3887
Gulf Systems
    Arlington, TX 817-261-1915
Herche Warehouse
    Denver, CO 303-371-8186
Highland Plastics Inc
    Mira Loma, CA 800-368-0491
Innovative Molding
    Sebastopol, CA 707-829-2666
IPEC
    New Castle, PA 800-377-4732
Ipec
    New Castle, PA 800-377-4732
Ives-Way Products
    Round Lake Beach, IL 847-740-0658
J L Clark Corp
    Rockford, IL. 815-962-8861
J.E. Roy
    St Claire, QC 418-883-2711
Kapak Corporation
    Minneapolis, MN 952-541-0730
Keystone Adjustable Cap Co Inc
    Pennsauken, NJ 800-663-5439
KWIK Lok Corp
    Yakima, WA 800-688-5945
L&H Wood Manufacturing Company
    Farmington, MI 248-474-9000
Label Makers
    Pleasant Prairie, WI 800-208-3331
Landis Plastics
    Alsip, IL 708-396-1470
Leco Plastic Inc
    Hackensack, NJ. 201-343-3330
LMK Containers
    Centerville, UT 626-821-9984
Metal Container Corporation
    St Louis, MO. 314-957-9500
Mold-Rite Plastics LLC
    Twinsburg, OH 330-425-4206
Molded Container Corporation
    Portland, OR 503-233-8601
Montebello Packaging
    Hawkesbury, ON. 613-632-7096
National Novelty Brush Co
    Lancaster, PA 717-299-5681
New Jersey Wire Stitching Machine Company
    Cherry Hill, NJ 856-428-2572
Nyman Manufacturing Company
    Rumford, RI 401-438-3410
Olcott Plastics
    St Charles, IL 888-313-5277
On-Hand Adhesives
    Lake Zurich, IL. 800-323-5158
Orca Inc
    New Britain, CT 860-223-4180
Owens-Illinois Inc
    Perrysburg, OH. 567-336-5000
Package Containers Inc
    Canby, OR. 800-266-5806
Packaging Associates
    Randolph, NJ 973-252-8890
PAR-Kan
    Silver Lake, IN 800-291-5487
Paradigm Packaging Inc
    Upland, CA. 909-985-2750
Parkway Plastic Inc
    Piscataway, NJ 800-881-4996
Parta
    Kent, OH. 800-543-5781
Perl Packaging Systems
    Middlebury, CT. 800-864-2853
Phoenix Closures Inc
    Naperville, IL. 630-544-3475
Qosina Corporation
    Ronkonkoma, NY 631-242-3000
Reotemp Instrument Corp
    San Diego, CA 800-648-7737
Richards Packaging
    Memphis, TN 800-583-0327
Rieke Packaging Systems
    Auburn, IN 260-925-3700

Romatic Manufacturing Co
    Southbury, CT. 203-264-3442
Scheidegger
    Yorktown Heights, NY 914-245-7850
Schiffmayer Plastics Corp.
    Algonquin, IL 847-658-8140
Signature Packaging
    West Orange, NJ 800-376-2299
Silgan Plastic Closure Sltns
    Downers Grove, IL 800-727-8652
Silgan Plastic Closure Sltns
    Downers Grove, IL 800-767-8652
Silgan Plastics Canada
    Chesterfield, MO 800-274-5426
Silgan White Cap LLC
    Downers Grove, IL 800-515-1565
Smith-Lee Company
    Oshkosh, WI. 800-327-9774
Sonoco Paperboard Specialties
    Norcross, GA 800-264-7494
Staplex Co Inc
    Brooklyn, NY 800-221-0822
Stoffel Seals Corp
    Tallapoosa, GA. 800-422-8247
Stormax International
    Concord, NH. 800-874-7629
T & T Industries Inc
    Fort Mohave, AZ 800-437-6246
Techform
    Mount Airy, NC 336-789-2115
Tipper Tie Inc
    Apex, NC 919-362-8811
Trent Corp
    Trenton, NJ 609-587-7515
Ultrapak
    Dunkirk, NY 800-228-6030
Us Bottlers Machinery Co Inc
    Charlotte, NC 704-588-4750
Van Blarcom Closures Inc
    Brooklyn, NY 718-855-3810
Wheaton Plastic Containers
    Millville, NJ 856-825-1400
Zero Manufacturing Inc
    North Salt Lake, UT 800-959-5050

Containers

A La Carte
    Chicago, IL 800-722-2370
A Snow Craft Co Inc
    New Hyde Park, NY 516-739-1399
A-A1 Aaction Bag
    Denver, CO 800-783-1224
A-Z Factory Supply
    Schiller Park, IL 800-323-4511
Abbott Industries
    Paterson, NJ
Accurate Paper Box Co Inc
    Knoxville, TN 865-690-0311
Ace Manufacturing & Parts Co
    Sullivan, MO. 800-325-6138
Aco Container Systems
    Pickering, ON 800-542-9942
Acryline
    North Attleboro, MA 508-695-7124
Adpro
    Solon, OH 440-542-1111
Aero Tec Laboratories/ATL
    Ramsey, NJ 800-526-5330
Alcan Packaging
    Baie D'Urfe, QC. 514-457-4555
All American Container
    Miami, FL 305-887-0797
All American Poly
    Piscataway, NJ 800-526-3551
Allflex Packaging Products
    Ambler, PA 800-448-2467
Alpack
    Centerville, NA. 774-994-8086
Althor Products
    Bethel, CT. 800-688-2693
Amco Metals Indl
    City Of Industry, CA. 626-855-2550
American Box Corporation
    Lisbon, OH 330-424-8055
American Production Co Inc
    Redwood City, CA 650-368-5334
Americraft Carton Inc
    St Paul, MN. 651-227-6655
Ample Industries
    Franklin, OH. 888-818-9700
Anchor Packaging
    Ballwin, MO 800-467-3900

Anova
St Louis, MO. 800-231-1327
Arena Products
Rochester, NY 844-762-0127
Arkansas Glass Container Corp
Jonesboro, AR. 800-527-4527
Armbrust Paper Tubes Inc
Chicago, IL 773-586-3232
Arthur Corporation
Huron, OH. 419-433-7202
Artistic Carton
Auburn, IN 800-735-7225
Artistic Carton Co
Elgin, IL 847-741-0247
ATD-American Co
Wyncote, PA 800-523-2300
Atlas Case Inc
Denver, CO 888-325-2199
Atlas Equipment Company
Kansas City, MO. 800-842-9188
Atlas Packaging Inc
Opa Locka, FL 800-662-0630
Auto Pallets-Boxes
Lathrup Village, MI 800-875-2699
B C Holland Inc
Dousman, WI 262-965-2939
B F Nelson Cartons Inc
Savage, MN. 800-328-2380
B.A.G Corporation
Richardson, TX. 800-331-9200
Bakers Choice Products
Beacon Falls, CT. 203-720-1000
Bal/Foster Glass Container Company
Port Allegany, PA 814-642-2521
Ball Corp
Broomfield, CO 303-469-3131
Ball Foster Glass
Fairfield, CA 707-863-4061
Ball Foster Glass Container Company
Sapulpa, OK 918-224-1440
Ball Glass Container Corporation
El Monte, CA 626-448-9831
Bardes Plastics Inc
Milwaukee, WI 800-558-5161
Bayhead Products Corp.
Dover, NH. 800-229-4323
Bell Packaging Corporation
Marion, IN. 800-382-0153
Belleview
Brookline, NH. 603-878-1583
Bennett Manufacturing Company
Alden, NY 800-345-2142
Berenz Packaging Corp
Menomonee Falls, WI. 262-251-8787
Bergen Barrel & Drum Company
Kearny, NJ. 201-998-3500
Berlin Fruit Box Company
Berlin Heights, OH. 800-877-7721
Berlon Industries
Hustisford, WI 800-899-3580
Berry Global
Evansville, IN 800-343-1295
Bertels Can Company
Belcamp, MD 410-272-0090
Best
Brunswick, OH. 800-827-9237
Boelter Industries
Winona, MN 507-452-2315
Boise Cascade Corporation
Burley, ID 208-678-3531
Bonar Plastics
West Chicago, IL 800-295-3725
Boxes.com
Livingston, NJ. 201-646-9050
Brenner Tank LLC
Fond Du Lac, WI 800-558-9750
Brewer-Cantelmo Inc
New York, NY 212-244-4600
Brooks Barrel Company
Baltimore, MD 800-398-2766
Brown International Corp LLC
Winter Haven, FL 863-299-2111
Bruni Glass Packaging
Lachine Montreal, QC 877-771-7856
Buckhorn Canada
Brampton, ON. 800-461-7579
Buckhorn Inc
Milford, OH 800-543-4454
Buffet Enhancements Intl
Point Clear, AL 251-990-6119
Bulk Lift International, LLC
Carpentersville, IL 800-879-2247

Bulk Pack
Monroe, LA. 800-498-4215
Bulk Sak Intl Inc
Malvern, AR 501-332-8745
Burd & Fletcher
Independence, MO 800-821-2776
Burgess Mfg. - Oklahoma
Guthrie, OK. 800-804-1913
Burrows Paper Corp
Little Falls, NY 800-272-7122
C & L Wood Products Inc
Hartselle, AL. 800-483-2035
Calzone Case Co
Bridgeport, CT 800-243-5152
Cambro Manufacturing Co
Huntington Beach, CA 800-833-3003
Can Corp Of America Inc
Blandon, PA 610-926-3044
Cantwell-Cleary Co Inc
Elkridge, MD 301-773-9800
Cantwell-Cleary Co Inc
Richmond, VA. 804-329-9800
Capital City Container Corporation
Buda, TX. 512-312-1222
Capitol Carton Company
Sacramento, CA 916-388-7848
Capitol City Container Corp
Indianapolis, IN 800-233-5145
Cardinal Packaging
Evansville, IN 800-343-1295
Cardinal Packaging Prod LLC
Crystal Lake, IL 866-216-4942
Carlisle Food Svc Products Inc
Oklahoma City, OK 800-654-8210
Carolina Container
High Point, NC 800-627-0825
Carpet City Paper Box Company
Amsterdam, NY 518-842-5430
Carrier Corp
Farmington, CT. 800-227-7437
Carson Industries
Pomona, CA 800-735-5566
Carton Service Co
Shelby, OH 800-533-7744
Ccw Products
Arvada, CO 303-427-9663
Cecor
Verona, WI 800-356-9042
Cedar Box Co
Minneapolis, MN 612-332-4287
Century Box Company
Chicago, IL 773-847-7070
Chambers Container Company
Gastonia, NC. 704-377-6317
Champlin Co
Hartford, CT. 800-458-5261
Charles Engineering & Service
Belcamp, MD 410-272-1090
Chem-Tainer Industries Inc
West Babylon, NY 800-275-2436
Chem-Tainer Industries Inc
West Babylon, NY 800-938-8896
Cherry's Industrial Eqpt Corp
Elk Grove Vlg, IL 800-350-0011
Chili Plastics
Rochester, NY 585-889-4680
Cin-Made Packaging Group
Norcross, GA 800-264-7494
Cincinnati Foam Products
Cincinnati, OH 513-741-7722
City Box Company
Aurora, IL 773-277-5500
CKS Packaging
Atlanta, GA. 800-800-4257
Clawson Container Company
Clarkston, MI 800-325-8700
Clearwater Paper Corporation
Spokane, WA. 877-847-7831
Cleveland Canvas Goods Mfg Co
Cleveland, OH 216-361-4567
Clorox Company
Oakland, CA 510-271-7000
Coast Paper Box Company
San Bernardino, CA 909-382-3475
Coastal Pallet Corp
Bridgeport, CT 203-333-6222
Colbert Packaging Corp
Lake Forest, IL 847-367-5990
Cold Chain Technologies
Holliston, MA 800-370-8566
Collectors Gallery
St Charles, IL 800-346-3063

Color Box
Richmond, IN 765-966-7588
Color Carton Corp
Bronx, NY. 718-665-0840
Columbus Paperbox Company
Columbus, OH 800-968-0797
Commencement Bay Corrugated
Orting, WA 253-845-3100
Commercial Corrugated Co Inc
Baltimore, MD 800-242-8861
Complete Packaging & Shipping
Freeport, NY 877-269-3236
Conductive Containers Inc
Minneapolis, MN 800-327-2329
Conn Container Corp
North Haven, CT. 203-248-0241
Consolidated Container Co
New Castle, PA. 724-658-0549
Constar International
Plymouth, MI 734-455-3600
Containair Packaging Corporation
Paterson, NJ 888-276-6500
Container Specialties
Melrose Park, IL 800-548-7513
Container Supply Co
Garden Grove, CA 562-594-0937
Containment Technology
St Gabriel, LA. 800-388-2467
Contico Container
Norwalk, CA 562-921-9967
Continental Plastic Container
Dallas, TX. 972-303-1825
Contour Packaging
Philadelphia, PA 215-457-1600
Convoy
Canton, OH. 800-899-1583
Corbett Timber Co
Wilmington, NC 800-334-0684
Corbox-Meyers Inc
Cleveland, OH 800-321-7286
Cornish Containers
Maumee, OH. 419-893-7911
Corpak
San Juan, PR 787-787-9085
Corr Pak Corp
Mc Cook, IL 708-442-7806
Corrobilt Container Company
Livermore, CA 925-373-0880
Corrugated Inner-Pak Corporation
Conshohocken, PA 610-825-0200
Corrugated Packaging
Sarasota, FL 941-371-0000
Corson Manufacturing Company
Lockport, NY 716-434-8871
Craft Corrugated Box Inc
New Bedford, MA 508-998-2115
Crate Ideas by Wilderness House
Cave Junction, OR 800-592-2206
Cream of the Valley Plastics
Arvada, CO 303-425-5499
Creative Packaging
Hayward, CA 510-785-6500
Crespac Incorporated
Tucker, GA 800-438-1900
Crown Manufacturing Corporation
Waterford, CT 860-442-4325
CTK Plastics
Moose Jaw, SK 800-667-8847
Cumberland Container Corp
Monterey, TN 931-839-2227
Curtis Packaging
Sandy Hook, CT 203-426-5861
Cush-Pak Container Corporation
Henderson, TX 903-657-0555
Custom Bottle of Connecticut
Naugatuck, CT 203-723-6661
Custom Stamping & Manufacturing
Portland, OR 503-238-3700
D & W Fine Pack
San Bernardino, CA 800-232-5959
D & W Fine Pack
Lake Zurich, IL 800-323-0422
Dakota Corrugated Box
Sioux Falls, SD 605-332-3501
Dallas Container Corp
Dallas, TX. 800-381-7148
Dart Container Corp.
Mason, MI 800-248-5960
Davis Brothers Produce Boxes
Evergreen, NC 910-654-4913
Davis Core & Pa
Cave Spring, GA. 800-235-7483

Day Lumber Company
Westfield, MA.............413-568-3511
Day Manufacturing Company
Sherman, TX.............903-893-1138
De Ster Corporation
Atlanta, GA.............800-237-8270
DEL-Tec Packaging Inc
Greer, SC.............800-747-8683
Deline Box Co
Denver, CO.............303-376-1283
Delta Container Corporation
New Orleans, LA.............800-752-7292
Delta Wire And Mfg.
Harrow, ON.............800-221-3794
Design Plastics Inc
Omaha, NE.............800-491-0786
Designers Folding Box Corp
Buffalo, NY.............716-853-5141
Despro Manufacturing
Cedar Grove, NJ.............800-292-9906
Diamond Packaging
Rochester, NY.............800-333-4079
Display One
Hartford, WI.............262-673-5880
Dixie Printing & Packaging
Glen Burnie, MD.............800-433-4943
Donnelly Industries, Inc
Wayne, NJ.............973-672-1800
Dorado Carton Company
Dorado, PR.............787-796-1670
Douglas Stephen Plastics Inc
Paterson, NJ.............973-523-3030
Drescher Paper Box Inc
Buffalo, NY.............716-854-0288
Dufeck Manufacturing Co
Denmark, WI.............888-603-9663
Dusobox Company
Haverhill, MA.............978-372-7192
Duval Container Co
Jacksonville, FL.............800-342-8194
Dynabilt Products
Readville, MA.............800-443-1008
E K Lay Co
Philadelphia, PA.............800-523-3220
Eagle Box Company
Farmingdale, NY.............212-255-3860
Eastern Container Corporation
Mansfield, MA.............508-337-0400
EB Box Company
Richmond Hill, ON.............800-513-2269
Economy Folding Box Corporation
Chicago, IL.............800-771-1053
Edco Industries
Bridgeport, CT.............203-333-8982
EGA Products Inc
Brookfield, WI.............800-937-3427
EGW Bradbury Enterprises
Bridgewater, ME.............800-332-6021
Eichler Wood Products
Laurys Station, PA.............610-262-6749
Elberta Crate & Box Company
Carpentersville, IL.............888-672-9260
Elm Packaging Company
Memphis, TN.............901-795-2711
Elopak Americas
Wixom, MI.............248-486-4600
Emco Industrial Plastics
Cedar Grove, NJ.............800-292-9906
Enterprise Box Company
Montclair, NJ.............973-509-2200
Erie Container
Cleveland, OH.............216-631-1650
ERO/Goodrich Forest Products
Tualatin, OR.............800-458-5545
Erwyn Products Inc
Morganville, NJ.............800-331-9208
ES Robbins Corp
Muscle Shoals, AL.............800-633-3325
Eureka Paper Box Company
Williamsport, PA.............570-326-9147
Expert Industries Inc
Brooklyn, NY.............718-434-6060
F G Products Inc
Rice Lake, WI.............800-247-3854
F N Smith Corp
Oregon, IL.............815-732-2171
F.E. Wood & Sons
West Baldwin, ME.............207-286-5003
Fabri-Kal Corp
Kalamazoo, MI.............800-888-5054
Fabricated Components Inc
Stroudsburg, PA.............800-233-8163

Fabricon Products Inc
River Rouge, MI.............313-841-8200
Faribault Manufacturing Co
Faribault, MN.............800-447-6043
Farmer's Co-Op Elevator Co
Hudsonville, MI.............800-439-9859
Faubion Central States Tank Company
Shawnee Mission, KS.............800-450-8265
Felco Packaging Specialist
Baltimore, MD.............800-673-8488
Ferguson Containers
Phillipsburg, NJ.............908-454-9755
Fibre Containers Inc
City Of Industry, CA.............626-968-5897
Finn Industries
Ontario, CA.............909-930-1500
Fitzpatrick Container Company
North Wales, PA.............215-699-3515
Flashfold Carton Inc
Fort Wayne, IN.............260-423-9431
Fleetwood International Paper
Vernon, CA.............323-588-7121
Flex Products
Carlstadt, NJ.............800-526-6273
Flexible Foam Products
Elkhart, IN.............800-678-3626
Flow of Solids
Westford, MA.............978-392-0300
Foam Concepts Inc
Uxbridge, MA.............508-278-7255
Foam Pack Industries
Springfield, NJ.............973-376-3700
Foam Packaging Inc
Vicksburg, MS.............800-962-2655
Fold-Pak Corporation
Newark, NY.............315-331-3159
Fold-Pak South
Columbus, GA.............706-689-2924
Folding Carton/Flexible Packaging
North Hollywood, CA.............818-896-3449
Food Pak Corp
San Mateo, CA.............650-341-6559
Foster Forbes Glass
Marion, IN.............765-668-1200
Four M Manufacturing Group
San Jose, CA.............408-998-1141
Franklin Crates
Micanopy, FL.............352-466-3141
Frankston Paper Box Company of Texas
Frankston, TX.............903-876-2550
Frem Corporation
Worcester, MA.............508-791-3152
Fremont Die Cut Products
Fremont, OH.............800-223-3177
Fresno Pallet, Inc.
Sultana, CA.............559-591-4111
Friend Box Co
Danvers, MA.............978-774-0240
Friendly City Box Co Inc
Johnstown, PA.............814-266-6287
Fruit Growers Package Company
Grandville, MI.............616-724-1400
Frye's Measure Mill
Wilton, NH.............603-654-6581
Fuller Box Co
North Attleboro, MA.............508-695-2525
Fuller Industries LLC
Great Bend, KS.............800-522-0499
Fuller Packaging Inc
Central Falls, RI.............401-725-4300
Fulton-Denver Co
Denver, CO.............800-521-1414
Fun-Time International
Philadelphia, PA.............800-776-4386
Gabriel Container Co
Santa Fe Springs, CA.............323-685-8844
Galbreath LLC
Winamac, IN.............574-946-6631
Gatewood Products LLC
Parkersburg, WV.............800-827-5461
Gaylord Container Corporation
Tampa, FL.............813-621-3591
Geerpres Inc
Muskegon, MI.............231-773-3211
General Bag Corporation
Cleveland, OH.............800-837-9396
General Industries Inc
Goldsboro, NC.............888-735-2882
Genesee Corrugated
Flint, MI.............810-228-3702
Genpak
Peterborough, ON.............800-461-1995

Genpak LLC
Charlotte, NC.............800-626-6695
Georg Fischer Central Plastics
Shawnee, OK.............800-654-3872
Georgia-Pacific LLC
Atlanta, GA.............800-283-5547
Gibbs Brothers Cooperage
Hot Springs, AR.............501-623-8881
Gibraltar Packaging Group Inc
Hastings, NE.............402-463-1366
Gillis Associated Industries
Prospect Heights, IL.............847-541-6500
Glaro Inc
Hauppauge, NY.............631-234-1717
Glasko Plastics
Santa Ana, CA.............714-751-7830
Global Equipment Co Inc
Port Washington, NY.............888-628-3466
Goldenwest Sales
Cerritos, CA.............800-827-6175
Goldman Manufacturing Company
Detroit, MI.............313-834-5535
Graff Tank Erection
Harrisville, PA.............814-385-6671
Graham Engineering Corp
York, PA.............717-848-3755
GranPac
Wetaskiwin, AB.............780-352-3324
Graphic Packaging Corporation
Golden, CO.............800-677-2886
Graphic Packaging International
Atlanta, GA.............770-240-7200
Graphic Packaging Intl
Elk Grove Vlg, IL.............847-437-1700
Great Lakes-Triad Package Corporation
Grand Rapids, MI.............616-241-6441
Great Northern Corp
Chippewa Falls, WI.............800-472-1800
Great Northern Corp.
Appleton, WI.............800-236-3671
Great Southern Industries
Jackson, MS.............877-638-3667
Green Bay Packaging Inc.
Kalamazoo, MI.............269-552-1000
Green Bay Packaging Inc.
Tulsa, OK.............918-446-3341
Green Bay Packaging Inc.
Green Bay, WI.............920-433-5111
Green Brothers
Barrington, RI.............401-245-9043
Greenfield Packaging
White Plains, NY.............914-993-0233
Greenfield Paper Box Co
Greenfield, MA.............413-773-9414
Greif Brothers Corporation
Cleveland, OH.............800-424-0342
Greif Inc
Delaware, OH.............740-549-6000
Grigsby Brothers Paper Box Manufacturers
Portland, OR.............866-233-4690
Gulf Arizona Packaging
Humble, TX.............800-364-3887
Gulf Packaging Company
Safety Harbor, FL.............800-749-3466
Gulf Systems
Brownsville, TX.............800-217-4853
Gulf Systems
Humble, TX.............800-364-3887
Gulf Systems
Arlington, TX.............817-261-1915
H S Inc
Oklahoma City, OK.............800-238-1240
H. Arnold Wood Turning
Tarrytown, NY.............888-314-0088
Hager Containers Inc
Carrollton, TX.............972-416-7660
Hampton Roads Box Company
Suffolk, VA.............757-934-2355
Hanson Box & Lumber Company
Wakefield, MA.............617-245-0358
Harbor Pallet Company
Anaheim, CA.............714-871-0932
Hardi-Tainer
South Deerfield, MA.............800-882-9878
Hardy Systems Corporation
Northbrook, IL.............800-927-3956
Harpak-ULMA Packaging LLC
Ball Ground, GA.............770-345-5300
Hartford Containers
Terryville, CT.............860-584-1194
Hartford Plastics
Omaha, NE

Harvard Folding Box Company
Lynn, MA 781-598-1600
Hedstrom Corporation
Ashland, OH 700-765-9665
Hedwin Division
Baltimore, MD 800-638-1012
Henry Ira L Co
Watertown, WI 920-261-0648
Herche Warehouse
Denver, CO 303-371-8186
Heritage Packaging
Victor, NY 585-742-3310
Herkimer Pallet & Wood Products Company
Herkimer, NY 315-866-4591
Highland Plastics Inc
Mira Loma, CA 800-368-0491
Hinchcliff Products Company
Strongsville, OH 440-238-5200
Hinkle Manufacturing
Perrysburg, OH 419-666-5367
Hodge Manufacturing Company
Springfield, MA 800-262-4634
Hodges
Vienna, IL 800-444-0011
Hoffmaster Group Inc.
Oshkosh, WI 800-558-9300
Holmco Container Manufacturing, LTD
Baltic, OH 330-897-4503
Hood Packaging
Madison, MS 800-321-8115
Hoover Materials Handling Group
Houston, TX 800-844-8683
Hope Paper Box Company
Pawtucket, RI 401-724-5700
Hot Food Boxes
Mooresville, IN 800-733-8073
Hunter Packaging Corporation
South Elgin, IL 800-428-4747
Hunter Woodworks
Carson, CA 800-966-4751
Hurri-Kleen Corporation
Birmingham, AL 800-455-8265
IBC Shell Packaging
New Hyde Park, NY 516-352-5138
Ideas Etc Inc
Louisville, KY 800-733-0337
Il Valley Container Inc
Peru, IL 815-223-7200
IMO Foods
Yarmouth, NS 902-742-3519
Imperial Containers
City of Industry, CA 626-333-6363
Imperial Industries Inc
Rothschild, WI 800-558-2945
Imperial Packaging Corporation
Pawtucket, RI 401-753-7778
Impress Industries
Emmaus, PA 610-967-6027
Incinerator International Inc
Houston, TX 713-227-1466
Independent Can Co
Belcamp, MD 410-272-0090
Indiana Bottle Co
Scottsburg, IN 800-752-8702
Indiana Vac Form Inc
Warsaw, IN 574-269-1725
Indianapolis Container Company
Indianapolis, IN 800-760-3318
Industrial Container Corp
High Point, NC 336-886-7031
Industrial Contracting & Rggng
Mahwah, NJ 888-427-7444
Industrial Hardwood
Perrysburg, OH 419-666-2503
Industrial Lumber & Packaging
Spring Lake, MI 616-842-1457
Industrial Nameplate Inc
Warminster, PA 800-878-6263
Industrial Woodfab & Packaging
Riverview, MI 734-284-4808
Inland Consumer Packaging
Harrington, DE 302-398-4211
Inland Paper Company
Ontario, CA 909-923-4505
Inland Paperboard & Packaging
Rock Hill, SC 803-366-4103
Innovative Folding Carton Company
South Plainfield, NJ 908-757-0205
Instabox
Calgary, AB 800-482-6173
Inter-Pack Corporation
Monroe, MI 734-242-7755

International Wood Industries
Snohomish, WA 800-922-6141
IPL Plastics
Edmundston, NB 800-739-9595
IPS International
Snohomish, WA 360-668-5050
Ivarson Inc
Milwaukee, WI 414-351-0700
J&J Corrugated Box Corporation
Franklin, MA 508-528-6200
J&J Mid-South Container Corporation
Augusta, GA 800-395-1025
Jackson Corrugated Container
Middletown, CT 860-346-9671
Jacksonville Box & Woodwork Co
Jacksonville, FL 800-683-2699
Jamestown Container Corporation
Buffalo, NY 855-234-4054
Jarisch Paper Box Company
North Adams, MA 413-663-5396
Jenike & Johanson Inc
Tyngsboro, MA 978-649-3300
Jescorp
Des Plaines, IL 847-299-7800
Jesse Jones Box Corporation
Philadelphia, PA 215-425-6600
Jessup Paper Box
Brookston, IN 765-490-9043
John Henry Packaging
Penngrove, CA 800-327-5997
Jordan Box Co
Syracuse, NY 315-422-3419
Jordan Paper Box Co
Chicago, IL 773-287-5362
Juice Merchandising Corp
Kansas City, MO 800-950-1998
Juice Tree
Omaha, NE 714-891-4425
Jupiter Mills Corporation
Roslyn, NY 800-853-5121
Just Plastics Inc
New York, NY 212-569-8500
K & L Intl
Ontario, CA 888-598-5588
K B Systems Inc
Bangor, PA 610-588-7788
K&H Container
Wallingford, CT 203-265-1547
Kadon Corporation
Milford, OH 937-299-0088
Karyall Telday Inc
Cleveland, OH 216-281-4063
Kaufman Paper Box Company
Providence, RI 401-272-7508
Kelley Wood Products
Fitchburg, MA 978-345-7531
Kendel
Countryside, IL 800-323-1100
Key Container Company
South Gate, CA 323-564-4211
Key Material Handling Inc
Simi Valley, CA 800-539-7225
Key Packaging Co
Sarasota, FL 941-355-2728
KHM Plastics Inc
Gurnee, IL 847-249-4910
Killington Wood ProductsCompany
Rutland, VT 802-773-9111
Kimball Companies
East Longmeadow, MA 413-525-1881
King Bag & Mfg Co
Cincinnati, OH 800-444-5464
King Plastic Corp
North Port, FL 800-780-5502
Knapp Container
Beacon Falls, CT 203-888-0511
Knight Paper Box Company
Chicago, IL 773-585-2035
Koch Container
Victor, NY 585-924-1600
Kontane
Charleston, SC 843-352-0011
Konz Wood Products Co
Appleton, WI 877-610-5145
Label Makers
Pleasant Prairie, WI 800-208-3331
Lakeside Container Corp
Plattsburgh, NY 518-561-6150
Lakeside Manufacturing Inc
Milwaukee, WI 888-558-8565
Laminated Paper Products
San Jose, CA 408-888-0880

Landis Plastics
Alsip, IL 708-396-1470
Larose & Fils Lte
Laval, QC 877-382-7001
Laval Paper Box
Pointe Claire, QC 450-669-3551
Lawrence Paper Co
Lawrence, KS 785-843-8111
LBP Manufacturing LLC
Cicero, IL 708-652-5600
Leclaire Packaging Corp
Ixonia, WI 920-206-9902
Leggett & Platt Storage
Vernon Hills, IL 847-816-6246
Lester Box & Mfg Div
Long Beach, CA 562-437-5123
Letica Corp
Rochester Hills, MI 800-538-4221
Levin Brothers Paper
Cicero, IL 800-545-6200
Lewis Steel Works Inc
Wrens, GA 800-521-5239
Lewisburg Container Co
Lewisburg, OH 937-962-0101
Lexel
Fort Worth, TX 817-332-4061
Lima Barrel & Drum Company
Lima, OH 419-224-8916
Lin Pac Plastics
Roswell, GA 770-751-6006
LinPac
San Angelo, TX 800-453-7393
Linpac Materials Handling
Dallas, TX 214-599-9023
Linvar
Hartford, CT 800-282-5288
Liquitane
Berwick, PA 570-759-6200
Little Rock Crate & Basket Co
Little Rock, AR 800-223-7823
LMK Containers
Centerville, UT 626-821-9984
Lone Star Container Corp
Irving, TX 800-552-6937
Longview Fibre Co
Longview, WA 800-929-8111
Longview Fibre Company
Beaverton, OR 503-350-1600
Lowell Paper Box Company
Nashua, NH 603-595-0700
Loy Lange Box Co
St Louis, MO 800-886-4712
LTI Printing Inc
Sturgis, MI 269-651-7574
Luce Corp
Hamden, CT 800-344-6966
Luke's Almond Acres
Reedley, CA 559-638-3483
Lunn Industries
Glen Cove, NY 516-671-9000
M & G Packaging Corp
Floral Park, NY 800-240-5288
M & H Crate Inc
Jacksonville, TX 903-683-5351
M&L Plastics
Easthampton, MA 413-527-1330
Mack-Chicago Corporation
Chicago, IL 800-992-6225
MacMillan Bloedel Packaging
Montgomery, AL 800-239-4464
Madsen Wire Products Inc
Orland, IN 260-829-6561
Malco Manufacturing Co
Los Angeles, CA 866-477-7267
Mall City Containers Inc
Kalamazoo, MI 800-643-6721
Mannkraft Corporation
Newark, NJ 973-589-7400
Marco Products
Adrian, MI 517-265-3333
Marcus Carton Company
Melville, NY 631-752-4200
Marfred Industries
Sun Valley, CA 800-529-5156
Marion Paper Box Co
Marion, IN 765-664-6435
Maro Paper Products Company
Bellwood, IL 708-649-9982
Marpac Industries
Philmont, NY 888-462-7722
Marshall Boxes Inc
Rochester, NY 585-458-7432

Massachusetts Container Corporation
North Haven, CT 203-248-2161
Massillon Container Co
Navarre, OH 330-879-5653
Master Containers
Mulberry, FL 800-881-6847
Master Package Corporation
Menomonie, WI 800-347-4144
Maull-Baker Box Company
Brookfield, WI 414-463-1290
Maypak Inc
Wayne, NJ 973-696-0780
Measurex/S&L Plastics
Nazareth, PA 800-752-0650
MeGa Industries
Burlington, ON 800-665-6342
Mello Smello LLC
Minneapolis, MN 888-574-2964
Melmat Inc
Huntington Beach, CA 800-635-6289
Melville Plastics
Haw River, NC 336-578-5800
Menasha Corp
Neenah, WI 800-558-5073
Merchants Publishing Company
Kalamazoo, MI 269-345-1175
Meyer Packaging
Palmyra, PA 717-838-6300
Michael Leson Dinnerware
Youngstown, OH 800-821-3541
Michiana Corrugate Products
Sturgis, MI 269-651-5225
Michigan Box Co
Detroit, MI 888-642-4269
Michigan Pallet Inc
St Charles, MI 989-865-9915
Micro Qwik
Cross Plains, WI 608-798-3071
Micro Wire Products Inc
Brockton, MA 508-584-0200
Mid Cities Paper Box Company
Downey, CA 877-277-6272
Mid-States Mfg & Engr Co Inc
Milton, IA 800-346-1792
Midland Manufacturing Co
Monroe, IA 800-394-2625
Midwest Aircraft Products Co
Lexington, OH 419-884-2164
Midwest Box Co
Cleveland, OH 216-281-3980
Midwest Paper Products Company
Louisville, KY 502-636-2741
Midwest Paper Tube & CanCorporation
New Berlin, WI 262-782-7300
Midwest Rubber Svc & Supply
Minneapolis, MN 800-537-7457
Milan Box Corporation
Milan, TN 800-225-8057
Miller Hofft Brands
Indianapolis, IN 317-638-6576
Modern Paper Box Company
Providence, RI 401-861-7357
Molded Container Corporation
Portland, OR 503-233-8601
Moli-International
Denver, CO 800-525-8468
Montebello Container Corp
La Mirada, CA 714-994-2351
Montebello Packaging
Hawkesbury, ON 613-632-7096
Morphy Container Company
Brantford, ON 519-752-5428
Morris Transparent Box Co
East Providence, RI 401-438-6116
Mountain Safety Research
Seattle, WA 800-877-9677
Mt Vernon Packaging Inc
Mt Vernon, OH 888-397-3221
Mullnix Packages Inc
Fort Wayne, IN 260-747-3149
Multibulk Systems International
Wendell, NC 919-366-2100
MultiFab Plastics
Boston, MA 888-293-5754
Muth Associates
Springfield, MA 800-388-0157
Nagel Paper & Box Company
Saginaw, MI 800-292-3654
Nefab Packaging Inc.
Coppell, TX 800-322-4425
Nefab Packaging, Inc.
Coppell, TX 800-322-4425

Neff Packaging
Simpsonville, KY 800-445-4383
Nelson Container Corp
Germantown, WI. 262-250-5000
NEPA Pallet & Container Co
Snohomish, WA 360-568-3185
New England Wooden Ware
Gardner, MA 800-252-9214
New Lisbon Wood ProductsManufacturing Company
New Lisbon, WI 608-562-3122
New Mexico Products Inc
Albuquerque, NM 877-345-7864
New York Corugated Box Co
Paterson, NJ 973-742-5000
North American Container Corp
Marietta, GA 800-929-0610
North American Packaging Corp
New York, NY 800-499-3521
Northeast Box Co
Ashtabula, OH 800-362-8100
Northeast Container Corporation
Dumont, NJ. 201-385-6200
Nosco
Waukegan, IL 847-360-4806
Novelis Foil Products
Atlanta, GA 800-776-8701
NPC Display Group
Newark, NJ 973-589-2155
Nu-Trend Plastics Thermoformer
Jacksonville, FL 904-353-5936
Oak Barrel Winecraft
Berkeley, CA 510-849-0400
Oakes Carton Co
Kalamazoo, MI 269-381-6022
Ockerlund Industries
Addison, IL 708-771-7707
Olcott Plastics
St Charles, IL 888-313-5277
Old Dominion Box Co Inc
Madison Heights, VA 434-929-6701
Old Dominion Box Company
Burlington, NC 336-226-4491
Oracle Packaging
Winston Salem, NC. 800-952-9536
ORBIS
Oconomowoc, WI. 262-560-5000
ORBIS
Oconomowoc, WI. 800-890-7292
Original Packaging & Display Company
Saint Louis, MO 314-772-7797
OTD Corporation
Hinsdale, IL 630-321-9232
Ott Packagings
Selinsgrove, PA. 570-374-2811
Owens-Illinois Inc
Perrysburg, OH 567-336-5000
Pacific Paper Box Co
Cudahy, CA. 323-771-7733
Pack-Rite
Newington, CT 860-953-0120
Packaging Associates
Randolph, NJ 973-252-8890
Packaging Corporation of America
Lake Forest, IL 800-456-4725
Packaging Design Corp
Burr Ridge, IL 630-323-1354
Packaging Dynamics International
Caldwell, OH 740-732-5665
Packaging Solutions
Los Altos Hills, CA 650-917-1022
Packing Material Company
Southfield, MI. 248-489-7000
Packing Specialities
Warren, MI 586-758-5240
Packrite Packaging
Archdale, NC. 336-431-1111
Pactiv LLC
Lake Forest, IL 800-476-4300
Pak-Sher
Kilgore, TX. 903-984-8596
Pallet One Inc
Bartow, FL. 800-771-1148
Palmer Distributors
St Clair Shores, MI 800-444-1912
Pan Pacific Plastics Inc
Hayward, CA 888-475-6888
Paper Systems Inc
Des Moines, IA. 800-342-2855
Paper Works Industries Inc
Baldwinsville, NY 800-847-5677
PAR-Kan
Silver Lake, IN 800-291-5487

Par-Pak
Houston, TX 713-686-6700
Par-Pak
Houston, TX 888-727-7252
Paradigm Packaging Inc
Upland, CA. 909-985-2750
Paragon Packaging
Ferndale, CA 888-615-0065
Parkway Plastic Inc
Piscataway, NJ 800-881-4996
Parlor City Paper Box Co Inc
Binghamton, NY. 607-772-0600
Parta
Kent, OH. 800-543-5781
Paul T. Freund Corporation
Palmyra, NY 800-333-0091
Pelco Packaging Corporation
Stirling, NJ 908-647-3500
Pell Paper Box Company
Elizabeth City, NC 252-335-4361
Penn Bottle & Supply Company
Philadelphia, PA 215-365-5700
Penn Products
Portland, CT 800-490-7366
Penny Plate
Haddonfield, NJ 856-429-7583
Pentwater Wire Products Inc
Pentwater, MI 877-869-6911
Performance Packaging
Trail Creek, IN 219-874-6226
Peter Pepper Products Inc
Compton, CA 310-639-0390
Phoenix Industries Corp
Madison, WI 888-241-7482
Pine Point Wood Products Inc
Osseo, MN 763-428-4301
Pinn Pack Packaging LLC
Oxnard, CA. 805-385-4100
Pioneer Packaging & Printing
Anoka, MN 800-708-1705
Pioneer Plastics Inc
Dixon, KY. 800-951-1551
Pittsburgh Tank Corp
Monongahela, PA 800-634-0243
Plastic Assembly Corporation
Ayer, MA
Plastican Corporation
Fairfield, NJ 973-227-7817
Plastics Inc
Greensboro, AL 334-624-8801
Plastics Industries
Athens, TN 800-894-4876
Plastipak Packaging
Plymouth, MI 734-354-3510
Plastiques Cascades Group
Montreal, QC 888-703-6515
Plaxall Inc
Long Island City, NY 800-876-5706
Podnar Plastics Inc
Kent, OH. 800-673-5277
Pohlig Brothers
N Chesterfield, VA 804-275-9000
Polar Tech Industries Inc
Genoa, IL 800-423-2749
Polar Ware Company
Sheboygan, WI 800-237-3655
Poliplastic
Granby, QC 450-378-8417
Poly One Corp
Avon Lake, OH 866-765-9663
Poly Processing Co
French Camp, CA 877-325-3142
Polybottle Group
Surrey, BC. 604-594-4999
Polycon Industries
Chicago, IL 773-374-5500
Portland Paper Box Company
Portland, OR 800-547-2571
PPC Perfect Packaging Co
Perrysburg, OH 419-874-3167
Prairie Packaging Inc
Mooresville, NC 704-660-6600
Precision Wood of Hawaii
Vancouver, WA 808-682-2055
Precision Wood Products
Vancouver, WA 360-694-8322
Premier Packages
Saint Louis, MO 800-466-6588
Premium Foil Products Company
Louisville, KY 502-459-2820
President Container Inc
Moonachie, NJ 212-244-0345

Prestige Plastics Corporation
Delta, BC. 604-930-2931
Pretium Packaging
Chesterfield, MO 314-727-8673
Pretium Packaging
Hazle Twp, PA 570-459-1800
Pride Container Corporation
Chicago, IL 773-227-6000
Princeton Shelving
Cedar Rapids, IA 319-369-0355
Priority Plastics Inc
Grinnell, IA 800-798-3512
Progressive Plastics
Cleveland, OH 800-252-0053
Prolon
Port Gibson, MS 888-480-9828
Propak
Burlington, ON 800-263-4872
Pruitt's Packaging Services
Grand Rapids, MI 800-878-0553
Quality Container Company
Ypsilanti, MI 734-481-1373
Quality Containers
Weston, ON 416-749-6247
Quality Packaging Inc
Fond Du Lac, WI 800-923-3633
Quantum Storage Systems Inc
Miami, FL 800-685-4665
Quintex Corp
Nampa, ID 208-467-1113
R C Molding Inc
Greer, SC. 864-879-7279
Ram Equipment Co
Waukesha, WI 262-513-1114
Rand-Whitney Group LLC
Worcester, MA 508-791-2301
Rand-Whitney Packaging Corp
Portsmouth, NH 508-791-2301
RAPAC Inc
Oakland, TN 800-280-6333
RDA Container Corp
Gates, NY 585-247-2323
Regal Plastic Company
Mission, KS 800-852-1556
Regal Plastic Supply Co
Kansas City, MO. 800-444-6390
Reliable Container Corporation
Downey, CA 562-745-0200
Reliance Product
Winnipeg, MB. 800-665-0258
Reliance-Paragon
Philadelphia, PA 215-743-1231
Remcon Plastics Inc
Reading, PA 800-360-3636
Revere Packaging
Shelbyville, KY 800-626-2668
Rez-Tech Corp
Kent, OH 800-673-5277
Rhoades Paper Box Corporation
Springfield, OH. 800-441-6494
Rice Packaging Inc
Ellington, CT 800-367-6725
Richard Read Construction Company
Arcadia, CA 888-450-7343
Ritz Packaging Company
Brooklyn, NY 718-366-2300
Rjr Technologies
Oakland, CA 510-638-5901
RMI-C/Rotonics Manaufacturing
Bensenville, IL 630-773-9510
Romanow Container
Westwood, MA 781-320-9200
Ronnie's Ceramic Company
San Francisco, CA 800-888-8218
Ropak
Oak Brook, IL 800-527-2267
Round Paper Packages Inc
Erlanger, KY 859-331-7200
Rownd & Son
Dillon, SC. 803-774-8264
Roy's Folding Box
Cleveland, OH. 216-464-1191
Royal Group
Cicero, IL 708-656-2020
Rubbermaid
High Point, NC 888-895-2110
Rudd Container Corp
Chicago, IL 773-847-7600
Ruffino Paper Box Co
Hackensack, NJ. 201-487-1260
Rusken Packaging
Cullman, AL 256-775-0014

S.S.I. Schaefer System International Limited
Brampton, ON. 905-458-5399
Sabert Corp
Sayreville, NJ 732-721-5546
Sabert Corp
Sayreville, NJ 800-722-3781
Saeplast Canada
St John, NB 800-567-3966
Sanchelima International
Miami, FL 305-591-4343
Schermerhorn Inc
Chicopee, MA 413-598-8348
Schiefer Packaging Corporation
Syracuse, NY 315-422-0615
Schwarz Supply Source
Morton Grove, IL 800-323-4903
Scope Packaging
Orange, CA 714-998-4411
Scott & Daniells
Portland, CT 860-342-1932
Seaboard Carton Company
Downers Grove, IL 708-344-0575
Seattle-Tacoma Box Co
Kent, WA. 253-854-9700
Sebring Container Corporation
Salem, OH. 330-332-1533
Security Packaging
North Bergen, NJ 201-854-1955
Semco Plastic Co
St Louis, MO. 314-487-4557
Sertapak Packaging Corporation
Woodstock, ON 800-265-1162
Set Point Paper Company
Mansfield, MA 800-225-0501
Setco
Monroe Twp, NJ 609-655-4600
Setco
Anaheim, CA 714-777-5200
Seville Flexpack Corp
Oak Creek, WI 414-761-2751
Seymour Woodenware Company
Seymour, WI 920-833-6551
Sfb Plastics Inc
Wichita, KS 800-343-8133
SFBC, LLC dba Seaboard Folding Box
Fitchburg, MA 800-225-6313
Sharpsville Container Corp
Sharpsville, PA 800-645-1248
Shaw-Clayton Corporation
San Rafael, CA 800-537-6712
Sheboygan Paper Box Co
Sheboygan, WI 800-458-8373
Shelby Co
Westlake, OH 800-842-1650
Shillington Box Co LLC
St Louis, MO. 636-825-6471
Shipmaster Containers Ltd.
Markham, ON. 416-493-9193
Shippers Supply
Saskatoon, SK. 800-661-5639
Shippers Supply, Labelgraphic
Calgary, AB. 800-661-5639
Shore Paper Box Co
Mardela Springs, MD 410-749-7125
Shorewood Packaging
Carlstadt, NJ 201-933-3203
Sigma Industries
Elkhart, IN. 574-295-9660
Silgan Plastics Canada
Chesterfield, MO 800-274-5426
Simkins Industries Inc
East Haven, CT 203-787-7171
Sirco Systems
Birmingham, AL. 205-731-7800
Smith Packaging
Mississauga, ON 905-564-6640
Smurfit Kappa
Carson, CA 310-537-8190
Smurfit Stone
Norcross, GA 314-656-5300
Smurfit Stone Container
St Louis, MO. 314-679-2300
Smurfit-Stone Container Corp
Santa Fe Springs, CA 714-523-3550
Smyrna Container Co
Atlanta, GA. 800-868-4305
Snapware
Fullerton, CA 800-334-3062
Snyder Crown
Marked Tree, AR 870-358-3400
Snyder Industries Inc.
Lincoln, NE. 800-351-1363

Sobel Corrugated Containers
Cleveland, OH 216-475-2100
Somerville Packaging
Toronto, ON 416-754-7228
Somerville Packaging
Mississauga, ON 905-678-8211
Sonderen Packaging
Spokane, WA. 800-727-9139
Sonoco ThermoSafe
Arlington Heights, IL 800-323-7442
SOPAKCO Foods
Mullins, SC 800-276-9678
Southern Champion Tray LP
Chattanooga, TN 800-468-2222
Southern Metal Fabricators Inc
Albertville, AL 800-989-1330
Southern Missouri Containers
Springfield, MO 800-999-7666
Southern Packaging Machinery
Athens, GA 706-208-0814
Spartanburg Steel Products Inc
Spartanburg, SC 800-974-7500
Spartech Plastics
Portage, WI 800-998-7123
Spring Cove Container Div
Roaring Spring, PA 814-224-5141
Spring Wood Products
Geneva, OH. 440-466-1135
Springport Steel Wire Products
Elkhart, IN. 574-295-9660
SQP
Schenectady, NY 800-724-1129
St Joseph Packaging Inc
St Joseph, MO. 800-383-3000
Stand Fast Pkgng Prods Inc
Addison, IL. 630-543-6390
Standard Folding Cartons Inc
Flushing, NY. 718-396-4522
Star Container Company
Phoenix, AZ 480-281-4200
Star Container Corporation
Leominster, MA 978-537-1676
State Container Corp
Moonachie, NJ 201-933-5200
Stearnswood Inc
Hutchinson, MN 800-657-0144
Step Products
Round Rock, TX 800-777-7837
Steril-Sil Company
Bowmansville, PA. 800-784-5537
Stone Container
Moss Point, MS 502-491-4870
Streator Dependable Mfg
Streator, IL 800-798-0551
Stronghaven Containers Co
Matthews, NC 800-222-7919
Suburban Corrugated Box Company
Indianhead Park, IL 630-920-1230
Superfos Packaging Inc
Cumberland, MD 800-537-9242
T J Smith Box Co
Fort Smith, AR 877-540-7933
T&S Blow Molding
Scarborough, ON 416-752-8330
Tap Packaging Solutions
Cleveland, OH 800-827-5679
Taylor Box Co
Warren, RI. 800-304-6361
Technibilt/Cari-All
Newton, NC 800-233-3972
Technipac
Le Sueur, MN 507-665-6658
TEMP-TECH Company
Springfield, MA 800-343-5579
Temple-Inland
Memphis, TN 901-419-9000
Tenneco Packaging
Westmont, IL. 630-850-7034
TEQ
Huntley, IL 800-874-7113
TGR Container Sales
San Leandro, CA. 800-273-6887
THARCO
San Lorenzo, CA. 800-772-2332
Thermo Wisconsin
De Pere, WI. 920-766-7200
Thermodynamics
Commerce City, CO 800-627-9037
Thermodyne International LTD
Ontario, CA. 909-923-9945
Thornton Plastics
Salt Lake City, UT 800-248-3434

Tinwerks Packaging Co
Addison, IL............................630-628-8600
Titan Plastics
East Rutherford, NJ................201-935-7700
TMS
San Francisco, CA...................800-447-7223
Tolco Corp
Toledo, OH...........................800-537-4786
Trade Fixtures
Little Rock, AR.......................800-872-3490
Traex
Dane, WI.............................800-356-8006
Transparent Container Co
Addison, IL..........................630-458-9031
Traub Container Corporation
Cleveland, OH.......................216-475-5100
Treen Box & Pallet Inc
Bensalem, PA........................215-639-5100
Trent Corp
Trenton, NJ..........................609-587-7515
Tri-State Plastics
Henderson, KY.......................270-826-8361
Trilla Steel Drum Corporation
Chicago, IL..........................773-847-7588
Triple A Containers
Buena Park, CA......................714-521-2820
Triple Dot Corp
Santa Ana, CA.......................714-241-0888
True Pac
New Castle, DE......................800-825-7890
Tucson Container Corp
Tucson, AZ...........................520-746-3171
Tupperware Brands Corporation
Orlando, FL..........................800-366-3800
Ultratainer
St Jean-Sur-Richelie, QC...........514-359-3651
Unarco Industries LLC
Wagoner, OK.........................800-654-4100
Unipak Inc
West Chester, PA....................610-436-6600
Unique Boxes
Chicago, IL..........................800-281-1670
Universal Container Corporation
Odessa, FL...........................800-582-7477
Universal Folding Box
East Orange, NJ.....................973-482-4300
Universal Folding Box Company
Hoboken, NJ.........................201-659-7373
Universal Paper Box
Seattle, WA..........................800-228-1045
US Can Company
Rosedale, MD........................800-436-8021
Utah PaperBox Company
Salt Lake City, UT...................801-363-0093
Valley Container Inc
Bridgeport, CT.......................203-368-6546
Van Dereems Mfg Co
Hawthorne, NJ......................973-427-2355
Victory Box Corp
Roselle, NJ...........................908-245-5100
Victory Packaging, Inc.
Houston, TX..........................800-486-5606
Viking Packaging & Display
San Jose, CA.........................408-998-1000
VIP Real Estate LTD
Chicago, IL..........................773-376-5000
Visual Packaging Corp
Haskell, NJ...........................973-835-7055
VitaMinder Company
Providence, RI.......................800-858-8840
Volk Packaging Corp
Biddeford, ME.......................207-282-6151
Wald Imports
Kirkland, WA........................800-426-2822
Wastequip Teem
Charlotte, NC........................877-468-9278
Waymar Industries
Burnsville, MN.......................888-474-1112
Weber Display & Packaging Inc
Philadelphia, PA.....................215-426-3500
Webster Packaging Corporation
Loveland, OH........................513-683-5666
Welbilt Inc.
New Port Richey, FL.................877-375-9300
WES Plastics
Richmond Hill, ON..................905-508-1546
West Rock
Atlanta, GA..........................770-448-2193
Westeel
Saskatoon, SK.......................306-931-2855
Wheaton Plastic Containers
Millville, NJ..........................856-825-1400

Willamette Industries
Beaverton, OR.......................503-641-1131
Willamette Industries
Louisville, KY........................800-465-3065
Willard Packaging Co
Gaithersburg, MD...................301-948-7700
Winchester Carton
Eutaw, AL............................205-372-3337
Winzen Film
Taylor, TX............................800-779-7595
Wisconsin Box Co
Wausau, WI..........................715-842-2248
Wisconsin Box Co
Wausau, WI..........................800-876-6658
WNA Hopple Plastics
Florence, KY.........................800-446-4622
Woodson Pallet Co
Anmoore, WV........................304-623-2858
Woodstock Plastics Co Inc
Marengo, IL..........................815-568-5281
World Kitchen
Rosemont, IL........................847-678-8600
Wright Brothers Paper Box Company
Fond Du Lac, WI....................920-921-8270
Xtreme Beverages, LLC
Dana Point, CA......................949-495-7929
York Container Co
York, PA..............................717-757-7611
Zero Manufacturing Inc
North Salt Lake, UT.................800-959-5050

Chicken, Prepared

Flexo Transparent Inc
Buffalo, NY..........................877-993-5396
Foam Packaging Inc
Vicksburg, MS.......................800-962-2655

Paper

Accurate Paper Box Co Inc
Knoxville, TN.........................865-690-0311
Adpro
Solon, OH............................440-542-1111
Alcan Packaging
Baie D'Urfe, QC......................514-457-4555
Ample Industries
Franklin, OH.........................888-818-9700
Apache Inc
Cedar Rapids, IA.....................800-553-5455
Armbrust Paper Tubes Inc
Chicago, IL...........................773-586-3232
Artistic Carton
Auburn, IN...........................800-735-7225
Artistic Carton Co
Elgin, IL..............................847-741-0247
Bell Packaging Corporation
Marion, IN............................800-382-0153
Boelter Industries
Winona, MN..........................507-452-2315
Boxes.com
Livingston, NJ........................201-646-9050
Brewer-Cantelmo Inc
New York, NY........................212-244-4600
Burrows Paper Corp
Little Falls, NY.......................800-272-7122
Capitol Carton Company
Sacramento, CA......................916-388-7848
Cardinal Packaging Prod LLC
Crystal Lake, IL......................866-216-4942
Carpet City Paper Box Company
Amsterdam, NY......................518-842-5430
Cedar Box Co
Minneapolis, MN.....................612-332-4287
Chambers Container Company
Gastonia, NC.........................704-377-6317
Cin-Made Packaging Group
Norcross, GA.........................800-264-7494
Coast Paper Box Company
San Bernardino, CA.................909-382-3475
Colbert Packaging Corp
Lake Forest, IL.......................847-367-5990
Collectors Gallery
St Charles, IL........................800-346-3063
Color Box
Richmond, IN........................765-966-7588
Color Carton Corp
Bronx, NY............................718-665-0840
Columbus Paperbox Company
Columbus, OH.......................800-968-0797
Commencement Bay Corrugated
Orting, WA...........................253-845-3100

Commercial Corrugated Co Inc
Baltimore, MD.......................800-242-8861
Complete Packaging & Shipping
Freeport, NY.........................877-269-3236
Conn Container Corp
North Haven, CT.....................203-248-0241
Corbox-Meyers Inc
Cleveland, OH.......................800-321-7286
Corpak
San Juan, PR.........................787-787-9085
Corr Pak Corp
Mc Cook, IL..........................708-442-7806
Corrobilt Container Company
Livermore, CA........................925-373-0880
Corrugated Packaging
Sarasota, FL..........................941-371-0000
Creative Packaging
Hayward, CA.........................510-785-6500
Cumberland Container Corp
Monterey, TN........................931-839-2227
Curtis Packaging
Sandy Hook, CT......................203-426-5861
Dallas Container Corp
Dallas, TX............................800-381-7148
Day Manufacturing Company
Sherman, TX.........................903-893-1138
Designers Folding Box Corp
Buffalo, NY...........................716-853-5141
Diamond Packaging
Rochester, NY........................800-333-4079
Dixie Printing & Packaging
Glen Burnie, MD.....................800-433-4943
Dorado Carton Company
Dorado, PR...........................787-796-1670
Drescher Paper Box Inc
Buffalo, NY...........................716-854-0288
Dusobox Company
Haverhill, MA........................978-372-7192
Duval Container Co
Jacksonville, FL......................800-342-8194
Eagle Box Company
Farmingdale, NY.....................212-255-3860
Eastern Container Corporation
Mansfield, MA........................508-337-0400
EB Box Company
Richmond Hill, ON..................800-513-2269
Economy Folding Box Corporation
Chicago, IL...........................800-771-1053
Enterprise Box Company
Montclair, NJ.........................973-509-2200
Erie Container
Cleveland, OH.......................216-631-1650
Eureka Paper Box Company
Williamsport, PA.....................570-326-9147
Fabricon Products Inc
River Rouge, MI......................313-841-8200
Felco Packaging Specialist
Baltimore, MD.......................800-673-8488
Fibre Containers Inc
City Of Industry, CA.................626-968-5897
Finn Industries
Ontario, CA...........................909-930-1500
Fitzpatrick Container Company
North Wales, PA.....................215-699-3515
Flashfold Carton Inc
Fort Wayne, IN......................260-423-9431
Folding Carton/Flexible Packaging
North Hollywood, CA................818-896-3449
Food Pak Corp
San Mateo, CA.......................650-341-6559
Four M Manufacturing Group
San Jose, CA..........................408-998-1141
Frankston Paper Box Company of Texas
Frankston, TX........................903-876-2550
Friend Box Co
Danvers, MA.........................978-774-0240
Friendly City Box Co Inc
Johnstown, PA.......................814-266-6287
Fuller Box Co
North Attleboro, MA................508-695-2525
Fuller Packaging Inc
Central Falls, RI......................401-725-4300
Gabriel Container Co
Santa Fe Springs, CA................323-685-8844
Goldman Manufacturing Company
Detroit, MI...........................313-834-5535
Graphic Packaging International
Atlanta, GA...........................770-240-7200
Graphic Packaging Intl
Elk Grove Vlg, IL.....................847-437-1700
Great Northern Corp
Chippewa Falls, WI..................800-472-1800

Green Bay Packaging Inc.
Tulsa, OK 918-446-3341
Green Bay Packaging Inc.
Green Bay, WI.................920-433-5111
Green Brothers
Barrington, RI 401-245-9043
Greenfield Paper Box Co
Greenfield, MA.................413-773-9414
Greif Brothers Corporation
Cleveland, OH 800-424-0342
Greif Inc
Delaware, OH 740-549-6000
Grigsby Brothers Paper Box Manufacturers
Portland, OR 866-233-4690
Gulf Packaging Company
Safety Harbor, FL 800-749-3466
Hager Containers Inc
Carrollton, TX.................972-416-7660
Harvard Folding Box Company
Lynn, MA 781-598-1600
Henry Ira L Co
Watertown, WI.................920-261-0648
Hoffmaster Group Inc.
Oshkosh, WI...................800-558-9300
Hood Packaging
Madison, MS...................800-321-8115
Hope Paper Box Company
Pawtucket, RI 401-724-5700
Hunter Packaging Corporation
South Elgin, IL................800-428-4747
Il Valley Container Inc
Peru, IL 815-223-7200
Imperial Containers
City of Industry, CA 626-333-6363
Imperial Packaging Corporation
Pawtucket, RI 401-753-7778
Impress Industries
Emmaus, PA 610-967-6027
Industrial Container Corp
High Point, NC................336-886-7031
Industrial Nameplate Inc
Warminster, PA 800-878-6263
Inland Consumer Packaging
Harrington, DE 302-398-4211
Inland Paper Company
Ontario, CA...................909-923-4505
Inland Paperboard & Packaging
Rock Hill, SC 803-366-4103
Instabox
Calgary, AB...................800-482-6173
Ivarson Inc
Milwaukee, WI................414-351-0700
J&J Mid-South Container Corporation
Augusta, GA..................800-395-1025
Jamestown Container Corporation
Buffalo, NY...................855-234-4054
Jarisch Paper Box Company
North Adams, MA 413-663-5396
Jesse Jones Box Corporation
Philadelphia, PA...............215-425-6600
Jessup Paper Box
Brookston, IN 765-490-9043
Jordan Box Co
Syracuse, NY..................315-422-3419
Jupiter Mills Corporation
Roslyn, NY....................800-853-5121
K&H Container
Wallingford, CT 203-265-1547
Kaufman Paper Box Company
Providence, RI 401-272-7508
Kendel
Countryside, IL................800-323-1100
Knight Paper Box Company
Chicago, IL...................773-585-2035
Koch Container
Victor, NY....................585-924-1600
Lakeside Container Corp
Plattsburgh, NY 518-561-6150
Levin Brothers Paper
Cicero, IL 800-545-6200
Lewisburg Container Co
Lewisburg, OH.................937-962-0101
Lone Star Container Corp
Irving, TX 800-552-6937
Longview Fibre Co
Longview, WA..................800-929-8111
Lowell Paper Box Company
Nashua, NH...................603-595-0700
Loy Lange Box Co
St Louis, MO..................800-886-4712
Mack-Chicago Corporation
Chicago, IL...................800-992-6225

MacMillan Bloedel Packaging
Montgomery, AL................800-239-4464
Mall City Containers Inc
Kalamazoo, MI 800-643-6721
Marcus Carton Company
Melville, NY...................631-752-4200
Marfred Industries
Sun Valley, CA 800-529-5156
Marion Paper Box Co
Marion, IN....................765-664-6435
Maro Paper Products Company
Bellwood, IL...................708-649-9982
Maypak Inc
Wayne, NJ....................973-696-0780
Merchants Publishing Company
Kalamazoo, MI 269-345-1175
Meyer Packaging
Palmyra, PA...................717-838-6300
Michiana Corrugate Products
Sturgis, MI 269-651-5225
Michigan Box Co
Detroit, MI....................888-642-4269
Mid Cities Paper Box Company
Downey, CA...................877-277-6272
Midwest Paper Tube & CanCorporation
New Berlin, WI.................262-782-7300
Modern Paper Box Company
Providence, RI 401-861-7357
Morphy Container Company
Brantford, ON.................519-752-5428
Mt Vernon Packaging Inc
Mt Vernon, OH 888-397-3221
Muth Associates
Springfield, MA 800-388-0157
Nagel Paper & Box Company
Saginaw, MI 800-292-3654
Neff Packaging
Simpsonville, KY 800-445-4383
New England Wooden Ware
Gardner, MA 800-252-9214
New York Corrugated Box Co
Paterson, NJ...................973-742-5000
North American Packaging Corp
New York, NY..................800-499-3521
Northeast Box Co
Ashtabula, OH 800-362-8100
Northeast Container Corporation
Dumont, NJ...................201-385-6200
NPC Display Group
Newark, NJ...................973-589-2155
Oakes Carton Co
Kalamazoo, MI 269-381-6022
Ockerlund Industries
Addison, IL....................708-771-7707
Old Dominion Box Co Inc
Madison Heights, VA 434-929-6701
Oracle Packaging
Winston Salem, NC.............800-952-9536
Original Packaging & Display Company
Saint Louis, MO................314-772-7797
Ott Packagings
Selinsgrove, PA.................570-374-2811
Pacific Paper Box Co
Cudahy, CA...................323-771-7733
Packaging Corporation of America
Lake Forest, IL.................800-456-4725
Packaging Design Corp
Burr Ridge, IL..................630-323-1354
Packing Material Company
Southfield, MI..................248-489-7000
Packrite Packaging
Archdale, NC..................336-431-1111
Paper Works Industries Inc
Baldwinsville, NY...............800-847-5677
Paragon Packaging
Ferndale, CA 888-615-0065
Parlor City Paper Box Co Inc
Binghamton, NY................607-772-0600
Parta
Kent, OH.....................800-543-5781
Paul T. Freund Corporation
Palmyra, NY...................800-333-0091
Pell Paper Box Company
Elizabeth City, NC..............252-335-4361
Performance Packaging
Trail Creek, IN 219-874-6226
Phoenix Industries Corp
Madison, WI...................888-241-7482
Pioneer Packaging & Printing
Anoka, MN...................800-708-1705
Pohlig Brothers
N Chesterfield, VA 804-275-9000

Portland Paper Box Company
Portland, OR...................800-547-2571
Premier Packages
Saint Louis, MO 800-466-6588
Pride Container Corporation
Chicago, IL...................773-227-6000
Quality Packaging Inc
Fond Du Lac, WI 800-923-3633
R.N.C. Industries
Lawrenceville, GA 888-844-3864
Rand-Whitney Group LLC
Worcester, MA.................508-791-2301
Rand-Whitney Packaging Corp
Portsmouth, NH...............508-791-2301
RDA Container Corp
Gates, NY....................585-247-2323
Reliable Container Corporation
Downey, CA...................562-745-0200
Reliance-Paragon
Philadelphia, PA................215-743-1231
Rhoades Paper Box Corporation
Springfield, OH.................800-441-6494
Rice Packaging Inc
Ellington, CT 800-367-6725
Ritz Packaging Company
Brooklyn, NY..................718-366-2300
Rjr Technologies
Oakland, CA...................510-638-5901
Romanow Container
Westwood, MA.................781-320-9200
Round Paper Packages Inc
Erlanger, KY...................859-331-7200
Roy's Folding Box
Cleveland, OH.................216-464-1191
Ruffino Paper Box Co
Hackensack, NJ................201-487-1260
Rusken Packaging
Cullman, AL...................256-775-0014
Schermerhorn Inc
Chicopee, MA..................413-598-8348
Schwarz Supply Source
Morton Grove, IL...............800-323-4903
Scope Packaging
Orange, CA...................714-998-4411
Scott & Daniells
Portland, CT 860-342-1932
Seaboard Carton Company
Downers Grove, IL..............708-344-0575
Sebring Container Corporation
Salem, OH....................330-332-1533
Security Packaging
North Bergen, NJ...............201-854-1955
Set Point Paper Company
Mansfield, MA 800-225-0501
SFBC, LLC dba Seaboard Folding Box
Fitchburg, MA 800-225-6313
Shelby Co
Westlake, OH 800-842-1650
Shillington Box Co LLC
St Louis, MO..................636-825-6471
Shippers Supply
Saskatoon, SK 800-661-5639
Shippers Supply, Labelgraphic
Calgary, AB...................800-661-5639
Shore Paper Box Co
Mardela Springs, MD............410-749-7125
Shorewood Packaging
Carlstadt, NJ..................201-933-3203
Simkins Industries Inc
East Haven, CT.................203-787-7171
Smurfit Kappa
Carson, CA...................310-537-8190
Smurfit Stone
Norcross, GA..................314-656-5300
Smurfit-Stone Container Corp
Santa Fe Springs, CA...........714-523-3550
Smyrna Container Co
Atlanta, GA...................800-868-4305
Somerville Packaging
Toronto, ON..................416-754-7228
Sonderen Packaging
Spokane, WA..................800-727-9139
Southern Champion Tray LP
Chattanooga, TN...............800-468-2222
Southern Missouri Containers
Springfield, MO................800-999-7666
Southern Packaging Machinery
Athens, GA...................706-208-0814
Spring Cove Container Div
Roaring Spring, PA..............814-224-5141
SQP
Schenectady, NY...............800-724-1129

St Joseph Packaging Inc
St Joseph, MO 800-383-3000
Stand Fast Pkgng Prods Inc
Addison, IL 630-543-6390
Standard Folding Cartons Inc
Flushing, NY 718-396-4522
Stearnswood Inc
Hutchinson, MN 800-657-0144
Stone Container
Moss Point, MS 502-491-4870
Stronghaven Containers Co
Matthews, NC 800-222-7919
Suburban Corrugated Box Company
Indianhead Park, IL 630-920-1230
T J Smith Inc
Fort Smith, AR 877-540-7933
Taylor Box Co
Warren, RI 800-304-6361
Tenneco Packaging
Westmont, IL 630-850-7034
THARCO
San Lorenzo, CA 800-772-2332
Traub Container Corporation
Cleveland, OH 216-475-5100
Trent Corp
Trenton, NJ 609-587-7515
Tucson Container Corp
Tucson, AZ 520-746-3171
Unipak Inc
West Chester, PA 610-436-6600
Unique Boxes
Chicago, IL 800-281-1670
Universal Folding Box
East Orange, NJ 973-482-4300
Universal Folding Box Company
Hoboken, NJ 201-659-7373
Universal Paper Box
Seattle, WA 800-228-1045
Utah PaperBox Company
Salt Lake City, UT 801-363-0093
Victory Box Corp
Roselle, NJ 908-245-5100
Victory Packaging, Inc.
Houston, TX 800-486-5606
Viking Packaging & Display
San Jose, CA 408-998-1000
VIP Real Estate LTD
Chicago, IL 773-376-5000
Volk Packaging Corp
Biddeford, ME 207-282-6151
West Rock
Atlanta, GA 770-448-2193
Willamette Industries
Beaverton, OR 503-641-1131
Winchester Carton
Eutaw, AL 205-372-3337
Woodson Pallet Co
Anmoore, WV 304-623-2858
Wright Brothers Paper Box Company
Fond Du Lac, WI 920-921-8270
York Container Co
York, PA 717-757-7611

Plastic

Abbott Industries
Paterson, NJ
Aco Container Systems
Pickering, ON 800-542-9942
All American Container
Miami, FL 305-887-0797
All American Poly
Piscataway, NJ 800-526-3551
Alpack
Centerville, NA 774-994-8086
Anchor Packaging
Ballwin, MO 800-467-3900
Arena Products
Rochester, NY 844-762-0127
Arthur Corporation
Huron, OH 419-433-7202
Atlas Equipment Company
Kansas City, MO 800-842-9188
Bardes Plastics Inc
Milwaukee, WI 800-558-5161
Belleview
Brookline, NH 603-878-1583
Bergen Barrel & Drum Company
Kearny, NJ 201-998-3500
Berry Global
Evansville, IN 800-343-1295

Bonar Plastics
West Chicago, IL 800-295-3725
Brown International Corp LLC
Winter Haven, FL 863-299-2111
Buckhorn Canada
Brampton, ON 800-461-7579
Buckhorn Inc
Milford, OH 800-543-4454
Bulk Lift International, LLC
Carpentersville, IL 800-879-2247
Cardinal Packaging
Evansville, IN 800-343-1295
Carson Industries
Pomona, CA 800-735-5566
Ccw Products
Arvada, CO 303-427-9663
Chem-Tainer Industries Inc
West Babylon, NY 800-275-2436
Chem-Tainer Industries Inc
West Babylon, NY 800-938-8896
Chili Plastics
Rochester, NY 585-889-4680
CKS Packaging
Atlanta, GA 800-800-4257
Clawson Container Company
Clarkston, MI 800-325-8700
Conductive Containers Inc
Minneapolis, MN 800-327-2329
Consolidated Container Co
New Castle, PA 724-658-0549
Constar International
Plymouth, MI 734-455-3600
Container Specialties
Melrose Park, IL 800-548-7513
Container Supply Co
Garden Grove, CA 562-594-0937
Continental Plastic Container
Dallas, TX 972-303-1825
Contour Packaging
Philadelphia, PA 215-457-1600
Convoy
Canton, OH 800-899-1583
Creative Packaging
Hayward, CA 510-785-6500
Crespac Incorporated
Tucker, GA 800-438-1900
CTK Plastics
Moose Jaw, SK 800-667-8847
Cube Plastics
Concord, Ontario, ON 877-260-2823
Custom Bottle of Connecticut
Naugatuck, CT 203-723-6661
Dahl-Tech Inc
Stillwater, MN 800-626-5812
Dart Container Corp.
Mason, MI 800-248-5960
De Ster Corporation
Atlanta, GA 800-237-8270
DEL-Tec Packaging Inc
Greer, SC 800-747-8683
Design Plastics Inc
Omaha, NE 800-491-0786
Douglas Stephen Plastics Inc
Paterson, NJ 973-523-3030
Edco Industries
Bridgeport, CT 203-333-8982
Emco Industrial Plastics
Cedar Grove, NJ 800-292-9906
Engineered Products
Hazelwood, MO 314-731-5744
ES Robbins Corp
Muscle Shoals, AL 800-633-3325
Fabri-Kal Corp
Kalamazoo, MI 800-888-5054
Finn Industries
Ontario, CA 909-930-1500
Flex Products
Carlstadt, NJ 800-526-6273
Frankston Paper Box Company of Texas
Frankston, TX 903-876-2550
Fuller Industries LLC
Great Bend, KS 800-522-0499
Gary Plastic Packaging Corporation
Bronx, NY 800-221-8151
Genpak
Peterborough, ON 800-461-1995
Genpak LLC
Charlotte, NC 800-626-6695
Georg Fischer Central Plastics
Shawnee, OK 800-654-3872
Glasko Plastics
Santa Ana, CA 714-751-7830

Graham Engineering Corp
York, PA 717-848-3755
GranPac
Wetaskiwin, AB 780-352-3324
Greenfield Packaging
White Plains, NY 914-993-0233
Gulf Packaging Company
Safety Harbor, FL 800-749-3466
Hartford Plastics
Omaha, NE
Hedstrom Corporation
Ashland, OH 700-765-9665
Hedwin Division
Baltimore, MD 800-638-1012
Highland Plastics Inc
Mira Loma, CA 800-368-0491
Indiana Bottle Co
Scottsburg, IN 800-752-8702
Indiana Vac Form Inc
Warsaw, IN 574-269-1725
Indianapolis Container Company
Indianapolis, IN 800-760-3318
Inmark, Inc
Austell, GA 800-646-6275
Intertech Corp
Greensboro, NC 800-364-2255
IPL Plastics
Edmundston, NB 800-739-9595
Jarisch Paper Box Company
North Adams, MA 413-663-5396
Jescorp
Des Plaines, IL 847-299-7800
Juice Merchandising Corp
Kansas City, MO 800-950-1998
Juice Tree
Omaha, NE 714-891-4425
Jupiter Mills Corporation
Roslyn, NY 800-853-5121
Just Plastics Inc
New York, NY 212-569-8500
K & L Intl
Ontario, CA 888-598-5588
Kadon Corporation
Milford, OH 937-299-0088
Key Packaging Co
Sarasota, FL 941-355-2728
KHM Plastics Inc
Gurnee, IL 847-249-4910
Kimball Companies
East Longmeadow, MA 413-525-1881
King Plastic Corp
North Port, FL 800-780-5502
Landis Plastics
Alsip, IL 708-396-1470
Letica Corp
Rochester Hills, MI 800-538-4221
Lin Pac Plastics
Roswell, GA 770-751-6006
Linvar
Hartford, CT 800-282-5288
Liquitane
Berwick, PA 570-759-6200
LMK Containers
Centerville, UT 626-821-9984
Lunn Industries
Glen Cove, NY 516-671-9000
M&L Plastics
Easthampton, MA 413-527-1330
Marco Products
Adrian, MI 517-265-3333
Marpac Industries
Philmont, NY 888-462-7722
Melmat Inc
Huntington Beach, CA 800-635-6289
Melville Plastics
Haw River, NC 336-578-5800
Micro Qwik
Cross Plains, WI 608-798-3071
Midland Manufacturing Co
Monroe, IA 800-394-2625
Molded Container Corporation
Portland, OR 503-233-8601
Morris Transparent Box Co
East Providence, RI 401-438-6116
Mullnix Packages Inc
Fort Wayne, IN 260-747-3149
North American Packaging Corp
New York, NY 800-499-3521
Nu-Trend Plastics Thermoformer
Jacksonville, FL 904-353-5936
Ockerlund Industries
Addison, IL 708-771-7707

Olcott Plastics
St Charles, IL 888-313-5277
ORBIS
Oconomowoc, WI. 262-560-5000
ORBIS
Oconomowoc, WI. 800-890-7292
Owens-Illinois Inc
Perrysburg, OH 567-336-5000
Pacific Paper Box Co
Cudahy, CA .323-771-7733
Packaging Associates
Randolph, NJ 973-252-8890
Pactiv LLC
Lake Forest, IL 800-476-4300
Pan Pacific Plastics Inc
Hayward, CA 888-475-6888
Par-Pak
Houston, TX .713-686-6700
Par-Pak
Houston, TX .888-727-7252
Paradigm Packaging Inc
Upland, CA. .909-985-2750
Paragon Packaging
Ferndale, CA 888-615-0065
Pelco Packaging Corporation
Stirling, NJ 908-647-3500
Penn Bottle & Supply Company
Philadelphia, PA 215-365-5700
Penn Products
Portland, CT 800-490-7366
Pinckney Molded Plastics
Howell, MI 800-854-2920
Pioneer Plastics Inc
Dixon, KY 800-951-1551
Plastic Assembly Corporation
Ayer, MA
Plastics Inc
Greensboro, AL 334-624-8801
Plastics Industries
Athens, TN 800-894-4876
Plastipak Packaging
Plymouth, MI 734-354-3510
Plastiques Cascades Group
Montreal, QC 888-703-6515
Podnar Plastics Inc
Kent, OH. 800-673-5277
Poliplastic
Granby, QC. .450-378-8417
Poly Plastic Products Inc
Delano, PA 570-467-3000
Poly Processing Co
French Camp, CA 877-325-3142
Polybottle Group
Surrey, BC 604-594-4999
Polycon Industries
Chicago, IL 773-374-5500
Prairie Packaging Inc
Mooresville, NC 704-660-6600
Prestige Plastics Corporation
Delta, BC. 604-930-2931
Pretium Packaging
Chesterfield, MO 314-727-8673
Pretium Packaging
Hazle Twp, PA 570-459-1800
Pretium Packaging, LLC.
Chesterfield, MO 314-727-8200
Printsource Group
Wakefield, RI 401-789-9339
Priority Plastics Inc
Grinnell, IA 800-798-3512
Progressive Plastics
Cleveland, OH 800-252-0053
Prolon
Port Gibson, MS 888-480-9828
Promens
St. John, NB .800-295-3725
Quality Container Company
Ypsilanti, MI .734-481-1373
Quantum Storage Systems Inc
Miami, FL. 800-685-4665
Quintex Corp
Nampa, ID. 208-467-1113
R C Molding Inc
Greer, SC. 864-879-7279
RAPAC Inc
Oakland, TN .800-280-6333
Regal Plastic Company
Mission, KS .800-852-1556
Reliance Product
Winnipeg, MB. 800-665-0258
Reliance-Paragon
Philadelphia, PA 215-743-1231

Rez-Tech Corp
Kent, OH. 800-673-5277
Richard Read Construction Company
Arcadia, CA .888-450-7343
RMI-C/Rotonics Manaufacturing
Bensenville, IL 630-773-9510
Ropak
Oak Brook, IL 800-527-2267
S.S.I. Schaefer System International Limited
Brampton, ON 905-458-5399
Sabert Corp
Sayreville, NJ 800-722-3781
Saeplast Canada
St John, NB .800-567-3966
Semco Plastic Co
St Louis, MO. 314-487-4557
Set Point Paper Company
Mansfield, MA 800-225-0501
Setco
Monroe Twp, NJ 609-655-4600
Setco
Anaheim, CA 714-777-5200
Sfb Plastics Inc
Wichita, KS. .800-343-8133
Sharpsville Container Corp
Sharpsville, PA 800-645-1248
Shaw-Clayton Corporation
San Rafael, CA 800-537-6712
Sheboygan Paper Box Co
Sheboygan, WI 800-458-8373
Silgan Plastics Canada
Chesterfield, MO 800-274-5426
Snapware
Fullerton, CA 800-334-3062
Snyder Industries Inc.
Lincoln, NE. .800-351-1363
Spartanburg Steel Products Inc
Spartanburg, SC 800-974-7500
Spartech Plastics
Portage, WI .800-998-7123
Star Container Company
Phoenix, AZ .480-281-4200
Step Products
Round Rock, TX 800-777-7837
Stock America Inc
Grafton, WI .262-375-4100
Superfos Packaging Inc
Cumberland, MD 800-537-9242
T&S Blow Molding
Scarborough, ON 416-752-8330
TEQ
Huntley, IL 800-874-7113
Thermodynamics
Commerce City, CO 800-627-9037
Thermodyne International LTD
Ontario, CA .909-923-9945
Thornton Plastics
Salt Lake City, UT 800-248-3434
Titan Plastics
East Rutherford, NJ 201-935-7700
Tri-State Plastics
Henderson, KY 270-826-8361
Triple Dot Corp
Santa Ana, CA 714-241-0888
Tupperware Brands Corporation
Orlando, FL. .800-366-3800
Universal Container Corporation
Odessa, FL 800-582-7477
Visual Packaging Corp
Haskell, NJ 973-835-7055
WES Plastics
Richmond Hill, ON. 905-508-1546
Willamette Industries
Louisville, KY 800-465-3065
Wiltec
Leominster, MA 978-537-1497
Winzen Film
Taylor, TX. 800-779-7595
WNA
Lancaster, TX. 800-334-2877
WNA Hopple Plastics
Florence, KY. 800-446-4622
Woodstock Plastics Co Inc
Marengo, IL .815-568-5281
World Kitchen
Rosemont, IL. 847-678-8600
Zero Manufacturing Inc
North Salt Lake, UT 800-959-5050

Corks

Crown

Cork Specialties
Miami, FL 305-477-1506
Fetzer Vineyards
Hopland, CA 800-846-8637
Palace Packaging Machines Inc
Downingtown, PA. 610-873-7252

Crates

Bottle

Langer Manufacturing Company
Cedar Rapids, IA. 800-728-6445
Tulip Molded Plastics Corp
Milwaukee, WI 414-963-3120

Egg

Eggboxes Inc
Deerfield Beach, FL 800-326-6667
Jacksonville Box & Woodwork Co
Jacksonville, FL 800-683-2699

Wooden Shipping

American Box Corporation
Lisbon, OH 330-424-8055
American Pallet Inc
Oakdale, CA 209-847-6122
Babcock Co
Bath, NY 607-776-3341
Brooks Barrel Company
Baltimore, MD 800-398-2766
Burgess Mfg. - Oklahoma
Guthrie, OK. .800-804-1913
C & L Wood Products Inc
Hartselle, AL. 800-483-2035
Cassel Box & Lumber Co Inc
Grafton, WI .262-377-9503
Corbett Timber Co
Wilmington, NC 800-334-0684
Corrugated Inner-Pak Corporation
Conshohocken, PA 610-825-0200
Creative Packaging
Hayward, CA 510-785-6500
Denver Reel & Pallet Company
Denver, CO .303-321-1920
Eichler Wood Products
Laurys Station, PA 610-262-6749
Elberta Crate & Box Company
Carpentersville, IL 888-672-9260
Farmer's Co-Op Elevator Co
Hudsonville, MI 800-439-9859
Fehlig Brothers Box & Lbr Co
St Louis, MO. 314-241-6900
Fox Valley Wood Products Inc
Kaukauna, WI. 920-766-4069
Franklin Crates
Micanopy, FL 352-466-3141
Fruit Growers Package Company
Grandville, MI 616-724-1400
Gatewood Products LLC
Parkersburg, WV. 800-827-5461
Goeman's Wood Products
Hartford, WI .262-673-6090
Greene Industries
East Greenwich, RI. 401-884-7530
H. Arnold Wood Turning
Tarrytown, NY 888-314-0088
Hampton Roads Box Company
Suffolk, VA 757-934-2355
Heritage Packaging
Victor, NY 585-742-3310
Herkimer Pallet & Wood Products Company
Herkimer, NY 315-866-4591
Hinchcliff Products Company
Strongsville, OH 440-238-5200
Hunter Woodworks
Carson, CA .800-966-4751
Industrial Contracting & Rggng
Mahwah, NJ 888-427-7444
Industrial Crating & Packing
Tukwila, WA .800-942-0499
Industrial Lumber & Packaging
Spring Lake, MI 616-842-1457
Industrial Woodfab & Packaging
Riverview, MI 734-284-4808

Jacksonville Box & Woodwork Co
Jacksonville, FL 800-683-2699
Killington Wood ProductsCompany
Rutland, VT 802-773-9111
Kontane
Charleston, SC .843-352-0011
Konz Wood Products Co
Appleton, WI 877-610-5145
Lawson Industries
Holden, MO 816-732-4347
Lester Box & Mfg Div
Long Beach, CA 562-437-5123
Lexel
Fort Worth, TX .817-332-4061
Little Rock Crate & Basket Co
Little Rock, AR .800-223-7823
Luke's Almond Acres
Reedley, CA 559-638-3483
Lumber & Things
Keyser, WV 800-296-5656
M & H Crate Inc
Jacksonville, TX 903-683-5351
Maull-Baker Box Company
Brookfield, WI .414-463-1290
Michiana Box & Crate
Niles, MI 800-677-6372
Michigan Box Co
Detroit, MI 888-642-4269
Milan Box Corporation
Milan, TN 800-225-8057
Moorecraft Box & Crate
Tarboro, NC 252-823-2510
Nefab Packaging Inc.
Coppell, TX 800-322-4425
Nefab Packaging, Inc.
Coppell, TX 800-322-4425
New Lisbon Wood ProductsManufacturing Company
New Lisbon, WI 608-562-3122
New Mexico Products Inc
Albuquerque, NM 877-345-7864
Oak Creek Pallet Company
Milwaukee, WI .414-762-7170
Original Lincoln Logs
Chestertown, NY 800-833-2461
Packing Material Company
Southfield, MI .248-489-7000
Pallets Inc
Fort Edward, NY 518-747-4177
Pine Point Wood Products Inc
Osseo, MN 763-428-4301
PPC Perfect Packaging Co
Perrysburg, OH 419-874-3167
Precision Wood of Hawaii
Vancouver, WA 808-682-2055
Precision Wood Products
Vancouver, WA 360-694-8322
Rand-Whitney Group LLC
Worcester, MA .508-791-2301
Remmey Wood Products
Southampton, PA 215-355-3335
Roddy Products Pkgng Co Inc
Aldan, PA 610-623-7040
Royal Group
Cicero, IL 708-656-2020
Seattle-Tacoma Box Co
Kent, WA 253-854-9700
Smith Pallet Co Inc
Hatfield, AR 870-389-6184
Southern Pallet
Christchurch, NZ 901-942-4603
Spring Wood Products
Geneva, OH 440-466-1135
Stearnswood Inc
Hutchinson, MN 800-657-0144
Tampa Pallet Co
Tampa, FL 813-626-5700
Thunder Pallet Inc
Theresa, WI 800-354-0643
Wisconsin Box Co
Wausau, WI 715-842-2248
Wisconsin Box Co
Wausau, WI 800-876-6658
Wnc Pallet & Forest Pdts Co
Candler, NC 828-667-5426
Xtreme Beverages, LLC
Dana Point, CA 949-495-7929

Cups

Paper

A-A1 Aaction Bag
Denver, CO 800-783-1224
Acme International
Maplewood, NJ 973-416-0400
AJM Packaging Corporation
Bloomfield Hills, MI 248-901-0040
Bynoe Printers
New York, NY .212-662-5041
Chinet Company
Laguna Niguel, CA 949-348-1711
Creative Converting Inc
Clintonville, WI 800-826-0418
Dart Canada Inc.
Toronto, ON 800-465-9696
Dart Container Corp.
Mason, MI 800-248-5960
Durango-Georgia Paper
Tampa, FL 813-286-2718
Fort James Canada
Toronto, ON 416-784-1621
Four M Manufacturing Group
San Jose, CA 408-998-1141
Hoffmaster Group Inc.
Oshkosh, WI 800-558-9300
Insulair
Vernalis, CA 800-343-3402
International Paper Co.
Memphis, TN
James River Canada
North York, ON 416-789-5151
Jones-Zylon Co
West Lafayette, OH 800-848-8160
Letica Corp
Rochester Hills, MI 800-538-4221
Nyman Manufacturing Company
Rumford, RI 401-438-3410
Primary Liquidation
Bohemia, NY 631-244-1410
Rockline Industries
Sheboygan, WI 800-558-7790
Scan Group
Appleton, WI 920-730-9150
Solo Cup Company
Lake Forest, IL
Tenneco Specialty Packaging
Smyrna, GA 800-241-4402

Plastic

A-A1 Aaction Bag
Denver, CO 800-783-1224
Arthur Corporation
Huron, OH 419-433-7202
C R Mfg
Waverly, NE 877-789-5844
Carlisle Food Svc Products Inc
Oklahoma City, OK 800-654-8210
Carthage Cup Company
Longview, TX .903-238-9833
Chinet Company
Laguna Niguel, CA 949-348-1711
Creative Converting Inc
Clintonville, WI 800-826-0418
Dart Canada Inc.
Toronto, ON 800-465-9696
Dart Container Corp.
Mason, MI 800-248-5960
De Ster Corporation
Atlanta, GA 800-237-8270
Design Specialties Inc
Hamden, CT 800-999-1584
Donoco Industries
Huntington Beach, CA 888-822-8763
Elliot Lee
Cedarhurst, NY 516-569-9595
Fabri-Kal Corp
Kalamazoo, MI 800-888-5054
Filmpack Plastic Corporation
Dayton, NJ 732-329-6523
Fort James Canada
Toronto, ON 416-784-1621
Genpak
Peterborough, ON 800-461-1995
Highland Plastics Inc
Mira Loma, CA 800-368-0491
Hoffmaster Group Inc.
Oshkosh, WI 800-558-9300

HPI North America/ Plastics
Eagan, MN 800-752-7462
Huhtamaki Food Service Plastics
Lake Forest, IL 800-244-6382
Image Plastics
Houston, TX 800-289-2811
James River Canada
North York, ON 416-789-5151
Jones-Zylon Co
West Lafayette, OH 800-848-8160
Kendrick Johnson & Assoc Inc
Minneapolis, MN 800-826-1271
King Plastic Corp
North Port, FL .800-780-5502
Letica Corp
Rochester Hills, MI 800-538-4221
Master Containers
Mulberry, FL 800-881-6847
MDR International
North Miami, FL 305-944-5019
NCC
Groveland, FL .800-429-9037
Nyman Manufacturing Company
Rumford, RI 401-438-3410
OWD
Tupper Lake, NY 800-836-1693
Party Yards
Casselberry, FL 877-501-4400
Peter Gray Corporation
Andover, MA 978-470-0990
Plaxall Inc
Long Island City, NY 800-876-5706
Polar Plastics
St Laurent, QC .514-331-0207
Prairie Packaging Inc
Mooresville, NC 704-660-6600
Set Point Paper Company
Mansfield, MA 800-225-0501
Spirit Foodservice, Inc.
Andover, MA 800-343-0996
Techform
Mount Airy, NC 336-789-2115
Tenneco Specialty Packaging
Smyrna, GA 800-241-4402
Thermo Service
Dallas, TX 800-635-5559
Ullman, Shapiro & UllmanLLP
New York, NY .212-755-0299
Whirley Industries Inc
Warren, PA 800-825-5575
Wiltec
Leominster, MA 978-537-1497
WNA
Lancaster, TX .800-334-2877
Wna Comet West Inc
City Of Industry, CA 800-225-0939

Film

Cellulose Acetate

Emco Industrial Plastics
Cedar Grove, NJ 800-292-9906
Modern Plastics
Shelton, CT 800-243-9696
Pater & Associates
Cincinnati, OH
Star Poly Bag Inc
Brooklyn, NY 718-384-7034
Teepak LLC
Lisle, IL 800-621-0264
UCB Inc
Smyrna, GA 770-970-8338

Plastic

A-A1 Aaction Bag
Denver, CO 800-783-1224
Achilles USA
Everett, WA 425-353-7000
AEP Industries
South Hackensack, NJ 800-999-2374
AEP Industries Inc
Mankato, MN .800-999-2374
Aep Industries Inc.
South Hackensack, NJ 800-999-2374
American Renolit Corp LA
Commerce, CA 323-721-2720
Anchor Packaging
Ballwin, MO 800-467-3900
Atlantis Plastics Linear Film
Tulsa, OK 800-324-9727

Bagcraft Papercon
   Chicago, IL 800-621-8468
Beayl Weiner/Pak
   Pacific Palisades, CA 310-454-1354
Blako Industries
   Dunbridge, OH 419-833-4491
Bollore Inc
   Dayville, CT 860-774-2930
Brentwood Plastics In
   St Louis, MO 314-968-1135
Carlisle Plastics
   Minneapolis, MN 952-884-1309
Cello Bag Company
   Bowling Green, KY 800-347-0338
Champion Plastics
   Clifton, NJ 800-526-1230
Cincinnati Convertors Inc
   Cincinnati, OH 513-731-6600
Cleveland Plastic Films
   Elyria, OH 800-832-6799
Cleveland Specialties Co
   Loveland, OH 513-677-9787
Colonial Transparent Products Company
   Hicksville, NY 516-822-4430
Command Packaging
   Vernon, CA 800-996-2247
Cortec Aero
   St Paul, MN 800-426-7832
COVERIS
   Tomah, WI 608-372-2153
Coveris
   Excelsior Springs, MO
Crayex Corp
   Piqua, OH 800-837-1747
Crystal-Flex Packaging Corporation
   Rockville Centre, NY 888-246-7325
Danafilms Inc
   Westborough, MA 508-366-8884
Dynamic Packaging
   Minneapolis, MN 800-878-9380
Ellehammer Industries
   Langley, BC 604-882-9326
Farnell Packaging
   Dartmouth, NS 800-565-9378
Film X
   Dayville, CT 800-628-6128
Film-Pak Inc
   Crowley, TX 800-526-1838
Filmco Inc
   Aurora, OH 800-545-8457
FLEXcon Company
   Spencer, MA 508-885-8200
Flexo Transparent Inc
   Buffalo, NY 877-993-5396
Formflex
   Bloomingdale, IN 800-255-7659
Fredman Bag Co
   Milwaukee, WI 800-945-5686
Gbs
   North Canton, OH 800-552-2427
Gemini Plastic Films Corporation
   Garfield, NJ 800-789-4732
General Films Inc
   Covington, OH 888-436-3456
Gloucester Engineering
   Gloucester, MA 978-281-1800
Goodwrappers Inc
   Halethorpe, MD 800-638-1127
Greenfield Packaging
   White Plains, NY 914-993-0233
Gulf Arizona Packaging
   Humble, TX 800-364-3887
Gulf Systems
   Brownsville, TX 800-217-4853
Gulf Systems
   Humble, TX 800-364-3887
Harpak-ULMA Packaging LLC
   Ball Ground, GA 770-345-5300
Hedwin Division
   Baltimore, MD 800-638-1012
Herche Warehouse
   Denver, CO 303-371-8186
Holo-Source Corporation
   Livonia, MI 888-995-7799
Home Plastics Inc
   Des Moines, IA 515-265-2562
Hudson Poly Bag Inc
   Hudson, MA 800-229-7566
Huntsman Packaging
   South Deerfield, MA 413-665-2145
Huntsman Packaging Corporation
   Birmingham, Bi. 205-328-4720

Inmark, Inc
   Austell, GA 800-646-6275
Inteplast Bags & Films Corporation
   Delta, BC 604-946-5431
Jescorp
   Des Plaines, IL 847-299-7800
Karolina Polymers
   Hickory, NC 828-328-2247
Klockner Pentaplast of America
   Gordonsville, VA 540-832-3600
KM International Corp
   Kenton, TN 731-749-8700
Kurz Transfer Products LP
   Charlotte, NC 800-333-2306
L&H Wood Manufacturing Company
   Farmington, MI 248-474-9000
Longhorn Packaging Inc
   San Antonio, TX 800-433-7974
Luetzow Industries
   South Milwaukee, WI 800-558-6055
M S Plastics & Packaging Inc
   Butler, NJ 800-593-1802
Mark Products Company
   Denville, NJ 973-983-8818
Marshall Plastic Film Inc
   Martin, MI 269-672-5511
Mason Transparent Package Company
   Armonk, NY 718-792-6000
Merix Chemical Company
   Chicago, IL 312-573-1400
Microplas Industries
   Dunwoody, GA 800-952-4528
Mitsubishi Polyester Film, Inc.
   Greer, SC 864-879-5000
Modern Plastics
   Shelton, CT 800-243-9696
Mohawk Northern Plastics
   Auburn, WA 800-426-1100
Multi-Plastics Extrusions Inc
   Hazleton, PA 570-455-2021
National Poly Bag Manufacturing Corporation
   Brooklyn, NY 718-629-9800
Northeast Packaging Materials
   Monsey, NY 845-426-2900
Now Plastics Inc
   East Longmeadow, MA 413-525-1010
Occidental Chemical Corporation
   Dallas, TX 800-733-3665
OMNOVA Solutions
   Fairlawn, OH 330-869-4200
Packaging Materials Inc
   Cambridge, OH 800-565-8550
Packing Material Company
   Southfield, MI 248-489-7000
Pactiv LLC
   Lake Forest, IL 800-476-4300
Pak-Sak Industries I
   Sparta, MI 800-748-0431
Parade Packaging
   Mundelein, IL 847-566-6264
Pater & Associates
   Cincinnati, OH
Plascal Corp
   Farmingdale, NY 800-899-7527
Plastic Craft Products Corp
   West Nyack, NY 800-627-3010
Plastic Suppliers Inc
   Columbus, OH 800-722-5577
Poly Plastic Products Inc
   Delano, PA 570-467-3000
Portco Corporation
   Vancouver, WA 800-426-1794
Printpack Inc.
   Atlanta, GA 404-460-7000
Quality Films
   Three Rivers, MI 269-679-5263
Quantum Performance Films
   Streamwood, IL 800-323-6963
Rjr Technologies
   Oakland, CA 510-638-5901
Robbie Manufacturing Inc
   Lenexa, KS 800-255-6328
Roll-O-Sheets Canada
   Barrie, ON 888-767-3456
Roplast Industries Inc
   Oroville, CA 800-767-5278
Rowland Technologies
   Wallingford, CT 203-269-9500
Rutan Poly Industries Inc
   Mahwah, NJ 800-872-1474
Seal-Tite Bag Company
   Philadelphia, PA 717-917-1949

Sealed Air Corp
   Charlotte, NC 800-391-5645
Senior Housing Options Inc
   Denver, CO 800-659-2656
Shields Bag & Printing Co
   Yakima, WA 800-541-8630
Ship Rite Packaging
   Bergenfield, NJ 800-721-7447
Shippers Supply
   Saskatoon, SK 800-661-5639
Sommers Plastic Product Co Inc
   Clifton, NJ 800-225-7677
Southern Film Extruders
   High Point, NC 800-334-6101
Spartech Plastics
   Wichita, KS 316-722-8621
Spartech Plastics
   Portage, WI 800-998-7123
Spartech Poly Com
   Clayton, MI 888-721-4242
Specialty Films & Associates
   Hebron, KY 800-984-3346
Star Poly Bag Inc
   Brooklyn, NY 718-384-7034
Stone Container
   Chicago, IL 312-346-6600
Sungjae Corporation
   Irvine, CA 949-757-1727
Teknor Apex Co
   City Of Industry, CA 800-556-3864
Terphane Inc
   Bloomfield, NY 800-724-3456
Trident Plastics
   Ivyland, PA 800-222-2318
Trinity Packaging
   Cheektowaga, NY 800-778-3111
Trio Packaging Corp
   Ronkonkoma, NY 800-331-0492
Triune Enterprises
   Gardena, CA 310-719-1600
Tyco Plastics
   Lakeville, MN 800-328-4080
UCB Inc
   Smyrna, GA 770-970-8338
Ultrapak
   Dunkirk, NY 800-228-6030
Uniplast Films
   Palmer, MA 800-343-1295
V C 999 Packaging Systems
   Kansas City, MO 800-728-2999
Vacumet Corporation
   Austell, GA 800-776-0865
VIFAN Canada
   Lanoraie, QC 800-557-0192
Virginia Plastics Co
   Roanoke, VA 800-777-8541
Viskase Co Inc
   Darien, IL 800-323-8562
Western Plastics
   Portland, TN 615-325-7331
Western Plastics
   Calhoun, GA 800-752-4106
Wisconsin Film & Bag Inc
   Shawano, WI. 800-765-9224
Wright Plastics Company
   Prattville, AL 800-874-7659
Zimmer Custom-Made Packaging
   Indianapolis, IN 317-263-3436

Pressure Sensitive

Amcor
   Oshkosh, WI 800-544-4672
CL&D Graphics
   Oconomowoc, WI 800-777-1114
Creative Coatings Corporation
   Nashua, NH 800-229-1957
FLEXcon Company
   Spencer, MA 508-885-8200
General Formulations
   Sparta, MI 800-253-3664
MAC Tac LLC
   Stow, OH 866-262-2822
Multi-Color Corp
   Green Bay, WI. 800-236-8208
Shippers Supply
   Winnipeg, NB 800-661-5639
Tyco Plastics
   Lakeville, MN 800-328-4080

Foil

Aluminum

All Foils Inc
  Strongsville, OH 800-521-0054
Alufoil Products Co Inc
  Hauppauge, NY 631-231-4141
Burrows Paper Corp
  Little Falls, NY 800-272-7122
Holo-Source Corporation
  Livonia, MI 888-995-7799
JW Aluminum
  Mt Holly, SC 800-568-1100
Norandal
  Franklin, TX 615-771-5700
Novelis Foil Products
  Atlanta, GA 800-776-8701
Packaging Dynamics International
  Caldwell, OH 740-732-5665
Republic Foil
  Danbury, CT 800-722-3645
Rjr Technologies
  Oakland, CA 510-638-5901
Somerville Packaging
  Mississauga, ON 905-678-8211
Source for Packaging
  New York, NY 800-223-2527
Tilly Industries
  St Laurent, QC 514-331-4922
Trinidad Benham Corporation
  Denver, CO 303-220-1400
Unifoil Corp
  Fairfield, NJ 973-244-9990
Western Plastics
  Portland, TN 615-325-7331
Western Plastics
  Calhoun, GA 800-752-4106

Pressure Sensitive

Advanced Labelworx
  Anderson, SC 865-966-8711
MAC Tac LLC
  Stow, OH 866-262-2822

Printed & Laminated

Advanced Labelworx
  Anderson, SC 865-966-8711
All Foils Inc
  Strongsville, OH 800-521-0054
Alufoil Products Co Inc
  Hauppauge, NY 631-231-4141
Bagcraft Papercon
  Chicago, IL 800-621-8468
Catty Inc
  Harvard, IL 815-943-2288
Cincinnati Convertors Inc
  Cincinnati, OH 513-731-6600
Clearwater Paper Corporation
  Spokane, WA 877-847-7831
Formflex
  Bloomingdale, IN 800-255-7659
Hampden Papers Inc
  Holyoke, MA 413-536-1000
Kurz Transfer Products LP
  Charlotte, NC 800-333-2306
Label Makers
  Pleasant Prairie, WI 800-208-3331
Milprint
  Oshkosh, WI 920-303-8600
Norandal
  Franklin, TX 615-771-5700
Pakmark
  Chesterfield, MO 800-423-1379
Paper Products Company
  Cincinnati, OH 513-921-4717
Pater & Associates
  Cincinnati, OH
Tolas Health Care Packaging
  Feasterville Trevose, PA 215-322-7900
Unifoil Corp
  Fairfield, NJ 973-244-9990

General

A & G Foods
  Chicago, IL 773-783-1672
Americasia International
  Hillsborough, NJ 609-608-6886
Barrington Packaging Systems Group
  Harrison, NY 888-814-7999

Carmi Flavor & Fragrance Company
  Commerce, CA 800-421-9647
CFC International, Inc.
  Chicago Heights, IL 708-891-3456
CHEP Pallecon Solutions
  Livonia, MI 888-873-2277
Cougar Packaging Concepts, Inc.
  St. Charles, IL 630-689-4050
Cougar Packaging Solutions
  Lemont, IL 630-231-7800
DuPont
  Wilmington, DE 800-441-7515
Groeb Farms
  Onsted, MI 800-530-9969
Harpak-Ulma
  Taunton, MA 800-813-6644
Horton Fruit Co Inc
  Louisville, KY 800-626-2245
Jowat Corp.
  High Point, NC 800-322-4583
Kalle USA Inc
  Gurnee, IL 847-775-0781
Khs USA Inc
  Waukesha, WI 262-797-7200
MonoSol
  Merrillville, IN 219-762-3165
ProMach
  Covington, KY 866-776-6224
Tecnocap
  Glen Dale, WV 800-999-2567
Weyauwega Star Dairy
  Weyauwega, WI 888-813-9720

Inks

Indelible

Chicago Ink & Research Co
  Antioch, IL 847-395-1078
Ideal Stencil Machine & Tape Company
  Marion, IL 800-388-0162
Organic Products Co
  Irving, TX 972-438-7321
Trident
  Brookfield, CT 203-740-9333
Volk Corp
  Farmington Hills, MI 800-521-6799
Wichita Stamp & Seal Inc
  Wichita, KS 316-263-4223

Marking & Coding

ABM Marking
  Belleville, IL 800-626-9012
Carteret Coding Inc
  Clark, NJ 732-574-0900
Chicago Ink & Research Co
  Antioch, IL 847-395-1078
Colorcon Inc
  Harleysville, PA 215-256-7700
Custom Rubber Stamp Co
  Crosby, MN 888-606-4579
Dixie Rubber Stamp & Seal Company
  Atlanta, GA 404-875-8883
Domino Amjet Inc
  Gurnee, IL 800-444-4512
Easterday Fluid Technologies
  Saint Francis, WI 414-482-4488
Federal Stamp & Seal Manufacturing Company
  Atlanta, GA 800-333-7726
Ferro Corporation
  Mayfield Heights, OH 216-875-5600
Fox Stamp Sign & Specialty
  Menasha, WI 920-725-2683
Fraser Stamp & Seal
  Chicago, IL 800-540-8565
Frost Manufacturing Corp
  Worcester, MA 800-462-0216
Garvey Products
  Cincinnati, OH 513-771-8710
Graphic Impressions of Illinois
  River Grove, IL 708-453-1100
Hartford Stamp Works
  Hartford, CT 860-249-6205
Hiss Stamp Company
  Columbus, OH 614-224-5119
Ideal Stencil Machine & Tape Company
  Marion, IL 800-388-0162
Imaje
  Kennesaw, GA 678-594-7153
Independent Ink
  Gardena, CA 800-446-5538

Innovative Ceramic Corp
  East Liverpool, OH 330-385-6515
Koehler-Gibson Marking
  Buffalo, NY 800-875-1562
Marsh Company
  Belleville, IL 800-527-6275
Mastermark
  Kent, WA 206-762-9610
Modern Stamp Company
  Baltimore, MD 800-727-3029
Muskogee Rubber Stamp & Seal Company
  Fort Gibson, OK 918-478-3046
Organic Products Co
  Irving, TX 972-438-7321
Quick Stamp & Sign Mfg
  Lafayette, LA 337-232-2171
Richardson's Stamp Works
  Houston, TX 713-973-0314
Sohn Manufacturing
  Elkhart Lake, WI. 920-876-3361
Southern Rubber Stamp
  Tulsa, OK 888-826-4304
Starkey Chemical Process Company
  La Grange, IL 800-323-3040
Tharo Systems Inc
  Brunswick, OH 800-878-6833
Trident
  Brookfield, CT 203-740-9333
Videojet Technologies Inc
  Wood Dale, IL. 800-843-3610
Volk Corp
  Farmington Hills, MI 800-521-6799

Meat Branding

Ideal Stencil Machine & Tape Company
  Marion, IL. 800-388-0162
Service Stamp Works
  Chicago, IL 312-666-8839

Jars

Canning & Preserving

Alcoa - Massena Operations
  Massena, NY
Delta Plastics
  Hot Springs, AR 501-760-3000

Glass

All American Container
  Miami, FL 305-887-0797
Arkansas Glass Container Corp
  Jonesboro, AR 800-527-4527
Bal/Foster Glass Container Company
  Port Allegany, PA 814-642-2521
Ball Glass Container Corporation
  El Monte, CA 626-448-9831
Gessner Products
  Ambler, PA 800-874-7808
Greenfield Packaging
  White Plains, NY 914-993-0233
Indiana Glass Company
  Columbus, OH 800-543-0357
Indianapolis Container Company
  Indianapolis, IN 800-760-3318
LMK Containers
  Centerville, UT 626-821-9984
Louisville Container Company
  Indianapolis, IN 888-539-7225
Olcott Plastics
  St Charles, IL 888-313-5277
Promens
  St. John, NB 800-295-3725
Richards Packaging
  Memphis, TN 800-583-0327
World Kitchen
  Elmira, NY 800-999-3436

Plastic

Delta Plastics
  Hot Springs, AR 501-760-3000

Labels

A-1 Business Supplies Inc
  Dover, NJ 800-631-3421
Aabbitt Adhesives
  Chicago, IL 800-222-2488
About Packaging Robotics
  Thornton, CO 303-449-2559

AC Label Company
  Provo, UT 801-642-3500
Accuform Manufacturing, Inc.
  Vacaville, CA 800-233-3352
Ad Mart Identity Group
  Danville, KY. 800-354-2102
Adhesive Label
  Minneapolis, MN 763-546-1182
Adhesive Products Inc
  Vernon, CA 800-669-5516
Adhesives Research
  Glen Rock, PA. 800-445-6240
Adstick Custom Labels Inc
  Denver, CO 800-255-7314
Advanced Labelworx
  Anderson, SC 865-966-8711
Advanced Labelworx Inc
  Oak Ridge, TN 864-224-2122
Ahlstrom Filtration LLC
  Madisonville, KY 270-821-0140
Aigner Index
  New Windsor, NY. 800-242-3919
ALLIED Graphics Inc
  St Michael, MN. 800-490-9931
Altrua Marketing & Design
  Tallahassee, FL 800-443-6939
AM Graphics
  Edina, MN. 612-341-2020
American Forms & Labels
  Boise, ID 800-388-3554
American Labelmark Co
  Chicago, IL 800-621-5808
Andrew H Lawson Co
  Philadelphia, PA 800-411-6628
Andy Printed Products
  Lagrangeville, NY 845-223-5101
Appleson Press
  Syosset, NY. 800-888-2775
Artistic Packaging Concepts
  Massapequa Pk, NY 516-797-4020
ASCENT Technics Corporation
  Brick, NJ 800-774-7077
ATK
  Chicago, IL 800-522-3582
ATL-East Tag & Label Inc
  West Chester, PA. 866-381-8744
Atlas Labels
  Montreal, QC 514-852-7000
Atlas Packaging Inc
  Opa Locka, FL 800-662-0630
Atlas Tag & Label Inc
  Neenah, WI. 800-558-6418
Auburn Label & Tag Company
  New York, NY 212-971-0338
Avery Dennison Corporation
  Glendale, CA 626-304-2000
Axon Styrotech
  Raleigh, NC 800-598-8601
Baltimore Tape Products Inc
  Sykesville, MD 410-795-0063
Barkley Filing Supplies
  Hattiesburg, MS 800-647-3070
Baur Tape & Label Co
  San Antonio, TX 877-738-3222
Bedford Industries
  Worthington, MN 800-533-5314
Bertek Systems Inc
  Fairfax, VT 800-367-0210
Born Printing Company
  Baltimore, MD 410-646-7768
Burford Corp
  Maysville, OK. 877-287-3673
Bynoe Printers
  New York, NY 212-662-5041
C-P Flexible Packaging
  Newtown, PA 800-448-8183
Carlton Industries
  La Grange, TX 800-231-5988
CCL Label Inc
  Cold Spring, KY 800-422-6633
Cellotape, Inc.
  Newark, CA 510-651-5551
Central Decal
  Burr Ridge, IL. 800-869-7654
Central Package & Display
  Minneapolis, MN 763-425-7444
Christman Screenprint Inc
  Springfield, MI 800-962-9330
Church Offset Printing Inc
  Albert Lea, MN. 800-345-2116
CL&D Graphics
  Oconomowoc, WI 800-777-1114

Coast Label Co
  Fountain Valley, CA 800-995-0483
Colonial Transparent Products Company
  Hicksville, NY 516-822-4430
Comm-Pak
  Opelika, AL. 334-749-6201
Computerized Machinery Systs
  Maple Grove, MN. 763-493-0099
Computype Inc
  St Paul, MN. 800-328-0852
Conimar Corp
  Ocala, FL. 800-874-9735
Consolidated Label Company
  Longwood, FL 800-475-2235
Continental Identification
  Sparta, MI 800-247-2499
Covergent Label Technology
  Tampa, FL 800-252-6111
Creative Label Designers
  Lees Summit, MO. 816-537-8757
Crown Label Company
  Santa Ana, CA 800-422-3590
Cucamonga Sign Shop LLC
  Rancho Cucamonga, CA 909-945-5888
Cummins Label Co
  Kalamazoo, MI 800-280-7589
Curtis 1000
  Duluth, GA 877-287-8715
Curzon Promotional Graphics
  Omaha, NE 800-769-7446
Custom Card & Label Corporation
  Lincoln Park, NJ 973-492-0022
Custom Stamp Company
  Anza, CA. 323-292-0753
D A C Labels & Graphic
  Dallas, TX. 800-483-1700
Dana Labels
  Beaverton, OR 800-255-1492
Darson Corp
  Detroit, MI 800-783-7781
Data Visible Corporation
  Charlottesville, VA 800-368-3494
Daydots
  Fort Worth, TX 800-321-3687
Daymark Safety Systems
  Bowling Green, OH 419-353-2458
De Leone Corp
  Redmond, OR 541-504-8311
Deadline Press
  Kennesaw, GA 770-419-2232
Decal Techniques Inc
  West Babylon, NY 800-735-3322
Deco Labels & Tags
  Toronto, ON 888-496-9029
Decorated Products Company
  Westfield, MA. 413-568-0944
Design Label Manufacturing
  East Lyme, CT. 800-666-1575
Design-Mark Industries
  Wareham, MA. 800-451-3275
Donnick Label Systems
  Jacksonville, FL 800-334-7849
Dot-It Food Safety Products
  Arlington, TX 800-642-3687
Double Envelope Corp
  Roanoke, VA 540-362-3311
Dow Industries
  Wilmington, MA. 800-776-1201
Drs Designs
  Bethel, CT. 888-792-3740
Eaton Manufacturing Co
  Houston, TX 800-328-6610
Ebel Tape & Label
  Cincinnati, OH 513-471-1067
Economy Label Sales Company
  Daytona Beach, FL. 386-253-4741
Emedco
  Williamsville, NY 877-765-8386
Engraving Services Co.
  Woodville South, SA
EPI World Graphics
  Midlothian, IL. 708-389-7500
Epsen Hillmer Graphics Co
  Omaha, NE 800-228-9940
ERS International
  Norwalk, CT 800-377-4685
Esselte Meto
  Morris Plains, NJ 800-645-3290
Farnell Packaging
  Dartmouth, NS 800-565-9378
Fast Bags
  Fort Worth, TX 800-321-3687

Federal Label Systems
  Elmhurst, NY 800-238-0015
Fernqvist Labeling Solutions
  Mountain View, CA 800-426-8215
Ferro Corporation
  Mayfield Heights, OH 216-875-5600
FFR Merchandising Inc
  Twinsburg, OH 800-422-2547
Fleming Packaging Corporation
  Peoria, IL. 309-676-7657
FLEXcon Company
  Spencer, MA 508-885-8200
Flexible Tape & Label Co
  Memphis, TN 901-522-1410
Flexo Graphics
  Amarillo, TX. 866-533-5396
Forest Manufacturing Co
  Twinsburg, OH 330-425-3805
Fort Dearborn Company
  Elk Grove, IL 847-357-9500
Fotel
  Lombard, IL 800-834-4920
Foxon Co
  Providence, RI 800-556-6943
France Personalized Signs
  Cleveland, OH 216-241-2198
Frost Manufacturing Corp
  Worcester, MA 800-462-0216
Garvey Products
  Cincinnati, OH 513-771-8710
Garvey Products
  West Chester, OH 800-543-1908
Gbs
  North Canton, OH. 800-552-2427
GCA
  Huntington Beach, CA 714-379-4911
General Press Corp
  Natrona Heights, PA 724-224-3500
General Tape & Supply
  Wixom, MI 800-490-3633
General Trade Mark Labelcraft
  Staten Island, NY 718-448-9800
Gintzler Graphics Inc
  Buffalo, NY. 716-631-9700
Globe Ticket & Label Company
  Warminster, PA 800-523-5968
GM Nameplate
  Seattle, WA 800-366-7668
Grand Rapids Label
  Grand Rapids, MI 616-776-2778
Grand Valley Labels
  Grand Rapids, MI
Graphic Impressions of Illinois
  River Grove, IL. 708-453-1100
Graphic Packaging Corporation
  Golden, CO 800-677-2886
Graphic Technology
  New Century, KS 800-767-9920
Graphics Unlimited
  San Diego, CA 858-453-4031
Green Bay Packaging Inc.
  Green Bay, WI. 920-433-5111
Greenbush Tape & Label Inc
  Albany, NY 518-465-2389
Gulf Arizona Packaging
  Humble, TX 800-364-3887
H B Fuller Co
  St. Paul, MN 651-236-5900
Hal Mather & Sons
  Woodstock, IL. 800-338-4007
Halpak Plastics
  Deer Park, NY. 800-442-5725
Hano Business Forms
  Wilbraham, MA 413-781-7800
Harris & Company
  Salem, OH. 330-332-4127
Herche Warehouse
  Denver, CO 303-371-8186
Holo-Source Corporation
  Livonia, MI 888-995-7799
Home Plastics Inc
  Des Moines, IA 515-265-2562
Hub Labels Inc
  Hagerstown, MD 800-433-4532
Hurst Labeling Systems
  Chatsworth, CA 800-969-1705
Imprinting Systems Specialty
  Charlotte, NC 800-497-1403
Industrial Nameplate Inc
  Warminster, PA 800-878-6263
Inland Label & Marketing Svc
  La Crosse, WI 800-657-4413

Innovative Folding Carton Company
South Plainfield, NJ 908-757-0205
Innovative Packaging Solution
Martin, MI. 616-656-2100
Inovar Packaging Group
Arlington, TX 800-285-2235
Intermec Technologies Corporation
Everett, WA. .425-348-2600
Interstate Packaging
White Bluff, TN 800-251-1072
Itac Label & Tag Corp
Brooklyn, NY 718-625-2148
J M Packaging Co
Warren, MI. .586-771-7800
J.V. Reed & Company
Louisville, KY 877-258-7333
John Henry Packaging
Penngrove, CA 800-327-5997
KAPCO
Kent, OH. 800-843-5368
Kemex Meat Brands
Washington, DC 301-277-2444
Kennedy Group
Willoughby, OH 440-951-7660
KHS Co
West Simsbury, CT 860-658-9454
KWIK Lok Corp
Yakima, WA .800-688-5945
L & N Label Co
Clearwater, FL 800-944-5401
L G I Intl Inc
Portland, OR 800-345-0534
Label Art
Tucker, GA 800-652-1072
Label House
Fullerton, CA 800-499-5858
Label Products Inc
Burnsville, MN 877-370-0688
Label Specialties Inc
Placentia, CA 800-635-2386
Label Systems
Bridgeport, CT 203-333-5503
Label Systems
Newmarket, ON 905-836-7844
Label Systems & Solutions
Bohemia, NY 800-811-2560
Label Systems Inc
Addison, TX .800-220-9552
Label Technology Inc
Merced, CA. .800-388-1990
Labelmart
Maple Grove, MN. 888-577-0141
Labelmax Inc
Laredo, TX 956-722-6493
Labelprint America
Newburyport, MA. 978-463-4004
Labelquest Inc
Elmhurst, IL .800-999-5301
Labels By Pulizzi Inc
Williamsport, PA. 570-326-1244
Lacroix Packaging
St-Placide, Quebec, QC 450-258-2262
Lawrence Schiff Silk Mills
New York, NY 800-272-4433
Leathertone
Findlay, OH. .419-429-0188
Lewis Label Products Corporation
Fort Worth, TX 800-772-7728
Lewisburg Printing
Lewisburg, TN 800-559-1526
Liberty Label
Liberty, MO. .800-783-5285
License Ad Plate Co
Cleveland, OH 216-265-4200
Lifeline Technology Inc
Morris Plains, NJ 973-984-0525
Lion Labels Inc
South Easton, MA. 800-875-5300
Lone Peak Labeling Systems
West Valley City, UT 800-658-8599
Long Island Stamp Corporation
Flushing, NY. 800-547-8267
Lord Label Group
Charlotte, NC 800-341-5225
Los Angeles Label Company
Commerce, CA 800-606-5223
Louis Roesch Company
Foster City, CA 415-621-4700
LPI Imports
Chicago, IL 877-389-6563
LTI Printing Inc
Sturgis, MI 269-651-7574

Lustrecal
Lodi, CA 800-234-6264
Mail-Well Label
Sparks, NV 775-359-1703
Mail-Well Label
Baltimore, MD 800-637-4879
Mar-Boro Printing & Advertising Specialties
Brooklyn, NY 718-336-4051
Mark-It Rubber Stamp & Label Company
Stamford, CT. 203-348-3204
Marklite Line
Bellwood, IL .708-668-4900
Master Tape & Label Printers
Chicago, IL 800-621-5801
Mateer Burt
Exton, PA 800-345-1308
Mc Court Label Co
Lewis Run, PA 800-458-2390
Merchants Publishing Company
Kalamazoo, MI 269-345-1175
Meyer Label Company
Fort Myers, FL 239-489-0342
Meyers Printing Co
Minneapolis, MN 763-533-9730
Miami Systems Corporation
Blue Ash, OH 800-543-4540
Mid South Graphics
Nashville, TN 615-331-4210
Middleton Printing & Label Co
Grand Rapids, MI 800-952-0076
Mister Label, Inc
Bluffton, SC .800-732-0439
Modern Stamp Company
Baltimore, MD 800-727-3029
Morris Industries
Forestville, MD 301-568-5005
Moss Inc
Elk Grove Vlg, IL 800-341-1557
Multi-Color Corp
Green Bay, WI. 800-236-8208
Nameplate
St Paul, MN. .651-228-1522
Nashua Corporation
Nashua, NH. .603-661-2004
Nashua Corporation
Park Ridge, IL. 800-323-4265
National Emblem
Carson, CA 800-877-5325
National Label Co
Lafayette Hill, PA 610-825-3250
National Marking Products Inc
Henrico, VA .800-482-1553
National Printing Converters
Encino, CA 818-906-7936
National Tape Corporation
New Orleans, LA 800-535-8846
Nationwide Pennant & Flag Mfg
San Antonio, TX. 800-383-3524
Neal Walters Poster Corporation
Bentonville, AR 501-273-2489
New England Label
Barre, VT 800-368-3932
New Era Label Corporation
Belleville, NJ 973-759-2444
North American Packaging Corp
New York, NY 800-499-3521
Northern Berkshire Tourist
North Adams, MA 413-663-9204
Nosco
Waukegan, IL 847-360-4806
Old English Printing & Label Company
Delray Beach, FL 561-997-9990
Ozark Tape & Label Co
Springfield, MO 417-831-1444
Pace Labels Inc
Williamston, SC 800-789-1592
Package Containers Inc
Canby, OR. 800-266-5806
Package Service Company of Colorado
Northmoor, MO 800-748-7799
Package Systems Corporation
Danielson, CT. 800-522-3548
Packaging Materials Co
El Paso, TX. .800-325-4195
Packaging Solutions
Los Altos Hills, CA 650-917-1022
Paco Label Systems Inc
Tyler, TX. 800-346-4185
Pakmark
Chesterfield, MO 800-423-1379
Pamco Label Co Inc
Des Plaines, IL 847-803-2200

Panther Industries Inc
Highlands Ranch, CO 800-530-6018
Paper Product Specialties
Waukesha, WI. 262-549-1730
Parisian Novelty Company
Homewood, IL 773-847-1212
Paxar
Paterson, NJ .973-684-6564
Pharmaceutic Litho & Label Co.
Simi Valley, CA. 800-882-9743
Phenix Label Co
Olathe, KS. 800-274-3649
Philipp Lithographing Co
Grafton, WI. .800-657-0871
Photo Graphics Co
Grandview, MO. 816-761-3333
Pierrepont Visual Graphics Inc
Rochester, NY. 585-235-5620
Pioneer Labels Inc
Denver, CO 877-744-1606
Pittsfield Weaving Company
Pittsfield, NH 603-435-8301
Plasti Print Inc
Burlingame, CA 650-652-4950
Precision Printing & Packaging
Clarksville, TN 800-500-4526
Premier Southern Ticket Co
Cincinnati, OH 800-331-2283
Prestige Label Company
Burgaw, NC .800-969-4449
Prestolabels.Com
Tipp City, OH 800-201-7120
Primera Technology
Plymouth, MN. 800-797-2772
Print & Peel
New York, NY 800-451-0807
Print-O-Tape Inc
Mundelein, IL 800-346-6311
Printsource Group
Wakefield, RI 401-789-9339
Pro-Ad-Co Inc
Portland, OR 800-287-5885
Promo Edge
Wall Township, NJ 732-938-4242
Qsx Labels
Everett, MA. .800-225-3496
Quali-Tech Tape & Label
Denver, CO
R R Donnelley
Chicago, IL 800-742-4455
Racine County Court Cmmssnr
Racine, WI 800-242-4202
Randall Printing
Brockton, MA 508-588-3830
Raypress Corp
Hoover, AL 800-423-3731
Recco International
West Columbia, SC 800-334-3008
Regency Label Corporation
Wood Ridge, NJ 201-342-2288
Reid Graphics Inc
Andover, MA 800-887-7461
Reidler Decal Corporation
Saint Clair, PA. 800-628-7770
Rhode Island Label Work Inc
West Warwick, RI 401-828-6400
Rice Packaging Inc
Ellington, CT 800-367-6725
Richmond Printed Tape & Label
Hatfield, PA. .800-522-3525
Robinson Tape & Label
Branford, CT. 800-433-7102
Rose City Label
Portland, OR 800-547-9920
Rothchild Printing Company
Flushing, NY. 800-238-0015
Royal Label Co
Dorchester, MA. 617-825-6050
RSI ID Technologies
St. Paul, MN .888-364-3577
S Walter Packaging Corp
Philadelphia, PA 888-429-5673
Samuels Products Inc
Blue Ash, OH 800-543-7155
San Miguel Label Manufacturing
Ciales, PR 787-871-3120
Sancoa International
Lumberton, NJ 609-953-5050
Seal-Tite Bag Company
Philadelphia, PA 717-917-1949
Seneca Tape & Label
Cleveland, OH 800-251-0514

Sesame Label System
New York, NY 800-551-3020
Seton Indentification Products
Branford, CT. 800-571-2596
SFBC, LLC dba Seaboard Folding Box
Fitchburg, MA 800-225-6313
Shippers Supply
Saskatoon, SK. 800-661-5639
Shippers Supply, Labelgraphic
Calgary, AB. 800-661-5639
Signature Packaging
West Orange, NJ 800-376-2299
Smurfit Stone Container
St Louis, MO. 314-679-2300
Smyth Co
Bedford, VA 800-950-7011
Smyth Co LLC
St Paul, MN. 800-473-3464
Sohn Manufacturing
Elkhart Lake, WI. 920-876-3361
Source for Packaging
New York, NY 800-223-2527
Southern Atlantic Label Co
Chesapeake, VA 800-456-5999
Southern Imperial Inc
Rockford, IL 800-747-4665
Steven Label Corp
Santa Fe Springs, CA 800-752-4968
Stoffel Seals Corp
Tallapoosa, GA 800-422-8247
Storad Tape Company
Marion, OH. 740-382-6440
Stratix Corp
Peachtree Cor, GA 800-883-8300
Stricker & Co
La Plata, MD. 301-934-8346
Stripper Bags
Henderson, NV 800-354-2247
Superior Products Company
Saint Paul, MN 800-328-9800
Swan Label & Tag Co
Coraopolis, PA 412-264-9000
Syracuse Label Co
Liverpool, NY. 315-422-1037
System Graphics Inc
St Louis, MO. 800-221-7858
T & T Industries Inc
Fort Mohave, AZ 800-437-6246
TAC-PAD
Irvine, CA 800-947-1609
Tape & Label Converters
Santa Fe Springs, CA 888-285-2462
Tape & Label Engineering
St Petersburg, FL 800-237-8955
Tarason Packaging, LLC.
Conover, NC. 828-464-4743
TeleTech Label Company
Fort Collins, CO 888-403-8253
Tharo Systems Inc
Brunswick, OH. 800-878-6833
Three P
Salt Lake City, UT 801-486-7407
Thunderbird Label Corportion
Fairfield, NJ 973-575-6677
Timely Signs Inc
Elmont, NY 800-457-4467
Timemed Labeling Systems
Valencia, CA 818-897-1111
Toledo Ticket Co
Toledo, OH. 800-533-6620
Trident
Brookfield, CT 203-740-9333
Trumbull Nameplates
New Smyrna Beach, FL 386-423-1105
Twin City Pricing & Label
Minneapolis, MN 800-328-5076
Typecraft Wood & Jones
Pasadena, CA 626-795-8093
United Ad Label
Downers Grove, IL 800-423-4643
United Label Corp
Newark, NJ 800-252-0917
United Seal & Tag Corporation
Port Charlotte, FL 800-211-9552
Universal Tag Inc
Dudley, MA. 800-332-8247
University Products
Holyoke, MA 800-628-9281
US Label Corporation
Greensboro, NC 336-332-7000
Vacumet Corp
Wayne, NJ. .973-628-1067

Varitronic Systems
Brooklyn Park, MN. 763-536-6400
Vetter Vineyards Winery
Westfield, NY 716-326-3100
Viking Identification Product
Hopkins, MN 952-935-5245
Viking Label Inc
Nisswa, MN 800-247-6573
Vomela/Harbor Graphics
St Paul, MN. 800-645-1012
Wallace Computer Services
Chicago, IL .888-925-8324
Walle Corp
New Orleans, LA 800-942-6761
Wishbone Utensil Tableware Line
Wheat Ridge, CO 866-266-5928
Worthen Industries Inc
Nashua, NH. 603-888-5443
WS Packaging Group Inc
Dallas, TX. .214-330-7770
WS Packaging Group Inc
Algoma, WI. 800-236-3424
WS Packaging Group Inc
Rochester, NY 800-836-8186
WS Packaging Group Inc
Oak Creek, WI 800-837-3838
WS Packaging Group Inc
Green Bay, WI. 877-977-5177
WS Packaging Group Inc
Neenah, WI. 888-532-3334
Wt Nickell Co
Batavia, OH. 888-899-1991
Yerecic Label Co
New Kensington, PA. 724-334-3300
Yeuell Name Plate & Label
Woburn, MA 781-933-2984

Pressure Sensitive

AC Label Company
Provo, UT 801-642-3500
Accuform Manufacturing, Inc.
Vacaville, CA 800-233-3352
Ad Mart Identity Group
Danville, KY. 800-354-2102
Adhesive Products Inc
Vernon, CA .800-669-5516
Adstick Custom Labels Inc
Denver, CO. 800-255-7314
Advanced Labelworx
Anderson, SC 865-966-8711
Advanced Labelworx Inc
Oak Ridge, TN 864-224-2122
ALLIED Graphics Inc
St Michael, MN. 800-490-9931
AM Graphics
Edina, MN. .612-341-2020
American Forms & Labels
Boise, ID 800-388-3554
American Labelmark Co
Chicago, IL .800-621-5808
Andy Printed Products
Lagrangeville, NY. 845-223-5101
Appleson Press
Syosset, NY. 800-888-2775
ATL-East Tag & Label Inc
West Chester, PA. 866-381-8744
Atlas Tag & Label Inc
Neenah, WI. 800-558-6418
Auburn Label & Tag Company
New York, NY 212-971-0338
Avery Dennison Corporation
Glendale, CA 626-304-2000
Baltimore Tape Products Inc
Sykesville, MD 410-795-0063
Barkley Filing Supplies
Hattiesburg, MS 800-647-3070
Bertek Systems Inc
Fairfax, VT .800-367-0210
CCL Label Inc
Cold Spring, KY 800-422-6633
Cellotape, Inc.
Newark, CA 510-651-5551
Central Decal
Burr Ridge, IL. 800-869-7654
CL&D Graphics
Oconomowoc, WI. 800-777-1114
Comm-Pak
Opelika, AL. 334-749-6201
Computerized Machinery Systs
Maple Grove, MN. 763-493-0099

Consolidated Label Company
Longwood, FL 800-475-2235
Creative Label Designers
Lees Summit, MO. 816-537-8757
Cucamonga Sign Shop LLC
Rancho Cucamonga, CA 909-945-5888
Cummins Label Co
Kalamazoo, MI. 800-280-7589
Custom Card & Label Corporation
Lincoln Park, NJ 973-492-0022
Custom Stamp Company
Anza, CA. 323-292-0753
D A C Labels & Graphic
Dallas, TX. .800-483-1700
Dana Labels
Beaverton, OR 800-255-1492
De Leone Corp
Redmond, OR 541-504-8311
Deadline Press
Kennesaw, GA 770-419-2232
Deco Labels & Tags
Toronto, ON 888-496-9029
Design Label Manufacturing
East Lyme, CT 800-666-1575
Double Envelope Corp
Roanoke, VA 540-362-3311
Dow Industries
Wilmington, MA 800-776-1201
Drs Designs
Bethel, CT. .888-792-3740
Eagles Printing & Label
Eau Claire, WI 715-835-6631
Ebel Tape & Label
Cincinnati, OH 513-471-1067
Economy Label Sales Company
Daytona Beach, FL 386-253-4741
Elmark Packaging Inc
West Chester, PA. 800-670-9688
Emedco
Williamsville, NY. 877-765-8386
Epsen Hillmer Graphics Co
Omaha, NE 800-228-9940
Farnell Packaging
Dartmouth, NS 800-565-9378
Federal Label Systems
Elmhurst, NY 800-238-0015
FLEXcon Company
Spencer, MA 508-885-8200
Flexible Tape & Label Co
Memphis, TN 901-522-1410
Flexo Graphics
Amarillo, TX. 866-533-5396
Forest Manufacturing Co
Twinsburg, OH 330-425-3805
Foxon Co
Providence, RI 800-556-6943
Garvey Products
Cincinnati, OH 513-771-8710
Garvey Products
West Chester, OH 800-543-1908
Gbs
North Canton, OH. 800-552-2427
General Tape & Supply
Wixom, MI 800-490-3633
General Trade Mark Labelcraft
Staten Island, NY 718-448-9800
Gintzler Graphics Inc
Buffalo, NY. 716-631-9700
Globe Ticket & Label Company
Warminster, PA. 800-523-5968
Grand Rapids Label
Grand Rapids, MI. 616-776-2778
Grand Valley Labels
Grand Rapids, MI
Graphic Impressions of Illinois
River Grove, IL. 708-453-1100
Graphic Technology
New Century, KS 800-767-9920
Greenbush Tape & Label Inc
Albany, NY. 518-465-2389
Greenfield Packaging
White Plains, NY 914-993-0233
Gulf Arizona Packaging
Humble, TX 800-364-3887
Herche Warehouse
Denver, CO 303-371-8186
Houston Label
Pasadena, TX 800-477-6995
Hub Labels Inc
Hagerstown, MD. 800-433-4532
Hurst Labeling Systems
Chatsworth, CA 800-969-1705

Imprinting Systems Specialty
Charlotte, NC 800-497-1403
Innovative Folding Carton Company
South Plainfield, NJ 908-757-0205
Innovative Packaging Solution
Martin, MI 616-656-2100
Interstate Packaging
White Bluff, TN 800-251-1072
Itac Label & Tag Corp
Brooklyn, NY 718-625-2148
KAPCO
Kent, OH.......................800-843-5368
KHS Co
West Simsbury, CT 860-658-9454
L & N Label Co
Clearwater, FL 800-944-5401
L G I Intl Inc
Portland, OR 800-345-0534
Label House
Fullerton, CA 800-499-5858
Label Products Inc
Burnsville, MN 877-370-0688
Label Specialties Inc
Placentia, CA 800-635-2386
Label Systems
Bridgeport, CT 203-333-5503
Label Systems
Newmarket, ON 905-836-7844
Label Systems & Solutions
Bohemia, NY 800-811-2560
Label Systems Inc
Addison, TX 800-220-9552
Label Technology Inc
Merced, CA.....................800-388-1990
Label-Aire Inc
Fullerton, CA 714-441-0700
Labelmart
Maple Grove, MN...............888-577-0141
Labelmax Inc
Laredo, TX 956-722-6493
Labelprint America
Newburyport, MA...............978-463-4004
Labels By Pulizzi Inc
Williamsport, PA................570-326-1244
Lewis Label Products Corporation
Fort Worth, TX 800-772-7728
Liberty Label
Liberty, MO....................800-783-5285
License Ad Plate Co
Cleveland, OH 216-265-4200
Lion Labels Inc
South Easton, MA...............800-875-5300
Long Island Stamp Corporation
Flushing, NY....................800-547-8267
M & M Display
Philadelphia, PA.................800-874-7171
Marklite Line
Bellwood, IL....................708-668-4900
Master Tape & Label Printers
Chicago, IL.....................800-621-5801
Mc Court Label Co
Lewis Run, PA..................800-458-2390
Metspeed Labels
Levittown, PA...................888-886-0638
Meyer Label Company
Fort Myers, FL 239-489-0342
Meyers Printing Co
Minneapolis, MN 763-533-9730
Mid South Graphics
Nashville, TN 615-331-4210
Middleton Printing & Label Co
Grand Rapids, MI...............800-952-0076
Mister Label, Inc
Bluffton, SC 800-732-0439
Morris Industries
Forestville, MD..................301-568-5005
Moss Inc
Elk Grove Vlg, IL...............800-341-1557
MPI Label Systems
Sebring, OH 800-837-2134
Multi-Color Corp
Green Bay, WI..................800-236-8208
Nashua Corporation
Nashua, NH....................603-661-2004
Nashua Corporation
Park Ridge, IL..................800-323-4265
National Printing Converters
Encino, CA.....................818-906-7936
National Tape Corporation
New Orleans, LA 800-535-8846
Neal Walters Poster Corporation
Bentonville, AR 501-273-2489

New England Label
Barre, VT 800-368-3932
New Era Label Corporation
Belleville, NJ 973-759-2444
NJM Packaging
Lebanon, NH....................800-432-2990
Ozark Tape & Label Co
Springfield, MO 417-831-1444
Pace Labels Inc
Williamston, SC 800-789-1592
Package Service Company of Colorado
Northmoor, MO 800-748-7799
Package Systems Corporation
Danielson, CT...................800-522-3548
Packaging Materials Co
El Paso, TX.....................800-325-4195
Pakmark
Chesterfield, MO 800-423-1379
Pamco Label Co Inc
Des Plaines, IL..................847-803-2200
Paper Product Specialties
Waukesha, WI..................262-549-1730
Pierrepont Visual Graphics Inc
Rochester, NY..................585-235-5620
Plasti Print Inc
Burlingame, CA.................650-652-4950
Premier Southern Ticket Co
Cincinnati, OH 800-331-2283
Print & Peel
New York, NY 800-451-0807
Print-O-Tape Inc
Mundelein, IL...................800-346-6311
Printsource Group
Wakefield, RI 401-789-9339
Promo Edge
Wall Township, NJ 732-938-4242
Quali-Tech Tape & Label
Denver, CO
R R Donnelley
Chicago, IL.....................800-742-4455
Racine County Court Cmmssnr
Racine, WI 800-242-4202
Raypress Corp
Hoover, AL.....................800-423-3731
Regency Label Corporation
Wood Ridge, NJ.................201-342-2288
Rhode Island Label Work Inc
West Warwick, RI 401-828-6400
Rice Packaging Inc
Ellington, CT 800-367-6725
Richmond Printed Tape & Label
Hatfield, PA.....................800-522-3525
Robinson Tape & Label
Branford, CT....................800-433-7102
Rose City Label
Portland, OR 800-547-9920
Royal Label Co
Dorchester, MA..................617-825-6050
Samuels Products Inc
Blue Ash, OH 800-543-7155
Sancoa International
Lumberton, NJ 609-953-5050
Seneca Tape & Label
Cleveland, OH 800-251-0514
Seton Indentification Products
Branford, CT....................800-571-2596
Smyth Co
Bedford, VA 800-950-7011
Smyth Co LLC
St Paul, MN....................800-473-3464
Source for Packaging
New York, NY 800-223-2527
Southern Atlantic Label Co
Chesapeake, VA 800-456-5999
Steven Label Corp
Santa Fe Springs, CA 800-752-4968
Stoffel Seals Corp
Tallapoosa, GA 800-422-8247
Storad Tape Company
Marion, OH.....................740-382-6440
Stratix Corp
Peachtree Cor, GA 800-883-8300
Stripper Bags
Henderson, NV 800-354-2247
Swan Label & Tag Co
Coraopolis, PA 412-264-9000
Syracuse Label Co
Liverpool, NY 315-422-1037
System Graphics Inc
St Louis, MO....................800-221-7858
TAC-PAD
Irvine, CA......................800-947-1609

Tape & Label Converters
Santa Fe Springs, CA 888-285-2462
Tape & Label Engineering
St Petersburg, FL 800-237-8955
Tarason Packaging, LLC.
Conover, NC....................828-464-4743
TeleTech Label Company
Fort Collins, CO 888-403-8253
Tharo Systems Inc
Brunswick, OH 800-878-6833
Three P
Salt Lake City, UT 801-486-7407
Thunderbird Label Corportion
Fairfield, NJ 973-575-6677
Timemed Labeling Systems
Valencia, CA....................818-897-1111
Trident
Brookfield, CT 203-740-9333
Trumbull Nameplates
New Smyrna Beach, FL 386-423-1105
United Ad Label
Downers Grove, IL 800-423-4643
United Seal & Tag Corporation
Port Charlotte, FL 800-211-9552
Universal Tag Inc
Dudley, MA.....................800-332-8247
University Products
Holyoke, MA 800-628-9281
Viking Identification Product
Hopkins, MN 952-935-5245
Vomela/Harbor Graphics
St Paul, MN.....................800-645-1012
Wallace Computer Services
Chicago, IL.....................888-925-8324
Wishbone Utensil Tableware Line
Wheat Ridge, CO 866-266-5928
WS Packaging Group Inc
Dallas, TX......................214-330-7770
WS Packaging Group Inc
Algoma, WI.....................800-236-3424
WS Packaging Group Inc
Rochester, NY 800-836-8186
WS Packaging Group Inc
Oak Creek, WI..................800-837-3838
Wt Nickell Co
Batavia, OH.....................888-899-1991
Yerecic Label Co
New Kensington, PA.............724-334-3300

Private Label

Adrienne's Gourmet Foods
Santa Barbara, CA 800-937-7010
Alewel's Country Meats
Warrensburg, MO 800-353-8553
Baldwin Richardson Foods
Oakbrook Terrace, IL 866-644-2732
Bunzl Distribution USA
St. Louis, MO...................888-997-5959
Century Foods Intl LLC
Sparta, WI 800-269-1901
Old Mansion Inc
Petersburg, VA 800-476-1877
Treofan America LLC
Winston Salem, NC..............800-424-6273

Linings

Box, Carton, Case & Crate

Atlantic Foam & Packaging Company
Sanford, FL.....................407-328-9444
Chalmur Bag Company, LLC
Philadelphia, PA.................800-349-2247
Conwed Global Netting Sltns
Roanoke, VA....................800-368-3610
Grayling Industries
Alpharetta, GA 800-635-1551
Greenfield Packaging
White Plains, NY 914-993-0233
Gulf Arizona Packaging
Humble, TX 800-364-3887
Herche Warehouse
Denver, CO 303-371-8186
IB Concepts
Elizabeth, NJ 888-671-0800
J A Heilferty & Co
Teaneck, NJ.....................201-836-5060
Midco Plastics
Enterprise, KS 800-235-2729
Naltex
Austin, TX......................800-531-5112

Paper Pak Industries
La Verne, CA 909-392-1750
Powertex Inc
Rouses Point, NY 800-769-3783
Target Industries
North Salt Lake, UT 866-617-2253
Weyerhaeuser Co
Seattle, WA 800-525-5440

Can, Drum & Barrel

Carson Manufacturing Company
Petaluma, CA 800-423-2380
CDF Corp
Plymouth, MA. 800-443-1920
Chalmur Bag Company, LLC
Philadelphia, PA 800-349-2247
Enerfab Inc.
Cincinnati, OH 513-641-0500
Fabohio Inc
Uhrichsville, OH. 740-922-4233
Fortifiber Building Systs Grp
Fernley, NV. 800-773-4777
Greenfield Packaging
White Plains, NY 914-993-0233
Gulf Arizona Packaging
Humble, TX 800-364-3887
Hedwin Division
Baltimore, MD 800-638-1012
Herche Warehouse
Denver, CO. 303-371-8186
Home Plastics Inc
Des Moines, IA. 515-265-2562
Indiana Vac Form Inc
Warsaw, IN 574-269-1725
Inteplast Bags & Films Corporation
Delta, BC. 604-946-5431
J A Heilferty & Co
Teaneck, NJ. 201-836-5060
Mello Smello LLC
Minneapolis, MN 888-574-2964
Midco Plastics
Enterprise, KS 800-235-2729
Nosaj Disposables
Paterson, NJ 800-631-3809
Packaging Dynamics International
Caldwell, OH 740-732-5665
Powertex Inc
Rouses Point, NY 800-769-3783
Pres-On Products
Addison, IL. 800-323-7467
Scholle IPN
Merced, CA. 209-384-3100
Target Industries
North Salt Lake, UT 866-617-2253
Tri-Seal
Blauvelt, NY 845-353-3300

Markers, Pens & Pencils

Amsterdam Printing & Litho Inc
Amsterdam, NY 800-203-9917
Dri Mark Products
Port Washington, NY 800-645-9118
Elliot Lee
Cedarhurst, NY 516-569-9595
Garland Writing Instruments
Coventry, RI 401-828-9582
Gold Bond Inc
Hixson, TN 423-842-5844
Gotham Pen Co Inc
Bronx, NY. 800-334-7970
Hub Pen Company
Quincy, MA. 617-471-9900
Industries of the Blind
Greensboro, NC 336-274-1591
Listo Pencil Corp
Alameda, CA. 800-547-8648
Markwell Manufacturing Company
Norwood, MA. 800-666-1123
Micropoint
Mountain View, CA 650-969-3097
National Pen Co
San Diego, CA 858-675-3000
Pelican Products Inc
Bronx, NY. 800-552-8820
Visual Planning Corp
Champlain, NY. 800-361-1192
Volk Corp
Farmington Hills, MI 800-521-6799

Packaging

Aseptic

Century Foods Intl LLC
Sparta, WI 800-269-1901
Elopak Americas
Wixom, MI 248-486-4600
Green Spot Packaging
Claremont, CA 800-456-3210
Innovative Food Solutions LLC
Columbus, OH 800-884-3314
JCS Controls, Inc.
Rochester, NY. 585-227-5910
Power Packaging Inc
Rosendale, WI. 920-872-2181
Pressure Pack
Williamsburg, VA 757-220-3693
Professional Marketing Group
Seattle, WA 800-227-3769
Scholle IPN
Merced, CA. 209-384-3100

Blister

Accurate Paper Box Co Inc
Knoxville, TN 865-690-0311
Ace Technical Plastics Inc
East Hartford, CT 860-278-2444
Artistic Packaging Concepts
Massapequa Pk, NY 516-797-4020
California Vibratory Feeders
Anaheim, CA 800-354-0972
Dynamic Pak LLC
Syracuse, NY 315-474-8593
Gulf Arizona Packaging
Humble, TX 800-364-3887
Gulf Packaging Company
Safety Harbor, FL 800-749-3466
Gulf Systems
Brownsville, TX 800-217-4853
Gulf Systems
Humble, TX 800-364-3887
Gulf Systems
Arlington, TX 817-261-1915
H.J. Jones & Sons
London, ON 800-667-0476
Hannan Products
Corona, CA 800-954-4266
Harpak-ULMA Packaging LLC
Ball Ground, GA 770-345-5300
Herche Warehouse
Denver, CO. 303-371-8186
In-Touch Products
North Salt Lake, UT 801-298-4466
Jay Packaging Group Inc
Warwick, RI 401-244-1300
Key Packaging Co
Sarasota, FL 941-355-2728
Kord Products Inc.
Brantford, ON. 800-452-9070
Leal True Form Corporation
Freeport, NY 516-379-2008
Maro Paper Products Company
Bellwood, IL. 708-649-9982
Packaging & Processing Equipment
Ayr, ON. 519-622-6666
Pinn Pack Packaging LLC
Oxnard, CA 805-385-4100
Plastech Corp
Atlanta, GA. 404-355-9682
Power Packaging Inc
Rosendale, WI. 920-872-2181
Professional Marketing Group
Seattle, WA 800-227-3769
Rohrer Corp.
Wadsworth, OH. 800-243-6640
Rose City Printing & Packaging
Vancouver, WA 800-704-8693
Scott Packaging Corporation
Philadelphia, PA 215-925-5595
Sheboygan Paper Box Co
Sheboygan, WI. 800-458-8373
TEQ
Huntley, IL 800-874-7113
Thermex Thermatron
Louisville, KY 502-493-1299
Woodstock Plastics Co Inc
Marengo, IL 815-568-5281

Flexible Materials

A-A1 Aaction Bag
Denver, CO. 800-783-1224
Ace Technical Plastics Inc
East Hartford, CT 860-278-2444
Achilles USA
Everett, WA. 425-353-7000
Aladdin Transparent Packaging
Hauppauge, NY 631-273-4747
Alcon Packaging
Weston, ON. 416-742-8910
All Foils Inc
Strongsville, OH 800-521-0054
All Sorts Premium Packaging
Buffalo, NY. 888-565-9727
Alufoil Products Co Inc
Hauppauge, NY 631-231-4141
Amcor
Oshkosh, WI. 800-544-4672
American Printpak Inc
Sussex, WI 800-441-8003
American Renolit Corp LA
Commerce, CA 323-721-2720
Anchor Packaging
Ballwin, MO 800-467-3900
Arbee Transparent Inc
Elk Grove Vlg, IL 800-642-2247
Archer Daniels Midland Company
Chicago, IL 312-634-8100
Atlantis Plastics Linear Film
Tulsa, OK 800-324-9727
B.A.G. Corporation
Richardson, TX. 800-331-9200
Bagcraft Papercon
Chicago, IL 800-621-8468
Beayl Weiner/Pak
Pacific Palisades, CA 310-454-1354
Blako Industries
Dunbridge, OH 419-833-4491
Brentwood Plastics In
St Louis, MO 314-968-1135
Bryce Corp
Memphis, TN 800-238-7277
Burrows Paper Corp
Little Falls, NY 800-272-7122
Can Creations
Pembroke Pines, FL 954-581-3312
Carlisle Plastics
Minneapolis, MN 952-884-1309
Catty Inc
Harvard, IL 815-943-2288
Cello Bag Company
Bowling Green, KY 800-347-0338
Central Bag Co
Leavenworth, KS 913-250-0325
Champion Plastics
Clifton, NJ. 800-526-1230
Cincinnati Convertors Inc
Cincinnati, OH 513-731-6600
Circle Packaging Machinery Inc
De Pere, WI. 920-983-3420
CL&D Graphics
Oconomowoc, WI. 800-777-1114
Clear Lam Packaging
Elk Grove Village, IL 847-439-8570
Cleveland Plastic Films
Elyria, OH. 800-832-6799
Cleveland Specialties Co
Loveland, OH 513-677-9787
Conn Container Corp
North Haven, CT. 203-248-0241
Continental Packaging Corporation
Elgin, IL 847-289-6400
Continental Products
Mexico, MO 800-325-0216
CoolBrands International
Ronkonkoma, NY. 631-737-9700
Coveris
Excelsior Springs, MO
Crystal-Flex Packaging Corporation
Rockville Centre, NY 888-246-7325
Danafilms Inc
Westborough, MA. 508-366-8884
Design Packaging Company
Glencoe, IL 800-321-7659
Dynamic Packaging
Minneapolis, MN 800-878-9380
Ensinger Inc
Washington, PA. 800-243-3221
Excelsior Transparent Bag Manufacturing
Yonkers, NY 914-968-1300

Fabricon Products Inc
River Rouge, MI 313-841-8200
Farnell Packaging
Dartmouth, NS 800-565-9378
Film X
Dayville, CT 800-628-6128
Filmco Inc
Aurora, OH 800-545-8457
Flexicon
Cary, IL 847-639-3530
Flexo Transparent Inc
Buffalo, NY 877-993-5396
Foam Pack Industries
Springfield, NJ 973-376-3700
Food Pak Corp
San Mateo, CA 650-341-6559
Formflex
Bloomingdale, IN 800-255-7659
Gemini Plastic Films Corporation
Garfield, NJ 800-789-4732
General Films Inc
Covington, OH 888-436-3456
Gibraltar Packaging Group Inc
Hastings, NE .402-463-1366
Glopak
St Leonard, QC 800-361-6994
Gulf Arizona Packaging
Humble, TX 800-364-3887
Gulf Systems
Brownsville, TX 800-217-4853
Gulf Systems
Humble, TX 800-364-3887
Gulf Systems
Arlington, TX .817-261-1915
H&H Lumber Company
Amarillo, TX 806-335-1813
Hedwin Division
Baltimore, MD 800-638-1012
Herche Warehouse
Denver, CO 303-371-8186
Home Plastics Inc
Des Moines, IA 515-265-2562
Hudson Poly Bag Inc
Hudson, MA 800-229-7566
Huntsman Packaging Corporation
Birmingham, Bi. 205-328-4720
In-Line Corporation
Hopkins, MN .952-938-0046
Interstate Packaging
White Bluff, TN 800-251-1072
J A Heilferty & Co
Teaneck, NJ 201-836-5060
Jif-Pak Manufacturing
Vista, CA 800-777-6613
JW Aluminum
Mt Holly, SC 800-568-1100
Kapak Corporation
Minneapolis, MN 952-541-0730
KAPCO
Kent, OH 800-843-5368
Karolina Polymers
Hickory, NC 828-328-2247
KHL Engineered Packaging
Montebello, CA 323-721-5300
Klockner Pentaplast of America
Gordonsville, VA 540-832-3600
KM International Corp
Kenton, TN 731-749-8700
Label Technology Inc
Merced, CA. 800-388-1990
Longhorn Packaging Inc
San Antonio, TX. 800-433-7974
LPS Industries
Moonachie, NJ 800-275-4577
Luetzow Industries
South Milwaukee, WI 800-558-6055
M&R Flexible Packaging
Springboro, OH. 800-543-3380
MAC Tac LLC
Stow, OH. 866-262-2822
Maco Bag Corp
Newark, NY 315-226-1000
Mark Products Company
Denville, NJ 973-983-8818
Marshall Plastic Film Inc
Martin, MI. 269-672-5511
Masternet, Ltd
Mississauga, ON 800-216-2536
Microplas Industries
Dunwoody, GA. 800-952-4528
Milprint
Oshkosh, WI. .920-303-8600

Mimi et Cie
Seattle, WA 206-545-1850
Mohawk Northern Plastics
Auburn, WA 800-426-1100
Mohawk Western Plastics Inc
La Verne, CA 909-593-7547
Morris Industries
Forestville, MD 301-568-5005
Multi-Plastics Extrusions Inc
Hazleton, PA 570-455-2021
Multibulk Systems International
Wendell, NC 919-366-2100
National Poly Bag Manufacturing Corporation
Brooklyn, NY .718-629-9800
Net Pack Systems
Oakland, ME. .207-465-4531
Northeast Packaging Materials
Monsey, NY 845-426-2900
Now Plastics Inc
East Longmeadow, MA 413-525-1010
OMNOVA Solutions
Fairlawn, OH. .330-869-4200
Outlook Packaging
Neenah, WI. 920-722-1666
Packaging Enterprises
Rockledge, PA. 800-453-6213
Packaging Products Corp
Mission, KS 913-262-3033
Paco Manufacturing
Clarksville, IN. 812-283-7963
Pak-Sak Industries I
Sparta, MI 800-748-0431
Pater & Associates
Cincinnati, OH
PDMP
Leesburg, VA .703-777-8400
Phoenix Closures Inc
Naperville, IL .630-544-3475
Plascal Corp
Farmingdale, NY 800-899-7527
Plastic Craft Products Corp
West Nyack, NY 800-627-3010
Plastic Packaging Technologies
Kansas City, KS 800-468-0029
Plastic Suppliers Inc
Columbus, OH 800-722-5577
Poly Shapes Corporation
Elyria, OH 800-605-9359
Polyplastics
Austin, TX. 800-753-7659
Portco Corporation
Vancouver, WA 800-426-1794
Power Packaging Inc
Rosendale, WI. 920-872-2181
Print & Peel
New York, NY 800-451-0807
Printpack Inc.
Atlanta, GA. 404-460-7000
Professional Marketing Group
Seattle, WA 800-227-3769
Quality Films
Three Rivers, MI. 269-679-5263
Quantum Performance Films
Streamwood, IL. 800-323-6963
Ray C. Sprosty Bag Company
Wooster, OH .330-264-8559
Rico Packaging Company
Chicago, IL 773-523-9190
Rjr Technologies
Oakland, CA. .510-638-5901
Rohrer Corp.
Wadsworth, OH. 800-243-6640
Roll-O-Sheets Canada
Barrie, ON. 888-767-3456
Rollprint Packaging Prods Inc
Addison, IL. 800-276-7629
Roplast Industries Inc
Oroville, CA. .800-767-5278
Rowland Technologies
Wallingford, CT 203-269-9500
Rutan Poly Industries Inc
Mahwah, NJ 800-872-1474
Schwab Paper Products Co
Romeoville, IL 800-837-7225
Seal-Tite Bag Company
Philadelphia, PA 717-917-1949
Sealed Air Corp
Charlotte, NC .800-391-5645
Seiler Plastics
St Louis, MO. .888-673-4537
Seville Flexpack Corp
Oak Creek, WI 414-761-2751

Shields Bag & Printing Co
Yakima, WA 800-541-8630
Shields Products Inc
West Pittston, PA. 570-655-4596
Ship Rite Packaging
Bergenfield, NJ 800-721-7447
Shippers Supply
Saskatoon, SK .800-661-5639
Shippers Supply, Labelgraphic
Calgary, AB. 800-661-5639
Southern Film Extruders
High Point, NC 800-334-6101
Spartech Poly Com
Clayton, MI. 888-721-4242
Specialty Films & Associates
Hebron, KY. 800-984-3346
Star Poly Bag Inc
Brooklyn, NY .718-384-7034
Sterling Novelty Products
Northbrook, IL 847-291-0070
Stock America Inc
Grafton, WI. 262-375-4100
Sungjae Corporation
Irvine, CA 949-757-1727
Sunland Manufacturing Company
Minneapolis, MN 800-790-1905
Terphane Inc
Bloomfield, NY 800-724-3456
Trans Flex Packagers Inc
Unionville, CT 860-673-2531
Trico Converting Inc
Fullerton, CA .714-563-0701
Trident Plastics
Ivyland, PA 800-222-2318
Trinity Packaging
Cheektowaga, NY 800-778-3111
Trio Packaging Corp
Ronkonkoma, NY 800-331-0492
Tyco Plastics
Lakeville, MN .800-328-4080
UCB Inc
Smyrna, GA 770-970-8338
Ultrapak
Dunkirk, NY 800-228-6030
Unifoil Corp
Fairfield, NJ 973-244-9990
Union Industries
Providence, RI 800-556-6454
Uniplast Films
Palmer, MA. 800-343-1295
United Flexible
Westbury, NY .516-222-2150
Vacumet Corp
Wayne, NJ 973-628-1067
Vacumet Corporation
Austell, GA. 800-776-0865
Vacuum Depositing Inc
Louisville, KY .502-969-4227
VIFAN Canada
Lanoraie, QC. .800-557-0192
Viskase Co Inc
Darien, IL 800-323-8562
Western Plastics
Portland, TN 615-325-7331
Western Plastics
Calhoun, GA. .800-752-4106
Winpak Technologies
Toronto, ON 416-421-1700
Witt Plastics
Greenville, OH 800-227-9181
Wraps
East Orange, NJ 973-673-7873
Zimmer Custom-Made Packaging
Indianapolis, IN 317-263-3436

Food Protective

A-A1 Aaction Bag
Denver, CO 800-783-1224
Accurate Flannel Bag Company
Paterson, NJ 800-234-9200
Alkar Rapid Pak
Lodi, WI 608-592-3211
Allflex Packaging Products
Ambler, PA 800-448-2467
American Excelsior Co
Arlington, TX .800-777-7645
Ample Industries
Franklin, OH .888-818-9700
Anchor Packaging
Ballwin, MO .800-467-3900

Arbee Transparent Inc
Elk Grove Vlg, IL 800-642-2247
Bag Masters
St Petersburg, FL 800-330-2247
BEI
Goleta, GA 800-350-2727
Bryce Corp
Memphis, TN 800-238-7277
Burrows Paper Corp
Little Falls, NY 800-272-7122
Catty Inc
Harvard, IL 815-943-2288
Ccw Products
Arvada, CO 303-427-9663
Central Coated Products Inc
Alliance, OH 330-821-9830
Central Fine Pack Inc
Fort Wayne, IN 260-432-3027
Cincinnati Convertors Inc
Cincinnati, OH 513-731-6600
Colbert Packaging Corp
Lake Forest, IL 847-367-5990
Collectors Gallery
St Charles, IL 800-346-3063
Crystal-Flex Packaging Corporation
Rockville Centre, NY 888-246-7325
Curwood Specialty Films
Oshkosh, WI 800-544-4672
Custom Foam Molders
Foristell, MO. 636-441-2307
Design Plastics Inc
Omaha, NE 800-491-0786
Elmo Rietschle - A Gardner Denver Product
Qunicy, IL 217-222-5400
Ensinger Inc
Washington, PA. 800-243-3221
Fabri-Kal Corp
Kalamazoo, MI 800-888-5054
Flexo Transparent Inc
Buffalo, NY. 877-993-5396
Foam Concepts Inc
Uxbridge, MA. 508-278-7255
Free Flow Packaging Corporation
Redwood City, CA 800-888-3725
Glopak
St Leonard, QC 800-361-6994
Greenfield Paper Box Co
Greenfield, MA. 413-773-9414
Gulf Arizona Packaging
Humble, TX 800-364-3887
Gulf Systems
Brownsville, TX 800-217-4853
Gulf Systems
Humble, TX 800-364-3887
Gulf Systems
Arlington, TX 817-261-1915
Handy Wacks Corp
Sparta, MI 800-445-4434
Harpak-ULMA Packaging LLC
Ball Ground, GA. 770-345-5300
Herche Warehouse
Denver, CO 303-371-8186
Hubco Inc
Hutchinson, KS. 800-563-1867
Indian Valley Industries
Johnson City, NY 800-659-5111
Jewel Case Corp
Cranston, RI 800-441-4447
K & L Intl
Ontario, CA. 888-598-5588
Kalco Enterprises
New York, NY 800-396-6600
King Plastic Corp
North Port, FL. 800-780-5502
Lenkay Sani Products Corporation
Brooklyn, NY. 718-927-9260
Letica Corp
Rochester Hills, MI. 800-538-4221
Maco Bag Corp
Newark, NY 315-226-1000
Mullnix Packages Inc
Fort Wayne, IN 260-747-3149
Multisorb Technologies Inc
Buffalo, NY. 800-445-9890
Norpak Corp
Newark, NJ 800-631-6970
ORBIS
Oconomowoc, WI. 800-890-7292
Osgood Industries
Oldsmar, FL 813-855-7337
Packaging Progressions
Collegeville, PA 610-489-9096

Packing Material Company
Southfield, MI. 248-489-7000
Pacquet Oneida
Charlotte, NC 800-631-8388
Pater & Associates
Cincinnati, OH
Patty Paper Inc
Plymouth, IN. 800-782-1703
Plastilite Corporation
Omaha, NE 800-228-9506
Polytainers
Toronto, ON 800-268-2424
Professional Marketing Group
Seattle, WA 800-227-3769
Promarks
Ontario, CA. 909-923-3888
Roll-O-Sheets Canada
Barrie, ON. 888-767-3456
Roplast Industries Inc
Oroville, CA 800-767-5278
Rownd & Son
Dillon, SC 803-774-8264
Rutan Poly Industries Inc
Mahwah, NJ 800-872-1474
Saeplast Canada
St John, NB 800-567-3966
Salinas Valley Wax Paper Co
Salinas, CA. 831-424-2747
Schroeder Machine
San Marcos, CA 760-591-9733
Schwab Paper Products Co
Romeoville, IL 800-837-7225
Schwarz Supply Source
Morton Grove, IL 800-323-4903
Shields Products Inc
West Pittston, PA. 570-655-4596
SIG Combibloc USA, Inc.
Chester, PA 610-546-4200
Southern Film Extruders
High Point, NC 800-334-6101
Sun Plastics
Clearwater, MN. 800-862-1673
T D Sawvel Co
Maple Plain, MN. 877-488-1816
TEMP-TECH Company
Springfield, MA. 800-343-5579
Tenneco Packaging
Westmont, IL. 630-850-7034
Trans World Services
Melrose, MA. 800-882-2105
Trevor Owen Limited
Scarborough, ON 866-487-2224
Tri-State Plastics
Henderson, KY 270-826-8361
Triune Enterprises
Gardena, CA. 310-719-1600
Union Industries
Providence, RI 800-556-6454
Unipac Shipping
Jamaica, NY 800-586-2711
United Desiccants
Reno, NE. 888-659-1377
Urnex Brands Inc
Elmsford, NY 800-222-2826
Valley Packaging Supply Co
Green Bay, WI. 920-336-9012
Viscofan USA Inc
Montgomery, AL. 800-521-3577
Vista Internatlonal Packaging
Kenosha, WI. 800-558-4058
West-Pak
Dallas, TX. 214-337-8984
Wisconsin Converting Inc
Green Bay, WI. 800-544-1935

Plastic

A-A1 Aaction Bag
Denver, CO 800-783-1224
Ace Technical Plastics Inc
East Hartford, CT 860-278-2444
Acme Bag Co
Chula Vista, CA 800-275-2263
AEP Industries
South Hackensack, NJ 800-999-2374
AEP Industries Inc
Mankato, MN 800-999-2374
Alcoa - Massena Operations
Massena, NY
Alkar Rapid Pak
Lodi, WI 608-592-3211

Anchor Packaging
Ballwin, MO. 800-467-3900
Arbee Transparent Inc
Elk Grove Vlg, IL 800-642-2247
Atlantis Plastics Linear Film
Tulsa, OK 800-324-9727
Automated Packaging Systems
Streetsboro, OH 800-527-0733
Beayl Weiner/Pak
Pacific Palisades, CA 310-454-1354
Blako Industries
Dunbridge, OH 419-833-4491
Brechteen
Chesterfield, MI 586-949-2240
Brentwood Plastics In
St Louis, MO. 314-968-1135
Buckhorn Inc
Milford, OH 800-543-4454
Bunzl Distribution USA
St. Louis, MO. 888-997-5959
C-P Flexible Packaging
Newtown, PA 800-448-8183
Ccw Products
Arvada, CO. 303-427-9663
CDF Corp
Plymouth, MA. 800-443-1920
Central Fine Pack Inc
Fort Wayne, IN 260-432-3027
Century Foods Intl LLC
Sparta, WI. 800-269-1901
Champion Plastics
Clifton, NJ. 800-526-1230
Chem-Tainer Industries Inc
West Babylon, NY 800-275-2436
Chester Plastics
Chester, NS. 902-275-3522
Cincinnati Convertors Inc
Cincinnati, OH 513-731-6600
Clawson Container Company
Clarkston, MI. 800-325-8700
Clorox Company
Oakland, CA 510-271-7000
Conn Container Corp
North Haven, CT. 203-248-0241
Consolidated Container Co LLC
Atlanta, GA. 888-831-2184
Contour Packaging
Philadelphia, PA 215-457-1600
Covestro LLC
Sheffield, MA 800-628-5084
Crayex Corp
Piqua, OH. 800-837-1747
Creative Packaging
Hayward, CA 510-785-6500
CTK Plastics
Moose Jaw, SK 800-667-8847
Custom Foam Molders
Foristell, MO. 636-441-2307
Danafilms Inc
Westborough, MA. 508-366-8884
Davis Core & Pa
Cave Spring, GA. 800-235-7483
Decker Plastics
Council Bluffs, IA. 866-869-6293
Denice & Filice LLC
Hollister, CA. 831-637-7492
Design Packaging Company
Glencoe, IL 800-321-7659
Design Plastics Inc
Omaha, NE 800-491-0786
Dub Harris Corporation
Pomona, CA 909-596-6300
Eaton Manufacturing Co
Houston, TX 800-328-6610
Fabri-Kal Corp
Kalamazoo, MI. 800-888-5054
Farnell Packaging
Dartmouth, NS 800-565-9378
Film X
Dayville, CT 800-628-6128
Flexo Transparent Inc
Buffalo, NY. 877-993-5396
Fredman Bag Co
Milwaukee, WI 800-945-5686
Fremont Die Cut Products
Fremont, OH. 800-223-3177
Fulton-Denver Co
Denver, CO 800-521-1414
Gary Plastic Packaging Corporation
Bronx, NY. 800-221-8151
Gary Plastic Packaging Corporation
Bronx, NY. 800-227-4279

Gateway Plastics Inc
Mequon, WI 262-242-2020
Genpak LLC
Lakeville, MN 800-328-4556
Gibraltar Packaging Group Inc
Hastings, NE 402-463-1366
Goex Corporation
Janesville, WI 608-754-3303
Golden West Packaging Concept
Lake Forest, CA 949-855-9646
Goodwrappers Inc
Halethorpe, MD 800-638-1127
Greif Inc
Delaware, OH 740-549-6000
Gulf Arizona Packaging
Humble, TX 800-364-3887
Gulf Coast Plastics
Tampa, FL 800-277-7491
Gulf Systems
Brownsville, TX 800-217-4853
Gulf Systems
Humble, TX 800-364-3887
Gulf Systems
Arlington, TX 817-261-1915
H&H Lumber Company
Amarillo, TX 806-335-1813
Handy Wacks Corp
Sparta, MI 800-445-4434
Herche Warehouse
Denver, CO 303-371-8186
Hinkle Manufacturing
Perrysburg, OH 419-666-5367
Hood Packaging
Burlington, ON 877-462-6627
Hubco Inc
Hutchinson, KS 800-563-1867
Hudson Poly Bag Inc
Hudson, MA 800-229-7566
Huntsman Packaging
South Deerfield, MA 413-665-2145
Indianapolis Container Company
Indianapolis, IN 800-760-3318
Inline Plastic Corp
McDonough, GA 678-466-3467
Inline Plastic Corp
Shelton, CT 800-826-5567
Interstate Packaging
White Bluff, TN 800-251-1072
IPL Plastics
Edmundston, NB. 800-739-9595
IVEX Packaging Corporation
Longueuil, QC 450-651-8887
J A Heilferty & Co
Teaneck, NJ 201-836-5060
Jomar Plastics Industry
Nanty Glo, PA 800-681-4039
K & L Intl
Ontario, CA 888-598-5588
Kimball Companies
East Longmeadow, MA 413-525-1881
Klockner Pentaplast of America
Gordonsville, VA 540-832-3600
KM International Corp
Kenton, TN 731-749-8700
Kord Products Inc.
Brantford, ON 800-452-9070
L&H Wood Manufacturing Company
Farmington, MI. 248-474-9000
Letica Corp
Rochester Hills, MI. 800-538-4221
Luetzow Industries
South Milwaukee, WI. 800-558-6055
M S Plastics & Packaging Inc
Butler, NJ 800-593-1802
Maco Bag Corp
Newark, NY 315-226-1000
Marpac Industries
Philmont, NY 888-462-7722
Marshall Plastic Film Inc
Martin, MI. 269-672-5511
Mason Transparent Package Company
Armonk, NY 718-792-6000
Masternet, Ltd
Mississauga, ON 800-216-2536
Maypak Inc
Wayne, NJ 973-696-0780
Melville Plastics
Haw River, NC 336-578-5800
Microplas Industries
Dunwoody, GA 800-952-4528
Midco Plastics
Enterprise, KS 800-235-2729

Mohawk Western Plastics Inc
La Verne, CA 909-593-7547
Mullnix Packages Inc
Fort Wayne, IN 260-747-3149
National Poly Bag Manufacturing Corporation
Brooklyn, NY 718-629-9800
Net Pack Systems
Oakland, ME. 207-465-4531
Nolon Industries
Mantua, OH. 330-274-2283
North American Packaging Corp
New York, NY 800-499-3521
Noteworthy Company
Amsterdam, NY 800-696-7849
ORBIS RPM
Madison, WI. 608-852-8840
Packaging Materials Inc
Cambridge, OH. 800-565-8550
Packing Material Company
Southfield, MI 248-489-7000
Papelera Puertorriquena
Utuado, PR 787-894-2098
Par-Pak
Houston, TX 713-686-6700
Pater & Associates
Cincinnati, OH
Pelco Packaging Corporation
Stirling, NJ 908-647-3500
Pilant Corp
Bloomington, IN 800-366-3525
Pioneer Plastics Inc
Dixon, KY 800-951-1551
Plascal Corp
Farmingdale, NY 800-899-7527
Plastic Suppliers Inc
Columbus, OH 800-722-5577
Plastipak Packaging
Plymouth, MI 734-354-3510
Poly Plastic Products Inc
Delano, PA 570-467-3000
Portco Corporation
Vancouver, WA 800-426-1794
Power Packaging Inc
Rosendale, WI 920-872-2181
Prairie Packaging Inc
Mooresville, NC 704-660-6600
Pretium Packaging
Hazle Twp, PA 570-459-1800
Printpack Inc.
Atlanta, GA. 404-460-7000
Professional Marketing Group
Seattle, WA 800-227-3769
Quality Transparent Bag Co
Bay City, MI 989-893-3561
Quantum Performance Films
Streamwood, IL 800-323-6963
Quintex Corp
Nampa, ID. 208-467-1113
Reliance Product
Winnipeg, MB. 800-665-0258
Ropak
Oak Brook, IL 800-527-2267
Roplast Industries Inc
Oroville, CA 800-767-5278
Ross & Wallace Inc
Hammond, LA 800-854-2300
Rowland Technologies
Wallingford, CT 203-269-9500
Rutan Poly Industries Inc
Mahwah, NJ 800-872-1474
Saeplast Canada
St John, NB 800-567-3966
Samuel Strapping Systems Inc
Woodridge, IL 800-323-4424
San Miguel Label Manufacturing
Ciales, PR 787-871-3120
Sealed Air Corp
Charlotte, NC 800-391-5645
Shamrock Plastics
Mt Vernon, OH 800-765-1611
Shields Bag & Printing Co
Yakima, WA 800-541-8630
Shields Products Inc
West Pittston, PA. 570-655-4596
Ship Rite Packaging
Bergenfield, NJ 800-721-7447
Shippers Supply
Saskatoon, SK 800-661-5639
Snapware
Fullerton, CA 800-334-3062
Spartec Plastics
Conneaut, OH 800-325-5176

Star Container Company
Phoenix, AZ 480-281-4200
Steel City Corporation
Youngstown, OH. 800-321-0350
Stock America Inc
Grafton, WI 262-375-4100
Stripper Bags
Henderson, NV 800-354-2247
Sun Plastics
Clearwater, MN. 800-862-1673
Sungjae Corporation
Irvine, CA 949-757-1727
T&S Blow Molding
Scarborough, ON 416-752-8330
Target Industries
North Salt Lake, UT 866-617-2253
Templock Corporation
Santa Barbara, CA 800-777-1715
Terphane Inc
Bloomfield, NY 800-724-3456
Tolas Health Care Packaging
Feasterville Trevose, PA 215-322-7900
Trans Flex Packagers Inc
Unionville, CT 860-673-2531
Trident Plastics
Ivyland, PA 800-222-2318
Trio Products
Elyria, OH 440-323-5457
Ultrapak
Dunkirk, NY 800-228-6030
Union Industries
Providence, RI 800-556-6454
Uniplast Films
Palmer, MA 800-343-1295
United Flexible
Westbury, NY 516-222-2150
United Seal & Tag Corporation
Port Charlotte, FL. 800-211-9552
Vacumet Corporation
Austell, GA 800-776-0865
VIFAN Canada
Lanoraie, QC 800-557-0192
Virginia Plastics Co
Roanoke, VA 800-777-8541
Western Plastics
Calhoun, GA 800-752-4106
Witt Plastics
Greenville, OH 800-227-9181
Woodstock Plastics Co Inc
Marengo, IL 815-568-5281
Zimmer Custom-Made Packaging
Indianapolis, IN 317-263-3436

Private Label

Agropur MSI, LLC
La Crosse, WI 800-359-2345
Bridgewell Resources LLC
Clackamas, OR 800-481-3557
C-P Flexible Packaging
Newtown, PA 800-448-8183
Cache Creek Foods LLC
Woodland, CA. 530-662-1764
Calhoun Bend Mill
Libuse, LA 800-519-6455
Century Foods Intl LLC
Sparta, WI 800-269-1901
Couprie Fenton
Augusta, GA 706-650-7017
Penguin Natural Food Inc
Vernon, CA 323-727-7980
Professional Image
Tulsa, OK 800-722-8550
The Rubin Family of Wines
Sebastopol, CA 707-887-8130
TRFG Inc
Springfield, OH 937-322-2040
Tri-Connect
Oak Park, IL 708-660-8190
Truitt Bros Inc
Salem, OR. 800-547-8712
Vetter Vineyards Winery
Westfield, NY 716-326-3100

Shrink

Adpro
Solon, OH 440-542-1111
AEP Industries Inc
Mankato, MN 800-999-2374
Audion Automation
Carrollton, TX. 972-389-0777

Campbell Wrapper Corporation
De Pere, WI. .920-983-7100
Can Creations
Pembroke Pines, FL 800-272-0235
Can Creations
Pembroke Pines, FL 954-581-3312
Central Bag Co
Leavenworth, KS 913-250-0325
Chem Pack Inc
Cincinnati, OH 800-421-2700
CiMa-Pak Corp.
Dorval, QC 877-631-2462
Collectors Gallery
St Charles, IL 800-346-3063
Coveris
Excelsior Springs, MO
Crayex Corp
Piqua, OH 800-837-1747
ESS Technologies
Blacksburg, VA 540-961-5716
Flexo Transparent Inc
Buffalo, NY 877-993-5396
Gulf Arizona Packaging
Humble, TX 800-364-3887
Gulf Systems
Humble, TX 800-364-3887
Gulf Systems
Arlington, TX 817-261-1915
Halpak Plastics
Deer Park, NY 800-442-5725
Herche Warehouse
Denver, CO 303-371-8186
Ilapak Inc
Newtown, PA 215-579-2900
M S Plastics & Packaging Inc
Butler, NJ 800-593-1802
Mark Products Company
Denville, NJ 973-983-8818
Marshall Plastic Film Inc
Martin, MI 269-672-5511
Mimi et Cie
Seattle, WA 206-545-1850
Oaklee International
Ronkonkoma, NY 800-333-7250
Pack Line Corporation
Racine, WI 800-248-6868
Packaging Materials Inc
Cambridge, OH. 800-565-8550
Power Packaging Inc
Rosendale, WI. 920-872-2181
Preferred Packaging Systems
San Dimas, CA 800-378-4777
Quantum Performance Films
Streamwood, IL. 800-323-6963
Seal-O-Matic Corp
Jacksonville, OR 800-631-2072
Shippers Supply
Saskatoon, SK 800-661-5639
Shrinkfast Marketing
Newport, NH. 800-867-4746
Sungjae Corporation
Irvine, CA. 949-757-1727
Templock Corporation
Santa Barbara, CA 800-777-1715
Tri-Sterling
Altamonte Spgs, FL 407-260-0330
Ultrapak
Dunkirk, NY. 800-228-6030
United Flexible
Westbury, NY 516-222-2150
Willow Specialties
Batavia, NY. 800-724-7300

Packaging & Containerizing Products

A La Carte
Chicago, IL 800-722-2370
A-A1 Aaction Bag
Denver, CO 800-783-1224
A-Z Factory Supply
Schiller Park, IL 800-323-4511
Aabbitt Adhesives
Chicago, IL 800-222-2488
Abbott Industries
Paterson, NJ
Abond Plastic Corporation
Lachine, QC 800-886-7947
AC Label Company
Provo, UT 801-642-3500
Accurate Flannel Bag Company
Paterson, NJ 800-234-9200
Accurate Paper Box Co Inc
Knoxville, TN 865-690-0311

Ace Manufacturing & Parts Co
Sullivan, MO. 800-325-6138
Ace Technical Plastics Inc
East Hartford, CT 860-278-2444
Acme Bag Co
Chula Vista, CA 800-275-2263
Aco Container Systems
Pickering, ON 800-542-9942
Adcapitol
Monroe, NC. 800-868-7111
Adhesive Applications
Easthampton, MA 800-356-3572
Adpro
Solon, OH 440-542-1111
Adstick Custom Labels Inc
Denver, CO 800-255-7314
Advanced Poly-Packaging Inc
Akron, OH. 800-754-4403
Advantage Puck Technologies
Corry, PA. 814-664-4810
AEP Industries Inc
Mankato, MN 800-999-2374
Aero Tec Laboratories/ATL
Ramsey, NJ 800-526-5330
AJM Packaging Corporation
Bloomfield Hills, MI 248-901-0040
Aladdin Transparent Packaging
Hauppauge, NY 631-273-4747
Alcan Packaging
Baie D'Urfe, QC 514-457-4555
Alcoa - Massena Operations
Massena, NY
Alger Creations
Miami, FL. 954-454-3272
All American Container
Miami, FL. 305-887-0797
All American Poly
Piscataway, NJ 800-526-3551
All Foils Inc
Strongsville, OH 800-521-0054
All Sorts Premium Packaging
Buffalo, NY. 888-565-9727
Allflex Packaging Products
Ambler, PA 800-448-2467
Alpack
Centerville, NA 774-994-8086
Alpha Packaging
St Louis, MO. 800-421-4772
Althor Products
Bethel, CT. 800-688-2693
Altira Inc
Miami, FL. 305-687-8074
Amcel
Watertown, MA. 800-225-7992
Amco Metals Indl
City Of Industry, CA. 626-855-2550
American Advertising & Shop Cap Company
Old Tappan, NJ 800-442-8837
American Bag & Burlap Company
Chelsea, MA 617-884-7600
American Box Corporation
Lisbon, OH 330-424-8055
American Containers Inc
Plymouth, IN. 574-936-4068
American Labelmark Co
Chicago, IL 800-621-5808
American Pallet Inc
Oakdale, CA 209-847-6122
American Production Co Inc
Redwood City, CA 650-368-5334
Americraft Carton Inc
St Paul, MN. 651-227-6655
Americraft Carton Inc
Prairie Village, KS 913-387-3700
Ameriglobe LLC
Lafayette, LA 337-234-3211
Ample Industries
Franklin, OH 888-818-9700
Anchor Packaging
Ballwin, MO. 800-467-3900
Appleson Press
Syosset, NY. 800-888-2775
Archer Daniels Midland Company
Chicago, IL 312-634-8100
Arena Products
Rochester, NY 844-762-0127
Arkansas Glass Container Corp
Jonesboro, AR. 800-527-4527
Armbrust Paper Tubes Inc
Chicago, IL. 773-586-3232
Art Poly Bag Co
Brooklyn, NY 800-278-7659

Artistic Carton
Auburn, IN 800-735-7225
Artistic Carton Co
Elgin, IL 847-741-0247
Artistic Packaging Concepts
Massapequa Pk, NY 516-797-4020
Atlantis Plastics Linear Film
Tulsa, OK 800-324-9727
Atlas Case Inc
Denver, CO 888-325-2199
Atlas Packaging Inc
Opa Locka, FL 800-662-0630
Atlas Tag & Label Inc
Neenah, WI 800-558-6418
Aurora Design Associates, Inc.
Salt Lake City, UT. 801-588-0111
Auto Pallets-Boxes
Lathrup Village, MI 800-875-2699
Automatic Electronic Machines Company
Brooklyn, NY 718-384-3211
Automatic Liquid Packaging Solutions
Arlington Heights, IL 847-264-5349
Automatic Specialties Inc
Marlborough, MA. 800-445-2370
Avantage Group Inc
Redondo Beach, CA 310-379-3933
Avon Tape
Chestnut Hill, MA 508-584-8273
B F Nelson Cartons Inc
Savage, MN. 800-328-2380
B.A.G. Corporation
Richardson, TX. 800-331-9200
Babcock Co
Bath, NY 607-776-3341
Bag Company
Kennesaw, GA 800-533-1931
Bag Masters
St Petersburg, FL 800-330-2247
Bagcraft Papercon
Chicago, IL 800-621-8468
Bakers Choice Products
Beacon Falls, CT. 203-720-1000
Bal/Foster Glass Container Company
Port Allegany, PA 814-642-2521
Ball Corp
Broomfield, CO 303-469-3131
Ball Foster Glass
Fairfield, CA. 707-863-4061
Ball Foster Glass Container Company
Sapulpa, OK 918-224-1440
Bancroft Bag Inc
West Monroe, LA 318-387-2550
Barbour Threads
Anniston, AL 256-237-9461
Bardes Plastics Inc
Milwaukee, WI 800-558-5161
Baskets Extraordinaires
Westbury, NY 800-666-1685
Bayard Kurth Company
Detroit, MI 313-891-0800
Beayl Weiner/Pak
Pacific Palisades, CA 310-454-1354
BEI
Goleta, GA 800-350-2727
Bell Container
Newark, NJ 973-344-6997
Bell Packaging Corporation
Marion, IN. 800-382-0153
Belleview
Brookline, NH. 603-878-1583
Bennett's Auto Inc
Neenah, WI. 800-215-5464
Berenz Packaging Corp
Menomonee Falls, WI. 262-251-8787
Bergen Barrel & Drum Company
Kearny, NJ. 201-998-3500
Berlin Fruit Box Company
Berlin Heights, OH 800-877-7721
Berlon Industries
Hustisford, WI 800-899-3580
Berry Global
Evansville, IN 800-343-1295
Bertels Can Company
Belcamp, MD 410-272-0090
Blackhawk Molding Co Inc
Addison, IL. 630-458-2100
Blako Industries
Dunbridge, OH. 419-833-4491
Boelter Industries
Winona, MN 507-452-2315
Boise Cascade Corporation
Burley, ID 208-678-3531

Bonar Plastics
West Chicago, IL 800-295-3725
Bonar Plastics
Ridgefield, WA 800-972-5252
Boxes.com
Livingston, NJ 201-646-9050
Brechteen
Chesterfield, MI 586-949-2240
Brewer-Cantelmo Inc
New York, NY 212-244-4600
Brooks Barrel Company
Baltimore, MD 800-398-2766
Brown International Corp LLC
Winter Haven, FL 863-299-2111
Brown Paper Goods Co
Waukegan, IL 847-688-1450
Bryce Corp
Memphis, TN 800-238-7277
Buckeye Group
South Charleston, OH 937-462-8361
Buckhorn Canada
Brampton, ON 800-461-7579
Buckhorn Inc
Milford, OH 800-543-4454
Bulk Lift International, LLC
Carpentersville, IL 800-879-2247
Bulk Pack
Monroe, LA 800-498-4215
Bulk Sak Intl Inc
Malvern, AR 501-332-8745
Burgess Mfg. - Oklahoma
Guthrie, OK 800-804-1913
Burrows Paper Corp
Little Falls, NY 800-272-7122
C & L Wood Products Inc
Hartselle, AL 800-483-2035
C R Daniels Inc
Ellicott City, MD 800-933-2638
C-P Flexible Packaging
Newtown, PA 800-448-8183
Calzone Case Co
Bridgeport, CT 800-243-5152
Cambro Manufacturing Co
Huntington Beach, CA 800-833-3003
Can Corp Of America Inc
Blandon, PA 610-926-3044
Can Creations
Pembroke Pines, FL 954-581-3312
Cannon Equipment Company
Cannon Falls, MN 800-825-8501
Cantwell-Cleary Co Inc
Elkridge, MD 301-773-9800
Cantwell-Cleary Co Inc
Richmond, VA 804-329-9800
Capital City Container Corporation
Buda, TX 512-312-1222
Capitol Carton Company
Sacramento, CA 916-388-7848
Capitol City Container Corp
Indianapolis, IN 800-233-5145
Caraustar Industries, Inc.
Archdale, NC 800-223-1373
Caravan Packaging Inc
Brookpark, OH 440-243-4100
Cardinal Container Corp
Indianapolis, IN 800-899-2715
Cardinal Packaging
Evansville, IN 800-343-1295
Cardinal Packaging Prod LLC
Crystal Lake, IL 866-216-4942
Caristrap International
Laval, QC 800-361-9466
Carlisle Food Svc Products Inc
Oklahoma City, OK 800-654-8210
Carlisle Plastics
Minneapolis, MN 952-884-1309
Carpenter-Hayes Paper Box Company
East Hampton, CT 203-267-4436
Carpet City Paper Box Company
Amsterdam, NY 518-842-5430
Carrier Corp
Farmington, CT 800-227-7437
Carroll Co
Garland, TX 800-527-5722
Carson Industries
Pomona, CA 800-735-5566
Carton Service Co
Shelby, OH 800-533-7744
Castle Bag Co.
Wilmington, DE 302-656-1001
CCL Container
Toronto, ON 416-756-8500

Ccw Products
Arvada, CO 303-427-9663
CDF Corp
Plymouth, MA 800-443-1920
Cedar Box Co
Minneapolis, MN 612-332-4287
Cello Bag Company
Bowling Green, KY 800-347-0338
Centennial Moldings
Hastings, NE 888-883-2189
Central Bag Co
Leavenworth, KS 913-250-0325
Central Missouri Sheltered Enterprises
Columbia, MO 573-442-6935
Central Ohio Bag & Burlap
Columbus, OH 800-798-9405
Central Package & Display
Minneapolis, MN 763-425-7444
Central Paper Box
Kansas City, MO 816-753-3126
Century Foods Intl LLC
Sparta, WI 800-269-1901
Chalmur Bag Company, LLC
Philadelphia, PA 800-349-2247
Chambers Container Company
Gastonia, NC 704-377-6317
Champion Plastics
Clifton, NJ 800-526-1230
Checker Bag Co
St Louis, MO 800-489-3130
Chem-Tainer Industries Inc
West Babylon, NY 800-275-2436
Chem-Tainer Industries Inc
West Babylon, NY 800-938-8896
Cherry's Industrial Eqpt Corp
Elk Grove Vlg, IL 800-350-0011
Chester Plastics
Chester, NS 902-275-3522
Chili Plastics
Rochester, NY 585-889-4680
Cin-Made Packaging Group
Norcross, GA 800-264-7494
Cincinnati Foam Products
Cincinnati, OH 513-741-7722
City Box Company
Aurora, IL 773-277-5500
CKS Packaging
Atlanta, GA 800-800-4257
Clawson Container Company
Clarkston, MI 800-325-8700
Clayton L. Hagy & Son
Philadelphia, PA 215-844-6470
Clear Lam Packaging
Elk Grove Village, IL 847-439-8570
Clear View Bag Co Inc Of Nc
Albany, NY 800-458-7153
Clear View Bag Company
Thomasville, NC 336-885-8131
Clearwater Paper Corporation
Spokane, WA 877-847-7831
Cleveland Canvas Goods Mfg Co
Cleveland, OH 216-361-4567
Cleveland Plastic Films
Elyria, OH 800-832-6799
Cleveland Specialties Co
Loveland, OH 513-677-9787
CMD Corporation
Appleton, WI 920-730-6888
Coast Label Co
Fountain Valley, CA 800-995-0483
Coast Paper Box Company
San Bernardino, CA 909-382-3475
Coast Scientific
Rancho Santa Fe, CA 800-445-1544
Coastal Pallet Corp
Bridgeport, CT 203-333-6222
Coffee Sock Company
Eugene, OR 541-344-7698
Colbert Packaging Corp
Lake Forest, IL 847-367-5990
Cold Chain Technologies
Holliston, MA 800-370-8566
Collectors Gallery
St Charles, IL 800-346-3063
Colonial Transparent Products Company
Hicksville, NY 516-822-4430
Color Box
Richmond, IN 765-966-7588
Color Carton Corp
Bronx, NY 718-665-0840
Columbus Paperbox Company
Columbus, OH 800-968-0797

Commencement Bay Corrugated
Orting, WA 253-845-3100
Commercial Corrugated Co Inc
Baltimore, MD 800-242-8861
Complete Packaging & Shipping
Freeport, NY 877-269-3236
Conductive Containers Inc
Minneapolis, MN 800-327-2329
Conn Container Corp
North Haven, CT 203-248-0241
Consolidated Can Co
Paramount, CA 888-793-2199
Consolidated Container Co
New Castle, PA 724-658-0549
Consolidated Container Co LLC
Atlanta, GA 888-831-2184
Consolidated Plastics Co Inc
Stow, OH 800-858-5001
Consolidated Thread Mills, Inc.
Fall River, MA 508-672-0032
Constar International
Plymouth, MI 734-455-3600
Containair Packaging Corporation
Paterson, NJ 888-276-6500
Container Specialties
Melrose Park, IL 800-548-7513
Container Supply Co
Garden Grove, CA 562-594-0937
Containment Technology
St Gabriel, LA 800-388-2467
Contico Container
Norwalk, CA 562-921-9967
Continental Extrusion Corporation
Cedar Grove, NJ 800-822-4748
Continental Packaging Corporation
Elgin, IL 847-289-6400
Continental Plastic Container
Dallas, TX 972-303-1825
Continental Products
Mexico, MO 800-325-0216
Continental-Fremont
Tiffin, OH 419-448-4045
Contour Packaging
Philadelphia, PA 215-457-1600
Convoy
Canton, OH 800-899-1583
Conwed Global Netting Sltns
Roanoke, VA 800-368-3610
Corbett Timber Co
Wilmington, NC 800-334-0684
Corbox-Meyers Inc
Cleveland, OH 800-321-7286
Corfab
Chicago, IL 708-458-8750
Corinth Products
Corinth, ME 207-285-3387
Cornish Containers
Maumee, OH 419-893-7911
Corpak
San Juan, PR 787-787-9085
Corr Pak Corp
Mc Cook, IL 708-442-7806
Corrobilt Container Company
Livermore, CA 925-373-0880
Corrugated Inner-Pak Corporation
Conshohocken, PA 610-825-0200
Corrugated Packaging
Sarasota, FL 941-371-0000
Corrugated Specialties
Plainwell, MI 269-685-9821
Corrugated Supplies Co.
Bedford, IL 888-826-2738
Corson Manufacturing Company
Lockport, NY 716-434-8871
Cortec Aero
St Paul, MN 800-426-7832
COVERIS
Tomah, WI 608-372-2153
Covestro LLC
Sheffield, MA 800-628-5084
Craft Corrugated Box Inc
New Bedford, MA 508-998-2115
Crane Carton Corporation
Chicago, IL 773-722-0555
Crate Ideas by Wilderness House
Cave Junction, OR 800-592-2206
Crayex Corp
Piqua, OH 800-837-1747
Cream of the Valley Plastics
Arvada, CO 303-425-5499
Creative Packaging
Hayward, CA 510-785-6500

Creative Packaging Corporation
Buffalo Grove, IL 847-459-1001
Creative Techniques
Auburn Hills, MI 800-473-0284
Crespac Incorporated
Tucker, GA 800-438-1900
Cresthill Industries
Yonkers, NY 914-965-9510
Crown Cork & Seal Co Inc
Philadelphia, PA 215-698-5100
Crystal-Flex Packaging Corporation
Rockville Centre, NY 888-246-7325
CTK Plastics
Moose Jaw, SK 800-667-8847
Cumberland Container Corp
Monterey, TN 931-839-2227
Curtis Packaging
Sandy Hook, CT 203-426-5861
Cush-Pak Container Corporation
Henderson, TX 903-657-0555
Custom Bottle of Connecticut
Naugatuck, CT 203-723-6661
Custom Card & Label Corporation
Lincoln Park, NJ 973-492-0022
Custom Foam Molders
Foristell, MO 636-441-2307
Custom Pack Inc
Exton, PA 800-722-7005
Custom Packaging Inc
Richmond, VA 804-232-3299
Custom Poly Packaging
Fort Wayne, IN 800-548-6603
Custom Stamping & Manufacturing
Portland, OR 503-238-3700
D & W Fine Pack
San Bernardino, CA 800-232-5959
D & W Fine Pack
Lake Zurich, IL 800-323-0422
D&M Pallet Company
Neshkoro, WI 920-293-4616
Dahl-Tech Inc
Stillwater, MN 800-626-5812
Dairyland Plastics Company
Colfax, WI 715-962-3425
Dakota Corrugated Box
Sioux Falls, SD 605-332-3501
Dallas Container Corp
Dallas, TX 800-381-7148
Dart Container Corp.
Mason, MI 800-248-5960
Dashco
Gloucester, ON 613-834-6825
Davis Brothers Produce Boxes
Evergreen, NC 910-654-4913
Davis Core & Pa
Cave Spring, GA 800-235-7483
Davron Technologies Inc
Chattanooga, TN 423-870-1888
Day Lumber Company
Westfield, MA 413-568-3511
Day Manufacturing Company
Sherman, TX 903-893-1138
Dayton Bag & Burlap Co
Dayton, OH 800-543-3400
DBE Inc
Concord, ON 800-461-5313
De Ster Corporation
Atlanta, GA 800-237-8270
Deccofelt Corp
Glendora, CA 800-543-3226
Decker Plastics
Council Bluffs, IA 866-869-6293
Deco Labels & Tags
Toronto, ON 888-496-9029
Decorated Products Company
Westfield, MA 413-568-0944
DEL-Tec Packaging Inc
Greer, SC 800-747-8683
Deline Box Co
Denver, CO 303-376-1283
Delta Container Corporation
New Orleans, LA 800-752-7292
Delta Plastics
Hot Springs, AR 501-760-3000
Delta Wire And Mfg.
Harrow, ON 800-221-3794
Denver Reel & Pallet Company
Denver, CO 303-321-1920
Desert Box & Supply Corporation
Thermal, CA 760-399-5161
Design Plastics Inc
Omaha, NE 800-491-0786

Designers Folding Box Corp
Buffalo, NY 716-853-5141
Despro Manufacturing
Cedar Grove, NJ 800-292-9906
Detroit Forming
Southfield, MI 248-440-1317
Development Workshop Inc
Idaho Falls, ID 800-657-5597
Diamond Packaging
Rochester, NY 800-333-4079
Die Cut Specialties Inc
Savage, MN 952-890-7590
Display One
Hartford, WI 262-673-5880
Dixie Poly Packaging
Greenville, SC. 864-268-3751
Dixie Printing & Packaging
Glen Burnie, MD 800-433-4943
Donnelly Industries, Inc
Wayne, NJ 973-672-1800
Dorado Carton Company
Dorado, PR 787-796-1670
Dordan Manufacturing Co
Woodstock, IL 800-663-5460
Douglas Stephen Plastics Inc
Paterson, NJ 973-523-3030
Drake Co
Houston, TX 800-299-5644
Drescher Paper Box Inc
Buffalo, NY. 716-854-0288
Dub Harris Corporation
Pomona, CA 909-596-6300
Dubuque Steel Products Co
Dubuque, IA 563-556-6288
Dufeck Manufacturing Co
Denmark, WI. 888-603-9663
Durango-Georgia Paper
Tampa, FL 813-286-2718
Dusobox Company
Haverhill, MA 978-372-7192
Duval Container Co
Jacksonville, FL 800-342-8194
Dynamic Packaging
Minneapolis, MN 800-878-9380
Dynamic Pak LLC
Syracuse, NY 315-474-8593
Dzignpak LLC Englander
Waco, TX 888-314-5259
E K Lay Co
Philadelphia, PA 800-523-3220
E2M
Duluth, GA 800-622-4326
Eagle Box Company
Farmingdale, NY 212-255-3860
Eastern Container Corporation
Mansfield, MA 508-337-0400
Eastern Plastics
Pawtucket, RI 800-442-8585
Eastern Poly Packaging   Company
Brooklyn, NY 800-421-6006
Eaton Manufacturing Co
Houston, TX 800-328-6610
EB Box Company
Richmond Hill, ON 800-513-2269
EB Eddy Paper
Port Huron, MI 810-982-0191
Eco-Bag Products
Ossining, NY 800-720-2247
Economy Folding Box Corporation
Chicago, IL 800-771-1053
EGA Products Inc
Brookfield, WI 800-937-3427
EGW Bradbury Enterprises
Bridgewater, ME. 800-332-6021
Eichler Wood Products
Laurys Station, PA 610-262-6749
El Dorado Packaging Inc
El Dorado, AR 870-862-4977
Elberta Crate & Box Company
Carpentersville, IL 888-672-9260
Electrol Specialties Co
South Beloit, IL 815-389-2291
Elegant Packaging
Cicero, IL 800-367-5493
Ellehammer Industries
Langley, BC 604-882-9326
Elm Packaging Company
Memphis, TN 901-795-2711
Elopak Americas
Wixom, MI 248-486-4600
Emoshun
Rancho Cucamonga, CA 909-484-9559

Engineered Products
Hazelwood, MO 314-731-5744
Ensinger Inc
Washington, PA 800-243-3221
Enterprise Box Company
Montclair, NJ 973-509-2200
Epsen Hillmer Graphics Co
Omaha, NE 800-228-9940
Erie Container
Cleveland, OH 216-631-1650
ERO/Goodrich Forest Products
Tualatin, OR 800-458-5545
Erwyn Products Inc
Morganville, NJ 800-331-9208
ES Robbins Corp
Muscle Shoals, AL 800-633-3325
Eureka Paper Box Company
Williamsport, PA 570-326-9147
Excelsior Transparent Bag Manufacturing
Yonkers, NY 914-968-1300
Expert Industries Inc
Brooklyn, NY 718-434-6060
F C MEYER Packaging LLC
Jeannette, PA 724-523-5565
F G Products Inc
Rice Lake, WI 800-247-3854
F N Smith Corp
Oregon, IL 815-732-2171
F&G Packaging
Yulee, FL 904-225-5121
F.E. Wood & Sons
West Baldwin, ME 207-286-5003
Fabohio Inc
Uhrichsville, OH 740-922-4233
Fabri-Kal Corp
Kalamazoo, MI 800-888-5054
Fabricated Components Inc
Stroudsburg, PA 800-233-8163
Fabriko
Altavista, VA 888-203-8098
Fan Bag Company
Chicago, IL 773-342-2752
Faribault Manufacturing Co
Faribault, MN 800-447-6043
Farmer's Co-Op Elevator Co
Hudsonville, MI 800-439-9859
Fast Bags
Fort Worth, TX 800-321-3687
Fehlig Brothers Box & Lbr Co
St Louis, MO. 314-241-6900
Felco Packaging Specialist
Baltimore, MD 800-673-8488
Ferguson Containers
Phillipsburg, NJ 908-454-9755
Fibre Containers Inc
City Of Industry, CA. 626-968-5897
Film X
Dayville, CT 800-628-6128
Film-Pak Inc
Crowley, TX 800-526-1838
Finn Industries
Ontario, CA. 909-930-1500
First Midwest of Iowa Corporation
Des Moines, IA 800-247-8411
Fischer Paper Products Inc
Antioch, IL 800-323-9093
Fitec International Inc
Memphis, TN 800-332-6387
Fitzpatrick Container Company
North Wales, PA 215-699-3515
Flashfold Carton Inc
Fort Wayne, IN 260-423-9431
Flex Products
Carlstadt, NJ 800-526-6273
FLEXcon Company
Spencer, MA 508-885-8200
Flexible Foam Products
Elkhart, IN. 800-678-3626
Flexicon
Cary, IL 847-639-3530
Flexo Transparent Inc
Buffalo, NY. 877-993-5396
Flint Boxmakers Inc
Flint, MI 810-743-0400
Flour City Press-Pack Company
Minneapolis, MN 952-831-1265
Foam Concepts Inc
Uxbridge, MA 508-278-7255
Foam Pack Industries
Springfield, NJ 973-376-3700
Foam Packaging Inc
Vicksburg, MS 800-962-2655

Foamex
Cornelius, NC 704-892-8081
Foamold Corporation
Oneida, NY 315-363-5350
Fold-Pak Corporation
Newark, NY 315-331-3159
Fold-Pak South
Columbus, GA 706-689-2924
Folding Carton/Flexible Packaging
North Hollywood, CA 818-896-3449
Food Pak Corp
San Mateo, CA 650-341-6559
Formel Industries
Franklin Park, IL 800-373-3300
Fortune Plastics, Inc
Old Saybrook, CT 800-243-0306
Four M Manufacturing Group
San Jose, CA 408-998-1141
Franklin Crates
Micanopy, FL 352-466-3141
Frankston Paper Box Company of Texas
Frankston, TX 903-876-2550
Fredman Bag Co
Milwaukee, WI 800-945-5686
Freedom Packaging
Watsonville, CA 831-722-3565
Frem Corporation
Worcester, MA 508-791-3152
Fremont Die Cut Products
Fremont, OH 800-223-3177
Fresno Pallet, Inc.
Sultana, CA 559-591-4111
Friedman Bag Company
Manhattan Beach, CA 213-628-2341
Friend Box Co
Danvers, MA 978-774-0240
Friendly City Box Co Inc
Johnstown, PA 814-266-6287
Frobisher Industries
Waterborough, NB 506-362-2198
Frontier Bag
Kansas City, MO 816-765-4811
Frontier Bag Co Inc
Omaha, NE 800-278-2247
Fruit Growers Package Company
Grandville, MI 616-724-1400
Frye's Measure Mill
Wilton, NH 603-654-6581
Fuller Box Co
North Attleboro, MA 508-695-2525
Fuller Industries LLC
Great Bend, KS 800-522-0499
Fuller Packaging Inc
Central Falls, RI 401-725-4300
Fulton-Denver Co
Denver, CO 800-521-1414
Gabriel Container Co
Santa Fe Springs, CA 323-685-8844
Garvey Products
Cincinnati, OH 513-771-8710
Gary Plastic Packaging Corporation
Bronx, NY 800-221-8151
Gates
West Peterborough, NH 888-543-6316
Gateway Packaging Co
Kansas City, MO 816-483-9800
Gateway Packaging Corp
Export, PA 888-289-2693
Gatewood Products LLC
Parkersburg, WV 800-827-5461
Gaylord Container Corporation
Tampa, FL 813-621-3591
Gemini Plastic Films Corporation
Garfield, NJ 800-789-4732
General Bag Corporation
Cleveland, OH 800-837-9396
General Films Inc
Covington, OH 888-436-3456
General Press Corp
Natrona Heights, PA 724-224-3500
Genesee Corrugated
Flint, MI .810-228-3702
Genpak
Peterborough, ON 800-461-1995
Genpak LLC
Lakeville, MN 800-328-4556
Genpak LLC
Charlotte, NC 800-626-6695
Georg Fischer Central Plastics
Shawnee, OK 800-654-3872
Georgia-Pacific LLC
Atlanta, GA 800-283-5547

Gessner Products
Ambler, PA 800-874-7808
Gibbs Brothers Cooperage
Hot Springs, AR 501-623-8881
Gibraltar Packaging Group Inc
Hastings, NE 402-463-1366
Gilchrist Bag Co Inc
Camden, AR 800-643-1513
Glasko Plastics
Santa Ana, CA 714-751-7830
Glopak
St Leonard, QC 800-361-6994
Goeman's Wood Products
Hartford, WI 262-673-6090
Goergen-Mackwirth Co Inc
Buffalo, NY 800-728-4446
Golden West Packaging Concept
Lake Forest, CA 949-855-9646
Goldenwest Sales
Cerritos, CA 800-827-6175
Goldman Manufacturing Company
Detroit, MI 313-834-5535
Goldmax Industries
City Of Industry, CA 626-964-8820
GP Plastics Corporation
Medley, FL 305-888-3555
Graff Tank Erection
Harrisville, PA 814-385-6671
Graham Engineering Corp
York, PA .717-848-3755
Grand Valley Labels
Grand Rapids, MI
GranPac
Wetaskiwin, AB 780-352-3324
Graphic Impressions of Illinois
River Grove, IL 708-453-1100
Graphic Packaging Corporation
Golden, CO 800-677-2886
Graphic Packaging International
Atlanta, GA 770-240-7200
Graphic Packaging Intl
Elk Grove Vlg, IL 847-437-1700
Great Lakes-Triad Package Corporation
Grand Rapids, MI 616-241-6441
Great Northern Corp
Chippewa Falls, WI 800-472-1800
Great Northern Corp
Racine, WI 800-558-4711
Great Northern Corp.
Appleton, WI 800-236-3671
Great Southern Industries
Jackson, MS 877-638-3667
Green Bay Packaging Inc.
Kalamazoo, MI 269-552-1000
Green Bay Packaging Inc.
Tulsa, OK 918-446-3341
Green Bay Packaging Inc.
Green Bay, WI 920-433-5111
Green Brothers
Barrington, RI 401-245-9043
Green Seams
Maple Grove, MN 612-929-3213
Greenfield Packaging
White Plains, NY 914-993-0233
Greenfield Paper Box Co
Greenfield, MA 413-773-9414
Greif Brothers Corporation
Cleveland, OH 800-424-0342
Greif Inc
Delaware, OH 740-549-6000
Greif Inc
Delaware, OH 800-476-1635
Gribble Stamp & Stencil Co
Houston, TX 713-228-5358
Grigsby Brothers Paper Box Manufacturers
Portland, OR 866-233-4690
Gulf Coast Plastics
Tampa, FL 800-277-7491
Gulf Packaging Company
Safety Harbor, FL 800-749-3466
H S Inc
Oklahoma City, OK 800-238-1240
H. Arnold Wood Turning
Tarrytown, NY 888-314-0088
H.J. Jones & Sons
London, ON 800-667-0476
H.P. Neun
Fairport, NY 585-388-1360
Hager Containers Inc
Carrollton, TX 972-416-7660
Hampton Roads Box Company
Suffolk, VA 757-934-2355

Handgards Inc
El Paso, TX 800-351-8161
Hank Rivera Associates
Dearborn, MI 313-581-8300
Hanson Box & Lumber Company
Wakefield, MA 617-245-0358
Harbor Pallet Company
Anaheim, CA 714-871-0932
Hardi-Tainer
South Deerfield, MA 800-882-9878
Hardy Systems Corporation
Northbrook, IL 800-927-3956
Harpak-ULMA Packaging LLC
Ball Ground, GA 770-345-5300
Hartford Containers
Terryville, CT 860-584-1194
Hartford Plastics
Omaha, NE
Harvard Folding Box Company
Lynn, MA 781-598-1600
Hawkeye Corrugated Box
Cedar Falls, IA 319-268-0407
Hedstrom Corporation
Ashland, OH 700-765-9665
Hedwin Division
Baltimore, MD 800-638-1012
Henry Ira L Co
Watertown, WI 920-261-0648
Heritage Bag Co
Roanoke, TX 800-527-2247
Heritage Packaging
Victor, NY 585-742-3310
Herkimer Pallet & Wood Products Company
Herkimer, NY 315-866-4591
Hibco Plastics
Yadkinville, NC 800-849-8683
Highland Plastics Inc
Mira Loma, CA 800-368-0491
Hinchcliff Products Company
Strongsville, OH 440-238-5200
Hinkle Manufacturing
Perrysburg, OH 419-666-5367
Hodge Manufacturing Company
Springfield, MA 800-262-4634
Hodges
Vienna, IL 800-444-0011
Holmco Container Manufacturing, LTD
Baltic, OH 330-897-4503
Home Plastics Inc
Des Moines, IA 515-265-2562
Hood Packaging
Madison, MS 800-321-8115
Hood Packaging
Burlington, ON 877-462-6627
Hoover Materials Handling Group
Houston, TX 800-844-8683
Hope Paper Box Company
Pawtucket, RI 401-724-5700
Hub Folding Box Co
Mansfield, MA 508-339-0102
Hubco Inc
Hutchinson, KS 800-563-1867
Hudson Poly Bag Inc
Hudson, MA 800-229-7566
Hunter Packaging Corporation
South Elgin, IL 800-428-4747
Huntsman Packaging Corporation
Birmingham, Bi. 205-328-4720
Hurri-Kleen Corporation
Birmingham, AL. 800-455-8265
IB Concepts
Elizabeth, NJ 888-671-0800
IBC Shell Packaging
New Hyde Park, NY 516-352-5138
Ideal Wire Works
Alhambra, CA 626-282-0886
Il Valley Container Inc
Peru, IL 815-223-7200
Imperial Containers
City of Industry, CA 626-333-6363
Imperial Industries Inc
Rothschild, WI 800-558-2945
Imperial Packaging Corporation
Pawtucket, RI 401-753-7778
Impress Industries
Emmaus, PA 610-967-6027
In-Touch Products
North Salt Lake, UT 801-298-4466
Incinerator International Inc
Houston, TX 713-227-1466
Independent Can Co
Belcamp, MD 410-272-0090

Indian Valley Industries
Johnson City, NY 800-659-5111
Indiana Bottle Co
Scottsburg, IN...................800-752-8702
Indiana Carton Co Inc
Bremen, IN 800-348-2390
Indiana Vac Form Inc
Warsaw, IN 574-269-1725
Indianapolis Container Company
Indianapolis, IN 800-760-3318
Industrial Container Corp
High Point, NC 336-886-7031
Industrial Contracting & Rggng
Mahwah, NJ 888-427-7444
Industrial Crating & Packing
Tukwila, WA 800-942-0499
Industrial Hardwood
Perrysburg, OH 419-666-2503
Industrial Lumber & Packaging
Spring Lake, MI 616-842-1457
Industrial Nameplate Inc
Warminster, PA 800-878-6263
Industrial Woodfab & Packaging
Riverview, MI 734-284-4808
Inland Consumer Packaging
Harrington, DE 302-398-4211
Inland Paper Company
Ontario, CA.....................909-923-4505
Inland Paperboard & Packaging
Rock Hill, SC 803-366-4103
Inline Plastic Corp
McDonough, GA 678-466-3467
Innova Envelopes
La Salle, QC 514-595-0555
Innovative Folding Carton Company
South Plainfield, NJ 908-757-0205
Instabox
Calgary, AB.....................800-482-6173
Inteplast Bags & Films Corporation
Delta, BC.......................604-946-5431
International Wood Industries
Snohomish, WA 800-922-6141
Interstate Packaging
White Bluff, TN 800-251-1072
Intertape Polymer Group
Sarasota, FL 888-898-7834
Intertech Corp
Greensboro, NC 800-364-2255
IPL Inc
Saint-Damien, QC 800-463-4755
IPL Plastics
Edmundston, NB..................800-739-9595
IPS International
Snohomish, WA 360-668-5050
ITW Angleboard
Villa Rica, GA...................770-459-5747
ITW Hi-Cone
Itasca, IL.......................630-438-5300
Ivarson Inc
Milwaukee, WI 414-351-0700
IVEX Packaging Corporation
Longueuil, QC 450-651-8887
J A Heilferty & Co
Teaneck, NJ.....................201-836-5060
J L Clark Corp
Rockford, IL 815-962-8861
J M Packaging Co
Warren, MI 586-771-7800
J&J Corrugated Box Corporation
Franklin, MA 508-528-6200
J&J Mid-South Container Corporation
Augusta, GA.....................800-395-1025
J.C. Products Inc.
Haddam, CT 860-267-5516
J.V. Reed & Company
Louisville, KY 877-258-7333
Jackson Corrugated Container
Middletown, CT 860-346-9671
Jacksonville Box & Woodwork Co
Jacksonville, FL 800-683-2699
James Thompson
New York, NY 212-686-5306
Jamestown Container Corporation
Buffalo, NY.....................855-234-4054
Jamison Plastic Corporation
Allentown, PA...................610-391-1400
Jarisch Paper Box Company
North Adams, MA 413-663-5396
Java Jacket
Portland, OR....................800-208-4128
Jayhawk Boxes
Fremont, NE 800-642-8363

Jeb Plastics
Wilmington, DE 800-556-2247
Jeco Plastic Products LLC
Plainfield, IN....................800-593-5326
JEM Wire Products
Middletown, CT 860-347-0447
Jesco Industries
Litchfield, MI 800-455-0019
Jescorp
Des Plaines, IL 847-299-7800
Jesse Jones Box Corporation
Philadelphia, PA 215-425-6600
Jessup Paper Box
Brookston, IN 765-490-9043
Jewel Case Corp
Cranston, RI 800-441-4447
Jewell Bag Company
Dallas, TX......................214-749-1223
Johnson Corrugated Products Corporation
Thompson, CT 860-923-9563
Jomar Plastics Industry
Nanty Glo, PA...................800-681-4039
Jordan Box Co
Syracuse, NY 315-422-3419
Jordan Paper Box Co
Chicago, IL 773-287-5362
JP Plastics, Inc.
Foxboro, MA 508-203-2420
Juice Tree
Omaha, NE 714-891-4425
Jupiter Mills Corporation
Roslyn, NY 800-853-5121
K & H Corrugated Corp
Walden, NY.....................845-778-3555
K&H Container
Wallingford, CT 203-265-1547
K-C Products Company
Van Nuys, CA...................818-267-1600
Kadon Corporation
Milford, OH 937-299-0088
Kal Pac Corp
Montgomery, NY 800-852-5722
KANE Bag Supply Co
Baltimore, MD 410-732-5800
KAPCO
Kent, OH.......................800-843-5368
Karyall Telday Inc
Cleveland, OH 216-281-4063
Kaufman Paper Box Company
Providence, RI 401-272-7508
Keeper Thermal Bag Co
Bartlett, IL......................800-765-9244
Kelley Wood Products
Fitchburg, MA 978-345-7531
Kelly Box & Packaging Corp
Fort Wayne, IN 260-432-4570
Kelman Bottles LLC
Glenshaw, PA 412-486-9100
Kendel
Countryside, IL 800-323-1100
Kerrigan Paper Products Inc
Haverhill, MA 978-374-4797
KETCH
Wichita, KS.....................800-766-3777
Key Container Company
South Gate, CA..................323-564-4211
Key Packaging Co
Sarasota, FL 941-355-2728
Keystone Packaging Svc Inc
Phillipsburg, NJ 800-473-8567
KHM Plastics Inc
Gurnee, IL......................847-249-4910
Killington Wood ProductsCompany
Rutland, VT 802-773-9111
Kimball Companies
East Longmeadow, MA 413-525-1881
King Plastic Corp
North Port, FL...................800-780-5502
KM International Corp
Kenton, TN 731-749-8700
Knapp Container
Beacon Falls, CT.................203-888-0511
Knight Paper Box Company
Chicago, IL 773-585-2035
Koch Container
Victor, NY......................585-924-1600
Koch Equipment LLC
Kansas City, MO.................816-931-4557
Kole Industries
Miami, FL 305-633-2556
Kontane
Charleston, SC 843-352-0011

Konz Wood Products Co
Appleton, WI 877-610-5145
L & C Plastic Bags
Covington, OH 937-473-2968
L&H Wood Manufacturing Company
Farmington, MI 248-474-9000
Label Makers
Pleasant Prairie, WI 800-208-3331
Label Systems Inc
Addison, TX 800-220-9552
Lakeside Container Corp
Plattsburgh, NY 518-561-6150
Lakeside Manufacturing Inc
Milwaukee, WI 888-558-8565
Laminated Paper Products
San Jose, CA....................408-888-0880
Landis Plastics
Alsip, IL........................708-396-1470
Langer Manufacturing Company
Cedar Rapids, IA. 800-728-6445
Langston Co Inc
Memphis, TN 901-774-4440
Lansing Corrugated Products
Lansing, MI.....................517-323-2752
Laval Paper Box
Pointe Claire, QC 450-669-3551
Lawrence Paper Co
Lawrence, KS 785-843-8111
Lawrence Schiff Silk Mills
New York, NY 800-272-4433
LBP Manufacturing LLC
Cicero, IL 708-652-5600
Leaman Container
Fort Worth, TX 817-429-2660
Leclaire Packaging Corp
Ixonia, WI......................920-206-9902
Leggett & Platt Storage
Vernon Hills, IL 847-816-6246
Lengsfield Brothers
New Orleans, LA 504-529-2235
Lenkay Sani Products Corporation
Brooklyn, NY 718-927-9260
Lester Box & Mfg Div
Long Beach, CA 562-437-5123
Letica Corp
Rochester Hills, MI...............800-538-4221
Levin Brothers Paper
Cicero, IL 800-545-6200
Lewis Steel Works Inc
Wrens, GA......................800-521-5239
Lewisburg Container Co
Lewisburg, OH 937-962-0101
Lexel
Fort Worth, TX 817-332-4061
Liberty Carton Co.
Golden Valley, MN 800-328-1784
Lima Barrel & Drum Company
Lima, OH 419-224-8916
Lin Pac Plastics
Roswell, GA.....................770-751-6006
LinPac
San Angelo, TX 800-453-7393
Linvar
Hartford, CT 800-282-5288
Liqui-Box
Richmond, VA...................804-325-1400
Liquitane
Berwick, PA 570-759-6200
Little Rock Crate & Basket Co
Little Rock, AR..................800-223-7823
LMK Containers
Centerville, UT 626-821-9984
Lone Star Container Corp
Irving, TX 800-552-6937
Longview Fibre Co
Longview, WA...................800-929-8111
Longview Fibre Company
Beaverton, OR 503-350-1600
Los Angeles Paper Box & Board Mills
Los Angeles, CA.................323-685-8900
Lowell Paper Box Company
Nashua, NH.....................603-595-0700
Loy Lange Box Co
St Louis, MO....................800-886-4712
LPS Industries
Moonachie, NJ 800-275-4577
LTI Printing Inc
Sturgis, MI 269-651-7574
Luce Corp
Hamden, CT 800-344-6966
Luetzow Industries
South Milwaukee, WI.............800-558-6055

Luke's Almond Acres
   Reedley, CA 559-638-3483
Lunn Industries
   Glen Cove, NY 516-671-9000
Lustrecal
   Lodi, CA 800-234-6264
M & G Packaging Corp
   Floral Park, NY 800-240-5288
M & H Crate Inc
   Jacksonville, TX 903-683-5351
M O Industries Inc
   Whippany, NJ 973-386-9228
M&L Plastics
   Easthampton, MA 413-527-1330
M&R Flexible Packaging
   Springboro, OH 800-543-3380
Mack-Chicago Corporation
   Chicago, IL 800-992-6225
MacMillan Bloedel Packaging
   Montgomery, AL 800-239-4464
Maco Bag Corp
   Newark, NY 315-226-1000
Madsen Wire Products Inc
   Orland, IN 260-829-6561
Malco Manufacturing Co
   Los Angeles, CA 866-477-7267
Mall City Containers Inc
   Kalamazoo, MI 800-643-6721
Malnove Of Nebraska
   Omaha, NE 800-228-9877
Malpack Polybag
   Ajax, ON 905-428-3751
Mannkraft Corporation
   Newark, NJ 973-589-7400
Manufacturers Corrugate Box
   Flushing, NY 718-894-7200
Manufacturers Wood Supply Company
   Cleveland, OH 216-771-7848
Mar-Boro Printing & Advertising Specialties
   Brooklyn, NY 718-336-4051
Marco Products
   Adrian, MI. 517-265-3333
Marcus Carton Company
   Melville, NY 631-752-4200
Marden Edwards
   Antioch, CA 800-332-1838
Marfred Industries
   Sun Valley, CA 800-529-5156
Marion Paper Box Co
   Marion, IN. 765-664-6435
Mark Container Corporation
   San Leandro, CA. 510-483-4440
Maro Paper Products Company
   Bellwood, IL 708-649-9982
Marpac Industries
   Philmont, NY 888-462-7722
Marshall Boxes Inc
   Rochester, NY 585-458-7432
Marshall Plastic Film Inc
   Martin, MI. 269-672-5511
Mason Transparent Package Company
   Armonk, NY 718-792-6000
Massachusetts Container Corporation
   North Haven, CT. 203-248-2161
Massillon Container Co
   Navarre, OH 330-879-5653
Master Containers
   Mulberry, FL 800-881-6847
Master Package Corporation
   Menomonie, WI 800-347-4144
Master Paper Box Co
   Chicago, IL 877-927-0252
Maull-Baker Box Company
   Brookfield, WI 414-463-1290
Maypak Inc
   Wayne, NJ. 973-696-0780
McDowell Industries
   Memphis, TN 800-622-3695
McGraw Box Company
   Mc Graw, NY 607-836-6465
Meadwestvaco Corp
   Richmond, VA. 804-444-1000
MeGa Industries
   Burlington, ON 800-665-6342
Mello Smello LLC
   Minneapolis, MN 888-574-2964
Melmat Inc
   Huntington Beach, CA 800-635-6289
Melville Plastics
   Haw River, NC 336-578-5800
Memphis Delta Tent & Awning
   Memphis, TN 901-522-1238

Menasha Corp
   Neenah, WI 800-558-5073
Merchants Publishing Company
   Kalamazoo, MI 269-345-1175
Meriden Box Company
   Southington, CT 860-621-7141
Metal Container Corporation
   St Louis, MO. 314-957-9500
Meyer Packaging
   Palmyra, PA. 717-838-6300
Michiana Box & Crate
   Niles, MI 800-677-6372
Michiana Corrugate Products
   Sturgis, MI 269-651-5225
Michigan Box Co
   Detroit, MI 888-642-4269
Michigan Pallet Inc
   St Charles, MI 989-865-9915
Micro Qwik
   Cross Plains, WI 608-798-3071
Micro Wire Products Inc
   Brockton, MA 508-584-0200
Microplas Industries
   Dunwoody, GA 800-952-4528
Mid Cities Paper Box Company
   Downey, CA 877-277-6272
Mid-States Mfg & Engr Co Inc
   Milton, IA 800-346-1792
Midco Plastics
   Enterprise, KS. 800-235-2729
Midland Manufacturing Co
   Monroe, LA 800-394-2625
Midlands Packaging Corp
   Lincoln, NE. 402-464-9124
Midvale Paper Box
   Wilkes Barre, PA 570-824-3577
Midwest Aircraft Products Co
   Lexington, OH 419-884-2164
Midwest Box Co
   Cleveland, OH 216-281-3980
Midwest Fibre Products Inc
   Viola, IL 309-596-2955
Midwest Paper Products Company
   Louisville, KY 502-636-2741
Midwest Paper Tube & Can Corporation
   New Berlin, WI. 262-782-7300
Midwest Rubber Svc & Supply
   Minneapolis, MN 800-537-7457
Midwest Wire Specialties
   Chicago, IL 800-238-0228
Milan Box Corporation
   Milan, TN 800-225-8057
Millhiser
   Richmond, VA. 800-446-2247
Milprint
   Oshkosh, WI 920-303-8600
Mimi et Cie
   Seattle, WA 206-545-1850
Mini-Bag Company
   Farmingdale, NY 631-694-3325
Mmi Engineered Soultions Inc.
   Saline, MI 800-825-2566
Modern Packaging Inc
   Deer Park, NY 631-595-2437
Modern Paper Box Company
   Providence, RI 401-861-7357
Mohawk Northern Plastics
   Auburn, WA 800-426-1100
Mohawk Western Plastics Inc
   La Verne, CA 909-593-7547
Molded Container Corporation
   Portland, OR 503-233-8601
Monte Package Co
   Riverside, MI 800-653-2807
Montebello Container Corp
   La Mirada, CA 714-994-2351
Montebello Packaging
   Hawkesbury, ON. 613-632-7096
Moore Paper Boxes Inc
   Dayton, OH 937-278-7327
Moorecraft Box & Crate
   Tarboro, NC 252-823-2510
Morgan Brothers Bag Company
   Richmond, VA. 804-355-9107
Morphy Container Company
   Brantford, ON. 519-752-5428
Morris Industries
   Forestville, MD. 301-568-5005
Morris Transparent Box Co
   East Providence, RI. 401-438-6116
Moser Bag & Paper Company
   Cleveland, OH 800-433-6638

Mountain Safety Research
   Seattle, WA 800-877-9677
Mt Vernon Packaging Inc
   Mt Vernon, OH 888-397-3221
Mullnix Packages Inc
   Fort Wayne, IN 260-747-3149
Multibulk Systems International
   Wendell, NC 919-366-2100
MultiFab Plastics
   Boston, MA 888-293-5754
Murray Envelope Corporation
   Hattiesburg, MS 601-583-8292
Muth Associates
   Springfield, MA 800-388-0157
Nagel Paper & Box Company
   Saginaw, MI 800-292-3654
Naltex
   Austin, TX. 800-531-5112
Nameplate
   St Paul, MN. 651-228-1522
NAP Industries
   Brooklyn, NY 877-635-4948
Nashua Corporation
   Nashua, NH. 603-661-2004
National Marking Products Inc
   Henrico, VA. 800-482-1553
National Poly Bag Manufacturing Corporation
   Brooklyn, NY 718-629-9800
Neal Walters Poster Corporation
   Bentonville, AR 501-273-2489
Nefab Packaging Inc
   Elk Grove Vlg, IL 847-787-0340
Nefab Packaging Inc.
   Coppell, TX 800-322-4425
Nefab Packaging, Inc.
   Coppell, TX 800-322-4425
Neff Packaging
   Simpsonville, KY 800-445-4383
Nelson Container Corp
   Germantown, WI. 262-250-5000
Neos
   Elk River, MN. 888-441-6367
Net Pack Systems
   Oakland, ME. 207-465-4531
New England Wooden Ware
   Gardner, MA 800-252-9214
New Era Label Corporation
   Belleville, NJ 973-759-2444
New Lisbon Wood Products Manufacturing Company
   New Lisbon, WI. 608-562-3122
New Mexico Products Inc
   Albuquerque, NM 877-345-7864
New York Corugated Box Co
   Paterson, NJ 973-742-5000
New York Folding Box Co Inc
   Stanhope, NJ 973-347-6932
Nolon Industries
   Mantua, OH. 330-274-2283
Nordic Printing & Packaging
   New Hope, MN. 763-535-6440
North American Container Corp
   Marietta, GA 800-929-0610
North American Packaging Corp
   New York, NY 800-499-3521
Northeast Box Co
   Ashtabula, OH 800-362-8100
Northeast Container Corporation
   Dumont, NJ. 201-385-6200
Northeast Packaging Co
   Presque Isle, ME. 207-764-6271
Northeast Packaging Materials
   Monsey, NY 845-426-2900
Northern Box Co Inc
   Elkhart, IN. 574-264-2161
Northern Package Corporation
   Minneapolis, MN 952-881-5861
Nosco
   Waukegan, IL 847-360-4806
Noteworthy Company
   Amsterdam, NY 800-696-7849
Nottingham Spirk
   Cleveland, OH 216-231-7830
Novelis Foil Products
   Atlanta, GA 800-776-8701
NOVOLEX
   Glendale, AZ 800-243-0306
Now Plastics Inc
   East Longmeadow, MA 413-525-1010
NPC Display Group
   Newark, NJ 973-589-2155
Nu-Trend Plastics Thermoformer
   Jacksonville, FL 904-353-5936

O.C. Adhesives Corporation
Ridgefield, NJ 800-662-1595
Oak Barrel Winecraft
Berkeley, CA 510-849-0400
Oak Creek Pallet Company
Milwaukee, WI 414-762-7170
Oakes Carton Co
Kalamazoo, MI 269-381-6022
Occidental Chemical Corporation
Dallas, TX 800-733-3665
Ockerlund Industries
Addison, IL .708-771-7707
Okura USA Inc
Lenexa, KS .800-772-1187
Olcott Plastics
St Charles, IL 888-313-5277
Old Dominion Box Co Inc
Madison Heights, VA 434-929-6701
Old Dominion Box Company
Burlington, NC 336-226-4491
Old English Printing & Label Company
Delray Beach, FL 561-997-9990
Olive Can Company
Elgin, IL 847-468-7474
Oracle Packaging
Winston Salem, NC 800-952-9536
Orange Plastics
Compton, CA 310-609-2121
Oration Rubber Stamp Company
Columbus, NJ 908-496-4161
ORBIS
Oconomowoc, WI 262-560-5000
ORBIS
Oconomowoc, WI 800-890-7292
Original Lincoln Logs
Chestertown, NY 800-833-2461
Original Packaging & Display Company
Saint Louis, MO 314-772-7797
Osterneck Company
Lumberton, NC 800-682-2416
OTD Corporation
Hinsdale, IL 630-321-9232
Owens-Illinois Inc
Perrysburg, OH 567-336-5000
P M Plastics
Pewaukee, WI 262-691-1700
P&E
Altamonte Spgs, FL 800-438-0674
Pacific Paper Box Co
Cudahy, CA 323-771-7733
Pack-Rite
Newington, CT 860-953-0120
Package Containers Inc
Canby, OR .800-266-5806
Packaging Associates
Randolph, NJ 973-252-8890
Packaging Corporation of America
Lake Forest, IL 800-456-4725
Packaging Design Corp
Burr Ridge, IL 630-323-1354
Packaging Dynamics International
Caldwell, OH 740-732-5665
Packaging Enterprises
Rockledge, PA 800-453-6213
Packaging Solutions
Los Altos Hills, CA 650-917-1022
Packaging Technologies
Tuckahoe, NY 914-337-2005
Packing Material Company
Southfield, MI 248-489-7000
Packing Specialities
Warren, MI 586-758-5240
Packrite Packaging
Archdale, NC 336-431-1111
Pacquet Oneida
Charlotte, NC 800-631-8388
Pactiv LLC
Lake Forest, IL 800-476-4300
Pak-Sak Industries I
Sparta, MI .800-748-0431
Pak-Sher
Kilgore, TX .903-984-8596
Pakmark
Chesterfield, MO 800-423-1379
Pallet One Inc
Bartow, FL .800-771-1148
Pallets Inc
Fort Edward, NY 518-747-4177
Pallox Incorporated
Onsted, MI 517-456-4101
Palmer Distributors
St Clair Shores, MI 800-444-1912

Palmetto Packaging
Florence, SC 843-662-5800
Pan Pacific Plastics Inc
Hayward, CA 888-475-6888
Papelera Puertorriquena
Utuado, PR 787-894-2098
Paper Box & Specialty Co
Sheboygan, WI 888-240-3756
Paper Products Company
Cincinnati, OH 513-921-4717
Paper Systems Inc
Des Moines, IA 800-342-2855
Paper Works Industries Inc
Baldwinsville, NY 800-847-5677
PAR-Kan
Silver Lake, IN 800-291-5487
Par-Pak
Houston, TX 713-686-6700
Par-Pak
Houston, TX 888-727-7252
Parade Packaging
Mundelein, IL 847-566-6264
Paradigm Packaging Inc
Upland, CA 909-985-2750
Paragon Packaging
Ferndale, CA 888-615-0065
Parisian Novelty Company
Homewood, IL 773-847-1212
Park Custom Molding
Linden, NJ .908-486-8882
Parkway Plastic Inc
Piscataway, NJ 800-881-4996
Parlor City Paper Box Co Inc
Binghamton, NY 607-772-0600
Parsons Manufacturing Corp.
Menlo Park, CA 650-324-4726
Parta
Kent, OH 800-543-5781
Parvin Manufacturing Company
Los Angeles, CA 800-648-0770
Paul T. Freund Corporation
Palmyra, NY 800-333-0091
PBC
Mahwah, NJ 800-514-2739
Peace Industries
Rolling Meadows, IL 800-873-2239
Peacock Crate Factory
Jacksonville, TX 800-657-2200
Peerless Cartons
Bartlett, IL .312-226-7952
Peerless Packages
Cleveland, OH 216-464-3620
Pel-Pak Container
Pell City, AL 800-239-2699
Pelco Packaging Corporation
Stirling, NJ .908-647-3500
Pelican Displays
Homer, IL .800-627-1517
Pell Paper Box Company
Elizabeth City, NC 252-335-4361
Peninsula Plastics
Auburn Hills, MI 800-394-8698
Penn Bottle & Supply Company
Philadelphia, PA 215-365-5700
Penn Products
Portland, CT 800-490-7366
Penny Plate
Haddonfield, NJ 856-429-7583
Pentwater Wire Products Inc
Pentwater, MI 877-869-6911
Performance Packaging
Trail Creek, IN 219-874-6226
Peter Dudgeon International
Honolulu, HI 808-841-8211
Peter Pepper Products Inc
Compton, CA 310-639-0390
Peterboro Basket Co
Peterborough, NH 603-924-3861
Petoskey Plastics
Morristown, TN 423-586-8917
Pexco Packaging Corporation
Toledo, OH 800-227-9950
Pfeil & Holding Inc
Woodside, NY 800-247-7955
Phoenix Closures Inc
Naperville, IL 630-544-3475
Phoenix Industries Corp
Madison, WI 888-241-7482
Pilant Corp
Bloomington, IN 800-366-3525
Pine Point Wood Products Inc
Osseo, MN 763-428-4301

Pinn Pack Packaging LLC
Oxnard, CA 805-385-4100
Pioneer Packaging
Chicopee, MA 413-378-6930
Pioneer Packaging & Printing
Anoka, MN 800-708-1705
Pioneer Plastics Inc
Dixon, KY .800-951-1551
Pittsburgh Tank Corp
Monongahela, PA 800-634-0243
Plastic Assembly Corporation
Ayer, MA
Plastican Corporation
Fairfield, NJ 973-227-7817
Plastics Inc
Greensboro, AL 334-624-8801
Plastics Industries
Athens, TN 800-894-4876
Plastilite Corporation
Omaha, NE 800-228-9506
Plastipak Packaging
Plymouth, MI 734-354-3510
Plastiques Cascades Group
Montreal, QC 888-703-6515
Plaxall Inc
Long Island City, NY 800-876-5706
Pohlig Brothers
N Chesterfield, VA 804-275-9000
Polar Tech Industries Inc
Genoa, IL 800-423-2749
Poly One Corp
Avon Lake, OH 866-765-9663
Poly Plastic Products Inc
Delano, PA 570-467-3000
Poly Processing Co
French Camp, CA 877-325-3142
Poly Shapes Corporation
Elyria, OH .800-605-9359
Polybottle Group
Surrey, BC .604-594-4999
Polycon Industries
Chicago, IL 773-374-5500
Polyplastics
Austin, TX .800-753-7659
Polytainers
Toronto, ON 800-268-2424
Pop Tops Co Inc
South Easton, MA 800-647-8677
Portco Corporation
Vancouver, WA 800-426-1794
Portland Paper Box Company
Portland, OR 800-547-2571
Power Packaging Inc
Rosendale, WI 920-872-2181
PPC Perfect Packaging Co
Perrysburg, OH 419-874-3167
PPI
Baton Rouge, LA 225-330-4602
Prairie Packaging Inc
Mooresville, NC 704-660-6600
Pratt Industries
New Orleans, LA 504-733-7292
Pratt Industries
Conyers, GA 800-428-9269
Pratt Industries
Raleigh, NC 919-334-7400
Precision Printing & Packaging
Clarksville, TN 800-500-4526
Precision Wood of Hawaii
Vancouver, WA 808-682-2055
Precision Wood Products
Vancouver, WA 360-694-8322
Premier Packages
Saint Louis, MO 800-466-6588
Premium Foil Products Company
Louisville, KY 502-459-2820
President Container Inc
Moonachie, NJ 212-244-0345
Prestige Plastics Corporation
Delta, BC 604-930-2931
Pretium Packaging
Chesterfield, MO 314-727-8673
Pretium Packaging
Hazle Twp, PA 570-459-1800
Pretium Packaging
Hermann, MO 573-486-2811
Pride Container Corporation
Chicago, IL 773-227-6000
Priority Plastics Inc
Grinnell, IA 800-798-3512
Pro-Gram Plastics Inc
Geneva, OH 440-466-8080

ProAmpac
Cincinnati, OH 800-543-7030
Process Solutions
Riviera Beach, FL. 561-840-0050
Professional Marketing Group
Seattle, WA 800-227-3769
Progressive Plastics
Cleveland, OH 800-252-0053
Promo Edge
Wall Township, NJ 732-938-4242
Propac Marketing Inc
Addison, TX 972-733-3199
Propak
Burlington, ON 800-263-4872
Pruitt's Packaging Services
Grand Rapids, MI 800-878-0553
Prystup Packaging Products
Livingston, AL 205-652-9583
Q Pak Inc
Newark, NJ 973-483-4404
Quality Container Company
Ypsilanti, MI 734-481-1373
Quality Containers
Weston, ON. 416-749-6247
Quality Containers of New England
Yarmouth, ME. 800-639-1550
Quality Packaging Inc
Fond Du Lac, WI 800-923-3633
Quality Plastic Bag Corporation
Flushing, NY. 800-532-2247
Quality Transparent Bag Co
Bay City, MI 989-893-3561
Quantum Storage Systems Inc
Miami, FL. 800-685-4665
Quintex Corp
Nampa, ID. 208-467-1113
R C Molding Inc
Greer, SC. 864-879-7279
R&R Corrugated Container
Terryville, CT 860-584-1194
R.N.C. Industries
Lawrenceville, GA 888-844-3864
Racine Paper Box Manufacturing
Chicago, IL 773-227-3900
Ram Equipment Co
Waukesha, WI 262-513-1114
Rand-Whitney Group LLC
Worcester, MA 508-791-2301
Rand-Whitney Packaging Corp
Portsmouth, NH 508-791-2301
RAPAC Inc
Oakland, TN 800-280-6333
Ray C. Sprosty Bag Company
Wooster, OH 330-264-8559
RDA Container Corp
Gates, NY 585-247-2323
Reading Box Co Inc
Reading, PA. 610-372-7411
Red River Lumber Company
Saint Helena, CA 707-963-1251
Regal Box Corp
Milwaukee, WI 414-562-5890
Regal Plastic Company
Mission, KS 800-852-1556
Regal Plastic Supply Co
Kansas City, MO. 800-444-6390
Regency Label Corporation
Wood Ridge, NJ 201-342-2288
Reliable Container Corporation
Downey, CA 562-745-0200
Reliance Product
Winnipeg, MB. 800-665-0258
Reliance-Paragon
Philadelphia, PA 215-743-1231
Remcon Plastics Inc
Reading, PA 800-360-3636
Remmey Wood Products
Southampton, PA 215-355-3335
Rex Carton Co Inc
Chicago, IL 773-581-4115
Rez-Tech Corp
Kent, OH. 800-673-5277
Rhoades Paper Box Corporation
Springfield, OH. 800-441-6494
Rice Packaging Inc
Ellington, CT 800-367-6725
Rice Paper Box Company
Colorado Springs, CO. 303-733-1000
Richard Read Construction Company
Arcadia, CA 888-450-7343
Richards Packaging
Memphis, TN 800-583-0327
Richmond Corrugated Box Company
Richmond, VA. 804-222-1300
Ritz Packaging Company
Brooklyn, NY 718-366-2300
Rjr Technologies
Oakland, CA 510-638-5901
RMI-C/Rotonics Manaufacturing
Bensenville, IL 630-773-9510
Robinette Co
Bristol, TN 423-968-7800
Robinson Industries Inc
Coleman, MI 989-465-6111
Rock-Tenn Company
Norcross, GA 608-223-6272
Roddy Products Pkgng Co Inc
Aldan, PA 610-623-7040
Roll-O-Sheets Canada
Barrie, ON. 888-767-3456
Romanow Container
Westwood, MA 781-320-9200
Rondo of America
Naugatuck, CT 203-723-7474
Ropak
Oak Brook, IL. 800-527-2267
Roplast Industries Inc
Oroville, CA 800-767-5278
Rose City Printing & Packaging
Vancouver, WA 800-704-8693
Ross & Wallace Inc
Hammond, LA 800-854-2300
Round Paper Packages Inc
Erlanger, KY 859-331-7200
Rownd & Son
Dillon, SC 803-774-8264
Roy's Folding Box
Cleveland, OH. 216-464-1191
Royal Group
Cicero, IL 708-656-2020
Royal Paper Box Co
Montebello, CA 323-728-7041
RubaTex Polymer
Middlefield, OH 440-632-1691
Rudd Container Corp
Chicago, IL 773-847-7600
Ruffino Paper Box Co
Hackensack, NJ. 201-487-1260
Rusken Packaging
Cullman, AL 256-775-0014
RXI Silgan Specialty Plastics
Triadelphia, WV 304-547-9100
S.S.I. Schaefer System International Limited
Brampton, ON. 905-458-5399
Sabert Corp
Sayreville, NJ 800-722-3781
Sacramento Bag Manufacturing
Woodland, CA. 530-662-6130
Saeplast Canada
St John, NB 800-567-3966
San Diego Paper Box Company
Spring Valley, CA 619-660-9566
San Miguel Label Manufacturing
Ciales, PR 787-871-3120
Sanchelima International
Miami, FL. 305-591-4343
Santa Fe Bag Company
Vernon, CA 323-585-7225
Saunders West
Azusa, CA. 888-932-8836
Save-A-Tree
Berkeley, CA. 510-843-5233
Scheb International
North Barrington, IL. 847-381-2573
Schermerhorn Inc
Chicopee, MA. 413-598-8348
Schiefer Packaging Corporation
Syracuse, NY 315-422-0615
Schiffenhaus Industries
Newark, NJ 973-484-5000
Schiffmayer Plastics Corp.
Algonquin, IL 847-658-8140
Schoeneck Containers Inc
New Berlin, WI. 262-786-9360
Scholle IPN
Merced, CA. 209-384-3100
Schroeder Machine
San Marcos, CA 760-591-9733
Schwab Paper Products Co
Romeoville, IL 800-837-7225
Schwarz Supply Source
Morton Grove, IL 800-323-4903
Scope Packaging
Orange, CA. 714-998-4411
Scott & Daniells
Portland, CT 860-342-1932
Scott Packaging Corporation
Philadelphia, PA 215-925-5595
Seaboard Bag Corporation
Richmond, VA
Seaboard Carton Company
Downers Grove, IL. 708-344-0575
Seaboard Folding Box Corp
Fitchburg, MA 800-255-6313
Seal-Tite Bag Company
Philadelphia, PA 717-917-1949
Sealed Air Corp
Charlotte, NC 800-391-5645
Sealstrip Corporation
Boyertown, PA 610-367-6282
Seattle Plastics
Seattle, WA 800-441-0679
Seattle-Tacoma Box Co
Kent, WA. 253-854-9700
Sebring Container Corporation
Salem, OH. 330-332-1533
Seco Industries
Commerce, CA 323-726-9721
Security Packaging
North Bergen, NJ 201-854-1955
Sekisui TA Industries
Brea, CA 800-258-8273
Semco Plastic Co
St Louis, MO. 314-487-4557
Sertapak Packaging Corporation
Woodstock, ON. 800-265-1162
SerVend International
Sellersburg, IN 800-367-4233
Service Manufacturing
Aurora, IL 888-325-2788
Servin Company
New Baltimore, MI. 800-824-0962
Set Point Paper Company
Mansfield, MA 800-225-0501
Setco
Monroe Twp, NJ 609-655-4600
Setco
Anaheim, CA 714-777-5200
Seton Indentification Products
Branford, CT. 800-571-2596
Setterstix Corp
Cattaraugus, NY 716-257-3451
Seville Flexpack Corp
Oak Creek, WI 414-761-2751
Seymour Woodenware Company
Seymour, WI. 920-833-6551
Sfb Plastics Inc
Wichita, KS. 800-343-8133
SFBC, LLC dba Seaboard Folding Box
Fitchburg, MA 800-225-6313
Shamrock Plastics
Mt Vernon, OH 800-765-1611
Sharpsville Container Corp
Sharpsville, PA 800-645-1248
Shaw-Clayton Corporation
San Rafael, CA 800-537-6712
Sheboygan Paper Box Co
Sheboygan, WI 800-458-8373
Shelby Co
Westlake, OH 800-842-1650
Shields Bag & Printing Co
Yakima, WA 800-541-8630
Shillington Box Co LLC
St Louis, MO. 636-825-6471
Ship Rite Packaging
Bergenfield, NJ 800-721-7447
Shipley Basket Mfg Co
Dayton, TN 800-251-0806
Shipmaster Containers Ltd.
Markham, ON. 416-493-9193
Shippers Paper Products Co
Sheridan, AR. 800-468-1230
Shippers Supply
Saskatoon, SK. 800-661-5639
Shippers Supply, Labelgraphic
Calgary, AB. 800-661-5639
Shore Paper Box Co
Mardela Springs, MD 410-749-7125
Shorewood Packaging
Carlstadt, NJ 201-933-3203
Shouldice Brothers SheetMetal
Battle Creek, MI 269-962-5579
Sicht-Pack Hagner
Dornstetten/ Hallwangen, QC 800-454-5269
SIG Combibloc USA, Inc.
Chester, PA 610-546-4200

Sigma Industries	Spring Cove Container Div	Technipac
Elkhart, IN 574-295-9660	Roaring Spring, PA 814-224-5141	Le Sueur, MN 507-665-6658
Signature Packaging	Spring Wood Products	TEMP-TECH Company
West Orange, NJ 800-376-2299	Geneva, OH 440-466-1135	Springfield, MA 800-343-5579
Silgan Plastic Closure Sltns	SQP	Temple-Inland
Downers Grove, IL 800-727-8652	Schenectady, NY 800-724-1129	Memphis, TN 901-419-9000
Silgan Plastics Canada	Squire Corrugated Container Company	Tenneco Inc
Chesterfield, MO 800-274-5426	South Plainfield, NJ 908-561-8550	Lake Forest, IL 800-403-3393
Silgan Plastics LLC	SSW Holding Co Inc	Tenneco Packaging
Chesterfield, MO 800-274-5426	Elizabethtown, KY 270-769-5526	Westmont, IL 630-850-7034
Silver State Plastics Inc	St Joseph Packaging Inc	Tenneco Specialty Packaging
Greeley, CO 970-346-8667	St Joseph, MO 800-383-3000	Smyrna, GA 800-241-4402
Simkins Industries Inc	St. Louis Carton Company	TEQ
East Haven, CT 203-787-7171	Saint Louis, MO 314-241-0990	Huntley, IL 800-874-7113
Sirco Systems	St. Pierre Box & Lumber Company	Tesa Tape Inc
Birmingham, AL 205-731-7800	Canton, CT 860-693-2089	Charlotte, NC 800-429-8273
Skd Distribution Corp	Stand Fast Pkgng Prods Inc	TGR Container Sales
Jamaica, NY 800-458-8753	Addison, IL 630-543-6390	San Leandro, CA 800-273-6887
Smalley Package Company	Standard Folding Cartons Inc	THARCO
Berryville, VA 540-955-2550	Flushing, NY 718-396-4522	San Lorenzo, CA 800-772-2332
Smith Pallet Co Inc	Star Container Company	Thermal Bags By Ingrid Inc
Hatfield, AR 870-389-6184	Phoenix, AZ 480-281-4200	Gilberts, IL 800-622-5560
Smith-Lee Company	Star Container Corporation	Thermodynamics
Oshkosh, WI 800-327-9774	Leominster, MA 978-537-1676	Commerce City, CO 800-627-9037
Smith-Lustig Paper Box Manufacturing	Star Poly Bag Inc	Thermodyne International LTD
Cleveland, OH 216-621-0454	Brooklyn, NY 718-384-7034	Ontario, CA 909-923-9945
Smurfit Kappa	State Container Corp	Thermos Company
Carson, CA 310-537-8190	Moonachie, NJ 201-933-5200	Schaumburg, IL 800-243-0745
Smurfit Stone	Steel City Corporation	Thomas Tape & Supply Co Inc
Norcross, GA 314-656-5300	Youngstown, OH 800-321-0350	Springfield, OH 937-325-6414
Smurfit Stone Container	Step Products	Thornton Plastics
St Louis, MO 314-679-2300	Round Rock, TX 800-777-7837	Salt Lake City, UT 800-248-3434
Smurfit-Stone Container Corp	Steril-Sil Company	Thunder Pallet Inc
Santa Fe Springs, CA 714-523-3550	Bowmansville, PA 800-784-5537	Theresa, WI 800-354-0643
Smyrna Container Co	Sterling Net & Twine Company	Tin Box Co Of America Inc
Atlanta, GA 800-868-4305	Cedar Knolls, NJ 800-342-0316	Farmingdale, NY 800-888-8467
Smyth Co	Sterling Novelty Products	Tipper Tie Inc
Bedford, VA 800-950-7011	Northbrook, IL 847-291-0070	Apex, NC 919-362-8811
Snapware	Sterling Paper Company	TMS
Fullerton, CA 800-334-3062	Ohio, PA 800-282-1124	San Francisco, CA 800-447-7223
Snyder Crown	Stewart Sutherland Inc	Tni Packaging Inc
Marked Tree, AR 870-358-3400	Vicksburg, MI 269-649-0530	West Chicago, IL 800-383-0990
Snyder Industries Inc.	Stock America Inc	Tolan Machinery Company
Lincoln, NE 800-351-1363	Grafton, WI 262-375-4100	Rockaway, NJ 973-983-7212
Sobel Corrugated Containers	Stoffel Seals Corp	Tolco Corp
Cleveland, OH 216-475-2100	Tallapoosa, GA 800-422-8247	Toledo, OH 800-537-4786
Solve Needs International	Stone Container	Trade Fixtures
White Lake, MI 800-783-2462	Chicago, IL 312-346-6600	Little Rock, AR 800-872-3490
Somerville Packaging	Stone Container	Trans Flex Packagers Inc
Toronto, ON 416-754-7228	Moss Point, MS 502-491-4870	Unionville, CT 860-673-2531
Somerville Packaging	Stoneway Carton Company	Trans World Services
Mississauga, ON 905-678-8211	Mercer Island, WA 800-498-2185	Melrose, MA 800-882-2105
Sommers Plastic Product Co Inc	Streator Dependable Mfg	Transparent Container Co
Clifton, NJ 800-225-7677	Streator, IL 800-798-0551	Addison, IL 630-458-9031
Sonderen Packaging	Stretch-Vent Packaging System	Traub Container Corporation
Spokane, WA 800-727-9139	Ontario, CA 800-822-8368	Cleveland, OH 216-475-5100
Sonoco ThermoSafe	Stripper Bags	Tree Saver
Arlington Heights, IL 800-323-7442	Henderson, NV 800-354-2247	Englewood, CO 800-676-7741
SOPAKCO Foods	Stronghaven Containers Co	Treen Box & Pallet Inc
Mullins, SC 800-276-9678	Matthews, NC 800-222-7919	Bensalem, PA 215-639-5100
Source for Packaging	Stryco Wire Products	Trent Corp
New York, NY 800-223-2527	North York, ON 416-663-7000	Trenton, NJ 609-587-7515
Source Packaging Inc	Suburban Corrugated Box Company	Trevor Owen Limited
Mahwah, NJ 888-665-9768	Indianhead Park, IL 630-920-1230	Scarborough, ON 866-487-2224
Southern Champion Tray LP	Sun Plastics	Tri-Seal
Chattanooga, TN 800-468-2222	Clearwater, MN 800-862-1673	Blauvelt, NY 845-353-3300
Southern Film Extruders	Sunland Manufacturing Company	Tri-State Plastics
High Point, NC 800-334-6101	Minneapolis, MN 800-790-1905	Henderson, KY 270-826-8361
Southern Metal Fabricators Inc	Superfos Packaging Inc	Tri-Sterling
Albertville, AL 800-989-1330	Cumberland, MD 800-537-9242	Altamonte Spgs, FL 407-260-0330
Southern Missouri Containers	Superior Uniform Group	Trident Plastics
Springfield, MO 800-999-7666	Seminole, FL 800-727-8643	Ivyland, PA 800-222-2318
Southern Packaging Machinery	Supply One Inc	Trinidad Benham Corporation
Athens, GA 706-208-0814	Tulsa, OK	Denver, CO 303-220-1400
Southern Pallet	Surfine Central Corporation	Trinity Packaging
Christchurch, NZ 901-942-4603	Pine Bluff, AR 870-247-2387	Cheektowaga, NY 800-778-3111
Spartanburg Steel Products Inc	T & T Industries Inc	Trio Packaging Corp
Spartanburg, SC 800-974-7500	Fort Mohave, AZ 800-437-6246	Ronkonkoma, NY 800-331-0492
Spartech Plastics	T J Smith Box Co	Trio Products
Portage, WI 800-998-7123	Fort Smith, AR 877-540-7933	Elyria, OH 440-323-5457
Specialized Packaging London	T&S Blow Molding	Triple A Containers
London, ON 519-659-7011	Scarborough, ON 416-752-8330	Buena Park, CA 714-521-2820
Specialty Films & Associates	Tampa Corrugated Carton Company	Triple Dot Corp
Hebron, KY 800-984-3346	Tampa, FL 813-623-5115	Santa Ana, CA 714-241-0888
Specialty Packaging Inc	Tampa Pallet Co	True Pac
Fort Worth, TX 800-284-7722	Tampa, FL 813-626-5700	New Castle, DE 800-825-7890
Specialty Paper Bag Company	Tampa Sheet Metal Co	Tucson Container Corp
City of Industry, CA 800-962-2247	Tampa, FL 813-251-1845	Tucson, AZ 520-746-3171
Spectape Inc	Target Industries	Tudor Pulp & Paper Corporation
Erlanger, KY 859-283-2044	North Salt Lake, UT 866-617-2253	Prospect, CT 203-758-4494
Spectrum Plastics	Taylor Box Co	TULSACK
Las Vegas, NV 702-876-8650	Warren, RI 800-304-6361	Tulsa, OK 800-228-1936

Tupperware Brands Corporation
Orlando, FL.........................800-366-3800
Tyco Plastics
Lakeville, MN......................800-328-4080
Ultratainer
St Jean-Sur-Richelie, QC...........514-359-3651
Union Camp Corporation
Denver, CO.........................303-371-0760
Union Industries
Providence, RI.....................800-556-6454
Unipac Shipping
Jamaica, NY........................800-586-2711
Unipak Inc
West Chester, PA...................610-436-6600
Uniplast Films
Palmer, MA.........................800-343-1295
Unique Boxes
Chicago, IL........................800-281-1670
United Bags Inc
St Louis, MO.......................800-550-2247
United Flexible
Westbury, NY.......................516-222-2150
United Seal & Tag Corporation
Port Charlotte, FL.................800-211-9552
Universal Container Corporation
Odessa, FL.........................800-582-7477
Universal Folding Box
East Orange, NJ....................973-482-4300
Universal Folding Box Company
Hoboken, NJ........................201-659-7373
Universal Paper Box
Seattle, WA........................800-228-1045
Universal Plastics
Holyoke, MA........................800-553-0120
Upham & Walsh Lumber
Hoffman Estates, IL................847-519-1010
Urnex Brands Inc
Elmsford, NY.......................800-222-2826
US Can Company
Rosedale, MD.......................800-436-8021
US Plastic Corporation
Swampscott, MA.....................781-595-1030
US Tsubaki Holdings Inc
Wheeling, IL.......................800-323-7790
Utah PaperBox Company
Salt Lake City, UT.................801-363-0093
Vacumet Corporation
Austell, GA........................800-776-0865
Valley Container Corporation
Saint Louis, MO....................314-652-8050
Valley Container Inc
Bridgeport, CT.....................203-368-6546
Valley Packaging Supply Co
Green Bay, WI......................920-336-9012
Van Dereems Mfg Co
Hawthorne, NJ......................973-427-2355
Vermont Bag & Film
Bennington, VT.....................802-442-3166
Vermont Container Corp
Bennington, VT.....................802-442-5455
Victory Box Corp
Roselle, NJ........................908-245-5100
Victory Packaging, Inc.
Houston, TX........................800-486-5606
VIFAN Canada
Lanoraie, QC.......................800-557-0192
Viking Packaging & Display
San Jose, CA.......................408-998-1000
VIP Real Estate LTD
Chicago, IL........................773-376-5000
Virginia Plastics Co
Roanoke, VA........................800-777-8541
Visual Packaging Corp
Haskell, NJ........................973-835-7055
VitaMinder Company
Providence, RI.....................800-858-8840
Volk Packaging Corp
Biddeford, ME......................207-282-6151
Vonco Products LLC
Lake Villa, IL.....................800-323-9077
VPI Manufacturing
Draper, UT.........................801-495-2310
Wagner Brothers Containers
Baltimore, MD......................410-354-0044
Walker Bag Mfg Co
Louisville, KY.....................800-642-4949
Warner Electric Inc
South Beloit, IL...................800-234-3369
Warren Packaging
San Bernardino, CA.................909-888-7008
Wasserman Bag Company
Center Moriches, NY................631-909-8656

Wastequip Teem
Charlotte, NC......................877-468-9278
Waymar Industries
Burnsville, MN.....................888-474-1112
WCB Ice Cream
Philadelphia, PA...................215-425-4320
Weber Display & Packaging Inc
Philadelphia, PA...................215-426-3500
Webster Packaging Corporation
Loveland, OH.......................513-683-5666
Wedlock Paper ConvertersLtd.
Mississauga, ON....................800-388-0447
Welch Packaging Group Inc
Elkhart, IN........................574-295-2460
Werthan Packaging
White House, TN....................615-672-3336
West Rock
Atlanta, GA........................770-448-2193
Westeel
Saskatoon, SK......................306-931-2855
Western Container Company
Kansas City, MO....................816-924-5700
Westvaco Corporation
Newark, DE.........................302-453-7200
Weyerhaeuser Co
Seattle, WA........................800-525-5440
Wilks Precision Instr Co Inc
Union Bridge, MD...................410-775-7917
Willamette Industries
Beaverton, OR......................503-641-1131
Willamette Industries
Louisville, KY.....................800-465-3065
Willard Packaging Co
Gaithersburg, MD...................301-948-7700
Winchester Carton
Eutaw, AL..........................205-372-3337
Wins Paper Products
Springtown, TX.....................800-733-2420
Winzen Film
Taylor, TX.........................800-779-7595
Wisconsin Box Co
Wausau, WI.........................800-876-6658
Wisconsin Converting Inc
Green Bay, WI......................800-544-1935
Wisconsin Film & Bag Inc
Shawano, WI........................800-765-9224
WNA
Lancaster, TX......................800-334-2877
WNA Hopple Plastics
Florence, KY.......................800-446-4622
Wnc Pallet & Forest Pdts Co
Candler, NC........................828-667-5426
Woodson Pallet Co
Anmoore, WV........................304-623-2858
Woodstock Plastics Co Inc
Marengo, IL........................815-568-5281
Workman Packaging Inc.
Saint-Laurent, QC..................800-252-5208
World Kitchen
Rosemont, IL.......................847-678-8600
Wrap Pack
Yakima, WA.........................800-879-9727
Wright Brothers Paper Box Company
Fond Du Lac, WI....................920-921-8270
WS Packaging Group Inc
Green Bay, WI......................877-977-5177
Yerecic Label Co
New Kensington, PA.................724-334-3300
Yeuell Name Plate & Label
Woburn, MA.........................781-933-2984
York Container Co
York, PA...........................717-757-7611
Zenith Specialty Bag Co
City Of Industry, CA...............800-962-2247
Zero Manufacturing Inc
North Salt Lake, UT................800-959-5050
Zip-Pak
Manteno, IL........................800-488-6973

Packing House Supplies

Acme Scale Co
San Leandro, CA....................888-638-5040
Actionpac Scales Automation
Oxnard, CA.........................800-394-0154
All Power Inc
Sioux City, IA.....................712-258-0681
Allflex Packaging Products
Ambler, PA.........................800-448-2467
Auto Pallets-Boxes
Lathrup Village, MI................800-875-2699
Barrette Outdoor Living
Cleveland, OH......................800-336-2383

Belco Packaging Systems
Monrovia, CA.......................800-833-1833
Bennett Box & Pallet Company
Winston, NC........................800-334-8741
C.J. Machine
Fridley, MN........................763-767-4630
Carton Closing Company
Butler, PA.........................724-287-7759
Cincinnati Foam Products
Cincinnati, OH.....................513-741-7722
Columbia Machine Inc
Vancouver, WA......................800-628-4065
Columbus McKinnon Corporation
Getzville, NY......................800-888-0985
Cozzini Inc
Algona, IA.........................888-295-1116
Crown Equipment Corp.
New Bremen, OH.....................419-629-2311
Cutler Brothers Box & Lumber
Fairview, NJ.......................201-943-2535
Dearborn Mid-West Conveyor Co
Overland Park, KS..................913-384-9950
Dorell Equipment Inc
Somerset, NJ.......................732-247-5400
Douglas Machine Inc
Alexandria, MN.....................320-763-6587
Dynabilt Products
Readville, MA......................800-443-1008
Edson Packaging Machinery
Hamilton, ON.......................800-493-3766
Elite Storage Solutions Inc
Monroe, GA.........................800-367-0572
Elliott Manufacturing Co Inc
Fresno, CA.........................559-233-6235
Exact Equipment Corporation
Morrisville, PA....................215-295-2000
F.E. Wood & Sons
West Baldwin, ME...................207-286-5003
Fabricating & Welding Corp
Chicago, IL........................773-928-2050
Fabrication Specialties
Centerville, TN....................931-729-2283
Florida Knife Co
Sarasota, FL.......................800-966-5643
Food Equipment Manufacturing Company
Bedford Heights, OH................216-672-5859
Frazier Industrial Co
Long Valley, NJ....................800-859-1342
FreesTech
Sinking Spring, PA.................717-560-7560
Fresno Pallet, Inc.
Sultana, CA........................559-591-4111
Gemini Plastic Films Corporation
Garfield, NJ.......................800-789-4732
Genesee Corrugated
Flint, MI..........................810-228-3702
Girard Wood Products Inc
Puyallup, WA.......................800-532-0505
Goldco Industries
Loveland, CO.......................970-663-4770
Goldman Manufacturing Company
Detroit, MI........................313-834-5535
Gram Equipment Of America
Tampa, FL..........................813-248-1978
H.J. Jones & Sons
London, ON.........................800-667-0476
Halpak Plastics
Deer Park, NY......................800-442-5725
Halton Packaging Systems
Oakville, ON.......................905-847-9141
Hanson Box & Lumber Company
Wakefield, MA......................617-245-0358
Hudson Control Group Inc
Springfield, NJ....................973-376-8265
Iman Pack
Westland, MI.......................800-810-4626
Industrial Hardwood
Perrysburg, OH.....................419-666-2503
Industrial Lumber & Packaging
Spring Lake, MI....................616-842-1457
International Paper Box Machine Company
Nashua, NH.........................603-889-6651
J.M. Rogers & Sons
Moss Point, MS.....................228-475-7584
Jetstream Systems
Wichita, KN........................855-861-6916
Kimball Companies
East Longmeadow, MA................413-525-1881
Kisters Kayat
Sarasota, FL.......................386-424-0101
Konz Wood Products Co
Appleton, WI.......................877-610-5145

233

Krones
Franklin, WI 800-752-3787
L&H Wood Manufacturing Company
Farmington, MI 248-474-9000
Landis Plastics
Alsip, IL 708-396-1470
Le Fiell Co
Reno, NV 402-592-9993
Load King Mfg
Jacksonville, FL 800-531-4975
Longford Equipment US
Glastonbury, CT 416-298-6622
M&R Flexible Packaging
Springboro, OH 800-543-3380
Market Forge Industries Inc
Everett, MA 866-698-3188
Matthiesen Equipment
San Antonio, TX 800-624-8635
Michiana Box & Crate
Niles, MI 800-677-6372
Millwood Inc
Vienna, OH 330-393-4400
New Age Industrial
Norton, KS 800-255-0104
New Jersey Wire Stitching Machine Company
Cherry Hill, NJ 856-428-2572
Old English Printing & Label Company
Delray Beach, FL 561-997-9990
Packaging & Processing Equipment
Ayr, ON 519-622-6666
Packaging Dynamics
Walnut Creek, CA 925-938-2711
Pallet Pro
Moss, TN 800-489-3661
PDC International
Austin, TX 512-302-0194
Pneumatic Scale Angelus
Cuyahoga Falls, OH 330-923-0491
Precision Printing & Packaging
Clarksville, TN 800-500-4526
Premier Packages
Saint Louis, MO 800-466-6588
Premium Pallet
Philadelphia, PA 800-648-7347
Priority One America
Oshkosh, WI 920-235-5562
Production Systems
Marietta, GA 800-235-9734
PTI Packaging
Portage, WI 800-501-4077
RAM Center
Red Wing, MN 800-309-5431
Ratcliff Hoist Company
San Carlos, CA 650-595-3840
Refrigiwear Inc
Dahlonega, GA 800-645-3744
Remcon Plastics Inc
Reading, PA 800-360-3636
Rennco LLC
Homer, MI 800-409-5225
Rockford-Midland Corporation
Rockford, IL 800-327-7908
Saeplast Canada
St John, NB 800-567-3966
Sapac International
Fond Du Lac, WI 800-257-2722
Seal-O-Matic Corp
Jacksonville, OR 800-631-2072
Seattle-Tacoma Box Co
Kent, WA 253-854-9700
Sekisui TA Industries
Brea, CA 800-258-8273
Shields Products Inc
West Pittston, PA 570-655-4596
Shippers Supply
Saskatoon, SK 800-661-5639
Sinco
Red Wing, MN 800-243-6753
Solve Needs International
White Lake, MI 800-783-2462
Sonoma Pacific Company
Montebello, CA 323-838-4374
Sperling Industries
Omaha, NE 800-647-5062
Standard-Knapp Inc
Portland, CT 800-628-9565
Steel King Industries
Stevens Point, WI 800-553-3096
Studd & Whipple Company
Conewango Valley, NY. 716-287-3791
Swift Creek Forest Products
Jetersville, VA. 804-561-4498

Technibilt/Cari-All
Newton, NC 800-233-3972
Thiele Technologies-Reedley
Reedley, CA 800-344-8951
Tier-Rack Corp
Ballwin, MO 800-325-7869
Trenton Mills Inc
Trenton, TN. 731-855-1323
Trident Plastics
Ivyland, PA 800-222-2318
Triple-A Manufacturing Company
Toronto, ON 800-786-2238
Unirak Storage Systems
Taylor, MI 800-348-7225
UPACO Adhesives
Richmond, VA. 800-446-9984
Upham & Walsh Lumber
Hoffman Estates, IL 847-519-1010
UPN Pallet Company
Penns Grove, NJ 856-299-1192
Vertical Systems Intl
Lakeside Park, KY 859-485-9650
Viking Pallet Corp
Maple Grove, MN 763-425-6707
W.G. Durant Corporation
Whittier, CA 562-946-5555
WE Killam Enterprises
Waterford, ON. 519-443-7421
Western Plastics
Portland, TN 615-325-7331
Whallon Machinery Inc
Royal Center, IN 574-643-9561
Williamsburg Millwork
Ruther Glen, VA 804-994-2151
Woodson Pallet Co
Anmoore, WV. 304-623-2858
Wrap Pack
Yakima, WA 800-879-9727
Zed Industries
Vandalia, OH. 937-667-8407

Paper

Candy Wrapping

Alufoil Products Co Inc
Hauppauge, NY 631-231-4141
ESS Technologies
Blacksburg, VA. 540-961-5716
IB Concepts
Elizabeth, NJ. 888-671-0800

Corrugated

Clearwater Paper Corporation
Spokane, WA. 877-847-7831
Corfab
Chicago, IL 708-458-8750
Corrugated Specialties
Plainwell, MI 269-685-9821
Corrugated Supplies Co.
Bedford, IL 888-826-2738
Graphic Packaging Intl
Elk Grove Vlg, IL 847-437-1700
Inter-Pack Corporation
Monroe, MI 734-242-7755
IVEX Packaging Corporation
Longueuil, QC 450-651-8887
Lumber & Things
Keyser, WV 800-296-5656
Marshall Paper Products
East Norwich, NY
National Packaging
Rumford, RI 401-434-1070
RTS Packaging
Hillside, IL 708-338-2800
Shipmaster Containers Ltd.
Markham, ON. 416-493-9193

Glassine

Brooklace
Oshkosh, WI. 800-572-4552
Simkins Industries Inc
East Haven, CT. 203-787-7171

Grease & Oil Resistant

Brooklace
Oshkosh, WI. 800-572-4552
Central Coated Products Inc
Alliance, OH 330-821-9830

Pepperell Paper Company
Lawrence, MA 978-433-6951
Printpack Inc.
Atlanta, GA. 404-460-7000
Simkins Industries Inc
East Haven, CT. 203-787-7171
Sorg Paper Company
Middletown, OH. 513-420-5300
Tudor Pulp & Paper Corporation
Prospect, CT 203-758-4494

Heat Sealing

Hazen Paper Co
Holyoke, MA 413-538-8204
Paper Product Specialties
Waukesha, WI. 262-549-1730
Printpack Inc.
Atlanta, GA. 404-460-7000

Kraft

Durango-Georgia Paper
Tampa, FL. 813-286-2718
Lumber & Things
Keyser, WV 800-296-5656
Meadwestvaco Corp
Richmond, VA. 804-444-1000
Pepperell Paper Company
Lawrence, MA 978-433-6951
Salinas Valley Wax Paper Co
Salinas, CA 831-424-2747
Shamrock Paper Company
Saint Louis, MO 314-241-2370

Label

Graphic Impressions of Illinois
River Grove, IL 708-453-1100
Harris & Company
Salem, OH. 330-332-4127
Print & Peel
New York, NY 800-451-0807
Southern Imperial Inc
Rockford, IL 800-747-4665
Vande Berg SCALES/Vbs Inc
Sioux Center, IA 712-722-1181

Laminated

Alufoil Products Co Inc
Hauppauge, NY 631-231-4141
Burrows Paper Corp
Little Falls, NY 800-272-7122
Fibre Converters Inc
Constantine, MI 269-279-1700
Fortifiber Building Systs Grp
Fernley, NV 800-773-4777
Hampden Papers Inc
Holyoke, MA 413-536-1000
Hazen Paper Co
Holyoke, MA 413-538-8204
Henschel Coating & Laminating
New Berlin, WI. 800-866-5683
Lamcraft Inc
Lees Summit, MO. 800-821-1333
Laminated Papers
Holyoke, MA 413-533-3906
Mail-Well Label
Baltimore, MD 800-637-4879
Norpak Corp
Newark, NJ 800-631-6970
Packaging Dynamics International
Caldwell, OH 740-732-5665
Salinas Valley Wax Paper Co
Salinas, CA 831-424-2747
Sorg Paper Company
Middletown, OH. 513-420-5300
Trinity Packaging
Cheektowaga, NY 800-778-3111
West Rock
Atlanta, GA. 770-448-2193
Zimmer Custom-Made Packaging
Indianapolis, IN 317-263-3436

Lining

Cellier Corporation
Taunton, MA 508-655-5906
Gardiner Paperboard
Gardiner, ME 207-582-3230
International Tray Pads
Aberdeen, NC 910-944-1800

Salinas Valley Wax Paper Co
Salinas, CA 831-424-2747

Plastic Coated

Central Coated Products Inc
Alliance, OH 330-821-9830
Fibre Leather Manufacturing Company
New Bedford, MA 800-358-6012
Henschel Coating & Laminating
New Berlin, WI .800-866-5683
International Tray Pads
Aberdeen, NC 910-944-1800
Jen-Coat, Inc.
Westfield, MA 877-536-2628
Salinas Valley Wax Paper Co
Salinas, CA 831-424-2747
Zimmer Custom-Made Packaging
Indianapolis, IN 317-263-3436

Pressure Sensitive

KAPCO
Kent, OH 800-843-5368
MAC Tac LLC
Stow, OH 866-262-2822
Print & Peel
New York, NY .800-451-0807

Waxed

Burrows Paper Corp
Little Falls, NY 800-272-7122
Clearwater Paper Corporation
Spokane, WA 877-847-7831
Fabricon Products Inc
River Rouge, MI 313-841-8200
Framarx Corp
S Chicago Hts, IL 800-336-3936
Handy Wacks Corp
Sparta, MI 800-445-4434
Norpak Corp
Newark, NJ 800-631-6970
Patty Paper Inc
Plymouth, IN 800-782-1703
Rochester Midland Corp
Rochester, NY .800-387-7174
Salinas Valley Wax Paper Co
Salinas, CA 831-424-2747
Schwab Paper Products Co
Romeoville, IL .800-837-7225
Shields Products Inc
West Pittston, PA 570-655-4596

Wet Strength

SCA Hygiene Paper
San Ramon, CA 800-992-8675
Shawano Specialty Papers
Shawano, WI 800-543-5554
Sorg Paper Company
Middletown, OH 513-420-5300

Wrapping

Alufoil Products Co Inc
Hauppauge, NY 631-231-4141
Dorado Carton Company
Dorado, PR 787-796-1670
ESS Technologies
Blacksburg, VA 540-961-5716
Hampden Papers Inc
Holyoke, MA 413-536-1000
Jupiter Mills Corporation
Roslyn, NY 800-853-5121
Mimi et Cie
Seattle, WA 206-545-1850
Norpak Corp
Newark, NJ 800-631-6970
North American Packaging Corp
New York, NY .800-499-3521
Paper Service
Hinsdale, NH 603-239-6344
Patty Paper Inc
Plymouth, IN 800-782-1703
Pepperell Paper Company
Lawrence, MA .978-433-6951
Robinette Co
Bristol, TN 423-968-7800
Salinas Valley Wax Paper Co
Salinas, CA 831-424-2747
Shamrock Paper Company
Saint Louis, MO 314-241-2370

Sorg Paper Company
Middletown, OH 513-420-5300
St. Clair Pakwell
Bellwood, IL 800-323-1922

Plastic

Alcoa Corp
Pittsburgh, PA .412-315-2900

Biodegradable, Recyclable

Arbee Transparent Inc
Elk Grove Vlg, IL 800-642-2247
Gateway Plastics Inc
Mequon, WI 262-242-2020
Hinkle Manufacturing
Perrysburg, OH 419-666-5367
International Polymers Corp
Allentown, PA .800-526-0953
Stock America Inc
Grafton, WI 262-375-4100
Tectonics
Westmoreland, NH 603-352-8894
Tolas Health Care Packaging
Feasterville Trevose, PA 215-322-7900

Retorts

Canning

A.K. Robins
Baltimore, MD 800-486-9656
Allpax Products
Covington, LA 888-893-9277
Dixie Canner Machine Shop
Athens, GA 706-549-0592
Innovative Food Solutions LLC
Columbus, OH 800-884-3314
Melco Steel Inc
Azusa, CA 626-334-7875
Reid Boiler Works
Bellingham, WA 360-714-6157
Stock America Inc
Grafton, WI 262-375-4100

Seals

Bottle & Jar

American National Rubber
Ceredo, WV 304-453-1311
Crown Closures Machinery
Lancaster, OH .740-681-6593
Crown Holdings, Inc.
Yardley, PA 215-698-5100
Dickey Manufacturing Company
St Charles, IL .630-584-2918
Greenfield Packaging
White Plains, NY 914-993-0233
Pack Line Corporation
Racine, WI 800-248-6868
Phoenix Closures Inc
Naperville, IL .630-544-3475
Romatic Manufacturing Co
Southbury, CT 203-264-3442
Simolex Rubber Corp
Plymouth, MI .734-453-4500
Tri-Seal
Blauvelt, NY 845-353-3300
Ultrapak
Dunkirk, NY 800-228-6030

Box Strapping

Gulf Arizona Packaging
Humble, TX 800-364-3887
Herche Warehouse
Denver, CO 303-371-8186
L&H Wood Manufacturing Company
Farmington, MI 248-474-9000

Pressure Sensitive

Cantech Industries Inc
Johnson City, TN 800-654-3947
City Stamp & Seal Co
Austin, TX 800-950-6074
Coleman Rubber Stamps
Daytona Beach, FL 386-252-8597
Cummins Label Co
Kalamazoo, MI 800-280-7589

Deco Labels & Tags
Toronto, ON 888-496-9029
Grand Rapids Label
Grand Rapids, MI 616-776-2778
Innovative Packaging Solution
Martin, MI 616-656-2100
Long Island Stamp Corporation
Flushing, NY .800-547-8267
M & M Display
Philadelphia, PA 800-874-7171
New Era Label Corporation
Belleville, NJ .973-759-2444
Reotemp Instrument Corp
San Diego, CA 800-648-7737
Rhode Island Label Work Inc
West Warwick, RI 401-828-6400
Schwaab, Inc
Milwaukee, WI 800-935-9877
Stoffel Seals Corp
Tallapoosa, GA 800-422-8247
Timemed Labeling Systems
Valencia, CA .818-897-1111

Price Tag

General Trade Mark Labelcraft
Staten Island, NY 718-448-9800
House Stamp Works
Chicago, IL 312-939-7177
Muskogee Rubber Stamp & Seal Company
Fort Gibson, OK 918-478-3046
Stoffel Seals Corp
Tallapoosa, GA 800-422-8247

Shakers

Salt & Pepper

Amco Metals Indl
City Of Industry, CA 626-855-2550
Browne & Company
Markham, ON .905-475-6104
C R Mfg
Waverly, NE 877-789-5844
Carlisle Food Svc Products Inc
Oklahoma City, OK 800-654-8210
Coley Industries
Wayland, NY .716-728-2390
Gril-Del
Mankato, MN .800-782-7320
Liberty Ware LLC
Clearfield, UT 888-500-5885
Michael Leson Dinnerware
Youngstown, OH 800-821-3541
Reiner Products
Waterbury, CT 800-345-6775
Superior Products Company
Saint Paul, MN 800-328-9800
Tablecraft Products Co Inc
Gurnee, IL 800-323-8321
Traex
Dane, WI 800-356-8006

Sleeves

Bottle

Flexo Transparent Inc
Buffalo, NY 877-993-5396
Ultrapak
Dunkirk, NY 800-228-6030
Wilkens-Anderson Co
Chicago, IL 800-847-2222

Stamps

Dating & Numbering

A.D. Johnson Engraving Company
Kalamazoo, MI 269-342-5500
A.D. Joslin Manufacturing Company
Manistee, MI .231-723-2908
ABC Stamp Signs & Awards
Boise, ID 208-375-4470
Accent Mark
Palmdale, CA .661-274-8191
American Art Stamp
Gardena, CA 310-965-9004
Century Rubber Stamp Company
New York, NY 212-962-6165
City Stamp & Seal Co
Austin, TX 800-950-6074

Des Moines Stamp Mfg Co
Des Moines, IA 888-236-7739
Drs Designs
Bethel, CT 888-792-3740
Durable Engravers
Franklin Park, IL 800-869-9565
E C Shaw Co
Cincinnati, OH 866-532-7429
Fleming Packaging Corporation
Peoria, IL 309-676-7657
Fraser Stamp & Seal
Chicago, IL 800-540-8565
G&R Graphics
West Orange, NJ 813-503-8592
Hartford Stamp Works
Hartford, CT 860-249-6205
Hiss Stamp Company
Columbus, OH 614-224-5119
Innovative Ceramic Corp
East Liverpool, OH 330-385-6515
Joyce Engraving Co Inc
Dallas, TX 214-638-1262
L&L Engraving Company
Gilford, NH 888-524-3032
Mecco Marking & Traceability
Cranberry Township, PA 888-369-9190
Modern Stamp Company
Baltimore, MD 800-727-3029
Nameplate
St Paul, MN 651-228-1522
National Metal Industries
West Springfield, MA 800-628-8850
Pinquist Tool & Die Company
Brooklyn, NY 800-752-0414
Plastimatic Arts Corporation
Mishawaka, IN 800-442-3593
R.P. Childs Stamp Company
Ludlow, MA 413-733-1211
Schwaab, Inc
Milwaukee, WI 800-935-9877
South Well Co
San Antonio, TX 210-223-1831
Southern Atlantic Label Co
Chesapeake, VA 800-456-5999
United Ribtype Co
Fort Wayne, IN 800-473-4039
Volk Corp
Farmington Hills, MI 800-521-6799

Rubber

ABC Stamp Signs & Awards
Boise, ID 208-375-4470
Accent Mark
Palmdale, CA 661-274-8191
Ace Stamp & Engraving
Lakewood, WA 253-582-3322
Allmark Impressions LTD
Fort Worth, TX 817-834-0080
American Art Stamp
Gardena, CA 310-965-9004
Ameristamp/Sign-A-Rama
Evansville, IN 800-543-6693
Atlas Rubber Stamp & Printing
York, PA 717-751-0459
Century Rubber Stamp Company
New York, NY 212-962-6165
Chattanooga Rubber Stamp & Stencil Works
Sale Creek, TN 800-894-1164
City Stamp & Seal Co
Austin, TX 800-950-6074
Coleman Rubber Stamps
Daytona Beach, FL 386-252-8597
Corpus Christi Stamp Works
Corpus Christi, TX 800-322-4515
Crown Marking
Minneapolis, MN 800-305-5249
Custom Rubber Stamp Co
Crosby, MN 888-606-4579
Custom Stamp Company
Anza, CA 323-292-0753
Dayton Marking Devices Company
Dayton, OH 937-432-0285
Des Moines Stamp Mfg Co
Des Moines, IA 888-236-7739
Detroit Marking Products
Detroit, MI 800-833-8222
Dixie Rubber Stamp & Seal Company
Atlanta, GA 404-875-8883
Drs Designs
Bethel, CT 888-792-3740

East Memphis Rubber Stamp Company
Bartlett, TN 901-384-0887
Ed Smith's Stencil Works LTD
New Orleans, LA 504-525-2128
Ehrgott Rubber Stamp Company
Indianapolis, IN 317-353-2222
Everett Rubber Stamp
Everett, WA 425-258-6747
Federal Stamp & Seal Manufacturing Company
Atlanta, GA 800-333-7726
Fleming Packaging Corporation
Peoria, IL 309-676-7657
Flint Rubber Stamp Works
Flint, MI 810-235-2341
Fox Stamp Sign & Specialty
Menasha, WI 920-725-2683
Franklin Rubber Stamp Co
Wilmington, DE 302-654-8841
Fraser Stamp & Seal
Chicago, IL 800-540-8565
Frost Manufacturing Corp
Worcester, MA 800-462-0216
G&R Graphics
West Orange, NJ 813-503-8592
Glover Rubber Stamp & Crafts
Wills Point, TX 214-824-6900
Granite State Stamps Inc
Manchester, NH 800-937-3736
Grays Harbor Stamp Works
Aberdeen, WA 800-894-3830
Gribble Stamp & Stencil Co
Houston, TX 713-228-5358
Grueny's Rubber Stamps
Little Rock, AR 501-376-0393
Hartford Stamp Works
Hartford, CT 860-249-6205
Hathaway Stamps
Cincinnati, OH 513-621-1052
Hiss Stamp Company
Columbus, OH 614-224-5119
House Stamp Works
Chicago, IL 312-939-7177
Houston Stamp & Stencil Company
Houston, TX 713-869-4337
Huntington Park Rbr Stamp Co
Huntington Park, CA 800-882-0029
Ideal Office Supply & Rubber Stamp Company
Kingsport, TN 423-246-7371
Innovative Ceramic Corp
East Liverpool, OH 330-385-6515
Jim Lake Companies
Dallas, TX 214-741-5018
Justrite Rubber Stamp & Seal
Kansas City, MO 800-229-5010
JVC Rubber Stamp Company
Elkhart, IN 574-293-0113
L&L Engraving Company
Gilford, NH 888-524-3032
Lakeland Rubber Stamp Company
Lakeland, FL 863-682-5111
Lakeview Rubber Stamp Co
Chicago, IL 773-539-1525
Larry B Newman Printing
Knoxville, TN 888-835-4566
Lobue's Rubber Stamp Co
Houston, TX 713-652-0031
Long Island Stamp Corporation
Flushing, NY 800-547-8267
Mankuta Bros Rubber Stamp Co
Bohemia, NY 800-223-4481
Mansfield Rubber Stamp
Mansfield, OH 419-524-1442
Mark-It Rubber Stamp & Label Company
Stamford, CT 203-348-3204
Marking Devices Inc
Cleveland, OH 216-861-4498
Martco Engravers
Fremont, NH 603-895-3561
Mastermark
Kent, WA 206-762-9610
Modern Stamp Company
Baltimore, MD 800-727-3029
Moore Efficient Communication Aids
Denver, CO 303-433-8456
Muskogee Rubber Stamp & Seal Company
Fort Gibson, OK 918-478-3046
My Serenity Pond
Cold Spring, MN 320-363-0411
Nameplate
St Paul, MN 651-228-1522
National Marking Products Inc
Henrico, VA 800-482-1553

Northern Berkshire Tourist
North Adams, MA 413-663-9204
O.K. Marking Devices
Regina, SK 306-522-2856
OK Stamp & Seal Products
Oklahoma City, OK 405-235-7853
Oration Rubber Stamp Company
Columbus, NJ 908-496-4161
Plastimatic Arts Corporation
Mishawaka, IN 800-442-3593
Printcraft Marking Devices Inc
Buffalo, NY 716-873-8181
Quick Stamp & Sign Mfg
Lafayette, LA 337-232-2171
R.P. Childs Stamp Company
Ludlow, MA 413-733-1211
Rebel Stamp & Sign Co
Baton Rouge, LA 800-860-5120
Richardson's Stamp Works
Houston, TX 713-973-0314
Royal ACME
Cleveland, OH 216-241-1477
Rubber Stamp Shop
Accokeek, MD 800-835-0839
Schwaab, Inc
Milwaukee, WI 800-935-9877
Service Stamp Works
Chicago, IL 312-666-8839
Sioux Falls Rbr Stamp Works
Sioux Falls, SD 855-334-5990
South Well Co
San Antonio, TX 210-223-1831
Southern Rubber Stamp
Tulsa, OK 888-826-4304
Spectrum Enterprises
Evansville, IN 812-425-1771
Spencer Business Form Company
Spencer, WV 304-372-8877
Sutherland Stamp Company
San Diego, CA 858-233-7784
United Ribtype Co
Fort Wayne, IN 800-473-4039
Volk Corp
Farmington Hills, MI 800-521-6799
Walker Co
Oklahoma City, OK 800-522-3015
Welch Stencil Company
Scarborough, ME 800-635-3506
Wichita Stamp & Seal Inc
Wichita, KS 316-263-4223
Wildes Printing Co Inc
White Plains, MD 301-870-4141
Winmark Stamp & Sign
Salt Lake City, UT 800-438-0480

Stands

Tray

C R Mfg
Waverly, NE 877-789-5844
Carlisle Food Svc Products Inc
Oklahoma City, OK 800-654-8210
Creative Essentials
Ronkonkoma, NY 800-355-5891
Duke Manufacturing Co
St Louis, MO 800-735-3853
Ex-Cell KAISER LLC
Franklin Park, IL 847-451-0451
Fixtur World
Cookeville, TN 800-634-9887
Gaychrome Division of CSL
Crystal Lake, IL 800-873-4370
Glaro Inc
Hauppauge, NY 631-234-1717
International Patterns, Inc.
Bay Shore, NY 631-952-2000
Marston Manufacturing
Cleveland, OH 216-587-3400
MLS Signs Inc
Chesterfield, MI 586-948-0200
Quality Highchairs
Pacoima, CA 800-969-9635
R.R. Scheibe Company
Newton Center, MA 508-584-4900
Superior Products Company
Saint Paul, MN 800-328-9800
US Seating Products
Ocala, FL 800-999-2589
WES Plastics
Richmond Hill, ON 905-508-1546

Sticks

Candy

Automated Food Systems
Waxahachie, TX................469-517-0470
Jarden Home Brands
Daleville, IN....................800-392-2575
Saunder Brothers
Bridgton, ME...................207-647-3331
Setterstix Corp
Cattaraugus, NY................716-257-3451

Ice Cream

Global Sticks, Inc.
Surrey, BC.....................866-433-5770
Hardwood Products Co LP
Guilford, ME...................800-289-3340
Jarden Home Brands
Cloquet, MN....................218-879-6700
Norse Dairy Systems
Columbus, OH...................800-338-7465
Solon Manufacturing Company
North Haven, CT................800-341-6640

Tags

Cellulose & Fiber

Atlas Tag & Label Inc
Neenah, WI.....................800-558-6418
Connecticut Laminating Co Inc
New Haven, CT..................800-753-9119
Labelprint America
Newburyport, MA................978-463-4004

Pressure Sensitive

Advanced Labelworx
Anderson, SC...................865-966-8711
ATL-East Tag & Label Inc
West Chester, PA...............866-381-8744
Carlton Industries
La Grange, TX..................800-231-5988
D A C Labels & Graphic
Dallas, TX.....................800-483-1700
Deco Labels & Tags
Toronto, ON....................888-496-9029
Emedco
Williamsville, NY..............877-765-8386
Gbs
North Canton, OH...............800-552-2427
Grand Valley Labels
Grand Rapids, MI
Itac Label & Tag Corp
Brooklyn, NY...................718-625-2148
Label House
Fullerton, CA..................800-499-5858
Label Technology Inc
Merced, CA.....................800-388-1990
Labelmart
Maple Grove, MN................888-577-0141
Labelprint America
Newburyport, MA................978-463-4004
Metspeed Labels
Levittown, PA..................888-886-0638
Mid South Graphics
Nashville, TN..................615-331-4210
Multi-Color Corp
Green Bay, WI..................800-236-8208
Nameplate
St Paul, MN....................651-228-1522
Ozark Tape & Label Co
Springfield, MO................417-831-1444
Paper Product Specialties
Waukesha, WI...................262-549-1730
Royal Label Co
Dorchester, MA.................617-825-6050
Seton Indentification Products
Branford, CT...................800-571-2596
Southern Atlantic Label Co
Chesapeake, VA.................800-456-5999
Stoffel Seals Corp
Tallapoosa, GA.................800-422-8247
Swan Label & Tag Co
Coraopolis, PA.................412-264-9000
TAC-PAD
Irvine, CA.....................800-947-1609
Three P
Salt Lake City, UT.............801-486-7407

Universal Tag Inc
Dudley, MA.....................800-332-8247

Price

Andrew H Lawson Co
Philadelphia, PA...............800-411-6628
Bedford Industries
Worthington, MN................800-533-5314
Clamp Swing Pricing Co Inc
Oakland, CA....................800-227-7615
Esselte Meto
Morris Plains, NJ..............800-645-3290
Federal Label Systems
Elmhurst, NY...................800-238-0015
General Trade Mark Labelcraft
Staten Island, NY..............718-448-9800
Intermec Technologies Corporation
Everett, WA....................425-348-2600
KHS Co
West Simsbury, CT..............860-658-9454
Labelprint America
Newburyport, MA................978-463-4004
Los Angeles Label Company
Commerce, CA...................800-606-5223
National Marking Products Inc
Henrico, VA....................800-482-1553
Plasti-Clip Corp
Milford, NH....................800-882-2547
Plastic Tagtrade Check
Essexville, MI.................989-892-7913
Reeve Store Equipment Co
Pico Rivera, CA................800-927-3383
Rothchild Printing Company
Flushing, NY...................800-238-0015
Royal Label Co
Dorchester, MA.................617-825-6050
SFBC, LLC dba Seaboard Folding Box
Fitchburg, MA..................800-225-6313
Stoffel Seals Corp
Tallapoosa, GA.................800-422-8247
United Seal & Tag Corporation
Port Charlotte, FL.............800-211-9552

Tea Bag

Cincinnati Convertors Inc
Cincinnati, OH.................513-731-6600
Stoffel Seals Corp
Tallapoosa, GA.................800-422-8247

Tapes

Adhesive

Adhesive Applications
Easthampton, MA................800-356-3572
Afassco
Minden, NV.....................775-783-3555
Cantech Industries Inc
Johnson City, TN...............800-654-3947
Deccofelt Corp
Glendora, CA...................800-543-3226
Dunrite Inc
Fremont, NE....................800-782-3061
Felco Packaging Specialist
Baltimore, MD..................800-673-8488
FFR Merchandising Inc
Twinsburg, OH..................800-422-2547
Glue Dots International
New Berlin, WI.................888-688-7131
Gulf Arizona Packaging
Humble, TX.....................800-364-3887
Herche Warehouse
Denver, CO.....................303-371-8186
International Adhesive Coating
Windham, NH....................800-253-4450
Jupiter Mills Corporation
Roslyn, NY.....................800-853-5121
Label Systems & Solutions
Bohemia, NY....................800-811-2560
Levin Brothers Paper
Cicero, IL.....................800-545-6200
Master Tape & Label Printers
Chicago, IL....................800-621-5801
Miller Studio
New Philadelphia, OH...........800-332-0050
Nashua Corporation
Nashua, NH.....................603-661-2004
National Tape Corporation
New Orleans, LA................800-535-8846
O.C. Adhesives Corporation
Ridgefield, NJ.................800-662-1595

On-Hand Adhesives
Lake Zurich, IL................800-323-5158
Quali-Tech Tape & Label
Denver, CO
Recco International
West Columbia, SC..............800-334-3008
Saunders West
Azusa, CA......................888-932-8836
Sekisui TA Industries
Brea, CA.......................800-258-8273
Spectape Inc
Erlanger, KY...................859-283-2044
Tesa Tape Inc
Charlotte, NC..................800-429-8273
Thomas Tape & Supply Co Inc
Springfield, OH................937-325-6414
US Label Corporation
Greensboro, NC.................336-332-7000
Wasserman Bag Company
Center Moriches, NY............631-909-8656
Worthen Industries Inc
Nashua, NH.....................603-888-5443
WS Packaging Group Inc
Green Bay, WI..................877-977-5177

Freezer

Gulf Arizona Packaging
Humble, TX.....................800-364-3887
Herche Warehouse
Denver, CO.....................303-371-8186
Verilon Products Co
Wheeling, IL...................800-323-1056

Gummed

Adhesive Products Inc
Vernon, CA.....................800-669-5516
Cantech Industries Inc
Johnson City, TN...............800-654-3947
Ebel Tape & Label
Cincinnati, OH.................513-471-1067
Gulf Arizona Packaging
Humble, TX.....................800-364-3887
Herche Warehouse
Denver, CO.....................303-371-8186
Intertape Polymer Group
Menasha, WI....................800-558-5006
Keena Corporation
Newton, MA.....................617-244-9800
Master Tape & Label Printers
Chicago, IL....................800-621-5801
Rexford Paper Company
Racine, WI.....................262-886-9100
Rudd Container Corp
Chicago, IL....................773-847-7600
Thomas Tape & Supply Co Inc
Springfield, OH................937-325-6414
Timemed Labeling Systems
Valencia, CA...................818-897-1111
Volk Corp
Farmington Hills, MI...........800-521-6799

Heat Sealing

International Adhesive Coating
Windham, NH....................800-253-4450
National Tape Corporation
New Orleans, LA................800-535-8846
Rexford Paper Company
Racine, WI.....................262-886-9100

Marking

Carlton Industries
La Grange, TX..................800-231-5988
Felco Packaging Specialist
Baltimore, MD..................800-673-8488
Master Tape & Label Printers
Chicago, IL....................800-621-5801
National Tape Corporation
New Orleans, LA................800-535-8846

Pressure Sensitive

Adhesive Products Inc
Vernon, CA.....................800-669-5516
Adstick Custom Labels Inc
Denver, CO.....................800-255-7314
Advanced Labelworx
Anderson, SC...................865-966-8711
Advanced Labelworx Inc
Oak Ridge, TN..................864-224-2122

237

Avon Tape
Chestnut Hill, MA 508-584-8273
Baltimore Tape Products Inc
Sykesville, MD.................410-795-0063
Cantech Industries Inc
Johnson City, TN 800-654-3947
D A C Labels & Graphic
Dallas, TX.................800-483-1700
Deccofelt Corp
Glendora, CA 800-543-3226
Ebel Tape & Label
Cincinnati, OH 513-471-1067
Emco Industrial Plastics
Cedar Grove, NJ.................800-292-9906
Fibre Leather Manufacturing Company
New Bedford, MA 800-358-6012
Gulf Arizona Packaging
Humble, TX 800-364-3887
Henkel Consumer Adhesive
Avon, OH 800-321-0253
Herche Warehouse
Denver, CO.................303-371-8186
International Adhesive Coating
Windham, NH.................800-253-4450
Intertape Polymer Group
Menasha, WI.................800-558-5006
J M Packaging Co
Warren, MI 586-771-7800
Jupiter Mills Corporation
Roslyn, NY.................800-853-5121
KAPCO
Kent, OH.................800-843-5368
Label Systems & Solutions
Bohemia, NY 800-811-2560
Marklite Line
Bellwood, IL.................708-668-4900
Master Tape & Label Printers
Chicago, IL.................800-621-5801
Merryweather Foam Inc
Sylacauga, AL.................256-249-8546
Miller Studio
New Philadelphia, OH 800-332-0050
NAP Industries
Brooklyn, NY.................877-635-4948
National Tape Corporation
New Orleans, LA 800-535-8846
Ozark Tape & Label Co
Springfield, MO 417-831-1444
Pakmark
Chesterfield, MO 800-423-1379
Pamco Label Co Inc
Des Plaines, IL.................847-803-2200
Print-O-Tape Inc
Mundelein, IL.................800-346-6311
Raypress Corp
Hoover, AL.................800-423-3731
Rexford Paper Company
Racine, WI.................262-886-9100
Richmond Printed Tape & Label
Hatfield, PA.................800-522-3525
Robinson Tape & Label
Branford, CT.................800-433-7102
Saunders West
Azusa, CA.................888-932-8836
Sekisui TA Industries
Brea, CA.................800-258-8273
Shippers Supply
Saskatoon, SK.................800-661-5639
Shippers Supply, Labelgraphic
Calgary, AB.................800-661-5639
Source for Packaging
New York, NY.................800-223-2527
Spectape Inc
Erlanger, KY.................859-283-2044
Tape & Label Engineering
St Petersburg, FL 800-237-8955
Tesa Tape Inc
Charlotte, NC 800-429-8273
Thomas Tape & Supply Co Inc
Springfield, OH.................937-325-6414
Volk Corp
Farmington Hills, MI 800-521-6799

Tea Packaging Materials

Cin-Made Packaging Group
Norcross, GA.................800-264-7494
Packaging Dynamics
Walnut Creek, CA.................925-938-2711
PPI
Baton Rouge, LA 225-330-4602
Xtreme Beverages, LLC
Dana Point, CA.................949-495-7929

Ties

Bag

Arbee Transparent Inc
Elk Grove Vlg, IL.................800-642-2247
Bedford Industries
Worthington, MN 800-533-5314
Cavert Wire Co
Rural Hall, NC 800-245-4042
Gulf Arizona Packaging
Humble, TX 800-364-3887
Herche Warehouse
Denver, CO 303-371-8186
Leco Plastic Inc
Hackensack, NJ.................201-343-3330
Package Containers Inc
Canby, OR.................800-266-5806
Superior Products Company
Saint Paul, MN 800-328-9800
T & T Industries Inc
Fort Mohave, AZ 800-437-6246

Bundle, Package

Bedford Industries
Worthington, MN 800-533-5314
Cavert Wire Co
Rural Hall, NC 800-245-4042
Emco Industrial Plastics
Cedar Grove, NJ.................800-292-9906
Gulf Arizona Packaging
Humble, TX 800-364-3887
Herche Warehouse
Denver, CO 303-371-8186
Indeco Products Inc
San Marcos, TX 888-246-3326
Jilson Group
Lodi, NJ.................800-969-5400
Leco Plastic Inc
Hackensack, NJ.................201-343-3330
Package Containers Inc
Canby, OR.................800-266-5806
QMS International, Inc.
Mississauga, Ontario, ON. 905-820-7225
T & T Industries Inc
Fort Mohave, AZ 800-437-6246

Trays

Ace Technical Plastics Inc
East Hartford, CT 860-278-2444
Bayhead Products Corp.
Dover, NH.................800-229-4323
Collectors Gallery
St Charles, IL 800-346-3063
DEL-Tec Packaging Inc
Greer, SC.................800-747-8683
Douglas Stephen Plastics Inc
Paterson, NJ 973-523-3030
In-Touch Products
North Salt Lake, UT 801-298-4466
IVEX Packaging Corporation
Longueuil, QC 450-651-8887
Jay Packaging Group Inc
Warwick, RI 401-244-1300
K & L Intl
Ontario, CA.................888-598-5588
Key Packaging Co
Sarasota, FL 941-355-2728
Leal True Form Corporation
Freeport, NY 516-379-2008
Madsen Wire Products Inc
Orland, IN.................260-829-6561
Mmi Engineered Soultions Inc
Saline, MI 800-825-2566
Nelipak
Phoenix, AZ 602-269-7648
Nu-Trend Plastics Thermoformer
Jacksonville, FL 904-353-5936
Olive Can Company
Elgin, IL 847-468-7474
Packaging Solutions
Los Altos Hills, CA 650-917-1022
Pactiv LLC
Lake Forest, IL 800-476-4300
Palace Packaging Machines Inc
Downingtown, PA.................610-873-7252
Parlor City Paper Box Co Inc
Binghamton, NY.................607-772-0600
Pinn Pack Packaging LLC
Oxnard, CA.................805-385-4100

Revere Group
Seattle, WA 206-545-1850
Schroeder Machine
San Marcos, CA 760-591-9733
Scott Packaging Corporation
Philadelphia, PA 215-925-5595
Seal Pac USA
Richmond, VA.................804-261-0580
Tenneco Inc
Lake Forest, IL 800-403-3393
Tenneco Specialty Packaging
Smyrna, GA 800-241-4402
V C 999 Packaging Systems
Kansas City, MO.................800-728-2999
WNA Hopple Plastics
Florence, KY.................800-446-4622
Xtreme Beverages, LLC
Dana Point, CA.................949-495-7929

Wax

Cheese Coating

Frank B Ross Co Inc
Rahway, NJ 732-669-0810
International Group Inc
Oshkosh, WI 920-233-5500

Paraffin

Hollowick Inc
Manlius, NY.................800-367-3015

Sealing

Frank B Ross Co Inc
Rahway, NJ.................732-669-0810
Stevenson-Cooper Inc
Philadelphia, PA.................215-223-2600

Wrappers

Frozen Food

Campbell Wrapper Corporation
De Pere, WI.................920-983-7100
Schwab Paper Products Co
Romeoville, IL 800-837-7225

Paper

Alufoil Products Co Inc
Hauppauge, NY 631-231-4141
Burrows Paper Corp
Little Falls, NY.................800-272-7122
Campbell Wrapper Corporation
De Pere, WI.................920-983-7100
Gardiner Paperboard
Gardiner, ME 207-582-3230
Handy Wacks Corp
Sparta, MI 800-445-4434
Patty Paper Inc
Plymouth, IN.................800-782-1703
Printpack, Inc.
Atlanta, GA.................404-460-7000
Ross & Wallace Inc
Hammond, LA 800-854-2300
Salinas Valley Wax Paper Co
Salinas, CA.................831-424-2747
Schwab Paper Products Co
Romeoville, IL 800-837-7225
Signature Packaging
West Orange, NJ.................800-376-2299
Stewart Sutherland Inc
Vicksburg, MI.................269-649-0530
Wrap Pack
Yakima, WA 800-879-9727

Transparent

Arbee Transparent Inc
Elk Grove Vlg, IL.................800-642-2247
Campbell Wrapper Corporation
De Pere, WI.................920-983-7100
Flexo Transparent Inc
Buffalo, NY.................877-993-5396
Goodwrappers Inc
Halethorpe, MD 800-638-1127
M S Plastics & Packaging Inc
Butler, NJ.................800-593-1802
MSK Covertech
Marietta, GA 770-928-1099

Trans World Services
  Melrose, MA 800-882-2105

Refrigeration & Cooling Equipment

Cabinets

Freezer & Frozen Foods

AAA Mill
Austin, TX.........................512-385-2215
Andgar Corp
Ferndale, WA.....................360-366-9900
Arkfeld Mfg & Distributing Co
Norfolk, NE.......................800-533-0676
Bacchus Wine Cellars
Houston, TX......................800-487-8812
Bettag & Associates
O Fallon, MO.....................800-325-0959
Bevles Company
Dallas, TX........................800-441-1601
C Nelson Mfg Co
Oak Harbor, OH..................800-922-7339
Crown Manufacturing Corporation
Waterford, CT....................860-442-4325
Cryochem
St Simons Island, GA............800-237-4001
Delfield Co
Mt Pleasant, MI..................800-733-8821
Duke Manufacturing Co
St Louis, MO.....................800-735-3853
EPCO
Murfreesboro, TN................800-251-3398
Eskay Metal Fabricating
Buffalo, NY.......................800-836-8015
Everidge
Plymouth, MN....................888-227-1629
Fogel Jordon Commercial Refrigeration Company
Philadelphia, PA.................800-523-0171
Food Warming Equipment Co
Crystal Lake, IL..................800-222-4393
Foster Refrigerator Corporation
Kinderhook, NY..................888-828-3311
G A Systems Inc
Huntington Beach, CA............714-848-7529
Habco
Concord, CA......................925-682-6203
Hoshizaki America Inc
Peachtree City, GA...............800-438-6087
IMC Teddy Food Service Equipment
Amityville, NY....................800-221-5644
J.H. Carr & Sons
Seattle, WA.......................800-523-8842
Kedco Wine Storage Systems
Farmingdale, NY.................800-654-9988
LA Rosa Refrigeration & Equip
Detroit, MI.......................800-527-6723
Lauritzen Makin Inc
Fort Worth, TX...................817-921-0218
Lyon LLC
Montgomery, IL..................630-892-8941
Master-Bilt
New Albany, MS..................800-647-1284
Merric
Bridgeton, MO...................314-770-9944
Metal Master Sales Corp
Glendale Heights, IL..............800-488-8729
Normandie Metal Fabricators
Port Washington, NY.............800-221-2398
Ojeda USA
Spartanburg, SC..................864-574-6004
Omicron Steel Products Company
Jamaica, NY......................718-805-3400
Piper Products Inc
Wausau, WI......................800-544-3057
Sefi Fabricators Inc
Amityville, NY....................631-842-2200
Shammi Industries
Corona, CA.......................800-417-9260
Silver King Refrigeration Inc
Minneapolis, MN.................800-328-3329
St. Louis Stainless Service
St Louis, MO.....................800-735-3853
Super Sturdy
Weldon, NC.......................800-253-4833
Talbert Display
Fort Worth, TX...................817-429-4504
Texican Specialty Products
Houston, TX......................800-869-5918
Valad Electric Heating Corporation
Tarrytown, NY....................914-631-4927

Welbilt Corporation
Stamford, CT.....................203-325-8300
Western Laminates
Omaha, NE.......................402-556-4600
Wine Chillers of California
Santa Ana, CA....................800-331-4274
Zero Manufacturing Inc
North Salt Lake, UT...............800-959-5050

Chillers

Blast

Advance Energy Technologies
Halfmoon, NY....................800-724-0198
Alkar Rapid Pak
Lodi, WI..........................608-592-3211
Chillers Solutions
Pompton Plains, NJ...............800-526-5201
Elliott-Williams Company
Indianapolis, IN..................800-428-9303
Gea Intec, Llc
Durham, NC......................919-433-0131
Glastender
Saginaw, MI......................800-748-0423
Henny Penny, Inc.
Eaton, OH........................800-417-8417
Pacific Pneumatics
Rancho Cucamonga, CA...........800-221-0961
Superior Products Company
Saint Paul, MN...................800-328-9800
USECO
Murfreesboro, TN................615-893-4820
Williams Refrigeration
Hillsdale, NJ......................800-445-9979

Compressors

GEA FES, Inc.
York, PA..........................025-119-1051
GEA Refrigeration North America
York, PA..........................800-888-4337
Tecumseh Products Co.
Ann Arbor, MI...................734-585-9500

Coolers

Beverage

Advance Energy Technologies
Halfmoon, NY....................800-724-0198
Alkar Rapid Pak
Lodi, WI..........................608-592-3211
Aurora Design Associates, Inc.
Salt Lake City, UT................801-588-0111
Bar Equipment Corporation of America
Downey, CA......................888-870-2322
Berkshire PPM
Litchfield, CT....................860-567-3118
Beverage Air
Winston Salem, NC...............800-845-9800
Chester-Jensen Co., Inc.
Chester, PA.......................800-685-3750
Cleland Sales Corp
Los Alamitos, CA.................562-598-6616
Convay Systems
Minnetonka, MN.................800-334-1099
Cool-Pitch Co
Jacksonville, FL..................800-938-0128
Cramer Products
New York, NY....................212-645-2368
Duke Manufacturing Co
St Louis, MO.....................800-735-3853
Elwood Safety Company
Buffalo, NY.......................866-326-6060
Felix Storch Inc
Bronx, NY........................800-932-4267
FleetwoodGoldcoWyard
Romeoville, IL....................630-759-6800
Fogel Jordon Commercial Refrigeration Company
Philadelphia, PA.................800-523-0171
Foster Refrigerator Corporation
Kinderhook, NY..................888-828-3311
Girard Spring Water
North Providence, RI..............800-477-9287

Glastender
Saginaw, MI......................800-748-0423
Hebeler Corp
Tonawanda, NY..................800-486-4709
Hoshizaki America Inc
Peachtree City, GA...............800-438-6087
Ilc Dover
Frederica, DE....................800-631-9567
International Patterns, Inc.
Bay Shore, NY....................631-952-2000
Ojeda USA
Spartanburg, SC..................864-574-6004
Perlick Corp
Milwaukee, WI...................800-558-5592
Pro-Flo Products
Cedar Grove, NJ..................800-325-1057
QBD Modular Systems
Santa Clara, CA..................800-663-3005
RubaTex Polymer
Middlefield, OH..................440-632-1691
Rubbermaid
High Point, NC...................888-895-2110
Summit Commercial
Bronx, NY........................800-932-4267
Superior Products Company
Saint Paul, MN...................800-328-9800
True Food Service Equipment, Inc.
O Fallon, MO.....................800-325-6152
Wine Chillers of California
Santa Ana, CA....................800-331-4274
Wine Well Chiller Co
Milford, CT.......................203-878-2465

Bread

Advance Energy Technologies
Halfmoon, NY....................800-724-0198
Fred D Pfening Co
Columbus, OH....................614-294-5361
I J White Corp
Farmingdale, NY.................631-293-2211
Industrial Air Conditioning Systems
Chicago, IL.......................773-486-4236
Peerless Food Equipment
Sidney, OH.......................937-492-4158

Butchers'

Advance Energy Technologies
Halfmoon, NY....................800-724-0198

Candy (Confectioners')

Advance Energy Technologies
Halfmoon, NY....................800-724-0198
Applied Thermal Technologies
San Marcos, CA..................800-736-5083
Hebeler Corp
Tonawanda, NY..................800-486-4709
Komline-Sanderson Engineering
Peapack, NJ.......................800-225-5457

Canners'

Advance Energy Technologies
Halfmoon, NY....................800-724-0198
Berkshire PPM
Litchfield, CT....................860-567-3118
Custom Food Machinery
Stockton, CA......................209-463-4343
Hebeler Corp
Tonawanda, NY..................800-486-4709
Horix Manufacturing Co
Mc Kees Rocks, PA...............412-771-1111
Nercon Engineering & Manufacturing
Oshkosh, WI.....................920-233-3268
South Valley Mfg Inc
Gilroy, CA........................408-842-5457

Ice

Eskay Metal Fabricating
Buffalo, NY.......................800-836-8015
Hoshizaki America Inc
Peachtree City, GA...............800-438-6087
Igloo Products Corp
Katy, TX..........................866-509-3503

Majestic
Bridgeport, CT 203-367-7900
Mid-Lands Chemical Company
Omaha, NE 800-642-5263
Midwest Aircraft Products Co
Lexington, OH 419-884-2164
Northfield Freezing Systems
Northfield, MN 800-426-1283
Olde Country Reproductions Inc
York, PA 800-358-3997
Plastilite Corporation
Omaha, NE 800-228-9506
Presence From Innovation LLC
St Louis, MO. 314-423-9777
Rubbermaid
High Point, NC 888-895-2110
Semco Manufacturing Company
Pharr, TX. 956-787-4203
Superior Products Company
Saint Paul, MN 800-328-9800

Ice Cream

Advance Energy Technologies
Halfmoon, NY. 800-724-0198
Jack Langston Manufacturing Company
Dallas, TX. 214-821-9844
Manufacturing Warehouse
Miami, FL 305-635-8886
Superior Products Company
Saint Paul, MN 800-328-9800
WA Brown & Son
Salisbury, NC 704-636-5131

Ingredient Water

Advance Energy Technologies
Halfmoon, NY. 800-724-0198
Applied Thermal Technologies
San Marcos, CA 800-736-5083
Bevistar
Oswego, IL 877-238-7827
Filtrine Manufacturing
Keene, NH. 800-930-3367
Girard Spring Water
North Providence, RI 800-477-9287
Komline-Sanderson Engineering
Peapack, NJ. 800-225-5457
Koolant Koolers
Kalamazoo, MI 800-968-5665
Perfect Equipment Inc
Gurnee, IL 800-356-6301
Wine Well Chiller Co
Milford, CT. 203-878-2465

Milk & Cream

Advance Energy Technologies
Halfmoon, NY. 800-724-0198
Applied Thermal Technologies
San Marcos, CA 800-736-5083
Beverage Air
Winston Salem, NC. 800-845-9800
C E Rogers Co
Mora, MN 800-279-8081
Carrier Vibrating Equip Inc
Louisville, KY 502-969-3171
Chester-Jensen Co., Inc.
Chester, PA 800-685-3750
Foster Refrigerator Corporation
Kinderhook, NY 888-828-3311
Gea Us
Galesville, WI. 608-582-3081
Hebeler Corp
Tonawanda, NY 800-486-4709
Precision
Miami, FL. 800-762-7565
Viatec
Victoria, BC 800-942-4702

Walk-In

Advance Energy Technologies
Halfmoon, NY. 800-724-0198
American Panel Corp
Ocala, FL. 800-327-3015
Arctic Industries
Medley, FL. 800-325-0123
Bally Refrigerated Boxes Inc
Morehead City, NC 800-242-2559
C.M. Lingle Company
Henderson, TX 800-256-6963

Crown Tonka Walk-Ins
Minneapolis, MN 800-523-7337
Dade Engineering
Tampa, FL 800-321-2112
David A Lingle & Son Mfg
Russellville, AR 479-968-2500
Elliott-Williams Company
Indianapolis, IN 800-428-9303
Emjac
Hialeah, FL. 305-883-2194
Erickson Industries
River Falls, WI. 800-729-9941
Everidge
Plymouth, MN. 888-227-1629
FleetwoodGoldcoWyard
Romeoville, IL 630-759-6800
Flo-Cold
Wixom, MI 248-348-6666
Harford Duracool LLC
Aberdeen, MD 410-272-9999
Heatcraft Worldwide Refrig
Columbus, GA 800-866-5596
International Cold Storage
Andover, KS 800-835-0001
Jack Langston Manufacturing Company
Dallas, TX. 214-821-9844
KEMCO
Wareham, MA 800-231-5955
Kolpak
Parsons, TN. 800-826-7036
Kolpak Walk-ins
Parsons, TN. 800-826-7036
Kysor Panel Systems
Fort Worth, TX 800-633-3426
Kysor/Kalt
Portland, OR. 503-235-0776
M&S Manufacturing
Arnold, MO. 636-464-2739
Manufacturing Warehouse
Miami, FL 305-635-8886
Marquis Products
Concord, ON. 800-268-1282
Mollenberg-Betz Inc
Buffalo, NY. 716-614-7473
Nor-Lake
Salem, NH. 603-893-9701
Pacific Refrigerator Company
San Bernardino, CA 909-381-5669
Penn Refrigeration Service Corporation
Wilkes Barre, PA. 800-233-8354
Perley-Halladay Assoc
West Chester, PA. 800-248-5800
Polar King Transportation
Fort Wayne, IN 888-541-8330
Portable Cold Storage
Edison, NJ. 800-535-2445
QBD Modular Systems
Santa Clara, CA 800-663-3005
Refrigeration Engineering
Grand Rapids, MI 800-968-3227
Superior Products Company
Saint Paul, MN 800-328-9800
Tafco Inc
Hyde, PA. 800-233-1954
US Cooler Company
Quincy, IL. 800-521-2665
WA Brown & Son
Salisbury, NC 704-636-5131
Zero Temp
Santa Ana, CA 714-538-3177

Doors

Cold Storage

Advance Energy Technologies
Halfmoon, NY. 800-724-0198
Advanced Insulation Concepts
Florence, KY. 800-826-3100
Air-Lec Industries, Inc
Madison, WI. 608-244-4754
Aleco Food Svc Div
Muscle Shoals, AL 800-633-3120
Aluma Shield
Deland, FL 877-638-3266
Andgar Corp
Ferndale, WA 360-366-9900
Apple-A-Day Nutritional Labeling Service
San Clemente, CA. 949-855-8954
Berner International Corp
New Castle, PA 800-245-4455

C.M. Lingle Company
Henderson, TX 800-256-6963
Carlson Products
Maize, KS 800-234-1069
Chase Doors
Cincinnati, OH 800-543-4455
Coldmatic Refrigeration
Concord, ON. 905-326-7600
Dade Engineering
Tampa, FL 800-321-2112
David A Lingle & Son Mfg
Russellville, AR 479-968-2500
Dole Refrigerating Co
Lewisburg, TN 800-251-8990
Kingspan Insulated Panels, Ltd.
Langley, BC 877-638-3266
Manufacturing Warehouse
Miami, FL 305-635-8886
Products A Curtron Div
Pittsburgh, PA. 800-888-9750
Rytec Corporation
Milwaukee, WI 888-467-9832
Therm L Tec Building Systems
Basehor, KS 913-728-2662

Freezer

Advance Energy Technologies
Halfmoon, NY. 800-724-0198
Advanced Insulation Concepts
Florence, KY. 800-826-3100
Air-Lec Industries, Inc
Madison, WI. 608-244-4754
Aleco Food Svc Div
Muscle Shoals, AL 800-633-3120
Berner International Corp
New Castle, PA. 800-245-4455
Chase Doors
Cincinnati, OH 800-543-4455
Dole Refrigerating Co
Lewisburg, TN 800-251-8990
Jamison Door Co
Hagerstown, MD. 800-532-3667
Kingspan Insulated Panels, Ltd.
Langley, BC 877-638-3266
Products A Curtron Div
Pittsburgh, PA. 800-888-9750
Rytec Corporation
Milwaukee, WI 888-467-9832
Superior Products Company
Saint Paul, MN 800-328-9800

Refrigerated Display Case

Advance Energy Technologies
Halfmoon, NY. 800-724-0198
Kedco Wine Storage Systems
Farmingdale, NY 800-654-9988
Ojeda USA
Spartanburg, SC 864-574-6004
Seville Display Door
Temecula, CA. 800-634-0412
Superior Products Company
Saint Paul, MN 800-328-9800

Refrigerator

Advance Energy Technologies
Halfmoon, NY. 800-724-0198
Advanced Insulation Concepts
Florence, KY. 800-826-3100
Aleco Food Svc Div
Muscle Shoals, AL 800-633-3120
Berner International Corp
New Castle, PA. 800-245-4455
Carlson Products
Maize, KS 800-234-1069
Chase Doors
Cincinnati, OH 800-543-4455
Coldmatic Refrigeration
Concord, ON. 905-326-7600
Dole Refrigerating Co
Lewisburg, TN 800-251-8990
Illinois Tool Works
Glenview, IL. 224-661-8870
JUMO Process Control Inc
East Syracuse, NY 800-554-5866
Kason Industries
Newnan, GA 770-254-0553
Pro Refrigeration
Auburn, WA 253-735-1189
Products A Curtron Div
Pittsburgh, PA. 800-888-9750

Seville Display Door
Temecula, CA 800-634-0412
Therm L Tec Building Systems
Basehor, KS 913-728-2662

Freezers

Advance Energy Technologies
Halfmoon, NY 800-724-0198
Advanced Equipment
Richmond, BC 604-276-8989
American Food Equipment
Miami, FL 305-377-8991
APV Americas
Delavan, WI 800-252-5200
Arctic Air
Eden Prairie, MN 800-853-3508
Arctic Industries
Medley, FL 800-325-0123
Attias Oven Corp
Brooklyn, NY 800-928-8427
Bally Refrigerated Boxes Inc
Morehead City, NC 800-242-2559
Berndorf Belt Technology USA
Gilberts, IL 800-393-8450
C Nelson Mfg Co
Oak Harbor, OH 800-922-7339
C.M. Lingle Company
Henderson, TX 800-256-6963
Carbonic Reserves
San Antonio, TX 800-880-1911
Carpigiani Corporation of America
Winston Salem, NC. 800-648-4389
Cci Industries-Cool Curtain
Costa Mesa, CA 800-854-5719
Checker Machine
Minneapolis, MN 888-800-5001
Chrysler & Koppin Co
Detroit, MI 800-441-0038
Cloudy & Britton
Mountlake Ter, WA 425-775-7424
Coldstream Products Corporation
Crossfield, AB 888-946-4097
Crown Tonka Walk-Ins
Minneapolis, MN 800-523-7337
Cryochem
St Simons Island, GA 800-237-4001
Dade Engineering
Tampa, FL 800-321-2112
David A Lingle & Son Mfg
Russellville, AR 479-968-2500
Delfield Co
Mt Pleasant, MI. 800-733-8821
Dole Refrigerating Co
Lewisburg, TN 800-251-8990
Duke Manufacturing Co
St Louis, MO. 800-735-3853
Elliott-Williams Company
Indianapolis, IN 800-428-9303
Emjac
Hialeah, FL 305-883-2194
Empire Bakery Equipment
Hicksville, NY 800-878-4070
Erickson Industries
River Falls, WI 800-729-9941
Esco Products Inc
Houston, TX 800-966-5514
Everidge
Plymouth, MN. 888-227-1629
Felix Storch Inc
Bronx, NY. 800-932-4267
Flo-Cold
Wixom, MI 248-348-6666
Fogel Jordon Commercial Refrigeration Company
Philadelphia, PA. 800-523-0171
Food Engineering Unlimited
Fullerton, CA 714-879-8762
Foster Refrigerator Corporation
Kinderhook, NY 888-828-3311
FreesTech
Sinking Spring, PA 717-560-7560
Frigidaire Co.
Charlotte, NC 866-449-4200
Frigoscandia
Redmond, WA. 800-423-1743
Frigoscandia Equipment
Northfield, MN. 800-426-1283
Galley
Jupiter, FL 800-537-2772
Gch Internatonal
Louisville, KY 502-636-1374
Gem Refrigerator Company
Philadelphia, PA 215-426-8700

General Electric Company
Fairfield, CT 203-373-2211
Glastender
Saginaw, MI 800-748-0423
Gold Star Products
Oak Park, MI. 800-800-0205
Gram Equipment Of America
Tampa, FL. 813-248-1978
HABCO Beverage Systems
Toronto, ON 800-448-0244
Heatcraft Worldwide Refrig
Columbus, GA 800-866-5596
Howard-Mccray
Philadelphia, PA 800-344-8222
I J White Corp
Farmingdale, NY 631-293-2211
IMECO Inc
Polo, IL 815-946-2351
International Cold Storage
Andover, KS 800-835-0001
Jack Langston Manufacturing Company
Dallas, TX. 214-821-9844
JBT Food Tech
Lakeland, FL 863-683-5411
Jordon Commercial Refrigerator
Philadelphia, PA 800-523-0171
KEMCO
Wareham, MA. 800-231-5955
Kold Pack
Jackson, MI. 800-824-2661
Kolpak
Parsons, TN. 800-826-7036
Kolpak Walk-ins
Parsons, TN. 800-826-7036
Kysor/Kalt
Portland, OR 503-235-0776
LA Rosa Refrigeration & Equip
Detroit, MI 800-527-6723
Manufacturing Warehouse
Miami, FL 305-635-8886
Mar-Con Wire Belt
Richmond, BC 877-962-7266
Marc Refrigeration Mfg Inc
Miami, FL 305-691-0500
Marquis Products
Concord, ON. 800-268-1282
Martin Cab Div
Cleveland, OH 216-377-8200
Martin/Baron
Irwindale, CA 626-960-5153
Master-Bilt
New Albany, MS. 800-647-1284
McCormack Manufacturing Company
Lake Oswego, OR. 800-395-1593
Migali Industries
Camden, NJ. 800-852-5292
Mollenberg-Betz Inc
Buffalo, NY. 716-614-7473
National Hotpack
Stone Ridge, NY 800-431-8232
Nor-Lake
Salem, NH. 603-893-9701
Northfield Freezing Systems
Northfield, MN. 800-426-1283
Northland Corp
Greenville, MI. 800-223-3900
Nothum Food Processing Systems
Springfield, MO 800-435-1297
Odenberg Engineering
West Sacramento, CA 800-688-8396
Ojeda USA
Spartanburg, SC 864-574-6004
Pacific Refrigerator Company
San Bernardino, CA 909-381-5669
Penn Refrigeration Service Corporation
Wilkes Barre, PA. 800-233-8354
Perley-Halladay Assoc
West Chester, PA. 800-248-5800
Polar King Transportation
Fort Wayne, IN 888-541-8330
Praxair Inc
Danbury, CT. 800-772-9247
Ransco Industries
Ventura, CA. 805-487-7777
Refrigerated Warehousing
Jasper, GA. 800-873-2008
Reliable Food Service Equipment
Concord, ON. 416-738-6840
Rival Manufacturing Company
Kansas City, MO. 816-943-4100
Ron Vallort & Associates
Oak Brook, IL. 630-734-3821

Ross Industries Inc
Midland, VA 540-439-3271
Russell
Scottsboro, AL 800-288-9488
Sandvik Process Systems
Sweden, NJ 973-790-1600
SaniServ
Mooresville, IN. 800-733-8073
Seattle Refrigeration & Manufacturing
Seattle, WA 800-228-8881
Semco Manufacturing Company
Pharr, TX. 956-787-4203
Silver King Refrigeration Inc
Minneapolis, MN 800-328-3329
SP Industries Inc
Warminster, PA 800-523-2327
Stafford-Smith Inc
Kalamazoo, MI 800-968-2442
Starlite Food Service Equipment
Detroit, MI 888-521-6603
Summit Commercial
Bronx, NY. 800-932-4267
Superior Products Company
Saint Paul, MN 800-328-9800
Supreme Corporation
Goshen, IN. 800-642-4889
Systemate Numafa
Canton, GA. 800-240-3770
Tafco Inc
Hyde, PA. 800-233-1954
Thermo King Corp
Bloomington, MN. 888-887-2202
Traulsen & Co
Fort Worth, TX 800-825-8220
True Food Service Equipment, Inc.
O Fallon, MO 800-325-6152
U-Line Corporation
Milwaukee, WI 800-779-2547
US Cooler Company
Quincy, IL 800-521-2665
Utility Refrigerator Company
Los Angeles, CA. 800-884-5233
Victory Refrigeration
Cherry Hill, NJ 856-428-4200
WA Brown & Son
Salisbury, NC 704-636-5131
Waukesha Cherry-Burrell
Louisville, KY 502-491-4310
WCB Ice Cream
Philadelphia, PA 215-425-4320
Welbilt Inc.
New Port Richey, FL 877-375-9300
White Mountain Freezer
Kansas City, MO. 816-943-4100
Wilch Manufacturing
Topeka, KS 785-267-2762
Zero Temp
Santa Ana, CA 714-538-3177

Ice Cream

Advance Energy Technologies
Halfmoon, NY. 800-724-0198
C Nelson Mfg Co
Oak Harbor, OH 800-922-7339
Carpigiani Corporation of America
Winston Salem, NC. 800-648-4389
Delfield Co
Mt Pleasant, MI. 800-733-8821
Eischen Enterprises
Fresno, CA 559-834-0013
Felix Storch Inc
Bronx, NY. 800-932-4267
FreesTech
Sinking Spring, PA 717-560-7560
Glastender
Saginaw, MI 800-748-0423
Howard-Mccray
Philadelphia, PA 800-344-8222
LA Rosa Refrigeration & Equip
Detroit, MI 800-527-6723
Manufacturing Warehouse
Miami, FL 305-635-8886
Marc Refrigeration Mfg Inc
Miami, FL 305-691-0500
Rival Manufacturing Company
Kansas City, MO. 816-943-4100
SaniServ
Mooresville, IN. 800-733-8073
Schroeder Machine
San Marcos, CA 760-591-9733

Stainless Fabrication Inc
Springfield, MO 800-397-8265
Summit Commercial
Bronx, NY. .800-932-4267
White Mountain Freezer
Kansas City, MO. 816-943-4100
Wilch Manufacturing
Topeka, KS .785-267-2762

Quick Freezing

Advance Energy Technologies
Halfmoon, NY. 800-724-0198
Advanced Equipment
Richmond, BC 604-276-8989
Carbonic Reserves
San Antonio, TX 800-880-1911
Dole Refrigerating Co
Lewisburg, TN 800-251-8990
Foster Refrigerator Corporation
Kinderhook, NY 888-828-3311
FreesTech
Sinking Spring, PA 717-560-7560
Frigoscandia
Redmond, WA. 800-423-1743
Gch Internatonal
Louisville, KY 502-636-1374
Manufacturing Warehouse
Miami, FL. .305-635-8886
Mar-Con Wire Belt
Richmond, BC 877-962-7266
Mayekawa USA, Inc.
Chicago, IL .773-516-5070
McCormack Manufacturing Company
Lake Oswego, OR. 800-395-1593
Stainless Fabrication Inc
Springfield, MO 800-397-8265
Witte Brothers Exchange Inc
Troy, MO. 800-325-8151

Sub-Zero

Advance Energy Technologies
Halfmoon, NY. 800-724-0198
C.M. Lingle Company
Henderson, TX 800-256-6963
Cryochem
St Simons Island, GA 800-237-4001
Fogel Jordon Commercial Refrigeration Company
Philadelphia, PA 800-523-0171
Foster Refrigerator Corporation
Kinderhook, NY 888-828-3311
Frigidaire Co.
Charlotte, NC 866-449-4200
Hoshizaki America Inc
Peachtree City, GA 800-438-6087
Howard-Mccray
Philadelphia, PA 800-344-8222
IMECO Inc
Polo, IL 815-946-2351
Martin/Baron
Irwindale, CA 626-960-5153
McCormack Manufacturing Company
Lake Oswego, OR. 800-395-1593
Portable Cold Storage
Edison, NJ .800-535-2445
Ransco Industries
Ventura, CA. 805-487-7777
Ron Vallort & Associates
Oak Brook, IL. 630-734-3821
Semco Manufacturing Company
Pharr, TX. .956-787-4203
SP Industries Inc
Warminster, PA 800-523-2327

Walk-In

Advance Energy Technologies
Halfmoon, NY. 800-724-0198
Arctic Industries
Medley, FL .800-325-0123
Bally Refrigerated Boxes Inc
Morehead City, NC 800-242-2559
C.M. Lingle Company
Henderson, TX 800-256-6963
Chrysler & Koppin Co
Detroit, MI .800-441-0038
Coldstream Products Corporation
Crossfield, AB 888-946-4097
Crown Tonka Walk-Ins
Minneapolis, MN 800-523-7337
Dade Engineering
Tampa, FL. .800-321-2112

David A Lingle & Son Mfg
Russellville, AR 479-968-2500
Elliott-Williams Company
Indianapolis, IN 800-428-9303
Emjac
Hialeah, FL. 305-883-2194
Foster Refrigerator Corporation
Kinderhook, NY 888-828-3311
Gem Refrigerator Company
Philadelphia, PA 215-426-8700
HABCO Beverage Systems
Toronto, ON 800-448-0244
Howard-Mccray
Philadelphia, PA 800-344-8222
International Cold Storage
Andover, KS 800-835-0001
Jack Langston Manufacturing Company
Dallas, TX. .214-821-9844
Jordon Commercial Refrigerator
Philadelphia, PA 800-523-0171
KEMCO
Wareham, MA 800-231-5955
Kolpak
Parsons, TN. 800-826-7036
Kolpak Walk-ins
Parsons, TN. 800-826-7036
Kysor/Kalt
Portland, OR 503-235-0776
Manufacturing Warehouse
Miami, FL. .305-635-8886
Martin Cab Div
Cleveland, OH 216-377-8200
Nor-Lake
Salem, NH. .603-893-9701
Pacific Refrigerator Company
San Bernardino, CA 909-381-5669
Penn Refrigeration Service Corporation
Wilkes Barre, PA. 800-233-8354
Polar King Transportation
Fort Wayne, IN 888-541-8330
Portable Cold Storage
Edison, NJ .800-535-2445
Russell
Scottsboro, AL 800-288-9488
Semco Manufacturing Company
Pharr, TX. .956-787-4203
Superior Products Company
Saint Paul, MN 800-328-9800
Tafco Inc
Hyde, PA. 800-233-1954
US Cooler Company
Quincy, IL .800-521-2665
WA Brown & Son
Salisbury, NC 704-636-5131
Zero Temp
Santa Ana, CA 714-538-3177

Insulation

Refrigeration & Cold Storage

Advanced Insulation Concepts
Florence, KY. 800-826-3100
Andgar Corp
Ferndale, WA 360-366-9900
Cellofoam North America
Conyers, GA. 800-241-3634
David A Lingle & Son Mfg
Russellville, AR 479-968-2500
Foam Pack Industries
Springfield, NJ 973-376-3700
Modular Panel Company
New Bedford, MA 508-993-9955
Reilly Foam Corporation
Conshohocken, PA 610-834-1900
Republic Refrigeration Inc
Monroe, NC 704-225-0410
Ron Vallort & Associates
Oak Brook, IL. 630-734-3821
Therm L Tec Building Systems
Basehor, KS 913-728-2662
WA Brown & Son
Salisbury, NC 704-636-5131

Lockers

Frozen Food

Cayne Industrial Sales Corp
Bronx, NY. .718-993-5800
Remcon Plastics Inc
Reading, PA 800-360-3636

Welch Brothers
Bartlett, IL. 847-741-6134

Refrigerating & Cooling Rooms

Advance Energy Technologies
Halfmoon, NY. 800-724-0198
AeroFreeze, Inc.
Richmond, BC, BC 604-278-4118
American Panel Corp
Ocala, FL. 800-327-3015
Arctic Industries
Medley, FL .800-325-0123
Bakery Refrigeration & Services
Lake Park, FL 561-882-1655
C.M. Lingle Company
Henderson, TX 800-256-6963
Cool Care
Boynton Beach, FL 561-364-5711
David A Lingle & Son Mfg
Russellville, AR 479-968-2500
Elliott-Williams Company
Indianapolis, IN 800-428-9303
Erickson Industries
River Falls, WI 800-729-9941
Fogel Jordon Commercial Refrigeration Company
Philadelphia, PA 800-523-0171
Heatcraft Worldwide Refrig
Columbus, GA 800-866-5596
Kysor Panel Systems
Fort Worth, TX 800-633-3426
Kysor/Kalt
Portland, OR 503-235-0776
M&S Manufacturing
Arnold, MO. 636-464-2739
Master-Bilt
New Albany, MS. 800-647-1284
Mollenberg-Betz Inc
Buffalo, NY. 716-614-7473
National Hotpack
Stone Ridge, NY 800-431-8232
Pacific Refrigerator Company
San Bernardino, CA 909-381-5669
Perley-Halladay Assoc
West Chester, PA. 800-248-5800
QBD Modular Systems
Santa Clara, CA 800-663-3005
Ransco Industries
Ventura, CA. 805-487-7777
Refrigerated Warehousing
Jasper, GA. .800-873-2008
Refrigerator Manufacturers LLC
Cerritos, CA 562-926-2006
RMF Companies
Grandview, MO. 816-839-9258
Ron Vallort & Associates
Oak Brook, IL. 630-734-3821
Tafco Inc
Hyde, PA. 800-233-1954
Thermal Technologies
Broomall, PA. 610-353-8887
US Cooler Company
Quincy, IL .800-521-2665
Zero Temp
Santa Ana, CA 714-538-3177

Refrigerating Equipment & Machinery

ABCO Industries Limited
Lunenburg, NS 866-634-8821
Advance Energy Technologies
Halfmoon, NY. 800-724-0198
Advanced Equipment
Richmond, BC 604-276-8989
Advanced Insulation Concepts
Florence, KY. 800-826-3100
AeroFreeze, Inc.
Richmond, BC, BC 604-278-4118
AGA Gas
Cleveland, OH 216-642-6600
Aleco Food Svc Div
Muscle Shoals, AL 800-633-3120
Alkar Rapid Pak
Lodi, WI 608-592-3211
Alto-Shaam
Menomonee Falls, WI. 800-329-8744
Aluma Shield
Deland, FL .877-638-3266
American Food Equipment
Miami, FL 305-377-8991

American Panel Corp
Ocala, FL 800-327-3015
American Systems Associates
Hampton Bays, NY. 800-584-3663
Applied Thermal Technologies
San Marcos, CA 800-736-5083
Arctic Air
Eden Prairie, MN 800-853-3508
Arctic Industries
Medley, FL 800-325-0123
Arctica Showcase Company
Cayuga, ON. 800-839-5536
Attias Oven Corp
Brooklyn, NY 800-928-8427
Baltimore Aircoil Co
Jessup, MD .410-799-1300
Bar Equipment Corporation of America
Downey, CA .888-870-2322
Bar-Maid Corp
Garfield, NJ .800-227-6243
Barker Company
Keosauqua, IA 319-293-3777
Beacon Specialties
New York, NY 800-221-9405
Benko Products
Sheffield Vlg, OH. 440-934-2180
Berg Chilling Systems
Toronto, ON, ON 416-755-2221
Berner International Corp
New Castle, PA 800-245-4455
Beverage Air
Winston Salem, NC. 800-845-9800
BNW Industries
Tippecanoe, IN 574-353-7855
Buffalo Technologies Corporation
Buffalo, NY. 800-332-2419
Buhler Inc.
Plymouth, MN. 763-847-9900
Bush Refrigeration Inc
Pennsauken, NJ 800-220-2874
C&R Refrigeration
Center, TX. .800-438-6182
C.M. Lingle Company
Henderson, TX 800-256-6963
Caddy Corporation of America
Bridgeport, NJ. 856-467-4222
Carbonic Reserves
San Antonio, TX 800-880-1911
Carpigiani Corporation of America
Winston Salem, NC. 800-648-4389
Carrier Corp
Farmington, CT. 800-227-7437
Carter-Hoffmann LLC
Mundelein, IL 800-323-9793
Carts Food Equipment
Brooklyn, NY 718-788-5540
Cci Industries-Cool Curtain
Costa Mesa, CA 800-854-5719
Century Refrigeration
Pryor, OK 918-825-6363
Checker Machine
Minneapolis, MN 888-800-5001
Chrysler & Koppin Co
Detroit, MI .800-441-0038
Cloudy & Britton
Mountlake Ter, WA. 425-775-7424
Coldmatic Refrigeration
Concord, ON. 905-326-7600
Coldstream Products Corporation
Crossfield, AB 888-946-4097
ColdZone
Anaheim, CA
Continental Refrigerator
Bensalem, PA 800-523-7138
Control Beverage
Adelanto, CA 330-549-5376
Cool Care
Boynton Beach, FL. 561-364-5711
Cornelius Inc.
Osseo, MN .800-238-3600
Cornell Pump Company
Portland, OR 503-653-0330
Craig Manufacturing
Irvington, NJ 800-631-7936
Cramer Products
New York, NY 212-645-2368
Cres Cor
Mentor, OH. 877-273-7267
Crown Tonka Walk-Ins
Minneapolis, MN 800-523-7337
Cryochem
St Simons Island, GA 800-237-4001

Custom Diamond International
Laval, QC 800-363-5926
Davenport Machine
Rock Island, IL 309-786-1500
David A Lingle & Son Mfg
Russellville, AR 479-968-2500
Dole Refrigerating Co
Lewisburg, TN 800-251-8990
Doucette Industries
York, PA 800-445-7511
Duke Manufacturing Co
St Louis, MO. 800-735-3853
Econofrost Night Covers
Shawnigan Lake, BC 800-519-1222
Eliason Corp
Portage, MI .800-828-3655
Elliott-Williams Company
Indianapolis, IN 800-428-9303
Elwood Safety Company
Buffalo, NY. 866-326-6060
Emjac
Hialeah, FL .305-883-2194
Empire Bakery Equipment
Hicksville, NY 800-878-4070
EPCO
Murfreesboro, TN 800-251-3398
Erickson Industries
River Falls, WI 800-729-9941
EVAPCO Inc
Taneytown, MD 410-876-3782
F G Products Inc
Rice Lake, WI. 800-247-3854
Federal Industries
Belleville, WI 800-356-4206
Felix Storch Inc
Bronx, NY 800-932-4267
Flakice Corporation
Everett, WA. 800-654-4630
Flat Plate Inc
York, PA 888-854-2500
FleetwoodGoldcoWyard
Romeoville, IL 630-759-6800
Flo-Cold
Wixom, MI .248-348-6666
Food Engineering Unlimited
Fullerton, CA 714-879-8762
Food Warming Equipment Co
Crystal Lake, IL 800-222-4393
FreesTech
Sinking Spring, PA. 717-560-7560
FRICK by Johnson Controls
Milwaukee, WI 855-270-5546
Frigidaire Co.
Charlotte, NC 866-449-4200
Frigoscandia
Redmond, WA. 800-423-1743
Galley
Jupiter, FL. .800-537-2772
Gates Manufacturing Company
Saint Louis, MO 800-237-9226
Gch Internatonal
Louisville, KY 502-636-1374
Gem Refrigerator Company
Philadelphia, PA 215-426-8700
Gold Star Products
Oak Park, MI. 800-800-0205
Governair Corp
Oklahoma City, OK 405-525-6546
H A Phillips & Co
Dekalb, IL 630-377-0050
Hackney Brothers
Washington, NC 800-763-0700
Hall Manufacturing Co
Ringwood, NJ 973-962-6022
Hansen Technologies Corporation
Bolingbrook, IL 800-426-7368
Harford Duracool LLC
Aberdeen, MD 410-272-9999
Harford Systems Inc
Havre De Grace, MD 800-638-7620
Harvey W Hottel Inc
Gaithersburg, MD. 301-921-9599
Heatcraft Refrigeration Prods
Stone Mountain, GA 770-465-5600
Heatcraft Worldwide Refrig
Columbus, GA 800-866-5596
Hoshizaki America Inc
Peachtree City, GA 800-438-6087
Howard-Mccray
Philadelphia, PA 800-344-8222
Howe Corp
Chicago, IL .773-235-0200

Hussmann Corp
Bridgeton, MO 314-291-2000
Hydro-Miser
San Marcos, CA 800-736-5083
IMECO Inc
Polo, IL 815-946-2351
International Cold Storage
Andover, KS 800-835-0001
International Cooling Systems
Richmond Hill, ON. 888-213-5566
Interstate Showcase & Fixture Company
West Orange, NJ 973-483-5555
Jack Langston Manufacturing Company
Dallas, TX. .214-821-9844
Jade Products Co
Brea, CA 800-884-5233
Johnson Refrigerated Truck
Rice Lake, WI. 800-922-8360
Jordon Commercial Refrigerator
Philadelphia, PA 800-523-0171
KaiRak
Anaheim, CA 714-870-8661
Kason Central
Columbus, OH 614-885-1992
Kason Industries
Newnan, GA 770-254-0553
Kedco Wine Storage Systems
Farmingdale, NY 800-654-9988
KEMCO
Wareham, MA 800-231-5955
Kold Pack
Jackson, MI. 800-824-2661
Kold-Hold
Edgefield, SC 803-637-3166
Kolpak
Parsons, TN. 800-826-7036
Kolpak Walk-ins
Parsons, TN. 800-826-7036
Koolant Koolers
Kalamazoo, MI 800-968-5665
Krewson Enterprises
Cleveland, OH 800-521-2282
Kysor Panel Systems
Fort Worth, TX 800-633-3426
Kysor/Kalt
Portland, OR 503-235-0776
LA Rosa Refrigeration & Equip
Detroit, MI .800-527-6723
Letrah International Corp
Fort Atkinson, WI 920-563-6597
Liberty Machine Company
York, PA 800-745-8152
Little Squirt
Toronto, ON 416-665-6605
M&S Manufacturing
Arnold, MO. 636-464-2739
Mannhardt Inc
Sheboygan Falls, WI. 800-423-2327
Manufacturing Warehouse
Miami, FL 305-635-8886
Marc Refrigeration Mfg Inc
Miami, FL 305-691-0500
Marquis Products
Concord, ON. 800-268-1282
Martin Cab Div
Cleveland, OH 216-377-8200
Martin/Baron
Irwindale, CA 626-960-5153
Master-Bilt
New Albany, MS. 800-647-1284
McCormack Manufacturing Company
Lake Oswego, OR. 800-395-1593
MCM Fixture Co
Hazel Park, MI 248-547-9280
Migali Industries
Camden, NJ. 800-852-5292
MMR Technologies
Mountain View, CA 855-962-9620
Mollenberg-Betz Inc
Buffalo, NY. 716-614-7473
Mycom Group
Richmond, BC 604-270-1544
National Drying Machry Co Inc
Philadelphia, PA 215-464-6070
Niagara Blower Company
Buffalo, NY. 800-426-5169
Nor-Lake
Salem, NH. .603-893-9701
Noren Products Inc
Menlo Park, CA 866-936-6736
Northfield Freezing Systems
Northfield, MN 800-426-1283

Northland Corp
Greenville, MI 800-223-3900
Odenberg Engineering
West Sacramento, CA 800-688-8396
Omnitemp Refrigeration
Downey, CA 800-423-9660
Pacific Refrigerator Company
San Bernardino, CA 909-381-5669
Paragon Electric Company
Two Rivers, WI 920-793-1161
Parkland
Houston, TX 713-926-5055
Peerless of America
Lincolnshire, IL 847-634-7500
Penn Refrigeration Service Corporation
Wilkes Barre, PA 800-233-8354
Perley-Halladay Assoc
West Chester, PA 800-248-5800
Perlick Corp
Milwaukee, WI 800-558-5592
Pioneer Manufacturing Co Inc
Cleveland, OH 800-877-1500
Pittsburgh Corning Corp
Pittsburgh, PA 724-327-6100
PMI Food Equipment Group
Troy, OH 937-332-3000
Polar King Transportation
Fort Wayne, IN 888-541-8330
Praxair Inc
Danbury, CT 800-772-9247
Precision
Miami, FL 800-762-7565
Premium Air Systems Inc
Troy, MI 877-430-0333
Presence From Innovation LLC
St Louis, MO 314-423-9777
Pro-Flo Products
Cedar Grove, NJ 800-325-1057
Process Engineering & Fabrication
Afton, VA 800-852-7975
R T C
Rolling Meadows, IL 847-640-2400
Randall Manufacturing Inc
Elmhurst, IL 800-323-7424
Randell Manufacturing Unified Brands
Weidman, MI 888-994-7636
Ransco Industries
Ventura, CA 805-487-7777
Refrigerated Design Tech
Waxahachie, TX 800-736-9518
Refrigerated Warehousing
Jasper, GA 800-873-2008
Refrigeration Engineering
Grand Rapids, MI 800-968-3227
Refrigeration Research
Brighton, MI 810-227-1151
Reliable Food Service Equipment
Concord, ON 416-738-6840
Ron Vallort & Associates
Oak Brook, IL 630-734-3821
Rubbermaid
High Point, NC 888-895-2110
Sandvik Process Systems
Sweden, NJ 973-790-1600
Schmidt Progressive
Lebanon, OH 800-272-3706
Scroll Compressors LLC
Sidney, OH 937-498-3011
Seattle Refrigeration & Manufacturing
Seattle, WA 800-228-8881
Seidman Brothers
Chelsea, MA 800-437-7770
Semco Manufacturing Company
Pharr, TX 956-787-4203
Servco Equipment Co
St Louis, MO 314-781-3189
Silver King Refrigeration Inc
Minneapolis, MN 800-328-3329
South Shore Controls Inc
Perry, OH 440-259-2500
SP Industries Inc
Warminster, PA 800-523-2327
Spartan Showcase
Union, MO 800-325-0775
Spinco Metal Products Inc
Newark, NY 315-331-6285
Standard Refrigeration Co
Wood Dale, IL 708-345-5400
Starlite Food Service Equipment
Detroit, MI 888-521-6603
Summit Commercial
Bronx, NY 800-932-4267
Superflex Limited
Brooklyn, NY 800-394-3665
Supreme Corporation
Goshen, IN 800-642-4889
Sure Kol Refrigerator
Brooklyn, NY 718-625-0601
Tecumseh Products Co.
Ann Arbor, MI 734-585-9500
Tetra Pak
Vernon Hills, IL 847-955-6000
Therm L Tec Building Systems
Basehor, KS 913-728-2662
Thermo King Corp
Bloomington, MN 888-887-2202
Thermo-KOOL/Mid-South Ind Inc
Laurel, MS 601-649-4600
Toromont Process Systems
North Salt Lake, UT 801-292-1747
Tranter INC
Wichita Falls, TX 940-723-7125
Traulsen & Co
Fort Worth, TX 800-825-8220
Trimen Foodservice Equipment
North York, ON 877-437-1422
True Food Service Equipment, Inc.
O Fallon, MO 800-325-6152
US Cooler Company
Quincy, IL 800-521-2665
USECO
Murfreesboro, TN 615-893-4820
Utility Refrigerator Company
Los Angeles, CA 800-884-5233
Victory Refrigeration
Cherry Hill, NJ 856-428-4200
Vilter Manufacturing Corporation
Cudahy, WI 414-744-0111
VT Kidron
Washington, NC 800-763-0700
WA Brown & Son
Salisbury, NC 704-636-5131
Welbilt Inc.
New Port Richey, FL 877-375-9300
West Star Industries
Stockton, CA 800-326-2288
Wilevco Inc
Billerica, MA 978-667-0400
Williams Refrigeration
Hillsdale, NJ 800-445-9979
Wine Chillers of California
Santa Ana, CA 800-331-4274
Wine Well Chiller Co
Milford, CT 203-878-2465
Wittemann Company
Palm Coast, FL 386-445-4200
York Refrigeration Marine US
Norman, OK 877-874-7378

Refrigerating Units

Truck, Trailer & Refrigerator Car

Advance Distribution Svc
Louisville, KY 502-449-1720
American Food Equipment
Miami, FL 305-377-8991
Carrier Corp
Farmington, CT 800-227-7437
Collins Manufacturing Company Ltd
Langley, BC 800-663-6761
Dole Refrigerating Co
Lewisburg, TN 800-251-8990
Hackney Brothers
Washington, NC 800-763-0700
Johnson Refrigerated Truck
Rice Lake, WI 800-922-8360
Kold-Hold
Edgefield, SC 803-637-3166
Martin Cab Div
Cleveland, OH 216-377-8200
National FABCO Manufacturing
St Louis, MO 314-842-4571
New Centennial
Columbus, GA 800-241-7541
Portable Cold Storage
Edison, NJ 800-535-2445
Supreme Corporation
Goshen, IN 800-642-4889
Thermo King Corp
Bloomington, MN 888-887-2202
VT Kidron
Washington, NC 800-763-0700

Refrigerators

Adamatic
Auburn, WA 800-578-2547
Advance Energy Technologies
Halfmoon, NY 800-724-0198
Arctic Air
Eden Prairie, MN 800-853-3508
Arctic Industries
Medley, FL 800-325-0123
Attias Oven Corp
Brooklyn, NY 800-928-8427
Bally Refrigerated Boxes Inc
Morehead City, NC 800-242-2559
Bar Equipment Corporation of America
Downey, CA 888-870-2322
Bar-Maid Corp
Garfield, NJ 800-227-6243
Benko Products
Sheffield Vlg, OH 440-934-2180
C.M. Lingle Company
Henderson, TX 800-256-6963
Carts Food Equipment
Brooklyn, NY 718-788-5540
Caselites
Hialeah, FL 305-819-7766
Chrysler & Koppin Co
Detroit, MI 800-441-0038
Cloudy & Britton
Mountlake Ter, WA 425-775-7424
Coldstream Products Corporation
Crossfield, AB 888-946-4097
Continental Refrigerator
Bensalem, PA 800-523-7138
Craig Manufacturing
Irvington, NJ 800-631-7936
Custom Diamond International
Laval, QC 800-363-5926
Delfield Co
Mt Pleasant, MI 800-733-8821
Duke Manufacturing Co
St Louis, MO 800-735-3853
Elliott-Williams Company
Indianapolis, IN 800-428-9303
Empire Bakery Equipment
Hicksville, NY 800-878-4070
EPCO
Murfreesboro, TN 800-251-3398
Erickson Industries
River Falls, WI 800-729-9941
Eskay Metal Fabricating
Buffalo, NY 800-836-8015
Everidge
Plymouth, MN 888-227-1629
Felix Storch Inc
Bronx, NY 800-932-4267
Fogel Jordon Commercial Refrigeration Company
Philadelphia, PA 800-523-0171
Follett Corp
Easton, PA 800-523-9361
Foster Refrigerator Corporation
Kinderhook, NY 888-828-3311
Gates Manufacturing Company
Saint Louis, MO 800-237-9226
Gem Refrigerator Company
Philadelphia, PA 215-426-8700
HABCO Beverage Systems
Toronto, ON 800-448-0244
Helmer
Noblesville, IN 317-773-9082
Hoshizaki America Inc
Peachtree City, GA 800-438-6087
Howard-Mccray
Philadelphia, PA 800-344-8222
Hussmann Corp
Bridgeton, MO 314-291-2000
International Cold Storage
Andover, KS 800-835-0001
Jack Langston Manufacturing Company
Dallas, TX 214-821-9844
Jade Products Co
Brea, CA 800-884-5233
Jordon Commercial Refrigerator
Philadelphia, PA 800-523-0171
Kolpak Walk-ins
Parsons, TN 800-826-7036
Lockwood Manufacturing
Livonia, MI 800-521-0238
Marc Refrigeration Mfg Inc
Miami, FL 305-691-0500
Master-Bilt
New Albany, MS 800-647-1284

Mayekawa USA, Inc.
Chicago, IL 773-516-5070
MCM Fixture Co
Hazel Park, MI 248-547-9280
National Hotpack
Stone Ridge, NY 800-431-8232
Nor-Lake
Salem, NH 603-893-9701
Northland Corp
Greenville, MI 800-223-3900
Parkland
Houston, TX 713-926-5055
Polar King Transportation
Fort Wayne, IN 888-541-8330
Portable Cold Storage
Edison, NJ 800-535-2445
QBD Modular Systems
Santa Clara, CA 800-663-3005
Randell Manufacturing   Unified Brands
Weidman, MI 888-994-7636
Ransco Industries
Ventura, CA 805-487-7777
Seidman Brothers
Chelsea, MA 800-437-7770
Servco Equipment Co
St Louis, MO 314-781-3189
Silver King Refrigeration Inc
Minneapolis, MN 800-328-3329
Spartan Showcase
Union, MO 800-325-0775
Springer-Penguin
Mount Vernon, NY 800-835-8500
Stafford-Smith Inc
Kalamazoo, MI 800-968-2442
Summit Commercial
Bronx, NY 800-932-4267
Superior Products Company
Saint Paul, MN 800-328-9800
Sure Kol Refrigerator
Brooklyn, NY 718-625-0601
Tafco Inc
Hyde, PA 800-233-1954
Thermo-KOOL/Mid-South Ind Inc
Laurel, MS 601-649-4600
Toromont Process Systems
North Salt Lake, UT 801-292-1747
Traulsen & Co
Fort Worth, TX 800-825-8220
Triad Scientific
Manasquan, NJ 800-867-6690
Tru Form Plastics
Gardena, CA 800-510-7999

True Food Service Equipment, Inc.
O Fallon, MO 800-325-6152
U-Line Corporation
Milwaukee, WI 800-779-2547
USECO
Murfreesboro, TN 615-893-4820
Utility Refrigerator Company
Los Angeles, CA 800-884-5233
Victory Refrigeration
Cherry Hill, NJ 856-428-4200
Welbilt Inc.
New Port Richey, FL 877-375-9300
Williams Refrigeration
Hillsdale, NJ 800-445-9979

Grilles

Gea Intec, Llc
Durham, NC 919-433-0131
Liberty Machine Company
York, PA 800-745-8152

Racks

ABI Limited
Concord, ON 800-297-8666
Caddy Corporation of America
Bridgeport, NJ 856-467-4222
ColdZone
Anaheim, CA
Dubuque Steel Products Co
Dubuque, IA 563-556-6288
Eagle Wire Works
Cleveland, OH 216-341-8550
Hewitt Manufacturing Co
Waldron, IN 765-525-9829
Houston Wire Works, Inc.
South Houston, TX 800-468-9477
Kedco Wine Storage Systems
Farmingdale, NY 800-654-9988
Metro Corporation
Wilkes Barre, PA 800-992-1776
Olson Wire Products Co
Baltimore, MD 410-242-7900
Straits Steel & Wire Co
Ludington, MI 231-843-3416
Unirak Storage Systems
Taylor, MI 800-348-7225
Universal Coatings
Twinsburg, OH 330-963-6776
Wald Wire & Mfg Co
Oshkosh, WI 800-236-0053

Trays

Kaines West Michigan Co
Ludington, MI 231-845-1281
Nelipak
Phoenix, AZ 602-269-7648
Olson Wire Products Co
Baltimore, MD 410-242-7900
Spot Wire Works Company
Philadelphia, PA 215-627-6124
World Kitchen
Elmira, NY 800-999-3436

Valves

Refrigeration

C & D Valve Mfg Co
Oklahoma City, OK 800-654-9233
Doering Co
Clear Lake, MN 320-743-2276
EVAPCO Inc
Taneytown, MD 410-876-3782
H A Phillips & Co
Dekalb, IL 630-377-0050
Hansen Technologies Corporation
Bolingbrook, IL 800-426-7368
Parker-Hannifin Corp
Cleveland, OH 800-272-7537
Vilter Manufacturing Corporation
Cudahy, WI 414-744-0111

Vats

Dairy Cooling

Dubuque Steel Products Co
Dubuque, IA 563-556-6288
Falco Technologies
La Prairie, QC 450-444-0566

Vender & Visi-Cooler Installation Systems

Ultra Lift Corp
San Jose, CA 800-346-3057

Safety & Security Equipment & Supplies

Alarm Systems

Acromag Inc.
Wixom, MI 248-624-1541
Alarm Controls Corp
Deer Park, NY 800-645-5538
AMSECO
Carson, CA 800-421-1096
Christy Industries Inc
Brooklyn, NY 800-472-2078
CMT
Hamilton, MA 978-768-2555
Control Products Inc
Chanhassen, MN 800-947-9098
Electro Alarms
Tiffin, OH 800-261-9174
Ellenco
Brentwood, MD 301-927-4370
Faraday
Tecumseh, MI 517-423-2111
Flair Electronics
Pomona, CA 800-532-3492
Gamewell Corporation
Northborough, MA 888-347-3269
George Risk Industries Inc
Kimball, NE 800-445-5218
Globe Fire Sprinkler Corp
Standish, MI 800-248-0278
Gralab Instruments
Centerville, OH 800-876-8353
Harford Systems Inc
Havre De Grace, MD 800-638-7620
Honeywell International
Charlotte, NC 877-841-2840
Iconics Inc
Foxboro, MA 800-946-9679
King Research Laboratory
Maywood, IL 708-344-7877
Krewson Enterprises
Cleveland, OH 800-521-2282
Liquid Scale
New Brighton, MN 888-633-2969
Long Range Systems
Addison, TX 800-577-8101
Napco Security Systems Inc
Amityville, NY 631-842-0253
Optex
Chino, CA 800-966-7839
Permaloc Security Devices
Silver Spring, MD 301-681-6300
Quantis Secure Systems
Hanover, MD 800-325-6124
Raco Mfg & Engineering Co
Emeryville, CA 800-722-6999
Sargent & Greenleaf
Nicholasville, KY 800-826-7652
Security Link
Danville, IL 217-446-4871
Sensidyne
St. Petersburg, FL 800-451-9444
Silent Watchman Security Services LLC
Danbury, CT 800-932-3822
Simplex Time Recorder Company
Santa Ana, CA 800-746-7539
Star Micronics
Edison, NJ 800-782-7636
Sterling Corp
Glendora, CA 800-932-9561
Ultrak
Westminster, CO 303-428-9480
Viking Corp
Hastings, MI 800-968-9501
W L Jenkins Co
Canton, OH 330-477-3407

Containment Systems

Arcoplast Wall & Ceiling Systems
St Peters, MO 888-736-2726
Blome International
O Fallon, MO 636-379-9119
Modutank Inc
Long Island City, NY 800-245-6964

Detectors

Detectamet Inc
Richmond, VA 844-820-7244

Gas Leak

Amerex
Trussville, AL 205-655-3271
American Gas & Chemical Co LTD
Northvale, NJ 800-288-3647
Chlorinators Inc
Stuart, FL 800-327-9761
Control Instruments Corp
Fairfield, NJ 973-575-9114
Gems Sensors & Controls
Plainville, CT 860-747-3000
Q A Supplies LLC
Norfolk, VA 800-472-7205
Rosemount Analytical Inc
Irvine, CA 800-543-8257
Sensidyne
St. Petersburg, FL 800-451-9444
Teledyne Benthos Inc
North Falmouth, MA 508-563-1000

Metal

Accu-Pak
Akron, OH
Accu-Ray Inspection Services
Elmhurst, IL 800-378-1226
Advanced Detection Systems
Milwaukee, WI 414-672-0553
Andgar Corp
Ferndale, WA 360-366-9900
Berkshire PPM
Litchfield, CT 860-567-3118
Bunting Magnetics Co
Newton, KS 800-835-2526
Cintex of America
Carol Stream, IL 800-424-6839
Eriez Magnetics
Erie, PA 800-346-4946
Friskem Infinetics
Wilmington, DE 302-658-2471
Geo. Olcott Company
Scottsboro, AL 800-634-2769
Leeman Labs Inc
Hudson, NH 800-634-9942
Lock Inspection Systems
Fitchburg, MA 800-227-5539
Loma International
Carol Stream, IL 800-872-5662
Magnetic Products Inc
Highland, MI 800-544-5930
Mettler-Toledo Safeline Inc
Lutz, FL 800-638-8537
Ohio Magnetics Inc
Maple Heights, OH 800-486-6446
TNA Packaging Solutions
Coppell, TX 972-462-6500
Vande Berg SCALES/Vbs Inc
Sioux Center, IA 712-722-1181

Shoplifting

Engineered Security System Inc
Towaco, NJ 800-742-1263
Friskem Infinetics
Wilmington, DE 302-658-2471
King Research Laboratory
Maywood, IL 708-344-7877
Protex International Corp.
Bohemia, NY 800-835-3580
Se Kure Controls Inc
Franklin Park, IL 800-250-9260
Silent Watchman Security Services LLC
Danbury, CT 800-932-3822

Detectors & Alarms

Fire, Heat & Smoke

Alarm Controls Corp
Deer Park, NY 800-645-5538

Amerex
Trussville, AL 205-655-3271
CMT
Hamilton, MA 978-768-2555
Krewson Enterprises
Cleveland, OH 800-521-2282
Migatron Corp
Woodstock, IL 888-644-2876
Napco Security Systems Inc
Amityville, NY 631-842-0253
Protectowire Co Inc
Pembroke, MA 781-924-5384
Silent Watchman Security Services LLC
Danbury, CT 800-932-3822
Simplex Time Recorder Company
Santa Ana, CA 800-746-7539
Sterling Corp
Glendora, CA 800-932-9561

Fire Alarm Systems

Carroll Manufacturing International
Florham Park, NJ 800-444-9696
Charles Gratz Fire Protection
Philadelphia, PA 215-235-5800
Christy Industries Inc
Brooklyn, NY 800-472-2078
Duke Manufacturing Co
St Louis, MO 800-735-3853
Ellenco
Brentwood, MD 301-927-4370
Faraday
Tecumseh, MI 517-423-2111
Gamewell Corporation
Northborough, MA 888-347-3269
Globe Fire Sprinkler Corp
Standish, MI 800-248-0278
Grinnell Fire ProtectionSystems Company
Sauk Rapids, MN 320-253-8665
Honeywell International
Charlotte, NC 877-841-2840
Monroe Extinguisher Co Inc
Rochester, NY 585-235-3310
Napco Security Systems Inc
Amityville, NY 631-842-0253
Protectowire Co Inc
Pembroke, MA 781-924-5384
Quantis Secure Systems
Hanover, MD 800-325-6124
Scientific Fire Prevention
Long Island City, NY 718-433-3880
Signal Equipment
Seattle, WA 800-542-0884
Silent Watchman Security Services LLC
Danbury, CT 800-932-3822
Simplex Time Recorder Company
Santa Ana, CA 800-746-7539
Simplex Time Recorder Company
Santa Ana, CA 949-724-5000
Sterling Corp
Glendora, CA 800-932-9561
Tyco Fire Protection Products
Marinette, WI 800-862-6785
Viking Corp
Hastings, MI 800-968-9501
W L Jenkins Co
Canton, OH 330-477-3407

Fire Extinguishers

Amerex
Trussville, AL 205-655-3271
Charles Gratz Fire Protection
Philadelphia, PA 215-235-5800
Greenheck Fan Corp
Schofield, WI 715-359-6171
Grinnell Fire ProtectionSystems Company
Westminster, MA 800-746-7539
Kidde Residential & Commercial
Mebane, NC 919-563-5911
National Foam
Exton, PA 610-363-1400
Pacific Scientific
Radford, VA 815-226-3100
Pyro-Chem
Marinette, WI 800-526-1079

Scientific Fire Prevention
Long Island City, NY 718-433-3880
Tyco Fire Protection Products
Marinette, WI 800-862-6785
United Fire & Safety Service
Yonkers, NY 914-968-4459

Flashlights

Rechargable

Natale Machine & Tool Co Inc
Carlstadt, NJ 800-883-8382

General

A&B Safe Corporation
Glassboro, NJ 800-253-1267
Accuform Manufacturing, Inc.
Vacaville, CA 800-233-3352
Afassco
Minden, NV 775-783-3555
AIB International
Manhattan, KS 800-633-5137
Alarm Controls Corp
Deer Park, NY 800-645-5538
Alvarado Manufacturing Co Inc
Chino, CA 800-423-4143
Amerex
Trussville, AL 205-655-3271
American Louver Co
Skokie, IL 800-772-0355
American Store Fixtures
Skokie, IL
AMSECO
Carson, CA 800-421-1096
Analogic Corp.
Peabody, MA 978-326-4000
Applied Robotics Inc
Schenectady, NY 800-309-3475
Ashcroft Inc
Stratford, CT 800-328-8258
Atlantic Rubber Products
East Wareham, MA 800-695-0446
Atlas Equipment Company
Kansas City, MO 800-842-9188
Ballymore Company
West Chester, PA 610-696-3250
Banner Engineering Corp
Minneapolis, MN 888-373-6767
Best Value Textiles
North Charleston, SC 800-858-8589
Bmh Equipment Inc
Sacramento, CA 800-350-8828
Boston Retail
Medford, MA 800-225-1633
Bullet Guard Corporation
West Sacramento, CA 800-233-5632
CCP Industries, Inc.
Cleveland, OH 800-321-2840
Cesco Magnetics
Rohnert Park, CA 877-624-8727
Charles Gratz Fire Protection
Philadelphia, PA 215-235-5800
Christy Industries Inc
Brooklyn, NY 800-472-2078
Cintex of America
Carol Stream, IL 800-424-6839
Claude Neon Signs
Baltimore, MD 410-685-7575
Continental Commercial Products
Bridgeton, MO 800-325-1051
Control Instruments Corp
Fairfield, NJ 973-575-9114
Conveyor Components Co
Croswell, MI 800-233-3233
Conveyor Components Co
Croswell, MI 800-552-3337
Corporate Safe Specialists
Posen, IL 800-342-3033
Creative Industries Inc
Indianapolis, IN 800-776-2068
Dalloz Safety
Smithfield, RI 800-977-9177
Detex Corp
New Braunfels, TX 830-629-2900
Diamond Electronics
Lancaster, OH 800-443-6680
Dickey Manufacturing Company
St Charles, IL 630-584-2918
Diversified Lighting Diffusers Inc
Copiague, NY 800-234-5464

Dometic Mini Bar
Elkhart, IN. 800-301-8118
Dri Mark Products
Port Washington, NY 800-645-9118
Duke Manufacturing Co
St Louis, MO. 800-735-3853
Durable Corp
Norwalk, OH. 800-537-1603
Dynamic Storage Systems Inc.
Brooksville, FL 800-974-8211
EJ Brooks Company
Atlanta, GE 800-458-7325
Ellenco
Brentwood, MD 301-927-4370
Elwood Safety Company
Buffalo, NY 866-326-6060
Emedco
Williamsville, NY 877-765-8386
Empire Safe Company
New York, NY 212-226-2255
Engineered Security System Inc
Towaco, NJ 800-742-1263
Etube & Wire
Shrewsbury, PA 800-618-4720
Firematic Sprinkler Devices
Shrewsbury, MA 800-225-7288
Flair Electronics
Pomona, CA 800-532-3492
Flame Gard
Lakewood, NJ 800-526-3694
Folding Guard Co
Chicago, IL 800-622-2214
Friskem Infinetics
Wilmington, DE 302-658-2471
Gamewell Corporation
Northborough, MA 888-347-3269
Gaylord Industries
Tualatin, OR 800-547-9696
George Risk Industries Inc
Kimball, NE 800-445-5218
Gilbert Insect Light Traps
Jonesboro, AR. 800-643-0400
Glaro Inc
Hauppauge, NY 631-234-1717
Globe Fire Sprinkler Corp
Standish, MI 800-248-0278
Grecon
Tigard, OR 503-641-7731
Grinnell Fire ProtectionSystems Company
Sauk Rapids, MN 320-253-8665
Grinnell Fire ProtectionSystems Company
Westminster, MA 800-746-7539
Halton Company
Scottsville, KY 800-442-5866
Harford Systems Inc
Havre De Grace, MD 800-638-7620
HD Electric Co
Park City, IL 847-473-4882
Hodge Manufacturing Company
Springfield, MA 800-262-4634
Honeywell International
Charlotte, NC 877-841-2840
Iconics Inc
Foxboro, MA 800-946-9679
Idesco Corp
New York, NY 800-336-1383
Inficon
East Syracuse, NY. 315-434-1100
Jesco Industries
Litchfield, MI 800-455-0019
JL Industries Inc
Bloomington, MN. 800-554-6077
Kason
Lewis Center, OH 740-549-2100
Kidde Residential & Commercial
Mebane, NC 919-563-5911
King Research Laboratory
Maywood, IL. 708-344-7877
Koke Inc
Queensbury, NY 800-535-5303
Krewson Enterprises
Cleveland, OH 800-521-2282
KTG
Cincinnati, OH 888-533-6900
Larco
Brainerd, MN 800-523-6996
Lavi Industries
Valencia, CA 800-624-6225
LDJ Electronics
Troy, MI 248-528-2202
Lima Sheet Metal
Lima, OH. 419-229-1161

Linde North America
Murray Hill, NJ 908-464-8100
Lixi, Inc.
Huntley, IL 847-961-6666
Locknetics
Carmel, IN
Lomont IMT
Mt. Pleasant, IA 800-776-0380
Long Range Systems
Addison, TX 800-577-8101
Loyal Manufacturing
Indianapolis, IN 317-359-3185
McGunn Safe Company
Chicago, IL 800-621-2816
Metro Corporation
Wilkes Barre, PA. 800-992-1776
Mettler-Toledo Safeline Inc
Lutz, FL. 800-638-8537
Micro Affiliates
Fairfax, VA 800-430-1099
Mirror Tech Mfg Co Inc
Yonkers, NY 914-423-1600
Monroe Extinguisher Co Inc
Rochester, NY. 585-235-3310
Nalge Process Technologies Group
Rochester, NY. 585-586-8800
Napco Security Systems Inc
Amityville, NY 631-842-0253
National Foam
Exton, PA 610-363-1400
National Marker Co Inc
North Smithfield, RI 800-453-2727
National Stock Sign Co
Santa Cruz, CA 800-462-7726
Nelson-Jameson Inc
Marshfield, WI 800-826-8302
New Pig Corp
Tipton, PA 800-468-4647
Newstamp Lighting Factory
North Easton, MA 508-238-7073
Niroflex, USA
Deerfield, IL 847-400-2638
Nrd LLC
Grand Island, NY 800-525-8076
O'Brien Bros Inc
West Springfield, MA 800-343-0949
Omicron Steel Products Company
Jamaica, NY 718-805-3400
Optex
Chino, CA. 800-966-7839
Our Name is Mud
New York, NY 877-683-7867
Pacific Scientific
Radford, VA 815-226-3100
Pak 2000 Inc
Mirror Lake, NH 603-569-3700
Patlite Corp
Torrance, CA. 888-214-2580
Penco Products
Skippack, PA 800-562-1000
Permaloc Security Devices
Silver Spring, MD. 301-681-6300
Plasticard-Locktech Intl
Asheville, NC 800-752-1017
Pro-Com Security Systems
Lehi, UT 877-776-2669
Protectowire Co Inc
Pembroke, MA 781-924-5384
Protex International Corp.
Bohemia, NY 800-835-3580
QUIKSERV Corp
Houston, TX 800-388-8307
R & D Brass
Wappingers Falls, NY 800-447-6050
Raco Mfg & Engineering Co
Emeryville, CA. 800-722-6999
Reidler Decal Corporation
Saint Clair, PA. 800-628-7770
Remcon Plastics Inc
Reading, PA 800-360-3636
Rocky Shoes & Boots Inc
Nelsonville, OH 866-442-4908
Roni LLC
Charlotte, NC 866-543-8635
Rosco Inc
Jamaica, NY 800-227-2095
Safety Light Corporation
Bloomsburg, PA 570-784-4344
Sargent & Greenleaf
Nicholasville, KY 800-826-7652
Scientific Fire Prevention
Long Island City, NY 718-433-3880

Se Kure Controls Inc
Franklin Park, IL 800-250-9260
Security Link
Danville, IL 217-446-4871
Sensidyne
St. Petersburg, FL 800-451-9444
Server Products Inc
Richfield, WI 800-558-8722
Seton Indentification Products
Branford, CT 800-571-2596
Shelden, Dickson, & Steven Company
Omaha, NE 402-571-4848
SICK Inc
Bloomington, MN 800-325-7425
Signal Equipment
Seattle, WA 800-542-0884
Silent Watchman Security Services LLC
Danbury, CT 800-932-3822
Simplex Time Recorder Company
Santa Ana, CA 800-746-7539
Simplex Time Recorder Company
Santa Ana, CA 949-724-5000
Sinco
Red Wing, MN 800-243-6753
Sipco Products
Peoria Heights, IL 309-682-5400
Slip Not
Detroit, MI 800-754-7668
Stanley Access Technologies
Farmington, CT 800-722-2377
Star Micronics
Edison, NJ 800-782-7636
Steel King Industries
Stevens Point, WI 800-553-3096
Sterling Corp
Glendora, CA 800-932-9561

Stoffel Seals Corp
Tallapoosa, GA 800-422-8247
Technibilt/Cari-All
Newton, NC 800-233-3972
Tepromark International
Osseo, MN 800-645-2622
Theta Sciences
San Diego, CA 760-745-3311
Tomsed Corporation
Lillington, NC 800-334-5552
Torbeck Industries
Harrison, OH 800-333-0080
Tucker Industries
Colorado Springs, CO 800-786-7287
Tyco Fire Protection Products
Lansdale, PA 800-558-5236
Tyco Fire Protection Products
Marinette, WI 800-862-6785
Tyco Retail Solutions
Boca Raton, FL 561-912-6000
UAA
Chicago, IL 800-813-1711
Ultrak
Westminster, CO 303-428-9480
United Fire & Safety Service
Yonkers, NY 914-968-4459
Valeo
Elmsford, Ny. 800-634-2704
Vent Master
Mississauga, ON 800-565-2981
Viking Corp
Hastings, MI 800-968-9501
W L Jenkins Co
Canton, OH 330-477-3407
Wearwell/Tennessee Mat Company
Nashville, TN 615-254-8381

Weinbrenner Shoe Co
Merrill, WI 800-826-0002
Wiginton Corp
Sanford, FL 407-585-3200
World Wide Safe Brokers
Woodbury, NJ 800-593-2893
Wylie Systems
Mississauga, ON 800-525-6609
YottaMark
Redwood City, CA 866-768-7878

Ladder Covers

Slip Not
Detroit, MI 800-754-7668

Ladder Rungs

Slip Not
Detroit, MI 800-754-7668

Mats

Electric Alarm

Floor

Larco
Brainerd, MN 800-523-6996

Metal Detectors

Industrial Magnetics
Boyne City, MI 800-662-4638

Sanitation Equipment & Supplies

Ammonia

Bottled for Cleaning

James Austin Co
Mars, PA 724-625-1535
KIK Custom Products
Salem, VA 540-389-5401
Laundry Aids
Carlstadt, NJ 201-933-3500
Patterson Laboratories
Detroit, MI 313-843-4500
Rooto Corp
Howell, MI 517-546-8330

Bleaches

Bio Pac Inc
Incline Village, NV 800-225-2855
Blue Cross Laboratories
Santa Clarita, CA
Country Save Products Corp
Arlington, WA .360-435-9868
Delta Chemical Corporation
Baltimore, MD .800-282-5322
Diamond Chemical Co Inc
East Rutherford, NJ 800-654-7627
Dover Chemical Corp
Dover, OH 800-321-8805
Hilex Company
Eagan, MN 651-454-1160
Hydrite Chemical Co
Brookfield, WI .262-792-1450
James Austin Co
Mars, PA 724-625-1535
KIK Custom Products
Salem, VA 540-389-5401
Kuehne Chemical
Kearny, NJ 973-589-0700
Patterson Laboratories
Detroit, MI 313-843-4500
Rooto Corp
Howell, MI 517-546-8330
Venturetech Corporation
Knoxville, TN .800-826-4095

Borax

Ceramic Color & Chemical Mfg
New Brighton, PA 724-846-4000

Brooms

Abco Products
Miami, FL 888-694-2226
Amarillo Mop & Broom Company
Amarillo, TX 800-955-8596
American Broom Co
Mattoon, IL 217-235-1992
American Brush Company
Portland, OR 800-826-8492
American Water Broom
Doraville, GA .800-241-6565
Anderson Products
Cresco, PA 800-729-4694
Birmingham Mop Manufacturing Company
Birmingham, AL 205-942-6101
Bouras Mop Manufacturing Company
Saint Louis, MO 800-634-9153
Bruske Products
Tinley Park, IL .708-532-3800
Carlisle Food Svc Products Inc
Oklahoma City, OK 800-654-8210
Carolina Mop
Anderson, SC .800-845-9725
Chickasaw Broom Mfg Co Inc
Little Rock, AR 501-562-0311
Cleveland Mop Manufacturing Company
Cleveland, OH 800-767-9934
Cornelia Broom Company
Cornelia, GA .800-228-2551
Cosgrove Enterprises Inc
Miami Lakes, FL 800-888-3396
Costa Broom Works
Tampa, FL 813-385-1722
Crystal Lake Mfg Inc
Autaugaville, AL 800-633-8720

Culicover & Shapiro
Bay Shore, NY 631-918-4560
Detroit Quality Brush Mfg Co
Livonia, MI 800-722-3037
Fuller Industries LLC
Great Bend, KS 800-522-0499
Furgale Industries Ltd.
Winnipeg, NB .800-665-0506
Greenwood Mop & Broom Inc
Greenwood, SC 800-635-6849
H. Arnold Wood Turning
Tarrytown, NY .888-314-0088
Harper Brush Works Inc
Fairfield, IA 800-223-7894
Hoge Brush Company
New Knoxville, OH 800-494-4643
Howard Overman & Sons
Baltimore, MD 410-276-8445
Hub City Brush Co
Petal, MS 800-278-7452
Imperial Broom Company
Richmond, VA 888-353-7840
Industries For The Blind
Milwaukee, WI 800-642-8778
Industries of the Blind
Greensboro, NC 336-274-1591
J.I. Holcomb Manufacturing
Independence, OH 800-458-3222
John L. Denning & Company
Wichita, KS 316-264-2357
Labpride Chemicals
Bronx, NY 800-467-1255
Libman Co
Arcola, IL 877-818-3380
Lighthouse for the Blindin New Orleans
New Orleans, LA 504-899-4501
Little Rock Broom Works
Little Rock, AR 501-562-0311
LMCO
Rosenberg, TX 281-342-8888
Luco Mop Co
St Louis, MO .800-522-5826
Messina Brothers Manufacturing Company
Brooklyn, NY .800-924-6454
Michigan Brush Mfg Co
Detroit, MI 800-642-7874
Milwaukee Dustless Brush Co
Delavan, WI 323-724-7777
Minuteman Power Boss
Aberdeen, NC 800-323-9420
Nationwide Wire & Brush Manufacturing
Lodi, CA 209-334-9660
Newton Broom Co
Newton, IL 618-783-4424
O'Dell Corp
Ware Shoals, SC 800-342-2843
O-Cedar
Aurora, IL 800-543-8105
Perfex Corporation
Poland, NY 800-848-8483
Quality Mop & Brush Manufacturers
Needham, MA 617-884-2999
Quickie Manufacturing Corp
Cinnaminson, NJ 856-829-7900
Reit-Price ManufacturingCompany
Union City, IN. 800-521-5343
RidgeView Products LLC
La Crosse, WI 888-782-1221
Royal Broom & Mop Factory Inc
New Orleans, LA 800-537-6925
S&M Manufacturing Company
Cisco, TX 800-772-8532
Tucel Industries, Inc.
Forestdale, VT 800-558-8235
Waco Broom & Mop Factory
Waco, TX 800-548-7716
Warren E. Conley Corporation
Carmel, IN. 800-367-7875
Whitley Manufacturing Company
Midland, NC .704-888-2625
Young & Swartz Inc
Buffalo, NY. 800-466-7682

Brushes

Bottle

Braun Brush Co
Albertson, NY 800-645-4111
Carlisle Food Svc Products Inc
Oklahoma City, OK 800-654-8210
Justman Brush Co
Omaha, NE 800-800-6940
Volckening Inc
Brooklyn, NY .800-221-0276

Floor, Sweeping, Polishing & Waxing

Abco Products
Miami, FL 888-694-2226
Anderson Products
Cresco, PA. 800-729-4694
Braun Brush Co
Albertson, NY 800-645-4111
Bruske Products
Tinley Park, IL .708-532-3800
Carlisle Food Svc Products Inc
Oklahoma City, OK 800-654-8210
Carlisle Sanitary Mntnc Prods
Oklahoma City, OK 800-654-8210
Cornelia Broom Company
Cornelia, GA .800-228-2551
Costa Broom Works
Tampa, FL 813-385-1722
Culicover & Shapiro
Bay Shore, NY 631-918-4560
Detroit Quality Brush Mfg Co
Livonia, MI 800-722-3037
Fox Brush Company
Oxford, ME. 207-539-2208
Fuller Industries LLC
Great Bend, KS 800-522-0499
Harper Brush Works Inc
Fairfield, IA 800-223-7894
Hoge Brush Company
New Knoxville, OH 800-494-4643
Kiefer Brushes, Inc
Franklin, NJ 800-526-2905
Labpride Chemicals
Bronx, NY 800-467-1255
Lighthouse for the Blindin New Orleans
New Orleans, LA 504-899-4501
Michigan Brush Mfg Co
Detroit, MI 800-642-7874
Microtron Abrasives
Pineville, NC. .800-476-7237
Milwaukee Dustless Brush Co
Delavan, WI 323-724-7777
O'Dell Corp
Ware Shoals, SC 800-342-2843
O-Cedar
Aurora, IL 800-543-8105
Perfex Corporation
Poland, NY 800-848-8483
Reit-Price ManufacturingCompany
Union City, IN. 800-521-5343
Superior Brush Company
Cleveland, OH 216-941-6987
Tucel Industries, Inc.
Forestdale, VT 800-558-8235
Walker Brush Inc
Webster, NY .585-545-4748
Wilen Professional Cleaning Products
Atlanta, GA. 800-241-7371
Young & Swartz Inc
Buffalo, NY. 800-466-7682
Zephyr Manufacturing Co
Sedalia, MO .660-827-0352

Carts

Housekeeping

Amco Metals Indl
City Of Industry, CA. 626-855-2550
Bmh Equipment Inc
Sacramento, CA 800-350-8828
Geerpres Inc
Muskegon, MI. 231-773-3211

James Varley & Sons
Saint Louis, MO 800-325-8891
Lakeside Manufacturing Inc
Milwaukee, WI 888-558-8565
Princeton Shelving
Cedar Rapids, IA. 319-369-0355

Caustic Soda

ATOFINA Chemicals
Philadelphia, PA 800-225-7788

Chlorine

Liquid

ATOFINA Chemicals
Philadelphia, PA 800-225-7788
Delta Chemical Corporation
Baltimore, MD 800-282-5322
Selig Chemical Industries
Atlanta, GA. 404-876-5511

Cleaners

Bottle (Compounds)

American Formula
Atlanta, GA. 800-282-1215
American Municipal Chemical
Milwaukee, WI 800-598-3106
APR Associates Inc
Memphis, TN 800-238-5150
Champion Chemical Co
Whittier, CA 800-621-7868
Church & Dwight Co., Inc.
Ewing, NJ 800-833-9532
Diamond Chemical Co Inc
East Rutherford, NJ 800-654-7627
ELF Machinery
La Porte, IN. 800-328-0466
Essential Industries Inc
Merton, WI 800-551-9679
Hy-Trous/Flash Sales
Woburn, MA 781-933-5772
James Varley & Sons
Saint Louis, MO 800-325-8891
Lubar Chemical
Kansas City, MO. 816-471-2560
Magnuson Products
Clifton, NJ. 973-472-9292
Mertz L. Carlton Company
Bedford Park, IL 708-594-1050
National Interchem Corporation
Blue Island, IL 800-638-6688
Oakite Products
New Providence, NJ 800-526-4473
Occidental Chemical Corporation
Houston, TX 713-215-7000
Pneumatic Scale Angelus
Cuyahoga Falls, OH 330-923-0491
Seatex Ltd
Rosenberg, TX 800-829-3020
Shepard Brothers Co
La Habra, CA 800-645-3594
Warren E. Conley Corporation
Carmel, IN. 800-367-7875
Warsaw Chemical Co Inc
Warsaw, IN 800-548-3396

Coffee Pot

Urnex Brands Inc
Elmsford, NY 800-222-2826

Dairy

GEA North America
Naperville, IL 630-369-8100
Hoge Brush Company
New Knoxville, OH 800-494-4643
Hy-Ko Enviro-MaintenanceProducts
Salt Lake City, UT 801-973-6099
Lechler Inc
St Charles, IL 800-777-2926
Magnuson Products
Clifton, NJ. 973-472-9292
Winn-Sol Products
Oshkosh, WI 920-231-2031

Grain & Seed

A C Horn & Co Sheet Metal
Dallas, TX. 800-657-6155
A T Ferrell Co Inc
Bluffton, IN. 800-248-8318
A.K. Robins
Baltimore, MD 800-486-9656
Carter-Day International Inc
Minneapolis, MN 763-571-1000
Cleland Manufacturing Company
Columbia Heights, MN. 763-571-4606
Crippen Manufacturing Co
St Louis, MI 800-872-2474
DMC-David Manufacturing Company
Mason City, IA 641-424-7010
En-Hanced Products Inc
Westerville, OH. 800-783-7400
Forster & Son
Ada, OK 580-332-6021
Grain Machinery Mfg Corp
Miami, FL. 305-620-2525
Lewis M Carter Mfg Co Inc
Donalsonville, GA 800-332-8232
NECO/Nebraska Engineering
Omaha, NE 800-367-6208

Hand

Afassco
Minden, NV 775-783-3555
Amodex Products
Bridgeport, CT 877-866-1255
Athea Laboratories
Milwaukee, WI 800-743-6417
Buckeye International
Maryland Heights, MO 314-291-1900
CCP Industries, Inc.
Cleveland, OH 800-321-2840
Chef Revival
North Charleston, SC 800-248-9826
Coleman Manufacturing Co Inc
Everett, MA. 617-389-0380
Concord Chemical Co Inc
Camden, NJ. 800-282-2436
Crc Industries Inc
Warminster, PA 800-556-5074
Cresset Chemical Company
Weston, OH. 800-367-2020
Critzas Industries Inc
St Louis, MO. 800-537-1418
Crown Chemical Products
Mississauga, ON. 905-564-0904
DCL Solutions LLC
Philadelphia, PA 800-426-1127
Deb Canada
Waterford, ON. 888-332-7627
Development Workshop Inc
Idaho Falls, ID 800-657-5597
Diamond Wipes Intl Inc
Chino, CA 800-454-1077
Dober Chemical Corporation
Midlothian, IL. 800-323-4983
Dreumex USA
York, PA 800-233-9382
Du-Good Chemical Laboratory & Manufacturing
Company
Saint Louis, MO 314-773-5007
Emulso
Tonawanda, NY 716-854-2889
Essential Industries Inc
Merton, WI 800-551-9679
Fishers Investment
Cincinnati, OH 800-833-5916
Galaxy Chemical Corp
Sarasota, FL 941-755-8545
GOJO Industries Inc
Akron, OH. 800-321-9647
Hallberg Manufacturing Corporation
Tampa, FL. 800-633-7627
Hewitt Soap Company
Dayton, OH. 800-543-2245
Hill Manufacturing Co Inc
Atlanta, GA. 404-522-8364
Hy-Ko Enviro-MaintenanceProducts
Salt Lake City, UT 801-973-6099
Hy-Trous/Flash Sales
Woburn, MA 781-933-5772
Industrial EnvironmentalPollution Control
Bronx, NY. 718-585-2410
Inksolv 30, LLC.
Emerson, NE. 515-537-5344

ITW Dymon
Olathe, KS. 800-443-9536
J C Whitlam Mfg Co
Wadsworth, OH. 800-321-8358
J.I. Holcomb Manufacturing
Independence, OH 800-458-3222
James Austin Co
Mars, PA 724-625-1535
James Varley & Sons
Saint Louis, MO 800-325-8891
Kildon Manufacturing
Ingersoll, ON 800-485-4930
Kleen Products Inc
Oklahoma City, OK 800-392-1792
L&M Chemicals
Tampa, FL 800-362-3331
Lee Products Co
Minneapolis, MN 952-300-2908
Man-O Products
Cincinnati, OH 888-210-6266
Martin Laboratories
Owensboro, KY 800-345-9352
Micro-Brush Pro Soap
Rockwall, TX 800-776-7627
Milburn Company
Detroit, MI 313-259-3410
Mione Manufacturing Company
Mickleton, NJ 800-257-0497
Mission Laboratories
Los Angeles, CA 888-201-8866
Nice-Pak Products Inc
Orangeburg, NY 800-444-6725
Nosaj Disposables
Paterson, NJ 800-631-3809
Nuance Solutions Inc
Chicago, IL 800-621-8553
R&C Pro Brands
Wayne, NJ. 973-633-7374
Rochester Midland Corp
Rochester, NY 800-535-5053
Rochester Midland Corp
Rochester, NY 800-836-1627
S & S Soap Co
Bronx, NY 718-585-2900
Sanitek Products Inc
Los Angeles, CA. 818-242-1071
Savogran Co
Norwood, MA. 800-225-9872
SCA Hygiene Paper
San Ramon, CA 800-992-8675
Simoniz USA Inc
Bolton, CT 800-227-5536
Starkey Chemical Process Company
La Grange, IL 800-323-3040
Steiner Company
Holland, IL 800-222-4638
Steiner Industries Inc
Chicago, IL 800-621-4515
Stone Soap Co Inc
Sylvan Lake, MI 800-952-7627
Sunbeam Products Co LLC
Toledo, OH 419-691-1551
Telechem Corp
Atlanta, GA. 800-637-0495
Tropical Soap Company
Carrollton, TX. 800-527-2368
Verax Chemical Co
Snohomish, WA 800-637-7771
W.M. Barr & Co Inc.
Memphis, TN 901-775-0100
Whisk Products Inc
Wentzville, MO. 800-204-7627

Silver

Burnishine Products
Gurnee, IL. 800-818-8275
Casabar
Morristown, NJ 877-745-8700
Copper Clad
Reading, PA 610-375-4596
Dynynstyl
Delray Beach, FL 800-774-7895
George Basch Company
Freeport, NY 516-378-8100
Swisher Hygiene
Charlotte, NC 800-444-4138

Cleaning Equipment & Supplies

9-12 Corporation
Caguas, PR 787-747-0405

A J Funk & Co
Elgin, IL 877-225-3865
A&L Laboratories
Minneapolis, MN 800-225-3832
A.K. Robins
Baltimore, MD 800-486-9656
Abco Products
Miami, FL 888-694-2226
Abicor Binzel
Frederick, MD 800-542-4867
Absorbco
Walterboro, SC 888-335-6439
Ace-Tex Enterprises
Detroit, MI 800-444-3800
Acme Sponge & Chamois Co Inc
Tarpon Springs, FL 727-937-3222
Acro Dishwashing Svc Co
Kansas City, KS 913-342-4282
ACS Industries, Inc.
Lincoln, RI 866-783-4838
Activon Products
Beaver Dam, WI 800-841-0410
Adamation
Commerce, CA 800-383-8800
ADCO
Albany, GA 800-821-7556
Advance Cleaning Products
Milwaukee, WI 800-925-5326
Air-Scent International
Pittsburgh, PA 800-247-0770
Airosol Co Inc
Neodesha, KS 800-633-9576
Akron Cotton Products
Akron, OH 800-899-7173
Alconox Inc
White Plains, NY 914-437-7585
Alex E Fergusson Co Inc
Chambersburg, PA 800-345-1329
Alkota Cleaning Systems Inc
Alcester, SD 800-255-6823
All American Container
Miami, FL 305-887-0797
Alumin-Nu Corporation
Lyndhurst, OH 800-899-7097
Amarillo Mop & Broom Company
Amarillo, TX 800-955-8596
Amco Metals Indl
City Of Industry, CA 626-855-2550
Ameri-Khem
Port Orange, FL 800-224-9950
American Broom Co
Mattoon, IL 217-235-1992
American Brush Company
Portland, OR 800-826-8492
American Formula
Atlanta, GA 800-282-1215
American Municipal Chemical
Milwaukee, WI 800-598-3106
American Textile Mills Inc
Kansas City, MO 816-842-2909
American Water Broom
Doraville, GA 800-241-6565
American Wax Co Inc
Long Island City, NY 718-361-4820
Ametek Technical & Industrial Products
Kent, OH 215-256-6601
Amodex Products
Bridgeport, CT 877-866-1255
Andersen 2000
Peachtree City, GA 800-241-5424
Anderson Products
Cresco, PA 800-729-4694
APR Associates Inc
Memphis, TN 800-238-5150
Aquafine Corp
Valencia, CA 800-423-3015
Aquionics Inc
Erlanger, KY 800-925-0440
ARC Specialties
Valencia, CA 661-775-8500
Arden Companies
Southfield, MI 248-415-8500
Argo & Company
Spartanburg, SC 864-583-9766
Armaly Brands
Commerce Twp, MI 800-772-1222
Armstrong Hot Water
Three Rivers, MI 269-279-3602
Armstrong Manufacturing
Mississauga, ON 866-627-6588
Arrow-Magnolia Intl Inc
Dallas, TX 800-527-2101

Assembled Products Corp
Rogers, AR 800-548-3373
Associated Products Inc
Glenshaw, PA 800-243-5689
Athea Laboratories
Milwaukee, WI 800-743-6417
Atlantic Mills
Lakewood, NJ 800-242-7374
ATOFINA Chemicals
Philadelphia, PA 800-225-7788
Auto Chlor Systems
Memphis, TN 800-477-3693
Banner Chemical Co
Orange, NJ 973-676-0105
Bar Keepers Friend Cleanser
Indianapolis, IN 800-433-5818
Bar Maid Corp
Pompano Beach, FL 954-960-1468
Beam Industries
Webster City, IA 800-369-2326
Beaumont Products
Kennesaw, GA 800-451-7096
Bel-Art Products
Wayne, NJ 800-423-5278
Bete Fog Nozzle Inc
Greenfield, MA 800-235-0049
Bethel Engineering & Equipment Inc
New Hampshire, OH 800-889-6129
BEX Inc
Ann Arbor, MI 734-464-8282
Bi-O-Kleen Industries
Portland, OR 503-224-6246
Bio Cide Intl Inc
Norman, OK 800-323-1398
Bio Industries
Luxemburg, WI 920-845-2355
Bio Pac Inc
Incline Village, NV 800-225-2855
Bio Zapp Laboratories
Sarasota, FL 941-922-9199
Birko Corporation
Olathe, KS 800-444-8360
Birmingham Mop Manufacturing Company
Birmingham, AL 205-942-6101
Black Bear Corp
Roanoke, VA 800-223-1284
Black's Products of HighPoint
High Point, NC 336-886-5011
Blue Cross Laboratories
Santa Clarita, CA
Blue Feather Products Inc
Ashland, OR 800-472-2487
Blue Ridge Converting
Asheville, NC 800-438-3893
Bouras Mop Manufacturing Company
Saint Louis, MO 800-634-9153
Boyer Corporation
La Grange, IL 800-323-3040
Bradford Soap Works Inc
West Warwick, RI 401-821-2141
Branson Ultrasonics Corp
Danbury, CT 203-796-0400
Braun Brush Co
Albertson, NY 800-645-4111
Bro-Tex Inc
St Paul, MN 800-328-2282
Brulin & Company
Indianapolis, IN 800-776-7149
Bruske Products
Tinley Park, IL 708-532-3800
Buckeye International
Maryland Heights, MO 314-291-1900
Bunzl Distribution USA
St. Louis, MO 888-997-5959
Burnishine Products
Gurnee, IL 800-818-8275
Butterworth Inc
Houston, TX 281-821-7300
C P Industries
Salt Lake City, UT 800-453-4931
C&H Chemical
St Paul, MN 651-227-4343
C&R Refrigation Inc,
Center, TX 800-438-6182
Cadie Products Corp
Paterson, NJ 973-278-8300
Cal Ben Soap Co
Oakland, CA 800-340-7091
Cam Spray
Iowa Falls, IA 800-648-5011
Candy & Company/Peck's Products Company
Chicago, IL 800-837-9189

Cantol
Markham, ON 800-387-9773
Canton Sterilized Wiping Cloth
Canton, OH 330-455-8157
Carbon Clean Industries Inc
Kingston, PA 570-288-1155
Carhoff Company
Cleveland, OH 216-541-4835
Carlisle Food Svc Products Inc
Oklahoma City, OK 800-654-8210
Carlisle Sanitary Mntnc Prods
Oklahoma City, OK 800-654-8210
Carnegie Textile Co
Cleveland, OH 800-633-4136
Carolina Mop
Anderson, SC 800-845-9725
Carroll Co
Garland, TX 800-527-5722
Casabar
Morristown, NJ 877-745-8700
CC Custom Technology Corporation
Cleveland, OH 216-662-5500
CCP Industries, Inc.
Cleveland, OH 800-321-2840
Central Solutions Inc
Kansas City, KS 800-255-0262
Century Chemical Corp
Elkhart, IN 800-348-3505
Ceramic Color & Chemical Mfg
New Brighton, PA 724-846-4000
Chad Co Inc
Olathe, KS 800-444-8360
Champion America Inc
Branford, CT 800-521-7000
Champion Chemical Co
Whittier, CA 800-621-7868
Champion Industries Inc
Winston Salem, NC 800-532-8591
Chef Revival
North Charleston, SC 800-248-9826
Chemclean Corp
Jamaica, NY 800-538-2436
Chemdet Inc
Sebastian, FL 800-645-1510
Chemifax
Santa Fe Springs, CA 800-527-5722
Chickasaw Broom Mfg Co Inc
Little Rock, AR 501-562-0311
Cincinnati Industrial Machry
Mason, OH 800-677-0076
Claire Manufacturing Company
Addison, IL 800-252-4731
Clarke American Sanders
Minneapolis, MN 800-253-0367
Clarkson Supply
Williamsport, PA 800-326-9457
Clayton L. Hagy & Son
Philadelphia, PA 215-844-6470
Clean-All Pool Svc
Syracuse, NY 315-472-7665
Cleanfreak
Appleton, WI 888-722-5508
Cleveland Mop Manufacturing Company
Cleveland, OH 800-767-9934
Clorox Company
Oakland, CA 510-271-7000
Cloud Inc
San Luis Obispo, CA 800-234-5650
Clyde Bergemann Eec
Halethorpe, MD 410-712-4280
Cma Dishmachines
Garden Grove, CA 800-854-6417
Coast Scientific
Rancho Santa Fe, CA 800-445-1544
Cobitco Inc
Denver, CO 303-296-8575
Coburn Company
Whitewater, WI 800-776-7042
Coleman Manufacturing Co Inc
Everett, MA 617-389-0380
Colgate-Palmolive Professional Products Group
North York, ON 800-468-6502
Colonial Paper Company
Silver Springs, FL 352-622-4171
Command Belt Cleaning Systems
Hammond, IN 800-433-7627
Common Sense Natural Soap & Bodycare Products
Rutland, VT 802-773-0582
Compliance Control Inc
Hyattsville, MD 800-810-4000
Composition Materials Co Inc
Milford, CT 800-262-7763

Concord Chemical Co Inc
Camden, NJ.........................800-282-2436
Continental Commercial Products
Bridgeton, MO....................800-325-1051
Continental Equipment Corporation
Milwaukee, WI....................414-463-0500
Continental Girbau Inc
Oshkosh, WI......................800-256-1073
Conveyor Components Co
Croswell, MI......................800-233-3233
Copper Brite
Santa Barbara, CA................805-565-1566
Copper Clad
Reading, PA......................610-375-4596
Core Products Co
Canton, TX.......................800-825-2673
Cornelia Broom Company
Cornelia, GA.....................800-228-2551
Cosgrove Enterprises Inc
Miami Lakes, FL..................800-888-3396
Costa Broom Works
Tampa, FL........................813-385-1722
Cougar Packaging Concepts, Inc.
St. Charles, IL...................630-689-4050
Country Save Products Corp
Arlington, WA....................360-435-9868
Crc Industries Inc
Warminster, PA...................800-556-5074
Cresset Chemical Company
Weston, OH.......................800-367-2020
Critzas Industries Inc
St Louis, MO.....................800-537-1418
Crown Chemical Products
Mississauga, ON..................905-564-0904
Crystal Lake Mfg Inc
Autaugaville, AL.................800-633-8720
Culicover & Shapiro
Bay Shore, NY....................631-918-4560
D R Technology Inc
Freehold, NJ.....................732-780-4664
D W Davies & Co
Racine, WI.......................800-888-6133
D&M Products
Santa Monica, CA.................800-245-0485
Damas Corporation
Trenton, NJ......................609-695-9121
Damon Industries
Alliance, OH.....................800-362-9850
Damp Rid
Memphis, TN......................888-326-7743
DCL Solutions LLC
Philadelphia, PA.................800-426-1127
De Laval
Kansas City, MO..................816-891-7700
De Royal Textiles
Camden, SC.......................800-845-1062
Deb Canada
Waterford, ON....................888-332-7627
Delta Carbona
Fairfield, NJ....................888-746-5599
Delta Chemical Corporation
Baltimore, MD....................800-282-5322
Dema Engineering Co
St Louis, MO.....................800-325-3362
Detroit Quality Brush Mfg Co
Livonia, MI......................800-722-3037
Development Workshop Inc
Idaho Falls, ID..................800-657-5597
Diablo Chemical
Kingston, PA.....................800-548-1384
Dial Corporation
Scottsdale, AZ...................480-754-3425
Diamond Chemical Co Inc
East Rutherford, NJ..............800-654-7627
Diamond Wipes Intl Inc
Chino, CA........................800-454-1077
Dirt Killer Pressure Washer
Gwynn Oak, MD....................800-544-1188
Distribution Results
Akron, OH........................800-737-9671
DL Enterprises
Etters, PA.......................717-938-1292
Dober Chemical Corporation
Midlothian, IL...................800-323-4983
Donaldson Co Inc
Bloomington, MN..................952-887-3131
Dorden & Co
Detroit, MI......................313-834-7910
Douglas Machines Corp.
Clearwater, FL...................800-331-6870
Dover Chemical Corp
Dover, OH........................800-321-8805

Dover Parkersburg
Follansbee, WV
Downeast Chemical
Westbrook, ME....................800-287-2225
DPC
Norristown, PA...................800-220-9473
Drackett Professional
Cincinnati, OH...................513-583-3900
Dreumex USA
York, PA.........................800-233-9382
Du-Good Chemical Laboratory & Manufacturing
Company
Saint Louis, MO..................314-773-5007
Dynablast Manufacturing
Mississauga, ON..................888-242-8597
Dynynstyl
Delray Beach, FL.................800-774-7895
Eagle Home Products
Huntington, NY...................631-673-3500
Ecolo Odor Control Systems Worldwide
North York, ON...................800-667-6355
Economy Paper & Restaurant Co
Clifton, NJ......................973-279-5500
Ecover
Los Angeles, CA..................323-720-5730
Electro-Steam Generator Corp
Rancocas, NJ.....................866-617-0764
ELF Machinery
La Porte, IN.....................800-328-0466
Elgene
Hamden, CT.......................800-922-4623
Emulso
Tonawanda, NY....................716-854-2889
Erie Cotton Products
Erie, PA.........................800-289-4737
Essential Industries Inc
Merton, WI.......................800-551-9679
Ettore
Alameda, CA......................510-748-4130
Eureka Company
Bloomington, IL..................800-282-2886
Ex-Cell KAISER LLC
Franklin Park, IL................847-451-0451
Excel Chemical Company
Jacksonville, FL.................904-356-0446
Faciltec Corporation
Elgin, IL........................800-284-8273
Falls Chemical Products
Oconto Falls, WI.................920-846-3561
Fast Industries
Fort Lauderdale, FL..............800-775-5345
Feather Duster Corporation
Amsterdam, NY....................800-967-8659
Fiebing Co
Milwaukee, WI....................800-558-1033
Fishers Investment
Cincinnati, OH...................800-833-5916
Fitzpatrick Brothers
Pleasant Prairie, WI.............800-233-8064
FleetwoodGoldcoWyard
Romeoville, IL...................630-759-6800
Flo-Matic Corporation
Belvidere, IL....................800-959-1179
Floor Master Inc
Chattanooga, TN..................423-867-4525
Flow International Corp.
Kent, WA.........................800-446-3569
Fuller Industries LLC
Great Bend, KS...................800-522-0499
Furgale Industries Ltd.
Winnipeg, NB.....................800-665-0506
FX-Lab Company
Union, NJ........................908-810-1212
Galaxy Chemical Corp
Sarasota, FL.....................941-755-8545
Gamajet Cleaning Systems
Exton, PA........................800-289-5387
Gamecock Chemical Co Inc
Sumter, SC.......................803-773-7391
Gardner Denver Inc.
Milwaukee, WI
Garman Co Inc
Valley Park, MO..................800-466-5150
Geerpres Inc
Muskegon, MI.....................231-773-3211
Gemtek Products LLC
Phoenix, AZ......................800-331-7022
General Floor Craft
Little Silver, NJ................973-742-7400
General Steel Fabricators
Joplin, MO.......................800-820-8644

General, Inc
Weston, FL.......................954-202-7419
Geo. Olcott Company
Scottsboro, AL...................800-634-2769
George Basch Company
Freeport, NY.....................516-378-8100
Georgia Pacific
Green Bay, WI....................920-435-8821
Ghibli North American
Wilmington, DE...................302-654-5908
Girton Manufacturing Co
Millville, PA....................570-458-5521
Glass Pro
Addison, IL......................888-641-8919
Glastender
Saginaw, MI......................800-748-0423
Glit Microtron
Bridgeton, MO....................800-325-1051
Glover Latex
Anaheim, CA......................800-243-5110
GOJO Industries Inc
Akron, OH........................800-321-9647
Golden Star
N Kansas City, MO................800-821-2792
Goodman Wiper & Paper Co
Auburn, ME.......................207-784-5779
Goodway Technologies Corp
Stamford, CT.....................800-333-7467
Goodwin Co
Garden Grove, CA.................714-894-0531
Grace-Lee Products
Minneapolis, MN..................612-379-2711
Graco Inc
Minneapolis, MN..................877-844-7226
Great Western Chemical Company
Portland, OR.....................800-547-1400
Greenwood Mop & Broom Inc
Greenwood, SC....................800-635-6849
Griffin Bros Inc
Salem, OR........................800-456-4743
Guardsman
Grand Rapids, MI.................616-940-2900
Guest Supply
Monmouth Jct, NJ.................800-448-3787
H F Staples & Co Inc
Merrimack, NH....................800-682-0034
H. Arnold Wood Turning
Tarrytown, NY....................888-314-0088
H.L. Diehl Company
South Windham, CT................860-423-7741
Hallberg Manufacturing Corporation
Tampa, FL........................800-633-7627
Hamilton Soap & Oil Products
Paterson, NJ.....................973-225-1031
Hanco Manufacturing Company
Memphis, TN......................800-530-7364
Hardt Equipment Manufacturing
Lachine, QC......................888-848-4408
Hardwood Products Co LP
Guilford, ME.....................800-289-3340
Harper Brush Works Inc
Fairfield, IA....................800-223-7894
Haviland Enterprises Inc
Grand Rapids, MI.................800-456-1134
Hedgetree Chemical Manufacturing
Savannah, GA.....................912-691-0408
Hewitt Soap Company
Dayton, OH.......................800-543-2245
Hibrett Puratex
Pennsauken, NJ...................800-260-5124
Hilex Company
Eagan, MN........................651-454-1160
Hill Manufacturing Co Inc
Atlanta, GA......................404-522-8364
Hillyard Inc
St Joseph, MO....................800-365-1555
Hodges
Vienna, IL.......................800-444-0011
Hoge Brush Company
New Knoxville, OH................800-494-4643
Hohn Manufacturing Company
Fenton, MO.......................800-878-1440
Holland Applied Technologies
Burr Ridge, IL...................630-325-5130
Holland Chemicals Company
Windsor, ON......................519-948-4373
Hollowell Products Corporation
Wyandotte, MI....................734-282-8200
Hoover Company
Glenwillow, OH...................330-499-9499
Hope Chemical Corporation
Pawtucket, RI....................401-724-8000

Hosch Properties
Oakdale, PA 800-695-3310
Howard Overman & Sons
Baltimore, MD 410-276-8445
Howell Brothers Chemical Laboratories
Philadelphia, PA 215-477-0260
Hub City Brush Co
Petal, MS 800-278-7452
Hy-Ko Enviro-MaintenanceProducts
Salt Lake City, UT 801-973-6099
Hy-Trous/Flash Sales
Woburn, MA 781-933-5772
Hydrite Chemical Co
Brookfield, WI 262-792-1450
Idexx Laboratories Inc
Westbrook, ME 800-548-6733
IFC Disposables Inc
Brownsville, TN 800-432-9473
Imperial Broom Company
Richmond, VA 888-353-7840
Indian Valley Industries
Johnson City, NY 800-659-5111
Indiana Wiping Cloth
Mishawaka, IN 800-446-9645
Industries For The Blind
Milwaukee, WI 800-642-8778
Industries of the Blind
Greensboro, NC 336-274-1591
Insect-O-Cutor Inc
Stone Mountain, GA 800-966-8480
Interlab
The Woodlands, TX 888-876-2844
International Environmental Solutions
South Pasadena, FL 800-972-8348
Iron Out
Fort Wayne, IN 888-476-6688
ITW Dymon
Olathe, KS 800-443-9536
J C Whitlam Mfg Co
Wadsworth, OH 800-321-8358
J.I. Holcomb Manufacturing
Independence, OH 800-458-3222
J.V. Reed & Company
Louisville, KY 877-258-7333
Jacks Manufacturing Company
Mendota, MN 800-821-2089
James Austin Co
Mars, PA 724-625-1535
James Varley & Sons
Saint Louis, MO 800-325-8891
JAS Manufacturing Company
Carrollton, TX 972-380-1150
John L. Denning & Company
Wichita, KS 316-264-2357
Johnson International Materials
Brownsville, TX 956-541-6364
Justman Brush Co
Omaha, NE 800-800-6940
Kafko International LTD
Skokie, IL 800-528-0334
Kent Co
North Miami, FL 800-521-4886
Kiefer Brushes, Inc
Franklin, NJ 800-526-2905
KIK Custom Products
Salem, VA 540-389-5401
Kilgore Chemical Corporation
Layton, UT 801-546-9909
Kimberly-Clark Corporation
Irving, TX 972-281-1200
King of All Manufacturing
Clio, MI 810-564-0139
Kleen Products Inc
Oklahoma City, OK 800-392-1792
KMT Aqua-Dyne Inc
Baxter Springs, KS 800-826-9274
Knapp Manufacturing
Fresno, CA 559-251-8254
Knight Equipment International
Lake Forest, CA 800-854-3764
Kuehne Chemical
Kearny, NJ 973-589-0700
L&M Chemicals
Tampa, FL 800-362-3331
Labpride Chemicals
Bronx, NY 800-467-1255
Labtech Industries
Detroit, MI 800-525-8667
Lake Process Systems Inc
Lake Barrington, IL 800-331-9260
Lakeside Manufacturing Inc
Milwaukee, WI 888-558-8565

Lamco Chemical Co Inc
Chelsea, MA 617-884-8470
Larose & Fils Lte
Laval, QC 877-382-7001
Laundry Aids
Carlstadt, NJ 201-933-3500
Laundrylux
Inwood, NY. 800-645-2205
Lavo Company
Milwaukee, WI 414-353-2140
Layflat Products
Shreveport, LA 800-551-8515
Lechler Inc
St Charles, IL 800-777-2926
Lee Products Co
Minneapolis, MN 952-300-2908
Lee Soap Company
Commerce City, CO 800-888-1896
Leedal Inc
Northbrook, IL 847-498-0111
Leggett & Platt Storage
Vernon Hills, IL 847-816-6246
Letraw Manufacturing Company
Rockford, IL 815-987-9670
Lexidyne of Pennsylvania
Pittsburgh, PA 800-543-2233
Libman Co
Arcola, IL 877-818-3380
Lighthouse for the Blindin New Orleans
New Orleans, LA 504-899-4501
Lite-Weight Tool & Mfg Co
Sun Valley, CA 800-859-3529
Little Rock Broom Works
Little Rock, AR 501-562-0311
LMCO
Rosenberg, TX 281-342-8888
LPI Imports
Chicago, IL 877-389-6563
Lubar Chemical
Kansas City, MO 816-471-2560
Luco Mop Co
St Louis, MO 800-522-5826
Luseaux Labs Inc
Gardena, CA 800-266-1555
M D Stetson Co
Randolph, MA 800-255-8651
Machem Industries
Delta, BC. 604-526-5655
Magic American Corporation
Cleveland, OH 800-321-6330
Magnuson Products
Clifton, NJ 973-472-9292
Mahoney Environmental
Joliet, IL 800-892-9392
Mainline Industries Inc
Springfield, MA 800-527-7917
Majestic Industries Inc
Macomb, MI 586-786-9100
Manhattan Truck Lines
Paterson, NJ 800-370-7627
Mar-Len Supply Inc
Hayward, CA 510-782-3555
Marcal Paper Mills
Elmwood Park, NJ 800-631-8451
Marko Inc
Spartanburg, SC 866-466-2726
Martin Laboratories
Owensboro, KY 800-345-9352
Mastercraft Industries Inc
Newburgh, NY 800-835-7812
Maxi-Vac Inc.
Dundee, MI 855-629-4538
Mba Suppliers Inc.
Bellevue, NE. 800-467-1201
Mcbrady Engineering Co
Rockdale, IL 815-744-8900
Mednik Wiping Materials Co
St Louis, MO. 800-325-7193
Meguiar's Inc
Irvine, CA 949-752-8000
Mercury Floor Machines Inc
Englewood, NJ 888-568-4606
Meritech
Golden, CO 800-932-7707
Mertz L. Carlton Company
Bedford Park, IL 708-594-1050
Messina Brothers Manufacturing Company
Brooklyn, NY 800-924-6454
Metalloid Corp
Huntington, IN 800-686-3201
Metcraft
Grandview, MO. 800-444-9624

MGF.com
Atlanta, GA 770-444-9686
Mia Rose Products
Newport Beach, CA 800-615-2767
Michigan Brush Mfg Co
Detroit, MI 800-642-7874
Micro-Brush Pro Soap
Rockwall, TX 800-776-7627
Microbest Inc
Waterbury, CT 800-426-4246
Microtron Abrasives
Pineville, NC 800-476-7237
MIFAB Inc
Chicago, IL 800-465-2736
Mil-Du-Gas Company/Star Brite
Fort Lauderdale, FL 800-327-8583
Mill Wiping Rags Inc
Bronx, NY 718-994-7100
Milsek Furniture Polish Inc.
North Lima, OH 330-542-2700
Milwaukee Dustless Brush Co
Delavan, WI 323-724-7777
Minuteman Power Boss
Aberdeen, NC 800-323-9420
Mione Manufacturing Company
Mickleton, NJ 800-257-0497
Mission Laboratories
Los Angeles, CA. 888-201-8866
Moly-XL Company
Westville, NJ 856-848-2880
Momar
Atlanta, GA 800-556-3967
Motom Corporation
Bensenville, IL 630-787-1995
Moyer Diebel
Winston Salem, NC. 336-661-1992
Murk Brush Company
New Britain, CT 860-249-2550
Murnell Wax Company
Springfield, MA 781-395-1323
N & A Mfg
Mallard, IA 712-425-3512
Nation/Ruskin
Montgomeryville, PA 800-523-2489
National Conveyor Corp
Commerce, CA 323-725-0355
National Interchem Corporation
Blue Island, IL 800-638-6688
National Purity LLC
Brooklyn Center, MN 612-672-0022
National Scoop & Equipment Company
Spring House, PA 215-646-2040
National Towelette
Bensalem, PA 215-245-7300
Nationwide Wire & Brush Manufacturing
Lodi, CA 209-334-9660
Navy Brand
St Louis, MO. 800-325-3312
New Klix Corporation
South San Francisco, CA 800-522-5544
New Pig Corp
Tipton, PA 800-468-4647
Newell Brands
Atlanta, GA
Newton Broom Co
Newton, IL 618-783-4424
Newton OA & Son Co
Bridgeville, DE 800-726-5745
Nice-Pak Products Inc
Orangeburg, NY 800-444-6725
Northwind Inc
Alpena, AR 877-937-2585
Nosaj Disposables
Paterson, NJ 800-631-3809
Nova Hand Dryers
Herndon, VA 703-615-3636
Novus
St. Paul, MN 800-328-1117
Nu-Tex Styles, Inc.
Somerset, NJ. 732-485-5456
Nu-Towel Co
Kansas City, MO. 800-800-7247
Nuance Solutions Inc
Chicago, IL 800-621-8553
NuTone
Cincinnati, OH 888-336-3948
Nyco Products Co
Countryside, IL 800-752-4754
O'Dell Corp
Ware Shoals, SC 800-342-2843
O-Cedar
Aurora, IL 800-543-8105

Occidental Chemical Corporation
Houston, TX 713-215-7000
Oerlikon Balzers Coating USA
Elgin, IL 847-695-5200
Ohio Soap Products Company
Wickliffe, OH 440-585-1100
Omni Lift Inc
Salt Lake City, UT 801-486-3776
Opie Brush Company
Independence, MO 800-877-6743
Oreck Manufacturing Co
Cookeville, TN 800-989-3535
Ostrem Chemical Co. Ltd
Edmonton, AB 780-440-1911
Pacific Oasis Enterprise Inc
Santa Fe Springs, CA 800-424-1475
Packaging & Processing Equipment
Ayr, ON 519-622-6666
Packaging Distribution Svc
Des Moines, IA 515-243-3156
Pagoda Industries Inc
Reading, PA 610-678-8096
Paley-Lloyd-Donohue
Elizabeth, NJ 908-352-5835
Panasonic Commercial Food Service
Newark, NJ
Paper Pak Industries
La Verne, CA 909-392-1750
Parachem Corporation
Des Moines, IA 515-280-9445
Paragon Group USA
St Petersburg, FL 800-835-6962
Patterson Laboratories
Detroit, MI 313-843-4500
Paxton Products Inc
Blue Ash, OH 800-441-7475
PCI Inc
St Louis, MO. 800-752-7657
Pepper Mill
Mobile, AL 800-669-5175
Perfex Corporation
Poland, NY 800-848-8483
Pioneer Chemical Co
Gardena, CA 310-366-7393
Pioneer Manufacturing Co Inc
Cleveland, OH 800-877-1500
PM Chemical Company
San Diego, CA 619-296-0191
Portion-Pac Chemical Corp.
Chicago, IL 312-226-0400
Potlatch Corp
Spokane, WA. 509-835-1500
Pretty Products
Wauconda, IL 800-726-4849
Pro-Tex-All Co
Evansville, IN 800-755-5458
Productos Familia
Santurce, PR 787-268-5929
Proffitt Manufacturing Company
Dalton, GA 800-241-4682
ProRestore Products
Pittsburgh, PA 800-332-6037
ProTeam
Boise, ID 800-541-1456
Puritan/Churchill Chemical Company
Marietta, GA 800-275-8914
Purity Products
Plainview, NY 800-256-6102
Quaker Chemical Company
Columbia, SC 800-849-9520
Quality Mop & Brush Manufacturers
Needham, MA. 617-884-2999
Quickie Manufacturing Corp
Cinnaminson, NJ. 856-829-7900
R R Street & Co
Naperville, IL 630-416-4244
R&C Pro Brands
Wayne, NJ. 973-633-7374
Ready White
Holyoke, MA 413-534-4864
Rebel Green
Mequon, WI 262-240-9992
Reeno Detergent & Soap Company
Saint Louis, MO. 314-429-6078
Reit-Price ManufacturingCompany
Union City, IN. 800-521-5343
REM Ohio Inc
Cincinnati, OH 513-381-3700
Remco Products Corp
Zionsville, IN 800-585-8619
Rex Chemical Corporation
Miami, FL. 877-634-5539

RHG Products Company
Castle Rock, CO 800-553-8131
Rjs Carter Co Inc
New Brighton, MN 651-636-8818
Robby Vapor Systems
Sunrise, FL 800-888-8711
Rochester Midland Corp
Rochester, NY. 800-535-5053
Rochester Midland Corp
Rochester, NY. 800-836-1627
Rockford Chemical Co
Belvidere, IL 815-544-3476
Rockline Industries
Sheboygan, WI 800-558-7790
Ronell Industries
Roselle, NJ 908-245-5255
Rooto Corp
Howell, MI 517-546-8330
Roxide International
Larchmont, NY 800-431-5500
Royal Broom & Mop Factory Inc
New Orleans, LA 800-537-6925
Royal Chemical Co Inc
Albemarle, NC 800-650-6346
Royal Paper Products
Coatesville, PA 800-666-6655
Royal Welding & Fabricating
Fullerton, CA 714-680-6669
Royce Rolls Ringer Co
Grand Rapids, MI 800-253-9638
Rubbermaid Commercial Products
Cleveland, TN. 423-476-4544
S & S Soap Co
Bronx, NY. 718-585-2900
S&M Manufacturing Company
Cisco, TX 800-772-8532
San Aire Industries
Fort Worth, TX 800-757-1912
San Joaquin Pool Svc & Supply
Stockton, CA. 209-952-0680
Sangamon Mills
Cohoes, NY 518-237-5321
Sani-Matic
Madison, WI. 800-356-3300
Sanitech Inc
Lorton, VA 800-486-4321
Sanitek Products Inc
Los Angeles, CA. 818-242-1071
Sasib Beverage & Food North America
Plano, TX 800-558-3814
Saunders Manufacturing Co.
N Kansas City, MO 800-821-2792
Savogran Co
Norwood, MA. 800-225-9872
SCA Hygiene Paper
San Ramon, CA. 800-992-8675
SCA Tissue
Philadelphia, PA 866-722-8675
SCA Tissue North America
S Glens Falls, NY 518-743-0240
Schlueter Company
Janesville, WI 800-359-1700
Scot Young Research LTD
St Joseph, MO. 816-233-4898
Scott's Liquid Gold-Inc
Denver, CO 800-447-1919
Seatex Ltd
Rosenberg, TX 800-829-3020
Sedalia Janitorial & Paper Supplies
Sedalia, MO. 660-826-9899
Selig Chemical Industries
Atlanta, GA. 404-876-5511
Seneca Environmental Products
Tiffin, OH 419-447-1282
Shen Manufacturing Co Inc
Conshohocken, PA 610-825-2790
Shepard Brothers Co
La Habra, CA 800-645-3594
Sierra Dawn Products
Santa Rosa, CA. 707-535-0172
Sioux Corp
Beresford, SD 888-763-8833
Snee Chemical Co
New Orleans, LA 800-489-7633
Solvit
Monona, WI 888-314-1072
Solvox Manufacturing Company
Milwaukee, WI. 414-774-5664
Sonicor
West Babylon, NY 800-864-5022
Southend Janitorial Supply
Los Angeles, CA. 323-754-2842

Spartan Tool LLC
Mendota, IL 800-435-3866
Specialty Equipment Company
Mendota Heights, MN 651-452-7909
Spencer Turbine Co
Windsor, CT 800-232-4321
Spontex
Columbia, TN 800-251-4222
Sprayway Inc
Addison, IL 800-332-9000
Spurrier Chemical Companies
Atlanta, GA. 800-795-9222
SQP
Schenectady, NY. 800-724-1129
Squar-Buff
Oakland, CA. 800-525-6955
ST Restaurant Supplies
Delta, BC. 888-448-4244
Stampendous
Anaheim, CA 800-869-0474
Stanford Chemicals
Dallas, TX. 972-682-5600
Star Pacific Inc
Union City, CA 800-227-0760
Starkey Chemical Process Company
La Grange, IL 800-323-3040
State Industrial Products Corp
Mayfield Heights, OH 877-747-6986
Stearns Packaging Corp
Madison, WI 608-246-5150
Stearns Technical Textiles Company
Cincinnati, OH 800-543-7173
Steiner Company
Holland, IL 800-222-4638
Steiner Industries Inc
Chicago, IL 800-621-4515
Sterling Novelty Products
Northbrook, IL 847-291-0070
Stero Co
Petaluma, CA 800-762-7600
Stewart Laboratories
Strattanville, PA 800-640-7869
Stone Soap Co Inc
Sylvan Lake, MI 800-952-7627
Stoner
Quarryville, PA 800-227-5538
Strahman Valves Inc
Bethlehem, PA 877-787-2462
Sun Paints & Coatings
Tampa, FL. 800-247-9691
Sunbeam Products Co LLC
Toledo, OH 419-691-1551
Sunpoint Products
Lawrence, MA 978-794-3100
Superior Brush Company
Cleveland, OH 216-941-6987
Superior Distributing Co
Louisville, KY 800-365-6661
Superior Linen & Work Wear
Kansas City, MO. 800-798-7987
Surco Products
Pittsburgh, PA 800-556-0111
Sure Clean Corporation
Two Rivers, WI 920-793-3838
Surtec Inc
Tracy, CA 800-877-6330
Swisher Hygiene
Charlotte, NC 800-444-4138
Swissh Commercial Equipment
Montreal, QC 888-794-7749
Synthron Inc.
Morganton, NC 828-437-8611
T & S Brass & Bronze Work
Travelers Rest, SC 800-476-4103
Tate Western
Goleta, CA 800-903-0200
Techni-Chem
Boise, ID 800-635-8930
Telechem Corp
Atlanta, GA. 800-637-0495
Tennant Co.
Minneapolis, MN 800-553-8033
Texas Refinery Corp
Fort Worth, TX 817-332-1161
Textile Buff & Wheel
Charlestown, MA 617-241-8100
Textile Products Company
Anaheim, CA 714-761-0401
Thamesville Metal Products Ltd
Thamesville, ON 519-692-3963
The Procter & Gamble Company
Cincinnati, OH 800-692-0132

Theochem Laboratories Inc
Tampa, FL..............................800-237-2591
Therma Kleen
Plainfield, IL.........................800-999-3120
Thermaco Inc
Asheboro, NC......................800-633-4204
Time Products
Atlanta, GA..........................800-241-6681
Tolco Corp
Toledo, OH..........................800-537-4786
Trap-Zap Environmental
Wyckoff, NJ.........................800-282-8727
TRC
Middlefield, OH....................440-834-0078
TRITEN Corporation
Houston, TX.........................832-214-5000
Tropical Soap Company
Carrollton, TX.......................800-527-2368
Tucel Industries, Inc.
Forestdale, VT......................800-558-8235
Tuchenhagen
Columbia, MD......................410-910-6000
Turtle Wax
Westmont, IL........................905-470-6665
Tuway American Group
Rockford, OH........................800-537-3750
Twi Laq
Bronx, NY............................800-950-7627
U B KLEM Furniture Co Inc
St Anthony, IN......................800-264-1995
Ulmer Pharmacal
Park Rapids, MN...................800-848-5637
United Floor Machine Co
Chicago, IL...........................800-288-0848
United Textile Distribution
Garner, NC...........................800-262-7624
Universal Stainless
Aurora, CO...........................800-223-8332
Universal Stainless & Alloy
Titusville, PA........................800-295-1909
Upright
St Louis, MO........................800-248-7007
Urnex Brands Inc
Elmsford, NY........................800-222-2826
US Chemical
Watertown, WI......................800-558-9566
US Industrial Lubricants
Cincinnati, OH......................800-562-5454
Valspar Paint
Cleveland, OH.......................877-825-7727
Vector Technologies
Milwaukee, WI......................800-832-4010
Venturetech Corporation
Knoxville, TN........................800-826-4095
Verax Chemical Co
Snohomish, WA.....................800-637-7771
Vulcan Materials Co
Vestavia, AL.........................205-298-3000
W.M. Barr & Co Inc.
Memphis, TN.........................901-775-0100
Waco Broom & Mop Factory
Waco, TX.............................800-548-7716
Wal-Vac
Wyoming, MI........................616-241-6717
Warren E. Conley Corporation
Carmel, IN...........................800-367-7875
Warsaw Chemical Co Inc
Warsaw, IN...........................800-548-3396
Waste Minimization/Containment
Cleveland, OH.......................216-696-8797
Wave Chemical Company
New York, NY........................973-243-5852
Waxine
Bow, NH..............................603-228-8241
WCS Corp
Hayward, CA.........................510-782-8727
West Agro
Kansas City, MO....................816-891-7700
Whisk Products Inc
Wentzville, MO......................800-204-7627
White Mop Wringer Company
Tampa, FL.............................800-237-7582
Whitley Manufacturing Company
Midland, NC..........................704-888-2625
Wilen Professional Cleaning Products
Atlanta, GA...........................800-241-7371
Wilson AL Chemical Co
Kearny, NJ............................800-526-1188
Windsor Industries Inc
Englewood, CO......................800-444-7654
Windsor Wax Co Inc
Charlestown, RI.....................800-243-8929

Winn-Sol Products
Oshkosh, WI..........................920-231-2031
Wipe-Tex International Corp
Bronx, NY............................800-643-9607
Wipeco Inc
Hillside, IL............................708-544-7247
World Dryer Corp
Berkeley, IL...........................800-323-0701
Y-Pers Inc
Philadelphia, PA.....................800-421-0242
Young & Swartz Inc
Buffalo, NY...........................800-466-7682
Zealco Industries
Calvert City, KY.....................800-759-5531
Zephyr Manufacturing Co
Sedalia, MO..........................660-827-0352
Zipskin
Dexter, MI............................734-426-5559

Cloths

Chamois

Acme Sponge & Chamois Co Inc
Tarpon Springs, FL..................727-937-3222
Blue Feather Products Inc
Ashland, OR..........................800-472-2487
Clayton L. Hagy & Son
Philadelphia, PA.....................215-844-6470

Dish

Arden Companies
Southfield, MI........................248-415-8500
Bro-Tex Inc
St Paul, MN...........................800-328-2282
Charles Craft Inc
Laurinburg, NC......................910-844-3521
Letraw Manufacturing Company
Rockford, IL..........................815-987-9670
Mednik Wiping Materials Co
St Louis, MO.........................800-325-7193
Nu-Tex Styles, Inc.
Somerset, NJ.........................732-485-5456
Sangamon Mills
Cohoes, NY...........................518-237-5321
Shen Manufacturing Co Inc
Conshohocken, PA..................610-825-2790
Standard Terry Mills
Souderton, PA........................215-723-8121
Wipe-Tex International Corp
Bronx, NY............................800-643-9607

Dusting

Cadie Products Corp
Paterson, NJ..........................973-278-8300
CCP Industries, Inc.
Cleveland, OH.......................800-321-2840
Champion America Inc
Branford, CT.........................800-521-7000
Clayton L. Hagy & Son
Philadelphia, PA.....................215-844-6470
Lexidyne of Pennsylvania
Pittsburgh, PA.......................800-543-2233
Majestic Industries Inc
Macomb, MI..........................586-786-9100
Mednik Wiping Materials Co
St Louis, MO.........................800-325-7193
Mill Wiping Rags Inc
Bronx, NY............................718-994-7100
Nu-Tex Styles, Inc.
Somerset, NJ.........................732-485-5456
Ready White
Holyoke, MA.........................413-534-4864
Shen Manufacturing Co Inc
Conshohocken, PA..................610-825-2790
Superior Distributing Co
Louisville, KY........................800-365-6661
Tuway American Group
Rockford, OH........................800-537-3750
Wipe-Tex International Corp
Bronx, NY............................800-643-9607

Wire

Champion America Inc
Branford, CT.........................800-521-7000
Cleveland Wire Cloth & Mfg Co
Cleveland, OH.......................800-321-3234
F.P. Smith Wire Cloth Company
Northlake, IL.........................800-323-6842

Newark Wire Cloth Co
Clifton, NJ............................800-221-0392

Compounds

Dishwashing

American Municipal Chemical
Milwaukee, WI......................800-598-3106
Cal Ben Soap Co
Oakland, CA..........................800-340-7091
Clarkson Supply
Williamsport, PA....................800-326-9457
D W Davies & Co
Racine, WI............................800-888-6133
Emulso
Tonawanda, NY.....................716-854-2889
Essential Industries Inc
Merton, WI...........................800-551-9679
Falls Chemical Products
Oconto Falls, WI....................920-846-3561
Fishers Investment
Cincinnati, OH......................800-833-5916
J.I. Holcomb Manufacturing
Independence, OH..................800-458-3222
Labpride Chemicals
Bronx, NY............................800-467-1255
Magnuson Products
Clifton, NJ............................973-472-9292
Rochester Midland Corp
Rochester, NY.......................800-535-5053
Simoniz USA Inc
Bolton, CT............................800-227-5536
Swisher Hygiene
Charlotte, NC........................800-444-4138
Texas Refinery Corp
Fort Worth, TX......................817-332-1161

Sweeping

American Municipal Chemical
Milwaukee, WI......................800-598-3106
APR Associates Inc
Memphis, TN.........................800-238-5150
Floor Master Inc
Chattanooga, TN....................423-867-4525
Gamecock Chemical Co Inc
Sumter, SC............................803-773-7391
Grayling Industries
Alpharetta, GA......................800-635-1551
Mission Laboratories
Los Angeles, CA....................888-201-8866
Waxine
Bow, NH..............................603-228-8241
Windsor Wax Co Inc
Charlestown, RI.....................800-243-8929

Washing

American Municipal Chemical
Milwaukee, WI......................800-598-3106
C&H Chemical
St Paul, MN...........................651-227-4343
Candy & Company/Peck's Products Company
Chicago, IL...........................800-837-9189
Elgene
Hamden, CT..........................800-922-4623
Essential Industries Inc
Merton, WI...........................800-551-9679
Fishers Investment
Cincinnati, OH......................800-833-5916
Garman Co Inc
Valley Park, MO.....................800-466-5150
Hibrett Puratex
Pennsauken, NJ......................800-260-5124
Hill Manufacturing Co Inc
Atlanta, GA...........................404-522-8364
Hohn Manufacturing Company
Fenton, MO...........................800-878-1440
Hy-Ko Enviro-MaintenanceProducts
Salt Lake City, UT..................801-973-6099
J.I. Holcomb Manufacturing
Independence, OH..................800-458-3222
KIK Custom Products
Salem, VA............................540-389-5401
Labpride Chemicals
Bronx, NY............................800-467-1255
Magnuson Products
Clifton, NJ............................973-472-9292
Manhattan Truck Lines
Paterson, NJ..........................800-370-7627
Ostrem Chemical Co. Ltd
Edmonton, AB.......................780-440-1911

R&C Pro Brands
Wayne, NJ.....................973-633-7374
Solvit
Monona, WI....................888-314-1072
Stanford Chemicals
Dallas, TX.....................972-682-5600
Swisher Hygiene
Charlotte, NC..................800-444-4138
Techni-Chem
Boise, ID......................800-635-8930
Windsor Wax Co Inc
Charlestown, RI................800-243-8929

Detergents

Household, Consumer

9-12 Corporation
Caguas, PR.....................787-747-0405
A&L Laboratories
Minneapolis, MN................800-225-3832
Abicor Binzel
Frederick, MD..................800-542-4867
American Wax Co Inc
Long Island City, NY...........718-361-4820
APR Associates Inc
Memphis, TN....................800-238-5150
Auto Chlor Systems
Memphis, TN....................800-477-3693
Bar Maid Corp
Pompano Beach, FL..............954-960-1468
Bio Industries
Luxemburg, WI..................920-845-2355
C P Industries
Salt Lake City, UT.............800-453-4931
Cal Ben Soap Co
Oakland, CA....................800-340-7091
Cantol
Markham, ON....................800-387-9773
Chef Revival
North Charleston, SC...........800-248-9826
Chemifax
Santa Fe Springs, CA...........800-527-5722
Clarkson Supply
Williamsport, PA...............800-326-9457
Clorox Company
Oakland, CA....................510-271-7000
Cobitco Inc
Denver, CO.....................303-296-8575
Concord Chemical Co Inc
Camden, NJ.....................800-282-2436
Country Save Products Corp
Arlington, WA..................360-435-9868
DCL Solutions LLC
Philadelphia, PA...............800-426-1127
De Vere Co Inc
Janesville, WI.................800-833-8373
Diablo Chemical
Kingston, PA...................800-548-1384
Diamond Chemical Co Inc
East Rutherford, NJ............800-654-7627
Downeast Chemical
Westbrook, ME..................800-287-2225
Du-Good Chemical Laboratory & Manufacturing
Company
Saint Louis, MO................314-773-5007
Essential Industries Inc
Merton, WI.....................800-551-9679
Falls Chemical Products
Oconto Falls, WI...............920-846-3561
Fitzpatrick Brothers
Pleasant Prairie, WI...........800-233-8064
Fuller Industries LLC
Great Bend, KS.................800-522-0499
Goodwin Co
Garden Grove, CA...............714-894-0531
Grace-Lee Products
Minneapolis, MN................612-379-2711
Griffin Bros Inc
Salem, OR......................800-456-4743
Hamilton Soap & Oil Products
Paterson, NJ...................973-225-1031
Hanco Manufacturing Company
Memphis, TN....................800-530-7364
Hohn Manufacturing Company
Fenton, MO.....................800-878-1440
Holland Chemicals Company
Windsor, ON....................519-948-4373
James Austin Co
Mars, PA.......................724-625-1535
Knapp Manufacturing
Fresno, CA.....................559-251-8254

L&M Chemicals
Tampa, FL......................800-362-3331
Labpride Chemicals
Bronx, NY......................800-467-1255
Laundry Aids
Carlstadt, NJ..................201-933-3500
Lee Soap Company
Commerce City, CO..............800-888-1896
Lubar Chemical
Kansas City, MO................816-471-2560
MGF.com
Atlanta, GA....................770-444-9686
Mione Manufacturing Company
Mickleton, NJ..................800-257-0497
National Purity LLC
Brooklyn Center, MN............612-672-0022
New Klix Corporation
South San Francisco, CA........800-522-5544
Nyco Products Co
Countryside, IL................800-752-4754
Ostrem Chemical Co. Ltd
Edmonton, AB...................780-440-1911
Portion-Pac Chemical Corp.
Chicago, IL....................312-226-0400
Reeno Detergent & Soap Company
Saint Louis, MO................314-429-6078
REM Ohio Inc
Cincinnati, OH.................513-381-3700
Rochester Midland Corp
Rochester, NY..................800-535-5053
S & S Soap Co
Bronx, NY......................718-585-2900
Snee Chemical Co
New Orleans, LA................800-489-7633
Star Pacific Inc
Union City, CA.................800-227-0760
Stearns Packaging Corp
Madison, WI....................608-246-5150
Stone Soap Co Inc
Sylvan Lake, MI................800-952-7627
Sunbeam Products Co LLC
Toledo, OH.....................419-691-1551
Sure Clean Corporation
Two Rivers, WI.................920-793-3838
Swisher Hygiene
Charlotte, NC..................800-444-4138
Synthron Inc.
Morganton, NC..................828-437-8611
Telechem Corp
Atlanta, GA....................800-637-0495
Texas Refinery Corp
Fort Worth, TX.................817-332-1161
The Procter & Gamble Company
Cincinnati, OH.................800-692-0132
Theochem Laboratories Inc
Tampa, FL......................800-237-2591
Twi Laq
Bronx, NY......................800-950-7627
Ulmer Pharmacal
Park Rapids, MN................800-848-5637
US Industrial Lubricants
Cincinnati, OH.................800-562-5454
Venturetech Corporation
Knoxville, TN..................800-826-4095
Wave Chemical Company
New York, NY...................973-243-5852
West Chemical Products
Princeton, NJ..................609-921-0501
Wilson AL Chemical Co
Kearny, NJ.....................800-526-1188

Industrial

9-12 Corporation
Caguas, PR.....................787-747-0405
A&L Laboratories
Minneapolis, MN................800-225-3832
Abicor Binzel
Frederick, MD..................800-542-4867
Alconox Inc
White Plains, NY...............914-437-7585
American Wax Co Inc
Long Island City, NY...........718-361-4820
Auto Chlor Systems
Memphis, TN....................800-477-3693
Bio Industries
Luxemburg, WI..................920-845-2355
Bradford Soap Works Inc
West Warwick, RI...............401-821-2141
Church & Dwight Co., Inc.
Ewing, NJ......................800-833-9532

Clarkson Supply
Williamsport, PA...............800-326-9457
Colgate-Palmolive Professional Products Group
North York, ON.................800-468-6502
Country Save Products Corp
Arlington, WA..................360-435-9868
Diablo Chemical
Kingston, PA...................800-548-1384
Dial Corporation
Scottsdale, AZ.................480-754-3425
Falls Chemical Products
Oconto Falls, WI...............920-846-3561
Fitzpatrick Brothers
Pleasant Prairie, WI...........800-233-8064
Hope Chemical Corporation
Pawtucket, RI..................401-724-8000
Hydrite Chemical Co
Brookfield, WI.................262-792-1450
King of All Manufacturing
Clio, MI.......................810-564-0139
Knapp Manufacturing
Fresno, CA.....................559-251-8254
Labpride Chemicals
Bronx, NY......................800-467-1255
Lubar Chemical
Kansas City, MO................816-471-2560
Luseaux Labs Inc
Gardena, CA....................800-266-1555
Manhattan Truck Lines
Paterson, NJ...................800-370-7627
Mione Manufacturing Company
Mickleton, NJ..................800-257-0497
Pagoda Industries Inc
Reading, PA....................610-678-8096
Patterson Laboratories
Detroit, MI....................313-843-4500
PM Chemical Company
San Diego, CA..................619-296-0191
Reeno Detergent & Soap Company
Saint Louis, MO................314-429-6078
Seatex Ltd
Rosenberg, TX..................800-829-3020
Snee Chemical Co
New Orleans, LA................800-489-7633
Spurrier Chemical Companies
Atlanta, GA....................800-795-9222
Stewart Laboratories
Strattanville, PA..............800-640-7869
Swisher Hygiene
Charlotte, NC..................800-444-4138
US Industrial Lubricants
Cincinnati, OH.................800-562-5454
Whisk Products Inc
Wentzville, MO.................800-204-7627

Dish Washing Machinery

Acro Dishwashing Svc Co
Kansas City, KS................913-342-4282
Adamation
Commerce, CA...................800-383-8800
Ali Group
Winston Salem, NC..............800-532-8591
American Dish Service
Edwardsville, KS...............800-922-2178
Attias Oven Corp
Brooklyn, NY...................800-928-8427
Blakeslee, Inc.
Addison, IL....................630-532-5021
Burns Chemical Systems
Cleveland, OH..................724-327-7600
Champion Industries Inc
Winston Salem, NC..............800-532-8591
Cma Dishmachines
Garden Grove, CA...............800-854-6417
Colonial Paper Company
Silver Springs, FL.............352-622-4171
Convay Systems
Minnetonka, MN.................800-334-1099
Custom Diamond International
Laval, QC......................800-363-5926
Douglas Machines Corp.
Clearwater, FL.................800-331-6870
Hartstone Pottery Inc
Zanesville, OH.................740-452-9999
Insinger Co
Philadelphia, PA...............800-344-4802
Jackson Msc LLC
Gray, KY.......................888-800-5672
Knight Equipment Canada
Mississauga, ON................800-854-3764
Knight Equipment International
Lake Forest, CA................800-854-3764

Moyer Diebel
Winston Salem, NC 336-661-1992
National Hotpack
Stone Ridge, NY 800-431-8232
Stero Co
Petaluma, CA 800-762-7600
Swissh Commercial Equipment
Montreal, QC 888-794-7749
The Procter & Gamble Company
Cincinnati, OH 800-692-0132
TNN-Jeros, Inc.
Byron, IL 815-978-2210
Vanguard Technology Inc
Eugene, OR 800-624-4809

Dishwasher

Racks

Amco Metals Indl
City Of Industry, CA 626-855-2550
Blakeslee, Inc.
Addison, IL 630-532-5021
Carlisle Food Svc Products Inc
Oklahoma City, OK 800-654-8210
Duke Manufacturing Co
St Louis, MO 800-735-3853
Marlin Steel Wire Products
Baltimore, MD 877-762-7546
Metro Corporation
Wilkes Barre, PA 800-992-1776
Micro Wire Products Inc
Brockton, MA 508-584-0200
Straits Steel & Wire Co
Ludington, MI 231-843-3416
Superior Products Company
Saint Paul, MN 800-328-9800
Traex
Dane, WI 800-356-8006

Disinfectants & Germicides

Accommodation Mollen
Philadelphia, PA 800-872-6268
ADCO
Albany, GA 800-821-7556
Afassco
Minden, NV 775-783-3555
American Wax Co Inc
Long Island City, NY 718-361-4820
Bio Cide Intl Inc
Norman, OK 800-323-1398
Burnishine Products
Gurnee, IL 800-818-8275
Candy & Company/Peck's Products Company
Chicago, IL 800-837-9189
Carroll Co
Garland, TX 800-527-5722
Central Solutions Inc
Kansas City, KS 800-255-0262
Chemifax
Santa Fe Springs, CA 800-527-5722
Church & Dwight Co., Inc.
Ewing, NJ 800-833-9532
Claire Manufacturing Company
Addison, IL 800-252-4731
Cobitco Inc
Denver, CO 303-296-8575
Colgate-Palmolive Professional Products Group
North York, ON 800-468-6502
Concord Chemical Co Inc
Camden, NJ 800-282-2436
Crown Chemical Products
Mississauga, ON 905-564-0904
Damon Industries
Alliance, OH 800-362-9850
DCL Solutions LLC
Philadelphia, PA 800-426-1127
De Vere Co Inc
Janesville, WI 800-833-8373
Diamond Chemical Co Inc
East Rutherford, NJ 800-654-7627
Emulso
Tonawanda, NY 716-854-2889
GERM-O-RAY
Stone Mountain, GA 800-966-8480
Griffin Bros Inc
Salem, OR 800-456-4743
Hanco Manufacturing Company
Memphis, TN 800-530-7364
Hilex Company
Eagan, MN 651-454-1160

Hill Manufacturing Co Inc
Atlanta, GA 404-522-8364
Hy-Ko Enviro-MaintenanceProducts
Salt Lake City, UT 801-973-6099
Hydrite Chemical Co
Brookfield, WI 262-792-1450
Insect-O-Cutor Inc
Stone Mountain, GA 800-966-8480
ITW Dymon
Olathe, KS 800-443-9536
J.I. Holcomb Manufacturing
Independence, OH 800-458-3222
James Austin Co
Mars, PA 724-625-1535
Knapp Manufacturing
Fresno, CA 559-251-8254
L&M Chemicals
Tampa, FL 800-362-3331
Labpride Chemicals
Bronx, NY 800-467-1255
Larose & Fils Lte
Laval, QC 877-382-7001
Lubar Chemical
Kansas City, MO 816-471-2560
Marko Inc
Spartanburg, SC 866-466-2726
MGF.com
Atlanta, GA 770-444-9686
Mission Laboratories
Los Angeles, CA 888-201-8866
Nuance Solutions Inc
Chicago, IL 800-621-8553
Paley-Lloyd-Donohue
Elizabeth, NJ 908-352-5835
Pioneer Chemical Co
Gardena, CA 310-366-7393
ProRestore Products
Pittsburgh, PA 800-332-6037
Puritan/Churchill Chemical Company
Marietta, GA 800-275-8914
R&C Pro Brands
Wayne, NJ 973-633-7374
Rochester Midland Corp
Rochester, NY 800-535-5053
Rochester Midland Corp
Rochester, NY 800-836-1627
San Joaquin Pool Svc & Supply
Stockton, CA 209-952-0680
Sanco Products Co Inc
Greenville, OH 937-548-2225
Seatex Ltd
Rosenberg, TX 800-829-3020
Selig Chemical Industries
Atlanta, GA 404-876-5511
Simoniz USA Inc
Bolton, CT 800-227-5536
State Industrial Products Corp
Mayfield Heights, OH 877-747-6986
Sunpoint Products
Lawrence, MA 978-794-3100
Swisher Hygiene
Charlotte, NC 800-444-4138
The Procter & Gamble Company
Cincinnati, OH 800-692-0132
Ulmer Pharmacal
Park Rapids, MN 800-848-5637
Verax Chemical Co
Snohomish, WA 800-637-7771
Vulcan Materials Co
Vestavia, AL 205-298-3000
West Chemical Products
Princeton, NJ 609-921-0501
Whisk Products Inc
Wentzville, MO 800-204-7627

Dispensers

Cleaning Compound

Auto Chlor Systems
Memphis, TN 800-477-3693
Carbon Clean Industries Inc
Kingston, PA 570-288-1155
Crc Industries Inc
Warminster, PA 800-556-5074
Eurodispenser
Decatur, IL 217-864-4061
GOJO Industries Inc
Akron, OH 800-321-9647
Graco Inc
Minneapolis, MN 877-844-7226

Hygiene-Technik
Beamsville, ON 905-563-4987
Knight Equipment Canada
Mississauga, ON 800-854-3764
Knight Equipment International
Lake Forest, CA 800-854-3764
Labpride Chemicals
Bronx, NY 800-467-1255
Steiner Industries Inc
Chicago, IL 800-621-4515
Tate Western
Goleta, CA 800-903-0200

Soap

Best Sanitizers Inc
Penn Valley, CA 888-225-3267
Deb Canada
Waterford, ON 888-332-7627
Dema Engineering Co
St Louis, MO 800-325-3362
Dreumex USA
York, PA 800-233-9382
Eurodispenser
Decatur, IL 217-864-4061
GOJO Industries Inc
Akron, OH 800-321-9647
Hygiene-Technik
Beamsville, ON 905-563-4987
Micro-Brush Pro Soap
Rockwall, TX 800-776-7627
Milburn Company
Detroit, MI 313-259-3410
Parachem Corporation
Des Moines, IA 515-280-9445
Steiner Company
Holland, IL 800-222-4638
Steiner Industries Inc
Chicago, IL 800-621-4515
Superior Products Company
Saint Paul, MN 800-328-9800
Tate Western
Goleta, CA 800-903-0200
Tolco Corp
Toledo, OH 800-537-4786
Whisk Products Inc
Wentzville, MO 800-204-7627
World Dryer Corp
Berkeley, IL 800-323-0701

Dryer Systems

A & B Process Systems Corp
Stratford, WI 888-258-2789
A&J Mixing International
Oakville, ON 800-668-3470
Amerivap Systems Inc
Dawsonville, GA 800-763-7687
Ametek Technical & Industrial Products
Kent, OH 215-256-6601
Applied Chemical Technology
Florence, AL 800-228-3217
Bepex International LLC
Minneapolis, MN 800-607-2470
BFM Equipment Sales
Fall River, WI 920-484-3341
Brothers Metal Products
Santa Ana, CA 714-972-3008
Buffalo Technologies Corporation
Buffalo, NY 800-332-2419
Carman Industries Inc
Jeffersonville, IN 800-456-7560
Casso-Solar Corporation
Nanuet, NY 800-988-4455
Chief Industries
Kearney, NE 800-359-8833
Convay Systems
Minnetonka, MN 800-334-1099
Crown Iron Works Company
Roseville, MN 888-703-7500
Damas Corporation
Trenton, NJ 609-695-9121
Davenport Machine
Rock Island, IL 309-786-1500
Davron Technologies Inc
Chattanooga, TN 423-870-1888
Dito Dean Food Prep
Charlotte, NC 866-449-4200
Evaporator Dryer Technologies
Hammond, WI. 715-796-2313
Fitzpatrick Co
Elmhurst, IL 630-592-4425

Flodin
Moses Lake, WA....................509-766-2996
Fluid Energy Processing & Eqpt
Hatfield, PA.......................215-368-2510
Gardner Denver Inc.
Milwaukee, WI
Gaston County Dyeing Mach Co
Mt Holly, NC......................704-822-5000
Glatt Air Techniques Inc
Ramsey, NJ........................201-825-8700
Grain Machinery Mfg Corp
Miami, FL.........................305-620-2525
Hankison International
Canonsburg, PA....................724-746-1100
Hoyt Corporation
Westport, MA......................508-636-8811
Insinger Co
Philadelphia, PA..................800-344-4802
International Reserve Equipment Corporation
Clarendon Hills, IL...............708-531-0680
Kinergy Corp
Louisville, KY....................502-366-5685
Laundrylux
Inwood, NY........................800-645-2205
LIST
Acton, MA.........................978-635-9521
Littleford Day
Florence, KY......................800-365-8555
Louisville Dryer Company
Louisville, KY....................800-735-3613
M-E-C Co
Neodesha, KS......................620-325-2673
Midbrook Inc
Jackson, MI.......................800-966-9274
National Drying Machry Co Inc
Philadelphia, PA..................215-464-6070
National Hotpack
Stone Ridge, NY...................800-431-8232
NECO/Nebraska Engineering
Omaha, NE.........................800-367-6208
Nemeth Engineering Assoc
Crestwood, KY.....................502-241-1502
Niro
Hudson, WI........................715-386-9371
Paget Equipment Co
Marshfield, WI....................715-384-3158
Patterson Industries
Scarborough, ON...................800-336-1110
Patterson-Kelley   Hars Company
East Stroudsburg, PA..............570-421-7500
Paul O. Abbe
Bensenville, IL...................630-350-2200
Paxton Products Inc
Blue Ash, OH......................800-441-7475
Procedyne Corp
New Brunswick, NJ.................732-249-8347
Professional Engineering Assoc
Louisville, KY....................502-429-0432
Radio Frequency Co Inc
Millis, MA........................508-376-9555
San Aire Industries
Fort Worth, TX....................800-757-1912
Shanzer Grain Dryer
Sioux Falls, SD...................800-843-9887
Spencer Turbine Co
Windsor, CT.......................800-232-4321
Spray Drying
Sykesville, MD....................410-549-8090
Steri Technologies Inc
Bohemia, NY.......................800-253-7140
Tuthill Vacuum & Blower Systems
Springfield, MO...................800-825-6937
United Mc Gill Corp
Groveport, OH.....................614-829-1200
Vector Corp
Marion, IA........................319-377-8263
Vortron Smokehouse/Ovens
Iron Ridge, WI....................800-874-1949
Wittemann Company
Palm Coast, FL....................386-445-4200
World Dryer Corp
Berkeley, IL......................800-323-0701
Zeeco Inc
Broken Arrow, OK..................918-258-8551

Dust Collectors

Chicago Conveyor Corporation
Addison, IL.......................630-543-6300
Paget Equipment Co
Marshfield, WI....................715-384-3158
Spencer Turbine Co
Windsor, CT.......................800-232-4321

Temp Air Inc
Burnsville, MN....................800-836-7432

Dust Pans

Carlisle Food Svc Products Inc
Oklahoma City, OK.................800-654-8210
Ex-Cell KAISER LLC
Franklin Park, IL.................847-451-0451
J.V. Reed & Company
Louisville, KY....................877-258-7333
Superior Products Company
Saint Paul, MN....................800-328-9800

Floor Cleaning Machinery

Polishing, Refinishing, Sanding & Scrubbing

Clarke American Sanders
Minneapolis, MN...................800-253-0367
Cleanfreak
Appleton, WI......................888-722-5508
Dynamic Coatings Inc
Fresno, CA........................559-225-4605
Larose & Fils Lte
Laval, QC.........................877-382-7001
Mercury Floor Machines Inc
Englewood, NJ.....................888-568-4606
Microtron Abrasives
Pineville, NC.....................800-476-7237
Squar-Buff
Oakland, CA.......................800-525-6955
Surtec Inc
Tracy, CA.........................800-877-6330
United Floor Machine Co
Chicago, IL.......................800-288-0848
Windsor Industries Inc
Englewood, CO.....................800-444-7654

Garbage Bags

All American Poly
Piscataway, NJ....................800-526-3551
Arbee Transparent Inc
Elk Grove Vlg, IL.................800-642-2247
Brown Paper Goods Co
Waukegan, IL......................847-688-1450
Carlisle Plastics
Minneapolis, MN...................952-884-1309
COVERIS
Tomah, WI.........................608-372-2153
Custom Poly Packaging
Fort Wayne, IN....................800-548-6603
Dashco
Gloucester, ON....................613-834-6825
Development Workshop Inc
Idaho Falls, ID...................800-657-5597
East Coast Group New York
Springfield Gardens, NY...........718-527-8464
GP Plastics Corporation
Medley, FL........................305-888-3555
Himolene
Carrollton, TX....................800-777-4411
J A Heilferty & Co
Teaneck, NJ.......................201-836-5060
KM International Corp
Kenton, TN........................731-749-8700
Lakeside Manufacturing Inc
Milwaukee, WI.....................888-558-8565
Luetzow Industries
South Milwaukee, WI...............800-558-6055
Marshall Plastic Film Inc
Martin, MI........................269-672-5511
Nosaj Disposables
Paterson, NJ......................800-631-3809
NOVOLEX
Glendale, AZ......................800-243-0306
Package Containers Inc
Canby, OR.........................800-266-5806
Pactiv LLC
Lake Forest, IL...................800-476-4300
Pan Pacific Plastics Inc
Hayward, CA.......................888-475-6888
Paradise Plastics
Brooklyn, NY......................718-788-3733
S&O Corporation
Gallaway, TN......................800-624-7858
Schroeder Machine
San Marcos, CA....................760-591-9733
Servin Company
New Baltimore, MI.................800-824-0962

Star Poly Bag Inc
Brooklyn, NY......................718-384-7034
Tree Saver
Englewood, CO.....................800-676-7741
Valley Packaging Supply Co
Green Bay, WI.....................920-336-9012
Wisconsin Converting Inc
Green Bay, WI.....................800-544-1935

Garbage Compactors

Chicago Trashpacker Corporation
Marengo, IL.......................800-635-5745
Compactors Inc
Hilton Head Isle, SC..............800-423-4003
Consolidated Baling Machine Company
Jacksonville, FL..................800-231-9286
Dempster Systems
Toccoa, GA........................706-886-2327
Enterprise Company
Santa Ana, CA.....................714-835-0541
Galbreath LLC
Winamac, IN.......................574-946-6631
Incinerator International Inc
Houston, TX.......................713-227-1466
Logemann Brothers Co
Milwaukee, WI.....................414-445-3005
Marathon Equipment Co
Vernon, AL........................800-269-7237
Maren Engineering Corp
South Holland, IL.................800-875-1038
Multi-Pak
Hackensack, NJ....................201-342-7474
Orwak
Minneapolis, MN...................800-747-0449
PAC Equipment Company
Garfield, NJ......................973-478-1008
PTR Baler & Compactor Co
Philadelphia, PA..................800-523-3654
Robar International Inc
Milwaukee, WI.....................800-279-7750
Schleicher & Company of America
Sanford, NC.......................800-775-7570
Schloss Engineered Equipment
Aurora, CO........................303-695-4500
SP Industries
Hopkins, MI.......................800-592-5959
Universal Handling Equipment
Hamilton, ON......................877-843-1122
Waste Away Systems
Newark, OH........................800-223-4741
Wastequip Inc
Charlotte, NC.....................704-366-7140
Wayne Engineering
Cedar Falls, IA...................319-266-1721

Garbage Control Units & Systems

Chicago Trashpacker Corporation
Marengo, IL.......................800-635-5745
Compactors Inc
Hilton Head Isle, SC..............800-423-4003
Consolidated Baling Machine Company
Jacksonville, FL..................800-231-9286
Convay Systems
Minnetonka, MN....................800-334-1099
Fabwright Inc
Garden Grove, CA..................800-854-6464
Harmony Enterprises
Harmony, MN.......................800-658-2320
Jwc Environmental
Costa Mesa, CA....................800-331-2277
Lodal Inc
Kingsford, MI.....................800-435-3500
Maren Engineering Corp
South Holland, IL.................800-875-1038
Mell & Co
Niles, IL.........................800-262-6355
Multi-Pak
Hackensack, NJ....................201-342-7474
Our Name is Mud
New York, NY......................877-683-7867
PAC Equipment Company
Garfield, NJ......................973-478-1008
PTR Baler & Compactor Co
Philadelphia, PA..................800-523-3654
Robar International Inc
Milwaukee, WI.....................800-279-7750
Tema Systems Inc
Cincinnati, OH....................513-792-2840
U B KLEM Furniture Co Inc
St Anthony, IN....................800-264-1995

Universal Handling Equipment
Hamilton, ON 877-843-1122
Wastequip Inc
Charlotte, NC 704-366-7140
Wayne Engineering
Cedar Falls, IA 319-266-1721

Garbage Disposal Units

Anaheim Manufacturing Company
Anaheim, CA 800-767-6293
Anova
St Louis, MO 800-231-1327
Blower Application Co Inc
Germantown, WI 800-959-0880
Consolidated Baling Machine Company
Jacksonville, FL 800-231-9286
Convay Systems
Minnetonka, MN 800-334-1099
Dempster Systems
Toccoa, GA 706-886-2327
Dover Parkersburg
Follansbee, WV
Dynabilt Products
Readville, MA 800-443-1008
Fabwright Inc
Garden Grove, CA 800-854-6464
General Electric Company
Fairfield, CT 203-373-2211
Harmony Enterprises
Harmony, MN 800-658-2320
In Sink Erator
Racine, WI 800-558-5700
Insinger Co
Philadelphia, PA 800-344-4802
Ken Coat
Bardstown, KY 888-536-2628
Larose & Fils Lte
Laval, QC 877-382-7001
Lewis Steel Works Inc
Wrens, GA 800-521-5239
Maren Engineering Corp
South Holland, IL 800-875-1038
Old Dominion Wood Products
Lynchburg, VA 800-245-6382
PAC Equipment Company
Garfield, NJ 973-478-1008
Pack-A-Drum
Satellite Beach, FL 800-694-6163
Robar International Inc
Milwaukee, WI 800-279-7750
Salvajor Co
Kansas City, MO 800-SAL-AJOR
Tema Systems Inc
Cincinnati, OH 513-792-2840
U B KLEM Furniture Co Inc
St Anthony, IN 800-264-1995
Universal Handling Equipment
Hamilton, ON 877-843-1122
Wastequip Inc
Charlotte, NC 704-366-7140
White Mop Wringer Company
Tampa, FL 800-237-7582

General

9-12 Corporation
Caguas, PR 787-747-0405
A & B Process Systems Corp
Stratford, WI 888-258-2789
A.K. Robins
Baltimore, MD 800-486-9656
Activon Products
Beaver Dam, WI 800-841-0410
Air-Scent International
Pittsburgh, PA 800-247-0770
Airosol Co Inc
Neodesha, KS 800-633-9576
Alconox Inc
White Plains, NY 914-437-7585
All American Container
Miami, FL 305-887-0797
Alumin-Nu Corporation
Lyndhurst, OH 800-899-7097
Ameri-Khem
Port Orange, FL 800-224-9950
Amerivap Systems Inc
Dawsonville, GA 800-763-7687
Ampco Pumps Co Inc
Milwaukee, WI 800-737-8671
Andco Environmental Processes
Amherst, NY 716-691-2100

Aquafine Corp
Valencia, CA 800-423-3015
Aquionics Inc
Erlanger, KY 800-925-0440
Archon Industries Inc
Suffern, NY 800-554-1394
Ashcroft Inc
Stratford, CT 800-328-8258
Atlantic Ultraviolet Corp
Hauppauge, NY 866-958-9085
ATOFINA Chemicals
Philadelphia, PA 800-225-7788
Bake Star
Somerset, WI 763-427-7611
Bar Maid Corp
Pompano Beach, FL 954-960-1468
Bennett Manufacturing Company
Alden, NY 800-345-2142
Bio Cide Intl Inc
Norman, OK 800-323-1398
Bio Zapp Laboratories
Sarasota, FL 941-922-9199
Birko Corporation
Olathe, KS 800-444-8360
Black Bear Corp
Roanoke, VA 800-223-1284
C&R Refrigation Inc,
Center, TX 800-438-6182
Cadie Products Corp
Paterson, NJ 973-278-8300
Candy & Company/Peck's Products Company
Chicago, IL 800-837-9189
Carroll Co
Garland, TX 800-527-5722
Cashco Inc
Ellsworth, KS 785-472-4461
Century Chemical Corp
Elkhart, IN 800-348-3505
Cesco Magnetics
Rohnert Park, CA 877-624-8727
Champion America Inc
Branford, CT 800-521-7000
Champion Chemical Co
Whittier, CA 800-621-7868
Chore-Boy Corporation
Centerville, IN 765-855-5434
Clean Water Systems
Klamath Falls, OR 866-273-9993
Coburn Company
Whitewater, WI 800-776-7042
Colgate-Palmolive Professional Products Group
North York, ON 800-468-6502
Compliance Control Inc
Hyattsville, MD 800-810-4000
Contec, Inc.
Spartenburg, SC 800-289-5762
Control Beverage
Adelanto, CA 330-549-5376
Cosgrove Enterprises Inc
Miami Lakes, FL 800-888-3396
Crown Chemical Products
Mississauga, ON 905-564-0904
Culinary Depot
Monsey, NY 888-845-8200
D R Technology Inc
Freehold, NJ 732-780-4664
Damon Industries
Alliance, OH 800-362-9850
Damrow Company
Fond Du Lac, WI 800-236-1501
DH/Sureflow
Portland, OR 800-654-2548
Diamond Wipes Intl Inc
Chino, CA 800-454-1077
Dipwell Co
Northampton, MA 413-587-4673
Discovery Chemical
Marietta, GA 800-973-9881
DL Enterprises
Etters, PA 717-938-1292
Donaldson Co Inc
Bloomington, MN 952-887-3131
Dorden & Co
Detroit, MI 313-834-7910
Driall Inc
Attica, IN 765-295-2255
Ecolo Odor Control Systems Worldwide
North York, ON 800-667-6355
Electro-Steam Generator Corp
Rancocas, NJ 866-617-0764
Electrol Specialties Co
South Beloit, IL 815-389-2291

Elgene
Hamden, CT 800-922-4623
Encompass Supply
Kalispell, MT 888-852-7590
Essential Industries Inc
Merton, WI 800-551-9679
Faciltec Corporation
Elgin, IL 800-284-8273
Falls Chemical Products
Oconto Falls, WI. 920-846-3561
FX-Lab Company
Union, NJ 908-810-1212
Gamajet Cleaning Systems
Exton, PA 800-289-5387
Geerpres Inc
Muskegon, MI 231-773-3211
Graco Inc
Minneapolis, MN 877-844-7226
Gralab Instruments
Centerville, OH 800-876-8353
Great Western Chemical Company
Portland, OR 800-547-1400
Haviland Enterprises Inc
Grand Rapids, MI 800-456-1134
Hill Brush, Inc.
Baltimore, MD 800-998-1515
Hoge Brush Company
New Knoxville, OH 800-494-4643
Hubbell Electric Heater Co
Stratford, CT 800-647-3165
Hydrite Chemical Co
Brookfield, WI 262-792-1450
Insect-O-Cutor Inc
Stone Mountain, GA 800-966-8480
Interlab
The Woodlands, TX 888-876-2844
ITW Dymon
Olathe, KS 800-443-9536
James Varley & Sons
Saint Louis, MO 800-325-8891
Joneca Corp
Anaheim, CA 714-993-5997
Justman Brush Co
Omaha, NE 800-800-6940
KES Science & Technology Inc
Kennesaw, GA 800-627-4913
Kimberly-Clark Corporation
Irving, TX 972-281-1200
Knapp Manufacturing
Fresno, CA 559-251-8254
Labpride Chemicals
Bronx, NY 800-467-1255
Lake Process Systems Inc
Lake Barrington, IL 800-331-9260
Laundry Aids
Carlstadt, NJ 201-933-3500
Lechler Inc
St Charles, IL 800-777-2926
Little Giant Pump Company
Fort Wayne, IN 260-824-2900
Luseaux Labs Inc
Gardena, CA 800-266-1555
M D Stetson Co
Randolph, MA 800-255-8651
Manhattan Truck Lines
Paterson, NJ 800-370-7627
Metcraft
Grandview, MO 800-444-9624
Midbrook Inc
Jackson, MI 800-966-9274
Mil-Du-Gas Company/Star Brite
Fort Lauderdale, FL 800-327-8583
Milsek Furniture Polish Inc.
North Lima, OH 330-542-2700
Mission Laboratories
Los Angeles, CA 888-201-8866
Moly-XL Company
Westville, NJ 856-848-2880
Navy Brand
St Louis, MO 800-325-3312
Netzsch Pumps North America
Exton, PA 610-363-8010
Nilfisk, Inc.
Morgantown, PA 800-645-3475
Northwind Inc
Alpena, AR 877-937-2585
Nuance Solutions Inc
Chicago, IL 800-621-8553
Oakite Products
New Providence, NJ 800-526-4473
Omni Controls Inc
Tampa, FL 800-783-6664

Orwak
  Minneapolis, MN 800-747-0449
PAC Equipment Company
  Garfield, NJ. 973-478-1008
Parachem Corporation
  Des Moines, IA. 515-280-9445
Paragon Group USA
  St Petersburg, FL 800-835-6962
Paramount Packaging Corp
  Melville, NY. 516-333-8100
Paxton Corp
  Bristol, RI. 401-396-9062
Pioneer Chemical Co
  Gardena, CA 310-366-7393
Pioneer Manufacturing Co Inc
  Cleveland, OH 800-877-1500
Portion-Pac Chemical Corp.
  Chicago, IL. 312-226-0400
Potlatch Corp
  Spokane, WA. 509-835-1500
Pretty Products
  Wauconda, IL 800-726-4849
ProRestore Products
  Pittsburgh, PA. 800-332-6037
Purolator Facet Inc
  Greensboro, NC 800-852-4449
PVI Industries LLC
  Fort Worth, TX 800-784-8326
Quikwater Inc
  Sand Springs, OK 918-241-8880
Radiation Processing Division
  Parsippany, NJ. 800-442-1969
Rea UltraVapor
  Ancaster, ON. 800-323-3865
RHG Products Company
  Castle Rock, CO 800-553-8131
Rochester Midland Corp
  Rochester, NY. 800-535-5053
Rochester Midland Corp
  Rochester, NY. 800-836-1627
Ronell Industries
  Roselle, NJ 908-245-5255
Royal Paper Products
  Coatesville, PA 800-666-6655
Royce Rolls Ringer Co
  Grand Rapids, MI 800-253-9638
Ryter Corporation
  Saint James, MN 800-643-2184
Sanitech Inc
  Lorton, VA 800-486-4321
Sanitor Manufacturing Co
  Portage, MI 800-379-5314
SCA Tissue
  Philadelphia, PA 866-722-8675
SCA Tissue North America
  S Glens Falls, NY 518-743-0240
Sedalia Janitorial & Paper Supplies
  Sedalia, MO 660-826-9899
Selig Chemical Industries
  Atlanta, GA 404-876-5511
Seneca Environmental Products
  Tiffin, OH 419-447-1282
Shamrock Foods Co
  Phoenix, AZ 800-289-3663
Sigma Engineering Corporation
  White Plains, NY 914-682-1820
Snee Chemical Co
  New Orleans, LA 800-489-7633
Southend Janitorial Supply
  Los Angeles, CA. 323-754-2842
Spartan Tool LLC
  Mendota, IL 800-435-3866
Spurrier Chemical Companies
  Atlanta, GA. 800-795-9222
Sterling Novelty Products
  Northbrook, IL 847-291-0070
Swisher Hygiene
  Charlotte, NC 800-444-4138
T & S Brass & Bronze Work
  Travelers Rest, SC 800-476-4103
Telechem Corp
  Atlanta, GA. 800-637-0495
Tennant Co.
  Minneapolis, MN 800-553-8033
Thermaco Inc
  Asheboro, NC 800-633-4204
TRITEN Corporation
  Houston, TX 832-214-5000
Tuchenhagen
  Columbia, MD 410-910-6000
Uni First Corp
  Wilmington, MA. 800-455-7654

United Electric Controls Co
  Watertown, MA. 617-926-1000
United Floor Machine Co
  Chicago, IL 800-288-0848
Upright
  St Louis, MO. 800-248-7007
US Industrial Lubricants
  Cincinnati, OH 800-562-5454
Waco Broom & Mop Factory
  Waco, TX 800-548-7716
Warren E. Conley Corporation
  Carmel, IN. 800-367-7875
Warsaw Chemical Co Inc
  Warsaw, IN 800-548-3396
Waste Away Systems
  Newark, OH 800-223-4741
Water Sciences Services, Inc.
  Jackson, TN 973-584-4131
Water System Group
  Santa Clarita, CA 800-350-9283
West Chemical Products
  Princeton, NJ. 609-921-0501
Zipskin
  Dexter, MI. 734-426-5559

Holders

Broom

Geerpres Inc
  Muskegon, MI. 231-773-3211

Incinerators

Garbage & Waste

Andersen 2000
  Peachtree City, GA 800-241-5424
Brown Fired Heater
  Elyria, OH. 440-323-3291
Chesmont Engineering Co Inc
  Exton, PA 610-594-9200
Driall Inc
  Attica, IN. 765-295-2255
Incinerator International Inc
  Houston, TX 713-227-1466
Incinerator Specialty Company
  Houston, TX 713-681-4207
Industronics Service Co
  South Windsor, CT 800-878-1551
Jarvis-Cutter Company
  Boston, MA. 617-567-7532
Outotec USA Inc
  Jessup, MD 301-543-1200
Process Heating Corp
  Shrewsbury, MA 508-842-5200
Therm-Tec Inc
  Sherwood, OR. 800-292-9163
Zeeco Inc
  Broken Arrow, OK 918-258-8551

Insecticides & Insect Control Systems

Accommodation Mollen
  Philadelphia, PA 800-872-6268
Actron
  Tarzana, CA 800-866-8887
Air-Scent International
  Pittsburgh, PA 800-247-0770
Airosol Co Inc
  Neodesha, KS 800-633-9576
All Weather Energy Systems
  Plymouth, MI 888-636-8324
APR Associates Inc
  Memphis, TN 800-238-5150
Arrow-Magnolia Intl Inc
  Dallas, TX. 800-527-2101
Atlas Equipment Company
  Kansas City, MO. 800-842-9188
Bacon Products Corp
  Chattanooga, TN. 800-251-6238
Bell Laboratories Inc
  Madison, WI. 608-241-0202
Berner International Corp
  New Castle, PA 800-245-4455
Cantol
  Markham, ON 800-387-9773
Cardinal Professional Products
  Woodland, CA. 800-548-2223
Cci Industries-Cool Curtain
  Costa Mesa, CA 800-854-5719

Claire Manufacturing Company
  Addison, IL 800-252-4731
Commercial Dehydrator Systems
  Eugene, OR. 800-369-4283
Contech Enterprises Inc
  Grand Rapids, MI 800-767-8658
Copper Brite
  Santa Barbara, CA 805-565-1566
Discovery Chemical
  Marietta, GA 800-973-9881
Entech Systems Corp
  Kenner, LA 800-783-6561
Envirolights Manufacturing
  Concord, ON. 905-738-0357
Gardner Manufacturing Inc
  Horicon, WI 800-242-5513
Gilbert Industries, Inc
  Jonesboro, AR. 800-643-0400
Gilbert Insect Light Traps
  Jonesboro, AR. 800-643-0400
Grant Laboratories
  San Leandro, CA. 510-483-6070
Hanco Manufacturing Company
  Memphis, TN 800-530-7364
Insect-O-Cutor Inc
  Stone Mountain, GA. 800-966-8480
Insects Limited Inc
  Westfield, IN. 800-992-1991
J.I. Holcomb Manufacturing
  Independence, OH 800-458-3222
Kincaid Enterprises
  Nitro, WV 800-951-3377
L ChemCo Distribution
  Louisville, KY 800-292-1977
Mars Air Products
  Gardena, CA 800-421-1266
Matson LLC
  North Bend, WA 800-308-3723
Mclaughlin Gormley King Co
  Minneapolis, MN 800-645-6466
Nozzle Nolen Inc
  Palm Springs, FL 800-226-6536
P.F. Harris Manufacturing Company
  Alpharetta, GA 800-637-0317
Paraclipse
  Columbus, NE 800-854-6379
Pioneer Manufacturing Co Inc
  Cleveland, OH 800-877-1500
Prentiss
  Alpharetta, GA 770-552-8072
Research Products Co
  Salina, KS 785-825-2181
Rochester Midland Corp
  Rochester, NY. 800-535-5053
Rochester Midland Corp
  Rochester, NY. 800-836-1627
Roxide International
  Larchmont, NY 800-431-5500
Safety Fumigant Co
  Hingham, MA 800-244-1199
Sanco Products Co Inc
  Greenville, OH 937-548-2225
Selig Chemical Industries
  Atlanta, GA 404-876-5511
Solvit
  Monona, WI 888-314-1072
Sprayway Inc
  Addison, IL 800-332-9000
Surco Products
  Pittsburgh, PA 800-556-0111
Temp Air Inc
  Burnsville, MN 800-836-7432
Terminix
  Flushing, NY 866-319-6528
Venturetech Corporation
  Knoxville, TN 800-826-4095
Walco-Link Company
  Bellingham, WA 800-338-2329
Warren E. Conley Corporation
  Carmel, IN. 800-367-7875
West Chemical Products
  Princeton, NJ. 609-921-0501
Western Exterminator Co
  Irvine, CA 949-954-8023
Whitmire Microgen Research Lab
  St Louis, MO. 800-777-8570

Isopropyl Alcohol

Afassco
  Minden, NV 775-783-3555
Dow Packaging
  Midland, MI 800-331-6451

Hydrite Chemical Co
Brookfield, WI 262-792-1450

Maintenance

Bunzl Processor Distribution LLC
Riverside, MO. 816-448-4300

Mop Wringers

Geerpres Inc
Muskegon, MI. 231-773-3211
Royce Rolls Ringer Co
Grand Rapids, MI 800-253-9638
Superior Products Company
Saint Paul, MN 800-328-9800

Mops

Abco Products
Miami, FL. 888-694-2226
Amarillo Mop & Broom Company
Amarillo, TX. 800-955-8596
Argo & Company
Spartanburg, SC 864-583-9766
Birmingham Mop Manufacturing Company
Birmingham, AL. 205-942-6101
Bouras Mop Manufacturing Company
Saint Louis, MO 800-634-9153
Bro-Tex Inc
St Paul, MN. 800-328-2282
Carlisle Food Svc Products Inc
Oklahoma City, OK 800-654-8210
Carnegie Textile Co
Cleveland, OH 800-633-4136
Carolina Mop
Anderson, SC 800-845-9725
Chickasaw Broom Mfg Co Inc
Little Rock, AR. 501-562-0311
Cleveland Mop Manufacturing Company
Cleveland, OH 800-767-9934
Continental Commercial Products
Bridgeton, MO 800-325-1051
Cornelia Broom Company
Cornelia, GA. 800-228-2551
Cosgrove Enterprises Inc
Miami Lakes, FL. 800-888-3396
Costa Broom Works
Tampa, FL. 813-385-1722
Crystal Lake Mfg Inc
Autaugaville, AL 800-633-8720
Dover Parkersburg
Follansbee, WV
Drackett Professional
Cincinnati, OH 513-583-3900
Fuller Industries LLC
Great Bend, KS. 800-522-0499
Furgale Industries Ltd.
Winnipeg, NB 800-665-0506
Golden Star
N Kansas City, MO. 800-821-2792
Greenwood Mop & Broom Inc
Greenwood, SC. 800-635-6849
H. Arnold Wood Turning
Tarrytown, NY 888-314-0088
Harper Brush Works Inc
Fairfield, IA 800-223-7894
Hub City Brush Co
Petal, MS. 800-278-7452
Industries of the Blind
Greensboro, NC 336-274-1591
J.I. Holcomb Manufacturing
Independence, OH 800-458-3222
Kiefer Brushes, Inc
Franklin, NJ 800-526-2905
Labpride Chemicals
Bronx, NY. 800-467-1255
Layflat Products
Shreveport, LA 800-551-8515
Libman Co
Arcola, IL 877-818-3380
Lighthouse for the Blindin New Orleans
New Orleans, LA 504-899-4501
Little Rock Broom Works
Little Rock, AR. 501-562-0311
LMCO
Rosenberg, TX 281-342-8888
Luco Mop Co
St Louis, MO. 800-522-5826
Majestic Industries Inc
Macomb, MI. 586-786-9100
Messina Brothers Manufacturing Company
Brooklyn, NY 800-924-6454

Milwaukee Dustless Brush Co
Delavan, WI 323-724-7777
Newton Broom Co
Newton, IL 618-783-4424
O'Dell Corp
Ware Shoals, SC 800-342-2843
Perfex Corporation
Poland, NY 800-848-8483
Pioneer Manufacturing Co Inc
Cleveland, OH 800-877-1500
Quaker Chemical Company
Columbia, SC 800-849-9520
Quality Mop & Brush Manufacturers
Needham, MA. 617-884-2999
Quickie Manufacturing Corp
Cinnaminson, NJ. 856-829-7900
Reit-Price ManufacturingCompany
Union City, IN. 800-521-5343
Royal Broom & Mop Factory Inc
New Orleans, LA 800-537-6925
Rubbermaid Commercial Products
Cleveland, TN. 423-476-4544
S&M Manufacturing Company
Cisco, TX 800-772-8532
Saunders Manufacturing Co.
N Kansas City, MO. 800-821-2792
Shen Manufacturing Co Inc
Conshohocken, PA 610-825-2790
Superior Products Company
Saint Paul, MN 800-328-9800
Tuway American Group
Rockford, OH 800-537-3750
Uni First Corp
Wilmington, MA 800-455-7654
Verax Chemical Co
Snohomish, WA 800-637-7771
Waco Broom & Mop Factory
Waco, TX 800-548-7716
Whitley Manufacturing Company
Midland, NC 704-888-2625

Oils

Cleaning

Gemtek Products LLC
Phoenix, AZ 800-331-7022
Labpride Chemicals
Bronx, NY. 800-467-1255
Moly-XL Company
Westville, NJ. 856-848-2880
Oak International
Sturgis, MI 269-651-9790
Stoner
Quarryville, PA 800-227-5538
US Industrial Lubricants
Cincinnati, OH 800-562-5454

Pest Control

Exterminators

Nozzle Nolen Inc
Palm Springs, FL 800-226-6536
Western Exterminator Co
Irvine, CA 949-954-8023

Pest Control Systems & Devices

Actron
Tarzana, CA 800-866-8887
Air-Scent International
Pittsburgh, PA 800-247-0770
All Weather Energy Systems
Plymouth, MI 888-636-8324
Bacon Products Corp
Chattanooga, TN. 800-251-6238
Bell Laboratories Inc
Madison, WI 608-241-0202
Cardinal Professional Products
Woodland, CA. 800-548-2223
Claire Manufacturing Company
Addison, IL 800-252-4731
Contech Enterprises Inc
Grand Rapids, MI 800-767-8658
Copesan
Menomonee Falls, WI. 800-267-3726
Envirolights Manufacturing
Concord, ON. 905-738-0357
Gardner Manufacturing Inc
Horicon, WI 800-242-5513

Gilbert Insect Light Traps
Jonesboro, AR. 800-643-0400
Grant Laboratories
San Leandro, CA. 510-483-6070
Insect-O-Cutor Inc
Stone Mountain, GA 800-966-8480
Insects Limited Inc
Westfield, IN. 800-992-1991
Kincaid Enterprises
Nitro, WV 800-951-3377
L ChemCo Distribution
Louisville, KY 800-292-1977
Matson LLC
North Bend, WA 800-308-3723
Mclaughlin Gormley King Co
Minneapolis, MN 800-645-6466
Nozzle Nolen Inc
Palm Springs, FL 800-226-6536
P.F. Harris Manufacturing Company
Alpharetta, GA 800-637-0317
Paraclipse
Columbus, NE. 800-854-6379
Pioneer Manufacturing Co Inc
Cleveland, OH 800-877-1500
Prentiss
Alpharetta, GA 770-552-8072
Q A Supplies LLC
Norfolk, VA. 800-472-7205
Rochester Midland Corp
Rochester, NY. 800-535-5053
Roxide International
Larchmont, NY 800-431-5500
Selig Chemical Industries
Atlanta, GA 404-876-5511
Sprayway Inc
Addison, IL 800-332-9000
Superior Products Company
Saint Paul, MN 800-328-9800
Surco Products
Pittsburgh, PA 800-556-0111
Temp Air Inc
Burnsville, MN 800-836-7432
Terminix
Flushing, NY. 866-319-6528
Truly Nolen Pest Control
Tucson, AZ 877-977-1553
Walco-Link Company
Bellingham, WA 800-338-2329
Warren E. Conley Corporation
Carmel, IN. 800-367-7875
Western Exterminator Co
Irvine, CA 949-954-8023
Whitmire Microgen Research Lab
St Louis, MO. 800-777-8570

Traps

Rat & Mouse

Bell Laboratories Inc
Madison, WI 608-241-0202
Nozzle Nolen Inc
Palm Springs, FL 800-226-6536
Roxide International
Larchmont, NY 800-431-5500

Plumbing & Drainage Equipment

A B T Inc
Troutman, NC. 800-438-6057
Advanced Detection Systems
Milwaukee, WI. 414-672-0553
Alkota Cleaning Systems Inc
Alcester, SD 800-255-6823
All Power Inc
Sioux City, IA 712-258-0681
Alumin-Nu Corporation
Lyndhurst, OH 800-899-7097
Ampco Pumps Co Inc
Milwaukee, WI. 800-737-8671
Andco Environmental Processes
Amherst, NY. 716-691-2100
Athea Laboratories
Milwaukee, WI. 800-743-6417
Atlas Minerals & Chemicals Inc
Mertztown, PA 800-523-8269
Beacon Specialties
New York, NY 800-221-9405
Boyer Corporation
La Grange, IL 800-323-3040
Browne & Company
Markham, ON 905-475-6104

Carts Food Equipment
Brooklyn, NY 718-788-5540
Continental Industrial Supply
South Pasadena, FL 727-341-1100
Corp Somat
Lancaster, PA 800-237-6628
Croll-Reynolds Engineering Company
Trumbull, CT 203-371-1983
DH/Sureflow
Portland, OR 800-654-2548
Drehmann Paving & Flooring Company
Pennsauken, NJ 800-523-3800
Enpoco
Richmond, VA 800-338-2581
FX-Lab Company
Union, NJ 908-810-1212
G K & L Inc
Dickerson, MD 301-948-5538
Hankison International
Canonsburg, PA 724-746-1100
Hi-Temp Inc
Tuscumbia, AL 800-239-5066
Hydrite Chemical Co
Brookfield, WI 262-792-1450
IMC Teddy Food Service Equipment
Amityville, NY 800-221-5644
Interlab
The Woodlands, TX 888-876-2844
Josam Co
Michigan City, IN 800-365-6726
Kason Central
Columbus, OH 614-885-1992
King of All Manufacturing
Clio, MI 810-564-0139
Kraissl Co Inc
Hackensack, NJ 800-572-4775
Krogh Pump Co
Benicia, CA 800-225-7644
M-One Specialties
Salt Lake City, UT 800-525-9223
Metcraft
Grandview, MO 800-444-9624
MIFAB Inc
Chicago, IL 800-465-2736
Netzsch Pumps North America
Exton, PA 610-363-8010
Newstamp Lighting Factory
North Easton, MA 508-238-7073
Northland Process Piping
Isle, MN 320-679-2119
PCI Inc
St Louis, MO 800-752-7657
Plastipro
Los Angeles, CA 800-779-0561
Rochester Midland Corp
Rochester, NY 800-836-1627
Rockford Sanitary Systems
Rockford, IL 800-747-5077
Sefi Fabricators Inc
Amityville, NY 631-842-2200
StainlessDrains.com
Greenville, TX 888-785-2345
Stogsdill Tile Co
Huntley, IL 800-323-7504
Trap-Zap Environmental
Wyckoff, NJ 800-282-8727
Van Air Systems
Lake City, PA 800-840-9906
Vaughan Co Inc
Montesano, WA 888-249-2467
Viking Corp
Hastings, MI 800-968-9501
Warren E. Conley Corporation
Carmel, IN 800-367-7875
Watts Regulator Co
North Andover, MA 978-688-1811
World Dryer Corp
Berkeley, IL 800-323-0701
Zurn Industries LLC
Erie, PA 855-663-9876

Polish

Floor

ADCO
Albany, GA 800-821-7556
Advance Cleaning Products
Milwaukee, WI 800-925-5326
American Wax Co Inc
Long Island City, NY 718-361-4820

Bar Keepers Friend Cleanser
Indianapolis, IN 800-433-5818
Boyer Corporation
La Grange, IL 800-323-3040
Brulin & Company
Indianapolis, IN 800-776-7149
Buckeye International
Maryland Heights, MO 314-291-1900
Cantol
Markham, ON 800-387-9773
Chemifax
Santa Fe Springs, CA 800-527-5722
Claire Manufacturing Company
Addison, IL 800-252-4731
Cobitco Inc
Denver, CO 303-296-8575
Concord Chemical Co Inc
Camden, NJ 800-282-2436
D W Davies & Co
Racine, WI 800-888-6133
Dial Corporation
Scottsdale, AZ 480-754-3425
Emulso
Tonawanda, NY 716-854-2889
Essential Industries Inc
Merton, WI 800-551-9679
Fuller Industries LLC
Great Bend, KS 800-522-0499
Golden Star
N Kansas City, MO 800-821-2792
Griffin Bros Inc
Salem, OR 800-456-4743
H F Staples & Co Inc
Merrimack, NH 800-682-0034
Hill Manufacturing Co Inc
Atlanta, GA 404-522-8364
Hillyard Inc
St Joseph, MO 800-365-1555
Holland Chemicals Company
Windsor, ON 519-948-4373
Hy-Ko Enviro-MaintenanceProducts
Salt Lake City, UT 801-973-6099
J.I. Holcomb Manufacturing
Independence, OH 800-458-3222
James Varley & Sons
Saint Louis, MO 800-325-8891
Knapp Manufacturing
Fresno, CA 559-251-8254
Lamco Chemical Co Inc
Chelsea, MA 617-884-8470
Larose & Fils Lte
Laval, QC 877-382-7001
Lavo Company
Milwaukee, WI 414-353-2140
Lubar Chemical
Kansas City, MO 816-471-2560
M D Stetson Co
Randolph, MA 800-255-8651
Magic American Corporation
Cleveland, OH 800-321-6330
Marko Inc
Spartanburg, SC 866-466-2726
Meguiar's Inc
Irvine, CA 949-752-8000
Microbest Inc
Waterbury, CT 800-426-4246
Mission Laboratories
Los Angeles, CA 888-201-8866
Murnell Wax Company
Springfield, MA 781-395-1323
Pioneer Manufacturing Co Inc
Cleveland, OH 800-877-1500
Portion-Pac Chemical Corp.
Chicago, IL 312-226-0400
Quaker Chemical Company
Columbia, SC 800-849-9520
R&C Pro Brands
Wayne, NJ 973-633-7374
Rochester Midland Corp
Rochester, NY 800-535-5053
Rochester Midland Corp
Rochester, NY 800-836-1627
Sanitek Products Inc
Los Angeles, CA 818-242-1071
Selig Chemical Industries
Atlanta, GA 404-876-5511
Twi Laq
Bronx, NY 800-950-7627
Valspar Paint
Cleveland, OH 877-825-7727
Verax Chemical Co
Snohomish, WA 800-637-7771

Warren E. Conley Corporation
Carmel, IN 800-367-7875
West Chemical Products
Princeton, NJ 609-921-0501
Windsor Wax Co Inc
Charlestown, RI 800-243-8929

Furniture

ADCO
Albany, GA 800-821-7556
Bar Keepers Friend Cleanser
Indianapolis, IN 800-433-5818
Black's Products of HighPoint
High Point, NC 336-886-5011
Burnishine Products
Gurnee, IL 800-818-8275
Claire Manufacturing Company
Addison, IL 800-252-4731
Golden Star
N Kansas City, MO 800-821-2792
H F Staples & Co Inc
Merrimack, NH 800-682-0034
Hohn Manufacturing Company
Fenton, MO 800-878-1440
M D Stetson Co
Randolph, MA 800-255-8651
Meguiar's Inc
Irvine, CA 949-752-8000
Milsek Furniture Polish Inc.
North Lima, OH 330-542-2700
Novus
St. Paul, MN 800-328-1117
Scott's Liquid Gold-Inc
Denver, CO 800-447-1919

Powder

Cleaning & Scouring

Bar Keepers Friend Cleanser
Indianapolis, IN 800-433-5818
Church & Dwight Co., Inc.
Ewing, NJ 800-833-9532
Fitzpatrick Brothers
Pleasant Prairie, WI 800-233-8064
Hill Manufacturing Co Inc
Atlanta, GA 404-522-8364
J.I. Holcomb Manufacturing
Independence, OH 800-458-3222
Rochester Midland Corp
Rochester, NY 800-836-1627
Savogran Co
Norwood, MA 800-225-9872

Pressure Washers

Aaladin Industries Inc
Elk Point, SD 800-356-3325
Alkota Cleaning Systems Inc
Alcester, SD 800-255-6823
Cam Spray
Iowa Falls, IA 800-648-5011
Clarke American Sanders
Minneapolis, MN 800-253-0367
D&M Products
Santa Monica, CA 800-245-0485
Davron Technologies Inc
Chattanooga, TN 423-870-1888
Dirt Killer Pressure Washer
Gwynn Oak, MD 800-544-1188
General Tank
Berwick, PA 800-435-8265
Goodway Technologies Corp
Stamford, CT 800-333-7467
Hector Delorme & Sons
Farnham, QC 450-293-5310
Industrial Washing Machine Corporation
Jackson, NJ 732-304-9203
Kew Cleaning Systems
Clearwater, FL 800-942-1690
Kewanee Washer Corporaton
Findlay, OH 419-435-8269
Larose & Fils Lte
Laval, QC 877-382-7001
Lechler Inc
St Charles, IL 800-777-2926
Mart CART-Smt
Rogers, AR 800-548-3373
Maxi-Vac Inc.
Dundee, IL 855-629-4538
N & A Mfg
Mallard, IA 712-425-3512

Pro Scientific Inc
Oxford, CT 800-584-3776
Sani-Matic
Madison, WI 800-356-3300
Sioux Corp
Beresford, SD 888-763-8833
Therma Kleen
Plainfield, IL 800-999-3120
Windsor Industries Inc
Englewood, CO. 800-444-7654

Sanitary Wall

AlphaBio Inc
Rancho Santa Maragarita, CA 800-966-0716
Arcoplast Wall & Ceiling Systems
St Peters, MO 888-736-2726
Zeroloc
Kirkland, WA 425-823-4888

Sanitizers

A&L Laboratories
Minneapolis, MN 800-225-3832
Activon Products
Beaver Dam, WI 800-841-0410
Air-Scent International
Pittsburgh, PA 800-247-0770
Atlantic Mills
Lakewood, NJ 800-242-7374
Bar Maid Corp
Pompano Beach, FL 954-960-1468
Best Sanitizers Inc
Penn Valley, CA 888-225-3267
Birko Corporation
Olathe, KS. 800-444-8360
Burnishine Products
Gurnee, IL 800-818-8275
Candy & Company/Peck's Products Company
Chicago, IL 800-837-9189
Century Chemical Corp
Elkhart, IN. 800-348-3505
Colgate-Palmolive Professional Products Group
North York, ON. 800-468-6502
Discovery Chemical
Marietta, GA 800-973-9881
Electro-Steam Generator Corp
Rancocas, NJ. 866-617-0764
Falls Chemical Products
Oconto Falls, WI. 920-846-3561
Glass Pro
Addison, IL 888-641-8919
Hilex Company
Eagan, MN 651-454-1160
Hydrite Chemical Co
Brookfield, WI 262-792-1450
James Varley & Sons
Saint Louis, MO 800-325-8891
Labpride Chemicals
Bronx, NY. 800-467-1255
Lee Industries
Philipsburg, PA 814-342-0461
Luseaux Labs Inc
Gardena, CA. 800-266-1555
M D Stetson Co
Randolph, MA 800-255-8651
Machem Industries
Delta, BC. 604-526-5655
Meritech
Golden, CO. 800-932-7707
Nelson-Jameson Inc
Marshfield, WI 800-826-8302
Nice-Pak Products Inc
Orangeburg, NY 800-444-6725
Nuance Solutions Inc
Chicago, IL 800-621-8553
Oakite Products
New Providence, NJ 800-526-4473
Paxton Corp
Bristol, RI 401-396-9062
Portion-Pac Chemical Corp.
Chicago, IL 312-226-0400
Pretty Products
Wauconda, IL 800-726-4849
ProRestore Products
Pittsburgh, PA 800-332-6037
REM Ohio Inc
Cincinnati, OH 513-381-3700
Rochester Midland Corp
Rochester, NY. 800-836-1627
Shepard Brothers Co
La Habra, CA 800-645-3594

Vulcan Materials Co
Vestavia, AL 205-298-3000
Water Sciences Services, Inc.
Jackson, TN 973-584-4131

Scouring Pads

ACS Industries, Inc.
Lincoln, RI 866-783-4838
Arden Companies
Southfield, MI 248-415-8500
Argo & Company
Spartanburg, SC 864-583-9766
Armaly Brands
Commerce Twp, MI 800-772-1222
Banner Chemical Co
Orange, NJ 973-676-0105
Carlisle Food Svc Products Inc
Oklahoma City, OK 800-654-8210
Glit Microtron
Bridgetown, MO. 800-325-1051
Mainline Industries Inc
Springfield, MA 800-527-7917
Microtron Abrasives
Pineville, NC. 800-476-7237
Pacific Oasis Enterprise Inc
Santa Fe Springs, CA 800-424-1475
Quickie Manufacturing Corp
Cinnaminson, NJ. 856-829-7900
Royal Paper Products
Coatesville, PA 800-666-6655
Stearns Technical Textiles Company
Cincinnati, OH 800-543-7173
Thamesville Metal Products Ltd
Thamesville, ON. 519-692-3963
Tucel Industries, Inc.
Forestdale, VT 800-558-8235
Tuway American Group
Rockford, OH 800-537-3750
Wilen Professional Cleaning Products
Atlanta, GA. 800-241-7371

Scrubbers

Andersen 2000
Peachtree City, GA 800-241-5424

Silverware Cleaning Machinery

Washing, Drying & Polishing

Adamation
Commerce, CA. 800-383-8800
Vanguard Technology Inc
Eugene, OR. 800-624-4809

Skin Cream & Lotions

Cold Cream

Milburn Company
Detroit, MI 313-259-3410

Lotion

Milburn Company
Detroit, MI 313-259-3410

Skin Cream

Milburn Company
Detroit, MI 313-259-3410
The Procter & Gamble Company
Cincinnati, OH 800-692-0132

Sneeze Guards

Advanced Design Mfg
Concord, CA. 800-690-0002
Brass Smith
Denver, CO. 800-662-9595
Carlisle Food Svc Products Inc
Oklahoma City, OK 800-654-8210
Custom Plastics Inc
Decatur, GA 404-373-1691
Duke Manufacturing Co
St Louis, MO. 800-735-3853
Emco Industrial Plastics
Cedar Grove, NJ 800-292-9906
English Manufacturing Inc
Rancho Cordova, CA 800-651-2711
Hanson Brass Rewd Co
Sun Valley, CA 888-841-3773

K & I Creative Plastics & Wood
Jacksonville, FL 904-387-0438
Lavi Industries
Valencia, CA. 800-624-6225
Precision Plastics Inc
Beltsville, MD. 800-922-1317
R & D Brass
Wappingers Falls, NY. 800-447-6050
Sneezeguard Solutions
Columbia, MO. 800-569-2056
Superior Products Company
Saint Paul, MN 800-328-9800

Soap

Advance Cleaning Products
Milwaukee, WI 800-925-5326
Akron Cotton Products
Akron, OH. 800-899-7173
American Wax Co Inc
Long Island City, NY 718-361-4820
APR Associates Inc
Memphis, TN 800-238-5150
Beaumont Products
Kennesaw, GA 800-451-7096
Bi-O-Kleen Industries
Portland, OR. 503-224-6246
Bio Pac Inc
Incline Village, NV 800-225-2855
Blue Cross Laboratories
Santa Clarita, CA
Bradford Soap Works Inc
West Warwick, RI 401-821-2141
Buckeye International
Maryland Heights, MO. 314-291-1900
Cal Ben Soap Co
Oakland, CA. 800-340-7091
Cantol
Markham, ON. 800-387-9773
Carroll Co
Garland, TX 800-527-5722
Chef Revival
North Charleston, SC 800-248-9826
Colgate-Palmolive Professional Products Group
North York, ON. 800-468-6502
Common Sense Natural Soap & Bodycare Products
Rutland, VT 802-773-0582
Concord Chemical Co Inc
Camden, NJ. 800-282-2436
Crc Industries Inc
Warminster, PA. 800-556-5074
Critzas Industries Inc
St Louis, MO. 800-537-1418
Crown Chemical Products
Mississauga, ON. 905-564-0904
DCL Solutions LLC
Philadelphia, PA 800-426-1127
Deb Canada
Waterford, ON. 888-332-7627
Diablo Chemical
Kingston, PA. 800-548-1384
Dial Corporation
Scottsdale, AZ. 480-754-3425
Dirt Killer Pressure Washer
Gwynn Oak, MD. 800-544-1188
Dober Chemical Corporation
Midlothian, IL. 800-323-4983
Dreumex USA
York, PA 800-233-9382
Economy Paper & Restaurant Co
Clifton, NJ. 973-279-5500
Emulso
Tonawanda, NY 716-854-2889
Essential Industries Inc
Merton, WI. 800-551-9679
Falls Chemical Products
Oconto Falls, WI. 920-846-3561
Fiebing Co
Milwaukee, WI. 800-558-1033
Fishers Investment
Cincinnati, OH 800-833-5916
GOJO Industries Inc
Akron, OH. 800-321-9647
Hallberg Manufacturing Corporation
Tampa, FL. 800-633-7627
Hamilton Soap & Oil Products
Paterson, NJ 973-225-1031
Hanco Manufacturing Company
Memphis, TN 800-530-7364
Hewitt Soap Company
Dayton, OH. 800-543-2245
Hohn Manufacturing Company
Fenton, MO. 800-878-1440

Hy-Trous/Flash Sales
Woburn, MA 781-933-5772
Inksolv 30, LLC.
Emerson, NE. 515-537-5344
J.I. Holcomb Manufacturing
Independence, OH 800-458-3222
James Austin Co
Mars, PA .724-625-1535
James Varley & Sons
Saint Louis, MO 800-325-8891
Kildon Manufacturing
Ingersoll, ON 800-485-4930
Larose & Fils Lte
Laval, QC .877-382-7001
Lavo Company
Milwaukee, WI 414-353-2140
Lee Soap Company
Commerce City, CO 800-888-1896
M D Stetson Co
Randolph, MA 800-255-8651
Man-O Products
Cincinnati, OH 888-210-6266
Martin Laboratories
Owensboro, KY 800-345-9352
Meritech
Golden, CO 800-932-7707
Micro-Brush Pro Soap
Rockwall, TX 800-776-7627
Milburn Company
Detroit, MI 313-259-3410
Mione Manufacturing Company
Mickleton, NJ 800-257-0497
Mission Laboratories
Los Angeles, CA. 888-201-8866
National Purity LLC
Brooklyn Center, MN 612-672-0022
Nuance Solutions Inc
Chicago, IL 800-621-8553
Ohio Soap Products Company
Wickliffe, OH 440-585-1100
Parachem Corporation
Des Moines, IA 515-280-9445
Pioneer Chemical Co
Gardena, CA 310-366-7393
PM Chemical Company
San Diego, CA 619-296-0191
R R Street & Co
Naperville, IL 630-416-4244
Rochester Midland Corp
Rochester, NY. 800-535-5053
Rochester Midland Corp
Rochester, NY. 800-836-1627
Rooto Corp
Howell, MI 517-546-8330
S & S Soap Co
Bronx, NY. 718-585-2900
San Joaquin Pool Svc & Supply
Stockton, CA. 209-952-0680
Sanitek Products Inc
Los Angeles, CA. 818-242-1071
SCA Hygiene Paper
San Ramon, CA 800-992-8675
Selig Chemical Industries
Atlanta, GA. 404-876-5511
Sierra Dawn Products
Santa Rosa, CA 707-535-0172
Simoniz USA Inc
Bolton, CT 800-227-5536
Snee Chemical Co
New Orleans, LA 800-489-7633
State Industrial Products Corp
Mayfield Heights, OH 877-747-6986
Steiner Company
Holland, IL 800-222-4638
Steiner Industries Inc
Chicago, IL 800-621-4515
Stone Soap Co Inc
Sylvan Lake, MI 800-952-7627
Sunbeam Products Co LLC
Toledo, OH 419-691-1551
Sunpoint Products
Lawrence, MA 978-794-3100
Sure Clean Corporation
Two Rivers, WI. 920-793-3838
The Procter & Gamble Company
Cincinnati, OH 800-692-0132
Tropical Soap Company
Carrollton, TX. 800-527-2368
Twi Laq
Bronx, NY. 800-950-7627
Ulmer Pharmacal
Park Rapids, MN. 800-848-5637

Uni First Corp
Wilmington, MA. 800-455-7654
US Industrial Lubricants
Cincinnati, OH 800-562-5454
Venturetech Corporation
Knoxville, TN 800-826-4095
Verax Chemical Co
Snohomish, WA 800-637-7771
Whisk Products Inc
Wentzville, MO. 800-204-7627

Powder

Hallberg Manufacturing Corporation
Tampa, FL. 800-633-7627

Vegetable Oil

National Purity LLC
Brooklyn Center, MN 612-672-0022
US Industrial Lubricants
Cincinnati, OH 800-562-5454

Sponges

Acme Sponge & Chamois Co Inc
Tarpon Springs, FL. 727-937-3222
ACS Industries, Inc.
Lincoln, RI 866-783-4838
Armaly Brands
Commerce Twp, MI 800-772-1222
Carlisle Food Svc Products Inc
Oklahoma City, OK 800-654-8210
Distribution Results
Akron, OH. 800-737-9671
Glit Microtron
Bridgetown, MO. 800-325-1051
Labpride Chemicals
Bronx, NY. 800-467-1255
Nation/Ruskin
Montgomeryville, PA 800-523-2489
Quickie Manufacturing Corp
Cinnaminson, NJ. 856-829-7900
Royal Paper Products
Coatesville, PA 800-666-6655
Spontex
Columbia, TN 800-251-4222
Tee-Jay Corporation
Shelton, CT 203-924-4767
Tucel Industries, Inc.
Forestdale, VT 800-558-8235

Sprinkling Systems

American Fire Sprinkler Services, Inc
Hialeah, FL. 305-628-0100
APEC
Lake Odessa, MI. 616-374-1000
Corrigan Corporation of America
Gurnee, IL. 800-462-6478
Doering Co
Clear Lake, MN 320-743-2276
Fire Protection Industries
Bensalem, PA 215-245-1830
Firematic Sprinkler Devices
Shrewsbury, MA. 800-225-7288
Globe Fire Sprinkler Corp
Standish, MI 800-248-0278
Grinnell Fire ProtectionSystems Company
Sauk Rapids, MN. 320-253-8665
Muellermist Irrigation Company
Broadview, IL 708-450-9595
Storm Industrial
Shawnee Mission, KS. 800-745-7483
Tyco Fire Protection Products
Lansdale, PA. 800-558-5236
Viking Corp
Hastings, MI 800-968-9501
Wiginton Corp
Sanford, FL 407-585-3200

Squeegees

Carlisle Food Svc Products Inc
Oklahoma City, OK 800-654-8210
Continental Commercial Products
Bridgeton, MO. 800-325-1051
Dorden & Co
Detroit, MI 313-834-7910
Ettore
Alameda, CA. 510-748-4130
Harper Brush Works Inc
Fairfield, IA 800-223-7894

Kiefer Brushes, Inc
Franklin, NJ 800-526-2905
Labpride Chemicals
Bronx, NY. 800-467-1255
Lite-Weight Tool & Mfg Co
Sun Valley, CA 800-859-3529
Milwaukee Dustless Brush Co
Delavan, WI 323-724-7777
Perfex Corporation
Poland, NY 800-848-8483
Reit-Price ManufacturingCompany
Union City, IN. 800-521-5343
Superior Products Company
Saint Paul, MN 800-328-9800
Warren E. Conley Corporation
Carmel, IN. 800-367-7875

Sterilizers

A.K. Robins
Baltimore, MD 800-486-9656
Allpax Products
Covington, LA 888-893-9277
American Ultraviolet Co
Lebanon, IN 800-288-9288
API Heat Transfer Inc
Buffalo, NY. 877-274-4328
Atlantic Ultraviolet Corp
Hauppauge, NY 866-958-9085
Burnishine Products
Gurnee, IL 800-818-8275
Cleaver-Brooks Inc
Thomasville, GA. 800-250-5583
Electro-Steam Generator Corp
Rancocas, NJ. 866-617-0764
GERM-O-RAY
Stone Mountain, GA. 800-966-8480
Hess Machine Intl
Ephrata, PA 800-735-4377
Littleford Day
Florence, KY. 800-365-8555
Market Forge Industries Inc
Everett, MA. 866-698-3188
Melco Steel Inc
Azusa, CA. 626-334-7875
National Hotpack
Stone Ridge, NY 800-431-8232
San Joaquin Pool Svc & Supply
Stockton, CA. 209-952-0680
Schlueter Company
Janesville, WI 800-359-1700
Severn Trent Svc
Colmar, PA 215-822-2901
South Valley Mfg Inc
Gilroy, CA. 408-842-5457
SP Industries Inc
Warminster, PA 800-523-2327
TMI-USA
Reston, VA 703-668-0114
Triad Scientific
Manasquan, NJ 800-867-6690

Tissue

Cleansing

Carhoff Company
Cleveland, OH 216-541-4835
Georgia Pacific
Green Bay, WI. 920-435-8821
Kimberly-Clark Professional
Roswell, GA. 800-241-3146
Marcal Paper Mills
Elmwood Park, NJ 800-631-8451
Potlatch Corp
Spokane, WA. 509-835-1500
Productos Familia
Santurce, PR 787-268-5929
SCA Hygiene Paper
San Ramon, CA 800-992-8675
SCA Tissue
Philadelphia, PA 866-722-8675
Sorg Paper Company
Middletown, OH 513-420-5300
SQP
Schenectady, NY 800-724-1129
The Procter & Gamble Company
Cincinnati, OH 800-692-0132
Vermont Tissue Paper Company
North Bennington, VT 802-447-7558

Vaccum Bags

Cretel Food Equipment
Holland, MI 616-786-3980

Vacuum Cleaners

Industrial

Beam Industries
Webster City, IA 800-369-2326
Clarke American Sanders
Minneapolis, MN 800-253-0367
DL Enterprises
Etters, PA 717-938-1292
Eureka Company
Bloomington, IL 800-282-2886
Gardner Denver Inc.
Milwaukee, WI
General Floor Craft
Little Silver, NJ 973-742-7400
Goodway Technologies Corp
Stamford, CT. 800-333-7467
H.L. Diehl Company
South Windham, CT 860-423-7741
Hollowell Products Corporation
Wyandotte, MI 734-282-8200
Hoover Company
Glenwillow, OH 330-499-9499
Mastercraft Industries Inc
Newburgh, NY 800-835-7812
Mercury Floor Machines Inc
Englewood, NJ 888-568-4606
Multivac
Union Grove, WI 800-640-4213
Oreck Manufacturing Co
Cookeville, TN 800-989-3535
ProTeam
Boise, ID 800-541-1456
Spencer Turbine Co
Windsor, CT 800-232-4321
Superior Products Company
Saint Paul, MN 800-328-9800
United Floor Machine Co
Chicago, IL 800-288-0848
Vector Technologies
Milwaukee, WI 800-832-4010
Windsor Industries Inc
Englewood, CO. 800-444-7654

Washing Machinery

A.K. Robins
Baltimore, MD 800-486-9656
Aaladin Industries Inc
Elk Point, SD 800-356-3325
Adamation
Commerce, CA 800-383-8800
Ali Group
Winston Salem, NC. 800-532-8591
Alkota Cleaning Systems Inc
Alcester, SD 800-255-6823
Ametek Technical & Industrial Products
Kent, OH. 215-256-6601
Andgar Corp
Ferndale, WA 360-366-9900
Assembled Products Corp
Rogers, AR 800-548-3373
Atlas Pacific Engineering
Pueblo, CO 719-948-3040
Attias Oven Corp
Brooklyn, NY 800-928-8427
Bar Maid Corp
Pompano Beach, FL 954-960-1468
Bete Fog Nozzle Inc
Greenfield, MA. 800-235-0049
Bethel Engineering & Equipment Inc
New Hampshire, OH. 800-889-6129
BFM Equipment Sales
Fall River, WI 920-484-3341
Burns Chemical Systems
Cleveland, OH 724-327-7600
Cam Spray
Iowa Falls, IA 800-648-5011
Cannon Equipment Company
Cannon Falls, MN 800-825-8501
Chad Co Inc
Olathe, KS. 800-444-8360
Champion Industries Inc
Winston Salem, NC. 800-532-8591
Chemdet Inc
Sebastian, FL 800-645-1510

Cincinnati Industrial Machry
Mason, OH 800-677-0076
Cloud Inc
San Luis Obispo, CA 800-234-5650
Cma Dishmachines
Garden Grove, CA 800-854-6417
Colonial Paper Company
Silver Springs, FL. 352-622-4171
Commercial Dehydrator Systems
Eugene, OR. 800-369-4283
Commercial Manufacturing
Fresno, CA 559-237-1855
Component Hardware Group Inc
Lakewood, NJ. 800-526-3694
Continental Equipment Corporation
Milwaukee, WI 414-463-0500
Continental Girbau Inc
Oshkosh, WI 800-256-1073
Convay Systems
Minnetonka, MN. 800-334-1099
Cugar Machine Co
Fort Worth, TX 817-927-0411
Custom Diamond International
Laval, QC 800-363-5926
Custom Food Machinery
Stockton, CA 209-463-4343
D&M Products
Santa Monica, CA. 800-245-0485
Damas Corporation
Trenton, NJ 609-695-9121
Davron Technologies Inc
Chattanooga, TN. 423-870-1888
Dirt Killer Pressure Washer
Gwynn Oak, MD. 800-544-1188
Diversified Metal Engineering
Charlottetown, PE. 902-628-6900
Douglas Machines Corp.
Clearwater, FL 800-331-6870
Dynablast Manufacturing
Mississauga, ON 888-242-8597
FleetwoodGoldcoWyard
Romeoville, IL 630-759-6800
Flo-Matic Corporation
Belvidere, IL 800-959-1179
Gamajet Cleaning Systems
Exton, PA 800-289-5387
Geo. Olcott Company
Scottsboro, AL 800-634-2769
Ghibli North American
Wilmington, DE 302-654-5908
Girton Manufacturing Co
Millville, PA 570-458-5521
Glass Pro
Addison, IL. 888-641-8919
Glastender
Saginaw, MI 800-748-0423
Harold F Haines Manufacturing Inc
Presque Isle, ME. 207-762-1411
Hector Delorme & Sons
Farnham, QC 450-293-5310
Horix Manufacturing Co
Mc Kees Rocks, PA. 412-771-1111
Hoyt Corporation
Westport, MA 508-636-8811
Hughes Co
Columbus, WI 866-535-9303
IMC Teddy Food Service Equipment
Amityville, NY 800-221-5644
Industrial Washing Machine Corporation
Jackson, NJ. 732-304-9203
Kew Cleaning Systems
Clearwater, FL 800-942-1690
Kewanee Washer Corporaton
Findlay, OH. 419-435-8269
Key Technology Inc.
Walla Walla, WA. 509-529-2161
Knight Equipment International
Lake Forest, CA 800-854-3764
Krones
Franklin, WI 800-752-3787
Krowne Metal Corp
Wayne, NJ. 800-631-0442
Kuhl Corporation
Flemington, NJ 908-782-5696
Larose & Fils Lte
Laval, QC 877-382-7001
Laundrylux
Inwood, NY. 800-645-2205
Lechler Inc
St Charles, IL 800-777-2926
Leedal Inc
Northbrook, IL 847-498-0111

Leon C. Osborn Company
Houston, TX 281-488-0755
LPS Technology
Grafton, OH 800-586-1410
Ltg Inc
Spartanburg, SC 864-599-6340
Magnuson
Pueblo, CO 719-948-9500
Mart CART-Smt
Rogers, AR 800-548-3373
Matcon Americas
Elmhurst, IL 856-256-1330
Maxi-Vac Inc.
Dundee, IL 855-629-4538
Mcbrady Engineering Co
Rockdale, IL 815-744-8900
Meritech
Golden, CO 800-932-7707
Metal Equipment Company
Cleveland, OH 800-700-6326
Metcraft
Grandview, MO. 800-444-9624
Midbrook Inc
Jackson, MI 800-966-9274
Moyer Diebel
Winston Salem, NC. 336-661-1992
N & A Mfg
Mallard, IA 712-425-3512
Namco Machinery
Maspeth, NY
National Conveyor Corp
Commerce, CA 323-725-0355
Paxton Products Inc
Blue Ash, OH 800-441-7475
Pellerin Milnor Corporation
Kenner, LA 800-469-8780
PMI Food Equipment Group
Troy, OH 937-332-3000
Pneumatic Scale Angelus
Cuyahoga Falls, OH 330-923-0491
Puritan/Churchill Chemical Company
Marietta, GA 800-275-8914
Roto-Jet Pump
Salt Lake City, UT 801-359-8731
Sani-Matic
Madison, WI 800-356-3300
Sanitech Inc
Lorton, VA 800-486-4321
Sasib Beverage & Food North America
Plano, TX 800-558-3814
Schlueter Company
Janesville, WI 800-359-1700
Sioux Corp
Beresford, SD 888-763-8833
Sonicor
West Babylon, NY 800-864-5022
Specialty Equipment Company
Mendota Heights, MN 651-452-7909
Spraying Systems Company
Wheaton, IL 630-655-5000
Stero Co
Petaluma, CA 800-762-7600
Superior Food Machinery Inc
Pico Rivera, CA 800-944-0396
Swissh Commercial Equipment
Montreal, QC 888-794-7749
Therma Kleen
Plainfield, IL 800-999-3120
Tri-Pak Machinery Inc
Harlingen, TX 956-423-5140
Us Bottlers Machinery Co Inc
Charlotte, NC 704-588-4750
Waring Products
Torrington, CT 800-492-7464
Washing Systems
Loveland, OH 800-272-1974
Windsor Industries Inc
Englewood, CO. 800-444-7654
Zealco Industries
Calvert City, KY 800-759-5531

Waste Handling & Disposal Equipment

Abel Pumps
Sewickley, PA 412-741-3222
Adamation
Commerce, CA 800-383-8800
Aeration Industries Intl LLC
Chaska, MN 800-328-8287
Aeromix Systems
Minneapolis, MN 800-879-3677

Ali Group
Winston Salem, NC 800-532-8591

Alkota Cleaning Systems Inc
Alcester, SD 800-255-6823

Alloy Hardfacing & Engineering
Jordan, MN 800-328-8408

Ameri-Khem
Port Orange, FL 800-224-9950

Ampco Pumps Co Inc
Milwaukee, WI 800-737-8671

Anaheim Manufacturing Company
Anaheim, CA 800-767-6293

Andco Environmental Processes
Amherst, NY 716-691-2100

Anova
St Louis, MO 800-231-1327

Apache Stainless Equipment
Beaver Dam, WI 800-444-0398

API Industries
Tulsa, OK 918-664-4010

Armstrong International
Three Rivers, MI 269-273-1415

Athea Laboratories
Milwaukee, WI 800-743-6417

Bennett Manufacturing Company
Alden, NY 800-345-2142

Betz Entec
Horsham, PA 800-877-1940

Biothane Corporation
Camden, NJ 856-541-3500

Blower Application Co Inc
Germantown, WI 800-959-0880

Brown Fired Heater
Elyria, OH 440-323-3291

C E Rogers Co
Mora, MN 800-279-8081

C S Bell Co
Tiffin, OH 888-958-6381

Can & Bottle Systems, Inc.
Milwaukie, OR 866-302-2636

Cavert Wire Co
Rural Hall, NC 800-245-4042

Chesmont Engineering Co Inc
Exton, PA 610-594-9200

Chicago Trashpacker Corporation
Marengo, IL 800-635-5745

Clean Water Systems
Klamath Falls, OR 866-273-9993

Compactors Inc
Hilton Head Isle, SC 800-423-4003

Consolidated Baling Machine Company
Jacksonville, FL 800-231-9286

Continental Commercial Products
Bridgeton, MO 800-325-1051

Convay Systems
Minnetonka, MN 800-334-1099

Corenco
Santa Rosa, CA 888-267-3626

Cornell Pump Company
Portland, OR 503-653-0330

Corp Somat
Lancaster, PA 800-237-6628

Dempster Systems
Toccoa, GA 706-886-2327

Driall Inc
Attica, IN 765-295-2255

Ertelalsop
Kingston, NY 800-553-7835

Erwyn Products Inc
Morganville, NJ 800-331-9208

Evoqua Water Technologies
Thomasville, GA 800-841-1550

Fabwright Inc
Garden Grove, CA 800-854-6464

Foremost Machine Builders Inc
Fairfield, NJ 973-227-0700

Frem Corporation
Worcester, MA 508-791-3152

Galbreath LLC
Winamac, IN 574-946-6631

Garb-El Products Co
Lockport, NY 716-434-6010

General Electric Company
Fairfield, CT 203-373-2211

General, Inc
Weston, FL 954-202-7419

Glaro Inc
Hauppauge, NY 631-234-1717

Harmony Enterprises
Harmony, MN 800-658-2320

Himolene
Carrollton, TX 800-777-4411

Hines III
Jacksonville, FL 904-398-5110

Hodge Manufacturing Company
Springfield, MA 800-262-4634

Hygiene-Technik
Beamsville, ON 905-563-4987

In Sink Erator
Racine, WI 800-558-5700

Incinerator International Inc
Houston, TX 713-227-1466

Incinerator Specialty Company
Houston, TX 713-681-4207

Industronics Service Co
South Windsor, CT 800-878-1551

Insect-O-Cutor Inc
Stone Mountain, GA 800-966-8480

Insinger Co
Philadelphia, PA 800-344-4802

International Reserve Equipment Corporation
Clarendon Hills, IL 708-531-0680

Intrex
Bethel, CT 203-792-7400

J C Industries Inc
West Babylon, NY 800-322-1189

J.V. Reed & Company
Louisville, KY 877-258-7333

Joneca Corp
Anaheim, CA 714-993-5997

Jones Environmental
Fullerton, CA 714-449-9937

Jwc Environmental
Costa Mesa, CA 800-331-2277

Kew Cleaning Systems
Clearwater, FL 800-942-1690

Komline-Sanderson Engineering
Peapack, NJ 800-225-5457

Krogh Pump Co
Benicia, CA 800-225-7644

Lenser Filtration
Lakewood, NJ 732-370-1600

Lewis Steel Works Inc
Wrens, GA 800-521-5239

Load King Mfg
Jacksonville, FL 800-531-4975

Lodal Inc
Kingsford, MI 800-435-3500

Logemann Brothers Co
Milwaukee, WI 414-445-3005

Ludell Manufacturing Co
Milwaukee, WI 800-558-0800

Mahoney Environmental
Joliet, IL 800-892-9392

Marathon Equipment Co
Vernon, AL 800-269-7237

Maren Engineering Corp
South Holland, IL 800-875-1038

Mell & Co
Niles, IL 800-262-6355

Metal Equipment Company
Cleveland, OH 800-700-6326

Midbrook Inc
Jackson, MI 800-966-9274

Miller Manufacturing Co
Turlock, CA 209-632-3846

Multi-Pak
Hackensack, NJ 201-342-7474

National Conveyor Corp
Commerce, CA 323-725-0355

Netzsch Pumps North America
Exton, PA 610-363-8010

Oil Skimmers Inc
Cleveland, OH 800-200-4603

Old Dominion Wood Products
Lynchburg, VA 800-245-6382

Orwak
Minneapolis, MN 800-747-0449

Our Name is Mud
New York, NY 877-683-7867

Outotec USA Inc
Jessup, MD 301-543-1200

PAC Equipment Company
Garfield, NJ 973-478-1008

Pack-A-Drum
Satellite Beach, FL 800-694-6163

Paradise Plastics
Brooklyn, NY 718-788-3733

Parallel Products Inc
Louisville, KY 800-883-9100

Parkson Corp
Vernon Hills, IL 847-816-3700

Peter Pepper Products Inc
Compton, CA 310-639-0390

Plymold
Kenyon, MN 800-759-6653

PMI Food Equipment Group
Troy, OH 937-332-3000

PTR Baler & Compactor Co
Philadelphia, PA 800-523-3654

R.G. Stephens Engineering
Long Beach, CA 800-499-3001

Respirometry Plus, LLC
Fond Du Lac, WI 800-328-7518

Reyco Systems Inc
Caldwell, ID 208-795-5700

Robar International Inc
Milwaukee, WI 800-279-7750

Rubbermaid Commercial Products
Pottsville, PA 800-233-0314

Salvajor Co
Kansas City, MO 800-SAL-AJOR

Schleicher & Company of America
Sanford, NC 800-775-7570

Schloss Engineered Equipment
Aurora, CO 303-695-4500

Scienco Systems
Saint Louis, MO 314-621-2536

Seating Concepts Inc
Rockdale, IL 800-421-2036

Serfilco
Northbrook, IL 800-323-5431

Shepard Brothers Co
La Habra, CA 800-645-3594

SP Industries
Hopkins, MI 800-592-5959

Star Filters
Timmonsville, SC 800-845-5381

Tema Systems Inc
Cincinnati, OH 513-792-2840

Terminix
Flushing, NY 866-319-6528

Therm-Tec Inc
Sherwood, OR 800-292-9163

TLB Corporation
Ellicott, MD 410-773-9443

U B KLEM Furniture Co Inc
St Anthony, IN 800-264-1995

Universal Handling Equipment
Hamilton, ON 877-843-1122

US Filter
Palm Desert, CA 760-340-0098

US Filter Dewatering Systems
Holland, MI 800-245-3006

V-Ram Solids
Albert Lea, MN 888-373-3996

Vaughan Co Inc
Montesano, WA 888-249-2467

Vescom America
Henderson, NC 252-436-9067

Waste Away Systems
Newark, OH 800-223-4741

Wastequip Inc
Charlotte, NC 704-366-7140

Waterlink/Sanborn Technologies
Canton, OH 800-343-3381

Waymar Industries
Burnsville, MN 888-474-1112

Wayne Engineering
Cedar Falls, IA 319-266-1721

White Mop Wringer Company
Tampa, FL 800-237-7582

WITT Industries Inc
Mason, OH 800-543-7417

Worcester Industrial Products
Worcester, MA 800-533-5711

Zeeco Inc
Broken Arrow, OK 918-258-8551

Wastewater Treatment Systems

Anaerobic & Aerobic

ADI Systems Inc
Fredericton, NB 800-561-2831

AERTEC
North Andover, MA 978-475-6385

Biothane Corporation
Camden, NJ 856-541-3500

FRC Systems International
Roswell, GA 770-534-3681

GW&E Global Water & Energy
Austin, TX 512-697-1930

Hach Co.
Loveland, CO 800-227-4224

M-Vac Systems Inc
  Bluffdale, UT 801-523-3962
Oakite Products
  New Providence, NJ 800-526-4473
Radiant Industrial Solutions
  Houston, TX 713-972-0196
SPX Flow Inc
  Rochester, NY...................585-436-5550
World Water Works
  Oklahoma City, OK 800-607-7973

Wipers

Disposable

Absorbco
  Walterboro, SC 888-335-6439
Akron Cotton Products
  Akron, OH.......................800-899-7173
Atlantic Mills
  Lakewood, NJ...................800-242-7374
Blue Ridge Converting
  Asheville, NC 800-438-3893

Bro-Tex Inc
  St Paul, MN......................800-328-2282
Casabar
  Morristown, NJ..................877-745-8700
CCP Industries, Inc.
  Cleveland, OH 800-321-2840
Coast Scientific
  Rancho Santa Fe, CA 800-445-1544
De Royal Textiles
  Camden, SC 800-845-1062
DPC
  Norristown, PA..................800-220-9473
Georgia Pacific
  Green Bay, WI...................920-435-8821
Goodman Wiper & Paper Co
  Auburn, ME 207-784-5779
ITW Dymon
  Olathe, KS.......................800-443-9536
Johnson International Materials
  Brownsville, TX.................956-541-6364
Lexidyne of Pennsylvania
  Pittsburgh, PA...................800-543-2233

Mainline Industries Inc
  Springfield, MA 800-527-7917
Mednik Wiping Materials Co
  St Louis, MO.....................800-325-7193
Mill Wiping Rags Inc
  Bronx, NY........................718-994-7100
Nosaj Disposables
  Paterson, NJ 800-631-3809
Nu-Towel Co
  Kansas City, MO.................800-800-7247
Packaging Distribution Svc
  Des Moines, IA...................515-243-3156
Rockline Industries
  Sheboygan, WI...................800-558-7790
SCA Hygiene Paper
  San Ramon, CA 800-992-8675
Textile Products Company
  Anaheim, CA 714-761-0401
United Textile Distribution
  Garner, NC 800-262-7624
Wipeco Inc
  Hillside, IL 708-544-7247

Transportation & Storage

Automated Guided Vehicles

John Bean Technologies Corp
Chalfont, PA 888-362-3622

Beer Keg Movers

Powered

Ultra Lift Corp
San Jose, CA 800-346-3057

Box Cutters

Charles Beck Machine Corporation
King of Prussia, PA 610-265-0500
Garvey Products
West Chester, OH 800-543-1908
Handy Roll Company
San Marcos, CA 760-471-6214
Listo Pencil Corp
Alameda, CA 800-547-8648
Safe-T-Cut Inc
Monson, MA 413-267-9984

Carts

Hand

Alliance Products LLC
Murfreesboro, TN 800-522-3973
Amco Metals Indl
City Of Industry, CA 626-855-2550
ARC Specialties
Valencia, CA 661-775-8500
Art Wire Works Co
Chicago, IL 708-458-3993
Atlas Equipment Company
Kansas City, MO 800-842-9188
Baking Machines
Livermore, CA 925-449-3369
Barrette Outdoor Living
Cleveland, OH 800-336-2383
Bennett Manufacturing Company
Alden, NY 800-345-2142
Bessco Tube Bending & Pipe Fabricating
Thornton, IL 800-337-3977
Bmh Equipment Inc
Sacramento, CA 800-350-8828
Burgess Enterprises, Inc
Renton, WA 800-927-3286
C Nelson Mfg Co
Oak Harbor, OH 800-922-7339
C R Daniels Inc
Ellicott City, MD 800-933-2638
Caddy Corporation of America
Bridgeport, NJ 856-467-4222
California Caster & Handtruck
San Francisco, CA 800-950-8750
Cambro Manufacturing Co
Huntington Beach, CA 800-833-3003
Cannon Equipment Company
Cannon Falls, MN 800-825-8501
Carlisle Food Svc Products Inc
Oklahoma City, OK 800-654-8210
Clark Caster Company
Cave In Rock, IL 800-538-0765
Conveyance Technologies LLC
Cleveland, OH 800-701-2278
Corsair Display Systems
Canandaigua, NY 800-347-5245
Custom Diamond Intl.
Laval, QC 800-326-5926
Decoren Equipment
Willowbrook, IL 708-789-3367
Dubuque Steel Products Co
Dubuque, IA 563-556-6288
Dutro Co
Logan, UT 866-388-7660
EPCO
Murfreesboro, TN 800-251-3398
Equipment Design & Fabrication
Charlotte, NC 800-949-0165
Exel
Lincolnton, NC 704-735-6535
Fabricated Components Inc
Stroudsburg, PA 800-233-8163

Fetco
Lake Zurich, IL 800-338-2699
Forbes Industries
Ontario, CA 909-923-4549
Galbreath LLC
Winamac, IN 574-946-6631
Galley
Jupiter, FL 800-537-2772
Gillis Associated Industries
Prospect Heights, IL 847-541-6500
Glowmaster Corporation
Clifton, NJ 800-272-7008
Hodges
Vienna, IL 800-444-0011
Houston Wire Works, Inc.
South Houston, TX 800-468-9477
Item Products
Houston, TX 800-333-4932
Jesco Industries
Litchfield, MI 800-455-0019
KEMCO
Wareham, MA 800-231-5955
Key Material Handling Inc
Simi Valley, CA 800-539-7225
Lakeside Manufacturing Inc
Milwaukee, WI 888-558-8565
Lambertson Industries Inc
Sparks, NV 800-548-3324
Leggett & Platt Storage
Vernon Hills, IL 847-816-6246
Line-Master Products
Cocolalla, ID 208-265-4743
Linett Company
Blawnox, PA 800-565-2165
Load King Mfg
Jacksonville, FL 800-531-4975
M & E Mfg Co Inc
Kingston, NY 845-331-2110
Metal Equipment Company
Cleveland, OH 800-700-6326
Metal Master Sales Corp
Glendale Heights, IL 800-488-8729
Metro Corporation
Wilkes Barre, PA 800-992-1776
Mid-States Mfg & Engr Co Inc
Milton, IA 800-346-1792
Midwest Aircraft Products Co
Lexington, OH 419-884-2164
Miller Metal Fabrication
Bridgeville, DE 302-337-2291
MIT Poly-Cart Corp
New York, NY 800-234-7659
Moseley Realty LLC
Franklin, MA 800-667-3539
Mosshaim Innovations
Jacksonville, FL 888-995-7775
New Age Industrial
Norton, KS 800-255-0104
Newell Brands
Atlanta, GA
Nexel Industries Inc
Port Washington, NY 800-245-6682
Normandie Metal Fabricators
Port Washington, NY 800-221-2398
Norris Products Corp   oration
Cincinnati, OH 877-543-2278
Nu-Star Inc
Shakopee, MN 800-800-9274
Omicron Steel Products Company
Jamaica, NY 718-805-3400
Ortmayer Materials Handling
Brooklyn, NY 718-875-7995
Palmer Snyder
Brookfield, WI 800-762-0415
Piper Products Inc
Wausau, WI 800-544-3057
Polar Beer Systems
Sun City, CA 951-928-8174
Princeton Shelving
Cedar Rapids, IA 319-369-0355
Pucel Enterprises Inc
Cleveland, OH 800-336-4986
Reelcraft Industries Inc
Columbia City, IN 800-444-3134
Royce Rolls Ringer Co
Grand Rapids, MI 800-253-9638

Schlueter Company
Janesville, WI 800-359-1700
Shammi Industries
Corona, CA 800-417-9260
Sharpsville Container Corp
Sharpsville, PA 800-645-1248
Shouldice Brothers SheetMetal
Battle Creek, MI 269-962-5579
Solve Needs International
White Lake, MI 800-783-2462
Super Sturdy
Weldon, NC 800-253-4833
Superior Products Company
Saint Paul, MN 800-328-9800
Technibilt/Cari-All
Newton, NC 800-233-3972
Travelon
Elk Grove Vlg, IL 800-537-5544
Traycon Manufacturing Co
Carlstadt, NJ 201-939-5555
Tri-Boro Shelving & Partition
Farmville, VA 800-633-3070
Westfield Sheet Metal Works
Kenilworth, NJ 908-276-5500
White Mop Wringer Company
Tampa, FL 800-237-7582
Wilder Manufacturing Company
Port Jervis, NY 800-832-1319

Utility

Amco Metals Indl
City Of Industry, CA 626-855-2550
Antrim Manufacturing Inc
Brookfield, WI 262-781-6860
ARC Specialties
Valencia, CA 661-775-8500
Bmh Equipment Inc
Sacramento, CA 800-350-8828
Caddy Corporation of America
Bridgeport, NJ 856-467-4222
Cannon Equipment Company
Cannon Falls, MN 800-825-8501
Continental Commercial Products
Bridgeton, MO 800-325-1051
Duke Manufacturing Co
St Louis, MO 800-735-3853
Food Warming Equipment Co
Crystal Lake, IL 800-222-4393
Galley
Jupiter, FL 800-537-2772
Hodge Manufacturing Company
Springfield, MA 800-262-4634
Hot Food Boxes
Mooresville, IN 800-733-8073
InterMetro Industries
Wilkes-Barre, PA 570-825-2741
Lakeside Manufacturing Inc
Milwaukee, WI 888-558-8565
Leggett & Platt Storage
Vernon Hills, IL 847-816-6246
Linett Company
Blawnox, PA 800-565-2165
Princeton Shelving
Cedar Rapids, IA 319-369-0355
Technibilt/Cari-All
Newton, NC 800-233-3972

Casters

Albion Industries Inc
Albion, MI 800-835-8911
Atlas Equipment Company
Kansas City, MO 800-842-9188
Beacon Specialties
New York, NY 800-221-9405
Berlon Industries
Hustisford, WI 800-899-3580
Bmh Equipment Inc
Sacramento, CA 800-350-8828
California Caster & Handtruck
San Francisco, CA 800-950-8750
Clark Caster Company
Cave In Rock, IL 800-538-0765
Colson Caster Corp
Jonesboro, AR 800-643-5515

Component Hardware Group Inc
  Lakewood, NJ.....................800-526-3694
Darcor Casters
  Toronto, ON 800-387-7206
Faultless Caster
  Evansville, IN 800-322-7359
FFR Merchandising Inc
  Twinsburg, OH 800-422-2547
Hamilton Caster
  Hamilton, OH 888-699-7164
Jarvis Caster Company
  Jackson, TN 800-995-9876
Jilson Group
  Lodi, NJ 800-969-5400
Lakeside Manufacturing Inc
  Milwaukee, WI 888-558-8565
LPI Imports
  Chicago, IL 877-389-6563
Metro Corporation
  Wilkes Barre, PA..................800-992-1776
Mid-State Metal Casting & Mfg
  Fresno, CA 559-445-1974
Monarch-McLaren
  Weston, ON 416-741-9675
PAR-Kan
  Silver Lake, IN 800-291-5487
Roll Rite Corp
  Hayward, CA 800-345-9305
Solve Needs International
  White Lake, MI....................800-783-2462
Standex International Corp.
  Salem, NH. 603-893-9701
Tente Casters Inc
  Hebron, KY 800-783-2470

Clutches & Brakes

Industrial

Warner Electric Inc
  South Beloit, IL 800-234-3369

Cordage, Rope & Twine

A&A Line & Wire Corporation
  Flushing, NY......................800-886-2657
Barbour Threads
  Anniston, AL 256-237-9461
Caristrap International
  Laval, QC 800-361-9466
Consolidated Thread Mills, Inc.
  Fall River, MA 508-672-0032
Crown Industries
  East Orange, NJ 877-747-2457
Fitec International Inc
  Memphis, TN 800-332-6387
Fulton-Denver Co
  Denver, CO........................800-521-1414
James Thompson
  New York, NY.....................212-686-5306
January & Wood Company
  Maysville, KY......................606-564-3301
John E. Ruggles & Company
  New Bedford, MA 508-992-9766
Pensacola Rope Company
  Slidell, LA. 850-968-9760
Rose City Awning Co
  Portland, OR 800-446-4104
Terkelsen Machine Company
  Hyannis, MA. 508-775-6229
US Line Company
  Westfield, MA.....................413-562-3629
Woodstock Line Co
  Putnam, CT. 860-928-6557

Drums

Acra Electric Corporation
  Tulsa, OK 800-223-4328
Bergen Barrel & Drum Company
  Kearny, NJ. 201-998-3500
Centennial Moldings
  Hastings, NE......................888-883-2189
Containair Packaging Corporation
  Paterson, NJ 888-276-6500
Dubuque Steel Products Co
  Dubuque, IA 563-556-6288
Greenfield Packaging
  White Plains, NY 914-993-0233
Greif Inc
  Delaware, OH 740-549-6000
Independent Stave Co
  Lebanon, MO 417-588-4151

Jupiter Mills Corporation
  Roslyn, NY.........................800-853-5121
Lima Barrel & Drum Company
  Lima, OH 419-224-8916
M O Industries Inc
  Whippany, NJ 973-386-9228
Munson Machinery Co
  Utica, NY 800-944-6644
Myers Container
  Hayward, CA 510-785-8235
Process Solutions
  Riviera Beach, FL 561-840-0050
Pucel Enterprises Inc
  Cleveland, OH 800-336-4986
Remcon Plastics Inc
  Reading, PA 800-360-3636
RMI-C/Rotonics Manufacturing
  Bensenville, IL 630-773-9510
Sharpsville Container Corp
  Sharpsville, PA 800-645-1248
Sirco Systems
  Birmingham, AL...................205-731-7800
Trilla Steel Drum Corporation
  Chicago, IL........................773-847-7588

Food Storage Supplies

Abel Manufacturing Co
  Appleton, WI 920-734-4443
Accent Store Fixtures
  Kenosha, WI 800-545-1144
Acrison Inc
  Moonachie, NJ 800-422-4266
Advance Energy Technologies
  Halfmoon, NY. 800-724-0198
Aero Tec Laboratories/ATL
  Ramsey, NJ 800-526-5330
AFGO Mechanical Svc Inc
  Astoria, NY. 800-438-2346
Alliance Products LLC
  Murfreesboro, TN..................800-522-3973
Allied Engineering
  North Vancouver, BC 877-929-1214
Althor Products
  Bethel, CT. 800-688-2693
Amco Metals Indl
  City Of Industry, CA. 626-855-2550
Anderson-Crane Company
  Minneapolis, MN 800-314-2747
Apache Stainless Equipment
  Beaver Dam, WI....................800-444-0398
ARC Specialties
  Valencia, CA.......................661-775-8500
Avalon Manufacturer
  Corona, CA 800-676-3040
Barker Company
  Keosauqua, IA 319-293-3777
Barker Wire
  Keosauqua, IA 319-293-3176
Bennett Manufacturing Company
  Alden, NY..........................800-345-2142
Bergen Barrel & Drum Company
  Kearny, NJ.........................201-998-3500
Bertels Can Company
  Belcamp, MD 410-272-0090
Bowers Process Equipment
  Stratford, ON. 800-567-3223
Brenner Tank LLC
  Fond Du Lac, WI 800-558-9750
Brisker Dry Food Crisper
  Oldsmar, FL 800-356-9080
Buckhorn Canada
  Brampton, ON. 800-461-7579
Buckhorn Inc
  Milford, OH 800-543-4454
Bulk Pack
  Monroe, LA........................800-498-4215
C Nelson Mfg Co
  Oak Harbor, OH 800-922-7339
Cal-Mil Plastic Products Inc
  Oceanside, CA 800-321-9069
Cambro Manufacturing Co
  Huntington Beach, CA.............800-833-3003
Cardinal Packaging
  Evansville, IN......................800-343-1295
Carlisle Food Svc Products Inc
  Oklahoma City, OK 800-654-8210
Carter-Hoffmann LLC
  Mundelein, IL 800-323-9793
Ccw Products
  Arvada, CO 303-427-9663
Central Fabricators Inc
  Cincinnati, OH 800-909-8265

Chem-Tainer Industries Inc
  West Babylon, NY 800-275-2436
Chem-Tainer Industries Inc
  West Babylon, NY 800-938-8896
Clayton & Lambert Manufacturing
  Buckner, KY 800-626-5819
Columbian TecTank
  Parsons, KS........................800-421-2788
Commercial Kitchen Co
  Los Angeles, CA....................323-732-2291
Containair Packaging Corporation
  Paterson, NJ 888-276-6500
Containment Technology
  St Gabriel, LA......................800-388-2467
Continental Commercial Products
  Bridgeton, MO 800-325-1051
Continental-Fremont
  Tiffin, OH 419-448-4045
Conwed Global Netting Sltns
  Roanoke, VA 800-368-3610
Cozzini Inc
  Algona, IA 888-295-1116
Cramer Products
  New York, NY......................212-645-2368
Cres Cor
  Mentor, OH 877-273-7267
Crown Custom Metal Spinning
  Concord, ON 800-750-1924
Cruvinet Winebar Co LLC
  Sparks, NV 800-278-8463
Culinary Depot
  Monsey, NY 888-845-8200
Custom Diamond Intl.
  Laval, QC 800-326-5926
Custom Metal Crafts
  Springfield, MO 417-862-9324
Custom Systems Integration Co
  Carlsbad, CA.......................760-635-1099
Den Mar Corp
  North Dartmouth, MA 508-999-3295
Denstor Mobile Storage Systems
  Walker, MI 800-234-7477
Design Plastics Inc
  Omaha, NE 800-491-0786
Despro Manufacturing
  Cedar Grove, NJ 800-292-9906
Dubuque Steel Products Co
  Dubuque, IA 563-556-6288
Duke Manufacturing Co
  St Louis, MO. 800-735-3853
E-Z Shelving Systems Inc
  Shawnee, KS. 800-353-1331
Easyup Storage Systems
  Tukwila, WA 800-426-9234
Eaton Sales & Service
  Denver, CO.........................800-208-2657
Edwards Fiberglass
  Sedalia, MO 660-826-3915
Eldorado Miranda Manufacturing Company
  Largo, FL 800-330-0708
Electrol Specialties Co
  South Beloit, IL 815-389-2291
Eliason Corp
  Portage, MI 800-828-3655
Ellett Industries
  Port Coquitlam, BC. 604-941-8211
Enerfab Inc.
  Cincinnati, OH 513-641-0500
Engineered Products Corp
  Greenville, SC. 800-868-0145
EPCO
  Murfreesboro, TN..................800-251-3398
Epic Products
  Santa Ana, CA 800-548-9791
ES Robbins Corp
  Muscle Shoals, AL 800-633-3325
Fab-X/Metals
  Washington, NC 800-677-3229
Fabricated Components Inc
  Stroudsburg, PA 800-233-8163
Faribault Manufacturing Co
  Faribault, MN 800-447-6043
Fato Industries
  Kankakee, IL 815-932-3015
Faubion Central States Tank Company
  Shawnee Mission, KS...............800-450-8265
Federal Industries
  Belleville, WI.......................800-356-4206
First Plastics Co Inc
  Leominster, MA 978-840-6908
Flexible Material Handling
  Suwanee, GA 800-669-1501

Flow of Solids
Westford, MA 978-392-0300
Forbes Industries
Ontario, CA 909-923-4549
FreesTech
Sinking Spring, PA 717-560-7560
G.F. Frank & Sons
Fairfield, OH 513-870-9075
Gates Manufacturing Company
Saint Louis, MO 800-237-9226
General Industries Inc
Goldsboro, NC 888-735-2882
Gillis Associated Industries
Prospect Heights, IL 847-541-6500
Grayline Housewares Inc
Columbus, OH 800-222-7388
H S Inc
Oklahoma City, OK 800-238-1240
Hall-Woolford Wood Tank Co Inc
Philadelphia, PA 215-329-9022
Harmar
Sarasota, FL 800-833-0478
Hedstrom Corporation
Ashland, OH 700-765-9665
Hewitt Manufacturing Co
Waldron, IN 765-525-9829
Hodges
Vienna, IL 800-444-0011
Hoover Materials Handling Group
Houston, TX 800-844-8683
Houston Wire Works, Inc.
South Houston, TX 800-468-9477
Howard Fabrication
City of Industry, CA 626-961-0114
Hughes Co
Columbus, WI 866-535-9303
IMC Teddy Food Service Equipment
Amityville, NY 800-221-5644
Industrial Air Conditioning Systems
Chicago, IL .773-486-4236
International Machinery Xchnge
Deerfield, WI 800-279-0191
IPL Plastics
Edmundston, NB. 800-739-9595
Irby
Rocky Mount, NC 252-442-0154
Item Products
Houston, TX 800-333-4932
J.H. Carr & Sons
Seattle, WA .800-523-8842
Jack Stack
Inwood, NY. 800-999-9840
Jenike & Johanson Inc
Tyngsboro, MA. 978-649-3300
Jesco Industries
Litchfield, MI 800-455-0019
JH Display & Fixture
Greenwood, IN 317-888-0631
K & I Creative Plastics & Wood
Jacksonville, FL 904-387-0438
Kason
Lewis Center, OH 740-549-2100
Kedco Wine Storage Systems
Farmingdale, NY 800-654-9988
KHM Plastics Inc
Gurnee, IL 847-249-4910
Kisco Manufacturing
Port Alberni, BC 604-823-7456
Kold-Hold
Edgefield, SC 803-637-3166
LA Rosa Refrigeration & Equip
Detroit, MI .800-527-6723
Lakeside Manufacturing Inc
Milwaukee, WI 888-558-8565
Langer Manufacturing Company
Cedar Rapids, IA. 800-728-6445
Langsenkamp Manufacturing
Indianapolis, IN 877-585-1950
Leggett & Platt Storage
Vernon Hills, IL 847-816-6246
Liberty Machine Company
York, PA 800-745-8152
Lodi Metal Tech
Lodi, CA 800-359-5999
Loyal Manufacturing
Indianapolis, IN 317-359-3185
LPI Imports
Chicago, IL .877-389-6563
Luce Corp
Hamden, CT 800-344-6966
Lyon LLC
Montgomery, IL 630-892-8941

M & E Mfg Co Inc
Kingston, NY 845-331-2110
Machine Ice Co
Houston, TX 800-423-8822
Madix Inc
Terrell, TX. .800-776-2349
Madsen Wire Products Inc
Orland, IN 260-829-6561
Marineland Commercial Aquariums
Blacksburg, VA 800-322-1266
Material Storage Systems
Gadsden, AL 877-543-2467
McMillin Manufacturing Corporation
Los Angeles, CA 323-268-1900
Melville Plastics
Haw River, NC 336-578-5800
Metal Equipment Company
Cleveland, OH 800-700-6326
Metal Master Sales Corp
Glendale Heights, IL. 800-488-8729
Metaline Products Co Inc
South Amboy, NJ 732-721-1373
Metro Corporation
Wilkes Barre, PA 800-992-1776
Meyer Machine & Garroutte Products
San Antonio, TX 210-736-1811
Michiana Box & Crate
Niles, MI 800-677-6372
Midwest Aircraft Products Co
Lexington, OH 419-884-2164
Miller Metal Fabrication
Bridgeville, DE 302-337-2291
MultiFab Plastics
Boston, MA. 888-293-5754
Myers Container
Hayward, CA 510-785-8235
Nalge Process Technologies Group
Rochester, NY. 585-586-8800
Nelipak
Phoenix, AZ 602-269-7648
New Age Industrial
Norton, KS .800-255-0104
Newell Brands
Atlanta, GA
Nexel Industries Inc
Port Washington, NY 800-245-6682
Normandie Metal Fabricators
Port Washington, NY 800-221-2398
NST Metals
Louisville, KY 502-584-5846
Oak Barrel Winecraft
Berkeley, CA. 510-849-0400
Omega Industries
St Louis, MO. 314-961-1668
Omicron Steel Products Company
Jamaica, NY 718-805-3400
Overhead Conveyor Co
Ferndale, MI 800-396-2554
Pallet One Inc
Bartow, FL .800-771-1148
Paltier
Michigan City, IN 800-348-3201
Paul Mueller Co Inc
Springfield, MO 800-683-5537
PBC
Mahwah, NJ 800-514-2739
Peterboro Basket Co
Peterborough, NH. 603-924-3861
Peterson Manufacturing Company
Plainfield, IL 800-547-8995
Piper Products Inc
Wausau, WI. 800-544-3057
Plastic Supply Inc
Londonderry, NH 800-752-7759
Plastilite Corporation
Omaha, NE .800-228-9506
Plastocon
Oconomowoc, WI 800-966-0103
Polar Ware Company
Sheboygan, WI 800-237-3655
Precision
Miami, FL 800-762-7565
Process Solutions
Riviera Beach, FL 561-840-0050
Prolon
Port Gibson, MS 888-480-9828
Pruitt's Packaging Services
Grand Rapids, MI 800-878-0553
QBD Modular Systems
Santa Clara, CA 800-663-3005
RAS Process Equipment Inc
Trenton, NJ .609-371-1220

Ridg-U-Rak
North East, PA. 866-479-7225
Rose City Awning Co
Portland, OR 800-446-4104
Royal Display Corporation
Middletown, CT 800-569-1295
Royce Corp
Glendale, AZ. 602-256-0006
S.S.I. Schaefer System International Limited
Brampton, ON 905-458-5399
Saeplast Canada
St John, NB. 800-567-3966
Scheb International
North Barrington, IL. 847-381-2573
Scherping Systems
Winsted, MN 320-485-4401
Schiefer Packaging Corporation
Syracuse, NY 315-422-0615
Schlueter Company
Janesville, WI 800-359-1700
Seattle Plastics
Seattle, WA .800-441-0679
Sefi Fabricators Inc
Amityville, NY. 631-842-2200
Shammi Industries
Corona, CA .800-417-9260
Shelley Cabinet Company
Shelley, ID. .208-357-3700
Silver King Refrigeration Inc
Minneapolis, MN 800-328-3329
Sims Machinery Co Inc
Lanett, AL. .334-576-2101
Southern Ag Co Inc
Blakely, GA. 229-723-4262
Spartan Showcase
Union, MO .800-325-0775
Specific Mechanical Systems
Victoria, BC. 250-652-2111
SPG International
Covington, GA 877-503-4774
SSW Holding Co Inc
Elizabethtown, KY 270-769-5526
St. Louis Stainless Service
St Louis, MO. 800-735-3853
Stainless Steel Fabricators
Tyler, TX. 903-595-6625
Stearnswood Inc
Hutchinson, MN 800-657-0144
Steel City Corporation
Youngstown, OH 800-321-0350
Steelmaster Material Handling
Marietta, GA 800-875-9900
Stock America Inc
Grafton, WI 262-375-4100
Storage Unlimited
Nixa, MO 800-478-6642
Stryco Wire Products
North York, ON. 416-663-7000
Super Sturdy
Weldon, NC. 800-253-4833
Superior Products Company
Saint Paul, MN 800-328-9800
Supreme Metal
Alpharetta, GA 800-645-2526
Tag-Trade Associated Group
Chicago, IL .800-621-8350
Teilhaber Manufacturing Corp
Broomfield, CO 800-358-7225
Tennsco Corp
Dickson, TN 800-251-8184
Thermal Bags By Ingrid Inc
Gilberts, IL .800-622-5560
Tosca Ltd
Green Bay, WI. 920-617-4000
Traex
Dane, WI. 800-356-8006
Triple-A Manufacturing Company
Toronto, ON 800-786-2238
Tupperware Brands Corporation
Orlando, FL. 800-366-3800
United States Systems Inc
Kansas City, KS 888-281-2454
Universal Stainless
Aurora, CO .800-223-8332
Universal Stainless & Alloy
Titusville, PA 800-295-1909
Upham & Walsh Lumber
Hoffman Estates, IL 847-519-1010
Valad Electric Heating Corporation
Tarrytown, NY 914-631-4927
Vermillion Flooring
Springfield, MO 417-862-3785

Viatec
  Victoria, BC 800-942-4702
Vollrath Co LLC
  Sheboygan, WI 800-624-2051
Wag Industries
  Skokie, IL 800-621-3305
Walker Stainless Equipment Co
  New Lisbon, WI 608-562-7500
Weiss Sheet Metal Inc
  Avon, MA 508-583-8300
Welbilt Corporation
  Stamford, CT....................203-325-8300
Welbilt Inc.
  New Port Richey, FL.............877-375-9300
Westfield Sheet Metal Works
  Kenilworth, NJ 908-276-5500
Wilder Manufacturing Company
  Port Jervis, NY 800-832-1319
Wine Chillers of California
  Santa Ana, CA 800-331-4274
Wire Products Mfg
  Merrill, WI 715-536-7884
Woerner Wire Works
  Omaha, NE 402-451-5414
WR Key
  Scarborough, ON 416-291-6246
Yorkraft
  York, PA 800-872-2044
Zero Manufacturing Inc
  North Salt Lake, UT 800-959-5050

Hoists & Lifting Equipment

A C Horn & Co Sheet Metal
  Dallas, TX.......................800-657-6155
A-Z Factory Supply
  Schiller Park, IL 800-323-4511
Abell-Howe Crane
  Amherst, NY.....................800-888-0985
Ace Engineering Company
  Fort Worth, TX 800-431-4223
Advance Lifts Inc
  St Charles, IL 800-843-3625
Air Technical Industries
  Mentor, OH 888-857-6265
Airfloat LLC
  Decatur, IL 800-888-0018
American Crane & Equip Corp
  Douglassville, PA 610-385-6061
American Lifts
  Guthrie, OK.....................877-360-6777
American Solving Inc.
  Brook Park, OH 800-822-2285
AMF CANADA
  Sherbrooke, QC 800-255-3869
Anchor Crane & Hoist Service Company
  Houston, TX 800-835-2223
Anderson-Crane Company
  Minneapolis, MN 800-314-2747
ANVER Corporation
  Hudson, MA 800-654-3500
Anver Corporation
  Hudson, MA 800-654-3500
Apache Stainless Equipment
  Beaver Dam, WI 800-444-0398
Atlas Equipment Company
  Kansas City, MO 800-842-9188
Autoquip Corp
  Guthrie, OK.....................877-360-6777
Baking Machines
  Livermore, CA 925-449-3369
Ballymore Company
  West Chester, PA.................610-696-3250
Basiloid Products Corp
  Elnora, IN 866-692-5511
Benko Products
  Sheffield Vlg, OH................440-934-2180
BEVCO
  Canada, BC 800-663-0090
Bishamon Industry Corp
  Ontario, CA.....................800-358-8833
Bmh Equipment Inc
  Sacramento, CA 800-350-8828
Bolzoni Auramo
  Homewood, IL 800-358-5438
Bradley Lifting
  York, PA 717-848-3121
Buffalo Technologies Corporation
  Buffalo, NY.....................800-332-2419
Burns Industries
  Line Lexington, PA...............800-223-6430
Bushman Equipment Inc
  Menomonee Falls, WI............800-338-7810

C.J. Machine
  Fridley, MN.....................763-767-4630
Caldwell Group
  Rockford, IL 800-628-4263
Century Crane & Hoist
  Dravosburg, PA..................888-601-8801
Chester Hoist
  Lisbon, OH 800-424-7248
Cleasby Manufacturing Co
  San Francisco, CA 800-253-2729
Columbus McKinnon Corporation
  Getzville, NY 800-888-0985
Commercial Manufacturing
  Fresno, CA 559-237-1855
Conveyance Technologies LLC
  Cleveland, OH 800-701-2278
Conveyor Components Co
  Croswell, MI 800-552-3337
Corn States Metal Fabricators
  West Des Moines, IA 515-225-7961
Crown Equipment Corp.
  New Bremen, OH 419-629-2311
Currie Machinery Co
  Santa Clara, CA 408-727-0422
Custom Conveyor & Supply Corp.
  Racine, WI 262-634-4920
Custom Metal Design Inc
  Oakland, FL 800-334-1777
Delta Machine & Maufacturing
  St Rose, LA......................504-949-8304
Demag Cranes & Components Corp
  Cleveland, OH 440-248-2400
Deshazo Crane Company
  Alabaster, AL 205-664-2006
Downs Crane & Hoist Co Inc
  Los Angeles, CA..................800-748-5994
Duplex Mill & Mfg Co
  Springfield, OH..................937-325-5555
Electro Lift Inc
  Clifton, NJ 973-471-0204
En-Hanced Products Inc
  Westerville, OH..................800-783-7400
Equipment Outlet
  Meridian, ID 208-887-1472
Frazier & Son
  Conroe, TX 800-365-5438
GEM Equipment Of Oregon Inc
  Woodburn, OR 503-982-9902
Gorbel Inc
  Victor, NY 585-924-6262
Gough-Econ Inc
  Charlotte, NC 800-204-6844
Grain Machinery Mfg Corp
  Miami, FL 305-620-2525
Harrington Hoists Inc
  Manheim, PA 800-233-3010
Hayes & Stolz Indl Mfg LTD
  Fort Worth, TX 800-725-7272
Howes S Co Inc
  Silver Creek, NY.................888-255-2611
Industrial Hoist Service
  Angleton, TX 800-766-7077
Innovation Moving Systems
  Oostburg, WI....................800-619-0625
Joyce Dayton Corp
  Moraine, OH 800-523-5204
Keenline Conveyor Systems
  Omro, WI 920-685-0365
Key Material Handling Inc
  Simi Valley, CA..................800-539-7225
Knight Ind
  Auburn Hills, MI 248-377-4950
Komatsu Forklift USA
  Rolling Meadows, IL..............847-437-5800
KWS Manufacturing Co LTD
  Burleson, TX....................800-543-6558
Landoo Corporation
  Horsham, PA....................785-562-5381
Lift Rite
  Mississauga, ON.................905-456-2603
Liftomatic Material Handling
  Buffalo Grove, IL.................800-837-6540
Linde Material Handling
  Summerville, SC..................843-871-0312
Matot - Commercial GradeLift Solutions
  Bellwood, IL 800-369-1070
Meyer Machine & Garroutte Products
  San Antonio, TX 210-736-1811
NACCO Materials HandlingGroup
  Fairview, OR.....................503-721-6205
O'Brien Installations
  Ontario, CA.....................905-336-8245

OTP Industrial Solutions
  Terre Haute, IN 860-953-7632
Pa R Systems Inc
  St Paul, MN......................800-464-1320
Parkson Corp
  Fort Lauderdale, FL 908-464-0700
Pucel Enterprises Inc
  Cleveland, OH 800-336-4986
Quality Corporation
  Denver, CO 800-383-3018
R.G Stephens Engineering
  Long Beach, CA..................800-499-3001
Ratcliff Hoist Company
  San Carlos, CA 650-595-3840
Raymond Corp
  Greene, NY 800-235-7200
Remstar International
  Westbrook, ME..................800-639-5805
Richards Industries Systems
  West Caldwell, NJ................973-575-7480
Sackett Systems
  Bensenville, IL 800-323-8332
Saturn Overhead Equipment
  Somerset, NJ 800-631-4473
Screw Conveyor Corp
  Hammond, IN 219-931-1450
Shepard Niles Parts
  Montour Falls, NY 800-727-8774
Sidney Manufacturing Co
  Sidney, OH 800-482-3535
SIT Indeva Inc
  Charlotte, NC 704-357-8811
Smetco
  Aurora, OR 800-253-5400
Solve Needs International
  White Lake, MI...................800-783-2462
Southern Ag Co Inc
  Blakely, GA......................229-723-4262
Southworth Products Corp
  Falmouth, ME...................800-743-1000
Spanco Crane & Monorail Systems
  Morgantown, PA.................800-869-2080
Sperling Industries
  Omaha, NE 800-647-5062
Stertil Alm Corp
  Streator, IL 800-544-5438
TC/American Monorail
  Saint Michael, MN 763-497-7000
Theimeg
  Sharpsville, PA 724-962-3571
Toter Inc
  Statesville, NC 800-772-0071
Unidex
  Warsaw, NY 800-724-1302
Unimove LLC
  Palmerton, PA 610-826-7855
UniTrak Corporation
  Port Hope, ON 866-883-5749
Valley Craft Inc
  Lake City, MN 800-328-1480
Vertical Systems Intl
  Lakeside Park, KY 859-485-9650
Ward Ironworks
  Welland, ON 888-441-9273
Wastequip Inc
  Charlotte, NC 704-366-7140
Weigh Right Automatic Scale Co
  Joliet, IL 800-571-0249
Whit-Log Trailers Inc
  Wilbur, OR 800-452-1234
Yargus Manufacturing Inc
  Marshall, IL 217-826-8059
Zenar Corp
  Oak Creek, WI 414-764-1800
Zimmerman Handling Systems
  Madison Heights, MI 800-347-7047

Material Handling & Distribution Equipment

A C Horn & Co Sheet Metal
  Dallas, TX.......................800-657-6155
A T Ferrell Co Inc
  Bluffton, IN.....................800-248-8318
A-Z Factory Supply
  Schiller Park, IL 800-323-4511
A.K. Robins
  Baltimore, MD 800-486-9656
A.M. Loveman Lumber & Box Company
  Nashville, TN 615-297-1397
AAMD
  Liverpool, NY 800-887-4167

Abel Manufacturing Co
Appleton, WI 920-734-4443
Abel Pumps
Sewickley, PA 412-741-3222
Abell-Howe Crane
Amherst, NY 800-888-0985
ACCO Systems
Warren, MI 800-342-2226
Accutek Packaging Equipment
Vista, CA 800-989-1828
Ace Engineering Company
Fort Worth, TX 800-431-4223
Ace Specialty Mfg Co Inc
Rosemead, CA 626-444-3867
ACLAUSA Inc
Cranberry Twp, PA 724-776-0099
ACO
Moore, OK 405-794-7662
Acrison Inc
Moonachie, NJ 800-422-4266
Action Engineering
Liburn, GA 800-228-4668
Adamation
Commerce, CA 800-383-8800
Advance Engineering Co
Canton, MI 800-497-6388
Advance Lifts Inc
St Charles, IL 800-843-3625
Advance Weight Systems Inc
Grafton, OH 440-926-3691
Advanced Detection Systems
Milwaukee, WI 414-672-0553
Advanced Uniflo Technologies
Wichita, KS 800-688-0400
Aerocon
Langhorne, PA 215-860-6056
Aerowerks
Mississauga, ON 888-774-1616
AFCO Manufacturing
Cincinnati, OH 800-747-7332
Air Technical Industries
Mentor, OH 888-857-6265
Airfloat LLC
Decatur, IL 800-888-0018
Albion Industries Inc
Albion, MI. 800-835-8911
All Power Inc
Sioux City, IA 712-258-0681
All Star Carts & Vehicles
Bay Shore, NY 800-831-3166
Allflex Packaging Products
Ambler, PA 800-448-2467
Alliance Industrial Corp
Lynchburg, VA 800-368-3556
Alliance Products LLC
Murfreesboro, TN 800-522-3973
Allied Uniking Corp Inc
Memphis, TN 901-365-7240
Alloy Products Corp
Waukesha, WI 800-236-6603
Amark Packaging Systems
Kansas City, MO. 816-965-9000
Amco Metals Indl
City Of Industry, CA. 626-855-2550
American Box Corporation
Lisbon, OH 330-424-8055
American Crane & Equip Corp
Douglassville, PA 610-385-6061
American Extrusion Intl
South Beloit, IL 815-624-6616
American Food Equipment Company
Hayward, CA 510-783-0255
American Lifts
Guthrie, OK. 877-360-6777
American Pallet Inc
Oakdale, CA 209-847-6122
American Solving Inc.
Brook Park, OH 800-822-2285
Ametek Technical & Industrial Products
Kent, OH. 215-256-6601
AMF CANADA
Sherbrooke, QC 800-255-3869
Ampco Pumps Co Inc
Milwaukee, WI 800-737-8671
Anchor Crane & Hoist Service Company
Houston, TX 800-835-2223
Anderson Machine Sales
Fort Lee, NJ
Anderson Tool & Engineering Company
Anderson, IN. 765-643-6691
Anderson-Crane Company
Minneapolis, MN 800-314-2747

ANDRITZ Inc
Muncy, PA. 704-943-4343
Ann Arbor Computer
Farmington Hills, MI 800-526-9322
Antrim Manufacturing Inc
Brookfield, WI 262-781-6860
ANVER Corporation
Hudson, MA 800-654-3500
Anver Corporation
Hudson, MA 800-654-3500
AP Dataweigh Inc
Cumming, GA 877-409-2562
Apache Stainless Equipment
Beaver Dam, WI 800-444-0398
Apollo Sheet Metal
Kennewick, WA 509-586-1104
Applied Chemical Technology
Florence, AL. 800-228-3217
ARC Specialties
Valencia, CA 661-775-8500
Arpac LP
Schiller Park, IL 847-678-9034
Art Wire Works Co
Chicago, IL 708-458-3993
Asgco Manufacturing Inc
Allentown, PA 800-344-4000
Ashworth Bros Inc
Winchester, VA 800-682-4594
Assembly Technology & Test
Livonia, MI 734-522-1900
Atlas Equipment Company
Kansas City, MO. 800-842-9188
Auto Pallets-Boxes
Lathrup Village, MI 800-875-2699
Automated Flexible Conveyors
Clifton, NJ 800-694-7271
Automated Production Systems Corporation
New Freedom, PA. 888-345-5377
Automatic Handling Int
Erie, MI. 734-847-0633
Automotion Inc
Oak Lawn, IL 708-229-3700
Autoquip Corp
Guthrie, OK. 877-360-6777
AZO Food
Memphis, TN 901-794-9480
Baking Machines
Livermore, CA 925-449-3369
Balemaster
Crown Point, IN 219-663-4525
Ballymore Company
West Chester, PA. 610-696-3250
Bamco Belting
Greenville, SC. 800-258-2358
Barrette Outdoor Living
Cleveland, OH 800-336-2383
Basiloid Products Corp
Elnora, IN 866-692-5511
Bay Area Pallet Company/IFCO Systems
Houston, TX 877-430-4326
Bayhead Products Corp.
Dover, NH. 800-229-4323
Bc Wood Products
Ashland, VA 804-798-9154
Bedford Enterprises Inc
Santa Maria, CA 800-242-8884
Beech Engineering
Ashland, OH 419-281-0894
Belco Packaging Systems
Monrovia, CA 800-833-1833
Bell Packaging Corporation
Marion, IN. 800-382-0153
Belt Technologies Inc
Agawam, MA 413-786-9922
Benko Products
Sheffield Vlg, OH. 440-934-2180
Bennett Box & Pallet Company
Winston, NC 800-334-8741
Bergen Barrel & Drum Company
Kearny, NJ. 201-998-3500
Berndorf Belt Technology USA
Gilberts, IL 800-393-8450
Bessco Tube Bending & Pipe Fabricating
Thornton, IL 800-337-3977
Best
Brunswick, OH 800-827-9237
Best Diversified Products
Jonesboro, AR. 800-327-9209
Bettendorf Stanford Inc
Salem, IL. 800-548-2253
BEUMER Corp
Somerset, NJ. 732-893-2800

BEVCO
Canada, BC. 800-663-0090
Bevles Company
Dallas, TX. 800-441-1601
Bilt-Rite Conveyors
New London, WI 920-982-6600
Biner Ellison Packaging Systs
Vista, CA. 800-733-8162
Bishamon Industry Corp
Ontario, CA. 800-358-8833
Black River Pallet Co
Zeeland, MI. 800-427-6515
Blue Giant Equipment Corporation
Brampton, ON. 800-668-7078
Bluff Manufacturing Inc
Fort Worth, TX 800-433-2212
BMH
City of Industry, CA 909-349-2530
Bmh Equipment Inc
Sacramento, CA 800-350-8828
Bolzoni Auramo
Homewood, IL 800-358-5438
Bowman Hollis Mfg Corp
Charlotte, NC 888-269-2358
Bradley Lifting
York, PA 717-848-3121
Branford Vibrator Company
Peru, IL 800-262-2106
Brothers Metal Products
Santa Ana, CA 714-972-3008
Brute Fabricators
Castroville, TX 800-777-2788
Bryant Products Inc
Ixonia, WI 800-825-3874
Buckhorn Canada
Brampton, ON. 800-461-7579
Buffalo Technologies Corporation
Buffalo, NY. 800-332-2419
Buhler Inc.
Plymouth, MN. 763-847-9900
Bulldog Factory Svc LLC
Madison Heights, MI 248-541-3500
Bunting Magnetics Co
Newton, KS 800-835-2526
Burgess Enterprises, Inc
Renton, WA. 800-927-3286
Burgess Mfg. - Oklahoma
Guthrie, OK. 800-804-1913
Burns Industries
Line Lexington, PA. 800-223-6430
Bushman Equipment Inc
Menomonee Falls, WI. 800-338-7810
Busse/SJI Corp
Randolph, WI 800-882-4995
BW Container Systems
Romeoville, IL 630-759-6800
C & L Wood Products Inc
Hartselle, AL. 800-483-2035
C H Babb Co Inc
Raynham, MA 508-977-0600
C Nelson Mfg Co
Oak Harbor, OH 800-922-7339
C R Daniels Inc
Ellicott City, MD. 800-933-2638
C S Bell Co
Tiffin, OH 888-958-6381
C&R Refrigation Inc,
Center, TX. 800-438-6182
C.J. Machine
Fridley, MN. 763-767-4630
Caddy Corporation of America
Bridgeport, NJ. 856-467-4222
Caldwell Group
Rockford, IL 800-628-4263
California Caster & Handtruck
San Francisco, CA 800-950-8750
Caljan America
Denver, CO. 303-321-3600
Cambelt International Corporation
Salt Lake City, UT 801-972-5511
Can Lines Engineering Inc
Downey, CA 562-861-2996
Cannon Equipment Company
Cannon Falls, MN. 800-825-8501
Cantley-Ellis Manufacturing Company
Kingsport, TN 423-246-4671
Carbis Inc
Florence, SC 800-948-7750
Carleton Helical Technologies
Doylestown, PA 215-230-8900
Carman Industries Inc
Jeffersonville, IN 800-456-7560

Carrier Vibrating Equip Inc
Louisville, KY 502-969-3171
Carron Net Co Inc
Two Rivers, WI.................800-558-7768
Carson Industries
Pomona, CA 800-735-5566
Cassel Box & Lumber Co Inc
Grafton, WI....................262-377-9503
Casso-Solar Corporation
Nanuet, NY 800-988-4455
Cattron Group International
Sharpsville, PA 724-962-1629
Cayne Industrial Sales Corp
Bronx, NY 718-993-5800
Cedar Box Co
Minneapolis, MN 612-332-4287
Century Crane & Hoist
Dravosburg, PA.................888-601-8801
Century Industries Inc
Sellersburg, IN 800-248-3371
Challenger Pallet & Supply Inc
Idaho Falls, ID 800-733-0205
Chantland Company, The
Humboldt, IA 515-332-4040
Charles Tirschman Pallet Co
Dundalk, MD 410-282-6199
Charlton & Hill
Lethbridge, AB 403-328-3388
Chase-Logeman Corp
Greensboro, NC 336-665-0754
Checker Machine
Minneapolis, MN 888-800-5001
Chem-Tainer Industries Inc
West Babylon, NY 800-938-8896
Cherry's Industrial Eqpt Corp
Elk Grove Vlg, IL 800-350-0011
Chester Hoist
Lisbon, OH 800-424-7248
Chicago Conveyor Corporation
Addison, IL 630-543-6300
Chief Industries
Kearney, NE 800-359-8833
CHL Systems
Souderton, PA 215-723-7284
Chocolate Concepts
Hartville, OH 330-877-3322
Christianson Systems Inc
Blomkest, MN..................800-328-8896
Christy Machine Co
Fremont, OH 888-332-6451
Cimino Box & Pallet Co
Cleveland, OH 216-961-7377
Cintex of America
Carol Stream, IL 800-424-6839
Citra-Tech
Lefkosia, CY
Clamp Swing Pricing Co Inc
Oakland, CA 800-227-7615
Clark Caster Company
Cave In Rock, IL................800-538-0765
Cleasby Manufacturing Co
San Francisco, CA 800-253-2729
CLECO Systems
Marietta, GA 770-392-0330
Cleveland Vibrator Co
Cleveland, OH 800-221-3298
Climax Packaging Machinery
Hamilton, OH 513-874-1664
Clipper Belt Lacer Company
Grand Rapids, MI...............616-459-3196
Coastal Pallet Corp
Bridgeport, CT 203-333-6222
Coblentz Brothers Inc
Apple Creek, OH 330-857-7211
Coddington Lumber Co
Frostburg, MD 301-689-8816
Collins Manufacturing Company Ltd
Langley, BC 800-663-6761
Colson Caster Corp
Jonesboro, AR 800-643-5515
Columbia Machine Inc
Vancouver, WA.................800-628-4065
Columbus McKinnon Corporation
Getzville, NY 800-888-0985
Commercial Manufacturing
Fresno, CA 559-237-1855
Conesco Conveyor Corporation
Clifton, NJ.....................973-365-1440
Continental Commercial Products
Bridgeton, MO 800-325-1051
Control & Metering
Mississauga, ON................800-736-5739

Control Chief Holdings Inc
Bradford, PA...................814-362-6811
Conveyance Technologies LLC
Cleveland, OH 800-701-2278
Conveying Industries
Denver, CO 877-600-4874
Conveyor Accessories
Burr Ridge, IL 800-323-7093
Conveyor Components Co
Croswell, MI 800-233-3233
Conveyor Components Co
Croswell, MI 800-552-3337
Conveyor Dynamics Corp
St Peters, MO 636-279-1111
Conveyor Supply Inc
Deerfield, IL 847-945-5670
Corinth Products
Corinth, ME 207-285-3387
Corn States Metal Fabricators
West Des Moines, IA............515-225-7961
Coss Engineering Sales Company
Rochester Hills, MI..............800-446-1365
Cotter Brothers Corp
Danvers, MA...................978-777-5001
Cozzini Inc
Algona, IA 888-295-1116
Craft Industries
Long Island City, NY 252-753-3152
Creative Foam Corp
Fenton, MI 810-629-4149
Creative Techniques
Auburn Hills, MI 800-473-0284
Crippen Manufacturing Co
St Louis, MI 800-872-2474
Crown Equipment Corp.
New Bremen, OH 419-629-2311
Cryovac
Charlotte, NC 800-391-5645
CSS International Corp
Philadelphia, PA 800-278-8107
Cugar Machine Co
Fort Worth, TX 817-927-0411
Cumberland Box & Mill Co
Cumberland, MD 301-724-1010
Currie Machinery Co
Santa Clara, CA 408-727-0422
Custom Conveyor & Supply Corp.
Racine, WI 262-634-4920
Custom Diamond Intl.
Laval, QC 800-326-5926
Custom Food Machinery
Stockton, CA 209-463-4343
Custom Metal Crafts
Springfield, MO 417-862-9324
Custom Metal Design Inc
Oakland, FL 800-334-1777
Custom Millers Supply Co
Monmouth, IL 309-734-6312
Custom Systems Integration Co
Carlsbad, CA 760-635-1099
Cutler Brothers Box & Lumber
Fairview, NJ 201-943-2535
Cutter Lumber Products
Livermore, CA 925-443-5959
Cyclonaire Corp
York, NE 800-445-0730
D&M Pallet Company
Neshkoro, WI 920-293-4616
Dairy Conveyor Corp
Brewster, NY 845-278-7878
Damrow Company
Fond Du Lac, WI 800-236-1501
Daniel Boone Lumber Industries
Morehead, KY 606-784-7586
Darcor Casters
Toronto, ON 800-387-7206
Darnell-Rose Inc
City Of Industry, CA.............800-327-6355
Davis Core & Pa
Cave Spring, GA................800-235-7483
Davron Technologies Inc
Chattanooga, TN 423-870-1888
Day Lumber Company
Westfield, MA..................413-568-3511
Dearborn Mid-West Conveyor Co
Taylor, MI 734-288-4400
Dearborn Mid-West Conveyor Co
Overland Park, KS 913-384-9950
Decoren Equipment
Willowbrook, IL 708-789-3367
DEL-Tec Packaging Inc
Greer, SC.....................800-747-8683

Delta Machine & Maufacturing
St Rose, LA....................504-949-8304
Delta Wire And Mfg.
Harrow, ON....................800-221-3794
Delta/Ducon
Malvern, PA 800-238-2974
Demag Cranes & Components Corp
Cleveland, OH 440-248-2400
Dematic USA
Grand Rapids, MI...............877-725-7500
Dempster Systems
Toccoa, GA 706-886-2327
Denver Reel & Pallet Company
Denver, CO 303-321-1920
Descon EDM
Brocton, NY 716-792-9300
Deshazo Crane Company
Alabaster, AL 205-664-2006
Design Systems Inc
Farmington Hills, MI 800-660-4374
Design Technology Corporation
Lexington, MA 800-597-7063
Development Workshop Inc
Idaho Falls, ID 800-657-5597
Dillin Automation Systems Corp
Perrysburg, OH 419-666-6789
Diversified Capping Equipment
Perrysburg, OH 419-666-2566
Diversified Metal Engineering
Charlottetown, PE 902-628-6900
DMC-David Manufacturing Company
Mason City, IA 641-424-7010
Dominion Pallet Inc
Mineral, VA....................800-227-5321
Donahower & Company
Olathe, KS....................913-829-2650
Doosan Industrial Vehicle America Corp
Buford, GA 678-745-2200
Douglas Machine Inc
Alexandria, MN 320-763-6587
Douglas Machines Corp.
Clearwater, FL 800-331-6870
Downs Crane & Hoist Co Inc
Los Angeles, CA................800-748-5994
Dubuque Steel Products Co
Dubuque, IA 563-556-6288
Dufeck Manufacturing Co
Denmark, WI...................888-603-9663
Duke Manufacturing Co
St Louis, MO...................800-735-3853
Dunkley International Inc
Kalamazoo, MI 800-666-1264
Dunrite Inc
Fremont, NE 800-782-3061
Duplex Mill & Mfg Co
Springfield, OH.................937-325-5555
Dupps Co
Germantown, OH 937-855-0623
Durable Corp
Norwalk, OH 800-537-1603
Durand-Wayland Inc
Lagrange, GA 800-241-2308
Durant Box Factory
Durant, OK 580-924-4035
Dutro Co
Logan, UT.....................866-388-7660
Dyco
Bloomsburg, PA 800-545-3926
Dyna-Veyor Inc
Newark, NJ 800-326-5009
Dynabilt Products
Readville, MA..................800-443-1008
Dynamet
Kalamazoo, MI 269-385-0006
Dynamic Air Inc
St Paul, MN....................651-484-2900
Dynamic Automation LTD
Simi Valley, CA.................805-584-8476
Dynamic Storage Systems Inc.
Brooksville, FL 800-974-8211
E F Bavis & Assoc Inc
Maineville, OH 513-677-0500
E-Z Lift Conveyors
Denver, CO 800-821-9966
E2M
Duluth, GA 800-622-4326
Earl Soesbe Company
Romeoville, IL 219-866-4191
Eckels Bilt
Fort Worth, TX 800-343-9020
Edmeyer
Minneapolis, MN 651-450-1210

Edson Packaging Machinery
Hamilton, ON 800-493-3766
Edwards Products
Cincinnati, OH 800-543-1835
EGA Products Inc
Brookfield, WI 800-937-3427
Eichler Wood Products
Laurys Station, PA 610-262-6749
Eisenmann Corp USA
Crystal Lake, IL 815-455-4100
Elba Pallets Company
Elba, AL 334-897-6034
Elberta Crate & Box Company
Carpentersville, IL 888-672-9260
Electrical Engineering & Equip
Windsor Heights, IA 800-955-3633
Electro Lift Inc
Clifton, NJ 973-471-0204
ELF Machinery
La Porte, IN 800-328-0466
Elite Storage Solutions Inc
Monroe, GA 800-367-0572
Elwell Parker
Coraopolis, PA 800-272-9953
Emc Solutions
Celina, OH 419-586-2388
Emtrol
York, PA 800-634-4927
En-Hanced Products Inc
Westerville, OH 800-783-7400
Engineered Products Corp
Greenville, SC 800-868-0145
Enrick Co
Zumbrota, MN 507-732-5215
Equipment Design & Fabrication
Charlotte, NC 800-949-0165
Equipment Outlet
Meridian, ID 208-887-1472
Eriez Magnetics
Erie, PA 800-346-4946
Ermanco
Norton Shores, MI 231-798-4547
ERO/Goodrich Forest Products
Tualatin, OR 800-458-5545
Eugene Welding Company
Marysville, MI 810-364-7421
Excalibur Miretti Group LLC
Fairfield, NJ 973-808-8399
Exel
Lincolnton, NC 704-735-6535
F & A Fabricating Inc
Battle Creek, MI 269-965-8371
F N Smith Corp
Oregon, IL 815-732-2171
F.E. Wood & Sons
West Baldwin, ME 207-286-5003
Fabreeka International
Boise, ID 800-423-4469
Fabricated Components Inc
Stroudsburg, PA 800-233-8163
Fabricating & Welding Corp
Chicago, IL 773-928-2050
Fabrication Specialties
Centerville, TN 931-729-2283
Fairborn USA Inc
Upper Sandusky, OH 800-262-1188
Fata Automation
Sterling Heights, MI 586-323-9400
Faultless Caster
Evansville, IN 800-322-7359
Fehlig Brothers Box & Lbr Co
St Louis, MO 314-241-6900
FEI Inc
Mansfield, TX 800-346-5908
Felco Packaging Specialist
Baltimore, MD 800-673-8488
Fenner Dunlop Americas Inc
Pittsburgh, PA 412-249-0700
Fetco
Lake Zurich, IL 800-338-2699
Fibre Converters Inc
Constantine, MI 269-279-1700
Filler Specialties
Zeeland, MI 616-772-9235
Filling Equipment Co Inc
Flushing, NY 800-247-7127
Fillit
Kirkland, QC 514-694-2390
Fishmore
Melbourne, FL 321-723-4751
Fleet Wood Goldco Wyard
Cockeysville, MD 410-785-1934
Fleetwood Systems
Orlando, FL 800-432-5433
FleetwoodGoldcoWyard
Romeoville, IL 630-759-6800
Flexco
Downers Grove, IL 800-323-3444
Flexible Material Handling
Suwanee, GA 800-669-1501
Flexicon
Bethlehem, PA 888-353-9426
Flodin
Moses Lake, WA 509-766-2996
Flow of Solids
Westford, MA 978-392-0300
Fogg Filler Co
Holland, MI 616-786-3644
Food Engineering Unlimited
Fullerton, CA 714-879-8762
Food Machinery Sales
Bogart, GA 706-549-2207
Food Processing Equipment Co
Santa Fe Springs, CA 562-802-3727
Forbo Siegling LLC
Huntersville, NC 800-255-5581
Foremost Machine Builders Inc
Fairfield, NJ 973-227-0700
Fox Valley Wood Products Inc
Kaukauna, WI 920-766-4069
FPEC Corporation
Santa Fe Springs, CA 562-802-3727
Frazier & Son
Conroe, TX 800-365-5438
Frazier Industrial Co
Long Valley, NJ 800-859-1342
Fred D Pfening Co
Columbus, OH 614-294-5361
FreesTech
Sinking Spring, PA 717-560-7560
Frelco
Stephenville, NL 709-643-5668
Fresno Pallet, Inc.
Sultana, CA 559-591-4111
Frost Food Handling Products
Grand Rapids, MI 800-253-9382
G L Packaging Products Inc
West Chicago, IL 866-935-8755
G.F. Frank & Sons
Fairfield, OH 513-870-9075
Galbreath LLC
Winamac, IN 574-946-6631
Garvey Corp
Hammonton, NJ 800-257-8581
Gates Manufacturing Company
Saint Louis, MO 800-237-9226
Gatewood Products LLC
Parkersburg, WV 800-827-5461
Gbn Machine & Engineering
Woodford, VA 800-446-9871
Gch Internatonal
Louisville, KY 502-636-1374
GE Appliances
Louisville, KY 877-959-8688
Gebo Conveyors, Consultants & Systems
Laval, QC 450-973-3337
Gebo Corporation
Bradenton, FL 941-727-1400
GEM Equipment Of Oregon Inc
Woodburn, OR 503-982-9902
General Corrugated Machinery Company
Palisades Park, NJ 201-944-0644
General Machinery Corp
Sheboygan, WI 888-243-6622
General Steel Fabricators
Joplin, MO 800-820-8644
General Tank
Berwick, PA 800-435-8265
Georgia Duck & Cordage Mill
Scottdale, GA 404-297-3170
Gerrity Industries
Monmouth, ME 877-933-2804
Gillis Associated Industries
Prospect Heights, IL 847-541-6500
Girard Wood Products Inc
Puyallup, WA 800-532-0505
Glatt Air Techniques Inc
Ramsey, NJ 201-825-8700
Goeman's Wood Products
Hartford, WI 262-673-6090
Goergen-Mackwirth Co Inc
Buffalo, NY 800-728-4446
Goldco Industries
Loveland, CO 970-663-4770
Gorbel Inc
Victor, NY 585-924-6262
Gough-Econ Inc
Charlotte, NC 800-204-6844
Graco Inc
Minneapolis, MN 612-623-6000
Graham Pallet Co Inc
Tompkinsville, KY 888-525-0694
Grain Machinery Mfg Corp
Miami, FL 305-620-2525
Gram Equipment Of America
Tampa, FL 813-248-1978
Gray Woodproducts
Tacoma, WA 253-752-7000
Graybill Machines Inc
Lititz, PA 717-626-5221
Green Belt Industries Inc
Buffalo, NY 800-668-1114
Green Tek
Janesville, WI 800-747-6440
Greitzer
Elizabeth City, NC 252-338-4000
H G Weber & Co
Kiel, WI 920-894-2221
H&H Lumber Company
Amarillo, TX 806-335-1813
H&H Wood Products
Hamburg, NY 716-648-5600
Habasit America
Suwanee, GA 800-458-6431
Habasit America Plastic Div
Reading, PA 800-445-7898
Hackney Brothers
Washington, NC 800-763-0700
Halton Packaging Systems
Oakville, ON 905-847-9141
Hamilton Caster
Hamilton, OH 888-699-7164
Hampton Roads Box Company
Suffolk, VA 757-934-2355
Handling Specialty
Niagara Falls, NY 800-559-8366
Hanel Storage Systems
Pittsburgh, PA 412-787-3444
Hannay Reels
Westerlo, NY 877-467-3357
Hanson Box & Lumber Company
Wakefield, MA 617-245-0358
Hapman Conveyors
Kalamazoo, MI 800-968-7722
Harbor Pallet Company
Anaheim, CA 714-871-0932
Hardy Systems Corporation
Northbrook, IL 800-927-3956
Harold F Haines Manufacturing Inc
Presque Isle, ME 207-762-1411
Harper Trucks Inc
Wichita, KS 800-835-4099
Harrington Hoists Inc
Manheim, PA 800-233-3010
Hart Design & Mfg
Green Bay, WI 920-468-5927
Hartness International
Greenville, SC 800-845-8791
Hawkeye Pallet Co
Johnston, IA 515-276-0409
Hayes & Stolz Indl Mfg LTD
Fort Worth, TX 800-725-7272
HDT Manufacturing
Salem, OH 800-968-7438
Hectronic
Oklahoma City, OK 405-946-3574
Herkimer Pallet & Wood Products Company
Herkimer, NY 315-866-4591
Hevi-Haul International LTD
Menomonee Falls, WI 800-558-0577
HHP Inc
Henniker, NH 603-428-3298
Hi Roller Enclosed Belt Conveyors
Sioux Falls, SD 800-328-1785
Hildreth Wood Products Inc
Wadesboro, NC 704-826-8326
Hinchcliff Products Company
Strongsville, OH 440-238-5200
Hodge Manufacturing Company
Springfield, MA 800-262-4634
Hodges
Vienna, IL 800-444-0011
Hoffmeyer Corp
San Leandro, CA 888-744-1826
Hoppmann Corporation
Elkwood, VA 800-368-3582

Hormann Flexan Llc
Leetsdale, PA 800-365-3667
Hot Food Boxes
Mooresville, IN 800-733-8073
Hotshot Delivery System
Bloomingdale, IL 630-924-8817
Houston Wire Works, Inc.
South Houston, TX 800-468-9477
Hovair Systems Inc
Kent, WA 800-237-4518
Howes S Co Inc
Silver Creek, NY 888-255-2611
Hunter Woodworks
Carson, CA 800-966-4751
Hurt Conveyor Equipment Company
Los Angeles, CA 323-541-0433
Hyster Company
San Diego, CA 855-804-2118
ICB Greenline
Charlotte, NC 800-331-5312
IEW
Niles, OH 330-652-0113
Iman Pack
Westland, MI 800-810-4626
Incinerator International Inc
Houston, TX 713-227-1466
Industrial Automation Systems
Santa Clarita, CA 888-484-4427
Industrial Hardwood
Perrysburg, OH 419-666-2503
Industrial Kinetics
Downers Grove, IL 800-655-0306
Industrial Lumber & Packaging
Spring Lake, MI 616-842-1457
Industrial Woodfab & Packaging
Riverview, MI 734-284-4808
Innovation Moving Systems
Oostburg, WI. 800-619-0625
Inter-City Welding & Manufacturing
Independence, MO 816-252-1770
Interlake Mecalux
Chicago, IL 708-344-9999
InterMetro Industries
Wilkes-Barre, PA 570-825-2741
International Wood Industries
Snohomish, WA 800-922-6141
Interroll Corp
Wilmington, NC 800-830-9680
Intralox LLC
Harahan, LA 800-535-8848
Irby
Rocky Mount, NC. 252-442-0154
Item Products
Houston, TX 800-333-4932
J C Ford Co
La Habra, CA 714-871-7361
J L Becker Co
Plymouth, MI 800-837-4328
J.H. Thornton Company
Olathe, KS. 913-764-6550
J.M. Rogers & Sons
Moss Point, MS 228-475-7584
Jantec
Traverse City, MI 800-992-3303
Jarke Corporation
Prospect Hts, IL 800-722-5255
Jarvis Caster Company
Jackson, TN 800-995-9876
Jervis B WEBB Co
Novi, MI. 248-553-1000
Jesco Industries
Litchfield, MI 800-455-0019
Jetstream Systems
Wichita, KN 855-861-6916
Jilson Group
Lodi, NJ. 800-969-5400
John Rock Inc
Coatesville, PA 610-857-4809
Johnston Equipment
Delta, BC. 800-237-5159
Joyce Dayton Corp
Moraine, OH. 800-523-5204
K-Tron
Salina, KS 785-825-1611
K.F. Logistics
Cincinnati, OH 800-347-9100
Kadon Corporation
Milford, OH 937-299-0088
Kamflex Corp
Chicago, IL 800-323-2440
KAPS All Packaging
Riverhead, NY 631-727-0300

Kasel Industries Inc
Denver, CO. 800-218-4417
Kaufman Engineered Systems
Waterville, OH 419-878-9727
Kauling Wood Products Company
Beckemeyer, IL. 618-594-2901
Keenline Conveyor Systems
Omro, WI 920-685-0365
Kelley Wood Products
Fitchburg, MA 978-345-7531
Kelly Dock Systems
Milwaukee, WI 414-352-1000
Kent District Library System
Comstock Park, MI. 616-784-2007
KETCH
Wichita, KS. 800-766-3777
Key Material Handling Inc
Simi Valley, CA. 800-539-7225
Key Technology Inc.
Walla Walla, WA 509-529-2161
Killington Wood ProductsCompany
Rutland, VT. 802-773-9111
Kimball Companies
East Longmeadow, MA 413-525-1881
Kinder Morgan Inc
Houston, TX 713-466-0496
Kinergy Corp
Louisville, KY 502-366-5685
Kinetic Equipment Company
Appleton, WI 806-293-4471
Kinsley Inc
Doylestown, PA 800-414-6664
Kisco Manufacturing
Port Alberni, BC 604-823-7456
KISS Packaging Systems
Vista, CA. 888-522-3538
Klippenstein Corp
Fresno, CA. 888-834-4258
Knight Ind
Auburn Hills, MI 248-377-4950
Koke Inc
Queensbury, NY 800-535-5303
Komatsu Forklift USA
Rolling Meadows, IL 847-437-5800
Konz Wood Products Co
Appleton, WI 877-610-5145
Kornylak Corp
Hamilton, OH 800-837-5676
Krones
Franklin, WI 800-752-3787
KUKA Robotics Corp
Shelby Township, MI 800-459-6691
Kusel Equipment Company
Watertown, WI 920-261-4112
KWS Manufacturing Co LTD
Burleson, TX. 800-543-6558
L T Hampel Corp
Germantown, WI. 800-681-6979
L&H Wood Manufacturing Company
Farmington, MI. 248-474-9000
L&S Pallet Company
Houston, TX 281-443-6537
La Crosse
Onalaska, WI. 800-345-0018
LA Marche Mfg Co
Des Plaines, IL 847-299-1193
La Menuiserie East Angus
East Angus, QC. 819-832-2746
Laidig
Mishawaka, IN 574-256-0204
Lake Michigan Hardwood Company
Leland, MI. 231-256-9811
Lakeside Manufacturing Inc
Milwaukee, WI 888-558-8565
Lakeside-Aris Manufacturing
Milwaukee, WI 800-558-8565
Lambert Material Handling
Syracuse, NY 800-253-5103
Landoo Corporation
Horsham, PA 785-562-5381
Laros Equipment Co Inc
Portage, MI 269-323-1441
Larson Pallet Company
Ogema, WI 715-767-5131
Laughlin Sales Corp
Fort Worth, TX 817-625-7756
Lawson Industries
Holden, MO 816-732-4347
Le Fiell Co
Reno, NV 402-592-9993
Lear Romec
Elyria, OH. 440-323-3211

Lee Engineering Company
Pawtucket, RI 401-725-6100
Leeds Conveyor Manufacturer Company
Guilford, CT 800-724-1088
Leggett & Platt Storage
Vernon Hills, IL 847-816-6246
Lesco Design & Mfg Co
La Grange, KY 502-222-7101
Lester Box & Mfg Div
Long Beach, CA 562-437-5123
Lewco Inc
Sandusky, OH 419-625-4014
Lewis M Carter Mfg Co Inc
Donalsonville, GA 800-332-8232
Lexington Logistics LLC
Portage, WI 800-356-8150
Leyman Manufacturing   Corporation
Cincinnati, OH 866-539-6261
Liberty Machine Company
York, PA 800-745-8152
Lift Rite
Mississauga, ON 905-456-2603
Liftomatic Material Handling
Buffalo Grove, IL 800-837-6540
Linde Material Handling
Summerville, SC 843-871-0312
Line-Master Products
Cocolalla, ID. 208-265-4743
Linett Company
Blawnox, PA 800-565-2165
Lista International Corp
Holliston, MA 800-722-3020
Load King Mfg
Jacksonville, FL 800-531-4975
LoadBank International
Orlando, FL. 800-458-9010
Lock Inspection Systems
Fitchburg, MA 800-227-5539
Logemann Brothers Co
Milwaukee, WI 414-445-3005
Long Reach ManufacturingCompany
Westport, CT. 800-285-7000
Longford Equipment US
Glastonbury, CT 416-298-6622
Longview Fibre Co
Longview, WA. 800-929-8111
Lorenz Couplings
Cobourg, ON. 800-263-7782
Louisville Dryer Company
Louisville, KY 800-735-3613
LPI Imports
Chicago, IL. 877-389-6563
LPS Technology
Grafton, OH 800-586-1410
Lumsden Flexx Flow
Lancaster, PA 800-367-3664
M & E Mfg Co Inc
Kingston, NY 845-331-2110
M & H Crate Inc
Jacksonville, TX 903-683-5351
M G Newell Corp
Greensboro, NC 800-334-0231
M O Industries Inc
Whippany, NJ 973-386-9228
Madison County Wood Products
St Louis, MO. 314-772-1722
Madsen Wire Products Inc
Orland, IN. 260-829-6561
Magline Inc
Standish, MI 800-624-5463
Magna Power Controls
Milwaukee, WI 800-288-8178
Magnuson
Pueblo, CO 719-948-9500
Magsys Inc
Milwaukee, WI 414-543-2177
Manufacturers Wood Supply Company
Cleveland, OH 216-771-7848
Mar-Con Wire Belt
Richmond, BC 877-962-7266
Marion Body Works Inc
Marion, WI 715-754-5261
Marion Pallet Company
Marion, OH 800-432-4117
Mark Slade ManufacturingCompany
Seymour, WI. 920-833-6557
Marlen International
Astoria, OR 800-862-7536
Marshall Boxes Inc
Rochester, NY 585-458-7432
Martin Cab Div
Cleveland, OH 216-377-8200

Martin Engineering
Neponset, IL 800-766-2786
Martin/Baron
Irwindale, CA 626-960-5153
Matcon Americas
Elmhurst, IL 856-256-1330
Material Storage Systems
Humble, TX 800-881-6750
Material Systems Engineering
Stilesville, IN 800-634-0904
Materials Transportation Co
Temple, TX 800-433-3110
Mathews Conveyor
Danville, KY 800-628-4397
Matot - Commercial GradeLift Solutions
Bellwood, IL 800-369-1070
Matthiesen Equipment
San Antonio, TX 800-624-8635
Maull-Baker Box Company
Brookfield, WI 414-463-1290
May-Wes Manufacturing Inc
Hutchinson, MN 800-788-6483
MBX Packaging Specialists
Wausau, WI 715-845-1171
McCormick Enterprises
Arlington Heights, IL 800-323-5201
Mccullough Industries Inc
Kenton, OH 800-245-9490
Mcintosh Box & Pallet Co
East Syracuse, NY 800-219-9552
Mcneilly Wood Products Inc
Campbell Hall, NY 845-457-9651
McNichols Conveyor Company
Southfield, MI 800-331-1926
MeGa Industries
Burlington, ON 800-665-6342
Melcher Manufacturing Co
Spokane Valley, WA 800-541-4227
Merco/Savory
Mt. Pleasant, MI 800-733-8821
Meriden Box Company
Southington, CT 860-621-7141
Meriwether Industries
Bloomfield, NJ 800-332-2358
MERRICK Industries Inc
Lynn Haven, FL 800-271-7834
Metal Equipment Company
Cleveland, OH 800-700-6326
Metko Inc
New Holstein, WI 920-898-4221
Metro Corporation
Wilkes Barre, PA 800-992-1776
Metzgar Conveyors
Comstock Park, MI 888-266-8390
Meyer Machine & Garroutte Products
San Antonio, TX 210-736-1811
Michaelo Espresso
Seattle, WA 800-545-2883
Michiana Box & Crate
Niles, MI 800-677-6372
Michigan Box Co
Detroit, MI 888-642-4269
Michigan Industrial Belting
Livonia, MI 800-778-1650
Michigan Pallet Inc
St Charles, MI 989-865-9915
Micro Solutions Ent Tech & Dev
Van Nuys, CA 800-673-4968
Mid-States Mfg & Engr Co Inc
Milton, IA 800-346-1792
Mid-West Wire Products
Ferndale, MI 800-989-9881
Midwest Metalcraft & Equipment
Windsor, MO 800-647-3167
Midwest Wire Specialties
Chicago, IL 800-238-0228
Milan Box Corporation
Milan, TN 800-225-8057
Millard Manufacturing Corp
La Vista, NE 800-662-4263
Miller Hofft Brands
Indianapolis, IN 317-638-6576
Miller Metal Fabrication
Bridgeville, DE 302-337-2291
Millwood Inc
Vienna, OH 330-393-4400
MIT Poly-Cart Corp
New York, NY 800-234-7659
Modern Metals Industries
El Segundo, CA 800-437-6633
Molding Automation Concepts
Woodstock, IL 800-435-6979

Moline Machinery LLC
Duluth, MN 800-767-5734
Momence Pallet Corp
Momence, IL 815-472-6451
Monarch-McLaren
Weston, ON 416-741-9675
Moorecraft Box & Crate
Tarboro, NC 252-823-2510
Morse Manufacturing Co Inc
East Syracuse, NY 315-437-8475
Moseley Realty LLC
Franklin, MA 800-667-3539
Motom Corporation
Bensenville, IL 630-787-1995
Mt Valley Farms & Lumber Prods
Biglerville, PA 717-677-6166
Multivac
Union Grove, WI 800-640-4213
Mumper Machine Corporation
Butler, WI 262-781-8908
Murata Automated Systems
Charlotte, NC 800-428-8469
NACCO Materials HandlingGroup
Fairview, OR 503-721-6205
Namco Controls Corporation
Cleveland, OH 800-626-8324
National Conveyor Corp
Commerce, CA 323-725-0355
National Distributor Services
Aurora, CO 303-755-4411
National Drying Machry Co Inc
Philadelphia, PA 215-464-6070
National Scoop & Equipment Company
Spring House, PA 215-646-2040
Native Lumber Company
Wallingford, CT 203-269-2625
Navco
Houston, TX 800-231-0164
Necedah Pallet Co Inc
Necedah, WI 800-672-5538
NECO/Nebraska Engineering
Omaha, NE 800-367-6208
Nefab Packaging Inc.
Coppell, TX 800-322-4425
Nefab Packaging, Inc.
Coppell, TX 800-322-4425
Nelson Co
Sparrows Point, MD 410-477-3000
Neos
Elk River, MN 888-441-6367
NEPA Pallet & Container Co
Snohomish, WA 360-568-3185
Nercon Engineering & Manufacturing
Oshkosh, WI 920-233-3268
Net Material Handling
Milwaukee, WI 800-558-7260
Nevlen Co. 2, Inc.
Wakefield, MA 800-562-7225
New Age Industrial
Norton, KS 800-255-0104
New England Machinery Inc
Bradenton, FL 941-755-5550
New England Pallets & Skids
Ludlow, MA 413-583-6628
New Lisbon Wood ProductsManufacturing Company
New Lisbon, WI 608-562-3122
New London Engineering
New London, WI 800-437-1994
New Mexico Products Inc
Albuquerque, NM 877-345-7864
New Pig Corp
Tipton, PA 800-468-4647
New South Co Inc
Myrtle Beach, SC 843-236-9399
Newcastle Co Inc
New Castle, PA 724-658-4516
Newell Brands
Atlanta, GA
Newton OA & Son Co
Bridgeville, DE 800-726-5745
Nexel Industries Inc
Port Washington, NY 800-245-6682
Norris Products Corp oration
Cincinnati, OH 877-543-2278
North Star Ice EquipmentCorporation
Seattle, WA 800-321-1381
Northwest Products
Archbold, OH 419-445-1950
Northwind Inc
Alpena, AR 877-937-2585
Norwalt Design Inc
Randolph, NJ 973-927-3200

Nothum Food Processing Systems
Springfield, MO 800-435-1297
NST Metals
Louisville, KY 502-584-5846
Nu-Con Equipment
Chanhassen, MN 877-939-0510
Nu-Star Inc
Shakopee, MN 800-800-9274
Nucon Corporation
Deerfield, IL 877-545-0070
Nutec Manufacturing Inc
New Lenox, IL 815-722-5348
O'Brien Installations
Ontario, CA 905-336-8245
Oak Creek Pallet Company
Milwaukee, WI 414-762-7170
Occidental Chemical Corporation
Dallas, TX 800-733-3665
Ohio Magnetics Inc
Maple Heights, OH 800-486-6446
Ohio Rack Inc
Alliance, OH 800-344-4164
Omega Design Corp
Exton, PA 800-346-0191
Omicron Steel Products Company
Jamaica, NY 718-805-3400
Omni Lift Inc
Salt Lake City, UT 801-486-3776
Omni Metalcraft Corporation
Alpena, MI 989-358-7000
OnTrack Automation Inc
Waterloo, ON 519-886-9090
ORBIS
Oconomowoc, WI 262-560-5000
ORBIS
Oconomowoc, WI 800-890-7292
Original Lincoln Logs
Chestertown, NY 800-833-2461
Orion Packaging Systems Inc
Alexandria, MN 800-333-6556
Ortmayer Materials Handling
Brooklyn, NY 718-875-7995
OTD Corporation
Hinsdale, IL 630-321-9232
OTP Industrial Solutions
Terre Haute, IN 860-953-7632
Otto Braun Bakery Equipment
Buffalo, NY 716-824-1252
Ouellette Machinery Systems
Fenton, MO 800-545-7619
Our Name is Mud
New York, NY 877-683-7867
Overhead Conveyor Co
Ferndale, MI 800-396-2554
Pa R Systems Inc
St Paul, MN 800-464-1320
Pacific Pneumatics
Rancho Cucamonga, CA 800-221-0961
Pacific Process Technology
La Jolla, CA 858-551-3298
Pacific Tank
Adelanto, CA 800-449-5838
Package Conveyor Co
Fort Worth, TX 800-792-1243
Packaging & Processing Equipment
Ayr, ON 519-622-6666
Packaging Equipment & Conveyors, Inc
Elkhart, IN 574-266-6995
Packaging Machinery
Montgomery, AL 334-265-9211
Packaging Systems Intl
Denver, CO 303-244-9000
Packing Material Company
Southfield, MI 248-489-7000
Paco Manufacturing
Clarksville, IN 812-283-7963
Paget Equipment Co
Marshfield, WI 715-384-3158
Palace Packaging Machines Inc
Downington, PA 610-873-7252
Pallet Management Systems
Lawrenceville, VA 800-446-1804
Pallet Masters
Los Angeles, CA 800-675-2579
Pallet One Inc
Mocksville, NC 336-492-5565
Pallet One Inc
Bartow, FL 800-771-1148
Pallet Pro
Moss, TN 800-489-3661
Pallet Service Corp
Maple Grove, MN 888-391-8020

Pallets Inc
  Fort Edward, NY...................518-747-4177
Pallister Pallet
  Wapello, IA......................319-523-8161
Pallox Incorporated
  Onsted, MI.......................517-456-4101
Paltier
  Michigan City, IN................800-348-3201
Paper Systems Inc
  Des Moines, IA...................800-342-2855
Paradigm Technologies
  Eugene, OR.......................541-345-5543
Parkson Corp
  Vernon Hills, IL.................847-816-3700
Parkson Corp
  Fort Lauderdale, FL..............908-464-0700
Paul Hawkins Lumber Company
  Mannington, WV...................304-986-2230
Paxton Products Inc
  Blue Ash, OH.....................800-441-7475
Payne Controls Co
  Scott Depot, WV..................800-331-1345
Peerless Conveyor & Mfg Corp
  Kansas City, KS..................913-342-2240
Peerless Food Equipment
  Sidney, OH.......................937-492-4158
Peerless-Winsmith Inc
  Springville, NY..................716-592-9310
Pelco Packaging Corporation
  Stirling, NJ.....................908-647-3500
Penda Form Corp
  New Concord, OH..................800-837-2574
Pengo Attachments Inc
  Cokato, MN.......................800-599-0211
Peregrine Inc
  Lincoln, NE......................800-777-3433
Peterson Fiberglass Laminates
  Shell Lake, WI...................715-468-2306
Phelps Industries
  Little Rock, AR..................501-568-5550
Piab Vacuum Products
  Hingham, MA......................800-321-7422
Pine Bluff Crating & Pallet
  Pine Bluff, AR...................866-415-1075
Pine Point Wood Products Inc
  Osseo, MN........................763-428-4301
Piper Products Inc
  Wausau, WI.......................800-544-3057
PlexPack Corp
  Toronto, ON......................855-635-9238
Pneumatic Conveying Inc
  Ontario, CA......................800-655-4481
Polar Beer Systems
  Sun City, CA.....................951-928-8174
Pomona Service & Pkgng Co LA
  Yakima, WA.......................509-452-7121
Port Erie Plastics Inc
  Harborcreek, PA..................814-899-7602
Portec Flowmaster
  Canon City, CO...................800-777-7471
Porter & Porter Lumber
  Fort Gay, WV.....................304-648-5133
Positech Corp
  Laurens, IA......................800-831-6026
Power Electronics Intl Inc
  East Dundee, IL..................800-362-7959
Power-Pack Conveyor Co
  Willoughby, OH...................440-975-9955
Poweramp
  Germantown, WI...................800-643-5424
Ppm Technologies LLC
  Newberg, OR......................800-246-2034
Prater Industries
  Bolingbrook, IL..................877-247-5625
Precision Wood of Hawaii
  Vancouver, WA....................808-682-2055
Precision Wood Products
  Vancouver, WA....................360-694-8322
Premium Pallet
  Philadelphia, PA.................800-648-7347
Presence From Innovation LLC
  St Louis, MO.....................314-423-9777
Priority One America
  Oshkosh, WI......................920-235-5562
Priority One Packaging
  Waterloo, ON.....................800-387-9102
Pro Line Co
  Haverhill, MA....................978-521-2600
Process Engineering & Fabrication
  Afton, VA........................800-852-7975
Process Solutions
  Riviera Beach, FL................561-840-0050

Prodo-Pak Corp
  Garfield, NJ.....................973-777-7770
Production Equipment Co
  Meriden, CT......................800-758-5697
Production Systems
  Marietta, GA.....................800-235-9734
Professional Engineering Assoc
  Louisville, KY...................502-429-0432
Progressive Tractor & Implement Co.
  Parks, LA........................337-845-5080
Pruitt's Packaging Services
  Grand Rapids, MI.................800-878-0553
Psc Floturn Inc
  Union, NJ........................908-687-3225
PTI Packaging
  Portage, WI......................800-501-4077
PTR Baler & Compactor Co
  Philadelphia, PA.................800-523-3654
Pucel Enterprises Inc
  Cleveland, OH....................800-336-4986
Puritan Manufacturing Inc
  Omaha, NE........................800-331-0487
Quality Corporation
  Denver, CO.......................800-383-3018
Quality Fabrication & Design
  Coppell, TX......................972-304-3266
R.G Stephens Engineering
  Long Beach, CA...................800-499-3001
Rahmann Belting & Industrial Rubber Products
  Gastonia, NC.....................888-248-8148
Ralph L. Mason,
  Newark, MD.......................410-632-1766
Ralphs Pugh Conveyor Rollers
  Benicia, CA......................800-486-0021
RAM Center
  Red Wing, MN.....................800-309-5431
Rand-Whitney Group LLC
  Worcester, MA....................508-791-2301
Repat Corp
  Hawley, MN.......................800-325-6377
Rapid Industries Inc
  Louisville, KY...................800-787-4381
Rapid Pallet
  Jermyn, PA.......................570-876-4000
Rapid Rack Industries
  City of Industry, CA.............800-736-7225
Ratcliff Hoist Company
  San Carlos, CA...................650-595-3840
Raymond Corp
  Greene, NY.......................800-235-7200
Reading Plastic Fabricators
  Reading, PA......................610-926-3245
Redding Pallet Inc
  Redding, CA......................530-241-6321
Reelcraft Industries Inc
  Columbia City, IN................800-444-3134
Reese Enterprises Inc
  Rosemount, MN....................800-328-0953
Regina USA
  Oak Creek, WI....................414-571-0032
Reinke & Schomann
  Milwaukee, WI....................414-964-1100
Reis Robotics
  Carpentersville, IL..............847-741-9500
Remco Products Corp
  Zionsville, IN...................800-585-8619
Remcon Plastics Inc
  Reading, PA......................800-360-3636
Remmey Wood Products
  Southampton, PA..................215-355-3335
Remstar International
  Westbrook, ME....................800-639-5805
Renold Products
  Westfield, NY....................800-879-2529
RETROTECH, Inc
  West Henrietta, NY...............866-915-2777
Rexnord Corporation
  Milwaukee, WI....................866-739-6673
Reyco Systems Inc
  Caldwell, ID.....................208-795-5700
Rhodes Machinery International
  Louisville, KY...................502-213-3865
Richards Industries Systems
  West Caldwell, NJ................973-575-7480
Rigidized Metal Corp
  Buffalo, NY......................800-836-2580
RMI-C/Rotonics Manaufacturing
  Bensenville, IL..................630-773-9510
Roberts Pallet Co
  Ellington, MO....................573-663-7877
Robinson Industries Inc
  Coleman, MI......................989-465-6111

Roechling Engineered Plastics
  Gastonia, NC.....................800-541-4419
Roll Rite Corp
  Hayward, CA......................800-345-9305
Rome Machine & Foundry Co
  Rome, GA.........................800-538-7663
Ron Vallort & Associates
  Oak Brook, IL....................630-734-3821
Ross Technology Corp
  Leola, PA........................800-345-8170
Roto-Jet Pump
  Salt Lake City, UT...............801-359-8731
Royal Ecoproducts
  Vaughan, ON......................800-465-7670
Royce Corp
  Glendale, AZ.....................602-256-0006
Royce Rolls Ringer Co
  Grand Rapids, MI.................800-253-9638
Ruiz Flour Tortillas
  Riverside, CA....................909-947-7811
S & W Pallet Co
  Camden, TN.......................800-640-0522
Sackett Systems
  Bensenville, IL..................800-323-8332
Sadler Conveyor Systems
  Montreal, QC.....................888-887-5129
Saeplast Canada
  St John, NB......................800-567-3966
Samuel Pressure Vessel Group
  Marinette, WI....................715-453-5326
San Fab Conveyor
  Sandusky, OH.....................419-626-4465
Sapac International
  Fond Du Lac, WI..................800-257-2722
Sardee Industries Inc
  Orlando, FL......................407-297-6362
Sardee Industries Inc
  Lisle, IL........................630-824-4200
Sasib Beverage & Food North America
  Plano, TX........................800-558-3814
Saturn Overhead Equipment
  Somerset, NJ.....................800-631-4473
Savanna Pallets
  McGregor, MN.....................218-768-2077
Savanna Pallets
  Cloquet, MN......................218-879-8553
Schaeff
  Bridgeview, IL...................888-436-7867
Scheb International
  North Barrington, IL.............847-381-2573
Schenck Process
  Whitewater, WI...................888-742-1249
Schloss Engineered Equipment
  Aurora, CO.......................303-695-4500
Schlueter Company
  Janesville, WI...................800-359-1700
Schroeder Machine
  San Marcos, CA...................760-591-9733
Scientific Process & Research
  Kendall Park, NJ.................800-868-4777
Scott Pallets Inc
  Amelia Court Hse, VA.............800-394-2514
Screw Conveyor Corp
  Hammond, IN......................219-931-1450
Semco Manufacturing Company
  Pharr, TX........................956-787-4203
Sencorp White
  Hyannis, MA......................508-771-9400
Sertapak Packaging Corporation
  Woodstock, ON....................800-265-1162
Servco Equipment Co
  St Louis, MO.....................314-781-3189
Sfb Plastics Inc
  Wichita, KS......................800-343-8133
Shammi Industries
  Corona, CA.......................800-417-9260
Shelby Pallet & Box Company
  Shelby, MI.......................231-861-4214
Shelcon Inc
  Ontario, CA......................909-947-4877
Sheldon Wood Products
  Toano, VA........................757-566-8880
Shepard Niles Parts
  Montour Falls, NY................800-727-8774
Shick Esteve
  Kansas City, MO..................877-744-2587
Shiffer Industries
  Kihei, HI........................800-642-1774
Shingle Belting
  King Of Prussia, PA..............800-345-6294
Shippers Supply
  Saskatoon, SK....................800-661-5639

Shippers Supply, Labelgraphic
Calgary, AB. 800-661-5639
Shouldice Brothers SheetMetal
Battle Creek, MI 269-962-5579
Shuttleworth North America
Huntington, IN 800-444-7412
SI Systems Inc
Easton, PA. 800-523-9464
Sidney Manufacturing Co
Sidney, OH. 800-482-3535
Sigma Industries
Elkhart, IN. 574-295-9660
Simplex Filler Co
Napa, CA. 800-796-7539
Simplimatic Automation
Forest, VA. 800-294-2003
Sinco
Red Wing, MN 800-243-6753
SIT Indeva Inc
Charlotte, NC 704-357-8811
Slip-Not Belting Corporation
Kingsport, TN. 423-246-8141
Smalley Manufacturing Co Inc
Knoxville, TN. 865-966-5866
Smalley Package Company
Berryville, VA. 540-955-2550
Smetco
Aurora, OR 800-253-5400
Smith Pallet Co Inc
Hatfield, AR 870-389-6184
Solve Needs International
White Lake, MI. 800-783-2462
Sonoma Pacific Company
Montebello, CA 323-838-4374
Sould Manufacturing
Winnepeg, NB. 204-339-3499
South Shore Controls Inc
Perry, OH 440-259-2500
Southern Ag Co Inc
Blakely, GA. 229-723-4262
Southern Pallet
Christchurch, NZ 901-942-4603
Southworth Products Corp
Falmouth, ME. 800-743-1000
SP Industries
Hopkins, MI 800-592-5959
Span Tech LLC
Glasgow, KY 270-651-9166
Spanco Crane & Monorail Systems
Morgantown, PA. 800-869-2080
Sparks Belting Co
Grand Rapids, MI 800-451-4537
Speedways Conveyors
Lancaster, NY. 800-800-1022
Spencer Turbine Co
Windsor, CT 800-232-4321
Sperling Industries
Omaha, NE 402-556-4070
SPG International
Covington, GA 877-503-4774
Spring Wood Products
Geneva, OH. 440-466-1135
Springport Steel Wire Products
Elkhart, IN. 574-295-9660
Spudnik Equipment Co
Blackfoot, ID 208-684-4120
Spurgeon Co
Ferndale, MI 800-396-2554
St. Pierre Box & Lumber Company
Canton, CT 860-693-2089
Stainless Specialists Inc
Wausau, WI. 800-236-4155
Stainless Steel Fabricator Inc
La Mirada, CA. 714-739-9904
Stearnswood Inc
Hutchinson, MN 800-657-0144
Steel King Industries
Stevens Point, WI 800-553-3096
Steel Storage Systems Inc
Commerce City, CO 800-442-0291
Steinmetz Machine Works Inc
Stamford, CT. 203-327-0118
Sterling Net & Twine Company
Cedar Knolls, NJ. 800-342-0316
Stewart Systems Baking LLC
Plano, TX 972-422-5808
Stiles Enterprises Inc
Rockaway, NJ 800-325-4232
Stokes Material Handling Systs
Doylestown, PA 215-340-2200
Storax
Bromsgrove, UK. 845-130-3090

Stratis Plastic Pallets
Indianapolis, IN 800-725-5387
Streator Dependable Mfg
Streator, IL 800-798-0551
Studd & Whipple Company
Conewango Valley, NY. 716-287-3791
Suffolk Iron Works Inc
Suffolk, VA. 757-539-2353
Summit Machine Builders Corporation
Denver, CO. 800-274-6741
Super Sturdy
Weldon, NC. 800-253-4833
Superior Industries
Morris, MN 800-321-1558
Svedala Industries
Colorado Springs, CO. 719-471-3443
Sweet Manufacturing Co
Springfield, OH. 800-334-7254
SWF Co
Reedley, CA 800-344-8951
Swift Creek Forest Products
Jetersville, VA. 804-561-4498
Swisslog Logistics Inc
Newport News, VA. 800-777-6862
Tampa Pallet Co
Tampa, FL 813-626-5700
Tasler Inc
Webster City, IA 515-832-5200
TC/American Monorail
Saint Michael, MN 763-497-7000
TDF Automation
Cedar Falls, IA 800-553-1777
Technibilt/Cari-All
Newton, NC 800-233-3972
Technipac
Le Sueur, MN 507-665-6658
Technistar Corporation
Denver, CO. 303-651-0188
Tecweigh
St Paul, MN. 800-536-4880
Tennessee Mills
Red Boiling Springs, TN. 615-699-2253
The National Provisioner
Deerfield, IL 847-763-9534
Theimeg
Sharpsville, PA. 724-962-3571
Thermodynamics
Commerce City, CO 800-627-9037
Thiele Technologies Inc
Minneapolis, MN 612-782-1200
Thomas L. Green & Company
Robenosia, PA. 610-693-5816
Thombert
Newton, IA 800-433-3572
Thorco Industries LLC
Lamar, MO 800-445-3375
Thoreson Mc Cosh Inc
Troy, MI 800-959-0805
Thunder Pallet Inc
Theresa, WI. 800-354-0643
Timbertech Company
Milton, NH 800-572-5538
Titan Industries Inc
New London, WI 800-558-3616
TKF Inc
Cincinnati, OH 513-241-5910
Torbeck Industries
Harrison, OH. 800-333-0080
Toter Inc
Statesville, NC 800-772-0071
Tower Pallet Co Inc
De Pere, WI. 920-336-3495
Transbotics Corp
Charlotte, NC 704-362-1115
Transnorm System Inc
Grand Prairie, TX 800-259-2303
Travelon
Elk Grove Vlg, IL. 800-537-5544
Traycon Manufacturing Co
Carlstadt, NJ 201-939-5555
Treen Box & Pallet Inc
Bensalem, PA 215-639-5100
Tri-Pak Machinery Inc
Harlingen, TX 956-423-5140
Tri-State Plastics
Glenwillard, PA. 724-457-6900
Tri-Tronics
Tampa, FL. 800-237-0946
Triad Pallet Co Inc
Greensboro, NC 336-292-8175
Tridyne Process Systems
South Burlington, VT 802-863-6873

Triple S Dynamics Inc
Breckenridge, TX 800-527-2116
Triple-A Manufacturing Company
Toronto, ON 800-786-2238
TWM Manufacturing
Leamington, ON 888-495-4831
Uhrden
Sugarcreek, OH. 800-852-2411
Unarco Material Handling Inc
Pandora, OH 800-448-0784
Unex Manufacturing Inc
Lakewood, NJ. 800-334-8639
Uni Carriers Americas Corp
Marengo, IL 800-871-5438
Unidex
Warsaw, NY 800-724-1302
United Pentek
Indianapolis, IN 800-357-9299
United States Systems Inc
Kansas City, KS 888-281-2454
UniTrak Corporation
Port Hope, ON 866-883-5749
Universal Die & Stampings
Prairie Du Sac, WI 608-643-2477
Universal Industries Inc
Cedar Falls, IA 800-553-4446
Universal Labeling Systems Inc
St Petersburg, FL 877-236-0266
Universal Packaging Inc
Houston, TX 800-324-2610
Upham & Walsh Lumber
Hoffman Estates, IL 847-519-1010
UPN Pallet Company
Penns Grove, NJ 856-299-1192
Us Rubber
Brooklyn, NY 718-782-7888
USECO
Murfreesboro, TN. 615-893-4820
V-Ram Solids
Albert Lea, MN 888-373-3996
Vac-U-Max
Belleville, NJ 800-822-8629
Van Dereems Mfg Co
Hawthorne, NJ 973-427-2355
Vancouver Manufacturing
Washougal, WA. 360-835-8519
Vande Berg SCALES/Vbs Inc
Sioux Center, IA 712-722-1181
Vaughn Belting Co-Main Acct
Spartanburg, SC 800-533-9086
Versa Conveyor
London, OH 740-852-5609
Vertical Systems Intl
Lakeside Park, KY 859-485-9650
Vescom America
Henderson, NC 252-436-9067
Videojet Technologies Inc
Wood Dale, IL. 800-843-3610
W A Powers Co
Fort Worth, TX 800-792-1243
W.G. Durant Corporation
Whittier, CA 562-946-5555
Waldon Manufacturing LLC
Fairview, OK. 800-486-0023
Walker Magnetics Group Inc
Worcester, MA 800-962-4638
Wall Conveyor & Manufacturing
Huntington, WV 800-456-1335
Walters Brothers
Radisson, WI. 715-945-2646
Ward Ironworks
Welland, ON 888-441-9273
Wardcraft Conveyor & Quick Die
Spring Arbor, MI 800-782-2779
Warren Pallet Co Inc
Bloomsbury, NJ. 908-995-7172
Wastequip Inc
Charlotte, NC 704-366-7140
Wayne Engineering
Cedar Falls, IA 319-266-1721
WEBB-Stiles Co
Valley City, OH. 330-273-9222
Weigh Right Automatic Scale Co
Joliet, IL 800-571-0249
Welch Packaging Group Inc
Elkhart, IN. 574-295-2460
Wesley International Corp
Scottdale, GA 800-241-8649
Westfield Sheet Metal Works
Kenilworth, NJ 908-276-5500
Wetterau Wood Products
Burlington, MA. 800-986-0958

Whallon Machinery Inc
Royal Center, IN 574-643-9561
Whirl Air Flow
Big Lake, MN 800-373-3461
Whit-Log Trailers Inc
Wilbur, OR 800-452-1234
White Mop Wringer Company
Tampa, FL 800-237-7582
White Mountain Lumber Co
Berlin, NH 603-752-1000
Wilder Manufacturing Company
Port Jervis, NY 800-832-1319
Wilkie Brothers Conveyor Inc
Marysville, MI 810-364-4820
Williams Pallet
West Chester, OH 513-874-4014
Williamsburg Millwork
Ruther Glen, VA 804-994-2151
Williamson & Co
Greer, SC 800-849-3263
Wilson Steel Products Company
Memphis, TN 901-527-8742
Win-Holt Equipment Group
Syosset, NY 800-444-3595
Wire Belt Co Of America
Londonderry, NH 603-644-2500
Wireway Husky Corp
Denver, NC 800-438-5629
Wittco Foodservice Equipment
Milwaukee, WI 800-821-3912
Witte Co Inc
Washington, NJ 908-689-6500
Wnc Pallet & Forest Pdts Co
Candler, NC 828-667-5426
Woodson Pallet Co
Anmoore, WV 304-623-2858
Yakima Wire Works
Reedley, CA 800-344-8951
Yargus Manufacturing Inc
Marshall, IL 217-826-8059
Yerger Wood Products
East Greenville, PA 215-679-4413
York River Pallet Corporation
Shacklefords, VA 804-785-5811
YW Yacht Basin
Easton, MD 410-822-0414
Z-Loda Systems Engineering Inc
Stamford, CT 203-325-8001
Zenar Corp
Oak Creek, WI 414-764-1800
Zimmerman Handling Systems
Madison Heights, MI 800-347-7047
Ziniz
Louisville, KY 502-955-6573
Zoia Banquetier Co
Cleveland, OH 216-631-6414

Pallet Handling Equipment

Advanced Uniflo Technologies
Wichita, KS 800-688-0400
Air Technical Industries
Mentor, OH 888-857-6265
Anver Corporation
Hudson, MA 800-654-3500
Automated Production Systems Corporation
New Freedom, PA 888-345-5377
Bayhead Products Corp.
Dover, NH 800-229-4323
Bmh Equipment Inc
Sacramento, CA 800-350-8828
Burgess Mfg. - Oklahoma
Guthrie, OK 800-804-1913
Bushman Equipment Inc
Menomonee Falls, WI 800-338-7810
Cannon Equipment Company
Cannon Falls, MN 800-825-8501
Cherry's Industrial Eqpt Corp
Elk Grove Vlg, IL 800-350-0011
CLECO Systems
Marietta, GA 770-392-0330
Conveyance Technologies LLC
Cleveland, OH 800-701-2278
Currie Machinery Co
Santa Clara, CA 408-727-0422
Douglas Machine Inc
Alexandria, MN 320-763-6587
Dynabilt Products
Readville, MA 800-443-1008
Edson Packaging Machinery
Hamilton, ON 800-493-3766
Equipment Design & Fabrication
Charlotte, NC 800-949-0165

Eugene Welding Company
Marysville, MI 810-364-7421
Fibre Converters Inc
Constantine, MI 269-279-1700
FreesTech
Sinking Spring, PA 717-560-7560
Goldco Industries
Loveland, CO 970-663-4770
Halton Packaging Systems
Oakville, ON 905-847-9141
Johnston Equipment
Delta, BC 800-237-5159
Krones
Franklin, WI 800-752-3787
KUKA Robotics Corp
Shelby Township, MI 800-459-6691
Lexington Logistics LLC
Portage, WI 800-356-8150
Load King Mfg
Jacksonville, FL 800-531-4975
Long Reach ManufacturingCompany
Westport, CT 800-285-7000
Metal Equipment Company
Cleveland, OH 800-700-6326
Metzgar Conveyors
Comstock Park, MI 888-266-8390
Mitsubishi Caterpillar Mcfa
Houston, TX 800-228-5438
Ohio Rack Inc
Alliance, OH 800-344-4164
Priority One Packaging
Waterloo, ON 800-387-9102
PTI Packaging
Portage, WI 800-501-4077
RAM Center
Red Wing, MN 800-309-5431
Reis Robotics
Carpentersville, IL 847-741-9500
Sadler Conveyor Systems
Montreal, QC 888-887-5129
San Fab Conveyor
Sandusky, OH 419-626-4465
Sfb Plastics Inc
Wichita, KS 800-343-8133
Shrinkfast Marketing
Newport, NH 800-867-4746
Sigma Industries
Elkhart, IN 574-295-9660
Smetco
Aurora, OR 800-253-5400
Solve Needs International
White Lake, MI 800-783-2462
Springport Steel Wire Products
Elkhart, IN 574-295-9660
Steel King Industries
Stevens Point, WI 800-553-3096
Unarco Material Handling Inc
Pandora, OH 800-448-0784
WEBB-Stiles Co
Valley City, OH 330-273-9222
Wesley International Corp
Scottdale, GA 800-241-8649
Wireway Husky Corp
Denver, NC 800-438-5629

Palletizers

Automated Production Systems Corporation
New Freedom, PA 888-345-5377
Bell Packaging Corporation
Marion, IN 800-382-0153
Berkshire PPM
Litchfield, CT 860-567-3118
BEUMER Corp
Somerset, NJ 732-893-2800
Busse/SJI Corp
Randolph, WI 800-882-4995
Cannon Equipment Company
Cannon Falls, MN 800-825-8501
Chantland Company, The
Humboldt, IA 515-332-4040
Columbia Machine Inc
Vancouver, WA 800-628-4065
Conveying Industries
Denver, CO 877-600-4874
Currie Machinery Co
Santa Clara, CA 408-727-0422
Custom Metal Design Inc
Oakland, FL 800-334-1777
Dearborn Mid-West Conveyor Co
Overland Park, KS 913-384-9950
Douglas Machine Inc
Alexandria, MN 320-763-6587

Edmeyer
Minneapolis, MN 651-450-1210
FleetwoodGoldcoWyard
Romeoville, IL 630-759-6800
FreesTech
Sinking Spring, PA 717-560-7560
General Corrugated Machinery Company
Palisades Park, NJ 201-944-0644
Goldco Industries
Loveland, CO 970-663-4770
Halton Packaging Systems
Oakville, ON 905-847-9141
Iman Pack
Westland, MI 800-810-4626
ITW Angleboard
Villa Rica, GA 770-459-5747
Jetstream Systems
Wichita, KN 855-861-6916
Krones
Franklin, WI 800-752-3787
KUKA Robotics Corp
Shelby Township, MI 800-459-6691
Kusel Equipment Company
Watertown, WI 920-261-4112
Lambert Material Handling
Syracuse, NY 800-253-5103
Lexington Logistics LLC
Portage, WI 800-356-8150
Magnuson
Pueblo, CO 719-948-9500
Mathews Conveyor
Danville, KY 800-628-4397
Newcastle Co Inc
New Castle, PA 724-658-4516
Nitech
Columbus, NE. 800-237-6496
Ocme America Corporation
York, PA 717-843-6263
Ouellette Machinery Systems
Fenton, MO 800-545-7619
Packaging & Processing Equipment
Ayr, ON 519-622-6666
Packaging Systems Intl
Denver, CO 303-244-9000
PASCO
St Louis, MO. 800-489-3300
Priority One America
Oshkosh, WI 920-235-5562
Priority One Packaging
Waterloo, ON 800-387-9102
Production Systems
Marietta, GA 800-235-9734
PTI Packaging
Portage, WI 800-501-4077
R.G. Stephens Engineering
Long Beach, CA 800-499-3001
RAM Center
Red Wing, MN 800-309-5431
Reis Robotics
Carpentersville, IL 847-741-9500
Sapac International
Fond Du Lac, WI 800-257-2722
Sardee Industries Inc
Orlando, FL 407-297-6362
Sardee Industries Inc
Lisle, IL 630-824-4200
Sasib Beverage & Food North America
Plano, TX 800-558-3814
Simplimatic Automation
Forest, VA 800-294-2003
Southworth Products Corp
Falmouth, ME. 800-743-1000
Technistar Corporation
Denver, CO 303-651-0188
Thiele Technologies Inc
Minneapolis, MN 612-782-1200
W.G. Durant Corporation
Whittier, CA 562-946-5555
Whallon Machinery Inc
Royal Center, IN 574-643-9561

Pallets

A.M. Loveman Lumber & Box Company
Nashville, TN 615-297-1397
Advance Engineering Co
Canton, MI 800-497-6388
Allflex Packaging Products
Ambler, PA 800-448-2467
American Box Corporation
Lisbon, OH 330-424-8055
American Pallet Inc
Oakdale, CA 209-847-6122

Auto Pallets-Boxes
  Lathrup Village, MI 800-875-2699
Barrette Outdoor Living
  Cleveland, OH 800-336-2383
Bay Area Pallet Company/IFCO Systems
  Houston, TX 877-430-4326
Bc Wood Products
  Ashland, VA 804-798-9154
Bell Packaging Corporation
  Marion, IN. 800-382-0153
Bennett Box & Pallet Company
  Winston, NC 800-334-8741
Bergen Barrel & Drum Company
  Kearny, NJ. 201-998-3500
Black River Pallet Co
  Zeeland, MI. 800-427-6515
Buckhorn Canada
  Brampton, ON. 800-461-7579
Buckhorn Inc
  Milford, OH 800-543-4454
Burgess Mfg. - Oklahoma
  Guthrie, OK. 800-804-1913
C & L Wood Products Inc
  Hartselle, AL. 800-483-2035
Cantley-Ellis Manufacturing Company
  Kingsport, TN 423-246-4671
Carson Industries
  Pomona, CA 800-735-5566
Cascade Wood Components
  Cascade Locks, OR. 541-374-8413
Cassel Box & Lumber Co Inc
  Grafton, WI. 262-377-9503
Cedar Box Co
  Minneapolis, MN 612-332-4287
Challenger Pallet & Supply Inc
  Idaho Falls, ID 800-733-0205
Charles Tirschman Pallet Co
  Dundalk, MD 410-282-6199
Cimino Box & Pallet Co
  Cleveland, OH 216-961-7377
Coblentz Brothers Inc
  Apple Creek, OH 330-857-7211
Coddington Lumber Co
  Frostburg, MD 301-689-8816
Corinth Products
  Corinth, ME 207-285-3387
Cutler Brothers Box & Lumber
  Fairview, NJ 201-943-2535
Cutler Lumber Products
  Livermore, CA 925-443-5959
D&M Pallet Company
  Neshkoro, WI 920-293-4616
Daniel Boone Lumber Industries
  Morehead, KY 606-784-7586
Davis Core & Pa
  Cave Spring, GA 800-235-7483
Day Lumber Company
  Westfield, MA. 413-568-3511
Denver Reel & Pallet Company
  Denver, CO 303-321-1920
Development Workshop Inc
  Idaho Falls, ID 800-657-5597
Dufeck Manufacturing Co
  Denmark, WI. 888-603-9663
Durant Box Factory
  Durant, OK 580-924-4035
Eichler Wood Products
  Laurys Station, PA 610-262-6749
Elba Pallets Company
  Elba, AL .334-897-6034
Elberta Crate & Box Company
  Carpentersville, IL 888-672-9260
ERO/Goodrich Forest Products
  Tualatin, OR. 800-458-5545
F.E. Wood & Sons
  West Baldwin, ME 207-286-5003
Fabricated Components Inc
  Stroudsburg, PA 800-233-8163
Fabrication Specialties
  Centerville, TN 931-729-2283
Fehlig Brothers Box & Lbr Co
  St Louis, MO. 314-241-6900
Felco Packaging Specialist
  Baltimore, MD 800-673-8488
Fresno Pallet, Inc.
  Sultana, CA 559-591-4111
G L Packaging Products Inc
  West Chicago, IL 866-935-8755
Gatewood Products LLC
  Parkersburg, WV. 800-827-5461
Gbn Machine & Engineering
  Woodford, VA. 800-446-9871

Gemini Plastic Films Corporation
  Garfield, NJ. 800-789-4732
Gerrity Industries
  Monmouth, ME. 877-933-2804
Girard Wood Products Inc
  Puyallup, WA 800-532-0505
Goeman's Wood Products
  Hartford, WI 262-673-6090
Graham Pallet Co Inc
  Tompkinsville, KY 888-525-0694
Gray Woodproducts
  Tacoma, WA 253-752-7000
Green Tek
  Janesville, WI 800-747-6440
H&H Lumber Company
  Amarillo, TX 806-335-1813
H&H Wood Products
  Hamburg, NY 716-648-5600
Hampton Roads Box Company
  Suffolk, VA 757-934-2355
Hanson Box & Lumber Company
  Wakefield, MA 617-245-0358
Harbor Pallet Company
  Anaheim, CA 714-871-0932
Hawkeye Pallet Co
  Johnston, IA 515-276-0409
Herkimer Pallet & Wood Products Company
  Herkimer, NY 315-866-4591
HHP Inc
  Henniker, NH 603-428-3298
Hildreth Wood Products Inc
  Wadesboro, NC. 704-826-8326
Hinchcliff Products Company
  Strongsville, OH 440-238-5200
Hunter Woodworks
  Carson, CA 800-966-4751
Industrial Hardwood
  Perrysburg, OH 419-666-2503
Industrial Lumber & Packaging
  Spring Lake, MI 616-842-1457
Industrial Woodfab & Packaging
  Riverview, MI 734-284-4808
International Wood Industries
  Snohomish, WA 800-922-6141
ITW Plastic Packaging
  Denver, CO 303-316-6816
J.M. Rogers & Sons
  Moss Point, MS 228-475-7584
Jarke Corporation
  Prospect Hts, IL 800-722-5255
Jeco Plastic Products LLC
  Plainfield, IN. 800-593-5326
John Rock Inc
  Coatesville, PA 610-857-4809
Kadon Corporation
  Milford, OH 937-299-0088
Kauling Wood Products Company
  Beckemeyer, IL. 618-594-2901
Kelley Wood Products
  Fitchburg, MA 978-345-7531
KETCH
  Wichita, KS 800-766-3777
Killington Wood ProductsCompany
  Rutland, VT. 802-773-9111
Kimball Companies
  East Longmeadow, MA 413-525-1881
Konz Wood Products Co
  Appleton, WI 877-610-5145
L T Hampel Corp
  Germantown, WI. 800-681-6979
L&H Wood Manufacturing Company
  Farmington, MI. 248-474-9000
L&S Pallet Company
  Houston, TX 281-443-6537
La Menuiserie East Angus
  East Angus, QC. 819-832-2746
Lake Michigan Hardwood Company
  Leland, MI. 231-256-9811
Larson Pallet Company
  Ogema, WI 715-767-5131
Lawson Industries
  Holden, MO 816-732-4347
Lester Box & Mfg Div
  Long Beach, CA 562-437-5123
Lexington Logistics LLC
  Portage, WI. 800-356-8150
Load King Mfg
  Jacksonville, FL 800-531-4975
Longview Fibre Co
  Longview, WA 800-929-8111
Lumber & Things
  Keyser, WV. 800-296-5656

Lydall
  Doswell, VA 804-266-9611
M & H Crate Inc
  Jacksonville, TX 903-683-5351
M O Industries Inc
  Whippany, NJ. 973-386-9228
Madison County Wood Products
  St Louis, MO. 314-772-1722
Marion Pallet Company
  Marion, OH 800-432-4117
Mark Slade ManufacturingCompany
  Seymour, WI. 920-833-6557
Marshall Boxes Inc
  Rochester, NY 585-458-7432
Mason Ways Indestructible
  West Palm Beach, FL 800-837-2881
Maull-Baker Box Company
  Brookfield, WI 414-463-1290
Mayco Inc
  Dallas, TX 214-638-4848
MBX Packaging Specialists
  Wausau, WI 715-845-1171
Mcintosh Box & Pallet Co
  East Syracuse, NY 800-219-9552
Mcneilly Wood Products Inc
  Campbell Hall, NY 845-457-9651
Meriden Box Company
  Southington, CT 860-621-7141
Michiana Box & Crate
  Niles, MI. 800-677-6372
Michigan Box Co
  Detroit, MI 888-642-4269
Michigan Pallet Inc
  St Charles, MI 989-865-9915
Millwood Inc
  Vienna, OH 330-393-4400
Momence Pallet Corp
  Momence, IL. 815-472-6451
Moorecraft Box & Crate
  Tarboro, NC 252-823-2510
Mt Valley Farms & Lumber Prods
  Biglerville, PA. 717-677-6166
Native Lumber Company
  Wallingford, CT 203-269-2625
Necedah Pallet Co Inc
  Necedah, WI 800-672-5538
Nefab Packaging Inc.
  Coppell, TX 800-322-4425
Nefab Packaging, Inc.
  Coppell, TX 800-322-4425
Nelson Co
  Sparrows Point, MD 410-477-3000
NEPA Pallet & Container Co
  Snohomish, WA 360-568-3185
New England Pallets & Skids
  Ludlow, MA 413-583-6628
New Lisbon Wood ProductsManufacturing Company
  New Lisbon, WI 608-562-3122
New Mexico Products Inc
  Albuquerque, NM 877-345-7864
New South Co Inc
  Myrtle Beach, SC 843-236-9399
Newcourt, Inc.
  Madison, IN. 800-933-0006
Northwest Products
  Archbold, OH 419-445-1950
Nucon Corporation
  Deerfield, IL. 877-545-0070
Oak Creek Pallet Company
  Milwaukee, WI 414-762-7170
Occidental Chemical Corporation
  Dallas, TX. 800-733-3665
ORBIS
  Oconomowoc, WI. 262-560-5000
ORBIS
  Oconomowoc, WI. 800-890-7292
Original Lincoln Logs
  Chestertown, NY 800-833-2461
OTD Corporation
  Hinsdale, IL. 630-321-9232
Packing Material Company
  Southfield, MI. 248-489-7000
Pallet Management Systems
  Lawrenceville, VA 800-446-1804
Pallet Masters
  Los Angeles, CA. 800-675-2579
Pallet One Inc
  Bartow, FL. 800-771-1148
Pallet Pro
  Moss, TN. 800-489-3661
Pallet Service Corp
  Maple Grove, MN. 888-391-8020

Pallets Inc
Fort Edward, NY..................518-747-4177
Pallister Pallet
Wapello, IA.......................319-523-8161
Pallox Incorporated
Onsted, MI.......................517-456-4101
Paper Systems Inc
Des Moines, IA...................800-342-2855
Paul Hawkins Lumber Company
Mannington, WV.................304-986-2230
Penda Form Corp
New Concord, OH...............800-837-2574
Pinckney Molded Plastics
Howell, MI.......................800-854-2920
Pine Bluff Crating & Pallet
Pine Bluff, AR...................866-415-1075
Pine Point Wood Products Inc
Osseo, MN.......................763-428-4301
Port Erie Plastics Inc
Harborcreek, PA.................814-899-7602
Porter & Porter Lumber
Fort Gay, WV....................304-648-5133
Precision Wood of Hawaii
Vancouver, WA..................808-682-2055
Precision Wood Products
Vancouver, WA..................360-694-8322
Premium Pallet
Philadelphia, PA.................800-648-7347
Pruitt's Packaging Services
Grand Rapids, MI................800-878-0553
Ralph L. Mason,
Newark, MD.....................410-632-1766
Rapid Pallet
Jermyn, PA......................570-876-4000
Redding Pallet Inc
Redding, CA......................530-241-6321
Remcon Plastics Inc
Reading, PA......................800-360-3636
Remmey Wood Products
Southampton, PA................215-355-3335
Roberts Pallet Co
Ellington, MO....................573-663-7877
Robinson Industries Inc
Coleman, MI.....................989-465-6111
Rotonics Manufacturing
Gardena, CA.....................310-327-5401
Royal Ecoproducts
Vaughan, ON....................800-465-7670
S & W Pallet Co
Camden, TN......................800-640-0522
Saeplast Canada
St John, NB......................800-567-3966
Savanna Pallets
McGregor, MN...................218-768-2077
Savanna Pallets
Cloquet, MN.....................218-879-8553
Scott Pallets Inc
Amelia Court Hse, VA............800-394-2514
Sertapak Packaging Corporation
Woodstock, ON..................800-265-1162
Sfb Plastics Inc
Wichita, KS......................800-343-8133
Shelby Pallet & Box Company
Shelby, MI.......................231-861-4214
Sheldon Wood Products
Toano, VA........................757-566-8880
Sigma Industries
Elkhart, IN.......................574-295-9660
Smalley Package Company
Berryville, VA....................540-955-2550
Smith Pallet Co Inc
Hatfield, AR......................870-389-6184
Sonoma Pacific Company
Montebello, CA..................323-838-4374
Southern Pallet
Christchurch, NZ.................901-942-4603
Spring Wood Products
Geneva, OH......................440-466-1135
Springport Steel Wire Products
Elkhart, IN.......................574-295-9660
St. Pierre Box & Lumber Company
Canton, CT.......................860-693-2089
Stearnswood Inc
Hutchinson, MN.................800-657-0144
Sterling Net & Twine Company
Cedar Knolls, NJ.................800-342-0316
Stratis Plastic Pallets
Indianapolis, IN..................800-725-5387
Streator Dependable Mfg
Streator, IL.......................800-798-0551
Studd & Whipple Company
Conewango Valley, NY...........716-287-3791

Swift Creek Forest Products
Jetersville, VA....................804-561-4498
Tampa Pallet Co
Tampa, FL........................813-626-5700
Tasler Inc
Webster City, IA..................515-832-5200
Technipac
Le Sueur, MN....................507-665-6658
Thermodynamics
Commerce City, CO..............800-627-9037
Thunder Pallet Inc
Theresa, WI......................800-354-0643
Timbertech Company
Milton, NH.......................800-572-5538
Tower Pallet Co Inc
De Pere, WI......................920-336-3495
Treen Box & Pallet Inc
Bensalem, PA....................215-639-5100
Triad Pallet Co Inc
Greensboro, NC..................336-292-8175
Upham & Walsh Lumber
Hoffman Estates, IL...............847-519-1010
UPN Pallet Company
Penns Grove, NJ.................856-299-1192
Vancouver Manufacturing
Washougal, WA..................360-835-8519
Viking Pallet Corp
Maple Grove, MN................763-425-6707
Walters Brothers
Radisson, WI.....................715-945-2646
Warren Pallet Co Inc
Bloomsbury, NJ..................908-995-7172
Welch Packaging Group Inc
Elkhart, IN.......................574-295-2460
Wetterau Wood Products
Burlington, MA...................800-986-0958
White Mountain Lumber Co
Berlin, NH........................603-752-1000
Williams Pallet
West Chester, OH................513-874-4014
Williamsburg Millwork
Ruther Glen, VA..................804-994-2151
Wnc Pallet & Forest Pdts Co
Candler, NC......................828-667-5426
Woodson Pallet Co
Anmoore, WV....................304-623-2858
Yerger Wood Products
East Greenville, PA...............215-679-4413
York River Pallet Corporation
Shacklefords, VA.................804-785-5811

Lift Truck

Bmh Equipment Inc
Sacramento, CA..................800-350-8828
Cantley-Ellis Manufacturing Company
Kingsport, TN....................423-246-4671
Central Pallet Mills Inc
Central City, KY..................270-754-2900
Dominion Pallet Inc
Mineral, VA.......................800-227-5321
Hanson Box & Lumber Company
Wakefield, MA...................617-245-0358
L T Hampel Corp
Germantown, WI.................800-681-6979
Paul Hawkins Lumber Company
Mannington, WV.................304-986-2230

Live Skid

L T Hampel Corp
Germantown, WI.................800-681-6979
Load King Mfg
Jacksonville, FL...................800-531-4975

Plastic

Barrette Outdoor Living
Cleveland, OH....................800-336-2383
Buckhorn Inc
Milford, OH.......................800-543-4454
Burgess Mfg. - Oklahoma
Guthrie, OK......................800-804-1913
Emco Industrial Plastics
Cedar Grove, NJ..................800-292-9906
Fresno Pallet, Inc.
Sultana, CA.......................559-591-4111
Green Tek
Janesville, WI....................800-747-6440
Gulf Arizona Packaging
Humble, TX.......................800-364-3887
Gulf Systems
Oklahoma City, OK..............800-364-3887

Harbor Pallet Company
Anaheim, CA.....................714-871-0932
Herche Warehouse
Denver, CO.......................303-371-8186
Kadon Corporation
Milford, OH.......................937-299-0088
Kimball Companies
East Longmeadow, MA...........413-525-1881
L T Hampel Corp
Germantown, WI.................800-681-6979
Lexington Logistics LLC
Portage, WI......................800-356-8150
Lumber & Things
Keyser, WV.......................800-296-5656
MBX Packaging Specialists
Wausau, WI......................715-845-1171
Nucon Corporation
Deerfield, IL......................877-545-0070
Occidental Chemical Corporation
Dallas, TX........................800-733-3665
ORBIS
Oconomowoc, WI................262-560-5000
ORBIS
Oconomowoc, WI................800-890-7292
Pallet Management Systems
Lawrenceville, VA.................800-446-1804
PDQ Plastics Inc
Bayonne, NJ......................800-447-7141
Penda Form Corp
New Concord, OH...............800-837-2574
Port Erie Plastics Inc
Harborcreek, PA.................814-899-7602
Robinson Industries Inc
Coleman, MI.....................989-465-6111
Royal Ecoproducts
Vaughan, ON....................800-465-7670
Saeplast Canada
St John, NB......................800-567-3966
Sfb Plastics Inc
Wichita, KS......................800-343-8133
Stearnswood Inc
Hutchinson, MN.................800-657-0144
Stratis Plastic Pallets
Indianapolis, IN..................800-725-5387
Thermodynamics
Commerce City, CO..............800-627-9037
TMF Corporation
Havertown, PA...................610-853-3080
Upham & Walsh Lumber
Hoffman Estates, IL...............847-519-1010

Wooden

A.M. Loveman Lumber & Box Company
Nashville, TN.....................615-297-1397
American Box Corporation
Lisbon, OH.......................330-424-8055
Auto Pallets-Boxes
Lathrup Village, MI...............800-875-2699
Bay Area Pallet Company/IFCO Systems
Houston, TX......................877-430-4326
Bc Wood Products
Ashland, VA......................804-798-9154
Burgess Mfg. - Oklahoma
Guthrie, OK......................800-804-1913
C & L Wood Products Inc
Hartselle, AL.....................800-483-2035
Cantley-Ellis Manufacturing Company
Kingsport, TN....................423-246-4671
Cascade Wood Components
Cascade Locks, OR...............541-374-8413
Cedar Box Co
Minneapolis, MN.................612-332-4287
Coastal Pallet Corp
Bridgeport, CT....................203-333-6222
Coblentz Brothers Inc
Apple Creek, OH................330-857-7211
Corinth Products
Corinth, ME......................207-285-3387
Cutler Brothers Box & Lumber
Fairview, NJ......................201-943-2535
D&M Pallet Company
Neshkoro, WI....................920-293-4616
Daniel Boone Lumber Industries
Morehead, KY....................606-784-7586
Day Lumber Company
Westfield, MA....................413-568-3511
Development Workshop Inc
Idaho Falls, ID...................800-657-5597
Dufeck Manufacturing Co
Denmark, WI.....................888-603-9663

Durant Box Factory
Durant, OK 580-924-4035
Eichler Wood Products
Laurys Station, PA 610-262-6749
Elba Pallets Company
Elba, AL 334-897-6034
ERO/Goodrich Forest Products
Tualatin, OR 800-458-5545
F.E. Wood & Sons
West Baldwin, ME 207-286-5003
Fabrication Specialties
Centerville, TN 931-729-2283
Fehlig Brothers Box & Lbr Co
St Louis, MO 314-241-6900
Fox Valley Wood Products Inc
Kaukauna, WI 920-766-4069
Fresno Pallet, Inc.
Sultana, CA 559-591-4111
G L Packaging Products Inc
West Chicago, IL 866-935-8755
Girard Wood Products Inc
Puyallup, WA 800-532-0505
Goeman's Wood Products
Hartford, WI 262-673-6090
Graham Pallet Co Inc
Tompkinsville, KY 888-525-0694
H&H Lumber Company
Amarillo, TX 806-335-1813
H&H Wood Products
Hamburg, NY 716-648-5600
Hanson Box & Lumber Company
Wakefield, MA 617-245-0358
Harbor Pallet Company
Anaheim, CA 714-871-0932
Hawkeye Pallet Co
Johnston, IA 515-276-0409
Herkimer Pallet & Wood Products Company
Herkimer, NY 315-866-4591
HHP Inc
Henniker, NH 603-428-3298
Hildreth Wood Products Inc
Wadesboro, NC 704-826-8326
Hinchcliff Products Company
Strongsville, OH 440-238-5200
Hunter Woodworks
Carson, CA 800-966-4751
Industrial Hardwood
Perrysburg, OH 419-666-2503
Industrial Woodfab & Packaging
Riverview, MI 734-284-4808
International Wood Industries
Snohomish, WA 800-922-6141
John Rock Inc
Coatesville, PA 610-857-4809
Kauling Wood Products Company
Beckemeyer, IL 618-594-2901
Kelley Wood Products
Fitchburg, MA 978-345-7531
KETCH
Wichita, KS 800-766-3777
Killington Wood ProductsCompany
Rutland, VT 802-773-9111
L&S Pallet Company
Houston, TX 281-443-6537
La Menuiserie East Angus
East Angus, QC 819-832-2746
Lake Michigan Hardwood Company
Leland, MI 231-256-9811
Lumber & Things
Keyser, WV 800-296-5656
Lydall
Doswell, VA 804-266-9611
M & H Crate Inc
Jacksonville, TX 903-683-5351
Madison County Wood Products
St Louis, MO 314-772-1722
Marion Pallet Company
Marion, OH 800-432-4117
Mark Slade ManufacturingCompany
Seymour, WI 920-833-6557
Marshall Boxes Inc
Rochester, NY 585-458-7432
Maull-Baker Box Company
Brookfield, WI 414-463-1290
Mayco Inc
Dallas, TX 214-638-4848
Mcintosh Box & Pallet Co
East Syracuse, NY 800-219-9552
Mcneilly Wood Products Inc
Campbell Hall, NY 845-457-9651
Meriden Box Company
Southington, CT 860-621-7141

Michigan Pallet Inc
St Charles, MI 989-865-9915
Millwood Inc
Vienna, OH 330-393-4400
Momence Pallet Corp
Momence, IL 815-472-6451
Moorecraft Box & Crate
Tarboro, NC 252-823-2510
Mt Valley Farms & Lumber Prods
Biglerville, PA 717-677-6166
Native Lumber Company
Wallingford, CT 203-269-2625
Nefab Packaging, Inc.
Coppell, TX 800-322-4425
Nelson Co
Sparrows Point, MD 410-477-3000
New England Pallets & Skids
Ludlow, MA 413-583-6628
New Lisbon Wood ProductsManufacturing
New Lisbon, WI 608-562-3122
New Mexico Products Inc
Albuquerque, NM 877-345-7864
New South Co Inc
Myrtle Beach, SC 843-236-9399
Northwest Products
Archbold, OH 419-445-1950
Oak Creek Pallet Company
Milwaukee, WI 414-762-7170
Original Lincoln Logs
Chestertown, NY 800-833-2461
Packing Material Company
Southfield, MI 248-489-7000
Pallet Management Systems
Lawrenceville, VA 800-446-1804
Pallet One Inc
Mocksville, NC 336-492-5565
Pallet One Inc
Bartow, FL 800-771-1148
Pallets Inc
Fort Edward, NY 518-747-4177
Pallister Pallet
Wapello, IA 319-523-8161
Pallox Incorporated
Onsted, MI 517-456-4101
Paul Hawkins Lumber Company
Mannington, WV 304-986-2230
Pine Bluff Crating & Pallet
Pine Bluff, AR 866-415-1075
Pine Point Wood Products Inc
Osseo, MN 763-428-4301
Porter & Porter Lumber
Fort Gay, WV 304-648-5133
Precision Wood of Hawaii
Vancouver, WA 808-682-2055
Precision Wood Products
Vancouver, WA 360-694-8322
Pruitt's Packaging Services
Grand Rapids, MI 800-878-0553
Ralph L. Mason,
Newark, MD 410-632-1766
Redding Pallet Inc
Redding, CA 530-241-6321
Remmey Wood Products
Southampton, PA 215-355-3335
Roberts Pallet Co
Ellington, MO 573-663-7877
S & W Pallet Co
Camden, TN 800-640-0522
Scott Pallets Inc
Amelia Court Hse, VA 800-394-2514
Sheldon Wood Products
Toano, VA 757-566-8880
Smith Pallet Co Inc
Hatfield, AR 870-389-6184
Sonoma Pacific Company
Montebello, CA 323-838-4374
Southern Pallet
Christchurch, NZ 901-942-4603
Spring Wood Products
Geneva, OH 440-466-1135
St. Pierre Box & Lumber Company
Canton, CT 860-693-2089
Stearnswood Inc
Hutchinson, MN 800-657-0144
Studd & Whipple Company
Conewango Valley, NY 716-287-3791
Tampa Pallet Co
Tampa, FL 813-626-5700
Tasler Inc
Webster City, IA 515-832-5200
Technipac
Le Sueur, MN 507-665-6658

Tennessee Mills
Red Boiling Springs, TN 615-699-2253
Thunder Pallet Inc
Theresa, WI 800-354-0643
Treen Box & Pallet Inc
Bensalem, PA 215-639-5100
Triad Pallet Co Inc
Greensboro, NC 336-292-8175
Upham & Walsh Lumber
Hoffman Estates, IL 847-519-1010
UPN Pallet Company
Penns Grove, NJ 856-299-1192
Vancouver Manufacturing
Washougal, WA 360-835-8519
Viking Pallet Corp
Maple Grove, MN 763-425-6707
Warren Pallet Co Inc
Bloomsbury, NJ 908-995-7172
White Mountain Lumber Co
Berlin, NH 603-752-1000
Williams Pallet
West Chester, OH 513-874-4014
Williamsburg Millwork
Ruther Glen, VA 804-994-2151
Wnc Pallet & Forest Pdts Co
Candler, NC 828-667-5426
Yerger Wood Products
East Greenville, PA 215-679-4413
York River Pallet Corporation
Shacklefords, VA 804-785-5811

Racks

Barrel & Drum Draining

Bmh Equipment Inc
Sacramento, CA 800-350-8828
Key Material Handling Inc
Simi Valley, CA 800-539-7225
Triple-A Manufacturing Company
Toronto, ON 800-786-2238

Bottle

Cannon Equipment Company
Cannon Falls, MN 800-825-8501
Dunn Woodworks
Shrewsbury, PA 877-835-8592
Houston Wire Works, Inc.
South Houston, TX 800-468-9477
Metro Corporation
Wilkes Barre, PA 800-992-1776
Olson Wire Products Co
Baltimore, MD 410-242-7900
Polymer Solutions International
Newtown Square, PA 877-444-7225
Supreme Metal
Alpharetta, GA 800-645-2526
Triple-A Manufacturing Company
Toronto, ON 800-786-2238
Vermillion Flooring
Springfield, MO 417-862-3785
Western Square Industries
Stockton, CA 800-367-8383
Xtreme Beverages, LLC
Dana Point, CA 949-495-7929

Can

Amco Metals Indl
City Of Industry, CA 626-855-2550
ARC Specialties
Valencia, CA 661-775-8500
EPCO
Murfreesboro, TN 800-251-3398
Grayline Housewares Inc
Columbus, OH 800-222-7388
Lakeside Manufacturing Inc
Milwaukee, WI 888-558-8565
Leggett & Platt Storage
Vernon Hills, IL 847-816-6246
Metro Corporation
Wilkes Barre, PA 800-992-1776
New Age Industrial
Norton, KS 800-255-0104
Storage Unlimited
Nixa, MO 800-478-6642
Superior Products Company
Saint Paul, MN 800-328-9800
Triple-A Manufacturing Company
Toronto, ON 800-786-2238
Xtreme Beverages, LLC
Dana Point, CA 949-495-7929

Cold Storage Room

ABI Limited
Concord, ON 800-297-8666
Ace Manufacturing & Parts Co
Sullivan, MO 800-325-6138
Bmh Equipment Inc
Sacramento, CA 800-350-8828
Carlisle Food Svc Products Inc
Oklahoma City, OK 800-654-8210
ColdZone
Anaheim, CA
Jarke Corporation
Prospect Hts, IL 800-722-5255
Kaines West Michigan Co
Ludington, MI 231-845-1281
Marlin Steel Wire Products
Baltimore, MD 877-762-7546
Metal Equipment Company
Cleveland, OH 800-700-6326
Metro Corporation
Wilkes Barre, PA 800-992-1776
Ridg-U-Rak
North East, PA 866-479-7225
Ron Vallort & Associates
Oak Brook, IL 630-734-3821
RTI Shelving Systems
Elmhurst, NY 800-223-6210
Superior Products Company
Saint Paul, MN 800-328-9800
Triple-A Manufacturing Company
Toronto, ON 800-786-2238

Kitchen

Advance Tabco
Edgewood, NY 800-645-3166
Amco Metals Indl
City Of Industry, CA 626-855-2550
American Housewares
Bronx, NY 718-665-9500
ARC Specialties
Valencia, CA 661-775-8500
Archer Wire Intl Corp
Chicago, IL 708-563-1700
Bevles Company
Dallas, TX 800-441-1601
Bmh Equipment Inc
Sacramento, CA 800-350-8828
California Caster & Handtruck
San Francisco, CA 800-950-8750
Dubuque Steel Products Co
Dubuque, IA 563-556-6288
Grayline Housewares Inc
Columbus, OH 800-222-7388
H A Sparke Co
Shreveport, LA 318-222-0927
Hodges
Vienna, IL 800-444-0011
Jack Stack
Inwood, NY 800-999-9840
Lavi Industries
Valencia, CA 800-624-6225
LPI Imports
Chicago, IL 877-389-6563
M & E Mfg Co Inc
Kingston, NY 845-331-2110
Metro Corporation
Wilkes Barre, PA 800-992-1776
New Age Industrial
Norton, KS 800-255-0104
Princeton Shelving
Cedar Rapids, IA 319-369-0355
Quipco Products Inc
Sauget, IL 314-993-1442
Storage Unlimited
Nixa, MO 800-478-6642
Thermal Bags By Ingrid Inc
Gilberts, IL 800-622-5560
United Showcase Company
Wood Ridge, NJ 800-526-6382
Universal Stainless
Aurora, CO 800-223-8332
Universal Stainless & Alloy
Titusville, PA 800-295-1909
Vermillion Flooring
Springfield, MO 417-862-3785
Westfield Sheet Metal Works
Kenilworth, NJ 908-276-5500
Wilder Manufacturing Company
Port Jervis, NY 800-832-1319

Packing House

Bmh Equipment Inc
Sacramento, CA 800-350-8828
Cannon Equipment Company
Cannon Falls, MN 800-825-8501
Cozzini Inc
Algona, IA 888-295-1116
Market Forge Industries Inc
Everett, MA 866-698-3188
New Age Industrial
Norton, KS 800-255-0104
Tier-Rack Corp
Ballwin, MO 800-325-7869
Unirak Storage Systems
Taylor, MI 800-348-7225
United Steel Products Company
East Stroudsburg, PA 570-476-1010
Westfield Sheet Metal Works
Kenilworth, NJ 908-276-5500
Xtreme Beverages, LLC
Dana Point, CA 949-495-7929

Pallet

Ace Manufacturing & Parts Co
Sullivan, MO 800-325-6138
Atlas Equipment Company
Kansas City, MO 800-842-9188
Bmh Equipment Inc
Sacramento, CA 800-350-8828
Brute Fabricators
Castroville, TX 800-777-2788
Delta Wire And Mfg.
Harrow, ON 800-221-3794
Durham Manufacturing Co
Durham, CT 800-243-3744
Dynamic Storage Systems Inc.
Brooksville, FL 800-974-8211
Elite Storage Solutions Inc
Monroe, GA 800-367-0572
Engineered Products Corp
Greenville, SC. 800-868-0145
Equipment Design & Fabrication
Charlotte, NC 800-949-0165
Eugene Welding Company
Marysville, MI 810-364-7421
Frazier Industrial Co
Long Valley, NJ. 800-859-1342
Global Equipment Co Inc
Port Washington, NY 888-628-3466
Key Material Handling Inc
Simi Valley, CA. 800-539-7225
Lumber & Things
Keyser, WV. 800-296-5656
Mason Ways Indestructible
West Palm Beach, FL 800-837-2881
Material Storage Systems
Humble, TX 800-881-6750
Omicron Steel Products Company
Jamaica, NY 718-805-3400
Penco Products
Skippack, PA. 800-562-1000
Princeton Shelving
Cedar Rapids, IA 319-369-0355
Ross Technology Corp
Leola, PA 800-345-8170
Sackett Systems
Bensenville, IL 800-323-8332
Sigma Industries
Elkhart, IN. 574-295-9660
Solve Needs International
White Lake, MI. 800-783-2462
Steel King Industries
Stevens Point, WI 800-553-3096
Steelmaster Material Handling
Marietta, GA 800-875-9900
Teilhaber Manufacturing Corp
Broomfield, CO 800-358-7225
Triple-A Manufacturing Company
Toronto, ON 800-786-2238
Unirak Storage Systems
Taylor, MI 800-348-7225
Wireway Husky Corp
Denver, NC 800-438-5629

Spice

Metro Corporation
Wilkes Barre, PA. 800-992-1776
Storage Unlimited
Nixa, MO 800-478-6642

Xtreme Beverages, LLC
Dana Point, CA. 949-495-7929

Stock

Acme Display Fixture Company
Los Angeles, CA. 800-959-5657
Advance Storage Products
Garden Grove, CA 888-478-7422
ARC Specialties
Valencia, CA 661-775-8500
Bayhead Products Corp.
Dover, NH 800-229-4323
Bennett Manufacturing Company
Alden, NY 800-345-2142
Bmh Equipment Inc
Sacramento, CA 800-350-8828
Cres Cor
Mentor, OH 877-273-7267
Edwards Products
Cincinnati, OH 800-543-1835
Faribault Manufacturing Co
Faribault, MN 800-447-6043
Flexible Material Handling
Suwanee, GA 800-669-1501
Hodge Manufacturing Company
Springfield, MA 800-262-4634
Hodges
Vienna, IL 800-444-0011
Interlake Mecalux
Chicago, IL 708-344-9999
Irby
Rocky Mount, NC 252-442-0154
Item Products
Houston, TX 800-333-4932
Lodi Metal Tech
Lodi, CA 800-359-5999
Metro Corporation
Wilkes Barre, PA 800-992-1776
Omicron Steel Products Company
Jamaica, NY 718-805-3400
Paltier
Michigan City, IN 800-348-3201
Princeton Shelving
Cedar Rapids, IA. 319-369-0355
Pucel Enterprises Inc
Cleveland, OH 800-336-4986
Rapid Rack Industries
City of Industry, CA 800-736-7225
RW Products
Edgewood, NY 800-345-1022
Southern Metal Fabricators Inc
Albertville, AL 800-989-1330
Speedrack Products Group LTD
Sparta, MI 616-887-0002
SPG International
Covington, GA 877-503-4774
Tier-Rack Corp
Ballwin, MO 800-325-7869
Unirak Storage Systems
Taylor, MI 800-348-7225
United Steel Products Company
East Stroudsburg, PA 570-476-1010
W.A. Schmidt Company
Oaks, PA 800-523-6719
Wirefab Inc
Worcester, MA 877-877-4445

Wine

Amco Metals Indl
City Of Industry, CA. 626-855-2550
Cannon Equipment Company
Cannon Falls, MN. 800-825-8501
Cramer Products
New York, NY 212-645-2368
Dunn Woodworks
Shrewsbury, PA. 877-835-8592
Epic Products
Santa Ana, CA 800-548-9791
Harmar
Sarasota, FL 800-833-0478
Houston Wire Works, Inc.
South Houston, TX 800-468-9477
Kedco Wine Storage Systems
Farmingdale, NY 800-654-9988
Leggett & Platt Storage
Vernon Hills, IL 847-816-6246
Metro Corporation
Wilkes Barre, PA 800-992-1776
Tag-Trade Associated Group
Chicago, IL 800-621-8350

Triple-A Manufacturing Company
Toronto, ON 800-786-2238
Vermillion Flooring
Springfield, MO 417-862-3785
Wine Chillers of California
Santa Ana, CA 800-331-4274
Wineracks by Marcus
Costa Mesa, CA 714-546-4922
Xtreme Beverages, LLC
Dana Point, CA 949-495-7929

Wire

Ace Manufacturing & Parts Co
Sullivan, MO. 800-325-6138
Advanced Plastic Coating Svc
Parsons, KS. 620-421-1660
Aero Manufacturing Co
Clifton, NJ. 800-631-8378
Amco Metals Indl
City Of Industry, CA. 626-855-2550
American Housewares
Bronx, NY. 718-665-9500
Automatic Specialties Inc
Marlborough, MA. 800-445-2370
Avalon Manufacturer
Corona, CA 800-676-3040
Barker Wire
Keosauqua, IA 319-293-3176
Better Bilt Products
Addison, IL. 800-544-4550
Complex Steel & Wire Corp
Wayne, MI. 734-326-1600
Cramer Products
New York, NY 212-645-2368
Dubuque Steel Products Co
Dubuque, IA 563-556-6288
Eagle Wire Works
Cleveland, OH 216-341-8550
Embro Manufacturing Company
East Canton, OH 330-489-3500
Emco Industrial Plastics
Cedar Grove, NJ. 800-292-9906
FMI Display
Elkins Park, PA 215-663-1998
Gillis Associated Industries
Prospect Heights, IL 847-541-6500
Grayline Housewares Inc
Columbus, OH 800-222-7388
Harmar
Sarasota, FL 800-833-0478
Hewitt Manufacturing Co
Waldron, IN. 765-525-9829
HMG Worldwide In-Store Marketing
New York, NY 212-736-2300
Hodges
Vienna, IL 800-444-0011
Houston Wire Works, Inc.
South Houston, TX 800-468-9477
Indiana Wire Company
Fremont, IN. 877-786-6883
J.C. Products Inc.
Haddam, CT 860-267-5516
Jarke Corporation
Prospect Hts, IL 800-722-5255
JEM Wire Products
Middletown, CT 860-347-0447
Kaines West Michigan Co
Ludington, MI. 231-845-1281
Key Material Handling Inc
Simi Valley, CA. 800-539-7225
Leggett & Platt Storage
Vernon Hills, IL 847-816-6246
Liberty Machine Company
York, PA .800-745-8152
Load King Mfg
Jacksonville, FL 800-531-4975
LPI Imports
Chicago, IL. 877-389-6563
Lynch-Jamentz Company
Lakewood, CA 800-828-6217
Marlin Steel Wire Products
Baltimore, MD 877-762-7546
McMillin Manufacturing Corporation
Los Angeles, CA. 323-268-1900
Metaline Products Co Inc
South Amboy, NJ 732-721-1373
Metro Corporation
Wilkes Barre, PA. 800-992-1776
Micro Wire Products Inc
Brockton, MA. 508-584-0200

Midwest Wire Products LLC
Sturgeon Bay, WI 800-445-0225
Midwest Wire Specialties
Chicago, IL. 800-238-0228
Nashville Wire Products
Nashville, TN 615-743-2480
New Age Industrial
Norton, KS 800-255-0104
Northern Metal Products
St Cloud, MN 800-458-5549
Olson Wire Products Co
Baltimore, MD 410-242-7900
Pentwater Wire Products Inc
Pentwater, MI 877-869-6911
Pinquist Tool & Die Company
Brooklyn, NY 800-752-0414
Princeton Shelving
Cedar Rapids, IA. 319-369-0355
R.I. Enterprises
Hernando, MS. 662-429-7863
Racks
San Diego, CA 619-661-0987
Randware Industries
Prospect Heights, IL 847-299-8884
Riverside Wire & Metal Co.
Ionia, MI 616-527-3500
Royal Display Corporation
Middletown, CT 800-569-1295
Schlueter Company
Janesville, WI 800-359-1700
Selma Wire Products Company
Selma, IN 765-282-3532
SEMCO
Ocala, FL. 800-749-6894
Sipco Products
Peoria Heights, IL 309-682-5400
Spot Wire Works Company
Philadelphia, PA 215-627-6124
SSW Holding Co Inc
Elizabethtown, KY 270-769-5526
Steel City Corporation
Youngstown, OH. 800-321-0350
Straits Steel & Wire Co
Ludington, MI. 231-843-3416
Superior Products Company
Saint Paul, MN 800-328-9800
Tennsco Corp
Dickson, TN 800-251-8184
Toledo Wire Products
Toledo, OH 888-430-7445
Trepte's Wire & Metal Works
Bellflower, CA 800-828-6217
Triple-A Manufacturing Company
Toronto, ON 800-786-2238
Victone Manufacturing Company
Chicago, IL. 312-738-3211
W J Egli & Co
Alliance, OH. 330-823-3666
Wahlstrom Manufacturing
Fontana, CA 909-822-4677
Wald Wire & Mfg Co
Oshkosh, WI. 800-236-0053
Wire Products Mfg
Merrill, WI 715-536-7884
Wirefab Inc
Worcester, MA 877-877-4445
Wiremaid Products Div
Coral Springs, FL 800-770-4700
Woerner Wire Works
Omaha, NE 402-451-5414
Yeager Wire Works
Berwick, PA 570-752-2769

Ramps

Delivery Truck

Hormann Flexan Llc
Leetsdale, PA 800-365-3667
Melcher Manufacturing Co
Spokane Valley, WA 800-541-4227

Shelving

Steel

Ace Manufacturing & Parts Co
Sullivan, MO. 800-325-6138
Advance Tabco
Edgewood, NY 800-645-3166
Allied Engineering
North Vancouver, BC 877-929-1214

Amco Metals Indl
City Of Industry, CA. 626-855-2550
Amscor Inc
West Babylon, NY 800-825-9800
ARC Specialties
Valencia, CA 661-775-8500
ATD-American Co
Wyncote, PA 800-523-2300
Atlas Equipment Company
Kansas City, MO. 800-842-9188
Bmh Equipment Inc
Sacramento, CA 800-350-8828
Borroughs Corp
Kalamazoo, MI. 800-748-0227
Cleveland Metal Stamping Company
Berea, OH 440-234-0010
Commercial Kitchen Co
Los Angeles, CA. 323-732-2291
Custom Diamond Intl.
Laval, QC 800-326-5926
Den Mar Corp
North Dartmouth, MA 508-999-3295
Despro Manufacturing
Cedar Grove, NJ 800-292-9906
Duluth Sheet Metal
Duluth, MN 218-722-2613
Durham Manufacturing Co
Durham, CT 800-243-3744
E-Z Shelving Systems Inc
Shawnee, KS 800-353-1331
Eagle Group
Clayton, DE. 800-441-8440
Easyup Storage Systems
Tukwila, WA 800-426-9234
Eldorado Miranda Manufacturing Company
Largo, FL 800-330-0708
Emco Industrial Plastics
Cedar Grove, NJ 800-292-9906
Global Equipment Co Inc
Port Washington, NY 888-628-3466
Hodges
Vienna, IL 800-444-0011
IMC Teddy Food Service Equipment
Amityville, NY 800-221-5644
Infra Corp
Waterford, MI 888-434-6372
Institutional Equipment Inc
Bolingbrook, IL 630-771-0990
InterMetro Industries
Wilkes-Barre, PA 570-825-2741
Jarke Corporation
Prospect Hts, IL 800-722-5255
Kent Corp
Birmingham, AL. 800-252-5368
Key Material Handling Inc
Simi Valley, CA. 800-539-7225
Lambertson Industries Inc
Sparks, NV 800-548-3324
Leggett & Platt Storage
Vernon Hills, IL 847-816-6246
Linvar
Hartford, CT 800-282-5288
Lista International Corp
Holliston, MA 800-722-3020
Loyal Manufacturing
Indianapolis, IN 317-359-3185
LPI Imports
Chicago, IL. 877-389-6563
Lyon LLC
Montgomery, IL 630-892-8941
M & E Mfg Co Inc
Kingston, NY 845-331-2110
Madix Inc
Terrell, TX. 800-776-2349
Market Forge Industries Inc
Everett, MA. 866-698-3188
Marlin Steel Wire Products
Baltimore, MD 877-762-7546
Metal Kitchen Fabricators Inc
Houston, TX. 713-683-8375
Metro Corporation
Wilkes Barre, PA. 800-992-1776
New Age Industrial
Norton, KS 800-255-0104
Nexel Industries Inc
Port Washington, NY 800-245-6682
Omicron Steel Products Company
Jamaica, NY 718-805-3400
OSF
Toronto, ON 800-465-4000
Princeton Shelving
Cedar Rapids, IA. 319-369-0355

Pucel Enterprises Inc
Cleveland, OH 800-336-4986
Quantum Storage Systems Inc
Miami, FL 800-685-4665
Republic Storage Systems LLC
Canton, OH 800-477-1255
Royce Corp
Glendale, AZ 602-256-0006
RTI Shelving Systems
Elmhurst, NY 800-223-6210
Sefi Fabricators Inc
Amityville, NY 631-842-2200
Solve Needs International
White Lake, MI 800-783-2462
Spot Wire Works Company
Philadelphia, PA 215-627-6124
Stainless Fabricating Company
Denver, CO 800-525-8966
Stainless Steel Fabricators
Tyler, TX 903-595-6625
Starlite Food Service Equipment
Detroit, MI 888-521-6603
Steelmaster Material Handling
Marietta, GA 800-875-9900
Streater Inc
Albert Lea, MN 800-527-4197
Stryco Wire Products
North York, ON 416-663-7000
Travis Manufacturing Corp
Alliance, OH 330-875-1661
Tri-Boro Shelving & Partition
Farmville, VA 800-633-3070
Triple-A Manufacturing Company
Toronto, ON 800-786-2238
Universal Stainless
Aurora, CO 800-223-8332
Universal Stainless & Alloy
Titusville, PA 800-295-1909
Weiss Sheet Metal Inc
Avon, MA 508-583-8300
Western Pacific Stge Solutions
San Dimas, CA 800-888-5707

Wire

Ace Manufacturing & Parts Co
Sullivan, MO 800-325-6138
Advance Tabco
Edgewood, NY 800-645-3166
Amco Metals Indl
City Of Industry, CA 626-855-2550
Atlas Equipment Company
Kansas City, MO 800-842-9188
Barker Wire
Keosauqua, IA 319-293-3176
Bettag & Associates
O Fallon, MO 800-325-0959
Bmh Equipment Inc
Sacramento, CA 800-350-8828
Coast Scientific
Rancho Santa Fe, CA 800-445-1544
Despro Manufacturing
Cedar Grove, NJ 800-292-9906
Enterprise Products
Bell Gardens, CA 562-928-1918
Etube & Wire
Shrewsbury, PA 800-618-4720
Gillis Associated Industries
Prospect Heights, IL 847-541-6500
Global Equipment Co Inc
Port Washington, NY 888-628-3466
Hodge Manufacturing Company
Springfield, MA 800-262-4634
Hodges
Vienna, IL 800-444-0011
Indiana Wire Company
Fremont, IN 877-786-6883
JEM Wire Products
Middletown, CT 860-347-0447
Kaines West Michigan Co
Ludington, MI 231-845-1281
Kotoff & Company
San Dimas, CA 626-443-7115
Langer Manufacturing Company
Cedar Rapids, IA 800-728-6445
Leggett & Platt Storage
Vernon Hills, IL 847-816-6246
LPI Imports
Chicago, IL 877-389-6563
Luckner Steel Shelving
Flushing, NY 800-888-4212

Madix Inc
Terrell, TX 800-776-2349
Madsen Wire Products Inc
Orland, IN 260-829-6561
Marlin Steel Wire Products
Baltimore, MD 877-762-7546
McMillin Manufacturing Corporation
Los Angeles, CA 323-268-1900
Metaline Products Co Inc
South Amboy, NJ 732-721-1373
Metro Corporation
Wilkes Barre, PA 800-992-1776
Midwest Wire Products LLC
Sturgeon Bay, WI 800-445-0225
Nexel Industries Inc
Port Washington, NY 800-245-6682
Ortmayer Materials Handling
Brooklyn, NY 718-875-7995
Pacific Northwest Wire Works
Dupont, WA 800-222-7699
Pentwater Wire Products Inc
Pentwater, MI 877-869-6911
Princeton Shelving
Cedar Rapids, IA 319-369-0355
Riverside Wire & Metal Co.
Ionia, MI 616-527-3500
Royal Display Corporation
Middletown, CT 800-569-1295
Royce Corp
Glendale, AZ 602-256-0006
RTI Shelving Systems
Elmhurst, NY 800-223-6210
Sefi Fabricators Inc
Amityville, NY 631-842-2200
Spaceguard Products
Seymour, IN 800-841-0680
Spot Wire Works Company
Philadelphia, PA 215-627-6124
Springport Steel Wire Products
Elkhart, IN 574-295-9660
Straits Steel & Wire Co
Ludington, MI 231-843-3416
Stryco Wire Products
North York, ON 416-663-7000
Superior Products Company
Saint Paul, MN 800-328-9800
Swanson Wire Works Industries, Inc.
Mesquite, TX 972-288-7465
Technibilt/Cari-All
Newton, NC 800-233-3972
Tennsco Corp
Dickson, TN 800-251-8184
Triad Scientific
Manasquan, NJ 800-867-6690
Triple-A Manufacturing Company
Toronto, ON 800-786-2238
Wirefab Inc
Worcester, MA 877-877-4445
Wiremaid Products Div
Coral Springs, FL 800-770-4700

Skids

American Box Corporation
Lisbon, OH 330-424-8055
American Pallet Inc
Oakdale, CA 209-847-6122
Bay Area Pallet Company/IFCO Systems
Houston, TX 877-430-4326
Bennett Box & Pallet Company
Winston, NC 800-334-8741
Black River Pallet Co
Zeeland, MI 800-427-6515
Burgess Mfg. - Oklahoma
Guthrie, OK 800-804-1913
Cassel Box & Lumber Co Inc
Grafton, WI 262-377-9503
Cedar Box Co
Minneapolis, MN 612-332-4287
Charles Tirschman Pallet Co
Dundalk, MD 410-282-6199
Cotter Brothers Corp
Danvers, MA 978-777-5001
Cumberland Box & Mill Co
Cumberland, MD 301-724-1010
Cutter Lumber Products
Livermore, CA 925-443-5959
D&M Pallet Company
Neshkoro, WI 920-293-4616
Daniel Boone Lumber Industries
Morehead, KY 606-784-7586
Day Lumber Company
Westfield, MA 413-568-3511

Denver Reel & Pallet Company
Denver, CO 303-321-1920
Durant Box Factory
Durant, OK 580-924-4035
Eichler Wood Products
Laurys Station, PA 610-262-6749
F.E. Wood & Sons
West Baldwin, ME 207-286-5003
Fabricating & Welding Corp
Chicago, IL 773-928-2050
Fabrication Specialties
Centerville, TN 931-729-2283
Fresno Pallet, Inc.
Sultana, CA 559-591-4111
Gatewood Products LLC
Parkersburg, WV. 800-827-5461
Gerrity Industries
Monmouth, ME. 877-933-2804
Girard Wood Products Inc
Puyallup, WA 800-532-0505
Global Equipment Co Inc
Port Washington, NY 888-628-3466
Goeman's Wood Products
Hartford, WI 262-673-6090
Graham Pallet Co Inc
Tompkinsville, KY 888-525-0694
Gray Woodproducts
Tacoma, WA 253-752-7000
Hanson Box & Lumber Company
Wakefield, MA 617-245-0358
Harbor Pallet Company
Anaheim, CA 714-871-0932
Hildreth Wood Products Inc
Wadesboro, NC 704-826-8326
Hinchcliff Products Company
Strongsville, OH 440-238-5200
Industrial Hardwood
Perrysburg, OH 419-666-2503
Industrial Lumber & Packaging
Spring Lake, MI 616-842-1457
International Wood Industries
Snohomish, WA 800-922-6141
J.M. Rogers & Sons
Moss Point, MS 228-475-7584
Jarke Corporation
Prospect Hts, IL 800-722-5255
Kauling Wood Products Company
Beckemeyer, IL 618-594-2901
Kelley Wood Products
Fitchburg, MA 978-345-7531
Kent District Library System
Comstock Park, MI 616-784-2007
Kimball Companies
East Longmeadow, MA 413-525-1881
Konz Wood Products Co
Appleton, WI 877-610-5145
L&H Wood Manufacturing Company
Farmington, MI 248-474-9000
Lester Box & Mfg Div
Long Beach, CA 562-437-5123
Load King Mfg
Jacksonville, FL 800-531-4975
Lumber & Things
Keyser, WV. 800-296-5656
Maull-Baker Box Company
Brookfield, WI 414-463-1290
May-Wes Manufacturing Inc
Hutchinson, MN 800-788-6483
Mcintosh Box & Pallet Co
East Syracuse, NY 800-219-9552
Mcneilly Wood Products Inc
Campbell Hall, NY 845-457-9651
Michiana Box & Crate
Niles, MI 800-677-6372
Michigan Pallet Inc
St Charles, MI 989-865-9915
Mt Valley Farms & Lumber Prods
Biglerville, PA. 717-677-6166
Necedah Pallet Co Inc
Necedah, WI 800-672-5538
Nefab Packaging, Inc.
Coppell, TX 800-322-4425
Nelson Co
Sparrows Point, MD 410-477-3000
New England Pallets & Skids
Ludlow, MA 413-583-6628
New Lisbon Wood ProductsManufacturing Company
New Lisbon, WI 608-562-3122
Original Lincoln Logs
Chestertown, NY 800-833-2461
Ortmayer Materials Handling
Brooklyn, NY 718-875-7995

Packing Material Company
Southfield, MI................248-489-7000
Pallet One Inc
Mocksville, NC...............336-492-5565
Pallets Inc
Fort Edward, NY..............518-747-4177
Pallox Incorporated
Onsted, MI..................517-456-4101
Pine Bluff Crating & Pallet
Pine Bluff, AR..............866-415-1075
Pine Point Wood Products Inc
Osseo, MN...................763-428-4301
Porter & Porter Lumber
Fort Gay, WV................304-648-5133
Premium Pallet
Philadelphia, PA............800-648-7347
Pruitt's Packaging Services
Grand Rapids, MI............800-878-0553
Rand-Whitney Group LLC
Worcester, MA...............508-791-2301
Remmey Wood Products
Southampton, PA.............215-355-3335
S & W Pallet Co
Camden, TN..................800-640-0522
Savanna Pallets
McGregor, MN................218-768-2077
Shelby Pallet & Box Company
Shelby, MI..................231-861-4214
Sheldon Wood Products
Toano, VA...................757-566-8880
Smith Pallet Co Inc
Hatfield, AR................870-389-6184
Sonoma Pacific Company
Montebello, CA..............323-838-4374
St. Pierre Box & Lumber Company
Canton, CT..................860-693-2089
Streator Dependable Mfg
Streator, IL................800-798-0551
Swift Creek Forest Products
Jetersville, VA.............804-561-4498
Technipac
Le Sueur, MN................507-665-6658
Thunder Pallet Inc
Theresa, WI.................800-354-0643
Tower Pallet Co Inc
De Pere, WI.................920-336-3495
Treen Box & Pallet Inc
Bensalem, PA................215-639-5100
Triad Pallet Co Inc
Greensboro, NC..............336-292-8175
Upham & Walsh Lumber
Hoffman Estates, IL.........847-519-1010
Van Dereems Mfg Co
Hawthorne, NJ...............973-427-2355
Westfield Sheet Metal Works
Kenilworth, NJ..............908-276-5500
Wetterau Wood Products
Burlington, MA..............800-986-0958
Williams Pallet
West Chester, OH............513-874-4014
Wnc Pallet & Forest Pdts Co
Candler, NC.................828-667-5426

Storage & Holding Equipment

A&B Safe Corporation
Glassboro, NJ...............800-253-1267
A-Z Factory Supply
Schiller Park, IL...........800-323-4511
Accent Store Fixtures
Kenosha, WI.................800-545-1144
Acme Display Fixture Company
Los Angeles, CA.............800-959-5657
Aco Container Systems
Pickering, ON...............800-542-9942
Acrison Inc
Moonachie, NJ...............800-422-4266
Adapto Storage Products
Hialeah, FL.................305-499-4800
Advance Fittings Corp
Elkhorn, WI.................262-723-6699
Advance Storage Products
Garden Grove, CA............888-478-7422
Advance Tabco
Edgewood, NY................800-645-3166
Aero Manufacturing Co
Clifton, NJ.................800-631-8378
AFGO Mechanical Svc Inc
Astoria, NY.................800-438-2346
Agspring
Leawood, KS.................913-333-3035
Allegheny Bradford Corp
Bradford, PA................800-542-0650

Alliance Products LLC
Murfreesboro, TN............800-522-3973
Allied Engineering
North Vancouver, BC.........877-929-1214
Alloy Products Corp
Waukesha, WI................800-236-6603
Althor Products
Bethel, CT..................800-688-2693
Amco Metals Indl
City Of Industry, CA........626-855-2550
Amscor Inc
West Babylon, NY............800-825-9800
Anderson-Crane Company
Minneapolis, MN.............800-314-2747
ANDRITZ Inc
Muncy, PA...................704-943-4343
Apache Stainless Equipment
Beaver Dam, WI..............800-444-0398
Apollo Sheet Metal
Kennewick, WA...............509-586-1104
APV Americas
Delavan, WI.................800-252-5200
ARC Specialties
Valencia, CA................661-775-8500
Arizona Store Equipment
Phoenix, AZ.................800-624-8395
Arkfeld Mfg & Distributing Co
Norfolk, NE.................800-533-0676
Art Wire Works Co
Chicago, IL.................708-458-3993
Art-Phyl Creations
Hialeah, FL.................800-327-8318
ATD-American Co
Wyncote, PA.................800-523-2300
Atlas Equipment Company
Kansas City, MO.............800-842-9188
Atlas Minerals & Chemicals Inc
Mertztown, PA...............800-523-8269
Automatic Specialties Inc
Marlborough, MA.............800-445-2370
B C Holland Inc
Dousman, WI.................262-965-2939
Bacchus Wine Cellars
Houston, TX.................800-487-8812
Bailly Showcase & Fixture Company
Las Vegas, NV...............702-947-6885
Baldewein Company
Lake Forrest, IL............800-424-5544
Barker Company
Keosauqua, IA...............319-293-3777
Barker Wire
Keosauqua, IA...............319-293-3176
Baxter Manufacturing Inc
Orting, WA..................800-777-2828
Bayhead Products Corp.
Dover, NH...................800-229-4323
Bennett Manufacturing Company
Alden, NY...................800-345-2142
Bergen Barrel & Drum Company
Kearny, NJ..................201-998-3500
Best
Brunswick, OH...............800-827-9237
Bevles Company
Dallas, TX..................800-441-1601
BMH
City of Industry, CA........909-349-2530
Bonar Plastics
West Chicago, IL............800-295-3725
Bonar Plastics
Ridgefield, WA..............800-972-5252
Borroughs Corp
Kalamazoo, MI...............800-748-0227
Bowers Process Equipment
Stratford, ON...............800-567-3223
Brenner Tank LLC
Fond Du Lac, WI.............800-558-9750
Brisker Dry Food Crisper
Oldsmar, FL.................800-356-9080
Brothers Manufacturing
Hermansville, MI............888-277-6117
Buckhorn Inc
Milford, OH.................800-543-4454
Buhler Inc.
Plymouth, MN................763-847-9900
Bulk Pack
Monroe, LA..................800-498-4215
Bulk Sak Intl Inc
Malvern, AR.................501-332-8745
Bush Tank Fabricators Inc
Newark, NJ..................973-596-1121
C E Rogers Co
Mora, MN....................800-279-8081

C Nelson Mfg Co
Oak Harbor, OH..............800-922-7339
C&H Store Equipment Company
Los Angeles, CA.............800-648-4979
C&R Refrigation Inc,
Center, TX..................800-438-6182
Cal-Coast Manufacturing
Turlock, CA.................209-668-9378
Calzone Case Co
Bridgeport, CT..............800-243-5152
Carter-Hoffmann LLC
Mundelein, IL...............800-323-9793
Cayne Industrial Sales Corp
Bronx, NY...................718-993-5800
Central Fabricators Inc
Cincinnati, OH..............800-909-8265
Chart Industries Inc
Cleveland, OH...............800-247-4446
Chem-Tainer Industries Inc
West Babylon, NY............800-938-8896
Chester-Jensen Co., Inc.
Chester, PA.................800-685-3750
Chicago Conveyor Corporation
Addison, IL.................630-543-6300
Clayton & Lambert Manufacturing
Buckner, KY.................800-626-5819
Coast Scientific
Rancho Santa Fe, CA.........800-445-1544
Columbian TecTank
Parsons, KS.................800-421-2788
Commercial Kitchen Co
Los Angeles, CA.............323-732-2291
Complex Steel & Wire Corp
Wayne, MI...................734-326-1600
Containair Packaging Corporation
Paterson, NJ................888-276-6500
Containment Technology
St Gabriel, LA..............800-388-2467
Continental Commercial Products
Bridgeton, MO...............800-325-1051
Continental-Fremont
Tiffin, OH..................419-448-4045
Corbox-Meyers Inc
Cleveland, OH...............800-321-7286
Coss Engineering Sales Company
Rochester Hills, MI.........800-446-1365
COW Industries Inc
Columbus, OH................800-542-9353
Cozzini Inc
Algona, IA..................888-295-1116
Cres Cor
Mentor, OH..................877-273-7267
Crown Custom Metal Spinning
Concord, ON.................800-750-1924
Cruvinet Winebar Co LLC
Sparks, NV..................800-278-8463
Custom Diamond Intl.
Laval, QC...................800-326-5926
Custom Metal Crafts
Springfield, MO.............417-862-9324
DBE Inc
Concord, ON.................800-461-5313
DCI, Inc.
St Cloud, MN................320-252-8200
Dematic USA
Grand Rapids, MI............877-725-7500
Denstor Mobile Storage Systems
Walker, MI..................800-234-7477
Despro Manufacturing
Cedar Grove, NJ.............800-292-9906
Dubuque Steel Products Co
Dubuque, IA.................563-556-6288
Duke Manufacturing Co
St Louis, MO................800-735-3853
Dunn Woodworks
Shrewsbury, PA..............877-835-8592
Durham Manufacturing Co
Durham, CT..................800-243-3744
Dynamic Storage Systems Inc.
Brooksville, FL.............800-974-8211
E2M
Duluth, GA..................800-622-4326
Eagle Group
Clayton, DE.................800-441-8440
Earl Soesbe Company
Romeoville, IL..............219-866-4191
Eastern Plastics
Pawtucket, RI...............800-442-8585
Easyup Storage Systems
Tukwila, WA.................800-426-9234
Eaton Sales & Service
Denver, CO..................800-208-2657

Edwards Fiberglass
  Sedalia, MO 660-826-3915
Edwards Products
  Cincinnati, OH 800-543-1835
EGA Products Inc
  Brookfield, WI 800-937-3427
Eldorado Miranda Manufacturing Company
  Largo, FL 800-330-0708
Electrol Specialties Co
  South Beloit, IL 815-389-2291
Ellett Industries
  Port Coquitlam, BC. 604-941-8211
Enerfab Inc.
  Cincinnati, OH 513-641-0500
Engineered Products Group
  Madison, WI 800-626-3111
Eskay Metal Fabricating
  Buffalo, NY.....................800-836-8015
Etube & Wire
  Shrewsbury, PA 800-618-4720
Eugene Welding Company
  Marysville, MI 810-364-7421
Expert Industries Inc
  Brooklyn, NY 718-434-6060
F.E. Wood & Sons
  West Baldwin, ME 207-286-5003
Fab-X/Metals
  Washington, NC 800-677-3229
Fabricated Components Inc
  Stroudsburg, PA 800-233-8163
Faribault Manufacturing Co
  Faribault, MN 800-447-6043
Feldmeier Equipment Inc
  Syracuse, NY 315-454-8608
Flexible Material Handling
  Suwanee, GA 800-669-1501
Flow of Solids
  Westford, MA 978-392-0300
Follett Corp
  Easton, PA. 800-523-9361
Foster Forbes Glass
  Marion, IN......................765-668-1200
Fourinox Inc
  Green Bay, WI. 920-336-0621
Frazier Industrial Co
  Long Valley, NJ. 800-859-1342
Frelco
  Stephenville, NL. 709-643-5668
G A Systems Inc
  Huntington Beach, CA 714-848-7529
G.F. Frank & Sons
  Fairfield, OH....................513-870-9075
Gch Internatonal
  Louisville, KY 502-636-1374
Geerpres Inc
  Muskegon, MI. 231-773-3211
General Industries Inc
  Goldsboro, NC 888-735-2882
General Steel Fabricators
  Joplin, MO 800-820-8644
Gibbs Brothers Cooperage
  Hot Springs, AR 501-623-8881
Goldenwest Sales
  Cerritos, CA 800-827-6175
Graff Tank Erection
  Harrisville, PA. 814-385-6671
Greene Industries
  East Greenwich, RI. 401-884-7530
Greif Inc
  Delaware, OH 740-549-6000
Hall-Woolford Wood Tank Co Inc
  Philadelphia, PA.................215-329-9022
Handy Manufacturing Co Inc
  Newark, NJ. 800-631-4280
Hanel Storage Systems
  Pittsburgh, PA...................412-787-3444
Hardware Components Inc
  New Matamoras, OH 740-865-2424
Hardy Systems Corporation
  Northbrook, IL 800-927-3956
Hedstrom Corporation
  Ashland, OH....................700-765-9665
Hewitt Manufacturing Co
  Waldron, IN.....................765-525-9829
Hodge Manufacturing Company
  Springfield, MA 800-262-4634
Hodges
  Vienna, IL 800-444-0011
Hoover Materials Handling Group
  Houston, TX....................800-844-8683
Houston Wire Works, Inc.
  South Houston, TX...............800-468-9477

Howard Fabrication
  City of Industry, CA 626-961-0114
Hughes Co
  Columbus, WI....................866-535-9303
Hydro-Miser
  San Marcos, CA 800-736-5083
Hyster Company
  San Diego, CA 855-804-2118
Ideal Wire Works
  Alhambra, CA...................626-282-0886
IMC Teddy Food Service Equipment
  Amityville, NY...................800-221-5644
Imperial Industries Inc
  Rothschild, WI 800-558-2945
Indeco Products Inc
  San Marcos, TX 888-246-3326
Indiana Wire Company
  Fremont, IN.....................877-786-6883
Interlake Mecalux
  Chicago, IL 708-344-9999
InterMetro Industries
  Wilkes-Barre, PA 570-825-2741
International Machinery Xchnge
  Deerfield, WI 800-279-0191
International Tank & Pipe Co
  Clackamas, OR 888-988-0011
Interroll Corp
  Wilmington, NC 800-830-9680
Item Products
  Houston, TX....................800-333-4932
J.H. Carr & Sons
  Seattle, WA 800-523-8842
JBC Plastics
  St Louis, MO....................877-834-5526
JEM Wire Products
  Middletown, CT 860-347-0447
Jenike & Johanson Inc
  Tyngsboro, MA..................978-649-3300
Jesco Industries
  Litchfield, MI 800-455-0019
JH Display & Fixture
  Greenwood, IN 317-888-0631
Jupiter Mills Corporation
  Roslyn, NY 800-853-5121
JW Leser Company
  Los Angeles, CA. 323-731-4173
K & I Creative Plastics & Wood
  Jacksonville, FL 904-387-0438
Kadon Corporation
  Milford, OH.....................937-299-0088
Kedco Wine Storage Systems
  Farmingdale, NY 800-654-9988
Key Material Handling Inc
  Simi Valley, CA. 800-539-7225
KHM Plastics Inc
  Gurnee, IL. 847-249-4910
Kisco Manufacturing
  Port Alberni, BC. 604-823-7456
La Crosse
  Onalaska, WI....................800-345-0018
Laidig Inc
  Mishawaka, IN 574-256-0204
Lakeside Manufacturing Inc
  Milwaukee, WI..................888-558-8565
Lambertson Industries Inc
  Sparks, NV 800-548-3324
Langsenkamp Manufacturing
  Indianapolis, IN 877-585-1950
Leggett & Platt Storage
  Vernon Hills, IL 847-816-6246
Liberty Machine Company
  York, PA 800-745-8152
Linvar
  Hartford, CT 800-282-5288
LoadBank International
  Orlando, FL.....................800-458-9010
Lodi Metal Tech
  Lodi, CA 800-359-5999
Longview Fibre Company
  Beaverton, OR 503-350-1600
Loyal Manufacturing
  Indianapolis, IN 317-359-3185
LPI Imports
  Chicago, IL 877-389-6563
Luckner Steel Shelving
  Flushing, NY 800-888-4212
Ludell Manufacturing Co
  Milwaukee, WI..................800-558-0800
Lyon LLC
  Montgomery, IL 630-892-8941
M & E Mfg Co Inc
  Kingston, NY 845-331-2110

M O Industries Inc
  Whippany, NJ 973-386-9228
Madsen Wire Products Inc
  Orland, IN......................260-829-6561
Mannhardt Inc
  Sheboygan Falls, WI. 800-423-2327
Marineland Commercial Aquariums
  Blacksburg, VA..................800-322-1266
Marlin Steel Wire Products
  Baltimore, MD 877-762-7546
Material Storage Systems
  Humble, TX 800-881-6750
Material Storage Systems
  Gadsden, AL 877-543-2467
Mccullough Industries Inc
  Kenton, OH 800-245-9490
MeGa Industries
  Burlington, ON 800-665-6342
Melmat Inc
  Huntington Beach, CA 800-635-6289
Merric
  Bridgeton, MO 314-770-9944
Metal Equipment Company
  Cleveland, OH 800-700-6326
Metal Master Sales Corp
  Glendale Heights, IL. 800-488-8729
Metro Corporation
  Wilkes Barre, PA. 800-992-1776
Meyer Machine & Garroutte Products
  San Antonio, TX 210-736-1811
Michiana Box & Crate
  Niles, MI. 800-677-6372
Micro Wire Products Inc
  Brockton, MA 508-584-0200
Midwest Aircraft Products Co
  Lexington, OH 419-884-2164
Midwest Stainless
  Menomonie, WI 715-235-5472
Miller Hofft Brands
  Indianapolis, IN 317-638-6576
Miller Metal Fabrication
  Bridgeville, DE 302-337-2291
Modar
  Benton Harbor, MI 800-253-6186
Modern Brewing & Design
  Santa Rosa, CA. 707-542-6620
Modern Metals Industries
  El Segundo, CA 800-437-6633
MultiFab Plastics
  Boston, MA.....................888-293-5754
Murata Automated Systems
  Charlotte, NC 800-428-8469
Myers Container
  Hayward, CA 510-785-8235
Nalge Process Technologies Group
  Rochester, NY 585-586-8800
National Bar Systems
  Huntington Beach, CA 714-848-1688
Nefab Packaging Inc
  Elk Grove Vlg, IL 847-787-0340
Nelipak
  Phoenix, AZ 602-269-7648
NEPA Pallet & Container Co
  Snohomish, WA 360-568-3185
New Pig Corp
  Tipton, PA 800-468-4647
Newell Brands
  Atlanta, GA
Nexel Industries Inc
  Port Washington, NY 800-245-6682
Oak Barrel Winecraft
  Berkeley, CA....................510-849-0400
Omicron Steel Products Company
  Jamaica, NY 718-805-3400
Pacific Store Designs Inc
  Garden Grove, CA 800-772-5661
Pacific Tank
  Adelanto, CA 800-449-5838
Pallet One Inc
  Bartow, FL 800-771-1148
Paltier
  Michigan City, IN 800-348-3201
Paramount Manufacturing Company
  Wilmington, MA.................978-657-4300
PBC
  Mahwah, NJ....................800-514-2739
Pelican Displays
  Homer, IL 800-627-1517
Penco Products
  Skippack, PA 800-562-1000
Pentwater Wire Products Inc
  Pentwater, MI 877-869-6911

Peter Gray Corporation
Andover, MA 978-470-0990
Peterson Manufacturing Company
Plainfield, IL 800-547-8995
Piper Products Inc
Wausau, WI 800-544-3057
Pittsburgh Tank Corp
Monongahela, PA 800-634-0243
Plastic Supply Inc
Londonderry, NH 800-752-7759
Plastilite Corporation
Omaha, NE 800-228-9506
Plastocon
Oconomowoc, WI. 800-966-0103
Ppm Technologies LLC
Newberg, OR 800-246-2034
Prestige Skirting & Tablecloths
Orangeburg, NY 800-635-3313
Prince Castle Inc
Carol Stream, IL 800-722-7853
Princeton Shelving
Cedar Rapids, IA 319-369-0355
Process Solutions
Riviera Beach, FL 561-840-0050
Production Packaging & Processing Equipment Company
Savannah, GA 912-856-4281
Proluxe
Paramount, CA 800-594-5528
Pucel Enterprises Inc
Cleveland, OH 800-336-4986
QBD Modular Systems
Santa Clara, CA 800-663-3005
Quantum Storage Systems Inc
Miami, FL 800-685-4665
R & D Brass
Wappingers Falls, NY 800-447-6050
Ram Equipment Co
Waukesha, WI 262-513-1114
Ransco Industries
Ventura, CA. 805-487-7777
Rapid Rack Industries
City of Industry, CA 800-736-7225
Reflex International
Norcross, GA 800-642-7640
Remcon Plastics Inc
Reading, PA 800-360-3636
Remstar International
Westbrook, ME 800-639-5805
Republic Storage Systems LLC
Canton, OH 800-477-1255
RETROTECH, Inc
West Henrietta, NY 866-915-2777
Ridg-U-Rak
North East, PA. 866-479-7225
Rolland Machining & Fabricating
Moneta, VA 973-827-6911
Rosenwach Tank Co LLC
Long Island City, NY 212-972-4411
Ross Technology Corp
Leola, PA. 800-345-8170
Royal Welding & Fabricating
Fullerton, CA 714-680-6669
RTI Shelving Systems
Elmhurst, NY 800-223-6210
Rubicon Industries
Brooklyn, NY 800-662-6999
Saeplast Canada
St John, NB 800-567-3966
Sanchelima International
Miami, FL. 305-591-4343
Scheb International
North Barrington, IL. 847-381-2573
Seattle Plastics
Seattle, WA 800-441-0679
Sefi Fabricators Inc
Amityville, NY 631-842-2200
SEMCO
Ocala, FL. 800-749-6894
SerVend International
Sellersburg, IN 800-367-4233
Sharpsville Container Corp
Sharpsville, PA 800-645-1248
Shelley Cabinet Company
Shelley, ID. 208-357-3700
Silver King Refrigeration Inc
Minneapolis, MN 800-328-3329
Sirco Systems
Birmingham, AL 205-731-7800
Smalley Manufacturing Co Inc
Knoxville, TN 865-966-5866

Snyder Crown
Marked Tree, AR 870-358-3400
Solve Needs International
White Lake, MI. 800-783-2462
Southern Imperial Inc
Rockford, IL 800-747-4665
Spacesaver Corp
Fort Atkinson, WI. 800-492-3434
Spartanburg Steel Products Inc
Spartanburg, SC 800-974-7500
Specific Mechanical Systems
Victoria, BC. 250-652-2111
Speedrack Products Group LTD
Sparta, MI 616-887-0002
SPG International
Covington, GA 877-503-4774
Spirit Foodservice, Inc.
Andover, MA 800-343-0996
Springport Steel Wire Products
Elkhart, IN. 574-295-9660
SSW Holding Co Inc
Elizabethtown, KY 270-769-5526
St. Louis Stainless Service
St Louis, MO. 800-735-3853
Stackbin Corp
Lincoln, RI 800-333-1603
Stainless Fabrication Inc
Springfield, MO 800-397-8265
Stainless Specialists Inc
Wausau, WI. 800-236-4155
Stainless Steel Fabricators
Tyler, TX 903-595-6625
Starlite Food Service Equipment
Detroit, MI 888-521-6603
Stearnswood Inc
Hutchinson, MN 800-657-0144
Steel King Industries
Stevens Point, WI 800-553-3096
Stor-Loc
Kankakee, IL. 800-786-7562
Storage Unlimited
Nixa, MO 800-478-6642
Strong Hold Products
Louisville, KY 800-880-2625
Summit Commercial
Bronx, NY. 800-932-4267
Super Sturdy
Weldon, NC. 800-253-4833
Supreme Fabricators
Artesia, CA 323-583-8944
Supreme Metal
Alpharetta, GA 800-645-2526
Tag-Trade Associated Group
Chicago, IL 800-621-8350
Tampa Sheet Metal Co
Tampa, FL. 813-251-1845
Technibilt/Cari-All
Newton, NC 800-233-3972
Tennsco Corp
Dickson, TN 800-251-8184
TGR Container Sales
San Leandro, CA. 800-273-6887
Thermal Bags By Ingrid Inc
Gilberts, IL 800-622-5560
Thermo Wisconsin
De Pere, WI. 920-766-7200
Thermodynamics
Commerce City, CO 800-627-9037
Tier-Rack Corp
Ballwin, MO. 800-325-7869
TMS
San Francisco, CA 800-447-7223
Traex
Dane, WI. 800-356-8006
Travis Manufacturing Corp
Alliance, OH 330-875-1661
Tri-Boro Shelving & Partition
Farmville, VA 800-633-3070
Triad Scientific
Manasquan, NJ 800-867-6690
Tupperware Brands Corporation
Orlando, FL. 800-366-3800
Turbo Refrigerating Company
Denton, TX 940-387-4301
Unex Manufacturing Inc
Lakewood, NJ 800-334-8639
Unirak Storage Systems
Taylor, MI 800-348-7225
United Industries Group Inc
Lake Forest, CA 949-759-3200
United Showcase Company
Wood Ridge, NJ 800-526-6382

United States Systems Inc
Kansas City, KS 888-281-2454
United Steel Products Company
East Stroudsburg, PA 570-476-1010
Universal Stainless
Aurora, CO 800-223-8332
Universal Stainless & Alloy
Titusville, PA 800-295-1909
Upham & Walsh Lumber
Hoffman Estates, IL 847-519-1010
Vac-U-Max
Belleville, NJ 800-822-8629
Valad Electric Heating Corporation
Tarrytown, NY 914-631-4927
Valley Fixtures
Sparks, NV 775-331-1050
Victone Manufacturing Company
Chicago, IL 312-738-3211
Vorti-Siv
Salem, OH. 800-227-7487
W.A. Schmidt Company
Oaks, PA 800-523-6719
Walker Stainless Equipment Co
New Lisbon, WI 608-562-7500
Waukesha Cherry-Burrell
Louisville, KY 502-491-4310
WCB Ice Cream
Philadelphia, PA 215-425-4320
Welbilt Corporation
Stamford, CT. 203-325-8300
Welbilt Inc.
New Port Richey, FL 877-375-9300
Welliver Metal Products Corporation
Salem, OR 503-362-1568
Westeel
Saskatoon, SK. 306-931-2855
Western Pacific Stge Solutions
San Dimas, CA 800-888-5707
Westfield Sheet Metal Works
Kenilworth, NJ 908-276-5500
Wilder Manufacturing Company
Port Jervis, NY 800-832-1319
Wiltec
Leominster, MA 978-537-1497
Wine Chillers of California
Santa Ana, CA 800-331-4274
Winekeeper
Santa Barbara, CA 805-963-3451
Winston Industries
Louisville, KY 800-234-5286
Wirefab Inc
Worcester, MA 877-877-4445
Woerner Wire Works
Omaha, NE 402-451-5414
Workman Packaging Inc.
Saint-Laurent, QC. 800-252-5208

Storage Units

Temperature Controlled

Advance Energy Technologies
Halfmoon, NY. 800-724-0198
Agspring
Leawood, KS. 913-333-3035
American Panel Corp
Ocala, FL. 800-327-3015
B C Holland Inc
Dousman, WI 262-965-2939
Bacchus Wine Cellars
Houston, TX 800-487-8812
Baltimore Aircoil Co
Jessup, MD 410-799-1300
Bmh Equipment Inc
Sacramento, CA 800-350-8828
Cool Care
Boynton Beach, FL. 561-364-5711
Cramer Products
New York, NY 212-645-2368
Creative Mobile Systems Inc
Manchester, CT. 800-646-8364
Cruvinet Winebar Co LLC
Sparks, NV 800-278-8463
Dade Engineering
Tampa, FL. 800-321-2112
Davis Core & Pa
Cave Spring, GA 800-235-7483
Edwards Fiberglass
Sedalia, MO 660-826-3915
Elliott-Williams Company
Indianapolis, IN 800-428-9303

Eskay Metal Fabricating
Buffalo, NY..........................800-836-8015
Faubion Central States Tank Company
Shawnee Mission, KS..............800-450-8265
Graff Tank Erection
Harrisville, PA.....................814-385-6671
HABCO Beverage Systems
Toronto, ON.......................800-448-0244
Hoshizaki America Inc
Peachtree City, GA................800-438-6087
Interstate Showcase & Fixture Company
West Orange, NJ...................973-483-5555
Johanson Transportation Svc
Fresno, CA........................800-742-2053
Kold-Hold
Edgefield, SC.....................803-637-3166
La Crosse
Onalaska, WI......................800-345-0018
National Bar Systems
Huntington Beach, CA.............714-848-1688
Portable Cold Storage
Edison, NJ........................800-535-2445
Refrigerator Manufacturers LLC
Cerritos, CA......................562-926-2006
Starlite Food Service Equipment
Detroit, MI.......................888-521-6603
Superior Products Company
Saint Paul, MN....................800-328-9800
TMS
San Francisco, CA.................800-447-7223
Tolan Machinery Company
Rockaway, NJ......................973-983-7212
Tranter INC
Wichita Falls, TX.................940-723-7125
Winekeeper
Santa Barbara, CA.................805-963-3451
Zero Temp
Santa Ana, CA.....................714-538-3177

Tanks

Holding, Storage

A & B Process Systems Corp
Stratford, WI.....................888-258-2789
Abalon Precision Manufacturing Corporation
Bronx, NY.........................800-888-2225
Aco Container Systems
Pickering, ON.....................800-542-9942
Advance Fittings Corp
Elkhorn, WI.......................262-723-6699
AFGO Mechanical Svc Inc
Astoria, NY.......................800-438-2346
Allegheny Bradford Corp
Bradford, PA......................800-542-0650
Alloy Products Corp
Waukesha, WI......................800-236-6603
Anderson-Crane Company
Minneapolis, MN...................800-314-2747
Andgar Corp
Ferndale, WA......................360-366-9900
Apache Stainless Equipment
Beaver Dam, WI....................800-444-0398
Apollo Sheet Metal
Kennewick, WA.....................509-586-1104
APV Americas
Delavan, WI.......................800-252-5200
Arrow Tank Co
Buffalo, NY.......................716-893-7200
Atlas Minerals & Chemicals Inc
Mertztown, PA.....................800-523-8269
Baldewein Company
Lake Forrest, IL..................800-424-5544
Bayhead Products Corp.
Dover, NH.........................800-229-4323
Berkshire PPM
Litchfield, CT....................860-567-3118
Bonar Plastics
Ridgefield, WA....................800-972-5252
Bowers Process Equipment
Stratford, ON.....................800-567-3223
Brenner Tank LLC
Fond Du Lac, WI...................800-558-9750
Brothers Manufacturing
Hermansville, MI..................888-277-6117
Bush Tank Fabricators Inc
Newark, NJ........................973-596-1121
C&R Refrigation Inc,
Center, TX........................800-438-6182
Cal-Coast Manufacturing
Turlock, CA.......................209-668-9378

Centennial Moldings
Hastings, NE......................888-883-2189
Central Fabricators Inc
Cincinnati, OH....................800-909-8265
Chart Industries Inc
Cleveland, OH.....................800-247-4446
Chem-Tainer Industries Inc
West Babylon, NY..................800-275-2436
Chem-Tainer Industries Inc
West Babylon, NY..................800-938-8896
Chester-Jensen Co., Inc.
Chester, PA.......................800-685-3750
Clayton & Lambert Manufacturing
Buckner, KY.......................800-626-5819
Coastline Equipment Inc
Bellingham, WA....................360-734-8509
Columbian TecTank
Parsons, KS.......................800-421-2788
Cozzini Inc
Algona, IA........................888-295-1116
Davron Technologies Inc
Chattanooga, TN...................423-870-1888
DCI, Inc.
St Cloud, MN......................320-252-8200
Eaton Sales & Service
Denver, CO........................800-208-2657
Electrol Specialties Co
South Beloit, IL..................815-389-2291
Emco Industrial Plastics
Cedar Grove, NJ...................800-292-9906
Enerfab Inc.
Cincinnati, OH....................513-641-0500
Engineered Products Group
Madison, WI.......................800-626-3111
Expert Industries Inc
Brooklyn, NY......................718-434-6060
Falco Technologies
La Prairie, QC....................450-444-0566
General Industries Inc
Goldsboro, NC.....................888-735-2882
General Tank
Berwick, PA.......................800-435-8265
Graff Tank Erection
Harrisville, PA...................814-385-6671
Howard Fabrication
City of Industry, CA..............626-961-0114
Hughes Co
Columbus, WI......................866-535-9303
Imperial Industries Inc
Rothschild, WI....................800-558-2945
International Tank & Pipe Co
Clackamas, OR.....................888-988-0011
JW Leser Company
Los Angeles, CA...................323-731-4173
Langsenkamp Manufacturing
Indianapolis, IN..................877-585-1950
Melmat Inc
Huntington Beach, CA.............800-635-6289
Miller Metal Fabrication
Bridgeville, DE...................302-337-2291
Modern Brewing & Design
Santa Rosa, CA....................707-542-6620
Nalge Process Technologies Group
Rochester, NY.....................585-586-8800
Northland Process Piping
Isle, MN..........................320-679-2119
Northwind Inc
Alpena, AR........................877-937-2585
Pacific Tank
Adelanto, CA......................800-449-5838
PBC
Mahwah, NJ........................800-514-2739
Pittsburgh Tank Corp
Monongahela, PA...................800-634-0243
Polar Process
Plattsville, ON...................877-896-8077
Poly Processing Co
French Camp, CA...................877-325-3142
Process Solutions
Riviera Beach, FL.................561-840-0050
Production Packaging & Processing Equipment
Company
Savannah, GA......................912-856-4281
PVI Industries LLC
Fort Worth, TX....................800-784-8326
RAS Process Equipment Inc
Trenton, NJ.......................609-371-1220
Remcon Plastics Inc
Reading, PA.......................800-360-3636
Rolland Machining & Fabricating
Moneta, VA........................973-827-6911

Rosenwach Tank Co LLC
Long Island City, NY..............212-972-4411
Royal Welding & Fabricating
Fullerton, CA.....................714-680-6669
Rubicon Industries
Brooklyn, NY......................800-662-6999
Sanchelima International
Miami, FL.........................305-591-4343
Scherping Systems
Winsted, MN.......................320-485-4401
Sharpsville Container Corp
Sharpsville, PA...................800-645-1248
Sims Machinery Co Inc
Lanett, AL........................334-576-2101
Snyder Crown
Marked Tree, AR...................870-358-3400
Southern Metal Fabricators Inc
Albertville, AL...................800-989-1330
Specific Mechanical Systems
Victoria, BC......................250-652-2111
Stainless Specialists Inc
Wausau, WI........................800-236-4155
Sterling Process Engineering
Columbus, OH......................800-783-7875
Supreme Fabricators
Artesia, CA.......................323-583-8944
Tampa Sheet Metal Co
Tampa, FL.........................813-251-1845
Thermo Wisconsin
De Pere, WI.......................920-766-7200
Tolan Machinery Company
Rockaway, NJ......................973-983-7212
United Industries Group Inc
Lake Forest, CA...................949-759-3200
Vorti-Siv
Salem, OH.........................800-227-7487
Waukesha Cherry-Burrell
Louisville, KY....................502-491-4310
WCB Ice Cream
Philadelphia, PA..................215-425-4320
Welliver Metal Products Corporation
Salem, OR.........................503-362-1568

Modular

Modutank Inc
Long Island City, NY..............800-245-6964

Stainless Steel

G & F Mfg
Oak Lawn, IL......................800-282-1574

Trailers

Refrigerated

All A Cart Custom Mfg
Columbus, OH......................800-695-2278
Fruehauf Trailer Services
St Louis, MO......................314-822-1113
Great Dane LP
Chicago, IL.......................773-254-5533
Manufacturers Railway Company
Saint Louis, MO...................314-577-1775
New Centennial
Columbus, GA......................800-241-7541
Portable Cold Storage
Edison, NJ........................800-535-2445
Texas Corn Roasters
Granbury, TX......................800-772-4345

Trucks

Factory, Warehouse, Shop & Industrial

A-Z Factory Supply
Schiller Park, IL.................800-323-4511
Ace Engineering Company
Fort Worth, TX....................800-431-4223
AFCO Manufacturing
Cincinnati, OH....................800-747-7332
All Power Inc
Sioux City, IA....................712-258-0681
Bell & Howell Company
Lincolnwood, IL...................800-647-2290
Bessco Tube Bending & Pipe Fabricating
Thornton, IL......................800-337-3977
Bishamon Industry Corp
Ontario, CA.......................800-358-8833
C R Daniels Inc
Ellicott City, MD.................800-933-2638

Caddy Corporation of America
Bridgeport, NJ. 856-467-4222
California Caster & Handtruck
San Francisco, CA 800-950-8750
Cannon Equipment Company
Cannon Falls, MN. 800-825-8501
Cayne Industrial Sales Corp
Bronx, NY. 718-993-5800
Collins Manufacturing Company Ltd
Langley, BC 800-663-6761
Continental Commercial Products
Bridgeton, MO 800-325-1051
Conveyance Technologies LLC
Cleveland, OH 800-701-2278
Crown Equipment Corp.
New Bremen, OH 419-629-2311
Doosan Industrial Vehicle America Corp
Buford, GA 678-745-2200
Dubuque Steel Products Co
Dubuque, IA 563-556-6288
Dutro Co
Logan, UT. 866-388-7660
Dynabilt Products
Readville, MA. 800-443-1008
Edwards Products
Cincinnati, OH 800-543-1835
Elwell Parker
Coraopolis, PA 800-272-9953
Excalibur Miretti Group LLC
Fairfield, NJ 973-808-8399
Exel
Lincolnton, NC 704-735-6535
General Truck Body Mfg
Houston, TX 800-395-8585
Hackney Brothers
Washington, NC 800-763-0700
Hamilton Caster
Hamilton, OH 888-699-7164
Harper Trucks Inc
Wichita, KS 800-835-4099
HDT Manufacturing
Salem, OH. 800-968-7438
Hotshot Delivery System
Bloomingdale, IL 630-924-8817
Hyster Company
San Diego, CA 855-804-2118
Incinerator International Inc
Houston, TX 713-227-1466
Industrial Equipment Company
Derry, NH 603-432-2037
Jarke Corporation
Prospect Hts, IL 800-722-5255
Jesco Industries
Litchfield, MI 800-455-0019
John Bean Technologies Corp
Chalfont, PA 888-362-3622
Johnston Equipment
Delta, BC. 800-237-5159
Kent District Library System
Comstock Park, MI. 616-784-2007
Komatsu Forklift USA
Rolling Meadows, IL 847-437-5800
Lakeside Manufacturing Inc
Milwaukee, WI. 888-558-8565
Landoo Corporation
Horsham, PA. 785-562-5381
Leyman Manufacturing   Corporation
Cincinnati, OH 866-539-6261
Linde Material Handling
Summerville, SC. 843-871-0312
Load King Mfg
Jacksonville, FL 800-531-4975
Long Reach ManufacturingCompany
Westport, CT. 800-285-7000
Marion Body Works Inc
Marion, WI. 715-754-5261
Metal Equipment Company
Cleveland, OH 800-700-6326
Mid-States Mfg & Engr Co Inc
Milton, IA 800-346-1792
Mitsubishi Caterpillar Mcfa
Houston, TX 800-228-5438
NACCO Materials HandlingGroup
Fairview, OR. 503-721-6205
National Scoop & Equipment Company
Spring House, PA 215-646-2040
Net Material Handling
Milwaukee, WI. 800-558-7260
Nevlen Co. 2, Inc.
Wakefield, MA 800-562-7225
New Age Industrial
Norton, KS 800-255-0104

Nexel Industries Inc
Port Washington, NY 800-245-6682
Ortmayer Materials Handling
Brooklyn, NY 718-875-7995
Peregrine Inc
Lincoln, NE. 800-777-3433
Pucel Enterprises Inc
Cleveland, OH 800-336-4986
Raymond Corp
Greene, NY 800-235-7200
Royce Corp
Glendale, AZ. 602-256-0006
Schaeff
Bridgeview, IL 888-436-7867
Solve Needs International
White Lake, MI. 800-783-2462
Technibilt/Cari-All
Newton, NC 800-233-3972
Thermo King Corp
Bloomington, MN. 888-887-2202
Thombert
Newton, IA 800-433-3572
Uni Carriers Americas Corp
Marengo, IL 800-871-5438
Valley Craft Inc
Lake City, MN 800-328-1480
Waldon Manufacturing LLC
Fairview, OK. 800-486-0023
Wesley International Corp
Scottdale, GA 800-241-8649

Food & Restaurant

All A Cart Custom Mfg
Columbus, OH 800-695-2278
All Star Carts & Vehicles
Bay Shore, NY 800-831-3166
Alliance Products LLC
Murfreesboro, TN. 800-522-3973
Amco Metals Indl
City Of Industry, CA. 626-855-2550
ARC Specialties
Valencia, CA. 661-775-8500
Bmh Equipment Inc
Sacramento, CA 800-350-8828
Century Industries Inc
Sellersburg, IN 800-248-3371
Creative Mobile Systems Inc
Manchester, CT. 800-646-8364
Custom Sales & Svc Inc
Hammonton, NJ 800-257-7855
Hackney Brothers
Washington, NC 800-763-0700
Holstein Manufacturing
Holstein, IA. 800-368-4342
Lakeside Manufacturing Inc
Milwaukee, WI. 888-558-8565
Lakeside-Aris Manufacturing
Milwaukee, WI. 800-558-8565
Leggett & Platt Storage
Vernon Hills, IL 847-816-6246
M & E Mfg Co Inc
Kingston, NY 845-331-2110
Metro Corporation
Wilkes Barre, PA. 800-992-1776
Technibilt/Cari-All
Newton, NC 800-233-3972
Wag Industries
Skokie, IL 800-621-3305
Worksman 800 Buy Cart
Ozone Park, NY 800-289-2278

Hand

ARC Specialties
Valencia, CA. 661-775-8500
Bmh Equipment Inc
Sacramento, CA 800-350-8828
California Caster & Handtruck
San Francisco, CA 800-950-8750
Clamp Swing Pricing Co Inc
Oakland, CA 800-227-7615
Clark Caster Company
Cave In Rock, IL. 800-538-0765
Enrick Co
Zumbrota, MN 507-732-5215
Hamilton Caster
Hamilton, OH 888-699-7164
Hodge Manufacturing Company
Springfield, MA 800-262-4634
Innovation Moving Systems
Oostburg, WI. 800-619-0625

Magline Inc
Standish, MI 800-624-5463
Net Material Handling
Milwaukee, WI. 800-558-7260
Otto Braun Bakery Equipment
Buffalo, NY. 716-824-1252
Roll Rite Corp
Hayward, CA 800-345-9305
Ultra Lift Corp
San Jose, CA 800-346-3057
Valley Craft Inc
Lake City, MN 800-328-1480

Meat

Dubuque Steel Products Co
Dubuque, IA 563-556-6288
Techform
Mount Airy, NC 336-789-2115

Packing House

Bessco Tube Bending & Pipe Fabricating
Thornton, IL 800-337-3977
Bmh Equipment Inc
Sacramento, CA 800-350-8828
Cannon Equipment Company
Cannon Falls, MN. 800-825-8501
Dc Tech
Kansas City, MO. 877-742-9090
Elwell Parker
Coraopolis, PA 800-272-9953
Key Material Handling Inc
Simi Valley, CA. 800-539-7225
Le Fiell Co
Reno, NV 402-592-9993
Wesley International Corp
Scottdale, GA 800-241-8649

Pallet Handling

Bishamon Industry Corp
Ontario, CA 800-358-8833
Bmh Equipment Inc
Sacramento, CA 800-350-8828
Cannon Equipment Company
Cannon Falls, MN. 800-825-8501
Elwell Parker
Coraopolis, PA 800-272-9953
Key Material Handling Inc
Simi Valley, CA. 800-539-7225
Landoll Corp
Marysville, KS 785-562-5381
Lift Rite
Mississauga, ON 905-456-2603
Long Reach ManufacturingCompany
Westport, CT. 800-285-7000
Lumber & Things
Keyser, WV. 800-296-5656
NACCO Materials HandlingGroup
Fairview, OR. 503-721-6205
Net Material Handling
Milwaukee, WI. 800-558-7260
Sackett Systems
Bensenville, IL 800-323-8332
Wesley International Corp
Scottdale, GA 800-241-8649

Tilt

Bayhead Products Corp.
Dover, NH. 800-229-4323
Bmh Equipment Inc
Sacramento, CA 800-350-8828
Pucel Enterprises Inc
Cleveland, OH 800-336-4986
RMI-C/Rotonics Manaufacturing
Bensenville, IL 630-773-9510

Utility Vault Covers

Slip Not
Detroit, MI 800-754-7668

Vats

Cheese

A & B Process Systems Corp
Stratford, WI. 888-258-2789
Damrow Company
Fond Du Lac, WI 800-236-1501

DCI, Inc.
  St Cloud, MN 320-252-8200
Dubuque Steel Products Co
  Dubuque, IA 563-556-6288
Peterson Fiberglass Laminates
  Shell Lake, WI 715-468-2306
Rosenwach Tank Co LLC
  Long Island City, NY 212-972-4411

Warehouses

Insulated

Advance Energy Technologies
  Halfmoon, NY.....................800-724-0198

Wine Storage Units

Advance Energy Technologies
  Halfmoon, NY.....................800-724-0198
Bacchus Wine Cellars
  Houston, TX 800-487-8812
Cramer Products
  New York, NY 212-645-2368
Cruvinet Winebar Co LLC
  Sparks, NV 800-278-8463
Dufeck Manufacturing Co
  Denmark, WI.....................888-603-9663
Falco Technologies
  La Prairie, QC...................450-444-0566
International Patterns, Inc.
  Bay Shore, NY 631-952-2000

Kedco Wine Storage Systems
  Farmingdale, NY 800-654-9988
Lockwood Manufacturing
  Livonia, MI.....................800-521-0238
Metro Corporation
  Wilkes Barre, PA................800-992-1776
PBC
  Mahwah, NJ 800-514-2739
Summit Commercial
  Bronx, NY......................800-932-4267
Winekeeper
  Santa Barbara, CA 805-963-3451
Wineracks by Marcus
  Costa Mesa, CA 714-546-4922

18000 3D Instruments LLC
2900 E White Star Ave
Anaheim, CA 92806-2627
714-399-9200
Fax: 714-399-9221 www.3dinstruments.com
Quality Control: Charlene L Lah
VP: Garey Cooper
Manager: Felix Brockmeyer
fbrockmeyer@3dinstruments.com
Estimated Sales: $50-100 Million
Number Employees: 100-249

18001 3DT, LLC
N114 W18850 Clinton Dr
Germantown, WI 53022
262-253-6700
Fax: 262-253-6977 888-326-7662
sales@3dtllc.com www.3dtllc.com
Corona treaters
President: Morten Jorgensen
Sales/Marketing Manager: S. Erik Kiel
Estimated Sales: $2.5-5 Million
Number Employees: 20-49

18002 3Greenmoms LLC
Po Box 59033
Potomac, MD 20859-9033
301-802-9390
Fax: 888-236-9043 kirsten@3greenmoms.com
www.lunchskins.com
Maker of reuseable decorative sandwich bags.

18003 (HQ)3M
3M Center
St. Paul, MN 55144-1000
888-364-3577
www.3m.com
Food safety products
Chairman & CEO: Michael Roman
SVP, Innovation & CTO: John Banovetz
EVP, Safety & Industrial Business Group: Michael Vale
EVP, Enterprise Operations: Eric Hammes
EVP, Consumer Business Group: Paul Keel
SVP & General Counsel: Ivan Fong
SVP & Chief Financial Officer: Nicholas Gangestad
SVP, Corporate Affairs: Denise Rutherford
Year Founded: 1902
Estimated Sales: $32.7 Billion
Number Employees: 93,516
Other Locations:
  3M Indianapolis
  Indianapolis IN
  3M Medina
  Medina OH
Brands:
  Post-it
  Scotch-Brite
  Scotch
  Nexcare
  Filtrete
  Command
  Scotch Painter's Tape
  FUTURO
  ACE
  3M Littman

18004 4front Entrematic
1612 Hutton Dr # 140
Suite 140
Carrollton, TX 75006-6642
972-236-2400
Fax: 972-389-4752 sales@sercocompany.com
www.4frontes.com
President: Keith Moore
keith.moore@4frontes.com
Estimated Sales: C
Number Employees: 100-249

18005 518 Corporation
518 Martin Luther King Jr.
Savannah, GA 31401-4881
912-232-1141
Fax: 912-236-7969
President: Louis C Mathews III
Estimated Sales: $5-10 Million
Number Employees: 10-19

18006 7 Seas Submarine
11216 S Michigan Ave
Chicago, IL 60628-4910
773-785-0550
Fax: 312-942-0236
Owner: Natibad Cortez
natibadcortez@hrblock.com

Estimated Sales: Less Than $500,000
Number Employees: 1-4

18007 9-12 Corporation
HC-1 Box 29030
Department 388
Caguas, PR 00725
787-747-0405
Fax: 787-747-0318
Manufacturers of elevate enhanced fiber water beverages.
President/CEO: Joe Lazoff
Estimated Sales: $1-5 Million
Number Employees: 10
Square Footage: 40000
Type of Packaging: Consumer, Food Service, Private Label
Brands:
  Apres
  Pirel

18008 915 Labs
9200 E Mineral Ave.
Centennial, CO 80112
855-915-5227
info@915Labs.com www.915labs.com
Offers microwave food processing technology to the food industry.
CEO: Michael Locatis
Year Founded: 2014
Number Employees: 10-20

18009 99 Ranch Market
1625 S Azusa Ave
Hacienda Heights, CA 91745-3832
626-839-2899
Fax: 626-839-2127 www.99ranch.com
Asian American groceries
Founder/CEO: Roger Chen
Year Founded: 1984
Estimated Sales: $500,000
Number Employees: 50-99
Other Locations:
  Manufacturing Facility-Sugarland
  Sugarland TX

18010 A & B Process Systems Corp
201 S Wisconsin Ave
P.O. Box 86
Stratford, WI 54484
715-687-4332
Fax: 715-687-3225 888-258-2789
www.abprocess.com
Manufacturer and exporter of ASME U stamps, process systems, tanks, vessels and custom components.
Chairman/Co-Founder: Ajay Hilgemann
Chief Executive Officer: Paul Kinate
pkinate@abprocess.com
Sales & Marketing Manager: Andrea Wiese
Health & Safety Manager: Bill Thompson
Year Founded: 1973
Estimated Sales: $120 Million
Number Employees: 50-99
Square Footage: 175000
Type of Packaging: Food Service, Bulk
Brands:
  Oc Guide Bearing
  Vacushear

18011 A & D Sales
145 E Colt Dr
Fayetteville, AR 72703-2847
479-521-8665
Fax: 479-521-0841
President: Jim Stockland
jim@adchicken.com
Treasurer: Pam Stockland
Estimated Sales: $5-10 Million
Number Employees: 5-9

18012 A & E Conveyor Systems Inc
121 P Rickman Industrial Dr
Canton, GA 30115-9099
770-345-7300
Fax: 770-345-7391 info@ae-conveyor.com
www.ae-conveyor.com
Waterless container cleaning systems, container handling, conveying systems
President: Raymond Young
ryoung@ae-conveyor.com
Estimated Sales: Below $5 000,000
Number Employees: 10-19

18013 A & G Foods
6945 S State St
Chicago, IL 60637-4528
773-783-1672
Fax: 773-994-9623
Owner: Sam Johnson
Estimated Sales: $3-5 Million
Number Employees: 10-19

18014 A & K Development Co
410 Chambers St
Eugene, OR 97402-4375
541-686-0012
Fax: 541-485-2892 akdco@akdco.net
Sweet corn processing equipment: power huskers, power orienter, vibratory receiving conveyors, steam wilters, elevators, distribution systems, automatic feeding and lubrication systems, roll washers, short piece graders, scalpers, andsilage choppers
President and R&D: Ronald L Anderson
akdevelop@akdco.com
CFO: Bob King
Marketing Director: Zack Zachemtmayer
Office Manager: Darla Vicksie
Estimated Sales: $1-2.5 Million
Number Employees: 20-49

18015 A A A Awning Co Inc
8810 Madie Dr
Houston, TX 77022-2617
800-281-6193
Fax: 713-694-0863 800-281-6193
www.aaaawning.net
Commercial awnings
Owner: Paul Yee
VP: Randy Deaton
Estimated Sales: $2.5-5 Million
Number Employees: 5-9

18016 A A Label Co
350 Stevenson Blvd # 2
New Kensington, PA 15068-5944
USA
724-335-5505
888-290-6012
customerservice@aalabel.com www.aalabel.com
Print and design of labels, gift wrap, boxes, containers
President: Mark Fisher
mfisher@aalabel.com
Estimated Sales: 700,000
Number Employees: 10-19

18017 A Allred Marketing
401 Graymont Ave W
Birmingham, AL 35204-4007
205-251-3700
Fax: 205-251-3706 allredpromos@gmail.com
Advertising specialties, signs, uniforms, shirts, caps, jackets, menus, flag poles and promotional items; also, custom printing and embroidery available.
President: Larry Allred
allredpromos@gmail.com
Estimated Sales: $500,000-$1 Million
Number Employees: 5-9
Parent Co: Promotional Products

18018 A B T Inc
259 Murdock Rd
Troutman, NC 28166-9695
704-528-9806
Fax: 704-528-5478 800-438-6057
sales@abtdrains.com
Pre-engineered drainage systems
President: Ralph Brafford
National Sales Manager: Jim DelRe
Estimated Sales: $2.5-5 Million
Number Employees: 50-99
Other Locations:
  ABT
  Lexington KY
Brands:
  Polydrain
  Polyduct
  Trench Former System

18019 A C Birox
200 Centennial Ave # 209
Piscataway, NJ 08854-3950
732-457-0015
Fax: 732-457-0016 800-242-2599
Biosensor-based instrument: quantifying folic acid and biotin levels

President: Jerry Williamson
CFO: George Hogan
National Account Manager: Thomas Grace
Contact: Anders Felt
anders.falt@biacore.com
Estimated Sales: $3-5 Million
Number Employees: 10-19

18020 A C Horn & Co Sheet Metal
1269 Majesty Dr
Dallas, TX 75247-3917

    214-630-3311
Fax: 214-905-1365 800-657-6155
www.achornco.com
Food processing, packaging, and material handling
equipment.
President: Doug Horn
CEO: Ricardo Pounds
rpounds@achornmfg.com
Vice President: Mark Ritter
Research/Development: Paul Lima
Quality Control: Paul Lima
Director Marketing/Sales: Mark Ritter
Public Relations: Michael Horn, Jr
Plant/Production Manager: Tommy Galloway
Purchasing: Elizabeth Durban
Estimated Sales: $10-20 Million
Number Employees: 50-99
Square Footage: 240000
Parent Co: A.C. Horn & Company
Brands:
  Radiant Ray
  Ray-O-Matic

18021 A C Tool & Machine Co
3711 Nobel Ct
Louisville, KY 40216-4113

    502-447-5505
Fax: 502-447-2305 www.actoolandmachine.com
Sausage processing and packaging equipment; re-
building of food processing equipment and replace-
ment parts.
President: Matthew Thoben
mthoben@actoolandmachine.com
Estimated Sales: $1-2.5 Million
Number Employees: 10-19
Square Footage: 48000
Type of Packaging: Food Service
Brands:
  Ac Slit & Trim

18022 A G Russell Knives
2900 S 26th St
Rogers, AR 72758-8571

    479-631-0130
Fax: 479-631-8734 800-255-9034
ag@agrussell.com www.agrussell.com
Manufacturer and exporter of household knives
Owner: A G Russell
goldie@agrussell.com
CFO: Michael Donnovan
Sales Exec: Goldie Russell
Estimated Sales: $20-50 Million
Number Employees: 20-49
Brands:
  Camillus Classic Cartridge
  Cartridge
  Dura-Tool
  Promaster
  Silver Sword
  Sword
  Western
  Woodcraft
  Yello-Jacket

18023 (HQ)A J Antunes & Co
180 Kehoe Blvd
Carol Stream, IL 60188-1814

    630-784-1000
Fax: 630-784-1650 800-253-2991
scott.march@antunes.com
Manufacturer and exporter of stainless steel food
service equipment for restaurants and concession
operations including tables and serving equipment in
addition to filtration products that remove
particulates, bacteria, and virusesfrom water.
President: Glenn Bullock
CEO: Juan Arzate
juan.arzate@ajantunes.com
CFO: Bill Nelson
Executive VP: William Hickey
Director New Business Development: Scott March
VP Sales/Marketing: Tom Krisch

Estimated Sales: $50-100 Million
Number Employees: 100-249
Type of Packaging: Food Service
Brands:
  Antunes Control
  Roundup

18024 A J Funk & Co
1471 Timber Dr
Elgin, IL 60123-1898

    847-741-6760
Fax: 847-741-6767 877-225-3865
info@glasscleaner.com
www.sparkle-glasscleaner.com
Glass cleaner. Also supply product and service to
distributors and end-users
President: Patrick Funk
Director of Sales: Lou Carlotti
Estimated Sales: $4 Million
Number Employees: 5-9
Square Footage: 48000
Type of Packaging: Consumer, Food Service
Brands:
  Sparkle

18025 A La Carte
5610 W Bloomingdale Ave
Chicago, IL 60639-4110

    773-237-3000
Fax: 773-237-3075 800-722-2370
service@alacarteline.com
Custom promotional products including hard candy
and popcorn in decorative tins, jars, boxes, etc.
President: Michael Shulkin
CEO: Adam Robins
Sales Director: James Janowski
Purchasing: Marly Robins
Estimated Sales: $10-20 Million
Number Employees: 50-99
Parent Co: David Scott Industries
Type of Packaging: Food Service, Private Label,
Bulk

18026 A Legacy Food Svc
12683 Corral Pl
Santa Fe Springs, CA 90670-4748

    562-320-3100
Fax: 888-604-1066 800-848-4440
info@alegacy.com www.alegacy.com
Manufacturer and exporter of top-of-range alumi-
num cookware. Also, restaurant supplies and
epuipment
President: Brett Gross
Sales Director: Eric Gross
Manager: Eric Gross
egross@alegacy.com
Estimated Sales: $1-5 Million
Number Employees: 5-9
Square Footage: 320000
Other Locations:
  Leonard, Harold, & Co.
  Chicago IL
Brands:
  Alegacy
  Eagleware

18027 A Line Corporation
5410 Powerhouse Court
Concord, NC 28027

    704-793-1602
Fax: 704-793-1603 sales@aline1.com
www.aline1.com
Top-Load Carton Forming and Closing machinery
President: Maria Naas
Marketing: Jan Stull
Estimated Sales: $5-10 Million
Number Employees: 5-9

18028 A M S Filling Systems
2500 Chestnut Tree Rd
Glenmoore, PA 19343

    610-942-3056
Fax: 610-942-7123 800-647-5390
sales@amsfilling.com www.amsfilling.com
Auger filling equipment for powder, granules, liq-
uids and pastes
President/CEO: Andy Baker
Sales: Mark Pezone
Estimated Sales: $3,000,000
Number Employees: 20-49
Square Footage: 140000
Brands:
  Ams

18029 A M Source Inc
261 Narragansett Park Dr
Rumford, RI 02916-1043

    401-431-4080
Fax: 401-431-0606 800-556-6254
info@ajksales.com
Manufacturers' representative for disposable paper
and plastic food service products and packaging;
serving all markets
President: Arthur Kaufman
spritchard@amsourcellc.com
Controller: H John Madden
VP: Allan Kaufman
Marketing Sales Manager: Kenneth McAuliffe
Sales Exec: Scott Prichard
Estimated Sales: $20-50 Million
Number Employees: 50-99
Type of Packaging: Food Service
Brands:
  Aep Institutional Products
  Austins
  Cascades
  Cascades Ifc Disposables
  Destiny Plastics
  Disposable Products Company
  Dopaco
  Fabri-Kal Corporation
  Fold Pak Company
  Genpak
  Handi-Foil of America
  Johnsondiversey
  McNarin Packaging
  Morgro
  Plastirun Corporation
  Poliback Plastics America
  Quality Paper Products
  Stewart Sutherland
  Tradex International

18030 A O A C Intl
481 N Frederick Ave
Suite 500
Gaithersburg, MD 20877-2417

    301-924-7087
Fax: 301-924-7089 800-379-2622
aoac@aoac.org www.aoac.org
CFO: Joyce Schumacher
Executive Director: James Bradford
Contact: Don Bark
dbark@aoac.org
Estimated Sales: $1-5 Million
Number Employees: 20-49

18031 A One Mfg Co
549 Evergreen Rd
Strafford, MO 65757-8810

    417-736-2195
Fax: 417-736-2833 www.a-onemfg.com
Conveyors and accessories, pressure washers, blend-
ers, massagers and tumblers
President: David Cobb
d.cobb@a-onemfg.com
Estimated Sales: $5-10 000,000
Number Employees: 50-99

18032 A Snow Craft Co Inc
200 Fulton Ave
PO Box 829
New Hyde Park, NY 11040-5306

    516-739-1399
Fax: 516-739-1637 snowcraft1@aol.com
www.snowcraft.com
Insulated shipping containers
President: Ron Pelesko
rpelesko@skydyne.com
Secretary: William Hess
Estimated Sales: $5-10 Million
Number Employees: 20-49

18033 A T C Inc
4037 Guion Ln
Indianapolis, IN 46268-2564

    317-429-1099
Fax: 317-328-2686 hsagi@atcinc.net
www.atcinc.net
President: Hemi Sagi
Estimated Sales: Less Than $500,000
Number Employees: 1-4

18034 A T Ferrell Co Inc
1440 S Adams St
Bluffton, IN 46714-9793
260-824-3400
Fax: 260-824-5463 800-248-8318
www.atferrell.com
Manufacturer and exporter of automatic electric feed mills, augers, pneumatic feed conveyors and aluminum beverage can crushers
President: Steve Stuller
bsstuller@atferrell.com
Estimated Sales: $1-2.5 Million
Number Employees: 50-99
Number of Brands: 2
Brands:
Modern Mill
Monarch Can Crushers

18035 A T Ferrell Co Inc
1440 S Adams St
Bluffton, IN 46714-9793
260-824-3400
Fax: 260-824-5463 800-248-8318
info@atferrell.com www.atferrell.com
Manufacturer and exporter of grain and seed cleaners and separators, hammer and roller mills, grain and feed coolers and vibrator and air conveyors
President: Steve Stuller
bsstuller@atferrell.com
CFO: Roger Stackhouse
Vice President: Phillip Petrakos
Research & Development: Dan Johnson
Sales Director: John Hay
Plant Manager: Howard Vaughn
Purchasing Manager: Brian Dynes
Estimated Sales: $5-10 Million
Number Employees: 50-99
Square Footage: 100000
Other Locations:
Clipper Separation Technologies
Bluffton IN
Ferrell-Ross Division
Amarillo TX
Brands:
Clipper
Ferrell-Ross
Mix-Mill

18036 A T Information Products Inc
575 Corporate Dr # 401
Mahwah, NJ 07430-3703
201-529-0202
Fax: 201-529-5603 www.atip-usa.com
Ink jet printing systems
President: Joseph Traut
joseph.traut@atip-usa.com
Estimated Sales: Below $5 000,000
Number Employees: 10-19

18037 A T Scafati Inc
417 W 44th St # A
New York, NY 10036-4402
212-695-4944
Fax: 212-695-4944
Doorman, bellboy, waiter uniforms
President: Joe Scafati
Estimated Sales: Below $5 Million
Number Employees: 10-19

18038 A Tec Technologic
5335 Progress Boulevard
Bethel Park, PA 15102-2545
412-835-6270
Fax: 412-835-6205
President: Philip Bochicchio

18039 A&A International
544 Central Dr Ste 110
Virginia Beach, VA 23454
757-463-1446
Fax: 757-463-4917 800-252-1446
info@aaawnings.com www.aaawnings.com
Commercial awnings
Manager: Rhonda Yarborough
Estimated Sales: $1-2,500,000
Number Employees: 20-49

18040 A&A Line & Wire Corporation
5118 Grand Ave Ste 10
Flushing, NY 11378
718-456-2657
Fax: 718-366-8284 800-886-2657
jlach@aalinewire.com
Manufacturer, importer and exporter of rope, twine and doormats, also sausage and pastella twine

President: Wally Greenburg
Treasurer: F Lach
Contact: Robert Giragosian
rgiragosian@aalinewire.com
Estimated Sales: Below $5 Million
Number Employees: 10-19
Square Footage: 32000
Parent Co: Long Island Import Center
Brands:
Coco
Crown
Queen O Mat

18041 A&A Manufacturing Company
2300 S Calhoun Rd
New Berlin, WI 53151-2708
414-906-4200
Fax: 262-786-3280 sales@gortite.com
www.gortite.com
Protective walk-on covers
President: Jim O'Rourke
CEO: Jerry O'Rourke
CFO: Larry Kean
VP: Tom Schanover
Quality Control: Darol Varter
Marketing Manager: Ken Sczyzkwski
Contact: Mike Adler
mike.adler@aaman.com
Estimated Sales: $20-50 Million
Number Employees: 100-249
Parent Co: Standalone

18042 A&B Safe Corporation
114 Delsea Dr S
Glassboro, NJ 08028
856-863-1186
Fax: 856-863-1208 800-253-1267
info@a-bsafecorp.com www.a-bsafecorp.com
Manufacturer, importer and exporter of depository, burglary and insulated safes and chests; also, insulated filing cabinets, safes and locks
President: Edward Dornisch
Sales Director: Edward C Dornisch
Operations Manager: Mildred Dornisch
Estimated Sales: $.5-1 million
Number Employees: 1-4
Number of Brands: 20
Square Footage: 10000
Brands:
A&B

18043 A&D Weighing
1756 Automation Pkwy
San Jose, CA 95131-1873
408-263-5333
Fax: 408-263-0119 800-726-3364
scales@andweighing.com www.andonline.com
Manufacturer and exporter of balances, scales and indicators
President: Paul Huber
President, Chief Executive Officer: Teruhisa Moriya
CEO: Peru Moriya
Marketing Communications Coordinator: Regina Starzyk
Director Sales: Dan Ashton
dashton@andweighing.com
Estimated Sales: $20-50 Million
Number Employees: 20-49
Square Footage: 3000

18044 A&D Weighing
1756 Automation Pkwy
San Jose, CA 95131-1873
408-263-5333
Fax: 408-263-0119 scales@andweighing.com
www.andonline.com
President: Paul Huver
President, Chief Executive Officer: Teruhisa Moriya
Quality Control: Maggie Tan
CEO: Peru Moriya
Contact: Dan Ashton
dashton@andweighing.com
Estimated Sales: $20-50 Million
Number Employees: 20-49

18045 A&F
5355 115th Avenue N
Clearwater, FL 33760-4840
727-572-7753
Fax: 727-573-0367
Filling and sealing machinery
President: Paul Desocio
Contact: Paul De Socio
paul@autoprodinc.com

Estimated Sales: $10-20 Million
Number Employees: 50-100
Parent Co: Jagenberg

18046 A&F Automation
1210 Campus Dr
Morganville, NJ 07751-1262
732-536-8770
Fax: 732-536-8850 www.oystarusa.com
President: Charles Ravalli
Estimated Sales: $3-5 Million
Number Employees: 10-19
Parent Co: IWKA Company

18047 A&G Machine Company
50 Dunnell Lane
Pawtucket, RI 02860-5828
401-726-4180
Fax: 401-723-2333
Aerators, candy making equipment including stringers and cookers, batch and continuous cooking equipment, cream machines, heat exchangers, kettle lifters and marshmallow equipment
President: Paul Desocio
Estimated Sales: $300,000-500,000
Number Employees: 1-4

18048 A&J Mixing International
8-2345 Wyecroft Road
Oakville, ON L6L 6L8
Canada
905-827-7288
Fax: 905-827-5045 800-668-3470
lyndon@ajmixing.com www.ajmixing.com
Manufacturer and exporter of food dry ingredient mixers, mixing sytems, vacuum coaters, dryers and continuous mixers.
President: A Flower
Sales: Lyndon Flower
Estimated Sales: $2.5 Million
Square Footage: 5000
Other Locations:
Sycamore IL
Brands:
Phlauer High Performance Mixers

18049 A&K Automation
1010 N Ashland Avenue
Aurora, ON L4G4R6
Canada
905-713-3429
Fax: 920-432-4356 info@akautomation.ca
www.akautomation.ca
Bakery products and pizza crust equipment
President: Randy Charles
CFO: Jim Charles
R & D: Dennis Dolski
Estimated Sales: Below $5 Million
Number Employees: 10
Square Footage: 1600

18050 A&L Laboratories
1001 Glenwood Ave
Minneapolis, MN 55405
612-374-9141
Fax: 612-374-5426 800-225-3832
Detergents and sanitizers
President: Guy Pochard
VP: Gabreiele Wittenburg
Contact: Roger Beers
beers@aandl-labs.com
Estimated Sales: $20-50 Million
Number Employees: 20-49

18051 A&L Western Ag Lab
1311 Woodland Avenue
Suite 1
Modesto, CA 95351-1221
209-529-4080
Fax: 209-529-4736 www.al-labs-west.com
Testing laboratory providing sanitation and nutritional analysis for product labeling
President and Laboratory Director: Robert Butterfield
Estimated Sales: $1-2.5 Million
Number Employees: 10-19
Square Footage: 26000

18052 A&M Industries
3610 North Cliff Avenue
Sioux Falls, SD 57104
605-332-4877
Fax: 605-338-6015 800-888-2615
amindustries@amindustries.com
www.amindustries.com

Manufacturer and exporter of rebuilt packaging, food processing and confectionery machinery, carton over-wrappers and specialty tooling
Owner: Richard Miller
Estimated Sales: Below $5 Million
Number Employees: 1-4
Square Footage: 20000
Type of Packaging: Consumer, Food Service, Private Label

18053 A&M Process Equipment
487 Westney Rd.
S., Unit #1
Ajax, ON L1S 6W7
Canada

905-619-8001
Fax: 905-619-8816
Food processing equipment including powder mixing and size reduction; exporter of ribbon, conical and twin shell blenders
President: John Lang
Number Employees: 4
Square Footage: 8000

18054 A&M Thermometer Corporation
17 Piney Park Road
Asheville, NC 28806-1727

828-251-9092
Fax: 828-254-5611 800-685-9211
Manufacturer and exporter of glass thermometers
President: M Pflaumbaum
R&D: Armin Pflaumbaum
Marketing: Kathy Toomey
Production: Armin Pflaumbaum
Purchasing Director: M Pflaumbaun
Estimated Sales: $2.5-5 Million
Number Employees: 10-19
Type of Packaging: Private Label, Bulk
Brands:
  Accutest
  Asico

18055 A&R Ceka North America
1755 North Brown Road
Suite 200
Lawrenceville, GA 30043-8196

770-623-8235
Fax: 770-623-8236 www.ar-carton.com
Supplier of carton packaging solutions.
President, Chief Executive Officer: Harald Schulz
Vice President, Chief Financial Officer: Niclas Nystrom
Senior Vice President of Sales and Marke: Jean-Francois Roche

18056 A-1 Booth Manufacturing
375 S 250 E
Burley, ID 83318-3718

208-678-2877
Fax: 800-952-3285 800-820-3285
sales@a1booth.com www.a1booth.com
Manufacturer and exporter of tables, chairs and seats
President: Robert Silcock
Estimated Sales: $1-2.5 Million
Number Employees: 5-9
Type of Packaging: Food Service
Brands:
  Patriot Plus
  Patriot Series

18057 A-1 Business Supplies Inc
158 W Clinton St # N
Dover, NJ 07801-3411

973-366-3690
800-631-3421
Tags, price tags, day dots and labels including inventory control
Manager: Janet Larkin
VP: Janet Larkin
Sales Manager: Dick Burbaum
Estimated Sales: $1-2,500,000
Number Employees: 5-9

18058 A-1 Refrigeration Co
1720 E Monticello Ct
Ontario, CA 91761-7740

909-930-9910
Fax: 909-930-9026 800-669-4423
custserv@a1flakeice.com www.a1flakeice.com
Ice machines.
Plant Manager: Tony Gallinucci
Estimated Sales: Less Than $500,000
Number Employees: 1-4
Number of Products: 10

Brands:
  A-1

18059 A-A1 Aaction Bag
5601 Logan St
Denver, CO 80216-1301

303-297-9955
Fax: 303-297-9960 800-783-1224
www.centralbag.com
Manufacturer and wholesaler/distributor of packaging materials including paper and plastic bags, deli containers, cups and packaging for meats and seafood; also, custom printed and plain bags available
President: Esther Seaman
CEO: Elly Zussman
elly@centralbag.com
CFO: David Fine
Vice President: Morton Zussman
VP, Marketing: Morty Zussman
Sales: Chuck Fine
Operations Manager: David Zussman
Estimated Sales: $5 Million
Number Employees: 10-19
Square Footage: 70000
Parent Co: Al-AAction Bag Company
Type of Packaging: Consumer, Food Service, Private Label, Bulk

18060 A-A1 Aaction Bag
5601 Logan St
Denver, CO 80216-1301

303-297-9955
Fax: 303-297-9960 800-783-1224
searichcorp@aol.com www.centralbag.com
Manufacturer and exporter of bags including plastic, burlap and cotton; also, plastic film; importer of burlap and woven polypropylene bags
President: Esther Seaman
Partner: Elly Zussman
elly@centralbag.com
VP: Lewis Bradford
Sales Director: Morton Seaman
Estimated Sales: $500,000-$1 Million
Number Employees: 10-19
Square Footage: 48000
Parent Co: Sea-Rich Corporation
Type of Packaging: Bulk

18061 A-B-C Packaging MachineCorp
811 Live Oak St
Tarpon Springs, FL 34689-4199

727-937-5144
Fax: 727-938-1239 800-237-5975
sales@abcpackaging.com www.abcpackaging.com
Manufacturer and exporter of packaging machinery
President: Donald G Reichert
Director Sales/Marketing: Bryan Sinicrope
Estimated Sales: $10-20 Million
Number Employees: 50-99
Square Footage: 200000

18062 A-L-L Magnetics Inc
2831 E Via Martens
Anaheim, CA 92806-1751

714-632-1754
Fax: 714-632-1757 800-262-4638
sales@allmagnetics.com www.allmagnetics.com
Manufacturer, exporter and importer of magnets used for holding, separating and water treatment
President: John Nellessen
john@allmagnetics.com
CFO: John Nellessen
Sales: Rosemary Kute
Estimated Sales: Below $5 Million
Number Employees: 10-19
Square Footage: 80000
Brands:
  Magnet Source, The

18063 A-Z Factory Supply
10512 United Pkwy
Schiller Park, IL 60176-1716

847-261-0620
Fax: 800-233-4512 800-323-4511
sales@azsupply.com www.azsupply.com
Manufacturer and exporter of material handling and storage equipment, shelving, carts, shelf trucks, boxes, bins, hoppers, corrugated steel containers, conveyors, lifts, hoists, etc
Manager: Henry Bolden
henry@azsupply.com
VP: R Hannesson
Sales Manager: B Spurling

Estimated Sales: Below $5,000,000
Number Employees: 10-19

18064 A. Klein & Company
P.O.Box 670
Claremont, NC 28610

828-459-9261
Fax: 828-459-9608
Custom made boxes for the confectionery industry
President: Jesse Salwen
Estimated Sales: $50-100 Million
Number Employees: 100-249

18065 A.A. Pesce Glass Company
216 Birch St
Kennett Square, PA 19348-3606

610-444-5065
Fax: 610-444-3358
Scientific and laboratory glassware
Manager: Mike Carroll
Estimated Sales: $1-2.5 Million
Number Employees: 5-9

18066 A.B. Sealer, Inc.
N 7212 Farwell Road
PO Box 635
Beaver Dam, WI 53916-0635

920-885-9299
Fax: 920-885-0288 877-885-9299
sales@absealer.com www.absealer.com
Manufacturer and exporter of packaging machinery including portable case erectors and sealers and custom equipment systems
Owner: Lou Stikowsky
CEO: Russell Quandt
Estimated Sales: $1-2.5 Million
Number Employees: 50-99
Brands:
  Aantek
  Series 9000

18067 A.C. Legg
6330 Highway 31
PO Box 709
Calera, AL 35040-5131

205-324-3451
Fax: 205-324-5971 800-422-5344
sales@aclegg.com www.aclegg.com
Processor of custom-blended seasonings for meat, poultry, seafood and snack foods.
President/CEO: James Purvis
jpurvis@aclegg.com
EVP: Charles Purvis
EVP: Sandra Purvis
Year Founded: 1923
Estimated Sales: $20-50 Million
Number Employees: 100-249
Number of Brands: 1
Square Footage: 131000
Type of Packaging: Food Service, Private Label, Bulk
Brands:
  Legg's Old Plantation

18068 A.D. Cowdrey Company
1442 Angie Avenue
Modesto, CA 95351-4952

209-538-4677
Fax: 209-538-6087 cvpsdp@aol.com
www.adcowdrey.com
Canners' and packers' knives, aprons and corers
President: David Racher
VP: John Hassapakis
Contact: Dave Racher
d.racher@adcowdrey.com
Estimated Sales: Below $5 Million
Number Employees: 20
Parent Co: Central Valley Professional Service

18069 A.D. Johnson Engraving Company
229 Woodward Ave
Kalamazoo, MI 49007-3221

269-342-5500
Fax: 269-342-5511
Engraving and embossing dies and stamps; also, engraving for premium goods and advertising novelties
President: Donovan J Kindle
Estimated Sales: $500,000-$1 Million
Number Employees: 1-4

18070 A.D. Joslin Manufacturing Company
33 Artic St
Manistee, MI 49660
231-723-2908
Fax: 231-723-2908 www.manistee.com/joslin
Manufacturer and exporter of handheld and electric seal embossing machinery, dating machinery, steel code marking stamps, ticket validators and handheld case numbering machines
General Manager: Norman Ware
Office Manager: Carol Westberg
Estimated Sales: $3-5 Million
Number Employees: 10-19
Parent Co: Cosco Industries

18071 A.K. Robins
4100 Pistorio Road
Baltimore, MD 21229-5509
410-247-4000
Fax: 410-247-9165 800-486-9656
Manufacturer and exporter of cleaners, cookers, cutters, exhausters, extractors, etc.; also, CAD engineering and design and USDA services available
Sales Manager: Steve Ward
Operations Manager: Ken Vogel
Number Employees: 50

18072 A.M. Loveman Lumber & Box Company
PO Box 40123
Nashville, TN 37204-0123
615-297-1397
Wooden boxes and pallets
President: Andrew M Loveman
Estimated Sales: $500,000-$1 Million
Number Employees: 8
Square Footage: 24000

18073 A.M. Manufacturing
14151 Irving Ave
Dolton, IL 60419
708-841-0959
Fax: 708-841-0975 800-342-6744
www.ammfg.com
Baking equipment
Owner: Claudia Kunis
Co-owner: Holly Rentner
Contact: Wojciechows Mentz
wojo2424@aol.com
Estimated Sales: $5-10 Million
Number Employees: 20-49
Square Footage: 28000

18074 A.O. Smith Water Products Company
600 E John Carpenter Fwy # 200
Irving, TX 75062-3985
972-792-4371
Fax: 972-719-5967 800-527-1953
techctr@hotwater.com www.hotwater.com
Manufacturer and exporter of tank-type water heaters and boilers and booster heaters
Chairman, Chief Executive Officer: Paul Jones
Vice President, Controller: Daniel Kempken
President, Chief Operating Officer: Ajita Rajendra
Project Manager: Will Harris
Number Employees: 50-99
Square Footage: 4000000
Parent Co: A.O. Smith Corporation
Brands:
Burkay
Cyclone Xhe
Dura-Max
Legend
Master Fit

18075 A.P.M.
1500 Hillcrest Rd
Norcross, GA 30093-2617
770-921-6300
Fax: 770-925-7801 800-226-5557
www.apminc.org
President: James R Sabourin
Estimated Sales: $3-5 Million
Number Employees: 10-19

18076 A.T. Foote Woodworking Company
726 Windsor Street
Hartford, CT 06120
860-249-6821
Fax: 860-249-6192
Store fixtures
President: Arthur Foote, Sr.
VP: Arthur Foote, Jr.
Estimated Sales: $20-50 Million
Number Employees: 4

18077 A1 Tablecloth Co
450 Huyler St # 102
South Hackensack, NJ 07606-1563
201-727-4364
Fax: 201-727-8988 800-727-8987
a1@a1tablecloth.com www.a1tablecloth.com
Manufacturer and exporter of tablecloths, napkins, table skirting, chair covers and drapes
Owner: Robert Fox
Contact: Pearle Adam
ap@a-1tablecloth.com
Estimated Sales: $10-50,000,000
Number Employees: 1-4

18078 AAA Electrical Signs
2407 E Business Highway 83
Donna, TX 78537-3545
956-546-2735
Fax: 956-464-2408 800-825-5376
tesoro@tesorocorporation.net www.3asigns.com
Custom electrical signs, brass plaques, illuminated letters and time and temperature units; also, electronic message centers and color elcetronic signs, we sell and lease.
President: Paul Sullivan
paulsullivan@3asigns.com
General Manager: Steve Smith
Plant Manager: Ken Bailey
Estimated Sales: $4 Million
Number Employees: 20-49
Square Footage: 20000
Parent Co: Tesoro Corporation

18079 AAA Flag & Banner Manufacturing
8955 National Blvd
Los Angeles, CA 90034-3307
310-836-3341
Fax: 310-836-7253 800-266-4222
www.aaaflag.com
Flags, pennants, banners and signs
Controller: Carol Hettiger
CEO: Howard Furst
Estimated Sales: $20-50 Million
Number Employees: 500-999

18080 AAA Mill
812 Airport Blvd
Austin, TX 78702-4106
512-385-2215
Fax: 512-385-0860
Wood and plastic laminated freezer cabinets and store fixtures
President: David Bockhorn
General Manager: David Bockhorn
Estimated Sales: Below $5 Million
Number Employees: 5 to 9
Square Footage: 20000

18081 AAMD
7342 Tomwood Dr
Liverpool, NY 13090-3747
315-451-0951
Fax: 315-451-8740 800-887-4167
Manufacturer, importer and exporter of packaging machinery including tamper evident sealing equipment, closure lining equipment, assembly machines, metal closure threaders, tamper evident cap slitting machines, etc.; also, consultingservices available
VP Sales/Marketing: Eugene Orr
Estimated Sales: $1-3 Million
Number Employees: 1-4
Square Footage: 52000

18082 AANTEC
3116 N Pointer Rd
Appleton, WI 54911
920-830-9723
Fax: 920-830-9840

Packaging equipment; case packers, palletizers, tray packers/formers, case erectors/sealers, napkin folders, towel and tissue interfolders, tissue rewinders, napkin wrappers and bundlers, roll wrappers, conveyors, grip per elevatorsand lowerators, high-speed case-packers
President: Robert Schuh
VP: Corben Hoffman
Sales: Jeffrey Aissen
Public Relations: Julia Kirsch
Operations: Paul Tassoul
Estimated Sales: $5-10 Million
Number Employees: 10-19
Type of Packaging: Consumer, Food Service, Private Label, Bulk
Brands:
Involvo
Tmc

18083 AB McLauchlan Company
P.O.Box 12006
Salem, OR 97309-0006
503-363-8611
Fax: 503-364-5546
Blenders, food processing, conveying, size grading, cleaning, slicing, sorting, filling, and mixing equipment, mixers
President: John Layton
Estimated Sales: $1-2.5 Million
Number Employees: 5-9

18084 AB6
17190 Grant Road
Cypress, TX 77429
713-824-7275
Fax: 775-366-0516 john@ab6.net
www.ab6.net
President: John de Penne rouge

18085 ABB
North American Headquarters
305 Gregson Dr
Cary, NC 27511
440-585-7804
Fax: 919-666-1377 800-435-7365
contact.center@us.abb.com new.abb.com
Manufacturer and exporter of presses and drives for high-pressure food processing equipment for pasteurization and sterilization, generators, control systems, drives, motors, instrumentation and metering.
CEO: Peter Voser
Managing Director, U.S.: Maryrose Sylvester
CFO, U.S.: Michael Gray
Year Founded: 1891
Estimated Sales: $27.9 Billion
Number Employees: 147,000
Parent Co: ABB Group

18086 (HQ)ABC Laboratories
7200 E. ABC Lane
Columbia, MO 65202
573-443-9000
Fax: 573-777-6033 800-538-5227
info@abclabs.com www.abclabs.com
Laboratory offering analysis, testing and field research to the food service industry
President/CEO: John D Bucksath
R&D: Eric Lawerence
VP: Kristein King
VP, Business Dev.: Amy Mize
Contact: Ambroise Akue
akuea@abclabs.com
Estimated Sales: $10-20 Million
Number Employees: 100-249
Square Footage: 300000

18087 ABC Letter Art
1623 S Vermont Ave
Los Angeles, CA 90006
323-733-0191
Fax: 323-733-6505 888-261-5367
Displays and signs including interior and exterior graphics, wood, metal, plastic and 3-D letters; also, installation services available
CEO: Mark Shear
Sales Director: Jerry Eckert
Estimated Sales: $1-2.5 Million
Number Employees: 10-19
Brands:
A Sign of Good Taste

18088 ABC Research Corp
3437 SW 24th Ave
Gainesville, FL 32607-4599

352-372-0436
Fax: 352-378-6483 866-233-5883
info@abcr.com
Certified, third-party, independent contract food laboratory specializing in microbiological and chemical analyses of commercial food products.
President: William Brown
CEO: George Baker
george.baker@abcr.com
VP: James Kennedy
Marketing Director: Larry Clement
COO/Executive Director: Gillian Folkes
Estimated Sales: $5 Million
Number Employees: 100-249
Square Footage: 99000

18089 ABC Scales
240 Boone Ave
Marion, OH 43302-3356

740-382-0551
Fax: 740-387-4869
Estimated Sales: $1-3 Million
Number Employees: 1-4
Parent Co: Fairfield Engineering Company

18090 ABC Stamp Signs & Awards
407 N Orchard St
Boise, ID 83706-1976

208-375-4470
Fax: 208-377-3509 abcstamp@abcstamp.com
www.abcstamp.com
Rubber stamps
President: Richard Paulson
abcstamp@abcstamp.com
Estimated Sales: Below $5 Million
Number Employees: 10-19
Square Footage: 12800

18091 ABCO Industries
2675 E Us Highway 80
Abilene, TX 79601

915-677-2011
Fax: 915-677-1420 800-530-4060
Estimated Sales: Below $500,000
Number Employees: 20-49

18092 ABCO Industries Limited
PO Box 1120
Lunenburg, NS B0J 2C0
Canada

902-634-8821
Fax: 902-634-8583 866-634-8821
www.abco.ca
Manufacturer and exporter of aluminum and stainless steel food processing equipment including steam blanchers evaporative coolers
President: John Meisner
CEO: J Eisenhauer
Marketing Director: Graham Gerhardt
Sales Director: Dan Croft
Number Employees: 50-99
Square Footage: 120000
Brands:
Abco

18093 ABCO Laboratories Inc
2450 S Watney Way
Fairfield, CA 94533-6730

707-432-2200
Fax: 707-432-2240 800-678-2226
www.abcolabs.com
Nutraceutical products-liquids, tablets, capsules, powder blends. Foods-spices, dry blends, seasonings, functional food blends.
President: David Baron
Founder: Allen Baron
abaron@abcolabs.com
R&D: Dr Muhammed Al-Nasassrah
Quality Control: Rich Hale
Marketing: Greg Northam
Sales: Victoria Gonzales
Operations: Richard Snowden
Plant Manager: Dick Snowden
Purchasing Director: Carl Falcone
Number Employees: 100-249
Number of Brands: 10
Number of Products: 5000
Square Footage: 800000
Type of Packaging: Consumer, Food Service, Private Label, Bulk

Brands:
Nutra Naturally Essentials

18094 ABG Industries
1051 Clinton St
Buffalo, NY 14206-2823

716-853-6132
Fax: 905-479-9752 www.abgindustries.com
Owner: Martin Malthouse
CFO: Ken Pice
Manager: Richard Dipchon
Estimated Sales: Below $5 Million
Number Employees: 5-9

18095 ABI Limited
8900 Keele Street, Unit 1
Concord, ON L4K 2N2
Canada

905-738-6070
Fax: 905-738-6085 800-297-8666
info@abiltd.com
ABI Ltd. manufacturers automated food processing equipment with the emphasis on performance, durability, reliability and simplicity in maintenance.
President: Alex Kuperman
Marketing: Regine Kuperman
Production VP: Mike Kuperman
Number Employees: 20
Square Footage: 60000
Brands:
Belt Saver 2000
Bpl 10000
Bpl 12000
Bpl 24000
Bpl 6000
Bpl 8600
Df 5000
Superformer

18096 ABIC International Consultants
24 Spielman Rd
Fairfield, NJ 07004-3412

973-227-7060
Fax: 973-227-0172 www.abic-consulting.com
Consultant providing product development, evaluation and improvement of current products and processing and implementation of cost efficiencies; also, expertise in food science, process engineering and sensory evaluation
President: Abraham Bakal
CEO: Penny Cash
Contact: Fifi Bakal
fbakal@abic-consulting.com
Estimated Sales: Less Than $500,000
Number Employees: 1-4
Square Footage: 32000

18097 ABJ/Sanitaire Corporation
9333 N 49th St
Milwaukee, WI 53223-1472

414-365-2200
Fax: 414-365-2210 www.sanitaire.com
Manufacturer and exporter of anaerobic wastewater systems including sequencing batch reactors
President: Tom Pokovsky
CFO: Tom Thompson
Finance Executive: Scott Tysen
R&D: Joe Krall
Marketing: Laurie Besch
Manager Sales/Marketing: Roger Byrne
Public Relations: Laurie Besch
Customer Service Manager: Ken George
Production: Loras Lux
Purchasing: Loras Lux
Estimated Sales: $50 Million
Number Employees: 100-249
Square Footage: 7000
Brands:
Iceas

18098 ABLOY Security Inc
6005 Commerce Dr # 330
Irving, TX 75063-2664

972-753-1127
Fax: 972-753-0792 800-367-4598
info@abloyusa.com www.abloyusa.com
High security locks, T-handle cylinders, padlocks, key-ring padlocks, cam locks
President: Martha Bartley
mbartley@abloy.com
CFO and QC and R&D: Jeff Carpenter
Sales Manager: Martha Bartley

Estimated Sales: $1-2.5 Million
Number Employees: 10-19
Parent Co: Assa Abloy

18099 ABM Marking
2799 S Belt W
Belleville, IL 62226-6777

618-277-3773
Fax: 618-277-3782 800-626-9012
abmmarking@aol.com www.abmmarking.com
Manufacturer and exporter of ink jet printers and coding inks for porous and nonporous surfaces including coated, plastic and polyethylene; importer of tape dispensers and machines
Owner: Al Merchiori
Sales Manager: Alberto Merchiori
abmmarking@aol.com
Operations: Roger Schaefer
Estimated Sales: $3-5 Million
Number Employees: 5-9
Square Footage: 24000
Brands:
Abm
Abm's Safemark

18100 ABO Industries
13620 Lindamere Ln
San Diego, CA 92128

858-566-9750
Fax: 858-566-9590
Manufacturer, exporter and importer of industrial progressive cavity, peristaltic, gear, metering and air operated diaphragm pumps
President: Joseph Schulman
VP: Ming Li
Estimated Sales: $1-5 Million
Number Employees: 5-9
Square Footage: 5000
Brands:
Carmine
Carminic Acid

18101 AC Dispensing Equipment
100 Dispensing Way
Lower Sackville, NS B4C 4H2
Canada

902-865-9602
Fax: 902-865-9604 888-777-9990
sales@sureshotdispensing.com
www.sureshotdispensing.com
Electronic portion controlled dispensers for cream, sugar, milk and oil
President: Michel Duck
R&D: Ian Maclen
CFO: Ian Tramble
Director Sales/Marketing: W William Morris
Number Employees: 80
Brands:
Sureshot

18102 AC Label Company
2101 Eest VallyVistaWay
Provo, UT 84606

801-642-3500
Fax: 801-642-3510
Bottling equipment and supplies, computer software, labeling and packaging machinery and packaging materials; also, printer, bar code, pressure sensitive and security labels
Manager: Matt Schwanbeck
VP: Jim DiBona
Estimated Sales: $10-20,000,000
Number Employees: 50-99
Parent Co: Impaxx

18103 ACCO Systems
12755 E 9 Mile Rd
Warren, MI 48089

845-456-2236
Fax: 586-758-1901 800-342-2226
www.accosystems.co.uk
Manufacturer and exporter of material handling systems and equipment
President: Anthony Gore
Director Sales/Marketing: Mark Murray
Contact: Glenn Clannell
gclannell@andek.com
Number Employees: 250-499
Parent Co: Durr GmbH

18104 ACH Rice Specialties
7171 Goodlett Farms Pkwy
Cordova, TN 38016-4909
901-381-3000
Fax: 901-381-2968 800-691-1106
information@achfood.com
President: Dan Antonelli
CFO: Jeff Atkins
R&D and Quality Control: Pete Sriedman
Estimated Sales: $20-30 Million
Number Employees: 1,000-4,999

18105 ACI
3731b San Gabriel River Pkwy
Pico Rivera, CA 90660-1404
562-699-4999
Fax: 562-699-0919
Industrial ink jet printers

18106 ACLAUSA Inc
509 Thomson Park Dr
Cranberry Twp, PA 16066-6425
724-776-0099
Fax: 724-776-0477
Manufacturer and exporter of material handling
equipment including rollers, tires, wheels, bumpers
and seals
President: Andy Mc Intyre
andym@aclausa.com
Estimated Sales: $1-2.5 Million
Number Employees: 1-4
Parent Co: ACLA

18107 ACMA/GD
501 Southlake Blvd
Richmond, VA 23236-3078
804-794-6688
Fax: 804-379-2199 800-525-2735
paul.smith@gidi.it www.acmavolpak.com
Manufacturer, importer and exporter of liquid filling
machinery and vertical and horizontal form/fill/seal
equipment
CEO: Guiseppe Venturi
Marketing: Glen Coater
Estimated Sales: Below $500,000
Number Employees: 250-499
Square Footage: 800000

18108 ACME Sign Corp
3 Lakeland Park Dr
Peabody, MA 01960-3835
978-535-6600
Fax: 978-536-5051 info@acmesigncorp.com
www.acmesigncorp.com
Custom sign manufacturer and supplier
President: Darius Aleksas
darius@acmesigncorp.com
Estimated Sales: $1 Million
Number Employees: 1-4
Square Footage: 16000

18109 ACME-McClain & Son
4759 Durfee Avenue
Pico Rivera, CA 90660-2037
562-692-0026
Fax: 800-428-2263

18110 ACO
501 SW 19th St
Moore, OK 73160-5427
405-794-7662
Fax: 405-236-4014 www.mcdonalds.com
Manufacturer and exporter of material handling
boxes, trays and racks
Founder: Ray Kroc
Estimated Sales: $1-2.5 Million
Number Employees: 10-19

18111 ACO Polymer Products
12080 Ravenna Road
Chardon, OH 44024-7008
440-285-7000
Fax: 440-285-7005
President: Derek Humphries
Contact: Ben Aulick
baulick@aco-online.com
Number Employees: 50-99

18112 ACR Systems
#210-15110 54A Avenue
Surrey, BC V3S 5X7
Canada
604-591-1128
Fax: 604-591-2252 800-663-7845
sales@acrsystems.com www.acrsystems.com
Data loggers-measure and record temperature and
humidity, current, power quality, pressure, process
signals and more
President: Albert C Rock
CFO: David McDougall
Director of Operations: Wayne Thompson
Number Employees: 30
Type of Packaging: Private Label
Brands:
   Acr Jr.
   Acr Powerwatch
   Owl
   Smartvision
   Smartreader
   Smartreader Plus
   Trendreader

18113 ACS Industries, Inc.
One New England Way
Lincoln, RI 02865
866-783-4838
Fax: 401-333-2294 acsind@acsind.com
www.acsindustries.com
Stainless steel sponges, nylon scouring pads,
screens, filter cones and grill cleaning systems; also,
nonsulphate antioxidants
President: Steven N Buckler
Contact: Ryan Abranovic
rabranovic@acsind.com
Estimated Sales: $5-10 Million
Number Employees: 1,000-4,999
Square Footage: 1200000
Brands:
   Acs Industries, Inc. Scrubble

18114 ACUair/York Refrigeration
5757 N. Green Bay Ave
P.O. Box 591
Milwaukee, WI 53201
414-524-1200
Fax: 305-887-7853 414-524-1200
www.johnsoncontrols.com
Chairman, President and Chief Executive: Alex A.
Molinaroli
EVP and Chief Financial Officer: R. Bruce
McDonald
Human Resources: William Hyland
VP and Chief Marketing Officer: Kim
Metcalf-Kupres
Estimated Sales: Below $500,000
Parent Co: Johnson Controls, Inc.

18115 AD Products
2919 Industrial Park Dr
Finksburg, MD 21048
800-743-8815
Fax: 410-833-8817 800-743-8815
sales@adprods.com www.adprods.com
Material handling equipment-dollies, racks, carts,
baskets, trays (stock and custom)
Manager: Nick Hailston
CFO: Ami Markle
R & D: William Fauntleroy
Sales: Nick Hailstone
Estimated Sales: Below $5 000,000
Number Employees: 10-19

18116 ADCO
P.O.Box 999
Sedalia, MO 65302-0999
660-826-3300
Fax: 660-826-1361 sales@adco-inc.com
www.adco-inc.com
President: Charles M Van Dyne
Quality Control: Archie Shrieman
Contact: Juanita Salmons
salmons@adco-inc.com
Estimated Sales: $10-20 Million
Number Employees: 50-99
Parent Co: AlliedSignal Company

18117 ADCO
1909 West Oakridge
Albany, GA 31707
660-826-3300
Fax: 660-826-1361 800-821-7556
sales@adco-inc.com www.adco-inc.com

Disinfectants, polishes and dry cleaning compounds
Chief Executive Officer: Mark Grimaldi
EVP/Business Operations: Yalda Harris
Quality/Compliance Manager: Scott Stanfill
Chief Products/Technology Officer: Jim Schreiner
National Sales Manager: Greg Reinhardt
Contact: James Schreiner
schreiner@adco-inc.com
Estimated Sales: $5-10 Million
Number Employees: 50-99

18118 ADCO Manufacturing Inc
2170 Academy Ave
Sanger, CA 93657-3795
559-875-5563
Fax: 559-875-7665 sales@adcomfg.com
www.adcomfg.com
Manufacturer and exporter of packaging machinery
for cartons
President: Frank Hoffman
CEO: Kate King
kking@adcomfg.com
VP Marketing: Scott Reed
VP Sales: Paul Kessock
Human Resources Manager: Maureen Say
Operations/Plant Manager: Dale Kingen
Purchasing Director: Juanita Johnson
Estimated Sales: $24 Million
Number Employees: 100-249
Square Footage: 76000
Type of Packaging: Consumer, Food Service, Pri-
vate Label

18119 ADCO Manufacturing Inc
2170 Academy Ave
Sanger, CA 93657-3795
559-875-5563
Fax: 559-875-7665 sales@adcomfg.com
www.adcomfg.com
Packaging machinery
President: Frank Hoffman
CEO: Kate King
kking@adcomfg.com
CFO: Kate King
CEO: Kate King
Estimated Sales: $20-50 Million
Number Employees: 100-249

18120 ADD Testing & Research
19 Addison Pl
Valley Stream, NY 11580
516-568-9197
Fax: 516-568-3147 info@addtestinglab.com
www.addtestinglab.com
Laboratory providing research, development, food
testing, spice analysis, sanitation testing, etc
President: Michael Schenoude
Owner: Aida Shenouga
Estimated Sales: Below 1 Million
Number Employees: 1-4
Square Footage: 6000

18121 ADDCHEK Coils
1285 Jim Wilson Rd
Fort Mill, SC 29715-7605
803-547-7566
Fax: 803-547-5250
Heat transfer equipment using aluminum, copper,
cupro nickel and stainless steel
President: Anna D Wood
Corporate Secretary: Helen Wood
Estimated Sales: $5-10 Million
Number Employees: 10-19

18122 ADE Inc
1430 E 130th St
Chicago, IL 60633-2399
773-646-3400
Fax: 773-646-3919 800-222-0221
info@ade-usa.com www.ade-usa.com
Protective packaging alternatives, package designs
using elastomeric film
Manager: Lewis Lofgren
CEO: L Lofgren
llotgren@ade-usa.com
Estimated Sales: $5-10 000,000
Number Employees: 20-49

18123 ADI Systems
370 Wilsey Rd
Fredericton, NB E3B 6E9
Canada

506-452-7307
Fax: 506-452-7308 800-561-2831
systems@adi.ca www.adisystemsinc.com
Wastewater treatment and water reuse.
President: Graham Brown
CFO: Hazen Hawker

18124 ADI Systems Inc
370 Wilsey Road
Fredericton, NB E3B 6E9
Canada

506-452-7307
Fax: 506-452-7308 800-561-2831
systems@adi.ca www.adisystemsinc.com
ADI offers proprietary anaerobic and aerobic industrial wastewater treatment and waste-to-energy tech-
nologies, biogas cleaning and utilization, plus
complete design-build services. ADI also conducts
treatability studies, pilot testingbench-scale studies,
operator training, and aftercare services to customers
who need to anaerobically or aerobically treat
industrial wastewater.
President: Graham Brown
CEO: Hazen Hawker
VP Technology: Shannon Grant
Marketing Assistant: Connie Smith
Manager Business Development: Scott Christian
Marketing & Communications Manager: Sarah
Brown
Estimated Sales: $10-20 Million
Number Employees: 25
Square Footage: 4000
Parent Co: ADI Group
Other Locations:
  Wolfeboro NH
Brands:
  Adi-Anmbr
  Adi-Bvf Digester
  Adi-Hybrid
  Adi-Mbr
  Adi-Sbr

18125 ADM/Matsutani LLC
4666 Faries Pkwy
Decatur, IL 62526

847-418-1615
Manufacturer of soluable dietary fiber ingredients,
specifically Fibersol®.
Senior Sales Manager: Barbara Brojack
Contact: Bob Heard
bheard97@aol.com
General Manager: George Perujo
Number Employees: 3
Parent Co: ADM
Brands:
  Fibersol 2

18126 ADMIX
234 Abby Rd
Manchester, NH 03103-3332

603-627-2340
Fax: 603-627-2019 800-466-2369
mixing@admix.com www.admix.com
Sanitary mixing and dispersion, and particle size re-
duction equipment
General Manager: L Beaudette
President: Louis Beaudette
Sales Manager: P Leitner
Contact: Jerry Baresich
jbaresich@admix.com
Operations Manager: P Foskitt
Estimated Sales: Below $5 Million
Number Employees: 20-49
Square Footage: 60000
Brands:
  Admixer
  Boston Shearpump
  Dynashear
  Oprishear
  Optifeed
  Rotomixx
  Rotosolver
  Rotostat
  Vacushear

18127 ADSI Inc
22971 State Road 78
Durant, OK 74701-1130

580-924-4461
Fax: 580-924-7375 adsi@adsiinc.com
Manufacturer & exporter of commercial egg break-
ing machinery, egg washing & sanitizing machines.
President, Sales, & Operations: Mike Maynard
VP, Sales, Production & Plant Mgr.: Steve Maynard
Estimated Sales: Below $5 Million
Number Employees: 10-19
Type of Packaging: Food Service
Brands:
  Centri-Matic Iii
  Egg Valet
  Sew 400
  Sew 800

18128 ADT Inc
1501 NW 51st St
Boca Raton, FL 33431-4438

800-521-1734
www.adt.com
Wholesaler/distributor of general merchandise in-
cluding burglar and fire alarm systems, access con-
trol systems, security equipment and closed circuit
TV.
Chief Executive Officer: Jim DeVries
Chief Financial Officer: Jeff Likosar
Chief Administration Officer: Dan Bresingham
Chief Legal Officer: P. Gray Finney
Chief Customer Officer: Jamie Rosand Haenggi
Chief Information Officer: Donald Young
Year Founded: 1874
Estimated Sales: Over $1 Billion
Number Employees: 18,000
Parent Co: Apollo Global Management

18129 AEP Industries
125 Phillips Ave
South Hackensack, NJ 07606

201-641-6600
Fax: 201-807-2567 800-999-2374
info@aepinc.com www.aepinc.com
Plastic sheeting, stretch films and liners and polyeth-
ylene products including bags, packaging and film
Manager: Don Drafford
Logistics Manager: Stacy LeMaster
Executive VP Sales/Marketing: Robert Cron
Contact: Glenny Adames
adamesg@aepinc.com
Estimated Sales: $75 Million-1 Billion
Number Employees: 2900

18130 AEP Industries Inc
1970 Excel Dr
Mankato, MN 56001-5903

507-386-4420
Fax: 507-388-4420 800-999-2374
www.aepinc.com
Manufacturer and exporter of disposable gloves,
aprons, bibs, table covers, specialty bags and films
including cling, polyethylene, stretch and shrink
President: Jenny Pherson
Research & Development: Thea Ellingson
Marketing Director: Mike Sauer
Sales Director: Ken Christensen
Operations/Purchasing: Mike Ellis
Estimated Sales: $20-50 Million
Number Employees: 100-249
Parent Co: Atlantis Plastics
Type of Packaging: Consumer, Food Service, Bulk
Other Locations:
  Mankato-Institutional Operations
  Mankato MN
Brands:
  Linear
  Sta-Dri

18131 AEP Texas
539 N Carancahua
Corpus Christi, TX 78478

877-373-4858
www.aeptexas.com
Electric utility systems.
President & COO: Judith Talavera
VP, Regulatory & Finance: Leigh Anne Strahler
VP, External Affairs: Julio Reyes
Year Founded: 1906
Estimated Sales: K
Parent Co: American Electric Power

18132 AERCO International Inc
100 Oritani Dr
Blauvelt, NY 10913-1022

845-580-8000
Fax: 845-580-8090 800-526-0288
Water heaters, condensing boilers and steam genera-
tors
President: Fred Depuy
CEO: Patricia Abrahamsen
pabrahamsen@aerco.com
VP: Fred F Campagna
Marketing Director: Mark Croche
Estimated Sales: $10-20 Million
Number Employees: 10-19

18133 AERTEC
P.O.Box 488
North Andover, MA 01845-0488

978-475-6385
Fax: 978-475-6387 info@aertec.com
www.aertec.com
Waste and water aeration
President: R Gary Gilbert
Estimated Sales: $1-5 Million
Number Employees: 5-9

18134 AES Corp
3412 Center Point Rd NE
Suite A
Cedar Rapids, IA 52402-5529

319-432-7365
Fax: 319-395-7693 info@aescorp.com
www.aescorp.com
Design and installation of aseptic processing and
packaging systems specialize in fruit and vegetables;
dairy; pharmaceuticals
Manager: David Garrelts
Estimated Sales: $1-5 Million
Number Employees: 50-99

18135 AET Films
15 Reads Way
New Castle, DE 19720-1648

302-326-5500
Fax: 302-326-5501 800-688-2044
ODP film for flexible packaging and labeling
President: David Terhuna
CFO: Bryan Crescenzo
CEO: Thomas Mohr
Contact: Mike Demchinski
mdemchinski@aetinc.com
Estimated Sales: $20-50 Million
Number Employees: 500-999

18136 AEW Thurne
1148 Ensell Road
Lake Zurich, IL 60047-1539

847-726-8000
Fax: 847-726-1600 800-239-7297
chicago@aewdelford.com www.aewdelford.com
Manufacturer and exporter of high-speed bandsaws
and automated portion control slicing systems
President: Chris Mason
Chief Operating Officer, Chief Executive: Sigsteinn
Gretarsson
Regional Sales Manager: David Bertelsen
Estimated Sales: $300,000-500,000
Number Employees: 9
Square Footage: 32000
Brands:
  Aew

18137 AFA Systems
8 Tilbury Court.
Brampton
Ontario, CA L6T 3T4

905-456-8700
Fax: 905-456-2343 info@afasystemsinc.com
www.afasystemsinc.com
Liquid fillers, software
Estimated Sales: $.5-1 million
Number Employees: 1-4

18138 AFCO
5121 Coffey Ave
Chambersburg, PA 17201-4127

813-684-6362
Fax: 610-644-8240 800-345-1329
sourcethree@afco.net www.afcocare.com
Cleaning and sanitizing soaps and chemicals
President: Michael Hinkle
Estimated Sales: Below $5 Million
Number Employees: 10-19

18139 AFCO Manufacturing
7007 Valley Lane
Cincinnati, OH 45244-3031

859-261-3585
Fax: 859-261-3590 800-747-7332
www.afcomanufacturing.com
Baking equipment including bakery pan racks, pan
trucks, dough troughs, custom dollies and flow racks
President: Frank Eberle
CEO: Peter Sullivan
Sales Manager: Brion Walter
Estimated Sales: Below $5 Million
Number Employees: 25
Square Footage: 100000

18140 AFGO Mechanical Svc Inc
3614 32nd St
Astoria, NY 11106-2325

718-389-2354
Fax: 718-476-2222 800-438-2346
info@afgo.com
Heaters, heat exchangers and stainless steel tanks;
also, repair services available
President/COO: Blaine Udell
blaine@afgo.com
CEO: Glenn S. Udell
Vice President: Gregory Oro
Director of Operations: Michael McGuire
Estimated Sales: $5-10 Million
Number Employees: 20-49
Square Footage: 280000
Parent Co: Heat Transfer

18141 AFL Industries
1751 W 10th St
West Palm Beach, FL 33404-6431

561-844-5200
Fax: 561-844-5246 800-807-2709
www.rwlwater.com
Manufacturer and exporter of oil and water separa-
tors for wastewater treatment systems
CEO: Tom Bieneman
CEO: Thomas Bieneman
tbieneman@aflindustries.com
Sales Manager: Ray Lopez
Administrative VP: Beverly Willcox
Estimated Sales: $1-2.5 Million
Number Employees: 10-19
Square Footage: 80000

18142 AFT Advanced Fiber Technologies
72 Queen Street
Sherbrooke, QC J1M 2C3
Canada

819-562-4754
Fax: 819-562-6064 800-668-7273
info@aikawagroup.com www.aft-global.com
Manufacturer, importer and exporter of custom made
screen and extraction plates
President: Roch Leblanc
CFO: Norman Pogdin
R&D: Robert Gooding
Quality Control: Serge Turcotte
Sales Manager: Jean Marc Brousseau
Number Employees: 175
Square Footage: 436560
Parent Co: CAE
Brands:
  Cae Profile
  Cae Select
  Durachrome

18143 AG Beverage
7031 Cahill Rd
Minneapolis, MN 55439

952-943-8148
Markets beverages for the food and beverage
industy
Estimated Sales: $2.5-5 000,000
Number Employees: 9

18144 AGA Gas
P.O.Box 94737
Cleveland, OH 44101-4737

216-642-6600
Fax: 216-642-6625 www.airgas.com
Cryogenic gas packaging and freezing equipment;
also, industrial gases including oxygen, nitrogen, ar-
gon and carbon dioxide for the food industry

President: Bob Bradshaw
Applications Engineer: Keith Davis
Vice President of HR: Ann Rice
Sales Manager: Jay Loo
Vice President of Operations: Don Goldschmidt
Estimated Sales: $1-5 Million
Number Employees: 100-249
Parent Co: AGA Gas AB

18145 AGC
10129 Piper Ln
Bristow, VA 20136-1418

703-257-1660
Fax: 703-330-7940 800-825-8820
info@agcengineering.com
www.agcheattransfer.com
Manufacturer and exporter sanitary plate heat
exchangers and replacement parts
President: Tamika Carter
cartert@agc.org
Director, Resaerch & Development: George Tholl
Director, Sales & Marketing: John C. Bohn
Office Manager-Western Factory: Jill Davis
Estimated Sales: $3-$5 Million
Number Employees: 20-49
Square Footage: 160000
Type of Packaging: Bulk

18146 AGC Engineering Portland
9109 SE 64th Avenue
Portland, OR 97206-9505

503-774-7342
Fax: 503-774-2550 800-715-8820
wadec@agcengineering.com
www.agcengineering.com
Manufacturers of heat exchangers
President: Robert Bohn
Plant Manager: Patrick Palmer
Estimated Sales: $2.5-5 Million
Number Employees: 20-49

18147 AGET Manufacturing Co
1408 E Church St
PO Box 248
Adrian, MI 49221-3437

517-263-5781
Fax: 517-263-7154 sales@agetmfg.com
www.agetmfg.com
Cleaners and dust and mist collectors
President: Ray Wakefield
rwakefield@agetmfg.com
CFO: Chuck Morrow
VP/Owner: Rich Olsaver
Sales: Rich Olsaver
Estimated Sales: $5-10 Million
Number Employees: 20-49
Square Footage: 200000
Brands:
  Dustkop
  Mistkup

18148 AGM Container Controls Inc
3526 E Fort Lowell Rd
Tucson, AZ 85716-1705

520-881-2130
Fax: 520-881-4983 800-995-5590
sales@agmcontainer.com
Container breather valves, tie-down straps and
shelving and portable wheelchair lifts
President: Howard Stewart
IT: Ellen Howlett
sales@custompowersystems.us
Estimated Sales: Less Than $500,000
Number Employees: 1-4

18149 AIB International
P.O. Box 3999
1213 Bakers Way
Manhattan, KS 66505-3999

785-537-4750
Fax: 785-537-1493 800-633-5137
info@aibonline.org www.aibinternational.com
Offers various food quality and safety services in-
cluding inspections and business consultations. Of-
fers training programs.
President & CEO: Andre Biane
CFO: Tom Ogle
VP, Global Sales: Steve Robert
VP, Operations, America: Stephanie Lopez
Year Founded: 1919
Number Employees: 300-500

18150 AIB International, Inc.
1213 Bakers Way
P.O. Box 3999
Manhattan, KS 66505-3999

785-537-4750
Fax: 785-537-1493 800-633-5137
info@aibonline.org www.aibonline.org
Food safety education guides and classes for the
packaging, distribution and food service operations
industries
President: Virgil Smail
Contact: Leslie Ackerman
lackerman@aibonline.org
Estimated Sales: $10-20 Million
Number Employees: 100-249

18151 AIDCO International
P.O.Box 15339
Cincinnati, OH 45215-339

Fax: 517-265-2131 www.aidcoint.com
Palletizers, depalletizers
Estimated Sales: $5-10 000,000
Number Employees: 10-19

18152 AIM
One Landmark North
20399 Route 19, Suite 203
Cranberry Township, PA 16066

724-742-4473
Fax: 724-742-4476 info@aim-na.org
President: Dan Mullen
COO: Mary Bosco
Number Employees: 6

18153 AIMCAL
201 Springs St
Fort Mill, SC 29715-1723

803-802-7820
Fax: 803-948-9471 aimcal@aimcal.org
www.aimcal.org
Executive Director: Craig Sheppard
aimcal@aimcal.org
Number Employees: 5-9

18154 AIS Container Handling
7000 Dutton Ind Pk Dr SE
Dutton, MI 49316

616-554-1000
Fax: 616-554-1008 800-253-4621
Manufacturer and exporter of bagging and
debagging equipment, conveyor, inspection and
analysis systems for plastic containers
President: Jerry Pollard
Sales Manager: Jim McDonald
Production Manager: Gary Shaw
Purchasing Manager: Mark Luebs
Estimated Sales: $5-10 000,000
Number Employees: 20-49
Square Footage: 25000

18155 AJM Packaging Corporation
E-4111 Andover Rd
Bloomfield Hills, MI 48302

248-901-0040
Fax: 248-901-0062 sales@ajmpack.com
www.ajmpack.com
Paper plates, cups, bowls and bags.
President: Robert Epstein
Chief Financial Officer: Terry Jackson
VP, Sales & Marketing: Bill Baumann
National Sales Manager: Michael Pickman
Year Founded: 1957
Estimated Sales: $111 Million
Number Employees: 1,000
Square Footage: 12000
Brands:
  Designer's Choice
  Green Label
  Original Heavyweight
  Penthouse

18156 AK Robbins
4030 Benson Avenue
Baltimore, MD 21227-1408

410-247-4000
Fax: 410-247-9165 800-486-9656
www.akrobins.com
Meat slicers, cooling tank elevators, tramp metal
eliminators, length and diameter grading equipment,
cutting equipment, vibratory and belt conveyors,
pack-off tables, hydrators, jar washers, chemical
peelers, laminar-flo liquidfiller, washers, cleaners
Estimated Sales: $2.5-5 Million
Number Employees: 19

18157 AK Steel Corp
9227 Centre Pointe Dr
West Chester, OH 45069

513-425-5000
833-505-1899
www.aksteel.com

Manufacturer of carbon, stainless steel, electrial products, mechanical tubing, and steel stamping.
President & Chief Operating Officer: Kirk Reich
Chief Executive Officer: Roger Newport
roger_newport@aksteel.com
Interim Chief Financial Officer: Christopher Ross
VP/General Counsel/Secretary: Joseph Alter
Year Founded: 1899
Estimated Sales: $6.8 Billion
Number Employees: 9,500
Parent Co: Cleveland-Cliffs, Inc

18158 AL Systems
385 Franklin Ave
Suite C
Rockaway, NJ 07866

973-586-8500
Fax: 973-586-8865 888-960-8324

Manufacturer and exporter of automated control systems and software
President: Paul Lightfoot
Contact: Hilary Galt
hilary@cardiomedicalproducts.com
Director Operations: Gary Oriani
Director of Product Management: Gary Clemens
Estimated Sales: $1-5 Million
Number Employees: 20-49

18159 (HQ)ALCO Designs
407 E Redondo Beach Blvd
Gardena, CA 90248

310-353-2300
Fax: 310-353-2301 800-228-2346
www.alcodesigns.com

Manufacturer and exporter of water treatment systems including outdoor fogging and standard and reverse osmosis misting, fogging and humidification
President: Samuel Cohen
Owner: Sam Cohen
CFO: Sam Cohen
VP: Issac Cohen
Marketing: Dick Wardlaw
Administrator: Liz Luna
Estimated Sales: $3-5 Million
Number Employees: 20-49
Square Footage: 5000
Other Locations:
  Vege Mist
  Tucker GA

18160 ALCO Designs
407 E Redondo Beach Blvd
Gardena, CA 90248

310-353-2300
Fax: 310-353-2301 800-228-2346
www.alcodesigns.com

Vacuum-molded risers, step-ups, trays and extenders for produce, meat and deli/dairy cases and dry tables; also, wooden display items available
President: Sam Cohen
Quality Control: Carlos Sanchez
Director Marketing: Bob Matsie
Estimated Sales: Below $5 Million
Number Employees: 20-49
Parent Co: Vege Mist

18161 ALL-CON World Systems
P.O.Box 647
Seaford, DE 19973

302-628-3380
Fax: 302-628-3390 sales@all-con.com
www.all-con.com

Feeding, weighing and conveying of dry powder ingredients for food and baking industries
President: G Barry Slater
Sales Director: Mark Allen
Estimated Sales: Below $5 Million
Number Employees: 10

18162 ALLCAMS Machine Company
116 Sycamore Ave
Folsom, PA 19033

610-534-9004
Fax: 610-534-7517 sales@allcams.net
www.allcams.net

Manufactures and designs CAMs for automated industrial machinery
Number Employees: 10

18163 ALLIED Graphics Inc
16290 54th St NE
St Michael, MN 55376-3471

763-428-8365
Fax: 763-428-8366 800-490-9931
sales@allied-graphics.com
www.allied-graphics.com

Pressure sensitive decals
President: Patrick Kohler
Estimated Sales: $1-2.5 Million
Number Employees: 10-19
Square Footage: 40000

18164 ALP Lighting & Ceiling Products
6965 Airport Highway Ln
Pennsauken, NJ 08109

856-663-0095
Fax: 856-661-0870 800-633-7732
www.alplighting.com

Manufacturer, importer and exporter of lighting fixtures including louvers, lens, fluorescent fixture diffusers and components
VP: Steven Dix
Contact: William Foley
b.foley@alplighting.com
Estimated Sales: $1-5,000,000
Number Employees: 100-249
Square Footage: 120000

18165 (HQ)ALPI Food Preparation Equipment
511 Piercey Road
Bolton, ON L7E 5B8
Canada

905-951-1067
Fax: 905-951-1608 800-928-2574
www.alpiinc.com

Manufacturer, exporter and importer of stainless steel convection/steam ovens, pasta cookers, pizza equipment, exhaust hoods, etc; consultant specializing in restaurant equipment design services
President: Pier Luigi Odorico
VP: Gian Paolo O'Dorico
National Sales Manager: Nazareno Cavallaro
Number Employees: 2
Square Footage: 28000
Type of Packaging: Food Service
Other Locations:
  ALPI Food Preparation Equipme
  Fort Lauderdale FL

18166 ALY Group of New York
70 Memorial Plaza
Pleasantville, NY 10570-2931

603-493-8088
Fax: 603-428-4280 alygroup@comcast.net
www.alygroup.com

Consultant and designer of restaurant interiors; also, space planning available.
President: Dolores Jones
CEO: A Eric Arctandfer
Estimated Sales: Less than $500,000
Number Employees: 5
Square Footage: 125000

18167 AM Graphics
5249 W. 73rd St.
Edina, MN 55439

612-341-2020
Fax: 612-333-3295
AMGraphics@AMGraphicsInc.com
www.amgraphicsinc.com

Pressure sensitive labels and promotional items including banners, decals and shirts
President: Craig Nygaard
Estimated Sales: Less than $500,000
Number Employees: 1-4

18168 AM Test Laboratories
13600 NE 126th Pl # C
Suite C
Kirkland, WA 98034-8720

425-885-1664
Fax: 425-820-0245
customerservice@amtestlab.com
www.amtestlab.com

Laboratory providing environmental testing, microbial and chemical food analysis and industrial hygiene services

President: Kathy Fugiel
kathyf@amtestlab.com
QA/QC Manager: Heidi Limmer
Vice President/Lab Manager: Aaron Young
Food Lab Director: Jim Pratt
General Manager: Mark Fugiel
Estimated Sales: Below $5 Million
Number Employees: 10-19
Square Footage: 80000

18169 AM-Mac
311 US Highway 46 # C
Fairfield, NJ 07004-2419

973-575-7567
Fax: 973-575-1956 800-829-2018
ammac1@aol.com www.am-mac.com

Manufacturer and exporter of meat and bread slicers, mixers, vegetable cutters and meat grinders; wholesaler/distributor of food handling and storage equipment, wire shelving and ovens
President: Judith Spritzer
ammac1@aol.com
Vice President: Jon Spritzer
Estimated Sales: $10-20,000,000
Number Employees: 10-19
Brands:
  Arimex
  Lan Elec

18170 AMAC Plastic Products Corp
740 Southpoint Blvd
Petaluma, CA 94954-7494

415-332-2170
Fax: 707-763-9500 800-852-7158
info@amacplastics.com www.catechiphoto.com

Rigid plastic containers for fine packaging; production and shopping of AMAC boxes to retail and manufacturing outlets worldwide
President: Jone Catechi
Contact: Gus Catechi
gcatechi@amacplastics.com
Estimated Sales: $2.5-5 Million
Number Employees: 10-19

18171 AMC Chemicals
93 Main St
Woodbridge, NJ 07095-2863

732-636-8720
Fax: 732-636-8727 www.amcchemical.com

Essential oils, aroma chemicals
Owner: Jerry Bozio
Estimated Sales: $1-5 Million
Number Employees: 1-4

18172 AMC Industries
12291 US 41 N
Palmetto, FL 33675-5006

941-479-7834
Fax: 941-981-3830

Restaurant furniture including bars, tables and booths; custom manufacturing available
President: Don Walstad
CEO: Gene Cornish
Accounting Controller: Richard Lee
Sales Director: John Ogden
Contact: Graham Bradford
gbradford@amcindustries.com
Estimated Sales: $10-20 Million
Number Employees: 50-99

18173 AME Engineering
209 Gateway Rd
Bensenville, IL 60106-1952

630-694-1828
Fax: 630-694-1827 www.ameengineering.com

Packaging systems for meat
Owner: M Epstein
ame1948@aol.com
Estimated Sales: $.5-1 000,000
Number Employees: 1-4

18174 AMEC
800 Marquett Ave
McGladrey Plaza Building, Suite 1200
Minneapolis, MN 55402

612-332-8326
Fax: 612-332-2423 iain.mcnerlin@amec.com
www.amec.com

Supplier of full service consulting, engineering and project management services to the following sectors: natural resources, clean energy, water and environmental.
Contact: Iain Mcnerlin
i_mcnerlin@amec.com

Estimated Sales: $1-5 Million
Number Employees: 22,000

18175 AMETEK Brookfield
11 Commerce Blvd
Middleboro, MA 02346-1031

508-946-6200
Fax: 508-946-6262 800-628-8139
MA-MID.websales@ametek.com
www.brookfieldengineering.com
Manufacturer and supplier of rotational viscometers and rheometers and also Texture Analyzers and powder flow testers.
CEO: David Zapico
Parent Co: AMETEK

18176 AMETEK Inc
1100 Cassatt Rd
PO Box 1764
Berwyn, PA 19312-1177

610-647-2121
Fax: 215-323-9337 800-473-1286
webmaster@ametek.com www.ametek.com
Controls, meters, transducers, temperature and chart recorders, calibrating devices, temperature and pressure transmitters
President: Frank Hermance
CEO: David A Zapico
david.zapico@ametek.com
Estimated Sales: Over $1 Billion
Number Employees: 10000+

18177 AMETEK Inc
8600 Somerset Dr
Largo, FL 33773-2700

727-536-7831
Fax: 727-538-2400 www.ametek.com
Force gauges, mechanical and motorized test stands, material test systems, packaging testers, puncture testers, peel strength testers, grips, fixtures and accessories
Manager: Mike Kern
mike.kern@ametek.com
Estimated Sales: $20-50 Million
Number Employees: 50-99

18178 AMETEK Inc
1100 Cassatt Rd
Berwyn, PA 19312-1177

610-647-2121
Fax: 215-323-9337 chatillon.fl-lar@ametek.com
www.ametek.com
Test and calibration instruments
President/GM: Timothy Jones
CEO: David A Zapico
david.zapico@ametek.com
VP: Tom Marecic
R&D: Mark Coppler
Quality Control: Dennis Petro
Estimated Sales: Over $1 Billion
Number Employees: 10000+

18179 AMETEK National Controls Corp
1725 Western Dr
West Chicago, IL 60185-1877

630-231-5900
Fax: 630-231-1377 800-323-5293
webmaster@ametek.com www.ameteknccc.com
Manufacturer and exporter of cooking computers, electronic timers and thermometers
COO: Tim Croal
tim.croal@ametek.com
VP: Tim Croal
General Manager: Nick Hoilds
Sales/Marketing Executive: John Meggesin
Sales Manager: Gerald Brown
Purchasing Manager: Cathy Porch
Number Employees: 20-49
Parent Co: Ametek
Brands:
Ncc

18180 AMF Bakery Systems Corp
2115 W Laburnum Ave
Richmond, VA 23227-4315

804-355-7961
Fax: 804-355-1074 800-225-3771
service-us@amfbakery.com www.amfbakery.com
Manufacturer and exporter of bakery and packaging equipment
President: Ken Newsome
CFO: Margaret Shaia
Director Product Marketing: Larry Gore
Sales Director: Richard MacArthur

Number Employees: 100-249
Square Footage: 400000
Parent Co: Bakery Holding
Type of Packaging: Consumer, Food Service, Private Label, Bulk
Other Locations:
AMF Bakery Systems
Sherbrooke, Quebec

18181 AMF CANADA
1025 Cabana Street
Sherbrooke, QC J1K 2M4
Canada

819-563-3111
Fax: 819-821-2832 800-255-3869
mbissonnette@amfcanada.com
www.amfbakery.com
Manufacturer and exporter of mixers, ovens, troughs, trough elevators, fermentation rooms, dividers, rounders, moulders, panners, final proofers, slicers and baggers for the baking industry
CFO: Manon Bissonnette
Vice President Sales & Marketing: Jason Ward
Research & Development: Alain Lemieux
Director of Sales & Marketing: Larry Gore
Public Relations: Marie-Eve Raqieot
Operations Manager: Claude La Jeunesse
Production Manager: Danny Morin
Purchasing Manager: Jean-Pierre Rosa
Number Employees: 180
Square Footage: 500000
Brands:
Etm
Etmw
Supermix
Supertilt
Versatilt

18182 AMI
PO Box 70520
Richmond, CA 94807-0520

510-234-5050
Fax: 510-234-5055 800-942-7466
www.amiincorporated.com
Manufacturer and exporter of food service serving carts, portable bars, mirror display products, cooking carts, maitre d' desks, etc
President: Kent Brown
CEO: Josh Yarrington
Sales: Lois Kitiuk
Plant Manager: Dang Nuygen
Number Employees: 10-19
Square Footage: 32000
Brands:
Ami

18183 AMI/RECPRO
4250 Northeast Expy
Atlanta, GA 30340-3304

770-458-9189
Fax: 770-454-7350 800-241-1833
www.ami-recpro.com

18184 AMISTCO Separation Products
23147 Highway 6 Alvin
Friendswood, TX 77512

281-331-5956
Fax: 281-585-1780 800-839-6374
amistco@amistco.com www.amistco.com
Owner: Mia Romar
Estimated Sales: $1-5 Million
Number Employees: 50-99
Square Footage: 210

18185 AMSECO
228 E. Star of India Lane
236
Carson, CA 90746-1418

310-538-4670
Fax: 310-538-9932 800-421-1096
Manufacturer and exporter of burglar and fire alarms, closed circuit televisions, annunciator systems and security equipment
President: Yukata Odawara
VP Sales: Tom Galvez
Advertising Manager: Sergio Galvez
Estimated Sales: $10-20 Million
Number Employees: 10-19
Parent Co: AMSECO
Brands:
Audeocam
Crimeshield
E2 D2
Pal
Select-A-Horn/Strobe

Select-A-Strobe
Shadow
Supershield

18186 AMSOIL Inc
925 Tower Ave
Superior, WI 54880-1582

715-392-7101
Fax: 715-392-5225 www.amsoil.com
Manufacturer and exporter of lubricating oils and greases, vitamins and filters including air and water
President: Albert Amatuzio
aamatuzio@amsoil.com
COO: Alan Amatuzio
Estimated Sales: G
Number Employees: 100-249

18187 ANDRITZ Inc
35 Sherman St
Muncy, PA 17756-1227

704-943-4343
www.andritz.com
Manufacturer and exporter of size reduction, screening, mixing, pelleting, material handling, conveyor, cereal cooking, dehydration, grading, barley, blending, milling, crushing, grinding, separating and storage equipment
President: Timothy J Ryan
timothy.ryan@andritz.com
Estimated Sales: $90 Million
Number Employees: 500-999
Square Footage: 400000
Parent Co: Andritz Maschinenfabrik AG
Brands:
Dynestene
Hydrasieve
Roto Shaker
Sonisift

18188 ANGUS Chemical Co
1500 E Lake Cook Rd
Buffalo Grove, IL 60089-6556

847-215-8600
Fax: 989-832-1465 www.angus.com
CEO: Kola Ajala
kola@angus.com
CEO: Mark Henning
Number Employees: 100-249

18189 ANKOM Technology
2052 Oneil Rd
Macedon, NY 14502-8953

315-986-8090
Fax: 315-986-8091 info@ankom.com
www.ankom.com
Instrumentation for the meat processing and food manufacturing industry.
President: Andrew Komarek
akomarek@ankom.com
Vice President, Manufacturing Operations: Shawn Ritchie
Vice President, Research and Development: Ronald Komarek
Director, Strategic Marketing: Greg Coutant
Technical Sales Manager: Nick Tedesche
Office Manager/Accounting: Scott Giali
Production Coordinator-Extraction System: Tom Bopp
Domestic Administrator: Mary Lou Williams
Number Employees: 50-99

18190 ANKOM Technology
2052 Oneil Rd
Macedon, NY 14502-8953

315-986-8090
Fax: 315-986-8091 www.ankom.com
www.ankom.com
Analytical instruments for analyzing foods, determinine solubility of dietary fiber contents, and increasing employee outputs.
President: Andrew Komarek
akomarek@ankom.com
Production Coordinator, RF Systems: Dave Lauber
VP Research & Development: Ronald Komarek
Quality Control Testing: Kurt Ouwenga
VP Marketing & Sales: Christopher Kelley
Technical Sales Manager: Nick Tedesche
Director, Strategic Marketing: Greg Coutant
VP Manufacturing Operations: Shawn Ritchie
Sr Design Engineer: Rick Giannetti
Estimated Sales: $3.3 Million
Number Employees: 50-99
Square Footage: 100000

18191 (HQ)ANVER Corporation
36 Parmenter Rd
Hudson, MA 1749
978-568-0221
Fax: 978-568-1570 800-654-3500
rfq13@anver.com www.anver.com
Manufacturer and exporter of FDA approved vacuum lifting equipment and parts including components, pumps and cups
President: Frank Vernooy
Contact: Anver Anderson
anver@anver.com
Estimated Sales: $10-20 Million
Number Employees: 50-99
Square Footage: 120000
Brands:
Anver
Vacu-Lift
Veribor

18192 (HQ)AP Dataweigh Inc
2730 Northgate Ct
Cumming, GA 30041-6482
678-679-8000
Fax: 678-679-8001 877-409-2562
www.checkweigh.com
Manufacturer and exporter of check weighers, in-motion conveyor scales and checkweighers.
President: Myrna Stanczak
myrnastanczak@apdataweigh.com
Operations Manager: Scott Gibson
Estimated Sales: $1 Million
Number Employees: 10-19
Number of Brands: 2
Number of Products: 14
Brands:
Ap Checkweigers

18193 APA
14536 Monroe Circle
Omaha, NE 68137-3962
402-290-5597
Fax: 402-390-2005 kathryn.a.hanson@ue.corp.com
www.omaha.apaleagues.com
Consultant specializing in conceptual and final design, scheduling and cost estimating, specification development, contract awards and construction oversight for food industry
CEO: Eddie Barvan
CFO: Ken Everett
VP: Bud Dose
VP: Ivan Vrtiska
Marketing Director: Kathryn Hanson
Contact: Russell East
russ@omahapoolplayers.com
Estimated Sales: $10 Million
Number Employees: 50-99
Square Footage: 30000
Other Locations:
APA
Dublin CA

18194 APEC
1201 4th Ave
Lake Odessa, MI 48849-1301
616-374-1000
Fax: 616-374-1010 sales@apecusa.com
www.apecusa.com
Process equipment including liquid scales, weighing and discharging systems, powder applicators, batch mixers, etc
President: Kendall Wilcox
kendallw@apecusa.com
Sales Director: Terry Stemler
Operations Manager: Garrett Billmire
Estimated Sales: $4,500,000
Number Employees: 50-99

18195 APG Cash Drawer
5250 Industrial Blvd NE
Fridley, MN 55421
763-571-5000
Fax: 763-571-5771 apginfo@apgcd.com
Heavy duty and standard duty cash draw for point of sales systems.
President: Mark Olson
Research & Development: Bob Daugs
Quality Control: Jan Leathers
Marketing Director: Bob Daugs
Sales Director: John Meilahn
Operations/Production: Dale Dahlberg
Plant Manager: Wally Szulga
Purchasing Manager: Sheila Weber

Estimated Sales: $22 Million
Number Employees: 100-249
Number of Brands: 12
Number of Products: 12
Square Footage: 60000
Parent Co: Upper Midwest Industries
Type of Packaging: Private Label
Brands:
Caddy
Series100
Series4000
Series6000c
Vasario

18196 API Foils
3841 Greenway Cir
Lawrence, KS 66046-5444
785-842-7674
Fax: 785-842-9748 800-255-4605
marketing@api-foils.com www.api-foils.com
Coding and marking foils
Estimated Sales: $50 Million
Number Employees: 50-99

18197 API Heat Transfer Inc
2777 Walden Ave # 1
Buffalo, NY 14225-4788
716-684-6700
Fax: 716-684-2155 877-274-4328
sales@apiheattransfer.com
www.apiheattransfer.com
Manufacturer and exporter of thermal processing equipment and systems including plate heat exchangers, pasteurizers, evaporators, sterilizers and de-alcoholization systems
President: Joseph Cordosi
CEO: Mike Laisure
mlaisure@apiheattransfer.com
CFO: Jeff Lennox
Quality Control: Barry Kent
R&D: David Sijas
Marketing Director: Gary Trumpfheller
General Manager: David Parrott
Estimated Sales: $50-100 Million
Number Employees: 500-999
Brands:
Advance Aroma System
Sigma Plates
Sigmastar
Sigmatec
Sigmatherm

18198 API Industries
6590 E 40th St
Tulsa, OK 74145
918-664-4010
Fax: 918-664-8741
Waste water pre-treatment systems
President: David Plumb
VP: John Roberds
Estimated Sales: $1-2.5 Million
Number Employees: 10-19
Square Footage: 10000
Brands:
Ech20
Point

18199 API Industries
560 Sylvan Avenue
Englewood Cliffs, NJ 07632-3119
201-569-1700
Fax: 201-569-8907 800-229-7659
Estimated Sales: $300,000-500,000
Number Employees: 1-4

18200 APM
7661 NW 68th Street
Miami, FL 33166-2850
305-888-0161
Estimated Sales: $1-3 Million
Number Employees: 10

18201 APM
441 Industrial Way
Benicia, CA 94510-1119
707-399-8706
Fax: 707-745-0371 800-487-7555
www.apmglobal.com
Packaging supplies, plastic lids, closures, metal and plastic capsules, wine corks, and imported and domestic specialty glass
Contact: Bert Loughmiller
b.loughmiller@lairdtech.com

Estimated Sales: $20-50 Million
Number Employees: 50-100

18202 APM/NNZ Industrial Packaging
805 Marathon Pkwy # 170
Lawrenceville, GA 30045-2890
770-921-9210
Fax: 770-682-7340 www.nnzusa.com
President: Marco Boot

18203 APN Inc
921 Industry Rd
Caledonia, MN 55921-1838
507-725-3392
Fax: 507-725-2073
Batch control systems, filtration equipment, piping, fittings and tubing
President: Richard Bever
rbever@apn-inc.net
Vice President: Neil Goetzinger
Estimated Sales: $2.5-5 000,000
Number Employees: 20-49

18204 APR Associates Inc
3915 Air Park St
Memphis, TN 38118-6007
901-363-5904
Fax: 901-375-3600 800-238-5150
sales@deltaforemost.com www.deltaforemost.com
Cleaning compounds, insecticides, germicidal soap, aerosols, etc
President: Ronald Cooper
rcooper@deltaforemost.com
CFO: John Trobaugh
R & D: Steve Cooper
Quality Control: Charles Autks
Director Sales: George Foust
VP Sales Administrator: Steven Cole
Plant Manager: Tim Martin
Estimated Sales: $10-20 Million
Number Employees: 50-99
Square Footage: 200000

18205 APS Packaging Systems
499 Parrot St.
San Jose, CA 95112-4118
408-286-7770
Fax: 408-286-3800 800-526-2276
aps@apspackaging.com www.apspackaging.com
Manual and automatic shrink wrap machinery
VP Sales: Eric Verbeke
Contact: Aron Blaustein
ablaustein@apspackaging.com
Estimated Sales: $2.5-5 Million
Number Employees: 10-19
Square Footage: 40000

18206 APS Plastic Systems
3 Bowerwalls Place
Crossmill Business Park, Gl G78 1BF
141-880-6688
info@apssafetysystems.com
www.apssafetysystems.com
Specialises in design and installation of fall protection systems and roof access systems.
President: Joe Carr
VP: Rick Roberts
Estimated Sales: $1-2.5 Million
Number Employees: 19

18207 APV Americas
611 Sugar Creek Road
Delavan, WI 53115
847-678-4300
Fax: 800-252-5012 800-252-5200
apvproducts.us@apv.com www.apv.com
Manufacturer and exporter of automation, process systems, heat exchangers, dryers, evaporizers, membrane filtration systems, tanks, mixers, blenders, evaporators, etc.; spray drying available
Marketing Director: Richard Johnston
Project Sales Manager: Enrique Hinojosa
Contact: Dick Powner
dick.powner@apv.com
Estimated Sales: $1-5 Million
Number Employees: 50-100
Square Footage: 1800000
Parent Co: Invensys

18208 APV Baker
1200 W Ash St
Goldsboro, NC 27530
919-736-4309
Fax: 919-735-5275 www.apvbaker.com

Manufacturer and exporter of baking equipment:
conveyors, ovens and mixers
VP Sales Bakery Machinery: Ricahrd Kirkland
Contact: Cindi Congdon
cindi.congdon@apv.com
Estimated Sales: $50-100 Million
Number Employees: 2800
Brands:
  Powerpro

18209 APV Engineered Systems
105 CrossPoint Pkwy
Getzville, NY 14068
800-462-6893
Fax: 716-692-6416 800-369-2782
apvservicena@apv.com www.apv.com
Agglomerators, custom fabrication, dryers, fluid
bed, spray filtration equipment, processing and
packaging
Project Sales Manager: Enrique Hinojosa
Contact: Maureen Ansell
ansell@apv.com
Estimated Sales: $1-5 Million

18210 APV Fluid Handling
100 S Cp Ave
Lake Mills, WI 53551-1726
920-648-8311
Fax: 920-648-1441 800-369-2782
www.apv.com
Sanitary and industrial rotary and centrifugal pumps,
pumping assemblies, sanitary valves, stainless steel
or rubber rotor pumps, W+ Series high efficiency
centrifugal pumps, mixproof double seat or single
seat, butterfly, diaphragmand control valves
Executive Director: Jim Keene
General Manager: Frank Wheelwright
Project Sales Manager: Enrique Hinojosa
Contact: Paul Beduze
pbeduze@apv.com
Estimated Sales: $50-100 Million
Number Employees: 100-249

18211 APV Heat Transfer
P.O.Box 1718
Goldsboro, NC 27533-1718
919-735-4570
Fax: 919-735-5275 800-369-2787
infous@apvbaker.com
Aseptic heat processing equipment
CEO: John Lucas
Contact: Kirt Jarrett
kirt.jarrett@apv.com
Estimated Sales: $10-25 Million
Number Employees: 250-499

18212 APV Mixing & Blending
100 S Cp Ave
Lake Mills, WI 53551-1726
920-648-8311
Fax: 920-648-1441 800-369-2782
ekiessli@apv.com
Mixing and blending equipment
Executive Director: Jim Keene
Marketing Communications Manager: Antonella
Crimi
Contact: Paul Beduze
pbeduze@apv.com
Estimated Sales: $20-50 Million
Number Employees: 100-249

18213 APV Systems
9525w Bryn Mawr Avenue
Rosemont, IL 60018-5205
847-678-4300
Fax: 847-678-4313 888-278-9087
answers@apv.com www.apv.com
Process to boardroom automation and systems for
food, dairy, beverage, brewery
Project Sales Manager: Enrique Hinojosa
Estimated Sales: $1-5 Million
Number Employees: 500

18214 APV Tanks & Fabricated Products
100 S Cp Ave
Lake Mills, WI 53551-1726
920-648-8311
Fax: 920-648-1441 888-278-4321
Auger feed units, food blenders, dual ribbon blenders, pumping assemblies for viscous products and
the multiverter that chops, mixes, heats and cools, in
one tank

Executive Director: Jim Keene
Marketing Communications Manager: Antonella
Crimi
Contact: Paul Beduze
pbeduze@apv.com
Estimated Sales: $20-50 Million
Number Employees: 100-249

18215 (HQ)APW Wyott Food Service Equipment Company
1938 Wyott Dr
Cheyenne, WY 82007-2102
307-634-5801
Fax: 307-637-8071 800-527-2100
www.apwwyott.com
Manufacturer and exporter of hardware, stainless
steel kitchen pans, bun toasters, hot plates, food
wells, broiling grills, dish dispensers and commer-
cial food warming equipment
President: Lawrence Rosenbloom
Director National Accounts: Bruce Deckard
VP: Jim Humphrey
VP Marketing: Jeff King
Estimated Sales: $20-50 Million
Number Employees: 100-249
Type of Packaging: Food Service
Other Locations:
  APW/WYOTT Food Service Equipment
  New Rochelle NY
Brands:
  Lowerraters

18216 ARBO Engineering
3 White Horse Road
Unit 5
Toronto, ON M3J 3G8
Canada
416-636-7057
Fax: 416-630-9135 800-689-2726
sgicza@arbo-feeders.com www.arbo-feeders.com
Manufacturer of feeding and closing equipment
President: Shlomo Gicza
Product Manager: David Gicza
Sales Manager: David Gicza
Estimated Sales: Below $5 Million
Number Employees: 10

18217 ARC Specialties
29120 Commerce Center Dr
Valencia, CA 91355-5404
661-775-8500
Fax: 661-775-1499 www.arc-specialties.com
Tables, racks, mobile storage equipment, cabinets,
dollies, hand trucks, carts, chafers, chafing dishes
and shelving
President: Jay Lateko
President, Chief Executive Officer: Steven DarnelL
Vice President of Business Development: Dave
Mack
VP Sales: Bill Gage
bgage@arcspecialties.com
Vice President of Operations: Bob Buehler
Estimated Sales: $10-20 Million
Number Employees: 20-49
Square Footage: 40000
Parent Co: Leggett & Platt

18218 ARPAC Group
9511 River St
Schiller Park, IL 60176
847-678-9034
Fax: 847-678-2109 info@arpac.com
www.arpac.com
Shrink wrap and pallett stretch wrappers
President: Michael Levy
Sales Manager: Greg Levy
Contact: Armando Agguire
aaguirre@arpac.com
Number Employees: 230
Square Footage: 180
Type of Packaging: Consumer, Food Service, Pri-
  vate Label, Bulk

18219 ARY
10301 Hickman Mills Dr Ste 200
Kansas City, MO 64137
816-761-2900
Fax: 816-761-0055 800-821-7849
Commercial manufacturer of Professional Cutlery
and Vacuum Packaging Equipment for the Food Processing and Food Service Industries

Administrator: David Philgreen
Marketing: Tracey Edwards
Sales: Gary Ralstin
Contact: Bernard Huff
ary@aryinc.com
General Manager: David Philgreen
Estimated Sales: $3-5 000,000
Number Employees: 5-9

18220 ASC Industries Inc
2100 International Pkwy
Canton, OH 44720-1373
330-899-0340
Fax: 330-899-0345 800-253-6009
www.asc-ind.com
President: Ted Swaldo
Contact: Alfred Cardoza
acardoza@ascind.com
Number Employees: 100-249

18221 ASCENT Technics Corporation
PO Box 981
Brick, NJ 08723-0981
732-279-0144
Fax: 732-255-3152 800-774-7077
Manufacturer and exporter of pressure sensitive la-
bel applicators including automatic, semi-automatic
and handheld, also; labels and packaging systems
President: Ched Greenhill
Estimated Sales: Below $5 Million
Number Employees: 15
Number of Products: 6
Square Footage: 20000
Brands:
  Air-Ply
  Atc
  Sharpshooter
  Smart 300

18222 ASI Data Myte
2800 Campus Dr # 60
Plymouth, MN 55441-2669
763-553-1040
Fax: 763-553-1041 800-455-4359
info@asidatamyte.com www.asidatamyte.com
Manufacturer and exporter of packaging and quality
control software
Chairman: Joel Ronning
President: Rick Bump
rickbump@asidatamyte.com
Global Financial Controller: Dave Nelson
CTO & VP Engineering: Raj Chauhan
R&D: Cecil Nelson
Quality Control: Douglas Stohr
VP Global Marketing: Mary Braunwarth
VP Sales: Rudiger Laabs
Customer Manager: Mike McCalley
Sr. Director, Global Operations: John Cullinane
Number Employees: 50-99
Brands:
  Applied Stats
  M-Ware

18223 ASI Electronics Inc
13006 Cricket Hollow Ln
Cypress, TX 77429-2262
281-373-3835
Fax: 281-256-1406 800-231-6066
www.asielectronics.com
Manufacturer, exporter and importer of process con-
trollers including level, weight and gate
Owner: William Jackson
Vice President: Alice Jackson
Sales: Bill Jackson
bjackson54@aol.com
Estimated Sales: $150,000
Number Employees: 1-4
Square Footage: 1000
Type of Packaging: Food Service, Bulk
Brands:
  Kasi-Weigh

18224 (HQ)ASI International Inc
10 Shawnee Dr # M
Suite B5
Watchung, NJ 07069-5803
908-753-4448
Fax: 908-753-1917 sales@info-asi.net
www.info-asi.net
Importer and distributor of bulk raw material ingredients to the nutritional, food, beverage and cosmetic industries.

Owner: Joseph Campis
joseph@info-asi.net
VP: Joseph Campis
Operations: John Wyckoff
Number Employees: 1-4
Type of Packaging: Bulk
Other Locations:
Padre Warehouse-California
Anaheim CA
Arco Warehouse-New Jersey
Passaic NJ

18225 ASI MeltPro Systems
PO Box 1085
Auburn, GA 30011-1085

800-366-0568
Fax: 770-339-1308
Hot melt tanks, heads, hoses and nozzles compatible with Nordson, Itw, slautterback at 50 % savings. M-Series applicator head modular that allows end user to adapt 1-2-3-4 modules and types, for carton, case sealing, non wovenapplication, replace all heads with one. Module types extrusion, spray, reduced cavity, zero cavity, and air on air off
Research & Development: Merk Morriseette
Sales Director: Steve Wages
Plant Manager: Jesse Owens
Estimated Sales: $1-2.5 Million
Number Employees: 19

18226 ASI Technologies
5848 N 95th Ct
Milwaukee, WI 53225

414-464-6200
Fax: 414-464-9863 800-558-7068
info@asidoors.com www.asidoors.com
Maunfacturer and exporter of cold storsge and industrial refrigerator doors including manual, powered, fiberglass and stainless steel
President: George C Balbach
CFO: Steve Contrucci
Estimated Sales: $5-10 000,000
Number Employees: 100-249
Square Footage: 60000

18227 ASI/Restaurant Manager
1734 Elton Rd Ste 219
Silver Spring, MD 20903

800-356-6037
Fax: 301-445-6104 800-356-6037
sales@actionsystems.com
The most compreensive and user-friendly POS system available. Improve service, reduce labor costs and makes faster, more informed decisions to boost your bottom line with powerful backoffice tracking. Choose the traditional touchscreen POS or give your servers the Write-On Handheld for the ultimate in imporved tableside service.
Owner: Smiley Shu
VP: Lisa Wilson
Sales/Marketing Director: Craig Bednarovsky
Contact: Rm Asi
asi.rm@rmpos.com
Estimated Sales: $1-3 Million
Number Employees: 10-19
Square Footage: 12000
Type of Packaging: Food Service
Brands:
Restaurant Manager

18228 ATAGO USA Inc
11811 NE First Street
Suite 101
Bellevue, WA 98005

425-637-2107
Fax: 425-637-2110 877-282-4687
customerservice@atago-usa.com www.atago.net
Suppliers of manufacturing equipment.
President: Yusuke Amamiya
Technical Sales Supervisor: Emerson Carillo
Marketing Director: Frank Young
Sales Director: Wesley LeMay, Jr.
Estimated Sales: A
Number Employees: 1-4

18229 ATD-American Co
135 Greenwood Ave
Wyncote, PA 19095-1396

215-576-1000
Fax: 215-576-1827 800-523-2300
american@atd.com www.atdamerican.com
Furniture, steel shelving, cabinets, bins, table linens and chef aprons; exporter of furniture, linens and food service equipment

President: Janet Wischnia
janet@atd.com
VP: S Zaslow
VP: A Zaslow
R&D: Eric Wischnia
Estimated Sales: $65Million
Number Employees: 100-249

18230 ATK
847 N Troy St
Chicago, IL 60622

773-826-0696 800-522-3582
Fax: www.andysthaikitchen.com
Labels
Estimated Sales: $500,000-$1 Million
Number Employees: 1-4

18231 ATL-East Tag & Label Inc
1244 W Chester Pike # 407
Suite 407, PO Box 3551
West Chester, PA 19382-5687

610-692-2999
Fax: 610-692-3044 866-381-8744
www.atl-east.com
Roll, pressure sensitive and continuous self-adhesive labels; also, shipping and multiport tags, nameplates and seals
President: James W Gordon
jgordon@atlas-tag.com
Estimated Sales: Less Than $500,000
Number Employees: 1-4
Parent Co: Bissell Corporation

18232 ATM Corporation
2450 S Commerce Dr
New Berlin, WI 53151

414-453-1100
Fax: 262-786-5074 800-511-2096
atm@execpc.com
Manufacturer and exporter of testing sieves and particle size measurement equipment
President: James Lang
VP: Stephen Kohl
VP of Marketing: Tony Romano
Contact: Eduardo Bolognesi
e.bolognesi@advantechmfg.com
Estimated Sales: $5-10,000,000
Number Employees: 20-49

18233 ATOFINA Chemicals
2000 Market St
Philadelphia, PA 19103-3231

215-419-7000
Fax: 215-419-7591 800-225-7788
bill.pernice@atofina.com
Manufacturer, importer and exporter of cleaning equipment and supplies including liquid chlorine and caustic soda
President: Doug Sharp
CFO: Larry Hartnett
R&D: Louis Hegedus
Contact: Francois Girin
francois.girin@atofina.com
Number Employees: 500-999

18234 ATS
5025-C N. Royal Atlanta Dr.
Tucker, GA 30084

770-270-1688
Fax: 770-270-5919 800-358-0212
Info@ATSfurniture.com www.atsfurniture.com
Tables and seating manufacturer
President: Sandra Xing
Estimated Sales: $10,000,000-$20,000,000
Number Employees: 50-90

18235 ATS Rheosystems
231 Crosswicks Rd # 7
Bordentown, NJ 08505-2602

609-298-2522
Fax: 609-298-2795 info@atsrheosystems.com
www.cannoninstrument.com
A comprehensive analytical instrumentation, rheological consulting and materials testing, technical support and services company. Rheometer and viscometer design, viscometers and viscosity measurements, research level rheometers andrheology measurements, capillary rheometers, dynamic shear rheometers for asphalt testing, and dynamic mechanical thermal analysis. Other materials characterization techniques are also available, including thermal analysis, surface tension, andcontact angle.

President/CEO: Steven Colo
Manager: Louise Colo
lc@atsrheosystems.com
Estimated Sales: Less Than $500,000
Number Employees: 1-4
Brands:
Dynalyser
Stresstech
Viscoanalyser

18236 ATW Manufacturing Company
4065 W. 11th Ave
Eugene, OR 97402-0029

800-759-3388
Fax: 541-484-1493 800-759-3388
sales@atwmfg.com www.atwmfg.com
Shrink-wrapping, shrink banding, labeling and heat sealing, shrink tunnels, vacuum packaging.
President and CEO: Thomas Drew
Sales: Jeff Spencer
Contact: Luminita Burmaster
luminita.burmaster@atwmfg.com
Operations: James Warren
Estimated Sales: $1-2.5 Million
Number Employees: 7

18237 ATZ Natural
7800 River Road
North Bergen, NJ 07047-6245

888-569-6449
Fax: 201-869-5655
Row materials for nutrition, health food and botanical industries

18238 AVC Industries Inc
20311 Valley Blvd
Suite H
Walnut, CA 91789

909-839-1188
Fax: 909-839-1060 info@avcfilms.com
www.avcfilms.com
POF Shrink Film and Cross Linked POF Film applications and uses of which include that of the food and beverage industry.
Owner: Bill Pan
Vice President Sales: Bill Pan

18239 AVG Automation
4140 Utica Ridge Rd
Bettendorf, IA 52722-1632

563-359-7501
Fax: 630-668-4676 800-TEC-ENGR
www.avg.net
Microprocessor based PLS, programmable limit switches, and revolver decoders for packaging machines
Plant Manager: Hyder Khan
Number Employees: 100-249

18240 AWP Butcher Block Inc
320 Cherry St
Horse Cave, KY 42749

270-786-2319
Fax: 270-786-2321 800-764-7840
Laminated butcher block tops including kitchen counter and island tops, table tops for restaurant, institutional and home use
Owner: Marcia Baugh
marciabaugh@awpbutcherblock.com
Estimated Sales: $1-2.5 Million
Number Employees: 20-49
Type of Packaging: Consumer

18241 AZO Food
4445 Malone Road
P.O.Box 181070
Memphis, TN 38181-1070

901-794-9480
Fax: 901-794-9934 info@azo.com
www.azo-inc.com
Pneumatic and automated handling equipment and systems for ingredients; also, mixers, hoppers, bins, batching and mixing controls and process control and weighing systems
President: Robert Moore
CFO: Jack Kerwin
Executive VP: Jim Cavender
Sales Manager: Kevin Pecha
Contact: Karl-Heinz Bubbach
bkh@azo.de
Estimated Sales: $10-20 Million
Number Employees: 50-99
Brands:
Componenter

Dositainer
Flexitainer
Ruberg

18242 Aabbitt Adhesives
2403 N Oakley Ave
Chicago, IL 60647-2093
773-227-2700
Fax: 773-227-2103 800-222-2488
info@aabbitt.com www.aabbitt.com
Manufacturer and exporter of hot melt and water
based labeling adhesives, casein-based ice proof la-
bel glue and resin emulsion systems
President: Benjamin Sarmas
ben@aabbitt.com
VP: Daniel Sarmas
Sales Manager: Greg Sarmas
General Manager/VP Sales: David Sarmas
Purchasing Director: Donna Hendrickson
Estimated Sales: $20-50 Million
Number Employees: 5-9
Square Footage: 150000

18243 (HQ)Aaburco Inc
17745 Atwater Ln
Grass Valley, CA 95949-7416
530-268-2734
Fax: 530-273-9312 800-533-7437
support@piemaster.com www.piemaster.com
Manufacturer, exporter and wholesaler/distributor of
food processing equipment including manually oper-
ated, semi-automatic and electro-pneumatic ma-
chines and dough rollers for calzones, empanadas
and pierogies
President: Edward Downs
aaburco@piemaster.com
CFO: F Burgard
Estimated Sales: Less Than $500,000
Number Employees: 1-4
Square Footage: 40000
Type of Packaging: Consumer, Food Service
Brands:
Mt20
Piemaster
Sa21

18244 Aaladin Industries Inc
32584 477th Ave
Elk Point, SD 57025-6700
605-356-3325
Fax: 605-356-2330 800-356-3325
info@aaladin.com www.aaladin.com
Manufacturer and exporter of portable, stationary
pressure and aqueous parts washers
President of Systems: Pat Wingen
pwingen@aaladin.com
Purchasing Manager: Don Klunder
Estimated Sales: $10-20 Million
Number Employees: 50-99
Square Footage: 450000
Brands:
Aaladin

18245 Aalint Fluid Measure Solutions
150 Venture Boulevard
Spartanburg, SC 29306-3805
864-574-8960
Fax: 864-578-7308 sales@venturemeas.com
www.venturemeas.com
President: Mark Earl
Number Employees: 50-99

18246 Aaron Equipment Co Div Areco
735 E Green St
P.O. Box 80
Bensenville, IL 60106-2549
630-350-2200
Fax: 630-350-9047 sales@aaronequipment.com
www.aaronequipment.com
Provider of new, used and reconditioned process
equipment and asset management services to the
chemical, plastics, pharmaceutical, food, mining and
related industries.
President: Jerrold V Cohen
Vice President of Business Development: Bruce
Baird
Estimated Sales: $20-50 Million
Number Employees: 5-9
Square Footage: 250000

18247 Aaron Fink Group
501 Mulberry Street
Newark, NJ 07114-2740
973-824-1414

President: Aaron Fink
Estimated Sales: Below $500,000
Number Employees: 2

18248 Aaron Thomas Co Inc
7421 Chapman Ave
Garden Grove, CA 92841-2115
714-894-4468
Fax: 714-373-8633 800-394-4776
www.packaging.com
Contract packager of promotional on-pack samples
and coupons; shrink wrapping, over wrappings and
display assemblies on pallets or racks available
President: Thomas Bacon
VP: Bob Cassens
CFO: James Chang
Quality Control: Danny Bacarrelaq
Sales Executive: Aaron Bacon
Purchasing Executive: Linda Bacon
Estimated Sales: $10-20 Million
Number Employees: 100-249
Square Footage: 700000

18249 Abacus Label Applications
20120 115a Avenue
Maple Ridge, BC V2X 0Z4
Canada
604-465-8633
Fax: 604-465-0818 888-595-8633
President: Roy Ashworth
Number Employees: 9

**18250 Abalon Precision Manufacturing
Corporation**
1040 Home Street
Bronx, NY 10459
718-589-5682
Fax: 718-589-0300 800-888-2225
info@abalonmfg.com
Manufacturer and exporter of fryer tanks, display
store racks and metal fabricated rack parts
President: Norman Orent
Estimated Sales: $2.5 Million
Number Employees: 25
Square Footage: 160000
Parent Co: Abalon Precision Manufacturing
Corporation

18251 Abanaki Corp
17387 Munn Rd
Chagrin Falls, OH 44023-5400
440-543-7400
Fax: 440-543-7404 800-358-7546
skimmers@abanaki.com www.abanaki.com
Manufacturer and exporter of oil and grease skim-
ming equipment including portable models and
multi-belt systems
President/Owner: Tom Hobson
tom@abanaki.com
Estimated Sales: $1-2.5 Million
Number Employees: 10-19
Square Footage: 20000
Brands:
Abanaki Concentrators
Abanaki Mighty Minn
Abanaki Oil Grabber
Abanaki Petro Extractor
Abanaki Tote-Its
Grease Grabber
Mighty Mini
Oil Concentrator
Oil Grabber
Oil Grabber Multi-Belt
Petroxtractor
Tote-It

18252 Abanda
PO Box 2028
Decatur, AL 35602-2028
205-340-1400
Fax: 205-340-5777

18253 Abatron Inc
5501 95th Ave
Kenosha, WI 53144-7499
262-653-2000
Fax: 262-653-2019 800-445-1754
www.abatron.com
Epoxy and plastic compounds, molds, adhesives,
protective coatings, sealants, wood and concrete restoration products
Owner: Marsha Caporaso
marsha.caporaso@abatron.com

Estimated Sales: $10-25 000,000
Number Employees: 20-49
Type of Packaging: Consumer, Bulk

18254 Abb Labels
1010 E 18th St
Los Angeles, CA 90021-3008
213-748-7480
Fax: 213-748-5838 888-22 -5 22
sales@abblabels.com www.abblabels.com
Labels and tags specialized in quick turnaround at
competitive prices
President: Pedram Fararooy
Owner: Albert Khoshbin
sales@abblabels.com
Sales: Pedram Fararooy
Estimated Sales: $10-20 Million
Number Employees: 50-99

18255 Abbeon Cal Inc
123 Gray Ave
Santa Barbara, CA 93101-1895
805-966-0810
Fax: 805-966-7659 800-922-0977
abbeoncal@abbeon.com www.abbeon.com
Manufacturer, exporter and importer of temperature,
humidity and moisture measurement instruments and
plastic cutting, bending & welding tools.
President: Alice Wertheim
CEO: Mark Tubbs
mtubbs@abbeon.com
CFO: Karen Barros
VP: Mara Hassenbein
Quality Control: Robyn Ramirez
Mktg/Sales/Pub Relations/Operations: Bob
Brunsman
Estimated Sales: $2.5-5 Million
Number Employees: 5-9
Square Footage: 40000

18256 Abbotsford Farms
301 Carlson Parkway
Suite 400
Abbotsford, WI 54405
877-203-7620
888-300-3447
nfo@abbotsfordfarms.com
Supplier of organic and cage free liquid eggs to the
food service industry.

18257 Abbott Industries
1-11 Morris St
Paterson, NJ 07501
Fax: 973-345-9154 abbott.harold@verizon.net
www.abbottind.com
Plastic bottles including extrusion, blow molded and
decoration
President: Leonard Grossman
Owner: Harold Sheck
VP: John Klandt
Operations Manager: Richard Lowe
Estimated Sales: $5-10 Million
Number Employees: 20-49
Square Footage: 19000
Brands:
Similac Toddler's Best

18258 Abbott Plastics & Supply Co
3302 Lonergan Dr
Rockford, IL 61109-2670
815-874-8500
Fax: 815-874-6297 800-850-8551
Sales@abbottplastics.com www.abbottplastics.com
Abbott Plastics is a plastics distributor the product
line of which includes sheets, rods, tubes or ma-
chined plastic parts that are applicable to a variety of
industries including dairy and food processing.
President: Roger Becknell
roger@abbottplastics.com
Sales Representative: Steve Forberg
Number Employees: 20-49

18259 Abco Automation
6202 Technology Dr
Browns Summit, NC 27214-9702
336-375-6400
Fax: 336-375-0090 contact@goabco.com
www.goabco.com
Serving industry since 1977. Our extensive experience, broad capabilities and strong technical aptitude
make ABCO a most capable supplier of automated
solutions

President: W Graham Ricks
Marketing: Terry Love
Sales: Paul Game
Purchasing: Tammy Murphy
Estimated Sales: $5-10 000,000
Number Employees: 100-249
Type of Packaging: Consumer

18260 Abco International
200 Broadhollow Rd # 400
Suite 400
Melville, NY 11747-4806
      631-427-9000
  Fax: 631-427-9001 866-240-2226
Tableware for the airline, cruise, and railroad industry
Manager: Bill Grannis
Estimated Sales: Below $500,000
Number Employees: 10-19
Parent Co: Oneida

18261 Abco International
163 Kenwood Ave
Oneida, NY 13421
      631-427-9000
  Fax: 631-427-9001 888-263-7195
    www.oneida.com
Manufacturer and exporter of dinnerware, flatware, glassware, holloware and ovenware
Manager: Bill Grannis
Managing Director: Peter Kranes
Estimated Sales: Below $500,000
Number Employees: 10-19
Parent Co: Delco Tableware International
Type of Packaging: Food Service
Brands:
 Abco International

18262 Abco Products
6800 NW 36th Ave
Miami, FL 33147-6504
      305-694-9465
  Fax: 305-694-0451 888-694-2226
Manufacturer and exporter of mops, brooms, brushes and dust control treatment systems
President: Mark Gray
m.gray@jea.com
VP of Sales: Jonathan Clark
Quality Control Manager: Bill Scheler
VP Sales/Marketing: Christopher Meaney
Customer Service Coordinator: Tiff Vereen
Estimated Sales: Below $500,000
Number Employees: 20-49
Type of Packaging: Food Service
Brands:
 Abco

18263 Abel Manufacturing Co
1100 N Mayflower Dr
Appleton, WI 54913-9656
      920-734-4443
  Fax: 920-734-1084 sales@abel-usa.com
    www.abelusa.com
Manufacturer and exporter of material handling equipment and batch weighing and bulk storage systems
President: Donald Abel
abel@abelusa.com
Estimated Sales: $5-10 Million
Number Employees: 10-19
Type of Packaging: Bulk

18264 Abel Pumps
79 N Industrial Park # 207
Sewickley, PA 15143
      412-741-3222
  Fax: 412-741-2599 mail@abelpumps.com
    www.abelpumps.com
Food processing pumps including solids handling, sanitary stainless steel centrifugal and positive displacement diaphragm
Manager: Carl Dawson
Manager Sales Support: Mark Neiderhauser
Contact: Ken Silay
jknight@abelpumps.com
Estimated Sales: $1-2.5 Million
Number Employees: 5-9
Square Footage: 96000
Parent Co: ABEL-Twiete 1
Brands:
 Abel

18265 Abell-Howe Crane
140 John James Audubon Parkway
Amherst, NY 14228-1197
      716-689-5400
  Fax: 630-972-0897 800-888-0985
   gree.rodriguez@ces-cranes.com
    www.cmworks.com
Overhead and stainless steel jib cranes
Sales: Eric Vach
Sales/Marketing Manager: Eric Vack
Number Employees: 50-99

18266 Abicor Binzel
650 Medimmune Ct # 110
Suite 110
Frederick, MD 21703-2602
      301-846-4196
  Fax: 301-846-4497 800-542-4867
   customerservice@abicorusa.com
    www.binzel-abicor.com
Dishwashing and laundry detergents
President: Gerry Anderson
andersongerry@binzel-abicor.com
VP, Finance & Administration: John R. Kuhn
Marketing Specialist: Megan Ensminger
Director of Sales/ Marketing: Paul Pfingston
VP Operations: Jutilda Binzel
Estimated Sales: Below $5 Million
Number Employees: 50-99

18267 Able Brands Inc
10540 72nd St
Largo, FL 33777-1500
      727-547-5222
  Fax: 727-541-3182 800-854-5019
   nutritionsale@hotmail.com
Owner: David Mc Cabe
Estimated Sales: $5-10 Million
Number Employees: 5-9

18268 Abond Plastic Corporation
10050 Chemin Cote de Liesse
Lachine, QC H8T 1A3
Canada
      514-636-7979
  Fax: 514-273-3155 800-886-7947
    info@abondcorp.com
Manufacturer and importer of tablecloths, oven mitts, place mats and vinyl bags
Sales Manager: R Katz
Estimated Sales: Below $500,000
Number Employees: 20

18269 About Packaging Robotics
2131 E 99th Pl
Thornton, CO 80229-2483
      303-449-2559
  Fax: 303-449-3420 aboutpr@apris.com
    www.apris.com
Open/fill/seal systems for pouches and bags; also, labeling machinery and applicators
President: Sal Beltrami
aboutpr@apris.com
CFO: Lynda Muhlbauer
Estimated Sales: $5-10 Million
Number Employees: 5-9
Square Footage: 5000
Brands:
 Labelmaster Applicator
 Pal Labelmaster
 Pouchmaster Abs System
 Pouchmaster Pac's System
 Pouchmaster Xii
 Thermal Printmaster
 Twin Abs Poucher

18270 Abresist Kalenborn Corp
5541 N State Road 13
Urbana, IN 46990-9548
      260-774-3327
  Fax: 260-774-8188 800-348-0717
  info@abresist.com www.abresist.com
Wear resistant linings to extend equipment life
President: Joe Acceta
CEO: Joe Accetta
Estimated Sales: $5-10 000,000
Number Employees: 20-49

18271 Absolute Custom Extrusions Inc
3868 N Fratney St
Milwaukee, WI 53212-1341
      414-332-8133
  Fax: 414-332-1827 info@ace-extrusions.com
    www.ace-extrusions.com
Cocktail stirrers and straws including custom size and color
President: Barbara Cupertino
IT Executive: Anthony Johnson
tony@ace-extrusions.com
Engineering/Technical: Mark Winiger
IT Executive: Anthony Johnson
tony@ace-extrusions.com
Estimated Sales: $500,000-$1 Million
Number Employees: 20-49
Type of Packaging: Food Service, Private Label, Bulk
Brands:
 Ace
 Rainbow of New Colors

18272 Absolute Process Instruments
1220 American Way
Libertyville, IL 60048-3936
      847-918-3510
  Fax: 800-942-7502 800-942-0315
    tgrimes@api-usa.com
Signal conditioners
President: William Sawyer
wsawyer@api-cecomp.net
Estimated Sales: $5-10 000,000
Number Employees: 20-49

18273 Absorbco
68 Anderson Road
Walterboro, SC 29488
   Fax: 843-538-8678 888-335-6439
    www.absorbco.com
Manufacturer and exporter of disposable wipers
VP: Scott Brown
Director Marketing: Randy Schubert
Number Employees: 107
Type of Packaging: Consumer, Food Service, Private Label, Bulk
Brands:
 Mighty Wipe

18274 Abundant Earth Corporation
495 Fernwood Dr
Ashland, OR 97520-1611
President: Brian Hoffman
Estimated Sales: $300,000-500,000
Number Employees: 1-4
Brands:
 Abundant

18275 Academy Awning
2080 Century Park E # 803
Los Angeles, CA 90067-2011
      310-277-8383
    Fax: 323-277-8370
Commercial awnings
President: James D Richman
Estimated Sales: $2,500,000-5,000,000
Number Employees: 10-19

18276 Accent Mark
345 Morningside Terrace
Palmdale, CA 93551-4445
      661-274-8191
Rubber date and number stamps including plastic and inspection
Owner: Mark Evans
Estimated Sales: Less than $500,000
Number Employees: 4
Brands:
 Baselock
 Cosco
 Ideal
 Just-Rite
 Pullman
 Ribtype
 X-Stamper

18277 Accent Store Fixtures
9629 58th Place
Kenosha, WI 53144
      262-857-9450
  Fax: 262-857-6620 800-545-1144
    sales@accentind.com
Checkout counters, displays, shelving and self-service displays; equipment service and installation available
Owner/President: Dave Shaw
Sales Executive: Chris Osborn
Estimated Sales: $5-10 Million
Number Employees: 55
Square Footage: 60000

Brands:
Accent

18278 Access Solutions
8705 Unicorn Dr Ste C302
Knoxville, TN 37923
865-531-0971
Fax: 865-531-3547 www.accesssolutionsinc.com
Manufacturer and exporter of advertising specialties
and forms; also, embroidery available
Owner: Randy Philipps
Estimated Sales: Below $5,000,000
Number Employees: 10-19

18279 Accessible Products Co
2122 W 5th Pl
Tempe, AZ 85281-7281
480-967-8888
Fax: 480-894-6255 800-922-5252
info@TechLite.net www.djtags.com
Foam insulation
Manager: Sean Pummer
seanp@techlite.net
Estimated Sales: $5,000,000-$10,000,000
Number Employees: 20-49

18280 Acco Systems
12755 E 9 Mile Rd
Warren, MI 48089
586-755-7501
Fax: 586-758-1901
Industrial conveyors, automated storage and re-
trieval systems and electrified monorail systems
President: Anthony Gore
Contact: Glenn Clannell
gclannell@andek.com
Estimated Sales: $10-25 000,000
Number Employees: 200
Parent Co: FKI Company

18281 Accommodation Mollen
2150 Kubach Road
Philadelphia, PA 19116-4203
215-739-2115
Fax: 215-739-4571 800-872-6268
sales@accommodation-mollen.com
Disinfectants and insecticides
President: Dave Potack
CFO: Sara Botoss
Quality Control: Ray Brand
Contact: Mark Berger
mberger@accommodation-mollen.com
General Manager: Dave Potack
Estimated Sales: Below $5 Million
Number Employees: 20-49
Brands:
3m
Buckeye
Chemspec
Taski

18282 Accommodation Program
120 Park Avenue
New York, NY 10017-5577
917-663-4048
Fax: 917-663-5544 800-929-1414
www.120parkhq.com
Consultant specializing in providing plans for desig-
nated and nondesignated smoking seats in food ser-
vice establishments
President: Tara Carraro
Senior Vice President: Diana L Biasotti
Number Employees: 20
Parent Co: Phillip Morris

18283 Accra Laboratory
2686 Lisbon Road
Cleveland, OH 44104-3145
216-721-4747
Fax: 216-721-8715 800-567-7200
Laboratory performing bacterial and nutritional
analysis on food and water, shelf-life studies, FDA
labeling, sanitation consulting and plant inspections
President: G Lancaster
Senior Microbiologist: Monique Panzeter
Estimated Sales: Below $500,000
Number Employees: 4
Square Footage: 15000
Parent Co: CWC Industries

18284 Accraply/Trine
3070 Mainway
Units 16-19
Burlington Ontario, ON L7M 3X1
Canada
905-336-8880
Fax: 905-335-5988 800-387-6742
sales@accraply.com www.accraply.com
Supplier of product identification and decorating
systems, offering pressure sensitive labeling sys-
tems, stand-alone label applicators, pritn and apply
labeling systems, trine roll-fed labeling systems,
shrink sleeve applicators andRFID solutions.
Manager: Peter Nicholson
Vice President: Rob Leonard
Sales Director: Stuart Moss
Operations Manager: Peter Nicholson
Number Employees: 100-249
Number of Brands: 5
Square Footage: 88000
Parent Co: Barry-Wehmiller Companies Inc
Brands:
Avery Dennison
Ccl Label
Collamat
Graham Sleeving
Mateer Burt
Novexx
Sato
Trine Labeling
Zebra

18285 Accro-Seal
316 Briggs St
Vicksburg, MI 49097-1162
269-649-1014
Fax: 269-649-1067 sales@accroseal.com
www.accroseal.com
Gaskets, seals, O-rings and machinery parts
President: Joe Messer
Sales/Marketing: Neil Patten
Estimated Sales: Below $5 000,000
Number Employees: 20-49

18286 Accu Place
1800 NW 69th Ave # 102
Plantation, FL 33313-4583
954-791-1500
Fax: 954-791-1501 www.accuplace.com
Labeling equipment
Owner: Jamie Schlinkmann
IT: Sharon Humphries
sharon.humphries@accuplace.com
Estimated Sales: $10-20 Million
Number Employees: 20-49

18287 Accu Seal Corp
225 Bingham Dr # B
San Marcos, CA 92069-1418
760-591-9800
Fax: 760-591-9117 800-452-6040
info@accu-seal.com www.accu-seal.com
Vacuum, modified-atmosphere, medical, validatable,
long-line, tube and hand-held sealers
Manager: Lesley Jensen
info@accu-seal.com
R&D: Chris Moore
General Manager: Roger Ricky
Estimated Sales: $1-2.5 000,000
Number Employees: 10-19

18288 Accu Temp Products Inc
8415 Clinton Park Dr
Fort Wayne, IN 46825-3197
260-490-5870
Fax: 260-493-0318 800-210-5907
sswogger@accutemp.net www.accutemp.net
Manufacturer and exporter of vacuum steam cookers
and flat top grills and griddles
President/CEO: Scott Swogger
sswogger@accutemp.com
CFO: Dave Ogram
Research & Development: Dean Stanley
Estimated Sales: $20 Million
Number Employees: 50-99
Square Footage: 45000
Brands:
Flipper the Robocook
Steam 'n' Hold
World's Best Griddle

18289 Accu-Labs Research
4663 Table Mountain Drive
Golden, CO 80403-1650
303-277-9514
Fax: 303-277-9512
Laboratory specializing in chemical and environ-
mental analysis
President: William Gilgren
Lab Manager: Christopher Shugarts
Marketing Director: Thomas Balka
Estimated Sales: $2.5-5 Million
Number Employees: 20-49
Square Footage: 108000

18290 Accu-Pak
2422 Prikel Rd
Akron, OH 44312
www.accu-pak.com
Vertical form/fill/seal packaging and metal detection
systems
President: Bill Frievalt
Vice President: Roy Allen
Operations Manager: Richard Camps
Production Manager: Curt Frievalt
Purchasing Manager: Ron Rendessy
Estimated Sales: $10-20,000,000
Number Employees: 50-99
Type of Packaging: Food Service

18291 Accu-Ray Inspection Services
211 Spangler Avenue
Elmhurst, IL 60126-1129
630-833-4027
800-378-1226
Inquires@accu-ray.com www.accu-ray.com
X-ray inspection services, X-ray rentals, metal de-
tector rentals, manufaturers of metal detection
equipment;, X-ray inspection services available
Manager: Doug Bierma
Contact: Fred Deruiter
fderuiter@accu-ray.com
Estimated Sales: Less than $500,000
Number Employees: 1-4
Brands:
Fortress Technology

18292 Accu-Sort Systems
511 School House Rd
Telford, PA 18969
Fax: 215-996-8249 800-227-2633
info@accusort.com www.accusort.com
Manufacturer and exporter of bar code scanners,
CCD cameras, RFID solutions, integrated solutions,
and data collection systems for material handling
applications
President: Bob Joyce
CFO: Greg Banning
Marketing: Mark Verheyden
Sales: Don De Lash
Contact: Melissa Barsuhn
melissa.barsuhn@accusort.com
Production: John Broderick
Estimated Sales: $50-100 Million
Type of Packaging: Bulk

18293 AccuLife
PO Box 218
Blanchester, OH 45107-0218
937-783-5565
Fax: 937-783-5574 acculift@compuserve.com

18294 Accubar
PO Box 6013
Suite 5
Newport News, VA 23606
757-873-9394
Fax: 757-873-8311
Distributor of Easy Bar
President: David Epps

18295 Accuflex Industrial Hose LTD
36663 Van Born Rd # 300
Romulus, MI 48174-4160
734-713-4100
Fax: 734-713-4190 sales@accuflex.com
www.accuflex.com
Manufacturer, exporter and importer of food and
beverage pressure and vacuum hoses and tubing;
NSF, FDA and USDA approved
President: Les Kraska
Estimated Sales: $5-10 Million
Number Employees: 10-19
Brands:
Accu-Clear

Accu-Flo
Accu-Poly
Bev-Flex
Bev-Seal
Bevlex
Kuni-Tec

18296 Accuform Manufacturing,Inc.
PO Box 6299
Vacaville, CA 95696-6299

707-452-1430
Fax: 707-452-1636 800-233-3352
www.accuform.com
Safety signs and pressure sensitive labels
Director of Product Development: Matt Johnson
Number Employees: 10

18297 Accura Tool & Mold
101 W Terra Cotta Ave
Crystal Lake, IL 60014-3507

815-459-5520
Fax: 815-459-4434
Die cast molds
Estimated Sales: $5-10 000,000
Number Employees: 50-99

18298 Accurate Flannel Bag Company
468 Totowa Ave. Ste 3
Paterson, NJ 07522-1573

973-720-1800
Fax: 973-689-6774 800-234-9200
Custom designed bags for ham, sea salt, spices,
flour, beverage mixes, candy, coffee beans, fruits
and vegetables
Executive VP: Fred Baron
Marketing Manager: Wanda Morales
Estimated Sales: $1-3 Million
Number Employees: 100
Square Footage: 50000
Brands:
Silverpak

18299 Accurate Paper Box Co Inc
2635 Byington Solway Rd
Knoxville, TN 37931-3253

865-690-0311
Fax: 865-690-0312 www.accuratepaperbox.com
Paper boxes, cartons, containers, blister packaging
and machinery including box making, cutting, fold-
ing, gluing, printing and sheeting
President: Carl B Hutchison
carl@accuratepaperbox.com
Chairman: Virgil Lawson
Sales Manager: Michael Cox
Estimated Sales: $1-2,500,000
Number Employees: 10-19

18300 Accutek Packaging Equipment
1399 Specialty Dr
Vista, CA 92081-8521

760-734-4177
Fax: 760-734-4188 800-989-1828
sales@accutekpackaging.com
Manufacturer of turnkey packaging solutions.
President: Edward Chocholek
ed@accutekpackagingequipment.com
VP: Darren Chocholek
Estimated Sales: $3-5 Million
Number Employees: 50-99
Square Footage: 80000
Brands:
Accucap
Accucapper
Accuvac
Auto Pinch-25
Auto Pinch-50
Auto-Mini
Handle Capper
Mini-6
Mini-Pinch
Mini-Punch
Pinch-25

18301 Ace Co Precision Mfg
4419 S Federal Way
Boise, ID 83716-5528

208-343-7712
Fax: 208-343-1237 800-359-7012
info@aceco.com www.aceco.com
Manufacturer and exporter of industrial knives and
water knife assemblies; also, custom cutting assemblies available

President: Sheng Vang
svang@acecosemicon.com
CFO: Sid Sullivan
VP: William Moynihan
Sales/Marketing: Joe Jensen
Technical Support: Larry Rupe
Estimated Sales: $10-20,000,000
Number Employees: 50-99
Brands:
Strapslicer System

18302 Ace Co Precision Mfg
4419 S Federal Way
Boise, ID 83716-5528

208-343-7712
Fax: 208-343-1237 800-359-7012
cut@aceco.com www.aceco.com
President: Brian Barber
bbarber@acecosemicon.com
CFO: Syd Sullivan
Estimated Sales: $10-20 Million
Number Employees: 50-99

18303 Ace Engineering Company
10200 Jacksboro Hwy
Fort Worth, TX 76135

817-237-7700
Fax: 817-237-2777 800-431-4223
tchapman@aceworldcompanies.com
www.aceworldcompanies.com
Manufacturer and exporter of hoists, load blocks and
end trucks
President: John Watson
CFO: Mike Harris
Vice President: Rick Reeves
Contact: Ellen Bellamy
ellen.bellamy@aceworldcompanies.com
Estimated Sales: $20-50 Million
Number Employees: 50-99

18304 Ace Fabrication
2715 Dauphin St
Mobile, AL 36606-4899

251-478-0401
Fax: 251-479-8080 acefab@bellsouth.com
Custom built stainless steel food serving equipment
President: Bill Stewart
bill@acefab.com
Estimated Sales: Below $5 Million
Number Employees: 20-49
Square Footage: 60000
Parent Co: Ace Fabrication
Type of Packaging: Food Service
Brands:
Design Series Counters

18305 Ace Manufacturing
5031 Winton Rd
Cincinnati, OH 45232-1506

513-541-2490
Fax: 513-541-2492 800-653-5692
Precision machining services
President: Linda Fullbeck
Contact: Mark Hess
mark.hess@acemanco.com
Number Employees: 10-19

18306 Ace Manufacturing & Parts Co
300 Ramsey Dr
Sullivan, MO 63080-1456

573-468-4181
Fax: 573-468-1711 800-325-6138
acesrmv@pacbell.net www.ace-mfg.com
Manufacturer and exporter of wire containers and
decks, shelving and racks:cantilever, pallet, drive-in
and push-back; also, repair services available
President: Richard Vartanian
HR Executive: Tina Cook
tcook@ace-mfg.com
Estimated Sales: $2.5-5 Million
Number Employees: 50-99
Square Footage: 92000

18307 Ace Signs
5512 Patterson Road
Little Rock, AR 72209-2450

501-562-0800
Fax: 501-423-2407 www.ace-sign.com
Decals, posters and banners
President: Sam Peters
Estimated Sales: $2.5-5 Million
Number Employees: 10

18308 Ace Specialty Mfg Co Inc
9616 Valley Blvd
Rosemead, CA 91770-1510

626-444-3867
Fax: 626-444-6395
Manufacturer and exporter of can ejectors.
President: Karl Anderson
Secretary/Treasurer: Keith Anderson
Estimated Sales: Less Than $500,000
Number Employees: 1-4
Square Footage: 12000
Brands:
Ace

18309 Ace Stamp & Engraving
10510 Bridgeport Way SW # 6
Lakewood, WA 98499-4846

253-582-3322
Fax: 253-582-1955
Corporate and recognition awards, medals, plaques,
seals, rubber stamps, signs, ID and name tags, seals.
Owner: Thomas Joseph
Estimated Sales: Less Than $500,000
Number Employees: 1-4
Square Footage: 2400

18310 Ace Technical Plastics Inc
150 Park Ave
East Hartford, CT 06108-4011

860-278-2444
Fax: 860-525-7000 www.acetechnicalplastics.com
Manufacturer, importer and exporter of packaging
materials including skin, blister, shrink, trays, etc
President: Robert Pomerantz
Estimated Sales: Below $5 Million
Number Employees: 5-9
Square Footage: 24000

18311 Ace-Tex Enterprises
7601 Central St
Detroit, MI 48210

313-834-4000
Fax: 313-834-0260 800-444-3800
info@ace-tex.com www.ace-tex.com
Wiping, lint free disposable and polyester cheese-
cloths.
President: Martin Laker
Year Founded: 1946
Estimated Sales: $23 Million
Number Employees: 75
Other Locations:
Ace Wiping Cloth
Detroit MI
Cross Wiping Cloth
Baltimore MD
Hamilton Wiping Cloth
Hamilton OH
Indiana Wiping Cloth
Mishawaka IN
Sanitary Wiping Cloth
Jamestown NY
Casselman Global
Toronto, Canada
Manufacturers Resource Group
St. Thomas, Canada
Windsor Wiping Cloth
Windsor, Canada

18312 Acebright Inc.
13-15 Deangelo Dr
Bedford, MA 01730

484-919-8980
deana.wang@acebright.com
Supplier and marketer of nutraceutical products such
as vitamin B2, B6, H; L-Lactic acid, Oxytetracycline
and Griseofulvin, etc.
President: Ying Kan
Estimated Sales: $700 Thousand
Number Employees: 7
Parent Co: Hegno Corporation
Type of Packaging: Bulk

18313 Achem Industry AmericaInc.
938 Hatcher Ave
City of Industry, CA 91748

626-839-0800
Fax: 562-802-5069 800-442-8273
www.achem-usa.com
Polyvinyl Chloride (PVC) and double-sided Pres-
sure Sensitive Tapes
Estimated Sales: $50-100 Million
Number Employees: 50-100
Other Locations:
ANCHEM Industry America
Chicago IL
ANCHEM Industry America

Charlotte NC
ANCHEM
China
ANCHEM
Taiwan
ANCHEM
South Asia
ANCHEM
Europe

18314 Achilles USA
1407 80th St SW
Everett, WA 98203-6295

425-353-7000
Fax: 425-348-6683 www.achillesusa.com
Manufacturer and exporter of flexible and semi-rigid
polyvinyl chloride film and sheeting
President: Hillary Askins
askins@achillesgroup.com
Vice President, Finance: Jestin Fought
Research & Development Manager: Bach Nguyen
Human Resources Manager/Safety Manager: Mike
Burrows
Quality Systems Manager: James Knosp
VP, Manufacturing Sales/Operations: Chad Turner
Estimated Sales: $34 Million
Number Employees: 50-99
Square Footage: 14910
Parent Co: Achilles Corporation
Type of Packaging: Bulk

18315 Acme
8563 Whittier Blvd
Pico Rivera, CA 90660

323-821-3930
Fax: 562-696-0026
Manufaturers of bakery and restaurant equipment
President: Mario Labat

18316 Acme Awning
210 N Main St
Salinas, CA 93901-2816

831-424-7134
Fax: 831-424-0328 info@acmeawn.com
www.acmeawnings.com
Commercial awnings, canopies and fabric products
Owner: Gale Rawitzer
grawitzer@gmail.com
Purchasing Manager: Jay Loiacono
Estimated Sales: Less Than $500,000
Number Employees: 5-9
Square Footage: 32000

18317 Acme Awning Co Inc
435 Van Nest Ave
Bronx, NY 10460-2876

718-409-1822
Fax: 718-824-3571 info@acmeawn.com
www.acmeawn.com
Commercial awnings
President: Julio Escalera
j.escalera@acmeawn.com
Estimated Sales: $1-2,500,000
Number Employees: 10-19
Square Footage: 50000

18318 Acme Bag Co
1031 Bay Blvd # T
Suite J
Chula Vista, CA 91911-1625

619-429-9800
Fax: 619-429-0969 800-275-2263
info@acmebag.com www.acmebag.com
Paper and plastic bags, also burlap and polypropy-
lene bags
President: Steve Short
acmebag@aol.com
Estimated Sales: $5-10 Million
Number Employees: 1-4

18319 Acme Control Svc Inc
6140 W Higgins Ave
Chicago, IL 60630-1845

773-774-9191
Fax: 773-774-3737 800-621-6427
info@acmecontrols.com www.acmecontrol.com
Reconditioner of boiler and burner controls
President: Steven R Huening
stevenh@acmecontrol.com
Estimated Sales: $5-10,000,000
Number Employees: 10-19

18320 Acme Display Fixture Company
1057 S Olive St
Los Angeles, CA 90015

800-379-9566
Fax: 213-749-9822 800-959-5657
sales@acmedisplay.com www.acmedisplay.com
Store fixtures including racks, display cases and
store buildouts
President: Lewis J Berenzweig
Director Marketing: Mitch Blumenfeld
Contact: Lindsay Berenzweig
lindsay.berenzweig@acmedisplay.com
Estimated Sales: $10-20,000,000
Number Employees: 50-99

18321 Acme Engineering & Mfg Corp
1820 N York St
Muskogee, OK 74403-1451

918-682-7791
Fax: 918-682-0134 marketing@acmefan.com
www.acmefan.com
Manufacturer and exporter of kitchen ventilation
systems and fans.
EVP, Sales & Marketing: Doug Yamashita
Year Founded: 1938
Estimated Sales: $50-100 Million
Number Employees: 500-999
Square Footage: 500000
Other Locations:
Acme Engineering & Manufacture
Fort Smith AR
Brands:
Centrimaster
Dynamaster
Propmaster
Sky Master
Tube Mastervent
Windmaster

18322 Acme Equipment Corporation
2202 Vondron Road
Madison, WI 53718-6732

608-222-6302
Fax: 608-222-2940 tmartin@mailbag.com
Agitation systems, milk and tank, continuous cook-
ers, fine savers, forks, cheese equipment, agitators,
custom fabrication, heat exchangers, plates, scraped
surface, tubular, piping, fittings and tubing
President: Todd Martin
Estimated Sales: $1-5 000,000
Number Employees: 30

18323 Acme Fixture Company
1057 S Olive Street
Los Angeles, CA 90015

888-388-2263
Fax: 213-749-9822 888-379-9566
www.acmedisplay.com
Store fixtures
Estimated Sales: Below $500,000
Number Employees: 20-50

18324 Acme International
1006 Chancellor Avenue
Maplewood, NJ 07040-3015

973-416-0400
Fax: 973-416-0499
Household kitchen gadgets and utensils including
baking cups, cutlery, cheese graters, egg slicers, gar-
lic presses, etc
President: Emil Gillotti
CEO: K Fischer
Contact: Alex Coutino
acoutino@acme-usa.com
Estimated Sales: $20-50 Million
Number Employees: 50-100
Square Footage: 150000

18325 Acme International Limited
115 West Avenue
Jenkintown, PA 19046-2031

215-885-7750
Fax: 215-885-5182 acmeintusa@aol.com
Estimated Sales: Below $500,000

18326 Acme Laundry Products Inc
21600 Lassen St
Chatsworth, CA 91311-4121

818-341-0700
Fax: 818-341-1546 info@hi-tecgarments.com
www.hi-tecgarments.com
Uniforms
President: Chris Collins
chris@peerless-acme.com

Estimated Sales: $5-10 Million
Number Employees: 100-249

18327 Acme Scale Co
1801 Adams Ave
PO Box 1922
San Leandro, CA 94577-1069

510-638-5040
Fax: 510-638-5619 888-638-5040
www.acmescales.com
Manufacturer, importer and exporter of scales in-
cluding butchers', counting, portable, portion con-
trol, warehouse, educational and laboratory
Owner: Lou Buran
CFO: Lou Buran
VP: Lou Buran
Quality Control: Ron Widgren
Sales Manager: Barbara Byrd
Manager: Jerry Anderson
janderson@acmescales.com
Estimated Sales: Below $5 Million
Number Employees: 20-49
Square Footage: 52000
Parent Co: Buran & Reed
Other Locations:
Acme Scale Co.
Santa Fe Springs CA
Brands:
Chatillon
Detecto
Homs
Ohaus
Toledo

18328 Acme Sponge & Chamois Co Inc
855 Pine St
Tarpon Springs, FL 34689-5902

727-937-3222
Fax: 727-942-3064 sales@acmesponge.com
www.acmespongeandchamoisonline.com
Manufacturer, distributor and exporter of chamois
and natural sponges
President: James Cantonis
CEO: George Cantonis
gcantonis@acmesponge.com
VP of Sales/Marketing: Steve Heller
Sales Manager: Nancy Troio
Estimated Sales: $5-10 Million
Number Employees: 50-99
Square Footage: 200000
Type of Packaging: Consumer, Food Service, Pri-
vate Label, Bulk
Brands:
Aqua
Careware
Duro
Tanners Select
Thenatura;

18329 Acme Wire Products Company
1 Broadway Ave
Mystic, CT 06355

860-572-0511
Fax: 860-572-9456 800-723-7015
www.acmewire.com
President: Mary Fitzgerald
Vice-President: Michael Planeta
VP Sales: Edward Planeta
Contact: John Montalbano
montalbanoj@bc-egan.com
Estimated Sales: $10-20 Million
Number Employees: 50-99

18330 Aco Container Systems
794 McKay Road
Pickering, ON L1W 2Y4
Canada

905-683-8222
Fax: 905-683-2969 800-542-9942
custserv@acotainers.com www.acotainers.com
Manufacturer and exporter of polyethylene tanks in-
cluding full draining, transportable and semi-bulk;
also, custom fabricator of liquid dispensing systems
President and CFO: Stefan Assmann
Order Desk: Kevin Wentzell
Quality Control: Dave Marsden
General Manager: Stephan Assman
Plant Manager: Mike Banas
Number Employees: 30
Square Footage: 50000

18331 Acorto
1287 120th Ave NE
Bellevue, WA 98005
425-453-2800
Fax: 425-453-2167 800-995-9019
contactus@concordiacoffee.com
www.concordiacoffee.com
Manufacturer and exporter of fully automatic
espresso, cappuccino and latte machines
President: David Isett
CFO: Ann Dimond
VP: Mike McLaughlin
Sales Director: Robin Mooney
Contact: Tony Grossi
tgrossi@acorto.com
VP, Operation: Wayne Stearns
Estimated Sales: $10-20 Million
Number Employees: 20-49
Square Footage: 32000
Brands:
  Acorto

18332 Acoustical Systems Inc
59 N Dixie Dr # C
Vandalia, OH 45377-2067
937-898-3198
Fax: 937-898-5043 info@acousticalsystems.com
www.acousticalsystems.com
President: Rick Seitz
rseitz@acousticalsystems.com
Estimated Sales: Below 1 Million
Number Employees: 1-4

18333 Acp Inc
225 49th Avenue Dr SW
Cedar Rapids, IA 52404-4772
319-368-8120
Fax: 319-622-8589 319-368-8198
commercialservice@acpsolutions.com
www.acpsolutions.com
Manufacturer and exporter of commercial micro-
wave and combination ovens.
Cio/Cto: Steve Gimse
sgimse@acp.com
Marketing Communications Manager: Wendy
Roltgen
Estimated Sales: $1-5 Million
Number Employees: 10-19
Square Footage: 7200000
Parent Co: Maytag Corporation
Type of Packaging: Food Service
Brands:
  Amana
  Menumaster
  Radarange
  Radarline

18334 Acra Electric Corporation
P. O. Box 9889
Tulsa, OK 74157
918-224-6755
Fax: 918-224-6866 800-223-4328
www.acraelectric.com
Manufacturer and exporter of electric heating ele-
ments for soup pots, food warmers, dispensers, pop-
corn machines and coffee brewing equipment; also,
drum and pail heaters
President: Robert Browne
Sales Director: Gary Marschke
Estimated Sales: $10-20 Million
Number Employees: 85
Brands:
  Acrawatt
  Wrap-It-Heat

18335 (HQ)Acraloc Corp
113 Flint Rd
Oak Ridge, TN 37830-7033
865-483-1368
Fax: 865-483-3500 acraloc@comcast.net
www.acraloc.com
Manufacturer and exporter of food processing
equipment, vacuum packaging equipment, robotic
saws, fixtures, etc
President: George Andre
CFO: Kent Park
R&D: Scott Andre
Quality Control: David Dyer
Director Corporate Development: Scott Andre
VP Engineering: Harry Ailey
Estimated Sales: $5-10 Million
Number Employees: 50-99
Square Footage: 100000

18336 (HQ)Acrison Inc
20 Empire Blvd
Moonachie, NJ 07074-1382
201-440-8301
Fax: 201-440-4939 800-422-4266
informal@acrison.com www.acrison.com
Manufacturer and exporter of metering equipment,
hoppers, blenders and microprocessor controls and
control systems.
President: Sam Berry
normajean.loftus@pearson.com
Marketing/Sales: John Shaw
Estimated Sales: $50-100 Million
Number Employees: 100-249
Square Footage: 130000
Other Locations:
  Acrison
  Manchester, England
Brands:
  Acrason
  Acri Lok
  Acrison
  Batch Lok
  Md-Ii
  Md-Ii-200

18337 Acro Dishwashing Svc Co
940 Miami Ave
Kansas City, KS 66105-1840
913-342-4282
Fax: 913-342-8006
Commercial low-temperature dishwashers
Manager: Scott Nelson
acroman940@gmail.com
Manager: Lisa Zane
Manager: Scott Nelson
acroman940@gmail.com
Estimated Sales: $1-2.5 Million
Number Employees: 5-9
Parent Co: Acro Manufacturing & Chemical
Company

18338 Acro Plastics
8630 Airport Hwy
Holland, OH 43528-8639
419-865-0256
Fax: 419-865-0256 wjllmi@megsinet.net
Plastic molds and products
President: William J Lowry
VP: Larry Lowry
Estimated Sales: $10-20 000,000
Number Employees: 5-9

18339 Acromag Inc.
30765 S Wixom Rd
P.O. Box 437
Wixom, MI 48393-2417
248-624-1541
Fax: 248-624-9234 sales@acromag.com
www.acromag.com
Manufactures measurement and control instrumenta-
tion, signal conditioning products, network I/O mod-
ules, VMEbus, PCI, and CompactPCI Bus Boards as
well as industry pack and PMC mezzanine modules
President: David Wolfe
Quality Control: Chuck Smith
Marketing: Robert Greenfield
Sales Director: Donald Lupo
Contact: Debbie Baron
dbaron@acromag.com
Plant Manager: Bret Stephenson
Purchasing Agent: Reg Crawford
Estimated Sales: $10-20 Million
Number Employees: 50-99
Brands:
  Intelli Pack

18340 Acrotech
4770 Chino Ave Ste E
Chino, CA 91710
909-465-0610
Fax: 909-465-0403
Industrial electronics for force, weight, pressure
management and control
President: Dan Blessum
d-b@acrotechinc.com
Estimated Sales: $1-2.5 000,000
Number Employees: 8

18341 Acryline
PO Box 872
North Attleboro, MA 2761
508-695-7124
Fax: 508-699-5636 rbaker@acryline.com
www.acryline.com
Merchandising displays
President: Russell Baker
Estimated Sales: $5-10 Million
Number Employees: 20-49

18342 Acta Health Products
380 N Pastoria Avenue
Sunnyvale, CA 94085-4108
408-732-6830
Fax: 408-732-0208 www.actaproducts.com
Processor and exporter of vitamins, minerals, herbal
extracts and other dietary supplements; importer of
raw materials
President: David Chang
david.chang@actaproducts.com
VP: K Y Chang
Director Quality Control: Michael Chang
Director Marketing/Sales: Cal Bewicke
Director Purchasing: Leo Liu
Estimated Sales: $3 Million
Number Employees: 30
Square Footage: 124000
Type of Packaging: Private Label, Bulk

18343 Acta Products Corporation
1131 N Fairoaks Avenue
Sunnyvale, CA 94089-2102
408-732-6830
Fax: 408-732-0208

18344 Action Engineering
4373 Lilburn Industrial Way
P.O. Box 505
Liburn, GA 30047
770-717-1000
Fax: 770-717-3000 800-228-4668
www.actionengineering.com
Manufacturer and exporter of oil skimmers, separa-
tors, wastewater equipment, corn bins, mixers,
heavy-duty, low-profile dollies and flexible tank
liners
President: Amos Broughton
CFO: Patricia Broughton
Estimated Sales: $.5-1 million
Number Employees: 5-9
Number of Brands: 3
Brands:
  Hi-Rise Lls Liquid Separator
  Hunter Oil Skimmer
  Tred-Ties Adjustable Railroad Ties

18345 Action Instruments Company
741 Miller Drive SE
Suite F1
Leesburg, VA 20175-8994
703-443-0000
Fax: 858-279-6290
Modules for measurement and control, electronic in-
strumentation
President: William Perry
Estimated Sales: $10-20 000,000
Number Employees: 100-250

18346 Action Lighting
310 Ice Pond Rd
Bozeman, MT 59715-5380
406-586-5105
Fax: 406-585-3078 800-248-0076
action@actionlighting.com
Manufacturer and exporter of lighting for restau-
rants, bars, casinos, etc
Owner: Jeff Buckley
jeff@actionlighting.com
CFO: Hubert Reid
General Manager: Robert Stone
Sales & Marketing: Allan Kottwitz
Manager: Dan Corthes
Estimated Sales: $5-10,000,000
Number Employees: 10-19
Type of Packaging: Food Service

18347 Action Packaging Automation
15 Oscar Dr
P.O.Box 190
Roosevelt, NJ 08555-7010
609-448-9210
Fax: 609-448-8116 800-241-2724
sales@apaiusa.com www.apaiusa.com
Manufacturer, exporter and importer of automatic packaging machinery for recloseable pouches including counters, scales and support equipment, high speed counting systems, blister packaging machines
Owner: John Wojnicki
Marketing Administrative Assistant: Robin Carroll
Sales Manager: John Wojnicki
Office Manager: Robin Carroll
robin.carroll@apai-usa.com
Estimated Sales: $2.5-5 Million
Number Employees: 20-49

18348 Action Signs By Stubblefield
2323 1st St NW
Albuquerque, NM 87102-1064
505-242-9802
Fax: 505-243-4187 ana@stubblefieldprint.com
www.stubblefieldprint.com
Emblems and decals
Owner: Patrick Segura
patrick@stubblefieldprint.com
Estimated Sales: Less Than $500,000
Number Employees: 5-9

18349 Action Technology
1150 First Avenue
Suite 500
Prussia, PA 19406
217-935-8311
Fax: 217-935-9132 Info@tekni-plex.com
www.tekni-plex.com
Manufacturer and exporter of extruded tubing for beverage dispensing and food handling, extruded coffee stirrers, cheese spreader applicators, sticks and tubing for frozen foods, etc
Sales Manager: Frank Lofrano
Plant Manager: Jason Gribbins
Number Employees: 100-249
Square Footage: 240000
Parent Co: Tekni-Plex
Other Locations:
Action Technology
City of Industry CA
Brands:
Ablex

18350 Actionpac Scales Automation
1300 Yarnell Pl
Oxnard, CA 93033-2457
805-486-5754
Fax: 805-487-0719 800-394-0154
info@actionpacscales.com
www.actionpacscales.com
Manufacturer and exporter of packaging machinery including automated bag filling; also, weighing machinery
President: John Dishion
john@actionpacscales.com
Sales & Services Manager: Johnathan Cantalupo
Sales Assistant: Jennifer Taylor
Purchasing Manager: Justin Pence
Estimated Sales: $500,000-$1 Million
Number Employees: 20-49
Square Footage: 8000

18351 Activon Products
123 Commercial Drive
Beaver Dam, WI 53916-1160
970-484-5560
Fax: 970-482-6184 800-841-0410
www.activon.com
Biodegradable sanitizers in tablet form
President: Todd Howe
Marketing Director: Jim Heeren
Parent Co: PR Pharmaceuticals

18352 Actron
PO Box 572244
Tarzana, CA 91357-2244
818-654-9744
Fax: 818-654-9788 800-866-8887
flymaster@actroninc.com
Manufacturer and exporter of flying-insect control systems and washable and decorative insect light and glue traps
Director Marketing: Abe Thomas

Estimated Sales: Below $500,000
Brands:
Actron
Efk
G-T 200/100 Ilt
Gardner
Haccp
Industrial
Wall Sconce
Ws-50/Ws-50 Bl

18353 Acuair
1700 Cannon Road
Northfield, MN 55057-1680
952-707-1286
Fax: 952-707-0914

Parent Co: York International

18354 Acumen Data Systems Inc
2223 Westfield St
West Springfield, MA 01089-2000
413-737-4800
Fax: 413-737-5544 888-816-0933
info@acumendatasystems.com
Manufacturer and exporter of computer software for bakery management including order, production, formulation, delivery, billing, etc
Owner: Edward W Squires
edward.squires@acumendatasystems.com
VP: Dan Coffey
Estimated Sales: $2.5-5,000,000
Number Employees: 10-19
Brands:
Clockview
Inview
Laborview
Opmview
Proview

18355 Ad Art Litho.
3133 Chester Ave
Cleveland, OH 44114
216-696-1460
Fax: 216-696-1463 800-875-6368
Menus and menu covers; also, printing and silk screening available
President: Felicia West
CFO: Felicia West
Director Operations: Felicia West
Estimated Sales: $1-2,500,000
Number Employees: 10

18356 (HQ)Ad Mart Identity Group
124 Daniel Dr
Danville, KY 40422-2527
859-236-7600
Fax: 859-236-9050 800-354-2102
www.admart.com
Flags, pennants, banners, labels and signs; also, design services available
President: Ed Cahoon
edcahoon@admart.com
Regional Sales Manager: Ed Cahoon
Office Manager: Dana Sheets
Estimated Sales: Less Than $500,000
Number Employees: 1-4
Square Footage: 10000

18357 Ad-Pak Systems Co
3545 North Pkwy
Cumming, GA 30040-5871
770-889-0033
Fax: 770-889-0189 www.adpaksystems.com
Labeling equipment
President: Ray Hawkins
r.hawkins@adpaksystems.com
Estimated Sales: $1-3 Million
Number Employees: 5-9

18358 Adam Electric Signs
1100 Industrial Ave SW
Massillon, OH 44647-7608
330-832-9844
Fax: 330-832-6999 888-886-9911
clevelandeast@adamsigns.com
www.adamsigns.com
Electric, neon, plastic and aluminum signs; also, interior graphics available, also message centers and reimaging
Owner: Kristal Dadisman
dadismankristal@adamsigns.com
Estimated Sales: $10-15 Million
Number Employees: 20-49
Square Footage: 140000

18359 Adamatic
814 44th St NW Ste 103
Auburn, WA 98001
206-322-5474
Fax: 206-322-5425 800-578-2547
info@adamatic.com www.adamatic.com
Manufacturer and exporter of bakers' equipment including ovens and machinery; also, refrigerators
General manager and Controller: Michael Hartnett
R&D: Walter Kopp
Quality Control: Michael Liberatore
Contact: Scott Ummel
scottu@belshaw-adamatic.com
General Manager: John Muldowney
Estimated Sales: $10-20 Million
Number Employees: 55
Parent Co: PMI Food Equipment Group
Type of Packaging: Consumer, Food Service

18360 Adamation
7039 E Slauson Ave
Commerce, CA 90040-3620
323-722-7900
Fax: 323-726-4700 800-383-8800
www.adamationinc.com
Manufacturer and exporter of dish washing and silver burnishing machinery, tray conveyors and food waste shredder disposal systems
Owner: Jeff Branstein
CEO: Hubert Perry, Jr.
CFO: Joe Braver
Operations Manager: John Onu
Plant Manager: Cliff Bergland
Purchasing Manager: Mike Schulng
Estimated Sales: $5 Million
Number Employees: 50-99
Square Footage: 84000
Parent Co: Winbro Group
Brands:
Adamation
Lusterator

18361 Adams Inc
2131 16th St N # C
Fargo, ND 58102-1840
701-277-9422
Fax: 701-277-9411 800-342-4748
info@adamsfargo.com www.adamsfargo.com
A leading maufacturers representative for hundreds of material handling and storage products.
Owner: Al Hagger
al@adamsfargo.com
Manager: Al Hager
Estimated Sales: $2.5-5 Million
Number Employees: 5-9
Square Footage: 12000
Type of Packaging: Consumer, Food Service, Private Label

18362 Adams Precision Screen
704 Whitney St
San Leandro, CA 94577-1118
510-632-8597
Fax: 510-632-1545 www.adamsscreenprint.com
Decals and screen printing and metal finishing available
Owner: Mark Adams
mark@adamsscreenprint.com
Estimated Sales: Less Than $500,000
Number Employees: 1-4
Square Footage: 12000

18363 Adapto Storage Products
PO Box 111600
Hialeah, FL 33011-1600
305-499-4800
Fax: 305-885-8677
Steel storage equipment
President: Joe Carignan
Quality Control: Elisa Hannna
Plant Manager: Ernie Ignaza
Purchasing: Jim Shutes
Number Employees: 70
Square Footage: 320000

18364 Adcapitol
1400 Goldmire Road
Monroe, NC 28111-5017
704-283-2147
Fax: 704-289-6857 800-868-7111
sales@adcapitol.com www.adcapitol.com
Cut and sew uniforms and promotional printed aprons, tote bags, tablecloths, napkins, lunch bags, banners and caps

President: Lance Dunn
Contact: Amanda Barnett
amanda.barnett@adcapitol.com
Estimated Sales: $50-100 Million
Number Employees: 300
Square Footage: 100000
Parent Co: Dunn Manufacturing
Type of Packaging: Bulk

18365 Adcraft
940 S Oyster Bay Rd
Hicksville, NY 11801

516-433-4534
Fax: 800-447-7751 800-223-7750
Sales@Hdsheldon.com www.admiralcraft.com
Equipment, utensils and supplies
President: Matthew Lobman
m.lobman@admiralcraft.com
Owner: Brett Ashley
EVP: Richard Powers
Estimated Sales: $
Number Employees: 44
Square Footage: 100000
Type of Packaging: Food Service
Brands:
Atlas
Hercules

18366 Adenna Inc
201 S Milliken Ave
Ontario, CA 91761-7832

909-510-6999
Fax: 909-510-8999 888-323-3662
info@adenna.com
Adenna markets and distributes a variety of hand
protection products including disposable polyethyl-
ene gloves for the food industry.
President: Maxwell Lee
Marketing Manager: Evangelene Cheng
Sales: Kevin Toshima
Estimated Sales: $3-5 Million
Number Employees: 10-19
Other Locations:
San Marc Liquidators
Philadelphia PA

18367 Adept Solutions, Inc.
990 Klamath Lane
Suite 6
Yuba City, CA 95993

530-751-5100
Fax: 530-313-5447 help@adept-solutions.net
www.adept-solutions.net
Specialty ingredients and technical services
President: Bud Sanchez
Owner: Jason Neukirchner
Contact: Kris Granger
kris@adept-solutions.net
Operations Manager: Geoffrey Granger
Estimated Sales: $370,000
Number Employees: 4
Square Footage: 2852
Type of Packaging: Consumer, Food Service

18368 Adept Technology
5960 Inglewood Dr Ste 300
Pleasanton, CA 94588

925-245-3400
Fax: 925-960-0452 www.adept.com
CEO: John Dulchinos
Contact: Jeffery Baird
jeff.baird@adeptechno.com
Estimated Sales: H
Number Employees: 100-249

18369 Adex Medical Inc
6101 Quail Valley Ct # D
Riverside, CA 92507-0764

951-653-9122
Fax: 951-653-9133 800-873-4776
info@adexmed.com www.adexmed.com
Manufacturer, wholesaler/distributor, importer and
exporter of disposable apparel including gloves,
goggles, aprons, hair nets, caps, masks, shoe covers,
etc.; also, towels, industrial safety products, emer-
gency preparednessproducts
President/CEO: Michael Ghafouri
mmg@adexmed.com
Estimated Sales: $5 Million
Number Employees: 20-49
Number of Brands: 3
Number of Products: 200
Square Footage: 44000
Type of Packaging: Consumer, Food Service, Pri-
vate Label

Brands:
Adex
Dispomed

18370 Adheron Coatings Corporation
16420 Kilbourne Ave
Oak Forest, IL 60452

708-687-0010

18371 Adhesive Applications
41 Oneil St
Easthampton, MA 01027-1103

413-527-7120
Fax: 413-527-7249 800-356-3572
Manufacturer and exporter of pressure sensitive
foam cloth adhesive tapes
President: Michael Schaefer
mschaefer@stikiiproducts.com
Sales Manager: David Premo
Sales Specialist: Judette Savino
Estimated Sales: $10-20 Million
Number Employees: 20-49
Parent Co: October Company

18372 Adhesive Label
2916 Nevada Ave N # 1
Minneapolis, MN 55427-2887

763-546-1182
Fax: 763-546-1182 www.adhesivelabelinc.com
Labels
President: Steve Ericcson
VP: Diane Hurley
Estimated Sales: $4 Million
Number Employees: 100-249
Square Footage: 14000

18373 Adhesive Products Inc
4727 E 48th St
Vernon, CA 90058-2799

323-589-5516
Fax: 323-589-6460 800-669-5516
www.adhesiveproductsinc.com
Resin emulsion, starch based and hot melt adhe-
sives, water activated paper and reinforced gummed
tapes and custom printed self adhesive labels and
tapes
President: Paul Shattuck
paul@ashesiveproducts.com
VP: W Shattuck
Operations Manager: William Almas
Estimated Sales: $2.5-5 Million
Number Employees: 5-9
Square Footage: 56000
Type of Packaging: Consumer, Bulk

18374 Adhesive Products Inc
945 S Doris St
Seattle, WA 98108-2729

206-762-7459
Fax: 206-762-9852 www.atwoodadhesives.com
Manager: Laurel Mangan
Estimated Sales: $5-10 Million
Number Employees: 10-19
Parent Co: Adhesive Products

18375 Adhesive Technologies Inc
3 Merrill Industrial Dr
Hampton, NH 03842-1995

603-929-5300
Fax: 603-926-1780 800-458-3486
marketing@adhesivetech.com
www.adhesivetech.com
Manufacturer, importer and exporter of applica-
tion-based systems: hot melts, sprays, solids, 2-part
reactives and a wide range of applicators (glue guns)
from craft to industrial.
Chief Executive Officer, Founder: Peter Melendy
pmelendy@adhesivetech.com
Marketing Director: Laura Scaccia
VP Sales: John Starer
Public Relations: Laura Scaccia
Estimated Sales: $20-50 Million
Number Employees: 20-49
Brands:
Crafty
Floralpro
Magic Melt

18376 Adhesives Research
400 Seaks Run Rd
Glen Rock, PA 17327

717-235-7979
800-445-6240
www.adhesivesresearch.com

High-performance, pressure-sensitive adhesives,
tapes, coatings, films and laminates
President/Owner: Richard Widden
Marketing: Deepak Hariharan
Sales: Dave Koppenhaver
Operations: Cameron Sterner
Year Founded: 1961
Number Employees: 300
Square Footage: 240000
Type of Packaging: Consumer

18377 Adhesives Research Inc
400 Seaks Run Rd
Glen Rock, PA 17327-9500

717-235-7979
Fax: 717-235-8320 800-445-6240
gandrews@arglobal.com
Armark Authentication Technologies develops custom authentication systems for use across a wide variety of brand owner applications. ARmark's covert
markers aid in brand protection, product surety and
risk mitigation to fight globalcounterfeiting and can
be combined with custom-developed delivery sys-
tems for application to a variety of goods, including
pharmaceuticals, packaging, food, apparel, currency,
bonds and documents.
President: Geoff Bennett
Vice President & General Manager: George Stolakis
Vice President & General Manager: Bill Stratton
Vice President of Sales: Rick Alexander
Vice President & General Manager: Beth Vondrak
Director & General Manager: Jeff Robertson
Marketing Manager: Greg Andrews
Vice President Commercial Development: George
Cramer
General Counsel & Secretary: Lynne Durbin
Controller: Gary Messersmith
Vice President Human Resources: Robert Valenti
Number Employees: 250-499

18378 Admatch Corporation
36 W 25th St
Fl 8
New York, NY 10010

212-696-2600
Fax: 212-696-0620 800-777-9909
ask@admatch.com www.admatch.com
Manufacturer, exporter and importer of wood and
paper matches with custom printed boxes and books,
wood toothpicks, paper napkins, place mats, coasters
and tissues
President: Mark Nackman
Sales Manager: Agatha Laura
Contact: King Chau
king@admatch.com
Estimated Sales: $10-20 Million
Number Employees: 10-19
Type of Packaging: Consumer, Food Service, Pri-
vate Label, Bulk
Brands:
Admatch
Promotissues

18379 Admix Inc.
234 Abby Rd
Manchester, NH 03103

603-627-2340
Fax: 603-627-2019 800-466-2369
mixing@admix.com www.admix.com
President: Louis Beaudette
Contact: Jerry Baresich
jbaresich@admix.com
Estimated Sales: $5-10 Million
Number Employees: 20-49

18380 Adolph Gottscho
835 Lehigh Ave
Union, NJ 07083-7631

908-688-2400
Fax: 908-687-9250 sales@gottscho.com
www.gottscho.com
President: Eva Gottscho
Contact: Paul Jancek
paul@gottscho.com
Estimated Sales: $5-10 Million
Number Employees: 20-49

18381 Adpro
30500 Solon Industrial Pkwy
Solon, OH 44139-4330

440-542-1111
www.ad-pro.net

Manufacturer and importer of boxes including folding, set-up and corrugated; shrink packaging available; also, designer of sales promotion and marketing materials
VP: Stephen Lebby
Estimated Sales: $2.5-5 Million
Number Employees: 20-49
Square Footage: 130000
Parent Co: ADPRO

18382 Adrienne's Gourmet Foods
849 Ward Dr
Santa Barbara, CA 93111
805-964-6848
Fax: 805-964-8698 800-937-7010
Organic and kosher cookies, crackers and high protein pastas.
President: John O'Donnell
Vice President: Adrienne O'Donnell
Contact: Sarah Guiginano
sarah@adriennes.com
Estimated Sales: $5-10 Million
Number Employees: 20-49
Type of Packaging: Consumer, Food Service, Private Label, Bulk
Brands:
  Appeteasers
  California Crisps
  Courtney's
  Courtney's Organic Water Crackers
  Darcia's Organic Crostini
  Lavosh HawaiiPapadina Pasta
  Papadini Hi-Protein

18383 Adstick Custom Labels Inc
11000 E 53rd Ave
Denver, CO 80239-2111
303-388-5821
Fax: 303-321-4536 800-255-7314
info@adstick.com www.adstick.com
Pressure sensitive tapes and labels
Owner: Daryl Leeson
dcleeson@adstick.com
CEO: R Stillahn
CEO: Brad Stillahn
General Manager: Robert Morland
Estimated Sales: $3-5 Million
Number Employees: 10-19
Square Footage: 28000

18384 Adstick Custom Labels Inc
3845 Forest St
Denver, CO 80207-1120
303-388-5821
Fax: 303-321-4536 brad@adstick.com
www.adstick.com
Labels
Owner: John Kiernan
jkiernan@adstick.com
Estimated Sales: $5-10 Million
Number Employees: 5-9

18385 Advance Adhesives
2403 N Oakley Ave
Chicago, IL 60647-2093
773-278-3988
Fax: 773-227-2103 www.aabbitt.com
President: Benjamin B Sarmas
Estimated Sales: $50-100 Million
Number Employees: 50-99

18386 Advance Automated Systems Inc
3775 14 Mile Rd NW
PO Box 476
Sparta, MI 49345-9362
616-887-0316
Fax: 616-887-8407
dale@advanceautomatedsystems.com
www.advanceautomatedsystems.com
Supplier of automated systems.
President: Dale Montgomery
dale@advanceautomatedsystems.com
Estimated Sales: $1-2.5 000,000
Number Employees: 1-4

18387 Advance Cleaning Products
PO Box 170950
Milwaukee, WI 53217-8086
414-937-8181
Fax: 414-344-3458 800-925-5326
Self-polishing floor polish and cleaners including all purpose, toilet bowl and liquid soap
President: Mark Halaska

Estimated Sales: Less than $1 Million
Number Employees: 10-19
Square Footage: 120000
Brands:
  Easy Strip
  Floor Suds
  Perma Shine
  Scrub 'n Shine
  Shine-Off
  Snappy
  Ultrashine

18388 Advance Distribution Svc
2349 Millers Ln
Louisville, KY 40216-5329
502-449-1720
Fax: 502-778-1718
contactADS@advancedistribution.com
www.advancedistribution.com
A packaging, warehouse and distributor company for the food industry
President: Brian Johnson
bjohnson@advancedistribution.com
R&D: J Perrier
Quality Control: L Defaint
Sales: Judy Jaedine
Operations: Aldo Dagnino
Plant Manager: Jorge Monge
Estimated Sales: $300,000-500,000
Number Employees: 50-99
Square Footage: 2400000
Type of Packaging: Consumer, Food Service

18389 Advance Energy Technologies
1 Solar Dr
Halfmoon, NY 12065-3402
518-371-2140
Fax: 518-371-0737 800-724-0198
sales@advanceet.com www.advanceet.com
Manufacturer and exporter of walk-in coolers and freezers, refrigerated warehouses, foam injected insulated panels, clean rooms and environmental chambers.
President: Timothy Carlo
sales@advanceet.com
General Manager: Dan Carlo
Estimated Sales: $10-20 Million
Number Employees: 20-49
Square Footage: 60000
Type of Packaging: Bulk

18390 Advance Engineering Co
7505 Baron Dr
Canton, MI 48187-2494
313-537-3500
Fax: 313-537-7389 800-497-6388
www.adveng.net
Plastic trays, pallets and packaging
President: Mike Baran
mbaran@adveng.net
Customer Service: Angela Frasher
General Manager: Gene Cook
Estimated Sales: $10-20,000,000
Number Employees: 50-99
Parent Co: L&W Engineering

18391 Advance Fittings Corp
218 W Centralia St
Elkhorn, WI 53121-1606
262-723-6699
Fax: 262-723-6643 advance@genevaonline.com
Manufacturer, importer and exporter of filtration equipment, fittings, clamps, tanks, sampling devices, tube and pipe supports, tubes and valves; also, custom fabrications available
President: Edward W Mentzer
ementzer@advancefittingscorp.com
VP: Roger Klemp
Marketing/Sales: Jeffery Klemp
VP of Sales: Peter Mentzer
Estimated Sales: $5-10 Million
Number Employees: 20-49

18392 Advance Grower Solutions
3343 Locke Ave
Suite 107
Fort Worth, TX 76107
503-646-5581
Fax: 503-646-0622 800-367-7082
sales@advgrower.com www.advgrower.com
Wine industry computer software
Owner: Dan Harris
Contact: Lucci Altman
lucci@advgrower.com

Estimated Sales: $3-5 Million
Number Employees: 10-19

18393 Advance Lifts Inc
701 Kirk Rd
St Charles, IL 60174-3428
630-584-9881
Fax: 630-584-9405 800-843-3625
sales@advancelifts.com
Hydraulic scissor lifts and recycling equipment
President: Henry Renken
hank@advancelifts.com
VP Sales: David Ferguson
Estimated Sales: $20-50 Million
Number Employees: 50-99
Square Footage: 120000

18394 Advance Storage Products
7341 Lincoln Way
Garden Grove, CA 92841-1428
714-902-9000
Fax: 714-902-9001 888-478-7422
asp@advstore.com
www.advancestorageproducts.com
Technology-driven company dedicated to developing the most efficient and economical solution to our customers' material storage needs. State-of-the-art engineering-providing turnkey systems. In business over 40 years
President: John Krummell
asp@advstore.com
CFO: Rick Callow
R&D: T J Imholte
Marketing/Public Relations: Judy Pugh
Sales Director: Adel Santner
Operations Manager: T Imholte
Purchasing Manager: Lisa Ramirez
Estimated Sales: $20-50 Million
Number Employees: 20-49
Brands:
  Pushback

18395 (HQ)Advance Tabco
200 Heartland Blvd
Edgewood, NY 11717-8379
631-242-8270
Fax: 631-242-6900 800-645-3166
www.advancetabco.com
Stainless steel sinks, worktables, shelving and dish tables; also, aluminum and racks and wire shelving
President: Penny Hutner
VP: Danny Schwartz
Estimated Sales: $50-100 Million
Number Employees: 250-499
Brands:
  Advance Tabco

18396 Advance Technology Corp
79 N Franklin Tpke
Suite 103
Ramsey, NJ 07446-2035
201-934-7127
Fax: 201-236-1891 sales@vetstar.com
www.vetstar.com
Manufacturer and exporter of laboratory information management system software
President: John Cummins
Sales Manager: Susan Cummins
IT: Eileen Costello
eeaston@vetstar.com
Number Employees: 10-19
Brands:
  V-Lims
  Vetstar

18397 Advance Weight Systems Inc
409 Main St
PO Box 6
Grafton, OH 44044-1205
440-926-3691
sales@advancew8.com
www.advancew8.com
Scales, weighers and conveyors for food packaging systems
President: Martha Noel
martha.noel@advancew8.com
VP Sales: John Koliha
Estimated Sales: Below $5 Million
Number Employees: 10-19

18398 Advanced Coating & Converting
1229 S Dickerson Rd
Goodlettsville, TN 37072-2802
615-851-2000
Fax: 615-851-5683 advancedcoating1@aol.com
Hot melt applicators and replacement parts, packaging
Owner: Gary Faulkner
advancedcoating1@aol.com
Estimated Sales: $1-3 Million
Number Employees: 10-19

18399 Advanced Coating & Converting
1229 S Dickerson Rd
Goodlettsville, TN 37072-2802
615-851-2000
Fax: 615-851-5683 advancedcoating1@aol.com
Owner: Gary Faulkner
advancedcoating1@aol.com
Number Employees: 10-19

18400 Advanced Control Technologies
6805 Hillsdale Ct
Indianapolis, IN 46250-2039
317-806-2750
Fax: 317-806-2770 800-886-2281
info@act-solutions.com
Manufacturer and exporter of HVAC controls
President: Gary Colip
gcolip@act-solutions.com
Estimated Sales: $5-10,000,000
Number Employees: 10-19

18401 Advanced Design Awning & Sign
1600 29th St
Cloquet, MN 55720-2886
612-870-7634
Fax: 218-879-2936 800-566-8368
www.advancedawning.com
Commercial awnings
Owner: Chris Mathews
camathews@advancedawning.com
Estimated Sales: Below $5 Million
Number Employees: 10-19

18402 Advanced Design Mfg
1281 Franquette Ave
Concord, CA 94520-5378
925-680-8764
Fax: 925-680-7252 800-690-0002
sales@sneezeguard.com www.sneezeguard.com
Stock and custom sneeze guards
Owner: David Murry
david@adc9001.com
CFO: Richard Harris
R & D: Peter Otool
Sales Director: Jeff Bigby
Production Director: Andy McGrath
Estimated Sales: $5-10 Million
Number Employees: 10-19
Square Footage: 88000

18403 Advanced Detection Systems
4740 W Electric Ave
Milwaukee, WI 53219-1626
414-672-0553
Fax: 414-672-5354 dsmith@adsdetection.com
www.adsdetection.com
Manufacturer and exporter of electronic metal detectors with reject devices, conveyors and pipeline systems; also, washdown severe-duty models
CFO: Matt Nagel
mnagel@adsdetection.com
Human Resources: Sue Medbed
Sales Manager: Dave Smith
Production Manager: Chuck Morgan
Estimated Sales: $10-20,000,000
Number Employees: 50-99
Parent Co: Venturedyne

18404 Advanced Equipment
2411 Vauxhall Place
Richmond, BC V6V 1Z5
Canada
604-276-8989
Fax: 604-276-8962 info@advancedfreezer.com
www.advancedfreezer.com
Manufacturer and exporter of freezers
President: Peter Pao
Purchasing Agent: Thomas Leung
Estimated Sales: Below $5 Million
Number Employees: 40
Square Footage: 80000

Brands:
Advanced Equipment

18405 Advanced Ergonomics Inc
7460 Warren Pkwy # 265
Suite 265
Frisco, TX 75034-4279
972-294-7506
Fax: 972-294-7620 800-682-0169
aei@advancedergonomics.com
www.advancedergonomics.com
Consultant providing pre-employment testing services and job site analysis
President: Harry Broxson
CEO: Terry Broxson
Manager: Mary Selan
mary.selan@advancedergonomics.com
Estimated Sales: Below $5,000,000
Number Employees: 5-9

18406 Advanced Food Equipment LLC
PO Box 470
Mt Vernon, OH 43050-0470
814-772-6396
Fax: 740-392-4785
Package spiral freezers and steam cookers, site-built spiral freezers, fluidized belt and tray freezers, car/dolley freezers, contact belt freezers, pouch water and prine chillers, case/box freezers and chillers
President: Michael Webber
R&D: John Webber
Estimated Sales: $1-5 000,000
Number Employees: 1-4

18407 Advanced Food Systems
2141 E Highland Ave # 10
Phoenix, AZ 85016-4736
602-522-8282
Fax: 602-522-1856 877-821-3007
ninad@afsi.com www.afsi.com
Equipment
CEO: Kurien Jacob
Number Employees: 50-99

18408 Advanced Food Systems
133 Lake Bluff Drive
Columbus, OH 43235
888-871-9885
Fax: 888-807-9632 sendmeinfo@afsusa.net
www.advancedfoodsys.com
President: Denny Vincent
Contact: Richelle Goldilla
rg@rvin.net
Estimated Sales: $300,000-500,000
Number Employees: 1-4

18409 Advanced Industrial Systems
21068 Bake Pkwy
Suite 200
Lake Forest, CA 92630-2185
208-237-2222
Fax: 949-597-9898 800-658-3850
www.advancedindustrial.com
Real-time process control systems, human-machine interfaces, supervisory and cell control-SCADA systems, statistical process control
President: Gene Kaplan
Estimated Sales: Below $500,000

18410 Advanced Ingredients, Inc.
401 N 3rd St
Suite 400
Minneapolis, MN 55401
Fax: 763-201-5820 888-238-4647
info@advancedingredients.com
www.advancedingredients.com
Specialty ingredients
President: Fred Greenland
Estimated Sales: $1-3 Million
Number Employees: 5-9
Brands:
Bakesmart®
Energysmart®
Energysource®
Fruitrim®
Fruitsavr®
Fruitsource®
Moisturlok®
Plus and Moisturlok®

18411 (HQ)Advanced Instruments Inc
2 Technology Way # 1
Norwood, MA 02062-2630
781-320-9000
Fax: 781-320-8181 800-225-4034
info@aicompanies.com www.aicompanies.com
Manufacturer and exporter of clinical, industrial laboratory and food and dairy quality control equipment.
CEO: John Coughlin
CFO: Jim Noris
jimn@aicompanies.com
Marketing Manager: Kristen Vuotto
Sales: John Ryder
Plant Manager: Mike Graham
Estimated Sales: $10-20 Million
Number Employees: 50-99
Number of Brands: 4
Number of Products: 6
Square Footage: 80000
Other Locations:
Advanced Instruments
Bethesda MD
Brands:
Advanced
Fiske
Fiske Associates
Fluorophos Test System

18412 Advanced Instruments Inc
2 Technology Way # 1
Norwood, MA 02062-2630
781-320-9000
Fax: 781-320-8181 800-225-4034
info@aicompanies.com www.aicompanies.com
Equipment for the dairy and food industry.
Director: Blanton Wiggin
CFO: Jim Noris
jimn@aicompanies.com
Vice President: Pierre Emond
Vice President Sales: John Ryder
Number Employees: 50-99

18413 Advanced Insulation Concepts
8055 Production Dr
Florence, KY 41042-3094
859-342-8550
Fax: 859-342-5445 800-826-3100
info@aicinsulate.com
www.advancedinsulationconcepts.com
Manufacturer and exporter of insulated panels and doors for refrigerated and other atmosphere-controlled rooms including horizontal sliding, bi-parting, vertical lift and swing. Also insulated fire wall panels
President: W Burton Lloyd
VP: Michael Lloyd
Sales: Michael Lloyd
Estimated Sales: $6-10 Million
Number Employees: 30
Square Footage: 124000
Brands:
Insulrock
Isowall
Regent

18414 Advanced Labelworx
2800 W Whitner St
Anderson, SC 29626-1035
865-966-8711
Fax: 865-813-9918
marketing@advancedlabelworx.com
www.advancedlabelworx.com
Pressure sensitive roll labels and printed tape, foils and tags
President: Gabrina Kelly
gkelly@tagandlabel.com
VP Marketing: Dennis Burt
VP Sales: Paul Neerhof
Plant Manager: John Kaser
Estimated Sales: $10-20 Million
Number Employees: 50-99
Square Footage: 125000

18415 (HQ)Advanced Labelworx Inc
1006 Larson Dr
Oak Ridge, TN 37830-8013
864-224-2122
Fax: 865-813-9918
marketing@advancedlabelworx.com
www.advancedlabelworx.com
Manufacturer and exporter of pressure sensitive paper labels and tapes

President: Lana Sellers
CFO: Clyde Duncan
HR Executive: Dan Piper
dpiper@advancedlabelworx.com
Quality Control: Gabrina Kelly
Number Employees: 50-99
Square Footage: 120000
Type of Packaging: Bulk

18416 Advanced Micro Controls
20 Gear Dr
Terryville, CT 06786

860-585-1254
Fax: 860-584-1973 sales@amci.com
www.amci.com
Hardware and software for packaging machinery
President: William Herbs
VP: Peter Serv
Contact: Laureen Archer
larcher@amci.com
Estimated Sales: $20-50 Million
Number Employees: 20-49
Brands:
 Ez Pack

18417 Advanced Organics
701 W Johnson St
Upper Sandusky, OH 43351

419-209-0216
Fax: 419-209-5010
Organic waste disposal service, sanitation
President: Doug Craig
Estimated Sales: $2.5-5 000,000
Number Employees: 20-49
Type of Packaging: Bulk

18418 Advanced Packaging Techniques Corporation
393 Bentley Place
Buffalo Grove, IL 60089-2500

847-808-9227
Fax: 630-887-0771
Packaging machinery soces consultants
President: Barbara Bloom
Number Employees: 2

18419 Advanced Plastic Coating Svc
1407 Corporate Dr
Parsons, KS 67357-4964

620-421-1660
Fax: 620-421-1662 adpowdergreg@par1.net
Custom manufacturer of plastic coated wire products including trays, ice cream cup holders and condiment holders for drive-in car service
President: Don Alexander
CFO: Don Alexander
R&D: Don Alexander
Quality Control: Don Alexander
Number Employees: 10-19
Square Footage: 40000
Brands:
 Serv-A-Car
 Wire Rite

18420 Advanced Poly-PackagingInc
1331 Emmitt Rd
Akron, OH 44306-3807

330-785-4000
Fax: 330-785-4010 800-754-4403
sales@advancedpoly.com www.advancedpoly.com
Bags including pre-opened and printed polyfilm and printers, ribbon and packaging equipment including automatic bagging
President: Stewart Baker
stewart@advancedpoly.com
VP of Sales: Stuart Baker
National Sales Manager: Dan Moute
Estimated Sales: $20-50 Million
Number Employees: 100-249
Brands:
 Advanced Polybagger

18421 Advanced Process Solutions
914 Springdale Dr
Jeffersonville, IN 47130

812-280-7450
888-294-8118
info@gotoaps.com
Provide food and beverage manufacturers with process engineering designs for aspetic, extended shelf life, pasteurization, hot fill, batching, blending and CIP equipment.

18422 Advanced Separation Technologies
5315 Great Oak Drive
Lakeland, FL 33815-3113

863-687-4460
Fax: 863-687-9362
Ion exchange, biotechnology, chromatography, fermentation, separators
President: Robert O'Brian
Estimated Sales: $5-10 Million
Number Employees: 60

18423 Advanced Separations andProcess Systems
6111 Pepsi Way
Windsor, WI 53598-9642

608-846-1130
Fax: 608-846-1144 800-879-8461
Software, systems integrator, membrane systems, resource recovery, separation equipment
Number Employees: 120

18424 Advanced Software Designs
1350 Elbridge Payne Rd Ste 150
Chesterfield, MO 63017

636-532-6021
Fax: 636-532-2935 info@asdsoftware.com
www.asdsoftware.com
Formula management software for nutritional labeling, production assistance and quality control measures
President: Ray Cook
Marketing Director: Stephanie Hanebrink
Account Executive: Ted Pliakos
Contact: Tom Galczynski
tom_galczynski@asdsoftware.com
Estimated Sales: $5-10 Million
Number Employees: 10-19
Brands:
 Product Vision

18425 Advanced Surfaces Corp
3355 Liberty Rd
Villa Rica, GA 30180

800-963-4632
www.advancedsurfacescorp.com
Specializing in flooring for the food and beverage industries.
President: Paul Patuka
paul@advancedsurfacescorp.com
Owner: Kerry Patuka
Year Founded: 1997
Estimated Sales: $5.67 million

18426 Advanced Uniflo Technologies
1850 N Ohio Ave
Wichita, KS 67214-1530

316-688-0000
Fax: 316-267-3387 800-688-0400
uniflo@gplains.com
Conveyor systems including small package, pallet handling, belt, chain, live roller and accumulation; also, steel fabrication services available
CEO: Steve Nulty
Sales Manager: Chuck Driskell
Marketing Technical Specialist: Brenda Salvati
Estimated Sales: $10-20 Million
Number Employees: 50-99
Square Footage: 160000
Brands:
 Uniflo

18427 Advantage Puck Technologies
1 Plastics Rd # 6
Corry, PA 16407-8538

814-664-4810
Fax: 814-663-6081 sales@advantagepuck.com
www.advantagepuck.com
Manufacturer and exporter of plastic product carriers for assembly line filling
President: Kurt Sieber
Estimated Sales: $1-2.5 Million
Number Employees: 1-4
Brands:
 Puck

18428 Advantage Puck Technologies
1 Plastics Rd # 6
Corry, PA 16407-8538

814-664-4810
Fax: 814-663-6081 800-396-7825
Sales@AdvantagePuck.com
www.advantagepuck.com
Pucks and puck handling machinery

Number Employees: 1-4

18429 Advantec Process Systems
95 Wyngate Dr
Newnan, GA 30265

770-253-1021
Fax: 770-251-3437
www.advantecprocesssystems.com
Supplier of process instrumentation for the food industry.
President: James Camp

18430 Advantek
7900 West 78th Street
Suite 180
Eden Prairie, MN 55439

952-746-9850
Fax: 952-938-1800 www.advantek.com
President: Bruce Bratten
CEO: Bruce Batten
CFO: Mike Eggers
Owner: Jared Koll
Quality Control: Mike Miller
Contact: Elena Nemirovsky
elena.nemirovsky@advantek.com
Number Employees: 250-499

18431 Advantus Corp.
12276 San Jose Blvd
Building 618
Jacksonville, FL 32223

904-482-0091
Fax: 904-482-0099 www.mcgillinc.com
Manufacturer and exporter of coin changers
President: Wayne Schwartzman
R&D: Becky McDaniel
VP Sales: Jim Booth
Estimated Sales: $5-10 Million
Number Employees: 10-19
Square Footage: 260000

18432 Advent Machine Co
6815 E Washington Blvd
Commerce, CA 90040-1905

323-728-5367
Fax: 323-728-2443 800-846-7716
info@adventmachine.net www.adventmachine.net
Pressure-sensitive or plain paper labels
Owner: Richard G Ealy
rgealy@fjsmith.com
Estimated Sales: $1-3 Million
Number Employees: 5-9

18433 Adwest Technologies
151 Trapping Brook Rd
Wellsville, NY 14895

585-593-1405
Fax: 585-593-6614
Air pollution control systems
President: Jack Preston
Sales: Brian Cannon
Number Employees: 50-100
Parent Co: Adwest Technologies

18434 Aei Corp
2641 Du Bridge Ave
Irvine, CA 92606-5001

949-474-3070
Fax: 949-474-0559
sales@patiocomfortheaters.com
www.patio-comfort.com
Outdoor and infrared patio heaters and outdoor heating equipment
Owner: Pete Arnold
p.arnold@aeicorporation.com
CFO: Fred Speicher
Estimated Sales: $5-10 Million
Number Employees: 10-19
Brands:
 Ducane
 Infratech
 Pgs
 Profire
 Sunglo
 Sunpak

18435 Aep Industries Inc.
125 Phillips Ave
South Hackensack, NJ 07606

201-641-6600
Fax: 201-807-6801 800-999-2374
www.aepinc.com
Plastic packaging film.

President/CEO/Chairman of the Board: J. Brendan
Barba
Managing Principal: Kenneth Avia
Executive VP/Finance/CFO: Paul M. Feeney
Vice President-Finance: Richard E. Davis
Vice President and Treasurer: James B. Rafferty
Executive Vice President, Sales/Marketin: John J.
Powers
Contact: Glenny Adames
adamesg@aepinc.com
Executive Vice President, Operations: Paul C.
Vegliante
Senior Vice President-Manufacturing: David J. Cron

18436 Aeration Industries Intl LLC
4100 Peavey Rd
Chaska, MN 55318-2353

952-448-6789
Fax: 952-448-7293 800-328-8287
aii@aireo2.com www.aireo2.com
Manufactures waste water treatment systems &
equipment, including the dual-process Triton aerator
and mixer to provide solutions for challenging
wastewater needs.
President: Daniel Durda
aiii@aireo2.com
VP: Brian Cohen
Estimated Sales: $10-20 Million
Number Employees: 20-49
Square Footage: 500000
Brands:
    Aire-02
    Aire-02 Triton
    Microfloat
    Turbo
    Unisystem

18437 Aeration Technologies Inc
11 Bartlet St
Andover, MA 01810-3655

978-475-6385
Fax: 978-475-6387 info@aertec.com
www.aertec.com
Wastewater aeration systems
Owner: R Gilbert
Office Manager: Linda Corners
Estimated Sales: Less Than $500,000
Number Employees: 1-4

18438 Aercology
8 Custom Drive
Old Saybrook, CT 06475-4009

860-399-7941
Fax: 860-399-7049 800-826-6123
www.aercology.com
Air filtration
Chairman, President, Chief Executive Off: Bill Cook
Estimated Sales: $5-10 Million
Number Employees: 50-100

18439 Aero Company
90 Mechanic St
Southbridge, MA 01550-2555

508-764-5500
Fax: 508-764-3350 800-678-4163
Manufactures and distributes safety equipment
President: Mike Mc Clain
Plant Manager: Earl Vancelette
Estimated Sales: $5-10 Million
Number Employees: 20-49
Parent Co: Aearo Company

18440 Aero Housewares
Ste C
600 Glynn St N
Fayetteville, GA 30214-6716

770-914-4240
Fax: 770-914-4236 www.aeroplastics.com
Injection molded plastic products including storage
containers, bowls, tableware, plates, tumblers, mi-
crowave containers, snack trays, etc
President: Jeffry Goldberg
CFO: Andrew Rice
Director Marketing/Sales: Heather Plaster
National Sales Manager: Steven Waugh
Regional Sales Manager: Keith Gouin
Estimated Sales: $20-50 Million
Number Employees: 20

18441 Aero Manufacturing Co
310 Allwood Rd
PO Box 1250
Clifton, NJ 07012-1786

973-473-5300
Fax: 973-473-3794 800-631-8378
sales@aeromfg.com www.aeromfg.com
Stainless steel sinks, tables, dishtables, cabinets,
shelving, and custom fabrication.
President/CEO: Wayne Phillips
kkreiss@aeromfg.com
Sales Exec: Ken Kreiss
Number Employees: 50-99
Square Footage: 600000
Brands:
    Aerospec

18442 (HQ)Aero Tec Laboratories/ATL
45 Spear Rd Industrial Park
Ramsey, NJ 07446-1251

201-825-1400
Fax: 201-825-1962 800-526-5330
atl@atlinc.com www.atlinc.com
Collapsible pillow-style storage tanks
President: Peter J Regna
VP, Contracts: I. Janeiro
VP, R&D: R. Clark
VP of Sales: David Dack
VP, Operations: L. Damico
Estimated Sales: $3-5 Million
Number Employees: 50-99
Square Footage: 280000
Other Locations:
    Aero Tec Laboratories/ATL
    Bletchley, Milton Keynes

18443 Aero-Motive Company
333 Knightsbridge Pkwy
Suite 200
Lincolnshire, IL 60069

847-353-2500
Fax: 847-353-2500 800-999-8559
wctechsup@molex.com
President: Micheal Gies
Number Employees: 100-249
Parent Co: Woodhead Industries

18444 Aero-Power Unitized Fueler
103 Smithtown Blvd
Smithtown, NY 11787

631-366-4362
Fax: 631-366-0905 info@areotank.com
www.areotank.com
Owner: Rudy Benit
Contact: Lou Benit
sales@areotank.com
Estimated Sales: $1-3 Million
Number Employees: 1-4

18445 AeroFreeze, Inc.
2551 Viking Way
Richmond, BC, BC V6V 1N4
Canada

604-278-4118
Fax: 604-278-4847 www.aerofreeze.com
Manufacturers of freezers, chillers and air cooling
products.

18446 Aerocon
1707 Langhorne Newtown Rd # 1
Langhorne, PA 19047

215-860-6056
Fax: 215-860-8606
Owner: Rosemary Caligiuri
Parent Co: Vac-U-Max

18447 Aerofreeze
P.O.Box 2439
Redmond, WA 98073

425-869-8889
Fax: 425-869-8839 www.aerofreeze.com
Freezing units, plate and belt freezers
Manager: Lars Johansson
Estimated Sales: $.5-1 000,000
Number Employees: 5-9

18448 Aerolator Systems
2716 Chamber Dr
Monroe, NC 28110

704-289-9585
Fax: 704-289-9580 800-843-8286
Hood systems; wholesaler/distributor of exhaust
fans; serving the food service market
President: Janet Griffen
Sales Manager: Steve Surratt

Estimated Sales: $10-20 Million
Number Employees: 50-99
Square Footage: 80000
Brands:
    Aerolator

18449 Aeromat Plastics Inc
801 Cliff Rd E # 104
Suite 104
Burnsville, MN 55337-1534

952-890-4697
Fax: 952-890-1814 888-286-8729
www.aero-mat.com
Manufacturer and exporter of plastic proofer trays
and machined plastic parts
President: Bruce Dahlke
bruce@aeromatplastics.com
Estimated Sales: $2.5 Million
Number Employees: 10-19
Square Footage: 34000

18450 Aeromix Systems
7135 Madison Ave W
Minneapolis, MN 55427

763-746-8400
Fax: 763-746-8408 800-879-3677
www.aeromix.com
Water and wastewater treatment equipment for the
municipal, industrial and freshwater markets. Also
offers a line of eco-friendly equipment that is com-
pletely powered by solar energy
President and CEO: Henry J. Charrabe
Contact: Limor Amar
lamar@nirosoft.com
Operations: Peter Gross
Estimated Sales: $5-10 Million
Number Employees: 25
Brands:
    Cyclone
    Hurricane
    Tornado
    Zephyr

18451 Aerotech Enterprise Inc
8511 Mulberry Rd
Chesterland, OH 44026

440-729-2616
Fax: 440-729-1620 amatic@aerotechcnc.com
www.aerotechcnc.com
Confectionery machinery
Owner: Andrea Maticci
Contact: Nicholas Tadic
ntadic@aerotechcnc.com
Office Manager: Elizabeth Krukowski
Estimated Sales: $500,000-$1 Million
Number Employees: 5-9

18452 Aerotech Laboratories
1501 W Knudsen Dr
Phoenix, AZ 85027

623-780-4800
Fax: 623-780-7695 800-651-4802
www.aerotechpk.com
Contact: Lori Thompson
al.yankulov@coat.com
Manager: Ben Sublasky

18453 (HQ)Aerovent Co
5959 Trenton Ln N
Minneapolis, MN 55442-3237

763-551-7500
Fax: 763-551-7501 aerovent_sales@aerovent.com
www.tcf.com
Industrial air handling equipment, fans and blowers
President: Zika Srejovic
CEO: Chuck Barry
cbarry@tcf.com
CEO: Chuck Barry
Marketing Manager: Timothy Clifford
Estimated Sales: $50-100 Million
Number Employees: 100-249
Brands:
    Axiad II
    Axico
    Axipal

18454 Aerovent Co
5959 Trenton Ln N
Minneapolis, MN 55442-3237

763-551-7500
Fax: 763-551-7501 aerovent_sales@aerovent.com
www.tcf.com
Manufacturer and exporter of fans

President: Charles Barry
CEO: Chuck Barry
cbarry@tcf.com
CFO: Julie Dale
VP Sales: Dave Laclerc
Estimated Sales: $50-75 Million
Number Employees: 100-249
Parent Co: Twin City Fan Company

18455 Aerowerks
6625 millcreek drive
Mississauga, ON L5M 5M4
Canada

905-363-6999
Fax: 905-363-6998 888-774-1616
aman@aero-werks.com www.aero-werks.com
Manufacturer and exporter of conveyors
President: Balbir Singh
Sales Manager: Aman Singh
Number Employees: 35
Parent Co: Aerotool
Brands:
  K-Flex Systems

18456 Aerzen USA Corp
108 Independence Way
Coatesville, PA 19320-1653

610-380-0244
Fax: 610-380-0278 800-444-1692
inquiries@aerzenusa.com www.aerzenusa.com
150 year old manufacturer of oil-free rotary lobe
blower packages and screw compressor packages
President: Michelle Abney
mabney@aerzenusa.com
CFO: Keith Rolfe
Marketing Manager: Ralph Wilton
Sales Manager: Darrel Hill
Production Manager: Steve Wark
Number Employees: 50-99
Square Footage: 60000
Parent Co: Aerzener/Maschinenfabrik

18457 Afassco
2244 Park Pl # C
Suite C
Minden, NV 89423-8632

775-783-3555
Fax: 775-783-3555 www.afassco.com
CEO: Don Schumaker
afassco@intercomm.com
Number Employees: 10-19

18458 Afeco
4300 West Bryn Mawr Ave
Chicago, IL 60646

773-478-9700
Fax: 773-478-8689 sales@cozzini.com
Contact: Bruce Keith
bkeith@afeco.com

18459 Affiliated Resource Inc
3839 N Western Ave
Chicago, IL 60618-3733

773-509-9300
Fax: 773-509-9929 800-366-9336
info@4ledsigns.com www.forledsigns.com
Manufacturer, wholesaler/distributor of indoor and
outdoor electronic signs
President: Stephen Stillman
stephen@yledsigns.com
National Sales Manager: Rick Markle
Regional Sales Manager: Pam Zayas
Estimated Sales: $1-3 Million
Number Employees: 1-4
Square Footage: 4000

18460 Aftermarket Specialties Inc
980 Cobb Place Blvd NW # 100
Kennesaw, GA 30144-4804

678-819-2274
Fax: 678-819-2275 800-438-5931
sales@aftermkt.com
Vending compressors, refrigeration compressors
President: Dallas Rohrer
CFO: Dallas Rohrer
Vice President: Dion Rohrer
Estimated Sales: $1-2.5 Million
Number Employees: 1-4

18461 Ag-Pak
8416 State Street
PO Box 304
Gasport, NY 14067

716-772-2651
Fax: 716-772-2555 info@agpak.com
www.agpak.com
Manufacturer and exporter of produce weighers and
bag fillers
President: Andy Currie
VP, Technical Support: Joe Gabree
Sales Manager: Greg Lureman
Plant Manager/ Engineering: Warren Farewell
Estimated Sales: Below $5 Million
Number Employees: 10-19

18462 AgTracker
2335 81st Ter
Vero Beach, FL 32966-1329

772-770-3293
Fax: 303-440-6162
Computer systems and software and weight control
systems
Estimated Sales: $1-5 000,000
Number Employees: 3

18463 Aggreko Rental
15600 J F Kennedy Blvd # 200
Houston, TX 77032-2343

281-848-1400
Fax: 713-852-4590 877-244-7356
aggreko@aggreko.com
As the world leader in temporary utility services we
are ready to satisfy your power, temperature and oil-
free compressed air needs. Our unique fleet of
equipment is custom designed and built for the rig-
ors of the diverse anddemanding temporary utility
industry
Manager: Gary Meador
gary.meador@aggreko.com
Estimated Sales: $.5-1 000,000
Number Employees: 20-49

18464 Agilysys, Inc.
1000 Windward Concourse
Suite 250
Alpharetta, GA 30005

770-810-7800
800-241-8768
sales@agilysys.com www.agilysys.com
A leading developer and marketer of proprietary enterprise software, services and solutions to the hospitality and retail industries. Specializes in
market-leading point-of-sale, property managerment,
inventory & procurement and mobile& wireless so-
lutions that are designed to streamline operations,
improve efficiency and enhance the consumer's
experience.
President & CEO: James Dennedy
Sr. VP, General Counsel & Secretary: Kyle C.
Badger
Senior Vice President, Chief Financial O: Janine
Seebeck
Senior Vice President, General Counsel a: Kyle C.
Badger
Senior Vice President and Chief Technolo: Larry
Steinberg
Sr. Vice President & General Manager: Paul Civils
Senior Vice President of Sales and Marke: Michael
Buckham-White
VP of Sales: Tony Ross
Estimated Sales: $5-10 Million
Number Employees: 50-99
Square Footage: 80000
Parent Co: Agilysys/Alpharetta GA
Brands:
  Infogenesis Gsa
  Infogenesis Hospitality
  Infogenesis Iqs
  Infogenesis Its
  Infogenesis Ticketing

18465 Agrana Fruit US Inc
6850 Southpointe Pkwy
Cleveland, OH 44141-3260

440-546-1199
Fax: 440-546-0038 800-477-3788
www.agrana.us
Sugar; starch; and processed fruits.
President/CEO: Johann Marihart
Board Member: Fritz Gattermeyer
Estimated Sales: $10-20 Million
Number Employees: 50-99
Parent Co: SIAS MPA

Type of Packaging: Food Service, Private Label,
Bulk

18466 Agri-Business Services
PO Box 1237
Lakeville, MN 55044-1237

952-469-6767

18467 Agri-Equipment International
493 Colonial Trace Dr
Longs, SC 29568

843-283-2583
Fax: 864-343-0076 877-550-4709
www.agri-equipmentonline.com
Manufacturer and wholesaler/distributor of release
(interleaver) sheets, thermometers, temperature data
loggers and probes
President: Tom Gaffney
VP Sales: Gary Gaffney
Estimated Sales: $1-2.5,000,000
Number Employees: 1-4

18468 Agri-Northwest
PO Box 230
Hope, AR 71802-0230

870-777-7105
Equipment Supply
Estimated Sales: Under $500,000
Number Employees: 20-49
Parent Co: Agri-Northwest

18469 Agri-Sales Assoc Inc
209 Louise Ave
Nashville, TN 37203-1811

615-329-1141
Fax: 615-329-2770 800-251-1141
info@agri-sales.com www.agri-sales.com
Manufacturer's Representative Group
President/Founder: Jerry Bellar
president@agri-sales.com
VP: Phillip Ferrell
Estimated Sales: Less than $500,000
Number Employees: 5-9

18470 AgriFiber Solutions
1011 Campus Dr.
Mundelein, IL 60060

847-549-6002
Fax: 847-549-6028 sales@agrfbr.com
www.agrifibersolutions.com
Offers agriculture solutions for corn and oat fiber,
including cost reduction, moisture retention, nutri-
tional value, gluten-free options, and more.
Senior Managing Partner: Jonathan Kahn
Type of Packaging: Food Service

18471 AgriTech
1989 W 5th Avenue
Columbus, OH 43212-1912

614-488-2772
Fax: 715-335-4390 agritech@iwaynet.net
Consultation firm offering market research and as-
sessment, operations analysis, technology transfer
and planning; specializing in food processing, agri-
cultural development, grains, dairy products and
foreign markets
President: William Riddle
Estimated Sales: less than $500,000
Number Employees: 1

18472 Agribuys Incorporated
3625 Del Amo Blvd
Suite 210
Torrance, CA 90503

310-944-9655
Fax: 310-944-9665 877-499-3052
Online supply chain integrator for the food industry
Quality Control: Le Vu
Manager: B J Asneck
Number Employees: 20-49

18473 Agricultural Data Systems
24331 Los Arboles Dr
Laguna Niguel, CA 92677-2196

949-363-5353
Fax: 949-495-7066 800-328-2246
sales@touchmemory.com www.touchmemory.com
Automatic harvesting and data collection equipment
President: Carl Gennaro
boss@touchmemory.com
VP: Carl Gennaro
National Sales Manager/Marketing: Paul Geisterfer
Estimated Sales: $3-5,000,000
Number Employees: 10-19

18474 Agricultural Research Service

Jamie L. Whitten Building
Washington, SW 20250

202-720-3656

Fax: 202-720-5427 www.ars.usda.gov

Government research center for fresh and processed foods; food development services available
Manager: Wendy H Kramer
Technical Transfer Coordinator: C Crawford
Director: John Cherry
Number Employees: 250-499
Parent Co: Agricultural Research Service/US Department of Agriculture

18475 Agriculture Consulting Services

New York City, NY

347-709-7587
jeffrey@agritecture.com
www.agritecture.com

Services include farm design, economic analysis, market research, techical assessment, and more.
Managing Director: Henry Gordon-Smith
Director of Business Development: Jeffrey Landau
Director of Operations: Yara Nagi *Year Founded:* 2014

18476 Agripac

PO Box 5110
Denver, CO 80217-5110

503-363-9255

Fax: 503-371-5666

Packaging of canned and frozen vegetables and fruit products
Number Employees: 150

18477 AgroFresh

510-513 Walnut St.
Ste. 1350
Philadelphia, PA 19106

866-850-6846
fusafna@agrofresh.com www.agrofresh.com

Offers technologies and solutions that support growers, packers, retailers, exporters and marketers. Focus is on fruits and vegetables.
CEO: Jordi Ferre
VP & General Counsel: Thomas Ermi
CFO: Graham Miao
Year Founded: 1996
Number Employees: 200-500

18478 Agropur MSI, LLC

2340 Enterprise Ave
La Crosse, WI 54603

800-359-2345
ingredients@agropur.com
www.agropuringredients.com

Supply the food, beverage and nutritional industries with contract manufacturing and private labelling services. Manufacture ingredients and additives: anticaking agents, dairy ingredients, egg replacers, gums, gydrocolloidsstabilizers, nutraceuticals, organic ingredients, proteins, whey and whey products.
Marketing & Communications Manager: Corrie Drellack

18479 Agspring

5101 College Blvd.
Leawood, KS 66211

913-333-3035
inquiry@agspring.com
agspring.com

Services include storage & handling, marketing & distribution, light processing, logistics, and risk management. Market focus is on grains & oilseeds, livestock feed ingredients, and food ingredients.
CEO: Mark Beemer
CFO: Bruce Chapin
VP, Merchandising: Brian Aust
VP, Marketing & Customer Engagement: Bradford Warner
VP, Sales: Mike Hallman
Director of Corporate Safety: Chris Stanger
AVP, Transportation & Supply Chain: Josh Skatvold
Plant Manager: Brady Eckart
Year Founded: 2012
Number Employees: 200-500

18480 Agtron Inc

9395 Double R Blvd
Reno, NV 89521-5919

775-850-4600

Fax: 775-850-4611 agtron@aol.com
www.agtron.net

Manufacturer and exporter of spectrophotometers used in the food industry to measure the degree of roasted, baked or fried goods or color grading of most food products.
President: Carl Staub
agtron@aol.com
CEO: Mike Rowley
CFO: Mike Rowley
Sales/Marketing: Kim Franke
Estimated Sales: $1-2.5 Million
Number Employees: 5-9
Square Footage: 80000
Brands:
  Agtron

18481 Agworld

1601 Pelican Lakes Pt.
Windsor, CO 80550

724-249-6753
www.agworld.com

Offers solutions and consultation concerning crops, farming staff, operation management, pre-season planning and more.
Co-Founder & President: Zach Sheely
Co-Founder & CEO: Doug Fitch
Year Founded: 2007
Number Employees: 65-100

18482 Ahlstrom Filtration LLC

215 Nebo Rd
P.O. Box 1708
Madisonville, KY 42431

270-821-0140

Fax: 270-326-3290 www.ahlstrom-munksjo.com

Filters, wallcovers, wipes, flooring, labels and food packaging.
President & CEO: Hans Sohlstrom
Deputy CEO & CFO: Sakari Ahdekivi
EVP, Filtration & Performance: Daniele Borlatto
EVP, Legal & General Counsel: Andreas Elving
EVP, People & Safety: Tarja Takko
Year Founded: 1851
Estimated Sales: $2.2 Billion
Number Employees: 6,000
Square Footage: 5000
Parent Co: Ahlstrom-Munksjo
Type of Packaging: Food Service

18483 Ahlstrom Nonwovens LLC

2 Elm St
Windsor Locks, CT 06096-2335

860-654-8300

Fax: 860-654-8301 www.ahlstrom.com

Tea and coffee industry filters (paper), pouch materials (cellophane, paper, films), teabag paper
Estimated Sales: K
Number Employees: 5000-9999
Parent Co: Ahlstrom-Munksjo

18484 Aibmr Life Sciences

4117 S Meridian
#202
Puyallup, WA 98373-3697

253-286-2888

Fax: 253-286-2451 info@aibmr.com
www.aibmr.com

Consulting firm specializing in nutraceutical research and product development.
Vice President: Connie Knapp
connie@aibmr.com
Chief Scientific Officer: John Endres
Vice President: Connie Knapp
connie@aibmr.com
Senior Director of Research: Alexander Schauss
Chief Operating/Financial Officer: Laura Schauss
Number Employees: 10-19

18485 Aidco International

P.O.Box 15339
Cincinnati, OH 45215-339

Fax: 517-265-2131 www.aidcoint.com

President: Salh Khan
Estimated Sales: $5-10000,000
Number Employees: 45

18486 Aidi International Hotels of America

1050-17th Street NW
Suite 600
Washington, DC 20036-

202-331-9299

Fax: 202-478-0367 sales@royalregencyhotels.com
www.royalregencyhotels.com

Engineering and marketing consultant specializing in construction, management, decoration and operations in overseas hotels; wholesaler/distributor and exporter of equipment, furniture and food
President: Ghassane Aidi
Chairman: Adnan Aidi
VP: Samia Aidi
Number Employees: 200
Square Footage: 28000
Parent Co: Aidi Group

18487 Aigner Index

P.O.Box 4084
New Windsor, NY 12553-0084

845-562-4510

Fax: 845-562-2638 800-242-3919
holdex@frontiernet.net

High quality plastic insertable label holders
President: Mark Aigner
maigner@aignerindex.com
Estimated Sales: $5-10 Million
Number Employees: 10-19

18488 Aim Blending Technologies Inc

4196 Suffolk Way
Pleasanton, CA 94588

925-484-5000

Fax: 925-484-5007 800-328-6060
pahelman@comcast.net www.aimblending.com

Premium quality dry powder blending equipment, ribbon, paddle, fluidicers, continuous, V, cone and numerous other dry powder blender.
President: Phil Helman
Marketing Director: Kassandra Cunningham
Sales Director: Phil Helman
Contact: Jesse Dornan
jdornan@aimblending.com
Estimated Sales: $5-10 000,000
Number Employees: 20-49
Square Footage: 20000

18489 Air Barge Company

26807 Springcreek Rd
Rancho Palos Verdes, CA 90275

310-378-2928

President: Carol Vaughen
R & D: Jack Vaughen
Estimated Sales: $5-10 Million
Number Employees: 1-4

18490 Air Economy Corporation

PO.Box 29
Flemington, NJ 08822-0029

908-782-8888

18491 Air Liquide USA, LLC

9811 Katy Freeway
Houston, TX 77024

713-624-8000
www.airliquide.com

Complete line of industrial gases, develops custom freezing, chilling, or gas packaging systems.
Chairman & CEO: Benoit Pottier
Executive Vice President: Michael Graff
Executive Vice President: Guy Salzgeber
Executive Vice President: Fabienne Lecorvaisier
Executive Vice President: Francois Jackow
CEO, Air Liquide USA, LLC: Sue Ellerbusch
Director, Marketing Supply Chain: Genevieve Matte
Chief Customer Officer: Rich Jahr
Year Founded: 1902
Estimated Sales: Over $1 Billion
Number Employees: 67,000
Parent Co: Air Liquide S.A.
Other Locations:
  San Francisco CA
  Los Angeles CA
  Dallas TX
  Chicago IL
  Baton Rouge LA
  Philadelphia PA

18492 Air Locke Dock Seal
549 W Indianola Ave
Youngstown, OH 44511-2460
330-788-6504
Fax: 330-788-6705 800-538-2388
www.airlocke.com
President: Larry O Neal
Marketing: Marijo Rischar
Estimated Sales: $1-5 Million
Number Employees: 5-9
Parent Co: O'Neal Tarpaulin & Awning Company

18493 Air Logic Power Systems
1745 S. 38th Street
Suite 100
Milwaukee, WI 53215
414-671-3332
Fax: 414-671-6645 800-325-8717
info@alpsleak.com www.alpsleak.com
On-line leak detection equipment for the plastic container manufacturing industry.
President: Roger Tambling
Sales Manager: Scott Heins
Contact: Pierre Aterianus
pierrea@alpsleak.com
Estimated Sales: $5-10 Million
Number Employees: 20-49
Square Footage: 80000
Brands:
Alps Model 7385
Alps Smart Test Module
Alps Sx-Flex
Alps Vision Plus

18494 Air Pak Products & Services
2976 Forsyth Road
Winter Park, FL 32792-6628
407-678-1847
Fax: 407-679-5655 800-824-7725
www.air-pakpsi.com
Designer/builder providing restaurant remodeling, renovation, cabinetry, millwork and HVAC services
President: David W McLeod
VP: Robert Nippes
Purchasing Manager: Sulyn McLeod
Estimated Sales: $20-50 Million
Number Employees: 100-249

18495 Air Products & Chemicals Inc
7201 Hamilton Blvd
Allentown, PA 18195-1501
610-481-4911
Fax: 610-481-5900 800-224-2724
www.airproducts.com
Gas production, storage, and handling equipment, including food freezers, oxy-fuel burners, and heat exchangers.
Chairman/President/CEO: Seifi Ghasemi
Executive Vice President: Dr. Samir Serhan
serhansj@airproducts.com
EVP/Chief Financial Officer: M. Scott Crocco
SVP/Chief Human Resources Officer: Victoria Brifo
EVP/General Counsel/Secretary: Sean Major
Year Founded: 1940
Estimated Sales: $9.8 Billion
Number Employees: 15,500
Other Locations:
Air Products and Chemicals Inc
Tempe AZ
Air Products and Chemicals Inc
Geismar LA
Air Products and Chemicals Inc
Carlsbad CA
Air Products and Chemicals Inc
Austin TX
Air Products and Chemicals Inc
Fountain Valley CA
Air Products and Chemicals Inc
Houston TX
Air Products and Chemicals Inc
Santa Clara CA
Air Products and Chemicals Inc
Irving TX
Brands:
Crustplus
Cryo Batch
Cyro Rotary
Cryo Dip
Cryo Quick
Freshpak
Vt Tune

18496 Air Quality Engineering
7140 Northland Dr N
Minneapolis, MN 55428-1520
888-883-3273
Fax: 763-531-9900 800-328-0787
info@air-quality-eng.com
www.air-quality-eng.com
Manufacturer and exporter of electronic and media air cleaners, parts and accessories
President & CEO: Heidi Oas
VP, Sales: Ira Golden
Estimated Sales: $5-10 Million
Number Employees: 50-75
Square Footage: 142800
Brands:
Smokemaster

18497 Air System Components Inc
605 Shiloh Rd
Plano, TX 75074
972-212-4888
www.airsysco.com
Market-leading supplier of heating, air conditioning and ventilation system components for commercial, industrial, and residential applications.
Estimated Sales: $212 Million
Number Employees: 1000-4999
Parent Co: Air Distribution Technologies Inc.
Brands:
Titus
Krueger
Tuttle & Bailey
Pennbarry
Superior Rex
Trion Indoor Air Quality
Koch Filter

18498 Air Technical Industries
7501 Clover Ave.
Mentor, OH 44060
440-951-5191
Fax: 440-953-9237 888-857-6265
ati@airtechnical.com www.airtechnical.com
Manufacturer and exporter of material handling equipment including floor cranes, fork lifts and pallet inverters and handlers; also, automatic wrappers and hydraulic lift tables
President: Pero Novak
VP: Jane Goff
Contact: Chad Aschbacher
chad@airtechnical.com
Estimated Sales: $10-20 Million
Number Employees: 50-99
Square Footage: 240000
Brands:
Articularm
Econo-Verter
Husky Master
Low Profile E-Z Wrap
Universal-Lift
V-Master

18499 Air-Knife Systems/PaxtonProducts Corporation
10125 Carver Rd
Cincinnati, OH 45242
513-891-7485
Fax: 513-891-4092 800-441-7475
sales@paxtonproducts.com
www.paxtonproducts.com
We off custom designed, complete air knife drying and blow-off cleaning systems.
General Manager: Barbara Stefl
Engineering Manager: Steve Pucciani
Sales Engineer: Jeem Newland
Operations Manager: Stan Coley
Number Employees: 30

18500 Air-Lec Industries, Inc
3300 Commercial Ave
Madison, WI 53714
608-244-4754
Fax: 608-246-7676 info@air-lec.com
www.air-lec.com
Quality door operating devices, track systems and door hardware, providing industry with reliable, productivity enhancing products since 1921.
President: John Lunenschloss
Contact: John Ganahl
john.ganahl@air-lec.com

Estimated Sales: $10-20,000,000
Number Employees: 10-19
Square Footage: 30000
Brands:
Air-Lec
Zephyr

18501 (HQ)Air-Scent International
290 Alpha Drive RIDC Industrial Park
Pittsburgh, PA 15238
412-252-2000
Fax: 412-252-1010 800-247-0770
info@airscent.com www.airscent.com
Manufacturer and exporter of air fresheners, sanitizers and odor control systems including aerosol dispensers and refills; also, aerosol insecticides
President: Arnold Zlotnik
Estimated Sales: Below $5 Million
Number Employees: 50-99
Square Footage: 160000
Brands:
Air-Scent
Ch
Nature Scent
Scent Flo
Surcotta

18502 Air/Tak Inc
107 W Main St
Worthington, PA 16262-2303
724-297-3416
Fax: 724-297-5189 airtak@airtak.com
www.airtak.com
President: Donald Burk
Manager: Gary Byers
gbyers@airtak.com
Estimated Sales: $3-5 Million
Number Employees: 10-19

18503 Airblast
2050 Pepper St
Alhambra, CA 91801-3162
626-576-0144
Fax: 626-289-2548 866-424-7252
sales@airblastinc.com www.airblastinc.com
President: Carl Von Wolffradt
Estimated Sales: Below 1 Million
Number Employees: 5-9

18504 Aire-Mate
17335 Us 31 N
Westfield, IN 46074-9119
317-896-2561
Fax: 317-896-3788 www.airemate.com
President: Conrad Mc Ginnis
Estimated Sales: $3-5 Million
Number Employees: 5-9

18505 Airflex
9919 Clinton Rd
Cleveland, OH 44144-1077
216-281-2211
Fax: 216-281-3890 edlunder@eaton.com
www.airflex.com
President: Alexander M Cutler
Executive: Ed Luehring
Estimated Sales: $20-50 Million
Number Employees: 100-249
Parent Co: Eaton Corporation

18506 Airfloat LLC
2230 N Brush College Rd
Decatur, IL 62526-5522
217-423-6001
Fax: 217-422-1049 800-888-0018
sales@airfloat.com www.airfloat.com
Manufacturer and designer of bulk handling machinery, conveyors and bucket elevators for the food industry
President: Jason Stoecker
Marketing Manager: Gary Mollohan
Director of Sales: Ken Adkins
Estimated Sales: $10-20 Million
Number Employees: 20-49

18507 Airfloat LLC
2230 N Brush College Rd
Decatur, IL 62526-5522
217-423-6001
Fax: 217-422-1049 800-888-0018
sales@alignprod.com
Manufacturer and exporter of lift, tilt and turn tables
President: Jason Stoecker
Marketing Manager: Kara Demarjian

Estimated Sales: $10-20 Million
Number Employees: 20-49

18508 Airflow Sciences Corp
12190 Hubbard St
Livonia, MI 48150-1737

734-525-0300
Fax: 734-525-0303 asc@airflowsciences.com
www.airflowsciences.com
Consultant specializing in product development testing, process trouble shooting, dryer, mixer, cooking, chilling and freezing reactions and computer simulations of heat transfer, fluid flow and chemical reactions
Manager: James C Paul
paul@ricardo.com
CEO: Robert Nelson
VP Western Office: James Paul
Manager: James Paul
paul@ricardo.com
Estimated Sales: $2.5-5 Million
Number Employees: 10-19
Square Footage: 16000
Parent Co: Airflow Science Corporation

18509 Airgas Carbonic
6340 Sugarloaf Pkwy Ste 300
Duluth, GA 30097

770-717-2200
Fax: 770-717-2222 800-241-5882
www.airgas.com
Water treatment, temperature controls, gas packaging, refrigeration systems
President: Phil Filer
Contact: John Cochran
john.cochran@airgas.com
Estimated Sales: $50 Million
Number Employees: 50-99

18510 Airgas Carbonic Inc
2530 Sever Rd # 300
Suite 300
Lawrenceville, GA 30043-4022

770-717-2200
Fax: 770-717-2222 www.airgas.com
Water pollution treatment and monitoring systems, cryogenics, carbon dioxide and nitrogen refrigeration systems, dry ice, blocks or pellets, freeze tunnels, refrigeration systems, trucks and trailers
President: Philip J Filer
philip.filer@airgas.com
Estimated Sales: $.5-1 million
Number Employees: 50-99

18511 Airlite Plastics Co
P.O. Box 8400
Omaha, NE 68108-0400

402-341-7300
888-228-3506
info@airliteplastics.com www.airliteplastics.com
Plastic injection molding and printing manufacturer product line; includes drink cups, polystyrene coolers, ICF (Insulating Concrete Form) building blocks, and customized plastic products. Also, in-mold labeling, shrink sleeving and offset printing.
Vice President & General Manager: John Bungert
Chief Financial Officer: Patrick Kenealy
Director of Engineering: Thomas Kinsella
Safety Manager: Jim Steele
Estimated Sales: $100-125 Million
Number Employees: 1000-4999
Square Footage: 325000

18512 (HQ)Airmaster Fan Co
1300 Falahee Rd # 5
Jackson, MI 49203-3548

517-764-2300
Fax: 517-764-3838 800-255-3084
sales@airmasterfan.com www.airmasterfan.com
Industrial and commercial fans, stainless steel fan guards, aluminum air circulator blades and explosion proof fans
President: Richard Stone
CEO: Robert Lazebrick
CFO: Ronald Johnson
Marketing: Maryann Talbot
Director Of Sales: Mike Pignataro
Product Manager: Mike Hemer
Estimated Sales: $10-20 Million
Number Employees: 20-49
Square Footage: 1500000
Brands:
　Airmaster

Chelsea
Nova
Powerline

18513 Airomat Corp
2916 Engle Rd
Fort Wayne, IN 46809-1198

260-747-7408
Fax: 260-747-7409 800-348-4905
airomat@airomat.com
Manufacturer and exporter of safety and fatigue relief matting
President: Joanne K Feasel
VP: Jody Feasel
Marketing/Sales: Claudia Logan
Operations Manager: Pam Peters
Plant Manager: John Solga
Estimated Sales: $1-3,000,000
Number Employees: 5-9
Square Footage: 6000
Brands:
　Airomat

18514 Airosol Co Inc
1206 Illinois St
Neodesha, KS 66757-1483

620-325-2666
Fax: 620-325-2602 800-633-9576
www.airosol.com
Aerosol propelled drain opener
Owner: Carl Stratemeier
Sales Coordinator: Linda Cushman
carls@airosol.com
Estimated Sales: $20-50 Million
Number Employees: 20-49
Parent Co: Airosol Company
Brands:
　Power Plumber

18515 (HQ)Airosol Co Inc
1101 Illinois St
Neodesha, KS 66757-1475

620-325-2666
Fax: 620-325-2602 800-633-9576
www.airosol.com
Manufacturer and exporter of insecticides and counter cleaners
President: Carl G Stratemeier
Marketing Specialist: Jim Leiker
VP Sales/Marketing: Don Gillen
Contact: Tim Bell
tbell@airosol.com
Estimated Sales: $20-50 Million
Number Employees: 10-19
Square Footage: 80000
Brands:
　Aero-Counter
　Blacknight

18516 Airsan Corp
4554 W Woolworth Ave
Milwaukee, WI 53218-1497

414-353-5800
Fax: 414-353-8402 800-558-5494
Manufacturer and exporter of filters including air and restaurant grease extractor
Owner: Randy Perry
Quality Control: Kurt Gleisner
VP Sales: Kurt Glaisner
randyperry@airsan.com
Estimated Sales: $5-10 Million
Number Employees: 10-19
Type of Packaging: Food Service
Brands:
　Airsan

18517 Ajinomoto Heartland Inc
8430 W Bryn Mawr Ave
Suite 650
Chicago, IL 60631-3421

773-380-7000
Fax: 773-380-7006 www.lysine.com
Feed-grade amino acids
President: Daniel Bercovici
Number Employees: 10-19
Parent Co: Ajinomoto Co., Inc.
Type of Packaging: Bulk
Brands:
　L-Lysine
　L-Threonine
　AjiLys®
　L-Tryptophan

AjiPro®-L
L-Valine

18518 Akers Group
1450 East North Blvd.
Suite 8
Leesburg, FL 34748

352-787-4112
Fax: 201-475-7667 877-253-7744
kendra@akersmediagroup.com
www.akersmediagroup.com
Computerized software for flavor and fragrance formula
Manager: Robert Sobel

18519 Akicorp
20145 NE 21st CT
N Miami Beach, FL 33179

786-426-5750
ysaac@akinin.com

Oilseeds
Manager: Ysaac Akinin
yakinin@akinin.com

18520 Akro-Mils
P.O.Box 989
Akron, OH 44309

330-848-3773
Fax: 330-761-6133 www.myersindustries.com
Molded plastic bins, cabinets and trays
President: John Orr
CFO: Gregory Stodnick
Quality Control: Guy Lyon
Marketing Director: Joseph Gluzyn
Estimated Sales: $75-100 Million
Number Employees: 1,000-4,999

18521 (HQ)Akron Cotton Products
437 W Cedar St
Akron, OH 44307-2321

330-434-7171
Fax: 330-434-7150 800-899-7173
akroncotton@akroncotton.com
www.akroncotton.com
Manufacturer filter bags: beer and winemaking
President: Michael L Zwick
mike@akroncotton.com
VP: Shawn Zwick
Estimated Sales: $1-3 Million
Number Employees: 10-19
Square Footage: 52000

18522 Alabama Bag Co Inc
230 Broadway Ave
Talladega, AL 35160-3659

256-362-4921
Fax: 256-362-1801 800-888-4921
www.alabamabag.com
Manufacturer and exporter of food bags, twine, uniforms, aprons, butcher frocks, disposable wipers, stockinettes, elastic netting, knit gloves, ham tubings, shrouds, money bags, courier bags, transit bags, locking bags and coin andcurrency bags, Poly money bags, coin wrappers, bill straps, tags, security seals.
President: Larkin Coker
wc@alabamabag.com
Number Employees: 10-19
Brands:
　U.S. Bag

18523 Alabama Power Company
PO Box 242
Birmingham, AL 35292

888-430-5787
www.alabamapower.com
Provides electricity to parts of Alabama and operates appliance stores.
Chairman/President/CEO: Mark Crosswhite
EVP/CFO: Philip Raymond
Customer Services: Gregory Barker
EVP, External Affairs: Zeke Smith
Year Founded: 1906
Estimated Sales: $6.1 Billion
Number Employees: 6,613
Parent Co: Southern Company

18524 Aladdin Label Inc
11301 W Forest Home Ave
Franklin, WI 53132-1402
USA

262-544-4455
Fax: 414-425-2384 www.aladdinlabel.com

Display fixtures, specialty food packaging: giftwrap, label, boxes, containers
President: Tony Heinl
Vice President: Rick Lichter
rickl@aladdinlabe.com
Sales Representative: Samantha Forster
Plant Manager: Aaron Dumke
Number Employees: 50-99

18525 Aladdin Temp-Rite, LLC
250 East Main Street
Hendersonville, TN 37075-2521
615-537-3600
Fax: 615-537-3634 800-888-8018
info@aladdin-atr.com www.aladdintemprite.com
Manufacturer and exporter of serving and heating equipment
President: Martin A. Rothshchild
VP Marketing: Marty Rothchild
VP Sales: Steve Avery
Contact: Kimmie Biggs
kbiggs@aladdin-atr.com
Estimated Sales: $300,000-500,000
Number Employees: 1-4
Parent Co: ENOCIS
Type of Packaging: Food Service
Brands:
    Heat on Demand
    Insul-Plus
    Temp-Rite Excel Ii

18526 Aladdin Transparent Packaging
115 Engineers Rd # 100
Hauppauge, NY 11788-4005
631-273-4747
Fax: 631-273-2523 www.aladdinpackaging.com
Cellophane, polyethylene and polypropylene bags, rolls and sheets; also, baking and candy cups/padding
Owner: Abe Mandel
abe@aladdinpackaging.com
Product Manager: Donny Uccellini
Plant Manager: Larry O'Connell
Estimated Sales: $10-20 Million
Number Employees: 20-49
Square Footage: 80000
Parent Co: Bleyer Industries
Other Locations:
    Aladdin Transparent Packaging
    Peoria IL
Brands:
    Pantry Bakers

18527 Alar Engineering Corp
9651 196th St
Mokena, IL 60448-9307
708-479-6100
Fax: 708-479-9059 info@alarcorp.com
www.alarcorp.com
Manufacturer and exporter of water pollution control equipment including filters for dewatering sludges, clarifiers, separators, carbon columns, drum compactors and holding tanks
President: Paula Jackfert
paulaj@alarcorp.com
CEO: Vickey Hassen
Estimated Sales: $5-10 Million
Number Employees: 20-49
Square Footage: 78000
Brands:
    Alar
    Auto-Vac
    Clar-O-Floc
    Flero Star
    Microklear
    Spiral Flow

18528 Alard Equipment Corp
6483 Lake Ave
PO Box 57
Williamson, NY 14589-9504
315-589-4511
Fax: 315-589-3871 sales@alard.com
www.alard.com
Buy, sell and refurbish food processing machinery and food packaging equipment for industrial fruit and vegetable canning, freezing, juice, bottling, and fresh cut applications, as well as all related packaging and labeling equipmentfor cans, jars, bottles, bags, etc.

President: Alvin E Shults
diane@alard.com
CEO: Susan Laird
VP: Edward Shults
Marketing Director: Michael Shults
Sales: Daryl Hoffman & Christopher Weigel
Purchasing: Diane Jenkins
Estimated Sales: $3 Million
Number Employees: 10-19
Square Footage: 40000

18529 Alarm Controls Corp
19 Brandywine Dr
Deer Park, NY 11729-5721
631-586-4220
Fax: 631-586-6500 800-645-5538
info@alarmcontrols.com www.alarmcontrols.com
Manufacturer and exporter of electronic burglar and smoke alarm systems and timers
President: Howard Berger
info@alarmcontrols.com
Sales Manager: John Benedetto
Estimated Sales: $5-10 Million
Number Employees: 10-19

18530 Albany International
975 Old Norcross Rd # A
Lawrenceville, GA 30045-4321
770-338-5000
Fax: 770-338-5024 800-252-2691
Contact: Joe Aiken
j.aiken@albanydoors.com
Plant Manager: Dan Garrau
Estimated Sales: $20-50 Million
Number Employees: 100-249

18531 Alberici Constructors Inc
8800 Page Ave
Overland, MO 63114-6106
314-733-2000
Fax: 314-733-2001 800-261-2611
gkozicz@alberici.com www.alberici.com
President/CEO: Gregory J. Kozicz
gkozicz@alberici.com
Vice President: Mark W. Okroy
Quality Control: Ron Rogge
Marketing Leader: Donald C. Oberlies
Estimated Sales: Over $1 Billion
Number Employees: 250-499

18532 Albion Industries Inc
800 N Clark St
Albion, MI 49224-1455
517-629-9441
Fax: 517-629-9501 800-835-8911
email@albioninc.com www.albioncasters.com
Casters and wheels.
President: Bill Winslow
CFO: Leanne Harbaugh
lharbaugh@albioninc.com
R&D: Rob Jorden
Sales: Mike Thorne
Estimated Sales: $35-45 Million
Number Employees: 50-99
Number of Brands: 10
Square Footage: 165000
Brands:
    Contender
    Prevenz
    Shockmaster
    Trionix

18533 Albion Machine & Tool Co
1001 Industrial Blvd
Albion, MI 49224-8551
517-629-9135
Fax: 517-629-6888
customercentral@albionconcepts.com
www.albionmachine.com
Manufacturer and exporter of specialty and reworked food processing equipment; repair services available
President: Robert Herwarth
CEO/Chairman: William Stoffer
wstoffer@albionmachine.com
VP: James Herwarth
Estimated Sales: $3-5 Million
Number Employees: 10-19

18534 Alburt Labeling Systems
3130 Pintail Ln
Signal Mountain, TN 37377
423-886-1664
Fax: 423-886-1676

Rollfed labeling, machines; foam labels
Owner: Alan Jones
Estimated Sales: less than $500,000
Number Employees: 1-4

18535 Alcan Foil Products
191 Evans Avenue
Etobicoke, ON M8Z 1J5
Canada
416-503-6709
Fax: 416-503-6720
President: Kevin Kindllan
Quality Control: Pierre Achim
Number Employees: 150

18536 Alcan Packaging
19701 Clark Graham Boulevard
Baie D'Urfe, QC H9X 3T1
Canada
514-457-4555
www.alcanpackaging.com
Folding cartons and paper boxes
President: Michael Rubensteil
CFO: Marcel Hetu
Research & Development: Martin Fogel
Plant Manager: Gilles Neron
Number Employees: 10
Square Footage: 300000
Parent Co: Algroup Wheaton Margo

18537 Alcoa-Lake Charles Carbon Plant
Lake Charles, LA 70605
337-480-7600
www.alcoa.com
Manufacturer of carbon.
Number Employees: 50

18538 Alcoa-Massena Operations
45 County Route 42
P.O. Box 5278
Massena, NY 13662
www.alcoa.com
Rod, billet, sow.
Number Employees: 480

18539 Alcoa-Warrick Operations
4400 State Route 66
P.O. Box 10
Newburgh, IN 47629-0010
812-853-6111
www.alcoa.com
Aluminum & sheet (litho and packaging)

18540 (HQ)Alcoa Corp
201 Isabella St
Suite 500
Pittsburgh, PA 15212-5858
412-315-2900
Production and conversion of flexible packaging, including plastic films and laminates and printed foils used by manufacturers within the pharmaceutical, tobacco, and food and beverage industries.
President & CEO: Roy Harvey
EVP & Chief Financial Officer: Bill Oplinger
EVP & Chief Operations Officer: John Slaven
EVP/General Counsel/Secretary: Jeff Heeter
EVP & Chief HR Officer: Tammi Jones
EVP & Chief Innovation Officer: Ben Kahrs
EVP & Chief Commercial Officer: Timothy Reyes
Year Founded: 1888
Estimated Sales: $11.6 Billion
Number Employees: 14,600
Brands:
    Mansi

18541 Alcon Packaging
130 Arrow Road
Weston, ON M9M 2M1
Canada
416-742-8910
Fax: 416-742-7118 www.alcon.com
Rotogravure printed flexible packaging laminations for food, beverage and personal care products
Technical Director: Don Iwacha
Number Employees: 10
Parent Co: Lawson Mardon Group
Brands:
    Mixpap

18542 Alconox Inc
30 Glenn St # 309
Suite 309
White Plains, NY 10603-3252

914-437-7585

Fax: 914-948-4088 cleaning@alconox.com
www.alconox.biz
Manufacturer and exporter of USDA approved detergents for critical cleaning applications including food preparation surfaces
President: Stewart Katz
skatz@alconox.com
CFO: Elliot Lebowitz
CEO: Elliot M Lebowitz
General Manager: Malcolm McLaughlin
Estimated Sales: $3-5 Million
Number Employees: 5-9
Type of Packaging: Food Service
Brands:
Alco Tabs
Alcojet
Alconox
Citranox
Det-O-Jet
Detergent 8
Liqui-Nox
Terg-A-Zyme

18543 Alconox Inc
30 Glenn St # 309
White Plains, NY 10603-3252

914-437-7585

Fax: 914-948-4088 cleaning@alconox.com
Cleaning detergents
President: Stewart Katz
skatz@alconox.com
CEO: Elliot M Lebowitz
Estimated Sales: $1-2.5 000,000
Number Employees: 5-9

18544 Alcor PMC
3730 S Kalamath Street
Englewood, CO 80110-3460

303-761-1535

Fax: 303-789-9300 www.pmc1.net
End liner technology for the food, beer and beverage packaging industry as well as its line of food equipment, which include stuffers, formers and portioners
President and Owner: David Groetsch
Sales: Tom Hoffmann
Contact: Jeff Isaacs
isaacs@stollemachinery.com
General Manager: Bob Geoffroy
Number Employees: 75
Number of Products: 20
Square Footage: 64000

18545 Aldo Locascio
1440 S Alvernon Way
Tucson, AZ 85711-5604

520-270-3059

Fax: 520-325-6776 800-488-8729
Consultant specializing in industrial design of commercial kitchens, concept dining rooms and food service operations, BBQ's, tabletop accessories
President: John Richards
Number Employees: 36
Number of Brands: 2
Number of Products: 40
Square Footage: 24000
Parent Co: Richards Manufacturing Company

18546 Aldon Co Inc
3410 Sunset Ave
Waukegan, IL 60087-3295

847-623-8800

Fax: 847-623-6139 e-rail@aldonco.com
www.aldonco.com
President: Joseph Ornig
e-rail@aldonco.com
CFO: Ralph V Switzer
Estimated Sales: $1-5 Million
Number Employees: 10-19

18547 Aleco Food Svc Div
2802 Avalon Ave
Muscle Shoals, AL 35661-2708

256-248-2400
Fax: 800-750-9616 800-633-3120
info@aleco.com www.aleco.com
PVC vinyl strip and impact-type doors for walk-in coolers, freezers; also, traffic doors
CEO: Edward Robbins III
VP Sales/Marketing: Stan Denton

Estimated Sales: $1-3 Million
Number Employees: 20-49
Type of Packaging: Food Service
Brands:
Clear-Flex Ii
Impacdor

18548 Aleco Food Svc Div
2802 Avalon Ave
Muscle Shoals, AL 35661-2708

256-248-2400
800-633-3120
info@aleco.com www.aleco.com
PVC door strips or walk-in coolers and freezers, impact doors for restaurants, insect control doors, air curtain doors.
Vice President: Stan Denton
rsdenton@aleco.com
CFO: Doug Sledge
Vice President: John Saylor
R&D/Quality Control: Steve Bacon
Marketing Director: Kelli Bush
Regional Account Manager: John Keddie
Public Relations: Bill May
Operations Manager: Ronald White
Production Manager: Jessie Hall
Plant Manager: Keith Rhodes
Purchasing Manager: Nancy Hamilton
Estimated Sales: $30,000,000
Number Employees: 20-49
Number of Brands: 10
Number of Products: 10
Square Footage: 100000
Parent Co: ER Robbins Corp
Type of Packaging: Food Service, Bulk
Brands:
Air Pro
Airflex
Clear-Flex Ii
Impacdoors
Maxbullet
Maxslide
Scratch-Guard

18549 Alef Custom Packaging
204 E Pennsylvania Blvd
Feastervl Trvs, PA 19053-7845

215-355-5200

Fax: 215-355-2577 800-453-2212
info@alefcustom.com www.alefcustom.com
President: Jeffrey Gottlieb
j.gottlieb@subway.com
Estimated Sales: $1-3 Million
Number Employees: 1-4

18550 Alegacy
12683 Corral Place
Santa Fe Springs, CA 90670

Fax: 888-604-1066 800-848-4440
info@alegacy.com www.alegacy.com
Cookware and small wares *Year Founded:* 1947
Brands:
EAGLEWARE

18551 Alewel's Country Meats
911 N Simpson Dr
Junction 13 & 50
Warrensburg, MO 64093-9277

660-747-8261
Fax: 660-747-1857 800-353-8553
ralewel@alewels.com www.country-meats.com
Dry, shelf stable, game and summer sausage, and game jerky including deer and buffalo.
Owner: Randy Alewel
alewels@sprintmail.com
Estimated Sales: $2.5-5 Million
Number Employees: 5-9
Square Footage: 20000
Type of Packaging: Consumer, Food Service, Private Label, Bulk
Brands:
Alewel's Country Meats
Grandpa A'S

18552 Alex Delvecchio Enterprises
PO Box 516
Troy, MI 48099-516

248-619-9600
Fax: 248-619-9688 sales@theimprintshop.com
www.theimprintshop.com
Promotional products including changeable letter bulletin boards, plaques, name plates, signs, matches and napkins; also, special clothing and uniforms

President: Alex Delvecchio Sr
CFO: Alex Delvecchio Jr
Estimated Sales: $5-10 Million
Number Employees: 10-19

18553 Alex E Fergusson Co Inc
800 Development Ave
Chambersburg, PA 17201

717-263-3132
Fax: 717-264-9182 800-345-1329
www.afcocare.info
Sanitizing and cleaning products including pressure cleaners, cleaning compounds and lubricants
President: Brett Bailey
brettbailey@afco.net
VP Sales: Joseph Woodring
Estimated Sales: $20-50 Million
Number Employees: 20-49
Square Footage: 80000
Brands:
Afco

18554 Alexander Machinery
P.O.Box 6446
Spartanburg, SC 29304

864-963-3624
Fax: 864-963-7018 alexcoair@aol.com
Manufacturer and exporter of pneumatic coalescer filters and system drainage equipment
President: Martin Cornelson
VP: W Spearman
Pneumatic Systems Design: Cliff Troutman
Estimated Sales: $20-50 Million
Number Employees: 20-49
Square Footage: 400000
Brands:
Alexco

18555 Alfa Chem
2 Harbor Way
Kings Point, NY 11024-2117

516-504-0059
Fax: 516-504-0039 800-375-6869
alfachem@gmail.com www.alfachem1.com
Provides raw materials to industries such as manufacturing, repackaging, research, pharmaceutical, food and cosmetics, as well as Universities and Hospitals.
President: Alfred Khalily
alfredkhalily@yahoo.com
Estimated Sales: $2.5 000,000
Number Employees: 1-4
Number of Products: 300
Square Footage: 7500
Type of Packaging: Private Label, Bulk

18556 Alfa Laval Ashbrook Simon-Hartley
10470 Deer Trail Dr
Houston, TX 77038

713-934-3160
ashbrook.sales@alfalaval.com
Manufacturer and exporter of liquid solid separation equipment (presses) and thickeners
Project Manager: Carl Boyd
Estimated Sales: $20-50 Million
Number Employees: 250-499
Parent Co: Alfa Laval Inc
Brands:
Aquabelt
Klampress
Winklepress

18557 Alfa Laval Inc
5400 International Trade Dr
Richmond, VA 23231

Fax: 804-236-3276 866-253-2528
customerservice.usa@alfalaval.com
www.alfalaval.us
Manufacturer and exporter of centrifuges including liquid/liquid and liquid/solid separators for edible oil, fish, meat, starch, protein, grain, yeast, wine, beer, coffee and sugar processing.
President & CEO: Tom Erixon
CFO: Jan Allde
Corporate Social Responsibility: Catarina Paulson
Senior VP, Communications: Peter Torstensson
Corporate General Counsel: Emma Adlerton
Executive VP, Global Sales & Service: Joakim Vilson
President, Operations: Mikael Tyden
Year Founded: 1883
Estimated Sales: $28 Billion

Number Employees: 17,000
Parent Co: Alfa Laval AB
Brands:
Sharples

18558 Alfa Systems Inc
522 Boulevard
Westfield, NJ 07090-3208

908-654-0255
Fax: 908-654-0256 www.alfasystems.biz
Manufacturer and exporter of custom automation equipment and packaging systems including tamper evident packaging, print registration systems, sealer mounted shrink tunnels, fragile product automatic infeeders, random product bar codescanning, etc
Owner: Steve Williams
Vice President: Chuck Holata
Estimated Sales: $1.25 Million
Number Employees: 10-19
Square Footage: 6000

18559 Alfacel
20w201 101st Street
Lemont, IL 60439-9674

630-783-9702
Fax: 630-783-9780
Casings, films, laminates, flexible packages, and shrink packaging materials
Estimated Sales: $1-2.5 000,000
Number Employees: 20-49

18560 Algene Marking Equipment Company
P.O. Box 410
Garfield, NJ 7026

973-478-9041
Fax: 973-473-3847
Manufacturer, importer and exporter of marking and printing equipment, coders, hand marking tools, air feed systems and indenters.
President: Milton Mann
VP/Production: Garry Mann
Plant Manager: Garry Mann
Estimated Sales: $1-1.5 Million
Number Employees: 5-9
Number of Brands: 19
Number of Products: 15
Square Footage: 10000
Brands:
Algene

18561 Alger Creations
P.O. Box 800604
Miami, FL 32380

954-454-3272
Fax: 954-239-5773 luisa@algercreations.com
Manufacturer and exporter of plastic bags, advertising specialties, displays and exhibits; importer of inflatable displays.
President: Alvin Brenner
Sales/Marketing: Ogden Farray
Contact: Luisa Maichel
luisa@algercreations.com
Estimated Sales: $2.5-5 Million
Number Employees: 20-49
Number of Brands: 1
Number of Products: 100
Square Footage: 40000
Type of Packaging: Private Label

18562 Algroup
17-17 State Route 208
Fair Lawn, NJ 07410-2820

201-794-2409
Fax: 201-794-2685 800-777-1875
www.algroupint.com
Chemicals, chemical manufacturing
CEO: Sergio Marchionne
CFO: Markus Hofer
VP: Michael Newman
Number Employees: 15
Parent Co: Algroup
Type of Packaging: Bulk

18563 Algus Packaging Inc
1212 E Taylor St
Dekalb, IL 60115-4507

815-756-1881
Fax: 815-758-2281 800-266-8581
algus@algus.com www.algus.com
Packaging service providing equipment and materials

Founder, President: Art Gustafson
CFO: Pat Stoner
pstoner@algus.com
Estimated Sales: $5-10 Million
Number Employees: 100-249

18564 (HQ)Ali Group
P.O.Box 4149
Winston Salem, NC 27115-4149

336-661-1556
Fax: 336-661-1979 800-532-8591
champion@championindustries.com
www.championindustries.com
Manufacturer and exporter of dishwashers, dish tables, manual and powered glass washers, pot and pan washers and waste disposal systems
President: Dexter Laughlin
CFO: Christian Miller
CEO: Hank Holt
Estimated Sales: $20-50 Million
Number Employees: 100-249
Brands:
Champion
Coldelite
Moyer Diebel

18565 Aline Heat Seal Corporation
13700 South Broadway
Los Angeles, CA 90061

310-715-6600
Fax: 310-715-6606 888-285-3917
alineinfo@sorbentsystems.com www.alinesys.com
Manufacturer and exporter of packaging machinery including shrink wrap, bundling, tube, bag and blister sealing and custom heat sealers for plastic films
President: Charles Schapira
Controller: Susanna Cano
VP: John Rydgren
Marketing and Sales: Charles Schapira
Customer Service: Pat Almanza
Plant Supervisor: Domingo Ayala
Estimated Sales: $5-10 Million
Number Employees: 10-19
Square Footage: 20000
Brands:
Aline

18566 Aline Systems Corporation
13700 South Broadway
Los Angeles, CA 90061

310-715-6600
Fax: 310-715-6606 888-825-3917
alineinfo@sorbentsystems.com www.alinesys.com
Semi and automatic binders, shrink wrappers, heat sealing, blister sealing and custom machinery
President: Charles Schapira
charles@alinesys.com
Controller: Susanna Cano
Vice President of Manufacturing: Julio Gonzalez
Estimated Sales: Below $5 Million
Number Employees: 10-19

18567 Alipack Americas
525 S Shore Dr
Osprey, FL 34229-9620

847-607-0591
Fax: 847-607-0592 info@alipack.it
www.alipack.it

18568 Alkar Rapid Pak
932 Development Dr
Lodi, WI 53555-1300

608-592-3211
Fax: 608-592-4039 marketing@alkar.com
www.alkar.com
Manufacturer and exporter of chillers including air blast, brine and glycol; also, smokehouses and continuous cook/chill systems.
President: Magdy Albert
Estimated Sales: $50-100 Million
Number Employees: 20-49
Square Footage: 80000

18569 Alkar Rapid Pak
932 Development Dr
PO Box 260
Lodi, WI 53555-1300

608-592-3211
Fax: 608-592-4039
daryl.shackelford@rapidpak.com
www.alkar.com
Form/fill/seal horizontal packaging equipment, rollstock machines

President: Jim Peterson
jim.peterson@rapidpak.com
CFO: Dave Smith
R&D: Bob Hanson
Quality Control: Dave Brathorst
Regional Sales Manager: Mike McCann
Estimated Sales: $5-10 Million
Number Employees: 20-49

18570 Alkar Rapid Pak
932 Development Dr
Lodi, WI 53555-1300

608-592-3211
Fax: 608-592-4039 www.alkar.com
Manufacturers of cooking and chilling systems for the food service industry.
President: Vic Addotta
addottavic@alkar1.com
Vice President/Sales: Timothy Moskal
Number Employees: 20-49

18571 Alkar Rapid Pak
932 Development Dr
PO Box 260
Lodi, WI 53555-1300

608-592-3211
Fax: 608-592-4039
Daryl.Shackelford@rapidpak.com
www.alkar.com
Food packaging machines for cook-in turkeys, hot dogs and string cheese.
President: Vic Addotta
addottavic@alkar1.com
Chief Financial Officer: Mary Jane Hansen
Research/Development: Seth Pulsfus
Marketing: Keith Shackleford
Plant Manager: Nick Cable
Number Employees: 20-49
Parent Co: Middleby Corporation

18572 Alkazone/Better Health Lab
200 S Newman St
Hackensack, NJ 07601-3124

201-880-7966
Fax: 201-880-7967 800-810-1888
contactus@alkazone.com www.alkazone.com
Manufacturer and exporter of antioxidant water and alkaline mineral supplement and water ionizers.
President: Robert Kim
Estimated Sales: $5-10 Million
Number Employees: 8
Square Footage: 80000
Type of Packaging: Consumer
Brands:
Alkaline
Alkazone
Alkazone Alkaline Booster Drops
Alkazone Antioxidant Water Ionizer
Alkazone Vitamins & Herbs
Antioxidant
Bhl
Better Health Lab

18573 Alkota Cleaning SystemsInc
105 Broad St
PO Box 288
Alcester, SD 57001-2120

605-934-2222
Fax: 605-934-1808 800-255-6823
info@alkota.com www.alkota.com
Manufacturer and exporter of high-pressure washers and parts, steam cleaners, water reclaim units and waste water/oil separators
President: Gary Scott
CEO: Jeff Burros
burrosjeff@spellcapital.com
CEO: Joseph Bjorkman
Head of Engineering: Roger Walz
Marketing Manager: Jim Scott
VP Sales: Jeff Burros
Estimated Sales: $10-20 Million
Number Employees: 50-99
Square Footage: 50000
Brands:
Alkota

18574 All A Cart Custom Mfg
2001 Courtright Rd
Columbus, OH 43232-4216

614-443-5544
Fax: 614-443-4248 800-695-2278
jjmorris@allacart.com

Manufacturer and exporter of vending carts, kiosks, trucks, mobile kitchens, catering vehicles and trailers
Owner: Jeff Morris
jjmorris@allacart.com
Estimated Sales: $5-10 Million
Number Employees: 20-49
Square Footage: 120000
Brands:
    All a Cart

18575 All About Furniture
6702 Jimmy Carter Blvd
Norcross, GA 30071
    Fax: 678-916-8383 800-893-0919
    www.aafllc.com
Seating products for the hospitality industry

18576 All American Container
9330 NW 110th Ave
Miami, FL 33178
    305-887-0797
Fax: 305-888-4133 sales@americancontainers.com
    www.allamericancontainers.com
Supplier of glass, plastic bottles and jars, can, pumps, sprayers and atomizers.
President: Remedios Diaz-Oliver
sales@americancontainers.com
Chief Executive Officer: Fausto Diaz-Oliver
Estimated Sales: $120 Million
Number Employees: 100-249
Square Footage: 100000
Other Locations:
    All American Containers
    Tampa FL

18577 All American Poly
40 Turner Pl
Piscataway, NJ 08854-3839
    732-752-2305
    Fax: 732-752-5570 800-526-3551
    steveb@allampoly.com www.allampoly.com
Extruders, converters and polyethylene bags including food, meat, shopping, plastic, shrink, liners and compactor
President: Jack Klein
jack@allampoly.com
Sales Manager: Joe Friedman
Estimated Sales: $20-50 Million
Number Employees: 50-99

18578 All American Seasonings
10600 E 54th Ave
Suite B
Denver, CO 80239-2132
    303-623-2320
    Fax: 303-623-1920
    www.allamericanseasonings.com
Baking mixes for bread, cakes, other pastries; assorted seasoned snacks including: chips, popcorn, nuts, & pretzels; sauces; variety of hot and cold beverages, energy drinks, and mixers.
Chairman: Andy Rodriguez
Director Of Quality Assurance: Mary Davis
Marketing Director: Joseph Gallagher
Year Founded: 1968
Estimated Sales: $12 Million
Number Employees: 20-49
Square Footage: 70000
Type of Packaging: Consumer, Food Service, Private Label, Bulk
Brands:
    All American

18579 All Bake Technologies
1930 Heck Avenue, Build 1
Suite 4
Neptune, NJ 07753
    732-988-0060
    Fax: 732-776-6418 info@allbaketech.com
    www.allbaketech.com
Mixing, proofing, baking, makeup equipment, retarding
President: Robert Hassell
Number Employees: 20-49

18580 All Fill Inc
418 Creamery Way
Exton, PA 19341-2536
    610-524-1918
    Fax: 610-524-7346 866-255-4455
    info@all-fill.com www.all-fill.com
Manufacturer and exporter of auger and Liouis filling and check weighing machinery

President/CEO: Ryan Edginton
ryane@allfill.com
CFO: Bill Egan
Executive VP/General Manager: Raymond Arra Jr
VP of Sales & Marketing: Kyle Edginton
Regional Sales Manager: Raymond Arra
All-Fill Operations Manager: Rick Brennecke
Purchasing Manager: Nick Dienno
Estimated Sales: $10-20 Million
Number Employees: 20-49
Square Footage: 110000

18581 All Fill Inc
418 Creamery Way
Exton, PA 19341-2536
    610-524-1918
    Fax: 610-524-7346 800-334-1529
    sales@all-fill.com www.all-fill.com
Powder and liquid filling machines and packaging equipment.
President: Ryan Edginton
ryane@allfill.com
Number Employees: 20-49
Square Footage: 55000

18582 All Foils Inc
16100 Imperial Pkwy
Strongsville, OH 44149-0600
    440-572-3645
    Fax: 440-378-0161 800-521-0054
    www.allfoils.com
Manufacturer and exporter of aluminum, foil and sheet gauges; importer of aluminum and copper; also, printing and laminating services available
President: Robert B Papp
rpapp@allfoils.com
Estimated Sales: $20-50 Million
Number Employees: 50-99
Square Footage: 140000
Brands:
    Metalix

18583 All Packaging MachineryCorp
90 13th Ave # 11
Unit 11
Ronkonkoma, NY 11779-6818
    631-588-7310
    Fax: 631-467-4690 800-637-8808
    sales@apmpackaging.com
    www.allpackagingmachinery.com
Manufacturer and exporter of packaging machinery and parts
President: Daniel Wood
Corp Comms: Lynn Miranda
lynn@allpackagingmachinery.com
Marketing/Sales: Lynn Miranda
Plant Manager: Dan Wood
Number Employees: 20-49
Square Footage: 80000
Parent Co: All Packaging Machinery & Supplies Corporation
Brands:
    Speedy Bag Packager

18584 All Power Inc
2228 Murray St
Sioux City, IA 51111-1148
    712-258-0681
    Fax: 712-258-6561 info@allpowerinc.com
    www.allpowerinc.com
Manufacturer and wholesaler/distributor of packing house equipment, trolleys, shackles and stainless steel conveyors; also, sludge pumps, pressure vessels, indexers, auto feeders and drives including electric motor, gear boxeshydraulics and line shafting
President: Eugene Anderson
General Manager: Gene Anderson, Jr.
Purchasing Manager: Jim Tucker
Estimated Sales: $10-20 Million
Number Employees: 50-99
Square Footage: 70000

18585 All Sorts Premium Packaging
2495 Main Street
Suite 548
Buffalo, NY 14214-2154
    716-831-1622
    Fax: 716-831-1630 888-565-9727
Gift basket wrap and bags
VP: Penny Duke
Estimated Sales: less than $500,000
Number Employees: 1-4

Brands:
    All Sorts

18586 All Southern Fabricators
5010 126th Ave N
Clearwater, FL 33760-4607
    727-571-1147
    Fax: 727-573-2360 800-878-2732
    asf@allsouthern.com
    www.allsouthernfabricators.com
Custom stainless steel food service equipment
President: Bernie Auer
bauer@allsouthern.com
CFO: Pav Willis
VP: Pavilyn Willis
Quality Control: Tom Richardson
Operations Manager: Tom Richardson
Estimated Sales: $10-20 Million
Number Employees: 50-99

18587 All Spun Metal Products
1877 Busse Hwy
Des Plaines, IL 60016
    847-824-4117
    Fax: 847-824-0419
Copper and stainless steel kettles; stainless steel sheet metal fabrication services available
President: Gianfranco Isaia
General Manager: Douglas Reed
Estimated Sales: $1-2.5 Million
Number Employees: 5-9
Parent Co: Spectracrafts

18588 All Star Carts & Vehicles
1565 5th Industrial Ct # B
Bay Shore, NY 11706-3434
    631-666-5581
    Fax: 631-666-1319 800-831-3166
    info@allstarcarts.com www.allstarcarts.com
Quality carts, kiosks, trailers and trucks for the food service and general merchandise industries
President: Stephen Kronrad
info@allstarcarts.com
Sales Director: Mark Weiner
VP: Robert Kronrad
Sales Executive: Michael Clark
Estimated Sales: $5-10 Million
Number Employees: 20-49
Square Footage: 50000

18589 All Star Dairy Foods
620 New Ludlow Rd
South Hadley, MA 01075-2669
    413-538-5240
    Fax: 413-532-4093 800-462-1129
    www.allstardairyfoods.com
Dairy products
Owner: Russ Sawyer
Inside Sales Manager: Lynne Sawyer
rsawyer@allstardairyfoods.com
Office Manager: Lynn Rivest
Estimated Sales: $7.5 Million
Number Employees: 20-49
Square Footage: 10400
Type of Packaging: Consumer
Other Locations:
    Schenkel's Dairy
    Fort Wayne IN

18590 All State Fabricators Corporation
1316 Tech Blvd
Tampa, FL 33619
    813-626-3166
    Fax: 800-867-3609 800-322-9925
    www.emiindustries.com
Stainless steel food service equipment including counters, hoods, tables, sinks, dishtables, display cases, mobile food carts and ventless fryers
Manager: Steven Rooney
General Manager: Steven Rooney
Estimated Sales: $10-20 Million
Number Employees: 50-99
Square Footage: 140000
Brands:
    Auto Fry

18591 All States Caster/F.I.R
Neils Thompson Drive
Suite 113
Austin, TX 78758-7653
    512-832-9821
    Fax: 512-832-9834 800-234-3882
    daves@allstatecasters.com
    www.allstatequip.com
President: Dave Spencer

Estimated Sales: $5-10 Million
Number Employees: 10-19

18592 All Valley Packaging
PO Box 63201
Colorado Springs, CO 80962-3201
Fax: 425-650-5090
Printed boxes, labels, bags, pouches, food service containers, pallets, janitorial maintenance supply
President: Cheryl Mikel
VP/Sales: Steve Hobden
Purchasing Manager: Cheryl Mikel
Number Employees: 5
Number of Brands: 100+
Number of Products: 1000
Type of Packaging: Food Service, Private Label
Brands:
3m
Clorox
Dixie
Dow
Dupont
Reynolds
Rubbermaid
Solo

18593 All Weather Energy Systems
PO Box 701064
Plymouth, MI 48170-0958
888-636-8324
Fax: 888-636-8304 escheatzle@aol.com
Door and dock leveler sealing systems, brushes, gaskets, containment seals, dust and infiltration control systems and pest control devices; design and installation services available
Owner/President: Elizabeth Scheatzle
Sales/Marketing Executive: Molly McCarville
Purchasing Agent: Mario Derrick
Number Employees: 5
Square Footage: 5000

18594 All-Clad METALCRAFTERS LLC
424 Morganza Rd
Canonsburg, PA 15317-5716
724-745-8300
Fax: 724-746-5035 800-255-2523
www.all-clad.com
Manufacturer and exporter of stainless steel, aluminum and copper cookware and utensils.
CEO: Peter Cameron
Manager: Hideyuki Nishizawa
hnishizawa@tubecityims.com
Estimated Sales: $20-50 Million
Number Employees: 100-249
Parent Co: Clad Metals
Brands:
Cop*R*Chef
Master Chef Ltd.
Stainless

18595 All-Right Enterprises
2307 Conciliation Lane
Green Cove Springs, FL 32043-8240
Canada
904-400-1245
Fax: 604-528-6103 lallright@aol.com
Principal: Vern Smith

18596 All-State Industries Inc
520 S 18th St
West Des Moines, IA 50265-6449
515-223-5843
Fax: 515-223-8305 800-247-4178
dsmsales@all-statebelting.com
www.all-stateind.com
Wholesaler/distributor of food handling belting for conveyors
President: Doug Berner
dberner@all-statebelting.com
Vice President: Casey Price
Research & Development: Doug Tibkin
Quality Control: Sherry Wilkinson
Estimated Sales: $20-50 Million
Number Employees: 10-19
Parent Co: All-State Industries

18597 All-State Industries Inc
520 S 18th St
West Des Moines, IA 50265-6449
515-223-5843
Fax: 515-223-8305 info@all-stateind.com
www.all-stateind.com
Food handling belting for conveyors and pulleys

President: Doug Berner
dberner@all-statebelting.com
Estimated Sales: $20-50 Million
Number Employees: 10-19
Square Footage: 120000

18598 AllPoints Foodservice
607 W Dempster St
Mt. Prospect, IL 60056
www.allpointsfps.com
Replacement parts and supplies for commercial cooking and refrigeration equipment
VP, Sales: Eric Trelstad
Year Founded: 1983
Number Employees: 51-200

18599 Alleghany Highlands Economic Development Authority
322 W Riverside St
Covington, VA 24426
540-862-6673
Fax: 540-962-8425 www.heartofva.org
Owner: Steve Bowers
Estimated Sales: $1-3 Million
Number Employees: 5-9

18600 Allegheny Bradford Corp
P.O. Box 200
Bradford, PA 16701
814-362-2590
Fax: 814-362-2574 800-542-0650
sales@alleghenybradford.com
www.alleghenybradford.com
Manufacturer and exporter of sanitary stainless steel heat exchangers, filter housings, tanks, pressure vessels, manifolds and modular process systems; custom fabrication available
President & CEO: Dan McCune
dmccune@alleghenybradford.com
Estimated Sales: $50-100 Million
Number Employees: 50-99
Square Footage: 40000

18601 Allegheny Technologies Inc
1000 Six PPG Place
Pittsburgh, PA 15222
412-394-2800
800-289-7454
www.atimetals.com
Manufacturer of titanium, nickle, cobalt and other materials; also, machine components.
Chair: Diane Creel
President & CEO: Robert Wetherbee
SVP, Finance & Chief Financial Officer: Don Newman
SVP & Chief Commercial/Marketing Officer: Kevin Kramer
EVP, High Performance Materials Segment: John Sims
VP, Environmental Affairs: Lauren McAndrews
VP, Investor Relations: Scott Minder
Year Founded: 1996
Estimated Sales: $4 Billion
Number Employees: 8,600

18602 Allen Coding & Marking Systems
501 90th Avenue NW
Minneapolis, MN 55433-8005
763-783-2734
Fax: 763-783-2580 877-611-1711
www.allencoding.com
Coding and marking equipment, hot stamp and thermal processes
Estimated Sales: $500,000-$1 Million
Number Employees: 10

18603 Allen Gauge & Tool Co
421 N Braddock Ave
Pittsburgh, PA 15208-2514
412-241-6410
Fax: 412-242-8877 info@allengauges.com
www.allengauges.com
Manufacturer and exporter of sausage linking machinery and other meat processing equipment
Owner: Charles Allen
Manager: C Moekle
Number Employees: 10-19
Parent Co: Allen Gauge & Tool Company

18604 (HQ)Allen Industries Inc
6434 Burnt Poplar Rd
Greensboro, NC 27409-9712
336-668-2791
Fax: 336-668-7875 800-967-2553
info@allenindustries.com
www.allenindustries.com
Menu boards, advertising and electric signs
President: Tom Allen
jenny.seamster@allenindustires.com
VP: John Allen
Estimated Sales: $10-20 Million
Number Employees: 250-499
Other Locations:
Allen Industries
Clearwater FL

18605 Allen Signs Co
2408 Chapman Hwy
Knoxville, TN 37920-1910
865-579-1683
Fax: 865-579-0356 800-844-3524
www.allensign.com
Manufacturer and exporter of advertising specialties, flags, pennants, banners, electric signs, lighting and flag poles, etc.; also, sign painting services available
Owner: Tom Allen
tom@allensign.com
CFO: Tom Allen
Public Relations: Scott Marshall
Operations Manager: Benjamin Booker
Plant Manager: Andrew Asbury
Estimated Sales: Below $5,000,000
Number Employees: 10-19
Square Footage: 7500

18606 Allenair Corp
255 E 2nd St
Mineola, NY 11501-3524
516-747-5450
Fax: 516-747-5481 info@allenair.com
All stainless steel air cylinders
Owner: John Allen
CFO: Linda Johanson
linda@allenair.com
Research Manager: Wayne Butner
Quality Control Director: Daniel Palladino
Sales Manager: Waler Scheid
Marketing Manager: Steve Santoriello
Human Resources Manager: Virginia Amato
Plant Manager: Stephen Werlinitsch
Purchasing Manager: Tin Byrnes
Estimated Sales: $12 Million
Number Employees: 100-249
Square Footage: 150000

18607 Allendale Cork Company
4 Walnut St
Rye, NY 10579
914-921-2787
Fax: 914-967-9605 800-816-2675
Manufacturer and exporter of wine and tapered cork stoppers and champagne corks; importer of cork
President: Dale Balun
Vice President: Ken Queen
Contact: Ken Queen
ken12564@aol.com
Estimated Sales: $1-2,500,000
Number Employees: 10-19

18608 Allergen Air Filter Corp
5205 Ashbrook Dr
Houston, TX 77081-2903
713-668-2371
Fax: 713-668-6815 800-333-8880
Air filters
President: Michael Horan
Estimated Sales: Below $5 Million
Number Employees: 5-9

18609 Allflex Packaging Products
105 Race St
Ambler, PA 19002-4423
215-542-9200
Fax: 215-643-3339 800-448-2467
sales@allflex.com www.allflex.com
Promotional sales kits, material handling totes, trays and bins, cases, insulated and hazardous material containers and protective packaging
President: Joel Cohen
Marketing Director: Kristine Koelzer
Purchasing Manager: Joy Rudegeair
Estimated Sales: $3-5 Million
Number Employees: 10-19

18610 Alliance Bakery Systems
130 Northpoint Court
Blythewood, SC 29016-8875
803-691-9227
Fax: 803-691-9239
Equipment: baking systems, dough handling, transport and sheeting lines
President: Cory Bolkestein
Estimated Sales: $10-20 Million
Number Employees: 19

18611 Alliance Industrial Corp
208 Tomahawk Industrial Park
Lynchburg, VA 24502-4153
434-239-2642
Fax: 434-239-5692 800-368-3556
www.allianceindustrial.com
Designer and manufacturer of conveying systems, material handling machinery, and controls. Spiral Conveyers for bulk and case, Depalletisers, Elevators, and Lowerators for can, bottle and case, rinsers, case switches, bulk case, andair conveyer systems and much more.
President: Bob Abbott
babbott@allianceindustrial.com
Marketing/Sales: David Loyd
Sales Manager: Wayne Walker
Purhasing: Todd Farrar
Estimated Sales: $20-50 Million
Number Employees: 100-249
Square Footage: 80000

18612 Alliance Knife Inc
124 May Dr
Harrison, OH 45030-2024
513-367-9000
Fax: 513-367-2233 800-852-7447
contactus@allianceknife.com
www.allianceknife.com
Produces and markets paper trimming knives, press knives, sheeters, slitter, granulator blades, woodworking knives, and packaging knives, as well as knives for the metal converting industry.
Owner: Lonnie Keith
akiknife@aol.com
Estimated Sales: $5-10 000,000
Number Employees: 20-49

18613 Alliance Products LLC
820 Esther Ln
Murfreesboro, TN 37129-5536
615-895-5333
Fax: 615-895-5334 800-522-3973
jparker@allianceproducts.com
www.allianceproducts.net
Custom and stock metal carts, nonpowered conveyors, heated cabinets, racks, heaters and proofers
President: Scott Marshall
smarshall@allianceproducts.net
Marketing Manager: Donna Sikes
Engineering Manager: Scott Marshall
Estimated Sales: $5-10 Million
Number Employees: 20-49
Square Footage: 80000
Parent Co: Win-Holt Equipment
Brands:
Alliance

18614 Alliance Rubber Co
210 Carpenter Dam Rd
Hot Springs, AR 71901-8219
501-262-2700
Fax: 501-262-5268 800-626-5940
sales@alliance-rubber.com www.rubberband.com
Manufacturer and exporter of imprinted rubber bands for brand identification, logos, produce, etc.; also, UPC imprinted tape for produce
Owner: Lance Gyldenege
Marketing Manager: Jason Risa
Sales Manager: Rachel Atkinson
lance_gyldenege@msn.com
Operations Manager: Brandon Hughes
Estimated Sales: $50-100 Million
Number Employees: 100-249
Number of Brands: 10
Number of Products: 4500
Square Footage: 160000
Type of Packaging: Consumer, Food Service, Private Label, Bulk
Brands:
Advantage
Alliance
Eco
Pale Crepe Gold

Protape
Sterling

18615 Alliance Shippers Inc
516 Sylvan Ave
Englewood Cliffs, NJ 07632-3022
201-227-0400
Fax: 201-227-1212 800-222-0451
www.alliance.com
President: Leona Allen
leona_allen@alliance.com
Estimated Sales: $10-20 Million
Number Employees: 20-49

18616 Alliance/PMS
267 Livingston St
Northvale, NJ 07647-1901
201-784-1101
Fax: 201-784-1116 www.wcbicecream.com
Encapsulation equipment, qualification, validation and rebuilding services
Owner: Neal White
Estimated Sales: $10-20 Million
Number Employees: 50-99
Square Footage: 34000
Parent Co: SBX

18617 Allied Adhesive Corporation
P.O.Box 1866
Baldwin, NY 11510-8566
718-846-3200
President: Steve Pollack
Estimated Sales: $1-3 Million
Number Employees: 5-9

18618 Allied Bakery and Food Service Equipment
12015 E. Slauson Ave
Suite K
Santa Fe Springs, CA 90670-8542
562-945-6506
Fax: 562-945-4282 info@alliedbake.com
www.alliedbake.com
Supplier of bakery equipment and systems
President: Roger Harsted
CFO: Phillis Markle
Estimated Sales: $5-10 Million
Number Employees: 10-19

18619 Allied Electric Sign & Awning
1920 S 900 W
Salt Lake City, UT 84104-1723
801-972-6837
Fax: 801-972-5670 www.allied-sign.com
Commercial awnings
President: Chris Blake
chris@allied-sign.com
Estimated Sales: Below $5 Million
Number Employees: 20-49

18620 (HQ)Allied Engineering
94 Riverside Drive
North Vancouver, BC V7H 2M6
Canada
604-929-1214
Fax: 604-929-5184 877-929-1214
sales@alliedboilers.com www.alliedboilers.com
Manufacturers of gas and electric boilers, tankless coils and electric boosters.
President: George Gilbert
Quality Control: Brad Gilbert
Marketing Director: Garry Epstein
Sales Director: T Weaver
Operations Manager: Urbano Pandin
Plant Manager: Howard Larlee
Purchasing Manager: Harry Bowker
Number Employees: 60
Square Footage: 340000
Brands:
Aae Series
E-Z-Rect
Mini-Gas Series
Saturn Series
Super Hot
Trim-Line
Type 1

18621 Allied Gear & Machine Company
1101 Research Blvd.
St Louis, MO 63132
314-991-5900
Fax: 314-991-5911 800-896-1989
Sales@alliedgear.com www.alliedgear.com

General Manager: Skip Liu
Technical Manager: Amy Zhang
Regional Sales Manager: Dan Jahn
Contact: Tom Serra
tom@alliedgear.com
Estimated Sales: $1-5 Million

18622 Allied Glove Corporation
433 E Stewart St
Milwaukee, WI 53207
414-481-0900
Fax: 414-481-0700 800-558-9263
Manufacturer, importer and exporter of safety products and disposable wear for food handlers including industrial gloves and X-ray protective materials
Manager: Sarah Cunningham
VP: Ray Sroka
Plant Manager: Dan Sroka
Estimated Sales: $1-3 Million
Number Employees: 10-19
Square Footage: 300000
Brands:
Security
Superguard
White Hawk

18623 Allied Metal Spinning
1290 Viele Ave
Bronx, NY 10474-7133
718-893-3300
Fax: 718-589-5780 800-615-2266
www.alliedmetalusa.com
Woks, cake rings, pizza screens, trays, cutters and bakery, pizza and chinese cooking utensils; also, pans including cake, pie, pizza, black nonstick, anodized, sheet extenders, etc. Importer of 2000 items to complement manufacturedline
Owner: Arlene Saunders
alliedsteam@aol.com
Plant Manager: Carlos Heredia
Purchasing Manager: Arlene Saunders
Number Employees: 20-49
Type of Packaging: Food Service, Private Label, Bulk

18624 Allied Purchasing Co
1334 18th St SW
Mason City, IA 50401-5602
641-423-1824
Fax: 641-423-2346 800-247-5956
brian@alliedpurchasing.com
www.alliedpurchasing.com
Equipment, supplies, ingredients and services for the dairy, soft drink, bottled water, water treatment and brewery industries.
President/CFO: Brian Janssen
brian@alliedpurchasing.com
EVP: Steve Husome
Customer Service: Angela Stadtlander
Senior Account Manager-Bottled Water: Kari Mondt
Number Employees: 10-19
Square Footage: 10500
Type of Packaging: Food Service

18625 Allied Trades of the Baking Industry
PO Box 1853
Sonoma, CA 95476-1853
847-920-9885
Fax: 847-920-9886 www.atbi.org

18626 Allied Uniking Corp Inc
4750 Cromwell Ave
Memphis, TN 38118-6367
901-365-7240
Fax: 901-365-7306
Conveyors including overhead monorail, overhead power and free and inverted power and free
President: Kenneth Anderson
CFO: Mike Baker
VP: Dolph Stritzel
Quality Control: Sharron Dean
IT Executive: Mark Coward
mcoward@allieduniking.com
Estimated Sales: $20-50 Million
Number Employees: 10-19
Square Footage: 100000

18627 Allione Agrifood USA
10390 Wilshire Boulevard
Apt 608
Los Angeles, CA 90024-6409
310-271-3663
Fax: 310-271-3664
Fruit processing, preparations, aromatic herbs, customized products, technology, quality control

18628 Allison Systems Inc
245 Regency Ct # L120
Suite 210
Brookfield, WI 53045-6157
262-522-9800
Fax: 262-522-9600 800-536-9077
info@allisonsystems.com
Owner: John Travares
j_travares@allisonblades.com
Estimated Sales: $1-5 Million
Number Employees: 5-9

18629 Allmark Impressions LTD
823 N Riverside Dr
Fort Worth, TX 76111-4249
817-834-0080
Fax: 817-838-2315 allmark7@aol.com
www.allmarkimpressions.com
Rubber stamps
President: Nancy Menchaca
allmark7@aol.com
Estimated Sales: $1-2.5 Million
Number Employees: 10-19

18630 Alloy Cast Products Inc
700 Swenson Dr
Kenilworth, NJ 07033-1326
908-245-2255
Fax: 908-245-3267 rexalloy@aol.com
www.alloycastproducts.com
President: Frank Panico
fpanico@alloycastproducts.com
Estimated Sales: $3-5 Million
Number Employees: 10-19

18631 Alloy Fab
200 Ryan St.
South Plainfield, NJ 07080-4208
908-753-9393
President: Larry Schillings
Estimated Sales: $10-20 Million
Number Employees: 50-99

18632 Alloy Hardfacing & Engineering
20425 Johnson Memorial Dr
Jordan, MN 55352-9518
952-492-5569
Fax: 952-492-3100 800-328-8408
juliek@alloyhardfacing.net
www.alloyhardfacing.com
Manufacturer and exporter of primary waste water
equipment, CIP-option pumps, heat exchangers and
custom cooking vessels
President: Mark Aulik
paulr@alloyhardfacing.net
Sales Director: Paul Rothenberger
Estimated Sales: $5-10 Million
Number Employees: 20-49

18633 Alloy Products Corp
1045 Perkins Ave
Waukesha, WI 53186-5249
262-542-6603
Fax: 262-542-5421 800-236-6603
info@alloyproductscorp.com
www.alloyproductscorp.com
Stainless steel pharmaceutical, bio-tech, specialty
chemicals and hygenic tanks; also, UN transport and
ASME portable pressure vessels
President: Joseph E. Vick
jvick@alloyproductscorp.com
CFO: Robert Rosenkranz
Executive VP: Betsy Bear Hoff
Engineering & Quality Assurance: Ray Woo
Sales & Customer Service: Pat Pajerski
Customer Service Representative: Matt Gamble
Estimated Sales: $10-20 Million
Number Employees: 100-249
Square Footage: 200000

18634 Alloy Wire Belt Company
2318 Tenaya Dr
Modesto, CA 95354
410-901-2660
Fax: 410-901-2680 877-649-7492
sales@cambridge-es.com www.alloywirebelt.com
Market Sales Manager: Cory Bloodsworth
Market Sales Manager: Melissa Lewis
Contact: Gene Ford
gene@alloywirebelt.com
Plant Manager: Gene Ford
Estimated Sales: $1-5 Million
Number Employees: 10-19

18635 Alloyd Brands
1401 Pleasant St
Dekalb, IL 60115-2663
815-756-8452
Fax: 815-756-5187 800-756-7639
info@alloyd.com www.tegrant.com
Formerly SCA Consumer Packaging, manufacturers
of light-gauge custom thermoformed retail packaging.
President: Ron Leach
Vice President of Business Development: Prakash
Mahesh
Marketing: Rob VanGilse
Contact: Joy Butzke
jbutzke@alloyd.com
Estimated Sales: $20-50 Million
Number Employees: 1-4
Type of Packaging: Bulk

18636 Allpac
P.O.Box 565685
Dallas, TX 75356-5685
214-630-8804
Fax: 214-630-3912
Horizontal fin seal wrapping machines
President: Lawrence D Lakey
VP of Sales/Marketing: Cheryl DiMarzio
Estimated Sales: $2.5-5 Million
Number Employees: 20-49

18637 Allpax Products
13510 Seymour Meyers Blvd
Covington, LA 70433-6879
985-893-9277
Fax: 985-893-9477 888-893-9277
info@allpax.com
Manufacturer and exporter of loading, unloading
and shuttle systems, retorts, autoclaves and control
software. Equipment manufactured for the following
products: dairy, meat, produce, seafood, and
beverages.
VP & General Manager: Greg Jacob
steveh@allpax.com
VP, Sales: Scott Williams
Estimated Sales: $30-40 Million
Number Employees: 50-99
Type of Packaging: Consumer, Food Service
Brands:
  2404
  Monitor
  Paxware
  Rotopax
  Stillpax

18638 Allsorts Premium Packaging
2495 Main St Ste 548
Buffalo, NY 14214
716-831-1622
Fax: 800-301-5301 888-565-9727
Gift basket packaging specialists, basket bags, candy
bags, tissue paper
Business Manager: Rosemarie Duke
Estimated Sales: Less than $500,000
Number Employees: 1-4

18639 Allstate Can Corporation
1 Woodhollow Rd
Parsippany, NJ 07054-2821
973-560-9030
Fax: 973-560-9217 tincans@allstatecan.com
www.allstatecan.com
Decorative stock tins, to include round, square and
rectangular shapes
President: Joseph Papera
CEO: Dave West
Estimated Sales: $5-10 Million
Number Employees: 50-99

18640 Allstate Food & Marketing Inc
2251 Lynx Lane
Suie 10
Orlando, FL 32804
321-400-5779
Foodservice sales and marketing agency focused on
manufacturers who sell to the restaurant and hospitality industries.
Year Founded: 1986
Estimated Sales: $50-100 Million
Number Employees: 100
Square Footage: 13400
Type of Packaging: Food Service

18641 Allstate Manufacturing Company
20 East Seventh Street
PO Box 326
Manchester, OH 45144
937-549-3133
Fax: 937-549-2709 800-262-2340
sales@allstatemfgco.com www.allstatemfgco.com
Portable display cases
President: Joel Birnbaum
Contact: Contactfirs Contactlastnam
jeff@solterra.us
Estimated Sales: $500,000-$1 Million
Number Employees: 5-9

18642 (HQ)Allstrong Restaurant Eqpt Inc
1839 Durfee Ave
South El Monte, CA 91733-3708
626-448-7878
Fax: 626-448-7838 800-933-8913
www.allstrong.com
Manufacturer and exporter of Chinese woks, exhaust
systems and stainless steel work and steam tables
President: Yuancansing Situ
Manager: Yuan Situ
yuan.situ@allstronginc.com
General Manager: Ken Situ
Estimated Sales: Less than $500,000
Number Employees: 20-49
Other Locations:
  Allstrong Restaurant Equipmen
  Alhambra CA
Brands:
  Allstrong

18643 Alltech Inc
3031 Catnip Hill Rd
Nicholasville, KY 40356-9765
859-885-9613
Fax: 859-887-3223 globalfoods@alltech.com
www.alltech.com
Bulk supplier and manufacture natural, safe, and environmental products that enhance crop production
President: T Pearse Lyons
Cmo: Elizabeth Bagby
ebagby@alltech.com
Product Manager: Elizabeth Graves
Estimated Sales: $20-50 Million
Number Employees: 500-999
Type of Packaging: Bulk

18644 Alluserv
4900 W Electric Ave
West Milwaukee, WI 53219
414-902-6400
Fax: 414-902-6446 800-558-8565
info@elakeside.com alluserv.com
Equipment for healthcare food service meal assembly and delivery
President/Owner: Joe Carlson
Principal: Larry Moon
General Manager: Tony Yenzer

18645 Allylix Inc
7220 Trade St
Suite 209
San Diego, CA 92121
858-909-0595
Fax: 858-909-0695 info@allylix.com
www.allylix.com
Terpene products and derivatives; food ingredients.
President & CEO: Carolyn Fritz
VP Business Development: Seth Goldblum
VP Research & Development: Richard Burlingame
sgoldblum@allylix.com
VP Sales & Marketing: Leandro Nonino
Contact: Seth Goldblum
sgoldblum@allylix.com
Estimated Sales: $280,000
Number Employees: 5-9

329

18646 Alnor Instrument Company
7555 Linder Avenue
Skokie, IL 60077-3223
800-424-7427
Fax: 847-677-3539 www.alnor-usa.com
Measuring equipment including air volume, air velocity, humidity, pressure and temperature
Marketing Communications Manager: Danielle Kenney
National Sales Manager: John Rose
General Manager: Alan Traylor
Number Employees: 50-99
Parent Co: TSI

18647 Aloe Hi-Tech
7921 NW South River Drive
Medley, FL 33166-2515
305-884-0399
Fax: 305-884-0365
Aloe vera raw materials
Estimated Sales: $1-5 000,000

18648 Alouf Plastics
4 Glenshaw St
Orangeburg, NY 10962-1207
845-512-8864
Fax: 845-365-2294 800-394-2247
ron.s@alufplastics.com www.alufplastics.com
Plastic and polyethylene bags
President: Reuven Rosenberg
Estimated Sales: $20-50 Million
Number Employees: 10-19
Parent Co: API Industries
Brands:
Commander

18649 Alpack
69 Holly Point Rd
Centerville, NA 2632
774-994-8086
Fax: 774-994-8170 info@alpackplastics.com
www.alpackplastics.com
Plastic boxes, bottles, jars and packaging components
President: Joseph Kopelman
Type of Packaging: Consumer

18650 Alpert/Siegel & Associates
3272 Motor Ave
Suite J
Los Angeles, CA 90034
310-571-0777
Fax: 310-826-8311 www.asaproperty.com
Consultant providing site selection for restaurants
Co Founder/ Chief Property Manager: Abe Skaletzky
Estimated Sales: $500,000-$1,000,000
Number Employees: 1-4

18651 Alpha Associates
2 Amboy Avenue
Woodbridge, NJ 07095-2699
732-634-5700
Fax: 732-634-1430 800-631-5399
ranton@alphainc.com www.alphainc.com
Industrial, coated, laminated and fiberglass insulation materials
President: Christopher Avallone
Contact: Kevin Burton
kburton@alphainc.com
Estimated Sales: $20-50 Million
Number Employees: 50-99

18652 Alpha Associates Inc
145 Lehigh Ave
Lakewood, NJ 08701-4527
732-634-5700
Fax: 732-634-1430 800-631-5399
www.alphainc.com
President: Christopher Avallone
cavallone@alphainc.com
Estimated Sales: $1-5 Million
Number Employees: 50-99

18653 Alpha Canvas & Awning Co
411 E 13th St
Charlotte, NC 28206-3310
704-333-1581
Fax: 704-333-1599 800-583-9179
www.alphacanvas.com
Commercial awnings

Owner: Angela Riggins
Quality Control: Eric Regans
VP: Brian Regans
Secretary: Jane Riggins
Estimated Sales: $1-2,500,000
Number Employees: 10-19
Square Footage: 8800

18654 Alpha Checkweigher
418 Creamery Way
Exton, PA 19341-2536
610-524-7350
Fax: 610-524-7346 www.all-fill.com
President: Glenn Edginton
Contact: Brian Jones
brianj@alphacheckweighers.com
Estimated Sales: $20-50 Million
Number Employees: 50-99

18655 Alpha Gear Drives Inc
1249 Humbracht Cir
Bartlett, IL 60103-1606
630-540-5300
Fax: 847-439-0755 888-534-1222
info@wittenstein-us.com
Motion control products and planetary gear reducers
President: Karl Heinz Schwarz
General Manager/VP: Tim Herbst
Marketing: Ronald Larsen
National Sales Manager: Ray Hamilton
Contact: Mike Anselmo
manselmo@alphagear.com
Estimated Sales: $15 000,000
Number Employees: 35

18656 Alpha MOS America
7502 Connelley Drive
Suite 110
Hanover, MD 21076-1075
410-553-9736
Fax: 410-553-9871 800-257-4249
www.alpha-mos.com
Importer of inspection and analysis instrumentation and systems including electronic nose for testing shelf life, spoilage & mishandling.
CEO: Jean-Paul Ansel
General Manager: Andrew Cowell
Estimated Sales: $1-2.5 Million
Number Employees: 5-9
Parent Co: Alpha MOS Sa

18657 (HQ)Alpha Omega Technology
14 Ridgedale Avenue #110
Cedar Knolls, NJ 07927-1106
973-537-0073
Fax: 973-292-4999 800-442-1969
info@karibafarms.com www.karibafarms.com
Designer, builder and wholesaler/distributor of turn-key facilities; also, irradiation processing facility for the sanitation and sterilization of food ingredients
CEO: Martin Welt
Office Manager: Ruth Welt
Estimated Sales: $500,000-$1 Million
Number Employees: 5-9
Square Footage: 120000

18658 Alpha Packaging
1555 Page Industrial Blvd
St Louis, MO 63132-1309
314-427-4300
Fax: 314-427-5445 800-421-4772
www.alphap.com
Manufacturer and exporter of jars, bottles and caps
CEO: David Spence
ds@alphaplastic.com
CFO: Jim Flower
VP: Dan Creston
R&D: Robert Wilson
Quality Control: Shane Vorden
Sales: Paul Bonastia
Operations Manager: Roy Allen
Plant Manager: Darren Viernes
Estimated Sales: $20-50 Million
Number Employees: 100-249
Square Footage: 210000

18659 Alpha Productions Inc
5800 W Jefferson Blvd
Los Angeles, CA 90016-3109
310-559-1364
Fax: 310-559-2151 800-223-0883
john@alphaproductions.com
www.alphaproductions.com

Retractable awnings
President: Missak Azirian
service@alphaproductions.com
Sales Manager: Howard Goldstein
Estimated Sales: $2.5-5 Million
Number Employees: 20-49

18660 Alpha Resources Inc
3090 Johnson Rd
Stevensville, MI 49127-1270
269-465-3629
Fax: 269-465-3629 800-833-3083
sales@alpharesources.com
www.alpharesources.com
Aftermarket parts Perkin Elmer, Leco & Specto machinery.
President: Phil Lunsford
alphares@aol.com
Number Employees: 20-49

18661 AlphaBio Inc
29816 Avenida De Las Banderas
Rancho Santa Maragarita, CA 92688
949-858-4999
Fax: 949-858-4994 800-966-0716
Sanitary pumps
Account Manager: Sean Pursaid
Estimated Sales: $25 Million
Number Employees: 100

18662 Alphabet Signs
91 Newport Rd # 102
Gap, PA 17527-9579
610-979-0174
Fax: 610-979-0066 800-582-6366
info@alphabetsigns.com www.alphabetsigns.com
Retailer of restaurant signs
President: Daniel Keane
Contact: Dan Keane
dan@alphabetsigns.com
Estimated Sales: Less Than $500,000
Number Employees: 1-4
Square Footage: 5000

18663 Alphasonics
15 Cottondale Rd
The Hills, TX 78738-1513
512-837-8088
Estimated Sales: $3-5 Million
Number Employees: 5-9

18664 Alpine Store Equipment Corporation
3710 10th St
Long Island City, NY 11101-6005
718-361-1213
Fax: 718-786-1220
Self-service food bars, restaurant counters and equipment
Estimated Sales: $2.5-5 Million
Number Employees: 20-49

18665 Alro Plastics
3100 E High St
Jackson, MI 49203-3467
517-787-5500
Fax: 517-787-6390 800-877-2576
aglick@alro.com www.alro.com
Engineering plastics parts and shapes, delrin, teflon, UHMW, nylon, polycarbonate, Ertalyte Pet-P & TX, fiberglass grating and structurals
President: Dean Davis
CEO: Al Glick
aglick@alro.com
Quality Control: Mike Mraz
CEO: Al Glick
Estimated Sales: $20 Million
Number Employees: 20-49
Parent Co: Alro Steel Corporation
Type of Packaging: Bulk

18666 Alstor America
PO Box 98
Stockbridge, WI 53088-0098
920-439-1777
Fax: 920-439-1002 pekaty1@fox.tds.net
Stainless steel, galvanized and epoxy coated bolted tanks, silos and bins for processing and storage of liquids, solids and semi-solids

Type of Packaging: Bulk

18667 Alta Refrigeration Inc
403 Dividend Dr
Peachtree City, GA 30269-1905
678-554-1100
Fax: 678-554-1111 alexg@cold4u.com
www.altarefrigeration.com
Owner: Rex Brown
alta@cold4you.com
Estimated Sales: $10-20 Million
Number Employees: 50-99

18668 Alteca Limited
731 Mccall Rd
Manhattan, KS 66502-5037
785-537-9773
Fax: 785-537-1800 alteca@alteca.com
Food and beverage research and inspection
President: Lynn Bates
info@alteca.com
Marketing/Advertising: Lisa Bardmment
Estimated Sales: $500,000
Number Employees: 5-9

18669 Altech
888 Gilbert Highway
Fairfield, CT 06824-1645
203-259-1525
Fax: 203-259-1527 www.altech.co.jp
Anti-microbial materials, long term anto-mite solu-
tion and anti-static agent for thermoplastic materials
President: Hirokazu Yuri

18670 Altech Packaging Company
330 Himrod St
Brooklyn, NY 11237
718-386-8800
Fax: 718-366-2398 800-362-2247
mitchell@altechpackaging.com
www.altechpackaging.com
Company is a wholesaler of packaging/recycling
management.
President: Mitchell Lomazow
chicoman57@aol.com
Estimated Sales: $4 000,000
Number Employees: 10-19
Number of Brands: 50
Number of Products: 300
Square Footage: 45000

18671 Altek Co
245 E Elm St
Torrington, CT 06790-5059
860-482-7626
Fax: 860-496-7113 info@altekcompany.com
www.altekcompany.com
Manufacturer and exporter of can testing equipment;
also, food and beverage can and bottle testing ser-
vices available
President: Stephen Altschuler
steve@altekcompany.com
Marketing: Brian Mazurkivich
Office Manager: David Altschuler
Estimated Sales: $10-20,000,000
Number Employees: 100-249
Square Footage: 46000
Brands:
　Tech

18672 Altek Industries Corporation
35 Vantage Point Drive
Rochester, NY 14624-1142
716-349-3500
Contact: John Devoldre
jdevoldre@altekcalibrators.com

**18673 Alternative Air & StoreFixtures
Company**
30 Echo Lane
Willingboro, NJ 08046
609-267-5870
Fax: 609-261-5531 aainfo@aafixtures.com
www.aafixtures.com
Display Fixtures
Contact: Mike Banks
mbanks@airalternative.com

18674 Althor Products
2 Turnage Lane
Bethel, CT 06801-2853
203-830-6060
Fax: 203-830-6064 800-688-2693
althor640@aol.com www.althor.com
FDA approved containers

President: Harold Shupack
Sales Manager: Judy Vivone
Estimated Sales: $1-2.5 Million
Number Employees: 5-9
Square Footage: 48000
Parent Co: American Hinge Corporation

18675 Altira Inc
3225 NW 112th St
Miami, FL 33167-3330
305-687-8074
Fax: 305-688-8029 sales@altira.com
www.altira.com
Manufacturer and exporter of blow molded plastic
bottles; also, silk screening, pressure sensitive label-
ing and hot stamping available
President: Ramon Poo
Vice President: Concepcion Alonso
alonso@altira.com
General Manager: Art Hammel
Estimated Sales: $10-20 Million
Number Employees: 100-249

18676 Altman Industries
699 Altman Road
Gray, GA 31032-3431
478-986-3116
Fax: 478-986-1699
Manufacturer and exporter of processing machinery
for peppers, citrus fruits, cabbage, cauliflower, car-
rots, celery, etc
President: James E Altman
OFC Administrator: Jeri Hastings
Secretary: Gwen Jones
Estimated Sales: Below $5 Million
Number Employees: 10
Square Footage: 40000

18677 Alto-Shaam
W164n9221 Water St
P.O. Box 450
Menomonee Falls, WI 53052
262-251-7067
800-329-8744
www.alto-shaam.com
Warming ovens, low temperature cook and holding
equipment, hot deli display cases, smokers, combi-
nation oven/steamers, quick chillers, fryers and con-
vection ovens.
President: Steve Maahs
stevem@alto-shaam.com
Director, Finance: Kevin Noonan
Vice President, Marketing: John Muldowney
Year Founded: 1950
Estimated Sales: $29 Million
Number Employees: 250-499
Number of Brands: 3
Number of Products: 200
Square Footage: 350000
Type of Packaging: Food Service
Brands:
　Combitherm
　Frytech
　Halo Heat
　Quickchiller

18678 Altra Industrial Motion Corp
300 Granite St.
Suite 201
Braintree, MA 02184
781-917-0600
Fax: 781-843-0709 info@altramotion.com
www.altramotion.com
Wide range of mechanical power transmission prod-
ucts.
Chairman/CEO: Carl Christenson
Vice President/CFO: Christian Storch
EVP, Legal & HR: Glenn Deegan
VP, Marketing & Business Development: Craig
Schuele
Year Founded: 2004
Estimated Sales: $1.8 Billion
Number Employees: 9,500
Number of Brands: 27
Brands:
　Ameridrives
　Bauer Gear Motor
　Bibby Turboflex
　Boston Gear
　Delroyd Worm Gear
　Formsprag Clutch
　Guardian Couplings
　Huco
　Industrial Clutch

　Inertia Dynamics
　Jacobs Vehicle Systems
　Kilian
　Kollmorgen
　Lamiflex Couplings
　Marland Clutch
　Matrix
　Nuttall Gear
　Portescap
　Stieber
　Stromag
　Svendborg Brakes
　TB Wood's
　Thomson
　Twiflex
　Warner Electric
　Warner Linear
　Wichita Clutch

18679 Altrafilters
200 Wanaque Ave # 401
Pompton Lakes, NJ 07442-2130
973-831-1010
Fax: 973-831-8181
Executive Director: Elaine Gordon

18680 Altrua Marketing & Design
3225 Hartsfield Rd
Tallahassee, FL 32303-3153
850-562-4564
Fax: 850-562-8511 800-443-6939
mfloyd@altrua.com www.wave94.com
Manufacturer and wholesaler/distributor of signs,
banners, flags, pennants, table displays, decals and
other printed promotional materials
President: Michael Floyd
msmelko@altrua.com
Sales Exec: Melode Smelko
Estimated Sales: $6 Million
Number Employees: 20-49
Square Footage: 160000

18681 Alturdyne Power Systems LLC
660 Steele St
El Cajon, CA 92020-1630
619-440-5531
Fax: 619-442-0481 info@alturdyne.com
www.alturdyne.com
President: Frank Dverbeke
CEO: James Eggert
Number Employees: 100-249

18682 Alufoil Products Co Inc
135 Oser Ave # 3
Hauppauge, NY 11788-3722
631-231-4141
Fax: 631-231-1435 sales@alufoil.com
www.alufoil.com
A supplier of aluminum foil, paper foil and foil
board for food packaging and laminating. Uses in-
clude ham & turkey wrap, confectioners foil and
general food service
President: Howard Lent
elliot@alufoil.com
VP: Elliot Lent
Estimated Sales: $3-5 000,000
Number Employees: 10-19
Square Footage: 40000
Type of Packaging: Food Service

18683 Aluma Shield
725 Summerhill Drive
Deland, FL 32724-2024
386-626-6789
877-638-3266
Manufacturer and exporter of cold storage panels
and doors
President: John Peters
Sales Director: Allen Rockafellow
Estimated Sales: $20-50 Million
Number Employees: 10

18684 Alumar
4809 N Armenia Avenue
Suite 05
Tampa, FL 33603-1447
813-870-0998
Fax: 813-870-0590
Food processing and can closing machinery
Estimated Sales: Below 1 Million
Number Employees: 1
Square Footage: 8000
Type of Packaging: Bulk

Brands:
Canco

18685 Alumaworks
16850-112 Collins Avenue #185
Sunny Isle Beach, FL 33160
305-635-6100
Fax: 866-790-2153 800-277-7267
rod@alumaworks.com www.alumaworks.com
Manufacturer and exporter of aluminum bakeware
and cookware including frying, sauce, saute, cake
and pizza pans, stock pots, deep fryers, pasta cook-
ers, roasters, steamers, etc
President: Rod Haber
Sales Manager: Rod Haber
Number Employees: 14
Square Footage: 40000
Brands:
Alumaworks

18686 Alumaworks
16850-112 Collins Avenue #185
Sunny Isles Bch, FL 33160-4238
305-635-6100
Fax: 866-790-2153 800-277-7267
sales@alumaworks.com www.alumaworks.com
Bakeware, cookware, pizza pans and accessories
President: Rod Haber
Estimated Sales: $2.5-5 Million
Number Employees: 5-9

18687 Alumin-Nu Corporation
PO Box 24359
Lyndhurst, OH 44124
216-421-2116
Fax: 216-791-8018 800-899-7097
aluminnu@aol.com www.aluminnu.com
Cleaners for drains, septics, ponds, lakes, fish, bird
bath cleaner, aluminum and vinyl doors, window,
gutters, siding and boats.
President/Purchasing Director: Howard Kaufman
aluminnu@aol.com
Plant Manager: Charles Moon
Number Employees: 3
Number of Products: 11
Square Footage: 30000
Type of Packaging: Consumer, Private Label, Bulk
Brands:
Alumin-Nu
Nice N Easy
Power

18688 Alusett Precision Manufacturing
3 Cecilia Ln
Pleasantville, NY 10570
914-769-4900
alusett@alusett-usa.com
www.alusett-usa.com
Estimated Sales: $1-3 Million
Number Employees: 1-4

18689 Alvarado Manufacturing Co Inc
12660 Colony Ct
Chino, CA 91710-2975
909-591-8431
Fax: 909-628-1403 800-423-4143
information@alvaradomfg.com
www.alvaradomfg.com
railings including ornamental, metal, brass, chrome
and color; also, bar railings and glass partitions and
stair and ramp rails
President: Jack Horener
CEO: Bret Armatas
barmatas@alvaradomfg.com
Chairman: James P Armatas
CEO: Bret Armatas
VP Sales/Marketing: Bret Armatas
Estimated Sales: $10-20 Million
Number Employees: 50-99
Brands:
Escort

18690 Amagic Holographics
1652 Deere Avenue
Irvine, CA 92606-4813
877-693-6457
Fax: 949-474-3979 800-262-4421
sales@amagicholo.com www.amagicholo.com
Vertically integrated holographic images including
holographic security labels, pressure sensitive stickers, PET/PVC/OPP film and hot stamping foil
President: Howard Chen
Marketing Manager: Susan Chiang

18691 Amano Artisan Chocolate
496 S 1325 W
Orem, UT 84058-5877
801-655-1996
amano@amanochocolate.com
www.amanochocolate.com
Chocolates
Owner: Art Pollard
Pastry Chef: Rebecca Millican
Number Employees: 20-49
Type of Packaging: Private Label
Brands:
Amano Ocumare
Amano Jenbrana

18692 Amarillo Mop & Broom Company
801 S Fillmore
Suite 205
Amarillo, TX 79101
806-372-8596
Fax: 806-379-8724 800-955-8596
Mop manufacturer
President: E Bryan
VP: Sue Ann Bryan
Estimated Sales: $2.5-5 Million
Number Employees: 10-19
Square Footage: 96000
Type of Packaging: Private Label, Bulk
Brands:
Amco
Trouble Shooter

18693 Amark Packaging Systems
4717 E. 119th Street
PO Box 9824
Kansas City, MO 64134
816-965-9000
Fax: 816-965-9003 amarkpkg@sprintmail.com
www.amarkpackaging.com
Manufacturer,exporter of conveyors,bag closers,
sewing machines, heat sealers,scales, and pinch
closers; custom fabrications available.
Owner: Bob Mc Cullough
Plant Manager: Jack Groblebe
Estimated Sales: $2.5-5 Million
Number Employees: 10
Number of Products: 15
Square Footage: 80000
Brands:
Amark/Simionato
Dura-Pak

18694 Amax Nutrasource Inc
1770 Prairie Rd
Eugene, OR 97402-9734
541-688-4944
Fax: 541-688-4866 800-893-5306
www.amaxnutrasource.com
Manufacturer and distributor of herbal extracts and
nutritional ingredients.
President: Larry Martinez
lm@amaxnutrasource.com
CFO: Daniel Rothwell
Business Development Manager: Steve Light
Production Manager: Charles Lofton
Number Employees: 10-19

18695 Ambaflex
2202 113th Street
Suite 112
Grand Prairie, TX 75050-1200
877-800-1634
Fax: 877-800-1635 877-800-1634
info@ambaflex.com www.ambaflex.com
Contact: Phil Miller
bcallanan@businessreadysolutions.net

18696 Amber Glo
4140 W Victoria St
Chicago, IL 60646-6727
773-604-8700
Fax: 773-604-4070 866-705-0515
info@emberglo.com www.emberglo.com
Manufacturer and exporter of commercial cooking
equipment including gas broilers and steam cookers
President: Teryl A Stanger
Marketing Director: J Kelderhouse
National Sales Manager: Karen Trice
Contact: Joseph Hrabovecky
karent@emberglo.com
Estimated Sales: $3,000,000
Number Employees: 100-249
Number of Brands: 1

Square Footage: 320000
Parent Co: Midco International
Type of Packaging: Food Service
Brands:
Ember-Glo

18697 Ambient Engineering Co
5 Crescent Ave # A-1
Rocky Hill, NJ 8553
609-279-6888
Fax: 609-279-9444 john@ambienteng.com
www.hydronics-env.com
President: Bruce Bruns
Estimated Sales: $.5-1 million
Number Employees: 1-4

18698 Ambitech Engineering Corp
1411 Opus Pl # 200
Downers Grove, IL 60515-1060
630-963-5800
Fax: 630-963-8099 www.ambitech.com
President: Alan Koenig
akoenig@ambitech.com
CFO: Christopher Hunt
Estimated Sales: $10-20 Million
Number Employees: 500-999

18699 Ambrose CM Co
2919 Fulton St
Everett, WA 98201-3733
425-317-9818
Fax: 425-317-8597
Manufacturer and exporterof liquid packaging
equipment including turnkey systems, pail denesters,
fillers, check weighters, conveyors, palletizers, con-
trols and engineering services
President: John Bowman
CFO: Cindy Annyas
Vice President: Jeff Bowman
Sales Director: John Bowman
Operations Manager: Jeff Bowman
Estimated Sales: $1.5 Million
Number Employees: 1-4
Number of Products: 12
Square Footage: 24000
Brands:
Ambrose

18700 Amcel
1 Galen Street
Watertown, MA 02472-4501
617-924-0800
Fax: 617-924-2931 800-225-7992
www.amcel.com
Producers of linear low density and high density
polyethylene liners, and stock-size polyethylene
bags for food packaging applications; also a leading
supplier of disposable plastic cutlery
President: Brad Gordon
Sales Manager: Mike Milich
Customer Service Manager: Laura Ott
Estimated Sales: $50-100 Million
Number Employees: 20-49
Square Footage: 18000
Brands:
Amcel

18701 Amco Mechanical
25915 Aldine Westfield Rd
Spring, TX 77373
281-353-2171
Fax: 281-353-2171 www.theamcogroup.com
Commercial contractor
President/Owner: Harold Herridge
VP: Kim Gabehart

18702 Amco Metals Indl
461 S 7th Ave
City Of Industry, CA 91746-3119
626-855-2550
Fax: 626-855-2551 info@amcocorporation.com
www.amcocorporation.com
Manufacturer and exporter of racks, utensils, carts,
dollies, trucks, mobile storage equipment, shelving,
etc
Owner: Fank Ko
amcocorporation@aol.com
Sales Director: Dennis Dominic
Estimated Sales: $20-50 Million
Number Employees: 10-19
Square Footage: 240000
Parent Co: Leggett & Platt Storage Products Group
Brands:
Amco

Amcoat
Amcoll
Amtrax
Challenger
Magic Wall
Mod-A-Flex
Plasteel
Plastic Plus
Polygard
Shelving By the Inch
Take 10
Ultra Density

18703 Amco Products Co
501 S Phoenix Ave
Fort Smith, AR 72916-8008
479-646-8949
Fax: 479-648-1032 www.amcoprod.com
Bottling machinery
President: Wendell Martin
Estimated Sales: $20-50 Million
Number Employees: 20-49
Square Footage: 65000

18704 Amco Warehouse & Transportation
1210 Kona Drive
Suite B
Compton, CA 90220-5405
310-635-1885
Fax: 310-604-9762
Samplers and weighing machinery

18705 Amcor
2200 Badger Ave
P.O. Box 2968
Oshkosh, WI 54904
920-527-7300
800-544-4672
NorthAmericaFlexibles@amcor.com
www.amcor.com
Major manufacturer of flexible packaging, rigid containers, specialty cartons, closures and other services
Managing Director/CEO: Ron Delia
President, Amcor Speciality Cartons: Jerzy Czubak
EVP & Chief Financial Officer: Michael Casamento
President, Amcor Rigid Packaging: Eric Roegner
President, Flexibles North America: Fred Stephan
Year Founded: 1860
Estimated Sales: $13 Billion
Number Employees: 50,000
Parent Co: Amcor plc
Brands:
Bemistape
Tension-Master Ii

18706 Amcor Group Limited
539 46th Avenue
Long Island City, NY 11101-5230
718-361-2700
Fax: 718-706-6058

18707 Ameranth Inc
5820 Oberlin Dr # 202
San Diego, CA 92121-3744
858-362-0150
Fax: 858-362-0151 888-263-7268
info@ameranth.com www.ameranth.net
Wireless provider
CEO: Keith McNally
Contact: Steve Brooks
sbrooks@ameranth.com
Estimated Sales: $20-50 Million
Number Employees: 20-49

18708 Amerex
7595 Gadsden Hwy
Trussville, AL 35173
205-655-3271
Fax: 800-654-5980 www.amerex-fire.com
Fire protection
President/Owner: Harrison Bishop
Year Founded: 1971
Estimated Sales: $100 Million
Number Employees: 500
Parent Co: McWane, Inc.

18709 Ameri Quest Transportation Svc
457 Haddonfield Rd # 220
Cherry Hill, NJ 08002-2201
800-608-0809
Fax: 856-773-0609 888-999-6957
feedback@fleetxchange.com
www.ameriquestcorp.com

President: Doug Clarck
CFO: Rich Spotts
CEO: Douglas W Clark
Estimated Sales: $50-75 Million
Number Employees: 10-19

18710 Ameri-Khem
530 New Town Road
PO Box 291907
Port Orange, FL 32129-1907
386-756-9950
800-224-9950
www.truckcompaniesin.com
Anti-bacterial drain cleaner and waste reduction equipment
President: George Huth
Number Employees: 1-4
Brands:
Nature's Best Liquid Live

18711 AmeriQual Foods
18200 Highway 41 N
Evansville, IN 47725
812-867-1444
Fax: 812-867-0278 www.ameriqual.com
Processor and contract packager of shelf stable entrees using retort processing
CEO: Dan Hermman
VP Sales/Marketing: Michael Billing
Contact: Casey Elliott
casey.elliott@thementornetwork.com
Senior VP Operations: Tim Brauer
Estimated Sales: $50-100 Million
Number Employees: 100-249
Square Footage: 100000

18712 America's Electric Cooperatives
4301 Wilson Boulevard
Arlington, VA 22203-1867
703-907-5707
Fax: 703-907-5531 nreca@nreca.coop
www.nreca.org
President: James Baker
Senior Vice President of Programs: Vivek Talvadkar

18713 American & Efird
24 American St
Mount Holly, NC 28120
704-827-4311
Fax: 704-861-8579
Industrial yarns
Contact: Melissa Carpenter
melissa.carpenter@amefird.com
Plant Manager: Chris McGuret
Estimated Sales: $20-50 Million
Number Employees: 100-249

18714 American Adhesives
1730 Evergreen St
Duarte, CA 91010
626-256-4417
Fax: 626-256-4427 800-557-4747
President: John S. Sepulveda
Owner: Tim Thornton
Estimated Sales: $1-5 Million
Number Employees: 1-4

18715 American Advertising & Shop Cap Company
48 Bi State Plaza
Suite 231
Old Tappan, NJ 07675-7003
845-639-1596
Fax: 845-639-1597 800-442-8837
Men's work headwear, imprinted painters' caps, aprons, cloth bags, baseball caps, t-shirts, tote bags sunvisors, golf shirts, sweatshirts and engineer caps.
President: Ronnie Ehrlich
Number Employees: 50

18716 American Agribusiness Assistance
2916 Dartmouth Road
Alexandria, VA 22314-4822
202-429-0500
Fax: 202-429-0525 agequip@aol.com
www.agribusiness.org.pk
Export broker of processing and packaging equipment for baked goods, sausage, vegetables, fruits, cheese, dairy products, etc.; consultant offering plant design and equipment installation
President: James Roberts
VP: Dick Verga
Number Employees: 1-4

18717 American Air Filter
4800 Hockaday Rd
Four Oaks, NC 27524
919-207-1376
Fax: 704-365-1975 800-600-5546
info@aafintl.com www.aafintl.com
Heating, cooling, ventilating, noise pollution control and air cleaning products and systems
Manager: Sam C Price
Sales/Marketing Director: Bob Sturges
APC Sales Manager: Chris O'Connor
Estimated Sales: Below 1 Million
Number Employees: 50-99

18718 American Apron Inc.
P.O.Box 318
Foxboro, MA 02035-0318
508-384-9600
Fax: 508-384-9601 800-262-7766
Aprons, safety vests and screen printing
President: James Holicker
VP: Connie Holicker
Estimated Sales: Less than $500,000
Number Employees: 1-4

18719 American Art Stamp
17803 South Harvard Street
Suite B
Gardena, CA 90248
310-965-9004
amartstamp@aol.com
Rubber, number, pre-inked and self-inking stamps; also, marking devices, signage and metal marking devices
Co-Owner: Robert Tepper
Estimated Sales: $300,000-500,000
Number Employees: 1-4
Square Footage: 6800

18720 American Association-Meat
1 Meating Pl
Elizabethtown, PA 17022-2883
717-367-1168
Fax: 717-367-9096 aamp@aamp.com
www.aamp.com
AAMP is a meat trade association which provides quality service, knowledge through education to it's members.
Manager: Jody Bartlett
jodi@aamp.com
Secretary: Marty Manion
Number Employees: 5-9

18721 American Auger & Accesories
325 Westtown Rd
Suite 8
West Chester, PA 19382
610-692-7811
Fax: 610-692-7886 866-219-9619
sales@americanauger.com
www.americanauger.com
Replacement augers and funnels for all make model of auger filling machines. We also make augers for conveyors and horizontal feeders
President: Jack Treptow
Estimated Sales: $.5-1 million
Number Employees: 1-4

18722 American Autoclaves Co
PO Box 430
Sumner, WA 98390-0080
253-863-5000
Fax: 253-863-1770 info@americanautoclave.com
President: Patty Stack
aautoclave@aol.com
Estimated Sales: Below $5 Million
Number Employees: 5-9

18723 American Autogard Corporation
5173 26th Avenue
Rockford, IL 61109
815-229-3190
Fax: 815-229-4615 www.autogard.com
Mechanical and pneumatic torque limiting/overload release clutches and monitors
Manager: Thomas Johnson
Contact: Bill Kuchler
autogarde@gmail.com
Operations Ex: Les Wodecki

18724 American Bag & Burlap Company

36 Arlington St
Chelsea, MA 2150

617-884-7600
Fax: 617-437-7917 info@cormanbag.com
www.cormanbag.com
Manufacturer and importer of bags including burlap, paper and plastic; also, weighing, filling and closing machinery
President: Elliot Corman
VP: Barry Corman
VP: Julie Corman
Estimated Sales: $12 Million
Number Employees: 10-19
Square Footage: 50000
Type of Packaging: Private Label

18725 American Bag & Linen Co

339 Airport Rd W
PO Box 8
Cornelia, GA 30531-5928

706-778-5377
Fax: 706-778-9118 abl@abl-sewing.com
www.abl-sewing.com
Aprons
Owner: Jim Harris
abl@windstream.net
Office Manager: Judy Porter
Plant Manager: Ramona Holt
Estimated Sales: $5-10 Million
Number Employees: 100-249

18726 American Bakery Equipment Company

435 Johnston St # B
PO Box 3135
Half Moon Bay, CA 94019

650-560-9970
Fax: 650-560-9971 800-341-5581
www.americanbakeryequipment.biz
Wholesaler/distributor of new and used bakery equipment for pastries, muffins, cookies, cakes, breads, pizzas, bagels, etc.; installation services available
Manager: John Candelori Jr
CEO: Ken Skelton
CFO: Norman Gwinn
VP: John Candelori, Jr.
Research & Development: Polly Vandersyde
CFO: Sabatino Compi
Estimated Sales: Below $5,000,000
Number Employees: 5-9
Number of Brands: 200
Number of Products: 1000
Square Footage: 4750

18727 American Box Corporation

PO Box 112
Lisbon, OH 44432-0112

330-424-8055
Fax: 330-424-7441 amboxcorp@aol.com
Custom, new and reconditioned wooden pallets, skids, boxes and crates
Estimated Sales: less than $500,000
Number Employees: 10

18728 American Broom Co

1200 Moultrie Ave
Mattoon, IL 61938-3123

217-235-1992
Fax: 217-234-9180 www.lucomop.com
Brooms
Manager: Clarence Gillispie
Manager: Clarence Gillispie
c.gillespie@lucomop.com
Manager: Clarence Gillispie
Estimated Sales: $1-2.5 Million
Number Employees: 5-9
Parent Co: Luco Mop Company

18729 American Brush Company

3150 NW 31st Avenue
Suite 3
Portland, OR 97210

503-234-5064
Fax: 503-234-1270 800-826-8492
info@americanbrush.com
www.americanbrush.com
Manufacturer and exporter of industrial and commercial brooms and brushes

President: Laddie M. Wirth, Sr.
CEO: John S. Martin
Vice President: Janine M. Wirth
Contact: Gladys Doern
gladys@americanbrush.com
Estimated Sales: $2.5-5 Million
Number Employees: 10-19
Square Footage: 40000

18730 American Cart Company

12 Eccleston Avenue
North Kingstown, RI 02852-7406

401-885-5055
Fax: 401-885-5057
Coffee and espresso carts

18731 American Casting & Mfg Corp

51 Commercial St
Plainview, NY 11803-2490

516-349-8389
Fax: 516-349-8389 800-342-0333
info@americancasting.com www.seals.com
Seals, security seals,cargo seals,ctpat seals,truch seals
President: Norman Wenk Iii
Cmo: Jim Wenk
jimwenk@americancasting.com
Number Employees: 50-99

18732 American Chocolate Mould Co.

1401 Church St
Suite 5
Bohemia, NY 11716-5016

631-589-5080
Fax: 516-908-3660 amerchoc@mindspring.com
www.americanchocolatemould.com
Chocolate equipment chocolate moulds, plain and printed aluminum foils, foil wrapping machines
President: Raymond J. Cote Jr.
amerchoc@mindspring.com
Sales Director: David Cote
Public Relations: Katie Cote
Estimated Sales: $500,000-$1,000,000
Number Employees: 5-9
Square Footage: 1700
Type of Packaging: Private Label, Bulk

18733 American Coaster Company

3685 Lockport Rd
Sanborn, NY 14132-9404

716-731-9193
Fax: 716-731-4138 888-423-8628
Custom designed beverage coasters
President: Tom Muraca
Sales Manager: Tammy Gorzka
Contact: Kristin Kinney
kkinney@katzamericas.com
Estimated Sales: $10-20 Million
Number Employees: 50-99
Parent Co: Gardei

18734 American Containers Inc

2526 Western Ave
Plymouth, IN 46563-1050

574-936-4068
Fax: 574-936-4036 info@acontainers.com
www.acontainers.com
Manufacturer and exporter of corrugated boxes
Owner: Leonard D Isban
misban@acontainers.com
CFO: Steve Tubes
Estimated Sales: $5-10 Million
Number Employees: 50-99

18735 American Conveyor Corporation

26-40 1st St.
Astoria, NY 11385-1002

718-386-0480
Fax: 718-456-1233
Supplier of belt and rollover conveyor, bagging & debagging, case packaging & unscrambling, case stackers, casers, checkweighers, corrugated case forming & top sealing, corrugated palletizing & banding, deunitizers, fillers, labeling &coding, metal detectors, palletizers, pushers, unitizers, unstackers, shrink wrap & stretch wrap, truck & dock leveling
Owner: Valdie Freidman
Estimated Sales: Below $5 Million
Number Employees: 20-49
Other Locations:
    American Conveyor Corporation
    Carlisle NY
    American Conveyor Corporation
    Overland Park KS
    American Conveyor Corporation

    Sarasota FL
    American Conveyor Corporation
    Uxbridge MA
    American Conveyor Corporation
    Murray KY
    American Conveyor Corporation
    St. Petersburg FL

18736 American Coolair Corp

3604 Mayflower St
Jacksonville, FL 32205-5378

904-389-3646
Fax: 904-387-3449 info@coolair.com
www.coolair.com
Manufacturer and exporter of ventilation fans and systems
President: Harry M Graves Jr
VP: Neal Taylor
Marketing/Sales Manager: Mark Fales
Estimated Sales: $20-50 Million
Number Employees: 100-249
Square Footage: 110000

18737 American Crane & Equip Corp

531 Old Swede Rd
Douglassville, PA 19518-1299

610-385-6061
Fax: 610-385-3191 info@americancrane.com
www.munckintl.com
Cranes and hoist trolleys
President: Oddvar Norheim
onorheim@americancrane.com
CFO: Dave Hope
Quality Control: Frank Yurich
VP of Sales: David Schaeffer
Purchasing Manager: Sandy Hoffman
Estimated Sales: $20-50 Million
Number Employees: 50-99
Square Footage: 60000

18738 American Creative Solutions

11145 Monroe Rd
Matthews, NC 28105

Fax: 731-925-3209 877-925-4406
info@amcreativesolutions.com
www.amcreativesolutions.com
Foodservice equipment manufacturer
President, Eagle Group: Larry McAllister
Parent Co: Eagle Group

18739 American Custom Dry Co

109 Elbow Ln
Burlington, NJ 08016-4123

609-387-3933
Fax: 609-387-7204
Spray drying and blending services
President: Richard Shipley
CFO: Michael Garger
Vice President: Svend Hansen
Quality Control: Fran Thornton
Public Relations: Jane Macey
Operations Manager: Larry Cutler
Estimated Sales: $10-20 Million
Number Employees: 50-99
Type of Packaging: Private Label, Bulk

18740 American Cut Edge Inc

480 Congress Park Dr
Dayton, OH 45459-4144

937-438-2390
Fax: 937-438-2398 888-252-3372
info@americancuttingedge.com
www.americancuttingedge.com
Industry standard blades and knives, high tolerant blades and safety knives
President: Chuck Biehn
cbiehn@americancuttingedge.com
CFO: Don Cain
Estimated Sales: $5-10 Million
Number Employees: 20-49
Square Footage: 400000
Parent Co: CB Manufacturing & Sales Company

18741 American Cylinder Co

481 S Governors Hwy
Peotone, IL 60468-9116

708-258-3935
Fax: 708-258-3980 amcyl@americancylinder.com
www.americancylinder.com
President: Joseph White
amcyl@americancylinder.com
Estimated Sales: $20-50 Million
Number Employees: 20-49

18742 American Design & Machinery
430 Cummings Avenue NW
Grand Rapids, MI 49534-7984
616-791-4856
Fax: 616-791-4898
Food processing machinery
Marketing Director: Robert Cisleil
Contact: Joe Cisler
j_cisler@hotmail.com
Estimated Sales: $1-2.5 000,000
Number Employees: 19
Square Footage: 23000

18743 American Design Studios
6353 Corte Del Abeto Ste A106
Carlsbad, CA 92011
760-438-8880
Fax: 760-438-8488 800-899-7104
Manufacturer and importer of shirts with names and
logos
President: Robert Peritz
Marketing Director: Judy Morrill
Contact: Mike Srtingfellow
mike@mss.net
Estimated Sales: $10-20 Million
Number Employees: 10-19
Brands:
American Terrain

18744 American Dish Service
900 Blake St
Edwardsville, KS 66111-3820
913-422-3700
Fax: 913-422-6630 800-922-2178
www.americandish.com
Commercial dishwashers
President: James Andrews
jamie@americandish.com
Estimated Sales: $20-50 Million
Number Employees: 100-249

18745 American Dixie Group
250 Osborne Rd
Albany, NY 12205-1300
518-453-9000
Packaging machinery
Owner: Beth Wade
Estimated Sales: $5-10 Million
Number Employees: 5-9

18746 American Eagle Food Machinery
3557 S Halsted St
Chicago, IL 60609
773-376-0800
Fax: 773-376-2010 888-390-0800
Info@AmericanEagleMachine.com
www.americaneaglemachine.com
Manufacturer, importer and exporter of bakery ma-
chinery including mixers, bread slicers and grinders-
meat tenderizer, dough sheets, dough roller, dividers
of rounders and dough molders.
Owner: Spencer Yang
Contact: Didicher Grace
grace@ameagle.biz
Estimated Sales: $1-2,500,000
Number Employees: 10-19
Brands:
American Eagle

18747 American Electric Power
1 Riverside Plaza
Columbus, OH 43215-2372
614-716-1000
800-277-2177
www.aep.com
Electric utility systems.
Chairman/President/CEO: Nicholas Akins
EVP & Chief Financial Officer: Brian Tierney
EVP/General Counsel/Secretary: David Feinberg
EVP & Chief Administrative Officer: Lana
Hillebrand
SVP & Chief Customer Officer: Bruce Evans
SVP, Governmental Affairs: Tony Kavanagh
SVP & Chief Customer Officer: Thomas Kirkpatrick
Year Founded: 1906
Estimated Sales: $15 Billion
Number Employees: 18,000

18748 American Electronic Components
1101 Lafayette St
Elkhart, IN 46516-2615
574-295-6330
Fax: 574-293-8013 888-847-6552

Vice President: Patrick Conway
pconway@aecsensors.com
Vice President: Patrick Conway
pconway@aecsensors.com
Number Employees: 10-19

**18749 American Engineering
Corporation**
PO Box 336
Collegedale, TN 37315-0336
423-396-3666
Fax: 423-396-3668
Food safety data collection
Estimated Sales: $5-10 Million
Number Employees: 3

**18750 American Environmental
International**
1325 Remington Road
Schaumburg, IL 60173-4834
847-342-8600
Fax: 847-342-8500 800-343-8601
jstandon@aol.com www.aei-inc.com
Environmental control and resource recovery equip-
ment, emission control, solvent recovery systems, air
pollution control
Estimated Sales: $500,000-$1 Million
Number Employees: 5-9

18751 American Equipment Co
1080 Hardees Dr
Aberdeen, MD 21001-2637
410-272-2626
Fax: 410-272-2011 www.seamers.com
Refurbisher of can seamers; also, parts available
President: Charles Adams
cadams@americanequipment.us
General Manager: Mike Mangone
Estimated Sales: Below $5 Million
Number Employees: 5-9

18752 American Equipment Systems Inc
5458 Louie Ln
Réno, NV 89511-1832
775-852-1114
www.aes-sorma.com
President: Robert G Sapeta
bob@aes-sorma.com
Estimated Sales: $3-5 Million
Number Employees: 1-4
Parent Co: American European Systems

18753 American European Systems
5456 Louie Lane
Reno, NV 89510-7061
775-852-1114
Fax: 775-852-1163 info@aes-sorma.com
www.aes-sorma.com
Importer and wholesaler/distributor of cutting, peel-
ing, bagging and weighing equipment
President: Robert Sapeta
Sales/Marketing Executive: Don Bergin
Estimated Sales: $3-5 Million
Number Employees: 5-9
Square Footage: 32000

18754 American Excelsior Co
850 Avenue H E
Arlington, TX 76011-7720
817-385-3500
Fax: 817-649-7816 800-777-7645
www.americanexcelsior.com
Manufacturer, custom molder and exporter of foam
packaging products including inserts, contours, pro-
tectors, pads, liners and fillers
President, Chief Executive Officer: Terry A.
Sadowski
tsadowski@americanexcelsior.com
VP, CFO: Todd A. Eblen
Vice President of Sales and Marketing: Ken Starrett
Vice President of Operations: Kevin Stew
Estimated Sales: $5-10 Million
Number Employees: 50-99

18755 American Excelsior Co
850 Avenue H E
Arlington, TX 76011-7720
817-385-3500
Fax: 817-649-7816 800-777-7645
www.americanexcelsior.com
Plastic packaging products, erosion control products, evaporative cooling products and foam padding

General Manager: Rice Lake
Chairman: Robert Gregerson
CEO: Terry A Sadowski
Vice President of Sales and Marketing: Ken Starrett
Vice President of Operations: Kevin Stew
Estimated Sales: $20-50 Million
Number Employees: 50-99

18756 (HQ)American Extrusion Intl
498 Prairie Hill Rd
South Beloit, IL 61080-2563
815-624-6616
Fax: 815-624-6628 rickw@americanextrusion.com
www.americanextrusion.info
Supplier and exporter of direct expansion extruders
and auxiliary equipment including forced air ovens,
fryers, seasoning systems, wear parts, reel cutters,
mixers, tumblers and conveyors
President: Richard J Warner
rickw@americanextrusion.com
R&D: Dr. Samir El-Shatter
Director of Sales: Rick Warner
Sales Director: Rick Warner
General Manager: Daniel Thompson
Estimated Sales: $.5-$1 million
Number Employees: 50-99
Square Footage: 54000
Other Locations:
American Extrusion Internatio
South Beloit IL
Brands:
American Extrusion International

18757 American Fabric Filter Co Inc
29807 State Road 54
Wesley Chapel, FL 33543-4507
813-991-9400
Fax: 813-991-9700 800-367-3591
info@americanfabricfilter.com
www.americanfabricfilter.com
Manufacturers of custom made filter bags, dust bags
and transfer sleeves for the food, wood, processing
and baking industries. Our products are made specifically to fit each application.
President: Derek Williams
CEO: Zoa Gomez
zgomez@americanfabricfilter.com
CFO: Tim Robinson
Estimated Sales: Below $5 Million
Number Employees: 10-19

18758 American Felt & Filter Co
361 Walsh Ave
New Windsor, NY 12553-6727
845-561-3560
Fax: 845-561-0967 questions@affco.com
www.affco.com
President/CEO: Wilson H. Pryne
wpryne@affco.com
Vice President: Scott H. Pryne
Sales Manager: Mark A. Pryne
Estimated Sales: $10-20 Million
Number Employees: 50-99

**18759 American Fire SprinklerServices,
Inc**
16221 NW 57th Ave
Hialeah, FL 33014-6709
305-628-0100
Fax: 305-628-3556 Sprinklerheads@bellsouth.net
www.americanfiresprinklers.com
Manufacturer and exporter of sprinkler systems
Owner: Anisa Oweiss
Contact: Omar Oweiss
sprinklerheads@bellsouth.net
Operations Director: Ken Oweis
Estimated Sales: $2.5-5 Million
Number Employees: 10-19
Type of Packaging: Consumer, Food Service

18760 American Flag & Banner Co Inc
28 S Main St
Clawson, MI 48017-2088
248-288-3010
Fax: 248-288-5630 800-892-5168
flagsetc@aol.com
Manufacturer and exporter of flags, pennants and
banners
President: William S Miles
flagsetc@aol.com
Sales Manager: Michelle Angle
Estimated Sales: Less Than $500,000
Number Employees: 1-4

18761 American Foam Corp
61 John St
Johnston, RI 02919-6210

401-944-4990
Fax: 401-944-0142 800-235-0010
www.americanfoam.com
Flocked foam packaging materials
Vice President: Chad Martin
chad@americanfoam.com
VP: Chad Martin
Estimated Sales: $20-50 Million
Number Employees: 50-99

18762 American Food Equipment
1301 N Miami Ave
Miami, FL 33136-2815

305-377-8991
Fax: 305-358-4328
michael@americanfoodequipment.com
www.americanfoodequipment.com
Manufacturer and supplier of restaurant equipment
such as coolers, freezers, and ice machines
Founder: Robert Green
President/Owner: Michael Clements
americanfoodequipment@gmail.com
Estimated Sales: $460,000
Number Employees: 5-9
Square Footage: 28000
Parent Co: American Grinding And Equipment
Company.
Type of Packaging: Consumer, Private Label, Bulk

18763 American Food Equipment Company
21040 Forbes Ave
Hayward, CA 94545-1116

510-783-0255
Fax: 510-783-0409 amfec@amfec.com
www.amfec.com
Manufacturer and exporter of mixers, dumpers, belt
and screw conveyors, vacuum stuffers, tumblers and
massagers
President: Michael Botto
Quality Control: Melvin Hauss
Contact: Leticia Alexandre
lalexandre@amfec.com
Controller: Simone Manos
Plant Manager: Ron Balthasar
Estimated Sales: $5-10 Million
Number Employees: 20-49
Square Footage: 80000
Brands:
  Amfec

18764 (HQ)American Forms & Labels
7448 W Mossy Cup St
Boise, ID 83709-2839

208-562-0750
Fax: 208-562-0151 800-388-3554
Pressure sensitive labels; also, bar code systems and
hardware
Owner: Kevin Curtin
Estimated Sales: $5-10 Million
Number Employees: 10-19
Square Footage: 60000

18765 American Formula
4720 Frederick Dr SW
Atlanta, GA 30336-1810

404-691-7940
Fax: 404-691-7943 800-282-1215
pvcnet@aol.com www.americanformula.com
Industrial cleaning compounds
President: Don Hamilton
dhamilton@americanformula.com
President: Phillip Consolino
General Manager: Michael Holtzman
Number Employees: 20-49
Parent Co: Holtco

18766 American Fruits & Flavors
10725 Sutter Ave
Pacoima, CA 91331

818-899-9574
SalesTeam@americanfruit.com
www.americanfruits-flavors.com
Custom flavors, fruit juice blends, natural sweeteners, juice concentrates and liquid powder blends.
Specializing in fruit, vegetable, sweet and savory
flavors, flavor bases, fruit concentrates, coconut
products, smoothies, andtropical blends.

President: Bill Haddad
CEO: Rodney Sacks
Corporate Controller: Michael Model
Senior Research & Development Chemist: Martin
Goldberg
Quality Control Chemist: Linda Valenzuela
VP of Marketing: Richard Linn
Director of Human Resources: Regina Rodriguez
Year Founded: 2016
Estimated Sales: $168 Million
Number Employees: 100-249
Square Footage: 20000
Parent Co: Monster Beverage Corporation

18767 American Fuji Seal
1051 Bloomfield Rd
Bardstown, KY 40004-9794

502-348-9211
Fax: 502-348-9558 800-533-3854
mlane@afseal.com www.fujiseal.com
Shrink sleeves and application equipment
President: Takeo Sonoda
Senior VP: Bill Hayworth
bhayworth@afseal.com
Estimated Sales: $20-50 Million
Number Employees: 250-499

18768 American Gas & Chemical Co LTD
220 Pegasus Ave
Northvale, NJ 07647-1904

201-767-7300
Fax: 201-767-1741 800-288-3647
contact@amgas.com www.amgas.com
Leak detection products and gas monitoring systems
President: Melanie Kershaw
mkershaw@amgas.com
Quality Control and CFO: Jim Zanosky
Controller: Jim Zanosky
R&D: Scott Bruce
Marketing Director: Gerald Anderson
Sales Manager: John Hamilton
Estimated Sales: $10-20 Million
Number Employees: 20-49
Square Footage: 50000
Brands:
  Flaw Finder
  Leak-Tec
  Pin Point

18769 American Gas Association
400 North Capitol Street
Washington, DC 20001

202-824-7000
Fax: 703-841-8406 www.aga.org
Gas dispensing systems
President: Christopher Johns
President, Chief Executive Officer: Dave McCurdy
Senior Vice President: Chris Hermann
Sales Director: Axel Nordwall
Contact: Nadia Anderson
nanderson@aga.org
President, Chief Operating Officer: Lawrence
Borgard
Estimated Sales: $1-5 Million
Number Employees: 5
Parent Co: Linde Technische

18770 American Gasket & Rubber Co
119 Commerce Dr
Schaumburg, IL 60173-5311

847-882-9333
Fax: 847-882-9333 www.tekni-plex.com
Number Employees: 100-249

18771 American Glass Research
349 Tomahawk Dr
Maumee, OH 43537-1611

419-897-9000
Fax: 419-897-9111
Laboratory providing analysis of packaging materi-
als, raw materials and problems such as foreign ma-
terials, package failure, etc
Manager: Diane Paskiet
Manager (Inorganic): James Hojuicki
Manager: Lindy Seagrave
lindyseagrave@yahoo.com
Estimated Sales: $2.5-5 Million
Number Employees: 20-49
Square Footage: 24000

18772 American Glass Research
615 Whitestown Rd
Butler, PA 16001-8703

724-482-2163
Fax: 724-482-2767 agrsales@agrintl.com
www.agrintl.com
Quality Assurance & Process Control Systems for
the Packaging Industry
CEO: Henry Dimmick Jr
Marketing: David Dineff
Operations: Robert Cowden
Estimated Sales: $20-50 Million
Number Employees: 100-249
Square Footage: 100000

18773 American Griddle Corp.
4416 New Haven Ave
Fort Wayne, IN 46803

260-428-2685
Fax: 260-428-2533 800-428-6550
steamshell@americangriddle.com
americangriddle.com
Steam griddle
Sales: Andy Garcia

18774 American Hawaiian Soy Company
274 Kalihi Street
Honolulu, HI 96819

808-841-8435
800-841-8435
Soybean
President: John Morita

18775 American Holt Corp
203 Carnegie Row
Norwood, MA 02062-5000

781-440-9993
Fax: 781-440-9994 sales@americanholt.com
www.americanholt.net
Replacement parts for industry
President: John Levy
jon@americanholt.com
Estimated Sales: $3-5 Million
Number Employees: 5-9

18776 American Housewares
755 E 134th St
Bronx, NY 10454-3419

718-665-9500
Fax: 718-292-0830
sales@americanhousewaresmfg.com
www.americanhousewaresmfg.com
Manufacturer and exporter of kitchen utensils and
equipment including strainers, colanders, basting
spoons, forks, pancake turners, mashers, fry baskets,
splatter screens, roast racks, kitchen tools and
gadgets
Owner: Paul Mayer
strainer4@juno.com
COO: Irving Spiegel
Estimated Sales: $5-10 Million
Number Employees: 50-99

18777 American Identification Industries
1319 Howard Drive
West Chicago, IL 60185-1625

630-231-4500
Fax: 630-231-4530 800-255-8890
Plastic cards
Sales Manager: Juan Sanjujo
Sales: Ginny Lacy
Sales Support: Sandy Brush
Estimated Sales: $5-10 Million
Number Employees: 5

18778 American Identity
1520 Albany Pl SE
Orange City, IA 51041

712-737-4925
Fax: 712-737-2408 800-369-2277
Manufacturer, importer and exporter of promotional
items including caps, jackets, uniforms, etc
Manager: Larry Sanson
Marketing Manager: Greg Ebel
Contact: Paul Awtry
paul.awtry@americanid.com
Estimated Sales: $50-100 Million
Number Employees: 250-499
Parent Co: American Marketing Industry
Brands:
  Glengate
  Identity
  K-Products
  Swingster

18779 American Industrial Supply Company
519 Potrero Ave
San Francisco, CA 94110-1431
415-826-1144
Fax: 415-552-3300
President: George Herbst
herbst@aiscmail.com
Estimated Sales: $50,000-1 Million
Number Employees: 1-4

18780 American Insulated Panel Co
75 John Hancock Rd
Taunton, MA 02780-1096
508-823-7003
Fax: 508-880-5476 800-924-2774
sales@aipanel.com
www.americaninsulatedpanel.com
Manufacturer and installer of walk in coolers and freezers, cold storage doors, and glass display doors.
President: John Lynch
CFO: John Lynch
R&D: John Lynch
Quality Control: John Lynch
IT: Judith Lynch
judylynch@aipanel.com
Estimated Sales: $5-10 Million
Number Employees: 20-49
Square Footage: 35000
Type of Packaging: Bulk

18781 American International Electric
2835 Pellissier Pl
City of Industry, CA 90601-1512
562-908-5058
Fax: 562-908-5059 800-732-5377
www.aieco.com
CEO: Charles Chen
cchen@fastdry.com
Estimated Sales: $3-5 Million
Number Employees: 10-19

18782 American International Tooling
2516 Business Parkway
Suite A
Minden, NV 89423
775-267-6939
Fax: 775-267-697 866-248-8665
sales@seamertooling.com
Manufacturer seamer tooling for canning and bottling industry
President: Lee Bertucci
Vice President Sales: John Konvicka
Contact: Cheryl Bertucci
cheryl@seamertooling.com
Production Manager: Anna Westmorland
Estimated Sales: $1-3 Million
Number Employees: 5-9

18783 American LEWA
132 Hopping Brook Road
Holliston, MA 01746
508-429-7403
Fax: 508-429-8615 888-539-2123
www.lewa.com
Manufacturer and exporter of precision metering and mixing pumps and systems for blending and proportioning all liquids; also, seal-less controlled volume pumps for process services and moderate high pressures
President/Owner: Mike Meraji
Contact: Larry Bell
houston@amlewa.com
Purchasing Director: Charlie Riordan
Number of Brands: 1
Number of Products: 4
Parent Co: OTT Holding Internationa GmbH
Brands:
    Lewa Ecodos
    Lewa Lab
    Lewa Modular
    Lewa Triplex

18784 (HQ)American Labelmark Co
5724 N Pulaski Rd
Chicago, IL 60646-6797
773-478-0900
Fax: 773-478-6054 800-621-5808
sales@labelmaster.com www.labelmaster.com
Manufacturer and exporter of signs including indoor, outdoor, painted and silk screened for restaurants, food manufacturers, etc

President: Alan Schoen
CFO: Ed Kaplan
VP/Marketing: Marilyn Paprocki
Estimated Sales: $30-50 Million
Number Employees: 100-249
Type of Packaging: Food Service

18785 American Led-Gible
1776 Lone Eagle St
Columbus, OH 43228-3655
614-851-1100
Fax: 614-851-1121 www.ledgible.com
Light emitting electronic display signs
President: George Smith
ledgible@ledgible.com
Senior Management of Sales: Candy Chlam
Senior Production Management: Charles Morrison
Estimated Sales: $1-2.5 Million
Number Employees: 5-9
Square Footage: 40000
Brands:
    American Led-Gible, Inc.

18786 American Lifts
P.O. Box 1058
Guthrie, OK 73044
405-282-5200
Fax: 405-282-8105 877-360-6777
sales@autoquip.com www.americanlifts.com
Manufacturer, importer and exporter of lifts including hydraulic scissor and stainless steel; also, hydraulic tilters, and pallet trucks
Manager: Clay Brinson
Estimated Sales: $10-20 Million
Number Employees: 50-99
Square Footage: 140000
Parent Co: Columbs McKinnon Corporation
Brands:
    Torklift

18787 American Liquid Pkgng Systs
440 N Wolfe Rd
Sunnyvale, CA 94085-3869
408-524-7474
Fax: 408-524-7470 alps@alps-aquaservice.com
Bottled water plants, accessories and plastic resin
Owner: Saeed Amidi
Estimated Sales: $20-50 Million
Number Employees: 1-4

18788 American Louver Co
7700 Austin Ave
Skokie, IL 60077-2603
847-470-3300
Fax: 847-470-0420 800-772-0355
Manufacturer and exporter of fluorescent lighting louvers, acrylic mirror sheets, handheld shopping baskets and convex security mirrors
President: Mark Comella
mcomella@plasticade.com
Chairman the Board: Walter Glass
VP: Barry Peterson
CFO: Lucy Polk
Marketing Manager: Butch Cavello
Estimated Sales: $20-50 Million
Number Employees: 50-99
Brands:
    Alumicube
    Paracube

18789 American Machinery Corporation
PO Box 3228
Orlando, FL 32802-3228
407-295-2581
Estimated Sales: $1-5 Million

18790 American Manufacturing-Engrng
4600 W 160th St
Cleveland, OH 44135-2630
440-899-9400
Fax: 440-899-9401 800-822-9402
info@ameco-usa.com www.ameco-usa.com
Steel and stainless steel fabricated beverage and liquid distribution/fillers, steam pressure vessels and mixer components; exporter of stainless and regular steel manufactured products
President and CEO: Michael Perkins
Sales/Marketing Manager: Fred Swanson
Sales Engineer: Tom Miller
Estimated Sales: $500,000-$1 Million
Number Employees: 20-49
Square Footage: 200000

18791 American Material Handling Inc
9013 Highway 165
PO Box 17878
N Little Rock, AR 72117-9728
501-375-6611
Fax: 501-375-8931 800-482-5801
sales@amermaterial.com www.amermaterial.com
Wholesaler/distributor and exporter of material handling systems; also, design consultant
Owner: Jackie Lackie
General Manager: Jay Carman
VP of Marketing: Albert Redding
Sales Manager: Adam Dickens
Manager: Adam Dickens
adam.dickens@amermaterial.com
Estimated Sales: $5-10 Million
Number Employees: 10-19
Square Footage: 80000
Parent Co: Cetrum Industries

18792 American Menu Displays
4862 36th Street
Long Island City, NY 11101-1918
561-544-8047
Fax: 561-544-8048 877-544-8046
sales@americandiscounttableware.com
www.americandiscounttableware.com
Display signs and menu boards
President: Robet Subaj
Estimated Sales: $10-20 Million
Number Employees: 100-249
Brands:
    Panel Lite

18793 American Metal Door Company
PO Box 2008
Richmond, IN 47375-2008
800-428-2737
Fax: 800-626-1490 800-428-2737
amdco@americanmetaldoor.com
www.americanmetaldoor.com
Stainless steel and galvanized sliding doors; also, high speed electric and pneumatic operators
Marketing Coordinator: Jennifer George
Sales Manager: Doug HolmesMidwest
Estimated Sales: $3 Million
Number Employees: 35
Square Footage: 108000
Brands:
    Doors
    Electric & Pneumatic Op.
    Hardware

18794 American Metal Stamping
1 Nassau Ave
Brooklyn, NY 11222-3115
718-384-1500
Fax: 718-384-1523
Heavy duty bakers' pans and trays, food strainers, institutional kitchen baking and roasting pans and equipment smallwares
President: Stephanie Eisenberg
Estimated Sales: $5-10 Million
Number Employees: 20-49

18795 American Metalcraft Inc
3708 River Rd
Suite 800
Franklin Park, IL 60131-2158
708-345-1177
Fax: 708-345-5758 info@amnow.com
www.amnow.com
Manufacturer, importer, exporter and wholesaler/distributor of stainless steel restaurant/bar tabletop supplies, funnels, pizza trays and food covers; serving the food service market
President: David Kahn
davidk@amnow.com
Sales Manager: Richard Packer
Estimated Sales: $10-20 Million
Number Employees: 50-99
Square Footage: 240000
Type of Packaging: Food Service
Brands:
    American Metalcraft

18796 American Municipal Chemical
1907 S 89th St
Milwaukee, WI 53227-1611
414-329-2920
Fax: 414-329-9043 800-598-3106
www.chemicalbargins.com
Cleaning compounds

President: Wayne Benz
wayne@wedor.com
VP: Eric Benz
Estimated Sales: $5-10 Million
Number Employees: 1-4
Square Footage: 60000

18797 American National Rubber
P.O. Box 878
Ceredo, WV 25507-6396

304-453-1311
Fax: 304-453-2347 www.anro.com
Manufacturer and exporter of sponge rubber including gaskets and seals
Sales Manager: Ed Littlehales
Estimated Sales: $20-50 Million
Number Employees: 250-500

18798 American Olean Tile Company
1000 N Cannon Ave
Lansdale, PA 19446

215-855-1111
Contact: Nancy Wilson
nancy_wilson@americanolean.com
Estimated Sales: $1-5 Million
Parent Co: Armstrong World Industries

18799 American Packaging Corporation
P.O.Box 16223
Philadelphia, PA 19114-0223

215-676-8888
Fax: 215-698-7119 bkemp@ampkcorp.com
www.swalter.com
Flexible packages
CEO: Peter Schottland
CFO: Tom May
CEO: Andrew N Wilson
Quality Control: Jim Carlson
Estimated Sales: $81.3 Million
Number Employees: 100-249

18800 American Packaging Machinery
2550 S Eastwood Dr
Woodstock, IL 60098-9112

815-337-8580
Fax: 815-337-8583 888-755-2705
sales@apm-machinery.com
www.americanpackagingmachinery.com
High speed servo controlled shrink wrapping systems and high speed shrink bundling equipment
Owner: Tadiya Peric
apmmachinery@aol.com
Estimated Sales: $10-20 000,000
Number Employees: 10-19
Type of Packaging: Bulk

18801 American Packaging Machinery
2550 S Eastwood Dr
Woodstock, IL 60098-9112

815-337-8580
Fax: 815-337-8583 sales@apm-machinery.com
www.americanpackagingmachinery.com
Owner: Tadiya Peric
apmmachinery@aol.com
Estimated Sales: Below $5 Million
Number Employees: 10-19

18802 American Pallet Inc
1001 Knox Rd
Oakdale, CA 95361-9463

209-847-6122
Fax: 209-847-6154
Pallets, skids, bins and crates
President: Bill Montey
bill@americanpallet.com
VP: John Fauria
VP: John Fauria
Estimated Sales: $20-50 Million
Number Employees: 20-49

18803 American Pallets
2069 New Castle Rd.
Box 201
Portersville, PA 16051

724-658-5747

18804 American Pan Co
417 E Water St # 2
PO Box 678
Urbana, OH 43078-2178

937-652-3232
Fax: 937-652-1384 800-652-2151
sales@americanpan.com www.americanpanuk.com
Commercial bakery pans

President: Gil T Bundy
gbundy@americanpan.com
Estimated Sales: $10-20 000,000
Number Employees: 50-99

18805 American Panel Corp
5800 SE 78th St
Ocala, FL 34472-3412

352-245-7055
Fax: 352-245-0726 800-327-3015
sales@americanpanel.com
www.americanpanel.com
Manufacturer and exporter of walk-in coolers and freezers, blast chillers, refrigerated warehouses and refrigeration systems
President: Danny E Duncan
danny@americanpanel.com
CEO: Marvin Duncan
VP: Harmon Lewis
Sales Manager: Kevin Graham
Sales Associate: Jenn Duncan
Estimated Sales: $20-50 Million
Number Employees: 100-249
Square Footage: 100000
Type of Packaging: Food Service
Brands:
    American Panel

18806 American Pasien Co
109 Elbow Ln
Burlington, NJ 08016-4123

609-387-3130
Fax: 609-387-7204 info@109elbow.com
www.amcocustomdrying.biz
Functional protein ingredients and protein polymers for edible applications
CEO: Jamil Ahmed
jamilahmed@americancasein.com
CEO: Dennis Bobker
CFO: Jack Pipala
Account Manager: Jane Macey
Sales Manager: Cliff Lang
Human Resources Manager/IT Manager: Ellen Iuliucci
Facilities Manager: Chris Lockard
Estimated Sales: $5.8 Million
Number Employees: 20-49
Square Footage: 120000
Type of Packaging: Bulk

18807 American Pistachio Growers
9 E River Park Pl E # 410
Suite 410
Fresno, CA 93720-1530

559-353-2023
Fax: 559-475-0624 info@pistachios.org
www.americanpistachios.org
Agricultural trade association representing members who are pistachio growers, processors and industry partners in California.
Executive Director: Richard Matoian
Director, Global Marketing: Judy Hirigoyen
Director, Member Services/Communications: Catherine Byrnes
Number Employees: 10-19

18808 American Plant & Equipment
4200 S Church Street Ext
Roebuck, SC 29376-2912

864-574-4000
Fax: 864-576-7204
apesales@americanplantandequipment.com
www.forkliftsworld.com
Owner: Victor Le Bron
americanplant@americanplantandequipment.com
Quality Control: Cindy Forster
Estimated Sales: Less Than $500,000
Number Employees: 5-9

18809 American Plywood
7011 S 19th St
Tacoma, WA 98466-5333

253-565-6600
Fax: 253-565-7265 www.apawood.org
President: David L Rogoway
Director: Dennis Hardman
Estimated Sales: F
Number Employees: 100-249

18810 American Printpak Inc
W225n6284 Village Dr
Sussex, WI 53089-3970

262-246-7300
Fax: 262-246-7388 800-441-8003
www.americanprintpak.com
Flexible packaging material including cohesive tape, foil, rolls and sheets; also, heat seal coated lidding and roll stock
President: Joseph Dollak
Director Sales/Marketing: Charles Holbrook
Customer Service: Anjanette Goetz
Estimated Sales: $5-10 Million
Number Employees: 20-49
Square Footage: 116000
Brands:
    Touchseal

18811 American Production Co Inc
2734 Spring St
Redwood City, CA 94063-3524

650-368-5334
Fax: 650-368-4547 www.americanproduction.com
Manufacturer and exporter of commercial and industrial stainless steel insulated food and beverage containers and thermal dispensers
Owner: Owen Conley
info@americanproduction.com
Estimated Sales: $2.5-5 Million
Number Employees: 5-9
Parent Co: Tilley Manufacturing Company
Brands:
    Super Chef

18812 American Profol Inc.
4333 C St SW
Cedar Rapids, IA 52404-7461

319-365-0599
Fax: 319-365-1696 sales@profol.com
Plastic industrial film
CEO: Mark Thoeny
mthoeny@profol.com
CEO: Mark Thoeny
Estimated Sales: $20-50 Million
Number Employees: 100-249

18813 American Radionic Co Inc
32 Hargrove Grade
Industrial Park
Palm Coast, FL 32137-5106

386-445-6000
Fax: 386-445-6871 800-445-6033
www.americanradionic.com
HVAC capacitors
President: Robert Stockman
crezarad@aol.com
Sales Exec: Carl Rezendes
Estimated Sales: $10-20 Million
Number Employees: 50-99

18814 American Range
13592 Desmond St
Pacoima, CA 91331-2315

818-897-0808
Fax: 818-897-1670 888-753-9898
info@americanrange.com
www.americanrange.com
Manufacturer and exporter of commercial cooking equipment including exhaust hoods, ranges, ovens, hot plates, open burners, stock pot stoves, broilers, griddles, woks, cheese melters, chicken rotisseries, etc
President: Courtney Cochran
courtney.cochran@fetzer.com
Quality Control: Cristie Merriot
Estimated Sales: $10-20 Million
Number Employees: 100-249
Square Footage: 70000
Brands:
    American Range

18815 American Renolit Corp LA
6900 Elm St
Commerce, CA 90040-2625

323-721-2720
Fax: 323-725-6466 www.renolit.com
Manufacturer and exporter of plastic materials including PVC films, compounds and roll stock for packaging and devices requiring food grade applications
President: Rich Sterndahl
rich.sterndahl@renolit.com
Finance Executive: Laurie Dunbar
VP Sales: Mark Stern

Estimated Sales: $10-20 Million
Number Employees: 100-249
Square Footage: 170000

18816 American Resin Corp
6250 Southwest Pkwy
Wichita Falls, TX 76310-2897

940-692-8011
Fax: 940-692-8014

President: John Vitek
jwvitek@aol.com
Estimated Sales: Less Than $500,000
Number Employees: 1-4

18817 American Roland Food Corp
71 West 23rd Street
New York, NY 10010

800-221-4030
Fax: 516-694-9177

Development, manufacture and sale of antioxidants
including ethoxyquin, propyl gallate and tocopherols
for feed, food and industrial uses
Contact: Tyrus Brailey
tyrus.r.brailey@jpmorgan.com

18818 American Safety Technologies
565 Eagle Rock Ave
Roseland, NJ 07068-1501

973-403-2600
Fax: 973-403-1108 800-645-7546
www.insulcast.com

Contact: Bob Gasson
bob@compenv.com
Operations: Don Motta
Number Employees: 50-99

18819 American Services Group
850 Ridge Lake Blvd
Memphis, TN 38120

800-333-6678
Fax: 630-271-2710
alison.boyle@servicemaster.com
www.servicemaster.com

Consultant providing energy and waste manage-
ment, sanitation, maintenance and pest control
services
CEO: Robert J Gillette
Senior Vice President, General Counsel: Greer
McMullen
Senior Vice President of Corporate Commu: Peter
Tosches

18820 American Society Of Brewing
3340 Pilot Knob Rd
Eagan, MN 55121-2055

651-454-7250
Fax: 651-454-0766 asbc@scisoc.org
www.asbcnet.org

Supplier of high quality malt based beverages and
ingredients
Executive Officer: Steve Nelson
snelson@scisoc.org
Member Public Relations Manager: Michelle
Bjerkness
VP Operations: Amy Hope
Number Employees: 50-99

18821 (HQ)American Solving Inc.
6519 Eastland Rd
Unit 5
Brook Park, OH 44142-1347

440-234-7373
Fax: 440-234-9112 800-822-2285
sales@solvinginc.com www.solvinginc.com

Manufacturer, importer and exporter of pneumatic
load-handling solutions
President: Andre Alho
andre.alho@solving.com
General Manager: Orley Aten
General Manager: Stanley Aten
Production Manager: Doug Eckert
Estimated Sales: $3-5 Million
Number Employees: 5-9
Square Footage: 12000
Brands:
American Solving
Numeri-Tech
Solving

18822 American Specialty Coffee & Culinary
204 14th Street NW
Atlanta, GA 30318-5304

404-607-1150
Fax: 404-876-1544

Espresso carts, espresso machines and accessories,
espresso pod machines

18823 American Specialty Machinery
456 Lake Hamilton Dr
Hot Springs, AR 71913-7424

713-828-2866
Fax: 713-926-2123

Owner: Jim West
Estimated Sales: $1-5 Million
Number Employees: 1-4

18824 American Star Cork Company
33-53 62nd Street
P.O. Box 770449
Woodside, NY 11377

718-335-3000
Fax: 718-335-3037 800-338-3581
www.amstarcork.com

Manufacturer, exporter and importer of cork and
cork products
President: Thomas Petrosino
amstarcork@gmail.com
Estimated Sales: $.5-1 million
Number Employees: 1-4

18825 American Store Fixtures
7700 Austin Avenue
Skokie, IL 60077-2603

Fax: 847-966-8074

Manufacturer and exporter of shopping baskets, se-
curity mirrors
CEO: Geoff Glass
CFO: Lucy Polk
Quality Control: Carol Salas
Marketing: Donna Kelner
Sales Manager: Debi Greenberg
Public Relations: Donna Kelner
Operations: Carol Salas
Plant Manager: Carol Salas
Estimated Sales: $1-5 Million
Number Employees: 100-250
Square Footage: 480000
Parent Co: American Louver

18826 American Style Foods
809 Riverside Drive
Old Hickory, TN 37138

615-847-0410

Consultant for food extrusion and product formula-
tion processes
President: Robert Garrison
Number Employees: 4

18827 American Sun Control Awnings
925 Mcfarland 400 Blvd
Alpharetta, GA 30004-3373

770-772-9900
Fax: 770-740-8668 800-245-6746

Commercial awnings
President: Glorio Patsy
Estimated Sales: $1-2,500,000
Number Employees: 10-19
Brands:
Fabri-Frame

18828 American Systems Associates
Leander Road
Hampton Bays, NY 11946

718-482-0408
800-584-3663

Gas powered cooking and refrigeration equipment;
also, food service design available
President: Johndavid Hensley
VP: Joyce Jones
Regional Director: Diane David
Number Employees: 1-4
Square Footage: 4000
Parent Co: FOOD

18829 American Technical Services Group
680 Oakbrook Parkway
Suite 165
Norcross, GA 30093

770-447-9444
Fax: 770-447-0319 800-893-1944
www.atsrmis.com

Service company providing instrumentation and
control system services including I/C installation,
ISO 9000 software, NIST calibration, integration,
maintenance and contract staffing
President: Robert Russo
Marketing Manager: Vicci Cogswell
VP Operations: Ray Green
Number Employees: 200
Parent Co: Strategic Distribution

18830 (HQ)American Textile Mills Inc
208 Bennington Ave
Kansas City, MO 64123-1914

816-842-2909
Fax: 816-842-8679

Disposable and reusable wiping towels
President: Dennis Wacknov
Estimated Sales: $5-10 Million
Number Employees: 10-19
Square Footage: 180000
Brands:
Nu-Wipes
Quik-Wipes

18831 American Time & Signal Co
140 3rd St
PO Box 707
Dassel, MN 55325-4511

320-275-2101
Fax: 320-275-2603 800-328-8996
theclockexperts@atsclock.com
www.american-time.com

Manufacturer and exporter of food preparation tim-
ers and clocks
President: Dieter Pape
dpape@atsclock.com
Estimated Sales: $10-20 Million
Number Employees: 50-99
Square Footage: 80000
Brands:
American Time & Signal
James Remind-O-Timer

18832 American Ultraviolet Co
212 S Mount Zion Rd
Lebanon, IN 46052-9479

765-483-9514
Fax: 765-483-9525 800-288-9288
www.americanultraviolet.com

Manufacturer and exporter of germicidal ultraviolet
air and water systems for air and water sterilization
President: Meredith C Stines
mstines@auvco.com
Estimated Sales: $10-20 Million
Number Employees: 100-249
Number of Brands: 4
Square Footage: 70000
Type of Packaging: Food Service
Brands:
Puritron
Ultra-Cool
Ultra-Gog
Ultra-Spec

18833 American Variseal
510 Burbank St
Broomfield, CO 80020-1604

303-465-1727
Fax: 303-469-4874

Manager: Tom Potosky
Contact: Clae Jrwall
claes.jorwall@trelleborg.com
Estimated Sales: $20-50 Million
Number Employees: 100-249

18834 American Ventilation Company
P.O.Box 227
Grafton, OH 44044-0227

440-365-4533
Fax: 440-365-5858 800-854-3267

Exhaust and make-up air fans for the food service
industry
Manager: Tammy Parron
General Manager: Michael Maynard
Estimated Sales: $1-2.5 Million
Number Employees: 5-9
Square Footage: 50000

18835 American Water Broom
3565 Mccall Pl
Doraville, GA 30340-2801

770-451-2000
Fax: 770-455-4478 800-241-6565
info@waterbrooms.com www.waterbrooms.com

Manufacturer and exporter of commercial and residential high pressure water brooms
Vice President: Archie Merlin
amerlin@waterbrooms.com
VP: Beverly Roberts
Number Employees: 5-9
Brands:
  Jetaway
  Squirt

18836 American Wax Co Inc
3930 Review Ave
PO Box 1943
Long Island City, NY 11101-2020
718-361-4820
Fax: 718-482-9366
solutions@cleaning-solutions.com
www.heathsprings.net
Manufacturer and exporter of detergents, deodorants, disinfectants, germicides, floor polish and soap
President: Michelle Devito
michelled@cleaning-solutions.com
Vice President: Ronald Ingber
Sales Manager: Allen Winik
Purchasing Manager: Ron Ingber
Estimated Sales: $2.5-5 Million
Number Employees: 20-49
Square Footage: 124000

18837 American Whey Company
12 N State Route 17
Paramus, NJ 07652-2644
201-587-1444
Fax: 201-587-0310

18838 American Wholesale Equipment
4001 Hamilton Ave
Cleveland, OH 44114-3839
216-426-8882
Fax: 216-426-8883 877-220-8882
info@awrco.com www.awrco.com
Refrigerating equipment and machinery
President: John Paris
Manager: Larry Treb
larry@awrco.com
Estimated Sales: Below $5 Million
Number Employees: 5-9

18839 American Wire Products
616 Industrial Park
Frankfort, KY 40601
502-695-0073
Manager: Carol Chamblain
Estimated Sales: $20-50 Million
Number Employees: 100-249

18840 American Wood Fibers
9841 Broken Land Pkwy # 302
Columbia, MD 21046-3073
410-290-8700
Fax: 410-290-6660 800-624-9663
www.awf.com
Sawdust, firelogs and wood floors
CEO: Ed Leland
eleland@awf.com
CEO: Ed Leland
General Manager: Mark Fahner
Estimated Sales: $1-5 Million
Number Employees: 20-49

18841 American-Newlong Inc
5310 S Harding St
Indianapolis, IN 46217-9575
317-787-9421
Fax: 317-786-5225
newlong@american-newlong.com
www.american-newlong.com
Automated packaging equipment and bagging systems.
President/General Manager: Gary Wells
gwells@american-newlong.com
CFO: Connie Perrin
North American Sales Manager: Garnet McMillian
Warehouse Manager: Mark Banholzer
Estimated Sales: $10-20 Million
Number Employees: 10-19

18842 (HQ)Americana Art China Company
PO Box 310
Sebring, OH 44672
330-938-6133
Fax: 330-938-9546 800-233-6133
amerimug@sbcglobal.net

Custom decorator of ceramic and glassware.
President/CEO: James Puckett
Research & Development: Lisa Cox
Manager of Quality Control: Wendy Davidson
Marketing Director: Jim Puckett
Operations: Jim Puckett
Estimated Sales: $1-3 Million
Number Employees: 32
Number of Products: 126
Square Footage: 80000
Type of Packaging: Private Label, Bulk
Other Locations:
  Americana Art China Co.
  Sebring OH

18843 Americana Marketing
840 Tourmaline Dr
Newbury Park, CA 91320
805-499-0451
Fax: 805-499-4668 800-742-7520
fdi@follmerdevelopment.com
www.follmerdevelopment.com
Aerosol nonstick cooking, baking and flavor sprays
President/CEO: Garrett Follmer
fdi@follmerdevelopment.com
Sales/Marketing VP: David McKenzie
Number Employees: 50-99
Type of Packaging: Consumer, Food Service, Private Label
Brands:
  Natural Lite
  Pure & Simple

18844 Americasia International
Hillsborough Business Center
1 Ilene Court, Building 8, Suite 12
Hillsborough, NJ 08844
609-608-6886
Fax: 908-262-2279 maria@americasia.net
americasia.net
Customized packaging and product displays
Other Locations:
  New Hampshire Office
  Dover NH

18845 Americo
601 E Barton Ave
West Memphis, AR 72301-2011
870-735-4848
Fax: 870-735-4129 800-626-2350
Laminated and vinyl table covers; also, upholstery fabrics
President: Ed Straub
ed@americo-inc.com
Chairman of the Board: Wallace Dunbar
Sales Director: Jerry Van Houten
Estimated Sales: $1-2.5 Million
Number Employees: 20-49

18846 Americode LLC
100 Redhaw Ct
Burleson, TX 76028-2540
817-447-9520
Fax: 817-447-3269 www.americodeusa.com
Printing systems
President: Jerry L Perry
Estimated Sales: $1-3 Million
Number Employees: 5-9

18847 Americraft Carton Inc
403 Fillmore Ave E
St Paul, MN 55107-1288
651-227-6655
Fax: 651-227-4713 www.americraft.com
Folding cartons
Manager: Jim Maher
jim.maher@americraft.com
General Manager: Jim Maher
Plnt Mngr: Brian Lewindowski
Estimated Sales: $10-20 Million
Number Employees: 100-249
Parent Co: Americraft Carton

18848 Americraft Carton Inc
7400 State Line Rd # 206
Suite 206
Prairie Village, KS 66208-3445
913-387-3700
www.americraft.com
Folding cartons
President: Rick N Johnson
rickj@americraft.com
Office Manager: L Large
Plant Manager: F Fess

Estimated Sales: $59 Million
Number Employees: 100-249
Square Footage: 135000
Parent Co: Americraft Carton Group

18849 Ameridia Innovative Solutions
20 Worlds Fair Dr
Suite F
Somerset, NJ 08873-1362
732-805-4003
Fax: 732-805-4008 dbar@ameridia.com
www.eurodia.com
Electrodialysis stacks and equipment; chromatography and ion exchange systems; micro-, ultra-, and non-afiltration systems
VP, Sales and Business Development: Daniel Bar
Estimated Sales: $5-10 Million
Number Employees: 5-9
Parent Co: Eurodia Industrie
Brands:
  STARS
  Aqualyzer

18850 Ameriglobe LLC
153 S Long St
Lafayette, LA 70506-3019
337-234-3211
Fax: 337-234-3213
marlener@ameriglobe-fibc.com
www.ameriglobe-fibc.com
Bulk bags and weigh/fill stations; also, bulk bag refurbishing services available
President: Daniel R Schnaars
dans@ameriglobe-fibc.com
CFO: Randy Girourard
Marketing Director: Blaine Beck
Sales Director: Marlene Rodrigue
Estimated Sales: $50-100 Million
Number Employees: 50-99

18851 Amerikooler Inc
575 E 10th Ave
Hialeah, FL 33010-4639
305-888-5071
Fax: 305-884-8330 800-627-5665
marylo@amerikooler.net www.amerikooler.com
Walk-in coolers, freezers and refrigerated warehouses
President: Renate M Alonso
Vice President: Renato J. Alonso
Vice President of Sales: Gian Carlo Alonso
Purchasing: Macbeth Araque
Estimated Sales: $5-10 Million
Number Employees: 50-99

18852 Ameripak Packaging Equipment
2001 County Line Rd
Warrington, PA 18976-2486
215-343-1530
Fax: 215-343-5293 www.opschuman.com
Packaging equipment including horizontal wrappers, filled tray sealers, rigid box and thermoforming; rebuilt equipment available; importer of thermoforming equipment; exporter of rigid box machinery and horizontal wrappers
President: William T Schuman
schumanwt@opschuman.com
VP Marketing/Sales: Phil Kelly
Estimated Sales: $5-10 Million
Number Employees: 20-49
Number of Products: 5
Square Footage: 240000
Parent Co: SKS Equipment Company

18853 Ameripak Packaging Equipment
2001 County Line Rd
Warrington, PA 18976-2486
215-343-1530
Fax: 215-343-5293 www.opschuman.com
Horizontal form fill seals, flowpak wrapper, fill tray sealers for plastic or paperboard trays
President: William T Schuman
schumanwt@opschuman.com
Estimated Sales: $5-10 Million
Number Employees: 20-49

18854 Ameripec
6965 Aragon Cir
Buena Park, CA 90620
714-994-2990
Fax: 714-562-0849 www.ameripecinc.com
Contract packing of PET bottles and glass bottles of juices, juice drink, flavored drink and water at acidified pH

Contact: Mathew Bamberger
mathew@ameripec.com
Director of Operations: D Delacruz
Estimated Sales: $20-50 Million
Number Employees: 150
Square Footage: 130000
Type of Packaging: Private Label

18855 Ameristamp/Sign-A-Rama
1300 N Royal Ave
Evansville, IN 47715-7808

812-477-7763
Fax: 812-477-7898 800-543-6693
websales@SignsOverAmerica.com
www.signsoveramerica.com
Manufacturer and exporter of marking devices, including rubber stamps
Owner: Walter Valiant
walter@signsoveramerica.com
VP of Public Relations: Grant Valiant
Estimated Sales: $1-2.5 Million
Number Employees: 10-19
Square Footage: 6000
Type of Packaging: Consumer, Food Service, Bulk

18856 Ameritech Laboratories
12817 20th Ave
Flushing, NY 11356-2401

718-461-0475
Fax: 718-461-0187
Consultant providing a complete range of chemical, microbiological and nutritional tests and product development services
President: John Bonnes
Estimated Sales: Below $5 Million
Number Employees: 5-9
Square Footage: 20000

18857 Ameritech Signs & Banners
3015 Pico Blvd
Santa Monica, CA 90405-2003

310-829-9359
Fax: 310-998-1109 ameritechsigns@verizon.net
www.ameritechsigns.com
Pennants, signs and banners
Owner: Bill Gabriel
ameritechsigns@earthlink.net
Estimated Sales: Less Than $500,000
Number Employees: 1-4

18858 Amerivacs
1518 Lancaster Point Way
San Diego, CA 92154-7700

619-498-8227
Fax: 619-498-8222 info@amerivacs.com
www.amerivacs.com
Clean room compatible chamber and retractable nozzle vacuum sealers with gas purge for all heat sealable bags, including all ESD bags by using quiet, nonparticle generating, maintenance-free compressed air-driven vacuum pumps. Standardimpulse sealers also available. One week trial period. Custom designs upon request. One year limited warranty. Made in the USA
President: Peter Tadlock
petertadlock@amerivacs.com
Estimated Sales: $1-2.5 Million
Number Employees: 1-4
Number of Brands: 1
Number of Products: 8
Square Footage: 8000
Brands:
    Amerivacs

18859 Amerivap Systems Inc
31 Successful Way
Dawsonville, GA 30534-6841

706-531-1509
Fax: 404-350-9214 800-763-7687
Dry steam cleaning and sanitizing systems.
President: Werner Diercks
werner.diercks@amerivap.com
CFO: Paula Marshal
VP Marketing: Dolly Diercks
VP Sales: Gabriel Perez
Estimated Sales: $3 Million
Number Employees: 10-19
Square Footage: 20000

18860 Ameron International
P.O.Box 1629
Brea, CA 92822-1629

714-256-7755
Fax: 714-256-7750 www.ameron.com

General Manager: Edwin Steenis
Chairman of the Board, Chief Executive O: James Marlen
Vice President: Christine Stanley
Vice Division President of Operations: David Jones
Plant Manager: Ron Johnson
Estimated Sales: $1-5 Million
Number Employees: 1-4

18861 Ames Engineering Corporation
805 E 13th St
Wilmington, DE 19802

302-658-6945
Fax: 302-658-6946 800-628-7128
telesonics@aol.com www.telesoniconline.com
Horizontal form-fill, three and four side seal sachet, stand-up pouch and stick pack portion packaging machinery
Owner: Bernard Katz
Contact: Steve Ames
steveames@telesoniconline.com
Estimated Sales: $5 000,000
Number Employees: 1-4

18862 Ametco Manufacturing Corp
4326 Hamann Pkwy
Willoughby, OH 44094-5626

440-951-4300
Fax: 440-951-2542 800-321-7042
ametco@ametco.com www.ametco.com
Iron and steel security fencing; also, perforated plastics and expanded, perforated, heavy weld and bar metal gratings
President: Greg Mitrovich
ametco@ametco.com
Sales Manager: Ludwig Weber
Estimated Sales: $5-10,000,000
Number Employees: 20-49

18863 Ametek
900 E Clymer Ave
Sellersville, PA 18960-2628

215-257-6531
Fax: 215-257-4711 chatillon.fl-lar@ametek.com
www.usgauge.com
Test and calibration instruments
Manager: Joe Karpov
Estimated Sales: $30-50 Million
Number Employees: 10-19

18864 Ametek
900 E Clymer Ave
Sellersville, PA 18960-2628

215-257-6531
Fax: 215-257-4711 chatillon.fl-lar@ametek.com
www.usgauge.com
Manufacturer and exporter of pressure and temperature gauges
Manager: Joe Karpov
Sales Manager: Amil Demicco
Estimated Sales: $1-5 Million
Number Employees: 500-999
Parent Co: Ametek
Brands:
    U.S. Gauge

18865 Ametek Drexelbrook
205 Keith Valley Rd
Horsham, PA 19044-1408

215-674-1234
Fax: 215-674-2731 800-553-9092
drexelbrook.info@ametek.com
www.drexelbrook.com
Test and calibration instruments
General Manager: Jim Visnic
VP: Dave Hernance
Number Employees: 50-99

18866 Ametek Technical & Industrial Products
627 Lake St
Kent, OH 44240

215-256-6601
Fax: 330-677-3306 www.ametektip.com
Air blowers and air knives for drying, dewatering and sterilization degassing applications; food grade products available, combustion blowers
Manager: Shannon Booth
Sales Director: Jay Jarboe
Contact: Chris Antwright
chris.antwright@ametek.com
Number Employees: 50-99
Parent Co: Ametek

18867 Ametek Us Gauge
205 Keith Valley Rd
Horsham, PA 19044-1408

215-674-1234
Fax: 215-323-9450 usg.sales@ametek.com
www.ametekusg.com
Test and calibration instruments
Manager: Joe Karpov
Number Employees: 20-49

18868 Amfec Inc
21040 Forbes Ave
Hayward, CA 94545-1116

510-780-0134
Fax: 510-783-0409
Food processing equipment.
Equipment Sales: Adam Quick
Contact: Melvin Huff
mhuff@amfec.com
Estimated Sales: Less Than $500,000
Number Employees: 1-4

18869 Amherst Milling Co
140 Union Hill Rd
Amherst, VA 24521-4053

434-946-7601
Grist mills
Manager: William H Wydner
General Manager/VP: Bill Wydner
Estimated Sales: $1-3 Million
Number Employees: 1-4
Square Footage: 6

18870 Amherst Stainless Fabrication
60 John Glenn Dr
Amherst, NY 14228

716-691-7012
Fax: 716-691-8202 www.amherstfab.com
Manufacturer of stainless steel equipment, parts and systems for the food and beverage industry
President/Owner: Gerald Bogdan
Square Footage: 45000

18871 Amiad Filtration Systems
120-J Talbert Road
Mooresville, NC 28117

704-662-3133
Fax: 704-662-3155 www.amiadusa.com
President: Tom Akehurst
Chief Executive Officer: Rami Molcho
Finance Executive: Inko Evrard
Sales Executive: Jim Lauria
Operations Executive: Jerry Weynand
Estimated Sales: $5-10 Million
Number Employees: 20-49

18872 Ammeraal Beltech
3720 3 Mile Rd NW
Grand Rapids, MI 49534-1270

616-791-0292
Fax: 616-791-1067 www.ammeraalbeltech.com
Process and conveyor belting equipment
President: Paul Hamilton
Manager: Jim Honeycutt
Sales Manager: Mike Wilde
Contact: Ron Jones
rjones@ammeraalbeltechusa.com
Technical Services Manager: Jim Honeycutt
Estimated Sales: $20-50 Million
Number Employees: 20-49
Parent Co: Ammeraal International

18873 Ammeraal Beltech Inc
7501 Saint Louis Ave
Skokie, IL 60076-4033

847-673-6720
Fax: 847-673-6373 800-323-4170
info@ammeraalbeltechusa.com
www.ammeraal-beltech.com
Manufacturer, importer and exporter of belts for packaging machinery and the processing of cookies, crackers, confectionery items, bread, rolls, meat and poultry
President: Jeffrey W Nank
Vice President: Jim Ekedahl
Estimated Sales: $20-50 Million
Number Employees: 50-99
Square Footage: 55000
Parent Co: Verseidag
Brands:
    Beltech
    Burtek
    Polytek
    Rapplon

Rapptex
Volta

18874 Ammeraal Beltech Inc
7501 Saint Louis Ave
Skokie, IL 60076-4033

847-673-6720
Fax: 847-673-6373 800-323-4170
info@ammeraalbeltechusa.com
www.ammeraal-beltech.com
Manufacturer, importer and exporter of belts for
packaging machinery and the processing of cookies,
crackers, confectionary items, bread, rolls, meat and
poultry
President: Jim Bateman
jbateman@ammeraalbeltechusa.com
CFO: Jan Marion
Marketing Director: Mark Wierzbinski
Estimated Sales: $20-50 Million
Number Employees: 50-99
Square Footage: 55000
Brands:
Beltech
Burtex
Polytek
Rapplon
Rapptex
Volta

18875 Amodex Products
PO Box 3332
Bridgeport, CT 6605

203-335-1255
Fax: 203-330-9988 877-866-1255
www.amodexink.com
Stain removers and all-purpose industrial and house-
hold cleaners for face and hands
President: Beverlee Fatse Dacey
Director, Finance & Technology: Nicolas Dacey
Director of Marketing: Alexander Dacey
Director of Operations: A. Peter Dacey
Estimated Sales: $.5-1 million
Number Employees: 1-4

18876 Amot Controls
401 1st Street
Richmond, CA 94801-2906

510-307-8300
info@amotusa.com
www.amot.com
President: James Mannebach
Contact: Lee Allen
lee.allen@amotusa.com
Estimated Sales: $5-10 Million
Number Employees: 20-49

18877 Ampac Packaging, LLC
12025 Tricon Road
Cincinnati, OH 45246

513-671-1777
Fax: 513-671-2920 800-543-7030
www.ampaconline.com
Flexible packaging and bags
Contact: Ward Alexander
ward.alexander@ourhouseinc.com
Brands:
Ab Sealers
All Packaging Machinery
Chantland
Fischbein Bag Closing
Fujy
Highlight Stretch Rappers
Lift Products
New London Eng
Vaculet Usa

18878 Ampak
4580 E 71st St
Cleveland, OH 44125

216-341-2022
Fax: 216-341-2163 800-342-6329
custserv@ampakco.com
www.heatsealco.com/about-ampak
Manufacturer and exporter of packaging machinery
including bag/cup wrapping, skin and die cutting
Southeast Equipment Sales Manager: Dan Barnes
Customer Service: Troy Roberts
General Manager: Les Szakallas
Estimated Sales: $5-10 Million
Number Employees: 20-49
Square Footage: 80000
Parent Co: Heat Sealing Equipment Manufacturing
Company

Brands:
Master
Maxima
Rotocut

18879 Ampco Pumps Co Inc
2045 W Mill Rd
Milwaukee, WI 53209-3444

414-540-1597
Fax: 414-643-4452 800-737-8671
ampcocs@ampcopumps.com
www.ampcopumps.com
Manufacturer and exporter of pumps including cen-
trifugal, sanitary, wastewater and water
Owner: Mike Nicholson
CFO: Loori Neisner
R&D: Loori Neisner
Quality Control: Oori Neisner
Midwestern Regional Manager: Matt Schultz
mnicholson@ampcopumps.com
Estimated Sales: $1-2.5 Million
Number Employees: 10-19

18880 Ample Industries
4000 Commerce Center Dr
Franklin, OH 45005

937-746-9700
Fax: 937-746-2234 888-818-9700
Carry-out containers, food trays, french fry and
pizza boxes and hot dog clam shells; exporter of
pizza boxes
Vice President Of Sales: David Ernst
Contact: Ty Gardner
tgardner@huhtamaki.com
General Manager: Robert Fairchild, Jr.
Plant Manager: Bill Bausmith
Estimated Sales: $50 Million
Number Employees: 100-249
Square Footage: 110000

18881 Amplexus Corporation
9 Commercial Blvd #150
Novato, CA 94949

415-897-3700
Fax: 415-897-4897 800-423-8268
info@adssolutions.com
www.softwarefordistributors.com
Software for restaurant supply and food equipment
distributors
President: Kenneth Levin
Marketing Manager: Rebecca Baker
Estimated Sales: $5-10 Million
Number Employees: 4
Brands:
Amplexus Advantage
Amplexus E3/Commerce

18882 Amri Inc
2045 Silber Rd # 100
Houston, TX 77055-2615

713-682-0000
Fax: 713-682-0080 info@amrivalves.com
President: William Leech
Manager: David Abbott
dabbott@amrivalves.com
Estimated Sales: $5-10 Million
Number Employees: 20-49

18883 Amscor Inc
119 Lamar St
West Babylon, NY 11704-1301

718-383-4900
Fax: 718-383-7787 800-825-9800
sales@amscorinc.com www.amscorinc.com
Steel shelving
President: Michael Silberglied
michael@amscorinc.com
Estimated Sales: $1-2.5 Million
Number Employees: 10-19
Square Footage: 20000
Parent Co: American Steel Corporation

18884 Amsler Equipment Inc
1245 Reid Street
Unit 1
Richmond Hill, ON, ON L4B 1G4
Canada

905-707-6704
Fax: 905-707-6707 877-738-2569
sales@amslerequipment.net
www.amslerequipment.net
Reheat stretch blow molding machines and related
equipment.

President/CEO: Werner Amsler
Quality Control: Jason Amsler
Sales: Heidi Amsler
Estimated Sales: $3 Million
Number Employees: 15

18885 Amstat Industries
3012 N Lake Terrace
Glenview, IL 60026-1335

847-998-6210
Fax: 847-998-6218 800-783-9999
info@amstat.com www.amstat.com
Manufacturer and distributor of static electricity
control products.
President: Larry Jacobson
Sales Director: Larry Jacobson
Estimated Sales: $3-5 Million
Number Employees: 10-19

18886 Amster-Kirtz Co
2830 Cleveland Ave NW
Canton, OH 44709-3204

330-535-6021
Fax: 330-437-2015 800-257-9338
www.amsterkirtz.com
Wholesaler/distributor of merchandise for conve-
nience stores including; candy and grocery items
President: James Ulery
jimu@amsterkirtzco.net
General Manager: Larry H
Sales Manager: Everett M
Number Employees: 50-99
Type of Packaging: Consumer, Bulk

18887 Amsterdam Printing & Litho Inc
166 Wallins Corners Rd
Amsterdam, NY 12010-1817

518-842-6000
Fax: 518-843-5204 800-203-9917
cs@amsterdamprinting.com
www.amsterdamprinting.com
Writing instruments including fine point, felt tip and
ball point pens; also, advertising specialties includ-
ing calendars, mugs, etc.; importer of roller ball pens
President: Robert Rosenthal
HR Executive: Donna Graham
dgraham@banyanincentives.com
Sales/Marketing: Jim Zuzzolo
Purchasing Manager: David Laemle
Estimated Sales: $10-20 Million
Number Employees: 500-999
Square Footage: 52000

18888 Amtab Manufacturing Corp
652 N Highland Ave
Aurora, IL 60506-2940

630-301-7600
Fax: 312-421-3448 800-878-2257
info@amtab.com www.amtab.com
Manufacturer and exporter of folding banquet tables
Owner: Greg Hanusiak
g_hanusiak@amtab.com
CEO: Chris Cornier
VP: Greg Hanusiak
Estimated Sales: $5-10 Million
Number Employees: 20-49
Square Footage: 70000
Type of Packaging: Food Service, Private Label

18889 Amtekco
1205 Refugee Rd
Columbus, OH 43207-2114

614-228-6590
Fax: 614-737-8017 800-336-4677
www.amtekco.com
Manufacturer and exporter of stainless steel tables,
commercial sinks, wood cabinets, fixtures, table
tops, bars and back bars.
President/Owner: Bruce Wasserstrom
brucewasserstrom@amtekco.com
CFO: Robert Hudgins
Research & Development: Roger Henry
Sales Manager: Nancy Green
Public Relations: Adena Bogdan
Plant Manager: Ron Fishking
Purchasing Manager: Hans Woschkolup
Estimated Sales: $18-20 Million
Number Employees: 100-249
Square Footage: 400000
Type of Packaging: Bulk

18890 Amwell
600 N Commons Dr # 116
Aurora, IL 60504-7928
630-898-6900
Fax: 630-898-1647 amwell@amwell-inc.com
www.amwell-inc.com
Owner: Art Benner
abenner@amwell-inc.com
Quality Control: Jim Martin
Estimated Sales: $3-5 Million
Number Employees: 10-19
Parent Co: McNish Corporation

18891 Amy Food Inc
3324 S Richey St
Houston, TX 77017-6259
713-910-5860
Fax: 713-910-4812 www.amyfood.com
Egg rolls, potstickers, empanadas and party platters,
natural and organic foods.
Owner: Phyllis Hsu
amyfood@aol.com
Number Employees: 50-99
Square Footage: 40000
Type of Packaging: Consumer, Food Service, Private Label
Brands:
Jamy's Three Dragon

18892 Anaheim Manufacturing Company
P.O. Box 4146
Anaheim, CA 92803-4146
714-524-7770
Fax: 714-996-7073 800-767-6293
www.anaheimmfg.com
Manufacturer and exporter of garbage disposal units
President: Tom Dugan
Sales Supervisor: Alicia Oregel
Commercial Sales Manager: Grevor Wainwright
Estimated Sales: $20-50 Million
Number Employees: 100-249
Square Footage: 60000
Parent Co: Western Industries
Brands:
Sinkmaster
Waste King
Whirlaway

18893 Analite
24 Newtown Plz
Plainview, NY 11803-4506
516-752-1818
Fax: 516-752-0554 800-229-3357
Manufacturer and exporter of relative humidity and
temperature probes, controllers and transmitters
President: Morris Wasser
Vice President: Julius Levin
Estimated Sales: $2.5-5 Million
Number Employees: 10-19
Square Footage: 15200
Brands:
A2000
Humitran
Humitran-C
Humitran-Dp
Humitran-T

18894 Analog Devices Inc
One Technology Way
P.O. Box 9106
Norwood, MA 02062
781-329-4700
800-262-5643
www.analog.com
Analog, mixed-signal and digital signal processing
integrated circuits for electronic equipment.
President & CEO: Vincent Roche
SVP, Finance & CFO: Prashanth Mahendra-Rajah
Chief Technology Officer: Dan Leibholz
Year Founded: 1965
Estimated Sales: $6.2 Billion
Number Employees: 16,000

18895 Analog Technology Corporation
5220 4th St # 18
Baldwin Park, CA 91706-6600
626-856-5690
Fax: 626-472-6069
Manufacturers of industrial-graphic, bar code forms
and label printers
President: James Lawrence
Estimated Sales: Below $5 Million
Number Employees: 1-4

18896 Analogic Corp.
8 Centennial Dr
Peabody, MA 01960
978-326-4000
Fax: 978-977-6809 www.analogic.com
Medical and security imaging products
President & CEO: Fred B. Parks
CFO: Michael Bourque
Quality Control: Albert C. Cefalo
Year Founded: 1967
Estimated Sales: $486 Million
Number Employees: 1,500

18897 Analytical Development
65 Cavender Run
Dahlonega, GA 30533
770-237-2330
Fax: 770-237-2332
Manufacturer and exporter of hand-held portable
luminometers
President: Ed Nemec
Estimated Sales: $500,000-$1 Million
Number Employees: 1-4
Brands:
Inspector

18898 Analytical Labs
1804 North 33rd Street Boise
Boise, ID 83703-5814
208-342-5515
Fax: 208-342-5591 800-574-5773
ali@analyticallaboratories.com
Laboratory specializing in microbiological and
chemical analysis of food, water, waste water and
fuel; also, nutritional labeling analysis and plant
GMP inspections available
President: Mike Moore
Estimated Sales: Below $5 Million
Number Employees: 20-49
Square Footage: 24000

18899 Analytical Measurements
22 Mountain View Drive
Chester, NJ 07930
800-635-5580
phmeter@verizon.net
www.analyticalmeasurements.com
Manufacturer/supplier of pH and ORP instrumentation, probes, and other related materials
President: W Richard Adey
Contact: Frank G Paully
frank@analyticalmeasurements.com
Estimated Sales: 500,000
Number Employees: 3
Square Footage: 2000
Brands:
Universal Ph Doser

18900 Analytical Technologies Inc
11 Holt St
Westfield, NY 14787-1118
716-326-6444
Fax: 716-326-6468 800-345-1357
sales@testmilk.com www.testmilk.com
Dairy, electronic milk testing equipment
President: David Gross
ati@testmilk.com
Estimated Sales: $500,000-$1 000,000
Number Employees: 5-9

18901 Analyticon Discovery LLC
9700 Great Seneca Hwy
Rockville, MD 20850-3307
240-406-1256
Fax: 240-453-6208 info@ac-discovery.com
www.ac-discovery.com
Natural active ingredients and products.
CEO/Co-Founder: Lutz Muller-Kuhrt
CFO/Co-Founder: Jochen Gatter
VP Research & Development: Karsten Siems
North American/UK Sales Representative: Andrea
Christes
Contact: Betsy Manikowski
b.manikowski@ac-discovery.com
VP Operations & Research: Martina Jaensch
Estimated Sales: $4.64 Million
Number Employees: 1-4

18902 Anbroco
7711 Old Plank Road
Stanley, NC 28164-7774
704-827-1255
Fax: 704-822-6266 800-228-4784

Agitators, aseptic processing equipment, blenders,
batching and blending systems
Sales Manager: Ken Fincham
Number Employees: 22

18903 Anchor Conveyor Products
6830 Kingsley St
Dearborn, MI 48126-1941
313-846-6000
Fax: 313-846-6004 800-959-1347
sales@anchorconveyor.com
www.anchorconveyor.com
President: Bill Farmer
bfarmer@anchorconveyor.com
Estimated Sales: $1-3 Million
Number Employees: 10-19

18904 Anchor Crane & Hoist Service Company
455 Aldine Bender Road
Houston, TX 77060
281-405-9048
Fax: 281-448-7500 800-835-2223
anchor@anchorcrane.com
www.proservanchor.com
Manufacturer and exporter of overhead crane systems
Manager: Greg Salinas
Contact: Tommy Cochran
cochran@proservanchor.com
Purchasing Manager: Bob Steward
Number Employees: 100-249
Parent Co: RPC

18905 Anchor Glass Container Corporation
401 East Jackson St.
Suite 1100
Tampa, FL 33602
813-884-0000
Fax: 813-882-7859 Info@AnchorGlass.com
www.anchorglass.com
Premium glass containers for beverages, beer, liquor,
and food products.
Chairman of the Board: Tom Kichler
President/CEO: Nipesh Shah
Executive VP/CFO: Steve Jackson
VP/General Counsel: Sam Hijab
Executive VP, Operations: Arlo Sims
Year Founded: 1983
Estimated Sales: $297 Million
Number Employees: 2,840
Parent Co: BA Glass B.V.

18906 Anchor Hocking Operating Co
519 N Pierce Ave
Lancaster, OH 43130-2969
740-681-6275
Fax: 740-681-6040 800-562-7511
consumerar@anchorhocking.com
www.anchorhocking.com
Manufacturer and exporter of glass tabletop products including beverageware, stemware, dinnerware,
ovenware and floral and table accessories
President: J David Reed
CEO: Mark Eichorn
Vice President Sales & Marketing: Jackie Sokol
Contact: Ben Baird
bb322801@ohiou.edu
Vice President Of Operations: Margaret Homers
Estimated Sales: Less Than $500,000
Number Employees: 1-4
Parent Co: Newell Rubbermaid
Other Locations:
Anchor Hocking Glass Co.
Richmond Hill ON
Brands:
Clarisse
Excellency
Florentine
Optic Florentine
Stackables

18907 Anchor Industries
P.O. Box 3477
Evansville, IN 47733-3477
812-867-2421
Fax: 812-867-1429 custdiv@anchorinc.com
www.anchorinc.com
Commercial awnings
Founder: Louis Daus
CFO: Mike Elliott
Contact: Hubert Clark
hclark@anchorind.com

Estimated Sales: $30-50 Million
Number Employees: 500-999

18908 (HQ)Anchor Packaging
13515 Barrett Parkway Dr # 100
Ballwin, MO 63021-5870
314-822-7800
Fax: 314-822-2035 800-467-3900
info@anchorpackaging.com
www.anchorpackaging.com
Manufacturer and exporter of plastic microwaveable packaging and container supplies including films, containers, trays, food protective and cling wrap.
President: Jeff Wolff
jeff.wolff@anchorpack.com
CFO: Steve Riek
CEO: Brad Jensen
Marketing: Michael Thaler
Sales: Frank Baumann
Public Relations: Michael Thaler
Operations: Staya Garg
Estimated Sales: $20-50 Million
Number Employees: 20-49
Type of Packaging: Food Service, Private Label
Brands:
   Aurity Wrap
   Bonfaire
   Culinary Classics
   Fresh View
   Micro Raves
   Purity Wrap
   Ultra Wrap

18909 Anco-Eaglin Inc
1420 Lorraine Ave
High Point, NC 27263-2040
336-855-7800
Fax: 336-855-7831 info@ancoeaglin.com
www.ancoeaglin.com
Batch rendering systems, continuous rendering systems, hydrolizing equipment, inedible rendering equipment and systems, prebreakers and presses
Owner: Clayton Eaglin
ancoeaglin@aol.com
US/European Sales: Brian Eaglin
Estimated Sales: Below $5 000,000
Number Employees: 20-49

18910 Andantex USA Inc
1705 Valley Rd
Ocean, NJ 07712-3949
732-493-2812
Fax: 732-493-2949 800-713-6170
info@andantex.com www.andantex.com
Power transmissions including robotic controls, speed reducers and right angle gear boxes
President: Mike Munn
mike@andantex.com
Vice President of Engineering: Dave Regiec
Systems Engineer: John Tashjian
VP of Marketing: Bruce Bradley
Sales Manager of Sales: Al Schwartz
Estimated Sales: $2.5-5 Million
Number Employees: 20-49

18911 Andco Environmental Processes
415 Commerce Dr
Amherst, NY 14228
716-691-2100
Fax: 716-691-2880 andco@localnet.com
www.localnet.com/~buffalo/customer/andco/andco
.htm
Manufacturer and exporter of waste and ground water pollution elimination systems
Sales Manager: Jack Reich
Chief Process Engineer: Michael Laschinger
Estimated Sales: less than $500,000
Number Employees: 5-9
Square Footage: 44000

18912 Andean Naturals LLC
393 Catamaran St
Foster City, CA 94404-2907
650-303-1780
Fax: 707-202-2838 info@andeannaturals.com
www.andeannaturals.com
Quinoa
Owner: Sergio Nunez De Arco
sergio_nunez@andeannaturals.com
Finance & Operations Manager: Marcos Guevara
Estimated Sales: $100 Thousand
Number Employees: 1-4
Type of Packaging: Bulk

18913 Andersen 2000
2011 Commerce Dr N
Peachtree City, GA 30269
770-486-2000
Fax: 770-487-5066 800-241-5424
Manufacturer and exporter of air pollution control systems for odor control, spray dryer dust and visible aerosol.
President/CEO: Jack Brady
CFO: Randall Morgan
CEO: Randall Morgan
Marketing/Sales: Tom Van Remmen
Contact: Randall Morgan
r.morgan@verantis.com
Purchasing Manager: Doug Topley
Number Employees: 50-99
Square Footage: 60000
Parent Co: Crown Andersen
Other Locations:
   Andersen 2000
   Sevenum

18914 Andersen Products Inc
3202 Caroline Dr
Haw River, NC 27258-9564
336-376-3000
Fax: 336-376-8153 www.anpro.com
President: H W Andersen
Quality Control: Lori Pfohl
HR Executive: Barbara England
bce@anpro.com
R&D: John Lindley
Estimated Sales: $20-50 Million
Number Employees: 100-249

18915 Andersen Sign Company
1580 French Pond Road
Woodsville, NH 03785
603-787-6806
Advertising specialties including signs
Owner: Don Bowman
Estimated Sales: Less than $500,000
Number Employees: 1-4
Square Footage: 2500

18916 Anderson American Precision
2511 Friday Rd.
Cocoa, FL 32926
321-637-0728
www.feedscrewdesigns.com
Estimated Sales: $300,000-500,000
Number Employees: 1-4

18917 Anderson Chemical Co
325 S Davis Ave
Litchfield, MN 55355-3106
320-693-2477
Fax: 320-693-8238 www.accomn.com
Cleaning/sanitation and water treatment chemical compounds
President: Terry Anderson
terryanderson@andersonchemco.com
Number Employees: 20-49
Type of Packaging: Food Service

18918 Anderson Dahlen Inc
6850 Sunwood Dr NW
Ramsey, MN 55303-3601
763-852-4700
Fax: 763-852-4795 877-205-0239
sales@andersondahlen.com
www.andersondahlen.com
President: Thomas Knoll
thomasknoll@andersondahlen.com
Estimated Sales: $20-50 Million
Number Employees: 100-249

18919 Anderson Instrument Company
156 Auriesville Rd
Fultonville, NY 12072
518-922-5315
Fax: 518-922-8997 800-833-0081
marc.cognetti@danaher.com
Sanitary temperature, pressure, liquid level monitoring and control instrumentation
President: Jennifer Honeycutt
Marketing Manager: Bill Wilson
Sales Manager: George Simok
Contact: Brigid Clare
brigid@shmaltzbrewing.com
Estimated Sales: $50-100 Million
Number Employees: 50-99
Parent Co: Danaher Corporation

18920 Anderson International Corp
4545 Boyce Pkwy
Stow, OH 44224-1770
216-641-1112
Fax: 216-641-0709 800-336-4730
www.expeller.info
Manufacturer and exporter of screw press machinery for the continuous extraction of vegetable oils and animal fats
President: Len Trocano
lenny.trocano@andersonintl.com
CFO: Kathleen O'Hearn
VP: Vincent Vavpot
Marketing: Vincent Vavpot
Sales: Bruce Brown
Plant Manager: Dave Botson
Estimated Sales: $10-20 Million
Number Employees: 50-99
Brands:
   Dox Expander
   Expeller
   Hivex Expander
   Solvex Expander

18921 Anderson Machine Sales
1066 Harvard Pl
P.O. Box 220
Fort Lee, NJ 07024-1630
Fax: 201-641-7952 amscapper@aol.com
Manufacturer and exporter of single spindle and rotary capping machines, pump placers and crimpers, conveyors and accumulating tables
Manager: Howard Cunningham
Estimated Sales: $2.5-5,000,000
Number Employees: 1-4
Parent Co: Anderson Machine Systems

18922 Anderson Products
1 Weiler Dr
Cresco, PA 18326-9804
508-755-6100
Fax: 508-755-4694 800-729-4694
info@andersonproducts.com
www.andersonproducts.com
Power, paint and maintenance brushes including wide face and strip, adapters, maintenance and hand, rollers and accessories, etc
President: Richard Gommel
VP Sales/Marketing: Robert Levine
Contact: Ed Frymier
efrymier@weilercorp.com
Estimated Sales: $20-50 Million
Number Employees: 100-249
Parent Co: Wilton Corporation

18923 Anderson Snow Corp
9225 Ivanhoe St
Schiller Park, IL 60176-2352
847-678-3823
Fax: 847-678-0413 800-346-2645
www.anscorcoils.com
Heating and cooling coils
President: Ted Campbell
tcamp5555@aol.com
Estimated Sales: $20-50 Million
Number Employees: 10-19

18924 Anderson Tool & Engineering Company
P.O.Box 1158
Anderson, IN 46015-1158
765-643-6691
Fax: 765-643-5022
Manufacturer and exporter of packaging, automation and material handling equipment; also, electrical design and assembly services available
President: Ted Fiock
Sales/Marketing Manager: David Keller
Operations Manager: Tom Tuterow
Purchasing Manager: Ron King
Estimated Sales: $10-20 Million
Number Employees: 100-249
Square Footage: 85000

18925 Anderson Wood Products
1381 Beech St
Louisville, KY 40211-3428
502-778-5591
Fax: 502-778-5599 kenl@andersonwood.com
www.andersonwood.com
Wooden butchers' blocks and restaurant tabletops

Vice President: David Anderson
davida@andersonwood.com
VP: David Anderson
Chairman Of The Board: Sidney W Anderson Jr
Estimated Sales: $20-50 Million
Number Employees: 100-249
Square Footage: 140000

18926 Anderson-Crane Company
1213-19 Harmon Pl
Minneapolis, MN 55403
612-332-0331
Fax: 612-332-0384 800-314-2747
minneapolis@anderson-crane.com
www.anderson-crane.com
Manufacturers of stainless steel screw conveyors @
screw feeders to food grade specs.
President: Bob Crane
Director Of Sales: Rob Crane
Contact: Steven Johnson
steven.johnson@screw-conveyor.com
Estimated Sales: $10-20 Million
Number Employees: 20-49
Square Footage: 60000

18927 Anderson-Negele
156 Auriesville Rd
Fultonville, NY 12072
518-922-5315
Fax: 518-922-8997 800-833-0081
info@anderson-negele.com
www.anderson-negele.com
sensors for food and life sciences.
General Manager: Parker Burke
Sr. Product and Marketing Manager: Paul Wagner
Director of Sales: Joe Gamradt
Estimated Sales: $50-60 Million
Number Employees: 100-249
Parent Co: Fortive Corporation

18928 Andex Corp
69 Deep Rock Rd
Rochester, NY 14624-3575
585-328-3790
Fax: 585-328-3792
Manufacturer and exporter of paper coffee filters
President: Andrew Cherre
andexcorp@aol.com
Estimated Sales: $1-2 Million
Number Employees: 20-49
Square Footage: 40000
Type of Packaging: Food Service, Private Label,
Bulk
Brands:
    Coffee's Choice
    Gourmay
    Tru Brew

18929 Andex Industries Inc
1911 4th Ave N
Escanaba, MI 49829-1435
906-786-6070
Fax: 906-786-3133 800-338-9882
andex@andex.net www.andex.net
Printed blister cards and skin boards
President: John Anthony
CEO: John T Anthony
Estimated Sales: $10-20 000,000
Number Employees: 50-99

18930 Andfel Corporation
2350 W Fulton Street
Chicago, IL 60612-2256
312-666-6375

18931 Andgar Corp
6920 Salashan Pkwy
Ferndale, WA 98248-8320
360-366-9900
Fax: 360-366-5800 corporate@andgar.com
www.andgar.com
Conveyors, belts, vibrating feeders, custom stainless
steel design and fabrication, packaging equipment,
metal detectors, separators, scanning and sorting
equipment, complete processing lines, refrigeration
and freezing equipmenttemperature controls, stairways, railings, catwalks, fabricated metal products
President: Gary Van Lou
garyv@andgar.com
CFO: Gary Van Lou
CEO: Gary Van Loo
Quality Control: Gary Van Lou
R&D: Gary Van Lou

Estimated Sales: $10-20 Million
Number Employees: 100-249
Number of Brands: 4
Square Footage: 45000
Brands:
    Andgar
    Lakewood
    Langser Camp
    Sateline

18932 Andre Robin And Associates
8630 Farley Way
Fair Oaks, CA 95628-5353
916-852-0177
Fax: 916-852-0192 800-998-6111
info@robin.com
President: Andre Robin
Estimated Sales: $5-10 Million
Number Employees: 10-19

18933 Andrea Basket
1401 Lakeland Ave
Bohemia, NY 11716-3317
631-231-4888
Fax: 631-231-5635 888-272-8826
info@andreabaskets.com
Various styles of decorative baskets
President: Andrea Lieberman
Estimated Sales: $3.4 Million
Number Employees: 5-9

18934 Andrew H Lawson Co
2927 W Thompson St
Philadelphia, PA 19121-4547
215-235-1119
Fax: 215-235-1727 800-411-6628
info@screengemsinc.com
www.screengemsinc.com
Tags, signs and labels
Owner: Edward Mitchell Sr
VP of Marketing: Regina Mitchell
Manager Operations: John Mitchell
Estimated Sales: $1-5 Million
Number Employees: 10-19
Square Footage: 40000

18935 Andrew W Nissly Inc
544 W Mill Ave
Lancaster, PA 17603-3426
717-393-3841
Fax: 717-397-6239
Signs; also, industrial finishing and silk screen print-
ing available
President: Andrew Nissly
General Manager: Andrew Nissley
Estimated Sales: $500,000-$1 Million
Number Employees: 5-9

18936 Andrew's Fixture Co
1720 Puyallup Ave
Tacoma, WA 98421-2616
253-627-8388
Fax: 253-627-8395
Store fixtures, custom cabinets and office furniture
President: Kenson Lee
afco25@gmail.com
Secretary/Treasurer: Andrea Lee
Estimated Sales: $1-2.5 Million
Number Employees: 5-9
Square Footage: 20000

18937 Andritz Separation Inc
1010 Commercial Blvd S
Arlington, TX 76001-7130
817-465-5611
Fax: 817-468-3961 www.andritz.com
Supplier of separation technologies in the municipal
and industrial sectors and of animal feed
technologies.
President: John Madden
john.madden@andritz.com
Estimated Sales: $10-20 000,000
Number Employees: 500-999

18938 Andy J. Egan Co.
2001 Waldorf NW
Grand Rapids, MI 49544
616-791-9952
Fax: 616-791-1037 800-594-9244
info@andyegan.com www.andyegan.com
Manufacturer processing equipment for the baking,
confectionery and snack food industries.

Owner: Tom Jasper
Vice President/Treasurer: Casey Schellenboom
Engineer: Eric Schippers
Contact: Jack Alexander
alexanderj@andyegan.com
Estimated Sales: 25 Million
Number Employees: 230
Square Footage: 70000

18939 Andy Printed Products
1258 Route 82
Lagrangeville, NY 12540-6015
845-223-5101
Fax: 845-223-7426
Pressure sensitive and gummed labels
Owner: Thakur Nandlal
Estimated Sales: Less than $500,000
Number Employees: 1-4
Square Footage: 4000

18940 Anetsberger
P.O. Box 501
Concord, NH 06062
603-225-6684
Fax: 603-225-8472
ANETS-Gas & Electric Fryers, Filter Systems,
Chrome Grills, Pasta Cookers
President: Paul Angrick
VP: Steve Spittle
VP Sales/Marketing: Bonnie Bolster
Contact: Tracy Doer
tdoer@anets.com
Estimated Sales: $10-20 Million
Number Employees: 50-99
Parent Co: Middleby Corp
Brands:
    Anets'

18941 (HQ)Anguil Environmental Systems
8855 N 55th St
Milwaukee, WI 53223
414-365-6400
Fax: 414-365-6410 800-488-0230
sales@anguil.com www.anguil.com
Manufacturer and exporter of air pollution abate-
ment and oxidation systems
President: Gene Anguil
CEO: Gene Anugil
Vice President: Chris Anguil
Marketing Director: Kevin Summ
Contact: Mathew Andrews
mathew.andrews@anguil.com
Estimated Sales: $20-25 Million
Number Employees: 50-99
Square Footage: 25000

18942 Anhydro Inc
20000 Governors Dr Ste 301
Olympia Fields, IL 60461
708-747-7000
Fax: 708-755-8815 anhydroinc@anhydro.com
www.anhydro.com
Manufacturer and exporter of food drying equipment
including spray, tower, flash, fluid bed and ring;
also, consulting, design and engineering services
available
President: Guy Lonergan
Contact: Dawn Braddy
d.braddy@anhydro.com
Number Employees: 20-49
Square Footage: 80000
Parent Co: Drytec

18943 Anixter Inc
2301 Patriot Blvd
Glenview, IL 60026-8020
224-521-8000
Fax: 224-521-8100 www.anixter.com
President: Bob Eck
bob.eck@anixter.com
CEO: Robert J Eck
CFO: Dennis Letham
Number Employees: 500-999

18944 Anko Food Machine USA Co LTD
390 Swift Ave # 2
S San Francisco, CA 94080-6221
650-624-8038
Fax: 650-624-8039 www.bakeryequsa.com
Owner: James Chung
james@bakeryequsa.com
Estimated Sales: Less Than $500,000
Number Employees: 1-4

18945 Anko Products Inc
6012 33rd St E
Bradenton, FL 34203-5402
941-749-1960
Fax: 941-748-2307 800-446-2656
sales@ankoproducts.com www.ankoproducts.com
Manufacture of contamination-proof peristaltic
pumps, and fractional horsepower gearmotors
Owner: Sharon Kottke
sharon@ankoproducts.com
Estimated Sales: $20-50 Million
Number Employees: 20-49
Brands:
Mitydrive
Mityflex

18946 Ann Arbor Computer
34375 W 12 Mile Road
Farmington Hills, MI 48331-3375
248-553-1000
Fax: 248-553-1228 800-526-9322
info@jerviswebb.com
Manufacturer and exporter of computer software in-
ventory control systems for warehouses and distribu-
tion centers; also, complete integrated control
systems for material handling and factory
automation
President & CEO: Brian Stewart
Sr. Vice President & CFO: John Doychich
Vice President Sales And Marketing: Bruce Buscher
Sales Manager: Art Fleischer
Vice President Of Operations: Lon McAllister
Number Employees: 80
Square Footage: 148000
Parent Co: Jervis B. Webb Company
Brands:
Basis
Pc/Aim

18947 Ann Clark, LTD
112B Quality Lane
Rutland, VT 05701
802-773-7886
Fax: 802-775-6864 800-252-6798
info@annclark.com www.annclark.com
Shaped and holiday themed cookie cutters
President: Ann Clark
VP: John Clark Jr
Sales Manager: Elizabeth Clark
Contact: Pat Buchanan
pat@annclark.com

18948 Annette's Donuts Ltd.
1965 Lawrence Ave W
Toronto, ON M9N 1H5
Canada
416-656-3444
Fax: 416-656-5400 888-839-7857
Bread, pastries and other bakery products
President: Nicolas Yannopoulos
Board Member: Ariadni Yannopoulos
Estimated Sales: $5.9 Million
Number Employees: 85
Square Footage: 124000
Type of Packaging: Consumer, Food Service, Bulk

18949 Annie's Frozen Yogurt
5200 W 74th St # A
Suite A
Minneapolis, MN 55439-2223
952-835-2110
800-969-9648
www.anniesyogurt.com
Soft serve equipment for frozen yogurt.
President: Lawrence Cerf
ldcerf@aol.com
Number Employees: 10-19
Brands:
Annie's

18950 Anova
211 N Lindbergh Blvd # 2
St Louis, MO 63141-7838
314-535-5005
Fax: 314-768-0835 800-231-1327
www.upbeat.com
Waste and recycling receptacles
President: William Gilbert
eric@anovafurnishings.com
CFO: John Mueller
Estimated Sales: $5-10 Million
Number Employees: 50-99

18951 Anresco Laboratories
1375 Van Dyke Ave
San Francisco, CA 94124-3312
415-822-1100
Fax: 415-822-6615 800-359-0920
info@anresco.com www.microtracers.com
Laboratory providing consulting and analytical ser-
vices including microbiology and food technology
Founder & President: David Eisenberg
Treasurer: Ngaly Frank
Lab Co-Direcotr: Mr. VuLam
Lab Co-Director: Ms. Cynthia Kushi
Quality Control Manager: Paleen Castenada
Marketing Director: Charleen Bizily
Purchasing Manager: Cynthia Kcohi
Estimated Sales: $3.85 Million
Number Employees: 50-99
Square Footage: 37600

18952 Anresco Laboratories
1375 Van Dyke Ave
San Francisco, CA 94124-3312
415-822-1100
Fax: 415-822-6615 info@anresco.com
www.microtracers.com
Analytical consultants for nutritional labeling, min-
erals, vitamins, sugars & sugar alcohols, fats & oils,
protein, proximates, aflatoxins, trans fatty acids, pre-
servatives, product stability and shelf life, extrane-
ous mattermicroscopy, microbiological pathogens,
dietary supplements and an extensive range of FDA
automatic detention tests on imported foods.
Owner: David Eisenberg
CEO: Norlinda Cuesta
CFO: Mai Vo
Chemist: Aileen Borbon
Associate Lab Director: Vu Lam
Director of Marketing: Charleene Min
Manager: Bill Li
Estimated Sales: $2.6 Million
Number Employees: 50-99
Square Footage: 22000

18953 Anritsu Industrial Solutions
1001 Cambridge Dr
Elk Grove Vlg, IL 60007-2453
847-419-9729
Fax: 847-419-8266
Food inspection equipment.
President: Erik Brainard
ebrainard@us.anritsu-industry.com
Number Employees: 20-49

18954 Ansell Healthcare Inc
111 Wood Ave S # 210
Iselin, NJ 08830-2700
732-345-5400
Fax: 732-219-5114 800-800-0444
info@ansell.com www.ansell.com
World's largest manufacturer of protective golves
and clothing for the food service and processing in-
dustries.
Senior VP: James Albetta
jamesalbetta@ansellpro.com
Manager: Willaim Gero
Number Employees: 100-249
Type of Packaging: Food Service

18955 Antek Industrial Instruments
PO Box 1130
Marble Falls, TX 78654-1130
830-693-5671
Fax: 830-798-8208 888-478-5387
www.antekhou.com
State-of-the-art testing and measurement of carbon
dioxide and sulfur levels commonly found in the
processing of soft drinks

18956 Anton Kimball Design
3777 SE Milwaukie Ave
Portland, OR 97202-3804
503-234-4777
Fax: 503-234-4687 heather@kimballdesign.com
www.bluestardecks.org
Specialty food packaging.
Owner: Anton C Kimball
info@kimballdesign.com
Marketing: Anton Kimball
Estimated Sales: Less Than $500,000
Number Employees: 5-9

18957 Anton Paar USA Inc
10215 Timber Ridge Dr
Ashland, VA 23005-8135
804-550-1051
Fax: 804-550-1057 800-722-7556
info.us@anton-paar.com www.anton-paar.com
Laboratory density and brix meters, process brix and
diet monitors, carbon dioxide monitors, laboratory
and process beer analyzers
President: Bart Arts
bart.arts@anton-paar.com
CEO: Niels Haggound
Product Manager: Thomas Luxbacher
Sales Manager: Erich Windischbacher
Estimated Sales: $2.5-5 Million
Number Employees: 50-99

18958 Antrim Manufacturing Inc
3530 N 127th St
Brookfield, WI 53005-2485
262-781-6860
Metal stampings and restaurant equipment including
ovens and utility carts
Owner: Dan Antrim
progrosup@aol.com
Office Manager: Patricia Antrim
Estimated Sales: $1-5 Million
Number Employees: 5-9

18959 Antunes Controls
180 Kehoe Blvd
Carol Stream, IL 60188-1814
630-784-1000
Fax: 630-784-1650 800-253-2991
www.ajantunes.com
Top Quality Counter Top Cooking Equipment, Ad-
vanced Membrane Filtration Equipment, Custom
Electronics, and Air and Gas Pressure Switches
CEO: Glenn Bullock
National Sales Manager: Dan Huizinga
Estimated Sales: $5-10 Million
Number Employees: 250-499

18960 Anver Corporation
36 Parmenter Rd
Hudson, MA 01749
978-568-0221
Fax: 978-568-1570 800-654-3500
rfq13@anver.com www.anver.com
Full range of vacuum system components, from suc-
tion cups and vacuum cups, air and electric vacuum
pumps and vacuum generations, and ergonomic vac-
uum lifters, to complete lifting systems
President: Anton Vernooy
CFO: Lynne Buttterworth
Marketing Director: Cully Murphy
Contact: Anver Anderson
anver@anver.com
Estimated Sales: $10 Million
Number Employees: 50-99
Square Footage: 60000

18961 Anzu Technology
3180 Imjin Rd # 155
Marina, CA 93933-5112
831-883-4400
Fax: 831-855-0220 twhite@anzutech.com
www.anzutech.com
Products and services include equipment for food
processing, inspection and packaging.
President: Tom White
twhite@anzutech.com
Number Employees: 5-9

18962 Aoki Laboratory America
1240 Landmeier Rd
Elk Grove Village, IL 60007
847-981-6000
Fax: 847-981-6105 info@aokiusa.com
www.aokitech.co.jp
Container manufacturer
President/Owner: Shuichi Koshi
Number Employees: 5-9

18963 Apa
7011 S 19th St
Tacoma, WA 98466-5333
253-565-6600
Fax: 253-565-7265 www.apawood.org
President: David L Rogoway
Director: Dennis Hardman
Contact: Jeff Wagner
jwagner@engineeredwood.org

Estimated Sales: F
Number Employees: 100-249

18964 Apache Inc
4805 Bowling St SW
Cedar Rapids, IA 52404-5021

319-365-0471
Fax: 319-365-2522 800-553-5455
info@apache-inc.com www.apache-inc.com
Wholesaler/distributor of hose and conveyor belting.
Products for the food industry.
President/CEO: Tom Pientok
Chief Financial Officer: Randy Walter
Controller: Eric Hentges
Quality Engineer: Rick Coyle
Marketing & Communications Manager: Jill Miller
VP, Operations: Kyle Gingrich
VP, Business Development: John Shafer
VP, Product Management: Tom Weisenstine
Purchasing Manager: Randy James
Estimated Sales: $75-85 Million
Number Employees: 100-249
Square Footage: 125000

18965 (HQ)Apache Stainless Equipment
200 Industrial Dr
Beaver Dam, WI 53916-1136

920-356-9900
Fax: 920-887-0206 800-444-0398
info@apachestainless.com
www.apachestainless.com
Manufacturer and exporter of stainless steel food
processing machinery including sanitary and ASME
pressure vessels, tanks, blenders, mixers, conveyors,
sanitary lifts, stuffers, dumpers and paced boning
systems
President and R&D: D Foulkes
CAO: Fern Core
fcore@apachestainless.com
CFO: D Seifert
VP: W Lynn
Quality Control: Jerome Scharrer
Plant Manager: Duane Crouse
Estimated Sales: $5-10 Million
Number Employees: 100-249
Square Footage: 200000
Other Locations:
Apache Stainless Equipment Co
Beloit WI
Brands:
Vortron

18966 Apache Stainless Equipment
200 Industrial Dr
PO Box 538
Beaver Dam, WI 53916-1136

920-356-9900
Fax: 920-887-0206 800-444-0398
dennis.buehring@mepaco.net
www.apachestainless.com
President: Duane Foulkes
CAO: Fern Core
fcore@apachestainless.com
V.P. of Sales & Marketing: Dennis Buehring
Estimated Sales: $5-10 Million
Number Employees: 100-249

18967 Apco/Valve & Primer Corporation
1420 Wright Blvd
Schaumburg, IL 60193

847-524-9000
Fax: 847-524-9007 factory@apcovalves.com
President: Robert Mauriello
r.mauriello@apcovalves.com
CEO: George Christofidis
CFO: Jack Mann
Engineering/Technical: Russell Voseurg
Estimated Sales: $10-20 Million
Number Employees: 50-99

18968 Apex Bakery Equipment
803 Main St
Belmar, NJ 07719-2783

888-571-3599
Fax: 954-364-6268 888-571-3599
sales@apex-equip.com www.apex-equip.com
President: Herbert Freedman
CFO: Barry McWatters
Quality Control: Mark Freedman
Contact: Jeffrey Liss
jeffreyliss@apex-equipment.com
Estimated Sales: $10-20 Million
Number Employees: 20-49

18969 Apex Fountain Sales Inc
1140 N American St
Philadelphia, PA 19123-1514

215-627-4526
Fax: 215-627-7877 800-523-4586
www.apexfountains.com
Manufacturer and exporter of champagne fountains,
chafing dishes, punch bowls, candelabra and food
stands
President: Abe Weinberg
info@apexfountains.com
Manager: Jody Clemente
Estimated Sales: $1-2.5 Million
Number Employees: 5-9

18970 Apex Machine Company
3000 NE 12th Ter
Oakland Park, FL 33334-4497

954-566-1572
Fax: 954-563-2844 email@apexmachine.com
www.apexmachine.com
Manufacturer and exporter, designs and engineers
customized part handling and printing-packaging so-
lutions for 3D products.
President: Todd Coningsby
CEO & Chairman: A. Robert Coningsby
toddc@apexmachine.com
Corp. Controller: Chris Bardelang
National Sales Manager: Russell Coningsby
Engineering Manager: Greg Coningsby
Director Production-Purchasing: Arthur Jordan
Estimated Sales: $5-10 Million
Number Employees: 50-99
Other Locations:
Capex Corporation
Fort Lauderdale FL
Desco Machine Company
Twinsburg OH

18971 Apex Packing & Rubber Co
1855 New Hwy # D
Farmingdale, NY 11735-1599

631-420-8150
Fax: 631-756-9639 800-645-9110
info@apexgaskets.com
Manufacturer and exporter of sanitary replacement
parts for the dairy, food, beverage and pharmaceuti-
cal industries
President: Ralph Oppenheim
ralph@apexgaskets.com
General Manager: Larry Hodes
Purchasing Agent: Leon Davidson
Estimated Sales: $2.5-5,000,000
Number Employees: 5-9
Brands:
Apex

18972 Apex Tool Works Inc
3200 Tollview Dr
Rolling Meadows, IL 60008

847-394-5810
Fax: 847-394-2739 apextool@apextool.com
www.apextool.com
Manufacturing equipment.
VP, Engineering: Edward Racutt
Estimated Sales: $5-10 Million
Number Employees: 20-49

18973 Apex Welding Inc
1 Industry Dr
Bedford, OH 44146-4413

440-232-6770
Fax: 440-232-6747 info@apex-bulkhandlers.com
www.apex-bulkhandlers.com
Bins
President: D J Warner
Manager: Gary Warner
info@apex-bulkhandlers.com
Estimated Sales: Less Than $500,000
Number Employees: 10-19

18974 Apigent Solutions
5 N McCormick Street
Oklahoma City, OK 73127-6620

405-946-8228
Fax: 405-946-8242 800-664-8228
Specializes in software products taht enhance busi-
ness performance and profitability by delivering
reaL-time information from legacy business systems
to site, field, and corporate personnel
CEO: Jim Melvin
Sales VP of the Americas: John Luidens
Public Relations: Ann Dickerson

18975 Aplen Sierra Coffee Company
2222 Park Place
Suite 1A
Minden, NV 89423

530-541-1053
Fax: 530-541-4412 800-531-1405
coffeentea@alpensierra.com www.alpensierra.com
Supplier of specialty coffees.
Contact: Christian Waskiewicz
coffeentea@alpensierra.com
Estimated Sales: $1-2.5 Million
Number Employees: 5-9

18976 Apogee Translite Inc
593 Acorn St # B
Deer Park, NY 11729-3613

631-254-6975
Fax: 631-254-3860 www.apogeetranslite.com
Manufacturer and exporter of lighting fixtures for
food processing range hoods, hose down and wet lo-
cations
President: Richard Nicolai
President: Mike Shada
Estimated Sales: $10-20,000,000
Number Employees: 20-49
Square Footage: 38000
Other Locations:
Apogee Lighting Group
Riverdale IL

18977 Apollo Acme Lighting Fixture
212 S 12th Ave
Mount Vernon, NY 10550

914-664-3600
Fax: 914-664-6091 800-833-9006
Fluorescent lighting fixtures
VP: Paul Verkleij
Estimated Sales: $1-2,500,000
Number Employees: 5-9
Square Footage: 33000

18978 Apollo Sheet Metal
1207 W Columbia Dr
Kennewick, WA 99336

509-586-1104
Fax: 509-586-3771 info@apollosm.com
www.apollosm.com
Food processing, handling and storage systems in-
cluding conveyors, tanks, blanchers, ovens and fry-
ers; also, installation services available.
President: Bruce Ratchford
CFO: Angie Haisch
VP: Keith Larson
Quality Control: Bill Meloy
Marketing Director: Connie Gillispie
Sales: Dan Briscoe
Contact: Emily Castle
ecastle@apollosm.com
Production: Cal Method
Estimated Sales: $20-50 Million
Number Employees: 250-499
Square Footage: 200000

18979 Apotheca Inc
201 Apple Boulevard
Woodbine, IA 51579

712-647-3133
Fax: 888-898-0401 800-736-3130
info@apothecacompany.com
www.apothecacompany.com
Homeopathics, botanical extracts, capsules, tablets
and sports nutritionals
President: Kathryn Simon
Contact: Mike Evans
mike@apothecacompany.com
Estimated Sales: $10-20 Million
Number Employees: 100
Square Footage: 140000

18980 Appalachian Power
P.O. Box 1986
Charleston, WV 25327

800-956-4237
www.appalachianpower.com
Electric utility systems.
President & COO: Chris Beam
VP, Regulatory & Finance: Steven Ferguson
VP, External Affairs: Brad Hall
Estimated Sales: K
Parent Co: American Electric Power

18981 Apparel Manufacturing Co Inc
5405 Webb Pkwy NW
Lilburn, GA 30047-5470
770-638-1100
Fax: 770-638-8030 800-366-1608
www.apparelmanufacturing.com
Advertising specialties and uniforms; importer of caps
President: Michelle Dance
m.dance@ipcabc.org
Administrative Assistant to President: Chelley Young
Estimated Sales: $5-10,000,000
Number Employees: 50-99

18982 Apple-A-Day Nutritional Labeling Service
103 1/2 Avenida Del Mar
San Clemente, CA 92672-4017
949-855-8954
Fax: 949-855-8954
Provides computerized nutrutional analysis based on submited recipes. Nutritional facts labeling for food manufacturers following FDA quidelines and regulations

18983 Applegate Chemical Company
1325 N Old Rand Road
Wauconda, IL 60084-9764
847-487-2651
Fax: 847-487-2654
President: Donald F Colby
Estimated Sales: $5-10 Million
Number Employees: 10

18984 Appleson Press
25 Tacoma Lane
Building 11
Syosset, NY 11791-6232
516-496-0004
Fax: 516-496-0006 800-888-2775
info@applesonpress.com www.applesonpress.com
Manufacturer of continuous business forms, envelopes and labels including printed cloth, linen, silk, pressure sensitive, promotional items; product labels
President: Kenneth Sands
CEO: Elyse Newman
Contact: Ken Sands
ksands@applesonpress.com
Plant Manager: John Samuels
Estimated Sales: $3-5 Million
Number Employees: 20-49
Square Footage: 40000
Type of Packaging: Food Service, Private Label, Bulk

18985 Applexion
9400 W Foster Avenue
Chicago, IL 60656-2860
773-243-0454
Fax: 773-243-0460 applexion@aol.com
Process engineering systems including ion exchange, chromatographic and membrane separation, fermentation, etc
President: Francois Rousset
Sales: Brian Burris
Production: Martha Turner
Estimated Sales: $1-2.5 Million
Number Employees: 1-4
Parent Co: Applexion S.A.
Brands:
Fast

18986 Application Software
211 Main St
New Paltz, NY 12561-1312
845-255-3226
Fax: 845-255-3295 800-888-9470
Bar code scanners, batching and blender systems
President: Greg Brandow
Estimated Sales: $1-3 Million
Number Employees: 1-4

18987 Applied Analytics
40 Kensington Cir
Chestnut Hill, MA 02467-2624
617-277-0906
Contact: Craig Miklencic
c.miklencic@a-a-inc.com

18988 Applied Chemical Technology
4350 Helton Dr
Florence, AL 35630
256-760-9600
Fax: 256-760-9638 800-228-3217
act@appliedchemical.com
www.appliedchemical.com
Manufacturer and exporter of fluid beds, feeders and granulators. Development and engineering of processing plants available
President: A Ray Shirley
CFO: Ginger Lewey
VP: Curtis Lewey
Quality Control: Curtis Lewey
Marketing: Alan Nix
Contact: Craig Arnett
carnett@appliedchemical.com
Purchasing Manager: Roger Kilburn
Estimated Sales: Below $5 Million
Number Employees: 50
Square Footage: 70000

18989 Applied Fabric Technologies
P.O.Box 575
Orchard Park, NY 14127-0575
716-662-0632
Fax: 716-662-0636 www.afti.com
Conveyor belting including endless felts, endless belts, rotary moulder belts and bakery belts
President: Peter Lane
Sales Director: Matt Severied
Contact: Carole Lane
oilfence@aol.com
Estimated Sales: $20-50 Million
Number Employees: 10-19

18990 Applied Handling NW
8531 South 222nd St
Kent, WA 98031
253-395-8500
Fax: 253-395-8585 888-395-3943
ahnwi@aol.com www.appliednw.com
Wholesaler/distributor of material handling equipment including package conveyors and pallet racks; rack jobber services available
President: Michael Tucker
Contact: Richard Chaffee
richc@appliednw.com
Estimated Sales: $5-10 Million
Number Employees: 10-19
Brands:
H.K. Systems
Prest Rack
Rapid Rack
Unarco
Western Pacific Storage Systems

18991 Applied Industrial TechInc
1 Applied Plz
Cleveland, OH 44115-2519
216-426-4000
Fax: 216-426-4845 877-279-2799
www.applied.com
CEO: Neil A Schrimsher
nschrimsher@ait-applied.com
CEO: David L Pugh
Estimated Sales: Over $1 Billion
Number Employees: 5000-9999

18992 Applied Membranes
2325 Cousteau Ct
Vista, CA 92081
760-727-3711
Fax: 760-727-4427 800-321-9321
sales@appliedmembranes.com
www.appliedmembranes.com
Reverse osmosis, ultrafiltration and nano filtration systems, RO membranes, filters, pressure vessels, residential and commercial components and resins
President: Gil Dhawan
Marketing: Jande Wysocki
Contact: Dorothy Adams
dadams@appliedmembranes.com
Estimated Sales: $5-10 000,000
Number Employees: 50-99

18993 Applied Product Sales
802 Angevine Court SW
Lilburn, GA 30047-4209
650-218-3104
Fax: 770-921-5814
info@appliedproductmarketing.com

Insulated shipping boxes and containers. Packaging and process machinery parts. Electro-mechanical power transmission components.
President: Tracey McHugh
CFO: Jim McHugh
Estimated Sales: $1.5 Million
Number Employees: 2
Number of Brands: 5
Type of Packaging: Food Service, Private Label, Bulk
Other Locations:
Applied Product Sales
Lilburn GA

18994 Applied Products Co
118 Sierra St
El Segundo, CA 90245-4117
310-322-5972
Fax: 310-640-2975 888-551-0447
appliedprods@att.net
Marking and numbering equipment
Owner: Richard Panacek
appliedprods@att.net
Estimated Sales: Less Than $500,000
Number Employees: 1-4

18995 Applied Robotics Inc
648 Saratoga Rd
Schenectady, NY 12302-5837
518-384-1000
Fax: 518-384-1200 800-309-3475
info@arobotics.com www.appliedrobotics.com
ARI is a leading provider of automation end-of-arm connectivity solutions designed to bring greater speed and flexibility to automation-based processes.
CEO: Michael F Quinn
mquinn@appliedrobotics.com
CEO: Tom Petronis
CFO: Paul Cullen
CEO: Thomas J Petronis
Research & Development: Clay Cooper
Quality Control: Mike Gallo
Marketing Director: Joanne Brown
Public Relations: Joanne Brown
Production Manager: Bob Butterfield
Plant Manager: John Sezfilippi
Estimated Sales: $10-20,000,000
Number Employees: 20-49
Square Footage: 18000
Brands:
Quickstop
Smartscan
Xchange

18996 Applied Technologies
16815 W Wisconsin Ave
Brookfield, WI 53005-5714
262-784-7690
Fax: 262-784-6847 info@ati-ae.com
www.ati-ae.com
Consultant specializing in water and wastewater management
President: Dennis Totzke
Vice President: Dennis Totzke
Quality Control: Frank Tiefert
Marketing Director: Dennis Totzke
Number Employees: 20-49

18997 Applied Thermal Technologies
906 Boardwalk Ste B
San Marcos, CA 92069-4071
760-744-5083
Fax: 442-744-5031 800-736-5083
Manufacturer and exporter of water chilling systems for batch cooling, food, confectionery and dairy products.
President: Kimberly Howard
khoward@appliedthermaltech.com
Plant Manager: Dale Anderson
Estimated Sales: $500,000-$1 Million
Number Employees: 1-4
Square Footage: 10000
Brands:
Hydro-Miser

18998 Apt-Li Specialty Brushes
231 Red Rose Rd
Kerrville, TX 78028-8957
830-995-5198
Fax: 830-995-4036
Brushes (for food and also for equipment) used in the food industry
Owner: Jerry O'Brien
Estimated Sales: $.5-1 million
Number Employees: 1-4

18999 Aptar Mukwonago
711 Fox St
Mukwonago, WI 53149-1419
262-363-7191
Fax: 262-363-3658 www.seaquistclosures.us
President: Eric Ruskoski
R & D: Jim Hammond
Data Processing: Michael Wedge
Manager: Asa Albritton
eem2rudy@aol.com
Number Employees: 250-499
Parent Co: Aptar Group

19000 Apv Crepaco Inc
395 Fillmore Ave
Tonawanda, NY 14150-2418
716-692-9967
Fax: 716-692-1715 800-828-7391
answers@invensys.com www.apv.com
Evaporators, dryers, membrane systems, distillation
Contact: Mamunur Rahman
mamunur.rahman@apv.com
Estimated Sales: $20-50 Million
Number Employees: 20-49

19001 Aqua Blast Corp Mfg
1025 W Commerce Dr
Decatur, IN 46733-7541
260-728-4433
Fax: 260-728-4517 800-338-7373
davidt@aquablast.com www.aquablast.com
High pressure cleaning systems. I order to meet certain food quality sterilization requirements, offers wash down motors, food grade oil and stainless steel.
President: Dave Tumbleson
abco@aquablast.com
Estimated Sales: $3-5 Million
Number Employees: 10-19

19002 Aqua Brew
3421 W Fordham Ave
Santa Ana, CA 92704
714-546-7117
Fax: 714-432-8802 800-888-BREW
sarah@cafejo.com www.aquabrew.com
Iced tea and coffee brewers, brewing devices and cleaners
Owner: Patrick Rolfes
Estimated Sales: $2.5-5 000,000
Number Employees: 20-49

19003 (HQ)Aqua Measure
9567 Arrow Rte # E
Suite E
Rancho Cucamonga, CA 91730-4550
909-941-7776
Fax: 909-941-6444 800-966-4788
sales@aquameasure.com www.finnagroup.com
Manufacturer and exporter of moisture meters and systems for measuring moisture content in solids for the food processing industry
Owner: John Lundrstrom
Sales: Gabriel Cote Jr
Contact: Steven Brunasso
sbrunasso@aquameasure.com
Estimated Sales: $2.5-5 Million
Number Employees: 5-9
Other Locations:
Aqua Measure InstrumentCo.
La Verne CA

19004 Aqua Tec Inc
1235 Shappert Dr
Machesney Park, IL 61115-1417
815-654-1500
Fax: 815-654-0038 rj.ryan@aquatecinc.com
www.aquatecinc.com
President: Richard Ryan
rj.ryan@aquatecinc.com
Estimated Sales: $3-5 Million
Number Employees: 20-49

19005 Aqua-Aerobic Systems Inc
6306 N Alpine Rd
Loves Park, IL 61111-4396
815-639-9803
Fax: 815-654-2508 800-940-5008
solutions@aqua-aerobic.com
www.aqua-aerobic.com

Manufacturer and exporter of water and wastewater treatment systems for both municipal and industrial market, including direct drive aerators, down draft mixers and sequencing batch reactors; also, shallow bed, gravity sand and clothmedia filtration equipment
President: Robert J Wimmer
rwimmer@aqua-aerobic.com
R&D: Lloyd Johnson
VP Marketing: Deb Lavelle
VP Sales: Steven Schupbach
VP International Sales: Sharon DeDoncker
Operations: Rick Reiland
Estimated Sales: $20-50 Million
Number Employees: 100-249
Square Footage: 100000
Brands:
Aqua Br
Aqua Cb12/24
Aqua Dm
Aqua Endura Disc
Aqua Endura Tube
Aqua Gf
Aqua-Jet Aerator
Aquadisk
Thermo F10

19006 Aquafine Corp
29010 Avenue Paine
Valencia, CA 91355-4198
661-257-4770
Fax: 661-257-2489 800-423-3015
techsupport@aquafineuv.com
www.aquafineuv.com
Ultra-violet water treatment equipment for pure and ultrapure applications. Aquafine meets the most stringent specifications in a variety of industries ranging from semiconductor to bio-pharmaceutical, food and beverage to powergeneration. The systems adhere to rigid industry standards of performance and are available with UL, CE and TUV specifications to meet all standards
Manager: Rick Clark
CEO: Michael Murphy
CFO: Steven Smith
VP Operations: John Maskaluk
Research & Development: Tony Ng
Quality Control: Robert Rivard
Sales/Marketing: Greg Hoffman
Contact: Lobefaro Angelo
l.angelo@aquafineuv.com
Human Resource Director: Julie Weith
Engineering: Mike Quinn
Purchasing Manager: Paul Contreras
Estimated Sales: $10-20 Million
Number Employees: 50-99
Square Footage: 220000

19007 Aquair
PO Box 777
Glen Ellen, CA 95442-0777
800-834-4474
Fax: 707-996-9234 www.aquair.com

19008 Aquathin Corporation
950 South Andrews Avenue
Pompano Beach, FL 33069
954-781-7777
Fax: 954-781-7336 800-462-7634
info@aquathin.com www.aquathin.com
Manufacturer and exporter of water purification systems including reverse osmosis, softening and filtration
President: Alfred Lipshultz
Estimated Sales: $5 -14 Million
Number Employees: 20-49
Square Footage: 130000
Brands:
Aqualite
Aquathin
Country Hutch
Lead Out
Megachar
Platinum 90
Sodia Lite
Soft N Clean
Yes

19009 Aquionics Inc
1455 Jamike Ave # 100
Suite 100
Erlanger, KY 41018-3147
859-341-0710
Fax: 859-341-0350 800-925-0440
sales@aquionics.com www.aquionics.com
Manufacturer and exporter of ultraviolet disinfection equipment
President: Oliver Lawal
oliver.law@aquionics.com
Manager: Rica Williams
Food/Beverage Sales Manager: Ralph Lopez
Number Employees: 20-49
Square Footage: 60000
Parent Co: Halma

19010 Aramark Uniform Svc
115 N First St # 203
Burbank, CA 91502-1857
818-973-3700
Fax: 818-973-3545 800-272-6275
www.aramarkuniform.com
Manufacturer and wholesaler/distributor of uniforms; serving the food service market
President: Brad Drummond
brad.drummond@uniform.aramark.com
CFO: David Solomon
VP Marketing: Judith Weiss
Estimated Sales: Over $1 Billion
Number Employees: 10000+
Parent Co: Aramark Services

19011 Aran USA
1704 Poplar Dr
Greer, SC 29651
864-479-0023
Fax: 864-479-0031 www.aran.co.il
Producer of bags for bag-in-box applications, including aseptic and non-aseptic liquid food.
Sales Manager North America: Mati Karni
Parent Co: Aran Group

19012 Arbee Transparent Inc
1450 Pratt Blvd
Elk Grove Vlg, IL 60007-5713
847-593-0400
Fax: 847-593-0291 800-642-2247
www.arbee.com
A supplier of Plastic Bags
President: Bob Harris
bagplastic@aol.com
Estimated Sales: $20-50 Million
Number Employees: 100-249
Square Footage: 25000

19013 (HQ)Arc Machines Inc
10500 Orbital Way
Pacoima, CA 91331-7129
818-896-9556
Fax: 818-890-3724 sales@arcmachines.com
www.arcmachines.com
Automatic orbital welding equipment
President: Mindegas E Gedgaudas
mindegas.gedgaudas@arcmachines.com
Estimated Sales: $30-50 Million
Number Employees: 100-249

19014 Arcar Graphics
450 Wegner Dr
West Chicago, IL 60185-2694
630-293-4453
Fax: 630-231-3716
President: Mark Denboer
Estimated Sales: Less Than $500,000
Number Employees: 1-4

19015 (HQ)Archer Daniels Midland Company
77 West Wacker Dr.
Suite 4600
Chicago, IL 60601
312-634-8100
www.adm.com
Food and feed ingredients, industrial chemicals and biofuels.
Chairman/CEO: Juan Luciano
Executive VP/CFO: Ray Young
Senior VP/General Counsel: D. Cameron Findlay
Year Founded: 1902
Estimated Sales: $64.3 Billion
Number Employees: 32,000

19016 Archer Wire Intl Corp

7300 S Narragansett Ave
Chicago, IL 60638-6020

708-563-1700

Fax: 708-563-1740 www.archerwire.com
Stainless steel fry and wire baskets, barbecue grills,
point of purchase displays, oven racks and stove
grates; also, metal stamping services available
Owner: Lawrence Svabek
larrysv@archerwire.com
VP Sales: Rick Svabek
National Sales Manager: Dale Brines
VP Finance: Larry Svabek
Estimated Sales: $10-20 Million
Number Employees: 100-249
Square Footage: 376000

19017 Archibald Frozen Desserts

990 Progress Blvd
New Albany, IN 47150-2259

812-941-8267

Fax: 812-941-5374
Soft serve ice cream and frozen yogurt
CEO: Ed Meyer
Executive VP: Greg Gilbert
greg.gilbert@archibaldfrozendesserts.com
Sales & Marketing Coordinator: Lindsay Usher
National Sales Manager: Alex Mohler
Warehouse/Service Manager: Tim Coy
Estimated Sales: Less Than $500,000
Number Employees: 1-4

19018 Architectural Products

1 Lockhart Ln
Highland, NY 12528

845-691-8500

Fax: 845-691-2501
Lighting fixtures and emergency lighting; also, en-
ergy consultants
President: Stephen Lockhart
Contact: Mark Manning
mmanning@archprod.com
Estimated Sales: $500,000-$1,000,000
Number Employees: 1-4
Brands:
 Api

19019 Architectural Sheet Metals LLC

1457 E 39th St
Cleveland, OH 44114-4198

216-361-9952

Fax: 216-431-6650 isminc@worldnet.att.com
www.architecturalsheetmetal.com
Sheet metal and stainless steel custom restaurant
equipment including cooking, heating and food pro-
cessing; also, store fixtures.
Owner: Art Petrauskis
Secretary/Treasurer: Donna Sens
Vice President: Jeff Dixon
Operations Manager: Guy DiSiena
Plant Manager: Guy DiSiena
Estimated Sales: $1-2.5 Million
Number Employees: 5-9
Square Footage: 24000

19020 Architectural Specialty Products

6312 W 74th St
Bedford Park, IL 60638

708-563-8510

Fax: 708-563-1860 800-388-0111
President: Rena Jahn
Owner: Lauren Jahn
Finance Executive: Tim Gibbons
Sales Executive: Warren Yoksas
Operations Executive: Pat Walsh
Estimated Sales: $1-5 Million
Number Employees: 20-49

19021 Architecture Plus Intl Inc

2709 N Rocky Point Dr # 201
Rocky Point, FL 33607-5562

813-281-9299

Fax: 813-281-9292 info@apiplus.com
www.apiplus.com
Manufacturer and exporter of aseptic packaging
equipment and components, over and shrink wrap-
pers and case packers, stackers and unstackers
President: Jean-Louis Limousin
CEO: Juan Romero
VP Sales: Keith Wennik
Number Employees: 50-99
Brands:
 Api
 Durajet

Duratech
Mastertech
Multitech
Versajet
Versatech

19022 Archon Industries

200 William Street
Rye Brook, NY 10573-4620

914-937-8030

Contact: Mario Faustini
sales@archonind.com
Estimated Sales: $1-5 Million
Number Employees: 20-50

19023 Archon Industries Inc

357 Spook Rock Rd
Suffern, NY 10901-5314

845-368-3600

Fax: 845-368-3040 800-554-1394
sales@archonind.com www.shoparchonind.com
Manufacturer, importer and exporter of washdown
stations, sanitary fittings and ball, butterfly, gage
and sanitary valves
CEO: Mario Faustini
Sales Manager: Linda Kyriakos
Engineering Manager: Konrad Mayer
Estimated Sales: $5-10 Million
Number Employees: 5-9

19024 Arco Coffee Co

2206 Winter St
Superior, WI 54880-1400

715-392-4771

Fax: 715-392-4776 800-283-2726
Pete@arcocoffee.com www.arcocoffee.com
Family owned coffee roasting company.
Owner: Don Andresen
donald@arcocoffee.com
Number Employees: 10-19
Type of Packaging: Consumer
Brands:
 Arco Coffee

19025 Arcobaleno Pasta Machines

160 Greenfield Rd
Lancaster, PA 17601-5815

717-394-1402
800-875-7096
www.arcobalenollc.com
Pasta machinery and bakery processing lines, continuous and general purpose mixers, pasta preparation machinery, dough cutters and sheeters,
pasteurizers, etc; exporter of calzone and pizza lines,
ravioli machines and dough sheeters
President: Antonio Adiletta
info@arcobalenollc.com
VP, Marketing & Sales: Maja Adijetta
Number Employees: 10-19
Square Footage: 80000
Brands:
 Arcobaleno

19026 Arcoplast Wall & Ceiling Systems

1873 Williamstown Drive
St Peters, MO 63376-8101

636-978-7781

Fax: 636-978-7782 888-736-2726
ghislain@arcoplast.com www.arcoplast.com
Integrated components necessary to design a contamination controlled environment. Product line includes ceilings, lights, air handling and microbial
control systems, load-bearing and airtight walls and
partitions, doors, windowspass-thru air locks, base-
boards, structures, fasteners and other accessories.
President: Ghislain Beauregard
beauregard@arcoplast.com
Estimated Sales: $1-$5 Million
Type of Packaging: Food Service, Bulk

19027 Arctic Air

6440 City West Pkwy Ste 2
Eden Prairie, MN 55344

952-941-2270

Fax: 952-941-3066 800-853-3508
info@arcticairco.com www.arcticairco.com
Manufacturer and exporter of refrigerators including
reach-in and NSF approved chest freezers.
Owner: Walter Broich Sr
wbroich@arcticairco.com
Estimated Sales: $10-20 Million
Number Employees: 4
Square Footage: 10000
Parent Co: Broich Enterprises

Brands:
 Arctic Air

19028 Arctic Glacier Premium Ice

625 Henry Avenue
Winnepeg, MB R3A 0V1
Canada

204-772-2473

Fax: 204-783-9857 888-783-9857
info@arcticglacier.com www.arcticglacier.com
Bagged ice.
Chief Financial Officer: Linda Davachi
Vice President: Jeremy Spencer
Year Founded: 1996
Estimated Sales: $100-500 Million
Number Employees: 650
Parent Co: H.I.G. Capital

19029 Arctic Industries

9731 NW 114th Way
Medley, FL 33178

305-883-5581

Fax: 305-883-4651 800-325-0123
rio@arcticwalk-ins.com www.arcticwalk-ins.com
Manufacturer and exporter of walk-in coolers, freez-
ers and cold storage facilities, as well as step-in
freezers and coolers.
President: Donald Goodstein
Vice President: Barbara Bowman
Sales Director: Rio Giardinieri
Contact: Gary Albright
galbright@arcticwalkins.com
Office Manager: Barbara Bowman
Estimated Sales: $5-100 Million
Number Employees: 100-249
Square Footage: 50000
Brands:
 Arctic
 Penguin

19030 Arctic Seal & Gasket

2796 SW Bridgeway St
Palm City, FL 34990-1451

772-283-0080

Fax: 772-220-7437 800-881-4663
gaskets@bellsouth.net
Gaskets and seals for refrigeration units
Owner: Fred Froberd
VP: Fred Froberg
Sales: I Micheal Roth
Estimated Sales: $1-2,500,000
Number Employees: 1-4

19031 Arctic Star

3540 W Pioneer Pkwy
Pantego, TX 76013-4699

817-274-1396

Fax: 817-277-4828 800-229-6567
www.arcticstar.com
Refrigerated store displays
Owner: Jim Dunnagan
jdunnagan@arcticstar.com
Estimated Sales: $10-20 000,000
Number Employees: 10-19

19032 Arctica Showcase Company

88 Talbot St. E
P.O.Box 130
Cayuga, ON N0A 1E0
Canada

905-772-5214

Fax: 905-772-3179 800-839-5536
info@cayugadisplays.com cayugadisplays.com
Supplier of Hot Food, Deli, Meat, Seafood, Bakery,
Candy Cafeteria showcases and more.
President: Rick Schotsman
Project Coordinator: Jennifer Zuidema
Vice President, Sales & Marketing: Chris
Schotsman
Sales Director: Kirk Bessey
Number Employees: 85
Square Footage: 188000
Parent Co: Cayuga Displays Inc.
Brands:
 Diamond 49 Series
 Diamond 52 Series
 M850 Series
 Maxima Series
 Omega 48 Series
 Omega 52 Series
 Omega Buffet Series

19033 Ardagh Group
8770 W Bryn Mawr Ave # 8
Chicago, IL 60631-3515

773-399-3000
Fax: 773-399-3354 www.ardaghgroup.com
Metal packaging manufacturer, aluminum can packaging
President: William Francois
CEO: Stephen Sefton
ssefton@rexambca.com
CEO: Harry Barto
Estimated Sales: $2.5-5 Million
Number Employees: 500-999

19034 Ardagh Group
1509 S Macedonia Ave
Muncie, IN 47302-3664

765-741-7000
Fax: 765-741-7012 www.ardaghgroup.com
Designs and manufactures glass containers for the food and beverage industries in North America.
CEO: Joseph R Grewe
joseph.grewe@saint-gobain.com
CEO: Joe Grewe
Marketing Director: Marilyn LaGrange
Sales Director: Jarrell Reeves
Estimated Sales: Over $1 Billion
Number Employees: 1000-4999
Parent Co: Ardagh Group S.A.

19035 Arde Inc
875 Washington Ave
Carlstadt, NJ 07072-3001

201-784-9880
Fax: 201-784-9710 800-909-6070
abmix@ardeinc.com www.ardeinc.com
Manufacturer and exporter of mixing equipment systems used to disperse gums and stabilizers to prepare emulsions
Manager: Sue Belaus
Sales/Engineering Manager: Roy Scott
Public Relations: Cindy Roehling
Purchasing: Tom Stephens
Estimated Sales: $5 Million
Number Employees: 50-99
Square Footage: 280000
Parent Co: Arde, Inc.

19036 Arde Inc
875 Washington Ave
Carlstadt, NJ 07072-3001

201-784-9880
Fax: 201-784-9710 800-909-6070
ABmix@Ardeinc.com www.ardeinc.com
Mixing equipment for beverage, sauces, preserves
Manager: Roy Scott
Manager: Kirk Sneddon
Estimated Sales: $2.5-5 000,000
Number Employees: 50-99
Square Footage: 20000

19037 Arden Companies
30400 Telegraph Road
Southfield, MI 48025

248-415-8500
Fax: 248-415-8520 www.ardencompanies.com
Manufacturer and exporter of aprons, chef coats, baker's mits, handle holders, cleaners, outdoor pads and cushions, grill covers, pot holders and oven mitts
President: Robert Sachs
CFO: John Connell
Sales/Marketing: William Sachs
Estimated Sales: $20-50 Million
Number Employees: 50-99
Square Footage: 675000
Type of Packaging: Consumer, Food Service

19038 Arena Products
2101 Mount Read Blvd
Rochester, NY 14615-3708

585-254-2180
Fax: 585-254-1046 844-762-0127
www.arenaproducts.com
Reusable, collapsible plastic containers for shipping liquid and cheese.
President: Anthony Arena
tarena@arenaproducts.com
Director of Marketing: Jim Roth
Plant Manager: Jeff Reeves
Estimated Sales: $5-10 Million
Number Employees: 5-9
Brands:
Arena 330 Shipper

Arena Shipper
Atlas 640 Shipper

19039 Argo & Company
182 Ezell Street
P.O. Box 2747
Spartanburg, SC 29304

864-583-9766
Fax: 864-585-5056 argosheen@bellsouth.net
Manufacturer and exporter of cleaning supplies including cotton pads, rug mops and carpet/upholstery chemicals and machines
President: Anne Sanders
Estimated Sales: $10-20 Million
Number Employees: 20-49
Square Footage: 200000
Brands:
Argomops
Argonaut
Argosheen

19040 Ari Industries Inc
381 S Ari Ct
Addison, IL 60101-4353

630-953-9100
Fax: 630-953-0590 800-237-6725
sales@ariindustries.com www.ariindustries.com
Manufacturer and exporter of temperature sensors and electric heaters
President: Dan Malcolm
brandi.crouch@lmco.com
VP Sales/Marketing: Dan Malcolm
Public Relations: Darlene Sosnowski
Operations: John Mulvey
Estimated Sales: $5-10 Million
Number Employees: 50-99
Square Footage: 56000

19041 Arizona Instrument LLC
3375 N Delaware St
Chandler, AZ 85225-1134

602-470-1414
Fax: 602-281-1745 800-528-7411
sales@azic.com www.azic.com
An ISO 9001:200 registered company that designs, manufactures, and markets Computrac precision moisture, solids, and ash analyzers and Jerome toxic gas analyzers.
President: George Hays
ghays@azic.com
Research & Development: Tom Hatfield
Quality Control: Blaine Nelson
Marketing: Shari Houtler
Operations Manager: Ben Brown
Estimated Sales: $10 Million
Number Employees: 50-99
Number of Brands: 4
Number of Products: 13
Brands:
Computrac Max
Computrac Vapor Pro
Jerome

19042 Arizona Store Equipment
2523 N 16th St
Phoenix, AZ 85006

602-252-4823
Fax: 602-258-3064 800-624-8395
Acrylic displays, showcases, slatwall, wall systems, shelving and store fixtures
Administrator: Bill James
Estimated Sales: $2.5-5,000,000
Number Employees: 1-4
Brands:
Cal Tuf
Diack
Discovery Plastics
Jahabow
Lozier
Marlite

19043 Arjo Wiggins
10901 Westlake Drive
Charlotte, NC 28273

704-587-3000
Fax: 704-587-1174 800-765-9278
www.polyart.com
Product and services are tag and label applications suitable for a variety of uses including that of: food labels; slaughterhouse meat tags; bar-coded labels, and self-adhesive labels.
Sales Representative: Chris Pelle
Contact: Bharath Chandra
bharath.chandra@arjobexamerica.com

19044 Arjobex
10901 Westlake Dr
Charlotte, NC 28273-3740

704-587-3000
Fax: 704-588-9506 800-POL-YART
www.polyart.com
Synthetic paper products
Vice President: David Brown
david.brown@arjobexamerica.com
VP: Vijay Yadav
Estimated Sales: $10-25 Million
Number Employees: 50-99

19045 Arkansas Glass Container Corp
516 W Johnson Ave
Jonesboro, AR 72401-1994

870-932-0168
Fax: 870-268-6217 800-527-4527
agcsalesdept@agcc.com www.agcc.com
Manufacturer and exporter of glass jars and bottles
CEO: Luann Sutton
lsutton@agcc.com
CEO: Anthony M Ramplex
VP Sales: Melton Harrison
VP Operations: Joel Sharp
Estimated Sales: $30-50 Million
Number Employees: 1-4
Square Footage: 450000

19046 Arkansas Poly
309 Phillips Rd
N Little Rock, AR 72117-4105

501-945-5763
Fax: 501-945-0276 800-342-7659
drew@arkpoly.com www.allampoly.com
Supplier of products for bottling, canning, food processing, and consumer packaging.
Manager: Jim Wilson
VP Sales/Marketing: Kip Johnson
Controller: Dave Robertson
Regional Sales Manager: Dave Schultz
Estimated Sales: $20-50 Million
Number Employees: 50-99
Brands:
Arkansas Poly

19047 Arkansas Tomato Shippers
106 N John C Moss III St
Warren, AR 71671-2510

870-463-8258
brooks@dakotacom.net
Distributor and processor of fresh produce
President: Charlie Sarcey
Estimated Sales: $1-5 Million
Number Employees: 6

19048 Arkfeld Mfg & Distributing Co
1230 W Monroe Ave
Norfolk, NE 68701-6664

402-371-9430
Fax: 402-371-5137 800-533-0676
arkfeldm@ncfcomm.com
Manufacturer, distributor and exporter of custom metal fabricated poultry scales, livestock dial scales and feed/grain hopper dial scales, custom automatic watering systems and security and frozen product storage cabinets.
President: Robert Arkfeld
CEO: Janet Arkfeld
CFO: Anthony Arkfeld
Sales Director: Janet Arkfeld
Sales: Robert Arkfeld
Number Employees: 10-19
Square Footage: 5000
Brands:
Arkfeld Instant Way Dial Scales
Arkfeld Security Cabinets
Bunker Boxes

19049 Arla Foods Ingredients
106 Allen Rd
4th Floor, The Offices at Liberty Cor.
Basking Ridge, NJ 07920

908-604-8551
Fax: 908-604-9310 ingredients@arlafoods.com
www.arlafoodsingredients.com
Specialist provider of advanced innovative solutions withing the milk-based ingredients industry such as dairy, ice cream, meat, ready meals/fine foods, bakery, infant nutrition and functional foods applications.

CEO: Henrick Anderson
CFO: Klaus Kristiansen
Director R&D: Kristian Albertsen
Key Account Manager: Courtney Lopez
Sales Director: Carsten Valentin
Sales Director: Anders Steen Jergensen
Contact: Kay Breyer
kbreyer@fultonbanknj.com
Account Manager: Nikolaj Beck
Product Manager: Adam Criscione
Estimated Sales: $5-10 Million
Number Employees: 5-9
Square Footage: 4000
Parent Co: Arla Foods Ingredients Group
Type of Packaging: Bulk
Brands:
    Capolac®Lacprodan®Miprodan®Nutrilac®

19050 Arlin Manufacturing Co
239 Industrial Ave E
Lowell, MA 01852-5113
    978-454-9165
Fax: 978-454-5265 sales@arlinmfg.com
    www.arlinmfg.com
Tear tapes, plastic film, plastic sheet
Owner: John Mitchell
sales@arlinmfg.com
Estimated Sales: $5-10 Million
Number Employees: 20-49

19051 Arlington Display Industries
19303 W Davison St
Detroit, MI 48223
    313-837-1212
Fax: 313-837-3425
Point-of-purchase displays
President: Carl Dumas
Number Employees: 50-99
Brands:
    Safe-Lode
    Traveler
    Versa-Panel

19052 Arlyn Johnson & Associates
1339 E Hanover St
Springfield, MO 65804-4232
    417-886-3367
Fax: 417-886-4859
Poultry, poultry products, primarily fresh & frozen
turkey [roducts or further processing
President: Rex Johnson
Estimated Sales: Below $5,000,000
Number Employees: 1-4

19053 (HQ)Armaly Brands
1900 Easy St
Commerce Twp, MI 48390-3220
    248-669-2100
Fax: 248-669-3505 800-772-1222
orderdesk207@armalybrands.com
    www.armalybrands.com
Manufacturer and exporter of sponges, scrubbers,
cotton cheesecloth and scouring pads
Owner: John Armaly
jwarmaly@armalybrands.com
VP: Gilbert Armaly
Estimated Sales: $1-5 Million
Number Employees: 20-49
Square Footage: 400
Type of Packaging: Consumer, Food Service, Private Label, Bulk
Brands:
    Auto Show
    Estracell
    Scourlite

19054 Armand Manufacturing Inc
2399 Silver Wolf Dr
Henderson, NV 89011-4431
    702-565-7500
Fax: 702-565-3838 sales@armandmfg.net
    www.armandmfg.com
President: Richard DE Heras
rich@armandmfg.net
Estimated Sales: $10-20 Million
Number Employees: 20-49

19055 Armato & Associates
7825 Carlisle Dr
Hanover Park, IL 60133-2405
    630-837-1886
Fax: 630-837-0813
Owner: Sam Armato

Estimated Sales: $1-5 Million
Number Employees: 1-4

19056 Armbrust Paper Tubes Inc
6255 S Harlem Ave # D
Chicago, IL 60638-3990
    773-586-3232
Fax: 773-586-8997 tubesrus@corecomm.net
    www.tubesrus.com
Manufacturer and exporter of packaging products
including paper tubes, cores, cans and push-ups for
frozen sherbet, gyros, etc.; also, containers for dry
goods
President: Bernard Armbrust
bernard@tubesrus.com
VP: Chris Armbrust
Marketing: Bill Constable
Sales: Marc Armbrust
Secretary: Dorothee Johnstone
Plant Manager: Mike Johnstone
Estimated Sales: $5-10 Million
Number Employees: 20-49
Square Footage: 170000
Type of Packaging: Food Service, Private Label
Brands:
    Artpak
    Pinched Tube
    Push-Pops

19057 Armco
385 Todhunter Road
Monroe, OH 45050-1113
    800-231-3748

19058 Armstrong Engineering Associates
PO Box 566
West Chester, PA 19381-0566
    610-436-6080
Fax: 610-436-0374 sales@armstrong-chemtec.com
    www.rmarmstrong.com
President: Richard M Armstrong Jr
Sales: Gail Justi
Contact: Janine Stein
janine@contentasia.tv
Estimated Sales: $1-5 Million
Number Employees: 50-99

19059 Armstrong Hot Water
221 Armstrong Blvd
Three Rivers, MI 49093-2374
    269-279-3602
Fax: 269-279-3150 www.armstrong-intl.com
Manufacturer and exporter of hose stations and ther-
mostatic mixing valves
President: David Armstrong
General Manager/Sales/Marketing Exec.: Paul
Knight
Purchasing Agent: Steven Shutes
Number Employees: 20-49
Parent Co: Armstrong International
Brands:
    Rada
    Steamix

19060 Armstrong International
900 Maple St
Three Rivers, MI 49093
    269-273-1415
Fax: 269-278-6555 marketing@armintl.com
    www.armstrong-intl.com
Steam traps, strainers, purgers, air vents, humidifiers
and liquid drainers, pressure reducing valves, instan-
taneous water heaters, radiator products, mixing
valves, hosestations, and heating and cooling coils
Chairman of the Board: Merrill Armstrong
Marketing Director: Tom Grubka
Estimated Sales: $50-100 Million
Number Employees: 250-499

19061 Armstrong Manufacturing
2485 Haines Road
Mississauga, ON L4Y 1Y7
Canada
    905-566-1395
Fax: 905-566-8195 866-627-6588
Industrial cleaning products
CEO: David Armstrong
Estimated Sales: $1-5 Million
Number Employees: 100-250

19062 Armstrong-Hunt
816 Maple Street
Three Rivers, MI 49093
    269-273-1415
Fax: 269-278-6555 www.armstrong-hunt.com
President, Chief Executive Officer: Patrick
Armstrong
Contact: Zac Findlay
zfindlay@armstronginternational.com

19063 Arneg LLC
750 Old Hargrave Rd
Lexington, NC 27295-7514
    336-956-5300
Fax: 610-746-9580 800-276-3487
    www.arnegusa.com
Display cases for meat, seafood, fish, cheese, deli
and frozen foods, etc
General Manager: Gianfrano Genovese
President: Rejean Lumiere
Sales Manager: Jim Christman
Manager: Louis Moschetta
lmoschetta@arnegusa.com
Secretary: Sharon Sherman
Estimated Sales: $10-20 Million
Number Employees: 50-99
Square Footage: 140000
Parent Co: Arneg
Brands:
    Arneg

19064 Arnold Equipment Co
24400 Highpoint Rd # 5
Cleveland, OH 44122-6027
    216-831-8485
Fax: 216-831-8414 800-642-1824
    www.arnoldeqp.com
Wholesaler/distributor and exporter of blenders, ov-
ens, agitators, filters, dryers, packaging plastic
granulators, centrifuges, pumps, evaporators, con-
densers, kettles, homogenizers and material handling
and laboratory testingequipment, etc
CEO: Jon Arnold
CFO: Seth Arnold
Estimated Sales: Less Than $500,000
Number Employees: 1-4
Square Footage: 120000

19065 Arol Closure Systems Spa
237 Graves Mill Road
Lynchburg, VA 24502-4203
    800-423-5822
Fax: 434-832-8352 info@belvac.com
    www.belvac.com

19066 Aroma Manufacturing Company
6469 Flanders Dr
San Diego, CA 92121
    858-558-8866
Fax: 858-558-7300 800-276-6286
    www.aroma-housewares.com
Rice and steam cookers; also, soup and rice warmers
Manager: David Kellerman
Marketing Director: Howard Ong
Contact: Peter Chang
pchang@aromaco.com
Estimated Sales: $3-5 Million
Number Employees: 5-9

19067 Aromascan PLC
14 Clinton Drive
Hollis, NH 03049-6595
    603-598-2922
    Fax: 603-595-9916
Instrumentation for the analysis of odors
Contact: Drwang Chong
drwang@aromascan.com
General Manager: Peter Debroczy
Estimated Sales: $1-2.5 Million
Number Employees: 24
Parent Co: Aromascan PLC
Brands:
    The Aromo Scanner

19068 Aromatech USA
5770 Hoffner Avenue
Suite 103
Orlando, FL 32822
    407-277-5727
Fax: 407-277-5725 americas@aromatech.fr
    www.aromatech.fr/en/f.usa.htm
Flavorings for beverages, candies, baking, snacks
and pastries.

19069 (HQ)Arpac LP
9511 River St
Schiller Park, IL 60176-1019
847-678-9034
Fax: 847-671-7006 info@arpac.com
www.arpac.com
One stop shop packaging solutions. Manufacture
shrink bundles, multipackers, horizontal shrin wrap-
pers, corrugated tray and case erectors, box formers,
corrugated board try and case packers, pallet stretch
wrappers and pallet stretchhooders.
President: Michael Levy
Marketing Manager: Greg Levy
VP Sales: Gary Ehmka
Contact: Stephen Archer
sarcher@arpac.com
Estimated Sales: $10-50 Million
Number Employees: 5-9
Square Footage: 260000
Brands:
    Brandpac
    Tray Star

19070 Arpac LP
9511 River St
Schiller Park, IL 60176-1019
847-678-9034
Fax: 847-671-7006 info@arpac.com
www.arpac.com
Shrink wrappers, case packers and tray loaders
President: Michael Levy
Contact: James Barry
jbarry@arpac.com
Estimated Sales: $25-50 Million
Number Employees: 5-9

19071 Arpeco Engineering Ltd
7095 Ordan Drive
Mississauga, ON L5T 1K6
Canada
905-564-5150
Fax: 905-564-2943 sales@arpeco.com
Owner: Allan Prittie

19072 Arro Corp
7440 Santa Fe Dr # A
Hodgkins, IL 60525-5076
708-639-9063
Fax: 708-352-5293 877-929-2776
Sales@arro.com www.arro.com
Corn, peanut, salad, soybean and vegetable oils.
Owner: Pat Gaughn
arrosales@aol.com
Sales Exec: Timothy Mcnicholas
Estimated Sales: $500,000-1 Million
Number Employees: 50-99
Type of Packaging: Food Service, Private Label,
    Bulk
Other Locations:
    Chicago IL
    Hodgkins IL

19073 Arro Corp
7440 Santa Fe Dr # A
Hodgkins, IL 60525-5076
708-639-9063
Fax: 708-352-5293 877-929-2776
sales@arro.com www.arro.com
Dry & liquid blending, dry & liquid processing, bulk
handling & storage.
Sales Exec: Timothy Mcnicholas
Number Employees: 50-99
Square Footage: 600

19074 Arrow Plastic Mfg Co
701 E Devon Ave
Elk Grove Vlg, IL 60007-6700
847-595-9000
Fax: 847-595-9122 info@arrowplastic.com
www.arrowplastic.com
Manufacturer and exporter of plastic cutting boards
President: Robert Kleckauskas
rkleck@arrowplastic.com
Estimated Sales: $20-50 Million
Number Employees: 100-249
Type of Packaging: Food Service

19075 Arrow Sign & Awning Company
18607 Highway 65 NE
East Bethel, MN 55304-6784
763-755-8873
Fax: 763-755-1473 800-621-9231
john@arrowfenceco.com www.arrowsignmn.com

Design manufacturer of lit and unlit fabric and metal
commercial awnings, neon signs and lighted channel
letters, also pylon signs, LED lighting, parking lot
lights, LED message centers.
President: Bruce Cardinal
CFO/VP: Connie Cardinal Ramberg
Research & Development: Kelli Keilty
Quality Control: Tony Ramberg
Marketing: Bruce Cardinal
Plant Manager: Tony Ramberg
Purchasing Manager: Ryan Thiede
Estimated Sales: $10 Million
Number Employees: 20-49
Square Footage: 72000

19076 Arrow Tank Co
16 Barnett Pl
Buffalo, NY 14215-3898
716-893-7200
Fax: 716-893-0693 sales@arrowtankco.com
www.arrowtankco.com
Manufacturer, exporter of wood tanks and tank
hoops
President: William H Wehr
sales@arrowtankco.com
Operations: W H Wehr
Plant Manager: R Willis
Estimated Sales: $1-3,000,000
Number Employees: 5-9
Square Footage: 25000

19077 Arrow-Magnolia Intl Inc
2646 Rodney Ln
Dallas, TX 75229-3425
972-247-7111
Fax: 972-484-2896 800-527-2101
info@arrowmagnolia.com
www.arrowmagnolia.com
Industrial insecticides, grill cleaners, drain cleaners
and deodorizers
President: Curtis Shaw
CEO: David Tippeconnic
Vice President of Sales: Jim Purcell
Operations Manager: Michael Campanaro
Number Employees: 50-99
Square Footage: 160000

19078 Art Craft Lighting
East Service Road
P.O. Box 1526
Champlain, NY 11919
718-387-8000
Fax: 516-593-9239 www.artcraftlighting.com
Electric lighting fixtures
President: Barry Spade
Estimated Sales: $1-2.5 Million
Number Employees: 5-9
Parent Co: Artcraft Lighting Company

19079 Art Poly Bag Co
70 Franklin Ave
Brooklyn, NY 11205-1504
718-243-9417
Fax: 718-422-8689 800-278-7659
Promotional poly tote bags
President: Erwin Katz
Estimated Sales: $500,000-$1 Million
Number Employees: 5-9

19080 Art Wire Works Co
6711 S Leclaire Ave
Chicago, IL 60638-6417
708-458-3993
Fax: 708-458-3008 dcollignon@artwireworks.com
www.artwireworks.com
Manufacturer and exporter of display racks, point of
purchase displays, back room trays and hand carts
President: David Collignon
dcollignon@artwireworks.com
CFO: Ksenia Nalysnyk
R&D/Quality Control: Danny Tomasevich
Sales: Gayle Blakeslee
Plant Manager: Wally Kaim
Purchasing: Gayle Blakeslee
Estimated Sales: $5 Million
Number Employees: 20-49
Square Footage: 80000

19081 Art's Welding
3902 230th St
PO Box 909
Winsted, MN 55395
320-485-2471
Fax: 320-485-4466 888-272-2600
customerservice@awimfg.com www.awimfg.com
President: Gary Scherping
Sales Manager: Brent Johnson
Estimated Sales: $1-3 Million
Number Employees: 20-49
Square Footage: 90

19082 Art-Phyl Creations
16250 NW 8th Avenue
Hialeah, FL 33014-6415
305-624-2333
Fax: 305-621-4093 800-327-8318
info@art-phyl.com
Manufacturer and exporter of store display fixtures,
peghooks, merchandising aids, point of purchase
displays, etc.
President: Arthur Hochman
CEO: S Gwinn
CFO: C Pomerantz
Sales: William Rodriguez
Estimated Sales: $5-10 Million
Number Employees: 20-49
Number of Products: 400
Square Footage: 200000
Brands:
    Kwik-Hook
    Kwik-Hub
    Poly-Pole
    Scan-A-Plate
    Short-Stop
    Super Hook

19083 Art-Tech Restaurant Design
30 Woodland Avenue
Rockville Centre, NY 11570
516-593-9130
Fax: 516-593-9239
Consultant and designer of restaurant/food service
interiors
President: Philip Starr
Consultant: Philip Starr
Estimated Sales: $1-2.5 Million
Number Employees: 5-9

19084 Artco Eq Co
40 Tillman St
Westwood, NJ 07675-2611
201-664-4455
Fax: 201-666-9243 800-664-5686
www.bagelbagel.com
Ovens, bagel machines, mixers, bagel kettles and
smallwares
President: Howard Goldberg
Estimated Sales: $1-2.5 Million
Number Employees: 5-9

19085 Artcraft Badge & Sign Company
3512 John Carroll Drive
Olney, MD 20832
301-519-2939
800-739-0709
Plastic custom imprinted identification badges and
interior signage. Produces personalized name
badges, identification tags, signs, and deskplates
Owner: Janet Dinerman
Bookkeeper: Shirley Bowker
General Manager: Arthur Dinerman
Shipping Manager: Reina Roeder
Estimated Sales: $2.5-5 Million
Number Employees: 9
Square Footage: 3600
Type of Packaging: Bulk

19086 Artel Packaging SystemsLimited
PO Box 335
Gromley, ON L0H 1G0
Canada
905-888-9800
Fax: 905-888-9804
President: Fred McCatrney
Estimated Sales: Below $5 Million
Number Employees: 10

19087 Artex International
1405 Walnut St
Highland, IL 62249
618-654-2113
Fax: 618-654-0200

Manufacturer and exporter of table linens including covers, skirts, napkins and place mats, restaurant design, linen processing, trade show listing, linen presentations
Manager: Mike Kirchoff
Estimated Sales: $50-100 Million
Number Employees: 50-99

19088 Arthur Corporation
1305 Huron Avery Rd
Huron, OH 44839
419-433-7202
Fax: 419-433-7088 arthurcorp.com
Plastic cups, trays and containers
President: Charles Hensel
Contact: Russell Gibboney
russell.gibboney@arthurcorp.com
Estimated Sales: $10-20 Million
Number Employees: 100-249
Square Footage: 150000

19089 (HQ)Arthur D Little Inc.
68 Fargo Street
Suite 2810
Boston, MA 02110
617-532-9550
Fax: 617-261-6630 www.adlittle.com
Consultant specializing in technology, product and marketing services; also, management, environmental, health, safety, product formulation, sensory evaluation, research and development.
CEO/Pres.: C LaMantia
Sr. VP: P Ranganath Nayak
VP/Managing Director: C Gail Greenwald
Estimated Sales: $.5-1 million
Number Employees: 1,000-4,999
Square Footage: 800000

19090 Arthur G Russell Co Inc
750 Clark Ave
P.O. Box 237
Bristol, CT 06010-4065
860-583-4109
Fax: 860-583-0686 agr@arthurgrussell.com
www.arthurgrussell.com
Manufacturer and exporter of automated packaging, counting, inspecting and assembling equipment for food and disposable manufacturers; custom design services available
President: Robert J Ensminger
robert.ensminger@arthurgrussell.com
Applications Engr.: John Picoli
Vice President Sales & Marketing: William Mis
Human Resources Manager: Shelly Bove
robert.ensminger@arthurgrussell.com
Operations Manager: Craig Churchill
Estimated Sales: $10-20 Million
Number Employees: 100-249
Square Footage: 166000
Brands:
  Uniplace
  Vibro-Block

19091 Arthur Products Co
1140 Industrial Pkwy
Medina, OH 44256-2486
330-725-4905
Fax: 330-722-2698 800-322-0510
apc@apclsq.com www.arthurproducts.com
Vent tubes and nozzles
Owner: Richard Rauckhorst
rlr@apclsq.com
Sales Manager: Bob Peck
Estimated Sales: Below $5 Million
Number Employees: 5-9
Square Footage: 20000

19092 Artisan Controls Corp
111 Canfield Ave # B-18
Bldg B15-18
Randolph, NJ 07869-1127
973-598-9400
Fax: 973-598-9410 800-457-4950
sales@artisancontrols.com
www.artisancontrols.com
Controllers including time/temperature, dispensing, scheduling for pasta machines, fryers, ovens, etc.
President: Jack Murray
adonnelly@artisancontrols.com
Vice President: Larry Affelt
Sales Manager: Mary Ann Peterson
Plant Manager: Jack Cooper
Purchasing Manager: Angie Donnelly

Estimated Sales: $3 Million
Number Employees: 50-99
Square Footage: 24000
Type of Packaging: Private Label, Bulk
Brands:
  Tyme Chef

19093 Artisan Industries
73 Pond St
Waltham, MA 02451-4594
781-893-6800
Fax: 781-647-0143 info@artisanind.com
www.artisanind.com
Equipment to purify, concentrate, deodorize or recover/remove solvents or fatty acids
President: Andrew Donevan
SVP/General Manager: Perry Alasti
Director Marketing/Sales: Richard Giberti
Contact: Louis Decker
lou@dectechassociates.com
Pilot Plant Services: Robert DiLoreto
Estimated Sales: $5-10 Million
Number Employees: 100
Brands:
  Rototherm

19094 Artist Coffee
51 Harvey Road
Unit D
Londonderry, NH 03053-7414
603-434-9385
Fax: 603-216-8029 866-440-4511
Producer of gourmet coffee, tea and candy for promotional trade. Specializing in Custom Labeling with very special products.
President: Tom Rushton
Marketing Director: Dan Sewell
Estimated Sales: $3-5 Million
Number Employees: 1-4
Type of Packaging: Consumer, Private Label
Other Locations:
  Lambent Technologies
  Gurnee IL
Brands:
  Cirashine
  Erucical
  Hodag
  Lamchem
  Lumisolve
  Lumisorb
  Lumulse
  Oleocal
  Polycal

19095 Artiste Flavor
35 Franklin Tpke
Waldwick, NJ 07463
201-447-1311
Ingredients, flavors, colors and additives
President: Joseph Raimondo
Contact: Tracy Hennig
thennig@artiste.us.com
Estimated Sales: $500,000- 1 Million
Number Employees: 5-9
Type of Packaging: Consumer

19096 Artistic Carton
1201 S Grandstaff Dr
Auburn, IN 46706-2660
260-925-6060
Fax: 260-925-1762 800-735-7225
customerserviceauburn@artisticcarton.com
www.artisticcarton.com
Folding cartons
President: Peter A Traeger
CFO: Mark Hopkinson
Manager: Brandy Aucunas
baucunas@artisticcarton.com
Estimated Sales: $10-20 Million
Number Employees: 50-99

19097 (HQ)Artistic Carton Co
1975 Big Timber Rd
Elgin, IL 60123-1139
847-741-0247
Fax: 847-741-8529 www.artisticcarton.com
Folding paper boxes and cartons
President: Peter A Traeger
CEO: Amanda Brown
brownamanda@artisticcarton.com
CFO: Mark Hopkinfon
Sales Manager: Patrick Driscoll
Estimated Sales: $20-50 Million
Number Employees: 20-49

19098 Artistic Packaging Concepts
PO Box 196
Massapequa Pk, NY 11762-0196
516-797-4020
Fax: 516-797-4020
Plain and printed plastic bags; also, blisters, blister cards, labels and paper printing foam envelopes
VP: S Falciana
Estimated Sales: $1-5 Million
Number Employees: 5

19099 Artkraft Strauss LLC
1776 Broadway # 1810
New York, NY 10019-2017
212-265-5156
Fax: 212-265-5262 info@artkraft.com
www.artkraft.com
Manufacturer and exporter of advertising signs
President: Tama Starr
CFO: Neil Vonknoblauch
Vice President Design & Engineering: Robert Jackowitz
VP Sales: Bob Neuberger
Manager: Amy Hu
alexandra.labrie@mercer.com
Estimated Sales: $10-20 Million
Number Employees: 5-9
Type of Packaging: Consumer, Food Service, Bulk

19100 Artx Limited
1770 W Lexington
Cincinnati, OH 45212-3508
513-631-0660
Fax: 513-631-3111 www.airtxinternational.com
President: Michael Rawlings
Estimated Sales: $5-10 Million
Number Employees: 1-4

19101 Asap Automation
503 S Westgate St # C
Suite C
Addison, IL 60101-4531
630-628-5830
Fax: 630-628-5831 800-409-0383
info@asapauto.com
Software and control systems
President: Steve Moore
sales@asap-automaticn.com
Board of Director: Bill Bastian
Marketing Manager: Lynsey Thomann
Sales Manager: Eric Cameron
Operations Manager: Hal Frary
Estimated Sales: Less Than $500,000
Number Employees: 1-4
Number of Products: 14
Type of Packaging: Private Label, Bulk

19102 Ascaso
524 North York Road
Bensenville, IL 60106
630-350-0066
Fax: 630-350-0005 info@expressoshoppe.com
www.expressoshoppe.com
Espresso equipment and espresso beans
Owner: David Dimbert
Estimated Sales: $300,000-500,000
Number Employees: 1-4
Parent Co: Ascaso Spa
Type of Packaging: Food Service
Brands:
  Ascaso

19103 Asepco
355 Pioneer Way # B
Mountain View, CA 94041-1542
650-691-4439
Fax: 650-691-9600 800-882-3886
www.asepco.com
President/CEO: Steve Joy
Executive Vice-President: Mark Embury
Quality Control Manager: Glenn Slusher
Contact: Arnold Brodskiy
arnoldbrodskiy@asepco.com
Purchasing: Ben Herbert
Estimated Sales: $3-5 Million
Number Employees: 10-19

19104 Aseptic Resources
10008 W 120th St
Overland Park, KS 66213-1647
913-897-4125
Fax: 913-327-5529
Consultant for aseptic systems
Estimated Sales: $1-5 Million

19105 (HQ)Asgco Manufacturing Inc
301 W Gordon St
Allentown, PA 18102-3136
610-821-0210
Fax: 610-778-8991 800-344-4000
info@asgco.com www.asgco.com
Conveyor and bulk material handling systems and components including impact beds, belt cleaner, conveyor components; also, lightweight belt for food applications
President: Todd Gibbs
CFO: George Anthony
Executive VP: George Anthony
ganthony@asgco.com
Research & Development: George Mott
Marketing: Peggy Anthony
Inside Sales Manager: Steve Strella
Plant Manager: Steve Schubert
Estimated Sales: $10-20 Million
Number Employees: 50-99
Square Footage: 200000
Other Locations:
    ASGCO Manufacturing
    Newburgh NY

19106 Ash Enterprises
801 N 7th St
Salina, KS 67401-2903
785-825-5280
Fax: 785-825-5072 888-825-5280
dave@ashenterprisesonline.com
www.ashenterprisesonline.com
Specializing in awnings, livestock curtains, tarps and sun shades.
CEO: Adrienne Ash
Estimated Sales: $5-9.9,000,000
Number Employees: 1-4
Brands:
    Chile Chews
    Hot Pops
    Jalea De Jalapeno
    Salsa Primo

19107 Ashcroft Inc
250 E Main St
Stratford, CT 06614-5145
203-212-5222
Fax: 203-385-0408 800-328-8258
info@ebro.com www.ashcroftinc.com
Ebro instruments can be used for applications in the food and beverage industries. Ebro products are high-precision measuring instruments for use in applications where reliability and performance are required. Ebro instruments canmeasure and store temperature, pressure, humidity, pH, oil quality, current/voltage, salt and RPM, as well as other physical units.
CEO: Steven A Culmone
steven.culmone@ashcroft.com
Managing Director: Wolfgang Klun
General Sales Manager: Iven Kruse
Quality Manager: Thomas Koch
Sales Manager USA: Frank Crisafulli
Marketing Manager: Norbert Niggl
Number Employees: 250-499
Number of Brands: 2
Square Footage: 325000
Brands:
    Ashcroft
    Ebro

19108 Ashland
8145 Blazer Dr
Wilmington, DE 19808
800-274-5263
www.ashland.com
Supplier of specialty resins, polymers, and adhesives. Ashland's Water Technologies unit provides papermaking chemicals and specialty chemicals to markets such as pulp and paper, food and beverage, municipal, and mining.
Chairman/Chief Executive Officer: Guillermo Novo
SVP/Chief Financial Officer: J. Kevin Willis
SVP/Chief Human Resources Officer: Anne Schumann
SVP/CTO: Osama Musa
SVP, Global Operations: Keith Silverman
Year Founded: 1924
Estimated Sales: $4.9 Billion
Number Employees: 6,500
Brands:
    Aqualon™
    Cellulose Gum
    HydraSperse™
    Polyclar™
    Aerowhip™
    Benecel™
    Klucel™
    Aquasorb™

19109 Ashland Nutritional Products
17751 Mitchell N
Irvine, CA 92614-6028
949-833-9500
Fax: 949-622-0954
Estimated Sales: $5-10 000,000
Number Employees: 5-9

19110 Ashlock Co
855 Montague St
P.O. Box 1676
San Leandro, CA 94577-4327
510-351-0560
Fax: 510-357-0329 info@ashlockco.com
www.ashlockco.com
Manufacturer and exporter of pitters for dates, prunes, cherries and olives. Also olive slicers
President: Tom Rettagliata
info@ashlockco.com
CFO: Sheryl Sullivan
R & D: Jeff Davis
Marketing Director: Alan Stender
Office Manager: S Sullivan
info@ashlockco.com
Manager, Operations: Jeff Davis
Estimated Sales: $5-10 Million
Number Employees: 10-19
Square Footage: 24800
Parent Co: Vistan Corporation
Brands:
    Ashlock

19111 Ashworth Bros Inc
450 Armour Dl
Winchester, VA 22601-3459
540-662-3494
Fax: 540-662-3150 800-682-4594
ashworth@ashworth.com www.ashworth.com
Manufacturer and exporter of conveyor belts
President: Keith Almryde
keith.almryde@ashworth.com
VP: Joe Lackner
Quality Control: Jonathan Lasecki
Commercial Support Manager: Kenneth King
Sales: Marty Tabaka
Estimated Sales: $20-50 Million
Number Employees: 100-249
Brands:
    All Plastic Belting
    Balanceo Weave
    Cbs Baking Band
    Flat Wire
    Fusion Grid
    Hybri Flex
    Hybri Grio
    Omni Grid
    Omniflex
    Washer Holddown Mats
    Woven Wire

19112 Asi Food Safety Consultants
7625 Page Ave
St Louis, MO 63133-1009
314-333-6201
Fax: 314-727-2563 800-477-0778
asi@asifood.com
Consultant specializing in food safety audits and training including manual and high pressure cleaning and sanitizing and foodborne illness prevention and pest control; also, HACCP literature, videos and training materials available
President: Tom Huge
CEO: Gary Huge
VP: Gary Huge
Quality Control: Michael Bushaw
Sales: Jeanette Huge
Number Employees: 50-99
Square Footage: 60000
Parent Co: Huge Company
Other Locations:
    ASI Food Safety Consultants
    Lakeland FL

19113 Asia and Middle East Food Traders
340 Pine Street
Suite 401
San Francisco, CA 94104
415-677-9700
Fax: 415-677-9711 info@arabellaadvisors.com
President: Lucy Bernholz
Number Employees: 10-19

19114 Aspect Engineering
7911 Linksview Cir.
Westerville, OH
614-638-7106
Fax: 614-416-6919
Consultant for product development and facility design; management advisory for food service companies and suppliers
Commun. Mgr.: Mark Wegner
Estimated Sales: $1-5 Million
Number Employees: 4
Square Footage: 4000

19115 Aspen Research Corp
8401 Jefferson Hwy
Maple Grove, MN 55369-4588
763-494-0273
Fax: 651-842-6199 answers@aspenresearch.com
Vice President: John Biesboer
john.biesboer@aspenresearch.com
Vice President-Research & Development: Roger Pearson, Ph.D.
Analytical Sales: Jan Fouks
VP of Manufacturing: Brian Woodman
Estimated Sales: $5-10 Million
Number Employees: 50-99

19116 Aspen Research Corporation
1800 Buerkle Rd
White Bear Lake, MN 55110
651-773-7961
Fax: 651-264-6270 answers@aspenresearch.com
www.aspenresearch.com
Contract applied research and development firm specializing in research on flavors, off-flavors, off odors and the interaction between food and food packaging
President: Andy Marine
VP Operations: Roger Worm
Estimated Sales: $20-50 Million
Number Employees: 50-99
Square Footage: 250000

19117 Aspen Systems
6930 E Chauncey Ln # 100
Suite 100
Phoenix, AZ 85054-5175
480-538-1970
Fax: 480-538-1971 800-767-1970
sales@aspen-systems.com
www.aspen-systems.com
Software developer for food industry
President: George Puype
CEO: Larry Andrews
landrews@aspen-systems.com
CFO: Jerry King
Quality Control: Stewart Ward
Estimated Sales: $10-20 000,000
Number Employees: 20-49

19118 Aspeon
16832 Red Hill Avenue
Irvine, CA 92606-4803
949-440-8000
Fax: 949-440-8087 800-574-1622
info@aspeon.com
Leading manufacturer and provider of point-of-sales systems, services and enterprise technology solutions for the retail and food markets

19119 Assembled Products Corp
112 E Linden St
Rogers, AR 72756-6035
479-636-5776
Fax: 479-636-5776 800-548-3373
techservice@assembledproducts.com
www.assembledproducts.com
Manufacturer and exporter of electric shopping carts for supermarkets and high pressure spray cleaning systems
President: Lori Barlar
lorib@martcart.com
Sr. VP Sales/Marketing: Steve Scroggine

Estimated Sales: $5-10 Million
Number Employees: 100-249
Square Footage: 256000
Parent Co: Assembled Products Corporation
Brands:
   Mart Cart
   Spray Master Technologies

19120 Assembly Technology & Test
12841 Stark Rd
Livonia, MI 48150-1525

734-522-1900
Fax: 734-522-9344

Designer and manufacturer of software for material handling implementation and electrified monorail systems for ingredient transport
Founder: Klaus Woerner
VP: James Diedrich
VP Sales/Marketing: Jim Anderson
Contact: Daniel Haubert
dhaubert@assembly-testww.com
Estimated Sales: $50-100 Million
Number Employees: 100-249
Square Footage: 200000
Parent Co: DT Industries

19121 Asset Design LLC
PO Box 3234
Mooresville, NC 28117

704-663-6170
Fax: 704-663-6177 888-293-1740

Consultant providing engineering solutions for process design and automation, plant design and operating procedures, feasibility studies, machine modifications and custom design. Also, project management, start-up assistance and efficiency training
Manager and R&D: Jeff Demback
Estimated Sales: $500,000-$1,000,000
Number Employees: 1-4

19122 Assmann Corp Of America
300 N Taylor Rd
Garrett, IN 46738-1844

260-357-3181
Fax: 260-357-3738 888-357-3181
info@assmann-usa.com www.assmann-usa.com

President: David Crager
dcrager@assmannusa.com
Quality Control: James Reynolds
Estimated Sales: $5-10 Million
Number Employees: 20-49

19123 Associated Bag Co
400 W Boden St
Milwaukee, WI 53207-6276

414-769-1000
Fax: 414-769-1820 800-926-6100
customerservice@associatedbag.com
www.associatedbag.com

Wholesaler/distributor of food grade stretch wrap and bags, gloves and shipping and packaging products
President: Herbert Rubenstein
hrubenstein@associatedbag.com
CFO: Sue Zelga
Quality Control: Mary Samanski
Marketing/Sales Director: Scott Pietila
Customer Service Manager: Philip Roedel
hrubenstein@associatedbag.com
Purchasing Manager: Sue Zylka
Estimated Sales: $20-50 Million
Number Employees: 100-249
Square Footage: 300000

19124 Associated Industrial Rubber
7550 West 2100 South
Magna, UT 84044

801-239-1670
Fax: 801-239-1675 800-526-6288
www.associated-rubber.com

Food handling hoses for beer, milk and juice
General Manager: Steve Williams
Controller: David George
Inside Sales: Steven Munz
Sales Agent: Wilson Dube
Branch Manager: Roger Morrison
Estimated Sales: $2.5-5 Million
Number Employees: 5-9
Square Footage: 120000
Parent Co: Associated Industrial Rubber

19125 Associated Packaging Enterprises
900 S Us Highway 1
Suite 207
Jupiter, FL 33477-6469

561-746-2414
Fax: 561-746-7192 info@aptechnologies.com

19126 Associated Packaging Equipment Corporation
70 Gibson Drive
Units 5 & 6
Markham, ON L3R 2Z3
Canada

905-475-6647
Fax: 905-479-9752

Manufacturer and exporter of roll fed labeling machinery
President: M Malthouse
Controller: Kenneth Bick
Sales Director: Klaus See
Plant Manager: John Malthouse
Purchasing Manager: R Manoharan
Estimated Sales: $1 Million
Number Employees: 15
Square Footage: 24000
Type of Packaging: Food Service, Private Label
Brands:
   Polyclad

19127 Associated Products Inc
1901 William Flynn Hwy
P.O. Box 8
Glenshaw, PA 15116-1742

412-486-2255
Fax: 412-486-7710 800-243-5689

Manufacturer and exporter of air fresheners, deodorants and deodorizers; importer of essential oils and aromatic chemicals
President: Ralph Simons
mrsimon@sani-air.com
CFO: Harlan Simons
Estimated Sales: $2.5-5 Million
Number Employees: 20-49
Number of Products: 100
Square Footage: 360000
Type of Packaging: Consumer, Private Label, Bulk
Brands:
   Ban Air
   Mini Scents
   Sani Air

19128 Association of Operative Millers
12351 w. 96th Terrace,
Suite 100
Lenexa, KS 66215

913-338-3377
Fax: 913-338-3553 aom@sky.net
www.iaom.info

Provider of educational resources and training for the milling industry.
Executive VP: Melinda Farris
Director (Association Services): Roger Gelsinger
Administration Assistant: Carole Smith
Number Employees: 1-4

19129 Association-Nutri
406 Surrey Woods Dr
St Charles, IL 60174-2386

630-587-6336
Fax: 630-587-6308 800-323-1908
info@anfponline.org www.anfponline.org

Dedicated to the practice of providing optimum nutritional care through foodservice management.
President: William S St John
nrubicz@anfponline.org
Quality Control: Pam Himrogh
Vice President of Development: Katherine Church
Marketing Manager: Kim Harden
Sales Exec: Nik Rubicz
Executive Vice President, Chief Operatin: Marla Isaacs
Estimated Sales: Below $5 Million
Number Employees: 20-49

19130 Astoria General Espresso
7912 Industrial Village Rd
Greensboro, NC 27409

336-393-0224
Fax: 336-393-0295 info@geec.com
www.usa.astoria.com

Manufacturer, importer and exporter of espresso and cappuccino machines, coffee grinders, espresso equipment accessories and sandwich grills

Owner: Roberto Daltio
CEO: Umberto Terreni
Accounting/Office Manager: Linda Sizemore
Sales & Marketing: Courtney Baber
Managing/Sales Director: Scott Gordon
Technical Support Specialist: Jimmy Wardell
Number Employees: 5-9
Number of Brands: 2
Number of Products: 36
Square Footage: 50000
Parent Co: CMA
Type of Packaging: Private Label
Brands:
   Astoria
   Grillmaster
   Llsa

19131 Astoria Laminations
19803 E 9 Mile Rd
St Clair Shores, MI 48080-1774

586-944-2294
Fax: 586-775-0010 800-526-7325
info@lamseal.com www.lamseal.com

Point of sales systems and equipment including bar coders and pricers; also, laminators including thermal, pouch and roll
President: Dennis Oster
doster@lamseal.com
R & D: Anthony Sagese
VP: Anthony Sagese
Estimated Sales: $5-10 Million
Number Employees: 1-4
Square Footage: 2600

19132 (HQ)Astra Manufacturing Inc
21520 Blythe St # A
Canoga Park, CA 91304-6609

818-340-1800
Fax: 818-340-5830 877-340-1800
sales@astramfr.com www.astramfr.com

Manufacturer and exporter of espresso and cappuccino equipment including coffee grinders
President: Richard Hourizadeh
richard@astramfr.com
Estimated Sales: $3 Million
Number Employees: 5-9
Square Footage: 40000
Type of Packaging: Food Service
Brands:
   Astra

19133 Astro Arc Polvsoude
W133n5138 Campbell Dr
Menomonee Falls, WI 53051

262-783-2720
Fax: 262-783-2730 www.igmusa.com

President: Hans-Peter Mariner
Principal: Lynn Marek
Estimated Sales: $1-5 Million
Number Employees: 5-9

19134 Astro Machine Corp
630 Lively Blvd
Elk Grove Vlg, IL 60007-2016

847-364-6363
Fax: 847-364-9898 www.astromachine.com

President: George Selak
gselak@astromachine.com
Estimated Sales: $5-10 Million
Number Employees: 20-49

19135 Astro Physic Inc
21481 Ferrero
Walnut, CA 91789-5233

909-598-5488
Fax: 909-598-5546 800-251-9750
sales@astrophysicsinc.com
www.astrophysicsinc.com

Owner: Francois Zayek
fzayek@xaytek.com
Estimated Sales: $1-3 Million
Number Employees: 20-49

19136 Astro Plastics
PO Box 665
Oakland, NJ 07436-0665

201-337-8170

Manufacturer and extruder of plastic film bags
President: Steven Ringley
Contact: Lenore Clark
lenore.clark@astroplastics.com
Estimated Sales: $5-10 Million
Number Employees: 25

19137 Astro Pure Water
1441 SW 1st Way
Deerfield Beach, FL 33441-6753

954-422-8966
Fax: 954-422-8966
Manufacturer and exporter of water purifiers and filters
President and CFO: Roger Stefl
VP Sales: Mary Munn
Office Manager: Miki Kaye
Estimated Sales: Below $5 Million
Number Employees: 10-19
Number of Brands: 1
Number of Products: 39
Square Footage: 6000
Type of Packaging: Consumer, Food Service, Private Label, Bulk
Brands:
    Astro-Pure

19138 Astro/Polymetron Zellweger
100 Park Avenue
League City, TX 77573-2446

281-332-2484
Fax: 970-669-2932 kcraig@hach.com
Water quality analyzers for silica, sodium, phosphate, chlorine, ozone, dissolved oxygen, hydrazine, pH/conductivity and on-line titrates
President: Tom Joyce
Marketing Manager: Karon Craig
Sales Mgr: Robert Blight
Number Employees: 500

19139 At-Your-Svc Software Inc
450 Bronxville Rd
Bronxville, NY 10708-1133

914-337-9030
Fax: 914-337-9031 888-325-6937
sales@costguard.com www.costguard.com
Develops Cost Guard restaurant and foodservice software
President: Matthew Starobin
CEO: Pamela Terr
Contact: Mathew Starobin
matt@costguard.com
Estimated Sales: $2.5-5 Million
Number Employees: 5-9
Brands:
    Cost Guard
    Smart Scaling
    Vendor Transport

19140 Athea Laboratories
7855 N Faulkner Rd
Milwaukee, WI 53224

414-354-6417
Fax: 414-354-9219 800-743-6417
info@athea.com www.athea.com
Manufacturer and exporter of chemical specialties including ground and sewer maintenance chemicals, insecticides, aerosol, liquid and waterless hand cleaners and lotion; packager of aerosol and other products
President: Steve Hipp
VP Technical: Pete Martin
National Sales Manager: Ron Lloyd
Contact: Zech Ashba
zech.ashba@athea.com
Estimated Sales: $20-50 Million
Number Employees: 10
Parent Co: Share Company

19141 Athena Controls Inc
5145 Campus Dr # 1
Plymouth Meeting, PA 19462-1195

610-828-2490
Fax: 610-828-7084 800-782-6776
sales@athenacontrols.com
www.athenacontrols.com
Manufacturer and exporter of temperature, power and process controls
Manager: Bob Schlegel
Sales/Marketing: Jennifer Klinedinst
Manager: C Bill
bc@athenacontrols.com
Estimated Sales: $10-20 Million
Number Employees: 50-99
Parent Co: Inductotherm Industries
Other Locations:
    Athena Controls
    Plymouth Meeting PA

19142 Atkins Jemptec
6911 NW 22nd St
Gainesville, FL 32653-1249

352-378-5555
Fax: 352-335-6736 sdiuguid@cooper-atkins.com
Estimated Sales: $20-50 Million
Number Employees: 50-99

19143 Atkins Technical
6911 NW 22nd St
Gainesville, FL 32653-1249

352-378-5555
Fax: 352-335-6736 800-284-2842
Temperature recorders, digital thermocouple and thermistor thermometers
President: Carol Wallace
Sales/Marketing Executive: Stelli Dounson
Estimated Sales: $10-20 Million
Number Employees: 50-99
Parent Co: Cooper Instrumental Corporation

19144 Atkinson Dynamics
2645 Federal Signal Dr
University Park, IL 60484-3167

708-534-3400
Fax: 708-534-4852 888-751-1500
www.atkinsondynamics.com
President: Peter Guile
Quality Control: Dennis Stanberry
Contact: Sandy Belk
sbelk@fedsig.com
Number Employees: 500-999
Parent Co: Federal Signal Company

19145 Atlanta Burning Bush
3781 Happy Valley Cir
Newnan, GA 30263

770-253-4443
Fax: 770-253-9941 800-665-5611
Hot sauces, BBQ sauce. Supplier of food related products
Owner: Marilyn Witt
Estimated Sales: $500,000-$1,000,000
Number Employees: 1-4
Type of Packaging: Consumer, Bulk
Brands:
    Atlanta Burning

19146 Atlanta SharpTech
403 Westpark Ct Ste 130
P.O. Box 11000
Peachtree City, GA 30269-3577

Fax: 404-752-9034 800-462-7297
Manufacturer and exporter of meat and bone cutting equipment including bandsaw blades, grinder plates, grinder knives, handsaw frames and handsaw blades
CEO: Tom Orelup
Estimated Sales: $20-50 Million
Number Employees: 100-249
Brands:
    Atlanta Sharptech
    Double Cut System
    Kam-Lok
    One Way Bands
    Powermate System
    Swift Tooth Bands

19147 Atlantic Coast CrushersInc
128 Market St
Kenilworth, NJ 07033-2026

908-259-9292
Fax: 908-259-9280 info@gocrushers.com
www.gocrushers.com
Owner: Jack Paddock
paddockj@gocrushers.com
Estimated Sales: $3-5 Million
Number Employees: 5-9

19148 Atlantic Foam & Packaging Company
2664 Jewett Ln
Sanford, FL 32771-1678

407-328-9444
Fax: 407-324-2299
Manufacturers and fabricators of polystyrene foam box liners for perishables and non perishables.
President: Peter Chorney
Estimated Sales: $2.5-5 Million
Number Employees: 10-19
Square Footage: 132000

19149 Atlantic Group Inc
16830 Barker Springs Rd # 405
Houston, TX 77084-5038

281-578-0366
info@agivalves.com
www.agivalves.com
CEO: Bobby Engelke
bengelke@agivalves.com
Estimated Sales: $1-5 Million
Number Employees: 5-9

19150 Atlantic Mills
1295 Towbin Ave
Lakewood, NJ 08701

732-363-9281
Fax: 732-363-4302 800-242-7374
Antimicrobial, sanitizing, disposable kitchen and industrial towels; also, aprons
President: Peter P Donnelly
Finance Executive: Warren Agate
Sales Director: Peter Donnelly
Contact: Cheryl Accoo
accoo@atlanticmills.com
Estimated Sales: $10-20,000,000
Number Employees: 20-49
Brands:
    Katelin
    Kerri Klean
    Simple Solutions

19151 Atlantic Rubber Products
3065 Cranberry Hwy 13
East Wareham, MA 02538-1325

508-291-1211
Fax: 508-291-1123 800-695-0446
Manufacturer, importer and exporter of rubber safety flooring for kitchens, bars and entrance ways
Owner: John Donahue
Sales Director: Susan Boyens
Contact: Susan Donahue
donahue@atlanticrubber.com
General Manager: Jerry Donahue
Estimated Sales: $5-10 Million
Number Employees: 10-19
Number of Products: 85
Square Footage: 56000
Type of Packaging: Consumer, Food Service, Bulk
Brands:
    Comfort Zone
    Enter Clean
    Modular Tile
    Ultimate Comfort
    Work Right
    Work Right Interlock
    Work Station Airlock

19152 Atlantic Ultraviolet Corp
375 Marcus Blvd
Hauppauge, NY 11788-2026

631-273-0500
Fax: 631-273-0771 866-958-9085
sales@atlanticuv.com www.ultraviolet.com
Manufacturer and exporter of ultraviolet sterilization products for air, water and surfaces
CEO: Hilary Boehme
CFO: Arlene Metzroth
VP: Thomas Dituro Sr.
Director of Marketing: Ann Wysocki
Estimated Sales: $10-20 Million
Number Employees: 20-49
Square Footage: 50000
Brands:
    Hygeaire
    Magnum
    Megatron
    Mighty-Pure
    Minipure
    Nutripure
    Sanitaire
    Sanitron
    Tank Master

19153 Atlantis Industries Inc
1 Park St
Milton, DE 19968-1108

302-684-8542
Fax: 302-684-3367 contact@atlantisusa.com
www.atlantisusa.com
Manufacturer and exporter of injection molded plastic tumblers, dessert dishes, bowls, salad bowls and mugs

President: Kenneth Orr
kenneth@atlantisusa.com
VP: Ken Orr
Sales: Judie Brasure
Estimated Sales: $2.5-5 Million
Number Employees: 20-49
Square Footage: 56000
Brands:
Sparkle-Lite

19154 Atlantis Pak USA Inc
75 Valencia Ave # 701
Coral Gables, FL 33134-6132

305-403-2603
Fax: 786-249-0454
customerservice@atlantis-pak.com
www.atlantis-pak.com
Meat Packing, manufacturer of acid free packing paper, and recycled paper for meat.
Principle: Vladimir Zhamgotsev
zhamgotsev@atlantis-pak.com
Number Employees: 1-4
Parent Co: Atlantis Pak

19155 Atlantis Plastics Linear Film
PO Box 9769
Tulsa, OK 74157-0769

918-446-1651
Fax: 918-227-2454 800-324-9727
paul.saari@atlantisplastics.com
Manufacturer and exporter of polyethylene stretch film
Manager: Randy Goodman
CFO: Paul G Saari
VP Sales: John Buchan
Estimated Sales: $10-20 Million
Number Employees: 100-249
Parent Co: Atlantis Films

19156 Atlas Bakery Machinery Company
4800 S.W. 51st Street
Suite 104
Davie, FL 33314-5511

954-316-6160
Fax: 954-316-1360 atlasbaker@aol.com
www.atlasshardwarecorp.com
Bread and roll make-up including dividers, rounders, proofers and mixers
President: Robert Atlass
Contact: Susan Baltus
sbaltus@atlasshardwarecorp.com
Estimated Sales: $2.5-5 Million
Number Employees: 5-9

19157 Atlas Body
PO Box 479
Amory, MS 38821-0479

601-256-5692
Fax: 601-256-2162 800-354-2192
Estimated Sales: $1-5 Million

19158 Atlas Case Inc
1380 S Cherokee St
Denver, CO 80223-3209

303-778-7058
Fax: 303-778-7102 888-325-2199
sales@atlascases.com www.atlascases.com
Trunks, cases and shipping containers
President: Randy Sabey
sales@atlascases.com
Estimated Sales: Below $5 Million
Number Employees: 5-9

19159 Atlas Copco Tools & Assembly
37735 Enterprise Court
Suite 300
Farmington Hills, MI 48331-3471

248-489-1260
Fax: 248-489-0130 800-359-3746
www.atlascopco.com
President: Frederik Moeller
Vice President of Corporate Communicatio: Annika Berglund

19160 Atlas Corporation
111 Ortona Court
Concord, ON L4K 3M3
Canada

905-669-6825
Fax: 905-669-8288 info@atlascorp.com

We are a construction company which offers the following services: General Contracting, Construction Management, Design Build, Project Management and LEED(Leadership in Engery and Environmental Design.
President: Andrew Famiglietti
VP Development: Adam Salehi
VP Operations: Eliseo Curto
Number Employees: 20-49

19161 Atlas Equipment Company
3111 Wyandotte St # 102
Kansas City, MO 64111-1369

816-842-9188
Fax: 816-842-9192 800-842-9188
2info@atlasequipment.com
www.atlasequipment.com
Wholesaler/distributor of storage and material handling systems, belt conveyors, steel shelving and pallet racks
President: Julie Duvall
Estimated Sales: $5-10 Million
Number Employees: 1-4
Square Footage: 600000

19162 Atlas Inspection
9001 Baltimore St NE
Minneapolis, MN 55449

763-783-7072
Fax: 763-783-7138
Xray inspection of food products
Founder: Ken Long
President: Jeffery Boisverg
Contact: Jeff Boisvert
atlas@atlasinspection.com
Estimated Sales: $2 Million
Number Employees: 5

19163 (HQ)Atlas Labels
11200 boul Pie 1X,
CP 280
Montreal, QC H1H 5L4
Canada

514-852-7000
Fax: 514-852-2000 info@cubart.com
Self-stick labels, silk screen, gold stampings, badges and folding boxes.
President: Rock Navy
Estimated Sales: $3 Million
Number Employees: 13
Number of Brands: 2
Number of Products: 114
Square Footage: 36000
Type of Packaging: Consumer, Food Service, Private Label, Bulk

19164 Atlas Match Company
45 Leadale Avenue
Toronto, ON M4G 3E9
Canada

416-929-8147
Fax: 416-961-3275 888-285-2783
nmackay11@rogers.com www.atlasmatch.com
Manufacturer, importer and exporter of custom designed wooden and book matches; also, reusable board coasters and cocktail and dinner napkins.
President: N Mackay
CFO: Sohan Kansal
Sales: W Teltz
Operations: Esther Tarahdmi
Number Employees: 5-9
Number of Brands: 2
Number of Products: 5
Square Footage: 8000
Type of Packaging: Food Service, Private Label, Bulk
Brands:
Atlas
Coasters Plus

19165 Atlas Match Corporation
1801 S Airport Cir
Euless, TX 76040

817-354-7474
Fax: 817-354-7478 800-628-2426
custserv@atlasmatch.com www.atlasmatch.com
Manufacturer, exporter and importer of matchbooks, box matches, scratchbooks and scratchpads
President: David Bradley
COO: Doug Lamb
Estimated Sales: $10-20 Million
Number Employees: 50-99
Square Footage: 130000

19166 Atlas Metal Industries
1135 NW 159th Dr
Miami, FL 33169

Fax: 305-623-0475 800-762-7565
atlasfoodserv.com
Cafeteria and restaurant counters, salad bars, food service tables and dispensers including cup, plate, self leveling, tray, bowl and napkin
President/Owner: David Meade
VP, Sales & Marketing: Jessica Meade DeMore
Year Founded: 1948
Estimated Sales: $10-20 Million
Number Employees: 100-249
Parent Co: Mercury Corporation
Brands:
Levelmatic
Precision
Set-N-Serve

19167 (HQ)Atlas Minerals & Chemicals Inc
1227 Valley Rd
P.O. Box 38
Mertztown, PA 19539-8827

610-682-7171
Fax: 610-682-9200 800-523-8269
sales@atlasmin.com www.atlasmin.com
Manufacturer and exporter of construction materials including floor plates, drains and coatings and corrosion prevention; also, tanks for processing and storage
President: Francis X Hanson
fhanson@atlasmin.com
Marketing: Scott Gallagher
Sales: Steve Abernathy
Number Employees: 50-99
Type of Packaging: Food Service, Private Label

19168 Atlas Minerals & Chemicals Inc
1227 Valley Rd
Mertztown, PA 19539-8827

610-682-7171
Fax: 610-682-9200 800-532-8269
sales@atlasmin.com www.atlasmin.com
Flooring products include coating, sealers, polymer toppings and tile and brick floors
President: Francis X Hanson
fhanson@atlasmin.com
Estimated Sales: $10-20 Million
Number Employees: 50-99

19169 (HQ)Atlas Pacific Engineering
1 Atlas Ave
P.O. Box 500
Pueblo, CO 81001-4833

719-948-3040
Fax: 719-948-3058 sales@atlaspacific.com
Manufacturer and exporter of decidious fruit and vegetable processing equipment including pitters, slicers, peelers, washers, cutters, sorters and scrubbers
President: Erik Teranchi
CFO: Don Freeman
VP Marketing: Robb Morris
Manager: Tom Ogrodny
tomo@atlaspacific.com
Estimated Sales: $20-50 Million
Number Employees: 100-249
Square Footage: 175000
Parent Co: Gulftech
Brands:
Magnupeeler
Magnuwasher
N.F. Peeler
Shufflo
Super Carrot Cutter
Super Cutter

19170 Atlas Packaging Inc
13165 NW 38th Ave
Opa Locka, FL 33054-4530

305-688-5096
Fax: 305-685-0843 800-662-0630
randy@atlaspackaginginc.com
www.atlaspackaginginc.com
Designer and manufacturer of all types of packaging, litho laminated boxes and displays. Also provides promotional items such as standers and casecards.
President: Penny Kroker
penny@flhosp.org
Sales Manager: Randy Macias

Estimated Sales: $5-10 Million
Number Employees: 50-99
Square Footage: 112000

19171 Atlas Restaurant Supply
3329 N Shadeland Ave
Indianapolis, IN 46226-6236

317-541-1111
Fax: 317-541-1404 877-528-5275
www.atlasrestaurantsupply.com
Manufacturers' representative for bar equipment,
carts, concession supplies, dishwashers, display
cases, ice machines, refrigerators, can openers,
steam tables, etc.; serving supermarket chains and
food service operators; kitchen andinterior design
services
President: Thomas S Vavul
Manager: Jimmy Gravel
rickv@atlasrs.com
Estimated Sales: Below $5,000,000
Number Employees: 10-19

19172 Atlas Rubber Stamp & Printing
3755 E Market St # 3
York, PA 17402-2700

717-751-0459
Fax: 717-751-0459 sales@atlasrubberstamp.com
www.atlasrubberstamp.com
Stamps and markers
Owner: Paul Sipe
sales@atlasrubberstamp.com
Co-Owner: Hally Fontaine
Estimated Sales: Below $5 Million
Number Employees: 10-19

19173 Atlas Tag & Label Inc
2361 Industrial Dr
Neenah, WI 54956-4884

920-722-1557
Fax: 920-720-7900 800-558-6418
www.atlas-tag.com
Heat sealed bags, labels and tags
President: Mark Bissell
CFO: Dennis Novell
VP: Jerry Bultt
Head of Marketing: Kent Salomon
Manager: Dennis Prett
Account Manager: Mark White
Estimated Sales: $10-20 Million
Number Employees: 100-249
Parent Co: Atlas Tag & Label

19174 Atlas-Stord
7011-F Albert Pick Road
Greensboro, NC 27409

816-799-0808
Fax: 816-799-0812 info-usa@haarslev.com
www.haarslev.com/
Manager: Denise Gardner
CFO: Brad Rodgers
Estimated Sales: Below $5 Million
Number Employees: 20-49
Parent Co: Haarslev Industries A/S

19175 Atomizing Systems Inc
1 Hollywood Ave # 1
Suite 1
Ho Ho Kus, NJ 07423-1438

201-447-1222
Fax: 201-447-6932 www.coldfog.com
President: Michael Elkas
info@coldfog.com
Estimated Sales: $3-5 Million
Number Employees: 5-9

19176 (HQ)Attias Oven Corp
926 3rd Ave
Brooklyn, NY 11232-2002

347-619-0314
Fax: 212-979-1423 800-928-8427
info@attiasco.com www.attiasco.com
Manufacturer and exporter of pizza ovens, rotisser-
ies, mixers, slicers, ice makers, refrigerators, freez-
ers, dishwashers, toasters, blenders, sheeters,
dividers and rounders
President: Simon Attias
Estimated Sales: $3-5 Million
Number Employees: 5-9

19177 Attracta Sign
14680 James Road
Rogers, MN 55374-9363

763-428-6377
Fax: 763-428-9097

Painted and electric signs
President: Greg Rendall
CFO: Greg Rendall
R&D/Quality Control: Greg Rendall
Estimated Sales: $1-2.5 Million
Number Employees: 10

19178 Attune Foods
535 Pacific Ave, 3rd Fl
San Francisco, CA 94133

415-486-2101
www.attunefoods.com
President: Rob Hurlbut
Director of Finance: Mike Centron
Director of Marketing: Daniel Wiser
Director of Sales: Steve Bernier
Contact: Idan Abada
iabada@piercecollege.edu
Production Manager: Marvin Malvar
Estimated Sales: $15 Million
Parent Co: Post Foods
Brands:
  UNCLE SAM
  SKINNER'S
  EREWHON
  ATTUNE

19179 AuNutra Industries Inc
5625 Daniels Street
Chino, CA 91710

909-628-2600
Fax: 909-628-8110 info@aunutra.com
www.aunutra.com
Manufacturer and supplier of botanicals and nutri-
tional ingredients
VP Sales/Marketing: Ken Guest
Regional Sales Manager: Tara Trainor
Contact: Jing Ang
jang@aunutra.com

19180 Auburn Label & Tag Company
225 W 34th St
New York, NY 10122-9001

212-971-0338
Fax: 212-244-4397 www.ragnewyork.com
Labels including pressure sensitive and nonpressure
sensitive
Owner: Max Greenstein
Vice President: Susan Alfender
Estimated Sales: $5-10 Million
Number Employees: 5-9

19181 Auburn Systems LLC
8 Electronics Ave # 1
Danvers, MA 01923-1045

978-777-8820
Fax: 978-777-8820 800-255-5008
sales@auburnsys.com
Auburn Systems, LLC designs, engineers, and man-
ufactures dust monitoring equipment and systems.
Auburn's product line ranges from simple broken
bag detectors, flow switches and dust monitors to
comprehensive bag leak detection systemsfor a wide
variety of applications.
President: Ron Dechene
rond@auburnsys.com
Director/Business Development: Justin Dechene
VP/Sales: Earl Parker
Number Employees: 5-9

19182 Auburn Systems LLC
8 Electronics Ave # 1
Danvers, MA 01923-1045

978-777-8820
Fax: 978-777-8820 800-255-5008
sales@auburnsys.com
President: Ron Dechene
rond@auburnsys.com
Number Employees: 5-9

19183 (HQ)Audion Automation
1533 Crescent Dr # 102
Carrollton, TX 75006-3642

972-389-0777
Fax: 972-389-0790 info@clamcopackaging.com
www.audionltd.com
Manufacturer and exporter of flexible packaging
machinery including bag opening, filling and heat
sealing; also, shrink packaging

President: Mark Goldman
markg@paçaids.com
CFO: David Johnson
Vice President Marketing & Sales: Dennis McGrath
Sales Manager: Bob Sorrentino
Operations Manager: David Bibb
Estimated Sales: $20-50 Million
Number Employees: 20-49
Square Footage: 56000
Brands:
  Sergeant
  Titan
  Vacumaster

19184 Audrey Signs
167 W 81st St
New York, NY 10024-7221

212-769-4992
Fax: 212-496-9649 audreysigns2@aol.com
www.audreysigns.com
Interior and exterior advertising signs including
brass, aluminum, bronze, plastic, neon, cold cathode
and cut-out letters; also, installation available
President and CEO: Harriet Black
audreysigns@aol.com
Estimated Sales: Below $5 Million
Number Employees: 10-19

19185 Audsam Printing
175 Park Blvd
Marion, OH 43302-3534

740-387-6252
Fax: 740-387-6251
Coupon books
President: J Saxby
VP: M Saxby
Secretary: S Saxby
Estimated Sales: $5-10 Million
Number Employees: 20-49

19186 Audubon Sales & Svc
850 Pennsylvania Blvd
Feastervl Trvs, PA 19053-7814

215-364-5377
Fax: 215-364-5538 800-523-0169
info@meshbelt.com www.meshbelt.com
President: Stephen I Weiss
accounting@meshbelt.com
Estimated Sales: $5-10 Million
Number Employees: 20-49

19187 Auger Fab
418 Creamery Way
Exton, PA 19341-2500

610-524-3350
Fax: 610-363-2821 800-334-1529
info@auger-fab.com www.augerfabrication.com
Manufacturer and exporter of stainless steel and
plastic liquid and powder filling equipment includ-
ing replacement augers and funnels
President: Erick Edginton
ericke@augerfab.com
CFO: Bill Egan
Regional Sales Manager: Allen Stewart
VP, Sales & Marketing: Kyle Edginton
Operations Manager: Rick Brennecke
Estimated Sales: $10-20 Million
Number Employees: 100-249
Square Footage: 100000

19188 Auger Fab
418 Creamery Way
Exton, PA 19341-2500

610-524-3350
Fax: 610-363-2821 800-334-1529
info@all-fill.com www.augerfabrication.com
Augers
President: Erick Edginton
ericke@augerfab.com
Estimated Sales: $10-20 000,000
Number Employees: 100-249

19189 Auger Manufacturing Spec
22 N Bacton Hill Rd # A
Malvern, PA 19355-1006

610-647-4677
Fax: 610-640-9085 800-544-1199
info@augermfgspec.com www.augermfgspec.com
Bag formers/fillers/sealers, cocoa packaging equipment, packaging machines, weighing machines and
augers
Owner: William E Day
info@augermfgspec.com

Estimated Sales: $5-10 000,000
Number Employees: 10-19

19190 August Thomsen Corp

36 Sea Cliff Ave
Glen Cove, NY 11542-3699

516-676-7100
Fax: 516-676-7108 800-645-7170
www.atecousa.com
Manufacturer, importer and exporter of pastry tubes,
pastry bags and other baking utensils
President: Jeffrey Schneider
jeff@atecousa.com
VP: Douglas Schneider
Estimated Sales: $10-20 Million
Number Employees: 20-49
Brands:
Ateco

19191 Aurora Air Products Inc

231c N Eola Rd
Aurora, IL 60502-9603

630-851-4515
Fax: 630-851-5165 ron@auroraair.com
www.auroraair.com
Owner: Rich Cibulskis
rich@auroraair.com
Quality Control: Don Cibulskis
Estimated Sales: $10-20 Million
Number Employees: 20-49

19192 Aurora Design Associates, Inc.

1308 South 1700 East
Suite 203
Salt Lake City, UT 84108

801-588-0111
Fax: 801-588-0333
Manufacturer and exporter of servers and ice buck-
ets for wine, water and champagne
President: Rob Norton
Contact: Robert Norton
robnorton1@att.net
Advertising Manager: Rick Daynes
Estimated Sales: Less than $500,000
Number Employees: 1-4
Number of Products: 6
Square Footage: 14000
Brands:
Chateau
Connoisseur
Evian Connoisseur

19193 Austin Brown Co

300 Reading Rd
Mason, OH 45040-1512

513-492-7933
Fax: 513-492-7932 800-421-9355
info@austinbrownco.com
www.austinbrownco.com
Manufacturers reps for insulated panels, cold storage
doors and high speed doors.
President: Doug Brown
doug@austinbrownco.com
Marketing: Douglas Brown
Inside Sales: Kevin Browning
Estimated Sales: $.5-1 million
Number Employees: 5-9
Number of Brands: 4

19194 Austin Co

6095 Parkland Blvd
Cleveland, OH 44124

440-544-2600
Fax: 440-544-2690 austin.info@theaustin.com
www.theaustin.com
Designing, engineering and construction architec-
tural firm that specializes in food and beverage pro-
cessing facilities including: production and bottling
plants; formulation and packaging plants for bulk in-
gredients; researchlaboratories; operations centers;
bulk storage warehouses; and automated distribution
centers.
Director & Executive Advisor: Mike Pierce
VP Food & Beverage: Robert Graham
Year Founded: 1916
Estimated Sales: $100-500 Million
Number Employees: 1000-4999
Parent Co: Kajima USA

19195 Authentic Biocode Corp

4355 Excel Parkway
Suite 100
Addison, TX 75001

469-737-4400
Fax: 469-737-4409 866-434-1402
www.authentix.com
Invisible inks and food markers
Chief Financial/Operations Officer and P: Jeff Kupp
Chairman and CEO: Bernard C Bailey
CAO, General Counsel and Secretary: Mark L
Weintrub
Senior Vice President: Kevin McKenna
Chief Technology Officer: Jeff Conroy, Ph.D.
Chief Sales and Marketing Officer: Ryon Packer
Director Business Development: Jeffrey Slocum
CPO, GM and President: Dr. Mohamed Lazzouni
Estimated Sales: $3-5 Million
Number Employees: 8

19196 Autio Co

93750 Autio Loop
Astoria, OR 97103-8400

503-458-6191
Fax: 503-458-6409 800-483-8884
office@autioco.com www.autioco.com
Manufacturer and exporter of grinders and pumps
President: Marvin Autio
marvin.autio@autioco.com
Office Manager: Marilyn Anderson
Estimated Sales: $1-3 Million
Number Employees: 10-19

19197 Auto Chlor Systems

1000 Ridgeway Loop Rd Ste 100
Memphis, TN 38120

901-684-0600
Fax: 901-684-0620 800-477-3693
Glass cleaner, dishwasher detergents and dispensers
H.R. Dir.: Marie Brain
VP: Kirk Northcutt
Contact: Lisa Boswe
lisa@autochlor.net
Estimated Sales: $1-5 Million
Number Employees: 20-49
Parent Co: Unilever USA
Brands:
Glass Klean
Laundry Detergent Ii
Machine Detergent Ii

19198 Auto Labe

3101 Industrial Avenue
Suite 2
Fort Pierce, FL 34946

772-465-4441
Fax: 772-465-5177 800-634-5376
info@autolabe.com www.autolabe.com
Manufacturer and exporter of labeling equipment for
fruits and vegetables, bottles, cans, boxes, cartons,
bar coding, etc
President: Robert Smith
Marketing/Sales: Bob Peterson
Public Relations: Roy Shepherd
Production/Plant Manager: Dean Stauffer
Estimated Sales: $10-20 Million
Number Employees: 50-99
Square Footage: 50000
Parent Co: Booth Manufacturing Company

19199 Auto Pallets-Boxes

28000 Southfield Rd Fl 2
Lathrup Village, MI 48076-2864

248-559-7744
Fax: 248-559-6584 800-875-2699
www.apallets.com
Manufacturer and recycler of wooden pallets and
boxes
Owner: Mitchell B Foster
VP: Mitchell Foster
Estimated Sales: $1-2.5 Million
Number Employees: 10 to 19

19200 Auto Quotes

4425 Merrimac Ave
Jacksonville, FL 32210

904-384-2279
Fax: 904-384-1736 kmotes@aqnet.com
www.aqnet.com
Software for the food service market

President: Michael Greenwald
Chief Executive Officer: Kent Motes
CFO: Rene Butcher
Executive Vice President: Rob Morgan
VP, Program Development: Bill Kessler
Marketing Director: Kate Schmidt
EVP, Sales: Rosemary Connor
Contact: Rene Butcher
rbutcher@aqnet.com
CFO, Database Manager: Martin Smith
Estimated Sales: $3-5 Million
Number Employees: 1-4
Square Footage: 9600

19201 Auto-Mate Technologies

34 Hinda Blvd
Riverhead, NY 11901-4804

631-727-8886
Fax: 631-369-3903 info@automatetech.com
www.auto-matetech.com
Bottle labeling systems, induction cap systems, and
complete bottle inspection systems.
Owner: Kenneth Herzog
info@automatetech.com
Estimated Sales: $9-12 Million
Number Employees: 20-49

19202 AutoPak Engineering Corporation

PO Box 9024155
San Juan, PR 00902-4155

787-723-8036
Fax: 787-745-0030 mailbox@autopak.com
www.autopak.com
President: Ignacio Munoz
CFO: Astrid Robriguze
Quality Control: Amarilys Rivera
Estimated Sales: $30-40 Million
Number Employees: 10

19203 Autobar Systems

1800 Bloomsbury Ave
Asbury Park, NJ 07712-3975

732-922-3355
Fax: 732-922-2221 autobarcorp@aol.com
Manufacturer and exporter of alcoholic beverage
dispensers and control equipment for bars, conven-
tion centers and restaurants
CEO: Donald Ullery
Estimated Sales: Below $5 Million
Number Employees: 5-9
Square Footage: 8000
Brands:
Autobar
Autopor
Beermatic
Underbar
Winematic

19204 Autobox NA/Jit Box Machines

218 N Broadway Rd
Azle, TX 76020-3708

817-270-1019
Fax: 817-270-8430
President: Jerry Jenkins
Estimated Sales: $10-20 Million
Number Employees: 10-19

19205 Autocon Mixing Systems

2360 Vallejo St
St Helena, CA 94574-2432

707-963-3998
Fax: 707-963-3978 800-225-6192
tom@theosten.com www.autoconsystems.com
Manufacturer and exporter of continuous solid/liq-
uid feeders and dry blending processing systems
President: Thomas Haas
info@autoconsystems.com
Estimated Sales: $5-10 Million
Number Employees: 20-49
Square Footage: 10000

19206 Autofry

10 Forbes Rd
Northborough, MA 01532-2501

508-460-9800
Fax: 508-393-5750 800-348-2976
www.autofry.com
Deep fryers
Mktg. Manager: Heather Guerriero
Regional Sales Manager: Laird Hansberger
Sales Manager: Gary Santos
Estimated Sales: Less Than $500,000
Number Employees: 1-4

Brands:
Autofry

19207 Autoline
23243 Clayton Ave
Reedley, CA 93654-9547

559-638-5432
Fax: 559-638-6189

Fruit sorting equipent
President: Clarence Rasmussen
R&D: Jack Wis
Sales: Kelvin Farris
Quality Control: Brudy Hieberp
Contact: Alex Cordero
a.cordero@aweta.us
Estimated Sales: $5-10 Million
Number Employees: 20-49

19208 Automated Business Products
50 Clinton Pl # 1
Hackensack, NJ 07601-4562

201-489-1440
Fax: 201-489-9443 800-334-1440

Manufacturer, importer and exporter of money processing and handling systems, packagers, sorters, counters and automatic wrappers; also, food stamp counters, endorsers and microencoders
President: Robert J Mahalik
bmahalik@aol.com
Estimated Sales: $1-2,500,000
Number Employees: 10-19

19209 Automated Container Corp
2758 Centennial Rd
Toledo, OH 43617-1829

419-536-8393
Fax: 419-536-9686
ezosales@automatedcontainer.com
www.automatedcontainer.com

President: John Morrison
Number Employees: 5-9

19210 Automated Control Concepts
3535 State Route 66
Neptune, NJ 07753

732-922-6611
Fax: 732-922-9611
sysmail@automated-control.com
www.automated-control.com

Owner: Robert Tomasetta
Estimated Sales: $10-20 Million
Number Employees: 50-99

19211 Automated Feeding & Alignment
1921 W Wilson Street
Suite A171
Batavia, IL 60510-1680

630-761-3104
Fax: 630-761-3105

Controlled pick and place system and packaging automation special purpose machinery
Estimated Sales: $.5-1 000,000
Number Employees: 1-4

19212 Automated Flexible Conveyors
55 Walman Ave
Clifton, NJ 07011-3416

973-340-1414
Fax: 973-340-8216 800-694-7271
www.afcsolutions.com

Spiral and volumetric feeders, cartridge type bag dump stations and bulk bag unloading equipment; exporter of spiral feeders
President: Kevin Devaney
kfdevaney@aol.com
Vice President: Grace Faria
Estimated Sales: Below $5 Million
Number Employees: 5-9
Square Footage: 88000
Brands:
Dump Clean
Spiralfeeder
True Flow

19213 Automated Food Systems
1000 Lofland Dr
Waxahachie, TX 75165-6200

469-517-0470
Fax: 469-517-0476 sales@afstexas.com
www.afstexas.com

Manufacturer, exporter and importer of production systems for corn dogs, kebabs, skewering, sausage sticking and funnel cakes. Fryers, mixers, pumps; special design

President: Robert Walser
robin@afstexas.com
CFO: Tina Walser
Marketing Director/Sales: Chris Consalus
Marketing Coordinator: Robin Seeton
Production Manager: Jerry Reidel
Plant Manager: Charles Stone
Purchasing Manager: Robert Walser
Estimated Sales: $2.5-5 Million
Number Employees: 10-19
Square Footage: 48000
Brands:
Cd-3 Vendor Cart
Fc-950
Kw-2001
Ptl-Condos Systems

19214 Automated Machine Technologies
10404 Chapel Hill Road
Suite 100
Morrisville, NC 27560-1186

919-361-0121
Fax: 919- 48- 212 Office@AMTLiquidFilling.com
www.amtliquidfilling.com

Packaging liquid filling equipment
Contact: David Kemnitz
dk@amtliquidfilling.com
Estimated Sales: $500,000-$1 Million
Number Employees: 2

19215 Automated Packaging Systems
10175 Philipp Pkwy
Streetsboro, OH 44241

330-342-2000
Fax: 330-342-2400 800-527-0733
info@autobag.com www.autobag.com

Manual, semi and fully automatic bagging equipment; also, customer training and graphic design services available.
Chairman: Hershey Lerner
Secretary & Chief Operating Officer: Daryl Manzetti
VP, Sales & Marketing: Brad Worman
Year Founded: 1962
Estimated Sales: $100-500 Million
Number Employees: 100-249
Brands:
Autobag

19216 Automated Production Systems Corporation
15556 Elm Dr
New Freedom, PA 17349

717-235-5220
Fax: 717-235-5274 888-345-5377

Conveyor systems, robotic palletizing and packing machinery, cappers and in-line fillers
President: William Donohue
Contact: Jason Cambia
jasonc@atsinc.org
Number Employees: 95

19217 Automated Retail Systems Inc
726 Boulevard # 18
Kenilworth, NJ 07033-1757

908-620-0008
Fax: 908-276-2214 800-355-0173
arsnj@aol.com www.arsnj.net

Distributor touch screen point of sale systems for restaurants, software and peripherals
President: Robert Meyn
Vice President: Grace Ann Meyn
Estimated Sales: Less Than $500,000
Number Employees: 5-9
Square Footage: 2400

19218 Automatic Bar Controls Inc
790 Eubanks Dr
Vacaville, CA 95688-9470

707-448-5151
Fax: 707-448-1521 800-722-6738
sales@wunderbar.com

Portable bars and dispensers including soft drink, liquor, juice, wine, beer and condiment; importer of beer dipensers; exporter of liquor, soft drink and condiment dipensers
President: Rick Martindale
rick.martindale@wunderbar.com
Sales/Marketing: Brent Baker
Purchasing Agent: Tim Schroeder
Estimated Sales: $50-100 Million
Number Employees: 100-249
Square Footage: 70000
Brands:
Wunder-Bar

19219 Automatic Electronic Machines Company
110 N 6th St
Brooklyn, NY 11211-3033

718-384-3211

Straw wrappers and automatic shears
Owner: Hannah Curtin
General Manager: George Casella
Estimated Sales: $1-5 Million
Number Employees: 1-4
Square Footage: 14000

19220 Automatic Feeder
921 Albion Ave
Schaumburg, IL 60193-4550

847-534-2300
Fax: 847-534-2354 888-534-2340
sales@automaticfeeder.com
www.automaticfeeder.com

Manufacturer, designer, and builder of specialty conveyor, feed (centrifugal linear and elevator) and assembly systems
President: Ken Eversole
VP: Kirk Verhasselt
VP: Jerry Kuntz
Marketing: Suzanne Eversole
Public Relations: Rochelle Verhasselt
Estimated Sales: $1-5 000,000
Number Employees: 10-19
Number of Brands: 4
Square Footage: 30000
Brands:
Auto-Slide
Flexlink
Hoppmann

19221 Automatic Filters Inc
2672 S LA Cienega Blvd
Los Angeles, CA 90034-2604

310-839-2828
Fax: 310-839-6878 800-336-1942
info@tekleen.com www.tekleen.com

Fully automatic, self cleaning water filters
President: Gideon Brunn
info@tekleen.com
Estimated Sales: Less than $10,000,000
Number Employees: 5-9

19222 Automatic Handling Int
360 LA Voy Rd
Erie, MI 48133-9436

734-847-0633
Fax: 734-847-1823 info@automatichandling.com
www.automatichandling.com

Manufacturer and exporter of conveyors and conveyor systems, platforms, walkways and stairs; also, custom fabrication and custom stainless steel machinery available
President: Daniel Pienta
dan.pienta@automatichandling.com
Operations Manager: Dennis Barutha
Estimated Sales: $1,5,000,000
Number Employees: 100-249
Square Footage: 66000
Parent Co: Automatic Handling

19223 Automatic Liquid Packaging Solutions
2445 E Oakton St
Arlington Heights, IL 60005

847-264-5349
Fax: 847-264-5348 www.alp-solutions.com

Manufacturer of sterile filling machines for sterile liquid packaging applications

19224 Automatic Products
PO Drawer 719
Williston, SC 29853

803-266-8891
Fax: 803-266-5150 800-523-8363
www.automaticproducts.com

Manufacturer and exporter of hot beverage vending machinery
President: Alan J Suitor
Sales Manager: Len McElhaney

19225 Automatic Products/Crane
165 Bridgepoint Dr
South St Paul, MN 55075-2500

651-288-2975
Fax: 651-224-5559 www.automaticproducts.com

Manufacturer and exporter of vending machinery including candy, pastry, snacks, coffee, hot drinks, ice cream and refrigerated/frozen foods

President: Robert J Sutter
CFO: Scott Edgergon
VP Marketing: James Radant
Quality Control: Randy Denver
Estimated Sales: Less Than $500,000
Number Employees: 1-4

19226 Automatic Specialties Inc

422 Northboro Road Central # 2
Marlborough, MA 01752-1895

508-481-2370
Fax: 508-485-6276 800-445-2370
sales@auspin.com www.automaticspecialties.com
Manufacturer and exporter of wire racks and baskets, stainless steel fry baskets, trays and food machinery parts
President: Wilfred Moineau
Vice President: Bill Moineau
Marketing/Sales: Jay Graham
Public Relations: Jay Graham
Estimated Sales: $3-5 Million
Number Employees: 20-49
Square Footage: 60000

19227 Automatic Timing & Controls

8019 Ohio Riv
8019 Ohio River Blvd.
Newell, WV 26050

304-387-1200
Fax: 304-387-1212 800-727-5646
customerRFQ@marshbellofram.com
www.marshbellofram.com
Manufacturer and exporter of controls including temperature, counters, timers and photoelectric sensors
President: Arnold Siemer
Cmo: Dwight Nafziger
dnafziger@marshbellofram.com
CFO: Roger Bailey
R&D: Tom Villano
Production Manager: J Tornetta
Production: E Allgyer
Estimated Sales: $10-20 Million
Number Employees: 50-99
Square Footage: 120000
Parent Co: Desco Corporation

19228 Automation Devices Inc

7050 W Ridge Rd
Fairview, PA 16415-2099
Canada

814-474-1818
Fax: 814-474-2131 sales@adlcan.com
www.autodev.com
Owner: Erdal Basaraner
erdal_basaraner@kibele-pims.com
CFO: Garry Projanowski
Estimated Sales: Below $5 Million
Number Employees: 20-49

19229 Automation Equipment

E. Notherwest Highway
Dailas, TX 75228

469-212-9212
Fax: 419-663-1187
Custom designed machinery, material handling systems, metal fabricating, printing presses and special automatic machinery
Estimated Sales: $5-10 Million
Number Employees: 20-49

19230 Automation Group

6100 Hillcroft Street
Suite 300
Houston, TX 77081-1010

713-860-5200
Fax: 713-860-5298 darrylh@tagsite.com
Process control and automation and networking software
President: Steven E Paulson
Business Development Manager: Darryl Hazlett
Estimated Sales: $5-10 Million
Number Employees: 120

19231 Automation Ideas Inc

9945 Greenland Ave NE
Rockford, MI 49341-9338

616-874-4041
Fax: 616-874-3454 877-254-3327
jerry@automationideas.com
www.automationideas.com
Equipment for the water bottling, dairy and food processing industries.

President: Jerry Bott
jerry@automationideas.com
Vice President: Mick Donahue
Sales, Midwest Region: Dave Westra
Operations Manager: Justin Bott
Parts orders / Purchasing / Logistics: Brandon Totten
Number Employees: 20-49

19232 Automation Intelligence

P.O.Box 704
Loganville, GA 30052-0704

404-241-1000
Fax: 770-497-8666 888-531-8213
Motion control
Owner: Jim Bowers
Estimated Sales: Below $5 Million
Number Employees: 5-9

19233 Automation Onspec Software

10923 Progress Ct # 743
Rancho Cordova, CA 95670-5667

916-362-5867
Fax: 916-362-5967 888-362-5867
sales@automationonspec.com
www.automationonspec.com
Provides SCADA/HMI software for process control and trending and reporting.
President: Mike McMann
CFO: Steve Schasser
Research & Development: Dedh Chisum
Quality Control: Mo Dhmed
Marketing Director: Ken Thompson
Sales Director: Ed Ireton
Estimated Sales: Below $5 Million
Number Employees: 5-9
Number of Brands: 1
Number of Products: 167

19234 Automation Packaging

6206 Benjamin Road
Suite 309
Tampa, FL 33634-5169

813-888-8488
Fax: 813-888-8113
Form, fill and seal wrappers, side-seal, lap-seal, shrink bundlers, automatic L-sealers and corrugated equipment
President: Jean Limousin
Estimated Sales: $5-10 000,000
Number Employees: 50-99

19235 Automation Products

8620 Richmond Ave # D
Houston, TX 77063-5649

713-785-3600
Fax: 713-869-7332 800-231-2062
www.packaging-online.com
Analyzers, tests, plant operations, total solids, batch control systems, chillers, filler monitoring systems, margarine processing equipment, meters, flow, milk, solids, process control
Owner: Vincent Gabory
National Sales Manager of Board: Brian Olesinski
Estimated Sales: $300,000-500,000
Number Employees: 1-4

19236 Automation Safety

24850 Drake Road
Farmington Hills, MI 48335-2506

248-473-1133
Fax: 248-473-3997 info@pilzusa.com
www.machinetoolsonline.com/doc/
Safety controls, industrial computers

19237 Automation Service

13871 Parks Steed Dr
Earth City, MO 63045-1406

314-785-6600
Fax: 314-785-6610 800-325-4808
info@automationservice.com
www.automationservice.com
Process control instrumentation
President: Rod Barnett
CEO: Wesley Rarick
wesleyr@automationservice.com
Quality Control: Bob Bokel
R&D: Alex Muller
Marketing Director: Deanna Coppeans
Sales Director: Curt Sykes
Operations Manager: Mike Brunts
Production Manager: Michael Pruett
Purchasing Manager: Rich Kruse

Estimated Sales: $10-20 Million
Number Employees: 100-249

19238 Automotion Inc

11000 Lavergne Ave
Oak Lawn, IL 60453-5500

708-229-3700
Fax: 708-229-3799
info@automotionconveyors.com
www.automotionconveyors.com
Conveyors and sortation equipment
President: Merle Davis
mdavis@autonotionconveyors.com
CFO: Dave Beesley
Vice President: John Hejmanowski
Marketing Director: Joe O'Connor
Estimated Sales: $20-50 Million
Number Employees: 100-249
Square Footage: 140000

19239 Autoprod

807 W Kimberly Rd
Davenport, IA 52806

563-391-1100
Fax: 563-391-0017
Manufacturer and exporter of packaging machinery for filling and closing pre-formed metallic, paper and plastic containers
President: Paul Desocio
CEO: Barry Shoulders
R & D: Hans Koule
Vice President Marketing & Sales: Tom Riggins
Sales: Barb Peeters
Trade Show Coordinator/Marketing: Mary Baltzell
Plant Manager: Larry Loftus
Purchasing Manager: Harvey Cassell
Number Employees: 50-99
Parent Co: IWKA Company
Type of Packaging: Consumer, Food Service, Private Label

19240 Autoquip Corp

1058 W Industrial Rd
Guthrie, OK 73044-6046

405-282-5200
Fax: 405-282-8105 877-360-6777
dcrabtree@autoquip.com www.autoquip.com
Manufacturer and exporter of material handling equipment including scissor lifts, turntables and tilters
President: Joe Robillard
jrobillard@autoquip.com
Plant Manager: Chris Curning
Manager, Marketing & Sales: Louis Coleman
Sales: Donnie Crabtree
Operations Director: Chris Kuehni
Engineering Director: Mike Adel
Supervisor, Parts & Services: Mike Calvert
Estimated Sales: $10-20 Million
Number Employees: 100-249
Parent Co: Autoquip Corporation

19241 Autosplice Inc

10121 Barnes Canyon Rd
San Diego, CA 92121-2725

858-678-3115
Fax: 858-535-0130 www.autosplice.com
President: Michael T Reagan
Contact: Jacques Belet
jbelet@psav.com
Estimated Sales: $50 Million
Number Employees: 50-99

19242 Autotron

195 W Ryan Rd
Oak Creek, WI 53154-4400

414-764-7500
Fax: 414-764-4298 800-527-7500
info@elwood.com www.elwood.com
Manufacturer and exporter of industrial photoelectric controls
President: Robert Larsen
Vice President/CFO: Terry Levin
Vice President: David Johnson
Quality Manager: John Hoeppner
Estimated Sales: $5-10 Million
Number Employees: 20-49
Square Footage: 60000

19243 Avalon Canvas & Upholstery Inc

4617 N Shepherd Dr
Houston, TX 77018-3315

713-607-9289
Fax: 713-697-9257 www.marygrove.com

Commercial awnings
Manager: Michael Falahee
Estimated Sales: Less Than $500,000
Number Employees: 1-4

19244 Avalon Foodservice
1 Avalon Drive
PO Box 536
Canal Fulton, OH 44614
330-854-4551
Fax: 330-854-7108 800-362-0622
marketing@avalonfoods.com
www.avalonfoods.com
Avalon is a member of UniPro Foodservice, Inc., a cooperative of distributors with collective annual sales of $58 billion. Avalon serves Ohio and parts of Pennsylvania and West Virginia.
Contact: Adam Ables
adam.ables@avalonfoods.com
Square Footage: 114000
Brands:
Nestle
Tyson
Stouffers

19245 Avalon Manufacturer
509 Bateman Cir
Corona, CA 92880-2012
951-340-0280
Fax: 951-340-0283 800-676-3040
info@avalonmfg.com www.avalonmfg.com
Manufacturer and exporter of fryers, glazers and stainless steel (aluminum) proof boxes
Owner: Troy Enger
troy@avalonmfg.com
VP: Troy Enger
Estimated Sales: $2.5-5 Million
Number Employees: 10-19
Square Footage: 80000

19246 Avantage Group Inc
250 N Harbor Dr # 311
Suite 311
Redondo Beach, CA 90277-2585
310-379-3933
Fax: 310-376-0591
Plastic bags
President: Mark E Daniels
Owner: Mark Daniels
mdaniels@avantage.nl
Estimated Sales: Below $5 Million
Number Employees: 5-9

19247 Avanti Polar Lipids
700 Industrial Park Dr
Alabaster, AL 35007-9105
205-663-0991
Fax: 205-663-0756 800-227-0651
info@avantilipids.com www.avantilipids.com
Analytical services, metal chellators, bulk products, diagnostic kits, natural lipids, sterols, synthetic lipids
President: Di Bush
dcl89@cornell.edu
VP: Rowena Shaw
Estimated Sales: $10-20 Million
Number Employees: 50-99

19248 Aveka Inc
2045 Wooddale Dr
St Paul, MN 55125-2904
651-730-1729
Fax: 651-730-1826 888-317-3700
aveka@aveka.com www.aveka.com
Contract manufacturer and research and development company that focuses on particle technology including spray drying, particle coating or microcapsule technologies.
Owner: John Anderson
aveka@avekamfg.com
CEO/Ownder: William Hendrickson
Environmental Manager: Shain Kroenecke
Process Engineer: Matthew Timmers
Number Employees: 50-99
Other Locations:
Aveka Manufacturing
Fredericksberg IA
Cresco Food Technologies
Cresco IA
Aveka Nutra Processing
Waukon IA
Aveka CCE Technologies
Cottage Grove MN

19249 Avena Foods Ltd.
316 1st Ave. E
Regina, SK S4N 5H2
Canada
306-757-3663
Fax: 306-757-1218 drichardson@avenafoods.com
www.avenafoods.com
Processor and supplier of gluten-free/wheat free oat products for private label/ingredients market. Aller-gen free plant with GFCO and OU Kosher Certification. Products include rolled oats, quick flakes, flour, steel cuts oats andbran.
Director: Kevin Meadows
Director: Maryellen Carlson
Quality Control: Nicole Gudmundsson
Sales: Dale Richardson
Operations: Rod Lechner
Plant Manager: Nathalie Paquin
Purchasing: Carryl Litzenberger
Estimated Sales: $746.93 Thousand
Number Employees: 26
Type of Packaging: Private Label, Bulk

19250 Aventics Corp
1953 Mercer Rd
Lexington, KY 40511-1021
859-254-8031
Fax: 859-281-3488 www.boschrexroth.com
Pneumatic and hydraulic cylinders and valves, electropneumatic control systems and actuators, vac-uum components
IT: Jerry Robinson
jerry.robinson@boschrexroth-us.com
Estimated Sales: $50-100 Million
Number Employees: 250-499

19251 Avery Dennison Corporation
207 N Goode Avenue
Suite 500
Glendale, CA 91203-1301
626-304-2000
www.averydennison.com
Manufacturer and exporter of pressure sensitive la-bels.
Chairman/President/CEO: Mitch Butier
SVP/Chief Financial Officer: Greg Lovins
SVP/Chief Human Resources Officer: Anne Hill
SVP/General Counsel/Secretary: Susan Miller
VP/General Manager, Retail Branding: Deon Stander
VP/Global Operations/Supply Chain: Kamran Kian
Year Founded: 1935
Estimated Sales: $7.5 Billion
Number Employees: 30,000
Other Locations:
Avery Research Center (AEM)
Irwindale CA
Business Media
Buffalo NY
Corporate
Framingham MA
Corporate Int'l Manufacturing
Covina CA
Corporate Office at Brea
Brea CA
Corporate Office at Framingham
Framingham MA
Corporate Shared EHS at Milford
Milford MA
Engineered Films Division
Greenfield IN
Engineered Films Division
Painesville OH

19252 Avery Filter Company
99 Kinderkamack Rd
Suite 209
Westwood, NJ 07675
201-666-9664
Fax: 201-666-3802 info@averyfilter.com
www.averyfilter.com
Supplier of used & reconditioned filter presses, pres-sure leaf, pressure plate and vacuum drum filtration equipment & parts; paper & cloth filter media; and technical consulting services.
Vice President Engineering & Sales: Ken Lindgren
Square Footage: 1000

19253 Avery Weigh-Tronix
1000 Armstrong Dr
Fairmont, MN 56031-1439
507-238-4461
Fax: 507-238-4195 877-368-2039
usinfo@awtxglobal.com
www.averyweigh-tronix.com
Manufacturer and exporter of industrial scales.

Estimated Sales: $533 Million
Number Employees: 5,500
Square Footage: 330000
Parent Co: Illinois Tool Works Inc.

19254 Avery Weigh-Tronix LLC
1000 Armstrong Dr
Fairmont, MN 56031-1439
507-238-4461
Fax: 507-238-4195 800-368-2039
usinfo@awtxglobal.com
www.averyweigh-tronix.com
Manufacturer, importer and exporter of point-of-sale interface scales that link to cash registers and com-puters; also, portion control scales
Cmo: Peggy Trimble
peggi.trimble@weigh-tronix.com
VP: Peggy Trimble
Worldwide Marketing Director: P Trimble
Sales Director: D Cone
Number Employees: 250-499
Square Footage: 130000
Parent Co: Weigh-Tronix
Other Locations:
Weigh-Tronix
Tonbridge, Kent
Brands:
Nci

19255 Avestin
2450 Don Reid Drive
Ottawa, ON K1H 1E1
Canada
613-736-0019
Fax: 613-736-8086 888-283-7846
avestin@avestin.com
Manufacturer and exporter of high pressure homoge-nizers, filters, extruders and liposome extruders
President: Mark Ruzbie
Vice President: Hilde Linder
Marketing Manager: Sophie Sommerer
Number Employees: 10
Brands:
Emulsiflex
Liposofast

19256 Avins Fabricating Co
60 John Glenn Dr
Amherst, NY 14228-2118
716-691-7990
Fax: 716-691-8202 888-735-6907
info@goe-avins.com www.amherstfab.com
President: Gerald Bogdan
ccornwall@avinsfab.com
Estimated Sales: $3-5 Million
Number Employees: 20-49

19257 Avne Packaging Services
PO Box 863
Bronx, NY 10457-0863
718-716-7600

19258 Avon Tape
79 Florence St Apt 310s
Chestnut Hill, MA 2467
508-584-8273
Manufacturer and exporter of pressure-sensitive tapes
President: Howard Shuman
Estimated Sales: $5-10 Million
Number Employees: 50-99

19259 Avondale Mills
506 S Broad St
Monroe, GA 30655
770-267-2226
Fax: 803-663-5839
Manufacturers of fabrics for awnings
Manager: Doug Johnson
VP: Kevin Crean
Estimated Sales: $20-50 Million
Number Employees: 100-249
Parent Co: Avondale Mills

19260 Avtec Industries
9 Kane Industrial Dr
Hudson, MA 01749-2905
978-562-2300
Fax: 978-562-8900 www.avtcindustries.com
President: Anthony Camarota
inquiries@avtcindustries.com
Estimated Sales: $1-5 Million
Number Employees: 1-4
Parent Co: Dover Industries

19261 Avure Technologies Svc & Sales
3721 Corporate Dr
Columbus, OH 43231-4964
614-891-3498
Fax: 614-891-4568
Isostatic presses and thermocouples
Manager: Melanie Harter
Manager: Toddington Harper
todd.harper@fuelcellmarkets.com
Estimated Sales: $1-5 Million
Number Employees: 20-49

19262 Aw Sheepscot Holding CoInc
8809 Industrial Dr
Franksville, WI 53126-9337
262-884-9800
Fax: 262-884-9810 800-850-6110
sales@aw-lake.com www.awcompany.com
Manufacturer and distributor of flow control products including positive displacement flow meters, turbine flow meters, electronic sensors, flow computers, on-line optical sensors and signal conditioners.
President: Roger Tambling
Contact: Greg Baldwin
gbaldwin@aw-lake.com
Estimated Sales: $5-10 Million
Number Employees: 1-4
Square Footage: 60000
Brands:
 Fluidpro
 Proscan
 Ta-3

19263 Award's of America's
The Cuisine Group 25 Kearny S
Suite 500
San Francisco, CA 94108
415-982-0701
Fax: 415-982-4580
Since 1985, has dedicated itself to the purveyance of taste and quality throughout the culinary industry and the search for the best of the best in food, beverage, and equipment. Expanded to include three division: American TestingInstitute, American Culinary Institute, and American Quality Institute

19264 Awb Engineers
1942 Northwood Dr
Salisbury, MD 21801-7824
410-742-7299
Fax: 410-742-0273 awbengs@aol.com
www.awbengineers.com
Consultant specializing in architecture, civil, constructural and mechanical engineering services for food processing facilities
President: Matt Smith
msmith@awbengineers.com
Director: John Shahan
Estimated Sales: $3-5 Million
Number Employees: 20-49
Square Footage: 23200

19265 Awmco Inc
11560 184th Pl
Orland Park, IL 60467-4904
708-478-6032
Fax: 708-478-6041 awmco@aol.com
www.awmcoinc.com
Manufacturer and exporter of baking decks and cooking stones for pizza, pretzel and bagel ovens
President: Mark O'Toole
Manager: Mark Otoole
Estimated Sales: $2 Million
Number Employees: 5-9
Number of Brands: 4
Number of Products: 12
Square Footage: 72000
Type of Packaging: Food Service
Brands:
 Fibrament Baking Stone
 Oven Stone

19266 Awning Co Inc
1668 Bhampton Sag Harbor Tpke
Sag Harbor, NY 11963-3706
631-725-3651
Fax: 631-725-7452 info@theawningcompany.com
www.theawningcompany.com
Commercial awnings
Owner: Michael Moody
michael.moody@awningcompany.com
Co-Ownr.: Susan Oi

Estimated Sales: $500,000-$1,000,000
Number Employees: 5-9

19267 Awning Enterprises
P.O.Box 1063
Frederick, MD 21702
301-631-0500
Fax: 301-695-7651 800-735-2453
awningenterprises@comcast.net
www.awningenterprises.com
Commercial awnings
Owner: Danny Baer
VP: Patrick O'Connell
Associate VP: Rita O'Connell
Estimated Sales: $.5-1,000,000
Number Employees: 1-4

19268 Awnings Plus
1405 W Bernard Dr # A
Suite A
Addison, IL 60101-4341
630-627-4700
Fax: 630-405-6105 888-627-4770
Commercial awnings
Owner: Kent Weber
CFO: Nancy Gomez
Marketing Director: Ken Miller
Sales Director: Erich Doering
kent@awningssigngroup.com
Purchasing Manager: Michael Moreth
Estimated Sales: Below $5,000,000
Number Employees: 20-49
Square Footage: 12000

19269 Awnings by Dee
24913 Northern Boulevard
Little Neck, NY 11362-1260
516-487-6688
Fax: 718-224-5614
Commercial awnings
Secretary: Laura Dee
Estimated Sales: $1-2,500,000
Number Employees: 10-19

19270 Axces Systems
265 Post Ave
Westbury, NY 11590-2233
516-333-8585
Fax: 516-333-4992 800-355-3534
www.access-systems.com
Consultant and marketing information specialist for companies with 3-tier distribution networks
Owner: Charlie Richgat
Estimated Sales: $1-2.5 Million
Number Employees: 5-9
Square Footage: 4000

19271 Axelrod, Norman N
445 E 86th St
New York, NY 10028-6433
212-369-2885
www.axelrodassociates.com
Manufacturer and exporter of optical sensing and vision systems for automated quality and process control systems for food processing and packaging. Consultant, market studies on optical sensing and control technologies
President: Norman N Axelrod, Phd
Manager of Systems Integration: C Chang
Manager Software Development: R Rolle
Estimated Sales: Less Than $500,000
Number Employees: 1-4

19272 Axia Distribution Corporation
247-2628 Granville Street
Vancouver, BC V6H 4B4
Canada
778-371-9885
Fax: 778-371-9000 info@axiadistribution.com
www.axiadistribution.com
Distributor & Manufacutuer of High Quality Rubber Mats. The Mats are molded with virgin rubber that offers durability, less odor, stability and anti-fatigue properties
Type of Packaging: Food Service

19273 Axiflow Technologies, Inc.
1955 Vaughn Road
Suite 103
Kennesaw, GA 30144
770-795-1195
Fax: 770-795-1342 www.axiflowtechnologies.com
Pumps, blenders and food processing machines for the food & beverage industries.

19274 Axiohm USA
2411 N Oak Street
Suite 203 C
Myrtle Beach, SC 29577
843-443-3155
Fax: 888-505-9555 namsales@Axiohm.com
www.axiohm.com
Manufacturer and exporter of magnetic strip card readers and thermal laser receipt printers
President and CEO: Lindsey Allen
Director Marketing/Communications: Mark Basla
Number Employees: 60
Brands:
 Axiohm

19275 Axon Styrotech
3080 Business Park Dr # 103
Raleigh, NC 27610-3094
919-772-8383
Fax: 919-772-5575 800-598-8601
info@axoncorp.com www.axoncorp.com
Tamper evident sleeve labels
President: H Lane
Quality Control: Andy Perry
Manager: George Albrecht
gealb@axoncorp.com
General Manager: Victor Menayan
Estimated Sales: $10-20,000,000
Number Employees: 20-49
Brands:
 E-Z Seal

19276 Axon Styrotech
3080 Business Park Dr # 103
Suite 103
Raleigh, NC 27610-3094
919-772-8383
Fax: 919-772-5575 800-598-8601
info@axoncorp.com www.axoncorp.com
Shrink and stretch sleeve labeling machines and systems
Sales Director: Ed Farley
Manager: George Albrecht
gealb@axoncorp.com
Estimated Sales: $1-2.5 Million
Number Employees: 20-49

19277 Axons Labeling
Gristmill Road
Wanaque, NJ 07465
973-616-7448
Fax: 973-616-7449
Labeling machines, labeling applicators/jar unscramblers

19278 Ay Machine Company
East King Street
PO Box 608
Ephrata, PA 17522-0608
717-733-0335
Fax: 717-733-2933 info@aymachine.com
www.aymachine.com
Custom built food processing machinery; also, spare parts and rebuilt equipment
President: Richard Ay
CEO: Rick Ay, Jr.
Estimated Sales: $2.5-5 Million
Number Employees: 10-19
Square Footage: 128000

19279 Ayer Sales Inc
2 Industrial Pkwy
Woburn, MA 01801-1997
781-933-1141
Fax: 781-933-3675 800-225-5736
customerservice@ayer.com www.ayer.com
Waste water treatment systems
Marketing Coordinator: Peter Quinn
Estimated Sales: $3-5 Million
Number Employees: 50-99
Parent Co: Ayer Sales

19280 Ayr King Corp
2013 Cobalt Dr
Louisville, KY 40299-2417
502-266-6270
Fax: 502-266-6274 866-266-6290
aurking@aol.com www.ayrking.com
Breading sifters, hoods and drive-thru windows
Owner: Don King
VP Engineering: Cha Harned
VP of Sales: James Bell
don@ayrking.com

Estimated Sales: $500,000-$1 Million
Number Employees: 5-9

19281 Azbar Plus
2755, av Dalton
Qu,bec, QC G1P 3T1
Canada

418-687-3672
Fax: 418-687-2987 azbar@total.net
azbarplus.com
Liquor and beverage control equipment and dispensers including electric and beverage
Estimated Sales: $1-5 Million

19282 Azco Corp
26 Just Rd
Fairfield, NJ 07004-3413

973-439-1428
Fax: 973-439-9411 cs@azcocorp.com
www.azcocorp.com
Dispensers, inserters, fan folders, cut-to-length assemblies
President: Andrew Zucaro
zucaro@azcocorp.com
Marketing: Tetie Milligan
Sales: John Perona
Estimated Sales: $1-2.5 Million
Number Employees: 20-49

19283 Azonix Corporation
101 Billerica Ave
Building 4
Billerica, MA 01862

978-670-6300
Fax: 978-670-8855 800-967-5558
www.azonix.com
President: Greg Balesta
Training/Sales Support: Craig Yelenick
Estimated Sales: $13 Million
Number Employees: 50-99

19284 Aztec Grill
PO Box 820037
Dallas, TX 75382

214-343-1897
Fax: 214-341-9996 800-346-8114
www.aztecgrill.com
Manufacturer and exporter of wood burning grills and rotisseries
Contact: Dennis Whiting
dennis@aztecgrill.com
Estimated Sales: $1-5 Million
Number Employees: 2
Square Footage: 16000
Type of Packaging: Food Service

19285 Azz/R-A-L
8500 Hansen Rd
Houston, TX 77075

713-943-0340
Fax: 713-943-8354 www.azz.com
Lighting fixtures for the food service industry.

19286 B & G Products
3631 44th St SE # E
Grand Rapids, MI 49512-3971

616-698-9050
Fax: 616-698-9271 sales@bgproducts.com
www.bgproducts.com
President: Kathleen Geddes
kgeddes@bgproducts.com
Vice President: Jacci Harding
Quality Control Manager: Mark Mastbergen
Sales: Paul Geddes
Estimated Sales: $5-10 Million
Number Employees: 10-19
Square Footage: 40000
Type of Packaging: Food Service

19287 (HQ)B & P Process Equipment
1000 Hess Ave
Saginaw, MI 48601-3729

989-757-1300
Fax: 989-757-1301 sales@bpprocess.com
www.bpprocess.com
Manufacturer and exporter of food processing machinery and equipment including automatic scales, sifters, etc
President: Alan Martin
alan@sandrofilm.com
R&D: Doug Hillman
Executive: Joe Flynn
CFO: Allen Martin

Estimated Sales: $20-50 Million
Number Employees: 50-99

19288 B & W Awning Co
219 Walton Ave
Lexington, KY 40502-1492

859-252-1619
Fax: 859-233-4354 lgille3607@aol.com
www.bwawning.com
Commercial awnings
President: Larry Gillespie
lgille3607@aol.com
Estimated Sales: $1-2,500,000
Number Employees: 5-9

19289 B C Holland Inc
45 Wilson Ave
Dousman, WI 53118-9369

262-965-2939
Fax: 262-965-3546 www.bcholland.net
Custom tanks and mixers
President: Brian Holland
CFO: Rom Able
VP: David Steward
Sales Manager: Jim Huth
VP Operations: Dave Stewart
Estimated Sales: $1-2.5 Million
Number Employees: 10-19
Square Footage: 20000

19290 B F Nelson Cartons Inc
12900 Eagle Creek Pkwy
Savage, MN 55378-1271

952-746-6300
Fax: 952-746-6399 800-328-2380
sales@bfnelson.com www.bfnelson.com
Folding cartons
President: Larry Ross
bfncartons@aol.com
Executive VP: Gary Sotebeer
VP Sales: Ron Anderson
Estimated Sales: $1-5 Million
Number Employees: 100-249

19291 B H Awning & Tent Co
2275 M 139
Benton Harbor, MI 49022-6190

269-925-2187
Fax: 269-925-2197 800-272-2187
sales@bhawning.com www.bhawning.com
Commercial awnings, banners, canopies and flags
President: Charles Dill
chuck@bhawning.com
Number Employees: 10-19

19292 B H Bunn Co
2730 Drane Field Rd
Lakeland, FL 33811-1325

863-647-1555
Fax: 863-686-2866 800-222-2866
info@bunntyco.com www.bunntyco.com
Bunn tying machines for poultry, pork and beef
Owner: John R Bunn
jbunn@bunntyco.com
Estimated Sales: $3-5 Million
Number Employees: 10-19
Square Footage: 68000
Brands:
    Bunn

19293 B J Wood Products Inc
400 W 9th St S
Ladysmith, WI 54848-9514

715-532-6626
Fax: 715-532-7774 pauls@bjwood.com
www.bjwood.com
Custom wood and acrylic casework, cabinets, displays, counters and store fixtures
President: Paul Sieg
pauls@bjwood.com
VP: John Sieg
Estimated Sales: $5-10 Million
Number Employees: 10-19
Square Footage: 95000

19294 B M T USA LLC
14532 169th Dr SE # 142
#142
Monroe, WA 98272-2936

360-863-2252
Fax: 360-863-2366 sales@bmtus.com
www.bmtus.com

Offers a wide range of equipment for the food laboratory, including stability chambers, incubators, sterilization ovens, vacuum and dry-heat ovens, small, medium, and large steam sterilizers, and clean steam generators
President: Jim Atkinson
jatkinson@bmtus.com
Number Employees: 10-19

19295 B R Machinery
3312 E 2153rd Rd
Wedron, IL 60557

815-434-0427
Fax: 815-434-0428 800-310-7057
info@brmachine.us www.brmachine.us
Portable propane and custom portable grills, gas grill carts, personalized custom canopy and grill accessories
Owner: Robert Rogowski
VP: Nancy Rogowski
VP of Sales: Tony Rogowski
robertr@wedrongrills.com
Production Manager: Sam Brown
Estimated Sales: Less Than $500,000
Number Employees: 5-9
Square Footage: 40000
Brands:
    Wedron Grills

19296 B S & B Safety Systems LLC
7455 E 46th St
Tulsa, OK 74145-6301

918-622-5950
Fax: 918-492-1559 800-272-3475
sales@bsbsystems.com www.bsbsystems.com
Manufactures overpressure protection safety products, pressure relief, both positive and vacuum with pressure relieving products including rupture disks.
VP: Dave Garrison
Number Employees: 5-9

19297 B S C Signs
7245 W 116th Pl
Broomfield, CO 80020-2955

303-464-0644
Fax: 303-464-0608 866-223-0101
sales@bscsigns.com www.bscsigns.com
Displays and signs including neon, lighted and nonilluminated; installation services available
President: Mike Nudd
VP: Jennifer Dent
Contact: John Dobie
john@bscsigns.com
Estimated Sales: Less Than $500,000
Number Employees: 1-4

19298 B T Engineering Inc
29 Bala Ave # 209
Bala Cynwyd, PA 19004-3269

610-664-9500
Fax: 610-664-0317 bte123123@aol.com
www.btengineering.com
Automated sanitary liquid food processing equipment and control systems including clean-in-place pipeline systems, pasteurizers and volumetric filling machines; exporter of skidded food systems; design services available
President/CEO: William Willard
CFO: Thomas Berger Sr
Secretary/Treasurer: Thomas Berger
Manager: W Willard
wilwillard@aol.com
Estimated Sales: $1-2.5 Million
Number Employees: 1-4
Square Footage: 5000
Type of Packaging: Food Service

19299 B W Cooney & Associates
28 Simpson Road
Bolton, Ontario, ON L7E 1G9
Canada

905-857-7880
Fax: 905-857-7883 info@bwcooney.com
www.bwcooney.ca
Shrink wrapping and tray stretch machines, flow wrappers, verticle form fill & seal systems, packaging film and retail food trays.
President: Brian Cooney
Number Employees: 2

19300 B&B Neon Sign Company
2305 Donley Dr # 116
Austin, TX 78758-4535

512-765-4470
Fax: 512-719-4490 800-791-6366
customerservice@everythingneon.com
www.everythingneon.com
Point of purchase displays including neon and plexi-glass signs; also, sign maintenance, refurbishing and repair services available
Owner: Tim O'Day
Estimated Sales: $300,000 -$500,000
Number Employees: 5-9

19301 B&G Machine Company
9124 S 53rd Ave
Oak Lawn, IL 60453-1665

708-499-1626
Fax: 631-589-9466 800-645-1191
www.bgmachine.com
Bins, hoppers, totes, ASME code vessels, storage tanks and mixing tanks
President: Barbara Ruehl
Vice President: Greg Ruehl
Estimated Sales: $5-10 Million
Number Employees: 5-9

19302 B&H Foods
P.O.Box 668568
Charlotte, NC 28266-8568

704-332-4106
Fax: 704-332-5980
Shellfish Shippers
President: Stan Bracey
Plant Manager: Dennis Frost
Estimated Sales: $20-50 Million
Number Employees: 50-99
Parent Co: B&H Foods

19303 B&H Labeling Systems
P.O.Box 247
Ceres, CA 95307

209-537-5785
Fax: 209-537-6854 marketing@bhlabeling.com
www.bhlabeling.com
Hot-melt roll-fed labeling machines capable of handling most container sizes, label substrates, and speeds for a diverse range of products and materials. Features and options include Computerized Registration System, Web TrackingOperator Alarms, Touch Screen Operation, Rapid Change Over Change Parts, ENDURA Shrink Labeling process, Precision Components
Owner: Carol Bright
CEO: Roman M Eckols
Contact: Lyn Bright
l.bright@bhlabeling.com
Plant Manager: Bruce Andrade
Number Employees: 100-249
Type of Packaging: Consumer, Food Service, Private Label

19304 B&J Machinery
11560 Rockfield Ct
Cincinnati, OH 45241-1919

513-771-7374
Fax: 513-771-3820 info@pe-us.com
www.pe-us.com
Packaging machinery and replacement parts
President: Bruno Negri
CFO: Bruno Negri
VP: Tom Kauffmann
Regional Sales Manager: Ryan Cooper
Estimated Sales: $10-20 Million
Number Employees: 20-49
Square Footage: 32000

19305 B&K Coffee
PO Box 1238
Oneonta, NY 13820-5238

607-432-1499
Fax: 607-432-1592 800-432-1499
www.bkcoffee.com
Manufacturer of coffee and tea.
Owner: Paul Karabinis
Owner: Gene Bettiol
Year Founded: 1991
Estimated Sales: $10-24.9 Million
Number Employees: 20-49
Number of Brands: 1
Type of Packaging: Private Label
Brands:
   B&K Coffee

19306 B&R Industrial Automation Corp
1250 Northmeadow Parkway
Suite 100
Roswell, GA 30076

770-772-0400
office.us@br-automation.com
www.br-automation.com
Machine and factory control systems
President: Patrick McDermott
Number Employees: 1,000-4,999
Parent Co: ABB Group

19307 B.A.G. Corporation
11510 Data Dr
Suite 170
Richardson, TX 75081

800-331-9200
Fax: 214-340-4598 800-331-9200
www.bagcorp.com
Manufacturer and exporter of the Super Sack container, a woven polypropylene FIBC for shipping, handling, and storing dry-flowable and fluid products
President: Karl Reimers
Estimated Sales: $5-10 Million
Number Employees: 20-49
Type of Packaging: Food Service, Bulk
Brands:
   Super Sack

19308 B.C.E. Technologies
616 S Ware Blvd
Tampa, FL 33619-4443

813-621-8128
Fax: 813-620-1206
President: Graham Lloyd
glloyd@bcetechnology.com
Number Employees: 20-49

19309 B.E. Industries
652 Glenbrook Rd # 4102
Stamford, CT 06906-1410

203-357-8055
Fax: 203-967-9537
Advertising specialties including key rings and magnets
President: Bruce Kahn
Estimated Sales: $2.5-5,000,000
Number Employees: 10-19

19310 B.E.S.T.
1071 Industrial Pkwy N
Brunswick, OH 44212

330-273-1277
Fax: 330-225-8740 sales@bestvibes.com
www.bestvibes.com
President: Ed Verbos
Estimated Sales: $5-10 Million
Number Employees: 20-49

19311 BAKERY Innovative Technology
139 N Ocean Ave
Patchogue, NY 11772-2018

631-758-3081
Fax: 631-758-3779
Software and automation: applying and installing computer and programmable controller automation for bakeries and food plants
Owner: Joe Vignati
joe.vignati@bit-corp.com
Estimated Sales: $2.5-5 Million
Number Employees: 10-19

19312 BAKERY Innovative Technology
139 N Ocean Ave
Patchogue, NY 11772-2018

631-758-3081
Fax: 631-758-3779
Owner: Mark Albert
mark.albert@bit-corp.com
Estimated Sales: $1-5 Million
Number Employees: 10-19

19313 BAW Plastics Inc
2148 Century Dr
Clairton, PA 15025-3654

412-384-2535
Fax: 412-384-2033 800-783-2229
www.allbrainscreateddreams.org
Coupon bags, transparent vinyl envelopes, vinyl checker aids, acrylic holders, lamination pouches, time and attendance badges and name tags, etc

Owner: Jim Slovonic
Sales Manager: Martin Slovonic
Sales Director: Francis Dusch
jslovonic@bawplastics.com
Estimated Sales: $10-20 Million
Number Employees: 100-249
Square Footage: 130000

19314 BBQ Pits by Klose
1355 Judiway Street #B
Houston, TX 77018-6005

713-686-8720
Fax: 713-686-8793 800-487-7487
www.bbqpits.com
Manufacturer, importer and exporter of barbecue equipment including grills and smokers; also, catering trailers; wood, charcoal and gas fired.
President: David Klose
Sales: Dana Harlow
Contact: Carla Hadley
carla.hadley@bbqpits.com
Estimated Sales: $1-3 Million
Number Employees: 10-19
Number of Products: 500
Square Footage: 24000
Type of Packaging: Consumer, Food Service, Bulk
Brands:
   Klose

19315 BCN Research Laboratories
2491 Stock Creek Blvd
Rockford, TN 37853-3056

865-573-7511
Fax: 865-573-7513 800-236-0505
emilia.rico@bcnlabs.com www.bcnlabs.com
Consultant providing laboratory and research services including sanitation, testing and analysis; also, plant audits and training available
President: Emilia Rico
emilia.rico@bcnlabs.com
VP: Shawn Johnson
Estimated Sales: $.5-1 million
Number Employees: 5-9
Square Footage: 12000

19316 BE&K Building Group
201 E McBee Ave
Suite 400
Greenville, SC 29601

864-250-5000
Fax: 864-250-5099 www.bekbg.com
Construction services
President & CEO: Frank Holley
EVP & Business Unit Leader: Mike Baumbach
Finance Controller: Kathy Harvey
VP, Preconstruction & Technology: Kevin Bredeson
SVP, Business Development: Jeff Thompson
VP, Human Resources: Candace Watson
Corporate Counsel: Leslie Sullivan
Marketing & Communications: Rick Helms
Year Founded: 1972
Estimated Sales: $2 Billion
Number Employees: 9,000
Other Locations:
   Atlanta GA
   Charlotte NC
   Greenville SC
   Brentwood TN
   Maitland FL
   Raleigh NC
   Vienna VA

19317 BEC International
2330 S Preston St
Louisville, KY 40217-2163

502-637-3852
Fax: 502-637-3803 877-232-4687
beci2001@hotmail.com
Consultant specializing in engineering and project management services
President: Richard Sorensen
Executive VP: James Winn
Number Employees: 1
Square Footage: 7200

19318 BEERCUP.COM
N22 W23685 Ridgeview Pkwy W
Waukesha, WI 53188

800-233-7287
Fax: 800-532-9287 beverage@boelter.com
BEERCUP.COM is an extension of The Boelter Companies' Beverage Group and provides the beverage industry with brand identified plastic cups, coasters, glassware, pitchers, buckets, and many other items used to serve beverage brands.

Director International Markets: Steve Dindorf

19319 BEI
1375 Kalamazoo St
South Haven, MI 49090
269-637-8541
Fax: 269-637-4233 800-364-7425
Manufacturer and exporter of berry harvesters and
packing equipment
President: William De Witt Jr
Vice President: Butch Greiffendorf
Contact: Rodney Tolbert
rtolbert@beiintl.com
Manager: J Greiffendorf
Estimated Sales: $5-10 Million
Number Employees: 20-49
Square Footage: 48000

19320 BEI
7230 Hollister Avenue
Goleta, GA 93117
805-968-0782
Fax: 805-968-3154 800-350-2727
beisales@beisensors.com www.beiresources.org
Insulated packaging
VP: Bob Belick
Marketing Manager: Bob Belick
Contact: Charles Crocker
charles@beiied.com
Estimated Sales: Less than $500,000
Number Employees: 1-4
Brands:
   Thermal Cor

19321 BEMA
7101 College Boulevard
Suite 1505
Overland Park, KS 66210-2087
847-920-1230
Fax: 847-920-1253 info@bema.org
www.bema.org
President, Chief Executive Officer: Kerwin Brown
Operations Manager: Gay Poteet
Number Employees: 10

19322 BEUMER Corp
800 Apgar Dr
Somerset, NJ 8873
732-893-2800
Fax: 732-563-0905 usa@beumer.com
www.beumer.com
Manufacturer, importer and exporter of material
handling equipment including automatic palletizing
systems and automatic shrink and stretch hood unit-
izing systems
President: Matthias Erdsmannadoerf
matthias.erdsmannadoerf@beumer.com
VP: Hanno Behm
Number Employees: 20-49
Square Footage: 10400
Parent Co: Beumer Maschinenfabrik GmbH &
Company KG

19323 BEVCO
9354-194th Street Surrey
Canada, BC V4N 4E9
Canada
604-888-1455
Fax: 604-888-2887 800-663-0090
info@bevco.net www.bevco.net
Manufacturer and exporter of material handling and
distribution equipment including accumulators, con-
veyors, conveyor systems, depalletizers and eleva-
tors; also, warmers and bottle rinsers
President: Brian Fortier
CEO: D Hargrove
CFO: Dianne Hargrove
Sales/Marketing Executive: Murray Kendrick
Estimated Sales: $5-10 Million
Number Employees: 45
Square Footage: 80000

19324 BEX Inc
836 Phoenix Dr
Ann Arbor, MI 48108-2221
734-464-8282
Fax: 734-389-0470 sales@bex.com
www.bex.com
Manufacture of spray nozzles and accessories for
parts cleaning, rinsing and food processing.
Number Employees: 5-9

19325 BFB Consultants
5995 River Grove Avenue
Mississauga, ON L5M 4Z8
Canada
905-819-9856
Fax: 905-819-9857
Consultant specializing in food packaging, labeling
and advertising in Canada and the U.S. in accor-
dance with government regulations
Regional Affairs: Laurel Bellissimo
Sr. Technical Director: Gary Gnirss
Estimated Sales: $1-5 Million

19326 BFD Corp
15544 E Hinsdale Cir
Centennial, CO 80112-4225
303-363-6288
Fax: 303-363-6844 www.bfdcorp.com
Depackaging soft products/soft tissue separation;
cutting-deboning-desinewing.
President: John Shook
bfdcorp@aol.com
CFO: Mark Thomas
Sales Director: Harold Hodges
Number Employees: 10-19

19327 BFM Equipment Sales
209 Steel Road
P.O. Box 117
Fall River, WI 53932-0117
920-484-3341
Fax: 920-484-3077 info@bfmequip.com
www.bfmequip.com
Manufacturer, importer, exporter and wholesaler/dis-
tributor of food processing machinery, can end
cleaners and dryers, replacement parts and supplies
Owner: Richard Bindley
Executive Manager: Russell Quandt
Contact: Leann Vick
lvick@bfmequip.com
Estimated Sales: Below $5 Million
Number Employees: 1-4
Square Footage: 40000
Brands:
   Bfm

19328 BFT
3513 Transmitter Rd
Panama City, FL 32404
850-784-1231
Fax: 850-784-1343 800-871-1481
Gripper style air cleaner, bi-directional accumulation
table, table top conveyors and a carry handle application machine for six-pack bottles and other containers and products
Estimated Sales: $2.5-5 000,000
Number Employees: 10

19329 BG Industries
305 Canal Street
Lemont, IL 60439-3603
630-257-1077
Fax: 630-257-0005 800-800-5761
www.bgindustry.com
Disposable plastic and metal catering products in-
cluding chafing dishes, soup terrines and beverage
urns
President: Paul Orednick
Estimated Sales: $1-2.5 Million
Number Employees: 9
Brands:
   Hot Buffet To Go
   Party Chafer

19330 BI Nutraceuticals
2550 El Presidio Street
Long Beach, CA 90810
310-669-2162
Fax: 310-637-3644
The largest supplier of botanical ingredients in the
United States, for use in food & beverage, dietary
supplements, personal care and pet care products.
Products include botanical powders, teas, extracts,
nutritional blends, vitaminsminerals, and more.
President/CEO: George Pontiakos
Chief Financial Officer: Christoph Kirchner
VP, North America: Bob Harvey
VP, Technical Services: Emilio Gutierrez
VP, Quality/Compliance: Rupa Das
Director, Marketing: Randy Kreienbrink
Contact: Patrisha Abergas
patrishaabergas@tmmc.com
Director, Extract Operations: Dr. Bill Meer

19331 BINDER Inc.
545-3 Johnson Avenue
Bohemia, NY 11716
631-224-4340
usa@binder-world.com
www.binder-world.com
A simulation chamber specialist. Drying ovens
Contact: Jerry Jiang
jerry.jiang@binder-world.com
Parent Co: BINDER GmbH

19332 BK Graphics
5270 Cub Cir Ste A
Morristown, TN 37814
423-581-4288
Fax: 423-581-9159 800-581-9159
www.bkgraphics.com
Advertising specialties; also, screen printing avail-
able
CEO: Brian Frankford
Quality Control: Kathy Frankford
Estimated Sales: $.5-1,000,000
Number Employees: 5-9

19333 BKI
1000 Broadway
Suite 410
Oakland, CA 94607
510-444-8707
Fax: 510-463-2690 contactus@bki.com
www.bki.com
Technical management consultants
President: Robert Knight
Vice President: Brian Gitt
Contact: Julie Foster
jfoster@bki.com
Number Employees: 10

19334 BKI Worldwide
2812 Grandview Dr
Simpsonville, SC 29680-6217
864-963-3471
Fax: 864-963-5316 800-927-6887
customerservice@bkideas.com www.bkideas.com
Manufacturer and exporter of rotisseries, ovens, fry-
ers, deli cases, ventless hood systems and food
warmers
President: Randy A Karns
Controller: Reggy Skelton
COO: Dave Korcsmaros
Quality Control Manager: Wade Pitts
Operations Manager: Reed Walpole
Production Manager: Reed Walpole
Purchasing Manager: Wade Pitts
Number Employees: 100-249
Parent Co: Standex International Corporation
Brands:
   Bar-B-Que King
   Whisperflow

19335 BLH Electronics
75 Shawmut Rd
Canton, MA 02021
781-821-2000
Fax: 781-828-1451 sales@blh.com
www.blh.com
Manufacturer and exporter of process weighing and
web tension systems, strain gauges and load sys-
tems/instruments
President: Robert E Murphy
Vice President: William Sheehan
Research & Development: David Scanlon
Sales Director: Art Koehler
Facilities Manager: Alan Sandman
Estimated Sales: $50-100 Million
Number Employees: 1-4
Square Footage: 55000
Parent Co: Spectra-Physics AB
Other Locations:
   BLH Electronics
   Toronto ON
Brands:
   Gate-Weigh

19336 BMH
19135 San Jose Avenue
City of Industry, CA 91748-1407
909-349-2530
Fax: 626-912-2477
Belt conveyors, automatic storage and handling sys-
tems and metal belting
Estimated Sales: $2.5-5,000,000
Number Employees: 20

19337 BMH Chronos Richardson
2 Stewart Place
Fairfield, NJ 07004-2202
973-227-3522
Fax: 973-227-8478 800-284-3644
info@premiertechchronos.com
www.bmhchronosrichardson.com
Contact: Bob Duran
info@chronosrichardson.com
Estimated Sales: $1-5 Million

19338 BNP Media
Beverage
Packaging Group
2401 W Big Beaver Rd, Su Troy
MI
480-4 -
248-362-3700
Henderson: Jim
Estimated Sales: www.bnpmedia.com
Type of Packaging: Food Service
Other Locations:
Deerfield IL
Marianna FL
New York NY
Paramus NJ
Pittsburgh PA
West Chester PA

19339 BNW Industries
7930 N 700 E
Tippecanoe, IN 46570-9613
574-353-7855
Fax: 574-353-8152 sales@norristhermal.com
Manufacturer and exporter of coolers and dehydrators; manufacturer of balance/single weave wire belts
Founder/President: Dan Norris
dnorris@bnwindustries.com
Vice President Sales: Aaron Norris
Purchasing Manager: Troy Eaton
Estimated Sales: $1-3 Million
Number Employees: 10-19
Square Footage: 52000
Parent Co: Lee Norris Construction & Grain Company
Brands:
Belt-O-Matic
Indiana Woven Wire

19340 BOC Gases
575 Mountain Ave
New Providence, NJ 07974
908-464-8100
Fax: 908-771-1701 800-742-4726
jobs@us.gases.boc.com www.boc.com
Full line of freezing and chilling equipment for beverage processing and carbonating needs
Marketing: Jon Lederman
Contact: Alexander Alvarado
alex.alvarado@boc.com
Estimated Sales: $5 000,000
Number Employees: 1,000-4,999

19341 BOC Plastics Inc
90 Piedmont Industrial Drive
Suite 100
Winston Salem, NC 27107
336-767-0277
Fax: 336-767-2338 800-334-8687
Plastic cutlery kits
President: Robert Bach
CFO: Aren Petersen
Estimated Sales: $5-10 Million
Number Employees: 20-49

19342 BP
501 Westlake Park Blvd
Houston, TX 77079
281-366-2000
www.bp.com/en_us/united-states/home.html
Packaging materials including FDA approved resins and film.
CEO: Bernard Looney
Chair/President, BP America: Susan Dio
CFO: Brian Gilvary
EVP, Safety & Operational Risk: Bob Fryar
EVP/COO: Andy Hopwood
Year Founded: 1908
Estimated Sales: $3.4 Billion
Number Employees: 74,000
Parent Co: BP plc
Brands:
Barex

19343 BPH Pump & Equipment
4126 W Orleans St
Mchenry, IL 60050-3972
815-578-0100
Fax: 815-578-0400 866-295-9161
www.sanitarypumpsandparts.com
Fluid handling equipment, system design, system fabrications, system engineering
Owner: Torres Beneth
torres.beneth@accenture.com
Estimated Sales: $2.5 000,000
Number Employees: 5-9

19344 BPM Inc
200 W Front St
Peshtigo, WI 54157-1406
715-582-4551
Fax: 715-582-4853 800-826-0494
www.bpmpaper.com
Bond, mimeograph, duplicator, computer, copier rolls, MG and MF manifold, laminating stock, printed and plain waxed papers
President: Ronald Swanson
Vice President: Mitchell Mekaelian
mm@bpmpaper.com
Plant Manager: Mark Bruemmer
Estimated Sales: $60 Million
Number Employees: 100-249

19345 BSI Instruments
101 Corporation Drive
Aliquippa, PA 15001-4859
724-378-1900
Fax: 724-378-1926 800-274-9851
bsischwa@sgi.net www.biospherical.com
On-line process control instrumentation including noninvasive level density systems
President: Bud Smith
VP of Marketing: Whit Little
Sales Manager: Aaron Tufts
Estimated Sales: $2.5-5 Million
Number Employees: 9
Square Footage: 60000

19346 BUCHI Corp
19 Lukens Dr # 400
Suite 400
New Castle, DE 19720-2787
302-652-8777
Fax: 302-225-2473 877-692-8844
us-sales@buchi.com www.buchi.com
Nutrition analysis systems
General Manager: Christopher Sopko
Finance Manager: Tony Casadei
Sales Director: John Pollard
Regional Sales Manager: Brad Miller
Regional Sales Manager: Charles Douglas
Estimated Sales: $5-10 Million
Number Employees: 20-49

19347 BUCHI Corp
19 Lukens Dr # 400
Suite 400
New Castle, DE 19720-2787
302-652-8777
Fax: 302-225-2473 877-692-8244
us-sales@buchi.com www.buchi.com
Lab instruments such as spray dryers, NIR spectroscopy instruments for quality control, solvent extraction equipment for food analysis, etc.
Finance Manager: Tony Casadei
Marketing Manager: Rudi Hartmann
Sales Director: John Pollard
Manager: Hodge Andy
h.andy@genealogygoldmine.com
General Manager: Vahe Iplikci
Estimated Sales: $6.3 Million
Number Employees: 20-49

19348 BVL Controls
661, The Pit
Bois-Des-Filion, QC J6Z 4T2
Canada
450-965-0502
Fax: 450-965-8751 866-285-2668
info@bvlcontrols.com www.bvlcontrols.com
Manufacturer, importer and exporter of portion control and cooling equipment and supplies for beer, wine, soft drinks and liquors
President: Alvin Guerette
Controller: Josee Merchand
Vice President: Gilles Guerette

Estimated Sales: $1-3 Million
Number Employees: 10-19
Square Footage: 48000
Brands:
Bvl
Oberdorfer
True Measure

19349 (HQ)BW Container Systems
1305 Lakeview Dr
Romeoville, IL 60446-3900
630-759-6800
Fax: 630-759-2299 sales@fleetinc.com
www.bwcontainersystems.com
Manufacturer and exporter of magnetic and specialized food handling and processing equipment including conveyors, capping, sealing, seaming, canning and food packing
Chairman of the Board: Robert H Chapman
CEO: Phil Ostapowicz
postapowicz@fgwa.com
CFO: David Brown
CEO: Phil Ostapowicz
VP Sales: Neil McConnellogue
Estimated Sales: $20-50 Million
Number Employees: 100-249
Square Footage: 200000
Parent Co: Barry-Wehmiller
Other Locations:
Fleetwood Systems
Orlando FL

19350 BW Controls
1080 North Crooks
Clawson, MI 48017
248-435-0700
Fax: 248-435-8120 800-635-0289
apt.orders@ametek.com www.ametekapt.com
Continuous and point level instruments, offering a line of 3-A approved magnetostictive level sensors
Manager: Bob Soeder
Bus Unit Manager: Robert Soeder
Business Development Director: Michael Geis
Estimated Sales: $5 Million
Number Employees: 100-249
Number of Brands: 4
Number of Products: 26
Square Footage: 520000

19351 BWI-PLC
1750 Corporate Drive
Suite 700
Norcross, GA 30093-2932
770-925-2004
800-605-6217
Packaging machinery, equipment and materials
Estimated Sales: $5-10 Million
Number Employees: 50

19352 BYK Gardner Inc
9104 Guilford Rd # 2
Columbia, MD 21046-2729
301-483-6500
Fax: 301-483-6555
Colors and color meters
VP: Mike Gogoel
Cio/Cto: Liza Wirkey
liza.wirkey@altana.com
General Manager: Mike Goegel
Estimated Sales: Over $1 Billion
Number Employees: 5000-9999

19353 Baader-Linco
2955 Fairfax Trfy
Kansas City, KS 66115-1317
913-621-3366
Fax: 913-621-1729 800-288-3434
www.baader.com
Designer, manufacturer and distributors of poultry and fish processing equipment.
President: Andy Miller
andy.miller@baaderna.com
Controller: Shaun Nicolas
Corporate Accounts/Sales Manager-US: Gehrig Chandler
Estimated Sales: $15.10 Million
Number Employees: 100-249
Square Footage: 13209
Parent Co: Baader Food Processing Machinery

19354 Babco International, Inc
911 S Tyndall
Tucson, AZ 85719

520-628-7596
Fax: 520-628-9622 contactus@babcotucson.com
www.babcotucson.com
Glassware, china, skirting, linen and silverware
Owner: Patrick Brodecky
patrick.brodecky@babcotucson.com
Marketing/Customer Service Director: Betsy Marco
Estimated Sales: $2.5-5 Million
Number Employees: 5-9
Brands:
 Snap Drape
 Syracuse

19355 Babcock & Wilcox MEGTEC
830 Prosper St
De Pere, WI 54115

920-336-5715
Manufacturer of environmental control technologies
Senior VP, B&W MEGTEC: Ken Zak
Parent Co: Babcock & Wilcox Enterprises

19356 Babcock & Wilcox Power Generation Group
20 S Van Buren Ave
Barberton, OH 44203-0351

330-753-4511
Fax: 330-860-1886 800-222-2625
slmccaulley@babcock.com www.babcock.com
Manufacturer and exporter of steam generation boilers and auxiliary equipment
President, COO: J. Randall Data
Senior Vice President, General Counsel,: James D. Canafax
SVP, CFO: Anthony S. Colatrella
SVP, Chief Administrative Officer: Kairus K. Tarapore
R&D Director: Stan Vecci
Manager Advertising: Phil Stillitano
Contact: Mel Albrecht
malbrecht@babcock.com
Director of Operation: Alan Nethery
Number Employees: 1,000-4,999
Parent Co: McDermott International

19357 Babcock Co
36 Delaware Ave
Bath, NY 14810-1607

607-776-3341
Fax: 607-776-7483 www.babcock.com
Manufacturer and exporter of small wooden crates
President: Marc Mc Connell
Sales/Marketing Executive: A Cranmer
Manager: Mike Bishop
Estimated Sales: $2.5-5 Million
Number Employees: 10-19
Square Footage: 154000

19358 Bacchus Wine Cellars
14027 Memorial Drive #228
Houston, TX 77079-9826

281-496-4495
Fax: 284-496-5855 800-487-8812
bacchuswinecellars.com
Manufacturer, importer and exporter of temperature and humidity controlled wine cellars, cabinets and storage equipment
President: Pierre Guinaudeau
Estimated Sales: Less than $500,000
Number Employees: 75
Square Footage: 40000
Brands:
 Le Cellier

19359 Bacharach Inc
621 Hunt Valley Cir
New Kensington, PA 15068-7074

724-334-5000
Fax: 724-334-5001 800-736-4666
Help@MyBacharach.com www.mybacharach.com
Estimated Sales: $1-5 Million
Number Employees: 100-249

19360 Back Tech
388 2nd Avenue.
459
New York, NJ 10010

973-279-0838
Fax: 212-673-0386 backtech@liftsolutions.com
www.liftsolutions.com
Lightweight electrical lifting cart for up to 500 pounds, mobil, handling rolls and totes

Plant Manager: E Rydstedt
Estimated Sales: $1 000,000
Number Employees: 1-4

19361 Back to Basics
PO Box 2780
West Bend, WI 53095-0278

801-523-6500
800-688-1989
www.backtobasicsproducts.com
Confections, candy, equipment
Estimated Sales: $5-10 Million
Number Employees: 50-99
Brands:
 Back To Basics
 Hawaiice
 Nutri Source
 Peel Away

19362 Backus USA
602 W Dubois Ave
Suite 9
Du Bois, PA 15801

814-375-6999
Estimated Sales: $1-5 Million

19363 Backwoods Smoker Inc
8245 Dixie Shreveport Rd
Shreveport, LA 71107-8439

318-220-0380
Fax: 318-220-9022 backwoodssmoker@hughes.net
Meat smokers
Owner: Mike Mc Gowan
backwoodssmoker@hughes.net
VP: Charlene McGowan
Secy.: Larie McGowan
Estimated Sales: $1-2.5 Million
Number Employees: 1-4
Square Footage: 6000
Type of Packaging: Private Label
Brands:
 Backwoods Smoker

19364 Bacon Products Corp
1605 Shepherd Rd
Chattanooga, TN 37421-2996

423-892-0414
Fax: 423-892-2065 800-251-6238
www.baconmail.com
Rodenticides and insecticides including pellets, glue traps, organic fly control products, ant, roach and spider spray, etc
Owner: Reed Bacon
jve@baconmail.com
R&D: Reed Bacon
Sales/Marketing: Karen Romito
VP of Production: James Edwards
Estimated Sales: $20-50 Million
Number Employees: 10-19
Brands:
 Ant, Roach & Spider
 Eagles-7
 Final Bite!
 Fly Eaters
 Fly Ribbons
 Last Step
 Roach Destroyer
 Septic Clean
 Spray-Kill With Nylar
 Wasp & Hornet Destroyer

19365 Baden Baden Food Equipment
3947 W Columbus Ave
Chicago, IL 60652

773-284-9009
Fax: 773-284-9109 877-368-8375
Sales of food and bakery equipment and wares
President: Vernon Condon
Contact: David Uhl
d.uhl@badenfoodequip.com
Estimated Sales: $1,500,000
Number Employees: 5-9
Square Footage: 12000

19366 Badger Meter Inc
4545 W Brown Deer Rd
P.O. Box 245036
Milwaukee, WI 53224

800-876-3837
www.badgermeter.com
Manufacturer and exporter of water meters and flowmeters.

President: Richard Meeusen
SVP & Chief Operating Officer: Kenneth Bockhorst
SVP, Finance/CFO/Treasurer: Richard Johnson
Vice President, Engineering: Fred Begale
VP/General Counsel/Secretary: Williams R.A. Bergum
VP, Business Development: Gregory Gomez
VP, Sales & Marketing: Kimberly Stoll
Vice President, Controller: Beverly L.P. Smiley
Vice President, Manufacturing: Raymond Serdynski
Vice President, Human Resources: Trina Jashinsky
Vice President, International Operations: Horst Gras
Year Founded: 1905
Estimated Sales: $100-500 Million
Number Employees: 1000-4999

19367 Badger Plug Co
N1045 Technical Dr
Greenville, WI 54942-8024

920-757-7300
Fax: 920-757-7339 sales@badgerplug.net
www.badgerplug.com
Plastic end plugs for cardboard tubes
President: Dan Voissem
dvoissem@badgerplug.net
Estimated Sales: $10-20 Million
Number Employees: 50-99

19368 Badger Wood Arts
PO Box 44698
Racine, WI 53404-7015

414-636-9902
Fax: 888-703-0383 800-331-9663
We design and produce food displays for retail point of sale
Estimated Sales: $1-5 Million

19369 Bag Company
1650 Airport Rd NW
Suite 104
Kennesaw, GA 30144-7039

770-422-4187
Fax: 800-417-7273 800-533-1931
www.bagco.com
Manufacturer and exporter of polyethylene and polypropylene bags; importer of plastic bags.
Director of Marketing: Katherine Remick
Estimated Sales: $13 Million
Number Employees: 10-19
Type of Packaging: Consumer

19370 Bag Masters
1540 19th St N
St Petersburg, FL 33713-5730

727-894-6797
Fax: 727-894-6734 800-330-2247
www.bagmastersusa.com
Converted and printed poly food and plastic bags
Owner: Eric Johannsen
eric@bagmastersusa.com
VP: Sandra Johannsen
General Manager: Eric Johannsen, Jr.
Estimated Sales: $1-2.5 Million
Number Employees: 10-19
Square Footage: 60000

19371 Bagcraft Papercon
3900 W 43rd St
Chicago, IL 60632-3490

773-254-8000
Fax: 773-254-8204 800-621-8468
www.bagcraft.com
Manufacturer and exporter of foil, film, paper, window and coffee bags and tin-tie
Vice President: Chuck Hathaway
chathaway@pkdy.com
Vice President, General Manager: Dan Vice
Director of Marketing: Barak Bright
Vice President of Sales: Chuck Hathaway
Customer Service Manager: Fredia Hess
chathaway@pkdy.com
Vice President-Operations: Grady Wetherington
Number Employees: 250-499
Square Footage: 1860000
Parent Co: Packaging Dynamics
Brands:
 Cameo
 Dubl-Fresh
 Dubl-View
 Dubl-Wax

19372 Bags Go Green
13 Ruths Place
Sequim, WA 98382

360-681-3876
Fax: 360-681-4877 info@bagsgogreen.com
www.bagsgogreen.com
Eco-friendly reusable bags
Marketing: Hena Marrero

19373 Bahnson Environmental Specs
4412 Tryon Rd
Raleigh, NC 27606-4246

919-829-9300
Fax: 919-833-9476 800-688-5859
jwalters@bahnson.com www.eschambers.com
Designs, manufactures, installs, and services a diverse line of controlled environmental chambers that maintain precise conditions. We also offer a range of envionmental test and stability chambers designed for high demand testing.Typical uses include stability, shelf life studies, freezing, refrigeration, freeze-thaw and other product testing and/or stability storage.
Business Development: John Walters
Number Employees: 50-99

19374 Bailey Moore Glazer Schaefer
16 Lunar Dr
Woodbridge, CT 06525-2397

203-397-7700
Fax: 203-397-7717 800-443-2362
www.baileymoore.com
Tea and coffee industry espresso machines and accessories, grinders
Partner: John Mooney
Manager: John J Mooney
Estimated Sales: Less than $500,000
Number Employees: 20-49

19375 Bailly Showcase & Fixture Company
2213 Paseo Ct
Las Vegas, NV 89117

702-947-6885
Fax: 323-232-6157
Store fixtures, cabinets and showcases
President: Gus Bailly
Estimated Sales: $1-2,500,000
Number Employees: 20

19376 (HQ)Baird & Bartlett Company
157 Green Street
Foxboro, MA 02035-2868

508-923-6400
Fax: 508-923-6060 800-752-4958
Cake collars and cardboard
President: Andrew Poce
CFO: George Whalen
Marketing Director: Andrew Londergan
Sales Director: Darck Ellwood
Plant Manager: Leo Sousa
Purchasing Manager: Lisa Omalley
Estimated Sales: $15 Million
Number Employees: 20
Square Footage: 60000
Type of Packaging: Consumer, Food Service, Private Label, Bulk
Other Locations:
 Baird & Bartlett Co.
 Edison NJ

19377 Bake Star
1881 County Road C
Somerset, WI 54025-7508

763-427-7611
Fax: 763-323-9821 www.bakestar.com
Manufacturer and wholesaler/distributor of chocolate spiral shavers, pre-depanners, semi-automatic strawberry cappers, surplus topping removers and UV surface sterilizers
CEO: Sherri Stumpl
President: Gary Hanson
R & D: Roger Hanson
Contact: Gary Hanson
grh230377@msn.com
General Manager: Laura Tuckner
Estimated Sales: Below $5 Million
Number Employees: 10
Square Footage: 36000

19378 Baker & Co
3541 Argonne Ave
Norfolk, VA 23509-2156

757-853-4325
Fax: 757-855-6252 800-909-4325
info@bakersheetmetal.com
www.bakersheetmetal.com
A fabrictor of custom and standard stainless steel products including worktables, sinks, tables, worktables and workstations, shelves and shelving, countertops, furniture, range hoods, cabinets, galley furniture, food service linespartitions
President: John Kronske
johnkronske@bakerco.com
Treasurer: Randy Bristow
CFO: R E Baker
Quality Control: C Winkler
Sales Director: John Kronske
Plant Manager: Paul Johnson
Estimated Sales: $10-20 Million
Number Employees: 50-99
Square Footage: 100000

19379 Baker Cabinet Co
2931 Grace Ln # C
Costa Mesa, CA 92626-4132

714-540-5515
Fax: 714-540-5515
Wood cabinets and store fixtures
Manager: Jim Thomas
bakercabinet@dslextreme.com
CEO: Tom Ouellette
Manager: Jim Thomas
bakercabinet@dslextreme.com
Estimated Sales: Less Than $500,000
Number Employees: 1-4

19380 Baker Concrete Construction
900 N Garver Rd
Monroe, OH 45050

513-539-4000
800-539-2224
www.bakerconcrete.com
Industrial concrete floor slab systems.
President: Brad Wucherpfennig
Excutive Vice President: Tom Bell
President, Baker DC: Kenneth Fender
President, Northern Region: Todd Fox
Administration: Ben Goodin
President, Southwest Region: Jeff Miller
Human Resources: Mike Schneider
Year Founded: 1968
Estimated Sales: $856.94 Million
Number Employees: 1000-4999
Square Footage: 750000

19381 Baker Foodservice Design Inc
2220 East Paris Ave SE
Grand Rapids, MI 49546-6129

616-942-4011
Fax: 616-940-1415 800-968-4011
Marketing@BakerGroup.com
www.bakergroup.com
Award-winning foodservice consulting firm that has provided expert support in evaluation, planning and design for over two decades.
President/Principal: James Sukenik
consult@bakergroup.com
Estimated Sales: $1-2.5 Million
Number Employees: 5-9

19382 Baker Hughes
17021 Aldine Westfield
Houston, TX 77073

www.bakerhughes.com
Manufacturer and exporter of centrifuges and filters for liquid/solid separations.
Chairman & CEO: Lorenzo Simonelli
CFO: Brian Worell
EVP, Turbomachinery & Process Solutions: Rod Christie
Chief Marketing & Technology Officer: Derek Mathieson
Year Founded: 1907
Estimated Sales: $22.8 Billion
Number Employees: 67,000

19383 Baker Perkins Inc
3223 Kraft Ave SE
Grand Rapids, MI 49512-2063

616-785-7500
Fax: 616-784-0973 800-458-2560
eriknadig@invensys.com www.bakerperkins.com

Manufacturer, importer and exporter of food processing equipment including bakers and confectioners, mixing, forming, baking and product handling equipment
Vice President: Paul Abbott
paul.abbott@bakerperkinsgroup.com
VP: John Lucas
R&D: Mark Glover
Marketing: Erik Nagig
VP Sales: Paul Abbott
Manager Process Optimization: Dan Smith
Number Employees: 50-99
Square Footage: 240000
Parent Co: APV plc

19384 Bakers Choice Products
4 Railroad Avenue Ext
Railroad Avenue Ext.
Beacon Falls, CT 6403

203-720-1000
Fax: 203-720-1004
Manufacturer, importer and exporter of sanitary food containers and cups for candy, cookie and baking; also, hot dog trays
Estimated Sales: $1-5 Million
Number Employees: 50-99
Square Footage: 120000
Parent Co: Reynolds Metals Company
Brands:
 Baker's Choice
 Chef's Choice

19385 Bakers Pride Oven Company
145 Huguenot St Ste Mz1
New Rochelle, NY 10801

914-576-0745
Fax: 914-576-0605 800-431-2745
sales@bakerspride.com www.bakerspride.com
Manufacturer and exporter of char-broilers and pizza and counter top ovens
President: Hylton Jonas
VP: Tom Marston
Technical Writer: Daniel J Rivera
Quality Manager: Jim Ponnwitz
Estimated Sales: $20-50 Million
Number Employees: 100-249
Parent Co: APW/WYOTT Food Service Equipment
Brands:
 Bakers Pride

19386 Bakery Associates
7 White Pine Ln
Setauket, NY 11733-3953

631-751-4156
Fax: 631-751-4156
Computerized bakery systems and commerical bakery equipment including ovens, oven loaders and unloaders
President: John Granger
wilcoven@aol.com
Estimated Sales: $1-2.5 Million
Number Employees: 10-19

19387 Bakery Crafts
P.O.Box 37
West Chester, OH 45071

513-942-0862
Fax: 513-942-3835 800-543-1673
info@bakerycrafts.com
Cake decorations: kits, edible decorations, candles, and bakery supplies
President: San Guttman
Head of Marketing: Anne Rueho
Head of Sales: Keith Murcum
Contact: Shelley Adamson
s.adamson@bakerycrafts.com
Estimated Sales: $5-10 Million
Number Employees: 100-249

19388 Bakery Equipment Svc
118 Nevin Ave
Richmond, CA 94801-2900

800-842-4005
Fax: 510-236-7600 800-842-4005
www.bakery-equip.com
President: Kenneth Lind
Contact: Russell Cook
rcook@bakery-equip.com
Estimated Sales: $5-10 Million
Number Employees: 1-4

19389 Bakery Machinery & Fabrication
307 Bakery Ave
Peru, IL 61354

815-224-1306
Fax: 815-224-1396 www.bakerymachine.com
New and remanufactured bakery machinery for the cookie, cracker, snack food and pet food industry
President: Cloyd Barnes
Estimated Sales: $1-2.5 000,000
Number Employees: 20-49

19390 Bakery Machinery Dealers
908 Colin Drive
Holbrook, NY 11741

631-567-6666
Fax: 631-567-6703
Bagel making and baking equipment
National Sales Manager: Rick Morrison
Number Employees: 12
Square Footage: 16000

19391 Bakery Refrigeration & Services
1125 Old Dixie Highway
Lake Park, FL 33403-2348

561-882-1655
Fax: 561-842-8106 waltman@flips.net
President: William Altman
Estimated Sales: Less than $500,000
Number Employees: 20-49

19392 Bakery Systems
7246 Beach Dr SW 1
Ocean Isle Beach, NC 28469

910-575-2253
Fax: 910-575-5057 800-526-2253
Importer, exporter and wholesaler/distributor of bakery equipment nd supplies
President: Hayden O'Neil
patzcuaro@juno.com
Sales Manager: Lee Wagner
Estimated Sales: $2.5 Million
Number Employees: 5-9
Square Footage: 2000

19393 Bakeware Coatings
2915 Wilmarco Avenue
Baltimore, MD 21223-3223

410-664-2211
Fax: 410-664-1766
Coatings for baking pans and equipment

19394 Baking Machines
4577b Las Positas Road
Livermore, CA 94551-9615

925-449-3369
Fax: 925-449-2144 www.bakingmachines.com
Bagel, roll and variety systems, sheeter makeup lines, tortilla equipment, troughs, elevators, baking pans and carts, reciprocators, dustets, reservoirs, etc.; also, custom design engineering services available
President: James Long
VP of Sales: J William Long
Estimated Sales: $10-20 Million
Number Employees: 50-99
Square Footage: 30000

19395 Baking Technology Systems
5243 Royal Woods Pkwy # 120
Tucker, GA 30084-3081

770-270-5911
Fax: 770-270-5913
VP: Bob Miller
Sales Project Manager: Ben Marcum
Vice President, Director of Operations: Robert Miller
Purchasing Manager: Glenda Arrington
Estimated Sales: $1 Million
Number Employees: 10-19

19396 Bakipan
9251 Van Horne Way
Richmond, BC V6X 1W2
Canada

604-278-1762
Fax: 604-278-3697
Estimated Sales: $1-5 Million

19397 Bakon Food Equipment
10117 Sepulveda Boulevard
Suite 205
Mission Hills, CA 91345-2600

818-895-7303
Fax: 818-892-1095 800-TRY-BAKO

Bakery equipment, glaze sprayers, chocolate machines, tartlet machine, whipping cream machine
Estimated Sales: 700000
Number Employees: 2

19398 Bal Seal Engineering Inc
19650 Pauling
Foothill Ranch, CA 92610-2610

949-460-2100
Fax: 949-460-2300 800-366-1006
sales@balseal.com www.balseal.com
Manufacturer and exporter of spring loaded PTFE seals
President: Rob Sjostedt
CEO: Rick Dawson
rdawson@balseal.com
Sales Director: Michael Anderson
Estimated Sales: $20-50 Million
Number Employees: 250-499

19399 Bal/Foster Glass Container Company
1 Glass Pl
Port Allegany, PA 16743-1154

814-642-2521
Fax: 814-642-3204 www.sgcontainers.com
Manufacturer and exporter of glass bottles and jars
Plant Manager: Ed Stewart
Estimated Sales: $1-5 Million
Number Employees: 250-499

19400 Balchem Corp
52 Sunrise Park Rd
New Hampton, NY 10958

845-326-5600
www.balchem.com
Extensive line of encapsulated ingredients.
Chairman & CEO: Ted Harris
CFO: Martin Bengtsson
General Counsel: Mark Stach
Year Founded: 1967
Estimated Sales: $100-500 Million

19401 Baldewein Company
9109 Belden Avenue
Lake Forrest, IL 60045

847-455-1686
Fax: 847-455-1706 800-424-5544
info@baldeweinco.com www.baldeweinco.com
Manufacturer and exporter of food processing equipment including sanitary fittings, pumps, valves, hose assemblies, brushes, steelware and steam and water mixers
President: Valentin R Baldewein Jr
Sales: Tina Sanders
Treasurer: Val Baldwewin
Estimated Sales: Below $5 Million
Number Employees: 10
Square Footage: 40000
Brands:
   Alpha Laval Flo
   Lightnin
   S.S.
   S.S. Ware
   Sani-Tech
   Sparta
   Strahman
   Thermo-Tech
   Tri-Clover
   Vollrath

19402 Baldor Electric Co
5711 Rs Boreham Jr St
P.O. Box 2400
Fort Smith, AR 72901-8394

479-646-4711
Fax: 479-648-5792 www.baldor.com
Marketers, designers and manufacturers of industrial electric motors, mechanical power transmission products, drive and generators, specializing in products for the food and pharmaceutical industries. A member of the ABB group since2011.
CEO: Ronald Tucker
rtucker@baldor.com
VP, Finance and Corporate Secretary: Larry Johnston
EVP: Edward Ralston
VP, Channel Management: Chris Keyser
VP Marketing: Tracy Long
Vice President, Sales: Randy Colip
COO, Baldor Operations: Wayne Thurman
Estimated Sales: Over $1 Billion
Number Employees: 5000-9999
Square Footage: 4000000

19403 Baldor Electric Co
5711 Rs Boreham Jr St
P.O. Box 2400
Fort Smith, AR 72901-8394

479-646-4711
Fax: 479-648-5792 800-241-2886
rjfleig@ra.rockwell.com www.baldor.com
Controls, energy management
CEO: Ronald E Tucker
rtucker@baldor.com
Chief Engineer: Alex McCutcheon
Estimated Sales: Over $1 Billion
Number Employees: 5000-9999

19404 Baldwin Richardson Foods
#2390, One Tower Lane
Oakbrook Terrace, IL 60181

866-644-2732
www.brfoods.com
Liquid ingredient manufacturer specializing in signature sauces, dessert toppings, beverage and pancake syrups, specialty fruit fillings and condiments. The company also offers processing options such as hot-fill, cold-fillhomogenization, and emulsion.
President & CEO: Eric Johnson
Chief Financial Officer: Evelyn White
Sr. Director of Sales: Cara Hughes
Year Founded: 1916
Estimated Sales: $5-10,000,000
Number Employees: 200-500
Square Footage: 900000
Type of Packaging: Consumer, Food Service, Private Label, Bulk
Other Locations:
   Macedon Manufacturing Facility
   Macedon NY
   Williamson Manufacturing
   East Williamson NY
Brands:
   Mrs. Richardson Toppings
   Nance's Mustards

19405 Baldwin Supply Co
2306 Washington Ave N
Minneapolis, MN 55411-2223

612-338-5070
Fax: 612-338-4877 800-897-1964
ghansen@baldwinsupply.com
www.baldwinsupply.com
President: Dave LA Rue
dave@baldwinsupply.com
Estimated Sales: $3-5 Million
Number Employees: 10-19

19406 Baldwin/Priesmeyer
1235 Hanley Industrial Ct
Saint Louis, MO 63144

314-535-2800
Fax: 314-535-2887 www.baldwinflags.com
Banners, flags, flagpoles and advertising specialties
Manager: Jim Schaper
CFO: Jannet Alexander
VP: Jim Schaper
Estimated Sales: $30-50 Million
Number Employees: 5-9
Parent Co: Baldwin Regalia

19407 Balemaster
980 Crown Ct
Crown Point, IN 46307-2732

219-663-4525
Fax: 219-663-4591 sales@balemaster.com
Automatic horizontal balers
President: Cornel Raab Jr
Cmo: Mike Connell
sales@balemaster.com
VP Sales/Marketing: Samuel Finlay
Estimated Sales: $300,000-500,000
Number Employees: 100-249

19408 Ball Corp
10 Longs Peak Dr
Broomfield, CO 80021

303-469-3131
info@ball.com
www.ball.com
Aluminum and steel beverage and food containers; also, lids, metal plastic food and beverage packaging, steel household packaging, plastic pails, ball aerospace.

Chairman/President/CEO: John Hayes
VP/General Counsel/Corporate Secretary: Charles Baker
VP/Controller: Nate Carey
SVP/Chief Financial Officer: Scott Morrison
SVP/Chief Operating Officer: Daniel Fisher
SVP: Robert Strain
SVP, Human Resources & Administration: Lisa Pauley
VP, Communications & Corp. Relations: Courtney Reynolds
Year Founded: 1880
Estimated Sales: $11 Billion
Number Employees: 18,300
Type of Packaging: Consumer, Food Service, Private Label

19409 Ball Design Group
1170 E Champlain Dr # 120
Suite 120
Fresno, CA 93720-5026
559-434-6100
Fax: 559-447-8596 john@balldesign.com
www.balldesign.com
Log and brand mark design, advertising website design, package and label design, and trade show displays for the produce and fruit industry
President: John Ball
john@balldesign.com
Estimated Sales: Less Than $500,000
Number Employees: 1-4

19410 Ball Foster Glass
5195 Fermi Drive
Fairfield, CA 94534-1607
707-863-4061
Fax: 707-863-4042
Glass bottles and containers for food, wine, liquor and beer
Estimated Sales: $50-100 Million
Number Employees: 100
Parent Co: Saint-Gobain

19411 Ball Foster Glass Container Company
1000 N Mission St
Sapulpa, OK 74066-3149
918-224-1440
Fax: 918-224-5280 us.verallia.com
Soft drink and tea glass bottles
Quality Control: Robert Beets
Plant Manager: Pat Hogan
Estimated Sales: $1-5 Million
Number Employees: 250-499
Square Footage: 4800000
Parent Co: American National Can Company

19412 Ball Glass Container Corporation
4000 Arden Drive
El Monte, CA 91731-1806
626-448-9831
Fax: 626-279-3225
Glass jars, bottles and containers
Plant Manager: Rich O'Neil
Estimated Sales: $50-100 Million
Number Employees: 250-499
Parent Co: St. Gobain

19413 (HQ)Ballantyne Food Service Equipment
4350 McKinley St
Omaha, NE 68112
402-453-4444
Fax: 402-453-7238 800-424-1215
www.ballantyne-omaha.com
Manufacturer and exporter of commercial restaurant equipment including electric pressure and gas pressure fryers, gourmet grills, cook and hold barbecue ovens, smokers and rotisseries
President/CEO: John Wilmers
Senior VP: Ray Boegner
VP: Michael Nulty
Estimated Sales: $1-5 Million
Number Employees: 100-249
Square Footage: 400000
Parent Co: Ballantyne of Omaha
Type of Packaging: Food Service, Private Label
Brands:
   Ballatyne
   Ballatyne Smokers
   Bpe 2000

19414 Ballard & Wolfe Company
519 Interstate 30 #102
Rockwall, TX 75087-5408
214-704-8451
Fax: 817-652-1245 dbruner@ballardwolfe.com
www.ballardwolfe.com
Ice cream equipment
Estimated Sales: Below 1 Million
Number Employees: 2

19415 Balluff Inc
8125 Holton Dr
Florence, KY 41042-3009
859-727-2200
Fax: 859-727-4823 800-543-8390
balluff@balluff.com
Sensor, transducers and ID systems for automation
CEO: Chad Bramer
cbramer@bannerengineering.com
CEO: Kent Howard
Number Employees: 100-249

19416 (HQ)Bally Block Co
30 S 7th St
30 South Seventh Street
Bally, PA 19503-9665
610-845-7511
Fax: 610-845-7726 bbc@ballyblock.com
www.butcherblock.com
Manufacturer and exporter of cutting benches, blocks, tables and boards
President: James Reichart
Vice President of Sales and Marketing: Joe Barbercheck
Vice President Sales & Marketing: Pat Stanley
Vice President, Production: Emmet Wood
Estimated Sales: $5-10 Million
Number Employees: 50-99
Square Footage: 500000

19417 Bally Refrigerated Boxes Inc
135 Little Nine Rd
Morehead City, NC 28557-8483
252-240-2829
Fax: 252-240-0384 800-242-2559
ballysales@ballyrefboxes.com
www.ballyrefboxes.com
Walk-in cooler and freezers, refrigerated buildings, modular structures, blast chillers and refrigeration for the foodservice and scientific industries.
President: Michael Coyle
cm@ballyrefboxes.com
Sales Manager: William Strompf
Plant Manager: Alan Summers
Purchasing Manager: William Stomps
Estimated Sales: $20-50 Million
Number Employees: 250-499
Parent Co: United Refrigeration
Type of Packaging: Food Service
Other Locations:
   Bally Refrigerated Boxes
   King of Prussia PA
Brands:
   Thermo-Plug

19418 Ballymore Company
220 Garfield Ave
West Chester, PA 19380-4512
610-696-3250
Fax: 610-593-8615 www.ballymore.com
Safety ladders, hydraulic lifts and special work platforms
Manager: Tom Richardson
Estimated Sales: $5-10 Million
Number Employees: 20-49

19419 Baltimore Aircoil Co
7600 Dorsey Run Rd
Jessup, MD 20794-9328
410-799-1300
Fax: 410-799-6416 info@baltimoreaircoil.com
www.baltimoreaircoil.com
Manufacturer and marketer of heat transfer and ice thermal storage products that conserve resources and respect the environment.
President: Steve Duerwachter
Contact: Glenn Babcock
amy@aafame.ccsend.com
Estimated Sales: $17 Million
Number Employees: 20-49
Parent Co: Amsted Industries
Brands:
   Bacount
   Bacross

Baltibond
Baltidrive
Easy Connect
Ejector
Energy Miser
High K
Ice Chiller
Ice Logic
Iobio
M Logic

19420 Baltimore Aircoil Co
7600 Dorsey Run Rd
Jessup, MD 20794-9328
410-799-1300
Fax: 410-799-6416 info@baltaircoil.com
www.baltaircoil.com
President: Steve Duerwachter
Quality Control: John Hawkins
CFO: Robert Landstra
Contact: Glenn Babcock
amy@aafame.ccsend.com
Number Employees: 20-49

19421 Baltimore Sign Company
472 Cedar Haven Road
Arnold, MD 21012-1167
410-276-1500
Fax: 410-675-2420 www.baltimoresign.com
Signs, banners, displays, etc.; also, screen process and offset printing and collation
President: John Ferretti
Plant Manager: Hank Barret
Account Director: Kathie Schisler
Estimated Sales: $5-10 Million
Number Employees: 50-99

19422 Baltimore Spice Inc
9740 Reisterstown Rd
Owings Mills, MD 21117-4155
410-363-3209
Fax: 410-363-6619 800-376-0316
www.fuchsna.com
Spices
President: Jack M Irvin Jr
CEO: Del Almonia
padc@pworld.com
R&D: Elizabeth Morris
Quality Control: Joe Walters
Estimated Sales: $5-10 Million
Number Employees: 1-4

19423 Baltimore Tape ProductsInc
27 W Obrecht Rd
Sykesville, MD 21784-7702
410-795-0063
Printed and converted pressure sensitive labels and tape
Owner: Jeff Remmel
jeff.remmel@trw.com
Estimated Sales: Less Than $500,000
Number Employees: 1-4
Square Footage: 2000

19424 Bambeck Systems Inc
1921 Carnegie Ave # 3a
Santa Ana, CA 92705-5510
949-250-3100
Fax: 949-757-1610 800-334-3101
webmaster@bambecksystems.com
www.bambecksystems.com
President: Robert Bambeck
rjbambeck@bambecksystems.com
CFO: Anthony Fazzio
Quality Control: Anthony Fazzio
Estimated Sales: $5-10 Million
Number Employees: 20-49

19425 Bamco Belting
6 Andrews St
PO Box 8678
Greenville, SC 29601-3902
864-269-9750
Fax: 864-269-9754 800-258-2358
sales@bamcobelting.com www.bamcobelting.com
Distributor of flat transmission belting and textile, conveyor belting, and hose belt conveyors
President: Leonard Chace
Estimated Sales: $5-10 Million
Number Employees: 10-19
Type of Packaging: Bulk

19426 Bancroft Bag Inc
425 Bancroft Blvd
West Monroe, LA 71292-5703
318-387-2550
Fax: 318-324-2318 bbisales@bancroftbag.com
www.bancroftbag.com
Paper bags
President: Louis Rothschild
lrothschild@bancroftbag.com
Executive Assistant: Teresa Lucas
Estimated Sales: $50-100 Million
Number Employees: 250-499

19427 Banner Chemical Co
111 Hill St
Orange, NJ 07050-3901
973-676-0105
Fax: 973-676-4564 info@bannerchemical.com
www.bannerchemical.com
Cleaning products and sanitary maintenance chemicals including glass cleaners, floor cleaners, wates and strippers, kitchen and bathroom cleaners, disinfectants and many other chemicals for food service and industry.
President: Stanley Reichel
bannerchem@aol.com
VP: David Herman
Estimated Sales: $2.5-5 Million
Number Employees: 5-9

19428 Banner Day
1840 N Michigan Ave # 1
Saginaw, MI 48602-5562
989-755-0584
Fax: 989-775-1309 info@banner-day.com
www.banner-day.com
CEO: Joseph Day
joeday@banner-day.com
Project Engineer: Brian Lewis
Estimated Sales: $5-10 Million
Number Employees: 10-19

19429 Banner Engineering Corp
9714 10th Ave N
Minneapolis, MN 55441-5093
763-544-3164
Fax: 763-544-3123 888-373-6767
www.bannerengineering.com
Photoelectric sensor, safety light curtains, ultrasonics, measurement and inspection sensors, safety modules, safety switches, fiber optics and vision sensors
President: Robert Fayfield
rfayfield@bannerengineering.com
CFO: Larry Evans
R&D: Neal Schumacher
Marketing: Christian E Benson
Sales: Charley Rapp
Estimated Sales: $50-100 Million
Number Employees: 250-499
Square Footage: 100000
Brands:
A Gage
Beam-Array
Beam-Tracker
Duo-Touch
Ez-Beam
Ez-Beam
Ez-Screen
Econo-Beam
L Gage
Machine-Guard
Maxi-Amo
Maxi-Beam
Micro-Amp
Micro-Screen
Mini-Array
Mini-Beam
Mini-Screen
Multi-Beam
Multi-Screen
Omni-Beam
Opto Touch
Pico Guard
Picodot
Presence Plus
Thin-Pak
Ultra-Beam
Ultra-Beam
Vall-Beam
Valu-Beam
World-Beam

19430 Banner Equipment Co
1370 Bungalow Rd
Morris, IL 60450-8929
815-941-9600
Fax: 815-941-9700 800-621-4625
internetsales@bannerbeer.com
www.bannerbeer.com
Manufacturer and exporter of draft beer tapping and dispensing equipment
President: Jim Groh
jgroh@bannerbeer.com
VP: Michael Tannhauser
Estimated Sales: $10-20 Million
Number Employees: 20-49
Square Footage: 80000
Brands:
Insta-Balance
Perfecta Line
Perfecta Pour

19431 Banner Idea
1400 Quail St
Newport Beach, CA 92660-2730
949-559-6600
Fax: 949-559-0861
Flags, pennants, banners and signs
Estimated Sales: less than $500,000
Number Employees: 5-9

19432 Bannerland
13360 Firestone Blvd Ste Ee
Santa Fe Springs, CA 90670-7040
Fax: 714-554-0579 800-654-0294
bannerland@aol.com
Banners, flags and poly pennants; also, silk screening available
Manager: Travis Townsend
Marketing/Sales: Terry Melanson
Plant Manager: Mike Slater
Estimated Sales: $26 Million
Number Employees: 10-19
Square Footage: 10000
Parent Co: AAA Flag & Banner

19433 Bar Equipment Corporation of America
7300 Flores Street
Downey, CA 90242
323-838-1770
Fax: 323-838-1778 888-870-2322
sales@lynxgrills.com www.lynxgrills.com
Bar equipment including undercounter refrigerators, bottle coolers, mug frosters and hand sinks
President: Michael Edwards
Director Sales: Dale Seiden
Estimated Sales: $3-5 Million
Number Employees: 5-9

19434 Bar Keepers Friend Cleanser
5240 Walt Pl
Indianapolis, IN 46254-5795
317-636-7760
Fax: 317-264-2192 800-433-5818
www.barkeepersfriend.com
Manufacturer and exporter of powdered and liquid cleansers for the removal of rust, lime, stains and mildew; also, polishes, bathroom and toilet bowl cleaners
President: Nick Childers
nchilders@barkeepersfriend.com
VP Sales: Tony Patterson
Estimated Sales: $20-50 Million
Number Employees: 20-49
Square Footage: 30000
Parent Co: SerVaas
Type of Packaging: Consumer, Private Label
Brands:
Bar Keepers Friend
Copper Glo
Just 'n Time
Shiny Sinks Plus

19435 Bar Maid Corp
2950 NW 22nd Ter
Pompano Beach, FL 33069-1045
954-960-1468
Fax: 954-960-1647 info@barmaidwashers.com
www.barmaidwashers.com
Manufacturer and exporter of portable, submersible and upright electric glass and muffin pan washers; also, low-sud detergents and sanitizers

President: George E Shepherd
CEO: Diane Michaud
diane@barmaidwashers.com
Marketing Director: Tammie Rice
Estimated Sales: Below $5 Million
Number Employees: 10-19
Number of Brands: 2
Square Footage: 16000
Brands:
Bar Maid
Losuds

19436 Bar NA, Inc.
PO Box 6599
Champaign, IL 61826-6599
217-687-4810
Fax: 217-687-4830 www.baraninc.com
Manufacturer, distribution and installation of small to medium capacity equipment for soy foods and vegetable oilseeds production and processing
President: Ramlakhan Boodram
Estimated Sales: $1-2.5 Million
Number Employees: 10-19

19437 Bar-B-Q Woods
800 E 14th Street
Newton, KS 67114-5700
316-284-0300
Fax: 316-283-8371 800-528-0819
www.flavorwood.com
Compressed wood in a can which is heated in a home Bar-B-Q grill to produce natural smoke blowing
President: Gary Hawkey
CEO: James Beery
Estimated Sales: $1-2,500,000
Number Employees: 4
Square Footage: 10000
Type of Packaging: Consumer, Food Service, Private Label, Bulk

19438 Bar-Maid Corp
362 Midland Ave # 1
Garfield, NJ 07026-1736
973-478-7070
Fax: 973-478-2106 800-227-6243
www.bar-maid.com
Refrigerators, minibars and freezers
President: George Steele
CEO: James Steele
Vice President: John Steele
Marketing Director: Ken Lasini
Sales Director: K Zanda
Public Relations: Mike Castle
Estimated Sales: $50-100 Million
Number Employees: 50-99
Square Footage: 80000
Brands:
Bar-Maids

19439 Bar-Ron Industries
58 Bryant Drive
Livingston, NJ 07039-1725
973-535-1406
Fax: 973-597-1996 www.grillit.com
Owner: Barry N Rein
Sales: Cindy Blanga
Sales: Rafi Blanga
Estimated Sales: $3-5 Million
Number Employees: 20-49
Brands:
Grillit 1200
Grillit 12x12

19440 Barbeque Wood Flavors Enterprises
141 Lyons Road
Ennis, TX 75119
972-875-8391
Fax: 972-875-8872
Manufacturer and exporter of wood firelogs
President and CEO: George C Wartsbaugh
Sales Manager: Charles Wartsbaugh
Estimated Sales: $5-10 Million
Number Employees: 10
Square Footage: 92000
Parent Co: Stephen Weber Production Company

19441 Barbour Threads
128 W 7th St
Anniston, AL 36201-5645
256-237-9461
Fax: 256-237-0646
Industrial nets and sports nets

President: Tony Foran
Plant Manager: Jim Landers
Estimated Sales: $5-10 Million
Number Employees: 50-99
Square Footage: 848000

19442 Barclay & Assoc PC
1525 Airport Rd # 101
Suite 101
Ames, IA 50010-8231

515-292-3023
Fax: 515-292-3053 tmbarclay@aol.com
Consultant providing automation solutions
President: T Michael Barclay
Contact: Dori Gass
dori@drbarclay.com
Estimated Sales: Less Than $500,000
Number Employees: 1-4
Brands:
 Margin Minder Software
 Watch Dog

19443 Barco Inc
3059 Premiere Pkwy
Duluth, GA 30097-4905

678-475-8000
Fax: 678-475-8100 www.barco.com
Optical and X-ray sorting inspection equipment
President: Mohammad Abu-Dalou
mohammad.abu-dalou@barco.com
Operations: Danny Claeys
VP Sales/Marketing: Richard McConeghy
Estimated Sales: $5-10 Million
Number Employees: 250-499
Parent Co: Barco
Brands:
 Elbicon
 Pulsarr

19444 Barco Inc
3078 Prospect Park Dr
Rancho Cordova, CA 95670-6000

888-414-7226
Fax: 916-376-0318 888-414-7226
www.ready2escape.com
President & Chief Executive Officer: Eric Van Zele
Chief Financial Officer: Carl Peeters
GM International Sales: Ney Corsino
Chief Human Resources Officer: Jan Van Acoleyen
Chief Operating Officer: Filip Pintelon
Estimated Sales: Less Than $500,000
Number Employees: 1-4
Parent Co: Barco

19445 Barcoding Inc
2220 Boston St # 2
Fl 2
Baltimore, MD 21231-3205

410-385-8532
Fax: 410-385-8559 888-412-7226
info@barcoding.com www.barcoding.com
Barcoding Inc works with companies within the
Food and Beverage Industry to streamline their op-
erations through the implementation of barcode and
RFID systems.
CEO: Jay Steinmetz
jays@barcoding.com
Media/Public Relations: Jon Stroz
Number Employees: 50-99
Type of Packaging: Consumer

19446 Bardes Plastics Inc
5225 W Clinton Ave
Milwaukee, WI 53223-4782

414-354-5300
Fax: 414-354-6331 800-558-5161
sales@bardesplastics.com
www.bardesplastics.com
Plastic and display boxes, lids, covers, food trays,
sleeves, beaded rounds and cylindrical trays
President: Michael Heyer
CEO: Randolph Hamner
Sales: Steve Kopiske
Estimated Sales: $5-10 Million
Number Employees: 20-49
Square Footage: 160000
Type of Packaging: Consumer, Food Service, Pri-
vate Label, Bulk

19447 Bardo Abrasives
1666 Summerfield St
Ridgewood, NY 11385

718-456-6400
Fax: 718-366-2104 www.bardoabrasives.com

Manufacturer and exporter of blending, finishing
and buffing wheels for food processing equipment
President: Edwin F Doyle
VP: Ted Wood
Estimated Sales: $20-50 Million
Number Employees: 100-249
Square Footage: 90000
Parent Co: Barker Brothers
Brands:
 Bardo Flex
 Bardo Flex Deburring Wheels
 Barker Buffs

19448 Bargreen Ellingson
6626 Tacoma Mall Blvd # B
Tacoma, WA 98409-9002

253-722-2600
Fax: 253-896-3620 800-322-4441
www.bargreen.com
Restaurant equipment and supplies; interior and en-
gineering design services available
Owner: Paul G Ellingson
paul.ellingson@bargreen.com
President: Paul G Ellingson
Estimated Sales: $20-50 Million
Number Employees: 10-19

19449 Bargreen Ellingson
2925 70th Avenue East
Fife, WA 98424

425-740-2424
Fax: 425-740-2432 866-722-2665
Restaurant equipment, restaurant supplies, kitchen
supplies, bar supplies, janitorial supplies,
disposables, and restaurant design services.
President: Howard Bargreen
Sales Manager: Josh Pugh
Contact: Brie Adair
b.adair@bargreen.com
Estimated Sales: $10-20 Million
Number Employees: 10-19
Parent Co: American Restaurant Supply
Brands:
 Bargreens
 Cafe Amore
 Golden Drip

19450 Barker Company
703 Franklin St
P.O. Box 478
Keosauqua, IA 52565

319-293-3777
Fax: 319-293-3776 sales@bakercompany.com
www.barkercompany.com
Manufacturer and importer of refrigerated, hot and
dry display cases
President: Pat Mahon
Contact: Amanda Brauns
amanda.brauns@barkercompany.com
Estimated Sales: $10-20,000,000
Number Employees: 250-499
Square Footage: 84000

19451 Barker Wire
708 Water St
Keosauqua, IA 52565-7711

319-293-3176
Fax: 319-293-3182 www.barkerwire.com
Custom wire shelves, baskets and racks
Sales Manager: Roy Abriani
Plant Manager: Larry Begley
Estimated Sales: $10-20 Million
Number Employees: 50-99
Square Footage: 580000
Parent Co: Angola Wire Products
Other Locations:
 Barker Wire Products
 Angola IN

19452 Barkley Filing Supplies
PO Box 15789
Hattiesburg, MS 39404-5789

601-545-2200
Fax: 800-423-7589 800-647-3070
Stationery including envelopes and pressure sensi-
tive labels
President: Joseph Compitello
Number Employees: 475

19453 Barksdale Inc
3211 Fruitland Ave
Vernon, CA 90058-3757

323-589-6181
Fax: 323-589-3463 mmueller@barksdale.com
www.barksdale.com

President: Ian Dodd
CFO: Dave Hefler
dave.hefler@barksdale.com
Estimated Sales: G
Number Employees: 100-249
Parent Co: Crane Company

19454 Barliant & Company
319 E Van Emmon St
Yorkville, IL 60560

630-553-6992
Fax: 630-553-6908 barliant@aol.com
www.barliant.com
Domestic and export broker of new and used food
processing equipment including meat and poultry, as
well as appraisals, liquidations, auctions and asset
management programs.
Owner: Scott Swanson
Sales Manager: Kevin Chapman
Contact: Tom Baumgartner
tom@centralice.com
Estimated Sales: $1.5 Million
Number Employees: 5
Square Footage: 152000

19455 Barlo Signs
158 Greeley St
Hudson, NH 03051-3422

603-880-8949
Fax: 603-882-7680 800-227-5674
www.barlosigns.com
Electric and interior point of purchase signs; also,
screen printing available
President: Arthur Bartlett
Estimated Sales: $10-20 Million
Number Employees: 250-499
Parent Co: Barlo Group

19456 Barn Furniture Mart
6206 Sepulveda Blvd
Van Nuys, CA 91411-1110

818-785-4253
Fax: 818-785-4564 888-302-2276
www.barnfurnituremart.com
Manufacturer and exporter of chairs, barstools, bars,
tables and booths; custom designing services avail-
able
Owner: Leon Tuberman
manya3@aol.com
VP: Leon Tuberman
Number Employees: 20-49
Square Footage: 840000

19457 Barnant Company
28092 W Commercial Ave
Lake Barrington, IL 60010

847-381-7050
Fax: 847-381-7053 800-637-3739
barnant@barnant.com www.barnant.com
Thermometers, tubing and vacuum pumps, control-
lers, data loggers, flow meters and mixers, and OEM
pumps
President: Duncan Ross
Marketing: Greg Johnson
Marketing Director: Gregg Johnson
Contact: Jan Stadt
stadtj@barnant.com
Estimated Sales: $20-50 Million
Number Employees: 100-249

19458 Barnes Machine Company
2462 Emerson Avenue S
Saint Petersburg, FL 33712-1644

727-327-9452
Fax: 727-323-8791
Packaging machinery including carton erecting,
closing, paper box, carton case, box sealing, etc
President: John Barnes
barnesmco@aol.com
CFO: Carla Barnes
Quality Control: John Barnes
Estimated Sales: Below $5 Million
Number Employees: 10 to 19
Square Footage: 30000
Brands:
 Barnes Machine Company Bamco

19459 Barnstead/Thermolyne Corporation
P.O.Box 797
Dubuque, IA 52004-0797

563-556-2241
Fax: 563-589-0516 800-553-0039
www.barnstead.com

Laboratory equipment
President: Duncan Ross
CEO: Guy Broadband
Quality Control: Mike Reagan
Marketing Communication Officer: Kathy Regan
Estimated Sales: $50-100 Million
Number Employees: 250-499

19460 Baron Spices Inc
1440 Kentucky Ave
St Louis, MO 63110-3817

314-535-9020
Fax: 314-535-7227 sales@baronspices.com
www.baronspices.com
Wholesaler/distributor and contract packager of
spices, seasonings, herbs, flavors and extracts
President: Tim Weigers
tewiegers@baronspices.com
Estimated Sales: $5-10 Million
Number Employees: 20-49
Number of Products: 300
Square Footage: 220000
Type of Packaging: Food Service, Private Label,
Bulk
Brands:
Baron

19461 Barr Engineering Co
4700 W 77th St # 200
Minneapolis, MN 55435-4820

952-832-2600
Fax: 952-832-2601 800-632-2277
askbarr@barr.com www.barrengineering.com
Consulting engineering services
President: Doug Connell
R&D: Karin Clemon
CEO: Doug Conell
CFO: Terry Krohnverg
Contact: Lisa Andrews
eandrews@barr.com
Estimated Sales: $20-30 Million
Number Employees: 1-4

19462 Barr Refrigeration
1423 Planeview Dr
Oshkosh, WI 54904-9101

920-231-1711
Fax: 920-231-1701 888-661-0871
info@barrinc.com www.barrinc.com
Refrigeration equipment
VP, Sales: Erick Alatorre
Estimated Sales: D
Number Employees: 20-49

19463 Barr Storage
1423 Planeview Dr
Oshkosh, WI 54904-9101

920-230-2600
Fax: 920-231-1701 888-661-0871
info@barrinc.com www.barrstorage.com
Refrigeration equipment
Owner: Thomas Barr
info@barrinc.com
Vice President: Jamie Barr
VP Marketing: Steve Morehead
Number Employees: 20-49

19464 Barr-Rosin
92 Boulevard Prevost
Boisbriand, QC J7G 2S2
Canada

450-437-5252
Fax: 450-437-6740 800-561-8305
sales.barr-rosin.ca@gea.com
President: Dell Lonvrgan
Quality Control: Haldgoudrvaulg Goudrvaulg
R & D: Paull Goudrvaulg
Number Employees: 10

19465 Barrette Outdoor Living
7830 Freeway Cir
Cleveland, OH 44130-6307

440-891-0790
Fax: 440-891-5267 800-336-2383
www.barretteoutdoorliving.com
Manufacturer and exporter of structural foam products, regular and tote trays, pallets, carts, plant displays, produce tables, lattice panels, plastic trellises,
plastic arbors and plastic fencing

President: Karin Golan
karin.golan@us.ebarrette.com
CFO: Nick Kokotovich
Vice President: William Goslin
Marketing Director: Ron Smith
Sales Director: John Payne
Product Manager: Mark Sprague
Purchasing Manager: Steve Armstrong
Number Employees: 1000-4999
Square Footage: 1400000

19466 Barrington Nutritionals
500 Mamaroneck Avenue
Harrison, NY 10528

914-381-3500
Fax: 914-381-2232 800-684-2436
info@barringtonchem.com
www.barringtonchem.com
Offers custom granulation, blending and particle
size reduction of products for the vitamin/nutrition
industry
Owner: Stuart Gelbard
Vice President: Vice President
Controller: Cathy Annattone
cathyannattone@barringtonnutritionals.com *Year
Founded:* 1991
Other Locations:
Utah Office
Bountiful UT

19467 Barrington Packaging Systems Group
500 Mamaroneck Ave # 201
Harrison, NY 10528-1636

914-381-3500
Fax: 914-381-2232 888-814-7999
sales@bpsgusa.com
Supplier of packaging equipment.
President: George Burny
Vice President-Marketing: Tom McClure
Sales Executive: Brian Fuller
Digital Data & eMarketing Director: Danny Lena
Chief Operating Officer: Larry Pence
Number Employees: 5-9

19468 Barrow-Agee Laboratories Inc
1555 Three Pl
Memphis, TN 38116-3507

901-332-1590
Fax: 901-398-1518 mhawkins@balabs.com
www.balabs.com
Analytical testing firm offering chemical and micro-
biological services
President: Lynn Hawkins
lhawkins@balabs.com
VP: Mike Hawkins
VP: John Peden
Estimated Sales: $2.5-5 Million
Number Employees: 20-49

19469 Barrow-Agee Laboratories Inc
1555 Three Pl
Memphis, TN 38116-3507

901-332-1590
Fax: 901-398-1518 customerservice@balabs.com
www.balabs.com
Private analytical laboratory
President and CEO: Lynn Hawkins
lhawkins@balabs.com
Estimated Sales: $5-10 Million
Number Employees: 20-49

19470 Barry Wehmiller DesignGroup
P.O.Box 245
New London, NH 3257

603-526-2585
Fax: 603-526-9468 866-526-2585
Full service engineering, architectural and construc-
tion management firm specializing in the food and
beverage industry
President: Robert Stahlman
VP: Scott Pribula
Marketing: Scott Pribula
Estimated Sales: $5-10 Million
Number Employees: 50-99
Square Footage: 15000

19471 Barry Wehmiller Design
1006 Windward Ridge Pkwy
Alpharetta, GA 30005

770-667-6250
Fax: 770-667-6251 800-667-6250
info@cadencetech.com www.cadencetech.com

Consultant and design engineer specializing in sys-
tems integration and project management; installa-
tion services available
Owner: G H Brink
VP: David Bryant
Estimated Sales: $5-10 Million
Number Employees: 20-49
Square Footage: 26000

19472 Barry-Wehmiller Companies
8020 Forsyth Blvd
Clayton, MO 63105

314-862-8000
Fax: 314-862-8858 www.barrywehmiller.com
Leader in the packaging automation industry,
world-wide provider of advanced technologies in
filling, closing, converting, labeling, conveying,
cartoning, case packing, and shrink-wrapping.
Chairman & CEO: Robert Chapman
Chief People Officer: Rhonda Spence
Group President, Paper & Converting: Tim Sullivan
Group President, Packaging: Carol O'Neill
Group President, Consulting: Joseph Wilhelm
Vice President, Finance: William Kuhn
Director, Marketing: Sarah Guptill
Director, Communications: Mary Rudder
Director, Organizational Development: Laurie
Ferrendelli
Director, Operations: Bruce Kuebler
Estimated Sales: $440 Million
Number Employees: 1000-4999

19473 Barry-Wehmiller Design Group
8020 Forsyth Blvd
St Louis, MO 63105-1707

314-862-8000
Fax: 314-862-2921 sales@barry-wehmiller.com
www.bwdesigngroup.com
Engineer consultant specializing in turnkey and line
monitoring systems and project site management;
also, feasibility studies, training programs, electrical
control panels, validation, servo-motion control sys-
tems, equipmentprocurement and installation
services available
Chairman/ CEO: Bob Chapman
VP/ CFO: Jim Lawson
Partner: Robyn Pikey
Director, Corporate Development: Jeff Giles
Chief Information Officer: Craig Hergenroether
Estimated Sales: F
Number Employees: 100-249
Square Footage: 16000
Parent Co: Barry-Wehmiller Company
Other Locations:
Barry-Wehmiller Design Group
Cuyahoga Falls OH

19474 Baruch Box Company
85 South Bragg Street
Suite 503
Alexandria, VA 22312

703-642-0472
Fax: 703-941-7645 800-242-6948
ahe@baruchco.com www.baruchco.com
Boxes, crates, and baskets made out of wood. Wire,
wicker and combination baskets, terra cotta, porce-
lain, silverplate
President: Andrew Eyck
ahe@baruchco.com
Estimated Sales: $2.5-5 000,000
Number Employees: 5-9

19475 Basic Adhesives
25 Knickerbocker Ave
Brooklyn, NY 11237

718-497-5200
Fax: 718-366-1425 info@basicadhesives.com
www.basicadhesives.com
President: Yale E Block Block
Contact: Michael Basch
mbasch@basicadhesives.com
Estimated Sales: $5-10 Million
Number Employees: 60

19476 Basic Concepts
6907 Mount Pleasant Dr
West Bend, WI 53090

262-247-2536
Fax: 262-673-2069 bio@execpc.com
www.execpc.com
SIS-Automatic saltine systems for cheese
President: James C Fischer
Estimated Sales: $1.6 000,000
Number Employees: 5-9

19477 (HQ)Basic Leasing Corporation
12a Port Kearny
Kearny, NJ 07032-4612
973-817-7373
Consultant specializing in the design of industrial kitchens; exporter of ice makers, dishwashers, etc.; importer of ice machines; wholesaler/distributor of equipment and fixtures and frozen drink machines and coffee machines
President: Harold Weber
VP: Johnathan Weber
Estimated Sales: $20-50 Million
Number Employees: 50-99
Square Footage: 28500

19478 Basic Polymers Industrial Flooring Systems
3628 W Holland Ave
Fresno, CA 93722-7808
559-230-1500
Fax: 559-266-6007 877-225-2549
www.basicpolymers.com/
Industrial flooring systems product line of which includes urethane, epoxy, MMA, flooring.
Owner: Jose Gonzalez
Sales Representative: Scott Hamilton

19479 Basiloid Products Corp
312 N East St
Elnora, IN 47529-3002
812-692-5511
Fax: 812-692-5512 866-692-5511
basiloid@dmrtc.net www.basiloid.net
Mechanical lift truck attachments
Owner: Rob French
rfrench@basiloid.com
Estimated Sales: $10-20 Million
Number Employees: 10-19

19480 Baskets Extraordinaires
1150 Shames Dr
Westbury, NY 11590
212-929-7259
Fax: 212-929-6124 800-666-1685
presentz@aol.com
Gift baskets
Owner: Michele Triester
Estimated Sales: less than $500,000
Number Employees: 5-9

19481 Batch
Boston, MA
617-416-1061
www.batchicecream.com
Manufacturer of natural ice cream.
Co-Owner: Susie Parish
Co-Owner: Veronica Janssens
Brands:
  batch

19482 Batching Systems
50 Jibsail Dr
Prince Frederick, MD 20678-3467
410-414-8111
Fax: 410-414-8121 800-311-0851
info@BatchingSystems.com
www.batchingsystems.com
Manufacturer and exporter of optical part counting, scanning, filling and batching machines.
Owner: Don Wooldridge
Marketing: Raven Easton
Sales: David Wooldridge
sales@batchingsystems.com
Estimated Sales: $10-20 Million
Number Employees: 20-49
Brands:
  Bagmaster
  Batchmaster

19483 Batchmaster
PO Box 1303
Fayetteville, AR 72702-1303
479-521-9208
Fax: 479-442-5860 sales@bmaster.com
Owner: Paul Reagan
sales@bmaster.com
Estimated Sales: $1-3 Million
Number Employees: 5-9

19484 Batchmasters Software
23191 LA Cadena Dr # 101
Suite 101
Laguna Hills, CA 92653-1429
949-583-1646
Fax: 949-296-0912 info@batchmaster.com
www.batchmaster.com
PC-based software products designed specifically for controlling inventory, production, formulation, costing, etc
Owner: David Stanyo
President, Chief Executive Officer: Sahib Dudani
sdudani@batchmaster.com
Vice President, General Manager: Ingrid Leon
VP of Sales: Christy Hudson
Technical Specialist: Jeremy Wheaton
Number Employees: 100-249
Brands:
  Batchmaster

19485 Baublys Control Laser
2419 Lake Orange Dr
Orlando, FL 32837
407-926-3500
Fax: 407-926-3590 866-612-8619
clcsales@controllaser.com www.controllaser.com
Fully integrated lasers and mechanical coding, marking, engraving, deep engraving, and 3D engraving systems and solution for the aerospace, automotive, coining and jewerly, consumer/commercial, electronic, medical, mold and diepackaging, tooling and trophy and awards industries. Our Laser Markink Systems are available: 10 Watt, 25 Watt, 50 Watt and CO2 with wigh power Nd:YAD and Nd:YLF lamp and diode pumped infrared, Green, UV and Deep UV systems.
President: Steve Graham
CEO: Antoine Dominic
Marketing Director: Monica Correal
Contact: Michele Fencik
mfencik@controllaser.com
Number Employees: 50-99
Number of Products: 20
Square Footage: 104000
Parent Co: Excel Technology
Brands:
  Instamark Script
  Instamark Signature
  Instamark Stylus

19486 Bauermeister
601 Corporate Woods Pkwy
Vernon Hills, IL 60061-3111
847-415-5293
Fax: 847-793-8611 info@bauermeisterusa.com
www.bauermeisterusa.com
Food processing and chocolate machinery
President: Jeff Soldan
Estimated Sales: Below $5 Million
Number Employees: 10

19487 Baumer Limited
122 Spring St # C6
Suite C6
Southington, CT 06489-1534
860-621-2121
Fax: 860-628-6280 www.baumernet.com
President: Mike Labieniec
labieniec@baumer.com.br
Owner: Ken Talentino
Estimated Sales: $1-5 Million
Number Employees: 20-49

19488 Baumuller LNI
117 W Dudley Town Rd
Bloomfield, CT 06002
860-243-0232
Fax: 860-286-3080 info@baumuller.com
www.baumuller.com
Contact: Chris Davis
c.davis@baumuller.com
Estimated Sales: $3-5 Million
Number Employees: 10-19

19489 Baur Tape & Label Co
130 Lombrano St
San Antonio, TX 78207-1832
210-738-3000
Fax: 210-738-0070 877-738-3222
baurlabel@swbell.net www.baurlabel.com
Manufacturer and exporter of shipping and metal labels

President: Leonard Humble
baurlabel@swbell.net
Sales Manager: Peter Humble
Estimated Sales: $1-2.5 Million
Number Employees: 5-9
Square Footage: 8000
Type of Packaging: Consumer, Food Service, Private Label, Bulk

19490 Baxter Manufacturing Inc
19220 State Route 162 E
Orting, WA 98360-9236
360-893-5554
Fax: 360-893-6836 800-777-2828
www.baxtermfg.com
Manufacturer and exporter of bakery and deli equipment including rack and revolving ovens, proof boxes, fryers, inventory supply items, ingredient bins, molders and dividers
Design/Marketing Manager: Laura Barrentine
Manager: Gabrielle Devault
gabrielle.devault@baxtermfg.com
Estimated Sales: $1-5 Million
Number Employees: 100-249
Square Footage: 228000
Parent Co: Hobart Corporation

19491 Bay Area Pallet Company/IFCO Systems
13100 Northwest Fwy # 625
Houston, TX 77040-6340
713-332-6145
Fax: 713-332-6146 877-430-4326
info@ifcosystems.com www.ifco-us.com
Re-manufacturer of wooden pallets and skids
President IFCO Systems North America: David Russell
Chairman: Bernd Malmstrom
Senior Vice President, Chief Financial O: Rich Hamlin
Senior VP: Mike Hachtman
Vice President of Sales: Dan Martin
Chief Operating Officer: Wolfgang Orgeldinger
Estimated Sales: $20-50 Million
Number Employees: 1,000-4,999
Parent Co: IFCO Systems

19492 Bayard Kurth Company
19321 Mount Elliott St
Detroit, MI 48234-2724
313-891-0800
Fax: 313-891-8966
Manufacturer and exporter of advertising displays, decalcomanias and packaging materials
President: Bayard Kurth Jr
VP: Bayard Kurth
Estimated Sales: $5-10 Million
Number Employees: 5-9
Type of Packaging: Consumer, Food Service, Bulk

19493 Bayer Environmental
95 Chestnut Ridge Road
Montvale, NJ 07645
201-307-9700
Fax: 201-307-3438
President: Helmut Schramm
Estimated Sales: Below $5 Million
Number Employees: 50-99

19494 Bayer/Wolff Walsrode
7330 S Madison St
Willowbrook, IL 60527-5588
630-789-8442
Fax: 630-789-8489 800-882-9987
Flexible packages, gas packaging materials, modified atmospheric packaging, vacuum packaging materials
CEO: Timothy McDivit
Estimated Sales: $5-10 000,000
Number Employees: 20-49

19495 Bayhead Products Corp.
173 Crosby Rd
Dover, NH 03820-4356
603-742-3000
Fax: 603-743-4701 800-229-4323
sales@bayheadproducts.com
www.bayheadproducts.com
Plastic and steel industrial items, tilt and box trucks, self-dumping hoppers, pallet containers, barrels, boxes, containment trays, totes, cases, tanks, steel racks and carts; exporter of tilt trucks and boxes
President: Elissa Moore
sales@bayheadproducts.com

Estimated Sales: $1.9 Million
Number Employees: 20-49
Square Footage: 50000
Type of Packaging: Bulk
Brands:
  Haul-All

19496 Bayou Container & Supply Inc
14021 Hemley Rd
Coden, AL 36523-3146

251-824-2658
Fax: 251-824-2670 www.bayoucontainer.com
Owner/President: Mike Frederick
Estimated Sales: Less Than $500,000
Number Employees: 1-4

19497 Bayou Packing
9155 Little River Rd
Bayou La Batre, AL 36509

251-824-7710
Fax: 251-824-4061
Packages seafood
Owner: Richard Roush

19498 Bayside Motion Group
27 Seaview Boulevard
Port Washington, NY 11050-4610

516-484-5482
Fax: 516-484-5496 800-305-4555
www.baysideinfo.com
Manufacturer and exporter of environmentally
sealed gear heads
Marketing Coordinator: Paul Gallagher
Estimated Sales: $5-10 Million
Number Employees: 150

19499 Bbc Industries
5 Capper Dr
Pacific, MO 63069-3603

636-343-5600
Fax: 636-343-3952 800-654-4205
info@bbcind.com www.hotyogaheaters.com
Industrial conveyor ovens and heaters
President and CFO: Ronald Vinyard
ron@bbcind.com
Head of R&D and Quality Control: Everett Graham
Estimated Sales: $5-10 Million
Number Employees: 10-19
Square Footage: 90400
Brands:
  Baker's Best

19500 Bc Wood Products
11364 Air Park Rd
Ashland, VA 23005-3283

804-798-9154
Fax: 804-798-2672 info@bcwoodonline.com
www.bcwoodonline.com
Wooden pallets
Owner: Gordon Murdock
sales@bcwoodonline.com
Sales/Marketing: Reynolds Cowardin
Secretary/Treasurer: Carolyn Barrett
Purchasing Manager: Richard Barrett
Estimated Sales: $3-5 Million
Number Employees: 50-99
Square Footage: 100000

19501 Be & Sco
1623 N San Marcos
San Antonio, TX 78201-6436

210-734-5124
Fax: 210-737-3925 800-683-0928
sales@bescomfg.com www.minom.com
Manufacturer and exporter of flour tortilla and ta-
male equipment and grills
President: Robert Escamilla
robert@bescomfg.com
VP: Rosie Ecamilla
Estimated Sales: $2.5-5 Million
Number Employees: 20-49
Square Footage: 120000
Brands:
  Beta Max
  Beta-900
  Mini-Wedge Press
  Wedge Press

19502 Beach Filter Products
P.O. Box 505
555 Centennial Ave
Hanover, PA 17331

717-698-1403
Fax: 717-698-1610 800-232-2485
sales@beachfilters.com www.beachfilters.com
Manufacturer and exporter of compressed air filters,
desiccant dehumidification bags, and breather filters.
President: Wesley Jones
abuckley@beachfilters.com
Sales Manager: Lori Prickitt
Production Manager: Leslie Doll
Plant Manager/Purchasing: Leslie Doll
Estimated Sales: $500 Thousand-$1 Million
Square Footage: 16000
Type of Packaging: Consumer, Bulk
Brands:
  Polyclear Ii

19503 Beacon Engineering Co
162 Don Westbrook Ave S
Jasper, GA 30143-1161

706-692-6411
Fax: 706-692-3227 beacon6411@aol.com
www.beaconcan.com
Batch spinners, conveyors, cooling equipment,
candy cutting machines, and automatic feeders
Owner: Susie Shields
susie@beaconcan.com
Estimated Sales: $1-2.5 000,000
Number Employees: 5-9

19504 Beacon Inc
12223 S Laramie Ave
Chicago, IL 60803-3129

708-544-9900
Fax: 708-544-9999 800-445-4203
www.beaconmetals.com
Stainless steel equipment for meat and poultry pro-
cessing.
President: Jim Niemiec
sales@beaconmetals.com
Number Employees: 5-9

19505 Beacon Specialties
345 Bloome Street
New York, NY 10013

800-221-9405
Food service equipment parts and supplies including
drains, casters, burners, grates, faucets, mixer parts,
gaskets, refrigeration hardware, etc
VP: Steven Levine
Sales Manager: L Levine
Estimated Sales: $1-5 Million
Number Employees: 10
Square Footage: 10000

19506 Beam Industries
1700 W 2nd St
Webster City, IA 50595

515-832-4620
Fax: 515-832-6659 800-369-2326
lars.hybel@beamvac.com www.beamvac.com
Manufacturer and exporter of central vacuum
cleaner systems and parts
President: Russell S Minick
CFO: Dave Thompson
Commercial Sales Manager: Bill Smith
Contact: Joel Fritz
joelfritz@beamsind.com
Estimated Sales: $20-50 Million
Number Employees: 100-249
Square Footage: 100000
Brands:
  Beam

19507 Bean Machines
18619 Middlefield Rd
Sonoma, CA 95476-1998

707-996-0706
Fax: 707-996-0704
Manufacturer and exporter of soybean processing
equipment used to produce soy milk, tofu, yogurt,
etc.; importer of multiple filter centrifuges
President: W Rogers
CEO: S Fiering
Estimated Sales: $350,000
Number Employees: 6
Square Footage: 5600
Type of Packaging: Food Service

19508 Beaufurn
5269 US Highway 158
Advance, NC 27006-6905

336-941-3446
Fax: 336-941-3568 888-766-7706
info@beaufurn.com www.beaufurn.com
Manufacturer, importer and exporter of chairs and
tables
President/CEO: Bill Bongaerts
bill@beaufurn.com
CFO: Monique De Proost
Sales: Lou Ann Bogulski
Public Relations: Janet Stanford
Estimated Sales: $3-4 Million
Number Employees: 20-49

19509 Beaumont Products
1560 Big Shanty Dr NW
Kennesaw, GA 30144-7040

770-514-7400
Fax: 770-514-7400 800-451-7096
cnatu31927@aol.com
www.beaumontproducts.com
Fruit and vegetable wash, citrus based and glycerine
hand soaps, air fresheners and cleaners
Owner: Robert Rice
Vice President: Mark Woods
mwoods@beaumontproducts.com
Public Relations: Wat Bagley
Office Manager: Peggy Dunne
Estimated Sales: $10-20 Million
Number Employees: 20-49
Number of Brands: 5
Number of Products: 20
Square Footage: 52000
Parent Co: Beaumont Products, Inc.
Type of Packaging: Consumer, Private Label
Brands:
  Clearly Natural

19510 Beaverite Corporation
9794 Bridge St
Croghan, NY 13327-2327

315-346-6011
Fax: 315-346-6221 800-424-6337
www.beaverite.com
Menu covers
Manager: Lucy Kniseley
Quality Control: Tom Becker
VP Manufacturing: Bob Burns
Estimated Sales: $20-50 Million
Number Employees: 20-49
Brands:
  Beaverite

19511 Beayl Weiner/Pak
610 Palisades Drive
Pacific Palisades, CA 90272-2849

310-454-1354
Fax: 310-459-6545 weinerb@aol.com
Manufacturer and importer of flexible packaging
materials including printed and laminated roll stock,
bags and pouches
Owner: Jeanne Weiner
Number Employees: 95
Square Footage: 200000
Type of Packaging: Food Service, Private Label,
Bulk

19512 Beckart Environmental Inc
6900 46th St
Kenosha, WI 53144-1779

262-656-7680
Fax: 262-656-7699 www.beckart.com
Wastewater treatment equipment
President: Arthur Fedrigon
CEO: Tom Fedrigon
dfedrigon@beckart.com
CFO: Shawn Jensen
Estimated Sales: $5-10 000,000
Number Employees: 20-49

19513 Becker Brothers Graphite Co
39 Legion St
Maywood, IL 60153-2321

708-410-0700
Fax: 708-410-0701 sales@beckergraphite.com
www.beckergraphite.com
Self-lubricating and heat resistant graphite bushings,
bearings, seals, rings and plates

President: Cheryl Ivanovich
sales@beckergraphite.com
Sales: Linda Egelhart
Customer Service: Linda Egelhart
Director Operations: Pedro Espinoza
Plant Manager: Pedro Espinoza
Estimated Sales: $2.5-5,000,000
Number Employees: 5-9
Square Footage: 20000

19514 Becker Foods
15136 Goldenwest Cir
Westminster, CA 92683-5235

714-891-9474
www.beckerfoods.com
Custom processor and packager of; fresh and frozen
poultry, beef, pork, lamb, veal, cheese products, and
more
President: Stan Becker
stan@beckerfoods.com
Vice President: Dian Vendel
Number Employees: 5-9
Type of Packaging: Food Service, Private Label

19515 Beckhoff Automation
12150 Nicollet Ave S
Burnsville, MN 55337

952-890-0000
Fax: 952-890-2888 www.beckhoffautomation.com
President: Gram Harris
R&D: Gram Harris
Quality Control: Gram Harris
Managing Director: Arnold Beckhoff
Contact: Dirk Bechtel
d.bechtel@beckhoff.com
Estimated Sales: $5-10 Million
Number Employees: 20-49

19516 Beckman Coulter Inc.
250 S. Kraemer Blvd.
Brea, CA 92821-6232

714-993-5321
Fax: 800-232-3828 800-526-3821
www.beckmancoulter.com
Diagnostic instruments for pharmaceutical compa-
nies.
President: Julie Sawyer Montgomery
Senior VP/Chief Financial Officer: Mark Kuhn
Year Founded: 1935
Estimated Sales: Over $1 Billion
Number Employees: 10000+

19517 Becton Dickinson & Co.
1 Becton Dr.
Franklin Lakes, NJ 07417-1880

201-847-6800
Fax: 201-847-6475 www.bd.com
Diagnostic tests and instruments for microbiology.
President/COO: Thomas Polen
Executive Chairman: Vincent Forlenza
vincent_forlenza@bd.com
Executive VP/CFO/CAO: Christopher Reidy
Executive VP/General Counsel: Samrat Khichi
Executive VP/Chief Quality Officer: Davide Shan
Executive VP/Chief Marketing Officer: Tony Ezell
EVP/Chief Human Resources Officer: Betty Larson
Year Founded: 1897
Estimated Sales: $17.2 Billion
Number Employees: 70,000+

19518 Bedford Enterprises Inc
1940 W Betteravia Rd
Santa Maria, CA 93455-5926

805-922-4977
Fax: 805-928-7241 800-242-8884
bedfordscrap@gmail.com www.beibedford.com
Manufacturer and exporter of stainless platforms,
hand railing, stair treads, ladders and decking;
wholesaler/distributor of fiberglass gratings; instal-
lation services available
Vice President: Hugh Bedford
bedford@tcsn.net
VP: David Thomas
Estimated Sales: $1-2.5 Million
Number Employees: 10-19
Brands:
Bestdeck
Bestread

19519 Bedford Industries
1659 Rowe Ave
P.O. Box 39
Worthington, MN 56187

507-376-4136
Fax: 507-376-6742 800-533-5314
www.bedfordind.com
Manufacturer and exporter of identification ties and
tags, twist ties, recloseable twist ties, and
ElasitTag® Products.
President: Kim Milbrandt
CEO: Bob Ludlow
Marketing Director: Deb Houseman
Sales Director: Martin Rickers
Estimated Sales: $20-50 Million
Number Employees: 100-249
Square Footage: 84000

19520 Bedrosian & Assoc
525 Veterans Blvd # 102
Suite 102
Redwood City, CA 94063-1140

650-367-0259
Fax: 650-367-0599 www.bedrosian-associates.com
Consultant for new product development
Owner: Ron Bedrosian
rbedrosian@bedrosian-associates.com
Estimated Sales: less than $500,000
Number Employees: 10-19

19521 Beech Engineering
1134 Turnpike Road 73
Ashland, OH 44805

419-281-0894
Fax: 419-281-0894 hello@bright.net
Transfer carts, lift tables, mobile work stations,
stocking systems, etc
General Manager: Tracy McBride
Number Employees: 7

19522 Beehive- Provisur
9950 191st St
Mokena, IL 60448

801-561-4211
Fax: 801-562-5857 800-621-8438
jim.varney@provisur.com
Food processing equipment, meat industry
President/CEO: Nick Lesar
Director: James Varney
Number Employees: 20-49

19523 Beehive/Provisur Technologies
9100 191st Street
Mokena, IL 60448

708-479-3500
Fax: 708-479-3598 www.provisur.com
Food processing equipment.

19524 Beemak-IDL Display
16711 Knott Ave
La Mirada, CA 90638-6013

714-367-5580
Fax: 310-764-0330 800-421-4393
info@beemak.com www.beemak-idl.com
Manufacturer and exporter of displays and holders
for recipe cards, brochures and pamphlets
President: Robert Gray
robert@warden.com
CEO: Thomas Quinn
Finance Executive: Christy Harp
Manager Sales: Julia Alty
Estimated Sales: $10-20 Million
Number Employees: 50-99
Square Footage: 72000
Parent Co: Jordon Industries

19525 Beer Magic Devices
20 Railway Street
Hamilton, ON L8R 2R3
Canada

905-522-3081
Fax: 905-522-1957
Manufacturer, wholesaler/distributor and importer of
portion control dispensing machines for beer, wine
and liquor
President: Fred Palermo
Number Employees: 4

19526 Beford Technology
PO Box 609
Worthington, MN 56187-0609

507-372-5558
Fax: 507-372-5726 mail@bedfordtech.com
www.bedfordtech.com

Contact: Larson Brian
larson.brian@bedfordtech.com
Estimated Sales: $1-5 Million
Number Employees: 25-49

19527 Behlen Manufacturing Co.
4025 E. 23rd St.
Columbus, NE 68601

402-564-3111
Fax: 402-563-7441 behlen@behlenmfg.com
www.behlenmfg.com
Grain storage bins, steel buildings, and grain dryers.
CEO: Phil Raimondo
Chairman: Tony Raimondo
Senior VP: Lyle Burbach
Year Founded: 1936
Estimated Sales: $98.6 Million
Number Employees: 1000-4999
Number of Products: 3
Square Footage: 850000
Brands:
Behlen Big Bin
Berico Dryers

19528 Behn & Bates/Haver Filling Systems
460 Gees Mill Business Ct NE
Conyers, GA 30013-1569

770-760-1130
Fax: 770-760-1181 sales@haverusa.com
www.haverusa.com
High speed and in-line packaging systems
VP: Thomas Reckersdrees
Estimated Sales: $10-20 Million
Number Employees: 10-19

19529 Behnke Lubricants/JAX
W134 N 5373 Campbell Dr
Menomonee Falls, WI 53051

262-781-8850
Fax: 262-781-3906 800-782-8850
info@jax.com www.jax.com
Manufacturer and exporter of food grade and high
temperature synthetic lubricants
President: Eric Peter
Manager Central Region: Carter Anderson
Manager Western Region: Mitch Clark
Estimated Sales: $10-20 Million
Number Employees: 20-49
Parent Co: JAX
Brands:
Jax

19530 Behrens Manufacturing LLC
1250 E Sanborn St
Winona, MN 55987

507-454-4664
Fax: 507-452-2106
customerservice@behrensmfg.com
www.behrensmfg.com
Steel and metal containers.
President: Keith Dau Schmidt
CEO: Steve Tuscic
Year Founded: 1911
Estimated Sales: $10-20 Million
Number Employees: 50-99
Number of Brands: 1
Type of Packaging: Bulk

19531 Beistle Co
1 Beistle Plz
Shippensburg, PA 17257-9684

717-532-2131
Fax: 717-532-7789 sales@beistle.com
www.beistle.com
New Year's Eve party goods
President: Tricia Lacy
VP Marketing: David Goode
Marketing Director: Michael Fague
Estimated Sales: $50-75 Million
Number Employees: 250-499
Number of Products: 4000
Type of Packaging: Private Label

19532 Beka Furniture
259 Bradwick Drive
Concord, ON L4K 1L5
Canada

905-669-4255
Fax: 905-669-3627 info@bekacasting.com
www.bekacasting.com
Tables, chairs and groupings
President: Maggie Dederian
National Sales Manager: Raffi Dayian

Parent Co: Beka Casting
Brands:
  Beka

19533 Bekum America Corp
1140 W Grand River Ave
Williamston, MI 48895-1394

517-655-4331
Fax: 517-655-4121 sales@bekumamerica.com
www.bekumamerica.com
Blow molding machinery
President: Martin Stark
admin@bekumamerica.com
President: Martin Stark
CEO: Martin Stark
CFO: Owen Johnston
Estimated Sales: $30-50 Million
Number Employees: 100-249

19534 (HQ)Bel-Art Products
661 State Route 23
Wayne, NJ 07470-6814

973-694-0500
Fax: 973-694-7199 800-423-5278
www.belart.com
Manufacturer and exporter of plastic laboratory supplies including sterile and nonsterile sampling devices and magnetic stirring bars; also, laboratory cleaning products
President: David Landsberger
CEO: William Downs
Estimated Sales: $10-20 Million
Number Employees: 100-249
Square Footage: 160000
Type of Packaging: Consumer, Private Label, Bulk
Other Locations:
  Bel-Art Products
  Pequannock NJ
Brands:
  Clavies
  Cleanware
  Spinbar
  Sterileware

19535 Bel-Ray Co LLC
1201 Bowman Ave
Wall Township, NJ 07727-3910

732-938-2421
Fax: 732-938-4232 belray@belray.com
www.belray.com
Formulated petroleum and synthetic oils and greases
President: Linda Kiefer
CEO: Carol Adams
adams@belray.com
CFO: Lauren Volk
CEO: Daryl Brosnan
R&D: Bill Shen
Quality Control: Victor Odueanjo
Manager (Industrial Division): Roy Provost
Estimated Sales: $75-100 Million
Number Employees: 100-249
Square Footage: 150000
Brands:
  Molyube
  No-Tox

19536 Bel-Terr China
1001 Country Way SW
Warren, OH 44481-9699
Fax: 330-457-7524 800-900-2371
Pottery
President: Edward Massey
VP: Paul Ramponi
Estimated Sales: $10-20 Million
Number Employees: 20-49

19537 Belcan Corp
10200 Anderson Way
Blue Ash, OH 45242-4718

513-891-0972
Fax: 513-793-8618 888-263-3165
dlajoie@belcan.com www.belcan.com
President: Todd Cross
CEO: Mike McCaw
Chief Financial Officer: Michael J. Wirth
Sr. Vice President: Leigh Ann Pagnard
COO: Cleve Campbell
Number Employees: 5000-9999

19538 Belco Packaging Systems
910 S Mountain Ave
Monrovia, CA 91016-3641

626-930-0366
Fax: 626-359-3440 800-833-1833
info@belcopackaging.com
www.belcopackaging.com
Manufacturer and wholesaler/distributor of shrink packaging equipment, carton sealers, shrink tunnels, conveyors and accumulating tables
President: Michael A. Misik
CEO: Helen Misik
R&D: Tom Bolby
Quality Control: Dave Macneil
National Sales Manager: Thomas Misik
Distributor Sales Manager: Bruce Miles
Estimated Sales: $10-20 Million
Number Employees: 20-49
Square Footage: 70000
Brands:
  Belco

19539 Belgian Electronic Sorting Technology USA
65 Inverness Dr E
Suite 300
Englewood, CO 80112-5141
Fax: 720-870-2241
President: Eddy De Reyes
CEO: Bert Van Der Auwera
VP: Johan Peters
R & D: Mark Ruynen
Manager: Johan Peeters
Estimated Sales: $3-5 Million
Number Employees: 5-9

19540 (HQ)Bell & Howell Company
6802 N McCormick Boulevard
Lincolnwood, IL 60712-2709

847-675-7600
800-647-2290
www.bellhowell.com
Weighing systems, inserting systems, automated guided mail delivery vehicles, remittance processing equipment, labeling machinery and sorters
Principal: Mike Swift
Quality Control: Josecer David
CFO: Tom Werner
President: John Lomdard
Number Employees: 160

19541 Bell Container
615 Ferry St
Newark, NJ 07105-4404

973-344-6997
Fax: 973-344-0817 www.bellcontainer.com
Corrugated boxes
President: John Weining
jweining@bellcontainers.com
Estimated Sales: $20-50 Million
Number Employees: 100-249

19542 Bell Flavors & Fragrances
500 Academy Dr
Northbrook, IL 60062-2497

847-291-8300
Fax: 847-291-1217 info@bellff.com
www.bellff.com
Manufacturer and exporter of natural and artificial flavoring extracts for food and beverages; also, spice compounds.
President: Jim Heinz
jheinz@bellff.com
Director of Marketing: Kelli Heinz
Year Founded: 1912
Estimated Sales: $39 Million
Number Employees: 50-99
Square Footage: 100000
Type of Packaging: Consumer, Food Service
Brands:
  Yuccafoam

19543 Bell Foods
134 Brookhollow Esplanade
New Orleans, LA 70123-5102

504-837-2355
Fax: 504-837-2365 info@bellfoods.net
www.bellfoods.net
Appetizers and prepared foods, USDA proteins, Louisiana seafood, chemicals, dairy, paper products

Owner: John Bellina
jb@bellfoods.net
Co-Owner/Dir., Sales: Shane Nicaud, Sr.
jb@bellfoods.net
Co-Owner/Dir., Operations: John Bellini III
Number Employees: 20-49

19544 Bell Laboratories Inc
3699 Kinsman Blvd
Madison, WI 53704

608-241-0202
Fax: 608-241-9631 www.belllabs.com
Rodent control products including rodenticides, glue traps and tamper resistant bait stations.
President: Steve Levy
Vice President, Sales-East: Sheila Haddad
Vice President, Sales-West: Patrick Lynch
Year Founded: 1974
Estimated Sales: $100-500 Million
Number Employees: 100-249
Square Footage: 5260000
Brands:
  Contrac
  Ditrac
  Final
  Protecta
  Trapper
  Zp

19545 Bell Packaging Corporation
3112 S Boots St
Marion, IN 46953

765-664-1261
Fax: 765-668-8127 800-382-0153
ryoung@prattindustries.com
www.prattindustries.com
Manufacturer corrugated shipping containers
President: Robert Young
Plant Manager: Terry Royal
Estimated Sales: $20-50 Million
Number Employees: 10
Square Footage: 250000
Parent Co: Pratt Industries

19546 (HQ)Bell-Mark Corporation
331 Changebridge Road
PO Box 2007
Pine Brook, NJ 7058

973-882-0202
Fax: 973-808-4616 info@bell-mark.com
www.bell-mark.com
Manufacturer and exporter of innovative coding and printing systems to the packaging and converting markets
President: John Marozzi
CFO: James Pontrella
VP: Tom Pugh
Marketing: Glenn Breslauer
Sales: Bob Batesko
Contact: Doug Buch
dbuch@bell-mark.com
Plant Manager: Dale Miller
Purchasing: Lou Ciccone
Estimated Sales: $16-20 Million
Number Employees: 50-99
Number of Brands: 5
Number of Products: 30
Square Footage: 90000
Brands:
  Easyprint
  Flexprint
  Intelijet

19547 Bella Vita
PO Box 93204
Phoenix, AZ 85070

877-827-3638
Fax: 480-827-7630 sales@bellavitabags.com
www.bellavitabags.com
Wine bags and gourmet bags

19548 Belle Isle Awning
20220 Cornillie Dr
Roseville, MI 48066-1746

586-294-6050
Fax: 586-294-2487 www.belleisleawning.com
Commercial awnings
Owner: Blair Belloumo
info@belleisleawning.com
Estimated Sales: $2.5-5,000,000
Number Employees: 20-49

19549 Belleco Inc
414 Hill St
Biddeford, ME 04005-4334
207-283-8006
Fax: 207-283-8080 sales@bellecocooking.com
www.bellecocooking.com
Customized toasters, conveyor Pizza Ovens and
Heat Lamps
President: Russ Bellerose
rbellerose@bellecocooking.com
CFO: Kevin Roche
Quality Control Manager: Gil Cole
Sales: Mike Clavet
Materials Manager: Ron Hevey
Number Employees: 10-19
Type of Packaging: Food Service

19550 Belleview
PO Box 122
Brookline, NH 3033
603-878-1583
Water and plastic milk cases
CEO: Alfred Stauble
Estimated Sales: $1-5 Million
Number Employees: 1-4

19551 Bellingham + Stanley
90 Horizon Dr
Suwanee, GA 30024
678-804-5730
Fax: 678-804-5729 800-678-8573
www.bellinghamandstanley.com
Manufactures refractometers and polarimeters
Administrator: Susan Davis
Parent Co: Bellingham + Stanley

19552 Belliss & Morcom
1800 Gardner expressway
Quincy, Il 62301
217-222-5400
Fax: 217-221-8728
belliss.red@gardnerdenver.com
www.belliss.com
High pressure oil-free air compressors for PET
stretch blow molding
Marketing/Sales: Wendy Johnson
Estimated Sales: $1-2.5 Million
Number Employees: 5-9

19553 Bellsola-Pan Plus
7326 NW 46th Street
Miami, FL 33166-6425
305-406-9662
Fax: 305-406-9664 maquipanit@msn.com
Director of Product Development: Kirk Crowder

19554 Belltown Boxing Company
1717 Market St
Tacoma, WA 98402-3246
253-274-9000
Fax: 253-274-9009
Creative custom, packaging for the retail and food
industries
President: Linda Ewing
VP: Andrew Levkass
Estimated Sales: $1-2.5 Million
Number Employees: 10-19
Type of Packaging: Private Label, Bulk

19555 Belly Treats, Inc.
210-200 Wellington St W
Toronto, ON M5V 3C7
Canada
416-418-3285
Fax: 905-479-4135 www.bellytreats.com
Candies and nuts
Owner/Sales & Marketing: George Tsioros
Estimated Sales: $1 Million
Number of Products: 500+
Type of Packaging: Bulk

19556 Belshaw Adamatic Bakery Group
814 44th St NW # 103
Suite 103
Auburn, WA 98001-1754
206-322-5474
Fax: 206-322-5425 800-578-2547
info@belshaw.com www.belshaw-adamatic.com
Machinery and production solutions for donut producers in every retail and wholesale category.
Doughnut systems fryers, glazers, and icers; also
pancake and batter depositers; and piston filler
depositers. One-hundred percentdedicated to the
donut and to donut-makers worldwide.

President: Roger Faw
roger_faw@belshaw.com
CFO: William Yee
Marketing Coordinator: Mike Baxter
Sales: John DeMarre
Estimated Sales: $20-50 Million
Number Employees: 100-249
Square Footage: 120000
Parent Co: Welbilt Corporation
Type of Packaging: Food Service

19557 Belson Outdoors Inc
111 N River Rd
North Aurora, IL 60542-1324
630-264-2396
Fax: 630-897-0573 800-323-5664
sales@belson.com www.belson.com
Manufacturer and distributor of the finest outdoor
cooking equipment available. Don't be misled, insist
on certified (ul, csa, nsf) safe equipment. product
line includes gas and charcoal grills, pig roasters,
steam tables, trailerpits, smokers and more.
Manager: John Hauptman
hj@belson.com
Number Employees: 20-49
Brands:
    Porta-Grills

19558 Belt Corporation of America
253 Castleberry Industrial Dr
Cumming, GA 30040
770-887-9725
Fax: 770-887-4138 800-235-0947
info@beltcorp.com www.beltcorp.com
Industrial belting, packing belts
Owner: Bill Levensalor
Estimated Sales: $5-10 000,000
Number Employees: 50-99
Type of Packaging: Consumer, Food Service, Pri-
vate Label, Bulk

19559 (HQ)Belt Technologies Inc
11 Bowles Rd
Agawam, MA 01001-3812
413-786-9922
Fax: 413-789-2786 www.belttechnologies.com
Manufacturer and exporter of pulleys and metal
belts used for conveyors, power transmissions, etc.;
importer of backed belts
President: Alan Wosky
Quality Control: John Robertson
Sales Manager: Timothy Potrikus
Human Resources: Cindy Gadbois
Estimated Sales: Below $5 Million
Number Employees: 20-49
Square Footage: 46000
Other Locations:
    Belt Technologies
    Durham City
Brands:
    Metrak
    Transback

19560 Beltek Systems Design
30 Englehart Street
Suite C
Dieppe, NB E1A 6P8
Canada
506-857-4196
Fax: 506-857-0194
Chief Executive Officer: Michel Belzile
Chief Financial Officer: David Pugsley
Chief Technology Officer: Jason Janes
Estimated Sales: $15,000,000
Number Employees: 99
Parent Co: HighJump Software, LLC.

19561 Beltram Foodservice Group
6800 N Florida Ave
Tampa, FL 33604-5558
813-239-1136
Fax: 813-238-6673 800-940-1136
bfgtampa@beltram.com www.beltram.com
Wholesaler/distributor of food service supplies and
equipment; serving the food service market
President: Dan Beltram
dan@beltram.com
CFO: Hal Herdman
VP: Allen Cope
VP: Kathy McCain
Purchasing Manager: John Zloch
Estimated Sales: $20-50 Million
Number Employees: 50-99
Parent Co: Beltram Foodservice Group

19562 Belvac Production Machinery
237 Graves Mill Rd
Lynchburg, VA 24502-4203
434-239-0358
Fax: 434-239-1964 800-423-5822
info@belvac.com www.belvac.com
Committed to provide our customers quality prod-
ucts, to be at the forefront of emerging technolo-
gies-to support our can makers and brands alike.
President: Richard S Steigerwald
CEO: Peggy Bell
peggy.bell@fema.gov
Director Marketing: Eric Hodge
Number Employees: 100-249

19563 Bematek Systems Inc
96 Swampscott Rd # 7
Salem, MA 01970-7004
978-744-5816
Fax: 978-922-7801 877-236-2835
bematek@bematek.com www.bematek.com
Manufacturer and exporter of food processing
equipment including in-line mixers, colloid mills,
homogenizers, grinders and dispersers; also, labora-
tory testing machinery for wet mixing and size re-
duction, continuous or batch
President: David Ekstrom
bematek@bematek.com
Technical Director: Stephen Masucci
Administration: Denise Raimo
Sales Manager: Lindsey Humphrey
Estimated Sales: $1-3 Million
Number Employees: 1-4
Square Footage: 8600
Brands:
    Bematek
    Colby
    Speco

19564 Ben H. Anderson Manufacturers
7848 Morrison St
Morrisonville, WI 53571
608-846-5474
Fax: 608-846-8878 bklucey@merr.com
www.benhanderson.com
Dairy processing equipment
President: Dale Victor
Number Employees: 10

19565 Benchmark Thermal
13185 Nevada City Ave
PO Box 1799
Grass Valley, CA 95945-9568
530-477-5011
Fax: 530-477-6507 800-748-6189
thermal@benchmarkthermal.com
www.benchmarkthermal.com
Heating elements
President: Gil Mathew
CEO: Myles McKelo
Estimated Sales: $5-10 Million
Number Employees: 10-19
Square Footage: 24000

19566 Bendow
1120 Federal Road
Brookfield, CT 06804-1122
203-775-6341
Fax: 203-746-3728
Tea and coffee filters
Estimated Sales: $1-5 000,000
Number Employees: 3

19567 Benier
351 Thornton Rd # 123
Lithia Springs, GA 30122-1589
770-745-2200
Fax: 770-745-0050 www.benierusa.com
Provider of bakery equipment
President: Mike Hartnett
Estimated Sales: $5-10 Million
Number Employees: 20-49
Brands:
    Benier
    Daub
    Diosna
    Kaak
    Oddy
    Spiromatic

19568 Benier USA
351 Thornton Rd # 123
Lithia Springs, GA 30122-1589
770-745-2200
Fax: 770-745-0050 www.benierusa.com
Supplier of equipment for the automated production
of bread, rolls, pizza crust and tortillas
President: Mike Hartnett
CFO: Ron Tabor
Estimated Sales: $5-10 Million
Number Employees: 20-49
Square Footage: 148000
Brands:
Benier
Daub
Diosna
Koak Oddy

19569 Benko Products
5350 Evergreen Pkwy
Sheffield Vlg, OH 44054-2446
440-934-2180
Fax: 440-934-4052 info@benkoproducts.com
www.benkoproducts.com
Manufacturer or revolutionary ergonomic beverage
cart that eliminates the need to bend when loading
and unloading.
President: John Benko
jbenko@benkoproducts.com
VP: Robert Benko
Sales/Marketing Manager: Laurie Benko
Estimated Sales: $10 Million
Number Employees: 50-99
Square Footage: 70000
Brands:
G-Raff
Sahara Hot Box

19570 Benner China & Glassware Inc
5329 Powers Ave
Jacksonville, FL 32207-8084
904-733-4620
Fax: 904-733-4622
Manufacturer, importer and exporter of glassware
and china
Vice President: Scott Miles
smiles@odyseyfl.com
VP: Marie Wang
General Manager: Edward Mills
Estimated Sales: $5-10 Million
Number Employees: 20-49
Square Footage: 100000
Parent Co: Jacksonville Ginter Box Company
Brands:
Odyssey

19571 Bennett Box & Pallet Company
200 River Street
Winston, NC 27968-9681
252-332-5026
Fax: 252-332-5799 800-334-8741
Skids and new and remanufactured pallets; also, pal-
let repair and removal services available
President: Barbara Perry
barbara.perry@bennettpackaging.com
VP of Marketing: Shirley Walker
Estimated Sales: $10-20 Million
Number Employees: 50-99
Square Footage: 170000

19572 Bennett Manufacturing Company
13315 Railroad St
Alden, NY 14004-1390
716-937-9161
Fax: 716-937-3137 800-345-2142
info@bennettmfg.com www.bennettmfg.com
Custom built metal cabinets, waste receptacles, jani-
tor carts, racks, frames, etc.
President: Steven Yellen
Estimated Sales: $5-10 Million
Number Employees: 50-99
Square Footage: 300000

19573 Bennett's Auto Inc
W8136 Winnegamie Dr
Neenah, WI 54956-9401
920-836-3534
Fax: 920-836-3873 800-215-5464
bauto@bennetts.com www.bennettsauto.com
Disposable polyethylene products including bags,
aprons and gloves; also, latex gloves

Owner: Lowell Bennett
Product Manager (Film Sales): Larry Stelow
National Sales Manager (Healthcare): William
Rusch
Product Manager (Food Service): Ronald Green
Estimated Sales: $3-5 Million
Number Employees: 5-9
Square Footage: 992000

19574 Bennington Furniture Corporation
1371 Historic Route 7A
Bennington, PA 5201
802-447-3212
Fax: 802-447-0360
sales@benningtonfurniture.com
www.benningtonfurniture.com
Cushioned chairs and bar stools
President/CEO: Michael Fiacco
VP: Joseph Bennington
VP: Robert Bennington
Sales: Peg Caron
Customer Service/Accounts Payable M: Marcy
Rodd
Estimated Sales: $2.5-5 Million
Number Employees: 50-99
Brands:
Bennington

19575 Bentley Instruments Inc
4004 Peavey Rd
Chaska, MN 55318-2344
952-448-7600
Fax: 952-368-3355 info@bentleyinstruments.com
www.bentleyus.com
Manufacturer and exporter of milk analyzers and
control systems
President: Bent Lyder
blyder@bentleyinstruments.com
Estimated Sales: $2.5-$5 Million
Number Employees: 10-19
Square Footage: 38000
Type of Packaging: Food Service, Bulk
Brands:
Bentley
Somacount

19576 Bepex International LLC
333 Taft St NE
Minneapolis, MN 55413-2885
612-259-0699
Fax: 612-627-1444 800-607-2470
info@bepex.com www.bepex.net
Provider of thermal processing, polymer processing,
drying, agglomeration, size reduction, compaction,
briquetting, mixing and blending for the food, chem-
ical and polymer markets
President: Teri Butler
t.butler@fairfieldinnandsuites.com
Estimated Sales: $20 Million
Number Employees: 50-99
Number of Brands: 4
Number of Products: 30+
Brands:
Alpine
Disintegrator
Extructor
Hosokawa
Kg
Mikropul
Rietz
Schugi
Strong Scott

19577 Berco
1120 Montrose Ave
St Louis, MO 63104-1828
314-772-4700
Fax: 314-772-6241 888-772-4788
info@bercoinc.com www.bercodesigns.com
Tables and components for the food service industry
President: Maxine Berkowitz
Human Resources: Angie Balencie
Estimated Sales: $5-10 Million
Number Employees: 50-99
Square Footage: 340000

19578 Berenz Packaging Corp
N93w16214 Megal Dr
N93 W16214 Megal Drive
Menomonee Falls, WI 53051-1555
262-251-8787
Fax: 262-251-4710 www.berenzpackaging.com
Corrugated containers

President: Tom Berenz
berenz@execpc.com
Sales Exec: Thomas Berenz
Estimated Sales: $10-20 Million
Number Employees: 20-49

19579 Berg Chilling Systems
51 Nantucket Blvd.
Toronto, ON, ON M1P 2N5
Canada
416-755-2221
Fax: 416-755-3874 bergsales@berg-group.com
www.berg-group.com
Manufacturer and exporter of industrial cooling
equipment, fluid recirculation, cold storage and
pumping systems, ice machines, chillers and cooling
towers
Chairman/CEO: Lorne Berggren
VP Sales: Stephanie Goudie
Estimated Sales: $20-50 Million
Number Employees: 100-249
Square Footage: 75000
Brands:
Berg

19580 Berg Chilling Systems
51 Nantucket Blvd.
Toronto, ON M1P 2N5
Canada
416-755-2221
Fax: 416-755-3874 bergsales@berg-group.com
www.berg-group.com
Manufacturer and exporter of process cooling equip-
ment, large ice-making machines, freeze dryers,
turnkey food processing/refrigeration systems and
brine chillers for meat
VP: S Goudie
Estimated Sales: $1-2.5 Million
Number Employees: 1-4
Parent Co: Berg Chilling Systems

19581 Berg Co
2160 Industrial Dr
Monona, WI 53713-4805
608-221-4281
Fax: 608-221-1416 sales@berg-controls.com
www.bergliquorcontrols.com
Liquor dispensers, beer equipment and beverage dis-
pensing systems
Estimated Sales: $2.5-5 Million
Number Employees: 10-19
Parent Co: DEC International
Brands:
All-Bottle
Berg
Infinity
Laser
Tap 1

19582 Bergen Barrel & Drum Company
43 Obrien Rd
Kearny, NJ 07032-4212
201-998-3500
Fax: 201-998-0414
Tanks, pallets and plastic drums
Sales Coordinator: Lisa Goldstein
Estimated Sales: $1-2.5 Million
Number Employees: 5-9

19583 Berger Lahr Motion Technology
8001 Knightdale Blvd
Knightdale, NC 27545-9023
734-459-8300
Fax: 734-459-8622
Electric motors and drive controls
President: Steve Seabaugh
Sales Manager: Frank Eble
Contact: Alexander Filippenko
alexander.filippenko@us.schneider-electric.com
Estimated Sales: $1-5 Million
Number Employees: 10

19584 Berghausen E Cheml Co
4524 Este Ave
Cincinnati, OH 45232-1763
513-541-5631
Fax: 530-683-4011 800-648-5887
www.berghausen.com
Processor and finisher of quillaja and yucca extracts
(powder and liquid forms) and food colors. Founded
in 1863.
President: Beth Baker
bbaker@berghausen.com
Quality Control Manager: Tom Davlin

Estimated Sales: $1-5 Million
Number Employees: 10-19

19585 Bergschrond
4458 51st Avenue SW
Seattle, WA 98116-4029

206-763-3502
Fax: 206-763-3767

Sereware
President: Karl Stephenson
VP of Marketing: Babette Easley
Estimated Sales: $1-2.5 Million
Number Employees: 20

19586 Bericap North America, Inc.
835 Syscon Court
CDN-Burlington, ON L7L 6C5
Canada

905-634-2248
Fax: 905-634-7780 info.na@bericap.com
www.bericap.com

Manufacturer, importer and exporter of tamper-evident pourer closures, capsules for bottled liquids and flat top dispensing closures
President: Scott Ambrose
Number Employees: 10
Square Footage: 58000
Parent Co: Rical SA

19587 Berkshire PPM
PO Box 59
Litchfield, CT 06759-0059

860-567-3118
Fax: 860-567-3014

Reconditioner and exporter of used food and beverage packaging, processing machinery and tanks
President: James Rindos
Estimated Sales: $3-5 Million
Number Employees: 3
Square Footage: 30000

19588 Berlekamp Plastics Inc
2587 County Road 99
Fremont, OH 43420-9316

419-334-4481
Fax: 419-334-9094 sales@berlekamp.com
www.berlekamp.com

Manufacturer and exporter of plastic signs and badges
President: Kenneth Berlekamp, Jr., CAS
Manager: Ken Berlekamp
ken@berlekamp.com
Estimated Sales: $1-2.5 Million
Number Employees: 20-49

19589 Berlin Foundry & Mach Co
489 Goebel St
P.O. Box 127
Berlin, NH 03570-2338

603-752-4550
Fax: 603-752-2798 htardiff@berlinfoundry.com
www.berlinfoundry.com

Manufacturer and exporter of wrapping and packaging machines for paper towels and toilet tissue.
Owner: Gary Hamel
Sales/Plant Manager: Gary Hamel
Manager: Helene Tardiff
foundry2@verizon.net
Operations: Gary Hamel
Estimated Sales: $1.5 Million
Number Employees: 10-19
Square Footage: 60000

19590 Berlin Fruit Box Company
PO Box 47
Berlin Heights, OH 44814-0047

419-588-2081
Fax: 419-588-2800 800-877-7721
contact@samuelpattersonbaskets.com

Wood veneer baskets for fruit and vegetables
President: Matthew Adelman
Contact: Anastasia Agee
anastasia.agee@samuelpattersonbaskets.com
Estimated Sales: $1-2.5 Million
Number Employees: 10-19
Square Footage: 160000
Brands:
  Family Heritage

19591 Berloc Manufacturing & Sign Company
8010 Wheatland Ave
Ste G
Sun Valley, CA 91352-5317

818-503-9823
Fax: 818-503-0934

Signs including aluminum, engraved and vinyl; also, letters, directories and bulletin boards
Owner: Joan Adams
VP: Harry Adams
Sales Manager: Diana Gleason
Estimated Sales: $1-3 Million
Number Employees: 10
Square Footage: 10000

19592 Berlon Industries
434 Rubicon St
Hustisford, WI 53034

920-349-3580
Fax: 920-349-3081 800-899-3580
www.berlon.com

Custom stainless steel products including boxes, casters and dairy equipment
President: Mike Ebben
CFO: Bill Olson
Contact: Cody Apfelbeck
capfelbeck@berlon.com
Director Operations: Steve Griep
Estimated Sales: $1-2.5 Million
Number Employees: 20-49
Square Footage: 17200

19593 Bermar America
42 Lloyd Ave # A
Malvern, PA 19355-3000

610-889-4900
Fax: 610-889-0289 888-289-5838
info@bermaramerica.com
www.bermaramerica.com

Manufacturer and importer of vacuum and pressure seal wine preservation systems
Owner: Aline Bouilland
alineb@bermaramerica.com
Estimated Sales: Less Than $500,000
Number Employees: 1-4

19594 Bernal Technology
2960 Technology Dr
Rochester Hills, MI 48309-3588

248-299-3600
Fax: 248-299-3601 800-237-6251
sales@bernalinc.com www.bernalinc.info

Manufacturer and exporter of die cutting and packaging machines for cereal, coffee, snack foods, etc
President: Luigi Pessarelli
CFO: Kelly Lang
lang@bernalinc.com
Director: Rey Hsu, Ph. D.
Vice President Sales & Marketing: Mark Voorhees
Sales Manager: Steven Leigh
Plant Manager: Frank Penksa
Estimated Sales: $20 Million
Number Employees: 20-49
Square Footage: 45000

19595 Bernard Wolnak & Associates
1721 Mission Hills Rd Apt 205
Northbrook, IL 60062-5715

847-480-0427
Fax: 847-480-0427

Consultant for the food processing industry providing consultation on food ingredients, processes, technology, planning, data acquisition and interpretation
President: Bernard Wolnak
Estimated Sales: $2.5-5 Million
Number Employees: 1 to 4
Square Footage: 9000

19596 Berndorf Belt Technology USA
59 Prairie Pkwy
Gilberts, IL 60136-4039

847-931-5264
Fax: 847-931-5299 800-393-8450
danielw@berndorf-usa.com
www.berndorf-usa.com

Manufacturer and service provider of solid steel belts, processing systems and complete turnkey plants for cooling, heat transfer, solidificationand casting applications.

VP: Larry Edwards
Marketing Director: Daniela Weiszhar
Contact: Brian Brown
brian.brown@berndorf-usa.com
Estimated Sales: Below $5 Million
Number Employees: 10-19
Square Footage: 23000
Parent Co: Berndorf Band Gesmb

19597 Berner International Corp
111 Progress Ave
New Castle, PA 16101-7601

724-652-7106
Fax: 724-652-0682 800-245-4455
sales@berner.com www.berner.com

Berner International Corp. has established itself as the leading manufacturer of air doors for insect and climate control and cooler/freezer applications. Berner also has its own line of patio heaters, arctic seal doors, strip doorsand bakery rack covers.
Owner: Georgia Berner
gberner@berner.com
Sales Manager: Michael Coscarelli
Estimated Sales: $10-20 Million
Number Employees: 50-99
Square Footage: 100000
Type of Packaging: Food Service
Brands:
  Aristocrat
  Berner
  Flystop
  Miniveil
  Posi-Flow
  Zephyr

19598 Berry Global
P.O. Box 959
Evansville, IN 47706-0959

812-424-2904
800-343-1295
www.berryglobal.com

Manufacturer and exporter of injection molded plastic containers and lids; also, container fillers.
Chairman & CEO: Tom Salmon
Chief Financial Officer: Mark Miles
SVP & Strategic Corp. Development: Brett Bauer
EVP & Chief Information Officer: Debbie Garrison
EVP, Operations: Rodgers Greenawalt
EVP/Chief Legal Officer/Secretary: Jason Greene
EVP, Human Resources: Ed Stratton
Year Founded: 1967
Estimated Sales: $13 Billion
Number Employees: 48,000
Other Locations:
  Berry Plastics
  Henderson NV

19599 Berryhill Signs
597 Vandalia St
Memphis, TN 38112

901-324-1730
Fax: 901-389-3610 patberryhill@msn.com
www.berryhillsigns.com

Commercial plastic signs and designs
President: Kenneth M Berryhill
Contact: Patricia Berryhill
patricia.berryhill@berryhillsigns.com
Manager: Debbie Faber
Estimated Sales: Below $5 Million
Number Employees: dd.berryhill@ao

19600 Bert Manufacturing
1276 Pit Rd # 3
Unit 3
Gardnerville, NV 89460-8723

775-265-3900
Fax: 775-265-3939 bertmfg2@aol.com
www.bertmanufacturing.com

Manufacturer and exporter of chucks and rolls for food processing machinery
Owner: Dennis Bertucci
bertmfg2@aol.com
Sales: Brian Bertucci
Technical Director: Paul Coleman
Engineering & Programming: Luis Martinez
Estimated Sales: Less Than $500,000
Number Employees: 1-4
Type of Packaging: Bulk

19601 (HQ)Bertek Systems Inc
133 Bryce Blvd
Fairfax, VT 05454-5491

802-752-3170
Fax: 802-868-3872 800-367-0210
www.berteksystems.com

Manufacturer and exporter of data processing and pressure sensitive labels
Owner: Sam Peters
Sales and Marketing Director: Peter Kvam
0: Ken Whitcomb
MIS Systems Manager: Mike Saunders
Sales/Marketing Manager: Peter Kvam
Sales Representative: Danielle Ryea
HR/Ex Assistant: Amy Kimball
General Manager: Barney Kijeh
Account Executive: Debbie Chadwick
Estimated Sales: $10-20 Million
Number Employees: 100-249

19602 Bertels Can Company
1300 Brass Mill Road
Belcamp, MD 21017

410-272-0090
sales@independentcan.com
www.independentcan.com
Manufacturer of specialty metal cans and lithography
President: Rick Huether
Director Of Sales: Neil DeFrancisco
Plant Manager: Frank Sorokach
Estimated Sales: $20-50 Million
Number Employees: 20-49
Square Footage: 60000
Parent Co: Independent Can Company

19603 Berthold Technologies
99 Widway Lane
Oak Ridge, TN 37830

865-483-1488
Fax: 865-425-4309 Berthold-US@berthold.com
www.berthold-us.com
Measurement gauges and analyzers

19604 Bertie County Peanuts
217 U.S. 13 North
Windsor, NC 27983

252-794-2138
Fax: 252-794-9267 800-457-0005
jon@pnuts.net www.pnuts.net
Sugar-free, other chocolate, other candy, health, fitness and energy bars, nuts, gift packs, private label.
Marketing: Jon Powell

19605 Beryl's Cake Decorating& Pastry Supplies
P.O.Box 1584
Springfield, VA 22151-0584

703-256-6951
Fax: 703-750-3779 800-488-2749
www.beryls.com
Specializes in mail order cake decorating and party supplies.
Owner: Beryl Loveland
Sales: Linda Howe
Public Relations: Mara Lee
Estimated Sales: $.5-1 million
Number Employees: 1-4
Number of Products: 6000

19606 Besco Grain Ltd
PO Box 166
30 Railway Avenue
Brunkild, MB R0G 0E0
Canada

204-736-3570
Fax: 204-736-3575 www.bescograin.ca
Grains
President: Renee Caners
Quality Control: Carol Schulz
International Sales: Anthony Krijger
Sales Manager: Fred Nicholson
Office Manager: Sheri Hiebert
Plant Manager: Jamie Stelmachowich

19607 Bessamaire Sales Inc
10145 Philipp Pkwy # B
Unit B
Streetsboro, OH 44241-4706

330-650-5001
Fax: 440-439-1625 800-321-5992
bill@bessamaire.com www.bessamaire.com
Manufacturer and exporter of indirect heating equipment for gas/oil, make-up air heating and summer evaporative cooling units.
Owner: Bill Sullivan
Marketing Director: Joseph Marg
Product Manager: Mark McGinty
Contact: Joseph Marg
marg@bessamaire.com

Estimated Sales: Less Than $500,000
Number Employees: 1-4
Number of Brands: 1
Number of Products: 9
Square Footage: 100000
Type of Packaging: Food Service
Brands:
  Bessam-Aire

19608 Bessco Tube Bending & Pipe Fabricating
18 Blackhawk Dr
Thornton, IL 60476-1127

708-339-3977
Fax: 708-339-9472 800-337-3977
Folding tables and trucks including hand, chair and table
President: Ed Eggebrecht
CEO: Ruth Hartman
Marketing Director: Theresa Eggebrecht
Purchasing Manager: Henry De Vries
Estimated Sales: $1-3 Million
Number Employees: 5-9
Square Footage: 40000
Brands:
  Handy-Cart
  Hercules Tables

19609 Best
1071 Industrial Pkwy N
Brunswick, OH 44212

330-273-1277
Fax: 330-225-8740 800-827-9237
sales@bestvibes.com www.bestvibes.com
Manufacturer and exporter of pneumatic and electric vibrators, bulk bag unloaders, bulk bag loaders, conveyors, tables, screeners and dry process systems.
President: Ed Verbos
VP of Engineering: Tim Conway
Marketing: S Fitzpatrick
Sales Manager: R Breudigam
Estimated Sales: $1-2,500,000
Number Employees: 10-19
Number of Products: 100+
Square Footage: 30000
Type of Packaging: Bulk

19610 Best & Donovan
5570 Creek Rd
Blue Ash, OH 45242-4004

513-791-9180
Fax: 513-791-0925 800-553-2378
info@bestanddonovan.com
www.bestanddonovan.com
Manufacturer and exporter of portable power meat saws, skinners, hock cutters, dehiders and dehorners
Owner: Scott Andre
info@bestanddonovan.com
Finance Executive: Ken Park
VP: Scott Andre
Estimated Sales: $5-10 Million
Number Employees: 20-49
Square Footage: 110000
Brands:
  B&D
  Best & Donovan

19611 Best Brands Home Products
20 W 33rd St # 5
New York, NY 10001-3305

212-684-7456
Fax: 212-684-7630 www.bestbrands.com
Manufacturer and importer of towels, tablecloths, place mats, pot holders, linen goods, display racks, vinyl & fabric table cloths and place mats, oven and barbecue mitts, barbecue aprons and vinyl coasters, all bath towel products
President: Jack Albert
CEO: Jack Kassin
jacksr@bestbrands.com
Vice President: Rodnie Gindi
Marketing Director: Cari Bennett
Sales Director: Rodnie Gindi
Secretary: David Meyer
Estimated Sales: $25 Million+
Number Employees: 20-49
Type of Packaging: Consumer, Private Label
Brands:
  American Greetings
  Cannon
  Norman Rockwell

19612 Best Buy Uniforms
500 E 8th Ave
Homestead, PA 15120-1904

412-461-4600
Fax: 412-461-4016 800-345-1924
customer-service@bestbuyuniforms.com
www.bestbuyuniforms.com
Manufacturer, wholesaler/distributor and importer of image apparel uniforms; also, custom T-shirts, table cloths, napkins and work uniforms; serving the food service market
Owner: David Frischman
davidf@bestbuyuniforms.com
CEO: Lester Frischman
Estimated Sales: $1-5 Million
Number Employees: 5-9
Square Footage: 24000
Type of Packaging: Food Service

19613 Best Cooking Pulses, Inc.
110 10th St NE
Portage la Prairie, MB R1N 1B5
Canada

204-857-4451
margaret@bestcookingpulses.com
www.bestcookingpulses.com
Peas, chickpea, lentil and bean flours and pea fiber. Certified Kosher, Halal, Conventional or Certified-Organic, free of all major allergens, and gluten free.
President: Trudy Heal
Director, Sales & Marketing: Jennifer Evancio
General Manager: Mike Gallais
Estimated Sales: $11.25 Million
Number Employees: 23
Type of Packaging: Bulk

19614 Best Diversified Products
107 Flint Street
Jonesboro, AR 72401-6717

870-935-0970
Fax: 870-935-3661 800-327-9209
www.bestconveyors.com
Manufacturer and exporter of conveyors including flexible, expandable, skatewheel and roller
President: James E Markley
Sales/Marketing Director: Charlie Appleby
Contact: Roger Haynes
rogerhaynes@bestconv.com
Estimated Sales: $20-50 Million
Number Employees: 100-249

19615 Best Label Co
13260 Moore St
Cerritos, CA 90703-2252

562-926-1432
Fax: 562-404-2076 800-404-2378
President: Donald Ingle
ingle@bestlabelinc.com
Estimated Sales: $10-20 Million
Number Employees: 100-249

19616 Best Manufacturers
6105 NE 92nd Dr
Portland, OR 97220-1321

503-253-1528
Fax: 503-253-0878 800-500-1528
sales@bestmfrs.com www.bestwhipsusa.com
Wire whips and mashers for beans and potatoes
Owner: Glennis Merrifield
VP Sales: Jeff Merrifield
glennis@bestmfrs.com
Estimated Sales: $2.5-5 Million
Number Employees: 1-4
Square Footage: 60000
Brands:
  Best

19617 Best Manufacturing
10 Exchange Pl Unit 5
Jersey City, NJ 07302

201-356-3800
Fax: 201-356-3816 www.bestmfg.com
Manufacturers of aprons, bathrobes, bedspreads and blankets, napkins, fabric, pillows, sheets and pillow cases tablecloths and napkins, towels, cotton or linen, uniforms, clothing
Manager: Eddie Chain
VP: Henry Garner
VP of Sales: Larry Miles
Number Employees: 100
Number of Products: 9

19618 Best Pack
10676 Fulton Ct
Rancho Cucamonga, CA 91730-4848
909-987-4258
Fax: 909-987-5189 sales@bestpack.com
www.bestpack.com
High speed carton erector without vacuum suction cups and fully automatic L-sealer with shrink tunnel
President: David Lim
dlim@bestpackpackagingsystems.com
Estimated Sales: $1-2.5 000,000
Number Employees: 10-19

19619 Best Restaurant Equip &Design
4020 Business Park Dr
Columbus, OH 43204-5023
614-488-2378
Fax: 614-488-4732 800-837-2378
www.bestrestaurant.com
Wholesaler/distributor of furniture, cookware and refrigeration, cooking and serving equipment; serving the food service market; installation and restaurant design services available
President: James Hanson
jhanson@betsrestaurant.com
CFO: Suzane Yosick
Estimated Sales: $10-20,000,000
Number Employees: 50-99

19620 Best Sanitizers Inc
17320 Penn Valley Dr
Penn Valley, CA 95946-9340
530-265-1800
Fax: 530-432-0752 888-225-3267
customerservice@bestsanitizers.com
www.gobrandstand.com
Hand sanitizing lotion, infrared no touch hand sanitizer dispensers and sinks
President: Hillard Witt
htw@bestsanitizers.com
VP Sales/Marketing: Ryan Witt
Marketing Manager: Suzette Pool
Number Employees: 10-19
Square Footage: 40000

19621 Best Value Textiles
7240 Cross Park Drive
North Charleston, SC 29418
262-723-6133
Fax: 843-767-0494 800-858-8589
customercare@chefrevival.com
www.chefrevival.com
Manufacturer, importer and exporter of chef/crew apparel and tools. Flame retardant items including gloves, table linens, aprons, uniforms and oven mitts
Manager: Alex Onda
CFO: Tone Long
R&D: Elizabeth Weiler
Marketing: Rob Johnson
Sales: Claude Brewer
Production: Arturo Gomez
Purchasing Director: Elizabeth Weiler
Estimated Sales: $15 Million
Number Employees: 20-49
Square Footage: 85000
Parent Co: The Coleman Group
Type of Packaging: Food Service
Brands:
  Gold Lion
  Kut-Guard
  Tri-Flex

19622 BestBins Corporation
1107 Hazeltine Blvd
Suite 470
Chaska, MN 55318
952-448-3114
Fax: 952-216-0155 866-448-3114
robert@bestbins.com
Provider of 'next generation' polycarbonate gravity bins for bulk foods such as coffee, candy and natural foods.
CEO: Robert Groenevelt
Vice President: Kyle McDonough
Estimated Sales: $1-3 Million
Number Employees: 1-4
Type of Packaging: Bulk

19623 Bestech Inc
442 S Dixie Hwy E
Pompano Beach, FL 33060-6910
954-785-4550
Fax: 954-785-4678 800-977-2378
bestek@aol.com
Manufacturer and exporter of water purification systems and vending machines
President: Gary Barr
bestek@aol.com
Director Sales: Gary Barr
Estimated Sales: $1-2.5 Million
Number Employees: 5-9
Square Footage: 20000

19624 Beta Screen Corp
707 Commercial Ave # A
Carlstadt, NJ 07072-2685
201-939-2400
Fax: 201-939-7656 800-272-7336
info@betascreen.com www.betascreen.com
Manufacturer and exporter of vinyl doors for automatic kitchen dining room access
President: Arnold Serchuk
info@betascreen.com
Public Relations Director: Stu Serchuk
Estimated Sales: $3-5 Million
Number Employees: 5-9
Parent Co: Beta Industries
Type of Packaging: Food Service
Brands:
  Betadoor

19625 Bete Fog Nozzle Inc
50 Greenfield St
Greenfield, MA 01301-1378
413-772-0846
Fax: 413-772-6729 800-235-0049
sales@bete.com www.bete.com
Manufacturer and exporter of nozzles for food and dairy processing and spray drying nozzles for food processing
President: Matthew Bete
mbete@bete.com
CEO: Lincoln Soule
Owner: David Bete
Research & Development: Dan Delesdernier
Quality Control: Tom Bassett
Sales Director: Susan Cole
Public Relations: Heidi Arnold
Estimated Sales: $15 Million
Number Employees: 100-249
Square Footage: 108000
Brands:
  Bete Spiral
  Mp Series
  Sa Series
  Xa Series

19626 Bethel Engineering & Equipment Inc
13830 McBeth Road
P.O.Box 67
New Hampshire, OH 45870
419-568-1100
Fax: 419-568-1807 800-889-6129
info@bethelengr.com www.bethelengr.com
Manufacturer and exporter of ovens, washers and spray booths
Owner: David Whitaker
Director Sales/Marketing: Tom Shield
Estimated Sales: $5-10 Million
Number Employees: 20-49
Parent Co: Finishing Systems Holdings

19627 Bethel Grain Company
4220 Commercial Way
Glenview, IL 60025-3597
847-635-9960
Fax: 847-635-6801
President: Steve Grubb
Estimated Sales: $1-3 Million
Number Employees: 5-9

19628 Betsy Ross Manufacturing Company
251 Broadway
Paterson, NJ 07501-2033
973-278-7700
Fax: 973-278-5903 877-238-7976
brossmfg@aol.com
Flags and banners
Sales: Stacey Jung
Manager: Zahia Chehadeh
Estimated Sales: $1-5 Million
Number Employees: 5-9
Square Footage: 40000

19629 Bettag & Associates
116 N Central Dr
O Fallon, MO 63366-2337
636-272-4400
Fax: 636-272-1405 800-325-0959
customerservice@rdmproducts.net
www.rdmproducts.net
Cabinet enclosures for refrigeration units, theft deterrent cages, UL listed panel shop
President/CEO: Mike Bettag
Marketing: Carrie Ellis
Estimated Sales: Below $5 Million
Number Employees: 10-19
Square Footage: 30000
Brands:
  Con-Pak
  Ez-Lok
  Pcu-2000

19630 Bettcher Industries Inc
6801 State Route 60
Wakeman, OH 44889-8509
440-965-4422
Fax: 440-965-4900 800-321-8763
sales@bettcher.com www.bettcher.com
Optimex® breading machine and power knife
President: Don Esch
Chairman and Chief Executive Officer: Laurence A. Bettcher
tclark@mobilityworks.com
Chief Financial Officer: Tim McNeil
Research/Development: Ed Steele
Quality Control: Mike Casteel
VP/Marketing: Paul Pirozzola
Public Relations: Wayne Daggett
Plant Manager: David Mears
Purchasing Director: Ed Gross
Number Employees: 100-249
Type of Packaging: Food Service

19631 Bettcher Industries Inc
6801 State Route 60
Wakeman, OH 44889-8509
440-965-4422
Fax: 440-965-4900 800-321-8763
vendas@bettcher.com.br www.bettcher.com
President: Laurence A Bettcher
Number Employees: 100-249

19632 Bettendorf Stanford Inc
1370 W Main St
Salem, IL 62881-3802
618-548-3555
Fax: 618-548-3557 800-548-2253
sales@bettendorfstanford.com
www.bettendorfstanford.com
Bread slicing and bagging equipment; also, cooling conveyors and slicing blades for bread, meat and fish
Manager: Matt Stanford
mstanford@bettendorfstanford.com
Sales: Chad Roberts
Shop Support: Merle Gwymon
Number Employees: 100-249

19633 Better Bilt Products
900 S Kay Avenue
Addison, IL 60101-4909
630-543-6767
Fax: 630-543-0524 800-544-4550
bbponline.com
Wire, metal and tubular products and point of purchase displays
President/Owner: Scott Camp
General Manager: Chris Wojcieszek
Year Founded: 1946
Estimated Sales: $50-100 Million
Number Employees: 51-100
Square Footage: 57000

19634 Better Packages
4 Hershey Dr
Ansonia, CT 06401
203-926-3700
800-237-9151
info@betterpackages.com
www.betterpackages.com
Carton-sealing systems and packaging solutions
President & CEO: Philip White
Vice President Sales & Marketing: Jeffrey Deacon
Director Research & Development: Allen Crowe
Marketing Director: Lynn Padell
Director of Sales: Marc Schaible
Operations Director: Paul Kromberg

Number Employees: 100-249
Brands:
- Better Pack
- Big Inch
- Code Taper
- Counterboy
- Express
- Packer
- Penetron
- Simplex
- Tape Culator
- Tape Shooter
- Tape Squirt

19635 Betz Entec
200 Witmer Road
Horsham, PA 19044-2213

215-674-9200
800-877-1940
www.hazard.com

Water treatment products, boilers, process cooling systems, cookers and waste water treatment systems; also, engineering service available
President: Joseph Perugini
VP of Sales: A Moisey
VP Technical: D Henderson
Number Employees: 300
Square Footage: 240000
Parent Co: Betz Labs

19636 (HQ)Beverage Air
3779 Champion Blvd
Winston Salem, NC 27105-2667

336-245-6400
Fax: 336-245-6453   800-845-9800
sales@bevair.com www.beverage-air.com
Manufacturer and exporter of commercial beverage coolers and food service refrigeration equipment
President: Philippo Berti
CEO: Filippo Berti
fberti@bevair.com
National Sales Manager: Bill Stowik
VP Sales/Marketing: Jack McDonald
National Service Manager: Loran Tucker
Estimated Sales: $1-5 Million
Number Employees: 500-999
Square Footage: 2000000
Parent Co: Specialty Equipment Companies
Type of Packaging: Food Service
Other Locations:
- Beverage-Air
- Honea Path SC
Brands:
- Bever Marketeer
- Bree
- Maxi Marketeer

19637 Beverage Flavors Intl
3150 N Campbell Ave
Chicago, IL 60618-7921

773-248-3860
Fax: 773-248-3862 info@beverageflavorsintl.com
www.beverageflavorsinternational.com
Beverage flavor emulsions and concentrates to bottlers. Flavor selection includes citrus punch, tropical fruit punch, pineapple-banana, mango peach, apple, strawberry-kiwi, aloha punch and pineapple-guava.
Manager: Daniel Manoogian
Contact: Gregg Goga
ggoga@beverageflavorsintl.com
Office Manager: Barbara Martinez
Estimated Sales: Less Than $500,000
Number Employees: 1-4
Type of Packaging: Bulk

19638 Bevistar
615 Vista Drive
Oswego, IL 60543-8129

847-758-1581
Fax: 847-758-1617   877-238-7827
Markets and distributes the newest technology in small-scale beverage dispensers and related consumable concentrate syrups. Specializes in systems comprised of patented technology ideal for the small volume account/establishment/workplace
Marketing Director: Lynda Filicette
Sales Director: Saul Strankus
Plant Manager: Joe Rosado
Estimated Sales: $1-5 Million
Number of Brands: 1
Number of Products: 15
Square Footage: 18400
Parent Co: Isoworth Limited

19639 Bevles Company
729 3rd Ave
Dallas, TX 75230-2098

214-421-7366
Fax: 214-565-0976   800-441-1601
info@apwwyott.com www.apwwyott.com
Manufacturer and exporter of kitchen equipment including heated holding, transport and storage cabinets, low temperature roast and hold ovens, proofing cabinets and racks
President: Hylcon Jonas
CFO: Don Wall
Quality Control: Jim Austin
Marketing Assistant: Martha Patino
VP of Sales/Marketing: John Kossler
Estimated Sales: $20-50 Million
Number Employees: 100-249
Square Footage: 45000
Brands:
- Climate 2000
- Tendertouch
- Transitray

19640 Bevsource
219 Little Canada Road East
St. Paul, MN 55117

651-797-0113
Fax: 651-482-1337   866-956-4608
sales@bevsource.com www.bevsource.com
Ingredients and packaging for the beverage industry, specifically sweeteners, vitamin blends, juice concentrates, and alcohol.

19641 Bevstar
615 Vista Drive
Oswego, IL 60543-8129

847-758-1581
Fax: 847-758-1617   877-238-7827
www.bevstar.com
A beverage dispenser that dispenses hot, cold and sparkling bottled or filtered water, as well as soft drinks, juices, coffees and teas
General Manager/VP: Allan Wasserman
Estimated Sales: $1-5 Million

19642 Bi-O-Kleen Industries
820 SW 2nd Ave # 200
Portland, OR 97204-3087

503-224-6246
Fax: 503-557-7818
Nonhazardous cleaning products including spray and glass cleaners, dish and laundry powders, enzyme stain and odor eliminator, carpet cleaning, dish soaps and laundry liquid
Owner: Robert C Kline Jr
CFO: Brian Barnett
VP Sales/Marketing: Cindy Rimer
Estimated Sales: $1.5 Million
Number Employees: 1-4
Number of Brands: 15
Number of Products: 15
Square Footage: 26000
Brands:
- Bac Out
- Bi-O-Kleen

19643 Bi-Star Enterprise
P.O.Box 14016
Torrance, CA 90503

310-532-5829
Fax: 310-532-4216
Decorative tin boxes
President: Daniel Hsieh
Contact: Bi-Star Corp
shirleylh@yahoo.com
Estimated Sales: $1-2.5 000,000
Number Employees: 1-4

19644 Bia Diagnostics
480 Hercules Dr
Colchester, VT 05446

802-540-0148
Fax: 802-540-0147 sales@biadiagnostics.com
www.biadiagnostics.com
A food testing facility, specializing in food allergens.
CEO/Co-Owner: Thomas Grace
CFO/Co-Owner: Robin Grace
Contact: Robin Grace
robingrace@biadiagnostics.com

19645 Bib Pak
3205 Sheridan Road
Racine, WI 53403-3662

262-633-5803
Fax: 262-633-2606
Disposable food service and catering equipment
President: John Geshay
Quality Control and R&D: Jim Geshay
VP Sales: Jim Geshay
Estimated Sales: Below $5 Million
Number Employees: 6
Square Footage: 56000
Parent Co: Standalone
Brands:
- The Party Servers

19646 Bicknell & Fuller Paperbox Company
5600 Highway 169 N
Minneapolis, MN 55428-3027

617-361-8484
Fax: 617-361-3716
Quality Control: Manuel Santos
General Manager: George Preston
Estimated Sales: $5-10 Million
Number Employees: 130

19647 Big Apple Equipment Corporation
PO Box 408
Yonkers, NY 10705-0408

914-376-9300
Fax: 914-376-9375   800-225-2626
Commercial refrigeration
President: Sheldon J Bess
Estimated Sales: $5-10 000,000
Number Employees: 15

19648 Big Basket Company
5382 Forty One Court
Lavergne, TN 37086

615-793-7779
Fax: 615-793-7487 rsaulters@bigbasketco.com
Shopping baskets and carts
Marketing: Phil Goodell

19649 Big Beam Emergency Systems Inc
290 E Prairie St
Crystal Lake, IL 60014-4415

815-459-6100
Fax: 815-459-6126 info@bigbeam.com
www.bigbeam.com
Emergency lights and exit signs
President: Nick Shah
nshah@bigbeam.com
Controller: Steve Loria
Quotations Manager: Pat Huber
Product Specialist: Frank Drew
Estimated Sales: $5-10 Million
Number Employees: 20-49
Brands:
- Big Beam

19650 Big Front Uniforms
4535 Huntington Dr S
Los Angeles, CA 90032-1940

323-227-4222
Fax: 323-227-4111   800-234-8383
info@bigfront.com
Uniforms
President: Karen Katz
info@bigfront.com
Marketing: Rou Pope
Estimated Sales: Less than $500,000
Number Employees: 20-49

19651 (HQ)Big John Corp
770 W College Ave
Pleasant Gap, PA 16823-7403

814-359-2755
Fax: 814-359-2621   800-326-9575
bjgrills@aol.com www.bigjohngrills.com
Barbecue grills including gas and charcoal
Owner: Jeff Derr
bjgrills@aol.com
Sales & Marketing: Scott Gray
Marketing & Sales Director: Steve McLaughlin
Office Manager: Randy Czekaj
Estimated Sales: $2.5-5 Million
Number Employees: 5-9
Square Footage: 40000
Other Locations:
- Big John Grills & Rotisseries
- Frisco CO

19652 Big State Spring Companyy

2738 S Port Avenue
PO Box 5255
Corpus Christi, TX 78405-2035

361-884-6232
Fax: 361-884-1112 800-880-0244
billwilltx@aol.com

Refurbisher of food mixer whips
President: Bill Willette
billwilltx@aol.com
Executive Officer: Armando Cantu
Craftsman: Manuel Ramos
billwilltx@aol.com
Number Employees: 1-4
Square Footage: 12000

19653 Big-D Construction Corp

404 W 400 S
Salt Lake City, UT 84101

801-415-6000
Fax: 801-415-6900 skieffer@big-d.com
www.big-d.com

Designer and engineer providing construction management to food processors and distributors; turn key projects included.
Chairman: Jack Livingood
jlivingood@big-d.com
Chief Executive Officer: Rob Moore
CFO: Blake Van Rosendaal
National President: Cory Moore
Executive Vice President & COO: Troy Thompson
President, Food & Beverage Group: Forrest McNab
Year Founded: 1967
Estimated Sales: $1 Billion
Number Employees: 1000
Square Footage: 15000000

19654 Bijur Lubricating Corporation

2250 Perimeter Park Dr.
Suite 120
Morrisville, NC 27560

919-465-4448
Fax: 919-465-0516 800-631-0168
info@bijurlube.com www.bijur.com

Manufacturer, exporter and importer of automatic lubricating equipment and fluid dispensers
CEO: Thomas Arndt
Marketing Communications Manager: Peter Sweeney
Sales: Kevin Ryan
Estimated Sales: $10-20 Million
Number Employees: 20-49
Square Footage: 160000
Parent Co: Vesper Corporation
Brands:
   Airmatic Lube
   Fluidflex
   Versa Iii Lub

19655 Bill Carr Signs

719 W 12th St
Flint, MI 48503-3851

810-232-1569
Fax: 810-232-6879 www.billcarrsigns.com

Vacuum formed, silk screened and advertising displays
President: Jeremy Elfstrom
CFO: Jergmy Elfstrom
Sales Executive: Mike Ellithorpe
Estimated Sales: $1-2.5 Million
Number Employees: 10-19

19656 Bill Davis Engineering

222 Hickman Drive
Suite 103
Sanford, FL 32771

407-328-1117
Fax: 407-330-5231 billdaviseng@bellsouth.net
www.davis-engineering.net

Packaging machinery
President: Rick Paulsen
Estimated Sales: $5-10 Million
Number Employees: 20-49
Parent Co: Davis Engineering

19657 Billie-Ann Plastics Packaging

360 Troutman St
Brooklyn, NY 11237-2614

718-497-3409
Fax: 718-497-6095 888-245-5432
info@billieannplastics.com
www.plasticcontainerswholesale-billieann.com

Cylinders and plastic boxes

Owner: Bill Rubenstein
info@billieannplastics.com
Marketing: Bill Rubenstein
Estimated Sales: $3 Million
Number Employees: 1-4

19658 Billington Welding & Mfg Inc

1442 N Emerald Ave
PO Box 4460
Modesto, CA 95351-1115

209-526-9312
Fax: 209-521-4759 800-932-9312
info@billington-mfg.com
www.billington-mfg.com

Food processing equipment
President: Frances Billington
HR Executive: Lindy Broome
lbroome@billington-mfg.com
Marketing Manager: Charles Billington
Estimated Sales: $5-10 Million
Number Employees: 20-49

19659 Bilt-Rite Conveyors

735 Industrial Loop Road
New London, WI 54961-3530

920-982-6600
Fax: 920-982-7750 www.bilt-rite.com

Manufacturer and exporter of stainless steel conveyors including belt, tabletop, chain and wire mesh
Owner: Jeffrey Bellig
R&D: Orlando Rojas
Contact: T Ramesh
trramesh@bilt.ae
Estimated Sales: $5-10 Million
Number Employees: 20-49
Parent Co: Titan Industies, Inc.
Brands:
   Bilt-Rite
   Brico
   Speed-Flow

19660 Bimba Manufacturing Co

25150 S Governors Hwy
University Park, IL 60484-8895

708-534-8544
Fax: 708-235-2014 800-442-4622
support@bimba.com www.bimba.com

Rodless cylinders, double bore rectangular cross-section cylinders, rack and pinion rotary actuators, linear thrusters, hydraulic cylinders, inport flow control valves and position sensing switches
President: Pat Ormsby
ormsbyp@bimba.com
VP: Randy Dunlap
Head of Marketing Department: Dennis Kennedy
Head Of Operations.: Randy Dunlap
Number Employees: 100-249

19661 Bimetalix

P.O.Box 8
Sullivan, WI 53178-0008

262-593-8066
Fax: 262-593-8067

A complete line of scraped surface heat exchanger cylinders for a variety of food processing
President: Forbes Hotchkiss

19662 Bindmax LLC

16595 W Stratton Dr
New Berlin, WI 53151-7301

262-796-2468
877-543-2463
tcolleton@bindmax.com

Protein products supplier utilized by meat, poultry and seafood companies to improve cook yield and flavor
Vice President: Tom Colleton
Contact: Rick Cassidy
rcassidy@bindmax.com
Estimated Sales: $1 Million
Number Employees: 5-9

19663 Biner Ellison PackagingSysts

2685 S Melrose Dr
Vista, CA 92081-8783

760-598-6500
Fax: 760-598-7600 800-733-8162
sales@binerellison.com www.accutekcapping.com

Manufacturer and exporter of bottle labeling, conveying, liquid filling and capping machinery and integrated packaging systems

President: Tom Ellison Jr
Contact: Timothy Hussman
timothy@newportmeat.com
Operations: Jeff Schwarz
Estimated Sales: $2.5-5 Million
Number Employees: 10-19

19664 Binks Industries Inc

1997a Aucutt Rd
Montgomery, IL 60538-1135

630-801-1100
Fax: 630-801-0819 info@binksindustries.com
www.binksindustries.com

Manufacturer and exporter of pin hole detection equipment
President: Carolyn Calkins
binksinc@binksindustries.com
Estimated Sales: Less Than $500,000
Number Employees: 1-4
Square Footage: 12000
Brands:
   Binks Industries, Inc.

19665 Bintz Restaurant SupplyCompany

P.O.Box 1350
Salt Lake City, UT 84110-1350

801-463-1515
Fax: 801-463-1693 800-443-4746
sales@bintzsupply.com www.bintzsupply.com

Wholesaler/distributor and design consultant of hotel and restaurant equipment and supplies
President: Roger Brown
CFO: Troy Hanson
Vice President: Brad Garner
Sales Manager: Michael Bailey
Purchasing Manager: Christie Smith
Estimated Sales: $10-20 Million
Number Employees: 20-49
Square Footage: 40000

19666 Bio Cide Intl Inc

2845 Broce Dr # A
Norman, OK 73072-2448

405-329-5556
Fax: 405-329-2681 800-323-1398
www.bio-cide.com

Manufacturer and exporter of chlorine dioxide based products for sanitization, disinfection, deodorization and water treatment
CEO: B C Danner
Sales Director: Damon Dickinson
Contact: Mark Cochran
mcochran@bio-cide.com
Chairman: B Danner
Estimated Sales: $1-2.5 Million
Number Employees: 20-49
Square Footage: 80000
Brands:
   Envirocon
   Odorid
   Oxine
   Purogene
   Sanogene

19667 Bio Huma Netics

1331 W Houston Ave
Gilbert, AZ 85233-1816

480-961-1220
Fax: 480-961-3501 480-961-1220
info@biohumanetics.com www.bhn.us

Odor control, sludge management, environmental compliance
President: Lyndon Smith
Contact: Rita Abi-Ghanem
rita@bhn.us
Estimated Sales: $5-10 Million
Number Employees: 10-19

19668 Bio Industries

112 4th St
Luxemburg, WI 54217-8396

920-845-2355
Fax: 920-845-2439

Industrial and household cleaners including detergents, degreasers, etc
President: Irvin Vincent
Office Manager: Nancy Vincent
Estimated Sales: $1-5 Million
Number Employees: 3
Number of Brands: 2
Square Footage: 8000
Parent Co: NEW Plastics Corporation

Brands:
Gp 101
Hazel's

19669 Bio Pac Inc
584 Pinto Ct
PO Box 5288
Incline Village, NV 89451-8118

775-831-9493
Fax: 866-628-1662 800-225-2855
ceh@bio-pac.com www.bio-pac.com
Laundry and dish cleaners including citrus cleaner
concentrates, liquid soap concentrate, laundry and
bleach powder
President: Collin Harris
Estimated Sales: $1 Million
Number Employees: 1
Square Footage: 2000
Brands:
Biopac
Oasis

19670 Bio Zapp Laboratories
PO Box 20127
Sarasota, FL 34276

941-922-9199
Fax: 210-805-9196 biozapp@biozapp.com
www.biozapp.com
Manufacturer and exporter of odor elimination sys-
tems, degreasers, glass ans surface cleaners
Founder: Miky Gershenson
miky@biozapp.com
Director Operations: Denise Novick
Estimated Sales: $5,000,000
Number Employees: 5-9
Number of Products: 20
Type of Packaging: Consumer, Food Service, Pri-
vate Label, Bulk
Brands:
Grease Off

19671 Bio-Rad Laboratories Inc.
1000 Alfred Nobel Dr.
Hercules, CA 94547

510-724-7000
Fax: 510-741-5817 www.bio-rad.com
Supplier of laboratory equiptment and other supplies
for the food industry.
Chairman/President/CEO: Norman Schwartz
norman_schwartz@bio-rad.com
Executive VP/CFO: Ilan Daskal
Executive VP/Chief Strategy Officer: Giovannni
Magni
Executive VP, Global Commercial Operat.: Mike
Crowley
Executive VP/COO: Andrew Last
Year Founded: 1952
Estimated Sales: $2 Billion
Number Employees: 8,205+

19672 BioAmber
3850 Annapolis Ln N
Suite 180
Plymouth, MN 55447

763-253-4480
kristine.weigal@bio-amber.com
Succinic acid, BDO, plasticizers, polymers and C6
chemicals
President & CEO: Jean-Francois HUC
CTO: Jim Millis
CFO: Andrew Ashworth
Executive VP: Mike Hartmann
Chief Commercial Officer: Babette Pettersen
Contact: Marie Beaumont
marie.beaumont@bio-amber.com
Chief Operations Officer: Fabrice Orecchioni
Estimated Sales: $560 Thousand
Number Employees: 74

19673 BioExx Specialty Proteins
33 Fraser Ave
Suite G11
Toronto, ON M6K 3J9
Canada

416-588-4442
Fax: 416-588-1999 www.bioexx.com
Oil and high-value proteins from Canola.
CEO & Director: Chris Schnarr
CFO: Greg Furyk
EVP: Samah Garringer
VP Operations: Clinton Smith

19674 BioSys
3810 Packard Street
Ann Arbor, MI 48108-2054

613-271-1144
Fax: 613-271-1148 800-458-5101
biosysinc@mail.com
E coliform
President: Brian Leek
Estimated Sales: $1-2.5 Million
Number Employees: 5-9

19675 BioTech Films, LLC
Ste 115
5370 College Blvd
Leawood, KS 66211-1884

813-628-0424
Fax: 813-628-0162 800-633-2611
Customized films made with food ingredients for
packaging uses; edible, water-soluble films; edible
plastic films; edible flakes for decoration
President: James Rossman
CEO: Graham Hind
Executive VP: Larry Shattles
Research & Development: Caroline Decker
Sales Director: Richard Fielder
VP Operations: George Tidy
Estimated Sales: $10 Million
Number Employees: 50-99
Number of Brands: 2
Number of Products: 20
Square Footage: 25000
Type of Packaging: Private Label, Bulk
Brands:
Aquafilm
Aquaflakes

19676 BioVittoria USA
357 N Milwaukee Rd
Libertyville, IL 60048

847-226-3467
Processor and supplier of monk fruit, a natural calo-
rie-free sweetener that is a new alternative to sugar
and artificial sweeteners.
President: Lan Fusheng
CEO: David Thorrold
CFO: Danny Wai Yen
VP: Garth Smith
VP Sales & Marketing: Paul Paslaski
Estimated Sales: $500 Thousand
Type of Packaging: Food Service, Private Label,
Bulk

19677 Bioclimatic Air Systems LLC
600 Delran Pkwy # D
Delran, NJ 08075-1255

856-764-4300
Fax: 856-764-4301 800-962-5594
mail@bioclimatic.com www.bioclimatic.com
Manufacturer and exporter of air purification sys-
tems
President: Michele Bottino
mbottino@bioclimatic.com
Estimated Sales: Below $5 Million
Number Employees: 20-49
Brands:
Aeromat
Aerotec

19678 (HQ)Biocontrol Systems Inc
12822 SE 32nd St
Bellevue, WA 98005-4340

425-603-1123
Fax: 425-603-0070 800-245-0113
bcs_us@biocontrolsys.com
www.biocontrolsys.com
Manufacturer and exporter of diagnostic microbiol-
ogy test kits and equipment
President: Phillip Feldsine
CEO: Khyati Shah
shahkhyati123@gmail.com
R&D: David Kerr
Sr. Vice President: Carolyn Feldsine
Quality Control: Julia Terry
Director Marketing: Maritta Ko
Marketing Assistant: Jennifer Hawton
Estimated Sales: $3-5 Million
Number Employees: 50-99
Other Locations:
Biocontrol Systems
Westbrook ME

19679 Bioenergetics Inc
PO Box 259096
Madison, WI 53725-9096

608-255-4028
Fax: 608-251-0658
Research on flavor and nutrition, consutation and
formulation
CEO: Roy Schenk
CFO: Roy Schenk
Estimated Sales: Less Than $500,000
Number Employees: 1-4

19680 Bioionix Inc
4603 Triangle St
Mc Farland, WI 53558-9445

608-838-0300
info@bioionix.com
www.bioionix.com
Disinfectants and oxidation systems for water treatment.
President/CEO: James Tretheway
Number Employees: 5-9

19681 Biolog Inc
21124 Cabot Blvd
Hayward, CA 94545-1130

510-785-2585
Fax: 415-782-4639 800-284-4949
csorders@biolog.com www.biolog.com
Manufacturer and exporter of microbiological iden-
tification products
President/CEO & CSO: Barry R Bochner
bbochner@biolog.com
Vice President Of Finance/CFO: Edwin R Fineman
Vice President Of Operations: Doug E Rife
Number Employees: 20-49
Brands:
Microlog
Microplate
Rainbow Agar

19682 Biological Services
10835 NW Ambassador Drive
Kansas City, MO 64153-1241

913-236-6868
Fax: 913-236-6868
Consultant offering testing services for all bacteria;
also, sanitation inspections and sampling
Estimated Sales: less than $500,000
Number Employees: 1-4

19683 Biomed Comm
2 Nickerson Street
Seattle, WA 98109-1652

206-284-3433
Fax: 206-284-6585 www.biomedcomm.com
Communications
CEO: Dr. Barbara Brewitt

19684 Biomerieux Inc
100 Rodolphe St
Durham, NC 27712-9402

919-620-2000
Fax: 800-968-9494 800-682-2666
www.biomerieux-usa.com
Manufacturer and exporter of food processing
equipment including aseptic, bacterial detection and
microbiological
Chairman: Jean Luc Belingard
CEO: Alexandre Merieux
CFO: Brian Armstrong
R&D: Brian Daniel
Quality Control: Katie Foushee
VP Sales: Harry Schrick
CVP, Human Resources & Communications: Michel
Baugenault
Estimated Sales: $5-10,000,000
Number Employees: 500-999
Parent Co: Azko Nobel

19685 Biomerieux Inc
595 Anglum Rd
Hazelwood, MO 63042-2320

314-731-7787
Fax: 314-731-8800 www.biomerieux-usa.com
BioM,rieux features a full range of diagnostic products for use in the food industry, including rapid, automated testing solutions for pathogen detection,
quality indicator enumeration, continuous bacterial
monitoring, identificationstrain typing, environmental monitoring and sample preparation equipment.

Vice President: Scott Remes
scott.remes@biomed.com
Vice President: Scott Remes
scott.remes@biomed.com
Number Employees: 500-999

19686 Biomist Inc
573 N Wolf Rd
Wheeling, IL 60090-3027
847-850-5530
Fax: 847-803-0875 prmartin@biomistinc.com
Biomist Power Disinfecting System Spray.
Director of Sales & Operations: Robert Cook
rlcook@biomistinc.com
Director of Sales & Operations: Robert Cook
Vice President Customer Service: Eileen Bowery
Director of Sales and Operations: Peter Martin
Number Employees: 5-9

19687 Biopath
2611 Mercer Avenue
West Palm Beach, FL 33401-7415
800-645-2302
Fax: 888-645-2302 800-645-2302
rchiger@rxir.com www.biopathholdings.com
President: Peter Nielsen

19688 Bioscience International Inc
11333 Woodglen Dr
Rockville, MD 20852-3071
301-231-7400
Fax: 301-231-7277 bioinfo@biosci-intl.com
www.biosci-intl.com
Manufacturer and wholesaler/distributor of micro-
bial air samplers for the food and beverage industry.
President: Don Queen
VP: Marsha Pratt
Customer Service: Don Queen
Number Employees: 1-4
Square Footage: 140000
Brands:
   Sas Super 90

19689 Biotek Instruments Inc
100 Tigan St
Winooski, VT 05404-1356
802-655-4040
Fax: 802-655-7941 sales@biotek.com
www.biotek.com
Test kits for vitamins, mycotoxins, antibiotics, ste-
roids/hormones, PSP, etc
President: Briar Alpert
CEO: Alpert Briar
briara@biotek.com
CFO: Klus Deutfcher
Quality Control: Mike Sevigny
R&D: Mike Kontorovich
Estimated Sales: $20-50 Million
Number Employees: 250-499

19690 Biotest Diagnostics Corporation
400 Commons Way
Rockaway, NJ 07866-2030
973-625-1300
Fax: 973-625-9454 800-522-0090
Manufacturer and exporter of environmental moni-
toring products
President: William Wiess
Quality Control: Lara Soltis
Marketing Director: Carol Julich
Contact: Angelene Atwal
angelene_atwal@bio-rad.com
Production Manager: Dan Behler
Estimated Sales: $10-20 Million
Number Employees: 20-49
Parent Co: Biotest AG
Type of Packaging: Bulk
Brands:
   Apc Particle Counters
   Hycom Contact Slides
   Rcs Air Samplers

19691 Biothane Corporation
2500 Broadway
Camden, NJ 08104
856-541-3500
Fax: 856-541-3366 sales@biothane.com
www.biothane.com
Manufacturer and exporter of anaerobic biological
waste water treatment systems

President: Robert Sax
VP: Jay Murphy
VP Marketing/Sales: Denise Johnston
Contact: William Donnell
b.odonnell@biothane.com
Estimated Sales: $3-5 Million
Number Employees: 30
Square Footage: 80000
Parent Co: Joseph Oat Corporation
Brands:
   Biopuric
   Biothane
   Biobed

19692 Biovail Technologies
3701 Concorde Pkwy Ste 800
Chantilly, VA 20151
703-995-2400
Fax: 703-995-2490 biovail@btl.com
Consultant offering technology including controlled
release and taste making applications, rapid dissolv-
ing tablets and long taste flavor systems
VP: Paul De Jardins
Contact: Myrna Gheen
myrna.gheen@biovail.com
Estimated Sales: $20-50 Million
Number Employees: 100-249
Square Footage: 32000

19693 Birko Corp
9152 Yosemite St
Henderson, CO 80640-8027
303-287-9604
Fax: 303-289-1190 800-525-0476
info@birkocorp.com
Inorganic industrial chemicals
President: Florence Powers
CEO: Josh Valdez
josh@seatosummit.com
CFO: Kelly Heffer
CEO: Mark Swanson
R&D and QC: Kerry McAninch
Estimated Sales: $20-50 Million
Number Employees: 50-99

19694 (HQ)Birko Corporation
19950 West 161st Street
Olathe, KS 66062
913-764-0321
Fax: 913-764-0779 800-444-8360
djohnson@birkocorp.com www.birkocorp.com
Manufactures 250 cleaning, sanitation and produc-
tion chemicals, and specialized chemical delivery
equipment for HACCP meat, poultry and food
plants.
President: Mike Gangel
CEO: Mike Swanson
VP, Business Development: Kelly Green
Research/Development VP: Terry MacAninch
VP sales: Philip Snellen
Customer Service: Rosey Hohendorf
Estimated Sales: $9 Million
Number Employees: 20-49
Other Locations:
   Birko Distribution Center
   Atlanta GA
   Birko Distribution Center
   Boise ID
   Birko Distribution Center
   Louisville KY
   Birko Distribution Center
   Modesto CA
   Birko Distribution Center
   Philadelphia PA
   Birko Distribution Center
   Phoenix AZ

19695 Birmingham Controls
11144 Business Cir
Cerritos, CA 90703-5523
909-825-7311
Fax: 562-402-0485 800-527-8326
sales@bermingham.com www.bermingham.com
President: Ernest Chavez
ernest.chavez@colostate.edu
Sales: Wes Selby
Number Employees: 50-99

19696 Birmingham Mop Manufacturing Company
115 Oxmoor Ln W
Birmingham, AL 35209-5901
205-942-6101
Fax: 205-942-6101
Mops, brooms, mopheads, etc

President: Glenn L Beacham Jr
glenn.beacham@afflink.com
CEO: Mary Williams
Secretary: Frank Beacham
Estimated Sales: Below $5 Million
Number Employees: 11
Square Footage: 13000

19697 Biro Manufacturing Co
1114 W Main St
Lakeside Marblhd, OH 43440-2099
419-798-4451
Fax: 419-798-9106 sales@birosaw.com
www.birosaw.com
Manufacturer and exporter of meat cutting and pro-
cessing equipment including grinders and mixer
grinders, vacuum tumblers, tenderizers, horizontal
slicing machines, cutters, meat mixers and industrial
power saws; also, frozen foodflakers
President: Theresa Bahm
tbahm@birosaw.com
VP of Sales & Marketing: D.L (Skip) Muir
Sales Manager: David Dursbacky
Estimated Sales: $5-10 Million
Number Employees: 50-99
Type of Packaging: Bulk
Brands:
   Biro

19698 Bishamon Industry Corp
5651 E Francis St
Ontario, CA 91761-3601
909-390-7093
Fax: 909-390-0060 800-358-8833
info@bishamon.com www.bishamon.com
Scissor and skid lifts, pallet trucks and manual level-
ers/positioners and mobile loading docks; exporter
of pallet levelers/positioners; importer of pallet jacks
President: Wataru Sugiura
wsugiura@bishamon.com
Quality Control: Margie Giordano
VP Sales/Marketing: Robert Clark
Sales Manager: Steve O'Connell
Estimated Sales: $10-20 Million
Number Employees: 20-49
Square Footage: 260000
Brands:
   Bishamon
   Ecoa
   Ez Loader
   Tad

19699 Bishop Machine Shop
2304 Hoge Ave
Zanesville, OH 43701-2166
740-453-8818
Fax: 740-453-6750 www.sprintermarking.com
Automatic contact ink marking machinery
Manager: Ron Barnhouse
Sales Manager: Bob Bishop
Estimated Sales: Less Than $500,000
Number Employees: 1-4
Brands:
   Ink-Koder

19700 Bismarck Caterers
1901 W Madison St
Chicago, IL 60612-2459
312-455-7500
Fax: 312-943-7898
Info@BismarckEnterprises.com
www.bismarckenterprises.com
Catering services, concessions
President: Peter Wirtz
Cmo: Erin Houlehen
ehoulehen@bismarck-enterprises.com
Estimated Sales: $7,600,000
Number Employees: 250-499

19701 Bison Gear & Engineering Corp.
3850 Ohio Ave
St. Charles, IL 60174
630-377-4327
Fax: 630-377-6777 800-282-4766
info@bisongear.com www.bisongear.com
Power transmission equipment
Chairman: Ron Bullock
CEO: John Burch *Year Founded:* 1960

19702 Bivac Enterprise
357 Lake Shore Drive
Brick, NJ 08723-6013
732-920-0080
Fax: 609-693-8637

Thermoplastic sealing, vacuum and gas packing equipment

19703 Bivans Corporation
2431 Dallas St
Los Angeles, CA 90031

323-225-4248
Fax: 323-225-7316 sales@bivans.com
www.bivans.com
Packaging equipment for the food industry

19704 Bizerba USA
5200 Anthony Rd # F
Suite F
Sandston, VA 23150-1929

804-649-2064
Fax: 804-649-2064 us.info@bizerba.com
www.bizerba.com
Packaging equipment
Vice President: Rainer Dallairosa
rainer.dallairosa@cporinc.com
CFO: Cheryll Ziemblicki
VP, Engineered Solutions: Rainer DallaRosa
Marketing Manager: Chuck Saje
Director Retail Systems: Robert Weisz
Operations Manager: Joanne Scuccimarri
Number Employees: 50-99

19705 Bizerba USA
31 Gordon Rd
Piscataway, NJ 08854

732-565-6000
Fax: 732-819-0429 www.bizerbausa.com
Retial scales, slicers, weigh price labeling equipment as well as checkweighers, industrial scales and software
President/CEO: Andreas Kraut
VP/Controller: Frank Thiry
Marketing Specialist: Gaudy Cruz
Contact: Manfred Beilharz
manfred.beilharz@bizerba.com
Operations Manager: Keith Aumiller
Estimated Sales: $10-$20 000,000
Number Employees: 20-49
Type of Packaging: Food Service, Bulk

19706 Bjm Pumps
123 Spencer Plain Rd # 1
Old Saybrook, CT 06475-4051

860-399-5937
Fax: 860-399-7784 www.bjmpumps.com
Pumps and pump accesories for food industry
Owner: Steve Bjorkman
sbjorkman@bjmcorp.com
Business Manager: Mike Bjorkman
Estimated Sales: $630,000
Number Employees: 10-19

19707 Black Bear Corp
2224 Buford Ave SW
Roanoke, VA 24015-5506

540-982-1061
Fax: 540-982-1066 800-223-1284
Specialty chemicals including municipal, institutional and industrial maintenance
President: Linda Jones
Estimated Sales: $2.5-5 Million
Number Employees: 1-4

19708 Black Bear Farm Winery
248 County Road 1
Chenango Forks, NY 13746-2208

607-656-9863
mamabear@blackbearwinery.com
www.blackbearwinery.com
Wines
President: Mark Stacey
Co-Owner: Sandy Stacey
Chief of Cider Production: Joe Stacey
Number Employees: 1-4

19709 (HQ)Black Brothers
501 9th Ave
PO Box 401
Mendota, IL 61342-1927

815-539-7451
Fax: 815-538-2451 800-252-2568
www.blackbros.com
Manufacturer and exporter of gluing, coating and laminating machines for packaging of food products

President: Matthew Carroll
CFO: Jeff Simonton
Director Sales/Service: Walter Weiland
Sales: Todd Phalen
IT: Jeffrey Simonton
rburkhart@reimersinc.com
Estimated Sales: $10-20 Million
Number Employees: 50-99
Other Locations:
   Black Brothers Co.
   Warsaw IN
Brands:
   Black

19710 Black Horse Mfg Co
601 Cumberland St # B
Chattanooga, TN 37404-1922

423-624-0798
Fax: 423-624-7557 bhorse1178@aol.com
Advertising specialties
President: Larry Shope
bhorse1178@aol.com
Estimated Sales: Below $5,000,000
Number Employees: 5-9

19711 Black River Caviar
0075 Sunset Dr
Breckenridge, CO 80424-7218

970-547-1542
Fax: 970-547-9707 888-315-0575
graham@blackrivercaviar.com
www.blackrivercaviar.com
Caviar
President: Graham Gaspard
Estimated Sales: $500 Thousand
Number Employees: 5
Type of Packaging: Consumer, Food Service

19712 Black River Pallet Co
410 E Roosevelt Ave
Zeeland, MI 49464-1342

616-772-6271
Fax: 616-772-6206 800-427-6515
bryan@blackriverpallet.com
www.blackriverpallet.com
Pallets and skids
President: Bryan Slagh
bryan@blackriverpallet.com
Estimated Sales: $1-2.5 Million
Number Employees: 20-49
Square Footage: 28000

19713 Black's Products of HighPoint
2800 Westchester Drive
High Point, NC 27262-8039

336-886-5011
Fax: 336-886-4734 blacks@highpoint.net
www.blacksfurniture.com
Manufacturer and exporter of leather and restaurant furniture polishes
Estimated Sales: $1-5 Million
Number Employees: 20-49
Square Footage: 40000
Brands:
   Antique Blend
   Apple Polisher
   Blodis
   Garde
   Leather Care
   Wood Care

19714 Blackhawk Molding Co Inc
120 W Interstate Rd
Addison, IL 60101

630-458-2100
Fax: 630-543-3904 www.blackhawkmolding.com
Manufacturer and exporter of Tamper-Evident closures for the dairy, juice, and bottled water industires
Human Resources Director: Roberto Castro
Director of Operations: Jeff Davis
Plastics Engineer: Robert Komperda
Automation Engineer: Andrew Dreasler
Year Founded: 1949
Estimated Sales: $100-500 Million
Number Employees: 100-249
Type of Packaging: Consumer, Food Service, Private Label, Bulk

19715 Blackmer Co
1809 Century Ave SW
Grand Rapids, MI 49503-8017

616-241-1611
Fax: 616-241-3752 info@blackmer.com
www.psgdover.com/blackmer

Pumps and compressors
President: Carmine Bosco
CFO: Tom Madden
VP: John Pepper
Quality Control: Dick Sowa
Sales Manager: Peter Sturgeon
IT: Stephen Brown
kenneth.paine@alcoa.com
Number Employees: 100-249

19716 Blackwing Ostrich MeatsInc.
19588 Il Route 173
Antioch, IL 60002-7206

847-838-4888
Fax: 847-838-4899 800-326-7874
roger@blackwing.com www.blackwing.com
Organic beef, chicken, buffalo, ostrich and game meats
President/Owner: Roger Gerber
VP: Beth Kaplan
bak@blackwing.com
Estimated Sales: $12 Million
Number Employees: 26
Number of Brands: 5
Number of Products: 140
Square Footage: 32000
Type of Packaging: Consumer, Food Service, Private Label, Bulk
Brands:
   Blackwing Organics
   Blackwing
   Solomon Glatt Kosher
   Sport Stick

19717 Blade Runners
P.O.Box 49
New London, WI 54961-0049

920-982-9974
Fax: 920-982-0580
Computer systems and software, used and rebuilt equipment, sausage linkers, smokehouses, accessories, stuffers and accessories, and vacuum pumps
Manager: John Mauthe
Estimated Sales: $1-2.5 000,000
Number Employees: 10-19

19718 Blake Corporation
W1902 Holy Hill Rd
Cecil, WI 54111

715-745-2700
Fax: 715-758-2080
Cheese equipment, cutters
Estimated Sales: $1-5 000,000
Number Employees: 1

19719 Blakeslee, Inc.
1228 Capital Drive
Addison, IL 60101

630-532-5021
Fax: 630-532-5020 blakeslee@blakesleeinc.com
www.blakesleeinc.com
Manufacturer and exporter of dishwashers, dishwasher racks, mixers, grinders, peelers and slicers
President: Pirjo Stafseth
CFO: Gary Stafseth
Executive VP: Chirs Berg
Marketing/Sales: Pirjo Stafsethh
Contact: Blakeslee Glass
blakeslee@hfse.com
Plant Manager: Gary Berg
Purchasing Manager: Ron Pentis
Square Footage: 400000
Parent Co: Blako
Brands:
   Blakeslee

19720 Blako Industries
P.O.Box 179
Dunbridge, OH 43414

419-833-4491
Fax: 419-833-5733
FDA and USDA approved low density polyethylene films and bags. Polyethylene plastic film and bags
President: Ed Long
Quality Control: Brad Kickle
VP: Chuck Hansen
Director Sales: Ronald Rummel
Estimated Sales: $5-10 Million
Number Employees: 20-49
Square Footage: 50000

19721 Blanc Industries
88 King St # 1
Dover, NJ 07801-3655

973-537-0090
Fax: 973-537-0906 888-332-5262
email@blancind.com www.blancind.com
Manufacture, design and print point of sale promotional signage, displays and fixtures for the food and retail industry. Founded in 1997.
President: Didier Blanc
dblanc@blancind.com
Operations: Dorothy Vitiello
Number Employees: 20-49

19722 Blancett
8635 Washington Ave
Racine, WI 53406-3738

262-639-6770
Fax: 262-417-1155 800-235-1638
info@blancett.com www.blancett.com
Manufacturer and exporter of 3-A sanitary liquid turbine flow meters
President: John Erskine
pascualespinoza@blancett.com
Sales: Pascual Espinoza
Purchasing Manager: Chuck Tucker
Estimated Sales: $3-5 Million
Number Employees: 100-249
Square Footage: 40000
Parent Co: Racine Federated
Type of Packaging: Bulk
Brands:
　Floclean

19723 Blanche P. Field, LLC
1 Design Center Pl
Boston, MA 02210

617-423-0715
Fax: 617-330-6876 800-895-0714
www.blanchefield.com
Manufacturer and exporter of custom lamp shades
President: Stephen G W Walk
CEO: Mitchell Massey
Estimated Sales: $2.5-5 Million
Number Employees: 20-49
Brands:
　Glanz French

19724 Blast It Clean
7800 E 12th St
Suite 7
Kansas City, MO 64126-2370

816-241-9199
Fax: 913-440-4725 877-379-4233
info@blast-it-clean.com www.blastitclean.com
Industrial cleaning solutions
Owner: Rick Dillon
rdillon@blast-it-clean.com
Owner: Rick Salgado
Marketing Director: Erica Chen
Estimated Sales: $1.7 Million
Number Employees: 23
Square Footage: 160000

19725 Blaze Products Corp
1101 Isaac Shelby Dr
Shelbyville, KY 40065-8171

502-633-0650
Fax: 502-633-0685 blazesales@blazeproducts.com
www.blazeproducts.com
Manufacture chafing dish fuel
COO: Cindy Foster
Number Employees: 1-4

19726 Blendco Inc
8 J M Tatum Industrial Dr
Hattiesburg, MS 39401-8341

601-544-9800
Fax: 601-544-5634 888-253-6326
csr@blendcoinc.com www.blendcoinc.com
Dry food manufacturer. Provide custom blending and packaging, as well as private labeling and contract packaging services.
President: Charles McCaffrey
Chief Financial Officer: Ken Hrdlica
Estimated Sales: $8 Million
Number Employees: 20-49
Number of Brands: 2
Type of Packaging: Food Service, Private Label,
　Bulk
Brands:
　Ezy Time
　Chicken-To-Go

19727 Blendex Co
11208 Electron Dr
Louisville, KY 40299-3875

502-267-1003
Fax: 502-267-1024 800-626-6325
www.blendex.com
Dry ingredients blending company specializing in batters, breadings, seasonings, seasonings and marinades. 12 distribution warehouses located across the US.
President: Jacquelyn Bailey
CEO: Ronald Pottinger
rpottinger@blendex.com
Director: Olin Cook
Executive Vice President: Tony Jessee
Vice President Research/Development: Jordan Stivers
Vice President of Sales: Ron Carr
Estimated Sales: $28.5 Million
Number Employees: 50-99
Type of Packaging: Food Service, Private Label,
　Bulk

19728 Blentech Corp
2899 Dowd Dr
Santa Rosa, CA 95407-7897

707-523-5949
Fax: 707-523-5939 info@blentech.com
Batch cookers, continuous batch cookers, mixer-blenders, vacuum tumble mixers, tilt and hi-lift dumpers, screw conveyors, pump feeders
President: Darrell Horn
CEO: Daniel Voit
Executive Vice President: Joe Yarnell
Estimated Sales: $5-10 Million
Number Employees: 50-99

19729 Blickman Supply Company
280 N Midland Avenue
Bldg M1
Saddle Brook, NJ 07663-5720

201-791-6680
Fax: 201-791-2288
Fry saver oil filtration machines for food service
Estimated Sales: $1-2.5 000,000
Number Employees: 19

19730 Blissfield Canning Company
PO Box 127
Blissfield, MI 49228-0127

517-486-3815
Fax: 517-486-4032
Canning
President: George Waigle
VP: Jerry Roessler
Estimated Sales: $2.5-5,000,000
Number Employees: 20-49

19731 Blodgett Co
10840 Seaboard Loop
Houston, TX 77099-3401

281-933-6195
Fax: 281-933-6196 info@theblodgettcompany.com
www.theblodgettcompany.com
Manufacturer and exporter of packaging equipment including scales, controls and vertical form/fill/seal, packaging machines
President: Amber Blodgett
ablodgett@theblodgettcompany.com
CFO and R&D: Bradley Blodgett
Purchasing Agent: Pete Duncan
Estimated Sales: $1-2.5 Million
Number Employees: 1-4
Square Footage: 11000

19732 Blodgett Corp
44 Lakeside Ave
Burlington, VT 05401-5242

802-658-6600
Fax: 802-864-0183 800-331-5842
literature@blodgett.com www.blodgett.com
Manufacturer and exporter of steamer ovens
President: Mark Pumphret
dreyn2@maytag.com
VP of Marketing: Des Hague
VP of Sales: Jeff Cook
Number Employees: 100-249
Parent Co: Maytag Corporation

19733 (HQ)Blodgett Oven Co
44 Lakeside Ave
Burlington, VT 05401-5274

802-860-3700
Fax: 802-864-0183 800-331-5842
literature@blodgett.com www.blodgett.com
Manufacturer and exporter of ovens including convection, range, deck, pizza and conveyor; also, steamers, fryers, kettles, grills, mobile food carts, charbroilers, catering equipment and filtering systems
President: Gary Mick
CFO: Gary Mick
IT Executive: Sarah Home
sarah@copelandfurniture.com
Director Corporate Communications: Ann Williams
IT Executive: Sarah Home
sarah@copelandfurniture.com
Number Employees: 100-249
Parent Co: Maytag Corporation
Brands:
　Blodgett
　Blodgett Combi
　Magikitch'n
　Pitco Frialator

19734 Bloemhof
1215 South Swaner Road
Salt Lake City, UT 84104
Canada

80- 42- 277
Fax: 801-973-6858 bert@bloemhof.com
www.bloemhof.com

19735 Blome International
1450 Hoff Industrial Ctr
O Fallon, MO 63366-1958

636-379-9119
Fax: 636-379-0388 support@blome.com
www.blome.com
Corrosion resistance coating materials.
President: Steven Blome
steven@blome.com
CEO: Steve Bloom
Number Employees: 5-9
Parent Co: Hempel

19736 (HQ)Blommer Chocolate Co
600 W Kinzie St
Chicago, IL 60654-5585

312-226-7700
Fax: 312-226-4141 800-621-1606
www.blommer.com
Processor and exporter of chocolate ingredients for the bakery, dairy and confectionery industries including milk and dark chocolate, confectioner and pastel coatings, cookie drops, chocolate liquor, cocoa butter, cocoa powder, icecream ingredients, etc. Founded in 1939.
President: Peter Blommer
Founder, Chairman & CEO: Henry Blommer
CFO: Jack S Larsen
jack@blommer.com
Vice President: Rich Blommer
Manager of Quality Assurance: Radka Kacena
Marketing & Purchasing Manager: Leanna Hicks
Sales Support: Chief Marketing Officer Kidd
VP of Operations: Rich Blommer
Plant Mnaager: Joe Chwala
Purchasing Manager: Faye Garcia
Estimated Sales: $38.4 Million
Number Employees: 1-4
Square Footage: 340000
Type of Packaging: Bulk
Other Locations:
　Union City CA
　East Greenville PA
　Campbellford ON

19737 Bloomfield Industries
10 Sunnen drive
St. Louis, MO 63143-3800

775-345-8200
Fax: 314-781-3445 888-356-5362
clientcare@wellsbloomfield.com
www.wellsbloomfield.com
Coffee and tea equipment including automatic and satellite brewers, airpots and thermal servers, decanters and accessories, coffee warmers and grinders and water filtration systems and filters
Vice President, Sales/Marketing, Wells-B: Paul Angrick
Senior VP: Dave Ek

Estimated Sales: $500,000-$1 Million
Number Employees: 1-4
Parent Co: Carrier Commercial Refrigeration
Brands:
    Cafe Elite
    Integrity
    Koffe King

19738 Blower Application Co Inc

N114w19125 Clinton Dr
PO Box 279
Germantown, WI 53022-3013
    262-255-5580
Fax: 262-255-3446 800-959-0880
sales@bloapco.com www.bloapco.com
Manufacturer and exporter of waste disposal systems and equipment shredders
President: John Stanislowski
bac@bloapco.com
Sales Director: Ric Johnson
Estimated Sales: $5-10 Million
Number Employees: 20-49
Square Footage: 80000
Brands:
    Blo Apco

19739 BluMetric EnvironmentalInc.

3108 Carp Road
P.O. Box 430
Ottawa, ON K0A 1L0
Canada
    613-839-3053
Fax: 613-839-5376 info@blumetric.ca
www.blumetric.ca
Manufacturer and exporter of food processing equipment including membrane and whey processing and brine systems; also, filtration equipment and water and waste water treatment systems.
President, Water: Dan L. Scroggins
CEO: Roger M. Woeller
Chief Financial Officer: Ian Malone, B.A. Hons.
Reaserch/Development: Sam Ali
Sales/Marketing: Gary Black
Director Process Development: Greg Choryhanna
Number Employees: 15
Square Footage: 34000
Type of Packaging: Bulk
Brands:
    Sepro Flow
    Sepro Kleen
    Sepro Pure

19740 Blue Bottle Coffee Co

300 Webster St
Oakland, CA 94607-4122
    510-653-3394
support@bluebottlecoffee.com
www.bluebottlecoffee.com
Coffee, coffee grinders and brewers
Number Employees: 20-49

19741 Blue Cross Laboratories

20950 Centre Pointe Pkwy
Santa Clarita, CA 91350
    bmahler@bc-labs.com
www.bc-labs.com
Cleaning products including air fresheners, nonchlorine bleach, anti-bacterial liquid soap, health and beauty care products.
President: Darrell Mahler
Formulation Development & Q.A.: Jagdish Koshti
Estimated Sales: $28 Million
Number Employees: 50-99
Number of Products: 150
Square Footage: 150000
Type of Packaging: Consumer, Private Label
Other Locations:
    Blue Cross Laboratories
    Phoenix AR
Brands:
    Admire
    Blue Too
    Capn Clean
    Carpet Scent
    Class
    Glass & More
    Glass Brite
    Mighty Pine
    Mr. John
    Now
    Pan Pal
    Royal Flush
    Scent Sation
    Sensation
    True Pine

    Ultra
    Wash & Clean

19742 Blue Diamond Growers

1802 C St.
Sacramento, CA 95811
    800-987-2329
www.bluediamond.com
Processor, grower and exporter of almonds, macadamians, pistachios and hazelnuts. Two thousand almond products in many cuts, styles, sizes and shapes for use in confectionery, bakery, dairy and processed foods. In house R/D for customproducts.
President/Chief Executive Officer: Mark Jansen
Chairman of The Board: Clinton Shick
CFO: Dean LaVallee
Vice Chairman: Dale Van Groningen
Quality Assurance Lab Manager: Steven Phillips
Director, Marketing: Al Greenlee
Manager, Communications: Cassandra Keyse
Manager, Operations: Bruce Lisch
Manager, Product Development: Mike Stoddard
Senior Vice President, Procurement: David Hills
Year Founded: 1910
Estimated Sales: $709 Million
Number Employees: 1,100
Type of Packaging: Consumer, Food Service, Private Label, Bulk
Brands:
    Almond Breeze
    Almond Toppers
    Blue Diamond
    Blue Diamond Almonds
    Blue Diamond Hazelnut
    Blue Diamond Macadamias
    Nut Thins
    Smokehouse
    California Nuts

19743 Blue Feather Products Inc

165 Reiten Dr
Ashland, OR 97520-9020
    541-482-5268
Fax: 541-482-2338 800-472-2487
www.blue-feather.com
Manufacturer, importer and exporter of synthetic chamois, magnetic picture frames and refrigerator magnets
Vice President: John R King
johninashland@charter.net
VP: John King
Marketing Manager: Ashley Black
Office Manager: Lisa Gentle
Estimated Sales: Less Than $500,000
Number Employees: 1-4
Square Footage: 8000
Type of Packaging: Consumer
Brands:
    Clipwell
    Cougar Cloth
    Magnamight
    Vpeez

19744 Blue Giant Equipment Corporation

85 Heart Lake Road South
Brampton, ON L6W 3K2
Canada
    905-457-3900
Fax: 905-457-2313 800-668-7078
sales@bluegiant.com www.bluegiant.com
Manufacturer and exporter of loading dock equipment, vehicle restraints, dock lifts, lift tables and industrial trucks and the Blue Genius Tech Control Panels
Chairman: Bill Kostenko
Director of Sales and Marketing: Steve Greco
VP of Sales/Marketing: Jeff Miller
Estimated Sales: $35 Million
Number Employees: 100-250
Square Footage: 85000

19745 Blue Lake Products

62 Greenmoor
Irvine, CA 92614-7476
    949-786-0108
Fax: 949-786-3108 800-257-3477
Power transmission belting and specialty belting: O-ring drive belts, flat woven endless belts, custom fabricated belts and foam covered belts
President: Dean Smeaton
dean@bluelakeproducts.com
Estimated Sales: $3-5 Million
Number Employees: 1-4

19746 Blue Line Foodservice Distr

24120 Haggerty Rd
Farmington Hills, MI 48335-2645
    248-478-6200
Fax: 248-442-4570 800-892-8272
Patricia.McGuire@bldcorp.com
www.bluelinedist.com
Restaurant equipment and supplies
Owner: Michael Ilitch
militch@bluelinedist.com
Number Employees: 50-99

19747 Blue Print Automation

16037 Innovation Dr
S Chesterfield, VA 23834-5951
    804-520-5400
Fax: 804-526-8164
sales@blueprintautomation.com
www.blueprintautomation.com
Fully integrated Turnkey Systems for applications that involve the loading of flexible and hard-to-handle packages into secondary containers such as cases, trays, cartons, crates and master bags
President: Peter Schneider
peter.schneider@blueprintautomation.com
CEO: Martin Prakken
CFO: Tom O'Connell
Director Sales/Marketing: John French
Sales Manager: John Kertesz
Operations Manager: David Schoon
Purchasing: Louis Spartano
Estimated Sales: $10-25 Million
Number Employees: 100-249
Square Footage: 160000

19748 Blue Print Automation

16037 Innovation Dr
S Chesterfield, VA 23834-5951
    804-520-5400
Fax: 804-526-8164
sales@blueprintautomation.com
www.blueprintautomation.com
Vision-guided robotics, case packing of flexible bags and rigid packages and complete turn-key packaging systems, taking control of the product in its naked state through packaging, utilizing and palletizing.
President: Mike Ganacoplos
Quality Control: Tom O'Connell
Marketing Director: Robbie Quinlin
Sales Manager: John Kertesz
Operations Manager: Jason Estes
Estimated Sales: $10-20 Million
Number Employees: 100-249
Square Footage: 40000

19749 Blue Ribbon Packaging Systems

4035 N 29th Ave
Hollywood, FL 33020-1011
    954-922-9292
Fax: 954-922-9977 800-433-4974
sales@brpack.com www.blueribbonlabel.com
Owner: Robert Schwartz
Estimated Sales: $3-5 Million
Number Employees: 20-49

19750 Blue Ridge Converting

100 Fairview Road
Asheville, NC 28803
    828-274-2100
Fax: 828-274-0000 800-438-3893
Manufacturer, importer and exporter of disposable and waterproof clothing and nonwoven wipers
CEO: Thomas Snell
Vice President: Daniel Neal
VP Sales: Daniel Neal
Purchasing: Jo Curtis
Estimated Sales: $2 Million
Number Employees: 24
Square Footage: 480000

19751 Blue Ridge Signs

1800 Barnett Dr
Weatherford, TX 76087-9440
    817-594-0353
Fax: 817-598-0025 800-659-5645
blueridgesigns@aol.com www.blueridgesigns.com
Indoor and outdoor painted signs including plywood, redwood and magnetic; also, display fixtures
Manager: Sherry Hamilton
Estimated Sales: Less Than $500,000
Number Employees: 1-4

19752 Blue Tech
PO Box 2674
Hickory, NC 28603
828-324-5900
Fax: 828-324-9712
Manufacturer and exporter of process control and air
swept grinding systems, mixers, ribbon blenders, air
filtration systems, etc
President: Dennis Harrow
VP: Charles Gero
Estimated Sales: $.5-1 million
Number Employees: 5-9
Square Footage: 16000

19753 BlueKey Inc
341 E Bay St
Charleston, SC 29401
843-628-6228
sales@bluekeyinc.com
www.bluekeyinc.com
Business consultants, areas of expertise include digi-
tal marketing, branding, web design and develop-
ment, and content strategy.
Founder & Strategist: Ben Cash
Business Development: John Mulvey
Director of Client Services: Stacey Bailey
Digital Strategist: Matt McDonald
Digital Project Manager: Liz Wall
Digital Marketing Manager: Christy Jones
Year Founded: 2000
Number Employees: 11-50

19754 Bluebird Manufacturing
6670 St. Patrick
Montreal, QC H8N 1V2
Canada
514-762-2505
800-406-2505
admin@bluebird.ca www.bluebird.ca
Manufacturer, exporter and importer of metal cookware including pots, pans, fry baskets, etc; also, custom services available
President: Harvey Engelberg
Brands:
Bluebird Products

19755 Bluegrass Packaging Industries
3651 Collins Ln
Louisville, KY 40245-1635
502-425-6442
Fax: 502-425-7201 800-489-3159
ellen@bluegrasspackaging.com
www.bluegrasspackaging.com
Co-packer of dried foods and snacks, beans, grain,
gum balls, candy, coffee, etc
Owner: Terry Waddle
twbpi@aol.com
CEO: Auggie Chick
Estimated Sales: $3-5 Million
Number Employees: 20-49
Square Footage: 100000

19756 Bluewater Environmental
704 Mara Street
Suite No. 201
Point Edward, ON N7V 1X4
Canada
519-337-0228
Fax: 519-337-9178 888-808-9782
eng@blueh2o.ca

19757 Bluff Manufacturing Inc
1400 Everman Pkwy # 156
Suite 156
Fort Worth, TX 76140-5034
817-293-3018
Fax: 817-293-7570 800-433-2212
jae@bluffmanufacturing.com
www.bluffmanufacturing.com
Manufacturers exporter of dockboards, dock plates
and edge-of-dock levelers
President: Phillip Amrozowicz
phillip@bluffmanufacturing.com
Director, Financing & Accounting: Bruce Parker
VP, Marketing: Amy Hamilton
Estimated Sales: $10-20 Million
Number Employees: 5-9

19758 Bluffton Motor Works
410 E Spring St
Bluffton, IN 46714-3737
260-827-2200
Fax: 260-827-2303 800-579-8527
mburgan@blmworks.com www.blmworks.com

Electric motors for the dairy, beverage, meat and
poultry industries.
CEO: Stacey Duncan
sduncan@bcbsks.com
Number Employees: 250-499

19759 Bluffton Slaw Cutter Company
331 N Main St Ste 1
Bluffton, OH 45817
419-358-9840
Fax: 419-358-9840 www.blufftonslawcutter.com
Manufacturer and exporter of lid removers, cheese
shredders, apple slicers and slaw cutters
President and CFO: Paul King
VP: T King
Quality Control: Louis Stier
Marketing Director: L King
Estimated Sales: Below $5 Million
Number Employees: 1-4
Square Footage: 2400
Brands:
Top Loose

19760 Blumer
800A Prospect Hill Road
Windsor, CT 06095-1570
860-688-1589
Fax: 860-688-1539 marketing@blumerusa.com
www.blumerusa.com
Banding and labeling production machines
President: Kevin Coyle
VP: David Olbria
Estimated Sales: $2.5-5 Million
Number Employees: 5-9

19761 Bma Inc
100 Springdale Rd # 110
Suite 110
Cherry Hill, NJ 08003-3300
609-239-3638
Fax: 610-455-1491 information@maskell.com
www.maskell.com
Consulting firm, serving the needs of manufacturers
and distributors
CFO: Nicholas S Katko
Contact: Bruce Baggaley
bbaggaley@maskell.com
Estimated Sales: $1-5 Million

19762 Bmh Equipment Inc
1217 Blumenfeld Dr
P.O. Box 162109
Sacramento, CA 95815-3903
916-922-8828
Fax: 916-922-8820 800-350-8828
www.bmhe.com
Distributor/exporter of custom material handling
equipment, hand trucks, casters, conveyor systems,
dollies, pallet jacks and racks, aluminum ramps,
dock boards, shelving and work tables; design and
engineering for nonstandard materialhandling
problems
President: Jack Alexander
jackalex@bmhequipment.com
VP: Jerry Berg
Conveyor Specialist: Richard Wales
Estimated Sales: $2.5-5 Million
Number Employees: 10-19
Square Footage: 20800

19763 Boardman Molded Products Inc
1110 Thalia Ave
Youngstown, OH 44512-1825
330-788-2401
Fax: 330-788-9665 800-233-4575
tbobonick@spacelinks1.com
www.boardmanmolded.com
Safety mats and flooring
Owner: Ron Kessler
Controller: Jim Bowser
QA Manager: Jeff Westlake
VP Marketing: Dan Kessler
VP of Sales: Tom Bobonick
rkessler@spacelinks1.com
Plant Manager: George Lolakis
Estimated Sales: $20-50 Million
Number Employees: 100-249
Brands:
Aisle Pro
Econo Pro
Entry Pro
Grip Top
Super Links
Water Pro

19764 Bodine Electric Co
201 Northfield Rd
Northfield, IL 60093-3311
773-478-3515
Fax: 773-478-3232 info@bodine-electric.com
www.bodine-electric.com
Components for food processing machinery includ-
ing fractional hp and gear motors and controls
President: John Bodine
CEO: John R Bodine
john.bodine@bodine-electric.com
CFO: Jeff Stahl
Marketing Manager: Edmund Glueck
Estimated Sales: $20-50 Million
Number Employees: 50-99
Square Footage: 250000
Type of Packaging: Private Label, Bulk

19765 Bodolay Packaging
2401 Airport Rd
Plant City, FL 33563-1101
813-754-9321
Fax: 813-754-9321 www.bodolaypackaging.com
Horizontal form, fill and seal packaging machines
President: Mostafa Farid
mostafa@bodolaypackaging.com
Estimated Sales: Less Than $500,000
Number Employees: 1-4
Number of Products: 2
Type of Packaging: Consumer

19766 Bodycote Materials Testing
7530 Frontage Rd
Skokie, IL 60077-3213
847-676-2100
Fax: 847-676-3065 800-323-3657
www.bodycote.com
Materials testing, food and drug testing, packaging
testing
Chief Executive Officer: Stephen Harris
CEO: Gordon Lawerance
Contact: Rebecca Alban
alban@bodycote.com
Estimated Sales: $2.5-5 Million
Number Employees: 50-99

19767 Boedeker Plastics Inc
904 W 6th St
Shiner, TX 77984-5608
361-594-2942
Fax: 361-594-2349 800-444-3485
info@boedeker.com www.boedeker.com
High performance engineering plastics such as
vespel, torlon, ultem, peek, nylon, teflon, and delrin,
in-house machine shop manufactures parts from
prints or samples
President: Ray Anderson
randerson@boedeker.com
Marketing Director: Mike Randall
Sales: Jake Jalufka
Estimated Sales: $5-10 Million
Number Employees: 50-99

19768 Boehringer Mfg. Co. Inc.
6500 Highway 9
Unit F
Felton, CA 95018
831-704-7732
Fax: 831-704-7731 800-630-8665
Manufacturer and exporter of burlap sack needles,
block scrapers, dough cutters, boning, meat hooks,
and specialty blades; custom plastic injection mold-
ings; also bbq tools and accessories
Secretary: Mark Fowles
Estimated Sales: $300-500,000
Number Employees: 5-9
Number of Products: 50
Square Footage: 2500
Parent Co: Boehringer Manufacturing Company
Type of Packaging: Consumer, Private Label

19769 Boekels
P.O.Box 7004
Oakland, NJ 07436-7004
201-651-0500
Fax: 201-651-0505
President: Mark Schultz

19770 Boelter Industries
202 Galewski Dr
Winona, MN 55987
507-452-2315
Fax: 507-452-2649
dboelter@boelterindustries.com

Folding cartons and special paper products
President: Dennis Boelter
CEO: Lester Boelter
VP: Dixie Breitenfeldt
R&D: Dean Boelter
Contact: Terrie Klug
tklug@boelterindustries.com
Estimated Sales: $20-50 Million
Number Employees: 130
Square Footage: 325000
Type of Packaging: Consumer, Food Service, Private Label, Bulk

19771 Bogner Industries
199 Trade Zone Drive
Ronkonkoma, NY 11779-7362
631-981-5123
Fax: 631-981-3792
Manufacturer, engineer and designer of hi-tech and high quality production of stainless steel processing and packaging equipment for the food and beverage industries.
Owner: Erwin Bogner
Owner: Ruediger Albrecht
Sales Director: Tina Hadizadeh
Type of Packaging: Food Service

19772 Bohler Bleche
11525 Brittmoore Park Drive
Houston, TX 77041-6916
800-852-8556
Fax: 281-856-5458 bohlr__jl@nol.net
www.iadd.org/LISTAD.HTM-101k
Specialty steel sheet and plate products used in producing knives for food processing
Head of Marketing Dept.: John Leonard
Operations Manager: John Leonard

19773 Bohn & Dawson
3500 Tree Court Industrial Blv
St Louis, MO 63122-6685
636-225-5011
Fax: 636-825-6111 800-225-5011
info@bohnanddawson.com
Manufacturer and exporter of metal fabricators, tubular parts and assemblies; also, tool and die services available
President: Steven L Hurster
Engineer: J Koopman
VP: R Wiele
CFO: Steve Leibach
Quality Control: Mike Schneider
Estimated Sales: $20-50 Million
Number Employees: 10-19

19774 Bohnert Construction Company
PO Box 34320
Kansas City, MO 64120-4320
816-231-2281
Fax: 816-241-5236 800-701-2281
Manager: Eric Limoges
Quality Control: Emmie Cobins
Estimated Sales: $5-10 Million
Number Employees: 10

19775 Boise Cascade Co
1111 W Jefferson St # 300
Suite 300
Boise, ID 83702-5389
208-384-6161
Fax: 208-384-7189 www.bc.com
Corrugated containers
President: Stanley Bell
Chief Executive Officer: Thomas Carlile
Chief Financial Officer: Wayne Rancourt
Senior Vice President: Thomas Corrick
Manager: Bill Bialkowsky
Vice President of Sales & Marketing: Dennis Huston
Vice President of Operations: Dan Hutchinson
Estimated Sales: Over $1 Billion
Number Employees: 5000-9999

19776 Boise Cascade Corporation
1544 W 27th St
Burley, ID 83318
208-678-3531
Fax: 208-677-7719 www.bc.com
Containers and boxes
Contact: Stan Allen
stanallen@boisepaper.com
Nnational Accounts Manager: Lee Gill

Estimated Sales: $50-100 Million
Number Employees: 100-249
Parent Co: Boise Cascade Corporation

19777 Boise Cold Storage Co
495 S 15th St
Boise, ID 83702-6846
208-344-8477
Fax: 208-344-8598 www.boisecoldstorage.com
Ice; warehouse providing cold, dry and freezer storage; also, distribution available
Owner: Tim Johnson
tfj@boisecold.com
Office Manager: B Grover
General Manager: M Tallent
Estimated Sales: $1-2,500,000
Number Employees: 20-49
Square Footage: 100000

19778 Boldt Co
2525 N Roemer Rd
Appleton, WI 54911-8623
920-739-6321
Fax: 920-739-4409 info@boldt.com
www.theboldtcompany.com
Offering consulting, construction and maintenance solutions throughout the United States
President/COO: Robert DeKoch
CEO: Thomas Boldt
thomas.boldt@boldt.com
CFO: Dale Von Behren
CEO: Thomas J Boldt
Chairman: Oscar Boldt
Marketing Director: Paula Wydeven
President, Chief Operating Officer: Bob DeKoch
Estimated Sales: $1-$3 Million
Number Employees: 1000-4999

19779 Boldt Technologies Corporation
812 10th Street
West Des Moines, IA 50265-3507
515-277-4848
Fax: 515-277-2775
Pouch machines, bag formers/fillers/sealers, cocoa packaging equipment, teabag machinery
President: Donald Vanoort
Estimated Sales: Less than $500,000
Number Employees: 25

19780 Bolling Oven & Machine Company
1101 Jaycox Road
Avon, OH 44011-1394
440-937-6112
Fax: 440-937-6875
Compact revolving tray baking ovens
VP: Lynn Bolling
Sales: Dennis Szalai
Estimated Sales: less than $500,000
Number Employees: 6
Square Footage: 22000

19781 Bollore Inc
60 Louisa Viens Dr
Dayville, CT 06241-1106
860-774-2930
Fax: 860-774-8895 sales@bolloreinc.com
www.bolphane.com
Tea, coffee filters (paper) and shrinkfilms
President: Stephen Brunetti
Estimated Sales: $20-50 Million
Number Employees: 50-99

19782 Bollore Inc
60 Louisa Viens Dr
Dayville, CT 06241-1106
860-774-2930
Fax: 860-774-8895 sales@bolloreinc.com
www.bolphane.com
Specialty plastic films; high performance multipurpose, specialty and cross-linked shrink packaging films. ISO 9001:2000 certified.
President: Stephen Brunetti
sbrunetti@seniorsnorth.com
CEO: Stephen Brunetti
Estimated Sales: $20-50 Million
Number Employees: 50-99

19783 Bolzoni Auramo
17635 Hoffman Way
Homewood, IL 60430-2186
708-957-8809
Fax: 708-957-8832 800-358-5438
sales.us@bolzoni-auramo.com
www.bolzoni-auramo.it
Manufacturer, importer and exporter of lift truck attachments
Vice President: Ad Artuso
eartuso@bolzoni-auramo.com
VP: Ad Artuso
VP Sales: Ronnie Keene
VP Operations: Ed Artuso
Plant Manager: Jose Cardonas
Purchasing Manager: Brian Cummings
Estimated Sales: $20 Million
Number Employees: 20-49
Square Footage: 14700
Parent Co: Bolzoni SPA

19784 Bolzoni Auramo
17635 Hoffman Way
Homewood, IL 60430-2186
708-957-8809
Fax: 708-957-8832 800-358-5438
sales.us@bolzoni-auramo.com
www.bolzoni-auramo.it
Manufacturer and exporter of lift truck attachments
President: Roberto Scotti
Vice President: Ad Artuso
eartuso@bolzoni-auramo.com
General Manager: Dick Fennessey
Estimated Sales: $5-10 Million
Number Employees: 20-49
Parent Co: Auramo O.Y.

19785 Bon Chef
205 State Route 94
Lafayette, NJ 07848-4617
973-383-8848
Fax: 973-383-1827 800-331-0177
info@bonchef.com www.bonchef.com
Food presentation items. Products include chafing dishes, coffee urns, sandstone servingware, buffet bars, custom counter-tops and more.
President: Salvatore Torre
Vice President: Anthony Lo Grippo
Director of Sales Administration: Amy Passafaro
Estimated Sales: $2.5-5 Million
Number Employees: 20-49

19786 Bonar Engineering & Constr Co
565 Edgewood Ave S
Jacksonville, FL 32205-5332
904-389-6700
Fax: 904-389-6003 henry3rd@bonareng.com
www.bonareng.com
Owner: Henry Bonar
hank@bonarengineering.com
Estimated Sales: $3-5 Million
Number Employees: 5-9

19787 Bonar Plastics
1005 Atlantic Dr
West Chicago, IL 60185
402-465-6497
Fax: 402-465-1220 800-295-3725
www.bonarplastics.com
Custom plastic rotational molded bulk bins, tanks, hoppers, drums, combo bins, etc
President: John Bielby
CFO: Don Layng
Quality Control: Gustavo Cuevas
Sales Director: Jerry Ankiewicz
jankiewicz@bonarplastics.com
Plant Manager: Gustavo Cuevas
Estimated Sales: Below $5 Million
Number Employees: 50-99
Square Footage: 200000

19788 Bonar Plastics
6111 S 6th Way
Ridgefield, WA 98642
360-887-2230
Fax: 360-887-3553 800-972-5252
www.bonarplastics.com
Bulk food handling bins
President: John Bielby
CFO: Lee Robinson
Sales/Marketing: Larry Hughes
Contact: Joel Carter
jcarter@bonarplastics.com
Plant Manager: Jeff Harms

Estimated Sales: $20-50 Million
Number Employees: 100-249
Square Footage: 100000
Parent Co: Low & Bonar
Brands:
Bonar
Payloader
Polar
Two-Can

19789 (HQ)Bonneau Company
3334 South Tech Boulevard
Miamisburg, OH 45342

937-886-9100
Fax: 937-886-9300 800-394-0678
www.bonneaucompany.com
Manufacturer, importer and exporter of commercial
and industrial dyes including paraffin,
microcrystalline waxes and blends
President: Timothy Muldoon
VP/Technical Director: Paul Guinn
Estimated Sales: $5-10 Million
Number Employees: 1-4
Square Footage: 60000
Brands:
Bonn Dye
Bonn Trace

19790 Bonnot Co
1301 Home Ave
Akron, OH 44310-2654

330-896-6544
Fax: 330-896-0822 info@thebonnotco.com
Manufacturer and exporter of extruders for food,
chemicals, ceramics, catalysts, etc
President: George Bain
CFO: Becky Goulden
VP: John Negrelli
Engineering Manager: Kurt Houk
General Manager: George W. Bain
Contact: Vince Damicone
damicone@thebonnotco.com
Controller: Becky Bouldon
Estimated Sales: $2.5-5 Million
Number Employees: 10-19
Square Footage: 160000

19791 Bonsai World
PO Box 2634
Union City, CA 94587-7634

510-784-8880
Fax: 510-784-8882 888-744-5444
Decorative water fountains
General Manager: Yoshi Nozawa
Marketing Manager: Francis Marsal
Number Employees: 7
Brands:
Fountainside

19792 Booth
2007 Royal Ln
Dallas, TX 75229-3263

972-243-0014
Fax: 912-243-8075 800-497-2958
Beverage dispensers
President: J Raulerson
Vice President: Robert Weeks
Marketing Director: JoAnn Leach
Sales Director: Jon Noble
Estimated Sales: $10-20 Million
Number Employees: 1-4
Parent Co: Welbilt Corporation

19793 Borgwaldt KC
7741 Whitepine Rd
N Chesterfield, VA 23237-2212

804-271-6471
Fax: 804-275-9070 www.borgwaldt.hauni.com
Wine industry pH valves and manufactures of ma-
chinery for tobacco industry
President: Michael Connor
michaelc@borgwaldt-kc.com
Managing Director: Shawn Maxwell
Estimated Sales: $2.5-5 Million
Number Employees: 20-49

19794 Bormioli Rocco Glass Company
41 Madison Ave
New York, NY 10010-2202

212-719-3605
Fax: 212-719-3605
lmonastero@bormiolirocco.com
www.bormiolirocco.com

Storage containers: jars, hermetic closures with wire
bail mechanism, terrines with wire bail closures,
bottles, decanters, vacuum jars
President: Greg Simone
Contact: Paolo Abbreviato
paolo_abbreviato@bormiolirocco.com
Estimated Sales: $10-20 Million
Number Employees: 5-9

19795 Born Printing Company
1125c Destro Rd #C
Baltimore, MD 21223-3222

410-646-7768
Fax: 410-644-6638
Can and bottle labels
President: Michael Born
VP: Timothy Born
VP: Richard Born
VP: Timothy Born
Estimated Sales: $1-2.5 Million
Number Employees: 10-19
Square Footage: 9600

19796 Borroughs Corp
3002 N Burdick St
Kalamazoo, MI 49004-3483

269-342-0161
Fax: 269-342-4161 800-748-0227
www.borroughs.com
Manufacturer and exporter of industrial and com-
mercial steel shelving, checkout counters and office
filing units
President: Timothy Tyler
ttyler@borroughs.com
Sales: Rick Stear
Estimated Sales: $20-50 Million
Number Employees: 250-499
Square Footage: 450000

19797 Bosch Packaging Svc
2440 Sumner Blvd
Raleigh, NC 27616-3275

919-877-0886
Fax: 919-877-0887 888-546-5744
www.siggroup.com
Bag and pouch sealers, bag filling and sealing ma-
chines, brush wrapping, foiling, carton machines:
closing, filling, forming, horizontal form and fill,
sear machines, robotics, pharmaceutical packaging
Vice President: Tod Torey
VP: Tod Torey
Estimated Sales: $5-10 Million
Number Employees: 50-99

19798 Bosch Packaging Technology
869 S Knowles Ave
New Richmond, WI 54017-1745

715-246-6511
Fax: 715-246-6539 sales@doboy.com
www.boschpackaging.com
Manufacturer and exporter of carton and tray form-
ing and sealing machines, horizontal wrappers and
bag closing machines
President: William Heilhecker
CFO: Julie Foss
Sales: Mike Wilcox
Director Sales: John Bowerman
Director Operations: Mark Hanson
Estimated Sales: $30-50 Million
Number Employees: 100-249
Parent Co: SIG
Brands:
At
Bd-Iii
Cbs-B
Cbs-Ch
Hd-900
J-Series
Microtronic
Mustang
Mustang Iv
Pc-1200
S-Ch
Scotty Ii
Servotronic
Super H
Super Mustang

19799 Bosch Packaging Technology Inc
8700 Wyoming Ave N
Minneapolis, MN 55445-1836

763-424-4700
Fax: 763-493-6776 www.boschpackaging.com
Phamaceutical and nutraceutical packaging

President: Don Demorett
CEO: Tom Mcdaniel
tom.mcdaniel@bosch.com
CFO: Jack Tsahalis
CEO: Tom McDaniel
R & D: Al Peterson
Quality Control: L S Gagnerls
Number Employees: 100-249

19800 Bosch Packaging Technology Inc
8700 Wyoming Ave N
Minneapolis, MN 55445-1836

763-424-4700
Fax: 763-493-6776
pharm-na@boschpackaging.com
www.boschpackaging.com
Supplier of filling, processing, and packaging technology for piece goods and bulk items in the food,
pharmaceutical, and confectionery sectors as well as
for health and hygiene products.
CEO: Tom Mcdaniel
tom.mcdaniel@bosch.com
Chief Executive Officer: Tom McDaniel
Number Employees: 100-249

19801 Bosch Packaging Technology
869 S Knowles Ave
New Richmond, WI 54017-1745

715-246-6511
Fax: 715-246-6539
sale.packaging-nrd@bosch.com
www.boschpackaging.com
Packaging machinery inclusing bag sealers, horizon-
tal flow wrappers, vertical form-fill-seal machines,
carton formers, carton closers, and delta robotics.
Sales: Mike Wilcox
Number Employees: 100-249
Parent Co: Robert Bosch GmbH

19802 Bosch Packaging Technology
9890 Red Arrow Hwy
Bridgman, MI 49106-9001

269-466-4000
Fax: 269-466-4040 vtnf@boschpackaging.com
www.boschpackaging.com
VP: John Staruch
Number Employees: 50-99

19803 Bosch Rexroth Corp
14001 S Lakes Dr
Charlotte, NC 28273-6791

800-739-7684
info@boschrexroth-us.com
www.boschrexroth-us.com
Linear actuators, linear guides, subassemblies, ma-
chine bases and frames.
President & CEO: Paul Cooke
EVP & CFO: Christoph Kleu
SEVP, Technical & Engineering: Matthias Aberle
EVP, Hydraulics: Erwin Wieckowski
Year Founded: 2001
Estimated Sales: $5.9 Billion
Number Employees: 33,100
Parent Co: Bosch Rexroth AG
Brands:
Star

19804 Boska Holland
40-4 Radio Circle Drive
Mt Kisco, NY 10549

914-241-3600
Fax: 914-663-5158 usa@boskaholland.com
www.boska.com
Cheese, accessories/supplies i.e. picninc baskets,
cooking implements/housewares, display fixtures.
Marketing: Esther Booth

19805 Boss Linerless Label Company
15990 N Greenway Hayden Loop
Suite 900
Scottsdale, AZ 85260-1655

480-348-6362
Fax: 480-348-6399 randkir@hotmail.com
Linerless label applicators for pressure sensitive la-
bels
Estimated Sales: $1-5 000,000

19806 Boss Manufacturing Co
1221 Page St
Kewanee, IL 61443-2159

309-852-2131
Fax: 309-852-0848 800-447-4581
custserv@bossgloves.com

Manufacturer, importer and exporter of gloves, boots, protective clothing and aprons
CEO: Louis Graziado
lgraziado@bossgloves.com
VP Sales/Marketing: Brian Wise
Sales Manager: Gerry Stockelman
Purchasing Manager: Summer Cohen
Estimated Sales: $40 Million
Number Employees: 50-99
Parent Co: Boss Holdings
Type of Packaging: Consumer, Food Service, Private Label, Bulk
Other Locations:
   Boss Manufacturing Co.
   Concord ON
Brands:
   Boss (Boots and Gloves)
   Tuff Grip (Gloves)

19807 Bossar
650 Hurricane Shoals Rd NW
Lawrenceville, GA 30046-4460
941-351-3023
Fax: 770-817-5031 ckoellner@bossar.com
Horizontal form, fill and seal pouch machines for three or four side seal sachets, gusset and stand-up pouches with recloseable zipper, spouts, valves, handles or a straw inside for fruit juices
Commercial Manager: Roger Stainton
CFO: Geanne Kaight
Contact: Ken Anderson
kanderson@bossar.com
Estimated Sales: $5-10 Million
Number Employees: 10-19
Parent Co: Bossar

19808 Bostik Inc
211 Boston St
Middleton, MA 01949-2128
978-777-0834
Fax: 978-750-7802 888-571-8558
info@booth.com
Adhesives in film, hot melt, liquid, web and Vitol resins
Key Person: Pat Lamb
CEO: Michael Klonne
michael.klonne@bostik-us.com
CEO: Mike Klonne
Number Employees: 100-249

19809 Boston Gear
229 Berkeley St
Suite 410
Boston, MA 02116
617-859-8439
Fax: 617-479-6238 888-999-9860
info@bostongear.com
www.bostongroundwater.org
The Colfax Power Transmission Group is a leading supplier of mechanical and electrical power transmission products to the food processing and packaging machinery industries. With hundreds of years of industry experience Colfax PT hasdeveloped some of the premier products, delivery programs and services available today.
Executive Director: Elliott Laffer
Marketing VP: Craig Schuele
Sales VP: Gerald Ferris
Estimated Sales: $5-10 Million
Number Employees: 20-49
Type of Packaging: Bulk
Brands:
   Boston Gear
   Bost-Kleen
   Centric Clutch

19810 Boston Rack
300 Main Street
223
North Easton, MA 02356
508-230-5755
Fax: 508-880-5449 800-640-5723
info@1stopmth.com www.bostonrack.com
Boston Rack is a nationwide storage and material handling systems integrator. The sales and engineering teams specialize in specific industries including Archive, Food and Beverage, Retail, 3rd Party Logistics, Petroleum, andGovernment.
President/Chief Executive Officer: Peter Murphy
Chief Financial Officer: Sean Medeiros
National Sales Engineer: Alex Hultron
Systems Enginer: Stephen Nolan
GSA Development Manager: Woody Farrow
Operations Manager: Jennifer Aguiar

19811 (HQ)Boston Retail
400 Riverside Ave
Medford, MA 02155-4949
781-395-2656
Fax: 781-395-0155 800-225-1633
info@bostonretail.com www.bostonretail.com
Manufacturer and exporter of space frame systems, damage control products, bumper guards, fixtures and display products
President & CEO: Russell Rubin
rrubin@bostonretail.com
CFO & Vice President: Victor Martin
Estimated Sales: $20-50 Million
Number Employees: 50-99
Other Locations:
   Boston Retail Products
   Youngstown OH
Brands:
   Boston Beam
   Boston Bumper
   Boston Colorguard
   Boston Tuffguard
   Carts

19812 Boston Shearpump
234 Abby Rd
Manchester, NH 03103-3332
603-627-2340
Fax: 603-627-2019 mixing@admix.com
www.admix.com
President: Lou Beaudette
Estimated Sales: $5-10 Million
Number Employees: 20-49

19813 Boston's Best Coffee Roasters
43 Norfolk Ave
South Easton, MA 02375-1190
508-238-8393
Fax: 508-238-6835 800-898-8393
sales@bostonsbestcoffee.com
www.bostonsbestcoffee.com
Coffee, mixers and filters
President: Jacqueline Dovner
CEO: Stephen Fortune
Director of Fundraising Sales: Erin Woodard
Contact: Mary Burke
marymb@bostonsbestcoffee.com
Production Manager: Rocky Raposa
Estimated Sales: Less Than $500,000
Number Employees: 5-9
Square Footage: 5692
Type of Packaging: Consumer, Food Service, Private Label, Bulk
Brands:
   David's Gourmet Coffee
   Gold Star Coffee
   Premier Coffee
   Tropical Coffee

19814 Bottom Line Processing Technologies, Inc.
901 Blue Sky Ridge
Snellville
Largo, GA 30078
678-344-7353
Fax: 678-623-9950 888-834-4552
Small scale candy making equipment, batch cookers, continuous cookers, chocolate makers and beverage processing equipment.

19815 Boulder Bar
2635 Ariane Drive
San Diego, CA 92117-3422
858-274-1049
Fax: 858-274-1207
Marketing & Advertising: Lorie Zapf

19816 Bouras Mop Manufacturing Company
1330 Dolman Street
Saint Louis, MO 63104-2908
314-241-5800
Fax: 314-241-9759 800-634-9153
virgil.bouras@sbcgobal.net
Manufacturer and exporter of corn brooms and brushes, mop heads, deck mops, dust mops and applicators
President: Virgil Bouras
R & D: James Bouras
Estimated Sales: Below $5 Million
Number Employees: 10
Square Footage: 200000

19817 Bower's Awning & Shade
366 N 9th St
Lebanon, PA 17046-3465
717-273-2351
Fax: 717-273-2351
Commercial awnings
Owner: Fred Bowers
Estimated Sales: Less Than $500,000
Number Employees: 1-4

19818 Bowers Process Equipment
487 Lorne Avenue E
Stratford, ON N5A 6T3
Canada
519-271-4757
Fax: 519-271-1092 800-567-3223
mail1@clemmersteelcraft.com www.steelcraft.ca
Manufacturer and exporter of agitators, blenders, bins, kettles, tube fillers, portable air-driven mixers and dairy equipment; also, tanks including mixing
President: Keith Zehr
Chief Executive Officer: Paul Summers
Quality Control: Roy Langford
Marketing: Chris Wyatt
Division Manager, Engineered Products Di: Darcy Vanneste
Operations Manager: Jayson Barlow
Number Employees: 150
Square Footage: 640000
Parent Co: Clemmer Steelcraft Technologies Inc.

19819 Bowlswitch
6580 Valley Center Dr # 6
Fairlawn, VA 24141-5691
540-633-6733
Fax: 540-633-6735 800-338-6733

19820 Bowman Hollis Mfg Corp
2925 Old Steele Creek Rd
Charlotte, NC 28208-6726
704-374-1500
Fax: 704-333-5520 888-269-2358
sbroadwell@bowmanhollis.com
www.bowmanhollis.com
A full service industrial distributor specializing in industrial belting of all types.
President: Tom Bowman
tbowman@bowmanhollis.com
Marketing/Sales: Steve Broadwell
Sales: Rick Siler
Production Manager: Tom Bowman
Estimated Sales: $5-10 Million
Number Employees: 20-49

19821 Bowtemp
5700 Cote De Liesse Road
Mont-Royal, QC H4T 1B1
Canada
514-735-5551
Fax: 514-735-0751
Thermometers
President: Sam Bern
Manager of Sales: Wayne Pregent
Purchasing Manager: David Parker
Number Employees: 100-249
Brands:
   Bowtemp

19822 Boxco
2326 Grissom Dr
St Louis, MO 63146-3311
314-569-9984
Fax: 314-567-4991 800-654-2932
sales@boxcoindustries.com
www.boxcoindustries.com
Specialty food packaging i.e. gift wrap/labels/boxes/containers.
Vice President: David Wolf
Vice President: David Wolf
Marketing: David Wolf
Number Employees: 1-4

19823 (HQ)Boxes.com
184 S Livingston Avenue
Suite 9
Livingston, NJ 07039
201-646-9050
Fax: 201-646-0990 www.boxes.com
Manufacturer and exporter of paper folding boxes, point of purchase displays and cardboard inserts
Estimated Sales: $1-5 Million
Number Employees: 19
Square Footage: 100000

Type of Packaging: Consumer, Food Service, Private Label
Brands:
　Quick 'n Easy
　Quik Lok
　Qwik Pak
　Swifty

19824 Boyd Lighting Company
30 Liberty Ship Way
Suite 3150
Sausalito, CA 94965

415-778-4300
Fax: 415-778-4319 info@boydlighting.com
www.boydlighting.com
Manufacturer, exporter and importer of decorative and architectural interior lighting; designing services available
President: John Sweet Jr
CEO: Jay Sweet
Design Director: Doyle Crosby
Director of Marketing: Erin Geiszler
Sales Manager: Jane Culligan
Estimated Sales: $10-20 Million
Number Employees: 50-99
Square Footage: 80000
Parent Co: Boyd Lighting Company
Other Locations:
　Boyd Lighting Co.
　Colorado Springs CO

19825 (HQ)Boyd's Coffee Co
Portland, OR 97230

800-735-2878
customerservicena@farmerbros.com
www.boydscoffeestore.com
Coffees, teas, cocoa, hot and frozen beverages
Senior Sales Manager: Gabriel Dominguez
VP of Manufacturing: Mitch Karstadt
Estimated Sales: $49 Million
Number Employees: 250-499
Number of Brands: 7
Parent Co: Farmer Bros Co
Type of Packaging: Food Service
Other Locations:
　Boyd's Coffee Company
　Coeur D Alene ID
Brands:
　Boyd's Coffee
　Coffee House Roasters
　Island Mist Iced Tea
　Italia D'Oro Coffee
　Techni-Brew
　Today
　Viaggio Coffee

19826 Boyer Corporation
PO Box 10
La Grange, IL 60525

708-352-2553
Fax: 708-352-2573 800-323-3040
www.boyercorporation.com
Liquid and dry drain openers, metal polishes, lubricants, etc
President: Harold Hurwitz
VP: James Burgener
Contact: Harold Herwitz
h.herwitz@boyercorporation.com
Estimated Sales: Less than $500,000
Number Employees: 1-4
Square Footage: 4000
Brands:
　Boyer

19827 Boyle Meat Company
1638 Saint Louis Ave
Kansas City, MO 64101-1130

816-221-6283
Fax: 816-221-3888 800-821-3626
theresa@boylescornedbeef.com
Steaks, corn beef, pastrami and pot roast
President: Don Wendl
Special Project Manager: James Crouch
VP: Christy Chester
Estimated Sales: $20-50 Million
Number Employees: 20-49
Square Footage: 10000
Type of Packaging: Food Service, Private Label, Bulk

19828 Brad's Raw Foods
PO Box 210
Pipersville, PA 18947-0210

215-766-3739
info@bradsrawfoods.com

Raw chips, crackers, kale and onion rings. Organic, gluten free, vegan, non gmo, and kosher.
Owner: Brad Gruno
Contact: Nancy Berger
execoffice@bradsrawchips.com
Number Employees: 5-9
Type of Packaging: Consumer

19829 Bradford A Ducon Company
N25 W23040 Paul Road
Pewaukee, WI 53072-2537
Fax: 800-789-4046 800-789-1718
info@bradfordfittings.com
www.bradfordfittings.com
Manufacturer and importer of stainless steel sanitary fittings, clamps, valves, machined castings and forgings
Quality Control: Bruce Anderson
Marketing: William Duyser
Sales: Jeff Casillo
Operations: Sally Besgrove
Number Employees: 5-9
Square Footage: 40000
Parent Co: Dixon Valve & Coupling

19830 Bradford Co
13500 Quincy St
Holland, MI 49424-9460

616-399-6538
Fax: 616-399-8989 info@bradfordco.com
www.bradfordco.com
Manufacturer of packaging products and material handling systems.
President: Hulda Grin
hgrin@championhealthandfitness.com
Estimated Sales: $2.5-5 Million
Number Employees: 100-249

19831 Bradford Derustit Corp
21660 Waterford Dr
Yorba Linda, CA 92887-2650

714-695-0899
Fax: 714-965-0840 877-899-5315
www.derustit.com
Chemical metal cleaners
President: Ann Denney
VP: Anne Denney
Number Employees: 1-4

19832 (HQ)Bradford Soap Works Inc
200 Providence St
West Warwick, RI 02893-2511

401-821-2141
Fax: 401-821-1660 info@bradfordsoap.com
www.bradfordsoap.com
Manufacturer and exporter of cake soap and industrial detergents
CEO: John H Howland
jhowland@bradfordsoap.com
CEO: John H Howland
VP Sales: Ed Windsor
Estimated Sales: $20-50 Million
Number Employees: 250-499
Type of Packaging: Private Label

19833 Bradley Industries
1 Westbrook Corp Ctr Ste 300
Westchester, IL 60154

815-469-2314
Fax: 815-469-7089
customerservice@atlantismatch.com
Matchbooks
President: Jon Bradley
Vice President: John Bradley
Estimated Sales: $5-10 Million
Number Employees: 50-99
Square Footage: 120000

19834 Bradley Lifting
1030 Elm St
York, PA 17403-2597

717-848-3121
Fax: 717-843-7102 www.bradleylifting.com
Manufacturer and exporter of material handling equipment including slab and ingot tongs, plate and sheet lifters and coil and paper roll grabs
President: Tom Thole
info@bradleylifting.com
CFO: Winfred Bradley
Estimated Sales: $5-10 Million
Number Employees: 20-49
Parent Co: Xtek, Inc.

19835 Bradley Ward Systems
635 Montauk Way
Alpharetta, GA 30022-4704

770-754-5899
Fax: 770-754-5876 www.bwsys.com
Manufacturing execution systems for packaging
President: Garry Diver

19836 Bradman Lake Inc
3050 Southcross Blvd
Rock Hill, SC 29730-9055

803-366-3688
Fax: 704-588-3302 usa@bradmanlake.com
www.bradman-lake.com
Specializes in the design and manufacture of packaging machinery
Manager: Steve Irwin
Marketing Director: Mervat El RaFei
Sales Director: Nick Bishop
Plant Manager: Sam Hunnicutt
Estimated Sales: Less Than $500,000
Number Employees: 1-4
Parent Co: Bradman Lake Ltd
Type of Packaging: Bulk
Other Locations:
　Bradman Lake Group
　Charlotte NC

19837 Brady Enterprises Inc
167 Moore Rd
East Weymouth, MA 02189-2332

781-337-5000
Fax: 781-337-9338 www.bradyenterprises.com
Manufacturer and exporter of cocktail, powdered drink, stuffing and meatloaf mixes and seasonings; importer of seasoning; also, spray drying and dish detergent
President: Kevin Maguire
Chairman/CEO: John Brady
CFO: Mary Gudalawicz
Director QC/R&D: Mike Waytowich
Director Sales/Marketing: Desi Gould
Human Resources: Jack Brady Jr.
Estimated Sales: $11.60 Million
Number Employees: 100-249
Number of Brands: 3
Number of Products: 16
Type of Packaging: Consumer, Food Service
Brands:
　Bar-Tenders
　Bells
　Dishwasher Glisten

19838 Brady Worldwide
P.O.Box 2131
Milwaukee, WI 53201

414-358-6600
Fax: 414-228-5979 www.whbrady.com
Safety signage and regulatory training products: pipe markers, floor marking materials, numbering and coding markers, aluminum, fiberglass and vinyl siding
President: Katherine Hudson
CEO: Frank Jaehnert
Estimated Sales: $50-100 Million
Number Employees: 100-249

19839 Bragard Professional Uniforms
201 E 42nd St # 1805
New York, NY 10017-5710

212-759-0202
Fax: 212-353-0318 800-488-2433
customersupport@bragardusa.com
www.bragardusa.com
Manufacturer, importer and exporter of uniforms and special clothing including aprons, linens, chef's hats and coats, footwear, cloth towels, etc.; complete embroidery services available
CEO: Lu Aranzamendez
lua@bragardusa.com
Vice President: Peter Isom
Chief Operating Officer: Benjamin Bragard
Estimated Sales: $1-2.5 Million
Number Employees: 1-4
Parent Co: Bragard SA
Brands:
　Bragard
　Cooking Star By Bargard

19840 Bran & Luebbe
1234 Remington Rd
Schaumburg, IL 60173-4812

847-882-8116
Fax: 847-882-2319 www.pumpsandprocess.com

Manufacturer and exporter of metering pumps, food blending systems and analyzers for determination of protein, fat, moisture and other parameters in food products
President: Robert Arcaro
Marketing Coordinator: Kelly Breitlando
Director Sales: Jim Hunson
Estimated Sales: $20-50 Million
Number Employees: 50-99
Square Footage: 36000
Parent Co: Bran & Luebbe GmbH

19841 Brand Castle
5111 Richmond Rd
Bedford, OH 44146-1354
216-292-7700
Fax: 216-292-7701 jimmyz@brandcastle.com
www.brandcastle.com
Cookie making kits and decorations
President/Founder: Jimmy Zeilinger
Marketing: Jimmy Zellinger
VP Sales/Marketing: Jim Shlonsky
Contact: Abby Barton
abby_barton@rand.org
Operations Manager: Jeff Berger
Estimated Sales: Less Than $500,000
Number Employees: 5-9

19842 Brand Specialists
PO Box 381146
Duncanville, TX 75138-1146
972-283-8491
Fax: 972-572-9292 888-323-3708
Consultant specializing in product development including frozen, fresh and dry items for the retail and food service markets
President: Dalton Lott
Member of the Board: Daniel F Pickering
VP of Operations: Jon Davies
Estimated Sales: $5-10 Million
Number Employees: 10

19843 Brandstedt Controls Corporation
3600 NW 115th Ave
Doral, FL 33178
305-477-0034
Fax: 305-477-0035 800-426-5488

19844 Branford Vibrator Company
3600 Cougar Drive
Peru, IL 61354-9336
815-224-1200
Fax: 815-224-1241 800-262-2106
www.cougarindustries.com
Manufacturer and exporter of pneumatic and electric vibrators
President: D Pedritti
Manager: T Zagorski
Estimated Sales: $20-50 Million
Number Employees: 50
Parent Co: Cougar Industries
Brands:
Branford

19845 Branson Ultrasonics Corp
41 Eagle Rd # 1
P.O. Box 1961
Danbury, CT 06810-4179
203-796-0400
Fax: 203-796-0450 www.emersonindustrial.com
The industry leader in the design, development, manufacture, and marketing of plastics joining, precision cleaning, ultrasonic processing, and ultrasonic metal welding equipment.
President: Ed M Boone
eboone@bransonultrasonics.com
VP Finance: Robert Tibbets
VP/General Manager-North America: Richard Gehrin
VP Sales: Rodger Martin
VP Operations: Anthony Prioreschi
Number Employees: 1000-4999

19846 Brass Smith
5125 Race Court
Denver, CO 80216
303-331-8777
Fax: 303-331-8444 800-662-9595
www.zguard.com
Manufacturer and exporter of sneeze guards, hot merchandising display cases, railing systems, crowd control posts, menu stands, etc

Human Resources: Dave Carr
Marketing: Wayne Sirmons
Regional Sales Manager: Benny Martinez
Contact: Michael Ackerman
mackerman@bsidesigns.com
Estimated Sales: $5-10 Million
Number Employees: 50-99
Square Footage: 400000
Parent Co: BSI
Brands:
Beltway
Brass Master
Lustre Rail
Z Guard

19847 Braun Brush Co
43 Albertson Ave
Albertson, NY 11507-2198
516-741-6000
Fax: 516-741-6299 800-645-4111
sales@brush.com
Manufacturer, importer and exporter of sanitary cleaning brushes used for baking, confectionery processing, etc
President: Lance Cheney
lance@brush.com
Business Development Director: Peter Lassen
Customer Service: Jerilyn Leis
Accounting: Joan Egidio
Estimated Sales: $2 Million
Number Employees: 20-49
Square Footage: 28000
Parent Co: Braun Industries
Type of Packaging: Consumer, Food Service, Private Label, Bulk
Brands:
Saniset

19848 Braun Brush Co
43 Albertson Ave
Albertson, NY 11507-2198
516-741-6000
Fax: 516-741-6299 800-645-4111
sales@brush.com
Manufacturer, importer and exporter of USDA standard and custom designed brushes
President: Lance Cheney
lance@brush.com
President: Max Cheney
Director of Business Development: Peter Lassen
Customer Service: Jerilyn Leis
Accounting: Joan Egidio
Estimated Sales: $2.5-5 Million
Number Employees: 20-49
Square Footage: 28000

19849 Brazilian Consulate
2601 S Bayshore Dr # 5
Miami, FL 33133-5417
305-446-3900
Fax: 305-461-4466 mhfeitosa@brazilmiami.org
Owner: Raul Arlacon

19850 Brechbuhler Scales
1414 Scales St SW
Canton, OH 44706
330-453-2424
Fax: 330-453-5322 www.brechbuhler.com
Manufacturer and exporter of scales including dormant, flour, warehouse, portable, etc
Contact: Mike Ambs
mambs@bscales.com
Manager: Roger Doerr
Branch Manager: Rick Spradling
Estimated Sales: $1-2.5 Million
Number Employees: 160
Parent Co: Brechbuhler Scales
Type of Packaging: Bulk

19851 Brechteen
30060 23 Mile Rd
Chesterfield, MI 48047-5718
586-949-2240
Manufacturer and importer of packaging materials including plastic, cellulose, collagen and fibrous; manufacturer of stuffing equipment
VP of Sales: Roger Allen
Number Employees: 100-249

19852 Brecoflex Co LLC
222 Industrial Way W
Eatontown, NJ 07724-2206
732-460-9500
Fax: 732-542-6725 888-463-1400
www.brecoflex.com
Manufacturer, and exporter of polyurethane, USDA and FDA approved timing belts, pulleys, and accessories
President: Bernie Fulleman
VP: Rudolf Schoendienst
Research & Development: Johnathan Weir
Quality Control: Dararith Son
Marketing Director: Joy Guigo
Estimated Sales: $2.5-5,000,000
Number Employees: 1-4
Brands:
Breco
Brecoflex
Esband

19853 Breddo Likwifier
1230 Taney N.
Kansas City, MO 64116
816-561-9050
Fax: 816-561-7778 800-669-4092
don.wolfe@corbion.com www.breddo.com
Manufacturer and exporter of high shear blender with scraped surface heat transfer
President: Ron Ashton
Sales: Don Wolfe
dwolfe@caravaningredients.com
Estimated Sales: $5 Million
Number Employees: 10-19
Parent Co: American Ingredients Company

19854 Bremer Manufacturing CoInc
W2002 County Road Q
Elkhart Lake, WI 53020-1109
920-894-2944
Fax: 920-894-2881 sales@bremermfg.com
www.bremermfg.com
Aluminum hand scoops
President: Tom Dolack
tdolack@bremermfg.com
Sales: Tim St Clair
Purchasing: Glen Leahn
Shipping Manager: J Thome
Estimated Sales: $10-20 Million
Number Employees: 100-249
Square Footage: 60000

19855 Bren Instruments
308 Century Court
Franklin, TN 37064-3918
615-794-6825
Fax: 615-794-7478 info@breninc.com
www.breninc.com
Automated decal and stencil systems
President: Murray O Wilhoite
bren308@msn.com
CFO: Brenda Wilhoite
Quality Control Manager: Phill Thomas
Director Marketing/VP: Murray Wilhoite
Estimated Sales: $500,000-$1 Million
Number Employees: 8

19856 (HQ)Brenner Tank LLC
450 Arlington Ave
Fond Du Lac, WI 54935-5571
920-922-5020
Fax: 920-922-3303 800-558-9750
sales@brennertank.com www.brennertank.com
Manufacturer, importer and exporter of stainless steel tank transports and intermodal tank containers
President: Bruce D Yakley
byakley@brennertank.com
Sales Manager: Thomas Ballon
Estimated Sales: $20-50 Million
Number Employees: 100-249
Square Footage: 300000
Parent Co: Wabash National Corp.

19857 Brenton Engineering Co
4750 County Road 13 NE
Alexandria, MN 56308-8022
320-852-7705
Fax: 320-852-7621 800-535-2730
bec@becmail.com
www.roboticpackagingsystems.com
Manufacturer and exporter of case packers, handling, robotics, and shrink wrappers

397

President: Jeff Bigger
Sales: Scott Leuschke
Marketing Director: Karen Kielmeyer
Vice President Sales: Troy Snader
Estimated Sales: $20-50 Million
Number Employees: 100-249
Parent Co: ProMach
Brands:
  Brenton

19858 Brentwood Plastics In
8734 Suburban Trak
PO Box 440160
St Louis, MO 63144-2734

314-968-1135
Fax: 314-968-4276

Polyethylene films
President: Sam Longstreth
Estimated Sales: $5-10 Million
Number Employees: 20-49
Square Footage: 80000

19859 Bresco
2428 6th Ave S
Birmingham, AL 35233-3322

205-252-0076
Fax: 205-323-8630 sales@brescoinc.com
www.brescoinc.com
Wholesaler/distributor of restaurant equipment and
supplies; design services available
President: George Tobia
gtobia@brescoinc.com
Estimated Sales: $10-20 Million
Number Employees: 50-99

19860 Brevard Restaurant Equipment
565 Gus Hipp Blvd.
Rockledge, FL 32955-48

321-631-0318
Fax: 321-631-6040
Wholesaler/distributor of new and used equipment;
serving the food service market; also, design and
layout plans
President: John Schneider
VP: Diana Schneider
General Manager: Glenn Pierson
Estimated Sales: $1-2.5 Million
Number Employees: 1-4
Square Footage: 30000

19861 Brewer-Cantelmo Inc
55 W 39th St # 205
New York, NY 10018-0573

212-244-4600
Fax: 212-244-1640 bc@brewer-cantelmo.com
www.brewer-cantelmo.com
Custom handed crafted menus, room directories, res-
ervation books, check presenters, wine lists, presen-
tation tools.
President: Niyazi Bozkurt
bozkurt@computeq.com
Vice President: David Kirschenbaum
Estimated Sales: $2 Million
Number Employees: 20-49
Square Footage: 37500

19862 Brewers Outlet-Chestnut Hill
7401 Germantown Ave
Philadelphia, PA 19119-1605

215-247-1265
Fax: 215-247-1855 info@mybrewersoutlet.com
www.mybrewersoutlet.com
Craft and specialty beers
Owner: Paul Egonopoulos
Estimated Sales: $2.5-5 Million
Number Employees: 5-9
Square Footage: 15000
Parent Co: Brewers Outlet

19863 Brewmatic Company
P.O.Box 2959
Torrance, CA 90509

310-787-5444
Fax: 310-787-5412 800-421-6860
Manufacturer and exporter of thermal coffee servers,
commercial and domestic drip brewing equipment
and accessories; importer of espresso machines
Manager: Ed Esteban
Research & Development: Traian Zaionciuc
Quality Control: Ron Mann
Marketing Director: Eddison Esteban
Sales Director: Cindi Watson Kramer
Plant Manager: John Galvin
Purchasing Manager: Frank Cherry

Number Employees: 50-99
Square Footage: 300000
Parent Co: Farmer Brothers Company
Type of Packaging: Food Service, Private Label
Other Locations:
  Brewmatic Company
  St. Louis MO
Brands:
  Brewmatic

19864 Bridge Machine Company
614 Kennedy Street
Palmyra, NJ 8065

856-829-1800
Fax: 856-786-8147 877-754-1800
sales@bridgeonline.com www.bridgeonline.com
Designs and manufactures a complete line of food
processing equipment such as patty formers, tender-
izers, dumpers/meat tubs, hand tenderizers, cutlet
flatteners, meatball formers, macerators, spreading
conveyors, dicers and stripcutters
President: Terry Bridge
Contact: David Hicks
david.hicks@bridgeonline.com
Estimated Sales: $10-20 Million
Number Employees: 50-99
Square Footage: 28000

19865 Bridgewell Resources LLC
124020 SE Carpenter Dr
Clackamas, OR 97015

800-481-3557
webinfo@bridgewellres.com
Edible oils, flours, grains and pulses.
President: Pat McCauley
CEO: Pat McCauley
Chief Financial Officer: Jay Wilson
Vice President of Human Resources: Donna Lesch
Food & Agriculture General Manager: Craig Mullen
Parent Co: Bridgewell Resources
Type of Packaging: Consumer, Food Service, Pri-
  vate Label, Bulk

19866 Briel America
3888 Bluffview Pt
Marietta, GA 30062

770-509-3006
Fax: 770-518-6624
Espresso machines, accessories, grinders
President: Wesley Smith
wesley@smithagy.net
Estimated Sales: $.5-1 000,000
Number Employees: 1-4

19867 Bright Technologies
127 N. Water Street
PO Box 296
Hopkins, MI 49328

269-793-7183
Fax: 269-793-8793 800-253-0532
www.brightbeltpress.com
De-packaging compactors, hydraulic cart dumpers,
factory direct installation, service, patented
Xtractors, patented HighDensity Extruders, patented
Belt Filter Presses, mobile, trailer mounted and sta-
tionary equipment.
President: Brent Sebright
R&D/Sales: Dennis Sprick
Marketing Director: Jeannie Jansma
Contact: Doug Sebright
doug@brightbeltpress.com
Operations: T Stuart Sebright
VP Purchasing: Lee Murray
Estimated Sales: $5-10 Million
Number Employees: 50-99
Number of Brands: 2
Number of Products: 80

19868 Bright of America
200 Greenbrier Rd
PO Box 460
Summersville, WV 26651

304-872-3000
Fax: 304-872-3040 www.brightwv.com
Place and counter mats
President: Steve Pridemore
Contact: John Whelan
jwhelan@brightwv.com
Estimated Sales: $10-20 Million
Number Employees: 20-49
Square Footage: 400000
Parent Co: Russ Berrie & Company

19869 Bril-Tech
1506 Baltimore Street
Defiance, OH 43512-1908

419-782-2430
Fax: 419-784-9717
Air pollution control, drying rooms, ovens, smoke-
houses, refrigeration systems and tempering systems

19870 Brill Manufacturing Co
715 S James St
Ludington, MI 49431-2368

231-843-2430
Fax: 231-845-9966 866-896-6420
www.brillcompany.com
Pine and oak tables, chairs and booths
President: David Field
dfield@brillcompany.com
Estimated Sales: $2.5-5 Million
Number Employees: 50-99
Square Footage: 192000

19871 Brimrose Corporation ofAmerica
19 Loveton Cir
Hunt Valley Loveton Center
Sparks Glencoe, MD 21152-9201

410-472-7070
Fax: 410-472-7960 office@brimrose.com
www.brimrose.com
Manufacturer of AOTF-NIR spectrometers for pro-
cess control with accelerated speeds of up to 16,000
wavelengths per second.
Vice President of Sales & Marketing: Benjamin
Fried

19872 (HQ)Brinkmann Corporation
4215 McEwen Rd
Dallas, TX 75244

972-387-4939
800-468-5252
Manufacturer and exporter of smokers and cookers;
also, lighting including portable emergency, flash-
lights, lanterns, electronic flashers and electronic
assemblies
President: Jon Brinkmann
VP: Erma Eddins
Contact: Brad Adams
badams@thebrinkmanncorp.com
Estimated Sales: $20-50 Million
Number Employees: 100-249

19873 Brinkmann Instruments, Inc.
6555 Pelican Creek Circle
Riverview, FL 33578-8653

813-316-4700
Fax: 516-334-7506 800-645-3050
info@brinkmann.com
Seward blenders, grinding mills and sievers, binders
and ovens, fat determination systems, universal sol-
vent extraction systems and lab equipment
President & Chief Executive Officer: Michael
Melingo
Contact: Felicia Nelson
f.nelson@metrohmusa.com
Estimated Sales: $20.40 Million
Number Employees: 143

19874 Brisker Dry Food Crisper
PO Box 7000
Oldsmar, FL 34677

813-854-5231
Fax: 800-854-3069 800-356-9080
Manufacturer and exporter of electric kitchen
countertop storage appliances designed to keep
crackers, chips, cereals, etc. free of humidity
CEO: Anita Rybicki
Estimated Sales: $1-5 Million
Number Employees: 7
Number of Brands: 1
Number of Products: 1
Square Footage: 48000
Type of Packaging: Consumer, Food Service
Brands:
  Brisker

19875 Bristol Associates Inc
5777 W Century Blvd # 855
Suite 865
Los Angeles, CA 90045-5671

310-670-0525
Fax: 310-670-4075 lstern@bristolassoc.com
www.bristolassoc.com
Executive recruitment firm serving the food industry

President: Ben Farber
Executive VP: Roberta Borer
rborer@bristolassoc.com
Director Marketing: Laurie Stern
Number Employees: 5-9

19876 Britt Food Equipment
684733 HWY 2
RR 3
Woodstock, ON N4S 7V7
Canada

519-533-0365
Fax: 519-533-6315
Equipment and machinery to the red meat, poultry,
fish and pet food industries
President: Brad Britton
Vice President: Greg Britton
Estimated Sales: $750,000
Number Employees: 3

19877 Britt's Barbecue
1678 Montgomery Highway
Suite 104
Birmingham, AL 35216

205-612-6538
info@brittsbarbecue.com
Stationery and trailer commercial smokers
Owner: James Britt

19878 Bro-Tex Inc
800 Hampden Ave
St Paul, MN 55114-1299

651-645-5721
Fax: 651-646-1876 800-328-2282
www.brotex.com
Polishing cloths, industrial paper and cloth wipers
and Turkish bar mops
President: Arlys Freeman
Secretary/Treasurer: Myra Greenberg
Senior Vice President: Ed Freeman
Director, Marketing: Erwin Rendall
Product Development Manager: Lee Gilbertson
Plant Manager: Greg Conroy
Purchasing Manager: Chris Keisling
Estimated Sales: $21 Million
Number Employees: 100-249
Square Footage: 200000
Brands:
  Bx-100
  Dual-Tex

19879 Broadcom Inc.
1320 Ridder Park
San Jose, CA 95131

learn@broadcom.com
www.broadcom.com
Software for systems, financial and warehouse man-
agement, etc.
President & CEO: Hock Tan
CFO: Tom Krause
Chief Legal Officer: Mark Brazeal
VP/Corporate Controller: Kristen Spears
Senior VP/Chief Sales Officer: Charlie Kawwas
Year Founded: 1961
Estimated Sales: $20.8 Billion
Number Employees: 15,000

19880 Broadmoor Baker
1301 5th Ave
Seattle, WA 98101-2603

206-624-3660
Fax: 206-464-1389
Consultant specializing in the development and mar-
keting of specialty bread recipes
Owner: Paul Suzman
Estimated Sales: less than $500,000
Number Employees: 1-4

19881 Broadway Companies
6161 Ventnor Ave
Dayton, OH 45414

937-890-1888
Fax: 937-890-5678 billbirch@aol.com
Innovations for custom molds, preforms and bottle
designs, prototyping and production, injection pre-
form models, blow molds, family molds that com-
bine multiple sizes and finishes
Owner: Bill Gaiser
Contact: Ken Enneking
kenneking@broadwayco.com
Estimated Sales: $10-20 000,000
Number Employees: 100-249

19882 Broaster Co LLC
2855 Cranston Rd
Beloit, WI 53511-3991

608-365-0193
Fax: 608-363-7957 800-365-8278
broaster@broaster.com
www.genuinebroasterchicken.com
Manufacturer and exporter of gas and electric pres-
sure fryers, ventless fryers, warmers, broilers and ro-
tisseries
President: Richard Schrank
rschrank@broaster.com
Vice President: Tracy Choppi
Marketing Director: Mark Markwardt
Sales Director: Randy McKinney
Plant Manager: Gene Halley
Purchasing Manager: Lee Blehinger
Number Employees: 50-99
Brands:
  Aristo-Ray
  Bro-Tisserie
  Broaster
  Broaster Chicken
  Broaster Foods
  Broaster Recipe
  Perfect Hold Deli Case
  Snack-Mate

19883 Brock Awnings LTD
211 E Montauk Hwy # 1
Hampton Bays, NY 11946-2035

631-728-3367
Fax: 631-728-0134 sales@brockawnings.com
www.brockawnings.com
Commercial awnings
President: Earl Brock
Estimated Sales: $500,000-$1,000,000
Number Employees: 5-9

19884 Brogdex Company
1441 W 2nd St
Pomona, CA 91766

909-622-1021
Fax: 909-629-4564
Manufacturer and exporter of cleaners and chemi-
cals for use in film/wax coatings for fresh fruits and
vegetables; exporter of fruit and vegetable process-
ing and handling equipment
President: Kirk Bannerman
Vice President: Greg Appel
Contact: Linda Smith
lindas@paceint.com
Number Employees: 50-99
Brands:
  Britex

19885 Brooklace
P.O.Box 2038
Oshkosh, WI 54903-2038

Fax: 203-937-4583 800-572-4552
www.brooklace.com
Manufacturer and exporter of paper, foil, glassine
and grease-proof doilies, place mats, tray covers,
baking cups, cake decorating triangles and hot dog
trays
President: Charles Foster
VP of Sales: Brian Schofield
VP of Manufacturing: James Stryker
Estimated Sales: $30-50 Million
Number Employees: 50-99
Square Footage: 50000
Parent Co: Hoffmaster
Brands:
  Brooklace

19886 Brooklyn Boys Pizza & Pasta
9967 Glades Rd
Boca Raton, FL 33434-3920

561-477-3663
Manufacturer and wholesaler of knives, cutlery,
china, dinnerware and related table-setting products
Owner: Carlos Sierra
Estimated Sales: $1-5 Million
Number Employees: 10-19

19887 Brooks Barrel Company
8 W Hamilton St
Baltimore, MD 21201-5008

410-228-0790
Fax: 410-221-1693 800-398-2766
brooksbarrel@shorenet.net www.brooksbarrel.com
Wooden barrels, kegs, planters and buckets; whole-
saler/distributor of bushel baskets and crates for
shipping and display

President: Kenneth Knox
Office Manager: Tammy Doege
Estimated Sales: $500,000-$1 Million
Number Employees: 15
Square Footage: 40000

19888 Brooks Instrument LLC
407 W Vine St
Hatfield, PA 19440-3000

215-362-3500
Fax: 215-362-3745 888-554-3569
brooksam@brooksinstrument.com
www.brooksinstrument.com
Manufacturer and exporter of measurement instru-
mentation for gas and liquid flow
President: Jim Dale
Cmo: Jim Hollis
jim.hollis@emersonprocess.com
CFO: Joe Doeters
Quality Control: Kevin Gallagher
R & D: Steve Glaudel
Marketing: T Hannigan
Sales: R Fravel
Number Employees: 100-249
Parent Co: Emerson Electric Company
Brands:
  Brooks

19889 Brookshire Grocery Company
PO Box 1411
Tyler, TX 75710-1411

903-534-3000
888-937-3776
www.brookshires.com
Regional supermarket chain in Texas, Louisiana and
Arkansas.
Chairman/CEO: Bradley Brookshire
Year Founded: 1928
Estimated Sales: $2.5 Billion
Number Employees: 14,000+
Brands:
  Brookshire's®
  Full Circle®
  Goldenbrook Farms®
  PAWS Premium™
  Tasty Bakery
  Top Care®
  Valu Time®
  World Classics™

19890 Brose Chemical Company
702 Bridge St
Twin Falls, ID 83301

208-733-1045
Fax: 208-733-1320
Manufactures chemicals for food processing and
mining industries
President: David Brose
Vice President: Susan Brose
Research & Development: Jim Brose
Sales Director: Ken Stewart
Production Manager: Dick Clarkson
Estimated Sales: 1-5 000,000
Number Employees: 10-19
Number of Brands: 1
Type of Packaging: Private Label, Bulk

19891 Brothers Manufacturing
PO Box 220
Hermansville, MI 49847-0220

906-498-7771
Fax: 906-498-2150 888-277-6117
Storage tanks and liquid handling systems
Operations Manager: Bob Triest
Estimated Sales: $10-20,000,000
Number Employees: 50-99
Square Footage: 33000

19892 Brothers Metal Products
1780 E McFadden Ave #117
Santa Ana, CA 92705-4648

714-972-3008
Fax: 714-632-5032
Manufacturer and exporter of vegetable slicers and
dryers; also, wash tank conveyors and packaging
and receiving tables
President: Gregory Siegmann
Estimated Sales: $600,000
Number Employees: 4
Square Footage: 22000
Type of Packaging: Food Service
Brands:
  Legrow

19893 Broughton Foods LLC
PO Box 961447
El Paso, TX 79996

740-373-4121
Fax: 740-373-2861 800-395-7004
www.dairypure.com
Milks, premium and homestyle ice cream, novelty
ice cream, juices and fruit drinks, cottage cheese,
sour cream, and chip dip.
Principle: Michael McCullum
General Manager: David Broughton
Executive Vice President: George Broughton
Manager of Sales: Neil Schilling
Plant Manager: Mike Depue
Purchasing Agent: Becci Becker
Estimated Sales: $46.6 Million
Number Employees: 100-249
Square Footage: 8000
Parent Co: Dean Foods
Type of Packaging: Consumer, Food Service, Bulk

19894 Brower
609 Main Street
P.O. Box 2000
Houghton, IA 52631

319-469-4141
Fax: 319-469-4402 800-553-1791
sales@hawkeyesteel.com www.hawkeyesteel.com
Manufacturer and exporter of poultry processing
equipment including scalders, pickers, evicerating
equipment and related accessories. Specialize in
small and medium plants.
President: Tom Wenstrand
VP Sales: Cindy Wellman
Estimated Sales: $10-20 Million
Number Employees: 50-99
Square Footage: 400000
Parent Co: Hawkeye Steel Products
Type of Packaging: Consumer
Brands:
　Batch Pik
　Brower
　Super Pik
　Super Scald

19895 Brower Equipment Co
3750 Getwell Cv
Memphis, TN 38118-5909

901-365-7991
Fax: 901-367-2925 info@browerequipment.net
www.browerequipment.net
Process tank, controls, installation pumps, fittings
and valve designs
President: Chandler Brower
cbrower@browerequipment.net
Estimated Sales: $5-10 000,000
Number Employees: 5-9

19896 Brown & Caldwell
201 N Civic Dr # 115
Suite 115
Walnut Creek, CA 94596-3865

925-937-9010
Fax: 925-932-9026 800-727-2224
info@brwncald.com
Environmental engineer and consultant offering san-
itation, waste water, testing and analytical services
President: Craig Goehring
Finance Administration Manager: Angela Ferrif
Director Marketing: Diana Levin
Contact: Norman Abrams
nabrams@conet.ucla.edu
Director Operations: Jim Meehan
Estimated Sales: $3-5 Million
Number Employees: 1-4

19897 Brown Chemical Co
302 W Oakland Ave
Oakland, NJ 07436-1381

201-337-0900
Fax: 201-337-9026 800-888-9822
sales@brownchem.com www.brownchem.com
Liquid packaging, contract warehousing, vendor
managed inventory programs, custom blending, reg-
ulatory compliance assistance, USP, food grade and
kosher packaging
Owner: Doug Blum
dougblum@subway.com
VP: Patrick Brown
VP Finance and Operations: Dave Lyle
Executive Secretary: Eileen Lyness
Office Manager: Doug Blum
Manager Information Systems: Rob Eckert
Operations Manager: Mark Donatiello

Estimated Sales: $20-50 Million
Number Employees: 10-19

19898 (HQ)Brown Fired Heater
300 Huron St
Elyria, OH 44035-4829

440-323-3291
Fax: 440-323-5734 www.enerconsystems.com
Manufacturer and exporter of process temperature
control systems, fluid heat systems and incinerators
President: David Hoecke
dhoecke@enerconsystemsinc.com
Vice President: John Somodi
Estimated Sales: $3 Million
Number Employees: 10-19
Square Footage: 100000
Brands:
　Consertherm
　Super-Trol
　Ventomatic

19899 Brown International Corp LLC
333 Avenue M NW
Winter Haven, FL 33881-2405

863-299-2111
Fax: 863-294-2688 info@brown-intl.com
www.brown-intl.com
Manufacturer and exporter of fruit and vegetable
processing equipment including extractors, pulpers,
finishers, dewaterers, sizers and processing lines
President: Scott Alexander
COO: Pete Devito
pete.d@brown-intl.com
VP: Ann Williams
Sales: Jim Sheppard
Operations: Bryce Adolph
Purchasing: Bruce Strong
Estimated Sales: $20-50 Million
Number Employees: 50-99
Number of Brands: 1
Number of Products: 85
Square Footage: 70000
Brands:
　Brown

19900 Brown International Corp LLC
333 Avenue M NW
Winter Haven, FL 33881-2405
Canada

863-299-2111
Fax: 863-294-2688 contact@brown-intl.com
www.brown-intl.com
Plastic bottles, closures and sprayers
President: Howard Bassel
COO: Pete Devito
pete.d@brown-intl.com
Number Employees: 50-99

19901 Brown Machine LLC
330 N Ross St
Beaverton, MI 48612

989-435-7741
Fax: 989-435-2821 877-702-4142
brownmachinegroup.com
Thermoforming machinery
Vice President, Operations & COO: Brian Keeley
Estimated Sales: $42 Million
Number Employees: 100-249
Number of Brands: 1
Square Footage: 140000

19902 Brown Manufacturing Company
125 New St Ste A
Decatur, GA 30030

404-378-8311
Fax: 404-378-8311 www.bottleopener.com
Manufacturer and exporter of stationary bottle open-
ers; custom imprinting available.
President: David Brim
Number Employees: 1-4
Square Footage: 5000
Brands:
　Starr

19903 Brown Paper Goods Co
3530 Birchwood Dr
Waukegan, IL 60085-8334

847-688-1450
Fax: 847-688-1458
jlabuda@brownpapergoods.com
www.brownpapergoods.com
Cake pan liners and bags including food, garbage,
greaseproof, paper, plastic and sandwich

President: Alan Mones
CEO: Allen Mons
amons@brownpapergoods.com
Estimated Sales: $20-50 Million
Number Employees: 100-249

19904 Brown Plastics & Equipment
683 Main Street # 1
Falmouth, MA 02540-3221

508-540-3990
Fax: 508-540-3963 www.falmouthlawyer.com
Partner: Paula M Barbosa
Estimated Sales: $300,000-500,000
Number Employees: 1-4

19905 Brown's Sign & Screen Printing
8299 Hazelbrand Road NE
Covington, GA 30014-3406

770-786-2257
Fax: 770-784-1324 800-540-3107
Manufacturer and exporter of flags, pennants, ban-
ners, signs and advertising specialties; screen print-
ing and lettering services available
President: Mike Brown
Estimated Sales: Less than $500,000
Number Employees: 4

19906 Brown/Millunzi & Associates
3305 Tampa St
Houston, TX 77021-1143

713-747-2870
Fax: 713-237-0761 800-460-3387
Consultant specializing in the design of food and
beverage facilities; also, project management ser-
vices available
Prin.: Daniel Brown
Prin.: Robert Millunzi
Prin.: Robert Pursell
Estimated Sales: $300,000-500,000
Number Employees: 1-4

19907 Browne & Company
100 Esna Park Drive
Markham, ON L3R 1E3
Canada

905-475-6104
Fax: 866-849-4719 sales@browneco.com
www.browneco.com
A leading supplier of glassware, dinnerware and
smallwares to the food service industry in Canada
President: Michael Browne
CFO: Alen Budish
Vice President: Brian Wood
Marketing Director: Katherine Dilk
Sales Director: Brian Wood
Number Employees: 10
Type of Packaging: Food Service

19908 Bruce Industrial Co Inc
4049 New Castle Ave
New Castle, DE 19720-1496

302-655-9616
Fax: 302-656-4327 866-866-4331
service@bruceindustrial.com
www.bruceindustrial.com
Wholesaler/distributor of material handling equip-
ment including overhead and modular lifts, enclo-
sures, rigging, etc
President: Clem Bason
sales@bruceindustrial.com
CEO: Doug Johnston
Estimated Sales: $10 Million
Number Employees: 50-99
Square Footage: 40000
Brands:
　Alm
　Akro-Mils
　Aleco
　Ballymore
　Bishamon
　Bluegiant
　Cm
　Cotterman
　Eagle
　Faultless
　Fred Silver
　Gorbel
　Hamilton
　Hytrol
　Keymaster
　Langley
　Lift-Rite
　Magline
　Omni Spaceguard

Palamatic
Presto
Republic

19909 Bruins Instruments
P.O. Box 1023
Salem, NH 03079

603-898-6527
Fax: 978-485-0055 info@bruinsinstruments.com
www.bruinsinstruments.com
NIR analyzers for the agricultural and food industries.
President: Hans Joachim Bruins
Contact: Hans Bruins
hans.bruins@bruinsinstruments.com

19910 Brulin & Company
2920 Dr Andrew J Brown Ave
Indianapolis, IN 46205

317-923-3211
Fax: 317-925-4596 800-776-7149
www.brulin.com
Manufacturer and exporter of sanitation products including disinfectants, hand care, food sanitation and floor care chemicals. ISO 9002 certified
President: Charles Pollnow
VP Sales/Marketing: Michael Falkowski
Marketing Coordinator: Janet Cleary Salisbury
Marketing Manager (Commerical Products): Garry Thornley
Estimated Sales: $10-20 Million
Number Employees: 100-249
Brands:
815 Mx
Quat Clean Sanitizer
Spotlight

19911 Bruni Glass
2750 Maxwell Way
Fairfield, CA 94534-9708

707-421-2946
Fax: 707-752-6201 877-278-6445
info@bruniglass.com
Glass packaging, specialty and custom glass jars and bottles
Contact: Samantha Bieganowski
samantha.bieganowski@bruniglass.com
Number Employees: 1-4

19912 Bruni Glass Packaging
1449 46TH Ave
Lachine Montreal, QC H8T 3C5
Canada

514-633-9247
Fax: 514-633-9878 877-771-7856
info@bruniglass.com www.bruniglass.com
Glass containers for food, pharmaceutical and related products; bottles for distillates, wine, oil and vinegar
President: Roberto Delbon
CEO: Gino Delbon
Marketing: Mark Bassel
Number Employees: 26

19913 Brush Research Mfg Co Inc
4642 Floral Dr
Los Angeles, CA 90022-1288

323-261-6162
Fax: 323-268-6587 info@brushresearch.com
Manufacturer and exporter of conveyor brushes.
President: Tara Rands
sales@brushresearch.com
VP: Robert Fowlie
General Manager: Don Didier
Estimated Sales: $5-10 Million
Number Employees: 50-99
Square Footage: 300000
Brands:
2-Flap
Flex-Hone
Nam Power

19914 Bruske Products
7447 Duvan Dr
Tinley Park, IL 60477-3714

708-532-3800
Fax: 708-532-3977
customersupport@bruskeproducts.com
www.bruskeproducts.com
Brushes and brooms

President: Steve Schafer
steve.schafer@bruskeproducts.com
Executive Administrator: Susan Bruske
Sales/Marketing Executive: David Cohea
Retail Sales Manager & VP: Steve Schafer
Estimated Sales: $10-20 Million
Number Employees: 50-99
Square Footage: 60000

19915 Brute Fabricators
PO Box 1621
Castroville, TX 78009-1621

210-648-2370
Fax: 210-648-5811 800-777-2788
www.bruterack.com
Manufacturer and exporter of heavy structural steel pallet racks including drive-in, drive-thru and cantilever drive-in
President: Fred Siebrecht
CEO: Brandie Siebrecht
CFO: Ben Cogdell
Number Employees: 20
Square Footage: 81000
Parent Co: Brute Fabricators
Brands:
Brute Rack

19916 Bry-Air Inc
10793 E State Route 37
Sunbury, OH 43074-9311

740-965-2974
Fax: 740-965-5470 877-379-2479
info@bry-air.com www.bry-air.com
Manufacturers of industrial dehumidifiers.
President/CEO: Mel Meyers
bryair1@bry-air.com
Executive VP: Doug Howery
Quality Control: Rick Frenier
Plant Manager: Ron Busch
Purchasing Director: Debra Kemmer
Estimated Sales: $5-10 Million
Number Employees: 20-49

19917 Bryan Boilers
783 Chili Ave
Peru, IN 46970

765-473-6651
Fax: 765-473-3074 inquires@bryansteam.com
www.bryanboilers.com
Manufacturer and exporter of boilers, blow down separators, boiler feed systems and de-aerators
President: Tom May
CEO: Dale Bowman
Sales/Marketing Manager: Dick Holmquist
Estimated Sales: G
Number Employees: 250-499
Parent Co: Bryan Steam LLC

19918 Bryant Glass
619 Main St
Wilmington, MA 01887-3215

978-988-9300
Fax: 978-988-9111 800-369-2782
bryantglass@verizon.net www.bryantglassco.com
High pressure pumps and homogenizers
Owner: Bob Bryant
Estimated Sales: Less Than $500,000
Number Employees: 1-4

19919 Bryant Products Inc
W1388 Elmwood Ave
Ixonia, WI 53036-9437

920-206-6920
Fax: 920-206-6929 800-825-3874
www.bryantpro.com
Manufacturer and exporter of tensioning devices for conveyors, straight and tapered rollers, machine grade conveyor pulleys
President: Fred Thimmel
Vice President: Dave Roessler
dave@bryantpro.com
Purchasing: Jody Mack
Estimated Sales: $20-50 Million
Number Employees: 20-49
Square Footage: 50000
Brands:
Airform
Telescoper
Tleltrack

19920 Bryce Corp
4505 Old Lamar Ave
P.O.Box 18338
Memphis, TN 38118-7063

901-369-4400
Fax: 901-367-5670 800-238-7277
www.brycecorp.com
Convertable flexible packaging including candy wrappers and potato chip bags
President: John Bryce
CEO: Tom Bryce
VP Sales: Paul Rickman
R & D: Mark Montsinger
Number Employees: 1000-4999

19921 Bubbla Inc
7931 Deering Ave
Canoga Park, CA 91304-5008

818-884-2000
Fax: 818-884-2164 www.bubbla.com
President: Andrew Cooper
Marketing: Cindy Daley
Estimated Sales: $3-5 Million
Number Employees: 1-4

19922 Buck Ice & Coal Co
2400 12th Ave
Columbus, GA 31901-1354

706-322-5451
Fax: 706-322-5453
Manufacturer and packager of ice. Private label packaging available
Owner: William C Buck
mailbucki@aol.com
CEO: W Buck, Jr.
Estimated Sales: $1-3 Million
Number Employees: 5-9
Number of Products: 1
Square Footage: 120000
Type of Packaging: Consumer, Food Service, Private Label
Brands:
Buck Ice

19923 Buck Knives
660 S Lochsa St
Post Falls, ID 83854-5200

208-262-0500
Fax: 208-262-0738 800-326-2825
www.buckknives.com
Manufacturer and exporter of fish fillet knives and cutlery.
Chairman: Charles Buck
CEO: Cj Buck
chuckbuck@buckknives.com
VP Sales/Marketing: Rob Morgan
Estimated Sales: $20-50 Million
Number Employees: 100-249
Square Footage: 200000
Brands:
Buck

19924 (HQ)Buckeye Group
4700 Wilmington Pike
South Charleston, OH 45368

937-462-8361
Fax: 937-462-7071
Wooden packaging including boxes
President: Sam McAdow
Estimated Sales: $10-20 Million
Number Employees: 50-99
Other Locations:
Buckeye Group
South Charleston OH

19925 Buckeye International
2700 Wagner Pl
Maryland Heights, MO 63043-3400

314-291-1900
Fax: 314-298-2850
www.buckeyeinternational.com
Manufacturer and exporter of cleaning chemicals including hand soap and floor polish for restaurants
President: Kristopher Kosup
Cio/Cto: Noel Haden
nhaden@buckeyeinternational.com
Estimated Sales: $20-50 Million
Number Employees: 100-249
Type of Packaging: Food Service, Bulk

19926 Buckhorn Canada
8028 Torbram Road
Brampton, ON L6T 3T2
Canada

905-791-6500
Fax: 905-791-9942 800-461-7579
sales@buckhorncanada.com
www.buckhorninc.com/
Manufacturer, importer and exporter of reusable
plastic pallets and boxes for storage, processing,
dipping and freezing
Sales Manager: Tim Walsh
Number Employees: 20
Square Footage: 180000
Parent Co: Myers Industries
Brands:
Akro-Bins
Ameri-Kart
Maxi-Bins
Nestier

19927 (HQ)Buckhorn Inc
55 W Techne Center Dr # A
Milford, OH 45150-9779

513-831-4402
Fax: 513-831-5474 800-543-4454
sales@buckhorninc.com www.buckhorninc.com
Manufacturer and exporter of reusable plastic pack-
aging systems, including plastic totes, bulk boxes,
containers, trays & pallets for shipping & in-process
use.
President: R. David Banyard
CEO: R. David Banyard
Dir. Engineering & Product Development: Jack
Fillmore
Director of Sales: Lane Pence
Director of Human Resources: Lorraine Gibbs
Parent Co: Meyers Industries Inc.
Brands:
Akro-Mils
Buckhoen

19928 Budget Blinds Inc
1927 N Glassell St
Orange, CA 92865-4313

714-637-2100
Fax: 714-637-1400 800-800-9250
corporateoffice@budgetblinds.com
www.budgetblinds.com
Manufacturer and exporter of decorative items in-
cluding centerpieces, candleabras, vases, candle-
sticks, etc
CEO: John Akins
centralbirmingham@budgetblinds.com
Executive VP: Mark Frankel
Office Manager: Cindy Mason
Number Employees: 1-4
Square Footage: 60000
Brands:
Band-It
Finesse
Franklinware
Garden Romance

19929 Buffalo China
658 Bailey Avenue
Buffalo, NY 14206-3003

716-824-8515
Fax: 716-825-5783 lester.rickard@oneida.com
www.oneida.com
Tabletop products and supplies including china
Sales Manager: Frank Fan
Manager: Charles Goehrig
VP Engineering: Paul Graeber
Estimated Sales: $1-5 Million
Number Employees: 500-999
Parent Co: Oneida Foodservice

**19930 (HQ)Buffalo Technologies
Corporation**
750 E Ferry Street
Buffalo, NY 14211-1106

716-895-2100
Fax: 716-895-8263 800-332-2419
sales@buflovak.com www.btcorp.com
Manufacturer and exporter of food dryers, flaking
drums, material handling and lifting equipment,
coolers, evaporators, heat exchangers, conveyors,
mills, etc
CEO/Chairman: Theodore Dann
Product Manager: Todd Murray
Production Manager: Patrick Scanlon

Estimated Sales: $10-20 Million
Number Employees: 2
Square Footage: 500000
Brands:
Bke
Bar Nun
Buflovak
Gump

19931 Buffalo Wire Works Co Inc
1165 Clinton St
Buffalo, NY 14206-2825

716-821-7866
Fax: 716-826-8271 800-828-7028
info@buffalowire.com www.buffalowire.com
Buffalo Wire Works offers screening media for in-
dustrial and food processing, including circular
screens, taped edge, hooked panel and rolled goods
for all major OEM's
CEO: Joseph Abramo
jabramo@buffalowire.com
CFO: George Ulrich
VP of Technalogy: Erich Steadman
R&D: Zach Hall
Quality Control: Rick Zimmer
Marketing: Melissa Kenneweg
Executive VP of Sales: Dominic Nasso
Customer Service: Beth Dajka
Operations: Kevin Shoemaker
Production: Terrie Battaglia
Plant Manager: Kevin Shoemaker
Purchasing Director: Tom Duriak
Estimated Sales: $10-20 Million
Number Employees: 100-249
Type of Packaging: Food Service

19932 Buffet Enhancements Intl
PO Box 1000
Point Clear, AL 36564

251-990-6119
Fax: 251-990-9373 www.buffetenhancements.com
Display products for banquets and catering includ-
ing decorative ice displays, illuminated ice displays,
food display trays, beverage housings and center-
piece trays; also, seafood display containers
Owner: Mike Anderson
Quality Control: Paul Lepiane
Marketing Director: Mike Anderson
Contact: Kevin Caldwell
kevinc@buffetenhancements.com
Estimated Sales: $10-20 Million
Number Employees: 50-99
Square Footage: 10000
Brands:
Banquet Boats
Chef Stone
Marquis Fountains

19933 (HQ)Buffet Partners
2701 E Plano Pkwy # 200
Plano, TX 75074

214-291-2900
Fax: 214-291-2467 888-626-6636
www.furrs.net
Food gift certificates
Manager: Jill Laird
CFO: Monty Standifer
Number Employees: 20-49

19934 Buhler Aeroglide Corp
100 Aeroglide Dr
Cary, NC 27511-6900

919-851-2000
Fax: 919-851-6029 www.buhlergroup.com
Design and manufacture of custom industrial dryers,
roasters, and coolers for food processing.
President: Fred Kelly
Senior VP: Mark Paulson
mpaulson@aeroglide.com
Sales Director: Tom Barber
Number Employees: 100-249

19935 Buhler Inc.
13105 12th Ave N
Plymouth, MN 55441-4509

763-847-9900
buhler.minneapolis@buhlergroup.com
www.buhlergroup.com
Supplies technologies and methods for processing
grain into flour and feed; the production of pasta &
chocolate; die casting, wet grinding & surface
coating.
President: Rene Steiner Jr
rene.steiner@buhlergroup.com

Number Employees: 100-249
Other Locations:
Buhler Inc
Minneapolis MN
Buhler Inc (Grinding & Dispersion)
Mahwah NJ
Buhler Aeroglide (Drying)
Cary NC
BuhlerPrince, Inc (Die Casting)
Holland MI
Buhler Inc (Optical Sorting)
Stockton CA
Buhler (Canada) Inc
Markham, Ontario
Buhler Mexico
Metepec, Mexico
Brands:
C.G. Sargent's Sons
Fec
National Drying Wachinery

19936 Bulk Lift International, LLC
1013 Tamarac Dr
Carpentersville, IL 60110-1967

847-428-6059
Fax: 847-428-7180 800-879-2247
www.bulklift.com
industrial bulk packaging, food packaging and bulk
shipping bag products.
President/CEO: Brian Kelly
VP of Sales & Product Development: Gary Nattrass
Marketing Manager: Elizabeth Prosser
Vice President of Sales & Marketing: Ron Lanier
Human Resources Manager: Brenda Kardys
Vice President of Operations: Mike Sanchez
Purchasing: James Morrow
Square Footage: 200000
Brands:
Bulklift
Ohmega
Sea Bag

19937 Bulk Pack
1025 N 9th St
Monroe, LA 71201

318-387-3260
Fax: 318-387-6362 800-498-4215
sales@bulk-pack.com www.bulk-pack.com
Manufacturer and exporter of bulk containers in-
cluding flexible and intermediate
President: Peter Anderson
Quality Control: Jane Burden
VP Marketing/Sales: Peter Anderson
Sales: Ron Shemwell
Estimated Sales: $1-3 Million
Number Employees: 5-9
Square Footage: 90000
Type of Packaging: Bulk

19938 (HQ)Bulk Sak Intl Inc
103 Industrial Dr
Malvern, AR 72104-2009

501-332-8745
Fax: 501-332-8438 bags@bulksak.com
www.bulksak.com
Bulk shipping containers; importer and exporter of
bulk bags
President: Grant Patterson
gpatterson@bulksak.com
VP: Grant Patterson
Vice President/Sales: David Whitt
Plant Manager: Mike Nissen
Estimated Sales: $8,000,000
Number Employees: 50-99
Square Footage: 48500
Type of Packaging: Bulk
Other Locations:
Bulk Sak
Memphis TN

19939 Bulldog Factory Svc LLC
25880 Commerce Dr
Madison Heights, MI 48071-4151

248-541-3500
Fax: 248-541-5095 bmullins@santannatool.com
www.bulldogfactory.com
Conveyors and mixing machinery
President: Joseph Newton
CEO: Jamilce Newton
jsnewton@santannatool.com
Sales: Brad Mullins
Estimated Sales: $5-10 Million
Number Employees: 20-49

19940 Bullet Guard Corporation
3963 Commerce Dr W
West Sacramento, CA 95691
916-373-0402
Fax: 916-373-0208 800-233-5632
Sheila@bulletguardmail.com
www.bulletguard.com
Manufacturer and exporter of drive-through and walk-up windows including bullet resistant; also, interior counter enclosures; installation and custom fabrication available
President: Karlin Lynch
CFO: Marcia Lynch
Vice President: Ken Lynch
Production Manager: Kevin Lynch
Marketing Director: Jeannine Ricci
Sales Manager: Sheila Lynch
Estimated Sales: $3-5 Million
Number Employees: 25
Square Footage: 30000
Brands:
    Bullet Guard
    Food Chute

19941 Bulman Products Inc
1650 Mcreynolds Ave NW
Grand Rapids, MI 49504-2091
616-363-4416
Fax: 616-363-0380 bulman@bulmanproducts.com
www.bulmandirect.com
Manufacturer and exporter of metal dispensers for rolled butcher paper, films, aluminum foil, bag sealing tape, etc.; importer of bag sealers
Owner: Ann Hall
akirkwoodhall@bulmanproducts.com
R&D: Marc Wierenga
Operations: Ann Kirkwood
Plant Manager/Purchasing: Nils Reichert
Estimated Sales: $3-4 Million
Number Employees: 20-49
Square Footage: 52000

19942 Bunge
1391 Timberlake Manor Pkwy.
Chesterfield, MO 63017
314-292-2000
news@bunge.com
www.bunge.com
Oilseed processing, supply milled wheat, corn and rice products to food processors, bakeries, brewers, foodservice companies and snack food producers. Offers distribution services.
CEO: Gregory Heckman
CFO: John Neppl
Chief Legal Officer: Joseph Podwika
Chief HR & Communications Officer: Deborah Borg
President, Global Operations: Raul Padilla
President, Global Supply Chain: Christos Dimopoulos
Year Founded: 1818
Number Employees: 24,000
Type of Packaging: Food Service

19943 (HQ)Bunn-O-Matic Corp
1400 Adlai Stevenson Dr
Springfield, IL 62703-4291
217-529-6601
Fax: 217-585-7699 800-352-2866
www.bunnautomatic.com
Manufacturer and exporter of coffee brewers, decanters, grinders and warmers as well as coffee and iced tea filters, hot water systems, iced tea brewers, water filtration systems, and hot powdered and frozen drink systems
President/CEO: Arthur Bunn
CFO: Gene Wilken
R&D: Robert Kobylarz
Quality Control: Kurt Powell
Sales: John Kielb
Public Relations: Melinda McDonald
Production: John Vanderveldt
Plant Manager: Doug Schwartz
Purchasing Director: John Essig
Estimated Sales: $10-20 Million
Number Employees: 500-999
Other Locations:
    Bunn-O-Matic Corporation
    Cerritos CA
Brands:
    Bunn
    Bunn-O-Matic
    Easy Pour
    Pour-O-Matic

19944 Bunn-O-Matic Corporation
280 Industrial Parkway S
Aurora, ON L4G 3T9
Canada
905-841-2866
Fax: 905-841-2775 800-263-2256
order.cdn@bunn.com www.bunn.com/canada
Coffee brewing equipment
VP of Sales: Ken Cox
General Manager: Ross Anderson
Estimated Sales: $1-5,000,000
Number Employees: 100
Parent Co: Bunn-O-Matic Corporation

19945 Bunting Magnetics Co
500 S Spencer Rd
Newton, KS 67114-4109
316-284-2020
Fax: 316-283-4975 800-835-2526
bmc@buntingmagnetics.com
www.buntingmagnetics.com
Magnetic and nonmagnetic conveyors in steel and aluminum extruded frames, magnetic separators and all metal detection equipment for both dry and wet lines
President: Robert J. Bunting
CEO: Matt Anderson
manderson@buntingeurope.com
CFO: Jana L. Davis
Vice President: Richard Meister
Marketing Director: Michael Wilks
Sales Director: Rod Henricks
General Manager: Barry Voorhees
Estimated Sales: $21.7 Million
Number Employees: 100-249
Square Footage: 122000
Other Locations:
    Bunting Magnetics Company
    Elk Grove Village IL
Brands:
    Mag Slide
    Powertrac

19946 Bunzl Distribution USA
One CityPlace Dr
Suite 200
St. Louis, MO 63141
314-997-5959
Fax: 314-997-1405 888-997-5959
www.bunzldistribution.com
Outsourced food packaging, disposable supplies, and cleaning and safety products to food processors, supermarkets, retailers, convenience stores and other users.
President & CEO: Patrick Larmon
Executive Vice President: Jeff Earnhart
Year Founded: 1981
Estimated Sales: Over $1 Billion
Number Employees: 5,000
Parent Co: Bunzl PLC
Type of Packaging: Food Service, Private Label, Bulk
Other Locations:
    Bunzl Distribution
    West Valley City UT

19947 Bunzl Processor Distribution LLC
5710 NW 41st St
Riverside, MO 64150
816-448-4300
Fax: 816-561-3286 www.bunzlpd.com
Leading supplier to the meat and food processing industry, providing everything from packaging materials to work and safety apparel. Also available is a private label product line called Prime Source, featuring various products for thefoodservice, janitorial, industrial and healthcare industries
Director, Marketing: Reese Naftel
International Sales Representative: Patricia Vargas
Number Employees: 500-999
Type of Packaging: Food Service, Private Label
Brands:
    Prime Source

19948 Burd & Fletcher
5151 E Geospace Dr
Independence, MO 64056-3321
816-257-0291
Fax: 816-257-9928 800-821-2776
info@burdfletcher.com www.burdfletcher.com
Carton containers for food products
Number Employees: 250-499
Type of Packaging: Food Service, Bulk

19949 Burdock Group
859 Outer Rd # 710
Orlando, FL 32814-6652
407-802-1400
Fax: 407-802-1405 info@burdockgroup.com
www.burdockgroup.com
Consulting team that provides clients with solutions to scientific and regulatory issues affecting FDA and USDA regulated products.
President: George Burdock, Ph.D
gburdock@burdockgroup.com
Director of Business Development: John Geisler
Marketing Coordinator: Alexandra Smith
Controller: Gina Radcliff
Estimated Sales: $300,000-500,000
Number Employees: 10

19950 Burford Corp
11284 Highway 74
Maysville, OK 73057-9669
405-867-4467
Fax: 405-867-4219 877-287-3673
cburford@burford.com
www.burford.publishpath.com
Bag and pouch sealers, bag labeling equipment, closing equipment, coders, daters, imprinters, computer systems, cooling equipment, cooling tunnels and computer programs
Executive VP: Fred Springer
fspringer@burford.com
CFO: Fred Speringr
Vice President: Don Ivey
R & D: Scott Clemons
Sales Manager: Teresa Ruder
Estimated Sales: $10-20 000,000
Number Employees: 50-99
Type of Packaging: Private Label, Bulk

19951 Burger Maker Inc
666 16th St
Carlstadt, NJ 07072-1922
201-939-0444
Fax: 201-939-1965 www.schweidandsons.com
Hamburger patties
Owner: David Schweid
davidschweid@burgermaker.com
EVP Operations: Brad Schweld
EVP Sales: Jamie Schweld
Regional Manager: Chip Crenshaw
Regional Manager: Bill Breslin
Regional Manager: John Jernagan
davidschweid@burgermaker.com
Number Employees: 100-249

19952 Burgess Enterprises, Inc
1000 SW 34th St
Bldg W2 Suite A
Renton, WA 98057
206-763-0255
Fax: 206-763-8039 800-927-3286
marketing@burgessenterprises.net
www.burgessenterprises.net
Carts and kiosks; importer and exporter of espresso machines
President/CEO: Robert S Burgess
CFO: Don Paschal
Sales: Robert Connor
Contact: Bob Connor
bconnor@burgessenterprises.net
Estimated Sales: Below $2.5 Million
Number Employees: 5-9
Number of Brands: 4
Number of Products: 12
Brands:
    Burgess
    Faema

19953 Burgess Mfg.-Oklahoma
1250 Roundhouse Rd
P.O. Box 237
Guthrie, OK 73044-4700
405-282-1913
Fax: 405-282-7132 800-804-1913
bmfg@sbcglobal.net www.burgesspallets.com
Manufacturer and exporter of pallets, boxes, crating and lumber; wholesaler/distributor of lumber, plywood, stretch film, plastic pallets, chipboard and plastic components
Plant Manager: Lee Williams
Estimated Sales: $3 Million
Number Employees: 20-49
Square Footage: 42000

19954 Burghof Engineering & Mfg Co
16051 W Deerfield Pkwy # 1
Prairie View, IL 60069-9629

847-634-0737
Fax: 847-634-0870

Automatic fillers and packers
President: Kaspar Kammerer
Manager: Jeff Mell
Estimated Sales: $2.5-5 Million
Number Employees: 10-19

19955 Burke Industrial Coatings
6200 NE Campus Drive
Suite B
Vancouver, WA 98661-6800

360-944-8465
Fax: 360-759-4989 800-348-3245
mickie@burkeindustrialcoatings.com

USDA accepted water base industrial coatings
President: James P Harris
Quality Control: Barreal Badertscher
Vice President: Darrell Badertscher
Estimated Sales: Below $5 Million
Number Employees: 10

19956 Burkert Fluid Control
2572 White Rd
Irvine, CA 92614-6236

949-251-1224
Fax: 949-223-3198 800-325-1405
marketing-usa@burkert.com www.burkert.com

Water treatment systems.
President: Harm Stratman
harm.stratman@burkert.com
Inside Sales: Ebert Bautista
Number Employees: 20-49

19957 Burling Instrument Inc
16 River Rd
P.O. Box 298
Chatham, NJ 07928-1988

973-635-9481
Fax: 973-635-9530 800-635-2526
www.burlinginstruments.com

Manufacturer and exporter of temperature controls,
limits and sensors; importer of thermostats
President: Bruce Freed
bfreed@burlinginstruments.com
Sr. VP: Roger Nation
VP of Sales: Michael Wetterer
Estimated Sales: $2.5-5 Million
Number Employees: 10-19
Square Footage: 44000

19958 Burnett Bros Engineering
20 Magnolia Via
Anaheim, CA 92801-1034

714-526-2448
Fax: 714-526-4961 info@burnettbros.com
www.burnettbros.com

Manufacturers and importers of machinery including
bunch and shrink wrappers, carton overwrappers,
colloid, roll-fed labelers for water, soft drink and
milk bottles. Also produce wrapper for cauliflower,
cabbage, iceberg lettuceetc
President: Malcolm Burnett
mfburnett@aol.com
Sales VP: Malcolm Burnett
Estimated Sales: Less Than $500,000
Number Employees: 1-4

19959 Burnishine Products
755 Tri State Pkwy
Gurnee, IL 60031

847-356-0222
Fax: 253-856-1003 800-818-8275
www.burnishine.com

Sanitizers, disinfectants, sterilants, cleaners and pol-
ishers
President: Carl Demasi
Human Resources: Laura Welch
Purchasing Manager: Michelle Hogan
Number Employees: 20-49
Number of Brands: 4
Number of Products: 250
Square Footage: 200000
Parent Co: Herbert Stanley Company
Type of Packaging: Consumer, Private Label, Bulk

19960 (HQ)Burns & Mcdonnell Inc
9400 Ward Pkwy
Kansas City, MO 64114-3319

816-333-9400
Fax: 816-333-3690 rdick@burnsmcd.com
www.burnsmcd.com

Consulting engineers and construction for various
industries including the food
General Manager: Ronald Colas
CEO: Ray Kowalik
rkowalik@burnsmcd.com
CEO: Greg Graves
Estimated Sales: $5 Million
Number Employees: 5000-9999

19961 Burns Chemical Systems
3100 Hamilton Ave
Cleveland, OH 44114-3701

724-327-7600
Fax: 724-327-8049

Dish washers
President: John Burns
Contact: Melissa Mitchell
mmitchell1@statechemical.com
Controller: Robert Rummel
Estimated Sales: $10-20,000,000
Number Employees: 100-249

19962 Burns Engineering Inc
10201 Bren Rd E
Hopkins, MN 55343-9066

952-935-4400
Fax: 952-935-8782 800-328-3871
info@burnsengineering.com
www.burnsengineering.com

Resistant thermometer devices (RTD) and thermo-
couple sanitary temperature sensors, transmitters and
thermowells; calibration services available
Owner: David Ciervo
Sales Director: Stefan Tudor
dciervo@burns-group.com
Purchasing Manager: Wendi Fetter
Estimated Sales: $10-20 Million
Number Employees: 50-99

19963 Burns Industries
1150 Bethlehem Pike
Line Lexington, PA 18932

215-822-8778
Fax: 215-822-1006 800-223-6430

Vacuum lifting systems
Manager: Tim Burns
Number Employees: 50
Square Footage: 60000
Brands:
  Vacuhoist

19964 Burrell Cutlery Company
100 Rockwell Ave.
Ellicottville, NY 14731

716-699-2343
Fax: 716-699-2683

Carving, culinary, fruit, slicing, steak, household,
specialty and kitchen knives
President: John Burrell
Estimated Sales: $2.5-5 Million
Number Employees: 10

19965 Burrows Paper Corp
501 W Main St # 1
Little Falls, NY 13365-1899

315-823-2300
Fax: 315-823-0867 800-272-7122
papersales@burline.com www.burrowspaper.com

Integrated paper manufacturer with operations in the
US and Europe.
President/CEO: R W Burrows
Corporate Secretary: Margaret Goldman
Corporate VP: Michael Lengvarsky
VP/General Manager: Hai Ninh
Vice President, Sales: Duane Judd
Estimated Sales: $20-50 Million
Number Employees: 1000-4999
Square Footage: 120000
Type of Packaging: Food Service
Brands:
  Plastawrap

19966 Burrows Paper Corp
501 W Main St # 1
Little Falls, NY 13365-1899

315-823-2300
Fax: 315-823-0867 800-272-7122
papersales@burrowspaper.com
www.burrowspaper.com

Pizza boxes, carry-out food containers, sandwich
wrap, and micro-flute packaging
President/CEO: R W Burrows
Cmo: Joe Healey
jhealey@burline.com
CFO: Philip Paras
Vice President: Hai Ninh
Research & Development: Terry McMillen
Quality Control: Melinda Bird
VP OF Sales: Duane Judd
Sales Director: Ed Amodei
Operations Manager: Jeffrey Hall
Production Manager: Jeffrey Hall
Plant Manager: Chris Kitchel
Purchasing Manager: Ralph Renzulli
Number Employees: 1000-4999
Type of Packaging: Consumer, Food Service, Pri-
vate Label

19967 Burry Foods
1750 E Main Street
Suite 160
Saint Charles, IL 60174

630-584-9976
www.burryfoodservice.com

Frozen food service supplier of Thomas', Boboli and
Entenmann's
CEO/Founder: Tony Hyler
CFO/VP Information Technology: Dave Phillips
Contact: Christopher Orlando
christopher.orlando@burryfoods.com
Operations Manager/VP Supply Chain: Gerard
Mitchell
Estimated Sales: $28.15 Million
Number Employees: 17
Square Footage: 7853
Type of Packaging: Food Service

19968 Busch LLC
516 Viking Dr
Virginia Beach, VA 23452-7316

757-463-7800
Fax: 757-463-7407 800-872-7867
marketing@buschinc.com www.buschusa.com

Vacuum packaging equipment, vacuum systems,
rendering pumps, vacuum pumps
President: Charles Kane
ckane@bushusa.com
CFO: Doug Clark
Quality Control: Kelly Wood
Marketing Director: Terry McMahan
VP of Engineering: Wayne Benson
Estimated Sales: $10-25 000,000
Number Employees: 100-249

19969 Bush Refrigeration Inc
1700 Admiral Wilson Blvd # A
Pennsauken, NJ 08109-3990

856-963-1801
Fax: 856-361-2772 800-220-2874
info@bushrefrigeration.com
www.bushrefrigeration.com

Manufacturer and exporter of walk in, display and
storage coolers and freezers. Refrigerated deli and
bakery display cases. Prep tables and under the
counter prep tables.
Owner: Alex Bush
abush@bushrefrigeration.com
Estimated Sales: $2.5-5 Million
Number Employees: 20-49

19970 Bush Tank Fabricators Inc
222 Thomas St
Newark, NJ 07114-2614

973-596-1121
Fax: 973-596-1662

Ribbon blenders, custom fabricated tanks, mixers,
agitators and hoppers
President: Thomas Horenburg
bushtank@aol.com
Vice President: Martin Koppel
Estimated Sales: $10-20,000,000
Number Employees: 5-9

19971 Bushman Equipment Inc
W133n4960 Campbell Dr
Menomonee Falls, WI 53051-7056
262-790-4200
Fax: 262-790-4202 800-338-7810
www.bushman.com
Manufacturer and exporter of material handling
equipment including cranes, hooks, coil, sheet and
pallet lifters, beams, spreaders, blocks and tongs
President: Ralph Deger
custinfo@bushman.com
Sales Manager: Chuck Nettesheim
Estimated Sales: $20-50 Million
Number Employees: 20-49

19972 Business Control Systems
1173 Green St
Iselin, NJ 08830-2011
732-283-1301
Fax: 732-283-1192 800-233-5876
www.businesscontrol.com
Point of sale systems and software
Owner: Alexander Want
alexw@businesscontrol.com
Number Employees: 10-19

19973 Business Facilities
44 Apple St # 3
Tinton Falls, NJ 07724-2672
732-842-7433
Fax: 732-458-6634 800-524-0337
dgoldstein@busfac.com
www.businessfacilities.com
Manager: Ted Coene
Manager: B Barbara
bbaldwin@americanrunning.org
Number Employees: 20-49

19974 Buss America
455 Kehoe Blvd
Carol Stream, IL 60188-5203
630-933-9100
Fax: 630-933-0400 info.us@busscorp.com
www.busscompounding.com
Kneading extruders
Contact: Ryan Buss
r.buss@summitradiology.com
Product Manager: Edmund Meier
Estimated Sales: $20-50 Million
Number Employees: 5-9
Square Footage: 66000
Parent Co: George Fisher

19975 Busse/SJI Corp
124 N Columbus St
Randolph, WI 53956-1204
920-326-3131
Fax: 920-326-3134 800-882-4995
inquiry@arrowheadsystems.com
www.arrowheadsystems.com
Manufacturer and exporter of palletizers and
depalletizers for glass, can and plastic beverage con-
tainers; also, retort crate loading and unloading
President: Thomas Young
tyoung@arrowheadsystems.com
Marketing Director: Nick Osterholt
Sales Manager: Dan Erdman
General Manager: George Vroom
Number Employees: 50-99
Parent Co: Arrowhead Systems
Other Locations:
Busse
Shelton CT
Brands:
Advantage
Eclipse
Turbo
Viper

19976 Busse/SJI Corp
124 N Columbus St
Randolph, WI 53956-1204
920-326-3131
Fax: 920-326-3134 www.arrowheadsystems.com
Conveyors
President: Thomas J Young
tyoung@arrowheadsystems.com
Estimated Sales: $10-25 Million
Number Employees: 50-99

19977 Butler Winery
6200 E Robinson Rtd
Bloomington, IN 47408
812-332-6660
vineyard@butlerwinery.com
www.butlerwinery.com
Wine and wine making supplies
President/CEO: James Butler
Secretary/Treasurer: Susan Butler
Manager: Amy Butler
Estimated Sales: $540,000
Number Employees: 5
Brands:
Butler

19978 Butterworth Inc
16737 W Hardy Rd
Houston, TX 77060-6241
281-821-7300
Fax: 281-821-5550 info@butterworth.com
www.butterworth.com
Tank cleaning machines
Owner: Daniel Elko
CFO: Craig Cooper
R & D: Dan Elko
Director Sales: James Slaughter
dabbuhl@repeatbusinesssystems.com
Estimated Sales: $1-2.5 Million
Number Employees: 20-49

19979 Buyers Laboratory Inc
108 John St
Hackensack, NJ 07601-4130
201-489-6439
Fax: 201-488-0461 info@buyerslab.com
www.buyerslab.com
Owner: Burt Meerow
Chief Executive Officer: Michael Danziger
Vice President of Sales: Patti Clyne
Chief Operating Officer: Mark Lerch
Estimated Sales: $.5-1 million
Number Employees: 5-9

19980 Buypass Corporation
360 Interstate North Pkwy SE
Atlanta, GA 30339-2204
770-953-2664
Fax: 770-916-3391 www.firstdata.com
Electronic payment systems for debit, credit, EBT
and check authorization purposes
Co- Founder: George Roberts
Chief Executive Officer, Chairman: Michael
Capellas
Vice President of Community Relations: Ellen
Sandberg
Client Executive: Rich Toland
Number Employees: 250-499
Parent Co: Electronic Payment Services

19981 Bynoe Printers
167 W 126th Street
New York, NY 10027-4412
212-662-5041
Manufacturer and wholesaler/distributor of advertis-
ing specialties including labels, raffle tickets and
paper cups
President: Mark Bynoe
Estimated Sales: $1-2,500,000
Number Employees: 1-4

19982 Byrton Dairy Products
28354 N Ballard Dr
Lake Forest, IL 60045
847-367-8300
Fax: 847-367-8332
President: Richard Tondi
Estimated Sales: $2.5-5 000,000
Number Employees: 5-9

19983 C & D Robotics
4780 S 23rd St
Beaumont, TX 77705-2632
409-840-5252
Fax: 409-840-4660 800-967-6268
www.cdrobot.com
Material handling for finished goods, industrial
contry robots, specialty machinery, conveyers and
material handling systems
President: Charles Davis
Estimated Sales: $10-20 000,000
Number Employees: 20-49

19984 C & D Valve Mfg Co
201 NW 67th St
Oklahoma City, OK 73116-8247
405-843-5621
Fax: 405-840-0443 800-654-9233
www.cdvalve.com
Manufacturer and exporter of valves for refrigera-
tion equipment
President: Brad Denning
bdenning@cdvalve.com
Estimated Sales: $5-10 Million
Number Employees: 20-49

19985 C & K Machine Co
56 Jackson St # 1
Holyoke, MA 01040-5582
413-536-8122
Fax: 413-532-9819 email@ckmachine.com
www.ckmachine.com
Manufacturer and exporter of nonshrink, conform-
ing wrapping machines for cookies, candies and
sandwiches; also, bakery slicing machines and gum
and candy cartoners
President: James Tallon
jjtallon@hge.net
Sales/Marketing: James Tallon
Estimated Sales: $1-3 Million
Number Employees: 1-4
Square Footage: 24000
Brands:
Redington
Wrap King

19986 C & L Wood Products Inc
62 Walnut Rd
Hartselle, AL 35640-5348
256-502-9650
Fax: 256-773-3238 800-483-2035
hbowman@clwoodproducts.com
www.clwoodproducts.com
Pallets and crates including hardwood and pine
Manager: Henry Bowman
hbowman@clwoodproducts.com
Plant Manager: Rodger Glaz
Estimated Sales: $2.5-5 Million
Number Employees: 50-99
Square Footage: 30000

19987 C & R Inc
5600 Clyde Moore Dr
Groveport, OH 43125-1081
614-497-1130
Fax: 614-497-1585 888-497-1130
www.crproducts.com
Fabrication and installation of stainless process
equipment and process piping; distributors of G and
H products and AMPCO centrifugal pumps, heat
exchangers, tubular, ice equipment, ice builders,
flow diversion stations, pipingfittings and tubing
President: R Murphy
Estimated Sales: $5-10 000,000
Number Employees: 20-49

19988 C E Rogers Co
1895 Frontage Rd
PO Box 118
Mora, MN 55051-7133
320-679-2172
Fax: 320-679-2180 800-279-8081
cerogers@cerogers.com www.cerogers.com
Manufacturer, exporter and importer of free-stand-
ing multi-effect and waste water evaporators, hori-
zontal and vertical spray dryers and related heating
and cooling equipment; installation service available
President/Sales: Howard Rogers
hrogers@cerogers.com
Chief Engineer: Steven Degeest
Parts: Carol Dutton
Estimated Sales: $5-10 Million
Number Employees: 20-49
Square Footage: 8000
Parent Co: CFR Group

19989 C F Napa Brand Design
2787 Napa Valley Corporate Dr
Napa, CA 94558-6216
707-265-1891
Fax: 707-265-1899 dschuemann@cfnapa.com
www.cfnapa.com
Designer of labels, containers, boxes, etc
Owner: David Schuemann
Principal: John Farrell
Marketing Director: Susan Rouzie

Estimated Sales: Below $5 Million
Number Employees: 10-19
Square Footage: 18000

19990 C H Babb Co Inc
445 Paramount Dr
Raynham, MA 02767-5178
508-977-0600
Fax: 508-977-1985 sales@chbabb.com
www.tunnelovens.com
Manufacturer and exporter of automated final proofers, tunnel ovens, cooling conveyors and complete systems for pizza, bagels, breads and rolls, pastries, pies, etc
President: Charles Foran
cforan@babbco.com
Sales Representative: William Foran
Number Employees: 20-49
Square Footage: 150000
Brands:
  Babbco

19991 C M Becker Inc
1604 Falcon Dr
PO Box 1022
Desoto, TX 75115-2418
972-228-1690
Fax: 972-224-2191 Info@CMBecker.com
www.cmbecker.com
Precision parts for the beverage industry
Owner: Michael Korkisch
Estimated Sales: Below $5 000,000
Number Employees: 1-4

19992 C M Processing Solutions
235 Benjamin Dr # 102
Suite 102
Corona, CA 92879-8098
951-808-4376
Fax: 951-808-8657 sales@cmpsolutions.net
www.cmpsolutions.net
Supplier of stainless steel hygiene equipment and food processing equipment for the beef, pork, poultry, seafood and produce industry
CEO: Mark Corser
Number Employees: 1-4

19993 C Nelson Mfg Co
265 N Lake Winds Pkwy
Oak Harbor, OH 43449-9012
419-898-3305
Fax: 419-898-4098 800-922-7339
nelsonoh@aol.com
Manufacturer and exporter of refrigerated pushcarts and ice cream storage cabinets
Owner: Kelley Smith
Sr. Engineer: Paul Cox
Sales Manager: Tammy Almendinger
nelsonoh@aol.com
Account Manager: Tammy Almendinger
Purchasing: Paul Zylka
Estimated Sales: $10-20 Million
Number Employees: 20-49
Square Footage: 40000

19994 C Nelson Mfg Co
265 N Lake Winds Pkwy
Oak Harbor, OH 43449-9012
419-898-3305
Fax: 419-898-4098
Manufacturer of ice cream cabinets, ice cream carts and related equipment.
Owner: Kelley Smith
nelsonoh@aol.com
Marketing/Sales: George Dunlap
Purchasing: Paul Zylka
Estimated Sales: $10-20 000,000
Number Employees: 20-49

19995 C P Industries
560 N 500 W
Salt Lake City, UT 84116-3429
801-521-0313
Fax: 801-539-0510 800-453-4931
info@cpindustries.net
Manufacturer and exporter of industrial and household cleaners, ice melters and detergents
Owner: Ann Lieber
ann@cpindustries.net
National Detergent Manager: Ted Olsen
Estimated Sales: $10-20 Million
Number Employees: 20-49
Square Footage: 500000

Type of Packaging: Consumer, Food Service, Private Label, Bulk
Brands:
  Generic Liquid Dish
  Generic Liquid Laundry
  Mountain White
  Power Clean
  Sparkle

19996 C Palmer Mfg Co Inc
5 Palmers Rd
West Newton, PA 15089-2014
724-872-8200
Fax: 724-872-8302 www.cpalmermfg.com
Pizelle irons
President: John Palmieri
CEO: John Palmeri
President: John Palmieri
VP: Kathryn Palmeri
CFO: Philpe Palmieri
Sales Manager: Parcy Smose
Estimated Sales: $1-2.5 Million
Number Employees: 5-9

19997 C R Daniels Inc
3451 Ellicott Center Dr
Ellicott City, MD 21043-4191
410-461-2100
Fax: 410-461-2987 800-933-2638
info@crdaniels.com www.crdaniels.com
Manufacturer and exporter of conveyor belting, trucks and plastic totes, carts, hampers and tubs; importer of cotton duck
President: Gary Abel
CEO: Gary V Abel
Vice President: Vic Keeler
Quality Control: J Singh
Estimated Sales: $20-50 Million
Number Employees: 100-249
Square Footage: 250000
Brands:
  Dandux

19998 C R Mfg
10240 Deer Park Rd
Waverly, NE 68462-1416
402-786-2000
Fax: 402-786-2096 877-789-5844
lisag@pmc-group.com
Manufacturer and exporter of plastic food spouts, scoops, spreaders, spatulas, funnels, knives, spoons, bowls, pitchers, corkscrews, tongs, etc
General Manager: Daryl Chapelle
Quality Control: Ace Dettinger
Vice President: Mary Gaber
mary.gaber@pmc-group.com
Estimated Sales: $5-10 Million
Number Employees: 100-249
Brands:
  Betterway
  Dispos-A-Way
  Exacto-Pour
  Ezy-Way
  Jigg-All
  Lidd Off
  Magic-Flo
  Magic-Mesh
  Margarita Made Easy
  Pop-N-Pull
  Posi-Pour
  Posi-Pour 2000
  Pour Mor
  Pour-Eaz
  Save-A-Nail
  Shooters Made Easy
  Table Lev'lr
  Whiskygate

19999 C R Mfg
10240 Deer Park Rd
Waverly, NE 68462-1416
402-786-2000
Fax: 402-786-2096 877-789-5844
Plastic supplies and smallwares to the food service, food prep, bakery, restaurant, scoop and scoop accessories, specialty items, pourers and pourer accessories, bar supply and bar accessories markets

Vice President: Mary Gaber
mary.gaber@pmc-group.com
Vice President: Mary Gaber
mary.gaber@pmc-group.com
Customer Service: Gary Knaub
Marketing/Sales: Sheila Camprecht
National Sales: Scott Donalds
Plant Manager: Bob Cooper
Estimated Sales: $20 Million
Number Employees: 100-249
Number of Brands: 27
Number of Products: 29
Square Footage: 120000
Parent Co: PMC Group Companies
Type of Packaging: Food Service, Private Label, Bulk
Brands:
  3-Cup Measurer
  Betterway Pourers
  Cr Scoops
  Cr Food Baskets
  Cake Comb
  Crystal Shooter Tubes
  Drip Catchers
  Econo Pourer
  Exacto-Pour Tester
  Ezy-Way Pourer
  Jigg-All
  Jumbo Straws
  Kover All Dust Cap
  Lid-Off Pail Opener
  Magic-Mesh
  Marga-Ezy
  Pizza Slicer
  Polar Pitcher
  Posi-Pour 2000 Pourer
  Posi-Pour Pourer
  Pour Mor
  Pro-Flo Pourer
  Roxi Rimming Supplies
  Roxi Sugar and Salt Spices/Flavors
  Shakers Prepackaged Accessories
  Shotskies Gelatin Mixes
  Steakmarkers
  Super Slicer
  Whisky Gate Pourer

20000 C S Bell Co
170 W Davis St
PO Box 291
Tiffin, OH 44883-1337
419-448-0791
Fax: 419-448-1203 888-958-6381
info@csbellco.com www.csbellco.com
Manufacturer and exporter of grist and hammer mills, conveyors and recycling and size reduction equipment; also, custom fabrication available.
President: Daniel White
Estimated Sales: Less Than $500,000
Number Employees: 5-9
Square Footage: 20000
Brands:
  Bell

20001 C W Cole & Co
2560 Rosemead Blvd
South El Monte, CA 91733-1593
626-443-2473
Fax: 626-443-9253 info@colelighting.com
www.colelighting.com
Custom lighting fixtures for cooking hoods, walk-in coolers and salad bar/pie cases; also, refrigerator door light switches
President: Stephen W Cole
scole@colelighting.com
Co-Owner: Donald Cole
Sales Manager: Sam Serrano
Sales Engineer: Kevin Brummett
Engineering & Design: Dan Wilkins
Plant Manager: Gustavo Castillo
Purchasing Manager: Jim Cotney
Estimated Sales: $5 Million
Number Employees: 20-49
Square Footage: 50000

20002 C&H Chemical
222 Starkey St
St Paul, MN 55107-1813
651-227-4343
Fax: 651-227-2485 www.secole.com
Cleaning compounds
President: Greg Elliott
Food Industry Specialist: John Jesmok

Estimated Sales: $5-10 Million
Number Employees: 20-49

20003 C&H Packaging Company
1401 W Taylor St
Merrill, WI 54452
715-536-5400
Fax: 715-536-4678 www.chpack.com
Flexographic printing, lamination, pouching
VP: Gene Wagner
Marketing: Bob Madderom
Sales: Bob Madderom
Operations: Larry Offerman
Plant Manager: Dave Welch
Estimated Sales: $3.5 000,000
Number Employees: 100-249
Type of Packaging: Consumer, Food Service, Private Label

20004 C&H Store Equipment Company
2530 S Broadway
Los Angeles, CA 90007
213-748-7165
Fax: 213-749-6135 800-648-4979
Manufacturer, wholesaler/distributor and exporter of store fixtures, office furniture, showcases, and metal shelving
CEO: Cheon Kim
Estimated Sales: $2.5-5,000,000
Number Employees: 10-19
Brands:
Lozier Reeve

20005 (HQ)C&R Refrigation Inc
PO Box 93
Center, TX 75935
936-598-2761
Fax: 936-598-7858 800-438-6182
www.crrefrig.com
Custom Metal Fabrication-3A tanks, process piping installation, platforms, flow panels, valve clusters, hoppers, skid systems, dryers, orbital welding. Distributor for Alfalaval, Ampco Pumps, Definix Valves.
President: Ronald Murphy
VP: Phillip McKitrick
Sales Manager: Jim McAnaul
Estimated Sales: $5-10 Million
Number Employees: 11
Square Footage: 160000
Other Locations:
C&R
Largo FL

20006 C&R Refrigeration
405 Center St
P.O. BOX 93
Center, TX 75935
936-598-2761
Fax: 409-598-7858 800-438-6182
crrefrig@netdot.com www.crrefrig.com
Rebuilt ammonia compressors, ice machines and other industrial refrigeration equipment
President: Robert Reeves
Founder: Willard Reeves
Estimated Sales: $10-20 Million
Number Employees: 50-99

20007 C-P Flexible Packaging
122 Penns Trl
Newtown, PA 18940-1815
215-860-7676
Fax: 215-860-6170 800-448-8183
Polyethylene sleeve labels, specialty bags and roll stock; also, polypropylene roll feed labels
COO: Gney Lane
Marketing VP/Sales: Art Bucci
Manager: Bill Owen
bowen@aa.com
Estimated Sales: $30 Million
Number Employees: 5-9

20008 C-P Flexible Packaging
15 Grumbacher Rd
York, PA 17406-8417
717-764-1193
Fax: 717-764-2039 www.cpflexpack.com
Snack food bags, cellophane lamination, polypropylene and polyethylene, slitting, resource recovery, quality assurance
President: Tony Vaudo
tvaudo@cpconverters.com
Information Technologist: Brad Gates
Estimated Sales: $20-50 Million
Number Employees: 100-249

Number of Products: 6
Square Footage: 120000

20009 C-P Flexible Packaging
122 Penns Trl
Newtown, PA 18940-1815
215-860-7676
Fax: 215-860-6170 800-448-8183
Polyethylene stretch sleeve labels, oriented polypropylene roll-fed labels, shrink sleeves, and shrink roll-fed labels.
Sales: Jennifer Hirsch
Manager: Bill Owen
bowen@aa.com
Estimated Sales: $15 Million
Number Employees: 5-9
Type of Packaging: Private Label

20010 C-Through Covers
4955 Curry Drive
San Diego, CA 92115-2631
619-286-0671
Fax: 619-286-7991
Reinforced vinyl and canvas covers for bakery rack, freezers, etc
Sales Manager: Marta Stulberger
Estimated Sales: $1-5 Million

20011 C. Cretors & Company
3243 N California Ave
Chicago, IL 60618
773-588-1690
Fax: 773-588-2171 800-228-1885
info@creators.com www.cretors.com
Manufacturer and exporter of popcorn machines and cotton candy equipment and supplies
President: Andrew Cretors
CFO: Dan Williams
Quality Control: Walter Karzak
Marketing Manager: Beth Cretors
Product Manager: John Concannon
Estimated Sales: $10-20 Million
Number Employees: 100-249
Square Footage: 106000
Brands:
Caramelizer
Cretors
Flo-Thru
Ringmaster I
Ringmaster Ii

20012 C.B. Dombach & Son
252 N Prince St
Lancaster, PA 17603
717-392-0578
Fax: 717-392-1210 info@cbdombach.com
www.cbdombach.com
Commercial awnings
President: Scott Underwood
Contact: Scott Pino
scott@cbdombach.com
Estimated Sales: $1-2.5 Million
Number Employees: 10-19

20013 C.F.F. Stainless Steels
1840 Burlington Street East
Hamilton, ON L8H 3L4
Canada
905-549-2603
Fax: 905-549-2994 800-263-4511
sales@cffstainless.com www.cffstainless.com
Supplier of stainless steel products to the pharmaceutical, chemical, beverage, mining, water purification, food and dairy industries
President: Brian McComb
Vice President Sales: John Burns

20014 C.H. Robinson Co.
14701 Charlson Rd
Eden Prairie, MN 55347-5076
952-683-2800
Fax: 952-933-4747 855-229-6128
solutions@chrobinson.com www.chrobinson.com
Provides: freight transportation (TL, intermodal, ocean, and air freight), cross docking, LTL, customs brokerage, freight forwarding and trucking services, fresh produce sourcing, and information services.
CEO: Bob Biesterfeld
President, NA Surface Transportation: Mac Pinkerton
CFO: Mike Zechmeister
President, Global Freight Forwarding: Michael Short

Year Founded: 1905
Estimated Sales: $14.87 Billion
Number Employees: 15,074
Type of Packaging: Consumer, Food Service, Bulk

20015 C.J. Machine
1183-73 1/2 Avenue NW
Fridley, MN 55432
763-767-4630
Fax: 763-767-4633
Conveyors, casers, stackers, dolly cart loaders and elevators
President: Chuck Voller
VP: Jeff Anderson
Number Employees: 10
Brands:
Built Rite

20016 C.J. Machine
11551 Eagle Street NW
Suite 1
Coon Rapids, MN 55448-3051
763-506-0968
Fax: 763-767-4633
Estimated Sales: $300,000-500,000
Number Employees: 1-4

20017 C.J. Zone ManufacturingCompany
1615 N 25th St
St Louis, MO 63106-2545
314-771-7107
Fax: 314-771-1292
Owner: Bud Zone
Estimated Sales: $10-20 Million
Number Employees: 20-49

20018 C.M. Lingle Company
100 Millard Drive
Henderson, TX 75652-5034
903-657-5557
Fax: 903-657-9749 800-256-6963
Walk-in coolers and freezers and cold storage doors
President: Fred Lingle
VP: James Lingle
Estimated Sales: $10-20 Million
Number Employees: 50-99
Square Footage: 140000

20019 C.W. Brabender Instruments
50 E Wesley St
P.O. Box 2127
South Hackensack, NJ 07606-1495
201-343-8425
Fax: 201-343-0608 foodsales@cwbrabender.com
www.cwbrabender.com
Instrumentation for testing physical properties and quality of various materials utilized in the food industry. Product line includes the world renowned Farinograph®, Extensograph®, as well as viscometers, mills andextruders.
President: Richard Thoma
VP of Sales & Marketing-Food Division: Sal Iaquez
Vice President of Customer Services: Kai Kunicke
Purchasing: Tony Grambone
Estimated Sales: $5-10 Million
Number Employees: 20-49
Brands:
Extensograph
Farinograph
Plasti-Corder

20020 C.W. Shasky & Associates Ltd.
2880 Portland Drive
Oakville, ON L4K 5P2
Canada
905-829-9414
Fax: 905-760-7715 www.shasky.com
Manufacturers' representative for foodservice, club and HMR segments
President: Michael Shasky
VP: James Shasky
Estimated Sales: $7.3 Million
Number Employees: 25
Brands:
Angostura Bitters
Au Pain Dore
Catania-Spagna
Dole Food Products
Eli's Cheesecake Company
Farmland Foods
Haagen-Dazs®
Japan Food Canada/Kikkoman
McIlhenny Company Tabasco®

Mimi Foods
Mission Foods
National Importers/Twinnings
Nestle Ice Cream
Norpac
Otis Spunkmeyer
Patak's
Rosina Food Products
Sea Watch International
Stanislaus Food Products
Tate & Lyle

20021 CA Griffith International
PO Box 1785
Huntington, NY 11743-0460

631-385-7521
Fax: 631-424-3639

Meat packaging
Estimated Sales: $5-10 000,000

20022 CAE Alpheus
9370 7th Street
Unit E
Rancho Cucamonga, CA 91730-5509
Fax: 513-831-3672 800-777-9101
info@coldjet.com www.dryiceblasting.com
Dry Ice blasting machines
Estimated Sales: $1-2.5 Million
Number Employees: 1-4

20023 CAL Controls
1675 Delany Road
Gurnee, IL 60031

800-866-6659
Fax: 847-782-5223 800-447-6690
NA@West-CS.com www.cal-controls.com
Temperature and process controllers for OEM and
Plant MRO
President: Alan Bates
Estimated Sales: $1-2.5 Million
Number Employees: 5-9

20024 CAM Campak/Technician
119 Naylon Ave
Livingston, NJ 07039-1005

973-597-1414
Fax: 973-992-4713 info@campak.com
www.campak.com
Thermoformers, intermittent motion horizontal
cartoners, automatic wrappers, automatic bundlers
and shrink tunnels
President: Thomas Miller
Estimated Sales: $5-10 Million
Number Employees: 10-19

20025 CANBERRA Industries Inc
800 Research Pkwy
Meriden, CT 06450-7169

203-238-2351
Fax: 203-235-1347 800-656-1114
www.canberra.com
Temperature recorders and monitors
Cmo: Bud Sielaff
bsielaff@canberra.com
Number Employees: 1000-4999

20026 (HQ)CB Mfg. & Sales Co.
4475 Infirmary Rd
Miamisburg, OH 45342

937-866-5986
Fax: 937-528-2006 800-543-6860
sales@cbmfg.com www.cbmfg.com
Manufacturer and distributor of industrial knives
and blades
Chief Executive Officer: Chuck Biehn
CFO: Don Cain
VP Manufacturing: Roger Adams
Contact: Jess Ahern
jahern@cbmfg.com
Purchasing Manager: Angie Matheney
Estimated Sales: $10-20 Million
Number Employees: 10
Square Footage: 200000
Type of Packaging: Private Label, Bulk
Other Locations:
    CB Manufacturing & Sales Company
    Centerville OH

20027 CBI Freezing Equipment
6202 214th St SW
Mountlake Terrace, WA 98043

425-775-7424
Fax: 425-775-1715

President: Ed Cloudy

Estimated Sales: $3-5 Million
Number Employees: 5-9

20028 (HQ)CBORD Group Inc
61 Brown Rd
Ithaca, NY 14850-1247

607-257-2410
Fax: 607-257-1902 sales@cbord.com
www.cbord.com
Looking for major food cost savings? Net-based
foodservice programs? Cashless cafeteria system to
increase revenue? The CBORD provides everything
from enterprise-wide food production management
to single-facility inventory tracking.Catering and
event modules are also available. NetNutrition provides nutrition information with just the click of a
mouse. The Nutrition Service Suite delivers support
tools to clinical services. Award winning 24/7 telephone support. CBORD offerssuccess w/out risk
President: Max Steinhardt
mxs@cbord.com
CEO: Tim Tighe
Director of Sales: Mohammad Ramzy
Estimated Sales: $10-20 Million
Number Employees: 250-499
Other Locations:
    CBORD Group
    Indianapolis IN
Brands:
    Catermate
    Foodservice Suite
    Gerimenu
    Nutrition Service Suite

20029 CBORD Group Inc
61 Brown Rd
Ithaca, NY 14850-1247

607-257-2410
Fax: 607-257-1902 800-982-4643
sales@cbord.com www.cbord.com
Manufacturer and exporter of computer software
that generates LTC food service, tickets, nourish-
ment labels, production tallies, recipes, inventory,
nutritional analysis, etc
President: Max Steinhardt
mxs@cbord.com
Vice President of Client Support and Edu: Nancy
Sullivan
Vice President of Human Resources: Lisa Patz
Executive Vice President: Bruce Lane
Director of Development, Odyssey Systems: Shane
Boyer
VP, Marketing: Cindy McCall
VP, Sales: Read Winkelman
Director of Contract Administration: Chris
Curkendall
Senior Director, Service Operations: Jodi Denman
Estimated Sales: Below $5 Million
Number Employees: 250-499
Parent Co: GeriMenu
Brands:
    Gerimenu

20030 CBS International
P.O.Box 70
Currituck, NC 27929-0070

252-232-3378
Fax: 252-232-3470
Manager: Spence Castello
Estimated Sales: $1-2.5 000,000
Number Employees: 1-4

20031 CBi Freezing Equipment
6202 214th St SW
Mountlake Terrace, WA 98043-2097

425-775-7424
Fax: 425-775-1715
President: Ed Cloudy
Estimated Sales: $3-5 Million
Number Employees: 20

20032 CC Custom Technology Corporation
18201 S Miles Road
Cleveland, OH 44128-4231

216-662-5500
Fax: 216-662-2623
Waxes and cleaners
President: April Esner
Quality Control: Don Pierce
VP Manufacturing: Charles Silk
Estimated Sales: $2.5-5 Million
Number Employees: 10

20033 CCL Container
1 Llodio Dr
Hermitage, PA 16148-9015

724-981-4420
Fax: 724-342-1116 www.cclcontainer.com
Collapsible metal tubes and plastic closures
Vice President: Karen Krebs
kkrebs@cclind.com
Vice President: Karen Krebs
kkrebs@cclind.com
Estimated Sales: $10-20 000,000
Number Employees: 100-249

20034 CCL Container
105 Gordon Baker Rd
Suite 500
Toronto, ON M2H 3P8
Canada

416-756-8500
ccl@cclind.com
www.cclind.com
Manufacturer and exporter of aluminum aerosol
cans and tubes
President & CEO: Geoffrey Martin
Executive Chairman: Donald Lang
Vice President, General Manager: Andy Iseli
Sales Manager: Joe Meldrew
Senior Vice President of Corporate Commu: Janis
Wade
Estimated Sales: $1-5 Million

20035 CCL Label Inc
1187 Industrial Rd
Cold Spring, KY 41076-8799

859-781-6161
Fax: 859-781-6339 800-422-6633
www.ccllabel.com
Pressure sensitive and promotional labels
President: Eric Schaffer
Cio/Cto: Marty Butherus
mbutherus@cclind.com
Quality Control: Liary Guys
Director Operations: Tom McDonald
Estimated Sales: $10-20 Million
Number Employees: 50-99
Brands:
    On-Pak

20036 CCL Label Inc
208 Spring Dr
St Charles, MO 63303-3118

636-946-2439
Fax: 314-724-4670 888-ETL-ABEL
www.cclind.com
Computerized numbering and bar coding devices;
pressure sensitive labels
President: Brian Madden
CEO: Chuck Jongeward
R & D: John Dultz
Quality Control: Steve Harding
Human Resources: Sheila Eicheo
Office Manager: Jeanne Hodges
Estimated Sales: $5-10 Million
Number Employees: 50-99

20037 CCL Labeling Equipment
1616 S California Avenue
Monrovia, CA 91016-4622

626-305-8056
Fax: 626-301-0405 800-423-6569
www.ccllabel.com
Stepper motor labeling heads with integrated electronics, in-line and rotary labeling systems, synchronous and transfer label applicators; prime and
promotional label designs including rotating labels
and multipanel labels

20038 CCP Industries, Inc.
26301 Curtiss-Wright Parkway
Cleveland, OH 44143

440-449-6550
Fax: 800-445-8366 800-321-2840
ccporders@ccpind.com www.ccpind.com
Industrial wiping materials, hand, glass and all pur-
pose cleaners, disposable clothing, uniforms and
safety products
President: Allen Menard
Quality Control: James Fulls
V.P.: Norman Sull
Marketing Manager: Dave Williams
Contact: Michael Alberico
michaelalberico@ccpind.com

Number Employees: 1,000-4,999
Square Footage: 500000
Parent Co: Tranzonic Companies

20039 CCR Data Systems
128 Airport Rd
Concord, NH 03301-5296

603-224-7757
Fax: 603-224-7709 800-633-6500
www.ccrdata.com
Supplier of software packages for retail applications
President: David Woetzel
Contact: Gerri Cote
gerri-cote@ncr.com
Estimated Sales: $20-50 Million
Number Employees: 50-99

20040 CCR USA LLC
5810 Wison Road
Suite 200
Houston, TX 77396

281-436-1121
Fax: 281-436-1108
mark.jumper@ccrcontainers.com
www.ccrcontainers.com
A global provider of stainless steel, portable containers to the food processing, cosmetics, pharmaceutical and chemical industries.

20041 CCS Creative, Inc.
3889 Chesswood Dr
Toronto, ON M3J 2R8
Canada

416-633-9733
Fax: 416-633-0677 888-633-2079
info@ccscreative.com ccscreative.com
Assisting with digital marketing, branding, menu and recipe development for restaurants.
President: Cynthia Hollidge
Vice President: Lesley Greenberg
Operations Manager: Steve Mauro
Number Employees: 7

20042 CCS Stone, Inc.
9-11 Caeser Place
Moonachie, NJ 07074-1702

201-933-1515
Fax: 201-933-5744 800-227-7785
info@ccsstone.com www.ccsstone.com
Manufacturer and importer of restaurant and bar furniture including chairs, barstools, marble and granite tabletops and bases
President: Donald Mitnick
Controller: Corey Mitnick
VP: John Mitnick
Purchasing Manager: Michael Rivkin
Estimated Sales: $5-10 Million
Number Employees: 20-49
Square Footage: 200000

20043 CCi Scale Company
PO Box 1767
Clovis, CA 93613

559-325-7900
Fax: 888-693-2792 800-900-0224
sales@cciscale.com www.cciscale.com
Manufacturer and importer of mechanical, electronic digital, portable, portion control, receiving, counting and battery operated scales
CEO: Tom Bouton
Sales Manager: Terri McGinn
Estimated Sales: Below $5 Million
Number Employees: 1-4
Brands:
Cci

20044 CDF Corp
77 Industrial Park Rd
Plymouth, MA 02360-4868

508-747-5858
Fax: 508-747-6333 800-443-1920
www.cdf1.com
Liners and other value added products used in industrial shipping and storage containers.CDF offers the following products: cheer pack; cheertainer bag in box; IBC aseptic; form-fit; pillow & high-barrier foil liners & accessories;DrumSaver liners for steel,plastic and fiber drums; PailSaver liners for steel & plastic pails & dust caps, cover sheets, lids and strainers for drums and pails.
President: Joe Sullivan
jsullivan@cdf1.com
Marketing: Amanda Verash-Morris
Operations: Buddy Morgan

Number Employees: 100-249
Type of Packaging: Food Service, Bulk

20045 CDI Service & Mfg Inc
2181 34th Way
Largo, FL 33771-3952

727-536-2207
Fax: 727-536-2208 www.cdimfg.com
Manufacturer and exporter of booths, tables and bars; also, custom design services available.
President: David Goudy
VP: Deborah Goudy
Sales Director: David Goudy
Estimated Sales: Less than $900,000
Number Employees: 5-9
Square Footage: 15200
Type of Packaging: Food Service, Private Label

20046 CE International Trading Corporation
13450 SW 134th Ave
Suite B-5
Miami, FL 33186-4530

305-254-3448
Fax: 305-254-3182 800-827-1169
edwin@ceinternationaltrading.com
http://ceinternational.marcorojas.com/index.htm
Vibratory and separation systems. Food and beverage usage includes batch operations to screen and scalp powders, granules, or liquids in different locations.
Sales Representative: Edwin Rojas
Contact: Vanessa Perez
vanessa@ceinternationaltrading.com

20047 CEA Instrument Inc
160 Tillman St # 2
Suite 1
Westwood, NJ 07675-2624

201-967-5660
Fax: 201-967-8450 888-893-9640
ceainstr@aol.com www.ceainstr.com
Manufacturer, importer and exporter of monitors for toxic and combustible gas and oxygen levels
Manager: Steven Adelman
ceainstr@aol.com
Vice President: Steve Adelman
General Manager: Martin Adelman
Estimated Sales: $2-3 Million
Number Employees: 5-9
Number of Brands: 4
Number of Products: 18
Square Footage: 8000
Brands:
Cea 266
Gas Baron
Gas Baron 2
Md-16
Series U

20048 CEM Corporation
3100 Smith Farm Rd
Matthews, NC 28104-5044

704-821-7015
Fax: 704-821-7894 800-726-3331
info@cem.com www.cem.com
Manufacturer and exporter of microwave instruments for moisture/solids, protein and fat analysis; also, digestion and solvent extraction systems and muffle furnaces.
Owner: Michael Collins
Senior Research & Development Scientist: Alicia Stell
Marketing Manager: Keller Barnhardt
Director of North American Sales: Bobbie McManus
Director of Manufacturing: Cathy McDonald
Estimated Sales: $20-30 Million
Number Employees: 100-249
Square Footage: 60000
Brands:
Fas-9001
Mars 5
Mars-X
Mas-7000
Profat 2
Smart System 5
Star Systems

20049 CERT ID LC
500 N 3rd St
Suite 204
Fairfield, IA 52556

641-209-1899
www.cert-id.com
Certifies food processing and packaging operations in which food is handled, processed, packed, stored or distributed.
Vice President of Business Development: Joan Moeller
General Manager: Lisa Eberman

20050 CF Chef
4030 Black Gold Dr
Dallas, TX 75247-6304

214-905-1518
Fax: 214-905-9817 800-332-8812
cfmails@cfchefs.com
Sell roux as an ingredient to chef and other food companies throughout the world
Owner: W R Seeds
R & D: Eugene Wisakowsky
Vice President, Controller: Campbell Tagg
Contact: Ann Geddes
ageddes@cfchefs.com
Director Operations: Donald Capone
ageddes@cfchefs.com
Vice President of Production: James Michel
Estimated Sales: $10-20 Million
Number Employees: 20-49
Brands:
Cf Chefs
Country Flavor Kitchens
Flavor Roux
Skillet Style

20051 CFC International, Inc.
500 State St
Chicago Heights, IL 60411-1293

708-891-3456
Fax: 708-758-5989 cfcinfo@cfcintl.com
www.cfcintl.com
Holographic patterns, images in laminating films, hot and cold stamp foils and other label materials.
Chairman: Roger Huby
President: Richard Grathwaite
Sales: Mark Mitravich
Estimated Sales: $10-25 000,000
Number Employees: 250-499
Parent Co: ITW

20052 CFS North America
3179 99th Street
Urbandale, IA 50322

515-278-1559
844-808-2063
www.camlinfs.com
Shelf life extension solutions
General Manager: Jennifer Igou

20053 CGI Processing Equipment
275 Innovation Drive
Romeoville, IL 60446

888-746-0275
Fax: 815-221-5301 info@cgimfg.com
www.cgimfg.com
Brine systems, bacon processing equipment and accesories, continuous sausage processing systems, cookers, smokehouses, accessories, trucks and cages
Sales Manager: Mike Willis
Estimated Sales: $5-10 Million
Number Employees: 60

20054 CH Imports
3410 Deep Green Dr
Greensboro, NC 27410

336-282-9734
Fax: 336-288-3375
Essential oils and aromatherapy supplies
Owner: Jack Bollini
Estimated Sales: Below $5 000,000
Number Employees: 1-4

20055 CHEP Pallecon Solutions
37564 Amrhein Rd
#100
Livonia, MI 48150

734-542-9150
Fax: 734-542-9628 888-873-2277
info.containers@chep.com
Provide food and beverage container rentals for dry or liquid products.

Business Development Manager: Katelyn Byrom
Marketing Specialist: Katie Hanka
Director of Technology Solutions: Keith Schall

20056 CHL Systems
476 Meetinghouse Rd
Souderton, PA 18964-2314
215-723-7284
Fax: 215-723-9115 sales@chlsystems.com
www.chlsystems.com
Food handling and conveyor systems, and material handling equipment; custom designed systems available
President: Dan Landis
dan.landis@chlsystems.com
CFO: Kevin Albvefer
Sales Manager: Leon Kartz
Estimated Sales: $20-50 Million
Number Employees: 100-249
Square Footage: 80000
Parent Co: Clayton H. Landis Company

20057 CHS Inc.
5500 Cenex Dr.
Inver Grove Hts., MN 55077
651-355-6000
800-328-6539
www.chsinc.com
Agriculture, energy, transportation and business services company, with food products through subsidiary Ventura Foods.
President/CEO: Jay Debertin
Executive VP/CFO: Olivia Nelligan
Executive VP/General Counsel: Jim Zappa
Estimated Sales: $32.6 Billion
Number Employees: 10000+
Type of Packaging: Consumer, Food Service, Private Label, Bulk

20058 CIDA
15895 SW 72nd Ave
Suite 200
Portland, OR 97224
503-226-1285
Fax: 503-226-1670 888-226-1285
www.cidainc.com
President: David G Welsh
Architect: Jennifer Beattie
Contact: Sam Corbin
samc@cidainc.com
Estimated Sales: $3-5 Million
Number Employees: 20-49

20059 CII Food Svc Design
545 N Saginaw St # A
Lapeer, MI 48446-2337
810-667-3100
Fax: 810-667-3101 JimP@CiiFSD.com
Consultant specializing in food service design
President: Jim Peterson
Estimated Sales: Less Than $500,000
Number Employees: 1-4

20060 CIM Bakery Equipment ofUSA
836 E Rand Road
Pmb 198
Arlington Heights, IL 60004-4008
847-818-8121
Fax: 847-818-8894 sales@cimbakery.com
www.cimbakery.com
Estimated Sales: $1-5 Million

20061 CK Products
310 Racquet Dr
Fort Wayne, IN 46825-4229
260-484-2517
Fax: 800-837-2686 800-424-6839
mail@ckproducts.com www.ckproducts.com
Cake decorating and candy making products
President: Orlie Brand
Contact: Steve Burdick
steve.burdick@ckproducts.com
Estimated Sales: $2.5-5 Million
Number Employees: 50-99

20062 CKS Packaging
350 Great SW Pkwy
Atlanta, GA 30336
404-691-8900
Fax: 404-691-0086 800-800-4257
www.ckspackaging.com
Clear plastic containers

Chairman: Charles K Sewell
President/CEO: John R Sewell
CFO: Dan Fischer
EVP: Dewayne Phillips
COO, Operations: Scott K Sewell
Estimated Sales: $10-20,000,000
Number Employees: 100-249
Parent Co: CKS Packaging

20063 CL&D Graphics
1101 Wests 2nd Street
Oconomowoc, WI 53066-0644
Fax: 262-569-4075 800-777-1114
marketing@cldgraphics.com
www.cldgraphics.com
Manufacturer and exporter of pressure sensitive labels and unsupported opp film
President: Mike Dowling
CFO: Scott Demski
Quality Control: Patrick Dillon
R&D: Greg McLain
Sales Manager: Ned Price
Estimated Sales: $20-50 Million
Number Employees: 100-249
Type of Packaging: Bulk

20064 CLARCOR Air Filtration Prods
100 River Ridge Cir
Jeffersonville, IN 47130-8974
502-969-2304
Fax: 502-961-0930 866-247-4827
mailbag@airguard.com www.clcair.com
Air filtration products including extended surface pleated, pocket and cartridges filter media, bag filters, fiberglass filter media, panel filters, streamline polyester filter medias, and synthetic automatic roll filter media, HEPAfilters
President: Rich Larson
rlarson@clcair.com
CFO: Jim Snoedy
R&D: Monroe Britt
Marketing Director: Gary Heilmann
Sales Director: Joe Hevekamp
Operations Manager: Tom Justire
Number Employees: 1000-4999
Brands:
    Clean-Pak
    Dp
    Mieloguard
    Powerguard
    Vari-Pak

20065 CLECO Systems
1395 S Marietta Pkwy SE
Bldg 750
Marietta, GA 30067-4440
770-392-0330
Fax: 770-795-8093 www.clecosys.com
Pallet and case handling systems and equipment
President: Kenneth Matson
Quality Control: Ban Santonato
Sales Manager: Paul Sartore
Estimated Sales: Below $5 Million
Number Employees: 10
Brands:
    Condor
    Maestro
    Raven
    Titan
    Viking

20066 CM Ambrose Company
PO Box 3037
Arlington, WA 98223-3037
360-435-1411
Fax: 360-435-8200 ambroseinc@aol.com
Liquid packaging equipment
Contact: John Bowman
john.bowman@ambroseco.com
Estimated Sales: $2.5-5 000,000
Number Employees: 19

20067 CM Packaging
800 Ela Rd
Lake Zurich, IL 60047
847-438-2171
Fax: 847-438-0369 800-323-0422
info@cmpackaging.com
President: Mark Faber
Contact: Jenny Bryan
j.bryan@packagingdirect.com

20068 CMA Group
61 Broadway
10th Floor
New York, NY 10006
212-382-1822
Fax: 212-382-2126 800-913-2531
www.cma.net
Corporate Financial Consultants
Contact: Ted Conwell
tconwell@lighthousefinance.no

20069 CMC America Corporation
208 South Center Street
Joliet, IL 60436
815-726-4337
Fax: 815-726-7138 Info@cmc-america.com
www.cmc-america.com
Bakery machinery including mixers, water handling equipment and cookie depositing systems
President: Edward Fay
Executive Consultant: James Fay
Plant Manager: Michael Baron
Estimated Sales: $3 Million
Number Employees: 10-19
Number of Brands: 1
Number of Products: 4
Square Footage: 80000
Brands:
    Champion

20070 CMD Corp
2901 E Pershing St
Appleton, WI 54911-8670
920-730-6888
Fax: 920-730-6880 info@cmd-corp.com
www.cmd-corp.com
High speed plastic film converting equipment for the production of trash can liners and bag rolls. Also vertical form fill and seal packaging equipment and modular pouch making systems.
President: Steve Sakai
steve.sakai@cmd-corp.com
Research & Development: Ron Buchinger
Quality Control: Curt Frievalt
Marketing/Public Relations: Lisa Kain
Sales: Margaret Valinski
Sales: Rich Camp
Operations Manager: Don Wiedenheft
Production Manager: Curt Frievalt
Plant Manager: Don Wiedenheft
Purchasing Manager: Colleen Frederick
Estimated Sales: $20-50 Million
Number Employees: 100-249
Number of Brands: 2
Number of Products: 40
Square Footage: 50000
Parent Co: CMD Corporation
Type of Packaging: Consumer, Food Service, Private Label, Bulk
Brands:
    Cmd Converting Solutions
    Cmd Packaging Systems
    Modular Pouch Machine
    Vffs Packaging System

20071 CMD Corp
2901 E Pershing St
Appleton, WI 54911-8670
920-730-6888
Fax: 920-730-6880 info@cmd-corp.com
www.cmd-corp.com
Vertical form, fill and seal packaging equipment, washdown equipment
President: Steve Sakai
steve.sakai@cmd-corp.com
CFO: Tim Lamerf
Quality Control: Mark Heindel
Regional Sales Manager: David Andrews
Director of Operations: Ron Buchinger
Number Employees: 100-249

20072 CMD Corporation
2901-3005 East Pershing Street
PO Box 1279
Appleton, WI 54912-1279
920-730-6888
Fax: 920-730-6880 info@cmd-corp.com
www.cmd-corp.com
Plastic bottles

President: John Smith
R & D: Larry Mikeosjy
Corporate Market Manager, Research and C: Lisa Karin
VP Marketing and Sales: Timothy B. Lewis
Regional Sales Manager: David Andrews
Contact: Christie Sweeney
christie.sweeney@cmd-corp.com
Director of Operations: Ron Buchinger
Product Line Manager: Scott Fuller
Number Employees: 10

20073 CMF Corp
1524 W 15th St
Long Beach, CA 90813-1207
562-437-2166
Fax: 562-495-1857 800-350-8979
info@jack-frost.com www.jack-frost.com
President: Larry Sackrison
Estimated Sales: $3-5 Million
Number Employees: 5-9

20074 CMS Fine Foods
4791 Dry Creek Rd
Healdsburg, CA 95448
707-473-9561
Fax: 707-473-9765 www.cmsfinefoods.com
sauces, dressings, mustards, marinades and other
condiments; offers co-packing and private label services.
Type of Packaging: Consumer, Food Service, Private Label, Bulk

20075 CMT
P.O.Box 297
Hamilton, MA 01936
978-768-2555
Fax: 978-768-2525 cmtinc@tiac.net
Manufacturer and exporter of temperature and humidity monitors, alarms and controls sustems for climate sensitive goods such as wine and cigars.
President: David C De Sieye
Estimated Sales: $500,000-$1 Million
Number Employees: 1-4
Number of Products: 50
Square Footage: 8000

20076 CNL Beverage Property Group
450 South Orange Avenue
Orlando, FL 32801-3383
407-650-1000
Fax: 407-316-0457 800-522-3863
www.cnl.com
President: Robert Bourne
CFO: Lynn Rose
CEO: James Seneff
R & D: Courtney Powell
Contact: Christian Abreu
christian@cnl.com
Number Employees: 10-19

20077 COMPRESSOR Engrg. Corp.
5440 Alder Dr
Houston, TX 77081-1798
713-664-7333
Fax: 713-664-6444 800-879-2326
sales@ceconet.com www.tryceco.com
President: Richard Hotze
CEO: Bruce R Hotze
bruceh@ceconet.com
CFO: Mark Hotze
Estimated Sales: $20-50 Million
Number Employees: 100-249

20078 COTT Technologies
14923 Proctor Ave
La Puente, CA 91746-3206
626-961-0370
Fax: 626-333-9307 800-373-1968
Sanitary Piston Pumps, Liquid Fillers, Custom Process Piping and machinery
Owner: Gilbert De Cardenas
Marketing: Dennis Gonzalez
Production: Westly Brown
Plant Manager: Westly Brown
Estimated Sales: $10-20 Million
Number Employees: 20-49
Number of Brands: 1
Brands:
    Cott

20079 COVERIS
501 Williams St
Tomah, WI 54660-1454
608-372-2153
Fax: 608-372-5702 www.coveris.com
Manufacturer and exporter of polyethylene film and bags
Quality Control: Don Bergum
President: Stan Bikulege
Sales Manager: Bruce Baker
Plant Manager: Terry Smith
Estimated Sales: $20-50 Million
Number Employees: 250-499
Parent Co: Union Camp Corporation
Type of Packaging: Consumer, Bulk

20080 COW Industries Inc
1875 Progress Ave
Columbus, OH 43207-1781
614-443-6537
Fax: 614-443-9600 800-542-9353
www.cowind.com
Bakers' equipment, flour hoppers, pans, racks, tanks, trays, etc
President: George Combs
gcombs@invacare.com
CFO: John Burns
Executive VP Sales: David Burns
VP Production: Rock Kauser
Estimated Sales: $20-50 Million
Number Employees: 20-49
Square Footage: 100000

20081 COX Technologies
69 McAdenville Rd
Belmont, NC 28012
704-825-8146
Fax: 704-825-4498 800-848-9865
www.coxtec.com
President: James L Cox
james.cox@coxtec.com
CFO: Jack Mason
Vice President: Dave Caskey
Quality Control: Bob Hiatt
Marketing/Sales: Maryy Norris
Operations/Production/Plant Manager: Margaret Hiatt
Purchasing Manager: Pamela Jackson
Estimated Sales: $10 000,000
Number Employees: 100
Parent Co: COX Technologies

20082 CPI Packaging
50 Jiffy Rd
Somerset, NJ 08873
732-431-3500
Fax: 732-568-0440 www.cpipkg.com
Foam and plastic packaging products
COO: Joseph Lomando
COO: Joseph Mormondo
Contact: Anthony Distefano
apiantieri@amrindustries.com
Estimated Sales: $20-50 Million
Number Employees: 10,000

20083 CPM Century Extrusion
2412 W Aero Park Ct
Traverse City, MI 49686-9102
231-947-6400
Fax: 231-947-8400 sales@centuryextrusion.com
www.centuryextrusion.com
Manufacturer & supplier of extruders and extrusion parts.
President: Bob Urtel
urtelb@centuryextrusion.com
General Manager: Charlie Spearing
Number Employees: 50-99
Parent Co: CPM Extrusion Group

20084 CPM Roskamp Champion
2975 Airline Cir
Waterloo, IA 50703-9631
319-232-8444
Fax: 319-236-0481 800-366-2563
www.cpm.net
Manufacturer and exporter of particle sizeing equipment including roller and hammer mills, flakers, crushers, pallet mills, coolers and crumblers for food processing; also, testing/lab facility available

President: Ted Waitman
CEO: Heath Hartwig
CFO: Doug Ostrich
Research & Development: Ron Fuller
Marketing Director: Scott Anderson
Sales Director: Linda Kruckenberg
Manager: J Manning
julie.manning@cpm.net
Operations Manager: Jim Hughes
Plant Manager: Terry Tackenberg
Purchasing Manager: Stuart Downs
Estimated Sales: $20 Million
Number Employees: 50-99
Square Footage: 50000
Parent Co: California Pellet Mill
Brands:
    Champion
    Roskamp

20085 (HQ)CPM Wolverine Proctor LLC
121 Proctor Ln
Lexington, NC 27292-7630
336-248-5181
Fax: 336-248-5118 www.wolverineproctor.com
Manufacturer and exporter of energy efficient equipment including conveyor dryers, roasters, toasters, coolers, ovens and the JETZONE fluidized dryers, puffers and toasters for the processing of fruits, vegetables, nuts, bakery, snackfoods, meat, poultry, pet foods, etc. Also offers batch drying equipment including tray, truck and laboratory dryers. Fully equipped Tech Centers available for demonstration purposes and development of new products and processes.
CEO: Steven Chilenski
CFO: Mark Brown
VP: Paul E Smith
Sales: Terry Midden
Estimated Sales: $15-25 Million
Number Employees: 50-99
Square Footage: 60000
Brands:
    Jetzone
    Proctor

20086 CPM Wolverine Proctor LLC
251 Gibraltar Rd
Horsham, PA 19044-2305
215-443-5200
Fax: 215-443-5206
sales@cpmwolverineproctor.com
www.wolverineproctor.com
Manufacturer and designer of processing equipment including energy efficient continuous dryers, roasters, toasters, coolers, impingement ovens, and jetzone fluid bed dryers for the processing of fruits, vegetables, nuts/seeds, bakerysnack foods, meat, poultry, pet foods, etc. Also batch drying equipment including tray, truck and laboratory dryers; ultra sanitary design conveyor dryer and new pizza infrared fuser/melter.
Lab Manager: Lisa Geck
Director of Sales & Marketing: Kevin Van Allen
Vice President, Sales & Marketing: Paul Smith
Vice President of Operations: Rick Diefes
General Manager: Paul Finnerty
Estimated Sales: $13.1 Million
Number Employees: 20-49
Square Footage: 180000
Parent Co: CPM Extrusion Group
Type of Packaging: Food Service
Other Locations:
    USA Operations Office
    Lexington NC
    European Office
    Glasgow, UK
    South American Office
    Sao Paulo, Brazil

20087 CPT
415 E Fulton St
Edgerton, WI 53534-1923
608-884-2244
Fax: 608-884-2288 info@cptplastics.com
www.cptplastics.com
Manufacturers of foamed polypropylene rollstock and trays for case-ready and other applications requiring extended shelf life; pre-formed trays and barrier shrink lidstock, foamed barrier PP is microwaveable, lightweight andeasy-to-form, specializes in
President: Linda Bracha

Estimated Sales: $10-20 Million
Number Employees: 20-49

20088 CRC Inc
3218 Nebraska Ave
Council Bluffs, IA 51501-7035

712-323-9477

Fax: 712-323-3573 www.bradley-refrigeration.com
Stainless steel variable speed blenders and mixers
Vice President: Jim Crossley
jimc@crcinconline.com
Secretary: Joan Collins
VP: Jim Crossley
Estimated Sales: $2.5-5,000,000
Number Employees: 5-9

20089 CRF Technologies
PO Box 32414
Charlotte, NC 28232-2414

704-554-2253

Fax: 704-554-3900 800-875-0275
Cut resistant gloves, apparel and uniforms
Estimated Sales: $1-5 000,000

20090 CRS Marking Systems
3315 NW 26th Ave #1
Portland, OR 97210-1856

503-228-7624

Fax: 503-228-2464 800-547-7158
info@crsdatasolutions.com
Manufacturer and wholesaler/distributor of marking,
coding, printing, labeling and bar code equipment
CEO: Julia Farrenkopf
Customer Service: Dwaine Brandson
COO: David Snmodgrass
Estimated Sales: $1-3 Million
Number Employees: 10 to 19

20091 CRT Custom Products Inc
7532 Hickory Hills Ct
Whites Creek, TN 37189-9289

615-876-5490

Fax: 615-876-0096 www.crtcustomproducts.com
Printing, packing, supplies
Sales: Ken Gereen
Estimated Sales: Less Than $500,000
Number Employees: 1-4

20092 CSAT America
7007 Johnson Cir
Longmont, CO 80503-7667

303-652-0370

Fax: 303-652-8736 888-904-2728
www.csat.de

20093 CSC Scientific Co Inc
2799 Merrilee Dr # B
Fairfax, VA 22031-4419

703-564-4306

Fax: 703-280-5142 800-621-4778
www.cscscientific.com
Manufacturer and exporter of sieves and laboratory
analyzers to measure water, moisture, filtration
equipment, solids, surface tension, particle size and
consistency; also, calibration services available
President: Al Gatenby
agatenby@cscscientific.com
Vice President: Tim Comwell
Marketing Director: Wendy Liu
Operations Manager: Theresa Andreoni
Estimated Sales: $2.5-5 Million
Number Employees: 20-49
Brands:
  Aquapal
  Cfc Dunouy Tensiometer
  Cfc Us Standard
  Digital Moisture Balance

20094 (HQ)CSC Worldwide
4401 Equity Dr
Columbus, OH 43228-3856

614-850-1460

Fax: 614-850-0741 800-848-3573
Manufacturer, designer and exporter of refrigerated
and heated display cases; also store fixtures
CEO: Carl J Aschinger Jr
Marketing: Jennier Bobbitt
Contact: Carl Aschinger
c.aschingerjr@cscworldwide.com
Estimated Sales: $20-50 Million
Number Employees: 100-249

20095 CSI Tools
2700 N Partnership Blvd
Springfield, MO 65803-8208

417-831-1411

Fax: 417-831-5314 800-258-0133
Leading provider of tube and pipe facing and cutting
equipment for the sanitary process piping industry;
also supply users of this equipment with top quality
consumables for these tools such as blades, bits
President: Mark Cook
CFO: Joe Reynolds
Vice President of Systems: Beth Ipock
Manager: Mark Wilson
Marketing Director: Ryan Tiller
Sales Manager: Liz Braden
Contact: Charlie Jockers
charlie@csitools.com
Vice President of Operations: Bryan Billmyer
Estimated Sales: $10-20 Million
Number Employees: 50-99
Type of Packaging: Food Service

20096 CSM Bakery Solutions
c/o Brill Inc
1912 Monteal Rd
Tucker, GA 30084

770-724-8200

info@brillinc.com
www.csmbakerysolutions.com
Develops, produces and sells a wide selection of
bakery ingredients and products to professional bak-
eries, top consumer food companies, grocers and re-
tailers. Products include brownies, cakes, cookies
croissants, fillings, glazesicing & toppings, mixes,
muffins, puff pastry, sweet rolls, filled pastries, and
turnovers.
President & CEO: Marianne Kirkegaard
SVP & Chief Administrative Officer: Michael
Delaney
SVP & Chief Financial Officer: Maarten Bok
SVP, Sales & Chief Commercial Officer: John
Lindsay
SVP & Chief Supply Chain Officer: Steve Jones
VP, Marketing: Val Burnett
SVP, Sales: Troy Hendricks
VP, Customer Solutions: James Mayer
VP, Manufacturing: John Doyle
Year Founded: 1919
Estimated Sales: $2.1 Billion
Number Employees: 7,000+
Other Locations:
  CSM Bakery Products
  Atlanta GA
  Caravan Ingredients
  Kansas City MO
  BakeMark USA
  Pico Rivera CA
Brands:
  Brill®
  Henry & Henry®
  Multifoods®
  Transmart™
  Sensibly Indulgent™ Cupcakes
  Thaw-N-Sell
  Scoop-N-Bake

20097 CSM Worldwide
1100 Globe Ave
Mountainside, NJ 07092

908-233-2882

Fax: 908-233-1064 www.csmworldwide.com
Tea and coffee industry pollution control equipment
President: Mike Torstup
Contact: Michael Sohnen
msohnen@csmworldwide.com
Estimated Sales: $2.5-5 000,000
Number Employees: 20-49

20098 CSPI
43 Manning Rd
Billerica, MA 01821-3925

978-663-7598

Fax: 978-663-0150 info@cspi.com
www.cspi.com
Scanning equipment
CEO: Alexander R Lupinetti
Marketing Coordinator: Bernard Pelon
Contact: Jim Duffy
jdufffy@cspi.com
Estimated Sales: $30-35 Million
Number Employees: 100-249

20099 CSS Inc
122 Rogers St
Hartsville, TN 37074

615-374-0601

Fax: 615-374-0610 choicecutsurplus@comcast.net
www.choicecut.net
Meat packing and food handling equipment
President: Randy Beach
Chief Executive Officer: Robert Paxton

20100 CSS International Corp
2061 E Glenwood Ave
PO Box 19560
Philadelphia, PA 19124-5674

215-533-6110

Fax: 215-288-8030 800-278-8107
sales@cssintl.com
Manufacturer and exporter of container handling
equipment and packaging machinery
Vice President: Eugene Fijalkowski
gene@cssintl.com
Vice President: Albert Andrew
VP Productions: Gene Fijalkowski
Number Employees: 20-49
Parent Co: CSS International Corporation
Type of Packaging: Consumer, Food Service, Pri-
vate Label

20101 CSV Sales
44450 Pinetree Dr
Plymouth, MI 48170-3869

734-453-4544

Fax: 248-669-3000 800-886-6866
info@nationalfoodgroup.com www.csvsales.com
Supplier of closeouts, surplus, salvage and liquidator
items including baked goods, poultry, meats and
off-grade, frozen and value added foods
President: Bud Zecman
Owner: Sean Zecman
Finance Executive: Scott Kaman
Sales Executive: Justin Sarrach
Contact: Tracey Daraban
tracey.daraban@nationalfoodgroup.com
Operations Manager: Justin Sarrach
Purchasing/Sales Support: Roger Cary
Estimated Sales: $5-10 Million
Number Employees: 5-9
Brands:
  Awrey's
  Bakery Chef
  House of Raeford
  Pierre
  Pilgrim's Pride
  Tyson

20102 CTC
11 York Ave
West Caldwell, NJ 07006-6486

973-228-2300

Fax: 973-228-7076 info@ctcint.com
www.ctcint.com
Supplier of automatic splicers for packaging lines.
President: Erwin L Herbert

20103 CTI Celtek Electronics
3609 Robertson St
Metairie, LA 70001-5844

504-832-0049

Fax: 504-832-8117
Level controls, inventory management
Owner: Jack Graves
Estimated Sales: $1-5 Million
Number Employees: 1-4

20104 CTK Plastics
1815 Stadacona Street W.
Moose Jaw, SK S6H 7K8
Canada

306-693-7075

Fax: 306-693-9944 800-667-8847
Plastic bottles and sheeting; importer of resin and
bottling equipment; exporter of plastic bottles and
rigid sheeting
President: Dennis Wastle
Sales/Marketing: Dennis Wastle
General Manager: Brian McGuigan
Supervisor: Bernice Larose
Number Employees: 10
Square Footage: 120000
Parent Co: CTK Developments

20105 CTS Bulk Sales
P.O.Box 8318
Northfield, IL 60093
847-267-0837
Fax: 847-267-0838
President: Charles L Brooks
R&D: Ginger Brooks
Estimated Sales: Below $5 000,000
Number Employees: 5-9

20106 CUTCO Corp
1116 E State St
Olean, NY 14760-3814
716-372-3111
Fax: 716-790-7160 www.cutco.com
Manufacturer and exporter of knives, forks and
spoons
President: Brent Driscoll
CEO: James E Stitt
jstitt@alcas.com
President: James Stitt
Executive Vice President of Eastern Regi: Amar
Dave
President, Chief Operating Officer: John Whelpley
Estimated Sales: H
Number Employees: 1000-4999
Parent Co: Alcas-Cutco Corporation
Type of Packaging: Consumer

20107 CVC Technologies Inc
10861 Business Dr
Fontana, CA 92337-8235
909-355-0311
Fax: 909-355-0411 sales@cvcusa.com
www.cvcusa.com
Labelers with automatic job set up, memory for 50
jobs and self-diagnostics. Also counters, cappers, in-
dexing cappers, cartoners and blister packers
Manager: Yulie Luo
Vice President: Andy Span
Quality Control: Oscar Esparza
Marketing Director: Brit Sten
Sales Director: Andy Span
Manager: Joseph Levy
jlevy@osgoodcapital.com
Plant Manager: Oscar Esparza
Estimated Sales: $7-12 000,000
Number Employees: 20-49
Number of Brands: 1
Number of Products: 9
Brands:
302 Hawk Labelers
Cvc 300

20108 CVP Systems Inc
2518 Wisconsin Ave
Downers Grove, IL 60515-4230
630-852-1190
Fax: 630-852-1386 800-422-4720
sales@cvpsystems.com www.cvpsystems.com
Manufacturer and exporter of cost effective, bags
and packaging machinery including microbial reduc-
tion units, wrap around label systems and vacuum
and modified atmosphere systems
President: Wesley Bork
VP: L Mykleby
Estimated Sales: $10-20 Million
Number Employees: 20-49
Type of Packaging: Consumer, Food Service, Pri-
vate Label, Bulk
Brands:
Cvp Fresh Vac
Dynarap

20109 CXR Co
2599 N Fox Farm Rd
PO Box 1114
Warsaw, IN 46580-6536
574-269-6020
Fax: 574-269-7140 800-817-5763
info@cxrcompany.com www.cxrcompany.com
Industrial x-ray machines; also, x-ray inspection ser-
vices available
President: Cassandra Stewart
cstewart@cxrcompany.com
Vice President: Paula Zeigler
Research & Development: Tim Murphy
Sales Manager: Scott Stewart
Plant Manager: John Sherman
Estimated Sales: $5-10 Million
Number Employees: 10-19
Square Footage: 32000
Brands:
Accuvue

20110 CXR Co
2599 N Fox Farm Rd
Warsaw, IN 46580-6536
574-269-6020
Fax: 574-269-7140 800-817-5763
info@cxrcompany.com
Safety X-ray inspection for contaminants
President: Cassandra Stewart
cstewart@cxrcompany.com
CEO: Barb Colbes
Vice President: Paula Zeigler
Research/Development: Tim Murphy
Sales: Scott Stewart
Plant Manager: John Sherman
Estimated Sales: $5-10 Million
Number Employees: 10-19

20111 CYBER BEARINGS, INC
4821 S. Eastern Ave
Bell, CA 90201
562-272-8032
Fax: 562-272-8588 888-288-9889
info@cyberbearings.com www.cyberbearings.com
Solid stainless steel bearing inserts with
theremoplastic housing, bearing units (pillow block,
flange), bearing inserts with nickel plated cast iron
housing, mast guide bearings, agricultural bearings
and ISO-9002 certified
President: Kevin Lee
Contact: Robyn Chung
robyn@cyberbearings.com

20112 Ca Polytechnic State/Alumni
1 Grand Ave
San Luis Obispo, CA 93407-0707
805-756-2586
Fax: 805-756-5052 lgay@calpoly.edu
www.calpolylink.com
President: Warren Baker
Manager: Dennis Elliot
delliot@calpoly.edu
Number Employees: 5-9

20113 Cab Technology Inc
87 Progress Ave # 1
Tyngsboro, MA 01879-1441
978-649-0293
Fax: 978-649-0294 info.us@cab.de
www.cab.de
President: Joachim Komus
Operations Executive: Mark Cavanaugh
Estimated Sales: Below $5 Million
Number Employees: 10-19

20114 Cabot Corp
2 Seaport Ln # 1300
Boston, MA 02210-2019
617-345-0100
Fax: 617-342-6312 www.cabot-corp.com
Manufacturer and exporter of treated and untreated
fumed silica
President/CEO: Patrick Prevost
CEO: Sean D Keohane
sean_keohane@cabot-corp.com
Executive Vice President/CFO: Eduardo Cordeiro
Vice President: James Belmont
Vice President, Research & Development: Yakov
Kutsovsky
National Sales Manager: James Litrun
Vice President, Operations: James Turner
Estimated Sales: Over $1 Billion
Number Employees: 1000-4999
Parent Co: Cabot Corporation
Brands:
Cab-O-Sil

20115 Cabot/Norit Americas Inc
3200 University Ave
Marshall, TX 75670-4842
903-923-1000
Fax: 903-938-9701 800-641-9245
mark@norit-americas.com www.norit.com
Activated carbon
Vice President: Nikki Gurule
ngurule@norit-americas.com
Vice President: Nikki Gurule
ngurule@norit-americas.com
Number Employees: 250-499

20116 Cabot/Norit Americas Inc
3200 University Ave
Marshall, TX 75670-4842
903-923-1000
Fax: 903-938-9701 800-641-9245
www.norit.com
Manufaturer activated carbon, a filter media
Vice President: Doug Dallmer
ddailmer@norit-americas.com
Vice President: Doug Dallmer
ddailmer@norit-americas.com
Number Employees: 250-499
Parent Co: Cabot Corp

20117 Cacao Prieto
218 Conover Street
Brooklyn, NY 11231
347-225-0130
www.cacaoprieto.com
Fine chocolates
President/CEO: Dan Preston
VP & Art Director: Michele Clark
Sales Director: Mike Dirksen
Contact: Michele Clark
michele@cacaoholdings.com
Chief Operating Officer: Dennis Walsh
Number Employees: 20

20118 Cache Box
2009 14th Street N
Suite 415
Arlington, VA 22201-2514
703-276-2500
Fax: 703-276-2504 800-603-4834
Manufacturer and exporter of touchscreen turn-key
point of sale systems
CEO: Lorenzo Salhi
VP Engineering: Murali Nagaraj
CTO: Dilip Ranade
VP, Technical Marketing: Shaloo Shalini
Contact: John Groff
john@cachebox.com
COO: John Groff
Estimated Sales: $5-10 Million
Number Employees: 20-49
Brands:
Chromium

20119 Cache Creek Foods LLC
411 N Pioneer Ave
Woodland, CA 95776-6122
530-662-1764
Fax: 530-662-2529 www.cachecreekfoods.com
Custom flavoring and wholesale manufacturing of
almond, cashew, pistachio, nut products and nut
butters
President: Nicholas Celek
ncelek@thelabb.com
CEO: Matthew Morehart
Sales and Marketing Executive: Mike Leonard
Office Manager: Connie Stephens
Production: Ana Contreras
Estimated Sales: $10 Million
Number Employees: 20-49
Number of Products: 75
Square Footage: 60000
Type of Packaging: Consumer, Food Service, Pri-
vate Label, Bulk
Brands:
Private Label

**20120 Cactus Mat
ManufacturingCompany**
4131 Arden Dr
El Monte, CA 91731-1999
626-579-6287
Fax: 626-401-2003 cactuskid@cactusmat.com
www.cactusmat.com
Floor mats including rigid wood, interlocking rub-
ber, entrance and rubber for food preparation areas
President: C W Hartranft Jr
CEO: Debra De Ring
CFO: Les De Ring
Contact: Debbie Dering
debbie@cactusmat.com
Estimated Sales: $5-10 Million
Number Employees: 20-49
Square Footage: 120000
Brands:
Cactus Kid
Contempo
Cushion Walk
Kaktus
Monterey

Softread
Vip
Vip Lite

20121 Caddy Corporation of America
509 Sharptown Road
Bridgeport, NJ 08014-0345
856-467-4222
Fax: 856-467-5511 mbodine@caddycorp.com
www.caddycorp.com
Manufacturer and exporter of food service equipment including conveyors, transport/delivery carts, kitchen ventilation hoods and utility distribution systems
President: Harry Schmidt
CEO: Craig Cohen
CFO: John McNamee
VP of Corporate Services: Al Scuderi
Vice President, Sales: Phil Bailis
National Sales Manager: Donald Morrison
Engineering Manager: Brad Wallace
Purchasing: Robin Corma
Estimated Sales: $5-10 Million
Number Employees: 50-99
Square Footage: 288000
Brands:
21c
Caddy
Caddy Cold
Caddy Connections
Caddy-Flex
Caddy-Veyor
Caddymagic
Circle-Air
Ds Special
Dura-San Belt
Fogg-It
Mega-Temp
Pacemaker
Servi-Shelf
Simplex
Speed-Lift
Temp-Lock
Temp-Lock Ii
Thermo-Lock
Xl-1

20122 Cadie Products Corp
151 E 11th St
Paterson, NJ 07524-1228
973-278-8300
Fax: 973-278-0303 www.cadieproducts.com
Manufacturer and exporter of cloths including dusting, polishing, cheese, pastry and sponge; also, cooking parchment, microwave cooking bags, seat covers, salad bags, ice cube bags, hamburger (patty) bags, and non-stick oven liner
President: Edwin Meyers
CFO: Bob Appelbaum
Vice President: Kenny Meyers
Estimated Sales: $20-50 Million
Number Employees: 20-49
Square Footage: 35000
Type of Packaging: Consumer, Private Label, Bulk
Brands:
Cadie
Chef's Favorite
Krazy Kloth
Super Power

20123 Cadillac Pallets
7000 15 Mile Rd
Sterling Heights, MI 48312-4520
586-264-2525
Fax: 248-879-7420

20124 Cadillac Plastics
2855 Coolidge Highway
Suite 300
Troy, MI 48084-3217
248-205-3100
Fax: 248-205-3173 800-488-1200
www.cadillacplastic.com
Engraved plastics: rods, sheets, tubes and film; adhesive and graphic arts products
Estimated Sales: D
Number Employees: 19

20125 Cadillac Products Inc
5800 Crooks Rd # 200
Troy, MI 48098-2830
248-879-5000
Fax: 248-879-7420 www.cadprod.com

Tea and coffee industry flexible packaging, bags and packaging film supplies materials
Chairman of the Board: Robert Williams Sr
CEO: Robert J Williams Jr
Estimated Sales: $50-100 Million
Number Employees: 250-499

20126 Cady Bag Co
41 Project Cir
Pearson, GA 31642-7428
912-422-3298
Fax: 912-422-3155 www.cadybag.com
Polypropylene, woven bags
President: William Cady
Vice President: John Moore
Estimated Sales: $20-50 Million
Number Employees: 100-249

20127 Cafe Del Mundo
229 E 51st Ave
Anchorage, AK 99503
907-562-2326
Fax: 907-562-3278 800-770-2326
www.cafedelmundo.com
Coffee, espresso equipment
Owner: Perry Merkel
Manager: Monique Johnston
Purchasing: Perry Merkel
Estimated Sales: $800,000
Number Employees: 12
Type of Packaging: Private Label, Bulk
Brands:
Cafe Del Mundo

20128 Cain Awning Co Inc
1301 3rd Ave S
Birmingham, AL 35233-1406
205-323-8379
Fax: 877-640-6739 info@cainawning.com
www.cainawning.com
Commercial awnings
Owner: Hank Lawson
info@cainawning.com
Estimated Sales: $1-2,500,000
Number Employees: 10-19

20129 Cal Ben Soap Co
9828 Pearmain St
Oakland, CA 94603-2312
510-638-7092
Fax: 510-638-7827 800-340-7091
calbenco@yahoo.com www.calbenpuresoap.com
Soaps including laundry, dish, etc.
President: Martin Schachter
calbenco@yahoo.com
Estimated Sales: Below $5 Million
Number Employees: 10-19

20130 Cal Controls
1675 Delany Road
Gurnee, IL 60031
Fax: 847-782-5223 800-866-6659
NA@West-CS.com www.cal-controls.com
Manufacturer and exporter of temperature and machine controllers for packaging and processing equipment
Sales Manager: Dave Chylstek
Estimated Sales: $15 Million
Number Employees: 21
Brands:
Cal
Calcomms
Calgrafix
Calogix

20131 Cal Western Pest Control
5417 Peck Road
Arcadia, CA 91006-5847
661-808-7378
Fax: 323-721-0377 800-326-2847
Consultant for pest and sanitation control programs for food processors and distributors
Owner: John Lemm
Manager: Dave Conner
General Manager: Marc Canipe
Estimated Sales: $2.5-5 Million
Number Employees: 50-99

20132 Cal-Coast Manufacturing
P.O.Box 1864
Turlock, CA 95381-1864
209-668-9378
Fax: 209-668-9382

Dairy equipment, storage tanks and auger systems. Also dairy construction and public scale
President: L Baptista
Controller: D Baptista
Estimated Sales: $1-3,000,000
Number Employees: 5-9

20133 Cal-Mil Plastic Products Inc
4079 Calle Platino
Oceanside, CA 92056-5805
760-630-5100
Fax: 760-630-5010 800-321-9069
www.calmil.com
Manufacturer, exporter and importer of acrylic counter top cabinets, mirrored displays, crocks, platters, risers, bowls, pedestals, tables, domes, etc. for the catering and banquet industries.
President: Barney Callahan
bcallahan@calmil.com
Marketing Director: Mike Juneman
Sales Director: Mike Juneman
Estimated Sales: $10-20 Million
Number Employees: 20-49
Number of Products: 1460
Type of Packaging: Bulk

20134 Calcium Chloride Sales Inc
713 W Main St
Grove City, PA 16127-1198
724-458-5778
Fax: 724-458-4250 800-228-3879
cacl2@zoominternet.net
www.calciumchloridesales.com
Food grade calcium chloride including liquid and flake
President: Jim Mc Lean
cacl2@zoominternet.net
Secretary: Larry Bowie
Estimated Sales: $2.5 Million
Number Employees: 5-9
Number of Products: 1
Square Footage: 16000
Type of Packaging: Private Label, Bulk

20135 Caldwell Group
5055 26th Avenue
Rockford, IL 61109
815-229-5667
Fax: 815-229-5686 800-628-4263
contact@caldwellinc.com www.caldwellinc.com
Manufacturer and exporter of crane lifting attachments
Owner: Howard Will
VP: William McLeod
Estimated Sales: $5-10 Million
Number Employees: 50-99

20136 Calgene
1920 5th St
Davis, CA 95616
530-753-6313
Fax: 530-753-1510 800-992-4363
rhonda.ryan@monsanto.com www.calgene.com
Research in genetics, and biotechnology of food
Contact: Julie Alvarez
julie.alvarez@monsanto.com
Estimated Sales: $10-15 000,000
Number Employees: 100-249

20137 Calgon Carbon
300 GSK Drive
Moon Township, PA 15108
412-787-6700
www.calgoncarbon.com
Activated carbon products
President & CEO: Randy Dearth
Estimated Sales: $555 Million
Number Employees: 1,100
Parent Co: Kuraray Co., Ltd.

20138 Calhoun Bend Mill
PO BOX 520
Libuse, LA 71348
318-640-0060
Fax: 318-339-9099 800-519-6455
sales@calhounbendmill.com
www.calhounbendmill.com
Fruit cobbler mixes, cornmeal and seafood coating.
President/CEO: Patrick Calhoun
Treasurer: Monica Calhoun
Vice President: Nathan Martin
Sales Manager: Emma Cash
Corporate Secretary: Martie Hoover

Estimated Sales: $400,000
Number Employees: 5
Number of Brands: 2
Number of Products: 25
Square Footage: 34000
Type of Packaging: Consumer, Food Service, Private Label, Bulk
Brands:
 Calhoun Bend Mill
 Orchard Mills

20139 Calia Technical
420 Jefferson Boulevard
Staten Island, NY 10312-2334
718-967-9757
Fax: 718-967-0275
Inspection, control systems, bar code verification systems, bottle and cap inspection and machine vision solutions; web bar code verification systems to verify multiple bar codes on thermoformer lidstock
President: Anthony Calia
VP: Robert Santagata
Engineer: Elias Hawileh
Estimated Sales: $.5-1 million
Number Employees: 1-4
Number of Products: 2

20140 Calico Cottage
210 New Hwy
Amityville, NY 11701-1116
631-841-2100
Fax: 631-841-2401 800-645-5345
www.calicocottage.com
Fudge mixes, flavors and colorings.
President & CEO: Mark Wurzel
m.wurzel@calicocottage.com
Chief Financial Officer: Michael Lobaccaro
Vice President: Larry Wurzel
Executive VP, Sales & Marketing: David Sank
Director, Human Resources & Admin: Barbara Stone-Carroll
Sr. VP, Operations & Technology: Thomas Montoya
Estimated Sales: $5 Million
Number Employees: 50-99
Square Footage: 45000
Type of Packaging: Consumer
Brands:
 Calico Cottage Fudge Mix
 Mister Fudge

20141 Calif Canning Peach Assn
2300 River Plaza Dr # 110
Sacramento, CA 95833-4241
916-925-9131
Fax: 916-925-9030 ccpa@calpeach.com
www.calpeach.com
Cooperative for cling peach processors providing marketing, price negotiation, etc
President: Rich Hudgins
rhudgins@calpeach.com
VP/COO: Rich Hudgins
Number Employees: 1-4

20142 California Blending Co
2603 Seaman Ave
El Monte, CA 91733-1929
626-448-1918
Fax: 626-448-1998
Pizza spices, dough mixes, dressing mixes, steak salts, and garlic blends. Also provided; custom blending
President: Bill Morehart
calblending@aol.com
Vice President: Roger Morehart
Estimated Sales: Less Than $500,000
Number Employees: 1-4
Square Footage: 14600
Type of Packaging: Private Label, Bulk

20143 California Caster & Handtruck
1400 17th St
San Francisco, CA 94107-2412
415-552-6750
Fax: 415-552-0463 800-950-8750
customerservice@californiacaster.com
Stainless steel hand trucks and carts, dollies, casters, leveling pads and oven and bun pan racks; wholesaler/distributor of casters
Owner: Alan Mc Clure
alanm@californiacaster.com
VP: Terry Cavannaugh
Estimated Sales: $5-10 Million
Number Employees: 10-19
Square Footage: 33000

Brands:
 Dareon
 Darnell
 Dutro
 Faultless
 Magline
 Meese
 Morton Kaciff
 Rack & Roll
 Vlier
 Werner

20144 California Hi-Lites
12500 Slauson Ave Ste C3
Santa Fe Springs, CA 90670-2631
562-696-1777
Fax: 562-696-8917 www.hilites.com
Co-packing, labeling, over wrapping, display construction, handwork, light assembly, bundling, gluing, collating, QC projects, order fulfillment, FDA approved cleanroom, alcoholic beverage license, organic food license and more
Owner: Hans Blom
Owner: Robert Landinl
Owner: Jim Yoder
Estimated Sales: $3-5 Million
Number Employees: 23
Square Footage: 80000
Type of Packaging: Consumer, Food Service, Private Label, Bulk
Brands:
 Feast of Eden
 Hi-Lites
 Nature's Candy
 Val Linda

20145 California League of Food Processors
1755 Creekside Oaks Drive
Suite 250
Sacramento, CA 95833
916-640-8150
Fax: 916-640-8156 www.clfp.com
Represents the business interest for California's food industry.
President/CEO: Rob Neenan
COO/Treasurer: Janet Planck
Marketing Manager: Amy Alcorn
Meetings & Events Manager: Alissa Dillon
Estimated Sales: $1-5 Million
Number Employees: 7

20146 California Milk Advisory
400 Oyster Point Blvd # 211
Suite 211
S San Francisco, CA 94080-1998
650-871-6455
Fax: 650-583-7328 jgiambroni@cmab.net
www.realcaliforniamilk.com
Other cold non-carbonated beverages, butter, cheese, other dairy and eggs, yogurt, ice cream/sorbet, foodservice, private label.
Manager: Jim Jones
CEO: Adri Boudewyn
Marketing: Jennifer Giambroni
Estimated Sales: $1-2.5 Million
Number Employees: 5-9

20147 California Saw & Knife Works
721 Brannan St
San Francisco, CA 94103-4927
415-861-0644
Fax: 415-861-0406 888-729-6533
calsaw@calsaw.com www.calsaw.com
Manufacturer and exporter of machine knives and circular saws for food processing equipment
President: Warren Bird
wbird@calsaw.com
CFO: Mike Weber
Vice President: Benson Joseph
VP Production: S Bird
Estimated Sales: $5-10 Million
Number Employees: 10-19
Square Footage: 36000
Brands:
 Calsaw

20148 California Toytime Balloons
554 West Seventh Street
PO Box 1876
San Pedro, CA 90733
310-548-1234
Fax: 310-548-1237

Printed advertising specialties including buttons, balloons, golf tees, bumper stickers and emery boards
Chairman: Bob Bershad
Sales: Richard Petrosino
Estimated Sales: $5-10 Million
Number Employees: 10-19
Parent Co: Bershad Advertising Products Company

20149 California Vibratory Feeders
1725 N Orangethorpe Park
Anaheim, CA 92801-1139
714-526-3359
Fax: 714-526-3515 800-354-0972
Custom design and build automation equipment
President: Donn Robinson
Marketing: Sandy Chester
Sales: Peter Speers
Operations: Kelly Reece
Estimated Sales: $5-10 Million
Number Employees: 20-49

20150 Caljan America
3600 E 45th Ave
Denver, CO 80216-6510
303-321-3600
Fax: 303-321-6767 www.caljan.com
Telescopic conveyors for trailer loading and unloading
President: Lonnie Watkins
Contact: Henrick Olsen
olsen@caljan.com
Estimated Sales: $5-10 Million
Number Employees: 20-49

20151 Callanan Company Alloy Company
1844 Brummel Avenue
Elk Grove Village, IL 60007-2121
847-364-4242
Fax: 847-364-4373 800-732-5123
alloyd@alloyd.com www.alloyd.com
Radio frequency heat sealing and packaging equipment
Estimated Sales: $5-10 Million
Number Employees: 40

20152 Calmar
501 South 5th Street
Richmond, VA 23219-0501
804-444-1000
Manufacturer and exporter of plastic pump dispensers
President: James Buzzard
Chairman/Chief Executive Officer: John Luke
Chief Financial Officer: Mark Rajkowski
Senior Vice President: Linda Schreiner
General Counsel/Secretary: Wendell Willkie
Vice President, Strategy & Marketing: Todd Fister
Communications: Donna Owens Cox
Supply Chain: Nik Hiremath
Estimated Sales: $50-100 Million
Number Employees: 200
Type of Packaging: Bulk

20153 Caloritech
1420 West Main Street
P.O. Box 146
Greensburg, IN 47240
812-663-4141
Fax: 812-663-4202 800-473-2403
info@ccithermal.com www.caloritech.com
Manufacturer and exporter of components for electrical cooking equipment, air heating immersion and clamp-on radiant equipment
President: Harold Roozen
VP Sales/Marketing: Bob Pender
Number Employees: 200
Square Footage: 440000
Parent Co: CCI Thermal Technologies
Brands:
 X-Max

20154 (HQ)Calzone Case Co
225 Black Rock Ave
Bridgeport, CT 06605-1204
203-367-5766
Fax: 203-336-4406 800-243-5152
www.calzonecase.com
Custom transporting cases including shipping and storage containers

President: Joe Calzone
joe.calzone-@calzonecase.com
CFO: Stephen Bajda
Executive VP: Vin Calzone
Marketing: Kim Bullard
Estimated Sales: $5-10,000,000
Number Employees: 50-99
Other Locations:
   Calzone Case Co.
   City of Industry CA

20155 Cam Spray
520 Brooks Rd
Iowa Falls, IA 50126-8005

                  641-648-5011
     Fax: 641-648-5013 800-648-5011
sales@camspray.com www.camspray.com
Manufacturer and exporter of high pressure washers;
importer of pumps
Manager: Jim Gillestie
CFO: Jim Gillispie
Estimated Sales: $5-10 Million
Number Employees: 20-49
Square Footage: 150000
Parent Co: Campbell Supplies
Brands:
   Cam Spray

20156 Cam Tron Systems
444 W Interstate Rd
Addison, IL 60101-4518

                  630-543-2884
             Fax: 630-543-8153
Pressure sensitive labeling equipment
President: Micheal Ahern
Contact: Mike Ahern
ahern_mike@hotmail.com
General Manager: Frank Ross
Estimated Sales: Below $5 Million
Number Employees: 20-49
Parent Co: Cameron Group
Brands:
   Cam Tron

20157 Cambelt International Corporation
2820 W 1100 S
Salt Lake City, UT 84104-4594

                  801-972-5511
     Fax: 801-972-5522 www.cambelt.com
Conveyor belt and automatic reclaiming systems
President: Colin Campbell
VP Marketing: Rex Wood
Estimated Sales: $20-50 Million
Number Employees: 50-99

20158 (HQ)Cambridge Intl. Inc.
105 Goodwill Rd
PO Box 399
Cambridge, MD 21613-2980

                  410-228-3000
     Fax: 410-221-1100 800-638-9560
info@cambridge-intl.com
www.cambridge-intl.com
Manufacturer and Exporter of conveyor belting, fil-
ters, vibration screens and filter leaves
Manager: Jody Padelko
CEO: Tracy Tyler
ttyler@cambridge-intl.com
International Sales Manager: Bart Shellabarger
Belt Sales Manager: Larry Windsor
Director of Sales: Larry Windsor
Customer Service Manager: Breanne Hemphill
Estimated Sales: $300,000-500,000
Number Employees: 250-499
Brands:
   Cam-Grid
   Cambri-Link
   Continu-Weld

20159 (HQ)Cambridge Viscosity, Inc.
101 Station Lndg
Medford, MA 02155-5134

                  781-393-6500
     Fax: 781-393-6515 800-554-4639
info@cambridgeviscosity.com
www.cambridgeapplied.com
Manufacturer and exporter of viscometers
President: Robert Kasameyer
Marketing Manager: Art MacNeill
Contact: Victoria Benea
beneavictoria@paclp.com
Director Engineering: Dan Airey

Estimated Sales: $1-2.5 Million
Number Employees: 20-49
Brands:
   Cambridge
   Visco Lab 400
   Visco Pro 1000
   Visco Pro 2000

20160 Cambro Manufacturing Co
5801 Skylab Rd
Huntington Beach, CA 92647-2056

                  714-848-1555
                800-833-3003
webmaster@cambro.com www.cambro.com
Food service equipment and supplies including bus
boxes, insulated food carriers, carts and beverage
containers, plastic insert pans, fiberglass trays and
polyethylene boxes.
President: Argyle Campbell
acampbell@cambro.com
Chief Financial Officer: David Capestro
Year Founded: 1951
Estimated Sales: $74 Million
Number Employees: 250-499
Type of Packaging: Food Service
Other Locations:
   Warehouse
   Brampton, Canada
   Customer Service Center
   Stuttgart, Germany
   Manufacturing Facility
   Mebane NC
Brands:
   Cambro

20161 Camco Chemicals
8150 Holton Dr
Florence, KY 41042-3010

                  859-727-3200
     Fax: 859-727-1508 800-554-1001
www.camco-chem.com
Contract packager of janitorial supplies, laundry de-
tergents, lubricants, soaps and cleaners
President: Thomas Cropper
CEO: Richard Rolfes
CFO: Richard Rolfes
CEO: Richard Rolfes
Estimated Sales: $20-50 Million
Number Employees: 100-249

20162 Camcorp Inc
8224 Nieman Rd
Overland Park, KS 66214-1507

                  913-831-0740
     Fax: 913-831-9271 info@camcorpinc.com
www.camcorpinc.com
Owner: Frank Hanwork
VP Sales/Marketing: Ted Remmers
Contact: Leydy Galindez
lgalindez@cam.com.co
Estimated Sales: $5-10 Million
Number Employees: 5-9

20163 Camel Canvas Shop
8910 Valgro Rd
Knoxville, TN 37920-9137

                  865-573-2804
     Fax: 865-573-9677 800-524-2704
www.camelcanvas.com
Commercial awnings, and custom canvas products
Owner: Christian Cain
Sales: Brad Young
ccain@camelcanvas.com
Plant Manager: Brenda Young
Purchasing: Rayma Stasen
Estimated Sales: $5-10 Million
Number Employees: 5-9
Square Footage: 6400

20164 Cameo Metal Products Inc
127 12th St
Brooklyn, NY 11215-3891

                  718-788-1106
   Fax: 718-788-3761 sales@cameometal.com
www.cameometal.com
Cameo Metal Products Manufactures metal closures
for the food and beverage industry.
President: Vito Di Maio
cameosales@cameometals.com
Finance Manager: Adolsopoll Cruz
Director of Sales/Plant Manager: Robert Geddis
Director of Operations: Anthony Di Maio
Estimated Sales: $5.8 Million
Number Employees: 20-49
Square Footage: 100000

20165 Cameron Intl. Corp.
Park Towers South
Houston, TX

                  281-285-4376
www.slb.com/companies/cameron
Manufacturer and exporter of oil-free centrifugal
compressors.
CEO, Schlumberger: Olivier Le Peuch
VP, Finance: Jeff Altamari
Year Founded: 1920
Estimated Sales: $9.8 Billion
Number Employees: 23,412
Parent Co: Schlumberger Limited
Brands:
   Joy

20166 Camerons Brewing Co.
1165 invicta Drive
Oakville, ON L6H 4M1
Canada

                  905-849-8282
   Fax: 905-849-5578 info@cameronsbrewing.com
www.cameronsbrewing.com
Manufacturer and exporter of micro brewing equip-
ment
President: Gary Deathe
Number Employees: 17

20167 Camie Campbell
9225 Watson Industrial Park
Saint Louis, MO 63126

                  314-968-3222
     Fax: 314-968-0741 800-325-9572
camie@camie.com www.camie.com
Lubricants, pressure sensitive adhesives, rust corro-
sion silicones, spray adhesive and silicone sealants
President: Vince Doder
CEO: Tom Shelby
CFO: Vincent Doder
Natl. Sales Rep.: Steve Hartley
Credit Manager: Claudia Grissin
Estimated Sales: $10-20 000,000
Number Employees: 20-49
Type of Packaging: Bulk

20168 Campak Inc
119 Naylon Ave
Livingston, NJ 07039-1005

                  973-597-1414
     Fax: 973-992-4713 info@campak.com
www.campak.com
Thermoformer, intermittent motion horiziontal car-
tons, automatic wrapper, automatic bundler and
shrink tunnel
CEO: Rugel Franz
rugel@campak.com
CEO: Thomas Miller
Estimated Sales: $5-10 Million
Number Employees: 10-19

20169 Campbell Wrapper Corporation
1415 Fortune Ave
De Pere, WI 54115-8104

                  920-983-7100
   Fax: 920-983-7300 www.campbellwrapper.com
Manufactures Horizontal Fin Seal Wrappers for food
and nonfood applications. On-Edge Wrappers for
cookies and crackers; In-line Feed Systems for con-
fectionery and bakery; Bar Distribution Systems for
health bars, confectionery, bakeryetc.
President: John Dykema
dykemaj@campbellwrapper.com
Chief Financial Officer: Todd Goodwin
Engineering Manager: Jeffrey Ginzl
Vice President Sales & Marketing: Don Stelzer
Regional Sales Manager: Steve Joosten
Service Manager: Marv Calaway
Materials Manager/Wrapper Assembly Mgr: Jeff
Jende
Estimated Sales: $10-20 Million
Number Employees: 50-99
Type of Packaging: Consumer

20170 Campbell-Hardage
305 Old Commerce Rd
Athens, GA 30607

                  706-548-4615
             Fax: 706-543-2139
Machinery for distribution systems and automatic
product loading
President: Tim Wayne Hardage
CFO: Ark Campbell
Estimated Sales: $2.5-5 000,000
Number Employees: 30

20171 Campus Collection, Inc.
PO Box 2904
Tuscaloosa, AL 35403

205-758-0678
Fax: 205-758-4848 800-289-8744
sales@campuscollection.net
www.campuscollection.net
Manufacturer and exporter of printed and embroidered T-shirts, hats
President: Chet Goldstein
Contact: Chris Ballard
chris@campuscollection.net

20172 Camstar Systems
100 Century Center Ct # 500
San Jose, CA 95112-4536

408-559-5700
Fax: 408-558-9350 800-237-2841
partners@camstar.com www.camstar.com
Production line software systems
President: James David Cone
President, Chief Executive Officer: Scott Toney
Vice President of Marketing: Karim Lokas
Chief Technical Officer: Scott Jones
Vice President of Sales: Jay Antonellis
Contact: Sean Henry
shenry@camstar.com
Estimated Sales: $20-50 Million
Number Employees: 100-249

20173 Camtech-AMF
2115 West Laburnum Avenue
Richmond, VA 23227-4315

804-355-7961
Fax: 804-355-1074 sales@amfbakery.com
www.amfbakery.com
Industrial baking equipment
President: Ken Newsome
Number Employees: 100-249

20174 Camtron Systems
444 W Interstate Rd
Addison, IL 60101-4518

630-543-2884
Fax: 630-543-8153
Labels and label applicators
Owner: Mike Ahern
ahern_mike@hotmail.com
Estimated Sales: $1-2.5 000,000
Number Employees: 20-49

20175 Can & Bottle Systems, Inc.
2525 SE Stubb St
Milwaukie, OR 97222-7323

503-236-9010
Fax: 503-232-8453 866-302-2636
www.canandbottle.com
Manufacturer, sales and service and exporter of reverse vending machines and systems for beverage container redemption and recycling. Can, plastic and glass beverage container crushers/recyclers
President: Bill Janner
Number Employees: 20-49
Number of Products: 15
Square Footage: 40000
Brands:
Cando

20176 Can Corp Of America Inc
326 June Ave
Blandon, PA 19510-9566

610-926-3044
Fax: 610-926-5041 www.cancorpam.com
Steel food cans.
President & CEO: Ronald Moreau
Vice President, Sales & Marketing: Phil Butler
Year Founded: 1975
Estimated Sales: $100-500 Million
Number Employees: 100-249
Square Footage: 150000
Other Locations:
Can Corp. of America
Reading PA

20177 Can Creations
PO Box 848576
Pembroke Pines, FL 33084

954-581-3312
Fax: 954-581-2523 800-272-0235
orders@cancreations.com www.cancreations.com
Bags, baskets and containers, boxes, cellophane, gift wrap, pull bows, shrink wrap.

20178 Can Creations
PO Box 8576
Pembroke Pines, FL 33084

954-581-3312
Fax: 954-581-2523 orders@cancreations.com
www.cancreations.com
Decorative boxes, shrink wrap, ribbons, bows and bags
Estimated Sales: $1-5 Million
Number Employees: 12
Brands:
Crystal Wrap

20179 Can Lines Engineering Inc
9839 Downey Norwalk Rd
P.O. Box 7039
Downey, CA 90241-7039

562-861-2996
www.canlines.com
Can and bottle handling conveyors.
President: Keenan Koplien
Director, Mechanical Engineering: Steve Lusa
Director, Operations: Darwin Smock
Year Founded: 1960
Estimated Sales: $20 Million
Number Employees: 10-19
Square Footage: 40000

20180 Can-Am Instruments
2851 Brighton Road
Oakville, ON L6H 6C9
Canada

905-829-0030
Fax: 905-829-4701 800-215-4469
psmyth@can-am.net www.can-am.net
Food machinery and equipment
President: Mark Reeves
Director: Richard Reeves
Director: Greg Reeves
Estimated Sales: $3 Million
Number Employees: 12

20181 CanPacific Engineering
7331 Vantage Way
Delta, BC V4G 1C9
Canada

604-946-1680
Fax: 604-946-1620 www.canpacific.com
Industrial can openers and can seam inspection equipment
President: Wun Chong
Number Employees: 5-9
Brands:
Canguard

20182 Canada Coaster
44 Head St.
Dundas, ON L9H 3H3
Canada

905-627-6910
Fax: 905-627-7608 866-233-7628
sales@canadacoaster.com www.canadacoaster.com
Manufacturers of beer and drink coasters
Type of Packaging: Food Service, Private Label, Bulk

20183 Canada Goose Wood Produc
2489 Del Zotto Avenue
Gloucester, ON K1T 3V6
Canada

613-822-2575
Fax: 613-822-2232 888-890-6506
www.canada-goose.com
Wooden cutting boards, butcherblocks, trays and fajita griddle underliners

20184 Canada Pure Water Company Ltd
7 Kodiak Crescent
Toronto, ON M3J 3E5
Canada

416-631-5800
Fax: 416-635-1711 800-361-2369
info@canadapure.com www.canadapure.com
Wholesaler/distributor of flavored spring water and teas
President: David Tavares
Marketing Assistant: Sophia Ahmed
Director Purchasing: Tracy Tavares
Number Employees: 10-19

20185 Canadian Display Systems
60 Corstate Ave
Concord, ON L4K 4X2
Canada

905-265-7888
Fax: 905-265-7692 800-895-5862
cds1@on.aibn.com
www.canadiandisplaysystems.com
Display coolers
President: Gary Sohi
Number Employees: 15

20186 Canarm, Ltd.
2157 Parkedale Avenue
PO Box 367
Brockville, ON K6V 5V6
Canada

613-342-5424
Fax: 800-263-4598 info@canarm.ca
www.canarm.ca
Manufacturer and importer of ceiling fans
President: James A. Cooper
Vice President-HVAC & Agri Products: Doug Matthews
Marketing Manager: John McBride
Sales Manager: Tim Sutton
Director Operations: Steven Read
Number Employees: 30
Type of Packaging: Consumer, Food Service, Private Label
Brands:
Four Seasons
Pleasantaire

20187 Candle Lamp Company
1880 Compton Avenue
Ste. 101
Corona, CA 92881

951-682-9600
Fax: 951-784-5801 877-526-7748
www.candlelamp.com
Chafing dish and lamp fuel; also, table lamps for the restaurant/hotel industry
President: Daniel Stoner
VP: L Murlin
Marketing Services: J Van Osdel
Contact: Karina Garcia
kgarcia@sternocandlelamp.com
Estimated Sales: $10-20 Million
Number Employees: 100-249
Brands:
Safe Heat
Soft Light

20188 Candy & Company/Peck's Products Company
4100 West 76th Street
Chicago, IL 60652

800-837-9189
daleyinternational.com/
Manufacturer and exporter of industrial disinfectant cleaners, janitorial supplies, sanitizers, laundry supplies and specialty cleaning chemicals
President: Joh Daley
Sales Manager: Joann Stoskoph
Estimated Sales: $1-5 Million
Number Employees: 1-4
Square Footage: 160000
Parent Co: J.F. Daley International
Brands:
Camagsolv
Pepcocide

20189 Candy Manufacturing Co
5633 W Howard St
Niles, IL 60714-4011

847-588-2639
Fax: 847-588-0055 info@candycontrols.com
www.candycontrols.com
Manufacturer and exporter of industrial timing controls including differentials, positioners, cam switches, timing hubs, and web handling systems
President: Robert Hendershot
Quality Control: Al Rosenow
Sales Director: Jacob Ninan
Estimated Sales: Below $5 Million
Number Employees: 5-9
Square Footage: 60000

20190 CandyMachines.com
27721 N Twin Oaks Valley Rd
San Marcos, CA 92069-9742
760-734-1414
Fax: 866-863-5867 800-853-3941
info@candymachines.com
www.candymachines.com
Distributor of gumball and candy vending machines,
sticker, capsule machines, and bulk products, and re-
fill supplies
Manager: Tonya Bryhie
CFO: Irving Korn
Vice President: Harris Harris
Marketing Director: Jerry Korn
Estimated Sales: Less Than $500,000
Number Employees: 1-4
Number of Brands: 500+
Number of Products: 5000
Parent Co: RM Electronics
Type of Packaging: Consumer, Bulk

20191 Canning & Filling
PO Box 7501
Burlingame, CA 94011
650-401-6654
Fax: 650-401-6535

20192 Cannon Equipment Company
324 W Washington St
Cannon Falls, MN 55009
507-263-6400
800-825-8501
info@cannonequipment.com
www.cannonequipment.com
Point-of-purchase displays, front-end merchandisers,
distribution and display carts, and material handling
equipment and system.
Business Unit Manager: Dan Rosa
General Manager: Shane Beaudin
Director of Sales: Jeff Stutz
Director, Human Resources & Safety: John Evans
Year Founded: 1981
Estimated Sales: $100-250 Million
Number Employees: 250-499
Number of Brands: 15
Number of Products: 100
Parent Co: IMI,PLC
Type of Packaging: Consumer, Food Service, Pri-
vate Label, Bulk
Other Locations:
Cannon Equipment Company
Passaic NJ
Cannon Equipment Company
College Point NY
Cannon Equipment Company
Chattanooga TN
Cannon Equipment Company
Garden Grove CA
Cannon Equipment Company
Cannon Falls MN
Brands:
Connect-A-Bench
Ez-Lock
Ez-Reach
Magna-Bar
Ship 'n Shop
Slip

20193 Canon Potato Company
P.O.Box 880
Center, CO 81125
719-754-3445
Fax: 719-754-2227 sales@canonpotato.com
www.canonpotato.com
Potatoes including Centennials, McClures,
Norkotahs, Nuggets, Reds, Russets, Sangres and Yu-
kon Gold.
Manager: Jim Tonso
Sales Representative: Matt Glowczewski
Sales Manager: David Tonso
d.tonso@canonpotato.com
General Manager: Jim Tonso
Office Manager: Sandy Tonso
Estimated Sales: $10-20 Million
Number Employees: 50-99
Square Footage: 865020
Type of Packaging: Consumer, Food Service, Bulk

20194 Canongate Technology
2045 S Arl Hts Rd Ste 109
Arlington Hts, IL 60005
847-593-1832
Fax: 847-593-1629 800-221-4051
sales@canongatetechnology.co.uk
www.canongatetechnology.com

Inline instruments and analyzers sensing dissolved
CO_2, O_2, % alcohol, O.G. and Brix
Group Managing Director: Robin Cuthbertson
VP: Ron Mc Rae
Estimated Sales: $500,000-$1 000,000
Number Employees: 1-4

20195 Cantech Industries Inc
2222 Eddie Williams Rd
Johnson City, TN 37601-2871
423-926-9748
Fax: 423-928-0311 800-654-3947
cii@cttgroup.com www.cantechtn.com
Manufacturer and exporter of pressure sensitive
tapes including duct, masking, box sealing, filament,
double-coated, and electrical for industrial, automo-
tive and retail markets
President: L Cohen
CFO: H Cohen
Research & Development: H Matsuura
VP Marketing/Sales: Ronald Jacobs
VP Sales: P Cohen
Plant Manager: Mark Patton
Estimated Sales: $50 Million
Number Employees: 50-99
Number of Brands: 2
Number of Products: 70
Square Footage: 100000
Parent Co: Canadian Technical Tape
Type of Packaging: Consumer, Food Service, Pri-
vate Label, Bulk
Brands:
Cantech
Clipper

**20196 Cantley-Ellis Manufacturing
Company**
1200 South Eastman Road
Kingsport, TN 37660-5408
423-246-4671
Wooden pallets
General Manager: Jim Cantley
Estimated Sales: $2.5-5 Million
Number Employees: 20-49

20197 Cantol
199 Steelcase Road West
Markham, ON L3R 2M4
Canada
905-475-6141
800-387-9773
info@cantol.com www.cantol.com
Liquid detergents, soaps, herbicides, insecticides, lu-
bricants, solvents and degreasers and floor care
products, drain treatment chemicals, turf products,
odor control, food processing and dietary chemicals
President & CEO: Ja Brightman
VP: Richard Petscha
Plant Manager: Ellwood Barth
Estimated Sales: $10-20 Million
Number Employees: 20-49
Number of Products: 13
Parent Co: Cantol
Type of Packaging: Private Label, Bulk

20198 (HQ)Canton Sign Co
222 5th St NE
Canton, OH 44702-1262
330-456-7151
Fax: 330-456-7152 cantonsign@aol.com
www.cantonsignco.com
Metal, electric, plastic and wood signs and displays
President: Timothy Franta
cantonsign@aol.com
VP: Mark Franta
VP: Timothy Franta
Estimated Sales: $500,000-$1 Million
Number Employees: 1-4

**20199 (HQ)Canton Sterilized Wiping
Cloth**
1401 Waynesburg Dr SE
Canton, OH 44707-2115
330-455-8157
Fax: 330-455-2003
Cheesecloth wiping rags
President: Robert Shapiro
Estimated Sales: $5-10 Million
Number Employees: 10-19

20200 (HQ)Cantwell-Cleary Co Inc
7575 Washington Blvd
Elkridge, MD 21075
301-773-9800
Fax: 301-773-9257 support@cantwellcleary.com
www.cantwellcleary.com
Distributors of corrugated boxes and containers.
Chairman/CEO: Vincent Cleary
Year Founded: 1914
Estimated Sales: $14 Million
Number Employees: 20-49
Square Footage: 45000

20201 Cantwell-Cleary Co Inc
4263-I Carolina Ave
Richmond, VA 23222
804-329-9800
Fax: 804-329-5780 support@cantwellcleary.com
www.cantwellcleary.com
Distributors of corrugated boxes and containers.
Chairman & CEO: Vincent Cleary
Year Founded: 1914
Estimated Sales: $14 Million
Number Employees: 20-49

20202 Canvas Products
580 25 Rd
Grand Junction, CO 81505-1230
970-242-1453
Fax: 970-241-4801 www.canvas-products.com
Commercial awnings
Owner: Greg L Coren
Estimated Sales: $1-2,500,000
Number Employees: 5-9

20203 CapSnap Equipment
2080 Brooklyn Road
Jackson, MI 49203
517-787-3481
Fax: 517-787-2349 sales@capsnapequipment.com
www.capsnapequipment.com
HOD water bottling equipment and service.

20204 Capaco Plastics
9231 Billy The Kid St
El Paso, TX 79907-4738
915-772-1395
Fax: 915-772-1396 sales@capcoplastics.com
www.capcoplastics.com
Thermoform company specializing in blister, clam-
shell and trifold packages.
President: Robert Arno
Vice President, General Manager: Bob Arno
Estimated Sales: Less Than $500,000
Number Employees: 1-4

20205 Cape Systems
100 Allentown Parkway
Suite 218
Allen, TX 75002
800-229-3434
Fax: 908-756-2332 www.capesystems.com
Pallets, load planning, optimization, transporta-
tion-software; warehouse management software or-
der fulfillment and inventory system
Executive Chairman: Hugo Biermann
Director/CEO/CFO: Nicholas Toms
CEO: Nicholas R Toms
International Marketing: Peter Ayling
Vice President Group Sales: Brad Leonard
Contact: Kennedy Allen
akennedy@capesystems.com
Chief Operating Officer/CTO: David Sasson
Vice President Software Sales: Heidi Larsen
Estimated Sales: Below $5 Million
Number Employees: 20-49
Number of Brands: 8

**20206 Capital City Container
Corporation**
150 Precision Drive
Buda, TX 78610
512-312-1222
Fax: 512-312-1349
Corrugated shipping containers
Manager: Mike McDonald
VP of Marketing: Doug King
Contact: Mike Mcdonald
m.mcdonald@boiseinc.com
Estimated Sales: $10-20 Million
Number Employees: 148

20207 Capital City Signs
2714 Industrial Dr
Monona, WI 53713-2250
608-222-1881
Fax: 608-222-1889
Luminous tube and plastic signs
President: Rosemary Zimmerman
info@capitalcitysigns.net
VP/Secretary: Rosemary Zimmerman
Estimated Sales: Below $5 Million
Number Employees: 5-9
Square Footage: 16000

20208 Capital Industries
PO Box 1693
Mattituck, NY 11952-0929
631-298-6300
Fax: 631-298-2077 info@kwikbond.com
www.kwikbond.com
Kwik-Bond, floor repair
Estimated Sales: $5-10 Million
Number Employees: 20-49

20209 Capital Packaging
PO Box 873
Panacea, FL 32346
229-228-0006
Fax: 912-228-6405
Packaging
C.E.O: Polybus B. Joseph
Secretary: Polybus T. Frances
Sales Manager: Randy Eason

20210 (HQ)Capital Plastics
15060 Madison Rd
Middlefield, OH 44062-9450
440-632-5800
Fax: 440-632-0012 collector@capitalplastics.com
www.capitalplastics.com
Manufacturer and exporter of custom plastic displays for acrylic cutting boards, clip boards, plaques and trophies
President: Lyle Schwartz
Estimated Sales: $2.5-5 Million
Number Employees: 10-19

20211 Capitol Awning Co Inc
10515 180th St
Jamaica, NY 11433-1818
718-454-6444
Fax: 718-657-8374 800-241-3539
www.capitolawning.com
Commercial awnings, banners, sign faces and graphics
President: Fred Catalano
Estimated Sales: $2.5-5,000,000
Number Employees: 20-49

20212 Capitol Carton Company
8333 24th Avenue
Sacramento, CA 95826
916-388-7848
Fax: 916-388-7840
Corrugated boxes
President: Neal Gurevitz
VP: Thomas Milligan
Plant Supervisor: James Wodarczyk
Estimated Sales: $1-5 Million
Number Employees: 5-9
Square Footage: 100000

20213 Capitol City Container Corp
8240 Zionsville Rd
Indianapolis, IN 46268-1627
317-875-0290
Fax: 317-876-6694 800-233-5145
Custom corrugated boxes and stock packaging supplies
President: Rich Purcell
rich@capcitycontainer.com
VP: Mike Purcell
Plant Manager: Jim Plank
Estimated Sales: $10-20 Million
Number Employees: 20-49
Square Footage: 130000

20214 Capitol Hardware, Inc.
402 N Main Street
P.O. Box 70
Middlebury, IN 46540-2573
800-327-6083
Fax: 800-544-4054

Manufacturer and exporter of retail store fixtures, peripheral display hardware and electric lighting fixtures
President: Joe Shelby
capitolhardware@leggett.com
Senior Vice President: David DeSonier
Executive Vice President of Sales: Joel Katterhagen
Executive Vice President of Operations: Ron McComas
Estimated Sales: $2.5-5 Million
Number Employees: 20-49
Square Footage: 1000000
Parent Co: Leggett & Platt Store Fixtures Group
Brands:
  Capitol Hardware

20215 Capitol Recruiting Group
712 Gum Rock Ct
Newport News, VA 23606-2524
757-812-8677
Executive search firm specializing in selection and placement of consumer packaged goods industry personnel including sales, marketing, category, broker and senior level management positions
Contact: Robyn Tragesser
robyn.tragesser@capitolrecruitinggroup.com
General Manager: Buford Sims
Number Employees: 10-19
Other Locations:
  Washington DC
  Boston MA
  New York NY

20216 Capitol Vial
151 Riverside Drive
Fultonville, NY 12072-1824
518-853-3377
Fax: 518-853-3409 sales@capitolvial.com
www.capitolvial.com
Contact: Jeff Steiger
jsteiger@capitolvial.com
Estimated Sales: $5-10 Million
Number Employees: 20-49

20217 Capmatic, Ltd.
12180 Boul. Albert-Hudon
Monreal North, QC H1G 3K7
Canada
514-332-0062
Fax: 514-322-0063 info@capmatic.com
www.capmatic.com
Manufacturer and exporter of packaging machinery and bottling equipment
President: Charles Lacasse
CFO: Nicole Murray
President: Alioscia Bassani
Sales Director: Christian Normandin
Number Employees: 20

20218 Capone Foods
14 Bow St. Union Square
Somerville, MA 02143
617-629-2296
Fax: 617-776-0318 albert@caponefoods.com
www.caponefoods.com
Producer of pasta and sauces. Some of their products include fresh pasta, ravioli, tortellini, gnocchi, pizza, entr,es, meatballs, sausage, empanadas and many more items. Their products can be found in several store locationsthroughout Massachusetts, such as Bedford, Boston, Brighton, Brookline, Cambridge, Concord, and other locations.
Owner: Albert Capone
Manager: Jennifer Capone
Estimated Sales: $320,000
Number Employees: 7
Brands:
  Capone Foods

20219 Capresso
81 Ruckman Rd
PO Box 775
Closter, NJ 07624-2102
201-564-7273
Fax: 201-767-9684 800-767-3554
contact@capresso.com www.capresso.com
Espresso machines and accessories, coffee makers, coffee grinders, coffee/espresso centers and toasters.
President: Michael Kramm
Manager: Barbara Leung
barbara@jura.com
Estimated Sales: $10-20 000,000
Number Employees: 10-19
Type of Packaging: Bulk

20220 Capricorn Coffees Inc
353 10th St
San Francisco, CA 94103-3804
415-621-8500
Fax: 415-621-9875 800-541-0758
www.capricorncoffees.com
Coffee, Tea, Accessories
Manager: Annie Ngo
Manager: Rachel Akins
rachel.akins@capricorncoffees.com
Estimated Sales: $1-2.5 Million
Number Employees: 10-19
Type of Packaging: Private Label

20221 Capricorn Coffees Inc
353 10th St
San Francisco, CA 94103-3804
415-621-8500
Fax: 415-621-9875 www.capricorncoffees.com
Espresso machines and accessories
Manager: Megan Patterson
CFO: Craig Edwards
Quality Control: Craig Edwards
Manager: Rachel Akins
rachel.akins@capricorncoffees.com
Estimated Sales: $1-2.5 000,000
Number Employees: 10-19

20222 Capway Conveyor Systems Inc
725 Vogelsong Rd
York, PA 17404-1765
717-843-0003
Fax: 717-843-1654 877-222-7929
sales@capwayusa.com www.capwayusa.com
Manufacturer and exporter of bakery and food processing equipment including depanners, proofers, coolers, pan storage systems, conveyors, etc
President: Frank Achterberg
fachterberg@capwayusa.com
General Manager: Frank Achterberg
Estimated Sales: $5-10 Million
Number Employees: 20-49
Square Footage: 72000
Parent Co: Capway Systems
Brands:
  Capway

20223 Cara Products Company
9192 Tara Boulevard
Jonesboro, GA 30236-4913
770-478-9802
Fax: 770-471-3715
Manufacturer and exporter of stainless steel, fiberglass and wood free standing and hot food counters. Custom stainless steel kitchen equipment, serving lines, buffets and salad bard, portable hot and cold carts and custom millwork
President: W Casey
VP: David Pearson
Marketing: Bill Steadman
Sales Manager: Bill Steadman
Purchasing: Dan Casey
Estimated Sales: $20-25 Million
Number Employees: 200

20224 Carando Technologies Inc
345 N Harrison St
Stockton, CA 95203-2801
209-948-6500
Fax: 209-948-6757 sales@carando.net
www.carando.net
Manufacturer and exporter of container production machinery
President: Sid Schuetz
CFO: Laura Keir
lkeir@carando.net
Sales Coordinator: Laura Keir
Estimated Sales: $5-10 Million
Number Employees: 10-19

20225 (HQ)Caraustar
5000 Austell Powder Springs Rd
Suite 300
Austell, GA 30106
770-948-3101
www.caraustar.com
Contract packager.
President & CEO: Mike Patton
Year Founded: 1938
Estimated Sales: $20-50 Million
Number Employees: 5000-9999
Other Locations:
  Consumer Packaging
  Pineville NC
  Chicago IL

Grand Rapids MI
Kingston Springs TN
Cleveland OH
Randleman NC
Burlington NC
Los Angeles CA
Industrial Products
Arlington TX
Atlanta GA
Augusta GA
Austell GA
Bay Minette AL

20226 Caraustar
115 Quail Road
Franklin, KY 42134
270-586-9565
info@caraustar.com
www.caraustar.com
Advertising novelties and specialties including plastic lids, tips and spouts
Division Manager: Mark Bamberger
Estimated Sales: $5-10 Million
Number Employees: 20-49

20227 Caraustar Industries, Inc.
3900 Comanche Drive
Archdale, NC 27263-3158
770-948-3101
800-223-1373
info@caraustar.com www.caraustar.com
Manufacturer and exporter of composite cans, tubes, metal ends and injection molded plastic products used for packaging wet and dry, hot fill and frozen products
Marketing Director: Andrew McGowan
Type of Packaging: Consumer, Food Service

20228 Caravan Company
237 Chandler St
Worcester, MA 01609
508-752-3777
Fax: 508-753-4717
Coffee
President/Treasurer: George Drapos
Vice President: Arthur Drapos
Clerk: Alex Drapos
Estimated Sales: $2.1 Million
Number Employees: 17

20229 Caravan Packaging Inc
6427 Eastland Rd
Brookpark, OH 44142-1305
440-243-4100
Fax: 440-243-4383 info@caravanpackaging.com
www.caravanpackaging.com
Manufacturer and exporter of wooden boxes and custom packaging
President: Fred Hitti
fred@caravanpackaging.com
Estimated Sales: $500,000-$1 Million
Number Employees: 1-4
Type of Packaging: Food Service, Bulk

20230 Carbis Inc
1430 W Darlington St
Florence, SC 29501-2124
843-669-6668
Fax: 843-662-1536 800-948-7750
sales@carbissolutions.com
Stainless steel products, including loading racks, arms, stairs, platforms and handrails
President: Sam Cramer
sam.cramer@carbissolutions.com
Marketing Director: Rob Cooksey
General Manager: Ron Bennett
Number Employees: 250-499
Square Footage: 1200000

20231 Carboline Co
2150 Schuetz Rd
St Louis, MO 63146-3517
314-644-1000
Fax: 314-644-4617 800-848-4645
www.carboline.com
High-performance, anti-corrosive coatings
President: Richard Wilson
richard_wilson@carboline.com
Estimated Sales: $87 Million
Number Employees: 10-19

20232 Carbon Clean Industries Inc
216 Courtdale Ave
Kingston, PA 18704-1123
570-288-1155
Fax: 570-288-1227 carbonclean@aol.com
Chemical cleaners for the removal of burnt and carbonized food products; also, dispensers
President: Ernest J Clamar
carbonclean@aol.com
CFO: Ernest J Clamar Sr
Estimated Sales: $5-10,000,000
Number Employees: 10-19

20233 Carbonic Machines Inc
2900 5th Ave S
Minneapolis, MN 55408-2497
612-824-0745
Fax: 612-824-1974 info@shamrockgroup.net
www.shamrockgroup.net
Ice machines and beer, wine and soda dispensing systems for restaurants
Owner: Nabil Gadros
nabil.gadros@bavaria.com
VP Marketing: Steven Kelly
Estimated Sales: $20-50 Million
Number Employees: 20-49

20234 Carbonic Reserves
4754 Shavano Oak # 102
San Antonio, TX 78249-4027
210-479-0100
Fax: 210-479-0070 800-880-1911
www.airgas.com
Freezers and cooling tunnels and spirals; processor of dry ice
President: Bob Bradshaw
Vice President of HR: Ann Rice
Sales Manager: Jay Loo
Vice President of Operations: Don Goldschmidt
Estimated Sales: $1-5 Million
Number Employees: 100-249
Brands:
Penguin Brand

20235 Card Pak Inc
29601 Solon Rd
Cleveland, OH 44139-3451
440-542-3100
Fax: 440-542-3399 800-824-3342
sgraham@cardpak.com
Owner: Shelby David
dshelby@cardpak.com
Estimated Sales: $20-50 Million
Number Employees: 100-249

20236 Cardan Design
227 Rutgers St
Maplewood, NJ 07040-3229
973-762-2186
Fax: 973-762-2753
Owner: Bert Ghavami
Contact: Cristi Mosco
cristimosco@techniedge.com
Estimated Sales: $1-5 000,000
Number Employees: 50-99

20237 Cardinal Container Corp
750 S Post Rd
Indianapolis, IN 46239-9745
317-898-2715
Fax: 317-899-6747 800-899-2715
www.cardinalcontainercorp.com
Corrugated cartons
President: Fred Beers
fbeers@cardinalcontainercorp.com
Controller: Mark Prosser
Estimated Sales: $10-20 Million
Number Employees: 20-49

20238 Cardinal Kitchens
165 Exeter Road
London, ON N6L 1A4
Canada
519-652-3295
Fax: 519-652-9853 800-928-0832
Laboratory providing food testing services
President: David M. Lucy
Parent Co: Cardinal Biologicals
Brands:
Snack Rite

20239 Cardinal Packaging
PO Box 959
Evansville, IN 47706-0959
812-424-2904
Fax: 330-562-4875 800-343-1295
www.berryplastics.com
Plastic round and rectangular containers
President: Ira Booth
CFO: Mike Cutnam
VP: Bill Regan
Quality Control: Warren Blazy
VP Sales: Bill Regan
Regional Manager: Norma Seevers
Plant Manager: Kurt Hamlin
Number Employees: 100-249
Square Footage: 760000
Parent Co: Cardinal Packaging

20240 Cardinal Packaging Prod LLC
300 Exchange Dr # A
Suite A
Crystal Lake, IL 60014-6290
815-444-6000
Fax: 815-444-6379 866-216-4942
info@cardinalpack.com www.cardinalpack.com
Manufacturer and exporter of set-up paper boxes, specialty folding cartons, incorporating domicut platforms, etc. Also hot leaf (foil) stamping
President: Bob Colletti
b.colletti@cardinalpkgproducts.com
Sales: Steve Overlee
Estimated Sales: Less Than $500,000
Number Employees: 1-4

20241 Cardinal Professional Products
57 Matmor Rd
Woodland, CA 95776-6008
530-666-1020
Fax: 530-666-3170 800-548-2223
info@cardinalproproducts.com
www.cardinalproproducts.com
Insecticides
President: John Sansone
Vice President: Ed Hosoda
ehosoda@cardinalproproducts.com
Estimated Sales: $.5-1 million
Number Employees: 10-19
Parent Co: Cal-Ag Industrial Supply

20242 Cardinal Rubber & Seal Inc
1545 Brownlee Ave SE
Roanoke, VA 24014-2609
540-982-0091
Fax: 540-982-6750 800-542-5737
sales@cardinalrubber.com
www.cardinalrubber.com
Manufacturer and exporter of rubber seals, gaskets, O-rings, hoses, etc.
CEO: Loren Bruffey, Sr.
Vice President: Pat Lawhorn
Inside Sales: Pat Worley
Purchasing: Connie Dowdy
Estimated Sales: $10-20 Million
Number Employees: 20-49

20243 Cardinal Scale Mfg Co
203 E Daugherty St
P.O. Box 151
Webb City, MO 64870-1929
417-673-4631
Fax: 417-673-5001 800-441-4237
cardinal@cardet.com www.cardinalscale.com
Manufacturer and exporter of scales
Owner: Brock Dawson
bdawson@detecto.com
CEO: W Perry
CFO: Charles Nasters
Vice President: Herbert Harwood
Estimated Sales: $50-100 Million
Number Employees: 500-999
Square Footage: 400000

20244 (HQ)Care Controls, Inc.
PO Box 12014
Mill Creek, WA 98082
425-745-1252
Fax: 425-745-8934 800-593-6050
info@carecontrols.com www.carecontrols.com
Manufacturer and exporter of on-line inspection systems including check weighers, vacuum and pressure detectors, etc

President: Ray Pynsky
Marketing: Rob Laroche
Contact: Brenda Ballard
brenda@carecontrols.com
Brands:
  Canalyzer
  Ivis
  Quantum

20245 (HQ)Cargill Inc.
P.O. Box 9300
Minneapolis, MN 55440-9300

800-227-4455
www.cargill.com
Stores, trades, processes and distributes grains, oil-
seeds, vegetable oils and meals; raises livestock and
produces animal feed; produces food ingredients
such as starches, glucose syrups, oils and fats.
Chairman/CEO: David MacLennan
CFO: David Dines
Chief Compliance Officer/General Counsel: Anna
Richo
Cheif Human Resources Officer: LeighAnne Baker
Business Operations & Supply Chain: Ruth
Kimmelshue
Year Founded: 1865
Estimated Sales: $114.6 Billion
Number Employees: 166,000
Type of Packaging: Bulk

20246 Cargill Kitchen Solutions Inc.
15407 McGinty Rd. W.
Wayzata, MN 55391

833-535-5205
CustomerService_Protein@Cargill.com
www.sunnyfresh.com
Eggs and breakfast products for foodservice
operatos, convenience stores, chain restaurants,
healthcare foodservice facilities, and schools.
Parent Co: Cargill Inc.
Type of Packaging: Bulk
Brands:
  Sunny Fresh™

20247 Carhartt
P.O.Box 600
Dearborn, MI 48121-0600

313-271-8460
Fax: 313-271-3455 800-358-3825
www.carhartt.com
CFO: Linda Hubbard
CEO: Mark Valade
Number Employees: 1,000-4,999

20248 Carhoff Company
13404 Saint Clair Ave
Cleveland, OH 44110

216-541-4835
Fax: 216-541-4022
Manufacturer and exporter of silicone and chemi-
cally treated cleansing tissues
V.P.: Jim Lauer
Estimated Sales: $5-10 Million
Number Employees: 10-19

20249 Carico Systems
4211 Clubview Dr
Fort Wayne, IN 46804

260-432-6738
Fax: 260-432-2461 800-466-6738
Material handling, wire carts, containers
President: Jon Marler
Estimated Sales: $500,000-$1 000,000
Number Employees: 1-4

20250 Caristrap International
1760 Fortin Boulevard
Laval, QC H7S 1N8
Canada

450-667-4700
Fax: 450-663-1520 800-361-9466
info@caristrap.com www.caristrap.com
Manufacturer and exporter of polyester cord strap-
ping
President: Audrey Karass
Operations: Gerry Elis
Plant Manager: Norm Stevenson
Number Employees: 150
Brands:
  Strapping

20251 Carl Strutz & Company
440 Mars-Valencia Road
PO Box 509
Mars, PA 16046

724-625-1501
Fax: 724-625-3570 info@strutz.com
www.strutz.com
Direct screen printing equipment for glass and plas-
tic containers
Director: Frank Strutz Jr
Director: James Strutz
President: Carl Strutz Jr
Contact: Larry Collingwood
lcollingwood@lovemystrutz.com
General Manager: Edward Zwigert
Estimated Sales: $5-10 Million
Number Employees: 10-19
Square Footage: 52000

20252 Carleton Helical Technologies
30 S Sand Rd
Doylestown, PA 18901-5123

215-230-8900
Fax: 215-230-8033 sales@feedscrew.com
www.carletonhelical.com
Container handling products and systems including
timing screws, invertors, inline air rinsers, carton
twisters, etc
President: Nick Carleton
ncarleton@feedscrew.com
Operations Manager: Connie McDermott
Production Manager: Mike Anrein
Production: Mark McDermott
Purchasing Manager: Edward Amrein
Estimated Sales: $2-3 Million
Number Employees: 10-19
Number of Brands: 5
Number of Products: 1
Square Footage: 52000

20253 Carleton Helical Technologies
30 S Sand Rd
Doylestown, PA 18901-5123

215-230-8900
Fax: 215-230-8033 sales@feedscrew.com
www.carletonhelical.com
Packaging and container handling
President: Nick Carleton
ncarleton@feedscrew.com
Engineering Dept./ Manager: Connie McDermott
Estimated Sales: Below $5 Million
Number Employees: 10-19

20254 Carleton Technologies Inc
10 Cobham Dr
Orchard Park, NY 14127-4195

716-662-0006
Fax: 716-662-0747 info@carltech.com
www.cobham.com
Manufacturer and exporter of testing equipment for
flexible package seal integrity and strength
President/CEO: Paddy Cawdery
Cmo: Stuart Buckley
stuart.buckley@cobham.com
Estimated Sales: $20-50 Million
Number Employees: 100-249
Square Footage: 93000
Parent Co: FR Group PLC
Brands:
  Test-A-Pack

20255 Carlin Manufacturing
466 West Fallbrook Avenue
Suite 106
Fresno, CA 93711

559-276-0123
Fax: 559-222-1538 888-212-0801
info@carlinmfg.com www.carlinmfg.com
Manufacturer and exporter of custom mobile kitch-
ens, military field kitchens and specialty vehicles.
Owner: Kevin Carlin
Sales/FMP/CEO: Bob Farrar
Contact: Robin Goldbeck
goldbeck@carlinmfg.com
Estimated Sales: $5-10 Million
Number Employees: 10-19
Number of Brands: 1
Square Footage: 74000

20256 Carlisle Food Svc Products Inc
4711 E Hefner Rd
Oklahoma City, OK 73131

405-475-5600
Fax: 800-872-4701 800-654-8210
customerservice@carlislefsp.com
www.carlislefsp.com
Dishware, tabletop accessories, coffee and tea sup-
plies, buffet service, food bars and accessories, food
service trays, bar supplies, catering equipment,
kitchen accessories, storage and handling and
cleaning tools.
President: Trent Freiberg
trentfreiberg@carlislefsp.com
Chief Financial Officer: Carolyn Ford
Vice President: Todd Manor
Vice President of Sales: Jim Calamito
Year Founded: 1946
Estimated Sales: $238.8 Million
Number Employees: 250-499
Number of Brands: 100
Number of Products: 1600
Square Footage: 150000
Type of Packaging: Food Service
Other Locations:
  Central Distribution Center
  Oklahoma City OK
  Western Distribution Center
  Reno NV
  Eastern Distribution Center
  Charlotte NC
Brands:
  Aria
  Bistro
  Bravo
  Catarcooler
  Celebration
  Che Series
  Classic
  Clutter Busters
  Coldmaster
  Crescendo
  Crystalite
  Delivers
  Designer Displpayer
  Elan
  Elegant
  Elegant Impressions
  Exceelibur
  Expressions
  Fall'n Go
  Festival Traus
  Flex-All
  Galaxy
  Glasted
  Griptite
  Hi-Lo
  Ice Sculptures
  Lexington
  Meteor
  Miracryl
  Mosar Design Displayware
  Munchie
  Napkin Deli
  Omni
  Orchid
  Perma-Sam
  Perma-Sil
  Petal Mist
  Poly-Tuf
  Poura-Clam
  Queen Anne
  Sani-Pail
  Save-All
  Signature Select
  Six Star
  Sleep'n Bag
  Sparta
  Spectrum
  Ssal 2000
  Stackable
  Star Plus
  Steclite
  Sted Stock Ii
  Steeluminum
  Store'n Pour
  Suds-Pail
  Supreme
  Symphony
  Textile Design Collection
  The Gotham Collection
  The Lions Head Collection
  The Mediterranean Collection
  The New World Collection
  The Oceana Collection

The Resort Collection
Thermoinsulator
Top Notch
Trimlina
Thermoinsulator
Top Notch
Trimlina
Tulip Deli
Universal
Weavewear

20257 Carlisle Plastics
1401 W 94th St
Minneapolis, MN 55431

952-884-1309
Fax: 952-884-6438

Polyethylene bags, film and sheeting; also, garbage bags
Number Employees: 250-499
Parent Co: Tyco International
Brands:
    Color Scents
    Film-Gard
    Ruffies
    Sure Sak

20258 Carlisle Sanitary Mntnc Prods
4711 E Hefner Rd
PO Box 53006
Oklahoma City, OK 73131-6114

405-475-5600
Fax: 405-475-5607   800-654-8210
www.carlislefsp.com

Manufacturer and exporter of custom-designed brushes including floor scrub, clean-up, fryers, nylon paddle scraper, grill, grease, glass and washing
CEO: Ruth Marciniec
ruthmarciniec@carlislefsp.com
Director Sales/Marketing: Christopher Meaney
General Manager: Robert Daley, Jr.
Estimated Sales: $200,000
Number Employees: 6
Square Footage: 16652
Type of Packaging: Food Service, Bulk
Brands:
    Broiler Master
    Galaxy
    Hercules
    Hi-Lo
    Long Reach
    Meteor
    Venus

20259 Carlo Gavazzi Inc
750 Hastings Dr
Buffalo Grove, IL 60089-6904

847-465-6100
Fax: 847-465-7373   sales@carlogavazzi.com
www.gavazzionline.com

Importer of solid-state relays, electronic plug-in control modules and sensors, digital electronic counters and meters
President: Fred Shirzadi
fshirzadi@carlogavazzi.com
Estimated Sales: $10-20 Million
Number Employees: 20-49

20260 Carlson Engineering Inc
505 NE 37th St
Fort Worth, TX 76106-3713

817-877-3815
Fax: 817-335-4712
office@carlsonengineeringinc.com
www.carlsonengineeringinc.com

Software development and systems integration
President: John Carlson
Estimated Sales: Below $5 000,000
Number Employees: 20-49

20261 Carlson Products
4601 N Tyler Rd
P.O. Box 429
Maize, KS 67101-8734

316-722-0265
Fax: 316-721-0158   800-234-1069
sales@carlsonproducts.com
www.carlsonproducts.com

Manufacturer and exporter of lightweight double-acting aluminum impact and sliding aluminum cooler and freezer doors; also pizza pans
President: Austin Peterson
austin@carlsonproducts.com
Sales Manager: Rich Dreiling

Estimated Sales: $5-10 Million
Number Employees: 50-99
Square Footage: 100000
Parent Co: Jay Ca

20262 Carlton Industries
PO Box 280
La Grange, TX 78945-0280

979-242-5055
Fax: 979-242-5058   800-231-5988
sales@carltonusa.com   www.carltonusa.com

Product identification labels, decals, tags, tapes, signs, placards, etc
President: Kay Carlton
Vice President: Richard Carlton
Marketing Director: Colette Merchant
Estimated Sales: Less Than $500,000
Number Employees: 1-4
Square Footage: 80000

20263 Carlyle Compressor
Carrier Parkway, TR-4
PO Box 4808
Syracuse, NY 13221

315-432-6000
Fax: 315-432-3274   800-462-2759
carlyle.compressor@carrier.utc.com
www.carlylecompressor.com

President: Richard Laubstein

20264 Carman And Company
12 Wilmington Rd
Burlington, MA 1803

781-221-3500
Fax: 781-221-3508

Counter display cabinets
Owner: Dan Carman
Contact: Seth Farmer
sfarmer@carmansite.com
Estimated Sales: $500,000-$1 Million
Number Employees: 5-9

20265 Carman Industries Inc
1005 W Riverside Dr
Jeffersonville, IN 47130-3143

812-288-4710
Fax: 812-288-4707   800-456-7560
info@carmanindustries.com
www.carmanindustries.com

Vibratory material handling and fluid-bed drying equipment including conveyors, feeders, bin dischargers and spiral elevators
President: Jim Hyslop
VP: Carl Porter
VP: Carl Porter
Estimated Sales: $2.5-5 Million
Number Employees: 50-99
Square Footage: 80000

20266 Carman Industries Inc
1005 W Riverside Dr
Jeffersonville, IN 47130-3143

812-288-4710
Fax: 812-288-4707   800-456-7560
info@carmanindustries.com
www.carmanindustries.com

Bulk material handling and processing equipment including vibrating feeders, vibrating conveyors, vibrating spiral elevators, vibrating bin dischargers and fluid bed dryers, heaters and coolers
President: Jim Hyslop
CFO: Jack Ising
Quality Control: Bill Whearthon
Estimated Sales: $2.5-5 000,000
Number Employees: 50-99

20267 Carmel Engineering
PO Box 67
Kirklin, IN 46050

317-896-9367
Fax: 765-896-5713   888-427-0497
sales@carmeleng.com
www.carmelengineering.com

Supplier of food processing equipment that include heat exchangers, product tubes, heat exchanger parts, resting tubes, dump tanks and accumulator tanks and convection systems
Owner: Randy Weaver
VP: Randy Weaver
Contact: Allan Roden
aroden@carmeleng.com
Estimated Sales: $1.5 Million
Number Employees: 10-19

20268 Carmel Engineering
PO Box 67
Kirklin, IN 46050

317-896-9367
Fax: 765-896-5713   888-427-0497
sales@carmeleng.com
www.carmelengineering.com

Supplier of food processing equipment that include heat exchangers, product tubes, heat exchanger parts, resting tubes, dump tanks and accumulator tanks and convection systems
Owner: Randy Weaver
VP: Randy Weaver
Contact: Allan Roden
aroden@carmeleng.com
Estimated Sales: $1.5 Million
Number Employees: 10-19

20269 (HQ)Carmi Flavor & Fragrance Company
6030 Scott Way
Commerce, CA 90040-3516

323-888-9240
Fax: 323-888-9339   800-421-9647
sales@carmiflavors.com   www.carmiflavors.com

High quality natural and artificial flavors in liquid or powder form; supplier of packaging products.
President: Eliot Carmi
CEO: Eliot Carmi
Chief Operating Officer: Dan Carmi
Estimated Sales: $12 Million
Number Employees: 40
Number of Brands: 1
Number of Products: 500
Square Footage: 60000
Type of Packaging: Private Label, Bulk
Other Locations:
    Carmi Flavor & Fragrance
    Port Coquitlam, Canada
    Midwest Office & Manufacturing
    Waverly IA
    Southern Office & Warehouse
    Lawrenceville GA
Brands:
    Carmi Flavors
    Flavor Depot

20270 Carmona Designs
737 3rd Ave
Chula Vista, CA 91910-5827

619-425-2800
Fax: 619-425-0225   carmonadgs@aol.com

Design consultant specializing in restaurants
President: Armando Carmona
General Manager: Armando Carmona
Estimated Sales: $1-2.5 Million
Number Employees: 10-19

20271 Carmun International
702 San Fernando Street
San Antonio, TX 78207-5041

210-224-1781
Fax: 210-227-5332   800-531-7907

Stainless steel fittings, aluminum cold plates, CO2 regulators and bar guns
Contact: Luther Cowden
luther.cowden@cornelius.com
General Manager: Luther Cowden
Estimated Sales: $20-50 Million
Number Employees: 250-499
Parent Co: IMI Cornelius

20272 Carnegie Manufacturing Company
20 Montesano Road
Fairfield, NJ 07004-3310

973-575-3449
Fax: 973-575-2575

Aluminum molds
President: Barbara Carnegie
Estimated Sales: $1-2.5 Million
Number Employees: 5-9

20273 Carnegie Textile Co
31100 Solon Rd # A
Cleveland, OH 44139-3463

440-542-1180
Fax: 440-542-1188   800-633-4136
kerry@carnegietextile.com
www.carnegietextile.com

Terry cloth wipes, bar mops, tablecloths, napkins and uniforms
Owner: Carren Kay
General Manager: Carren Kay

Estimated Sales: $10-20 Million
Number Employees: 10-19
Square Footage: 68000
Parent Co: Surgical Manufacturing Company
Type of Packaging: Bulk

20274 Carnes Company
PO Box 930040
Verona, WI 53593

608-845-6411
Fax: 608-845-6470 carnes@carnes.com
www.carnes.com
Carnes Company is a manufacturer of commercial HVAC equipment. Its product line offering includes registers, grilles, diffusers. terminal units, ventilation equipment, louvers, penthouses, fire and smoke dampers, steam humidifiers andenergy recovering ventilators. Carnes has been a supplier of HVAC equipment since 1939.
VP, Sales & Marketing: David Stankevich
dstankevich@carnes.com
Estimated Sales: $50-100 Million
Number Employees: 11-50
Square Footage: 93000

20275 Carolina Container
909 Prospect St
High Point, NC 27260-8273

336-883-7146
Fax: 336-883-7576 800-627-0825
www.carolinacontainer.com
Corrugated containers
President: Ronald Sessions
rsessions@carolinacontainer.com
CEO: Ron Sessions
General Sales Manager: David Mitchell
Estimated Sales: $20-50 Million
Number Employees: 100-249

20276 Carolina Cracker
P.O.Box 374
Garner, NC 27529-0374

919-779-6899
Fax: 919-779-6899 www.carolinacracker.net
Nut crackers for soft shell nuts, shelled pecans in bulk
President: Dot Woodruff
CEO: Harold Woodruff
Estimated Sales: $1-2.5 Million
Number Employees: 10-19
Number of Brands: 3
Square Footage: 4
Type of Packaging: Bulk
Brands:
  The Carolina Cracker

20277 Carolina Glove Co
116 S Mclin Creek Rd
PO Box 999
Conover, NC 28613-9024

828-464-1132
Fax: 828-464-1710 800-335-1918
sales@carolinaglovecompany.com
www.carolinaglove.com
Gloves including plastic, rubber, leather, cotton and knit
President: Robert Abernethy
rabernethy@carolinaglovecompany.com
National Sales Director: Marshall Fisher
Manager: Fred Abernethy
Estimated Sales: $5-10 Million
Number Employees: 20-49
Brands:
  Eagle
  Golden Hawk
  Master Rigger
  Patriot
  Tiger Tuff
  Tuff-Dot
  Warm Grip

20278 Carolina Knife
224 Mulvaney St
Asheville, NC 28803-1499

828-253-6796
Fax: 828-258-0693 800-520-5030
info@cknife.com
Manufacturer and exporter of machine knives
President: Walter Ashbrook
wally@cknife.com
Sales Manager: Paul Turner
Technical Rep.: Bart Loudermilk
Estimated Sales: $2.5-5 Million
Number Employees: 20-49

Square Footage: 12000
Parent Co: Hamilton Industrial Knife & Machine

20279 Carolina Mop
819 Whitehall Road
Anderson, SC 29625-2119

864-225-8351
Fax: 864-225-1917 800-845-9725
www.carolinamop.com
Manufacturer, importer and exporter of dust mops, wet mops, brooms and broom handles
President: Pam Ritter
Estimated Sales: $5-10 Million
Number Employees: 20-49
Square Footage: 100000
Brands:
  Camoco
  Cotton Queen

20280 Carolina Summit Mountain Spring Water
6557 Garden Road
Unit 9
Riviera Beach, FL 33404-6307

561-841-8841
Fax: 828-743-5483 water123@bellsouth.net
bottledwater123.com
Bottled water
President: Tom Mitchell
Estimated Sales: $1-2.5 Million
Number Employees: 10-19
Parent Co: Mountain Valley Spring Company

20281 Carometec Inc
8548 Kapp Dr
Peosta, IA 52068-9759

563-582-4230
Fax: 563-582-4130 js@carometec.com
www.carometec.com
Food equipment for carcass grading and quality control
President: Henrrick Anderson
Sales: Jeb Supple
Manager: Jeb Supple
js@carometec.com
Estimated Sales: Under $500,000
Number Employees: 1-4
Parent Co: Carometec

20282 Caron Products & Svc Inc
27640 State Route 7
P.O. Box 715
Marietta, OH 45750-5146

740-373-6809
Fax: 740-374-3760 800-648-3042
sales@caronproducts.com
www.caronproducts.com
Test chambers, temperature/humidity,photostability chambers,and reach in CO_
Manager: Terry St Peter
CEO: Steve Keiser
Vice President: Joyce Abicht
j.abicht@caronproducts.com
R&D: David Figel
Estimated Sales: Below $5 Million
Number Employees: 10-19
Square Footage: 20000

20283 Carotek Inc
700 Sam Newell Rd
Matthews, NC 28105-4515

704-847-4406
Fax: 704-847-5101 terri.smedley@carotek.com
www.carotek.com
Positive displacement pumps including internal and external rotary gear, magnetic drive and rotary lobe. air-operated double diaphragm pumps and abrasives, solids, corrosives and aggressive materials
President: Rebecca Adler
rebecca.adler@carotek.com
Sales Engineer: Mike Mercredy
Sales and Marketing Assistance: Terri Smedley
Quality Control: Mack A Stewart
Manager: Stephen Bell
Estimated Sales: $20-50 Million
Number Employees: 1-4

20284 Carpenter Advanced Ceramics
13395 New Airport Rd
Auburn, CA 95602

530-823-3401
Fax: 530-888-1087 800-288-8730
cacsales@cartech.com www.cartech.com

President: James West
Quality Control: Marc Fichou
Financial Controller: Sonia Souron
Contact: Janet Brown
jbrown@cartech.com
Estimated Sales: $20-30 Million
Number Employees: 100-249

20285 Carpenter Emergency Lighting
2 Marlen Drive
Hamilton, NJ 08691

609-689-3090
Fax: 609-689-3091 888-884-2270
sales@carpenterlighting.com
www.carpenterlighting.com
Manufacturer and exporter of emergency lighting equipment, emergency exit, portable and recharge-able lights
President: Avinash Diwan
National Sales Manager: Philip Salvatore
Contact: Evi Nash
info@carpenterlighting.com

20286 Carpenter-Hayes Paper Box Company
8 Walnut Avenue
East Hampton, CT 06424-1222

203-267-4436
Fax: 203-425-1769
Folding paper cartons
President: Bill Salinsky
CFO: Bill Salinsky
R&D: Bill Salinsky
Quality Control: Bill Salinsky
Estimated Sales: $5-10 Million
Number Employees: 15

20287 Carpet City Paper Box Company
36 Finlay Street
Amsterdam, NY 12010

518-842-5430
Paper set-up boxes for ravioli and nonperishable food products
Owner: John Bogdan
Estimated Sales: Less than $500,000
Number Employees: 4
Square Footage: 8400

20288 Carpigiani Corporation of America
3760 Industrial Drive
Winston Salem, NC 27105

336-661-9893
Fax: 336-661-9895 800-648-4389
info@carpigiani-usa.com www.carpigiani-usa.com
Manufacturer, importer and exporter of self serve frozen dessert and drink machines, whip cream dis-pensers and batch ice cream freezers
VP: Randy Karns
General Manager: Jim Hall
Sales Manager: Jim Marmion
Operations Manager: Bill Van Hine
National Sales Manager: Jerry Hoefer
Estimated Sales: $5-10 Million
Number Employees: 10-19
Square Footage: 80000
Parent Co: Carpigiani Viaemilia
Type of Packaging: Food Service
Other Locations:
  Coldelite Corp. of America
  Bologna
Brands:
  Coldelite
  Colore
  Kwik Whipper

20289 Carrageenan Company
200 E 61st St Apt 27a
New York, NY 10065-8580

Fax: 714-850-9865
sales@carrageenancompany.com
Processor, importer and exporter of gum and hydrocolloide blends; also, custom blending of carrageenan products for dairy, meat and poultry
President: Vincent Zaragoza
Executive Director: Javier Zaragoza
Marketing Director: Yolanda Zaragoza
Sales Director: Carla Gonzales
Public Relations: Cristina Gonzales
Managing Director: Vincente Zaragoza
Estimated Sales: Below $5 Million
Number Employees: 5-9
Type of Packaging: Private Label

Brands:
Carrabind
Carrafat
Carralite
Carralizer
Carraloc
Carravis

20290 Carrier Corp
1 Carrier Pl
Farmington, CT 06032-2562
800-227-7437
www.carrier.com
Manufacturer and exporter of refrigerating units for delivery trucks, marine containers and commercial refrigeration equipment.
President & CEO: Dave Gitlin
Executive VP & CFO: Tim McLevish
VP & Chief Legal Officer: Kevin O'Connor
VP, Communications & Marketing: Mary Milmoe
VP, Operations: Rishi Grover
Year Founded: 1902
Estimated Sales: $12.5 Billion
Number Employees: 55,000
Brands:
Automated Logic
Carrier
Noresco
UTEC
Autronica
Chubb
Delta Security Solutions
Det-tronics
Edwards
Fireye
GST
Interlogix
Kidde
Lenel-S2
Marioff
Onity
Sicli
Supra
Sensitech

20291 Carrier Rental Systems
9655 Industrial Dr
Bridgeview, IL 60455-2323
847-847-2220
Fax: 847-847-7330 800-586-8336
www.nutemp.com
Refrigeration, chiller sales, rentals and investment recovery
Manager: Laurie Werner
Marketing Manager: David Brockemeyer
Contact: Thomas Benedict
thomas.benedict@carrier.com
Estimated Sales: $5-10 Million
Number Employees: 50-99

20292 Carrier Transicold
1 Carrier Pl
Farmington, CT 06032-2562
www.carrier.com
Manufactures refridgerated units for trucks and trailers.
President: David Appel
Chief Financial Officer: Martha Ingram
Parent Co: Carrier Corporation

20293 (HQ)Carrier Vibrating EquipInc
3400 Fern Valley Rd
Louisville, KY 40213-3554
502-969-3171
Fax: 502-969-3172 cve@carriervibrating.com
www.carriervibrating.com
Manufacturer and exporter of custom designed screening conveyor systems and feeders, bin dischargers, stainless steel dairy dryers, coolers and bulk handling vibrating equipment
CEO: Brian M Trudel
CEO: Brian M Trudel
Sales Manager: Steve Baker
Estimated Sales: $30 Million
Number Employees: 100-249
Square Footage: 185000
Other Locations:
Carrier Europe
Nivelles, Belgium

20294 Carroll Chair Company
411 Mason Street
Onalaska, WI 54650
608-779-7505
Fax: 608-779-7508 800-331-4704
info@carrollchair.com www.carrollchair.com
Bar, restaurant and lounge seating
Member of the Board: Anthony Wilson
Contact: Bill Dykema
bill.dykema@carrollchair.com
General Manager: Keith Martin
Estimated Sales: $10-20 Million
Number Employees: 100-249
Parent Co: Hospitality International
Brands:
Carroll Chair

20295 Carroll Co
2900 W Kingsley Rd
Garland, TX 75041-2378
972-278-1304
Fax: 972-840-0678 800-527-5722
info@carrollco.com www.carrollconverting.com
Manufacturer and exporter of soap, cleaners, disinfectants and germicides
President: Kyle Ogden
CEO: Frank Antonacci
fantonacci@carrollco.com
VP Technical: Ron Cramer
VP Sales: Craig Neely
Estimated Sales: $20-50 Million
Number Employees: 500-999
Square Footage: 220000

20296 Carroll Co
2900 W Kingsley Rd
Garland, TX 75041-2378
972-278-1304
Fax: 972-840-0678 800-527-5722
www.carrollconverting.com
Plastic bags and rollstock; also, printing services available
President: Gene Stys
CEO: Frank Antonacci
fantonacci@carrollco.com
Sales Manager: Gary Denenak
Estimated Sales: $2.5-5 Million
Number Employees: 500-999

20297 Carroll Manufacturing International
23 Vreeland Rd
Florham Park, NJ 07932-1510
973-966-6000
Fax: 973-966-0315 800-444-9696
info@carrollmi.com www.carrollmi.com
Manufacturer and exporter of exhaust systems, fire protection equipment, heat reclaim units and utility distribution systems
Chairman of the Board: Barry J Carroll
VP Sales: Richard Moon
Contact: Bill Burrus
info@carrollmi.com
General Manager: Byron Read
Estimated Sales: $10-15 Million
Number Employees: 10-19
Square Footage: 150000
Parent Co: Carroll International Corporation
Brands:
Aquafire
Carroll
Environair
Hmr Merchandiser
Transporter
Udisco

20298 Carroll Packaging
PO Box 780
Dearborn, MI 48121-0780
313-584-0400
Fax: 313-584-2022
Plastic packaging equipment
President: Hazen Carroll
Estimated Sales: $10-20 Million
Number Employees: 50-99

20299 Carron Net Co Inc
1623 17th St
PO Box 177
Two Rivers, WI 54241-2995
920-793-2217
Fax: 920-793-2122 800-558-7768
sales@carronnet.com www.carronnet.com

Manufacturer and exporter of hardware and netting for racks and conveyors
President/CEO: Bill Kiel Jr
bkieljr@carronnet.com
EVP/CFO: Troy Christiansen
VP: Donald Schweiger
Estimated Sales: $5-10 Million
Number Employees: 20-49
Type of Packaging: Bulk

20300 Carry-All Canvas Bag Co.
1983 Coney Island Ave
Brooklyn, NY 11223-2328
718-375-4230
Fax: 718-375-4230 888-425-5224
sales@carryallbag.com www.carryallbag.com
Advertising specialties, bags and aprons; importer of tote bags; logo imprinting services available
Owner: Mitchel Kraut
Estimated Sales: $400,000

20301 Carson Industries
801 Corporate Center Dr
Pomona, CA 91768
909-592-6272
Fax: 909-592-7971 800-735-5566
info@carsonind.com www.carsonind.com
Plastic bulk containers and pallets
President: Richard Gardner
CEO: Richard Gordinier
Sales Coordinator: Roscoe Bes
Estimated Sales: $20-50 Million
Number Employees: 20-49
Brands:
Titan I
Titan Ii

20302 Carson Manufacturing Company
PO Box 750338
Petaluma, CA 94975-0338
707-778-3141
Fax: 707-778-8691 800-423-2380
sales@carsonmanufacturing.com
www.carsonmfg.com
Manufacturer and exporter of vinyl aprons
President: Curtis Lang
Number Employees: 10-19
Type of Packaging: Private Label, Bulk

20303 Cart Mart
PO Box 686
Itasca, IL 60143-0686
630-628-6655
Fax: 630-628-6855 800-628-3183
Material handling products including pallet rack, carts and used equipment
Estimated Sales: $1-2.5 000,000
Number Employees: 1-4

20304 Carter & Burgess Food and Beverage Division
777 Main Street
Fort Worth, TX 76102-5304
817-735-600
Fax: 817-735-6148
Carter & Burgess' Food & Beverage professionals specialize in the design, construction, and management of facilities for meat, poultry, RTE prepared foods, beverage, dairy, produce, bakery and seafood.
Senior Consultant Food Processing: Jim Short
Contact: Deepak Agarwal
deepak.agarwal@c-b.com

20305 Carter Products
2871 Northridge Dr NW
Grand Rapids, MI 49544-9109
616-647-3380
Fax: 616-647-3387 888-622-7837
sales@carterproducts.com
www.carterproducts.com
Manufacturer and exporter of guide line and inspection lights; also, bandsaw guides, wheels and tires
President: Peter Perez
perez@carterproducts.com
VP: Terry Camp
Marketing Director: Kip Walworth
Operations Manager: Jeff Folkert
Purchasing Manager: Char Mooney
Estimated Sales: $3-5 Million
Number Employees: 20-49
Square Footage: 30000
Brands:
Carter
Flip-Pod

Guidall
Inspecto-Light
Laser
Laser Diode
Micro-Precision

20306 Carter-Day International Inc
500 73rd Ave NE # 100
Minneapolis, MN 55432-3271

763-571-1000
Fax: 763-571-3012 bulldog@carterday.com
www.carterday.com
Manufacturer and exporter of grain cleaning and sizing equipment
President: Paul Ernst
HR Executive: Tim Ryan
bulldog@carterday.com
Director International Agribusiness: Matthew Ernst
Estimated Sales: $10-20 Million
Number Employees: 100-249

20307 Carter-Hoffmann LLC
1551 Mccormick Blvd
Mundelein, IL 60060-4491

847-362-5500
Fax: 847-367-8981 800-323-9793
sales@carter-hoffmann.com
www.carter-hoffmann.com
Manufacturer and exporter of stainless steel food carts including refrigerator, banquet and heated holding/transport
President: Bob Fortmann
jfagan@carter-hoffman.com
CFO: Jim Fagan
CEO: Robert Fortman
Research & Development: Jim Minard
Marketing Director: Kim Aaron
Sales Director: Mark Anderson
IT Executive: Jim Fagan
Production Manager: John Bartoski
Purchasing Manager: Vince Unger
Estimated Sales: $20-25 Million
Number Employees: 100-249
Number of Products: 300+
Brands:
Carter-Hoffmann

20308 Carteret Coding Inc
1431 Raritan Rd
Clark, NJ 07066-1230

732-574-0900
Fax: 732-574-9212 ccisales@carteretcoding.com
www.carteretcoding.com
Date and lot coding systems
Owner: Charles Vill
Number Employees: 1-4

20309 Carthage Cup Company
115 Kodak Blvd
Longview, TX 75602

903-238-9833
Plastic cups, plates, bowls, deli containers and portion cups; also, hotel/motel wrapped cups with printing capability available
President: C Mark Abernathy
VP Consumer Sales: William Tostlebe
VP Institutional Sales: Brent Abernathy
Number Employees: 1 to 4
Parent Co: John Waddington
Brands:
Carthage
Cool Cups
Holiday

20310 Carton Closing Company
P.O.Box 629
Butler, PA 16003-0629

724-287-7759
Fax: 724-287-2811
Industrial staples and staplers for corrugated carton closing
Marketing Manager: Mary Lawler
Sales Manager: Robert McHugh
Purchasing Manager: Paul Lucas
Estimated Sales: $1-5 Million
Number Employees: 100-249

20311 Carton Service Co
2 Franklin Ave
Shelby, OH 44875-1661

419-342-5010
Fax: 419-342-4804 800-533-7744
www.cartonservice.com

Boxes and cartons; contract packaging services available
Vice President: Scott Garverick
scott.ferguson@rauantiques.com
VP: Mike Robinette
Marketing/Sales: Scott Garverick
Estimated Sales: $20-50 Million
Number Employees: 250-499

20312 Cartonplast
609 Burton Blvd
De Forest, WI 53532-1289

608-846-2516
Fax: 608-849-4496 info@cartonplast.com
www.cartonplast.com
Plastic tier sheets, plastic layer pads, layer pad pool system
Estimated Sales: less than $500,000
Number Employees: 1-4

20313 Cartpac Inc
245 E North Ave
Carol Stream, IL 60188-2021

630-510-1100
Fax: 630-629-6575 www.fraingroup.com
Rebuilt cartoner and case filling equipment; repair services available
President: Richard Frain
rfrain@fraingroup.com
CEO: Rich Frain
CFO: Chris Hostert
Senior Engineer: Thomas Suchan
Sales Manager: Steve Norman
HR Director: Olga Sivek
General Manager: Kenneth Campbell
Manager Engineer: Len Thomsen
Estimated Sales: Below $5 Million
Number Employees: 50-99
Square Footage: 126000
Parent Co: Frain Industries

20314 Carts Food Equipment
113 8th St
Brooklyn, NY 11215-3115

718-788-5540
Fax: 718-788-4962 www.cartsfoodeqp.com
Sinks, reach-in and underbar refrigerators and marble top pizza and stainless steel work tables; exporter of mobile food vending carts
Owner: David Nadler
dave@cartsfoodeqp.com
CFO: Florence Rosenberg
VP: Dave Nadler
Estimated Sales: $2.5-5 Million
Number Employees: 10-19
Square Footage: 120000

20315 Carts Of Colorado Inc
5420 S Quebec St # 204
Suite 204
Greenwood Vlg, CO 80111-1902

303-329-0101
Fax: 303-329-6577 800-227-8634
carts@cartsofcolorado.com
www.cartsofcolorado.com
Manufacturer and exporter of mobile food carts, kiosks, and modular systems
President: Dan Gallery
dgallery@cartsofcolorado.com
Accountant: Bill Sheakin
Research & Development: Craig Green
Quality Control Manager: Jeff Clonk
Sales Director: John Gallery
Operations Manager: Jim Covey
Purchasing Manager: Deborah Gallery
Estimated Sales: $500,000-$1 Million
Number Employees: 10-19
Number of Brands: 4
Number of Products: 10
Square Footage: 240000
Brands:
Carts of Colorado
Mobile Merchandising Systems
Peckam Carts
Power Carts

20316 Casa Herrera
2655 Pine St
Pomona, CA 91767-2115

909-392-3930
Fax: 909-392-0231 800-624-3916
rudyh@casaherrera.com www.casaherrera.com

Manufacturer and exporter of tortilla and corn chip machinery including cookers, millers, sheeters, bakers, coolers, dividers, pressers, seasoners, etc
President: Michael Herrera
michaelh@casaherrera.com
CEO: Ron Meade
VP Sales: Christopher Herrera
Manager: Susana Herrera
Estimated Sales: $20-50 Million
Number Employees: 100-249
Square Footage: 100000

20317 Casa Herrera
2655 Pine St
Pomona, CA 91767-2115

909-392-3930
Fax: 909-392-0231 800-624-3916
alfredoj@casaherrera.com www.casaherrera.com
Food processing machines for commercial and industrial food makers
President: Michael Herrera
michaelh@casaherrera.com
Manager: Christopher Herrera
Mngr.: Susana Herrera
Estimated Sales: $20-50 Million
Number Employees: 100-249

20318 Casabar
42 Court St
Morristown, NJ 07960-5199

973-605-8995
Fax: 973-401-1519 877-745-8700
Instant Dip silver cleaner and polishing cloths
President: Mel Appelbaum
m3@casabar.com
Administrative Assistant: Irene Carpio
General Manager: Mel Sales
Estimated Sales: Less than $500,000
Number Employees: 1-4
Brands:
Instant Dip

20319 Cascade Earth Sciences
3511 Pacific Blvd SW
Albany, OR 97321-7727

541-926-7737
Fax: 503-967-7619 albany@cascade-earth.com
www.cascade-earth.com
President: Perry Rahe
CAO: Dayla Rabe
dayla@cascade-earth.com
CEO: Steel Maloney
Estimated Sales: G
Number Employees: 5000-9999

20320 Cascade Signs & Neon
2166 Wayside Ter NE
Salem, OR 97301-0323

503-378-0012
Fax: 503-362-8154 info@cascade-signs.com
www.cascade-signs.com
Electric neon signs
Owner: Jay Kinnee
jay@cascade-signs.com
Estimated Sales: $500,000-$1 Million
Number Employees: 5-9

20321 Cascade Wood Components
15 Herman Creek Road
Cascade Locks, OR 97014

541-374-8413
Fax: 541-374-9054
Wooden pallets
President: Gary Hegewald
Manager: Gene Shultz
gschultz@cascadewood.com
Sales Manager: Tim Todd
Office Manager: Gene Hill
Estimated Sales: $10-20 Million
Number Employees: 10 to 19

20322 Case Lowe & Hart Architects
2484 Washington Blvd # 510
Suite 510
Ogden, UT 84401-2346

801-399-5821
Fax: 801-399-0728 kevinl@clhae.com
www.clhae.com
President: Kevin Lewis
kevinl@clhae.com
Estimated Sales: $1-3 Million
Number Employees: 10-19

20323 Case Manufacturing Company
14304 29th Rd
Flushing, NY 11354-2312

914-965-5100
Fax: 914-965-2362 casestaty@aol.com
Tea and coffee industry coffee canisters
President: Jerome Sudnow
Estimated Sales: $1-5 000,000
Number Employees: 10

20324 Caselites
PO Box 161000
Hialeah, FL 33016-0017

305-819-7766
Fax: 305-819-8198 www.caselites.com
Lighting for steam tables, and refrigerated/nonrefrigerated cases. Also special lighting for food equipment
President: Barry Spade
R & D: Fred Morgan
Estimated Sales: $50-100 Million
Number Employees: 10
Square Footage: 10000

20325 Casella Lighting
10183 Croydon Way # C
Suite C
Sacramento, CA 95827-2103

916-363-2888
Fax: 888-489-9543 Info@CasellaLighting.com
www.casellalighting.com
Manufacturer and exporter of portable floor and table lamps, wall sconces, chandeliers and solid brass fixtures
Owner: Chuck Bird
chuck@casellalighting.com
Buyer: Margig Yaka
Office Manager: Ronda Simi
Estimated Sales: $5-10 Million
Number Employees: 5-9
Square Footage: 120000
Type of Packaging: Food Service
Brands:
    Casella
    Grag Studios

20326 Cash Caddy
PO Box 13770
Palm Desert, CA 92255-3770

760-772-8884
Fax: 760-772-8885 888-522-2221
cashcaddy@aol.com
Change, dinner check and tip trays
Sales Manager: Eddie Robinson
General Manager: Judy Wilkins
Number Employees: 30
Square Footage: 12000
Parent Co: Plastic By Design
Brands:
    Cash Caddy
    Dinner Check

20327 Cashco Inc
607 W 15th St
Ellsworth, KS 67439-1624

785-472-4461
Fax: 785-472-3539 sales@cashco.com
www.cashco.com
Regulators, control valves and sanitary biotechnological products for the food and pharmaceutical industry
President: Philip Rogers
philipr@cashco.com
National Sales Manager: Robert Schroeder
Estimated Sales: $10-20 Million
Number Employees: 100-249

20328 Cass Saw & Tool Sharpening
3916 N Cass Ave
Westmont, IL 60559-1103

630-968-1617
Fax: 630-968-7767
Saw and knife sharpeners, carbide retipping and chain and circular saws
Owner: Sam Robertson
Manager: Joseph Robertson
Estimated Sales: Less than $500,000
Number Employees: 1 to 4

20329 Cassel Box & Lumber Co Inc
1100 Falls Rd
Grafton, WI 53024-9728

262-377-9503
Fax: 262-377-4421 www.casselboxlumber.com

Wooden boxes, crates, skids and pallets
President: John Cassel
Vice President: Craig Cassel
craigcassel@casselboxlumber.com
Manager: John Cassel
Estimated Sales: $500,000-$1 Million
Number Employees: 10-19

20330 Casso-Solar Corporation
506 Airport Executive Park
P.O. Box 163
Nanuet, NY 10954

845-354-2010
Fax: 845-547-0328 800-988-4455
sales@cassosolartechnologies.com
www.cassosolar.com
Manufacturer and exporter of dryers, ovens, and electric and gas conveyor systems
President: Doug Canfield
VP Finance: Harry Lyons
Quality Control Manager: Alex Mankiewicz
VP Sales/Marketing: Frank Lu
Plant Manager: Jan Michalski
Purchasing Manager: John Moles
Estimated Sales: $10 Million
Number Employees: 20-49
Number of Products: 100
Square Footage: 50000
Brands:
    Solar Infrared Heater

20331 Cast Film Technology
7455 E Adamo Drive
Tampa, FL 33619-3433

847-487-8899
Fax: 847-487-7288
Edible plastic films, customized films made with food ingredients for packaging and barrier uses
President: James Rossman
Vice President: Scott Schaneville
Research & Development: Caroline Decker
Estimated Sales: $8 Million
Number Employees: 50
Number of Products: 15
Square Footage: 80000

20332 Cast Nylons LTD
4300 Hamann Pkwy
Willoughby, OH 44094-5626

440-269-2300
Fax: 440-269-2323 800-543-3619
cnlmail@castnylon.com
Manufacuturer of cast nylon materials
President: Jack Thorp
jackthorp@castnylon.com
CFO: Dan Welsh
VP: Steve Tischler
Quality Control: Tom Schaffer
Marketing Head: Shelly Pike
Sales: Traci Deiner
Estimated Sales: $10-20 000,000
Number Employees: 50-99
Type of Packaging: Bulk

20333 Castell Interlocks Inc
150 N Michigan Ave # 800
Sutie 800
Chicago, IL 60601-7585

312-360-1516
Fax: 312-268-5174 ussales@castell.com
www.castell.com
Dock locks
President: Bryan Gregory
bgregory@castell.com
Number Employees: 10-19

20334 Castella Imports Inc
120 A Wilshire Blvd
Brentwood, NY 11717

631-231-5500
Cheeses, spices, olives and olive oils
Estimated Sales: $100+ Million
Number Employees: 250-499
Square Footage: 66000

20335 Castino Restaurant Equipment
50 Utility Ct
Rohnert Park, CA 94928-1659

800-238-0404
Fax: 707-585-7306 800-238-0404
solutions@castinosolutions.com
www.castinosolutions.com

Wholesaler/distributor of restaurant equipment, kitchen equipment, furniture, refrigeration hood systems, chinaware, glassware, pots, pans, etc
President/CEO: David Castino
david_castino@castinosolutions.com
Purchasing Manager: Ron Nasuti
Estimated Sales: $8 Million
Number Employees: 5-9
Square Footage: 60000
Parent Co: Castino Refrigeration Company

20336 Castle Bag Co.
115 Valley Rd.
Wilmington, DE 19804

302-656-1001
Fax: 302-656-2830
sales@castlebagcompany.comcastbiz.net
www.castlebag.com
Polyethylene bags.
President/Owner: Harry Russell
castlebag@juno.com
VP/Secretary: Christine Ditzler
Year Founded: 1969
Estimated Sales: $750 Million
Number Employees: 1-4
Square Footage: 6000
Type of Packaging: Consumer, Food Service, Private Label, Bulk
Brands:
    Castle Bag

20337 Castrol Industrial
201 N Webster St
White Cloud, MI 49349-9678

231-689-0002
Fax: 231-689-0372 800-582-3266
lubeconcc@castrol.com www.lubecon.com
Lubrication equipment, conveyor cleaners, lubricants, machinery lubrication
BDM: Frank Langley
BDM: Ted Edwards
BDM: Jerry Robinson
Site Manager: Michael Bailey
michael.bailey@castrol.com
Production Manager: Kathy Crickmore
Purchasing Manager: Chris Warren
Estimated Sales: $10-20 Million
Number Employees: 10-19
Square Footage: 10000

20338 Cat Inc
201 S Erie Ave
Russellville, AR 72801-5265

479-890-3433
Fax: 479-967-2651 888-890-3433
www.gocatgo.biz
Supplier of chilling systems, whole muscle pumps, plant monitoring and weighing systems
CEO: Mike Miller
mike.miller@catsquared.com
CEO: Michael Miller
Principal: Dion Henson
Estimated Sales: $26 Million
Number Employees: 50-99

20339 Cat Pumps
1681 94th Ln NE
Minneapolis, MN 55449-4372

763-780-5440
Fax: 763-780-2958 techsupport@catpumps.com
www.catpumps.com
Manufacturer and exporter of pumps including high-pressure, positive displacement, piston and plunger, stainless steel, hightemp, custom designed power units, submersible and end-suction centrifugal
CEO: William Bruggeman
CEO: William Bruggeman
Marketing Director: Darla Jean Thompson
Sales: Scott Stelzner
Estimated Sales: $50-100 Million
Number Employees: 100-249
Square Footage: 130000
Brands:
    Cat Pumps

20340 (HQ)Catalent Pharma Solutions Inc
1100 Enterprise Dr
Winchester, KY 40391-9668

859-745-8679
Fax: 859-745-6636 www.catalent.com
Consultant offering agglomeration, instantizing, encapsulation and solids drying services

President: David Heyens
President, Chief Executive Officer: John Chiminski
Vice President of Audit: Charles Silvey
Senior Vice President of Quality: Sharon Johnson
Senior Vice President of Sales and Marke: Will Downie
Manager: Steve Havel
shavel@cardinalhealth.com
VP Business Development: Michael Valazza
Estimated Sales: $19.7 Million
Number Employees: 250-499
Square Footage: 200000
Other Locations:
International Processing Corp
Ramsey NJ

20341 Catalina Cylinders
7300 Anaconda Ave
Garden Grove, CA 92841-2930

714-890-0999
Fax: 714-890-1744 sales@catalinacylinders.com
www.catalinacylinders.com
Empty aluminum high pressure CO2 cylinders aluminum cylinders to the compressed gas industry
President: Tom Newell
Quality Control: Ward Dekker
Sales Director: Michael Krupsky
Manager: Doug Burtt
d.burtt@catalinacylinders.com
Estimated Sales: $10-20 000,000
Number Employees: 100-249

20342 Catalyst International
1285 101st Street
Lemont, IL 60439

630-972-9800
Fax: 630-972-9876 800-236-4600
info@cdcsupply.com www.cdcsupply.com
Manufacturer and exporter of computer software for warehouse management
President: J Scott Pearson
CEO: Mitchell Radar
CFO: Tim Ward
Office Manager: Laurie Goodwin
VP, Business Development: Thomas Geza Varga
Controller: Mike Grecco
Marketing Coordinator: Wendy Erwin
Director Of Sales: Bryan Gaines
VP Operations: James H Martin
Number Employees: 70
Type of Packaging: Bulk

20343 Catalytic Products IntlInc
980 Ensell Rd
Lake Zurich, IL 60047-1557

847-438-0334
Fax: 847-438-0944 info@cpilink.com
www.cpilink.com
Air pollution control equipment, baking oven emission control, catalytic and thermal oxidizers
President: Dennis Lincoln
Vice President: Scott Christopher
scott.christopher@cpilink.com
Marketing Manager: Jan Carlson
Estimated Sales: $1-2.5 000,000
Number Employees: 20-49

20344 CaterMate
61 Brown Road
Ithaca, NY 14850-1247

800-486-2283
Fax: 607-257-1902 www.catermate.com
Software for catering and event management
President: John Alexander
VP: Tim Tighe
Marketing: Susie Stephnson
Sales Manager: Ron Prorus
Contact: Peter Martini
petermartini@cbord.com
Number Employees: 10-19
Parent Co: The CBORD Group, Inc.
Type of Packaging: Food Service
Brands:
Eventmaster

20345 Catering Co
24833 Commercial Ave
Orange Beach, AL 36561-3845

251-974-5000
Fax: 251-974-5640 www.catering.com
Owner: J Schenck
hazels@gulftel.com
Vice President: J Hall Schenck
Estimated Sales: Below 1 Million
Number Employees: 10-19

20346 Cates Mechanical Corp
3901 Corporation Cir
Charlotte, NC 28216-3420

704-392-8932
Fax: 704-392-8932
ernest.cates@catesmechanical.com
www.catesmechanical.com
Packaging machinery
President: John Cates
tom.cates@catesmechanical.com
Estimated Sales: Below $5 000,000
Number Employees: 5-9

20347 Catskill Craftsmen Inc
15 W End Ave
Stamford, NY 12167-1296

607-652-7321
Fax: 607-652-7293 info@catskillcraftsmen.com
www.catskillcraftsmen.com
Manufacturer and exporter of butcher block tables, cutting boards, solid maple housewares and kitchen furniture and work counters
President: Duncan Axtel
catskill@telenet.net
Vice President: Kenneth Smith
Quality Control: John Locastro
VP Sales: Dick Carpenter
Purchasing Manager: Hank Cioccari
Estimated Sales: $5-10 Million
Number Employees: 50-99
Number of Products: 17
Square Footage: 208000
Type of Packaging: Consumer, Food Service, Private Label

20348 Cattron Group International
25 W Shenango St
Sharpsville, PA 16150-1123

724-962-1629
Fax: 724-962-4310
Cattron Group International, including the Cattron, Remtron, Theimeg and Vectran brands, provides industrial radio remote control systems for overhead cranes, hoists, conveyors, yard locomotives, overhead doors, boom trucks, concretepumps or anywhere the operator of equipment can be moved to a safer, more efficient location.
President/CEO: John Paul
CFO: Mike Pearson
Marketing/Public Relations: Amanda Bailey
Sales: Jeremy Pearson
Contact: Alan Anglemyer
aanglemyer@cattron-theimeg.com
Production: Rich Patterson
Estimated Sales: $10-20 Million
Number Employees: 100-249
Number of Brands: 6
Parent Co: Laird Technologies
Other Locations:
Cattron Group-Remtron
Escondido CA
Brands:
Cattron
Remtron
Theimeg
Vectran

20349 Catty Inc
6111 White Oaks Rd
Harvard, IL 60033-8307

815-943-2288
Fax: 815-943-4473 plawther@cattycorp.com
www.cattycorp.com
Manufacturer and exporter of flexible packaging including foil, foil/paper, poly structures, margarine and candy wraps and lidding
President: Vincent Jefferson
vince.jefferson@comcast.net
CFO: Bill Schmiederer
Marketing and Sales Coordinator: Kristen Dahm
Sales Manager: Sheri Morelli
Operations Manager: Chuck DiPietro
Vice President, Engineering: Ron Klint
Number Employees: 50-99
Square Footage: 270000

20350 Cavalla Inc
111 Union St
Hackensack, NJ 07601-4083

201-343-3338
Fax: 201-487-1096 www.cavalla.com
Equipment
President: Arthur Pisani
apisani@cavalla.net

Estimated Sales: $5-10 Million
Number Employees: 20-49

20351 Cavanna Packaging USA Inc
2150 Northmont Pkwy # A
Suite A
Duluth, GA 30096-5835

770-688-1501
Fax: 973-383-0741 www.cavanna.com
Wholesaler/distributor of horizontal flow wrapping machinery
President: William Stoebling
Contact: Adam Caplan
a.caplan@cavannagroup.com
Estimated Sales: Below $5 Million
Number Employees: 10-19

20352 (HQ)Cavert Wire Co
620 Forum Pkwy
Rural Hall, NC 27045-8934

336-969-2601
Fax: 336-969-2621 800-245-4042
cspittler@cavertwire.com www.cavertwire.com
Single loop wire bale ties used in supermarkets for waste corrugated boxes
Owner: Chuck Spittler
CFO: Harry Sages
VP Sales: Ben Shifler
cspittler@cavertwire.com
Estimated Sales: $20-50 Million
Number Employees: 20-49
Square Footage: 200000
Other Locations:
Cavert Wire Co.
Atlanta GA

20353 Cawley Co
1544 N 8th St
PO Box 2110
Manitowoc, WI 54220-1902

920-686-7000
Fax: 920-686-7080 800-822-9539
info@cawleyco.com www.thecawleyco.com
Manufacturer and exporter of engravable badges, plates, plaques and awards; also, electronic personalization systems for do-it-yourself engraving
President/CEO: Jim Peterson
CFO: Jerry Harris
HR Executive: Jean Slaby
jeans@thecawleyco.com
R & D: Jim Peterson
Quality Control: Paul Mueller
Marketing Director: Molly Peterson
Public Relations: Molly Peterson
Operations/Productions Manager: Paul Mueller
Plant Manager: Diane Fogltanz
Estimated Sales: Below $5 Million
Number Employees: 100-249
Square Footage: 112000
Parent Co: Contemporary
Brands:
Champ Awards
Chrom-A-Grav
Engravable Gifts

20354 Cayne Industrial Sales Corp
429 Bruckner Blvd
Bronx, NY 10455-5007

718-993-5800
Fax: 718-402-9465
Manufacturer and exporter of industrial racks, handling equipment and food lockers including custom plastic.
President: Steven Cayne
Manager: Hank Cayne
hankcayne@aol.com
Estimated Sales: Less Than $500,000
Number Employees: 1-4
Square Footage: 20000
Brands:
Uni-Steel Lockers

20355 Cci Industries-Cool Curtain
350 Fischer Ave # A
Costa Mesa, CA 92626-4508

714-662-3879
Fax: 714-662-0943 800-854-5719
www.coolcurtain.com
Freezer curtains, fly traps and broiler griddles
President: Michael Robinson
Sales Manager: Randy Wall
VP Production: Marion Mills
Estimated Sales: $5-10 Million
Number Employees: 1-4
Square Footage: 16000

Brands:
Clear Vu

20356 Ccw Products
5861 Tennyson St
Arvada, CO 80003-6902
303-427-9663
Fax: 303-427-1608 vickie.h@ccwproducts.com
www.ccwproducts.com
Manufacturer and exporter of clear wide-mouth
plastic containers used for food packaging and
point-of-purchase displays
President: David Teneyck
CEO: Mort Saffer
Sales Manager: Donald Johnston
Contact: Mirza Beg
beg@ccwproducts.com
Operations Manager: Roger Lamb
Estimated Sales: Less Than $500,000
Number Employees: 1-4
Number of Products: 300+
Square Footage: 160000
Type of Packaging: Consumer, Food Service, Private Label, Bulk

20357 Cecor
102 Lincoln St
Verona, WI 53593-1599
608-845-6771
Fax: 608-845-6792 800-356-9042
cecor@cecor.net www.chipcarts.net
Waste handling equipment including dumping containers, sump cleaners and filter units for separation
of solids from liquids
President: Dennis Johnson
djohnson@cecor.net
Production Manager: Paul Elmer
Estimated Sales: $2.5-5 Million
Number Employees: 5-9
Brands:
Cecor

20358 Cedar Box Co
2012 Cedar Ave S
Minneapolis, MN 55404-3199
612-332-4287
Fax: 612-332-8619 sales@cedarboxcompany.com
www.cedarboxcompany.com
Corrugated and wooden boxes, wooden pallets
skids, specialty wood bases, and specialty wood
blocking
President: Michael Mintz
mike@cedarboxco.com
Owner: Jefferey Migershone
CFO: Michael Mintz
Purchasing Agent: C Skjeveland
Estimated Sales: $5-10 Million
Number Employees: 20-49
Square Footage: 30000

20359 Ceilcote Air Pollution Control
7251 Engle Rd
Suite 300
Middleburg Hts, OH 44130
440-243-0700
Fax: 440-243-9854 800-554-8673
1us@verantis.com www.verantis.com
Manufacturer and exporter of air pollution control
equipment including fans, tower packing, blowers,
mist eliminators, resin systems and ionizing wet
scrubbers, turn key systems, emergency vapor spill
equipment
President: Larry Hein
CEO: Lars Buttkus
Sales: John Tonkewicz
Engineering Director: Nat Dickinson
Number Employees: 20-49
Square Footage: 100000
Brands:
Duracor
Iws
Tellerette

20360 Celebrity Promotions
P.O.Box 200
Remsen, IA 51050
712-786-1100
Fax: 712-786-2900 800-332-6847
sewncm@midlands.net
Aprons and re-usable cloth shopping bags inclduing
washable and poly-cotton; screen printing and embroidery available

CFO: Connie Mueller
QC and R&D: Paul Mueller
VP Marketing: Mark Mueller
Estimated Sales: Below $5 Million
Number Employees: 20-49
Square Footage: 36000
Brands:
Celebrity Stars

20361 Celite Corporation
2500 San Miguelito Rd
Lompoc, CA 93436
805-736-1221
Fax: 805-736-1222 info@worldminerals.com
www.worldminerals.com
Manufacturer and exporter of diatomite filter aids
and functional fillers; also, absorbents, synthetic calcium silicate and mineral fillers
CEO: John Oskam
Contact: George Christoferson
christofersong@worldminerals.com
Estimated Sales: $5-10 Million
Number Employees: 250-499

20362 Cell-O-Core Company
6935 Ridge Road
PO Box 342
Sharon Center, OH 44274-0342
330-239-4370
Fax: 330-239-4403 800-239-4370
cellocore@cellocore.com www.cellocore.com
Cocktail stirrers, straws and wooden and plastic
toothpicks
President: Craig Cook
Quality Control: Damm Damwillan
R&D: Mathew Willam
CFO: Creak Cook
Director: Hugh Alpeter
Director: Jill Hoffman
Contact: Thomas Allen
allenthomas@cellocore.com
(Distributor Service): Dede Beynon
Estimated Sales: $5-10 Million
Number Employees: 20-49
Square Footage: 60000
Brands:
Cell-O-Core

20363 Cellier Corporation
135 Robert Treat Paine Drive
Taunton, MA 02780-7266
508-655-5906
Fax: 508-653-2508
Paper coatings and kitchen lube oil
Acting General Manager: Stephen Noworski
Number Employees: 10

20364 Cello Bag Company
123 Willamette Lane
Bowling Green, KY 42101-9170
800-347-0338
Fax: 270-782-7478
Packaging materials including plastic bags and film
Number Employees: 25

20365 Cellofoam North America
1917 Rockdale Industrial Blvd
PO Box 406
Conyers, GA 30012
770-483-4491
Fax: 770-929-3608 800-241-3634
info@cellofoam.com www.cellofoam.com
Manufacturer and exporter of expanded polystyrene
foam insulation
President: Steve Gardner
VP Sales/Marketing: Cliff Hanson
Estimated Sales: $10-20 Million
Number Employees: 100-249
Brands:
Cello Foam
Permafloat
Permaspan
Poly Shield
Super Sheath

20366 Cellotape, Inc.
39611 Eureka Dr
Newark, CA 94560
510-651-5551
Fax: 510-651-8091 sales@cellotape.com
cellotape.com
Adhesive panels and pressure sensitive labels
President & CEO: Peter Offerman
VP, Sales: Steve Suppa

Estimated Sales: $50-100 Million
Number Employees: 100-249
Square Footage: 35000

20367 Cellox Corp
1200 Industrial St
Reedsburg, WI 53959-2154
608-524-2316
Fax: 608-524-2362 sales@cellox.com
www.cellox.com
Manufacturer and exporter of packaging supplies
and plastic molding for advertising displays
President: Craig Hutchison
Estimated Sales: $10-20 Million
Number Employees: 50-99

20368 (HQ)Cellucap Manufacturing Co
4626 N 15th St
Philadelphia, PA 19140-1197
215-324-1541
Fax: 215-324-1290 800-523-3814
sales@cellucap.com www.cellucap.com
Personal protective apparel with a full range of
headwear, disposable apparel, aprons and gloves
President: Jane Harris
cellucap@aol.com
Executive VP: Mark Davis
VP Sales: John Twamley
VP Sales: Nancy Lozoff
Operations Manager: David Richman
Estimated Sales: $2.5-5 Million
Number Employees: 20-49
Type of Packaging: Food Service

20369 Celplast Metallized Products Limited
67 Commander Boulevard
Unit 4
Toronto, ON M1S-3M7
Canada
416-293-4330
Fax: 416-293-9198 800-866-0059
jim@celplast.com http://cmp.celplast.com
Producer and manufacturer of metallized films for
the food industry.
President/Founder: Chuck Larsen
CEO: Dante Ferrari
Vice President: Bill Hellings
Technical Representative: Dante Ferrari
Technical Sales: Jim Lush
Account Manager: Naomi Panagrapka

20370 Celsis
400 W Erie St Ste 300
Chicago, IL 60654
312-476-1200
Fax: 312-476-1201 800-222-8260
ATP bioluminescence end product screening systems
CEO: Jay Le Coque
Contact: Lori Daane
ldaane@celsis.com
Estimated Sales: $5-10 000,000
Number Employees: 5-9

20371 Celsis Laboratory Group
600 W. Chicago Avenue
Suite 625
Chicago, IL 60654-2822
312-476-1282
Fax: 312-476-1201 800-222-8260
RDinfo@celsis.com www.celsis.com
Consultant and independent testing laboratory specializing in microbiology, analytical chemistry and
toxicology testing services
Chief Executive Officer: Jay Lecoque
Manager Marketing Development: Martin Gilman,
Ph.D.
Contact: Bhavna Solanki
bsolanki@celsis.com
Associate Director: William Gilman
Estimated Sales: $5-10 Million
Number Employees: 50-99
Square Footage: 140000
Parent Co: Celsis Laboratory Group

20372 Centennial Moldings
1830 Centennial Ave
1900 Summit Ave
Hastings, NE 68901-6712
402-462-2173
Fax: 402-461-3219 888-883-2189
www.centennialplastics.com
Manufacturer and exporter of plastic tanks and
drums

CEO: G Peter Konen
Sales Manager: Jeff Armstrong
Product Manager: Val Kopke
Plant Manager: Bob Shockey
Estimated Sales: $1 Million
Number Employees: 5-9
Number of Brands: 1
Number of Products: 3
Square Footage: 600000
Type of Packaging: Food Service, Private Label, Bulk
Brands:
 Pure-Life

20373 Centennial Transportation Industries
P.O.Box 708
Columbus, GA 31902-0708

706-323-6446
Fax: 706-327-9921

Manager: Bob Hudak
Estimated Sales: $10-20 Million
Number Employees: 50-99

20374 Centent Co
3879 S Main St
Santa Ana, CA 92707-5787

714-979-6491
Fax: 714-979-4241 info@centent.com
www.centent.com

Manufacturer and exporter of industrial controls for factory automation including computer guided multiple axis positioning systems
President: August Freimanis
august.freimanis@centent.com
Estimated Sales: $2.5-5 Million
Number Employees: 10-19

20375 Center for Packaging Education
358 Route 202
Somers, NY 10589-3234

914-276-0425
Fax: 914-276-0428

Consultant and educators in packaging, provide expert testimony in legal conflicts
President: Dr. Robert Goldberg
Vice President: Mark Goldsberg
Estimated Sales: Less than $500,000
Number Employees: 1-4
Square Footage: 4000

20376 Centi Mark Corp
401 Technology Dr # 2
Canonsburg, PA 15317-7538

724-514-8700
Fax: 724-743-7770 jason.meyers@centimark.com
www.centimark.com

Cleaners, flooring, floor grating, floor and wall coating materials, paints and enamels
President: Timothy Dunlap
Contact: Robert Detweiler
robert.detweiler@centimark.com
Estimated Sales: H
Number Employees: 20-49

20377 Central Bag Co
4901 S 4th St
Leavenworth, KS 66048-5003

913-250-0325
Fax: 913-727-1760 sales@centralbagcompany.com
www.centralbagcompany.com

Bags including burlap, cotton and polypropylene multi-wall; also, shrink wrap
President: Walter Cordova
waltercordova@centralbagcompany.com
Sales: Dog Cross
Estimated Sales: $5-10 Million
Number Employees: 50-99

20378 Central Coated ProductsInc
2025 Mccrea St
Alliance, OH 44601-2794

330-821-9830
Fax: 330-821-3114
www.centralcoatedproducts.com

Coated paper packaging materials
President: Thomas Tormey
sporter@centralcoatedproducts.com
VP: Steve Porter
Sales Exec: Steve Porter
Estimated Sales: $10-20 Million
Number Employees: 50-99

20379 Central Decal
6901 High Grove Blvd
Burr Ridge, IL 60527-7583

630-325-9892
Fax: 630-325-9878 800-869-7654
info@centraldecal.com www.centraldecal.com

Manufacturer and exporter of flexible nameplates, pressure sensitive labels and decals
President: Bob Keflin
bkeflin@centraldecal.com
CFO: Jennifer Loconte
VP: Robert Kaplan
Sales Manager: George Labine
Estimated Sales: $10-20 Million
Number Employees: 50-99
Square Footage: 60000

20380 Central Electropolishing Company
124 N Lawrence Ave
Anthony, KS 67003

620-842-3701
Fax: 620-842-3208 877-200-5488
steve@celcoinc.com www.celcoinc.com

Electropolishing, passivation and oxygen cleaning of stainless steel and other alloys
President: Kenneth Bellesine
CFO: Kim Bell
Quality Control: Jerry Smith
Estimated Sales: $2.5-5 000,000
Number Employees: 20-49

20381 Central Fabricators Inc
408 Poplar St
Cincinnati, OH 45214-2481

513-621-1240
Fax: 513-621-1243 800-909-8265
esales@centralfabricators.com
www.centralfabricators.com

Manufacturer and exporter of stainless and carbon steel pressure vessels, heat exchangers, storage tanks, condensers, cookers, evaporators and kettles; also, other alloys available
President: Mike Lewis
mlewis@centralfabricators.com
CEO: Dave Angner
CFO: Dan Meade
Vice President: Tim Maly
Operations Manager: Troy Black
Estimated Sales: $3-5 Million
Number Employees: 10-19
Square Footage: 40000

20382 Central Fine Pack Inc
7707 Vicksburg Pike
Fort Wayne, IN 46804-5549

260-432-3027
Fax: 260-432-9275 www.dwfinepack.com

Plastic disposable food packaging and trays
Director Sales/Marketing: David Brown
Plant Manager: Russ Stephens
Estimated Sales: $20-50 Million
Number Employees: 20-49

20383 Central Ice Machine Co
6279 S 118th St
Omaha, NE 68137-3574

402-731-4690
Fax: 402-731-0823 800-228-7213
customerservice@centralice.com
www.refrigerationsupplies.net

Compressors, control valves, hand valves, relief valves, condensers and evaporators, gauges, refrigeration controls, refrigeration pumps, purgers, X-pando pipe joint compound, MSA gas masks, sulphur sticks, litmus paper and neverseez
President: Don Erftmier
customerservice@centralice.com
Number Employees: 1-4

20384 Central Missouri Sheltered Enterprises
PO Box 10147
Columbia, MO 65205-4002

573-442-6935
Fax: 573-499-0586 www.cmse.org

Promotional items and packaging for barbecue sauce and rice cakes
Executive Director: Bruce Young
Executive Director: Bruce Young
Estimated Sales: $20-50 Million
Number Employees: 100-249

20385 Central Ohio Bag & Burlap
1000 E, Fifth Ave
Columbus, OH 43203

614-294-4495
Fax: 614-294-4362 800-798-9405
info@centralohiobagandburlap.com
www.centralohiobagandburlap.com

Bags and packaging materials
President: James Stout
Estimated Sales: $1-3,000,000
Number Employees: 5-9

20386 Central Package & Display
3901 85th Ave N
Minneapolis, MN 55443-1907

763-425-7444
Fax: 763-425-7917
customerservice@centralcontainer.com
www.centralpackage.com

Manufacturer and wholesaler/distributor of corrugated boxes, cushion packaging, flexible films, litho labels and static control products
President: James E Haglund
CEO: Mike Haglund
mhaglund@centralpackage.com
Sales: Steve Braun
VP Sales/Marketing: Steve Braun
General Manager: Jerry Condon
Estimated Sales: $10-20 Million
Number Employees: 100-249
Square Footage: 300000

20387 Central Pallet Mills Inc
5745 Paradise Rd
Central City, KY 42330

270-754-2900
Fax: 270-754-2902

Lift truck pallets
President: Jack Brewer
jackbrewer28@aol.com
Estimated Sales: $20-50 Million
Number Employees: 20-49

20388 Central Paper Box
2911 Belleview Avenue
Kansas City, MO 64108-3538

816-753-3126
Fax: 816-753-6923

Paper boxes including candy, paper and set-up; also, folding cartons
General Manager: Lon Wilkerson
Estimated Sales: $20-50 Million
Number Employees: 50-100
Square Footage: 125000

20389 Central Solutions Inc
401 Funston Rd
Kansas City, KS 66115-1213

913-621-6542
Fax: 913-621-7031 800-255-0262
markn@centralsolutions.com

Disinfectants and cleaners; also, custom formulating available
President: Mark Nobrega
CEO: Mike Noberga
HR Executive: Mike Nobrega
miken@centralsolutions.com
Estimated Sales: $10-20 Million
Number Employees: 50-99

20390 Central States Indl Eqpt & Svc
2700 N Partnership Blvd
Springfield, MO 65803-8208

417-831-1411
Fax: 417-831-5314 800-654-5635
sales@csidesigns.com

Fluid handling systems for food process and CIP
Owner: Bryan Billmyer
billmyerb@csitools.com
Estimated Sales: $10-20 000,000
Number Employees: 100-249

20391 Centrifuge Solutions
2232 S Main Street
Suite 357
Ann Arbor, MI 48103-6938

734-424-0713
Fax: 734-426-9016 sales@centrifugesolutions.com
www.centrifugesolutions.com

Custom blended seasonings.
President: Tom Czartoski
Sales: Ron Mederski

20392 Centrisys
9586 58th Pl
Kenosha, WI 53144-7805
262-654-6006
Fax: 262-654-6063 info@centrisys.us
www.centrisys.us
Centrifuges and separators; also, centrifuge services
available
President: Michael Copper
michael.copper@centrisys.us
Marketing Manager: Michael Kopper
Estimated Sales: $2.5-5 Million
Number Employees: 20-49
Brands:
Centrisys

20393 Century 21 Manufacturing
8008 Harney Street
Omaha, NE 68114-4451
402-391-2104
High quality vending machines
President: R Lebron

20394 Century Box Company
2412 W Cermak Road
Chicago, IL 60608-3704
773-847-7070
Fax: 773-847-7868 info@centurybox.com
www.centurybox.com
Wooden boxes
President: Daniel Leon
Estimated Sales: Less than $500,000
Number Employees: 1-4
Square Footage: 25000

20395 Century Chemical Corp
28790 County Road 20
Elkhart, IN 46517-1125
574-293-9521
Fax: 574-522-5723 800-348-3505
sales@centurychemical.com
Manufacturer and exporter of industrial and house-
hold deodorants and sanitizers; also, nontoxic
anti-freeze
President: Edward A Fetters
edfetters@centurychemical.com
Office Manager: Bobbi Holdeman
Plant Manager: David Eller
Estimated Sales: $1-2.5 Million
Number Employees: 5-9
Brands:
Travel-Jon

20396 Century Crane & Hoist
210 Washington Ave
Dravosburg, PA 15034
412-466-6987
Fax: 412-469-0813 888-601-8801
info@centurysteel.com www.centurysteel.com
Energy absorbing bumpers, overhead electric cranes
and hoists; also, repair services and OSHA inspections
President: Don Taylor
Sales Representative: Frank Marchese

20397 Century Foods Intl LLC
400 Century Ct
Sparta, WI 54656-2468
608-269-1900
Fax: 608-269-1910 800-269-1901
www.centuryfoods.com
Century Foods International is a manufacturer of nutritional powders and ready-to-drink beverages un-
der private label and contract manufacturing
agreements for food, sports, health and nutritional
supplement industries. Other servicesprovided in-
clude agglomeration, blending and instantizing, re-
search and development, analytical testing, and
packaging from bulk to consumer size.
President: Tom Miskowski
VP R&D: Julie Wagner
VP Sales/Marketing: Gene Quast
VP Operations: Wade Nolte
Number Employees: 250-499
Square Footage: 1680000
Parent Co: Hormel Foods Corporation
Type of Packaging: Private Label, Bulk
Brands:
Cenprem
Lacey Delite
Pizazz
Ready Cheese

20398 Century Glove Corp
145 John Bankston Dr
Summerville, GA 30747-5124
706-857-6444
Fax: 706-857-6446 www.centuryglove.com
Manufacturer and importer of cotton work and uni-
form gloves
Manager: Mary Seiler
Sales: Mary Seiler
Estimated Sales: less than $500,000
Number Employees: 20-49

20399 Century Industries Inc
299 Prather Ln
Sellersburg, IN 47172-1739
812-246-3371
Fax: 812-246-5446 800-248-3371
info@centuryindustries.com
www.centuryindustries.com
Manufacturer and exporter of mobile concession
trailers and kitchens
President: Robert Uhl
robertuhl@centuryindustries.com
VP: John Uhl
Sales Manager: Matt Gilland
Estimated Sales: $5-10 Million
Number Employees: 20-49
Type of Packaging: Food Service
Brands:
Goldrush

20400 Century Products
1 Doulton Place
Peabody, MA 01960-3817
978-535-9001
Fax: 978-535-9002 800-225-3472
info@poolcover.com www.poolcover.com
Air bubble cushioning materials and shipping bags
Estimated Sales: $10-20 Million
Number Employees: 100-249

20401 Century Refrigeration
P.O.Box 1206
Pryor, OK 74362-1206
918-825-6363
Fax: 918-825-0723 century@rae-corp.com
Commercial and industrial refrigeration equipment
including condensing units, unit coolers, product
coolers and chillers
President/CEO: Eric Swank
VP/CTO: Vickie Stephens
VP/Engineering: Jay Kindle
Manager of Quality: John Martin
Manager Marketing: Lisa Schrader
VP/Sales: Kevin Trowhill
Contact: Rawls Bill
robm@rae-corp.com
Vp/Operations: Jerry Salcher
Purchasing Manager: Jerry Douglas
Estimated Sales: $50-100 Million
Number Employees: 275
Square Footage: 125000
Parent Co: RAE Corporation

20402 Century Rubber Stamp Company
121 Fulton St Fl 2
New York, NY 10038
212-962-6165
Numbering machinery, stamps, stencils, etc
Manager: Harry Gold
Estimated Sales: $500,000-$1 Million
Number Employees: 5-9

20403 Century Sign Company
1622 Main Ave # E
Fargo, ND 58103-1553
701-235-5323
Fax: 701-235-5325 dwalstad@cooksignco.com
Neon and plastic signs
President: Matt Brasel
CFO: Steven Fliflet
Estimated Sales: $5-10 Million
Number Employees: 20-49

20404 Cenveo Inc
3001 N Rockwell St
Chicago, IL 60618-7917
773-267-3600
Fax: 773-267-2440 800-388-8406
www.cenveo.com
Envelopes including advertising clasp, string, window, postage saver, pressure sensitive, billing, etc

Chairman, CEO: Robert G. Burton Sr.
CFO: Scott Goodwin
VP: Ian Scheinmann
Estimated Sales: $1-2.5 Million
Number Employees: 100-249
Square Footage: 1080000

20405 Cepco
2400 Turner Avenue NW
Suite A
Grand Rapids, MI 49544-2004
616-364-8454
Fax: 616-364-8442
Management

20406 Ceramic Color & Chemical Mfg
13th St & 11th Ave
New Brighton, PA 15066
724-846-4000
Fax: 724-846-4123 www.ceramiccolor.com
Inorganic pigments
Owner: Bill Wenning
cccmfg@verizon.net
Sales Manager: Tom Knox
Sales/Shipping Coordinator: Sally Antonini
Estimated Sales: $20-50 Million
Number Employees: 10-19

20407 Ceramic Decorating Co Inc
4651 Sheila St
Commerce, CA 90040-1003
323-268-5135
Fax: 323-268-5108
sales@ceramicdecoratingco.com
www.ceramicdecoratingco.com
Supplier of custom made packaging labels.
President: Caitlyn Anaya
caitlyn@ceramicdecoratingco.com
CEO: Chad Johnson
Number Employees: 10-19

20408 Ceramica De Espana
7700 NW 54th St
Doral, FL 33166-4106
305-597-9161
Fax: 305-597-9161
Manufacturer and importer of ceramic tableware,
vases and candlesticks, bathroom, table top, cook-
ware, table accessories, pottery, garden pottery
President: Monica Ruiz
Estimated Sales: $5-10 Million
Number Employees: 5-9
Type of Packaging: Consumer, Food Service

20409 Cermex
5600 Sun Court
Norcross, GE 30092
678-221-3570
Fax: 678-221-3571 cermexinc.sales@sidel.com
Side loading case packer specifically developed for
pharmaceutical industry, pick and place robot for
plastic bottles, top loading machines, compact machine integrating case erection and high speed
shrinkwrapping machine of cans andbottles
Manager: Marc Daniel
Contact: Guy Ayel
guy.ayel@gebocermex.com

20410 Certified Grocers Midwest
1 Certified Dr
Hodgkins, IL 60525
708-579-2100
Fax: 708-354-7502 www.certisaver.com
Grocery supplier
President: James Bradley
CEO: Jim Denges
Number Employees: 100-249

20411 Certified Labs
200 Express St
Plainview, NY 11803-2423
516-576-1400
Fax: 516-576-1410 800-237-8522
corp@800certlab.com
www.certified-laboratories.com
Full service laboratory
General Manager: Martin Mitchell
mmitchell@certified-laboratories.com
Estimated Sales: $10-20 Million
Number Employees: 50-99

20412 Certified Labs Of California
6460 Dale St
Buena Park, CA 90621-3115
714-562-8622
Fax: 714-562-8799 888-366-3522
cflabs@certified-laboratories.com
www.certified-laboratories.com
Providing laboratory testing services for the food industry.
President: Martin Mitchell
mmitchell@800certlab.com
Vice President: Steven Mitchell
Estimated Sales: $5-10 Million
Number Employees: 20-49

20413 Certified Machinery Inc
3175 Princeton Pike # A
Lawrenceville, NJ 08648-2331
609-912-0300
Fax: 609-912-0144 www.certifiedmachinery.com
Inkjet and labeling product handling equipment including off line coding and labeling, base coding diverter, l-sealers and heat tunnels
President: Randy Camacho
randy.camacho@certifiedmachinery.com
Estimated Sales: Below $5 Million
Number Employees: 5-9
Square Footage: 50000

20414 Certified Piedmontese Beef
100 West Harvest Drive
PO Box 82545
Lincoln, NE 68521
402-458-4442
Fax: 402-458-4531 800-414-3487
info@piedmontese.com www.piedmontese.com
Prime cuts of beef
President: Billy Swain

20415 Cesco Magnetics
93 Utility Ct
Rohnert Park, CA 94928-1614
707-585-2402
Fax: 707-585-3886 877-624-8727
www.cescomagnetics.com
Manufacture magnetic separation equipment and sanitary valves
President: Alfred Truslow
Estimated Sales: $1-3 Million
Number Employees: 20-49
Brands:
Cesco

20416 Chad Co Inc
19950 W 161st St # A
Olathe, KS 66062-2717
913-764-0321
Fax: 913-764-0779 800-444-8360
Manufacturer and exporter of automated washing and pasteurizing equipment for meat slaughtering operations
President: Mike Gangel
mike@chadcompany.com
Estimated Sales: Below $5 Million
Number Employees: 10-19
Square Footage: 10400

20417 Chaffee Co
4111 Citrus Ave # 10
#10
Rocklin, CA 95677-4009
916-630-3980
Fax: 916-630-3987 chaffee@chaffeeco.com
Barrier laminate, cellophane and polyethylene sealers, and sealer systems.
President: Charlie Harper
Estimated Sales: $2.5-5 Million
Number Employees: 5-9
Brands:
Chaffee

20418 Chain Restaurant Resolutions
Suite 5
Toronto, ON M5S 1T8
Canada
416-934-4334
Fax: 416-934-4333
Consultant providing physical and financial restructuring to the restaurant and fast food industries
Estimated Sales: $1-5,000,000
Number Employees: 2

20419 (HQ)Chain Store Graphics
2220 E Logan Street
Decatur, IL 62526-5133
217-428-4695
Fax: 217-423-4010 800-443-7446
Advertising materials including paper and plastic signs, sign kits and decals; also, OEM decals and fleet markings
VP: Scott Bowers
Estimated Sales: $500,000-$1 Million
Number Employees: 4
Square Footage: 50000

20420 (HQ)Chaircraft
P.O.Box 608
Hickory, NC 28603-0608
828-326-8458
Fax: 828-326-8447 www.centuryfurniture.com
Chairs and bar stools
President: Cick Finch
Plant Manager: Kevin Boyle
Estimated Sales: $20-50 Million
Number Employees: 100-249
Parent Co: Century Furniture

20421 (HQ)Challenger Pallet & Supply Inc
24 N 3210 E
Idaho Falls, ID 83401-5174
208-523-1969
Fax: 208-523-1972 800-733-0205
www.challengerpallet.com
Pallets, stakes, wedges and saw dust
President: Tad Hegsted
just_hegs@yahoo.com
R&D: Justin Hegsted
VP Operations: Kelly Bennion
Estimated Sales: $5-10 Million
Number Employees: 20-49
Square Footage: 60000
Other Locations:
Challenger Pallet & Supply
Midvale UT

20422 Chalmur Bag Company, LLC
1426 Frankford Avenue
Philadelphia, PA 19125
215-425-0400
Fax: 215-425-4749 800-349-2247
chalmurbag@msn.com
chalmurbag.homestead.com/
Printed bags including polyethylene, cellophane, mini-lock and pre-opened on rolls, extruded narrow width tubing and cellophane sheets; also, carton and drum lining
Manager: Bob Livingston
blivingston@chalmurbag.com
Sales Manager: John Yarris
Plant Manager: Jon Ashley
Estimated Sales: $5-10 Million
Number Employees: 10-19
Square Footage: 64000

20423 (HQ)Chamberland Engineering
PO Box 817
West Warwick, RI 02893
800-687-1136
Fax: 401-615-7758 vibrate020@aol.com
www.chamberlandengineering.com
Vibrating screens, vibrating separators, vibrating sieves, bin and hopper vibrators, point and strip samplers, rotary tray dryers, ball valves, dust collectors, cyclones, scrubbers, electromechanical feeders, dosing feeders, air sweeprssystems, weigh belt feeders, bulk bag unloaders, BIC bins, blenders and mixers, ingredient dispensing systems
President: David Chamberland
VP: Steven Chamberland
R & D: Albert Bleau
Estimated Sales: $3.5 Million
Number Employees: 4
Number of Brands: 5
Number of Products: 27
Square Footage: 40000
Type of Packaging: Food Service

20424 Chambers Container Company
145 Bluedevil Dr
Gastonia, NC 28056-8610
704-377-6317
Fax: 704-864-4022
Corrugated boxes

Manager: Roger Powers
Controller: Beth Hudson
VP: Scott Chambers
Estimated Sales: $20-50 Million
Number Employees: 50-99
Square Footage: 54000

20425 Champaign Plastics Company
PO Box 6413
Champaign, IL 61822
217-359-3664
Fax: 217-359-0091 800-575-0170
products@champaignplastics.com
www.champaignplastics.com
Manufacturer and wholesaler/distributor of disposable aprons, gloves, boots, shoe covers, hats, beard restraints, sleeves, children's and adult bibs and banquet rolls
President: Donna Williams
Contact: Joseph Bateman
joseph.bateman@champaignplastics.com
Estimated Sales: Below $5,000,000
Number Employees: 1-4

20426 Champion America Inc
20 Flax Mill Rd
Branford, CT 06405-2803
203-315-1106
Fax: 203-488-4770 800-521-7000
www.champion-america.com
Signs, tags, labels, identification and safety products
Manager: Pascal Deman
Estimated Sales: $100+ Million
Number Employees: 500-999
Brands:
Saftex Flame-Retardant Mitts

20427 Champion Chemical Co
8319 Greenleaf Ave
Whittier, CA 90602-2998
562-945-1456
800-621-7868
service@championchemical.com
www.cleanthatpot.com
Manufacturer and exporter of carbon and grease removers
Owner: Andrew Ellis
service@championchemical.com
Estimated Sales: $1-5 Million
Number Employees: 10-19
Square Footage: 72000
Brands:
Sokoff

20428 Champion Industries Inc
3765 Champion Blvd
Winston Salem, NC 27105-2667
336-661-1556
Fax: 336-661-1979 800-532-8591
info@championindustries.com
www.championindustries.com
Manufacturer and exporter of commercial dishwashers, pot and pan washers and waste disposal systems
Owner: Luciano Berti
Chairman of the Board: Luciano Berti
CEO: Hank Holt
CFO: Christa Miller
R & D: Perry Money
Director Sales: Pete Michailo
Advertising Manager: Patrick Elworth
lberti@championindustries.com
Purchasing Manager: Donna Mealka
Estimated Sales: $20-50 Million
Number Employees: 100-249
Square Footage: 130000
Parent Co: Comenda-Alispa
Type of Packaging: Food Service
Brands:
Champion
Moyer Diebel

20429 Champion Plastics
220 Clifton Blvd
Clifton, NJ 07011
Fax: 800-526-1238 800-526-1230
sales@championplastics.com
www.championplastics.com
Manufacturer and exporter of polyethylene bags and films.
Founding Partner: John Callaghan
Year Founded: 1972
Estimated Sales: $20-30 Million
Number Employees: 100-249

20430 (HQ)Champion Trading Corporation
P.O.Box 227
Marlboro, NJ 07746
732-780-4200
Fax: 732-780-9839 info@champtrading.com
www.champtrading.com
Manufacturer and exporter of used and rebuilt processing and packaging machinery
Principal: David Matthews
Co-Owner: James Matthew
Co-Owner: Michael Matthews
Contact: Adrienne Schere
schere@champtrading.com
Plant Manager: S Bassett
Estimated Sales: $1-2,500,000
Number Employees: 5-9
Square Footage: 50000

20431 Champlin Co
236 Hamilton St
Hartford, CT 06106-2910
860-951-9217
Fax: 860-951-3464 800-458-5261
info@champlincompany.com
www.champlincompany.com
Wooden and corrugated boxes
President: Rory Poole
champlinco@snet.net
VP: W James Schumaker
Estimated Sales: $3-5 Million
Number Employees: 20-49

20432 Chandre Corporation
14 Catharine Street
Poughkeepsie, NY 12601-3104
845-473-8003
Fax: 845-473-8004 800-324-6252
www.chandre.com
Chocolate tempering machines
Estimated Sales: 700000
Number Employees: 10

20433 (HQ)Chaney Instrument Co
965 S Wells St
P.O. Box 70
Lake Geneva, WI 53147-2468
262-248-4449
Fax: 262-248-8707 800-777-0565
info@chaney-inst.com www.acurite.com
Manufacturer and exporter of digital and analog kitchen thermometers, timers and clocks
President: Valerie Wilson
v.wilson@laonastatebank.com
National Sales Manager Food Service: Allan Ahrens
Number Employees: 100-249
Square Footage: 95000
Type of Packaging: Consumer, Food Service, Private Label, Bulk
Other Locations:
Chaney Instruments
Lake Geneva WI
Brands:
Acu-Rite
Chaney Instrument

20434 Change Parts Inc
185 S Jebavy Dr
Ludington, MI 49431-2460
231-845-5107
Fax: 231-843-4907 www.changeparts.com
Custom designed changeover parts including fillers, cleaners, cappers, timing screws, stars and guides, nozzles, drive wheels and belts; also, remanufactured and used packaging equipment
President: Jeff Pelc
j.pelc@apcoe.com
CFO: Greg Simsa
VP: Greg Simsa
Marketing: Dori Bray
National Sales Manager: Jon Goad
Operations Manager: Andy Kmetz
Production: Andy Kmetz
Estimated Sales: $2.5-5 Million
Number Employees: 20-49
Square Footage: 90000

20435 Chantland Company, The
PO Box 69
Humboldt, IA 50548
515-332-4040
Fax: 515-332-4923 info@chantlandpulley.com
www.chantlandpulley.com
Manufacturer and exporter of belt conveyors, bag filling equipment and bag palletizers
CEO: Donald Sosnoski
Year Founded: 1943
Estimated Sales: $33 Million
Number Employees: 200
Square Footage: 140000

20436 Chapman Corp
3366 Tree Court Industrial Blv
St Louis, MO 63122-6688
636-225-5313
Fax: 636-825-2610 800-843-1404
sales@chapmanstl.com www.chapmanstl.com
Replacement knives, blades, slitters and perforators for processing and packaging equipment.
Executive VP: Mark Zumbehl
mzumbehl@chapmanstl.com
Estimated Sales: $2.5-5,000,000
Number Employees: 10-19

20437 Chapman Manufacturing Co Inc
481 W Main St
Avon, MA 02322-1695
508-587-7592
Fax: 508-587-7592 info@chapmanco.com
www.chapmanco.com
Manufacturer and exporter of lamps and lighting fixtures, encompasses table and floor lamps, chandeliers, sconces, accent furniture and decorative accessories. Authentic reproductions, traditional adaptations and transitional andoriginal contemporary designs
President: Richard Amaral
ramaral@chapmanco.com
Estimated Sales: $10-20 Million
Number Employees: 50-99

20438 Chapman Sign
23253 Hoover Rd
Warren, MI 48089-1934
586-758-1600
Fax: 586-758-1610
Electric signs
Manager: Harold Chapman
Estimated Sales: less than $500,000
Number Employees: 5

20439 Charles Beck Machine Corporation
400 W Church Road
King of Prussia, PA 19406-3185
610-265-0500
Fax: 610-265-5627 beckmachine@verizon.net
www.beckmachine.com
Manufacturer and exporter of set-up box lidders and rotary shear sheet cutters
President: Arthur Beck
Manager Parts/Service: Robert Pickell
Estimated Sales: Below $5 Million
Number Employees: 10

20440 Charles Beseler Company
2018 W Main St
P.O. Box 431
Stroudsburg, PA 18360
570-517-0400
Fax: 800-966-4515 800-237-3537
www.beselershrinkpackaging.com
Manufacturer and exporter of shrink wrap machinery.
Estimated Sales: $100-500 Million

20441 Charles Craft Inc
21381 Charles Craft Ln
Laurinburg, NC 28352
910-844-3521
Fax: 910-844-9846 www.charlescraftinc.com
Towels including dish, pot holders and aprons
President: Charles G Buie Jr
Cmo: Marybeth Zadel
mzadel@charlescraft.com
President: Clifton Buie
Estimated Sales: $50-100 Million
Number Employees: 100-249
Brands:
Charles Craft

20442 Charles E. Roberts Company
539 Fairmont Rd
Wyckoff, NJ 07481-1318
973-345-3035
Fax: 973-345-8516 800-237-2684
Manufacturer and exporter of embossed ribbon for awards, badges, prizes, contests, emblems, fairs and conventions
Owner/President: Bernard Gallant
Estimated Sales: $5-10 Million
Number Employees: 10-19
Square Footage: 28000

20443 Charles Engineering & Service
1 Tye Green Paddoc
Belcamp, MD 21017-0428
410-272-1090
Temperature sensitive containers; custom design available
Sr. VP: Charles Furlong
Estimated Sales: $300,000-500,000
Number Employees: 7
Square Footage: 32000

20444 Charles Gratz Fire Protection
241 W Oxford St
Philadelphia, PA 19122-3798
215-235-5800
Fax: 215-236-2510
Manfacturer of fire alarm systems and fire extinguishers
Owner: Harry Gratz
Office Manager: Deborah DeSimone
Estimated Sales: Below $5 Million
Number Employees: 5 to 9

20445 Charles H Baldwin & Sons
1 Center St
P.O.Box 372
West Stockbridge, MA 01266-9502
413-232-7785
Fax: 413-232-0114 www.baldwinextracts.com
Flavoring extracts and flavors, maple table syrup and supplier of baking supplies.
Owner: Jackie Moffatt
jackie@baldwinextracts.com
Estimated Sales: $500,000-$1 Million
Number Employees: 1-4
Brands:
Baldwin

20446 Charles Lapierre
56 Etna Road
Lebanon, NH 03766-1403
Canada
603-448-0300
Fax: 603-448-4810 800-432-2990
info@njmpackaging.com
President: Charles Lapierre
Vice President of Operations: Andre Caumartin
R&D: Louis Lasluer
Director of International Sales: Marc Lapierre
Number Employees: 25

20447 Charles Mayer Studios
105 E Market St
Suite 114
Akron, OH 44308-2037
330-535-6121
Fax: 330-434-2016
Manufacturer, exporter and importer of hotel and restaurant menu boards, white liquid chalk boards, bulletin boards, easels, trade show displays and today's specials boards, custom tables
Owner: Jeffrey Mayer
Executive VP: M Barton
Estimated Sales: $1-3 Million
Number Employees: 20-49
Square Footage: 210000
Type of Packaging: Food Service
Brands:
Mayer Hook N' Loop
Mayer Magna

20448 (HQ)Charles Ross & Son Co
710 Old Willets Path
Hauppauge, NY 11788-4193
631-234-0500
Fax: 631-234-0691 800-243-7677
mail@mixers.com www.mixers.com
Manufacturer, importer and exporter of mixing, blending and dispersion equipment

Square Footage: 96000
Parent Co: X-L Plastics
Brands:
Champtuf Polyethylene

President: Richard Ross
rross@mixers.com
Executive VP: Bogard Lagman
Estimated Sales: $20-50 Million
Number Employees: 100-249
Square Footage: 150000
Other Locations:
  Ross, Charles, & Son Co.
  Savannah GA
Brands:
  Double Planetary
  Powermix
  Ross
  X-Series

20449 Charles Ross & Son Co
710 Old Willets Path
Hauppauge, NY 11788-4193

631-234-0500
Fax: 631-234-0691 800-243-7677
sales@mixers.com www.mixers.com
Emulsifying equipment
President: Richard Ross
rross@mixers.com
Executive Vice President: Bogard Lagman
Product Manager: Shannon Wolf
Regional Sales Manager: Chip Nipps
Estimated Sales: $20-50 Million
Number Employees: 100-249

20450 Charles Tirschman Pallet Co
1936 Graves Ct
Dundalk, MD 21222-5508

410-282-6199
Pallets and skids
Owner: Charles Tirschman
Estimated Sales: $500,000-$1 Million
Number Employees: 5-9

20451 Charles Walker North America
2901 Stanley Ave
Fort Worth, TX 76110

817-922-9834
Fax: 817-922-9854 cissy@charlesalaninc.com
www.charlesalanfurniture.com
Furniture manufacturer
Owner: Margaret Sevadjian
Vice President: Jim Boston
Operations Manager: Steve McDonald
Square Footage: 120
Brands:
  Waiker Conveyor Belt & Equipment

20452 Charlotte Tent & Awning
5901 N Hill Cir
Charlotte, NC 28213-6237

704-921-8743
Fax: 704-921-3034
www.charlottetentandawning.com
Commercial awnings
President: Dale Michael
dale@charlottetentandawning.com
Estimated Sales: $1-2,500,000
Number Employees: 20-49

20453 Charlton & Hill
655 30th Street N
Lethbridge, AB T1H 5G5
Canada

403-328-3388
Fax: 403-328-3533 www.charltonandhill.com
Conveyors; wholesaler/distributor of ranges, coolers
and hot plates; serving the food service market; also,
metal fabrication available
Sales Manager: Dwayne Huber
Estimated Sales: $1-5 Million
Number Employees: 100-250

20454 Charm Sciences Inc
659 Andover St
Lawrence, MA 01843-1032

978-687-9200
Fax: 978-687-9216 info@charm.com
www.charm.com
Manufacturer and exporter of food safety diagnostic
instruments for antibiotic, aflatoxin and pesticide
residues, ATP sanitation/hygiene, pasteurization effi-
ciency and doneness in meat products
President: Dr Stanley Charm
VP Sales: Gerard Ruth
Contact: Rami Abraham
r.abraham@charm.com
Estimated Sales: Less Than $500,000
Number Employees: 1-4

Brands:
  Chef Test
  Cidelite
  Paslite
  Pathogel
  Pocketswab
  SI Test

20455 Chart Applied Technologies
3505 County Road 42 W
Burnsville, MN 55306-3803

952-882-5000
Fax: 952-882-5172 888-877-3093
www.mve-inc.com
VP: Eric M Rottier
Estimated Sales: $1-5 Million
Number Employees: 250-499

20456 (HQ)Chart Inc
407 7th St NW
New Prague, MN 56071-1010

952-758-4484
Fax: 952-758-8293 800-428-3777
aconrade@mve-inc.com www.chartindustries.com
Turnkey liquid nitrogen systems for food freezing,
turnkey liquid nitrogen injection systems for still
product manufacturing and bulk carbon dioxide sys-
tems for beverage carbonation
VP Industrial Gases Marketing: Ron' Stark
Manager: Bruce Lyman
bruce.lyman@chart-ind.com
VP Technical Engineering: Jon Wikstrom
VP Restaurant Products: Paul Plooster
Number Employees: 500-999
Square Footage: 844000
Other Locations:
  Minnesota Valley Engineering
  Canton GA

20457 (HQ)Chart Industries Inc
1 Infinity Corporate Ctr # 300
Cleveland, OH 44125-5370

440-753-1490
Fax: 440-753-1491 800-247-4446
mary.nelson@chart-ind.com
www.chartindustries.com
Manufacturer and exporter of CO2 storage tanks
used for carbonation in soda dispensing machines
President: John Wikstrom
CEO: William C Johnson
william.johnson@chart-ind.com
VP: Eric M Rottier
Marketing Director: Mary Nelson
Sales Director: Dick Mich
Estimated Sales: $20-50 Million
Number Employees: 1000-4999
Type of Packaging: Food Service

20458 Charter House
200 N Franklin St # B
Zeeland, MI 49464-1075

616-741-4301
Fax: 616-796-1199 800-314-7659
www.sperrysmoviehouse.com
Food service dining room furniture
President: Chuck Reid
Cmo: Scott Simpson
scott.simpson@charter-house.com
Finance Executive: Jacob Burroughs
Director/Managing Engineer: Bill Regan
Plant Manager: Harriet Trethewey
Purchasing Manager: Bill Forslund
Estimated Sales: $10-20 Million
Number Employees: 50-99
Square Footage: 80000
Parent Co: Franke

20459 Chase Doors
10021 Commerce Park Dr.
Cincinnati, OH 45246

513-860-5565
Fax: 800-245-7045 800-543-4455
Manual, electric sliding cold storage room, swing
and vertical lift doors for walk-in coolers and freez-
ers. Full line of parts. Commercial refrigeration
sales, service, and installation
Owner: Jeff Staples
Contact: Vicki Byrd
vbyrd@chasedoors.com
General Manager: David Canady
Estimated Sales: $2.5-5 Million
Number Employees: 1-4
Square Footage: 64000

20460 Chase Doors
10021 Commerce Park Dr
Cincinnati, OH 45246

513-860-5565
Fax: 800-245-7045 800-543-4455
info@chasedoors.com www.chasedoors.com
Impact traffic doors, service doors, flexible doors,
security doors, corrosion resistant doors, fire and
service doors, pharmaceutical doors, door opera-
tions, cold storage doors and dock seals and shelters
President: Jim Lindsay
CEO: Robert W Muir
Contact: Vicki Byrd
vbyrd@chasedoors.com
Estimated Sales: $10-25 000,000
Number Employees: 100-249

20461 Chase Industries Inc
10021 Commerce Park Dr
West Chester, OH 45246-1333

513-860-5565
Fax: 513-860-0933 800-543-4455
www.chasedoors.com
Chase Industries, Inc. manufactures a full line of
manual and semi-automatic L-Sealers, Shrink Tun-
nels, and Bar Sealers as well as fully automatic
Sleeve Wrappers, Bundlers, Blister Sealers, Clam
Shell Sealers, Curing Systems andFormfill equip-
ment. Our goal as a manufacturer, is to provide top
performance and top quality to the customer in as
many combinations of size and options as possible.
We like to work closely with our distributors and
their customers for the bestpossible standards
CEO: Robert W Muir
bmuir@chaseind.com
CEO: Elizabeth Braslow
CEO: Jim Braslow
R&D: James Braslow
Purchasing: Jose Garcia
Estimated Sales: $5-10 Million
Number Employees: 250-499
Number of Brands: 10
Square Footage: 30000
Brands:
  Chase
  Cii
  Ultrablister
  Ultrasealer

20462 (HQ)Chase-Doors
10021 Commerce Park Dr
Cincinnati, OH 45246

513-860-5565
Fax: 513-245-7045 800-543-4455
www.chasedoors.com
Manufacturer and exporter of vinyl and roll up
doors, fire and insulated doors, door operators and
air curtains
CEO: Dan O'Connor
CFO: Drew Bachman
CEO: Robert W Muir
R&D: Rory Falato
Marketing: Rory Falato
General Manager: Carl Johnson
Plant Manager: Rick Schweitzer
Purchasing Director: Diane Wells
Estimated Sales: $20-50 Million
Number Employees: 100-249
Number of Brands: 10
Number of Products: 35
Other Locations:
  Chase-Durus
  Memphis TN

20463 Chase-Logeman Corp
303 Friendship Dr
Greensboro, NC 27409-9332

336-665-0754
Fax: 336-665-0723 info@chaselogeman.com
Manufacturer and exporter of liquid filling, plugging
and screw capping machinery, tray loaders and
unloaders, conveyors, unscramblers, rotary tables,
accumulators and monoblocks; also, custom
designing available
President: Alan Gillespie
alang@chaselogeman.com
Vice President: Joel Slazyk
Quality Control: Louis Stier
Plant Manager: Lew Stier
Estimated Sales: $1 Million
Number Employees: 10-19
Square Footage: 36000
Brands:
  Chaselock

20464 (HQ)Chaska Chocolate
821 Oriole Lane
Chaska, MN 55318-1131
952-448-5699
Fax: 952-448-6719
Consultant for the oilseed extraction, fats and oils, chocolate and coffee industries; also, food technology research available
Contact: Phillip Arendt
parendt@aol.com
Estimated Sales: $1-5 Million
Number Employees: 2
Square Footage: 2200
Other Locations:
Chaska Chocolate
Chicago IL

20465 Chatelain Plastics
413 N Main St
PO Box 1464
Findlay, OH 45840-3541
419-422-4323
Fax: 419-422-1122 866-421-4323
sales@chatelainplastics.com
www.chatelainplastics.com
Advertising signs
Owner: Tom Klein
tom@chatelainplastics.com
President: Jim Chatelain
Estimated Sales: Below $5 Million
Number Employees: 1-4

20466 (HQ)Chatfield & Woods Sack Company
651 Enterprise Dr
Harrison, OH 45030-1691
513-202-9700
Fax: 513-202-0900
Paper sacks
President: Alan Bicknayer
General Manager: Mark Mitter
Number Employees: 5
Square Footage: 60000
Other Locations:
Chatfield & Woods Sack Co.
Harrison OH

20467 Chatillon
8600 Somerset Dr
Largo, FL 33773-2700
727-536-7831
Fax: 727-538-2400 chatillon.fl-lar@ametek.com
www.ametek.com
Mechanical and electronic calibration equipment for hydraulic, pneumatic, materials testers
Quality Control: Mike Guglicelli
Manager: Nick Hoiles
Estimated Sales: $10-20 Million
Number Employees: 50-99
Parent Co: Amatek

20468 Chattanooga Labeling Systems
P.O.Box 2492
Chattanooga, TN 37409-0492
423-825-2125
Fax: 423-825-2173 cls@cledeco.com
www.clsdeco.com
Pressure sensitive, heat transfer and shrink sleeve labels; glassware and plastic screen printing
President: Marvin Smith
CFO: Dave Houseman
Head Of Customer Service Dept.: Chris Gonzalez
Office Manager: Jenny Hughes
Production Manager: Don Gilbert
Estimated Sales: $20-30 Million
Number Employees: 20-49

20469 Chattanooga Rubber Stamp & Stencil Works
P.O.Box 443
Sale Creek, TN 37373-0443
423-894-1163
Fax: 423-894-1164 800-894-1164
crs4018@aol.com
Rubber stamps
President: John L McNair Jr
Estimated Sales: Less than $500,000
Number Employees: 3

20470 Chattin Awning Company
85 Newfield Ave
Edison, NJ 08837
732-225-8800
Fax: 732-225-2110 800-394-3500
mainattractions3500@gmail.com
www.mainattractions.com
Commercial awnings
President: Rocky Sconda
CEO: Kevin Bova
Contact: Theresa Ascolese
tascolese@mainattractions.com
Operations Manager: Dean Dialfonso
Estimated Sales: $5-10 Million
Number Employees: 20-49

20471 Chaucer Press Inc
535 Stewart Rd
Hanover Twp, PA 18706-1454
570-825-2005
Fax: 570-825-0535 www.chaucerpress.com
Communnicone and Xtenda-cone collars for on-pack promotion, folding cartons, pressure-sensitive and cut labels, and other printed materials
CEO: Patricia A. Frances
COO: Frank A. Franzo
Plant Manager: Al Saldy
Estimated Sales: $2.5-5 000,000
Number Employees: 20-49

20472 Check Savers Inc
529 Shepherd Dr
Garland, TX 75042-6830
972-272-7533
Fax: 972-276-8315 800-276-8315
Checks
President: R P Mc Nabb
CEO: Bret Woods
National Sales Rep.: Mike Voight
Number Employees: 20-49

20473 Checker Bag Co
10655 Midwest Industrial Blvd
St Louis, MO 63132-1281
314-423-3131
Fax: 314-423-1329 800-489-3130
www.checkerbag.com
Manufacturer, importer and exporter of polyethylene, polypropylene and cellophane bags including bakery, confection and gourmet
President: Robert Freund
VP: Al Stix
Number Employees: 20-49

20474 Checker Machine
2701 Nevada Ave N
Minneapolis, MN 55427-2879
763-544-5000
Fax: 763-544-1272 888-800-5001
cm@checkermachine.com
Spiral conveyors, ovens and freezers
President: Steve Lipinski
CFO: John Ackerman
Vice President: Steve Lipinski
Sales/Marketing Manager: Don Hockman
Production Manager: Brad Schmitt
Plant Manager: Steve Lipinski
Estimated Sales: $5-10 Million
Number Employees: 50-99
Square Footage: 400000
Parent Co: Checker Machine
Brands:
Checker
Stein/Checker

20475 Cheese Merchants of America
248 Tubeway Dr
Carol Stream, IL 60188
630-768-0317
Fax: 630-221-0584 johnp@cheesemerchants.com
www.cheesemerchants.com
Processors of custom blends of Italian cheeses, converters of hard Italian cheeses to grated, shredded, and shaved.
EVP/Managing Partner: Robert Greco
Director Purchasing/Quality Assurance: Paul DelleGrazie
Central Regional Sales Manager: Mark Lewis
EVP Sales: Jim Smart
Contact: Brian Barrett
brianb@cheesemerchants.com
Estimated Sales: $19.3 Million
Number Employees: 90
Square Footage: 105000

Type of Packaging: Consumer, Food Service, Bulk

20476 Cheese Outlet Fresh Market
400 Pine St
Burlington, VT 5401
802-863-3968
Fax: 802-865-1705 800-447-1205
www.freshmarketgourmetvt.com
Retail gourmet bakery of cheeses, produce and gourmet items, prepared foods, wine and Vermont products
President: Simon Pozirekides
Manager: Sherie Cyr
Estimated Sales: $5-10 Million
Number Employees: 20-49
Square Footage: 10000

20477 Cheesemakers Inc
2266 S Walker Rd
Cleveland, TX 77328-6336
281-593-1319
Fax: 281-593-2898 www.cheesemakers.com
General Manager: James Keliehor
jck@cheesemakers.com
Estimated Sales: $2.5-5 Million
Number Employees: 10-19

20478 Chef Revival
7240 Cross Park Drive
North Charleston, SC 29418
800-858-8589
Fax: 843-767-0494 800-248-9826
www.chefrevival.com
Manufacturer, importer and exporter of traditional and contemporary chef uniforms including jackets,aprons,pants, hats,clogs,as well as a full line of ladies and chilrens clothing.
President: Jerry Rosenblum
VP: Kim dela Villefromoy
Marketing Director: Kelly Gloor
Sales: Jack Kramer
Contact: Rob Johnson
rob@chefrevival.com
Production: Louis Nardella
Plant Manager: Paul Brady
Number Employees: 20
Square Footage: 16000
Type of Packaging: Consumer, Food Service
Brands:
Chef Revival
Chefcare
Chefcutlery
Knife & Steel

20479 Chef Specialties
411 W Water St
Smethport, PA 16749-1199
814-887-5652
Fax: 814-887-2021 800-440-2433
info@chefspecialties.com
www.chefspecialties.com
Manufacturer, exporter and importer of metal and wood kitchen specialties including peppermills, spice mills, salad bowls and cutting boards
Owner: Jack Pierotti
Sales: Mike Wagner
info@chefspecialties.com
Estimated Sales: $500,000-$1 Million
Number Employees: 5-9
Square Footage: 50000
Type of Packaging: Consumer, Food Service, Private Label, Bulk
Brands:
Chef

20480 Chef's Choice Mesquite Charcoal
1729 Ocean Oaks Rd
PO Box 707
Carpinteria, CA 93014-0707
805-684-8284
Fax: 805-684-8284
Manufacturer and importer of mesquite charcoal
Owner: Bill Lord
Number of Products: 2
Type of Packaging: Food Service
Brands:
Chef's Choice

20481 Chefwear
2300 W Windsor Ct # C
Addison, IL 60101-1491
312-427-6700
Fax: 630-396-8337 800-568-2433
info@chefwear.com www.chefwear.com

Manufacturer and exporter of culinary apparel and accessories
President: Rochelle Huppin Fleck
CEO: Gary Fleck
Vice President: Carol Mueller
carol.mueller@chefwear.com
VP Sales/Marketing: Carol Mueller
Sales Director: Glenn Woerz
General Manager: Rob James
Estimated Sales: Less than $500,000
Number Employees: 50-99
Square Footage: 24000
Brands:
    Chef-R-Alls
    Chefwear
    Pint Size Duds

20482 Cheil Jedang Corporation
105 Challenger Rd
Ridgefield Park, NJ 07660-2101
    201-229-6050
Fax: 201-229-6058 annie@cheiljedang.com
Flavor enhancers
President: Ben Heo
Estimated Sales: $10-20 Million
Number Employees: 50-99

20483 Chem Mark International
635 E Chapman Ave
Orange, CA 92866-1604
    714-633-8560
Fax: 310-557-1976
Broker of commercial dishwashing machines, chemicals, air purification equipment, bar glass washer and flying insect control products. Also exporter of commercial dishwashing machines
President: Darol Carlson
VP: Betty Carlson
Marketing Director: Jay Jaeger
Estimated Sales: $1-2.5 Million
Number Employees: 1 to4

20484 Chem Pack Inc
2261 Spring Grove Ave
Cincinnati, OH 45214-1797
    513-241-6616
Fax: 513-241-6664 800-421-2700
info@chem-pack.com www.chem-pack.com
Contract packager of multi-packaged food products, health and beauty aids, skin and blister packaging, shrink wrap, liquids, powders, etc.; also display assembly.
President: John Pierce
Contact: Sanya Mishevski
sanya@chem-pack.com
Estimated Sales: $1-2.5 Million
Number Employees: 20-49
Square Footage: 100000

20485 Chem Pruf Door Co LTD
5224 Ruben Torres Sr Blvd
5224 FM 802
Brownsville, TX 78526-5217
    956-544-1000
Fax: 956-544-7943 800-444-6924
info@chem-pruf.com www.chem-pruf.com
Noncorrosive fiberglass doors and wall windows, louver systems and fiberglass frames; also, stainless steel hardware available
Owner: Tony Mc Dermid
CFO: Bill Stirling
HR Executive: Mary Chapa
mary@chem-pruf.com
Estimated Sales: $10-20 Million
Number Employees: 50-99
Square Footage: 80000
Type of Packaging: Food Service, Private Label
Brands:
    Chem-Pruf

20486 Chem-Tainer Industries Inc
361 Neptune Ave
West Babylon, NY 11704-5800
    631-661-8300
Fax: 631-661-8209 800-275-2436
sales@chemtainer.com www.chemtainer.com
Manufacturer and exporter of plastic tanks and containers
President: James Glen
VP Marketing: Tony Lamb
Contact: Joan Flaxman
joanflaxman@chem-tainer.com

Estimated Sales: $5-10 Million
Number Employees: 1-4
Square Footage: 1000000
Brands:
    Haz Mat

20487 Chem-Tainer Industries Inc
361 Neptune Ave
West Babylon, NY 11704-5800
    631-661-8300
Fax: 631-661-8209 800-938-8896
sales@chemtainer.com www.chemtainer.com
Manufacturer and exporter of plastic tanks, containers and material handling equipment
President: James Glen
Executive VP: A Lamb
Contact: Joan Flaxman
joanflaxman@chem-tainer.com
Estimated Sales: $5-10,000,000
Number Employees: 1-4
Square Footage: 40000
Parent Co: Chem-Trainer Industries

20488 ChemTreat, Inc.
4461 Cox Rd
Glen Allen, VA 23060-3331
    804-935-2000
Fax: 804-965-0154 800-648-4579
cs_orders@chemtreat.com www.chemtreat.com
Manufacturer and exporter of water treatment chemicals for boilers and cooler, cooker and waste water treatment and clarification systems
Contact: Roy Arnett
arnett@chemtreat.com
Manager,Food Industry Marketing: David Anthony
Dierctor Food Industry Division: Dennis Martin
Purchasing Manager: Steve Hemmis
Estimated Sales: $300,000-500,000
Number Employees: 1-4

20489 Chemclean Corp
13045 180th St
Jamaica, NY 11434-4194
    718-525-4500
Fax: 718-481-6470 800-538-2436
info@chemclean.com www.chemclean.com
Manufacturer and exporter of industrial cleaners, degreasers, disinfectants, and deodorizers
President: Alberto Bodhert
alberto@chemclean.com
CEO: Frank Bass
Manager: S Emil Johnsen
Estimated Sales: $20-50 Million
Number Employees: 20-49
Square Footage: 20000
Brands:
    D-Carb 297
    D-Scale
    Multichlor
    Neutraclean
    Sparkleen 310

20490 Chemco Products Inc
1349 Grand Oaks Dr
Howell, MI 48843-8579
    517-546-7800
Fax: 517-546-5163 www.chemcoproducts.net
USDA sanitation chemicals, boiler, cooling tower and wastewater treatment; provides and installs related dispensing equipment, controllers, tanks, CIP systems, lube systems, pressure washers
President: Janis Utz
CFO: Elaine Cooper
CEO: Joe Mickunas
Quality Control: Elaine Cooper
VP Sales: Dave McCalo
Manager: Julie Blank
julieblankpt@aol.com
Estimated Sales: $10-20 000,000
Number Employees: 10-19

20491 Chemdet Inc
730 Commerce Center Dr # D
Sebastian, FL 32958-3128
    772-388-2755
Fax: 772-388-8813 800-645-1510
info@chemdet.com www.chemdet.com
Manufacturer and exporter of stainless steel tank washers
President: Phillip Joachim
Estimated Sales: $2.5-5 Million
Number Employees: 10-19
Brands:
    Chem Disc

Clip Disc
Fury
Rotaball
Spray Ball
Turbodisc

20492 Chemetall
675 Central Ave
New Providence, NJ 07974-1560
    908-464-6900
Fax: 908-464-4658 800-526-4473
mail@oakite.com www.chemetallna.com
President: Joris Merckx
joris.merckx@chemetall.com
Number Employees: 500-999

20493 Chemetrics Inc
4295 Catlett Rd
Midland, VA 22728-2003
    540-788-9026
Fax: 540-788-9302 800-356-3072
www.chemetrics.com
Water analysis test kits
President: Bruce Rampy
Cmo: Henry B Castaneda
henryc@chemetrics.com
International Business Manager: Shirley Ward
Estimated Sales: $20-50 Million
Number Employees: 50-99

20494 Chemex Division/International Housewares Corporation
11 Veterans Drive
Chicopee, MA 1022
    413-499-2370
Fax: 413-443-3546 800-243-6399
www.chemexcoffeemaker.com
Manufacturer, importer and exporter of drip coffee makers and filters
President: Eliza Grassy
Estimated Sales: $1-3 Million
Number Employees: 5-9
Type of Packaging: Consumer
Brands:
    Chemex

20495 Chemglass Life Sciences
3800 N Mill Rd
Vineland, NJ 08360-1528
    856-696-0014
Fax: 856-696-9102 800-843-1794
customer-service@cglifesciences.com
www.cglifesciences.com
Manufacturer of high quality laboratory glassware and equipment. Products include glassware and plastics, hotplates, overhead stirrers, stirrer bars, chromatography and reaction vials, beakers, cylinders, volumetric flasks, shakersvortexers, rotators, mini centrifuges, UV lamps, melting point apparatus, clamps, supports and bossheads.
Sales Exec: Craig Beesecker
Export Manager: Linnea Warren
Number Employees: 100-249

20496 Chemi-Graphic Inc
340 State St
PO Box 410
Ludlow, MA 01056-3439
    413-589-0151
Fax: 413-589-7448
customer.service@chemi-graphic.com
www.chemi-graphic.com
Etched, lithographed and silk screened name plates, dials and scales
President: Paul R Pohl
sales@chemi-graphic.com
Executive VP: Donald Devine
Estimated Sales: Below $5 Million
Number Employees: 50-99

20497 Chemicolloid Laboratories, Inc.
P.O.Box 251
New Hyde Park, NY 11040-0251
    516-747-2666
Fax: 516-747-4888
customersupport@colloidmill.com
www.colloidmill.com
Manufacturer and exporter of colloid mills used in applications to process materials being dispersed, suspended, emulsified, homogenized or comminuted, and process equipment.

VP: Robert Best
Marketing: Susan Okeefe
Sales Director: George Ryder
Purchasing: Steve Best
Estimated Sales: $3-5 Million
Number Employees: 20-49
Square Footage: 144000
Brands:
 Charlotte
 Colloid Mills

20498 Chemifax
11641 Pike St
Santa Fe Springs, CA 90670
  562-908-0405
 Fax: 562-908-0077 800-527-5722
 info@carrollco.com www.carrollco.com
Manufacturer and exporter of cleaning products including floor waxes, finishes, detergents, soaps and chemical specialties
Manager: Mohammed Nilchian
Sales Manager: Mike Greene
Contact: Eddie Ayala
eayala@carrollco.com
Sales Manager: Mike Meller
Estimated Sales: $20-50 Million
Number Employees: 50-99
Square Footage: 80000
Parent Co: Carroll Company
Brands:
 Airx
 Nature's Orange
 Show Patrol
 Shower Patrol Plus
 Solar System
 Trewax Hardware
 Trewax Industrial
 Trewax Janitorial

20499 (HQ)Chemindustrial Systems Inc
W 53 N 560 Highl & Dr
Cedarburg, WI 53012
  262-375-8570
 Fax: 262-375-8559 info@chemindustrial.com
  www.chemindustrial.com
Manufacturers of pH control, neutralizing process systems and hydrocyclones.
CEO: Michael Lloyd
mlloyd@chemindustrial.com
Sales Manager: Michael Lloyd
Estimated Sales: $5-10 Million
Number Employees: 10-19
Square Footage: 6000
Brands:
 Chemindustrial

20500 Chemineer
P.O.Box 1123
Dayton, OH 45401-1123
  937-454-3200
 Fax: 937-454-3379 chemineer@nov.com
  www.chemineer.com
Agitators and mixers
Manager: Patty Breig
Contact: Cherie Buhler
c.buhler@chemineer.com
Estimated Sales: $10-50 Million
Number Employees: 250-499

20501 Chemir Analytical Svc
2672 Metro Blvd
Maryland Heights, MO 63043-2412
  314-291-6620
 Fax: 314-291-6630 800-659-7659
  www.chemir.net
Provides investigative analytical services for the food & beverage industry. Services include contaminant identification, material/foreign object identification, off-colors/off-odors/off-flavors analysis, extractables/leachablestoxicological evaluations, packaging failure analysis and litigation support.
Chairman: Shri Thanedar
sthanedar@chemir.com
Number Employees: 50-99

20502 ChemtranUSA.com
5634 Shirley Ln
Houston, TX 77032-2640
  281-590-9400
 Fax: 763-476-8155 800-523-9033
 info@ChemTranUSA.com www.chemtranusa.com
Specialize in packaging for shipment of infectious substances; suppliers of UN Performance-Oriented Packaging

Owner: Randy Hill
randy@chemtranusa.com
Number Employees: 10-19

20503 Chemtreat
4461 Cox Rd # 106
Glen Allen, VA 23060-3331
  804-935-2000
 Fax: 804-965-6974 800-442-8292
 michaelk@chemtreat.com www.chemtreat.com
Contact: Jackie Allen
allen@chemtreat.com
Estimated Sales: $1-5 Million
Number Employees: 1-4

20504 Chemtura Corp
199 Benson Rd
Middlebury, CT 06762-3218
  203-573-2000
 Fax: 203-573-3711 800-295-2392
  www.chemtura.com
CEO: Ron Abbott
ron.abbott@chemtura.com
Estimated Sales: Over $1 Billion
Number Employees: 500-999

20505 Chep
8517 Southpark Cir # 100
Orlando, FL 32819-9062
  407-370-2437
 Fax: 407-355-6211 800-243-7872
President: Michael Lamb
Contact: Amanda Abbott
amanda.abbott@chep.com
Estimated Sales: Less Than $500,000
Number Employees: 1-4

20506 Cherry's Industrial Eqpt Corp
600 Morse Ave
Elk Grove Vlg, IL 60007-5102
  847-364-0200
 Fax: 800-350-8454 800-350-0011
 sales@cherrysind.com www.cherrysind.com
Manufacturer and exporter of aluminum shipping containers and pallet transfer machines, inverters and retrievers; importer of pallet inverters
President: David Novak
david@cherrysind.com
National Accounts Manager: James Woods
Estimated Sales: $500,000-$750,000
Number Employees: 10-19
Square Footage: 60000

20507 Cheshire Signs
201 Old Homestead Highway
Keene, NH 03431-4441
  603-352-5985
Neon and plastic signs
President: Anthony A Magaletta
Estimated Sales: $500,000-$1 Million
Number Employees: 1 to4

20508 Chesmont Engineering CoInc
619 Jeffers Cir
Exton, PA 19341-2540
  610-594-9200
 Fax: 610-594-1909 heatpro@aol.com
  www.chesmont-engineering.com
Fume incinerators for volatile organic compounds and odors; also, process heating systems, fuel and propane standby systems and baking ovens
Owner: Christopher Mohler
heatpro@aol.com
Office Administrator: Lois Lanza
VP: Christopher Mohler
Office Manager: Kathy Tiffany
Estimated Sales: Below $1Million
Number Employees: 1-4
Square Footage: 8000

20509 Chester Hoist
PO Box 449
Lisbon, OH 44432
  330-424-7248
 Fax: 330-424-3126 800-424-7248
  www.chesterhoist.com
Manufacturer and importer of hoists including manual chain, worm-drive and electrical low headroom; exporter of manual and electric chain hoists
Manager: Bob Burkey
Quality Control: Bob Eusanio
Sales Rep.: Chris Reynolds
Application Engineer: Vince Anderson
Product Manager: Joe Runyon

Estimated Sales: $10-20 Million
Number Employees: 50-99
Parent Co: Columbus McKinnon Corporation
Brands:
 Chester
 Model Am
 Zephyr

20510 Chester Plastics
Highway 3
P.O. Box 460
Chester, NS B0J 1J0
Canada
  902-275-3522
 Fax: 902-275-5002
Manufacturer and exporter of rigid plastic packaging and thermoformed plastic bottles; importer of plastic sheeting
President: George Nemskeri
General Manger: John Babiak
Marketing Manager: Ed Baker
General Manager: Michael Johnston
Number Employees: 90
Square Footage: 108000

20511 (HQ)Chester-Jensen Co., Inc.
345 Tilghman St
Chester, PA 19013-3432
  610-876-6276
 Fax: 610-876-0485 800-685-3750
 htxchng@chester-jensen.com
  www.chester-jensen.com
stainless steel food processing equipment, including sanitary chillers, ice builders (thermal storage), batch mixing processors, plate heat exchangers & cook-chill equipment.
President: Richard Miller
CEO: Steven Miller
Sales Director: Robert Skoog
Estimated Sales: $10-20 Million
Square Footage: 76000
Type of Packaging: Consumer, Food Service, Private Label, Bulk
Other Locations:
 Chester-Jensen Company
 Cattaraugus NY

20512 Chesterfield Awning Co
9301 S Western Ave
Chicago, IL 60643-6736
  773-239-1513
 Fax: 708-848-4309 800-339-6522
  www.chesterfieldawning.com
Commercial awnings
Owner: David Ausema
Vice President: Dave Ausema
dave@chesterfieldawnings.com
Estimated Sales: $1-3,000,000
Number Employees: 20-49

20513 Chesterfield Awning Co
16999 Van Dam Rd
South Holland, IL 60473-2660
  708-596-4434
 Fax: 708-596-9469 800-339-6522
 david@chesterfieldawning.com
  www.chesterfieldawning.com
Commercial awnings
President: David Ausema
dave@chesterfieldawning.com
Estimated Sales: Less Than $500,000
Number Employees: 1-4

20514 Chestnut Labs
3233 E. Chestnut Expressway
Springfield, MO 65802
  417-829-3788
 Fax: 417-829-3787 information@chestnutlabs.com
  www.chestnutlabs.com
Laboratory testing for food microbiology pathogens such as Salmonella and Listeria testing, and water analysis testing.
Contact: Kristen Acker
kristenacker@chestnutlabs.com

20515 Chevron Global Lubricants
555 Market Street
San Francisco, CA 94105-2800
  415-894-4646
 Fax: 415-894-1297
Number Employees: 10,000 +

20516 Chicago Automated Labeling Inc
44 N 450 E
Valparaiso, IN 46383-9310
219-531-0646
Fax: 219-462-8315 www.chicagoautolabel.com
Manufactuerers of labeling equipment
Owner: Mark Walker
sales@chicagoautolabel.com
CEO: Ken Walker
Estimated Sales: $2 000,000
Number Employees: 10-19

20517 Chicago Conveyor Corporation
330 S La Londe Avenue
Addison, IL 60101-3309
630-543-6300
Fax: 630-543-2308
Pneumatic conveying systems for powder or granu-
lar materials, storage spaces and related equipment,
weighing bathcing and controls
VP Sales: Tom Hodanovac
Contact: Mike Stogdill
mstogdill@chicagoconveyor.com
Purchasing Manager: Keith Stark
Estimated Sales: $5-10 Million
Number Employees: 20
Square Footage: 60000

20518 Chicago Dowel Co Inc
4700 W Grand Ave
Chicago, IL 60639-4695
773-622-2000
Fax: 773-622-2047 800-333-6935
sales@chicagodowel.com www.chicagodowel.com
Skewers for candy, apples, corn dogs and meat
President: Paul Iacono
piacono@chicagodowel.com
Sales Director: Jay Goodwin
Manager: George Iacono
Estimated Sales: $5-10 Million
Number Employees: 20-49
Square Footage: 100000

20519 Chicago Ink & Research Co
97 Ida Ave
Antioch, IL 60002-1887
847-395-1078
Fax: 847-395-3568
Industrial marking and rubber stamp inks
President: Charles Doty
sales@chicagoink.com
General Manager: F Arthur Doty
Estimated Sales: $1-2.5 Million
Number Employees: 5-9
Square Footage: 16000

20520 Chicago Scale & Slicer Company
2359 Rose St
Franklin Park, IL 60131-3504
847-455-3400
Fax: 847-455-3450
Manufacturer, importer and exporter of hand oper-
ated and electric slicers; also, grinders and knives
Owner: Eugene Dee
Estimated Sales: $1-5 Million
Number Employees: 10 to 19
Square Footage: 28000
Parent Co: Lawndale Corporation
Brands:
Digi
Globe

20521 Chicago Show Inc
851 Asbury Dr
Buffalo Grove, IL 60089-4525
847-955-0200
Fax: 847-955-9996 www.chicagoshow.com
Point of purchase advertising displays and signs;
also, fixtures
CEO: Andrew Prantner
prantner@mail.med.upenn.edu
CEO: James M. Snediker
CFO: B Fier
Estimated Sales: $5-10 Million
Number Employees: 50-99
Square Footage: 200000

20522 Chicago Stainless Eqpt Inc
1280 SW 34th St
Palm City, FL 34990-3308
772-781-1441
Fax: 772-781-1488 800-927-8575
www.chicagostainless.com

Since 1937, manufacturer of high quality sanitary
pressure gauges, homogenizer gauges and digital
thermometers
Manager: Jerry Williamson
VP of Marketing: Mark Mistarz
Sales Director: Jerry Williamson
Manager: John Kalousek
john@chicagostainless.com
Estimated Sales: $2.5-5 Million
Number Employees: 10-19
Brands:
Pharma-Flow
Sani-Flow

20523 Chicago Trashpacker Corporation
290 N Prospect St
Marengo, IL 60152-3235
815-568-5116
800-635-5745
Trash compactors, can and glass crushers
President/CEO: Fredrick Gohl
VP/R&D/Quality Control: Bill Phillips
Estimated Sales: Below $5 Million
Number Employees: 10
Number of Products: 12
Square Footage: 2000
Brands:
Trashpacker

20524 Chickadee Products
1208 N Swift Road
Addison, IL 60101-6104
773-523-7972
Fax: 773-523-9066 800-621-5046
donaldmk@aol.com
Custom blending
Estimated Sales: $5-10 Million
Number Employees: 10-19

20525 Chickasaw Broom Mfg Co Inc
7710 Jamison Rd
Little Rock, AR 72209-5541
501-562-0311
www.thehatchergroup.com
Brooms and mops
CEO: Everette Hatcher
ehatcher@thehatchergroup.com
Number Employees: 10-19

20526 Chief Industries
PO Box 848
Kearney, NE 68848-0848
308-237-3186
Fax: 308-237-2650 800-359-8833
agri@chiefind.com www.chiefind.com
Manufacturer and exporter of grain drying and han-
dling equipment; also, bins
President: Roger Townsend
Research & Development: Jim Moffit
Sales Director: Ed Benson
Plant Manager: Duene McCann
Purchasing Manager: Rob Morris
Estimated Sales: $20-50 Million
Number Employees: 100-249
Number of Brands: 3
Number of Products: 12
Square Footage: 90000
Parent Co: Chief Industries
Type of Packaging: Bulk
Brands:
Caldwell Manufacturing
Chief
York

20527 Chil-Con Products
PO Box 1385
Brantford, ON N3T 5T6
Canada
519-759-3010
Fax: 519-759-1611 800-263-0086
www.henrytech.com
Manufacturer and exporter of pressure vessels, oil
separators, condensers, process cooling heat
exchangers, direct expansion and flooded chillers
General Manager: Scott Rahmel
President, Chief Executive Officer: Michael
Giordano
Business Manager: Harry Stewart
Plant Manager: Myron Harasym
Number Employees: 95
Square Footage: 400000
Parent Co: Valve, Henry, Company

20528 Childres Custom Canvas Prods
711 E Highway 67
Duncanville, TX 75137-3407
972-298-4943
Fax: 972-709-7453 info@childresproducts.com
www.childresproducts.com
Awnings
Owner: Gary Childres
info@childresproducts.com
CFO: Linda Childres
Estimated Sales: $2,500,000
Number Employees: 20-49
Square Footage: 20000

20529 Chili Plastics
4 Pixley Industrial Pkwy
Rochester, NY 14624-2399
585-889-4680
Fax: 585-889-6199
Molded plastics including containers
Manager: Mike Curley
Estimated Sales: $.5-1 million
Number Employees: 5-9

20530 Chill Rite Mfg
2371 Gause Blvd W
Slidell, LA 70460-6501
985-641-4865
Fax: 985-641-0183 800-256-2190
www.chillrite32.com
Beverage dispensing and delivery systems
Owner: Buddy Abraham
info@chillrite32.com
Estimated Sales: $1-5 Million
Number Employees: 20-49
Brands:
Chill Rite
Desco

20531 Chillers Solutions
101 Alexander Ave # 3
Pompton Plains, NJ 07444-1854
973-835-2800
Fax: 973-835-3222 800-526-5201
www.edwards-eng.com
Manufacturer and exporter of heating/cooling equip-
ment and products, control components, hydronic
heating/cooling systems and vapor recovery units for
pollution and process control; also, packaged
industrial chillers
President: R Waldrop
VP Engineering: G Passaro
Manager: Aaron Herl
aherl@frhsd.com
Plant Manager: Jose Mercedes
Estimated Sales: $40 Million
Number Employees: 50-99
Brands:
Box'fin
Quiet' Slide

20532 Chilson's Shops Inc
8 Industrial Pkwy
Easthampton, MA 01027-1164
413-529-8062
Fax: 413-529-2022 chilsons@chilsons.com
www.chilsons.com
Commercial awnings
President and R&D and QC: Edward Ghareeb
chilsons@chilsons.com
Estimated Sales: $1-2,500,000
Number Employees: 10-19

20533 Chilton Consulting Group
PO Box 129
Rocky Face, GA 30740-0129
706-694-8325
Fax: 706-694-8316 info@chiltonconsulting.com
www.chiltonconsulting.com
Consulting firm providing HACCP development,
validation and training, food safety and quality au-
dits, crisis management, environmental sanitation
audits, employee safety training, etc
President: Jeff Chilton
General Manager: Brent Heldt
Contact: Jorge Acosta
jacosta@chiltonconsulting.com

20534 China D Food Service
2535 S Kessler Street
Wichita, KS 67217-1044
316-945-2323
Fax: 316-945-5557
Food service and management

Purchasing: Lisa Diez
Estimated Sales: $300,000-500,000
Number Employees: 1-4
Type of Packaging: Food Service

20535 China Food Merchant Corporation
1601 N Hale Avenue
Fullerton, CA 92831-1218
714-773-0803
Fax: 714-773-1082

20536 China Lenox Incorporated
1414 Radcliffe Street
Bristol, PA 19007-5413
267-525-7800
www.lenox.com
Manufacturer and exporter of fine china dinnerware and giftware
Contact: Nea Ahern
nea_ahern@msn.com
Human Resources Manager: Jim Haddix
Estimated Sales: $91 Million
Number Employees: 1,500
Square Footage: 9774
Parent Co: Brown-Foreman
Type of Packaging: Food Service

20537 Chinet Company
722 Barrington Circle
Winter Springs, FL 32708-6117
407-365-5372
Fax: 407-359-8381 800-539-3726
www.mychinet.com
Biodegradable disposable tableware; serving the food service industry
District Sales Manager: Marvin Tolley

20538 Chinet Company
27601 Forbes Rd # 59
Laguna Niguel, CA 92677-1242
949-348-1711
Fax: 949-489-2043
Disposable plastic and paper tableware
Owner: Xiao Qiu
Regional Sales Manager: Ronald Shillings
Estimated Sales: Less than $500,000
Number Employees: 10-19
Brands:
  Chinet

20539 Chino Works America Inc
22301 S Western Ave # 105
Sutie 105
Torrance, CA 90501-4155
310-787-8899
Fax: 310-787-8899 888-321-9118
info@chinoamerica.com www.chinoamerica.com
Recorders, controllers, infared technology (pyrometers) and noncontact moisture reading on line
President: Toshikazu Inden
Sales, OEM and Tech Support: Toshi Toshi
Vice President: Akemi Adachi
akemi@chinoamerica.com
Sales Engineer: Mike Matsuno
Estimated Sales: $500,000-$1 Million
Number Employees: 5-9
Number of Products: 100

20540 Chipmaker Tooling Supply
7352 Whittier Ave
Whittier, CA 90602-1131
562-698-5840
Fax: 562-698-5646 800-659-5840
chipmakerca@yahoo.com www.chip-makers.com
A major supplier of machines and parts to the food industry.
Manager: Patty Rivera
Contact: Stephen Smith
chipmakerca@yahoo.com
Office Manager/Purchasing Agent: Laura Kurbel
Estimated Sales: $3-5 Million
Number Employees: 1-4
Square Footage: 48000

20541 Chiquita Brands LLC.
DCOTA Office Center
1855 Griffin Rd., Suite C-346
Fort Lauderdale, FL 33004-2275
954-924-5700
www.chiquita.com
Fruit and vegetable grower and producer of fresh and prepared food products.

President: Carlos Lopez Flores
VP: Chris Dugan
Year Founded: 1899
Estimated Sales: $3 Billion
Number Employees: 20,000
Number of Brands: 3
Parent Co: Cutrale-Safra
Type of Packaging: Consumer, Food Service, Private Label, Bulk
Brands:
  Chiquita®
  Fresh Express®
  Bites

20542 Chlorinators Inc
1044 SE Dixie Cutoff Rd
Stuart, FL 34994-3436
772-288-4854
Fax: 772-287-3238 800-327-9761
regal@regalchlorinators.com
www.regalchlorinators.com
Manufacturer and exporter of gas chlorinators, waste water treatment systems, sulphonators, dual cylinder scales, chlorine gas detectors, flow pacing control valves and vacuum monitors
President: Diane Haskett
Vice President: Chris Myers
Marketing Manager: Jill Majka
Operations Manager: John Hentz
Estimated Sales: $3-5 Million
Number Employees: 20-49
Square Footage: 20000
Brands:
  Regal

20543 Chocolate Concepts
114 S Prospect Ave
Hartville, OH 44632-8906
330-877-3322
Fax: 330-877-1100 cc@dmpweb.net
Manufacturer, importer and exporter of chocolate equipment including tempering tanks, measuring pumps, vibrating tables, cooling conveying tunnels, coin machines and kettles; manufacturer and exporter of plastic standard and custommolds
Owner: Scott Huckestein
shuckestein@dmpweb.net
Estimated Sales: $1-2.5 Million
Number Employees: 5-9
Number of Products: 55
Square Footage: 120000
Parent Co: LCF
Brands:
  Chocolate Concepts

20544 (HQ)Choctaw-Kaul Distribution Company
540 Vinewood Avenue
Detroit, MI 48208
313-894-9494
Fax: 313-894-7977 jgreer@choctawkaul.com
www.choctawkaul.com
Gloves, personal protective equipment and safety related products
Estimated Sales: $21 Million
Number Employees: 125
Square Footage: 110000

20545 Choklit Molds LTD
23 Carrington St
Lincoln, RI 02865-1702
401-725-7377
Fax: 401-724-7776 800-777-6653
www.choklitmolds.com
Manufacturer and exporter of reusable plastic chocolate molds. Wholesaler of packaging supplies for the candy retail.
President: Lea Goyette
CEO: Richard Goyette
VP/Treasurer: Lea Goyette
Contact: Richard Oyette
choklitmolds@cox.net
Plant Manager: Chris Mottram
Purchasing: Kelly Mottram
Number Employees: 1-4
Square Footage: 20000
Type of Packaging: Bulk

20546 Chop-Rite Two Inc
531 Old Skippack Rd
Harleysville, PA 19438-2203
215-256-4620
Fax: 215-256-4363 800-683-5858
info@chop-rite.com www.chop-rite.com

Meat grinders, cherry stoners and juice extractors
Owner: Nancy Saeger
info@chop-rite.com
Estimated Sales: $5-10 Million
Number Employees: 10-19

20547 Chord Engineering
P.O.Box 518
Niwot, CO 80544
303-449-5812
Fax: 303-546-6405 www.chord.org
On-line inspection equipment for cans
Estimated Sales: Below $500,000
Number Employees: 2

20548 Chore-Boy Corporation
411 E Water Street
Centerville, IN 47330
765-855-5434
Fax: 765-855-1311
Sanitary pumps
President: Ronald Napier
Estimated Sales: $500,000-$1 Million
Number Employees: 5-9
Square Footage: 14000
Brands:
  Chore-Boy
  Kleen-Flo

20549 Chori America
154 Veterans Drive
Northvale, NJ 07647-2302
201-750-7050
Fax: 201-750-7055 866-420-7050
Flexible pouch filling and sealing equipment
Estimated Sales: $1-3 Million
Number Employees: 1-4
Brands:
  Hisaka Works Ltd
  Toyo Jidoki

20550 (HQ)Christianson Systems Inc
20421 15th St SE
PO Box 138
Blomkest, MN 56216-9706
320-995-6141
Fax: 320-995-6145 800-328-8896
info@christianson.com www.onyxrp.com
Manufacturer and exporter of pneumatic conveyors and ship and barge unloaders
President: Jim Gerhardt
jger@christianson.com
Marketing Manager: Barbara Gilberts
Sales: Tim Flaan
Estimated Sales: $5-10 Million
Number Employees: 50-99
Square Footage: 170000
Brands:
  Chem-Vac
  Handlair
  Push-Pac
  Superportable
  Supertower
  Vac-U-Vator

20551 Christman Screenprint Inc
2822 Wilbur St
Springfield, MI 49037-7954
269-962-6274
Fax: 269-962-9411 800-962-9330
dtc@christmanscreenprint.com
www.christmanscreenprint.com
Decals, labels, signs, aprons, shirts, jackets and hats
President: David Christman
dtc@christmanscreenprint.com
Secretary: Dana Christman
VP: Michael Christman
Estimated Sales: Less than $500,000
Number Employees: 1-4

20552 Christy Industries Inc
1812 Bath Ave # 1
Brooklyn, NY 11214-4690
718-236-0211
Fax: 718-259-3294 800-472-2078
www.christy-ind.com
Manufacturer and exporter of fire and burglar alarms; wholesaler/distributor of intercoms and television equipment including security and closed circuit
President: Statz Cheryl
s.cheryl@alarmdistributor.com

Estimated Sales: $1-3 Million
Number Employees: 5-9
Square Footage: 6000

20553 Christy Machine Co
118 Birchard Ave
P.O. Box 32
Fremont, OH 43420-3008
419-332-6451
Fax: 419-332-8800 888-332-6451
www.christymachine.com
Manufacturer and exporter of conveyers; also, filling, icing and glazing machinery
President: Randy L Fielding
cmc1@cros.net
Estimated Sales: $1-2.5 Million
Number Employees: 10-19

20554 Chroma Tone
P.O.Box 4
Saint Clair, PA 17970
214-321-8601
Fax: 214-320-3791 800-878-1552
Metal and plastic signs, decals, point of purchase displays and candy rail strips
President: Matthew Parulis
Marketing Director: Nan Merchant
Plant Manager: Jerry Watts
Estimated Sales: $2.5-5 Million
Number Employees: 20-49
Square Footage: 60000

20555 Chromalox Inc
103 Gamma Dr # 2
Pittsburgh, PA 15238-2981
412-967-3800
Fax: 412-967-3938 800-443-2640
www.chromalox.com
Manufacturer and exporter of electric heating elements for commercial cooking equipment
Managing Director: Steve Valentino
CEO: Anthony Deane
deanea@dmipartners.com
Chief Financial Officer/Secretary: Edward Cumberledge
Vice President: Peter Ranalli
Vice President, Engineering: Roger Ormsby
Quality Manager: Jack Foster
Marketing Manager: Paul Skidmore
Senior Vice President, Sales: John Halloran
Facilities Manager: Roger Iverson
Procurement Manager: Kristina McCann
Estimated Sales: $161 Million
Number Employees: 100-249
Square Footage: 20259
Parent Co: Emerson Electric Company
Brands:
Chromalox

20556 Chronos Richardson
2 Stewart Place
Fairfield, NJ 07004-2202
973-227-3522
Fax: 973-227-8478 800-284-3644
info@bmhchronosrichardson.com
www.bmhchronosrichardson.com
Bags, batching systems, form, fill and seal, palletizing
Mktg. Manager: Mike Hudak
Contact: Bob Duran
info@chronosrichardson.com
Number Employees: 415

20557 Chroust Associates International
22311 Ventura Boulevard
Suite 115
Woodland Hills, CA 91364-1555
818-348-1438
Fax: 818-348-1094 chroust@aol.com
www.members.aol.com/chroust/associates.html
Consultant specializing in engineering and design for restaurants, schools, hotels, casinos, schools and universities
Principal: Thomas Chroust
Product Manager: Ivan Benes
Number Employees: 3
Square Footage: 6000

20558 Chrysler & Koppin Co
7000 Intervale St
Detroit, MI 48238-2498
313-491-7100
Fax: 313-491-8769 800-441-0038
dkoppin@aol.com www.chryslerkoppin.com

Pre-fabricated walk-in refrigerators and freezers
President: Douglas G Koppin
CEO: Dean Koppin
CFO: Karen Oakley
kare@chryslerkoppin.com
Estimated Sales: $5-10 Million
Number Employees: 5-9

20559 Chu's Packaging Supplies
10011 Santa Fe Springs Rd
Santa Fe Springs, CA 90670-2921
562-944-6411
Fax: 562-944-7113 800-377-4754
www.chuspkg.com
Owner: Pao Chu
pao@movingpad.com
Estimated Sales: $10-20 Million
Number Employees: 10-19

20560 Chuppa Knife Manufacturing
133 N Conalco Drive
Jackson, TN 38301
731-424-1212
Fax: 731-424-8937 chuppak@aol.com
Manufacturer and exporter of stainless steel and aluminum handle cutlery
President: Elmer Rausch
Estimated Sales: $1-2.5 Million
Number Employees: 8
Number of Products: 350
Type of Packaging: Consumer, Food Service, Private Label

20561 Church & Dwight Co., Inc.
Princeton South Corporate Center
500 Charles Ewing Boulevard
Ewing, NJ 08628
609-806-1200
800-833-9532
www.churchdwight.com
Personal care, household cleaning, fabric care, and health and well-being products for the consumer market. Manufacturer of Arm & Hammer brand sodium bicarbonate (baking soda), and other leavening products for the baking industry.
Chairman/President/CEO: Matthew Farrell
Executive VP/CFO: Rick Dierker
Executive VP/General Counsel/Secretary: Patrick de Maynadier
Executive V, Global R&D: Carlos Linares
Executive VP/CMO: Britta Bomhard
Executive VP, U.S. Sales: Paul Wood
Executive VP, Global Operations: Rick Spann
Year Founded: 1846
Estimated Sales: $4.15 Billion
Number Employees: 4,700
Number of Brands: 34
Type of Packaging: Consumer, Food Service, Bulk
Brands:
ARM & HAMMER
Arrid
Answer
AIM
Batiste Dry Shampoo
Close-Up
Delicare
Feline Pine
First Response
KABOOM
Lady's Choice
Legatin
L'il Critters
Nair
Orajel
Orange Glo
OxiClean
PB 8
Pepsodent
Pre-Seed
RepHresh
Replens
Simply Saline
Spinbrush
Toppik
Trojan
Truly Radient
vitafusion
Viviscal
Waterpik
Wellgate
XTRA

20562 Church Offset Printing Inc
1731 Margaretha Ave
P.O. Box 988
Albert Lea, MN 56007-3270
507-373-6485
Fax: 507-373-2716 800-345-2116
sales@churchoffsetprinting.com
www.churchoffsetprinting.com
Labels for automatic or hand application; also, specializing in flexographic printing
Owner: Michael Kruse
mikek@churchoffsetprinting.com
Financial Manager: Dan Bodensteiner
Plant and Project Manager: Todd Hoenisch
Estimated Sales: Below $1 Million
Number Employees: 20-49

20563 (HQ)CiMa-Pak Corp.
50 Lindsay Ave
Dorval, QC H9P 2T8
Canada
514-631-6222
Fax: 514-631-7361 877-631-2462
info@cima-pak.com www.cima-pak.com
Trays and tray-sealing equipment
President: Tim Dawson
Sales Manager: Todd Trudel
Other Locations:
Mississauga, ON
Mooers NY

20564 Cielo Foods
9238 Bally Ct
Rancho Cucamonga, CA 91730-5313
909-945-2323
Fax: 909-945-9090 877-652-4356
www.cielousa.com
Frozen yogurt
Owner: Dan Kim
info@cielousa.com
Number Employees: 5-9

20565 Cimino Box & Pallet Co
8500 Clinton Rd # J
Cleveland, OH 44144-1000
216-961-7377
Fax: 216-961-4054
Pallets
Owner: Frank Ritson
ciminobox@aol.com
VP: Frank Ritson
Estimated Sales: Less Than $500,000
Number Employees: 5-9

20566 Cin-Made Packaging Group
3150 Clinton Ct
Norcross, GA 30071
770-476-9088
Fax: 513-541-5945 800-264-7494
info@cin-made.com
Manufacturer and exporter of paper composite cans and tubes for specialty markets including wine and spirits, fancy foods and teas.
Manager: Hartmut Geisselbrecht
CFO: John Ewalt
Quality Control: Erik Frey
Marketing Director: Hartmut Geisselbrecht
Sales Manager: Janet Pickerell
Plant Manager: Eric Frey
Purchasing Manager: Phyllis Dietrich
Estimated Sales: $10-20 Million
Number Employees: 20-49
Type of Packaging: Consumer, Private Label

20567 Cincinnati Convertors Inc
1730 Cleneay Ave
Cincinnati, OH 45212-3506
513-731-6600
Fax: 513-731-6605
info@cincinnaticonvertors.com
www.cincinnaticonvertors.com
Up to 6 color printed and plain flexible packaging for food, pharmaceutical and chemical applications: cellophane bags, confectioners' bags, heat sealed bags, food bags, plastic packaging, thermoformed cups, pouch lidding materials andtea bag tags
President: Donald Ellsworth Jr
VP: Donald Ellsworth, Jr.
Office Manager: Kristin Goltra
kristin@cincinnaticonvertors.com
COO: Kristin Goltra
Estimated Sales: $2.5-5 Million
Number Employees: 10-19

20568 Cincinnati Foam Products
3244 McGill Rd
Cincinnati, OH 45251

513-741-7722
Fax: 513-741-7723
Manufacture high quality foam shipping containers, protective packaging, molded EPS and fabricated foam.
Founder: Carl Welage
Plant Manager: John Shearer
Estimated Sales: Below $5 Million
Number Employees: 5-9
Square Footage: 20000
Type of Packaging: Consumer, Food Service, Private Label, Bulk

20569 Cincinnati Industrial Machry
4600 N Mason Montgomery Rd
Mason, OH 45040-9176

513-923-5600
Fax: 513-769-0697 800-677-0076
sales@cinind.com www.thearmorgroup.com
Warewashing equipment for bakeries, supermarkets, food processing, and institutions
Owner: Frank Ahaus
fahaus@cinind.com
Global Sales Director: George Shillcock
fahaus@cinind.com
Estimated Sales: $5-10 Million
Number Employees: 250-499
Number of Brands: 2
Square Footage: 320000
Parent Co: The Armor Group, Inc
Type of Packaging: Food Service

20570 Cincinnati Industrial Machry
4600 N Mason Montgomery Rd
Mason, OH 45040-9176

513-923-5600
Fax: 513-769-0697 800-677-0076
sales@cinind.com www.thearmorgroup.com
Manufacturer and exporter of baking ovens and can washing equipment; also turnkey finishing systems and cleaning/drying/curing systems
Owner: Frank Ahaus
fahaus@cinind.com
Marketing Director: Liz Chamberlain
Public Relations: Liz Chamberlain
Operations Manager: Joe Bohlen
Estimated Sales: $20-25 Million
Number Employees: 250-499
Square Footage: 317000

20571 Cinelli Esperia
380 Chrislea Road
Woodbridge, ON L4L 8A8
Canada

905-856-1820
albert@cinelli.com
www.gcinelli-esperia.com
Manufacturer and exporter of spiral mixers, bagel and roll machinery, steam proofers, baguette and bread molders, automatic bun dividers, rounders, sheeters, etc.; importer of coffee machines and revolving rack and convection ovens
President: Guido Cinnelli
Sales/Marketing Manager: Albert Cinelli
Number Employees: 50
Square Footage: 160000
Brands:
G. Cinelli-Esperia Corp.

20572 Cintas Corp
6800 Cintas Blvd
Cincinnati, OH 45262

Fax: 800-864-3888 800-864-3676
www.cintas.com
Business uniforms; also, rental uniform service available.
EVP/Chief Administrative Officer: Mike Thompson
Chairman & Chief Executive Officer: Scott Farmer
farmers@cintas.com
EVP/Chief Financial Officer: J. Michael Hansen
SVP/General Counsel/Secretary: Thomas Frooman
Vice President & Treasurer: Paul Adler
EVP/Chief Operating Officer: Todd Schneider
Year Founded: 1929
Estimated Sales: $4.9 Billion
Number Employees: 45,000

20573 Cintex of America
283 E Lies Rd
Carol Stream, IL 60188

630-588-0900
Fax: 425-962-4600 800-424-6839
www.centex.com
Manufacturer and exporter of metal detection check weighing equipment, x-ray inspection systems and vision systems
President: Anthony Divito
CEO: Simon Armstrong
CFO: Richard Harwood Smith
Marketing: Dan Izzard
Sales: Dan Izzaro
Production: Jeff Hoffman
Plant Manager: Jeff Hoffman
Purchasing: Sandy Sell
Estimated Sales: $10-20 Million
Number Employees: 50-99
Number of Brands: 10
Number of Products: 4
Square Footage: 60000
Brands:
Autosearch
Eclipse
Insight

20574 Cipriani
30271 Tomas
Rancho Sta Marg, CA 92688-2123

949-589-3978
Fax: 949-589-3979 www.ciprianicorp.com
Manufacturer, distributor and importer of hygienic stainless steel valves
President: Maria Carlo
mg@ciprianicorp.com
CEO: Robert Moreno
Vice President: Maria Grazia Cipriani
Marketing/Sales VP: Carlo Cipriani
Sales Manager: Chris P Winsek
Estimated Sales: $1,000,000
Number Employees: 5-9
Square Footage: 6000

20575 Ciranda Inc.
221 Vine St
Hudson, WI 54016

715-386-1737
Fax: 715-386-3277 www.ciranda.com
Global supplier of organic, non-GMO and fair trade ingredients, specializing in tapioca syrups; starches and derivatives; honey and agave; cocoa and chocolates; coconut; soy and sunflower lecithin; and various oils and fats.
Contact: Patty Gfrerer
pgfrerer@gmail.com
Chief Financial Officer: Mark Cross
Marketing Manager: Tonya Lofgren
Human Resources Manager: Karen Brabec
Director of Commerical Operations: Joe Rouleau

20576 Circle Packaging Machinery Inc
2020 American Blvd
De Pere, WI 54115-9139

920-983-3420
Fax: 920-983-3421 www.circlepackaging.com
Vertical and horizontal form/fill/seal machines.
F/F/S machines can be used to package a wide verity of liquids, tablet, capsules and other food and beverage products.
President: John Dykema
john@circlepackaging.com
VP Marketing & Sales: Don Stelzer
Product Manager: Craig Stelzer
Production Manager: Steve Joosten
Parts & Service Manager: Ralph Ruggiero
Estimated Sales: Less than $500,000
Number Employees: 20-49
Type of Packaging: Consumer

20577 Circuits & Systems Inc
59 2nd St
East Rockaway, NY 11518-1236

516-593-4607
Fax: 516-593-4607 800-645-4301
sales@arlynscales.com www.arlynscales.com
Manufacturer and exporter of electronic scales
President: Arnold Gordon
a.gordon@chaverware.com
Estimated Sales: Below $5 Million
Number Employees: 20-49
Square Footage: 20000

20578 Cisco Eagle
2120 Valley View Ln
Dallas, TX 75234-8911

972-331-3000
Fax: 972-406-9577 www.cisco-eagle.com
Carton erecting and sealing equipment; conveyors, conveyor systems, storage systems
President: Steve Strifler
steve.strifler@cisco-eagle.com
Chairman the Board: Warren W Gandall
CEO: Warren W Gandall
Office Manager: Marc Dewall
Estimated Sales: $20-50 Million
Number Employees: 50-99
Type of Packaging: Bulk

20579 Citadel Computer Corporation
60A State Route 101A
Amherst, NH 03031-2213

603-672-5500
Fax: 603-672-5590 www.citadelcomputer.com
Industrial computer systems for advanced information management and data collection applications in industrial warehousing, transportation and logistics-product configurations include integrated touchscreens and multilple displaysizes
President: Gregory Walker
CFO: Lesley Sillion
Manager: Andy Nacard
VP Sales: Brandy Herring
Estimated Sales: $10-25 Million
Number Employees: 2

20580 Citect Inc
30000 Mill Creek Ave Ste 300
Alpharetta, GA 30022

770-521-7511
Fax: 770-521-7512 sales-americas@citect.com
www.citect.com
Services include integrated solution systems that facilitate productivity, product quality and traceability. CitectSCADA Reports system includes advanced data management tools for tracking production and serving as a reporting tool anddata transfer engine. Ampla Suite system facilitates the streamlining of the production process thereby increasing throughput and eliminating downtime, reducing wastage, improving quality levels, tracking resource genealogy and achieving industrycompliance.
Manager: Scott Mack
Chief Technology Officer: Paul Francis
Chief Human Resources Officer: Andrea Bidwell
Global Director SCADA Systems: Stephen Flannigan
Global Director Ampla Systems: Colette Munro
Global Director Meta Systems: Kurt Lovell
Global Director S-Business Systems: James Cowie
Director Global Partner Programs: Brooke Mauro
Contact: Danie Badenhorst
daniebadenhorst@citect.com
Estimated Sales: $61.5 Million

20581 Citra-Tech
2 Prespas Street
Lefkosia, CY 33811

info@citra-tech.com
www.citra-tech.com
Manufacturer and exporter of fruit handling and processing machinery; consultant specializing in the design and construction of fresh and citrus fruit processing facilities
President: P M Irby
VP: P Irby, Jr.
Number Employees: 25
Square Footage: 8000

20582 Citrus and Allied Essences
3000 Marcus Ave, Ste 3e11
New Hyde Park, NY 11042

516-354-1200
Fax: 516-354-1502 www.citrusandallied.com
Supplier of essential oils, oleoresins, aromatic chemicals and specialty flavor ingredients.
President/CEO/Owner: Richard Pisano Jr.
Executive Vice President: Stephen Pisano
Sales Manager: Ann Heller
Contact: Jodi Adams
jadams@citrusandallied.com
Director Purchasing: Rob Haedrich
Number Employees: 100+
Type of Packaging: Food Service, Bulk

20583 City Box Company
4390 Liberty Street
Aurora, IL 60504-9502
773-277-5500
Fax: 773-277-9541
Corrugated cartons; also, inner packaging
Marketing/Sales: Mark Rosenhlatt
Estimated Sales: less than $500,000
Number Employees: 20
Square Footage: 178000

20584 City Canvas
750 W San Carlos St
San Jose, CA 95126-3532
408-287-2688
Fax: 408-287-1727 info@citycanvas.com
www.citycanvas.com
Commercial awnings, canopies, backyard products, custom projects and yards. Also custom fabrication and installation of the finest commercial and residential retractable styles
President: Johnny Cerrito
cccanvas@aol.com
Estimated Sales: $1-2,500,000
Number Employees: 10-19
Number of Brands: 25

20585 City Grafx
243 Grimes Street
Suite D
Eugene, OR 97402
541-345-1101
Fax: 541-345-1942 800-258-2489
www.citygrafx.com
Manufacturer and exporter of tabletop signs, table numbers, specialty merchandising boards, custom signs, menu boards and dimensional graphics
President: Jeff Phoenix
j.phoenix@citygrafx.com
VP: Mary Phoenix
Estimated Sales: Below $5 Million
Number Employees: 1-4
Square Footage: 16000

20586 City Neon Sign Company
3117 E Glass Ave Ste C
Spokane, WA 99217
509-483-5171
Advertising, neon, electric and plastic signs
Owner: Thomas Quigley
Estimated Sales: less than $500,000
Number Employees: 1-4

20587 City Sign Svc Inc
3914 Elm St
Dallas, TX 75226-1218
214-826-4475
Fax: 214-826-4722 css1956@aol.com
citysignservices.com
Signs including advertising, neon, painted, indoor and outdoor
President: Kenneth Waits
css1956@aol.com
CFO: Shelly Peters
Quality Control: Kenneth Waits
Estimated Sales: $2.5-5 Million
Number Employees: 20-49

20588 City Signs LLC
65 Bonwood Dr
Jackson, TN 38301-7785
731-424-5551
Fax: 731-427-9096 877-248-9744
Electric, plastic and neon signs, billboards and electronic message centers
Owner: John Mc Caskill
Marketing Director: Paul Anderson
National Sales Manager: Scott Rogers
Estimated Sales: $2.5-5 Million
Number Employees: 10-19

20589 City Stamp & Seal Co
1308 W Anderson Ln # A
Austin, TX 78757-1496
512-452-2578
Fax: 512-452-2979 800-950-6074
Rubber stamps, badges, wall signs and embossing seals
Owner: Spencer Daniel
Office Manager: Sharon Smith
orders@city-stamp.com
General Manager: Stacy Daniel

Estimated Sales: Less Than $500,000
Number Employees: 5-9
Square Footage: 8400

20590 City-Long Beach Pubc Library
101 Pacific Ave
Long Beach, CA 90822-1003
562-570-7500
Fax: 562-628-2312 sara@lbplfoundation.org
www.lbpl.org
Information
Executive Director: Sara Myers
Contact: Mario Adame
madame@lbpl.org
Number Employees: 10-19

20591 Claire Manufacturing Company
500 S Vista Ave
Addison, IL 60101
630-543-7600
Fax: 630-543-4310 800-252-4731
www.clairemfg.com
Cleaning compounds, glass cleaners, aerosols, disinfectants, polishers and insecticides
President: Tony Schwab
CFO: Roger Hayes
VP Sales/Marketing: Bob Potvin
Contact: Mark Kubiak
mkubiak@clairemfg.com
Estimated Sales: G
Number Employees: 250-499
Square Footage: 85000
Parent Co: Oakite Products
Brands:
　Dust Up
　Fast Kill
　Fly Jinx
　Gleme
　Mister Jinx

20592 Clamco Corporation
775 Berea Industrial Parkway
Berea, OH 44017
216-267-1911
Fax: 216-267-8713 www.clamcocorp.com
Manufacturer and exporter of shrink packaging machinery and bag sealers
Owner: Serge Bergun
CEO: Mark Goldman
VP: Dennis McGrath
R&D: Rob Patton
Marketing: Dennis McGrath
Sales Director: Bruce Howell
Contact: Sandy Waite
swaite@clamcocorp.com
General Manager: Larry Boyles
Purchasing: Bob Snyder
Estimated Sales: $5-10 Million
Number Employees: 40
Square Footage: 48000
Parent Co: PAC Machinery Group
Type of Packaging: Consumer, Food Service, Private Label, Bulk

20593 Clamp Swing Pricing Co Inc
8386 Capwell Dr
Oakland, CA 94621-2114
510-567-1600
Fax: 510-567-1830 800-227-7615
cspinfo@clampswing.com www.clampswing.com
Manufacturer and exporter of pricing tags, sign holders, display hooks, hand trucks, handheld plastic shopping baskets, etc
President: Trageser Ed
ed@clampswing.com
Sales/Marketing Executive: Kamran Faizi
Purchasing Manager: Ron Coffman
Estimated Sales: $3-5 Million
Number Employees: 20-49
Brands:
　Celographics
　Deligraphics
　Doubletalk
　Frameworks
　Fresh Facts
　Kick-Off
　Monorail
　Spacesaver
　Vari-Extenders
　View-Lok

20594 Clanton & Company
2204 E Vista Canyon Rd
Orange, CA 92867
714-282-7980
Fax: 714-978-7103 fssearch@aol.com
Executive recruitment firm specializing in the placement of sales and management personnel within the food and disposable manufacturing industry
Owner: Diane Clanton
Estimated Sales: Less than $500,000
Number Employees: 1-4

20595 (HQ)Claridge Products & Equipment
601 US 32
Harrison, AR 72602
Fax: 870-743-1908 orders@claridgeproducts.com
www.claridgeproducts.com
Manufacturer and exporter of menu signs and boards, display cases and cabinets, easels, chalkboards, markerboards, etc.; importer of raw materials
President: Helen Clavey
CFO: Leslie Eddings
VP: Paul Clavey
Purchasing Director: John Wilson
Number Employees: 250-499
Square Footage: 300000
Other Locations:
　Claridge Products & Equipment
　Mamaroneck NY
　Claridge Products & Equipment
　Palatine IL
　South Central Claridge
　Farmers Branch TX
　Claridge Products & Equipment
　San Leandro CA
Brands:
　Claridge Cork
　Fabricork
　Lcs
　Vitracite

20596 Clark Caster Company
RR 1 Box 210A
Cave In Rock, IL 62919
708-366-1913
Fax: 708-366-5103 800-538-0765
sales@clarkcaster.com www.clarkcaster.com
Casters, wheels
President: James Clark
Estimated Sales: $2.5-5 Million
Number Employees: 5-9
Square Footage: 12000

20597 Clark Richardson-Biskup
1251 NW Briarcliff Pkwy # 500
Suite 500
Kansas City, MO 64116-1795
816-880-9800
Fax: 816-880-9898 www.crbusa.com
A full-service network of engineers, architects, constructors and consultants assisting food, nutrition and consumer product organizations in the planning, design, construction and operations support of facilities across the globe.
President: Doyle Clark
VP, Facility Integration: Mark Von Stwolinski
Associate/Core Team Leader: Aaron Saggars
Process Specialist: Marc Pelletier
Senior Associate: J. Lee Emel
General Manager, Midwest Region: Larry Klein
Process Engineer/Senior Associate: Bill Jarvis
Number Employees: 50-99

20598 Clark-Cooper Division Magnatrol Valve Corporation
855 Industrial Highway
Unit 4
Cinnaminson, NJ 08077
856-829-4580
Fax: 856-829-7303 techsupport@clarkcooper.com
www.clarkcooper.com
Metering pumps and valves; exporter of pumps and skid systems
Manager: Brian White
CEO: Brian Hagan
CFO: Kevin Hagan
Contact: John Bush
johnb@clarkcooper.com
Plant Manager: John Chando
Estimated Sales: $3-5 Million
Number Employees: 10-19
Square Footage: 32000

Brands:
Chemtrol

20599 Clarke American Sanders
14600 21st Ave N
Minneapolis, MN 55447-4617
336-372-8080
800-253-0367
info@clarkeus.com www.americansanders.com
Floor maintenance equipment such as floor polishers, floor sanders, carpet extractors and vacuum cleaners
CEO: Mark Hefty
CFO: Niels Olsen
R&D: Tom Benton
Marketing: Rob Godlewski
Sales: John Castaldo
Estimated Sales: $10-20 Million
Number Employees: 300
Number of Products: 150
Square Footage: 500000
Parent Co: Incentive Group
Brands:
A.L. Cook Technology
American Sanders Technology
American-Lincoln Technology
Clarke Technology
Delco Technology
Kew Technology
Simpson Technology

20600 Clarkson Supply
213 Main St
Williamsport, PA 17702-7312
570-323-3631
Fax: 570-323-1899 800-326-9457
clarksonmurphy@gmail.com
www.clarksonsupply.com
Warewashing and laundry washing products; also, chemicals for hydro-therapy equipment
President: Michael I Stuempfle
mikes@clarksonchemical.com
Estimated Sales: $1-2.5 Million
Number Employees: 5-9

20601 Classic Signs Inc
13 Columbia Dr # 15
Amherst, NH 03031-2331
603-883-0384
Fax: 603-882-2962 800-734-7446
ptripp@classicsignsnh.com
www.classicsignsnh.com
Electric signs including interior, vehicle and changeable letter
President: Paul Tripp
ptripp@classicsignsnh.com
Estimated Sales: Below $5 Million
Number Employees: 5-9

20602 Classico Seating
801 N Clay St
Peru, IN 46970-1068
765-473-6691
Fax: 800-242-9787 800-968-6655
Manufacturer and exporter of metal chairs, barstools, dinettes, tables and table bases
President: Kim Regan
CFO: Hank Richardson
Estimated Sales: $20-50 Million
Number Employees: 100-249
Square Footage: 125000
Type of Packaging: Consumer, Food Service
Brands:
Classico Seating

20603 Classy Basket
9275 Trade Place
San Diego, CA 92126-6318
858-274-4901
Fax: 858-274-0795 888-449-4901
info@patent.org www.classybasket.com
Novelty food gift baskets
Estimated Sales: $1-5 Million
Number Employees: 2

20604 Claude Neon Signs
1808 Cherry Hill Rd
Baltimore, MD 21230-3522
410-685-7575
Fax: 410-837-3154
Electric, neon and fluorescent signs, floodlights and bullet resistant protection equipment
President: Alan Nethen

Estimated Sales: $1-2.5 Million
Number Employees: 20-49
Square Footage: 16000

20605 Clauss Tools
60 Round Hill Road
Fairfield, CT 6824
877-412-7467
Fax: 419-332-8077 800-835-2263
orders@shopatron.com www.claussco.com
Hand tools: ergonomic food processing shears
President: Scott Sprause
Marketing Director: William Miller
Sales Director: E Ted Miller
Estimated Sales: $5-10 Million
Number Employees: 10
Type of Packaging: Bulk

20606 Clawson Container Company
4545 Clawson Tank Dr
Clarkston, MI 48346
248-625-3921
Fax: 248-625-3066 800-325-8700
Complete line of steel, composite, and rotationally and blow molded polyethylene intermediate bulk containers. Container management services include daily rental program and ReturnNet System for the Passport IBC, which picks upreconditions and recycles the container for the customer; ISO 9001:200 certified.
President: Dick Harding
VP: Robert Harding
Quality Control: Peter Ricketts
Marketing: Carol Abid
Sales: Dave McKenna
Contact: Larry Bricco
lbricco@ibcna.com
Estimated Sales: $20-50 Million
Number Employees: 20-49
Type of Packaging: Bulk
Brands:
Enviroclean Gold
Jumbo Bin

20607 Clawson Machine Co Inc
12 Cork Hill Rd
Franklin, NJ 07416-1304
973-827-8209
Fax: 973-827-4613 800-828-4088
eclipse@nac.net www.clawsonmachine.com
Cole slaw cutters and ice crushers and shavers for sno-cones; exporter of ice crushers, ice shavers and slaw cutters
Owner: Charles Fletcher
Customer Service: Diane Olsen
eclipse@nac.net
Estimated Sales: $10-20 Million
Number Employees: 20-49
Square Footage: 20000
Parent Co: Technology General Corporation
Type of Packaging: Food Service
Brands:
Hail Queen
Plus Crusher
Princess Chipper
Snow Ball Ice Shavers

20608 Clayton & Lambert Manufacturing
3813 West Highway 146
Buckner, KY 40010
502-222-1411
Fax: 502-222-1415 800-626-5819
info@claytonlambert.com
www.claytonlambert.com
Manufacturer and exporter of galvanized and stainless steel tanks for storage
President: John Lambert
Estimated Sales: $2.5-5 Million
Number Employees: 10-19
Square Footage: 700000
Brands:
Herd King
Silver Shield

20609 Clayton Corp.
866 Horan Dr
Fenton, MO 63026-2416
636-349-5333
Fax: 636-349-5335 800-729-8220
rberger@claytoncorp.com www.claytoncorp.com
Aerosol Valves, Actuators, Dispensing Systems, Covers, Barrier Packaging and assorted plastic moulded parts

President & CEO: Barry Baker
bakerb@claycorp.com
Director of Sales: Ric Berger
Number Employees: 100-249
Type of Packaging: Bulk

20610 Clayton Industries
17477 Hurley St
City Of Industry, CA 91744-5106
626-435-1200
Fax: 626-435-0180 800-423-4585
sales@claytonindustries.com
www.claytonindustries.com
Manufacturer and exporter of steam generators
President: Boyd Calvin
boyd.calvin@claytonind.com
Chairman: William N
CFO: Boyd Calvin
Quality Control: Jess Alvear
Sales: Marsha Ashley
Plant Manager: Robin Pope
Purchasing Director: Maria Serna
Estimated Sales: $20-50 Million
Number Employees: 500-999

20611 Clayton L. Hagy & Son
5000 Paschall Ave
Philadelphia, PA 19143-5136
215-844-6470
Fax: 215-724-9983
Wiping cloths and cheesecloth
Owner: Andriea Bookbinder
Estimated Sales: $1-3 Million
Number Employees: 10 to 19
Parent Co: American By Products

20612 Clayton Manufacturing Company
7873 Catherine Street
Derby, NY 14047-9597
716-549-0392
Fax: 716-549-0392 claytonmfg@aol.com
www.claytonindustries.com
Pie crimpers and cake slicers
President: John Clayton
Vice President: Jim Oetinger
Square Footage: 70000
Type of Packaging: Food Service

20613 Clean Room Products
1800 Ocean Ave
Ronkonkoma, NY 11779-6532
631-588-7000
Fax: 631-588-7863 800-777-2532
pjcarcara@knfcorporation.com
www.knfcorporation.com
Clean rooms and equipment, controls, energy controls, piping, fittings and tubing, sanitary, processing and packaging
President: Phil Cacara
Sales Manager: Lee Gordon
General Manager: John Stuerzel
Estimated Sales: $10-20 Million
Number Employees: 50-99

20614 Clean That Pot
PO Box 5429
Whittier, CA 90607
909-674-8332
Fax: 909-674-8395 800-621-7868
service@championchemical.com
www.cleanthatpot.com
Provides effective solutions for the coffee industry's toughest cleaning challenges.
President: Andrew Ellis
VP: Dennis Hall
Estimated Sales: $1.4 Million
Number Employees: 8
Square Footage: 32000

20615 Clean Water Systems
2322 Marina Dr
PO Box 146
Klamath Falls, OR 97601-9110
541-882-9993
Fax: 541-882-9994 866-273-9993
info@cleanwatersysintl.com
www.cleanwatersysintl.com
Manufacturer and exporter of solid state ballasts, UV sensing, monitor and control system, ultraviolet water, and waste water treatment systems and air ozone units
President/CEO: Charles Romary
Estimated Sales: Less Than $500,000
Number Employees: 1-4

Square Footage: 6000
Parent Co: C G Romary & Son
Type of Packaging: Private Label
Brands:
  Cws

20616 Clean Water Technology
151 W 135th St
Los Angeles, CA 90061-1645

310-380-4658
Fax: 310-380-4658 info@cleanwatertech.com
www.cleanwatertech.com
Wastewater treatment systems
VP: Linda Englander Mills
Manager: Joanna Parra
jparra@cleanwatertech.com
Number Employees: 10-19
Parent Co: The Marvin Group
Brands:
  GEM System

20617 Clean-All Pool Svc
838 Erie Blvd W
Syracuse, NY 13204-2228

315-472-7665
Fax: 315-472-3904
Owner/President: Severino Gonnella
CEO/Finance Executive: August Gonnella
Sales Executive: August Gonnella
Manager: Severino Gonnella
Estimated Sales: Below $5 Million
Number Employees: 5-9

20618 Cleanfreak
3900 N Providence Ave
Appleton, WI 54913-8017

920-380-0777
Fax: 920-380-0878 888-722-5508
info@cleanfreak.com www.cleanfreak.com
Maufacturer and supplier of cleaning equipment and
supplies
Vice President: Steve Menzner
smenzner@pti-1.com
Number Employees: 10-19
Parent Co: Packaging Tape Inc.

20619 Clear Bags
4949 Windplay Dr # 100
Suite 100
El Dorado Hills, CA 95762-9318

916-933-4700
Fax: 916-933-4717 800-233-2630
sales@clearbags.com www.clearbags.com
Accessories/supplies i.e picnic baskets, specialty
food packaging i.e .gift wrap/labels/boxes/contain-
ers.
Marketing: Danielle Badeaux
Number Employees: 20-49

20620 Clear Lam Packaging
1950 Pratt Blvd
Elk Grove Village, IL 60007

847-439-8570
Fax: 847-439-8589 www.clearlam.com
Flexible and rigid packaging materials printed and
laminated films for form/fill/seal and lidding.
President: James Sanfilippo
Estimated Sales: $100-500 Million
Number Employees: 250-499

20621 Clear Products Inc.
6156 Mission Gorge Rd
Suite C
San Diego, CA 92120

619-521-0327
Fax: 619-283-3913 888-257-2532
mail@clearproductsinc.com
www.clearproductsinc.com
Manufacturing
Owner: Del Neville
Estimated Sales: $300,000-500,000
Number Employees: 1-4

20622 (HQ)Clear View Bag Co Inc Of Nc
5 Burdick Dr
Albany, NY 12205-6407

518-458-7153
Fax: 518-458-1401 800-458-7153
sales_info@clearviewbag.com
www.clearviewbag.com
Plastic bags

President: William Romer
CFO: Virginia Trimarchi
Quality Control: Todd Romer
Sales Manager: Trent Romer
General Manager: William Todd Romer
Estimated Sales: $10 Million
Number Employees: 50-99
Square Footage: 128000
Type of Packaging: Consumer, Food Service, Pri-
vate Label, Bulk
Other Locations:
  Clear View Bag Co.
  Thomasville NC

20623 Clear View Bag Company
7137 Prospect Church RD
Thomasville, NC 27360-8839

336-885-8131
Fax: 336-885-1044
Plastic bags
VP: Joe Romer
Manager: Daniel A Jones
Estimated Sales: $5-10 Million
Number Employees: 50-99
Parent Co: Clear View Bag Company

20624 ClearWater Tech LLC
P.O. Box 15330
San Luis Obispo, CA 93406

805-549-9724
Fax: 805-549-0306 800-262-0203
sales@cwtozone.com www.cwtozone.com
ClearWater Tech's water purification systems produce ozone-enriched water that uses few to no
chemicals in order to eliminate pathogens and many
other organic and inorganic contaminants, leaving
no residue in the water or on theproduct.
President: Cameron Tapp
Factory Representative: Ed Knueve
Factory Representative: John Dittbemer
Contact: Richard Camp
rcamp@cwtozone.com

20625 Clearr Corporation
6325 Sandburg Rd
Minneapolis, MN 55427-3629

763-398-5400
Fax: 763-398-0134 800-548-3269
www.clearrcorp.com
Pop displays, signage, light boxes, poster frames
President/Owner: Andy Steinfeldt
VP: Pete Nelson
Marketing: Ryan Lester
Sales: Darryl Helleman
Estimated Sales: $10 Million
Number Employees: 50-99
Number of Products: 15
Square Footage: 40000
Parent Co: Stylmark
Brands:
  Alcon Plus
  Edge Lite
  Luminate Ultra
  Moving Pix
  Pointframe
  Stretch Frame
  Tension
  Triad
  Triola

20626 Cleartec Packaging
409 Parkway Dr
Park Hills, MO 63601-4435

314-543-4150
Fax: 314-543-4054 800-817-8967
sales@cleartecpackaging.com
www.cleartecpackaging.com
Sales Manager: Michael Wester
Contact: Amanda Merritt
amerritt@mocap.com
Estimated Sales: $1-5 Million

20627 Clearwater Packaging Inc
615 Grand Central St # B
Clearwater, FL 33756-3438

727-442-2596
Fax: 727-447-3587 800-299-2596
www.clearwaterpackaging.com
Manufacturer and exporter of packaging machinery
President: Jon Hoover
sales@clearwaterpackaging.com
Estimated Sales: $5-10 Million
Number Employees: 20-49

20628 Clearwater Paper Corporation
Suite 1100
Spokane, WA 99201

509-344-5900
877-847-7831
www.clearwaterpaper.com
Manufacturer and exporter of paper packaging prod-
ucts
President/CEO: Linda Massman
Chief Financial Officer/SVP: John Hertz
SVP/General Counsel/Corporate Secretary: Michael
Gadd
SVP, Human Resources: Jackson Lynch
Facility Manager: Rick Tucker
Vice President, Procurement: Terry Borden
Estimated Sales: $1.87 Billion
Number Employees: 3,860
Parent Co: Bell Fibre Company
Type of Packaging: Consumer, Bulk
Brands:
  Rap-In-Wax
  Wax Tex

20629 Cleasby Manufacturing Co
1414 Bancroft Ave
PO Box 24132
San Francisco, CA 94124-3603

415-822-6565
Fax: 415-822-1843 800-253-2729
info@cleasby.com www.cleasby.com
Tar buckets, kettles, dump trailers and hoisting
equipment
President: John Cleasby
john@cleasby.com
Estimated Sales: $10-20 Million
Number Employees: 10-19

20630 Cleaver-Brooks Inc
221 Law St
Thomasville, GA 31792

229-226-3024
800-250-5583
info@cleaverbrooks.com cleaverbrooks.com
Manufacturer and exporter of packaged steam and
hot water boilers; applications include food process-
ing, packaging, sterilization, heating/ventilation/air
conditioning, etc.
President & CEO: Bart Aitken
President, Boiler Systems: Earle Pfefferkorn
Chief Financial Officer: Jimmy Sprouse
SVP, Sales & Marketing: Paul Anderson
Chairman Emeritus: P. Welch Goggins, Jr.
Year Founded: 1929
Estimated Sales: $100-500 Million
Number Employees: 1,400

20631 Cleco Systems
1395 S Marietta Pkwy SE
Bldg 750
Marietta, GA 30067-4440

770-392-0330
Fax: 770-795-8093
President: Kenneth Matson
R&D: Percy Nay
Quality Control: Ban Sandlnato
Estimated Sales: $5-10 Million
Number Employees: 15

20632 Cleland Manufacturing Company
2125 Argonne Dr NE
Columbia Heights, MN 55421-1317

763-571-4606
Fax: 763-571-4606
clelandmanufacturing@tcq.net
Manufacturer and exporter of grain/seed cleaners
and spiral separators
President: Robert Maxton
Quality Control: George Maxton
VP: Mary Maxton
Contact: Bob Maxton
glen@agmercury.com
Estimated Sales: Less than $500,000
Number Employees: 2
Square Footage: 6000
Brands:
  Expert Line

20633 (HQ)Cleland Sales Corp
11051 Via El Mercado
Los Alamitos, CA 90720-2878

562-598-6616
Fax: 562-598-3858
sales@blizzardbeersystems.com
www.blizzardbeersystems.com

Manufacturer, importer and exporter of automatic refill devices, beer chillers and beverage and dry powder dispensers.
President: Arlene Cleland
Vice President: Jimmy Cleland
Sales Director: Mike Pollock
Manager: Kevin Wesley
kevin@clelandsales.com
Estimated Sales: $1-3 Million
Number Employees: 5-9
Square Footage: 40000
Type of Packaging: Food Service
Other Locations:
  Cleland Sales Corp.
  Los Alamitos CA
Brands:
  Automate
  Automix
  Blizzard Beer Systems
  Choc-O-Lot
  Dove
  Starline

20634 Clements Industries Inc
50 Ruta Ct
South Hackensack, NJ 07606-1709
201-440-5500
Fax: 201-440-1455 800-222-5540
steven@tach-it.com www.tach-it.com
Tape and label dispensers, twist tie equipment and supplies
President: Alan Clements
alan@tach-it.com
CEO: Steven Clements
CFO: Steven Clements
Vice President: Steven Clements
Research & Development: Steven Clements
VP Marketing: Steven Clements
VP Sales: Steven Clements
Operations Manager: Steven Clements
Production Manager: Alan Clements
Plant Manager: Steven Clements
Purchasing: Marilyn Ring
Number Employees: 10-19
Parent Co: Tech-It

20635 Clerestory
1740 Ridge Avenue
Suite 117
Evanston, IL 60201
312-640-5777
Fax: 312-915-5933 www.clstory.com
Tea and coffee industry cans
Founding principal and managing partner: Linda Toops
Founding principal and partner: Michelle Kerr
Contact: Asad Ali
aali@clstory.com
Estimated Sales: Below $5 Million
Number Employees: 5-9

20636 Cleveland Canvas Goods Mfg Co
1960 E 57th St
Cleveland, OH 44103-3804
216-361-4567
Fax: 216-361-1728 sales@clevelandcanvas.com
www.clevelandcanvas.com
Insulated carrying cases and filter bags
President: Mark Howard
m.howard@clevelandcanvas.com
Treasurer: W Morton
m.howard@clevelandcanvas.com
VP Sales: M Howard
Estimated Sales: $2.5-5 Million
Number Employees: 20-49
Square Footage: 64000
Brands:
  The Coldholder

20637 Cleveland Menu Printing
1441 E 17th St
Cleveland, OH 44114-2012
216-241-5256
Fax: 216-241-5696 800-356-6368
web_sales@clevelandmenu.com
www.clevelandmenu.com
Manfacturer and exporter of menus and menu boards, covers, holders and displays
Owner: Thomas Ramella
tramella@clevelandmenuprinting.com
Estimated Sales: $2.5-5 Million
Number Employees: 20-49

20638 Cleveland Metal Stamping Company
1231 W Bagley Rd #1
Berea, OH 44017-2942
440-234-0010
Fax: 440-234-8050
Manufacturer and exporter of bottle openers, burner bowls for gas ranges and metal shelf extenders; also, barbecue utensils including spatulas and forks.
Manager: Frank Ghinga
CFO: Dorina Ghinga
VP: Pascu Ghinga
Estimated Sales: $1-3 Million
Number Employees: 50 to 99
Number of Products: 200
Square Footage: 86000
Type of Packaging: Private Label, Bulk

20639 Cleveland Mop Manufacturing Company
5261 W 161st St
Cleveland, OH 44142-1606
216-898-5866
Fax: 216-898-5867 800-767-9934
clevelandmop@hotmail.com
Wet mop heads, mop head handles, dust and bowl mops, floor machine pads, push brooms and broom handles
Owner: David Rhodes
Estimated Sales: $5-10 Million
Number Employees: 1-4
Square Footage: 40000
Brands:
  Dumor
  Eagle
  Kleen Mor

20640 Cleveland Motion Controls
7550 Hub Pkwy
Cleveland, OH 44125
216-524-8800
Fax: 216-642-2199 800-321-8072
www.cmccontrols.com
Electronic industrial controls and systems
President: E Wayne Foley
Marketing/Communications Director: Tim Schultz
Product Manager: Kenneth Bobick
Estimated Sales: $50-100 Million
Number Employees: 100-249
Parent Co: IMC

20641 Cleveland Plastic Films
41740 Schadden Road
Elyria, OH 44035-2294
440-324-2222
Fax: 440-324-2790 800-832-6799
Polyethylene films and printed and plain polyethylene bags for poultry, meat and pastries
CFO: Thomas Tyler
Vice President: James Hendershot
Sales Director: Frank Szabo
Plant Manager: Dan McDonald
Purchasing Manager: Paul Mirka
Estimated Sales: $5-10 Million
Number Employees: 100
Square Footage: 240000
Parent Co: Global Film & Packaging Corporation
Type of Packaging: Food Service, Bulk

20642 Cleveland Range
1333 E 179th St
Cleveland, OH 44110
216-481-4900
Fax: 216-481-3782 800-338-2204
www.clevelandrange.com
Manufacturer and exporter of steam cooking equipment including convection steamers, kettles, skillets, combi-ovens and cook-chill systems
President: Rick Cutler
rcutler@clevelandrange.com
Estimated Sales: $48 Million
Number Employees: 100-249
Square Footage: 150000
Parent Co: The Manitowac Company, Inc.
Type of Packaging: Food Service
Brands:
  Cleveland
  Combicraft
  Spectrum
  Steamcraft

20643 (HQ)Cleveland Specialties Co
6612 Miami Trails Dr
Loveland, OH 45140-8044
513-677-9787
Fax: 513-683-4132
Plastic closures, plastic shrink film, milk carton handles and polycoated paperboard products including folding boxes and cartons; importer of packaging products
President: Nancy Hartmann
Vice President: James Downing
Estimated Sales: Less Than $500,000
Number Employees: 1-4
Type of Packaging: Consumer, Food Service, Private Label, Bulk

20644 Cleveland Vibrator Co
2828 Clinton Ave
Cleveland, OH 44113-2998
216-241-7157
Fax: 216-241-3480 800-221-3298
cvc@clevelandvibrator.com
www.clevelandvibrator.com
Industrial vibrators including air piston, air ball, electromagnetic and rotary electric; also, air and electric brute force feeders and screeners and vibratory tables and conveyors
President: William Lee Gardner
CEO: Julia Hoverson
julia.hoverson@gmail.com
CFO: Mike Valore
VP: Glen Roberts
CEO: Jeff Chokel
Marketing: Susan Koblyski
Sales: Jack Steinbuch
Public Relations: Suasan Kobylski
Plant Manager: Mike Weisinger
Estimated Sales: Below $5 Million
Number Employees: 20-49
Square Footage: 56000
Type of Packaging: Bulk
Brands:
  Hybrute
  Vibra-Ball
  Vibra-Might

20645 Cleveland Wire Cloth & Mfg Co
3573 E 78th St
Cleveland, OH 44105-1596
216-341-1832
Fax: 216-341-1876 800-321-3234
cleveland@wirecloth.com www.wirecloth.com
Manufacturer, importer and exporter of woven wire cloth and wire cloth products.
President: C Crone
CFO: Joe Sarasa
VP Marketing: Larry Schrader
Estimated Sales: $5-10 Million
Number Employees: 20-49
Square Footage: 200000

20646 Cleveland-Eastern Mixers
4 Heritage Park Rd
Clinton, CT 06413-1836
860-669-1199
Fax: 860-669-7461 800-243-1188
Manufacturer and exporter of industrial fluid mixers
President: James Donkin
Sales Director: Sean Donkin
Estimated Sales: $10 Million
Number Employees: 20-49
Number of Brands: 30
Number of Products: 2
Square Footage: 50000
Parent Co: EMI Inc Technology Group
Brands:
  Cleveland
  Eastern

20647 Clevenger Frable Lavallee
39 Westmoreland Ave # 114
White Plains, NY 10606-1970
914-997-9660
Fax: 914-997-9671 marketing@cfldesign.com
www.cfldesign.com
Consultant specializing in the design of commercial food facilities
President: Foster Frable Jr
CFO: James Lavalle
VP: James LaVallee
Contact: David Bell
dbell@excelsior.edu

Estimated Sales: Less Than $500,000
Number Employees: 1-4
Square Footage: 8000

20648 Clextral USA
14450 Carlson Cir
Tampa, FL 33626

813-854-4434
Fax: 813-855-2269 www.clextral.com
Manufacturer and exporter of food processing machinery including twin screw extruders.
President: Jose Coelho
Sales Manager, North America: Justin Montgomery
Contact: Alice Albaret
aalbaret@clextral.com
Pilot Plant Manager: Julie Probst
Estimated Sales: Below $5 Million
Number Employees: 10-19
Parent Co: Clextral

20649 Climate Master Inc
7300 SW 44th St
Oklahoma City, OK 73179-4307

405-745-6000
Fax: 405-745-6058 877-436-0263
cyperry@climatemaster.com
www.climatemaster.com
Manufacturer and exporter of heat pumps, air conditioners, filters and controls
President: Daniel Ellis
CEO: Dan Ellis
dellis@climatemaster.com
Estimated Sales: H
Number Employees: 250-499
Parent Co: LSB Corporation
Brands:
    Climate Master

20650 Climax Industries
11836 Judd Ct
Suite 320
Dallas, TX 75243

972-881-8860
Fax: 972-424-0293 800-854-5063
Estimated Sales: $1-3 Million
Number Employees: 5-9

20651 Climax Packaging Machinery
25 Standen Dr
Hamilton, OH 45015-2209

513-874-1664
Fax: 513-874-3375 info@climaxpackaging.com
www.climaxpackaging.com
Manufacturer and exporter of uncasing and case packing equipment, bottle conveyors, lane dividers, tray stackers and carton and flap openers
President: William George
Marketing/Sales: Jack Bunce
Manager: Nick Jody
njody@climaxpackaging.com
Purchasing: Barb Ruthwell
Estimated Sales: $5-10 Million
Number Employees: 20-49
Square Footage: 40000
Parent Co: GL Industries
Brands:
    Air Cush'n
    Sof-Pac

20652 Clipco
5841 Melshire Drive
Dallas, TX 75230-2117

972-239-8028
Fax: 972-980-7552
Plastic containers

20653 Clippard Instrument LabInc
7390 Colerain Ave
Cincinnati, OH 45239-5396

513-521-4261
Fax: 513-521-4464 sales@clippard.com
www.clippard.com
President: Amy Dryer
clippardinstrumentlaboratoryinc@exhibitorinvites.com
R&D: Sid Hendry
Chairman of the Board: William L Clippard III
Estimated Sales: $20-50 Million
Number Employees: 100-249

20654 Clipper Belt Lacer Company
1995 Oak Industrial Dr NE
Grand Rapids, MI 49505

616-459-3196
Fax: 616-459-4976 info@flexco.com
www.flexco.com
Manufacturer and exporter of mechanical belt fastening systems for conveyors
Manager: Nancy Ayres
CFO: Lee Merys
Marketing Specialist: Beth Miller
Estimated Sales: $10-20 Million
Number Employees: 50-99
Square Footage: 304000
Parent Co: Flexco-Grand Rapids
Brands:
    Baler Belt Lacer
    Clipmark
    Clipper
    Microlacer
    Roller Lacer
    Unibar
    Valulacer

20655 Clock Associates
1629 SE 11th Ave
Portland, OR 97214-4795

503-234-0202
Fax: 503-238-0420 www.clockassociates.com
Manufactures food product machinery
Owner: Pat Clock
pclock@clockassociates.com
Estimated Sales: Less Than $500,000
Number Employees: 1-4

20656 (HQ)Clofine Dairy Products Inc
1407 New Rd
P.O. Box 335
Linwood, NJ 08221

609-653-1000
Fax: 609-653-0127 info@clofinedairy.com
www.clofinedairy.com
Fluid and dried dairy products; proteins, cheeses, milk replacement blends, tofu and soymilk powders, vital wheat gluten, etc.
Chairman: Larry Clofine
lclofine@clofinedairy.com
President & CEO: Frederick Smith
CFO: Butch Harmon
Warehouse Coordinator: Pamela Gerety
Estimated Sales: $20-50 Million
Number Employees: 10-19
Number of Brands: 2
Number of Products: 100
Type of Packaging: Food Service, Private Label, Bulk
Other Locations:
    Midwest Officer
    Chicago IL
Brands:
    Fine-Mix Dairy
    Food Blends
    Soy Products
    Soyfine
    Soymilk

20657 Clorox Company
1221 Broadway
Oakland, CA 94612

510-271-7000
corporate.communications@clorox.com
www.thecloroxcompany.com
Dips, dip mixes, bbq sauces, marinades, and dressings; plastic bags and wrap; disinfectants.
Chairman/CEO: Benno Dorer
EVP/General Counsel: Laura Stein
SVP, Corporate Business Development: Bill Bailey
SVP/Chief Innovation Officer: Denise Garner
SVP/Chief Financial Officer: Kevin Jacobsen
SVP/Chief Customer Officer: Troy Datcher
SVP/Chief People Officer: Kirsten Marriner
SVP/Chief Product Supply Officer: Andy Lowery
EVP, Household & Lifestyle: Eric Reynolds
Year Founded: 1913
Estimated Sales: $6.2 Billion
Number Employees: 8,800
Brands:
    Brita
    Clorox
    Glad Bags
    Kitchen Bouquet
    Hidden Valley
    Masterpiece
    Burt's Bees

Chux
Ever Clean
409
Fresh Step
Green Works
Kings Ford
Liquid PlumR
Poett
Renew Life
Scoop Away
S.O.S.
Tilex

20658 Closure Systems Intl Inc
7702 Woodland Dr # 200
Suite 200
Indianapolis, IN 46278-2709

317-390-5000
Fax: 317-390-5079 800-311-2740
www.csiclosures.com
Suppliers of closures for carbonated soft drinks, bottled water, juice & isotonic, milk and dairy products, alcoholic beverages, packaged foods and wine.
President: Rafael Pantigoso
rafael.pantigoso@csiclosures.com
President: Ruth Mack
VP Finance: Robert Smith
EVP: Lawrence Purtell
Quality Manager: Praveen Mathur
VP Human Resources: Arrigo Bodda
Number Employees: 1000-4999
Square Footage: 64000
Parent Co: Rank Group Limited

20659 Cloud Inc
4855 Morabito Pl
San Luis Obispo, CA 93401-8748

805-549-8093
Fax: 805-549-0131 800-234-5650
mkemp@cloudinc.com www.cloudinc.com
Manufacturer and exporter of rotary tank cleaning machines
Owner: Brian Buell
Product and Marketing Manager: Mike Kemp
Regional Sales Manager: Lee LaFond
brian@cloudinc.com
Division Manager: Greg Boege
Job Shop Division Mgr.: Richard Riggs
Manufacturing Mngr.: Brad Erickson
Estimated Sales: Less Than $500,000
Number Employees: 1-4
Brands:
    Cloud

20660 Cloudy & Britton
6202 214th St SW
Mountlake Ter, WA 98043-2097

425-775-7424
Fax: 425-775-1715
Refrigeration systems including industrial refrigerators, freezing tunnels and spiral and plate freezers
President: Edward Cloudy
Purchasing Agent: Gordon Derksema
Estimated Sales: $5-10 Million
Number Employees: 5-9
Brands:
    Cloudy & Britton

20661 Clyde Bergemann Eec
3700 Koppers St
Halethorpe, MD 21227-1019

410-712-4280
Fax: 410-368-6721
www.clydebergemannpowergroup.com
Air cleaning systems and air filters
President, Chief Executive Officer: Franz Bartels
Vice President & CFO: Graham Lees
Contact: Matt Rodgers
mrodgers@clydebergemanneec.com
VP Finance & Chief Operating Officer: Patrick von Hagen
Estimated Sales: Less Than $500,000
Number Employees: 1-4

20662 Cma Dishmachines
12700 Knott St
Garden Grove, CA 92841-3904

714-898-8781
Fax: 71- 89- 214 800-854-6417
sales@cmadishmachines.com
Manufacturer, importer and exporter of commercial dishmachines, glasswashers and dishtables

President: David Crane
Vice President: Mike Belleville
mike.belleville@cmadishmachines.com
Marketing Director: Matt Swift
Sales Assistant: Kimberly Feldstein
Plant Manager: Mike Belleville
Number Employees: 50-99
Square Footage: 135000
Parent Co: S.C. Johnson & Son
Brands:
  Energy Mizer

20663 Co-Rect Products Inc
7105 Medicine Lake Rd
Golden Valley, MN 55427-3675
763-542-9200
Fax: 763-542-9205 800-328-5702
customerservice@co-rectproducts.com
www.co-rectproducts.com
Bar and restaurant supplies; serving the food service market
President & CEO: Michael Pierce
Vice President: Steve Ess
Sales Manager: Bryan Mattson
Accounts Representative: Brian Mattson
Purchasing: Rose Bruhn
Estimated Sales: $10-20 Million
Number Employees: 20-49
Number of Brands: 20
Square Footage: 60000
Type of Packaging: Food Service, Private Label, Bulk

20664 Coast Controls Inc
7500 Commerce Ct
Sarasota, FL 34243-3217
941-355-7555
Fax: 941-359-2321 800-513-2345
sales@coastcontrols.com www.coastcontrols.com
Industrial process controls
President: Thomas Marks
tmarks@coastcontrols.com
Vice President: Kyle Koontz
Contact-Marketing/Sales: Rodney Shrock
Estimated Sales: Below $5 000,000
Number Employees: 10-19

20665 Coast Label Co
17406 Mount Cliffwood Cir
Fountain Valley, CA 92708-4101
714-426-1410
Fax: 714-426-1440 800-995-0483
sales@coastlabel.com www.coastlabel.com
Offset, letterpress, flexography and seal press printed labels
President: Craig Moreland
cmoreland@coastlabel.com
Chief Executive Officer: Craig Moreland
Quality Control: Dave Fox
VP Sales: Tom Miller
Estimated Sales: $1-2.5 Million
Number Employees: 20-49

20666 Coast Packing Co
3275 E Vernon Avenue
Vernon, CA 90058
323-277-7700
www.coastpacking.com
Quality shortening products for the restaurant, baking, and food industries. A supplier of animal fat and vegetable oil shortenings.
President: Ronald Gustafson
ronald.gustafson@coastpacking.com
CEO: Eric Gustafson
HR Manager: Washington Paredes
Director of Operations: Chavis Ferguson
Number Employees: 50-99
Type of Packaging: Consumer, Food Service
Brands:
  Bake Lite All Soy
  Bake Lite Soy/Cotton
  Coast Refined Lard
  Flavor King Blue
  Flavor King Red
  Gold Coast
  Golden Bake
  Supreme
  Viva Lard
  VIVA Manteca Mixta
  Viva Retail Lard

20667 Coast Paper Box Company
205 S Frank Bland Drive
San Bernardino, CA 92408
909-382-3475
Fax: 909-382-3481
Folding paper boxes
Number Employees: 50-99

20668 Coast Scientific
P.O. Box 185
Rancho Santa Fe, CA 92067
Fax: 800-791-8999 800-445-1544
www.medcosupplies.com
Manufacturer and exporter of adhesive mats, aprons, polyethylene bags, bouffant caps, carts, shelving, latex and vinyl gloves, convection ovens and disposable wipers
Manager: Alex Sardarian
Director Operations: Stacy Camp
Estimated Sales: $2.5-5 Million
Number Employees: 10-19

20669 Coast Signs & Graphics
520 Cypress Ave
Hermosa Beach, CA 90254
310-379-9921
Fax: 310-372-2160
Banners and signs of all types; also, screen printing, graphi design, digital, large and small format available
President: Bill Febbo
Owner: William Febbo
Marketing Director: Linda Hopkins
Art Director: Wayne Morris
Estimated Sales: Less than $500,000
Number Employees: 1-4
Square Footage: 6

20670 Coastal Canvas Products
73 Ross Rd
P.O.Box 22834
Savannah, GA 31405-1660
912-236-2416
Fax: 912-232-7884 800-476-5174
sales@coastalcanvas.net
Commercial canvas awnings, roll curtains, storon protection machinery covers, sunscreens, and strip curtians
Owner: Ellen Barber
ebarber@coastalcanvas.net
CFO: Marlene Wood
Vice President: Duane Wood
Estimated Sales: $2.5-5,000,000
Number Employees: 20-49

20671 Coastal Mechanical Svc Inc
33 Parker Ave
Stamford, CT 06906-1713
203-359-3070
Fax: 203-995-9129 www.coastalmechanical.com
Consultant specializing in design of HVAC and refrigeration systems; also, engineering and installation services available
President: David Besterfield
Estimated Sales: $1-2,500,000
Number Employees: 5-9

20672 Coastal Pallet Corp
135 E Washington Ave
Bridgeport, CT 06604-3607
203-333-6222
Fax: 203-333-1892 www.coastalpallet.com
Wooden pallets and boxes
President: Peter G. Standish
coastalpallet@msn.com
Estimated Sales: $1-2.5 Million
Number Employees: 20-49

20673 Coastal Products Company
PO Box 208
Westbrook, ME 04098-0208
207-854-5616
Fax: 207-854-2118
Chemicals
President: Herb Pressman

20674 Coastline Equipment Inc
2235 E Bakerview Rd
Bellingham, WA 98226-7153
360-734-8509
Fax: 360-734-9321 www.coastline-equipment.com
Designer and manufacturer of processing and handling equipment. A complete package from design to fabrication and start-up. Family owned for 30 years

President: Kurt Lunde
admin@coasteq.com
Sales Manager: Brian Claudon
Estimated Sales: $5-10 Million
Number Employees: 20-49
Square Footage: 128000

20675 Coating Technologies International
805 Birch Street
Algonquin, IL 60102-2213
847-854-9620
Fax: 847-854-9621 mrgintl@aol.com
Lolipop processing equipment, pans and pan lids

20676 Coats American Industrial
745 Gotham Pkwy
Carlstadt, NJ 07072-2413
201-935-0200
Fax: 201-804-9392
Tea and coffee industry packaging
Estimated Sales: $3-5 000,000
Number Employees: 5-9

20677 Coats North America
3430 Toringdon Way # 301
Charlotte, NC 28277-2576
704-329-5800
Fax: 704-329-5820 800-631-0965
www.coats.com
Thread
CFO: Donna Armstrong
CEO: Max Perks
max.perks@coats.com
CEO: Max Perks
CEO: Max Perks
Estimated Sales: $5-10 Million
Number Employees: 5000-9999

20678 Cobatco
1327 NE Adams St
Peoria, IL 61603
309-676-2663
Fax: 309-676-2667 800-426-2282
info@cobatco.com www.cobatco.com
Manufacturer and exporter of specialty baking equipment for waffles, waffle cones, doughnuts, edible shells, etc.; also, mixes including vanilla and chocolate waffle cone, regular and multigrain waffle and vanilla and chocolatedoughnut
President: Donald Stephens
Contact: Brett Crosthwaite
bcrosthwaite@cobatco.com
Estimated Sales: $2.5-5 Million
Number Employees: 10-19
Square Footage: 240000
Type of Packaging: Food Service
Brands:
  Cobatco
  Cobatco Olde Time

20679 Cobb & Zimmer
7900 Mack Avenue
Detroit, MI 48214-1766
313-923-0350
Fax: 313-923-1916
Bar fixtures, laminated counter and table tops and tables including wood and steel
Estimated Sales: $1-5 Million
Number Employees: 1
Square Footage: 30000

20680 Cobb Sign Co Inc
528 Elmira St
Burlington, NC 27217-1328
336-227-0181
Fax: 336-227-0206
Neon and plastic signs
President: Jody Speagle
jodys@cobbsignco.com
President: Kenneth Speagle
Manager: Jody Speagle
Estimated Sales: $1-2.5 Million
Number Employees: 5-9

20681 Cober Electronics, Inc.
151 Woodward Ave
Norwalk, CT 06854-4721
203-855-8755
Fax: 203-855-7511 800-709-5948
sales@cober.com www.cober.com

Manufacturer and exporter of batch and continuous conveyorized microwave ovens for the food scientist and production floor; also, laboratory and pilot plant services, process development and engineering design
CEO: Bernard Krieger
bern@cober.com
President: Martin Yonnone
VP Engineering: Martin Yonnone
Estimated Sales: $30-50 Million
Number Employees: 20-49
Square Footage: 39000

20682 Cobitco Inc
5301 Bannock St
Denver, CO 80216-1623

303-296-8575
Fax: 303-297-3029 info@cobitco.com
www.cobitco.com
Cobitco is a private label and branded chemical solutions provider with 20+ years experience and over 10,000 product formulations. Markets include jan-san, automotive, industrial, bulk, health care and marine.
President: Lee E Morgan
lee.morgan@cobitco.com
Marketing Director: Ray Harter
Sales Director: Greg Dauer
Number Employees: 10-19
Number of Brands: 10
Number of Products: 1200
Square Footage: 200000
Type of Packaging: Food Service, Private Label, Bulk
Brands:
    Car Chem
    Cobit+Care
    Enviro~Chem
    Enviro~Chem Gold
    Norseman
    Pressure Patch
    Pro-Magic
    Tidal Marine

20683 Coblentz Brothers Inc
7101 S Kohler Rd
Apple Creek, OH 44606-9613

330-857-7211
Fax: 330-857-4966 www.coblentzbros.com
Wooden pallets
President: Wayne Liechty
wayne@coblentzbros.com
Business Manager: Don Yoder
Vice President: Jonas Coblentz
Estimated Sales: $2.5-5 Million
Number Employees: 20-49
Square Footage: 40000

20684 (HQ)Coburn Company
P.O.Box 147
Whitewater, WI 53190-0147

262-473-2822
Fax: 262-473-3522 800-776-7042
www.coburn.com
Manufacturer and exporter of dairy equipment including milking and sanitation
President: Jim Coburn
Finance: Jason Alexander
Marketing: Ginny Coburn
Sales: Joe Coburn
Operations: Thayer Coburn
Export Manager: Jack Kolo
Purchasing: Jim Coburn
Estimated Sales: $5-10 Million
Number Employees: 20-49
Type of Packaging: Bulk

20685 Coca-Cola European Partners
Pemberton House
Bakers Road
Uxbridge, Middx, UB8 1EZ
UK

800-418-4223
comms@ccep.com www.cocacolaep.com
Coca-Cola brands products.
Chairman: Sol Daurella
CEO: Damian Gammell
CFO: Nik Jhangiani
Chief Public Affairs Officer: Lauren Sayeski
Estimated Sales: $10.9 Billion
Number Employees: 23,300
Number of Brands: 44
Type of Packaging: Consumer, Food Service, Bulk

Brands:
    5-Alive
    Abbey Well
    Apollinaris
    Appletiser
    aquaBona
    Aquarius
    Bonaqua
    Burn
    Capri-Sun
    Chaqwa
    Chaidfontaine
    Coca-Cola
    Coca-Cola Light/Diet
    Coca-Cola Zero
    Dr. Pepper
    Fanta Still
    Fanta Zero
    Fanta
    Fernandes
    Finley
    Fruit & Nadia
    Fruitopia
    Glaceau vitamin water
    Glaceau smart water
    Kia Ora
    Kinley
    Krystal
    Kuli
    Lift
    Lilt
    MER
    Mezzo Mix
    Minute Maid
    Monster Energy
    Nalu
    Nestea
    Nordic
    Oasis
    Ocean Spray
    Powerade
    Relentless Energy Drink
    Rosport Blue
    Schuss
    Schwepps
    Seagram's
    Sprite
    TAB X-tra
    Toscal
    Urge
    Vilas del Turbon
    ViO
    ViO BiO LiMO
    Viva

20686 Coconut Code
4490 N Federal Hwy
Lighthouse Point, FL 33064

954-786-0252
Fax: 954-481-9360
Software for financial reporting, inventory control, product/menu analysis, time and attendance for food service operations
Chairman Of Board: Jack Abdo
CEO/President: Mark Wotell
President: Mark Woterl
VP/R&D: E Wotell
Estimated Sales: $5-10 Million
Number Employees: 50-99
Square Footage: 14000
Brands:
    Coconut Code
    Food Service Management Systems
    Remotecontroller
    Timeware

20687 Coddington Lumber Co
19501 Shaft Rd SW
Frostburg, MD 21532-3723

301-689-8816
Fax: 301-689-1629
Pallets
President: Carl Mazer
pallets@allcolink.com
Estimated Sales: $2.5-5 Million
Number Employees: 5-9

20688 Codeck Manufacturing
PO Box 2940
Sausalito, CA 94966-2940

415-331-9509
Fax: 415-331-9469 800-878-5663
Manufactures coding equipment for various industries

Estimated Sales: $500,000-$1 000,000
Number Employees: 4

20689 Codema
11790 Troy Ln N
Maple Grove, MN 55369

763-428-2266
Fax: 763-428-4411 info@codemallc.com
Manufacturer, importer and exporter of processing equipment; packaging systems. Also have reconditioned and used equipment.
President: Heinz Baecker
h.baecker@codemallc.com
VP: Steve Parker
VP sales: Larry Yarger
VP Engineering: Rick Gilles
Estimated Sales: $1-2.5 Million
Number Employees: 5-9
Square Footage: 70000

20690 Coding Products
111 W Park Dr
Kalkaska, MI 49646-8794

231-258-5521
Fax: 231-258-6120 800-748-0525
www.codingproducts.com
Hot stamp ribbons, thermal transfer ribbons, inks and hot ink rollers for packaging applications
Sales Executive: Rob Fickling
Plant Manager: Ron Maxey
Estimated Sales: $50-100 Million
Number Employees: 50-99
Parent Co: Illinois Tool Works

20691 Cody Consulting Services
509 Whitney
Cedar Hill, TX 75104

972-291-7268
Customized quality and food safety program development. Food safety audits, audit preparation.
President: Deborah Cody
Number of Products: 4

20692 Coe & Dru Inc
589 W Terrace Dr
San Dimas, CA 91773-2915

909-599-5500
Fax: 909-599-2005 800-722-7538
inquiry@coedru.com www.coedru.com
Supplies baskets to those who make gift baskets.
President: Frank Chu
fchu@coedru.com
Sales Manager: Steve Wemane
Human Resources Manager: Lena Chu
Production Manager: Kwok Lai
Purchasing Manager: Kwonk Wong
Estimated Sales: $1.6 Million
Number Employees: 10-19

20693 Coextruded Packaging Technologies
3706 Enterprise Drive
Janesville, WI 53546

608-314-2020
Fax: 608-314-2021 info@cptplastics.com
www.cptplastics.com
Barrier foamed polypropylene trays
President: Linda Bracha
Contact: Katrina Bennett
katrina@cptgroup.com
Estimated Sales: $5-10 Million
Number Employees: 20-49

20694 Coffee Brothers Inc
1204 Via Roma
Colton, CA 92324-3909

909-370-1100
Fax: 909-370-1101 888-443-5282
info@coffeebrothers.com www.coffeebrothers.com
Coffee and espresso; importer and wholesaler/distributor of espresso machines
Owner: Cal Amodemo
cal@coffeebrothers.com
General Manager: Max Amodeo
Estimated Sales: $2.5-5 Million
Number Employees: 1-4
Square Footage: 44000
Type of Packaging: Private Label, Bulk
Brands:
    Coffee Brothers
    Il Caffe
    Sigma

20695 Coffee Enterprises
32 Lakeside Ave
Burlington, VT 05401-5242
802-865-4480
Fax: 802-865-3364 800-375-3398
www.coffeeenterprises.com
Coffee extracts and chilled coffee-based beverage concentrates; laboratory specializing in the testing and analyzing services for coffee; consultant specializing in the marketing and promotion of coffee
Owner/President: Daniel C Cox
dancox@coffee-ent.com
Administrative Assistant: Christine Hibma
Office Manager: Judy Mammorella
Estimated Sales: $1-3 Million
Number Employees: 10-19
Square Footage: 14000
Type of Packaging: Bulk

20696 Coffee Express RoastingCo
47722 Clipper St
Plymouth, MI 48170-2437
734-459-4900
Fax: 734-459-5511 800-466-9000
info@coffeeexpressco.com
www.coffeeexpressco.com
Wholesaler roaster of specialty coffees; distributors of associated products.
President: Tom Isaia
Office Manager: Joyce Novak
Contact: Genevieve Boss
g.boss@coffeeexpressco.com
Production: Scott Novak
Estimated Sales: Less Than $500,000
Number Employees: 1-4
Number of Brands: 8
Number of Products: 20
Square Footage: 32000
Type of Packaging: Consumer, Food Service, Private Label, Bulk
Brands:
  Coffee Express
  Mountain Country

20697 Coffee PER
111 Freeport Circle
Fallon, NV 89406-2823
775-423-8857
Fax: 775-423-8859 866-957-9233
coffee@phonewave.net www.coffeeper.com
Roasting machines
President: Sherman Dodd
CFO: Phyliss Dodd
Estimated Sales: $1-5 Million
Number Employees: 5-9

20698 Coffee Processing Systems
3666 Swenson Ave
St. Charles, IL 60174-3442
630-443-0034
Fax: 630-443-0049
Automatic controls, bin silo systems and storage, conveying equipment, elevators, machiners and buckets
Estimated Sales: Less than $500,000
Number Employees: 4

20699 Coffee Sock Company
PO Box 10023
Eugene, OR 97440-2023
541-344-7698
Fax: 541-344-7672
jason@coffeesockcompany.com
www.coffeesockcompany.com
Reusable cloth coffee filters and household storage products
Director Sales/Marketing: Robert Thomas
Estimated Sales: $5-10 Million
Number Employees: 5-9

20700 Coffee-Inns of America
3617 E La Salle St
Phoenix, AZ 85040
602-438-8286
Fax: 602-437-2270 800-528-0552
www.coffeeinns.com
Brewers
Owner: John Bergmann
john.bergmann@2mfg.com
Estimated Sales: $10-20 000,000
Number Employees: 100-249

20701 Cog-Veyor Systems, Inc.
371 Hanlan Road
Woodbridge, Ontario, ON L4L 3T1
Canada
416-798-7333
Fax: 416-743-7196 888-337-2358
frubino@ontariobelting.com www.cog-veyor.com
Conveyor's designed for use in the food processing, canning and bottling industries.
Production Manager: Brian Kilbride

20702 Cognitive
4403 Table Mountain Dr Ste A
Golden, CO 80403
303-273-1400
Fax: 303-273-1414 800-765-6600
sales@cognitive.com www.cogsol.com
Labelers, label printing equipment and printing systems
VP: Arthu Kennedy
Marketing Manager: Vic Barezyk
Estimated Sales: $20-50 Million
Number Employees: 100-249
Parent Co: Axiohm Transaction Solutions

20703 Colbert Packaging Corp
28355 N Bradley Rd
Lake Forest, IL 60045-1173
847-367-5990
Fax: 847-367-4403 847-367-5990
www.colbertpkg.com
Rigid paper heart-shaped candy boxes.
President: Jim Hamilton
jhamilton@colbertpkg.com
Chairman: Nancy Colbert MacDougall
Sales Manager: Dave Sult
Sales Representative: Michael Baker
General Manager: Tim Price
Estimated Sales: $10-20 Million
Number Employees: 100-249
Square Footage: 230000
Type of Packaging: Consumer

20704 Colbert Packaging Corp
28355 N Bradley Rd
Lake Forest, IL 60045-1173
847-367-5990
Fax: 847-367-4403 jhamilton@colbertpkg.com
www.colbertpkg.com
Rigid paper heart-shaped candy boxes
President: Jim Hamilton
jhamilton@colbertpkg.com
Sales Manager: Dave Sult
General Manager: Tim Price
Estimated Sales: $32 Million
Number Employees: 100-249
Square Footage: 115000
Parent Co: Colbert Packaging Corporation

20705 Colbert Packaging Corp
28355 N Bradley Rd
Lake Forest, IL 60045-1173
847-367-5990
Fax: 847-367-4403 www.colbertpkg.com
Rigid paper heart-shaped candy boxes
President: Jim Hamilton
jhamilton@colbertpkg.com
Sales Manager: Dave Sult
General Manager: Tim Price
Estimated Sales: $20-50 Million
Number Employees: 100-249
Square Footage: 115000
Parent Co: Colbert Packaging Corporation

20706 Colborne Foodbotics
28495 N Ballard Dr
Lake Forest, IL 60045-4510
847-724-5070
Fax: 847-724-5081 jenny@questequipment.co.uk
www.colbornefoodbotics.com
Cutting systems ideal for cutting sticky, fragile and difficult to cut products and bakery industry turnover systems
President: Richard Hoskins
Quality Control: Don Guther
Manager: Brenda Anderson
brendaa@colbornefoodbotics.com
Estimated Sales: $5-10 Million
Number Employees: 100-249

20707 Cold Chain Technologies
29 Everett St
Holliston, MA 1746
508-429-1395
Fax: 508-429-9056 800-370-8566
info@coldchaintech.com www.coldchaintech.com
Manufacturer and exporter of insulated shipping containers and refrigerant packs for perishable food shipments
President: Larry Gordon
VP, General Manager: Bob Bohne
R&D Manager: Richard Formato
VP Sales/Marketing: TJ Rizzo
Contact: Paul Anderson
panderson@coldchaintech.com
Number Employees: 100-249
Square Footage: 80000
Type of Packaging: Food Service, Private Label, Bulk
Brands:
  Fdc
  Koolit

20708 Cold Jet, LLC
455 Wards Corner
Loveland, OH 45140
513-831-3211
Fax: 513-831-1209 800-337-9423
service@coldjet.com www.coldjet.com
Manufacturer and exporter of dry ice cleaning solutions and dry ice production equipment.
President & CEO: Gene Cooke III
Vice President of Global Marketing: Christian Rogiers
Sr. Vice President of Sales: Brian Allen
Human Resources Manager: Jennifer Ellspermann
Chief Operating Officer: Scott Gatje
Estimated Sales: $1-2.5 Million
Number Employees: 1-4

20709 Cold Storage Building Products
510 Turtle Cove Boulevard
Suite 100
Rockwall, TX 75087-5374
972-771-7824
Fax: 972-771-7822 888-544-4225
Estimated Sales: $3-5 Million
Number Employees: 1-4

20710 ColdZone
8101 E Kaiser Blvd Ste 110
Anaheim, CA 92808-2661
Fax: 714-529-8503
Manufacturer and exporter of refrigeration equipment including remote racks and fluid coolers
President: Jim Grob
VP: Ken Falk
National Sales Manager: R Echols
Contact: Sherry Rister
sherry.rister@htpgusa.com
Product Manager: R Dotson
Estimated Sales: $20-50 Million
Number Employees: 100-249
Square Footage: 260000
Parent Co: Ardco
Type of Packaging: Food Service
Brands:
  C/Z
  Cold Saver
  Enviro-Cool
  Enviro-Therm
  Fc-Pack
  Mini-Pak
  Parallel-Pak
  Uni-Pak

20711 Colder Products Co
1001 Westgate Dr
St Paul, MN 55114-1092
651-645-0091
Fax: 651-645-6938 800-444-2474
brad.ferstan@colder.com www.cpcworldwide.com
Industrial connectors
President: Gary Rychley
gary.rychley@colder.com
Number Employees: 250-499

20712 Coldmatic Building Systems
8500 Keele Street
Concord, ON L4K 2A6
Canada
905-326-7600
Fax: 905-326-7600 800-668-4165
markgalea@rogers.com www.coldmatic.com

President: MARK GALEA
Sales Manager: DEREK FRANCIS
Estimated Sales: $1-5 Million

20713 Coldmatic Refrigeration
8500 Keel Street
Concord, ON L4K 2A6
Canada

905-326-7600
Fax: 905-326-7601 mark@summitproducts.com
www.coldmatic.com
Manufacturer and exporter of automatic and manual
doors including cold storage, double acting, plastic
and refrigerator
President: Mark Galea
CFO: Stafford Mass
VP: Rex Palmatier
Marketing Director: Dan Gregero
Sales Manager- Ontario & Eastern Canada: Mike
Robbie
Plant Manager: Derrick Lee
Estimated Sales: $1-3 Million
Number Employees: 5-9
Parent Co: Coldmatic Refrigeration

20714 Coldstream Products Corporation
10 McCool Crescent
P.O. Box 878
Crossfield, AB T0M 0S0
Canada

403-946-4097
Fax: 403-946-0148 888-946-4097
Manufacturer and exporter of coolers, freezers and
display cases
President: George Zafir
VP: Trevor Rees
VP Marketing: Trevor Rees
Director of Sales: Ken Savard
Operations: Rick Lewis
Purchasing: Les Lewis
Number Employees: 100-249
Number of Brands: s
Number of Products: 75
Square Footage: 1000000
Parent Co: Coldmatic Group of Companies
Brands:
   Cold Tech
   Coldstream

20715 Cole-Parmer Instrument Co LLC
625 Bunker Ct
Vernon Hills, IL 60061-1844

847-549-7600
Fax: 847-247-2929 800-323-4340
info@coleparmer.com www.coleparmer.com
Centrifuges, meters, flow, piping, fittings and tub-
ing, nonsanitary, sanitary
President: Andy Greenawalt
CEO: Bernd Brust
bbrust@coleparmer.com
Quality Control: Robert Czapla
Estimated Sales: $20-50 Million
Number Employees: 250-499

20716 Colecraft Commercial Furnishings
1021 Allen Street
Jamestown, NY 14701

716-488-2810
Fax: 716-488-2824 800-622-2777
www.colecraftcf.com
Plastic laminated food service tables
Manager: Dave Messinger
CEO: Robert Benzel
Vice President: Peter Cardinale
Contact: Martin Buescher
mbuescher@colecraftcf.com
Plant Manager: Neil Hergott
Purchasing Manager: Pat Cleary
Estimated Sales: $8 Million
Number Employees: 50-99
Square Footage: 400000
Parent Co: TR Manufacturing

20717 Coleman Manufacturing Co Inc
48 Waters Ave
Everett, MA 02149-2099

617-389-0380
Fax: 617-389-0769 www.coleman.com/home
Manufacturer and exporter of hand cleaners
President: Richard Coleman
dickcoleman@coleman.com
Estimated Sales: $1-2.5 Million
Number Employees: 5-9
Square Footage: 40000

20718 Coleman Resources
PO Box 8129
Greensboro, NC 27419-0129

336-852-4006
Fax: 336-854-8469
Business printed materials
Manager: Tom Byerly
Estimated Sales: Below $5 Million
Number Employees: 20-49

20719 Coleman Rubber Stamps
171 Madison Ave
Daytona Beach, FL 32114-2177

386-252-8597
Fax: 386-257-5301
Rubber stamps, signs, seals, etc
President: Carole C Ford
VP: Carole Ford
Estimated Sales: $5-10 Million
Number Employees: 5-9

20720 Coley Industries
11885 Granger Road
Wayland, NY 14572-9745

716-728-2390
Woodenware, wooden and gourmet salad bowls,
pepper grinders, salt and pepper shakers and
mounted/unmounted time and hour glasses
President: John Coley

**20721 Colgate-Palmolive Professional
Products Group**
895 Don Mills Rd
North York, ON M3C 1W3
Canada

800-468-6502
Manufacturer and exporter of cleaning supplies
Chairman, President & CEO: Ian Cook
Estimated Sales: $100-500 Million
Number Employees: 1,000-4,999
Type of Packaging: Food Service
Brands:
   Ajax
   Palmolive
   Murphy Oil Soap
   Irish Spring
   Fabuloso
   Softsoap
   Colgate

20722 Collectors Gallery
2601 E Main St
St Charles, IL 60174-4289

630-584-5235
Fax: 630-584-1224 800-346-3063
www.studiostyle.com
Extensive line of decorative boxes, bags and wraps
Executive Director: Kevin Hughes
kevinh@studiostyle.com
Project Manager: Sandy Peterman
Number Employees: 100-249

**20723 Collegeville Flag &
Manufacturing Company**
24 W 4th Avenue
Collegeville, PA 19426-2601

610-489-4131
Fax: 610-489-4164 800-523-5630
In store displays, flags and banners including U.S.,
custom logo, advertising, etc.; also, poles and acces-
sories
Chairman: Richard Doyle
Account Executive: Jennifer Engle
Estimated Sales: $10-20 Million
Number Employees: 50-99
Parent Co: Collegeville Flag & Banner

20724 Colliers International
3439 Brookside Rd # 108
Suite 108
Stockton, CA 95219-1754

209-475-5100
Fax: 209-475-5102 www.colliers.com
Partner: Michael Goldstein
Senior Vice President: Lisa Hodgson
lhodgson@colliersparrish.com
Vice President: Adam Lucatello
Operations Manager: Maria Marquez
Estimated Sales: Below $500,000
Number Employees: 10-19

20725 Collins & Aikman
1212 7th St SW
Canton, OH 44707

330-253-3826
Fax: 330-456-0849 800-321-0244
www.collinsaikman.com
Manufacturer and exporter of rubber and vinyl mat-
ting
Quality Control: Chris Carpenter
CEO: Mike Geaghan
Contact: Michelle Petruska
michellepetruska@devry.edu
VP Merchandising: Scot Landeis
Production Manager: Gary Taylor
Plant Manager: Todd Weber
Estimated Sales: $.5-1 million
Number Employees: 20-49
Type of Packaging: Food Service
Brands:
   Aqua Trap
   Cushion Ease

**20726 Collins Manufacturing Company
Ltd**
9835 199 A Street
Langley, BC V1M 2X7
Canada

604-888-2812
Fax: 604-888-7689 800-663-6761
www.collinsmfg.com
Refrigerated and dry freight van-bodies and
flat-decks ditributor of Maxon liftgates, Parco-Hesse
beverage bodies and Utilimaster walk-in bodies
President: Michael Sondergaard
Finance: Bobbie Hiscock
Director, Sales & Marketing: Guy Perrault
Account Manager: Brent Wilson
Plant Manager: Jerry Brownlee
Number Employees: 50-99
Brands:
   Collins
   Maxon
   Parco-Hesse
   Utilimaster

20727 Collins Technical
8330 Route a i a S
St Augustine, FL 32086

904-461-4546
Fax: 904-461-4539
Moulding equipment
Sales Manager: Jack Collins
Estimated Sales: $1-5 000,000
Number Employees: 6

20728 Colmac Coil Mfg Inc
370 N Lincoln St
Colville, WA 99114-2342

509-684-2595
Fax: 509-684-8331 800-845-6778
mail@colmaccoil.com www.colmaccoil.com
Owner: Scott Mc Millan
scott.mcmillan@colmac.ind.com
Sales Manager: Jeremy Olberding
scott.mcmillan@colmac.ind.com
Estimated Sales: $20-50 Million
Number Employees: 100-249
Square Footage: 225000

20729 Colmar Storage Co Warehouse
6695 NW 36th Ave
Miami, FL 33147-7519

305-696-1614
Fax: 305-836-5800
Storage of coffee (green coffee), samplers and
weighers
manager: Robert Olmedo
rolmedo@colmarstoragellc.com
Manager: Robert Olmedo
Estimated Sales: $2.5-5 000,000
Number Employees: 10-19
Type of Packaging: Private Label

20730 Colonial Marketing Assoc
400 Broadway
Freehold, NJ 07728-1494

732-462-2100
Fax: 732-431-3419
Marketing consultant for the egg industry
Owner: Abe Opatut
Partner: Henry Opatut
henry.opatut@nextfinancial.com
Number Employees: 5-9

20731 Colonial Paper Company
P.O.Box 310
Silver Springs, FL 34489-0310
352-622-4171
Fax: 352-422-7247 cpcweb@aol.com
Paper goods, disposable tabletop items and janitorial, dishwashing and warewashing equipment and supplies
President: William H Tuck Sr
Estimated Sales: $10-20 Million
Number Employees: 20-49

20732 Colonial Transparent Products Company
870 S Oyster Bay Road
mail.com
Hicksville, NY 11801-3576
516-822-4430
Fax: 516-822-4292
Plastic films, sleeve labels and polyethylene bags; also, design, printing and converting available
President: L Goldstein
VP: E Goldstein
Office Manager: C Bland
Estimated Sales: $5-10 Million
Number Employees: 20-49
Square Footage: 50000

20733 Colony Brands Inc
1112 7th Ave
Monroe, WI 53566-1364
608-328-8400
Fax: 608-328-8457 800-544-9036
www.colonybrands.com
Cakes, tortes & pies; cookies & bars; pastries; petits fours; candy & chocolate; boxed assortments of all kinds; cheeses; sausage, ham and other meats; nuts & pre-mixed snacks; home furniture; home d,cor; electronics; jewelry; fitnessequipment; unisex apparel; small appliances
CEO: John Baumann
Chairman: Pat Kubly
VP/CIO: Steve Cretney
Content Marketing Manager: Matt Stetler
Director of Strategic Planning: Ryan Kubly
Number Employees: 1000-4999
Square Footage: 13236
Parent Co: Colony Brands, Inc.
Brands:
   Swiss Colony Foods

20734 Color Ad Tech Signs
6500 S Washington St
Amarillo, TX 79118-7817
806-374-8117
Advertising signs
Owner: Truet Cargill
Estimated Sales: $1-3 Million
Number Employees: 5-9
Square Footage: 15000

20735 Color Box
623 S G St
Richmond, IN 47374
765-966-7588
Fax: 765-962-5584 www.gp.com
Manufacturer and exporter of paper boxes and cartons
Manager: Jeff Pobanz
VP Sales: Frank Mazzei
Contact: Michael Adams
madams@cskcorp.com
VP Manufacturing: Mike Roark
Estimated Sales: $20-50 Million
Number Employees: 250-499
Parent Co: Georgia Pacific
Type of Packaging: Consumer, Bulk

20736 Color Carton Corp
341 Canal Pl
Bronx, NY 10451-6091
718-665-0840
Fax: 718-993-1776
customerservice@colorcarton.com
www.colorcarton.com
Folding paper boxes
President: Debbie Loprinzi
dloprinzi@colorcarton.com
VP: Nicholas LoPrinzi
Treasurer: Vincent LoPrinzi
Estimated Sales: $5-10 Million
Number Employees: 20-49

20737 Color Communications Inc
4000 W Fillmore St
Chicago, IL 60624-3916
773-638-1400
Fax: 773-638-0887 www.ccicolor.com
Creates visual quality colors control standards and color tolerance to communicate your product
President: Steve Winter
hpham@ccicolor.com
VP: Steven Winter
General Manager: Harry Lerner
Marketing Director: Jill Goldstein
Estimated Sales: $50-100 Million
Number Employees: 250-499
Type of Packaging: Bulk

20738 Color-Box Inc
1275 S Granada Dr
Madera, CA 93637-4803
559-674-1049
Fax: 559-674-1050
Wine industry bag, box and carton packaging
Manager: Tim McCoy
VP: Barbara Fox
Manager: Brad Alling
bpalling@gapac.com
Number Employees: 50-99

20739 Colorado Nut Co
2 Kalamath St
Denver, CO 80223-1550
303-733-7311
800-876-1625
sales@coloradonutco.com
www.coloradonutco.com
Manufactures and Imports candies, chocolates, unique trail mixes, snack mixes, dried fruits and gift baskets for any occasion. Also roast nuts on site. Also offer products with private labeling and customized logos for a variety ofspecialized events.
Owner: Mark Goodman
mgoodman@coloradonutco.com
Owner: Roger Renaud
Estimated Sales: Less Than $500,000
Number Employees: 5-9
Type of Packaging: Consumer, Private Label

20740 Colorcon Inc
275 Ruth Rd
Harleysville, PA 19438-1952
215-256-7700
Fax: 215-661-2626 www.colorcon.com
Custom dispersed colorant systems, natural colorants, pearlescent color systems, barrier coatings, glazes, FD&C certified pigments, color blends and monogramming and nontoxic printing inks for food packaging applications; exporter offood colorants, coatings, inks, etc.
CEO: William Motzer
wmotzer@colorcon.com
Senior Business Manager-Naturals/Food: Lou Palermo
Business Manager-Food/Confectionary: John Jaworski
Estimated Sales: $50-100 Million
Number Employees: 250-499
Parent Co: Berwind Pharmaceutical Services
Type of Packaging: Bulk
Other Locations:
   NA Headquarters
   Westpoint PA
   Colorcon No-Tox Products
   Chalfont PA
   Colorcon, Inc.
   Irvine CA
   Colorcon, Inc.
   Indianapolis IN
   Colorcon, Inc.
   Stoughton WI
   Colorcon P.R., Inc.
   Humacao PR
   Colorcon, Inc.
   St. Laurent, Canada

20741 Colortec Associates Inc
28 Center St # 1
Clinton, NJ 08809-2632
908-735-2248
Fax: 908-236-7865 www.formulatorus.com
Develops and markets technologically advanced PC software and color instruments for industrial applications and point-of-sale merchandising; delivering color measuring instruments and nutritional labeling software to the food andagriculture industry.

President: James Degroff
jdegroff@color-tec.com
Vice President: C Womer
Estimated Sales: $1-3 Million
Number Employees: 5-9
Number of Brands: 3
Number of Products: 3

20742 Colson Caster Corp
3700 Airport Rd
Jonesboro, AR 72401-4463
870-932-4501
Fax: 870-932-1446 800-643-5515
info1@colsoncaster.com www.colsoncaster.com
Manufacturer and exporter of casters, wheels and bumpers
President: Don Laux
dlaux@colsoncaster.com
CEO: Jim Blankenship
Chairman the Board: Robert Pritzker
VP: Bill Blackley
Marketing: Cary Gillespie
Estimated Sales: $50-100 Million
Number Employees: 100-249

20743 Colter & Peterson
414 East 16th Street
Paterson, NJ 07514
973-684-0901
Fax: 973-684-0260 contact@colterpeterson.com
www.colter-peterson.com
New and rebuilt machinery for set-up, folding and corrugated boxes
Manager: Lawrence Harris
VP: Lawrence Harris
Contact: Bob Allan
ballan@colter-peterson.com
Assistant Manager: Jo Taylor
Estimated Sales: $1-2.5 Million
Number Employees: 5-9

20744 Columbia Equipment & Finance
586 Silver Lake Dr
Danville, CA 94526-6226
925-314-1242
Fax: 925-314-1240 800-733-3939
information@columbialeasing.com
www.columbialeasingusa.com
Equipment lease financing and small business loans
President: Stan Nathanson
Estimated Sales: $.5-1 million
Number Employees: 1-4

20745 (HQ)Columbia Jet/JPL
750 Almeda Genoa Road
Houston, TX 77047-4106
713-433-4511
Fax: 713-434-1397 800-876-4511
Lighting fixtures
Director Sales: Mack Pyle
Marketing Manager: Tom Scott
Sales Manager: Les Simpson
Estimated Sales: $1-5 Million

20746 Columbia Labeling Machinery
1580 Dale Ave
PO Box 5290
Benton City, WA 99320
Fax: 509-588-5080 888-791-9590
sales@rippedsheets.com www.columbialabel.com
Manufacturer and exporter of automatic and semi-automatic labeling machines and supplies; also, bar code printing and labeling equipment
President: Raymond MacNeill
Sales: Catherine Bryson
Estimated Sales: $1-2.5 Million
Number Employees: 4
Square Footage: 100000

20747 Columbia Lighting
701 Millennium Blvd.
Greenville, SC 29607
864-678-1000
Fax: 864-678-1740
www.hubbell.com/columbialighting/en
Lighting fixtures including electric and fluorescent.
Chairman/President/CEO: David Nord
Senior VP/CFO: William Sperry
Year Founded: 1897
Estimated Sales: $100-500 Million
Number Employees: 500-999
Number of Brands: 1
Square Footage: 680000
Parent Co: Hubbell Lighting

Brands:
 Columbia

20748 Columbia Machine Inc
107 Grand Blvd
Vancouver, WA 98661-7795

360-694-1501
Fax: 360-695-7517 800-628-4065
pallsales@colmac.com
www.columbiamachine.com
Floor, high level and robotic palletizers for cases,
bags, pails, bales and trays
President: Jerry Finolay
CEO: Rick Goode
ricgoo@colmac.com
CFO: Winston Asai
CEO: Rick Goode
Sales Director: Richard Armstrong
Estimated Sales: $50-100 Million
Number Employees: 100-249
Square Footage: 186530

20749 Columbia Okura LLC
301 Grove St
Vancouver, WA 98661

360-735-1952
Fax: 360-905-1707 taygoo@colmac.com
www.columbiamachine.com
Robotic palletizing experts.
President: Rick Goode
Contact: Robert Alley
robert.alley@columbiaokura.com
Estimated Sales: $20-50 Million
Number Employees: 10-19

20750 Columbian TecTank
2101 S 21st St
Parsons, KS 67357

620-421-0200
Fax: 620-421-9122 800-421-2788
www.columbiantectank.com
Manufacturer and exporter of bolted and welded car-
bon steel, stainless steel and aluminum storage tanks
and silos
Contact: Robert Baker
rwbaker@columbiantectank.com
Plant Manager: Steve Allen
Estimated Sales: $20-50 Million
Number Employees: 100-249
Brands:
 Aquastore
 Harvestove
 Peabody Tectank
 Seal Weld

20751 Columbus Instruments
950 N Hague Ave
Columbus, OH 43204-2121

614-279-9607
Fax: 614-276-0529 800-669-5011
sales@colinst.com www.colinst.com
Manufacturer and exporter of respirometers for mea-
suring the sterility, bacterial and fungal growth,
biodegradation and oxidation of fats; also, calorime-
ters, precision gas mixers and air dryers
President: Jan A Czekajewski
Manager: Frank Pence
frank.pence@service.colinst.com
Estimated Sales: $2.5-5 Million
Number Employees: 20-49
Square Footage: 40000
Brands:
 Micro-Oxymax
 Oxymax

20752 Columbus McKinnon Corporation
205 Crosspoint Pkwy.
Getzville, NY 14068

716-689-5400
800-888-0985
www.cmworks.com
Chains, hoists, forgings, lift tables, jib arms, manip-
ulators and conveyors.
Chairman: Richard Fleming
President/CEO: Mark Morelli
Vice President, Finance/CFO: Gregory Rustowicz
Vice President, Information Services: Mark
Paradowski
Year Founded: 1875
Estimated Sales: $597 Million
Number Employees: 3,328
Brands:
 Abell-Howe
 Alltec

Budgit
Cady
CES
Chester Hoist
CM
CMCO
Coffing
Duff Norton
Little Mule
Magnetek
Pfaff Silberblau
Shaw-Box
STAHL CraneSystems
STB Stahlhammer Bommern
Unified Industries
Yale

20753 Columbus Paperbox Company
595 Van Buren Dr
Columbus, OH 43223

419-628-2381
Fax: 419-628-3105 800-968-0797
info@globusprinting.com
www.globusprinting.com/
Folding cartons and rigid set-up boxes
President: William Reiber
VP: Robert Reiber
VP Sales: Thomas Kasle
Estimated Sales: $5-10 Million
Number Employees: 20-49
Square Footage: 240000
Parent Co: Globus Printing & Packaging, Inc.
Brands:
 Conoco Lubricants
 Conoco/Andero
 Hydroclear

20754 Com-Pac International Inc
800 W Industrial Park Rd
Carbondale, IL 62901-5514

618-529-2421
Fax: 618-529-2234 888-297-2824
compac@com-pac.com www.com-pac.com
In-line reclosable zipper system with air-tight seal
President: Greg Sprehe
greg.sprehe@com-pac.com
CEO: Don Wright
R&D: Chris Pemberton
Quality Control: Kendall Henkins
Marketing: Durrell McDannel
Sales: Darrell McDannel
Estimated Sales: Below $5 Million
Number Employees: 100-249
Number of Brands: 4
Number of Products: 20
Type of Packaging: Consumer, Food Service, Pri-
vate Label
Brands:
 Integra
 Integra Cm
 Integra T
 Rtr 1000
 Z Patch

20755 Com-Pak International
11615 Cardinal Circle
Garden Grove, CA 92843-3814

714-537-5772
Fax: 714-537-4326
Wholesaler/distributor of food and chemical pro-
cessing and packaging equipment
President: Billy Fielder
VP: David West
Estimated Sales: $1-3 Million
Number Employees: 7
Square Footage: 72000
Parent Co: Garden Grove
Other Locations:
 Com-Pak International
 Hemet CA

20756 Comalex
419-B Gordon Avenue
Van Buren, AR 72956

866-343-2594
renewberry@comalex.com www.comalex.com
Manufacturers computer software designed to auto-
mate Point-of-Sale (POS) food service operations in
K-12 public and private schools and colleges
President: Richard Newberry
Number Employees: 16
Square Footage: 12400

20757 Comark Instruments
P.O.Box 9029
Everett, WA 98206-9029

360-435-5571
Fax: 360-403-4243 800-555-6658
sales@comarkusa.com global.bayliner.com
Supplier of electronic measurement instruments
including food and industrial thermometers,
thermocouples, temperature probes, data loggers,
data management systems and timers plus humidity
and pressure instruments.
President: Jeff Behan
Marketing Manager: Alan Mellinger
National Sales Manager: Bob Bader
Estimated Sales: $5-10 Million
Number Employees: 1,000-4,999
Number of Brands: 1
Number of Products: 200
Parent Co: Brunsik Corporation
Type of Packaging: Food Service
Brands:
 Comark
 Kane-May/Km

20758 Comasec Safety, Inc.
8 Niblick Road
Enfield, CT 06082

860-749-0506
Fax: 860-741-0881 800-333-0219
Manufacturer and importer of gloves including
PVC/nitrile, knit lined latex, plastic, cotton/mesh
lined, heavy unlined rubber; exporter of knit lined
latex gloves
General Manager: P Gelinas
Tecnical Manager: Joe Krocheski
Estimated Sales: $5-10 Million
Number Employees: 10-19
Brands:
 Astroflex

20759 Comax Flavors
130 Baylis Rd
Melville, NY 11747-3808

631-420-0073
Fax: 631-249-9255 800-992-0629
info@comaxflavors.com www.comaxflavors.com
Supplier of flavors
President: Weisz Agneta
CEO: Peter Calabretta
CFO: Virginia Wyan
Vice President: Paul Calabretta
Sr. Flavor Chemist: Mike Crain
Quality Control: Frank Vollaro
EVP Sales & Marketing: Bill Graham
PR/Communications Manager: Laura Ferrante
VP Operations: Joe Piazza
Production Manager: Jorge Quintanilla
Plant Manager: Marion Cunningham
Purchasing Manager: Michael Keppel
Estimated Sales: $15 Million
Number Employees: 250-499

20760 Combake International
3050 Royal Boulevard S
Suite 150
Alpharetta, GA 30022-4454

770-667-4944
Fax: 770-677-3440 wpib@aol.com

20761 Combi Packaging Systems LLC
5365 E Center Dr NE
PO Box 9326
Canton, OH 44721-3734

330-456-9333
Fax: 330-456-4644 866-472-5236
sales@combi.com www.combi.com
30 year manufacturer of case erectors, case packers
and case sealers, robotic pick and place pakcers with
integrated case erectors; ergonomic hand packaging
stations and drop packers with integrated case
erectors.
President/CEO: John Fisher
jfisher@combi.com
CFO: Barb Karch
Research & Development: Bill Mitchell
Marketing Director: Sue Lewis
Sales Director: Mark Freidly
Plant Manager: Brian Miller
Estimated Sales: $10-20 Million
Number Employees: 100-249
Square Footage: 270000
Brands:
 Combi America

Laser 2000
Z-Ez

20762 Combined Computer Resource
2777 N Stemmons Fwy Ste 1046
Dallas, TX 75207

214-267-1010
Fax: 214-267-1019 800-956-1866
www.winocular.com
Suppliers of management software solutions that
solve problems with paper and electronic document
movement,retrieval,storage and archival or retention
Owner: Nick Sanders
Quality Control: Kim Roberts
VP: Rocky Chesnutt
VP: Kim Roberts
Estimated Sales: $4 000,000
Number Employees: 10-19

20763 Combustion Systems Sales
12946 SE Kent Kangley Road
300
Kent, WA 98030-7940

206-623-1141
Fax: 501-556-4104
Roasters (machines), conveying equipment (eleva-
tors, machiners and buckets), repair services

20764 Comco Signs
1624 Toal St
Charlotte, NC 28206-1522

704-375-2338
Fax: 704-333-3335
Signs
President: John W Ulery
Estimated Sales: Below $5 Million
Number Employees: 20 to 49

20765 Comet Signs
235 W Turbo Dr
San Antonio, TX 78216-3313

210-341-7244
Fax: 210-341-7279 info@cometsigns.com
www.cometsigns.com
Indoor and outdoor signs including advertising and
electric
President: Arthur Sitterle
CEO: Tim Edmonds
tim@cometneon.com
VP: Pete Sitterle
Estimated Sales: $5-10 Million
Number Employees: 50-99

20766 Comm-Pak
2406 Frederick Rd
Opelika, AL 36801-7222

334-749-6201
Fax: 334-749-1948
Point of purchase displays and pressure sensitive de-
cals and labels; also, custom printing of plastic
drinkware available
President: Trey Gafford
Estimated Sales: $1-2.5 Million
Number Employees: 10 To 19
Square Footage: 36000

20767 Command Belt Cleaning Systems
700 Hoffman Street
Hammond, IN 46327-1894

219-931-1450
Fax: 219-931-0209 800-433-7627
www.screwconveyor.com
Automated conveyor belt cleaning systems
Operations Manager: Frank Pennino
General Manager: John Rice
Number Employees: 20-49
Square Footage: 20000
Parent Co: Pari Industries

20768 Command Communications
14510 E Fremont Ave
Centennial, CO 80112-4233

304-839-4051
Fax: 303-792-0899 800-288-3491
Manufacturer and exporter of wireless, staff, guest,
hostess and waitress paging systems. Also communi-
cation products designed to reduce the number of
phone lines— saving monthly phone line expenses
President/CEO: Craig Hibbard
chibbard@commandcom.com
VP Operations: Mary Larson
Director of Communications/Online Mkting:
Michael Rose
National Accounts Sales Manager: Charla Martin

Estimated Sales: $3-5 Million
Number Employees: 10-19
Number of Products: 10
Type of Packaging: Consumer, Food Service, Pri-
vate Label, Bulk

20769 Command Electronics Inc
15670 Morris Industrial Dr
Schoolcraft, MI 49087-9628

269-679-4011
Fax: 269-679-5410
info@commandelectronics.com
www.commandelectronics.com
Manufacturer and exporter of fluorescent and incan-
descent lighting
President: Cary Campagna
Vice President: Dan Campagna
Estimated Sales: $1-5 Million
Number Employees: 10-19
Square Footage: 52000
Brands:
Porta-Lamp

20770 Command Line Corporation
1090 Kng Geo Pst Rd Ste 802
Edison, NJ 8837

732-738-6500
Fax: 732-738-6504 www.commandlinecorp.com
Customized purchasing, distribution and manufac-
turing management software systems for multi-site
inventory control, requisitions, receiving, bar cod-
ing, A/P interfaces, warehouse locator systems, etc
President: Donald Staffin
Estimated Sales: $1-2.5 Million
Number Employees: 10-19

20771 Command Packaging
3840 E 26th St
Vernon, CA 90058-4107

323-980-0918
Fax: 323-260-7047 800-996-2247
info@commandpackaging.com
www.commandpackaging.com
Elegant, upscale, and value added bags for retail
stores including, bakeries and delies, restaurants,
and grocery stores. We specialize in bags for restau-
rant carry out
President: Albert Halimi
CEO: Pete Grande
Vice President: Scott Ellingson
scottellingson@cox.net
Marketing Director: Vicki Stiling
Operations Manager: Carol Bullock
Estimated Sales: $10-20 Million
Number Employees: 100-249
Square Footage: 100000
Type of Packaging: Food Service

20772 (HQ)Commencement Bay Corrugated
13414 142nd Ave E
Orting, WA 98360-9560

253-845-3100
Fax: 253-445-0772 www.cbcbox.com
Manufacturer and exporter of corrugated paper
boxes
Manager: Paul Winber
Sales Coordinator: James Kressler
Manager: Steve Mc Donald
mcdonald@cbcbox.com
General Manager: Joe McQuade
Plant Manager: Randy Snow
Estimated Sales: $20-50 Million
Number Employees: 100-249
Square Footage: 130000

20773 Commercial Corrugated Co Inc
4101 Ashland Ave
Baltimore, MD 21205-2924

410-522-0900
Fax: 410-522-6184 800-242-8861
jpauly@commercialcorrugated.com
www.commercialwagner.com
Corrugated boxes and containers; also, point of pur-
chase displays
President: John Pauley Sr
Contact: Wanda Battaglia
wbattaglia@commercialwagner.com
Estimated Sales: $10-20 Million
Number Employees: 10-19
Type of Packaging: Private Label, Bulk

20774 Commercial Creamery Co
159 S Cedar St
Spokane, WA 99201

509-747-4131
sales@cheesepowder.com
www.cheesepowder.com
Dried cheese and yogurt powders; processor and exporter of snack seasoning and spray dried dairy flavors
Owner/VP Sales & Marketing: Megan Boell
mboell@cheesepowder.com
Year Founded: 1908
Estimated Sales: $28 Million
Number Employees: 5-9

20775 (HQ)Commercial Dehydrator Systems
256 Bethel Dr
Eugene, OR 97402-2504

541-688-5282
Fax: 541-688-5989 800-369-4283
darryl@dryer.com www.dehydrator.com
Berry crate washers, insect sterilization chambers,
roasters, cookers and dryers including continuous
belt, bin and tray; exporter of dryers/roasters and
sorting/grading belting.
President: David Stone
marketing@dryer.com
Vice President: David Stone
National Sales Manager: Darryl Hastings
Field Representative: Darryl Hastings
Estimated Sales: $1-2.5 Million
Number Employees: 50-99
Square Footage: 54000

20776 Commercial Envelope Manufacturing Company
350 Wireless Blvd Ste 102
Hauppauge, NY 11788-3947

Fax: 631-242-6935
Envelopes
President: Alan Kristel
Estimated Sales: $20-50 Million
Number Employees: 100-249

20777 (HQ)Commercial Furniture Group Inc
810 W Highway 25 70
Newport, TN 37821-8044

423-623-0031
Fax: 423-587-8872 800-873-3252
www.commercialfurnituregroup.com
Manufacturer and exporter of chairs, benches,
booths and tables
Manager: Bob Branstetter
CFO: Neal Restivo
Marketing Specialist: Teri Winters
IT: Stefanie Thompson
sthompson@commercialfurniture.com
Number Employees: 1000-4999
Type of Packaging: Food Service
Brands:
Epic
Falcon
Howe
Shelby Williams
Thonet

20778 Commercial Kitchen Co
3219 W Washington Blvd
Los Angeles, CA 90018-1249

323-732-2291
Fax: 323-732-2729 www.commercialkitchen.com
Stainless steel hoods, tables and shelving
President: Armando Carmona
commercialkitchen18@yahoo.com
Estimated Sales: $500,000-$1,000,000
Number Employees: 1-4

20779 Commercial Lighting Design
43 S Dudley St
Memphis, TN 38104

901-774-5771
Fax: 901-946-2478 800-774-5799
www.lumalier.com
Manufacturer and exporter of lighting fixtures
President: Charles Dunn
CEO: Charles Dunn, Sr.
VP: Charles Dunn, Jr.
Estimated Sales: $1-2,500,000
Number Employees: 10-19
Brands:
Lumalier

20780 Commercial Manufacturing
2432 S Railroad Ave
Fresno, CA 93706-5187
559-237-1855
Fax: 559-266-5149 info@commercialmfg.com
www.commercialmfg.com
Manufacturer and exporter of bin handling systems, conveyors, bucket elevators, air dryers, coolers and cleaners, washers, centrifuges, food pumps, graders and mix and blend systems
President: Larry Hagopian
info@commercialmfg.com
Sales Manager: Jack Kraemer
Sales Engineer: Jim MacKenzie
Sales Engineer: Bob Peschel
Estimated Sales: $10-20 Million
Number Employees: 50-99

20781 Commercial Packaging
8425 Fairway Pl
Middleton, WI 53562-2501
608-836-7181
Fax: 608-831-9632 800-500-9519
info@commercialpackaging.com
Packaging material
Manager: Bonnie Dahlk
bdahlk@commercialpackaging.com
VP: Aaron Egbers
Estimated Sales: $5-10 Million
Number Employees: 1-4
Parent Co: Commercial Packaging

20782 Commercial Printing Company
P.O.Box 10302
Birmingham, AL 35202-0302
205-251-9203
Fax: 205-251-6133 800-989-9203
Manufacturers of printers and printing related services like scanning, digital and conventional stripping, multicolor printing, bindery, on demand printing and elkote finishing
President: Thomas Arledge
Executive Vice President: Mike Leathers
Account Executive: Alex Berger
Contact: Don Thompson
dthompson@cprintingco.com
Estimated Sales: $10-20 Million
Number Employees: 50-99

20783 Commercial Refrigeration Service, Inc.
2501 West Behrend Drive
Suite 39
Phoenix, AZ 85027-4148
623-869-8881
Fax: 623-869-8882 www.comrefsvc.com
Manufacturer and exporter of beverage dispensers
Contact: Sandra Forsythe
s.forsythe@crhinc.com
Estimated Sales: $1-5 Million
Number Employees: 100-250
Square Footage: 240000
Type of Packaging: Food Service
Brands:
  Jet Spray

20784 Commercial Seating Specailists
481 Laurelwood Rd
Santa Clara, CA 95054-2416
408-453-8983
Fax: 408-453-8986 www.comseat.com
Booths and table tops.
Owner: Jim Day
CEO: Patricia Day
Marketing Director: Rich Buchner
Sales Director: Mike Alexander
jday@comseat.com
Purchasing Manager: Scott Wallace
Estimated Sales: $1-2.5 Million
Number Employees: 10-19

20785 Commercial Testing Lab Inc
514 Main St
Colfax, WI 54730-9001
715-962-3121
Fax: 715-962-4030 800-962-5227
ctlfoods@ctlcolfax.com
An analytical microbiology Testing Lab testing water, food, calibrations, and feed and forage.
President: Peter Klug
peterk@ctlcolfax.com
R&D: Cheryl Bean
Estimated Sales: $2.5-5 000,000
Number Employees: 20-49

20786 Commodity Traders International
101 E. Main Street
P.O. Box 6
Trilla, IL 62469-0006
217-235-4322
Fax: 217-235-3246 sales@commoditytraders.biz
www.commoditytraders.biz
Manufacturer and exporter of new and used milling, grain handling and seed processing machinery
Executive Trustee: Charles Stodden

20787 Common Sense Natural Soap & Bodycare Products
109 Lincoln Avenue
Rutland, VT 05701-3226
802-773-0582
Fax: 561-753-8207
Natural soap products
General Manager: Michael Delaney
Estimated Sales: $5-10 Million
Number Employees: 10-19

20788 Compacker Systems LLC
9104 N Zenith Ave
P.O. Box 2026
Davenport, IA 52806-6432
563-391-2751
Fax: 563-391-8598
Manufacturer and exporter of case packing and sealing equipment including case erectors, wrap-around and top and bottom sealers, traymakers, etc
President: Keith Tucker
CEO: John Curtis
compacker@compacker.com
Quality Control: Jane Bower
Marketing Manager: Michael Bower
General Manager: Keith Tucker
Estimated Sales: $5-10 Million
Number Employees: 10-19
Square Footage: 80000
Brands:
  Bottom Line
  Compacker Ii
  Compacker Ii Abf-3
  Compacker Iii
  Endpacker
  Rap-Up 90
  Tm1000

20789 Compact Industries Inc
3945 Ohio Ave
St Charles, IL 60174-5467
630-513-9600
Fax: 630-513-9655 800-513-4262
www.compactind.com
Private label and contract packager: dry product packaging, in-house blending, formulating
President/CEO: Michael Brown
CFO: Steve Zaruba
VP Sales: Gary Johnson
Estimated Sales: $9 Million
Number Employees: 100-249
Square Footage: 300000
Type of Packaging: Consumer, Food Service, Private Label, Bulk
Brands:
  Casa Verde
  Cool Off
  Geneva Freeze
  John Foster Green

20790 Compact Mold
3436 Turfway Road
Erlanger, KY 41018-3169
859-371-3250
Fax: 859-371-2290
Blow molds
Estimated Sales: $1-5 000,000
Number Employees: 12

20791 Compactors Inc
71 Lighthouse Rd # 221
Hilton Head Isle, SC 29928-7297
843-363-5077
Fax: 843-686-3290 800-423-4003
info@compactorsinc.com
www.compactorsinc.com
Manufacturer and exporter of can and bottle crushers, trash compactors and densifiers
President: Mike Pierson
mike@compactorsinc.com
VP: Bill Phillips
Estimated Sales: Below $5 Million
Number Employees: 1-4

Square Footage: 8000
Parent Co: Hilton Head SC
Brands:
  Pac Crusher I

20792 Compass Group Canada
1 Prologis Blvd
Suite 400
Mississauga, ON L5W 0G2
Canada
800-465-2203
www.compass-canada.com
Foodservices and support services for sports and leisure venues, executive dining rooms and cafes, schools, universities, seniors' residences, hospitals, remote camps and off-shore oil rigs.
CEO: Saajid Khan
CFO: Brent Mooney
SVP/General Counsel: Ian Baskerville
Chief Growth Officer, Canada: Peter Kourtis
Chief People & Culture Officer: Lauren Davey
Estimated Sales: $28 Billion
Number Employees: 25,000
Parent Co: Compass Group PLC
Type of Packaging: Food Service

20793 Compatible Components Corporation
1213 West Loop North
Suite 180
Houston, TX 77055
713-688-2008
Fax: 713-688-2993 sales@cccmix.com
www.compatible-components.com
Mixing/blending products and separating/dewatering products
President: Gerald Lott
Contact: Anthony Lerma
alerma@cccmix.com

20794 Complete Automation
1776 W Clarkston Rd
Lake Orion, MI 48362-2267
248-814-4967
Fax: 248-693-0503 marketing@completeco.com
www.completeco.com
Coolant filtration systems and filtration products.
President: Kenneth Matheis
IT: Ryan Rausch
rmrausch@completeco.com
Number Employees: 50-99
Square Footage: 45000

20795 (HQ)Complete Packaging & Shipping
83 Bennington Ave
Freeport, NY 11520-3913
516-546-2100
Fax: 516-546-0717 877-269-3236
johnc@completepackage.com
www.completesupplyusa.com
Corrugated boxes; exporter and importer of tapes, cartons, stretch film, impulse sealers and plastic strapping materials. 3000 box sizes in stock
Owner: Jeffery Berkowitz
Director Of Sales: Tom DiGiacomo
Estimated Sales: $10-20 Million
Number Employees: 10-19

20796 Complete Packaging Solutions
325 Curie Dr
Alpharetta, GA 30005-2264
770-751-7400
Fax: 770-751-0706 800-417-3178
info@kallfass-us.com www.kallfass.com
Fully automatic l-sealer, side sealers and sleeve wrapper, shrink tunnels and semiautomatic l-sealer
Owner: Bodo Goepfert
bodo@kallfass-us.com
Vice President: Bodo Goepfert
Marketing/Sales Manager: Cece Loft
Estimated Sales: $1-2.5 000,000
Number Employees: 5-9

20797 Complete Packaging Systems
2411 Loma Avenue
South El Monte, CA 91733-1415
626-579-4670
Fax: 626-579-2015
Prints blister cards and thermoforms blisters
President: Bruce Romfo
Estimated Sales: $10-20 000,000
Number Employees: 100-249

20798 Complex Steel & Wire Corp
36254 Annapolis St
Wayne, MI 48184-2094
734-326-1600
Fax: 734-326-7421 www.complexsteel.com
Wire rack decking and partitions.
President: Vincent Fedell
complexsteel@aol.com
Sales Manager: Gary Snarkas
Estimated Sales: $2.5-5 Million
Number Employees: 20-49

20799 Compliance Control Inc
1595 Cabin Branch Dr
Hyattsville, MD 20785-3816
301-773-6485
Fax: 301-773-4044 800-810-4000
info@hygenius.com www.tempgenius.com
Manufacturer and exporter of handwashing verification systems
President: Neil Segal
nsegal@compliancecontrolinc.com
Executive VP: Bill Karlin
Estimated Sales: $2.5-5 Million
Number Employees: 20-49
Type of Packaging: Food Service, Private Label
Brands:
Hygenius

20800 (HQ)Component Hardware Group Inc
1890 Swarthmore Ave
Lakewood, NJ 08701-4530
323-888-9395
Fax: 732-363-9864 800-526-3694
Manufacturer, importer and exporter of food service equipment including beverage preparation and serving products, dispensers, faucets, spray washers, water stations, tables including legs and bases, drains, grease filters, castersetc
President: Alfred Klein
VP Marketing: William Matthaei
VP Sales: Pat Campbell
Contact: Steve Bruno
sbruno@chgusa.com
Estimated Sales: Less Than $500,000
Number Employees: 1-4
Square Footage: 96000
Brands:
Encore
Standard-Keil

20801 Composite Can & Tube Institute
50 S Pickett St # 110
Alexandria, VA 22304-7206
703-823-7234
Fax: 703-823-7237
Representing the interests of manufacturers of composite paperboard cans, containers, canisters, tubes, cores, cones, fibre drums, spools, ribbon blocks, bobbins and related or similar composite products.
VP: Kristine Garland
ccti@cctiwdc.org
Estimated Sales: $2.5-5,000,000
Number Employees: 1-4

20802 Composition Materials Co Inc
249 Pepes Farm Rd
Milford, CT 06460-3671
203-874-6500
Fax: 203-874-6505 800-262-7763
info@compomat.com www.compomat.com
Plastic Blasting Media, a distributor of a multitude of filers and extenders, supplier of Walnut Shell grits and flours, and importer of birch wood flour from Sweden.
President: Alan Nudelman
nudelman@compomat.com
Chairman: Theodore Diamond
Sales Representative: Steven D. Essex
Product Operations Manager: David M. Elster
Estimated Sales: $2.5-5 Million
Number Employees: 10-19
Square Footage: 30000
Brands:
Clear-Cut
Cob Dry
Plasti-Grit
Resistat

20803 Compris Technologies
2651 Satellite Blvd
Duluth, GA 30096-5810
770-418-4616
Fax: 770-795-3333 800-615-3301
www.compristech.com
Manufacturer and exporter of computer software including point of sale, labor, inventory, scheduling, executive information and cash management
President: Alaa Pasha
Vice President, Development: Eric Kobres
Area VP Sales: Ron Small
Contact: Mills Bronson
brown.james@ncr.com
Estimated Sales: $5-10 Million
Number Employees: 100-249

20804 Compusense Inc.
P.O. Box 1116
Guelph, ON N1H 6n3
Canada
519-836-9993
Fax: 519-836-9898 800-367-6666
info@compusense.com www.compusense.com
A leader in sensory and consumer research, Compusense's software and services guide leading food and beverage companis in making informed business decisions.

20805 Computer Aid Inc
1390 Ridgeview Dr # 300
Allentown, PA 18104-9065
610-530-5000
Fax: 610-530-5298 800-327-4243
blake@computeraid-llc.com www.compaid.com
In-house payroll, automated time and attendance software
President: Joe Angronaco
CEO: Anthony J Salvaggio
tony_salvaggio@compaid.com
Program System Analyst: Kyle Bonney
Estimated Sales: $3-5 Million
Number Employees: 1000-4999
Square Footage: 3000
Brands:
Pay Master
Pay Master Plus

20806 Computer Aided Marketing
PO Box 4990
Chapel Hill, NC 27515-4990
919-401-0996
Fax: 919-489-4980
Restaurant back office software for frequent diners
VP Sales/Marketing: Bill Ryan
Number Employees: 6
Brands:
Cam Frequent Diners

20807 Computer Assocs. Intl.
2950 Express Dr S Ste 106
Central Islip, NY 11749
631-342-2984
Fax: 631-342-5329 800-225-5224
www.ca.com
Prepackaged software publishing
C.E.O: Sanjay Kumar
Quality Control: Douglas Robinson
C.T.O: Yogesh Gupta
G.M. Global Mkting.: Kenneth Fitzpatrick
Executive VP/GM: Stephen Richards
Exec. V.P. Administrative Services: Gary Quinn
Estimated Sales: $1-5 000,000
Number Employees: 1,000-4,999

20808 Computer Communications Specialists
2960 Shallowford Rd # 102
Marietta, GA 30066-3093
770-509-5321
888-231-4227
Designer and manufacturer of integrated information response systems
Manager: Andy Pereira
Marketing Specialist: David Gay
Estimated Sales: $10-20 Million
Number Employees: 1-4
Brands:
Acca
First Line

20809 Computer Controlled Machines
1 Magnuson Ave
Pueblo, CO 81001-4889
719-948-9500
Fax: 719-948-9540 sales@magnusoncorp.com
www.magnusoncorp.com
Manufacturer and exporter of vegetable processing equipment for sweet corn, green beans and peas
Owner: Bob Smith
VP/General Manager: Craig Furlo
Estimated Sales: $5-10 Million
Number Employees: 20-49
Parent Co: Atlas-Pacific Engineering

20810 Computer Group
4212 N Arlington Heights Rd
Arlington Hts, IL 60004-1372
847-818-9200
Fax: 847-818-9300 dsj@computer-group.com
Service computers and internet services
Owner: Dave Besser
Estimated Sales: $5-10 000,000
Number Employees: 10-19
Square Footage: 4500

20811 (HQ)Computerized Machinery Systs
11733 95th Ave N
Maple Grove, MN 55369-5551
763-493-0099
Fax: 763-493-0093 sales@cmsitechnologies.com
www.labelmart.com
Manufacturer and exporter of pressure sensitive labels; wholesaler/distributor and exporter of barcode printers, label scanners and applicators
Owner: Kate Jackson
Sales: Eric Sorensen
kate@labelmart.com
Estimated Sales: Below $5 Million
Number Employees: 20-49
Brands:
Dura-Kote

20812 Computerway Food Systems
635 Southwest Street
High Point, NC 27260
336-841-7289
Fax: 336-841-2594 sales@mycfs.com
www.mycfs.com
Our systems include overhead sizing, grading and weighing lines as well as fully integrated computerized production and inventory systems for food processing plants.
President: William Altenpohl
Contact: Elhanan Bone
ebone@mycfs.com
Estimated Sales: $2.5-5 000,000
Number Employees: 20-49

20813 Computrition
19808 Nordhoff Pl
Chatsworth, CA 91311
818-701-5544
Fax: 818-701-1702 800-222-4488
info@computrition.com www.computrition.com
Offers completely integrated food service and nutrition care management software systems for operations of all size. Software features include diet order, recipe, menu and inventory management, online order entry and nutrientanalysis
President: Luros Luros-Elson RD
CEO: Scott Saklad
R&D: Joseph Bibbo
Manager, Marketing: Marty Yadrick, RD
Sales: Scott Saklad
Contact: Bindu Amin
bamin@computrition.com
Operations: Kim Goldberg
Estimated Sales: $20-50 Million
Number Employees: 50-99
Square Footage: 17000
Type of Packaging: Food Service
Brands:
Hospitality Suite

20814 (HQ)Computype Inc
2285 County Road C W
St Paul, MN 55113-2567
651-633-0633
Fax: 651-633-5580 800-328-0852
www.computype.com
Manufacturer and exporter of bar code labels, printers and applicators

President: R Huntsinger
CEO: Sonia Artola
soniaartola@hotmail.com
VP: J Ammann
CEO: William Roche
Estimated Sales: $20-50 Million
Number Employees: 100-249
Other Locations:
  Computype
  Concord NH

20815 Comstar Printing Solutions

10175 Philipp Pkwy
Streetsboro, OH 44241-4706

330-528-2800
Fax: 330-528-2828 info@printpro.com
www.printpro.com
In-line and thermal transfer imprinters for in-line
packaging and table top labeling systems
Executive Assistant: Sharon Spaeth
Production Manager: Jeff Burke

20816 Comstock Castle Stove Co

119 W Washington St
Quincy, IL 62301-3860

410-829-4199
Fax: 217-223-0007 800-637-9188
sales@castlestove.com www.castlestove.com
Manufacturer, importer and exporter of cooking
equipment including gas broilers, deep fat fryers,
ovens, griddles, ranges, hot plates, etc
Vice President: Tim Spake
tspake@comstockcastlestoveco.com
Vice President: Timothy Spake
Marketing/Sales: Curtis Spake
Purchasing Manager: Bob Speckhart
Estimated Sales: $5-10 Million
Number Employees: 20-49
Square Footage: 170000
Type of Packaging: Food Service, Private Label
Brands:
  Castle
  Economy

20817 Comtec Industries

10210 Werch Dr
Suite 204
Woodridge, IL 60517

630-759-9000
Fax: 630-759-9009
feedback@comtecindustriesltd.com
www.comtecindustriesltd.com
Baking equipment and supplies including dough
formers for pot pies, hors d'oeuvres and top/bottom
crusts; also, dies and tooling for pies, tarts, cheese-
cakes, etc.; exporter of dough presses
President: James Reilly
Contact: Dolores Reilly
dreilly@comtecindustriesltd.com
Estimated Sales: $1-3 Million
Number Employees: 10
Square Footage: 8000
Brands:
  Comtec

20818 Comtek Systems

309 Breesport Street
San Antonio, TX 78216-2699

210-340-8253
Fax: 210-340-8255
Point of sale systems
President: Thomas Hayes
Plant Manager: M Hayes
Number Employees: 5-9
Square Footage: 5000
Brands:
  Comtek Supercharger

20819 Comus Restaurant Systems

9667 Fleetwood Court
Frederick, MD 21701

301-698-6208
Manufacturer and exporter of point of sale and full
back office software
Marketing: Fred Ihrer
Estimated Sales: $2.5-5 Million
Number Employees: 10
Square Footage: 4000
Parent Co: Comus Software
Brands:
  Comus Restaurant Systems

20820 Con-tech/Conservation Technology

2783 Shermer Rd
Northbrook, IL 60062-7708

847-559-5505
Fax: 847-559-5505 800-728-0312
www.con-techlighting.com
Manufacturer, importer and exporter of lighting
products and industrial fans
President: John Ranshaw
Secretary: Sandy Grossman
VP: John Ranshow
Sales/Marketing Executive: Olga Draqunsky
Contact: Sally Baybutt
sbaybutt@con-techlighting.com
Purchasing Agent: Larry Sabatino
Estimated Sales: $20-50 Million
Number Employees: 20-49
Square Footage: 36000
Brands:
  Con-Tech

20821 (HQ)Conagra Brands Inc

222 W. Merchandise Mart Plaza
Chicago, IL 60654

312-549-5000
877-266-2472
www.conagrafoods.com
Consumer brands.
President & CEO: Sean Connolly
Executive VP/CFO: David Marberger
Executive Vice President: Colleen Batcheler
Executive VP/Co-COO: Tom McGough
Estimated Sales: $11 Billion
Number Employees: 18,000
Number of Brands: 70
Type of Packaging: Consumer, Food Service, Bulk
Brands:
  ACT II®
  Alexia®
  Andy Capp's®
  Angie's BOOMCHICKAPOP®
  Armour Star®
  Aunt Jemima®
  Banquet®
  Bernstein's®
  Bertoli®
  BIGS®
  Birds Eye®
  Birds Eye C&W
  Birds Eye Voila
  Blake's®
  Blue Bonnet®
  Brooks®
  Celeste® Pizza for One
  Chef Boyardee®
  Crunch 'n Munch®
  DAVID® Seeds
  Dennison's®
  Duke's®
  Duncan Hines®
  Duncan Hines Comstock®
  Duncan Hies Wilderness®
  Earth Balance®
  Egg Beaters®
  Erin's®
  EVOL®
  Fiddle Faddle®
  Fleischmann's®
  Frontera®
  Gardein®
  Glutino®
  Gulden's®
  H.K. Anderson®
  Hawaiian Snacks®
  Healthy Choice®
  Hebrew National®
  Hungry-Man®
  Hunt's®
  Husman's®
  Jiffy Pop®
  Kangaroo®
  Kid Cuisine®
  La Choy®
  Lender's®
  Libby's®
  Log Cabin®
  Manwich®
  Marie Callender's®
  Mrs.Butterworth's®
  Mrs.Paul's®
  Nalley®
  Odom's Tennessee Pride®
  Open Pit®

Orville Redenbacher'S®
P.F. Chang's Home Menu®
PAM®
Parkay®
Penrose®
Peter Pan®
Poppycock®
Ranch Style Beans®
Reddi-wip®
RO*TEL®
Rosarita®
Reddi-wip®
RO*TEL®
Rosarita®
Sandwhich Bros. of Wisconsin®
Slim Jim®
Smart Balance®

20822 Conagra Foodservice

222 W. Merchandise Mart Plaza
Suite 1300
Chicago, IL 60654

312-549-5000
877-266-2472
www.conagrabrands.com
Supplies restaurants, retailers, commercial custom-
ers and other foodservice suppliers.
President/CEO: Sean Connolly
Executive VP/CFO: David Marberger
Executive VP/General Counsel: Colleen Batcheler
Executive VP/Co-COO: Tom McGough
Estimated Sales: K
Number Employees: 10,000+
Number of Brands: 70
Square Footage: 11042
Parent Co: Conagra Brands
Type of Packaging: Consumer, Food Service, Bulk
Other Locations:
  ConAgra Headquarters
  Kennewick WA
  ConAgra Headquarters
  Naperville IL
  Sales Office
  Anaheim CA
  Sales Office
  Mesa AR
  Sales Office
  San Antonio TX
  Sales Office
  Plano TX
  Sales Office
  Tampa FL
  Sales Office
  Baltimore MD
  Sales Office
  Mason OH
  Sales Office
  Troy OH
Brands:
  ACT II®
  Alexia®
  Andy Capp's®
  Angie's BOOMCHICKAPOP®
  Armour Star®
  Aunt Jemima®
  Banquet®
  Bernstein's®
  Bertoli®
  BIGS®
  Birds Eye®
  Birds Eye C&W
  Birds Eye Voila
  Blake's®
  Blue Bonnet®
  Brooks®
  Celeste® Pizza for One
  Chef Boyardee®
  Crunch 'n Munch®
  DAVID® Seeds
  Dennison's®
  Duke's®
  Duncan Hines®
  Duncan Hines Comstock®
  Duncan Hies Wilderness®
  Earth Balance®
  Egg Beaters®
  Erin's®
  EVOL®
  Fiddle Faddle®
  Fleischmann's®
  Frontera®
  Gardein®
  Glutino®
  Gulden's®
  H.K. Anderson®

Hawaiian Snacks®
Healthy Choice®
Hebrew National®
Hungry-Man®
Hunt's®
Husman's®
Jiffy Pop®
Kangaroo®
Kid Cuisine®
La Choy®
Lender's®
Libby's®
Log Cabin®
Manwich®
Marie Callender's®
Mrs.Butterworth's®
Mrs.Paul's®
Nalley®
Odom's Tennessee Pride®
Open Pit®
Orville Redenbacher'S®
P.F. Chang's Home Menu®
PAM®
Parkay®
Penrose®
Peter Pan®
Poppycock®
Ranch Style Beans®
Reddi-wip®
RO*TEL®
Rosarita®
Reddi-wip®
RO*TEL®
Rosarita®
Sandwhich Bros. of Wisconsin®
Slim Jim®
Smart Balance®

20823 Conam Inspection
192 Internationale Blvd
Glendale Heights, IL 60139-2094
630-681-0008
Fax: 630-681-0009
www.mistrasgroup.com/services/
Consultant providing nondestructive testing laboratory services, lubricant and fuel analysis and chemical and environmental testing
President: Laurie Todd
Contact: Stephen Bertolet
stephen.bertolet@conaminsp.com
Estimated Sales: $10-20 Million
Number Employees: 50-99

20824 Conatech Consulting Group, Inc
501 N Lindbergh Blvd Ste 105
Saint Louis, MO 63141
314-995-9767
Fax: 314-995-9766 rjbockserman@conatech.com
www.conatech.com
Consulting engineering firm, processing-packaging-distribution of food products. Product and package development, line integration, federal regulations, expert testimony trial, research and discovery; product liability, patentinfringement research and discovery, depositions, trial testimony
President: Robert Bockserman
Estimated Sales: $500,000-$1 Million
Number Employees: 42
Number of Products: 42

20825 Conax Buffalo Technologies
2300 Walden Ave
Buffalo, NY 14225-4779
716-684-4500
Fax: 716-684-7433 800-223-2389
conax@conaxtechnologies.com
www.conaxbuffalo.com
Manufacturer and exporter of measurement systems including temperature sensors, sealing devices and fiber optic systems
President: Robert Fox
Marketing Director: Richard Paluch
Director of Sales and Marketing: Michael Valachos
Purchasing: Joe Kelly
Estimated Sales: $10-20 Million
Number Employees: 50-99
Square Footage: 186000

20826 Conbraco Industries Inc
701 Matthews Mint Hill Rd
Matthews, NC 28105-1706
704-841-6000
Fax: 704-841-6020 www.apollovalves.com

Water gauge valves
President: Glenn Mosack
CFO: Eric Miller
Estimated Sales: Below $5 Million
Number Employees: 50-99

20827 Concept Foods Inc
141 Covington Dr
Bloomingdale, IL 60108-3107
630-539-3107
Fax: 630-539-3109 800-762-1734
www.cafortune.com
President: Dorothy Rzeszutko
Estimated Sales: $20-50 Million
Number Employees: 1-4

20828 Concept Hospitality Group
325 Cutwater
Foster City, CA 94404
650-357-1224
Fax: 760-323-0170 tomkelley@juno.com
Consultant specializing in image enhancement, product marketing and promotion for the hospitality and service markets
Managing Partner: Tom Kelley
Number Employees: 5

20829 Concepts & Design International, Ltd
203 Foxwood Road
West Nyack, NY 10994-2507
845-358-1558
Fax: 845-358-1558
Design and engineering consultant for food facilities including restaurants, schools and hotels.
President: Philip Amato
CFO: Adrienne Amato
Estimated Sales: $300,000-$500,000
Number Employees: 1
Square Footage: 156
Type of Packaging: Food Service

20830 Concord Chemical Co Inc
1700 Federal St
Camden, NJ 08105-1716
856-966-1526
Fax: 856-963-0246 800-282-2436
www.concordchemical.com
Producer of eco-friendly cleaners, soaps, lubricants, release agents, dust control products and more.
President/CEO: Miguel Castillo
VP Product Development: Jack Cram
VP Sales: Carol Griffiths
VP Purchasing: Lauren DeSilvio
Number Employees: 1-4
Square Footage: 120000
Parent Co: Seacord Corporation
Brands:
22 K Gold Finish
3-D Degreaser
Creamedic
Harley Activated Pine
Lemonee-8

20831 Conductive Containers Inc
4500 Quebec Ave N
Minneapolis, MN 55428-4915
763-537-2090
Fax: 763-537-1738 800-327-2329
info@corstat.com www.corstat.com
Manufacturer and exporter of containers including conductive fiberboard, corrugated, chipboard and plastic
President: Brad Ahlm
VP: Paul Granning
VP Operations/R&D: Robert Marlovits
Estimated Sales: $1-2.5 Million
Number Employees: 50-99
Square Footage: 100000
Brands:
Corstat

20832 ConeTech
1450 Airport Blvd Ste 180
Santa Rosa, CA 95403
707-577-7500
Fax: 707-577-7511 info@conetech.com
www.conetech.com
President: Anthony Dann
CFO: Robert E Williams
Estimated Sales: $1-2.5 000,000
Number Employees: 5-9

20833 Conesco Conveyor Corporation
953 Paulison Avenue
Clifton, NJ 07011-3641
973-365-1440
Fax: 973-365-1923 conesco@aol.com
Belt and chain conveyors
President: John Garratt
VP: Jim Garratt
Estimated Sales: Below $5 Million
Number Employees: 4
Square Footage: 40000

20834 Confection Art Inc
3636 North Williams Avenue
Portland, OR 97227
503-505-0481
info@chocolatecraftkits.com
www.chocolatecraftkits.com
Molded chocolates
President: Nancy Baggett
Master Pastry Chef: Pierre Herme
Number Employees: 8

20835 Conflex Incorporated
6637 N Sidney Pl
Germantown, WI 53022
262-512-2665
Fax: 262-512-1665 800-225-4296
jmorrissey@conflex.com www.conflex.com
President: Kevin Laird

20836 Conflex, Inc.
W130 N10751 Washington Drive
Germantown, WI 53022
262-512-2665
Fax: 262-512-1665 800-225-4296
info@conflex.com www.conflex.com
Manufacturer and exporter of shrink wrapping equipment
President: Bill Morrissey
CEO: Joe Morrissey
CFO: Jim Benton
Research & Development: Mark Kubisiak
Tech Services: Kevin Thomas
Product Manager: Joe Morrissey
Purchasing Manager: Bill Morrissey, Jr.
Number Employees: 20-49
Square Footage: 320000
Type of Packaging: Consumer, Food Service, Bulk

20837 Conflow Technologies, Inc.
18 Regan Road
Units 28 & 29
Brampton, ON L7A 1C2
Canada
905-840-6800
Fax: 905-840-6799 800-275-9887
sales@conflow.ca www.conflow.ca
Manufacturer and importer of food processing machinery including certified milk reception and loadout systems, in-plant sanitary flow meters and calibration services and batch and blend control systems; also, transport custodydispensing systems
President: Gary Collins
CFO: Anna Lynn Wiebe
Vice President: Gerry Camirand
Research & Development: Anna Lynn
Quality Control: Gerry Camirand
Number Employees: 7
Square Footage: 5400
Brands:
Contrec
Flowdata, Inc.
Hoffer Flow Controls Inc.
Proces-Data

20838 Congent Technologies
11140 Luschek Drive
Cincinnati, OH 45241-2434
513-469-6800
Fax: 513-469-6811
Bioluminescence lighting system
President: Jim Leroy
Estimated Sales: $2.5-5 000,000
Number Employees: 5-9
Square Footage: 2000

20839 Conifer Paper Products
4911 Central Avenue
Richmond, CA 94804-5842
510-527-8222
Fax: 510-526-3376
Tea and coffee industry bags and packaging film supplies

Number Employees: 104

20840 Conimar Corp
1724 NE 22nd Ave
Ocala, FL 34470-4702

352-732-3262
Fax: 352-732-6888 800-874-9735
corp@conimar.com www.conimar.com
Beverage coaster, flexible cutting mats and bamboo cutting boards
Owner: Terry Crawford
CFO: Eric Robinson
VP: Ron Dampier
Marketing: Terry Putty
Estimated Sales: $10-15 Million
Number Employees: 50-99
Square Footage: 140000
Type of Packaging: Private Label

20841 (HQ)Conn Container Corp
455 Sackett Point Rd
North Haven, CT 06473-3199

203-248-0241
Fax: 203-248-0241 www.unicorr.com
Corrugated boxes, containers, displays, foam and plastic packaging
President: Harry Perkins
hperkins@unicorr.com
President: Lawrence Perkins
Sales Manager: B Etra
Estimated Sales: $20-50 Million
Number Employees: 250-499

20842 Connecticut Culinary Institute
230 Farmington Avenue
Suite 5
Farmington, CT 06032-1973

860-677-7869
Fax: 860-676-0679 ct.culinary.inst@snet.net
Consulting firm providing assistance for food service operators
President: David Tine
Contact: Tad Handley
admissions@ctculinary.com
Number Employees: 20-49
Square Footage: 20000
Parent Co: Hartine Corporation

20843 Connecticut Laminating Co Inc
162 James St
New Haven, CT 06513-3845

203-787-2184
Fax: 203-787-4073 800-753-9119
info@ctlaminating.com www.ctlaminating.com
Manufacturer and exporter of plastic laminated advertising signs, place mats, tags, menus and cards
President: Henry Snow
henry@ctlaminating.com
VP: Steve Snow
Estimated Sales: $10 Million+
Number Employees: 100-249
Square Footage: 110000

20844 Connerton Co
1131 E Wakeham Ave
Santa Ana, CA 92705-4145

714-547-9218
Fax: 714-547-1969 sales@connertoncompany.com
www.connertoncompany.com
Commercial gas cooking equipment including broilers, hot plates, griddles, stock pot stoves and over/under broilers
Vice President: Craig Reynolds
sales@connertoncompany.com
VP: Craig Reynolds
Number Employees: 10-19
Brands:
 Connerton

20845 Conpac
131 Industrial Dr
Warminster, PA 18974

215-322-2755
Contract packaging
President: Sam Gerbino
Estimated Sales: Less than $500,000
Number Employees: 1-4

20846 Conquest International LLC
1108 SW 8th St
Plainville, KS 67663-3106

785-434-2483
Fax: 785-434-2736 conquest@ruraltel.net
www.envirolyteconquestusa.com

Water treatment and purification systems. Turn-key bottled water plants and water stores.
President: Ned Colburn
CFO: Jeffrey Van Dyke
Estimated Sales: A
Number Employees: 1-4
Square Footage: 40000
Brands:
 Natural Pure

20847 Consolidated Baling Machine Company
P.O.Box 6922
Jacksonville, FL 32236-6922

904-358-3812
Fax: 904-358-7013 800-231-9286
sales@intl-baler.com www.intl-baler.com
Manufacturer and exporter of balers, compactors and drum crushers/packers
President: William Nielsen
CEO: Roger Griffin
Sales Manager: Jerry Wise
Estimated Sales: F
Number Employees: 50-99
Square Footage: 8000
Parent Co: Waste Technology Corporation
Brands:
 Cmbc
 Consolidated Baling Machine Co.
 Ibc
 Ips
 International Baler Corp.
 International Press & Shear
 Wpc

20848 Consolidated Can Co
15725 Illinois Ave
Paramount, CA 90723-4112

562-634-5245
Fax: 562-634-8689 888-793-2199
www.consolidatedcan.com
Manufacturer and exporter of tin cans; also, tops, bottoms, plugs and caps for containers
Owner: Doug Lampson
consilidatedcan@aol.com
CFO: Doug Lampson
Estimated Sales: $1-2.5 Million
Number Employees: 1-4
Square Footage: 6000
Type of Packaging: Bulk

20849 Consolidated Commercial Controls
200 International Way
Winsted, CT 6098

860-738-7112
Fax: 860-738-7140 800-227-1511
CustServ@AllPointsFPS.com
www.allpointsfps.com
Manufacturer and exporter of commercial cooking and refrigeration equipment parts; importer of cast iron parts and supplies.
CEO: John Hanby
CFO: Dan Cox
Vice President: Azie Kahn
Research & Development: Azie Kahn
Marketing Director: John McDermott
Sales Director: Phil Wisehart
Contact: Rick Hernandez
rhernandez@allpointsfps.com
Purchasing Manager: Linda Feichtl
Estimated Sales: $15-20 Million
Number Employees: 20-49
Square Footage: 90000
Type of Packaging: Food Service

20850 Consolidated Container Co
221 Grove St
New Castle, PA 16101-4022

724-658-0549
Fax: 724-658-7427 www.cccllc.com
Plastic containers for liquids including orange juice and syrup
Sales Manager: John Wolfgang
General Manager: Joe Smarrelli
Plant Manager: Nick Shuler
Purchasing Manager: Bill Bullano
Estimated Sales: $20-50 Million
Number Employees: 50-99
Parent Co: Rostan Corporation

20851 (HQ)Consolidated Container Co LLC
3101 Towercreek Pkwy SE # 300
Suite 300
Atlanta, GA 30339-3256

678-742-4600
Fax: 678-742-4750 888-831-2184
www.cccllc.com
Manufacturer and exporter of blow molded plastic bottles
President/Director/CEO: Jeffrey Greene
jeffrey.greene@cccllc.com
Vice President, Human Resources: Bradley Newman
Estimated Sales: $237 Million
Number Employees: 1000-4999
Square Footage: 16000
Parent Co: Bain Capital, LLC

20852 Consolidated Container Co
8 Harbor View Rd
South Burlington, VT 05403-7850

802-658-6588
Fax: 802-658-6596
Plastic bottles
President: Eugene Torvend
etorvend@shelburneplastics.com
Vice President of Sales: John Wolfgang
Estimated Sales: $10-20 Million
Number Employees: 50-99

20853 Consolidated Container Co LLC
3101 Towercreek Pkwy SE # 300
Suite 300
Atlanta, GA 30339-3256

678-742-4600
Fax: 678-742-4750 888-831-2184
www.cccllc.com
Blow molded plastic packaging for the dairy, water, beverage and food industries.
President/CEO/Director: Jeffrey Greene
jeffrey.greene@cccllc.com
CFO: Richard Sehring
EVP Sales/Market Development: Kenneth Branham
VP Human Resources: Bradley Newman
COO: Robert Walton
Number Employees: 1000-4999
Square Footage: 16000
Type of Packaging: Consumer, Food Service

20854 Consolidated Display CoInc
1210 US Highway 34
Oswego, IL 60543-8939

630-851-8666
Fax: 630-851-8756 888-851-7669
buzzp@aol.com www.letitsnow.com
Food props for displays
President: Sebastian Puccio
VP: Anthony Puccio
Estimated Sales: Below $5 Million
Number Employees: 10-19
Square Footage: 60000

20855 Consolidated Label Company
925 Florida Central Pkwy
Longwood, FL 32750

407-339-2626
Fax: 407-331-1711 800-475-2235
liz@consolidatedlabel.com
www.consolidatedlabel.com
Manufacturer and exporter of pressure sensitive labels and tags
President: Joel Carmany
National Sales Manager: Beau Bowman
Plant Manager: Dick St Hilaire
Estimated Sales: $20-50 Million
Number Employees: 50-99
Square Footage: 35000
Type of Packaging: Private Label, Bulk

20856 Consolidated Plastics Co Inc
4700 Prosper Rd
Stow, OH 44224-1068

330-689-3000
Fax: 800-858-5001 800-858-5001
www.consolidatedplastics.net
Blow molded plastic bottles
Number Employees: 50-99

20857 Consolidated Thread Mills, Inc.
P.O. Box 1107
Fall River, MA 02722

508-672-0032
Fax: 508-674-3773
www.consolidatedthreadmills.com

Manufacturer and exporter of bounded and waxed industrial twine including nylon, polyester, rayon and cotton
Owner: Colleen Pacheco
Estimated Sales: $1-5 Million
Number Employees: 5-9

20858 Consorcio, MG SA DE CV
4812 N 10th Street
Apt 503
McAllen, TX 78504-2880

956-664-9793
Fax: 956-664-9793

20859 Constantia Colmar
92 County Line Rd
Colmar, PA 18915-9606

215-997-6222
Fax: 215-997-3976
Manufacturer and exporter of foil, juice and yogurt lids, butter wrappers, etc
CEO: Jerry Decker
jerryd@hnpack.com
CEO: Jerry Decker
Estimated Sales: $50-100 Million
Number Employees: 50-99
Parent Co: H&N Packaging
Type of Packaging: Bulk

20860 Constantia Colmar
92 County Line Rd
Colmar, PA 18915-9606

215-997-6222
Fax: 215-997-3976
CEO: Jerry Decker
jerryd@hnpack.com
CEO: Jerry Decker
Estimated Sales: $20-50 Million
Number Employees: 50-99

20861 Constar International
41605 Ann Arbor Road
Plymouth, MI 48170

734-455-3600
info@plastipak.com
Plastic containers and bottles for soft drinks, mustard, edible oils, wine and liquors
President: Mike Hoffman
CFO: Bill Rymer
R&D: Don Deual
Production: Craig Renton
Estimated Sales: $2.5-5 Million
Number Employees: 20
Parent Co: Crown Cork & Seal

20862 Consulting Nutritional Services
26500 Agoura Road
Suite 210
Calabasas, CA 91302-3550

818-880-6774
Fax: 818-880-6797 cns@foodsafe.com
www.foodsafe.com

20863 Consumer Cap Corporation
PO Box 7259
New Castle, PA 16107-7259

724-657-9440
Fax: 724-654-8573 800-545-5504
Plastic closures
Number Employees: 100

20864 Consumers Packing Company
Plum & Liberty Street
Lancaster, PA 17603

717-397-6141
Fax: 717-397-0322
Packaging supplies
Estimated Sales: $1-3 Million
Number Employees: 5-9

20865 Contact Industries
9200 SE Sunnybrook Blvd # 200
Suite 200
Clackamas, OR 97015-5767

503-228-7361
Fax: 503-221-1340 800-345-2232
sales@contactind.com www.contactind.com
Contract packager of aerosols, adhesives, cements, insecticides, room deodorants and oven cleaners
President: Frank Pearson
Quality Control: Leo Hu
Estimated Sales: $10-20 Million
Number Employees: 1-4
Parent Co: Safeguard Chemical Corporation
Type of Packaging: Food Service, Private Label

20866 Containair Packaging Corporation
37 E 6th St
Paterson, NJ 7524

973-523-1800
Fax: 973-523-1818 888-276-6500
Manufacturer and exporter of semi-bulk containers for food ingredients; also, slotted cartons and graphic displays available
CEO/President: Lawrence Taylor
VP: Paul Davis
Plant Manager: Ken Kutner
Estimated Sales: $2.5-5 Million
Number Employees: 20-49
Square Footage: 94000
Brands:
  K Box
  Kl Box

20867 Container Handling Systs Corp
621 E Plainfield Rd
Countryside, IL 60525-6913

708-482-9900
Fax: 708-482-8960 sales@chsc1.com
www.containerhandlingsystems.com
Conveyors and conveyor systems
President: Matt Nalbach
neco@nalbach.com
R&D: David Haskell
Estimated Sales: $5-10 000,000
Number Employees: 20-49

20868 Container Machinery Corporation
1060 Broadway
Albany, NY 12204

518-694-3310
Fax: 608-719-8380 www.cmc-kuhnke.com
High speed notching presses; exporter of seam quality inspection and measuring systems; importer of can making machinery
Managing Director: Thomas Duve
VP: Alex Grossjohann
Technical Service Manager: Markus Kellner
Marketing Manager: Aura Marcks
Sales Manager Southeast Asia: Ning Qian
Customer Service Manager: Jose Rodriguez
Vice President, Managing Director: Alex Grossjohann
Estimated Sales: $1-3 Million
Number Employees: 5-9
Square Footage: 60000
Brands:
  Bertil-Ohlsson
  Imeta
  Krupp (Sig Cantech)
  Lanico
  Mbt (Lubeca)
  Mh Press Systems
  Sanyu
  Wegro Metal Crown

20869 Container ManufacturingInc
50 Baekeland Ave
Middlesex, NJ 08846-2601

732-563-0100
Fax: 732-563-0704 www.containermfg.com
Plastic containers
President: David Jennings
Estimated Sales: $5-10 000,000
Number Employees: 20-49

20870 Container Services Company
PO Box 1115
Warrenton, OR 97146-1115

503-861-3338
Fax: 503-861-0287 cscastoria@aol.com
Estimated Sales: $1-5 Million

20871 Container Specialties
1950 N Mannheim Rd
Melrose Park, IL 60160

708-615-1400
Fax: 708-615-0381 800-548-7513
www.midwestcan.com
Plastic bottles and sanitary cans
Owner: John Trippi Sr
CFO: Janet Johnson
Quality Control: John Trippi Jr
Sales/Marketing: Alan Trippi
Estimated Sales: $10-20 Million
Number Employees: 20-49
Square Footage: 160000
Parent Co: Midwest Can Company

20872 Container Supply Co
12571 Western Ave
Garden Grove, CA 92841-4012

562-594-0937
Fax: 714-892-3824
tbertoglio@containersupplycompany.com
www.containersupplycompany.com
Manufacturer and exporter of tin cans and plastic pails and containers
Owner: Robert Hurtt
cscmaster@aol.com
Quality Control: C Bonnet
Regional Sales Manager: T Carlson
Director Sales: Tony Bertoglio
Export Sales: F Ceja
Estimated Sales: $20-50 Million
Number Employees: 100-249
Square Footage: 160000

20873 Container Testing Lab
607 Fayette Ave
Mamaroneck, NY 10543

914-381-2600
Fax: 914-381-0143 800-221-5170
Laboratory and consulting service specializing in container materials and systems including package engineering, related material handling and package testing certification
President: Vasilis Morfoupolous
Contact: Anton Cotaj
sales@packagelab.com
Lab Manager: S Brooks
Technical Director: C Coleman, Ph.D.
Estimated Sales: Less than $500,000
Number Employees: 5 to 9
Square Footage: 43500

20874 Container-Quinn TestingLab
170 Shepard Ave # A
Wheeling, IL 60090-6061

847-537-9470
Fax: 847-537-9098 spowell@container-quinn.com
Consultant offering package testing, design development, engineering and systems services
President: Todd R Nelson
Manager: Steven Powell
spowell@containerquinn.com
Lab Director: Stephen Powell
Estimated Sales: less than $500,000
Number Employees: 1-4

20875 (HQ)Containment Technology
1105 Highway 30
St Gabriel, LA 70776-5011

225-642-3963
Fax: 225-642-9629 800-388-2467
contectun.bin@aol.com
FDA approved steel containers for liquid and dry hazardous and nonhazardous materials
President: Robert Allen
Vice President: Sylvia Allen
Marketing: Roderick Franklin
VP Sales: Gerald Scruggs
Estimated Sales: $1-2.5 Million
Number Employees: 10-19
Square Footage: 40000
Type of Packaging: Bulk
Other Locations:
  Material Containment
  City of Commerce CA
Brands:
  Blend Tanks
  Fda Steel Container
  Greane Bins

20876 Contec, Inc.
2680 New Cut Rd
Spartenburg, SC 29303

864-503-8333
Fax: 864-503-8444 800-289-5762
www.contecinc.com
Designer and manufacturer of science based cleaning products for food manufacturing facilities.
Estimated Sales: $2.5-5 Million
Number Employees: 5-9
Other Locations:
  Contec, Inc.-Automotive Division
  Toledo OH
  Contec Cleanroom Technology Co, Ltd
  Suzhou, China
  Contec
  France

20877 Contech Enterprises Inc
314 Straight Ave SW
Grand Rapids, MI 49504-6439

616-818-1520
Fax: 616-459-4140 800-767-8658

Manufacturer and exporter of pesticide-free insect trapping adhesives
President and CEO: Mark Grambart
VP of Sales and Marketing: Allen Spigelman
VP of Sales and Marketing: Allen Spigelman
Contact: John Borden
john.borden@contech-inc.com
VP of Operations: Bill Jones
Estimated Sales: $2.5-5 Million
Number Employees: 5-9
Square Footage: 80000
Type of Packaging: Private Label
Brands:
Tangle-Trap
Tanglefoot

20878 Contemporary Product Inc
273 Hein Dr
Garner, NC 27529-7221

919-779-4228
Fax: 919-779-9734

Manufacturer and importer of award plaques and shields, trophies and cup bases
VP: David Hamilton
Manager: Joan Squillini
Manager: Joan Squillini
Estimated Sales: $1-5 Million
Number Employees: 1-4

20879 (HQ)Contico Container
15510 Blackburn Ave
Norwalk, CA 90650

562-921-9967
Fax: 562-926-4979 www.contico.com

Manufacturer and exporter of polyethylene containers
Engineering-R&D: Michael Angelo
Contact: Nick Man
nickm@conticospraychem.com
Estimated Sales: $20-50 Million
Number Employees: 100-249
Parent Co: Contico International

20880 Continental Carbonic Products
2985 East Harrison Avenue
Decatur, IL 62526

217-428-2068
Fax: 217-424-2325 800-379-4232
www.continentalcarbonic.com

Specializes in the manufacture and distribution of dry ice and liquid carbon dioxide, along with sales and rental of dry ice blasting equipment.
President: John Funk
Vice President/Chief Financial Officer: Randy Spitz
General Manager, Manufacturing: Phil Wood
Vice President, Business Development: David Butts
Vice President, Distribution: Jason Taulbee
VP, Manufacturing & Distribution: Mark Hatton

20881 Continental Cart by Kullman Industries
1 Kullman Corporate Campus Dr
Lebanon, NJ 08833-2163

908-236-0220
Fax: 908-236-0848 888-882-2278

Manufacturer and exporter of carts and kiosks; also, modular construction for diners, schools and correctional facilities
President: Amy Marks
CEO: Avi Telyas
Vice President of Operations: Michael Hathaway
Vice President of Production: Bobby Pohlman
Estimated Sales: $50-60 Million
Number Employees: 250-499

20882 Continental Commercial Products
305 Rock Industrial Park Dr.
Bridgeton, MO 63044

314-656-4301
Fax: 800-327-5492 800-325-1051
janics@contico.com
www.continentalcommercialproducts.com

Wastebaskets, recycle collection and trash receptacles, utility carts, liners, mopping equipment, squeegees, trigger sprayers, caution signs, plastic shelves, food service products and mobile equipment

President: Mike Boland
VP: Jim Dunn
Contact: Gary Anton
ganton@continentalcommercialproducts.com
Number Employees: 250-499
Square Footage: 12000000
Parent Co: Katy Industries
Brands:
Guardsboy
Guardsmen
Huskee
King Kan
Kleen Aire
Kleen Mist
Roun' Top
Snapoff
Steeline
Structolene
Swing Top
Tip Top
Wall Hugger

20883 Continental Disc Corp
3160 W Heartland Dr
Liberty, MO 64068-3385

816-792-1500
Fax: 816-792-2277 pressure@contdisc.com
www.contdisc.com

Food processing machinery parts including rupture discs for overpressure protection
President: Kenneth R Shaw
CEO: David Brown
dbrown@contdisc.com
Estimated Sales: $20-50 Million
Number Employees: 100-249

20884 Continental Envelope
1700 Averill Rd
Geneva, IL 60134-1668

630-578-3300
Fax: 630-262-1450 800-621-8155
sales@continentalenvelope.com
www.continentalenvelope.com

Custom made printed flexo and lithographed envelopes
President: Fred Margulies
fred@convelope.com
Estimated Sales: $20-50 Million
Number Employees: 100-249
Square Footage: 120000

20885 Continental Equipment Corporation
P.O.Box 18662
6103 N. 76th Street
Milwaukee, WI 53218

414-463-0500
Fax: 414-463-3199 www.ceceq.com

Manufacturer and exporter of custom washing machinery
President: Will Leistikow
Manager: Mark Kelso
VP Sales: Doug Piszczek
Engineer: Brennen Cullen
Estimated Sales: $3-5 Million
Number Employees: 20-49
Square Footage: 60000
Brands:
Aqucous Washing Systems

20886 Continental Extrusion Corporation
11 Cliffside Drive
Cedar Grove, NJ 07009-1234

973-239-4030
Fax: 973-239-9289 800-822-4748

Bags including specialty squared bottom HDPE and SOS style
VP Sales/Marketing: Ronald Basso
Estimated Sales: $10-20 Million
Number Employees: 100
Square Footage: 266
Brands:
Superbag
Superbag Jr.

20887 Continental Girbau Inc
2500 State Road 44
Oshkosh, WI 54904-8914

920-231-8222
Fax: 920-231-4666 800-256-1073
www.cgilaundry.com

Manufacturer and exporter of commercial and industrial laundry equipment

President: Mike Floyd
mike.floyd@continentalgirbau.org
VP Sales & Customer Service: Joel T Jorgensen
Director Human Resources: Kelly Zabel
Number Employees: 20-49
Parent Co: Girbau S.A.
Brands:
Continental

20888 Continental Identification
140 E Averill
Sparta, MI 49345

616-887-7341
Fax: 616-887-0154 800-247-2499
cipinfo@continentalid.com
www.continentalid.com

Manufacturer and exporter of counter mats, screen printed decals and cooler doors danglers
President: James Clay
Contact: John Begerow
jbegerow@continentalid.com
Operations Manager: Dave Clay
Estimated Sales: $10-20 Million
Number Employees: 100-249
Parent Co: Celia Corporation

20889 Continental Industrial Supply
6935 Grande Vista Way S
South Pasadena, FL 33707-4702

727-341-1100
Fax: 727-343-3606

Flooring, trenchdrains, gratings and water conditioners and steamers (dry steamers)
Owner: Mike Marshall
Brands:
Kitchen Best
Never Scale
Polycast

20890 Continental Packaging Corporation
1327-29 Gateway Drive
Elgin, IL 60124

847-289-6400
Fax: 847-289-9048 info@continentalpkg.com
www.continentalpkg.com

Custom flexible packaging materials including bags and printed and plain overwrap
President: Rory Lent
CEO: Christian Krupsha
Contact: Joseph Barsano
joseph@continentalpkg.com
Estimated Sales: $5 Million
Number Employees: 20-50
Square Footage: 60000

20891 Continental Plastic Container
2515 McKinney Avenue
Suite 850
Dallas, TX 75201-7617

972-303-1825
Fax: 972-303-1829

Blow molded plastic bottles
Director Marketing: John Murphy
VP Sales/Marketing: John Roesch

20892 Continental Products
2000 W Boulevard St
Mexico, MO 65265-1209

573-581-5568
Fax: 573-581-8711 800-325-0216
mail@adbags.com www.continentalproducts.com

Plastic and cloth shopping bags
Owner: Pat Mcguire
National Sales Manager: Thad Fisher
Estimated Sales: $1-2.5 Million
Number Employees: 100-249

20893 Continental Refrigeration
539 Dunksferry Rd
Bensalem, PA 19020

215-244-1400
Fax: 215-244-9579 800-523-7138
www.continentalrefrigerator.com

Commercial foodservice refrigeration equipment.
Year Founded: 1989
Estimated Sales: $50-100 Million
Number Employees: 100-249

20894 (HQ)Continental Refrigerator
539 Dunksferry Rd
Bensalem, PA 19020-5908
215-244-1400
Fax: 215-244-9579 800-523-7138
www.nrproducts.com
Refrigeration and air conditioning equipment
Cmo: Tara Migatz
tmigatz@nrac.com
CEO: Brian Kelly
Marketing Director: Tara Montvydas
Sales Manager: Mike Coyle
Operations Manager: Ed Carruthers
Purchasing Manager: Amy Ahern
Estimated Sales: $50-100 Million
Number Employees: 100-249
Square Footage: 87000
Brands:
   Continental Refrigerator
   Hvac

20895 Continental Refrigerator
539 Dunksferry Rd
Bensalem, PA 19020-5908
215-244-1400
Fax: 215-244-9579 800-523-7138
www.nrproducts.com
President: Brian Kelly
Cmo: Tara Migatz
tmigatz@nrac.com
Estimated Sales: $50-100 Million
Number Employees: 100-249

20896 Continental Terminals
112 Port Jersey Blvd
Jersey, NJ 07305
973-578-2702
Fax: 973-578-2795
infonj@continentalterminals.com
www.continentalterminals.com
Tea and coffee industry reconditioners, samplers and weighers
Owner: Vito Difalco
Estimated Sales: Less than $500,000
Number Employees: 10-19

20897 Continental-Fremont
Airport Industrial Park 1685 S. County
PO Box 489
Tiffin, OH 44883
419-448-4045
Fax: 419-448-4048
Manufacturer and exporter of carbon and stainless steel storage tanks, plating, bins, hoppers, and silos; sanitary and metal fabrication services available
President: C William Harple
CFO: Melissa Hoover
Quality Control: Ron Ranson
Marketing/Sales: Don Harple
Operations Manager: Ron Ransom
Estimated Sales: Below $5 Million
Number Employees: 20-49
Square Footage: 100000

20898 Contour Packaging
637 W Rockland St
Philadelphia, PA 19120
215-457-1600
Fax: 215-457-5040
Manufacturer and exporter of stand-up pouches and blow molded plastic bottles and containers; also, screen printing and hot foil stamping services available
President: Stephen D Mannino
Sales Engineer: Mark Rysak
Estimated Sales: $10-20 Million
Number Employees: 50-99

20899 Contour Products
4001 Kaw Dr
Kansas City, KS 66102
913-321-4114
Fax: 913-321-8063 800-638-3626
Molded foam
President: Richard Nickloy
Sales Manager: E Brandt
Contact: Mark Deal
mdeal@contourliving.com
Estimated Sales: $2.5-5 Million
Number Employees: 1-4

20900 Contract Chemicals
201 Concourse Boulevard
Suite 102
Glen Allen, VA 23059-5640
804-967-9761
Fax: 804-967-9764
Specialty chemicals
Estimated Sales: $1-2.5 Million
Number Employees: 4

20901 Contract Comestibles
2004 Beulah Ave
East Troy, WI 53120-1202
262-642-9400
Fax: 262-642-9404 www.execpc.com
Packagers
Owner: Matt Nitz
mnitz@contractcomestibles.com
Purchasing: Matthew Nitz
Estimated Sales: $1-2,500,000
Number Employees: 5-9

20902 Contrex Inc
8900 Zachary Ln N
Maple Grove, MN 55369-4018
763-424-7800
Fax: 763-424-8734 info@contrexinc.com
www.contrexinc.com
Manufacturer and exporter of electronic controls including universal motor speed, universal motor synchronizing, rotary die/knife synchronizing, cut-to-length/indexing and digital DC motor
President: Gary C Hansen
VP: Glen Gauvin
Estimated Sales: $5-10 Million
Number Employees: 10-19
Brands:
   M-Cut
   M-Drive
   M-Rotary
   M-Shuttle
   M-Track
   M-Traverse
   M-Trim

20903 Control & Metering
6500 Kestrel Road
Mississauga, ON L5T 1Z6
Canada
905-795-9696
Fax: 905-795-9654 800-736-5739
sales@candm.ca
Manufacturer and exporter of dry material handling equipment including bulk bag dischargers, fillers and controls
President: Chris Gadula
COO: Don Mackrill
Marketing Manager: Don Mackrill
Operationa Manager: Carmine Cacciarro
Number Employees: 15

20904 Control Beverage
PO Box 578
Adelanto, CA 92301-0578
330-549-5376
Fax: 330-549-9851
Manufacturer and exporter of drink dispensers including liquor and soft drink; also, portable bars
President: P Beeghly
VP/Division Manager: Glenn Lewis
Sales Director: Kenneth Wogberg
Manager Technical Services: Dan Pershing
Purchasing Manager: Glenn Lewis
Estimated Sales: $1-3 Million
Number Employees: 6
Square Footage: 10000
Parent Co: International Carbonic
Brands:
   Bevcon

20905 Control Chief Holdings Inc
200 Williams St
Bradford, PA 16701-1411
814-362-6811
Fax: 814-368-4133 sales@controlchief.com
www.controlchief.com
Wireless industrial remote control manufacturer
President: Doug Bell
CEO: Greg Caggiano
gcaggiano@controlchief.com
CFO: David Dedionisio
R&D: David Higgs
Quality Control: Christine Foster
Marketing Director: Allison Ambrose
Sales: Brian Landries
Operations: Paul McCord
Production: Jack Zelina
Purchasing Director: Dan Johnston
Estimated Sales: $10-20 Million
Number Employees: 20-49

20906 Control Concepts Inc.
18760 Lake Dr E
Chanhassen, MN 55317-9384
952-474-6200
Fax: 952-474-6070 800-765-2799
www.ccipower.com
Manufacturer and exporter of electric temperature process controls. Not to be confused with Control Concepts, Inc. located in Putnam, CT.
President: Gary Gretenhuis
CEO: Stan Kintigh
CEO: Stanley S Kintigh
Director Sales Support: William Rovick
Contact: Lynn Abraham
lynn@controlconcepts.net
Operations Manager: Don Christomer
Production Manager: Linh Nguyen
Number Employees: 20
Square Footage: 28000

20907 Control Concepts, Inc.
100 Park St
Putnam, CT 06260
860-928-6551
Fax: 860-928-9450 sales@controlconceptsusa.com
controlconceptsusa.com
Productivity equipment, including Airsweep Systems, SpeedSwitch Devices and AcoustiClean Sonic Horns. Not to be confused with Control Concepts Inc. located in Chanhassen, MN.
President: Henry Tiffany III

20908 Control Instrument Service
3607 Ventura Drive E
Lakeland, FL 33811-1229
863-644-9838
Fax: 863-644-8608 800-644-9839
Instrumentation, valves, weighing equipment including temperature, pressure, level, flow and weight
Chairman: John Benedict
Estimated Sales: $1-2.5 Million
Number Employees: 9
Type of Packaging: Bulk

20909 Control Instruments Corp
25 Law Dr # 1
Fairfield, NJ 07004-3295
973-575-9114
Fax: 973-575-0013 info@controlinstruments.com
www.controlinstruments.com
Manufacturer and exporter of hazardous gas detection systems
CEO: Chris Schaeffer
cschaeffer@controlinstruments.com
CEO: Chris Schaeffer
Marketing Manager: Patty Gardner
Sales Director: Debra Woods
Estimated Sales: $5-10 Million
Number Employees: 50-99
Type of Packaging: Private Label

20910 Control Module
89 Phoenix Ave
Enfield, CT 6082
860-745-2433
Fax: 860-741-6064 800-722-6654
info@controlmod.com www.controlmod.com
Manufacturer and exporter of bar code data collection equipment including label printers, laser scanners, data collection terminals and cluster buffers
President: James Bianco
VP: John Fahy
VP Marketing/Sales: James Bianco
Contact: Denise Batalha
dbatalha@controlmod.com
Estimated Sales: $10-20 Million
Number Employees: 50-99
Square Footage: 80000
Brands:
   Bioscan Ii

Linc
Savetime
Securcode Ii

20911 Control Pak Intl
11494 Delmar Dr # 100
Suite #100
Fenton, MI 48430-9018

810-735-2800
Fax: 734-761-2880 info@controlpak.com
www.controlpak.com
Manufacturer and exporter of energy management
control systems for temperature, humidity and
HVAC applications
Owner: Tim Glinke
Office Manager: Julie Bodziak
Engineer: Len Poma
Estimated Sales: Less Than $500,000
Number Employees: 5-9

20912 Control Products Inc
1724 Lake Dr W
Chanhassen, MN 55317-8580

952-448-2217
Fax: 952-448-1606 800-947-9098
www.protectedhome.com
Digital electronic temperature, humidity and pres-
sure controls including timers, alarms, indicators
and controllers; also, custom design available
President: Chris Berghoff
VP Operations: Paul Carlson
IT Executive: John Abbott
jabbott@controlproductsinc.com
Director Foodservice Industry: Jerry Brown
Marketing Manager: Mark Bjornstad
National Sales Manager: Greg Colvin
IT Executive: John Abbott
jabbott@controlproductsinc.com
Estimated Sales: $20-50 Million
Number Employees: 100-249

20913 Control Systems Design
PO Box 647
Forest Hill, MD 21050-0647

410-296-0466
Fax: 410-337-8360
www.controlsystemsdesign.com
Industrial control and data acquisition systems
President: Eldon Hiebert
Part Owner: Jay King
Estimated Sales: $1-2.5 Million
Number Employees: 9
Square Footage: 6000

20914 Control Techniques
7078 Shady Oak Rd
Eden Prairie, MN 55344

952-995-8000
Fax: 952-995-8020 800-893-2321
info.cta@mail.nidec.com acim.nidec.com
Supplier of intelligent drives for commercial and in-
dustrial motor control applications. Products help in-
crease productivity, save energy and reduce
operating costs.
Parent Co: Nidec Motor Corp.
Other Locations:
Grand Island NY
York PA
Fort Meyers FL
Portland OR
Salt Lake City UT
Cleveland OH
Toronto, ON
Calagary AB Canada

20915 Control Technology Corp
25 South St # E
Hopkinton, MA 01748-2231

508-435-9596
Fax: 508-435-2373 800-282-5008
sales@ctc-control.com
www.controltechnologycorp.com
Designs, manufactures and markets products that en-
able electronic automation device to be controlled,
configured, or reprogrammed over the internet
and/or internets.
President: Kenneth Crater
crater@powermotionsales.com
Controller: Lisa St George
Director of Research & Development: Kevin
Halloran
Quality Control: Tim Leavitt
Sales Director: Karl Chambers
Operations Manager: Tim Leavitt

Estimated Sales: $4-5 Million
Number Employees: 20-49
Other Locations:
Control Technology Corporation
Mequon WI

20916 Convay Systems
9800 Bren Road East
Suite 300
Minnetonka, MN 55343
Canada

905-279-9970
Fax: 888-329-1099 800-334-1099
Manufacturer and exporter of washing and drying
systems, pasteurizers, coolers, warmers and dry trash
removal systems for the food, beverage and dairy
industries
President: Roger Potts
Controller: Carol Ruggiero
Engineering Manager: Michael Voss
Number Employees: 18
Square Footage: 28000

20917 Convectronics
111 Neck Rd
Ward Hill Industrial Park
Haverhill, MA 01835-8027

978-374-7714
Fax: 978-374-7794 800-633-0166
info@convectronics.com www.convectronics.com
Manufacturer and exporter of electric air heaters and
thermocouples
President: Philip G Aberizk Jr
VP/Quality Control: Steve Becker
sbecker@connectronics.com
R&D: Bryce Budrow
Sales: Leslie Woodfall
Estimated Sales: Below $5 Million
Number Employees: 10-19
Square Footage: 40000

20918 Convergent Label Technology
620 S Ware Blvd
Tampa, FL 33619

813-621-8128
Fax: 813-620-1206 800-252-6111
Manufacturer and exporter of weigh price labeling
equipment and labels
President: Graham Lloyd
Marketing Director: Paula Nelson
Sales/Marketing: Chris Walker
Contact: Nancy Solman
n_solman@discovery-academy.org
Purchasing Manager: Steve Halbrook
Estimated Sales: $60 Million
Number Employees: 100-249
Square Footage: 166000
Type of Packaging: Food Service

20919 Conveyance Technologies LLC
24803 Detroit Rd
Cleveland, OH 44145

440-899-7440
Fax: 440-835-3107 800-701-2278
billwalzer@conveyancecart.com
www.conveyancecart.com
Manufacturer, importer and exporter of material
handling products including mobile loading docks,
stocking systems, hydraulic lifts, nestable warehouse
carts, stocking carts, conveyors, pallet carriers and
platform trucks
President: William Walzer
Sales Manager: Sam Aquino
Estimated Sales: $1-2 Million
Number Employees: 20-49
Square Footage: 220000
Brands:
Roll-A-Bench
Thru-Put
Uni-Cart
Uni-Lift

20920 Conveying Industries
3795 Paris St # B
Denver, CO 80239-3369

303-373-2035
Fax: 303-373-5149 877-600-4874
info@conveyind.com www.palletizing.us
Conveyors and palletizers
Manager: Don Simmonds
Sales Manager: Bob Carr
Manager: Bill Priday
billpriday@conveyind.com
Estimated Sales: $5-10 Million
Number Employees: 10-19

20921 Conveyor Accessories
7013 High Grove Blvd
Burr Ridge, IL 60527-7593

630-655-4205
Fax: 630-655-4209 800-323-7093
cai@conveyoraccessories.com
www.conveyoraccessories.com
Manufacturer and exporter of conveyor belt fasten-
ers, tools and accessories
President: Thomas Richardson
sales@conveyoraccessories.com
Estimated Sales: $10-20 Million
Number Employees: 20-49
Square Footage: 60000

20922 Conveyor Components Co
130 Seltzer Road
Croswell, MI 48422-9180

810-679-4211
Fax: 810-679-4510 800-233-3233
info@conveyorcomponents.com
www.conveyorcomponents.com
Quality engineered conveyor accessories including
emergency stop switches & pull cords, compact stop
controls, belt mi-alignment switches, tripper position
switches, bucket elevator alignment switches, dam-
aged belt detectors, bulkmaterial flow switches, mo-
tion controls and zero speed switches, aeration pads,
level controls including rotating paddles and tilt
switches, skirtboard clamps, a rotary brush style belt
cleaner as well as a wide variety of other conveyor
beltcleaners.
President/CEO: Clint Stimpson
General Manager: Barb Stimpson
Sales Manager: Rich Washkevich
Purchasing Coordinator: Sandy VanBrande
Estimated Sales: $5-10 Million
Number Employees: 50-99
Square Footage: 80000
Brands:
Insul-Air
Insul-Glare

20923 Conveyor Components Co
130 Seltzer Rd
Croswell, MI 48422-9180

810-679-4211
Fax: 810-679-4510 800-552-3337
info@cotterman.com
www.conveyorcomponents.com
Manufacturer and exporter of rolling safety and
fixed ladders including powder-coated and alumi-
num; also, portable elevating work platforms
President/CEO: C Stimpson
CFO: B Stimpson
Research & Development: J Kerr
Sales Manager: David Taylor
Manufacturing Manager: Robert Stimpson
Production Manager: L Higgins
Purchasing Manager: G Smith
Estimated Sales: $20-50 Million
Number Employees: 50-99
Square Footage: 60000
Parent Co: Material Control
Brands:
Maxi-Lift
Stockmaster
Tiltnroll
Workmaster

20924 Conveyor Dynamics Corp
7000 W Geneva Dr
St Peters, MO 63376-5712

636-279-1111
Fax: 636-279-1121
info@conveyordynamicscorp.com
www.conveyordynamicscorp.com
Manufacturer and exporter of vibratory processing
machinery for bulk and material handling applica-
tions
President: Michael Didion
info@conveyordynamicscorp.com
Engineer: Scott Milsark
Estimated Sales: $500,000-$1,000,000
Number Employees: 1-4
Square Footage: 72000

20925 Conveyor Equipment Manufacturers Association
6724 Lone Oak Blvd
Naples, FL 34109-6834

239-514-3441
Fax: 239-514-3470 bob@cemanet.org
www.cemanet.org

461

Serves the manufacturers and designers of conveyor equipment worldwide.
President: George Huber III
Executive VP: Robert Reinfried
Marketing/Membership Manager: Kim MacLaren
Contact: Phil Hannigan
phil@cemanet.org
Executive Secretary: Philip Hannigan
Estimated Sales: $500,000-$800,000
Number Employees: 1-4

20926 Conveyor Mart
3972 S Us Highway 45
Oshkosh, WI 54902-7351
920-233-2724
Fax: 920-233-3159
On-line conveyors and conveyor parts
President: James L Nerenhausen
Quality Control: Kurt Frank
Estimated Sales: Below $5 Million
Number Employees: 50-99

20927 Conveyor Supply Inc
1334 Dartmouth Ln
Deerfield, IL 60015-4066
847-945-5670
Fax: 847-945-5676 conveyorsupply2@att.net
Conductors and conveyor systems
Owner: Walter Weiss
CEO: Keith Weiss
Number Employees: 1-4
Square Footage: 8000

20928 Conveyor Systems & Components
21 Norman Ave
Riverside, NJ 08075-1009
856-461-8084
Fax: 856-764-9367 info@conveyorsystems.com
www.conveyorsystems.com
Conveyors and conveyor systems
Owner: Thomas Mc Larney
Estimated Sales: $5-10 Million
Number Employees: 1-4

20929 Conveyor Technologies Intergraded
1001 W Waukau Ave
Oshkosh, WI 54902
920-233-2756
Fax: 920-233-3159
Material handling equipment, packaging machinery, material handling and conveyor equipment
Number Employees: 5-9

20930 Conviron
572 S 5th St
Suite 2
Pembina, ND 58271-4309
701-280-9635
Fax: 204-786-7736 800-363-6451
sales@conviron.com
Refrigerated structures, walk-in coolers and freezer building and construction consultants, meat distributing center
President: Steve J Kroft
steve@conviron.com
Estimated Sales: $1-2.5 Million
Number Employees: 100-249

20931 Convoy
PO Box 8589
Canton, OH 44711
330-453-8163
Fax: 330-453-8181 800-899-1583
Manufacturer and exporter of plastic collapsible containers and plastic tote boxes
President: Phillip Dannemiller
National Sales Manager: Daren Newman
Estimated Sales: $2.5-5 Million
Number Employees: 10-19
Type of Packaging: Bulk

20932 Conwed Global Netting Sltns
530 Gregory Ave NE
Roanoke, VA 24016-2129
540-981-0879
Fax: 540-345-8421 800-368-3610
www.conwedplastics.com
Manufacturer and exporter of bags including vented plastic netting and netting header, onion netting, mesh linings and netting pallet wrap for fruits, vegetables and meats; also, fruit and vegetable juice filter support cartridges

President: Lawrance Ptaschek
Sales Manager: Michael Woldanski
Controller: Del Ramsey
Plant Manager: Charlie Boxler
Estimated Sales: $10-20 Million
Number Employees: 50-99
Parent Co: Siemens Corporation
Brands:
　Polynet

20933 Conwed Plastics LLC
2810 Weeks Ave SE
Minneapolis, MN 55414-2835
612-623-1700
Fax: 612-623-2500 800-426-0149
contact@conwedplastics.com
www.conwedplastics.com
Netting
Manager: John Burke
CEO: Chris Hatzenbuhler
chris.hatzenbuhler@conwedplastics.com
Quality Control: Tim Downes
Estimated Sales: $5-10 Million
Number Employees: 50-99

20934 Conxall Corporation
601 E Wildwood Ave
Villa Park, IL 60181
630-834-7504
Fax: 630-834-8540 sales@conxall.com
www.conxall.com
Custom nonmetallic product connectors and cable assemblies for processing and controls
President: Keith Bandolik
CFO: Dave Bandolik
Quality Control: Jim Collado
Plant Manager: Rob Smith
Estimated Sales: $20-50 Million
Number Employees: 100-249
Square Footage: 45000
Brands:
　Maxi-Con
　Mega-Con
　Micro-Con
　Mil-E-Qual
　Mini-Con
　Multi-Con

20935 Cook & Beals Inc
221 S 7th St
Loup City, NE 68853-8041
308-745-0154
Fax: 308-745-0154 www.cooknbeals.com
Manufacturer and exporter of honey processing equipment including rotary knife uncappers, spin float honey-wax separators, heat exchange units, honey pumps, wax melters, etc
President: Patrick Kuehl
info@cooknbeals.com
Secretary: Carol Kuehl
VP: Lawrence Kuehl
Estimated Sales: $1-2.5 Million
Number Employees: 5-9

20936 Cook Associates
212 W Kinzie St
Second Floor
Chicago, IL 60654
312-329-0900
Fax: 312-329-1528
Executive search firm for the food and beverage industry
President: Arnie Kins
CEO: Mary Kier
VP: Jessica Gentile
Contact: Joe Bilanzic
jbilanzic@cookma.com
Division Manager: Walter Rach
Estimated Sales: $2.5-5 Million
Number Employees: 50-99

20937 Cook Neon Signs
5382 New Manchester Hwy
Tullahoma, TN 37388-6783
931-455-0944
Fax: 931-455-4536 800-488-0944
rhonda@cookneon.com www.cookneon.com
Internally illuminated signs
Owner: Charles Callaway
charles@cookneon.com
Estimated Sales: Below $5 Million
Number Employees: 10-19

20938 CookTek
156 N. Jefferson Street
Suite 300
Chicago, IL 60661-1436
312-563-9600
Fax: 312-432-6220 888-266-5835
www.cooktek.com
Manufacturer and exporter of induction cooking systems
President: Robert Wolters
Quality Control: Robbe Gibb
Marketing Director: Tricia Cleary
Contact: Steven Lopez
slopez@cooktek.com
Estimated Sales: $.5-1 million
Number Employees: 1-4
Number of Brands: 1
Number of Products: 5
Square Footage: 100000
Parent Co: Wolters Group International
Brands:
　Cooktek

20939 Cookie Kingdom
1201 E Walnut St
Oglesby, IL 61348-1344
815-883-3331
Fax: 815-883-3332 ckingdomoffice@gmail.com
www.cookiekingdom.com
Manufacturer of cookies, ice cream wafers and dairy inclusions; co-packer for private label companies; and builder and upgrader of dairy equipment for lease or purchase.
President: Cliff Sheppard
ckingdom@ivnet.com
Director: Patty Smith
Estimated Sales: $13 Million
Number Employees: 100-249
Type of Packaging: Consumer, Private Label, Bulk

20940 Cooking Systems International
76 Pelican Ln
Redwood City, CA 94065
650-556-6222
Fax: 203-377-8187 info@mysck.com
www.sck.com
Manufacturer and exporter of rethermalizing units for cook chill, sous vide, precooked and frozen food
Chairman: B Koether
Executive VP: Scott Wakeman
VP Sales/Marketing: George Koether
Part Time Controller: Scott C Kennedy
Estimated Sales: $10-20 Million
Number Employees: 25
Square Footage: 80000
Type of Packaging: Food Service
Brands:
　Csi

20941 Cookshack
2304 N Ash St
Ponca City, OK 74601-1109
580-765-3669
Fax: 580-765-2223 800-423-0698
info@cookshack.com www.cookshack.com
Sauces & spices, smoking wood accessories for better barbeque, Cookshack smoked foods cookbooks, electric smoker ovens, pellet fired smokes, charbroilers, pellet grills
President: Brent Matthews
CEO: Sara Birch
j.kenney@varde.com
VP: Edward Aguiar Jr
Marketing Coordinator: Cayley Armstrong
Finance/Marketing/Sales Manager: John Shiflet
General Manager: Stuart Powell
Production Manager: Jim Linnebur
Estimated Sales: $4 Million
Number Employees: 20-49
Number of Brands: 2
Number of Products: 1
Square Footage: 44000
Type of Packaging: Consumer, Food Service, Private Label, Bulk
Brands:
　Fast Eddy's

20942 Cookson Plastic Molding
787 Watervliet Shaker Road
Latham, NY 12110-2285
518-951-1000
Fax: 518-783-0004 888-738-8800
www.pacificpools.com

President: Bruce Quay
Technical Services Manager: Peter Morgan

20943 Cool Care
4020 Thor Drive
Boynton Beach, FL 33426-8407
561-364-5711
Fax: 561-364-5766 www.coolcarehvac.com
Manufacturer, importer and exporter of ripening
rooms for produce with cold storage and controlled
atmosphere; also, vacuum coolers, ice injectors, etc.;
installation services available
President: Mike Bianco
Director Sales: Ron Roberts
Engineering Manager: Bob Windecker
Number Employees: 20-49
Square Footage: 100000
Parent Co: Dole Food Company

20944 Cool Cargo
5324 Georgia Highway 85
Forest Park, GA 30297-2475
770-994-0338
Temperature control systems.
President: Burt Pedowitz

20945 Cool-Pitch Co
5948 Rocky Mount Dr
Jacksonville, FL 32258-5415
904-260-1876
800-938-0128
www.cool-pitch.com
Pitcher coolers
President: William Coker
Estimated Sales: $1-3,000,000
Number Employees: 5-9
Brands:
Cool-Pitch

20946 CoolBrands International
4175 Veterans Memorial Highway
3rd Floor
Ronkonkoma, NY 11779-7639
631-737-9700
Fax: 631-737-9792 www.eskimopie.com
Distributor of frozen desserts including ice cream,
also flexible packaging
CFO: Gary Stevens
Estimated Sales: $35 Million
Number Employees: 35
Type of Packaging: Food Service, Bulk
Brands:
Breyers
Care Bears
Chipwich
Crayola
Disney
Dogsters
Eskimo Pie
Fruit a Freeze
Godiva Ice Cream
No Pudge
Snapple
The Sopranos
Trix
Tropicana
Wholefruit
Yoplait

20947 Cooling Products Inc
500 N Pecan Ave
Broken Arrow, OK 74012-2333
918-251-8588
Fax: 918-251-8837 coolprod@gorilla.net
Manufacturer and exporter of heat exchangers, radi-
ators, finned tubes and condensers
Manager: Steve Chalmers
schalmers@coolprod.com
Production: Harold Gordon
Sales Manager: Stephen Chalmers
Estimated Sales: $20-50 Million
Number Employees: 50-99

20948 Cooling Technology Inc
1800 Orr Industrial Ct
Charlotte, NC 28213-6342
704-596-4109
Fax: 704-597-8697 800-872-1448
info@coolingtechnology.com
www.coolingtechnology.com
Manufacturer and exporter of temperature controllers, chillers and evaporative cooling and pumping
systems.

Owner: Chrystel Baker
Marketing Director: Chris Fore
Director of Sales and Marketing: Laura Walker
cbaker@coolingtech.gd
Operations Manager: Sheetal Desai
Estimated Sales: $3-5 Million
Number Employees: 20-49
Number of Products: 20
Square Footage: 40000

20949 Cooper Decoration Company
PO Box 81
Weston, MA 02493-0005
315-475-1661
Fax: 315-475-1664 tsmallcoop@aol.com
Christmas lights and decorations; also, food show
decorator
President: Jon Cooper
VP: Lou Galtieri
Operations Manager: Jim Cooper
Estimated Sales: $1-2.5 Million
Number Employees: 10
Parent Co: Cooper Drapery Company

20950 Cooper Instrument Corporation
P.O.Box 450
Middlefield, CT 06455-0450
860-349-3473
Fax: 860-349-8994 800-835-5011
sbennett@cooperinstrument.com
www.cooper-atkins.com
CEO: Carol P Wallace
Director of Marketing: Cherylann Hunt
Estimated Sales: $1-5 Million
Number Employees: 100-249

20951 Cooperheat/MQS
P.O.Box 123
Alvin, TX 77512-0123
281-331-6154
Fax: 281-331-4107 800-526-4233
cooperheat-mqs@2isi.com
Manufacturer and exporter of heat treating equip-
ment, accesories and services, heat tracing equip-
ment and services; also, induction equipment and
nondestructive testing
President: Kenneth Tholan
VP Sales: Charels Silver
VP International Sales: Jim Campbell
Number Employees: 20-49
Square Footage: 160000
Parent Co: International Industrial Services
Brands:
Eagle
Versatrace

20952 Copack International
1270 Belle Ave # 115
Winter Springs, FL 32708-1905
407-699-7507
Fax: 407-699-7543 padamission@copack.com
www.copack.com
Food packaging materials
President: Paul J Adamission
Contact: Paul Adamission
p.adamission@copack.com
Estimated Sales: $4 Million
Number Employees: 50-99
Square Footage: 400000
Type of Packaging: Consumer, Food Service, Pri-
vate Label, Bulk

20953 Cope Plastics Inc
4441 Industrial Dr
Alton, IL 62002-5939
618-466-0221
Fax: 618-466-7975 800-851-5510
mi@copeplastics.com www.copeplastics.com
FDA, 3A and USDA compliant plastic components
President & CEO: Jane Saale
CEO: Grant Benner
grant@thegoalieclub.com
VP of Finance: John Theen
Quality Manager: Mike Chism
Director of Marketing: Cindy Smalley
VP of Sales: John Lee
VP of Operations: Josh Kuhnash
Manufacturing Manager: Jerry Dunnagan
Estimated Sales: $1-2.5 Million
Number Employees: 100-249
Parent Co: Cope Plastics

20954 Coperion Corp
590 Woodbury Glassboro Rd
Sewell, NJ 08080-4558
854-253-3265
info@coperionktron.com
www.coperion.com
Provide process automation, equipment, systems and
solutions for bulk material handling.
Vice President: Thomas Hummel
Vice President: Thomas Hummel
Business Development Manager-Food: Sharon
Nowark
Number Employees: 100-249

20955 Copesan
W175n5711 Technology Dr
Menomonee Falls, WI 53051-5673
262-783-6261
Fax: 262-783-6267 800-267-3726
info@copesan.com www.copesan.com
Provides effective pest management services for all
your pest management needs, including insect, ro-
dent stored product pest, bird and weed control, and
fumigations
President: Deni Naumann
Vice President of Finance: Kevin Fixel
Vice President: Mike Campbell
Quality Control: Jim Snkiele
Technical Advisor: Jim Snkiele
Marketing Director: Elizabeth Johnson
VP, Sales: Aric Schroeder
Director, HR: Jessica Janiszewski
Operations Manager: Carl Griswold
Estimated Sales: $2.5-5 Million
Number Employees: 20-49

20956 Copper Brite
PO Box 50610
Santa Barbara, CA 93150-0610
805-565-1566
Fax: 805-565-1394
Manufacturer and exporter of insecticides and wood
rot fungicides; also, cleaner and polish for copper,
brass and stainless steel
President/ CEO: Alan D. Brite
CFO: Alan Brite
Executive VP: Terry Brite
R&D: Alan Brite
Quality Control: Terry Brite
Estimated Sales: $2.5-5 Million
Number Employees: 1-4
Brands:
Copper Brite
Roach Prufe
Termite Prufe

20957 Copper Clad
600 S 9th St
Reading, PA 19602-2506
610-375-4596
Fax: 610-375-3557
Metal polish cleaners including silver, brass, copper
and stainless steel
President: Thomas Ziemer
Estimated Sales: $10-20 Million
Number Employees: 10-19
Square Footage: 144000
Brands:
Farberware
Revere

20958 Copper Hills Fruit Sales
4337 N Golden State Boulevard
Suite 102
Fresno, CA 93722-3801
559-432-5400
Fax: 559-432-5620
Packers of peaches, plums, nectarines, apricots,
pomegranates, and persimmons
Managing Member: Wilma J. Deniz

20959 Copperwood InternationalInc
9249 S Broadway
Unit 200-238
Highland Ranch, CO 80129-5692
303-683-1234
Fax: 303-683-0933 800-411-7887
copperwoodfoods@aol.com
Broker of a wide variety of closeout, excess and dis-
counted food items
Sales Director: Michael Casey
Estimated Sales: $5,000,000
Number Employees: 4
Number of Brands: 76

Number of Products: 127
Square Footage: 50000

20960 Coral LLC
5576 Bighorn Dr # B
Carson City, NV 89701-1474

775-883-9853
Fax: 775-883-9858   800-882-9577
sales@coralcalcium.com www.coralcalcium.com
Natural minerals
Sales Director: Alberto Galdamez
Contact: Matt Cuhadar
matt@coralcalcium.com
Number Employees: 5-9

20961 Corben Packaging & Display
976 Grand Street
Brooklyn, NY 11211-2707

718-388-7666
Fax: 718-388-6592 packitgood@aol.com
Full service contract packaging includes shrink
wrapping, poly bagging, blister packaging, custom
packaging, clam shells and folding boxes
Estimated Sales: $1-2.5 000,000
Number Employees: 12

20962 Corbett Timber Co
1200 Castle Hayne Rd
Wilmington, NC 28401-8885

910-763-9991
Fax: 910-763-3426   800-334-0684
Wooden wirebound crates
President: Scott Corbett
Partner: William Corbett
Sales Manager (Containers): Donald Williamson
Estimated Sales: $10-20 Million
Number Employees: 50-99
Square Footage: 300000

20963 Corbox-Meyers Inc
6701 Hubbard Ave
Cleveland, OH 44127-1475

216-441-0150
Fax: 216-441-4213   800-321-7286
info@corbox.com www.corbox.com
Shipping containers, bins and storage boxes
Owner: Kathy Zenisek
VP: Clyde Zenisek
Estimated Sales: $1-2.5 Million
Number Employees: 20-49
Square Footage: 96000
Parent Co: Corbox

20964 Corby Hall
3 Emery Ave
Randolph, NJ 07869-1308

973-366-8300
Fax: 973-366-9833 info@corbyhall.com
www.corbyhall.com
Manufacturer and exporter of stainless steel and sil-
ver plated flatware and holloware; importer of
flatware
Vice President: Bill Adams
bill.adams@hollowick.com
CFO: Alan Millward
Vice President: Adrian Millward
Quality Control: Andrew Millward
VP Marketing: Andrew Millward
Estimated Sales: $500,000-$1 Million
Number Employees: 5-9
Square Footage: 30000
Type of Packaging: Food Service
Brands:
  Algarve
  Corby Hall
  Riviera
  St. Morirz

20965 Cord Tex
136 Industrial Ave
New Orleans, LA 70121-2902

504-834-2862
Fax: 504-837-7645
Distributor, importer and exporter of manila, sisal
and synthetic rope and twine
President: Carl Ruch
VP: Gerard Ruch
Estimated Sales: $1-3 Million
Number Employees: 5-9

20966 Core Products Co
401 Industrial Park
PO Box 669
Canton, TX 75103-2817

903-567-1341
Fax: 903-567-1346   800-825-2673
www.coreproductsco.com
Manufacturer and exporter of odor control agents,
carpet and upholstery cleaning products, stain and
rust removers, degreasers and cleaners for tub, tile,
glass, chrome and stainless steel
President: Brent Crawford
core@coreproductsco.com
CFO: Debbie Crawford
VP: Debbie Crawford
Sales Manager: Brian Hawkins
Estimated Sales: $500,000-$1 Million
Number Employees: 10-19
Square Footage: 80000
Brands:
  Believe It
  Beta-Kleen
  Bonnet Buff
  De-Foamer
  Hot Water Extract
  Incredible Blue
  Juice Out
  Leather Magic
  Mal-X
  Perfect Image
  Plus Ii
  Preconditioner Traffic Lane
  Rust Bust'r
  Tann-X
  Unbelievable Green
  Unbelievable!

20967 Corenco
3275 Dutton Ave
Santa Rosa, CA 95407-7891

707-824-9868
Fax: 707-528-3197   888-267-3626
ngorsuch@corenco.biz www.corenco.biz
Manufactures size reduction equipment for the food
processing industry.
President/CEO: Chris Cory
ccory@corenco.biz
Corporate Secretary/Accounting: Saraj Cory
VP/COO: Jeff Boheim
Inside Machinery Sales: Neil Gorsuch
Production Manager: Matt Young
Estimated Sales: $1-2.5 Million
Number Employees: 5-9
Number of Brands: 1
Number of Products: 14
Square Footage: 14000
Brands:
  Corenco

20968 Corfab
6700 S Sayre Avenue
Chicago, IL 60638

708-458-8750
Corrugated paperboard partitions, boxes, file folders
and displays
President: R Izenstark
VP: Sy Ginsberg
Plant Manager: Frank Fandl
Estimated Sales: $20-50 Million
Number Employees: 50-99

20969 Corinth Products
74 Hob Rd
Corinth, ME 4427

207-285-3387
Fax: 207-285-7738
Wooden pallets and boxes
President/CEO: Peter Higgins
Estimated Sales: Below $5 Million
Number Employees: 10

20970 Cork Specialties
1454 NW 78th Ave #305
Miami, FL 33126

305-477-1506
Fax: 305-591-0593 corkspec@aol.com
Manufacturer, importer and exporter of corks and
plastic top stoppers
President: Rafael Figueroa
VP: Orlando Barranco
Estimated Sales: Below $5 Million
Number Employees: 5-9

20971 Corman & Assoc Inc
881 Floyd Dr
Lexington, KY 40505-3694

859-233-0544
Fax: 859-253-0119 ted@cormans.com
www.cormans.com
Point of purchase displays and store fixtures
President: Ted Corman
ted@cormans.com
Estimated Sales: $5-10 Million
Number Employees: 50-99
Square Footage: 220000

20972 Corn States Metal Fabricators
1323 Maple St
PO Box 65635
West Des Moines, IA 50265-4397

515-225-7961
Fax: 515-225-9382 www.cornstates.com
Conveyors and elevators
President and CEO: Randall Golay
Vice President: Mitch Golay
mitchg@cornstates.com
Estimated Sales: $5-10 Million
Number Employees: 20-49
Square Footage: 60000

20973 Cornelia Broom Company
756 Hoyt St
Cornelia, GA 30531

706-778-4434
Fax: 706-778-9814 800-228-2551
Brushes, brooms, mops and handles
President: Joby Scroggs
Secretary: Fran Chastain
VP: Marcia Scroggs
Estimated Sales: $5-10 Million
Number Employees: 24
Square Footage: 40000

20974 Cornelius
2421 15th SW
Mason City, IA 50401

641-424-3601
800-238-3600
www.cornelius.com
Manufacturer and exporter of ice makers and dis-
pensers.
Year Founded: 1931
Estimated Sales: $100-$500 Million
Number Employees: 4,500
Type of Packaging: Food Service

20975 Cornelius Inc.
101 Broadway St. W
Osseo, MN 55369

763-488-8200
Fax: 763-488-4298 800-238-3600
publications@cornelius.com
www.cornelius-usa.com
Beverage dispensing and ice making equipment.
President: Tim Hubbard
Year Founded: 1931
Estimated Sales: $241.8 Million
Number Employees: 4,500+
Number of Brands: 4
Number of Products: 6
Parent Co: Marmon Beverage Technologies Inc.
Type of Packaging: Food Service
Other Locations:
  IMI Cornelius
  Norwood MA
Brands:
  Cornelius
  Jet Spray
  Rencor
  Wilshire

20976 Cornelius Wilshire Corporation
2401 N Palmer Dr
Schaumburg, IL 60196-0001

847-397-4600
Fax: 847-539-6960 www.cornelius-usa.com
Ice makers and juice dispensers
President: Tim Hubbard
Sales/Marketing: Michael Orlando
Brands:
  Wilshire

20977 Cornell Machine Co
45 Brown Ave
Springfield, NJ 07081-2992

973-379-6860
Fax: 973-379-6854 info@cornellmachine.com
www.cornellversator.com

Manufacturer and exporter of food processing equipment including homogenizers, emulsifiers, mixers, oxygen removers, deaerators and defoaming equipment
President: Martin Huska
Contact: Alan Huska
ajhuska@cornellmachine.com
Estimated Sales: $1-2.5 Million
Number Employees: 5-9
Brands:
    Cornell Versator

20978 Cornell Pump Company
P.O.Box 6334
Portland, OR 97228-6334
                          503-653-0330
    Fax: 503-653-0338 info@cornellpump.com
                    www.cornellpump.com
Manufacturer, importer and exporter of pumps for food product handling, hot oil circulation, refrigeration and waste handling
President: Jeff Markham
Marketing: Brenda Case
Number Employees: 100-249
Parent Co: Roper Industries
Brands:
    Cycloseal
    Redi-Prime

20979 Cornerstone
750 Patrick Pl
Brownsburg, IN 46112-2211
                          317-852-6522
    Fax: 317-852-6433 800-659-7699
        info@cornerstoneflooring.com
www.cornerstoneflooring.com/industries/industrie
                    s.shtml
Manufacturer and installer of high performance polymer flooring, lining and coating materials for a variety of industries including that of food and beverage.
President: Dann Hess
Sales Manager: Tracy Figley
Contact: Charles Joslin
cjoslin@cornerstoneflooring.com
Estimated Sales: $1-5 000,000
Number Employees: 20-49

20980 Corniani
501 Southlake Blvd
Richmond, VA 23236-3042
                          804-794-6688
              Fax: 804-794-6187
President: Giuseppe Venturi
gventuri@middleburgbank.com
Number Employees: 100-249

20981 Corning Life Sciences
836 North Street
Tewksbury, MA 01876
                          978-442-2200
                          800-492-1110
                  inquiries@corning.com
www.corning.com/worldwide/en/products/life-scie
                    nces.html
Pyrex Laboratory glassware, Corning brand instruments and equipment, and Cornin and Costar brand plasticware.
Chairman & CEO: Wendell Weeks
Vice Chairman/Corporate Development: Lawrence McRae
Senior VP & GM, Life Sciences: Ronald Verkleeren
Executive VP & CFO: Tony Tripeny
Estimated Sales: $10.5 Billion
Number Employees: 45,000
Parent Co: Corning Inc
Brands:
    Checkmate
    Checkmite
    Corex Ii
    Corning
    Costar
    Pyrex
    Pyrex Plus
    Scholar
    Vycor

20982 Cornish Containers
205 W Sophia Street
Maumee, OH 43537-2166
                          419-893-7911
              Fax: 419-893-5146
Chest and door type insulated and refrigerated containers

CEO: Jody Holbrook
Sales Director: Tim McNulty
Estimated Sales: $1-2.5 Million
Number Employees: 6
Square Footage: 50000
Brands:
    Frigi-Top
    Transafe

20983 Coronet Chandelier Originals
12 Grand Blvd # 16
Brentwood, NY 11717-5195
                          631-273-1177
              Fax: 631-273-1247
Manufacturer and exporter of custom chandeliers; importer of chandelier crystals, wrought iron tables, wall solders, pendents
President: Irwin Goldberg
Estimated Sales: $1-3 Million
Number Employees: 10-19
Square Footage: 60000

20984 Corp Somat
165 Independence Ct
Lancaster, PA 17601-5838
                          717-392-6714
    Fax: 717-291-0877 800-237-6628
                  www.somatcompany.com
Manufacturer and exporter of waste pulping and dewatering systems for processing and reduction of food service wastes
Manager: Scott Witmer
R&D: Steve Eno
Marketing: Lin Sensenig
Food Service Equipment Sales: Herman Williams
Contact: Dolores Alexander
dalexander@somat.com
Production: Barry Alexander
Plant Manager: Rich Zimmerman
Number Employees: 5-9
Square Footage: 78000
Brands:
    Somat Classic
    Somat Evergreen

20985 Corpak
PO Box 364747
San Juan, PR 00936-4747
                          787-787-9085
              Fax: 787-740-5230
Paperboard boxes
VP Sales: Minerva Medina
Estimated Sales: $1-5 Million
Number Employees: 50-99

20986 Corporate Safe Specialists
14800 S Mckinley Ave
Posen, IL 60469-1547
                          708-371-4200
    Fax: 708-371-3326 800-342-3033
                  curreyj@corporatesafe.com
CSS is an industry leader providing innovative security solutions to the restaurant and retail industries globally. CSS safes, smart safes and kiosks can be configured to provide closed-loop cash management to deter armed robbery burglary and internal theft.
President: Edward McGunn
CEO: Ed McGunn
CFO: Lisa Marsh
Vice President: Rosemary Leonard
Marketing Director: Peter Muiznieks
Sales Director: James Currey
Operations Manager: Adam Saggese
Estimated Sales: $35 Million
Number Employees: 5-9
Square Footage: 60000
Brands:
    Power Lever
    Quik Lock Ii

20987 Corpus Christi Stamp Works
502 S Staples St
Corpus Christi, TX 78401-3333
                          361-884-4801
    Fax: 361-884-1038 800-322-4515
                  sales@ccstampworks.com
                  www.ccswsignsystems.com
Marking devices, rubber and pre-inked stamps and engraved signs and name badges
President: Harry Lee Chester
hches92383@aol.com
VP: Catherine Ray
Office Manager: Mildred Ashmore

Estimated Sales: $2.5-5 Million
Number Employees: 20-49
Square Footage: 10000

20988 Corr Pak Corp
8000 Joliet Rd # 100
Mc Cook, IL 60525-3256
                          708-442-7806
    Fax: 708-442-0467 haltaylor@corr-pak.com
Corrugated boxes, containers and point of purchase displays; silk screen printing available
President: Jim Hagenseker
hagensekerjim@corr-pak.com
VP, Display Division: Jim Hagenseker
Sales: Barry Smith
Estimated Sales: Below $5 Million
Number Employees: 20-49

20989 Corrections Dept
1920 Technology Pkwy
Mechanicsburg, PA 17050-8507
                          717-728-2573
    Fax: 717-975-2242 ra-contactdoc@pa.gov
                    www.cor.state.pa.us
Industrial school
Manager: Franklin Tennis
Quality Control: Carroll Healey
Manager: John E Wetzel
jowetzel@state.pa.us
Number Employees: 10000+

20990 Corrigan Corporation of America
104 Ambrogio Dr
Gurnee, IL 60031-3373
                          847-263-5955
    Fax: 847-263-5944 800-462-6478
    sales@corriganmist.com www.corriganmist.com
Produce misting, meat humidification and water filtration systems
Owner: J Michael Corrigan
Account Manager: Charles Noland
Estimated Sales: $3-5 Million
Number Employees: 10-19
Parent Co: Corrigan Corporation of America
Brands:
    Hypersoft
    Optimist
    Ultramist
    Vaporplus

20991 Corro-Shield International Inc
7059 Barry St
Rosemont, IL 60018-3401
                          847-298-7770
    Fax: 847-298-7784 800-298-7637
                    www.corroshield.com
Industrial floors and wall coatings.
Manager: Bret Snider
bsnider@corroshield.com
Number Employees: 5-9

20992 Corrobilt Container Company
7888 Marathon Dr
Livermore, CA 94550-9325
                          925-373-0880
              Fax: 209-249-3130
Corrugated containers
President: Edward Childe
Number Employees: 5 to 9
Type of Packaging: Bulk

20993 Corrugated Inner-Pak Corporation
51 Washington Street
Conshohocken, PA 19428
                          610-825-0200
              Fax: 610-828-0907
Corrugated paper and foam plastic packaging specialties and wooden boxes and crates; contract packaging available for the government and commercial industries
President: Robert E Doyoe
Treasurer: Ben Watson
VP: John McCarthy
Estimated Sales: Below $5 Million
Number Employees: 9
Parent Co: Inter-Pack Corporation

20994 Corrugated Packaging
1683 Cattlemen Rd
Sarasota, FL 34232
                          941-371-0000
              Fax: 941-378-5637

Packaging materials including corrugated boxes, pads, folders and die cuts
Owner: Nancy James
President: Arthur James Jr
Marketing Director: Herbert Markham
Purchasing Manager: Robert Mecall
Estimated Sales: $2.5-5 Million
Number Employees: 10
Square Footage: 53000

20995 Corrugated Specialties
352 12th St # 2
Plainwell, MI 49080-1154
    269-685-9821

Corrugated paper and boxes
Owner: Jim Skrobot
President: James Skrobot
Estimated Sales: $1-2.5 Million
Number Employees: 1 to4

20996 Corrugated Supplies Co.
5043 W 67th St
Bedford, IL 60638
    708-458-5525
    Fax: 708-458-0013 888-826-2738
    www.corrugatedsuppliescompany.com
Manufacturer of corrugated cardboard sheets
CEO: John Potocsnak
Estimated Sales: $21 Million
Number Employees: 50-99
Square Footage: 100000
Type of Packaging: Consumer, Food Service, Bulk

20997 Corrupad Protective Packaging
89 Oleary Dr
Bensenville, IL 60106-2270
    630-238-8090
    Fax: 630-238-8096
Recycled paper packaging materials
President: Norman Lynn
Estimated Sales: $10-25 Million
Number Employees: 20-49

20998 Corsair Display Systems
5560 Airport Rd
Canandalgua, NY 14424
    585-396-3480
    Fax: 585-396-5953 800-347-5245
sales@corsairdisplay.com www.corsairdisplay.com
Merchandising stations, pastry cases, carts, kiosks, menu systems and bulkhead signs
President: David Mansfield
Vice President: Alison Leet
Marketing/Sales: Bruce Meckling
Operations Manager: Cindy DeRycke
Purchasing Manager: Eric Rands
Estimated Sales: $3-5 Million
Number Employees: 20-49
Square Footage: 80000

20999 Corson Manufacturing Company
20 Michigan Street
24
Lockport, NY 14094-2628
    716-434-8871
    Fax: 716-434-8801
Paper boxes for cereal, snacks, cookies, etc
CEO: Anthony Gioia
Estimated Sales: $3-5 Million
Number Employees: 230

21000 Corson Rubber Products Inc
105 Smith St
Clover, SC 29710-1333
    803-222-7779
    Fax: 803-222-9022 info@corsonrubber.com
    www.corsonrubber.com
Color coded sanitation was FDA compliant knobby mats.
President: Denis Garvey
Plant Manager: Terry Wallace
Estimated Sales: $9-15 Million
Number Employees: 10-19
Type of Packaging: Consumer, Food Service, Private Label, Bulk
Brands:
  Corson

21001 Cortec Aero
4119 White Bear Pkwy
St Paul, MN 55110-7634
    651-429-1100
    Fax: 651-429-1122 800-426-7832
info@cortecvci.com www.cortecvci.com

Polyethylene film and bags including plain and printed
General Manager: Usama Jacir
CEO: Boris Miksic
bmiksic@cortecvci.com
Vice President of Sales: Cliff Cracauer
Regional Sales Manager: Ashlee Meints
Plant Manager: Tim Bliss
Estimated Sales: $1-3 Million
Number Employees: 100-249
Square Footage: 106400

21002 Cortec Aero
4119 White Bear Pkwy
St Paul, MN 55110-7634
    651-429-1100
    Fax: 651-429-1122 800-426-7832
    info@cortecvci.com www.cortecvci.com
Cortec Corporation is a pioneer of environmentally friendly, corrosion protection Vapor Phase Corrosion Inhibitors(VpClin), a Migratory corrosion Inhibitors(MCI) Technologies for the packaging industry.
ISO 9001:2000 & 14001Registered
President: Boris Miksic
bmiksic@cortecvci.com
Estimated Sales: $10-20 000,000
Number Employees: 100-249
Number of Brands: 5
Number of Products: 400+
Type of Packaging: Consumer, Food Service, Private Label, Bulk

21003 Cosco Home & Office Products
2525 State St
Columbus, IN 47201
    Fax: 636-745-1005 800-628-8321
    customer.service@coscoproducts.com
    www.coscoproducts.com
Manufacturer and exporter of home and office furniture.
President: Troy Franks
tfranks@coscoproducts.com
Year Founded: 1939
Estimated Sales: $100-500 Million
Number Employees: 1000-4999
Parent Co: Dorel Home Furnishings
Type of Packaging: Food Service
Brands:
  Cosco

21004 Cosense Inc
155 Ricefield Ln
Hauppauge, NY 11788-2031
    631-231-0735
    Fax: 631-231-0838 sales@cosense.com
Designs and manufactures lliquid level sensors utilizing patented ultrasonic technology.
Owner: Naim Dam
Sales Director: Kevin Conlin
Contact: Bill Allhusen
ballhusen@cosense.com
Estimated Sales: $5-10 Million
Number Employees: 20-49
Square Footage: 20000
Brands:
  Millennuim
  Pointsense
  Sentio
  Sonic Eye

21005 Cosgrove Enterprises Inc
14300 NW 77th Ct
Miami Lakes, FL 33016-1534
    305-820-5600
    Fax: 305-623-6935 800-888-3396
    orders@e-cosgrove.com
    www.cosgroveenterprises.com
Manufacturer, exporter and importer of cleaning equipment and janitorial supplies including brooms, brushes and paper products
President: Robert Cosgrove
robert@cosgroveenterprises.com
Quality Control: Louides Cohen
VP: Randy Shelton
Estimated Sales: $500,000-$1 Million
Number Employees: 20-49
Square Footage: 220000

21006 Cosmic Co
151 Haskins Way # A
S San Francisco, CA 94080-6200
    650-742-0888
    Fax: 650-742-6777 cosmic@cosmicco.us
    www.cosmicco.us

Boxes, thermal-formed trays, compartments, semi-rigid clear containers
VP: Agnes Cheung
Estimated Sales: $2.5-5 000,000
Number Employees: 10-19

21007 Cosmo/Kabar
140 Schmitt Blvd
Farmingdale, NY 11735-1461
    631-694-6857
    Fax: 631-694-6846 info@cosmos-kabar.com
    www.cosmos-kabar.com
President: Bruce McKee
R&D: Bryan Matty
CFO: Bruce McKee
Contact: Paolo Bruschi
pbruschi@cosmos-kabar.com
Estimated Sales: $2 Million
Number Employees: 20-49

21008 Cosmos International
PO Box 7740
Burbank, CA 91510-7740
    626-330-8499
    Fax: 626-333-4210
Canned fruit
Office Manager: Janet Muna

21009 Coss Engineering Sales Company
3943 S Creek Drive
Ts
Rochester Hills, MI 48306-4729
    248-370-0707
    Fax: 248-370-9211 800-446-1365
Manufacturer and exporter of pneumatic conveying systems, surge hoppers and storage silos
CEO and President: Carter Coss
Estimated Sales: Less than $500,000
Number Employees: 4

21010 Costa Broom Works
3606 E 4th Ave
Tampa, FL 33605-5835
    813-385-1722
    Fax: 813-247-6060
Brooms, mops, mop heads and brushes; importer of related products for cleaning
Owner: Frank J Costa
Estimated Sales: $1-2.5 Million
Number Employees: 20-30
Type of Packaging: Food Service, Bulk

21011 Cott Technologies
14923 Proctor Ave
La Puente, CA 91746-3206
    626-961-0370
    Fax: 626-333-9307
Automated vacuum packaging machines and refrigerator display cases
Owner: Gilbert De Cardenas
Estimated Sales: $10-20 Million
Number Employees: 20-49
Brands:
  Vari-Pack

21012 Cotter Brothers Corp
8 Southside Rd
Danvers, MA 01923-1409
    978-777-5001
    Fax: 978-750-6219 info@cotterbrothers.com
    www.cotterbrothers.com
High purity process piping and skid mounted systems; also, installation available
President: Randolph Cotter
randy@cotterbrothers.com
VP: David Cotter
Director Business Development: Frank Armstrong
Estimated Sales: $10-20 Million
Number Employees: 20-49

21013 (HQ)Cotton Goods Mfg Co
259 N California Ave
Chicago, IL 60612-1903
    773-265-0088
    Fax: 773-265-0096 cotton2@earthlink.net
    www.cottongoodsmfg.com
Manufacturer and exporter of table skirts and linens
President/CEO: Edward Lewis
cotton2@earthlink.net
Sales Manager: Kevin Higgins
Estimated Sales: $3-5 Million
Number Employees: 10-19
Square Footage: 20000

Brands:
  Grip Clips

21014 Couch & Philippi
10680 Fern Ave
PO Box A
Stanton, CA 90680-2600

714-527-2261
Fax: 714-827-2077 800-854-3360
sales@couchandphilippi.com
Designing and producing innovative products for restaurants and beverage copmanies nationwide.
President: Steve Ellsworth
sellsworth@primus-group.com
Estimated Sales: $5-10 Million
Number Employees: 50-99

21015 Cougar Packaging Concepts, Inc.
612 Stetson Ave
St. Charles, IL 60174

630-689-4050
www.cougarpackaging.com
Developer of packaging systems to help food safety and shelf life extension. Creator of a Modified Atmosphere Packaging (AMP) process combined with Pulsed Ultra Violet (PUV) light technology that creates a sanitization method to cleanproduct lines, packaging and even food products, without adversely affecting the taste of the products.
President: Mark Cottone
CEO: Tiffany DeSalvo
Marketing & Admin/Sales Support: Brooke Shipbaugh
Vice President of Tech Sales: Steve Kligis

21016 Cougar Packaging Solutions
12301 New Ave
Unit E
Lemont, IL 60439

630-231-7800
Fax: 630-231-1286 sales@cougargroup.com
www.cougargroup.com
Provides packaging services, including Modified Atmosphere Packaging equipment, thermoformed trays and lidded films.
President: John Senese
Senior Account Executive: Pam Anderson
Vice President of Sales: Dan Ferguson

21017 Country Save Products Corp
19704 60th Ave NE
Arlington, WA 98223-4736

360-435-9868
Fax: 360-435-0896 info@countrysave.com
www.countrysave.com
Manufacturer and exporter of phosphate-free laundry detergent and dishwashing powder; also, chlorine-free powdered bleach
President: Kris Anderson
krisa@countrysave.com
Estimated Sales: $2.5-5 Million
Number Employees: 5-9
Brands:
  Country Save

21018 County Neon Sign Corporation
PO Box 504
Plainview, NY 11803-0504

516-349-9550
Fax: 516-349-0090
Lighting fixtures and electric and neon signs
President: George Schneider
VP: Joe Miller
Estimated Sales: $2.5-5,000,000
Number Employees: 20-49

21019 Couprie Fenton
4282 Belair Frontage Rd
Suite 5
Augusta, GA 30909

706-650-7017
Fax: 706-868-1534
Crab, conch, crabmeat, dogfish, full line seafood, halibut, lobster, lobster meat
Manager: Yves Latremouille
Estimated Sales: $.5-1 million
Number Employees: 1-4

21020 Courtesy Signs
3101 S Fillmore St
Amarillo, TX 79110-1025

806-373-6609
Fax: 806-373-2953 courtesy@arn.net
www.bestsigns.com

Window signs, over-the-wire banners, point of purchase markers, aisle product signs, pennant banners, flags, etc
Manager: Bruce Milton
CFO: Wesley Ninemire
Sales: Dixie Flaherty
Manager: Victor Newton
Estimated Sales: Below $5 Million
Number Employees: 5-9
Square Footage: 148000

21021 Courtright Companies
26749 S. Governors Hwy.
Monee, IL 60449-8095

708-534-8400
Fax: 708-534-9140 sales@right-tape.com
www.right-tape.com
Manufacturer & exporter of reusable shipping containers, Teflon tapes, shellac adhesives, tensilized polypropylene and stretch film
Owner: Patricia Schoenbeck
Sales Director: Ted Bachand
Purchasing Manager: Ted Bachand
Estimated Sales: $3-5 Million
Number Employees: 6
Square Footage: 40000
Type of Packaging: Food Service, Private Label

21022 Cousins Packaging
105 Claireport Crescent
Etobicoke, ON M9V 6P7
Canada

416-743-1341
Fax: 416-743-1831 888-209-4344
info@cousinspackaging.com
www.cousinspackaging.com
Number Employees: 50

21023 Covance Inc.
210 Carnegie Center
Princeton, NJ 08540-6233

609-452-4440
Fax: 609-452-9375 888-268-2623
www.covance.com
Analytical testing services to the food, dietary supplement and biotechnology industries.
Executive Chairman: David King
CEO: Adam Schechter
Executive VP/CFO: Glenn Eisenberg
Senior VP/Global General Counsel: Sandra van der Vaart
Chief Human Resources Officer: Judi Seltz
Year Founded: 1996
Estimated Sales: Over $1 Billion
Number Employees: 50,000
Parent Co: LabCorp

21024 Cove Four
195 E Merrick Rd
Freeport, NY 11520-4012

516-379-4232
Fax: 516-379-4563 www.covefour.com
Wire products including corkscrews and custom; also, forming available
President: Barry Jaffe
erikcovefour@aol.com
VP Marketing: Bill Freedman
Sales Exec: Erik Christopher
Estimated Sales: $10-20 Million
Number Employees: 50-99

21025 Cove Woodworking
20 Kettle Cove Lane
Gloucester, MA 01930

978-526-4755
Fax: 978-526-4188 800-273-0037
whit33@msn.com
Restaurant tables, bars, bar stools, booths, chairs, bases, built-ins and custom work.
President: Andrew Marques
CFO: Patty Kenaedy
Production Manager: Paul Hargreaves
Estimated Sales: $1 Million
Number Employees: 10-19
Square Footage: 17000
Type of Packaging: Food Service

21026 Covergent Label Technology
620 S Ware Boulevard
Tampa, FL 33619-4443

800-252-6111
Fax: 813-620-1206
Weighing and labeling systems

Contact: Nancy Solman
n_solman@discovery-academy.org
Estimated Sales: $20-25 Million
Number Employees: 100-250

21027 Coveris
1701 Johnson Industrial Dr
Excelsior Springs, MO 64024

contact.rigidna@coveris.com
Rigid packaging solutions
CEO: Jakob Mosser
Brands:
  Aqua Crystal
  Instabowl
  Repellence
  Safe-T-Strip
  Serve-N-Seal
  Slide-Rite

21028 Covestro LLC
119 Salisbury Rd
Sheffield, MA 01257-9706

413-229-8711
Fax: 413-229-8717 800-628-5084
www.covestro.com
Extruded plastic sheets for window glazing, signs, displays, architectural products and industrial applications
President: Dennis Duff
Cmo: Kurt Glaser
curt.glaser@bayerbms.com
CFO: David Martin
Quality Control: Sherley Alarie
Estimated Sales: $20-50 Million
Number Employees: 100-249
Square Footage: 160000
Parent Co: Bayer Corporation

21029 Coy Laboratory ProductsInc
14500 Coy Dr
Grass Lake, MI 49240-9207

734-433-9296
Fax: 734-475-1846 sales@coylab.com
www.coylab.com
Glove boxes, anaerobic chambers, controlled environment
President: Richard Coy
Cmo: Brian Coy
brian@coylab.com
Estimated Sales: $2.5-5 000,000
Number Employees: 20-49

21030 Cozzini Inc
2400 Highway 18 E
Algona, IA 50511-7204

515-295-7234
Fax: 515-295-9568 888-295-1116
sales@afeco.com www.cozzini.com
Vat and barrel dumpers, belt and screw conveyors, curing and blending systems, pallet lifts, platforms, tables, tanks, and smokehouse racks
President: Jeffrey Christensen
Director Sales/Marketing: Mike Rooney
Manager: Mike Broughton
mike.broughton@afeco.com
Manager Production/Engineering: Jeffery Philips
Number Employees: 50-99
Square Footage: 200000

21031 (HQ)Cozzini LLC
4300 W Bryn Mawr Ave
Chicago, IL 60646-5943

773-478-9700
Fax: 773-478-8689 sales@cozzini.com
www.rapidpaktec.com
Manufacturer and exporter of meat processing equipment and blades
President: Peter J Samson
psamson@cozzini.com
VP: Oscar Cozzini
R&D: Greg Grady
Quality Control: Mario Lucchesi
Catalog Sales Technical Assistance: Pete Pierazzi
Estimated Sales: $20 Million
Number Employees: 100-249
Square Footage: 65000
Other Locations:
  Cozzini
  Soucy
Brands:
  Cozzini
  Ergo
  Primedge
  Suspentec

21032 Cozzini LLC
4300 W Bryn Mawr Ave
Chicago, IL 60646-5943
773-478-9700
Fax: 773-478-8689 888-295-1116
cozzini@cozzini.com
Meat processing and packaging equipment: chutes,
boning systems, canning systems, custom machinery
President: Peter J Samson
psamson@cozzini.com
Estimated Sales: $5-10 Million
Number Employees: 100-249

21033 Cozzoli Machine Co
50 Schoolhouse Rd
Somerset, NJ 08873-1289
732-564-0400
Fax: 732-564-0444 www.cozzoli.com
Designs and manufactures integrated precision pack-
aging systems solutions.
President: Frank Cozzoli
General Manager: Fred Hart
Controller: Michael Shanker
Marketing Director: Crystal Basiluk
Sales: Bruce Teeling
Purchasing Manager: Steve Turkus
Estimated Sales: $10-20 Million
Number Employees: 5-9
Number of Brands: 2
Number of Products: 200
Square Footage: 180000
Parent Co: Cozzoli Machine Company
Type of Packaging: Food Service
Brands:
    Inline Fill-To-Level Filler
    Inline Piston Filler
    Rotary Fill-To-Level Filler
    Rotary Piston Filler
    Versa-Cap
    Versa-Fil

21034 Craft Corrugated Box Inc
4674 Acushnet Ave
New Bedford, MA 02745-4736
508-998-2115
Fax: 508-998-8112
Corrugated boxes and other corrugated products
President: Ronald Mardula
Estimated Sales: Below $5 Million
Number Employees: 5-9

21035 Craft Industries
26-35 47th Avenue
Long Island City, NY 11101
252-753-3152
Fax: 252-753-3154
Portable LP gas cookers and trailers for caterers;
also, custom made cookers and trailers available
President and CFO: Jim Craft Jr
VP Financing: Sylvia Craft
Estimated Sales: Below $5 Million
Number Employees: 1-4
Square Footage: 80000
Brands:
    Craftmaster
    Steelcraft

21036 Craig Manufacturing
30 Loretto St
Irvington, NJ 7111
973-923-3211
Fax: 973-923-1767 800-631-7936
buycraig@aol.com
Deli cases, steam tables, back bars, refrigerators and
sandwich units
President: Craig Dubov
Estimated Sales: $5-10 Million
Number Employees: 50-99
Square Footage: 150000
Type of Packaging: Food Service

21037 Crain Walnut Shelling, Inc.
10695 Decker Ave
Los Molinos, CA 96055-9628
530-529-1585
Fax: 530-529-1458 crainwalnut@crainwalnut.com
www.crainwalnut.com
Shelled walnuts supplying industrial ingredient
needs.

President: Grant Skognes
gskognes@ridefox.com
Owner: Harold Crain
Vice President of Sales & Logistics: Vicki Lapera
Quality Assurance: Devan Wilson
Sales Administrator: Kimberly Gonsalves
Number Employees: 100-249
Type of Packaging: Bulk

21038 Cramer Company
105 Nutmeg Rd S
South Windsor, CT 6074
877-684-6464
Fax: 860-610-0897
customer-service@mhrhodes.com
Manufacturer and exporter of motors and timers for
process control systems
President: Kenneth Mac Cormac
VP: Wayne Taylor
Director Operations: Frank Darmig
Estimated Sales: $3-5 Million
Number Employees: 5-9
Square Footage: 220000
Parent Co: Owosso Corporation
Type of Packaging: Bulk

21039 Cramer Inc
1523 Grand Blvd
Kansas City, MO 64108-1403
816-471-4433
Fax: 816-471-7188 800-366-6700
nick@cramerinc.com www.cramerinc.com
Industrial steel seating, step stools and ladders
President: Nick Christianson
nick@cramerinc.com
CEO: Jason Rann
Director Marketing: J Sanders
VP Sales/Marketing: Jeff Meyer
Director Product Development: Lee Denny
Estimated Sales: $10-20 Million
Number Employees: 10-19
Parent Co: Rotherwood Corporation

21040 Cramer Products
381 Park Ave S
New York, NY 10016-8806
212-645-2368
Fax: 212-242-6799 www.abpaonline.org
Manufacturer and exporter of temperature controlled
storage units, humidors, wire and wood storage
racks and cooling panels for wine and cheese
President: Richard Rothschild
Treasurer: Valerie Tomaselli
Vice President: Nancy Hall
Estimated Sales: Less than $500,000
Number Employees: 1-4
Brands:
    Cmc
    Cool-Kit
    Cool-Safe
    Cramarc
    Well Tempered

21041 Crandall Filling Machinery
80 Gruner Rd
Buffalo, NY 14227-1007
716-897-3486
Fax: 716-897-3488 800-280-8551
cai@conveyoraccessories.com www.crandall.com
Manufacturer and exporter of filling, packaging and
closing machinery
Owner: Scott Reed
Technician: Scott Reed
VP sales: Charles Wood
dave@crandall.com
Estimated Sales: $1-3 Million
Number Employees: 1-4
Square Footage: 16000

21042 Crane Carton Corporation
555 N Tripp Avenue
Chicago, IL 60624-1079
773-722-0555
Fax: 773-722-3510
Folding paper boxes
Estimated Sales: $20-50 Million
Number Employees: 100-249

21043 Crane Composites Inc
23525 W Eames St
Channahon, IL 60410-3220
815-467-8600
Fax: 815-467-8666 800-435-0080
sales@cranecomposites.com
www.cranecomposites.com
Fiber-reinforced composite materials.
President: Thomas Jeff Craney
Cmo: Cleve Madlock
cmadlock@cranecomposites.com
VP of Building Products: Kelly Erdmann
Eastern Regional Sales Manager: Kevin Bellinger
Western Regional Sales Manager: Chris Schamer
Number Employees: 100-249

21044 Crane Environmental
2650 Eisenhower Ave Ste 100a
Norristown, PA 19403
610-631-7700
Fax: 610-631-6800 800-633-7435
www.cranenv.com
Manufacturer and exporter of water treatment equip-
ment including reverse osmosis, demineralizers,
softeners, filters, CB pumps, deaerators and steam
specialty items
Manager: Russ Burke
Marketing Manager: Russell Burke
Purchasing Agent: Sandra Bisci
Estimated Sales: $20-30 Million
Number Employees: 1-4
Square Footage: 100000
Parent Co: Crane Company
Brands:
    Accu-Spray
    Delta
    Epro
    Spiraflow
    Uni-Mod
    Uni-Pac

21045 Crane National Vendors
12955 Enterprise Way
Bridgeton, MO 63044
314-298-0055
Fax: 314-298-3534 www.cranems.com
Tea and coffee industry dispensers
President: Brad Ellis
Contact: Anne Barks
abarks@cranems.com
Estimated Sales: $50-100 Million
Number Employees: 100-249

21046 Crane Pumps & Systems
420 Third St
Piqua, OH 45356
937-778-8947
Fax: 937-773-7157 cranepumps@cranepumps.com
www.cranepumps.com
Manufacturer and exporter of pumps for the agricul-
tural and food processing industries.
Year Founded: 1946
Estimated Sales: $100-$500 Million
Number Employees: 250-499
Square Footage: 400000
Parent Co: Crane Pumps & Systems
Brands:
    Midland
    Weinman

**21047 (HQ)Crane Research &
Engineering**
617 Regional Dr
Hampton, VA 23661-1800
757-826-1707
Fax: 757-838-3728
Crab processing, picking and cleaning machinery
Owner: John Biggs
john.biggs@craftbearing.com
Plant Manager: Dan Schrum, Jr.
Estimated Sales: $5-10 Million
Number Employees: 20-49
Square Footage: 33000
Brands:
    Quik-Pik

21048 Crate Ideas by Wilderness House
P.O.Box 675
Cave Junction, OR 97523-0675
541-592-2106
Fax: 541-592-6670 800-592-2206
Custom wooden and decorative gift crates
President: Eugene Schreiber
Sales Director: Sarah Peiffer

Estimated Sales: $1-3 Million
Number Employees: 10-19

21049 Crawford Packaging
1609 N Capitol Avenue
Indianapolis, IN 46202-1202

317-924-2494
Fax: 317-283-1817

Estimated Sales: $1-5 000,000
Number Employees: 20-49

21050 Crayex Corp
1747 Commerce Dr
Piqua, OH 45356-2601

937-773-7000
Fax: 937-773-4823 800-837-1747
crayex@crayex.com www.crayex.com
Low density polyethylene film and bags for shrink
packaging and wrapping
President: Mimi Crawford
mimi.crawford@crayex.com
Founder & CEO: Clifford R. Alexander
CFO: Lori Webster
Quality Control: Jeff Gower
Manager: Keith Killingsworth
Estimated Sales: $10-20 Million
Number Employees: 50-99
Square Footage: 180000

21051 Crc Industries Inc
885 Louis Dr
Warminster, PA 18974-2869

301-843-5226
Fax: 215-674-2196 800-556-5074
kcantwell@crcindustries.com
www.crc-industries.com
Manufacturer and exporter of cleaners, degreasers,
lubricants, corrosion inhibitors, hand cleaners, adhe-
sives and sealants; also, cleaning compound
dispensers
President & Chief Executive Officer: Dennis Conlon
Contact: Tony Arends
tony.arends@unisys.com
Estimated Sales: $91 Million
Number Employees: 10-19
Brands:
3-36
Hydroforce
Mechanix Orange
Power Lube
Screwloose
Super

21052 Cream of the Valley Plastics
5750 Lamar Street
Arvada, CO 80002

303-425-5499
Fax: 303-425-0734
Milk and juice containers
Plant Supervisor: Bart Hurley
Estimated Sales: $2.5-5 Million
Number Employees: 10-19
Parent Co: Southern Foods

21053 Creamery Plastics Products, Ltd
8989 Charles Street
Chilliwack, BC V2P 2V8
Canada

604-792-0232
Fax: 604-792-1890 www.icechiller.net
Cream and condiment dispensers; also, buffet dis-
plays and ice chillers to keep foods & beverages
chilled for many hours.
President: Lucy Vales
CEO: Tony Rapaz
Purchasing Agent: Tony Rapaz
Number Employees: 4

21054 Creative Automation
5404 Jedmed Court
Saint Louis, MO 63129-2221

800-745-9539
Fax: 314-845-7779

Contact: Paul Habinstript
ph@creative-automation.com

21055 Creative Automation
61 Willet St Ste 3b
Passaic, NJ 7055

973-778-0061
Fax: 973-614-8336

Manufacturer and exporter of automatic feeders, bar
code verification equipment, turnkey systems, leaflet
inserters and outserters, vertical, form, fill and seal
equipment
President: John Calabrese
jcalabrese@creative-auto.com
CEO: John Bartlo
VP: John Calabrese
Estimated Sales: $1-2.5 Million
Number Employees: 1-4

21056 Creative Canopy Design
4272 Columbus Dr
Hernando Beach, FL 34607

866-970-5200
Fax: 303-424-0172 866-970-5200
Portable canopies/shade structures, commercial
tents, banner flags, screen printing and dyesub print-
ing.
Owner: Laura Uribe

21057 Creative Coatings Corporation
28 Charron Avenue
1165
Nashua, NH 03063-1783

603-889-8040
Fax: 603-889-3780 800-229-1957
flocking@aol.com
Packaging materials including laminated vinyls,
metallized barrier and pressure sensitive films, etc.;
importer of bakery and confectionery mixers and
homogenizers
CEO: Robert Borowski
Customer Service Manager: Barbara Landry
Number Employees: 5
Square Footage: 20000

21058 Creative Converting Inc
255 Spring St
Clintonville, WI 54929-1159

715-823-3104
Fax: 715-823-5232 800-826-0418
www.creativeconverting.com
Paper table cloths, napkins, plates and cups
CEO: Rory Leyden
rory.leyden@creativeconverting.com
Estimated Sales: $50-100 Million
Number Employees: 100-249
Square Footage: 105000
Parent Co: Hoffmaster Group, Inc.
Brands:
Every Occasion

21059 Creative Cookie
8673 Commerce Dr
Suite 7
Easton, MD 21601

410-819-0091
Fax: 410-819-0255 800-451-4005
www.creativecookieetc.com
Manufacturer and exporter of themed fortune cook-
ies and candy boxes
Owner: Marty Schwartz
Vice President: Joan Schwartz
General Manager: Martin Schwartz
Estimated Sales: Less than $500,000
Number Employees: 1-4
Number of Products: 80
Type of Packaging: Consumer, Food Service, Pri-
vate Label, Bulk
Brands:
A World of Good Fortune
Anniversary
Baseball Trivia
Bible Verse
Birthday
Calling Card
Christmas
Congratulations!
Doctor's
Easter
Executive
For Kid's Only
Get Well
Golfer's
Halloween
Holiday Greetings
Housewarming
Irish
It's a Baby!
Italian
Jewish
Millenium Message
Mother's Day

Movie Trivia
Naughty But Nice!
Over the Hill
Romantic
Sports Trivia
Teachers
Thank You
Trivia
Valentine
Wedding
Year 2000
You're the Greatest!

21060 Creative Enterprises
12 Rochelle Drive
Kendall Park, NJ 08824-1405

732-422-0300
Fax: 732-422-0008
Platforms, point of purchase and store displays,
dump tables and cabinets
President: S Y Goldberg
Estimated Sales: Below $5 Million
Number Employees: 2

21061 Creative Essentials
2155 5th Ave
Ronkonkoma, NY 11779-6908

631-467-8370
Fax: 631-467-4255 800-355-5891
sales@menudesigns.com
Manufacturer and exporter of menu covers, acrylic
stands, placemats, recipe holders, menus and check
presenters
President: Allen Fischer
Sales Manager: Jonathan Sunshine
Sales: Karen Chalson
Number Employees: 20-49
Square Footage: 64000

21062 Creative Foam Corp
300 N Alloy Dr
Fenton, MI 48430-2649

810-629-4149
Fax: 810-629-7368 www.creativefoam.com
Manufacturer and exporter of packaging and mate-
rial handling systems
President: David Swallow
daswallow@creativefoam.com
Sales Manager: David Rosser
Estimated Sales: $20-50 Million
Number Employees: 100-249
Type of Packaging: Bulk

21063 Creative Forming
PO Box 128
Ripon, WI 54971-0128

920-748-7285
Fax: 920-748-9466 www.creativeforming.com
Manufacturer and exporter of thermoformed plastic
trays
President: Glen Yurjevich
General Manager: John Beard
Estimated Sales: $20-50 Million
Number Employees: 100-249
Parent Co: Wellman
Type of Packaging: Consumer, Food Service, Bulk

21064 Creative Impressions
7697 9th St
Buena Park, CA 90621-2898

714-521-4441
Fax: 714-522-2733 800-524-5278
email@emenucovers.com
Clear and soft plastic menu covers in 30 colors and
textures; also, inserts available
President: Marc Abbott
email@emenucovers.com
Estimated Sales: $5-10 Million
Number Employees: 20-49

21065 Creative Industries Inc
1024 Western Dr
Indianapolis, IN 46241-1437

317-248-2068
Fax: 317-247-4953 800-776-2068
mike.clark@creativeind.com www.creativeind.com
Pass- and talk-thru, plastic laminated and bulletproof
windows
President: Mark Clark
Estimated Sales: Below $5 Million
Number Employees: 5-9
Type of Packaging: Private Label

21066 Creative Label Designers
3890 SW Harbor Drive
Lees Summit, MO 64082-4679
816-537-8757
Fax: 816-537-8757
Pressure sensitive printed and thermal bar code labels
President: Dale G Wheat
Number Employees: 4
Square Footage: 8000

21067 Creative Mobile SystemsInc
189 Adams St
Manchester, CT 06042-1919
860-649-6272
Fax: 860-643-2830 800-646-8364
cms189@ntplx.net www.hotdog325.com
Catering trucks, hot dog carts and concession trailers
President: Brian Smith
rlumpkin@cmsc.com
CFO: Mary Davis
VP: Richard Lumpkin
VP: Richard Lumpkin
Purchasing Manager: John Izzo
Estimated Sales: Below $5 Million
Number Employees: 1-4
Square Footage: 24000
Brands:
   Cms, Inc.

21068 Creative Packaging
2249 Davis Ct
Hayward, CA 94545-1113
510-785-6500
Fax: 510-785-6349
www.cpccreativepackaging.com
Wooden crates and containers including corrugated, foam, urethane and styrofoam
Owner: Jim Oliver
jim@ivccreativepackaging.com
General Manager: J Hunter
Estimated Sales: $5-10 Million
Number Employees: 10-19
Square Footage: 190000

21069 Creative Packaging Corporation
700 Corporate Grove Dr
Buffalo Grove, IL 60089
847-459-1001
Fax: 847-325-3919
Manufacturer and exporter of dispensing closures
President: John Weeks
CFO: Mike Farreoo
Quality Control: Samantha Gibson
VP Sales/Marketing: Jeff Teth
Corporate Manager: Robert Giles
Estimated Sales: $50-75 Million
Number Employees: 10
Square Footage: 1100000
Parent Co: Courtesy Corporation
Brands:
   Shear Pak
   Sports Cap

21070 Creative Printing Co
200 Lakewood Cir
Burr Ridge, IL 60527-6340
630-734-3244
www.creativeprinting.net
Menus
Owner: Rick Styfer
Estimated Sales: $500,000-$1 Million
Number Employees: 10-19

21071 Creative Signage System
9101 51st Place
College Park, MD 20740
301-345-3700
Fax: 301-220-0289 800-220-7446
creative@creativesignage.com
www.creativesignage.com
Plastic signs
President: John Mayer
Sales: Peter Van Allen
Estimated Sales: $2.5-5 Million
Number Employees: 20-49

21072 Creative Storage Systems
2700 Barr Lks Blvd NW Ste 500
Kennesaw, GA 30144
770-514-0711
Fax: 770-514-0622 888-370-8810
marketing@creativestorage.com
www.creativestorage.com
High density dynamic warehouse storage systems, conveyors/gravity, flow-through pallet systems, pallets/racks, racks/storage, storage
President: Robert Lawless
Estimated Sales: $10-20 000,000
Number Employees: 20-49

21073 Creative Techniques
2441 N Opdyke Rd
Auburn Hills, MI 48326
248-373-3050
Fax: 248-373-3458 800-473-0284
www.creativetechniques.com
Manufacturer and exporter of packaging and material handling products
President: Richard Yeakey
Sales Manager: Stanley Shore
Contact: Joe Banfield
banfieldj@creativetechniques.com
Estimated Sales: $20-50 Million
Number Employees: 100-249

21074 Creegan Animation Company
508 Washington St
Steubenville, OH 43952-2140
740-283-3708
Fax: 740-283-4117
Manufacturer and exporter of animations, costume characters and audio-animatronics
Owner: George Creegan
Contact: Sandy Baumgard
sandy.baumgard@creegans.com
Estimated Sales: $1-5 Million
Number Employees: 20-49

21075 Creekstone Farms Premium Beef
604 Goff Industrial Park Rd
PO Box 869
Arkansas City, KS 67005-8880
620-741-3100
Fax: 620-741-3353 www.creekstonefarms.com
Their own line of Creekstone Farms Natural and Premium Black Angus Beef marketed under the USDA Process-Verified Tender Beef label.
President: John Stewart
Genetics Division: Joe Bill Meng
Bull and Semen Sales: Danny Rankin
Feeder Calf Program: Ryan Meyer
Natural Beef Program: Matt Bode
Number Employees: 500-999
Type of Packaging: Food Service

21076 Crepas & Associates
15w725 Virginia Lane
Elmhurst, IL 60126-1259
630-833-4880
Fax: 630-833-0580
Consultant providing structural engineering services for facility renovations new contruction renovation specialize in floors concrete and epoxy
President: Robert Crepas
Estimated Sales: Less than $500,000
Number Employees: 4

21077 Cres Cor
5925 Heisley Rd
Mentor, OH 44060-1833
440-350-1100
Fax: 440-350-7267 877-273-7267
www.crescor.com
A complete line of quality mobile food service equipment including hot cabinets, utility cabinets and racks, banquet cabinets, dish dollies, ovens and more. Since 1936...There is no equal.
President: Clifford D Baggott
cbaggott@crescor.com
VP: Rio DeGennaro
Director of Engineering: Heather Stewart
Sales/Marketing Director: Michael Capretta
Number Employees: 100-249
Brands:
   Cres Cor

21078 Cresco Food Technologies
717 2nd Ave SE
Cresco, IA 52136-1703
563-547-4241
Fax: 563-547-4504 cft@iowatelecom.net
www.aveka.com
Nutraceutical and food processing facility.
Manager: John Anderson
john_@iowatelecom.net
Number Employees: 50-99
Parent Co: Aveka, Inc.

21079 Crespac Incorporated
5032 N Royal Atlanta Drive
Tucker, GA 30084
770-938-1900
Fax: 770-939-4900 800-438-1900
info@crespac.com
Disposable thermoformed food trays and containers; exporter of produce and food containers
CEO: Jeff Moon
Estimated Sales: $5-10 Million
Number Employees: 50-99
Square Footage: 400000
Brands:
   Big Green

21080 Cresset Chemical Company
One Cresset Center
PO Box 367
Weston, OH 43569
419-669-2041
Fax: 419-669-2200 800-367-2020
cresset@cresset.com www.cresset.com
Manufacturer and exporter of hand cleaners, release agents and admixtures
President: Mike Baty
CFO: Roger Davis
Vice President: Mike Baty
Quality Control: Rick Reynolds
Inside Sales Representative: Shanelle Scott
Estimated Sales: Below $5 Million
Number Employees: 10
Brands:
   Crete-Lease
   Crete-Trete
   Han-D
   Sol-Zol
   Spatter-Cote
   Super Strip
   Super-Trete

21081 Crest Foods Inc
905 Main St.
Ashton, IL 61006
877-273-7893
www.crestfoods.com
Established in 1941. Processor of food ingredients including emulsifying agents, proteins, caseinates, whey, stabilizers and flavors for dips, bases and seasonings; contract packaging available
President: Jeff Meiners
VP of Corporate Sales: Steve Meiners
VP Manufacturing: Mike Meiners
Contact: Rebecca Henson
bhenson@crestfoods.com
Estimated Sales: $20-50 Million
Number Employees: 250-499
Type of Packaging: Consumer, Food Service, Private Label

21082 Cresthill Industries
196 Ashburton Ave
Yonkers, NY 10701-4001
914-965-9510
Fax: 914-965-9534 www.whereorg.com
Manufacturer and exporter of bag closures
President: Christopher Rie
Treasurer: J Rie
Contact: Rhoda Needelman
rhoda@cresthillindustries.com
Estimated Sales: $10-20 Million
Number Employees: 50-99
Parent Co: Cresthill Industries
Brands:
   Kisco Bip

21083 Crestware
520 N Redwood Rd
PO Box 540210
North Salt Lake, UT 84054-2747
801-292-0656
Fax: 801-295-5732 800-345-0513
sales@crestware.com www.crestware.com
Manufacturer and importer of china, flatware, steamtable pans, chafers, pots, pans, smallwares, thermometers and scales
President: Hal Harrison
Vice President: Julie Jackson
jjackson@crestware.com
VP Marketing: Stephen Jordan
VP Operations: Greg Harrison
Estimated Sales: $10-20 Million
Number Employees: 10-19
Square Footage: 160000

Brands:
  Crestware

21084 Cretel Food Equipment
303 Little Station Road
Holland, MI 49424-2618

616-786-3980
Fax: 616-786-0299

Bags for beef, ham, bacon and sausage; films, laminates, flexible packages, vacuum packaging materials and equipment, processing equipment, skinning machines, fish processing equipment, plant layout and product flow
Owner: James Smith
Estimated Sales: $1-3 Million
Number Employees: 5
Number of Brands: 4
Number of Products: 10
Type of Packaging: Consumer, Food Service

21085 Cretorr
3243 N California Ave
Chicago, IL 60618-5890

773-588-1690
Fax: 773-588-2171 800-228-1885
marketing@cretors.com www.cretors.com

Popcorn machines
President: Charles D Cretors
Quality Control: Wally Krzak
Vice President of Sales and Marketing: Shelly Olesen
Estimated Sales: $10-20 Million
Number Employees: 100-249

21086 Crippen Manufacturing Co
400 Woodside Dr
St Louis, MI 48880-1057

989-681-4323
Fax: 989-681-3818 800-872-2474
www.crippenmfg.com

Grain separators, polishers and conveyors
President: Darren Losey
darrenl@crippenmfg.com
System Technician: Daniel Kelley
CFO: Shane Gascho
V P/Sales: Douglas Clark
V P and Mktg: Kevin Kennedy
Conveying and Systems Product Mgr: Jerry Valch
Density Specialist: William Donnell
New Equipment Sales: Kevin Vogt
Customer Service: Kevin Vogt
Design Eng'r /Air Screen Equipment: James Strawder
Design Eng'r/Density Equipment: Robert Gilbert
Materials Mgr: Darren Losey
Product Specialist: Steve Galgoczi
Estimated Sales: $1-2.5 Million
Number Employees: 20-49
Square Footage: 260000

21087 Crisci Food Equipment Company
P.O.Box 8327
New Castle, PA 16107-8327

724-654-6609
Fax: 724-654-9266

Stainless steel food services equipment, ladders, step stools and conveyors
President: Sally Firmi
Estimated Sales: $2.5-5 000,000
Number Employees: 10-19

21088 Crispy Lite
10 Sunnen Drive
St. Louis, MO 63143-3800

775-689-5700
Fax: 314-781-5445 888-356-5362
clientcare@wellsbloomfield.com
www.wellsbloomfield.com

Manufacturer and exporter of display cases, filters, pressure fryers, fans, hoods and food warmers
Vice President, Sales/Marketing, Wells-B: Paul Angrick
VP Sales/Marketing: David Moore
Mngr: D Joseph Lambert
Number Employees: 250-499
Square Footage: 248000
Parent Co: Wells Bloomfield Company
Type of Packaging: Food Service

21089 Critzas Industries Inc
4041 Park Ave Frnt
St Louis, MO 63110-2391

314-773-8510
Fax: 314-773-4837 800-537-1418
goop@earthlink.net www.goophandcleaner.com

Manufacturer and exporter of premium waterless hand cleaner.
President/Treasurer: John Critzas
Contact: Gerald Pogue
critzas@aol.com
Estimated Sales: $10-20 Million
Number Employees: 10-19
Square Footage: 120000
Brands:
  Goop

21090 Criveller East
6935 Oakwood Drive
Niagara Falls, ON L2E 6S5
Canada

905-357-2930
Fax: 905-374-2930 888-894-2266
info@criveller.com www.criveller.com

President: Mario Criiveller
CFO: Jim Farlane
Number Employees: 10

21091 Croll Reynolds Inc
6 Campus Dr # 5
Suite 1
Parsippany, NJ 07054-4406

908-232-4200
Fax: 908-232-2146

Manufacturer and exporter of food processing machinery including combined evactor/condenser/liquid ring vaccum, vapor recovery and vacuum cooling systems and ejectors
Vice President: Philip Reynolds
preynolds@croll.com
CEO: Samuel W. Croll
CEO: Samuel W Croll Iii
Division Manager: Henry Hage
Plant Manager: Ellis Production/Shipping
Estimated Sales: $5-10 Million
Number Employees: 20-49
Brands:
  Chill-Vactor
  Core-Chill
  Evactor
  Rotajector
  Scrub-Vactor

21092 Croll-Reynolds Engineering Company
2400 Reservoir Ave
Trumbull, CT 06611-4793

203-371-1983
Fax: 203-371-0615 creco@att.net

Design and manufacture backwashable, liquid pressure, tubular element polishing type filters and strainers.
President/CEO: John Quinlan
Sales Manager: Louis Ancillai
Estimated Sales: $200,000
Number Employees: 3
Number of Brands: 3
Number of Products: 3
Square Footage: 10000
Brands:
  Clarite
  Flexodisc
  Flexoleed

21093 Crompton Corporation
One American Lane
Greenwich, CT 06831-2560

203-573-2000
Fax: 203-552-2010 800-295-2392

Chemical ingredients and food additives
Chairman/ President/ CEO: Craig A. Rogerson
CFO/ SVP: Stephen C. Forsyth
VP/ Corporate Controller/ Principal Acco: Laurence Orton
Global Market Manager: Bob Ruckle
Sales Director: Rick Beitel
Contact: Paul Ellis
paul.ellis@chemtura.com
Number Employees: 20-49

21094 Crosfield Company
111 Ingalls Ave
Joliet, IL 60435-4373

815-727-3651
Fax: 815-774-2804 www.ineossilicas.com

Manufacturer and exporter of silicon dioxide gels and precipitates; also, silica hydrogel
Plant Manager: Pat Murphy
Estimated Sales: $1-5 Million
Number Employees: 100-249
Brands:
  Gasil
  Neosyl

21095 Crossroads Espresso
P.O.Box 23610
Eugene, OR 97402

541-344-4600
Fax: 541-344-8992

Espresso parts and espresso machines
President: James Glang
Contact: Susan Schultheis
sue@crossroads-espresso.com
Estimated Sales: $1-5 000,000
Number Employees: 10-19

21096 Crosswind Foods
P.O.Box 29
Sabetha, KS 66534

785-284-3462
Fax: 785-284-3940 www.crosswindindustries.com

Contract food manufacturing
President: Ken Matson
Vice President: Bob Niehues
Quality Control: Gary Lierz
Plant Manager: Chris Shelly
Estimated Sales: $5-10 000,000
Number Employees: 20-49
Type of Packaging: Consumer, Private Label, Bulk
Other Locations:
  Crosswind Industries
  Kansas City MO

21097 Crouch Dairy Supply
305 S Main St
Fort Worth, TX 76104-1226

817-332-2118
Fax: 817-332-6511 800-825-1110
k.kertis@crouchinc.com www.crouchinc.com

Distribution of process and refrigeration equipment, supplies and services
Vice President: Mike Davis
Vice President: Mike Davis
Sales: Karyn Kertis
Number Employees: 10-19

21098 Crouse-Hinds
1201 Wolf St
Syracuse, NY 13208

Fax: 315-477-5179 866-764-5454
crousecustomerctr@eaton.com
www.cooperindustries.com/content/public/en/crouse-hinds.html

Manufacturer and exporter of outdoor and emergency lighting
President/Owner: Scott Hearn
Estimated Sales: $135 Million
Number Employees: 1,300
Parent Co: Eaton

21099 Crouzet Corporation
3237 Commander Drive
Carrollton, TX 75006-2506

972-620-7713
Fax: 972-250-3865 800-677-5311
www.crouzet.com

Manufacturer and exporter of OEM products for packaging and processing equipment: timers, proximity sensors, counters, control relays, solid state relays and temperature controllers
President: Gerald Vincent
VP Marketing: Phillipe Dubois
Contact: Rosemary Martinez
martinezr@us.crouzet.com
Estimated Sales: $20-50 Million
Number Employees: 100-249
Parent Co: Crouzet
Brands:
  Crouzet
  Gordos
  Syrelec

21100 Crown Battery Mfg
1445 Majestic Dr
Fremont, OH 43420-9190
419-334-7181
Fax: 419-334-7416 800-487-2879
www.crownbattery.com
Manufacturer and exporter of industrial batteries
used in lift trucks and food service equipment
President: Hal Hawk
Senior VP: Bill Bessire
bbessire@crownbattery.com
Director Marketing: Mark Kelley
Estimated Sales: $20-50 Million
Number Employees: 250-499
Square Footage: 200000

21101 Crown Chemical Products
6125 Netherhart Road
Mississauga, ON L5T 1G5
Canada
905-564-0904
Fax: 905-564-0906 crownchemical@bellnet.ca
Sanitation and janitorial chemicals including hand
cleaners, degreasers, disinfectants, deodorants,
plumbing and carpet chemicals, etc.; custom
blending available
President: Keith Chan
Quality Control: Annie Chan
Number Employees: 10
Square Footage: 30000
Type of Packaging: Food Service, Private Label

21102 Crown Closures Machinery
1765 W Fair Ave
Lancaster, OH 43130-2325
740-681-6593
Fax: 740-681-6527 sheila.heath@crowncork.com
www.crowncork.com
Capping/sealing equipment since 1913. Formerly
known as Anchor Hocking Packaging. Member of
Crown Cork and Seal family of corporations. Preci-
sion CNC machining capabilities. Machine building
and rebuilding
CAO: Amanda Marutz
amanda.marutz@crowncork.com
Operations Manager: Sheila Heath
Plant Manager: Ed Schott
Purchasing Manager: Greg Henwood
Estimated Sales: Below $5 Million
Number Employees: 20-49
Square Footage: 192000
Parent Co: Crown Cork & Seal

21103 Crown Controls Inc.
2316 Crown Point Executive Drive
Charlotte, NC 28227
704-841-1622
Fax: 704-841-1655 800-541-7874
crowncontrols@windstream.net
www.crowncontrols.com
Manufacturer and exporter of level controls and
open channel flow meters; also, food processing
equipment
President: Charles Stevens
Number Employees: 20-49
Brands:
  Capaciagage
  Sonargage
  Sonarswitch

21104 Crown Cork & Seal Co Inc
1 Crown Way
Philadelphia, PA 19154-4599
215-698-5100
Fax: 215-698-5201 www.crowncork.com
Metal cans
CEO: John W Conway
john.conway@crowncork.com
Sales Department: Bill Keith
Number Employees: 100-249

21105 Crown Custom Metal Spinning
1-176 Creditstone Road
Concord, ON L4K 4H7
Canada
416-243-0112
Fax: 416-243-0112 800-750-1924
sales@crowncookware.ca www.crowncookware.ca
Manufacturer and exporter of bakery racks and aluminum cookware including stockpots and cake and
pizza pans; importer of stainless steel mixing bowls

President: David P Vella
CFO: Franco Mazzuca
Customer Service: Carmen D'Cruze
Administrator: Gilda Leib
Number Employees: 10
Square Footage: 80000
Type of Packaging: Consumer, Food Service, Bulk

21106 Crown Equipment Corp.
44 S. Washington St.
New Bremen, OH 45869
419-629-2311
Fax: 419-629-2900 www.crown.com
Lift trucks.
Chairman/Chief Executive Officer: James Dicke
President: James Dicke
VP: Keith Sinram
Senior Vice President: James Mozer
Senior Vice President: Timothy Quellhorst
Senior Vice President: John Tate
Vice President, Sales: Christopher Rahe
Vice President, Engineering: Steven Dues
Vice President, Design: Michael Gallagher
Vice President, Manufacturing Operations: David
Beddow
Year Founded: 1945
Estimated Sales: $3.48 Billion
Number Employees: 16,100

21107 Crown Holdings, Inc.
770 Township Line Rd.
Yardley, PA 19067
215-698-5100
ir@crowncork.com
www.crowncork.com
Bottle caps, can tops, crowns and cans including tin,
beer and ale; also, bottling machinery
Chairman: John Conway
President/CEO: Timothy Donahue
Senior VP/CFO: Thomas Kelly
VP/Treasurer: Kevin Clothier
Executive VP/COO: Gerard Gifford
Year Founded: 1892
Estimated Sales: $11.7 Billion
Number Employees: 33,000
Type of Packaging: Consumer, Food Service, Pri-
  vate Label, Bulk
Other Locations:
  Crown Cork & Seal Co.
  Apopka FL

21108 Crown Industries
155 N Park St
East Orange, NJ 7017
973-672-2277
Fax: 973-672-7536 877-747-2457
www.4rails.com
Furniture including railings and fittings: brass; also,
crowd control stanchion and ropes; tables, easels
and dance floors
President: Gene Loebner
VP: Mario Camerota
Contact: Mario Camerota
mario.camerota@crowncork.com
VP: Carmen Ware
Estimated Sales: $500,000-$1 Million
Number Employees: 5-9
Square Footage: 56000

21109 (HQ)Crown Iron Works Company
2500 County Road C W # A
Roseville, MN 55113-2523
651-639-8900
Fax: 651-639-8051 888-703-7500
sales@crowniron.com www.crowniron.com
Manufacturer and exporter of oil extractors, oil/fat
processing systems and dryer/cooler systems.
Product Sales Manager: Richard Ozer
General Manager: Bill Antilla
Estimated Sales: $1-5 Million
Number Employees: 50-99
Brands:
  Crown
  Wurster & Sanger

21110 Crown Jewels Marketing
423 W Fallbrook Ave # 203
Suite 204
Fresno, CA 93711-6138
559-438-2335
Fax: 559-438-2341
mail@crownjewelsproduce.com
www.crownjewelsproduce.com

President: Rob Mathias
robm@crownjewelsmarketing.com
Sales: Rob Mathias
Administration: Danell Wright
Estimated Sales: $5-10 Million
Number Employees: 20-49

21111 Crown Label Company
663 Young Street
Santa Ana, CA 92750
714-557-3830
Fax: 714-557-0401 800-422-3590
sales@crownlabel.com www.crownlabel.com
Labels, decals and tags; also, silk screening avail-
able
Owner: Gary Siposs
Estimated Sales: $1-2,500,000
Number Employees: 10-19

21112 Crown Manufacturing Corporation
147 Cross Rd
Waterford, CT 06385-1216
860-442-4325
Fax: 860-442-9658
Cabinets and boxes
President: David Parker
crownmanufacturing@snet.net
Estimated Sales: $1-2.5 Million
Number Employees: 5 to 9
Type of Packaging: Bulk

21113 Crown Marking
1000 Boone Ave. N.
Suite 680
Minneapolis, MN 55427
763-543-8243
Fax: 800-488-4034 800-305-5249
sales@crownmarking.com
www.crownmarking.com
Stamps, stamp pads and name plates, signs and ID
badges
CEO: Gregg Prest
VP: Thomas Knauer
Contact: Karen Prest
kprest@crownmarking.com
Estimated Sales: $1-2.5 Million
Number Employees: 5-9
Square Footage: 9200
Brands:
  Bates
  Cosco
  X-Stamper

21114 Crown Metal Manufacturing Company
765 South State
Route 83
Elmhurst, IL 60126-4228
630-279-9800
Fax: 630-279-9807 ca-sales@crownmetal.com
www.crownmetal.com
Manufacturer and exporter of store fixtures includ-
ing wall standards, brackets, showcase hardware and
sign holders
Manager: Mike Volosin
Operations Manager: Mike Volosin
Estimated Sales: Less than $500,000
Number Employees: 1-4
Parent Co: Crown Metal

21115 (HQ)Crown Metal Mfg Co
8768 Hellman Ave
Rancho Cucamonga, CA 91730-4418
909-291-8585
Fax: 909-291-8587 ca-sales@crownmetal.com
www.crownmetal.com
Manufacturer and exporter of metal store fixtures,
pegboard equipment and sign holders
Manager: Mike Volosin
Vice President: Glenn Dalglerish
Research & Development: Steve Varon
Sales Director: Scott Durham
Manager: Chris Montoya
cmontoya@crownmetal.com
Production Manager: Wayne Baker
Estimated Sales: Less Than $500,000
Number Employees: 1-4
Number of Brands: 8
Number of Products: 500
Square Footage: 340000
Type of Packaging: Bulk

Other Locations:
    Crown Metal Manufacturing Co.
    Rancho Cucamonga CA

21116 Crown Packaging
17854 Chesterfield Airport Road
Chesterfield, MO 63005
636-681-8000
Fax: 636-681-9600 800-883-9400
www.crownpack.com
Wholesaler/distributor of packaging machinery and
materials
Estimated Sales: $70 Million
Number Employees: 95
Square Footage: 18800
Other Locations:
    Atlanta GA
    Baltimore MD
    Baton Rouge LA
    Boston MA
    Charlotte NC
    Cincinnatti OH
    Cleveland OH
    Dallas/Ft. Worth TX
    Des Moines IA
    Evansville IN
    Indianapolis IN
    Knoxville TN
    Lenexa KS

21117 Crown Plastics Inc
12615 16th Ave N
Minneapolis, MN 55441-4609
763-557-6000
Fax: 763-557-6638 800-423-2769
www.crystalpalacecupcaketree.com
Tea and coffee industry dispensers; whisper blend
sound enclosures.
CEO: Tom Van Beusekon
Estimated Sales: $2.5-5 000,000
Number Employees: 20-49
Number of Brands: 1
Number of Products: 1
Square Footage: 30000
Type of Packaging: Food Service, Bulk

21118 Crown Steel Mfg
177 Newport Dr # A
San Marcos, CA 92069-1470
760-471-1188
Fax: 760-471-1189 info@crownsteelmfg.net
www.crownsteelmfg.net
Kitchen and restaurant equipment including tables
and sinks
President: Dave Carr
carrdj@pacbell.net
VP: David Carr
Estimated Sales: $3-5 Million
Number Employees: 20-49
Square Footage: 80000

21119 Crown Tonka Walk-Ins
15600 37th Ave N # 100
Minneapolis, MN 55446-3204
763-541-1410
Fax: 763-541-1563 800-523-7337
sales@crowntonka.com www.crowntonka.com
Manufacturer and exporter of walk-in coolers and
freezers
President: Mike Kahler
mikek@crowntonka.com
Senior Vice President Sales & Marketing: Greg
Sullens
Estimated Sales: $5-10 Million
Number Employees: 50-99
Type of Packaging: Consumer, Food Service

21120 Crown Verity
37 Adams Boulevard
Brantford, ON N3S 7V8
Canada
519-751-1800
Fax: 519-751-1802 888-505-7240
info@crownverity.com www.crownverity.com
Manufacturer and exporter of stainless steel barbe-
cues
President: William Verity
Founder: Bill Verity
CFO: Tracy McIngrrey
Quality Control: Allan Frennett
R & D: William Verity
Sales Manager: John Foulger
Number Employees: 10
Square Footage: 48000
Brands:
    Chef's Choice

21121 Crown-Simplimatic
1200 S Newkirk Street
Baltimore, MD 21224-5308
410-563-6700
Fax: 410-563-6782

21122 Crownlite Manufacturing Corporation
1546 Ocean Ave
Bohemia, NY 11716-1916
631-589-9100
Fax: 631-589-4584
Manufacturer and exporter of fluorescent and HID
lighting fixtures and supplies; specializing in super-
market lighting
President: William Siegel
Sales Executive: Lois Carbonaro
Sales Manager: C Longo
Estimated Sales: $5-10 Million
Number Employees: 50 to 99

21123 Crucible Chemical Co
10 Crucible Ct
Greenville, SC 29605-5411
864-277-1284
Fax: 864-299-1192 800-845-8873
www.cruciblechemical.com
Food grade defoamers
President: Mark Chandler
markchandler.ccc@gmail.com
Assistant to the President: Kathryn Stroud
Lab Manager: Danny Hawkins
Estimated Sales: $10-20 Million
Number Employees: 20-49
Brands:
    Foamkill

21124 Crunch Time Information Systems
129 Portland Street
Boston, MA 02114
857-202-3000
www.crunchtime.com
Purchasing and inventory control information sys-
tems
President: Bill Bellissimo
Chief Operating Officer: David Daugherty
Vice President of Client Services: Jean Fogarty
VP, Prodcut Development: James Krawcynski
Director of Marketing: Chris Bauer
Sales Manager: Michelle Bullock
Contact: Elizabeth Russo
erusso@crunchtime.com
Chief Operating Officer: David Daugherty
Estimated Sales: $500,000-$1 Million
Number Employees: 1-4

21125 Cruvinet Winebar Co LLC
610 S Rock Blvd # 115
Sparks, NV 89431-8118
775-827-4044
Fax: 800-873-7894 800-278-8463
info@cruvinetsys.com www.cruvinetsys.com
Manufacturer, importer and exporter of wine dis-
pensing/preserving systems, nitrogen-based preserv-
ing systems and wine storage cases; also, service,
repair and preventative maintenance for all makes
and models of wine dispensing andcellaring systems
President/CEO: Matt Kuchnis
Vice President: Jennifer Kuchnis
Director of Sales: Matt Kuehnis
Production: Matt Kuehnis
Estimated Sales: Less Than $500,000
Number Employees: 1-4
Square Footage: 19960
Brands:
    Cruvinet Collector
    Cruvinet Estate
    Le Cavernet
    Le Grand Cruvinet
    Le Grand Cruvinet Mobile
    Le Grand Cruvinet Premier
    Le Sommelier
    Petite Sommelier
    Petite Sommelier Cruvinet
    The Cruvinet
    Ultra Cruvinet

21126 Cryochem
PO Box 20268
St Simons Island, GA 31522-8268
912-262-0033
Fax: 912-262-9990 800-237-4001
sales@cryochem.com www.cryochem.com

Manufacturer and exporter of cryogenic freezing and
chilling equipment including single and tri-deck
freezers, immersion and batch cabinets; also, cus-
tom-designed systems
Marketing Manager: Bryan Smith
General Manager: Frank Grillo
Estimated Sales: $1-5 Million
Number Employees: 18
Square Footage: 120000
Parent Co: Cryogenic Industries
Brands:
    Kryospray

21127 Cryogenic Systems Equipment
2363 136th St
Blue Island, IL 60406-3233
708-385-4216
Fax: 708-385-4390 dsink@cryobrain.com
www.cryobrain.com
Cryogenic food processing equipment, exhaust,
parts
President: Brian Sink
bsink@cryobrain.com
CFO: Devin Sink
Marketing Director: Todd Czernik
Sales Director: Brian Sink
Operations Manager: Peter Kruse
Purchasing Manager: Gary Magdziarz
Estimated Sales: $3.2 Million
Number Employees: 10-19
Number of Products: 15
Square Footage: 30

21128 Cryopak
6818 Jarry Street E
St. Leonard, QC H1P 1W3
Canada
514-324-4720
Fax: 514-324-9623 888-423-7251
bstapleton@cryopak.com www.cryopak.com
A wide range of gel packs and insulated containers
for shipping perishables
President: Maurice Barakat
VP: Raj Gill
Marketing/Sales: Bruce Stapleton
Estimated Sales: $1-5 Million

21129 Cryovac
2415 Cascade Pointe Blvd
Charlotte, NC 28208
980-430-7000
800-391-5645
www.sealedair.com
Micro-layered shrink films.
President & CEO: Ted Doheny
SVP & Chief Commercial Officer: Karl Deily
VP & Chief Human Resources Officer: Susan
Edwards
VP & Chief Human Resources Officer: Angel Willis
SVP & Chief Strategy Officer: Sergio Pupkin
SVP & Chief Financial Officer: Jim Sullivan
SVP & Chief Supply Chain Officer: Emile
Chammas
Estimated Sales: K
Number Employees: 10-19
Parent Co: Sealed Air Corp

21130 Crystal Chem Inc.
1536 Brook Dr
Suite A
Downers Grove, IL 60515
630-889-9003
Fax: 630-889-9021 sales@crystalchem.com
www.crystalchem.com
Food allergen and vitamin kits for easy to use detec-
tion of allergens in both raw and processed food.
President: Priyavadan Shah
VP: Hema Shah
Safety Manager: Robert Kyle
Sales Manager: Sachin Shah
Contact: Dawn Conklin
dawn@crystalchem.com
Estimated Sales: $3 Million

21131 Crystal Creative Products
PO Box 450
Middletown, OH 45042
513-423-0731
Fax: 513-423-0516 800-776-6762
Manufacturer, importer and exporter of tissue in-
cluding wrapping and industrial

President: James Akers
Vice President: John Crider
Sales Director: Ed Miller
Purchasing Manager: Randy Clark
Estimated Sales: $20-50 Million
Number Employees: 100-249
Brands:
    Crystal
    Crystalized
    Fantasy Wrap
    Radiant Wrap
    Tiara

21132 Crystal Lake Mfg Inc
2225 Highway 14 W
Autaugaville, AL 36003-2541

    334-365-3342
Fax: 334-365-3332 800-633-8720
customerservice@crystallakemfg.com
www.homeworkclean.com
Manufacturer and exporter of brooms, mops and handles
President: James Pearson
james.pearson@crystallakemfg.com
Chairman: Theresa Dunn
Chairman the Board: Theresa Dunn
Sales Director: Ron Poole
Estimated Sales: $10-20 Million
Number Employees: 100-249
Square Footage: 406000
Type of Packaging: Consumer, Food Service, Private Label, Bulk
Brands:
    Crystal Lake

21133 Crystal-Flex Packaging Corporation
10 Oxford Road
Rockville Centre, NY 11570-2122

    770-218-3556
Fax: 732-967-9839 888-246-7325
sales@crystalflex.com www.crystalflex.com
Manufacturer and exporter of polyethylene bags, plastic and barrier film, food packaging, pouches and laminations
President: Lesley Craig Litt
Number Employees: 6
Brands:
    Flexbarrier
    Oven Pak

21134 Crystal-Vision Packaging Systems
23870 Hawthorne Blvd
Torrance, CA 90505-5908

    310-373-6057
Fax: 310-373-6157 800-331-3240
don@crystalvisionpkg.com
www.crystalvisionpkg.com
Shrink film; printed shrink labels; dry food weigh/fill machines; packaging machines and bag sealers; food bags; & printed stand-up food bags.
President/CEO/CFO: Donald Hilmer
Quality Control: Emilio Diaz
Sales: Karl Behrens
Contact: Mark Bayless
mbayless@drbayless.com
General Manager: Jeff Hilmer
Purchasing: Bernie Johnson
Estimated Sales: $5 Million
Number Employees: 11
Square Footage: 60000
Parent Co: AID Corporation
Brands:
    Aie
    Cal Vac
    Crystal Vision
    Curwocd
    Good Year
    Multivac

21135 Cube Plastics
190 Maplecrete Road
Concord, Ontario, ON L4K 2B6
Canada

    905-669-8669
Fax: 905-669-8646 877-260-2823
Microwavable food containers in a variety of sizes.

21136 Cucamonga Sign Shop LLC
9223 Archibald Ave # A
Rancho Cucamonga, CA 91730-5237
    909-945-5888
Fax: 909-941-7395 www.signshopofrc.com

Custom vinyl banners, wood and metal signs, name plates, labels, etc.; also, screen printing and lettering services available
Owner: Andy Megaw
sales@signshopofrc.com
Estimated Sales: Less Than $500,000
Number Employees: 1-4
Brands:
    The Bob-O-Bear

21137 Cuerden Sign Co
PO Box 187
Conway, AR 72033-0187

    501-375-7705
Fax: 501-327-3438 cuerden@swbell.net
Signs including interior, outdoor and electric
Owner: Jasper Burton
cuerden@nwbell.net
VP Sales: Jap Burton
Estimated Sales: $1-2.5 Million
Number Employees: 10-19
Square Footage: 20000

21138 Cugar Machine Co
3579 Mccart Ave
Fort Worth, TX 76110-4694

    817-927-0411
Fax: 817-927-0473 www.cugarmachine.com
Food processing machinery including bin dumpers, trimlines, pivot conveyors, catwalks, washing systems, onion peelers, etc
President: Gary Greene
Estimated Sales: $1-2.5 Million
Number Employees: 5-9

21139 Culicover & Shapiro
220 S Fehrway
Bay Shore, NY 11706-1208

    631-918-4560
Fax: 631-918-4561
Floor brooms and brushes
President: Richard Shapiro
Marketing: David Shaw
Estimated Sales: $500,000-$1 Million
Number Employees: 5 to 9
Square Footage: 16000

21140 Culinar
4945 Ontario Rue E
Montreal, QC H1V 1M2
Canada

    514-255-2811
Fax: 514-251-2184
Consultant providing research and development for cookies
Director Sales: Daniel Merci
Estimated Sales: $1-5 Million
Parent Co: Culinar Canada

21141 Culinart Inc
7609 Production Dr
Cincinnati, OH 45237-3208

    513-244-2999
Fax: 513-244-2555 800-333-5678
Tallow sculptures and specialty candles; also, bulk tallow in white, butter, cheddar and chocolate available
President/ Culinary Artist: Dominic Palazzolo
culinart@yahoo.com
Estimated Sales: $500,000-$1 Million
Number Employees: 1-4
Type of Packaging: Bulk

21142 Culinary Collective
12407-B Mukilteo Speedway
Suite 245
Lynnwood, WA 98087

    425-398-9761
Fax: 425-398-9765 info@culinarycollective.com
www.culinarycollective.com
Spanish and Peru foods
Co-Founder: Betsy Power
Co-Founder: Pere Selles
Sales Manager: Marion Sproul
Estimated Sales: $3-5 Million
Number Employees: 5-9

21143 (HQ)Culinary Depot
2 Melnick Dr.
Monsey, NY 10952

    Fax: 845-352-2700 888-845-8200
customerservice@culinarydepot.biz
www.culinarydepotinc.com

Kitchen and restaurant equipment, janitorial supplies, restaurant furniture and food storage and transport materials
Founder/President: Sholem Potash
CEO: Michael Lichter

21144 Culinary Papers
10 Maybrook Dr
Toronto, ON M1V 4B6
Canada

    416-757-6768
Fax: 416-757-5183
Accessories/supplies i.e. picnic baskets, cooking implements/housewares.
Marketing: Bill Benson

21145 Culligan Company
1 Culligan Parkway
Northbrook, IL 60062-6287

    847-205-6000
Fax: 847-205-6030 800-527-8637
feedback@culligan.com www.culligan.com
Manufacturer and exporter of commercial/industrial water softeners, filters, deionizers, dealkalizers and reverse osmosis units
President: Tim Tousignant
Sales Director: Doug Dickinson
Contact: Nisha Aggarwal
naggarwal@culligan.com
Estimated Sales: $35-40 Million
Number Employees: 250-500
Square Footage: 120000
Brands:
    Bruner
    Bruner-Matic
    Iqs/3
    Salt-Master

21146 Culligan International Co
9399 W Higgins Rd # 1100
Suite 1100
Rosemont, IL 60018-4940

    847-430-2800
Fax: 732-512-0166 800-231-9283
www.culligan.com
Water Systems, Water
Manager: Bob Prigen
President: Scoot Levy
Chairman: Peter Dixon
Estimated Sales: Under $500,000
Number Employees: 5000-9999
Parent Co: Culligan Water Technologies

21147 Culmac
720 Hanford St # 2
Geneseo, IL 61254

    309-944-6494
Fax: 309-944-6495
Flexographic printing presses
President: Archie Cullen
Estimated Sales: $1-2.5 000,000
Number Employees: 10-19

21148 Cumberland Box & Mill Co
215 W Elder St
Cumberland, MD 21502-4606

    301-724-1010
Fax: 301-777-0700
Wooden skids and lids
President: James L Ketterman
Estimated Sales: $1-2.5 Million
Number Employees: 5-9

21149 Cumberland Container Corp
1027 N Chestnut St
Monterey, TN 38574-1062

    931-839-2227
Fax: 931-839-3971
service@cumberlandcontainer.com
www.cumberlandcontainer.com
Corrugated containers
President: Eugene Jared
CFO: Tim Dunn
Quality Control: Patti Davis
Sales Manager: Randy Swallows
Computer: Randall Hardison
Plant Manager: Chris Landers
Estimated Sales: Less than $500,000
Number Employees: 100-249

21150 Cumberland Farms
100 Crossing Blvd
Framingham, MA 01702
781-828-4900
Fax: 781-828-9012 www.cumberlandfarms.com
Milk and ice cream
Chairman: Lily Bentas
VP: George Haseotes, Sr.
Senior VP: Don Holt
Sales Director: Barbara Paidy
Contact: Ahmed Ali
aali@cumberlandfarms.com
VP Manufacturing: Emanuel Cavaco
Number Employees: 250-499
Parent Co: Suiza Foods

21151 Cummings
PO Box 23194
Nashville, TN 37202-3194
615-673-8999
Fax: 615-782-6699
stacey.hawke@cummingssigns.com
Manufacturer and exporter of electric signs and marquees
President: Stephen R Kerr
Sr VP: Bruce Cornett
Contact: T Cummings
t.cummings@thesign.com
Executive VP National Accounts: Jerry Morrison
Estimated Sales: $20-50 Million
Number Employees: 50-99
Square Footage: 175000

21152 Cummins Label Co
2230 Glendenning Rd
Kalamazoo, MI 49001-4189
269-345-3386
Fax: 269-345-6657 800-280-7589
customerservice@cumminslabel.com
www.cumminslabel.com
Pressure sensitive labels and seals
President: Phil Nagel
pnagel@cumminslabel.com
Vice President: Kevin Nagel
Chairman: Gordon Nagle
Marketing/Sales Executive: Len Boekhoven
Estimated Sales: $5-10 Million
Number Employees: 20-49
Type of Packaging: Private Label, Bulk

21153 Cummins Power Generation Inc.
500 Jackson St.
Columbus, IN 47201
812-377-5000
www.cummins.com
Electric generators and engines.
Chairman/CEO: Tom Linebarger
Vice President/CFO: Mark Smith
Vice President/General Counsel: Sharon Barner
President/COO: Tony Satterthwaite
Year Founded: 1919
Estimated Sales: $23.77 Billion
Number Employees: 58,600

21154 Cunningham LP Gas
400 Carswell Ave
Daytona Beach, FL 32117-4418
386-672-2507
Fax: 386-254-5007
paul@cunninghamresearch.com
Sensory research for the food industry
President: Stacy Cunningham
General Manager: Tom Brett
VP Corporate Operations: Frankie Tonelli
Number Employees: 50-99

21155 Cup Pac Packaging Inc
777 Progressive Ln
South Beloit, IL 61080-2618
815-624-7060
Fax: 815-624-8170 877-347-9725
info@cuppac.com www.cuppac.com
Manufacturer and exporter of machinery for filling,
tamper-evident sealing, lidding and code dating
plastic cups; contract packaging available
President: Dennis James
Vice President: Jim Philipp
VP Sales: Russell James
Estimated Sales: $4 Million
Number Employees: 20-49
Square Footage: 68000
Type of Packaging: Consumer, Food Service, Private Label, Bulk

21156 Cup Pac Packaging Inc
777 Progressive Ln
South Beloit, IL 61080-2618
815-624-7060
Fax: 815-624-8170 info@cuppac.com
www.cuppac.com
President: Dennis James
Vice President: Jim Philipp
Estimated Sales: $20-50 Million
Number Employees: 20-49

21157 Currie Machinery Co
1150 Walsh Ave
Santa Clara, CA 95050-2647
408-727-0422
Fax: 408-727-8892 currieco@aol.com
www.curriepalletizers.com
Manufacturer and exporter of material handling
equipment including automatic palletizers, case elevators, beverage pallet stackers and powered discharge conveyors; also, dispensers including pallet,
slip and tier sheet
President: Bradley Patrick
b.patrick@curriepalletizers.com
Marketing Director: Gerry Haase
Estimated Sales: $5-10 Million
Number Employees: 1-4
Square Footage: 160000

21158 Curry Enterprises
1248 Zonolite Road NE
Atlanta, GA 30306-2006
404-873-1163
800-241-7308
Screen printed point of purchase displays and merchandising systems
Sales Manager: Steve Cornett
Estimated Sales: $1-5 Million
Number Employees: 17

21159 (HQ)Curtainaire
6000-T S. Gramercy Place
Los Angeles, CA 90047
323-753-4266
Fax: 323-753-6460
Air curtains
President: Ken Burns
VP Sales: Gary Burns
Estimated Sales: $5-10 Million
Number Employees: 19
Square Footage: 64000
Brands:
Curtainaire

21160 Curtis 1000
1725 Breckinridge Pkwy
Suite 500
Duluth, GA 30096-8994
770-925-4500
877-287-8715
www.curtis1000.com
Labels; digital and commercial printing
President/Owner: Steve Geiger
Contact: Kelli Hayes
kmhayes@curtis1000.com
Estimated Sales: $50-75 Million
Number Employees: 20-49

21161 Curtis Packaging
44 Berkshire Rd
Sandy Hook, CT 06482-1499
203-426-5861
Fax: 203-426-2684 www.curtispackaging.com
Manufacturer and exporter of folding paper boxes;
also, hot stamping and UV coating available
Chairman, President & CEO: Donald Droppo
Estimated Sales: $35 Million
Number Employees: 100-249
Square Footage: 150000

21162 Curtis Restaurant Equipment
P.O.Box 7307
Springfield, OR 97401
541-746-7480
Fax: 541-746-7384 sales@curtisresteq.com
www.curtisresteq.com
Consultant specializing in design for the food service market; wholesaler/distributor of equipment
and supplies; serving the food service market
CEO: Daniel Curtis
Chief Financial Officer: Bill Kettas
Estimated Sales: $20-30 Million
Number Employees: 50-99
Square Footage: 38000

21163 Curwood Specialty Films
2200 Badger Ave
PO Box 2968
Oshkosh, WI 54904-9118
920-303-7300
Fax: 920-303-7309 800-544-4672
curwood@bemis.com www.curwood.com
Supplier of films, trays, lids and other packaging
materials for the food and beverage industries.
Founder: Howard Curler
Founder: Bob Woods
Contact: Tom Bordona
tsbordona@bemis.com
Estimated Sales: Less Than $500,000
Number Employees: 5-9

21164 Curzon Promotional Graphics
1013 S 75th St
Omaha, NE 68114-4658
402-393-2020
Fax: 402-393-1502 800-769-7446
Banners, posters, decals and screen printed point of
purchase displays
President: Kirby Smith
CFO: E J Stanek
Sales Manager: Bob Drake
Product Manager: Ray Serfass
Estimated Sales: $2.5-5 Million
Number Employees: 10-19
Square Footage: 80000

21165 Cush-Pak Container Corporation
904 State Highway 64 W
Henderson, TX 75652-5516
903-657-0555
Corrugated and wooden boxes and containers
Estimated Sales: $20-50 Million
Number Employees: 20-49

21166 Cusham Enterprises
441 Commonwealth Avenue
Erlanger, KY 41018-1425
859-727-9727
Fax: 859-727-9796
Buys and sells food equipment and companies and
then resells their machinery and parts
Estimated Sales: $1-5 Million

21167 Custom Baking Products
111 Erick Street
Suite 129
Crystal Lake, IL 60014-1314
877-455-4938
Fax: 815-455-2735
info@custombakingproducts.com
www.custombakingproducts.com

21168 Custom Bottle of Connecticut
P.O.Box 979
Naugatuck, CT 06770-0979
203-723-6661
Fax: 203-723-6687 sales@bottles.com
www.custombottle.com
Plastic blow molded bottles and extruded containers
Vice President of Engineering: William Padgett
Vice President of Sales: Ed Jacquette
Contact: William Padgett
padgett@custombottle.com
Executive Vice President, Chief Operatin: Richard
Allen
Estimated Sales: $30-50 Million
Number Employees: 100-249
Square Footage: 75000

21169 Custom Brands Unlimited
PO Box 500
Solebury, PA 18963-0500
215-297-9842
Fax: 215-297-0161
Private-label gourmet mixes, candy, tea, snack items
and fruit
Owner: David Vissor

21170 (HQ)Custom Business Interiors
1701 Athol Avenue
Henderson, NV 89011-4072
702-564-6661
Fax: 702-564-6767 cbilv@aol.com
Store fixtures
General Manager: John Filar
Estimated Sales: $1-5 Million
Number Employees: 20
Other Locations:
Custom Business Interiors
Ventura CA

21171 Custom Business Solutions
12 Morgan
Irvine, CA 92618
949-380-7674
Fax: 949-380-7644 800-551-7674
info@cbsnorthstar.com www.cbsnorthstar.com
Point of sale hardware and software
Founder & CEO: Art Julian
Chief Financial Officer: Michael Block
VP, Software Development: Joseph Castillo
VP, Sales & Marketing: Gary Stotko
Inside Sales: Jason Perovich
Contact: Cyndy Allen
cyndy.allen@custombusinesssolutions.com
Square Footage: 16528
Other Locations:
San Diego CA
Dallas TX

21172 Custom Card & Label Corporation
P.O.Box 433
Lincoln Park, NJ 07035-0433
973-492-0022
Fax: 973-492-0022
Pressure sensitive labels
Owner: John Miller
Sales Manager: John Miller
Estimated Sales: $1-2.5 Million
Number Employees: 1-4

21173 Custom Color Corp
14320 W 101st Ter
Lenexa, KS 66215-1123
816-595-6800
Fax: 913-730-9301 888-605-4050
info@customcolor.com www.customcolor.com
Menu boards
CEO: Matthew Keith
Director Strategic Marketing: Jan Ray
Corporate Sales Rep.: Joe Goodwin
Estimated Sales: $5-10 Million
Number Employees: 50-99

21174 Custom Control Products
1300 N Memorial Dr
Racine, WI 53404
262-637-9225
Fax: 262-637-5728 800-279-9225
Batch control systems, cleaning equipment, distributed control systems, expert systems, flow diverson stations, instruments/sensors, process control, process software, heat exchangers, plate, scraped surface, tubular
Estimated Sales: $1-5 000,000
Number Employees: 15

21175 Custom Conveyor & Supply Corp.
PO Box 668
Racine, WI 53401-0668
262-634-4920
Fax: 262-634-1787
Manufacturer and designer of belt and chain conveyors and lifts
President: George Seater, Jr.
VP: Thomas Fountas
Estimated Sales: $1-2.5 Million
Number Employees: 9

21176 Custom Craft Laminates
4705 N Manhattan Ave
Tampa, FL 33614-6981
813-877-7100
Fax: 813-877-5285 800-486-4367
mblanton@Humidorstore.com
www.mycabinetcompany.com
Store fixtures
Owner: James E Blanton
james@mycabinetcompany.com
Estimated Sales: $5-10 Million
Number Employees: 10-19

21177 Custom Diamond International
895 Munck Avenue
Laval, QC H7S 1A9
Canada
450-668-0330
Fax: 450-662-1326 800-363-5926
info@diamond-group.com
www.diamond-group.com
Refrigerators, work tables, buffets, ovens, dispensers, glass washers, etc

President: Ron Diamond
CFO: Craig Aronoff
Quality Control: Hilly Diamond
Number Employees: 50
Parent Co: The Diamond Group

21178 Custom Diamond Intl.
895 Munck Avenue
Laval, QC H7S 1A9
Canada
450-668-0330
Fax: 450-662-1326 800-326-5926
Smokers, ovens, combi-oven systems, food transport systems, heated and refrigerated stainless steel tables, counters, carts, dollies, feeding systems, etc.; exporter of food service equipment including ovens, prison food carts, andrethermalization food systems
President/CEO: Ron Diamond
CFO: D Bucci
Vice President: Allan Weber
R&D: Jason B
Marketing: Alex Malikian
Sales/Public Relations: Nick V
Production/Plant Manager: Paul Nesi
Plant Manager: H Diamond
Purchasing: George D
Square Footage: 204000
Type of Packaging: Bulk
Brands:
Brute
Custom
Diamond

21179 Custom Extrusion Technologies
1650 Corporate Rd W
Lakewood, NJ 08701-5920
732-367-5511
Fax: 732-367-2908 coburn@aol.com
www.cetfilms.com
President: Roger Jacobs
Cmo: Guy Leigh
gleigh@cetfilms.com
Vice President: James Putvinski
Number Employees: 20-49

21180 (HQ)Custom Fabricating & Repair
1932 E 26th St
Marshfield, WI 54449-5500
715-387-6598
Fax: 715-384-3768 800-236-8773
dawn.isenberg@gotocfr.com www.gotocfr.com
Stainless steel filtration and cheese processing equipment; wholesaler/distributor of fittings, valves and pumps
President: Kyle Balcom
kyle.balcom@gotocfr.com
VP: Dawn Isenberg
Sales Director: Jay Moore
Estimated Sales: $7 Million
Number Employees: 50-99
Square Footage: 130000
Other Locations:
Custom Fabricating & Repair
Fridley MN
Brands:
Custom Fab

21181 Custom Foam Molders
122 Mulberry St
Foristell, MO 63348-0100
636-441-2307
Packaging including expandable polystyrene, food protective and thermal insulation
VP: Mike Loyet
Estimated Sales: $500,000-$1 Million
Number Employees: 1-4
Square Footage: 32000

21182 (HQ)Custom Food Machinery
1881 E Market Street
Stockton, CA 95205-5673
209-463-4343
Fax: 209-463-3831
Rebuilder, importer and exporter of machinery including canning, beverage and beer bottling, fruit and vegetable, processing, filling, sterilization, can closing, packaging, cartoning, etc
President: Ron McNiel Sr
VP Sales/Advertising (Inventory): Richard Gomez-Stockton
VP Operations: Ron McNiel, Jr.
Estimated Sales: $10-20 Million
Number Employees: 50-99

Other Locations:
Custom Food Machinery
Sampron Nakornpathom

21183 Custom ID Systems
3506 E Venice Ave
Venice, FL 34292-2535
941-488-8430
Fax: 941-485-1969 800-242-8430
order@custom-id.com
Signs, displays and name badges
Quality Control: Jerry Barnes
j.barns@custom-id.com
Estimated Sales: Less Than $500,000
Number Employees: 1-4

21184 Custom Lights & Iron
3101 Hoover Ave
National City, CA 91950-7221
858-274-7070
Fax: 619-474-8596 www.customlightsandiron.com
Lighting fixtures
Owner: Paul Bell
paul@customlightsandiron.com
Sales Manager: Joe Campbell
Estimated Sales: Less Than $500,000
Number Employees: 1-4
Square Footage: 24000

21185 Custom Machining Inc
1204 Hale Rd
P.O. Box 192
Shelbyville, IN 46176-2371
317-392-2328
Fax: 317-398-8856 www.custommachininginc.com
Pumpkin processing equipment, including washers, cutters, deseeders and dryers; tapered auger dryer, pork cutter depositor
Owner: Darrell Mollenkotpf
mike@custommachininginc.com
Sales Exec: Mike Walker
Estimated Sales: Less than $500,000
Number Employees: 20-49

21186 Custom Metal Crafts
2332 E Division St
Springfield, MO 65803-5197
417-862-9324
Fax: 417-864-7575
cmcsales@custom-metalcraft.com
www.custom-metalcraft.com
Process vessels and food processing equipment including material handling systems.
President: Dwayne Holden
dwayneh@custom-metalcrafts.com
CEO: Jerry Cowan
CFO: Sharon Saunders
Marketing Director: Nikki Holden
Sales Director: Drew Holden
Production Manager: Scott Higgins
Purchasing Manager: Tom Georges
Estimated Sales: $30 Million
Number Employees: 10-19
Number of Brands: 35
Square Footage: 125000
Brands:
Cm-L Lifters
Flex Bag
Invert-A-Bin
Transchem
Transitainer
Transtore
Voyager

21187 Custom Metal Design Inc
921 W Oakland Ave
Oakland, FL 34760-8855
407-656-7771
Fax: 407-656-6230 800-334-1777
sales@custommetaldesigns.com
www.custommetaldesigns.com
Manufacturer and exporter of material handling equipment including conveyors and systems, depalletizers, elevators, accumulators and bagging equipment and supplies
President: Dennis Bankowitz
dennis@custommetaldesigns.com
Estimated Sales: $10-20 Million
Number Employees: 20-49
Type of Packaging: Bulk

21188 Custom Metalcraft, Architectural Lighting
65 Sprague Street
Boston, MA 02136
617-242-0868
Fax: 617-242-0743 info@custommetalcraft.com
www.custommetalcraft.com
Electric lighting fixtures
Owner: Mike Elson
Sales/ Quotations: Mike Elson
Contact: Guil Dasilva
gds@custommetalcraft.com
Estimated Sales: $1-2.5 Million
Number Employees: 5-9

21189 Custom Millers Supply Co
511 S 3rd St
Monmouth, IL 61462-2235
309-734-6312
Fax: 309-734-7466
Grain processing equipment including corn cutters, hammer mills and trailers
President: L Howard White
Secretary: Wanda White
VP: Loran White
Estimated Sales: $1-2.5 Million
Number Employees: 1-4
Square Footage: 20000
Brands:
  Big Chief
  White

21190 Custom Mobile Food Equipment
275 South 2nd Road
Hammonton, NJ 08037-0635
609-561-6900
Fax: 609-567-9318 800-257-7855
info@foodcart.com
www.customsalesandservice.com
President: William Sikora
Estimated Sales: $5-10 Million
Number Employees: 100-249

21191 (HQ)Custom Molders
PO Box 7100
Rocky Mount, NC 27804-0100
919-688-8061
Fax: 919-688-8439
Injection custom-molded plastics including trays
President/CEO: Hwa-Yong Jo
Contact: George Perfon
gperfon@custommolders.com
VP Manufacturing: Chung-Yong Jo
Estimated Sales: $20-30 Million
Number Employees: 100-250
Other Locations:
  Custom Molders
  Morrisville NC

21192 Custom Pack Inc
662 Exton Cmns
Exton, PA 19341-2446
610-363-1900
Fax: 610-321-2526 800-722-7005
sales@custompackinc.com
www.custompackinc.com
Converter of plastic films, bags, and lidding stick
President: Frank Menichini
sales@cpispecimen.com
Estimated Sales: $6 Millon
Number Employees: 20-49
Square Footage: 54000
Brands:
  Poleguards

21193 Custom Packaging Inc
1003 Commerce Rd
Richmond, VA 23224-7007
804-232-3299
Fax: 804-232-6230 www.custompack.com
Manufacturer and exporter of corrugated boxes and point of purchase displays
President: Ed Beadels
custompackaging@verizon.net
VP: Jackie Cowden
VP Sales: Gary West
Estimated Sales: $20-50 Million
Number Employees: 10-19

21194 Custom Packaging Systems
200 W North Avenue
Northlake, IL 60164-2402
231-723-5211
Fax: 231-723-6301 800-968-5211
scholle@scholle.com www.scholle.com
Rhino spouted form-fit dry liners; multiply liquid liners; liquid squeeze bags for fill and discharge of highly viscous products; bulk bags; Rhino protecto tank and the Rhino mussle pack bag-in-box
President: Lee Lefleur
Estimated Sales: $10-20 Million
Number Employees: 150

21195 Custom Plastics Inc
250 Laredo Dr
Decatur, GA 30030-2294
404-373-1691
Fax: 404-373-8605 www.custom-plasticsinc.com
Acrylic sneeze guards for salad bars, indoor plastic signs and skylights; also, custom acrylic fabrication available
President: Scarlett Luke
scarlett@custom-plasticsinc.com
Estimated Sales: $1-2.5 Million
Number Employees: 5-9
Square Footage: 24000

21196 Custom Poly Packaging
3216 Congressional Pkwy
Fort Wayne, IN 46808-4417
260-483-4008
Fax: 260-484-5166 800-548-6603
info@custompoly.com www.custompoly.com
Polyethylene, polypropylene, trash, shopping and laboratory bags; importer of sample bags
Owner: Michael Carpenter
info@custompoly.com
Estimated Sales: $2.5-5,000,000
Number Employees: 10-19
Square Footage: 13000

21197 Custom Pools Inc
373 Shattuck Way
Portsmouth, NH 03801-2828
603-431-7800
Fax: 603-431-5109 800-323-9509
info@custompools.com www.custompools.com
Manufacturer and wholesaler/distributor of ultraviolet disinfection equipment for opaque fluids, juices, etc
President: Kelsey Hemming
kelsey.hemming@gmail.com
Vice President: Darrel Short
VP: David Short
Estimated Sales: $3-5 Million
Number Employees: 20-49

21198 Custom Quality Products
1645 Blue Rock St
Cincinnati, OH 45223
513-541-1191
Fax: 513-541-1192 800-477-4720
www.cqpinc.com
Temperature controls, cold storage doors and hardware
President: George White
Contact: Chuck Lovinski
chuckl@cqpinc.com
Estimated Sales: $2.5-5 000,000
Number Employees: 20-49

21199 Custom Rubber Stamp Co
326 5th St NE
Crosby, MN 56441-1513
218-545-4977
Fax: 866-485-9205 888-606-4579
orders@crstamp.com www.crstamp.com
Manufacturer, exporter and importer of custom rubber stamps, self-inking and pre-inked stamps, embossers, engraved plastic signs, name tags and inks
President: James Grimes
Co-Owner: Jean Grimes
Employee: Paula Steigauf
Estimated Sales: Less Than $500,000
Number Employees: 1-4
Square Footage: 4000
Brands:
  2000 Plus
  Aero
  Albany
  Base Lock
  Brailltac
  Brooklyn

Comet
Cooke
Cosco
Dapon
Eagle Zephyr
Imprintz
Quik
Rowmark
Triumph
X-Stamper

21200 Custom Sales & Svc Inc
275 S 2nd Rd
Hammonton, NJ 08037-8445
609-561-6900
Fax: 609-567-9318 800-257-7855
info@foodcart.com
Manufacturer and exporter of mobile food equipment including trucks, trailers, vans and cart systems
CEO: William Sikora
VP Sales/Marketing: Lynda Sikora
IT: Jay Celona
jay.celona@foodcart.com
Estimated Sales: $5-10 Million
Number Employees: 100-249
Square Footage: 140000

21201 (HQ)Custom Stamp Company
37449 Regal Blue Trail
Anza, CA 92539-8806
323-292-0753
Fax: 323-292-0754
Manufacturer and exporter of pressure sensitive labels, rubber stamps, name plates, stencils, daters, marking products, metal tags and serial numbering on metal
President: Jack Coleman
Sales Manager: Steve Glass
Number Employees: 8
Square Footage: 7200
Type of Packaging: Food Service
Brands:
  Cosco
  Custom
  Dymo
  Garvey
  Jrs
  Melind
  Roovers

21202 (HQ)Custom Stamping & Manufacturing
1340 SE 9th Ave
PO Box 14340
Portland, OR 97293-0340
503-238-3700
Fax: 503-238-3742
Custom metal stampers and foil food containers
Owner: Dave Stoudt
General Manager: D Stoudt
Engineer: D Marcotte
Estimated Sales: $10-20 Million
Number Employees: 50-99
Square Footage: 240000

21203 Custom Systems Integration Co
PO Box 130414
Carlsbad, CA 92013-0414
760-635-1099
Fax: 760-766-3307 bill@csicinc.com
Machinery and services for the packaging and automation industries serving the food and beverage markets. Including feeders, conveyors and custom automation
Owner: Bill Davis
feeders@att.net
Estimated Sales: $500,000-$1 Million
Number Employees: 1-4
Square Footage: 20000
Type of Packaging: Food Service, Private Label
Brands:
  Archimedes

21204 Custom Table Pads
455 Hayward Ave N
St Paul, MN 55128-5374
651-714-5720
Fax: 651-501-9246 800-325-4643
Table pads and cloths; also, place mats
Owner: Steve Mc Kay
Estimated Sales: $10-20 Million
Number Employees: 20-49

21205 Custom Tarpaulin Products Inc
8095 Southern Blvd
Youngstown, OH 44512-6336
330-758-1801
Fax: 330-758-9872 888-394-5054
info@customtarpaulin.com
www.customtarpaulin.com
Commercial awnings
President: Gerald Robinson
Estimated Sales: $10-20 Million
Number Employees: 10-19

21206 Customized Equipment SE
4186 Railroad Ave
Tucker, GA 30084-4484
770-934-9300
Fax: 770-934-0610
Manufacturer and exporter of packaging machinery
including automatic and semi-automatic baggers and
sealers; also, random and fixed size carton taping
machinery
President: Kermit Cooper
Sales Director: Bruce Cooper
Estimated Sales: $1-5 Million
Number Employees: 10 to 19
Square Footage: 40000

21207 (HQ)Cutler Brothers Box & Lumber
711 W Prospect Ave
PO Box 217
Fairview, NJ 07022-1523
201-943-2535
Fax: 201-943-8532 cutler711@aol.com
www.cutlerpallets.com
Wooden and reconditioned pallets; also, scrap wood
removal and pallet repair services available
Owner: Greg Cutler
cutler711@aol.com
VP: Greg Cutler
VP: Jed Cutler
Estimated Sales: $12 Million
Number Employees: 50-99
Square Footage: 60000
Other Locations:
Cutler Brothers Box & Lumber
Woodland PA

21208 Cutler Industries
8300 Austin Avenue
Morton Grove, IL 60053-3209
847-965-3700
Fax: 847-965-8585 800-458-5593
Manufacturer and exporter of revolving tray, rack
and utility ovens and under counter proofers
Director Marketing Support: Kathleen Casey
Estimated Sales: $1-5 Million
Number Employees: 50-99
Square Footage: 340000

21209 Cutler-Hammer
811 Green Crest Drive
Westerville, OH 43081-2838
614-882-3282
Fax: 614-895-7111 www.ch.cutler-hammer.com
Open control and automation solutions including
software, logic products, operator interface, sensors,
acuators, and industrial PC's
Estimated Sales: $30-50 Million
Number Employees: 250-500

21210 Cutrite Company
PO Box 851
Fremont, OH 43420-0851
419-332-1380
Fax: 419-334-2383 800-928-8748
sales@arius-eickert.com
Manufacturer and exporter of cooking knives, poul-
try shears and meat processing specialty tools and
utensils
Sales Manager: Ramon Eickert
General Manager: Becky Smith
Estimated Sales: $3-5 Million
Number Employees: 20-50
Square Footage: 100000
Parent Co: A. Eickert Company
Brands:
Arius-Eickert
Cutrite
Proline

21211 Cutter Lumber Products
10 Rickenbacker Cir
Livermore, CA 94551-7211
925-443-5959
Fax: 925-443-0648 sales@cutterlumber.com
www.cutterlumber.com
Pallets and skids
President: Tony Palma
tony@cutterlumber.com
Sales Manager: Todd Samuels
Estimated Sales: $1-2.5 Million
Number Employees: 1-4
Other Locations:
Cutter Lumber Products
Willits CA

21212 Cyborg Equipment Corporation
8 Graham St
Wareham, MA 02571
508-291-0999
Fax: 781-297-0097
Packaging, vacuum, tumblers, crede machine, form,
fill and seal machines, temp monitoring device
Manager: Jennifer Lawrence
Estimated Sales: $1-2.5 000,000
Number Employees: 1-4

21213 Cyclamen Collection
2140 Livingston St
Oakland, CA 94606
510-434-7620
Fax: 510-434-7624 CYCLAMENCOLL@aol.com
www.cyclamencollection.com
Manufacturer and exporter of dinnerware,
serveware, bakeware and vitrified stoneware, pitch-
ers, vases, and lamps
Owner: Julie Sanders
julie.sanders@cyclamencollection.com
Sales: Julie Sanders
julie.sanders@cyclamencollection.com
Estimated Sales: $500,000-$1,000,000
Number Employees: 5-9
Number of Products: 200+
Type of Packaging: Bulk
Brands:
Calla
Cyclamen
Ergo
Fallingwater
Fiamma
Forma
Mosaica
Nelson
Nova
Patchwork
Stella

21214 Cycle Computer Consultants
95 Jerusalem Ave
Hicksville, NY 11801
516-733-1892
Fax: 516-935-0697
Consultant offering computer services for food dis-
tributors
Owner: Anthony Manzillilo
Marketing Manager: Frank Berelson
Number Employees: 10-19
Parent Co: Tomark-Cyber Associates

21215 Cyclonaire Corp
2922 N Division Ave
P.O.Box 366
York, NE 68467-9775
402-362-2000
Fax: 402-362-2001 800-445-0730
sales@cyclonaire.com www.cyclonaire.com
Manufacturer and exporter of pneumatic conveying
equipment and accessories
President: Dan Reckner
dreckner@ddreckner.com
CEO: Don Baker
VP: Scott Schmidt
Sales: Joe Morris
Plant Manager: Deryl Kliewer
Purchasing: Sheila Miller
Estimated Sales: $10-20 Million
Number Employees: 20-49
Square Footage: 80000
Brands:
Cyclojet
Cyclolift
Cyclolok
Cyclonaire
Vibra Pad

21216 Cynter Con Technology Adviser
656 Quince Orchard Road
7th Floor
Gaithersburg, MD 20878-1409
301-208-3958
Fax: 301-990-3434 800-287-1811
Consultant specializing in technology for the food
service and retail industries
Business Development Manager: Francis Carmello
Number Employees: 12
Square Footage: 40000

21217 (HQ)Cyntergy Corporation
400 E Gude Dr
Rockville, MD 20850-1365
301-315-8610
Fax: 301-315-8611 800-825-5787
info@cyntergy.com www.cyntergy.com
Consultant specializing in project management,
training, implementation/training and documentation
for the food service and retail industries
President: Mitchell Rambler
Chairman/CEO: Rob Grimes
VP Sales/Marketing: Cort Grey
Estimated Sales: $5-10 Million
Number Employees: 50-99
Type of Packaging: Bulk

21218 Cyplex
6311 Primrose Ave Apt 18
Los Angeles, CA 90068-4413
Fax: 323-436-0190 www.cyplex.net
Developer of point of sale hardware and software
Estimated Sales: $1-2,500,000
Number Employees: 10-19
Brands:
Alliance

21219 Cypress Systems
40365 Brickyard Dr # 101
Suite 101
Madera, CA 93636-9520
559-229-7850
Fax: 559-225-9007 800-235-2436
www.cypsystems.com
Electrochemical instrumentation
President: Paul Willis
paul.willis@cypsystems.com
Business Manager: Huei Chi Alice Sutherland
Estimated Sales: Less Than $500,000
Number Employees: 1-4

21220 Cyprus Embassy Trade Ctr
13 E 40th St
New York, NY 10016-0110
212-213-9100
Fax: 212-213-2918 ctcny@cyprustradeny.org
www.cyprustradeny.com
Agency/Trade Organization.
Marketing: Aristos Constantine
Manager: Aristos Constantine
ctcny@aol.com
Number Employees: 1-4

21221 Cyrk
14224 167th Avenue
Monroe, WA 98272
Fax: 800-545-8840 800-426-3125
Manufacturer and exporter of advertising novelties
including screen printed promotional materials
Sales Manager: Steve Paradiso
Contact: Kathy Heineman
kheineman@cyrk.com
Estimated Sales: $40 Million
Number Employees: 250-500
Type of Packaging: Food Service

21222 Cyro Industries/Degussa
P.O.Box 677
Parsippany, NJ 07054-0677
973-541-8000
Fax: 973-541-8445 800-631-5384
cyro@degussa.com www.cyro.com
Manufacturer and exporter of molding and extrusion
compounds for food bins and displays
President: Thomas Bates
Marketing Director: Cynthia Zey
Public Relations: Gail Wood
Number Employees: 500-999
Parent Co: Cytec Industries/Rohm GmbH
Brands:
Cyrolite G-20
Xt

21223 Cyvex Nutrition
1851 Kaiser Ave
Irvine, CA 92614

949-622-9030
Fax: 949-622-9033 888-992-9839
sales@cyvex.com www.cyvex.com
High quality, reliable and accurate refractometers
and polarimeters for liquid concentration control
Director, Operations: Quang La
R&D: Denise Lam
Marketing: Charlene Lee
Contact: Michelle Adelman
michelle.adelman@reachlocal.com
Number Employees: 5-9
Number of Brands: 1
Number of Products: 3
Square Footage: 15000
Brands:
　Atago Brand

21224 D & F Equipment
8641 Highway 227 North
PO Box 275
Crossville, AL 35962

256-528-7842
Fax: 256-528-7171 800-282-7842
terrycleghorn@dfequip.com www.dfequip.com
Equipment and machinery for meat processing
Owner: Larry Fortenberry
Owner: Lynn Fortenberry
Owner: Dawn Knox
SVP: Greg Cagle
Director of Engineering: Gary Cambron
Corporate Purchasing/Marketing: Gene Pledger
Sales Manager: Terry Cleghorn
Contact: Joey Knott
projects@dfequip.com
VP of Operations & Service: Joey Knott
Accounts Receivable: Cathy Sims
Accounts Payable: Towania Williams
Number Employees: 20

21225 D & L Manufacturing
1818 S 71st St
Milwaukee, WI 53214

414-256-8160
Fax: 414-476-0564 sales@kempsmith-dl.com
www.kempsmith-dl.com
Manufacturer and exporter of machinery including
file folder, paper converting, cutting, creasing, fold-
ing carton, folding and glueing, laminating, printing,
embossing and rotary die cutting
President: Brett Burris
CEO: Robert Burris
Sales Director: Judy Lewis
Estimated Sales: $10-20 Million
Number Employees: 20-49
Square Footage: 116000

21226 D & S Mfg
14 Sword St # 4
Auburn, MA 01501-2170

508-799-7812
Fax: 508-753-3468
Knives; also, screens for granulators and choppers
President: Graham Scarsbrook
Contact: Robert Johnson
dsmanufacturing@aol.com
Estimated Sales: $1-2.5 Million
Number Employees: 10-19
Parent Co: L. Hardy

21227 D & W Fine Pack
800 Ela Rd
Lake Zurich, IL 60047-2340

847-438-2171
Fax: 847-438-0369 800-323-0422
www.dwfinepack.com
Manufacturer and exporter of metal baking pans for
muffins, cupcakes, breads, baguettes, pizza, cakes,
pies, buns and rolls; also, aluminum foil containers,
plastic domes, plastic containers, and plastic
clamshells
President & CEO: Dave Randall
Cio/Cto: Mike Jenkins
CFO, VP Finance: Tom Nickele
VP, CIO: Michael Casula
VP Sales Grocery & Processor: Rick Barton
SVP Operations: Jay DuBois
Number Employees: 100-249
Square Footage: 1200000
Type of Packaging: Consumer, Food Service, Pri-
vate Label, Bulk

Brands:
　Bakalon
　Bake King
　Chicago Metallic
　Cm Packaging
　Sure-Bake
　Sure-Bake & Glaze
　Ultraslik
　Village Bakers

21228 D & W Fine Pack
4162 Georgia Blvd
San Bernardino, CA 92407-1852

909-880-1781
Fax: 909-474-4384 800-232-5959
www.dwfinepack.com
Disposable food containers
President: Andrew Falcon
Controller: Rick Blanton
rickb@cmfinepack.com
Estimated Sales: G
Number Employees: 100-249
Brands:
　Fine Pak

21229 D A Berther Inc
9000 W Becher St
Milwaukee, WI 53227-1510

414-328-1995
Fax: 414-328-1818 877-357-9622
info@daberther.com www.daberther.com
Stainless steel food equipment, supplies, tables and
sinks
President/CEO: David A. Berther
jeff@daberther.com
CFO: David Berther
Vice President/Sales Consultant: Jeff Berther
Inside Sales/Rental Manager: Jim Lidwin
Estimated Sales: $1-2.5 Million
Number Employees: 10-19
Square Footage: 42000

21230 D A C Labels & Graphic
10491 Brockwood Rd
Dallas, TX 75238-1641

214-340-2055
Fax: 214-340-2272 800-483-1700
daclbl@aol.com www.daclabels.com
Printed labels and tags; wholesaler/distributor of
thermal transfer printers and ribbons
Vice President: Judy Benson
daclbl@aol.com
CEO: Jay Fair
R & D: Greg Swindle
VP: Judy Vinson
Marketing Manager: Greg Towers
Customer Support: Michelle Ywhite
Estimated Sales: $5-10 Million
Number Employees: 10-19

21231 D D Bean & Sons Co
207 Peterborough St
Jaffrey, NH 03452-5868

603-532-8311
Fax: 603-532-6001 800-326-8311
info@ddbean.com www.ddbean.com
Manufacturer and exporter of matchbooks
President: D Bean
CEO: Delcie D Bean
dbean@ddbean.com
VP: Peter Leach
Manager: Terry Fecto
Estimated Sales: $20-50 Million
Number Employees: 50-99
Square Footage: 100000
Type of Packaging: Food Service, Private Label

21232 D D Williamson & Co Inc
1901 Payne St
Louisville, KY 40206-1902

502-895-2438
Fax: 502-895-7381
Global manufacturer of natural colour for the food
and beverage industries with facilities in Africa,
Asia, Europe and North and South America.
Chairman & CEO: Ted Nixon
Type of Packaging: Bulk

21233 D F Ingredients Inc
127 Elm St # 200
Suite 200
Washington, MO 63090-2140

636-583-0802
Fax: 630-583-4877 888-583-0802
michael@dfingredients.com
www.dfingredients.com
Ingredients and dairy products
President: Michael Husmann
Vice President: Larry Rice
Sales Rep: Richard Kuddes
Sales Rep: Kenneth Johnson
Sales Rep: Jim Wesselschmidt
Manager: Megan Bade
megan@dfingredients.com
Number Employees: 1-4

21234 D I Mfg LLC
13335 C St
Omaha, NE 68144-3601

402-330-5650
info@dimanufacturing.com
www.dimanufacturing.com
Specialty food products including gluten free foods,
garlic bread, wrapped breads, pizza, cookie dough
Contact: Zack Best
zbest@dimanufacturing.com
Number Employees: 10-19
Type of Packaging: Food Service, Bulk

21235 D M Sales & EngineeringCo
1325 Sunday Dr
Indianapolis, IN 46217-9334

317-783-5493
Fax: 317-787-5642 www.dmsales-eng.com
Decorative and thermoforming plastic molding and
plastic packaging products
President: Dave Mickel
davemickel@dmsaleseng.com
Estimated Sales: $2.5-5 Million
Number Employees: 20-49

21236 D R Technology Inc
73 South St
Freehold, NJ 07728-2317

732-780-4664
Fax: 732-780-1545 sales@DRTechnologyInc.com
www.drtechnologyinc.com
Manufacturer and exporter of wet scrubbers used to
control atmospheric emissions in food manufactur-
ing plants
President: Richard Schwartz
CEO: Doris Schwartz
drtinfo@aol.com
Marketing Director: Debra Kruggen
Estimated Sales: $.5-1 million
Number Employees: 5-9
Square Footage: 5000

21237 D W Davies & Co
3200 Phillips Ave
Racine, WI 53403-4309

262-637-6133
Fax: 262-637-3933 800-888-6133
dwdavies@dwdavies.com www.dwdavies.com
Chemicals, cleaners, floor finishes, boiler com-
pounds and dishwashing detergents.
Owner: D J Davies
dwdavies@dwdavies.com
President: Daniel Davies
CFO: David Rubenstein
Estimated Sales: $10-20 Million
Number Employees: 20-49
Square Footage: 40000
Type of Packaging: Consumer, Private Label
Brands:
　D.W. Concentrate

21238 D&D Sign Company
6232 Southwest Pkwy
Wichita Falls, TX 76308-0803

940-692-4643
Fax: 940-692-1344
Metal, electric, neon, plexiglass and wooden signs;
also, installation and services available
Co-Owner: Mark Patterson
Estimated Sales: $1-2.5 Million
Number Employees: 5-9

21239 D&L Manufacturing
1818 S 71st St
Milwaukee, WI 53214
414-256-8160
Fax: 414-476-0564 sales@kempsmith-dl.com
www.kempsmith-dl.com
Bottle washers and fillers
President: Les Johnson
CEO: Robert E Burris
Estimated Sales: $10-20 Million
Number Employees: 20-49

21240 D&M Pallet Company
118 Morris St
Neshkoro, WI 54960-9599
920-293-4616
Fax: 920-293-4660
Pallets, skids, crates and boxes
President: David Heinzelman
Estimated Sales: $500,000-$1 Million
Number Employees: 1 to4

21241 D&M Products
2310 Michigan Avenue
Santa Monica, CA 90404
310-453-0485
Fax: 310-828-9670 800-245-0485
sales@dm-products.com www.dm-products.com
Hydro-air pressure guns for cold stream cleaning
President and CFO: Karl Hirzel
Contact: Dennis Markle
dennis@dmproducts.net
Estimated Sales: Below $5 Million
Number Employees: 1-4
Brands:
  D&M

21242 D'Ac Lighting
420 Railroad Way
PO BOX 262
Mamaroneck, NY 10543-2257
914-698-5959
Fax: 914-698-6061 www.daclighting.com
Manufacturer and importer of lighting fixtures in-
cluding electric and flourescent
President: Robert N Haidinger
Customer Service: Peggy Guglielmo
General Manager: Moshe Toledo
Estimated Sales: $1-2.5 Million
Number Employees: 50-99
Square Footage: 100000

21243 D'Addario Design Associates
123 W 44th Street
New York, NY 10036-4000
212-302-0059
Fax: 212-764-7262
Design consultant specializing in labels, cartons, lo-
gos, wooden boxes and POS and merchandising aids
President: Thomas D'Addario
VP: Adam D'Addario
Estimated Sales: Less than $500,000
Number Employees: 1-4
Square Footage: 4000

21244 D'Lights
533 West Windsor Road
Glendale, CA 91204
818-956-5656
Fax: 818-956-2157 slsmgr@dlights.com
www.dlights.com
Manufacturer and exporter of lighting fixtures and
food warmers
President: Kent Erle Sokolow
General Manager: Steve Sink
Estimated Sales: Below $5 Million
Number Employees: 10

21245 D. Picking & Company
119 S Walnut St
Bucyrus, OH 44820
419-562-6891
Fax: 419-562-0078
Copper kettles for use in the processing of apple
butter and decorative items
Owner: Helen Picking-Neff
Office Manager: Steve Schifer
Director: Sylvia Cooper
Estimated Sales: $5-10 Million
Number Employees: 5-9

21246 D.A. Colongeli & Sons
16 Pomeroy Street
Cortland, NY 13045-2241
607-753-0888
Fax: 607-756-2997 800-322-7687
Established in 1970; purveyors of fine foods.
President: Donald Colongeli
Number Employees: 1
Square Footage: 4000
Type of Packaging: Food Service
Brands:
  Fancy
  Fine
  Gourmet
  Haco Foods
  Knorr

21247 D.D.& D. Machinery
7620 Seneca St
East Aurora, NY 14052-9457
716-652-4410
Fax: 716-652-0677
President: Norbert Gerhard
Estimated Sales: $3-5 Million
Number Employees: 1-4

21248 D.R. McClain & Son
7039 E Slauson Ave
Commerce, CA 90040-3620
323-722-7900
Fax: 323-726-4700 800-428-2263
Bakery equipment including dough rollers, sheeters
and molders
Owner: Jeff Branstein
National Sales Manager: Norm Gwinn
Estimated Sales: $1-5 Million
Number Employees: 50-99
Square Footage: 76000

21249 D2 Ingredients, LP.
1244 Enterprise Dr
De Pere, WI 54115
920-425-8870
Fax: 920-964-0116 info@d2ingredients.com
d2ingredients.com
Functional ingredients and products, including
smoke flavorings, alginate products, extrudable
yeast-less doughs and savory fillings; spice blends,
caramelized sugars and commodities; injection and
tumbling products for poulty andmeat. Also provide
Vice President of Sales & Marketing: Dan Rose
Type of Packaging: Private Label, Bulk

21250 (HQ)DBE Inc
310 Rayette Road
Concord, ON L4K 2G5
Canada
905-738-0353
Fax: 905-738-7585 800-461-5313
www.dbe-vsi.com
Manufacturer, importer and exporter of seafood
equipment including commercial fish/lobster tanks,
electrical fish sealers, customized seafood tanks
President: Fima Dreff
Marketing Director: Lesya Sklyarenko
Sales Director: Joe Albis
Public Relations: Lesya Sklyarenko
Plant Manager: Jean-Pierre Paquette
Estimated Sales: $10-20 Million
Number Employees: 15
Number of Brands: 6
Square Footage: 100000
Other Locations:
  DBE Food Equipment
  Kyiv
Brands:
  Dde

21251 (HQ)DCI, Inc.
600 54th Ave N
St Cloud, MN 56303-2043
320-252-8200
Fax: 320-252-0866 sales@dciinc.com
www.dciinc.com
Manufacturer and exporter of stainless steel process-
ing and storage tanks as well as OEM components
(tank heads, manways, mixers/agitators,parts). Also
offering DCI Site-Fab (field fabrication of any size
tank up to 500,00 gallons).
Chief Financial Officer: Chad Leither
Executive Vice President: Chad Leither
Estimated Sales: $20-50 Million
Number Employees: 100-249
Square Footage: 88000

Other Locations:
  Manufacturing/Site-Fab Facility
  Sparta MO
  Manufacturing/Site-Fab Facility
  Fresno CA

21252 (HQ)DCL Solutions LLC
4201 Torresdale Ave
Philadelphia, PA 19124-4701
215-743-4201
Fax: 215-288-0847 800-426-1127
sales@dclsolutions.com www.big3packaging.com
Manufacturer and exporter of floor finishes, strip-
pers, oven/grill cleaners, hand soaps, degreasers and
portion control water soluble packets
Owner: Steve Seneca
sseneca@pakit.com
CFO: Bill Harry
VP: Bill Paris
Estimated Sales: $5-10 Million
Number Employees: 50-99
Square Footage: 120000
Brands:
  Chemical Service
  Pak It
  Vapguard

21253 DCM Tech Corp
4455 Theurer Blvd
PO Box 1304
Winona, MN 55987-1593
507-452-4043
Fax: 507-452-7970 800-533-5339
interest@dcm-tech.com www.dcm-tech.com
Supplier of metal cutting tools and machines
President: Chris Arnold
chris@luminet.net
Financial Controller: Jennifer Fruth
Technical Specialist: Mike Anderson
Engineering Manager: Jerry Lawson
Purchasing Manager: Denise Aitken
Estimated Sales: $4 Million
Number Employees: 50-99

21254 DCS IPAL Consultants
1043 Autoroute Chomedey
Laval, QC J7W 4V3
Canada
450-973-3338
Fax: 450-973-3339 www.sidel.com
Consultant specializing in packaging and process
engineering
Engineering & Material Handling: Marc Aury
Controls and Automation Dir.: Franck Klotz
Director Operations: Alex Gieysztor
Number Employees: 250
Square Footage: 56000
Parent Co: Gebo Industries

21255 DCS Sanitation Management
7864 Camargo Rd
Cincinnati, OH 45243
513-271-9300
Fax: 513-271-5710 800-837-8737
www.pssi.co
Consultants and sanitation programs for the meat industry; sanitation supplies and equipment, including
cleaning compounds and solutions, cleaning and
washing equipment and accessories, and sanitizers
President: Tom Murray
Estimated Sales: $1-5 Million
Number Employees: 1-4

21256 DCV BioNutritionals
3521 Silverside Road
Wilmington, DE 19810-4900
800-641-2001
Fax: 302-695-5188 800-641-2001
Microencapsulation of nutrition, baking and spe-
cialty food ingredients: choline and betaine salts
Contact: Becky Price
becky.price@airepel.com
Estimated Sales: $50-100 Million
Number Employees: 50-99

21257 DECI Corporation
One Todd Drive
Burgettstown, PA 15021
724-947-3300
Fax: 724-947-3621
Consultant specializing in food processing plant en-
gineering and design
Vice President: Bruce Mahoney
Contact: Michael Gialames
michael.gialames@deccorp.com

Estimated Sales: $2.5-5 Million
Number Employees: 20-50
Square Footage: 29824

21258 DEFCO
165 Sawmill Road
Landenberg, PA 19350-9302

215-274-8245
Fax: 610-274-0342
Fiberglass reinforced thermoset plastic process
equipment; also, installation and maintenance
available
VP: John Field
Estimated Sales: $1-2.5 Million
Number Employees: 10-19
Square Footage: 32000

21259 DEL-Tec Packaging Inc
4020 Pelham Ct
Greer, SC 29650-4804

864-288-7390
Fax: 864-288-7237 800-747-8683
sales@del-tec.com www.del-tec.com
Totes, bins, trays and vacuum and thermoformed
plastic containers
Owner: Robert Kocis
VP Finance: Jere Davis
VP Sales: Bob Kocis
rkocis@mainstay.net
Customer Service: Joy McCullough
Plant Manager: Tim Shea
Estimated Sales: $1-2.5 Million
Number Employees: 20-49
Square Footage: 260000

21260 DEMACO
411 S Ebenezer Road
Florence, SC 29501-7916

407-952-6600
Fax: 407-952-6683

21261 DFL Laboratories
111 E. Wacker Dr.
Suite 2300
Chicago, IL 60601

312-938-5151
Fax: 209-521-1005
Consultant specializing in chemical and microbio-
logical testing services
Manager: Stephanie Campbell
Estimated Sales: $10-20,000,000
Number Employees: 100-249

21262 DH/Sureflow
402 SE 31st Avenue
Portland, OR 97214-1929

503-236-9263
Fax: 503-236-9264 800-654-2548
sureflow@dhsales.com
Manufacturer and exporter of drain cleaning ma-
chinery and power snakes
Owner and President: Doug Hemenway
VP: Geoff Hemenway
Number Employees: 3
Square Footage: 10000
Brands:
  Sureflow

21263 DHM Adhesives Inc
509 S Wall St # A
Calhoun, GA 30701-2536

706-629-7960
Fax: 706-625-2819 800-745-1346
www.dhmadhesives.com
Pressure sensitive and hot melt adhesives
President: Matt Devine
mdevine@dhmadhesives.com
CFO: Bill Matthews
Vice President of Procurement: Bob Goodman
Vice President of Sales and Marketing: Bob
Shumaker
Plant Manager: David Chase
Purchasing Manager: Milton Bryson
Estimated Sales: $5-10 Million
Number Employees: 20-49

21264 DHP
1911 Rustic Pl
Farmington, NM 87401

Fax: 505-327-2934 877-711-4347
info@dhptraining.com www.dhptraining.com
Water treatment, training, products and service
Founder & President: David Paul

Year Founded: 1988
Estimated Sales: $100-200 Million
Number Employees: 20-49

21265 DIC International
35 Waterview Blvd Ste 100
Parsippany, NJ 07054-1270

Fax: 201-836-4962
www.dic.co.jp/eng/products/pps/global.html
Manufacturer, importer and exporter of a natural
nontoxic chlorophyll colorant
President: Shintaro Asada
CFO: Yuzi Koike
Marketing Manager: Y Akiyama
Contact: Christine Medordi
christine@dica.com
Number Employees: 20-49
Parent Co: Dainippou Ink & Chemicals
Brands:
  Co-Enzyme Q-10
  Linablue A
  Pantethine
  Sqvalene

21266 DIPIX Technologies
1051 Baxter Road
Ottawa, ON K2C 3P2
Canada

613-596-4942
Fax: 613-596-4914 info@dipix.com
www.dipix.com
President: Anton Kitai
Director of Sales: Geoff Evans
Chief Operating Officer: Peter Wakeman
Estimated Sales: $1-5 Million
Number Employees: 20-50

21267 DL Enterprises
399 Cameron St
Etters, PA 17319-9775

717-938-1292
Fax: 717-938-5110
www.panetwork.com/aisle-a-gator
Battery powered wet/dry vacuum cleaners for gro-
cery warehouses, distribution centers, food proces-
sors, warehouses and retail stores
President: Dick Lewis
Estimated Sales: $300,000-500,000
Number Employees: 1-4
Square Footage: 10000
Brands:
  The Aisle-A-Gator

21268 DLX Industries
1609 Roote 202
Pomona, NY 10970-2902

845-517-2200
www.dlxonline.com
Manufacturer and exporter of vinyl-imprinted adver-
tising specialties and promotional items
Estimated Sales: $78,000
Number Employees: 2
Number of Products: 120
Square Footage: 12804
Parent Co: DLX

21269 DMC-David ManufacturingCompany
1600 12th Street NE
Mason City, IA 50401-2543

641-424-7010
Fax: 641-424-7017
Manufacturer and exporter of grain-handling equip-
ment including cleaners and dryers; also, moisture
sensing devices for flowing or moving material
CEO and President: Wes Cagle
Sales/Marketing Manager: Jim Balk
Estimated Sales: $20-50 Million
Number Employees: 100-249
Square Footage: 157000
Brands:
  Cal-Cu-Dri
  Calc-U-Dryer
  Hi-Cap
  Stirator

21270 DMG Financial Inc
950 S Cherry St # 424
Suite 424
Denver, CO 80246-2612

303-756-1794
Fax: 303-756-9484 888-331-3882
info@dmgfinancial.com www.dmgfinancial.com

Management consultants specializing in management consulting, mergers and acquisitions, financial
services
President: Douglas Bilenski
dbilenski@dmgfinancial.com
Estimated Sales: Less Than $500,000
Number Employees: 1-4

21271 DMN Inc
220 S Woods St
West Memphis, AR 72301-4304

870-733-9100
Fax: 870-733-9101 www.dmnwestinghouse.com
Rotary valves, diverter valves
Owner: Rob Kabel
rkabel@dmn-inc.com
Estimated Sales: Below $5 Million
Number Employees: 5-9

21272 DOWL LLC
4041 B St
Anchorage, AK 99503-5906

907-562-2000
Fax: 907-563-3953 800-478-3695
Glycine, chelating agents, surfactants, dispersing
agents and emulsion polymers
President: Stewart G Osgood
sosgood@dowlhkm.com
CEO: Andrew Liveris
Executive VP: Geoffery Merszel
Marketing Manager: Art Paulidis
Commercial Manager: Mark DeGeorge
Estimated Sales: $2.5-5 Million
Number Employees: 250-499

21273 DPC
21 W Fornance St # 150
Norristown, PA 19401-3300

610-277-3000
Fax: 610-277-1264 800-220-9473
Disposable and nonwoven counter and table wipers
in folded, roll and portion control dispenser box
form
President: Jim Drucker
CFO: Daniel Chojnacki
VP: Jeff Berk
Director Marketing: D Bancroft
Estimated Sales: $1-2.5 Million
Number Employees: 50-99
Square Footage: 600000
Parent Co: RTR Industries
Other Locations:
  D.P.C.
  Greenville SC

21274 DPI Specialty Foods Inc.
601 Rockefeller Ave.
Ontario, CA 91761

909-975-1019
Fax: 909-975-7238 www.dpispecialtyfoods.com
Gourmet, natural, organic, gluten free, local and eth-
nic foods.
CEO: Russ Blake
Chief Financial Officer: Marc Barth
Chief Information Officer: Nadia Rosseels
Chief Operating Officer: Christopher Erklenz
Year Founded: 1963
Estimated Sales: Over $1 Billion
Number Employees: 1000-4999

21275 DR McClain & Son
PO Box 95
Pico Rivera, CA 90660-0095

562-699-4542
Fax: 562-692-0026 800-428-2263
Dough rollers and sheeters

21276 DSA Software
34 School St # 201
Foxboro, MA 02035-2318

508-543-0400
Fax: 508-543-0856 sales@dsasoft.com
www.dsasoft.com
Warehouse management software
President: David Petri
lpetri@dsasoft.com
Estimated Sales: Below $5 Million
Number Employees: 5-9
Brands:
  Foxware Dc Label
  Foxware Dc Manager
  Foxware Edi Manager
  Foxware Rf Manager

21277 DSI
15304 NE 95th St
Redmond, WA 98052

425-885-5223
Fax: 425-882-2025 rich_kish@fmc.com
Cutting, boning devices and processing equipment, defatting machines, trimming devices, dicers, and slicers
President: Jim Heber
Estimated Sales: $5-10 000,000
Number Employees: 20-49

21278 DSI Process Systems
4630 W Florissant Ave
St Louis, MO 63115-2233

314-382-1525
Fax: 314-382-5234 800-342-5374
jack@dsiprocess.com www.statco-dsi.com
Conveyor systems, stainless steel food processing equipment, tanks, and sanitary piping
President: Robert Goetz
rgoetz@statco-dsi.com
Marketing Contact: Jack Luechtefeld
Estimated Sales: $10-20 Million
Number Employees: 50-99

21279 DSM Nutritional Products LLC
45 Waterview Blvd
Parsippany, NJ 07054

info.dnp@dsm.com
www.dsm.com/corporate/about/businesses/dsm-nutritional-products.html
Supplier of vitamins, carotenoids and other fine chemicals to the feed, food, pharmaceutical and personal care industries.
President: Chris Goppelsroeder
Year Founded: 1902
Estimated Sales: K
Number Employees: 10,000+
Parent Co: Koninklijke DSM N.V.
Type of Packaging: Bulk

21280 DSO Fluid Handling Company
300 McGaw Drive,
Raritan Center Edison
Irvington, NJ 08837

732-225-9100
Fax: 732-225-9101 1 8-0 5-7 68
Owner: Darrin Oppenheim
Estimated Sales: $10-20 000,000
Number Employees: 10-19

21281 DSW Converting Knives
1504 8th Avenue N
Birmingham, AL 35203

205-322-2021
Fax: 205-322-2576
Manufacturer and exporter of machine knives
President: Chris Mc Ilvaine
Estimated Sales: Below $5 Million
Number Employees: 10-19
Type of Packaging: Bulk

21282 DT Converting Technologies-Stokes
207 Mill St
Bristol, PA 19007-4808

215-788-3500
Fax: 215-781-1122 800-635-0036
stokes-info@dtindustries.com
www.dtindustries.com
Manufacturer tablet presses, granulators, tablet deduster, tornado mills
President: Ken Peterson
Vice President: George Graff
Research & Development: Dave Breen
Marketing Director: Barb McDevitt
Sales Director: George Graff
Number Employees: 20-49
Parent Co: DT Industries
Brands:
Genesis Removable Head Press
Tablet Press 328
Valitah 3000

21283 (HQ)DT Industrials
949 S McCord Rd
Holland, OH 43528

567-703-8550
Fax: 419-866-4656 sales@dtindustrials.com
dtindustrials-lubricants.com
Food grade oils and greases
Sales & Marketing: Erica Jaspers

21284 DT Packaging Systems
18105 Trans Canada
Kirkland, QC H9J 3Z4
Canada

514-694-2390
Fax: 514-694-6552 888-384-3343
lvilleneuve@kalishdti.com www.dtindustries.com

21285 DT Packaging Systems
7 New Lancaster Road
Leominster, MA 01453-5224

978-537-8534
Fax: 978-840-0730 800-851-1518
Line integration conveyors, online quality assurance, filling by count, bulk handling
President: Jim Ririe
Contact: Burckhart Cory
stewart.harvey@imanova.com
Plant Manager: Stewart Harvey
Estimated Sales: $5-10 Million
Number Employees: 100-249

21286 DWL Industries Company
65 Industrial Road
Lodi, NJ 07644

973-916-9958
Fax: 973-916-9959 888-946-2682
cs@wincous.com www.wincodwl.com
Wholesaler/distributor, importer and exporter of knives, utensils and tableware; serving the food service market
President: David Li
Officer: Jieyui Ding
VP Sales: Steve Chang
Contact: Steven Chu
1and1admin@wincous.com
Number Employees: 15
Square Footage: 40000

21287 Dabrico Inc
1555 Commerce Dr
Bourbonnais, IL 60914-4600

815-939-7798
Fax: 815-939-7798 888-439-0580
sales@dabrico.com www.dabrico.com
President: Efrain A Davila
efrain@dabrico.com
Marketing Manager: Maria Carter
Director of Sales and Marketing: Chuck Goranson
Purchasing Manager: Mario Trevino
Estimated Sales: $3-5 Million
Number Employees: 10-19

21288 Dacam Corporation
PO Box 310
Madison Heights, VA 24572-0310

434-929-4001
Fax: 434-847-4487 www.dacammachinery.com
Manufacturer and exporter of packaging machinery
President: Ed Tolle
Sales And Marketing: Dean Hargis
Director Engineering: David Vaughan
Estimated Sales: $2.5-5 Million
Number Employees: 20-49
Square Footage: 80000
Brands:
Dacam

21289 Dacam Machinery
113 N Amherst Highway
Madison Heights, VA 24572

434-369-1259
Fax: 434-369-1949
Produces high quality packaging and material handling equipment for the food and beverage industries.
Estimated Sales: $2.5-5 Million
Number Employees: 20-49

21290 Dadant & Sons Inc
51 S 2nd St # 2
Hamilton, IL 62341-1397

217-847-3324
Fax: 217-847-3660 888-922-1293
dadant@dadant.com www.dadant.com
Injection molded hardware and honey handling and processing equipment; also, chocolate melters
President: Tim Dadant
Cio/Cto: Terry Avis
dadant@dadant.com
CFO: Tom Ross
VP: T Ross
Quality Control: Gary Stanspery

Estimated Sales: $1-2.5 Million
Number Employees: 100-249

21291 Dade Canvas Products Company
12067 Tech Road
Silver Spring, MD 20904

301-680-2500
Fax: 301-680-0851 thomasawning@prodigy.net
www.thomasawning.com
Commercial awnings
Owner: Michael Riley
Estimated Sales: $1-2.5 Million
Number Employees: 1-4

21292 Dade Engineering
15150 Nighthawk Drive
Tampa, FL 33625

813-264-2273
Fax: 813-343-8117 800-321-2112
richard@starsouth.us www.daeco.net
Manufacturer and exporter of walk-in coolers and freezers and cold storage doors
President: Joanne Goodstein
Estimated Sales: $5-10 Million
Number Employees: 10-19
Square Footage: 80000
Brands:
Daeco

21293 Daesang America Inc
1 University Plz # 505
Hackensack, NJ 07601-6203

201-488-4010
Fax: 201-488-4625 www.daesangamerica.com
President: David Park
Contact: Han Chang
chan@daesangamerica.com
Estimated Sales: $20-50 Million
Number Employees: 5-9

21294 Daga Restaurant Ware
500 Alakawa St Rm 220c
Honolulu, HI 96817

808-847-3100
Fax: 808-843-2977
Restaurant supplies
Owner: Noreen Quirk
Vice President: Alfred Coscina
Estimated Sales: $2.5-5 000,000
Number Employees: 1-4

21295 Dagher Printing
11775 Marco Beach Dr
Jacksonville, FL 32224-7616

904-998-0921
Fax: 904-998-0921 www.dagher.com
Commercial printer of business stationery; color printing available
Owner: Anthony Fredrickson
afredrickson@dagherprintingonline.com
Treasurer: Mouma Khourly
VP: Sam Dagher
Estimated Sales: $1-2.5 Million
Number Employees: 10-19
Square Footage: 16000

21296 Dahl-Tech Inc
5805 Saint Croix Trl N
Stillwater, MN 55082-6593

651-439-2946
Fax: 651-439-2976 800-626-5812
daltechinc@qwestoffice.net
www.dahltechplastics.com
Custom blew molding company and manufacturer of plastic containers, devices, and hollow structures for the food packaging, chemical, automotive, agricultural, healthcare, recreational, and household products industries.
President: Bob Dahlke
bob.dahlke@dahltechplastics.com
Sales: Nichole Blekum
Plant Manager: Brian Hell
Estimated Sales: $5 Million
Number Employees: 50-99
Square Footage: 128000
Type of Packaging: Consumer, Food Service, Private Label, Bulk

21297 Dahmes Stainless
6300 County Road 40
New London, MN 56273

320-354-5711
Fax: 320-354-5712 info@dahmes.com
www.dahmes.com

President: Forrest Dahmes
CFO: Dan DeGeest
Sales Director: Steve Frank
Production Manager: Jeff Kampsen
Purchasing Manager: Brad Doyle
Estimated Sales: $5-10 000,000
Number Employees: 20-49
Type of Packaging: Consumer, Bulk

21298 Daido Corp
1031 Fred White Blvd
Portland, TN 37148-8369

615-323-4020
Fax: 615-323-4015 866-219-9972
www.daidocorp.com

President: Mike Kato
carrierl@daidocorp.com
CEO: Steve Pudles
Sales Exec: Lee Carrier
Estimated Sales: $10-20 Million
Number Employees: 20-49

21299 Daily Printing Inc
2333 Niagara Ln N
Plymouth, MN 55447-4712

763-475-2333
Fax: 763-449-6320 800-622-6596
info@dailyprinting.com www.dailyprinting.com
Manufacturer and exporter of size reduction equipment for grinding, deagglomerating and pulverizing feeds, foods, spices, etc
President: Pete Jacobson
pjacobson@dailyprinting.com
CFO: Ken Rein
EVP: Don Bergeron
VP of Sales and Marketing: Tom Moe
Estimated Sales: $10-20 Million
Number Employees: 50-99
Square Footage: 200000

21300 DairiConcepts
3253 E Chestnut Expy
Springfield, MO 65802-2540

417-829-3400
Fax: 417-829-3401 877-596-4374
mwilliams@dairiconcepts.com
www.dairiconcepts.com

CEO: Jeff Miyake
jeffmiyake@dairiconcepts.com
Number Employees: 1-4

21301 Dairiconcepts
3253 E Chestnut Expy
Springfield, MO 65802-2540

417-829-3400
Fax: 417-829-3401 877-596-4374
mwilliams@dairiconcepts.com
www.dairiconcepts.com

CEO: Jeff Miyake
jeffmiyake@dairiconcepts.com
Number Employees: 1-4

21302 (HQ)Dairy Conveyor Corp
38 Mount Ebo Rd S
Brewster, NY 10509-4005

845-278-7878
Fax: 845-278-7305 info@dairyconveyor.com
www.dairyconveyor.com
Manufacturer and exporter of material handling equipment for dairies and ice cream plants
President: Karl Kleinschrod
CEO: Karl Kleinsahrod
Southeast Regional Sales Manager: Greg Reid
Eastern Regional Sales Manager: Tony Gomez
Estimated Sales: $12 Million
Number Employees: 100-249
Square Footage: 24000

21303 Dairy Foods
1050 IL Route 83
Suite 200
Bensenville, IL 60106

630-694-4341
Fax: 630-227-0527 www.bnp.com
Publications
Market Analyst: Jerry Dryer
Contact: M Sarah
kennedys@dairyfoods.com
Estimated Sales: Below $5 Million
Number Employees: 10

21304 Dairy Service & Mfg
1818 Linn St
Kansas City, MO 64116-3627

816-472-0011
Fax: 816-472-7935 800-825-0011
dsikc@dsiprocess.com
Custom fabrication, processing and packaging
Owner: Jack W Luechtefeld
Controller: Charlie Siebert
Accounts Manager: Gordon Gosejohan
Vice President: Gary Rinck
Technical Sevices/Refrigeration Manager: Dave Smith
Customer service: Brandon Barr
Marketing Manager: Lori Collier
Inside Sales: Nicole Wohletz
Customer Service: Dawn Jinson
Operations Manager: Georgia Pilla
Project Engineer: Paul Wallace
Estimated Sales: $2.5-5 000,000
Number Employees: 1-4

21305 Dairy Services Inc
450 W Meadow St
Stratford, WI 54484-9498

715-687-8091
800-221-3947
dsistratford@dairyservicesinc.com
Owner: Barb Nikolai
barb.nikolai@gmail.com
Number Employees: 10-19
Square Footage: 32000

21306 Dairy Specialties
8536 Cartney Ct
Dublin, OH 43017

614-764-1216
Fax: 614-855-3114 dsibrown@aol.com
Exporter, importer and wholesaler/distributor of milk proteins, flavor producing enzymes and dried dairy ingredients
President: David Brown
d.brown@dsm.com
CEO: V Brown
Estimated Sales: $2 Million
Number Employees: 1-4
Square Footage: 6000
Type of Packaging: Bulk

21307 Dairyland Plastics Company
N 8986 County Rd
Colfax, WI 54730-4500

715-962-3425
Plastic bags
Owner: David Haugle

21308 Dakota Blenders
1350 South Kingshighway
St. Louis, MO 63110

314-898-9926
Fax: 314-531-3789 800-383-0958
www.dakotablenders.net
A leading supplier of quality blends for top wholesale bakeries, as well as numerous other divisions of the industry.

21309 Dakota Corrugated Box
4501 N 2nd Ave
Sioux Falls, SD 57104-0676

605-332-3501
Fax: 605-332-3496
Corrugated containers
President: Robert Bittner
CFO: Bob Bittner
Sales Manager: Mike Bartlett
General Manager: Mike Bartlett
Estimated Sales: $2.5-5 Million
Number Employees: 20 to 49

21310 Dakota Valley Products,Inc.
419 3rd St.
Willow Lake, SD 57278

605-625-2526
Fax: 605-352-0558
Agricultural products marketing company
Estimated Sales: $1-5 Million
Number Employees: 4

21311 Dalare Associates Inc
217 S 24th St
Philadelphia, PA 19103-5593

215-567-1953
Fax: 215-567-1168 info@dalarelab.com
www.dalarelab.com

Analytical and Environmental analysis through a full range of laboratory services.
President: Joseph J Strug Jr
Estimated Sales: $500,000-$1 Million
Number Employees: 5-9

21312 Daleco
1000 Wilmont Mews
5th Floor
West Chester, PA 19382

610-429-0181
Fax: 610-429-0818 www.dalecoresources.com
Steamed cheeseburger making machines
President: Robert Gattilia
Estimated Sales: $.5-1 million
Number Employees: 1-4
Brands:
Burg'r Tend'r

21313 Dalemark Industries
575 Prospect St
Bldg. 211
Lakewood, NJ 08701-5040

732-367-3100
Fax: 732-367-7031 sales@dalemark.com
www.dalemark.com
Manufacturer and exporter of coding, imprinting and labeling equipment
President: Michael Delli Gatti
CFO: Kathy Scalzo
Research & Development: Thurman Becker
Marketing: Maria Rau
Sales: Maria Rau
Purchasing: Maria Rau
Estimated Sales: $1 Million
Number Employees: 10-19
Number of Brands: 15
Number of Products: 25
Square Footage: 24000
Type of Packaging: Food Service
Brands:
Codaire
Dotmark

21314 (HQ)Dallas Container Corp
8330 Endicott Ln
Dallas, TX 75227-2305

214-381-7148
Fax: 214-381-8279 800-381-7148
www.dallascontainer.com
Corrugated containers
President & Owner: Rod Turnipseed
rturnipseed@dallascontainer.net
Plant Manager: James Cullen
Estimated Sales: $10-20 Million
Number Employees: 50-99
Other Locations:
Dallas Container Corp.
Albuquerque NM

21315 Dallas Group of America Inc
374 US Highway 22
Whitehouse, NJ 08888-9800

908-534-7800
Fax: 908-534-0084 800-367-4188
info@dallasgrp.com
Magnesium silicate, frying oil purifiers, filter aids and absorbents; exporter of magnesium silicate
Owner: Bob Dallas Sr
Estimated Sales: $10-20,000,000
Number Employees: 20-49
Type of Packaging: Food Service, Bulk
Brands:
Dalsorb
Haze-Out
Magnesol
Xl

21316 Dallas Roth Young
100 N Cottonwood Drive
Suite 108
Richardson, TX 75080-4772

972-233-5000
Fax: 972-235-5210
Executive search firm specializing in selection and placement of food industry personnel
President: Ben Dickerson
Sales/Marketing Manager: Chad Dickerson
Number Employees: 3
Square Footage: 1600
Parent Co: Winston Franchise Corporation

21317 Dalloz Safety
10 Thurber Blvd
Smithfield, RI 02917-1858

401-233-0333
Fax: 401-232-1830 800-977-9177
jwomer@dallozsafety.com
Ear muffs, laser eyewear, safety spectacles, goggles
and disposable and reusable respirators and ear
plugs
Director Marketing Communication: Elizabeth
Antry
Director Sales: Scott Walker
Estimated Sales: $50-100 Million
Number Employees: 10-19
Brands:
  Bilsom
  Gpt
  Glendale

21318 Dalls Semiconductor
160 Rio Robles
San Jose, CA 95134

972-702-9250
Fax: 972-371-3748 888-629-4642
sales-us@maximintegrated.com
www.maxim-ic.com
President and Chief Executive Officer: Tun‡ Doluca
SVP and Chief Financial Officer: Bruce E. Kiddoo
President; Chief Executive Officer; Dire: Tunc
Doluca
Vice President, Test Engineering: Rob Georges
Vice President, Quality: Bryan Preeshl
Vice President of Sales and Marketing: Walter
Sangalli
Vice President of Human Resources: Steve
Yamasaki
SVP of Manufacturing Operations: Vivek Jain
Estimated Sales: $1-5 Million
Parent Co: Maxim Integrated

21319 Dalmec North America
469 Fox Ct
Bloomingdale, IL 60108-3110

630-307-8426
Fax: 630-307-8436 800-935-8686
sales@dalmecusa.com www.dalmec-na.com
Industrial manipulators for handling rolls, barrels,
boxes, pails or custom product manufacture highly
ergonomic manipulators, combined with bispoke
tooling heads, custom-built to handle a specific
product
Manager: Al Izzo
Sales Manager: Al Killian
Branch Manager: Allan Izzo
Estimated Sales: $2.5-5 000,000
Number Employees: 10-19

21320 Dalton Electric HeatingCo
28 Hayward St
Ipswich, MA 01938-2096

978-356-9844
Fax: 978-356-9846 dalton@daltonelectric.com
www.daltonelectric.com
Industrial heating products-Wall-Flex® Cartridge
Heaters.
Owner: Thomas A Shields
tshields@daltonelectricheatingco.com
Sales: E W Whitney III
tshields@daltonelectricheatingco.com
Plant Manager: Steve Lounes
Estimated Sales: $5-10 000,000
Number Employees: 20-49
Square Footage: 17000

21321 Damas Corporation
1977 N Olden Avenue Ext
Suite 289
Trenton, NJ 08618-2112

609-695-9121
Fax: 609-695-9225
Manufacturer and exporter of washing and drying
equipment for laboratory glassware, trays, tote bins,
tubs, pallets and carts
President: David M Smith
Engineer: Dave Smith
Estimated Sales: $1-2,500,000
Number Employees: 5-9
Brands:
  Aquasan
  Thermajet

21322 Damascus/Bishop Tube Company
795 Reynolds Industrial Park Road
Greenville, PA 16125-4203

724-646-1500
Fax: 724-646-1514
FDA approved steel stainless pipe and tubing for
dairy processors
President: Brent Ward
Estimated Sales: $1-5 Million
Number Employees: 100-249

21323 Damon Industries
12435 Rockhill Ave NE
Alliance, OH 44601

Fax: 330-821-6355 800-362-9850
info@damonq.com damonq.com
Manufacturer cleaning chemicals and disinfectants;
consultant specializing in food safety and HACCP
President/Owner: Amy Damon
Executive Vice President: Scott Butterfield
Estimated Sales: $50-100 Million
Number Employees: 100-249
Square Footage: 45000

21324 Damons Graoo
11 Green Pond Road
Rockaway, NJ 07866-2001

973-664-1000
Fax: 973-664-1305
Manufacture high pressure enjection molded prod-
ucts for food and agriculture
Estimated Sales: $300,000-500,000
Number Employees: 10

21325 Damp Rid
W.M. Barr
P.O. Box 1879
Memphis, TN 38101-6948

407-851-6230
Fax: 407-851-6246 888-326-7743
www.damprid.com
Manufacturer and exporter of mildew preventatives,
moisture absorbers and odor eliminators
President: Darien Jalka
CFO: Ken Lasseter
Quality Control: Oliver Cunanan
Sales Director: Darin Galka
Purchasing Manager: Roy Rosado
Estimated Sales: $5-10 Million
Number Employees: 10
Square Footage: 288000
Parent Co: Tetra Technologies Incorporated
Type of Packaging: Consumer
Brands:
  Damp Rid
  Fresh-All
  Magic Disk

21326 Damrow Company
894 S Military Rd
Fond Du Lac, WI 54935

920-922-1500
Fax: 920-922-1502 800-236-1501
Dairy and food processing equipment including
cheese making, automated control systems, process
and storage tanks, evaporators, CIP systems and pro-
cess piping; exporter of cheese making equipment
Manager: Gary Ring
Sales Director: Mark Steffens
Operations: Todd Martin
Estimated Sales: $10-20 Million
Number Employees: 5-9
Square Footage: 300000
Parent Co: Carlisle Process Systems

21327 Dan Mar Co
2131 N Collins St
B433-738
Arlington, TX 76011

817-822-5767
Fax: 218-338-5909 danmarco1@msn.com
www.danmarco.net
Supplier of products in antimicrobial control for
beef, pork and poultry industries
President: Paul Edwards
Estimated Sales: Under $500,000
Number Employees: 1-4

21328 Dan-D Foods Ltd
11760 Machrina Way
Richmond, BC V7A 4V1
Canada

604-274-3263
Fax: 604-274-3268 800-633-4788
www.dan-d-pak.com
Fine food importer, manufacturer and distributor of
cashews, dried fruits, rice crackers, snack foods,
spices etc. from around the world.
Chairman/President/CEO/Founder: Dan On
Number Employees: 500
Type of Packaging: Food Service, Bulk

21329 (HQ)Dana Labels
7778 SW Nimbus Ave
Beaverton, OR 97008-6423

503-646-7933
Fax: 503-641-4728 800-255-1492
Labels and labeling machines
Owner: Wilfredo Rabanal
Sales Manager: Dave Pancoast
Estimated Sales: $20-50 Million
Number Employees: 20-49
Brands:
  Axcess

21330 Dana S. Oliver & Associates
21 Island Drive
Savannah, GA 31406-5238

912-354-1455
Fax: 912-354-2455
Consultants for executive searches and placement in
the food and beverage industry
President: Dana Oliver

21331 (HQ)Danafilms Inc
5 Otis St
Westborough, MA 01581-3311

508-366-8884
Fax: 508-898-0106 www.danafilms.com
Manufacturer and exporter of polyethylene films for
packaging.
President: Sherman Olson
solson@danafilms.com
VP Sales: Bob Simoncini
Marketing Director: Steve Crimmin
Sales Manager: Steve Crimmin
General Manager: Alan Simoncini
Purchasing Manager: Alan Simoncini
Estimated Sales: $20-30 Million
Number Employees: 50-99
Square Footage: 40000
Type of Packaging: Consumer, Food Service, Pri-
  vate Label, Bulk
Other Locations:
  Danafilms
  Hopedale MA

21332 Danbury Plastics
239 Castleberry Industrial Dr
Cumming, GA 30040-9051

678-455-7391
Fax: 203-790-6801 info@danburyplastics.com
www.danburyplastics.com
Manufacturer, importer and exporter of compression
and injection molded bottle caps as well as linings
and gaskets
President: Michael Da Cruz
Quality Control: Diana Cepada
Sales: Donna Dyke
Plant Manager: Rocco Grosse
Estimated Sales: $2.5-5 Million
Number Employees: 10-19
Square Footage: 18000
Type of Packaging: Consumer, Private Label

21333 Dandelion Chocolate
740 Valencia St
San Francisco, CA 94110-1735

415-349-0942
800-785-2301
www.dandelionchocolate.com
Chocolates
Owner: Maggi Mcconnell
maggi.m@gmail.com
CEO: Todd Masonis
Number Employees: 5-9

21334 Danfoss Drives
2995 Eastrock Drive
Rockford, IL 61109-1737

815-398-2770
Fax: 815-398-2869

CEO: Jergen Clausen
Executive VP & CFO: Frederik Lotz
Estimated Sales: $1-5 Million

21335 Danfoss Drives
4401 N Bell School Rd
Loves Park, IL 61111

888-326-3677
www.danfossdrives.com
Electronic AC motor controls.
President & CEO: Kim Fausing
EVP & Chief Financial Officer: Jesper Christensen
President, Power Solutions: Eric Alstrom
President, Cooling: Jurgen Fischer
President, Drives: Vesa Laisi
President, Heating: Lars Tveen
Year Founded: 1933
Estimated Sales: Over $1 Billion
Number Employees: 26,000
Parent Co: Danfoss

21336 Danger Men Cooking
3 Lumen Ln
Highland, NY 12528-1903

845-691-7029
Fax: 845-691-2852
BBQ accesories and gear for men
President: Peter Rooney
Estimated Sales: $10-20 Million
Number Employees: 10-19
Brands:
Bbq Sauce
Danger Men Cooking
Hot Sauce
Ketchupepper
Steak Sauce
Tough Guy's
Wussy Hot Sauce

21337 Daniel Boone Lumber Industries
1375 Clearfork N
Morehead, KY 40351

606-784-7586
Fax: 606-783-1858
New and reconditioned wooden pallets and skids
President: Gail Lincoln
Regional Sales Manager: Mike Coburn
Sales Manager: Mike Coburn
Plant Supervisor: Elvis Middleton
Estimated Sales: Below $5 Million
Number Employees: 10-19
Square Footage: 50000

21338 Daniel J. Bloch & Company
PO Box 263
Essex, CT 06426-0263

860-767-8204
Fax: 860-767-8205
Roasters and roasting machines
Owner: Daniel Bloch

21339 Daniel Woodhead Company
3411 Woodhead Drive
Northbrook, IL 60062-1892

847-272-7990
Fax: 847-272-8133
General packing house electrical and safety equipment and devices; AC Waterlite plugs and connectors, quick disconnect molded control connectors, temporary lighting, portable outlet boxes, electric reels, wire mesh grips, DC batteryconnectors and push b
Contact: Debbie Dickinson
ddickinson@danielwoodhead.com
Estimated Sales: $2.5-5 000,000
Number Employees: 10-19

21340 Danieli Awnings
2530 Oak St
Napa, CA 94559-2227

707-257-6100
Fax: 707-257-0318
Commercial awnings
President: Charles Gibson
charles@danielis.com
Estimated Sales: $500,000-$1,000,000
Number Employees: 5-9

21341 Daniels Food Equipment
310 N Clayborn Ave
PO Box 341
Parkers Prairie, MN 56361-4748

218-338-5000
Fax: 218-338-5909 danielsfood@midwestinfo.net
www.danielsfood.com
Supplier of stainless steel products for meat industry; including grinders, stuffers, grinders, mixers, etc
President: Gary Haavig
garyhaavig@midwestinfo.net
President: Marty Weibye
Estimated Sales: $2 Million
Number Employees: 1-4

21342 Danish Food Equipment
1633 E Madison St
Petaluma, CA 94954-2320

707-763-0110
Fax: 707-763-1303
Owner: Flemming Maersk
Vice President: Flemming Maersk
Estimated Sales: $1-5 Million

21343 Daniso USA
PO Box 653
Pine Brook, NJ 07058-0653

201-784-9300
Fax: 201-784-0604
Estimated Sales: $1-5 Million

21344 Danlac Inc
1917 Twilight Ln
Hudson, WI 54016-9271

715-381-5575
Fax: 715-381-5576
Butter processing and dairy equipment
Owner: Liane Hoier
liane@danlacinc.com
Estimated Sales: less than $500,000
Number Employees: 1-4

21345 Danmark Packaging Systems
PO Box 560901
Lewisville, TX 75056-6901

972-625-8311
Fax: 972-370-9113
Shrink packaging machinery including semi and fully automatic L-sealers and shrink tunnel combinations, horizontal form, fill, seal machines and semi and fully automatic sleeve wrap and bundling systems with in-line and multi-packcollating capabilities

21346 Dansk International Designs
P.O. Box 2006
Suite 301
Bristol, PA 19007-0806

914-697-6400
Fax: 914-697-6464 www.dansk.com
China, crystal, housewares, tabletop items, giftware, etc
President: David Herman
VP Merchandising: Jeanne Allen
Estimated Sales: $1-5 Million
Number Employees: 250-500
Parent Co: Lenox

21347 Danville Economic Development
427 Patton St # 203
Danville, VA 24541-1215

434-793-1753
Fax: 434-797-9606
Manager: Jeremy Stratton
Number Employees: 5-9

21348 Dap Technologies Corporation
8945 South Harl Avenue
Suite 112
Tempe, AR 85284

813-969-3271
Fax: 813-969-3334 800-229-2822
www.daptech.com
Packaging equipment specializing in bar code scanner technology
President: Yzes Oaroctue
CEO: Michel Oatointe
Contact: Jim Higgins
jimhiggins@daptech.com
Estimated Sales: $2.5-5 Million
Number Employees: 9

21349 Dapec
1000 Evenflo Dr
Ball Ground, GA 30107

770-345-2841
Fax: 770-345-5926
Processing equipment
President: Scott Russell
Chairman of the Board: Jack Hazenbroek
Estimated Sales: $20-50 Million
Number Employees: 20-49

21350 Dapec/Numafa
1000 Evenflo Dr
Ball Ground, GA 30107-4544

770-345-2841
Fax: 770-345-5926 www.dapec.com
Conveyor systems and accessories, sanitation supplies, temperature control equipment
President: Scott Russell
Estimated Sales: $10-20 Million
Number Employees: 20-49

21351 Dar-B-Ques Barbecue Equipment
2300 Minnehaha Ave S
Minneapolis, MN 55404

612-724-7425
www.coastalseafoods.com
Barbecue grills and pig roasters
President: Freddrew Freddrew
Estimated Sales: Below $5 Million
Number Employees: 1-4
Square Footage: 150000
Brands:
Dar-B-Ques

21352 Darcor Casters
7 Staffordshire Place
Toronto, ON M8W 1T1
Canada

416-255-8563
Fax: 416-251-6117 800-387-7206
casters@darcor.com www.darcor.com
Manufacturer and exporter of casters and wheels
President: Rob Hilborn
Controller: Dan Watson
Engineering Manager: Adrian Steenson
Director of Marketing: Kirk Tobias
Number Employees: 75
Square Footage: 320000
Parent Co: Darcor Casters
Brands:
Carpet Master
Cartwashable
Solid Elastomer

21353 Darcy Group
1350 Home Ave Ste L
Akron, OH 44310

330-633-4700
Fax: 330-633-8779
Manager: Jodi Westphal
Quality Control: Bob Tredd
Estimated Sales: $2.5-5 000,000
Number Employees: 50-99

21354 Darfill
750 Green Crest Dr
Westerville, OH 43081-2837

614-890-3274
Fax: 614-890-4230 info@darifill.com
www.darifill.com
Equipment that offers a variety of filling, packaging styles and sealing methods for the dairy and ice cream industries.
President: Lisa Aspery
lisa@darifill.com
Number Employees: 10-19

21355 Dari Farms Ice Cream Inc
1501 State St
Bridgeport, CT 06605-2010

203-384-0820
Fax: 203-336-3235
www.dairyfarms.com/error.html
Manager: Richard Corraro
rcorraro@dairyfarms.com
General Manager: Michael Carraro
Estimated Sales: $3-5 Million
Number Employees: 20-49

485

21356 Darlington Dairy Supply Co Inc
17332 State Road 81
Darlington, WI 53530-9257
608-776-4064
Fax: 608-776-4092 800-877-4064
daveg@ddsco.com www.ddsco.com
Heat exchangers, plate, tubular, process control
President: Mae Thuli
dds@mhtc.net
Marketing: Torry Thuli
Estimated Sales: $5-10 000,000
Number Employees: 10-19

21357 Darlington Sign Awning & Neon
221 Jefferson Blvd
Warwick, RI 02888-3818
401-734-5800
Fax: 401-231-1481 custserv@aathriftysign.com
www.aathriftysign.com
Neon signs and awnings; installation services available
Owner: David Solomon
Operations Manager: Tom Grenga
Estimated Sales: $5-10 Million
Number Employees: 20-49
Square Footage: 20000

21358 Darmex Corporation
71 Jane Street
Roslyn Heights, NY 11577-1359
516-621-3000
Fax: 516-621-3627 800-645-6368
info@fuchs.com
Sanitary lubricants
Estimated Sales: $50-100 Million
Number Employees: 140

21359 Darnell-Rose Inc
17915 Railroad St
City Of Industry, CA 91748-1113
626-912-1688
Fax: 626-912-3765 800-327-6355
www.casters.com
Manufacturer and exporter of casters and wheels, including stainless steel models and other mobility products
President: Brent Bargar
bbargar@casters.com
Research & Development: Bob Siegried
Quality Control: Phil Mazzolini
Marketing Director: Brent Bargar
Sales Director: Bob Siegried
Operations Manager: Richard Martinez
Purchasing Manager: Robbie McCullah
Estimated Sales: $10-20 Million
Number Employees: 50-99
Square Footage: 170000
Type of Packaging: Food Service, Bulk

21360 Darson Corp
7650 Chrysler Dr # 150
Suite 150
Detroit, MI 48211-1734
313-875-7781
Fax: 313-875-1666 800-783-7781
www.thedarsoncorp.com
Screen printed decals, labels and name plates
President: Mary Ellen Darge
Controller: Shirley Lyle
Production Manager: David Breuhan
Estimated Sales: $1-2.5 Million
Number Employees: 10-19

21361 Dart Canada Inc.
2121 Markham Rd.
Toronto, ON M1B 2W3
Canada
416-293-2877
800-465-9696
canadainfo@dartcanada.ca
www.dartcontainer.com/ca
Paper, plastic and foam cups and plates; also, plastic knives, forks and spoons.
Estimated Sales: K
Number Employees: 5,000-9,999
Parent Co: Dart Container Corp.
Brands:
　Lily

21362 Dart Container Corp.
500 Hogsback Rd.
Mason, MI 48854
Fax: 517-676-3883 800-248-5960
sales@dart.biz www.dartcontainer.com

Disposable tabletop supplies including foam cups, containers and lids, plastic cups and lids, fusion cups, foam plastic dinnerware, foam hinged lid containers, clear containers, portion containers and lids, and plastic cutlery.
President: Jim Lammers
Executive VP/CFO: Christine Waltz
Executive VP, Sales: Robert Novak
Year Founded: 1960
Estimated Sales: Over $1 Billion
Number Employees: 15,000
Number of Brands: 37
Brands:
　J Cup®
　LX®
　ThermoGlaze®
　Trophy®
　Solo®
　Bare® by Solo®
　Conex ClearPro®
　Conex ProMotions®
　Galaxy®
　MicroGreen™
　Duo Shield®
　Anthora™
　ThermoGuard™
　Fusion®
　Impulse®
　PresentaBowls®
　ClearPac®
　StayLock®
　SafeSeal™
　Conex Complements®
　MicroGourmet®
　M-Line™
　SoloServe®
　Eco Expressions™
　Expressions®
　Creative Carryouts®
　Flexstyle®
　Concord®
　Quiet Classic®
　Silent Service®
　Guildware®
　Reliance®
　Impress™
　Regal™
　Ready Roll®
　Traveler®
　Prima™

21363 Dashco
17 Westpark Drive
Gloucester, ON K1B 3G6
Canada
613-834-6825
Fax: 613-834-6826
Manufacturer and exporter of degradable plastic carry-out/check-out bags
President: Dave Paul
Number Employees: 2
Brands:
　Biosolo
　Dashco

21364 Data 2
1099 Essex Ave
Richmond, CA 94801-2112
510-232-6200
Fax: 510-235-2176 800-227-2121
www.data2.com
Wine industry UPC bar code labels
Manager: Alan Gaber
alan@data2.com
Estimated Sales: $1-5 Million
Number Employees: 20-49

21365 Data Consultants
P.O.Box 180
Pleasant Hill, MO 64080
805-748-3427
Fax: 703-330-2436 info@dataconsultantsinc.com
www.dataconsultantsinc.com
PCs and management of and access to critical business information
Owner: Mike Mc Neall
Accountant and Public Relations: Shelly Haines
Marketing: Mark Frund
Contact: Aaron Donatello
aaron.donatello@dciasp.com

21366 Data Consulting Associates
18000 Coleman Valley Rd
Occidental, CA 95465-9236
707-874-3067
Fax: 707-874-3848
Wine industry computer software
Owner: Carey Dubbert
Estimated Sales: $1-3 Million
Number Employees: 1-4

21367 Data Management
1 Time Clock Drive
San Angelo, TX 76904
325-223-9500
Fax: 325-223-9104 800-749-8463
www.timeclockplus.com
Software for restaurants including programs for recording and calculating payroll hours, taking orders, customer service, P.O.S., delivery systems, time, attendance and scheduling packages
President: Jorge Ellis
Director Marketing: Scott Turner
Sales/Technical Manager: Mark Moorman
Estimated Sales: $1-2.5 Million
Number Employees: 10-19
Square Footage: 3400
Brands:
　Timeclock Plus

21368 Data Scale
42430 Blacow Rd
Fremont, CA 94539-5621
510-651-7350
Fax: 510-651-6343 800-651-7350
sales@datascale.com www.datascale.com
Liquid drum and pail filling systems
Owner: Terry B Lowe
tlowe@datascale.com
Sales Director: Tim DuClos
Estimated Sales: $1-2,500,000
Number Employees: 10-19
Type of Packaging: Consumer, Food Service
Brands:
　Data Scale

21369 Data Specialists
1021 Proctor Dr # 1
Elkhorn, WI 53121-2027
262-723-5726
Fax: 262-723-5767 800-211-1545
info@dataspecialist.com www.dataspecialists.com
Manufacutrer of computers and software designed for the dairy industry including production, costing, inventory, distribution, payroll, etc.; installation and start-up services available
President: Sherrie Mertes
Estimated Sales: $2.5-5 Million
Number Employees: 20-49

21370 Data Specialists
1021 Proctor Dr # 1
Elkhorn, WI 53121-2027
262-723-5726
Fax: 262-723-5767 www.dataspecialists.com
Process accountablity and reconciliatoin business software for food and dairy industry
President: Sherrie Mertes
Estimated Sales: $2.5-5 Million
Number Employees: 20-49

21371 Data Visible Corporation
PO Box 7767
Charlottesville, VA 22906-7767
434-296-5608
Fax: 434-977-1076 800-368-3494
www.datavisible.com
Quick reference cash register units, flip cards, job-aids for bulk pricing and instructions, color coded folders, labels, filing cabinets, etc
President: A Patton Janssen Jr
Executive VP: Gary Sloan
Number Employees: 10
Brands:
　Data Visible
　Dataflex

21372 Datalogic ADC
959 Terry St
Eugene, OR 97402-9150
541-683-5700
Fax: 541-687-7998 800-929-3221
info.adc.us@datalogic.com www.datalogic.com

Sensors, capacitive sensors, photoelectrics, linear transducers and identification for packaging and electronic sensors for automation manufacturer of both CCD and LASER bar code reading technologies
President: Darrell Owens
CFO: Mack Ruacker
Estimated Sales: $5-10 000,000
Number Employees: 20-49

21373 (HQ)Datapaq
187 Ballardvale St
Wilmington, MA 01887-1082

978-988-9000
Fax: 978-988-0666 800-326-5270
websales@datapaq.com www.datapaq.com
Monitors the temperature profiles of a food product as it passes through continuous cook, bake, chill, freeze, and fry processes. A Datapaq system is comprised of four major components: a data logger, a protective thermal barrier toprotect the logger, thermocouple probes, and easy-to-use software to analyze and store temperature data collected during a process. Detailed graphical information gives a complete picture of the continuous process
President: Michael E White
Marketing Director: Kathleen Higgins
Sales Director: Bill Adaschik
Contact: D Abbrat
abbrat@datapaq.com
Estimated Sales: $5-10 Million
Number Employees: 10-19
Square Footage: 19200
Other Locations:
  Datapaq
  Cambridge
Brands:
  Datapaq Multi-Tracker System

21374 Datapax
11225 North 28th Drive
Suite D-102
Phoenix, AZ 85029

602-212-9202
Fax: 602-274-1476 877-328-2729
Computer programming, management systems and services for bakeries and food processing in modular and integrated system format
Owner: Tyson Philippi
Estimated Sales: $2.5-5 000,000
Number Employees: 5-9

21375 Datu Inc
159 Maxwell Ave
Geneva, NY 14456-1538

315-787-2240
Fax: 315-787-2284
GCO systems for analysis of odors
President: Terry Accree
CEO: Stephen Wyckoff
Manager: Steve Wyckoff
Number Employees: 1-4

21376 Daubert Cromwell LLC
12701 S Ridgeway Ave
Alsip, IL 60803-1526

708-293-7750
Fax: 708-293-7765 info@daubertcromwell.com
Rust inhibiting paper, film and paper converting
President: Francis Houlihan
CEO: Oscar Abello
oabello@daubert.com
CEO: Martin J Simpson
Estimated Sales: $5-10 000,000
Number Employees: 50-99

21377 Daubert VCI
1333 Burr Ridge Pkwy Ste 200
Burr Ridge, IL 60527

630-203-6800
Fax: 630-203-6900 800-535-3535
www.daubert.com
Corrosion-preventive packaging products paper, film, emitters
President: M Lawrence Garman
CFO: Peter Miehl
Estimated Sales: H
Number Employees: 100-249

21378 Dave's Imports
6824 N Main Street
Jacksonville, FL 32208-4726

904-764-6886
Fax: 904-764-7131 800-553-2837
Advertising specialties

Graphic Artist/Admin.: Kimberly Pratt
Estimated Sales: less than $500,000
Number Employees: 1

21379 Davenport Machine
301 Second St
PO Box 6635
Rock Island, IL 61201

309-786-1500
Fax: 309-786-0771
Manufacturer and exporter of rotary dryers and coolers, foundry equipment and continuous dewatering presses
President: R Nixon Jr
General Sales Manager: Lauren Reimer
Chief Engineer: R Bateman
Estimated Sales: $5-10 Million
Number Employees: 20-50
Square Footage: 172000
Parent Co: Middle States Corporation

21380 David A Lingle & Son Mfg
104 S Knoxville Ave
Russellville, AR 72801-5315

479-968-2500
Fax: 479-968-1998
Walk-in coolers and freezers, cold storage doors and insulated specialties
Owner: David L Lingle
Partner: Larry Lingle
CFO: Jean Harbison
Estimated Sales: $1-3 Million
Number Employees: 20-49
Square Footage: 40000

21381 (HQ)David Dobbs EnterpriseInc.
4600 US 1 N
St Augustine, FL 32095

904-824-6171
Fax: 904-824-9989 800-889-6368
sales@menudesigns.com www.menudesigns.com
Vinyl and leather menu covers, wine lists and guest service directories; also, promotional items including hats, T-shirts, tote bags, aprons and pizza bags
President: David Dobbs
CFO: Peggy Dobs
Executive VP: Jay Maguire
Quality Control: Terry Sechen
Sales Manager: J Michael Davis
Estimated Sales: $10-20 Million
Number Employees: 50-99

21382 David E. Moley & Associates
PO Box 920
Wrightsville Beach, NC 28480

910-256-3826
Fax: 910-256-8639 moleyusa@aol.com
Executive search consultant for food service manufacturers seeking sales and marketing executives
VP: Gloria Moley
Estimated Sales: less than $500,000
Number Employees: 5

21383 David's Goodbatter
PO Box 102
Bausman, PA 17504-0102

717-872-0652
Fax: 717-872-8152
Processor, packager and exporter of organic pancakes and baking mixes, pasta, couscous, Irish oatmeal, dried beans, bean blends and gluten-free and wheat-free foods; importer of maple candies and syrup; also, custom packaging andprivate labeling available
Owner: Jane David
Estimated Sales: $1-2.5 Million appx.
Number Employees: 1-4
Square Footage: 52000
Type of Packaging: Consumer, Food Service, Private Label, Bulk
Brands:
  David's Goodbatter
  Gabriel & Rose

21384 Davidson's Safest Choice Eggs
2963 Bernice Road
Lansing, IL 60438

708-418-8500
Fax: 708-418-1235 800-410-7619
info@safeeggs.com www.safeeggs.com
Pasteurized eggs
President: Greg West
CFO: Michael Smith

21385 Davis & Small Decor
1888 Clements Ferry Rd
Charleston, SC 29492

843-881-8990
Fax: 800-227-7398 800-849-5082
orders@dsdecor.com
Manufacturer and exporter of decorative wall items for restaurants
President: Thomas M Davis
Estimated Sales: $3-5 Million
Number Employees: 20-49

21386 Davis Brothers Produce Boxes
8264 Haynes Lennon Highway
Evergreen, NC 28438-0069

910-654-4913
Packaging material including wooden containers and boxes
President: Bedford S David Jr
Estimated Sales: $1-5 Million
Number Employees: 20

21387 Davis Core & Pa
1140 Davis Rd SW
Cave Spring, GA 30124-2422

706-777-3675
Fax: 706-777-8690 800-235-7483
sales@daviscore.com www.daviscore.com
Custom molded expanded polystyrene packaging materials, cold storage shipping containers and disposable shipping pallets; industrial sizes available
President: Joel Davis
joel@daviscore.com
Estimated Sales: $5 Million
Number Employees: 20-49
Square Footage: 60000
Brands:
  Kol-Boy Products

21388 Davlynne International
3383 E Layton Ave Stop 3
Cudahy, WI 53110

414-481-1011
Fax: 414-481-3155 800-558-5208
Manufacturer and exporter of strip curtains and doors, custom cart covers and enclosures
President: Kristin Larson
CEO: Randall Larson
Marketing Director: Krista Larson
Estimated Sales: $2.5-5 Million
Number Employees: 7
Square Footage: 13000
Brands:
  Glare-Eze
  Inhibidor

21389 Davron Technologies Inc
4563 Pinnacle Ln
Chattanooga, TN 37415-3811

423-870-1888
Fax: 423-870-1108 sales@davrontech.com
www.davrontech.com
Manufacturer and exporter of all types of custom process equipment including, but not limited to, ovens, conveying systems, washing systems and frying systems
President: Ronald Speicher
Director Sales/Marketing: Jimmy Evans
Contact: Bobby Bishop
bbishop@davrontech.com
Equipment Design Manager: David Craft
Estimated Sales: $10-20 Million
Number Employees: 50-99

21390 Day & Zimmermann Group Inc
1500 Spring Garden St # 500
Philadelphia, PA 19130-4070

215-299-8000
Fax: 215-299-8208 800-523-0786
media.relations@dayzim.com www.dayzim.com
Electrical, electronic and construction engineering equipment and services for food and beverage industry
President: Steve Selfridge
sselfridge@davita.com
Vice President: Anthony Bosco Jr.
Marketing Manager: Tamara Dean
Chief Operating Officer: Michael McAreavy
Estimated Sales: Over $1 Billion
Number Employees: 10000+

21391 Day & Zimmermann International
610 Minuet Lane
Charlotte, NC 28217-2723
704-943-5007
Fax: 704-943-5112 www.dayzim.com
CEO: Harold Yoh III
Vice President And CIO: Anthony Bosco Jr.
Marketing Manager: Tamara Dean
Chief Operating Officer: Michael McAreavy

21392 Day Basket Factory
PO Box 724
North East, MD 21901
410-398-5150
Fax: 410-287-8835
daybasketcompany@gmail.com
www.daybasketfactory.com
Hand-made white oak baskets including grocery and shopping
Owner: Robert Fredrick
Estimated Sales: $500,000-$1 Million
Number Employees: 1-4
Type of Packaging: Private Label

21393 Day Lumber Company
34 South Broad Street
Westfield, MA 01085
413-568-3511
Fax: 413-568-6668 allen@daylumber.com
www.daylumber.com
Wooden skids and pallets; also, plywood containers
President: Arthur Grodd
VP Sales / General Manager: Allen Nadler
Operations Manager: Lee Krieg
Estimated Sales: $2.5-5 Million
Number Employees: 10-19

21394 Day Manufacturing Company
419 E Lamar St
Sherman, TX 75090
903-893-1138
Fax: 903-892-0218
Folding cartons
President: Herald W Totten
VP: Curry Vogelsang
Operations Manager: Rick Smith
Estimated Sales: $10-20 Million
Number Employees: 20-49
Square Footage: 107000
Parent Co: Washington Iron Works

21395 Day Nite Neon Signs
PO Box 2716
Dartmouth, NS B3B 1E3
Canada
902-469-7095
Fax: 902-469-2124
Illuminated and architectural signs and interior graphics
President: Chris Boone Jr
CFO: Allen Fraser
Sales Director: Wayne Stewart
Number Employees: 10

21396 Day-O-Lite
126 Chestnut St
Warwick, RI 02888-2104
401-467-8232
Fax: 401-941-2960 sales@dayolite.com
www.dayoliteled.com
Fluorescent lighting fixtures
President: Steven Weisman
steve@dayolight.com
Estimated Sales: $20-50 Million
Number Employees: 50-99
Square Footage: 4000

21397 Dayco
4681 107th Circle N
Clearwater, FL 33762-5006
727-573-9330
Fax: 727-573-2879 www.daycoindia.com
Stainless steel custom chef lines and tables
President: James Ashbaugh
Sales Director: Ron Rogers
Estimated Sales: $2.5-5 Million
Number Employees: 10
Square Footage: 60000

21398 Daydots
1801 Riverbend West Dr
Fort Worth, TX 76118
817-590-4500
Fax: 817-590-4501 800-321-3687
sales@daydots.com www.daydots.com
A goal of making the world a safer place to eat. Daydots offers more than 4,000 products and services including original day of the week food safety labels. Produce and distribute products for food rotation, temperture control;cross-contamination prevention; personal hygiene and sanitation and cleaning, employee safety and food safety education.
President/Owner: Mark Smith
Marketing: Paul McGinnis
Sales: Laura Manatis
Contact: Shawn Blazuir
shawnb@daydots.com
Operations: Chad Logan
Number Employees: 50-99
Number of Products: 4000
Square Footage: 200000
Type of Packaging: Food Service, Private Label
Brands:
Coders
Daydots

21399 Daymark Safety Systems
12830 S Dixie Hwy
Bowling Green, OH 43402-9697
419-353-2458
Fax: 419-354-0514 corgan@daymarklabel.com
www.daymarksafety.com
Manufacturer, importer and exporter of dissolve-a-way food labels, coding, dating and marking equipment, label applicators and food rotation systems
VP/General Manager: Jeff Palmer
jpalmer@daymarsafety.com
Estimated Sales: $1-3 Million
Number Employees: 5-9
Square Footage: 172000
Parent Co: CMC Group
Brands:
Daymark
Dissolve-A-Way

21400 Daymark Safety Systems
12830 S Dixie Hwy
Bowling Green, OH 43402-9697
419-353-2458
Fax: 419-354-0514 866-517-0490
international@daymarklabel.com
www.daymarksafety.com
President: Jeff Palmer
jpalmer@daymarsafety.com
Vice President: Tammy Corral
Director, Inside Sales: Heidi Chambers
Estimated Sales: $1-3 Million
Number Employees: 5-9

21401 Daystar
12530 Manor Road
Glen Arm, MD 21057-9503
410-592-3106
Fax: 410-592-3362 800-494-6537
sales@lenoxlaser.com www.lenoxlaser.com
Micro leaks for can and bag testing valves for gas handling, laser systems, rapid prototyping and small hole drilling services
Quality Control: John Whelan
General Manager: Gary Thornton
Number Employees: 10
Square Footage: 18000
Parent Co: Lenox Laser
Brands:
Microleak

21402 Daytech Limited
70 Disco Road
Toronto, ON M9W 1L9
Canada
416-675-1195
Fax: 416-675-7183 877-329-1907
info@daytechlimited.com
www.daytechlimited.com
Illuminated and nonilluminated signage shelters, parking lot kiosks, shopping cart corrals, smoking shelters and covered walkways
President, COO: Dion McGuire
VP Operations: Dave Bradley
Sales & Marketing Manager: John Duthie
Purchasing Manager: Rick Rankin

Estimated Sales: $5-10 Million
Number Employees: 25

21403 Dayton Bag & Burlap Co
322 Davis Ave
Dayton, OH 45403-2900
937-258-8000
Fax: 937-258-0029 800-543-3400
info1@daybag.com www.daybag.com
Manufacturer and exporter of bags including burlap, feed, grain, greaseproof, paper, paper lined, plastic and polypropylene for shipping commodities
President: Samuel Lumby
slumby@daybag.com
VP Marketing: Sue Spiegel
Industrial Sales Manager: Sue Spiegel
Customer Service: Delilah Oda
Estimated Sales: $1-3 Million
Number Employees: 100-249
Square Footage: 150000
Type of Packaging: Bulk

21404 Dayton Marking Devices Company
1681 Ladera Trl
Dayton, OH 45459-1401
937-432-0285
Fax: 937-254-9638
Rubber stamps, printing dies, steel stamps and dies, engraved/etched nameplates, time equipment and signaling devices
Owner: Michael Dunham
Estimated Sales: Below $5 Million
Number Employees: 10

21405 Dayton Reliable Tool
618 Greenmount Blvd
Dayton, OH 45419
937-298-7391
Fax: 937-298-7190 postoffice@drtusa.com
www.drtusa.com
Specializes in the design of conversion systems for all types of easy-open end applications including SOT, ringpull and full aperture, spare parts tooling for all types of cans including conversion systems, shell systems and cuppers
President: Gary Van Gundy
CFO: James Sass
CEO: Gary L Vangundy
Quality Control: George Kloos
R & D: Paul Klips
Contact: David Geis
david.geis@drtusa.com
Estimated Sales: $20-50 Million
Number Employees: 100-249

21406 Dayton Wire Products
7 Dayton Wire Pkwy
Dayton, OH 45404-1282
937-236-8000
Fax: 937-236-8300 888-265-1711
www.daytonwireproducts.com
Wire store display racks
Owner: Brian Schissler
Estimated Sales: $10-20 Million
Number Employees: 50-99

21407 Dc Tech
619 E 19th St
Kansas City, MO 64108-1743
816-842-9090
Fax: 816-842-4121 877-742-9090
sales@dctech-inc.com www.dctech-inc.com
Meat packing and food processing equipment including carts, tables, smokehouse trucks and vats. Manufacturer of grocery store and restaurant equipment, and custom stainless steel fabrication. Polished aluminum performance car partsbattery covers and turbo shields
President: Buddy Mitchum
buddy@dctech-inc.com
Sales/Marketing Executive: Buddy Mitchum
Purchasing Manager: Robert Mitchum
Estimated Sales: $3-5 Million
Number Employees: 10-19
Square Footage: 148000

21408 De Felsko Corp
802 Proctor Ave
Ogdensburg, NY 13669-2205
315-393-4450
Fax: 315-393-8471 800-448-3835
techsale@defelsko.com www.defelsko.com
Automatic liquor pourers

President: David Bamish
davidbamish@defelsko.com
Estimated Sales: $5-10 Million
Number Employees: 20-49
Brands:
    Accupour

21409 De Iorio's Foods Inc
2200 Bleecker St
Utica, NY 13501-1739

    315-732-7612
Fax: 315-732-7621 800-649-7612
www.deiorios.com
Manufacturer of dough products. Products include
dough balls, flats, shells, self rise, breads and sub
rolls, breadsticks, and more.
Chairman & CEO: Robert Ragusa
VP, Business Development: Robert Horth
Manager: Fabio Faro
ffaro@deiorios.com
Manager: Donald King
Estimated Sales: $5-10,000,000
Number Employees: 100-249
Number of Brands: 1
Number of Products: 87
Type of Packaging: Consumer, Food Service, Private Label
Other Locations:
    De-Iorio's Frozen Dough
    Utica NY
Brands:
    Delorio's

21410 De Laval
11100 N Congress Ave
Kansas City, MO 64153-1222

    816-891-7700
Fax: 816-891-1606
www.delavalcleaningsolutions.com
Manufacturer and suppliers of cleaning and sanitizing products for the dairy, food, and beverage processing industies.
Number Employees: 100-249

21411 De Leone Corp
1258 SW Lake Rd
Redmond, OR 97756-8611

    541-504-8311
Fax: 541-504-8411 sam@deleone.com
www.cascadelabel.com
Manufacturer and exporter of pressure sensitive and
custom labels; wholesaler/distributor of label
dispensers
President: Samuel A DE Leone
steve@deleone.com
General Manager: David Hawes
Sales Director: Diana Jibiden
Estimated Sales: $5-10 Million
Number Employees: 20-49

21412 De Leone Corp
1258 SW Lake Rd
Redmond, OR 97756-8611

    541-504-8311
Fax: 541-504-8411 sam@deleone.com
www.cascadelabel.com
Labels and labeling material
President: Samuel A DE Leone
steve@deleone.com
Quality Control: David Hawes
Sales Representative: Diana Jibiden
Estimated Sales: $5-10 000,000
Number Employees: 20-49

21413 De Leone Corp
1258 SW Lake Rd
Redmond, OR 97756-8611

    541-504-8311
Fax: 541-504-8411 www.cascadelabel.com
President: Samuel A DE Leone
steve@deleone.com
Estimated Sales: $5-10 Million
Number Employees: 20-49

21414 De Paul Industries
4950 NE M L King Blvd
Portland, OR 97211-3354

    503-281-1289
Fax: 503-284-0548 800-518-6637
www.depaulindustries.com
DePaul Industries provides food and consumer
goods packaging services.

CEO: Dave Shaffer
dshaffer@depaulindustries.com
CEO: Bennett Johnson
Foods & Consumer Goods Packaging Manager:
Chris Cusack
Business Development Manager: Lori Fletcher
Number Employees: 10-19
Type of Packaging: Consumer

21415 De Royal Textiles
100 E York St
Camden, SC 29020

    803-432-1103
Fax: 803-425-4566 800-845-1062
textiles@deroyal.com www.deroyaltextiles.com
Wipers and cheesecloth
President: Steve Ward
Quality Control: John Getting
VP: E Steven Ward
Sales Manager: Jay Green
Plant Manager: John Gettys
Estimated Sales: Below $5 Million
Number Employees: 1-4
Square Footage: 550000
Brands:
    Hermitex
    Idealfold
    Jiffy Roll

21416 De Ster Corporation
225 Peachtree Street
Suite 400
Atlanta, GA 30303-1727

    404-659-9100
Fax: 404-659-5116 800-237-8270
info@dester.com www.dester.com
Manufacturer, importer and exporter of disposable
and reusable trays, plates, flatware, containers, cups
and cutlery
Executive VP: Gerrit de Kiewit
Director Marketing/Development: John Squire
Senior VP Sales: Dan Whitehead
Estimated Sales: $5-10 Million
Number Employees: 150-200
Square Footage: 640000
Parent Co: De Ster Holding BV
Type of Packaging: Consumer, Food Service, Private Label, Bulk
Brands:
    Isobox
    Microstar
    Octaview

21417 De Vere Co Inc
1923 Beloit Ave
Janesville, WI 53546-3028

    608-752-0576
Fax: 608-752-6625 800-833-8373
www.deverechemical.com
Cleaning and sanitizing chemicals including
dishwashing detergents
President: Cynthia Shackelford
cshackelford@deverechemical.com
VP: Frank Drew
Estimated Sales: Below $5 Million
Number Employees: 10-19
Square Footage: 52000

21418 Deacom
950 W Valley Rd
Wayne, PA 19087-1824

    610-971-2278
Fax: 610-971-2279
Technology software
President: Jay Dookins
Marketing Manager: Susan Shaw
Sales Manager: Jim Reilly
Contact: Dave Beyel
dbeyel@deacom.com
Estimated Sales: $300,000-500,000
Number Employees: 1-4

21419 Deadline Press
1652 N Roberts Road NW
Suite C-2
Kennesaw, GA 30144-3634

    770-419-2232
Fax: 770-419-2933
Advertising specialties, flags, pennants, banners and
labels
Owner: Susan Lester
Other Locations:
    Deadline Press
    Atlanta GA

21420 Dean Custom Awning
529 Route 303
Orangeburg, NY 10962-1303

    845-425-6678
Fax: 845-425-6678
mail@deancustomawnings.com
www.deancustomawnings.com
Commercial awnings
President: Charles Collishaw
deancustomawning@aol.com
Estimated Sales: Less Than $500,000
Number Employees: 1-4

21421 (HQ)Dean Foods Co.
2711 N. Haskell Ave.
Suite 3400
Dallas, TX 75204

    800-395-7004
deanfoods@casupport.com www.deanfoods.com
Milk, ice cream, cultured dairy products, juices, teas
and bottled water.
President/CEO: Eric Beringause
Interim CFO/SVP, Finance & Strategy: Gary Rahlfs
SVP/General Counsel: Kristy Waterman
SVP/Chief Commercial Officer: Thomas Murray
Year Founded: 1925
Estimated Sales: $7.7 Billion
Number Employees: 16,000+
Number of Brands: 35
Type of Packaging: Food Service, Private Label
Brands:
    Alta Dena
    Barber's®
    Berkeley Farms
    Broughton®
    Brown's Dairy®
    Country Fresh™
    Creamland
    Dairy Pure®
    Dean's™
    Friendly's®
    Fruit Rush™
    Gandy's
    Garelick Farms®
    Hygeia®
    Jilbert
    Land O Lakes®
    Lehigh Valley®
    Mayfield Creamery™
    Mayfield®
    McArthur Dairy®
    Meadow Brook®
    Meadow Gold®
    Model Dairy
    Oak Farms Dairy
    Orchard Pure™
    PET®
    Price's
    Purity
    Ready Leaf
    Reiter Dairy™
    Swiss Premium®
    T.G. Lee
    TruMoo
    Tuscan™
    Uncle Matt's®

21422 Dean Industries
14501 S Broadway
Gardena, CA 90248

    310-353-5000
Fax: 310-327-3343 800-995-1210
salesmkt@frymaster.com
Manufacturer and exporter of fryer baskets and deep
fat fryers
Owner: Jimmy Dean
General Manager: Al Cote
Estimated Sales: $300,000-500,000
Number Employees: 1-4
Parent Co: ENODIS

21423 Dearborn Mid-West Conveyor Co
8245 Nieman Rd # 123
Overland Park, KS 66214-1509

    913-384-9950
Fax: 913-261-2470
Manufacturer and exporter of material handling sys-
tems including conveyors, palletizers and palletizing
systems
President, CEO: Tony Rosati
Executive VP: Sudy Ohra
sudyv@dmwcc.com
Manager of Sales: Gerry Cohen
Number Employees: 20-49

489

21424 Dearborn Mid-West Conveyor Co
20334 Superior Rd
Taylor, MI 48180-6301

734-288-4400
Fax: 734-288-1914 jwp@dmwcc.com
www.dmwcc.com
Automated material handling systems
President: Jeff Homenik
jeffh@dmwcc.com
CEO: Tony Rosati
Controller: Sherry Gavito
VP: Jeff Homenik
Quality Control: Mark Duxter
Director, Marketing & Sales: John Confer
Human Resources: Kelly Schafer
Plant Manager: Bruce Mazarowski
Purchasing: Katarina Katsavrias
Estimated Sales: $500,000-$1 Million
Number Employees: 50-99
Number of Products: 5

21425 Deb Canada
42 Thompson Rd W
Waterford, ON N0E 1Y0
Canada

519-443-8697
Fax: 519-443-5160 888-332-7627
www.debgroup.com/us/contact-us/global-contact
Hand and body cleansers, protective creams,
anti-bacterial, gel, heavy duty and waterless soaps
and soap dispensers
Controller: Dan Balan
General Manager: Didier Bauton
Asst. to General Manager: Theresa Sulisz
Number Employees: 50-99
Square Footage: 80000
Parent Co: Deb Group
Type of Packaging: Private Label
Brands:
  Debba
  Ensuite
  Florafree
  Great White
  Hands
  Heiress
  Hypor
  Inhibit
  Lanimol
  Maxipor
  Mitzi
  Quick Shift
  Sceptre
  Suprega
  Tiv Plus
  Tuf'n Ega

21426 Debbie Wright Sales
5852 E Berry St
PO Box 15554
Fort Worth, TX 76119-1803

817-429-8282
Fax: 817-429-8882 800-935-7883
www.debbiewrightsales.net
Manufacturer and wholesaler/distributor of stud
welding equipment and supplies
Owner: Debbie Wright
Sls. Rep.: Allan Yarber
Estimated Sales: $1-2.5 Million
Number Employees: 5-9

21427 Debelak Technical Systems
W6390 Quality Drive
Greenville, WI 54942-8015

920-757-9980
Fax: 920-757-9987 800-888-4207
Control systems including clean-in-place, instrument
monitoring, pasteurization and temperature for the
food and dairy industries
President: William Debelak
Production Manager: Lee Fintelmann
Estimated Sales: $5-10 Million
Number Employees: 10

21428 Debelis Corp
5000 70th Ave
Kenosha, WI 53144-1762

262-657-5000
Fax: 262-656-8326 800-472-7462
www.puratos.com
R&D: Gloria Brandes
Quality Control: Eillen Walo
Contact: Brian Hogan
bhogan@puratos.com
Manager: Benoit Keppenne

Estimated Sales: $10-20 Million
Number Employees: 20-49

21429 Deborah Sales LLC
109 Meeker Ave
Newark, NJ 07114-1300

973-344-8466
Fax: 973-344-3981 crei@deborahsales.us
Advertising specialties and premiums
President: Carlos Rei
crei@deborahsales.us
Estimated Sales: $1-2.5 Million
Number Employees: 1-4

21430 Decade Products
3910 Plainfield Ave NE
Grand Rapids, MI 49525-1602

616-365-2887
Fax: 616-956-9492 www.decadeproducts.com
Owner: Cindy Douthett

21431 Decagon Devices Inc
2635 NE Hopkins Court
Pullman, WA 99163

509-332-2756
Fax: 509-332-5158 800-755-2751
sales@aqualab.com www.aqualab.com
Scientific instruments.
Research/Development: Brady Carter
Product Design: Ken Byers
Marketing Assistant: Tyler Zollinger
Sales Support: John Russell

21432 Decal Techniques Inc
25 Mahan St # A
West Babylon, NY 11704-1306

631-491-1800
Fax: 631-491-1816 800-735-3322
decalinfo@earthlink.net www.decaltech.com
Silk screened labels, posters, banners and displays
President: Gene Snyder
Contact: Eugene Snyder
e.snyder@decaltech.com
Estimated Sales: $1-2.5 Million
Number Employees: 10-19
Square Footage: 10000

21433 Decartes Systems Group
120 Randall Drive
Waterloo, ON N2V 1C6
Canada

519-746-8110
Fax: 519-747-0082 info@descartes.com
www.descartes.com
Computer accounting systems for the dairy, bever-
age and food industries
Executive Vice President of Information: Raimond
Diederik
Regional Manager: Rick Spencer
Estimated Sales: $1-5 Million
Type of Packaging: Bulk

21434 Deccofelt Corp
555 S Vermont Ave
Glendora, CA 91741-6206

626-963-8511
Fax: 626-914-2734 800-543-3226
sales@deccofelt.com
www.greenmoisturebarrier.com
Industrial tapes including adhesive coated, heat acti-
vated and laminated
President: Jerry Heinrich
jheinrich@deccofelt.com
Director Sales: Kathy Smith
Estimated Sales: $5-10 Million
Number Employees: 20-49
Square Footage: 120000

21435 Decernis
1250 Connecticut Avenue NW
Suite 200
Washington, DC 20036

240-428-1800
Fax: 301-990-1086 www.decernis.com
Provides regulatory compliance, supply chain tracking and information management systems for food
additives, food contact materials and consumer
product manufacturers.

Chief Executive Officer: Andrew Waldow
Director, International Business Dev.: Jacques
Desarnauts
Director, Data Services: Clive Raven
Director, System Development: Yong Zou
Chief Operating Officer: Kevin Kenny
VP, Business Development Americas: Craig Henry

21436 (HQ)Decision Analyst Inc
604 Avenue H E
Arlington, TX 76011-3119

817-649-5241
Fax: 817-640-6567 800-262-5974
jthomas@decisionanalyst.com
Consultant performing consumer testing and adver-
tising pre-testing; market researcher including new
product development and strategy
President: Jerry W. Thomas
CEO: Vivian Allan
vallan@secondarydata.com
EVP: Bonnie Kenoly
Marketing Director: Cristi Johnson
Number Employees: 100-249
Square Footage: 100000
Brands:
  Copytest
  Optima

21437 Decker Plastics
1104 2nd Ave
Council Bluffs, IA 51501-4012

712-323-9995
Fax: 712-328-8617 866-869-6293
www.deckerplastics.com
Polyethylene bags, tubes and sheeting
President: Robert A Decker
CFO: Sherry Deckar
sherrydeckar@deckerplastics.com
Estimated Sales: $1-2.5 Million
Number Employees: 20-49
Square Footage: 50000

21438 Decker Tape Products Inc
6 Stewart Pl
Fairfield, NJ 07004-2202

973-227-5350
Fax: 973-808-9418 800-227-5252
www.deckertape.com
Pressure sensitive tapes and stock labels and
in-house converting services include custom imprinting 2-color, die cutting, spooling, laminating, sheeting, narrow width and long length rolls
Owner: Jack Decker
jdecker@deckertape.com
Estimated Sales: $20-50 Million
Number Employees: 50-99

21439 Decko Products Inc
2105 Superior St
Sandusky, OH 44870-1891

419-626-5757
Fax: 419-626-3135 800-537-6143
shumphrey@decko.com www.decko.com
Edible cake and candy decorations and packaged
rings, gels
President: F William Niggemyer
Marketing Director: Sara Humphrey
Estimated Sales: $10 Million
Number Employees: 50-99
Square Footage: 105000
Type of Packaging: Private Label
Brands:
  Royal Icing Decoration

21440 Deco Labels & Tags
28 Greensboro Drive
Toronto, ON M9W 1E1
Canada

416-247-7878
Fax: 416-247-9030 888-496-9029
www.decolabels.com
Pressure sensitive labels, shipping tags, stickers, de-
cals and seals; also, silk screening, data processing
and hot stamping available
President: Doug Ford
Quality Control: Brian Burke
General Manager: Douglas Ford
Assistant Manager: Robbie Ford
Number Employees: 10
Square Footage: 72000
Brands:
  Data-Tabs
  Hard-Tac
  Sof-Tac

21441 Deco Pac Inc
3500 Thurston Ave # 100
Anoka, MN 55303-1061
763-574-0091
Fax: 763-574-1060 tana.krona@decopac.com
President: Christine McKenna
CEO: Mike Mcglynn
mike.mcglynn@decopac.com
CFO: Mike McGlynn
Quality Control: Kim Roy
Estimated Sales: $10-20 Million
Number Employees: 100-249

21442 Decolin
9150 Parc Avenue
Montreal, QC H2N 1Z2
Canada
514-384-2910
Fax: 514-382-1305 www.decolin.com
Table cloths and runners; also, place mats
President: Leonard Mendel
CFO: Alissa Ratpatort
Number Employees: 50

21443 Decorated Products Company
PO Box 580
Westfield, MA 01086-0580
413-568-0944
Fax: 413-568-1875
Labels including food product, carton and computer
pin feed
President: Mike Goepfert
Sales Manager: Joe Menh
Contact: William Chevalier
wchevalier@decorated.com
Operations Manager: Stafford Springs
Number Employees: 10
Square Footage: 180000

21444 Decoren Equipment
133 Chaucer Court
Willowbrook, IL 60527-8418
708-789-3367
Fax: 708-789-3367
Carts including specialty, china and plate
Marketing Manager (West): Howard Charles
Administrative Manager: Jule Arvans
Estimated Sales: $1-5 Million

21445 Dedert Corporation
20000 Governors Dr # 3
Olympia Fields, IL 60461-1034
708-747-7000
Fax: 708-755-8815 info@dedert.com
www.anhydro.com
Manufacturer and exporter of evaporators, filters,
centrifuges and liquid/solid separation equipment;
importer of filters, liquid/solid separation equipment
and centrifuges
President: Guy Lonergan
Marketing Director: John Ruhl
Contact: Pat Baumgartner
p.baumgartner@dedert.com
Estimated Sales: $20-50 Million
Number Employees: 20-49
Brands:
　Dedert
　Lfc
　Reineveld

21446 Defontaine of America
16720 W Victor Rd
New Berlin, WI 53151
262-754-4665
Fax: 262-797-5735 sternw2@earthlink.net
Sanitary butterfly, check valves, air-operated valves,
pigging systems, mixproof valves
President: William Stern
Marketing: Wayne Johnson
Estimated Sales: $1-2.5 000,000
Number Employees: 1-4

21447 (HQ)Defranco Co
1000 Lawrence St
Los Angeles, CA 90021-1620
213-627-8575
Fax: 213-627-9837 800-992-3992
Defrancomp@aol.com www.defrancoandsons.com
We are a family owned business that offers fresh
produce and nuts.

Manager: Paul De Franco
CEO: Paul DeFranco
CFO: Jerry De Franco
VP: Gerald DeFranco
R&D: Salvatore DeFranco
Estimated Sales: $15 Million
Number Employees: 20-49
Square Footage: 150000
Type of Packaging: Consumer, Food Service, Private Label, Bulk
Brands:
　Sunripe

21448 Defreeze Corporation
PO Box 330
Southborough, MA 1772
508-485-8512
Fax: 508-481-1491 albezanson@defreeze.com
www.defreeze.com
Industrial microwave processing and frozen fish
slicing equipment
President: Allan Bezanson
Estimated Sales: $1-3 Million
Number Employees: 1-4

21449 Degussa BioActives
P.O.Box 1609
Waukesha, WI 53187-1609
262-547-5531
Fax: 262-547-0587 800-342-5724
Estimated Sales: $1-5 Million
Number Employees: 50-99

21450 Degussa Flavors
1000 Redna Ter
Cincinnati, OH 45215-1187
513-771-4682
Fax: 513-771-8748 888-771-2448
flavors.us@degussa.com
Number Employees: 20-49

21451 Dehyco Company
1000 Kansas Street
Memphis, TN 38106-1925
901-774-3322
Fax: 901-774-2076
Manufacturer and exporter of hammer mills, custom
grinders, pulverizers, separators and packaging
machinery
President: Mike Broussard
VP: Albert Harris, Jr.
Estimated Sales: $10-20 Million
Number Employees: 20-49

21452 Dehydration & Environmental System
864 Saint Francis Way
Rio Vista, CA 94571-1250
707-374-7500
Fax: 707-374-7505 800-992-9113
sales@desllc.biz www.desllc.biz
Dewatering and drying equipment; by-product used
to process both food and waste
President: Dan Simpson
Estimated Sales: $2.5-5 Million
Number Employees: 5-9

21453 Deibel Laboratories
407 Cabot Rd
South San Francisco, CA 94080
650-952-4209
Fax: 650-952-4518 Sales@DeibelLabs.com
www.deibellabs.com
Analytical laboratory specializing in chemical and
microbiological food testing including nutrition labeling, dietary fiber, cholesterol, sulfites, vitamins,
trace minerals, sugar profiles, etc
President and CEO: Dr. Robert Deibel
Research & Development: Dr. Lawrence Rosner
Manager: Dean Reed
Contact: Judy Tran
southsanfrancisco@deibellabs.com
Plant Manager: Dan Coules
Number Employees: 10
Square Footage: 14000

21454 Deibel Laboratories
3530 NW 97th Blvd
Gainesville, FL 32606
352-331-3313
Fax: 352-332-2050 www.deibellabs.com

Analytical laboratory specializing in chemical and
microbiological food testing including nutrition labeling, dietary fiber, cholesterol, sulfites, vitamins,
trace minerals, sugar profiles, etc
Research & Development: Dr Lawrence Rosner
Manager: Kirsten Hunt
Manager: Dean Reed
Plant Manager: Dan Coules
Estimated Sales: $.5-1 million
Number Employees: 1-4
Square Footage: 7000

21455 Deibel Laboratories Inc
103 S 2nd St
Madison, WI 53704-5216
608-241-1177
Fax: 608-241-2252 madison@deibellabs.com
www.deibellabs.com
Analytical laboratory specializing in chemical and
microbiological food testing including nutrition labeling, dietary fiber, cholesterol, sulfites, vitamins,
trace minerals, sugar profiles, etc
President: Robert H Deibel
Contact: Richard Boehme
deibelmad@ameritech.net
Director of Operations: Kristen A. Hunt
Plant Manager: Dan Coules
Estimated Sales: $3-5 Million
Number Employees: 20-49
Square Footage: 14000

21456 Deibel Laboratories Inc
7165 Curtiss Ave
Sarasota, FL 34231-8012
941-925-1579
Fax: 941-925-2130 SarasotaLab@DeibelLabs.com
www.deibellabs.com
Analytical laboratory specializing in chemical and
microbiological food testing including nutrition labeling, dietary fiber, cholesterol, sulfites, vitamins,
trace minerals, sugar profiles, etc
President: Robert H Deibel
Research & Development: Dr. Lawrence Rosner
Manager: Dean Reed
Plant Manager: Dan Coules
Estimated Sales: $300,000-500,000
Number Employees: 1-4
Square Footage: 7000

21457 Deibel Laboratories Of Il
7120 N Ridgeway Ave
Lincolnwood, IL 60712-2622
847-329-9900
Fax: 847-329-9903
LincolnwoodLab@DeibelLabs.com
www.deibellabs.com
Analytical laboratory specializing in chemical and
microbiological food testing including nutrition labeling, dietary fiber, cholesterol, sulfites, vitamins,
trace minerals, sugar profiles, etc
President: Charles Deibel
charlesdeibel@deibellabs.com
Research & Development: Dr. Lawrence Rosner
Manager: Dean Reed
Plant Manager: Dan Coules
Estimated Sales: $1-3 Million
Number Employees: 10-19
Square Footage: 7000

21458 Deibel Laboratories Of Il
7120 N Ridgeway Ave
Lincolnwood, IL 60712-2622
847-329-9900
Fax: 847-329-9903
LincolnwoodLab@DeibelLabs.com
www.deibellabs.com
Analytical laboratory specializing in chemical and
microbiological food testing including nutrition labeling, dietary fiber, cholesterol, sulfites, vitamins,
trace minerals, sugar profiles, etc
President: Charles Deibel
charlesdeibel@deibellabs.com
Research & Development: Dr. Lawrence Rosner
Manager: Dean Reed
Plant Manager: Dan Coules
Number Employees: 10-19
Square Footage: 14000

21459 Deitz Company
1750 Route 34
PO Box 1108
Wall, NJ 07719

732-681-0200
Fax: 732-681-8468 800-394-2709
www.deitzco.com

Machinery
President: James L Deitz
VP Engineering: John Deitz
Estimated Sales: $2.5-5 000,000
Number Employees: 10-19

21460 (HQ)Del Monte Fresh Produce Inc.
PO Box 149222
Coral Gables, FL 33114-9222

305-520-8400
Fax: 305-567-0320 800-950-3683
contact-us-executive-office@freshdelmonte.com
www.freshdelmonte.com

Fresh and fresh-cut fruit and vegetables.
President/COO: Youssef Zakharia
Chairman/CEO: Mohammad Abu-Ghazaleh
mabughazaleh@freshdelmonte.com
Senior VP/CFO: Eduardo Bezerra
Senior VP/General Counsel/Secretary: Marlene Gordon
Senior VP, North America Operations: Annunciata Cerioli
Year Founded: 1886
Estimated Sales: $3.9 Billion
Number Employees: 45,000
Number of Brands: 11
Type of Packaging: Consumer, Food Service
Other Locations:
  Del Monte Fresh Plant
  Forest Park GA
  Del Monte Fresh Plant
  Kankakee IL
  Del Monte Fresh Plant
  Jessup MD
  Del Monte Fresh Plant
  Kansas City MO
  Del Monte Fresh Plant
  Bloomfield NJ
  Del Monte Fresh Plant
  Mappsville VA
  Del Monte Fresh Plant
  Canton MA
  Del Monte Fresh Plant
  Mulberry FL
  Del Monte Fresh Plant
  Richmond CA
  Del Monte Fresh Plant
  Eddystone PA
  Del Monte Fresh Plant
  Chicago IL
  Del Monte Fresh Plant
  Plant City FL
  Del Monte Fresh Plant
  Columbus OH
Brands:
  Del Monte Fresh®
  Mann's®
  Rosy®
  Fruitini
  Golden Ripe®
  Just Juice
  Mission®
  MAG® Melon
  UTC®
  National Poultry Company
  De L'Ora®

21461 Del Monte Fresh Produce Inc.
9880 S Dorchester Ave
Chicago, IL 60628

773-221-9480
Fax: 773-221-9388 www.freshdelmonte.com
Distribution center providing a variety of services including ripening, sorting, re-packing, fresh cut processing, and delivery of fruits and vegetables
Type of Packaging: Consumer, Food Service

21462 Del Monte Fresh Produce Inc.
2200 Westbelt Dr
Columbus, OH 43228-3820

614-527-7398
Fax: 614-527-8575 800-348-8878
www.freshdelmonte.com
Distribution center providing a variety of services including ripening, sorting, re-packing, fresh cut processing, and delivery of fruits and vegetables
Type of Packaging: Consumer, Food Service

21463 Del Monte Fresh Produce Inc.
1400-1500 Parker St
Dallas, TX 75215

214-428-3600
Fax: 214-428-8836 800-428-3600
www.freshdelmonte.com
Distribution center providing a variety of services including ripening, sorting, re-packing, fresh cut processing, and delivery of fruits and vegetables
Type of Packaging: Consumer, Food Service

21464 Del Monte Fresh Produce Inc.
3101 SW 42nd St
Fort Lauderdale, FL 33312-6802

954-791-4828
Fax: 954-583-8648 www.freshdelmonte.com
Distribution center providing a variety of services including ripening, sorting, re-packing, fresh cut processing, and delivery of fruits and vegetables
Type of Packaging: Consumer, Food Service

21465 Del Monte Fresh Produce Inc.
7780 Westside Industrial Dr
Unit 5
Jacksonville, FL 32219-3287

904-378-0051
Fax: 904-378-0260 www.freshdelmonte.com
Distribution center providing a variety of services including ripening, sorting, re-packing, fresh cut processing, and delivery of fruits and vegetables
Type of Packaging: Consumer, Food Service

21466 Del Monte Fresh Produce Inc.
6311 Deramus Ave
Kansas City, MO 64120-1358

816-241-6242
Fax: 816-483-4050 www.freshdelmonte.com
Distribution center providing a variety of services including ripening, sorting, re-packing, fresh cut processing, and delivery of fruits and vegetables
Type of Packaging: Consumer, Food Service

21467 Del Monte Fresh Produce Inc.
1001 Industrial Hwy
Building D
Eddystone, PA 19022-1529

610-499-0343
Fax: 610-499-9042 www.freshdelmonte.com
Distribution center providing a variety of services including ripening, sorting, re-packing, fresh cut processing, and delivery of fruits and vegetables
Type of Packaging: Consumer, Food Service

21468 Del Monte Fresh Produce Inc.
3602 W Washington St
Suite 1
Phoenix, AZ 85009-4767

Fax: 602-252-8265 800-226-4758
www.freshdelmonte.com
Distribution center providing a variety of services including ripening, sorting, re-packing, fresh cut processing, and delivery of fruits and vegetables
Type of Packaging: Consumer, Food Service

21469 Del Monte Fresh Produce Inc.
14550 W La Estrella
Goodyear, AZ 85338-3615

623-925-0900
Fax: 623-932-7999 www.freshdelmonte.com
Distribution center providing a variety of services including ripening, sorting, re-packing, fresh cut processing, and delivery of fruits and vegetables
Type of Packaging: Consumer, Food Service

21470 Del Monte Fresh Produce Inc.
3306 Sydney Rd
Plant City, FL 33566

813-752-5145
Fax: 813-759-8625 www.freshdelmonte.com
Distribution center providing a variety of services including ripening, sorting, re-packing, fresh cut processing, and delivery of fruits and vegetables
Type of Packaging: Consumer, Food Service

21471 Del Monte Fresh Produce Inc.
10730 Patterson Pl
Santa Fe Springs, CA 90670-4025

562-777-1127
Fax: 562-777-9498 www.freshdelmonte.com
Distribution center providing a variety of services including ripening, sorting, re-packing, fresh cut processing, and delivery of fruits and vegetables
Type of Packaging: Consumer, Food Service

21472 Del Monte Fresh Produce Inc.
504 42nd St NE
Suite 101
Auburn, WA 98002-1416

253-850-3190
Fax: 253-850-3182 www.freshdelmonte.com
Distribution center providing a variety of services including ripening, sorting, re-packing, fresh cut processing, and delivery of fruits and vegetables
Type of Packaging: Consumer, Food Service

21473 Del Monte Fresh Produce Inc.
7970 Tar Bay Dr
Jessup, MD 20794-9416

410-799-4440
Fax: 410-799-3828 www.freshdelmonte.com
Distribution center providing a variety of services including ripening, sorting, re-packing, fresh cut processing, and delivery of fruits and vegetables
Type of Packaging: Consumer, Food Service

21474 Del Monte Fresh Produce Inc.
105 Shawmut Rd
Shamut Industrial Park
Canton, MA 02021-1438

781-830-2600
Fax: 781-830-2699 www.freshdelmonte.com
Distribution center providing a variety of services including ripening, sorting, re-packing, fresh cut processing, and delivery of fruits and vegetables
Type of Packaging: Consumer, Food Service

21475 Del Monte Fresh Produce Inc.
15845 E 32nd Ave
Suite D
Aurora, CO 80011-1570

720-857-9678
Fax: 720-857-9956 www.freshdelmonte.com
Distribution center providing a variety of services including ripening, sorting, re-packing, fresh cut processing, and delivery of fruits and vegetables
Type of Packaging: Consumer, Food Service

21476 Del Monte Fresh Produce Inc.
6532 Judge Adams Rd
Suite 170
Whitsett, NC 27377

336-446-2031
Fax: 336-446-6590 www.freshdelmonte.com
Distribution center providing a variety of services including ripening, sorting, re-packing, fresh cut processing, and delivery of fruits and vegetables
Type of Packaging: Consumer, Food Service

21477 Del Monte Fresh Produce Inc.
C/O Holt Marine Terminal
701 North Broadway
Gloucester City, NJ 08030

856-742-9202
Fax: 856-742-9209 www.freshdelmonte.com
Distribution center providing a variety of services including ripening, sorting, re-packing, fresh cut processing, and delivery of fruits and vegetables
Type of Packaging: Consumer, Food Service

21478 Del Monte Fresh Produce Inc.
9243 N Rivergate Blvd
Portland, OR 97203-6615

503-285-0992
Fax: 503-285-1040 www.freshdelmonte.com
Distribution center providing a variety of services including ripening, sorting, re-packing, fresh cut processing, and delivery of fruits and vegetables
Type of Packaging: Consumer, Food Service

21479 Del Monte Fresh Produce Inc.
1810 Academy Ave
Sanger, CA 93657-3739

559-875-5000
Fax: 559-875-1301 www.freshdelmonte.com
Distribution center providing a variety of services including ripening, sorting, re-packing, fresh cut processing, and delivery of fruits and vegetables
Type of Packaging: Consumer, Food Service

21480 Del Monte Fresh Produce Inc.
P.O. Box 755
Galveston, TX 77553

409-762-4638
Fax: 409-762-5358 www.freshdelmonte.com
Distribution center providing a variety of services including ripening, sorting, re-packing, fresh cut processing, and delivery of fruits and vegetables
Type of Packaging: Consumer, Food Service

21481 Del Monte Fresh Produce Inc.
300 Broadacres Drive
Suite 205
Bloomfield, NJ 07003
973-338-8591
Fax: 973-338-1523 www.freshdelmonte.com
Distribution center providing a variety of services
including ripening, sorting, re-packing, fresh cut
processing, and delivery of fruits and vegetables
Type of Packaging: Consumer, Food Service

21482 Del Monte Fresh Produce Inc.
P.O. Box 520
Port Hueneme, CA 93044
805-488-0881
Fax: 805-488-2428 www.freshdelmonte.com
Distribution center providing a variety of services
including ripening, sorting, re-packing, fresh cut
processing, and delivery of fruits and vegetables
Type of Packaging: Consumer, Food Service

21483 Del Monte Fresh Produce Inc.
200 Del Monte Way
Palmetto, FL 34221-6609
941-722-3060
Fax: 941-722-7075 www.freshdelmonte.com
Distribution center providing a variety of services
including ripening, sorting, re-packing, fresh cut
processing, and delivery of fruits and vegetables
Type of Packaging: Consumer, Food Service

21484 Del Monte Fresh Produce Inc.
118-A Forest Pkwy
Forest Park, GA 30297
404-366-3699
Fax: 404-366-6945 www.freshdelmonte.com
Distribution center providing a variety of services
including ripening, sorting, re-packing, fresh cut
processing, and delivery of fruits and vegetables
Type of Packaging: Consumer, Food Service

21485 Del Monte Fresh Produce Inc.
14 Stuart Dr
Kankakee, IL 60901
815-936-7400
Fax: 815-936-7409 www.freshdelmonte.com
Distribution center providing a variety of services
including ripening, sorting, re-packing, fresh cut
processing, and delivery of fruits and vegetables
Type of Packaging: Consumer, Food Service

21486 Del Monte Fresh Produce Inc.
15141 Finney Mason Lane
Mappsville, VA 23407
www.freshdelmonte.com
Distribution center providing a variety of services
including ripening, sorting, re-packing, fresh cut
processing, and delivery of fruits and vegetables
Type of Packaging: Consumer, Food Service

21487 Del Monte Fresh Produce Inc.
5050 State Route 60 W
Mulberry, FL 33860
863-844-5836
www.freshdelmonte.com
Distribution center providing a variety of services
including ripening, sorting, re-packing, fresh cut
processing, and delivery of fruits and vegetables
Type of Packaging: Consumer, Food Service

21488 Del Monte Fresh Produce Inc.
14516 Heathrow Forest Pkwy
Houston, TX 77032
281-912-6900
Fax: 281-912-6931 www.freshdelmonte.com
Distribution center providing a variety of services
including ripening, sorting, re-packing, fresh cut
processing, and delivery of fruits and vegetables
Type of Packaging: Consumer, Food Service

21489 Del Monte Fresh Produce Inc.
3151 Regatta Blvd
Suite E
Richmond, CA 94804
510-236-2719
Fax: 510-236-2029 www.freshdelmonte.com
Distribution center providing a variety of services
including ripening, sorting, re-packing, fresh cut
processing, and delivery of fruits and vegetables
Type of Packaging: Consumer, Food Service

21490 Del Monte Fresh Produce Inc.
936 Bankhead Hwy
Winder, GA 30680
770-307-4013
Fax: 770-307-2960 www.freshdelmonte.com
Distribution center providing a variety of services
including ripening, sorting, re-packing, fresh cut
processing, and delivery of fruits and vegetables
Type of Packaging: Consumer, Food Service

21491 Del Monte Fresh Produce Inc.
940 Thornton Rd S
Oshawa, ON L1J 7E2
Canada
905-743-5900
Fax: 905-743-5935 www.freshdelmonte.com
Distribution center providing a variety of services
including ripening, sorting, re-packing, fresh cut
processing, and delivery of fruits and vegetables
Type of Packaging: Consumer, Food Service

21492 Del Monte Fresh Produce Inc.
1570 rue Ampere
Suite 501
Boucherville, QC J4B 7L4
Canada
450-641-7373
Fax: 450-641-2269 www.freshdelmonte.com
Distribution center providing a variety of services
including ripening, sorting, re-packing, fresh cut
processing, and delivery of fruits and vegetables
Type of Packaging: Consumer, Food Service

21493 Del Packaging Inc
18113 Telge Rd
Cypress, TX 77429-1301
281-653-0099
Fax: 281-653-0077 sales@delpackaging.com
www.delpackaging.com
Packaging equipment
President: Dwayne Harthorn
dharthorn@delpackaging.com
Quality Control: Paro Patrick
CFO: Patrick Paro
Estimated Sales: Below $5 000,000
Number Employees: 50-99

21494 Delavan Spray Technologies
PO Box 969
Bamberg, SC 29003-0969
803-245-4347
Fax: 803-245-4146 800-982-6943
delavansales@goodrich.com www.delavaninc.com
Manufacturer, importer and exporter of spray noz-
zles and accessories including flat spray, straight
stream, hollow and solid cone, etc
EVP: Terrence G Linnert
Senior VP: Stephen R Huggins
VP: Joseph F Andolino
Contact: Allen Priester
allen.priester@goodrich.com
Plant Manager: Roger Young
Estimated Sales: $1-5 Million
Number Employees: 100-249

21495 Delavan Spray Technologies
2730 W Tyvola Rd # 600
Charlotte, NC 28217-4578
704-423-7000
Fax: 704-423-4098 www.goodrich.com
Manufacturer, importer and exporter of spray noz-
zles and accessories including flat spray, straight
stream, hollow and solid cone, etc
President: Ray Davis
Division Controller: Carolin Kirsch
CEO: Marshall O Larsen
Contact: Tom Barrow
tom.barrow@utas.utc.com
Executive Vice President of Operation: Jerry
Witowski
Estimated Sales: $5-10 Million
Number Employees: 10,000
Parent Co: Coltec Industries
Brands:
Mini Sdx
Sdx
Sdx Iii

21496 Delavan-Delta
11 Rado Drive
Naugatuck, CT 06770-2220
203-720-5610
Fax: 203-720-5616
Manufacturer and exporter of level controls

Sales/Marketing Manager: Dean Cheramie
Number Employees: 65
Parent Co: Coltec Industries

21497 (HQ)Delco Tableware
19 Harbor Park Dr
Port Washington, NY 11050-4657
516-484-7965
Fax: 516-625-0859 800-221-9557
info@delcointl.com
Flatware, hollowware, steak knives and chinaware
Executive VP: Robert Delman
VP Distributor Sales: Holly Newme
Other Locations:
Delco Tableware
Port Washington NY
Brands:
Atlantic
Ceramicor
Delco
Hotel America
Table De France

21498 Delfield Co
980 S Isabella Rd
Mt Pleasant, MI 48858
989-773-7981
Fax: 800-669-0619 800-733-8821
www.delfield.com
Manufacturer and exporter of freezers and cabinets,
display cases, cafeteria/restaurant serving counters,
dispensers, ventilation systems, commercial refriger-
ators, mobile cafeteria systems, salad bars, pizza ta-
bles and stationary andmobile hot tables.
Year Founded: 1949
Estimated Sales: $100-500 Million
Number Employees: 500-999
Parent Co: The Manitowoc Company
Brands:
Air Tech
Mark V
Shelleyglass
Shelleymatic

21499 Delfin Design & Mfg
23301 Antonio Pkwy
Rancho Sta Marg, CA 92688-2664
949-888-4644
Fax: 949-888-4626 800-354-7919
john@delfinfs.com www.delfinfs.com
Manufacturer and exporter of plastic displayware in-
cluding crocks, bowls, platters, trays, domes and
covers
President: John Rief
john@delfinff.com
VP Sales: Gary Mazzone
Estimated Sales: $2.5-5,000,000
Number Employees: 20-49
Square Footage: 25000

21500 Deli-Boy Inc
100 Matthews Ave
Syracuse, NY 13209-1500
315-488-4411
Fax: 315-488-4155 www.deli-boy.com
Owner: Lon Frocione
lon.frocione@deli-boy.com
Estimated Sales: $20-50 Million
Number Employees: 50-99
Brands:
Grande
Premier/Nugget

21501 Delice Global Inc
150 Roosevelt Pl
Palisades Park, NJ 07650-1153
201-438-0300
Fax: 201-947-0320 info@deliceusa.com
www.deliceglobal.com
Baking equipment
Number Employees: 10-19

21502 Deline Box Co
3700 Lima St
Denver, CO 80239-3309
303-376-1283
Fax: 303-373-2325 webmaster@delinebox.com
Corrugated boxes
President: Dade Deline
Sales Manager: Jim Davis
Contact: Ricardo Alvarez
alvarez.ricardo@delinebox.com
Estimated Sales: $10-20 Million
Number Employees: 20-49

21503 Delkor Systems, Inc
8700 Rendova St NE
Minneapolis, MN 55014

763-783-0855
Fax: 763-783-0875 800-328-5558
sales@delkorsystems.com
www.delkorsystems.com

Provides end-of-line packaging systems that deliver robust, innovative solutions for carton forming, loading, and closing, top load case and tray packing, flat pad shrink wrapping, and robotic palletizing. Delkor's packaging solutionsare engineered for maximum versatility and flexibility to help customers meet ever-changing market requirements while preserving their capital investments.
Owner: Dale Andersen
CFO: Terry Cook
Contact: Dave Ackley
dackley@delkorsystems.com
Estimated Sales: $10-20 Million
Number Employees: 50-99

21504 Dell Marking Systems
721 Wanda St
Ferndale, MI 48220

248-547-7750
Fax: 248-544-9115 info@dellid.com
www.dellid.com

Marking and identification systems
President: Michael Grattan
sales@dellid.com
Estimated Sales: $1-2.5 000,000
Number Employees: 10-19

21505 Delmonte Fresh
3151 Regatta Ave
Suite E
Richmond, CA 94804-6411

510-236-8968
Fax: 510-236-2029
contact-us-executive-office@freshdelmonte.com
www.freshdelmonte.com

Distribution center providing a variety of services including ripening, sorting, re-packing, fresh cut processing, and delivery of fruits and vegetables.
President/Chief Operating Officer: Hani El-Naffy
Chief Executive Officer/Chairman: Mohammad Abu-Ghazaleh
SVP/Chief Financial Officer: Richard Contreras
SVP/General Counsel & Secretary: Bruce Jordan
VP/Research-Development Agricultural Svs: Thomas Young
efiroozabady@freshdelmonte.com
SVP/North American Sales & Product Mgmt: Emanuel Lazopoulos
VP/Human Resources: Marissa Tenazas
SVP/North American Operations: Paul Rice
Number Employees: 10-19
Parent Co: Del Monte Fresh Produce Company
Type of Packaging: Consumer, Food Service

21506 Delmonte Fresh Produce Co
118 Forest Pkwy
Forest Park, GA 30297-2008

404-366-2112
Fax: 404-366-3996
contact-us-executive-office@freshdelmonte.com
www.freshdelmonte.com

Distribution center providing a variety of services including ripening, sorting, re-packing, fresh cut processing, and delivery of fruits and vegetables.
President: Mike Ford
mford@freshdelmonte.com
Chief Executive Officer/Chairman: Mohammad Abu-Ghazaleh
mford@freshdelmonte.com
SVP/Chief Financial Officer: Richard Contreras
SVP/General Counsel & Secretary: Bruce Jordan
VP/Research-Development Agricultural Svs: Thomas Young
mford@freshdelmonte.com
SVP/North American Sales & Product Mgmt: Emanuel Lazopoulos
VP/Human Resources: Marissa Tenazas
SVP/North American Operations: Paul Rice
Site Manager: Mike Ford
Number Employees: 10-19
Parent Co: Del Monte Fresh Produce Company
Type of Packaging: Consumer, Food Service

21507 Delphi Food Machinery
625 S Smith Rd # 21
Suite 21
Tempe, AZ 85281-2967

480-483-8361
Fax: 480-483-8396 foodmachinery@delphifm.com
www.delphifm.com

Dealers of used processing equipment
Owner: Peter Yioulos
Estimated Sales: $.5-1 million
Number Employees: 1-4

21508 Delran Label Corporation
1829 Underwood Boulevard
Suite 10
Delran, NJ 08075-1241

856-764-1336
Fax: 856-764-3470

Wine industry labels

21509 Delta Carbona
376 Hollywood Ave # 208
Fairfield, NJ 07004-1807

973-808-6260
Fax: 973-808-5661 888-746-5599
www.carbona.com

Stain removers
President: Tim Wells
dbudhan@carbona.com
Marketing Director: Sherry Polevoy
Purchasing Manager: Eileen Hirschfield
Estimated Sales: $1-2.5 Million
Number Employees: 5-9
Square Footage: 80000
Brands:
    Carbona Cleanit! Oven Cleaner
    Carpet Wizard
    Color Run Remover
    Pet Stain & Odor Remover
    Stain Devils
    Stain Stop
    Stain Wizard
    Stain Wizard Wipes

21510 Delta Chemical Corporation
P.O.Box 73054
Baltimore, MD 21273-3054

410-354-3253
Fax: 410-354-1021 800-282-5322
jack@deltachemical.com www.deltachemical.com

Chlorine liquid bleaches
President: John Besson
CEO: Rebecca Besson
Director of Technology: Jim Dulko
Natl Sls Mgr: Jack Colgan
Director of Technology: Jim Dulko
Sales Manager (South): Joe Shemanski
Northern Regional Sales: Dan Moyer
Western/Caribbean Regional Sales Manager: Ed Penick
Vice President, Marketing & Sales: Terry Badwak
Estimated Sales: $20-50 Million
Number Employees: 100-249

21511 Delta Container Corporation
220 Plantation Rd
New Orleans, LA 70123

504-733-7292
Fax: 504-734-8920 800-752-7292
www.prattindustries.com

Corrugated containers
President: Gary Byrd
CEO: Brian McPheely
CFO: Gary Byrd
Quality Control: Mark May
COO: David Dennis
Estimated Sales: $10-20 Million
Number Employees: 50-99
Square Footage: 170000
Parent Co: Pratt Industries

21512 Delta Cooling Towers Inc
41 Pine St # 103
Suite 103
Rockaway, NJ 07866-3139

973-586-2201
Fax: 973-586-2243 800-289-3358
sales@deltacooling.com www.deltacooling.com

Polyethylene non-corroding cooling towers and air strippers
President: John Flaherty
Sales: David Jurgensen
Contact: Frank Przyhocki
fprzyhocki@deltacooling.com

Estimated Sales: Above $10MM
Number Employees: 5-9
Brands:
    Paragon
    Pioneer
    Premier
    Vanguard

21513 Delta Cyklop Orga Pac
2601 Westinghouse Blvd
Charlotte, NC 28273-6517

704-588-2510
Fax: 704-588-6838 800-446-4347
www.itwpbna.com

Polyester, steel, cord and polypropylene strapping; also, tape dispensers, strapping machines and elastic string tying equipment
VP Sales/Marketing: James Prieb
Estimated Sales: $10-20 Million
Number Employees: 20-49
Parent Co: Illinois Tool Works

21514 Delta Engineering Corporation
3 Freedom Way
Walpole, MA 02081

781-729-8650
Fax: 781-729-6149
info@deltaengineeringcorp.com
www.deltaengineeringcorp.com

Electronic counting and weighing systems, boxing and bagging equipment
Manager: Peter Knobel
R&D: Herb Mac Rae
Sales: Steve Hill
Production: Richard Pooler
Plant Manager: Pete Knobel
Estimated Sales: $2.5-5 000,000
Number Employees: 1-4
Number of Products: 25
Type of Packaging: Consumer, Food Service, Bulk

21515 Delta F Corporation
4 Constitution Way Ste I
Woburn, MA 01801

781-935-4600
Fax: 781-938-0531

Oxygen analyzers
VP: John Swyers
Sales Manager: Margaret Lanoue
Contact: John Swyers
j.swyers@delta-f.com
Estimated Sales: $50-100 Million
Number Employees: 50-99
Parent Co: TGE Group

21516 Delta Industrial Services
11501 Eagle St NW
Coon Rapids, MN 55448

800-279-3358
Fax: 763-755-7799 800-279-3358
www.deltaind.com

Narrow web converting, packaging
Contact: Greg Sorensen
gsorensen@deltaind.com
Estimated Sales: $1-5 000,000
Number Employees: 50-99

21517 Delta Machine & Maufacturing
137 Teal St
St Rose, LA 70087-4022

504-949-8304
Fax: 504-467-0071 debra@deltamachinemfg.com

Manufacturer and exporter of bakery equipment including trough elevators
President/Owner: Dale Kessler
CEO: Andrew Kessler, Jr.
CFO: Debra Kessler
Estimated Sales: Below $1 Million
Number Employees: 1-4

21518 Delta Plastics
106 Delta Pl
Hot Springs, AR 71913

501-760-3000
Fax: 501-760-3005 sales@deltaplastics.com
www.deltaplastics.com

Packaging supplies for the food industry. Rexam PLC has now acquired the company as of September 2005
CEO: Lothar Schweigert
VP: Kurt Nyberg
VP Sales: Kurt Nyberg
Contact: Leanne Mitchell
lmitchell@deltapl.com

Estimated Sales: $50 Million
Number Employees: 250-499
Parent Co: Rexam PLC
Type of Packaging: Food Service

21519 Delta Pure Filtration Corp
11011 Richardson Rd
Ashland, VA 23005-3418

804-798-2888
Fax: 804-798-3923 800-785-9450
tfurbee@deltapure.com www.deltapure.net
Manufacturer and exporter of active carbon cartridge filters for water, juice, vegetable oil, etc
President: Todd Furbee
tfurbee@deltapure.com
Operations Manager: Frank Williams
Number Employees: 20-49
Square Footage: 36000
Type of Packaging: Bulk
Brands:
 Aquatrust
 Delta Pure

21520 Delta Signs
1802 Hickory Dr
Haltom City, TX 76117

817-838-0213
Fax: 817-665-0167 866-643-3582
deltasigns@delta-sign.com
Electric signs and awnings; also, installation available with crane service
Owner: Steve Jessup
CEO: Sergio Contreras
CFO: Steve Jessup
Quality Control: N Cao
Estimated Sales: Below $5 Million
Number Employees: 5-9
Square Footage: 20800

21521 Delta Systems Inc
535 W Dyke Rd
Rogers, AR 72758-6443

479-631-2210
Fax: 479-631-2217 800-631-2214
www.delta-systems-inc.com
Horizontal flow wrapping machinery, turnkey packaging systems, automatic feeding equipment, distribution equipment
President: Jake Bushey
CEO: Charles Bruce
c.bruce@delta-systems-inc.com
Director of Sales: Liam Buckley
Estimated Sales: $5-10 Million
Number Employees: 20-49

21522 Delta T Construction
10838 Old Mill Rd # A
Omaha, NE 68154-2649

402-333-0830
Fax: 402-333-6635 info@deltatconstruction.com
www.deltatconstruction.com
Cold storage doors and hardware, insulated building panels, insulation-floors, ceilings, and refrigerated structures
Manager: Ty Kestel
tyk@deltatconstuction.com
Estimated Sales: Less Than $500,000
Number Employees: 1-4

21523 Delta Technology Corp
1602 Townhurst Dr
Houston, TX 77043-3283

713-464-7407
Fax: 713-461-6753 info@deltatechnology.com
www.deltatechnology.com
Electronic color sorting equipment
VP/Sales: Eduardo Libin
Estimated Sales: $5-10 Million
Number Employees: 10-19

21524 Delta Trak
PO Box 398
Pleasanton, CA 94566-0039

925-249-2250
Fax: 925-249-2251 800-962-6776
salesinfo@deltatrak.com www.deltatrak.com
Innovator of cold chain managament and food safety solutions. Product line includes a wide range of temperature, humidity, and pH monitoring and recodring devices such as data loggers, wireless systems, and a variety of professionalthermometers.

President/Founder: Fredrick Wu
R&D Director: George Krasten
Marketing/Business Development Director: Ray Caron
Operations Director: Steve Hibbs
Production Manager: Satwant Chand
Estimated Sales: $10-15 000,000
Number Employees: 70+
Number of Brands: 4
Number of Products: 220+
Square Footage: 6000
Brands:
 Air Repair
 Coldtrak
 Flash Link
 Temp Dot
 Thermotrace

21525 Delta Wire And Mfg.
29 Delta Drive
Harrow, ON N0R 1G0
Canada

519-738-3514
Fax: 519-738-3468 800-221-3794
contact@deltawire.com www.deltawire.com
Manufacturer and exporter of welded wire mesh products including pallet racks and containers
President: Geoffrey Scully
CFO: Geoffrey Scully
National Sales Manager: Larry Cunningham
Estimated Sales: $10-20 Million
Number Employees: 10-19

21526 Delta/Ducon
Three Tun Center
33 Sproul Road
Malvern, PA 19355

610-695-9700
Fax: 610-695-9724 800-238-2974
sales@deltaducon.com www.deltaducon.com
Pneumatic conveying equipment for flour, unloading rail cars, in-plant transfer and dust capture systems.
Manager: Gini Krisciunas
Sales Director: Ron Tempesta
Engineering: Dave Lizzi
Purchasing Manager: Cathy Heinser
Estimated Sales: $5 Million
Number Employees: 10-19
Brands:
 Perma/Flo
 Perma/Lok
 Spira/Flo
 Xl Airlock

21527 DeltaTrak
P.O.Box 398
Pleasanton, CA 94566

925-249-2250
Fax: 925-249-2251 800-962-6776
salesinfo@deltatrak.com www.deltatrak.com
DeltaTrak, Inc. is a leading innovator of cold chain management and temperature monitoring solutions. DeltaTrak offers a wide range of temperature and humidity data loggers and wireless systems. DeltaTrak develops and manufactures highquality portable test instruments that monitor/record temperature and humidity. DeltaTrak's comprehensive cold chain management systems also include professional digital probe and infrared thermometers.
Quality Assurance Manager: Tony Trapolino
VP Marketing & Business Development: Ray Carson
Director, Operations: Rick Delgado
Estimated Sales: $8,000,000
Number Employees: 250
Number of Brands: 20
Number of Products: 80+
Type of Packaging: Food Service, Private Label, Bulk
Brands:
 Flash Link
 Thermotrace

21528 Delux Manufacturing Co
4650 Airport Rd
PO Box 1027
Kearney, NE 68847-3761

308-237-2274
Fax: 308-234-3765 800-658-3240
info@deluxmfg.com www.deluxmfg.com
Manufacturer and exporter of grain dryers
President: Eric D Michel
eric.dm@deluxmfg.com
VP/Sales Manager: Bob Schultz

Estimated Sales: $2.5-5 Million
Number Employees: 20-49
Square Footage: 144000

21529 Deluxe Equipment Company
P.O.Box 11390
4414 28th St. West
Bradenton, FL 34207

941-753-3184
Fax: 941-753-4529 800-367-8931
deluxe@gte.net www.deluxeovens.com
Manufacturer and exporter of ovens, proofers, warmers.
President: Gib Smith
CFO: Sandra Smith
VP/Sales: Russ D'Aiuto
Estimated Sales: $2.5-5 Million
Number Employees: 10-19
Square Footage: 50000
Brands:
 Convect a Ray
 Deluxe

21530 (HQ)Dema Engineering Co
10020 Big Bend Rd
St Louis, MO 63122-6457

314-966-3533
Fax: 314-965-8319 800-325-3362
sales@demaeng.com
Manufacturer and exporter of warewash, laundry and liquid soap dispensers including injectors, proportioning detergent feeders, rinse pumps and foamers
President: Jonathan Deutsch
jonathand@demaeng.com
VP, Marketing: Dan Gillespie
SVP, Global Sales: Ron Dickerson
Purchasing Manager: David Deutsch
Estimated Sales: $10-20 Million
Number Employees: 20-49
Square Footage: 56000
Other Locations:
 Dema Engineering Co.
 Gerald MO

21531 Demaco
4645 Metropolitan Ave
Ridgewood, NY 11385
Fax: 718-417-9264 www.demaco.nl/en/
Manufacturer and exporter of pasta equipment
President: Leonard Defrancisci
VP: John Deluca
Mngr: Amy Casaburri
Estimated Sales: $10-20 Million
Number Employees: 20-49
Parent Co: Howden Food Equipment

21532 Demag Cranes & Components Corp
29201 Aurora Rd
Cleveland, OH 44139-1895

440-248-2400
Fax: 440-248-3086 www.demagcranes.us
Manufacturer and exporter of cranes and hoists
President: John Paxton
Corp Comms: Dan Konstantinovsk
Administrative Assistant: Maureen Tilly
Estimated Sales: H
Number Employees: 250-499
Parent Co: Demag Material Handling

21533 Demarle Inc
8 Corporate Dr # 1
Cranbury, NJ 08512-3630

609-395-0219
Fax: 609-395-1027 888-353-9726
info@demarleusa.com www.sasademarle.com
Silicone applied mold and trays for baking and freezing
President: Hatsuo Takeuchi
Vice President: Pierre Bonnet
pierre@sasademarle.com
Sales Manager: Eliane Feiner
Estimated Sales: $5-10 000,000
Number Employees: 10-19
Brands:
 Flexipan
 Silform
 Silpat

21534 Dematic Corp
8012 Tower Point Dr
Charlotte, NC 28227-7726

704-845-1110
Fax: 704-845-1111

President: Mats Herrstromer
CEO: Terry Dunn
CFO: Bob Consoli
Quality Control: Janet Hill
Estimated Sales: $10-20 Million
Number Employees: 20-49

21535 Dematic Corp
2855 S James Dr
New Berlin, WI 53151-3662

262-860-7000
Fax: 262-860-7010   800-424-7365
www.dematic.com

Chairman of the Board: John Splude
Cmo: Mike Kotecki
mike.kotecki@dematic.com
Vice President and CFO: James P Purko
Vice President, Corporate Marketing: Cheryl Falk
Estimated Sales: $20-30 Million
Number Employees: 250-499

21536 Dematic USA
507 Plymouth Ave NE
Grand Rapids, MI 49505-6029

616-451-6200
Fax: 616-913-7701   877-725-7500
logisticsresults@dematic.com www.dematic.com
Material handling, systems and management.
President/ CEO: Ulf Henriksson
CEO: David Abbey
david.abbey@dematic.com
CFO: Richard Paradise
EVP/ General Counsel: Ben Clark
EVP R&D: Jim Strollberg
EVP Human Resources: Dutch Burfield
EVP Global Operations: Robert Arguelles
Number Employees: 20-49
Parent Co: Siemens Dematic AG
Brands:
Dematic
Direct It
Pick Director
Q-Can
Rapid Sort
Rapistan
Siplace
Sort Director
Staging Director

21537 Dembling & Dembling Architects
307 Washington Ave
Albany, NY 12206-3074

518-463-8066
Fax: 518-463-8610 daved@ddarch.com
www.ddarch.com
Consultant specializing in the design of food service
and hospitality establishments
President: Daniel Dembling
dand@ddarch.com
Partner: David Dembling
Estimated Sales: Below $5 Million
Number Employees: 5-9

21538 Demeyere Na, Llc
3 Dorchester Dr
Westport, CT 06880-4037

203-255-2402
Fax: 203-255-2406   800-338-7304
dem.breeden@prodigy.net
Commercial stainless steel cookware with seven ply
construction, industry rated for all energy sources
especially efficient induction
President: John Walters
Contact: John Breeden
info@demeyere.be
Estimated Sales: $50 Million+
Number Employees: 1-4
Number of Brands: 11
Number of Products: 1700
Square Footage: 120000

21539 Dempster Systems
PO Box 1388
Toccoa, GA 30577-1424

706-886-2327
Fax: 706-886-0088

Manufacturer and exporter of refuse handling systems
President: John Boonstra

Estimated Sales: $20-50 Million
Number Employees: 100-249
Parent Co: Technology
Type of Packaging: Consumer, Food Service, Bulk

21540 Demptos Glass Corporation
2300 Cordelia Rd
Fairfield, CA 94534

707-422-9999
Fax: 707-422-1242 david@demptos.com
Manufacturers of wine bottles, champagne bottles,
spirits bottles, beer bottles etc
Manager: John Symank
COO: Rob Belke
rob@demptos.com
General Manager: John Symank
Estimated Sales: $20-50 Million
Number Employees: 50-99

21541 (HQ)Den Mar Corp
1005 Reed Rd
North Dartmouth, MA 02747-1567

508-999-3295
Fax: 508-999-6108 henrydenmar@corp.com
www.denmar-corp.com
Stainless steel and wood tables including dish, work
and steam; also, shelving and sinks
President: George Henriques
Partner: Henry Martin
henry@denmar-corp.com
Production Manager: Aaron Magrath
Estimated Sales: $1-2.5 Million
Number Employees: 10-19
Square Footage: 56000
Other Locations:
Denmar Corp.
North Dartmouth MA
Brands:
Aqua-Vent
Denmar
Simplex

21542 Den Ray Sign Company
1057 Whitehall St
Jackson, TN 38301

731-427-5466
Fax: 731-427-5473   800-530-7291
sales@denraysign.com www.denraysign.com
Plastic and neon signs; custom designs, service and
maintenance available
President: Rhea Deming
Estimated Sales: $500,000-$1 Million
Number Employees: 10-19

21543 Denair Trailer Company
P.O. Box 1389enue
Yuma, AZ 85366

928-627-4716
Fax: 928-627-4717 denairtrailer.com
Wine industry agricultural trailers.
Estimated Sales: $100-500 Million
Number Employees: 10-19

21544 Denice & Filice LLC
10001 Fairview Rd
Hollister, CA 95023-9209

831-637-7492
Fax: 831-637-4174

Contact: Vince Brigantino
vince.brigantino@denicefilice.com
Estimated Sales: $20-50 Million
Number Employees: 20-49

21545 Denman Equipment
2020 Satinwood Dr
Memphis, TN 38119-5631

901-755-7135
Fax: 901-754-0105 www.denserv.com
Dealer of used and rebuilt food processing equipment for the meat and poultry industry
Owner: Pierce Denman
Estimated Sales: $.5-1 million
Number Employees: 1-4

21546 Dennis Engineering Group
1537 Main St # 2
Springfield, MA 01103-1463

413-787-1785
Fax: 413-787-1786 info@dennisgrp.com
www.dennisgrp.com
Offers complete planning, design, architectural, engineering and construction management services.

President: Calen Burr
burr@dennisgrp.com
Principal: Tan McCreary
VP: John Lapinksi
Finance Executive/HR Director: Alissa Boudreau
Number Employees: 10-19
Square Footage: 32000

21547 (HQ)Dennsi Group
1537 Main St
Springfield, MA 01103-1458

413-737-1353
Fax: 413-787-1786 info@dennisgrp.com
www.dennisgroup.com
Full-Service architectural, engineering, process design and construction management firm providing
total project solutions, from conception through
start-up, exclusively to the food and beverags
industries.
President: Thomas Dennis
Sales: Dan McCreary
Estimated Sales: Less Than $500,000
Number Employees: 1-4
Other Locations:
Salt Lake City UT
San Diego CA
Wheaton IL
Toronto, Canada

21548 Denstor Mobile Storage Systems
2966 Wilson Drive NW
Walker, MI 49534

616-735-9100
Fax: 616-988-4045   800-234-7477
sales@pippmobile.com www.denstor.com
High density mobile storage systems
President, CEO: Craig J. Umans
Chief Financial Officer: Keith Carpentier
Director of Retail Sales: Len Kowalski
lkowalski@denstor.com
Operations Manager: Tom French
Estimated Sales: $5-10 Million
Number Employees: 20
Parent Co: Pipp Mobile Storage Systems, Inc

21549 DentalOne Partners
17300 Dallas Parkway
Suite 1070
Dallas, TX 75248-7725

972-755-0800
Fax: 972-387-9774
Printing materials, film coextruded, film laminated,
film LLDPE, film LDPE, stand-up pouch, film
stretch, film shrink, film oriented polxprotylene, film
coated
CEO: R Kirk Huntsman
Contact: Robert Anders
robert.anders@dental-one.com
Estimated Sales: $3-5 Million
Number Employees: 20-49

21550 Denver Instrument Company
5 Orville Dr.
Bohemia, NY 11716

303-431-7255
Fax: 303-423-4831   800-321-1135
info@denverinstrument.com
www.denverinstrumentusa.com
Balances, multiple weighing units
Manager: Karen Ware
Contact: Denice Pracht
denice@denverinstrument.com
Estimated Sales: Below $5 Million
Number Employees: 10-19
Brands:
Apex

21551 Denver Mixer Company
6565 Vine Ct
Denver, CO 80229

303-287-0025
Fax: 303-287-0924
President: Chris Barnhill
Estimated Sales: $2.5-5 000,000
Number Employees: 5-9

21552 Denver Reel & Pallet Company
4600 Monaco Parkaway
Denver, CO 80216

303-321-1920
Fax: 303-321-1949 denverreel@aol.com
www.denverreelandpallet.com
Pallets, reels, skids, boxes and crates

President: Kurt Heimbrock
CFO: Kurt Heimbrock
VP: Darold Herrera
R&D: Kurt Heimbrock
Quality Control: Kurt Heimbrock
VP of Sales: Dareld Herrera
Estimated Sales: $2.5-5 Million
Number Employees: 20-49
Square Footage: 32000
Brands:
 Dratco

21553 Dependable Machine, Inc.
308 S. 14th St.-Coeur
d'Alene, ID 83814

973-239-7800
Fax: 973-239-7855 866-967-0146
dmi-cnc.com
Manufacturer, importer and exporter of screen and
pad printing equipment, printing inks and accesso-
ries
President: Thomas Skeels
VP: Brett Skeels
Estimated Sales: $2.5-5 Million
Number Employees: 10-19
Square Footage: 40000

21554 (HQ)Derse Inc
3800 W Canal St
Milwaukee, WI 53208-4150

414-977-0002
Fax: 414-257-3798 800-562-2300
ezeum@derse.com www.derse.com
Custom exhibits and highway business signs
CEO: William Haney
CEO: Aaron Bartelt
abartelt@derse.com
President: Adam Beckett
VP Sales/Marketing: Kent Jones
Estimated Sales: $10-20 Million
Number Employees: 100-249
Other Locations:
 Derse
 Carrollton TX

21555 Des Moines Stamp Mfg Co
851 6th Ave
Des Moines, IA 50309-1229

515-288-7245
Fax: 515-288-0418 888-236-7739
info@dmstamp.com www.dmstamp.com
Rubber stamps, notary seals and stencils
Owner: Tom Child
tchild@dmstamp.com
Estimated Sales: $2.5-5 Million
Number Employees: 20-49
Square Footage: 80000

21556 Desco Equipment Corporation
1903 Case Pkwy
Twinsburg, OH 44087-2343

330-405-1581
Fax: 330-405-1584 desco@descoequipment.com
www.descoequipment.com
Innovators of high quality, cost-efficient printing
systems for the container and closure industry.
President: Leo Henry
Contact: Phyllis Faiken
pfaiken@descoequipment.com
Purchasing Manager: Dennis Sweeney
Estimated Sales: $3.7 Million
Number Employees: 26
Square Footage: 200000
Brands:
 Desco

21557 Descon EDM
54 W Main St
PO Box 189
Brocton, NY 14716

716-792-9300
Fax: 716-792-9363 us.kompass.com/
Manufacturer and exporter of material handling
equipment including vibrating and belt conveyors,
graders, etc
CEO: David Beehler
R&D: Christopher Beehler
General Manager: C Beehler
Estimated Sales: Below $5 Million
Number Employees: 1-4
Square Footage: 20000

21558 Desert Box & Supply Corporation
P.O.Box 281
Thermal, CA 92274-281

760-399-5161
Wooden boxes, packaging materials and corrugated
boxes
President: Michael Wills
Co-Owner: Ann Wills
Estimated Sales: Less than $500,000
Number Employees: 10

21559 Deshazo Crane Company
P.O.Box 1450
Alabaster, AL 35007-2062

205-664-2006
Fax: 205-664-3668 www.deshazo.com
Manufacturer and exporter of cranes including over-
head bridge, gantry and semi-gantry
CEO: Guy K Mitchell Jr
Estimated Sales: $20-50 Million
Number Employees: 100-249
Type of Packaging: Bulk

21560 Desiccare
10600 Shoemaker Avenue
Suite C
Santa Fe Springs, CA 90670-4073

888-932-0405
Fax: 562-903-2272 800-446-6650
desiccant@desiccare.com www.desicare.com
Silica gel, clay, molecular sieve and activated carbon
desiccants ranging in size from 0.25 grams to 2,500
grams
President: Ken Blankenhorn
Contact: Wayne Pelletier
wpelletier@desiccare.com
Estimated Sales: $10-20 Million
Number Employees: 50-99

21561 Design Group
1002 S Prospect Ave
Clearwater, FL 33756-4042

727-441-2825
Fax: 727-446-0388
thedesigngroup@tampabay.rr.com
www.thedesigngroupincusa.com
Interior design services for hospitality-hotels and
restaurants. Licensed in the state of Florida
(ID-0001657, IBC-000317)
President: Jeanette Brewer
thedesigngroupinc@verizon.net
Vice President: Delayna Cowley Nestell
Marketing: Jeanetter Brewer
Sales: Delayna Nestell
Production: Irene Bishop
Purchasing Manager: Delayna Cowley Nestell
Estimated Sales: Less than $500,000
Number Employees: 1-4
Square Footage: 12000
Brands:
 Daniel Paul
 Flexsteel Contract
 Lexmark Carpet
 McI Group
 Mtj Seating
 Shelly Williams Seating

21562 Design Ideas
2521 Stockyard Rd
P.O.Box 2967
Springfield, IL 62702-1437

217-753-3081
Fax: 217-753-3080 800-426-6394
designideas@designid.com
Containers, gift packaging, and candle holders
Owner: Court Hager
chager@designideas.net
Director Sales/Marketing: Christine Netznik
Number Employees: 50-99
Number of Products: 1500

21563 Design Label Manufacturing
7 Capitol Dr
East Lyme, CT 6333

860-739-6266
Fax: 860-739-7659 800-666-1575
sales@designlabel.com www.designlabel.com
Pressure sensitive and promotional labels, clam shell
and polystyrene inserts and coupons
President: Jeff P Dunphy
Controller: Kim Dunphy
Contact: David Arroyo
darroyo@designlabel.com

Estimated Sales: $10-20 Million
Number Employees: 20-49

21564 Design Packaging Company
100 Hazel Ave
Glencoe, IL 60022-1731

773-486-8100
Fax: 773-486-2160 800-321-7659
Polypropylene and polyethylene bags and sheets;
importer of polyethylene and polyproplyne bags; ex-
porter of polyethylene sleeves and bags
President: Myron Horvitz
CFO: Greg Horvitz
VP: Randy Block
Sales Representative: Greg Horvitz
Contact: Conrad Capulong
conrad.capulong@designpackaging.net
Purchasing Agent: Randy Block
Estimated Sales: $5-10 Million
Number Employees: 20-49
Square Footage: 80000
Brands:
 Designbags
 Foiltex
 Kristalene

21565 Design Plastics Inc
3550 Keystone Dr
Omaha, NE 68134-4800

402-572-7177
Fax: 402-572-0500 800-491-0786
www.designplastics.com
Plastic packaging and containers for dry and frozen
foods
President: Rick Breden
HR Executive: Nancy Janne
njanne@designplastics.com
Director Marketing: Sylvio Rebolloso
Estimated Sales: $10-20 Million
Number Employees: 50-99

21566 Design Specialties Inc
1890 Dixwell Ave # 200
Hamden, CT 06514-3171

203-288-3587
Fax: 203-288-3594 800-999-1584
design@duralux4you.com www.duralux4you.com
Reusable plastic tableware including flatware, trays,
dishes, tumblers, mugs and bowls; also, insulated
trays and high temperature dishes available for
cooking and chilling
Owner: Patricia Whitlock
design@duralux4you.com
VP: Patricia Whitlock
Estimated Sales: $5-10 Million
Number Employees: 5-9
Number of Brands: 1
Number of Products: 40
Brands:
 Duralux

21567 Design Systems Inc
38799 W 12 Mile Rd # 100
Farmington Hills, MI 48331-2903

248-489-4300
Fax: 248-489-4321 800-660-4374
pmunzenberger@dsidsc.com www.dsidsc.com
Process engineering company specializing in lean
manufacturing and controls integration, through put
simulation
Manager: Steve Puranen
Sales Director: Paul Munzenberger
Manager: David Goings
dgoing@ofisolutions.com
Estimated Sales: $35 Million
Number Employees: 100-249

21568 Design Technology Corporation
5 Suburban Park Drive
Billerica, MA 01821-3904

978-663-7000
Fax: 978-663-6841
Custom designed and built food processing, material
handling, packaging, inspection and assembly
equipment
President: Marvin Menzin
Estimated Sales: $5-10 Million
Number Employees: 20-49
Square Footage: 120000

21569 Design Technology Corporation
26 Mason Street
Lexington, MA 02421
781-862-5107
Fax: 303-440-5127 800-597-7063
Manufacturer and exporter of material handling equipment, food processing machinery and process control systems
President: Marvin Menzin
Estimated Sales: $1-2,500,000
Number Employees: 4

21570 Design-Mark Industries
3 Kendrick Rd
Wareham, MA 02571-1093
508-295-9591
Fax: 508-295-6752 800-451-3275
sales@design-mark.com www.design-mark.com
Manufacturer and exporter of labels, nameplates and membrane switch panels
President: Carl Burquist
Cmo: Denise Shurtleff
denise@design-mark.com
Quality Control: Jim Brawders
Operations: Jon Winzler
Marketing Director: Denise Shurtley
Estimated Sales: $14 Million
Number Employees: 50-99
Square Footage: 40000
Type of Packaging: Bulk

21571 Designers Folding Box Corp
84 Tennessee St
Buffalo, NY 14204-2797
716-853-5141
Fax: 716-853-5149
sales@designersfoldingbox.com
www.designersfoldingbox.com
Folding paper boxes and carry-out trays and boxes; also, die cut inserts
President: Jeffrey Winney
CSR: Teri McAndrews
Manager: Eugene Zilka
ezilka@designers.com
PA: Donald Rounds
Estimated Sales: $5-10 Million
Number Employees: 20-49
Type of Packaging: Consumer, Food Service, Private Label, Bulk

21572 Designers Plastics
12880 Automobile Blvd # G
Suite G-I
Clearwater, FL 33762-4711
727-573-1643
Fax: 727-572-7078 sales@designersplastics.com
www.designersplastics.com
Acrylic displays
President: Bruce Ely
desplastic@aol.com
CFO and Quality Controller: Penny Carrigan
Estimated Sales: $1-2.5 Million
Number Employees: 5-9

21573 Designpro Engineering
20092 Edison Circle East
Clearwater, MN 55320
320-558-6000
Fax: 320-558-6110 800-221-4144
www.franklinoutdoor.com
Poultry cutting machinery
Owner: Keith Franklin
Director: John Boughner
Head Technical Department: Jon Boughner
Estimated Sales: $500,000-$1 Million
Number Employees: 1-4
Square Footage: 28000

21574 Despro Manufacturing
PO Box 2503
Cedar Grove, NJ 07009-2503
973-239-0202
Fax: 973-239-1595 800-292-9906
mailbox@emcoplastics.com
www.emcoplastics.com
Acrylic bulk food containers and bins, steel shelving, display racks, point of purchase displays, awnings and pastry cases
President: James Mc Namara
VP: Mark Mercadante
Estimated Sales: $20-50 Million
Number Employees: 100-249
Square Footage: 40000
Parent Co: Emco Industrial Plastics

21575 Detectamet Inc
5111 Glen Alden Dr
Richmond, VA 23231
804-303-1983
844-820-7244
sales@us.detectamet.com www.detectamet.com
Designer and manufacturer of tools and equipment used to detect plastic contamination in food products.
Group Managing Director: Angela Musson-Smith
CEO: Sean Smith
Managing Director: James Chrismas
Parent Co: Detectamet

21576 Detecto Scale Co
203 E Daugherty St
Webb City, MO 64870-1929
417-673-4631
Fax: 417-673-5001 800-641-2008
detecto@cardet.com www.detecto.com
Manufacturer and exporter of scales including portion control, top loading, price computing, bench, platform, counter, pre-packaging, hanging and receiving
President: David Perry
Chief Financial Officer: Elise Crume
Vice President: Larry Hicks
Research And Development: Tony Herrin
Quality Control: Ginger Harper
Marketing Director: Jonathan Sabo
Sales Exec: Brock Dawson
Advertising Manager: Jonathan Sabo
brockdawson@detecto.com
Estimated Sales: $50-60 Million
Number Employees: 10-19
Square Footage: 400000
Parent Co: Cardinal Scale Manufacturing Company
Type of Packaging: Food Service
Brands:
    Cardinal
    Detecto

21577 Detecto Scale Co
203 E Daugherty St
Webb City, MO 64870-1929
417-673-4631
Fax: 417-673-5001 800-641-2008
detecto@cardet.com www.detecto.com
Weighing scales
President: David H Perry
brockdawson@detecto.com
Chief Financial Officer: Elise Crume
Vice President: Larry Hicks
Research/Development: Tony Herrin
Quality Control: Ginger Harper
Marketing: Jonathan Sabo
Sales Exec: Brock Dawson
Operations/Production: Matt Stovern
Estimated Sales: $45 Million
Number Employees: 10-19
Square Footage: 350000
Parent Co: Cardinal Scale Manufacturing Company

21578 Detex Corp
302 Detex Dr
New Braunfels, TX 78130-3099
830-629-2900
Fax: 830-620-6711 www.detex.com
Security locks, alarms, panels, switches and electric and manual guard tour clocks
President: John Blodgett
dta@detex.com
Chairman of the Board: Philip Haselton
R & D: George Val
Director Sales/Marketing: Gary Hackney
National Accounts Sales Manager: Ken Khueler
IT: David Alexander
Production Manager (Hardware): Greg Drake
Estimated Sales: $5-10 Million
Number Employees: 100-249

21579 Detroit Forming
19100 W 8 Mile Rd
Southfield, MI 48075-5792
248-440-1317
Fax: 248-352-0445 sales@detroitforming.net
www.detroitforming.com
Manufacturer and exporter of plastic food trays for meat, produce, ice cream and cookies
President: Leigh Rodney
leigh.rodney@detroitforming.net
National Sales Manager: Ken Sherry
Estimated Sales: $10-20 Million
Number Employees: 100-249

Type of Packaging: Food Service

21580 Detroit Marking Products
15100 Castleton St
Detroit, MI 48227
313-838-9760
Fax: 800-831-4243 800-833-8222
www.dmpco.com
Rubber stamps
President: William Foerg
Contact: Joe Foerg
jfoerg@dmpco.com
Estimated Sales: $1-2.5 Million
Number Employees: 10-19

21581 Detroit Quality Brush Mfg Co
32165 Schoolcraft Rd
Livonia, MI 48150-1833
734-525-5660
Fax: 734-525-0437 800-722-3037
sales@dqb.com www.dqb.com
Manufacturer and exporter of brooms and brushes
Owner: Donald Weinbaum
don@gqb.com
Manufacturing Manager: Mike Lindemoth
Estimated Sales: $2.5-5 Million
Number Employees: 50-99
Square Footage: 200000
Parent Co: Erco Housewares
Type of Packaging: Consumer, Food Service, Private Label, Bulk

21582 Devar Inc
706 Bostwick Ave
Bridgeport, CT 06605-2396
203-368-6751
Fax: 203-368-3747 800-566-6822
sales@devarinc.com www.devarinc.com
Process control instruments including indicators, data acquisition recorders and temperature transmitters, alarms and panel meters; also, pH analyzers and instrument calibrators
President: A J Ruscito
jhead@devarinc.com
VP Engineering: A Gura
VP Sales: Terry Tomasko
Estimated Sales: $2.5-5 Million
Number Employees: 20-49
Square Footage: 40000
Brands:
    Smart Chart

21583 Developak Corporation
2525 Pioneer Ave
Vista, CA 92081-8419
760-598-7404
Fax: 760-598-7402
Custom packaging machinery
President: Brian Pike
Executive VP: Annette Watson
Estimated Sales: Less than $500,000
Number Employees: 1-4
Square Footage: 4000

21584 Development Workshop Inc
555 W 25th St
Idaho Falls, ID 83402-4527
208-524-1550
Fax: 208-523-3148 800-657-5597
www.dwinc.org
Plastic trash liners and specialty and grain bags; also, hand cleaners and wooden pallets
President: Dwight Whittaker
VP: Gerald Hodges
CFO: Bruce Cook
CEO: Michael O'Bleness
Mktg Mgr and Sales Mgr and Pub Relns Mgr: Gregg Katainen
Operations Mgr: Mike O'Bleness
Prodn Mgr: Joe Hodge
VP Operations: Gerry Hodges
VP Upper Valley Industries: Rose Murphy
Estimated Sales: $2.5-5 Million
Number Employees: 250-499

21585 Deville Technologies
8515 Bourassa West
St Laurent, QC 4Y5 1P7
Canada
514-366-4545
Fax: 514-366-9606 866-404-4545
info@devilletechnologies.com
www.devilletechnologies.com

Manufacturers of high capacity food reduction equipment such as shredders, graters, dicers, strip cutters
President: Angelo Penta
Marketing: Lou Penta
Sales: Terry Baggott
Number Employees: 15

21586 Dewatering Equipment Company
6002 SW Texas Court
Portland, OR 97219-1175
503-246-8899
Fax: 503-248-7016 800-426-1723
Number Employees: 4

21587 Dewey & Wilson Displays
5635 Bancroft Avenue
Lincoln, NE 68506-4517
402-489-0868
Advertising signs, posters and emblems
President: Lynn Wilson
Estimated Sales: $500,000-$1 Million
Number Employees: 1-4

21588 (HQ)Dewied International Inc
5010 Interstate 10 E
San Antonio, TX 78219-3352
210-661-6161
Fax: 210-662-6112 800-992-5600
www.dewied.com
Natural and synthetic sausage casings specializing in hog, sheep and beef casings
President: Phil Bohlender
philb@dewiedint.com
VP Sales: George Burt
Estimated Sales: $10-20 Million
Number Employees: 50-99
Brands:
    Dewied

21589 Dex-O-Tex Crossfield Products Corporation
3000 E Harcourt St
Compton, CA 90221-5589
310-886-9100
Fax: 310-886-9119 jodih@cpcmail.net
www.crossfieldproducts.com
Seamless sanitary flooring
President/CEO: Bradford Watt
CFO: David Johnson
Marketing Director: Jodi Hood
Estimated Sales: $30 Million
Number Employees: 100-249
Number of Brands: 3
Number of Products: 25

21590 Dexter Laundry Inc
2211 W Grimes Ave
Fairfield, IA 52556
641-472-5131
800-524-2954
www.dexter.com
Laundry machines.
President: Craig Kirchner
Year Founded: 1894
Estimated Sales: $100-500 Million
Number Employees: 100-249

21591 Dexter Russell Inc
44 River St
Southbridge, MA 01550-1834
508-765-0201
Fax: 508-764-2897 800-343-6042
sales@dexter1818.com www.dexter1818.com
Manufacturer and exporter of knives, turners and spatulas
President: Alan Peppel
apeppel@dexter1818.com
Sales: Kevin Clark
Estimated Sales: $10-20 Million
Number Employees: 250-499
Brands:
    Connoisseur
    Dexter Russell
    Russell Green River
    Russell International
    Sani-Safe
    Sofgrip

21592 Di Engineering
1658 Cole Blvd # 290
Lakewood, CO 80401-3304
303-235-0050
Fax: 303-231-0050 www.diec-group.com

Export and import of cans and end making machinery, fill line equipment, spare parts, and associated technologies, equipment sales and service
VP: Patty Locke
Estimated Sales: $2.5-5 Million
Number Employees: 1-4

21593 Diablo Chemical
216 Court Dale Ave
Kingston, PA 18704
Fax: 570-288-1227 800-548-1384
diablochemicalco@aol.com
Manufacturer and exporter of soaps, detergent and oven cleaners
President: Ernest Clamar
VP, Sales & Marketing: E.J. Clamar

Estimated Sales: $2.8 Million
Number Employees: 1-4
Brands:
    Diablo

21594 Diablo Valley Packaging
2373 N Watney Way
Fairfield, CA 94533-6746
707-422-4300
Fax: 707-422-4545
Wine industry bottles and packaging
Owner: Jeffrey Jones
jeffj@dvpackaging.com
VP: William Bronson
Estimated Sales: $25 Million
Number Employees: 20-49

21595 Dial Corporation
19001 N Scottsdale Rd
Scottsdale, AZ 85255
480-754-3425
Fax: 480-754-1098 www.henkelna.com
Cleaning products including bath and liquid soaps, floor polish and detergents
President: Jeffery C, Piccolomini
Corporate SVP: Alan Syzdek
Senior VP Research & Development: Richard Theiler
Senior VP Sales: Tracy VanBibber
Number Employees: 775
Parent Co: Henkel KGaA
Brands:
    Armour Star Canned Foods

21596 Diamond & Lappin
20-21 Wagaraw Road
Bldg 30a
Fair Lawn, NJ 07410-1322
973-636-9550
Fax: 973-636-9590 877-527-7461
Consultant specializing in private label designing including photography, pre-press and print, digital and conventional production. Package design and manufacture, labeling
Estimated Sales: $1-5 Million
Number Employees: 5
Square Footage: 16000
Parent Co: Lappin Marketing Group

21597 Diamond Automation
23550 Haggerty Rd
Farmington Hills, MI 48335
248-426-9394
Fax: 248-476-0849 www.diamondsystems.com
Manufacturer and exporter of automated packaging equipment; also, egg production and processing equipment
President: Michel Defenbau
Estimated Sales: $20-50 Million
Number Employees: 1-4

21598 Diamond Chain
402 Kentucky Ave
Indianapolis, IN 46225-1174
317-635-8422
Fax: 317-633-2243 800-872-4246
custsvc@diamondchain.com
www.diamondchain.com
Manufacturer and exporter of transmission chains and chain drives

President: Mike Fwiderski
VP Operations: Jerry Randich
CFO: Sheeley Faback
Quality Control: Joe Fossard
VP Sales/Marketing: Douglas Bademoch
Contact: Kristen Abbott
kabbott@diamondchain.com
VP Operations: Pat Taylor
Purchasing Manager: Barbara Heacock
Number Employees: 1-4
Parent Co: Amsted Industries

21599 Diamond Chemical & Supply Co
524 S Walnut St # B
Wilmington, DE 19801-5243
302-656-7786
Fax: 302-656-3039 800-355-7786
sales@diamondchemical.com
www.diamondchemical.com
Wholesaler/distributor of paper products, commercial dishwashing and laundry chemicals, floor maintenance and janitorial equipment and insecticides
President: Susan Hartzel
susan@diamondchemical.com
CFO: Saeed Malik
VP: Richard Ventresca
Sales Manager: Gene Mirolli
Warehouse: Ryan Rynar
Estimated Sales: $5 Million
Number Employees: 20-49
Square Footage: 52000

21600 Diamond Chemical Co Inc
Union Ave & Dubois St
East Rutherford, NJ 7073
201-935-4300
Fax: 201-935-6997 800-654-7627
sales@diamondchem.com www.diamondchem.com
Manufacturer and exporter of detergents and cleaners for meat and poultry plants; also, laundry detergent and bleach
President: Harold Diamond
hdiamond@diamondchem.com
CFO: R Diamond
Estimated Sales: $20-50 Million
Number Employees: 100-249
Square Footage: 137000
Brands:
    Diamond

21601 Diamond Electronics
2530 E Main St
Lancaster, OH 43130-8490
800-700-2791
Fax: 740-687-4201 800-443-6680
www.diamondpower.com
Closed circuit camera and discreet dome surveillance systems
Director Marketing: Pat Kula
Customer Service Manager: Lee Montgomery
Estimated Sales: $1-5 Million
Number Employees: 10-19

21602 Diamond Machining Technology
85 Hayes Memorial Dr # 1
Marlborough, MA 01752-1892
508-481-5944
Fax: 508-485-3924 800-666-4368
www.dmtsharp.com
Manufacturer and exporter of knife sharpeners
President: Christine Miller
Chairman: Elizabeth Powell
R&D: Stan Watson
Sales Manager: George Pettee
Manager: Kris Byron
dmtcustomercare@dmtsharp.com
Estimated Sales: $1-2.5 Million
Number Employees: 1-4
Square Footage: 40000
Brands:
    Diamond

21603 (HQ)Diamond Packaging
111 Commerce Dr
Rochester, NY 14623-3503
585-334-8030
Fax: 585-334-9141 800-333-4079
sales@diamondpkg.com
www.diamondpackaging.com
Folding carton manufacturing and contract packaging services

President/Owner: Kirsten Werner
CEO/Owner: Karla Fichter
kfichter@diamondpkg.com
CFO: Keith Robinson
CEO: Karla Fichter
Research & Development: Dave Ziemba
Quality Control: Heidi Ingersol
Director of Marketing: Dennis Bacchetta
Director of Business Development: Sue Julien
Director of Business Development: Dave Semrau
Plant Manager: Dan Gurbacki
Estimated Sales: $20-50 Million
Number Employees: 100-249
Square Footage: 90000
Type of Packaging: Consumer, Private Label
Other Locations:
   Diamond Packaging Company
   Rochester NY

21604 Diamond Pheonix Corporation
P.O.Box 1608
Lewiston, ME 04241-1608

207-784-1381
Fax: 207-786-0271

President: E Strayhorn
CFO: Peter Pacetti
President, Chief Executive Officer: Tom Coyne
Director of Sales: Dennis Duell
Estimated Sales: $20-50 Million
Number Employees: 50-99

21605 Diamond Roll-Up Door
295 Commerce Way
Upper Sandusky, OH 43351-9079

419-294-3373
Fax: 419-294-3329
diamondinfo@australmonsoon.com
www.diamondrollupdoor.com
Tractor trailer and cargo van roll-up doors; industrial
roll-up doors
President: Ray Vangunten
rvangunten@diamonddoor.com
Admin Manager: Sheri Gatchell
Estimated Sales: $10-20 000,000
Number Employees: 20-49

21606 Diamond Sign Co
2950 Airway Ave # D9
Costa Mesa, CA 92626-6002

714-545-1440
Fax: 714-545-1449 diamondsignco@aol.com
Flags, pennants, banners, signs, displays and exhib-
its; screen printing service available
Owner: John Kasell
diamondsignco@aol.com
Partner: Nancy Gill
Estimated Sales: Less Than $500,000
Number Employees: 1-4
Square Footage: 3000

21607 Diamond Water Conditioning
PO Box 39
Hortonville, WI 54944-0039

920-779-9940
Fax: 920-779-9950 800-236-8931
info@diamondh2o.com www.diamondh2o.com
Water treatment and purification systems including
filters, softeners, etc
President: Tom Griesbach
Sales Commercial/Industrial: Bill Calabria
Estimated Sales: Below $5 Million
Number Employees: 10
Square Footage: 20000

21608 Diamond Wipes Intl Inc
4651 Schaefer Ave
Chino, CA 91710-5542

909-230-9888
Fax: 909-230-9885 800-454-1077
info@diamondwipes.com
www.diamondwipes.com
Manufacturer and exporter of pre-moistened paper
towels
Founder, Owner & President: Eve Yen
eyen@diamondwipes.com
R&D: Map Taing
Quality Control: Anthony Castro
Marketing: Anthony Reyes
Estimated Sales: $5-10 Million
Number Employees: 50-99
Square Footage: 15000
Brands:
   Diamond Wipes
   La Fresh
   With Our Compliment

21609 Diazteca Inc
993 E Frontage Rd
Rio Rico, AZ 85648-6234

520-761-4621
Fax: 520-281-1024 www.diazteca.com
Processor and distributor of Mexican fresh mangos,
fresh hot peppers, granulated cane sugar, refriger-
ated and frozen lean beef, frozen shrimp, frozen IQF
fruits and vegetables, aseptic fruit purees and other
food products.
Owner/President: Ismael Diaz
Vice President: Roderigo Diaz
Estimated Sales: Less Than $500,000
Number Employees: 5-9
Type of Packaging: Consumer, Private Label, Bulk

21610 Dibpack USA
196 Coolidge Avenue
Englewood, NJ 07631-4522

201-871-8787
Fax: 201-871-8908 800-990-3424
Packaging, graphic and printing services
President: Ira Dermanski
CEO: Peter Quercia
CFO: Ira Dermanski
Number Employees: 20

21611 Dickey Manufacturing Company
3632 Stem Avenue
St Charles, IL 60174

630-584-2918
Fax: 630-584-0261 info@securityseals.com
www.securityseals.com
Manufacturer and exporter of security and tamper
proof seals for containers, rail cars, trucks, etc.; also,
locking devices
Manager: Terry Mauger
Sales: Dan Bemis
General Manager: Terry Mauger
Estimated Sales: Below $5,000,000
Number Employees: 20-49
Square Footage: 80000

21612 Dicks Packing Plant
7745 State Route 37 E
New Lexington, OH 43764-9512

740-342-4150
Fresh meats
Owner: Dick Knipe
regina_knipe@yahoo.com
Partner: Blanche Knipe
Partner: Rex Knipe
Estimated Sales: $320,000
Number Employees: 5-9
Square Footage: 11865
Type of Packaging: Consumer, Food Service, Bulk

21613 Dickson
930 S Westwood Ave
Addison, IL 60101-4917

630-543-3747
Fax: 630-543-0498 800-757-3747
dicksoncsr@dicksondata.com
www.dicksondata.com
High temperature stainless steel data loggers for
tracking, sterilization, pasteurization, autoclave and
oven temperatures
President: Michael Unger
CFO: Mike Kohlmeier
Quality Control: Dan Gawel
Contact: Eugene Deleplanque
edeleplanque@dickson-constant.com
Estimated Sales: Below $5 Million
Number Employees: 50-99

21614 Dickson Company
930 S Westwood Ave
Addison, IL 60101-4917

630-543-3747
Fax: 630-543-0498 800-757-3747
dicksoncsr@dicksondata.com
www.dicksondata.com
Data loggers, chart recorders and indicators.
President: Michael Unger
Marketing: Kathy Donovan
Contact: Eugene Deleplanque
edeleplanque@dickson-constant.com
Estimated Sales: $5-10 Million
Number Employees: 50-99

21615 Die Cut Specialties Inc
12543 Rhode Island Ave
Savage, MN 55378-1136

952-890-7590
Fax: 952-890-7590
Manufacturer and exporter of packaging materials
and bulk boxes for sugar, cocoa etc
President: Robert Jones
Plant Manager: Mike Jones
Estimated Sales: $500,000-$1 Million
Number Employees: 10-19
Square Footage: 20000
Type of Packaging: Bulk

21616 Diebel Manufacturing Company
6505 Oakton Street
Morton Grove, IL 60053-2736

847-967-5678
Fax: 847-967-0655 jeffs@diebel.com
www.diebel.com
President and CEO: Richard H Schaefer Sr
Chief Executive Officer: Mike Chester
Quality Control: Victor Rivera
Contact: Jeffrey Schaefer
jschaefer@diebel.com
Estimated Sales: $10-20 Million
Number Employees: 40

21617 Diebolt & Co
100 Halls Rd
Old Lyme, CT 06371-1456

860-434-2222
Fax: 860-434-0370 800-343-2658
sales@dieboltco.com www.heatedhose.com
Steam transfer and Teflon hoses for filtering cooking
oil
President: Mark Diebolt
mdiebolt@diebold.com
Sales Manager: Terrence Murphy
Estimated Sales: Below $5,000,000
Number Employees: 5-9
Brands:
   Electroflo
   Kleenflo
   Steamflo

21618 Diehl Food Ingredients
136 Fox Run Dr
Defiance, OH 43512

419-782-5010
Fax: 419-783-4319 800-251-3033
Lactose free beverages, powdered fat, coffee cream-
ers and whip topping bases.
President: Charles Nicolais
CFO: Darren Lane
CEO: Peter Diehl
Research & Development: Joan Hasselman
Quality Control: Kelly Roach
Marketing Director: Dennis Reid
Sales Director: Jim Holdrieth
Number Employees: 100-249
Parent Co: Diehl
Type of Packaging: Consumer, Food Service, Bulk
Brands:
   Chocomite
   Vitamite

21619 Diequa Inc
180 Covington Dr
Bloomingdale, IL 60108-3105

630-980-1133
Fax: 630-980-1232 info@diequa.com
www.diequa.com
Power transmission and drive components
President: Michael Quaas
mquaas@diequa.com
Estimated Sales: $10-20 000,000
Number Employees: 20-49

21620 Diequa Inc
180 Covington Dr
Bloomingdale, IL 60108-3105

630-980-1133
Fax: 630-980-1232 800-480-1095
info@diequa.com www.diequa.com
President: Michael Quaas
mquaas@diequa.com
CFO: Norman Quaas
Marketing Coordinator: Jeff Gibbons
Inside Sales Manager: Jeff White
Motion Products Manager: Tom Kahn
Number Employees: 20-49

21621 Dietzco
6 Bigelow St
Hudson, MA 01749-2697
508-481-4000
Fax: 508-481-4004 www.entwistleco.com
Spiral winding equipment for production of composite, paper and fiber cans; exporter of paper converting equipment
President: H Corkin
CEO: V Robinson
VP: R J Heidel
Estimated Sales: G
Number Employees: 100-249
Square Footage: 200000
Parent Co: Entwistle Company

21622 Digatex
4301 Westbank Drive
Suite B
Austin, TX 78746-4400
512-346-8090
Fax: 512-328-3556 800-285-1636
sales@digatex.com www.digatex.com
Complete route accounting software solutions for Direct Store Distribution companies. Includes accounting routing, production, sales, inventory and more!
Estimated Sales: $2.5-5 Million
Number Employees: 10-19

21623 Digital Design
67 Sand Park Rd
Cedar Grove, NJ 07009-1281
973-857-0900
Fax: 973-857-9375 800-469-2205
edg@ddiworldwide.com
Marking devices
Manager: Richard Coventryu
Manager: Michael Liddawi
mike@ddiworldwide.com
Estimated Sales: $5-10 000,000
Number Employees: 20-49

21624 Digital Dining
7370 Steel Mill Dr
Springfield, VA 22150-3600
703-912-3000
Fax: 703-912-4305 moconnor@menusoft.com
Point of sale software
Owner: Carol Boden
carol.boden@menusoft.com
Estimated Sales: $5-10 Million
Number Employees: 5-9
Brands:
Digital Dining

21625 Digital Dynamics Inc
5 Victor Sq
Scotts Valley, CA 95066-3531
831-438-4444
Fax: 831-438-6825 800-765-1288
sales@digitaldynamics.com
www.digitaldynamics.com
Wash down safe industrial computers, and computer work stations
President: James B Jerde
jjerde@digitaldynamics.com
Vice President Engineering: Craig Nelson
Sales Manager: Steve Wait
Estimated Sales: $5-10 Million
Number Employees: 20-49
Number of Brands: 4
Square Footage: 200000

21626 Digital Image & Sound Corporation
11 Denonville Rdge
Rochester, NY 14625
585-381-0410
Fax: 585-381-0428 jfroom@aol.com
Computer hardware, software and systems for dairy and food processors; also, package design consultant
President: James Froom
Treasurer: Kathryn Froom
Sales Manager: Chris Ince
Contact: Jim Froom
jfroom@aol.com
Estimated Sales: Less than $500,000

21627 Dilley Manufacturing Co
215 E 3rd St
Des Moines, IA 50309-2095
515-288-7289
Fax: 515-288-4210 800-247-5087
www.dilleymfg.com
Menu covers
President: David Dilley
CEO: Robert Dilley
kflagg@dilleymfg.com
Estimated Sales: $5-10 Million
Number Employees: 10-19

21628 Dillin Automation Systems Corp
8030 Broadstone Rd
Perrysburg, OH 43551-4856
419-666-6789
Fax: 419-666-4020 www.dillinautomation.com
Accumulators and conveyor systems; merge, divert, elevate and orientation equipment; caselifts; gripper lifts; air conveyor and accumulation
President: David Smith
david.smith@dillinautomation.com
Estimated Sales: $10-20,000,000
Number Employees: 50-99
Square Footage: 80000
Brands:
Air Deck
Over-The-Top
Roe-Lift

21629 Dillin Automation Systems Corp
8030 Broadstone Rd
Perrysburg, OH 43551-4856
419-666-6789
Fax: 419-666-4020 www.dillinautomation.com
Engineered conveyor systems, vertical accumulators, case lifts and compression belts
President: David Smith
david.smith@dillinautomation.com
Estimated Sales: $10-20 Million
Number Employees: 50-99

21630 Dillons Food Stores
2700 E 4th Ave
Hutchinson, KS 67501-1903
620-665-5511
Fax: 620-669-3167 www.dillons.com
Supermarket chain
President: Colleen Juergensen
colleen.juergensen@kroger.com
Plant Manager: Albert Garcia
Number Employees: 100-249
Parent Co: Kroger

21631 Dimension Graphics Inc
800 Burton St SE
Grand Rapids, MI 49507-3320
616-245-1447
Fax: 616-245-2899 855-476-1281
dime@dimensiongraphics.com
www.dimensiongraphics.com
Advertising signs including banners, point of purchase and silk-screened
President: Ken Blessing
dime@dimensiongraphics.com
Estimated Sales: $500,000-$1 Million
Number Employees: 5-9

21632 Dimensional Insight
111 S Bedford St
Burlington, MA 01803-6807
781-229-9111
Fax: 781-229-9113 info@dimins.com
www.dimins.com
Integrated data visualization, analysis and reporting solution that delivers information with unparalleled speed and simplicity
President: Frederick A Powers
CEO: Nancy Berkowitz
nberkowitz@dimins.com
CFO: Cathy Sweet
R&D: Stan Zanarotti
Estimated Sales: $10-20 000,000
Number Employees: 20-49

21633 Dimplex Thermal Solutions
2625 Emerald Dr
Kalamazoo, MI 49001-4542
269-349-6800
Fax: 269-349-8951 bbutch@dimplexthermal.com
www.dimplexthermal.com
Supplier of cooling solutions
President: Steve Cummings
scummings@dimplexthermal.com
National Sales Manager: William Butch
Director of Operations: Mark Siegfried
Estimated Sales: $34 Million
Number Employees: 100-249

21634 Dinex International
4711 E. Hefner Rd
Oklahoma City, OK 73131
800-872-4701
Fax: 405-475-5600 800-654-8210
customerservice@carlislefsp.com www.dinex.com
CEO: Kick Dzuvin
Chairman of the Board: Barry Taintor
VP: Jacqueline Gustafson
Quality Control: Marc Ginnett
Estimated Sales: $3-5 Million
Number Employees: 50-99

21635 Dings Co Magnetic Group
4740 W Electric Ave
Milwaukee, WI 53219-1626
414-672-7830
Fax: 414-672-5354 magnets@dingsco.com
www.dingsmagnets.com
Manufacturer and exporter of magnetic separators for the removal of ferrous metal contaminants from free-flowing powders and granular materials
President: Harold Bolstad
CEO: Brian Nahey
Manager: Gene Poker
Estimated Sales: $10-20 Million
Number Employees: 50-99

21636 Dinosaur Plastics
2815 Gulf Fwy
Houston, TX 77003
713-923-2278
Fax: 713-923-4454
Plastic signs, name badges and buttons, T-shirts, multi-color counter cards, window posters, pennants, banners, promotional products and give-aways; also, letters including plastic, metal and zip change
Owner: Jinny Stephens
Marketing: Chris Conrad
Estimated Sales: Less than $500,000
Number Employees: 5-9
Square Footage: 6000
Brands:
Gemini
Wagner

21637 Dinovo Produce Company
135 Wilson Street
Newark, OH 43055-4921
740-345-4025
Fax: 740-349-7276
Fruit and vegetables
President: Mark Dinovo
Estimated Sales: $2.5-5 000,000
Number Employees: 4
Type of Packaging: Private Label, Bulk

21638 Dipix Technologies
1051 Baxter Road
Ottawa, ON K2C 3P2
Canada
613-596-4942
Fax: 613-249-7341 info@dipix.com
www.dipix.com
Manufacturer and exporter of two dimensional and three dimensional vision inspection systems for the detection of defects in the color, size and shape of baked goods
President: Anton Kitai
Chairman And Acting CEO: Don Gibbs
VP Engineering: Andy Peters
VP Marketing/Sales: John Lawrence
Director of Sales: Geoff Evans
Chief Operating Officer: Peter Wakeman
Square Footage: 60000
Brands:
Dipix Vision Inspection Systems

21639 Dipwell Co
106 Industrial Dr
Northampton, MA 01060-2327
413-587-4673
Fax: 413-587-4609 rinse@dipwell.com
www.dipwell.com

Manufacturer and exporter of food processing equipment including creamery, ice cream, mashed potatoes, butter, sour cream, cole slaw and peas; also, stainless steel running water wells to keep scoops sanitary
Owner: Tom Baird
rinse@dipwell.com
President: Lynn Perry-Alstadt
VP: Fred Perry, Jr.
Estimated Sales: Less Than $500,000
Number Employees: 1-4
Square Footage: 5000
Type of Packaging: Food Service
Brands:
    Collar-Dip
    Dipwell

21640 Direct Fire Technical
45 Bounty Road W
Benbrook, TX 76132-1043
    817-568-8778
Fax: 817-568-8784 888-920-2468
Manufacturer and exporter of industrial hot water heaters and steam generators
President: J Baker
VP: Jack Nichols
Estimated Sales: $1-2,500,000
Number Employees: 20-49
Brands:
    Dft Series
    Direct Fire Technical, Inc.

21641 Direct South
P.O.Box 2445
Macon, GA 31203-2445
    478-746-3518
Fax: 478-745-5668
Food service equipment
Chairman of the Board: Danny Truelove
danny.truelove@directsouth.com
Estimated Sales: $5-10 Million
Number Employees: 20-49

21642 Dirt Killer Pressure Washer
1708 Whitehead Rd # 103
Gwynn Oak, MD 21207-4021
    410-944-9966
Fax: 410-944-8866 800-544-1188
info@dirtkiller.com www.dirtkiller.com
Manufacturer and wholesaler/distributor of pressure washers, accessories and cleaning soaps
President: Jeffrey Paulding
jpaulding@dirtkiller.com
Sales Director: Ken Rankin
Estimated Sales: $3-5 Million
Number Employees: 5-9
Square Footage: 60000
Brands:
    China-Brite
    Dirt Killer
    Kranzle

21643 Discovery Chemical
2141 Carlyle Drive
Marietta, GA 30062-5836
    770-973-5661
    800-973-9881
Wastewater treatment chemicals, sanitizers, insecticides, degreasers, etc
Estimated Sales: $2.5-5,000,000
Number Employees: 2

21644 Discovery Products Corporation
13619 Mukilteo Speedway # 1180
Lynnwood, WA 98087-1626
    425-267-9577
Fax: 425-267-9156
President: Dennis A Clark
Vice President of Sales and Marketing: David Muir
Estimated Sales: $300,000-500,000
Number Employees: 1-4

21645 Diskey Architectural Signs
450 E Brackenridge St
Fort Wayne, IN 46802-3521
    260-424-0233
Fax: 260-424-0668 Orders@DiskeySign.com
    www.diskeysign.com
Interior and exterior signs
Owner: Stacie Breen
sbreen@diskeysign.com
Estimated Sales: $1-3 Million
Number Employees: 10-19

21646 Dispensa-Matic Label Dispense
28220 Playmor Beach Road
Rocky Mount, MO 65072
    573-392-7684
Fax: 573-392-1757 800-325-7303
info@dispensamatic.com www.dispensamatic.com
Pressure sensitive label dispensers for roll labels and computer printouts
President: David Pocost
Marketing: Richard Shannon II
Sales Manager: Rich Laycob
Contact: Richard Shannon
richard@dispensamatic.com
Estimated Sales: $5-10 Million
Number Employees: 1-4
Parent Co: Commercial Mailing Accessories

21647 Dispense Rite
2205 Carlson Dr
Northbrook, IL 60062
    847-753-9595
Fax: 847-753-9648 800-772-2877
sales@dispense-rite.com www.dispense-rite.com
Dispensing equipment for the foodservice industry
President: Robert Gapp
R&D: Robert Riley
Quality Control: Don Hitchcock
VP Marketing/Sales: Ronald Klein
Contact: Donald Hitchcock
dhitchcock@dispense-rite.com
Plant Manager: Don Hitchcok
Purchasing Agent: Robert Gapp
Estimated Sales: $3-5,000,000
Number Employees: 20-49
Number of Brands: 1
Number of Products: 250
Parent Co: Diversified Metal Products
Brands:
    Dispense Rite

21648 Display Concepts
Rr 3
Trenton, ME 04605
    207-667-3386
Fax: 207-667-4103 800-446-0033
Store decor letters and signs including neon; also, aisle markers, trim and graphics
President: S Shelton
CEO: K Shelton
Number Employees: 20-49
Square Footage: 120000
Brands:
    Iridescents
    Neoneon

21649 Display Craft Mfg Co
3939 Washington Blvd
Halethorpe, MD 21227-4185
    410-242-0400
Fax: 410-242-0475 sales@displaycraft.com
    www.displaycraftmfg.com
Store fixtures
CEO: Ronald Weitzmann
ron@storesbydc.com
CEO: Ronald Weitzman
Estimated Sales: $5-10 Million
Number Employees: 50-99

21650 Display Creations
PO Box 70449
Brooklyn, NY 11207-0449
    718-257-2300
Fax: 718-257-2558 ron@displaycreations.com
Manfacturer of lucite displays, store fixtures and point of purchase displays
President: Ronald Newman
Sales Director: Michael Mathless
Purchasing Manager: Jeffry Baum
Estimated Sales: $5-10 Million
Number Employees: 50-99
Square Footage: 320000

21651 Display One
621 N Wacker Dr
Hartford, WI 53027-1001
    262-673-5880
Fax: 262-670-2008 info@menasha.com
    www.menasha.com
Corrugated boxes and containers including shipping and display

CFO: Arthur Huge
President, Chief Executive Officer: James Kotek
Vice President of Corporate Development: Evan Pritz
Sales Manager: Mike Waite
Estimated Sales: $20-50 Million
Number Employees: 100-249
Parent Co: Menasha Corporation

21652 Display Pack Inc
1340 Monroe Ave NW # 1
Grand Rapids, MI 49505-4604
    616-451-3061
Fax: 616-451-8907 info@displaypack.com
Contract packaging and materials, vacuum and thermoformed plastics, printed packaging and phone-card packaging
President: Roger Hansen
CEO: Victor Hansen
vhansen@displaypack.com
Estimated Sales: $20-50 Million
Number Employees: 250-499
Square Footage: 400000
Type of Packaging: Private Label, Bulk

21653 Display Studios Inc
5420 Kansas Ave
Kansas City, KS 66106-1143
    913-754-8900
Fax: 913-754-8901 800-648-8479
    www.displaystudios.com
Manufacturer and exporter of displays and exhibits
President: John Mc Coy
jmccoy@displaystudios.com
Estimated Sales: $2.5-5 Million
Number Employees: 20-49

21654 Display Technologies
11101 14th Ave
College Point, NY 11356-1405
    914-699-2666
Fax: 718-939-4034
info@display-technologies.com
www.display-technologies.com
Computer display, monitors and systems
President: Glenn Affonso
gaffonso@display-technologies.com
CFO: Leslie Tannenbaum
Estimated Sales: $30-50 Million
Number Employees: 50-99

21655 Display Tray
5475 Royalmount Avenue
Mont-Royal, QC H4P 1J3
Canada
    514-735-2988
Fax: 514-735-8933 800-782-8861
displaytray@hotmail.com
Manufacturer and exporter of high impact styrene food display and market trays; also, plastic proof and bagel boards
President: Gail Cantor
CEO: Simy Oliel
Sales: Yoel Acoca
Number Employees: 4
Square Footage: 8000

21656 Dispoz-O Plastics
3736 Abercrombie Rd
Fountain Inn, SC 29644
    864-862-4004
Fax: 864-862-4511 pgehrels@dispozo.com
    www.dispozo.com
Plastic cutlery
President: Joseph D Lancia
CFO: Todd Linecerger
Estimated Sales: $75-100 Million
Number Employees: 500-999

21657 Distaview Corp
121 E Wooster St # 201
Bowling Green, OH 43402-2920
    419-353-6080
Fax: 419-353-6080 800-795-9970
    sales@distaview.com
Manufacturer and exporter of liquid and material process controllers
President: Rick Kramer
rkramer@distaview.com
Estimated Sales: Less Than $500,000
Number Employees: 5-9
Square Footage: 27200
Brands:
    2point

Levelair
Liquavision
Twoview
Vacview

21658 Distillata

1608 E 24th Street
Cleveland, OH 44114

800-999-2906
www.distillata.com

Bottler of spring and distilled water, as well as water filtration systems, water coolers, water fountains, and pool filling services.
Owner: Kevin Schroeder
Head of Sales: Adam Schroeder
Operations Manager: Heather Schroeder
Estimated Sales: $10-20 Million
Number Employees: 100-249
Type of Packaging: Consumer, Food Service, Private Label, Bulk
Brands:
   Distillata

21659 Distinctive Embedments

110 Kenyon Ave
Pawtucket, RI 2861

401-729-0770
Fax: 401-729-0772

Advertising novelties including key tags and paper weights
President: Mario Carosi
General Manager: Mario Carosi
Estimated Sales: $10-20 Million
Number Employees: 20 to 49

21660 Distributed Robotics

172 Lockrow Rd
Troy, NY 12180-9622

518-279-3419
Fax: 518-279-3611
derbys@distributedrobotics.com
www.distributedrobotics.com

President: Steven Derby
Contact: Stephen Derby
sderby1@gmail.com
Estimated Sales: Below $5 Million
Number Employees: 5-9

21661 Distribution Results

900 Moe Dr
Akron, OH 44310-2519

330-633-0727
Fax: 330-633-0728 800-737-9671
sales@icsponge.com www.icsponge.com

Manufacturer, importer and exporter of cellulose sponges for the bakery, dairy and candy industries
Owner: Larry Rowlands
VP: Larry Rowlands
Research & Development: Jeff Shaffer
Quality Control: Carol Schaffer
Sales: Sherwood Shoemaker
Contact: Dotty Barrett
dotty@icsponge.com
Operations: Dotty Barrott
Estimated Sales: $1 Million
Number Employees: 10-19
Square Footage: 60000
Parent Co: Distribution Results

21662 Dito Dean Food Prep

10200 David Taylor Drive
Charlotte, NC 28262

916-652-5824
Fax: 704-547-7401 866-449-4200
dito-foodservice@electrolux.com
professional.electroluxusa.com

Manufacturer and exporter of blenders, cheese shredding and cubing equipment, cutters, slicers, food and vegetable processors, salad dryers and verticle cutters and mixers
President: Gary Probert
Estimated Sales: $1-2.5 Million
Number Employees: 5-9
Parent Co: WCI
Type of Packaging: Food Service

21663 Ditting USA

1000 Air Way
Glendale, CA 91201-3030

818-247-9479
Fax: 818-247-9722 800-835-5992
info@ditting.com www.ditting.com

Manufacturer, importer and exporter of commercial coffee grinders

President: Albert Bezjian
nancy@ditting.com
CEO: Nancy Wideman
CFO: Mike Hatun
Estimated Sales: Below $5 Million
Number Employees: 5-9
Number of Brands: 1
Square Footage: 16000
Brands:
   Ditting

21664 Divercon Inc

9684 N 109th Ave
Omaha, NE 68142-1124

402-571-5115
Fax: 402-571-1742 www.scottent.com

Consultant specializing in the design and engineering of food manufacturing, warehouse and distribution facilities
President: Scott Seaton
Executive VP: S Shain Humphrey
Vice President: Tim Wood
Estimated Sales: $5-10 Million
Number Employees: 5-9
Square Footage: 40000

21665 Diversified Capping Equipment

8030 Broadstone Road
Perrysburg, OH 43551-4856

419-666-2566
Fax: 419-666-0275

Manufacturer and exporter of closure application machines, cap sorters and cap conveying equipment
VP: Jack Weber
Engineering Manager: John Louy
Estimated Sales: $2.5-5 Million
Number Employees: 10-19
Square Footage: 128000
Brands:
   Diversified (Dce)

21666 Diversified Label Images

136 Industrial Dr
Birmingham, AL 35211-4466

205-942-4791
Fax: 205-942-4896 800-777-4791
www.diversifiedlabel.com

Point of sale for beer, beverage and snack industry; also labels
President: Greg Boggis
gboggis@diversifiedlabel.com
Marketing Director: Jennifer Davis
Sales Director: Chad Johnson
Number Employees: 20-49

21667 Diversified Lighting Diffusers Inc

175-B Liberty St
Copiague, NY 11726

631-842-0099
Fax: 631-980-7668 800-234-5464
info@receilit.com www.1800ceiling.com

Manufacturer and distributor of fluorescent safety sleeves and vapor-tight lenses; also, custom fabrication of acrylic and lexan diffusers
CEO: Joe Broser
COO: Colleen Baum
Estimated Sales: $1-3 Million
Number Employees: 5-9
Square Footage: 100000

21668 Diversified Metal Engineering

54 Hilstrom Ave.
PO Box 553
Charlottetown, PE C1E 2C6
Canada

902-628-6900
Fax: 902-628-1313 info@dmeinternational.com

Manufacturer and exporter of washers, cookers, conveyors, graders and coolers for fish; also, brewery and dairy tanks, potato and vegetable shapers, turnkey microbrewery systems, portion packing equipment and piping systems and conveyors for dairy products, pressure vessels, complete skid systems and tanks.
President: Peter Toombs
VP Marketing/Sales: Barry MacLeod
Marketing Director: Kelly Lantz
Director of Sales and Marketing: David Campbell
Production Manager: Blair MacKinnon
Purchasing Manager: Ralph MacDonald
Estimated Sales: $7 Million
Number Employees: 50-99
Square Footage: 80000

Brands:
   Dme

21669 Diversified Metal Manufacturing

2661 Alvarado St
San Leandro, CA 94577-4304

510-667-9900
Fax: 510-667-9700

Tea and coffee industry carts
Owner: Shawn O'Leary
Estimated Sales: Less than $500,000
Number Employees: 1-4

21670 Diversified Metal Products Inc

2205 Carlson Dr
Northbrook, IL 60062-6705

847-753-9595
Fax: 847-753-9648 800-772-2877
sales@dispense-rite.com www.dispense-rite.com

Dispensing equipment for the foodservice industry
President: Robert Gapp
rgapp@dispense-rite.com
CFO: Paul Gapp
R&D: Robert Riley
Quality Control: Don Hitchcok
Marketing Director: Ronald Klein
Sales Administration Manager: Ronald Klein
Plant Manager: Don Hitchcock
Purchasing Manager: Robert Gapp
Estimated Sales: $3-5 Million
Number Employees: 20-49
Number of Brands: 3
Number of Products: 350
Square Footage: 60000
Brands:
   Dispense-Rite

21671 Diversified Panel Systems

2345 Statham Blvd
Oxnard, CA 93033-3911

805-487-9241
Fax: 805-988-4630

President: Richard C Bell
rich@dpspanels.com
Estimated Sales: $1-3 Million
Number Employees: 10-19

21672 Diversified Plastics Corp

120 W Mount Vernon St
Nixa, MO 65714-7827

417-725-2622
Fax: 417-725-5925 sales@dpcap.com
www.dpcap.com

Custom molded polystyrene packaging materials, plastic molding and foam fabricating
President: Justin Carter
jcarter@divplast.com
Quality Control: Shane Boston
Estimated Sales: $20-50 Million
Number Employees: 250-499

21673 Diversified Products

1460 Kings Wood Lane
Eagan, MN 55122

651-269-9091
Fax: 651-454-8079 800-942-2282
www.divprod.com

Wine industry packaging
President: James Crea
Contact: Jeff Knight
jeff@select-a-vision.com
Estimated Sales: $500,000-$1 Million
Number Employees: 1-4

21674 Diversiplast Products

7425 Laurel Ave
Minneapolis, MN 55426-1501

763-540-9700
Fax: 763-540-9709 800-828-6114
www.diversiplast.com

Corrugated plastic sheets and containers
Manager: Lanny Jass
Estimated Sales: $2.5-5 000,000
Number Employees: 20-49

21675 Dividella

14501 58th Street North
Clearwater, FL 33760

727-532-6509
Fax: 727-532-6537 info@kmedipak.com
www.dividella.com

Carton packaging for vials, ampoules, cartridges, syringes, tablet blisters, blistercards, sachets and similar products and automatic tray and carton loading systems for vials
Contact: Christoph Hammer
c.hammer@dividella.ch
Estimated Sales: $1-5 Million

21676 Divis Laboratories
325 Columbia Tpk
3rd Fl Suite 305
Florham Park, NJ 07932
973-993-1060
Fax: 973-993-1070 usmail@divislaboratories.com
www.divislaboratories.com
Carotenoids and specialty vitamins
CEO: Murali Krishna Prasad Divi
Director of Research & Development: Gundu Rao Padakandla
Contact: Punna Aml
punnarao@divislaboratories.com
Head of Manufacturing: Madhusudana Rao Divi
Number Employees: 5000

21677 Dixie Canner Machine Shop
326 Commerce Blvd
Athens, GA 30606-0824
706-549-0592
Fax: 706-549-0137 sales@dixiecanner.com
www.dixiecanner.net
Manufacturer and exporter of low-volume canning equipment including seamers, retorts, exhausters and vacuum closers; also, blanchers, pulpers/finishers and lye peelers
President: B Gentry
Chairman: W Stapleton Sr
VP Manufacturing: J Campbell
VP Sales: Parrish Stapleton
Contact: Bill Gentry
bill@dixiecanner.com
Estimated Sales: $1-2.5 Million
Number Employees: 5-9
Square Footage: 24000
Brands:
  Dixie

21678 Dixie Flag Mfg Co
1930 N Interstate 35
San Antonio, TX 78208-1925
210-227-5039
Fax: 210-227-5920 800-356-4085
dixieflg@dixieflag.com www.dixieflag.com
Manufacturer and exporter of flags, street net banners and pennants
President: Henry P Van Deputte Jr
pete@dixieflag.com
VP: Sally Van de Putte
VP: Glenda Krueger
Estimated Sales: $5-10 Million
Number Employees: 20-49

21679 Dixie Graphics
636 Grassmere Park
Nashville, TN 37211-3697
615-832-7000
Fax: 615-832-7621 info@dixiegraphics.com
www.dixiegraphics.com
Rubber printing plates, photo engraving and color separations
President: J R Meadows
jmeadows@dixiegraphic.com
Estimated Sales: $10-20 000,000
Number Employees: 50-99

21680 Dixie Maid Ice Cream Company
206 E 2nd St
Deridder, LA 70634-5004
337-463-8835
Ice cream novelties
Owner: L C Kern
Estimated Sales: $5-10 Million
Number Employees: 7
Type of Packaging: Consumer

21681 Dixie Neon Company
3001 W Granada St
Tampa, FL 33629
813-248-2531
Fax: 813-247-6230
Signs including advertising, electric and plastic
Owner: Freddie Hevia Iii
Estimated Sales: $1-2.5 Million
Number Employees: 5-9

21682 Dixie Poly Packaging
916 Tanner Road
Greenville, SC 29607-6036
864-268-3751
Fax: 864-268-0511
Polyethylene poultry bags
Owner: Whit Jordan
Estimated Sales: $5-10 Million
Number Employees: 20-49

21683 Dixie Printing & Packaging
7354-58 Baltimore-Annapolis Blvd
Glen Burnie, MD 21061
410-766-1944
Fax: 410-761-4032 800-433-4943
www.primepkg.com
Folding paper boxes
Owner: A Newth Morris Iii
VP Sales: Bill Linchan
General Manager: Raymond Bedell
Estimated Sales: $15-20 Million
Number Employees: 100-249
Square Footage: 135000
Type of Packaging: Consumer, Food Service, Private Label

21684 Dixie Rubber Stamp & Seal Company
PO Box 54616
Atlanta, GA 30308-0616
404-875-8883
Fax: 404-872-3504 plates@dixieseal.com
Rubber stamps and ink products
President: Jack Anders
Plant Manager: Brad Grice
Estimated Sales: $10-20 Million
Number Employees: 80

21685 Dixie Search Associates
316 Audubon Place
Dauphin Island, AL 36528
770-675-7300
Fax: 770-850-9295 dsa@dixiesearch.com
www.dixiesearch.com
Executive search agency specializing in supermarket, food sales/marketing, manufacturing and hospitality industries
President: Clifford G Fill
clifford.fill@dixiesearch.com
Senior VP: Ellyn Fill
Estimated Sales: $300,000-500,000
Number Employees: 10-19
Square Footage: 6000
Parent Co: Fill Corporation

21686 Dixie Signs Inc
2930 Drane Field Rd
Lakeland, FL 33811-1329
863-644-3521
Fax: 863-644-3524 www.dixiesignsinc.com
Interior and exterior signs and graphics
President: Roger Snyder
Estimated Sales: $2.5-5 Million
Number Employees: 20-49

21687 Dixon Lubricants & Specialty Pro Group
P.O.Box 144
Asbury, NJ 08802-0144
908-537-2155
Fax: 908-537-2908 sendinfo@asbury.com
www.asbury.com
Chief Executive Officer: Stephen Riddle
Vice President of Manufacturing: Gary Ziegler
Quality Manager: Ken Newton
Sales Manager: Debra Nowacki
Plant Manager: Michael Mares
Estimated Sales: $1-5 Million
Number Employees: 500-999

21688 Dize Co
1512 S Main St
Winston Salem, NC 27127-2707
336-722-5181
Fax: 336-761-1334 800-583-8243
Commercial awnings, tarps, window coverings, and food cart covers
President: Cr Skidmore
CFO: Mike Durr
Marketing/Sales: Carl Livengood
Operations Manager: Jim Shaver
Estimated Sales: Less Than $500,000
Number Employees: 1-4
Square Footage: 160000

Type of Packaging: Bulk

21689 Do-It Corp
1201 Blue Star Hwy
PO Box 592
South Haven, MI 49090-9784
269-639-2600
Fax: 269-637-7223 800-426-4822
sales@do-it.com www.do-it.com
Manufacturer, importer and exporter of self-adhesive plastic hangers and hang tabs; also, contract packaging available
President: Mark Mc Clendon
sales@do-it.com
Director Marketing: John Deschaine
VP Sales: Chuck Miller
Estimated Sales: $5-10 Million
Number Employees: 50-99
Square Footage: 80000
Brands:
  Do-It

21690 Dober Chemical Corporation
14461 S Waverly Ave
Midlothian, IL 60445
630-410-7300
Fax: 630-410-7444 800-323-4983
doberinfo@dober-group.com
Liquid and powdered soap; also, cleaning chemicals for metal finishing
President: John G Dobrez
CFO: Jim Harper
SVP: Scott Smith
VP Sales: Tom Blakmore
Contact: Scott Dobrez
sdobrez@dobergroup.com
Estimated Sales: $10-20 Million
Number Employees: 50-99

21691 Doering Co
6343 River Rd SE
Clear Lake, MN 55319-9611
320-743-2276
Fax: 320-743-3723 info@doering.com
www.doering.com
Stainless steel valves for high pressure directional control, manually operated stainless steel pumps for high pressure hydraulic service and manually activated hand wash water valves UHMW and stainless construction
President: Jon Boughner
jonb@doering.com
Sales Director: Kris King
Estimated Sales: $3-5 Million
Number Employees: 10-19
Square Footage: 20000
Brands:
  Doering
  Water Miser

21692 Doering Machines Inc
2121 Newcomb Ave
San Francisco, CA 94124-1300
415-526-2131
Fax: 415-526-2136 sales@doeringmachines.com
www.doeringmachines.com
Manufacturer and exporter of pumping, extruding, portioning, metering, cartoning and wrapping systems for high viscosity products including dough, butter, cheese and polymers
President: Richard Doering
richard.doering@doeringmachines.com
CEO: Tim Doering
Estimated Sales: $2.5-5 Million
Number Employees: 5-9
Square Footage: 60000

21693 Dolcera
155 Bovet Rd # 302
Real #505
San Mateo, CA 94402-3111
650-269-7952
Fax: 866-690-7517 info@dolcera.com
Provides clients with the technical, intellectual property and business information they need to develop new products and ideas, and to understand the competitive landscape and market environment.
Chief Executive Officer: Samir Raiyani
info@dolcera.com
Founder: Lakshmikant Goenka
Founder: Ed Rozenberg
Number Employees: 1-4

21694 Dolco Packaging Co
2110 Patterson St
Decatur, IN 46733-1892

260-728-2161
Fax: 260-728-9958 www.tekni-plex.com
Manufacturer and exporter of polystyrene foam packaging
CEO: Steve Harvey
steve.harvey@tekni-plex.com
Vice President: Norm Patterson
Quality Control: Doug Keller
Marketing Director: Phil Laughlin
Public Relations: Amy Geradoj
Production Manager: Jeff Brown
Plant Manager: Roger Lichtle
Purchasing Manager: Terry Alberson
Estimated Sales: $20-50 Million
Number Employees: 100-249
Parent Co: Tekni Plex
Type of Packaging: Food Service

21695 (HQ)Dole Refrigerating Co
1420 Higgs Rd
Lewisburg, TN 37091-4402

931-359-6211
Fax: 931-359-8664 800-251-8990
sales@doleref.com www.kencoplastics.com
Manufacturer and exporter of truck refrigeration units including eutectic plate and blower; also, quick freeze plates for food processing, double contact quick freezing freezers and fiberglass coolers
President: John Cook
johnjr@doleref.com
CFO: Joe Mulliniks
Sales Manager: Bobby Dunnivant
Chief Engineer: Rod Hardy
Estimated Sales: $20-50 Million
Number Employees: 50-99
Square Footage: 55000
Brands:
   Cold-Cel
   Freze-Cel

21696 DomainMarket
9812 Falls Road Ste.
Suite 290
Potomac, MD 20854

973-366-7500
Fax: 973-366-7453 888-694-6735
contact@DomainMarket.com
Manufacturer and exporter of converting equipment for food packaging
CEO: John Wilkes
Estimated Sales: $10-20 Million
Number Employees: 50-99

21697 Dometic Mini Bar
P.O.Box 490
Elkhart, IN 46515-0490

574-294-2511
Fax: 574-293-9686 800-301-8118
In-room refreshment products including honor bars, automated systems, carts, safes, etc
CEO: John Waters
National Sales Manager: Tyler Ellendorff
Contact: Bryan Bergin
bryan.bergin@dometicusa.com
General Manager: Hans Disch
Estimated Sales: F
Number Employees: 20-49
Parent Co: A.B. Electrolux

21698 Dominion Pallet Inc
9644 Cross County Rd
Mineral, VA 23117-2915

540-894-5401
Fax: 540-894-0108 800-227-5321
info@dominionpallet.com
www.dominionpallet.com
Lift truck pallets
Owner: Dan Yancey
dompal@aol.com
CFO: Bernon Aenos
Buyer (Lumber): Scott Walton
General Manager: Vernon Jones
Estimated Sales: $10-20 Million
Number Employees: 20-49

21699 Dominion Regala
4 Overlea Blvd
Toronto, ON M4H 1A4
Canada

416-752-9987
Fax: 416-752-9986 866-423-4086
info@dominionregalia.com
www.dominionregalia.com
Patio umbrellas, flags, banners and continously printed ribbons
President: Ross Chafe
Quality Control: Summer Zurawski
Director Marketing: Connie Murphy
Number Employees: 10

21700 Domino Amjet Inc
1290 Lakeside Dr
Gurnee, IL 60031-2499

847-244-2501
Fax: 847-244-1421 800-444-4512
service@domino-na.com
www.dominodigitalprinting.com
Digital printing solutions used for date coding, product markings, serialization and variable printing.
President: Michael Brown
Chief Executive Officer: Brian McGarry
Chief Financial Officer: David Hollister
Chairman of the Board: Nigel Bond
Research & Development: Chris Gehring
Quality Assurance Manager: Barbara Diliberti
Vice President, Marketing: Carl Traynor
Vice President, Sales: David Ellen
Product Manager: Adem Kulauzovic
Estimated Sales: $39 Million
Number Employees: 1000-4999
Square Footage: 72000
Parent Co: Domino Printing Sciences PLC

21701 Don Lee
1114 W. Berks St.
Philadelphia, PA 19122-6090

760-745-0707
Fax: 760-746-2856 connieberry@aol.com
www.don-lee.com
Dough cutters and dividers.
President: Lee Berry
CFO: Kim Key
Vice President: Connie Berry
Number Employees: 20-49
Number of Products: 2
Square Footage: 20000
Type of Packaging: Private Label
Brands:
   Cloverleaf
   Roll Former/Divider

21702 Don Walters Company
11630 Western Ave
Stanton, CA 90680

714-892-0275
Fax: 714-901-1852 donwaltersco@aol.com
www.donwatersinc.com
Wholesaler/distributor of restaurant equipment; also, design consulting available
President/CEO: Roger Criswell
CFO/VP: Mindy Criswell
Estimated Sales: $1-2,500,000
Number Employees: 5-9
Type of Packaging: Food Service

21703 (HQ)Donahower & Company
15615 S Keeler Ter
Olathe, KS 66062-3509

913-829-2650
Fax: 913-829-5494
Manufacturer and exporter of conveyors including package handling, flat top chain and material handling; also, lidding and capping machinery and bottle rotators
President: Carol Brooks
Vice President: Ken Koelzer
Estimated Sales: $1-2.5 Million
Number Employees: 5-9
Square Footage: 10000

21704 Donalds & Associates
3900 Kilroy Airport Way # 190
Long Beach, CA 90806-6815

562-290-8440
Fax: 562-438-2668
Consultant specializing in restaurant conceptualization
President: Steve Donalds

21705 Donaldson Co Inc
1400 W 94th St
Bloomington, MN 55431

952-887-3131
www.donaldson.com
Manufacturer, importer and exporter of dust control and filtration equipment.
Chairman, President & CEO: Tod Carpenter
tod.carpenter@donaldson.com
Senior VP & CFO: Scott Robinson
Year Founded: 1915
Estimated Sales: $2.85 Billion
Number Employees: 11,700
Brands:
   Dce Dalamatic
   Dce Siloair
   Dce Sintamatic
   Dce Unicell
   Dce Unimaster

21706 Dong Us I
2590 Main St
Irvine, CA 92614-6227

949-251-1768
Fax: 949-251-8865 888-580-0088
info@dongyu.us www.dongyu.us
Manufacturer and distributor of L-Carnitine products, amino acids, vitamins, sweeteners, sports nutrition ingredients, food and beverage ingredients
Manager: Weili Zhang
Number Employees: 10-19
Square Footage: 40000

21707 Donnelly Industries, Inc
557 Route 23 South
Wayne, NJ 07470

973-672-1800
Fax: 973-323-8699
info@donnellyconstruction.com
www.donnellyconstruction.com
Wooden boxes
President: Gerard J Donnelly Jr
CEO: Rod Donnelly
VP: Christopher Powers
Estimated Sales: $1-2.5 Million
Number Employees: 5-9

21708 Donnick Label Systems
1450 Lane Ave N
Jacksonville, FL 32254

Fax: 904-786-7301 800-334-7849
Direct thermal scale and product labels, thermal printers and ribbons
President: Jerry Smith
Owner: Anne Smith
ms@donnick.com
CFO: Anne Smith
Sales/Marketing: David Frederick
Estimated Sales: $.5-1 million
Number Employees: 5-9
Square Footage: 14000

21709 Donoco Industries
P.O. Box 3208
Huntington Beach, CA 92605

714-893-7889
Fax: 714-897-7968 888-822-8763
info@encoreplastics.com www.encoreplastics.com
Manufacturer and exporter of plastic mugs and tumblers
President: Richard Harvey
Estimated Sales: $5-10 Million
Number Employees: 25
Brands:
   Encore

21710 Dontech Industries Inc
76 Center Dr
Gilberts, IL 60136-9712

847-428-8222
Fax: 847-428-6855 rap@micropure.com
www.dontechindustriesinc.com
Ultraviolet disinfection systems for food processing, sanitation, water and wastewater treatment
Owner: Bill Cataldo
w.cataldo@hotmail.com
Estimated Sales: $1-2.5 Million
Number Employees: 5-9

21711 Doosan Industrial Vehicle America Corp

2475 Mill Center Parkway
Suite 400
Buford, GA 30518

678-745-2200
Fax: 678-745-2250 www.doosanlift.com
Manufacturer, importer and exporter of industrial
trucks.
VP & CEO: Tony Jones
National Sales Director: Jeff Powell
Year Founded: 1962
Estimated Sales: $7 Billion
Number Employees: 7,728
Square Footage: 150000
Parent Co: Doosan Group

21712 Dorado Carton Company

Carr 693
Dorado, PR 00646-0546

787-796-1670
Fax: 787-796-2988
Paper, pizza and food service boxes, doilies, place
mats and shelf and wrapping paper; also, coated
stock available
President: Keneth Schulman
VP F.C. Meyer Division: Paul Robinson
Business Manager: Nazira Wightman
Number Employees: 16
Square Footage: 44000
Parent Co: Frank C. Meyer Company/Mafcote In-
dustries

21713 Doran Scales Inc

1315 Paramount Pkwy
Batavia, IL 60510-1460

630-879-1200
Fax: 630-879-0073 800-365-0084
sales@doranscales.com www.doranscales.com
Stainless steel washdown safe scales.
President: Mark Podl
markp@doranscales.com
Chairman/CEO: William Podl
CEO: William Podl
Marketing Coordinator: Mark Anderson
Applications Engineer: Mark Podl
Estimated Sales: $5-10 Million
Number Employees: 20-49
Square Footage: 80000
Brands:
    Digibar

21714 Dordan Manufacturing Co

2025 Castle Rd
Woodstock, IL 60098-9271

815-334-0087
Fax: 815-334-0089 800-663-5460
sales@dordan.com www.dordan.com
Heat sealing and plastic vacuum formed packaging
products
President: Oney Pineda
opineda@coppersmith.com
Estimated Sales: $2.5-5 Million
Number Employees: 20-49

21715 Dorden & Co

7446 Central St
Detroit, MI 48210-1037

313-834-7910
Fax: 313-834-1178 www.dordensqueegee.com
All types of rubber floor and window squeegees
CEO: Bruce M Gale
bgale@dordensqueegee.com
Public Relations: Bruce Gale
Purchasing: Bruce Gale
Estimated Sales: $.5-1 million
Number Employees: 1-4
Square Footage: 30000
Type of Packaging: Food Service, Private Label,
Bulk

21716 (HQ)Dorell Equipment Inc

80 Veronica Ave # 60
Somerset, NJ 08873-3498

732-247-5400
Fax: 732-247-5700
Food and beverage packaging equipment including
tray and case erectors, and loaders, shrink wrapping
systems, collation and stacking systems.

Manager: Lu Mado
Vice President: Joseph Minond
Marketing/Sales: Jon Levin
Sales Representative: Eli Schloss
Plant Manager: Ray Jenito
Purchasing Manager: Tami Minond
Estimated Sales: $2.5-5 Million
Number Employees: 20-49
Type of Packaging: Bulk
Other Locations:
    Dorell Equipment Company
    Cincinati OH
    Dorell Equipment Company
    Atlanta GA
Brands:
    Dorell

21717 Dormont Manufacturing Co

6015 Enterprise Dr
Export, PA 15632-8969

724-733-4800
Fax: 724-733-4808 800-367-6668
info@dormont.com www.dormont.com
Safety system flexible stainless steel gas appliance
connectors and gas connection accessories; also,
pre-rinse assemblies and faucets
Vice President: Joey Kelly
joey@rynopro.com
CEO: Evan Segal
VP: Mark Humenansky
Marketing Manager: Judi D'Amico
VP Sales: David Berstein
Purchasing Manager: Norman Czarnecki
Estimated Sales: H
Number Employees: 100-249
Square Footage: 70000
Parent Co: Watts Water Technologies
Type of Packaging: Food Service, Private Label,
Bulk
Brands:
    Cimfast
    Hi-Psi-Flex(Water)
    Power Force
    Supr Swivel
    Supr-Safe (Gas)

21718 Dorner Manufacturing Corp

975 Cottonwood Ave
975 Cottonwood Ave
Hartland, WI 53029-2461

262-367-7600
Fax: 262-367-5827 800-397-8664
www.dornerconveyors.com
Belt conveyors
President: Werner Dorner
President: Scott Lucas
CFO: Dale Visgar
Engineering Manager: Michael Hosch
Marketing Director: Gary Wemmert
Sales Director: Mark Wedell
Operations Manager: Randy Meis
Purchasing Manager: Greg Sipek
Estimated Sales: $10-20 Million
Number Employees: 100-249

21719 Dorpak

1780 Dreman Avenue
Cincinnati, OH 45223-2456

513-681-2323
Fax: 513-541-5945 info@cin-made.com
High graphic, re-closable, rectangular paperboard
drums
President: Robert Fry
CFO: John Ewalt
Quality Control: Brian Kilpatrick
Estimated Sales: Below $5 Million
Number Employees: 10

21720 Dorton Incorporated

3436 N Kennicott Ave
Arlington Hts, IL 60004-7814

847-577-8600
Fax: 847-392-6212 800-299-8600
www.dortongroup.com
President: Ed Collins
CFO: Al Nowak
VP: Marie Collins
R&D: Milt Lynn
Marketing: Micki Bagnuolo
Sales: Micki Bagnuolo
Public Relations: Ed Collins
Operations Manager: Michelle Gilbert
Production: M Levinberg
Purchasing: Cindy Byrne

Number Employees: 10-19
Number of Brands: 2
Number of Products: 12
Square Footage: 15200
Type of Packaging: Food Service
Brands:
    Dor-Blend
    Dor-Mixer
    Dor-Opener
    Dorton

21721 Dosatron International Inc

2090 Sunnydale Blvd
Clearwater, FL 33765-1201

727-443-5404
Fax: 727-447-0591 800-523-8499
mailbox@dosatronusa.com
www.swinemedicator.com
Distributor of Dosatron water powered chemical injectors used int he food processind sanitation process. They are easy to adjust and automatically
compensate for changes in water pressure or flow,
allowing for a fine tuned chemical mixthat provides
improved results and reduced waste.
President: Edward Kelly
Contact: Courtney Boettcher
c.boettcher@dosatronusa.com
Number Employees: 20-49

21722 Dot-It Food Safety Products

2011 E Randol Mill Rd
Arlington, TX 76011

817-275-7714
Fax: 817-275-0122 800-642-3687
Labels and tags
Manager: Ben Nicholson
Director Sales: Robert Galan
General Manager: Sonya Peterson
Estimated Sales: $1-3 Million
Number Employees: 5-9
Square Footage: 72000
Parent Co: Craftmark Label Graphics

21723 Double E Co LLC

319 Manley St # 301
West Bridgewater, MA 02379-1034

508-588-8099
Fax: 508-580-2915 doublee@doubleusa.com
www.ee-co.com
Core chucks anad core shafts for packaging and pa-
per, film and foil converting
President: Mark Fortin
mfortin@doubleeusa.com
CEO: Redward Flagg
Estimated Sales: $10-20 000,000
Number Employees: 100-249

21724 Double E Co LLC

319 Manley St # 301
West Bridgewater, MA 02379-1034

508-588-8099
Fax: 508-580-2915 www.ee-co.com
Engineering
President: Mark Fortin
mfortin@doubleeusa.com
Estimated Sales: $10-20 Million
Number Employees: 100-249

21725 (HQ)Double Envelope Corp

7702 Plantation Rd
Roanoke, VA 24019-3225

540-362-3311
Fax: 540-366-8401 www.double-envelope.com
Pressure sensitive labels, bind-in order forms and
envelopes
Sales Manager: Jim Long
Manager: Bill Howell
bhowell@double-envelope.com
Estimated Sales: $20-50 Million
Number Employees: 100-249

21726 Double H Plastics

50 W Street Rd
Warminster, PA 18974-3203

215-674-4100
Fax: 215-674-4109 800-523-3932
phaney@doublehplastics.com
www.doublehplastics.com
President: Harry J Harp Iii
phaney@doublehplastics.com
Sales Exec: Peter Haney
Estimated Sales: $20-50 Million
Number Employees: 100-249

21727 Double Wrap Cup & Container
728 W Jackson Blvd
Ste 1002
Chicago, IL 60661
312-337-0072
Fax: 847-777-0586
High quality,low cost insulated wrap for paper coffee cups.
CEO: Ted Alpert
VP: Ted Alpert
Marketing Director: Ted Alpert
Sales Director: Ted Alpert
Public Relations: Ted Alpert
Operations Manager: Ted Alpert
Estimated Sales: $3-5 Million
Number Employees: 10-19
Type of Packaging: Food Service

21728 Doucette Industries
20 Leigh Dr
York, PA 17406-8474
717-718-8944
Fax: 717-845-2864 800-445-7511
info@doucetteindustries.com
www.doucetteindustries.com
Manufacturer and exporter of suction line and vented double wall heat exchangers, CO2 Vaporizers, coaxial coils, counterflow condensers and vibration absorbers for air conditioning, refrigeration and hydronic applications
President: John Lebo
johnl@doucetteindustries.com
Number Employees: 20-49

21729 DoughXpress
1201 E 27th Terrace
Pittsburg, KS 66762
620-231-8568
Fax: 620-231-1598 800-835-0606
sales@hixcorp.com www.doughxpress.com
Bakery equipment including bread slicers, dough dividers, rounders, air compressors, release agents, storage carts, dough dockers, dual heated, presses, air automatic pizza presses, flat grills, and meat presses
President: Doug Condra
Chairman: Jack Deboer
Treasurer: Kay Stroud
Marketing & Product Manager: Tim McNally
Sales & Marketing Manager: Lorin Rigby
National Sales Manager: Willie Anderson
Contact: Isabel Ianieri
isabel.ianieri@doughxpress.com
Plant Manager: Jim Mattson
Purchasing Manager: Dave Gromer
Estimated Sales: $8.2 Million
Number Employees: 60
Square Footage: 222000
Parent Co: Hix Corporation
Type of Packaging: Food Service, Bulk

21730 Doughmakers, LLC
PO Box 10034
Terre Haute, IN 47801
812-299-8750
Fax: 812-299-7788 888-386-8517
www.doughmakers.com
Manufacturer and distributor of bakeware pans, sheets, and tins
Quality Control: Tony Buck
Manager: Robert Bossar
Estimated Sales: $5-10 Million
Number Employees: 20-49

21731 Doughpro
20281 Harvill Ave
Perris, CA 92570
800-624-6717
Fax: 562-869-7715 800-594-5528
Pizza presses and wood fired ovens
President: Eugene Raio
Contact: Michael Cole
mcole@doughpro.com
Number Employees: 10

21732 Douglas Battery Manufacturing Company
1255 Creekshire Way
Suite 221
Winston Salem, NC 27103
800-368-4527
info@douglasbattery.com
www.douglasbattery.com
Industrial batteries & generators.

Chief Executive Officer: Thomas Douglas III
Year Founded: 1921
Estimated Sales: $100-500 Million

21733 (HQ)Douglas Machine Inc
3404 Iowa St
Alexandria, MN 56308-3399
320-763-6587
Fax: 320-763-5754 info@douglas-machine.com
www.douglas-machine.com
Manufacturer and exporter of packaging machinery including high speed continuous and multi-range intermittent motion case packers, case openers, bottom sealers, integrated conveyor systems, shrink wrappers, tray formers, palletizerssleeves, cartoners, multipackers and provide rebuild/conversion services
Chairman: Vernon Anderson
COO/President: Rick Paulsen
EVP: Paul Anderson
VP Manufacturing: Chris Haugen
Estimated Sales: $94 Million
Number Employees: 500-999
Square Footage: 218000
Parent Co: Douglas
Type of Packaging: Consumer, Food Service, Private Label, Bulk

21734 Douglas Machine Inc
3404 Iowa St
Alexandria, MN 56308-3399
320-763-6587
Fax: 320-763-5754 info@douglas-machine.com
www.douglas-machine.com
Standard, custom continuous and intermittent-motion cartoners, automatic placers, robotic palletizers, etc
President: Vernon Anderson
CEO: John Ballou
Marketing Director: Jon Ballone
Sales Director: Mike Huss
Operations Manager: Bill Lawrence
Estimated Sales: $20-50 Million
Number Employees: 500-999
Square Footage: 85000
Parent Co: Douglas Machine

21735 Douglas Machines Corp
2101 Calumet St
Clearwater, FL 33765-1310
727-461-3477
Fax: 727-449-0029 800-331-6870
info@dougmac.com www.dougmac.com
Douglas Machines Corporation specializes in the design and manufacture of automated industrial and commercial washers and sanitizing equipment for all containers commonly found in the Bakery, Food Processing, Food Service andDistribution industries.
President: Gerri Boyce
boyce@jea.com
Executive Vice President: Kevin Lemen
Vice President Finance & Accounting: Susan Mader
Engineering Manager: Josef Weinberger
Service Manager: Dale Breedlove
Sales & Marketing Coordinator: Rosie Rachel
Operations Manager: Jim Beadling
Technical Support Specialist: John Jurski
Purchasing Manager: Karen McCrae
Number Employees: 50-99

21736 Douglas Machines Corp.
4500 110th Ave North
Clearwater, FL 33762
727-461-3477
Fax: 727-449-0029 800-331-6870
info@dougmac.com www.dougmac.com
Automated industrial and commercial washing and sanitizing equipment
President/Owner: Dave Ward
VP, Finance: Susan Mader
Marketing Manager: Darcel Schouler
Sales Manager: Kevin Quinn
Operations Manager: Dale Breedlove
Estimated Sales: $5-10 Million
Number Employees: 50-99
Number of Brands: 3
Number of Products: 40
Square Footage: 50000
Brands:
Douglas

21737 (HQ)Douglas Products
1550 E Old State Route 210
Liberty, MO 64068-9459
816-781-4250
Fax: 816-781-1043 800-223-3684
info@douglasproducts.com
Custom packager of liquid products
President: Jerry McCaslin
CEO: Bill R Fuller
bill.fuller@douglasproducts.com
CEO: Bill R Fuller
General Manager: Jim Osment
Estimated Sales: $10-20 Million
Number Employees: 20-49
Square Footage: 110000
Type of Packaging: Private Label, Bulk

21738 Douglas Stephen Plastics Inc
22 Green St # 36
Paterson, NJ 07501-2825
973-523-3030
Fax: 973-523-0643
bmccullough@douglasstephen.com
www.douglasstephen.com
Plastic containers and trays
President and CFO: Stewart Graff
Cmo: Ellen Sciancalepore
esciancalepore@douglasstephen.com
National Sales Manager: Brian McCullough
VP Operations: Doug Graff
Estimated Sales: $10-20 Million
Number Employees: 100-249

21739 Dove Screen Printing Co
18 Salem Rd
Royston, GA 30662-7406
706-245-4975
Fax: 706-245-7500 www.dovescreenprinting.com
Manufacturer and exporter of advertising specialties, signs and restaurant aprons; importer of caps and coffee mugs
Owner: Ronny Dove
ronnydove@aol.com
Estimated Sales: Less Than $500,000
Number Employees: 1-4

21740 Dover Chemical Corp
3676 Davis Rd NW
Dover, OH 44622-9771
330-343-7711
Fax: 330-364-1579 800-321-8805
www.doverchem.com
Manufacturer and exporter of bleaches, muratic acids and antioxidants
President: Kevin Burke
burke@cranechempharma.com
CFO: Mike Caffrey
Quality Control: Dave Schlarb
Quality Issues: Carol Churilla
Marketing Coordinator: Wendy Finch
US Sales Manager: Chad McGlothlin
Purchasing Agent: Robert Ren
Number Employees: 100-249
Parent Co: ICC Industries
Brands:
Dover Phos Foods

21741 Dover Hospitality Consulting
6 Tallforest Crescent
Etobicoke, ON M9C 2X2
Canada
416-622-9294
Fax: 416-622-5944
Consultant specializing in chain restaurant marketing and operations
President: Bill Dover
Number Employees: 1

21742 Dover Industries
3005 Highland Parkway
Downers Grove, IL 60515
630-541-1540
Fax: 630-743-2671 www.doverind.com
President: Michael Zhang
President, Chief Executive Officer: Robert Livingston
CFO: Robert Scheuer
Vice President, Treasurer: Brian Moore
Operations Manager of Sales: Greg Smith
Contact: Marcel Berkhout
mberkhout@dovergrp.com
Estimated Sales: $1.2 Million
Number Employees: 1,000-4,999

21743 Dover Metals
4768 Hwy M-63
Coloma, MI 49038
269-849-1411
Fax: 269-849-2903
Accessories and supplies for the food service and
hospitality industry
President/Owner: Deborah Bedwell
VP: Nick Anders
Estimated Sales: $2.8 Million
Number Employees: 8

21744 Dover Parkersburg
PO Box 610
Follansbee, WV 26037-610
Fax: 304-485-3214
Manufacturer and importer of tinware including bak-
ing pans, garbage cans, buckets, tubs, wringers and
mopping equipment
Sales: Donna Burns
Director Operations: William Cusack, Jr.
Estimated Sales: $10-20 Million
Number Employees: 50-99
Parent Co: Louis Berkman
Type of Packaging: Bulk

21745 Dover Products Company
607 W Jefferson St # 1
Bloomington, IL 61701-8208
309-821-1271
Fax: 502-633-3798 800-351-5582
Grease, oil and tallow
President: Egerton M Dover
Plant Manager: Robert Kepfer
Estimated Sales: $500,000-$1 Million
Number Employees: 5 to 9

21746 Dow Agro Sciences LLC
9330 Zionsville Rd
Indianapolis, IN 46268-1053
317-337-3000
Fax: 317-337-4140 800-258-3033
www.dowagro.com
Wine industry vineyard chemicals
Director: Rogelio Lara
CEO: Jerry Britt
jlbritt@dow.com
Estimated Sales: Over $1 Billion
Number Employees: 5000-9999

21747 Dow Cover Co Inc
373 Lexington Ave
New Haven, CT 06513-4061
203-469-5394
Fax: 203-469-0742 800-735-8877
mark@dowcover.com www.dowcover.com
Canvas covers and aprons including custom logo,
screenprint and embroidery
President: Mark Steinhardt
mark@dowcover.com
Estimated Sales: $5-10 Million
Number Employees: 50-99
Square Footage: 68000
Brands:
Dowsport America

21748 Dow Industries
271 Ballardvale St
Wilmington, MA 01887-1081
978-658-8200
Fax: 978-658-2307 800-776-1201
sales@dowindustries.com www.smythco.com
Manufacturer and exporter of pressure sensitive la-
bels and automatic labeling equipment
President: Walter Dow
CEO: Andy Farquharson
CFO: John Morrison
Quality Control: Scott Boucher
Senior VP: Bill Donovan
Operations Manager: D Apgar
Estimated Sales: $20 Million
Number Employees: 50-99
Square Footage: 64000
Type of Packaging: Consumer, Private Label

21749 Dow Packaging
2211 H.H. Dow Way
Midland, MI 48674
989-636-1000
Fax: 989-382-1456 800-331-6451
www.dow.com
Processor and exporter of ethylene oxide/ethylene
glycol, coating materials, industrial performance
chemicals, polyolefin resins and compounds, sol-
vents intermediates and monomers, UCAR emulsion
systems, specialty polymers andproducts.
Chairman & CEO: Andrew Liveris
President & COO: James Fitterling
Vice Chairman & CFO: Howard Underleider
EVP & General Counsel: Charles Kalil
Controller/VP of Controllers & Tax: Ron Edmonds
Year Founded: 1917
Number Employees: 2,300
Parent Co: The Dow Chemical Company
Type of Packaging: Bulk

21750 Dow Water and Process Solutions
7600 Metro Boulevard
Edina, MN 55439
800-447-4369
www.dowwaterandprocess.com
Product line includes food grade ion exchange res-
ins, adsorbents and membranes used to recover, iso-
late and purify nutritional ingredients such as
polyphenols, taste mask unwanted flavors, stabilize
victims, immobilize enzymesdecolorize juice
streams, produce clean water, efficiently reduce
waste and more.
Director, Finance: Ken Swanson
Director, Business Unit Ion Exchange: Rajat Mehta
Director, Communications: Kimberly Kupiecki
Director, Business Unit Reverse Osmosis: Lance
Johnson
Director, Research & Development: Dr. George
Barclay
Director, Business Manufacturing/Tech: Vicky
Biedenstein
Legal Counsel: Janaki Catanzarite
Global Business Director: Snehal Desai
Contact: Randy Blom
rblom@dow.com
Director, Human Resources: Kim Fisher
Global Supply Chain Director: Christophe
Gay-Bellile

21751 Dowling Signs Inc
1801 Princess Anne St
Fredericksburg, VA 22401-3544
540-373-6675
Fax: 540-371-7543 800-572-2100
www.dowlingsignsinc.com
Signs specializing in ADA (American Disabilities
Act) approved including illuminated and
nonilluminated identification
President: Allen Malocha
signsdsi@aol.com
Secretary and Treasurer: Susanne Bradley
General Manager: Allen Malocha
Production Manager: Charles Ward
Estimated Sales: $2.5-5 Million
Number Employees: 20-49
Square Footage: 60000

21752 Downeast Chemical
88 Scott Dr
Westbrook, ME 04092-1927
207-773-9668
Fax: 207-773-0832 800-287-2225
Detergents, degreasers and boiler treatment com-
pounds; also, custom blending
President: Joseph Brita
VP: John Bowns
Customer Service: Heather Bowns
Estimated Sales: $1-3 Million
Number Employees: 9
Square Footage: 16800

21753 Downs Crane & Hoist Co Inc
8827 Juniper St
Los Angeles, CA 90002-1899
323-589-6061
Fax: 323-589-6066 800-748-5994
sales@downscrane.com www.downscrane.com
Manufacturer and exporter of lifting devices includ-
ing grabs, tongs, spreaders, manipulators, hooks,
cranes and crane wheels and assemblies
President: John W Downs Jr
Number Employees: 5-9
Type of Packaging: Bulk
Brands:
Grabmaster

21754 Doyen Medipharm
4030 S Pipkin Rd Ste 102
Lakeland, FL 33811
863-683-6335
Fax: 863-683-6857
Packaging machinery for food industry
President: Ray Johnson
VP: Martin Beriswill
Estimated Sales: $2.5-5 000,000
Number Employees: 20-49

21755 Doyle Signs Inc
232 W Interstate Rd
Addison, IL 60101-4563
630-543-9490
Fax: 630-543-9493 info@doylesigns.com
www.doylesigns.com
Interior and exterior electric identification signs;
also, design, installation and maintenance services
available
President: Terrence J Doyle
terrence@doylesigns.com
VP: P Doyle
Sales Director: J Doyle
Estimated Sales: $10 Million
Number Employees: 50-99
Square Footage: 74000

21756 Doyon Equipment
1255 Rue Principale
Liniere, QC G0M 1J0
Canada
418-685-3431
Fax: 418-685-3948 800-463-4273
sales@nu-vu.com www.doyon.qc.ca
Baking equipment
President: Karl Doyon
Research & Development: Pierre Poirier
Marketing Director: Jennifer Letourneau
Regional Sales Director: John Herbert
Regional Sales Director: Jim Markee
Estimated Sales: $10-20 Million
Number Employees: 20
Brands:
Doyon
Jet Air

21757 Drackett Professional
8600 Governors Hill Drive
Cincinnati, OH 45249-1360
513-583-3900
Fax: 513-583-3968
Cleaners and mops
National Sales Director: Steve Moser
Director Advertising/PR: Diego Esquibel
General Manager: Terry Conlon
Number Employees: 20-49
Parent Co: S.C. Johnson Wax
Brands:
Beer Clean
Draino
Easy Paks
Glade
Ice-Foe
Raid
Windex

21758 Draeger Safety Inc
101 Technology Dr
Pittsburgh, PA 15275-1005
412-787-8383
Fax: 412-787-2207 800-922-5518
www.draeger.com
Develops safety technology for manufacturing in-
dustry.
President: Ralf Drews
CFO: Graeme Roberts
Contact: Elaine Adie
elaine.adie@draeger.com
Estimated Sales: $50-100 Million
Number Employees: 100-249

21759 Draiswerke Inc
40 Whitney Rd
Mahwah, NJ 07430-3130
201-847-0600
Fax: 201-847-0606 800-494-3151
www.buhlergroup.com
Tea and coffee industry mills for micro wet grinding
and dispersing, mixers, dryers, reactors, and compounding systems
President: Gilbert Schall
gschall@draiswerke-inc.com

Estimated Sales: $10-20 000,000
Number Employees: 20-49

21760 Drake Co
1401 Greengrass Dr
Houston, TX 77008-5005

713-869-9121
Fax: 713-869-3512 800-299-5644

Manufacturer and exporter of corrugated boxes and lithographic displays
CEO: John Carrico
CFO: Shelley Golden
sgolden@drakecompany.com
Sales/Service Manager: Kevin Fiedler
Estimated Sales: $1-5 Million
Number Employees: 100-249

21761 Drapes 4 Show
12811 Foothill Blvd
Sylmar, CA 91342-5316

818-838-0852
Fax: 818-222-7469 800-525-7469

staff@drapes.com www.drapes.com
Tabletop accessories including napkins, table skirting and table linens
CEO: Karen Honigberg
Customer Service: Kathryn Pereyra
Estimated Sales: Below $5 Million
Number Employees: 20-49
Square Footage: 12800

21762 Dreaco Products
172 Reaser Court
Elyria, OH 44035-6285

440-366-7600
Fax: 440-365-5858 800-368-3267

Manufacturer and exporter of exhaust hoods and fans; also, make-up air fans
Owner and President: Robert Gargasz
Sales/Marketing Executive: Karen Kauk
Purchasing Agent: Michael Gargasz
Estimated Sales: $2.5-5 Million
Number Employees: 20-49
Square Footage: 100000
Brands:
  Dreaco

21763 DreamPak LLC
4717 Eisenhower Avenue
Alexandria, VA 22304

703-751-3511
877-687-4662

info@dreampak.com www.dreampak.com
On-the-go beverages
President/CEO: Dr. Aly Gamay
Executive Vice President: Terry Schneider
Contact: Taufeeque Ali
tali@dreampak.com
Vice President, Operations: Randy Cook
Brands:
  Fruitslim
  Soluflex
  Dogflex
  Trimma
  Enhance To Go
  Joker's Wild Energy
  Chocolate Slim
  Zeniht

21764 Drehmann Paving & Flooring Company
847 Bethel Ave
Pennsauken, NJ 08110-2605

856-486-0202
Fax: 856-486-0808 800-523-3800

Manufacturer and exporter of brick floor coatings, plates and drains; installation services available
President: William Varra
VP: J Kline, Jr.
Executive VP: Horace Furman
Research & Development: M Bojesuk
Quality Control: S Furman
Contact: J Kline
kklinejr@drehmann.com
Estimated Sales: $5,000,000
Number Employees: 75-100
Number of Brands: 1
Number of Products: 10
Square Footage: 36000
Type of Packaging: Private Label

21765 Drehmann Paving & Flooring Company
2101 Byberry Road
Philadelphia, PA 19116-3017

215-464-7700
Fax: 215-673-9755 800-523-3800
www.drehmann.com

Industrial brick flooring, epoxy, joint materials, expansion joints,cast iron floor drains and stainless steel floor drains

21766 Drescher Paper Box Inc
459 Broadway St
Buffalo, NY 14204-1697

716-854-0288
Fax: 716-854-1920 jb@drescherpuzzle.com

Rigid set-up paper boxes, jigsaw puzzles, board games
President: Jb Langworthy
CEO: Joyce MacLeod
Estimated Sales: $10-20 Million
Number Employees: 10-19
Square Footage: 96000

21767 Dresco Belting Co Inc
122 East St
PO Box 890026
East Weymouth, MA 02189-2198

781-335-1350
Fax: 781-340-0500 sales@drescobelt.com
www.drescobelt.com

Manufacturer and exporter of conveyor and transmission belting
Owner: James Dresser
jim.dresser@drescobelt.com
VP, Manufacturing & Technology: James G. Dresser
VP, Sales: Norman K. Dresser
Estimated Sales: $1-2.5 Million
Number Employees: 1-4
Square Footage: 40000

21768 Dreumex USA
3445 Board Rd
York, PA 17406-8409

717-767-6881
Fax: 717-767-6888 800-233-9382
dreumex@dreumex.com www.dreumex.com

Manufacturer and exporter of waterless gel and lotion hand cleaners and liquid soap; also, hand and multi-purpose wipes, dispensing systems, and car/truck wash
President/CEO: Jim Strickler
Research & Development: Gail Shermeyer
Quality Control: Gail Shermeyer
Marketing Director: Karen Hansen
Sales Director: Jim Strickler
Contact: Craig Bennett
c.bennett@dreumex.com
Operations Manager: Jeff Strickler
Production Manager: Jim Mitzel
Plant Manager: Jim Mitzel
Purchasing Manager: Bob Keyser
Estimated Sales: $5-10 Million
Number Employees: 20-49
Number of Brands: 13
Number of Products: 13
Square Footage: 160000
Type of Packaging: Private Label
Brands:
  Citrus
  Gent-L-Kleen
  Grime Grabber
  Power Wipes Formula Z
  Premium Blue
  Pumicizied Advantage Plus
  Skin Armor
  Zapper

21769 Dri Mark Products
15 Harbor Park Dr
Port Washington, NY 11050

516-484-6200
Fax: 516-484-6279 800-645-9118
www.drimark.com

Manufacturer and exporter of pens including nylon, felt and plastic tip, ball point, roller ball and counterfeit detector; also, watercolor and permanent markers, highlighters and drawing sets
President: Charles Reichmann
CFO: Cathy Owens
VP Sales: Mark Dobbs
Purchasing Manager: Mickey Cirrani

Estimated Sales: $20-50 Million
Number Employees: 100-249
Square Footage: 70000
Brands:
  Buffalo
  Color Graphic
  Communication
  Mr. Doodler
  Perma Graphic

21770 Driall Inc
1144 E 800 N
Attica, IN 47918-8027

765-295-2255
Fax: 317-272-1097

Manufacturer and exporter of grain dryers and air curtain destructors for controlled open residue burning
Manager: Dave Scott
Estimated Sales: Less Than $500,000
Number Employees: 1-4
Type of Packaging: Food Service, Bulk

21771 Driam USA Inc
181 Access Rd
Spartanburg, SC 29303-1775

864-579-7850
Fax: 864-579-7852 info@driamusa.com

Confectionary and candy sorting and inspection machinery. Coating equipment for the pharmeceutical and confectionary industry
Owner: Marilyn Drumm
Sales Manager: Hans Peter Schwendeler
Manager: Rose Michael
rosemichael@driamusa.com
Estimated Sales: Less Than $500,000
Number Employees: 1-4
Parent Co: Driam

21772 Dried Ingredients, LLC.
9010 NW 105th Way
Miami, FL 33178

786-999-8499
Fax: 888-893-6595 info@driedingredients.com
www.driedingredients.com

Maufacturer of organic, precooked pulses (beans, lentils, peas); also teas, tea ingredients, herbs, spices, essential oils & dried vegetables. Provide product development & logistics services.
President: Armin Dilles
armin.dilles@driedingredients.com
Sales Manager: Maria Rosello
Parent Co: Dried Ingredients GmbH
Type of Packaging: Food Service, Bulk

21773 Driscoll Label Company
19 West Street
East Hanover, NJ 07936

973-585-7291
Fax: 973-585-7295 craguso@driscolllabel.com
www.driscolllabel.com

Wine industry pressure sensitive labels
President: John Riguso
Vice President: Patricia Biava
Sales Director: Patricia Vargas
Contact: Gail Chill
gailchill@driscolllabel.com
Estimated Sales: $10-20 000,000
Number Employees: 20-49

21774 Drives Incorporated
901 19th Ave
Fulton, IL 61252

815-589-2211
Fax: 815-589-4420 custserv@drivesinc.com

Power transmission products, conveyor chain, screw conveyors
President: David J Vogel
CFO: Michael Landers
Contact: Steven Eggemeyer
eggemeyers@drivesinc.com
Estimated Sales: $50-100 Million
Number Employees: 250-499

21775 Drs Designs
217 Greenwood Ave
Bethel, CT 06801-2113

203-744-2858
Fax: 203-743-4389 888-792-3740
www.drsdesigns.com

Rubber stamps, engraved signs and pressure sensitive labels; also, general printing, laminating and hot stamping services available

Manager: Samantha Conrad
Manager: Dave Spence
dspence@drsdesigns.com
Estimated Sales: $500,000-$1 Million
Number Employees: 1-4
Square Footage: 2400

21776 Drum-Mates Inc.
PO Box 636
Lumberton, NJ 08048-0636

609-261-1033
Fax: 609-261-1034 800-621-3786
info@drummates.com www.drummates.com
Manufacturer and supplier of sanitary duty drum and
IBC heaters, mixers, pumps, hand dispensing noz-
zles, bung equipment, fittings, global
ThreadConverters and adapters.
Technical Sales: David Marcmann
Estimated Sales: $1-5 Million
Number Employees: 20
Square Footage: 100000
Brands:
   Drum-Mate
   Quikmix
   Threadconverter
   Threadguard

21777 Drying Technology Inc
500 Highway 327 E
Silsbee, TX 77656-5018

409-385-6422
Fax: 409-385-6537 drying@moisturecontrols.com
www.moisturecontrols.com
Moisture controls
President: John Robinson
Estimated Sales: Below $5 000,000
Number Employees: 1-4

21778 Dryomatic
7924 Reco Avenue
Frederick, MD 70814

301-668-8200
Fax: 225-612-7407 sales@dryomatic.com
www.dryomatic.com
Parent Co: Airflow Company

21779 Dsl
6504 Mayfair St
Houston, TX 77087-3422

713-645-9177
Fax: 713-645-9131 800-460-3164
sales@dslformers.com www.dslformers.com
Forming collars to fit draw bar, pull belt, vacuum
pull belt and continuous motion baggers and pack-
aging machinery
President: Louis Posada
R & D: Simon Gonales
Marketing Manager: Simon Gondales
Contact: Simon Gonzales
sg@dslformers.com
Estimated Sales: Below $5 000,000
Number Employees: 5-9

21780 Dsr Enterprises
38404 Hidden Creek Way
Mechanicsville, MD 20659-7203

301-472-4990
Fax: 610-942-4273 800-238-0310
dsr@dsrenterprises.com www.dsrenterprises.com
Electrical panel management schedules and esti-
mates loads
Partner: Randy Junkins
President: David Groh
Estimated Sales: Less Than $500,000
Number Employees: 1-4
Square Footage: 1500
Type of Packaging: Private Label

21781 Du Bois Chemicals
3630 E Kemper Rd
Cincinnati, OH 45241-2046

513-326-8800
Fax: 513-326-8309
charlie.weber@diverseylever.com
www.duboischemicals.com
CEO: Mike Gallico
mikeg@johnson-company.com
Estimated Sales: $1-5 Million
Number Employees: 100-249

21782 Du-Good Chemical Laboratory & Manufacturing Company
1215 S Jefferson Ave
Saint Louis, MO 63104-1992

314-773-5007
Fax: 314-773-5007 dugood@stlnet.com
Dishwashing detergent and waterless hand cleaning
products
President: Lincoln I Diuguid
VP: Lewis Diuguid
Manager: V Diuguid
Estimated Sales: $.5-1 million
Number Employees: 5 to 9
Square Footage: 13150
Brands:
   Du-Good
   Rainbow Delight

21783 DuBois Chemicals
3630 E Kemper Rd
Sharonville, OH 45241-2011

800-438-2647
www.duboischemicals.com
Supplier of cleaning and hygiene systems for dairy,
beverage, brewing and food industries.
President & CEO: Jeff Walsh
Technical Advisor: Michael Askren
VP, Operations: James Walker
Year Founded: 1920
Estimated Sales: $2 Billion
Number Employees: 150
Square Footage: 105000

21784 (HQ)DuPont
939 Centre Rd.
Wilmington, DE 19807

302-774-1000
800-441-7515
info@dupont.com www.dupont.com
Collaborates with equipment manufactureres, con-
verters, brand owners and retailers to develop appli-
cation-specific packaging solutions; tecnologies
include packging resins and sealants, anti-counter-
feit solutions, non-wovensubstrates, grease-resistant
coatings and liquid packaging solutions.
Executive Chairman/CEO: Edward Breen
CFO: Lori Koch
Senior VP/General Counsel: Erik Hoover
President, Nutrition & Biosciences: Matthias
Heinzel
Senior VP/Chief Operations & Engineering: Daryl
Roberts
Year Founded: 1802
Estimated Sales: $25 Biliion
Number Employees: 34,000
Number of Brands: 169

21785 DuPont Nutrition & Biosciences
4 New Century Pkwy
New Century, KS 66031

913-764-8100
www.food.dupont.com
Ingredients for baking, bars, beverages, confection-
ery, culinary, diary, frozen desserts, fruit applica-
tions, meat alternatives, meat/poultry/seafood, oils
and fats, and pet food
President, Nutrition & Biosciences: Matthias
Heinzel
Estimated Sales: $4.4 Billion
Number Employees: 10,000
Parent Co: DuPont
Type of Packaging: Consumer, Bulk
Other Locations:
   Central Soya Company-Processing
   Decatur IN
   Central Soya Company-Processing
   Gibson City IL
   Central Soya Company-Processing
   Marion OH
   Central Soya Company-Grain Plant
   Indianapolis IN
   Central Soya Company-Processing
   Bellevue OH
   Central Soya Company-Grain Plant
   Cincinnati OH
   Central Soya Company-Processing
   Delphos OH
   Central Soya Company-Mfg
   Remington IN
   Central Soya Company-Processing
   Morristown IN
   Central Soya Company-Grain
   Jeffersonville OH
   Central Soya Company-Grain
   Waterloo IN
   Central Soya Company-Bulk Oil

Pawtucket RI
Central Soya Company-Mfg
New Bremen OH
Brands:
   Fibrim
   Solae
   V8 Splash
   Gardenburgers
   Mori-Nu
   Yves Veggie Cuisine
   Medifast

21786 Dual Temp
4301 S Packers Ave
Chicago, IL 60609-3311

773-254-9800
Fax: 773-254-9840 800-255-9801
sales@dualtempcompanies.com
www.dualtempcompanies.com
President: Mary Akers
marya@dualtempcompanies.com
Estimated Sales: $1-5 Million
Number Employees: 20-49

21787 Dualite Sales & Svc Inc
1 Dualite Ln
Williamsburg, OH 45176-1121

513-724-7100
Fax: 513-724-9029 dualite@dualite.com
www.dualite.com
National account sign manufacturer
President: Frank W Schube
fschube@dualite.com
Executive VP Administration: E Lynn Webb
R&D: Pat Seggerson
National Sales Manager: Robert Stephany
Plant Manager: Jerry Hinnenkamp
Purchasing: Greg Hoffer
Estimated Sales: $35-50 Million
Number Employees: 250-499
Square Footage: 600000
Parent Co: Dualite

21788 Dub Harris Corporation
2875 Metropolitan Place
Pomona, CA 91767

909-596-6300
Fax: 909-596-6336 dubharris@dubharris.com
www.dubharris.com
Plastic bags; wholesaler/distributor of corrugated
boxes and packaging materials
President: Maurice Harris
Contact: Ming Yu
dubharris@dubharris.com
Estimated Sales: $2.5-5 Million
Number Employees: 5-9

21789 Dubor GmbH
4801 Harbor Pointe Dr.
Suite 1305
North Myrtle Beach, SC 29016-9458

803-691-8941
Fax: 803-754-7755
benmuller@mullerinternational.com
www.mullerinternational.com

21790 Dubuit Of America Inc
70 Monaco Dr
Roselle, IL 60172-1955

630-894-9500
Fax: 847-647-1796 www.dubuit.com
Printers and screen printing equipment
President: Pierre Crozet
pcrozet@dubuitamerica.com
Estimated Sales: $3 000,000
Number Employees: 5-9

21791 Dubuque Steel Products Co
1500 Radford Rd
Dubuque, IA 52002-2115

563-556-6288
Fax: 563-583-7365
www.dubuquesteelproducts.com
Stainless steel tubs, trucks, dollies, racks, drums and
vats
President: Thomas A Geisler
sales@dubuquesteelproducts.com
CEO: Dave Geisler
Vice President: Todd Geisler
Estimated Sales: $2.5-5 Million
Number Employees: 5-9
Parent Co: Geisler Brothers Company

21792 Duck Waok
44535 Main Road
PO Box 962
Water Mill, NY 11976-0962
631-765-3500
Fax: 631-765-3509 www.duckwalk.com
Wines
Owner: Alexander Damianos
VP and General Manager: Alex Zamianos
Estimated Sales: Below $5 Million
Number Employees: 10-19

21793 Duct Sox Corp
9866 Kapp Ct
Peosta, IA 52068-9451
563-588-5300
Fax: 563-588-5330 866-563-7729
cpinkalla@ductsox.com www.ductsox.com
Fabric air dispersion systems
President: Cary Pinkalla
cpinkalla@ductsox.com
Key Person: Lou Wiegand
Number Employees: 250-499

21794 Dudson USA Inc
5604 Departure Dr
Raleigh, NC 27616-1841
919-877-0200
Fax: 919-877-0300 800-438-3766
usasales@dudson.com
Importer and wholesaler/distributor of dinnerware
including china; serving the food service market
President: Elmer Carr
VP: Lorraine Delois
VP Marketing/Sales: Joel DeNoble
VP Corporate Accounts: Maire-Anne Bassil
Manager: Steve Abourisk
Estimated Sales: $1-2.5 Million
Number Employees: 10-19
Square Footage: 180000
Parent Co: Dudson Company
Type of Packaging: Food Service

21795 Duerr Packaging Co Inc
892 Steubenville Pike
Burgettstown, PA 15021-9510
724-947-1234
Fax: 724-947-4321 sales@duerrpack.com
www.duerrpack.com
Rigid paper boxes, transformed plastics
CEO: Samuel Duerr Jr
sam@duerrpack.com
CFO: Wayne Albroght
VP: David Duerr
Sales Exec: Sam Duerr
Estimated Sales: $2.5-5 Million
Number Employees: 20-49

21796 Dufeck Manufacturing Co
210 Maple St
Denmark, WI 54208
920-863-2354
Fax: 920-863-2054 888-603-9663
info@dufeckwood.com www.dufeckwood.com
Wooden cheese and wine boxes, custom display
units, containers, gift boxes and baskets and wooden
pallets
President: Paul Dufeck
paul@dufeckwood.com
Finance: Jeanette Dufeck
R&D: Junette Dufeck
Plant Manager: Al Bouressa
Estimated Sales: $10-20 Million
Number Employees: 50-99
Square Footage: 40000

21797 Dugussa Texturant Systems
3582 McCall Pl
Atlanta, GA 30340-2802
770-455-3603
Fax: 770-986-6216 800-241-9485
texturants@degussa.com
President: Ed Baranski
Number Employees: 50-99

21798 Dukane Corp
2900 Dukane Dr
St Charles, IL 60174-3395
630-797-4900
Fax: 630-797-4949 usservice@dukcorp.com
www.dukane.com
Ultrasonic food cutting

President: Jean Stone
CEO: Michael W Ritschdorff
mritschdorff@dukcorp.com
CEO: Michael W Ritschdorff
Marketing Communications: Kathy Jensen
Sales Director: Joe Re
Estimated Sales: G
Number Employees: 250-499
Brands:
Ultrasonic Equipment

21799 Dukane Corp
2900 Dukane Dr
St Charles, IL 60174-3395
630-797-4900
Fax: 630-797-4949 usuntl@dukane.com
www.dukane.com
CEO: Michael W Ritschdorff
mritschdorff@dukcorp.com
CEO: Michael W Ritschdorff
Estimated Sales: $1-5 Million
Number Employees: 250-499

21800 Duke Manufacturing Co
2305 N Broadway
St Louis, MO 63102-1420
314-231-1130
Fax: 314-231-5074 800-735-3853
www.dukemfg.com
Manufacturer and exporter of ingredient bins, cabi-
nets, sneeze guards, conveyors, counters, filters,
freezers, ovens, steam tables, pans, racks, coolers,
kiosks, fire extinguishing systems, sinks, carts, etc
President: Jack Hake
jhake@dukemfg.com
CFO: Larry Reader
Quality Control: Art Lamley
Estimated Sales: $20-50 Million
Number Employees: 100-249
Square Footage: 300000

21801 Duluth Sheet Metal
P.O.Box 16582
Duluth, MN 55816-0582
218-722-2613
Fax: 218-727-8870
Stainless steel tables, stands, shelves, counter tops,
cabinets, sinks and vapor hoods; custom fabricator
of conveyors, platforms, tanks, etc
President: Mark Jam
Contact: Barney Revier
revier@duluthsheetmetal.com
Estimated Sales: $1-2.5 Million
Number Employees: 10-19
Square Footage: 24000

21802 Dunbar Co
1186 Walter St
Lemont, IL 60439-3993
630-257-2900
Fax: 630-257-3434 dunbar@dunbarsystems.com
www.dunbarsystems.com
Producer of serpentine baking systems for cookies,
cakes, biscuits, bread, pies, pastries, muffins and
puddings.
President/Owner: Mark Dunbar
CEO/Owner: Mike Dunbar
Senior Sales Engineer: Chuck Kazen
Manager: George Dunbar
george@dunbarsystems.com
Vice President of Operations: Doug Hale
Estimated Sales: $9.7 Million
Number Employees: 10-19
Type of Packaging: Food Service

21803 Dunbar Manufacturing Co
390 N Gilbert St
South Elgin, IL 60177-1398
847-741-6394
Fax: 847-741-6394
www.dunbarmanufacturing.com
Manufacturer and exporter of caramel and regular
popcorn equipment including mixers, tumblers,
poppers and sprayers
President: Ray Goode Jr
rgoode4@gmail.com
Estimated Sales: Less than $500,000
Number Employees: 1-4
Number of Products: 40
Square Footage: 12000
Brands:
Popt-Rite

**21804 Dunhill Food Equipment
Corporation**
PO Box 496
Armonk, NY 10504
718-625-4006
Fax: 718-625-0155 800-847-4206
sales@dunhill-esquire.net
Manufacturer and exporter of cafeteria and kitchen
equipment including cashier stands, serving coun-
ters, sinks, refrigerated display cases and tables
President: Geoffrey Thaw
VP: Larry Dubow
Estimated Sales: $5-10 Million
Number Employees: 10-19
Square Footage: 100000
Parent Co: Esquire Mechanical Group
Type of Packaging: Food Service
Brands:
Dunhill

21805 Dunkin' Brands Inc.
130 Royall St.
Canton, MA 02021
781-737-3000
800-859-5339
www.dunkinbrands.com
Coffee, baked goods and premium ice cream.
President/CEO: David Hoffmann
CFO: Kate Jaspon
Chief Marketing Officer: Tony Weisman
Chief Operating Officer: Scott Murphy
Year Founded: 2004
Estimated Sales: $860 Million
Number Employees: 1,163
Number of Brands: 2
Type of Packaging: Food Service
Brands:
Baskin-Robbins®
Dunkin' Donuts®

21806 Dunkley International Inc
1910 Lake St
Kalamazoo, MI 49001-3274
269-343-5583
Fax: 269-343-5614 800-666-1264
Manufacturer and exporter of pitters, de-stemmers
and electronic sorters, inspection systems and con-
veyors
President: Richard L Bogard
Manager: Nick Hatzinikolis
nhatzinikolis@dunkleyinyl.com
General Manager: Ernest Kenneway
Plant Manager: Rob Prange
Estimated Sales: $1-3 Million
Number Employees: 10-19
Square Footage: 120000
Parent Co: Cherry Central

21807 Dunn Woodworks
536 S Main Street
Shrewsbury, PA 17361-1739
717-235-1144
Fax: 717-227-2828 877-835-8592
woodpilot@aol.com
Manufacturer, broker and wholesaler/distributor of
custom designed displays, kiosks, racks, P.O.P,
P.O.S. and merchandisers. Custom designed wine
racks and display headers. Over ten thousand dis-
plays made annually
Owner: Henry Dunn
Estimated Sales: $1-3,000,000
Number Employees: 5
Square Footage: 10000

21808 Dunrite Inc
3405 N Yager Rd
Fremont, NE 68025-7880
402-721-3061
Fax: 402-721-3040 800-782-3061
www.dunrite.com
Pneumatic grain conveyors, grain elevator vacuums
and accessories including respirators, dust masks
and duct tape
Manager: Leroy Klinzing
VP: Leroy Klinzing
Estimated Sales: $2.5-5 Million
Number Employees: 5-9
Brands:
Buckskin Bill
Harvestvac

21809 Duo-Aire
39 Third Street SW
Suite 606
Winter Haven, FL 33880

863-294-2272
Fax: 863-294-2704 info@duoaire.com
www.duoaire.com
Commercial kitchen ventilation systems
President: Gary Smith
Accounting: Jan Smith
Sales & Parts: Jody Reynolds
Estimated Sales: $470,000
Number Employees: 4
Square Footage: 14836
Parent Co: Ventilation Marketing Services

21810 Duplex Mill & Mfg Co
415 Sigler St
Springfield, OH 45506-1144

937-325-5555
Fax: 937-325-0859 www.dmmc.com
Diverter valves and mixing, blending, conveying, elevating, size reduction and slide gate machinery; exporter of mixers, conveyors and hammer mills
CEO: Eric Wise
eww@dmmc.com
Sales Manager: Eric Wise
Production Manager: Eric Brickson
Plant Manager: Eric Brickson
Estimated Sales: $2-3 Million
Number Employees: 10-19
Square Footage: 320000
Brands:
  Kelly Duplex

21811 Dupps Co
548 N Cherry St
Germantown, OH 45327-1185

937-855-0623
Fax: 937-855-6554 info@dupps.com
www.dupps.com
Manufacturer and exporter of process equipment and protein waste recovery systems including cookers and dryers; also, computerized control and information systems, screw presses, conveyor systems, high viscosity material pumps and sizereduction equipment
President: John A Dupps Jr
VP: Frank Dupps
frank.dupps@dupps.com
Quality Control: Tim Seebach
Marketing Manager: Rich Hollmeyer
Estimated Sales: $20-50 Million
Number Employees: 100-249
Square Footage: 120000
Brands:
  Equacookor
  Precrushor
  Pressor
  Ring Dryer

21812 Dupuy Storage & Forwarding LLC
4300 Jourdan Rd
New Orleans, LA 70126-3731

504-245-7600
Fax: 504-245-7643 www.dupuygroup.com
Tea and coffee industry bulk silo services, reconditioners, samplers and weighers
President: Allan B Colley
abcolley@dupuystorage.com
Estimated Sales: $50-100 Million
Number Employees: 50-99

21813 Dur-Able Aluminum Corporation
1555 Barrington Rd
Hoffman Estates, IL 60169-1019

847-843-1100
Fax: 847-843-0764
Manufacturer and exporter of aluminum foil bakeware including pans, plates, trays and cooking and baking utensils
Estimated Sales: $20-50 Million
Number Employees: 1-4
Type of Packaging: Food Service, Bulk

21814 Dura Electric Lamp Company
64 E Bigelow Street
Newark, NJ 07114-1699

973-624-0014
Fax: 973-624-3945
Manufacturer and exporter of incandescent and fluorescent lamps and starters

---

President: Lawrence Portnow
General Manager: A Gross
Estimated Sales: $2.5-5 Million
Number Employees: 5-9
Square Footage: 80000
Brands:
  Dura
  Durelco

21815 Dura-Flex
95 Goodwin St
East Hartford, CT 06108-1146

860-528-9838
Fax: 860-528-2802 877-251-5418
contact_us@dur-a-flex.com
Commercial and seemless industrial flooring systems and wall coatings and polymer components-epoxies, urethanes and methyl methacrylates (MMA) plus premium colored quartz aggregates.
CEO: Robert Smith
roberts@dur-a-flex.com
Marketing: Mark Paggioli
Number Employees: 50-99
Square Footage: 260000
Brands:
  Cryl-A-Chip
  Cryl-A-Flex
  Cryl-A-Floor
  Cryl-A-Quartz
  Poly-Crete

21816 Dura-Pack Inc.
7641 Holland Rd
Taylor, MI 48180

313-299-9600
Fax: 313-299-9988 sales@dura-pack.com
dura-pack.com
Custom bags and packaging; machinery for bagging
President: Tim Harrison
Year Founded: 1971
Estimated Sales: $550,000
Number Employees: 20

21817 (HQ)Dura-Ware Company of America
PO Box 53006
Oklahoma City, OK 73152-3006

405-475-5600
Fax: 405-475-5607 800-664-3872
customerservice@carlislefsp.com
www.carlislefsp.com
Manufacturer, importer and exporter of commercial cookware and servingware including stock pots, frying pans, sauce pans, pasta cookers, chafers, etc
President: David Shannon
VP Sales: David Wasserman
Estimated Sales: $20-50 Million
Number Employees: 50-99
Square Footage: 70000
Brands:
  Celebration
  Dura-Ware
  Signature
  Ssal
  Symphony

21818 Durable Corp
75 N Pleasant St
Norwalk, OH 44857-1218

419-668-8138
Fax: 419-668-8068 800-537-1603
sales@durablecorp.com www.durablecorp.com
Dock bumpers, wheel chocks and floor mats and matting
President: Thomas Secor
CEO: Hilary Alexander
alexander@durablecorp.com
Sales Director: Phil Lorcher
Estimated Sales: $20-50 Million
Number Employees: 50-99
Type of Packaging: Private Label

21819 Durable Engravers
521 S County Line Rd
Franklin Park, IL 60131

630-766-6420
Fax: 630-766-0219 800-869-9565
www.durable-tech.com
Manufacturer and exporter of steel and brass codes, logo blocks and holders for the food and pharmaceutical industries
CEO: Gary Berenger
g.berenger@durable-tech.com
VP: Jim Maybach

Estimated Sales: $1-2.5 Million
Number Employees: 20-49
Square Footage: 20000
Type of Packaging: Food Service, Bulk

21820 Durable Packaging Corporation
5117 Dansher Rd
Countryside, IL 60525-6905

708-387-2253
Fax: 708-387-2211 800-700-5677
www.okcorp.com
Case erectors and sealers
Manager: Adam Kwiek
Sales/Marketing Manager: Carol Crouse
General Information: Leslie Hickey
Estimated Sales: $5-10 Million
Number Employees: 10-19

21821 Duralite Inc
15 School St
Riverton, CT 06065-1013

860-379-3113
Fax: 860-379-5879 888-432-8797
sales@duralite.com www.duralite.com
Manufacturer and exporter of quartz tubes for heating/cooking equipment with element enclosed is tube or wrapped around tube, also heating elements (electric) heating and cooking, coiled or not
Owner: Mark Jessen
markj@duralite.com
CEO: Elliott Jessen
Chairman: Elliot Jessen
Sales Director: Barbara Asselin
markj@duralite.com
Estimated Sales: $1 Million+
Number Employees: 10-19
Square Footage: 15000

21822 (HQ)Durand-Wayland Inc
101 Durand Rd
Lagrange, GA 30241-2501

706-882-8161
Fax: 706-882-0052 800-241-2308
sales@durand-wayland.com
www.durand-wayland.com
Manufacturer and exporter of fruit processing and packing machinery including conveyors, cleaners, sizers, sorters, blemish graders and sprayers
President: Brooks Lee
brooksl@durand-wayland.com
VP Sales: Ray Perry
Marketing Director: Ashley Scott
Sales Manager: Suzanne Bryan
Purchasing Manager: Savral Patel
Number Employees: 100-249
Other Locations:
  Durand-Wayland
  Reedley CA

21823 (HQ)Durango-Georgia Paper
4301 Anchor Plaza Parkway
Suite 360
Tampa, FL 33634

813-286-2718
Fax: 912-576-0713
Manufacturer and exporter of bleached boards for folding cartons; also, grease resistant decorative paper plates and lightweight cups, bleached and natural kraft paper
VP Marketing: Joseph Meighan
Estimated Sales: $1-5 Million
Parent Co: Corporation Durango.

21824 Durant Box Factory
916 Crooked Oak Dr
Durant, OK 74701-2218

580-924-4035
Fax: 580-924-7276
Hardwood pallets and skids
Estimated Sales: $1-2.5 Million
Number Employees: 20
Square Footage: 50000

21825 Durashield USA
601 W Cherry St
Sunbury, OH 43074-9803

740-965-3008
Fax: 740-965-4485 www.americanpan.com
Non-stick coatings
Operations Manager: Brad Moore
bradmoore@richardsapex.com
Estimated Sales: $1-2.5 000,000
Number Employees: 10-19

21826 (HQ)Durasol Awnings
225 Tower Dr
Middletown, NY 10941

845-692-1100
Fax: 845-692-1101 800-444-6131
Custom-made awnings and awning products
President: Rich Lemond
Contact: Lauri Blake
lblake@durasol.com
Estimated Sales: $50-100 Million
Number Employees: 50-99
Square Footage: 50000
Other Locations:
  Durasol
  Tolleson AZ

21827 Durastill Export Inc
86 Reservoir Park Dr
Rockland, MA 02370-1062

781-878-5577
Fax: 781-878-2224 800-449-5260
sales@durastill.com www.durastill.com
Manufacturer and exporter of water distillation systems
Owner: M Anthony
Director Sales: Horace Mansfield
Sales: Jeff Thompson
Estimated Sales: Less Than $500,000
Number Employees: 1-4
Parent Co: Master Pitching Machine Company

21828 Durham Manufacturing Co
201 Main St
Durham, CT 06422-2108

860-349-3427
Fax: 860-349-8572 800-243-3744
info@durhammfg.com www.durhammfg.com
Manufacturer and exporter of pallet rack and industrial duty steel shelving
President: Paul H Frick Jr
Sales/Marketing Administrative Manager: David Massie
Estimated Sales: $2.5-5 Million
Number Employees: 100-249

21829 Duske Drying Systems
6901 Industrial Loop
Greendale, WI 53129-2445

414-529-0240
Fax: 414-529-0362 www.uzelacind.com
Drying systems
President: Mike Uzelac
Estimated Sales: $2.5 000,000
Number Employees: 10-19

21830 Dusobox Company
233 Neck Rd
Haverhill, MA 01835-8029

978-372-7192
Fax: 978-372-7198
Corrugated boxes
Manager: Peter Grogan
General Manager: Peter Grogan
Estimated Sales: $2.5-5 Million
Number Employees: 10 to 19
Parent Co: Dusobox Company

21831 Dutchess Bakers' Machinery Co
302 Grand Ave
Superior, WI 54880-1243

715-394-2387
Fax: 715-394-6199 800-777-4498
www.dutchessbakers.com
Dutchess Bakers' Machinery Company has been manufacturing high quality dough dividers and dough divider rounders for the foodservice industry since 1886! We are the originator and most respected & recognized name in the world for thiskind of equipment; also offers the bun & bagel slicer.
President: Kent Phillips
Marketing Director: Tony Marino
Plant Manager: John Skandel
Estimated Sales: $3-5 Million
Number Employees: 20-49
Square Footage: 120000
Parent Co: Superior-Lidgerwood-Mundy Corporation
Brands:
  Dutchess

21832 Dutro Co
675 N 600 W # 2
Logan, UT 84321-3197

435-752-3921
Fax: 435-752-6360 866-388-7660
contact@dutro.com www.dutro.com
Manufacturer and exporter of carts, dollies and trucks
President: Josh Adams
j.adams@dutro.com
CEO: William Dutro
Estimated Sales: $17,483,702
Number Employees: 50-99
Number of Products: 16

21833 Dutter's Food
2700 Lord Baltimore Drive
Baltimore, MD 21244-2648

410-298-3663
Fax: 410-298-1625
Food Plans & Programs and Grocery stores
President: Vernon Mules
Estimated Sales: $10-20 Million
Number Employees: 10-19

21834 Duval Container Co
91 S Myrtle Ave
Jacksonville, FL 32204-2117

904-355-0711
Fax: 904-350-9709 800-342-8194
www.duvalcontainer.com
Corrugated boxes; wholesaler/distributor of containers and packaging materials
President: Richard L Gills
CFO: Mary Geller
Contact: William Erwin
william@duvalcontainer.com
Estimated Sales: $10-20 Million
Number Employees: 20-49

21835 Dwinell's Central Neon
101 Butterfield Rd
Yakima, WA 98901-2008

509-248-3772
Fax: 509-457-8026 800-932-8832
Indoor and outdoor signs including advertising, electric, neon and painted
President: Chuck Colmenero
President: Glenn Terrell
Estimated Sales: $5-10 Million
Number Employees: 50-99

21836 Dwyer Instruments Inc
102 Indiana Highway 212
Michigan City, IN 46360-1956

219-879-8000
Fax: 219-872-9057 800-872-3141
info@dwyer-inst.com www.dwyer-inst.com
Manufacturer and exporter of HVAC instruments including air filter gauges, thermostats, air velocity transmitters, temperature and process controllers and mercury switches
President: Steve Clark
CFO: Tom Dhaeze
Quality Control: Don Goad
Manager: Dave Lange
dlange@love-controls.com
Purchasing Manager: Dave Pilarski
Estimated Sales: $50-100 Million
Number Employees: 250-499

21837 Dycem Limited
83 Gilbane St
Warwick, RI 02886-6901

401-738-4420
Fax: 401-739-9634 800-458-0060
Contamination control systems including contamination mats for entranceways dealing with heavy pedestrian flow and wheeled machinery. Also, detergents and cleaners, cleaning equipment (vacuums, mops, buckets), and also stabilizing matsfor laboratory use.
President: Mark Dalziel
VP: Leo Lake
Research Microbiologist: Caroline Clibbon
Quality Officer: Cherie Jackson
Marketing Coordinator: Emma Truby
Sales Manager: Thomas Mulligan
Contact: Katlyn Babb
katlynn.babb@dycemusa.com
Purchasing: Lee Hamilton
Number Employees: 5-9

21838 Dyco
50 Naus Way
Bloomsburg, PA 17815-8784

570-752-2757
Fax: 570-752-7366 800-545-3926
sales@dyco-inc.com www.dyco-inc.com
Manufacturer and exporter of material handling equipment including case conveyors, car conveyors, diverter gates, fittings, and can rinsers
President: David M Rauscher
VP Sales/Marketing: David Rauscher, Jr.
Manager: Lewis Abram
labram@dyco-inc.com
Office Manager: Lea Ann O'Quinn
Estimated Sales: $2.5-5 Million
Number Employees: 50-99
Square Footage: 10000

21839 Dyco
50 Naus Way
Bloomsburg, PA 17815-8784

570-752-2757
Fax: 570-752-7366 800-545-3926
sales@dyco-inc.com www.dyco-inc.com
Conveyers, bagger and debagger machines
Finance Executive: Dan Bierdziewski
Manager: Lewis Abram
labram@dyco-inc.com
Estimated Sales: $1-5 Million
Number Employees: 50-99

21840 Dyco
6951 Naus Way
Bloomsburg, PA 17815

570-752-2757
Fax: 570-752-7366 800-545-3926
sales@dyco-inc.com www.dyco-inc.com
Provides custom engineered container handling solutions
President: Peter Yohe
Finance Executive: Dan Bierdziewski
Sales Manager: Kevin John
Contact: John Petty
jpetty@dyco-inc.com
Operations Manager: John Wittman
Number Employees: 50-99

21841 Dylog USA Vanens
7213 Sandscove Court
Suite 5
Winter Park, FL 32792-6901

407-265-9385
Fax: 407-265-9003

21842 Dyna-Veyor Inc
10 Hudson St
Newark, NJ 07103-2804

973-484-1119
Fax: 973-484-7790 800-326-5009
dynaveyor@aol.com www.dyna-veyor.com
Manufacturer and exporter of plastic conveyor chain belting, sprockets, idlers and corner tracks for the food processing, beverage, canning, pharmaceutical, packaging and container industries
Owner: Tony Ayre
dynaveyor@aol.com
Estimated Sales: $5-10 Million
Number Employees: 10-19

21843 Dynabilt Products
31 Industrial Drive
Readville, MA 02136-2355

617-364-1200
Fax: 617-364-7643 800-443-1008
http://dynabilt.com
Pallet racking and mezzanine systems, floor trucks and refuse and recycling containers
President: Charles Burtman
VP: Mark Goodman
National Sales Manager: Paul Venini
Estimated Sales: $10-20 Million
Number Employees: 50-99
Square Footage: 240000
Parent Co: Burtman Iron Works

21844 Dynablast Manufacturing
94 Riverside Drive
Mississauga, ON V5N 7K5
Canada

905-567-4126
Fax: 905-567-4330 888-242-8597
sales@dynablast.com www.dynablast.com
Gas fired pressure washers for kitchen degreasing and hot water and steam drain cleaning

President: Max Minkhorst
CFO: Don Kent
General Manager: William Duff
Purchasing Manager: Harry Bowker
Number Employees: 10
Square Footage: 340000
Brands:
    Dynablast

21845 Dynaclear Packaging
500 W Main St
Suite 12
Wyckoff, NJ 07481-1439

          201-337-1001
    Fax: 201-337-5001 gerard@shrinkfilm.com
        www.shrinkfilm.com
Manufacturer and supplier of packaging equipment
and supplies.
Chairman/CEO: Peter Quercia
peterquercia@gmail.com
Manager: Jim Quercia
CFO: Barbara Kaywork
Manager of Sales: Michael Kintzley
Estimated Sales: $3.4 Million
Number Employees: 5-9
Other Locations:
    Warehouse & Shipping
    Wyckoff NJ

21846 Dynaco USA
935 Campus Dr
Mundelein, IL 60060-3830

         847-562-4910
    Fax: 847-562-4917 800-459-1930
       dynaco@dynacodoor.us
High performance roll-up doors.
President: Bryan Gregory
CEO: Dirk Wouters
d.wouters@dynacodoor.us
Estimated Sales: Below $5 Million
Number Employees: 20-49

21847 Dynalab Corp
175 Humboldt St # 300
Suite 300
Rochester, NY 14610-1058

         585-334-2060
    Fax: 585-334-0241 800-828-6595
   labinfo@dyna-labware.com www.dynalon.com
Distributor of a full line of plastic lab supplies in-
cluding world renowned brands such as Azlon,
Cowie, Kartell, and Sterilin.
President: Martin Davies
martin@dyna-labware.com
Number Employees: 20-49

21848 Dynalon Labware
175 Humboldt St
Suite 300
Rochester, NY 14610

         585-334-2064
    Fax: 585-334-0241 800-334-7585
   dynaloninfo@dyna-labware.com
      www.dynalabcorp.com
Wholesaler and distributor of plastic lab supplies
President & CEO: Martin Davies
Data Processing: Brian Genter
Product Manager: Steve Yudicky
Human Resources Director: Patti Zimmer
Engineering Manager: William Potter
Manager: Christine Leskovar
Plant Manager: Robert Pfeil
Estimated Sales: $6.7 Million
Number Employees: 35
Square Footage: 100000
Brands:
    Stuart
    Ads Laminaire
    Burkle
    Kartell
    Azlon
    Baritainer ® Jerry Cans
    Bio-Bin® Waste Disposal
    Sterilin
    Delrin®
    Noryl®
    Sintra®
    Kydex®
    Kynar®
    Ultem®

21849 Dynamet
7687 N 6th St
Kalamazoo, MI 49009-8865

         269-385-0006
   Fax: 269-385-4750 dynamet@net-link.net
Specialty bulk material handling conveyors includ-
ing flexible screw, tubular drag and oscillating; also,
hydraulic dumpers
President: Robert Sutton
Estimated Sales: $1-3 Million
Number Employees: 10 to 19
Square Footage: 10000

21850 Dynamic Air Inc
1125 Willow Lake Blvd
St Paul, MN 55110-5193

         651-484-2900
   Fax: 651-484-7015 info@dynamicair.com
       www.dynamicair.com
Pneumatic conveying of bulk solids for the process-
ing industries.
President: James Steele
james.steele@dynamicair.com
National Sales Manager: Tom Acheson
Estimated Sales: $20-50 Million
Number Employees: 100-249

21851 Dynamic Automation LTD
4525 Runway St
Simi Valley, CA 93063-3479

         805-584-8476
   Fax: 805-584-8479 info@dynamicautomation.com
      www.dynamicautomation.com
Bottling, bag closing, food and dairy processing,
packaging, material handling and conveyor systems
and equipment
Owner: Marc Freedman
mark@dynamicautomation.com
Sales Executive: Randy Gray
Estimated Sales: $2.5-5,000,000
Number Employees: 10-19

21852 Dynamic Coatings Inc
3315 W Sussex Way
Fresno, CA 93727-1320

         559-225-4605
   Fax: 559-225-4606 info@dynamiccoatingsinc.net
Product and service line is concrete restoration and
protective coating products for floors and walls ap-
plications of which include that of food processing
plants, kitchens, wineries, dairies, bakeries and
breweries.
Owner: Jose A Gonzales
President: Scott Hamilton
Sales Representative: Jose Gonzalez
Estimated Sales: $857,000
Number Employees: 12

21853 Dynamic Cooking Systems
5900 Skylab Rd
Huntington Beach, CA 92647-2061

         714-372-7000
   Fax: 714-372-7096 800-433-8466
  info@dcsappliances.com www.dcsappliances.com
Manufacturer and exporter of ranges, broilers, coun-
ter equipment, drop-in-cook tops, wall and convec-
tion ovens, ventilation hoods, outdoor barbecues and
patio heaters
President: Mike Goadby
President: Michael Markowich
VP: Randy Rummel
CFO: Jeff Elder
Quality Control: Chillie Waiemas
Marketing Manager: Scott Davies
Contact: Vince Barott
vince.barott@fisherpaykel.com
Estimated Sales: $5-10 Million
Number Employees: 500-999
Square Footage: 66000
Brands:
    Professional

21854 Dynamic International
PO Box 3322
Champlain, NY 12919-3322

         514-956-0127
   Fax: 877-668-6623 800-267-7794
    info@dynamicmixers.com
     www.dynamicmixers.com

Contact: Tony Tsirigoris
tony@dynamicmixers.com

21855 Dynamic Packaging
5725 International Pkwy
Minneapolis, MN 55428-3079

         763-535-8669
   Fax: 763-535-8768 800-878-9380
      www.dynamicpkg.com
Printed and laminated flexible packaging films, roll
stock and bags including simplex style and wicketed
side-weld polyethylene; importer of polypropylene
and polyester packaging films
Owner: George Butgusaim
VP Sales: James Pater, Jr.
Contact: Cindy Carr
ccarr@packaging-specialties.com
VP Production: Thoams Guerity
Estimated Sales: $1-2.5 Million
Number Employees: 10-19
Square Footage: 80000

21856 Dynamic Pak LLC
102 W Division St # 100
Suite 100
Syracuse, NY 13204-1428

         315-474-8593
   Fax: 315-474-8795 www.dynamicpak.us
Thermoforming and contract packaging including
labeling andpackaging.
President: Tm Coyne
tcoyne@dynamicpak.us
Sales Executive: Herman Garcia
Estimated Sales: $1-3 Million
Number Employees: 5-9

21857 Dynamic Storage SystemsInc.
15315 Flight Path Dr.
Brooksville, FL 34604

   Fax: 254-221-4106 800-974-8211
 info@dynamicstorage.com www.hi-linerack.com
Sales storage and pallet racks, belt conveyors, canti-
levers and guided rail entries
VP Sales: Robert Egner
Estimated Sales: $2.5-5 Million
Number Employees: 20-49
Brands:
    Flexi-Guide
    Gold Shield
    Hi-Line
    Hipir Kart

21858 Dynapar Corp
1675 N Delany Rd
Gurnee, IL 60031-1237

         847-662-2666
   Fax: 847-662-6633 800-873-8731
   dancon@dancon.com www.dynapar.com
Industrial controls, counters, encoders, tachometers,
temperative controllers
Vice President: Susan Ottmann
sottmann@dancon.com
VP: Susan Ottmann
Estimated Sales: $20-50 Million
Number Employees: 1000-4999
Number of Products: 8

21859 Dynaric Inc
5740 Bayside Rd
Virginia Beach, VA 23455-3004

         757-460-3725
   Fax: 757-363-8016 800-526-0827
   gd@d-y-c.com www.dynaric.com
Manufacturer and exporter of strapping machinery
and nonmetallic strapping
President: Joseph Martinez
CEO: Mike Moses
CFO: John Guzdus
Plant Manager: Vernon Wilson
Assistant Marketing Manager: Brian Cosgrove
Manager: Dennis Fuller
dennisf@dynaric.com
Plant Manager: Dennis Fuller
Number Employees: 100-249
Square Footage: 200000
Type of Packaging: Consumer, Food Service, Pri-
vate Label, Bulk
Brands:
    Durastrap
    Dynaric
    Dynastrap

21860 Dynasty Transportation
4021 Ambassador Caffery Prkwy
Suite 200 Bldg A
Lafayette, LA 70503
337-291-6700
Fax: 811-764-9229 866-626-3845
uvlwebsitesupport@uvlogistics.com
www.uvlogistics.com
Refrigerated and dry less than truckload and truck-
load service
Sales Director: Garland Hutson
Estimated Sales: $1-3 Million
Number Employees: 10-19
Parent Co: UV Logistics Holding Corp.

21861 Dynasys Technologies
2106 Drew Street
Suite 104
Clearwater, FL 34698-7880
727-443-6600
Fax: 727-443-4390 800-867-5968
dynasys@dyna-sys.com www.dyna-sys.com
Products for automatic identification datacapture,
temperature indicators, and other products
President: Robert Scher
CEO/owner: Bobby Burkett
Director of R&D/COO: Tomas Grajales
Contact: Darrick Olson
darrickolson@dyna-sys.com
Estimated Sales: $5-10 Million
Number Employees: 20-49

21862 Dynatek Laboratory Inc
105 E 4th St
Galena, MO 65656-9649
417-357-6155
Fax: 417-357-6327 800-325-8252
www.dynateklabs.com
Texture analysis and adhesive testing
President: Elaine R Strope
Estimated Sales: $1-5 000,000
Number Employees: 10-19

21863 (HQ)Dynic USA Corp
4750 NE Dawson Creek Dr
Hillsboro, OR 97124-5799
503-693-1070
Fax: 503-648-1185 800-326-1249
enrique@dynic.com www.dynic.com
Labeling and printing products
President: Gwen Robinson
leej@smccd.edu
CEO/President: Shigeru Tamura
Director of Marketing: Mindy Nybert
Sales Engineer: Cesar Santa
Customer Service Rep: James Brandow
Estimated Sales: $25 Million
Number Employees: 50-99
Parent Co: Dynic Corporation
Other Locations:
  Dynic UK Ltd
  Cardiff, South Wales UK
  Dynic Corporation
  Minatoku, Tokyo, Japan HK
Brands:
  Cabin Air Filters
  Cetus Textile Fabrics
  Oled Desiccant
  Sirius Ttr

21864 (HQ)Dynynstyl
855 NW 17th Avenue
Suite A
Delray Beach, FL 33445-2520
561-547-5585
Fax: 561-547-0993 800-774-7895
Manufacturer and exporter of china, flatware, hol-
lowware, chafing dishes, trays, buffetware, etc.;
also, polishers, burnishers, silver cleaners and
canned fuel for chafing dishes, etc.; silver and stain-
less steel repair servicesavailable
CEO: Dennis Paul
Vice President: Debra Cosner
Estimated Sales: $1-5 Million
Number Employees: 10
Brands:
  Dynynstyl
  Eco Lamp
  Eco Pure Aqua Straw
  Ecofuel
  Emperor
  Empress
  Fold Flat

21865 Dzignpak LLC Englander
701 Texas Central Pkwy
Waco, TX 76712-6507
254-776-2360
Fax: 254-776-1213 888-314-5259
info@englanderdzp.com www.englanderdzp.com
Corrugated boxes
Chairman of the Board: Louis Englander
Chief Executive Officer: Marty Englander
Chief Financial Officer: Hal Whitaker
Executive Vice President: Steve Hager
Executive Vice President: Carl Renner
Customer Service Director: Sydney Williams
Logistics Manager: Tim Luke
Estimated Sales: $23 Million
Number Employees: 50-99
Square Footage: 100000

21866 E & E Process Instrumentation
4-40 North Rivermede Road
Concord, Ontario, ON L4K 2H3318
Canada
905-669-4857
Fax: 905-669-2158 info@eeprocess.com
www.eeprocess.com
Manufacturer, importer and exporter of thermome-
ters, hygrometers and hydrometers. Instruments for
quality control and research and development. Nist
certification of test instruments for FDA & USDA
compliance
President: Todd Teichert
Estimated Sales: $1-2.5 Million
Number Employees: 5-9
Square Footage: 16000
Parent Co: E & E Process Instrumentation
Brands:
  Brooklyn

21867 E & M Electric & Machinery Inc
126 Mill St
Healdsburg, CA 95448-4438
415-392-4834
Fax: 707-431-2558 www.eandm.com
Wine industry machinery
President: Judith Deas
steve.deas@enm.com
Sales Exec: Steven Deas
Estimated Sales: $20-50 Million
Number Employees: 50-99

21868 E A Bonelli & Assoc
8450 Edes Ave
Oakland, CA 94621-1306
510-740-0155
Fax: 510-740-0160 marco@eabonelli.com
President: Marco Di Gino
marco@eabenelli.com
Estimated Sales: $3-5 Million
Number Employees: 20-49

21869 E C Shaw Co
1242 Mehring Way
Cincinnati, OH 45203-1836
513-721-6334
Fax: 513-721-6350 866-532-7429
johnpinkley@ecshaw.com www.ecshaw.com
Flexographic plates, marking devices, nameplates,
brass dies and steel stamps
President: Joseph C Grome
ajgrome@ecshaw.com
Rubber Stamp Sales: Marilyn Schalk
Customer Service Manager: Diana Randolph
Plant Manager: Joe Moffitt
Estimated Sales: $3-5 Million
Number Employees: 20-49

21870 E F Bavis & Assoc Inc
201 Grandin Rd
Maineville, OH 45039-9762
513-677-0500
Fax: 513-677-0552 info@bavis.com
www.bavis.com
Manufacturer and exporter of drive-thru and vertical
conveyor systems including transaction cash
drawers
President: William Sieber
wps@bavis.com
R&D: Mike Brown
Director Marketing/Sales: Terry Roberts
Estimated Sales: $5-10 Million
Number Employees: 20-49
Number of Products: 2
Type of Packaging: Food Service

Brands:
  Transaction Drawer
  Vittleveyor

21871 E F Engineering
9710 Humboldt Ave S
Minneapolis, MN 55431-2623
952-888-6596
Fax: 952-888-3619 sales@efengineering.com
www.efengineering.com
Owner: Eyal Fine
eyalf@chemserv.com
Number Employees: 10-19

21872 E H Wachs Co
600 Knightsbridge Pkwy
Lincolnshire, IL 60069-3617
847-537-8800
Fax: 847-520-1147 800-323-8185
sales@ehwachs.com www.ehwachs.com
President: Ken Morency
VP Finance: Nate Drucker
Quality Control: Peter Mullally
Marketing: John Geis
Sales: Chris Bauer
Public Relations: John Geis
Plant Manager: Craig Lewandowski
Purchasing: Ken Jarasz
Estimated Sales: $10-20 000,000
Number Employees: 100-249

21873 E J Mckernan Co
800 S Rock Blvd
Reno, NV 89502-4122
775-356-6111
Fax: 775-356-2181 800-787-7587
surplus@mckernan.com www.mckernan.com
President: Timothy Mckernan
timm@mckernan.com
Chief Operating Officer: Frank Maggio
Estimated Sales: $20-50 Million
Number Employees: 20-49

21874 E K Lay Co
3469 Belgrade St
Philadelphia, PA 19134-5419
215-739-1141
Fax: 215-739-7470 800-523-3220
info@eklay.com www.eklay.com
Cutlery, utensils, foam plates and hinge take-out
containers and cups
President: Jim O'Brien
job@eklay.com
VP: James O'Brien
Sales: William Gallen
Estimated Sales: $10-20 Million
Number Employees: 10-19

21875 E-Control Systems
5170 Sepulveda Blvd
Suite 240
Sherman Oaks, CA 91403
818-783-5229
Fax: 818-783-5219 888-384-3274
sales@econtrolsystems.com
www.econtrolsystems.com
CEO: Abraham Bernstein
Estimated Sales: $10-20 Million
Number Employees: 50-99

21876 E-Cooler
4320 S. Knox Avenue
Chicago, IL 80632
773-284-9975
Fax: 773-284-9973 866-955-3266
www.e-cooler.com
Supplier of corrugated boxes and custom designed
boxes for the meat, seafood and produce industries.

21877 E-J Industries Inc
1275 S Campbell Ave
Chicago, IL 60608-1013
312-226-5023
Fax: 312-226-5976 www.e-jindustries.com
Manufacturers of contract commercial seating and
cabinetry for the hospitality industry.
Vice President: Bill Colles
bcolles@ejindus.com
CEO/CFO: Keith Weitzman
VP: Keith Weitzman
Quality Control: W Nowak
Estimated Sales: $7 Million
Number Employees: 50-99
Square Footage: 240000

21878 E-Lite Technologies
2285 Reservoir Ave
Trumbull, CT 06611
203-371-2070
Fax: 203-371-2078 877-520-3951
Manufacturer and exporter of electroluminescent
lamps
President: Mark Appelberg
President: Mark Appelberg
VP/COO: Mark Appelberg
Contact: Paul Burge
pburge@elitetechnologies.uk.com
Office Manager: Judith Sepelak
Estimated Sales: Below $5,000,000
Number Employees: 10-19
Brands:
  Flatlite

21879 E-Pak Machinery
1555 S State Road 39
La Porte, IN 46350
219-393-5541
Fax: 219-324-2884 800-328-0466
sales@epakmachinery.com
www.epakmachinery.com
President: Lyle Lucas
CEO: Ron Sarto
Vice-President: Chris Ake
Contact: Brandon Pudlo
brandonpudlo@epakmachinery.com
Purchasing Director: Susie Nehal
Estimated Sales: $10-20 Million
Number Employees: 50-99

21880 E-Quip Manufacturing
230 Industry Ave
Frankfort, IL 60423-1641
815-464-0053
Fax: 815-464-0059 www.e-quipmfg.com
OEM stainless steel equipment for food applications
President: Milt Minyard
sales@e-quipmfg.com
CFO: Marge Minyard
Estimated Sales: $2.5-5 000,000
Number Employees: 20-49

21881 E-Saeng Company
17316 Edwards Rd # 240
Cerritos, CA 90703-2450
562-404-1844
Fax: 562-404-1774 esaeng@wcis.com
Plastic bottle, container and tray, multi-layer plastic
sheet, flexible package, co-extruded
VP: K J Chang
Estimated Sales: $1-3 000,000
Number Employees: 1-4

21882 E-Z Dip
2048 S State Road 39
Frankfort, IN 46041-7655
317-575-1088
Fax: 765-659-9687 866-347-3279
Electric ice cream scoop dips hard ice cream quickly
and easily. Ideal for caterers, convention centers, ho-
tels, cruise ships. Commercial grade, cast aluminum
President: Tom Shoup
Vice President: Amy Mennem
Marketing Director: Katherine Russell
Estimated Sales: $150,000
Number Employees: 5
Number of Brands: 1
Number of Products: 1
Square Footage: 9600
Brands:
  E-Z Dip

21883 E-Z Edge Inc
6119 Adams St
West New York, NJ 07093-1505
201-295-1171
Fax: 201-295-1115 800-232-4470
order@e-zedge.com www.e-zedge.com
Manufacturer, exporter and importer of food pro-
cessing equipment including shears, knives and
grinders for meat, fish and poultry; importer of
stainless steel fish shears, bowl cutter knives and
cutlery
Owner: Michael Maffei
ezedgeusa@aol.com
VP: Michael Maffei
Manager: Paul Povinelli
Estimated Sales: Less Than $500,000
Number Employees: 1-4
Square Footage: 15000

Brands:
  Finney
  Giesser
  Speco
  Steffens
  Triumph
  Victorianox
  Zico

21884 E-Z Edge Inc
6119 Adams St
West New York, NJ 07093-1505
201-295-1171
Fax: 201-295-1115 800-232-4470
order@e-zedge.com www.e-zedge.com
Supplier of custom made blades and saws, injector
needles, packing blades, bowl choppers, etc
Owner: Michael Maffei
ezedgeusa@aol.com
Manager: April Carazani
Estimated Sales: Less Than $500,000
Number Employees: 1-4

21885 E-Z Lift Conveyors
2000 S Cherokee St
Denver, CO 80223-3917
303-733-5642
Fax: 303-733-5642 800-821-9966
ez@ezliftconveyors.com
www.ezliftconveyors.com
Manufacturer and exporter of lightweight conveyors
for beans, fruits, nuts and vegetables including
troughing belt, belt bucket, bottom dump car un-
loader and floor-to-floor
President: Kenneth B Drost
Estimated Sales: $1-2.5 Million
Number Employees: 10-19
Square Footage: 20000
Brands:
  E-Z Lift

21886 E-Z Shelving Systems Inc
5538 Merriam Dr
Shawnee, KS 66203-2548
913-384-1331
Fax: 913-384-3399 800-353-1331
info@e-zshelving.com
www.walkincooler-shelving.com
Heavy duty cantilever shelving systems for walk-in
coolers, back room storage and sales areas
President: Ralph Larkin
ralph.larkin@e-zshelving.com
Estimated Sales: $1-2.5 Million
Number Employees: 10-19
Square Footage: 16000
Type of Packaging: Consumer, Food Service, Pri-
vate Label, Bulk

21887 E.G. Staats & Company
608 N Iris Rd
Mount Pleasant, IA 52641
319-385-2116
Fax: 319-385-2429 800-553-1853
info@staatsawards.com www.staatsawards.com
Custom award ribbons
Contact: Rick Garbers
rick@staatsbikes.com
General Manager: Robert Mendenhall
Manager: Andy Zinkle
Estimated Sales: $5-10 Million
Number Employees: 20-49
Parent Co: Midwest Publishing Company

21888 (HQ)E.L. Nickell Company
385 Centreville St
Constantine, MI 49042
269-435-2475
Fax: 616-435-8216
Manufacturer and exporter of pressure vessels and
heat exchangers
President: Brian Hicks
Sales Manager: Roger Bainbridge
Estimated Sales: $5-10 Million
Number Employees: 20-49
Square Footage: 60000

21889 E2M
3300 Breckinridge Blvd
Duluth, GA 30096-8983
770-449-7383
Fax: 770-328-2880 800-622-4326
fskwira@e2m.com

Specializing in the integration of people, machines,
controls, procedures, materials and laytout into
seamless highly efficient packaging systems
President: Waye Young
Vice President of Development: Don Baldwin
General Manager: Fran Skwira
Estimated Sales: $20-50 Million
Number Employees: 50-99

21890 EAS Consulting Group LLC
1700 Diagonal Rd # 750
Suite 750
Alexandria, VA 22314-2841
703-548-3270
Fax: 703-684-4428 877-327-9808
esteele@easconsultinggroup.com
www.easconsultinggroup.com
A leading provider of regulatory services to the
food, dietary supplement, cosmetic, pharmaceutical,
medical device, and tobacco industries.
President/Chief Operating Officer: Dean Cirotta
Chairman/Chief Executive Officer: Edward Steele
esteele@easconsultinggroup.com
Chief Financial Officer: Brett Steele
Director, Regulator Info & Submissions: Charles
Celeste
Number Employees: 1-4

21891 EB Box Company
20 Pollard Street
Unit #3
Richmond Hill, ON L4B 1C3
Canada
905-889-5600
Fax: 905-889-5602 800-513-2269
sales@ebbox.com www.ebbox.com
Paper boxes for fish and chips, Chinese food,
doughnuts andpatties, auto parts, computer parts,
health products, cosmetics, garments, innerboxes,
trays and custom boxes
Number Employees: 5-9

21892 EB Eddy Paper
P.O. Box 5003
Port Huron, MI 48061-5003
810-982-0191
Fax: 810-982-4057 www.domtar.com
Manufacturer and exporter of packaging and spe-
cialty coated papers
Vice President: Mark Ushpol
Marketing Manager: Rob Belanger
Contact: John Beecroft
johnbeecroft@domtar.com
Production Manager: David Rushton
Estimated Sales: $30-50 Million
Number Employees: 20-49
Parent Co: Domtar

21893 EB Metal Industries
Poultney St
Whitehall, NY 12887-0149
518-499-1222
Fax: 518-499-2220
Vending equipment, zinc die castings and sheet
metal fabrication
Sales Director: Stu Tesser
Purchasing Director: Patti Abbott

21894 EBM Technology
641 Keeaumoku Street
Suite 5
Honolulu, HI 96814
330-929-8929
Fax: 808-945-3105 866-212-6127
info@ebmtech.com www.ebmtech.com
Fully automated, highspeed collating and packing
system which will top load or side load with gantry
robots, two axis robots or pushers
President: Martin Dannenberg
Contact: Bell Hsu
bell@ebmtech.com
Number Employees: 5200

21895 EBS
14657 Pebble Bend Drive
Houston, TX 77068
713-939-1000
Fax: 281-444-7900 www.ebs-next.com
Software for material handling systems
President/ COO: Ron Rogers
VP, Development & Software Support: Jay Spencer
Director, Business Development: Kim Prevost
Contact: Steve Benedict
steve@ebsoftware.com

Estimated Sales: $1-3,000,000
Number Employees: 30

21896 ECHO Inc
400 Oakwood Rd
Lake Zurich, IL 60047-1564
Fax: 847-540-9670 800-432-3246
www.echo-usa.com
Wine industry hoses and sprayers.
President: Tim Dorsey
Year Founded: 1950
Estimated Sales: $220 Million
Number Employees: 500-999

21897 ECOM Agroindustrial Corporation Ltd
Av Etienne Guillemin 16
PO Box 64
Pully, CH-1009
Switzerland
www.ecomtrading.com
Cotton, cocoa, coffee and sugar.
CFO: Daniel Willett
Year Founded: 1849
Estimated Sales: $5.1 Billion
Number Employees: 6,000
Type of Packaging: Consumer, Food Service, Private Label, Bulk

21898 EDT Corp
1006 NE 146th St # J
Vancouver, WA 98685-1411
360-574-7294
Fax: 360-574-3834 edtsales@edtcorp.com
www.edtcorp.com
Sanitary bearings and bearings for extreme environments
President: Carl Klinge
Manager: Carl G Klinge
carl@edtcorp.com
Estimated Sales: $1-5 000,000
Number Employees: 10-19

21899 EFA Processing EquipmentCompany
13308 C St
Omaha, NE 68144-3602
402-592-9360
Fax: 402-592-9366
Cutters, boning devices and slaughtering equipment, skinning machines and stunning apparatus
Manager: Donald Novonty
Estimated Sales: $500,000-$1 000,000
Number Employees: 1-4

21900 EFCO Products Inc
130 Smith St
Poughkeepsie, NY 12601
800-284-3326
info@efcoproducts.com www.efcoproducts.com
Leading supplier of mixes, fruit and creme style fillings, jellies, jams and concentrated icing fruits to the baking industry.
CEO: David Miller
Vice President: Andy Herzing
Senior Director of Sales & Marketing: Mark Lowman
Director of Manufacturing Operations: Veronica Miller
Year Founded: 1903
Estimated Sales: $2.5-5 Million
Number Employees: 50-99

21901 EFP Corp
223 Middleton Run Rd
Elkhart, IN 46516-5488
574-295-4690
Fax: 574-295-6512 www.efpcorp.com
Molders and fabricators of expanded polystyrene for packing, insulation, flotation and foundry patterns
President: Bill B Flint
Cmo: Joann Phillips
jphillips@efpcorp.com
Estimated Sales: G
Number Employees: 50-99

21902 EG&G Instruments
100 Midland Rd
Oak Ridge, TN 37830
Fax: 865-483-0396 800-251-9750
info@signalrecovery.com www.ortec-online.com
Modular research instrumentation; gamma and alpha semiconductor detectors
VP: Jon P Kidder

Estimated Sales: $25-50 Million
Number Employees: 250-499

21903 EGA Products Inc
4275 N 127th St
Brookfield, WI 53005-1890
262-781-7899
Fax: 262-781-3586 800-937-3427
johnk@egaproducts.com www.egaproducts.com
Material handling equipment; also, cabinets, racks and containers
President: David Young
Marketing/Sales: John Kuhnz
Estimated Sales: $10-20 Million
Number Employees: 50-99

21904 EGS Electrical Group
7770 Frontage Rd
Skokie, IL 60077
847-679-7800
Fax: 847-268-6011
Manufacturer and exporter of electrical products including controls, switches and lighting fixtures
President: Eric Meyer
CFO: Michael Bryant
Quality Control: L Engler
Marketing Communication Manager: Michelle Miller
Contact: Peter Strong
pstrong@egseg.com
Estimated Sales: $20-50 Million
Number Employees: 100-249
Parent Co: EGS Electrical Group

21905 EGW Bradbury Enterprises
479 US Highway 1
PO Box 129
Bridgewater, ME 04735-0129
207-429-8141
Fax: 207-429-8188 800-332-6021
info@bradburybarrel.com
www.bradburybarrel.com
Manufacturer and exporter of tongue and groove white cedar barrels, tubs and barrelcraft and wooden display fixtures; also, custom wooden displays, fixtures and accessories
President/CEO: Adelle Bradbury
Sales/Marketing Manager: Wayne Bradbury
Office Manager: Jennifer Griffin
Estimated Sales: $5-10 Million
Number Employees: 20-49

21906 EIT
532 W Lake St
Elmhurst, IL 60126-1408
630-279-3400
Fax: 630-279-3420 eitpromo@aol.com
Manufacturer and exporter of flags and promotional products
Owner: Mark Tober
CFO: Lucille Tobor
VP: Mark Tobor
Quality Control: Beth Pirc
Chairman of the Board: Earl Tobor
Estimated Sales: Below $5 Million
Number Employees: 5 to 9
Square Footage: 32000

21907 EJ Brooks Company
2727 Paces Ferry Road
Atlanta, GE 30339
973-597-2900
Fax: 973-597-2919 800-458-7325
info@tydenbrooks.com www.tydenbrooks.com
Security seals and locking devices.
President/CEO: John Roessner
Sales Director: Paul Dietlin
Director Purchasing: George Weber
Estimated Sales: $5-10 Million
Number Employees: 250-499

21908 EKATO Corporation
700 C Lake St
St Ramsey, NJ 07436
201-825-4684
Fax: 201-825-9776 jerry.baresich@ekato.com
Manufacturer and exporter of industrial mixers and agitators for fluids and solids
President: Paul Dwelle
Sales Director: Michael Starer
Estimated Sales: $5-10,000,000
Number Employees: 10-19
Parent Co: EKATO Ruhr Und Mischtechnik-GmbH

Brands:
Esd
Ekato
Fluid
Unimix

21909 ELAU-Elektronik Automatiions
4201 W Wrightwood Avenue
Chicago, IL 60639-2095
773-342-8400
Fax: 773-342-8404 sales@elau.com
www.elau.com
Motion control systems
CEO: Thomas Cord
Business Manager: Ronda Dade
Estimated Sales: $2.5-5 Million
Number Employees: 1-4
Parent Co: Elau Germany

21910 ELBA
4717 Sweden Road
Charlotte, NC 28273-5935
704-643-5777
Fax: 704-643-2010
Complete bag making systems, ice cube bags, systems for producing extruded netting and systems to produce mesh bags from extruded material
President: Carlo Louni
CFO: Angle Louni
Contact: Paolo Azimonti
paolo@elba-spa.it
Warehouse Manager: Bill Lebact
Estimated Sales: $3-5 000,000
Number Employees: 10

21911 ELF Machinery
1555 S State Road 39
La Porte, IN 46350-6301
219-325-3060
Fax: 219-324-2884 800-328-0466
www.elfmachines.com
Manufacturer and exporter of liquid packaging equipment including fillers, cappers, labelers, induction sealers, coders, bottle cleaners, unscramblers, conveyors, turntables, etc
President: Thomas Ake Reed
CEO: Ron Sarto
International Sales Manager: Eric Thorgren
Number Employees: 100-249
Square Footage: 320000
Type of Packaging: Food Service
Brands:
Elf

21912 ELISA Technologies, Inc.
2501 NW 66th Ct
Gainesville, FL 32653-1693
352-337-3929
Fax: 352-337-3928 info@elisa-tek.com
www.elisa-tek.com
Developed of enzyme immunoassay technology for use in the food industry.
Scientific Director: Justin Bickford
justin.bickford@elisa-tek.com
Sales & Marketing: Nick Lafferman
Administrative Director: Natalie Rosskopf
Estimated Sales: $500,000-$1 Million
Number Employees: 10-19

21913 ELP Inc
366 Grant St
Elizabeth, CO 80107
303-688-2240
Fax: 303-688-2240
Packer of meat including beef, lamb, goat and pork
President: Mike Hundley
VP: Robert Hundley
Estimated Sales: $1-2.5 Million
Number Employees: 10-19
Type of Packaging: Consumer

21914 EM Industries
480 S Democrat Rd
Gibbstown, NJ 08027-1239
914-592-4660
Fax: 914-592-9469
Specialty chemicals
Contact: Kalyan Nuguru
knuguru@emindustries.com
Estimated Sales: $10-15 Million
Number Employees: 50-99

21915 EMCO
170 Monarch Ln
Miamisburg, OH 45342
661-294-9966
Fax: 937-865-6605 800-722-3626
www.emcolabels.com
Manufacturer and exporter of code labelers and printers for price marking and UPC/EAN code printing
President: Robert H Hay
Sales Manager: Morris Bargorch
Estimated Sales: $5-10 Million
Number Employees: 10
Brands:
    Coronet
    Mark Ii
    Medalist
    Regal
    Signet

21916 EMCO Packaging
2100 Commonwealth Ave
North Chicago, IL 60064
847-689-2200
Fax: 847-689-8470 www.emcochem.com
Contract packager of detergents
President & CEO: Edward Polen
Estimated Sales: $31 Million
Number Employees: 385
Parent Co: Emco Chemical Distributors, Inc.

21917 EMD Performance Materials
One International Plaza
#300
Philadelphia, PA 19113
908-591-7496
Fax: 484-652-5749 888-367-3275
Specialty testing products for the Food and Beverage industry including Microbiology Culture Media featuring granulated media for safety and convenience; the MAS-100 Eco, a lightweight, portable air sampling instrument; the HYLiTE 2system, a portable system for determining the cleanliness of surfaces and work spaces; and Test Strip Kits for rapid testing of Ions and pH measurement. Manufactures a mineral based line of colors for use in foods, dietary supplements and drugs.
President/CEO: Meiken Krebs
Contact: Matthew Girard
mgirard@emdchemicals.com
CFO: Klaus Rueth
Vice President: Octavio Diaz
Research & Development: Jim Morgera
Quality Control: Stephen Bates
Marketing Director: Rebecca Vaiarelli
Key Account Manager: Taina Franke
Public Relations: Rina Spatafore
Operations Manager: Thorsten Hartis
Production Manager: John Alestra
Plant Manager: Bob Jones
Purchasing Manager: Ron Wisda
Estimated Sales: $10-25 Million
Number Employees: 500-999
Parent Co: Merck KgaA Darmstadt

21918 EMD Products
33 Zarpa Way
Hot Springs Village, AR 71909-7108
847-549-8308
Fax: 501-922-4873 800-910-4000
emdproduct@aol.com www.emdproducts.com
Servo motion control products, single axis positioning brushless servo systems, multi-axis controllers and analog and digital brushless servo systems and software
Member: Ray Eimerman
emdproduct@aol.com

21919 EMI
4 Heritage Park Rd
Clinton, CT 06413
860-669-1199
Fax: 860-669-7461 800-243-1188
info@clevelandmixer.com
Fluid mixing and blending, wine industry tank mixers
President: Emmett Barker
Contact: Jullian Anderson
janderson@emi1.com
Estimated Sales: $10-20 000,000
Number Employees: 20-49

21920 ENJAY Converters Limited
495 Ball Street
Cobourg, ON K9A 3J6
Canada
905-372-7373
Fax: 905-377-8066 800-427-5517
sales@enjay.com www.enjay.com
Manufactures complete line of laminated and grapped cake circles and sheets

21921 ENM Co
5617 N Northwest Hwy
Chicago, IL 60646-6177
773-775-8400
Fax: 773-775-5968 enmco@aol.com
www.enmco.com
Manufacturer and exporter of counting and number devices and hour meters; also, mechanical, electro-mechanical and electronic digital counters
Owner: Nicholas Polydoris
npolydoris@enmco.com
Sales Manager: Dale Hall
Sales Manager: Lee Bryant
Sales Engineer: Megan Fitzgerald
Estimated Sales: $20-50 Million
Number Employees: 50-99

21922 ENSCO Inc
5400 Port Royal Rd
Springfield, VA 22151-2312
703-321-9000
Fax: 703-321-4529 williams.susan@ensco.com
www.ensco.com
Vision based food product color verification inspection systems; instantaneous feedback process control for food processing applications
President: Gregory B Young
gregory.young@ensco.com
CEO: Paul W Broome Iii
Director Marketing: Tom Cirillo
Estimated Sales: $80 Million
Number Employees: 100-249

21923 EP Minerals LLC
9785 Gateway Dr # 1000
Reno, NV 89521-2991
775-824-7600
Fax: 775-824-7601 www.epminerals.com
Wine industry filter aids
President: Randy Moore
CEO: David Treadwell
Vice President of Technology: Greg Miller
Director of Quality Assurance: Forrest Reed
Estimated Sales: H
Number Employees: 20-49

21924 EPCO
P.O.Box 20428
Murfreesboro, TN 37129-0428
615-893-8432
Fax: 615-890-3196 800-251-3398
www.useco.com
Manufacturer and exporter of food service equipment including bun racks, heater/proofer cabinets, banquet carts, can racks and air curtain refrigerators
Controller: Philip Keller
VP/General Manager: Thomas Taylor
VP Sales/Marketing: James Jean
Number Employees: 10-19
Square Footage: 400000
Parent Co: Standex International Corporation
Type of Packaging: Food Service

21925 EPD Technology Corporation
14 Hayes St
Elmsford, NY 10523-2502
914-592-1233
Fax: 914-347-2181 800-892-8926
Steam management products, software and services; also, infrared thermometers and ultrasonic test instruments.
President: Gary Mohr
CEO: Helen Clint
VP Marketing: Alan Bardes
Estimated Sales: $5-10 Million
Number Employees: 20-49
Square Footage: 40000
Parent Co: UE Systems

21926 EPI Labelers
1145 E Wellspring Rd
New Freedom, PA 17349-8426
717-235-8344
Fax: 717-235-0608 800-755-8344
sales@epilabelers.com www.epilabelers.com
Pressure sensitive label applicators and premium inserting equipment
President: Randy Cottalier
sales@epilabelers.com
Co-Owner: Lynn Vonderhorst
R&D: Linda Fulginiti
General Manager: Linda Fulginiti
Estimated Sales: $5-10 Million
Number Employees: 10-19

21927 EPI World Graphics
3824 147th St Ste F
Midlothian, IL 60445-3460
708-389-7500
Fax: 708-389-7522
Nameplates and labels; also, imprinting services available
President: Nancy Kolar
VP: Karen R Steffey
Purchasing: Chuck Tanner
Estimated Sales: $5-10 Million
Number Employees: 5 to 9
Square Footage: 50000

21928 EPL Technologies
237 Lancaster Avenue
Suite 2002
Devon, PA 19333
610-254-8600
Fax: 610-521-5985 800-637-3743
www.bloomberg.com
Consultant providing technology, products and services to maintain the quality of fresh cut produce
President: Paul L. Devine
CEO: Antony E. Kendall
VP Technology: William R. Romig
Commercial Manager: Lisa Herickhoff
Number Employees: 221

21929 ERC Parts Inc
4001 Cobb International Blvd N
Kennesaw, GA 30152-4374
770-984-0276
Fax: 770-951-1875 800-241-6880
marketing@erconline.com www.erconline.com
Drive-thru displays, recording devices and timers and battery chargers; importer of cash register parts; exporter of point of sale systems, parts and software; wholesaler/distributor of VAR products; serving the food service market
Owner: Chuck Rollins
cerollins@erconline.com
CFO: Stuart Dobson
Vice President: Charles Barnes
Research & Development: Timothy Adams
Marketing Director: Bryon Finkel
Parts/Manufacturing Division: Eric Hart
Purchasing Manager: Rob Haight
Estimated Sales: $1-2.5 Million
Number Employees: 50-99
Square Footage: 180000
Other Locations:
    ERC Parts
    Louisville KY
    ERC Parts
    Lexington KY
    ERC Parts
    Cleveland OH
    ERC Parts
    Las Vegas NV
    ERC Parts
    Baltimore MD
    ERC Parts
    Greensboro NC
    ERC Parts
    Raleigh NC

21930 ERO/Goodrich Forest Products
19255 SW 65th Ave # 110
Tualatin, OR 97062-9717
503-885-9414
Fax: 503-625-5825 800-458-5545
Manufacturer and exporter of plywood shipping containers and pallets
Manager: Elizabeth Brashear
Sales Manager: Harry Nelson
Estimated Sales: $1-5 Million
Number Employees: 16
Type of Packaging: Bulk

21931 ERS International
488 Main Avenue
Norwalk, CT 06851-1008

203-849-2500
Fax: 203-849-2501 800-377-4685
Electronic displays and shelf labels
CEO and President: Bruce Failing
Number Employees: 50-99
Square Footage: 20000
Brands:
Shelfnet

21932 ES Robbins Corp
2802 Avalon Ave
Muscle Shoals, AL 35661-3748

256-248-2400
Fax: 256-248-2410 800-633-3325
info@esrchairmats.com www.esrobbins.com
Expandable and collapsible reusable beverage and
food storage containers, plastic measuring caps and
canisters
Owner: Amanda Berryman
CFO: Ron Mansel
CEO: Edward S Robbins Iii
VP Sales/Marketing: Steve Doerr
berryman@esrchairmats.com
Purchasing Manager: Nancy Hamilton
Estimated Sales: $10-20 Million
Number Employees: 100-249
Parent Co: E.S. Robbins Corporation
Brands:
Flex-Flo
Kleer-Measure
Poptite

21933 ESD Energy Saving Devices
1751 Highway 36 E
St Paul, MN 55109-2108

651-222-0849
Fax: 651-222-4626
Commercial and industrial fluorescent and vapor
tight lighting fixtures
President: Kerry Petersen
VP: Mike Holder
Estimated Sales: Below $5 Million
Number Employees: 5-9

21934 ESD Waste2water Inc
495 Oak Rd
Ocala, FL 34472-3005

352-680-9134
Fax: 352-867-1320 800-277-3279
info@waste2water.com www.waste2water.com
Manufacturer and exporter of water treatment equip-
ment
Manager: Kevin Hawkins
Estimated Sales: $2.5-5 Million
Number Employees: 20-49
Square Footage: 100000
Parent Co: Zentox
Brands:
Cascade

21935 ESE Inc
3600 Downwind Dr
Marshfield, WI 54449-8656

715-387-4778
Fax: 715-387-0125 800-236-4778
sudat@ese1.com www.eseautomation.com
Owner: Mark Weber
CEO: Michael Richart
richartm@ese1.com
Director of Sales: Brandon Teachman
Director of Operations: Justin Hobson
Estimated Sales: $2.5-5 Million
Number Employees: 20-49

21936 ESE, Inc
PO Box 1107
Marshfield, WI 54449-7107

715-387-4778
Fax: 715-387-0125 800-236-4778
sudat@ese1.com www.ese1.com
Process control systems; also, specialty applications
and integration services available for PC based
systems
President: Mark Weber
Director of Sales: Brandon Teachman
Contact: Gwen Irvan
irvang@ese1.com
Director of Operations: Justin Hobson
Estimated Sales: $5-10 Million
Number Employees: 5-9
Square Footage: 68000

21937 ESI Group
950 Walnut Ridge Dr
Hartland, WI 53029-9388

262-369-3535
Fax: 262-369-3536 866-369-3535
sales@esigroupusa.com www.esigroupusa.com
ESI is an industry leading design-build firm focused
on the new construction, expansion and renovation
of foodservice facilities. Our single source approach
streamlines the building process allowing the team
at ESI to remain focusedon the needs of the customer, the success of their project and their financial
bottom line.
President: Brad Barke
bbarke@esigroupusa.com
Number Employees: 50-99

21938 ESI Qual Intl
968 Washington St # 2
Stoughton, MA 02072-2973

781-344-6344
Fax: 781-341-3978 800-443-0511
info@esiqual.com www.esiqual.com
Enviromental services and equipment, laboratory
testing equipment, sanitation supplies and equip-
ment, environmental, occupational, and food safety
consultants.
President/CEO: Phil Ventresca
info@esiqual.com
Vice President: Vince Vantresca
Estimated Sales: Below 1 Million
Number Employees: 5-9

21939 ESKAY Corporation
5202 D Corrigan Way Ste 100
Salt Lake City, UT 84116

801-363-6100
Fax: 801-359-9911 800-253-1003
info@eskay.com
Designs, sells, installs, and supports a complete line
of world-class logistics systems for automated material handling in factory, distribution, and cleanroom
environments. Full range of advanced-technology
products forrefrigerated/frozen food distribution includes conveyors, sortation systems, transport vehicles, order-picking systems, automated storage
buffers, and real-time warehouse management
software (WMS)
President: Itsud Oyamatsu

21940 ESS Technologies
3160 State St
Blacksburg, VA 24060-6603

540-961-5716
Fax: 540-961-5721 info@esstechnologies.com
www.esstechnologies.com
Supplier of packaging equipment including
overwrapping and bundling; shrinkwrapping, stretch
banding, automatic cartoning and case packing;
candy wrapping equipment; filling and packaging
equipment; turnkey lines and integrationservices.
President: Kevin Browne
Vice President: Linda Browne
Director, Global Business Development: Walter
Langosch
Estimated Sales: $1-2.5 Million

21941 ESummits
PO BOX 27946
Scottsdale, AZ 90831-0002

562-983-8050
Fax: 562-983-8051 800-643-0797
www.esummits.com
Marketing company, promote food products globally
Chief Executive Officer, Director: Paul Ortman
Estimated Sales: Below $500,000
Number Employees: 1-4

21942 ET International Technologies
3705 Kipling Street
Suite 103
Wheat Ridge, CO 80033

303-854-9087
Fax: 303-722-7379 855-412-5726
Manufacturer and exporter of hot tapping machines
for the HVAC/R and piping industries
President: Greg Apple

21943 ETS Laboratories
899 Adams St # A
St Helena, CA 94574-1160

707-963-4806
Fax: 707-963-1054 info@etslabs.com
www.etslabs.com
Wine, beer, and spirits testing, ISO Guide 25 accred-
ited
President: Gordon Burns
gburns@etslabs.com
Estimated Sales: $1-2.5 000,000
Number Employees: 20-49

21944 EVAPCO Inc
5151 Allendale Ln
Taneytown, MD 21787-2155

410-876-3782
Fax: 410-756-6450 marketing@evapco.com
www.evapco.com
Manufacturer and exporter of industrial refrigeration
equipment including evaporative condensers, cool-
ing towers, evaporators, vessels, valves, recirculator
packages, rooftop hygienic air systems, and closed
curcuit coolers
President: Bill Bartley
bbartley@evapco.com
CFO: Harold Walsh
VP: Joseph Mondato
VP Marketing/Sales: Dave Rule
Number Employees: 5-9
Square Footage: 360000

21945 EXE Technologies
8787 N Stemmons Fwy
Dallas, TX 75247

214-775-6000
Fax: 214-775-0900 800-393-8324
Warehouse management systems, supply chain dis-
tribution
CEO: Raymond Hood
Senior VP Professional Services/CFO: Michael
Burstein
Contact: Miroslav Buran
miroslav.buran@exe.sk
Director: Adam Belsky
Estimated Sales: $35-40 Million
Number Employees: 100

21946 EZ-Tek Industries
7041 Boone Avenue
Brooklyn Park, MN 55428

800-835-9344
Fax: 763-795-8867 800-796-3279
info@eztek.com www.eztek.com
Manufacturer and exporter of case sealers, tapers,
material handling and packaging equipment; im-
porter of case sealers, tapers and strappers
President: Bob Kops
CFO: Bob Kops
Estimated Sales: $1 Million
Number Employees: 4
Brands:
Easy Gluer
Easy Strapper
Easy Taper

21947 EZE-Lap Diamond Products
3572 Arrowhead Dr
Carson City, NV 89706-2006

775-888-9500
Fax: 775-888-9555 800-843-4815
sales@eze-lap.com www.eze-lap.com
Sharpeners and sharpening stones for knives, slicing
wheels, saw chains and pizza cutters; also, grinding
equipment
President: Jack Fletcher
sales@eze-lap.com
Sales Coordinator: Donna Long
Office Manager: Lisa Fletcher
sales@eze-lap.com
General Manager: Ralph Johnson
Estimated Sales: $1-20,000,000
Number Employees: 10-19
Brands:
Diamond

21948 Eagle Bakery Equipment
9989 Lickinghole Road
Ashland, VA 23005

804-798-8920
Fax: 804-752-6828
support@eaglebakeryequipment.com
www.eaglebakeryequipment.com
Bun, bread make-up lines and equipment, dough
pumps, tortillia and speciality equipment
Manager: Paul Peebles
CFO: Wd David Abbott
R&D: Howard Brandon
Quality Control: Howard Brandon
Sales: Mac Broddus

Estimated Sales: Below $5 000,000
Number Employees: 1-4

21949 Eagle Box Company
1 Adams Blvd Ste 1
Farmingdale, NY 11735

212-255-3860
Fax: 212-249-4517 info@eaglebox.com
www.eaglebox.com
Printed folding paperboard cartons
Owner: Jay Hoffman
Sales Director: Jim Fahlgren
Plant Manager: Steve Williamson
Estimated Sales: $10 Million
Number Employees: 20-49
Square Footage: 160000

21950 Eagle Foodservice Equipment
100 Industrial Blvd
Clayton, DE 19938

302-653-3000
Fax: 302-653-2065 800-441-8440
answers@eaglegrp.com www.eaglegrp.com
Manufacturer and exporter of wire, solid and polymer shelving, work tables, sinks, handsinks, countertop equipment, underbar equipment, bun pans, as well as custom fabricated items
Owner: Larry N McAllister
Sales Director: Linda Donavon
Number Employees: 250-499
Type of Packaging: Food Service

21951 Eagle Group
100 Industrial Blvd
Clayton, DE 19938-8903

302-653-3000
Fax: 302-653-2065 800-441-8440
customerservice@eaglegrp.com
Manufacturer and exporter of stainless steel food service equipment including shelving, sinks, tables, cookers, warmers and bar equipment
Owner: Larry Mccallister
Sales: Linda Donavon
lmccallister@eaglegroup.com
Estimated Sales: $50-75 Million
Number Employees: 250-499
Parent Co: Eagle Group
Brands:
    Lifestore
    Panco

21952 Eagle Home Products
1 Arnold Dr # 1
Huntington, NY 11743-3981

631-673-3500
Fax: 631-673-6700 www.eaglehomeproducts.com
Manufacturer, importer and exporter of cleaning aids and rubber gloves
Owner: Robert Chemtob
rchemtob@eaglehomeproducts.com
Vice President: Andre Chemtob
Estimated Sales: $5-10 Million
Number Employees: 20-49
Square Footage: 20000
Brands:
    Denta Brite
    Diamond Brite
    Diamond Grip
    Eagle
    Eagle Absolute
    Soft Touch

21953 Eagle Labeling
1741 Industrial Dr
Sterling, IL 61081-9290

815-625-1858
Fax: 815-625-8554 800-527-7549
Custom label applicators, labeling in-line, label dispensors, automation
Estimated Sales: Below $500,000
Number Employees: 5-9

21954 Eagle Packaging Corp
2100 Dennison St
Oakland, CA 94606-5236

510-533-3000
Fax: 510-534-3000 800-824-EAGL
pesales@parsons-eagle.com www.eaglepack.net
Vice President: Russ Davis
r.davis@eaglepack.net
Vice President: Russ Davis
r.davis@eaglepack.net
Estimated Sales: $20-50 Million
Number Employees: 10-19

21955 Eagle Packaging Corp
2100 Dennison St
Oakland, CA 94606-5236

510-533-3000
Fax: 510-534-3000 800-824-3245
info@eaglepack.net
President: Peter Hatchell
Vice President: Pierce Butler
Product Manager: Jeff Reed
Vice President of Sales: Pete Butler
Estimated Sales: $10 Million
Number Employees: 10-19

21956 Eagle Products Company
P.O.Box 431601
Houston, TX 77243-1601

713-690-1161
Fax: 713-690-7661 info@eaglechair.com
www.eaglechair.com
Quality manufacturer and exporter of booths, chairs, bar stools, tabletops and bases
Executive Director: Maximillian Yurgulich
CEO: Natalia Jurcic-Koc
CFO: Nathalai Kac
Contact: Max Yuglich
max@eaglechair.com
Director of Operations: Max Yuglich
Estimated Sales: $5-10 Million
Number Employees: 10-19
Square Footage: 80000
Parent Co: Eagle Chair
Type of Packaging: Food Service
Brands:
    Eagle Chair

21957 Eagle Research Inc
2375 Bush St
San Francisco, CA 94115-3123

415-495-3131
Fax: 415-441-6709 info@xeaglex.com
www.xeaglex.com
Custom software for any indsutry
President: Allen Gleazer
allen@xeaglex.com
Vice President: Nina Rosa carino
Vice President: Nina Carino
Estimated Sales: $1-5 000,000
Number Employees: 1-4

21958 Eagle Wire Works
3173 E 66th St
Cleveland, OH 44127

216-341-8550
Fax: 216-341-6460
Refrigerator racks and stands and racks to hold plastic bags
President: James J Malik
Contact: Jim Bartolotta
jimb@eaglewireworks.com
Estimated Sales: $1-2.5 Million
Number Employees: 5-9

21959 Eagle-Concordia Paper Corporation
1 Adams Blvd
Farmingdale, NY 11735-6611

212-255-3860
Fax: 212-249-4530 info@eaglebox.com
www.eaglebox.com
Wholesaler/distributor of boxes, cartons, packaging tape, bubble wrap, etc.; also, package design services available
Owner: Michael Hoffman
Estimated Sales: $10-20 Million
Number Employees: 20-49

21960 Eagles Printing & Label
1206 International Dr
Eau Claire, WI 54701-7052

715-835-6631
Fax: 715-835-1601 eagles@eaglesprinting.com
www.eaglesprinting.com
Commercial printing and labels
President: Barb Sands
eagles@eaglesprinting.com
Estimated Sales: $1-2.5 Million
Number Employees: 20-49

21961 Eagleware Manufacturing
12683 Corral Pl
Santa Fe Springs, CA 90670

562-20 -100
Fax: 314-527-4314

Contact: J Gross
j.gross@alegacy.com
Parent Co: Harold Leonard & Company

21962 Eagleware Manufacturing
2835 E Ana Street
Compton, CA 90221-5601

310-604-0404
Fax: 310-604-1748
Manufacturer and exporter of cookware
President: Jesse Gross
Vice President: Brett Gross
Estimated Sales: Below $5,000,000
Number Employees: 10
Square Footage: 140000
Parent Co: Harold Leonard & Company
Brands:
    Eagleware

21963 Eam
19 Pomerleau St
Biddeford, ME 04005-9457

207-283-3001
Fax: 207-283-3023 info@eaminc.com
www.eaminc.com
Owner: John Grondin
Outside Sales: Kevin Call
jgrondin@prescottmetal.com
Estimated Sales: $3-5 Million
Number Employees: 20-49

21964 Eam-Mosca Corporation
675 Jaycee Dr
Hazle Township, PA 18202

570-459-3426
Fax: 570-455-2442 info@eammosca.com
www.eammosca.com
Plastic strapping systems for pallets, off-line and in-line strappers, side-seal pallet strappers, drive-thru pallet strappers and horizontal pallet strapper
President: Daniel Dreher
Regional Sales Manager: Jim Gum
Contact: Sal Carsia
america2@americanpigeonracing.com
Sales Coordinator: Denise Casanova
Estimated Sales: $30-50 Million
Number Employees: 50-99

21965 Earl Soesbe Company
1347 Enterprise Drive
Romeoville, IL 60446-1015

219-866-4191
Fax: 219-866-7979
Bulk material handling equipment including self-dumping hoppers
President: Jerry Schlottmann
Sales Manager: Claas Schlottmann
Estimated Sales: $2.5-5 Million
Number Employees: 10-19
Square Footage: 106000

21966 Earthstone Wood-Fire Ovens
6717 San Fernando Rd
Glendale, CA 91201-1704

818-553-1134
Fax: 818-553-1133 800-840-4915
info@earthstoneovens.com
www.earthstoneovens.com
Manufacturer/exporter of wood and gas fire ovens including pre-assembled, commercial kit and residential; also, wood fire training available
Principal: Maurice Yotnegparian
Principal: Jean-Paul Yotnegparian
Estimated Sales: $3-5 Million
Number Employees: 15
Square Footage: 60000
Brands:
    Earthstone

21967 Earthy Delights
1161 E Clark Road
Suite 260
Dewitt, MI 48820

517-668-2402
Fax: 517-668-1213 800-367-4709
info@earthy.com www.earthy.com
Specialty foods
President: Ed Baker
eb@earthy.com
Marketing: Angie Pacgett
Estimated Sales: $2.5 Million
Number Employees: 12

21968 Eash Industries
120 Rush Ct
Elkhart, IN 46516
574-295-4450
Fax: 574-389-1190
High gloss bar tops and tables; also, custom logos
and inlaid graphics available
President: Todd Eash
Contact: Lisa Eash
eashindustries@hotmail.com
Estimated Sales: $2.5-5,000,000
Number Employees: 5-9
Brands:
Diamond Clear

21969 East Bay Fixture Co
941 Aileen St
Emeryville, CA 94608-2805
510-652-4421
Fax: 510-652-5915 800-995-4521
rick@ebfc.com www.eastbayfixture.com
Store fixtures
Owner: Richard Laible
rick@ebfc.com
Estimated Sales: $5-10 Million
Number Employees: 20-49

21970 East Coast Group New York
23209 Merrick Boulevard
Springfield Gardens, NY 11413-2116
718-527-8464
Fax: 718-527-8498
Garbage, insulated, multi-wall and plastic bags and
packaging materials
Sr Partner: Trevor Ford
Estimated Sales: $500,000-$1,000,000
Number Employees: 9
Brands:
East Coast

21971 East Coast Mold Manufacturing
30 Eastern Ave # 1
Deer Park, NY 11729-3100
631-253-2397
Fax: 631-254-6682 800-933-9533
Candy and confectionery equipment
President: Sebastian Piccione
Number Employees: 5-9

21972 East Memphis Rubber Stamp Company
6246 Acorn Dr
Bartlett, TN 38134-4608
901-384-0887
Fax: 901-384-3507
Rubber stamps
President: Buddy Good
VP Marketing: Buddy Good
Estimated Sales: Below $5 Million
Number Employees: 1 to4

21973 Easterday Belting Company
1400 E Touhy Ave # 409
Des Plaines, IL 60018-3341
847-297-8200
Fax: 847-803-9290
Thermal and solid color jet inks, for small character
jet printers
Owner: Azam Nizamudiz
Estimated Sales: $5-10 000,000
Number Employees: 10-19

21974 Easterday Fluid Technologies
4343 S Kansas Ave
Saint Francis, WI 53235
414-482-4488
Fax: 414-482-3720
Supplies the food processing industry thermal sensi-
tive coding links. Manufactures thermal sensitive,
solid color, and UV jet inks for noncontact jet print-
ers for tough, reliable product codes on retorted food
containers andpasteurization processes of the beer
and beverage industry
President: Max Baum
Director Operations: Lee Robbins
National/International Services Manager: Paul
Oetlinger
Estimated Sales: $1-3 Million
Number Employees: 5-9
Square Footage: 12000
Brands:
Easterday

21975 Eastern Bakery Co
475 Stevens Rd
York Haven, PA 17370-9236
717-938-8278
Fax: 717-938-3060
Manufacturers of bakery equipment
President and R&D: Ken Johson
CFO: Cindy Ng
Quality Control: Jeff Love
Manager: Jeff Love
jlove@eb-sys.com
Plant Manager: Jeff Love
Estimated Sales: Below $5 000,000
Number Employees: 10-19
Parent Co: Gemini Bakery Equipment Company

21976 Eastern Cap & Closure Company
726 N Kresson Street
Baltimore, MD 21205-2907
410-327-5640
Fax: 410-522-6068
Caps and closures for bottles and jars
Manager: John Lepus
Number Employees: 30
Square Footage: 98000
Parent Co: Penn Bottle & Supply Company

21977 Eastern Container Corporation
60 Maple St
Mansfield, MA 02048-1505
508-337-0400
Fax: 508-339-8493 www.smurfitstone.com
Corrugated shipping containers and displays
General Manager: Randy Thrasher
Estimated Sales: $5-10 Million
Number Employees: 250-499
Parent Co: Eastern Container
Brands:
Radio Pack

21978 Eastern Design & Development Corporation
PO Box 440
Hershey, PA 17033-0440
717-533-2452
Fax: 717-533-2036
Confectionary and baking equipment
Estimated Sales: $1-2.5 000,000
Number Employees: 20-49

21979 Eastern Envelope
5 Laurel Dr
Flanders, NJ 07836-4701
973-584-3311
Fax: 973-584-4125
Envelopes
President: Jerome Kessler
Estimated Sales: $1-2.5 Million
Number Employees: 5-9

21980 Eastern Machine
80 Turnpike Dr # 2
Middlebury, CT 06762-1830
203-598-0066
Fax: 203-598-0068
Manufacturer and exporter of capping machinery for
metal and plastic screw and snap caps; also, cap
tighteners, fitment applicators and trigger sprayers
President: David Baker
Number Employees: 5-9
Square Footage: 20000

21981 Eastern Plastics
PO Box 1266
Pawtucket, RI 02862-1266
401-724-8050
Fax: 401-728-3770 800-442-8585
Clear acrylic products including bulk food bins, step
up racks, product displays, bag holders, description
holders, literature dispensers, recipe card holders,
etc
President: Jim Rosenthal
Sales Representative: Irene Champagne
Number Employees: 20
Square Footage: 20000

21982 Eastern Poly Packaging Company
53 Prospect Park W
Brooklyn, NY 11215-2629
718-788-4700
Fax: 718-788-5463 800-421-6006
www.easternpoly.com
Printed and plain bags including polypropylene and
polyethylene

Owner: Stephen Somers
General Manager: Tran Van Lam
Director: Tran Minh Tam
Estimated Sales: $2.5-5 Million
Number Employees: 20-49
Parent Co: X

21983 Eastern Tabletop Mfg
1943 Pitkin Ave
Brooklyn, NY 11207-3312
718-240-9595
Fax: 718-240-9797 888-422-4142
sales@easterntabletop.com
www.easterntabletop.com
High quality silver plated and stainless steel food
service equipment including chafing dishes, coffee
urns, trays, serving and tabletop accessories,
punchbowls and candelabras
President: Sol Basch
sol@easterntabletop.com
Estimated Sales: $10-20 Million
Number Employees: 10-19
Brands:
Eastern

21984 Eastey Enterprises
7041 Boone Avenue
Brooklyn Park, MN 55428
800-835-9344
Fax: 763-795-8867 800-835-9344
parts_eastey@dgi.net www.eastey.com
Electric or air operated L-sealers, shrink tunnels,
high speed tunnels, banding tunnels, bundling tunnels and manual or automatic sleeve wrapping
systems
President: Jeff Eastey
Contact: John Belden
john@eastey.com
Estimated Sales: $4 Million
Number Employees: 20-49

21985 Easy Lift Equipment Co Inc
2 Mill Park Ct
Newark, DE 19713-1986
302-737-8784
Fax: 302-737-7333 800-233-1800
sales@easylifteqpt.com www.easylifteqpt.com
Manufacturers of Drum & Roll handling Equipment
President: Lorea Eastbrun
eastbrun@easylifteqpt.com
Estimated Sales: $5-10 Million
Number Employees: 5-9

21986 Easy-Care Environs
7002 Maplewood Court SW
Olympia, WA 98512-2031
360-754-1013
Fax: 360-754-1013
Specialty walls and ceilings (glass, FRP)

21987 Easybar Corp
19799 SW 95th Ave # A
Suite A
Tualatin, OR 97062-7584
503-624-6744
Fax: 503-624-6741 888-294-7405
info@easybar.com www.easybar.com
Manufacturer and exporter of liquor, beer, wine and
soda dispensers.
President: Gorham Nicol
gnicol@easybar.com
CEO: James Nicol
Marketing: Sarah Puglia
Sales: Margo Winquist
Estimated Sales: $5-10 Million
Number Employees: 20-49
Brands:
Easybar

21988 (HQ)Easyup Storage Systems
18271 Andover Park W
Tukwila, WA 98188-4706
206-394-3330
Fax: 206-575-6829 800-426-9234
www.easyupusa.com
Boltless steel storage and shelving systems
President: Dave Saman
VP: Kyle Jones
VP/C-Store Manager: Ken Davis
Estimated Sales: Less Than $500,000
Number Employees: 1-4
Square Footage: 56000
Brands:
Easy Up

21989 Eatec Corporation
1900 Powell St
Suite 230
Emeryville, CA 94608
510-594-9011
Fax: 510-549-1959 877-374-4783
info@agilysys.com www.agilysys.com
A provider of enterprise back-office software and services for the foodservice and hospitality industries. EatecNetX, Eatec's proven software solution, is recognized as a state-of-the-art foodservice management system that iscentralizzed, scalable, web-centric and user-friendly for food and beverage operators of every variety.
Contact: Scot Benbow
s.benbow@eatec.com
Manager: Jeff Gebhardt
Estimated Sales: $5-10 Million
Number Employees: 20-49
Brands:
  Catertec
  Clubtec
  Eatec Netx
  Eatec System

21990 Eatem Foods Co
1829 Gallagher Dr
Vineland, NJ 08360-1548
856-692-1663
Fax: 856-692-0847 800-683-2836
sales@eatemfoods.com
Food base manufacturing; supplier of savory flavor systems, flavor concentrates, broth concentrates and seasoning bases.
Vice President: Gerrie Bouchard
gerriebouchard@gmail.com
Chief Technical Officer: John Randazzi
Chief Financial Officer: Danine Freeman
Vice President, Treasurer: Mario Riviello
Director, R&D: Bill Cawley
Marketing Manager: Gerrie Bouchard
Vice President, Sales: Don Witherspoon
Director of Operations: Jerry Santo
Estimated Sales: $14 Million
Number Employees: 50-99
Square Footage: 12916
Type of Packaging: Consumer, Food Service, Bulk
Brands:
  Eatem

21991 (HQ)Eaton Corporation
1000 Eaton Blvd
Beachwood, OH 44122
800-386-1911
www.eaton.com
Manufacturer and exporter of emergency, indoor and outdoor lighting
Chairman & CEO: Craig Arnold
Vice Chairman & CFO: Richard Fearon
Executive VP & General Counsel: April Miller Boise
Executive VP, Supply Chain Management: Rogerico Branco
Estimated Sales: $21.4 Billion
Number Employees: 97,000

21992 Eaton Electrical Sector
1000 Cherrington Pkwy
Moon Township, PA 15108
877-386-2273
www.eaton.com/Eaton/ProductsServices/Electrical
Controls and control systems, electrical distribution, electronics components, lighting, metering, monitoring and protection.
President & COO, Electrical Sector: Uday Yadav
President, Americas: Brian Brickhouse
Parent Co: Eaton Corporation

21993 Eaton Equipment
5210 State Road 133
PO Box 55
Boscobel, WI 53805-9134
608-375-2256
Fax: 608-375-2256 www.mwt.net
Homoginizers, cheese equipment, custom fabrication, heat exchangers, plate, agitators, cookers, ford, hoop washers, hoops, knives, molds, automatic presses, manual presses, piping, fittings and sanitary tubing
President: Don Eaton
eatoneq@mwt.net
Estimated Sales: $500,000-$1 Million
Number Employees: 1-4

21994 Eaton Filtration, LLC
44 Apple Street
Tinton Falls, NJ 07724
732-212-4700
Fax: 952-906-3706 800-859-9212
www.filtration.eaton.com
Manufacturer and exporter of fluid filters and strainers
Chairman & CEO: Craig Arnold
President & COO, Industrial Sector: Heath Monesmith
Vice Chairman & CFO: Richard H. Fearon
Number Employees: 50-99
Parent Co: Eaton Corporation
Brands:
  Ronningen-Petter

21995 Eaton Manufacturing Co
1201 Holly St
Houston, TX 77007-6241
713-223-2331
Fax: 713-223-2342 800-328-6610
www.eatonmfg.com
Manufacturer and exporter of labels, laminated films, cash control envelopes and bags including polyethylene, polypropylene and ice
President: Tom B Eaton Jr
General Manager: Joe Williams
Estimated Sales: $5-10 Million
Number Employees: 20-49
Square Footage: 100000

21996 Eaton Quade Plastics & Sign Co
1116 W Main St
Oklahoma City, OK 73106-7854
405-236-4475
Fax: 405-236-4520 doug@eatonquade.com
www.eatonquade.com
Custom formed plastics including sneeze protectors, displays, food display covers, etc
President: Doug Swindell
doug@eatonquade.com
Estimated Sales: $1-2.5 Million
Number Employees: 5-9
Square Footage: 30000

21997 (HQ)Eaton Sales & Service
PO Box 16405
Denver, CO 80216
303-296-4800
Fax: 303-296-5749 800-208-2657
sales@eatonmetal.com www.eatonmetalsales.com
Atmospheric and pressure tanks; also, installation services available
President: Timothy J Travis
CFO: Dorothy Martin
General Manager Administration: Kirby Boutelle
Estimated Sales: $20-50 Million
Number Employees: 50-99

21998 Ebel Tape & Label
1832 Westwood Ave
Cincinnati, OH 45214-1347
513-471-1067
Fax: 513-471-5657
Tapes including gummed and pressure sensitive; also, pressure sensitive labels
President: Greg Dulle
CFO: James Dulle
Contact: Larry Heidemann
ebellabel@fuse.net
Estimated Sales: Below $5 Million
Number Employees: 5 to 9

21999 Ebenezer Flag Company
64 Spring St
Newport, RI 02840-6803
401-846-1891
Fax: 401-849-1640
Flags and banners
President: Tina Croce
Estimated Sales: less than $500,000
Number Employees: 1 to4

22000 Eberbach Corp
505 S Maple Rd
Ann Arbor, MI 48103-3836
734-665-8877
Fax: 734-665-9099 800-422-2558
info@eberbachlabtools.com
www.eberbachlabtools.com
Laboratory and pilot-plant equipment, instruments, apparatus, shakers, mixers, homogenizers and blenders

President: Ralph O Boehnke Jr
CFO: Ralph O Boehnke Jr
R&D: Chris Boehnke Jr
Quality Control: Ralph O Boehnke Jr
Estimated Sales: Below $5 000,000
Number Employees: 10-19

22001 EcFood.Com
4655 Old Ironsides Dr
Santa Clara, CA 95054-1808
408-496-2900
Fax: 408-566-6148 877-532-7253
Estimated Sales: $1-5 Million
Number Employees: 1-4

22002 EcFood.com
410 Jessie St
San Francisco, CA 94103-1834
415-869-6100
Fax: 415-869-6148 877-532-7253
President: Dave Laukat
Estimated Sales: $10-20 Million
Number Employees: 20-49

22003 Eckels Bilt
7700 Harwell St
Fort Worth, TX 76108-1806
817-246-4555
Fax: 817-246-7139 800-343-9020
info@eckelsbilt.com www.eckelsbilt.com
Manufacturer and exporter of conveyor belt automatic tracking systems
President: John Mic Kunas
johnm@eckelsbilt.com
Sales Manager: Tony Keeton
Estimated Sales: $5-10 Million
Number Employees: 10-19
Square Footage: 15000
Brands:
  True Tracker

22004 Ecklund-Harrison Technologies
11000 Metro Pkwy # 40
Fort Myers, FL 33966-1245
239-936-6032
Fax: 239-936-6327 www.ecklund-harrison.com
Manufacturer and exporter of heat penetration equipment and pasteurization monitor computers
President: Daneil Highbaugh
kathy@ecklund-harrison.com
Estimated Sales: $500,000
Number Employees: 1-4

22005 Eclipse Electric Manufacturing
6512 Walker St
St Louis Park, MN 55426
952-929-2500
Fax: 952-929-0024 emailchico@aol.com
Electric custom lighting fixtures
President: David Jenkins
emailchico@aol.com
VP Marketing: Dave Jenkins
Estimated Sales: $1-2.5 Million
Number Employees: 5-9
Square Footage: 40000

22006 Eclipse Espresso Systems
1733 Westlake Avenue N
Seattle, WA 98109-3014
206-587-3767
Fax: 206-587-0339
members.aol.com/eclsystm/parts.htm
Tea and coffee industry blending and mixing equipment, dryers and feeders, evaporators
Estimated Sales: $500,000-$1 Million
Number Employees: 5

22007 Eclipse Innovative Thermal Solutions
5040 Enterprise Blvd
Toledo, OH 43612
419-729-9726
Fax: 419-729-9705 800-662-3966
sales@exothermics.com
Industrial air-to-air heat exchangers and heat recovery equipment; exporter of industrial heat exchangers
Manager: Paul Wilde
R&D: Bob Shaffer
Contact: Sheryl Holbrook
sholbrook@eclipsenet.com
Number Employees: 20-49
Square Footage: 70000
Parent Co: Eclipse

22008 Eclipse Systems Inc
943 Hanson Ct
Milpitas, CA 95035-3166

408-263-2201
Fax: 408-559-2252
Manufacturer and exporter of mixers including electric and pneumatic drive
Owner: Jerry Grose
CFO: Helen Fletcher
Sales Director: Diane Olsen
jerrygrose@eclipsesystems.com
Estimated Sales: $20-50 Million
Number Employees: 1-4
Square Footage: 30000
Parent Co: Technology General Corporation
Brands:
Pneumix

22009 Eco Fish Inc
340 Central Ave # 303
Suite 305
Dover, NH 03820-3770

603-834-6034
Fax: 603-430-9929 comments@ecofish.com
www.ecofish.com
Distributor and promoter of ecologically sound seafood
President: Henry Lovejoy
henry@ecofish.com
Manager: Hector Gudino
Estimated Sales: $1-3 Million
Number Employees: 5-9

22010 Eco-Air Products
7466 Carroll Rd # 101
San Diego, CA 92121-2356

858-271-8111
Fax: 858-578-3816 800-284-8111
pcurrie@shoreline.com
Manufacturer and exporter of air, rangehood and grease filters
President: Wesley Measamer
CFO: John Hodson
Vice President of Division: Charlie Kwiatkowski
Manager: Robert Jaquay
Quality Control: Bill Stevens
VP Marketing: Bill O'Brien
Director of Sales: Bill Cawley
Senior Vice President of Operations: Kirk Dominick
Estimated Sales: $30-50 Million
Number Employees: 20-49
Square Footage: 110000

22011 Eco-Bag Products
23-25 Spring St, #302
Ossining, NY 10562

914-944-4556
Fax: 914-271-4867 800-720-2247
sales@ecobags.com www.eco-bags.com
Manufacturer, importer and exporter of natural and organic cotton bags including shopping and promotional tote, lunch and produce; printing services available
President: Sharon Rowe
Marketing: Ellen Ornato
PR & Communications: Rob Bradey
Estimated Sales: Below $5 Million
Number Employees: 1-4
Type of Packaging: Consumer, Food Service, Bulk
Brands:
Eco-Bags

22012 Eco-Pak Products Engineering
P.O.Box 179
Fenton, MO 63026-0179

636-305-9800
Fax: 636-305-9800
Multi-packaging for beverage and food products, customizing packaging with or without full color graphics
President: Helly Miller
Estimated Sales: Less than $500,000
Number Employees: 1-4

22013 Ecodyne Water Treatment, LLC
1270 Frontenac Rd
Naperville, IL 60563

630-961-5043
Fax: 630-671-8846 800-228-9326
Manufacturer and exporter of water treatment equipment including softeners, filters and reverse osmosis systems

President: Patrick O'Neill
Finance Executive: Todd Mc Gee
Research & Development: Wayne Simpson
Quality Control: Mark Thenhaus
Sales Director: Patrick O'Neill
Public Relations: Patrick O'Neill
Operations Manager: Mark Thenhaus
Production Manager: Mark Thenhaus
Plant Manager: Mark Thenhaus
Purchasing Manager: Mark Thenhaus
Estimated Sales: $5-10,000,000
Number Employees: 20-49
Square Footage: 50000
Brands:
Red Line

22014 Ecolab Inc
1 Ecolab Place
St. Paul, MN 55102-2233

Fax: 651-225-3098 800-352-5326
institutionalorders@ecolab.com www.ecolab.com
Cleaning and sanitizing products, equipment, systems and services for the agribusiness, beverage, brewery, pharmaceutical, dairy, meat, poultry and food processing industries.
Chairman & Chief Executive Officer: Douglas Baker, Jr.
President & Chief Operating Officer: Christophe Beck
Chief Financial Officer: Daniel Schmechel
EVP & President, Global Institutional: Timothy Mulhere
EVP & GM, Global Food & Beverage: Nicholas Alfano
EVP & President, Global Nalco Water: Christophe Beck
EVP & Chief Information Officer: Anil Arcalgud
EVP & Chief Technical Officer: Dr. Larry Berger
EVP & Chief Supply Chain Officer: Mike Duijser
EVP, Corporate Strategy: Angela Busch
SVP & Corporate Controller: Scott Kirkland
Year Founded: 1923
Estimated Sales: $13.84 Billion
Number Employees: 48,400
Square Footage: 24135
Type of Packaging: Food Service

22015 Ecolo Odor Control Systems Worldwide
59 Penn Drive
North York, ON M9L 2A6
Canada

416-740-3900
Fax: 416-740-3800 800-667-6355
info@ecolo.com www.ecolo.com
Manufacturer and exporter of odor control systems and air solutions to deodorize washrooms, garbage rooms, transfer stations, waste water treatment plants, etc
President: Calvin Sager
Vice President: Ian Howard
Marketing Director: Cindy Pickard
Director Manufacturing: John Linthwaite
Number Employees: 20
Square Footage: 60000
Parent Co: Sager Industries
Brands:
Air Solution
Ecolo

22016 Ecological Labs Inc
13 Hendrickson Ave
Lynbrook, NY 11563-1201

516-823-3441
Fax: 516-379-3632 800-645-2976
info@propump.com www.microbelift.com
Live bacterial cultures
President: Barry Richter
barryrichter@microbelist.com
Estimated Sales: $5-10 Million
Number Employees: 10-19
Type of Packaging: Bulk

22017 Econo Equipment
PO Box 250
Westfield, WI 53964-0250

608-296-3646
Fax: 608-296-4029
Packaging equipment
President: Michael Johnson
Estimated Sales: $1-2.5 000,000
Number Employees: 19

22018 Econo Frost Night Covers
PO Box 40
Shawnigan Lake, BC V0R 2W0
Canada

250-743-1222
Fax: 250-743-1221 800-519-1222
info@econofrost.com www.mgvinc.com
Manufacturer, importer and exporter of color corrected lighting and night covers for refrigerated display cases
President: Mark Granfar
Marketing: Samantha Criddle
International Sales Director: Carlos Paniagua
Product Development: Trevor Brien
Number Employees: 20-49
Number of Products: 1
Square Footage: 6000
Parent Co: MGV Inc
Type of Packaging: Food Service
Brands:
Econofrost
Instamark
Mgv
Mr16
Multichrome
Promolux
Samark

22019 Econocorp Inc
72 Pacella Park Dr
Randolph, MA 02368-1791

781-986-7500
Fax: 781-986-1553 www.econocorp.com
Manufacturer and exporter of carton sealing machinery
President: Wayne Goldberg
wayne@econocorp.com
Quality Control: Richard Norton
VP: Mark Jacobson
Estimated Sales: $10-20 Million
Number Employees: 50-99
Square Footage: 42000
Brands:
Econoseal

22020 Econofrost Night Covers
Box 40
Shawnigan Lake, BC V0R 2W0
Canada

250-743-1222
Fax: 250-743-1221 800-519-1222
info@econofrost.com www.econofrost.com
Night covers for the refrigerated display cases in supermarkets.
President: Mark Granfar
Marketing: Lyn Rose
Sales: Trevor Brian
Sales: Scott Werhun
Sales: Jamie Farr
International Sales: Carlos Paniagua
Number Employees: 15
Number of Brands: 2
Square Footage: 3000
Type of Packaging: Private Label
Brands:
Econofrost

22021 Economic Sciences Corp
1516 Le Roy Ave
Berkeley, CA 94708-1914

510-841-6869
Fax: 510-644-1943
Computer software
President: Bill F Roberts
bill@econsci.com
VP: Helen Chin
Estimated Sales: Less Than $500,000
Number Employees: 1-4

22022 Economy Folding Box Corporation
2601 S La Salle St
Chicago, IL 60616

312-225-2000
Fax: 312-225-3082 800-771-1053
Manufacturer and exporter of paper boxes
President: Michael M Mitchel
CEO: Clifford Moos
guizhou@yahoo.com
VP/Treasurer: Michael Mitchel
Purchasing Officer: Marie Hernandez
Sales Manager: Joseph Moos

Estimated Sales: $10-20 Million
Number Employees: 50-99
Square Footage: 330000
Type of Packaging: Consumer, Food Service, Private Label

22023 Economy Label Sales Company
515 Carswell Ave
Daytona Beach, FL 32117-4411
386-253-4741
Fax: 386-238-0775
Manufacturer and exporter of flexible plastic and vinyl labels including pressure sensitive, plain, hot-stamped and printed
Estimated Sales: $5-10 Million
Number Employees: 50-99
Parent Co: Meadow USA

22024 Economy Novelty & Printing Co
407 Park Ave S # 26a
Suite 26A
New York, NY 10016-8420
212-481-3022
Fax: 212-481-4514 info@thinkideas.com
www.thinkideas.com
Manufacturer and importer of advertising specialties including badges, medals, decals and ribbons
President: Robert Becker
einfo@thinkideas.com
VP: Warren Becker
Estimated Sales: Less Than $500,000
Number Employees: 1-4
Square Footage: 2000
Parent Co: Economy Novelty
Brands:
   Thinkideas

22025 Economy Paper & Restaurant Co
180 Broad St
Clifton, NJ 07013-1299
973-279-5500
Fax: 973-279-4140 sales@economysupply.com
www.economysupply.com
Soaps, degreasers and custom fabricated equipment; wholesaler/distributor and exporter of food service equipment, disposables, janitorial supplies, smallwares, glassware, flatware and china; installation and consulting available
President: L J Konzelman
CFO: Susan Majors
VP: Micheal Konzelman
R&D: Alex Nasarone
Public Relations: Susan Majors
Purchasing: Kevin Konzelman
Estimated Sales: $3-5 Million
Number Employees: 10-19
Square Footage: 50000
Type of Packaging: Food Service
Brands:
   Econo-Flash
   Econo-Suds

22026 Economy Tent Intl
2995 NW 75th St
Miami, FL 33147-5943
305-694-1234
Fax: 305-835-7098 800-438-3226
sales@economytent.com www.mmicreateweb.com
Supplier and exporter of party tents for the food service industry
Owner: Hal Lapping
hlapping@economytent.com
VP Marketing: Hal Lapping
Estimated Sales: $1-2.5 Million
Number Employees: 20-49
Type of Packaging: Food Service

22027 Ecover
PO Box 911058
Los Angeles, CA 90091-1058
323-720-5730
Fax: 323-720-5732 www.ecover.com
Natural bases, environmentally safe cleaning products.
CEO: Philip Malmberg
Sales Manager: Maureen Davis
Estimated Sales: $3-5 Million
Number Employees: 5-9

22028 Ecs Warehouse
2381 Fillmore Ave
Buffalo, NY 14214-2129
716-833-7380
Fax: 716-833-7386 permerling@emerfood.com
www.ecswarehouse.com
A warehouse that understands your needs. Frozen, dry, refrigerated warehouse on Canadian border, within 500 miles of 70% of the entire Canadian population and 55% of the entire USA population. Services include: pick & pack, crossdocking, express service, repacking, distribution, TL & LTL, rail, consolidation, salvage, quick access to NYC, Boston, D.C., Cleveland, Buffalo, Toronto, Rockland, Syracuse, Detroit and Cincinnati. If you have special product needs, call us.
CEO: Peter Emerling
pemerling@emerfood.com
Number Employees: 10-19
Square Footage: 500000
Type of Packaging: Bulk
Brands:
   Chocolate Moose
   Flathead Lake Monster Gourmet Soda
   Havana Cappuccino
   Hill-Tween Farms
   Ocean Spray

22029 Ed Smith's Stencil Works LTD
4315 Bienville St
P O Box 791837
New Orleans, LA 70119-4621
504-525-2128
Fax: 504-525-2157 sales@edsmiths.net
www.edsmiths.net
Marking devices, rubber stamps, checks, name badges, price markers, stencils and plastic signs
Owner: Mike Rowan
VP: Ronald Schaefer
Assistant Sales Manager: Michael Rowan
mike@edsmiths.net
Estimated Sales: $1-2.5 Million
Number Employees: 10-19
Square Footage: 27168

22030 Edco Industries
203-249 Dekalb Ave
Bridgeport, CT 6607
203-333-8982
Fax: 203-333-7950 www.edcoindustries.com
Molded plastic products including housewares, ice buckets, tumblers, trays, coasters, etc.; also, hot stamping available
President: John Thomas Szalan
VP: Anna Marie Szalan
Plant Manager: Hector Mendez
Estimated Sales: $1 Million
Number Employees: 10-19
Square Footage: 26800

22031 Edco Supply Corp
323 36th St
Brooklyn, NY 11232-2599
718-499-7005
Fax: 718-788-7481 800-221-0918
info@edcosupply.com www.edcosupply.com
Antistatic packaging including antistatic bags, commercial translucent static shielding materials, desiccant, indicator cards, caution labels and VCI papers
Owner: Sylvia Freyer
sylvia@edcosupply.com
Estimated Sales: $5-10 000,000
Number Employees: 20-49

22032 Ederback Corporation
505 South Maple Road
Ann Arbor, MI 48103
734-665-8877
Fax: 734-665-9099 800-422-2558
info@eberbachlabtools.com
www.eberbachlabtools.com
Manufacturer and exporter of laboratory equipment including shakers, mixers, homogenizers and blenders
President: Ralph Boehnke Jr
Estimated Sales: $3-5 Million
Number Employees: 10-19

22033 Edge Resources
1 Menfi Way
Unit 20
Hopedale, MA 01747-1542
508-634-8214
Fax: 508-634-9888 888-849-0998
info@edgeresources.com www.edgeresources.com
Manufacturer and importer of food service equipment and supplies; consultant specializing in marketing and sales services
President/CEO: Frank Curty
Estimated Sales: $500,000-$1 Million
Number Employees: 5-9
Square Footage: 16000

22034 Edgecraft Corp
825 Southwood Rd
Avondale, PA 19311-9765
610-268-0500
Fax: 610-268-3545 800-342-3255
val.gleason@edgecraft.com www.chefschoice.com
Manufacturer and exporter of manual and power driven sharpeners slicer and cutlery
President: Samuel Weiner
samuel.weiner@edgecraft.com
CEO: Daniel Friel Sr
Estimated Sales: G
Number Employees: 100-249
Brands:
   Chef's Choice

22035 Edgemold Products
37031 E Wisconsin Ave
PO Box 88
Oconomowoc, WI 53066
262-567-9313
Fax: 262-567-9339 800-450-0051
info@fiberesin.com www.edgemold.com
Urethane-edged tables and tabletops
President & CEO: Mike MacDougal
National Sales Manager: Lonie Wise
Director of Manufacturing: Jeff Bahr
Estimated Sales: $1-5 Million
Number Employees: 10-19
Parent Co: Fibersin Industries
Brands:
   Edgemold

22036 Edgerton Corporation
22560 Lunn Rd
Strongsville, OH 44149
440-268-0000
Fax: 440-268-0300 www.edgerton.com
Computer systems for material handling
President: Bob Walters
CFO: Susan Sponsler
Executive VP: Barry Zimmerman
COO: Jed Cavadas
Estimated Sales: $10-20,000,000
Number Employees: 20-49

22037 Edhard Corp
279 Blau Rd
Hackettstown, NJ 07840-5221
908-850-8444
Fax: 908-850-8445 888-334-2731
meter@edhard.com www.edhard.com
Bakers' equipment and supplies including plastic injection molds and dies
President: Ed Bars
ed@edhard.com
CFO: Joe Englert
Sales Manager: Nancy Neri
Estimated Sales: $2.5-5 Million
Number Employees: 20-49
Brands:
   Edhard Injectors & Depositors

22038 Edible Software
3603 Westcenter Dr # 100
Suite 100
Houston, TX 77042-5222
713-592-8200
Fax: 832-200-8001 sales@ediblesoftware.com
www.ediblesoftware.com
Accessories/supplies i.e. picnic baskets
CEO: Trevor Morris
info@ediblesoftware.com
President, Chief Executive Officer: Henri Morris
Senior Vice President: Trevor Morris
Number Employees: 20-49

22039 Edison Price Lighting
4150 22nd St
Long Island City, NY 11101-4815
718-685-0700
Fax: 718-786-8530 jlattanzio@epl.com
Manufacturer and exporter of architectural, energy efficient, recessed and surface mounted lighting fixtures
President: Emma Price
eprice@epl.com
Finance: MaryAnna Romano
R&D: Richard J. Shaver
Sales/Marketing: Joel Seigel
Sales Service: Joanie Lattanzio
Customer Service: Stephanie Smith
Administration: James D. Vizzini
purchasing/operations: George H. Closs
Number Employees: 100-249
Brands:
Anglux
Artima
Autotrak
Bablux
Duplux
Multipurpose
Sight Line
Simplux
Spredlite
Triples

22040 Edl Packaging Engineers
1260 Parkview Rd
Green Bay, WI 54304-5619
920-336-7744
Fax: 920-336-8585 sales@edlpackaging.com
www.edlpackaging.com
Manufacturer and exporter of shrink and stretch bundling machinery
President: Ken Carter
sales@edlpackaging.com
Director Of Sales: Larry D Cozine
Product Manager/Bagged Product: Jariath Harkin
Estimated Sales: $5-10,000,000
Number Employees: 50-99
Number of Products: 4
Square Footage: 50000
Parent Co: EDL UK
Type of Packaging: Consumer, Food Service, Private Label, Bulk

22041 Edlund Co
159 Industrial Pkwy
Burlington, VT 05401-5494
802-862-9661
Fax: 802-862-4822 800-772-2126
scrane@edlundco.com www.edlundco.com
Develops and manufactures operator-oriented stainless steel equipment for the food service industry product line of which includes can crushers; manual, electric and air-powered can openers; high speed industrial systems; mechanical and digital portion control scales; mechanical and digital receiving scales; knife sharpeners; knife racks; and tongs.
President: Willett S Foster Iv
Cmo: Peter Nordell
pnordell@edlundco.com
Vice President: Peter Nordell
Vice President of Sales and Marketing: David Sebastianelli
Estimated Sales: $10-25 Million
Number Employees: 100-249
Brands:
Edlund

22042 Edmeyer
315 27th Ave NE
Minneapolis, MN 55418-2715
651-450-1210
Fax: 651-450-0003 www.edmeyerinc.com
Manufacturer and exporter of casers, conveyors, case packers and palletizers
President: Larry Smith
VP: Jerry Kisch
Sales Manager: Greg Reid
Estimated Sales: $20-50 Million
Number Employees: 20-49
Square Footage: 12000

22043 Edson Packaging Machinery
215 Hempstead Drive
Hamilton, ON L8W 2E6
Canada
905-385-3201
Fax: 905-385-8775 800-493-3766
value@edson.com www.edson.com
Manufacturer and exporter of robotic top load packers, packaging machinery including case openers, robotic palletizers, stretch bundlers, sealers and automatic packers
CEO: Robert Hattin
Vice President, General Manager: Gary Evans
Engineering Manager: Bob Krouse
Quality Control: Bob Krause
Account Manager: Scott Killins
Estimated Sales: $10 Million
Number Employees: 70
Number of Brands: 5
Square Footage: 96600
Type of Packaging: Consumer, Food Service
Brands:
Edson

22044 (HQ)Educational Products Company
P.O. Box 295
Hope, NJ 07844
908-459-4220
Fax: 908-459-4770 800-272-3822
cookiecutters1947@hotmail.com
www.cookiecutters.com
3-D cookie cutters
President: Christopher Maier
Manager: Lucy Kise
Estimated Sales: $500,000-$1 Million
Number Employees: 1-4
Brands:
Cookie Craft

22045 Edward & Sons Trading Co
4420 Via Real # C
Carpinteria, CA 93013-1635
805-684-8500
Fax: 805-684-8220 www.edwardandsons.com
Innovative natural and organic vegetarian foods
President: Joel Dee
edwardsons@aol.com
Number Employees: 10-19

22046 Edwards Fiberglass
P.O.Box 1252
Sedalia, MO 65302-1252
660-826-3915
Fax: 660-827-2793 www.edwardsfiberglass.com
Above and below ground fiberglass storage tanks
President: Robert L Edwards
VP: Shane Edwards
Sales: Donna Schoolman
Estimated Sales: $20-50 Million
Number Employees: 20-49
Square Footage: 31000

22047 Edwards Products
1223 Budd St
Cincinnati, OH 45203
513-851-3000
Fax: 513-851-9300 800-543-1835
Stock trucks and storage racks
President: Thomas Reilly
Quality Control: Kevin Reilly
General Manager: John Sloniker
Estimated Sales: $20-50 Million
Number Employees: 20-49
Square Footage: 30000

22048 Efficient Frontiers
2021 W.Las Positas Ct.Ste 127
Livermore, CA 94551
925-456-6700
Fax: 925-456-6701 888-433-4725
Automated software for event sales, dining reservations and club membership
Director Sales/Marketing: Beth Goodell
Contact: Ron Goodell
ron.goodell@reserveinteractive.com
Brands:
Efficient Frontiers
Reserve

22049 Eggboxes Inc
PO Box 8651
Deerfield Beach, FL 33443
954-410-5565
Fax: 954-783-3456 800-326-6667
www.eggboxes.com
Egg cartons, baskets, egg washing supplies, hatchery supplies, bird care, incubating trays, feeders, scales, and nest accessories
President: James Tongle

22050 Ehmke Manufacturing
4200 Macalester St
Philadelphia, PA 19124-6014
215-324-4200
Fax: 215-324-4210
www.ehmkemanufacturing.com
Commercial awnings
President: Louis Verna
CEO: Bob Rosania
Manager, Quality Assurance: Richard Ludwig
Director, Sales & Marketing: Brad Milnes
Sales Manager: Brad Daniels
COO: Cliff Stokes
Number Employees: 100-249

22051 Ehrgott Rubber Stamp Company
4615 E 10th St
Indianapolis, IN 46201-2823
317-353-2222
Fax: 317-357-7750 www.ehrgott.com
Rubber stamps, engraved signs and name tags
President and CFO: Mary Clevenger
Estimated Sales: $500,000-$1 Million
Number Employees: 1-4

22052 Eichler Wood Products
5477 Mauser Street
Laurys Station, PA 18059-1317
610-262-6749
Fax: 610-262-4454
Wooden pallets, boxes, crates and skids
Owner: Henry Taylor
Business Manager: Thomas R Nemeth
Estimated Sales: $1-3 Million
Number Employees: 30
Square Footage: 40000

22053 Eide Industries Inc
16215 Piuma Ave
Cerritos, CA 90703-1528
562-402-8335
Fax: 562-924-2233 800-422-6827
info@eideindustries.com www.eideindustries.com
Manufacturer and exporter of commercial awnings, canopies, tension structures and custom fabric covers
President: Luis Barragan
barraganl@gmail.com
VP Manufacturing/ Chairman: Jesse Borrego
Secretary/VP Marketing: Joe Belli
VP Sales & Marketing: Dan Neill
Human Resources: Lourdes Jordan
Production Coordinator: Ignacio Pellegrin
Chairman/VP Manufacturing: Jesse Borrego
Estimated Sales: $8 Million
Number Employees: 50-99
Square Footage: 82000

22054 Einson Freeman
200 Robin Road
Paramus, NJ 7652
201-221-2800
Fax: 201-226-9262 info@cafsnj.org
www.cafsnj.org
Manufacturer and exporter of point of purchase displays, exhibits and sales promotion items
President & CEO: Jerrold B. Binney
Treasurer & CFO: Joanne Mandry
EVP & Chief Development Officer: Elizabeth Mason
Senior Project Manager: Jeff Shapiro
Estimated Sales: $10-20 Million
Number Employees: 50-99
Parent Co: WPP Group PLC

22055 Eirich Machines
4033 Ryan Rd
Gurnee, IL 60031-1255
847-336-2444
Fax: 847-336-0914 eirich@eirichusa.com
www.eirich.com/en/eirich-machines

Manufacturer and exporter of high speed, ribbon, paddle, plow and fluidized zone mixers, finishers, bag dump work stations, viscous pumps, blenders and hoppers
Co-President: Paul Eirich
VP Sales: Richard Zak
Estimated Sales: $10-20 Million
Number Employees: 100-249
Square Footage: 150000
Parent Co: Maschinenfabrik G. Eirich GmbH

22056 Eirich Machines
4033 Ryan Rd
Gurnee, IL 60031-1255

847-336-2444
Fax: 847-336-0914 eirich@eirichusa.com
www.eirichusa.com
High quality mixers, dryers, reactors and ancillary equipment
Sales: Richard Zak
VP Sales: Richard Zak
Estimated Sales: $20-50 Million
Number Employees: 100-249
Parent Co: Elrich Machines

22057 Eisai
3 University Plz
Hackensack, NJ 07601-6208

201-692-0999
Fax: 201-692-1972 www.eisaiusa.com
Fully automated inspection machines for parenteral products
President: Micheal De La Montaign
Contact: Stephen Breckenridge
emu@eisai.com
Estimated Sales: $10-15 Million
Number Employees: 10-19

22058 Eischen Enterprises
10111 S Cedar Ave
Fresno, CA 93725-9107

559-834-0013
Fax: 559-834-9183 veischen@aol.com
www.eischenenterprisesinc.com
Sell food processing equipment, used and reconditioned.
President: Virgil Eischen
Marketing: Janice Jepsen
Sales: Virgil Eischen
Estimated Sales: Less Than $500,000
Number Employees: 1-4

22059 Eisenmann Corp USA
150 E Dartmoor Dr
Crystal Lake, IL 60014-8710

815-455-4100
Fax: 815-455-1018 www.eisenmann.com
Manufacturer and exporter of turnkey material handling systems including electrified monorail systems and belt, power, chain, overhead chain and free conveyors; system design services available
VP: Craig Benner
Manager: Jeff Wehner
info@eisenmann.com
General Manager (General Industry): R Trenn
Estimated Sales: $50-100 Million
Number Employees: 20-49
Square Footage: 300
Parent Co: Eisenmann Corporation
Type of Packaging: Bulk

22060 El Cerrito Steel
1424 Kearney St
El Cerrito, CA 94530-2397

510-230-4709
Fax: 510-233-0116
Steel canning and preserving kettles
President: John Kim
Estimated Sales: $1-2.5 Million
Number Employees: 1-4

22061 El Dorado Packaging Inc
204 Prescolite Dr
El Dorado, AR 71730-6677

870-862-4977
Fax: 870-862-8520 www.eldoradobag.com
Manufacturer and exporter of paper bags
President: Louis Hall
CEO: Louis T Hall Iii
Estimated Sales: $20-50 Million
Number Employees: 100-249
Type of Packaging: Consumer

22062 Elan Vanilla Co
268 Doremus Ave
Newark, NJ 07105-4879

973-344-8014
Fax: 973-344-5880 www.elanvanilla.com
Organic kosher certified vanilla extract, flavoring and synthetic and natural aromatic chemicals
President: Jocelyn Manship
jmanship@elan-chemical.com
Quality Control Manager: Phil Kapp
VP Sales: David Pimentel
Director of Customer Service: Marilyn Santiago
Estimated Sales: $20-50 Million
Number Employees: 50-99
Type of Packaging: Bulk

22063 Elanco Food Solutions
2500 Innovation Way
PO Box 708
Greenfield, IN 46140

317-276-9846
800-428-4441
www.elanco.com
Food safety products and services
President: Jeff Simmons
Contact: Summer Amado
summeramado@hotmail.com
Number Employees: 2,500

22064 Elba Pallets Company
PO Box 276
Elba, AL 36323-0276

334-897-6034
Fax: 334-897-6421
Wooden pallets
President: L Little
Estimated Sales: $5-10 Million
Number Employees: 19

22065 Elberta Crate & Box Company
231 W Main Street
Suite 207
Carpentersville, IL 60110-1769

847-426-3491
Fax: 847-426-3520 888-672-9260
Manufacturer and exporter of wirebound boxes, crates and expendable pallets
CEO: Ramsay Simmons
Sales Director: Walter Eschenbach
Public Relations: Todd Mills
Estimated Sales: $1-5 Million
Number Employees: 1-4
Parent Co: Elberta Crate & Box Company
Type of Packaging: Food Service, Bulk
Brands:
 Elberta
 Skee
 Woodkor

22066 Eldetco
20 Anson Road
Burlingame, CA 94010-7226

650-579-7655
Fax: 650-579-7650
Conveyors and conveying equipment
President: Don Lunghi
Estimated Sales: $1 000,000
Number Employees: 9

22067 Eldorado Miranda Manufacturing Company
1744 12th St SE Ofc
Largo, FL 33771

727-586-0707
Fax: 727-585-4797 800-330-0708
www.eldoradomfg.com
UL listed ventmatic hoods; also, stainless steel work tables, square corner sinks, shelving and commercial dishwasher tables
President: Andrew Miranda Jr
Quality Control: Cora Miranda
VP: Andrew Miranda
Estimated Sales: Below $5 Million
Number Employees: 5-9
Square Footage: 90000
Brands:
 Eldorado Miranda

22068 Elecro-Craft/Rockwell Automation
6950 Washington Ave S
Eden Prairie, MN 55344-3407

952-942-3600
Fax: 612-942-3636 800-752-6946
eesemea@ra.rockwell.com www.electro-craft.com
Programmable limit switches and electornic rotary cam switches used to control food processing and packaging machinery
General Manager: Philip Martin
President, Chief Executive Officer: James Elsner
Senior VP: William Calisse
Vice President of Business Development: Rob Kerber
VP: David Dorgan
Vice President of Sales: Tom Ouellette
Plant Manager: Rick Roberts
Estimated Sales: $50-100 Million
Number Employees: 100-249
Number of Products: 4
Square Footage: 279000
Type of Packaging: Bulk

22069 Electra-Gear
1110 N Anaheim Boulevard
Anaheim, CA 92801-2502

714-535-6061
Fax: 714-535-2489
Manager: Katherine Garrison
Human Resoures and Administration: Anna Alvarez
Estimated Sales: $3-5 Million
Number Employees: 1
Parent Co: Regal-Beloit Company

22070 Electric City Signs & Neon Inc.
701 US Hwy 28 By Pass
PO Box 656
Anderson, SC 29622

864-225-5351
Fax: 864-225-9050 800-270-5851
www.electriccitysigns.com
Plastic and neon signs
Owner: Darrell Ridgeway
Secretary and Treasurer: Patricia Ridgeway
Contact: Chad Ridgeway
cridgeway@electriccitysigns.com
Production Manager: Chris Bowser
Estimated Sales: $2 Million
Number Employees: 20-49
Square Footage: 60000

22071 Electric Contract Furniture
450 Fashion Ave # 2710
Suite 2701
New York, NY 10123-2710

212-967-5504
Fax: 212-760-8823 888-311-6272
eclecticinc@aol.com www.eclecticcontract.com
Tables, chairs, booths and barstools
Owner: Junior Ferma
junior@eclecticcontract.com
Estimated Sales: Less than $500,000
Number Employees: 1-4

22072 Electrical Engineering & Equip
953 73rd St
Windsor Heights, IA 50324-1031

515-273-0100
Fax: 515-273-0101 800-955-3633
www.3e-co.com
Conveyors, elevators, bins and other material handling systems
President/ CEO: Jeff Stroud
CFO: Dave Moench
EVP: John Pilmer
Corporate Marketing Director: Tim Pruch
SVP, Sales & Operations: Steve VanBrocklin
Sr. Director of Operations: Barry Tegels
Estimated Sales: $10-20 Million
Number Employees: 250-499

22073 Electro Alarms
24 S Washington St
Tiffin, OH 44883

419-447-3062
800-261-9174
Broker of burglar and fire alarm systems. Repair and installation services available
Owner: Howard Beisner
Sales Director: Howard Beisner
Estimated Sales: $1-2.5 Million
Number Employees: 1-4

22074 Electro Cam Corp
13647 Metric Rd
Roscoe, IL 61073-9717
815-389-2620
Fax: 815-389-3304 800-228-5487
info@electrocam.com www.electrocam.com
Manufacturer and exporter of packaging and food processing controls and software including programmable and electric switches
President: Donald Davis
application@electrocam.com
Quality Control: Mike Engevretson
Marketing Manager: Barbara Scheeberger
Sales Manager: John Straw
Estimated Sales: $5-10 Million
Number Employees: 20-49
Brands:
  Plus
  Plusnet
  Slimline

22075 Electro Freeze
2116 8th Ave
East Moline, IL 61244
309-755-4553
Fax: 309-755-9858 sales@electrofreeze.com
www.hcduke.com
Manufacturer, importer and exporter of soft serve ice cream, slush, shake and frozen yogurt equipment
Marketing: Joe Clark
Contact: Shane Allen
sallen@electrofreeze.com
Estimated Sales: $20-50 Million
Number Employees: 100-249
Square Footage: 115000
Parent Co: H.C. Duke & Son

22076 Electro Lift Inc
204 Sargeant Ave
Clifton, NJ 07013-1932
973-471-0204
Fax: 973-471-2814 info2@electrolift.com
www.electrolift.com
Manufacturer and exporter of hoists for monorail, dual rail, hatchway or base-mounted applications
Owner: Deborah Rechtschaffer
debbie@electrolift.com
Estimated Sales: $5-10 Million
Number Employees: 20-49
Type of Packaging: Bulk

22077 Electro-Lite Signs
9155 Archibald Ave # 303
Rancho Cucamonga, CA 91730-5258
909-945-3555
Fax: 909-945-9805 www.els4signs.com
Electric signs
Owner: Ken Brown
els4signs@aol.com
Estimated Sales: $500,000-$1,000,000
Number Employees: 5-9

22078 Electro-Sensors Inc
6111 Blue Circle Dr
Minnetonka, MN 55343-9108
952-930-0100
Fax: 952-930-0130 1 8-0 3-8 61
sales@electro-sensors.com
www.electro-sensors.com
Electro-Sensors, Inc. manufactures a complete line of motion monitoring and speed control systems for industrial machinery including: Speed Sensors, Speed Sensitive Switches, Tachometers, Counters, Speed to Analog Converters, DigitalPulse Generators, Closed Loop Motor Speed Control Systems, and Material Level Controls
President/CEO': Brad Slyle
CEO: David L Klenk
dklenk@electro-sensors.com
CFO: Gloria Grundhoefer
Marketing/Sales: Philip Rae
Estimated Sales: $5-10 000,000
Number Employees: 20-49

22079 Electro-Sensors Inc
6111 Blue Circle Dr
Minnetonka, MN 55343-9108
952-930-0100
Fax: 952-930-0130 800-323-6170
sales@electro-sensors.com
www.electro-sensors.com
Speed monitoring systems, speed switches, tachometers, counters, speed to analog converters, ratemeters

CEO: David L Klenk
dklenk@electro-sensors.com
CEO: Brad Flye
CEO: Bradley D Slye
Manager: Mike Kroening
Number Employees: 20-49
Number of Products: 14

22080 Electro-Steam GeneratorCorp
50 Indel Ave
PO Box 438
Rancocas, NJ 8073
609-288-9071
Fax: 609-288-9078 866-617-0764
sales@electrosteam.com www.electrosteam.com
Manufacturer all-electric steam generators that are used in industry for ovens, proofers, kettles, and for cleaning, sanitizing, and heating
President: Robert Murnane
Cio/Cto: Sal Negro
sal@electrosteam.com
Quality Control: Barbara Aikens
Marketing/National Sales Manager: Jack Harlin
Operations: Jack Harlin
Manufacturing Executive: Sal Negro
Plant Manager: Barbara Aikens
Purchase Executive: Gary Lango
Estimated Sales: $1-3 Million
Number Employees: 10-19
Number of Brands: 4
Square Footage: 52000
Type of Packaging: Private Label
Brands:
  Baby Giant
  Little Giant
  Low Boy
  Space Savers

22081 (HQ)Electrodex
4554 19th St Ct E
Bradenton, FL 34203
941-753-5663
Fax: 941-753-7049 800-362-1972
Manufacturer and exporter of lighting fixtures
President: Mike Guritz
Sales Manager: Warren Dalton
Estimated Sales: $2.5-5 Million
Number Employees: 10-19
Type of Packaging: Food Service

22082 Electrol Specialties Co
441 Clark St
South Beloit, IL 61080-1363
815-389-2291
Fax: 815-389-2294 esc@jvlnet.com
www.esc4cip.com
Clean-in-place, computer and control systems, sanitation equipment, transfer panels and tanks; custom fabrication services available
President: Nicholas Amsbaugh
nick@amsbaugh.net
Quality Control: Roger Schwartz
VP/General Manager: John Franks
Senior Sales Engineer: Dick Gleed
Estimated Sales: $5-10,000,000
Number Employees: 50-99
Square Footage: 100000
Type of Packaging: Bulk

22083 Electron Machine Corp
15824 County Road 450
P.O. Box 2349
Umatilla, FL 32784-8176
352-669-3101
Fax: 352-669-1373 sales@electronmachine.com
www.electronmachine.com
Microprocessor refractometers
President: C A Vosburg
ca@electronmachine.com
Estimated Sales: $2.5-5 000,000
Number Employees: 20-49

22084 Electronic Development Labs
244 Oakland Drive
Danville, VA 24540
434-799-0807
Fax: 434-799-0847 800-342-5335
sales@edl-inc.com www.edl-inc.com

Provides products and service, the most reliable precision temperature meassuring sensors, equipment, accessories, and calibrators; customized to customer specifications as needed. EDL offers an extensive line of calibratorsthermocouples, RTD's, thermistors, wire, high temperature bore thru compression fittings, bimetals, lab thermometers, recorders, infrared, high temperature insulations, over 10,000 sensors, and a full range of precision handheld pyrometers.
President and CFO: Donald Polsky
Quality Control: Steve Winnes
Marketing: Kristen Gusler
Sales: Jean Moore
Contact: John Lollar
jlollar@emory.edu
Purchasing: Stephanie King
Number Employees: 35

22085 Electronic Filling Systems
574 Barrow Park Drive
Winder, GA 30680-3416
770-621-9200
Fax: 770-934-0959
In-line liquid filling systems including volumetric piston liquid fillers, stainless steel tabletop chain conveyors, rotary unscramblers and accumulators and ink jet imagers
Estimated Sales: $5-10 000,000
Number Employees: 10-19

22086 Electronic Liquid Fillers
P.O.Box 387
Kingsbury, IN 46345-0387
219-393-5571
Fax: 219-393-5283 800-328-0466
Owner: Mitch Juszkiewicz
CEO and CFO: Ronald Sarto
Number Employees: 50-99

22087 Electronic Machine Parts
400 Oser Ave # 2000
Hauppauge, NY 11788-3658
631-434-3700
Fax: 631-434-3718 www.empregister.com
Registration controls, rebuilding labeling machines
President: Maureen Mc Adam
loubier_gabriel@jpmorgan.com
Estimated Sales: $10-20 Million
Number Employees: 10-19

22088 Electronic Weighing Systems
664 Fisherman Street
Opa Locka, FL 33054
305-685-8067
Fax: 305-685-2440
Manufacturer and exporter of electronic scales for receiving, counter, heavy duty, warehouse and crane scale
VP: Victor Perez, Jr.
Estimated Sales: $2.5-5 Million
Number Employees: 7
Square Footage: 84000
Brands:
  Ews

22089 Electrostatics Inc
352 Godshall Dr
Harleysville, PA 19438-2017
215-513-0850
Fax: 215-513-0855 888-782-8427
sales@electrostatics.com www.electrostatics.com
Static neutralizing-generating and related contamination control equipment including static measuring locator and meter, high and low pressure guns, nozzles and blowers, static neutralizing bars, power units, static inducingequipment
President: Peter Mariani
ken@electrostatics.com
Marketing: Maryjane Vielhauer
Sales: Maryjane Vielhauer
Director Engineering: Bob Meyers
Production: Keri Farrington
Purchasing: Janet Benfield
Estimated Sales: $2.5-5 000,000
Number Employees: 20-49

22090 Electrotechnology Applications Center
3835 Green Pond Rd
Bethlehem, PA 18020
610-861-4552
Fax: 610-861-5060 877-862-3696
www.etctr.com

Infrared, ultraviolet, microwave, and radiofrequency energy to improve heating, drying, curing, and coating processes

Number Employees: 9

22091 Elegant Awnings
13831 Oaks Avenue
Chino, CA 91710-7009

626-575-3556
Fax: 626-575-3567 800-541-9011
Commercial awnings
President: Mike Chiovare
CFO: Tony Chiovare
sales manager: Mike Chiovare
Estimated Sales: Below $5 Million
Number Employees: 10-19

22092 Elegant Packaging
5253 W Roosevelt Rd
Cicero, IL 60804-1222

708-652-3400
Fax: 708-652-6444 800-367-5493
www.elegantpackaging.com
Manufacturer and designers of customized rigid specialty boxes, presentation binders, soft sewn packaging and compression thermal forming.
Manager: Carlos Iriarte
iriarte_carlos@jpmorgan.com
Estimated Sales: $11 Million
Number Employees: 50-99
Square Footage: 96000
Type of Packaging: Consumer, Food Service, Private Label, Bulk

22093 Elemental Containers
860 Springfield Rd
Union, NJ 07083-8614

908-687-7720
Fax: 908-687-5157 800-577-7624
www.aluminumbottles.com
Industrial aluminum bottles used for liquids, viscous and solid products, keeping out light, moisture and oxidation.
President: Luc Tournaire
Account Manager: Patricia Cataldo
Sales & Marketing Manager: Benoit Ramet
Director of Operations: Madeline Cicalese
Estimated Sales: $6 Million
Number Employees: 5-9
Square Footage: 44000

22094 Elementar Americas Inc
520 Fellowship Rd # D408
Suite D-408
Mt Laurel, NJ 08054-3409

856-787-0022
Fax: 856-787-0055 www.elementaramericas.com
Represents the worldwide leading German manufacturer of analytical instrumentation for non-metallic elements like carbon, nitrogen, hydrogen, oxygen and chlorine in all organic materials. Also offers isotope ratio massspectrometers.
President: Georg Schick
sandy_hughes@elementar-inc.com
Number Employees: 10-19

22095 Elettric 80 Inc
8100 Monticello Ave
Skokie, IL 60076-3326

847-329-7717
Fax: 847-329-9923 www.elettric80.com
Robotic palletizers, laser-guided vehicle systems
President: Johan Castegren
Vice President: Marco Ferrarini
ferrarini.m@electric80.it
Estimated Sales: Below $5 Million
Number Employees: 50-99

22096 Elgene
299 Welton St
Hamden, CT 06517-3938

203-562-9948
Fax: 203-562-2053 800-922-4623
answers@elgene.com www.chargar.com
Industrial cleaning compounds
President: Tim Reason
VP: Giulio Fraenza
Estimated Sales: $1-3 Million
Number Employees: 1-4
Number of Brands: 22
Number of Products: 22
Square Footage: 60000
Parent Co: Chargar Corporation

Brands:
Fabulene

22097 (HQ)Eliason Corp
9229 Shaver Rd
Portage, MI 49024-6799

269-327-7003
Fax: 269-327-7006 800-828-3655
doors@eliasoncorp.com
Manufacturer and exporter of swing doors and night covers for open refrigerated cases and freezers.
Owner: Edwanda Eliason
CEO: Doug Morrison
dmking851027@gmail.com
Marketing Director: Michael Woolsey
Estimated Sales: $5-10 Million
Number Employees: 50-99
Square Footage: 350000
Other Locations:
Eliason Corporation
Woodland CA
Brands:
Easy Swing
Econo-Cover
Eliason

22098 Elite Forming Design Solutions
15 Commerce Ct SE
Rome, GA 30161-6848

706-232-3021
Fax: 706-232-3121 info@eliteforming.com
www.eliteforming.com
Manufacturer and supplier of OEM plates and parts.
Owner: Jim Mauer
Number Employees: 10-19

22099 Elite Spice Inc
7151 Montevideo Rd
Jessup, MD 20794-9308

410-796-1900
Fax: 410-379-6933 800-232-3531
jbrandt@elitespice.com www.elitespice.com
Spice, seasoning, capsicum, oil & oleoresin, and dehydrated vegetable producer.
President & CEO: Isaac Samuel
CFO/Human Resources Director: Debbie Ingle
R&D Director: Leslie Krause
Quality Control Directory: Dave Anthony
Marketing Executive: Kathy Lyons
VP, Sales: Paul Kurpe
VP/Plant Manager: George Mayer
Purchasing Manager: Margie Schneidman
Year Founded: 1988
Estimated Sales: $20-50 Million
Number Employees: 100-249
Square Footage: 11000
Type of Packaging: Private Label

22100 Elite Storage SolutionsInc
1118 W Spring St
Monroe, GA 30655-1755

770-207-0002
Fax: 770-207-0101 800-367-0572
www.basemfg.com
Pallet rack systems; also, design and installation available
President: Steve South
ssouth@elitena.com
Chairman of the Board: Dan South
VP Sales: Lee Bissell
Estimated Sales: $10-20 Million
Number Employees: 250-499
Square Footage: 360000

22101 Elkay Plastics Co Inc
6000 Sheila St
Commerce, CA 90040-2405

323-722-7073
Fax: 323-869-3911 800-809-8393
www.sirane.biz
Manufacturer and distributor of flexible polyethylene packaging
President: Louis Chertkow
CFO: Stuart Hortwiz
Quality Control: Christina Lucas
IT: Raul Cruz
r.cruz@elkayplastics.com
Estimated Sales: $20-50 Million
Number Employees: 10-19

22102 Ellab
1299 Del Mar Ave
San Jose, CA 95128-3548

408-938-0506
Fax: 408-280-0979 888-533-5588
www.phfspec.com
Estimated Sales: $300,000-500,000
Number Employees: 1-4

22103 Ellab
Trollesmindealle 25
Hilleroed, DK 3400

454-452-0500
Fax: 454-453-0505 info@ellab.com
www.ellab.com
Temperature, pressure and relative humidity monitoring
Estimated Sales: $1-2.5 Million
Number Employees: 1-4

22104 Ellehammer Industries
20146 100 A Avenue
Langley, BC V1M 3G2
Canada

604-882-9326
Fax: 604-882-9703
Manufacturer and exporter of plastic bags and film
Quality Control: Jack Tucker
Plant Manager: Ralph Schnitzer
Number Employees: 50

22105 Ellenco
4419 41st Street
Brentwood, MD 20722-1515

301-927-4370
Fax: 301-927-4376
Manufacturer and exporter of fire alarm systems
VP: Bob Harding
Estimated Sales: $1-5 Million
Number Employees: 20-50

22106 Ellett Industries
1575 Kingsway Avenue
Port Coquitlam, BC V3C 4E5
Canada

604-941-8211
Fax: 604-941-6854
Manufacturer and exporter of fabricated alloy metal, tanks, stills, heat exchangers, vessels, stainless steel and titanium pipes and fittings
President/CEO: J Ellett
Vice President: Bob Gill
Sales Director: L Osberg
Production Manager: David Clift
Purchasing Manager: Don Young
Estimated Sales: $20 Million
Number Employees: 100-250
Square Footage: 120000

22107 Ellingers Agatized WoodInc
923 S 21st St
Sheboygan, WI 53081-4702

920-457-7746
Fax: 920-457-2972 888-287-8906
jenny@ellingerswoodproducts.com
www.agatized.com
Manufacturer and exporter of wood bowls, bar trays, cutting boards and wood bowl gift sets.
President: Joyce Neese
jennye@bytehead.com
Sales Director: Jennifer Stafford
Estimated Sales: $800,000
Number Employees: 10-19
Number of Products: 35
Square Footage: 25000
Type of Packaging: Consumer, Food Service

22108 Elliot Horowitz & Co
675 3rd Ave
New York, NY 10017-5704

212-972-7500
Fax: 212-972-7050 ehorowitz@elliothorowitz.com
www.elliothorowitz.com
Manufacturers' representative for food service equipment and supplies including smallwares and heavy cooking and freezing equipment
Owner: Elliot Horowitz
Estimated Sales: $.5-1 million
Number Employees: 5-9
Type of Packaging: Food Service
Brands:
Brewmatic
Doyen
Piper Industries

22109 Elliot Lee

445 Central Ave Unit 100
Cedarhurst, NY 11516

516-569-9595
Fax: 516-569-8088 sales@misterpromotion.com
www.misterpromotion.com
Manufacturer, importer and wholesaler/distributor of
advertising specialties including sign holders,
awards, badges, bags, cups, pens and plaques
President/CFO: Victor Deutsch
CFO: Elliot Deutsch
Marketing Director: Elliot Deutsch
Estimated Sales: Below $5 Million
Number Employees: 5-9

22110 Elliott Bay Espresso

950 NW Elford Drive
Seattle, WA 98177-4125

206-467-6838
Fax: 206-467-6819
Espresso machines and accessories

22111 Elliott Manufacturing Co Inc

2664 S Cherry Ave
Fresno, CA 93706-5494

559-233-6235
Fax: 559-233-9833 elliottmfg@elliott-mfg.com
www.elliott-mfg.com
Manufacturer and exporter of date and raisin pro-
cessing machinery and olive, date and prune pitters;
also, packaging machinery including erectors, seal-
ers, cartoners and case packers
President, Chief Executive Officer: Terry Aluisi
National Sales Manager: John Rea
Estimated Sales: $1-5 Million
Number Employees: 20-49
Square Footage: 120000

22112 Elliott-Williams Company

3500 E 20th St
Indianapolis, IN 46218

317-635-1660
Fax: 317-453-1977 800-428-9303
Manufacturer and exporter of blast chillers, walk-in
coolers, freezers and refrigerators; also, pre-fabri-
cated refrigerated warehouses
Owner: Stuart Mc Keehan
CFO: R Scott
Contact: Michael Elliott
mark.m.elliott@williams.com
Purchasing Manager: K McCoy
Estimated Sales: $20-50 Million
Number Employees: 100-249
Square Footage: 100000
Brands:
    Correctchill
    Faster Freezer

22113 Ellis Corp

1400 W Bryn Mawr Ave
Itasca, IL 60143-1384

630-250-9222
Fax: 630-250-9241 800-611-6806
ksiriano@elliscorp.com www.elliscorp.com
President: Robert H Fesmire
rfesmire@elliscorp.com
Chief Executive Officer: Bob Fesmire
CEO: Robert H Fesmire
Estimated Sales: $10-20 Million
Number Employees: 50-99

22114 Elm Packaging Company

5837 Distribution Dr
Memphis, TN 38141-8204

901-795-2711
Fax: 901-795-8035 www.tekni-plex.com
Foam carry out containers
President: Kenneth Baker
CFO: Glean Davis
Plant Manager: Rick Nelson
Estimated Sales: $20-30 Million
Number Employees: 100-249

22115 Elmar Industries

200 Gould Ave
Depew, NY 14043-3138

716-681-5650
Fax: 716-681-4660 800-433-3562
www.elmarworldwide.com
Filling machines: rotary piston (both rotary and vertical valve), bottom fill, gravity, true monoblock volumetric pocket, and vacuum syruper product fillers

President: Mark Dahlquist
Cio/Cto: Unggit Tjitradjaja
unggitt@elmarworldwide.com
Estimated Sales: $10-20 000,000
Number Employees: 100-249

22116 Elmar Worldwide

200 Gould Avenue
P.O.Box 245
Depew, NY 14043-0245

716-681-5650
Fax: 716-681-4660 800-433-3562
elmar@elmarworldwide.com
www.elmarworldwide.com
Manufacturer, exporter and designer of rotary valve
piston fillers, multi-flex particulate fillers, vacuum
syrupers and monoblock systems; also, re-manufac-
turing, R&D, computer/electronic line control sys-
tems, product testing andflush-in place systems
President: Mark Dahlquist
CEO: Martin Jolden, Jr.
CFO: Linda Gregorio
Sales: Tom Depczynski
Estimated Sales: $10-20 Million
Number Employees: 50-99
Brands:
    Elmar

22117 Elmark Packaging Inc

901 S Bolmar St # 1j
West Chester, PA 19382-4550

610-692-2455
Fax: 610-692-8793 800-670-9688
sales@elmarkpkg.com www.elmarkpkg.com
Provider of equipment, products and knowledge to
enable customers to add information to their prod-
ucts and packages in plant, on-line with self-adhe-
sive labels and/or all forms of printing
President: Heather Skerlak
apar@elmarkpkg.com
Estimated Sales: Below $5 Million
Number Employees: 5-9
Square Footage: 16400
Brands:
    Mini-Pro

22118 Elmeco SRL

5700 Ferguson Road
Suite 8
Bartlett, TN 38134-4557

901-385-0490
Fax: 901-373-7091
Slush machines
President: David Roberts
Number Employees: 4

22119 Elmo Rietschle-A Gardner Denver Product

1800 Gardner Expressway
Qunicy, IL 62305

217-222-5400
Fax: 217-228-8243
Compressors and pumps for the beverage and food
production industries.
President & CEO: Barry Pennypacker
Chairman Board Of Directors: Frank Hansen
frank.hansen@garnerdenver.com

22120 Elmwood Sensors

500 Narragansett Park Dr
Pawtucket, RI 00861

401-727-1300
Fax: 401-728-5390 800-356-9663
linda.lundgren@invensys.com
www.elmwoodsensors.com
Manufacturer and exporter of thermostats and con-
trols
VP/General Manager: Steven Fof
Estimated Sales: $50-100 Million
Number Employees: 100-250
Square Footage: 160000
Parent Co: Fasco

22121 Elo Touch Systems

301 Constitution Dr
Menlo Park, CA 94025-1110

650-361-4800
Fax: 650-361-4721 800-557-1458
eloinfo@elotouch.com www.elotouch.com
Manufacturer and exporter of operator interfaces
and point of sale systems

General Manager: Mark Mendenhall
Chief Executive Officer: Craig Witsoe
CFO: Roxi Wen
Vice President, Chief Technical Officer: Bruno
Thuillier
VP, Corporate Development: Sharon Segev
VP, Global Quality: Anita Chang
Manager of Marketing: Fumiko Sasaki
Vice President of Global Sales: Sean Miller
Contact: Thuillier Bruno
bruno.thuillier@elotouch.com
Vice President of Operations: Mike Moran
Number Employees: 500-999
Parent Co: Amp
Type of Packaging: Food Service
Brands:
    Ad-Touch
    Info Board
    Smart Frame
    Total Touch
    Touch In a Box

22122 Elopak Americas

46962 Liberty Dr
Wixom, MI 48393

248-486-4600
www.elopak.com
Cartons, aseptic and plastic pouches, form/fill/seal
systems and packaging equipment for paper and
plastic; importer of filling machinery.
Director, National Accounts, Americas: Julia Viter
Year Founded: 1906
Estimated Sales: $13 Billion
Number Employees: 2,800
Square Footage: 175000
Parent Co: Ferd Groups
Brands:
    Elopouch
    Pure-Pak
    Unifill

22123 Elreha Controls Corporation

2510 Terminal Drive South
St Petersburg, FL 33712

727-327-6236
Fax: 727-323-7336 sales@elreha.com
www.elreha.com
Electronic timers, cooking computers and thermom-
eters
President: Abdul Hamadeh
Contact: Junis Hamadeh
jhamadeh@elreha.com
General Manager: Bonnie DelGrosso
Estimated Sales: $5-10 Million
Number Employees: 100-249
Square Footage: 260000

22124 Elrene Home Fashions

261 5th Ave
New York, NY 10016-7794

212-213-0425
Fax: 212-481-1738
Place mats and tablecloths including plastic and fab-
ric
CEO: Mark Siegel
CFO and QC: Ron Selber
Estimated Sales: $2.5-5 Million
Number Employees: 100-249
Parent Co: Elrene Manufacturing Company

22125 (HQ)Elro Signs

400 W Walnut St
Gardena, CA 90248-3137

310-380-7444
Fax: 310-380-7452 800-927-4555
sales@elrosigns.com www.elrosigns.com
Electric, plastic, neon and metal signs; installation
service available nationwide
President: Max Rhodes
VP: Frank Rhodes
Manager: Dan Materman
sales@elrosigns.com
Estimated Sales: $4 Million
Number Employees: 20-49
Square Footage: 72000
Other Locations:
    Elro Sign Co.
    Marietta GA

22126 Elwell Parker

4200 Casteel Drive
Coraopolis, PA 15108

216-432-0638
Fax: 216-881-7555 800-272-9953
nick@elwellparker.com www.elwellparker.com

Manufacturer and exporter of material handling equipment including rider style, electric fork and platform trucks
Sales and Marketing: Nick Marshall
VP Sales/Marketing: Jeff Leggett
Manager Sales/Parts/Service/Support: Curt Roupe
Estimated Sales: $3-5 Million
Number Employees: 5-9

22127 Elwood Safety Company
2180 Elmwood Ave
Buffalo, NY 14216

716-308-0573
Fax: 716-874-2110 866-326-6060
leslie@elwoodsafety.com www.elwoodsafety.com
Manufacturer and exporter of protective clothing including aprons, coveralls, sweatbands, lab coats and flame retardant clothing; also, voltage testers, food and beverage coolers and filtration systems
VP/ Sr. Sales Representative: Leslie Meyers
Estimated Sales: $1-5 Million
Number Employees: 10-19
Square Footage: 30000

22128 Embee Sunshade Co
722 Metropolitan Ave # 1
Brooklyn, NY 11211-3722

718-387-8566
Fax: 718-782-2642 info@embeesunshade.com
www.embeesunshade.com
Umbrellas for carts and tables
Owner: Barnett S Brickner
info@embeesunshade.com
Estimated Sales: $2.5-5 Million
Number Employees: 10-19
Square Footage: 48000

22129 Emblem & Badge
123 Dyer Street
Suite 2
Providence, RI 02903-3907

401-365-1265
Fax: 401-365-1263 800-875-5444
sales@recognition.com www.recognition.com
Manufacturer, importer and exporter of plaques, trophies, advertising novelties, name badges, desk sets, glassware, custom awards, etc
President: David Resnik
Vice President: Mike Hersherits
Sales: RI Johnston
Contact: Dinna Finnegan
dinna@recognition.com
Number Employees: 50-99
Square Footage: 100000
Type of Packaging: Bulk
Brands:
    Awards America
    Emblem & Badge

22130 Embro Manufacturing Company
400 Nassau Street E
East Canton, OH 44730-1330

330-489-3500
Fax: 330-488-3131
O.E.M. wire forms, point of purchase and displays
Customer Service: Joni Nelson
Production Manager: Gary Wilson
Estimated Sales: $2.5-5 Million
Number Employees: 20-49
Square Footage: 136000

22131 Emc Solutions
302 S Ash St
Celina, OH 45822-2210

419-586-2388
Fax: 419-586-3311 sales@emcconveyor.com
www.emcconveyor.com
Stainless steel and painted overhead trolley conveyors.
Owner: Jeffrey Hazel
econo-mfg@bright.net
Estimated Sales: Less Than $500,000
Number Employees: 1-4
Square Footage: 20000
Type of Packaging: Food Service

22132 Emco Industrial Plastics
99 Commerce Rd
Cedar Grove, NJ 07009

973-239-0202
Fax: 973-239-1595 800-292-9906
mailbox@emcoplastics.com
www.emcoplastics.com

Supplier of plastic sheet, rod, tubing and films including plexiglass, cutting boards, and vinyl door strip. Manufacturer of plastic point of purchase displays including bulk food containers, bagel bins, pastry cases, candy binsframes, sign holders, and sneeze guards.
President: James Mc Namara
Vice President: Mark Mercadante
Sales Manager: Jim McNamara
Estimated Sales: $20-50 Million
Number Employees: 50-99
Square Footage: 50000
Type of Packaging: Food Service

22133 Emedco
2491 Wehrle Dr
Williamsville, NY 14221-7141

716-626-1616
Fax: 716-626-1630 877-765-8386
customerservice@emedco.com www.emedco.com
Signs and marking and safety devices including warning flags, tags, convex mirrors and laminated metal and pressure sensitive labels
President: David Ewert
Quality Control: Bill Meehen
Marketing Director: Kathleen Brunner
Sales Manager: Joseph Reinhart
Manager: Pascal Deman
Estimated Sales: $10-20 Million
Number Employees: 100-249
Square Footage: 140000
Brands:
    Economarks
    Kwik-Koils

22134 Emerald City Closets Inc
301-30th St. NE, #106
Auburn, WA 98002

425-497-8808
Fax: 425-497-8311 800-925-1521
www.emeraldcc.com
Manufacturer, importer and exporter of induction ranges and ovens
Owner: John Pearson
johnp@emeraldcc.com
Purchasing Manager: Winston Chiu
Estimated Sales: $2.5-5 Million
Number Employees: 1-4
Square Footage: 30000
Type of Packaging: Food Service, Private Label
Brands:
    Fuji Electric

22135 Emerald Packaging Inc
33050 Western Ave
Union City, CA 94587-2157

510-429-5700
Fax: 510-429-5715 www.empack.com
Polyethylene bags
President: Kevin Kelly
CEO: Esmeralda Barriga
ebarriga@cisco.com
Estimated Sales: $20-50 Million
Number Employees: 100-249

22136 Emerling International Foods
2381 Fillmore Ave
Suite 1
Buffalo, NY 14214-2197

716-833-7381
Fax: 716-833-7386 pemerling@emerfood.com
www.emerlinginternational.com
Bulk ingredients including: Fruits & Vegetables; Juice Concentrates; Herbs & Spices; Oils & Vinegars; Flavors & Colors; Honey & Molasses. Also produces pure maple syrup.
President: J Emerling
jemerling@emerfood.com
Sales: Peter Emerling
Public Relations: Jenn Burke
Year Founded: 1988
Estimated Sales: $10-20 Million
Number Employees: 20-49
Square Footage: 500000

22137 Emerson Industrial Automation
7078 Shady Oak Rd
Eden Prairie, MN 55344

952-995-8000
800-893-2321
info.us@mail.nidec.com
Automation solutions.
Contact: Steve Burts
steve.burts@emersonct.com

Number Employees: 100-249
Parent Co: Emerson Electric Co.

22138 Emerson Process Management
7070 Winchester Cir
Boulder, CO 80301-3506

303-527-5200
Fax: 303-530-8459 800-522-6277
flowcustomercare.americas@emerson.com
www2.emersonprocess.com
Measurement and process controls for the food and beverage industry, as well as solutions for water and wastewater treatments.
Business Leader: Steven Sonnenberg
Number Employees: 500-999

22139 Emery Thompson Machine &Supply Company
15350 Flight Path Drive
Brooksville, FL 34604-6861

718-588-7300
Fax: 352-796-0720
STEVE@EMERYTHOMPSON.COM
www.emerythompson.com
Manufacturer, importer and exporter of ice cream, Italian ice, frozen lemonade and frozen custard making machinery
President: Steve Thompson
CEO: Ted Thompson
Estimated Sales: $2.5-5 Million
Number Employees: 20-49
Square Footage: 180000

22140 Emery Winslow Scale Co
73 Cogwheel Ln # A
Seymour, CT 06483-3930

203-881-9333
Fax: 203-881-9477 www.emerywinslow.com
Industrial scale manufacturer
Owner/CEO: Walter Young
CEO: Rudi Baisch
emeryscale@aol.com
CFO/President: Bill Fischer
VP/Marketing: Rudi Baisch
Research & Development: Sam Sagarsee
Sales: David Young
Operations Manager: Bill Rosser
Plant Manager: Jim Evinger
Purchasing Manager: Jonathan Young
Estimated Sales: $20 Million+
Number Employees: 20-49
Number of Brands: 3
Square Footage: 120000
Other Locations:
    Pennsylvania Scale Company
    Lancaster PA
Brands:
    Emery
    Flattop
    Genesis
    Hydrostatics
    Hytronics
    Lifemount
    Totalizer
    Weighsquare
    Winslow

22141 Emico
13570 Larwin Circle
Santa Fe Springs, CA 90670

562-926-9600
Fax: 562-926-9611 info@emicoinc.com
www.emicoinc.com
Magnetic pan indexer, dough maker, zig-zag board rotary and boards, bread moulder, up-down pan indexer, wet onion applicator, bread and bun cooler, and screw pan; parts and service
Contact: Ron Fender
rfender@emicoinc.com
Estimated Sales: $1-5 Million

22142 Emiliomiti
219 9th St
San Francisco, CA 94103-3806

415-621-1909
Fax: 415-621-4613 866-867-2782
info@pastabiz.com www.pastabiz.com
Wholesaler/distributor of espresso coffee machines, pasta machines and wood burning brick pizza ovens; serving the food service market
CEO: Emilio Mitidieri
Estimated Sales: 900000
Number Employees: 10-19
Number of Brands: 5

Number of Products: 16
Square Footage: 12000
Brands:
 Capitani
 Emiollomiti
 Libitalia
 Pastabiz
 Technomachine

22143 Emjac
1075 Hialeah Dr
Hialeah, FL 33010-5551
 305-883-2194
 Fax: 305-883-2197 www.emjacindustries.com
Walk-in coolers and freezers
President: David Dorta
davidd@emjacindustries.com
Estimated Sales: $20-50 Million
Number Employees: 100-249

22144 Emmeti
101 Sherwood Drive
Boalsburg, PA 16827-1612
 816-466-2781
 Fax: 816-466-2782 emmeti@nauticom.net
Fully automatic, floor level, bulk palletizers, intelligent bottle stacker, automatic layer pad, top frame and empty pallet inserters
President: Kevin Zarnick
Marketing Manager/Owner: Fausto Savazzi
Sales Manager and PET Industry: Paolo Biondi
V P: Beth Zarnick-duffy
Sales Manager: Fabrizio Boschi
Technical Manager: Luis Garcia

22145 Emmeti USA
7320 East Fletcher Avenue
Tampa, FL 33637
 813-490-6252
 Fax: 813-490-6253 www.emmetiusa.com
President: Kevin Zarnick
Vice President: Fausto Savazzi
USA Sales Manager: Beth Zarnick-Duffy

22146 Emoshun
10022 6th Street
Rancho Cucamonga, CA 91730-5746
 909-484-9559
 Fax: 909-484-9560
Insulated bags and bottles
Estimated Sales: $1-5 Million

22147 Empire Bakery Equipment
1 Enterprise Pl # C
Hicksville, NY 11801-5347
 516-681-1500
 Fax: 516-681-1510 800-878-4070
 info@empirebake.com
Distributor of mixers, dough dividers, rounders, moulders, stampers, bagel machines, retarders, freezers, refrigerators, ovens, display cases, tables, slicers, etc
Owner: S Wechsler
info@empirebake.com
VP: C Zarate
Estimated Sales: Below $8 Million
Number Employees: 10-19
Square Footage: 64000

22148 Empire Candle Mfg LLC
2925 Fairfax Trfy
Kansas City, KS 66115-1317
 913-621-4555
 Fax: 913-621-3444 800-231-9398
Candles including scented and seasonal citronella
Owner: Rick Langley
rlangley@langleyempirecandle.com
CEO: Drummond Crews
CFO: Mick Buttress
Marketing: Brenda Cherpitel
Operations Manager: Eric Coulter
Purchasing: Larry Palmer
Estimated Sales: $10-20 Million
Number Employees: 50-99

22149 Empire Safe Company
6 E 39th St
New York, NY 10016-0112
 212-226-2255
 Fax: 212-684-5550 info@empiresafe.com
 www.empiresafe.com
Safes including burglar resistant and cash depositing

President: Richard Krasilovsky
CFO: Andy Genett
Contact: Tom Iacobellis
tom@empiresafe.com
Director of Operations: Mark Rubin
Estimated Sales: $5-10 Million
Number Employees: 5-9
Square Footage: 80000

22150 Empire Screen Printing Inc
N5206 Marco Rd
Onalaska, WI 54650-8818
 608-783-3301
 Fax: 608-783-3306 www.empirescreen.com
Empire is a leader in the latest printing processes including flexographic, screen & digital printing, as well as doming. Empire is a supplier to the appliance, retail, food, and beverage industries. Products include retail signagepackage labels, and marketing support items.
President: Johns Freismuth
CEO: James Brush
jamesbr@empirescreen.com
Vice President: James Schwinefus
Research & Development: Keith Cole
Quality Control: Steve Johnson
Marketing Director: Douglas Billings
Sales Director: Kathleen Cuellar
Public Relations: Douglas Billings
Operations Manager: John Johnsonth
Plant Manager: Lee Vieth
Purchasing Manager: Lori Taube
Estimated Sales: $25 Million
Number Employees: 250-499
Number of Brands: 2
Square Footage: 150000
Type of Packaging: Food Service, Private Label

22151 Emtrol
425 E Berlin Rd
York, PA 17408-8810
 717-846-4000
 Fax: 717-846-3624 800-634-4927
cgales@emtrol.com www.weldonmachinetool.com
Manufacturer, importer and exporter of material handling equipment and controls, plant automation equipment and custom warehouse/inventory software
President: George Sipe
Executive VP: Matthew Anater
VP Sales/Marketing: Nicholas Selch
Estimated Sales: $20-50 Million
Number Employees: 50-99
Square Footage: 52000

22152 Emulso
2750 Kenmore Ave
Tonawanda, NY 14150-7707
 716-854-2889
 Fax: 716-854-2809 info@emulso.com
 www.emulso.com
General and specialty cleaning compounds
President/Owner: Chris Miller
Estimated Sales: $10 Million
Number Employees: 25
Square Footage: 34000
Type of Packaging: Private Label, Bulk
Brands:
 Emulso

22153 En-Hanced Products Inc
229 E Broadway Ave
Westerville, OH 43081-1656
 614-882-7400
 Fax: 614-882-7549 800-783-7400
 www.en-hancedproducts.com
Food grade elevators and conveyors; also, hand and power seed cleaners.
President: James Hance
jhance@en-hancedproductsinc.com
Sales Director: Dennis James
Production Manager: Tim Woodruff
Purchasing Manager: Dennis James
Estimated Sales: $750,000
Number Employees: 5-9
Square Footage: 28000

22154 EnWave Corporation
744 W Hastings St
Suite 425
Vancouver, BC V6C 1A5
Canada
 604-806-6110
 info@enwave.net
 www.enwave.net
Dehydration of food, live or active bulk liquids, and sensitive pharmaceuticals.
President & CEO: Tim Durance
Executive Chairman: John P.A. Budreski
Chief Financial Officer: Dan Henriques
SVP, Research & Development: Dr. John Zhang
SVP, Technical Services & Director: Dr. Gary Sandberg
Director, R&D, Biomaterials: Dr. Rehaineh Noorbakhsh
SVP, Sales & Business Development: Brent Charleton
SVP, Manufacturing & Chief Engineer: Leon Fu
Year Founded: 1996
Estimated Sales: $14.9 Million
Number Employees: 35

22155 Encapsulation Systems
1489 Baltimore Pike
Suite 109
Springfield, PA 19064-3958
 610-543-0800
 Fax: 610-543-0688
Manufacturers of specially controlled release products for use in the pharmaceutical and medical-device field
President and CEO: Bruce Retting
Executive Vice President, Licensing: Cyril Burke
Number Employees: 10

22156 Encompass Supply
3505 Autumn Ct
Kalispell, MT 59901
 406-756-5900
 Fax: 406-756-1203 888-852-7590
 info@encompass-supply.com
 encompass-supply.com
Commercial janitorial supply company

22157 Encore Glass
4345 Industrial Way
Benicia, CA 94510
 707-745-4444
 Fax: 707-748-4444 sales@Encoreglass.com
 www.encoreglass.com
Wine industry recycled equipment
Sales Director: Dave Hammond
Contact: Rannie Dada
rannie.dada@encoreglass.com
Estimated Sales: $5-10 000,000
Number Employees: 40

22158 Encore Image Inc
303 W Main St
Ontario, CA 91762-3843
 909-986-4632
 Fax: 909-988-6376 800-791-1187
 info@encoreimage.com www.encoreimage.com
Exterior and interior electric and neon signs; also, menus and awnings
Chairman of the Board: Terry Wilkins
HR Executive: Sarah Quevada
s.quevada@encoreimage.com
VP Sales: Corey Northncott
Estimated Sales: $3-4,000,000
Number Employees: 20-49
Square Footage: 30000

22159 Encore Plastics
P.O.Box 3208
Huntington Beach, CA 92605
 714-893-7889
 Fax: 714-897-7968 888-822-8763
 info@encoreplastics.com www.encoreplastics.com
Manufacturer and exporter of beverageware and plastic stemware
President: Richard Harvey
Quality Control: David Martin
VP: Donald Okada
Contact: Donald Okada
dokada@encoreplastics.com
Estimated Sales: $500,000-$1 Million
Number Employees: 10
Parent Co: Donoco Industries

22160 Endress & Hauser
P.O.Box 246
Greenwood, IN 46142-0246

317-535-7138
Fax: 317-535-1489 800-428-4344
info@us.endress.com www.us.endress.com
Electronic process control instruments
Manager: Todd Lucey
VP Controller: Nancy Winter
Executive VP: Joseph Schaffer
Contact: David Jackson
david.jackson@us.endress.com
VP Manufacturing: Phil Tumey
Estimated Sales: $20-50 Million
Number Employees: 250-499
Square Footage: 78000
Parent Co: Endress & Hauser Consult

22161 Endurart Inc
20 W 22nd St
New York, NY 10010-5804

212-779-8522
Fax: 212-691-4751
Advertising novelties and specialties including
awards, trophies, embedments and coins
Manager: William Kalsman
Estimated Sales: $5-10 Million
Number Employees: 1-4

22162 Enercon
PO Box 773
Menomonee Falls, WI 53052-0773

262-255-6070
Fax: 262-255-7784 www.enerconind.com
Corona treaters and power supplies
Owner: Don Nimmer
CEO: Donald Nimmer
Contact: Sarah Bauer
sbauer@enerconmail.com
Estimated Sales: $10-20 000,000
Number Employees: 100-249

22163 Enerfab Inc.
4955 Spring Grove Ave.
Cincinnati, OH 45232

513-641-0500
enerfab.com
Stainless and carbon steel tanks, bulk aseptic storage
systems, epoxy tank linings, sanitary manways and
gasket materials.
President: Aaron Landolt
CEO: Scott Anderson
COO: Shawn Peck
Year Founded: 1901
Estimated Sales: $251 Million
Number Employees: 1000-4999
Square Footage: 250000
Brands:
  Lastiglas/Munkadur

22164 Energy Sciences Inc
42 Industrial Way # 1
Wilmington, MA 01887-3471

978-658-3731
Fax: 978-694-9046 www.ebeam.com
Manufacturer and exporter of electron beam pro-
cessing machinery used for drying and curing pack-
aging materials, printed foil, etc
President: Tsuneo Kobayashi
Manager: Harvey Clough
Accounts: Sharon Lagos
Chief Operating Officer: Ed Maguire
Estimated Sales: $7 Million
Number Employees: 50-99
Square Footage: 52000
Parent Co: Iwasaki Electric

22165 Energy Sciences Inc
42 Industrial Way # 1
Wilmington, MA 01887-3471

978-658-3731
Fax: 978-694-9046 tmclaughlin@ebeam.com
www.ebeam.com
Manufactures laser bean machinery that are used to
make bags used in the food industry
President: Harvey Clough
CEO: Gsunio Kadayashi
Sales Director: Brian Sullivan
Estimated Sales: $50-100 Million
Number Employees: 50-99

22166 Energymaster
105 Liberty St
Walled Lake, MI 48390

248-624-6900
Fax: 248-624-6975 www.energymasterusa.com
Manufacturer and exporter of energy conservation
equipment for heating and cooling, summer/winter
ventilation and make-up air
President: Erik Hall
Estimated Sales: $2.5-5 Million
Number Employees: 10-19
Square Footage: 3600
Type of Packaging: Consumer, Food Service
Brands:
  Energymaster
  Seasonmaster
  Ventilation

22167 Enerquip Inc
611 North Rd
611 North Road
Medford, WI 54451-1154

715-748-5888
Fax: 715-748-6484 ronherman@enerquip.com
www.enerquip.com
Designer and fabricator of stainless steel shell and
tube heat exchangers and custom components.
President & CEO: Jeannie Deml
Parts and Service: Sue Rhyner
Quality Control: John Barna
Director of Sales & Marketing: Ron Herman
Thermal Design and Inside Sales: Ron Herman
Manager: Ryan Ballinger
ryanballinger@enerquip.com
Number Employees: 20-49

22168 Engineered Automation
19 Pomerleau St.
Suite 101
Biddeford, MI 4005

207-200-8301
Fax: 207-283-3023 www.eaminc.com
Packaging machinery including rotary lidders, puck
inserters and removers and rotary overcappers
National Sales Manager: Suzanne Farrell
Number Employees: 20

22169 Engineered Food Systems
PO Box 821
Aurora, OR 97002-0821

503-699-6682
Fax: 503-699-6658
Equipment for Tortilla, Snack, Bakery and Packag-
ing industries

22170 Engineered Plastics Inc
211 Chase St
PO Box 227
Gibsonville, NC 27249-2877

336-449-4121
Fax: 336-449-6352 800-711-1740
engplas@triad.rr.com www.engplas.com
Illuminated buffet and ice sculpture display equip-
ment, acrylic serving bowls and trays and specialty
display items
President: Dwight M Davidson
engplas@triad.rr.com
Sales Manager: Robert Ratliff
Food Service Manager: W Mottinger
Estimated Sales: $2.5-5 Million
Number Employees: 20-49
Square Footage: 150000
Brands:
  Glo-Ice

22171 Engineered Products
12202 Missouri Bottom Rd
Hazelwood, MO 63042-2318

314-731-5744
Fax: 314-731-5744 800-474-1474
tdaugherty@enprod.com
President: Dave Wendel
Estimated Sales: $10-20 Million
Number Employees: 50-99

22172 (HQ)Engineered Products
12202 Missouri Bottom Rd
Hazelwood, MO 63042-2318

314-731-5744
Fax: 314-731-5744 www.epico.com
Custom plastic injection molding including contain-
ers
President: Dave Wendel
VP/General Manager: Ron McGee

Estimated Sales: $10-20 Million
Number Employees: 50-99
Square Footage: 96000
Other Locations:
  Engineered Products
  Dequeen AR

22173 Engineered Products Corp
355 Woodruff Rd # 204
Greenville, SC 29607-3494

864-234-4888
Fax: 864-234-4860 800-868-0145
sales@engprod.com www.engprod.com
Manufacturer and exporter of pallet storage racks,
gravity flow storage systems and conveyors; also,
turnkey warehouse engineering services available
Manager: David Shupe
Sales/Marketing Executive: Charles Rouse
Manager: Andre Butler
asbutler@epco.com
Purchasing Agent: Allen Griffith
Estimated Sales: $5-10 Million
Number Employees: 100-249
Square Footage: 400000
Parent Co: Gower
Brands:
  Deepflo
  Durabit
  Pushbak Cart
  Selectrak
  Traytrak

22174 Engineered Products Group
P.O.Box 8050
Madison, WI 53708

608-222-3484
Fax: 608-222-9314 800-626-3111
www.boumatic.com
Manufacturer and exporter of heat transfer equip-
ment, jacketed shells, troughs, baffles and tanks,
plates for fluid bed coolers and heaters, process ves-
sels and storage and mixing tanks; also, carbon steel,
stainless stell, titaniumand other alloys available
Owner: John Kotts
Sales: R Albrecht
Estimated Sales: $1-2.5 Million
Number Employees: 250-499
Parent Co: DEC International

22175 Engineered Security System Inc
1 Indian Ln
Towaco, NJ 07082-1015

973-257-0555
Fax: 973-257-0550 800-742-1263
info@engineeredsecurity.com
www.engineeredsecurity.com
Manufacturer and exporter of computer based secu-
rity systems; closed circuit TV monitoring available
Owner: David George
dgeorge@engineeredsecurity.com
Estimated Sales: $20-50 Million
Number Employees: 50-99
Square Footage: 8500

22176 Engineered Systems & Designs
119 Sandy Dr # A
Newark, DE 19713-1148

302-456-0446
Fax: 302-456-0441 esd@esdinc.com
www.esdinc.com
Wine industry laboratory equipment
President: Robert Spring
Estimated Sales: Below $5 Million
Number Employees: 1-4

22177 Engineered Textile Products
715 Loeffler St
Mobile, AL 36607-1317

251-476-8001
Fax: 251-476-0956 800-222-8277
ken@etpinfo.com www.etpinfo.com
Commercial awnings
President: Kenneth Robinson
ken@etpinfo.com
Estimated Sales: $1-2.5 Million
Number Employees: 20-49
Brands:
  Artcraft

22178 Engineering & Mgmt Consultants
742 Butternut Dr
Franklin Lakes, NJ 07417-2243

201-847-0748
Fax: 201-847-0748 rhmeeremc@aol.com

Consultant specializing in plant operations, production and inventory control, laboratory and technical activities, marketing, regulatory and financial affairs, processing functions, certification, etc
President: Richard H Meer
rhmeeremc@aol.com
Estimated Sales: Less Than $500,000
Number Employees: 1-4

22179 England Logistics
4701 West 2100 South
Salt Lake City, UT 84120
801-972-2712
Fax: 801-977-5795 800-887-0764
info@englandlogistics.com
www.englandlogistics.com
Transportation firm providing local, short and long haul trucking; also, contract warehousing available
President: Dan England
CEO: Dean England
Senior Vice President Chief Financial Of: Keith Wallace
Vice President: Brandon Harrison
Executive Vice President of Corporate Sa: David Kramer
Contact: Rolina Camello
rolina.camello@crengland.com

22180 English Manufacturing Inc
11292 Sunrise Park Dr
Rancho Cordova, CA 95742-6599
916-638-9902
Fax: 916-638-9961 800-651-2711
www.englishmfg.com
Stainless steel sneeze gaurds and food guards, glass racks and partition posts.
President: Doug English
CFO: Diana English
Vice President: Jennifer Kogler
Research & Development: Shawn Rice
Quality Control: A J Wells
Marketing Director: Andrew Nelson
Sales Director: Cindy Lucas
Contact: Mark Dallara
markdallara@freudenbergmedical.com
Operations Manager: Mike Richardson
Production Manager: Sara Stefanik
Estimated Sales: Less Than $500,000
Number Employees: 1-4
Number of Brands: 2
Number of Products: 12
Square Footage: 10000
Type of Packaging: Food Service, Private Label
Brands:
Matrix Sneezegaurd

22181 Engraph Label Group
1187 Industrial Rd
Cold Spring, KY 41076-8799
859-781-6161
Fax: 859-781-6339 800-422-6633
Wine industry label printers
President: Eric Schaffer
Estimated Sales: $3-5 Million
Number Employees: 10-19

22182 Engraving Services Co.
818 Port Road
Woodville South, SA 05011
engrave@engravingservices.com.au
www.engravingservices.com.au
Manufacturer and exporter of labels, nameplates, decals and engraved plastic and electric signs
Sales/Marketing Director: Peter Vasic
Production Manager: Jamie Smale
Estimated Sales: $5-10 Million
Number Employees: 50-99
Type of Packaging: Bulk

22183 Engraving Specialists
503 N Washington Ave
Royal Oak, MI 48067-1756
248-542-2244
Fax: 248-542-1847
Engraved promotional items, award plaques and name badges; also, signage including ADA, directional, label, vinyl letter and logo available
Owner: Marc Milosevich
VP/Secretary/Treasurer: Dick Lang
Estimated Sales: $500,000-$1 Million
Number Employees: 1-4
Square Footage: 5600

22184 Enhance Packaging Technologies
201 S Blair Street
Whitby, ON L1N 5S6
Canada
905-668-5811
Fax: 905-666-7005 www.packagingdigest.com
Liquid pouch form/fill/seal equipment including pasteurized and aseptic fillers; also, films matched to application and equipment
Marketing Development Manager (US Dairy): Harry Akamphuber
Marketing Development: Wayne Naumowich
Marketing Development: Joe Shields
Parent Co: DuPont Canada
Brands:
Mini-Sip

22185 Enjay Converters Ltd.
495 Ball Street
Cobourg, ON K9A
Canada
905-372-7373
Fax: 905-377-8066 800-427-5517
sales@enjay.com www.enjay.com
Manufactures a complete line of laminated and wrapped cake circles and shieets
President: Jay Cassidy
Number Employees: 10

22186 Ennio International
1005 N. Commons Drive
Aurora, IL 60504-4100
630-851-5808
Fax: 630-851-7744 www.enniousa.com
Manufacturer and supplier of high quality netting and casings for the meat and poultry industries.
Director Of Sales: Ralph Schuster
Contact: Ennio Hand
ennio.hand@enniousa.com

22187 Ennis Inc.
2241 Presidential Pkwy.
Midlothian, TX 76065
972-775-9801
Fax: 800-645-8339 800-972-1069
HOTLine@ennis.com www.ennis.com
Restaurant supplies including menus, place mats and paper items.
Chairman/CEO/President: Keith Walters
Vice President, Finance/CFO: Richard Travis
Executive Vice President/Secretary: Michael Magill
Vice President, Administration: Ronald Graham
Year Founded: 1909
Estimated Sales: $370 Million
Number Employees: 2,300+
Number of Brands: 33
Brands:
Allen-Bailey™
Adams McClure®
Admore®
Atlas Tag & Label®
B&D Litho of Arizona®
Block Graphics®
Calibrated®
ColorWorx®
Ennis®
Falcon Business Forms®
Forms Manufacturers™
Folder Express®
GenForms®
General Financial Supply®
Hayes Graphics®
Hoosier Data Forms®
Independant Folders®
Kay Toledo Tag™
Major Business Systems™
Mutual Graphics™
National Imprint Corporation®
Northstar®
Printegra®
Print Graphics®
PrintXcel®
Royal®
Special Service Partners™
Specialized Printed Forms®
Star Award Ribbon Co.®
Trade Envelopes®
Tri-C Business Forms™
Wisco Envelope®
Witt Printing™

22188 Enotech Corporation
PO Box 576
Palo Alto, CA 94302-0576
650-851-2040
Fax: 650-851-2034 info@enotechusa.com
Wine industry equipment

22189 Enpoco
4263 Carolina Avenue
Suite J
Richmond, VA 23222-1400
804-228-9934
Fax: 703-668-1400 800-338-2581
Grease interceptors
CEO: Patrick Okeefe
Interceptor Production Manager: Roy Hetzler
Estimated Sales: $2.5-5 Million
Number Employees: 10-19
Parent Co: Watts Industries

22190 Enrick Co
150 E 1st St
PO Box 37
Zumbrota, MN 55992-1552
507-732-5215
Fax: 507-625-6570 rollorkari@yahoo.com
www.enrickco.com
Manufacturer and exporter of hand trucks, dollies and carts
Owner: Vince Small
Estimated Sales: $1-2.5 Million
Number Employees: 5-9

22191 Ensign Ribbon Burners LLC
101 Secor Ln
Pelham, NY 10803-2791
914-813-0815
Fax: 914-738-0928 info@erbensign.com
Industrial gas burners
President: John F Cavallo
Vice President: Mario Anelich
mario@erbensign.com
Estimated Sales: $2.5-5 Million
Number Employees: 10-19

22192 Ensign Ribbon Burners LLC
101 Secor Ln
PO Box 8369
Pelham, NY 10803-2791
914-813-0815
Fax: 914-738-0928 info@erbensign.com
Vice President: Mario Anelich
mario@erbensign.com
Vice President: James Pezzuto
Director of Sales: Mario Anelich
Estimated Sales: $3-5 Million
Number Employees: 10-19

22193 Ensinger Inc
365 Meadowlands Blvd
Washington, PA 15301-8900
724-746-6050
Fax: 724-746-9078 800-243-3221
sales@ensinger-ind.com www.ensinger-inc.com
Manufacturer and exporter of plastic packaging materials
President: Frank Bavaro
fbavaro@ensinger-inc.com
Director Sales/Marketing: Bruce Dickinson
Technical Director: Ken Schwartz
Estimated Sales: $10-20 Million
Number Employees: 20-49
Parent Co: Dana Her Corporation
Type of Packaging: Bulk

22194 Entech Instruments Inc.
2207 Agate Court
Simi Valley, CA 93065
805-527-5939
www.entechinst.com
Developer and manufacturer of analytical instruments.
Founder & Presdient: Dan Cardin
Director, Marketing & Information System: John Quintana
Customer Care & Service Manager: Tom Wilber
National Service Manager: Tim Raub

22195 Entech Systems Corp
607 Maria St
Kenner, LA 70062-7400
504-469-6541
Fax: 504-465-9192 800-783-6561
entech@msn.com www.entech.com

Manufacturer and exporter of automatic ULV insect fogging systems for killing crawling and flying insects; also, semi-automatic and portable systems, sanitation audits and insecticides
President: Robert Drude
robert.drudge@entech.cc
Corporate Secretary: Gail Stumpf
Purchasing Manager: Marcus Curtis
Estimated Sales: Below $5 Million
Number Employees: 5-9
Square Footage: 16000
Brands:
Auto Fog
Entech Fog

22196 Entergy's Teamwork Louisiana
4809 Jefferson Highway
Jefferson, LA 70121-3126
504-840-2562
Fax: 504-840-2512 800-968-8243
laed@entergy.com www.entergy.com
Chairman of the Board; Chief Executive O: Wayne Leonard
Senior Vice President: Donna Jacobs
Contact: Cain Merite
cmerite@entergy.com
Estimated Sales: $1-5 Million

22197 Enterprise
7800 Sovereign Row
Dallas, TX 75247-4887
214-688-5223
Fax: 214-638-2016 800-527-9431
Contact: Frederick Goes
fred@goesent.com
Estimated Sales: $10-20 000,000
Number Employees: 5-9

22198 Enterprise Box Company
10 Burnside Street
Montclair, NJ 07043-1325
973-509-2200
Fax: 973-509-1910
Paper boxes and envelopes
VP: Lenore Klein
Estimated Sales: Less than $500,000
Number Employees: 1-4

22199 Enterprise Company
616 S Santa Fe
Santa Ana, CA 92705
714-835-0541
Fax: 714-543-2856
Manufacturer and exporter of baling presses
President: Orval Gould
VP: Albert Gould
Marketing Director: John Gould
Contact: Dan Scott
dan@enterpriseco.com
Estimated Sales: $2.5-5 Million
Number Employees: 50-99
Type of Packaging: Bulk

22200 Enterprise Dynamics Corporation
1577 N Technology Way # A
Orem, UT 84097-2395
801-224-6914
Fax: 801-224-6984
Software
Owner: Bill Nordgren
Estimated Sales: $1-3 Million
Number Employees: 10-19

22201 Enterprise Envelope Inc
920 Ken O Sha Ind Park Dr SE
Grand Rapids, MI 49508-8215
616-247-1301
Fax: 616-247-1343 800-422-4255
orders@enterpriseenvelope.com
www.enterpriseenvelope.com
Envelopes including lithographed, commercial catalog, special size and window; up to four color process
President: Gary Helmholdt
gary@enterpriseenvelope.com
Estimated Sales: $1-3 Million
Number Employees: 10-19
Square Footage: 42000

22202 Enterprise Products
6875 Suva St
Bell Gardens, CA 90201-1998
562-928-1918
Fax: 562-927-8413

Wire display racks and shelving; also, tubing goods and stampings
CEO: Ron Spicer
Contact: Stephanie Happel
stephanie.happel@georgfischer.com
Estimated Sales: $20-50 Million
Number Employees: 100-249

22203 Enting Water Conditioning Inc
3211 Dryden Rd Frnt
Moraine, OH 45439-1400
937-456-5151
Fax: 937-294-5485 800-735-5100
sales@enting.com www.enting.com
Manufacturer and exporter of water treatment systems including softeners, reverse osmosis, cartridge filters and ultra-violet purifiers
President: Mel Entingh
President/COO: Dan Entingh
info@enting.com
Estimated Sales: $5-10 Million
Number Employees: 10-19
Square Footage: 86800
Brands:
Aquamate
Enting
Kane
Watermate

22204 Entoleter LLC
251 Welton St
Hamden, CT 06517-3944
203-787-3575
Fax: 203-787-1492 800-729-3575
info@entoleter.com www.entoleter.com
Manufacturer, exporter of centrifugal impact mills, wet scrubbers and wet electrostatic precipitators
President: Ernie Carr
ecarr@entoleter.com
Sales Manager: Todd Gardner
Sales Manager: Dick Steinsuaag
ecarr@entoleter.com
Estimated Sales: $5-10 000,000
Number Employees: 20-49
Square Footage: 62000
Parent Co: Spinnaker Industries
Brands:
Centrified
Centrimil
Eid
Esa

22205 Enviro Doors By ASI Technologies
5848 N. 95th Court
Milwaukee, WI 53225-2613
414-464-6200
Fax: 414-464-9863 800-558-7068
sales@asidoors.com www.asidoors.com
President: George C Balbach
Estimated Sales: $6 Million
Number Employees: 100-249

22206 Enviro-Clear Co
152 Cregar Rd
High Bridge, NJ 08829-1003
908-638-5507
Fax: 908-638-4636 info@enviro-clear.com
www.enviro-clear.com
Manufacturer and exporter of clarifiers and belt and pressure filters and separators
President: Joe Muldowney
sales@enviro-clear.com
VP Marketing: Cindy Meyer
Sales: James Grau
Estimated Sales: $3-5 Million
Number Employees: 5-9
Square Footage: 40000
Brands:
Enviro-Clear
Pronto

22207 Enviro-Pak
15450 SE For Mor Ct
PO Box 1569
Clackamas, OR 97015
503-655-7044
Fax: 503-655-6368 800-223-6836
sales@enviro-pak.com www.enviro-pak.com

Manufactures food processing ovens, smokers, dryers, steam cabinets and chillers for further processing of meat, fish and poultry. Products are also now being used in different industries such as pet foods, fruits, vegetables, tofubakery products, mushrooms, and more.
Owner: Gil Martini
Contact: Kim Bryant
kim.bryant@enviropak.com
Estimated Sales: $10-20 Million
Number Employees: 20-49

22208 Enviro-Safety Products
8248 West Doe Ave
Visalia, CA 93291-9263
559-625-5592
Fax: 559-651-1320 800-637-6606
info@envirosafetyproducts.com
www.envirosafetyproducts.com
Wine industry powdered spray and sulfur helmets, protective clothing, respirators of all types
Manager: Scott Newton
R & D: Peggy Dahlvang
Contact: Bob Brussel
b.brussel@envirosafetyproducts.com
Estimated Sales: $500,000
Number Employees: 20-49
Brands:
3m
Aearo/Peltor
Paulson
Sas

22209 Enviro-Test/Perry Laboratories
8102 Lemont Rd Ste 1500
Woodridge, IL 60517-7776
630-324-6685
Fax: 630-734-9534 www.envirotest-perry.com
Laboratory testing and analysis firm
President: Maria Lenos
VP Sales: Detrie Zacharias
Lab Director: George Lenos
Estimated Sales: Less than $500,000
Number Employees: 10 to 19
Square Footage: 9000

22210 Enviro-Ware
100 Sandusky Street
2nd Floor
Pittsburgh, PA 15212-5822
412-642-2222
Fax: 412-642-2223 888-233-7857
www.enviro-ware.com
Manufacturers of biodegradable dinnerware and packing
Estimated Sales: $1-5 Million
Brands:
Enviro-Ware

22211 Envirolights Manufacturing
50 Viceroy Road
Concord, ON L4K 2L8
Canada
905-738-0357
Fax: 905-738-0647
Pest and insect control systems and devices including industrial electrocution and glue board type insect light traps
President: Ken Nayler
VP: Douglas Nayler
Number Employees: 5-9
Parent Co: Envirolights Manufacturing
Brands:
Electri-Fly
Flintrol
The Flylight

22212 Enviromental Structures
950 Walnut Ridge Dr
Hartland, WI 53029-9388
262-369-3535
Fax: 262-369-3536
President: Brad Barke
Contact: Kathryn Macdonald
kathryn.macdonald@aurora.org
Estimated Sales: $10-20 Million
Number Employees: 20-49

22213 Environmental Consultants
391 Newman Ave
Clarksville, IN 47129-3247
812-282-8481
Fax: 812-282-8554

Environmental consultants specializing in pollution control, testing and analysis
President: Robert Fuchs
Office Manager: Patti Kinchlow
Estimated Sales: $1-2.5 Million
Number Employees: 5 to 9

22214 Environmental Express
2345 Charleston Regional Pkwy
Charleston, SC 29492-8405

843-881-6560
Fax: 843-881-3964 800-343-5319
suggestions@envexp.com www.envexp.com
Supplier of environmentally safer laboratory equipment for the food and beverage research & developent industry.
CEO: Dennis Pope
CFO: Nikki Truman
nikkit@envexp.com
Vice President: Paul Strickler
Technical Sales Representative: Allison Ditullio
Manager: Paula Borgstedt
Estimated Sales: $5.2 Million
Number Employees: 50-99

22215 Environmental Products
730 Commerce Dr
Venice, FL 34292

941-486-1325
Fax: 941-480-9201 800-828-2447
www.cranenv.com/index1
Reverse osmosis based water purification equipment, including pre-treatment and post-treatment systems
Estimated Sales: $10-20 000,000
Number Employees: 50-99

22216 (HQ)Environmental Products Corp
99 Great Hill Rd
Naugatuck, CT 06770-2227

203-720-4059
Fax: 203-720-9302 800-275-3861
Reverse-vending machinery; also, container accounting and collection services available
President: Bhajun G Santchurn
CFO: Pilraj Chuwla
Sales: Bill Donnelly
Contact: David Baltimore
davidb@envipco.com
Operations Manager: Charles Ricey
Plant Manager: Harry Yerrick
Estimated Sales: $.5-1 million
Number Employees: 5-9
Square Footage: 160000
Other Locations:
Environmental Products Corp.
Fairfax VA

22217 Environmental Products Company
197 Poplar Place #3
North Aurora, IL 60542-8191

630-892-2414
Fax: 630-892-2467 800-677-8479
Manufacturer and exporter of polyvinyl chloride strip doors, heat recycling fans and welding screens
Manager: Kurt Pfoutz
kpfoutz@hotmail.com
Office Manager: Kurt Pfoutz
Estimated Sales: $5-10 Million
Number Employees: 10 to 19
Square Footage: 30000
Parent Co: Material Control

22218 Environmental Systems
218 N Main St
Culpeper, VA 22701-2620

540-825-6660
Fax: 540-825-4961 800-541-2116
info@ess-services.com www.ess-services.com
Consultant specializing in dairy and sanitation testing, quality control and analysis including water, wastewater, microbiological and shelf-life
President: Robert Jebson
robertj@ess-services.com
VP: Donald Hearl
Estimated Sales: $5-10 Million
Number Employees: 20-49
Square Footage: 20000

22219 Environmizer Systems Corporation
25 W Highland Avenue
Atlantic Highlands, NJ 07716-2804

732-291-4700
Fax: 732-291-4720
Magnetic scale removal in evaporators, separators, pasteurizers
Estimated Sales: Less than $500,000
Number Employees: 4

22220 Enviropak Corp
4203 Shoreline Dr
Earth City, MO 63045-1209

314-739-1202
Fax: 314-739-2422 info@enviropak.com
www.enviropak.com
Molded pulp packaging
President: John Wichlenski
CEO: Chris Miget
chris@enviropak.com
Estimated Sales: $5-10 000,000
Number Employees: 50-99

22221 Enviropak Corp
4203 Shoreline Dr
Earth City, MO 63045-1209

314-739-1202
Fax: 314-739-2422 sales@enviropak.com
www.enviropak.com
Pulp packaging for numerous industries including that of food and beverage.
President: John Wichlenski
CEO: Chris Miget
chris@enviropak.com
Treasurer: Joseph Walsh
VP: Jon Smith
Vice President Sales & Marketing: Bill Noble
Sales Coordinator: Kay Walsh
Vice President Manufacturing: Rodney Heenan
Estimated Sales: $4 Million
Number Employees: 50-99
Square Footage: 40000

22222 Epcon Industrial Systems
17777 I-45 South
Conroe, TX 77385

936-273-3300
Fax: 936-273-4600 800-447-7872
sales@epconlp.com www.epconlp.com
Manufacturer and exporter of air pollution control systems for enclosures, odor control systems and oxidizers; also, general bake ovens
President and R&D: Aziz Jamaluddin
CFO: Sunny Naidu
Quality Control: Mike Paddie
Sales Engineer: Brad Morello
Engineer Designer: Nedzad Hadzajlic
Estimated Sales: $5-10 Million
Number Employees: 50-99
Square Footage: 400000

22223 Epic Industries
1007 Jersey Ave
New Brunswick, NJ 08901

732-249-6867
Fax: 732-249-7683 800-221-3742
www.epicindustries.com
Institutional and industrial cleaning
President and CFO: Ted Bustany
Quality Control: John Nelson
Director: Sam Levine
Estimated Sales: $1-2.5 000,000
Number Employees: 50-99
Square Footage: 55000

22224 Epic Products
2801 S Yale St
Santa Ana, CA 92704

714-641-8194
Fax: 714-641-8217 800-548-9791
info@epicproductsinc.com
www.epicproductsinc.com
Bar supplies including plastic wine glasses, acrylic glassware, servingware, wine racks, cork pullers and drink stirrers
Owner: Ardeen Dubow
VP: Matt DuBow
Contact: Rocio Brooks
brooks@epicproductsinc.com
Estimated Sales: $5-10 Million
Number Employees: 20-49

22225 Epsen Hillmer Graphics Co
13748 F St
Omaha, NE 68137-1166

402-342-7000
Fax: 402-342-9284 800-228-9940
www.ehg.net
Manufacturer and exporter of labels including pressure sensitive, glue applied litho, in-mold and PET beverage
President: Tom Hillmer
thillmer@ehg.net
VP Opers.: Thomas Hillmer
VP Sales/Marketing: R Craig Cunran
VP Operations: Thomas Hillmer
Estimated Sales: $.5-1 million
Number Employees: 50-99

22226 Epsilon Industrial
2215 Grand Avenue Pkwy
Austin, TX 78728

512-251-1500
Fax: 512-251-1593
Provides food technologists with instrumentation to perform multicomponent analysis on clear or cloudy liquids, slurries, powders, solids
Estimated Sales: $1-2.5 000,000
Number Employees: 5-9

22227 Epsilon-Opti Films Corporation
132 Case Dr
South Plainfield, NJ 07080-5109

908-791-1732
Fax: 908-791-1030 800-235-8383
Polyolefin shrink films
Number Employees: 20-49

22228 Epstein
600 W Fulton St # 9
Chicago, IL 60661-1253

312-454-9100
Fax: 312-559-1217 information@epstein-isi.com
www.epsteinglobal.com
Design and construction of food manufacturing and distribution facilities
President: John Patelski
CFO: Jim Jirsa
jimjirsa@epstein-isi.com
Executive VP: Allen L Pomerance
Quality Control: Darrin McCormies
R&D: Andrea Velasquez
Estimated Sales: $20-50 Million
Number Employees: 250-499

22229 Epstein
600 W Fulton St # 9
Chicago, IL 60661-1253

312-454-9100
Fax: 312-559-1217 information@epstein-isi.com
www.epsteinglobal.com
CFO: Jim Jirsa
jimjirsa@epstein-isi.com
Executive VP: Allen L Pomerance
Estimated Sales: $20-50 Million
Number Employees: 250-499

22230 Equichem International Inc
510 Tower Blvd
Carol Stream, IL 60188-9426

630-784-0432
Fax: 630-784-0436 mail@equichem.com
www.equichem.com
Custom vitamin and mineral premixes and enzyme blends.
President: Luis C Lovis
llovis@equichem.com
Research/Development Director: Luis J Lovis
Sales Director: Anna Lovis
Number Employees: 5-9
Type of Packaging: Bulk

22231 Equilon Lubricants
1111 Bagby Street
Houston, TX 77002-2551

713-752-6695
Fax: 713-752-4678 800-645-8237
www.shell-lubricants.com
Synthetic and mineral based fluids and greases for food or beverage processing plants
Chief Executive Officer: Peter Voser
Research & Development: Kris Kaushik
Marketing Director: David Rowe
Sales Director: Larry Cekella
Parent Co: Shell International Petroleum Company

535

Brands:
Cassida Fluids and Greasers
Cyenus Fluids and Greasers
Shell Fm Fluids and Greasers

22232 Equipex Limited
765 Westminster St
Providence, RI 02903-4018
401-273-3300
Fax: 401-273-3328 800-649-7885
sales@equipex.com www.equipex.com
Manufacturer and exporter of ovens and restaurant
equipment
President: Loretta Clark
lorettac@equipex.com
VP: Val Ginzburg
Sales/Marketing Division: Irina Mirsky-Zayas
Operations: Loretta Fortier
Estimated Sales: $2.5-5,000,000
Number Employees: 1-4

22233 Equipment Design & Fabrication
722 N Smith St
Charlotte, NC 28202-1454
704-372-4513
Fax: 704-372-4514 800-949-0165
Materials handling, railroad maintenance, textile &
furniture manufacturing equipment
President: Terry D Miller
edfterry@bellsouth.net
Purchasing Manager: Tony Walkins
Number Employees: 5-9

22234 Equipment Distributing of America
1776 Country Road M
PO Box 213
Wahoo, NE 68066
402-592-9360
Fax: 402-443-1384 efa.efa-usa@windstream.net
www.efa-germany.de
Supplier of meat processing machines and industrial
tools
Manager: David Weinert
Estimated Sales: Under $500,000
Number Employees: 1-4
Parent Co: EFA Germany

22235 Equipment Enterprises
6670 E Harris Blvd
Charlotte, NC 28215-5101
704-568-3001
Fax: 704-536-3259 800-221-3681
sales@wardtank.com www.wardtank.com
Water treatment systems
President: Donald Ward
President, Chief Executive Officer: Jon Ward
President, Chief Executive Officer: Jon Ward
Operations Sales Manager: Rick Shepherd
Vice President of Operations: Bob Besh
Estimated Sales: $5-10 Million
Number Employees: 20-49
Square Footage: 64000
Parent Co: Ward Tank & Heat Exchanger

22236 Equipment Enterprises
1875 Graves Road
Norcross, GA 30093-1022
770-368-9789
Fax: 770-368-0587 800-221-3681
Water treatment systems including lime coagulation,
direct filtraton, membranes, carbon purifiers, filters,
ozanators, and ultraviolet units
Estimated Sales: $1-5 000,000
Number Employees: 9

22237 Equipment Equities Corporation
866 United Nations Plaza
Suite 440
New York, NY 10017-1838
212-688-8800
Fax: 212-688-0061
Estimated Sales: $3-5 Million
Number Employees: 1-4

22238 Equipment Exchange Co
10042 Keystone Dr
Lake City, PA 16423-1060
814-774-0888
Fax: 814-774-0880 info@eeclink.com
Buyers and sellers of used food process machinery.
Choppers, grinders, patty, meat forming and portion,
smokehouses and accessories, seasonings, ingredients, batters and breading

President: Robert J Breakstone
info@eeclink.com
Estimated Sales: $2.5-5 Million
Number Employees: 10-19
Square Footage: 120000

22239 Equipment Express
60 Wanless Court
Ayr, ON N0B 1E0
Canada
519-740-8008
Fax: 519-740-6297 800-387-9791
carrief@equipmentexpress.com
equipmentexpress.com
Unscramblers, air and wet bottle cleaners, convey-
ors, fillers, cappers, induction sealers, labelers, cod-
ers, tapers, case erectors, case packers, palletizer,
bundlers, pallet warppers, turnkey bottled water
plants, including watertreatment systems, specialty
machines
President: Jeff Ake
VP Marketing: Liliana Ake
Production Manager: Kurt Organ
Plant Manager: John Naughton
Purchasing Manager: Teresa Mago
Estimated Sales: $1-4 Million
Number Employees: 20

22240 Equipment Innovators
800 Industrial Park Dr
Marietta, GA 30062-2498
770-427-9467
Fax: 678-391-9120 800-733-3434
sales@equipmentinnovators.com
www.equipmentinnovators.com
President: Richard C McCamey
CEO: Joe Rubin
Vice President: Doug Edwards
dedwards@equipmentinnovators.com
Estimated Sales: $10-20 Million
Number Employees: 20-49

22241 Equipment Outlet
199 N Linder Road
Meridian, ID 83642-2440
208-887-1472
Fax: 208-887-4874
Supplier of packaging equipment materials
Salesman: Brian Maglecic
Estimated Sales: $1-2.5 Million
Number Employees: 10

22242 Equipment Specialists Inc
9489 Hawkins Dr
Manassas, VA 20109-3907
703-361-2227
Fax: 703-361-4965
www.equipmentspecialistsinc.com
Manufacturer and exporter of new and used food
processing and packaging equipment
Owner: Allan Tousha
CEO: Beverly Gordon
Vice President: Jeremy Gordon
Sales Director: Mariano Montealegre
allan@esitrucks.com
Operations Manager: Jose Macy
Plant Manager: Reinaldo Mendoza
Purchasing Manager: Eric Ball
Estimated Sales: $10-20 Million
Number Employees: 10-19
Square Footage: 300000
Type of Packaging: Food Service

22243 Equipment for Coffee
71 Lost Lake Ln
Campbell, CA 95008-6642
650-259-7801
Fax: 650-259-7603
Tea and coffee industry colorimeters, pollution con-
trol equipment, vacuum packaging machinery
Contact: Robert Hensley
rh@specialtycoffee.com
Plant Manager: Gordon McNeil
Estimated Sales: Less than $500,000
Number Employees: 1-4
Square Footage: 3000

22244 Erb International
290 Hamilton Road
New Hamburg, ON N3A 1A2
Canada
519-662-2710
Fax: 519-662-3316 800-665-2653
werb@erbgroup.com www.erbgroup.com

President: Vernon D Erb
CFO: Kevin Copper
Number Employees: 10

22245 Erca-Formseal
1210 Campus Dr
Morganville, NJ 07751-1262
732-536-8770
Fax: 732-536-8850 www.oystarusa.com
President: Charles Ravalli
Estimated Sales: $3-5 Million
Number Employees: 10-19

22246 Erell Manufacturing Co
2678 Coyle Ave
Elk Grove Vlg, IL 60007-6404
847-427-3000
Fax: 847-663-9970 800-622-6334
Plastic aprons; exporter and manufacturer of vinyl
industrial and promotional products
President: Randy Silton
randy@erell.com
Estimated Sales: $1-2.5 Million
Number Employees: 10-19
Square Footage: 34000
Brands:
Plasti-Guard

22247 Ergonomic Handling Systems
PO Box 338
Line Lexington, PA 18932-0338
215-822-8778
Fax: 215-822-8088 800-223-6430
General and CNC machining, drilling, boring, cut-
ting and honing, general welding, fabricating and
material handling
Sales Director: Tim Burns
Estimated Sales: $1-2.5 Million
Number Employees: 20-50

22248 Erickson Industries
717 Saint Croix St
River Falls, WI 54022
715-426-9700
Fax: 715-426-9701 800-729-9941
Manufacturer and exporter of refrigerators, freezers,
walk-in coolers and pre-fabricated cooling and
freezing warehouses; also, manufacturer of tubular
towers and planter grids
Owner: Paul Erickson
Sales: Debbie Huppert
Sales Engineering: Joel Johnson
Advertising Manager: H Walsh
Estimated Sales: $1-2.5 Million
Number Employees: 1-4
Square Footage: 80000
Brands:
Chill-Air
Erickson
Kool-Rite

22249 Erie Container
4700 Lorain Ave
Cleveland, OH 44102-3443
216-631-1650
Fax: 216-631-1249
Paper tubes and containers
President: Frank Lipinski
flipinski@containers-cases.com
VP: Joseph Lipinski
Estimated Sales: $5-10 Million
Number Employees: 5-9

22250 Erie Cotton Products
1112 Bacon St
Erie, PA 16511-1732
814-459-6644
Fax: 814-453-7816 800-289-4737
sales@eriecotton.com www.eriecotton.com
Towels including burlap, cheesecloth, nonwovens,
dish, glass, bar and disposable; also, janitorial sup-
plies, gloves, disposable aprons and hair caps
President: Gregory Rubin
rags@eriecotton.com
CFO: Louise Clemens
General Manager: Rick Gore
Estimated Sales: $5-10 Million
Number Employees: 20-49

22251 (HQ)Erie Foods Intl Inc
401 7th Ave
PO Box 648
Erie, IL 61250

309-659-2233
Fax: 309-659-2822 glindsey@eriefoods.com
www.eriefoods.com
Co-dried and concentrated milk proteins; also so-
dium, calcium, combination and acid-stable
caseinates and dairy blends; importer of milk
proteins
President/CEO: David Reisenbigler
dreisenbigler@eriefoods.com
CFO: Mark Delaney
COO: Jim Klein
Technical Services Manager: Craig Air
Quality Manager: Rene Perla
Purchasing Manager: Jake VanDeWostine
Process Development Manager: Jim Jacoby
Purchasing Manager: Shawn Larson
Estimated Sales: $1-2.5 Million
Number Employees: 10-19
Square Footage: 120000
Parent Co: Erie Foods International Inc
Type of Packaging: Bulk
Other Locations:
  Erie Foods International
  Beenleigh QLD
Brands:
  Ecco
  Erie

22252 Eriez Magnetics
4700 W 23rd St
Erie, PA 16506

Fax: 814-838-4960 800-346-4946
eriez@eriez.com www.eriez.com
Manufacturer and exporter of vibratory feeders and
conveyors, magnetic separators, metal detectors, vi-
bratory and material-sizing screeners, lifting mag-
nets and magnetic conveyors.
Chairman: R Merwin
President/CEO: Tim Shuttleworth
Treasurer: M Mandel
Quality Control: J Snyder
Marketing: K Jones
VP Sales/Marketing: C Ingram
VP Operations: M Mankosa
Plant Manager: J Kiehl
Estimated Sales: $50-100 Million
Number Employees: 250-499
Square Footage: 110000
Brands:
  E-Z Tec
  Hi-Vi
  Metalarm
  Safehold

22253 Erika Record LLC
37 Atlantic Way
Clifton, NJ 07012-1141

973-614-8500
Fax: 973-614-8503 800-682-8203
max@erikarecord.com www.bake-easier.com
Bun divider and rounder, bakery equipment
President: Max Oehler
Manager: Austin Archdeacon
austin@erikarecord.com
Estimated Sales: Below $5 000,000
Number Employees: 10-19
Type of Packaging: Bulk

22254 Ermanco
6870 Grand Haven Rd
Norton Shores, MI 49456

231-798-4547
Fax: 231-798-8322 info@ermanco.com
www.ermanco.com
Manufacturer and exporter of conveyors including
belt/live roller, lineshaft driven, belt driven and
sortation; also, turnkey systems
President: Leon Kirschner
Quality Control: Bob Dorgan
VP of Marketing: Lee Schomberg
VP of Sales: Gordon Hellberg
Contact: Tom Bergy
tombergy@ermanco.com
Estimated Sales: $30-50 Million
Number Employees: 100-249
Square Footage: 100000
Parent Co: Paragon Technologies
Brands:
  Accurol
  Ers Sorter

Intellorol
Nbs Sorter
Swing Arm Diverter
Xenopressure Xenorol

22255 Ernest F Mariani Co
573 W 2890 S
Salt Lake City, UT 84115-3456

801-359-3744
Fax: 801-531-9615 800-453-2927
sales@efmco.com www.efmco.com
Accumulating of bottling supplies and equipment
President: Wil Fiedler
wil@efmco.com
Finance Manager: Clay Dalton
Estimated Sales: $5-10 Million
Number Employees: 10-19

22256 Ernst Timing Screw Co
1534 Bridgewater Rd
Bensalem, PA 19020-4508

215-639-1438
Fax: 215-639-2873 ernstime@comcat.com
www.ernsttiming.com
Feed screws, change parts, star wheels, center guides
President: Suzanne Cannon
t.cannon@ernsttiming.com
CEO: Lee Cannon
Estimated Sales: $1-2,500,000
Number Employees: 10-19

22257 Ertelalsop
132 Flatbush Ave
Kingston, NY 12401-2202

845-331-4552
Fax: 845-339-1063 800-553-7835
sales@ertelalsop.com www.ertelalsop.com
Manufacturer and exporter of filtration equipment,
filter media and mixers for liquids; also, glass crush-
ing equipment
President: George Quigley
VP: George Quigley
Marketing Manager Food & Beverage: Mike Kelly
VP Sales/Marketing: William Kearney
Estimated Sales: $5-10 Million
Number Employees: 50-99
Brands:
  Alpha-Media
  Bottle-Buster
  Micro-Deck
  Micro-Media
  Vapor-Master

22258 Erving Industries
97 East Main Street
Erving, MA 01344

413-422-2700
Fax: 413-422-2710 www.ervingpaper.com
Custom printed and plain paper products including
napkins, placemats, traycovers and table covers
Estimated Sales: $50-100 Million
Number Employees: 1-4
Square Footage: 130000
Brands:
  Savlin

22259 Erwin Food Service Equipment
2915 Horton Rd
Fort Worth, TX 76119-5635

817-535-0021
Fax: 817-535-2999
Stainless steel cooking and heating equipment, ta-
bles, sinks, counters and hoods
President: Al Erwin
Office Manager: Barbara Vandever
Estimated Sales: $500,000-$1 Million
Number Employees: 1 to4
Square Footage: 20000

22260 Erwyn Products Inc
200 Campus Dr # C
Morganville, NJ 07751-2101

732-972-1440
Fax: 732-972-1263 800-331-9208
steve@erwyn.com www.erwyn.com
Manufacturer, importer and exporter of waste paper
baskets and ice buckets
President: Randy Grant
randy.grant@erwyn.com
Estimated Sales: $10-20 Million
Number Employees: 20-49

**22261 Esbelt of North America: Divison
of ASGCO**
301 W Gordon Street
Allentown, PA 18102-3136

610-821-0216
Fax: 610-778-8991 rlehman@asgco.com
www.asgco.com
Heavyweight conveyor belts
Estimated Sales: $1-5 Million

22262 Escher Mixers, USA
2770 W Commerce Street
Suite 100
Dallas, TX 75212-4913

214-572-7777
Fax: 214-572-8888

22263 Esco Manufacturing Inc
2020 4th Ave SW
Watertown, SD 57201-3413

605-886-9668
Fax: 605-882-1205 800-843-3726
wholesale@escomfg.com
www.escomanufacturing.com
Signs and displays
President: Mark Stein
mstein@escomfg.com
Senior Account Manager of Sales: Rob Fjerstad
Manufacturing Manager: Kevin Morris
Resources Manager of Purchasing: Laurie Gates
Estimated Sales: $10-20 Million
Number Employees: 100-249

22264 Esco Manufacturing Inc
2020 4th Ave SW
PO Box 1237
Watertown, SD 57201-3413

605-886-9668
Fax: 605-882-1205 800-843-3726
wholesale@escomfg.com
www.escomanufacturing.com
Indoor and outdoor signs including neon, electric
and painted
Owner: Mark Stein
mstein@escomfg.com
Engineering Manager/Account Representati: Dave
Bartels
Paint Supervisor: Jeremy Raap
Manufacturing Manager: Kevin Morris
Resources Manager: Laurie Gates
Senior Account Manager: Rob Fjerstad
Estimated Sales: less than $500,000
Number Employees: 100-249
Parent Co: Esco

22265 Esco Products Inc
5325 Glenmont Dr # D
Suite D
Houston, TX 77081-2050

832-649-5684
Fax: 713-666-5877 800-966-5514
www.escopro.com
Rebuilt and reconditioned food processing equipment, dashers, freezer barrels, thermometers, homo
blocks, piston plungers, pumps, etc.; also, OEM,
machining and grinding services available
President: Chris Haught
chaught@escopro.com
Number Employees: 10-19

22266 Esha Research
4747 Skyline Rd S # 100
Suite 100
Salem, OR 97306-5700

503-540-7518
Fax: 503-585-5543 800-659-3742
info@esha.com www.esha.com
Software for formulation development and nutrition
labeling; exporter of nutritional labeling software
CEO: Craig Bennett
c@esha.com
CEO: Robert Geltz
Vice President: David Hands
Sales Director: Scott Hadsall
Estimated Sales: $2 Million
Number Employees: 20-49
Number of Brands: 6
Number of Products: 6
Square Footage: 1000
Brands:
  Genesis R&D

22267 Eskay Metal Fabricating
83 Doat St
Buffalo, NY 14211-2048
716-893-3100
Fax: 716-893-0443 800-836-8015
www.specialtystainless.com
Food preparation equipment including sinks, chef's
tables, restaurant, cafeteria, serving and specialty
counters, etc.; also, cabinets, coolers and self con-
tained mobile hot dog and display carts.
President: Jeff Subra
Public Relations: Kathy Bristol
Engineering Manager: Ken White
Estimated Sales: $1 Million
Number Employees: 5-9
Square Footage: 32000
Parent Co: Schuler-Subra
Brands:
Buffalo Grill

22268 Espresso Carts and Supplies
429 United States Avenue
Lindenwold, NJ 08021-2658
856-782-1775
Fax: 856-782-1775 74274.60@compuserve.com
Carts, espresso carts, espresso machines and acces-
sories, bars, kiosks displays
Vie President of Sales/Marketing: Anthony
Santangelo
Estimated Sales: 250000
Number Employees: 3
Type of Packaging: Bulk

22269 Espresso Roma
1310 65th St
Emeryville, CA 94608-1119
510-420-8898
Fax: 510-420-8980 800-437-1668
sandydboyd@aol.com
www.sweetonyouberkeley.com
Processor and wholesaler/distributor of roast coffee;
manufacturer and wholesaler/distributor of espresso
machines and restaurant equipment
President: Sandy Boyd
VP: Pat Weigt
Sales Manager: Sandy Boyd
Estimated Sales: $1-2.5 Million
Number Employees: 10-19

22270 Esquire Mechanical Corp.
PO Box 496
Armonk, NY 10504
718-625-4006
Fax: 718-625-0155 800-847-4206
sales@dunhill-esquire.net
www.dunhill-esquire.com
Manufacturer and exporter of cafeteria and kitchen
equipment including cashier stands,serving coun-
ters,sinks,refrigerated display cases,tables and bbq
and rotisserie machines.
President: Geoffrey Thaw
Estimated Sales: $1-5 Million
Number Employees: 10-19
Square Footage: 240000
Parent Co: Dunhill Food Equipment
Type of Packaging: Food Service

22271 Esselte Meto
1200t American Road
Morris Plains, NJ 07950-2453
973-359-0947
Fax: 201-455-7492 800-645-3290
Manufacturer and exporter of handheld labeling and
merchandising systems, thermal and laser bar code
printers and supplies, tags and labels
President: Travis Howe
VP Marketing: Bob Cantono
VP Sales: Bob Evans
Estimated Sales: $300,000-500,000
Number Employees: 50-99
Square Footage: 270000
Parent Co: Esselte AB
Type of Packaging: Consumer, Private Label
Brands:
Essette Meto
Laser-Link
Meto
Meto/Primark
Price Marquee
Take a Number
Turn-O-Matic

22272 Essential Industries Inc
28391 Essential Rd
Merton, WI 53056
262-538-1122
Fax: 262-538-1354 800-551-9679
sales@essind.com www.essind.com
Manufacturer and exporter of household and indus-
trial hand, glass and window cleaners, liquid and
powder dishwashing compounds and soap, deter-
gents and floor polish
President: Michael Wheeler
mwheeler@essind.com
Chief Executive Officer: Jim Coddington
Controller: Carol Sanchez
Senior Vice President: Nick Contos
Quality & Safety Regional Manager: Maureen Smith
Vice President, Sales & Marketing: Ed Zgrabik
Vice President, Operations: Thomas Gitzlaff
Production Manager: Brandon Coulter
Director, Purchasing: Kathleen Leemon
Estimated Sales: $15 Million
Number Employees: 50-99
Square Footage: 110000
Type of Packaging: Private Label, Bulk
Brands:
Durabrite
Silhouette
Sport Kote
Superbase
Trust

22273 Essentra Packaging Inc.
1625 Ashton Park Drive
Suite D
Colonial Heights, VA 23834-5908
804-518-1803
Fax: 804-518-1809 800-849-0633
info@essentrapackaging.com
Pressure sensitive tear tape
President: Bob Donnahoo
Contact: Jame Belton
jamesbelton@payne-worldwide.com
Estimated Sales: $5-10 Million
Number Employees: 30

22274 Esstech
13911 NW 3rd Court
Vancouver, WA 98685-5703
360-546-5662
Fax: 360-546-5664
Boxes, multi-wall and plastic bags designed to elim-
inate or reduce the use of banding and stretch wrap-
ping without damaging package graphics or
appearance
President: Paul Mazi
Estimated Sales: $500,000-$1 000,000
Number Employees: 1-4
Type of Packaging: Bulk

22275 Ester International
29 Junction Pond Lane
Monmouth Junction, NJ 08852-2924
732-967-0561
Fax: 732-967-0563
Plain, corona treated, chemically treated film, poly-
ester film, milky white film, colored film and differ-
ent types of polyester resins
General Manager: S Shridhar
Number Employees: 4
Number of Brands: 1

22276 Esterle Mold & Machine Co Inc
1539 Commerce Dr
Stow, OH 44224-1783
330-686-1685
Fax: 330-686-9434 800-411-4086
info@esterle.com www.esterle.com
Peel boards made from 100% long-lasting high im-
pact, virgin and prime rigid plastic; standard 18 in. x
26 in. and custom sizes. Hygienic and FDA ap-
proved; 100% recyclable
President: Richard Esterle
resterle@esterle.com
VP: Kathleen Sawyer
Vice President: Kathleen Sawyer
Chairman: Adam Esterle
Sales Director: Patrick Miller
Operations Manager: Mark Starnes
Purchasing Manager: Steve Staszak
Estimated Sales: Below $5 Million
Number Employees: 50-99
Square Footage: 120000

22277 Et Oakes Corp
686 Old Willets Path
Hauppauge, NY 11788-4102
631-232-0002
Fax: 631-232-0170 info@oakes.com
Food processing equipment including mixers, de-
positors, blenders, controllers, creme injectors, agi-
tators, emulsifiers, extruders, homogenizers, fillers
and ladders, and cake depositors
President: W Peter Oakes
Vice President: Bob Peck
Marketing Director: Karen Oakes
Sales Director: Chris Oakes
Estimated Sales: Below $5 Million
Number Employees: 20-49

22278 Etched Images
1758 Industrial Way # 101
Napa, CA 94558-3302
707-252-5450
Fax: 707-252-2666 www.etchedimages.com
Wine industry applications; bottle design
Owner: Stu Mc Farland
stu@etchedimages.com
Estimated Sales: $20-50 Million
Number Employees: 20-49

22279 Etna Sales
1112 W Barkley Avenue
Orange, CA 92868-1213
714-520-5204
Fax: 714-563-0339
Brewing devices, coffee urn cleaners

22280 Ettore
2100 N Loop Rd
Alameda, CA 94502-8010
510-748-4130
Fax: 510-638-0928 info@ettore.com
Manufacturer and exporter of window and floor
squeegees and window washing equipment
Chairman of the Board: Michael Smahlik
michael.smahlik@ettore.com
VP Sales/Marketing: Patrick Murphy
National Sales Manager: Herman Miron
Estimated Sales: $1-2.5 Million
Number Employees: 50-99
Type of Packaging: Consumer, Food Service, Bulk
Brands:
Ehore

22281 Etube & Wire
50 W Clearview Dr
Shrewsbury, PA 17361-1103
717-227-0280
Fax: 717-428-2974 800-618-4720
sales@etubeandwire.com www.etubeandwire.com
Wire fryer baskets, displays, hooks, hangers, rings,
screens, grills, filters, guards, fan guards, and shelv-
ing
Owner: Glenn Eyster
General Manager: Larry Krumrine
Contact: Jed Beckman
jbeckman@eysters.com
Manager: Larry Krumrwe
Estimated Sales: $2.5 Million
Number Employees: 20-49
Square Footage: 120000

22282 Euchner-USA
6723 Lyons St
East Syracuse, NY 13057-9332
315-701-0315
Fax: 315-701-0319 info@euchner-usa.com
www.euchner-usa.com
Suppliers of sensors for automation, safety and
man-machine interface products including safety interlocking swithces, enabling switches, trip dogs
and rails, encoders, read & write coding systems,
read only identification systemsjoysticks and
operator panels.
President & CEO: Mike Ladd
Customer Service Supervisor: Margie Krayenhof
Operations Manager: Doug Hatch
Number Employees: 500-1000

22283 Eugene Welding Company
2420 Wills St
Marysville, MI 48040
810-364-7421
Fax: 810-364-4347
Manufacturer and exporter of racks including pallet
storage, drive-in, push back and cantilever

President: Charles Vamella
CEO: Jim Bradshaw
Sales: Scott Samples
Public Relations: Dawne Kimberley
Plant Maanger: Wes Boyne
Purchasing: Dave Campa
Estimated Sales: $20-50 Million
Number Employees: 250-499
Square Footage: 120000
Parent Co: Eugene Welding Company
Brands:
   Spacerak

22284 Eunice Locker Plant
1232 Main Street
Eunice, NM 88231

            505-394-2060
Slaughterer and packer of beef and pork
Owner: Louie Miller
Estimated Sales: $1-2.5 Million
Number Employees: 1-4
Type of Packaging: Consumer

22285 Eureka Company
807 N Main St
Bloomington, IL 61701

            309-828-2367
   Fax: 309-823-5335 800-282-2886
kathy.luedke@eureka.com www.eureka.com
Manufacturer and exporter of commercial vacuums
including canisters, uprights, built-ins and rechargeable
President: John Case
CEO: Jan Wolansky
VP Advertising: Don Johnson
Quality Control: Steve Knuth
Contact: Bruce Gold
bruce.gold@electrolux.com
Number Employees: 250-499
Parent Co: White Consolidated Industries
Type of Packaging: Consumer
Brands:
   Eureka

22286 Eureka Door
PO Box 276
Ballwin, MO 63022-0276

            314-256-1949
            800-673-8735

22287 Eureka Ice & Cold Storage Company
12 Waterfront Dr
Eureka, CA 95501-0368

            707-443-5663
      Fax: 707-443-6481
   http://eurekaice.com/index.html
Warehouse providing freezer and cooler storage and
a manufacturer of ice. Eureka Ice also offers Blast
Freezing, a quick freezing of up to 80 tons of product in a short time.
Manager: Tom Devere
Manager: Tom Devero
Estimated Sales: $2.5-5 Million
Number Employees: 5-9
Square Footage: 140000

22288 (HQ)Eureka Paper Box Company
PO Box 1476
Williamsport, PA 17703-1476

            570-326-9147
      Fax: 570-326-7239
Custom paper folding cartons
Co-Owner: Jim Waters
Co-Owner: John McInerney
CFO: Bob Bernaski
Production Manager: Joseph Cioffi
Estimated Sales: $5-10 Million
Number Employees: 80
Square Footage: 212000
Other Locations:
   Eureka Paper Box Co.
   Syracuse NY

22289 Euro-Pol Bakery Equipment
2770 W Commerce St
Dallas, TX 75212-4913

            214-637-2253
      Fax: 214-637-2257
President: Mariusz B. Bandurski

22290 Eurobar Sales Corporation
12b W Main Street
Elmsford, NY 10523-2401

            914-592-5770
      Fax: 914-592-6004
Espresso machines and accessories

22291 Eurodib
PO Box 1798
1320 State Route 9
Champlain, NY 12919

            450-641-8700
   Fax: 451-641-8705 888-956-6866
shaun@eurodib.com www.eurodib.com
Importer of citrus and centrifugal juicers, dispensers,
coffee grinders, blenders, vegetable cutters, grills,
mandolines, cookware, and dishwashers
President: Jean Yves Dumaine
VP: Shaun McDonald
Marketing: Shaun McDonald
Contact: Shaun Mcdonald
jydumaine@eurodib.com
Purchasing Manager: Robert Perrier
Number Employees: 14
Number of Brands: 15
Number of Products: 500
Square Footage: 176000

22292 Eurodispenser
6480 Majors Lane
Decatur, IL 62521-9697

            217-864-4061
      Fax: 217-864-6722
Quality dispensing equipment including condiments,
sauces, toppings, syrups, soap and cleaning
compounds
Estimated Sales: $1-2.5 Million
Number Employees: 1-4

22293 Eurofins DQCI
5205 Quincy St
St Paul, MN 55112-1438

            763-785-0484
 Fax: 763-785-0584 dqciinfo@eurofinsus.com
           www.dqci.com
Laboratory providing chemical analysis and testing
services to the dairy industry; also, calibration
standards
Owner: Tom Janas
tom@dqci.com
Estimated Sales: $5-10,000,000
Number Employees: 20-49

22294 Eurofins S-F AnalyticalLabs
2345 S 170th St
New Berlin, WI 53151-2701

            262-754-5300
   Fax: 262-754-5310 800-300-6700
sales@sflabs.com www.eurofinsus.com
Laboratory performing chemical analysis and micro-
biological testing of food and food related products.
Nutritional labeling anf USDA Fat Claims are
specialties.
President/CEO: David Kliber
Manager: Bryan Dieckelman
bdieckelman@sflabs.com
Number Employees: 20-49
Type of Packaging: Food Service

22295 (HQ)Eurofins Scientific Inc
2200 Rittenhouse St # 150
Suite 175
Des Moines, IA 50321-3157

            515-265-1461
   Fax: 515-266-5453 800-841-1110
ENACclientservices@eurofinsus.com
     www.eurofins.com/food
Laboratory offering nutrition labeling, food analysis,
microbiology, nutritional bioassays, toxicology and
independent testing
President: Brandi Augustine
augustine@eurofinsus.com
Quality Assurance Director: Rhonda Krick
VP Sales/Marketing: Michael Meyers
Client Services Representative: Sophies Holbrook
Account Manager: Charles Hecht
Estimated Sales: $5-10 Million
Number Employees: 100-249
Parent Co: Eurofins Group
Other Locations:
   Eurofins Scientific
   Teltow/Berlin

22296 Eurofins Scientific Inc.
4500 Wadsworth
Suite 110
Dayton, OH 45414

            937-276-7800
   Fax: 937-276-7805 800-880-1038
info@eurofinsus.com www.eurofinsus.com/food
Laboratory specializing in nutrition analysis for
amino acids, dietary fibers, microbiological, proxi-
mate and vitamins; also, pesticide and residue test-
ing, mycotoxin screening, authenticity, and
GMO/ONA testing
President: Gary Wnorowski
CFO: Jean-Denis Giraudet
Quality Assurance Director: Rhonda Krick
Marketing Director: Lori Overstreet
Sales Director: Jay Kurmaski
Contact: Jennifer Durando
jenniferdurando@eurofinsus.com
Estimated Sales: $1-2.5 Million
Number Employees: 5-9

22297 Europa Company
11289 Slater Ave
Fountain Valley, CA 92708-5421

            714-432-0112
   Fax: 714-432-7246 www.europa-co.com
Espresso machines and accessories, grinders
Estimated Sales: Less than $500,000
Number Employees: 1-4

22298 European Gift & Houseware
514 S 5th Ave
Mt Vernon, NY 10550-4408

            914-664-3448
   Fax: 914-664-3257 800-927-0277
sales@europeangift.com www.europeangift.com
Espresso machines and accessories.
Owner: Angelo Forzano
afsales@europeangift.com
Estimated Sales: $5-10 Million
Number Employees: 5-9

22299 European Packaging Machinery
PO Box 40
Tennent, NJ 07763-0040

            732-845-3557
   Fax: 732-845-3844 www.epmincorporated.com
Packaging form-fill-seal, fill-seal, filling, inspection
equipment, special engineering and customized han-
dling and assembling equipment
President: Klans Huenecke
Brands:
   Asg
   Alfa-Kortogleu
   Deltamat
   Siebler

22300 Eurosicma
36 Lake St
Wilmington, MA 01887-3708

            978-657-8841
   Fax: 978-657-8847 www.eurosicma.it
Pillow pack wrapping machine for hard boiled
candy, chewing-gum balls, deposited candies and
milk tablets
Estimated Sales: $1-5 Million
Number Employees: 1-4

22301 Eurotherm
44621 Guilford Dr # 100
Ashburn, VA 20147-6070

            703-726-0138
   Fax: 703-724-7301 info@eurotherm.com
          www.eurotherm.com
Supplier of precision process and temperature con-
trol instrumentation including single and multiloop
digital controllers, alarms and indicators.
President: John Searle
Executive: Dan Dudici
Marketing Director: Al Betz
Sales Director: Al Betz
IT: Terry Ackerman
terry.wolfe@invensys.com
Estimated Sales: $50 Million
Number Employees: 50-99
Number of Brands: 5
Number of Products: 1000
Parent Co: Invensys Intelligent Automation

22302 Eutek Systems
2925 NW Aloclek Dr
Hillsboro, OR 97124-7523
503-601-0843
Fax: 503-615-2906
Manufacturer and exporter of wastewater reclamation and reuse equipment; also, grit removers
Operations: Steve Tansley
Contact: Mohamed Abu
mabu@hydro-int.com
Estimated Sales: Less Than $500,000
Number Employees: 1-4

22303 Eval Company of America
1001 Warrenville Rd # 110
Lisle, IL 60532-1392
312-347-0126
Fax: 312-893-8510 800-423-9726
Plastic containers for food applications like ketchup or juice, coextruded films for flexible packaging of food, coextruded plastic tubing, coated paperboard and films in both standard and biaxially oriented forms
Owner: Rodger Bloch
Vice President Of Sales: George Avdey
Director Of Sales: Jim Claggett
Estimated Sales: $20-50 Million
Number Employees: 10-19

22304 Evans Adhesive Corp LTD
925 Old Henderson Rd
Columbus, OH 43220-3779
614-451-9778
Fax: 614-451-1373 800-868-0925
orders@evansadhesive.com
www.evansadhesive.com
Packaging adhesives for all applications
President: Rusty Thompson
Estimated Sales: $10 Million
Number Employees: 20-49

22305 Evanston Awning Co
2801 Central St
Evanston, IL 60201-1200
847-864-4520
Fax: 847-864-5886 www.evanstonawnings.com
Commercial awnings
President: Edward Hunzinger Jr
Estimated Sales: $1-2,500,000
Number Employees: 10-19

22306 Evant
2300 Windy Ridge Parkway
10th Floor
Atlanta, GA 30339
770-955-7070
Fax: 770-955-0302 877-596-9208
Management software for manufacturers and wholesalers in the food industry used to optimize purchasing. Manhattan Associates has now acquired this company who is a provider of supply chain planning and replenishment solutions
President/CEO: Eddie Capel
EVP and CFO: Dennis Story
Chief Marketing Officer: Jonathan Colehower
Senior Vice President, Americas Sales: Bob Howell
SVP and Chief Human Resources Officer: Terry Geraghty
SVP, International Operations: Steve Smith
Parent Co: Manhattan Associates, Inc

22307 Evaporator Dryer Technologies
1805 Ridgeway St
Hammond, WI 54015-5044
715-796-2313
Fax: 715-796-2378 info@evapdryertech.com
www.evapdryertech.com
Engineering and supply of custom evaporators and spray drying systems, heat recovery, dust collection, and exclusive sanitary designed components: liquid-activated, retractable CIP spray nozzles and systems, fire suppression systemssanitary, heavy-duty manways and inspection ports
Owner: Peter Jensen
info@evapdryertech.com
Purchasing: Jeff Derrick
Estimated Sales: $3-10 Million
Number Employees: 10-19
Square Footage: 13000
Other Locations:
    Stainless Steel Machining Division
    Fond du Lac WI

22308 Ever Extruder Co
7 Goodwin Dr
Festus, MO 63028-4122
636-937-8830
Fax: 636-937-6111
Custom designer & manufacturer of new extruder bases, power transmissions, barrel assemblies and dischargers to fit existing aftermarket extruder systems.
President: Tommy Davis
tommydavis@everextruder.com
Chief Engineer: Steve Stewart
Number Employees: 100-249

22309 (HQ)Everbrite LLC
4949 S. 110th St.
Greenfield, WI 53228
414-529-3500
800-558-3888
sales@everbrite.com www.everbrite.com
Signs and displays including indoor, outdoor, neon, electric and menu boards.
Vice President, Sales/Marketing: Jay Jensen
Year Founded: 1927
Estimated Sales: $74.8 Million
Number Employees: 500-999
Square Footage: 1000000
Type of Packaging: Food Service

22310 Everedy Automation
345 Renninger Rd
Frederick, PA 19435
610-754-1775
Fax: 610-754-1108
Manufacturer and exporter of bakery machinery for batter, scaling, cake cutting, icing, splitting, slicing, cake sandwich, pie, custard and fruit filling and meringue/cream topping; also, raisin cleaning and stemming equipmentavailable.
President: Irv Fisher
Sales Director: Irv Fisher
Number Employees: 2
Square Footage: 31200

22311 Everest Interscience
2102 N.Forbes Blvd.
Suite 107
Tucson, AZ 85705-6429
Fax: 520-792-4545 www.everestinterscience.com
Wine industry infrared thermometers
President: Charles Everest
sales@everestinterscience.com
CFO: Marilin Everest
Estimated Sales: $1-5 000,000
Number Employees: 5-9

22312 Everett Rubber Stamp
2933 Wetmore Ave
Everett, WA 98201-4016
425-258-6747
Fax: 425-252-8858
Rubber stamps and plastic signs
Owner: Jeff Hathaway
everettstamp@frontier.com
Owner: Jeffrey Hathaway
Estimated Sales: Less Than $500,000
Number Employees: 1-4

22313 Everfilt Corp
3167 Progress Cir
Mira Loma, CA 91752-1112
951-360-8380
Fax: 951-360-8384 800-360-8380
everfilt@everfilt.com www.everfilt.com
Water and waste water filtration and separation equipment for food processing plants, packing houses, etc
Contact: Barbara Andrew
b.andrew@everfilt.com
Operations Manager: Brian Tolson
Estimated Sales: $2.5-5 Million
Number Employees: 5-9
Square Footage: 21200
Brands:
    Everfilt

22314 Evergreen Packaging
5350 Poplar Ave
Suite 600
Memphis, TN 38119
901-821-5350
evergreenpackaging.com
Gable top packaging equipment and gable top cartons.

President & CEO: John Rooney
Estimated Sales: $5.5 Billion
Number Employees: 3,800
Square Footage: 40000
Type of Packaging: Consumer, Food Service

22315 Everidge
15600 37th Ave N
Suite 100
Plymouth, MN 55446
888-227-1629
www.everidge.com
ThermalRite division manufactures commercial refrigeration systems
President & CEO: Chris Kahler
CFO: Mike Polis
SVP, Foodservice Sales & Marketing: Steve Gill
President & COO: Mike Kahler
Brands:
    CROWNTONKA
    ICS
    THERMALRITE

22316 Everpure, LLC
1040 Muirfield Drive
Hanover Park, IL 60133
630-307-3000
Fax: 630-307-3030 info@everpure.com
www.everpure.com
Manufacturer and exporter of water filters
Contact: Peter Gorr
gorr@everpure.com
Estimated Sales: $35-40 Million
Number Employees: 1-4
Parent Co: Culligan International Company

22317 Everson Spice Co
2667 Gundry Ave
Signal Hill, CA 90755-1808
562-595-4785
Fax: 562-988-0219 800-421-3753
customerservice@eversonspice.com
www.eversonspice.com
Seasonings, dry rubs, stuffing mixes and marinades
Owner: Tom Everson
tomeverson@eversonspice.com
President: Ken Hopkins
CEO: Kim Everson
Estimated Sales: $2.5-5 Million
Number Employees: 50-99
Type of Packaging: Food Service

22318 Evonik Corporation North America
299 Jefferson Rd
Parsippany, NJ 07054
973-929-8000
corporate.evonik.us
Precipitated and fumed silica used to improve the flow properties of food products, prevent caking, transfer liquids into free-flowing powders, improve dispersability, and function as processing aids in spray drying and millingapplications.
President, North America Region: John Rolando
Estimated Sales: $3.5 Billion
Number Employees: 4,800
Parent Co: Evonik Industries AG
Other Locations:
    Production/Health & Nutrition
    Blair NE
    Production/Inorganic Materials
    Clavert City KY
    Production/R&D
    Chester PA
    Production/Coatings & Additives
    Deer Park TX
    Production/Performance Polymers
    Fortier LA
    Production/Advanced Intermediates
    Galena KS
    Production/Consumer Specialties
    Garyville LA
    Production/R&D
    Greensboro NC
    Production/Coatings & Additives
    Hopewell VA
    Production/Coatings & Additives
    Horsham PA
    Production/Consumer Specialties
    Janesville WI
    Customer Services/Health/Nutrition
    Kennesaw GA
    Tippecanoe Laboratories
    Lafayette IN

22319 Evoqua Water Technologies
1828 Metcalf Ave
Thomasville, GA 31792-6845
229-226-5733
Fax: 229-226-4793 800-841-1550
www.evoqua.com
Water and wastewater treatment equipment.
President: Roger Radke
radker@kusfilter.com
CEO: Roger Radke
Marketing Manager: Doug Davis
Estimated Sales: $50-100 Million
Number Employees: 100-249
Square Footage: 40000

22320 Ex-Cell KAISER LLC
11240 Melrose Ave
Franklin Park, IL 60131-1332
847-451-0451
Fax: 847-451-0458 service@ex-cell.com
www.ex-cell.com
Manufacturer and exporter of metal check order
rails, long handle dust pans, handheld dust pans,
waste receptacles, bus tub and water carts, bar speed
rails, bottlecap catchers, mobile coat racks, condi-
ment trays, luggage racks, andluggage carriers
Owner: Tom Berg
tom@processdisplays.com
Managing Member: Janet Kaiser
Vice President/General Manager: Jeffrey Speizman
Human Resources/Purchasing: Elaine Abba
Estimated Sales: $8 Million
Number Employees: 100-249
Square Footage: 70000
Brands:
    Banquet Series
    Ex-Cell
    Landscape Series
    Note Minder
    Quicksilver
    Safeguard
    Service Solutions Series

22321 Ex-Tech Plastics
11413 Burlington Road
PO Box 576
Richmond, IL 60071
847-829-8100
Fax: 847-829-8190 sales@extechplastics.com
www.extechplastics.com
Extruded, plastic film and sheet PVC, PET, COPP,
HOPP, and PLA
President: Jeff Fidler
Marketing: Laura Pichon
Contact: Lettitia Kokan
lkokan@extechplastics.com
Estimated Sales: $10-20 000,000
Number Employees: 50-99

22322 Exact Equipment Corporation
20 N Pennsylvania Ave
Morrisville, PA 19067-1110
215-295-2000
Fax: 215-295-2080 www.exactequipment.com
Automatic and manual wrapping equipment, indexer
labelers, scales and printers
Manager: Rich Lee
National Sales Manager: F Basil
VP Operations: S Smith
Estimated Sales: $5-10 Million
Number Employees: 50-99
Brands:
    Exact Weight
    Power Pack
    Pre-Pac
    Speedmaster
    Work Horse

22323 Exact Mixing Systems Inc
4739 S Mendenhall Rd
Memphis, TN 38141-8202
901-362-8501
Fax: 901-362-5479 jwarren@exactmixing.com
www.readingbakery.com
Continuous dough mixers and ingredient metering
systems
President: Jim Warren
CFO and Corporate Secretary: Cheryl Followell
Chairman/VP: Robert Followell
Estimated Sales: $2.5-5 Million
Number Employees: 5-9
Square Footage: 40000

22324 Exact Mixing Systems Inc
4739 S Mendenhall Rd
Memphis, TN 38141-8202
901-362-8501
Fax: 901-362-5479 exactmix@aol.com
Mixing equipment
President: Jim Warren
Estimated Sales: $5-10 Million
Number Employees: 5-9

22325 Exact Packaging
1145 E Wellspring Rd
New Freedom, PA 17349-8426
717-235-8345
Fax: 717-235-0608 800-755-8344
President: Randy Cotteleer
Contact: Bill Berg
bberg@epilabelers.com

22326 Exaxol Chemical Corp
14325 60th St N
Clearwater, FL 33760-2708
727-524-7732
Fax: 727-532-8221 800-739-2965
info@exaxol.com www.exaxol.com
Manufacturer and exporter of food quality control
laboratory chemicals
Owner: Joe Papa
Estimated Sales: $1-2,500,000
Number Employees: 1-4

22327 Excalibur Bagel & Bakery Eqpt
4-01 Banta Pl
Fair Lawn, NJ 07410-3026
201-797-2788
Fax: 201-797-2711 excaliburequip@aol.com
www.excaliburequipment.com
Manufacturing ovens, mixers (spiral), two-arm mix-
ers, bagel machines
Owner: Richard Zinn
excaliburequip@aol.com
Estimated Sales: $1-2.5 000,000
Number Employees: 10-19

22328 Excalibur Miretti Group LLC
285 Eldridge Rd
Fairfield, NJ 07004-2508
973-808-8399
Fax: 973-808-8398 sales@exequipment.com
www.exequipment.com
Explosion-proof forklifts, electric and forklift
trucks, exporter of forklifts
President: Angelo Miretti
Number Employees: 20-49
Square Footage: 88000
Brands:
    Go Getters
    Gregory

22329 Excalibur Seasoning
1800 Riverway Dr
Pekin, IL 61554-9307
309-347-1221
Fax: 309-347-9086 800-444-2169
sales@excaliburseasoning.com
www.excaliburseasoning.com
Seasoning
President: Jay Hall
CEO: Blake Taylor
btaylor@lumc.edu
Estimated Sales: $5-10 Million
Number Employees: 50-99

22330 Excel Chemical Company
2385 Corbett St
Jacksonville, FL 32204-1705
904-356-0446
Fax: 904-356-1906
Cleaning compounds
President: William D Gladney
Contact: Joan Gladney
joan.gladney@americanchemical.net
Number Employees: 5 to 9

22331 Excel Engineering
100 Camelot Dr
Fond Du Lac, WI 54935-8333
920-926-9800
Fax: 920-926-9801 info@excelengineer.com
www.excelengineer.com
Architectural design, surveyor and engineering resources

President: Jeff Quast
CEO: Steve Soodsma
Business Development Director: Tony LeShay
Estimated Sales: Less Than $500,000
Number Employees: 1-4

22332 Excel-A-Tec Inc
3695 N 126th St # N
Brookfield, WI 53005-2424
262-252-3600
Fax: 262-252-3664 www.excelatec.com
Heat recovery systems, homogenizers, aseptic pro-
cessing equipment, cheese equipment, blenders,
deactators, heat exchangers, piping, fittings and tub-
ing, sanitary, process control, process software
President: Herve Bronnert
Vice President: Joan Bronnert
Estimated Sales: $5-10 Million
Number Employees: 10-19

22333 Excell Products Inc
2500 Enterprise Blvd
Choctaw, OK 73020-8400
405-390-4491
Fax: 405-390-4493 800-633-7670
sales@excellproducts.com
Screen painting, offset painting, signing systems,
aisle markers, plastic extruding, spiral painting
systems
President and CFO: Merle Medcalf
merle@excellproducts.com
Estimated Sales: $500,000-$1 Million
Number Employees: 20-49

22334 Excellence Commercial Products
1750 N University Dr
Pompano Beach, FL 33071-8903
954-752-0010
Fax: 954-752-0080 800-441-4014
howard@stajac.com www.stajac.com
Wholesaler/distributor, importer and exporter of
coolers, freezers and ice cream cabinets
President: Howard Noskowicz
Quality Control: Catherina Derr
Number Employees: 1-4
Parent Co: Stajac Industries

22335 Excellent Bakery Equipment Co
315 Fairfield Rd
Fairfield, NJ 07004-1930
973-244-1664
Fax: 973-244-1696 staff@excellent-bagels.com
www.excellent-bagels.com
Bakery machinery, graters and shredders, triple action mixers, spiral mixers, rack ovens, formers and
dividers, removable owl and self tipping mixers, bagel ovens and kettles, deck ovens, and volumetric
dough dividers
President: Karin Seruga
Estimated Sales: $5-10 000,000
Number Employees: 10-19

**22336 Excelsior Transparent Bag
Manufacturing**
159 Alexander St
Yonkers, NY 10701-2520
914-968-1300
Fax: 914-968-6567
Printed flexible packaging and laminated materials,
bags and envelopes
President: Arleen Neustein
CFO: Ron Shenesh
VP: Cynthia Gaines
Contact: Jeff Marger
info@yonkerschamber.com
Estimated Sales: $10-20 Million
Number Employees: 50 to 99

22337 ExecuChef Software
862 Sir Francis Drake Boulevard
Suite 282
San Anselmo, CA 94960-1914
415-488-9600
Fax: 415-488-9690
Computer software including back-of-the-house
management, inventory, cost, etc
Brands:
    Chef Apprentice
    Chef Explosion
    Execuchef Pro

22338 Executive Line
30 Church St
Chatham, NY 12037-0352

518-392-5761
Fax: 518-392-5156 800-333-5761
Advertising specialties including tags, badges, pins, magnets, name plates, calendars, rulers, etc
President: Danny Crellin
VP Finance: Bernie Rizzo
Sales Manager: Jane Ryan
Estimated Sales: $2.5-5 Million
Number Employees: 1 to49
Square Footage: 5000

22339 Executive Match Inc
PO Box 693
Salem, OH 44460-0693

330-332-2674
Fax: 330-332-2673 800-860-2674
President: William Penfold
exmatch@neo.rr.com
Estimated Sales: Less Than $500,000
Number Employees: 1-4

22340 Executive Referral Services
5440 N Cumberland Ave
Chicago, IL 60656-1490

773-693-6622
Fax: 773-693-8466 866-466-3339
info@facilitec-sw.com www.facilitec-sw.com
International consultant specializing in operations and sales management positions for grocery, convenience store, retail, food service and manufacturing organizations
Owner: Bruce Freier
Vice President: Mark Gray
Accounting Executive: Garry Chesla
Estimated Sales: $1-2.5 Million
Number Employees: 5-9

22341 Exel
509 Lee Ave
Lincolnton, NC 28092-2522

704-735-6535
Fax: 704-735-4899 www.excelhandling.com
Manufacturer and exporter of industrial hand, flat deck, order picking and specially fabricated trucks. Also, material handling carts, dollies, pin trucks, and yarn and beam transports
President/CEO: Charles Eurey
ceurey@excelcontainer.com
VP Administration/Sales: Jim Eurey
Estimated Sales: $20-50 Million
Number Employees: 10-19
Square Footage: 65000

22342 Exhausto
PO Box 720651
Atlanta, GA 30358-2651

770-587-3238
Fax: 770-587-4731 800-255-2923
steenh@exhausto.com www.exhausto.com
Manufacturer, importer and exporter of kitchen exhaust/grease fans
President: Steen Hagensen
Marketing Director: Kelly Johnson
Sales Director: Mark Sylvia
Purchasing Manager: Joan Chenier
Estimated Sales: $40 Million
Number Employees: 100
Number of Brands: 1
Square Footage: 18000
Parent Co: Exhausto A/S
Type of Packaging: Bulk
Brands:
    Exhausto

22343 Exhibitron Co
505 SE H St
Grants Pass, OR 97526-3262

541-471-7400
Fax: 541-471-7200 800-437-4571
info@exhibitroncorp.com
www.exhibitroncorp.com
Screen printing commercial signage, and decor products and garments, aisle markers for grocery and retail stores; also, general fabrication and screen printing available
Owner: Ken Northrup
exhibitron@uci.net
CEO: Kenneth Northup
Vice President: Marlene King

Estimated Sales: Less Than $500,000
Number Employees: 1-4
Square Footage: 13000

22344 Exhibits & More Shopworks
7843 Goguen Dr
Liverpool, NY 13090-2514

315-652-0383
Fax: 315-652-8020 888-326-9100
bobd@exhibitsandmore.com
Store fixtures
Owner: Bob Davidson
bobd@exhibtsandmore.com
CEO: Frank Carnovale
VP of Sales: Valerie Low
bobd@exhibtsandmore.com
COO: Jeff Vandeyacht
Estimated Sales: $500,000-$1 Million
Number Employees: 10-19
Other Locations:
    Victor NY

22345 (HQ)Eximco Manufacturing Company
5311 N Kedzie Ave
Chicago, IL 60625-4711

773-463-1470
Fax: 773-583-5131
Fluorescent lighting fixtures, light bulbs, energy-saving lighting, alkaline batteries and fluorescent ballasts; importer and exporter of lamps
President: R Ramsden
General Manager: John Perell
Estimated Sales: $2.5-5 Million
Number Employees: 20-49
Square Footage: 40000
Other Locations:
    Eximco Manufacturing Co.
    Chicago IL

22346 Expanko Cork Co
180 Gordon Dr # 113
Suite 113
Exton, PA 19341-1340

610-363-0735
Fax: 610-363-0735 800-345-6202
sales@expanko.com www.expanko.com
Wine industry corks and closures
President: Rob Mc Kee
Estimated Sales: $2.5-5 000,000
Number Employees: 5-9

22347 Expert Industries Inc
848 E 43rd St
Brooklyn, NY 11210-3502

718-434-6060
Fax: 718-434-6174 www.rubiconhx.com
Custom fabricated ribbon blenders, tanks, hoppers, mixers, dispersers, agitators, batch containers, cooling towers, half pipe coils, reactors, polishing pans, liquid and powder transporting bins, etc
Manager: Matt Rubinberg
Sales: E Senatore
General Manager: M Sterling
Estimated Sales: $10-20,000,000
Number Employees: 20-49

22348 Expo Displays
3401 Mary Taylor Rd
Birmingham, AL 35235-3234

205-439-8284
Fax: 205-439-8201 800-367-3976
www.expodisplays.com
Manufacturer and exporter of portable and modular displays and exhibits for tradeshow exhibition and marketplace display
Owner: Jeff Colton
jeff@expodisplays.com
CEO: Jeff Culton
VP: Jay Burkette
Marketing: Sara Mathews
Public Relations: Jay Burkette
Estimated Sales: $10-20 Million
Number Employees: 50-99
Square Footage: 60000
Brands:
    2001
    Airlite
    Eclipse
    Expoaire
    Expoframe
    Odyssey
    Quantum
    Visions

22349 Expo Instruments
1122 Aster Ave Ste E
Sunnyvale, CA 94086

408-554-8822
Fax: 408-554-8822 800-775-EXPO
info@expoinstruments.com
www.expoinstruments.com
Custom liquid level sensors, moniters, controls
President: George Rauchwerger
Estimated Sales: Below $5 000,000
Number Employees: 1-4

22350 Express Card & Label CoInc
2012 NE Meriden Rd
Topeka, KS 66608-1737

785-233-0369
Fax: 785-233-2763 absales@expresscl.com
Labeling equipment
President: John George
CEO: Stephen Atha
CFO: Mark Tillings
HR Executive: Pam Whitfield
express@expresscl.com
Estimated Sales: $5-10 Million
Number Employees: 50-99

22351 Express Packaging
Highway 67
PO Box 1333
Pembroke, GA 31321

912-653-2800
Fax: 912-653-2801 www.expresspkg.com
President: John Reardon
Vice President/Sales Manager: Mike Reardon
Estimated Sales: $10-20 Million
Number Employees: 20-49

22352 Expresso Shoppe Inc
524 N York Rd
Bensenville, IL 60106-1607

630-350-0066
Fax: 336-393-0295 info@expressoshoppe.com
www.expressoshoppe.com
Owner: David Dimbert
david@expressoshoppe.com
Estimated Sales: Below $5 Million
Number Employees: 1-4

22353 Expro Manufacturing
2800 Ayers Avenue
Vernon, CA 90058

323-415-8544
Fax: 323-268-4060
Manufacturer and packager of food ingredients, including custom dry powder blends
President: Peter Ernster
CEO: Douglas Kantner
R&D: Greg Rowland
VP Sales: Michele Mullen
Contact: Daniel Diaz
ddiaz@expromfg.com
Purchasing: James Ernster
Number Employees: 20

22354 Exquis Confections
17629 Wheat Fall Drive
Derwood, MD 20855-1151

301-926-7043
Fax: 301-926-6432

22355 Extech Instruments
285 Bear Hill Rd
Waltham, MA 02451

781-890-7440
Fax: 781-890-7864 extech@extech.com
www.extech.com
Test and measurement instruments
Marketing Coordinator: Tracy Milhomme
Number Employees: 50-99

22356 Extrutech Plastics Inc
5902 W Custer St
Manitowoc, WI 54220-9790

920-684-2065
Fax: 920-684-4344 888-818-0118
info@epiplastics.com www.epiplastics.com
Plastic panels that are lightweight and easy to install. Panels can be used both indoors and out for dairy barns, foodplants, car washes and will not rust, peel, rot or corrode and are very easy to clean.

President/CEO/CFO: Greg Sheehy
Research/Development: Mike Sheehy
Quality Control: Ashley Shulz
Marketing: Greg Sheehy
Sales Representative: Scott Charles
Senior Project Engineer: Chuck Grozis
Estimated Sales: $10 Million
Number Employees: 5-9

22357 Exxon Mobil
5959 Las Colinas Blvd
Irving, TX 75039-2298

972-940-6000
www.exxonmobil.com
Industrial fuels and lubricants, among other business
divisions.
Chairman & CEO: Darren Woods
SVP: Jack Williams
SVP & Principal Financial Officer: Andrew Swiger
SVP: Neil Chapman
Estimated Sales: $279.3 Billion
Number Employees: 71,000

22358 Exxon Mobil Chemical Company
22777 Springwoods Village Prkw
Spring, TX 77389-1425

www.exxonmobilchemical.com
Pressure sensitive oriented polypropylene labels, roll
stock cut and stack.
Chairman & Chief Executive Officer: Darren Woods
President, ExxonMobil Chemical: Karen McKee
Year Founded: 1999
Estimated Sales: $279.3 Billion
Number Employees: 71,000
Parent Co: Exxon Mobil Corporation
Brands:
Label-Lyte

22359 Ez Box Machinery Company
6126 Brookshire Blvd Ste E
Charlotte, NC 28216

704-399-0727
Fax: 704-393-3629 sales08@ezbox.com
www.ezbox.com
Box machines, slitters, corrugated boxes
President: Andrew Dunn
Sales Director: Johnnie Quinn
Contact: Jim Rasmussen
jimrasmussen@ezbox.com
Number Employees: 1-4

22360 F & A Fabricating Inc
104 Arbor St
Battle Creek, MI 49015-3068

269-965-8371
Fax: 269-965-8371 www.fa-fabricating.com
Manufacturer and exporter of stainless steel fabri-
cated products including belt conveyors
President: Hiep Nguyen
Estimated Sales: $2.5-5 Million
Number Employees: 20-49
Type of Packaging: Food Service, Bulk

22361 F & F and A. Jacobs & Sons, Inc.
1100 Wicomico St
Baltimore, MD 21230

410-727-6397
Fax: 800-426-4595 www.rjuniform.com
Military, commercial and institutional uniforms
President: Robert Friedlander
Estimated Sales: $1-5 Million
Number Employees: 20-49

22362 F & S Awning & Sign Co
13 Coral St
Edison, NJ 08837-3242

732-738-4110
Fax: 732-738-7255 www.fsawning.com
Commercial awnings
Owner: Bob Trotte
Estimated Sales: $1-2,500,000
Number Employees: 10-19

22363 F & S Engraving Inc
1620 W Central Rd
Mt Prospect, IL 60056-2269

847-870-8400
Fax: 847-870-8414 fsengrav@aol.com
www.fandsengraving.com
Bronze rotary cookie and cracker molds, and steel
dye engraving
President: Jim Fromm
fsengrav@aol.com

Estimated Sales: $5-10 000,000
Number Employees: 50-99

22364 F C MEYER Packaging LLC
2531 Thomas St
Jeannette, PA 15644-1876

724-523-5565
Fax: 724-527-3575 www.mafcote.com
Paper boxes for pasta, frozen poultry, pizza, etc
Manager: Tracey Moranduzzo
Manager: Paul Parisi
pparisi@spc.cc
Estimated Sales: $20-50 Million
Number Employees: 10-19

22365 F G Products Inc
3000 Pioneer Ave
Rice Lake, WI 54868-2433

715-234-2334
Fax: 715-234-6259 800-247-3854
info@fgproducts.com www.fgproducts.com
Insulated and return air bulkheads and center parti-
tion systems for the refrigerated transportation
industry
Owner: Chad Nelson
Marketing Director: Matthew Nelson
Sales Manager: Ron Hagen
info@fgproducts.com
Estimated Sales: $10-20 Million
Number Employees: 50-99
Square Footage: 50000

22366 (HQ)F I L T E C-Inspection Systems
3100 Fujita St
Torrance, CA 90505-4007

310-325-5633
Fax: 310-530-1000 888-434-5832
www.filtec.com
Manufacturer and exporter of automatic inspection
systems for empty bottles, cases, missing caps, la-
bels, filler/seamer monitors and packaging line
detectors
President/Chief Executive Officer: Steve Calhoun
Managing Director: Reginaldo Pereira
Chief Financial Officer: Dan Leo
Manager, Research & Development: Kendall
Hudson
Vice President, Sales & Marketing: Joanie Natisin
Chief Operating Officer: Bob Catalanotti
Purchasing Agent: Bill Herich
Estimated Sales: $44 Million
Number Employees: 250-499
Square Footage: 155000
Type of Packaging: Food Service
Other Locations:
Industrial Dynamics Co.Ltd.
Hamburg 30, West
Brands:
Dairyvision
Ebi-Ultraline
Ft-50
Omnivision 1200
Omnivision 900

22367 F N Sheppard & Co
1261 Jamike Ave
P. O. Box 18520
Erlanger, KY 41018-3115

859-525-2358
Fax: 859-525-8467 800-733-5773
beltinfo@fnsheppard.com www.fnsheppard.com
Manufacturer and exporter of industrial belting for
packaging including custom, flat, surreys and power
transmission; also, design assistance, custom fabri-
cation, field service, splicing tools and equipment
available
CEO: James E. Reilly
Vice President: Frank Klaene
R&D: Tim Reilly
Quality Control: Bob Black
Marketing Director: Flint Coltharp
Sales Director: Wayne Siemer
Manufacturing Executive: Dan Martin
Plant Manager: Jim Reilly, Jr.
Purchasing Manager: Jack Fassel
Estimated Sales: $10-20 Million
Number Employees: 50-99
Square Footage: 40000

22368 F N Smith Corp
1200 S 2nd St
P.O. Box 179
Oregon, IL 61061-2330

815-732-2171
Fax: 815-732-6173 fnsmith@fnsmithcorp.com
www.fnsmithcorp.com
Bins, conveyors, packaging and extrusion equip-
ment, knives, cartoning equipment and forming rolls
for flaking/forming food; exporter of oat hullers and
grain steamers
President: Ed Smith
CEO: Fred Smith
fnsmith@fnsmithcorp.com
CFO: Fred Smith
VP: Edward Smith
Estimated Sales: $2.5-5 Million
Number Employees: 20-49
Square Footage: 70000

22369 F P Intl
1090 Mills Way
Redwood City, CA 94063-3120

650-261-5300
Fax: 650-361-1713 800-866-9946
www.fpintl.com
Manufactures cushioning material for protective
packaging
President: Joe Nezwek
joenezwek@fpintl.com
CFO: Dennis Fernandes
Marketing: Larry Lenhart
Estimated Sales: $30-50 Million
Number Employees: 5-9

22370 F R Drake Co
1410 Genicom Dr
Waynesboro, VA 22980-1956

540-949-6215
Fax: 540-949-8363 sales@drakeloader.com
www.drakeloader.com
Designs and manufactures automatic loading sys-
tems for cylindrical products and frozen patties.
Frankfurters and other cylindrical products are
loaded into packages at speeds up to 1,800 pieces
per minute
President: Russ Martin
Vice President of Engineering: George Reed
Sales Manager of North America: Tyrone Beatty
Number Employees: 50-99
Type of Packaging: Food Service, Bulk

22371 F&G Packaging
US Highway 17
Yulee, FL 32097

904-225-5121
Fax: 904-225-9500
Paper bags
General Manager: Allan Young
Number Employees: 177
Parent Co: Stone Container

22372 F-D-S Mfg Co
2200 S Reservoir St
Pomona, CA 91766-6408

909-591-1733
Fax: 909-591-1571 custserv@fdsmfg.com
www.fdsmfg.com
Fruit and vegetable packaging
Chairman: Sameul Stevenson
Cmo: Dan Stevenson
dstevenson@fdsmfg.com
Estimated Sales: $20-50 Million
Number Employees: 100-249

22373 F.B. Leopold
227 S Division St
Zelienople, PA 16063

724-452-6300
Fax: 724-452-1377 sales@fbleopold.com
Wine industry filtration equipment
VP: Robert M Clements
Contact: Francis Daugherty
pdaugherty@fbleopold.com
Estimated Sales: $1-5 Million
Number Employees: 50-99

22374 F.B. Pease Company
1450 E Henrietta Road
Rochester, NY 14623-3184

585-475-1870
Fax: 716-475-9621

Paring, coring, slicing and conveying machinery for apples, kiwifruit, potatoes, squash and eggplant; exporter of apple parers, corers and slicers
Chairman: Warren Pease
President: Dudley Pease
Export Manager: Vivian Bubel
Estimated Sales: $2.5-5 Million
Number Employees: 19
Square Footage: 88000
Parent Co: Pease Development Company

22375 F.E. Wood & Sons
5 Brown Road
West Baldwin, ME 4091
207-286-5003
Fax: 207-787-2575 info@fewoodenergy.com
www.fewoodenergy.com
Wooden pallets, bins and skids
CEO: Tony Wood
VP: Anthony Wood
Contact: Dean Wood
dean@fewoodenergy.com
Head, Procurement & Logistics: Dean Wood
Estimated Sales: $1-2.5 Million
Number Employees: 20-49

22376 F.M. Corporation
1360 SW 32nd Way
Deerfield Beach, FL 33442-8110
954-570-9860
Fax: 954-570-9865
Manufacturer and exporter of kitchen ventilation equipment including oven hoods
Plant Manager: Twayn Katz
Estimated Sales: $1-5,000,000
Number Employees: 20-50
Parent Co: Hood Depot
Type of Packaging: Food Service

22377 F.P. Smith Wire Cloth Company
11700 W Grand Avenue
Northlake, IL 60164-1373
708-562-3344
Fax: 800-310-8999 800-323-6842
Manufacturer and exporter of woven and welded wire cloth
VP of Manufacturing: John Crupper
VP Sales: Ted Kapp
VP Manufacturing: Dr. John Crupper
Estimated Sales: $2.5-5 Million
Number Employees: 500
Square Footage: 114000
Brands:
Metaloom

22378 FAN Separator
466 Randy Road
Carol Stream, IL 60188-2120
922-793-8400
Fax: 922-793-8444 800-451-8001
info@fan-separator.de www.fan-separator.de
Liquids, solid separation
President: Friedrich Wiegand
Estimated Sales: $1-2.5 Million
Number Employees: 2

22379 FASTCORP LLC
22 Shelter Rock Lane
Danbury, CT 06810
973-455-0400
Fax: 973-455-7401 888-457-0716
fastcorp1@aol.com www.fastcorpvending.com
Contact: Jay Bender
jay.bender@fastcorpvending.com
Estimated Sales: $3-5 Million
Number Employees: 20-49

22380 FBM/Baking Machines Inc
1 Corporate Drive
Cranbury, NJ 08512
800-449-0433
Fax: 609-860-0576 800-449-0433
info@fbmbakingmachines.com
www.fbmbakingmachines.com
Ovens and machines, VMI mixers, Panimatic retarders/proofers and ovens
President: Oliver Frot
CFO: Beatrice Harmett
Contact: Frank Signorile
fsignorile@fbmbakingmachines.com
Number Employees: 5-9

22381 FCD Tabletops
812 Snediker Ave
Brooklyn, NY 11207
718-649-1002
Fax: 800-938-0818 800-822-5399
Manufacturer and exporter of table, bar and counter tops
Sales Manager: Eric Grossman
VP Sales: Peter Stagg
Estimated Sales: $5-10,000,000
Number Employees: 20-49
Square Footage: 35000

22382 FCF Ginseng, LLC
3225 Halder Dr
Mosinee, WI 54455
715-693-3166
Fax: 715-693-5541
President: Lawrence Murray
CFO: Yvonne Murray
Estimated Sales: Below $5 Million
Number Employees: 1-4

22383 FCI Inc
4661 Giles Rd
Cleveland, OH 44135-3794
216-251-5200
Fax: 216-251-5206 800-321-1032
www.fci-usa.com
Change parts for bottle fillers and cappers, replacement parts fore beverage equipment, vent tubes
President: Kenneth J Edgar
Operations Manager: Mike Peronek
Estimated Sales: $10-20 Million
Number Employees: 20-49

22384 FCN Publishing
1725 K St NW # 506
Washington, DC 20006-1401
202-887-6320
Fax: 202-887-6339
Publish food chemical news, food tracebility report newsletter, lawyers, regulators, food industry execs. In bulk commodities
Manager: David Acord
Estimated Sales: $3-5 Million
Number Employees: 5-9

22385 FDL/Flair Designs
P.O.Box 606
Kokomo, IN 46903-0606
765-452-6000
Fax: 765-452-5882 www.fdlinc.com
Chairs, cushions, pads and bar/counter stools
Contact: Stephen Striebel
stephen.striebel@eyeweardesigns.com
Estimated Sales: $1-2.5 Million
Number Employees: 20-49

22386 FECO/MOCO
1745 Overland Avenue
Warren, OH 44483
330-372-8511
Fax: 330-372-8608 800-547-1527
www.ajaxtocco.com
Custom designing and manufacturing industrial ovens and thermal processing equipment Engineering and design capabilities include the unique ability to combine heat-processing and curing technologies with material handling andconveying methods
President: Dave Ekers
Project Manager Conveyors: Jim Hercik
Project Manager Ovens: Alan Semetana
Purchasing Manager: Jack Specker
Estimated Sales: $10-20 Million
Number Employees: 10
Square Footage: 240000
Parent Co: Park Ohio Company

22387 FEI Co
1125 Berryhill St # 2
Harrisburg, PA 17104-1704
717-232-2310
Fax: 888-381-6910
Warehouse providing cooler, freezer, humidity-controlled and dry storage
Manager: Greg Shipe
Estimated Sales: Less Than $500,000
Number Employees: 5-9
Square Footage: 160000
Type of Packaging: Consumer, Food Service

22388 FEI Inc
934 S 5th Ave
Mansfield, TX 76063-2794
817-473-3344
Fax: 817-473-3124 800-346-5908
sales@feiconveyors.com www.feiconveyors.com
Manufacturer and exporter of sanitary and anti-corrosive conveyors including gravity, powered and stainless steel skate wheels; also, conveyor components
President: Duane Murray
duane@feiconveyors.com
VP: David Murray
Estimated Sales: $5-10 Million
Number Employees: 20-49
Square Footage: 68000

22389 FES West
2617 Willowbrook Ln
Aptos, CA 95003-6022
831-462-6603
Fax: 831-462-9781 800-251-6603
Wine industry refrigeration systems
Owner: Harold Paul
Estimated Sales: $1-2.5 Million
Number Employees: 1-4

22390 (HQ)FFE Transportation Services
P.O.Box 655888
Dallas, TX 75265-5888
Fax: 214-819-5625 800-569-9200
ir@ffex.net www.ffex.net
To get to any information for the other FFE sites please visit the web address in this listing, transportation firm providing refrigerated local, long and short haul trucking and van service, LTL, and TL
CEO: Stoney M Stubbs Jr
Contact: Leonard Bartholomew
lbartholmew@ffex.net
Estimated Sales: D
Number Employees: 250-499
Other Locations:
FFE Transportation Services
Oakland CA

22391 FFI Corporation
P.O. Box 20
1004 East Illinois Street
Assumption, IL 62510
217-226-5100
Manufacturer and exporter of continuous flow commercial and industrial grain dryers
Estimated Sales: $50-100 Million
Number Employees: 250-499

22392 FFR Merchandising Inc
8181 Darrow Rd
Twinsburg, OH 44087-2303
440-505-6919
Fax: 440-505-6900 800-422-2547
info@ffr.com www.ffr.com
Since 1962, has been developing innovative merchandising systems and accesories to effectively position brands at retail. Offers custom design services and fullfillment
President/CEO: Donald Kimmel
CEO: Stanley Burson
stanley.burson@ffr.com
CFO: Nathaniel Smith
CEO: Stanley Burson
Research & Development: Daniel Kump
Marketing Director: Paul Bloom
Sales Director: Michael DeJohn
Operations Manager: Drew Phillips
Estimated Sales: $50-100 Million
Number Employees: 100-249
Number of Brands: 40
Number of Products: 1700
Square Footage: 100000

22393 FIB-R-DOR
10021 Commerce Park Dr.
P.O.Box 13268
Cincinnati, OH 45246
501-758-9494
Fax: 501-758-9496 800-342-7367
fibrdor@fibrdor.com www.fibrdor.com
Manufacturer and exporter of fiberglass doors, etc.
President: Jason Dileo
Marketing Director: Wes Lacewell
Sales Director: Mike Ferrell
Estimated Sales: $2.5 Million
Number Employees: 10-19
Number of Products: 3

Square Footage: 50000
Parent Co: Advance Fiberglass
Type of Packaging: Bulk
Brands:
    Fib-R-Dor

22394 FJC International
2418 Hilton Way
Gainesville, GA 30501-6192
    770-718-0100
Fax: 770-718-0909 info@fjcinternational.com
    www.fjcinternational.com
Provides equipment and turnkey operations for poultry processing plants
President: Juan Chiarella
info@fjcinternational.com
Estimated Sales: $1.3 Million
Number Employees: 5-9

22395 (HQ)FLEXcon Company
1 FLEXcon Industrial Park
Spencer, MA 01562-2642
    508-885-8200
Fax: 508-885-8400 www.flexcon.com
Pressure sensitive film and adhesive products
President & CEO: Neil McDonough
CEO: Neil McDonough
Number Employees: 1,000-4,999

22396 FMB Company
RR 1
Box 564
Broken Bow, OK 74728-9780
    580-513-5309
Fax: 580-584-2971 fmbco@octm.com
Consultant providing design and building services for food and industrial plants
President: Fred Bray
Director Marketing: Tonya Laffey
Estimated Sales: Below $5 Million
Number Employees: 1
Square Footage: 6400

22397 FMC Corporation
2929 Walnut St
Philadelphia, PA 19104
    215-299-6000
Fax: 215-299-5998 www.fmc.com
Natural soda ash for sodium bicarbonate, sodium cyanide, sodium sesquicarbonate and caustic soda, hydrogen peroxide, active oxidants, phosphorus chemicals and phosphoric acid.
Chairman/CEO: Pierre Brondeau
EVP & CFO: Andrew Sandifer
EVP/General Counsel/Secretary: Michael Reilly
President & CEO-Elect: Mark Douglas
Year Founded: 1883
Estimated Sales: Over $1 Billion
Number Employees: 7,000

22398 FMC Fluid Control
103 E Maple Street
Hoopeston, IL 60942-1699
    217-283-8300
    Fax: 217-283-8424
Wine industry vineyard sprayers
Co- Owner: Thomas Hamilton
Chairman, President, Chief Executive Off: John Gremp
Vice President of Infrastructure: Barry Glickman
Regional Sales Manager: Ellen Hao
Contact: Lavonda Sherrill
lavonda_sherrill@fmc.com
Estimated Sales: $10-20 Million
Number Employees: 50-99

22399 FMI Display
360 Glen Way
Elkins Park, PA 19027-1740
    215-663-1998
    Fax: 215-763-7099
Wire display racks and point of purchase displays including paper and plastic; also, screen printing services available
President: Kenneth Hoffman
Number Employees: 10
Square Footage: 10000

22400 FMI Fluid Metering
5 Aerial Way
Suite 500
Syosset, NY 11791-5593
    516-922-6050
Fax: 516-624-8261 800-223-3388
pumps@fmipump.com www.fmipump.com
Dispensers, ingredients, lubricant, ingredient feeders
President: Harry Pinkerton
Contact: Hank Pinkerton
pumps@fmipump.com
Number Employees: 50-99

22401 FMS
328 Commerce Blvd # 8
Bogart, GA 30622-2200
    706-549-2207
Fax: 706-548-1724 fmssales@fmsathens.com
    www.fmsathens.com
Manager: Eric Gunderson
Estimated Sales: $10-20 Million
Number Employees: 20-49

22402 FMS Company
338 Alana Drive
New Lenox, IL 60451-1784
    815-485-4955
Fax: 815-485-4011 800-992-2814
Wine industry financial software
Estimated Sales: $2.5-5 000,000
Number Employees: 1-4

22403 FOODesign from tna
29103 SW Kinsman Rd
Wilsonville, OR 97070-8701
    503-685-5030
Fax: 503-685-5034 info@foodesign.com
    www.foodesign.com
Supplier of commercial and industrial cooking & baking equipment, fryers, Cryo-Jet, cooling units, coating & seasoning equipment, food grade bulk packaging handling conveyers and specialty cooking equipment.
Vice President: Daniel Luna
Project Manager: Jason Heisler
Estimated Sales: $5-10 million
Number Employees: 20
Parent Co: tna

22404 FORT Hill Sign ProductsInc
13 Airport Rd
Hopedale, MA 01747-1547
    781-321-4320
Fax: 781-397-0452 fh@forthillsigns.com
    www.forthillsigns.com
Plastic cut letters and logos, name plates and signs
Owner: Amy Clark
amy.clark@forthillsigns.com
Estimated Sales: $3-5 Million
Number Employees: 5-9

22405 FP Packaging Company
193 Camino Dorado
Napa, CA 94558-6213
    707-258-3940
Fax: 707-258-3949 www.collopack.com
Wine industry packaging and wine corks
CEO: Gregory Fulford
Founder, Executive Vice President Sales: Phil Giacalone
Founder, Vice President of Sales: Joe Mironicki
Estimated Sales: $10-20 Million
Number Employees: 10-19
Type of Packaging: Bulk

22406 FPC Corp
355 Hollow Hill Rd
Wauconda, IL 60084-9794
    847-487-4583
Fax: 847-487-0174 www.surebonderindustrial.com
Glue sticks, staples and staple guns
President: Michael Kamins
glueguns@aol.com
CFO: Patrick Kamins
Quality Control: M Bernard Kamins
Estimated Sales: $10-20 000,000
Number Employees: 20-49

22407 FPEC Corp
2216 Ford Ave
Springdale, AR 72764-4722
    479-751-9392
Fax: 479-751-9399 salesark@fpec.com
    www.fpec.com

Processing equipment for beef, chicken, sausage, fish and ham
President: Alan Davison
Estimated Sales: $5-10 Million
Number Employees: 20-49

22408 FPEC Corporation
13623 Pumice St
Santa Fe Springs, CA 90670-5105
    562-802-3727
Fax: 562-802-8621 salescal@fpec.com
    www.fpec.com
Manufacturer and exporter of food processing equipment including blenders, conveyors and vacuum tumblers
President: Alan Davison
Contact: Laura Flynn
flynnl@fpec.com
Plant Manager: Dwayne Lee
Estimated Sales: $5-10 Million
Number Employees: 20-49
Square Footage: 212000
Brands:
    Fpec

22409 FRC Environmental
1635 Oakbrook Dr
Gainesville, GA 30507
    770-534-3681
    Fax: 770-535-1887
Manufacturer and exporter of stainless steel waste water treatment equipment and systems
President: Lonnie Finley
Estimated Sales: $2,600,000
Number Employees: 25
Square Footage: 72000
Type of Packaging: Bulk

22410 FRC Systems International
1770 Ridgefield Drive
Roswell, GA 30075
    770-534-3681
Fax: 770-992-2289 info@FRCsystems.com
    www.frcsystems.com
Water and wastewater treatment systems for the dairy, poultry, meat & seafood processing industries.

22411 FRICK by Johnson Controls
5757 N Green Bay Ave
P.O. Box 591
Milwaukee, WI 53201
    414-524-1200
    855-270-5546
    www.jci.com/frick
Industrial refrigeration, food and beverage, petrochemical, oil and gas extraction.
Chairman & CEO: George Oliver
EVP & Chief Financial Officer: Brian Stief
EVP & General Counsel: John Donofrio
R&D: Joe Pillis
VP, Corporate Controller: Bob VanHimbergen
EVP & Chief Human Resources Officer: Lynn Minella
Estimated Sales: $100-500 Million
Number Employees: 500
Parent Co: Johnson Controls

22412 FRS Industries
1021 Center Ave.
Moorhead, MN 56560
    701-365-1000
Fax: 218-287-2907 800-747-4795
    art@kiefers.com www.frsind.com
Advertising novelties and specialites including award ribbons, rosettes, trophies, promotional buttons, imprinted T-shirts, jackets, caps, etc
Owner: Sheri Larson
Controller: Timothy Dockter
Sales Manager: Sheri Larson
Contact: Eric Bacon
ebacon@heatsoftware.com
Estimated Sales: $5-10 Million
Number Employees: 20-49

22413 FSFG Capital
814 Fontana Avenue
Richardson, TX 75080-3002
    972-783-0611
    Fax: 972-235-5310
Investment firm for food companies
Vice President: Richard Harju

22414 FTC International Consulting
19021 Mitchell Road
Pitt Meadows, BC V3Y 1Y1
Canada
604-288-2719
Fax: 604-288-8565 contact@ftcinternational.com
www.ftcinternational.com
Consulting: product development, nutrition analysis,
regulatory consulting, quality programs
President: Walter Dullemond
Operations Manager: Eva Savova

22415 FTI International Automation Systems
10914 N 2nd Street
Machesney Park, IL 61115-1400
815-877-4080
Fax: 815-877-0073
www.ftiautomationsystems.com

22416 FTL/Happold Tensil Structure Design & Engineering
44 East 32nd Street
3rd Floor
New York, NY 10016
212-732-4691
Fax: 212-385-1025 ngoldsmith@ftlstudio.com
www.ftlstudio.com
Commercial tents, fabric structures
Owner: Todd Dalland
Genetics Department: Andre Chaszar
Engineer: Wayne Rendeley
Estimated Sales: $1-5 Million
Number Employees: 20-49
Parent Co: Buro Happold

22417 FTR Processing Equipment
2101 Troy Ave
South El Monte, CA 91733-2535
626-452-1870
Fax: 626-452-1857 ftrequipment@yahoo.com
ftrequipment.com
Packaging, processing and slaughtering equipment
Owner: Francisco Prejo
ftrprocessingequipment@yahoo.com
Vice President: Gloria Trejo
Sales Director: Jair Trejo
Estimated Sales: Below $5 000,000
Number Employees: 10-19
Number of Brands: 55

22418 FX Technology & Products
900 Factory Rd
PO Box 547
Fremont, NE 68026
402-727-5222
Fax: 402-721-5154 866-938-8388
Proteins
Regional Sales Manager: Rick Young
Office Manager: Debbie Vacha
Estimated Sales: Under $500,000
Number Employees: 10-19

22419 FX-Lab Company
725 Lehigh Avenue
Union, NJ 07083-7642
908-810-1212
Fax: 908-810-1630
Manufacturer and exporter of beneficial bacterial
cleaning compounds and liquefiers for septic tanks
and cesspools
President: George Weinik
Number Employees: 5
Square Footage: 4800

22420 Fab-X/Metals
PO Box 1903
Washington, NC 27889-1903
252-977-3229
Fax: 252-977-6605 800-677-3229
Manufacturer and wholesaler/distributor of chairs,
ovens, sinks, spoons, tables, etc.; also, supermarket
equipment including store fixtures and racks; serv-
ing the food service market
President: Jonathan Turner
COO: Cyrus Watson
Quality Control: Carol Causeway
Estimated Sales: $10-20 Million
Number Employees: 10
Square Footage: 200000

22421 Fabco
PO Box 754
Albertville, AL 35950-0012
256-878-5010
Fax: 256-878-7879 www.fabcoinc.com
CEO: Rocky Frazier
Director of Sales: Stephen Frazier
Manufacturing Manager: Phillip Murphree
Estimated Sales: $20-50 Million
Number Employees: 20-49

22422 Fabick CAT
11200 W Silver Spring Rd
Milwaukee, WI 53225-3118
414-461-9100
Fax: 414-461-8899 sal@fabco.com
Disinfection of pumpable foods and drinking water
CEO: Jere Fabick
j.fabick@fabco.com
Estimated Sales: $500,000-$1 Million
Number Employees: 50-99

22423 Fabohio Inc
521 E 7th St
Uhrichsville, OH 44683-1613
740-922-4233
Fax: 740-922-4785 www.fabohio.com
Manufacturer and exporter of protective clothing
and products including drum liners, meat cutters'
aprons and smocks and shoe covers. Also custom
fabrication available.
President: Don Coy
dcoy@fabohio.com
CEO: Kurt Shelley
CFO: Kurt Shelley
Purchasing Manager: Dennis Sautters
Estimated Sales: $1-3 Million
Number Employees: 20-49
Square Footage: 50000

22424 Fabreeka International
315 Ruthar Dr
Newark, DE 19711
302-452-2500
Fax: 302-452-2505 www.derco.com
Equipment
Manager: Paul O'Connor
Estimated Sales: $3-5 Million
Number Employees: 10-19

22425 Fabreeka International
696 W Amity Rd
Boise, ID 83705-5401
208-342-4681
Fax: 208-343-8043 800-423-4469
www.beltservice.com
Manufacturer and exporter of lightweight custom
conveyor belting including food grade, food grade
incline, special profile, harvester, PVC and
polyurethane
Branch Manager: Bob Holda
General manager: Toby Grindstaff
Division Manager: Toby Grindstaff
Assistant Division Manager: Mitz Pellicciotta
Estimated Sales: Below $5 Million
Number Employees: 10-19
Square Footage: 400000
Parent Co: Fabreeka International
Other Locations:
Fabreeka International
Oakville ON
Brands:
Fablene
Fablon
Fabreeka
Fabsyn

22426 Fabreeka International Inc
1023 Turnpike St
Stoughton, MA 02072-1156
781-341-3655
Fax: 781-341-3983 800-322-7352
info@fabreeka.com www.fabreeka.com
Integrally molded cleated and special profile rubber
belting and European style thermoplastics belting
President: Pat Norton
pnorton@fabreeka.com
Estimated Sales: $25-30 Million
Number Employees: 1-4

22427 Fabri-Kal Corp
600 Plastics Pl
Kalamazoo, MI 49001-4882
269-385-5050
Fax: 269-385-0197 800-888-5054
info@fabri-kal.com www.fabri-kal.com
Thermoformed plastic containers and cups including
custom designed, prototype, production, stock food
service line, clear or colored and FDA certified
CEO: Scott Abel
sabel@f-k.com
CEO: Robert P Kittredge
Marketing Manager: Scott Tindall
Estimated Sales: $10-20 Million
Number Employees: 50-99
Brands:
Kal-Tainer

22428 Fabricated Components Inc
2018 W Main St
PO Box 431
Stroudsburg, PA 18360
570-421-4110
Fax: 570-421-2553 800-233-8163
info@fabricatedcomponents.com
www.fabricatedcomponents.com
Manufacturer and exporter of pallets, dollies, carts,
cabinetry and containers
President: Bob Deinarowicz
Estimated Sales: $2.5-5 Million
Number Employees: 20-49
Square Footage: 200000
Type of Packaging: Private Label

22429 Fabricating & Welding Corp
12246 S Halsted St
Chicago, IL 60628-6400
773-928-2050
Fax: 773-928-4950
www.fabricatingandwelding.com
Steel skids, base plates and motor bases
President: Greg Delcotto
gregdelcotto@fabricatingandwelding.com
CFO: Elizabeth Pecora
Research & Development: Steven Samecak
Production Manager: Jim Foley
Purchasing Manager: Robert Del Cotto
Estimated Sales: $5-10 Million
Number Employees: 10-19
Square Footage: 60000

22430 Fabrication Specialties
2898 Crestridge Dr
Centerville, TN 37033-5941
931-729-2283
Fax: 931-729-2585
www.fabricationspecialties.com
Wood pallets and shipping skids
Owner: Mike Goodpasture
fabspec@hughes.net
VP: William Goodpasture
Estimated Sales: $2.5-5 Million
Number Employees: 20-49
Square Footage: 40000

22431 Fabrichem Inc
2226 Black Rock Tpke # 206
Fairfield, CT 06825-3240
203-366-1820
Fax: 203-366-1850 sales@fabricheminc.com
www.fabricheminc.com
Aspartame, amino acids, L-Tyrosine, botanical ex-
tracts, L-theanine, Lutein, D-Glucuronolactone
Owner: Jacob Tallathra
Estimated Sales: $5-10 000,000
Number Employees: 10
Number of Brands: 4
Number of Products: 50

22432 Fabricon Products Inc
1721 W Pleasant St
River Rouge, MI 48218-1099
313-841-8200
Fax: 313-841-4819 bdinda@fabriconproducts.com
www.fabriconproducts.com
Manufacturer, importer and exporter of flexible
packaging materials including printed waxed and
coated paper, films, frozen/novelty food packaging
and wrapping, preformed paper bags and film laminated pouches; also, package designservices
available

President: Bruce Dinda
bdinda@fabriconproducts.com
CFO: Roland David
Sales Director: Bruce L Dinda
Customer Service: Becky Smith
Production Manager: Mike Aslanian
Plant Manager: John Kuzawinski
Purchasing Manager: Colleen Loweifer
Estimated Sales: $9 Million
Number Employees: 50-99
Square Footage: 302000
Type of Packaging: Consumer, Food Service, Private Label, Bulk

22433 Fabriko
P.O.Box 67
Altavista, VA 24517-0067
434-369-1170
Fax: 434-369-1169 888-203-8098
afbriko@voyager.net www.fabriko.com
Manufacturer and importer of barbecue and waist aprons, coolers and bags including lunch, grocery and shopping
Owner: Ranata Allbeck
Sales Manager: Jerry Fischer
Estimated Sales: $3-5 Million
Number Employees: 10-19

22434 Fabwright Inc
13912 Enterprise Dr
Garden Grove, CA 92843-4021
714-554-5544
Fax: 714-554-5545 800-854-6464
Manufacturer and exporter of custom stainless steel kitchen equipment fabrication; complete line of commercial food waste disposers
Owner: Della Williams
della@fabwrightinc.com
Vice President: J Wright
Purchasing Manager: D Yeardley
Number Employees: 10-19
Type of Packaging: Food Service

22435 Facilitec
73 S Riverside Dr
Elgin, IL 60120-6425
847-931-9500
Fax: 847-931-9629
Estimated Sales: $1-5 Million
Parent Co: Ecolab

22436 Facilities Design Inc
100 Brubaker Rd
Lititz, PA 17543-8662
717-626-1880
Fax: 717-285-3102 www.facilitiesdesign.net
Full-service design capabilities including construction services with special expertise in cold storage warehousing and food processing facilities, complete architectural engineering and materials handling design
President: Joe Shaffer
Marketing Director: Jack Stone
Estimated Sales: Less Than $500,000
Number Employees: 1-4

22437 Facility Group
2233 Lake Park Dr SE Ste 100
Smyrna, GA 30080
770-437-2700
Fax: 770-437-3900 www.facilitygroup.com
Fully integrated planning, engineering and construction management firm specializing in turn-key services for the food processing and distribution industries. Refrigeration engineering and insulation technology, materials handling equipment selection
CEO: Ennis Parker
Estimated Sales: $50
Number Employees: 250-499

22438 Faciltec Corporation
73 S Riverside Dr
Elgin, IL 60120-6425
847-931-9500
Fax: 847-931-9629 800-284-8273
Manufacturer and exporter of a rooftop grease containment system for food service and industrial markets; also, cleaning services available
Executive VP: Christopher Barry
National Sales/Service Manager: Patrick Molloy
Estimated Sales: $1-5 Million
Number Employees: 50-99
Square Footage: 104000
Type of Packaging: Food Service

Brands:
Afc
G2 Grease Guard
Grease Guard

22439 Factory Cat
1509 Rapids Drive
Racine, WI 53404-2383
262-681-3583
Fax: 262-632-3335 800-634-4060
www.factorycat.com
Industrial, walk-behind and rider sweepers and scrubbers

22440 FactoryTalk
1201 S 2nd St
Milwaukee, WI 53204
414-382-2000
www.rockwellautomation.com/en_NA/products/factorytalk
Software to support advanced industrial applications, including system design, operations, plant maintenance, and analytics.
VP, Architecture & Software: Fran Wlodarczyk
Parent Co: Rockwell Automation Inc

22441 Fair Publishing House
15 Schauss Ave
PO Box 350
Norwalk, OH 44857-1851
419-668-3746
Fax: 419-663-3247 orders@fairsupplies.com
www.fairpublishing.com
Manufacturer and exporter of award ribbons, tickets and signs including advertising
President: Kevin Doyle
kevin@fairsupplies.com
Sales Director: Charles Doyle
Production Manager: Kenneth Kosie
Estimated Sales: $3-5 Million
Number Employees: 20-49
Square Footage: 50000
Parent Co: Rotary Printing Company
Other Locations:
Fair Publishing House
Norwalk OH

22442 Fairbanks Scales
821 Locust St
Kansas City, MO 64106-1925
816-471-0231
Fax: 816-471-0241 800-451-4107
www.fairbanks.com
Manufacturer and exporter of stainless steel hostile environment scales including bench, unirail, omnicells, digital indicators, bench and portable scales, and bar code dataprinter
President: Richard Norden
rnorden@fairbanks.com
Chairman: F.A. Norden
Chief Financial Officer: Steve Wurtzler
Vice President, Engineering: Tom Luke
Quality Assurance Manager: Craig Schnepf
Vice President, Sales & Marketing: Bob Jozwiak
Director, Product Development: Derrick Mashaney
Plant Manager: Wayne Gaboriault
Purchasing Manager: Keith George
Estimated Sales: $81 Million
Number Employees: 20-49
Square Footage: 12000
Parent Co: Fancor, Inc.

22443 Fairborn USA Inc
205 Broadview St
Upper Sandusky, OH 43351-9628
419-294-4987
Fax: 419-294-4980 800-262-1188
info@fairbornusa.com www.fairbornusa.com
Manufacturer and exporter of truck and rail loading dock enclosures
President: Mark Dillon
dillonm@fairbornusa.com
General Manager: Mark Dillon
Number Employees: 100-249

22444 Fairchester Snacks Corp
100 Lafayette Ave
White Plains, NY 10603-1612
914-761-2824
www.nysnacks.com
Salty biscuits
Owner: John Barisano
Estimated Sales: $300,000-500,000
Number Employees: 5-9

22445 Fairchild Industrial Products
3920 Westpoint Blvd
Winston Salem, NC 27103-6727
336-659-3400
Fax: 336-659-9323 800-334-8422
sales@fairchildproducts.com www.soldousa.com
Manufacturer and exporter of industrial controls including electro-pneumatic transducers and pneumatic pressure regulators; also, mechanical power transmission equipment including differential and draw transmissions
President: Mark Cuthbert
CEO: Bryan Buono
bryan.buono@rotork.com
Director, Finance: David C. Velten
VP Industrial Controls: Thomas McNichol
Quality Control: Greg Argrabright
R&D: Andy Askew
Director of Sales: Claudio Borges
VP Power Transportation Equipment: Jack Dunivant
Estimated Sales: $10-20 Million
Number Employees: 100-249
Square Footage: 176000
Brands:
Cubic
Fairchild
Harmonic
Specon
Vari-Chain

22446 Fairfield Line Inc
605 W Stone Ave
PO Box 500
Fairfield, IA 52556-2223
641-472-3191
Fax: 641-472-3194 800-247-3383
www.fairfieldlineinc.com
Manufacturer, importer and exporter of work gloves including cotton, leather, leather-palm, coated and string knits
President: Nicole Vivacqua
nvivacqua@fairfieldline.com
VP: Larry Sheffler
Sales Manager: Larry Ray Sheffler
Estimated Sales: $5-10 Million
Number Employees: 20-49
Parent Co: Fairfield Line

22447 Falco Technologies
1245 Rue Industrielle
La Prairie, QC J5R 2E4
Canada
450-444-0566
Fax: 450-444-2227 www.falcotechnologies.com
Manufacturer and exporter of stainless steel food processing equipment including silos, tanks, hoppers, mixing kettles, wine storage units, brewery machinery, dairy processing equipment and custom fabrication turn key solutions to simple and complex problems-from tank installation to complete process
Co-President: Bertrand Blanchette
Co-President: Marc Regnaud
Quality Control: Andre Pichette
Marketing/Sales: Nicolas Courchesne
Vice President of Sales and Marketing: Stephane Audy
Production/Plant Manager: Jonathan Gingras
Purchasing: Susan Hynes
Estimated Sales: $10 Million
Number Employees: 75
Square Footage: 130000
Parent Co: Falco
Brands:
Falco

22448 Falcon Belting
8338 SW 15th Street
Oklahoma City, OK 73128-9594
405-495-7563
Fax: 405-495-7911 800-922-0878
Plastic belts
Estimated Sales: $5-10 000,000
Number Employees: 60

22449 Falcon Fabricators Inc
422 Allied Dr
Nashville, TN 37211-3304
615-832-0027
Fax: 615-832-0048 www.falconnashville.com
Stainless steel work tables, hot fat filters, chicken marinators, etc.; also, replacement parts available

President: Gary Heckle
gheckle@falconnashville.com
President: Gary Heckle
Account Manager: Jan Wilson
Estimated Sales: $20-50 Million
Number Employees: 10-19
Square Footage: 50000
Parent Co: Trendco

22450 Fallas Automation Inc.
7000 Imperial Dr
Waco, TX 76712-6816

254-772-9524
Fax: 254-751-1242 sales@fallasautomation.com
www.fallasautomation.com
Automatic packaging machinery
President: Dave Fallas
dfallas@fallasautomation.com
Vice President: Mark McAninch
Sales Manager: Chris Calebrese
Spare Parts Manager: Curtis Gross
Estimated Sales: $10-20 Million
Number Employees: 50+
Square Footage: 130000
Type of Packaging: Consumer, Food Service, Private Label, Bulk

22451 Falls Chemical Products
123 Caldwell Ave
Oconto Falls, WI 54154

920-846-3561
Fax: 920-846-4830 fallschemical@ez-net.com
Cleaners, sanitizers, soaps and dish washing detergent for restaurant, bar and janitorial services; also, dairy chemicals
Owner/President: Sam Scimemi
Number Employees: 2

22452 Falls Filtration Technologies
115 E Steels Corners Rd
Stow, OH 44224-4919

330-928-4100
Fax: 330-928-0122 info@fallsfti.com
Air and oil filters
President: David Casper
dcasper@fallsfti.com
CFO: Bradley Lane
Quality Manager: Jeff Patrick
Director of Commercial Marketing: Andy Blair
Director of Sales: Andy Blair
Customer Service Rep.: Simone Edwards
Senior Buyer: Jean Balcer
Estimated Sales: $10-20 Million
Number Employees: 20-49

22453 Fallshaw Wheels & Casters
6848 Moorhen Place
Oceanside, CA 92009

760-476-9713
Fax: 760-476-9714 jdavitt@fallshaw.com.au
Estimated Sales: $1 Million
Number Employees: 1

22454 Fallwood Corp
75 S Broadway
Suite 494
White Plains, NY 10601-4413

914-304-4065
Fax: 914-304-4063 ana@fallwoodcorp.com
www.fallwoodcorp.com
Manufacturer and supplier of all natural nutraceutical ingredients and raw materials. All glanulars-Bovine and Porcine Enzymes
President/CEO: Jorge Millan
Vice President: Graciela Rocchia
Sales: Wayne Battenfield
Manager: Anne-Marie Rodriguez
anna@fallwoodcorp.com
Adminstration: Anne Marie Rodriguez
Estimated Sales: Under $500,000
Number Employees: 1-4
Parent Co: Loboratorio Opoterapico Argentino

22455 Famco Automatic SausageLinkers
P. O. Box 8647
Pittsburgh, PA 15221

412-241-6410
Fax: 412-242-8877 info@famcousa.com
www.famcousa.com
Linking machines for sausage and frankfurter production
President: Charles Allen
Vice President: R. Robert Allen
Sales: Dick Carson

22456 Famco Sausage Linking Machines
421 N Braddock Ave
Pittsburgh, PA 15208-2514

412-241-6410
Fax: 412-242-8877 info@famcousa.com
www.famcousa.com
Sausage linkers
Owner: Bob Allen
VP: R Robert Allen
Estimated Sales: $1-5 Million
Number Employees: 20-49

22457 Family Farms Group
31832 Dehli Rd.
Brighton, IL 62012

618-372-7400
877-221-3276
www.familyfarmsgroup.com
Services including coaching and management consulting, networking, human resources, cost savings, crop financing, and crop marketing.
CEO: Jeff Haferkamp
EVP: Harold Birch
Director, Sales & Marketing: Dave Bryden
Year Founded: 2006
Number Employees: 50-200

22458 Family Tree Farms
41646 Road 62
Reedley, CA 93654-9124

559-591-8394
Fax: 559-595-7795 866-352-8671
www.familytreefarms.com
Plumcots, white peaches and nectarines, donut peaches and nectarines, yellow peaches and nectarines, apricots, apriums, plums, blueberries, cherries, satsumas
President: David Jackson
djackson@familytreefarms.com
CFO: Dan Clenney
Executive Director of Global Development: Gerome Raco
Director of Research & Development: Eric Wuhl
Quality Control: Mary Ortiz
Director of Marketing: Don Goforth
Estimated Sales: $20-50 Million
Number Employees: 250-499
Brands:
    Eat Smart
    Great Whites
    Flavor Safari
    Farmers Market
    Summerripe
    River Run

22459 Famous Software LLC
8080 N Palm Ave # 210
Suite 210
Fresno, CA 93711-5797

559-431-8100
Fax: 559-447-6339 support@FamousSoftware.com
www.famoussoftware.com
Wine industry computer systems
President: Kirk Parrish
kirkp@famoussoftware.com
CFO: Rick Desehr
Estimated Sales: $5-10 Million
Number Employees: 50-99

22460 Fan Bag Company
4307 W Division St
Chicago, IL 60651-1714

773-342-2752
Fax: 773-342-4413
Plastic bags
CEO: Florian Nocek
VP Marketing: Carl Nocek
Estimated Sales: $5-10 Million
Number Employees: 25

22461 Fantapak
12150 Merriman Rd
Livonia, MI 48150-1914

734-838-1300
Fax: 248-743-2970 800-856-3803
sales@fantapak.com www.fantapak.com
President: Chia Chang
j.chang@fantapakinternational.com
Estimated Sales: $5-10 Million
Number Employees: 20-49

22462 Faraday
805 S Maumee St
Tecumseh, MI 49286-2053

517-423-2111
Fax: 517-423-2320 www.faraday.com
Manufacturer and exporter of fire alarm systems
Manager: Tim Wertz
Contact: Hugo Hortiz
hugo@faradaybikes.com
Estimated Sales: $20-50 Million
Number Employees: 100-249
Parent Co: Cerberus Pryotronics
Brands:
    Faraday

22463 Fargo Automation
969 34th St N
Fargo, ND 58102-3071

701-239-1656
Fax: 701-232-1929 888-616-0188
sales@fargoautomation.com
www.fargoautomation.com
Owner: Kevin Biffert
kevin.biffert@fargoautomation.com
Estimated Sales: $20-50 Million
Number Employees: 20-49

22464 Faribault Foods, Inc.
3401 Park Ave. NW
Fairbault, MN 55021

507-331-1400
ConsumeResponse@faribaultfoods.com
www.faribaultfoods.com
Canned vegetables, sauced beans, refried beans, baked beans, pasta, soup, chili, and organic and Mexican specialties.
President/CEO: Reid MacDonald
CFO: Mike Weber
Executive VP, Sales/Marketing: Frank Lynch
Year Founded: 1888
Estimated Sales: $164 Million
Number Employees: 5
Number of Brands: 8
Parent Co: Arizona Canning Company, LLC
Type of Packaging: Consumer, Private Label, Bulk
Other Locations:
    Faribault Foods Distribution
    Faribault MN
    Faribault Foods Plant
    Cokato MN
Brands:
    Butter Kernel®
    Chilliman®
    Kuner's®
    Luck's®
    Mrs. Grimes®
    SunVista®
    Pride®
    S & W Beans®

22465 Faribault ManufacturingCo
820 20th St NW
Faribault, MN 55021-2396

507-334-0464
Fax: 507-334-0674 800-447-6043
tcook.sales@faribomfg.com www.faribomfg.com
Plastic light globes, food containers, dunnage racks and ingredient bins; also, custom roto molded components available.
President: Timothy M. Hoschette
National Sales/Marketing Manager: Tom Cook
National Sales/Marketing Manager: Kristy Hoffstatter
kristy.orders@faribomfg.com
Purchasing Manager: Tim Hoschette
Estimated Sales: $2.5-5 Million
Number Employees: 10-19
Number of Brands: 2
Number of Products: 150+
Square Footage: 108000
Parent Co: Hoschette Enterprises

22466 Farmer Direct Foods, Inc
PO Box 326
511 Commercial
Atchison, KS 66002

913-367-4422
Fax: 913-367-4443 800-372-4422
www.farmerdirectfoods.com
Provides white and whole wheat baking products, bread recipes, and tips for using bread machines.
Chief Executive Officer: Kent Symns
sales@farmerdirectfoods.com
Director: Dave Pfefer
Operations Director: Marcia Walters

Estimated Sales: $2.5-5 Million
Number Employees: 20-49

22467 Farmer's Co-Op ElevatorCo
3302 Prospect St
P.O. Box 219
Hudsonville, MI 49426-1420
616-669-9596
Fax: 616-669-0490 800-439-9859
info@fcelevator.com www.fcelevator.com
Corrugated cartons and wooden shipping crates,
boxes and baskets
President: Jim Roskam
jroskam@fcelevator.com
General Manager: Jim Roskam
Estimated Sales: $1-5 Million
Number Employees: 20-49
Parent Co: Farmer's Cooperative Elevator Co., Inc.

22468 Farnell Packaging
30 Ilsley Avenue
Dartmouth, NS B3B 1L3
Canada
902-468-9378
Fax: 902-468-3192 800-565-9378
sales@farnell.ns.ca www.farnell.ns.ca
Flexible packaging, plastic films and pressure sensi-
tive labels
President: Donald Farnell
CFO: Bill Morash
Quality Control: Danny Christianson
Sales/Marketing Manager: D Stanfield
General Manager: H Christianson
Number Employees: 160
Square Footage: 75000

22469 Fas-Co Coders
422 Thornton Rd # 103
Lithia Springs, GA 30122-1581
770-739-7798
Fax: 480-545-1998 800-478-0685
Manufacturer and exporter of coding and marking
equipment
Owner: Victor Er
CFO: Roger Van Steenkiste
VP: Dan Piercy
Quality Control: Ty Martin
Estimated Sales: $6,000,000
Number Employees: 20-49
Square Footage: 30000

22470 Fashion Industries
1120 Everee Inn Rd
Griffin, GA 30224
770-412-9214
Fax: 770-412-1124
Table cloths
CEO: William Shapard
Contact: Tamika Huff
huff@fgi.org.gr
Estimated Sales: $50-100 Million
Number Employees: 250-499

22471 Fasson Employee FCU
250 Chester St
Painesville, OH 44077-4118
440-358-2100
Fax: 440-358-2102 www.fasson.com
Wine industry labeling equipment
Manager: Laurie Hall
lhall@fasson.com
Estimated Sales: Less Than $500,000
Number Employees: 1-4

22472 Fast Bags
2501 Ludelle Street
Fort Worth, TX 76105-1036
817-534-9950
Fax: 817-534-1771 800-321-3687
Paper and plastic bags and labels
Estimated Sales: $1-5,000,000
Parent Co: Daydots International

22473 Fast Industries
1850 NW 49th St
Fort Lauderdale, FL 33309-3304
954-776-0066
Fax: 954-776-5387 800-775-5345
Manufacturer and exporter of label placement systems, sign holders and merchandising aids; also,
cleaning supplies including stain, laundry, rust and
odor removers
President: Jacob Fast
Market Manager: Mike Brinkman

Estimated Sales: $10-15 Million
Number Employees: 100 to 249
Square Footage: 190000
Brands:
Carpet Gun
Ez View
Frontrunner
One Drop
One Spray
Rust Gun
Sell Strip
Smoking Gun
Stain Gun

22474 Fast Stuff Packaging
2 Village Road
Suite 10
Horsham, PA 19044-3816
877-388-3278
Fax: 215-830-9332
Void fill packaging system

22475 Fastcorp
1 Cory Road
Morristown, NJ 07960-3103
973-455-0400
Fax: 201-939-0255
Estimated Sales: $500,000-$1 000,000
Number Employees: 5-9

22476 Fata Automation
6050 19 Mile Rd
Sterling Heights, MI 48314
586-323-9400
Fax: 248-553-6013 www.fatainc.com
Conveyors, integrated systems and controls
President: Piero Bugnone
Sales Manager: Ron Benish
Contact: Anthony Calabrese
acalabrese@fatainc.com
Estimated Sales: $75 Million
Number Employees: 100
Square Footage: 65000
Parent Co: Fata Automation Group

22477 Fato Industries
462 S 5000w Rd
Kankakee, IL 60901-7905
815-932-3015
Fax: 815-932-9839 fatoindustries@gmail.com
Fiberglass and polyethylene tanks, covers, trays and
totes
President: Thomas Fato
otaf226@yahoo.com
CFO: Chris Fato
Quality Control: Tom Fato
R&D: Tom Fato
Estimated Sales: Below $5,000,000
Number Employees: 1-4
Square Footage: 20000

**22478 Faubion Central States Tank
Company**
P.O.Box 26085
Shawnee Mission, KS 66225-6085
913-681-0069
Fax: 913-681-0150 800-450-8265
dfaubion@faubiontank.com www.faubiontank.com
Food grade and heated stainless steel storage tanks
Owner: Dan Faubion
VP: Tom Thompson
Plant Manager: Dave Hill
Estimated Sales: $1-2.5 Million
Number Employees: 5-9
Square Footage: 160000

22479 Faulkenberg Inc
3660 2nd St
Hubbard, OR 97032-9560
503-981-3200
Fax: 503-981-9143 www.falkenberginc.net
High pressure pumps, nozzles and accessories
Owner: Gary Faulkenberg
Estimated Sales: $2.5-5 000,000
Number Employees: 5-9

22480 Faultless Caster
1421 N Garvin Street
Evansville, IN 47711-4687
866-316-2163
Fax: 800-322-9329 800-322-7359
www.faultlesscaster.com
Casters and wheels

Sales Manager: Matt Olson
Contact: Mary Heskett
mheskett@iupui.edu
Manager (Industrial Distribution): Brian Robb
Sales/Production Manager: Denny Garness
Number Employees: 250-499
Parent Co: FKI Industries
Brands:
Dynatred
Heavy Metal
K-Wheel
Rt

22481 Favorite Foods Inc
29 Interstate Dr
Somersworth, NH 03878-1227
603-692-4990
Fax: 603-692-4993 800-NUT-S4YO
favorite99@aol.com
www.midtownfavoritebeef.com
Vertical mixers, moulding and nut processing equip-
ment
Owner: Fred Lewin
CEO: Chris Barstow
VP: Tom Myers
Estimated Sales: $2.5-5 Million
Number Employees: 20-49

22482 Fawema Packaging Machinery
1701 Desoto Road
Palmetto, FL 34221-3066
941-351-9597
Fax: 941-351-4673 www.fawema.com
Manufacturer, importer and exporter of bag packag-
ing systems including formers, fillers and closers;
also, control modules, checkweighers and hot melt
glue applicators
Customer Service Manager: Frank Potvin
Estimated Sales: $1-2.5 Million
Number Employees: 1-4
Square Footage: 20000
Parent Co: Fawema Maschinenfabrik GmbH
Brands:
Allen Bradley
Electro Cam
Emerson
Hi-Speed
Nordson

22483 Fax Foods
1205 Activity Dr
Vista, CA 92081-8510
760-599-6030
Fax: 760-599-6040
Manufacturer and exporter of plastic food replica.
Owner: Judy Preston
Square Footage: 60000
Parent Co: Fax Plastics
Type of Packaging: Food Service
Brands:
Foodart By Francesco
Replikale

22484 Fay Paper Products
124 Washington St # 101
Foxboro, MA 02035-1368
781-769-4620
Fax: 781-769-8522 800-765-4620
Manufacturer and exporter of cash register rolls and
stationery items
President: Gregory Steele
VP: Peter Steele
Estimated Sales: $5-10 Million
Number Employees: 20-49
Brands:
Fay-Vo-Rite

22485 Feather Duster Corporation
10 Park St
Amsterdam, NY 12010-4214
518-842-3690
Fax: 518-842-3754 800-967-8659
Manufacturer, importer and exporter of dusters in-
cluding ostrich feather and wool; also, applicator
pads
President and CFO: Neil Stravitz
Quality Control: Susan Spagnola
Plant Manager: Susan Spagnola
Estimated Sales: Below $5 Million
Number Employees: 5-9
Square Footage: 20000

22486 Fedco Systems
500 S Vandemark Road
Sidney, OH 45365-8991
813-920-6641
Fax: 813-920-3564   800-922-6641
Rollerbar mixer

22487 Federal Engineered Systems
141 Ben Burton Cir
Bogart, GA 30622-1791
706-543-8101
Fax: 706-543-7934
Owner: Micheal Van Drunen
mvandurnen@federalengineeredsystems.com
Estimated Sales: Less Than $500,000
Number Employees: 1-4

22488 Federal Heath Sign Co LLC
3609 Ocean Ranch Blvd # 204
Suite #204
Oceanside, CA 92056-8601
760-901-7447
Fax: 760-727-2279   800-527-9495
marketing@federalheath.com
www.federalheath.com
Manufacturer and exporter of custom interior and
exterior signs including plastic and metal; also, in-
stallation and maintenance available
CEO: Kevin Stotmeister
kstotmeister@fedsign.com
Account Executive: Randy Cearlock
Estimated Sales: $1-2.5 Million
Number Employees: 100-249
Square Footage: 300000
Parent Co: Federal Signal Corporation

22489 Federal Industries
215 Federal Ave
Belleville, WI 53508-9201
608-424-3331
Fax: 608-424-3234   800-356-4206
geninfo@federalind.com   www.federalind.com
Refrigerated and nonrefrigerated display cases for
bakery and deli products
National Sales Manager (Food Service): Bill Rice
Plant Manager: Gary Hamburg
Estimated Sales: $20-50 Million
Number Employees: 50-99
Parent Co: Standex International Corporation

22490 Federal Industries Inc
2550 Niagara Ln N
Minneapolis, MN 55447-8761
763-476-1500
Fax: 763-476-8155   800-523-9033
chemtran@aol.com   www.chem-tran.com
Shipping systems for hazardous materials
President: Chuck Goldman
chemtran@aol.com
Estimated Sales: $1-2.5 000,000
Number Employees: 1-4

22491 Federal Label Systems
7920 Barnwell Avenue
Elmhurst, NY 11373-3727
718-899-2233
Fax: 718-397-1921   800-238-0015
Product merchandising tags, pressure sensitive la-
bels, on-product coupons, display and card
packaging
President: Alan Rothchild
Co-Chairman: Herbert Rothchild
Executive VP: Paul Rothchild
Estimated Sales: $10-20 Million
Number Employees: 100-249
Square Footage: 90000
Parent Co: Rothchild Printing Group

22492 Federal Machine Corp
8040 University Blvd
Clive, IA 50325-1118
515-274-1555
Fax: 515-274-9256   800-247-2446
www.vending.com
Manufacturer and exporter of vending machines for
snacks, candy, pastries, milk, canned drinks, gum,
mints, hot beverages, frozen foods and ice cream;
also machine parts (full line vending equipment
manufacturing company).

President: Todd Wiggins
twiggins@wittern.com
CFO: Ray Lantz
CEO: F A Wittern Jr
Sales: Gary Bahr
Director Operations: Gary Bahr
Estimated Sales: $5-10 Million
Number Employees: 5-9
Number of Brands: 10
Number of Products: 20
Square Footage: 1400000
Type of Packaging: Food Service, Private Label
Brands:
  Fs1
  Us1

22493 Federal Mfg Co
201 West Walker Street
Milwaukee, WI 53204
414-384-3200
Fax: 414-384-8704 www.federalmfg.com
Designers and Manufacturers of bottle filling and
capping systems and specialty products for the
Dairy, Juice, Water, Food, and Pharmaceutical
Industries.
President: Otis Cobb
CEO: Marjorie Fee
Contact: Gilbert Alba
galba@federalmfg.com
Estimated Sales: $5-10 Million
Number Employees: 50-99
Square Footage: 240000

22494 Federal Sign
135 Dean St
PO Box 1
Providence, RI 02903-1603
401-421-9643
Fax: 401-351-2233 federalsigns@cox.net
www.federalsigns.net
Advertising signs including electric, luminous and
billboards.
Manager: Frank Benell
federalsigns@cox.net
VP: William Benell
Estimated Sales: Less Than $500,000
Number Employees: 5-9
Square Footage: 60000
Parent Co: Hub Sign Company

22495 Federal Sign
135 Dean St
Providence, RI 02903-1603
401-421-9643
Fax: 401-351-2233 www.federalsigns.net
Manufacturer, designer and installer of electrical
signs
President: Frank Benell Jr
federalsigns@cox.net
VP: William Benell
Estimated Sales: Less Than $500,000
Number Employees: 5-9
Square Footage: 34000
Parent Co: Federal Sign Company

22496 Federal Stamp & Seal Manufacturing Company
2210 Marietta Blvd NW
Atlanta, GA 30318-2020
404-525-6103
Fax: 404-525-3320   800-333-7726
info@fessco.net www.fessco.net
Pre-inked and self-inking rubber stamps; also, en-
graved signs, seals, numbering machines, ink and
ink pads
President: Don Bradshaw
fesco@fescogroup.net
Plant Manager: Gary D'Andrea
Purchasing Manager: Mick Mortensen
Number Employees: 20-49

22497 Federated Mills
3620 Tamiami Trl N
Naples, FL 34103-3705
239-659-5450
Fax: 518-734-5805   888-692-6226
fedmills@mhcable.com
Mold inhibitors for mycoban calcium propionate,
mycoban sodium propionate, supreme brand dykon
(sodium diacetate), potassium sorbate, sorbic acid,
sodium citrate, sodium benzoate, xantham gum,
citric acid
VP: Douglas Sweet
VP: Doug Sweet

Estimated Sales: Below $5 Million
Number Employees: 1-4

22498 Feed The Party
2055 Nelson Miller Pkwy
Louisville, KY 40223
partyon@feedtheparty.com
feedtheparty.com
Supplier of the finest butcher shop quality meats, in-
cluding steak, pork, chicken, and lamb.
President & Founder: Matt Kenney
Estimated Sales: $100+ Million
Number Employees: 2-10
Square Footage: 89000
Type of Packaging: Food Service, Bulk
Brands:
  A. Thomas Meats
  Berkwood Farms
  Border Springs Farm Lamb
  Shire Gate
  Shuckman's Fish Co. & Smokery, Inc.
  Joyce Farms
  Big Fork

22499 Feedback Plus
2222 W Spring Creek Pkwy
#114
Plano, TX 75023
972-661-8989
Fax: 972-661-5414   800-882-7467
www.feedbackplusinc.com
Consulant offering market research
CEO: Vickie Henry
VP Marketing: Bill Waston
Food Service Sales Representative: Kelly Heatly
Contact: Sharon Karlebach
sharon.karlebach@gofeedback.com
VP Of Store Operations: Monica Rattay
Estimated Sales: $2.5-5,000,000
Number Employees: 10-19

22500 Fehlig Brothers Box & Lbr Co
1909 Cole St
St Louis, MO 63106-3506
314-241-6900
Fax: 314-436-0315 fehligbrothers@sbcglobal.net
www.fehligbrotherslumber.com
Custom made wooden crates, boxes and pallets
President: John Oleary
markf10355@aol.com
Treasurer: Tim O'Leary
Estimated Sales: Below $5 Million
Number Employees: 20-49
Square Footage: 152000

22501 Felco Packaging Specialist
4001 E Baltimore St
Baltimore, MD 21224-1544
410-675-2664
Fax: 410-276-2367   800-673-8488
Manufacturer, importer and exporter of corrugated
boxes, tapes, burlap, canvas, pallets, paper products
and bags
President: Jeffrey Feldman
jeff@felcoinc.com
Controller: Sherry Feldman
Estimated Sales: $5-10 Million
Number Employees: 10-19
Square Footage: 150000

22502 (HQ)Feldmeier Equipment Inc
6800 Townline Rd
Syracuse, NY 13211-1325
315-454-8608
Fax: 315-454-3701 sstanks@feldmeier.com
www.feldmeier.com
Manufacturer and exporter of heat exchangers,
pasteurizers, stainless steel tanks, processing ves-
sels, strainers, and stainless steel ice builders
President: John Feldmeier
CEO: Robert Feldmeier
CFO: Margaret Feldmeier
VP: Robert Feldmeier
Estimated Sales: $40 Million
Number Employees: 100-249
Other Locations:
  Feldmeier Equipment
  Little Falls NY
  Feldmeier Equipment
  Reno NV
  Feldmeier Equipment
  Cedar Falls IA
Brands:
  Across-The-Line

Feldmeier
Torpedo

22503 Felins USA Inc
8306 W Parkland Ct
Milwaukee, WI 53223-3832

414-355-7747
Fax: 414-355-7559 800-343-5667
sales@felins.com www.felins.com
Manufacturer, importer and exporter of manual and
automatic bundling, tying, wrapping, strapping and
banding equipment; also, automated banding sys-
tems for multi-packing food products
Manager: Bruce Bartelt
Owner: James Chisholm
CFO: Ron Kuzia
Marketing: Peter Chapman
Sales: Mark Meyer
Public Relations: Neal Donding
Production: Bruce Lanham
Estimated Sales: $8.5 Million
Number Employees: 20-49
Square Footage: 50000
Brands:
Flexstrap
Loop Plus
Pak Tyer 2000

22504 Felix Storch Inc
770 Garrison Ave
Bronx, NY 10474-5603

718-328-8101
Fax: 718-842-3093 800-932-4267
sales@summitappliance.com
www.summitappliance.com
Manufacturer, importer and exporter of beer taps,
wine coolers, ice cream freezers and beverage mer-
chandisers, minibars and coolers
President: Floria Lee
lee.floria@gmail.com
Vice President of Marketing: Steve Ross
R&D: Phil Yacht
Quality Control: Jeff Musnikow
Sales Director: Stephen Ross
Vice President: Paul Storch
Estimated Sales: $25 Million
Number Employees: 100-249
Square Footage: 140000
Parent Co: Felix Storch
Brands:
Summit

22505 Fell & Co Intl Inc
3266 Winbrook Dr
Memphis, TN 38116-3644

901-332-6669
Fax: 901-332-6433 800-356-8588
info@fellcoinc.com www.fellcoinc.com
Cocoa and chocolate preparation equipment including batch kneaders, block shavers, conches,
enrobing, refiners, cooling equipment and cooling
tunnels, cream machines, depositors and nut processing equipment, bean cleaners,
roasterswinnowers, liquor grinders, cocoa powder
systems, mixer/kneaders, pre-refiners, continuous
conches, storage and pumps/piping, moulding
machine
President/CEO/CFO: Marc Fell
fellandcompany@aol.com
Sales Manager: Mike Dunn
Sales/ Operations Manager: Marc Fell
Estimated Sales: $1-2.5 Million
Number Employees: 1-4
Square Footage: 48000

22506 Femc
22201 Aurora Rd
Cleveland, OH 44146-1273

216-663-1208
Fax: 216-663-9337 info@femc.com
www.femc.com
President: Dan Auvil
dauvil@femc.com
Estimated Sales: $5-10 Million
Number Employees: 20-49

22507 Fenco
2210 County A
Three Lakes, WI 54562

715-546-8077
Fax: 715-546-3561
Conveyor components, plastic conveyor belt, and
wearstrips

Estimated Sales: Less Than $500,000
Number Employees: 1-4

22508 Fenner Drives
311 W Stiegel St
Manheim, PA 17545-1747

717-665-2421
Fax: 717-665-2649 800-243-3374
info@fennerdrives.com
Industrial transmission conveyor belts
President: Debbie Adler
d.adler@phillyjcc.com
CEO: Nick Hobson
Marketing Director: Robin Palmer
Sales Director: Craig Harris
Estimated Sales: $50+ Million
Number Employees: 100-249
Type of Packaging: Private Label, Bulk
Brands:
Orange Belt

22509 Fenner Drives
311 W Stiegel St
Manheim, PA 17545-1747

717-665-2421
Fax: 717-665-2649 800-327-2288
info@fennerdrives.com
Industrial belting, power transmission and motion
control components, maintains extensive engineer-
ing, development, and testing facilities
President: Debbie Adler
d.adler@phillyjcc.com
CEO: Nick Hobson
Marketing Director: Robin Palmer
Sales Director: Craig Harris
Estimated Sales: $30-50 Million
Number Employees: 100-249
Number of Products: +0
Type of Packaging: Bulk
Brands:
Clear-Go
Minikeeper
Orange-Go
Powertwist
Quik-Go
Red-Go
Torquekeeper
Trantorque
Veelos

22510 Fenner Dunlop Americas Inc
1000 Omega Dr # 1400
Pittsburgh, PA 15205-5001

412-249-0700
Fax: 412-249-0701
www.fennerdunlopamericas.com
Conveyors and elevator belting
President: Cassandra Pan
CEO: David Jones
david.jones@fennerdunlop.com
Chief Financial Officer: William Mooney
Chief Operating Officer: Mark Hardwick
Estimated Sales: $1-5 Million
Number Employees: 250-499
Brands:
Duratrax

22511 Fenster Consulting Inc
29 Davis Rd
Port Washington, NY 11050-3935

516-944-7108
Fax: 516-944-7953 fred@fensterconsulting.com
www.fensterconsulting.com
Consultant specializing in factory, warehouse and
material handling, packaging and storage system
design
President: Fred Fenster
fensterf@fensterconsulting.com
Vice President: Linda Necroto
Sales Director: Jordan Fenster
Purchasing Manager: Sandra Lee
Number Employees: 5-9
Square Footage: 20000

22512 Fenton Art Glass Company
700 Elizabeth St
Williamstown, WV 26187

304-375-6122
Fax: 304-375-7833 800-933-6766
askfenton@fentonartglass.com
www.fentonartglass.com
Manufacturer and exporter of decorative glassware
and lamps

President: George Fenton
CFO: Stan Van Lanqingham
VP: Tom Fenton
R&D: Nancy Fenton
Quality Control: Tom Bobbitt
Sales VP: Scott Fenton
Public Relations: Terry Nutter
Purchasing Director: Mike Fenton
Estimated Sales: $25-30 Million
Number Employees: 250-499
Type of Packaging: Consumer, Bulk
Brands:
Fenton Art Glass

22513 Ferguson Containers
20 Industrial Rd
Phillipsburg, NJ 08865-4081

908-454-9755
Fax: 908-454-7144 mail@fergusoncontainers.com
www.fergusoncontainers.com
Corrugated boxes and containers
Owner: Stuart Ferguson
ferguson@silo.com
General Manager: Ed Reichard
Estimated Sales: $5 Million
Number Employees: 20-49
Square Footage: 42000

22514 Ferm-Rite Equipment
PO Box 1233
Woodbridge, CA 95258-1233

209-794-2700
Fax: 209-794-8164
Wine industry bungs
President: Martyn Nastasian
Bookkeeper: Jil Nastasian
Number Employees: 2

22515 Fernholtz Engineering
15471 Victory Boulevard
Van Nuys, CA 91406-6241

818-785-5800
Fax: 818-785-8406
Manufacturer and exporter of mills, sifting and
screening machinery, wet and dry magnetic separa-
tors, mixers, blenders and agitators
President: Vivian Fernholtz
VP: Frank Fernholtz
Estimated Sales: $500,000-$1 Million
Number Employees: 1-4

22516 Fernqvist Labeling Solutions
2544 Leghorn St
Suite C
Mountain View, CA 94043-1614

650-967-3766
Fax: 650-428-1615 800-426-8215
customercare@fernqvist.com www.fernqvist.com
Label and bar code printing systems, labels, thermal
transfer ribbons, dispensers, bar code verifiers, scan-
ners, etc
President: Per Fernqvist
VP: Bill Goodman
Manufacturing Manager: Richard Hernandez
Estimated Sales: Below $5 Million
Number Employees: 1-4
Square Footage: 7000
Brands:
Fernqvist Prodigy Max

22517 Fernqvist Labeling Solutions
2544 Leghorn St
Mountain View, CA 94043-1614

650-967-3766
Fax: 650-428-1615 800-426-8215
sales@fernqvist.com www.fernqvist.com
Digital and flexo labels provided nationally, thermal
transfer printers, labling software, TT ribbons, and
other labling supplies.
President: Per Fernqvist
Operations/Production Officer: Richard Hernandez
Estimated Sales: $3-5 Million
Number Employees: 1-4

22518 Ferrell-Ross
PO Box 50669
Amarillo, TX 79159

806-359-9051
Fax: 806-359-9064 800-299-9051
info@ferrellross.com www.ferrellross.com
Manufacturer and exporter of grinding and flaking
mills for breakfast cereals, spices and snack foods;
also, grain and cereal blenders, grain and seed cleaning machinery

President: David Ibach
Vice President: Philip Petrakos
Sales Director: Clay Gerber
Estimated Sales: $10-20 Million
Number Employees: 10
Square Footage: 50000
Parent Co: Bluffton Agri Industrial Corporation
Other Locations:
  Ferrell-Ross
  Bluffton IN
Brands:
  Clipper Precision
  Ferrell-Ross

22519 Ferrer Corporation
415 Calle San Claudio
San Juan, PR 00926-4206

787-761-5151
Fax: 787-755-0450
Manufacturer and exporter of interior and exterior signs including electric, metal, neon and plastic
President: Juan Ferrer Davila
Controller: Jose Vazquez
Sales Manager: Enid Cintron
Number Employees: 50
Square Footage: 80000
Brands:
  Rotulos Ferrer

22520 Ferrite Components Inc
165 Ledge St
Nashua, NH 03060-3061

603-881-5234
Fax: 603-881-5406 info@ferriteinc.com
www.ferriteinc.com
President: Richard Wolfe
CEO: Ron Clark
ascholder@digcommunications.com
Quality Control: Bill Tabonnu
Estimated Sales: $50-100 Million
Number Employees: 5-9

22521 Ferro Corporation
6060 Parkland Blvd
Suite 250
Mayfield Heights, OH 44124

216-875-5600
Fax: 216-875-5627 www.ferro.com
Manufacturer and exporter of printing inks, labels and label supplies.
Chairman/President/CEO: Peter Thomas
VP/Chief Financial Officer: Ben Schlater
VP/General Counsel/Secretary: Mark Duesenberg
VP/Human Resources: Pepe Tortajada
Year Founded: 1919
Estimated Sales: $1,075 Million
Number Employees: 4,846
Parent Co: Ferro Corporation

22522 Festo Corp
395 Moreland Rd
Hauppauge, NY 11788-3900

631-435-0800
Fax: 631-435-8026 800-99F-ESTO
www.festo.com
Offers one of the largest selections of pneumatic components and controls available from a single source. Select from over 90 product families, including pneumatic valves, cylinders and controls. Festo has the engineering expertiseto design and build
President: Hans Zobel
CFO: Sven Doerge
sven.doerge@us.festo.com
Estimated Sales: $20-50 Million
Number Employees: 250-499

22523 Fetco
600 Rose Rd
Lake Zurich, IL 60047-1560

847-719-3000
Fax: 847-719-3001 800-338-2699
info@fetco.com
Manufacturer, importer and exporter of food service equipment including coffee carts, tea brewing equipment servers, commissary systems and coffee and tea equipment
President: Zbigniew Lassota
zlassota@fetco.com
CFO: Zeel Lasoda
VP: Christopher Nowak
VP of Marketing and Sales: Richard Baggett
Estimated Sales: $10-20 Million
Number Employees: 100-249

22524 Fettig Laboratories
900 Godfrey Ave SW
Grand Rapids, MI 49503

616-245-3000
Fax: 616-245-3299 radonman01@aol.com
Laboratory providing nutritional analysis and labeling, bacteriological testing, QC/QA program design and management, shelf life testing, contamination/adulteration identification and witness service
President: Patricia Fettig
Marketing Director: Gregory Painter
Estimated Sales: $500,000-$1 Million
Number Employees: 5-9

22525 Fetzer Vineyards
12901 Old River Rd
Hopland, CA 95449-9813

707-744-1250
Fax: 707-744-7605 800-846-8637
Fernando.Avalos@fetzer.com www.fetzer.com
Manufacturer and exporter of table wines, barrels and corks
Head Operations: Pat Voss
Manager: Tim Nall
Director Winemaking: Dennis Martin
Estimated Sales: $19.2 Million
Number Employees: 250-499
Parent Co: Brown-Forman Corporation
Type of Packaging: Consumer, Food Service, Private Label, Bulk
Brands:
  Bel Arbors
  Bon Terra
  Fetzer

22526 Fiber Does
1470 N 4th Street
San Jose, CA 95112-4715

408-453-5533
Fax: 408-453-9303
Manufacturer and exporter of fiber optic lighted signs including indoor, outdoor and window display
CEO: Song Lee
Sales/Customer Service Manager: Rick Perez
Estimated Sales: $3,000,000
Number Employees: 20-50
Brands:
  Fiberpro
  Optickles

22527 Fibercell Packaging LLC
46 Brooklyn St
Portville, NY 14770-9529

716-933-8703
Fax: 716-933-6948 800-545-8546
www.fibercel.com
Bulk packaging
General Manager: Mitch Gray
Sales Administrator: Geoff Buckner
Manager: Bruce Olson
bolson@fibercel.net
Estimated Sales: $20-50 Million
Number Employees: 50-99

22528 Fibergrate Composite Strctrs
5151 Belt Line Rd # 1212
Dallas, TX 75254-6740

972-250-1633
Fax: 972-250-1530 800-527-4043
info@fibergrate.com www.fibergrate.com
Manufacture fiberglass, reinforced plastic, gratings and products for the food and beverage industry
President: Eric Breiner
ebreiner@fibergrate.com
CFO: Sean Lovison
Operations Manager: Wendell Hollingsworth
Estimated Sales: $10-25 Million
Number Employees: 20-49
Brands:
  Chemgrate
  Fibergrate
  Rigirtex0

22529 Fibergrate Composite Strctrs
5151 Belt Line Rd # 1212
Suite 1212
Dallas, TX 75254-6740

972-250-1633
Fax: 972-250-1530 800-527-4043
www.fibergrate.com
President: Eric Breiner
ebreiner@fibergrate.com
CFO: Travis Kirsch
Quality Control: Ray Blackshear

Number Employees: 20-49

22530 Fiberich Technologies
3280 Gorham Ave Ste 202
St Louis Park, MN 55426

952-920-8054
Fax: 952-920-8056
Pea fiber, vegetable fiber, bean and lentil precooked whole and powders
President: Edward Schmidt
edward.schmidt@popp.net
Estimated Sales: $1-2.5 000,000
Number Employees: 1-4
Type of Packaging: Bulk

22531 Fiberich Technologies
3280 Gorham Ave
Suite 202
St Louis Park, MN 55426

952-920-8054
Fax: 952-920-8056 fiberichtech@popp.net
Processes and markets peas, beans and lentil based ingredients
President: Ed Schmidt
Contact: Edward Schmidt
edward.schmidt@popp.net
Type of Packaging: Consumer, Bulk

22532 Fibertech Inc
11744 Blue Bell Rd
Elberfeld, IN 47613-9455

812-983-2642
Fax: 812-983-4953 800-304-4600
www.fibertechinc.net
President: William Scott
Contact: Tabitha Devasier
tdevasier@fibretechinc.net
Estimated Sales: Less Than $500,000
Number Employees: 1-4

22533 Fibertech Inc
11744 Blue Bell Rd
Elberfeld, IN 47613-9455

812-983-2642
Fax: 812-983-4953 800-304-6400
www.fibertechinc.net
Supplies fiber materials used in food industry manufacturing
Contact: Tabitha Devasier
tdevasier@fibretechinc.net
Estimated Sales: Less Than $500,000
Number Employees: 1-4

22534 Fibre Containers Inc
15250 Don Julian Rd
City Of Industry, CA 91745-1001

626-968-5897
Fax: 626-330-0870 www.fleetwood-fibre.com
Corrugated shipping containers
President: Tony Pietrangelo
Vice President: Mark White
white@fibrecontainers.com
Director Sales: Lloyd Kennedy
Estimated Sales: $20-50 Million
Number Employees: 5-9

22535 Fibre Converters Inc
1 Industrial Park Dr
PO Box 130
Constantine, MI 49042-8735

269-279-1700
jamey.southland@fibreconverters.com
www.fibreconverters.com
Manufacturer and exporter of die cut slip sheets for replacement of pallets as well as special laminated or solid fibre paperboard
Owner: Jim Stuck
st@net-link.net
Chairman: David T Stuck
Operations Manager: Stephen Reed
Estimated Sales: $25 Million
Number Employees: 50-99
Square Footage: 160000
Brands:
  Fiber-Pul
  Fico
  Valdor

22536 Fibre Leather Manufacturing Company
686 Belleville Avenue
New Bedford, MA 02745-6093

508-997-4557
Fax: 508-997-7268 800-358-6012

Manufacturer and exporter of latex-impregnated and coated paper for box coverings; also, base stock for pressure sensitive tapes and jean label stock.
President: Daniel Finger
fibreleather@earthlink.net
VP: Louis Finger
Production Manager: Ellen Hull
Shipping Manager: Charles Hull
Estimated Sales: $10-20 Million
Number Employees: 50-99
Square Footage: 400000

22537 Fibreform Containers Inc
N115w19255 Edison Dr
Germantown, WI 53022-3092
262-251-1901
Fax: 262-251-1941
customersupport@fibreforminc.com
www.fibreforminc.com
Model pulp protective packaging
President: Edward Gratz
jeffgratz@fibreforminc.com
Sales Exec: Jeff Gratz
Estimated Sales: $20-50 Million
Number Employees: 20-49

22538 (HQ)Fiebing Co
421 S 2nd St
Milwaukee, WI 53204-1612
414-271-5011
Fax: 414-271-3769 800-558-1033
custserv@fiebing.com www.fiebing.com
Manufacturer and exporter of soap and waterproofers
President: Richard Chase
jchase@fiebing.com
R&D: Mansur Abul
VP: Dennis Kendall
Estimated Sales: $10-20 Million
Number Employees: 5-9
Square Footage: 140000
Brands:
Fiebing
Kelly
Snow Proof

22539 Fiedler Technology
84 Malmo Court
Units 13-15
Maple, ON L6A 1R4
Canada
905-832-0493
Primary and secondary packaging machinery for nonstandard packages
President: Edgar Fiedler
Number Employees: 5-9
Square Footage: 12000

22540 Field Manufacturing Corporation
2535 Maricopa St.
Torrance, CA 90503
310-781-9292
Fax: 310-781-9386 www.fieldmfg.com
Plastic molded store fixtures
President: Steven Fields
Vice President: Mary McWilliams
Research & Development: Omar Balley
Contact: Katarina Field
katarina.field@norcomfg.com
Estimated Sales: $5-10 Million
Number Employees: 100

22541 Fife Corp
222 W Memorial Rd
Oklahoma City, OK 73114-2317
405-755-1600
Fax: 405-755-8425 800-639-3433
fife@fife.com www.maxcessintl.com
Automatic process controls
President: Terry Brookes
CFO: Merlyn Devries
mdevries@fife.com
CEO: Bruce Ryan
CEO: Bruce E Ryan
Estimated Sales: $20-50 Million
Number Employees: 100-249

22542 Filet Menu
P.O.Box 352161
Los Angeles, CA 90035
310-202-8000
Fax: 310-559-0917

Manufacturer and designer of menus, point of purchase displays, table cards, dinner napkins, place mats, etc
Owner: Michael Le Vine
Marketing: Marcia Petersen
Estimated Sales: $2.5-5,000,000
Number Employees: 20-49
Type of Packaging: Food Service

22543 Filler Specialties
440 100th Ave
Zeeland, MI 49464-2061
616-772-9235
Fax: 616-772-4544 filler@filler-specialties.com
www.filler-specialties.com
Manufacturer and exporter of capping and closing equipment, conveyor systems and fillers and filling equipment
President: Ron Slagh
rslagh@filler-specialties.com
Sales Manager: Jim Grant
Estimated Sales: $5-10,000,000
Number Employees: 10-19

22544 Filling Equipment Co Inc
1539 130th St
Flushing, NY 11356-2481
718-445-2111
Fax: 718-463-6034 800-247-7127
filling@fillingequipment.com
www.fillingequipment.com
Manufacturer and exporter of packaging equipment, tables, conveyors, automatic cap tighteners, etc
President: Robert Hampton
Sales: G Hite
Sales: J Popper
Estimated Sales: $1-2.5 Million
Number Employees: 10-19

22545 Fillit
18105 Trans Canada Highway
Kirkland, QC H9J 3Z4
Canada
514-694-2390
Fax: 514-694-6552 rzajko@kalishdti.com
Manufacturer and exporter of conveying, filling, capping and counting equipment
President/Owner: ý
Production Manager: Richard Zajko
Number Employees: 100-249
Brands:
Fillit
Fillkit
Kapit
Power Fillit
Torquit

22546 Film X
20 Louisa Viens Dr
Dayville, CT 6241
860-779-3403
Fax: 860-779-3406 800-628-6128
Packaging materials including film; also, extrusion coating and slitting services available
Manager: Michael Quarry
Sr. Account Manager: Peter Hendrickson
Contact: Steve English
senglish@webindustries.com
General Manager: Jon Pluff
Estimated Sales: $5-10 Million
Number Employees: 1-4
Parent Co: Web Industries

22547 Film-Pak Inc
201 S Magnolia St
Crowley, TX 76036-3110
817-297-4341
Fax: 817-572-7568 800-526-1838
www.film-pak.com
Film and plain and printed bags
President: Rossi Callender
Sales Manager: Chris Walters
Manager: Melissa Blyleo
Estimated Sales: $5-10 Million
Number Employees: 20-49
Square Footage: 32000

22548 Filmco Inc
1450 S Chillicothe Rd
Aurora, OH 44202-9264
330-562-6111
Fax: 330-562-2740 800-545-8457
www.linpac.com
Manufacturer and exporter of PVC film

President: Rolland Castellanos
Customer Service: Marianne Martone
General Manager: Richard Pohland
Purchasing Manager: Susan Burkholder
Estimated Sales: $20-50 Million
Number Employees: 50-99
Parent Co: Linpac Plastics Inc.
Brands:
Britepak
Crustpak

22549 (HQ)Filmpack Plastic Corporation
266 Ridge Rd
Dayton, NJ 8810
732-329-6523
Fax: 732-329-8543
Plastic translucent polystyrene cold drinking cups
President: Morris Herman
VP: Moric O'Streicher
Estimated Sales: $5-10 Million
Number Employees: 20-49

22550 Filter Equipment Co
1440 State Route 34
Wall Township, NJ 07753-6807
732-938-3312
Fax: 732-938-3312 800-445-9775
sales@filter-equipment.com
www.filter-equipment.com
Filtration equipment
Owner: Herman Groh
herman@filter-equipment.com
VP: Scott Groh
Estimated Sales: $5-10 000,000
Number Employees: 10-19

22551 Filter Products
8314 Tiogawoods Dr
Sacramento, CA 95828
916-689-2328
Fax: 916-689-1035
Wine industry filtration equipment
President: Paris Rivera
Estimated Sales: $5-10 000,000
Number Employees: 20-49

22552 Filtercarb LLC/ Filtercorp
9805 NE 116th St
Suite A-200
Kirkland, WA 98034-4245
425-820-4850
Fax: 425-820-2816 800-473-4526
rbernard@filtercorp.com www.filtercorp.com
President: Robin Bernard
Estimated Sales: $5-10 Million
Number Employees: 10-19

22553 Filtercold Corporation
1840 E University Drive
Suite 2
Tempe, AZ 85281-7760
800-442-2941
Tea and coffee industry filtration equipment

22554 (HQ)Filtercorp
2585 S Sarah Street
Fresno, CA 93706-5034
559-495-3140
Fax: 559-495-3145 800-473-4526
www.filtercorp.com
Manufacturer, importer and exporter of nonwoven cellulose fiber filter pads used for cooking fats and oils
President: Don Eskes
sales@filtercorp.com
Estimated Sales: $500,000-$1 Million
Number Employees: 4
Square Footage: 24000
Brands:
Supersorb
Unifit

22555 Filtration Solutions
4361 Charlotte Hwy # 301
Suite 301
Lake Wylie, SC 29710-7063
803-831-8379
Fax: 803-931-8476 800-598-1897
sales@filtrationsolutions.com
www.filtrationsolutions.com
Filtration products and systems.

President: Billie Wells
billie@filtrtionsolutions.com
Office Manager: Tamara Hartman
Engineerig Consultant: Larry Seitz
Sales Representative: April Sadler
Sales Representative: Pete Dawes
Customer Service Representative: Robbie Putnam
Number Employees: 5-9

22556 Filtration Systems
10304 NW 50th St
Sunrise, FL 33351-8007

954-572-2700
Fax: 954-572-3401 service@filtsys.com
www.filtrationsystems.com
Liquid filters, pressure vessels and filter media
President: Sidney Goldman
VP: Michael Goldman
Contact: Michael Goldman
mgoldman@filtsys.com
Estimated Sales: $2.5-5 Million
Number Employees: 10-19
Parent Co: Mechanical Manufacturing Corporation

22557 Filtration Systems Prods Inc
8506 Herrington Ct
Pevely, MO 63070-1601

314-721-2888
Fax: 314-721-4519 800-444-4720
info@fsptbm.com www.fsptbm.com
OEM filter products including cartridges, bags, paper rolls, pressure plates, HVAC and frame sheets.
Vice President: David Harrell
dharrell@fsptbm.com
VP: David Harrell
Research & Development: Andy Burns
Sales Director: Dave Kassabaum
Production: Russell Brown
Estimated Sales: $5-10 Million
Number Employees: 20-49
Square Footage: 100000

22558 Filtrine Manufacturing
15 Kit St
Keene, NH 03431-5911

603-352-5500
Fax: 603-352-0330 800-930-3367
www.filtrine.com
Water filtration systems and ingredient water coolers for baked goods, confections, brewing, etc
Chairman: John Hansel
President: Peter Hansel
Sales: Philip Tussing
IT: David Hansel
dhansel@filtrine.com
Estimated Sales: $10-20 Million
Number Employees: 50-99
Square Footage: 500000
Brands:
 Filtrine
 Larco
 Steri-Flo
 Taste Master

22559 Final Filtration
139 Columbia Dr.
Williamsville, NY 14221

716-568-8080
Fax: 716-568-8079 800-454-2357
info@cleanerpools.net www.cleanerpools.net
Filtration for wine and beverages
President: David Privitera
Estimated Sales: $500,000-$1 Million
Number Employees: 5-9

22560 Fine Cocoa Products
224 48th St
Brooklyn, NY 11220-1012

201-244-9210
Fax: 201-244-8555 info@cocoasupply.com
www.cocoasupply.com
Importers and distributors of conventional, organic, and kosher cocoa and other ingredients. Some of their products include Cocoa Powders, Cacao Nibs & Beans, Cocoa Butter, Cocoa Liquor/Mass, Chocolate Couvertures and more.
Estimated Sales: Less Than $500,000
Number Employees: 2-10
Type of Packaging: Consumer, Food Service, Private Label, Bulk
Brands:
 Bergenfield Cocoa
 Cafiesa
 Doncella Chocolates
 Eve's Organic Cocoa

22561 Fine Foods Intl
9907 Baptist Church Rd
St Louis, MO 63123-4903

314-842-4473
Fax: 314-843-8846 ffinylp@aol.com
www.dek.de
Tea and coffee industry bags (brick packs), coffee and cappuccino mixes
Manager: Carole Garnett
cagarnett1@aol.com
VP: Keith Sheller
Operations: Carole Garnett
Estimated Sales: Less Than $500,000
Number Employees: 1-4
Type of Packaging: Bulk

22562 Fine Woods Manufacturing
2413 East Jones
Phoenix, AZ 85040

602-258-3868
Fax: 602-258-3868 800-279-2871
info@finewoodsmfg.com www.finewoodsmfg.com
Store fixtures including steel, wood and laminate cabinet displays
President: Dennis Thomas
Estimated Sales: $5-10,000,000
Number Employees: 20-49

22563 Fingerlakes Construction Co
10269 Old Route 31
Clyde, NY 14433-9742

315-923-7777
Fax: 315-923-9158 800-328-3522
www.fingerlakesconstruction.com
Winery construction
President: Rex Brigham
rbrigham@fingerlakesconstruction.com
Estimated Sales: $50-100 Million
Number Employees: 50-99

22564 (HQ)Finlays
10 Blackstone Valley Place
Lincoln, RI 02865

401-333-3300
800-288-6272
americas@finlays.net www.finlays.net
Roaster and extractor of gourmet coffee and tea; also, coffee extracts, syrups, concentrates, iced cappuccino, iced coffee, espresso and smoothies available; services include retail, distributor, OCS, food service and foodingredients
Managing Director: Guy Chambers
Finance Director: Julian Rutherford
Technical Director: Wolfgang Tosch
Year Founded: 1895
Number Employees: 100-249
Square Footage: 180000
Parent Co: Swire
Type of Packaging: Consumer, Food Service, Private Label
Brands:
 Autocrat
 Eclipse
 Newport Coffee Traders

22565 Finn & Son's Metal Spinning Specialists
PO Box 72
South Lebanon, OH 45065-0072

513-494-2898
Fax: 513-494-2885
Metal spun professional bowls and pans
Estimated Sales: $500,000-$1,000,000
Number Employees: 3
Square Footage: 5000

22566 Finn Industries
1921 S Business Pkwy
Ontario, CA 91761

909-930-1500
Fax: 909-930-1510
PVC containers, folding cartons and rigid boxes
President: William Finn
Contact: Wes Biel
wbiel@finnindustriesinc.com
Estimated Sales: $5-10,000,000
Number Employees: 20-49

22567 Fiore Di Pasta
4776 E Jensen Ave
Fresno, CA 93725-1704

559-457-0431
Fax: 559-457-0164 info@fioredipasta.com
www.fioredipasta.com
Fresh and frozen organic pastas, sauces, and entrees
Owner: Shanaz Ahmed
ahmed.sarah81@gmail.com
Chief Operating Officer: Benedetta Primavera
Vice President: Anthony Primavera
Purchasing Director: John Day
Number Employees: 20-49
Square Footage: 120000

22568 Fioriware
333 Market Street
Zanesville, OH 43701-3429

740-454-7400
Fax: 740-454-7790
Flatware
President: Howard Peller
Estimated Sales: $.5-1 million
Number Employees: 10
Brands:
 Fioriware

22569 Fire & Flavor
375 Commerce Blvd
Athens, GA 30606-0825

706-369-9466
Fax: 706-369-9468 866-728-8332
info@fireandflavor.com www.fireandflavor.com
Grilling planks, grilling papers, brine mixes, rubs & sals, skewers & spice
CEO: Genevieve Knox
CFO: Davis Knox
Contact: George Carlton
george@fireandflavor.com
Estimated Sales: Less Than $500,000
Number Employees: 1-4

22570 Fire Protection Industries
1765 Woodhaven Dr
Bensalem, PA 19020-7107

215-245-1830
Fax: 215-245-8819 ausmfpi@cswebmail.com
Fire sprinkler systems; installation available
President: Aus Marburger
Sales Manager: Galen Young
Contact: David Herron
david_herron@thebluebook.com
Estimated Sales: $5-10 Million
Number Employees: 100-249
Parent Co: Williard Company

22571 Firebird Artisan Mills
500 North St W
Harvey, ND 58341-1012

701-324-4330
Fax: 701-324-4334 www.firebirdmills.com
Manufactuere of gluten free flour and mixes; custom blending available.
President Sales & Procurement: Chris Cairo
Plant Manager: Don Franke
Number Employees: 20-49
Parent Co: Agspring LLC
Type of Packaging: Consumer, Food Service, Private Label, Bulk

22572 (HQ)Firematic Sprinkler Devices
900 Boston Turnpike
Shrewsbury, MA 1545

508-845-2121
Fax: 508-842-3523 800-225-7288
Manufacturer and exporter of fire protection devices and control valves
Sales Manager: Greta Heath
Estimated Sales: $10-20 Million
Number Employees: 20-49

22573 Firl Industries Inc
321 W Scott St
Fond Du Lac, WI 54937-2121

920-921-6942
Fax: 920-921-7329 800-558-4890
info@firlindustries.com www.firlindustries.com
Manufacturer and exporter of doors and accessories including vinyl strip-traffic.
President: John M Buser
Estimated Sales: Less Than $500,000
Number Employees: 10-19
Brands:
 Roll-Up

22574 Firmenich Inc.
250 Plainsboro Rd.
Plainsboro, NJ 08536
609-452-1000
Fax: 609-520-9780 800-257-9591
www.firmenich.com
Flavors and fragrances.
Chairman: Patrick Firmenich
CEO: Gilbert Ghostine
President, Perfumery & Ingredients: Armand de
Villoutreys
Chief Research Officer: Genevieve Berger
President, Flavors: Emmanuel Butstraen
COO: Eric Nicolas
Chief Supply Chain Officer: Boet Brinkgreve
Year Founded: 1895
Estimated Sales: $4 Billion
Number Employees: 8,000
Other Locations:
Firmenich Chemical Plant
Newark NJ
Fermenich Citrus Center
Safety Harbor FL

22575 First Bank of Highland P
633 Skokie Blvd
3rd Floor
Northbrook, IL 60062-2871
847-272-1300
Fax: 847-562-2000 www.firstbankhp.com
Consultant specializing in market research, strategic
planning, direct marketing and point of sale mer-
chandising; manufacturer of food display magnetic
base counter signs
Chief Executive Officer: Randy L. Green
Estimated Sales: $.5-1 million
Number Employees: 1-4
Square Footage: 3200

22576 First Choice Sign & Lighting
610 Rock Springs Rd
Escondido, CA 92025-1623
760-746-5069
Fax: 760-746-5393 800-659-0629
Neon lighting, channel letters and architectural and
electrical monument signs
Owner: Noel Johnson
Manager: Robby Seeds
Estimated Sales: Less than $500,000
Number Employees: 1-4

22577 First DataBank
1111 Bayhill Dr # 350
San Bruno, CA 94066-3056
650-827-4555
Fax: 650-588-6867 800-633-3453
cs@firstdatabank.com www.firstdatabank.com
Software programs for analyzing diets, menus, for-
mulations and individual food items for nutrient
content
President: Joe Hirshman
VP Sales/Marketing: Jim Wilson
Sales Representative: Michele O'Reilly-Kim
Contact: Ron Ross
rross@fdbhealth.com
Production Manager: Judy Lichtman
Estimated Sales: $20-50 Million
Number Employees: 100-249
Parent Co: Hearst Corporation/First Data Bank
Brands:
Nutritionist Iv

**22578 First Midwest of Iowa
Corporation**
616 10th Street
Des Moines, IA 50309-2621
515-243-0768
Fax: 515-243-8103 800-247-8411
Multi-wall paper bags
Estimated Sales: $2.5-5 Million
Number Employees: 50-99
Square Footage: 110000

22579 First Plastics Co Inc
22 Jytek Rd
Leominster, MA 01453-5966
978-840-6908
Fax: 978-840-6908 ed@firstplastics.com
Plastic restaurant supplies including cake keepers,
round platters and salad tongs
Owner: Ed Mazzaferro
CEO: Mary Anne Taylor
Office Manager: Lisa Butler

Estimated Sales: Below $5 Million
Number Employees: 50-99
Square Footage: 120000
Parent Co: Art Plastics Manufacturing Corporation
Type of Packaging: Consumer
Brands:
Handy-Home Helpers

22580 First Source LLC
3612 LA Grange Pkwy
Toano, VA 23168-9347
757-566-5360
Fax: 757-566-5379 800-296-0273
www.wythewill.com
Distributor of specialty foods and fine confections
across the US
President: Keith McDaniel
Owner: John McCurry
CFO & VP Finance: Rod Hogan
VP: Belton Joyner
Director of Sales & Marketing: David Mastricola
Director of Human Resources: Lisa Weakland
Operations Manager: Bill Hall
Purchasing Manager: Nanette Ross
Estimated Sales: $8.9 Million
Number Employees: 50-99
Square Footage: 200000
Type of Packaging: Consumer, Bulk

22581 Fischbein LLC
151 Walker Rd
Statesville, NC 28625-2535
704-838-4600
Fax: 704-872-3303 sales@fischbein.com
www.fischbein.com
Manufacturer and exporter of bag closing equipment
including bag closing, sealing and flexible material
handling
President: Craig Blaske
cblaske@fischbein.com
VP Of Sales/Marketing: Lee Thompson
Manager: Mike Hersey
VP Sales/Marketing: Sean O'Flynn
Sales Development Manager: Tom Conroy
Operations Manager: Lynn McDonald
Purchasing Manager: Curt Poppe
Estimated Sales: $5,000,000
Number Employees: 100-249
Number of Brands: 3
Number of Products: 21
Square Footage: 56000
Parent Co: AXIA
Brands:
Fischbein
Inglett
Saxon

22582 Fischer Paper Products Inc
179 Ida Ave
Antioch, IL 60002-1838
847-395-6060
Fax: 847-395-8619 800-323-9093
bags@fischerpaperproducts.com
www.fischerpaperproducts.com
Specialty paper bags for foodservice, prescription,
merchandise and industrial applications.
President: Josh Fischer
jfischer@fischerpaperproducts.com
Vice President: William Fischer
VP Sales: William Fischer
Estimated Sales: $10-15 Million
Number Employees: 50-99
Square Footage: 140000
Type of Packaging: Food Service

22583 Fish Oven & Equipment Co
120 Kent Ave
PO Box 875
Wauconda, IL 60084-2441
847-526-8686
Fax: 847-526-7447 877-526-8720
info@fishoven.com www.fishoven.com
Manufacturer and exporter of mechanical revolving
tray, rotating rack, and woodburning ovens for bak-
ing, roasting, supermarket, food service and
institutions.
President: James M Campbell III
j.campbell@browardschools.com
Sales Manager: Sandra Bradley
Estimated Sales: $2.5-5 Million
Number Employees: 20-49
Square Footage: 160000
Parent Co: Campbell International

22584 Fisher Manufacturing Company
1900 South O Street
PO Box 60
Tulare, CA 93274
559-685-5200
Fax: 800-832-8238 800-421-6162
info1@fisher-mfg.com www.fisher-mfg.com
Manufacturer and exporter of stainless steel faucets,
spray washers and water stations
President: Ray Fisher Jr
Quality Control: Delbert Poole
CFO: Rudy Fernandes
Contact: Michael Emoff
michael.emoff@outtathebox.com
Estimated Sales: $10-20 Million
Number Employees: 50-99
Type of Packaging: Food Service

22585 Fisher Scientific Company
2000 Park Lane Dr
Pittsburgh, PA 15275-1104
412-490-8300
Fax: 412-490-8759 www.fishersci.com
Manufacturer and exporter of food grade laboratory
chemicals
Contact: Lawrence Crooks
larry.cook@fishersci.com
Estimated Sales: $50-100 Million
Number Employees: 500-999
Parent Co: Fisher Scientific International

22586 Fisher Scientific Company
2844 Soquel Ave
Santa Cruz, CA 95062-1411
831-425-7240
Fax: 800-926-1166 800-766-7000
www.fisherscientific.com
Wine industry laboratory equipment
Owner: William Fisher
Estimated Sales: $.5-1 million
Number Employees: 1-4

22587 Fishers Investment
8950 Rossash Road
Cincinnati, OH 45236-1210
513-731-3400
Fax: 513-731-8113 800-833-5916
Manufacturer and exporter of cleaning equipment
and supplies including glass cleaners, hand soap,
dishwashing and washing compounds
Number Employees: 10
Type of Packaging: Food Service, Private Label

22588 Fishmore
1231 East New Haven Avenue
PO Box 24018
Melbourne, FL 32901
321-723-4751
Fax: 321-726-0939
Manufacturer, exporter and importer of custom fish
processing equipment including automatic scaling,
heading and gutting machines, glazers, conveyors,
cutting tables etc
President: Al Sebastian
VP: Tim Cojocari
Estimated Sales: $300,000-500,000
Number Employees: 4
Square Footage: 12000
Brands:
Simor

22589 Fiskars Brands Inc.
PO Box 320
Baldwinsville, NY 13027-0320
315-635-9911
Fax: 315-635-1089 consumeraffairs@fiskars.com
www.fiskars.com
Manufacturer and exporter of casual resin and alu-
minum furniture for restaurants and cafes; also,
clocks, plaques and wall mirrors
President: Ray Carrock
R&D: Melisa Rader
CFO: Michael Read
Quality Control: Tom Norgrack
Number Employees: 250-499

22590 Fiske Brothers RefiningCo
129 Lockwood St
Newark, NJ 07105-4782
973-589-9150
Fax: 973-589-4432 800-733-4755
info@lubriplate.com www.lubriplate.com

USDA H-1/H-2/FDA lubricants for use in food and beverage processing, petroleum-based and synthetic lubricants
President: Richard McCouskey
CEO: Richard T Mccluskey
richardm@lubriplate.com
CEO: Richard T Mc Cluskey
Sales/Marketing: James Girarg
Estimated Sales: G
Number Employees: 50-99
Brands:
    Lubriplate

22591 Fitec International Inc
3525 Ridge Meadow Pkwy # 200
Suite 200
Memphis, TN 38115-4081
901-366-9144
Fax: 901-366-9446 800-332-6387
www.castnets.com
Manufacturer, importer and exporter of cotton and nylon mesh bags; also, netting, twine and rope
President: Mark Hall
hall@castnets.com
Sales: Mark Hall
Estimated Sales: $5-10 Million
Number Employees: 5-9
Type of Packaging: Bulk

22592 Fittings Inc
3300 Fisher Ave
Fort Worth, TX 76111-4506
817-332-3300
Fax: 817-332-5102 800-473-3301
sales@fitandcp.com
Stainless steel fittings and cold plates for premix and postmix dispensing equipment
Owner: Mark Gannon
mark@fitandcp.com
Partner: Mark Gannon
mark@fitandcp.com
Estimated Sales: $5-10 000,000
Number Employees: 50-99

22593 Fitzpatrick Brothers
10700 88th Ave
Pleasant Prairie, WI 53158
773-722-3100
Fax: 773-722-5133 800-233-8064
boconnor@oldsfitz.com
Manufacturer and exporter of scouring powders, cleansers and detergents
General Manager/VP: Odie Ramien
VP: William O'Connor
VP: Tim McAvoy
Plant Manager: Vic Luburich
Estimated Sales: $.5-1 million
Number Employees: 1-4
Parent Co: Olds Products Company
Brands:
    Babo
    Kitchen Klenzer
    Old Dutch
    Tip Top

22594 Fitzpatrick Co
832 N Industrial Dr
Elmhurst, IL 60126-1179
630-592-4425
Fax: 630-530-0832 info@fitzmill.com
www.fitzmill.com
Manufacturer and exporter of grinder and hammer mills, fluid bed dryers, roll compactors and continuous mixers
President: Scott Patterson
Quality Control: Jose Molimar
CFO: Gary Minta
R&D: Scott Waemmnerstrun
Director Development/Marketing: Scott Wennerstrum
Manager, Sales: Tom Kendrick
Plant Manager: Al Cedno
Estimated Sales: $20-50 Million
Number Employees: 100-249
Square Footage: 150000
Brands:
    Chilsonator
    Fitzmill
    Guiloriver
    Malaxator

22595 Fitzpatrick Container Company
6923 Schantz Rd.
North Wales, PA 19454
215-699-3515
Fax: 215-699-7603 contain@fitzbox.com
www.fitzbox.com
Corrugated containers and point of purchase displays
President: Thomas J Shallow Jr
VP: Thomas Shallow
Estimated Sales: $2.5-5 Million
Number Employees: 50-99

22596 Five Continents
P.O.Box 2134
Darien, IL 60561-7134
773-927-0100
Fax: 773-927-5113
Marketing Manager: Marilyn Mara
Estimated Sales: $30-35 Million
Number Employees: 100-250

22597 Five-M Plastics Company
178 N State Street
Allentown, PA 18106
610-628-4291
Fax: 610-395-7336
Manufacturer and instalation, indoor/outdoor signs and displays
Owner: John Chapman
Sales Manager: Phil George
Estimated Sales: $500,000-$1 Million
Number Employees: 9

22598 Fixtur World
1555 Interstate Dr
Cookeville, TN 38501-4124
931-528-7259
Fax: 931-528-9214 800-634-9887
www.fixturworld.com
Manufacturer and exporter of wooden and stainless steel furniture including stands, benches, booths, chairs, cushions, pads, counters/tabletops and hot food tables; custom fabrications available
President: Randy Dyer
rdyer@fixturworld.com
Sales Director: Bobby Hull
General Manager: Al Paker
Estimated Sales: $10-20 Million
Number Employees: 100-249
Square Footage: 240000

22599 Fixtures Furniture
4121 Rushton Street
Florence, AL 35630
855-321-4999
Fax: 800-831-9821 icare@izzyplus.com
www.izzyplus.com
Tables, stools and benches
Founder/CEO: Chuck Saylor
Estimated Sales: $2.5-5 Million
Number Employees: 50
Parent Co: JSJ Corp.
Brands:
    Albi
    Astro
    Baby Bola
    Bola
    D Chair
    Encore
    Jazz
    Ole
    Romo

22600 Flair Electronics
212 Mercury Cir
Pomona, CA 91768-3212
626-963-6077
Fax: 626-335-2080 800-532-3492
www.flairsecurity.com
Glass break detectors, water sensors and door annunciators and contacts
Estimated Sales: $1-2.5 Million
Number Employees: 10-19
Type of Packaging: Bulk

22601 Flair Flexible Packaging Corp
2605 S Lakeland Dr
Appleton, WI 54915-4193
920-574-3121
Fax: 920-574-3122 www.flairpackaging.com

Flair Flexible Packaging is a fully integrated packaging solutions company providing complete in-house services within the United States and Canada since 1992. Product line includes printing and manufacturing of rolls and bags:multilayer lamination; dry lamination; extrusion lamination and tandem extrusion lamination.
Director/Operations: Cheryl Miller Balster
cheryl@flairpackaging.com
Number Employees: 50-99
Type of Packaging: Consumer

22602 Flakice Corporation
6920 Seaway Blvd
Everett, WA 98203
425-347-6100
Fax: 425-446-5116 800-654-4630
www.fluke.com
Manufacturer and exporter of fluid chillers and industrial ice machines
President: Antoine Hajjar
Vice President: Robert Butler
Chairman: William Adelman
Number Employees: 25
Square Footage: 50000
Brands:
    Flakice
    Instant-Ice
    Liquid Freeze

22603 Flambeau Inc
100 Grace Dr
Weldon, NC 27890-1200
252-536-2171
Fax: 252-536-2201 800-344-5716
info@flambeau.com www.flambeau.com
Plastic blow molded and injection molded packaging
Plant Manager: David Burke
Estimated Sales: $1-5 Million
Number Employees: 100-249
Square Footage: 5600000

22604 Flame Gard
1890 Swarthmore Avenue
PO Box 2020
Lakewood, NJ 08701
800-526-3694
Fax: 732-364-8110 sales@flamegard.com
www.flamegard.com
Manufacturer and exporter of UL classified and commercial grease extracting filters, baffles for kitchen exhaust hoods and grease containment products
President: Lawrence Capalbo
CFO: Gary Barros
VP: Gary Barros
Estimated Sales: Below $5 Million
Number Employees: 20-49
Square Footage: 48000
Parent Co: Component Hardware Group, Inc.
Brands:
    Flame Gard
    Flame Gard Iii

22605 Flamingo Food Service Products
3095 E 11th Ave
Hialeah, FL 33013
305-691-4641
Fax: 305-696-7342 800-432-8269
info@flamingopaper.com
www.flamingopaper.com
Manufacturer and exporter of paper napkins
President: Tonny Arias
Operations Manager: Evelyn Hernandez
Estimated Sales: $1-5 Million
Number Employees: 10-19
Type of Packaging: Consumer, Food Service

22606 Flanders Corp
531 Flanders Filter Rd
Washington, NC 27889-7805
252-946-8081
Fax: 252-946-3425 800-637-2803
customerservice@flanderscorp.com
www.flanderscorp.com
Air filters for heating, air conditioning and ventilation systems
President: John Oakley
joakley@flanderscorp.com
Chief Executive Officer: Harry L. Smith, Jr.
SVP: Charlie Kwiatkowski
Senior Vice President of Sales: Travis Stephenson
Number Employees: 1000-4999

22607 FlashBake Ovens Food Service
47817 Fremont Boulevard
Fremont, CA 94538-6506
510-498-4200
Fax: 510-498-4224 800-843-6836
Cooking and heating equipment including visible
light wave ovens
Director Sales/Marketing: Nora Romo
VP Sales: Rick Schoenberg
Estimated Sales: $300,000-500,000
Number Employees: 1-4
Parent Co: Quadlux

22608 Flashfold Carton Inc
1140 Hayden St
Fort Wayne, IN 46803-2040
260-423-9431
Fax: 260-423-4351
Folding cartons
Contact: Ralph Clanton
rclanton@gppkg.com
Estimated Sales: $20-50 Million
Number Employees: 100-249

22609 Flat Plate Inc
2161 Pennsylvania Ave
York, PA 17404-1793
717-767-9060
Fax: 717-767-9160 888-854-2500
www.flatplate.com
Manufacturer and exporter of brazed plate heat
exchangers
President: Steven Wand
CEO: Charles Schmidt
CFO: Mike Losties
Quality Control: Brian Emery
R&D: Brian Emery
Marketing Head: Steve Wand
Estimated Sales: Less Than $500,000
Number Employees: 1-4

**22610 Flatten-O-Matic: Universal
Concepts**
1147 SW 1st Way
Deerfield Beach, FL 33441-6640
954-327-0194
Fax: 954-792-4502 flattenomatic@aol.com

22611 Flavor Burst
499 Commerce Dr
Danville, IN 46122-7848
317-745-2952
Fax: 317-745-2377 800-264-3528
support@flavorburst.com www.flavorburst.com
Owner: Ernie Gerber
erniegerber@flavorburst.com
Estimated Sales: $5-10 Million
Number Employees: 10-19

22612 Flavor Wear
28425 Cole Grade Road
Valley Center, CA 92082-6572
760-749-1332
Fax: 760-749-6164 800-647-8372
www.flavorwear.com
Manufacturer and exporter of uniform accessories
including ties, vests, hair accessories, hats, suspend-
ers, bows, shirts and aprons
President: Lawrence Schleif
Owner/CEO: Martin Anthony
Vice President: Annie Smith
Estimated Sales: $2 Million
Number Employees: 23
Number of Brands: 2
Number of Products: 50
Square Footage: 40000
Parent Co: Anthony Enterprises
Type of Packaging: Food Service, Private Label
Brands:
   Designs By Anthony
   Flavor Classics
   Flavor Touch
   Flavor Trim
   Flavor Wear
   Flavor Weave

22613 Flavorseal
35179 Avon Commerce Pkwy
Avon, OH 44011
440-937-3900
Fax: 440-937-3901 877-827-5962
www.flavorseal.com
Supplies shring bags, cooking bags, netting, casings
and other accessories
Principal: Ron Mitchell
Contact: Eric Aites
aites.eric@flavorseal.com
Estimated Sales: $1-2.5 Million
Number Employees: 50-99
Square Footage: 133
Parent Co: Carroll Manufacturing and Sales

22614 Flavourtech Americas
9505 N. Congress Ave
Kansas City, MO 64153-1811
816-880-9321
Fax: 707-829-6211 www.flavourtech.com
President: Anthony Dann
Number Employees: 19

22615 Fleet Wood Goldco Wyard
10615 Beaver Dam Rd
Cockeysville, MD 21030-2204
410-785-1934
Fax: 410-785-2909 service@fgwa.com
www.barrywehmiller.com
Manufacturer and exporter of mechanical conveyors
and low pressure accumulating conveying and
blending systems; also, package line engineering
and integration of systems
President: Tom Spangenberg
VP: John Molite
R&D: Tom Spangenberg
Marketing: Dee Yakel
Sales: Michael Tymowezak
Contact: Don Powell
dpowell@bwcontainersystems.com
Operations: Bob Jones
Estimated Sales: $30 Million
Number Employees: 20-49
Square Footage: 50000
Type of Packaging: Consumer, Food Service, Pri-
vate Label, Bulk
Brands:
   Air Flow
   Ambec 10
   Ambec 10r
   Can Jet
   Double Density Miniroller
   Isometric
   Lite Touch
   Ring Jet

22616 Fleetwood InternationalPaper
2721 E 45th Street
Vernon, CA 90058-2301
323-588-7121
Fax: 323-588-9219
Corrugated cartons and displays
Marketing Manager: Clive Costa
Contact: Mike Hinton
hinton@fleetwoodcontainer.com
Estimated Sales: $20-50 Million
Number Employees: 100-249

22617 Fleetwood Systems
1264 La Quinta Dr
Orlando, FL 32809-7724
407-855-2282
Fax: 407-857-4453 800-432-5433
www.hardwareimagination-tech.com
Material handling systems and components includ-
ing conveyor belts, chains, vacuums, elevators and
lowerators
Sales Applications: Norman Nissen
General Manager: Gerald Janesek
Number Employees: 50-99
Square Footage: 120000
Parent Co: Fleetwood Systems
Type of Packaging: Private Label, Bulk

22618 FleetwoodGoldcoWyard
1305 Lakeview Dr
Romeoville, IL 60446
630-759-6800
Fax: 630-759-2299 www.fgwa.com
Manufacturer and exporter of depalletizers, brewery
pasteurizers, warmers, coolers, complete turnkeys,
conveyors and rinsers; also, engineering and installation services available

President: David Brown
CEO: Phil Ostapowicz
R&D: Neil McConnellogue
Chairman of the Board: Robert Chapman
General Sales Manager: Richard Witte
Contact: Ronald Burns
rburns@bwcontainersystems.com
Number Employees: 100-249
Square Footage: 200000
Parent Co: Barry-Wehmiller Co.
Brands:
   Ez-Just

22619 Fleming Packaging Corporation
411 Hamilton Blvd # 1518
Peoria, IL 61602-1185
309-676-7657
Fax: 309-676-8776
Partner: John Fleming
CEO: Ken Lyons
CFO: Paul Wayvon
General Manager: J Willard Briggs
Estimated Sales: $1-3 Million
Square Footage: 164000

22620 Flex Pack USA
6321 Emperor Dr
Orlando, FL 32809-5513
407-857-2883
Fax: 407-857-6970
Packaging/bags
Owner: Mark Dorey
Estimated Sales: $5-10 Million
Number Employees: 50-99

22621 Flex Products
640 Dell Rd # 1
Carlstadt, NJ 07072-2202
201-933-3030
Fax: 201-933-2396 800-526-6273
www.flex-products.com
Manufacturer and exporter of plastic extruded tube
containers, closures and caps
President: Ed Friedhoff
Vice President: Bill Rooney
Sales Director: Darby Rosa
Plant Manager: Chris Smolar
Estimated Sales: $5-10 Million
Number Employees: 10-19
Square Footage: 130000
Brands:
   Flexshape

22622 Flex Sol Packaging Corp
1531 NW 12th Ave
Pompano Beach, FL 33069-1730
954-941-6333
Fax: 954-956-4200 877-353-9765
www.flexsolpackaging.com
Custom industrial extruder of flexible packaging
film and bag
President: Brian Stevenson
bstevenson@flexsolpackaging.com
Estimated Sales: $43 Million
Number Employees: 250-499
Type of Packaging: Food Service, Bulk
Other Locations:
   Flex Sol Packaging
   Chicago IL
   Flex Sol Packaging
   Newark NJ
   Flex Sol Packaging
   Nashville TN
   Flex Sol Packaging
   Marshville NC

22623 Flex Sol Packaging Corp
1531 NW 12th Ave
Pompano Beach, FL 33069-1730
954-941-6333
Fax: 954-956-4200 800-231-4191
www.flexsolpackaging.com
Plastic film and bags
President: Brian Stevenson
bstevenson@flexsolpackaging.com
Number Employees: 250-499

22624 Flex-Hose Co Inc
6801 Crossbow Dr
East Syracuse, NY 13057-1026
315-437-1611
Fax: 315-437-1903 sales@flexhose.com
www.flexhose.com

Manufacturer and exporter of hoses including Teflon, stainless steel and rubber flexible; also, couplings and expansion joints
President: Philip Argersinger
pbargersinger@flexhose.com
VP: Philip Argersinger
Quality Assurance: Chuck Phillips
Sales Management: Philip Argersinger
Operations Coordinator: Charles Phillips
Purchasing: Bill Wells
Estimated Sales: Below $5 Million
Number Employees: 10-19
Square Footage: 20000
Brands:
  Flexzorber
  Guideline
  Pumpsaver
  Te-Flex
  Tri-Flex Loop

22625 Flex-O-Glass
1100 N Cicero Ave # 1
Chicago, IL 60651-3213
773-379-7878
Fax: 773-261-5204 www.flexoglass.com
Ionomer skin packaging film
Owner: Harold Warp
Manager: Jeff Whittington
Estimated Sales: $10-20 000,000
Number Employees: 5-9

22626 FlexBarrier Products
5350 Campbells Run Road
Pittsburgh, PA 15205
412-787-9750
Fax: 412-787-3665 800-888-9750
Manager: Rick M Rochelle
Estimated Sales: $1-3 Million
Number Employees: 5-9
Parent Co: TMI, LLC

22627 Flexco
2525 Wisconsin Ave
Downers Grove, IL 60515-4241
630-971-0150
Fax: 630-971-1180 800-323-3444
info@flexco.com www.flexco.com
Single source for light-duty endless and mechanical belt splicing solutions.
President/CEO: Richard White
CFO: Glen Paradise
EVP/COO: Tom Wujek
Marketing: Mike Stein
Sales: Dick Reynolds
Public Relations: Kelly Clancy
Estimated Sales: $20-50 Million
Number Employees: 250-499
Square Footage: 175000
Other Locations:
  Australia
  Chile
  China
  England
  Germany
  Mexico
  India
  Singapore
  South Africa
Brands:
  Alligator
  Clipper
  Flexco
  Novitool

22628 Flexco
2525 Wisconsin Ave
Downers Grove, IL 60515-4241
630-971-0150
Fax: 630-971-1180 800-541-8028
info@flexco.com www.flexco.com
Fasteners for conveyor belts, endless splicing products and other products that improve conveyor productivity.
President: Richard White
EVP: Tom Wujek
VP Marketing: Michael Stein
Sales Manager: Richard Reynolds
PR Specialist: Kelly Clancy
Estimated Sales: $20-50 Million
Number Employees: 250-499
Other Locations:
  Grand Rapids MI

22629 Flexco
2525 Wisconsin Ave
Downers Grove, IL 60515-4241
630-971-0150
Fax: 630-971-1180 800-323-3444
info@flexco.com www.flexco.com
Supplier of belt conveyor products
President: Richard White
Number Employees: 250-499

22630 (HQ)Flexible Foam Products
1900 W Lusher Ave
Elkhart, IN 46517
574-294-7694
Fax: 574-522-4823 800-678-3626
Foamed polyurethane plastic products including containers; also, custom cutting to specific shapes available
General Manager: Jerry Egan
Contact: Beckie Smith
bsmith@flexiblefoam.com
Chemist: Karl Baier
Plant Manager: John Noble
Estimated Sales: $20-50 Million
Number Employees: 100-249

22631 Flexible Material Handling
410 Horizon Dr Ste 200
Suwanee, GA 30024
216-587-1575
Fax: 216-587-2833 800-669-1501
www.flexmh.com
Conveyors including portable, flexible gravity and powered; also, portable storage racks
Sales Administration: Nancy Stohlman
Sales/Marketing Manager: Karl Dearnley
Contact: Teresa Blanton
tblanton@flexmh.com
Estimated Sales: $20-50 Million
Number Employees: 50-99
Parent Co: Axia

22632 Flexible Tape & Label Co
243 Jefferson Ave
Memphis, TN 38103-2376
901-522-1410
Fax: 901-523-0073 art@flexiblelabel.com
www.flexiblelabelgroup.com
Printed pressure sensitive labels
Owner: Alan Magnus
orderlabel@aol.com
VP: Melanie Magnus
Estimated Sales: $1-2.5 Million
Number Employees: 5-9

22633 Flexicell Inc
10463 Wilden Dr
Ashland, VA 23005-8134
804-550-7300
Fax: 804-550-4898 www.flexicell.com
Manufacturer and exporter of robotic packaging machinery for case packing, collating, palletizing and conveying
President: Hans Dekoning
hdekoning@flexcon.com
R & D: Jack Morris
VP of Sales: Stuart Cooper
Operations Manager: Allen Bancroft
Manufacturing Specialist: Jack Mouris
Plant Manager: John Architzel
Purchasing Manager: Jim Golob
Estimated Sales: Below $5 Million
Number Employees: 20-49
Square Footage: 48000
Brands:
  Flexi-1850
  Flexi-Cell
  Flexilinear
  Flexiloader

22634 (HQ)Flexicon
2400 Emrick Blvd
Bethlehem, PA 18020-8006
610-814-2400
Fax: 610-814-0600 888-353-9426
sales@flexicon.com www.flexicon.com
Manufacturer and exporter of flexible screw conveyor systems, bulk bag dischargers, weigh batching systems and bulk handling systems with automated controls
CEO: William S Gill
Number Employees: 50-99

Other Locations:
  Flexicon Corporation
  Kent
Brands:
  Batch-Con
  Bev-Con
  Flow-Flexer
  Pop-Top

22635 Flexicon
165 Chicago St
Cary, IL 60013
847-639-3530
Fax: 847-639-6828
Flexible packaging materials for the food and pharmaceutical industries, supplied in rollstock for thermoforming, lidding, and form fill and seal applications. Preformed pouches are also supplied. Specializing in rollstock orpouches for boil and freeze applications.
President: Robert Biddle
CEO: Greg Baron
Estimated Sales: $20 Million
Number Employees: 50-99
Type of Packaging: Consumer, Food Service, Private Label

22636 Flexlink Systems Inc
6580 Snowdrift Rd # 200
Allentown, PA 18106-9331
610-954-7000
Fax: 610-973-8345 800-782-1399
us1.marketing@flexlink.com www.flexlink.com
Plastic chain conveyor systems and automation components
President: Dave Clark
CFO: Nino Dipietroo
IT: Jeff Russo
jeff.roth@flexlink.com
Estimated Sales: $20-50 Million
Number Employees: 50-99

22637 Flexlume Sign Corp
1464 Main St
Buffalo, NY 14209-1780
716-884-2020
Fax: 716-881-0361 info@flexlume.com
www.flexlume.com
Indoor and outdoor signs
Owner: Curtis Martin
cmartin@signweb.com
Estimated Sales: Below $5 Million
Number Employees: 5-9

22638 Flexo Graphics
900 S Georgia St
Amarillo, TX 79102-1204
806-374-5363
Fax: 806-371-7104 866-533-5396
Labels including die-cut and pressure sensitive
Owner: Kevin Ahrens
flexo@arn.net
Sales: Ray Clark
Office Manager: Dylan Clark
Estimated Sales: $500,000-$1 Million
Number Employees: 1-4
Square Footage: 7000

22639 Flexo Printing Equipment Corp
416 Hayward Ave N
St Paul, MN 55128-5379
651-731-9499
Fax: 651-731-0525 www.flexo-siat.com
Die cutting and slitting capability for tape and labels
President: Wynn Lidell
wynn@flexo-siat.com
Estimated Sales: Below $5 000,000
Number Employees: 1-4

22640 Flexo Transparent Inc
28 Wasson St
Buffalo, NY 14210-1544
716-825-7710
Fax: 716-825-0139 877-993-5396
Flexographic printer, manufacturer and exporter of custom designed and printed plastic films up to ten colors including process print. Flexible packaging materials including: bags, rollstock, bottle sleeves, sheeting, reclosablezipper, resealable tape, pallet covers, specialty prepared foods totes, custom shaped packaging, etc. EDI and VMI capable; Just in Time Deliveries; Fast turnaround shipments.

President: Ronald Mabry
HR Executive: Debbi Gauthier
dgauthier@flexotransparent.com
Sales: Mark Barrile
Estimated Sales: $20-50 Million
Number Employees: 50-99
Number of Brands: 4
Square Footage: 84000
Type of Packaging: Consumer, Food Service, Private Label, Bulk
Brands:
    Chicken Keeper
    Crispy Keeper
    Rotisserie Keeper
    Safti Keeper

22641 (HQ)Flint Boxmakers Inc
2490 E Bristol Rd
Flint, MI 48529-1325
    810-743-0400
Fax: 810-743-9577 www.michiganmall.com
Corrugated boxes
President: Steve Landaal
Number Employees: 5-9

22642 Flint Rubber Stamp Works
3518 Fenton Rd
Flint, MI 48507
    810-235-2341
Fax: 810-235-3919 rodzinaind@aol.com
Marking and coding devices including rubber stamps
President: Robert Cross Jr
Estimated Sales: $500,000-$1 Million
Number Employees: 5-9
Parent Co: Rodzina Industries

22643 Flo-Cold
29290 Wall St,
PO Box 930317
Wixom, MI 48393
    248-348-6666
Fax: 248-348-6667
Coolers, freezers and racked modular refrigeration systems
President: Dean M Koppin
Engineer: Albert Durand
Estimated Sales: $2.5-5 Million
Number Employees: 60
Parent Co: Chrysler & Koppin Company
Brands:
    Flo-Cold

22644 Flo-Matic Corporation
1982t Belford North Drive
Belvidere, IL 61008-8565
    815-547-5650
Fax: 815-544-2287 800-959-1179
Manufacturer and exporter of washers and washing systems
Chief Engineer: Edward Herman
Estimated Sales: $1-5,000,000

22645 Floaire
1730 Walton Rd # 203
Suite # 203
Blue Bell, PA 19422-2301
    484-530-2601
Fax: 610-239-8941 800-726-5623
sales@floaire.com www.floaire.com
Ventilation equipment and commercial cookware
President: Clark S Fuller
Marketing Administration: Dawn Kearny
VP Sales Food Service: Richard Kinzler
Manager: Cory Scott
sales@floaire.com
Estimated Sales: Less Than $500,000
Number Employees: 1-4
Parent Co: Ralph Kearney & Sons

22646 Flodin
PO Box 1578
Moses Lake, WA 98837-0245
    509-766-2996
Fax: 509-766-0157
Manufacturer and exporter of potato processing equipment including conveyors, dumpers, friers, dryers and frozen concertrate, thawing and breaker systems, etc
Sales Executive: Bill Flodin
Purchasing Agent: Rod Wright
Estimated Sales: $2.5-5 Million
Number Employees: 10-19
Square Footage: 92000

Brands:
    Flodin

22647 Flojet
20 Icon
Foothill Ranch, CA 92610-3000
    949-859-4945
Fax: 949-859-1153 www.flojet.com
Manufacturer, importer and exporter of bag-in-box packaging pumps, motor pump units and power sprayers for soda, beer, cider, wine, condiments and water
President: Russ Davis
Marketing Director: Brud LeTourneav
Sales Director: Jon Byrd
Estimated Sales: $50-100 Million
Number Employees: 250

22648 Flomatic International
2100 Future Drive
Sellersburg, IN 47172
    503-775-2550
Fax: 812-246-7020 800-367-4233
www.manitowocbeverage.com
Manufacturer and exporter of post-mix soft drink dispensing valves
VP: John Cochran
Estimated Sales: $10-20 Million
Number Employees: 20-49
Square Footage: 43200
Parent Co: Manitowoc Foodservice Group
Brands:
    Flomatic

22649 Floor Master Inc
1157 Hooker Rd
Chattanooga, TN 37407-3248
    423-867-4525
Fax: 423-867-4563 www.floormasterinc.net
Floor sweeping compounds
President: Johnny Bailey
floormaster@bellsouth.net
Estimated Sales: $2.5-5 Million
Number Employees: 10-19
Square Footage: 20000

22650 Florart Flock Process
13870 W Dixie Hwy
North Miami, FL 33161-3343
    305-643-3900
Fax: 305-981-9929 800-292-3524
www.flagusa.com
Manufacturer and exporter of flags, flagpoles, pennants, indoor flag sets and banners
Owner: Barbara Dabney
CEO: Stephanie Ledlow
Number Employees: 5-9
Square Footage: 20800
Brands:
    Annin
    Cf
    Eder
    Valley Forge

22651 Florida Knife Co
1735 Apex Rd
Sarasota, FL 34240-9386
    941-371-2104
Fax: 941-378-9427 800-966-5643
sales@florida-knife.com www.florida-knife.com
Manufacturer and exporter of knives for ice, candy and packaging; also, food processing machine knife blades
President: Tom Johanning
tjohanning@florida-knife.com
Sales: Tom Johanning Jr
Personnel: Debbie Dean
Estimated Sales: $2.5-5 Million
Number Employees: 10-19
Square Footage: 48000

22652 Florida Plastics Intl
10200 S Kedzie Ave
Evergreen Park, IL 60805-3735
    708-499-0400
Fax: 708-499-4620 800-499-0400
salessupport@keyser-group.com
Manufacturer and exporter of point of purchase displays, signs and menu boards
Owner: Bill Kaiser
bkaiser@keyser-group.com
CEO: Donald Keyser
Quality Control: Tom Page

Estimated Sales: $10-20 Million
Number Employees: 1-4
Square Footage: 120000
Type of Packaging: Food Service

22653 Florida Seating
6100 Mears Ct
Clearwater, FL 33760-2337
    727-540-9802
Fax: 727-540-9403 www.floridaseating.com
Manager: Jeremy Williams
Manager: Joe Bonnetti
joe@floridaseating.com
Estimated Sales: $1-5 Million
Number Employees: 20-49

22654 Florin Box & Lumber Company
PO Box 292338
Sacramento, CA 95829-2338
    916-383-2675
Fax: 916-383-1397 800-767-2675
Wine industry gift boxes, packaging, wood crates
Estimated Sales: $5-10 000,000
Number Employees: 20-49

22655 Flour City Press-Pack Company
P.O.Box 398198
Minneapolis, MN 55439-8198
    952-831-1265
Fax: 612-378-9441
Paper boxes including set-up and folding
Owner: Gene N Fuller
Quality Control: Richard Hall
Estimated Sales: $300,000-500,000
Number Employees: 1-4

22656 Flow Aerospace
1635 Production Rd
Jeffersonville, IN 47130-9624
    812-283-7888
Fax: 812-284-3281 www.flowwaterjet.com
Manufacturer and exporter of positioning systems for waterjet cutting pick and place robots
Manager: Anthony Neeley
Vice President of Global Sales: Dick LeBlanc
Manager: Kent Eubank
keubank@flowcorp.com
General Manager: Gerald Malmrose
Chief Engineer: Mark Saberton
Estimated Sales: $1-5 Million
Number Employees: 100-249
Square Footage: 108000
Parent Co: Flow International

22657 (HQ)Flow International Corp.
23150 64th Ave. S
Kent, WA 98032
    253-850-3500
Fax: 253-813-9377 800-446-3569
info@flowcorp.com www.flowwaterjet.com
Food processing and high-pressure waterjet cutting and cleaning equipment.
President/CEO: Marc Michael
Year Founded: 1974
Estimated Sales: $200 Million
Number Employees: 680
Square Footage: 150000
Brands:
    Fresher Under Pressure

22658 Flow Technology
P.O.Box 52103
Phoenix, AZ 85072-2103
    480-240-3400
Fax: 480-240-3401 800-528-4225
ftimarket@ftimeters.com www.ftimeters.com
Instrumetation and controls, flow meters
President: Alan Eschbach
Quality Control: Randy Larrison
Estimated Sales: $10-20 Million
Number Employees: 50-99

22659 Flow Technology Inc
8930 S Beck Ave # 107
Suite #107
Tempe, AZ 85284-2864
    480-240-3400
Fax: 480-240-3401 800-833-2448
ftimarket@ftimeters.com www.ftimeters.com
Positive displacement and turbine flow meters
President: C Foran, Jr.
Vice President: Ralph Duffill
Number Employees: 50-99
Square Footage: 60000

Brands:
Decathlon Series
Exact Series

22660 Flow of Solids
1 Technology Park Drive
Westford, MA 01886-3139
978-392-0300
Fax: 978-392-9980 www.jenike.com
Portable and stationery containers including silos, bins, hoppers, feeders, tumble blenders, chutes, solid pumps and slide gates
Director Sales/Marketing: Roderick Hossfeld
National Sales Manager: Brian Pittenger
Estimated Sales: $3-5 Million
Number Employees: 20-49
Parent Co: Jenike & Johanson

22661 Fluid Air Inc
2580 Diehl Rd # E
Aurora, IL 60502-5309
630-665-5001
Fax: 630-851-1244 fluidairinfo@spray.com
www.fluidairinc.com
Manufacturer and exporter of milling equipment for fine grinding and dryers/agglomerators for drying, agglomerating, coating and encapsulating foods and flavors
President: Martin Bender
CEO: Thomas Tappen
Director Process Development: Donald Verbarg
Estimated Sales: $5-10 Million
Number Employees: 20-49
Square Footage: 64000
Parent Co: Spraying Systems Company

22662 Fluid Energy Processing& Eqpt
2629 Penn St
Hatfield, PA 19440-2344
215-368-2510
Fax: 215-368-6235 sales@fluidenergype.com
www.fluidenergype.com
Manufacturer and exporter of jet/micronizing grinding mills, pulverizers and flash drying equipment
President: Jerry Leimkuhler
Estimated Sales: $5-10 Million
Number Employees: 50-99
Brands:
Jet-O-Mizer
Micro-Jet
Roto-Jet
Roto-Sizer
Thermajet

22663 Fluid Imaging Technologies Inc
200 Enterprise Dr
Scarborough, ME 04074-7636
207-846-6100
Fax: 207-846-6110 info@fluidimaging.com
www.fluidimaging.com
Continuous-imaging particle analysis instruments for food and beverage research and development and inspection.
President: Chris Sieracki
CEO: Kent Peterson
kent@fluidimaging.com
Marketing Assistant: Faith Baker
Estimated Sales: $2.5 Million
Number Employees: 20-49

22664 Fluid Metering Inc
5 Aerial Way # 500
Syosset, NY 11791-5593
516-922-6050
Fax: 516-624-8261 800-223-3388
pumps@fmipump.com www.fmipump.com
Manufacturer and exporter of metering pumps, dispensers and accessories including valveless and variable positive displacement piston pumps
President: Hank Pinkerton
hank.pinkerton@fmipump.com
Marketing Manager: Herb Werner
VP Sales: David Peled
Purchasing Director: Anthony Mennella
Estimated Sales: $10-20 Million
Number Employees: 10-19
Square Footage: 24000
Brands:
Fmi
Micro-Petter
Ratiomatic

22665 Fluid Systems
10054 Old Grove Rd
San Diego, CA 92131
858-695-3840
Fax: 858-695-2176 800-525-4369
Crossflow membrane filtration processes and systems for the industrial, good, water, chemical, and biotechnology markets
CFO: William Colins
Contact: William Liht
fluid.systems@ksb.com

22666 Fluted Partition Inc
850 Union Ave
Bridgeport, CT 06607-1137
203-368-2548
Fax: 203-367-5266 www.valleycontainer.com
Fluted partitions, corrugated and solid fiber boxes
Owner: Arthur W Vietze Jr
VP: Richard Jackson
Vice President: Rudolph Niedermeier
cellpak@aol.com
Estimated Sales: $5-10 000,000
Number Employees: 10-19
Number of Products: 1
Type of Packaging: Private Label, Bulk

22667 Flux Pumps Corporation
4330 Commerce Cir SW
Atlanta, GA 30336
404-691-6010
Fax: 404-691-6314 800-367-3589
contact-flux-usa@flux-pumpen.de
Manufacturer and exporter of pumps including centrifugal, pneumatic, positive displacement, progressive cavity and sanitary
President: L G Eastman
Vice President: Mike O'Toole
Contact: Fred Bryant
fbryant@flux-pumps.com
Estimated Sales: $1-2.5,000,000
Number Employees: 5-9
Parent Co: Flux Pumps Corporation
Type of Packaging: Bulk

22668 Flynn Burner Corporation
425 5th Ave
New Rochelle, NY 10801
914-636-1320
Fax: 914-636-3751 800-643-8910
www.flynnburner.com
Industrial gas burners for baking and surface treating (3D and flat web), paper, plastic
CEO: Edward S Flynn
Number Employees: 50-99
Type of Packaging: Food Service, Private Label

22669 Foam Concepts Inc
44 Rivulet St
PO Box 410
Uxbridge, MA 01569-3134
508-278-7255
Fax: 508-278-3623 sales@foamconcepts.com
www.foamconcepts.com
Manufacturer and exporter of custom molded insulated foam shipping containers and custom packaging for perishables
Owner: Mark Villamaino
mvillamaino@filmconcepts.com
VP Sales: Philip Michaelson
mvillamaino@filmconcepts.com
Estimated Sales: $5-10 Million
Number Employees: 20-49
Square Footage: 160000

22670 Foam Fabricator-Corp
8722 E San Alberto Dr # 200
Scottsdale, AZ 85258-4353
480-607-7330
Fax: 480-607-7333
scottsdale@foamfabricatorsinc.com
www.foamfabricatorsinc.com
Custom molded polystyrene packaging materials, expanded polystyrene, expanded polypropylene, expanded polyethylene
President: Jeffrey Askins
jaskins@foamfabricatorsinc.com
CFO: James Hughes
Estimated Sales: $5-10 Million
Number Employees: 10-19

22671 Foam Pack Industries
72 Fadem Rd
Springfield, NJ 07081-3116
973-376-3700
Fax: 973-467-9850 foampack@verizon.net
www.foampackindustries.com
Polystyrene packaging materials and containers; also, ice packs
President: Harvey Goodstein
CFO: David Goodstein
Sales Manager: Lacy Seabrook
Estimated Sales: $5-10 Million
Number Employees: 5-9

22672 Foam Packaging Inc
35 Stennis Rd
Vicksburg, MS 39180-9175
601-638-4871
Fax: 601-636-2655 800-962-2655
info@foampackaging.com
www.foam-packaging.com
Manufacturer and exporter of food service trays and insulated food containers for eggs, poultry and produce
President: Ray B English
renglish@vicksburg.com
Estimated Sales: $1-2.5 Million
Number Employees: 1-4

22673 Foamex
18801 Old Statesville Rd
Cornelius, NC 28031-9306
704-892-8081
Fax: 704-892-0409 www.foamex.com
Polyurethane foam
General Manager: Fran Conard
Finance Executive: Jennifer Hughes
Contact: Richard Centeno
rcenteno@fxi.com
Manager of Laminated Products: L Peterson
Estimated Sales: $20-50 Million
Number Employees: 10-19

22674 Foamold Corporation
34 Birchwood Dr
PO Box 95
Oneida, NY 13421-0095
315-363-5350
Fax: 315-363-4518
Foam packaging materials
Plant Manager: Jay Rheinhardt

22675 Focke & Co Inc
5730 Millstream Rd
Whitsett, NC 27377-9789
336-449-7200
Fax: 336-449-5444 sales@fockegso.com
www.focke.com
Packaging machinery
Vice President: Johann Betschart
jbetschart@fockegso.com
Financial Controller: Alec Pratto
VP: Johann Betschart
Estimated Sales: $10-20 000,000
Number Employees: 50-99

22676 Focus
2852 Anthony Ln S
Minneapolis, MN 55418-3233
612-706-4444
Fax: 612-706-0544
food@focusexecutivesearch.com
www.focusexecutivesearch.com
Executive search firm specializing in personnel for general management, sales, research and development, operations, production and administration positions
President: Tim Mc Lafferty
CFO: Gayle Hope
Vice President: Tim Schultz
R & D: Nicholas Kallenbach
Sales Director: Tony Misum
Contact: Gayle Holt
gh@focusexecutivesearch.com
Estimated Sales: Below $5 Million
Number Employees: 5-9
Square Footage: 400000

22677 (HQ)Fogel Jordon CommercialRefrigeration Company
2501 Grant Avenue
Philadelphia, PA 19114-2307
215-535-8300
Fax: 215-289-1597 800-523-0171
Manufacturer and exporter of refrigerators, walk-in cabinets, refrigerated display cases, beverage coolers, cooling rooms, etc
Secretary/Treasurer: Gene Sterner
Sales Manager: Howard Smith
Estimated Sales: $20-50 Million
Number Employees: 50-99
Square Footage: 200000
Type of Packaging: Consumer, Bulk
Brands:
　Fogel
　Jordon
　Jordon Scientific

22678 Fogel Rubin & Fogel
44 W Flagler St # 350
Miami, FL 33130-6813
305-577-4905
Fax: 305-372-0936
Commercial refrigerators specifically designed for beverage and beer industries
Partner: Joel D Fogel
Estimated Sales: $300,000-500,000
Number Employees: 5-9

22679 Fogg Filler Co
3455 John F Donnelly Dr
Holland, MI 49424-9207
616-786-3644
Fax: 616-786-0350 info@foggfiller.com
Manufacturer and exporter of packaging machinery including bottle fillers and cappers, and rinsers for flowable liquid, and noncarbonated products
President: Mike Fogg
Vice President: Al Nienhuis
Marketing Director: Susan Lamar
Sales Director: Ben Fogg
Plant Manager: Randy Dewaard
Estimated Sales: $10-20 Million
Number Employees: 100-249
Square Footage: 80000
Type of Packaging: Consumer, Food Service, Private Label, Bulk
Brands:
　Clip Go Valve
　Easi-63
　Filt Pro 5000
　Ventraflow

22680 Foilmark Inc
5 Malcolm Hoyt Dr
Newburyport, MA 01950-4082
978-462-7300
Fax: 978-462-0831 sales@itwfoilmark.com
Wine industry fillers
President: David Bales
dbales@itwfoils.com
Estimated Sales: $50-100 Million
Number Employees: 100-249

22681 (HQ)Fold-Pak Corporation
Van Buren Street
Newark, NY 14513
315-331-3159
Fax: 315-331-0093
Manufacturer and exporter of folding ice cream and carry out food cartons
President/CEO: Karl De May
Senior VP Sales/Marketing: Robert Mullally
VP Sales: Max Richter
Estimated Sales: $50-100 Million
Number Employees: 100-249
Type of Packaging: Consumer, Private Label
Other Locations:
　Fold-Pak Corp.
　Hazleton PA

22682 Fold-Pak South
3961 Cusseta Rd
Columbus, GA 31903-2045
706-689-2924
Fax: 706-689-2308
Manufacturer and exporter of food trays, soup containers and wire-handled food pails including Oriental and microwaveable; available with or without pagoda design

Quality Control: Coral Vessel
Contact: April Butler
aprilb@fold-pak.com
Plant Manager: Carl Vessell
Estimated Sales: $10-10 Million
Number Employees: 20-49
Type of Packaging: Food Service
Brands:
　Bio-Pak

22683 Folding Carton/FlexiblePackaging
12323 Sherman Way
North Hollywood, CA 91605-5517
818-896-3449
Fax: 818-982-9039
Paper boxes, cartons, blister cards and skin sheets
General Manager: Tom Hiraishi
Number Employees: 60
Parent Co: Marfred Industries

22684 Folding Guard Co
5858 W 73rd St
Chicago, IL 60638-6216
708-924-1359
Fax: 312-829-3278 800-622-2214
Manufacturer and exporter of partitions, gates and lockers
Manager: J Lipa
jlipa@foldingguard.com
Operations Manager: Keith Stadwick
Estimated Sales: $10-20 Million
Number Employees: 50-99
Type of Packaging: Bulk
Brands:
　Quik-Fence

22685 Foley Sign Co
572 Mercer St
Seattle, WA 98109-4618
206-324-3040
Fax: 206-328-4953 www.foleysign.com
Manufacturer and exporter of signs
Owner: Mark Metcalf
mark@foleysign.com
Estimated Sales: $1-2.5 Million
Number Employees: 10-19

22686 Foley's Famous Aprons
3441 Filbert St
Wayne, MI 48184-1974
734-641-9507
Fax: 734-721-8426 800-634-3245
Work cloths, caps and aprons
Owner: Terrence Foley
Secretary: Kevin Foley
VP: Tom Foley
Estimated Sales: $300,000-500,000
Number Employees: 1-4
Square Footage: 10000

22687 Follett Corp
801 Church Ln
Easton, PA 18040-6637
610-252-7301
Fax: 610-250-0696 800-523-9361
www.follettice.com
Manufacturer and exporter of high quality, innovative ice storage bins, ice storage and transport systems, ice and water dispensers, ice and beverage dispensers, and Chewblet® ice nugget ice machines
President/CEO: Steven Follett
fsteven@follettice.com
CFO: Thomas Rohrbach
Executive VP: Robert Bryson
Marketing Director: Lois Schneck
VP Sales: Ed Barr
Manager, Marketing Services: Robin Porter
VP Operations: David Tumbusch
Manager, Materials: Jeff Craig
Number Employees: 100-249
Type of Packaging: Food Service

22688 Fona International
1900 Averill Rd
Geneva, IL 60134
630-578-8600
Fax: 630-578-8601 www.fona.com
Flavoring extracts and syrups.
Founder, Chairman & CEO: Joe Slawek
jslawek@fona.com
VP, Accounting & Finance: Chad Hall
EVP: TJ Widuch
EVP: Manon Daoust
COO: Jeremy Thompson

Estimated Sales: $100-500 Million
Number Employees: 100-249

22689 Fonda Group
PO Box 519
Goshen, IN 46527-0519
574-534-2515
Fax: 574-533-6330
Paper plates
President: William Lester
Principal: Meg Amadeo
Number Employees: 50

22690 Food & Agrosystems
1289 Mandarin Drive
Sunnyvale, CA 94087-2028
408-245-8450
Fax: 408-748-1826 www.foodagrosys.com
Consultant specializing in process engineering, product/process development, plant/process layout, equipment design, feasibility analysis, production problem-solving, management assistance, etc
President: Thomas Parks
VP Marketing: Robert Marquardt
Estimated Sales: $1-2.5 Million
Number Employees: 10

22691 Food & Beverage Consultants
1260 Oaklawn Ave
Cranston, RI 02920-2628
401-463-5784
Fax: 401-463-7931
Consultant specializing in food and beverage development, flavor modification, food service and institutional consulting, recipe and menu development, quality control, food labeling, sensory evaluation and training programs
President: Demetri Kazantzis
Contact: Abel Martinez
amartinez@hpaconsultants.co.uk
Estimated Sales: $.5-1 million
Number Employees: 1-4

22692 Food Allergy & Anaphylaxis Network
7925 Jones Branch Dr.
Suite 1100
McLean, VA 22102
703-691-3179
Fax: 703-691-2713 800-929-4040
afurlong@foodallergy.org www.foodallergy.org
To improve the quality of life and the health of individuals with food allergies.
Founder/CEO: Anne Munoz-Furlong
Contact: Alyssa Ackerman
aackerman@foodallergy.org
Number Employees: 10-19

22693 (HQ)Food Business Associates
PO Box J
Temple, ME 04984-0539
207-778-2251
Fax: 207-778-5097
Consultant and market development specialist providing growth strategy planning and consumer and trade acceptance research; also, supermarket supervisor training services available
President: Robert Bull
VP: Stephen Bull
Estimated Sales: Less than $500,000
Number Employees: 4

22694 Food Consulting Company
13724 Recuerdo Drive
Del Mar, CA 92014-3430
858-793-4658
Fax: 800-522-3545 800-793-2844
info@foodlabels.com www.foodlabels.com
Consultant specializing in nutrition analysis and food labeling
Contact: Susan Drew
jim.wurbel.b7hq@statefarm.com
Estimated Sales: Below $500,000
Number Employees: 1

22695 Food Development Centre
PO Box 1240
Portage La Prairie, NB R1N 3J9
Canada
306-933-7555
Fax: 306-933-7208 800-870-1044
info@foodcentre.sk.ca www.foodcentre.sk.ca

Consultant specializing in product development, packaging, equipment, food analyses, nutritional profiles, QC programs, food research and development, food processing, process engineering, etc.; full service food science and technologylibrary in house; also, seminars available
CEO: Dave Donaghy
Research & Development: AlPhonSus Utioh
Marketing Director: Markus Schmulgen
Number Employees: 25
Square Footage: 80000
Parent Co: Manitoba Agriculture & Food

22696 Food Engineering Network
1050 Il Route 83
Bensenville, IL 60106-1049

630-616-0200
Fax: 630-227-0204 www.bnpmedia.com
CEO: Jim Henderson
Contact: Joyce Fassi
fasslj@bnpmedia.com
Estimated Sales: $1-5 000,000

22697 Food Engineering Unlimited
1501 N Harbor Blvd Ste 103
Fullerton, CA 92835-4128

714-879-8762
Fax: 714-773-0911 feu@earthlink.net
Conveyors,material handling systems, bakery ovens, mixers and spiral freezers; also, installation services available
President: Russ Juergens
Contact: Rosalie Hofmaenner
rosalie.hofmaenner@food-eng.com
Estimated Sales: $1-2,500,000
Number Employees: 1-4

22698 Food Equipment BrokerageInc
PO Box 6541
Key West, FL 33041

800-968-8881
febinc@mo.net
We do turn key c-stores across the United States and Canada. We also export to Asia
CEO: Michael Hesse
Marketing: J R Kim
Sales: Dave Schuller
Number Employees: 110
Number of Brands: 400
Type of Packaging: Food Service, Private Label

22699 Food Equipment Manufacturing Company
22201 Aurora Rd
Bedford Heights, OH 44146

216-672-5859
Fax: 216-663-9337 info@femc.com
www.femc.com
Manufacturer and exporter of packaging machinery including fillers, de-stackers, sealers and slicers
President: Robert Sauer
rls@femc.com
CFO: Obert Sauer
VP: Joseph Lukes
Sales Manager: Daniel Auvil
Estimated Sales: $5-10 Million
Number Employees: 20-49
Square Footage: 120000

22700 Food Executives Network
10415 West Michigan Street
Milwaukee, WI 53226

414-962-7684
Fax: 414-962-6261
careers@foodexecsnetwork.com
Search firm speacializing in the selection and placement of executive, managerial and technical professionals.
President and CEO: Thomas Brenneman
VP: Kay Boxer
Business Manager: Christine Brennemen
Director of BD, SE Office: Kay Boxer
Contact: Tom Brenneman
chris.brenneman@gmail.com
Business Manager, Milwaukee Office: Christine Brenneman
Estimated Sales: $300,000-500,000
Number Employees: 1-4
Square Footage: 6000
Parent Co: Winston Franchise Corporation

22701 Food Handling Systems
8948 SW Barbur Boulevard
Suite 720
Portland, OR 97219-4047

877-266-6972
Fax: 503-691-0917
Gentle food handling, horizontal motion conveyors and vibratory equipment
Chairman: Richard Frank
President/CEO: Trevor Fagerskog
CFO: Steven Reiss
VP Sales/Marketing: Karen Orton Katz
Type of Packaging: Bulk

22702 (HQ)Food Industry ConsultingGroup
21050 SW 93rd Lane Road
Dunnellon, FL 34431-5802

352-489-8919
Fax: 352-489-8919 800-443-5820
Consultant specializing food service systems especially food procurement productivity in food preperation and service
CEO: J Hill
Operations: James Mixon
Estimated Sales: $1-5 Million
Number Employees: 6
Square Footage: 5000
Other Locations:
Food Industry Consulting Group
Silver Spring MD

22703 Food Industry Equipment
1121 W 14th Street
Lorain, OH 44052-3800

440-246-3150
Fax: 440-246-1739
Defattting machines, skinnning machines and accessories and trimming devices, deboning equipment/meat, knives/powered, sharpening systems, boning machines, meat and poultry, cutters/knives, cutters/trimmers, consultants/processingequipment and consultants/processing equipment
Manager Customer Support: Pam Agocki

22704 Food Insights
1100 Connecticut Avenue NW
Suite 430
Washington, DC 20036

202-296-6540
Fax: 901-755-1006 info@foodinsight.org
www.foodinsight.org
Consultant specializing in marketing research, operating systems and management strategy services, customer relationship management
CEO: Judy Patton
Marketing: Carolyn Thomas
Operations: Sandy Brickley
Purchasing: Larry Ruggles
Estimated Sales: $300,000-500,000
Number Employees: 1-4

22705 Food Institute
10 Mountainview Rd # S125
Suite S125
Upper Saddle Rvr, NJ 07458-1942

201-791-5570
Fax: 201-791-5222 brian.todd@foodinstitute.com
www.foodinstitute.com
A non-profit organization founded in 1928. Provides information covering the entire food industry issues and food industry news.
President: Brian Todd
HR Executive: Cathy Sloan
csloan@foodinstitute.com
Order Status/Billing: April Brendel
Estimated Sales: $2.5-5 Million
Number Employees: 10-19

22706 Food Instrument Corp
115 Academy Ave
Federalsburg, MD 21632-1202

410-754-8606
Fax: 410-754-8796 800-542-5688
kickout@verizon.net
www.foodinstrumentcorporation.com
Manufacturer, wholesaler/distributor and exporter of microprocessor based quality control instrumentation including closure seal testers, rejectors, data analyzers, can orienters and diverters
President: Richard V Kudlich
Sales Director: James Boehm
Estimated Sales: $1-5 Million
Number Employees: 1-4

Number of Brands: 1
Number of Products: 6
Square Footage: 40000
Brands:
Adr
Das Ii
Div-10
Vrr

22707 Food Machinery Sales
328 Commerce Blvd # 8
Bogart, GA 30622-2200

706-549-2207
Fax: 706-548-1724 fmssales@fmsathens.com
www.fmsathens.com
Manufacturer and exporter of product handling and packaging machinery for the biscuit and cracker industries
Manager: Eric Gunderson
Estimated Sales: $10-20 Million
Number Employees: 20-49

22708 Food Machinery of America
3115 Pepper Mill Court
Mississauga,, ON L5L 4X5
Canada

905-823-5522
Fax: 905-607-0234 800-465-0234
sales@omcan.com www.omcan.com
Estimated Sales: $1-5 Million

22709 Food Makers Equipment
16019 Adelante St
Irwindale, CA 91702-3255

626-358-1343
Fax: 626-358-1613 www.bakeryequipment.net
Owner: Tom Fowler
tom@fmbe.com
Estimated Sales: $10-20 Million
Number Employees: 20-49

22710 Food Management Search
235 State St # 326
Suite 326
Springfield, MA 01103-1749

413-732-2666
Fax: 413-732-6466
recruiters@foodmanagementsearch.com
www.foodmanagementsearch.com
Contingency firm specializing in recruiting food industry career professionals in the areas of food production, supermarket and distribution, food service, restaurant, culinary, hotel food and beverage and sales and marketingnationwide. Position salaries range between $40K and $150K
Contact: Allison Wellman
allisonw@chap-con.com
Estimated Sales: Less Than $500,000
Number Employees: 1-4

22711 Food Marketing Servises
419 Friday Rd
Pittsburgh, PA 15209

412-821-8960
www.leepercompanies.com
Provides sales and marketing services to manufacturers of Consumer Packaged Goods, sold generally through grocery, drug and mass merchant stores.
President: James Leeper
Year Founded: 1987
Estimated Sales: $20-50 Million
Number Employees: 100-249
Parent Co: Louis F Leeper

22712 (HQ)Food Pak Corp
2300 Palm Ave
San Mateo, CA 94403-1817

650-341-6559
Fax: 650-341-2110
Chili seasonings, board and food coatings; manufacturer and exporter of custom packaging products including flexible X-ray film, insulated and sandwich bags, containers, folding cartons, shopping bags, flexible packaging bags, paper &foil bags
CEO: Steve Kanaga
Estimated Sales: Less Than $500,000
Number Employees: 1-4
Square Footage: 14000
Type of Packaging: Food Service, Private Label, Bulk
Brands:
A.B. Curry's
Hyfroydol
Safety Pak

Scoop It
Sta-Hot
Zest

22713 Food Plant Companies
15945 N 76th Street
Scottsdale, AZ 85260-1781

480-991-6534
Fax: 480-991-1243

22714 Food Plant Engineering
PO Box 9906
Yakima, WA 98909-0906

509-248-5530
Fax: 509-453-3008

Meat industry services: architects and engineers, building and construction consultants, temperature controls, refrigerated structures and refrigeration systems

22715 Food Plant Engineering
10816 Millington Ct # 110
Cincinnati, OH 45242-4025

513-488-8888
Fax: 513-641-0057
mail@foodplantengineering.com
www.foodplantengineering.com

We specialize in facility design, engineering, architectural and construction management services for expansions, renovations and new construction. We provide master planning, production capacity studies, plant flow investigationprocess and equipment layouts, process design, lean manufacturing principle implementation and process simulation analysis. We offer a variety of project formats including competitive bidding, construction management and design build
President: Mark Redmond
Marketing Director: Jennifer Redmond
Project Manager: Michael Cowgill
Estimated Sales: D
Number Employees: 10-19

22716 Food Processing Concepts
4212 Happy Valley Cir
Newnan, GA 30263

628-478-4700
www.foodprocessingconcepts.com
Equipment for food industry used in the production process
Sales: David McKinney

22717 Food Processing Equipment Co
13623 Pumice St
Santa Fe Springs, CA 90670-5105

562-802-3727
Fax: 562-802-8621 salesark@fpec.com
www.fpec.com

Manufacturer and exporter of food processing and material handling equipment including vacuum tumblers, blenders and mixers, chilled massage blenders, conveyors, dumpers, screw conveyors, cart lifts, screw loaders, vacuum hoppers, openblenders and mixers, etc
Owner: Alan Davison
Sales Manager: Larry Butler
Estimated Sales: $5-10 Million
Number Employees: 1-4
Square Footage: 72000

22718 Food Processors Institute
1350 I St NW # 300
Washington, DC 20005-3377

202-393-0890
Fax: 202-639-5932 800-355-0983
Non-profit association that provides education for food processors and affiliated industries
CEO: Cal Dooley
Contact: Carla Mitchell
cmitchell@fpa-food.org
Executive Director: Lisa Weddnig
Number Employees: 1-4

22719 Food Products Lab
12003 NE Ainsworth Cir # 105
Portland, OR 97220-9034

503-253-9136
Fax: 503-253-9019 800-375-9555
www.fplabs.com

Manager: Nidel Kahl
Quality Control: Nadil Kahl
Estimated Sales: $3-5 Million
Number Employees: 20-49

22720 Food Resources International
250 Rayette Rd.
Units 13 & 14
Concord, ON L4K 2G6
Canada

905-482-8967
Fax: 905-482-8968 ifr@rogers.com
Manufacturer and exporter of food processing equipment including dairy machinery, membrane systems and spray dryers; also, reconditioned equipment available; importer of casein and whey and milk protein concentrates
President: Jon Chesnut
VP: Karen Chesnut
Number Employees: 10-19

22721 Food Safety Net Services Ltd
199 W Rhapsody Dr
San Antonio, TX 78216-3105

210-308-0675
Fax: 210-525-1702 888-525-9788
tcornett@food-safetynet.com www.fsns.com
Laboratory specializing in microbiological, nutritional, and chemical analysis, consulting and auditing, education and training
President: Gina R. Bellinger
CEO: John W. Bellinger
CFO/COO: Alan W. Uecker
VP of Operations: Dr. Randal Garrett
Quality Control: Micheal Devine
Marketing Director: Tesa Cornett
Business Development Manager: Tim Deary
Business Development Manager: Tony Nguyen
Lead Special Scientist: Amit Morey PhD
Estimated Sales: Below $5 Million
Number Employees: 50-99
Square Footage: 24000
Type of Packaging: Food Service
Other Locations:
  Food Safety Net Services
  Richardson TX

22722 Food Sanitation Svc Inc
64 Fulton St # 702
New York, NY 10038-2752

212-732-9540
Fax: 212-608-7862
Consultant specializing in food sanitation and safety
President: Barbara Kleiner
bkleiner@food-san.com
CEO: Martin Muchanic
CFO: Barbara Kleiner
Estimated Sales: $1-2.5 Million
Number Employees: 10-19

22723 Food Scene
P.O.Box 459
Colts Neck, NJ 07722

732-431-1132
Fax: 732-577-8445
Owner: Barry Kahn
Contact: John Pauciullo
jpauciullo@foodscene.com
Estimated Sales: $20-50 Million
Number Employees: 10-19

22724 Food Science Associates
PO Box 525
Crugers, NY 10521-0525

914-739-7541
Fax: 914-739-7541
Consultant providing product development, nutritional labeling, culinary assistance, regulatory compliance, etc
VP: Frank del Valle
Estimated Sales: $1-5 Million
Number Employees: 14

22725 Food Science Consulting
PO Box 30992
Walnut Creek, CA 94598-7992

925-947-6785
Fax: 925-947-2811 www.foodonline.com
Consultant for product formulation and development, process development, plant implementation, recipe development, food styling and commercialization of recipes
President: Dorothy Keefer
Number Employees: 1

22726 Food Service Equipment Corporation
727 Del Prado Boulevard N
Cape Coral, FL 33909-2254

941-574-7767
New and used hotel restaurant, deli, cafeteria equipment and heavy duty equipment and small wares
President: J Furdell
Estimated Sales: $500,000-$1 Million
Number Employees: 4

22727 Food Tech Structures LLC
10 Crescent Rd
Riverside, CT 06878

203-637-2471
Fax: 203-637-2527 800-880-0118

22728 Food Technologies
10001 Wayzata Boulevard
Golden Valley, MN 55405

763-544-8586
Fax: 763-544-0999
Consultant specializing in food product development, program design and marketing for food processors
President: William Drier, Ph.D.
Marketer: C Carroll Hicks
Production Developer: Gene Monroe
Number Employees: 3
Square Footage: 4000

22729 Food Technology Corporation
45921 Maries Rd
Suite 120
Sterling, VA 20166-9278

703-444-1870
Fax: 703-444-9860 info@foodtechcorp.com
www.foodtechcorp.com
Manufacturer and exporter of food texture testing systems and measurement equipment including texture profile analysis, pea tenderometers, peak force measurement systems, and kramer shear press
President: Shirl Lakeway
srkim@mcik.co.kr
Estimated Sales: $3 Million
Number Employees: 5
Square Footage: 6000
Brands:
  Kramer Shear Press
  Tenderometers
  Tenore Measurement Equipment

22730 Food Tools
315 Laguna St
Santa Barbara, CA 93101-1716

805-962-8383
Fax: 805-966-3614 877-836-6386
www.foodtools.com
Manufacturer and exporter of de-panners, cake slabbers, crumb spreaders and ultrasonic slicers and mechanical slicers
Owner: Marty Grano
martyg@foodtools.com
Vice President: Mike Christenson
Vice President: Doug Petrovich
VP of Engineering: Matt Browne
VP of Production: Gary Grand
Estimated Sales: $5-10 Million
Number Employees: 20-49
Square Footage: 78000

22731 Food Tools
315 Laguna St
Santa Barbara, CA 93101-1716

805-962-8383
Fax: 805-966-3614 877-836-6386
www.foodtools.com
Owner: Marty Grano
martyg@foodtools.com
Chairman of the Board: Martin Grano
Estimated Sales: $5-10 Million
Number Employees: 20-49

22732 Food Warming Equipment Co
338 Memorial Dr # 300
Crystal Lake, IL 60014-6262

815-444-6394
Fax: 815-459-7989 800-222-4393
www.fwe.com
Manufacturer and exporter of stainless steel heated and refrigerated utility carts and mobile cabinets

President: Chuck Deck
c-deck@fweco.net
CEO: Deron Lichte
CFO: Chris Huffman
VP Marketing/Sales: Curt Benson
Estimated Sales: $5-10 Million
Number Employees: 50-99
Square Footage: 280000
Brands:
　Prm-Ii (Prime Rib Master)
　Weather-All Bars

22733　Food and Dairy ResearchAssociates
107 Homer St
Commerce, GA 30529-1859

706-335-9703
Fax: 706-335-9704

Owner: Steve Green
Estimated Sales: $.5-1 000,000
Number Employees: 5-9

22734　Food-Tek
9 Whippany Rd Bldg C-2
Whippany, NJ 7981

973-257-4000
Fax: 973-257-5555　800-648-8114
info@foodtek.com www.foodtek.com
Consultant specializing in product development services for food manufacturers
President: Gilbert Finkel
CFO: Gilbert Finkel
Vice President: Victor Davila
R&D: Gilbert Finkel
Quality Control: Gilbert Finkel
Estimated Sales: $5-10 Million
Number Employees: 5-9
Square Footage: 10000

22735　FoodHandler
2301 Lunt Avenue
Elk Grove Village, IL 60007

516-338-4433
Fax: 516-338-4405　800-338-4433
www.foodhandler.com
Disposable gloves, aprons, hair restraints, bibs, worker protection and food safety training
Contact: Don Allegretti
dallegretti@foodhandler.com
Number Employees: 20-49

22736　FoodLogiQ
2655 Meridian Pkwy.
Durham, NC 27713

866-492-4468
info@foodlogiq.com www.foodlogiq.com
Solutions for all sectors of the food industry, including compliance and regulations, supplier management, recall management, safety and quality control, and blockchain management.
CEO: Sean O'Leary
CFO: Faith Kosobucki
Chief Marketing & Strategy Officer: Katy Jones
VP, Sales: Julie Hepner
Chief Product Officer: Todd Dolinsky
Year Founded: 2006
Number Employees: 80-200

22737　Foodchek Systems
1414　8 St SW
Suite 450
Calgary, AB T2R 1J6
Canada

403-269-9424
Fax: 403-263-6357　877-298-0208
info@foodcheksystems.com
www.foodcheksystems.com
Supplier of food safety pathogen tests
President: William Hogan
Estimated Sales: $500,000- 1 Million
Number Employees: 8

22738　Fooddesign Machinery & Systems
29103 SW Kinsman Rd
Wilsonville, OR 97070-8701

503-685-5030
Fax: 503-685-5034 sales@foodesign.com
President: Joseph Mistretta
joe.mistretta@foodesign.com
Estimated Sales: $5-10 Million
Number Employees: 1-4

22739　Fooddesign Machinery & Systems
29103 SW Kinsman Rd
PO Box 2449
Wilsonville, OR 97070-8701

503-685-5030
Fax: 503-685-5034 sales@foodesign.com
Supplier of heavy-duty precision built cooking and processing machines
President: Joseph Mistretta
joe.mistretta@foodesign.com
Sales Executive: Daniel Luna
Number Employees: 1-4

22740　Foodmark, Inc.
180 Linden Street
Wellesley, MA 02482

781-237-7088
Fax: 781-237-7455　800-535-3447
ggavris@foodmark.com
Offers prospective clients a variety of brand development and sales management possibilties, as well as capital investment opportunities when necessary.
Partner: George Gavris
Partner: Rob Simmons
Partner: Lee Gavris
Contact: George Banis
gbanis@foodmark.com
Estimated Sales: $950 Thousand
Number Employees: 10

22741　(HQ)Foodpro International
P.O.Box 1119
Stockton, CA 95202

209-943-8400
Fax: 408-227-4908　888-687-5797
bwashburn@foodpro.net www.foodpro.net
Consultant provides engineering services including studies, plans and specifications development, construction and equipment installation management; exporter of fruit fly extermination systems
President: M W Washburn
CEO: M Wm Washburn
CFO: Lou Kong
Research & Development: Olga Osipova
Marketing Director: Richard Jennings
Branch Manager: Alex Tarasov
Estimated Sales: $1-3 Million
Number Employees: 12

22742　Foods Research Laboratories
130 Newmarket Sq # 3
Boston, MA 02118-2675

617-442-3322
Fax: 617-442-2013
Laboratory providing microbiological and chemical analysis of food and nutrition labeling; also, consultant services include plant sanitation, quality control and HACCP audits and verifications
Owner: Andrea Fontaine
Lab Director: Andrea Fontaine
Chemist: Regina Pierce
Estimated Sales: Less than $500,000
Number Employees: 1-4

22743　Foodservice ConsultantsSociety International
P.O. Box 4961
Louisville, KY 40204

502-379-4122
Info@fcsi.org
www.fcsi.org
Promotion professionalism in foodservice and hospitality consulting.
President: Mr. Jonathan Doughty
Secretary, Treasurer: James Petersen
Estimated Sales: $5-10 Million
Number Employees: 50-99

22744　Foodservice Design Associates
10207 General Dr
Orlando, FL 32824-8529

407-896-4115
Fax: 407-895-7022
p.bean@foodservice-design.com
www.foodservice-design.com
Consultant specializing in architectural design and specification services for the food service industry
Principal: Philip Bean
Estimated Sales: $150,000
Number Employees: 1-4

22745　Foodservice East
197　8th St # 728
Charlestown, MA 02129-4234

617-242-2217
Fax: 617-742-5938　800-852-5212
susan@foodserviceeast.com
www.foodserviceeast.com
Estimated Sales: Less Than $500,000
Number Employees: 1-4

22746　Foodservice Equipment &pplie
110 Schiller
Suite 312
Elmhurst, IL 60126

847-390-2010
Fax: 800-630-4169　800-630-4168
maureen@zoombagroup.com www.fesmag.com
Contact: Cindy Cardinal
cindy@zoombagroup.com

22747　Foodservice Equipment Distributors Association
2250 Point Boulevard
Suite 200
Elgin, IL 60123

224-293-6500
Fax: 224-293-6505 feda@feda.com
www.feda.com
Trade association for foodservice and supplies dealers.
President: Brad Pierce
Executive Vice President: Raymond W. Herrick
Secretary: Jay Ringelheim
Number Employees: 5-9

22748　Foodservice Innovation Network
335 North River Street
Batavia, IL 60510

630-879-3006
Fax: 630-879-3014 info@airesconsulting.com

22749　Foodworks
400 N 4th Street
La Grange, KY 40031-1512

502-222-0135
Fax: 502-222-0135 easyhaccp@aol.com
Consultant providing HACCP training, food safety seminars, food plant sanitation and food safety auditing
President: Dotty Heady
Executive VP: Kazmer Wolkensperg
Number Employees: 4

22750　Foote & Jenks
1420 Crestmont Ave
Camden, NJ 08103-3182

856-966-0700
Fax: 856-966-6137
President: Castro Alexander
castro@footeandjenks.com
Estimated Sales: $20-50 Million
Number Employees: 10-19

22751　For Life
1811 W Mahalo Pl
Compton, CA 90220-5429

310-638-6386
Fax: 310-638-6305 info@forlifedesign.com
www.forlifedesign.com
Accessories/suplies i.e. picnic baskets, cooking implements,/housewares.
President: Masa Fujii
masa@forlifedesign.com
Number Employees: 5-9

22752　Foran Spice Inc
7616 S 6th St
P.O. Box 109
Oak Creek, WI 53154-2049

414-764-1220
Fax: 414-764-8803　800-558-6030
email@asenzya.com www.asenzya.com
Re-cleaned and sterilized spices, custom engineered seasonings, and value-added food products
President: Patty Goto
patty.goto@foranspice.com
CFO: Andy Gitter
Vice President: Joy Hauser
VP of Business Development & Marketing: Chris Anderson
VP Sales: Paul Duddleston
Engineer: Alan Goto

Estimated Sales: $19 Million
Number Employees: 100-249
Square Footage: 213000
Type of Packaging: Food Service, Private Label, Bulk

22753 Forbes Industries
1933 E Locust St
Ontario, CA 91761-7608

909-923-4549
Fax: 909-923-1969 sales@forbesindustries.com
www.forbesindustries.com
Manufacturer and exporter of banquet cabinets and carts, tables, sign stands, boards, easels, bins, carts, menus, etc.; also, bars including salad, soup and portable.
President: Tim Sweetland
tsweetland@forbesindustries.com
Estimated Sales: $50-100 Million
Number Employees: 100-249

22754 Forbes Products Corp
45 High Tech Dr
Rush, NY 14543-9746

585-334-4800
Fax: 585-334-6180 800-316-5235
www.forbesproducts.com
Customized vinyl office products and promotional items including pocket planners, binders, desk and carrying portfolios, proposal covers, clear envelopes and business card holders
President: Jim Mcdermott
jmcdermott@forbesproducts.com
VP Sales: Rick Blowers
Estimated Sales: $2.5-5 Million
Number Employees: 10-19
Square Footage: 300000

22755 (HQ)Forbo Siegling LLC
12201 Vanstory Dr
Huntersville, NC 28078-8395

704-948-0800
Fax: 704-948-0995 800-255-5581
siegling.us@forbo.com www.forbo.com
Transilon conveyor belts, extremultus flat transmission belts, transfer conveyor belting, prolink plastic modular belts, proposition high-efficiency timing belts and other related products specifically designed for the food andbeverage industry.
President: Wayne Hoffman
VP Sales/Marketing: John Casal
Research & Development: Jay Leighton
Quality Control: Natalie Deal
Marketing Director: Kitty Spence
National Sales Manager: Dany Bearden
Contact: Stacy Bennett
stacy.bennett@forbo.com
VP Production: Chris Flannigan
Number Employees: 500-999
Square Footage: 200000
Other Locations:
Siegling America
Wood Dale IL
Siegling America
Englewood NJ
Siegling America
Fullerton CA
Siegling America
Manteca CA
Siegling America
Kansas City MO
Siegling America
Mobile AL
Siegling America
Stone Mountain GA
Siegling America
Mansfield TX
Brands:
Extremultus
Transilon
Transtex

22756 Foreign Candy Company
1 Foreign Candy Dr
Hull, IA 51239-7499

712-439-1496
Fax: 712-439-3207 800-831-8541
www.foreigncandy.com
Developer and distributor of candy.
CEO, President & Owner: Peter De Yager
VP, Marketing & Sales: Bill Lange
HR Manager: Bethany Bosma
Estimated Sales: $5-10 Million
Number Employees: 11-50
Type of Packaging: Private Label

Brands:
Mega Warheads
Rips Toll

22757 Foreman Group
P.O.Box 189
Zelienople, PA 16063

724-452-9690
Fax: 724-452-0136 www.foremangroup.com
Owner: Phil Foreman
Contact: Mark Follen
m.follen@foremangroup.com
Estimated Sales: $10-20 Million
Number Employees: 50-99

22758 Foremost Machine Builders Inc
23 Spielman Rd
Fairfield, NJ 07004-3488

973-227-0700
Fax: 973-227-7307 sales@foremostmachine.com
Manufacturer and exporter of plastic scrap recovery and bulk material handling systems
President: Marlene Heydenreich
mheydenreich@foremostmachine.com
VP/General Manager: Clifford Weinpel
Assistant Sales Manager: Drew Schmid
Estimated Sales: $10-20 Million
Number Employees: 50-99
Square Footage: 110000

22759 Forest Manufacturing Co
1665 Enterprise Pkwy
Twinsburg, OH 44087-2284

330-425-3805
Fax: 330-425-9604
Manufacturer/exporter of flags, pennants, banners, pressure-sensitive product markings and decals
President: Forest Bookman
CFO: Bob Briggs
Sales Manager: Dick Dragonnette
General Manager: John Hammons
Estimated Sales: $20-30 Million
Number Employees: 50-99
Square Footage: 135000

22760 Formaticum
165 Court Street
Apt 104
Brooklyn, NY 11201

503-922-3866
Fax: 503-389-7675 800-830-0317
mark@formaticum.com www.formaticum.com
Accessories/supplies i.e. picninc baskets, cooking implements/housewares, dispaly fixtures, specialty food packaging i.e. gift wrap/labels/boxes/containers.
Marketing: Mark Goldman
Contact: Mark Goldman
mark@formaticum.com

22761 Formation Systems
144 Turnpike Rd Ste 310
Southborough, MA 01772

508-303-6200
Fax: 508-303-6250 info@formationsystems.com
www.formationsystems.com
A provider of product lifecycle management solutions for process manufacturing companies. Info, a large software provider has acquired this company
President: Trent Landreth
CFO: Leo Casey
Contact: G Casey
g.casey@formationsystems.com
Estimated Sales: $10-20 Million
Number Employees: 60
Parent Co: Infor

22762 Formel Industries
2355 N. 25th Ave
Franklin Park, IL 60131

847-455-3300
Fax: 847-928-9655 800-373-3300
www.formelinc.com
Cellophane bags
President: Don O' Malley
Sales/ Marketing: Sam O'Malley
Plant Manager: Mike Cinquepalmi
Estimated Sales: $5-10 Million
Number Employees: 20-49

22763 Former Tech
9367 Winkler Drive
Houston, TX 77017-5915

713-944-5336
Fax: 713-944-2194 800-843-8914
President and CEO: Ron Hokanson
Estimated Sales: $5-10 Million
Number Employees: 25

22764 Formers By Ernie
7905 Almeda Genoa Rd # B
Suite B
Houston, TX 77075-2007

713-991-3455
Fax: 713-991-0048 866-991-3455
www.formersbyernie.net
Metal and aluminum bag formers and packaging machinery equipment
President: Ernie Sanchez
sales@formersbyernie.com
CFO: Terry Sanchez
Quality Control: Ernie Jr Sanchez
R&D: Dennis Kokkins
Estimated Sales: $2 000,000
Number Employees: 10-19

22765 Formers of Houston
3533 Preston Ave
Pasadena, TX 77505

281-998-9570
Fax: 281-998-9692 800-468-5224
info@formers.com www.formers.com
Packaging machinery parts
President: John Dominguez Jr
Vice President: John Dominguez
Quality Control: Chico Marquez
Sales Director: Patty O'Neal
Contact: Cynthia Alaniz
cynthia@formers.com
Production Manager: Ben Dominguez
Estimated Sales: $5-10 000,000
Number Employees: 20-49
Square Footage: 9500
Type of Packaging: Consumer

22766 Formflex
70 N Main St
Bloomingdale, IN 47832

765-498-8900
Fax: 765-498-5200 800-255-7659
de@formflexsales.com
www.formflexproducts.com
Manufacturer and exporter of polyolefin sheets, signs, and packaging
CEO: Martha Alexander
kwformflex@bloomingdaletel.com
CEO: Brent Thompson
Marketing Director: David Elliott
Sales Director: Brent Thompson
Public Relations: Janice Stewart
Estimated Sales: $10-20 Million
Number Employees: 250-499
Square Footage: 60000
Parent Co: Futurex Industries
Type of Packaging: Bulk
Brands:
Formflex

22767 Formost Packaging Machines
19211 144th Ave NE
Woodinville, WA 98072

425-483-9090
Fax: 425-486-5656 sales@formostfuji.com
Manufacturer and exporter of high-speed automated horizontal and vertical bagging and wrapping machines including formers/fillers/sealers
President: Norm Formo
normf@formostpkg.com
CFO: Dan Semanskee
Executive VP: Norm Formo
VP Sales: Dennis Gunnell
Plant Manager: Al Shelton
Purchasing Manager: Michelle Richards
Number Employees: 50-99
Type of Packaging: Consumer, Food Service, Private Label, Bulk

22768 Formula Espresso
65 Commerce Street
Brooklyn, NY 11231-1642

718-834-8724
Fax: 718-834-9022 www.espressosystems.com
Manufacturer and exporter of commercial stainless steel espresso equipment

Owner: George Ilardo
Estimated Sales: $1-2.5 Million
Number Employees: 5-9
Type of Packaging: Food Service
Brands:
  Formula

22769 Formulator Software, LLC
28 Center St
Clinton, NJ 08809-2635

908-735-2248
Fax: 908-236-7865 jdegroff@formulatorus.com
www.formulatorus.com
Offering barcode solutions and products including
route accounting softwareand implementation, ware-
house management software and wireless
integration.
Managing Partner: James Degroff
Technical Manager: C Womer
Research & Development: C Longfield
Estimated Sales: $1-3 Million
Number Employees: 12
Number of Brands: 20
Number of Products: 8000
Brands:
  Eltron
  Hhp
  Symbol
  Zebra

22770 Forpack
16905 Neill Path
Hastings, MN 55033-8743

651-438-2115
Fax: 651-437-8755
President: Loyd Lowweden
CFO: Loyd Lowweden
Quality Control: Dave Lege
Estimated Sales: $3-5 Million
Number Employees: 10

22771 Forpak
16901 Neill Path
Hastings, MN 55033-8743

651-438-2115
Fax: 651-437-8755
President: Lloyd Lodewegen
CFO: Suzanne Lloyd
Estimated Sales: $1-2.5 000,000
Number Employees: 7

22772 Forrest Engraving Company
92 1st St
New Rochelle, NY 10801-6121

914-632-9892
Fax: 914-632-7416
Manufacturer and exporter of plastic and metal
nameplates and signs
President: Thomas Giordano
tom@forrestpermasigns.com
Manager: Tom Giordano
Estimated Sales: $500,000-$1 Million
Number Employees: 5 to 9

22773 Forster & Son
1900 B St
Ada, OK 74820-2831

580-332-6021
Fax: 580-332-6021
Flour and feed mill machinery; also, custom steel
fabrication, steel perforation and mining equipment
Owner: John Forster
jforster40@hotmail.com
Estimated Sales: Less Than $500,000
Number Employees: 1-4

22774 Fort Dearborn Company
1530 Morse Ave
Elk Grove, IL 60007

847-357-9500
Fax: 847-357-8726 info@fortdearborn.com
www.fortdearborn.com
Label supplier
CEO: Kevin Kwilinski
CFO: Timothy Trahey
COO: Bill Johnstone
Year Founded: 1925
Estimated Sales: $526 Million
Number Employees: 1,675

22775 Fort James Canada
137 Bentworth Avenue
Toronto, ON M6A 1P6
Canada

416-784-1621
Fax: 416-789-0170
Disposable cups including paper, plastic and foam
National Sales Manager: Phil Wahl
Number Employees: 500-999
Parent Co: James River Corporation

22776 Fort Lock Corporation
3000 River Road
River Grove, IL 60171-1097

708-456-1100
Fax: 708-456-9476
Manufacturing, electronic and mechanical locks for
the vending industry
President: Jay Fine
VP: Gary Myers
Estimated Sales: $10-20 000,000
Number Employees: 3

22777 Fort Wayne Awning
7105 Ardmore Ave
Fort Wayne, IN 46809-9541

260-478-1636
Fax: 260-747-0466 800-404-1636
mccawning@aol.com www.fortwayneawning.com
Commercial awnings
Owner: Mel Mc Clain
mccawning@aol.com
Estimated Sales: Below $5,000,000
Number Employees: 5-9

22778 Forte Technology
58 Norfolk Ave.
Suite 4
South Easton, MA 02375-1055

508-297-2363
Fax: 508-297-2314 info@forte-tec.com
www.forte-tec.com
Manufacturer and exporter of electronic moisture
measurement systems
President: Patricia White
Contact: Tom Gorman
t.gorman@forte-tec.com
Plant Manager: Mark Donohowski
Estimated Sales: $2.5-5 Million
Number Employees: 5-9
Square Footage: 28000
Brands:
  Forte

22779 Fortenberry Mini-Storage
3128 Fortenberry Rd
Kodak, TN 37764-2020

865-933-2568
Fax: 865-933-2568
Ice
President: Arvil Fortenberry
arvil@fortenberrymm.com
Estimated Sales: Less Than $500,000
Number Employees: 1-4

22780 Fortifiber Building Systs Grp
300 Industrial Dr
Fernley, NV 89408-8905

775-575-5557
Fax: 775-333-6411 800-773-4777
buildingproducts@fortifiber.com
www.fortifiber.com
Paper bags, building papers and linings
Manager: Bill Rieger
CEO: Stuart Yount
syount@fortifiber.com
Plant Manager: Greg Hobbs
Estimated Sales: $5-10 Million
Number Employees: 10-19
Brands:
  Fibreen Economy
  Super Bar

22781 Fortress Technology
51 Grand Marshall Drive
Scarborough, ON M1B 5N6
Canada

416-754-2898
Fax: 416-754-2976 888-220-8737
sales@fortresstechnology.com
www.fortresstechnology.com

Fortress Technology is a world leader in the design
and manufacture of the highest quality metal detec-
tor systems for the food processing, material han-
dling and packaging operations.
President: Steve Gidman
Marketing Director: Adam Lang
Sales Director: Steve Mason
Number Employees: 60
Number of Brands: 4
Number of Products: 20

22782 Fortress Technology
51 Grand Marshall Dr
Toronto, ON M1B 5N6
Canada

416-754-2898
Fax: 416-754-2976 888-220-8737
info@fortresstechnology.com
www.fortresstechnology.com
Food safety detector equipment

22783 Fortune Plastics, Inc
P.O Box 637
Williams Ln.
Old Saybrook, CT 06475
Fax: 860-388-9930 800-243-0306
Manufacturer and exporter of plastic bags
Contact: Jay Adamski
jadamski@fortuneplastics.com
Estimated Sales: $5-10 Million
Number Employees: 20-49
Parent Co: Hilex Poly Co. LLC

22784 Fortune Products Inc
2010 Windy Ter # A
Cedar Park, TX 78613-4559

512-249-0334
Fax: 830-693-6394 contact@accusharp.com
www.accusharp.com
Manufacturer and exporter of manually operated
knife and scissor sharpeners
President: Jay Cavanaugh
info@accusharp.com
VP: Dale Fortenberry Jr
Operations: Randy Fortenberry
Estimated Sales: Less Than $500,000
Number Employees: 5-9
Square Footage: 13000
Type of Packaging: Consumer, Food Service, Pri-
  vate Label, Bulk
Brands:
  Accusharp
  Sharp 'n' Easy
  Shear Sharp

22785 Fort, Products
4801 Main St
Suite 205
Kansas City, MO 64112

816-741-3000
www.forteproducts.com
Retail fixtures for the food service industry
CFO: Scott Morris

22786 Forum Lighting
900 Old Freeport Rd
Pittsburgh, PA 15238-3130

412-781-5970
Fax: 412-244-9032 www.forumlighting.com
Manufacturer and exporter of fluorescent and HID
linear lighting; custom designs available
Special Projects: Paula Garret
Controller: Julie McElhattan
Senior VP: Jonathan Garret
Special Projects: Paula Garret
Vice President of Sales: Steve Seligman
Plant Manager: Bill Dapper
Estimated Sales: $20-50 Million
Number Employees: 20-49
Square Footage: 70000

22787 Foss Nirsystems
12101 Tech Rd
Silver Spring, MD 20904-1915

301-755-5200
Fax: 301-236-0134
Manufacturer and exporter of rapid quality control
analysis equipment including moisture, fat, protein
and sugar for laboratory and in-plant application using near infrared technology
IT Executive: Dan Cipriaso
dcipriaso@foss.dk
IT Executive: Dan Cipriaso
dcipriaso@foss.dk

Estimated Sales: $20 Million
Number Employees: 1-4

22788 Foster Farms Inc.
1000 Davis St.
PO Box 306
Livingston, CA 95334

800-255-7227
www.fosterfarms.com
Poultry producer.
CEO: Dan Huber
Estimated Sales: Over $1 Billion
Number Employees: 10000+
Number of Brands: 6
Type of Packaging: Consumer, Food Service, Private Label, Bulk
Brands:
Foster Farms Fresh & Natural
Foster Farms Naturally Seasoned
Foster Farms Simply Raised
Foster Farms Organic
Foster Farms Always Natural
Foster Farms Saut, Ready

22789 Foster Forbes Glass
E Charles St
Marion, IN 46952

765-668-1200
Fax: 765-668-1389
Glass containers
Sr. VP Sales/Marketing: R Deneau
VP Operations/Service: J Fordham
Manager of Purchasing: T Moreland
Estimated Sales: $1-2.5 Million
Number Employees: 5-9
Parent Co: American National Can Company

22790 Foster Miller Inc
350 2nd Ave
Waltham, MA 02451-1196

781-684-4000
Fax: 781-290-0693 www.qinetiq-na.com
Custom food processing and vending equipment; design services available engineering and R&D services from 200+ engineers and scienctists
President: Michael G. Stolarik
CEO: Duane P. Andrews
Executive VP: David Shrum
david.shrum@qinetiq-na.com
Marketing: Peter Debakker
Number Employees: 20-49
Square Footage: 380000

22791 Foster Refrigerator Corporation
PO Box 718
Kinderhook, NY 12106

518-828-3311
Fax: 518-828-3315 888-828-3311
fosterusa@yahoo.com www.foster-us.com
Manufacturer and exporter of commercial refrigerators, freezers, coolers and ovens
Owner: James Dinardi
Estimated Sales: $1-5 Million
Number Employees: 1-4
Square Footage: 200000
Type of Packaging: Food Service
Brands:
Fosters

22792 Foster-Forbes Glass Company
4855 E 52nd Pl
Vernon, CA 90058

323-562-5100
Fax: 323-560-4165 800-767-4527
www.sgcontainers.com
Glass bottles
Plant Manager: Art Jones
Estimated Sales: $1-5 Million
Number Employees: 250-499
Parent Co: Sant' Gobian

22793 Fotel
1125 E St Charles Rd Ste 100
Lombard, IL 60148-2085

630-932-7520
Fax: 630-932-7610 800-834-4920
Bar code film masters, pre-printed bar code labels and equipment, RFID systems for manufacturing bar code verifiers.
President: John Nachtries
CEO: John Nachtrieb
Marketing Director: Beverly Nachtries
Operations Manager: Kevin Sousa
Plant Manager: Cathy Letza

Estimated Sales: $2.5-5 Million
Number Employees: 20-49
Square Footage: 40000

22794 Foth & Van Dyke
P.O.Box 19012
Green Bay, WI 54307-9012

920-497-2500
Fax: 920-497-8516 foth@foth.com
www.foth.com
Consultant for custom machine development and design, packaging line layout and design and modifications and upgrades to lines and equipment
CEO: Tim Weyenberg
CEO: Tim Weyenberg
Contact: Dorothi Cummings
dcummings@foth.com
Estimated Sales: $50 Million
Number Employees: 250-499

22795 Fountainhead
1726 Woodhaven Drive
Bensalem, PA 19020-7108

215-245-7300
Fax: 215-245-7390 800-326-8998
info@towelettes.com www.towelettes.com
Manufacturer and exporter of stainless steel beverage dispensers, fountains, hoods and fans
General Manager: Ralph Kearney
Number Employees: 50-99
Parent Co: Floaire

22796 Four Corners Ice
801 W Arrington St
Farmington, NM 87401-5530

505-325-3813
Ice
Owner: Shirley Whipple
Estimated Sales: $500,000-$1 Million
Number Employees: 5-9

22797 Four M Manufacturing Group
210 San Jose Avenue
San Jose, CA 95125-1033

408-998-1141
www. four m manufacturing.com
Paper products including plates, cups, partitions and corrugated cardboard boxes
President: Dennis Mechiel
Owner: Frank Martinez
Executive VP: Peter Mechiel
Estimated Sales: Less than $500,000
Number Employees: 4

22798 Four Seasons Produce Inc
400 Wabash Rd
PO Box 788
Ephrata, PA 17522-9100

717-721-2800
Fax: 717-721-2597 800-422-8384
www.sunrisetransportinc.com
Fruits and vegetables
Owner: David Hollinger
VP Finance: Loretta Radanovic
Quality Manager: Daniel Oloro
National Sales Manager: Stan Paluszewski
davidh@fsproduce.com
VP/General Manager: Rob Kurtz
Number Employees: 500-999
Square Footage: 261000

22799 Four Star Beef
Omaha, NE

www.fourstarbeef.com
Beef
Parent Co: JBS USA, LLC.
Other Locations:
Tolleson AZ
Green Bay WI
Plainwell MI
Souderton PA

22800 Fourinox Inc
1015 Centennial St
Green Bay, WI 54304-5562

920-336-0621
Fax: 920-336-0089 www.fourcorp.com
Manufacturer and exporter of ASME certified process vessels
President: Ben Meeuwsen
ben.meeuwsen@fourinox.com
Marketing/Sales: John Ruppel
Estimated Sales: $10-20 Million
Number Employees: 20-49
Square Footage: 110000

22801 Fowler Products Co LLC
150 Collins Industrial Blvd
Athens, GA 30601-1516

706-549-3300
Fax: 706-548-1278 877-549-3301
sales@fowlerproducts.com
www.fowlerproducts.com
Manufacturer and exporter of bottling, capping and packaging machinery
President: Don Cotney
Vice President: Randy Uebler
ruebler@fowlerproducts.com
VP Sales: Andy Monroe
Estimated Sales: Less Than $500,000
Number Employees: 1-4
Square Footage: 150000

22802 Fox Brush Company
29 Tiger Hill Road
Oxford, ME 4270

207-539-2208
Fax: 207-539-2208
Wholesaler/distributor of corn, road, push and street sweeper brooms and brushes; manufacturer of specialty brushes
Owner: Linda Cushman
Manager: Thomas Cushman
Estimated Sales: Below $5 Million
Number Employees: 1

22803 Fox Iv Technologies
6011 Enterprise Dr
Export, PA 15632-8969

724-387-3500
Fax: 724-387-3516 877-436-2434
www.foxiv.com
Labels and packing supplies
President/CEO: Rick Fox
Estimated Sales: $10-20 Million
Number Employees: 20-49

22804 Fox Stamp Sign & Specialty
618 W Airport Rd
Menasha, WI 54952-1407

920-725-2683
Fax: 920-725-2037 office@foxstamp.com
www.foxstamp.com
Rubber and pre-inked stamps, daters, stamp pads, inks, engraved signs and badges, notary and other embossers; also, advertising and political buttons
Owner: Jon Ceninger
jon@foxstamp.com
Sales Director: Steve Kryscio
Production Manager: Jason Burmeister
Purchasing Manager: Deb Zuck
Estimated Sales: Below $5 Million
Number Employees: 5-9
Square Footage: 4400
Parent Co: Fox Stamp, Sign & Specialty

22805 Fox Valley Wood Products Inc
W811 State Highway 96
Kaukauna, WI 54130-9653

920-766-4069
Fax: 920-766-1220
jeff@foxvalleywoodproducts.com
www.foxvalleywoodproducts.com
Pallets, crates and boxes
President: Dale Van Zeeland
jeff@foxvalleywoodproducts.com
VP: Dale Van Zeeland
Sales Manager/ Design/ Customer Service: Jeff Van Zeeland
Plant Manager: Travis Van Zeeland
Purchasing Manager/ Controller: Dale Van Zeeland
Estimated Sales: $1-2.5 Million
Number Employees: 20-49

22806 Fox-Morris Associates
9140 Arrow Point Boulevard
Suite 380
Charlotte, NC 28273-8140

704-522-8244
Fax: 704-529-1465 800-777-6503
Executive search firm specializing in the bakery and food industry
VP Executive Search: Toni Marie
Estimated Sales: $500,000-$1,000,000
Number Employees: 5-9

22807 FoxJet
P.O.Box 83
South Canaan, PA 18459-0083
570-937-4921
Fax: 570-937-3229 800-572-3434
info@loveshaw.com www.loveshaw.com
Marking and coding equipment and barcodes/label-ing equipment
Marketing Director: Mark Gilvey
Plant Manager: Mark Gilvy
Estimated Sales: $10-20 Million
Number Employees: 100-249
Parent Co: Illinois Tool Works
Brands:
Foxjet
Lablex
System Master
Waxjet

22808 Foxboro Company
10900 Equity Drive
Houston, TX 77041
713-329-1600
Fax: 508-543-8764 888-369-2676
ips.csc@invensys.com www.foxboro.com
Manufacturer and exporter of microprocessor based enterprise network systems, instruments and controls
President: Mike Caliel
Industry Consultant: John Blanchard
VP: Ken Brown
Contact: Alexander Johnson
ajohnson@foxboro.com
Manager: Joe Fillion
Number Employees: 6000
Parent Co: Siebe

22809 Foxcroft Equipment & Svc Co
2101 Creek Rd
Glenmoore, PA 19343-1421
610-942-2888
Fax: 610-942-2769 800-874-0590
sales@foxcroft.com www.foxcroft.com
Chlorine control equipment, on-line analyzers, gas pacing valves, loop (set point) controllers and toxic gas detectors
Owner: Roger W Irey Jr
General Manager: Sandra Moriarity
postoffice@foxcroft.com
Estimated Sales: $2.5-5 000,000
Number Employees: 10-19

22810 Foxfire Marketing Solutions
750 Dawson Drive
Newark, DE 19713
302-533-2240
Fax: 302-533-2241 800-497-0512
Point of purchase displays and sales aids including tissue decor kits, special event cards, contest boxes and parking lot pennants.
President: Gerry Senker
Marketing Director: Jeanne Nooney
Sales Director: Bob Wegbreit
Estimated Sales: $5-10 Million
Number Employees: 50-99

22811 Foxjet
2016 E Randol Mill Road
Suite 409
Arlington, TX 76011-8223
817-795-6056
Fax: 817-795-7101 800-369-5384
www.foxjet.com
Marketing Manager: Dina Garland
Sales Director: Steve Shoup
Contact: Debbie Arling
ddarling@foxjet.com

22812 Foxon Co
235 W Park St
Providence, RI 02908-4881
401-421-2386
Fax: 401-421-8996 800-556-6943
www.quicktest.com
Manufacturer and exporter of pressure sensitive, flexible and embossed/debossed foil and paper labels
President: William Ewing
wewing@foxonlabels.com
Estimated Sales: $10-20 Million
Number Employees: 20-49

22813 Fp Development
402 S Main St
Williamstown, NJ 08094-1729
856-875-7100
Fax: 856-875-6717 sales@fpdevelopments.com
www.fpdevelopments.com
Specialized packaging equipment
President: Fred Pfleger
fpfleger@fpdevelopments.com
Estimated Sales: $5-10 Million
Number Employees: 20-49

22814 Frain Industries
245 E North Ave
Carol Stream, IL 60188-2021
630-629-9900
Fax: 630-629-6575 847-629-6575
sales@fraingroup.com www.frainindustries.com
Wholesaler/distributor of used packaging and pro-cessing equipment; rental/leasing services
Owner: Richard Frain
rfrain@fraingroup.com
CEO: David Eggleston
Marketing Director: Suzanne Eaton
Estimated Sales: $14 Million
Number Employees: 50-99
Square Footage: 350000

22815 Framarx Corp
3224 Butler St
S Chicago Hts, IL 60411-5505
708-755-3530
Fax: 708-755-3617 800-336-3936
saus@framarx.com www.framarx.com
Manufacturer and exporter of waxed and coated pa-pers
Vice President: Cindy Cofran
ccofran@framarx.com
Vice President: Cindy Cofran
Marketing Coordinator: Julia Saeid
Sales: Deborah M
Operations Manager: Christopher Czaszwicz
Production Manager: Jim Merrell
Estimated Sales: $20-50 Million
Number Employees: 20-49
Type of Packaging: Food Service, Private Label, Bulk

22816 FranRica Systems
PO Box 30127
Stockton, CA 95213-0127
209-948-2811
Fax: 209-948-5198
Food processing and filling equipment, including heat exchangers (tubular, scraped surface, aseptic flash cooling, steam injection), hot break systems, evaporators, control panels, pre-made aseptic bag fillers, aseptic bulk storagesystems, complete syst
President: Eric Kurtz
CFO: Marty Menz
R&D: Bill Kreaner
Contact: Jerry Hougland
jerry.hougland@fmc.com
Estimated Sales: $20-30 Million
Number Employees: 125

22817 France Personalized Signs
1559 E 17th St
Cleveland, OH 44114-2921
216-241-2198
Fax: 216-771-5111
Signs, banners, decals, interior graphics and displays
President: Stephen Treitinick Jr
Estimated Sales: less than $500,000
Number Employees: 1-4

22818 (HQ)Francis & Lusky Company
1437 Donelson Pike
Nashville, TN 37217-2957
615-242-0501
Fax: 615-256-0862 800-251-3711
Manufacturer, importer and exporter of advertising calendars; distributor of promotional products
President: Richard Francis
VP Marketing: Eric Wittel
VP Sales: Jeff Brown
Estimated Sales: $20-50 Million
Number Employees: 20-49

22819 (HQ)Francorp
20200 Governors Dr
Olympia Fields, IL 60461
708-481-2900
Fax: 708-481-5885 800-327-6244
info@francorp.com www.francorp.com
Management consulting firm specializing in fran-chise development providing legal, financial, opera-tional and marketing services
CEO: Donald Boroian
President: L Patrick Callaway
Executive VP/COO: Mary Kennedy
Contact: Ahmed Alrefai
ahmad.alrefai@reedsunaidiexpo.com
COO: Mary Kennedy
Estimated Sales: $10-15 Million
Number Employees: 20-49
Square Footage: 26000
Other Locations:
Francorp
Seville

22820 Frank B Ross Co Inc
970 New Brunswick Ave # H
Rahway, NJ 07065-3814
732-669-0810
Fax: 732-669-0814 techinfo@rosswaxes.com
www.frankbross.com
Natural waxes and wax blends
President: Larry Powell
VP: Donald Ayerlee
Estimated Sales: $1-5 Million
Number Employees: 5-9
Square Footage: 160000

22821 Frank Haile & Assoc
2650 Freewood Dr
Dallas, TX 75220-2596
214-357-6659
Fax: 214-357-9321 800-544-2511
n4fh@aol.com www.fha-usa.net
Bulk and minor ingredients handling systems
President/CEO: Frank Haile
n4fh@aol.com
CFO: Dale Fehlman
Vice President: Elaine Cook
Estimated Sales: $2.5 000,000
Number Employees: 5-9
Square Footage: 6400

22822 Frank O Carlson & Co
3622 S Morgan St # 2r
Chicago, IL 60609-1576
773-847-6900
Fax: 773-847-6924 dcarlson@focarlson.com
www.focarlson.com
Indoor advertising signs and graphics
President: Rose Carlson
rcarlson@focarlson.com
Quality Control: Earl Raas
VP: Douglas Carlson
Number Employees: 5-9

22823 Frank Torrone & Sons
400 Broadway
Staten Island, NY 10310-2096
718-273-7600
Fax: 718-447-5103 atorrone@aol.com
Electric signs
Owner: Arthur Torrone
Estimated Sales: $1-2.5 Million
Number Employees: 10-19

22824 Franke Americas
3050 Campus Dr
Suite 500
Hatfield, PA 19440
215-822-6590
Fax: 800-789-6201 www.franke.com/us
Manufacturer of foodservice and coffee systems
President, Franke Coffee Systems NA: Corrie Byron
Parent Co: Franke Group

22825 Franklin Automation Inc
1981 Bucktail Ln
Sugar Grove, IL 60554-9609
630-466-1900
Fax: 630-466-1902 info@franklinautomation.com
www.franklinautomation.com
Form, fill and seal machine for packaging small con-sumer products
President: Frank Kigyos
frank@franklinautomation.com
Estimated Sales: $3-5 Million
Number Employees: 10-19

22826 Franklin Crates
P.O.Box 279
Micanopy, FL 32667
352-466-3141
Fax: 352-466-0708 fcrates@bellsouth.net
Fruit and vegetable wirebound crates
President: Ben O Franklin Iii
Secretary: W Davis
Estimated Sales: $5-10 Million
Number Employees: 50-99

22827 Franklin Equipment
P.O.Box 8246
Greenville, TX 75404-8246
903-883-2002
Fax: 903-883-3210 800-356-7591
www.thehenrygroup.com
Food plant construction services, stainless fabrica-
tion services, matching of replacement part for food
equipment
President, Chief Executive Officer, Owne: Troy
Henry
Estimated Sales: $10-25 Million
Number Employees: 100-249

22828 Franklin Machine Products
PO Box 992
Marlton, NJ 08053-0992
856-983-2500
Fax: 800-255-9866 800-257-7737
sales@fmponline.com www.fmponline.com
Wholesaler/distributor of parts and accessories:
serving the food service market
CEO: Carol Adams
Vice President: Michael Conte, Sr.
Estimated Sales: $20-50 Million
Number Employees: 100-249
Square Footage: 50000

22829 Franklin Rubber Stamp Co
301 W 8th St
Wilmington, DE 19801-1553
302-654-8841
Fax: 302-654-8860 orders@franklinstamps.com
www.franklinstamps.com
Rubber stamps and magnetic and engraved plastic
signs
President: Tom Tanzilli
Manager: Russell Protas
Estimated Sales: $1-2.5 Million
Number Employees: 10-19

22830 Franklin Uniform Corporation
3946 Cloverhill Rd
Baltimore, MD 21218-1707
410-235-8151
Fax: 410-347-7607
Uniforms and special clothing
Owner: Paula A Franklin
Estimated Sales: $1-2.5 Million
Number Employees: 1-4

22831 Frankston Paper Box Company of Texas
699 N Frankston Hwy
Frankston, TX 75763
903-876-2550
Fax: 903-876-4458
admin@frankstonpackaging.com
www.frankstonpackaging.com
Rigid set-up, paper, plastic and folding boxes
Owner: Norm Bollock
nbollock@frankstonpackaging.com
CFO: Norm Bullock
Quality Control: Edwin Adcock
Sales: D'Wayne Odom
Production Manager: Charles Montrose
Plant Manager: Bill McHam
Estimated Sales: $20-50 Million
Number Employees: 50-99
Square Footage: 45000

22832 Franmara
560 Work St
Salinas, CA 93901-4350
831-422-4000
Fax: 831-422-7000 800-423-5855
franksr@franmara.com www.modularackusa.com
Wine industry tasting room supplies
President: John Chiorazzi
johnc@franmara.com
Estimated Sales: $10-20 Million
Number Employees: 20-49
Number of Products: 19

22833 Franrica Systems
PO Box 30127
Stockton, CA 95213-0127
209-948-2811
Fax: 209-948-5198
Manufacturer, importer and exporter of aseptic fill-
ers, heat exchangers, tanks, pumps, evaporators,
flash coolers, tomato paste processing plants, etc
Director: Eric Curtz
Controller: Marty Menz
Contact: Jerry Hougland
jerry.hougland@fmc.com
Estimated Sales: $20-30 Million
Number Employees: 125
Square Footage: 70000
Parent Co: FMC Technologies
Brands:
Franrica

22834 Frantz Co Inc
12314 W Silver Spring Dr
Milwaukee, WI 53225-2918
414-462-8700
Fax: 414-462-6655 inform@frantzcompany.com
www.frantzcompany.com
Smokehouse sawdust
President: Steve Frantz
steve@frantzcompany.com
CFO: John Tesensky
Estimated Sales: $5-10 Million
Number Employees: 10-19

22835 Franz Haas Machinery-America
6207 Settler Rd
Henrico, VA 23231-6044
804-222-6022
Fax: 804-222-0217 sales-usa@haas.com
www.haasusa.com
Bakery machinery including ovens
Manager: Michael Fleetwood
Director Sales/Marketing: M Fleetwood
General Manager: Michael Fleetwood
Application Engineer: Bill Redden
Estimated Sales: $10-20 Million
Number Employees: 20-49
Parent Co: Franz Haas Machinery of America

22836 Fraser Stamp & Seal
215 N Desplaines St # 2n
Chicago, IL 60661-1073
312-922-4970
Fax: 312-922-2692 800-540-8565
fraserstamp@aol.com www.aerubberstamp.com
Sealing stamps, stamp pad inks and marking stencils
President: Phil DE Francisco
aerbrstamp@aol.com
Estimated Sales: Less Than $500,000
Number Employees: 1-4

22837 Frazier & Son
101 Longview St
Conroe, TX 77301-4075
936-494-4040
Fax: 936-494-4045 800-365-5438
info@frazierandson.com www.frazierandson.com
Manufacturer and exporter of power operated pack-
aging machinery including fillers for frozen food;
also, bucket elevators
Owner: Mark Frazier
Sales/Engineer: Robert Gennaro
Manager: Nicole Baird
nicole.baird@lrsus.com
Estimated Sales: $2.5-5 Million
Number Employees: 10-19
Square Footage: 20000
Brands:
Whiz-Lifter

22838 Frazier Industrial Co
91 Fairview Ave
Long Valley, NJ 07853-3381
908-876-3001
Fax: 908-876-3615 800-859-1342
frazier@frazier.com www.frazier.com
Structural steel pallet rack systems
CEO: William L Mascharka
wmascharka@frazier.com
Estimated Sales: $50-100 Million
Number Employees: 100-249

22839 Frazier Precision InstrCo
925 Sweeney Dr
Hagerstown, MD 21740-7128
301-790-2585
Fax: 301-790-2589 info@frazierinstrument.com
www.frazierinstrument.com
Manufacturer and exporter of test instruments and
measuring equipment
President: Thomas F Scrivener
Estimated Sales: $1-2.5 Million
Number Employees: 5-9

22840 Frazier Signs
1304 N 20th St
Decatur, IL 62521
217-429-2349
Fax: 217-429-2340
Signs including neon, plastic, metal, magnetic, vinyl
and pressure sensitive; also, maintainenance, instal-
lation and repair services available
Manager (Vinyl Graphics): Robert Frazier
Estimated Sales: less than $500,000
Number Employees: 1-4
Square Footage: 12000

22841 Fred Beesley's Booth & Upholstery
264 Brookfield Ln
Centerville, UT 84014-1474
801-364-8189
Restaurant booths, counters and tables
President: Fred Beesley
Marketing Director: Fred Beesley
Estimated Sales: Below $5 Million
Number Employees: 10

22842 (HQ)Fred D Pfening Co
1075 W 5th Ave
Columbus, OH 43212-2691
614-294-5361
Fax: 614-294-1633 sales@pfening.com
www.pfening.com
Manufacturer and exporter of bakers' machinery in-
cluding proof boxes, sifters and water metering de-
vices; also, material handling equipment
President: Fred Pfening
ebrackman@pfening.com
VP of Sales/Marketing: Norm Meulenberg
Sales Exec: Edward Brackman
Purchasing Agent: Patrick Inskeep
Estimated Sales: $10-20 Million
Number Employees: 50-99
Square Footage: 150000
Brands:
Wat-A-Mat

22843 Fredman Bag Co
5801 W Bender Ct
Milwaukee, WI 53218-1609
414-462-9400
Fax: 414-462-9409 800-945-5686
www.fredmanbag.com
Printed packaging materials including recloseable
polyethylene bags and breathable films
President: Charles Akins
charlesakins29@yahoo.com
Executive VP: Tim Fredman, Jr.
Number Employees: 50-99
Square Footage: 50000

22844 Fredrick Ramond Company
33000 Pin Oak Parkway
Avon Lake, OH 44012
440-653-5550
Fax: 440-653-5555 800-446-5539
service@hinkleylighting.com
www.fredrickramond.com
Manufacturer, importer and exporter of decorative
light fixtures
President: Fredrick Glassman
National Sales Manager: Alan Dubrow
Inside Sales: David Brusius
Support Manager: Carol Romero
Estimated Sales: $10-20 Million
Number Employees: 100-249
Brands:
F. Ramond
Palm Springs

22845 Free Flow Packaging Corporation
1090 Mills Way
Redwood City, CA 94063
650-261-5300
Fax: 650-361-1713 800-888-3725

Interior cushioning material for protective packaging; also, dispersing systems for loose-fill cushioning materials
President: Arthur Graham
Marketing Manager: Jim Jensen
National Sales Manager: Harry Reynolds
Contact: Jim Birkle
james.birkle@fpintl.com
Number Employees: 350
Brands:
Flo-Pak
Flo-Pak Bio 8

22846 Freedom Packaging
195 Aviation Way # 201
Watsonville, CA 95076-2059
831-722-3565
Fax: 831-724-0995 laura@freedompackaging.com
www.freedompackaging.com
Packaging supplies for frozen foods
Owner: Tom Prague
Owner/CEO: Thomas Sprague
CEO: Thomas Sprague
Contact: Paul Hurlburt
phurlburt@choc.org
Estimated Sales: Less Than $500,000
Number Employees: 1-4

22847 Freely Display
12401 Euclid Ave
Cleveland, OH 44106-4314
216-721-6056
Fax: 216-721-6081
Manufacturer and exporter of wood store fixtures and displays
Controller: Bernadette Gello
Operations Manager: Thomas Olechiw
Estimated Sales: $2.5-5 Million
Number Employees: 5-9

22848 Freeman Co
911 Graham Dr
Fremont, OH 43420-4086
419-334-9709
Fax: 419-334-3426 800-223-7788
info@freemancompany.com
www.freemancompany.com
Cutting equipment, presses, dies, tooling
President: Greg Defisher
COO: Mike Mullholand
mmullholand@freemancompany.com
CEO: Louis G Freeman III
CFO: Scott Clifford
Estimated Sales: $2.5-5 Million
Number Employees: 50-99

22849 Freeman Electric Co Inc
534 Oak Ave
Panama City, FL 32401-2648
850-785-7448
Fax: 850-747-1162
Plastic and neon signs
President: Tommy Duncan
freemanelectricc@bellsouth.net
Estimated Sales: $1-2.5 Million
Number Employees: 10-19

22850 FreesTech
PO Box 2156
Sinking Spring, PA 19608
717-560-7560
Fax: 717-560-7587 info@freestech.com
www.freestech.com
Palletizers, freezing and cooling systems, conveyors and storage and retrieval machines for warehouse applications.
Contact: Richard Greener
dgreener@freestech.com
Year Founded: 1967
Estimated Sales: $500 Million-$1 Billion
Number Employees: 10
Brands:
Auto-Pal
Fusion Cell
Milk-Stor
Tri-Flow
Tri-Stacker
Tri-Tray

22851 Frelco
PO Box 316
Stephenville, NL A2N 2Z5
Canada
709-643-5668
Fax: 709-643-3046
Manufacturer, importer and exporter of conveyors, hoppers, tables and cabinets

22852 Frem Corporation
60 Webster Place
Worcester, MA 01603-1920
508-791-3152
Fax: 508-791-7969
Manufacturer and exporter of injection molded plastic housewares including food storage bins, crates and waste baskets
CEO: M.L. Sherman
CFO: D.A. Denovellis
Vice President: J.J. Althoff
Manager: Tim Eunice
Parent Co: Ekco Group

22853 Fremont Die Cut Products
3177 E State St
Fremont, OH 43420
419-334-2626
Fax: 419-334-3327 800-223-3177
Corrugated plastic products including bulk and sleeve packs, sheets and containers
President: Les Mintz
Estimated Sales: $1-5 Million
Number Employees: 20-49
Square Footage: 320000

22854 French Awning & Screen Co Inc
4514 S Mcraven Rd
Jackson, MS 39204-2031
601-922-1132
Fax: 601-922-9671 800-898-1132
kerry@frenchcanvasawnings.com
www.frenchcanvasawnings.com
Commercial awnings
President: Kerry French
kerry@frenchcanvasawnings.com
Estimated Sales: Less Than $500,000
Number Employees: 1-4

22855 French Oil Mill Machinery Co
1035 W Greene St
P.O. Box 920
Piqua, OH 45356-1855
937-773-3420
Fax: 937-773-3424 sales@frenchoil.com
www.frenchoil.com
Manufacturer and exporter of vegetable oilseed processing equipment including cracking and flaking mills, conditioners, full, extruder and pre-presses, dewatering and drying presses, liquid-solid separation equipment and hydraulicpresses
President: Daniel French
CEO: Jason P Mcdaniel
jmcdaniel@frenchoil.com
CFO: Dennis Bratton
CEO: Jason P McDaniel
Quality Control: Jason McDaniel
Sales Director: James King
Public Relations: Eric Brockman
Estimated Sales: $10-20 Million
Number Employees: 50-99
Square Footage: 450000

22856 Fres-Co SYSTEM USA Inc
3005 State Rd
Telford, PA 18969-1021
215-256-4172
Fax: 215-721-0747 contact@fresco.com
www.fresco.com
Tea and coffee industry bag formers/fillers/sealers, bagging machines, bags and packaging film supplies, espresso pod machines, foil laminates, machinery for coffee roasters, packaging (flexible), vacuum packaging machinery, scalesteabag machinery, pac
President: Tullio Vigano
tvigano@fresco.com
Estimated Sales: $20-50 Million
Number Employees: 250-499

22857 Fresca Foods Inc.
195 CTC Blvd.
Louisville, CO 80027
303-996-8881
Fax: 303-645-4884 hello@frescafoodsinc.com
frescafoodsinc.com
Supply chain management services.
CEO: Todd Dutkin
CFO: Zan Powell
Chief Commercial Officer: Brandon Viar
CMO: Liz Myslik
COO: Mark Bible
Year Founded: 1993
Number Employees: 150-500

22858 Fresh Express, Inc.
P.O. Box 80599
Salinas, CA 93912
800-242-5472
www.freshexpress.com
Certified organic salads and lettuce, cole slaw & shreds, delicious kits, flavorful spinach, gourmet cafe salads, harvest originals, refreshing mixes, tasty greens mixes, and tender leaf mixes.
President: John Olivo
CEO: Kenneth Diveley
Year Founded: 1926
Estimated Sales: $368.3 Million
Number Employees: 5,000+
Square Footage: 20000
Parent Co: Chiquita Brands International, Inc
Type of Packaging: Bulk
Brands:
Fresh Express

22859 Fresh Mark Inc.
1888 Southway St. SW
Massillon, OH 44646
330-832-7491
Fax: 330-830-3174 www.freshmark.com
Bacon, ham, weiners, deli and luncheon meats, dry sausage and other specialty meat items.
CEO: Neil Genshaft
ngenshaft@freshmark.com
Year Founded: 1920
Estimated Sales: $219 Million
Number Employees: 500-999
Square Footage: 80000
Type of Packaging: Consumer, Food Service, Private Label
Brands:
Sugardale
Superior's Brand

22860 Freshloc Technologies
15443 Knoll Trail Dr
Suite 100
Dallas, TX 75248
972-759-0111
Fax: 972-759-0090 888-225-9458
sales@freshloc.com
President/CEO: Alan C Heller
Founder: Richard G. Fettig
Vice President of Sales & Operations: JD Donnelly
Sales Director: Donna Fettig
Contact: Larah Cooley
larah@freshloc.com
Estimated Sales: $2.5-5 Million
Number Employees: 10-19

22861 Freshway Distributors
50 Ludy St
Hicksville, NY 11801-5115
516-870-3333
www.freshway.com
Refrigerating company and also offers transportation services

22862 Fresno Neon Sign Co Inc
5901 E Clinton Ave
Fresno, CA 93727-8641
559-292-2944
Fax: 559-292-2980 www.fresnoneon.com
Signs including point of purchase, neon luminous tube and plastic
President: Ken Block
block@fresnoneon.com
Manager: Bill Kratt
Estimated Sales: $1-2.5 Million
Number Employees: 10-19

22863 Fresno Pallet, Inc.
PO Box 268
Sultana, CA 93666
559-591-4111
Fax: 559-591-6116
Fencing, skids, plywood bins and wooden and plastic pallets; also, rail and truck unloading services available
Owner: Steven Johnson
Sales Manager: Steve Johnson
Operations Manager: Michael Johnson
Estimated Sales: $2.5-5 Million
Number Employees: 10-19

22864 Fresno Tent & Awning
100 M St
Fresno, CA 93721-3117
559-264-4771
Fax: 559-485-5629 www.yahoo.com
Commercial awnings
President: Pat Haun
fresnotent@yahoo.com
Estimated Sales: $2.5-5,000,000
Number Employees: 1-4

22865 Freudenberg Nonwovens
2975 Pembroke Road
Hopkinsville, KY 42240
270-887-5115
Fax: 270-886-5069
HVAC@freudenberg-filter.com
www.freudenberg-filter.com
Manufacturer and importer of air and liquid filters; also, filtration media
Contact: Terezie Zapletalova
terezie.zapletalova@freudenberg-nw.com
Estimated Sales: $50-100 Million
Number Employees: 100-249
Brands:
Micronair
Viledon

22866 (HQ)Friedman Bag Company
865 Manhattan Beach Boulevard
Suite 204
Manhattan Beach, CA 90266-4955
213-628-2341
Fax: 213-687-9772
Manufacturer and exporter of burlap, cotton, polyethylene, open mesh bags; wholesaler/distributor of paper bags, cartons and packaging supplies
President: Al Lanfeld
VP/Operations Manager: David Friedman
Sales/Service: Diane Dal Porto
Estimated Sales: $20-50 Million
Number Employees: 250-499
Square Footage: 400000

22867 Friedr Dick Corp
33 Allen Blvd
Farmingdale, NY 11735-5611
631-454-6955
Fax: 631-454-6184 800-554-3425
www.fdick.us
Manufacturer and distributor of cutlery
Sales: Morgan
Manager: Steve Kurek
s.kurek@feiedrdick.us
Operations: Scott Belovin
Number Employees: 5-9
Number of Brands: 7
Number of Products: 600
Square Footage: 10000
Type of Packaging: Consumer, Food Service, Bulk
Brands:
Friedr. Dick

22868 Friedrich Metal Products
6204 Technology Dr
Browns Summit, NC 27214-9702
336-375-3067
Fax: 336-621-7901 800-772-0326
info@friedrichproducts.com
www.friedrichproducts.com
Manufacturer and exporter of smokehouses, bakery ovens, smokers, deli equipment, etc
President: Jennifer Prago
jprago@friedrichproducts.com
CFO: Bob Friedrich
Vice President: Laura Friedrich-Bargebuhr
Quality Control: Axel Dender
Estimated Sales: $1-3 Million
Number Employees: 20-49
Square Footage: 60000

22869 Friend Box Co
90 High St
Danvers, MA 01923-3196
978-774-0240
Fax: 978-777-7921 www.friendbox.com
Boxes including rigid paper and loose wrap candy
President: Debbie Bertolino
debbie@friendbox.com
Quality Control: Rich Lombardo
CEO: Charlie Walker
VP Sales: Fran Dollard
VP Operations: Larry Comeau
Estimated Sales: $5-10 Million
Number Employees: 50-99

22870 Friendly City Box Co Inc
520 Oakridge Dr
Johnstown, PA 15904-6915
814-266-6287
Fax: 814-266-9757
Folding paper cartons
Owner: Lance Blackburn
fcboxco@floodcity.net
Estimated Sales: $1-2.5 Million
Number Employees: 5-9

22871 Frigid Coil
13711 Freeway Drive
Santa Fe Springs, CA 90670-5688
562-921-4310
Fax: 562-921-6412
Manufactures refrigeration and air conditioning equipment for commercial use
President: David Myers
Quality Control: Thomas Serry
R & D: Gary Price
Estimated Sales: $1-2.5 Million
Number Employees: 10

22872 Frigidaire Co.
10200 David Taylor Dr.
Charlotte, NC 28262
866-449-4200
Fax: 704-547-7401 www.frigidaire.com
Freezers and fridges.
Contact: Kyle Crown
kyle.chown@electrolux.com
General Manager: Kyle Chown
Estimated Sales: $100-500 Million
Number Employees: 1000-4999
Parent Co: Electrolux
Brands:
Gibson
Kelvinator
White Westinghouse

22873 Frigoscandia
9577 153rd Ave NE
Redmond, WA 98052-2513
425-883-2244
Fax: 425-882-0948 800-423-1743
dave_faires@fmc.com
Freezing/refrigeration equipment including in-line quick freezing and spiral freezers, freezer control systems and pre-packaged refrigeration systems; also, steam pasteurization systems for carcasses
Vice President: Charlie Cannon
Director Sales: Mike Kish
Contact: Jared Larson
vijay_lamba@fmc.com
Number Employees: 20-49
Parent Co: FMC Corporation
Brands:
Flofreeze
Frigopak
Gyrocompact
Gyrostack
Lewis Iqf
Sps

22874 Frigoscandia Equipment
1700 Cannon Road
Northfield, MN 55057-1680
507-645-9546
Fax: 507-645-6148 800-426-1283
fmcfoodtech.info@fmcti.com
www.fmctechnologies.com
Manufacturers inline spiral freezer for food processing industry
President: Simoau Jeff
Quality Control: Chucks Moder
Regional Sales Manager: Ellen Hao
Estimated Sales: $20-50 Million
Number Employees: 100

22875 Frigoscandia Equipment
1700 Cannon Road
Northfield, MN 55057-1680
507-645-9546
Fax: 507-645-6148 800-426-1283
www.frigoscandia-equipment.com
Freezing systems, specializing in in-process line freezers, chillers, coolers, bakery proofers, dehydrators, bottle elevators, conveyors, fluidized belt freezers, trolley freezers
President: Joseph Nertherland
Marketing Manager: Larry DeBoer
Estimated Sales: $20-50 Million
Number Employees: 75

22876 Frisk Design
PO Box 504
Saint Helena, CA 94574-5004
707-944-1655
Fax: 707-944-1655
Wine industry bottle etching and design

22877 (HQ)Friskem Infinetics
PO Box 2330
Wilmington, DE 19899
302-658-2471
Fax: 302-658-2475
Manufacturer and exporter of detectors including metal, pilferage, passive magnetometer and active field
CEO: M Schwartz
Brands:
Friskem
Friskem-Af
Tellem

22878 Fristam Pumps USA LLP
2410 Parview Rd
Middleton, WI 53562-2521
608-831-5001
Fax: 608-831-8467 800-841-5001
fristam@fristampumps.com www.fristam.com
Manufacturer and exporter of stainless steel, centrifugal and positive displacement pumps, blenders and mixers.
President: Pete Herb
CEO: Wolfgang Stamp
VP: Pete Skora
Quality Control/Operations: Duane Ehlke
Marketing Supervisor: Dan Funk
Sales Director: Larry Cook
Public Relations: Wendy Andrew
Number Employees: 100-249
Number of Products: 80
Brands:
Fristam

22879 Fristam Pumps USA LLP
2410 Parview Rd
Middleton, WI 53562-2521
608-831-5001
Fax: 608-831-8467 sales@fristampumps.com
www.fristam.com
Centrifugal pumps, shear pumps, powder mixers and positive displacement pumps
President: Scott Haman
shaman@fristam.com
Number Employees: 100-249

22880 Fritsch
921 Proton Rd
San Antonio, TX 78258-4203
210-227-2726
Fax: 210-227-5550
Industrial bakery equipment (sheeting equipment) roll-fix USA (retail reversible sheeters)
President: Claus Fritsch
General Manager: Danny Kelly
Off. Mngr.: Joseph Mouyer
Estimated Sales: $300,000-500,000
Number Employees: 1-4

22881 Fritsch USA
2706 Treble Crk Ste 200
San Antonio, TX 78258
210-491-9309
Fax: 210-227-5550
Sheeting and laminating equipment
President/General Manager: Danny Kelly
Estimated Sales: $300,000-500,000
Number Employees: 1-4

22882 Frobisher Industries
6260 Rte 105
Waterborough, NB E4C 2Y4
Canada
506-362-2198
Fax: 506-362-9090
Manufacturer and exporter of hamper baskets, veneer and wooden boxes for fruits and vegetables
President: George Staples
CFO: George Lorriaine
Number Employees: 10
Square Footage: 48000

22883 (HQ)Frohling Sign Co
419 E Route 59
Nanuet, NY 10954-2908
845-623-2258
Fax: 845-623-2799 bocfrohlingsign@aol.com
Plastic, wood, interior, exterior, neon and metal signs; also, plaques
President: Brian O'Connor
brian@frohlingsign.com
Estimated Sales: $1-2.5 Million
Number Employees: 5-9

22884 Frommelt Safety Products& Ductsox Corporation
4343 Chavenelle Rd
Dubuque, IA 52002-2653
563-556-2020
Fax: 563-589-2776 800-553-5560
Fabric air dispersion products for open ceiling architecture
President: Cary Pinkalla
Sr. Sales Promotion Specialist: Mary Jo Kluesner
Contact: Lou Wiegand
l.wiegand@ritehite.com
Plant Manager: Lou Wiegand
Estimated Sales: $2 million
Number Employees: 5-9

22885 Frontage Enterprises
14111 Freeway Dr
Santa Fe Springs, CA 90670-5822
562-407-9345
Fax: 562-404-3602

22886 Frontier Bag
5720 E State Route 150
Kansas City, MO 64147-1003
816-765-4811
Fax: 816-765-6603 www.yellowbagpeople.com
Plastic, shrink and meat bags, polyethylene bag liners, pallet covers and sheeting; exporter of plastic bags; importer of polyethylene raw materials bager plain and printed
President: Mark Gurley
m.gurley@yellowbagpeople.com
Owner: Ron Gurley
VP Sales: Tom Hauser
VP Production: Ron Avery
Estimated Sales: $20-50 Million
Number Employees: 50-99
Square Footage: 90000

22887 Frontier Bag Co Inc
2420 Grant St
Omaha, NE 68111-3825
402-342-0992
Fax: 402-342-2107 800-278-2247
customerservice@frontierbagco.com
www.frontierbagco.com
Burlap and cotton bags; wholesaler/distributor of paper and plastic bags; serving the food service market
President: Judy Pearl-Lee
jplee@frontierbagco.com
Sales Manager: Judy Pearl-Lee
Estimated Sales: $1-2.5 Million
Number Employees: 10-19

22888 Frontier Packaging Company
1938 Occidental Avenue S
Seattle, WA 98134-1413
206-682-7800
Fax: 206-682-1669 800-737-7333
Wine industry packaging
Estimated Sales: $1-2.5 000,000
Number Employees: 19

22889 Frost ET Inc
2020 Bristol Ave NW
Grand Rapids, MI 49504-1402
616-301-2660
Fax: 616-453-2161 800-253-9382
frost.sales@frostinc.com www.frostinc.com
Overhead, inverted and converyor trolleys, guide rollers, conveyor roll bearings, and food processing components.
President: Chad Frost
cfrost@frostinc.com
Number Employees: 10-19

22890 Frost Food Handling Products
2020 Bristol Ave NW
Grand Rapids, MI 49504
616-453-7781
Fax: 616-453-2161 800-253-9382
frost@frostinc.com www.frostinc.com
Conveying components for food handling applications
CEO: Chad Frost
CFO: Fred Sytsma
Sales Director: Joe Jakeway
Estimated Sales: $10-20 Million
Number Employees: 50-99
Square Footage: 120000
Parent Co: Frost Industries
Brands:
Attachments
Blue Poly Trolleys
Sani-Link Chain
Sani-Trolley
Sani-Wheel
Stainless Steel Bearings
Stainless Steel Trolleys
Stainless Steel X-Chain
X-Chain

22891 Frost Manufacturing Corp
173 Grove St # 1
Worcester, MA 01605-1715
508-756-4685
Fax: 508-757-5604 800-462-0216
info@frostmanufacturing.com
www.frostmanufacturing.com
Rubber stamps, signs, name plates, stencils, menu boards, inks, labels, banners and name badges
President: Douglas Frost
dfrost@frostmanufacturing.com
VP Marketing: Julieane Frost
Estimated Sales: $1-2.5 Million
Number Employees: 5-9

22892 Frosty Factory Of America Inc
2301 S Farmerville St
Ruston, LA 71270-9042
318-255-1162
Fax: 318-255-1170 800-544-4071
dolph@frostyfactory.com www.frostyfactory.com
Manufacturer and exporter of frozen beverage, soft serve ice cream and shake machines
President: Heath Williams
ruston186@aol.com
Finance Executive: Penny Taylor
Sales/Marketing: Craig Moss
Sales Executive: Christopher Williams
Engineer: Ralph Pettijohn
Purchasing Manager: Ralph Pettijohn
Estimated Sales: $5 Million
Number Employees: 20-49
Square Footage: 80000
Brands:
Petite Sorbeteer
Soft-Serve Ice Cream
Sorbeteer

22893 Frozen Specialties Inc
8600 S Wilkinson Way
Suite G
Perrysburg, OH 43551
419-867-2005
www.frozenspecialties.com
Private label pizza and pizza bites, a multi-line supplier
President & CEO: Rich Alvarez
rich.alvarez@frc.com
Controller: Paul Nungester
Director of Marketing: Lori Hamilton
Vice President, Sales: Dan Burdick
Year Founded: 1969
Estimated Sales: $49.99 Million
Number Employees: 10-19
Number of Brands: 1

Number of Products: 6
Square Footage: 13395
Type of Packaging: Consumer, Private Label, Bulk
Brands:
Mr. P'S

22894 Fruehauf Trailer Services
12813 Flushing Meadows Dr
St Louis, MO 63131-1835
314-822-1113
Refrigerated trailers; service available
CEO: Derek Nagle
Director Marketing/Advertising: Steve Havens
Number Employees: 10-19
Parent Co: Wabash National Company
Brands:
Fruehauf

22895 Fruit Growers Package Company
4693 Wilson Avenue SW
Suite H
Grandville, MI 49418-8762
616-724-1400
Manufacturer and exporter of wood veneer products, craft baskets and wooden shipping crates for berries
President: Diane Taylor
VP: Dennis Palasek
Contact: Dennis Palasek
dennis.palasek@fruitgrowers.com
Estimated Sales: $600,000
Number Employees: 10
Square Footage: 80000
Type of Packaging: Consumer, Bulk

22896 Fruitcrown Products Corp
250 Adams Blvd
Farmingdale, NY 11735-6615
631-694-5800
Fax: 631-694-6467 800-441-3210
info@fruitcrown.com www.fruitcrown.com
Aseptic fruit flavors and bases for beverage, dairy and baking industries
President: Robert Jagenburg
orjagenburg@fruitcrown.com
Number Employees: 50-99
Type of Packaging: Bulk
Brands:
Asp
Exquizita
Fruitcrown
Huntingcastle

22897 Fruition Northwest LLC
29345 NW W Union Rd
PO Box 130
North Plains, OR 97133
503-880-5193
High-quality infused-dehydrated berry fruits to the wholesale market.
Owner: Alan Krassowski
Estimated Sales: $210 Thousand
Type of Packaging: Bulk

22898 Fruvemex
233 Paulin Ave
Calexico, CA 92231
760-203-1896
Fax: 760-203-2389 fcaballero@fruvemex.com
www.fruvemex.com
Refrigerated and frozen fruit and vegetable products
President: Gustavo Caballero
VP Sales/Marketing: Yvonne Brewer
Year Founded: 1986
Number Employees: 85
Square Footage: 180000
Type of Packaging: Bulk

22899 Fry Tech Corporation
4430 Dodge Street
Dubuque, IA 52003-2600
319-583-1559
Fax: 319-557-8602 frytech@mwci.net
Fryers including ventless counter-top and auto-lift fryers with built-in air filtration and fire suppression systems
Owner: Rod Christ
VP: Donna Christ
Number Employees: 2
Square Footage: 7000
Brands:
Alpaire
Fan-C-Fry
U-Fry-It

22900 Frye's Measure Mill
12 Frye Mill Rd
Wilton, NH 03086-5010

603-654-6581
Fax: 603-654-6103 www.fryesmeasuremill.com
Manufacturer and exporter of wooden dry measures, specialty packaging, veneer containers, colonial pantry and shaker boxes
President: Harley Savage
harleysavage@tds.net
Quality Control: Harley Savage
Estimated Sales: Below $5 Million
Number Employees: 5-9
Brands:
Frye's Measure Mill
Old Tyme

22901 Frymaster/Dean
8700 Line Ave
Shreveport, LA 71106-6800

318-865-1711
Fax: 318-868-5987 800-221-4583
webmaster@frymaster.com
Supplier of commercial fryers, frying systems, water-bath rethermalizers, pasta cookers, and of the equipment related to these technologies.
President: Gene Baugh
Cio/Cto: Bruce Arnold
bconnor@frymaster.com
Vice President & General Manager: Todd Phillips
Estimated Sales: $60 Million
Number Employees: 500-999
Square Footage: 180000
Parent Co: ENODIS
Type of Packaging: Food Service
Brands:
Frymaster
Master Jet

22902 Fsi Technologies
668 E Western Ave
Lombard, IL 60148-2005

630-932-9380
Fax: 630-932-0016 800-468-6009
info@fsinet.com www.fsinet.com
Machine vision and systems, automatic inspection systems, rotary shaft encoders, electronic counters and displays for motion variables, specialized photo-electric sensors.
President: Scott Tobey
scott@fsinet.com
VP: Fred Turek
Sales: Kim Jackson
Estimated Sales: $2.5-5 Million
Number Employees: 20-49
Brands:
Checker Vision System
Cirrus
Defender
Ese
Hde
Indicoder
Pulsar
Rse
Tuff-Coder

22903 Fuji Health Science/Inc
3 Terri Ln # 12
Unit 12
Burlington, NJ 08016-4903

609-386-3030
Fax: 609-386-3033 contact@fujihealthscience.com
www.fujichemicalusa.com
Markets and manufacturers natural specialty food ingredient, AstaReal astaxanthin, a powerful anti-oxidant
National Sales Manager: Joe Kuncewitch
kuncewitch@fujihealthscience.com
Estimated Sales: Under $500,000
Number Employees: 10-19

22904 Fuji Labeling Systems
2025 S Arl Hts Rd Ste 100
Arlington Heights, IL 60005

847-690-1725
Fax: 847-690-1734 fujiusa@aol.com
Standard series labels
Estimated Sales: $300,000-500,000
Number Employees: 1-4

22905 Fujitso Transaction Solutions
11085 N Torrey Pines Road
La Jolla, CA 92037-1015

858-457-9900
Fax: 858-457-2701 800-340-4425
Lightweight and rugged hand-held computers, route accounting, distributing
President: Hiroaki Kurokawa
Marketing Manager: Sandy Watts
Estimated Sales: $20-50 Million
Number Employees: 50

22906 Ful-Flav-R Foods
P.O.Box 82
Alamo, CA 94507

925-838-0300
Fax: 925-838-0310 www.fulflavr.com
Premium Ground Garlic, Minced Garlic (in oil & water), Ground and Minced Ginger, Ground Roasted Garlic, Ground Onion, diced Sweet Bell Peppers, Ground and Diced Jalepeno's, Fire Roasted Anaheim chili's, Ground Chili-Garlic Blends andother unique custom formulated blends. All of our products are pasteurized and pH controlled.
President: Joseph Farrell
Chief Operations Officer: Glen Farrell
Director Sales/Marketing: Steve Linzmeyer
Plant Manager: John Small
Estimated Sales: $1-2.5 Million
Number Employees: 5-9
Type of Packaging: Food Service, Bulk
Brands:
Ful-Flav-R

22907 Full-View Display Case
PO Box 79200
Fort Worth, TX 76179-0200

817-847-0775
Fax: 817-232-0214 800-252-1667
Refrigerated and nonrefrigerated display cases for the gourmet candy and bakery industries
Estimated Sales: $1-2.5 Million
Number Employees: 10-19

22908 Fuller Box Co
150 Chestnut St
North Attleboro, MA 02760-3205

508-695-2525
Fax: 508-695-2187 www.fullerbox.com
Cardboard and steel packaging and packaging machinery; also, metal stamping machinery
President: Peter C Fuller
CFO: John Backner
Vice President: A Fuller
Sales/Marketing Executive: Thomas Mercer
Estimated Sales: $10-20 Million
Number Employees: 100-249
Square Footage: 194000
Parent Co: Fuller Companies

22909 Fuller Flag Company
1092 Main Street
Holden, MA 01520-1247

508-829-6016
Fax: 508-829-7767 800-348-6723
tjaitken@earthling.net
Flags and pennants, retail and wholesale flags
Sales Manager: Samantha McDonald
Office Manager: Samatha McDonald
Estimated Sales: $300,000-500,000
Number Employees: 1-4

22910 Fuller Industries LLC
1 Fuller Way
Great Bend, KS 67530-2466

620-792-1711
Fax: 620-792-1906 800-522-0499
customer@fuller.com www.fullerindustriesllc.com
Manufacturer and exporter of detergents, mops, floor polish, brooms and plastic bottles
President: G Robert Gey
CEO: David Sabin
dsabin@fuller.com
VP: Lewis L Gray
VP Sales: Dolores McConnaughy
VP Sales: Bill McCoy
Number Employees: 250-499
Square Footage: 1000000

22911 Fuller Packaging Inc
1152 High St
PO Box 198
Central Falls, RI 02863-1506

401-725-4300
Fax: 401-726-8050
customerservice@fullerbox.com
www.fullerbox.com
Manufacturer, importer and exporter of boxes including paper and counter display
President: Peter Fuller
Product Development Manager: Alvin Fuller
Estimated Sales: $10-20 Million
Number Employees: 50-99
Square Footage: 154000

22912 Fuller Ultra Violet Corp
9416 Gulfstream Rd
Frankfort, IL 60423-2524

815-469-3301
Fax: 815-469-1438 www.fulleruv.com
Liquid sweetener tank storage, water purification
President: William Eckstrom
fulleruvcorp@mindspriomng.com
Number Employees: 10-19
Number of Brands: 1
Number of Products: 12
Square Footage: 16000

22913 Fuller Weighing Systems
1600 Georgesville Road
Columbus, OH 43228-3616

614-882-8121
Fax: 614-882-9594 www.fullerweighing.com
Manufacturer and exporter of bulk weighing systems, feeders and automatic net-weigh container filling systems for liquids and dry materials
VP Sales: Tim Schultz
General Manager: Karl Hedderich
Production: David Patterson
Number Employees: 50
Square Footage: 60000
Parent Co: Cardinal Scale Manufacturing Company

22914 Fulton Boiler Works Inc
3981 Port St
Pulaski, NY 13142-4604

315-298-5121
Fax: 315-298-6390 service@fulton.com
www.fulton.com
Process, heat, steam for baking, cooking, frying
President: Nathan Fulton
nathan@nathanfulton.com
Chairman: Ronald B Palm
Estimated Sales: $20 Million
Number Employees: 250-499

22915 (HQ)Fulton-Denver Co
3500 Wynkoop St
Denver, CO 80216-3650

303-294-9292
Fax: 303-292-9470 800-521-1414
www.fultondenver.com
Bags including burlap, mesh, poly, paper, bulk, cotton, vexar and wool; also, cartons, wrap, sheets, twine and thread
Manager: Steve Potter
spotter@fultondenver.com
President: Rhett Schuller
Estimated Sales: $5-10 Million
Number Employees: 1-4

22916 Fun City Popcorn
3211 Sunrise Ave
Las Vegas, NV 89101

702-367-2676
Fax: 702-876-1099 800-423-1710
www.funcitypopcorn.com
Caramel, cheese and butter popcorn; manufacturer of popcorn processing machinery
President/CEO: Richard Falk
CFO: Maryann Talavera
Estimated Sales: $1-3 Million
Number Employees: 5-9
Square Footage: 40000
Type of Packaging: Consumer, Food Service, Private Label, Bulk

22917 Fun-Time International
433 W Girard Ave.
Philadelphia, PA 19123

215-925-1450
Fax: 215-925-1884 800-776-4386
orders@krazystraws.com www.krazystraws.com

Manufacturer and exporter of novelty drinking straws, eating utensils and drinking containers; also, novelty candy items
Owner: Erik Lipson
Estimated Sales: $3-5 Million
Number Employees: 10-19
Square Footage: 2000
Brands:
Candy Bracelets
Connecter
Crazy Glasses
Funstraws
Krazy Koolers
Krazy Strawston
Krazy Utensils
Spookyware

22918 Funke Filters
P.O.Box 30097
Cincinnati, OH 45230-0097
513-528-5535
Fax: 513-528-5575 800-543-7070
Filters and filtration equipment
President: William F Funke
Estimated Sales: Below $5 000,000
Number Employees: 1-4

22919 Funny Apron Co
PO Box 1780
Lake Dallas, TX 75065-1780
940-498-3308
Fax: 800-515-8076 800-835-5802
info@funnyaprons.com www.funnyaprons.com
Imprinted aprons with humorous food themed designs
President: Ellice Lovelady
CFO: Charles Lovelady
Sales Director: Terri Whiting
Estimated Sales: Under $1 Million
Number Employees: 1-4
Number of Products: 90+
Parent Co: The Imagination Association LLC
Type of Packaging: Consumer

22920 Furgale Industries Ltd.
324 Lizzie Street
Winnipeg, NB R3A 0Y7
Canada
204-949-4200
Fax: 204-943-3191 800-665-0506
Provider of cleaning tools to the north american market-tools include: brooms, mops & brushes
President: Jim Furgale
VP: Terry Gibb
Customer Service: Kate Furgale
Number Employees: 70
Number of Brands: 10
Number of Products: 250
Square Footage: 280000
Type of Packaging: Consumer, Private Label
Brands:
Furgale
Home Commercial
No Name
Northwest Co
Pro Seris
Shop Master
Western Family

22921 Furnace Belt Company
2316 Delaware Avenue
Suite 217
Buffalo, NY 14216
Canada
Fax: 800-354-7215 800-354-7213
fbc@furnacebeltco.com www.furnacebeltco.com
Manufacturer and exporter of wire processing belts for heat treating, brazing, annealing, sintering, quenching, freezing and baking
President: J Tatone
Number Employees: 40
Square Footage: 90000

22922 Furniturelab
106 S Greensboro St # E
Carrboro, NC 27510-2266
919-913-0270
Fax: 919-913-0271 800-449-8677
sales@furniturelab.com www.furniturelab.com
Manufacturer and exporter of wood and laminated tables, tabletops, chairs and bases

President: Greg Rapp
sales@furniturelab.com
Marketing: Courtney Smith
Sales Director: Nathan Bearman
Estimated Sales: $1-3 Million
Number Employees: 10-19
Square Footage: 14000

22923 Futura 2000 Corporation
8861 SW 132nd Street
31
Miami, FL 33176-5926
305-256-5877
Fax: 718-349-2485
Menu boards and systems and point of purchase signage; also, retrofitting services available
VP: Diana Amengual
Sales Manager: Rocco Colafrancesco
Estimated Sales: $300,000-500,000
Number Employees: 1-4

22924 Futura Coatings
6614 Grant Road
Houston, TX 77066
281-397-0033
Fax: 281-397-6512
Wine industry tank linings and coating
CFO: David Wicks
Contact: Dannie Vickers
dvickers@futuracoatings.com
Estimated Sales: $5-10 000,000
Number Employees: 50-99

22925 Futura Equipment Corporation
460 McLaughlin Rd
Yakima, WA 98908-9659
509-972-3300
Fax: 509-972-3377 888-886-2233
President: Andy Briesmeister
Estimated Sales: $1-3 Million
Number Employees: 5-9

22926 Future Commodities IntlInc
10676 Fulton Ct
Rancho Cucamonga, CA 91730-4848
909-987-4258
Fax: 909-987-5189 888-588-2378
sales@bestpack.com www.bestpack.com
Manufacturer and exporter of carton sealers, erectors and end line packaging machinery
President: David Lim
VP: Chery Lim
Sales Manager: Patrick Brennan
Contact: Mike Byrne
mbyrne@bestpack.com
Estimated Sales: $5-10 Million
Number Employees: 1-4
Square Footage: 108000
Parent Co: Future Commodities International
Brands:
Bestpack

22927 Future Foods
945 W. Fulton Marke
Chicago, IL 60607
312-987-9342
Fax: 773-561-0307
Consultant providing marketing services to the food service industry; also, product development available
President: Andrew Patterson
VP Sales: Ron Gulyas
Estimated Sales: $.5-1,000,000
Number Employees: 1-4

22928 Futures
P.O.Box 60
Barrington, NH 03825-0060
603-664-5811
Fax: 603-664-5864 info@futuressearch.com
www.cri-mms.com
Executive search firm specializing in food service sales and marketing
Manager: Peter Dutton
VP: Richard Mazzola
Estimated Sales: $500,000-$1 Million
Number Employees: 5-9
Square Footage: 8000

22929 Fygir Logistic Information Systems
25 Mall Road
Suite 300
Burlington, MA 01803-4144
781-270-0683
Fax: 781-238-6725
Production planning for developing and monitoring production resources
Estimated Sales: Under $500,000

22930 Fyh Bearing Units USA Inc
285 Industrial Dr
Wauconda, IL 60084-1078
847-487-9111
Fax: 847-882-5360 www.fyhusa.com
Mounted bearing units and insert bearings; inch and metric shaft sizes, heavy duty, medium duty, standard duty, and light duty units; specialty series include solid stainless steel, bright white thermoplstic, clean series, taper borelocking UK-series
Manager: J Frasor
CFO: Rodney Jones
Executive VP: Tohru Yamashita
Contact: Jay Frasor
jfrasor@fyhusa.com
General Manager: Charles Horwitz
Estimated Sales: $10-20 000,000
Number Employees: 5-9
Type of Packaging: Private Label

22931 (HQ)G & C Packing Co
240 S 21st St
Colorado Springs, CO 80904-3304
719-634-1587
Fax: 719-636-1038
Supplier of slaughtering services only
President: Frank Grindinger
gcpack@qwestoffice.net
Estimated Sales: $7.6 Million
Number Employees: 20-49
Square Footage: 23850
Type of Packaging: Consumer, Food Service, Bulk

22932 G & D Chillers Inc
3498 W 1st Ave # 1
Eugene, OR 97402-5453
541-345-3903
Fax: 541-345-8835 800-555-0973
www.gdchillers.com
Wine industry, glycol and process chiller
Owner: Justin Thomas
justin@gdchillers.com
VP: Ray Tatum
Estimated Sales: Below $5 000,000
Number Employees: 5-9

22933 G & F Mfg
5555 W 109th St
Oak Lawn, IL 60453-5070
708-424-4170
Fax: 708-424-4922 800-282-1574
gandf@gandf.com www.gandf.com
Designing and manufacturing high quality chemical resistant, durable and rugged Stainless steel products such as steel tanks, filling machines, piston filters, cappers, and labeling.
President: Rob Bais
rbais@gfmfg.com
Purchasing Manager: Ron Bais
Number Employees: 10-19
Square Footage: 15000
Type of Packaging: Food Service

22934 G & J Awning & Canvas Inc
1260 10th St N
Sauk Rapids, MN 56379-2500
320-255-1733
Fax: 320-255-0130 800-467-1744
info@gjawning.com www.gjawning.com
Commercial awnings including interior and exterior
Owner: Gary Buermann
CEO: Janice Buermann
CFO: Janice Beurmann
Vice President: Janice Buermann
Manager: Beth Brenny
beth@gjawning.com
Estimated Sales: Below $5,000,000
Number Employees: 10-19
Square Footage: 19800

22935 (HQ)G & S Metal Products CoInc
3330 E 79th St
Cleveland, OH 44127-1878
216-441-0700
Fax: 216-441-0736 www.gsmetal.com
Aluminum and steel bakeware and housewares including pans
President: Anoop Govind
agovind@njtcs.com
Estimated Sales: $50-100 Million
Number Employees: 250-499
Brands:
Baker-Eze
Black Beauty
Ez Baker
Silverstone

22936 G A Systems Inc
17872 Gothard St
Huntington Beach, CA 92647-6217
714-848-7529
Fax: 714-841-2356 sales@gasystemsmfg.com
www.gasystemsmfg.com
Stainless steel food service equipment and display cabinets
President: Steve Anderson
Founder: Gordon Anderson
Chief Financial Officer: Pat Devalle
Vice President: Steven Anderson
Sales: Virginia Anderson
Estimated Sales: $2.5-5 Million
Number Employees: 10-19
Square Footage: 64000

22937 G C Evans Sales & Mfg Co
3300 S Woodrow St
Little Rock, AR 72204-6550
501-664-5095
Fax: 501-663-8690 800-382-6720
sales@gcevans.com www.gcevans.com
Cooling tunnels, warmers and pasteurizers
President: Gerald Mc Namer
jenniferb@gcevans.com
Sales/Marketing: Mark McNamer
Operations/Production: David McNamer
Estimated Sales: $5-10 000,000
Number Employees: 20-49
Square Footage: 50000

22938 G C Evans Sales & Mfg Co
3300 S Woodrow St
Little Rock, AR 72204-6550
501-664-5095
Fax: 501-663-8690 800-382-6720
sales@gcevans.com www.gcevans.com
Accumulating conveyors
President: Gerald Mc Namer
jenniferb@gcevans.com
Estimated Sales: $5-10 000,000
Number Employees: 20-49

22939 G K & L Inc
20910 Peach Tree Rd
Dickerson, MD 20842-9159
301-948-5538
Fax: 301-972-7641 GKandL@aol.com
www.gkandl.com
Grease interceptors, floor sinks and solid strainers for restaurants
Owner: Gene Wilkes
gkandl@aol.com
Estimated Sales: $1-2.5 Million
Number Employees: 1-4
Brands:
Renn

22940 G L Packaging Products Inc
1135 Carolina Dr
West Chicago, IL 60185-1713
630-231-5440
Fax: 630-231-5447 866-935-8755
info@glpackaging.com www.glpackaging.com
Corrugated and wooden pallets
President: Todd Tomala
toddt@glpackaging.com
Sales Director: Len Kats
Operations Manager: Dale Komarek
Estimated Sales: $5-10 Million
Number Employees: 20-49
Square Footage: 160000

22941 G Lighting
9777 Reavis Park Dr
St Louis, MO 63123-5315
314-631-6000
Fax: 314-631-7800 800-331-2425
sales@glighting.com www.glighting.com
Designer and manufacturer of decorative commercial lighting fixtures
President: Nick Gross
nick@glighting.com
CEO: Robert Gross
Executive Vice President: Linton Gross
Marketing/R&D: Brent Paiva
Marketing/R&D: Brent Paiva
President, Sales Manager: Nick Gross
Customer Service: Kara Gross
Office Manager, Purchasing Manager: Jenny Cole
Production Manager: Dan Dickinson
Office Manager, Purchasing Manager: Jenny Cole
Estimated Sales: $5-10 Million
Number Employees: 20-49
Square Footage: 16000

22942 G P 50 New York LTD
2770 Long Rd
Grand Island, NY 14072-1223
716-773-9300
Fax: 716-773-5019 meltsales@gp50.com
www.gp50.com
Controls: transducers and transmitters
President: Donald Less
don@gp50.com
Vice President: Ken Brodie
Director: Bob Atwood
Director: Bob Atwood
Estimated Sales: $10-20 000,000
Number Employees: 50-99
Square Footage: 30000

22943 G W Berkheimer Co
1011 E Wallace St
Fort Wayne, IN 46803-2591
260-744-4156
Fax: 260-456-2177 800-535-6696
webmaster@gwberkheimer.com
www.gwberkheimer.com
Heating equipment
Manager: Chris Wamsley
chriswamsley@gwberkheimer.com
Branch Manager: Curt Rees
Estimated Sales: $10-20,000,000
Number Employees: 20-49
Parent Co: G.W. Berkheimer Company

22944 G&H Enterprises
344 McLaws Cir
Williamsburg, VA 23185-5648
757-258-1230
Fax: 757-258-1231
Case packaging machinery, case packing, box erection, top sealing custom automated machinery and components
Estimated Sales: $1-2.5 000,000
Number Employees: 10-19

22945 G&K Vijuk Intern. Corp
715 Church Rd
Elmhurst, IL 60126
630-530-2203
Fax: 630-530-2245 info@guk-vijuk.com
Bindery finishing equipment, miniature folders
President: Joseph Vijuk
Contact: Steve Kozak
skozak@vijukequip.com
Estimated Sales: $10-20 Million
Number Employees: 35

22946 G&R Graphics
PO Box 7095
West Orange, NJ 7052
973-380-8317
Fax: 973-731-7438 813-503-8592
gnrstamp@aol.com
Manufacturer and exporter of rubber printing plates, corporate seals, rubber stamps, inks and pads
President: David Gonzalez
Contact: Anibal Gonzalez
agonzalez@grgraphicsinc.com
Estimated Sales: $1-5 Million
Number Employees: 5-9
Square Footage: 8000

22947 G-3 Enterprises
500 S Santa Rosa Ave
Modesto, CA 95354-3717
209-341-4100
Fax: 209-341-3034 888-264-3225
www.g3enterprises.com
Wine, Champagne, Beer, Soda, Water and Sake industries. Aluminum screw caps, corks, capsules
President, Chief Executive Officer: Robert Lubeck
Director Marketing/Sales: Lee McDonald
Customer Care Specialist: Jack Leguria
Estimated Sales: $20-50 Million
Number Employees: 100-249

22948 G.F. Frank & Sons
9075 LeSaint Dr Fairfield
Fairfield, OH 45014
513-870-9075
Fax: 513-870-0579 john@GFFrankAndSons.com
www.gffrankandsons.com
Manufacturer and exporter of meat hooks, skewers, trolleys and smokehouse shelving
President: George Frank
Vice President: John Frank
Estimated Sales: $10-20 Million
Number Employees: 10-19

22949 G.G. Greene Enterprises
2790 Pennsylvania Avenue
West Warren, PA 16365
814-723-5700
Fax: 814-723-3037
awillingham@greenegroup.com
www.greenegroup.com
Manufactures guns, howitzers, mortars & related equipment; manufactures small arms ammunition; manufactures stamped or pressed metal machine parts; plate metal fabricator
Manager: Brent Long
Estimated Sales: $4,500,000
Number Employees: 20-49
Square Footage: 850000
Type of Packaging: Consumer, Food Service

22950 G.V. Aikman Company
6312 Southeastern Avenue
Indianapolis, IN 46203-5828
317-353-8181
Fax: 317-352-7695 800-886-4029
Designer of commercial kitchens for schools, institutions, etc
Estimated Sales: $2.5-5,000,000
Number Employees: 20-49

22951 G.W. Dahl Company
8439 Triad Dr
Greensboro, NC 27409-9018
336-668-4444
Fax: 336-668-4452 800-852-4449
info@purolator-facet.com
www.purolator-facet.com
Filters including water, oil and air; also, I/P transducers, P/I transmitters and pneumatic relays
President: Bruss Stellfox
Quality Control: Stlee Bigary
Marketing Manager: John Mello
Sales Administration: Debbie Froelich
Number Employees: 100-249
Square Footage: 340000
Parent Co: Purolator Products Company

22952 GA Design Menu Company
28710 Wall Street
Wixom, MI 48393-3516
313-561-2530
Fax: 313-561-1049
Laminated menus including inserts and covers
Owner: Gary Anoshka
Number Employees: 3
Square Footage: 6000

22953 GAF Seelig Inc
5905 52nd Ave
Flushing, NY 11377-7480
718-899-5000
Fax: 718-803-1198
Wholesaler and distributor of juice, milk, cheese, yogurt, sour cream, purees, raviolis and pastas, oils and vinegars, chocolate and many more food service items.
President: Rodney Seelig
rseelig@gafseelig.com
Executive Vice President: Gary Lavery Sr.
Director of Sales: John Arena

Estimated Sales: $5-10 Million
Number Employees: 100-249

22954 GBS Foodservice Equipment, Inc.
951 Matheson Boulevard E
Mississauga, ON L4W 2R7
Canada

905-897-2333
Fax: 905-897-2334 888-402-1242
pdouglas@gbscooks.com www.gbscooks.com
Distributor of foodservice equipment including;
combi-ovens, open well fryers, rotisseries, blast
chillers, for hot & cold merchandisers
General Manager: S Jaffer
Estimated Sales: $1-5 Million
Number Employees: 10-20

22955 GCA
5122 Bolsa Ave # 104
Huntington Beach, CA 92649-1050

714-379-4911
Fax: 714-379-4913 julie@gcalabels.com
www.gcalabels.com
Bar code equipment and supplies, labels, packaging,
printers, software and marking devices; laser mark-
ing service available
Owner: Karen Schade
kschade@schoollane.org
Office Manager: Kim Benudict
Estimated Sales: Less Than $500,000
Number Employees: 1-4
Brands:
    Loftware
    Monarch

22956 GCJ Mattei Company
927 E Madison St
Louisville, KY 40204

502-583-4774
Fax: 502-583-4776
Displays
Owner: Louis Mattei
Estimated Sales: $500,000-$1 Million
Number Employees: 1-4
Square Footage: 24000

22957 GD Packaging Machinery
501 Southlake Blvd
Richmond, VA 23236-3078

804-794-9777
Fax: 804-794-6187
CFO: Lich Polchinski
Marketing: Glen Coater
Number Employees: 250-499

22958 GDM Concepts
15330 Texaco Ave
Paramount, CA 90723-3920

562-633-0195
Fax: 562-633-1561
Store fixtures
President: George Myers
info@gdmconcepts.com
Estimated Sales: $10-20,000,000
Number Employees: 20-49

22959 GE Appliances
Appliance Park
Louisville, KY 40225-0001

877-959-8688
www.geappliances.com
Appliances for home and businesses.
President & CEO: Kevin Nolan
VP & CFO: Marc Charnas
VP, Legal: Jason Brown
VP, Human Resources: Tom Quick
Chief Commercial Officer: Rick Hasselbeck
COO: Melanie Cook
Number Employees: 12,000
Parent Co: Haier Group Corporation
Brands:
    GE
    GE Profile
    Cafe
    Monogram
    Haier
    Hotpoint

22960 GE Interlogix Industrial
12345 SW Leveton Dr
Tualatin, OR 97062-6001

503-692-4052
Fax: 503-691-7377 800-247-9447
www.sentrol.com

Manufacturer and exporter of noncontract safety
switches, position sensors and safety relays
President: Greg Burge
Contact: Rich Laitta
rlaitta@berwind.com
Estimated Sales: $50-100 Million
Number Employees: 500-999
Square Footage: 140000
Parent Co: Interlogix
Brands:
    Failsafe Guardswitch
    Guardswitch

22961 GE Lighting
1975 Noble Rd
Cleveland, OH 44112-6300

800-435-4448
www.gelighting.com
Lighting and lighting fixtures including incandes-
cent, flourescent, HID, outdoor and mercury
CEO: Bill Lacey
bill.lacey@ge.com
Estimated Sales: $3 Billion
Number Employees: 17,000
Parent Co: General Electric Company
Other Locations:
    GE Lighting
    Elmwood Park NJ

22962 GEA Evaporation Technologies LLC
9165 Rumsey Rd
Columbia, MD 21045-1929

410-997-8700
Fax: 410-997-5021
President: Eric Bryars
Contact: Ramash Quasba
ramash.quasba@geagroup.com
Estimated Sales: $20 Million
Number Employees: 100-249

22963 GEA FES, Inc.
44840 Les SoriniŠres
York, PA 17406

025-119-1051
Fax: 024-005-7381 geneglace@gea.com
Industrial refrigeration components.
President: John Ansbro
Service Manager: Randy Keefer

22964 GEA Filtration
1600 Okeefe Rd
Hudson, WI 54016-2290

715-386-9371
Fax: 715-386-9376
President: Steve Kathleen
VP: Eric Bryars
Manufacturing Manager: Gerry Nelson
Sales: Bob Keefe
Contact: Jamie Atwell
jamie.atwell@gea.com
Estimated Sales: $20-50 Million
Number Employees: 100-249

22965 GEA Niro Soavi North America
10 Commerce Park North
Building 7
Bedford, NH 03110

603-606-4060
Fax: 603-606-4065
Manufacturer and supplier of high pressure pumps
and homoginizers for the food industry.

22966 (HQ)GEA North America
1880 Country Farm Dr
Naperville, IL 60563-1089

630-369-8100
Fax: 630-369-9875
Manufacturer and exporter of dairy farm equipment
including cleaners
President: John Ansbro
john.ansbro@geagroup.com
CEO: Dirk Hejnal
CFO: Dr. Ulrich Hullman
Sales: Vern Foster
Business Unit, Milking & Cooling: Dr. Armin
Tietjen
Estimated Sales: Below $5 Million
Number Employees: 100-249
Other Locations:
    Babson Brothers Co.
    Galesville WI
Brands:
    Surge

22967 GEA PHE Systems North America, Inc.
100 Gea Drive
York, PA 17406-8469

717-268-6200
Fax: 717-268-6162 800-774-0474
info.phe-systems.usa@gea.com
www.geaphena.com
Heat exchangers, industrial evaporating equipment,
spray dryers
Manager: Steve Lovell
VP Sales: Clemens Starzinski
Contact: Dave Berry
dave.berry@geagroup.com
Estimated Sales: $7 Million
Number Employees: 5-9

22968 GEA Refrigeration NorthAmerica
3475 Board Rd
York, PA 17406-8414

717-767-6411
Fax: 717-764-3627 800-888-4337
sales.gearna@gea.com www.gea.com
Industrial refrigeration equipment
President: John Ansbro
john.ansbro@geagroup.com
CFO: John Lutz
Quality Control: Jim Mesbitt
VP: Dennis Halsey
Marketing Manager: Teresa Sauble
Sales: John Miranda
Estimated Sales: $500,000-$1 Million
Number Employees: 250-499

22969 GEBO Corporation
6015 31st Street E
Bradenton, FL 34203-5382

941-727-1400
Fax: 941-727-1200
Packaging machinery
Marketing Director: George Rouli
Estimated Sales: $20-50 Million
Number Employees: 100-250

22970 GED, LLC
28107 Beaver Dam Branch Rd
Box 140
Laurel, DE 19956-9801

302-856-1756
Fax: 302-856-9888 gedllc@yahoo.com
Importers and exporters of cans, plus dealers of food
processing machines and parts
Estimated Sales: $1-5 Million
Number Employees: 3

22971 GEE Manufacturing
2200 S Golden State Blvd
P.O. Box 397
Fowler, CA 93625

559-834-2929
Fax: 559-834-1715 800-433-1620
info@geemanufacturing.com
www.geemanufacturing.com
Wine industry stainless steel tanks
President and Owner: Glen Gee
Estimated Sales: $5-10 000,000
Number Employees: 20-49

22972 GEI Autowrappers
700 Pennsylvania Drive
Exton, PA 19341-1129

610-321-1115
Fax: 610-321-1199
Manufacturer and exporter of electronic flow wrap-
pers
Sales Manager: Richard Landers
Number Employees: 120
Square Footage: 160000
Parent Co: GEI International

22973 GEI PPM
569 W Uwchlan Ave
Exton, PA 19341-1563

610-524-7178
Fax: 610-321-1199 800-345-1308
Manufacturer and exporter of pressure sensitive and
multi-head/in-line rotary labelers
Owner: Jin Guo
Estimated Sales: $1-5 Million
Number Employees: 1-4
Square Footage: 320000
Parent Co: GEI International

22974 GEI Turbo
700 Pennsylvania Drive
Exton, PA 19341-1129
610-321-1100
Fax: 610-321-1199 800-345-1308
Manufacturer and exporter of hand-held and automatic high and low temperature filling equipment
Estimated Sales: $1-5 Million
Parent Co: GEI International

22975 GEM Equipment Of OregonInc
2150 Progress Way
Woodburn, OR 97071-9765
503-982-9902
Fax: 503-981-6316 gem@gemequipment.com
www.gemequipment.com
Manufacturer and exporter of blanchers, conveyor systems and components, fryers, dumpers, mixers, preheaters and batter mix systems
President: Edward McKenney
CEO: Steve Ross
sross@gemequipment.com
COO: Steve Ross
Vice President of Sales: Jerry Bell
Plant Manager: Ray Rowe
Purchasing Manager: Ray Rowe
Estimated Sales: $20-50 Million
Number Employees: 50-99
Square Footage: 100000

22976 GEM Equipment Of OregonInc
2150 Progress Way
P.O.Box 2449
Woodburn, OR 97071-9765
503-982-9902
Fax: 503-981-6316 gem@gemequipment.com
www.gemequipment.com
President: Edward T McKenney
CEO: Steve Ross
sross@gemequipment.com
Vice President, Sales: Jerry Bell
R&D: Dill Larson
Quality Control: Tony Meehl
Technical Sales: Jim Caughlin
Estimated Sales: $10-20 Million
Number Employees: 50-99

22977 GENESTA
1850 E Interstate 30
Rockwall, TX 75087-6201
Canada
972-771-1653
Fax: 972-722-1179 info@genesta.com
www.genesta.com
Extruded formed fluorescent lighting fixtures and vacuum formed display components
Partner: Kelson Elam
kelam@genesta.com
VP: Merv Schwantz
Number Employees: 10-19

22978 GEO Graphics-Spegram
PO Box 305
Mystic, CT 06355-0305
860-572-8507
Fax: 860-536-3961 gspmystic@gsptoday.com
www.gsptoday.com
Wine industry labelers
CEO: Erik H Ljungberg
Contact: Erik Ljungberg
eljungberg@gsptoday.com
Estimated Sales: $10-20 Million
Number Employees: 10-19

22979 GERM-O-RAY
1641 Lewis Way
Stone Mountain, GA 30083-1107
770-939-2835
Fax: 770-621-0100 800-766-8480
sales@insect-o-cutor.com www.insect-o-cutor.com
Manufacturer and exporter of air disinfection fixtures and germicidal fluorescent, UV and UVC lamps; available in in-room, in-duct and custom styles
CEO: Bill Harris
Marketing Director: J Harris
Advertising: D Johnson
Systems Engineer: J Baum
Estimated Sales: $1-3 Million
Number Employees: 10-19
Brands:
   Germ-O-Ray

22980 GET Enterprises LLC
1515 W Sam Houston Pkwy N
Houston, TX 77043-3112
713-467-9394
Fax: 713-467-9396 800-727-4500
info@get-melamine.com www.get-melamine.com
Importer and wholesaler/distributor of dinnerware, high chairs, tray stands, tumblers, platters and soup and coffee mugs; serving the food service market
President: Glen Hou
HR Executive: Joyce Liu
joyceliu@get-melamine.com
VP Sales/Marketing: Eve Hou
Estimated Sales: $5-10 Million
Number Employees: 50-99
Square Footage: 40000

22981 GFI Stainless
2084 Lapham Dr # A
Building A
Modesto, CA 95354-3909
209-571-1684
Fax: 209-571-2445 800-221-2652
sales@gfistainless.com www.gfistainless.com
Wine industry fluid handling products
President: Gordon Fluker
g_fluker@gfistainless.com
Vice President: Fred Elwood
Estimated Sales: $1-2.5 Million
Number Employees: 10-19

22982 (HQ)GHM Industries Inc
100 Sturbridge Rd # A
Charlton, MA 01507-5323
508-248-3941
Fax: 508-248-0639 800-793-7013
sales@millerproducts.net www.millerproducts.net
Manufacturer and exporter of textile machinery including automatic roll wrappers and polywraps
President: Paul Jankovic
pjankovic@millerproducts.net
Estimated Sales: $2.5-5 Million
Number Employees: 5-9

22983 GJ Glass Company
1019 Lincoln Street
Cedar Falls, IA 50613-3248
319-266-4444
Fax: 319-266-2041 800-422-8807

22984 GKI Foods
7926 Lochlin Road
Brighton, MI 48116
248-486-0055
Fax: 248-486-9135 www.gkifoods.com
Milk chocolate, sugar free chocolate, yogurt and cards products, panned and enrobed, bulk or packaged. Also produces custom granola (all natural, highly nutritional, low in fat and fat free), trail mixes, etc. Custom formulation. Aidcertified, GMP and HACCP accreditation.
President: Sue Wilts
Contact: Nancy Fletcher
nancy.fletcher@gkifoods.com
General Manager: Jim Frazier
Number Employees: 20-49
Square Footage: 60000
Type of Packaging: Consumer, Private Label, Bulk

22985 (HQ)GM Nameplate
2040 15th Ave W
Seattle, WA 98119-2783
206-284-2200
Fax: 206-284-3705 800-366-7668
webnet@gmnameplate.com
www.gmnameplate.com
Manufacturer and exporter of nameplates, labels, membrane switches, injection and compression molding.
President: Brad Root
brad@gmnameplate.com
Chairman & CEO: Donald Root
New Product Manager: Dennis Cook
Research & Development: Debbie Anderson
Marketing Manager: Shannon Kirk
VP Sales & Marketing: Gerry Gallagher
Operations Executive: Mark Samuel
Plant/Production Manager: Marc Doan
Purchasing Agent: Jim Davis
Number Employees: 1000-4999
Square Footage: 560000
Other Locations:
   Elite Plastics Division
   Beaverton OR
   Canada Division
   Surrey BC
   California Division
   San Jose CA
   North Carolina Division
   Monroe NC
   SuperGraphics Division
   Seattle WA
Brands:
   Color Cal
   Mark Cal
   Poly Cal

22986 GMF
9201 NW 78th
St Weatherby Lake, MO 64152
816-505-9900
Fax: 816-505-9995 www.andritzgouda.com
GMF-Gouda supplies specialized machinery to the chemical and food industries.
President: Mark Mc Kee
Estimated Sales: $.5-1 million
Number Employees: 170
Parent Co: ANDRITZ Separation

22987 GN Thermoforming Equipment
345 Old Trunk 3
PO Box 710
Chester, NS B0J 1J0
Canada
902-275-3571
Fax: 902-275-3100 gn@gncanada.com
www.gnplastics.com
President: Georg Nemeskeri
Quality Manager: Curtis Dowe
Marketing Manager: Jerome Romkey
Sales Representative: Colin MacDonald
Number Employees: 100+

22988 GNTUSA Inc
660 White Plains Rd # 6
Tarrytown, NY 10591-5139
914-332-6663
Fax: 914-524-0681 877-468-8727
info@gntusa.com www.gnt-group.com
GNT manufactures Exberry natural colors and Nutrifood fuit and vegetable extracts.
President and CEO: Stefan Hake
gnt-orders@gntusa.com
Marketing: Jeannette O'Brien
Number Employees: 10-19
Parent Co: GNT International B.V.
Type of Packaging: Food Service, Private Label, Bulk

22989 GOBI Library Solutions
999 Maple St
Hopkinton, NH 03229-3374
603-746-3102
Fax: 603-746-5628 800-258-3774
service@ybp.com
Information resource
Director, Finance & Accounting: Andy Fries
Senior VP: Amy Alcorn
a_alcorn@salemstate.edu
Senior Vice President, Sales and Operati: Mark Kendall
Vice President, Operations: Nathaniel Bruning
Number Employees: 250-499

22990 GOJO Industries Inc
1 Gojo Plz # 500
Akron, OH 44311-1085
330-255-6000
Fax: 330-255-6119 800-321-9647
www.gojo.com
Manufacturer and exporter of hand cleaners and soap dispensers
President/Chief Operating Officer: Mark Lerner
Chief Executive Officer: Joe Kanfer
Managing Director: Adrian Coombes
Vice Chair: Marcella Rolnick
Research & Development: Thales De Nardo
Quality Control Assurance: Susan Jack
Vice President, Sales & Marketing: Jeff Buysse
Vice President, Sales: Greg Conner
Product Manager: Aaron Conrow
Lab Manager: Dan Willis
Purchasing: Debbie Topliff
Estimated Sales: $75 Million
Number Employees: 250-499
Square Footage: 500000
Brands:
   Derma-Pro
   Go-Jo

22991 GP Plastics Corporation
8900 NW 77th Court
Medley, FL 33166-2102
305-888-3555
Fax: 305-885-4204
Extruded polyethylene products including trash and produce bags
Division Manager: Pam Hauserman
Manager (Southeast): Elaine Kurau
Plant Manager: Bob Riber
Estimated Sales: $20-50 Million
Number Employees: 100-249

22992 GPI USA LLC.
10062 190th Place
Suite 107
Mokena, IL 60448
706-850-7826
Fax: 708-785-0608 800-929-4248
karen.haley@foodgums.com
Specialize in carageenan used for stabilization and as an additive for both dairy products and in the red meat and poultry industries.

22993 GSC Blending
3600 Atl Ind Pkwy NW
Atlanta, GA 30331
404-696-6200
Fax: 404-696-4546 800-453-9997
SShapiro@gaspiceco.com www.gaspiceco.com
President/Owner: Selma Shapiro
President: Robert S Shapiro
Estimated Sales: $10-20 Million
Number Employees: 16

22994 GSC Packaging
3715 Atlanta Industrial Pkwy
Atlanta, GA 30331-1049
404-505-9925
Fax: 404-696-2667 800-453-9997
www.gscpackaging.com
President and CEO: Robert Shapiro
Estimated Sales: $10-20 Million
Number Employees: 20-49

22995 GSMA Division of SWF Co
1949 E. Manning Avenue
Suite 5
Reedley, CA 93654
559-638-8484
Fax: 559-38 -478 800-344-8951
info@swfcompanies.com www.swfcompanies.com
Automated robotics, barcode scanners, proofreaders
President: Roland Parker
Vice President / General Manager: Ed Suarez
Product Manager-Robotics: Matt Garcia
AMP Manager: Mark Freitas
Product Manager: Craig Friesen
General Manager: Mark Senti
Estimated Sales: $1-5 Million
Number Employees: 10

22996 GSW Jackes-Evans Manufacturing Company
4427 Geraldine Avenue
Saint Louis, MO 63115-1217
314-385-4132
Fax: 314-385-0802 800-325-6173
Manufacturer, importer and exporter of barbecue equipment and accessories
President: Rob Harris
BBQ Products: Joe Fernandez
Director Sales (Heating Products): Ron Bailey
Number Employees: 200
Square Footage: 500000
Parent Co: GSW
Type of Packaging: Consumer, Private Label, Bulk
Brands:
    Chef Shop
    E-Z Fit Barbecue
    Party Chef
    Super Chef

22997 GT International
1400 Post Oak Boulevard
Suite 270
Houston, TX 77056-3008
713-494-8779
Fax: 713-629-8908
Plasic pallets, plastic crates, bottled water
Estimated Sales: $500,000-$1 000,000
Number Employees: 1-4

22998 GTCO CalComp
14557 N. 82nd Street
Scottsdale, AZ 85260
410-381-3450
Fax: 480-948-5508 800-856-0732
calcomp.sales@gtcocalcomp.com
Manufacturer and exporter of wide-format graphic printers and tablets
Sales Director: Kim Plasterer
VP Sales: Don Lightfoot
Contact: Debra Melcher
dmelcher@gtcocalcomp.com
Number Employees: 1,000-4,999
Parent Co: eInstruction
Type of Packaging: Food Service

22999 GTI
12650 W 64th Ave # F
Arvada, CO 80004-3887
303-420-6699
Fax: 303-420-6699 www.greatclips.com
Manufacturer and exporter of seamers
President: Charlie Simpson
Chairman of the Board: Ray Barton
Vice President: Michelle Sack
Senior Vice President of Operations: Steve Hockett
Estimated Sales: $1-5 Million
Brands:
    Ease Out

23000 GW&E Global Water & Energy
2404 Rutland Drive
Austin, TX 78758
512-697-1930
Fax: 512-697-1931
Supplier of wastewater treatment and bio-waste-to-energy solutions with sludge management, scrubbing & utilizations sytems, reuse/reclaim water systems, and biological treatments.
Contact: Jeff Faldyn
jfaldyn@globalwaterengineering.com

23001 Gabriel Container Co
8844 Millergrove Dr
Santa Fe Springs, CA 90670-2013
323-685-8844
Fax: 562-699-3284
Corrugated containers
President: Ron Gabriel
r.gabriel@gabrielcontainer.com
Estimated Sales: $20-50 Million
Number Employees: 100-249

23002 Gabriella Imports
5100 Prospect Ave
Cleveland, OH 44103
216-432-3651
Fax: 216-432-3654 800-544-8117
Manufacturer, importer and exporter of automatic espresso equipment and granita machines and products
Estimated Sales: $500,000-$1 Million
Number Employees: 35
Brands:
    Gabriella

23003 Gadren Machine Company
PO Box 117
Mount Ephraim, NJ 08059-0117
856-456-4329
Fax: 856-456-2238 800-822-4233
gadreninfo@comcast.net
Wine industry valves and fittings
Estimated Sales: $3 Million
Number Employees: 20

23004 Gaetano America
9460 Telstar Ave
El Monte, CA 91731-2904
626-442-2858
Fax: 626-401-1988 gaetanorf@aol.com
Manufacturer and exporter of ceramic bowls, platters, serving pieces and dinnerware
Owner: Irving Chait
VP Sales/Marketing: Rick Frovich

23005 Gafco-Worldwide
6302 Harrison Avenue
Suite 5
Cincinnati, OH 45247-6413
513-574-2257
Fax: 513-574-2362 gafcoww@aol.com

Accumulating conveyors and bar code scanners, spare parts, export management brewery and soft drink applications
President: Frank May
Estimated Sales: $5-10 000,000
Number Employees: 9

23006 Gage Industries
P.O.Box 1318
Lake Oswego, OR 97035
503-639-2177
Fax: 503-624-1070 800-443-4243
sales@gageindustries.com
Manufacturer and exporter of plastic thermoformed packaging products including freezable and dual-ovenable food trays, cutting trays, totes, plastic containers, etc
President: Jeff Gage
Executive VP: Lizbeth Gage
Sales: Scott Tullis
Estimated Sales: $50-100 Million
Number Employees: 250-499
Number of Brands: 3
Number of Products: 70
Square Footage: 200000
Type of Packaging: Consumer, Food Service, Private Label, Bulk
Brands:
    Gage

23007 Gainco Inc
1635 Oakbrook Dr
Gainesville, GA 30507-8492
770-534-0703
Fax: 770-534-1865 800-467-2828
Sales@gainco.com www.gainco.com
Automated weighing and sorting systems for the meat and poultry industry
Manager: Gene Parets
Manager: Joe Cowman
jcowman@gainco.com
Number Employees: 20-49
Parent Co: Bettcher Industries

23008 Gainco Inc
1635 Oakbrook Dr
Gainesville, GA 30507-8492
770-534-0703
Fax: 770-534-1865 800-467-2828
Sales@gainco.com www.gainco.com
Portion sizing and distribution equipment, sorting, counting, weighing, and bagging systems, as well as bench and floor scales for the poultry, meat and food processing industries.
Manager: Joe Cowman
jcowman@gainco.com
Number Employees: 20-49

23009 Gainesville Neon & Signs
1405 NW 53rd Ave
Gainesville, FL 32609-6104
352-376-2750
Fax: 352-373-5734 800-852-1407
sales@gainesvilleneon.com
www.gainesvilleneon.com
Lighted signs including neon, wooden, vinyl, luminous tube and billboard
Owner: Daryl Tomlinson
accounting@gainesvilleneon.com
General Manager: Robert Jammer
Estimated Sales: Below $5 Million
Number Employees: 10-19
Square Footage: 40000

23010 Gainesville Welding & Mntnc
37 Henry Grady Hwy
Dawsonville, GA 30534-5717
706-216-2666
Fax: 706-216-4282 www.gwrendering.com
Cookers, dryers, prebakers, presses, tanks and storage units
Owner: Terry Stephens
Estimated Sales: $500,000-$1 000,000
Number Employees: 10-19
Type of Packaging: Bulk

23011 Galaxy Chemical Corp
2041 Whitfield Park Ave
Sarasota, FL 34243-4085
941-755-8545
Fax: 941-751-9412 gccgps@aol.com
Manufacturer and exporter of hand cleaners

Owner: Allan M Sanger
gccgps@aol.com
Manager: Tim San
Estimated Sales: $5-10 Million
Number Employees: 10-19

23012 Galbraith Laboratories Inc
2323 Sycamore Dr
Knoxville, TN 37921-1700

865-546-1335
Fax: 865-546-7209 877-449-8797
labinfo@galbraith.com www.galbraith.com
Consultant specializing in chemical microanalyses
and analyses for all elements including trace analy-
ses, TOX, ION chromatography, ICP metal scans
and molecular weights
President: Brenda S Thornburgh
brendathornburgh@galbraith.com
CFO: Jim Cunnings
Senior VP: Lee Bates
Quality Control: Robert Logan
Estimated Sales: $10-20 Million
Number Employees: 50-99
Square Footage: 51000

23013 (HQ)Galbreath LLC
461 East Rosser Road
Winamac, IN 46996

574-946-6631
sales@wastequip.com
www.galbreath-inc.com
Manufacturer and exporter of detachable container
systems, roll-off hoists and recycling containers,
lugger boxes, self-dumping hoppers, dock carts, ma-
terial-handling equipment, compactors, utility,
trailers and balers
Chief Technology Officer: Lbehny Podell
Contact: Shawn Harper
sharper@wastequip.com
Estimated Sales: $10 Million
Number Employees: 75
Square Footage: 250000
Parent Co: Wastequip, Inc.
Other Locations:
Galbreath
Ider AL
Brands:
Combo-Pack
Pack-Man
Super Pack-Man

23014 Gallard-Schlesinger Industries
245 Newtown Road
Plainview, NY 11803-4316

516-683-6900
Fax: 516-683-6990 800-645-3044
Chemicals for food products
President: Karl Dorn
CFO: Jelle Westra
Quality Control: Henry Medello
Contact: Sandra Riquelme
sriquelme@gallard.com
Estimated Sales: $20-50 Million
Number Employees: 40

23015 Galley
50 South US Highway One
Jupiter, FL 33477-5107

561-748-5200
Fax: 561-748-5250 800-537-2772
galley@galleyline.com www.galleyline.com
Manufacturer and exporter of modular and mobile
cafeteria and buffet equipment, salad bars, hot food
tables and portable freezers
President: Alice Spritzer
CEO: Larry Spritzer
Estimated Sales: $500,000-$1 Million
Number Employees: 1-4
Square Footage: 11000
Brands:
Galley
Galley Line
Mate-Lock

23016 Gallimore Industries
PO Box 158
Lake Villa, IL 60046

847-356-3331
Fax: 847-356-6224 800-927-8020
mark@gallimoreinc.com
Manufacturer and exporter of in-pack coupons and
coupon inserters

President: Claris Gallimore
CEO: C Clay Gallimore
Quality Control: Mark Gallimore
Equip. VP/Production Manager: Kent Gallimore
Print VP/Production Manager: Mark Gallimore
Estimated Sales: Below $5 Million
Number Employees: 10-19
Square Footage: 42000

23017 Gallo
3600 S Memorial Dr
Racine, WI 53403-3822

262-752-9950
Fax: 262-752-9951
Manufacturer and exporter of resealable plastic bag
sealers
President: Mary Sollman
VP: Thomas Sollman
Estimated Sales: $1-2.5 Million
Number Employees: 10-19
Square Footage: 32000
Brands:
Easy-Lock

23018 Galvinell Meat Co Inc
461 Ragan Rd
Conowingo, MD 21918-1224

410-378-3032
galvinell@zoominternet.net
www.galvinell.com
Custom meat processor, also cooker services and
products and private label, custom slaughtering, and
party platters, salads, charcoal and ice also available.
Beef, pork, goat, and lamb.
President: Dennis Welsh
dennis@galvinell.com
Estimated Sales: $730 Thousand
Number Employees: 5-9
Type of Packaging: Consumer, Food Service, Private Label, Bulk

23019 Gamajet Cleaning Systems
604 Jeffers Circle
Exton, PA 19341-2524

610-408-9940
Fax: 610-408-9945 800-289-5387
sales@gamajet.com www.gamajet.com
Manufacturer and exporter of tank cleaning equip-
ment and CIP systems for fermenters, reactors, tank
trucks, storage tanks and industrial process vessels
Chairman: Robert Delaney
Sales/Customer Service: Linda Chappell
Estimated Sales: $1-2.5 Million
Number Employees: 10-19
Square Footage: 19200
Parent Co: Alfa Laval Group
Brands:
Gamajet

23020 Gamecock Chemical Co Inc
23 Plowden Mill Rd
Sumter, SC 29153-8909

803-773-7391
Fax: 803-775-8362
Sweeping compounds
Owner: George Self Jr
General Manager: Tommy Self
Estimated Sales: $1-2.5 Million
Number Employees: 5-9
Square Footage: 19000

23021 Gamewell Corporation
251 Crawford Street
Northborough, MA 01532-1234

508-231-1400
Fax: 508-231-0900 888-347-3269
www.gamewell.com
Manufacturer and exporter of fire alarm systems
President: Bill Abraham
Estimated Sales: $20-50 Million
Number Employees: 50-99

23022 Gamse Lithographing Co Inc
7413 Pulaski Hwy
Rosedale, MD 21237-2580

410-866-4700
Fax: 410-866-5672 gamse@gamse.com
www.gamse.com
Wine industry label design

President: Daniel Canzoniero
m.holland@bishophouse.com
CFO: Shelly Welling
Vice President: Ivan Sigris
Marketing Director: Joan Ziegler
Production Manager: Bob Markel
Estimated Sales: $20-50 Million
Number Employees: 100-249

23023 Ganau America Inc
21900 Carneros Oak Ln
Sonoma, CA 95476-2824

707-939-1774
Fax: 707-939-0671 800-694-CORK
www.ganau.com
Wine industry corks and cork stoppers
President: Mariella Ganau
mariella@ganauamerica.com
Sales Consultant: Kerry Smith
Accounting Manager: Gina Isi
Estimated Sales: $1-2.5 Million
Number Employees: 10-19

23024 Gann Manufacturing
1607 Wicomico St
Baltimore, MD 21230-1705

410-752-5040
Fax: 410-727-3521 800-922-9832
Safety products including gloves, liners, rainwear,
boots and disposable clothing
CEO: Stuart Levin
Exec. Sales: Grace Gracey
Estimated Sales: $2.5-5 Million
Number Employees: 1-4

23025 Gannett Outdoor of New Jersey
185 Us Highway 46
Fairfield, NJ 07004-2321

973-575-6900
Fax: 973-808-8316 www.viacomoutdoor.com
Outdoor advertising items including bulletins, post-
ers and backlights
VP: George Gross
Local Sales Manager: Gerald Allen
VP/General Sales Manager: Seth Bosin
Estimated Sales: $1-5 Million
Number Employees: 100-249
Parent Co: Gannett Company

23026 Ganz Brothers
12 Mulberry Ct
Paramus, NJ 7652

201-845-6010
Fax: 201-384-1329
Manufacturer and exporter of wrapping machinery
including high speed, paperboard, multipack and
shrink film for cans, bottles, cups and tubs
President: Christopher Ganz
cganz@ganz.com
VP: Jay Ganz
VP: Jay Ganz
Manager: Lisa Noch
Estimated Sales: $2.5-5 Million
Number Employees: 19
Square Footage: 24000

23027 Gar Products
170 Lehigh Ave
Lakewood, NJ 08701-4526

732-364-2100
Fax: 732-370-5021 800-424-2477
elliotb@garproducts.com www.garproducts.com
Manufacturer and exporter of indoor and outdoor
barstools, chairs, tables and bases; importer of chair
frames and table base castings
President: Jay Garfunkel
jaygar@garproducts.com
Vice President: Ellen Garfunkle
Quality Control: Sam Garfunkle
Sales Director: Elliot Bass
Operations Manager: Sam Garfunkle
Plant Manager: Jose Lopez
Purchasing Manager: Daniel Hyams
Number Employees: 20-49
Square Footage: 300000

23028 Garb-El Products Co
240 Michigan St # 1
Lockport, NY 14094-1797

716-434-6010
Fax: 716-434-9148 jcarbonejr@garb-el.com
www.garb-el.com
Manufacturer and exporter of food waste disposal
equipment and prep stations

President/ CEO: James M. Carbone, Jr.
VP: Deborah Carbone
Contact: Deborah Carbone
jcarbonejr@garb-el.com
Estimated Sales: $1-2.5 Million
Number Employees: 10-19
Square Footage: 30000
Brands:
Garb-El

23029 Garden City Community College

801 N Campus Dr
Garden City, KS 67846-6398

620-276-7611
Fax: 620-276-9573 www.gcccks.edu
President: Carol Ballantyne
Executive Vice President: Dee Wigner
Administrative Assistant: Ruth Drees
Number Employees: 250-499

23030 Gardenville Signs

4622 Hazelwood Ave
Baltimore, MD 21206-2812

410-485-4800
Fax: 410-485-4805

Electric signs
Owner: Conley D Reems
Marketing: Conley Reams
Estimated Sales: $500,000-$1 Million
Number Employees: 5 to 9

23031 Gardiner Paperboard

721 Water Street
Gardiner, ME 04345-2013

207-582-3230
Fax: 207-582-8207
Paper board
CEO: Jeffrey Hinderliter
Estimated Sales: $20-50 Million
Number Employees: 50-99
Parent Co: Newark Group

23032 Gardner Denver Inc.

222 E Erie St
Suite 500
Milwaukee, WI 53202

www.gardnerdenver.com
Compressed air, blower and vacuum applications.
President & CEO, Industrials Group: Vicente
Reynal
Parent Co: Ingersoll Rand Inc
Brands:
Gardner Denver
CompAir
Hydrovane
Elmo Rietschle
Robusch

23033 Gardner Manufacturing Inc

1201 W Lake St
Horicon, WI 53032-1819

920-485-4303
Fax: 920-485-4370 800-242-5513
www.gardnermfg.com
Manufacturer and exporter of insect electrocuting
systems, traps and lamps
Owner: John S Jones
johnjones@gardnermfg.com
Quality Control: Mark Sullivan
Sales Division: Robert Marschke
Estimated Sales: $10-20 Million
Number Employees: 100-249
Square Footage: 190000
Brands:
Zap

23034 Garland Commercial Ranges Ltd.

1177 Kamato Road
Mississauga, ON L4W 1X4
Canada

905-624-0260
www.garland-group.com
Manufacturer and exporter of commercial cooking
equipment including ranges, ovens, gas and electric
broilers and griddles; custom cooking equipment
available
CFO: Angelo Ascidne
CEO: Dale Kostick
Senior VP: Dale Kostick
Regional Manager: Jeff McGowan
Number Employees: 250-499
Number of Brands: 2
Number of Products: 1005

Square Footage: 904000
Parent Co: ENODIS

23035 Garland Commercial Ranges

1177 Kamato Road
Mississauga, ON L4W 1X4
Canada

905-624-0260
Fax: 905-624-5669 www.garland-group.com
Commercial holding, warming and cooking equip-
ment including ranges, ovens, gas and electric broil-
ers, griddles, steam cookers and fryers; also,
warming and ventilation equipment
President: Jack Seguin
CFO: Angelo Ascione
Quality Control: Keith Milmine
Group VP Sales/Marketing: Ian Osborne
Regional Manager: Jeff McGowan
Number Employees: 300
Parent Co: Welbilt Corporation

23036 Garland Floor Company

4500 Willow Pkwy
Cleveland, OH 44125-1042

216-883-4100
Fax: 216-883-9076 800-321-2395
Industrial flooring, thermal-shock/chemical resistant
flooring systems
CEO: Byron Smith
Estimated Sales: $10-20 Million
Number Employees: 20-49

23037 Garland Truffles, Inc.

3020 Ode Turner Rd
Hillsborough, NC 27278

919-732-3041
Fax: 919-732-6037 sheila@garlandtruffles.com
www.garlandtruffles.com
Mushrooms including rare truffle mushrooms, also,
truffle tree nursery
Estimated Sales: $1.6 Million
Number Employees: 11
Type of Packaging: Food Service

23038 Garland Writing Instruments

1 S Main St
Coventry, RI 2816

401-828-9582
Fax: 401-823-7460
customerservice@garlandpen.com
www.garlandpen.com
Quality writing instruments and accessories.
USA-made writing collections offer a full color logo
top. All writing instruments and accessories can be
customized
President: Louise Lanoie
VP: Kevin Bittle
Estimated Sales: $10-20 Million
Number Employees: 20-49
Number of Brands: 1
Square Footage: 130000

23039 Garman Co Inc

401 Marshall Rd
Valley Park, MO 63088-1817

636-923-2121
Fax: 636-923-2144 800-466-5150
nancyl@vapcoproducts.com
www.vapcoproducts.com
Ice machine cleaners.
President: Scott Garner
scottg@vapcoproducts.com
Research & Development: Dr Joseph Raible
Marketing Director: Nancy Leppo
Sales Director: Bill Taylor
Estimated Sales: $2.5-5 Million
Number Employees: 10-19
Type of Packaging: Private Label
Brands:
Blow Out
Foaming Coil

23040 Garman Routing Systems Inc

1612 Barthel Road
PO Box 1126
Taylor, TX 76574

410-561-8085
Fax: 410-561-8086 512-535-0178
www.garmanrouting.com

Route accounting and distribution software for all
route distribution applications including that of sales
order entry; sales analysis; inventory control; full
service vending; truck dispatch. Food industry uses
include soft drinkbottlers, bottled water delivery,
snack food distributors, dairy delivery, and coffee
delivery services.
Sales Manager: Chip Sturm

23041 Garrity Equipment Company

31 Georgia Trl
Medford, NJ 08055-8938

609-953-0007
Fax: 609-953-0022 markg8@yahoo.com
Dryers, drum, fluid bed, roller, spray, tunner, fillers,
filtration equipment, heat exchangers, homogenizers, ice cream equipment, margarine processing
equipment, custom fabrication, distributed control
systems, processing andpackaging, pilot plants
Estimated Sales: $500,000-$1 000,000
Number Employees: 1

23042 Garroutte

830 NE Loop 410 # 203
San Antonio, TX 78209-1207

210-826-2321
Fax: 210-824-5253 888-457-4997
Manufacturer and exporter of custom designed food
processing equipment
President: Bob Garrett
Sales Support Manager: Richard Knappen
International Rep.: John Wurster
Operations Manager: Dan Southwood
Estimated Sales: $5-10 Million
Number Employees: 5-9
Square Footage: 120000
Brands:
Waterfall Hydrochiller

23043 Garver Manufacturing Inc

224 N Columbia St
PO Box 306
Union City, IN 47390-1432

765-964-5828
Fax: 765-964-5828 www.garvermfg.com
Manufacture a wide variety of industrial centrifuges,
bottle shakers, and bottle washers as well as custom
equipment.
President: Michael Read
garvermfg@woh.rr.com
Estimated Sales: Less Than $500,000
Number Employees: 1-4
Number of Brands: 2
Number of Products: 5
Square Footage: 16000

23044 Garvey Corp

208 S Route 73
Hammonton, NJ 08037-9565

609-561-2450
Fax: 609-561-2328 800-257-8581
garvey@garvey.com www.garvey.com
Conveyors and accumulators; exporter of conveyor
systems and components; also, installation and
start-up services available
President: Mark Garvey
Cmo: Ruth Caldwell
rcaldwell@garvey.com
VP: William Garvey
Sales: Michael Earling
Estimated Sales: $20-50 Million
Number Employees: 50-99
Type of Packaging: Bulk

23045 Garvey Products

5428 Duff Dr
West Chester, OH 45246-1323

513-771-8710
Fax: 888-218-5551 800-543-1908
garveycares@garveyproducts.com
www.garveyproducts.com
A comprehensive supplier of handheld labeling
equipment, custom labels, safety box cutters,
handheld tagging equipment, handheld shopping
baskets and carts, stampers and ink refills, and a va-
riety of other retail supplies, for foodservice, deli or
retail.
President: Chad Heminover
Marketing Manager: Benita Dorn
Customer Service Manager: Douglas Kelly
Director of Operations: Richard Williams
Estimated Sales: $5 Million+
Parent Co: Cosco Industries

Type of Packaging: Consumer, Food Service, Private Label, Bulk
Brands:
 Garvey

23046 Garvey Products
871 Redna Terrace
Cincinnati, OH 45215-1174
513-771-8710
Fax: 513-771-5108 www.garveyproducts.com
Price marking equipment, pressure sensitive labels, ink cutters, blades and express baskets
President: Rick Gmoch
Quality Control: Dave Ramey
VP: Dennis Feltner
R&D: Dave Ramey
Marketing Director: Dan Cork
Estimated Sales: $5-10 Million
Number Employees: 60
Parent Co: Cosco Industries

23047 Garvin Industries
3700 Sandra St
Franklin Park, IL 60131-1114
847-455-0188
Fax: 773-276-5580 847-451-6500
Manufacturer and designer of fluorescent lighting fixtures, backlighted menu display systems and transparency illuminators
Owner: Raheel Baig
jim@ntisterling.com
Estimated Sales: $1-5 Million
Number Employees: 10-19

23048 Garvis Manufacturing Company
212 E 3rd Street
Des Moines, IA 50309-2006
515-243-8054
Fax: 515-243-1488
Steam cookers
President/Co-Owner: Robert Williams
VP/Co-Owner: Phillip Williams
Estimated Sales: Less than $500,000
Number Employees: 1-4
Parent Co: Fabricon

23049 Gary Manufacturing Company
2626 Southpoint Wat
Suite E
National City, CA 91950
619-429-4479
Fax: 619-429-4810 800-775-0804
www.garymanufacturing.com
Manufacturer and exporter of plastic and fabric table covers, aprons and napkins
Co-Owner: Helen Smith
Estimated Sales: $2.5-5 Million
Number Employees: 5-9
Square Footage: 20000

23050 Gary Plastic Packaging Corporation
3539 Tiemann Ave
Bronx, NY 10469-1636
718-231-4285
Fax: 203-629-1160 800-221-8151
sales@plasticboxes.com www.plasticboxes.com
Manufacturer and exporter of plastic boxes, containers and packaging materials; also, package design service available
Owner: Valerie A Gray
Sales: Rich Satone
Estimated Sales: 25-50 Million
Number Employees: 1-4

23051 Gary Plastic Packaging Corporation
3539 Tiemann Ave
Bronx, NY 10469-1636
718-231-4285
Fax: 203-629-1160 800-227-4279
sales@plasticboxes.com www.plasticboxes.com
Advertising specialties, plastic packaging and candy boxes; exporter of packaging products
Owner: Valerie A Gray
VP: Marilyn Hellinger
Sales: Rich Satone
Estimated Sales: $24 Million
Number Employees: 1-4
Square Footage: 4000
Brands:
 Garyline

23052 Gary Sign Co
3289 E 83rd Pl
Merrillville, IN 46410-6542
219-942-3191
Fax: 219-942-3077
Signs and advertising displays
Owner: Paul Grochowski
garysignco@verizon.net
Estimated Sales: $1-2.5 Million
Number Employees: 5-9

23053 Gary W. Pritchard Engineer
5082 Bolsa Ave Ste 112
Huntington Beach, CA 92649
714-893-5441
Fax: 714-893-8405
Food processing machinery and sanitary fittings
President: Gary Pritchard
Sales Manager: Lisa Carlson
Estimated Sales: $1-2,500,000
Number Employees: 19

23054 Gasser Chair Co Inc
4136 Logan Way
Youngstown, OH 44505-1797
330-759-2234
Fax: 330-759-9844 800-323-2234
sales@gasserchair.com www.gasserchair.com
Wood and metal chairs, barstools and tables
President: Gary Gasser
gary.gasser@gasserchair.com
CEO: George L Gasser
President: Mark Gasser
VP Sales/Marketing: Cindy Gasser
Estimated Sales: $10-20 Million
Number Employees: 50-99
Square Footage: 300000

23055 (HQ)Gaston County Dyeing Mach Co
1310 Charles Raper Jonas Hwy
Mt Holly, NC 28120-1234
704-822-5000
Fax: 704-822-0753 info@gaston-county.com
www.gaston-county.com
Heat exchangers, pressure vessels, tanks, dryers and electronic assemblies
President: Hubert Craig
Cmo: Ted J Hiley
thiley@gaston-county.com
CEO: Joseph Mahoney
Advertising Manager: Sally Davis
Operations: Scott Davis
Purchasing: Scott Jonas
Estimated Sales: $20-50 Million
Number Employees: 500-999
Square Footage: 370000

23056 Gastro-Gnomes
22 Brightview Drive
West Hartford, CT 06117-2001
860-236-0225
Fax: 860-236-7967 800-747-4666
Manufacturer and exporter of plastic and thematic menu stands, menus and pop-out menu inserts
President: Allan Grody
Vice President: Marjorie Grody
Number Employees: 4

23057 Gates
PO Box 90
West Peterborough, NH 03468-0090
603-924-3394
Fax: 603-924-9677 888-543-6316
Wooden boxes
President: Mike Herz
Marketing Manager: John Naylor
Estimated Sales: $1-2.5 Million
Number Employees: 10-19

23058 Gates Corp
1144 15th St
Denver, CO 80202
303-744-5800
www.gates.com
Application-specific fluid power and power transmission solutions.
Chief Executive Officer: Ivo Jurek
Chief Financial Officer: Brooks Mallard
Chief Operating Officer: Walt Lifsey
EVP, Human Resources: Roger Gaston
Chief Information Officer: Michael Rhymes
SVP/Chief Marketing Officer: Tom Pitstick

Year Founded: 1911
Estimated Sales: Over $1 Billion
Number Employees: 14,000
Square Footage: 234264

23059 Gates Manufacturing Company
6924 Smiley Avenue
Saint Louis, MO 63139
314-647-5662
Fax: 314-645-7003 800-237-9226
DWentzel@gatesmfg.com www.gatesmfg.com
Custom commercial kitchen equipment including bins, conveyors, dish tables, refrigerators and tray make-up systems
President: Earl Gates Jr
Marketing/Sales: Robert Martin
Estimated Sales: $5-10 Million
Number Employees: 50

23060 Gates Mectrol Inc
9 Northwestern Dr
Salem, NH 03079-4809
603-890-1515
Fax: 603-890-1616 800-394-4844
www.gatesmectrol.com
Urethane timing belts, speed reducers and motion controle components
President: Bret Morrison
Estimated Sales: $20-50 Million
Number Employees: 100-249
Square Footage: 45000

23061 Gates Mectrol Inc
9 Northwestern Dr
Salem, NH 03079-4809
603-890-1515
Fax: 603-890-1616 800-394-4844
contact@gatesmectrol.com www.gatesmectrol.com
Timing pulleys and polymer based automation components and synchronous timing belts.
President: Mark Appleton
appleton@gatesmectrol.com
Number Employees: 100-249

23062 Gateway Packaging Co
5910 Winner Rd
Kansas City, MO 64125-1626
816-483-9800
Fax: 618-876-4856
marketing@gatewaypackaging.com
Multiwall, small and specialty paper bags
Owner: Roger Miller
VP/CFO: Judy Samayda
Estimated Sales: $1-5 Million
Number Employees: 100-249
Square Footage: 300000

23063 Gateway Packaging Corp
2240 Boyd Rd
Export, PA 15632-8974
724-327-7400
Fax: 724-325-7447 888-289-2693
sales@gatepack.com www.gatepack.com
Corrugated boxes
President: Benjamin Getty
VP: Thomas Gill
Contact: Thomas Gill
gill@gatepack.com
General Manager: Scott Getty
Estimated Sales: $10-20 Million
Number Employees: 50-99
Square Footage: 196000

23064 Gateway Plastics Inc
5650 W County Line Rd
Mequon, WI 53092-4751
262-242-2020
Fax: 262-242-7262 www.gatewayplastics.com
Plastic caps and closures, custom plastic packaging
President: Carl Vogel
carl.vogel@gatewayplastics.com
Marketing/Sales: Bob Proudfoot
Estimated Sales: $20+ Million
Number Employees: 100-249
Number of Brands: 2
Square Footage: 200000
Type of Packaging: Consumer, Food Service, Private Label, Bulk
Brands:
 Gateway Closures
 Gateway Plastics

23065 Gateway Printing Company
3425 N Ridge Avenue
Arlington Heights, IL 60004-1496
847-394-0625
Fax: 847-727-1200 www.gateway-printing.com
Printing on skin and blister packaging board
General Manager: Bill Waters
CEO: John Rohrer
Estimated Sales: $10-20 Million
Number Employees: 50-99

23066 (HQ)Gatewood Products LLC
814 Jeanette St
3001 Gateman Drive
Parkersburg, WV 26101
304-422-5461
Fax: 304-485-2714 800-827-5461
Wood and wood-and-metal containers, pallets, skid
shocks and wire-bounds; also, dry warehousing and
transportation service available
President/CEO/Vice Chairman: Perry Smith
Estimated Sales: $20-50 Million
Number Employees: 20-49
Square Footage: 1150000

23067 Gavco Plastics Inc
9840 S 219th East Ave
Broken Arrow, OK 74014-5911
918-455-7888
Fax: 918-455-3695 info@GavcoPlastics.com
www.gavcoplastics.com
President: Randall Gavlik
randygavlik@gavcoplastics.com
Estimated Sales: $1-5 Million
Number Employees: 50-99

23068 Gaychrome Division of CSL
220 D Exchange Drive
Crystal Lake, IL 60014
815-459-6000
Fax: 815-459-6105 800-873-4370
sales@csltd.com www.csltd.com
Tray stands, high chairs, etc., for the hospitality and
food service industries.
President: Jay Maher
Director Sales: Rus Budde
Plant Manager: Joe Mancuso
Purchasing Manager: Sharri Kapaldo
Estimated Sales: $10-20 Million
Number Employees: 20-49
Type of Packaging: Consumer, Food Service, Pri-
vate Label

23069 Gaylord Container Corporation
8700 Adamo Dr
Tampa, FL 33619-3524
813-621-3591
Fax: 813-621-3318 www.templeinland.com
Manufacturer and exporter of corrugated shipping
containers, boxes and cartons
Manager: Wayne Parker
Controller: P Wilkins
General Manager: John Thrift
Production Supervisor: R Piepenbring
Estimated Sales: $20-50 Million
Number Employees: 100-249

23070 Gaylord Container Corporation
2301 Wilbur Ave
Antioch, CA 94509
925-779-3200
Fax: 925-779-4960 800-727-2699
Wine industry packaging
President: Michael Keough
CEO: Marvin Pomerantz
CFO: Daniel Casey
Senior VP: Lawrence Rogna

23071 Gaylord Industries
10900 SW Avery St
Tualatin, OR 97062-8578
503-691-2010
Fax: 503-692-6048 800-547-9696
www.gaylordventilation.com
or more than 75 years, Gaylord's ventilation systems
have been known for durability, dependability, and
meticulous attention to detail. They continue to rev-
olutionize the industry with groundbreaking new designs as well as an innovative approach to solving
the two main priorities facing foodservice operators:
enrg savings and labor optimization.

President: Dan Shoop
CFO: Jeana Randall
R&D: Biucazx Lukins
Sales Manager: Keven Hass
Estimated Sales: $10-20 Million
Number Employees: 100-249
Square Footage: 150000
Brands:
Gaylord

23072 Gaynes Labs Inc
9708 Industrial Dr
Bridgeview, IL 60455-2305
708-233-6655
Fax: 708-233-6985 gayneslabs@aol.com
www.gaynestesting.com
Consultant and testing laboratory for packaging ma-
terials
President: Yury Beyderman
gayneslabs@aol.com
Estimated Sales: $1-2.5 Million
Number Employees: 10-19
Square Footage: 33000

23073 Gbn Machine & Engineering
17073 Bull Church Rd
Woodford, VA 22580-2412
804-448-2033
Fax: 804-448-2684 800-446-9871
gbnmach@verizon.net www.nailerman.com
Manufacturer and exporter of pallet assembly sys-
tems, lumber stackers and conveyors
Vice President: Paul Bailey
paul@nailerman.com
Estimated Sales: Below $5 Million
Number Employees: 5-9

23074 Gbs
7233 Freedom Ave NW
North Canton, OH 44720-7123
330-494-5330
800-552-2427
marketing@gbscorp.com www.gbscorp.com
Manufacturer and exporter of plastic film, pressure
sensitive labels and tags
VP: Jim Lee
VP/General Manager: James Lee
Marketing Director: Jackie Davidson
Plant Manager: Bruce Budney
Estimated Sales: $4 Million
Number Employees: 1-4
Square Footage: 120000

23075 (HQ)Gch Internatonal
330 Boxley Ave
Louisville, KY 40209-1845
502-636-1374
Fax: 502-636-0125 www.gchintl.com
Manufacturer and exporter of surge bins, vibrating
sizing conveyors, enrobers and separators; also,
freezers including spiral, tunnel and trolley
Chief Operating Officer: Haldun Turgay
CEO: John Thornton
jthornton@gchintl.com
VP Business Development: Edward Ward
Sales Manager Food: Thomas Fahed
Estimated Sales: $1-2.5 Million
Number Employees: 50-99
Square Footage: 360000
Parent Co: GCH International
Other Locations:
Cardwell Machine Co.
Farnborough NH
Brands:
Spiro-Freeze
Trolly-Freeze
Uni-Freeze
Vibe-O-Bin
Vibe-O-Vey

23076 Ge-No's Nursery
12285 Road 25
Madera, CA 93637-9013
559-674-4752
Fax: 559-674-3724
Grapevines for wine industry
Manager: Martin Nonin
Estimated Sales: Below $5 000,000
Number Employees: 10-19

23077 Gea Intec, Llc
4319 S Alston Ave
Suite 105
Durham, NC 27713
919-433-0131
Fax: 919-433-0140
Single and variable retention time freezers/chillers
for the food and beverage industries.
Contact: Jennifer Shambley
jshambley@gearefrigeration.com
Parent Co: Intec USA

23078 Gea Process EngineeringInc
9165 Rumsey Rd
Columbia, MD 21045-1929
410-997-8700
Fax: 410-997-5021 gea-pe.us@gea.com
www.geapharmasystems.com
Liquid and powder processing equipment for the
dairy and food and beverage industries.
President: Steve Kaplan
steve.kaplan@geagroup.com
Number Employees: 100-249

23079 Gea Processing
1600 Okeefe Rd
Hudson, WI 54016-7206
715-386-9371
Fax: 715-386-9376 800-376-6476
Powder and liquid processing equipment for the
dairy and food & beverage industries.
Vice President: Ron Matzek
ron.matzek@geagroup.com
Vice President: Ron Matzek
ron.matzek@geagroup.com
Number Employees: 100-249

23080 Gea Us
20903 W Gale Ave
Galesville, WI 54630-7276
608-582-3081
Fax: 608-582-2581
Manufacturer, importer and exporter of dairy farm
equipment and machinery including milk meters,
processors and coolers
Manager: Ralph Rottier
Cio/Cto: Kathy Snyder
kathy.snyder@westfaliasurge.com
VP: Ralph Rottier
Estimated Sales: $20-50 Million
Number Employees: 100-249
Square Footage: 140000
Parent Co: Babson Brothers Company
Brands:
Surge
Tru-Test

**23081 Gebo Conveyors, Consultants &
Systems**
1045 Autoroute Chomedey
Laval, QC H7W 4V3
Canada
450-973-3337
Fax: 450-973-3336 www.sidel.com
Manufacturer and exporter of stainless steel tabletop
conveying systems and equipment including pack-
age line controls, pressure-free combiners, packer
infeed systems and line audits
President: Mark Aury
Sales Manager: Jean Dion
Project Director: Mike De Cotiis
Number Employees: 250
Square Footage: 260000
Parent Co: Gebo Industries
Brands:
Gebo

23082 Gebo Corporation
6015 31st Street E
Bradenton, FL 34203-5382
941-727-1400
Fax: 941-727-1200
Manufacturer, importer and exporter of conveyors
including air trans and cap feeder
President: Mark Aury
Marketing Director: George Louli
General Manager: Christian Fitsch-Mouras
Estimated Sales: $20-50 Million
Number Employees: 100-249
Square Footage: 40000
Parent Co: Sidel Corporation
Brands:
Flat Top
Garro

Magneroll
Uf Feeder

23083 Gecko Electronics
Riedtlistrasse 72
CH-8006
Zurich, SW G2E 5W6
Canada

418-872-4411
Fax: 418-872-0920 contact@gecko-research.com
www.gecko-research.com
President: Michel Authier
R&D: Bemoit Laslamme
Number Employees: 350

23084 Geerpres Inc
1780 Harvey St
Muskegon, MI 49442-5396

231-773-3211
Fax: 231-773-8263 sales@geerpres.com
www.geerpres.com
Manufactures cleaning tools for the maintenance
supply industry in a business-to-business environ-
ment: steel, stainless steel, plastic, microfiber and
metal components.
President: Scott Ribbe
scott@geerpres.com
CFO: Bryan Depree
R&D: Joe Fodrocy
Quality Control: Jeff Kulbe
Marketing Director: Megan Schihl
Sales Director: Ted Moon
Purchasing Manager: Barb McAttnen
Estimated Sales: Below $5 Million
Number Employees: 20-49
Square Footage: 340000

23085 Gehnrich Oven Sales Company
2675 Main Street
East Troy, WI 53120

262-642-3938
Fax: 262-363-4018 sales@wisoven.com
www.wisoven.com/gehnrich-oven
Manufacturer and exporter of convection baking and
cooking ovens
President: Richard Gehnrich
Treasurer: Leon Pedigo, Jr.
VP: Wayne Pedigo
Estimated Sales: $1-2.5 Million
Number Employees: 20-49
Square Footage: 45000
Parent Co: Nevo Corporation

23086 Gei International Inc
100 Ball St
East Syracuse, NY 13057-2359

315-463-9261
Fax: 315-463-9034 800-345-1308
info@geionline.com www.geionline.com
Complete food processing and packaging systems
Estimated Sales: $1-5 Million
Number Employees: 10-19

23087 Geiger Bros
70 Mount Hope Ave
Lewiston, ME 04240-1021

207-755-2000
Fax: 207-755-2422 geigerorders@geiger.com
www.geiger.com
Manufacturer and exporter of advertising specialties
Regional VP East: Fred Snyder
Owner, CEO: Gene Geiger
CFO: Bob Blaisdell
Owner, Executive Vice President: Peter Geiger
V.P. Marketing: Gary Biron
V.P. Sales & Marketing: Jim Habzda
Vice President of Operations: Sheila Olson
Estimated Sales: $500,000-$1 Million
Number Employees: 500-999
Square Footage: 40000
Brands:
Farmer's Almanac
Time By Design

23088 Gelberg Signs
6511 Chillum Pl NW
Washington, DC 20012-2192

202-882-7733
Fax: 202-882-1580 800-443-5237
sales@gelbergsigns.com www.gelbergsigns.com
Menu boards, signs and point of purchase displays

President: Neil Brami
nbrami@gelbergsigns.com
CFO: Bruce Gersh
Executive VP: Christopher Smith
Human Resource: Sarah Armour
Production Manager: Mark McCluney
Estimated Sales: Below $5 Million
Number Employees: 50-99
Square Footage: 50000

23089 Gem Electric Manufacturing Company
20 Commerce Dr
Hauppauge, NY 11788-3910

631-273-2230
Fax: 631-273-9876 800-275-4361
Electrical wiring devices and electrical lighting ac-
cessories
President: Harvey Cooper
Vice President: Peter Massa
Marketing Director: Neal Massa
Contact: Andy Aqkr
andy@btn.net
Plant Manager: Andy Aqkr
Estimated Sales: Over $10 Million
Number Employees: 30
Number of Brands: 1
Number of Products: 8000
Square Footage: 140000
Parent Co: Gem Electric Manufacturing Company
Type of Packaging: Consumer, Private Label

23090 Gem Refrigerator Company
7340 Milnor St
Philadelphia, PA 19136-4211

215-426-8700
Fax: 215-426-8731
Refrigerators and freezers including walk-in and
reach-in, also custom boxes
President: Bruce Gruhler
Sales: John Greenwood
Plant Manager/Sales: Tony Iacono
Estimated Sales: $5-10 Million
Number Employees: 20 to 49
Square Footage: 80000

23091 Gemini Bakery Equipment
9991 Global Rd
Philadelphia, PA 19115-1005

215-676-9508
Fax: 215-673-3944 800-468-9046
sales@geminibe.com www.geminibe.com
Manufacturer and importer of bakery equipment
CEO/ Founder: Mark Rosenberg
Marketing Coordinator: Laura Albright
Sales Exec: Lou Giliberti
Estimated Sales: $10-20 Million
Number Employees: 20-49

23092 Gemini Data Loggers Inc
3685 Lakeside Dr
Suite A
Reno, NV 89509-5280

406-721-1958
Fax: 877-799-5198 sales@geminidataloggers.com
www.geminidataloggers.com
Contact: Neil Vass
nvass@geminidataloggers.com
Number Employees: 5-9

23093 Gemini Plastic Films Corporation
535 Midland Ave
Garfield, NJ 7026

973-340-0700
Fax: 973-340-1045 800-789-4732
customerservice@geminiplasticfilms.com
www.geminiplasticfilms.com
FDA/USDA approved plastic bags, sheeting, tubing,
pallet covers and film
President: Richard Hulbert Jr
Marketing/Sales: Frank Fusaro
Maintenance Manager: Pasquale Pavillo
Contact: Gemini Corp
r.hulbert@geminiplasticfilms.com
Production Manager: Jack Pezdic
Purchasing Manager: Richard Primo
Estimated Sales: $5-10 Million
Number Employees: 20-49
Square Footage: 100000
Type of Packaging: Consumer, Food Service, Pri-
vate Label, Bulk

23094 Gems Sensors & Controls
1 Cowles Rd
Plainville, CT 06062-1107

860-747-3000
Fax: 860-793-4531 www.gemssensors.com
Manufacturer and exporter of conductance actuated
liquid level controls including sanitary probes and
fittings; also, underground leak detection services
available
President: Blue Lane
twanbentlage@yahoo.com
Marketing Specialist: Tony Mancin
Estimated Sales: H
Number Employees: 100-249
Square Footage: 29000
Parent Co: Danaher Corporation

23095 Gems Sensors & Controls
1 Cowles Rd
Plainville, CT 06062-1107

860-747-3000
Fax: 860-793-4531 800-378-1600
info@gemsensors.com www.gemssensors.com
Designs and manufacturers a broad portfolio of liquid level, flow and pressure sensors, miniature solenoid valves, and pre-assembled fluidic systems to
exact customer application and manufacturing
requirements.
President: Douglas Banks
douglas.banks@danaher.com
Estimated Sales: H
Number Employees: 100-249

23096 Gemtek Products LLC
3808 N 28th Ave
Phoenix, AZ 85017-4733

602-265-8586
Fax: 602-265-7241 800-331-7022
info@gemtek.com www.gemtek.com
Manufacturer and supplier of safe solvents, cleaners,
and lubrications
President: Sarah Kristoff
sarah.hunt@cdctn.org
Number Employees: 5-9
Other Locations:
Manufacturing Plant
Hayward CA
Manufacturing Plant
Mecedonia OH

23097 Genarom International
41 Mountain Blvd
Warren, NJ 07059-2630

908-753-8484
Fax: 908-753-9635 800-352-8672
Owner: Kenny Woo

23098 Genecor International
925 Page Mill Road
Palo Alto, CA 94304

650-846-7500
Fax: 585-256-6952 800-847-5311
www.genencor.com
Enzymes, such as amylases, cellulases, xylanases,
glucose-oxidase, catalase and proteases
Contact: Lilia Babe
lbabe@genencor.com
Number Employees: 73

23099 Genemco Inc
4455 Carter Creek Pkwy
Bryan, TX 77802-4416

979-268-7447
Fax: 979-268-7447 877-268-5865
sales@genemco.com
Agitation systems, milk and tank, cheese equipment,
vacuum chambers, centrifuges, chillers, dryers,
drum, fluid bed, roller, spray, tunnel, homogenizers,
ice equipment, ingredient feeders, fillers, air gravity,
milk, steam, filtrationequipment, flow div
Owner: Diane Lafving
blafving@gmail.com
Estimated Sales: $500,000-$1 Million
Number Employees: 10-19

23100 General Analysis Corporation
PO Box 528
Norwalk, CT 06856-0528

203-852-8999
Fax: 203-838-1551
Diet and carbonation monitors for soft drink, beer,
tea, and juice lines; lab testers for measuring CO2 in
packaged beverage products
Estimated Sales: $1-5 000,000
Number Employees: 20-50

583

23101 General Bag Corporation
3368 W 137th St
Cleveland, OH 44111

216-941-1190
Fax: 216-476-3401 800-837-9396
generalbag@aol.com
Manufacturer and distributor of all packaging materials paper bags, poly, mesh. Boxes all sizes, bulk and waxed produce cartons; also packaging machinery
President: Rob Sprosty
Sales Manager: Dan Juba
Sales Representative: Larry Sprosty
Contact: Robert Sprosty
generalbag@aol.com
Estimated Sales: $5-10 Million
Number Employees: 20-49
Square Footage: 160000

23102 General Cage
238 N 29th St
Elwood, IN 46036-1702

765-552-5039
Fax: 765-552-6962 800-428-6403
Manufacturer and exporter of wire products including forms, specialties, cages, display racks, partitions, grills, etc
Member: Bruce D Cook
Estimated Sales: $10-20 Million
Number Employees: 100-249
Square Footage: 216000

23103 General Chemical Corporation
90 E Halsey Rd Ste 301
Parsippany, NJ 07054

973-515-0900
Fax: 973-515-3232 info@genchemcorp.com
Industrial specialty and fine chemicals
CEO: William E Redmond Jr
Contact: Anny Ally
a.ally@gentek-global.com
Estimated Sales: G
Number Employees: 1,000-4,999

23104 General Conveyor Company
245 Industrial Parkway South
Auroua, ON L4G 4J9
Canada

905-727-7922
Fax: 905-841-1056 gccl@gccl.com
www.gccl.com
Design and manufacture a wide range of standard and customized conveyors, accumulators, end-of-line automation and custom machinery. Our primary focus is in the food, personal care, pharamceutical, beverage, irrafiation and plasticsmarkets.

23105 General Corrugated Machinery Company
269 Commercial Avenue
Palisades Park, NJ 07650-1154

201-944-0644
Fax: 201-944-7858 70451.2363@compuserve.com
Manufacturer and exporter of corrugated box formers; also, case formers, sealers, case packers and palletizers
Sales Manager: John Lavin
Estimated Sales: $1-5 Million
Brands:
    Galaxy
    Model Cf
    Nova

23106 General Cutlery Co
1918 N County Road 232
Fremont, OH 43420-9595

419-332-2316
Fax: 419-334-7119
Cutlery including knives
President: David Reitz
dreitz@generalcutlery.com
VP: David Reitz
Estimated Sales: Below $5 Million
Number Employees: 10-19
Square Footage: 40000
Brands:
    Hard-Edge

23107 General Data Co Inc
4354 Ferguson Dr
Cincinnati, OH 45245-1667

513-752-7978
Fax: 513-752-6947 www.general-data.com

President: Peter Wenzel
Quality Control: Marsha Doon
Estimated Sales: $20-30 Million
Number Employees: 100-249

23108 General Electric Company
3135 Easton Turnpike
Fairfield, CT 06828

203-373-2211
www.geconsumerandindustrial.com
Household appliances including freezers and garbage disposal units
President & Chief Executive Officer: Ferdinando Beccalli-Falco
CEO: Jeff Immelt
CEO: James P Campbell
VP Marketing: Bruce Albertsons
Estimated Sales: $500,000-$1 Million
Number Employees: 10,000

23109 General Electric Company
5 Necco St
Boston, MA 02210

617-443-3078
800-417-0575
directors@corporate.ge.com www.ge.com
Electricity provider, as well as other segments such as additive manufacturing.
Chairman & CEO: H. Lawrence Culp, Jr
VP & CEO, GE Additive: Jason Oliver
SVP & CFO: Carolina Dybeck Happe
SVP & General Counsel: Mike Holston
SVP & President & CEO, GE Power: Russell Stokes
Year Founded: 1892
Estimated Sales: $95.2 Billion
Number Employees: 205,000

23110 General Equipment & Machinery Company
1617 NW 79th Avenue
Doral, FL 33126-1105

305-471-0802
Fax: 305-471-6196
Machinery for PET stretch blow molding, form-fill seal, injection molding and film shrink wrap packing
Estimated Sales: $2.5-5 Million
Number Employees: 8

23111 General Espresso Equipment
7912 Industrial Village Rd
Greensboro, NC 27409-9691

336-393-0224
Fax: 336-393-0295 info@geec.com
www.astoriausaparts.com
Espresso machine cleaners, espresso machines/accessories, espresso pod machines
Owner: Roberto Daltio
Manager: Randy Brewer
Estimated Sales: $500,000-$1 000,000
Number Employees: 10-19

23112 General Films Inc
645 S High St
Covington, OH 45318-1182

937-473-3033
Fax: 937-473-2403 888-436-3456
www.generalfilms.com
Manufacturer and exporter of plastic bags, packaging coextruded films and bag-in-box bulk liquid packaging
President: Tim Weikert
Quality Control: Norman Slade
Sales (Food Pkg.): Linda Lyons
Sales Manager (Industrial Pkg.): Howard Stutzman
Sales (Bag-in-Box): Cindy Grogean
Estimated Sales: $20-50 Million
Number Employees: 50-99
Square Footage: 60000
Brands:
    Duratuf

23113 General Floor Craft
4 Heights Ter
Little Silver, NJ 07739-1323

973-742-7400
Fax: 973-742-0004
Manufacturer and exporter of vacuums and carpet cleaning machinery
Owner: Barry Gore
VP: Jeff Gore
Estimated Sales: $2.5-5 Million
Number Employees: 20-49
Square Footage: 54000

23114 General Formulations
309 S Union St
Sparta, MI 49345-1529

616-887-7387
Fax: 616-887-0537 800-253-3664
mclay@generalformulations.com
www.generalformulations.com
Manufacturer and exporter of self-adhesive and floor advertising films
CEO: James Clay
CEO: James Clay
Marketing Manager: Mike Clay
Regional Sales Manager: Jeff Balasko
Estimated Sales: $20-50 Million
Number Employees: 50-99
Square Footage: 100000
Brands:
    Permalar
    Traffic Graffic

23115 (HQ)General Grinding Inc
801 51st Ave
Oakland, CA 94601-5694

510-261-5557
Fax: 510-261-5567 800-806-6037
ggrind@aol.com www.generalgrindinginc.com
Knife sharpeners; also, replacement parts for machinery including curling and beading rings; repair services available
President: Michael Bardon
ggrind@aol.com
Sales Manager: Daniel Bardon
Estimated Sales: $5-10 Million
Number Employees: 20-49
Square Footage: 42000

23116 General Industries Inc
3048 Thoroughfare Rd
PO Box 1279
Goldsboro, NC 27534-7728

919-751-1791
Fax: 919-751-8186 888-735-2882
tanks@gitank.com www.gitank.com
Vaulted tire rated, mix/process, above ground and underground steel storage tanks and oil/water separators also carbon steel and stainless steel
President: John T Wiggins
tommyw@gitank.com
Sales Marketing: Nancy Lilly
Purchasing Manager: Jody Vernon
Estimated Sales: $6 Million
Number Employees: 20-49
Square Footage: 160000
Brands:
    Fireguard
    Permatank

23117 General Machinery Corp
1831 N 18th St
PO Box 717
Sheboygan, WI 53081-2312

920-458-2189
Fax: 920-458-8316 888-243-6622
sales@genmac.com www.genmac.com
Manufacturer and exporter of meat and cheese processing equipment including meat flakers, slicers, dicers, mechanical tenderizers, grinders, pork rind chippers and cheese cutters; also, cake and bun slabbers, pan washers and beltconveyors.
President: Michael Horwitz
CFO: Marsha Binversie
VP Operations: Robert Jeske
Production Manager: Gary Mueller
Estimated Sales: $2.5-5 Million
Number Employees: 10-19
Brands:
    Cannon
    Hydraucuber Super Slicer
    Hydrauflakers
    M-8 Slitter
    Multislicer
    Rotary Dicer
    S/M Flaker
    Sp-250 Flattener
    Tenderit
    Tu-Way

23118 General Magnaplate Corp
1331 W Edgar Rd
Linden, NJ 07036-6496

908-862-6200
Fax: 908-862-6110 800-852-3301
info@magnaplate.com www.magnaplate.com

Metal finishing, surface enhancement coatings for food and drug processing and packaging equipment, wear and corrosion resistant coatings for metal parts.
CEO: Candida Aversenti
caversenti@magnaplate.com
Estimated Sales: $12 Million
Number Employees: 100-249

23119 General Methods Corporation
3012 SW Adams Street
Peoria, IL 61602
309-497-3344
Fax: 309-497-3345
Manufacturer and exporter of coupon and premium dispensers; also, contract thermoform packaging and seal integrity verification equipment
President: Dale Kuykendall
Chief Tech.: Ken Brackett
Estimated Sales: Less than $500,000
Number Employees: 3
Square Footage: 26000

23120 General Neon Sign Co
900 Buena Vista St
San Antonio, TX 78207-4308
210-227-1203
Fax: 210-227-0067 www.generalsignsinc.com
Signs including neon, plastic, vinyl, advertising, electric, etc.; also, installation and repair services available
Owner: Jason Kaupert
Quality Control: Jason Kaupert
Estimated Sales: Below $5 Million
Number Employees: 10-19

23121 General Packaging Equipment Co
6048 Westview Dr
Houston, TX 77055-5420
713-686-4331
Fax: 713-683-3967 sales@generalpackaging.com
www.generalpackaging.com
Manufacturer and exporter of packaging machinery including bag forming and net weighers
President: Robert C Kelly
rkelly@generalpackaging.com
Director of Sales: Tom Wilson
Estimated Sales: $5-10 Million
Number Employees: 20-49
Square Footage: 66000
Type of Packaging: Consumer, Food Service, Private Label
Brands:
General Packager
Hydrafeed

23122 General Packaging Products Inc
1700 S Canal St
Chicago, IL 60616-1189
312-226-8380
Fax: 312-226-4027 800-621-1921
info@generalpk.com www.generalpk.com
Wrappers and protective packages for food industry
President: William K Kellogg III
william@generalpk.com
CFO: Tom Woods
CEO: William Kellogg
Quality Control: Eric Courtney
Sales (Central Region): Tim Schoolman
VPO: Volney Bunch
Plant Manager: Joe Bunch
Estimated Sales: $10-25 Million
Number Employees: 100-249
Type of Packaging: Private Label

23123 General Press Corp
110 Allegheny Dr
PO Box 316
Natrona Heights, PA 15065-1902
724-224-3500
Fax: 724-224-3934 www.generalpress.com
Manufacturer and exporter of die cut paper labels for food and beverage containers; also, heat seal foil lids for single serve jelly cups, injection mold labels and lightweight plastic labels.
President: Scott Poorbaugh
spoorbaugh@generalpress.com
Sales Manager: David Wolff
VP Operations: T Conroy
Estimated Sales: $5-10 Million
Number Employees: 50-99
Square Footage: 120000

23124 General Processing Systems
12838 Stainless Drive
Holland, MI 49424
616-399-2220
Fax: 616-399-7365 800-547-9370
jswiatlo@nbe-inc.com www.productsaver.com
Manufacturer and exporter of bag opening equipment and custom designed product recovery systems.
President: Ed Swiatlo
Sales Manager: Jeff Swiatlo
Contact: Joe Reed
todd@nbe-inc.com
Estimated Sales: $3-5 Million
Number Employees: 10-19
Square Footage: 40000
Parent Co: General Processing Systems

23125 General Resource Corporation
P.O.Box 470
Dassel, MN 55325-0470
952-933-7474
Fax: 952-933-9777
Airlock, gates, air slides
President: Joseph Pausch
VP: Jim Masterman
Estimated Sales: $1-3 Million
Number Employees: 1-4

23126 General Shelters Of Texas LTD
1639 State Highway 87 N
P.O. Box 2108
Center, TX 75935
936-598-3389
Fax: 936-598-1432 www.generalshelters.com
Manufacturer of portable buildings.
President: Rick Campbell
Year Founded: 1973
Estimated Sales: $50-100 Million
Number Employees: 100-249
Square Footage: 300000

23127 General Sign Co
2723 N Jackson Hwy
Sheffield, AL 35660-3430
256-383-3176
Fax: 256-383-3170 gensign@hiwaay.net
Identification and deco electrical signage
General Manager: Ted Martin
CEO/President: Lenn Scheibal
Controller: Kris Sneed
Engineer: Dean Precival
Sales Director: Kim Underwood
Estimated Sales: Less Than $500,000
Number Employees: 5-9
Square Footage: 280000
Type of Packaging: Bulk

23128 General Steel Fabricators
927 S Schifferdecker Ave
Joplin, MO 64801-3528
417-623-2224
Fax: 417-623-2204 800-820-8644
Tanks, bucket elevators and dust and cyclone collectors
Manager: Stan Rife
General Manager: Stan Rife
Assistant General Manager: Paul Howey
Purchasing Manager: Jim Cruzan
Estimated Sales: $10-20 Million
Number Employees: 50-99
Square Footage: 80400
Parent Co: Doane Pet Care

23129 General Tank
328 West Front Street
P O Box 488
Berwick, PA 18603-2138
570-752-4528
Fax: 570-752-6121 800-435-8265
Conveyors, fittings, pumps, valves, tanks, washers and control systems
President: Dan Bower
Contact: Gebby Bankoski
gbankoski@generaltank.com
Estimated Sales: Below 1 Million
Number Employees: 1-4

23130 General Tape & Supply
28505 Automation Blvd
Wixom, MI 48393-3154
248-357-2744
Fax: 248-357-2749 800-490-3633

Manufacturer and exporter of pressure sensitive labels
President: Mary Raden
COO: Jack Hooker
Research & Development: Debbie Wojcik
Sales Director: Julie Stallings
Estimated Sales: $2.5-5 Million
Number Employees: 30

23131 General Trade Mark Labelcraft
55 Lasalle St
Staten Island, NY 10303
718-448-9800
Fax: 718-448-9808
Embossed and printed labels, price tag seals and stickers; exporter of printed labels
Owner: Richard Capuozzo
CEO: V Kruse
Estimated Sales: $10-20 Million
Number Employees: 20-49
Square Footage: 40000
Brands:
Sure-Stik

23132 General Truck Body Mfg
7110 Jensen Dr
Houston, TX 77093-8703
713-692-5177
Fax: 713-692-0700 800-395-8585
www.generalbody.com
Truck bodies including van, slide-ins, cold plates and refrigerated
President: Barbara Paull
barbara.paull@generalbody.com
CEO: Barbara Paull
Sales: Clayton Price
Plant Manager: Tollan Maxwell
Estimated Sales: $10-20 Million
Number Employees: 50-99

23133 General Wax & Candle Co
6863 Beck Ave
North Hollywood, CA 91605-6206
818-765-5800
Fax: 818-764-3878 800-929-7867
www.generalwax.com
Manufacturer and exporter of candles
Owner: Jerry Baker
jbaker@generalwax.com
VP: Mike Tapp
Estimated Sales: $10-15 Million
Number Employees: 50-99
Type of Packaging: Food Service

23134 General, Inc
3355 Enterprise Ave.
Suite 160
Weston, FL 33331
954-202-7419
Fax: 954-202-7337 info@generalfoodservice.com
www.generalfoodservice.com
Manufacturer, importer and exporter of slicers, grinders and mixers; manufacturer of food and organic waste disposers
President: John Westbrook
VP Sales/Marketing: Harry Ristan
Purchasing Manager: Dean Council
Estimated Sales: $5-10 Million
Number Employees: 100-249
Square Footage: 80000
Parent Co: Standex International Corporation
Type of Packaging: Food Service
Brands:
General Slicing

23135 Genesee Corrugated
2022 North St
Flint, MI 48505
810-228-3702
Fax: 810-235-0350 www.genpackaging.com
Manufacturer and exporter of corrugated shipping containers and interior packing materials
President: Luella Kautman
lkautman@co.genesee.mi.us
Material Control: Bobbi Jackson
Estimated Sales: $23.1 Million
Number Employees: 20-49
Type of Packaging: Bulk

23136 Genesis Machinery Products
400 Eagleview Blvd Ste 100
Exton, PA 19341
610-458-4900
Fax: 610-458-4939 800-552-9980

585

President: Bruce Smith
CFO: Bill Seiler
Contact: Bill Bogle
bbogle@gen-techno.com
Estimated Sales: $5-10 000,000
Number Employees: 20-49

23137 Genesis Nutritional Labs
391 S Orange St
Salt Lake City, UT 84104-3524

801-973-8824
Fax: 801-973-8807 sales@gnlabs.net
www.gnlabs.net
Testing services offered for chemical and microbiological nutraceutical and food needs.
Managing Partner: Jeff Reynolds
Technical Account Manager: Melissa Robbins
Business Development: Rachelle Maass
On-Staff Physician: Joe Giacalone
edgar@genysislabs.com
Sr Laboratory Manager: Edgar Grigorian
Manager: Edgar Grigorian
edgar@genysislabs.com
Microbiology Manager: Scott Larsen
Number Employees: 1-4

23138 Genesis Total SolutionsInc
3524 Decatur Hwy # 104
Suite 104
Fultondale, AL 35068-1366

205-631-5334
Fax: 205-877-3224 gts@gts-genesis.com
www.gts-genesis.com
rovides quality software solutions to the Food & Beverage Industry for over 35 years. We have users located throughout the United States, in Canada and overseas. Our applications include Accounting, Distribution, Production, and OrderFulfillment. All of our applications were developed by, and are supported through our staff of responsive professionals. Our solutions were designed to address the specific requirements of the F/B industry and an be used by both large and smallbusinesses.
President and Owner: Bill Miller
bmiller@gts-genesis.com
Vice President: Chris Miller
Technical Director: Camille Bourque
Estimated Sales: Below $5 Million
Number Employees: 1-4
Square Footage: 6000

23139 Geneva Awning & Tent Works Inc
96 Lewis St
Geneva, NY 14456

315-789-3151
Fax: 315-789-2695 800-789-3151
tgenevaa@rochester.rr.com www.genevatent.com
Commercial awnings and tents,also rental and sales
Owner: Sam Heakel
VP: Dan Warder
Estimated Sales: $1-2.5 Million
Number Employees: 5-9

23140 Geneva Lakes Cold Storage
PO Box 39
Darien, WI 53114-0039

262-724-3295
Fax: 262-724-4200
Warehouse offering cooler, freezer and dry storage for frozen, refrigerated and nonperishable food items; transportation firm providing refrigerated truck and van services including local, short and long haul
Number Employees: 1-4

23141 Genflex Roofing Systems
250 West
96th Street
Indianapolis, IN 46260

972-233-4100
Fax: 817-588-3099 800-443-4272
info@fbpe.be www.genflex.com
Partner: Rick L Cohen
Sales Manager: Bob Marini
QBS Regional Manager: Brian Stevenson
Sales Manager: Tim Creagan
Sales Manager: Mike Melito
Customer Service Representative: Linda Monroe
Estimated Sales: $1-3 000,000
Number Employees: 5-9

23142 Genpak
25 Aylmer Street
P O Box 209
Peterborough, ON K9J 6Y8
Canada

705-743-4733
Fax: 705-743-4798 800-461-1995
info@genpak.com www.genpakca.com
Manufacturer and exporter of plastic containers, cups and lids; also, single-serve packaging machinery for butter, margarine, creamers, etc
Quality Control: Jennifer Seeley
R&D: Jennifer Seeley
National Sales Manager: Kevin Callahan
Production Manager: Bernie Logan
Plant Manager: Brian May
Number Employees: 60
Type of Packaging: Bulk
Brands:
　Purity Pat
　Sealcup

23143 Genpak LLC
8235 220th St W
Lakeville, MN 55044-8059

952-881-8673
Fax: 952-881-9617 800-328-4556
www.genpak.com
Plain and printed new and recycled polyethylene bags and film, flexible packaging, laminations and pouches for various food and snack food applications.
President: Kim Lenhardt
Sales: Kevin Callahan
Plant Manager: Russ Snyder
Estimated Sales: $20-50 Million
Number Employees: 100-249
Number of Products: 100+
Square Footage: 140000
Parent Co: Jim Pattison Group
Other Locations:
　Strout Plastics
　Lakeville MN
Brands:
　Bags Again
　Flip & Grip
　Mr. Neat
　Value Tough

23144 Genpak LLC
10601 Westlake Dr
Charlotte, NC 28273

800-626-6695
info@genpak.com www.genpak.com
Manufacturer and exporter of plastic and styrofoam take out containers including plates, bowls and take-out containers. Dual oven meal solutions and bakery trays in opet plastic for retail packs. Packaging for processor, food serviceand retail applications.
Vice Presdient, Marketing: Tawn Whittemore
Director of Product Innovation: Jeff Cole
Estimated Sales: $100-500 Million
Number Employees: 1000-4999

23145 Gensaco Marketing
1751 2nd Ave
New York, NY 10128-5388

212-876-1020
Fax: 212-876-1003 800-506-1935
espmachine@aol.com
Coffee bars, espresso and cappuccino machines; importer of grinders; exporter of espresso machines, ice cream machines-restaurant equipment
Partner: Edward V Giannasca
CEO: Al Elvino
VP Sales: Lawrence Coal
VP Purchasing: Carbone Lorenzo
Estimated Sales: $1 Million
Number Employees: 5-9
Square Footage: 34000
Parent Co: Gensaco
Brands:
　Gensaco

23146 Gentile Packaging Machinery
8300 Boettner Rd
Saline, MI 48176-9642

734-429-1177
Fax: 734-429-4714 info@gentilemachinery.com
www.gentilemachinery.com
Packaging machinery

President: Aliseo Gentile
al@xelapack.com
Vice President: Anthony Gentile
Plant Manager: Rob Wilkerson
Estimated Sales: $1-2.5 000,000
Number Employees: 50-99

23147 Geo. Olcott Company
PO Box 267
Scottsboro, AL 35768-0267

256-259-4937
Fax: 256-259-4942 800-634-2769
Manufacturer and exporter of glass bead blast-cleaning cabinets, degreasing tanks, magnetic detectors and jet spray washers
President: Richard Olcott
Vice President: Marilyn Olcott
Estimated Sales: $1-2.5 Million
Number Employees: 9
Square Footage: 16800
Brands:
　Olcott

23148 Georg Fischer Central Plastics
39605 Independence St
Shawnee, OK 74804-9203

405-273-6302
Fax: 405-273-5993 800-654-3872
www.centralplastics.com
Molded plastic boxes
Contact: Cameron Laplante
cameronlaplante@yahoo.com
Estimated Sales: $1-5 Million
Number Employees: 50-99

23149 Georg Fischer Disa PipeTools
PO Box 40
Holly, MI 48442-0040

248-634-8251
Fax: 248-634-2507
Pipe cutting and beveling equipment
CEO: Kurt Stirnemann
Estimated Sales: $20-50 Million
Number Employees: 100-249

23150 George Basch Company
PO Box 188
Freeport, NY 11520

516-378-8100
Fax: 516-378-8140 info@nevrdull.com
www.nevrdull.com
Metal cleaners and polishes
President: Laurie Basch-Levy
Vice President: Mark Ax
Estimated Sales: $5-10 Million
Number Employees: 10-19
Number of Brands: 1
Number of Products: 1
Brands:
　Nevr-Dull Polish

23151 George G. Giddings
61 Beech Road
Randolph, NJ 07869-4548

973-361-4687
Fax: 973-887-1476
Consultant for food processing preservation
Consultant: George Giddings, Ph.D.
Number Employees: 1

23152 George Glove Company, Inc
301 Greenwood Ave
Midland Park, NJ 07432

201-251-1200
Fax: 201-251-8431 800-631-4292
steve@georgeglove.com www.georgeglove.com
Importer of white gloves
President/CEO: Andrew Wilson
CFO: Andrew Wilson
Marketing Director: Roy Miller
Sales: Roy Miller
Contact: Sharon Jubelt
sjubelt@newconceptoffice.com
Operations Manager: Juan Mino
Estimated Sales: $2 Million
Number Employees: 7
Square Footage: 48000
Brands:
　Beauty
　Dermal
　While-U-Color

23153 George Gordon Assoc
12 Continental Blvd
Merrimack, NH 03054-4302
603-424-5204
Fax: 603-424-9031 sales@ggapack.com
www.ggamfg.com
Packaging machinery, kits packaging, pouching systems, case/carton/gaylord loaders
President: Don Blanger
VP Sales/Marketing: Ron Downing
Purchasing Manager: Maurice Demarais
Estimated Sales: $10-20 000,000
Number Employees: 5-9

23154 George Lapgley Enterprises
4988 E Rolling Glen Drive
Pipersville, PA 18947
267-221-2426
Fax: 215-766-1687
Specialist in food safety & security consulting. Liason with regulatory agencies. Production, retail, food service, HACCP Plans, food safety training, expert testimony, food safety audits

23155 George Lauterer Corp
310 S Racine Ave # 6
6th Floor North
Chicago, IL 60607-2841
312-913-1881
Fax: 312-913-1811 sales@lauterer.com
www.lauterer.com
Advertising novelties and specialties including flags, banners, badges and buttons
Owner: Earl Joyce
johnj@lauterer.com
VP Marketing: John Joyce
Sales Exec: John Joyce
Estimated Sales: $2.5-5 Million
Number Employees: 20-49

23156 George Risk Industries Inc
802 S Elm St
Kimball, NE 69145-1599
308-235-4645
Fax: 308-235-3561 800-445-5218
www.grisk.com
Reed-type panel mount pushbutton switches, burglar alarms, door, window and keyboard switches, alphanumeric keyboards and proximity systems
CEO: Stephanie Risk-McElroy
gricfo@embarqmail.com
CFO: Stephanie Risk
VP Sales: Mary Ann Brothers
Quality Control: Bonnie Heaton
Sales Administration: Sharon Westby
Estimated Sales: F
Number Employees: 100-249

23157 George's Bakery Svc
1525 Macarthur Blvd # 4
Suite 4
Costa Mesa, CA 92626-1413
714-437-7143
Fax: 714-437-1016 www.georgesbakery.com
Owner: George Grezaud
george@georgesbakery.com
Estimated Sales: Less Than $500,000
Number Employees: 1-4

23158 Georgia Cold Storage
503 Ship St
Tifton, GA 31794-9617
229-382-5800
Fax: 912-382-5803
Cold Storage
Estimated Sales: $300,000-500,000
Number Employees: 1-4

23159 (HQ)Georgia Duck & Cordage Mill
21 Laredo Drive
Scottdale, GA 30079
404-297-3170
Fax: 404-296-5165
Manufacturer and exporter of conveyor and elevator belting including vinyl, rubber and urethane
President: Raymond Willoch
VP Sales/Marketing: Ken Dangelo
Sales Manager/National Accounts: Jim Hinson
Sales Manager: Jim Panter
Number Employees: 490

23160 Georgia Pacific
P.O.Box 19130
Green Bay, WI 54307
920-435-8821
Fax: 920-496-9445 www.gp.com
Facial tissue, hand towels, napkins, wipers, dispensing systems and printed specialty products
VP: Russ Mc Collister
Sr. VP Sales: George Hartmann
VP Sales: Paul Farren
Contact: Dean Baumgartner
dean.baumgartner@gapac.com
Estimated Sales: $1-5 Million
Number Employees: 1,000-4,999
Brands:
  Adnaps
  Belnap
  Bevnaps
  Bi-Tex
  Billow
  Commander Ii
  Dari-Dri
  Dine-A-Wipe
  Dine-A-Wipe Plus
  Drize
  Dust 'n Clean
  Elfin
  Essence
  Fornap
  Fort Howard
  Generation Ii
  Handifold
  Hy-Tex
  Hynap
  Miltex
  Mini-Mornap
  Mornap
  Mynap
  Nornap Jr.
  Nu-Nap
  Pom
  Palmer
  Paperlux
  Perfection
  Plyfold
  Pom-Etts
  Prim
  Pul-A-Nap
  Ritenap
  Selford
  Shur-Wipe
  Sirnap
  So-Dri
  Sof-Knit
  Soft 'n Fresh
  Soft 'n Gentle
  Spread
  Staynap
  Studio Colors
  Stylene
  Texnap
  Tidynap Jr.
  Twin-Tex
  Ultra Wipe
  Wipe Away

23161 Georgia Tent & Awning
1356 English St NW
Atlanta, GA 30318
404-523-7551
Fax: 404-525-0601 800-252-2391
info@georgiatent.com www.georgiatent.com
Commercial awnings
President: Ken Spooner
Quality Control: Mike Hill
VP: Bob Spooner
CFO: Gary Meacher
Chairman of the Board: Robert Spooner
Contact: Leonard Buccellato
leonard.buccellato@georgiatent.com
Estimated Sales: $5-10,000,000
Number Employees: 50-99

23162 Georgia Watermelon Association
4109 Country Way
PO Box 1109
LaGrange, GA 30241
706-845-8575
Fax: 706-883-8215
Our purpose is watermelon promotion from production to consumption.
President: Ricky Tucker
Executive Secretary/Treasurer: Nancy Childers

Estimated Sales: $1-2.5 Million
Number Employees: 1-4

23163 Georgia-Pacific LLC
133 Peachtree St. NE
Atlanta, GA 30303
404-652-4000
800-283-5547
www.gp.com
Manufacturer and exporter of corrugated shipping cases.
President/Chief Executive Officer: Christian Fischer
SVP, Operations: Jeff Koeppel
SVP/Chief Financial Officer: Tyler Woolson
SVP/Communications, Gov't & Pub. Affairs: Sheila Weidman
Year Founded: 1927
Estimated Sales: Over $5 Billion
Number Employees: 30,000+
Parent Co: Koch Industries
Type of Packaging: Consumer

23164 Gerber Innovations
24 Industrial Park Rd W
Tolland, CT 6084
Fax: 978-694-0055 800-331-5797
www.gerberinnovations.com
Manufacturer and exporter of computer plotters and sample makers for packaging design
Director of Sales & Marketing: Don Skenderian
Vice President, Business Development: Mark Bibo
Technical Manager: Ken Hooks
VP Sales: Steven Gore
General Manager: W Staniewicz
Estimated Sales: $10-20 Million
Number Employees: 50-99
Parent Co: Data Technology

23165 Gerber Legendary Blades
14200 SW 72nd Ave.
Portland, OR 97224-8010
503-639-6161
Fax: 503-403-1102 800-950-6161
www.gerbergear.com
Culinary knives including steak, carving, slicing, etc.
Year Founded: 1939
Estimated Sales: $100 Million
Number Employees: 250-499
Parent Co: Fiskars

23166 Germantown Milling Company
6098 Brooksville Germantown Rd
Germantown, KY 41044-9060
606-728-5857
Fax: 606-883-3172
Feed
President: Jack Myrick
Estimated Sales: Below $5 Million
Number Employees: 2
Square Footage: 900000

23167 Gerrity Industries
PO Box 121
Monmouth, ME 04259
207-933-2804
Fax: 207-933-1081 877-933-2804
info@gerrityindustries.com
www.gerrityindustries.com
Pallets and skids
President: Peter Gerrity
Sales: Leo Moody
Contact: Wally Fish
fish@gerrityindustries.com
Estimated Sales: Below $5 Million
Number Employees: 20-49
Square Footage: 120000

23168 Gerstel Inc
701 Digital Dr # J
Suite J
Linthicum Hts, MD 21090-2236
410-609-0856
Fax: 410-247-5887 800-413-8160
info@gerstelus.com www.gerstelus.com
Gas chromatographic systems for analysis of complex samples in the flavoring and food additive business including thermal desorption, static headspace, fraction collectors and multi-column switching systems

President: Bob Collins
CFO: Robert Collins
Vice President: Robert Collins
R&D: Ed Pfannkoch
IT: Robert Collins
sales@gerstelus.com
Estimated Sales: Below $5 Million
Number Employees: 10-19
Parent Co: Gerstel GmbH
Brands:
  Gerstel

23169 Gervasi Wood Products
2611 W Beltline Highway
Madison, WI 53713-2349

608-274-6752

Counters
Estimated Sales: $500,000-$1 Million
Number Employees: 5-9

23170 Gessner Products
241 N Main St
PO Box 389
Ambler, PA 19002-4224

215-646-7667
Fax: 215-646-6222 800-874-7808
sales@gessnerproducts.com
www.gessnerproducts.com
Manufacturer and exporter of plastic ashtrays, credit card trays, coasters, signs, condiment jars, sugar caddies and restaurant smallwares
President: Edward H Gessner
Controller: Neo Brown
Executive VP: Geoffrey Ries
Quality Control: Steve Fuhrmeister
National Sales Manager: Michael Salemi
Production Manager: Chuck Denoncour
Estimated Sales: $5-10 Million
Number Employees: 100-249

23171 Geyersville Printing Company
21001 Geyersville Avenue
Geyserville, CA 95441

707-857-1704
Fax: 707-857-1705
Wine industry labels
Estimated Sales: less than $500,000
Number Employees: 6

23172 Ghibli North American
14 Germay Drive
Wilmington, DE 19804

302-654-5908
Fax: 302-652-7159 ghibli@frontiernet.net
Manufacturer and exporter of high pressure and hot water cleaning equipment
General Manager: Gordon Thomas
Estimated Sales: $1-5 Million
Number Employees: 5 to 9
Brands:
  Ghibli

23173 (HQ)Giant Gumball Machine Company
200 Macarthur Blvd
Grand Prairie, TX 75050-4739

972-262-2234
Fax: 972-262-3167
Manufacturer and exporter of vending machines
President: Dan Clemson
d.clemson@productsales.com
National Sales Manager: Bob Rogers
National Sales Manager: Dan Wright
Estimated Sales: $300,000-500,000
Number Employees: 1-4

23174 Giant Packaging Corporation
545 W Lambert Road
Suite F
Brea, CA 92821-3916

714-256-8498
Fax: 714-256-8499 giant@gus.net
Strapping and wrapping machines, carton sealers, impulse sealers, and strapping hand tools
Estimated Sales: $2.5-5 000,000
Number Employees: 1-4

23175 Gibbs Brothers Cooperage
113 Overton St
Hot Springs, AR 71901-6312

501-623-8881
Fax: 501-623-9610 gibbsbro@swbell.net
White oak wooden kegs and barrels

President: James Gibbs Sr
Manager: Jay Gibbs
Estimated Sales: $1-2.5 Million
Number Employees: 5-9
Square Footage: 48000

23176 (HQ)Gibraltar Packaging Group Inc
2000 Summit Ave
Hastings, NE 68901-6703

402-463-1366
Fax: 402-463-2467
Folding cartons, litho-laminated cartons, regular and corrugated cartons and flexible packaging including converted bags and rollstock
President and COO: Richard Hinrichs
rhinrichs@rosmarpackaging.com
CEO: Walter E Rose
Chairman of the Board: Walter E Rose
VP Sales: Mark Lessor
Corporate Marketing/Investor Rel. Mgr: Leslie Schroeder
Estimated Sales: Below $5,000,000
Number Employees: 100-249
Other Locations:
  Gibraltar Packaging Group
  Mount Gilead NC

23177 Giddings & Lewis
P.O.Box 1960
Fond Du Lac, WI 54936-1960

920-921-7100
Fax: 920-906-7669 800-558-4808
mwl@giddings.com
Automotion controls, measurement, sensing
Manager: Pete Winkelmann
President, Chief Executive Officer: Lawrence Culp
Estimated Sales: $50-100 Million
Number Employees: 100-249

23178 Giesecke & Devrient America
45925 Horseshoe Dr # 100
Dulles, VA 20166-6588

703-480-2000
Fax: 703-480-2060 800-856-7712
www.gi-de.com
Manufacturer and exporter of high speed currency counters, dispensers and endorsers
President: Scott Marquardt
scott.marquardt@gdai.com
Director Distribution: Bill Chamberlain
Estimated Sales: $50-100 Million
Number Employees: 250-499
Parent Co: G&D America

23179 Giffin International
1900 Brown Rd
Auburn Hills, MI 48326-1701

248-478-5115
Fax: 248-478-1321 info@giffinusa.com
Cooking and chilling systems; smoke houses, air chillers, batch and continuous systems
Owner: Shawn Drury
shawn.drury@giffinusa.com
Estimated Sales: Less Than $500,000
Number Employees: 1-4

23180 Gilbert Industries, Inc
5611 Krueger Drive
Jonesboro, AR 72401-6818

870-932-6070
Fax: 870-932-5609 800-643-0400
mailbox@gilbertinc.com www.gilbertinc.com
Electronic wall-mounted flytraps
President: David Gilbert
Sales: Stephen Goad
Sales: Libby Mackey
Estimated Sales: $1-5 Million

23181 Gilbert Insect Light Traps
5611 Krueger Dr
Jonesboro, AR 72401-6818

870-932-6070
Fax: 870-932-5609 800-643-0400
mailbox@gilbertinc.com www.gilbertinc.com
Manufacturer and exporter of professional flytraps, emergency lighting and LED exit signs; also, consultant on flying insect control
President/ILT Research/Customer Service: David Gilbert
ILT Sales/Customer Service: Stephen Goad
Executive Administrator/Customer Service: Libby Mackey

Estimated Sales: $1-3 Million
Number Employees: 20-49
Number of Brands: 2
Number of Products: 15
Square Footage: 152000
Parent Co: Gilbert Industries
Brands:
  Gilbert

23182 Gilchrist Bag Co Inc
907 Sharp Ave
Camden, AR 71701-2603

870-836-6416
Fax: 870-836-8379 800-643-1513
sales@gilchristbag.com www.gilchristbag.com
Manufacturer and exporters of a wide variety of quality paper bags, sacks and specialty supplies used by a variety of markets.
Owner: Tom Gilchrist
tgilchrist@gilchristbag.com
Director Operations Marketing: Randy Robertson
Plant/Production Manager: Larry Starnes
Plant Manager: Louis Hammond
Estimated Sales: $5-10,000,000
Number Employees: 20-49
Square Footage: 350000
Type of Packaging: Consumer, Food Service, Private Label

23183 (HQ)Giles Enterprises Inc
2750 Gunter Park Dr W
P.O.Box 210247
Montgomery, AL 36109-1098

334-272-1457
Fax: 334-239-4117 800-288-1555
intsales@gilesent.com www.gfse.com
Manufacturer and exporter of kitchen and deli equipment including ventless hood fryers
President: David Byrd
dbyrd@gfsequipment.com
Financial Director: Ken Robinson
Quality Control: Sheila Munday
VP Sales: David Byrd
Estimated Sales: $10-20 Million
Number Employees: 100-249
Square Footage: 160000
Brands:
  Chester Fried
  Giles

23184 Gillis Associated Industries
750 Pinecrest Dr
Prospect Heights, IL 60070-1806

847-541-6500
Fax: 847-541-0858 www.gillisindustries.com
Wire systems for shelving, carts, palletainer stacking wire containers, rack decking, high-density mobile storage and rivet rack with wire decking
President: Harvey Baker
President, Chief Executive Officer: Steven DarnelL
Vice President of Business Development: Dave Mack
VP Sales: Mark Jones
Vice President of Operations: Bob Buehler
Estimated Sales: $5-10 Million
Number Employees: 20-49

23185 Gilson Co Inc
7975 N Central Dr
Lewis Center, OH 43035-9409

740-548-5314
Fax: 740-548-5314 800-444-1508
www.globalgilson.com
Liquid handling
President: Trent R Smith
tsmith@gilsonco.com
CEO: Robert H Smith
Marketing Director: Carl Kramer
Technical Development Manager: Jim Bibler
Estimated Sales: $12-20 Million
Number Employees: 50-99
Brands:
  Fristch Mills
  Gilsonic Autosiever
  Ultra Siever

23186 Giltron Inc
61 Endicott St
PO Box 427
Norwood, MA 02062-3046

781-762-4310
Fax: 508-359-4317 sales@giltron.com
www.giltron.com
Induction heat cap foil sealers for bottles and jars

President: Fred Giltron
CFO: A Stanley Pittman
Quality Control: Bruce Green
R & D: Mike Sievert
Service Manager: William Koivu
VP Operations: Fred Pittman
Estimated Sales: Below $5 Million
Number Employees: 1-4
Square Footage: 14000
Brands:
    Giltron Foilsealer

23187 Ginnie Nichols Graphic Design
780 W Napa St
Sonoma, CA 95476-6452

        707-996-0164
    Fax: 707-938-3855 800-399-7890
Package design
President: Jenny Nichols
Estimated Sales: $300,000-500,000
Number Employees: 1-4

23188 Ginseng Up Corp
16 Plum St
Worcester, MA 01604-3600

        508-799-6178
    Fax: 508-799-0686 800-446-7364
info@ginsengup.com www.ginsengup.com
Natural soft drinks; contract packaging available
President: Sang Han
Manufacturing Executive: Courtney Craite
courtney@ginsengup.com
Estimated Sales: $3-5 Million
Number Employees: 10-19
Parent Co: One Up
Type of Packaging: Consumer
Brands:
    Cold/Hot Pack Tunnel Pasterized
    Flavor
    Ginseng Up

23189 Gintzler Graphics Inc
100 Lawrence Bell Dr
Buffalo, NY 14221-7089

        716-631-9700
    Fax: 716-631-0075 sales@gintzler.com
Pressure sensitive labels
President: Jeff Amato
amato.jeff@gintzler.com
Sales Manager: James Calamita
Estimated Sales: $20-50 Million
Number Employees: 50-99

23190 Girard Spring Water
1100 Mineral Spring Ave
North Providence, RI 02904-4104

        401-725-7298
    Fax: 401-725-7913 800-477-9287
Spring water and water coolers
President: John Ponton
Estimated Sales: $500,000-$1 Million
Number Employees: 1 to 4
Square Footage: 7500
Type of Packaging: Consumer, Private Label, Bulk

23191 Girard Wood Products Inc
802 E Main St
Puyallup, WA 98372-3364

        253-845-0505
    Fax: 253-845-5463 800-532-0505
    greg@girardwoodproducts.com
Wooden pallets and skids; also, pallet recycling services including retrieval, repair and disposal available
President: Anthony Hubbs
anthony@girardwoodproducts.com
VP of Sales: Greg Vipond
Sales Manager: Dave Loden
Operations Manager: Scott Vipond
Plant Manager: Virgil Vwngwirth
Purchasing Manager: Stan Henry
Estimated Sales: $10-20 Million
Number Employees: 20-49

23192 Girton Manufacturing Co
160 W Main St
Millville, PA 17846-5004

        570-458-5521
    Fax: 570-458-5589 info@girton.com
    www.girton.com

Manufactures stainless steel washing equipment for the Food & Dairy Processing Industries, including COP tanks, bin and tub washing systems for pallets, drums, cases, etc. Girton MFG co Inc also manufactures King Zeero Ice Builders.
President: Dean Girton
info@girton.com
Sales: Wm Bruce Michael
Plant Manager: Jim Eves
Purchasing Director: Donna Bender
Estimated Sales: $10-20 Million
Number Employees: 50-99
Square Footage: 45000
Brands:
    Girton King Zeero

23193 Giunta Brothers
2612 S 17th St
Philadelphia, PA 19145-4502

        215-389-9670
Culinary strainers and graters
Owner: Anthony P Giunta
Estimated Sales: less than $500,000
Number Employees: 1 to 4

23194 Gl Mezzetta Inc
105 Mezzetta Ct
American Canyon, CA 94503-9604

        707-648-1050
    Fax: 707-648-1060 800-941-7044
    www.mezzetta.com
Glass-packed peppers and olives
President: Jeff Mezzetta
Founder: Giuseppe Luigi Mezzetta
HR Executive: Maritza Monge
mmonge@mezzetta.com
General Manager: Ronald Mezzetta
Estimated Sales: $12.3 Million
Number Employees: 100-249

23195 Glamorgan Bakery
3919 Richmond Rd SW
Building 19
Calgary, AB T3E 4P2
Canada

        403-232-2800
    glamorganbakery@gmail.com
    www.glamorganbakery.com
Freshly baked goods
President/Owner: Douwe Nauta
General Manager: Don Nauta
Sales/Customer Service: Jeremy Nauta
Number Employees: 8

23196 Glaro Inc
735 Calebs Path # 1
Hauppauge, NY 11788-4201

        631-234-1717
    Fax: 631-234-9510 info@glaro.com
    www.glaro.com
Manufacturer and exporter of waste containers, engraved signs, aluminum tray stand equipment, crowd control stanchions, planters, coat racks, etc
Vice President: Robert Betensky
robert@glaro.com
CEO: Michael Glass
VP: Robert Betensky
Estimated Sales: $20-50 Million
Number Employees: 10-19
Square Footage: 50000

23197 Glasko Plastics
3123 W Alpine St
Santa Ana, CA 92704

        714-751-7830
    Fax: 714-751-4039
Plastic containers
Estimated Sales: $2.5-5 Million
Number Employees: 20-49

23198 Glass Industries America LLC
340 Quinnipiac St # 3
Wallingford, CT 06492-4050

        203-269-6700
    Fax: 203-269-8782 www.wallingfordglass.com
Manufacturer and exporter of lighting fixtures including bent and decorated glassware
Owner: George Sutherland
glass.industries@snet.net
Manager: Jack Jackson
Estimated Sales: $2.5-5 Million
Number Employees: 5-9
Parent Co: L.D. Kichler

23199 Glass Pro
2300 W Windsor Ct
Addison, IL 60101-1491

        630-268-9494
    Fax: 800-875-6243 888-641-8919
Manufacturer and exporter of glass washing machinery, sanitizers and accessories
President: Robert Joesel
CEO: Evelyn Joesel
R&D: Robert Joesel
Quality Control: Robert Joesel
Estimated Sales: Below $5 Million
Number Employees: 5-9
Number of Brands: 4
Number of Products: 3
Square Footage: 12000
Type of Packaging: Food Service, Private Label
Brands:
    Brush-Rite
    Glass Maid
    Glass Pro

23200 Glass Tech
23780 NW Huffman St # 101
Hillsboro, OR 97124-5976

        503-646-3989
    Fax: 503-626-2890 www.glasstechweb.com
Wine industry tasting room supplies
Contact: Patricia Patton
patricia@glasscellar.com
Estimated Sales: $1-2.5 000,000
Number Employees: 10-19

23201 Glassline Corp
28905 Glenwood Rd
Perrysburg, OH 43551-3020

        419-666-0857
    Fax: 419-666-1549 www.glasslinecompanies.com
Hot and cold seal packaging machinery
Owner: Tom Ziems
sales@glassline.com
Estimated Sales: $10-20 Million
Number Employees: 100-249

23202 Glastender
5400 N Michigan Rd
Saginaw, MI 48604-9700

        989-752-4275
    Fax: 989-752-4444 800-748-0423
    info@glastender.com
Manufacturer and exporter of bar and restaurant equipment including glass washers, cocktail stations, underbar and refrigerated backbar equipment, mug frosters, beer and soda line chillers, ice cream freezers and coolers
President: Todd Hall
thall@glastender.com
CFO: Jamie Rievert
VP Admin: Kim Norris
Quality Control: David Burk
VP Operations: Mark Norris
Plant Manager: Mark Norris
Purchasing Manager: Zoa May
Estimated Sales: $10-20 Million
Number Employees: 100-249
Square Footage: 200000

23203 Glatech Productions LLC
325 2nd St
Lakewood, NJ 08701-3329

        732-364-8700
    Fax: 732-370-0877 info@kosherGELATIN.com
    www.koshergelatin.com
Producer of Kolatin® Kosher gelatin and Elyon® kosher confectionery products.
CEO: Moshe Eider
glatech@gmail.com
Marketing: Chez Eider
Estimated Sales: $1-5 Million
Number Employees: 1-4
Number of Brands: 2
Type of Packaging: Bulk
Brands:
    Elyon
    Kolatin

23204 Glatfelter P H Co
96 S George St # 520
Suite 500
York, PA 17401-1434

        717-225-4711
    Fax: 717-846-7208 866-744-7680
    info@glatfelter.com www.glatfelter.com

Teabag paper, bags and packaging film supplies, coffeebag paper, coffeebag paper (metallized)
CEO: Dante C Parrini
dante.parrini@glatfelter.com
CEO: George Glatfelter
CFO: John Jacunski
Number Employees: 1000-4999

23205 Glatt Air Techniques Inc
20 Spear Rd
Ramsey, NJ 07446-1288
201-825-8700
Fax: 201-825-0389 info@glattair.com
Process controls, material handling equipment, coaters, fluid bed dryers, granulators, etc
EVP: Stephen Sirabian
General Manager Sales: John Carey
Vice President: Steve Sirabian
ssirabian@glattair.com
Director Business Development: Ted Wisniewski
VP Sales/Technical Operations: Stephen Sirabian
Estimated Sales: $30-50 Million
Number Employees: 100-249
Square Footage: 60000
Parent Co: Glatt GmbH
Other Locations:
Glatt Air Techniques
San Leandro CA

23206 Glawe Manufacturing Company
851 Zapata Dr
Fairborn, OH 45324-5165
937-754-0064
Fax: 937-754-1780 800-434-8368
bhughes@glaweawning.com
www.glaweawning.com
Commercial awnings
CEO: L Vernon Schaefer
Contact: L Schaefer
l.schaefer@glaweawnings.com
Estimated Sales: $2.5-5 Million
Number Employees: 20-49

23207 Gleason Industries
3013 Douglas Boulevard
Suite 230
Roseville, CA 95661-3847
916-784-1302
Fax: 310-679-5581
Converting box boards and layerboards for the candy and bakery industries
President: Michael Richards
CEO: Mike Richards
VP Finance: John Mahar
Sales Director: Carlene Milligan
Plant Manager: Tony Concad
Estimated Sales: $1-3 Million
Number Employees: 85
Other Locations:
Gleason Industries
Sacramento CA
Gleason Industries
Summer WA
Gleason Industries
Millwaukie OR
Gleason Industries
West Valley City UT
Gleason Industries
Rancho Cocamonca CA

23208 Gleeson Construct & Engineers
2015 7th St
P.O.Box 625
Sioux City, IA 51101-2003
712-258-9300
Fax: 712-277-5300 www.gleesonllc.com
Specializes in the construction of food processing facilities, freezers, cold storage facilities and distribution centers.
President: Harlan Vandezandschul
h.vandezandschul@gleesonllc.com
Number Employees: 1-4

23209 Glen Mills Inc.
220 Delawanna Ave
Clifton, NJ 07014-1550
973-777-0777
Fax: 973-777-0070 sales@glenmills.com
Laboratory and small-scale production equipment
Director: Stanley Goldberg
Marketing: Lisa McCormack
Sales Engineer: Ross Kaplan
Estimated Sales: $2.5-5 Million
Number Employees: 6
Square Footage: 48000

Brands:
Turbula
Kakuhunter
Retsch
SEPR

23210 Glen Raven Custom Fabrics LLC
1831 N Park Ave
Burlington, NC 27217-1137
336-227-6211
Fax: 336-226-8133 oford@glenraven.com
www.glenraven.com
Solutions dyed acrylic fabrics for awnings and umbrellas
Chairman/ CEO: Allen E Gant Jr
President/ COO: Leib Oehmig
SVP, CFO & Treasurer: Gary Smith
SVP, Secretary & General Counsel: Derek Steed
R&D: John Coates
Sales/Marketing Administration: Harry Gobble
National Sales Manager: Ocie Ford
Contact: Emily Eby
eeby@glenraven.com
Number Employees: 20-49
Parent Co: Glen Raven Custom Fabrics LLC
Type of Packaging: Food Service

23211 Glenmarc Manufacturing
2001 S.Blue Island Ave.
Chicago, IL 60608
312-243-0800
Fax: 312-243-4670 800-323-5350
glenmarc@aol.com
Manufacturer and exporter of adhesive dispensing equipment. Also 304/316 stainless steel pressure tanks
President: John Sims
Chairman, Chief Executive Officer: John Chen
CEO: Don Deloach
Senior Vice President of Operations: Billy Ho
Purchasing Manager: Steve Eichele
Estimated Sales: Below $500,000
Number Employees: 5-9
Square Footage: 26000

23212 (HQ)Glenro Inc
39 Mcbride Ave
Paterson, NJ 07501-1799
973-279-5900
Fax: 973-279-9103 888-453-6761
info@glenro.com www.glenro.com
Hot air and infrared ovens for food packaging
President: Bill Bacher
bbacher@glenro.com
Vice President: Jim Karrett
Sales Director: Jim Karrett
Estimated Sales: $10-15 Million
Number Employees: 10-19

23213 Glenroy Inc
1437 Wells Dr
Bensalem, PA 19020-4469
215-245-3575
Fax: 215-245-3589 800-441-2230
www.glenroylabels.com
Labeling technologies, bar code scanners
Owner: Patrick Larkin Jr
Vice President: Terry la Ruffa
CFO: Vince Laruffa
Estimated Sales: $5-10 000,000
Number Employees: 20-49

23214 Glit Microtron
305 Rock Industrial Park Dr
Bridgetown, MO 63044
877-947-7117
Fax: 800-327-5492 800-325-1051
CustomerService@contico.com
www.continentalcommercialproducts.com
Abrasive coated synthetic sponge, scour pads and scrub sponges
President: Gordan Kirsch
Research Manager: Alan Christopher
Number Employees: 250-499
Parent Co: Katy Industries

23215 Glit/Disco
13330 Lakefront Drive
Earth City, MO 63045-1513
314-770-9919
Fax: 800-327-5492 contmfg@contico.com
www.continental-mfg.com
Estimated Sales: $1-5 Million
Parent Co: Katy Company

23216 Glo Germ Company
P.O. Box 189
Moab, UT 84532
435-259-6034
Fax: 435-259-5930 800-842-6622
info@glogerm.com www.glogerm.com
Handwashing training
President: Joe D Kingsley
Estimated Sales: $1 000,000
Number Employees: 5-9
Type of Packaging: Consumer, Bulk
Brands:
Superior Systems

23217 Glo-Quartz Electric Heater
7084 Maple St
Mentor, OH 44060-4932
440-255-9701
Fax: 440-255-7852 800-321-3574
tstrokes@gloquartz.com www.gloquartz.com
Electric immersion heaters and tubular metal and quartz heating elements for food processing and packaging; also, temperature controls; exporter of electric heaters
President: George Strokes
VP: Thomas Strokes
Sales: John Paglia
Contact: Jeffrey Payne
jpayne@gloquartz.com
Plant Manager: Jeff Payne
Estimated Sales: $3-5 Million
Number Employees: 20-49
Square Footage: 88000
Brands:
Glo-Quartz

23218 Global Canvas Products
5000 Paschall Ave
Philadelphia, PA 19143-5136
267-634-6207
Fax: 610-284-4323 kanvasking@globecanvas.com
www.globecanvas.com
Wholesale manufacturer and distributor, with a diverse product mix comprised of 60% awning, 25% athletic pads for track and field, 10% industrial covers and 5% bags.
President: Kevin Kelly
kevin@globecanvas.com
Estimated Sales: $1-2.5 Million
Number Employees: 1-4
Square Footage: 72000

23219 Global Carts and Equipment
640 Herman Road
Suite 2
Jackson, NJ 08527-3068
732-899-9555
Fax: 732-899-1719 800-653-0881
foodman40@aol.com
Supplier of hot dog carts, soup carts and food.
Estimated Sales: $2.5-5 Million
Number Employees: 5-9
Square Footage: 104000

23220 Global Environmental Packaging
221 3rd Street
Newport, RI 02840-1087
401-847-4603
Fax: 401-847-4654 800-729-4210

23221 Global Equipment Co Inc
11 Harbor Park Dr
Port Washington, NY 11050-4646
516-608-7000
Fax: 516-625-8415 888-628-3466
www.globalindustrial.com
Manufacturer, exporter and importer of steel bins, benches, wire shelving and material handling equipment
President: Bob Dooley
bdooley@systemax.com
Chief Financial Officer: Lawrence Reinhold
Vice President: Bruce Leeds
Quality Control Assurance: Paul Betzold
Marketing Manager: Maureen Cronin
Director, Sales: Steve McNamara
Operations: Jack Kaserow
Product Manager: Elise Wong
Purchasing Manager: Eric Bertel
Estimated Sales: $28 Million
Number Employees: 100-249
Square Footage: 85000
Parent Co: Systemax

23222 Global Manufacturing
1801 E 22nd St
Little Rock, AR 72206-2501

501-374-7416
Fax: 501-376-7147 800-551-3569
www.globalmanufacturing.com
Manufacturer and exporter of vibrators including
hydraulic, pneumatic, electric, air blasters and
turbine
President: Catherine Janosky
cjanosky@globalmanufacturing.com
Quality Control: Wilfred Coney
Marketing: April Crocker
Sales: Perry Schnebelen
Operations: Tom Janosky
Production: Stan Kligman
Plant Manager: Rod Treat
Purchasing Director: Howard Stewart
Estimated Sales: $3-5,000,000
Number Employees: 10-19
Brands:
    Quiet Thunder
    Silver Sonic
    Yellow Jacket

23223 Global Marketing Enterprises
1801 S Canal St # C
Chicago, IL 60616-1522

312-733-0000
Fax: 312-733-8010
President: Eduardo Chua
echua@globalmsi.com
Estimated Sales: $5-10 Million
Number Employees: 10-19

23224 Global New Products DataBase
333 West Wacker Drive
Suite 1100
Chicago, IL 60606

312-932-0400
Fax: 312-932-0469 helpdesk@mintel.com
www.gnpd.com
Comprehensive database that monitors worldwide
product innovation in consumer packaged goods
markets
Manager: Jon Butcher
CFO: John Weeks
Estimated Sales: $5-10 Million
Number Employees: 20-49

23225 Global Nutrition Research Corporation
3120 S Potter Dr
Tempe, AZ 85282

602-454-2248
Fax: 602-454-2249
Provide a comprehensive database of herbal supple-
ments, health products, and herbal companies avail-
able on the internet. We are not only an information
provider, but also an herbal and alternative medicine
community site.
President: Ken Ardisson
Sales Contact: Shannon Purcell
Estimated Sales: $20-50 Million
Number Employees: 20-49

23226 Global Organics
68 Moulton St
Cambridge, MA 02138-1119

781-648-8844
Fax: 781-648-0774 info@global-organics.com
www.global-organics.com
Organic ingredients
President: Dave Alexander
Vice President: Roland Hoch
Account Manager: Dino Scarsella
Sales and Marketing Coordinator: Ravi Arori
Estimated Sales: Under $500,000
Number Employees: 25

23227 Global Package
PO Box 634
Napa, CA 94559

707-224-5670
Fax: 707-224-8170 info@globalpackage.net
www.globalpackage.net
International packaging solutions for wine, spirits
and food
CEO: Erica Harrop
Sales: Kathy Feder
Estimated Sales: $5 Million
Number Employees: 3
Type of Packaging: Food Service

23228 Global Packaging Machinery Company
1500 Cardinal Drive
Little Falls, NJ 07424

973-450-4601
Fax: 973-450-4603
global@globalpackmachinery.com
www.globalpackmachinery.com
President: Daniel Waldron
R & D: Mike Kurgyla
Vice President/Mechanical Engineer: Herman
Andrade
Contact: Michael Kurdyla
global@globalpackmachinery.com
Estimated Sales: Below $5 Million
Number Employees: 10

23229 Global Payment Tech Inc
170 Wilbur Pl # 4
Bohemia, NY 11716-2416

631-563-2500
Fax: 631-563-2630 www.gptx.com
Paper currency validators, lockable stackers for use
in the gaming, beverage and vending industries
President: Thomas Oliveri
CFO: William L Mcmahon
wmcmahon@gptx.com
Quality Control: Dede Lisa
Sales Director: Mary Russell
Number Employees: 20-49

23230 Global Product Development Group
3501 Woodhead Drive
Suite 10
Northbrook, IL 60062

847-504-0464
Fax: 608-224-0455 info@globalpdg.com
www.globalpdg.com
Laboratory providing research and development,
consulting and contract research services
President: Michael Maloney
Estimated Sales: $1-3 Million
Number Employees: 5-9
Square Footage: 15000

23231 Global Sticks, Inc.
13555-23A Avenue
Surrey, BC V4A 9V1
Canada

604-535-7748
Fax: 604-535-7749 866-433-5770
Wooden ice cream spoons & sticks, corn dog sticks
& coffee stirrers.
President: Reggie Nukovic
General Manager: Earl Metcalf

23232 Global USA Inc
1990 M St NW # 200
Washington, DC 20036-3468

202-296-2400
Fax: 202-296-2409 info@globalusainc.com
www.globalusainc.com
CEO: H Lottie
lottie@globalusainc.com
Chairman and Chief Executive Officer: Dr. Bo
Denysyk
Senior Vice President: David C. Fine
Director-Research and Analysis: Viktor Sulzynsky
Number Employees: 10-19

23233 Global Water & Energy
2404 Rutland Dr
Suite 200
Austin, TX 78758

512-697-1930
Fax: 512-697-1931 mail.usa@globalwe.com
www.globalwaterengineering.com
Industrial wastewater treatment and bio-waste-to-en-
ergy solution provider for food industries
Chairman/CEO: Jean-Pierre Ombregt
Contact: Erin Booth
ebooth@globalwaterengineering.com
Controller: Mike Herbert
Estimated Sales: $1 Million
Number Employees: 5
Parent Co: GLV

23234 Global Water Group Inc
8601 Sovereign Row
Dallas, TX 75247-4613

214-678-9866
Fax: 214-678-9811 info@globalwater.com
www.globalwater.com

Mobile, self-contained and fixed based water purifi-
cation systems, wastewater processing equipment,
and gray water recycling equipment
President: Alan Weiss
amweiss@globalwater.com
COO: Rick Stafford
CFO: Rd Stafford
Vice President: N Kanmer
Research & Development: Jacob Kupersztoch
Quality Control: Thomas Boutwell
Public Relations: Cherie Weiss
Estimated Sales: $10 Million
Number Employees: 20-49
Number of Brands: 6
Number of Products: 50
Square Footage: 40000

23235 (HQ)Globe Fire Sprinkler Corp
4077 Airpark Dr
Standish, MI 48658-9533

989-846-4583
Fax: 989-846-9231 800-248-0278
Bob733@aol.com www.globesprinkler.com
Manufacturer, importer and exporter of commercial,
industrial and residential fire sprinklers, de-
luge/preaction, alarm, dry pipe and check valves,
water motor alarms and accessories for sprinkler
systems
President: Steven R. Worthington, I.M.B..A
Chairman/ CEO: Robert C. Worthington, P.E.
bob733@aol.com
EVP: Buck Buchanan
Dir. Of Marketing & Information System: John D.
Corcoran
VP, Sales: Randy Lane
VP, Operations: Terry Bovee
Estimated Sales: $10-20 Million
Number Employees: 100-249
Square Footage: 80000
Brands:
    Globe
    Kennedy
    System Sensor

23236 Globe Food Equipment Co
2153 Dryden Rd
Moraine, OH 45439-1739

937-299-5493
Fax: 937-299-4147 800-347-5423
www.globefoodequip.com
Manufactures slicers, vegetable cutters, mixers,
choppers and scales
President: Hilton Gardner
hgardner@globeslicers.com
Marketing: Alicia Sanders
Sales: Bob Adams
Number Employees: 20-49
Brands:
    Chefmate
    Globe
    Protech

23237 Globe Machine
902 E E St
Tacoma, WA 98421-1839

253-572-9637
Fax: 253-572-9672 800-523-6575
sales@globemachine.com www.globemachine.com
Manufacturer and exporter of material handling
equipment including hydraulic lift tables, conveyors,
personnel carriers, tilters, dumpers and transfer cars
Special Projects Manager: Mark Allen
Operations Manager: Michael Natucci
Estimated Sales: $20-50 Million
Number Employees: 1-4
Square Footage: 225000
Parent Co: Globe Machine Manufacturing Company

23238 Globe Packaging Co
368 Paterson Plank Rd
Carlstadt, NJ 07072-2306

201-939-3335
Fax: 201-939-3325 888-221-0989
sales@globecasing.com www.globecasing.com
Natural casing for meat industries
Owner: Isreal Bank
issy@globecasing.com
VP: David Knoebel
Estimated Sales: $2 Million
Number Employees: 10-19

23239 (HQ)Globe Ticket & Label Company

300 Constance Dr
Warminster, PA 18974

215-443-7960
Fax: 215-956-2493 800-523-5968
www.globeticket.com
Tickets, coupons and labels including heat seal, pressure sensitive and EDP
COO: Randy Hicks
sales@globeticket.com
CFO: Don Schilling
Treasurer: Maddalena Krause
Estimated Sales: $20-50 Million
Number Employees: 100-249
Brands:
Tak-A-Number

23240 Globex America

2324 Shorecrest Dr
Dallas, TX 75235-1804

214-353-0328
Fax: 214-353-0074 jerry@globexamerica.net
Brewing devices
President: Bonnie Itzig
info@globexamerica.net
CFO: Jerry Itziq
R & D: Donnie Itziq
Estimated Sales: $1-3 Million
Number Employees: 5-9

23241 Glopak

4755 Boulevard De Grandes Prairies
St Leonard, QC H1R 1A6
Canada

514-323-4510
Fax: 514-323-5999 800-361-6994
www.glopak.com
Manufacturer and exporter of packaging equipment and supplies including bags, fillers, filling equipment, films, flexible packaging, pouches and wrapping material
President: Ritchie Baird
CEO: Harold Martin
CFO: John Mireault
Quality Control: Hens Pohl
R&D: Eves Quiten
Number Employees: 130
Type of Packaging: Bulk

23242 Gloucester Engineering

11 Dory Rd
Gloucester, MA 01931

978-281-1800
Fax: 978-282-9111
Film extrusion products
CEO: John Tattersfield
CFO: Bill Schmidt
VP, Operations: Amanda Oelschlegel
Year Founded: 1961
Estimated Sales: $100+ Million
Number Employees: 250-499

23243 Glover Latex

PO Box 167
Anaheim, CA 92815

714-535-8920
Fax: 714-535-3635 800-243-5110
Plastic, rubber and protective gloves
President: Paul Babcock
CEO: Sandra Robles
Sales Director: R Fisher
Estimated Sales: $2.5-5 Million
Number Employees: 20-49
Square Footage: 34000
Type of Packaging: Consumer, Food Service, Private Label, Bulk

23244 Glover Rubber Stamp & Crafts

1015 Goodnight Blvd
Wills Point, TX 75169-3134

214-824-6900
Fax: 214-824-6906 anna@gloverstamp.com
www.gloverstamp.com
Rubber stamps and signs
Manager: Anna Prile
anna@gloversstamps.com
Estimated Sales: $500,000-$1 Million
Number Employees: 1-4

23245 Glowmaster Corporation

312 Lexington Ave
Clifton, NJ 07011-2366

973-772-1112
Fax: 973-772-4040 800-272-7008
www.e-hospitality.com/storefronts/glowmaster.html
Manufacturer and importer of cooking and heating equipment including portable tabletop butane stoves and fuel, chafers, griddles, service carts and induction cooking systems; exporter of portable butane stoves
Owner: Juan Travezano
CFO: Linda Smith
Director Sales: Frank Palatiello
Number Employees: 10-19
Square Footage: 28000
Brands:
Chafermate
Glowmaster

23246 Glue Dots International

5515 S Westridge Dr
New Berlin, WI 53151

262-814-8500
Fax: 262-814-8505 888-688-7131
info@gluedots.com www.gluedots.com
Providing adhesive solutions to people, businesses and industries worldwide. Packaging/product assembly, printing and bindery, direct mail/sales promotion, gift baskets, balloon decorating, candlemaking, greeting cards, customproducts, kids and school, scrapbooking and rubber stamping and many more.
Manager: Paul Ellsworth
Marketing/Communications Manager: Jennie Staghano
Contact: Dave Angus
dangus@gluedots.com
Estimated Sales: $10-20 Million
Number Employees: 10-19
Type of Packaging: Consumer, Bulk

23247 Glue Fast

3535 State Route 66 # 1
Neptune, NJ 07753-2623

732-918-4600
Fax: 732-918-4646 800-242-7318
info@gluefast.com www.gluefast.com
Pressure sensitive adhesives, packaging adhesive, adhesive applicators, faux finish texture coating/texturizing products, hot melt glue systems, coating and laminating equipment, palletizing glue, mountin and laminating products andmuch more.
President: Lester Mallet
lmallet@gluefast.com
General Manager: Joe Benenati
Vice President: Amy Altman
Estimated Sales: $5-10 Million
Number Employees: 5-9

23248 Glue Fast

3535 State Route 66 # 1
Neptune, NJ 07753-2623

732-918-4600
Fax: 732-918-4646 800-242-7318
info@gluefast.com www.gluefast.com
Adhesives and applicators used for packaging, labeling, palletizing, gluing and hot melts
President: Lester Mallet
lmallet@gluefast.com
Vice President: Amy Altman
Estimated Sales: $2.8 Million
Number Employees: 5-9
Square Footage: 68000

23249 Gluemaster

12620 Wilmot Rd
Kenosha, WI 53142-7360

262-857-7212
Fax: 262-857-7430
Labeling and packaging machinery
President: Darlene Sanew
Contact: Sherri Longshore
slongshore@kamind.com
Estimated Sales: $1-2.5 Million
Number Employees: 5-9

23250 Godshall Paper Box Company

146 Algoma Boulevard
Oshkosh, WI 54901

920-235-4040
Fax: 920-235-2326
Candy boxes for chocolate candy manufacturers and cheese manufacturers

President: Patrick Kogutkiewiez
CEO: Terry Tormoen
Estimated Sales: $2.5-5 Million
Number Employees: 15
Square Footage: 42000

23251 Goebel Fixture Co

528 Dale St SW
Hutchinson, MN 55350-2397

320-587-2112
Fax: 320-587-2378 888-339-0509
www.gf.com
Wooden and plastic cutting boards and knife storage blocks
President: Matt Field
mfield@environmentsinc.com
VP: Richard Goebel
General Manager: Bob Croatt
Department Manager: Brian Koehler
Estimated Sales: $10-20 Million
Number Employees: 100-249
Square Footage: 200000

23252 (HQ)Goeman's Wood Products

PO Box 270240
5840 Highway 60 East
Hartford, WI 53027-0240

262-673-6090
Fax: 262-673-6459 info@gwp-inc.com
Shipping crates, pallets and skids
President: Danny Guzman
Chairman/ CEO: Danny Goeman
Controller: Rich Blair
CEO: Danny Goeman
Regional Sales Manager: Dale Cordy
General Manager: Don Woods
Purchasing: Gary Hyber
Estimated Sales: $10-20 Million
Number Employees: 50-99
Square Footage: 80000
Other Locations:
Goeman's Wood Products
Hartford WI

23253 Goergen-Mackwirth Co Inc

765 Hertel Ave
Buffalo, NY 14207-1992

716-874-4800
Fax: 716-874-4715 800-728-4446
sales@gomac.com www.goergenmackwirth.com
Stainless steel and aluminum custom metal bins; also, conveyors
President: Drew Fossum
djfossum@albanyhousing.org
Project Manager: Paul Kruger
Estimated Sales: $5-10 Million
Number Employees: 20-49
Square Footage: 48000

23254 Goex Corporation

2532 Foster Ave
Janesville, WI 53545

608-754-3303
Fax: 608-754-8976 goex@goex.com
www.goex.com
Manufacturer and exporter of packaging materials including rigid plastic sheet products
President: Joshua D Gray
Sales Manager: Richard Hamlin
Contact: Vicky Bladl
vbladl@goex.com
Estimated Sales: $50-100 Million
Number Employees: 50-99

23255 Gold Bond Inc

5485 Hixson Pike
Hixson, TN 37343-3235

423-842-5844
Fax: 423-842-7934 lisan@goldbondinc.com
www.goldbondinc.com
Advertising novelties including pencils, pens, rulers and wooden nickels; also, custom plastic injection molding available
CEO: Donald W Godsey
donaldg@goldbondinc.com
CEO: Donald W Godsey
Estimated Sales: $20-50 Million
Number Employees: 250-499

23256 Gold Medal Products Co

10700 Medallion Dr
Cincinnati, OH 45241-4807

513-769-7676
Fax: 513-769-8500 800-543-0862
info@gmpopcorn.com www.gmpopcorn.com

Manufacturer and exporter of food products and concession equipment including popcorn machines, supplies and staging cabinets, butter dispensers, caramel, kettle and cheese corn, cotton candy machines and supplies, shave ice & sno-conemachines, drinks and frozen beverages, fried foods & bakers, nachos & cheese dispensers, hot dog grills & cookers, candy & caramel apples, whiz bang carnival games and more.
President: Dan Kroeger
dkroeger@gmpopcorn.com
Senior VP: John Evans
National Sales: Chris Petroff
International Sales: David Garretson
Estimated Sales: $20-50 Million
Number Employees: 250-499
Square Footage: 325000
Type of Packaging: Consumer, Food Service, Private Label, Bulk
Brands:
Love My Popper

23257 Gold Star Products
21680 Coolidge Hwy
Oak Park, MI 48237-3109
248-548-9840
Fax: 248-548-9844 800-800-0205
info@goldstarmail.com
Restaurant equipment including refrigerators, stoves, freezers, etc.; also, trays, forks, napkins, etc
Owner: Frouke Bruinsma
frouke-bruinsma@g-star.com
Estimated Sales: $5-10,000,000
Number Employees: 20-49

23258 (HQ)Goldco Industries
5605 Goldco Dr
Loveland, CO 80538
970-663-4770
Fax: 970-663-7212 info@goldcointernational.com
www.goldcointernational.com
Manufacturer and exporter of container and material handling equipment including depalletizers, palletizers and container, case and pallet handling systems
President: Richard Vander Meer
Marketing: Jim Parker
Sales: Jim Parker
Contact: Sharon Hogan
sharon.hogan@fgwa.com
Estimated Sales: $1-3 Million
Number Employees: 5-9
Square Footage: 200000
Other Locations:
Goldco Industries
Appleton WI

23259 Golden Eagle ExtrusionsInc
1762 State Route 131
Milford, OH 45150-2649
513-248-8292
Fax: 513-248-8300 800-634-3355
info@goldeneagleextrusions.com
www.goldeneagleextrusions.com
Owner: Paul Eagle
info@goldeneagleextrusions.com
CEO: Jenny Eagle
CFO: Jenney Dunkin
Product Development: Pat Delany
Plant Supervisor: Joe Herzog
Estimated Sales: $3-5 Million
Number Employees: 5-9

23260 Golden Needles Knitting& Glove Company
1300 Walnut Street
Coshocton, OH 43812-2262
919-667-5102
Fax: 919-838-2753 www.ansell.com
Manufacturer and exporter of protective gloves
Managing Director, Chief Executive Offic: Magnus Nicolin
Senior Vice President, Director of Asia: Denis Gallant
Communications Director: Wouter Piepers
Senior Vice President of Operations: Steve Genzer
Estimated Sales: $1-5 Million
Number Employees: 1000
Type of Packaging: Consumer, Food Service, Private Label, Bulk
Brands:
Hotpan'zers
Polar Bear

23261 (HQ)Golden Star
PO Box 12539
N Kansas City, MO 64116
816-842-0233
Fax: 816-842-1129 800-821-2792
goldenstar@goldenstar.com www.goldenstar.com
Manufacturer and exporter of floor and furniture polish, mops, dry carpet cleaner solvent, mats and mattings
President: Gary Gradinger
Executive VP: Bill Gradinger
National Sales Manager: Steve Lewis
Contact: Heather Moll
moll@goldenstar.com
Estimated Sales: $20-50 Million
Number Employees: 20-49
Square Footage: 350000
Type of Packaging: Consumer, Food Service, Private Label
Brands:
Admiral
Barricade
Clencher
Comet Blend
Disposo-Treet
Dus-Trol
Golden Star
Healthcare
Infinity Twist
King
Performer
Quality
Quik-Change
Set-O-Swiv
Sno-White
Soil Sorb
Sta-Flat
Starborne
Wearever

23262 Golden West Packaging Concept
24342 Muirlands Blvd
Lake Forest, CA 92630-3679
949-855-9646
Fax: 949-645-7043
Custom and stock plastic packaging
General Manager: Connie Nash
Number Employees: 5-9
Square Footage: 10000

23263 Goldenwest Sales
16730 Gridley Rd
Cerritos, CA 90703-1730
562-924-7909
Fax: 562-924-7930 800-827-6175
info@gwsales.com www.gwsales.com
Manufacturer and exporter of tote boxes, magnetic flatware retriever systems and cutlery bins, covers, and rapid cooling flash chill bottles
Owner: Jitu Patel
jitu@sftech.com
Treasurer: Estee Edwards
Estimated Sales: $.5-1 million
Number Employees: 10-19
Square Footage: 60000
Brands:
The Chute
Tough Guy Totes

23264 Goldman Manufacturing Company
13697 Elmira St
Detroit, MI 48227-3015
313-834-5535
Fax: 313-834-0496
Cardboard boxes, box partitions and separator pads; also, die cutting services available
Owner: Cherrie L Goldman
Office Manager: Elaine Patterson
Estimated Sales: $2.5-5 Million
Number Employees: 10 to 19

23265 Goldmax Industries
17747 Railroad St
City Of Industry, CA 91748-1111
626-964-8820
Fax: 626-964-6629 sales@goldmax.com
Manufacturer and importer of wooden and bamboo toothpicks, chopsticks, stirrers, plastic bags, glove dispensers, skewers, disposable gloves and aprons; also, cocktail and party straws and picks

President: Helen Chen
helenchen@goldmax-polyking.com
COO: Marcelo Mancilla
Sales Director: David Wang
Production: Manuel De La Roja
Purchasing Manager: William Hsing
Estimated Sales: $1-2.5 Million
Number Employees: 10-19
Type of Packaging: Food Service

23266 (HQ)Gonterman & Associates
5411 S Grand Blvd
Saint Louis, MO 63111
314-771-0600
Fax: 314-771-0610
Manufacturer and exporter of custom calendars and other advertising specialties
Estimated Sales: $1-5 Million
Number Employees: 5
Square Footage: 6000000
Brands:
S-Line

23267 Good Idea
351 Pleasant St
PMB 224
Northampton, MA 01060
413-586-4000
Fax: 413-585-0101 800-462-9237
info@larien.com www.larien.com
Manufacturer and exporter of bagel slicers and replacement blades.
President: Rick Ricard
Sales/Marketing Executive: Jim Dodge
Contact: Elizabeth Devito
bdevito@larien.com
Estimated Sales: $1-3 Million
Number Employees: 1-4
Brands:
Bagel Biter
Smartblade

23268 Good Pack
500 E Plume Street
Suite 509
Norfolk, VA 23510-2312
757-627-8889
Fax: 757-627-8989
Steel cargo carrier shipping baskets
Estimated Sales: $1-5 000,000
Number Employees: 10

23269 Goodall Rubber Company
Quakerbridge Executive Drive
Lawrenceville, NJ 08648
609-799-2000
Fax: 609-799-4582 800-524-2650
Wine industry transfer and washing hoses
Estimated Sales: $1-5 000,000

23270 Goodell Tools
9440 Science Center Dr
New Hope, MN 55428-3624
763-531-0053
Fax: 763-531-0252 800-542-3906
Manufacturer and exporter of grill scrapers and ice picks
Owner: Rick Garon
Marketing/Sales: Linda Alexander
Estimated Sales: $5-10 Million
Number Employees: 20-49
Square Footage: 88000
Type of Packaging: Private Label, Bulk
Brands:
Goodell

23271 Goodman & Company
401 Cooper Street
Camden, NJ 8102
856-225-6070
Fax: 856-225-6559 www.cgoodman.com
Filter cloths for filter presses, centrifuges, others
President: Arnold H Goodman
Estimated Sales: $5-10 Million
Number Employees: 50

23272 Goodman Wiper & Paper Co
120 Mill St
Auburn, ME 04210-5647
207-784-5779
Fax: 207-777-1717 ken@goodmanwiper.com
www.goodmanwiper.com

New and recycled wiping cloths; distributor of paper towels, towel systems, trash liners, linen and terry towels, cleaners, gloves, oil absorbent pads and compounds.
Owner: Ken Goodman
CFO: Ken Goodman
VP/Plant Manager: Steve Goodman
Sales/Purchasing Director: Ken Goodman
kengoodman@goodmanwiper.com
Plant Manager: Steven Goodman
Estimated Sales: $10-20 Million
Number Employees: 10-19
Square Footage: 12000
Type of Packaging: Consumer, Food Service, Private Label

23273 Goodnature Products
3860 California Rd
Orchard Park, NY 14127
 716-855-3325
 Fax: 716-855-3328 800-875-3381
sales@goodnature.com www.goodnature.com
Manufacturer and exporter of food and juice processing equipment
President/Treasurer: Dale Wettlaufer
President: Diane Massett
Marketing: Angela Dedlin
Estimated Sales: $3.5 Million
Number Employees: 20-49
Number of Brands: 1
Number of Products: 21
Brands:
 Cmp Pasteurizer
 Juice-It
 Maximizer
 Squeezebox
 X-1

23274 Goodway Industries Inc
175 Orville Dr
Bohemia, NY 11716-2503
 631-567-2929
 Fax: 631-567-2423 800-943-4501
Manufacturer, importer and exporter of batch mixers, emulsifiers, dispersers, homogenizers, foamers, injectors, fillers, toppers and depositors
Director Sales/Marketing: Phillip Branning
Estimated Sales: $1-3,000,000
Number Employees: 5-9

23275 Goodway Technologies Corp
420 West Ave
Stamford, CT 06902-6329
 203-359-4709
 Fax: 203-359-9601 800-333-7467
goodway@goodway.com www.goodway.com
Manufacturer and exporter of tube cleaning equipment, vacuums and pressure washers
President: Per Reichdlin
CEO: Amanda Williams
awilliams@l1id.com
CFO: David Lobelson
CEO: Per K Reichborn
Director Marketing: Chris Van Name
Estimated Sales: $10-20,000,000
Number Employees: 50-99
Square Footage: 70000
Brands:
 Awt-100
 Jet Cleaner
 Rea-A-Matic
 Soot-A-Matic
 Soot-Vac

23276 (HQ)Goodwin Co
12102 Industry St
Garden Grove, CA 92841-2814
 714-894-0531
 Fax: 714-897-7673 www.goodwininc.com
Manufacturer and exporter of detergents
President: Tom Goodwin
tom.goodwin@goodwinlnc.com
General Manager: Rusty Peters
Estimated Sales: $20-50 Million
Number Employees: 50-99

23277 Goodwin-Cole Co Inc
8320 Belvedere Ave
Sacramento, CA 95826-5902
 916-381-8888
 Fax: 916-383-3499 800-752-4477
info@goodwincole.com www.goodwincole.com
Commercial awnings, party tents and flags

President: Roger Gilleland
roger@goodwincole.com
Estimated Sales: $1-2,500,000
Number Employees: 10-19

23278 Goodwrappers Inc
1920 Halethorpe Farms Rd
Halethorpe, MD 21227-4501
 410-536-0400
 Fax: 410-536-0484 800-638-1127
 www.goodwrappers.com
Manufacturer and exporter of pallet stretch wrapping systems, printed stretch and black, red, orange, green, blue and white opaque and color tinted films and stretch netting
President: Bea Parry
CEO: John Parry
VP Marketing: David Parry
Estimated Sales: $10-20 Million
Number Employees: 20-49
Brands:
 Goodwrappers Handwrappers
 Goodwrappers Identi-Wrap

23279 Goodyear Tire & Rubber Company
200 Innovation Way
Akron, OH 44316-0001
 330-796-2121
 Fax: 330-796-2222 800-321-2136
 www.goodyear.com
Tires for most applications.
Chairman, President & CEO: Richard Kramer
President, Americas: Steve McClellan
EVP & Chief Financial Officer: Darren Wells
SVP, Global Operations & Technology: John Bellissimo
SVP & Chief Technology Officer: Chris Helsel
SVP & Chief Human Resources Officer: Gary Vanderlind
SVP & Chief Communications Officer: Laura Duda
SVP & General Counsel: David Phillips
Year Founded: 1898
Estimated Sales: $15.3 Billion
Number Employees: 64,000

23280 Gorbel Inc
600 Fishers Run
Victor, NY 14564-9732
 585-924-6262
 Fax: 585-924-6273 www.gorbel.com
Manufacturer and exporter of aluminum and steel track cranes
President: David Reh
VP: David Butwid
Manager: Deb Rader
debrad@gorbel.com
Estimated Sales: $20.9 Million
Number Employees: 100-249
Parent Co: Raytek Group

23281 Gordon Graphics
15 Digital Drive
Suite A
Novato, CA 94949-5792
 415-883-0455
 Fax: 415-883-5124
Wine industry labels
President: Gordon Lindstron
Estimated Sales: $5-10 Millon
Number Employees: 10

23282 Gorilla Label
7466 E Monte Cristo Avenue
Scottsdale, AZ 85260-1208
 480-443-0303
 Fax: 480-368-7923 800-615-7277

23283 Goring Kerr
642 Blackhawk Dr
Westmont, IL 60559-1116
 847-842-2397
 Fax: 630-734-1497 866-269-0070
 www.goring-kerr.com
Manager: Aaron Soto
Estimated Sales: $1-5 Million
Number Employees: 1-4
Parent Co: Thermo Fisher Scientific Inc

23284 Goshen Dairy Company
1026 Cookson Ave SE
New Philadelphia, OH 44663-9500
 330-339-1959
 Fax: 330-339-2252

Distributer of ice cream.
President: Jerry Bichsel
Estimated Sales: $5-9.9,000,000
Number Employees: 20-49
Parent Co: Smith Dairy

23285 Gotham Pen Co Inc
1827 Washington Ave
Bronx, NY 10457-6203
 212-675-7904
 Fax: 718-294-9044 800-334-7970
 gothampen@aol.com
Pens and pencils; also, custom imprinting services available
Owner: Marshall Sutterman
Estimated Sales: Less Than $500,000
Number Employees: 5-9

23286 Gough-Econ Inc
9400 N Lakebrook Rd
Charlotte, NC 28214-9008
 704-399-4501
 Fax: 704-392-8706 800-204-6844
 sales@goughecon.com www.goughecon.com
Bucket elevator and conveyor systems; exporter of bucket elevator systems; also, multiple discharges available. Also manufacturer of complete line of vibratory conveyors, feeders, screens and belt conveyors
CEO: David Risley
drisley@goughecon.com
VP: Don Calvert
Marketing: Angela Gallagher
Sales: Andrew Leitch
Estimated Sales: $5-10 Million
Number Employees: 20-49
Square Footage: 160000

23287 Gourmet COFFEE Roasters
46956 Liberty Dr
Wixom, MI 48393-3693
 248-669-1060
 Fax: 248-669-1111 866-933-6300
 www.javamasters.com
In-store coffee roasters
President: Richard C Sewell
javausa@aol.com
VP Retail Development: Terry Immel
Estimated Sales: $10-20,000,000
Number Employees: 5-9
Square Footage: 34000

23288 Gourmet Display
6040 S 194th St # 102
Suite 102
Kent, WA 98032-1191
 206-767-4711
 Fax: 206-764-6094 800-767-4711
 info@gourmetdisplay.com
 www.gourmetdisplay.com
Mirrored and marble serving equipment for buffets and banquets
Owner: Precious Chuop
Vice President: Mark Vollmar
Marketing Manager: T Ecker
Sales Manager: Julien Chomette
pchuop@gourmetdisplay.com
General Manager: T Schueler
Estimated Sales: $2.5-5 Million
Number Employees: 5-9
Parent Co: Plastic Dynamics
Brands:
 Riser Rims
 Serving Stone
 Texture Tone

23289 Gourmet Foods Intl
255 Ted Turner Dr SW
Atlanta, GA 30303-3705
 404-954-7600
 Fax: 404-954-7672 800-966-6172
Full-line oils, full-line chocolate, cheese, frozen desserts, hors d'oeuvres/appetizers, full-line meat/game/pate, full-line spices, olives.
Owner: Russell Mc Call
rmccall@gfifoods.com
Marketing: Doug Jay
Number Employees: 250-499

23290 Gourmet Gear
1413 Westwood Blvd
Los Angeles, CA 90024-4911
 310-268-2222
 Fax: 310-301-4115 800-682-4635

Culinary apparel
Owner: Farhad Besharati
CEO: Newton Katz
Director Marketing: Marcee Katz
Estimated Sales: $500,000-$1 Million
Number Employees: 1-4

23291 Gourmet Table Skirts
9415 W Bellfort St
Houston, TX 77031-2308

713-666-0602
Fax: 713-666-0627 800-527-0440
gkammerman@gourmet-table-skirts.com
www.tableskirts.com
Manufacturer and exporter of table cloths, skirts and
runners, napkins, place mats and aprons
Owner: Glenn Kammerman
glenn@tableskirts.com
Estimated Sales: $2.5-5 Million
Number Employees: 50-99
Square Footage: 64000
Type of Packaging: Consumer, Food Service
Brands:
   Permalux
   Permanent Press
   Polytwill
   Visa

23292 Governair Corp
4841 N Sewell Ave
Oklahoma City, OK 73118-7820

405-525-6546
Fax: 405-528-4724 info@governair.com
Manufacturer and exporter of air handling units,
evaporative condensing package water chillers, etc
General Manager: Jim Durr
Quality Control: Bill Taylor
R & D: Mark Sly
Marketing: Mark Fly
Sales: Buddy Cross
Plant Manager: Brad Campbell
Purchasing: Vickey Hopper
Estimated Sales: $20-30 Million
Number Employees: 100-249
Square Footage: 150000
Parent Co: Nortek
Brands:
   Governair

23293 Government Food Service
P.O.Box 1500
Westbury, NY 11590-0812

516-334-3030
Fax: 516-334-3059 ebm-mail@ebmpubs.com
www.ebmpubs.com
President: Murry Greenwald
R & D: Fred Shaen
Estimated Sales: $10-20 Million
Number Employees: 20-49

23294 Grace Instrument Co
9434 Katy Fwy # 300
Houston, TX 77055-6309

713-783-1560
Fax: 713-974-7144 info@graceinstrument.com
www.graceinstrument.com
Manufacturer and importer of thermometers includ-
ing bi-metal, digital, pocket test, vapor tension dial,
refrigeration, oven, barbecue grill and deep fry
Owner: Hongfeng Bi
Marketing Manager: Michelle Dahm
Estimated Sales: $1-5 Million
Number Employees: 20-49

23295 Grace Tea Co
14 Craig Rd
Acton, MA 01720-5405

978-635-9500
Fax: 978-635-9701
customerservice@gracetea.com
www.gracetea.com
Teas
Owner: Hartley Johnson
hejohnson1@gracetea.com
VP: Richard Verdery
Operations Director: Richard Sanders
Estimated Sales: $48,000
Number Employees: 5-9
Number of Brands: 1
Number of Products: 20
Square Footage: 4000
Brands:
   China Yunnan Silver Tip Choice

Connoisseur Master Blend
Darjceling Superb 6000
Demitasse After Dinner Tea
Earl Grey Superior Mixture
Flowery Jasmine-Before the Rain
Formosa Oolong Champagne of Tea
Gun Powder Pearl Pinhead Green Tea
Lapsang Souchong Smoky #1 Blend
Mountain-Grown Fancy Ceylon
Owner's Blend Premium Congou
Pure Assam Irish Breakfast
Russian Caravan Original China
Winey Keemun English Breakfast

23296 Grace-Lee Products
2450 2nd Street NE
Minneapolis, MN 55418

612-379-2711
Fax: 763-789-6263
Detergents and institutional cleaning products
President: Barry Graceman
Executive VP: Sherman Gleekel
Institutional Sales Manager: Tom Pross
Number Employees: 75
Square Footage: 110000

23297 (HQ)Graco Inc
88 11th Ave NE
Minneapolis, MN 55413-1829

612-623-6000
Fax: 612-378-3505 877-844-7226
info@graco.com www.graco.com
Manufacturer and exporter of industrial and portable
cleaners, sanitary pumps and dispensers.
Chairman/President/CEO: David Roberts
Chief Administrative Officer: Mark Sheahan
Chief Financial Officer/Treasurer: James Graner
CEO: Patrick J McHale
Sales & Marketing Director: Rick Berkbigler
Vice President Operations: Charles Rescoria
Estimated Sales: Over $1 Billion
Number Employees: 1000-4999
Brands:
   Graco, Inc.

23298 Graco Inc
88 11th Ave NE
Minneapolis, MN 55413-1829

612-623-6000
Fax: 612-378-3505 www.graco.com
Manufacturer and exporter of conveyor lubrication
equipment and specialty lubricants
HR Manager: Kathy Buechel
CEO: Patrick J Mc Hale
pmchale@graco.com
Vice President, General Counsel, Secreta: Karen
Gallivan
Service Manager: Gary Knutson
Plant Manager: Ryan Eidenschink
Estimated Sales: Over $1 Billion
Number Employees: 1000-4999
Parent Co: IDEX

23299 Graff Tank Erection
RR 1
Box 246
Harrisville, PA 16038-9511

814-385-6671
Fax: 814-385-6657
Above-ground steel storage tanks, bins and hoppers;
field based erection and repair services available
Owner: William Graff
Controller: Rose Graff
Quality Control: Rose Graff
President: William Graff
Engineer Manager: Raymond Graff
Estimated Sales: $500,000-$1 Million
Number Employees: 10
Square Footage: 32000

23300 Grafoplast Wiremarkers Inc
6875 E 48th Ave
Denver, CO 80216-5310

303-321-5995
Fax: 303-399-5054 800-864-3874
sales@grafoplast.com www.grafoplast.com
Markers for terminal blocks, relays, wire, and cable
Manager: Maureen Wilkins
Manager: Priscilla Hobdell
priscilla@grafoplast.com
Estimated Sales: $1-2.5 Million
Number Employees: 1-4

23301 Grafoplast Wiremarkers Inc
6875 E 48th Ave
Denver, CO 80216-5310

303-321-5995
Fax: 303-399-5054 800-864-3874
www.grafoplast.com
Manager: Priscilla Hobdell
priscilla@grafoplast.com
Estimated Sales: $3-5 Million
Number Employees: 1-4

23302 (HQ)Graham Engineering Corp
1203 Eden Rd
York, PA 17402-1965

717-848-3755
Fax: 717-846-1931 www.grahamengineering.com
Manufacturer and exporter of blow-molded plastic
bottles and containers
President: Steven F Wood
CEO: Wendy Brown
wendy_brown@uscourts.gov
VP: Joe Spohr
CEO: Wolfgang Liebertz
CFO: Rich Rutkowski
VP Sales/Marketing: F White
Estimated Sales: $20-50 Million
Number Employees: 50-99

23303 Graham Ice & Locker Plant
328 Elm Street
Graham, TX 76450-2514

940-549-1975
Ice; slaughterer, processor and wholesaler/distribu-
tor of deer
Owner: James Black
Estimated Sales: Less than $500,000
Number Employees: 1 to 4
Type of Packaging: Consumer

23304 Graham Pallet Co Inc
3234 Celina Rd
Tompkinsville, KY 42167-8207

270-487-6609
Fax: 270-487-9420 888-525-0694
www.millwoodinc.com
Wooden pallets and skids
President: Rick Miller
Sales Exec: Mike Scoby
mscoby@grahampallet.com
Customer Service: Carolyn Turner
mscoby@grahampallet.com
General Manager: Terry Marr
Production Manager: Carolyn Grove
Plant Manager: Keith Ainsley
Estimated Sales: $5-10 Million
Number Employees: 50-99
Square Footage: 100000

23305 Grain Machinery Mfg Corp
1130 NW 163rd Dr
Miami, FL 33169-5816

305-620-2525
Fax: 305-620-2551 grainman@bellsouth.net
www.grainman.com
Manufacturer and exporter of grain elevators, dryers,
graders, cleaners, pea and bean hullers, casting and
rice machinery, bagging scales and conveyor belts;
importer of casting and rice machinery
Owner: Manny Diaz
grainman@bellsouth.net
Treasurer: Librada Dieguez
Vice President: Cary Dieguez
Sales Director: Jose Martinez
Purchasing Manager: Brissa Pichardo
Estimated Sales: $3-5 Million
Number Employees: 10-19
Square Footage: 86000
Brands:
   Cell-O-Matic
   Grainman
   Rimac

23306 (HQ)Gralab Instruments
900 Dimco Way
Centerville, OH 45458-2710

937-433-7600
Fax: 937-433-0520 800-876-8353
www.gralab.com
Electromechanical and electronic timing devices for
commercial cooking and baking applications, food
testing laboratories, process control systems and
sanitation; also, thermoset and thermoplastic compression and injection moldedproducts.

President & CEO: Michael Sieron
msieron@dimcogray.com
Treasurer: Terry Tate
Quality Control: Lyle Crum
Sales & Marketing Manager: Linda Raisch
Production: James Daulton
Number Employees: 50-99
Number of Brands: 1
Number of Products: 20
Parent Co: Dimco-Gray Corporation

23307 (HQ)Gram Equipment Of America
1212 N 39th St # 438
Tampa, FL 33605-5890

813-248-1978
Fax: 813-248-2314 www.gram-equipment.com
Box/carton formers, ice cream makers, feeders,
freezers and heat exchangers
President: Morten Borup
mgs@gram-equipment.com
Number Employees: 10-19
Type of Packaging: Food Service, Bulk

23308 GranPac
4709 39th Avenue
Wetaskiwin, AB T9A 2J4
Canada

780-352-3324
Fax: 780-352-3387 www.granpac.com.br
Polyethylene plastic food containers
Sales Manager: G Jacobson
Managing Director: J Patel
Estimated Sales: $1-5 Million
Number Employees: 20-50
Square Footage: 80000

23309 Granco Manufacturing Inc
2010 Crow Canyon Pl # 100
Suite 100
San Ramon, CA 94583-1344

510-652-8847
Fax: 510-652-1565 info@grancopump.com
www.grancopump.com
Manufacturer and exporter of hydraulically driven
and low shear pumping systems; also, rotary positive
pumps for displacement of viscous liquids.
President: Ivan Dimcheff
CEO: Michael Alessandro
Operations: Ivan Dimcheff
Production Manager: David Kenzler
Estimated Sales: $.5-1 million
Number Employees: 5-9
Square Footage: 64000
Parent Co: Challenge Manufacturing Company
Type of Packaging: Private Label
Brands:
    Grandco
    Hy-Drive Systems

23310 Grand Cypress
6087 NW 90th Avenue
Parkland, FL 33067-3722

954-255-5686
Fax: 954-255-5926 grandcypressintl@comcast.net
President: Bart Ostroff

23311 Grand Rapids Chair Company
625 Chestnut St SW
Grand Rapids, MI 49503

616-774-0561
Fax: 616-774-0563 tom@grandrapidschair.com
www.grandrapidschair.com
Chairs
Owner: Jill Miller
Contact: Aladin Brakic
abrakic@grandrapidschair.com
Estimated Sales: $5-10 Million
Number Employees: 20-49

23312 Grand Rapids Label
2351 Oak Industrial Dr NE
Grand Rapids, MI 49505-6017

616-776-2778
Fax: 616-459-4543 grlabel@grlabel.com
www.grlabel.com
Manufacturer and exporter of pressure sensitive and
heat seal labels including advertising and
supermarket
President: William Muir
CFO: John Laninga
R&D: Tony Maravalo
Quality Control: Christine Howlett
VP Sales: Tom Topel

Estimated Sales: $10-20 Million
Number Employees: 50-99
Type of Packaging: Bulk

23313 Grand Silver Company
289 Morris Avenue
Bronx, NY 10451-6198

718-585-1930
Fax: 718-402-4724 grandsilve@aol.com
Silver plated holloware, coffee pots, sugar bowls
and creamers; also, repairing and replating services
available
CEO: Barry Kostrinsky
Estimated Sales: $2.5-5 Million
Number Employees: 20-49

23314 Grand Valley Labels
4417 Broadmoor Ave SE
Grand Rapids, MI 49512-5367

Fax: 616-784-2915
Pressure sensitive labels, tags, envelopes, bar codes,
label printing systems, packaging, etc.
Estimated Sales: $5-10 Million
Number Employees: 1-4
Square Footage: 10000

23315 Grande Chef Company
21 Stewart Court
Orangeville, ON L9W 3Z9
Canada

519-942-4470
Fax: 519-942-4440
Manufacturer, importer and exporter of stainless
steel cooking equipment including cookers, kettles,
ovens and broilers
President: Frank Edmonstone
Sales/Marketing Executive: Lisa Ashton
Sales/Marketing Executive: Alex Mackay
Operations Manager: Lisa Ashton
Purchasing Manager: Frank Edmonstone
Number Employees: 5-9
Brands:
    Grande Chef

23316 Grande Ronde Sign Company
2302 Cove Avenue
La Grande, OR 97850-3907

541-963-5841
Fax: 541-963-4337 www.whereorg.com
Signs including neon, wood, plastic and vinyl
President: Mat Barber
Contact: Earl Barber
gabebarber@gmail.com
Office Manager: Jenne O'Daol
Estimated Sales: Below $5 Million
Number Employees: 1 to 4

23317 Granite State Stamps Inc
8025 S Willow St # 102
Manchester, NH 03103-2311

603-669-9322
Fax: 603-669-5182 800-937-3736
sales@granitestatestamps.com
www.granitestatestamps.com
Engraved name pins and rubber stamps
President: Lynn A Hale
lynn@granitestatestamps.com
VP Sales: Lynn Hale
Estimated Sales: $1-2.5 Million
Number Employees: 5-9
Square Footage: 20000

23318 Grant Chemicals
PO Box 13
New Hope, PA 18938-0013

215-331-3350
Fax: 215-331-2394
Wine industry chemicals

23319 Grant Laboratories
14688 Washington Ave
San Leandro, CA 94578-4218

510-483-6070
Fax: 510-483-9846
grant-laboratories-inc.san-leandro.ca.amfibi.compa
ny
Insecticides including ant and insect granular
CEO: William E Brown
COO: Louis Antonali
Sales Director: Samantha Sturdivant
COO: Quazui Iqbal
Estimated Sales: $5-10 Million
Number Employees: 5 to 9

Square Footage: 52000
Parent Co: Central Garden & Pet
Type of Packaging: Consumer
Brands:
    Grants Kill Ants

23320 Grant-Letchworth
110 Mullen Street
Tonawanda, NY 14150-5424

716-692-1000
Fax: 716-692-3638 response@letchworth.com
www.letchworth.com
Grinders, mixers and stuffers
President: W Keith Jackson
Sales Manager: James Smith
Estimated Sales: $1-2.5 Million
Number Employees: 4

23321 Granville ManufacturingCo
45 Mill Rd
Granville, VT 05747-9669

802-767-4747
Fax: 802-767-3107 800-828-1005
bowlmill@madriver.com www.woodsiding.com
One piece wooden bowls made from premium hard-
woods in Vermont
President: Robert Fuller
Vice President: Jeff Fuller
woodsiding@woodsiding.com
Marketing Director: Cindy Fuller
Purchasing Manager: Cindy Fuller
Estimated Sales: $1,000,000
Number Employees: 1-4
Square Footage: 10000

23322 Graphic Apparel
2365 Industrial Park Road
Inniasfil, ON L9S 3W1
Canada

705-436-6137
Fax: 705-436-6139 800-757-4867
Distributor of career apparel and promotions
President: Werner Syndikus
Sales Manager: Mitch Dawkins
Number Employees: 10
Square Footage: 32000
Type of Packaging: Food Service

23323 Graphic Arts Center
709 Silver Palm Ave
Suite H
Melbourne, FL 32901

321-725-0710
Fax: 321-984-3783 888-345-7436
gac@yourlink.net
Graphic designer of packages, labels, advertising
materials, cartons, displays, literature and trade
show displays
Owner: D D Rhem
Estimated Sales: $500,000-$1 Million
Number Employees: 1-4
Square Footage: 9600
Parent Co: Rhem Group
Type of Packaging: Consumer, Food Service, Pri-
vate Label, Bulk

23324 Graphic Calculator Company
234 James Street
Barrington, IL 60010-3388

847-381-4480
Fax: 847-381-5370
Manufacturer and exporter of advertising novelties
including slide rules, printed calculators and feature
demonstrators
President: Capron Gulbronsen
VP: Lorraine Gorski
Estimated Sales: $5-10 Million
Number Employees: 10

23325 Graphic Impressions of Illinois
8538 Grand Ave
River Grove, IL 60171

708-453-1100
Fdx: 708-453-1169
Quality flexographic labels and printing plates. Cus-
tom labels priced by specification. Complete design
for flexible packaging. ValueStar certified. A family
owned business since 1956
Estimated Sales: $1-2,500,000
Number Employees: 5-9

23326 Graphic Packaging Corporation
4455 Table Mountain Drive
Golden, CO 80403
720-497-4724
Fax: 303-273-2935 800-677-2886
www.graphicpkg.com
Labels, bottle carriers and beverage and carrier cartons
Chairman/ President/ CEO: David W. Scheible
CFO/ SVP: Daniel J. Blount
SVP, Flexible Division: R. Allen Ennis
Plant Manager: Jeffrey Coors
Estimated Sales: $1-5 Million
Number Employees: 100-249
Parent Co: Graphic Packaging Corporation

23327 Graphic Packaging International
1500 Riveredge Parkway NW
Atlanta, GA 30328
770-240-7200
www.graphicpkg.com
Paperboard containers
President & CEO: Michael Doss
EVP/Chief Financial Officer: Stephen Scherger
EVP, Human Resources: Stacey Panayiotou
EVP/General Counsel: Lauren Tashma
President, Americas: Joseph Yost
Estimated Sales: Over $1 Billion
Number Employees: 13,000
Parent Co: Graphic Pakaging Holding Company

23328 Graphic Packaging Intl
1500 Nicholas Blvd
Elk Grove Vlg, IL 60007-5516
847-437-1700
Fax: 847-956-9291 www.graphicpkg.com
Manufacturer and exporter of folding cartons
President: Larry Field
Cmo: Larry Janis
larry.janis@fieldcontainer.com
Number Employees: 250-499

23329 (HQ)Graphic Promotions
7418 SW 23rd Court
Topeka, KS 66614-6079
785-234-6684
Fax: 785-354-1519 gpromotion@aol.com
Consultant specializing in promotional services and support including point of purchase signage, labels, specialty items, fulfillment, creative art/graphics, design, inventory manangement and printing
VP: Kurt Oswald
Number Employees: 100-249
Square Footage: 144000
Other Locations:
   Graphic Promotions
   Topeka KS

23330 Graphic Technology
301 Gardner Dr
New Century, KS 66031
913-764-5550
Fax: 913-764-0320 800-767-9920
Manufacturer, exporter and importer of bar coded and nonbar coded shelf labels for product unit pricing; bar code printers and software; also, picking labels
VP Sales/Marketing: Tom Pooton
Contact: Robert Mccurdy
rob@graphictech.com
Estimated Sales: $1-5 Million
Number Employees: 500-999
Square Footage: 500000
Parent Co: Nitto Denko Corporation

23331 Graphics Unlimited
10477 Roselle St # B
San Diego, CA 92121-1593
858-453-4031
Fax: 858-453-5337
www.graphicsunlimitedusa.com
Decals, name plates and banners; also, screen printing available
Owner: Les Burge
les@unlimitedgraphics.com
Estimated Sales: $1-2,500,000
Number Employees: 5-9

23332 Graphite Metalizing Corp
1050 Nepperhan Ave
Yonkers, NY 10703-1421
914-968-8400
Fax: 914-968-8468 sales@graphalloy.com
www.graphalloy.com
Manufacturer and exporter of graphalloy high-temperature self-lubricating bearings for ovens
President: Eben Walker
Quality Control: Mohmed Youssef
Director Marketing: Eric Ford
Estimated Sales: $10-20 Million
Number Employees: 50-99
Square Footage: 50000
Brands:
   Graphalloy
   Graphilm

23333 Grasselli SSI
410 Charles St
Throop, PA 18512
570-489-8001
Fax: 570-485-8005 800-789-4353
info@grasselli-ssi.com www.grasselli-ssi.com
Processing equipment for meat and fish industries; slicing and skinning
President: David Atcherley
Vice President: Helga Harrington
Contact: Benjamin Conner
benc@grasselli-ssi.com
Estimated Sales: $8 Million
Number Employees: 12

23334 Grasso
1101 N Governor Street
Evansville, IN 47711-5069
812-465-6600
Fax: 812-465-6610 800-821-3486
grasso@fessystems.com
Industrial reciprocating and screw refrigeration compressors, custom-built refrigeration packages for any refrigerant including ammonia; self-limiting automatic purgers for refrigeration systems
President: Jake Grifford
Manager of Quality: Harald Wilke
Marketing Manager: Martina Chao
Manager of International Sales: Siegfried Pitsch
Estimated Sales: $20-50 Million
Number Employees: 10

23335 Grating Pacific Inc
3651 Sausalito St
Los Alamitos, CA 90720-2436
562-598-4314
Fax: 562-598-2740 800-321-4314
sales@gratingpacific.com www.gratingpacific.com
Distributor of industrial flooring.
President: Ron Robertson
ronrobertson@gratingpacific.com
Year Founded: 1971
Estimated Sales: $20-30 Million
Number Employees: 50-99

23336 Graver Technologies LLC
200 Lake Dr
Newark, DE 19702-3327
302-731-1700
Fax: 302-731-1707 800-249-1990
info@gravertech.com www.gravertech.com
Microfiltration membranes
President: John Almeida
jalmeida@gravertech.com
VP Finance and Administration: Sharon Gatta
VP and General Manager Liquid Filters: Bill Cummings
Product Manager: Scott Wittwer
Number Employees: 50-99

23337 Gray Woodproducts
297 Swetts Pond Rd
P.O. Box 7126
Tacoma, WA 98417
253-752-7000
Fax: 207-825-3200
www.graylumber.com/products.php
Pallets and skids
President/Sales Manager: Mac Gray
Treasurer/Secretary: Steve Gray
Vice President: W Douglas Gray, Jr.
Asst. Sales Manager: Jack deLeon
Operations Manager: Paul VanDyken
Estimated Sales: $500,000-$1 Million
Number Employees: 1-4

23338 Graybill Machines Inc
221 W Lexington Rd # 1
Lititz, PA 17543-9400
717-626-5221
Fax: 717-626-1886 info@graybillmachines.com
www.graybillmachines.com
Designs and builds custom food machinery, specializing in finishing systems, product registration/handling, process machinery and specialized packaging
President: David Fyock
dfyock@graybillmachines.com
Marketing Director: Matthew Randolph
Sales Director: John Stough
Estimated Sales: $2.5-$5 Million
Number Employees: 10-19
Square Footage: 44000

23339 Grayco Products Sales
100 Tec Street
Hicksville, NY 11801-3650
516-997-9200
Fax: 516-870-0510
Wholesaler/distributor and exporter of paper and disposable products including tabletop and industrial equipment, packaging and printing supplies
Owner: Helen Kushner
CEO: Adrienne Kushner
Vice President: Alan Kushner
Operations Manager: D Pascale
Estimated Sales: $1-5 Million
Number Employees: 2
Square Footage: 10000
Parent Co: ASK Sales

23340 Graydon Lettercraft
81 Cuttermill Rd
Great Neck, NY 11021-3153
516-482-0531
Fax: 516-482-5632
Advertising specialties and custom printed brochures and stationery
Owner: Pasquale Riccardi
VP: Ruth Theobald
Estimated Sales: $300,000-500,000
Number Employees: 1-4

23341 Grayline Housewares Inc
2711 International St
Suite 105
Columbus, OH 43228-4604
614-850-7000
Fax: 614-850-7111 800-222-7388
www.graylinehousewares.com
Coated-wire space savers and organizers including bag and pot holders, bars, wall grids and racks including can, kitchen and wire
President: Fred Rosen
Director: Paul Nearpass
Estimated Sales: $500,000-$1 Million
Number Employees: 10-19

23342 Grayling Industries
1008 Branch Dr
Alpharetta, GA 30004-3391
770-751-9095
Fax: 770-751-3710 800-635-1551
raymond.joyner@graylingmail.com
www.graylingindustries.com
Director of Sales: Raymond Joyner
Contact: Salvador Abreu
sabreu@graylingindustries.com
Estimated Sales: Less Than $500,000
Number Employees: 1-4
Parent Co: ILC Dover
Type of Packaging: Food Service, Bulk

23343 Grays Harbor Stamp Works
110 N G St
Aberdeen, WA 98520-5226
360-533-3830
Fax: 360-533-3210 800-894-3830
graysharborstamp@olynet.com
www.graysharborstamp.com
Promotional buttons, engraved signage and rubber stamps
Partner: Ronald Windell
Partner: Ron Windell
Partner: Kenneth Windell
Estimated Sales: $2.5-5 Million
Number Employees: 5-9

23344 Graytech Carbonic
9460 230th Street E
Lakeville, MN 55044-8137
952-461-8020
Fax: 952-461-8022
Estimated Sales: $1-2.5 000,000
Number Employees: 1-4

23345 Grease Master
608 Matthews Mint Hill # 105
Suite 105
Matthews, NC 28105-1763
704-844-6907
Fax: 704-844-8013 info@greasemaster.com
www.greasemaster.com
Kitchen ventilation systems including wall mounted
and exhaust only canopies
Division Manager: David Breidt
david.breidt@greasemaster.com
Sales Quotations Design: Harvey Worrell
Division Manager: David Breidt
Plant Manager: Nick Nakos
Estimated Sales: Less Than $500,000
Number Employees: 1-4
Square Footage: 92000
Parent Co: Custom Industries
Brands:
    Grease Master

23346 Great Dane LP
222 N LaSalle St
Suite 920
Chicago, IL 60601
773-254-5533
www.greatdane.com
Refrigerated tractor trailers.
President: Dean Engelage
Year Founded: 1900
Estimated Sales: $257.6 Million
Number Employees: 1000-4999
Brands:
    Great Dane

23347 Great Lakes Brush
6859 Audrain Road #9139
Centralia, MO 65240
573-682-2128
Fax: 573-682-2121
Manufacturer and importer of brushes and wire
drawn products
President: Matthew Kallas
Estimated Sales: $500,000-$1 Million
Number Employees: 1-4
Square Footage: 8000

23348 Great Lakes Cold Storage
6531 Cochran Rd
Cleveland, OH 44139-3959
440-248-3950
Fax: 440-248-4315   888-248-9600
info@glcsinc.com www.glcsinc.com
Terminal
President: Pat Gorbett
pgorbett@glcsinc.com
Accounts Payable and Receivable: Daphne
Bengough
Chief Engineer: Phil Watson
VP National Sales and Marketing: Ken Mossgrove
IT/HR Manager: Regina Twining
pgorbett@glcsinc.com
Director of Operations: Tom Johnson
Estimated Sales: $3-5 Million
Number Employees: 50-99

23349 Great Lakes Foods
1230 48th Ave
Menominee, MI 49858-1002
906-863-5503
Fax: 906-863-2102   800-800-7492
jvan@greatlakesfoods.com
Canned mushrooms; fruit and vegetable canning,
pickling and drying
President: Tom Ireland
Owner: Jerry Vandelaarschot
CFO: Don Kressin
dkressin@greatlakefood.com
Vice President: Johanne Ubbels
Estimated Sales: $1-2.5 Million
Number Employees: 50-99
Parent Co: Ubbelea Farms
Type of Packaging: Consumer, Food Service, Pri-
    vate Label
Brands:
    Chateau
    Riviera

23350 Great Lakes Scientific
2847 Lawrence St
Stevensville, MI 49127-1257
269-429-1000
www.glslab.com

An independent laboratory offering confidential testing services for food, water and environmental samples. A USDA recognized (microbiology) and
accredited (chemistry) laboratory.
President: Wayne Gleiber
gls@glslab.com
Estimated Sales: $1-2.5 Million
Number Employees: 20-49
Square Footage: 10000

23351 Great Lakes Software ofMichigan
P.O.Box 2222
Howell, MI 48844
517-548-4333
Fax: 517-548-4433 www.greatlakessoftware.com
C.I.M.S.(computerized inventory and logistic man-
agement system) designed for beverage industry
manufacturing, distribution, warehousing and sales
Owner: Gene Chandler
Estimated Sales: $1-2.5 000,000
Number Employees: 1-4

**23352 Great Lakes-Triad Package
Corporation**
3939 36th Street
Grand Rapids, MI 49512
616-241-6441
Fax: 616-241-4145 www.gltpackaging.com
Corrugated boxes and containers
Contact: Aleisha Baweja
abaweja@gltpkg.com
Estimated Sales: $50-100 Million
Number Employees: 50-99

23353 Great Northern Corp
421 Palmer St
Chippewa Falls, WI 54729-1449
715-723-1801
Fax: 715-723-7744   800-472-1800
www.greatnortherncorp.com
Corrugated shipping containers, inner packaging
partitions and point of purchase displays
CEO: John Kell
CEO: John Kell
Plant Production Manager: Rick Gates
Estimated Sales: $30-50 Million
Number Employees: 100-249
Square Footage: 250000

23354 Great Northern Corp
1800 South St
Racine, WI 53404-1518
262-639-4700
Fax: 262-639-8103   800-558-4711
www.greatnortherncorp.com
Corrugated boxes
HR Executive: Stacy Feest
sfeest@greatnortherncorp.com
Estimated Sales: $50-100 Million
Number Employees: 100-249
Square Footage: 70058
Parent Co: Great Northern Corporation
Type of Packaging: Bulk

23355 Great Northern Corp.
395 Stroebe Rd.
Appleton, WI 54914
800-236-3671
www.greatnortherncorp.com
Expandable polystyrene plastic packaging products
including boxes and containers.
President/CEO: John Davis
Chairman: William Raaths
Year Founded: 1962
Estimated Sales: $100-500 Million
Number Employees: 500-999
Type of Packaging: Bulk
Brands:
    Rollguard®
    StrataGraph®
    Laminations®
    Packaging
    Instore

23356 Great Plains Software
1 Lone Tree Road S
Fargo, ND 58104-3911
701-281-0550
Fax: 701-282-9243   800-456-0025
Backoffice accounting software
Sr. VP (Marketing Communications): Michael Olsen
Franchise Marketing Manager: Judy Felch

23357 Great Southern Corp
3595 Regal Blvd
Memphis, TN 38118-6117
901-365-1611
Fax: 901-365-4498   800-421-7802
sales@greatsoutherncorp.com
www.gsmemphis.com
Manufacturer, importer and exporter of licensed
gloves consisting of leather, cotton, plastic and rub-
ber gloves; also, rubber bands
President: Scott Vaught
Chairman: C Vaught
Manager: Jeff Harrell
j.harrell@greatsoutherncorp.com
Estimated Sales: $20-50 Million
Number Employees: 5-9
Square Footage: 48000
Parent Co: Great Southern Corporation
Brands:
    Sirco

23358 Great Southern Industries
PO Box 22488
Jackson, MS 39225
601-969-1434
Fax: 601-969-3838   877-638-3667
sales@netdoor.com netdoor.com
Corrugated shipping containers
President: Charles Ellis
President, Chief Executive Officer: Tom Tiernan
CFO: Nancy Hocutt
Executive Vice President, General Manage: Michael
Elia
Production Manager: Bill Dahlman
Estimated Sales: $10-20 Million
Number Employees: 100-249

**23359 Great Western Chemical
Company**
5200 SW Macadam Ave # 200
Portland, OR 97239-3800
503-228-2600
Fax: 503-228-8471   800-547-1400
Manufacturer and wholesaler/distributor of cleaning
and sanitation chemicals and food ingredients in-
cluding acidulants, preservatives, etc
Manager: Jason Keyes
Bus. Mgr.: Tom Cervenka
Bus. Mgr.: Andy Pollard
VP Marketing: Tami Mainero
Estimated Sales: $50-100 Million
Number Employees: 5-9

23360 Great Western Co LLC
30290 US Highway 72
Hollywood, AL 35752-6134
256-259-3578
Fax: 256-259-7087 www.gwproducts.com
Processor and exporter of popcorn, popping corn oil,
cotton candy, sno-cone syrup, candy apple coatings,
funnel cakes, waffle cones, corn dog mix, and other
concession items
Contact: Tim Ferguson
timf@gwproducts.com
Estimated Sales: Less Than $500,000
Number Employees: 1-4
Number of Brands: 6
Type of Packaging: Consumer, Food Service, Pri-
    vate Label, Bulk
Brands:
    Chillee Snow Cones
    Frostee Snow Cones
    Great Western Products Company
    Peter's Movie Time Products
    Premium America
    Sunglo

**23361 Great Western Manufacturing
Company**
2017 So. 4th Floor
PO Box 149
Leavenworth, KS 66048
913-682-2291
Fax: 913-682-1431   800-682-3121
sifter@gwmfg.com www.gwmfg.com
Screening machines, shakers, sifters, screens and
sieves.
CFO: Michael Bell
General Manager: Robert Ricklefs
Sales, Services & Applications Engineeri: Bob
Recklifs
Production Manager: Steve Wood
Purchasing Manager: Michael Glassford

Estimated Sales: $5-10 Million
Number Employees: 10
Type of Packaging: Food Service
Brands:
  Hs
  Tru Balance

23362 Grecon
15875 SW 74th Ave # 100
Suite 100
Tigard, OR 97224-7934
503-641-7731
Fax: 503-641-7508 sales@grecon-us.com
www.grecon-us.com
Spark detection and extinguishing systems, as well as quality assurance measuring systems.
Contact: Walter Crosson
wcrosson@grecon.us
Number Employees: 10-19

23363 Greeley Tent & Awning Co
2209 9th St # C
Greeley, CO 80631-3088
970-352-0253
Fax: 970-352-2013 info@greeleytadirect.com
Commercial awnings
Owner: Julie Heyer
greeleytentawning@gmail.com
CFO: Barbara Hendricks
Estimated Sales: Less than $500,000
Number Employees: 5-9

23364 Green Bag America Inc.
15430 Cabrito Road
Unit 1
Van Nuys, CA 91406
818-787-6223
Fax: 818-453-0316 877-224-2299
sales@greenbagamerica.com
www.greenbagamerica.com
Accesories/supplies i.e. picninc baskets, display fixtures, specialty food packaging i.e. gift wrap/labels/boxes/containers.
Marketing: Tom Maor
Contact: Richelle Kim
richellekim@greenbagamerica.com

23365 Green Bay Machinery
P.O. Box 19010
Green Bay, WI 54307
920-455-6749
Fax: 920-455-2203 www.gbm-co.com
Estimated Sales: $2.5-5 000,000
Number Employees: 250-499

23366 (HQ)Green Bay Packaging Inc.
1700 Webster Ct.
Green Bay, WI 54302
920-433-5111
Fax: 920-433-5471 www.gbp.com
Corrugated shipping containers and labels including coated and stock.
President/CEO: William Kress
bkress@gbp.com
Senior VP/General Counsel: Scott Wochos
Year Founded: 1933
Estimated Sales: $850 Million
Number Employees: 3,200
Type of Packaging: Consumer, Food Service, Private Label, Bulk

23367 Green Bay Packaging Inc.
5350 East Kilgore Ave.
Kalamazoo, MI 49048
269-552-1000
www.gbp.com
Printed and plain corrugated shipping containers
President: Will Kress
Year Founded: 1933
Estimated Sales: $20-30 Million
Number Employees: 50-99
Square Footage: 312000
Parent Co: Green Bay Packaging

23368 Green Bay Packaging Inc.
6106 W. 68th St.
Tulsa, OK 74131
918-446-3341
www.gbp.com
Corrugated boxes.
President: William Kress
Year Founded: 1933
Estimated Sales: $20-50 Million

Number Employees: 100-249
Parent Co: Green Bay Packaging

23369 Green Belt Industries Inc
45 Comet Ave
Buffalo, NY 14216-1710
716-873-6923
Fax: 716-873-1728 800-668-1114
www.greenbelting.com
Manufacturer and exporter of Teflon-coated conveyor belting for baking pans and trays
Manager: Gail Lipka
Marketing Director: Joe Smith
Manager: Sue King
sking@greenbelting.com
Operations Manager: Scott O Hearn
Purchasing Manager: Jennifer White
Estimated Sales: $5-10 Million
Number Employees: 20-49
Square Footage: 200000

23370 Green Brothers
43 Massasoit Avenue
Barrington, RI 2806
401-245-9043
Steel rule dies and paper boxes
President: James McClelland
Estimated Sales: $1-2.5 Million
Number Employees: 19

23371 Green Earth Bags
815C Tecumseh
Point-Claire, QC H9R 4B1
Canada
514-694-9440
Fax: 514-694-6311
keberwein@fiberlinkstextiles.com
www.fiberlinkstextiles.com
Accessories/supplies i.e. picninc baskets, specialty food packaging i.e. gift wrsp/labels/boxes/containers.
Marketing: Kassandra Eberwein

23372 Green Metal Fabricating
536 Houston St # A
West Sacramento, CA 95691-2253
916-371-2951
Fax: 916-371-7541
Sheet metal and stainless steel fabrications for use in restaurants
Owner: Harry Green Jr
hgreen32@yahoo.com
Estimated Sales: Below $5 Million
Number Employees: 5-9

23373 Green Mountain Awning Inc
36 Marble St
West Rutland, VT 5777
802-438-2951
Fax: 802-438-2774 800-479-2951
info@greenmountainawning.com
Flags, pennants and banners
President: Robert Pearo Sr
Vice President: Robert Pearo, Jr.
Marketing Director: Robert Pearo, Jr.
Estimated Sales: Less Than $500,000
Number Employees: 1-4

23374 Green Mountain Graphics
P.O.Box 1417
Long Island City, NY 11101
718-472-3377
Fax: 718-472-4040 www.gm-graphics.com
Manufacturer and wholesaler/distributor of signs, awards and promotional products
President: Eric Greenberg
VP Sales: Steve Goldman
Estimated Sales: $1-2,500,000
Number Employees: 10-19
Square Footage: 6000
Parent Co: Eastern Concepts

23375 Green Pond Development
92 Greenport Road
Rockaway, NJ 07866
973-983-1023
Land developers

23376 Green Seams
11605 100th Avenue N
Maple Grove, MN 55369-3203
612-929-3213
Fax: 612-929-3027
Totes, bags, uniforms and promotional garments
Owner: Francis Green

23377 Green Spot Packaging
100 S Cambridge Ave
Claremont, CA 91711-4842
909-625-8771
Fax: 909-621-4634 800-456-3210
info@greenspotusa.com www.lagunaliquid.com
Beverages, flavors and fragrances; aseptic packaging services available
CEO: John Tsu
Finance Executive: Don Koury
Sales Executive: Greg Faust
Chief Operating Officer: Dana Staal
Plant Manager: Roy Cooley
Estimated Sales: $6.5 Million
Number Employees: 20-49
Square Footage: 200000
Type of Packaging: Consumer, Food Service, Private Label, Bulk
Brands:
  Action Ade
  Apple Delight
  Apple Royal
  Awesome Orange
  Black Cherry Royal
  Citrus Royal
  Galactic Grape
  Good Buddies
  Green Spot
  Peach Royal
  Superstar Strawberry
  Tropical Royal

23378 Green Sustainable Solutions
1624 Staunton Ave # 101
Parkersburg, WV 26101-5073
304-422-5461
Fax: 304-428-7530 800-827-5461
custserv@gssllc.us.com www.gssllcus.com
CEO: Perry D. Smith
Marketing: Eric Watkins
Manager: Kristen Deem
kdeem@greenpak.com
Estimated Sales: $1-5 Million
Number Employees: 100-249

23379 Green Tek
3708 Enterprise Dr
Janesville, WI 53546-8737
608-754-7336
Fax: 608-754-7334 800-747-6440
greentek@green-tek.com www.green-tek.com
Plastic pallets and trays for oven use and manual heat sealers to package meals for ovens and microwaves. Manufacturer of disposable, dual-ovenable and microwavable food trays and lids.
President: Linda Bracha
lbrach@green-tek.com
CFO: Sandy Boyer
Sales Representative: Steve Guertin
General Manager: Paul Jacobson
Estimated Sales: $20-50 Million
Number Employees: 20-49
Square Footage: 10000
Brands:
  Green-Tek
  Polyziv
  Seal N' Serve

23380 Greenbush Tape & Label Inc
40 Broadway # 3
PO Box 1488
Albany, NY 12202-1020
518-465-2389
Fax: 518-465-5781 www.greenbushlabel.com
Manufacturer and exporter of pressure sensitive tapes and labels
President: James Chenot
Estimated Sales: Below $5 Million
Number Employees: 20-49
Type of Packaging: Consumer, Food Service, Private Label, Bulk

23381 Greene Brothers
134 Broadway
Brooklyn, NY 11211-6031
718-388-6800
Fax: 718-782-4123
Manufacturer and exporter of lighting fixtures
Fmn.: Matthew Santoro
Number Employees: 5-9
Parent Co: Greene's Lighting Fixtures

23382 Greene Industries
65 Rocky Hollow Rd
East Greenwich, RI 02818-3513
401-884-7530
Fax: 401-885-9370 rallengreene@aol.com
Plywood and fiberboard cases and wooden shipping crates
President: Allison Greene
agreene@greeneinc.org
Estimated Sales: Below $5 Million
Number Employees: 5-9

23383 Greener Corp
4 Helmly St
Bayville, NJ 08721-2188
732-269-0107
Fax: 732-286-7842 800-634-9933
custserve@greencorp.com www.greenercorp.com
Bag and pouch sealers, closing equipment: bag closure, heat seal
President: Ted Wojtech
IT Executive: Donna Pilla
donnap@greenercorp.com
R&D: Matt Wojtech
IT Executive: Donna Pilla
donnap@greenercorp.com
Estimated Sales: Below $5 000,000
Number Employees: 20-49

23384 Greenfield Disston
7345 W Friendly Ave # G
Greensboro, NC 27410-6252
336-855-4200
Fax: 336-299-0616
Industrial cutting tools including machine knives
CEO: Henry Libby
Marketing Manager: Holly Oakley
Estimated Sales: $3-5 Million
Number Employees: 10-19
Square Footage: 16000
Parent Co: Rule Industries

23385 Greenfield Packaging
39 Westmoreland Avenue
White Plains, NY 10606-1937
914-993-0233
Fax: 203-934-7172 gpind@aol.com
We sell stock and custom plastic, glass and aluminum bottles, jars and caps; also, print logos, hex-packs and drums available
President: Debra Greenfield
Executive VP: Barbara Greenfield
Estimated Sales: $1-5,000,000

23386 Greenfield Paper Box Co
55 Pierce St
Greenfield, MA 01301-1740
413-773-9414
Fax: 413-774-5134 gpbox123@verizon.net
Manufacturer and designer of set-up and folding boxes for candy, cookies, cereal, etc
President: Brian T Lowell
Vice President: Robert Fischlein
rfischlein@greenfieldpaperboxcoin.com
VP Marketing: Brian Lowell
VP Manufacturing: Robert Fischlein
Production Manager: Roger Phillips
Estimated Sales: $2.5-5 Million
Number Employees: 20-49
Square Footage: 40000
Type of Packaging: Private Label

23387 Greenheck Fan Corp
P.O. Box 410
Schofield, WI 54476
715-359-6171
info@greenheck.com
www.greenheck.com
Manufacturer and exporter of kitchen ventilation equipment including exhaust and supply fans, air units and exhaust hoods; also, pre-piped fire suppression systems including wet chemical and water spray.
Chairman & CEO: James McIntyre
President, Operations: Dave Kallstrom
Chief Financial Officer & Treasurer: Rich Totzke
VP, Manufacturing Execllence & Logistics: Scott Graf
Plant Manager: Mark Haase
Year Founded: 1947
Estimated Sales: $203.7 Million
Number Employees: 250-499
Square Footage: 1000000

Brands:
Greenheck

23388 Greensburg Manufacturing Company
513 N Depot Street
Greensburg, KY 42743-1300
270-932-5511
Fax: 270-932-7866
Cutting boards and butcher blocks with lacquer finishes
General Manager: Daryl Parnell
Estimated Sales: $1-3 Million
Number Employees: 160
Parent Co: Kimball International

23389 Greenville Awning Company
325 New Neely Ferry Rd
Mauldin, SC 29662
864-288-0063
Fax: 864-288-3683 www.greenvilleawning.com
Commercial awnings
President: Gerhard Kuhn
info@greenvilleawning.com
Estimated Sales: $10-20,000,000
Number Employees: 20-49

23390 Greenwood Mop & Broom Inc
312 Palmer St
Greenwood, SC 29646
864-227-8411
Fax: 864-227-3200 800-635-6849
gmb@emeraldis.com
www.greenwoodmopandbroom.com
Brooms, dry and wet mops, handles and brushes
CEO: Henry Bonds
Vice President of Finance: Craig Glanton
VP: Freida Bonds
VP Sales/Marketing: Sid Johnston
Chief Operating Officer: Sid G. Johnston
Estimated Sales: $10-20 Million
Number Employees: 20-49
Square Footage: 314000

23391 (HQ)Greer's Ferry Glass Work
PO Box 797
Dubuque, IA 52004-0797
501-589-2947
Fax: 800-310-0525 gfgw@hotmail.com
Manufacturer and exporter of thermometers, refractometers and hydrometers for testing salt, alcohol, sugar, etc
Sales: Brenda Marler
Operations: Bob Mallis
Estimated Sales: $1-2.5 Million
Number Employees: 5-9
Other Locations:
Greer's Ferry Glass Works
West Paterson NJ
Brands:
Brix
Salometers

23392 Greerco High Shear Mixers
125 Flagship Dr
North Andover, MA 01845-6119
978-687-0101
Fax: 978-687-8500 800-643-0641
inquiry@kenics.com www.chemineer.com
Homogenizers, colloid mills, laboratory homogenizers, self contained systems and high shear mixers
Manager: Mark Raymond
Estimated Sales: $20-50 Million
Number Employees: 20-49

23393 Grefco
23705 Crenshaw Blvd
Torrance, CA 90505-5236
310-660-8840
Fax: 213-517-0794
Wine industry filter acids
Estimated Sales: $2.5-5 Million
Number Employees: 10-19

23394 Gregg Industries Inc
5048 Vienna Dr
Waunakee, WI 53597-9746
608-846-5143
Fax: 608-846-5143 greggind@gregginc.com
www.smokehouseparts.com
Smokers, parts, and equipments
President: Wes Gillespie
greggind@gregginc.com

Estimated Sales: $300,000-500,000
Number Employees: 1-4

23395 Gregg Industries Inc
5048 Vienna Dr
Waunakee, WI 53597-9746
608-846-5143
Fax: 608-846-5143 greggind@gregginc.com
www.smokehouseparts.com
Industrial equipment for meat industries; smokehouse door air seals, wet bulb socks and silicone gasket
President: Wes Gillespie
greggind@gregginc.com
Vice President: Kathleen Triggs
Estimated Sales: Under $500,000
Number Employees: 1-4

23396 Gregor Jonsson Inc
13822 W Laurel Dr
Lake Forest, IL 60045-4529
847-247-4200
Fax: 847-247-4272 sales@jonsson.com
www.jonsson.com
Manufacturer and exporter of shrimp peeling systems
President: Frank Heurich
Vice President: Beth Dancy
Computer Support/Database Design: Ann Curry
Operations Manager: Scott Heurich
Operations Manager: Scott Heurich
Estimated Sales: $10-20 Million
Number Employees: 10-19
Square Footage: 80000

23397 Greif Brothers Corporation
3113 W 110th Street
Cleveland, OH 44111-2753
216-941-2021
Fax: 216-476-8209 800-424-0342
www.greif.com
Corrugated cartons
Product Manager: Rick Volker
Sales Manager: Michael Blatt
Plant Manager: Bob Dozer
Estimated Sales: $20-50 Million
Number Employees: 100-249

23398 Greif Inc
425 Winter Rd
Delaware, OH 43015-8903
740-549-6000
Fax: 740-549-6100 800-476-1635
www.greif.com
Specialty packaging, signage and displays including point of purchase
President, Chief Executive Officer: David B. Fischer
CEO: Peter G Watson
watson@greif.com
EVP: Gary R. Martz
COO: Peter G. Watson
Estimated Sales: Over $1 Billion
Number Employees: 10000+
Square Footage: 260000

23399 Greif Inc
425 Winter Rd
Delaware, OH 43015-8903
740-549-6000
Fax: 740-549-6100 www.greif.com
Bulk boxes, die cuts and curtain contained corrugated shipping containers
Manager: George Petzelt
CEO: Peter G Watson
watson@greif.com
VP Sales/Marketing: Dan Lautermilch
Sales Representative: David Mackson
Estimated Sales: Over $1 Billion
Number Employees: 10000+

23400 Greif Inc
425 Winter Rd
Delaware, OH 43015-8903
740-549-6000
Fax: 740-549-6100 www.greif.com
Fiber and plastic packaging, steel drums, corrugated containers, etc
CFO: Donald S Huml
CEO: Peter G Watson
watson@greif.com
CEO: Michael J Gasser
Product Manager: Rick Volker
Estimated Sales: Over $1 Billion
Number Employees: 10000+

23401 Greif Inc
4300 W 130th St
Alsip, IL 60803-2003
708-371-4777
Fax: 708-371-2047 800-233-0004
www.greif.com
Steel and plastic shipping containers and drums,
specialty containers, stainless steel batch containers
and process drums
President: Tony Riley
Estimated Sales: $49.5 Million
Number Employees: 100-249

23402 Greig Filters Inc
412 High Meadows Blvd
P.O.Box 91675
Lafayette, LA 70507-3417
337-237-3355
Fax: 337-233-9263 800-456-0177
gfi@greigfilters.com www.greigfilters.com
Manufacturer and exporter of filtration systems for
cooking oil and beverages
Owner: Alan Greig
gfi@greigfilters.com
Office Manager: Tammy Roy
Engineer: Shane Hulin
Estimated Sales: $1-2.5 Million
Number Employees: 5-9
Square Footage: 40000
Brands:
Greig Filters
Pressure Leaf Filter
Purifry

23403 Greitzer
P.O.Box 2008
Elizabeth City, NC 27906
252-338-4000
Fax: 252-338-5445 kevin@greitzer.com
Conveyors and ventilators
Owner: Kevin Gilroy
Estimated Sales: $300,000-500,000
Number Employees: 1-4

23404 Greydon Inc
391 Greendale Rd # 2
York, PA 17403-4638
717-848-3875
Fax: 717-843-6435 info@greydon.com
www.greydon.com
Inline printing for packaging
President: Gregory Rochon
Vice President: John Rochon
Sales Director: Leo Zitella
Plant Manager: Jim Buchmver
Purchasing Manager: Brian Newman
Estimated Sales: $2.5-5 000,000
Number Employees: 20-49

23405 Gribble Stamp & StencilCo
121 St Emanuel St
Houston, TX 77002-2355
713-228-5358
Fax: 713-228-2127
Rubber and steel stamps, stencils, engraved signs,
security seals and plaques
President: C W Gribble
sales@gribblestamp.com
President: C Gribble
Number Employees: 1-4

23406 Gridpath, Inc.
328 Glover Road
Stony Creek, ON L8E 5M3
Canada
905-643-0955
Fax: 905-643-6718 info@gridpathinc.com
High pressure processing equipment for non-thermal
pasteurization and packaging for the food processing
industry.
President: Rick Marshall

23407 Griffin Automation
240 Westminster Rd
Buffalo, NY 14224-1930
716-674-2300
Fax: 716-674-2309 sales@griffinautomation.com
www.griffinautomation.com
Design adn build automation machinery

CEO: Gerald Bidlack
VP Finance: John Shepherd
VP Engineering: Robert Kern
Sales: Richard Hacker
Manager: Randy Reed
rreed@griffinautomation.com
Plant Manager: Mike Baines
Purchasing Manager: Chuck Peskir
Estimated Sales: $5-10 000,000
Number Employees: 20-49
Number of Products: 20
Square Footage: 40000
Type of Packaging: Private Label

23408 (HQ)Griffin Bros Inc
3033 Industrial Way NE
Salem, OR 97301-0042
503-540-7886
Fax: 503-540-7929 800-456-4743
griffinbros1@yahoo.com
Manufacturer and exporter of disinfectants, polymer
floor finish, etc
President: Rod Bennett
rod@griffinbrothers.com
Account Sales Manager: Rod Bennett
Production Manager: Mike Allison
Estimated Sales: $1-3 Million
Number Employees: 5-9
Type of Packaging: Consumer, Food Service

23409 Griffin Food Co
111 S Cherokee St
Muskogee, OK 74403-5420
918-687-6311
Fax: 918-687-3579 800-866-6311
www.griffinfoods.com
Contract packager and wholesaler/distributor of
sauces, vegetables and condiments including jams
and syrups
Owner: John Griffin
johngriffin@griffinfoods.com
Vice President: David Needham
VP Sales/Marketing: Sam Ramos
Director Midwest Sales: D.C. Smith
Director Southeast Region Sales: Wayne Fuller
Estimated Sales: $16,000,000
Number Employees: 50-99
Square Footage: 648297
Type of Packaging: Consumer, Food Service, Pri-
vate Label, Bulk
Brands:
Cherokee Maid
Delta
Griffin
Lucky Dutch
Old Santa Fe
Olde Farm
Prize Taker

23410 Griffin Products
P.O.Box 90
Wills Point, TX 75169
903-873-6388
Fax: 903-873-6389 800-379-9709
sales@griffinproducts.com
www.griffinproducts.com
Stainless steel sinks and tables including work and
dish
President: Shane Griffin
CFO: Kenneth Fratcher
Sales: Janet Griffen
Sales: Mike Whitus
Estimated Sales: $2.5-5,000,000
Number Employees: 20-49

23411 Griffin Rutgers Co Inc
1170 Lincoln Ave # 12
Holbrook, NY 11741-2286
631-981-4141
Fax: 631-981-4171 800-237-6713
custserv@griffin-rutgers.com
www.griffinrutgers.com
Supplying printing
Owner: Jim Umbdenstock
jim@griffin-rutgers.com
Estimated Sales: $1-2.5 Million
Number Employees: 5-9

23412 Griffith Foods Inc.
1 Griffith Center
Alsip, IL 60803
708-371-0900
Fax: 708-371-4783 www.griffithfoods.com

Protein, side-dish and snack seasonings; sauces, gra-
vies, and soups mixes; salsa and condiments; and
bakery and dough blends.
Chairman: Brian Griffith
CEO: TC Chatterjee
Executive VP/CFO: Matt West
Year Founded: 1919
Estimated Sales: $286.8 Million
Number Employees: 1,000-4,999
Square Footage: 250000
Type of Packaging: Food Service, Private Label,
Bulk

23413 Grigg Box Company
18900 Fitzpatrick Street
Detroit, MI 48228-1428
313-273-9000
Fax: 313-273-9356 rocco@griggbox.com
www.griggbox.com
Packaging equipment
President: Rocco Franco
General Manager: R Gary Turnbull
Packaging Sales: Leon Cote
Contact: Alan Gentinne
alan@griggbox.com
Plant Manager: Ed Schlacht
Estimated Sales: $10-20 Million
Number Employees: 1-4

**23414 Grigsby Brothers Paper Box
Manufacturers**
817 NE Madrona Street
PO Box 11189
Portland, OR 97211
503-285-8341
Fax: 503-285-3334 866-233-4690
And folding cartons; package design and full service
printing available
President: Terry Grigsby
CFO: Jane Hewitt
VP: Terry Grigsby
R&D: Todd Grigsby
Estimated Sales: $2.5-5 Million
Number Employees: 10-19

23415 Gril-Del
400 Southbrook Circle
Mankato, MN 56001-4782
507-776-8275
Fax: 507-776-8276 800-782-7320
Manufacturer and exporter of outdoor cooking uten-
sils for the barbecue grill including spatulas, tongs
and knives; also, aprons, salt and pepper shakers,
handmade baskets, mitts and meat platters
President: Steven Saggau
VP: Connie Saggau
Number Employees: 10
Square Footage: 12000
Type of Packaging: Consumer, Food Service, Pri-
vate Label, Bulk
Brands:
Gril-Classics
Gril-Del

23416 Grill Greats
PO Box 568
Saxonburg, PA 16056-0568
724-352-1511
Fax: 724-352-1266 sales@du-co.com
www.du-co.com
Manufacturer and exporter of ceramic briquettes for
barbecue grills
President: Tom Arbanas
Quality Control: Paul Sekeras
Sales: Mike Carson
Estimated Sales: $50-100 Million
Number Employees: 100-249
Square Footage: 150000
Type of Packaging: Private Label, Bulk
Brands:
Grill Greats

23417 Grillco Inc
1775 Mallette Rd
Aurora, IL 60505-1319
630-906-0290
Fax: 630-906-0289 800-644-0067
Portable grills including charcoal, gas and pit barbe-
cue; also, rotisseries, hoods, shelves and racks
Sales Director: Brian Ruseitti
Manager: Brian Ruscitti
sales@grillcoinc.com
Estimated Sales: Less Than $500,000
Number Employees: 1-4

Brands:
  Grillco, Inc.

23418 Grills to Go
5659 W San Madele Avenue
Fresno, CA 93722-5066
559-645-8089
Fax: 559-645-8088 877-869-2253
Manufacturer, Distributor and Exporter of
commerical barbecue equipment, smoker ovens,
Southern Pride brand ovens and Rotisseries and
supplies
President: Michael Hall
CEO: Nora Hall
Estimated Sales: $1-2.5 Million
Number Employees: 1-4
Square Footage: 12000
Brands:
  Grills To Go

23419 Grimes Co
600 Ellis Rd N
Jacksonville, FL 32254-2801
904-786-5711
Fax: 904-786-7805 800-474-6378
www.grimescompanies.com
Heat sealers, tong welders, impulse sealers, impulse
bar sealers, and rotary hospital sealers
Owner: Nicole Adler
nadler@grimescompanies.com
Estimated Sales: Less than $500,000
Number Employees: 20-49

23420 (HQ)Grindmaster-Cecilware Corp
4003 Collins Ln
Louisville, KY 40245-1602
502-425-4776
Fax: 502-425-4664 800-695-4500
info@gmcw.com www.gmcw.com
Manufacturers of a complete line of hot, cold and
frozen beverage dispensing equipment.
CEO: Michael G Tinsley
mtinsley@grindmaster.com
CEO: Tom McDonald
Plant Manager: Jim Howell
Estimated Sales: $5-10 Million
Number Employees: 100-249
Brands:
  American Metal Ware
  Crathco
  Espressimo
  Grindmaster
  Wilch

**23421 Grinnell Fire ProtectionSystems
Company**
4985 Quail Rd NE
Sauk Rapids, MN 56379
320-253-8665
Fax: 320-253-4540
Fire protection and sprinkling systems
Branch Manager: Harry Ramler
Estimated Sales: $10-20 Million
Number Employees: 100
Parent Co: TYCO International Company

**23422 Grinnell Fire ProtectionSystems
Company**
50 Technology Drive
Westminster, MA 1441
320-253-8665
Fax: 320-253-4540 800-746-7539
www.tycosimplexgrinnell.com
Fire extinguishers and kitchen hood systems
Regional Manager: Don Molloy
VP Human Resource: Dana Smith
Estimated Sales: $10-20,000,000
Number Employees: 250
Parent Co: TYCO International Company

23423 Grocery Manufacturers Assn
1350 I St NW # 300
Washington, DC 20005-3377
202-639-5900
Fax: 202-639-5932 www.gmaonline.org
Representing the food products industry.
President: John Cady
CEO: Pamela G Bailey
pbailey@nfpa-food.org
CEO: Cal Dooley
Estimated Sales: $5-10 Million
Number Employees: 50-99

23424 Grocery Products Distribution
14 Ridgedale Ave # 106
Cedar Knolls, NJ 07927-1106
973-538-1035
Fax: 973-538-0944 richgpds@aol.com
Consultant specializing in distribution marketing
services for public grocery distribution centers
President: Rich Richards
richgpds@aol.com
VP: Florence Richards
Staff Assistant: Barbara Brown
Estimated Sales: $.5-1 million
Number Employees: 5-9

23425 Groeb Farms
10464 Bryan Hwy
Onsted, MI 49265-0269
517-467-2065
Fax: 517-467-2840 800-530-9969
Honey; UPC labeling, tamper-evident packaging,
re-closable cap, easy pour handle and shatterproof
containers
President & CEO: Ernest Groeb
VP & CFO: Jack Irvin Jr
VP/COO: Troy Groeb
Director Retail Sales: Jim McCoy
Chief Procurement Officer: Alison Tringale
Type of Packaging: Consumer, Food Service, Pri-
  vate Label, Bulk
Other Locations:
  Belleview FL
  Miller's American Honey
  Colton CA
Brands:
  Gourmet Jose
  Groeb Farms

23426 Groen Process Equipment
271 Country Commons Rd # F
Trout Valley, IL 60013-2545
847-462-1865
Fax: 847-462-1950 info@groen.com
Manager: Frank Lobes
flobes@gpeequipment.com
Estimated Sales: Below $5 Million
Number Employees: 250-499

23427 Groen-A Dover Industries Co
1055 Mendell Davis Dr
Byram, MS 39272-9788
601-371-4417
Fax: 601-373-9587 800-676-9040
info@groen.com www.unifiedbrands.net
Manufacturers of steam jacketed kettles, braising
pans, convection steamers, combi ovens, cook-chill
and continuous processing systems for food service
operators and industrial processors worldwide
President: Bill Strenglis
CFO: Scott Stevenson
R&D: Pam Holmes
Quality Control: Mike Blackwell
Sales/Marketing: Clay Thames
Estimated Sales: $10-20 Million
Number Employees: 50-99
Parent Co: Dover Industries

23428 Groen-A Dover Industries Co
1055 Mendell Davis Dr
Byram, MS 39272-9788
601-371-4417
Fax: 888-864-7636 webmaster@unifiedbrands.net
www.unifiedbrands.net
President: Bill Strenglis
CFO: Scott Stevenson
R&D: Pam Holmes
Quality Control: Mike Blackwell
V.P. of Sales and Marketing: Blair Alfdord
Estimated Sales: $10-20 Million
Number Employees: 50-99

23429 Grosfillex Inc
230 Old West Penn Ave
Robesonia, PA 19551-8904
610-693-6213
Fax: 610-693-5414 800-233-3186
info@grosfillexfurniture.com
www.grosfillexfurniture.com
Supplier, importer and exporter of commercial out-
door resin furniture
President: Kim Addington
kladdington@grosfillex.com
Estimated Sales: $50-100 Million
Number Employees: 100-249
Parent Co: Grosfillex SARL

Other Locations:
  Grosfillex Contract Furniture
  Chino CA
Brands:
  Grosfillex

23430 Gross & Co Licensed BusPro
1208 Sunset St
Middletown, OH 45042-2890
513-424-6035
Fax: 513-420-9260 www.grossinc.com
Chill rolls, hearto rolls and process water systems
Owner: M Dtannreuther
dtannreuther@grossinc.com
Estimated Sales: Less Than $500,000
Number Employees: 5-9

23431 Grote Co
1160 Gahanna Pkwy
Columbus, OH 43230-6615
614-868-8414
Fax: 614-863-1647 888-534-7683
www.grotecompany.com
Manufacturer and exporter of food processing
equipment including high yield slicer applicators,
multi-purpose slicers, cheese shredders, pizza top-
ping lines and paper sheeter systems
President: Jelff Rawef
aschneider@grotecompany.com
CEO: Bruce Hohl
Chairman: James Grote
Quality Control: Jon Feifeit
Marketing Communication/Sales Coord.: Terri
Hoover
Sales Exec: Andy Schneider
Estimated Sales: $10-20 Million
Number Employees: 100-249
Square Footage: 140000
Brands:
  Grote

23432 Groth Corp
13650 N Promenade Blvd
Stafford, TX 77477-3972
281-295-6800
Fax: 713-295-6999 800-354-7684
sales@grothcorp.com www.grothcorp.com
Consultant specializing in sales and marketing for
U.S. companies overseas through exclusive
distributorships and joint venture arrangements
President: David Brown
dbrown@grothcorp.com
Managing Director: Helen Groth
Estimated Sales: $1-5 Million
Number Employees: 50-99
Square Footage: 600

23433 Group One Partners
21 W 3rd St
Boston, MA 02127-1133
617-268-7000
Fax: 617-268-0209 info@grouponeinc.com
www.grouponeinc.com
Consultant specializing in food service design for
facilities including kitchens and restaurants; also,
food service programming and interior design
President: Mary Fraria
m_fraria@lysibishop.com
Principal: Kevin Mullin
Principal: Harry Wheeler
Director Food Service Design: William Stenstrom
Estimated Sales: $1-2.5 Million
Number Employees: 20-49

**23434 Gruenewald
ManufacturingCompany**
100 Ferncroft Rd Ste 204
Danvers, MA 1923
978-777-0200
Fax: 978-777-9432 800-229-9447
info@whipcream.com www.whipcream.com
Manufacturer, importer and exporter of dispensers
for food products, including ice cream and whipped
cream
Owner: Fredrick Gruenewald
fredrick@whipcream.com
Sales/Marketing: Kevin Muldoon
VP Sales: Thomas Muldoon
Sales: Joseph Ransom
Estimated Sales: $10-20 Million
Number Employees: 10-19
Square Footage: 30000
Type of Packaging: Food Service

Brands:
Refillo
River of Cream
Rocket

23435 Grueny's Rubber Stamps
210 S Gaines St
Little Rock, AR 72201-2218

501-376-0393
Fax: 501-376-6327

Price markers and rubber stanps
President and CFO: John Ward Jr
Quality Control: Bob Pinkerton
Sales Manager: Brit Wood
Estimated Sales: Less than $500,000
Number Employees: 1 to 4

23436 Guardsman
4999 36th St SE
Grand Rapids, MI 49512-2005

616-940-2900
Fax: 616-285-7870 www.guardsman.com

Carpet and fabric cleaners, degreasers and adhesive removers
Manager: Kate Bass
New Business Development Manager: Sandi Brogger
Estimated Sales: $10-20 Million
Number Employees: 100-249
Parent Co: Lilly Industries
Brands:
Afta
Carpet Guard
Goof Off
One-Wipe

23437 Guest Supply
P.O.Box 902
Monmouth Jct, NJ 08852

609-514-9696
Fax: 609-514-2692 800-448-3787
eservice@guestsupply.com www.guestsupply.com

Cleaning equipment and chemicals
President: Clifford Stanley
Number Employees: 100

23438 Gulf Arizona Packaging
7720 FM 1960 East
Humble, TX 77346

281-582-6700
Fax: 281-852-1590 800-364-3887

Manufacturer and wholesaler/distributor of packaging equipment and materials including bags, containers, closures, conveyors, labels, linings, tapes, ties, etc
Manager: Paul Corley
General Manager: Paul Corley
General Manager: Jay Crabb
Estimated Sales: $5-10 Million
Number Employees: 5-9
Parent Co: Gulf Systems

23439 Gulf Coast Plastics
9314 Princess Palm Ave
Tampa, FL 33619-1364

813-621-8098
Fax: 813-623-1408 800-277-7491
sales@gulfcoastplastics.com
www.gulfcoastplastics.com

Manufacturer and exporter of anti-static plastic bags
Owner: Karen Santiago
karens@gulfcoastplastics.com
CFO: Tom Coryn
Quality Control: Tom Coryn
Manager: Thomas Coryn
Estimated Sales: Below $5 Million
Number Employees: 20-49
Square Footage: 24000
Parent Co: Dairy Mix
Type of Packaging: Consumer, Food Service, Bulk

23440 Gulf Coast Sign Company
380 Clematis Street
Pensacola, FL 32503-2839

850-438-2131
Fax: 850-432-6367 800-768-3549
gulfcoastsign@hotmail.com

U.L. approved neon, plastic, electric and sandblasted signs; also, maintenance, repair and erection services
CEO: William Terry
Estimated Sales: $1-2.5 Million
Number Employees: 19
Square Footage: 40000

23441 Gulf Packaging Company
323 9th Avenue N
Safety Harbor, FL 34695

727-725-4424
Fax: 727-725-2885 800-749-3466

Folding, paper, set-up and transparent boxes; also, blister and skin cards
President: Jeffrey A Herran
Chairman: F Edward Herran
Plant Manager: Patrick Herran
Estimated Sales: $2.5-5 Million
Number Employees: 20
Square Footage: 32000

23442 Gulf Systems
801 E Fronton St
Brownsville, TX 78520

800-217-4853
Fax: 956-504-9800 www.gulfpackaging.com

Wholesaler/distributor of packaging equipment and materials
Manager: Blanca Puga
bpuga@gulfsys.com
CFO: Debby Malone
Customer Service Representative: Cathy Wyatt
Estimated Sales: Below $5,000,000
Number Employees: 5-9
Parent Co: Gulf Systems

23443 Gulf Systems
2109 Exchange Dr
Arlington, TX 76011

817-261-1915
Fax: 817-861-0092

Wholesaler/distributor of packaging equipment and materials
Manager: Denise Stiger
Contact: Todd Williams
todd_esala@lselectric.com
Estimated Sales: $20-50 Million
Number Employees: 20-49
Parent Co: Gulf Systems

23444 Gulf Systems
7720 fm 960 e
Humble, TX 77346

405-528-2293
Fax: 281-852-1590 800-364-3887
customerservicehumble@gulfpackaging.com
www.gulfpackaging.com

Wholesaler/distributor of packaging equipment and materials
Customer Service Representative: Cathy Wyatt
Estimated Sales: $2.5-5,000,000
Number Employees: 5-9
Parent Co: Gulf Systems

23445 Gulf Systems
7720 fm 960 e
Humble, TX 77346

405-528-2293
Fax: 281-852-1590 800-364-3887
customerservicehumble@gulfpackaging.com
www.gulfpackaging.com

Wholesaler/distributor of packaging equipment and materials
Customer Service Representative: Cathy Wyatt
Estimated Sales: $1-5,000,000
Number Employees: 5-9
Parent Co: Gulf Systems

23446 Gulf Systems
3815 N Santa Fe Ave
Oklahoma City, OK 73108

800-364-3887
Fax: 405-557-0903

Wholesaler/distributor of packaging equipment and materials
Customer Service Representative: Cathy Wyatt
Estimated Sales: $5-10,000,000
Number Employees: 5-9
Parent Co: Gulf Systems

23447 Gunter Wilhelm Cutlery
20-10 Maple Ave # 35g
Fair Lawn, NJ 07410-1591

201-569-6866
Fax: 201-369-4679 sales@gunterwilhelm.com
www.gunterwilhelm.com

Cookware, cooking implements
Founder: Paul Hellman
CEO: David Malek
Contact: Cherry Dan
sales@gunterwilhelm.com

Number Employees: 1-4

23448 Gusmer Enterprises Inc
81 M St
Fresno, CA 93721-3215

559-485-2692
Fax: 559-485-4254 866-213-1131
www.gusmerenterprises.com

Manufacturer and exporter of filter and fiber media for food and beverages
CEO: Marla Jeffrey
mjeffrey@gusmerenterprises.com
CEO: Marla Jeffrey
VP/Technical Sales: Phil Crantz
Estimated Sales: $5-10 Million
Number Employees: 50-99
Square Footage: 240000
Parent Co: Gusmer Enterprises
Other Locations:
Cellulo Co.
Crawford NJ
Brands:
Cellu Flo
Cellu Pore
Cellu Stacks
Kolor Fine
Oak Mor

23449 Gustave A Larson Co
W233n2869 Roundy Cir W
Pewaukee, WI 53072-6285

262-542-0200
Fax: 262-542-1400 www.galarson.com

Heating equipment
President: Devon Becker
devon.becker@jpmorgan.com
Branch Manager: John Hirsch
Estimated Sales: $2.5-5,000,000
Number Employees: 250-499
Parent Co: Indiana Supply Company

23450 Guth Lighting
PO Box 7079
Saint Louis, MO 63177

314-533-3200
Fax: 314-533-9127

Manufacturer and exporter of sealed and gasketed fluorescent and high-intensity discharge lighting equipment for use in water wash down and corrosive environments
Manager: Robert Catone
VP and Controller: Sue Pries
VP/General Manager: Robert Catone
Research & Development: Mike Kurtz
Estimated Sales: $20-50 Million
Number Employees: 50-99
Square Footage: 100000
Parent Co: JJI
Brands:
Duraclamp
Enviroguard
Kleenseal
Plascolume
Railtite
Steeltite

23451 H & H Metal FabricationInc
3066 Faulkner Rd
PO Box 1505
Belden, MS 38826-9649

662-489-4626
Fax: 662-489-4626 hhmetalfab@earthlink.net
www.hhmetalfab.com

Manufactures electrical enclosures & panels; residential & commercial fluorescent light fixtures; steel sheet metal fabricating; punch press work & welding
President: Michael Huey
hhmetalfab@earthlink.net
Number Employees: 10-19

23452 H & M Bay Inc
1600 Industrial Park Rd
Federalsburg, MD 21632

410-754-5167
Fax: 410-754-3495 800-932-7521
information@hmbayinc.net www.hmbayinc.net

Warehouse offering cooler and freezer storage of seafood; transportation firm providing refrigerated trucking services including local, short and long haul

Co-Owner: Walter Messick
CFO: Al Nulph
Marketing And Sales Manager: Scott Steinhardt
Manager: Randy Hind
rhind@hmbayinc.com
COO: Michael Ryan
Number Employees: 100-249

23453 H A Phillips & Co
770 Enterprise Ave
Dekalb, IL 60115-7904

630-377-0050
Fax: 630-377-2706 info@haphillips.com
www.haphillips.com
Manufacturer and exporter of float controls, valves
and pressure vessels for ammonia refrigeration sys-
tems; wholesaler/distributor and importer of pres-
sure regulating and solenoid valves
President/Chief Executive Officer: Michael R. Ryan
Executive Director: John Schroeder
Vice-President of Finance: Janet L. Jones
Vice-President of Engineering: Steve L. . Yagla, P.E
R&D/Quality Control: Mike Ryan
Sales/Marketing: Ed Murziuski
Corporate Sales Manager: Thomas W. Herman
Secretary/Vice President of Human Resour: Mary
Wright
Operations Manager: Andrew McCullough
Vice President of Manufacturing: Brian J. Youssi
Plant Manager: David Williams
Purchasing Manager: Rou Coleman
Estimated Sales: $4.2 Million
Number Employees: 20-49
Square Footage: 60000
Brands:
    Dump Trap
    Live Brine
    Phillips
    Phillips Level-Edge

23454 H A Sparke Co
1032 Texas Ave
PO Box 674
Shreveport, LA 71101-3341

318-222-0927
Fax: 318-222-2731 info@hasparke.com
www.hasparke.com
Manufacturer and exporter of restaurant fixtures in-
cluding pot, pan and utensil racks; also, guest check
handling equipment
President: Richard W Sparke
Estimated Sales: $1-2.5 Million
Number Employees: 5-9
Square Footage: 14000

23455 H A Stiles
386 Bridgton Rd # A1
Westbrook, ME 04092-3606

207-854-8458
Fax: 207-854-3863 800-447-8537
askhastiles@hastiles.com www.hastiles.com
Manufacturer and exporter of wooden kitchen uten-
sils and bread and cake boards; also, toothpicks
President: Ambrose Berry
Estimated Sales: Less Than $500,000
Number Employees: 10-19

23456 H B Fuller Co
1200 Willow Lake Blvd
P.O. Box 64683
St. Paul, MN 55164-0683

651-236-5900
www.hbfuller.com
Adhesives including hot melt, palletizing and low
temperature application.
President & Chief Executive Officer: Jim Owens
EVP & Chief Operating Officer: Ted Clark
EVP & Chief Financial Officer: John Corkrean
Year Founded: 1887
Estimated Sales: $2.8 Billion
Number Employees: 3,700
Brands:
    Adventra
    H.B. Fuller
    Palletite
    Potimelt

23457 H C Bainbridge Inc
718 N Salina St
Syracuse, NY 13208-2511

315-475-5313
Fax: 315-475-5469 bainbridgeflags@twcny.rr.com
Flags, flag poles and banners.

President: Marilyn Swetland
bainbridgeflags@twcny.rr.com
Estimated Sales: Less than $500,000
Square Footage: 8000

23458 H C Duke & Son Inc
2116 8th Ave
East Moline, IL 61244-1800

309-755-4553
Fax: 309-755-9858 sales@electrofreeze.com
www.electrofreeze.com
Manufacturer and exporter of soft serve ice cream
machines
Marketing: Joe Clark
VP Sales: Jim Duke
Estimated Sales: $20-50 Million
Number Employees: 100-249
Square Footage: 115000
Type of Packaging: Food Service
Brands:
    Electro Freeze
    H.C. Duke & Son

23459 H F Staples & Co Inc
9 Webb Dr # 5
PO Box 956
Merrimack, NH 03054-4876

603-889-8600
Fax: 603-883-9409 800-682-0034
info@hfstaples.com www.naturalfurniturecare.com
Manufacturer and exporter of wood filler, wax and
ladder accessories. Contract private label tube filling
of viscous products
President: John Murphy
john.murphy@staples.com
Vice President: Thomas Stratton
Estimated Sales: $5-10 Million
Number Employees: 5-9
Square Footage: 52000
Type of Packaging: Private Label

23460 H G Weber & Co
725 Fremont St
Kiel, WI 53042-1352

920-894-2221
Fax: 920-894-3786 info@hgweber.com
www.holwegweber.com
Manufacturer and exporter of paper and film bag
machinery, flexographic printers and vertical case
conveyors
President: Mike Odom
modom@hgweber.com
CFO: John Smith
Senior VP: Donald Ludwig
Marketing Director: Jeff Vogel
Sales Director: Brian Niemuth
Estimated Sales: $20-50 Million
Number Employees: 50-99
Square Footage: 130
Brands:
    Presto Flex
    Upender
    Weber-Univers

23461 H G Weber & Co
725 Fremont St
Kiel, WI 53042-1352

920-894-2221
Fax: 920-894-3786 info@hgweber.com
www.holwegweber.com
Bag making machines
President: Mike Odom
modom@hgweber.com
Estimated Sales: $20-50 Million
Number Employees: 50-99

23462 H H Franz Co
3201 Fallscliff Rd
Baltimore, MD 21211-2792

410-889-2975
Fax: 410-889-2160 www.hhfranzfillers.com
Packaging, bottle fillers
President: Bob Mintiens Jr
bmintiens@hhfranzco.com
Estimated Sales: $1-2.5 000,000
Number Employees: 1-4

23463 H H Franz Co
3201 Fallscliff Rd
Baltimore, MD 21211-2792

410-889-2975
Fax: 410-889-2160 800-731-3309
franz@qis.net www.hhfranzfillers.com
Food processing equipment

President: Bob Mintiens Jr
bmintiens@hhfranzco.com
Estimated Sales: $1-2.5 000,000
Number Employees: 1-4

23464 H P Mfg Co
3705 Carnegie Ave
Cleveland, OH 44115-2750

216-361-6500
Fax: 216-361-6508 info@hpmanufacturing.com
Plastic items including sheets, rods and tubes
President: John Melchiorre
CFO: Ken Lutke
Quality Control: Paul Glozer
Chairman of the Board: Terry Poltorek
VP Sales/Marketing: Bob Roman
Contact: Denise Arcangelini
darcangelini@hpmanufacturing.com
Estimated Sales: $5-10 Million
Number Employees: 10-19

23465 H S Crocker Co Inc
12100 Smith Dr
Huntley, IL 60142-9618

847-669-3600
Fax: 847-669-1170 www.hscrocker.com
Specialty, gravure, flexographic and letterpress
printing; paper and pressure sensitive labels; tickets;
pharmaceutical, portion pack, foil, juice and yogurt
lids
CFO: John Dai
CEO: Endilch Andy
endilch.andy@hscrocker.com
CFO: John Dai
CEO: Ron Giordano
Marketing Manager: Ron Giordano
Estimated Sales: $20-30 Million
Number Employees: 50-99

23466 H S Inc
1301 W Sheridan Ave
Oklahoma City, OK 73106-5233

405-239-6864
Fax: 405-239-2242 800-238-1240
sales@hsfoodservers.com
Thermal food containers for tabletop service
President: Esther Feiler
Owner: Ester Stephenson
estherstephenson@coxinet.net
Sales Manager: Sue Garcia
Estimated Sales: $2.5-5 Million
Number Employees: 10-19
Parent Co: ACO

23467 H T I Filtration
30241 Tomas
Rancho Sta Marg, CA 92688-2123

949-546-0745
Fax: 949-269-6438 877-404-9372
info@htifiltration.com
Manufacturer and exporter of filtration equipment
including oil, and hydraulic, specializing in water re-
moval from oils
CEO: Steven Parker
Technical Service: Ron Hart
r.hart@htifiltration.com
Estimated Sales: $1-5 Million
Number Employees: 10-19
Square Footage: 40000
Parent Co: Temcor
Type of Packaging: Private Label
Brands:
    H-F 201
    H-F 211
    H-S 410
    Hydra-Supreme
    Hydro-Fil

23468 H&H Lumber Company
11100 SE 3rd Ave
Amarillo, TX 79118

806-335-1813
Fax: 806-335-3734
Wooden pallets
Owner: Doyle Herring
Estimated Sales: Less than $500,000
Number Employees: 1-4
Square Footage: 12000

23469 (HQ)H&H Wood Products
5600 Camp Rd
Hamburg, NY 14075

716-648-5600
Fax: 716-648-3246 hhwood1@aol.com

Wooden pallets; heat treating service
President: William Heussler
williamheussler@voestalpine.com
Production Coordinator: Richard Perez
Estimated Sales: $3 Million
Number Employees: 20-49
Square Footage: 52000
Type of Packaging: Bulk
Other Locations:
    H&H Wood Products
    Hamburg NY

23470 H&H of the Americas
225 W 34th Street
Suite 1310
New York, NY 10122-1310
                          212-695-4980
    Fax: 212-695-7153 johntripas@msn.com
Processing equipment for the meat industry
President: Barbara Negron
CFO: Barbara Negron
Estimated Sales: Below $5 000,000
Number Employees: 6

23471 H. Arnold Wood Turning
220 White Plains Road
Suite 245
Tarrytown, NY 10591
                          914-381-0801
    Fax: 914-381-0804 888-314-0088
staff@arnoldwood.com www.arnoldwood.com
Wooden items including mini crates and boxes,
broom and mop handles, turned handles, rolling
pins, flag poles, skewers and dowels; importer of
broom and mop handles and dowels
VP: Johnathan Arnold
VP Sales: Jonathan Arnold
Contact: Ann Arnold
ann@arnoldwood.com
Estimated Sales: $500,000-$1 Million
Number Employees: 5-9

23472 H. Gartenberg & Company
260 Blackthorn Drive
Buffalo Grove, IL 60089-6341
                          847-821-7590
                     Fax: 773-268-6402
Commercial drying, pulverizing and blending equip-
ment for dried egg processing; also, dehydration ser-
vices available
President: Melvin Gartenberg
Estimated Sales: $2.5-5 Million
Number Employees: 10
Square Footage: 60000
Type of Packaging: Bulk

23473 H. Reisman Corporation
377 Crane St
Orange, NJ 07050
                          973-677-9200
    Fax: 973-675-2766 800-631-3424
President: David Holmes
Sales/Marketing Manager: Dillon McLellan
Estimated Sales: $5-10 000,000
Number Employees: 20-49

23474 H. Yamamoto
8 Hickory Road
Port Washington, NY 11050-1504
                          718-821-7700
                     Fax: 718-366-1619
Zinc and aluminum die castings

23475 H.B. Wall & Sons
1560 W Skyline Ave
Ozark, MO 65721
                          417-581-1902
    Fax: 417-581-2010 800-373-1616
scott@welhenerawning.com www.hbwall.com
Commercial awnings
Owner: Greg Casey
Estimated Sales: Below $5,000,000
Number Employees: 10-19

23476 H.C. Foods Co. Ltd.
6414 Gayhart St
Commerce, CA 90040
                          323-722-8648
                sales@hcfoods.net
                www.hcfoods.net
Asian foodstuffs, including rice and tea
President/Owner: Ken Hsiao
Co-Owner: Anthony Sher
Number of Products: 3000
Square Footage: 70000

23477 H.F. Coors China Company
PO Box 59
New Albany, MS 38652-0059
                          310-338-8921
    Fax: 310-641-9429 800-782-6677
Manufacturer and exporter of cookware and table-
ware including high strength china, health care ser-
vice dishes, cups and mugs; also, custom decorated,
colored, decal and banding available
Controller: George Holzheimer
General VP: Robert Gasbarro
Ceramics Engineer: Leo Suzuki
Number Employees: 50-99
Square Footage: 400000
Parent Co: Standex International Corporation
Type of Packaging: Food Service, Private Label,
    Bulk
Brands:
    Alox
    Chefsware
    Roca Beige

23478 H.J. Jones & Sons
1155 Dundas Street
London, ON N5W 3A9
Canada
                          519-451-5250
    Fax: 519-451-0545 800-667-0476
                jonesy@farmline.com
Packaging materials including stretch pak and blister
cards and folding cartons
President: Michael Jones
Controller: Scott Switzer
Vice President: Doug Jones
Marketing Director: Les Meeneil
Purchasing Manager: Glen Davies
Number Employees: 50

23479 (HQ)H.L. Diehl Company
9 Babcock Hill Rd
South Windham, CT 6266
                          860-423-7741
    Fax: 860-423-2654 info@giant-vac.com
                www.giant-vac.com
Manufacturer and exporter of power cleaning equip-
ment including industrial vacuum cleaners
President: Anton Janiak
anton.janiak@giant-vac.com
VP: Gail Marie Diehl
Estimated Sales: $10-20 Million
Number Employees: 50-99

23480 H.P. Neun
75 N Main St
Fairport, NY 14450
                          585-388-1360
                Fax: 585-388-0184
Manufacturer and exporter of foam products and pa-
per boxes including corrugated, folding, candy,
set-up and fancy.
President: Mike Hanna
Estimated Sales: $20-50 Million
Number Employees: 100-249

23481 HAABTEC Inc
116 Bohannon Park
Shacklefords, VA 23156
                          804-785-4408
                Fax: 804-785-3208
Packaging equipment
Owner: Robert Haab
eric@haabtec.com
Estimated Sales: $5-10 000,000
Number Employees: 5-9

23482 HABCO Beverage Systems
501 Gordon Baker Road
Toronto, ON M2H 2S6
Canada
                          416-491-6008
    Fax: 416-491-6982 800-448-0244
                info@habcotech.com
Manufacturer and exporter of reach-in refrigerators,
freezers, and merchandisers.
Vice President/Marketing: Scott Brown
EVP/Sales: Jim Maynard
Number Employees: 100
Number of Brands: 2
Number of Products: 27
Brands:
    Cold Space
    Habco
    Signature Series

23483 HAMBA USA, Inc
2050 Trade Center Dr E
Saint Peters, MO 63376
                Fax: 636-281-1503
Filler for still beverages and almost any liquid or
pasty product
President: Gary Pyles
VP: Ken Hicks
Number Employees: 10-19

23484 (HQ)HBD Industries
PO Box 948
Salisbury, NC 28145
                          704-636-0121
    Fax: 704-633-3880 800-438-2312
info@hbdthermoid.com www.hbdthermoid.com
Industrial hoses for nondairy or alcoholic applica-
tions
President: Robert Lyons
Manager: David Dockins
Customer Service Manager: Pat Stubbs
Contact: John Backscheider
j.backscheider@hbdthermoid.com
General Manager: Lou Smith
Plant Manager: Dave Dockins
Estimated Sales: $20-50 Million
Number Employees: 100-249
Square Footage: 300000

23485 HBD Thermoid, Inc.
1301 W Sandusky Ave
Suite 110
Bellefontaine, OH 43311-1082
                          614-526-7000
    Fax: 614-526-7027 800-543-8070
info@hbdthermoid.com www.hbdthermoid.com
industrial rubber products since 1883.
President & CEO: Tom Pozda
President, Rubber Products Group: Chris Denick
Vice President & CFO: Eric Houser
Finance Director, Rubber Products Group: Kent
    Carleton
Director, Sales & Marketing: David Schempp
Dir. of Marketing, Rubber Products Group: Subin
    Sethuram
Vice President, Human Resources: Emily Ritchey
Estimated Sales: $1-5 Million
Number Employees: 250-499
Type of Packaging: Consumer, Private Label, Bulk

23486 HCI Corp
28 S 5th St
Geneva, IL 60134-2111
                          630-208-3100
    Fax: 630-208-3111 www.hci-search.com
Executive search and placement firm
President: Frank Cianchetti
frankc@hci-search.com
Estimated Sales: Less Than $500,000
Number Employees: 5-9

23487 HCR
Highway 87 West
Lewistown, MT 59457
                          406-538-7781
    Fax: 406-538-5506 800-326-7700
contact@hcrdoors.com www.hcr-inc.com
President: Peter Smith
Estimated Sales: $10-20 Million
Number Employees: 20-49
Parent Co: The Jamison Door Company

23488 HD Barcode
334 4th Ave
Indialantic, FL 32903-4214
                          321-952-2490
    Fax: 321-952-2475 sales@hdbarcode.com
                www.hdbarcode.com
Barcoding technologies
President: Gary Parish
mbrandon@completeinspectionsystems.com
Marketing: Angela Kirshon
Sales Exec: Michael Brandon
Estimated Sales: $1-3 Million
Number Employees: 10+
Brands:
    HD Barcode
    HD SecureID
    HD SmartCode

23489 HD Electric Co
1475 S Lakeside Dr
Park City, IL 60085-8314
847-473-4882
Fax: 847-473-4981 www.hdeinnovations.com
Manufacturer and exporter of electrical test equipment and portable/emergency lighting products
CEO: M Hoffman
mhoffman@hdelectriccompany.com
CEO: M Hoffman
Marketing Manager: Kimberly Higgins
Sales: Berstrom
Estimated Sales: $2.5-5 Million
Number Employees: 20-49
Brands:
 Digivolt
 Halo
 Mark
 Quickcheck
 Versa-Lite

23490 HDT Manufacturing
RR 9
Salem, OH 44460
330-337-8565
Fax: 330-337-8576 800-968-7438
Manufacturer and exporter of industrial trailers and trucks
President: Dave Lawless
VP: Shawn Lawless
Purchasing Manager: Don Souce

23491 HH Controls Company
6 Frost Street
Arilington, MA 02474-1012
781-646-2626
Heat storage/exchange devices for full size convection ovens
Estimated Sales: Less than $500,000
Number Employees: 1-4

23492 (HQ)HHP Inc
14 Buxton Industrial Dr
PO Box 489
Henniker, NH 3242
603-428-3298
Fax: 603-428-3448 hhp@conknet.com
www.hhp-inc.com
Manufacturer and exporter of wooden pallets; also, saw mill
President: Ross D Elia
hhp@conknet.com
Sales: Nancy Kocsis
Estimated Sales: $5-10 Million
Number Employees: 50-99

23493 HI-TECH Filter
80 Myrtle Street
North Quincy, MA 02171-1728
617-328-7756
Fax: 617-773-4192 800-448-3249
Air filters

23494 HID Global
6533 Flying Cloud Dr # 1000
Eden Prairie, MN 55344-3334
952-942-5258
Fax: 952-941-7836 sales@fargo.com
www.fargo.com
ID CARD printers
President: Gary Holland
Cmo: Alan Fontanella
afontanella@hidglobal.com
Quality Control: Jeff Sasse
VP: Thomas C Platner
CFO: Paul Stephenson
Sales Manager: Mark Anderson
Number Employees: 100-249

23495 HMC Corp
284 Maple St
Hopkinton, NH 03229-3339
603-746-4691
Fax: 603-746-4819 petertaylor@hmccorp.com
www.hmccorp.com
Manufacturer and exporter of saw mill conveyors
President: Peter Taylor
petertaylor@hmccorp.com
Estimated Sales: $20-50 Million
Number Employees: 50-99

23496 HMG Worldwide
8710 Ferris Avenue
Morton Grove, IL 60053-2841
847-965-7100
Fax: 947-965-7141
Custom and stock in-store marketing programs and displays
President: Stephen Dopp
Number Employees: 50
Parent Co: Howard Marlboro Group

23497 (HQ)HMG Worldwide In-Store Marketing
371 7th Ave
New York, NY 10001-3984
212-736-2300
Fax: 212-564-3395
Manufacturer and exporter of point-of-sale displays, integrated merchandising systems and interactive electronics; also, in-store related research, market planning, package design and space management services available
CEO Director: Andrew Wahl
CEO: Michael Lipman
Estimated Sales: $1-5 Million
Number Employees: 5-9
Square Footage: 1200000
Other Locations:
 HMG Worldwide In-Store Market
 Chicago IL

23498 HPI North America/Plastics
900 Apollo Rd
Eagan, MN 55121-2477
651-454-2520
Fax: 651-229-5470 800-752-7462
Disposable plastic dinnerware including plates, tumblers, trays, coffee cups, barware, etc
Estimated Sales: $1-5 Million
Number Employees: 250-499
Parent Co: Newell Companies

23499 HPI North America/Plastics
4501 W 47th St
PO Box 2830
Chicago, IL 60632
773-890-0523
800-327-3534
homzinfo@homzproducts.com
www.homzproducts.com
Disposable plastic tableware and drinkware
President: Frank Biller
VP Merchandising: Jim Schmidt
Contact: George Haminton
ghamilton@homz.biz
Number Employees: 500-999
Parent Co: Newell Companies
Brands:
 Beverageware
 Dinnerware
 Flip-N-Fresh
 Gourmet To Go
 Hi-Heat
 Legacy
 Microproof
 Microware
 Pop-Tops
 Prestige
 Scrollware
 Stow Away
 Swirl

23500 HSI
9977 North 90th Street
Suite 300
Scottsdale, AZ 85258
480-596-5456
Fax: 480-707-6223 info@hsi-solutions.com
Hospitality application software
Controller: Ron McNamee
General Manager And VP: Cyndi Shepley
Contact: Hany Ahmed
hany.ahmed@oracle.com
Director of Operations: Norbert Holzmann
Purchasing Director: Jim Nicholas
Number Employees: 100-249

23501 HSI Company
3002 Hempland Rd
Lancaster, PA 17601-1992
717-392-2987
Fax: 717-392-0723
Ice cream hardening machinery and warehouse storage systems

Estimated Sales: $10-25 000,000
Number Employees: 10-19

23502 HW Theller Engineering
1540 Crown Rd
Petaluma, CA 94954-1487
707-762-3820
Fax: 707-769-0874
Hot tack heatsealer tester, mini tensile tester, precision heatsealer tester
Contact: Theller Hutton
mcaprara@bottinifuel.com
Estimated Sales: $1-2.5 Million
Number Employees: 5-9

23503 Haake
33 N Century Rd
Paramus, NJ 07652-2810
201-262-3628
Fax: 201-265-1977 800-631-1369
Rheological instrumentation including viscometers, rheometers, thermal analyzers and circulators/water baths
Sales Director: Stephen Dieter
Estimated Sales: $1-5 Million
Number Employees: 1-4
Brands:
 Minilab Micro Compouuder
 Polylab
 Rheostress Rs1
 Rheostress Rs300
 Rheostress Rv1
 Rheostress Rs150
 Vt-550

23504 Haarslev Inc
9700 NW Conant Ave
Kansas City, MO 64153-1832
816-799-0808
Fax: 816-799-0812 info-usa@haarslev.com
www.haarslev.com
Supplier of processing equipment to meat and fish industries
President: Matthew Aguilera
maguilera@haarslev.com
CEO: Hans Nissen
VP Sales: Bob McKay
Number Employees: 20-49

23505 Haas Tailoring Company
3425 Sinclair Ln
Baltimore, MD 21213-2030
410-732-3804
Fax: 410-732-9310
Clothes and service uniforms
Comptroller: Mark McLean
President Of Sales: Matthew Haas
Estimated Sales: $5-10 Million
Number Employees: 100-249

23506 Haban Saw Company
9301 Watson Industrial Park
St.Louis, MO 63126
314-968-3991
Fax: 314-968-1240 info@habansaw.com
www.habansaw.com
Manufacturer and exporter of butcher handsaws and blades
Estimated Sales: $1-2.5 Million
Number Employees: 4

23507 Habasit America
805 Satellite Blvd NW
Suwanee, GA 30024-2879
678-288-3600
Fax: 800-422-2748 800-458-6431
info.america@us.habasit.com www.habasit.com
Manufacturer, importer and exporter of belting
Chairman: Thomas Habegger
CEO: Andrea Volpi
CFO: Beat Stebler
Vice Chairman: Alice Habegger
R&D: Bill Humsby
Marketing: Allison Cox
National Sales Manager: Bert Fliegi
Segment Manager: Mike Creo
Head of Product Division Fabrics: Maarten Aarts
Estimated Sales: $5-10 Million
Number Employees: 100-249
Parent Co: Habasit-AG
Type of Packaging: Bulk

23508 Habasit America PlasticDiv
825 Morgantown Rd
Reading, PA 19607-9533
610-373-1400
Fax: 610-373-7448   800-445-7898
Manufacturers of modular plastic conveyor belts,
chains and flat top chains
President: Christopher Nigon
VP Marketing/Sales: Joe Gianfalla
Marketing: Galina Rodzirosky
Estimated Sales: F
Number Employees: 100-249
Type of Packaging: Bulk

23509 Habasit Belting
3453 Pierce Drive NE
Chamblee, GA 30341-2496
770-458-6431
Fax: 770-454-6164   800-458-6431
hbi.habasit@us.habasit.com www.habasitusa.com
Industrial flat belting
President: Harry Cardillo
Estimated Sales: $10-25 Million
Number Employees: 115

23510 Habasit Canada Limited
2275 Bristol Circle
Oakville, ON L6H 6P8
Canada
905-827-4131
Fax: 905-825-2612
Canada.CustomerCare@habasit.com
www.habasit.ca
Food handling conveyor belts, modular belts and flat
power transmission belts.
President: John Visser
Plant Manager: Marty Ahearn
Number Employees: 30
Square Footage: 100000
Parent Co: Habasit AG

23511 Habco
1262 Windermere Way
Concord, CA 94521-3344
925-682-6203
Fax: 925-686-2036
Custom kitchen and galley equipment including
steam tables, cabinets, counters and foodstands
Owner: Heidi Linder
CEO: Sarah Trissel
Estimated Sales: 500000
Number Employees: 1-4
Number of Brands: 50
Number of Products: 100
Square Footage: 2400

23512 Hach Co
5600 Lindbergh Dr
Loveland, CO 80538-8842
970-669-3050
Fax: 970-669-2932   800-227-4224
httc@hach.com www.hach.com
Supplier of water and wastewater analysis equipment, including products for laboratory and microbiology testing, on-line analysis, and flow and
sampling measurement equipment
President: Kevin Klau
kklau@hach.com
CFO: Jary Dreher
Number Employees: 1000-4999

23513 Hach Co
5600 Lindbergh Dr
Loveland, CO 80538-8842
970-669-3050
Fax: 970-669-2932   800-227-4224
info@gliint.com www.hach.com
Wine industry flow and level gauges
President: Kevin Klau
kklau@hach.com
Number Employees: 1000-4999

23514 Hach Co.
PO Box 389
Loveland, CO 80539-0389
970-669-3050
Fax: 970-669-2932   800-227-4224
techhelp@hach.com
Manufacturer of oxygen sensors and water analysis
products for the beverage and water bottling industries. Also manufactures, designs, and distributes
test kits for testing the quality of water in food
industry applications.

Contact: Leon Moore
lmoore@hach.com

23515 Hackney Brothers
911 West 5th Street
Box 880
Washington, NC 27889
252-946-6521
Fax: 252-975-8340   800-763-0700
kgodley@vthackney.com
www.hackneybeverage.com
Manufacturer and exporter of refrigerated truck bod-
ies and trailers; also, refrigeration systems and ice
cream vending carts
President/Chief Executive Officer: Michael Tucker
Managing Director: Leandro Rodriguez
President, International Division: R. Hodges
Hackney
Contact: Neal Dixon
ndixon@vthackney.com
Estimated Sales: $50-100 Million
Number Employees: 100-249
Square Footage: 220000
Type of Packaging: Food Service
Brands:
   Hackney
   Hackney Champion
   Hackney Classic
   Short Stop
   Sno Van
   Starlite
   Vari-Temp

23516 Haden Signs of Texas
1102 30th St
Lubbock, TX 79411
806-744-4404
Fax: 806-744-1327 hadensigns@nts-online.net
Illuminated and nonilluminated signs including
neon, plexiglass, metal and vinyl; also, electronic
message centers; service and installation available
President: Curt Jones
CFO: Delwin Jones
Estimated Sales: Below $5 Million
Number Employees: 5-9

23517 Hager Containers Inc
1015 Hayden Dr
Carrollton, TX 75006-5741
972-416-7660
Fax: 972-417-8875 www.englanderdzp.com
Corrugated boxes, partitions, point of purchase dis-
plays and value added packaging
President: Carl Renner
VP/General Manager: Carl Renner
Sales/Marketing Manager: Steve Main
Estimated Sales: $10-20 Million
Number Employees: 50-99

23518 Hagerty Foods
987 N Enterprise St
Suite J
Orange, CA 92867
714-628-1230
Condiments
President: Francisco Esquivel
Estimated Sales: $220,000
Number Employees: 3
Square Footage: 20000
Type of Packaging: Consumer, Food Service, Pri-
vate Label
Brands:
   Hagerty Foods
   La Napa
   Winemaker's Choice

23519 Hahn Laboratories
1111 Flora St
Columbia, SC 29201-4569
803-799-1614
Fax: 803-256-1417
Consultant and chemical analyst providing agricul-
tural and food service testing
Owner: Frank Hahn
hahnlab@bellsouth.net
Lab Manager: Frank Hahn
Estimated Sales: $500,000-$1 Million
Number Employees: 1-4

23520 Haier American Trading
1356 Broadway
New York, NY 10018-7300
212-594-3330
Fax: 212-594-3434 www.haieramerica.com

Owner: Michael Jamal
Contact: Sal Alberta
salberta@haieramerica.com
Estimated Sales: $1-5 Million
Number Employees: 5-9

23521 Haifa Chemicals
6800 Jericho Tpke
Suite 216w
Syosset, NY 11791-4488
516-921-0044
Fax: 516-921-0228   800-404-2368
Sales Manager: JoAnn Sprung
Estimated Sales: $2.5-5 Million
Number Employees: 9

23522 Haines Packing Company
5 Mile Mud Bay Rd.
PO Box 290
Haines, AK 99827
907-766-2883
harry@hainespacking.com
www.hainespacking.com
Salmon, crab, halibut, and shrimp.
President/CEO: William Weisfield
CFO/Controller: Bob Hall
Vice President /Owner: Jan Supler
Year Founded: 1917
Estimated Sales: 100 Million
Number Employees: 40
Square Footage: 5963
Type of Packaging: Consumer, Food Service, Bulk
Other Locations:
   Ward Cove Packing Co.
   Seattle WA
Brands:
   Northern Pride
   Pirate

23523 Hairnet Corporation of America
151 W 26th St # 2
New York, NY 10001-6810
212-675-5840
Fax: 212-685-6225
Manufacturer and exporter of hairnets
President: E Gard
Secretary: M Moron
VP: T Persad
Estimated Sales: $2.5-5 Million
Number Employees: 1-4
Square Footage: 3500
Brands:
   Jac-O-Net
   Lady Swiss
   Mirage

23524 Hal Mather & Sons
11803 Il Route 120
Woodstock, IL 60098-1900
815-338-4000
Fax: 815-338-3003   800-338-4007
Tags, labels and tickets
President: Douglas Mather
CFO: Paul Weathersby
VP: Jim Mather
General Manager: David Diverde
Estimated Sales: $5-10 Million
Number Employees: 1-4

23525 Hal-One Plastics
801 E Highway 56
Olathe, KS 66061-4999
913-782-3535
Fax: 913-764-7369   800-626-5784
Manufacturer and wholesaler/distributor of reusable
plastic tableware and trays
CEO: Joyce Stawarz
1st Executive VP Sales: Galen Soule
Estimated Sales: $10-20 Million
Number Employees: 50-99
Square Footage: 60000

23526 Hall China Co
1 Anna St
East Liverpool, OH 43920-3675
330-385-2900
Fax: 330-385-6185   800-445-4255
custserv@hallchina.com www.hlcdinnerware.com
Chinaware
President: Chuck Henderson
chenderson@hallchina.com
National Sales Manager: Jim Clunk
National Distributor Account Manager: Joe Owen
National Chain Account Manager: Joe Brice

607

Estimated Sales: $20-50 Million
Number Employees: 100-249

23527 Hall Manufacturing Co
297 Margaret King Ave
Ringwood, NJ 07456-1423

973-962-6022

Fax: 973-962-7652 kerry@hallmanufacturing.com
Manufacturer and exporter of extruded plastic tracks for refrigeration industry; also, co-extrusions and tubing
President: Mike Goceljak
kerry@hallmanufacturing.com
Sales Manager: Kerry Goceljak
Estimated Sales: $2.5-5 Million
Number Employees: 10-19
Square Footage: 42000

23528 Hall Manufacturing Company
1321 Industrial Drive
Henderson, TX 75652-5019

903-657-4501
Fax: 903-657-4502

Tote bags
Contact: Steve Strain
steve@hallmfgco.com
Estimated Sales: $1-2.5 Million
Number Employees: 5-9

23529 Hall Safety Apparel
1020 W 1st St
Uhrichsville, OH 44683-2210

740-922-3671
Fax: 740-922-4880 800-232-3671
www.hallssafety.com

Protective Clothin Manufacturing; Supplier, Importer and Exporter
President: Delores Schneider
delores.schneider@pro-am.com
VP: Delores Schneider
Public Relations: Arnold Ziffel
Estimated Sales: $1-3 Million
Number Employees: 5-9
Square Footage: 42000
Parent Co: Schneider Enterprises USA
Type of Packaging: Food Service, Private Label, Bulk
Brands:
Polytex
Solvaseal

23530 Hall-Woolford Wood TankCo Inc
5500 N Water St
Philadelphia, PA 19120-3093

215-329-9022
Fax: 215-329-1177 jackhillman@woodtank.com
www.woodtank.com

Manufacturer and exporter of noncorrosive wood tanks, vats and tubs; wholesaler/distributor of flexible tank liners; industrial wood products; all products FDA approved. Also industrial wood products
President: Scott Hochhauser
woodtanks@aol.com
Sales Manager: Jack Hillman
Operations Manager: Robert Riepen
Estimated Sales: $1-3 Million
Number Employees: 5-9
Square Footage: 38000

23531 Hallams
5204 N 10th Ave
Ozark, MO 65721

417-581-3786
Fax: 417-581-3786 rzkozark@yahoo.com

Owner: Robert Zoppelt
Vice President: Katherine Zoppelt
Marketing Director: Robert Zoppelt
Estimated Sales: 300000
Number Employees: 1-4
Number of Brands: 1
Square Footage: 1800
Type of Packaging: Private Label

23532 Hallberg Manufacturing Corporation
PO Box 23985
Tampa, FL 33623-3985

800-633-7627
Fax: 800-253-7323

Manufacturer and exporter of industrial hand soap
President: Charles Hallberg
VP: Linda Werlein
Estimated Sales: $300,000-500,000
Square Footage: 20000

Brands:
Aloe Jell Water Less
Citra Jell
Pumice Jell
Surety Pwd Hand Soap

23533 Hallmark Equipment Inc
11040 Monterey Rd
Morgan Hill, CA 95037-9362

408-782-2600
Fax: 408-782-2605 hallmark@heiusa.com
www.heiusa.com

Supplier of used packaging and food processing equipment
Owner: Ron Wilson
hallmark@heiusa.com
Estimated Sales: $1-3 Million
Number Employees: 5-9

23534 Hallock Fabricating Corp
324 Doctors Path
Riverhead, NY 11901-1509

631-727-2441
Fax: 631-369-6021

Stainless steel and carbon steel exhaust hoods and countertops; also, custom metal fabrication
Owner: Cory Hallock
hallockfabricating@gmail.com
Estimated Sales: $1-5 Million
Number Employees: 1-4
Square Footage: 18400

23535 Halmark Systems Inc
354 Page St
Stoughton, MA 02072-1104

781-344-8616
Fax: 781-341-4505 800-225-5823
sales@halmarksystems.net
www.halmarksystems.net

Price marking equipment, custom-printed labels, and date marking equipment
President: Mark Crean
mark@halmarksystems.net
Operations: Lisa Allen
Estimated Sales: $5-10 Million
Number Employees: 10-19

23536 Halpak Plastics
10 Burt Dr
Deer Park, NY 11729-5702

631-242-1100
Fax: 631-242-6150 800-442-5725

Shrink bands and labels
Marketing Director: Sande Kaplan
Estimated Sales: $5-10 Million
Number Employees: 20-49

23537 Halton Company
101 Industrial Dr
Scottsville, KY 42164

270-237-5600
Fax: 270-237-5700 800-442-5866

Manufacturer and exporter of stainless steel hoods, filters and fans; also, fire suppression and ventilation systems
President: Rick Bagwell
R&D: Andre Livchak
Controller: Chris Gentry
National Sales Manager: Rich Catan
Contact: Ben Barshaw
b.barshaw@petersoncat.com
Plant Manager: Phil Meredith
Purchasing Manager: Eric Key
Estimated Sales: $10-20 Million
Number Employees: 1250
Square Footage: 100000
Parent Co: Halton O.Y.
Brands:
Capture Jet
Capture Rey

23538 Halton Packaging Systems
1045 S Service Road W
Oakville, ON L6L 6K3
Canada

905-847-9141
Fax: 905-847-9145

Manufacturer and exporter of pallet packaging machinery including stretch wrapping, conveyors, and pallet handling machinery
President: Peter Hughes
Estimated Sales: $2 Million
Number Employees: 10-19
Square Footage: 120000

Brands:
Halton

23539 Hamer Inc
14650 28th Ave N
Plymouth, MN 55447-4821

763-231-0100
Fax: 763-231-0101 800-927-4674
packaging@hamerinc.com www.hamerinc.com

Form-fill-seal systems, bag closers, bag fillers, balers
President: Dan Brown
dan@hamerinc.com
Sales Manager: Jerome Eller
Estimated Sales: $5-10 Million
Number Employees: 20-49

23540 Hamersmith, Inc.
3200 NW 125 Street
Miami, FL 33167

305-685-7451
Fax: 305-681-6093 office@hamersmith.com
www.hamersmith.com

Shortenings, margarines, oils, puff paste, pan releases and spices; packaging services
President: Calvin Theobald
Sales Director: Gerald Delmonico
Estimated Sales: $2.5-5 Million
Number Employees: 10
Number of Brands: 20
Number of Products: 9
Square Footage: 60000
Type of Packaging: Food Service, Private Label, Bulk

23541 Hamilton Awning Co
469 Market St
Beaver, PA 15009-2130

724-774-7644
Fax: 724-775-4221

Commercial awnings
Owner: Dave Mulcahy
Estimated Sales: $1-2,500,000
Number Employees: 5-9

23542 Hamilton Beach Brands
261 Yadkin Rd
Southern Pines, NC 28387-3415

910-692-7676
Fax: 910-692-7959 800-851-8900
www.hamiltonbeach.com

Foodservice equipment for restaurant, bars, nursing homes, healthcare facilities, hotels, and more
CEO: Michael J Morecroft
Sales Director: Steve Sarfaty
Public Relations: Kirby Kriz
Estimated Sales: $1-5 Million
Number Employees: 100-249
Parent Co: Nacco Industries
Type of Packaging: Food Service
Brands:
Hamilton Beach
Proctor Silex

23543 Hamilton Caster
1637 Dixie Hwy
Hamilton, OH 45011-4087

513-896-3541
Fax: 513-863-5508 888-699-7164
info@hamiltoncaster.com
www.hamiltoncaster.com

Manufacturer and exporter of nonpowered material handling carts, hand trucks, trailers, industrial casters and wheels
Vice President: Steve Lippert
steve.lippert@hamiltoncaster.com
Executive VP: Steven Lippert
Quality Control: Mary Latimer
Marketing Director: Mark Lippert
Sales Director: James Lippert
Estimated Sales: $10-20 Million
Number Employees: 50-99
Brands:
Ace-Tuf
Aqualite
Bondalast
Cush-N-Aire
Cush-N-Flex
Cush-N-Tuf
Duralast
Ebonite
Eleva-Truck
Flexonite
Freightainer

Hi-Lo
Instoematic
Job-Built
Leader
Lite-N-Tuff
Lube-Gard
Maxi-Duty
Nu-Flex
Nu-Last
Plastex
Poly-Tech
Roll Models
Roll-N-Stor
Stack-N-Roll
Steeltest
Super-Flex
Superlast
Ultra-Lite
Unilast
Versa-Tech
Vulcalite

23544 Hamilton Kettles
2898 Birch Drive
Weirton, WV 26062-5142

304-794-9400
Fax: 304-794-9430 800-535-1882
sales@hamiltonkettles.com
Manufacturer and exporter of sanitary stainless steel
and steam jacketed kettles, mix-cookers, pressure
cookers, agitators, vacuum kettles and custom de-
signed processing kettles and mixers
President: Charles Friend
Quality Control: Ed Henderson
VP/General Manager: George Gruner
R&D: Ed Henderson
Sales Director: Peggy Miller
Production Manager: Kenneth Henderson
Estimated Sales: $5-10 Million
Number Employees: 25
Square Footage: 128000
Parent Co: Allegheny Hancock Corporation

23545 Hamilton Manufacturing Corp
1026 Hamilton Dr
Holland, OH 43528-8210

419-867-4858
Fax: 419-867-4850 888-723-4858
www.hamiltonmfg.com
Currency validators and changemakers
President: Pam Anderson
panderson@horstengineering.com
Sales: Tim Morgan
Estimated Sales: $10-20 Million
Number Employees: 50-99

23546 Hamilton Soap & Oil Products
51 Bleeker Street
Paterson, NJ 7524

973-225-1031
Fax: 973-225-0268
Soap and detergent; also, private label and contract
packaging services available
Estimated Sales: $1-5 Million

23547 Hammar & Sons
71 Bridge St
PO Box 184
Pelham, NH 03076-3479

603-635-2292
Fax: 603-635-7904 800-527-7446
info@hammarandsons.com www.signsnownh.com
Signs including neon, wood, sandblasted window,
in-store and aisle markers; also, banners and posters;
installation and repair services available
Owner: Al Hammar
VP: Mike Hammar
Estimated Sales: Less Than $500,000
Number Employees: 5-9
Square Footage: 24000
Brands:
Hammar

23548 Hammer Packaging Inc
200 Lucius Gordon Dr
West Henrietta, NY 14586

585-424-3880
Fax: 585-424-3886 www.hammerpackaging.com
Labels for the food and beverage industry;
holticulture, wine and spirits and household products.

President & CEO: James Hammer
Chief Financial Officer: Mike Guche
Senior Vice President: Lou Iovoli
Vice President, Research & Innovation: Hart
Swisher
Vice President, Manufacturing: Jason Hammer
Vice President, Sales: Gregg Ockun
Estimated Sales: $100-500 Million
Number Employees: 100-249
Square Footage: 92000
Type of Packaging: Consumer, Food Service, Pri-
vate Label

23549 Hammerstahl Cutlery
3232 Woodsmill Drive
Melbourne, FL 32934

561-373-1925
Fax: 321-253-0737 felipe.florida@netzero.com
www.hammerstahl.com
Contact: Zuleik Urquiola
zuleik.urquiola@hammerstahl.com

23550 Hampden Papers Inc
100 Water St
Holyoke, MA 01040-6298

413-536-1000
Fax: 413-532-9161 www.hampdenpapers.com
Embossed and plain foil and glazed, laminated and
gift wrapping paper, packaging components, FDA
compliant
President/COO: Richard Wells
CEO: Robert Fowler
HR Executive: Marylou Mccormick
mmccormick@hampdenpapers.com
Vice President of Sales and Marketing: Bob Adams
VP Operations: Michael Archambeault
Estimated Sales: $33 Million
Number Employees: 100-249
Square Footage: 400000

23551 Hampton Roads Box Company
619 E Pinner St
Suffolk, VA 23434

757-934-2355
Fax: 757-539-4918
Manufacturer and exporter of pallets, wooden boxes
and shipping crates
President: Mark Sullivan
Estimated Sales: $1.2 Million
Number Employees: 5-9

23552 Hampton-Tilley Associates
740 Goddard Ave
Chesterfield, MO 63005

636-537-3353
Fax: 636-536-4114 813-418-3340
info@dcreng.com www.dcreng.com
Consultant specializing in automation and engineer-
ing services; designer of software for recipes, cook-
ing, processing, packaging and quality
control/validation
Manager: Pat Finefield
VP: C Tilley
Estimated Sales: $5-10 Million
Number Employees: 10-19
Square Footage: 42000

23553 Hamrick Manufacturing &Svc
1436 Martin Rd
PO Box 5
Mogadore, OH 44260-1591

330-628-4877
Fax: 330-628-2180 800-321-9590
marketing@hamrickmfg.com
www.hamrickmfg.com
Manufacturer and exporter of packaging machinery
including case packers, case sealers, bottled water
case packers, lock tab pullers/breakers, liter tray
packers, four flap openers, uncasers, etc.; custom
built machinery available
President: Phil Hamrick
phamrick@hamrickmfg.com
CEO: Luther Hamrick
VP Sales: Tom Hamrick
VP of Production: Phil Hamrick
Purchasing Director: Kurt Kothmayer
Estimated Sales: $5-10 Million
Number Employees: 20-49
Number of Products: 18
Square Footage: 56000
Brands:
Hms

23554 Hanco Manufacturing Company
1301 Heistan Place
Memphis, TN 38104

901-725-7364
Fax: 901-726-5899 800-530-7364
Disinfectants, insecticides, cleaners and degreasers
VP: Scott Hanover
Estimated Sales: $1-2.5 Million
Number Employees: 19
Square Footage: 60000
Brands:
Hanco

23555 Hand Made Lollies
465 S Orlando Avenue
Suite 205
Maitland, FL 32751

877-784-2724
Fax: 877-249-6419 info@handmadelollies.com
www.handmadelollies.com
Handmade and personalized lollipops
President: Timothy Lang

23556 Handgards Inc
901 Hawkins Blvd
El Paso, TX 79915-1202

915-779-6606
Fax: 915-779-1312 800-351-8161
sales@handgards.com www.handgards.com
Manufacturer and exporter of disposable plastic
gloves, aprons and bags; importer of latex and PVC
gloves
CEO: Bob Mclellan
bmclellan@handgards.com
CEO: Bob McLellan
Estimated Sales: $500,000-$1,000,000
Number Employees: 250-499
Square Footage: 280000
Type of Packaging: Food Service, Private Label
Brands:
Handgards
Neatgards
Tuffgards
Valugards
Zipgards

23557 Handi-Foil Corp
135 E Hintz Rd
Wheeling, IL 60090-6059

847-520-8347
Fax: 847-229-8000 www.handi-foil.com
Foil wrap
CEO: Norton Sarnoff
nsarnoff@handi-foil.com
CEO: Norton Sarnoff
Estimated Sales: $1-3 Million
Number Employees: 20-49

23558 Handicap Sign Inc
1142 Wealthy St SE
Grand Rapids, MI 49506-1599

616-454-9416
Fax: 616-454-4999 800-690-4888
handicapsign@gmail.com www.hsisign.com
Custom screen printing, vinyl graphics and hand let-
tering for decals, signs, posters, banners and P.O.P
displays
President: Charles Tasma
handicapsign@gmail.com
VP: Kim Tasma
Estimated Sales: $500,000-$1 Million
Number Employees: 5-9
Square Footage: 15000

23559 Handling Specialty
PO Box 279
Niagara Falls, NY 14304-0279

716-694-6333
Fax: 716-694-6903 800-559-8366
info@handling.com www.handling.com
Manufacturer and exporter of material handling
equipment including lifting systems for very hot or
cold environments, tilters, rotators, fork truck ser-
vice lifts and robotic indexing tables
President: Thomas Beach
Marketing Director: Lydia Macugajlo
Direct Sales: Mike Roper
Contact: Linda Videto
lvideto@handling.com
Estimated Sales: C
Number Employees: 10-19
Parent Co: Handling Specialty
Brands:
Forklevator

23560 Handtmann
28690 N.
Ballard Drive
Lake Forest, IL 60045
847-808-1100
Fax: 847-808-1106 800-477-3585
www.handtmann.com
Vacuum fillers with in-line grinders, and high speed clipping machines
President: Steve Tennis
Sales Director: Robert Kors
Estimated Sales: $5-10 000,000
Number Employees: 20-49

23561 Handtmann Inc
28690 N Ballard Dr
Lake Forest, IL 60045-4500
847-808-1100
Fax: 847-808-1106 800-477-3585
www.handtmann.us
Filling, portioning and linking machines for the sausage and meat industries. Also manufacture deli product systems and grinding machines.
President: Tom Kittle
tom.kittle@handtmann.us
Number Employees: 20-49

23562 Handy Manufacturing Co Inc
337 Sherman Ave
Newark, NJ 07114-1507
973-242-1600
Fax: 973-733-2185 800-631-4280
www.handystorefixtures.com
Manufacturer and exporter of store and wall fixtures, show cases, gondolas and shelving units
President: Paul Kurland
richardkurland@handystorefixtures.com
CFO: Scott McClymont
Executive VP: Richard Kurland
VP Sales: Walter Pincus
Number Employees: 50-99
Square Footage: 1200000
Type of Packaging: Food Service

23563 Handy Roll Company
1236 Anna Lane
San Marcos, CA 92069-2160
760-471-6214
Carton cutters
Co-Owner: Glenn Spear
Co-Owner: Margaret Spear
Number Employees: 1
Brands:
Handy Blade

23564 Handy Wacks Corp
100 E Averill St
P.O. Box 129
Sparta, MI 49345
800-445-4434
customerserv@handywacks.com
www.handywacks.com
Waxed packaging products including sandwich and interfolded high density polyethylene wrap, baking cups, hot dog trays, and steak, freezer, locker, delicatessen and bakery tissue and paper.
CIS Director: Bruce Stevens
Sales Director: George Siwik
Purchasing Manager: Mike Moberly
Year Founded: 1929
Estimated Sales: $20-25 Million
Number Employees: 50+
Number of Brands: 12
Number of Products: 225
Square Footage: 90000
Type of Packaging: Food Service
Brands:
Handy Wacks

23565 Hanel Storage Systems
121 Industry Dr
Pittsburgh, PA 15275-1015
412-787-3444
Fax: 412-787-3744 info@hanel.us
www.hanel.us
Manufacturer, importer and exporter of vertical storage systems
President: Joachim Hanel
CEO: Brian Cohen
bcohen@hanel.us
Vice President: Brian Cohen
VP: Brian Cohen
Sales Director: Michael Fanning

Estimated Sales: $5-10 Million
Number Employees: 20-49
Parent Co: Hanel GmbH
Brands:
Hanel Lean-Lift
Hanel Vertical Carousels

23566 Hangzhou Sanhe USA Inc.
20536 Carrey Rd
Walnut, CA 91789
909-869-6016
Fax: 909-869-6015 www.sanheinc.com
Food ingredients and additives.
President: Aili Chen
Contact: Yun Qian
yunqian@sanheinc.com
Estimated Sales: $1 Million
Type of Packaging: Bulk

23567 Hank Rivera Associates
13600 W Warren Ave
Dearborn, MI 48126-1421
313-581-8300
Manufacturer and exporter of uniforms, aprons and pizza delivery equipment including heat retention/insulated food bags, nylon pan pullers, beverage carriers and pizza lid supports
President: Dante Rivera
Secretary/Treasurer: Hank Rivera
Number Employees: 10-19
Square Footage: 25000
Brands:
Hank's

23568 Hankin Specialty Elevators Inc
3237 Fitzgerald Rd
Rancho Cordova, CA 95742-6813
916-381-2400
Fax: 916-381-2481 800-831-8395
info@hankinspecialty.com
www.hankinspecialty.com
Wine industry pallet postitioners
President and QC: Neil Hankin
neilh@hankinspecialty.com
CFO: Mike Seebode
Estimated Sales: $5-10 Million
Number Employees: 10-19

23569 Hankison International
1000 Philadelphia St
Canonsburg, PA 15317-1700
724-746-1100
Fax: 724-745-6040 www.spx-hankison.de
Manufacturer and exporter of compressed air dryers, filters, condensate drains and air purifiers
Manager: Neal Horrigan
Marketing: Bill Kennedy
Sales: Rod Smith
Manager: Ken Gorman
Estimated Sales: $5-10 Million
Number Employees: 20-49
Square Footage: 808000
Parent Co: Hansen

23570 Hanley Sign Company
26 Sicker Rd
Latham, NY 12110
518-783-6183
Fax: 518-783-0128 ltymchyn@hanleysign.com
Signs and advertising displays
President: Lisa Tymchyn
Quality Control: Lisa Tymchyn
Contact: Kerry Blinn
kblinn@hanleysign.com
Estimated Sales: Below $5 Million
Number Employees: 20-49
Square Footage: 16000

23571 Hanna Instruments
584 Park E Dr
Woonsocket, RI 02895
401-765-7500
Fax: 401-765-7575 800-426-6287
info@hannainst.com
Manufacturer and exporter of electro-analytical instruments including sodium chloride and chlorine analyzers, conductivity, pH and relative humidity meters, temperature recorders and thermo hygrometers.
President: Martino Nardo
Vice President: Pamela Nardo
General Manager: Harry Lau
Year Founded: 1978
Estimated Sales: $100 Million

Number Employees: 20-49
Number of Products: 3000
Square Footage: 26000
Type of Packaging: Consumer, Food Service, Bulk
Brands:
Agricare
Bravo
Champ
Checker
Checktemp
Conmet
Elth
Food Care
Hydrocheck
Key
Micro Phep
Phandy
Phep
Piccolo
Temp Care
Temp Check

23572 Hannan Products
220 N Smith Ave
Corona, CA 92880-1740
951-735-1587
Fax: 951-735-0827 800-954-4266
sales@hannanpak.com
Manufacturer and exporter of machinery and materials for skin and blister packaging; also, for die cutting
President: Damon Lewis
damon@hannanpak.com
CFO and QC and R&D: Alfred Ramos
Sales Manager: Lawrence Jenkins
Estimated Sales: $5-10 Million
Number Employees: 20-49

23573 Hannay Reels
553 State Route 143
Westerlo, NY 12193-2691
518-797-3791
Fax: 518-797-3259 877-467-3357
reels@hannay.com
Metal reels for hose & cable, water, washdown, fluid handling
President: Eric Hannay
COO: Elaine Gruener
Quality Control: Ken Fritz
Marketing Manager: Jennifer Wing
Sales Manager: Mark Saker
Public Relations: Maureen Bagshaw
President/CEO: Eric Hannay
Production: Mike Ferguson
Facilities Manager: Walt Scram
Materials Manager: Dick Storm
Estimated Sales: $25-50 Million
Number Employees: 100-249
Square Footage: 118612

23574 Hannic Freight Forwarders Inc
16214 S Lincoln Hwy
PO Box 445
Plainfield, IL 60586-5146
815-436-4521
Fax: 815-436-1734 800-786-4521
www.hannic.net
Owner: Hans Maass
hans@hffi.net
Vice President: Hans Maass
Estimated Sales: $.5-1 million
Number Employees: 5-9

23575 Hano Business Forms
PO Box 275
Wilbraham, MA 01095-0275
413-781-7800
Fax: 413-781-7808 www.hano.com
Printed documents
CEO and President: John Sindstorm
VP: Jim Michill
Number Employees: 50

23576 Hansaloy Corp
820 W 35th St
Davenport, IA 52806-5800
563-386-1131
Fax: 563-386-7707 800-553-4992
sales@hansaloy.com www.hansaloy.com
Manufacturer and exporter of blades including slicing/dicing, band and reciprocating with scalloped and straight edges for slicing bread and boneless meat

Owner: Diane Artioli
CEO: Howard H Cherry Iii
Quality Control: Stephen Wright
VP Sales/Marketing: K Brenner
VP Sales: Allen Wright
d.artioli@hansaloy.com
Estimated Sales: $5-10 Million
Number Employees: 50-99
Square Footage: 80000

23577 Hansen Technologies Corporation

400 Quadrangle Dr Ste F
Bolingbrook, IL 60440

630-325-1565
Fax: 630-325-1572 800-426-7368
info@hantech.com www.hantech.com
Hansen Technologies Corporation offers an extensive line of components for industrial refrigeration systems including sealed motor valves, control valves, shut-off valves, pressure-relief valves, refrigerant pumps, air purgers, defrostcontrols, and liquid level controls
President: Jeffrey Nank
CEO: Jeff Markham
CFO: Mark Sebben
R&D: John Yencho
Marketing Manager: Denise Ernst
Sales: Harold Streicher
Contact: Phillip Beste
pbeste@hantech.com
Operations: Jim Flurry
Purchasing Director: Joe Reicher
Estimated Sales: $20-50 Million
Number Employees: 100-249
Number of Brands: 3
Number of Products: 300

23578 Hansen's Laboratory

N67w33880 Loghouse Ct
Oconomowoc, WI 53066-1936

262-966-4952
Fax: 414-607-5959
Culture research
Owner: Marsha Hanson
Estimated Sales: $1-3 000,000
Number Employees: 5-9

23579 Hanset Stainless Inc

1729 NE Argyle St
Portland, OR 97211-1801

503-283-8822
Fax: 503-283-8875 800-360-7030
info@hansetstainless.com
www.hansetstainless.com
Custom stainless steel food service equipment
President: Jim Hanset
jim@hansetstainless.com
Estimated Sales: $20-50 Million
Number Employees: 50-99
Square Footage: 25000

23580 Hanson Box & Lumber Company

12 New Salem Street
Wakefield, MA 01880-1979

617-245-0358
Fax: 781-245-8043
Plywood and pine boxes, shipping containers, pallets and skids
President: Kirk Hanson

23581 Hanson Brass Rewd Co

7530 San Fernando Rd
Sun Valley, CA 91352-4344

818-767-3501
Fax: 818-767-7891 888-841-3773
info@hansonbrass.com www.hansonhl.com
Sneeze guards, copper carts and brass, chrome and copper lamps; exporter of carving units, food displays; wholesaler/distributor of restaurant equipment and supplies; serving the food service market, alto shaam test kitchen
President: Tom Hanson
VP: Jim Hanson
CFO: Tom Hanson
info@hansonbrass.com
Vice President: Robert Hanson
Plant Manager: Mark Denny
Estimated Sales: $6-7 Million
Number Employees: 10-19
Number of Brands: 2
Square Footage: 32000
Brands:
  Hanson Brass

23582 Hanson Brass Rewd Co

7530 San Fernando Rd
Sun Valley, CA 91352-4344

818-767-3501
Fax: 818-767-7891 888-841-3773
info@hansonbrass.com www.hansonhl.com
President: Tom Hanson Jr
CEO: Jim Hanson
CFO: Tom Hanson Sr
VP: Robert Hanson
Plant Manager: Mark Denny
Number Employees: 10-19

23583 Hanson Lab Furniture Inc

814 Mitchell Rd
Newbury Park, CA 91320-2215

805-498-3121
Fax: 805-498-1855 info@hansonlab.com
www.hansonlab.com
Manufacturer and exporter of laboratory furniture, fume hoods and accessories; also, installation and lab planning services available
Owner: Joe Matta
joe@hansonlab.com
VP: Mike Hanson
Estimated Sales: $5-10 Million
Number Employees: 5-9
Parent Co: Norlab

23584 (HQ)Hantover Inc

10301 Hickman Mills Dr # 200
Kansas City, MO 64137-1600

816-761-7800
Fax: 816-761-0044 800-821-7849
contactus@hantover.com
Manufacturer and exporter of vacuum packaging machinery and stainless steel cutlery and utensils
Chairman: Bernard Huff
General Manager: David Philgreen
Estimated Sales: $20-50 Million
Number Employees: 100-249
Type of Packaging: Food Service
Other Locations:
  Hantover
  Kansas City MO

23585 Hapco Inc

390 Portage Blvd
Kent, OH 44240-7283

330-678-9353
Fax: 330-677-8282 800-345-9353
www.hapcoinc.com
Hot air tools, sealing equipment
Owner: Charles George
mike@hapcoinc.com
VP: Mike Harrison
Estimated Sales: $10-20 Million
Number Employees: 20-49

23586 Hapco Inc

390 Portage Blvd
Kent, OH 44240-7283

330-678-9353
Fax: 330-677-8282 800-345-9553
www.hapcoinc.com
Owner: Charles George
mike@hapcoinc.com
Estimated Sales: $10-20 Million
Number Employees: 20-49

23587 Hapman Conveyors

6002 E N Ave
Kalamazoo, MI 49048-9775

269-343-1675
Fax: 269-349-2477 800-968-7722
info@hapman.com www.hapman.com
Manufacturer and exporter of flexible screw, pneumatic and tubular drag conveyors, bulk bag unloaders, manual bag dump stations, batch weigh equipment and silo dischargers
President: Edward Thompson
info@hapman.com
Quality Control: Randy McBroom
Marketing: Greg Nowak
Estimated Sales: $20-50 Million
Number Employees: 50-99
Square Footage: 100000
Parent Co: Prab
Brands:
  Helix
  Mini-Vac

23588 Happy Chef Inc

22 Park Pl # 2
Suite 2
Butler, NJ 07405-1377

973-492-2525
Fax: 973-492-0303 800-347-0288
info@happychefuniforms.com
www.happychefuniforms.com
Manufacturer and wholesaler/distributor of uniforms and table linens for kitchen and waiter/waitress personnel. Serving the food service market
Vice President: Howard Curtin
info@happychefuniforms.com
VP: Howard Curtin
VP, Sales/Marketing: Howard Curtin
Estimated Sales: $10 Million
Number Employees: 20-49
Square Footage: 30000
Type of Packaging: Private Label

23589 Harbor Group Inc

1520 N Main Ave
Sioux Center, IA 51250-2111

712-722-1662
Fax: 712-722-1667 bdev@interstates.com
www.interstates.com
Electrical engineering, electrical construction and automation
Chairman of the Board: Larry Den Herder
CEO: Scott Peterson
scott.peterson@harborcg.com
CFO: Scott Peterson
Estimated Sales: $40-60 Million
Number Employees: 100-249
Number of Brands: 4

23590 Harbor Pallet Company

301 W Imperial Hwy
Anaheim, CA 90631

714-871-0932
Fax: 714-871-3483 pomonabox@att.net
www.harborpallet.com
Wooden and plastic pallets and skids and wooden boxes and containers
President: Ross Gilroy
Estimated Sales: $2.5-5 Million
Number Employees: 5-9

23591 Harborlite Corporation

PO Box 519
Lompoc, CA 93438-0519

800-342-8667
Fax: 805-735-5699 info@worldminerals.com
www.worldminerals.com
Manufacturer and exporter of perlite filter aids and functional fillers
Contact: Mike Mcdonald
mike.mcdonald@worldminerals.com
Type of Packaging: Food Service, Bulk

23592 Harborlite Corporation

P.O.Box 462908
Escondido, CA 92046-2908

760-745-5900
Fax: 760-745-6349
lemmonse@worldminerals.com
www.worldminerals.com
Wine industry filtration and wastewater systems
Manager: Darin Jackman
d.jackman@imerys.com
Estimated Sales: $2.5-5 Million
Number Employees: 10-19

23593 Harbour House Bar Crafting

737 Canal Street
Bldg 16
Stamford, CT 06902-5930

203-348-6906
Fax: 203-348-6190 800-755-1227
bigbars@snet.net www.harbourhouse.com
Manufacturer solid wooden bars, tables, booths and carts
President: Steven Kline
VP: Jeff Watkins
Estimated Sales: $1-2.5 Million
Number Employees: 10
Type of Packaging: Food Service

23594 Harbour House Furniture
37 Canal Street
Bldg 16
Stamford, CT 06902-5930
203-348-6906
Fax: 203-348-6190 bigbars@snet.net
www.harbourhouse.com
President: Steven Kline

23595 Harbro Packaging Co
2635 N Kildare Ave
Chicago, IL 60639-2051
773-489-6520
Fax: 773-489-6584 877-428-5812
www.purepoolcleaning.com
Distributor of tabletop and stand-alone vacuum machines
President: Hershcel Brohman
rand_thomas@harbro.net
CFO: Susan Thomas
Quality Control: Rand Thomas
Estimated Sales: $5-10 Million
Number Employees: 10-19

23596 Harco Enterprises
675 the Parkway
Peterborough, ON K9J 7K2
Canada
705-743-5361
Fax: 705-743-4312 800-361-5361
sales@harco.on.ca
Manufacturer, wholesaler/distributor and exporter of promotional items including hot stamping, pad printing, multi-color imprints, glow-in-the-dark custom products, coasters, swizzle sticks, toys, flyers, key tags, spoons, etc; servingthe food service market. Supplier of spare parts to the dairy and food industries
President: Ray Harris
VP Finance: Kathy Perry
VP: Terry Harris
VP Marketing: Kathy Perry
VP Administration: Joan Harris
Number Employees: 10
Square Footage: 64000
Type of Packaging: Food Service

23597 Harcros Chemicals Inc
5200 Speaker Rd
Kansas City, KS 66106-1048
913-321-3131
Fax: 913-621-7718 KansasCityCS@harcros.com
www.harcroschem.com
Surface active agents and medicinal chemicals
President, Chief Executive Officer: Kevin Mirner
kmirner@harcros.com
Vice President: Dan Larsen
Director of Operations: Dan Johnson
Number Employees: 250-499

23598 Hardi-Tainer
P.O.Box 201
South Deerfield, MA 01373-0201
413-665-2163
Fax: 413-665-4801 800-882-9878
hardiggacct@hardigg.com www.hardigg.com
Returnable and reusable intermediate bulk containers with wide mouth openings
President, Chief Executive Officer: Lyndon Faulkner
CEO: James S Hardigg
Vice President of Research: Kevin Deighton
Vice President of Sales: Mark Rolfes
Estimated Sales: $20-50 Million
Number Employees: 250-499
Square Footage: 100000
Parent Co: Hardigg Industries
Brands:
Hardi-Tainer

23599 Hardin Signs Inc
3663 N Meadowbrook Rd
Peoria, IL 61604-1214
309-688-4111
Fax: 309-688-3217
Signs including neon plastic; also, lettering, installation and maintenance services available
President: William Hardin
sales@hardinsigns.com
CFO: Marian Hardin
VP: James Hardin
Estimated Sales: $2.2 Million
Number Employees: 10-19
Square Footage: 48000

Type of Packaging: Bulk

23600 Hardt Equipment Manufacturing
1756 50th Avenue
Lachine, QC H8T 2V5
Canada
888-848-4408
www.hardt.ca
Designer and manufacturer of food service equipment including commercial rotisseries, heated merchandisers, counter-top healted display cases and a cleaning apparatus for cookin utensils and accessories.
Purchasing Manager: Tony Morrone
Number Employees: 75
Square Footage: 112000
Brands:
Inferno
Snack Zone
The Cleaning Solution
Zone

23601 Hardware Components Inc
1021 Park Ave
New Matamoras, OH 45767
740-865-2424
Fax: 740-865-2534 hci@hardwarecomponents.com
www.hardwarecomponents.com
Manufacturer and importer of ferrous and nonferrous castings, stampings, forgings, furniture and cabinets
Vice President: Dan Gautschi
hci@hardwarecomponents.com
VP/General Manager: Danny Gautschi
VP Sales: Chris Dickinson
Estimated Sales: $5-10,000,000
Number Employees: 1-4

23602 Hardwood Products Co LP
31 School St
Guilford, ME 04443-6388
207-876-3311
Fax: 207-876-3130 800-289-3340
info@hwppuritan.com www.hwppuritan.com
Manufacturer and exporter of wooden ice cream sticks and spoons, stir sticks and skewers; also, industrial cleaning swabs, cocktail forks, cocktail spears, corn dog sticks, flag sticks, fan paddles, dawels
Chief Finacial Officer: Scott Welman
Quality Control: William Young
Sales Manager: Ann Erickson
Sales Exec: Timothy Templet
CSR Rep: Jessica Brown
ttemplet@hwppuritan.com
VP of Operations: James Cartwright
Plant Manager: Bruce Jones
Purchasing Agent: Joseph Cartwright
Estimated Sales: $20-50 Million
Number Employees: 250-499
Square Footage: 600000
Type of Packaging: Consumer, Food Service, Private Label, Bulk
Brands:
Gold Bond
Puritan
Purswab
Trophy

23603 Hardy Diagnostics
1430 W Mccoy Ln
Santa Maria, CA 93455-1005
805-346-2766
Fax: 805-346-2760 800-266-2222
techservice@hardydiagnostics.com
www.hardydiagnostics.com
Owner: Jay Hardy
burksr@hardydiagnostics.com
CFO: Nathaniel Gragssle
Estimated Sales: $10-20 000,000
Number Employees: 100-249

23604 Hardy Process SolutionsInc
9440 Carroll Park Dr # 150
San Diego, CA 92121-5201
858-278-2900
Fax: 858-278-6700 800-821-5831
hardyinfo@hardyinst.com
www.hardysolutions.com

Designer and manufacturer of process weighin, tension control and vibration monitoring equipment serving the food, chemical, petrochemical, pharamatical, feed and grain, mining and metal, pulp and paper, oil and gas, and generalautomation industries.
Manager: Jim Ephraim
Sales: Jerry Samaniego
Manager: Steven Barron
sbarron@hardyinst.com
Number Employees: 50-99

23605 Hardy Systems Corporation
610 Anthony Trl
Northbrook, IL 60062
847-272-4400
Fax: 847-272-4471 800-927-3956
Manufacturer and exporter of bins, batching scales, conveying systems and flow control panels
President: Richard Walter
Sales Manager: J Soling
Head Engineer: D Acker
Estimated Sales: Below $5,000,000
Number Employees: 5-9

23606 Hardy-Graham
P.O.Box 487
Ambler, PA 19002
215-699-6111
Fax: 215-699-6106 800-445-4271
www.hardy-builtfastener.com
Knock-down, returnable, reusable crates and containers made of wood, metal, plastic
President: A Stuart Graham
CFO: A Stuart Graham
Contact: Diane Alexander
adiane@hardy-builtfastener.com
Estimated Sales: Below $5 Million
Number Employees: 5-9

23607 Harford Duracool LLC
P.O.Box 1026
Aberdeen, MD 21001-6026
410-272-9999
Fax: 410-272-8508
Walk-in coolers
President: Arley Mead
Operations: Charles Mike
Sales Manager: Scott Smith
Number Employees: 50-99
Parent Co: IPC Industries
Brands:
Harford Duracool

23608 Harford Systems Inc
2225 Pulaski Hwy
Havre De Grace, MD 21078-2145
410-272-3400
Fax: 410-273-7892 800-638-7620
pwatson@harfordsystems.com
www.harfordsystems.com
Manufacturer and exporter of alarm systems and refrigeration equipment and machinery
President: Ralph Ahrens
VP: George Gabriel
HR Manager: Kate Pelonquin
Estimated Sales: $20-50 Million
Number Employees: 100-249
Parent Co: Bio Medic Corporation
Brands:
Duracool

23609 Harlan Laws Corp
304 Muldee St
Durham, NC 27703-2332
919-596-2124
Fax: 919-596-0421 800-596-7602
sales@harlanlaws.com www.harlanlaws.com
Signs including electric and neon
Owner: Kenny Lester
klester@harlanlaws.com
VP: Gary Hester
Estimated Sales: $10-20 Million
Number Employees: 100-249
Square Footage: 100000

23610 Harland America
1803 Underwood Blvd
Delran, NJ 08075
856-764-9622
Fax: 856-764-9615 us.enquiries@harland-hms.com
Manager: John Lyall
Contact: Mike Habeck
mikehabeck@harland-hms.com

Estimated Sales: $2.5-5 Million
Number Employees: 10-19

23611 Harland Simon Control Systems USA

Windsor Office Plaza
210 West 22nd Street, Suite 138
Oakbrook, IL 60523

630-572-7650
Fax: 630-572-7653 sales@harlandsimon.com
Manufacturer and exporter of control systems including drive systems
Systems Sales Manager: Robert Picknell
National Sales Support Manager: Scott Mincher
Number Employees: 70
Square Footage: 164000
Parent Co: Monotype Systems
Brands:
  Micropower
  Micropower Ac
  Symtec

23612 Harmar

2075 47th St
Sarasota, FL 34234-3109

941-351-2776
Fax: 941-351-5801 800-833-0478
garys@harmar.com www.harmar.com
Custom wire displays and wire forms; also, bending spot welding and coated parts available
President: Robert Williams
Founder, President, Chief Executive Offi: Chad Williams
Vice President of Sales: Paul Johnson
Vice President of Operations: Todd Walters
Estimated Sales: $10-20 Million
Number Employees: 5-9
Square Footage: 90000

23613 Harmony Enterprises

704 Main Ave N
Harmony, MN 55939-8839

507-886-6666
Fax: 507-886-6706 800-658-2320
info@harmony1.com www.harmony1.com
Manufacturer and exporter of waste handling and recycling equipment including indoor and outdoor compactors, vertical balers, beverage extraction equipment and full product destruction equipment. Some of their brands include HarmonyPower Packer, Harmony Insite Wireless Monitoring, Harmony SunPak Solar Options, Harmony Equipment Rental, Harmony ExtractPack and more.
President: Steve Cremer
Office Manager & Finance: Lana Soppa
New Business Development Manager: Lane Powell
Vice President, Sales & Marketing: Brent Christiansen
National Sales Manager: Nick Roberts
Vice President, Operations: Ramon Hernandez
Purchasing: Sid Polley
Estimated Sales: $24 Million
Number Employees: 75
Other Locations:
  Harmony MN
Brands:
  Gpi

23614 Harold F Haines Manufacturing Inc

243 Main St
Presque Isle, ME 04769-2899

207-762-1411
Fax: 207-762-1412
Potato handling equipment, sizers and washers
Owner: Fred Haines
VP: Harold Haines
Estimated Sales: $2.5-5 Million
Number Employees: 10-19

23615 Harold Import Co Inc

747 Vassar Ave
Lakewood, NJ 08701-6908

732-367-2800
Fax: 732-364-3253 800-526-2163
info@haroldskitchen.com www.hickitchen.com
Paper, brewers (tea), filters (cloth, cotton), grinders.
President: Mildred Laub Polansky
mpolansky@haroldimport.com
Estimated Sales: $50-100 Million
Number Employees: 100-249

23616 Harold Leonard Southwest Corporation

1812 Brittmoore Road
Suite 230
Houston, TX 77043-2216

713-467-8105
Fax: 713-467-0072 800-245-8105
Manufacturer and wholesaler/distrbutor of smallwares
President: Carl Marcus
CEO: Herb Kelleher
Marketing Director: Roger Randall
Sales Representative: Jerry Williams
Estimated Sales: $1-2.5 Million
Number Employees: 6
Square Footage: 100000
Parent Co: Harold Leonard & Company
Brands:
  Eagleware

23617 Harold M. Lincoln Company

2130 Madison Ave
Suite 101
Toledo, OH 43604-5135

419-255-1200
Broker of confectionery and dairy/deli products, frozen foods, general merchandise, groceries, etc. Marketing, sales planning and promotional tracking services available
President: David Lincoln
Chairman: Harold Lincoln
VP/Account Manager: John Lincoln
Estimated Sales: $20-50 Million
Number Employees: 7
Square Footage: 7000

23618 Harold Wainess & Assoc

2045 N Dunhill Ct N
Arlington Hts, IL 60004-3179

847-259-6400
Fax: 847-259-6460 847-722-8744
kenderson@aol.com www.haroldwainess.com
Food safety consultant providing audits, food equipment evaluations and testing
V.P.: Kenneth Anderson
kenderson@aol.com
R&D: Erickson
Estimated Sales: Below $5 Million
Number Employees: 1-4

23619 Harpak-ULMA Packaging LLC

175 John Quincy Adams Rd
Taunton, MA 02780-1035

508-238-8884
Fax: 508-238-8885 www.harpak-ulma.com
Flexible packaging machinery
President: Linda Harlfinger
lindaharlfinger@harpak.com
VP: Harvey Fine
Number Employees: 20-49
Type of Packaging: Consumer, Food Service, Private Label, Bulk
Brands:
  Ulma

23620 Harpak-ULMA Packaging LLC

3035 Torrington Dr
Ball Ground, GA 30107-4543

770-345-5300
Fax: 770-345-5322 www.harpak-ulma.com
Packaging machines and packaging solutions such as traysealers, vertical and side seal packaging, blister packaging and film.
Manager: Ron Hartwig
ronhartwig@harpak-ulma.com
Number Employees: 10-19

23621 Harpak-Ulma

175 John Quincy Adams Rd
Taunton, MA 02780-1035

508-884-2500
Fax: 508-884-2501 800-813-6644
info@harpak-ULMA.com www.harpak-ulma.com
Supplier of engineered packaging equipment and complete automated systems.
Field Sales Manager: Jerry Rundle
Estimated Sales: $60 Million
Number Employees: 88
Type of Packaging: Food Service, Private Label, Bulk
Brands:
  Rama

23622 Harper Associates

31000 Northwestern Hwy # 240
Farmington Hills, MI 48334-2564

248-932-1170
Fax: 248-932-1214 Info@HarperJobs.com
www.harperjobs.com
Personnel placement specialist for the hospitality industry
President: Ben Schwartz
ben@harperjobs.com
Vice President: Cindy Kramer
CEO: Ben Schwartz
Estimated Sales: $500,000-$1 Million
Number Employees: 5-9

23623 Harper Brush Works Inc

400 N 2nd St
Fairfield, IA 52556-2416

641-472-5186
Fax: 641-472-3187 800-223-7894
info@harperbrush.com www.harperbrush.com
Manufacturer and exporter of brooms, brushes, mops and squeegees
CEO: Barry Harper
barry.harper@harperbrush.com
Marketing: Pat Adam
Sales: Jerry Armstrong
Public Relations: Pat Adam
Operations: Don Sander
Purchasing Director: Randy Rhoads
Estimated Sales: $20-50 Million
Number Employees: 100-249
Type of Packaging: Consumer, Food Service, Bulk

23624 Harper Trucks Inc

1522 S Florence St
Wichita, KS 67209-2634

316-942-1381
Fax: 316-942-8508 800-835-4099
www.harpertrucks.com
Manufacturer and exporter of industrial trucks
President: Phil G Ruffin
pruffin@harpertrucks.com
CFO: Phillip Ruffin
Vice President: Gary Leiker
Marketing Director: David Rife
Sales Director: Judy Darnell
Plant Manager: Hugh Sales
Purchasing Manager: Sonya Kellogg
Estimated Sales: $20 Million
Number Employees: 100-249
Number of Brands: 1
Square Footage: 350000

23625 Harrington Hoists Inc

401 W End Ave
Manheim, PA 17545-1703

717-665-2000
Fax: 717-665-2861 800-233-3010
www.harringtonhoists.com
Material handling equipment including hoists, lever pullers and cranes
President: Ned Hunter
Manager of Quality & Engineering: Drew Schoenberger
National Sales Manager: W David Merkel, Jr.
Customer Service Manager: Hope Arment
COO: Carlo Lonardi
Plant Manager: Guy Haney
Estimated Sales: $10-20 Million
Number Employees: 100-249
Parent Co: Kito Corporation

23626 Harrington's Equipment Co

475 Orchard Rd
Fairfield, PA 17320-9399

410-756-2506
Fax: 302-422-7149 800-468-8467
RSH5@live.com www.harringtonsequipment.com
Dealer of rebuilt can seamers, replacement parts and change parts
President: Thomas H Harrington Jr
Number Employees: 5-9

23627 Harris & Company

980 Salem Pkwy
Salem, OH 44460

330-332-4127
Fax: 330-332-9627 info@harrisandcompany.com
CIS labels, self adhesive labels in sheets, coated paper and printed boards

President: Charles M Day
Owner: Charles W. Harris
VP (Pre-Press): George Ritchie
VP Sales: Norm Ritchie
Contact: David Harris
davidh@hjpchartered.com
Estimated Sales: $1 Million
Number Employees: 5-9
Square Footage: 22000

23628 Harris Equipment Corp
2040 N Hawthorne Ave
Melrose Park, IL 60160-1106

708-343-0866
Fax: 708-343-0995   800-365-0315
customer_service@harrisequipment.com
www.harrisequipment.com
Heat exchangers; wholesaler/distributor of oil free
air compressors and compressed air filtration equip-
ment, oil flooded compresser air dryers, stainless
steel vavles, filter regulated lubricators
President: Gary Pollack
gpollack@harrisequipment.com
VP: John Pearson
Marketing: Tony Beaman
Purchasing Manager: Humer Lovett
Estimated Sales: $10-20 Million
Number Employees: 20-49
Square Footage: 56000

23629 Harris Specialty Chemicals
P.O.Box 2789
Jacksonville, FL 32203-2789

904-598-9808
Fax: 904-598-9833   800-537-4722
hsc@hsc-ss.com
Polymer floor systems
CEO: Ellen Harris
Estimated Sales: $1-5 Million
Number Employees: 5-9

23630 Harrison Electropolishing
13002 Brittmoore Park Dr
Houston, TX 77041-7231

832-467-3100
Fax: 832-467-3111   info@harrisonep.com
www.m.harrisonep.com
Specializes in mechanical, electropolishing and
passivation for brew kettles, fermenters and lagering
tanks.
President: Tom Harrison
Manager: Ginger Happacher
ginger@harrisonep.com
Number Employees: 50-99

23631 Harrison of Texas
7142 Siena Vista Dr
Houston, TX 77083-2938

281-498-8206
Fax: 713-981-9589   800-245-5707
Electropolishing and mechanical polishing service
for stainless steel food processing equipment; also,
oxygen cleaning and mil-spec passivation services
available
President: Tom Harrison
Office Manager: Patricia Bays
Operations Manager: Matt Buck
Estimated Sales: $300,000-500,000
Number Employees: 1-4
Square Footage: 60000

23632 Harro Hofliger Packaging Systems
4 W Oakland Ave # 2
Doylestown, PA 18901-4243

215-345-4256
Fax: 215-345-4994
Supplier of Packaging Equipment
President: Allen Shane
Contact: Seth Blau
sblau@hofliger.com
Estimated Sales: $1-3 Million
Number Employees: 5-9

23633 Harry Davis & Co
1725 Blvd Of The Allies
Pittsburgh, PA 15219-5991

412-765-1170
Fax: 412-765-0910   800-775-2289
sales@harrydavis.com www.harrydavis.com
CEO: Stanford Davis
sdavis@harrydavis.com
CEO: Martin Davis
Estimated Sales: $20-50 Million
Number Employees: 10-19

23634 Harsco Industrial IKG
1801 Forrest Park Dr
Garrett, IN 46738

260-357-6900
Fax: 260-357-0027   800-467-2345
salesikg@harsco.com www.harscoikg.com
Manufacturer and exporter of fiberglass grating used
for flooring in food processing plants
Marketing Manager: Tom Toler
VP Sales/Marketing: Ray Palombi
Contact: Heidi Malcolm
h.malcolm@ikgindustries.com
Estimated Sales: $1-5 Million

23635 (HQ)Hart Design & Mfg
1940 Radisson St
Green Bay, WI 54302-2092

920-468-5927
Fax: 920-468-5888 www.hartdesign.com
Designs and constructs specialty, standard and pro-
prietary equipment for use in the Food and Dairy in-
dustry. Our packaging machinery includes process
cheese wrappers, automatic puching, filling and
sealing lines for process and creamcheese, a ribbon
cheese casting, slitting, slice stacking equipment, au-
tomatic product feeders, and portion cutting equip-
ment for block and barrel cheese.
President: Timm Schaetz
CEO: John Adams
Founder/CEO: Gerald Schaetz
Marketing Manager: Dennis Adelmeyer
Sales Manager: Dennis Adelmeyer
Estimated Sales: $4 Million
Number Employees: 20-49
Square Footage: 80000
Brands:
  Hart

23636 (HQ)Hart Designs LLC
PO Box 1387
Ruston, LA 71273-1387

318-278-0473
Fax: 318-255-8328   800-592-3500
www.hart-designs.com
Electric lighting fixtures
CEO: Charles Hart
Quality Control: Sandra Hart
Sales: Amy Foster
Estimated Sales: Less Than $500,000
Number Employees: 1-4

23637 Hartford Containers
PO Box 399
Terryville, CT 06786-0399

860-584-1194
Fax: 860-582-5051
Corrugated containers
President: Bob Braverman
Estimated Sales: $20-50 Million
Number Employees: 50-99

23638 Hartford Plastics
10861 Mill Valley Rd
Omaha, NE 68154

Fax: 860-683-8484
Manufacturer and exporter of plastic bottles and
containers; also, custom blow molding, labeling, hot
stamping and silk screening available
VP Marketing: Anthony Roncaioli
Estimated Sales: $10-20 Million
Number Employees: 50-99
Parent Co: Comtrol

23639 Hartford Stamp Works
201 Locust Street
Hartford, CT 6114

860-249-6205
Fax: 860-409-4110
Rubber stamps, name plates, seals, name pins,
self-inking stamps, etc.; also, inks
CEO: Ramani Ayer
Contact: Kyle Shorty
hartfordstamp@aol.com
Office Manager: Sandy Williams
Estimated Sales: $1-2.5 Million
Number Employees: 10-19
Square Footage: 15000

23640 Harting Graphics
111 N Cleveland Ave
Wilmington, DE 19805-1714

302-622-8911
Fax: 302-622-8909   800-848-1373

Advertising signs and point of purchase posters and
banners
President: Theodore Harting
Sales/Marketing Executive: Susan Cuttance
Purchasing Agent: Kim Livermore
Estimated Sales: Below $5 Million
Number Employees: 5-9
Square Footage: 40000

23641 Hartness International
1200 Garlington Road
P.O. Box 26509
Greenville, SC 26509

864-297-1200
Fax: 864-297-4486   800-845-8791
www.hartness.com
Manufacturer and exporter of packaging equipment
and machinery including case packers, decasers, sin-
gle filers/laners and conveyor and mass product flow
systems
Managing Director: Jim Gordon
Chief Executive Officer: Bernard McPheely
Chief Financial Officer: Lamar Jordan
Vice President: Sean Hartness
Marketing Manager: Anne Elmerick
Vice President, Sales & Marketing: Scott Smith
Product Manager: Bill Gemmell
Director, Procurement: Dianne Hall
Estimated Sales: $50-75 Million
Number Employees: 250-499
Brands:
  Dynac

23642 Hartstone Pottery Inc
1719 Dearborn St
Zanesville, OH 43701-5299

740-452-9999
Fax: 800-506-9627
Manufacturer, importer and exporter of stoneware,
dinnerware, cookware, bakeware, tabletop accesso-
ries, oven dishwashers and microwave safe cookie
molds
Manager: Wess Foltz
wess@hartstonepottery.com
VP/General Manager: Patrick Hart
Sales Manager: Mike Flynn
Operations Manager: Shawn McGee
Estimated Sales: $7 Million
Number Employees: 20-49
Square Footage: 400000
Parent Co: Carlisle Companies
Type of Packaging: Consumer, Food Service
Brands:
  Hartstone
  The Original Cookie & Shortbread
  The Wine Tote

23643 Hartzell Fan Inc
910 S Downing St
Piqua, OH 45356

937-773-7411
Fax: 937-773-8994   800-336-3267
info@hartzellfan.com www.hartzell.com
Manufacturer and exporter of general and process
ventilation fans and centrifugal fans and blowers
President: George D Atkinson
CEO: Sean Steimle
customerservice@hartzell.com
Sales: George Atkins
Operations Manager: R Wallace
Estimated Sales: $20-50 Million
Number Employees: 100-249
Brands:
  Duct Axial

23644 Harvard Folding Box Company
71 Linden St
Lynn, MA 1905

781-598-1600
Fax: 781-598-2950 www.idealboxmakers.com
Manufacturer and exporter of folding paper boxes
President: Leon Simkins
VP: David Simkins
Logistics Manager: Tony Geraneo
Contact: Mike Hios
mhios@idealboxmakers.com
Operational Manager: Chris Robertson
Plant Manager: Jimmy Mc Gee
Estimated Sales: $10-20 Million
Number Employees: 100-249
Parent Co: Simkins Industries

23645 Harvey W Hottel Inc
18900 Woodfield Rd # A
Gaithersburg, MD 20879-6704
301-921-9599
Fax: 301-948-1892 jhottel@harveyhottel.com
www.harveyhottel.com
Air conditioning, heating and refrigeration items, financing, food service, HVAC, plumbing, design/build case study
President: Richard Hottel
CEO: Dick Hottel
VP: Jeff Hottel
VP Sales: Bernard Mejean
Estimated Sales: $10-20 Million
Number Employees: 100-249
Square Footage: 20000

23646 Harvey's Indian River Groves
3700 US Highway 1
Rockledge, FL 32955-4925
321-636-6072
Fax: 321-633-4132 800-327-9312
www.harveysgroves.com
Fruit gift baskets
President: Jim Harvey
Manager: Ann Manerino
Estimated Sales: $2.5-5 Million
Number Employees: 100-249

23647 Harwil Corp
541 Kinetic Dr
Oxnard, CA 93030-7923
805-988-6800
Fax: 805-988-6804 800-562-2447
www.harwil.com
Manufacturer and exporter of bag closing machinery, heat sealers and flow and liquid level switches. Also manufature fluid liquid level switches, liquid level pumpup/plumpdown controlles, pump emergency shutdown controllers andachemical feed pump interface module
VP: Bruce Bowman
Sales Exec: Ellis Anderson
Number Employees: 20-49

23648 Hasco Electric Corporation
84 S Water St Ste 1
Greenwich, CT 06830
203-531-9400
Fax: 203-531-9408
Lighting fixtures
Owner: Donna Sagona
VP: Brad Sagona
Estimated Sales: $5-10,000,000
Number Employees: 20-49
Square Footage: 58000

23649 Hassia USA
1210 Campus Dr
Morganville, NJ 07751-1262
732-536-8770
Fax: 732-536-8850
President: Charles Ravalli
Estimated Sales: $3-5 Million
Number Employees: 10-19

23650 Hastings Lighting Company
1206 Long Beach Ave
Los Angeles, CA 90021
213-622-2009
Fax: 213-622-9157
Fluorescent showcase lighting fixtures for use in show cases
President: Jim Culbertson
VP: Jeffrey Colby
Office Manager: Joan Culbertson
Estimated Sales: $1-2.5 Million
Number Employees: 1-4
Square Footage: 9600

23651 Hasty Bake Charcoal Grills
1313 S Lewis Ave
Tulsa, OK 74104-4215
918-665-8220
Fax: 918-665-8225 800-426-6836
info@hastybake.com www.hastybake.com
Charcoal ovens and barbecue accessories
Owner: Richard Alexander
ralexander@hastybake.com
Estimated Sales: $2.5-5 Million
Number Employees: 10-19

23652 Hatco Corp
635 S 28th St
Milwaukee, WI 53215-1298
414-671-6350
Fax: 414-615-1226 800-558-0607
www.hatcocorp.com
Manufacturer and exporter of heating, warming, toasting, cooking and equipment including display warmers, holding cabinets, low temperature and slow cookers and booster and sink heaters for hot water, toasters, etc
President: Dave Rolston
drolston@hatcocorp.com
Co-Founder: Lareine Hatch
Vice President-Sales: Michael Whiteley
National Sales Manager: Mark Pumphret
Number Employees: 50-99
Type of Packaging: Food Service
Brands:
    Chef System
    Flav-R-Fresh
    Flav-R-Savor
    Glo-Ray
    Hatco
    Toast King
    Toast Rite
    Toast-Qwik

23653 Hathaway Stamps
635 Main St # 1
Cincinnati, OH 45202-2524
513-621-1052
Fax: 513-621-7339 contact@hathawaystamps.com
www.hathawaystamps.com
Rubber stamps
Manager: Larry Schultz
VP: Robert Ruwe
Estimated Sales: $1-2.5 Million
Number Employees: 10-19
Square Footage: 8000
Parent Co: Volk Corporation

23654 Hatteras Packaging Systems
8753 S Highway A1a
Melbourne Beach, FL 32951-4008
321-728-0908
Fax: 321-984-7252 hatteraspk@aol.com
Number Employees: 10

23655 Haug Quality Equipment
18443 Technology Dr
Morgan Hill, CA 95037-2822
408-465-8160
Fax: 408-842-1265 sales@haugquality.com
www.haugquality.com
Leak detecting equipment for food packaging
President: Brian Haug
bhaug@haugmfg.com
Secretary: Gale Craft
Sales Manager: Thomas Hoffman
Estimated Sales: $1-3 Million
Number Employees: 10-19
Brands:
    Haug

23656 Haumiller Engineering Co
445 Renner Dr
Elgin, IL 60123-6991
847-695-9111
Fax: 847-695-2092 sales@haumiller.com
www.haumiller.com
Manufacturer and exporter of high-speed automatic custom assembly machines, flip top closure closing machines, cappers, spray tip and fitment applicators, reducer plug inserters and collar placers
President: Russ Holmer
rholmer@haumiller.com
VP Sales: John Giacopelli
Estimated Sales: $5-10 Million
Number Employees: 50-99
Square Footage: 90000

23657 Hauser Packaging
44 Exchange Street
Suite 202
Portland, ME 04101-5018
207-899-3306
Fax: 207-899-3970 888-600-2671
info@hauserpack.com www.hauserpack.com
Wine industry bottles
Contact: Thomas Houser
thouser@hauserpack.com

23658 Hautly Cheese Co
251 Axminister Dr
Fenton, MO 63026-2938
636-533-4400
Fax: 653-533-4401 info@hautly.com
www.hautly.com
Cheese, cheese products
Owner: Alan Hautly
a_hautly@hautly.com
Estimated Sales: Less than $500,000
Number Employees: 20-49

23659 Have Our Plastic Inc
6990 Creditview Road
Unit 4
Mississauga, ON L5N 8R9
Canada
905-821-7550
Fax: 905-821-7553 800-263-5995
sales@hop.ca
Manufacture and distrubute synthetic paper, plastic and wire binding products, laminating equipment and supplies, other equipment and supplies, restaurant menu covers, display and merchandising products and PVC.
Estimated Sales: $5,000,000
Number Employees: 16
Number of Brands: 1
Square Footage: 96000
Type of Packaging: Private Label, Bulk
Brands:
    E-Binder
    H.O.P.
    Hop-Syn
    Print Protector
    The Menu Roll

23660 Haven's Candies
87 County Rd
Westbrook, ME 04092-3807
207-772-1557
Fax: 207-775-0086 800-639-6309
info@havenscandies.com www.havenscandies.com
Chocolates and other confectionary; custom chocolate molding available
Owner: Andy Charles
Marketing Director: Krista Viola
Production Manager: Arthur Dillon
Estimated Sales: $1-2.5 Million
Number Employees: 20-49
Square Footage: 24000
Type of Packaging: Consumer, Private Label, Bulk

23661 Haviland Enterprises Inc
421 Ann St NW
Grand Rapids, MI 49504-2019
616-734-0250
Fax: 616-361-9772 800-456-1134
Industrial, food grade and U.S.P. specialty cleaners and wastewater treatment chemicals; wholesaler/distributor of various food grade and U.S.P. process chemicals
President: E Bernard Haviland
Cmo: Graham Torr
grahamt@havilandusa.com
CFO: Tom Simmons
Quality Control: Terry Schoew
Sales/Marketing Manager: Eric Earl
Estimated Sales: $20-50 Million
Number Employees: 100-249
Square Footage: 185000

23662 Haward Corporation
29 Porete Ave
North Arlington, NJ 7031
201-991-8777
Fax: 201-991-1903 800-342-9041
Metal finisher whose services include teflon and plastic coating and electropolishing of stainless steel
President: Dean Ward
Vice President: Keith Schumacher
Sales Director: Gary Horman
Estimated Sales: $5-10 Million
Number Employees: 20-49
Square Footage: 60000

23663 Hawkeye Corrugated Box
725 Ida St
Cedar Falls, IA 50613-2112
319-268-0407
Fax: 319-268-0057 www.buckeyecorrugated.com
Corrugated boxes
President: Matt Highland
highland@hawkeyebox.com

Estimated Sales: $20-50 Million
Number Employees: 20-49

23664 Hawkeye Pallet Co
6055 NW Beaver Dr
Johnston, IA 50131-1349
515-276-0409
Wooden pallets
Owner: Bill Haller
Estimated Sales: Less Than $500,000
Number Employees: 1-4

23665 Hayes & Stolz Indl Mfg LTD
3521 Hemphill St
PO Box 11217
Fort Worth, TX 76110-5212
817-926-3391
Fax: 817-926-4133 800-725-7272
sales@hayes-stolz.com www.hayes-stolz.com
Manufacturer and exporter of batch mixers, continuous blenders, liquid coaters, bucket elevators, valves and rotary screeners
President: B J Masters
marhay@hayes-stolz.com
VP: Mark Hayes
Chairman of the Board: Vernon Hayes
Sales Exec: Mark Hayes
Sales Engineer: Kris Helsley
Estimated Sales: $10-20 Million
Number Employees: 100-249

23666 Hayes Machine Co Inc
3434 106th Cir
Des Moines, IA 50322-3700
515-252-1216
Fax: 515-252-1316 800-860-6224
aandersen@hayesmachine.com
www.hayesmachine.com
Packaging and cartoning machines
President: Luca Berrone
CFO: John Stone
R & D: Allan Anderson
Inside Sales Manager: Julie Reincke
Manager: Allan Andersen
aandersen@sacmiusa.com
Plant Manager: Allan Anderson
Estimated Sales: Below $5 Million
Number Employees: 20-49
Square Footage: 32000
Parent Co: Gram Equipment of America

23667 Haynes Manufacturing Co
24142 Detroit Rd
Westlake, OH 44145-1528
440-871-2188
Fax: 440-871-0855 800-992-2166
info@haynesmfg.com www.haynesmfg.com
Manufacturer and exporter of food grade lubricants
Owner: Tammy Doctor
Sales and Marketing Coordinator: Tammy Doctor
tdoctor@haynesmfg.com
Estimated Sales: Less Than $500,000
Number Employees: 1-4
Type of Packaging: Food Service, Private Label, Bulk
Brands:
Haynes

23668 (HQ)Hayon Manufacturing
9682 Borgata Bay Blvd
Las Vegas, NV 89147-8080
702-562-3377
Fax: 702-562-3351 hayonmfg@aol.com
www.eggwashsprayer.com
Manufacturer and exporter of bakery machinery including automatic pan greasers and coaters, egg washers and icing/glaze applicators
Owner: Z Hayon
hayonmfg@aol.com
VP: Ziona Hayon
Estimated Sales: Below $500,000
Number Employees: 1-4
Brands:
Hayon Select-A-Spray

23669 Hayssen Flexible Systems
225 Spartangreen Blvd
Duncan, SC 29334-9400
864-486-4000
Fax: 864-486-4412 sales@hayssen.com
www.hayssen.com
Manufacturer and exporter of horizontal flow wrapping and horizontal and vertical form/fill/seal machinery

President: Daniel L Jones
Vice President: Dan Minor
dan.minor@hayssensandiacre.com
Vice President of Sales and Marketing: Dan Minor
Estimated Sales: $50 Million
Number Employees: 250-499
Parent Co: Barry Wehmiller Companies
Brands:
Edge
Rt
Servo Ii
Turbo
Ultima
Ultra

23670 Hayssen Flexible Systems
225 Spartangreen Blvd
Duncan, SC 29334-9400
864-486-4000
Fax: 864-486-4412 sandiacre.usa@molins.com
www.hayssen.com
Packaging machinery and machinery parts, vertical form fill and seal bagmakers and horzaontal flow wrappers
Founder: Herman Hayssen
General Manager: Troy Snader
Vice President: Dan Minor
dan.minor@hayssensandiacre.com
Vice President of Sales and Marketing: Dan Minor
Estimated Sales: $8-10 Million
Number Employees: 250-499
Parent Co: Molins Richmond

23671 Hayward Gordon
6660 Campobello Road
Mississauga, ON L5N 2L9
Canada
905-567-6116
Fax: 905-567-1706 info@haywardgordon.com
www.haywardgordon.com
President: John Hayward
CFO: Jeanne Gray
Number Employees: 10

23672 Hayward Industries Inc
1 Hayward Industrial Dr
Clemmons, NC 27012-9737
336-712-9900
Fax: 336-712-9523 www.haywardindustries.com
Manufacturer and exporter of cartridge filters, pipeline strainers, gas/liquid separators, plastic valves and flow meters
President: Robert Davis
HR Executive: Mathieu Bienvenue
mbienvenue@haywardnet.com
Marketing Communication Manager: D Treslan
Number Employees: 500-999
Brands:
Flosite
Loeffler
Qic
Strainomatic
Wright-Austin

23673 Hazen Paper Co
240 S Water St
Holyoke, MA 01040-5979
413-538-8204
Fax: 413-533-1420 customerservice@hazen.com
www.hazen.com
Paper including foil and metallized film laminations, heat sealing, fancy, printed and embossed paper
President: Royal Casino
sdximuhb@amazinhazen.org
Quality Control: Alfred Zuffoletti
R&D: Kyle Parent
VP Sales: Steve Smith
Purchasing Manager: Larry Hoague
Estimated Sales: $20-50 Million
Number Employees: 50-99

23674 Hazmat Business Ideas
1620 i St NW Ste 925
Washington, DC 20006
202-293-5800
Fax: 202-463-8998
Provides a forum for the gathering and exchange of information for the shipment and distribution of hazardous materials.
Number Employees: 20-49

23675 Hcs Enterprises
Plot No. 333, Rai Industrial Estate
Sonipat
Haryana, 131029
India
www.hcsbakerymachines.com
Manufacturer, supplier and exporter of a comprehensive range of bakery plants, machines and equipment including steel flour sifters, bread slicing machines, baking proofer ovens, planetary mixers, infrared ovens, rack ovens
Managing Director: Bhupinder Singh
Estimated Sales: $1 Million
Number Employees: 26-50

23676 Healdsburg Machine Company
2584 Rim Rock Way
Santa Rosa, CA 95404-1819
707-433-3348
Fax: 707-433-3340
Manufacturer and exporter of grape crushing and stemming machinery; also, special pumps for the canning industry
President: Arthur Rafanelli
yvette.moseman@mosemanlaw.com
VP: Ron Rafanelli
Marketing: Ron Rafanelli
Estimated Sales: $1-2.5 Million
Number Employees: 10
Square Footage: 180000
Parent Co: Healdsburg Machine Company

23677 Health Products Corp
1060 Nepperhan Ave
Yonkers, NY 10703-1432
914-423-2900
Fax: 914-963-6001 www.hpc7.com
Psyllium and nutritional herbs, tablets and capsules; contract packager of blending and filling powders
President: Joseph Lewin
zurion2@aol.com
Number Employees: 50-99
Brands:
Aspi-Cor
Khg-7
Lactalins
Malpotane
Tick Stop

23678 Health Star
80 Pacella Dr
Randolph, MA 02368
781-961-5400
Fax: 781-961-5456 800-545-3639
info@HealthStaronline.com
www.healthstaronline.com
New, and rebuilt processing and packaging machinery including liquid fillers
Marketing Manager: Bonnie Cote
Sales: Patl Lais
Estimated Sales: $2.5-5 Million
Number Employees: 50-99
Brands:
Level Star Ls Level Sensing Fillers
Purecop
Purefil

23679 HealthFocus
1140 Hightower Trail
Suite 201
Atlanta, GA 30350-2988
770-645-1999
Fax: 770-518-0630 www.healthfocus.net
Market research firm specializing in consumer health and nutrition trends
Marketing Director: Julie Johnson
Estimated Sales: $500,000-$1 Million
Number Employees: 1
Square Footage: 8000

23680 Healthline Products
100 N Santa Fe Avenue
Los Angeles, CA 90012-4021
213-620-8600
Fax: 213-620-8636 800-473-4003
Pot holders, gloves, towels, uniforms, etc
President: Courtney Sapin
National Sales Manager: Trina Brown
Customer Service: Rita Recio
Estimated Sales: $5-10,000,000
Number Employees: 19
Square Footage: 15000

23681 Healthstar Inc
1 Randolph Rd
Randolph, MA 02368-4321
781-961-5400
Fax: 781-961-5456 800-LIK-ENEW
info@healthstaronline.com
www.healthstaronline.com
Pre-owned, rebuilt, and new processing and packaging equipment
President: William Graboswki
CFO: Scott Johnson
Contact: Robert Bean
rbean@healthstaronline.com
Estimated Sales: $10-20 Million
Number Employees: 20-49

23682 Healthy Dining
4849 Ronson Ct Ste 115
San Diego, CA 92111
858-541-2049
Fax: 858-541-0508 800-266-2049
erica@healthy-dining.com
www.healthydiningfinder.com
Consultant specializing in marketing and promoting healthy restaurant menu items; also, computerized nutrition analysis of menu items available
President/ Founder: Anita Jones Mueller
VP/ Director Strategic Partnerships: Erica Bohm, M.S.
Research & Communications Coordinator: Nancy Snyder, M.S.
Director Nutrition, Quality Assurance: Lauren Rezende, M.P.H., R.D.
Contact: Rick Bayless
rick@healthydiningfinder.com
Director Operations: Andrew Packer, M.A.
Estimated Sales: Below $5,000,000
Number Employees: 5-9

23683 Healthy Grain Foods LLC
4125 Yorkshire Ln
Northbrook, IL 60062-2915
847-272-5576
Fax: 847-272-5576
Cereals; research and development
President: Harold Zukerman
haroldzukerman@gmail.com
Estimated Sales: $1-2,500,000
Number Employees: 5-9

23684 Heart Smart International
6702 E Clinton St
Scottsdale, AZ 85254-5254
480-948-7631
Fax: 480-948-9834 800-762-7819
www.heartsmartinternational.net
Consultant specializing in the computer analysis of menu items, product marketing and nutritional training assistance
Owner: Jay Philips
Director Customer Relations: Judy Peters
Production Manager: Joe Cox
Estimated Sales: less than $500,000
Number Employees: 1-4
Square Footage: 2000
Parent Co: Best of Taste

23685 Heart of Virginia
PO Box 937
Lynchburg, VA 24505-0937
804-847-1732
Fax: 804-847-2067 kbutler@region2000.org

23686 Hearthside Food Solutions
3500 Lacey Rd
Suite 300
Downers Grove, IL 60515
630-967-3600
info@hearthsidefoods.com
www.hearthsidefoods.com
Nutrition and energy bars, cookies, crackers, snack foods, cereal and granola, and food packaging.
Chairman/CEO & Co-Founder: Rich Scalise
Senior VP/CFO: Fred Jasser
Senior VP Human Resources: Steve England
Year Founded: 2009
Number Employees: 5000-9999
Type of Packaging: Consumer, Private Label

23687 Heartland Farms Dairy & Food Products, LLC
3668 South Geyer Road
Suite 205
St. Louis, MO 63127
314-965-1110
Fax: 314-965-1118 888-633-6455
info@heartlandfarmsdairy.com
www.heartlandfarmsdairy.com
Dairy products
President: Tom Jacoby
Marketing Assistant: Pat Hittmeier
Sales of Dry Products: Tim Fann
Contact: Christine Anderson
canderson@heartlandfarmsdairy.com
Weights and Tests: Jenn Jacoby
Type of Packaging: Consumer, Bulk

23688 Heartland Ingredients LLC
802 West College Street
Troy, MO 63379
Fax: 877-841-2067 800-557-2621
contactus@heartlandingredients.net
www.heartlandingredients.net
Ingredients, food and technical grade chemicals and colors, dairy products, meat products, sugar, artifical sweeteners, close dated finished products.

23689 Heartwood
5063 Arrow Hwy
Montclair, CA 91763-1304
909-626-8104
Fax: 909-626-7636
www.heartwoodcountertops.com
Solid surfacing materials and store fixtures
Estimated Sales: Less than $500,000
Number Employees: 1-4

23690 Heat Seal
4580 E 71st St
Cleveland, OH 44125-1048
216-341-2022
Fax: 216-341-2163 800-342-6329
custserv@heatsealco.com www.heatsealco.com
Horizontal form/fill/seal machines, shrink packaging systems, rotary blister packaging machinery, high speed shrink tunnels and vertical L-sealer bagger
Owner: Ron Skalsky
Contact: Brent Ferns
brferns@heatsealequipment.com
Estimated Sales: $20-50 Million
Number Employees: 100-249

23691 Heat-It Manufacturing
12050 Crownpoint Dr
San Antonio, TX 78233-5362
210-650-9112
Fax: 210-967-8345 800-323-9336
Manufacturer and exporter of canned heating fuels for buffets, catering, camping and emergencies
Manager: Lisa Garza
General Manager: Georgina Yoast
Estimated Sales: $.5-1 million
Number Employees: 1-4
Square Footage: 60000
Brands:
Heat-It

23692 Heatcraft Refrigeration Prods
2175 W Park Place Blvd
Stone Mountain, GA 30087-3535
770-465-5600
Fax: 770-465-5990
hrrdp.feedback@heatcraftrpd.com
www.heatcraftrpd.com
Manufacturer and exporter of commercial refrigeration equipment
Cmo: Grady Mcadams
VP: Ken Rothgeb
Director Marketing: Jeff Almond
Director Sales: Mark Westphal
General Manager: J Jones
Estimated Sales: $10-20,000,000
Number Employees: 100-249
Square Footage: 140000
Parent Co: Lennox International
Brands:
Bohn
Chandler
Climate Control
Larkin

23693 Heatcraft Worldwide Refrig
5201 Transport Blvd
Columbus, GA 31907-1961
706-568-1514
Fax: 706-568-8990 800-866-5596
marietta.oneill@heatcraftrpd.com
www.kysorwarren.com
Manufacturer and exporter of refrigerated display fixtures, walk-in coolers/freezers and refrigeration systems
President: Ralph Schmitt
Director of Sales-Eastern U.S. & Canada: Larry Norton
Director of Sales-Western U.S.: Robert Greene
Executive VP: Cliff Hill
Sales Manager: Brian Eddins
Dealer Development Manager: Oscar Stuart
Estimated Sales: $1-5 Million
Number Employees: 500-999
Square Footage: 980000
Parent Co: Heatcraft Worldwide Refrigeration
Brands:
Dual Jet
Kysor/Warren

23694 Heatec
P.O.Box 72760
Chattanooga, TN 37407
423-821-5200
Fax: 423-821-7673 800-235-5200
heatec@heatec.com www.heatec.com
Heaters, storage tanks and related products
President: Richard Dorris
VP/Marketing: Tom Wilkey
Sales: Jerry Vautrease
Parent Co: Astec Industries

23695 Heath & Company
3411 Johnson Ferry Road
Roswell, GA 30075-5205
770-650-2724
Fax: 678-623-3475 info@heathandco.com
www.heathandco.com
Signs including advertising, changeable letter, electric, luminous tube, etc
Founder & Managing Partner: David W. Health
Contact: Pooja Mehta
pooja@jkworld.net
Manager: Ken Plass
Number Employees: 150
Parent Co: Jim Patterson Group

23696 Heath & Company
3411 Johnson Ferry Road
Roswell, GA 30075-5205
770-650-2724
Fax: 678-623-3475 info@heathandco.com
www.heathandco.com
Signs including electric advertising, plastic and luminous tube
Founder & Managing Partner: David W. Health
Contact: Pooja Mehta
pooja@jkworld.net
Manager: Ken Plass
Estimated Sales: C
Number Employees: 150
Parent Co: Jim Patterson Group

23697 Heath Signs
278 Hillcrest Dr
Reno, NV 89509-3705
775-359-9007
Fax: 775-359-2527
Neon signs
President: Steve Scharfe
Secretary: Cathleen Wallman
Estimated Sales: Less than $500,000
Number Employees: 10

23698 Heatrex
P.O.Box 515
231 Chestnut St., Suite 410
Meadville, PA 16335-0515
814-724-1800
Fax: 814-333-6580 800-394-6589
sales@heatrex.com www.heatrex.com
Manufacturer and exporter of heaters including tubular/finned tubular, flanged/screw plug immersion, circulation, defrost, high temperature duct, infrared and radiant process; also, heater controls

Owner: Fred O'Polka
CFO: Fred O Polka
R&D: Larry Clever
Quality Control: Kim Lenhart
Marketing: Earl Pifer
Sales: Earl Pifer
Contact: Cindy Andrews
andrews@heatrex.com
Operations Manager: Earl Pifer
Plant Manager: Kim Lenhart
Estimated Sales: $10-20 Million
Number Employees: 50-99
Brands:
　Heatzone
　Quartzone

23699 Heatron Inc
3000 Wilson Ave
Leavenworth, KS 66048-4637
913-651-4420
Fax: 913-651-5352 chrisk@heatron.com
www.heatron.com
Custom designers and manufacturers of patented non-stick cartridge heaters, Max2000 mica band and strip heater, Ceramix ceramic bands, Extruheat tubular channel bands, aluminum and bronze cast in heaters, flexible silicone rubberetched-foil
CEO: Mike Keenan
mikek@heatron.com
CEO: Michael W Keenan
Estimated Sales: $5-10 000,000
Number Employees: 100-249

23700 (HQ)Hebeler Corp
2000 Military Rd
Tonawanda, NY 14150-6704
716-873-9300
Fax: 716-873-7538 800-486-4709
info@hebeler.com www.hebeler.com
Stainless steel food processing machinery including bakers' mixers, candy, syrup and beverage coolers, food dryers, deaerators, distillation units, evaporative condensers, separators, heat exchangers and preheaters
President: Brian Sullivan
Chairman: John Coleman
Vice President, Finance: James Breyer
Information Technology Manager: Dan Emma
Quality Assurance Manager: Lisa Glass
Vice President, Sales & Marketing: Cody Pinelli
Chief Operating Officer: Kristina Leibring
Production Supervisor: Christine Hockenberry
Purchasing: Lori Neidlinger
Estimated Sales: $25 Million
Number Employees: 100-249
Square Footage: 100000
Other Locations:
　Hebeler Corp.
　Vicksburg MS

23701 Hebenstreit GmbH
2465 Byron Station Dr. SW,
Suite B
Byron Center, MI 49315
616-583-1458
Fax: 616-583-1646 bryan@bainbridge-assoc.com
www.hebenstreit.de
Representative: Ross Brainbridge

23702 Hector Delorme & Sons
1631 Route 235
Farnham, QC J2N 2R2
Canada
450-293-5310
Fax: 450-293-5319
High pressure washers
President: Yves Cloutier
Number Employees: 5
Brands:
　Cyclone

23703 Hectronic
4300 Highline Blvd # 300
Oklahoma City, OK 73108-1843
405-946-3574
Fax: 405-946-3564 info@hetronic.com
www.hetronic.com
Manufacturer and exporter of material handling equipment including remote control systems

President: Dave Krueger
Executive VP: Torsten Rempe
VP: Torsten Rempe
Marketing: Laurel Benjamin
Sales: Bob Peddycoart
Contact: Stefan De
deboor@hectronic.com
Estimated Sales: $5-10 Million
Number Employees: 20-49
Parent Co: Hectronic

23704 Hedges Neon Sales
616 Reynolds St
Salina, KS 67401-1932
785-827-9341
Fax: 785-827-1411
Signs including luminous tube, painted, wooden, etc
President: Nancy Hedges
nhedges@hedgesonline.com
Estimated Sales: Less Than $500,000
Number Employees: 1-4

23705 Hedgetree Chemical Manufacturing
119 Prosperity Drive
Savannah, GA 31408-9551
912-691-0408
Fax: 912-692-0440
Organic and biodegradable household and industrial cleaning compounds; also, freezer, food and meat processing equipment cleaners
President: Larry Skinner Sr
Sales/Marketing: James Wallace
Estimated Sales: $1-2.5 Million
Number Employees: 7
Square Footage: 27200
Brands:
　U.N.L.O.C.C.

23706 Hedland Flow Meters
PO Box 081580
Racine, WI 53408
262-639-6770
Fax: 262-639-2267 800-433-5263
hedlandsales@racinefed.com www.hedland.com
President: John Erksine
Sales Manager: Mark Leveille
Estimated Sales: $10-20 Million
Number Employees: 100-249

23707 Hedstrom Corporation
1401 Jacobson Ave
Ashland, OH 44805
419-289-9310
Fax: 419-281-3371 700-765-9665
www.hedstrom.com
Rotationally molded polyethylene and vinyl bins, material handling containers, hoppers, etc
President: Jim Braeunit
VP: James Braeunig
VP (Industrial Sales): Marty Fickenscher
Sales Manager (Technical): Jim Cotter
Contact: Tommy Bauer
t.bauer@hedstrom.com
VP Operations: James Braeunig
Estimated Sales: $20-50 Million
Number Employees: 100-249
Square Footage: 300000
Parent Co: GAI Partners

23708 Hedwin Division
1600 Roland Heights Ave
Baltimore, MD 21211-1299
410-467-8209
Fax: 410-889-5189 800-638-1012
sales@hedwin.net www.hedwin.com
Manufacturer and exporter of plastic products including containers, film bags, shipping trays and drum protector lids; also, dispensing systems, drum and film liners, pails and flexible packaging
President: David E Rubley
CEO: Randy Wolfinger
rwolfinger@hedwin.com
Sales Service Manager: Wayne Deal
Number Employees: 500-999
Parent Co: A. Solvay America Company
Brands:
　Cubitainer
　Ecoset
　Hedliner
　Hedpak
　Payliner
　Topliner

Winliner
Winpak

23709 Heely-Brown Co Inc
1280 Chattahoochee Ave NW
Atlanta, GA 30318-3683
404-352-0022
Fax: 404-350-2693 800-241-4628
info@heely-brown.com www.heelybrown.com
President: Bill Brown
CEO: William H Brown
williamb@heelybrown.com
CFO: Mike Spencer
Estimated Sales: $20-50 Million
Number Employees: 50-99

23710 Hefferman Interactive
1196 Easton Road
Horsham, PA 19044-1405
610-517-2877
Fax: 215-441-5292
Estimated Sales: $500,000-$1 000,000
Number Employees: 1-4

23711 Heico Chemicals Inc
Route 611
Delaware Wtr Gap, PA 18327
570-420-3900
Fax: 570-421-9012 800-344-3426
www.vertellus.com
Organic and inorganic fine chemicals and organic performance chemicals
Vice President of Business Development: Dan Giambattisto
Manager of Corporate Sales: Joshua Kley
Estimated Sales: $10-25 Million
Number Employees: 20-49

23712 Heimann Systems Corporation
3203 Regal Dr
Alcoa, TN 37701
865-379-1670
Fax: 865-379-1677
President: Brad Mueller
Estimated Sales: $20-50 Million
Number Employees: 50-99

23713 Heinlin Packaging Svc
3121 South Ave
Toledo, OH 43609-1331
419-385-2681
Industrial and food packaging machinery
Manager: John Heinlin
VP: John Heinlin
Estimated Sales: $1-2.5 000,000
Number Employees: 5-9
Square Footage: 25000

23714 Heinrich Envelope Corp
925 Zane Ave N
Minneapolis, MN 55422-4692
763-544-3571
Fax: 763-544-6287 800-346-7957
information@heinrichenvelope.com
www.heinrichenvelope.com
Envelopes
President: Bill Berkner
Sales Manager: Don Schindle
Manager: Wesley Clerc
wfclerc@heinrichenvelope.com
Estimated Sales: $10-20 Million
Number Employees: 50-99
Parent Co: Taylor Corporation

23715 Heinzen Sales
405 Mayock Rd
Gilroy, CA 95020-7040
408-842-6678
Fax: 408-842-6678 hmisales@heinzen.com
www.heinzen.com
Manufacturer and exporter of food processing equipment including fruit peelers, dryers, dumpers, trim lines and conveyors with complete engineering service for new plant layout and equipment
President: Allan Heinzen
Sales: Gary M Hertzog
Estimated Sales: $10-20 Million
Number Employees: 1-4
Square Footage: 44000

23716 Heisler Machine & Tool Co
224 Passaic Ave
Fairfield, NJ 07004-3581
973-227-6300
Fax: 973-227-7627 heislersales@heislerind.com
www.heislerind.com
Packaging equipment amd 5 gallon pail handling
equipment; denesters, lid placers, lid closers, label-
ers, palletizers, case packers, gray packers,
lipstackers, line integration, pail orientation,
bail-o-matic,spcialty equipment.
President: Richard Heisler
rheisler@heislerind.com
VP Sales: James Lamb
Sales Administrator: Judy Vinson
Estimated Sales: $3-5 Million
Number Employees: 50-99
Number of Products: 12
Square Footage: 100000
Type of Packaging: Food Service, Bulk
Brands:
Casettraypackers
Denester
Lid Placers
Lid Press

23717 Helken Equipment Co
171 Erick St # Q1
Crystal Lake, IL 60014-4539
847-697-3690
Fax: 847-697-3692 info@helkenequipment.com
Used and rebuilt food processing equipment
Owner: Kent Redmond
kent@helkenequipment.com
Estimated Sales: $1-2.5 Million
Number Employees: 1-4
Square Footage: 29600

23718 Heller Truck Body Corp
138 US Highway 22
Hillside, NJ 07205-1888
973-923-9200
Fax: 973-923-9269 800-229-4148
dnovak2491@hotmail.com
Truck bodies, trailers, cargo containers, service and
repair all major brands of liftgates.
President: D Novak
contactus@hellertruck.com
Estimated Sales: $1-2.5 Million
Number Employees: 1-4

23719 Helm Software
4722 N 24th Street
Suite 225
Phoenix, AZ 85016-9140
602-522-2999
Fax: 602-522-8046
Provide trade spending and equipment program soft-
ware to food service manufacturing
President: Daniel Buckstaff
Executive VP: Doug McFetters
Quality Control: Douglas McFetters
Estimated Sales: Below $5 Million
Number Employees: 15

23720 Helman International
4196 Suffolk Way
Pleasanton, CA 94588-4119
925-484-5000
Fax: 925-484-5007 pahelman@attb.com
www.aimblending.com
Ribbon blenders
President: Phil Helman
Contact: Jessica Hanscom
jessicahanscom@aimblending.com
Estimated Sales: $2.5-5 Million
Number Employees: 20-49

23721 Helmer
14395 Bergen Blvd.
Noblesville, IN 46060
317-773-9073
Fax: 800-743-5637 317-773-9082
sales@helmerinc.com www.helmerinc.com
Refrigerators and freezers.
President: David Helmer
Market Integration Manager: Ann Marie Rohe
Contact: Steve Cloyd
scloyd@helmerinc.com

23722 Hemco Corp
711 S Powell Rd
Independence, MO 64056-2602
816-796-2900
Fax: 816-796-3333 800-779-4362
info@hemcocorp.com www.hemcocorp.com
Complete line of laboratory fume hoods, lab furni-
ture, countertops, sinks, and fixture plumbing op-
tions. Large floor mount hoods, ventilation
equipment, emergency shower decontamination
booths, and Modular Clearn Labs
class1,000-100,000.
President: David Campbell
Owner: Ron Hill
Marketing: Jerry Schwarz
Contact: Sue Chandler
suechandler@hemcocorp.com
Estimated Sales: 3 Million
Number Employees: 20-49
Square Footage: 60000
Brands:
UniMax Large Floor Mount Hoods
HazMax Enclosures
UniFlow SE
UniFlow Fume Hoods
UniLine Casework
EnviroMax Enclosures
CE AireStream Hoods

23723 Hench Control, Inc.
3701 Collins Avenue
Suite 8C
Richmond, CA 94806
510-741-8100
Fax: 510-307-9804 sales@henchcontrol.com
www.henchcontrol.com
Efficiently controlling compressors , condensers,
evaporaters, vessels, heat exchangers, pumps and total alarms.
Chief Executive Officer: Alex Daneman
Contact: Patrick Cardon
pcardon@lightpointe.com

23724 Hendee Enterprises Inc
9350 S Point Dr
Houston, TX 77054-3724
713-796-2322
Fax: 713-796-0494 800-231-7275
sales@hendee.com www.hendee.com
Commercial awnings
President: Robert Veasey
robertv@hendee.com
Quality Control: Buddy Teairfon
CEO: John Macfarlane
Sales: Kathy Davis
Estimated Sales: $10-20 Million
Number Employees: 50-99

23725 Henkel Consumer Adhesive
32150 Just Imagine Dr
Avon, OH 44011
440-937-7000
Fax: 440-937-7077 800-321-0253
ask.a.duck@us.henkel.com
Manufacturer and exporter of pressure sensitive
tapes including masking, strapping, packaging, iden-
tification, cloth, foil, electrical and specialty
President: Jack Kahle
CEO: John Kahle
Contact: Melanie Amato
melanie.amato@manco.com
Number Employees: 250-499
Type of Packaging: Consumer, Food Service

23726 Henkel Corp.
200 Elm St
Stamford, CT 06902-3800
475-210-0230
www.henkel-northamerica.com
Adhesive technologies
President/Owner: Jerry Perkins
Director, Operations: Drew Thaler
drew.thaler@henkel.com
Estimated Sales: $4.4 Billion
Number Employees: 8,200
Brands:
AQUENCE
BONDERITE
LOCTITE
TECHNOMELT
TEROSON

23727 (HQ)Henley Paper Company
4229 Beechwood Dr
Greensboro, NC 27410-8108
336-668-0081
Fax: 336-605-9366 Atlanta@AtlanticPkg.com
www.atlanticpkg.com
Manufacturer and wholesaler/distributor of die cut-
ting, hosiery inserts, slitting, rewinding, sheeting,
transfer tissue, electrical insulator paper
VP Sales/Marketing: Bill Parks
Estimated Sales: $10-20 Million
Number Employees: 50-99

23728 Henningsen Foods Inc
14334 Industrial Rd
Omaha, NE 68144-3398
402-330-2500
Fax: 402-330-0875 800-228-2769
davids@henningsenfoods.com
www.henningsenfoods.com
Dried meats and eggs; contract dehydration
President: Jerry Walker
CEO: Arnulfo Arevalo
arnulfoa@henningsenfoods.com
R&D: Jason Zhang
Vice President, Sales: Aaron Heironimus
Logistics Manager: Gina Blankenau
Estimated Sales: $10-49.9 Million
Number Employees: 100-249
Square Footage: 12000
Type of Packaging: Food Service, Private Label,
Bulk

23729 Henny Penny, Inc.
1219 US 35 W.
PO Box 60
Eaton, OH 45320
937-456-8400
Fax: 937-456-8402 800-417-8417
www.hennypenny.com
Pressure and open fryers, heated holding equipment,
combination convection and steamer ovens, rotisser-
ies, filters, etc.
CEO: Rob Connelly
Executive VP: Steve Maggard
Executive VP: Carolyn Wall
Year Founded: 1957
Estimated Sales: $200 Million
Number Employees: 600
Square Footage: 400000
Brands:
Climaplus
Hot N' Tender
Sure Chef
Sure Chef Climaplus Combi

23730 Henry & Sons Inc
58480 Frudden Rd
Bradley, CA 93426-9674
805-472-2600
Fax: 805-472-2626 800-752-7507
mark@dhenryandsons.com
www.dhenryandsons.com
Weight control systems, casing stuffer, extrudeers,
ham stuffing equipment, sausage linkers, stuffers
and accessories
Vice President: Mark Henry
mark@dhenryandsons.com
Vice President: Mark Henry
Estimated Sales: $1.5 Million
Number Employees: 1-4

23731 Henry Group
3734 State Highway 34 S
Greenville, TX 75402-5133
903-883-2002
Fax: 903-883-3210 www.thehenrygroup.com
Custom food processing equipment and food plant
reconstruction services
Owner: Troy Henry
troy@thg1.com
VP Business Development: Darren Jackson
Estimated Sales: $5-10 Million
Number Employees: 100-249

23732 Henry Hanger & Fixture Corporation of America
450 Seventh Ave 23rd Floor
New York City, NY 10123
212-279-0852
Fax: 212-594-7302 877-279-0852
www.henryhanger.com
Manufacturer and exporter of store fixtures and garment hangers

President: Henry Spitz
VP: Nancy Spitz Bittan
VP: Astrid Spitz Metsos
Estimated Sales: $5-10 Million
Number Employees: 50-99

23733 Henry Ira L Co
802 Elm St
Watertown, WI 53098-2538

920-261-0648
Fax: 920-261-3525 info@irabox.com
Custom set-up paper boxes and gameboards
Owner: Gregory Farado
Sales Director: Keith Thomas
Customer Service Manager: Joanne Duckworth
jduckworth@iralhenry.com
Design & Production Manager: Clark Farago
Plant Manager: Bob Wolfram
Estimated Sales: $1-3 Million
Number Employees: 20-49

23734 Henry Molded Products Inc
71 N 16th St
Lebanon, PA 17042-4502

717-273-3714
Fax: 717-274-3743 henry@henry-molded.com
Pressed and molded pulp goods, fiber containers and
custom packaging service, including pharmaceutical
and wine bottles, etc
President: J Brian
bj@henrymolded.com
CEO: Sue Wymann
CFO: Susan Weiman
Estimated Sales: $20-50 Million
Number Employees: 50-99
Brands:
  Stakker

23735 Henry Troemner LLC
201 Wolf Dr
West Deptford, NJ 08086-2245

856-686-1600
Fax: 856-686-1601 856-686-1600
www.troemner.com
Manufacturer and exporter of laboratory stirrers and
mixers for research and development and quality as-
surance applications
COO: Steve Butler
sbutler@troemner.com
Sales/Marketing: Linda Sears
Estimated Sales: $1-2.5 Million
Number Employees: 100-249
Brands:
  T-Line

23736 Henschel Coating & Laminating
15805 W Overland Dr
New Berlin, WI 53151-2814

262-786-1750
Fax: 262-786-3852 800-866-5683
warren@henschelcoating.com
www.henschelcoating.com
Coated and laminated paper
President: Warren Henschel
warren@henschelcoating.com
R & D: Brian Lemke
VP: Warren Henschel
Estimated Sales: Below $5 Million
Number Employees: 20-49

23737 Herbert Miller
1548 Old Skokie Rd
Highland Park, IL 60035-2704

847-831-2083
Fax: 847-831-2193
Aseptic processing systems, including packaging
and all forms of processing equipment
Owner: Herb Miller
Estimated Sales: Less than $500,000
Number Employees: 1-4

23738 Herche Warehouse
4735 Leyden Street
Denver, CO 80216-3301

303-371-8186
Manufacturer and wholesaler/distributor of packag-
ing equipment and materials including bags, con-
tainers, closures, conveyors, labels, linings, tapes,
ties, etc
Customer Service Representative: Cathy Wyatt
Estimated Sales: $1-5,000,000
Parent Co: Gulf Systems

23739 Herculean Equipment
4917 Encinita Ave
Temple City, CA 91780

626-286-7057
Fax: 626-286-7922 800-441-3455
Owner: Steven Law
Estimated Sales: $300,000-500,000
Number Employees: 1-4

23740 Hercules Food Equipment
145 Millwick Drive
Weston, ON M9L 1Y7
Canada

416-742-9673
Fax: 416-742-6486 hercules@interlog.com
Custom stainless steel sinks, counters and exhaust
canopies; also, refrigerated and heated display units,
barbecue ovens and Chinese cooking equipment;
wholesaler/distributor of food service equipment;
serving the food servicemarket
President: R Barron
CEO: M Lepage
Number Employees: 20-49
Square Footage: 34000

23741 Herdell Printing Inc
340 Mccormick St
St Helena, CA 94574-1457

707-963-3634
Fax: 707-963-5002 866-963-3634
www.herdellprinting.com
Wine industry labels
President: Mike Herdell
info@herdellprinting.com
VP: Michael Herdell
Quality Control: Steve Herdell
Estimated Sales: $2.5-5 000,000
Number Employees: 20-49

23742 Heritage Bag Co
501 Gateway Pkwy
Roanoke, TX 76262-3481

214-432-3644
Fax: 972-247-3843 800-527-2247
infot@heritage-bag.com www.hunt2recovery.com
Plastic trash bags
CEO: Carl Allen Jr
Contact: Adina Aghinitei
aaghinitei@heritage-bag.com
Estimated Sales: $10-20 Million
Number Employees: 500-999

23743 Heritage Corrugated BoxCorporation
454 Livonia Ave
Brooklyn, NY 11207

718-495-1500
Fax: 718-922-9553
Manufactures corrugated & solid fiber boxes
President: Jeff Schatz
jeff@heritagecontainer.com
Estimated Sales: $5.2 Million
Number Employees: 50-99
Type of Packaging: Bulk

23744 Heritage Equipment Co
9000 Heritage Dr
Plain City, OH 43064-8744

614-873-3941
Fax: 614-873-3549 800-282-7961
eric@heritage-equipment.com
www.heritage-equipment.com
Owner: Louis Castelli
VP: Lisa Zwirner
Ops Mgr: Lou Costillo
Estimated Sales: $5-10 Million
Number Employees: 20-49

23745 Heritage Packaging
625 Fishers Run
Victor, NY 14564-8905

585-742-3310
Fax: 585-742-3311 sales@heritagepackaging.com
www.heritagepackaging.com
Manufacturer and exporter of shipping containers
and packaging for equipment
President: William S Smith
sales@heritagepackaging.com
Estimated Sales: $1-2.5 Million
Number Employees: 50-99

23746 Herkimer Pallet & Wood Products Company
Arthur Street Extension
Herkimer, NY 13350-1440

315-866-4591
Fax: 315-866-4591
Wooden crates, boxes, pallets, etc
President: Michael Lennon
CFO: Karen Dass
VP Marketing: Dave Bass
Manager: Karen Bass
Estimated Sales: Below $5 Million
Number Employees: 1 to 4

23747 Hermann Laue Spice Company
119 Franklin Street
Uxbridge, ON L9P 1J5
Canada

905-852-5100
Fax: 905-852-1113 www.helacanada.ca
Custom blended spices; technical assistance avail-
able
President: Walter Knecht
Director of Sales and Marketing: Eric Nummelin
Number Employees: 35
Square Footage: 228000
Parent Co: Laue, Herman, GmbH
Type of Packaging: Food Service
Brands:
  Hela

23748 Herrmann Ultrasonics
1261 Hardt Cir
Bartlett, IL 60103-1690

630-626-1626
Fax: 630-626-1627 www.herrmannultrasonics.com
Ultrasonic packaging sealing equipment
President: Thomas Herrmann
Marketing Director: Emily Rutkoske
Number Employees: 20-49

23749 Hersey Measurement Company
PO Box 4585
Spartanburg, SC 29305-4585

864-574-8964
Fax: 864-578-7308 800-845-2102
hersey@worldnet.att.net
Batch control systems
Estimated Sales: $20-50 Million
Number Employees: 100-249

23750 Hershey Co.
19 E Chocolate Dr.
Hershey, PA 17033

800-468-1714
www.thehersheycompany.com
Chocolate, confectionery, snack, refreshment and
grocery products.
Chairman/President/CEO: Michele Buck
Senior VP/CFO: Steve Voskuil
Senior VP/General Counsel: Damien Atkins
Year Founded: 1894
Estimated Sales: $7.8 Billion
Number Employees: 15,360
Number of Brands: 31
Type of Packaging: Consumer, Food Service, Pri-
vate Label
Brands:
  Hershey's
  Reese's
  Hershey's Kisses
  Lancaster
  Hershey's Bliss
  Twizzlers
  Almond Joy
  Mounds
  York
  Kit Kat
  Pieces
  5th Avenue
  Brookside
  Cadbury
  Heath
  Whoppers
  Mr.Goodbar
  Krackel
  Take 5
  Whatchamacallit
  Skor
  Symphony
  Allan
  Good & Plenty
  Jolly Rancher
  breathsavers

Bubble Yum
Ice Breakers
Milk Duds
Payday
Rolo
Zagnut
Zero

23751 Hess Machine Intl
1040 S State St
Ephrata, PA 17522-2355
717-733-0005
Fax: 717-733-2255 800-735-4377
ozone@hessmachine.com www.hessmachine.com
Manufacturer and exporter of water treatment equipment including ozone analyzers, ozone generators and filteration equipment.
President: Richard Hess
Marketing Director: Lynn Martin
Manager: Terry Good
terry@ozonesolutions.com
Plant Manager: Calburn McEllheauey
Estimated Sales: Less Than $500,000
Number Employees: 1-4

23752 Heuft USA Inc
2820 Thatcher Rd
Downers Grove, IL 60515-4051
630-968-9011
Fax: 630-968-8767 edi.e.gilich@heuft.com
www.heuft.com
Container inspection equipment including online empty and full container inspectors, valve monitors and bottle sorting equipment
General Manager: Carl Bonnan
Marketing Manager: Bob Klien
Sales Manager: Carl Bonnan
Administrative Manager: Edi Gilch
Estimated Sales: $10-20 Million
Number Employees: 20-49
Parent Co: Heuft SystemTechnik GmbH

23753 Hevi-Haul InternationalLTD
N90w14555 Commerce Dr
Menomonee Falls, WI 53051-2338
262-502-0333
Fax: 262-502-0260 800-558-0577
www.langelift.com
Manufacturer and exporter of rollers and material handling equipment
President: Daniel Knaebe
sales@hevihaul.com
VP: S Knaebe
Sales/Marketing Executive: M Knaebe
Purchasing Agent: M Knaebe
Estimated Sales: $1-2.5 Million
Number Employees: 5-9

23754 Hewitt Manufacturing Co
5365 S 600 E
Waldron, IN 46182-9559
765-525-9829
Fax: 765-525-7185 hewittmfg@tds.net
www.hewittmfg.com
Wire goods including display and refrigerator racks
President: Donald Hewitt
hewittmfg@tds.net
Estimated Sales: $1-2.5 Million
Number Employees: 5-9

23755 Hewitt Soap Company
654 Residenz Pkwy # H
Dayton, OH 45429-6290
937-293-2697
Fax: 937-258-3123 800-543-2245
contact@hewittsoap.com www.hewittsoap.com
Manufacturer and exporter of bar soap
Vice President of Marketing: Deb McDonough
Estimated Sales: $33.9 Million
Number Employees: 1-4
Square Footage: 400000
Parent Co: ASR

23756 Hewlett-Packard
1000 NE Circle Blvd
Corvallis, OR 97330-4291
541-757-2000
Fax: 541-715-6925 www.hp.com
Printers, computers, desktops, laptops, printer ink
Estimated Sales: $20-50 Million
Number Employees: 5000-9999

23757 Hexion Inc
180 E Broad St
Columbus, OH 43215
614-986-2497
888-443-9466
www.hexion.com
Chemical manufacturer.
Chairman/President/CEO: Craig Rogerson
EVP & Chief Financial Officer: George Knight
EVP/General Counsel/Secretary: Douglas Johns
EVP, Human Resources: John Auletto
EVP, Environmental Health & Safety: Stephanie Couhig
EVP & Chief Procurement Officer: Nathan Fisher
EVP & Chief Administrative Officer: Matt Sokol
Year Founded: 2005
Estimated Sales: $3.8 Billion
Number Employees: 4,300
Brands:
    Prince

23758 Hi Roller Enclosed BeltConveyors
5100 W 12th St
Sioux Falls, SD 57107-0551
605-332-3200
Fax: 605-332-1107 800-328-1785
sales@hiroller.com www.hiroller.com
Manufacturer and exporter of enclosed belt conveyors and related accessories
Owner: Philip Clark
Controller: Sally Dieltz
Sales Manager: Mike Spillum
General Manager: John Nelson
General Manager: Steve Tweet
Estimated Sales: $10-20 Million
Number Employees: 20-49
Square Footage: 120000
Parent Co: Hansen Manufacturing Corporation
Brands:
    Hi Roller

23759 Hi-Tech Packaging Inc
1 Bruce Ave
Stratford, CT 06615-6102
203-378-2700
Fax: 203-378-1344 sales@hitechpackaging.net
www.hitechpackaging.com
Packaging machinery
Manager: Al Thibault
athibault@hitechpackaging.net
Estimated Sales: $1-5 000,000
Number Employees: 20-49

23760 Hi-Temp Inc
820 Mississippi St
PO Box 478
Tuscumbia, AL 35674-4741
256-383-5066
Fax: 256-383-5175 800-239-5066
hitemp@hitemp.net www.hitemp.biz
Check and plug valves, pump impellers, valve stems, plastic mallets, rubber pipe grommets, gaskets, dies and floor drains
CEO: Billy Rumbley
Plant Manager: Randy Inman
Estimated Sales: $5-10 Million
Number Employees: 20-49
Square Footage: 76200

23761 Hibco Plastics
1820 US 601 Hwy
PO Box 157
Yadkinville, NC 27055-6347
336-463-2391
Fax: 336-463-5591 800-849-8683
www.hibco.com
Plastic foam
President: Mark Pavlansky
Chairman Board/CEO: Dan Pavlansky
Quality Control: Landon Hardy
Sales: Chris Pavlansky
Accounts Receivable: Sharon Renegar
Purchasing Manager: Mike Russell
Estimated Sales: $10-20 Million
Number Employees: 50-99
Square Footage: 240000

23762 Hibrett Puratex
7001 Westfield Avenue
Pennsauken, NJ 8110
856-662-1717
Fax: 856-662-0550 800-260-5124
www.hibrettpuratex.com
Manufacturer and wholesaler/distributor of compound cleaning chemicals and water treatment products
CEO: Jerome Ellerbee
Sales: Nelissa Abreu
Contact: Stefanie Geoghegan
sgeoghegan@hibrettpuratex.com
Number Employees: 20
Number of Products: 1000
Square Footage: 42000
Parent Co: Hibrett Puratex
Type of Packaging: Private Label

23763 Hickory Industries
4900 W Side Ave
North Bergen, NJ 00047
201-223-4382
Fax: 201-223-0950 800-732-9153
www.hickorybbq.com
Manufacturer and exporter of cooking equipment including grills, warmers, ovens and rotisseries; also, barbecue machinery and accessories
President: Steven Maroti
VP Sales/Marketing: Joe Slusz
Contact: Beth Beyer
beth.beyer@hickorybbq.com
Estimated Sales: $20-50 Million
Number Employees: 100-249
Square Footage: 50000
Brands:
    Hickory
    Old Hickory

23764 Hickory Zesti Smoked Specialties
783 Old Hickory Boulevard
Suite 300
Brentwood, TN 37027-4508
615-373-8838
Fax: 615-371-1780 800-251-2076
www.hickoryspecialties.com
Liquid smoke products
President: Pat Moeller
Estimated Sales: $5-10 Million
Number Employees: 110

23765 Hiclay Studios
3015 Locust Street
St Louis, MO 63103-1328
314-533-8393
Fax: 314-533-8397
Displays and signs
President: Harold A Lutz Jr
Estimated Sales: $1-2.5 Million
Number Employees: 1-4

23766 High Ground of Texas
401 N. 3rd Street
PO Box 716
Stratford, TX 79084-0716
806-366-7510
Fax: 806-366-7511 www.highground.org
Estimated Sales: Below $500,000
Number Employees: 1-4

23767 High-Purity Standards
7221 Investment Drive
North Charleston, SC 29418
843-767-7900
Fax: 843-767-7906 866-767-4771
www.highpuritystandards.com
Manufactures single and multielement standards of extremely high purity for the calibration of analytical instruments such as the AAS, ICP, ICP-MS and IC.
President: Theodore Rains
CEO: Connie Hayes
Contact: Stephanie Audette
stephanie@hps.net
Estimated Sales: $1,904,757
Number Employees: 20-49
Square Footage: 40000

23768 Highland Plastics Inc
3650 Dulles Dr
Mira Loma, CA 91752-3260
951-360-9587
Fax: 951-360-9465 800-368-0491
mmurphy@hiplas.com www.hiplas.com
Lid capping equipment and containers, cups and closures; also, custom printing and labeling available
CEO: James Nelson
jnelson@hiplas.com
CEO: James Nelson
Marketing Director: Mark Murphy

Estimated Sales: $10-20 Million
Number Employees: 250-499
Square Footage: 162000

23769 Highland Sugarworks
49 Parker Rd
Wilson Industrial Park, P.O. Box 58
Websterville, VT 5678

802-479-1747
Fax: 802-479-1737 800-452-4012
jclose@highlandsugarworks.com
www.highlandsugarworks.com
Pure maple syrup and pancake mixes
President: Jim Mac Isaac
jim@highlandsugarworks.com
Sales/Marketing: Jim Close
Operations: Deb Frimodig
Estimated Sales: $500,000-$1 Million
Number Employees: 10-19
Square Footage: 60000
Type of Packaging: Consumer, Food Service, Private Label, Bulk
Brands:
Highland Sugarworks

23770 Highland Supply Corp
1111 6th St
Highland, IL 62249-1408

618-654-2161
Fax: 618-654-3911 800-472-3645
orderdesk@highlandsupply.com
www.billkreitzer.com
Converted printed, tinted and clear film; also, shredded material and pre-cut covers
President: Donald Weder
dweder@highlandsupply.com
Sales Service Manager: Scott Greathouse
Estimated Sales: $20-50 Million
Number Employees: 250-499
Brands:
Speed Cover

23771 Highlight Industries
2694 Prairie St SW
Wyoming, MI 49519-2461

616-531-2464
Fax: 616-531-0506 800-531-2465
info@highlightindustries.com
www.highlightindustries.com
Manufacturer and exporter of stretch wrapping machinery, case sealing, case strapping, and shrink wrap machinery
Owner: Kurt Riemenschneide
Estimated Sales: $10-20 Million
Number Employees: 50-99
Square Footage: 120000
Brands:
Freedom
Poly Packer
Revolver
Synergy

23772 Hilden Halifax
1044 Commerce Lane
P.O.Box 1098
South Boston, VA 24592-1098

434-572-3965
Fax: 434-572-4781 800-431-2514
www.hildenamerica.com
Manufacturer, importer and exporter of table linens and kitchen textiles
President: Russell Basch
Vice President of Sales: Tom Hall
Sales: Sharlene Gulley
Estimated Sales: $2.5-5 Million
Number Employees: 20-49
Square Footage: 160000
Parent Co: Hilden Manufacturing Company
Brands:
Village Square

23773 Hildreth Wood Products Inc
825 Mount Vernon Rd
Wadesboro, NC 28170-7108

704-826-8326
Fax: 704-826-8097
www.hildrethwoodproducts.com
Wooden pallets and skids
Owner: Blake E Hildreth Jr
bhildreth@hildrethwoodproducts.com
General Manager: Leon Hildreth
Estimated Sales: $3-5 Million
Number Employees: 20-49

23774 Hilex Company
990 Apollo Rd # A
Eagan, MN 55121-2390

651-454-1160
Fax: 651-454-2507
Bleaches, sanitizers and disinfectants
President: Tom Gates
COO: Ray Lee
Estimated Sales: $5-10 Million
Number Employees: 20 to 49
Square Footage: 120000
Brands:
Hilex 6-40

23775 Hill Brush, Inc.
811 Rolyn Ave
Baltimore, MD 21237

410-325-7000
Fax: 410-325-6477 800-998-1515
info@hillbrushinc.com
www.hillbrushinc.com/index.htm
Cleaning systems for hygienically sensitive areas within food and beverage production facilities, restaurants & kitchens, catering, dairies and hospitals. Color coded manual cleaning tools.
President: Philip Coward
Manager: Ernest Atkinson
VP: Peter Coward
National Sales Director: James Sokaitis
Contact: Lori Cain
lori@hillbrush.com
Manager: Margie Gessinger
Estimated Sales: $600 Thousand
Type of Packaging: Food Service, Bulk

23776 Hill Manufacturing Co Inc
1500 Jonesboro Rd SE
Atlanta, GA 30315-4085

404-522-8364
Fax: 404-522-9694 www.hillmfg.com
Manufacturer, importer and exporter of USDA cleaning products including hand cleaners, liquid washing and industrial cleaning compounds, germicide disinfectants and floor polish
President: Stewart Hillman
VP: Jack Hillman
Estimated Sales: $20-50 Million
Number Employees: 100-249
Square Footage: 110000
Type of Packaging: Bulk
Brands:
Hilco

23777 Hill Parts
211 Hogan Pond Ln
Ball Ground, GA 30107-4380

770-735-4181
Fax: 770-735-4494 800-241-4003
sales@hillparts.com www.hillparts.com
Equipment and parts for poultry processing
Owner: Donald Hill
Chief Executive: Billy Hill
Account Manager: Marty Lee
Number Employees: 5-9
Parent Co: Cooperatieve Meyn

23778 Hillards Chocolate System
275 E Center St
West Bridgewater, MA 02379-1813

508-587-3666
Fax: 508-587-3735 800-258-1530
sales@hilliardschocolate.com
www.hilliardschocolate.com
Candymaking utensils and manufacturers of chocolate machinery
President: James S Bourne
Contact: Daniel Andersen
dandersen@hilliardschocolate.com
Estimated Sales: $1 Million
Number Employees: 5-9
Type of Packaging: Bulk
Brands:
Hilliard

23779 Hilliard Corp
100 W 4th St
Elmira, NY 14901-2190

607-733-7121
Fax: 607-737-1108 hilliard@hilliardcorp.com
www.hilliardcorp.com
Motion control products, oil filtration and reclaiming equipment, starters for industrial gas, diesel engines and gas turbines, and plate and frame filter presses used in the food and beverage industry.

President: Paul Webb
CEO: Nelson Mooers Van Den
n.vandenblink@hilliardcorp.com
CEO: Nelson Mooers Van Den
CEO: Nelson Mooers Van Den Blink
Regional Sales Manager: Gerry Lachut
Estimated Sales: $50-75 Million
Number Employees: 500-999

23780 Hillside Metal Ware Company
1060 Commerce Ave
Union, NJ 07083-5026

908-964-3080
Fax: 908-964-3082
Manufacturer and exporter of aluminum cookware and bakeware including molds, black steel pizza, springform and cake pans
Estimated Sales: $2 Million
Number Employees: 20-49
Square Footage: 120000
Brands:
Hillware

23781 Hilltop Services LLC
6616 Fribay Road
Byron, IL 61010

815-234-8600
Fax: 815-234-3028 mmhilltop@verizon.net
Supplies prep equipment/machinery
President: Michael Lingel
CFO: Mary Lingel
Sales/PR: Mike Lingel

23782 Hillyard Inc
302 N 4th St
P.O. Box 909
St Joseph, MO 64501-1720

816-233-1321
Fax: 816-383-8414 800-365-1555
www.hillyard.com
Manufacturer and exporter of floor seals, finishes, waxes, polishes and cleaners
President: Jim Corolus
jcorolus@hillyard.com
Chief Financial Officer: Neil Ambrose
Executive Vice President: Scott Hillyard
Vice President, R&D: Stuart Hughes
Vice President, Sales: David Schauer
Operations Manager: Jon Gottlieb
Product Manager: Blake Roth
Purchasing Manager: Tom Armstrong
Estimated Sales: $66 Million
Number Employees: 500-999
Square Footage: 325600

23783 Hilter Stainless
614 Eau Placine Street
Stratford, WI 54484

715-387-8260
Fax: 715-387-0148
Estimated Sales: $1-2.5 Million
Number Employees: 15

23784 Himolene
1648 Diplomat Drive
Carrollton, TX 75006-6847

203-731-3600
Fax: 203-731-3620 800-777-4411
High density industrial can liners
VP/General Manager: Paul Hart
Marketing Manager: Dave Shewmaker
Estimated Sales: $1-2.5 Million
Number Employees: 5-9
Parent Co: First Brands Corporation
Brands:
Stick 'n Stay
Tie-Tie

23785 (HQ)Hinchcliff Products Company
13477 Prospect Road
Strongsville, OH 44149

440-238-5200
Fax: 440-238-5202 sales@hinchcliffproducts.com
www.hinchcliffproducts.com
Manufacturer and exporter of wooden pallets, skids, boxes, crates and containers
President: Jay D Phillips
VP of Sales: Don Phillips
Contact: Donald Phillips
sales@hinchcliffproducts.com
Purchasing Manager: Scott Phillips
Estimated Sales: $500,000-$1 Million
Number Employees: 1-4

Number of Products: 3
Square Footage: 200000

23786 Hinds-Bock Corp
2122 222nd St SE
Bothell, WA 98021-4430
425-885-1183
Fax: 425-885-1492 garyh@hinds-bock.com
www.hinds-bock.com
Manufacturer and exporter of standard and custom piston filling machines, depositors and transfer pumps for liquids and viscous products with delicate particulates
President: Gary Hinds
CFO: John Davis
VP Sales/Marketing: Lance Aasness
Estimated Sales: $5-10 Million
Number Employees: 20-49
Square Footage: 96000

23787 Hines III
1650 Art Museum Dr
Suite 18
Jacksonville, FL 32207-2188
904-398-5110
Fax: 904-396-1867
Fiberglass, steel and wood benches/seats; also, planters, ash and trash receptacles, tables, table tops and planter/bench combinations
CEO: Samuel Hines
Estimated Sales: Below $5 Million
Number Employees: 1-4
Square Footage: 64000

23788 Hinkle Manufacturing
5th & D Streets Ampoint Industrial Park
Perrysburg, OH 43551
419-666-5550
Fax: 419-666-5367 419-666-5367
klembke@hinklemfg.com www.hinklemfg.com
Corrugated boxes and recyclable plastic and foam packaging
Manger: Taber Hinkle
VP Marketing: Malcolm Eddy
General Manager: John Mayland
Estimated Sales: $10-20 Million
Number Employees: 50-99

23789 Hino Diesel Trucks
41180 Bridge Street
Novi, MI 48375
248-699-9300
Fax: 248-699-9310 daniels@hino.com
www.hino.com
VP: Francis Merz
IT Manager: Brad Czischke
VP Marketing and Dealer Operations: Glenn Ellis
SM, Human Resources and Administration: Joseph Whalen
VP of Service Operations: George M. Daniels

23790 Hishi Plastics
600 Ryerson Road
Lincoln Park, NJ 07035-2057
973-633-1230
Fax: 973-872-8381
customerservice@hishiplastics.com
www.hishiplastics.com
Food and HBA packaging materials
President: Shawn Kawazato
Contact: Kathy Ammirata
kammirata@hishiplastics.com
Estimated Sales: $5-10 Million
Number Employees: 50-99

23791 Hiss Stamp Company
100 N Grant Ave
Columbus, OH 43215-5119
614-224-5119
Fax: 614-224-0464
Manufacturer and wholesaler/distributor of stamps and FDA approved inks
Manager: Michael Gaborcik
Estimated Sales: Less than $500,000
Number Employees: 4
Square Footage: 7000
Parent Co: Cosco Industries

23792 Hitachi Maxco LTD
1630 Cobb International Blvd
Kennesaw, GA 30152-4353
770-424-9350
Fax: 770-424-9145 800-241-8209
twalker@hitmax.com www.hitmax.com

President: Martin Bando
mbando@hitmax.com
CFO: Douglas Roberts
Number Employees: 20-49

23793 Hitec Food Equipment
818 Lively Blvd
Wood Dale, IL 60191-1202
630-521-9460
Fax: 630-521-9466 information@hitec-usa.com
www.hitec-usa.com
Owner: Charles Chacon
cchacon@hitec-usa.com
CFO: Takeshi Kojima
Estimated Sales: Below $5 000,000
Number Employees: 5-9

23794 Hitec Food Equipment
818 Lively Blvd
Wood Dale, IL 60191-1202
630-521-9460
Fax: 630-521-9466 information@hitec-usa.com
www.hitec-usa.com
Food processing machines for the ham and sausage industry.
Owner: Charles Chacon
cchacon@hitec-usa.com
Number Employees: 5-9

23795 Hiwin Technologies Corporation
520 E Business Center Drive
Mt Prospect, IL 60056-2186
847-827-2270
Fax: 847-827-2291 info@hiwin.com
www.hiwin.com.tw
High quality linear motion products
President: Joe Jou
Sales Engineer: Fred Chevalau
Sales Engineer: Joe Long
Sales Engineer: Chuck Haas
Accounting Dept.: Geneva Wang
Inventory Control: Andrew Choi
Estimated Sales: $5-10 Million
Number Employees: 30

23796 Hixson Architecture Engrng
659 Van Meter St
Cincinnati, OH 45202-1568
513-241-1230
Fax: 513-241-1287 info@hixson-inc.com
www.hixson-inc.com
Hixson provides engineering and design solutions that enable food and beverage processors to increase production speed and thoughput, improve product quality and consistency, reduce costs, and deliver capital projects more effectively. Design capabilities include process, packaging, material handling, automation, electrical, HVAC, plumbing, refrigeration, civil and structural engineering, architecture, environmental, health and safety compliance, project management, constructionadministration.
President: Michael Follmer
m.follmer@hixson-inc.com
Sales: Jim Rivard
Sales: Mike Steur
Estimated Sales: $20-30 Million
Number Employees: 100-249

23797 Hixson Architecture Engrng
659 Van Meter St
Cincinnati, OH 45202-1568
513-241-1230
Fax: 513-241-1287 info@hixson-inc.com
www.hixson-inc.com
Engineering and design solutions that enable food and beverage processors to increase production speed and through-put, improve product quality and consistency, reduce costs, and deliver capital projects more effectively. Designcapabilities include process, packaging, material handling, automation, electrical, HVAC, plumbing, refridgeration, civil and structural. Hixson assists companies with renovations, expansion, site selection, master planning, utility improvements andmore.
President: Bryan Suutherly
bsuutherly@hixson-inc.com
Chief Financial Officer: Thomas Banker
Vice President: William Sander NCARB
Marketing/Sales: Mike Steur
Sales: Jim Rivard
Public Relations: Patricia Helmbrook
Estimated Sales: $20-30 Million
Number Employees: 100-249

23798 Hoarel Sign Co
819 NE 7th Ave
Amarillo, TX 79107-5417
806-373-2175
Fax: 806-373-2329 www.hoarelsign.com
Point of purchase displays and signs including advertising, changeable letter, electric, interchangeable, luminous tube and plastic
President: Gary Cox
Treasurer: Linda Cox
VP: Ray Cox
Estimated Sales: $1-2.5 Million
Number Employees: 10-19
Square Footage: 32000

23799 Hobart
701 S Ridge Ave
Troy, OH 45374-0001
888-378-1338
www.hobartcorp.com
Bakery machinery and equipment.
Year Founded: 1897
Estimated Sales: Above $5 Billion
Number Employees: 1,000-4,999
Parent Co: ITW Food Equipment Group LLC

23800 Hodge Design Assoc PC
22 Chestnut St
Evansville, IN 47713-1022
812-422-2558
Fax: 812-422-3337 info@hodgestructural.com
www.hodgedesign.com
Wine industry label design
Owner: Gray Hodge
ghodge@hodgedesign.com
Estimated Sales: $1-5 000,000
Number Employees: 5-9

23801 Hodge Manufacturing Company
55 Fisk Ave
Springfield, MA 01107
413-781-6800
Fax: 413-349-8235 800-262-4634
www.durhammfg.com
Steel work benches, carts, platforms, shelf and hand trucks, recycle receptacles, waste material containers, shelving racks, hook-on bins, storage cabinets, safety equipment, wire carts, etc
Manager: Bob Hall
Contact: Edwin Kossoy
e.kossoy@hodgemfg.com
Estimated Sales: $10-20,000,000
Number Employees: 50-99
Square Footage: 50000

23802 Hodges
PO Box 187
Vienna, IL 62995-0187
618-658-9070
Fax: 773-379-8102 800-444-0011
Racks, shelving, casters, dolly trucks, utilty carts and mobile storage equipment
National Sales Manager: Chris Geurden
Estimated Sales: $1-5,000,000
Number Employees: 100-249
Square Footage: 240000
Parent Co: Leggett & Platt Storage Products Group
Brands:
Postmaster

23803 Hoegger Alpina
PO Box 175918
Covington, KY 41017-5918
865-344-8642
Fax: 865-344-8743
Commerical meat processing machines, choppers, stuffers, and chip machines

23804 Hoegger Food Technology
3555 Holly Ln N # 10
Suite 10
Minneapolis, MN 55447-1285
763-233-6930
Fax: 802-223-5499 877-789-5400
info.usa@hoegger.com www.hoegger.com
Meat presses for bacon, pork and strip steaks, as well as post packaging pasteurization products for hams, sausage and other meat products as well as pasta and vegetables.
Manager: Mike Collins
Number Employees: 5-9

23805 Hoffer Flow Controls Inc
107 Kitty Hawk Ln
P.O.Box 2145
Elizabeth City, NC 27909-6756
252-331-1997
Fax: 252-331-2886 800-628-4584
info@hofferflow.com www.hofferflow.com
Manufacturer and exporter of sanitary turbine flowmeters for batch controlling, flow rate indication and totalization.
President: Bob Carrell
bcarrell@hofferflow.com
CEO: Ken Hoffer
CEO: Sandra Kelly
Quality Control: Wendy Brabble
Marketing Manager: Janna Critcher
Sales: Linda Markham
Production Manager: Deborah Blakeney
Purchasing: Melissa Stallings
Estimated Sales: $5-10 Million
Number Employees: 50-99
Square Footage: 80000
Brands:
  Hoffer

23806 Hoffman & Levy Inc Tasseldepot
3251 SW 13th Dr # 3
Deerfield Beach, FL 33442-8166
954-698-0001
Fax: 954-698-0009 info@tasseldepot.com
www.tasseldepot.com
Manufacturer and exporter of napkin rings and decorative items including tassles and chair tie-backs
President: Roger Leavy
info@tasseldepot.com
Marketing/Design: April Leavy
Estimated Sales: $1-2.5 Million
Number Employees: 50-99
Square Footage: 46000

23807 Hoffman Co
1306 Laredo St
Corpus Christi, TX 78401-3249
361-882-9281
Fax: 361-883-1677 sales@hoffman-co.com
www.hoffmanandcompany.com
Doors, cabinets and store fixtures
President: Bryan Hoffman
bhoff@hoffmancompany.com
Marketing Manager: Brian Hoffman
Estimated Sales: $5-10 Million
Number Employees: 20-49

23808 Hoffmann LA Roche
340 Kingsland St
Nutley, NJ 07110-1199
973-235-4761
Fax: 973-235-3775 800-526-6367
President: George B Abercrombie
Chief Financial Officer: Ivor MacLeod
Contact: Sophie Actis
sophie.actis@roche.com
Number Employees: 1-4
Parent Co: Roche Group

23809 Hoffmaster Group Inc
2920 N Main St
Oshkosh, WI 54901-1221
920-235-9330
Fax: 920-235-1642 800-367-2877
info@solocup.com www.hoffmaster.com
Institutional and consumer food service items: baking, eclair, portion, burger cups; hot dog trays; pan liners; bath mats/car mats; doilies; lace and linen placemats, printed and custom designed placemats; plain and printed napkins;tray sovers and table covers
President: Robert Korzenski
CEO: Dennis Mehiel
CFO: Haris Heinsen
VP Operations: Bryan Hollenbach
Marketing Director: Beth Dahlke
Sales Director: John Lewchenko
Public Relations: Jenny Leichtfuss
Plant Manager: Tom Glaeser
Purchasing Manager: Mike Marquardt
Number Employees: 500-999
Number of Brands: 9
Square Footage: 970000
Parent Co: SF Holdings Group
Other Locations:
  Fonda Group
  Lakeland FL
  Fonda Group
  Goshen IA

Fonda Group
Glens Falls NY
Fonda Group
Williamsberg PA
Fonda Group
St. Albans VT
Fonda Group
Appleton WI
Fonda Group
Augusta GA
Fonda Group
Indianapolis IA
Brands:
  American
  Budgetware
  Dollarwise
  Firmware
  Fonda
  Hoffmaster
  Linen-Like
  Sensations
  Smartware

23810 Hoffmaster Group Inc
2920 N Main St
Oshkosh, WI 54901-1221
Fax: 920-235-1642 800-327-9774
marketing@hoffmaster.com www.hoffmaster.com
Manufacturer and exporter of strip lace, place mats, baking cups, tray covers and doilies including paper lace, linen, glassine, grease-proof and foil
CEO: Rory Leyden
rory.leyden@creativeconverting.com
Customer Service Manager: Lori Hart-Noyes
General Manager: Wayne Grant
Number Employees: 500-999
Square Footage: 50000
Type of Packaging: Consumer, Private Label, Bulk
Brands:
  Gay 90's

23811 Hoffmaster Group Inc.
2920 N. Main St.
Oshkosh, WI 54901
800-558-9300
www.hoffmaster.com
Disposable tableware including plates, napkins, table covers, cups, bowls, trays, take-out containers, etc.
President/CEO: Rory Leyden
rory.leyden@creativeconverting.com
Year Founded: 1947
Estimated Sales: $100-500 Million
Number Employees: 500-999
Number of Brands: 17
Brands:
  Bello Lino®
  CaterWrap®
  Classy Kid®
  Combo Packs™
  Earth Wise Tree Free®
  Earth Wise®
  FashnPoint®
  Linen-Like Natural®
  Linen-Like Supreme®
  Linen-Like®
  Linen-Like® Select™
  Multipack®
  Party in a Box®
  Quickset®
  S!mply Baked®
  Spunbond®
  SturdyStyle™

23812 Hoffmeyer Corp
1600 Factor Ave
San Leandro, CA 94577-5618
510-895-9014
Fax: 510-895-9014 888-744-1826
sales@hoffmeyerco.com
Manufacturer and fabricator of conveyor belting, gaskets, seals, hoses, fittings and assemblies
Owner: Frederick O Shay
Chairman Board/CEO: Frederick Oshay
Chairman: Frederick Oshay
Contact: Mike Alberts
malberts@hoffmeyerco.com
Estimated Sales: $5-10 Million
Number Employees: 1-4
Square Footage: 34000

23813 Hoge Brush Company
701 S Main Street
State Route 29
New Knoxville, OH 45871
419-753-2351
Fax: 419-753-2893 800-494-4643
info@hoge.com www.hoge.com
Counter dusters, dairy, floor, sweeping, garage and window brushes, street brooms, etc
President: John Hoge
Sales/Marketing Executive: David Zwiep
Production Manager: Ray Slone
Plant Manager: Dave Zwiep
Purchasing Manager: David Zwiep
Estimated Sales: $1-3 Million
Number Employees: 5-9
Square Footage: 71484
Parent Co: Hoge Lumber Company
Brands:
  Hoge

23814 Hogshire Industries
2401 Hampton Blvd
Norfolk, VA 23517
757-877-2297
Fax: 757-624-2328 www.bigleycanvas.com
Commercial awnings
Estimated Sales: $1-2,500,000
Number Employees: 20-49

23815 Hogtown Brewing Company
2351 Royal Windsor Drive
Unit 6
Mississauga, ON L5J 4S7
Canada
905-855-9065
Fax: 905-822-0990 www.hogtownbrewers.org
Beers; bottling services
President: Maria Lopez
General Manager: Peter Lazaro
Number Employees: 5-9
Type of Packaging: Consumer, Food Service

23816 Hohn Manufacturing Company
200 Sun Valley Cir
Fenton, MO 63026
636-349-1400
Fax: 636-349-1440 800-878-1440
hohnmfginc@toast.net
Manufacturer and exporter of furniture polishes, cleaning compounds, soaps, detergents, tablets, etc
President: Larry Harrington
Estimated Sales: $1-4 Million
Number Employees: 5-9
Square Footage: 72000
Type of Packaging: Private Label
Brands:
  Vita Lustre

23817 Hohner Corporation
PO Box 3004
Beamsville, ON L0R 1B3
Canada
905-563-4924
Fax: 905-563-7209 800-295-5693
hohner@hohner.com www.hohner.com
President: Walter Bloechle
Number Employees: 10

23818 (HQ)Holcor
13603 S Halsted Street
Riverdale, IL 60827-1163
708-841-3800
Fax: 708-841-3941
Fluorescent, incandescent and mercury lighting
President: S Larson
Estimated Sales: $20-50 Million
Number Employees: 50-99
Square Footage: 5000

23819 (HQ)Holden Graphic Services
607 Washington Ave N
Minneapolis, MN 55401-1220
612-339-0241
Fax: 612-349-0433 holden@usinternet.com
Printed cash register tapes, coupons and business forms
President: George T Holden
CFO: Gary Plager
Sales Manager: Dave Brow
Contact: Craig Fixell
cfixell@holdenonline.com
Estimated Sales: $5-10 Million
Number Employees: 20-49

Other Locations:
Holden Graphic Services
Minneapolis MN

23820 Holland Applied Technologies
7050 High Grove Blvd
Burr Ridge, IL 60527-7595

630-325-5130
Fax: 630-654-2518 information@hollandapt.com
www.hollandapt.com
Packaging equipment and materials, clean-in-place
systems, filters, gauges, heat exchangers and valves
President: Dave Cheney
VP: Fred Kramer
Estimated Sales: $25 Million
Number Employees: 50-99

23821 Holland Chemicals Company
4590 Rhodes Drive
Windsor, ON N8W 5C2
Canada

519-948-4373
Fax: 519-945-2256 info@hollandcleaning.com
www.hollandcleaning.com
Floor finishes and detergents
Manager: Mike Shalub

23822 Holland Co Inc
153 Howland Ave
Adams, MA 01220-1199

413-743-1292
Fax: 413-743-1298 800-639-9602
info@hollandcompany.com
www.hollandcompany.com
Manufacturer and exporter of food grade additives
including ammonium, potassium and iron-free alu-
minum sulfates
President: Daniel J Holland
Estimated Sales: $10-20,000,000
Number Employees: 20-49

23823 Holland Manufacturing Co Inc
15 Main St
Succasunna, NJ 07876-1747

973-584-8141
Fax: 973-584-6845 www.hollandmfg.com
Converted paper products and packaging tapes
President: Jack Holland
CEO: Edelina Zajac
edelina@hollandmfg.com
CFO: Mitch Cantor
R&D: Donald Thoren
Estimated Sales: $20-50 Million
Number Employees: 50-99

23824 Hollander Horizon International
16 Wall St
Princeton, NJ 08540-1513

609-924-7577
Fax: 609-924-8626 www.hhisearch.com
Hollander Horizon International is the premier exec-
utive search firm specializing in the technical sector
of the food and consumer products industry. The ar-
eas we serve are: research and development, manu-
facturing and engineeringquality control, and quality
assurance.
East Coast Senior Partner: Michael Hollander
West Coast Senior Partner: Arnold Zimmerman
Contact: Sheri Baker
sbaker@hhisearch.com
Estimated Sales: $300,000-500,000
Number Employees: 5-9
Parent Co: Hollander Horizon International

23825 Hollandia Bakeries Limited
PO Box 100
Mt Brydges, ON N0L 1W0
Canada

519-264-1020
800-265-3480
www.hollandiacookies.com
Cookies
President: Joop De Voest Jr
Controller: Rick Bannister
Quality Control: Mike Hobley
VP Sales: Doug Smith
Brands:
  Kerleens
  Sugar Free Cookies
  Hard Cookies
  Soft Cookies
  Gourmet Specialty Cookies
  Mini Tubs
  Red Label

23826 Hollingsworth Custom Wood Products
284 N Street
Sault Ste. Marie, ON P6A 7B8
Canada

705-759-1756
Fax: 705-759-0275
Manufacturer and exporter of butchers' blocks, cut-
ting boards and wooden bakers' tops
Marketing Director: Paul Hollingsworth
Customer Service: Ruth Bradley
General Manager: Jim Webb
Estimated Sales: $1-5 Million
Number Employees: 15
Parent Co: Soo Mill Lumber
Brands:
  Woodwelded

23827 Hollowell Products Corporation
570 Central St
Wyandotte, MI 48192-7123

734-282-8200
Fax: 734-282-0678
Industrial vacuum cleaners including mobile, gas
and electric powered
President: John F Hollowell
Contact: John Hollowell
jhollowell@elephant-vac.com
Estimated Sales: Below $5 Million
Number Employees: 5-9

23828 Hollowick Inc
100 Fairgrounds Dr
Manlius, NY 13104-1699

315-682-2163
Fax: 315-682-6948 800-367-3015
info@hollowick.com
Manufacturer and exporter of liquid candle lamps,
lamp fuel, wax candles, chafing fuel and silk flowers
ceramic vases
President: Alan Menter
info@hollowick.com
CFO: Eugene Duffy
Marketing: Mike Cleveland
Sales: Mike Cleveland
Plant Manager: Tom Palmeter
Estimated Sales: $5-10 Million
Number Employees: 20-49
Brands:
  Easy Florals
  Easy Heat
  Select Wax

23829 Holly International
PO Box 265
Lake Elsinore, CA 92531-0265

909-678-8386
Fax: 909-678-7856
Equipment

23830 Hollymatic Corp
600 E Plainfield Rd
Countryside, IL 60525-6900

708-579-3700
Fax: 708-579-1057 hollyinfo@hollymatic.com
www.hollymatic.com
Manufacturer, exporter and importer of food pro-
cessing equipment and supplies including tenderiz-
ers, grinders, mixers/grinders/ patty machines, meat
saws, etc.
President: James Azzar
R&D: Hardev Somal
Marketing Manager: Rob Kovack
Manager: Jim Trejo
jtrejo@hollymatic.com
Estimated Sales: $5-10 Million
Number Employees: 20-49
Type of Packaging: Food Service
Brands:
  Hollymatic

23831 Hollywood Banners
539 Oak St
Copiague, NY 11726-3261

631-842-3000
Fax: 631-842-3148 800-691-5652
info@hollywoodbanners.com
www.hollywoodbanners.com
Manufacturer and exporter of indoor and outdoor
banners including plastic and cloth
President: Daniel F Mahoney
dmaoney@hollywoodbanners.com
Sales Exec: Daniel F Mahoney
Production Manager: Hugo Canedo

Estimated Sales: $1-3 Million
Number Employees: 20-49
Square Footage: 100000

23832 Holman Boiler Works
1956 Singleton Blvd
Dallas, TX 75212

214-637-0020
Fax: 214-637-2539 800-331-1956
dal-sales@holmanboiler.com
Manufacturer and exporter of watertube and firetube
boilers; also, burners
President: John Campollo
sales@holmanboiler.com
CEO: Richard Maxson
Quality Control: Greg Martinez
Manager Business Development: Gary Perskhini
Estimated Sales: $50-100 Million
Number Employees: 50-99
Parent Co: Copes-Vulcan
Brands:
  E.D.G.E.

23833 Holman Cooking Equipment
10 Sunnen Dr
Saint Louis, MO 63143-3800

888-356-5362
Fax: 800-264-6666
Food service equipment including conveyor toasters,
conveyor ovens and specialty/finishing ovens
CFO: Mike Barber
CEO: Frank Ricchio
VP Engineering: Doug Vogt
Marketing Manager: Candi Benz
Number Employees: 100-249
Square Footage: 80000
Parent Co: Star Manufacturing International

23834 Holmco Container Manufacturing, LTD
1501 TR 183
Baltic, OH 43804-9677

330-897-4503
Fax: 330-698-3200
Manufacturer and exporter of stainless steel milk
containers.
Owner: Eli Troyer
Number Employees: 2
Square Footage: 38400
Type of Packaging: Food Service

23835 Holo-Source Corporation
12280 Hubbard St
Livonia, MI 48150

734-427-1530
Fax: 734-525-8520 888-995-7799
sales@holo-source.com www.holo-source.com
Holographic materials for packaging and label appli-
cations
CEO: Rob Levy
VP, Operations: Craig Pomish
Year Founded: 1986
Estimated Sales: I
Number Employees: 51-200

23836 Holophane
P.O.Box 3004
Newark, OH 43058-3004

740-587-7218
Fax: 740-349-4451 sbacklund@holophane.com
www.holophane.com
Lighting and control equipment, glass reflectors and
HID lighting fixtures, emergency lighting systems,
and back-up power supplies
President: Crawford Lipsey
CFO: Daren Cox
Vice President: Bob Petro
Quality Control: Lowry Pierce
Manufacturing Director: Kim Lombardi
Contact: William Gordon
bgordon@holophane.com
Estimated Sales: $50-100 Million
Number Employees: 10-19

23837 Holsman Sign Svc
15002 Woodworth Rd
Cleveland, OH 44110-3310

216-761-4433
Fax: 216-761-4439
Signs including neon, electric, plastic, wood, vinyl,
metal, etc.; also, service and installation available
Branch Manager: J Burge
Estimated Sales: $1-5 Million
Number Employees: 10-19

Square Footage: 120000
Parent Co: Identitek

23838 Holstein Manufacturing
5368 110th St
Holstein, IA 51025-8131

712-368-4342
Fax: 712-368-2351 800-368-4342
hmi@pionet.net www.holsteinmfg.com
Barbecue equipment, portable grills and flatbed,
livestock and concession trailers
Vice President: Darrin Schmidt
dlshmidt@ruralwaves.us
VP: Darrin Schmidt
Estimated Sales: $1-2.5 Million
Number Employees: 5-9

23839 Home City Ice Co
6045 Bridgetown Rd # 1
Cincinnati, OH 45248-3047

513-598-3000
Fax: 513-574-5409 800-759-4411
www.homecityice.com
Packaged and block ice
Manager: Robert Everly
Estimated Sales: $1-2.5 Million
Number Employees: 20-49

23840 Home Plastics Inc
5250 NE 17th St
Des Moines, IA 50313-2192

515-265-2562
Fax: 515-265-8872 info@homeplastics.com
www.homeplastics.com
Manufacturer and exporter of polyethylene heat
sealed bags, tubes and liners; also, plastic film and
plain and printed slip-on sleeve labels, political
signs
President and QC: Samuel Siegel
Manager: Bob Rees
brees@homeplastics.com
Estimated Sales: $20-50 Million
Number Employees: 100-249
Type of Packaging: Consumer, Food Service, Pri-
vate Label, Bulk

23841 Home Rubber Co
31 Wolverton St
Trenton, NJ 08611-2429

609-394-1176
Fax: 609-396-1985 800-257-9441
info@homerubber.com www.homerubber.com
Manufacturer and exporter of industrial rubber food
and milk unloading hoses, belting, molded goods
and sheet rubber
President: Rich Balka
VP: Stephen Kelley
Estimated Sales: $10-20 Million
Number Employees: 20-49
Brands:
    Sterling

23842 (HQ)Homer Laughlin China Co
672 Fiesta Dr
Newell, WV 26050-1299

304-387-1300
Fax: 304-387-0593 800-452-4462
hlc@hlchina.com
Manufacturer and exporter of dinnerware china
President: Elizabeth Mc Ilvain
emcilvain@hlchina.com
CEO: Joseph Wells
Marketing Director: Kimberly Faloon
Production Manager: Wilbur Waigoneer
Plant Manager: John Bennley
Purchasing Manager: Otto Jirianni
Estimated Sales: Less Than $500,000
Number Employees: 5-9
Square Footage: 1700000
Brands:
    Ameriwhite
    Best China
    Fiesta
    Gothic
    Lyrica
    Milford
    Pristine
    Seville

23843 (HQ)Honeywell International
World Headquarters
Charlotte, NC 07950

877-841-2840
www.honeywell.com

Fire alarm systems and controls, among other safety
and productivity products.
Chairman/CEO: Darius Adamczyk
President, Safety & Productivity: John Waldron
Senior VP/Chief Financial Officer: Greg Lewis
Senior VP/General Counsel: Anne Madden
Senior VP, HR/Security & Communications: Mark
James
Year Founded: 1906
Estimated Sales: $41.8 Billion
Number Employees: 114,000
Square Footage: 15803

23844 Honeywell Sensing & Internet of Things

302-613-4491
800-537-6945
info.sc@honeywell.com sensing.honeywell.com
Switches and sensors for packaging lines (smart dis-
tributed systems): photoelectric, proximity, pressure,
cuttent and ultrasonic.
Chairman/CEO: Darius Admczyk
Estimated Sales: $500 Million-$1 Billion
Number Employees: 1000-4999
Parent Co: Honeywell International

23845 Honeywell UOP
25 E. Algonquin Road
P.O. Box 5017
Des Plaines, IL 60017-5017

847-391-2000
800-877-6184
www.uop.com
Treatment of food production-related wastewater.
President: John Gugel

23846 Honiron Corp
400 Canal St
Jeanerette, LA 70544-4504

337-276-6314
Fax: 337-276-3614 sales@honiron.com
www.honiron.com
Manufacturer and exporter of sugar machinery
Owner: John Deere
COO: Dennis Banta
dbanta@honiron.com
Estimated Sales: $1-5 Million
Number Employees: 50-99
Type of Packaging: Bulk

23847 (HQ)Hood Packaging
25 Woodgreen Pl
Madison, MS 39110

601-853-7260
Fax: 601-853-7299 800-321-8115
www.hoodpkg.com
Paper and plastic packaging supplies.
President: Robert Morris
Year Founded: 1978
Estimated Sales: $250-500 Million
Number Employees: 250

23848 Hood Packaging
2380 McDowell Road
Burlington, ON L7R 4A1
Canada

905-637-5611
Fax: 905-637-9954 877-462-6627
www.hoodpkg.com
Paper and plastic packaging supplies.
President: Robert Morris
Year Founded: 1978
Estimated Sales: $250-500 Million
Number Employees: 250

23849 Hoover Company
7005 Cochran Rd.
Glenwillow, OH 44139

330-499-9499
Fax: 330-497-5065 www.hoover.com
Extractors, vacuum cleaners and supplies including
bags, belts, air freshener tablets and steamvac clean-
ing solutions.
Year Founded: 1908
Estimated Sales: $350-400 Million
Number Employees: 1000-4999
Square Footage: 527000
Parent Co: Techtronic Industries

23850 Hoover Materials Handling Group
2135 Highway 6 S
Houston, TX 77077-4319

800-844-8683
Manufacturer and exporter of containers and tanks.

Year Founded: 1911
Estimated Sales: $103.2 Million
Parent Co: Hoover Group
Brands:
    Apr
    Bdi
    Bdii
    Bdiii
    Liquitote
    Mamor
    Suredrain

23851 Hop Growers Of Washington
301 W Prospect Rd
Moxee, WA 98936-9811

509-453-4749
Fax: 509-457-8561 info@usahops.org
Represents and promotes the interests of U.S. growers both domestically and internationally. As the national organization, HGA provides support,
coordination and communication to growers, brewers and the world hop industry in areas ofcommon
interest, including; marketing statistics, promotion,
education and research.
Administrator: Ann George
info@usahops.org
Public Relations: Michelle Palacios
Number Employees: 1-4

23852 Hope Chemical Corporation
PO Box 908
Pawtucket, RI 2862

401-724-8000
Fax: 401-724-8076
Industrial cleaning compounds
President: R Bernstein
Contact: Robert Bernstein
robert.bernstein@mannsvillechemical.com
Number Employees: 50

23853 Hope Industrial Systems
1325 Northmeadow Pkwy # 100
Suite 100
Roswell, GA 30076-3896

678-762-9790
Fax: 678-762-9789 877-762-9790
sales@hopeindustrial.com
Flat panel touchscreens and monitors for the food
processing and dairy industries.
Contact: Bo Bowling
bo.bowling@hopeindustrial.com
Number Employees: 5-9

23854 Hope Paper Box Company
33 India Street
Pawtucket, RI 02860-5510

401-724-5700
Corrugated paper boxes and partitions
President: Timothy H Hayes
VP: Gregory Yates
Estimated Sales: $2.5-5 Million
Number Employees: 20-49

23855 Hopp Co Inc
815 2nd Ave
New Hyde Park, NY 11040-4869

516-358-4170
Fax: 516-358-4178 800-889-8425
Sales@HoppCompanies.com
www.hoppcompanies.com
Plastic chips, strips, restocking tags, label backers
and covers used as label holders, overlays and deco-
rative coverings for shelf moldings
Owner: Robert Hopp
bob@hoppcompanies.com
CEO: Cani Hopp
CEO: Bob Hopp
Estimated Sales: $2.5-5 Million
Number Employees: 10-19
Number of Brands: 1

23856 Hoppmann Corporation
13129 Airpark Dr # 120
Elkwood, VA 22718-1761

540-825-2899
Fax: 540-829-1724 800-368-3582
sales@ShibuyaHoppmann.com
www.shibuyahoppmann.com
Manufacturer and exporter of assembly packaging
systems including feeders, pre-feeders, conveyors,
turnkey systems, etc.; also, integration services
available

President: Mark Flanagan
flanagan@hoppmann.com
CEO: Peter Hoppmann
Executive Vice President: Kazuhiro Miyamae
VP Finance: Maryanne Flusher
Product Manager: Chad Roberts
Sales Director: Dave Martin
Number Employees: 100-249

23857 Horix Manufacturing Co
1384 Island Ave
Mc Kees Rocks, PA 15136-2593

412-771-1111
Fax: 412-331-8599 info@horix.net
www.horix.info
Manufacturer, importer and exporter of liquid fill-
ing, capping, labeling and rinsing machinery for
cans and bottles
President: Linda Fzramowski
Plant Manager: Felgon Robert
Research & Development: Russell Myers
CEO: Linda M Szramowski
Sales Director: David Becki
Plant Manager: Robert Feltop
Purchasing Manager: Brad Barber
Estimated Sales: $5-10 Million
Number Employees: 20-49
Square Footage: 120000
Brands:
  Dura-Base
  Flo-Fil
  Hytamatic
  Posi-Sync
  Screen-Flo
  Ultra-Fil
  Var-I-Vol
  Volufil
  Weigh-Master

23858 Horizon Plastics
Northam Industrial Park, Bldg 3
PO Box 474
Cobourg, ON K9A5V7
Canada

905-372-2291
Fax: 905-372-9397 855-467-4066
info@horizonplastics.com
www.horizonplastics.com

23859 Horizon Software International
2915 Premiere Parkway
Suite 300
Duluth, GA 30097

770-554-6353
Fax: 770-554-6331 800-741-7100
Point of sale and back office solutions for all your
food service management needs
President: Randy Eckels
VP/Finance: Jason Hayes
Senior VP/R&D: Robbie Payne
VP/Sales: Sharon McGuire
Contact: Nikki Bridwell
nbridwell@horizonsoftware.com
Estimated Sales: $10-20 Million
Number Employees: 50-99
Brands:
  Fast Lane 2000
  Visual Boss

23860 Hormann Flexan Llc
20a Avenue C
Leetsdale, PA 15056-1305

412-749-0400
Fax: 412-749-0410 800-365-3667
Manufacturer and exporter of industrial/commercial
doors and loading dock equipment including deliv-
ery truck ramps.
President: Christoph Hormann
CEO: Charles A De La Porte
VP: Patrick Boyle
Marketing: Alic Permigiani
Contact: Peter Burnham
p.burnham@hormann-flexon.com
Plant Manager: Mark Permigiani
Purchasing: David Palmosina
Estimated Sales: $10-20 Million
Number Employees: 20-49
Square Footage: 180000
Parent Co: Hexon
Brands:
  Easy Hinge
  Flexidoor
  Weathershield

23861 Hormel Foods Corp.
1 Hormel Pl.
Austin, MN 55912

507-437-5611
www.hormelfoods.com
Meat and grocery products.
Chairman/President/CEO: Jim Snee
Executive VP/CFO: Jim Sheehan
Senior VP/General Counsel: Lori Marco
Senior VP, R&D: Kevin Myers
Vice President, Quality Management: Richard
Carlson
Year Founded: 1891
Estimated Sales: $9 Billion
Number Employees: 20,000
Number of Brands: 52
Type of Packaging: Consumer, Food Service, Pri-
vate Label
Other Locations:
  Manufacturing Facility
  Austin MN
  Manufacturing Facility
  Algona IA
  Manufacturing Facility
  Alma KS
  Manufacturing Facility
  Atlanta GA
  Manufacturing Facility
  Aurora IL
  Manufacturing Facility
  Barron WI
  Manufacturing Facility
  Beloit WI
  Manufacturing Facility
  Bondurant IA
  Manufacturing Facility
  Bremin GA
  Manufacturing Facility
  Browerville MN
  Manufacturing Facility
  Dayton OH
  Manufacturing Facility
  Dubuque IA
  Manufacturing Facility
  Eldridge IA
Brands:
  Applegate®
  Hormel®
  Jennie-O Turkey®
  Austin Blues BBQ®
  Bacon 1®
  Real Bacon Toppings
  Black Label Bacon®
  Bufalo®
  Burke®
  Cafe H®
  Chi-Chi's®
  Premium Chicken Breast®
  Hormel Chili®
  Columbus®
  Compleats®
  Cure 81®
  Dan's Prize®
  Del Fuerte®
  Deli Meats
  DiLusso Deli Company®
  Dinty Moore®
  Don Miguel®
  Doña María™
  Embasa®
  Evolve™
  Fire Braised Meats®
  Fontanini®
  Fuse Burger™
  Gatherings®
  Herbox®
  Herdez®
  Hormel Health Labs
  House of Tsang®
  Justin's®
  La Victoria®
  Little Sizzlers®
  Lloyds Barbeque Co®
  Mary Kitchen®
  Muscle Milk®
  Natural Choice®
  Not So Sloppy Joe®
  Old Smokehouse®
  Hormel Pepperoni®
  Refrigerated Entre,s
  Hormel Side Dishes
  Skippy®
  SPAM®
  Stagg Chili®
  Hormel Taco Meats®
  Valley Fresh®
  Vital Cuisine™
  Wholly Guacamole®

23862 Horn & Todak
10505 Judicial Dr # 101
Fairfax, VA 22030-5157

703-352-7330
Fax: 703-352-6940
Partner: Bob Horan
Estimated Sales: Below $5 Million
Number Employees: 5-9

23863 Horner International
5304 Emerson Drive
Raleigh, NC 27609

919-787-3112
Fax: 919-787-4272 sales@hornerintl.com
www.hornerinternational.com
Natural extracts and flavors
Contact: Ladiner Blaylock
ladiner.blaylock@hornerintl.com
Parent Co: Horner International

23864 Horton Fruit Co Inc
4701 Jennings Ln
Louisville, KY 40218-2967

502-969-1375
Fax: 502-964-1515 800-626-2245
Tomatoes, onions, spinach, kale, coleslaw, bananas,
avocados, pineapples and caramel apples
Chairman/CEO: Albert Horton
ahorton@hortonfruit.com
President/COO: Jackson Woodward
Treasurer: Steve Edelen
Vice President: Bill Benoit
Sales/Procurement: Tom Smith
Transportation Manager: Bobby Harlow
Number Employees: 100-249
Square Footage: 400000
Type of Packaging: Consumer, Food Service, Pri-
vate Label
Other Locations:
  Louisville Produce Terminal
  Louisville KY

23865 Hosch Properties
1002 International Dr
Oakdale, PA 15071-9226

724-695-3002
Fax: 724-695-3603 800-695-3310
hosch@hoschusa.com www.hoschusa.com
Scrapers for conveyor belt cleaning.
Owner: Kevin Carpol
kevinc@hoschusa.com
Operations: Grace Barkhurst
Estimated Sales: $5-10 Million
Number Employees: 20-49

23866 Hose Master Inc
1233 E 222nd St
Euclid, OH 44117-1121

216-481-2020
Fax: 216-481-7557 info@hosemaster.com
www.hosemaster.com
Manufacturer and exporter of gas, steam and water
connectors
CEO: Sam Foti
Quality Control: Mike Thompson
CEO: Sam J Foti
Estimated Sales: $20-50 Million
Number Employees: 250-499
Square Footage: 130000
Brands:
  Live Link
  Smart

23867 Hoshizaki
530 Lakeview Plaza Blvd # F
Worthington, OH 43085-4710

614-848-7702
Fax: 614-848-7706 800-642-1140
www.hoshizaki.com
VP: Gary Peffly
Estimated Sales: $1-5 Million
Number Employees: 5-9

23868 Hoshizaki America Inc
618 Highway 74 S
Peachtree City, GA 30269-3016

770-487-2331
Fax: 770-487-1325 800-438-6087
marketing@hoshizaki.com
www.hoshizakiamerica.com
Commercial ice machines and refrigeration equipment.

CEO: Youki Suzuki
Executive VP: Mark McClanahan
Quality Control: Carter Davis
Marketing Director: Carter Davis
Operations Manager: Jim Procuro
Production Manager: Jim Procuro
Plant Manager: Jim Procuro
Number Employees: 500-999
Parent Co: Hoshizaki Electric Company
Brands:
    Cleancycle 12
    Cyclesaver
    Evercheck
    Hoshizaki America
    Temp Guard

23869 Hosokawa Confectionery &Bakery Technology and Systems
10 Chatham Rd
Summit, NJ 07901-1310
908-273-6360
Fax: 908-273-7432 www.hosokawa.com
Agglomeration, size reduction, compaction/briquetting, mixing/blending, thermal reactors, disintegrators and drying and cooling machinery; consultant for process designs, engineering, research, testing, istallation, etc. available.Small scale food grade production agreements, AIG certified
Manager: Rob Vorhees
CEO: Masuo Hosokawa
Estimated Sales: $5-10 Million
Number Employees: 1,000-4,999
Parent Co: Hosokawa Micron Corporation

23870 Hosokawa Micron Powder Systems
10 Chatham Rd
Summit, NJ 07901-1310
908-273-6360
Fax: 908-273-7432 800-526-4491
info@hmps.hosokawa.com
www.hmicronpowder.com
Weighing machines and augers, blending and mixing equipment (coffee), brewing devices (urns, cleaners, coffeemakers), bulk silo services (green coffee), dryers, feeders, grinders, agglomeration, size reduction, compaction, thermalreactors and packaging
Manager: Rob Vorhees
Contact: Greg Boyer
gboyer@hmps.hosokawa.com
Estimated Sales: $10-25 Million
Number Employees: 1-4

23871 Hosokawa/Bepex Corporation
PO Box 880
Santa Rosa, CA 95402-0880
707-586-6000
Fax: 707-585-2325 info@hmfg.hosokawa.com
www.hosokawamicron.com
Food processing equipment including size reduction, liquid/solid separation, mixing/blending and thermal processing
CEO: Masuo Hosokawa
Vice President And COO: Kiyomi Miyata
Estimated Sales: $1-5 Million
Number Employees: 100-249
Brands:
    Rietz
    Strong-Scott

23872 Hospitality International
W6636 L B White Rd
Onalaska, WI 54650
608-783-2800
Fax: 608-783-6115 info@carrollchair.com
www.hospitalityinternational.com
President: Anthony Wilson
Vice President of Development: Ron Provus
Contact: Al Hebers
ahebers@hospitalityinternational.com
Estimated Sales: $10-20 Million
Number Employees: 100-249

23873 Hoss-S
12985 Dunnings Hwy
PO Box 219
Claysburg, PA 16625-8202
814-693-3453
Fax: 814-239-5922 800-438-7439
www.hosswares.com
Prepared foods
Owner: Bill Campbell
VP: Mark Spinazzola
Plant Manager: Rocky Rhodes

Estimated Sales: Less Than $500,000
Number Employees: 5-9

23874 Hot Food Boxes
451 East County Line Road
Mooresville, IN 46158
317-831-7030
Fax: 317-831-7036 800-733-8073
schirico@theramp.net www.secoselect.com
Manufacturer and exporter of insulated stainless steel and aluminum equipment for hot and cold foods; also, steam tables and heated bulk food carts for banquet service.
President: John Schirico
Vice President: Pat Darre
Estimated Sales: $2.5-5 Million
Number Employees: 20-49
Square Footage: 100000
Brands:
    Piper
    Road Warrior

23875 Hot Mama's Foods
134 Avocado St
Springfield, MA 01104
413-737-6572
Fax: 413-737-6793
Gourmet foods, including salsa, hummus, pesto, prepared salads, dips and ready-to-cook products; custom packaging and consulting
President: Matt Morse
Finance & Business Development: Herb Heller
Executive Chef: Josh Cooper
Director of Human Resources: Lisa Dufour
Director of Operations: Jim Boyle
Estimated Sales: $14.9 Million
Number Employees: 90
Square Footage: 13500

23876 Hotshot Delivery System
155 Covington Dr
Bloomingdale, IL 60108-3107
630-924-8817
Fax: 630-924-8819 sales@deliveryconcepts.com
www.hotshotdeliverysystems.com
Mobile vending trucks for hot, cold and refrigerated foods
Owner: Bernard Pfeiffer
hdsbernie@aol.com
General Sales Manager: Nick Prestia
Estimated Sales: $10-20 Million
Number Employees: 5-9

23877 Hotsy Corporation
10099 Ridgegate Pkwy # 280
Lone Tree, CO 80124-5534
303-792-5200
Fax: 303-792-0547 800-525-1976
info@hotsy.com www.hotsy.com
Pressure washers
Vice President Of Sales: Frank Rotondi
Estimated Sales: $1-5 Million
Number Employees: 50-99

23878 Houdini Inc
4225 N Palm St
Fullerton, CA 92835-1045
714-525-0325
Fax: 714-996-9605
www.winecountrygiftbaskets.com
Gourmet food, wine and gift baskets
Owner: Tim Dean
tdean@houdiniinc.com
Estimated Sales: $500,000-$1 Million
Number Employees: 10-19
Brands:
    California Pantry
    Wine Country

23879 House Stamp Works
20650 South Cicero
Chicago, IL 60443
312-939-7177
Fax: 312-939-8520 info@housestampworks.com
www.housestampworks.com
Stamps, dies, seals, etc
President: Edward Leppert
Estimated Sales: Less than $500,000
Number Employees: 1-4

23880 Houser Neon Sign Company
6411 Airline Dr
Houston, TX 77076-3507
713-691-5765

Lighted signs
Owner: Kimberly Mallett
Division Manager: Robert Betz
Estimated Sales: Less than $500,000
Number Employees: 1-4
Parent Co: Southwest Neon Signs

23881 Houston Atlas
1201 N Velasco Street
Angleton, TX 77515-3009
409-849-2344
Fax: 409-849-2166
Analytical instrumentation
President: Hammond Rrood
Estimated Sales: $5-10 000,000
Number Employees: 50

23882 Houston Label
909 Shaver St
Pasadena, TX 77506-4411
713-477-6995
Fax: 713-477-0023 800-477-6995
sales@houstonlabel.com www.houstonlabel.com
Manufacturer and exporter of labels including pressure sensitive, printed, unprinted, color processed, UPC and inventory automatic labeling equipment
Owner: Richard Ryholt
Executive VP: Hans Ryholt
Outside Sales Manager: Willie Hager
rryholt@houstonlabel.com
Estimated Sales: $5-10 Million
Number Employees: 50-99
Square Footage: 92000
Type of Packaging: Consumer, Food Service, Private Label, Bulk
Other Locations:
    Houston Tape & Label Co.
    Pasadena TX
Brands:
    3m
    Fasson
    Mactac
    Technicote

23883 Houston Stamp & Stencil Company
601 Jackson Hill St
Houston, TX 77007
713-869-4337
Fax: 713-869-4339 sales@houstonstamp.com
www.houstonstamp.com
Plastic signs, rubber stamps, nameplates and marking dies
President: Bruce La Roche
Contact: Bruce Laroche
roche@houstonstamp.com
Estimated Sales: $1-5 Million
Number Employees: 5-9

23884 Houston Wire Works, Inc.
1007 Kentucky
South Houston, TX 77587
713-946-2920
Fax: 713-946-3579 800-468-9477
info@houstonwire.com www.houstonwire.com
Manufacturer and exporter of water bottle display, refrigerator, wine and wire racks; also, steel platform ladders and hand carts; exporter of storage racks
President: Ken Legler
CEO: Barbara Leagler
VP Sales/Marketing: Steve Foster
Sales Director: Melanie Houser
Contact: Barbara Legler
barbaralegler@att.net
Sales Manager: Bill Watkins
Purchasing Manager: Raquel Garza
Estimated Sales: $3-5 Million
Number Employees: 45
Square Footage: 280000
Type of Packaging: Food Service
Brands:
    Hww
    Space-Saver

23885 Hovair Systems Inc
6912 S 220th St
Kent, WA 98032-1906
253-872-0405
Fax: 253-872-0406 800-237-4518
info@hovair.com www.hovair.com

Manufacturer and exporter of air film material handling equipment. Manufactures air bearing systems and air film products for a wide variety of applications, with particular emphasis on the movement of heavy loads and equipment withintoday's industry.
Manager: Betty Roberts
robertsb@hovair.com
Marketing: Betty Roberts
Operations: Betty Roberts
Plant Manager: Jeff Grow
Estimated Sales: $3-5 Million
Number Employees: 10-19

23886 Hovus Inc
272 Brodhead Rd # 200
Bethlehem, PA 18017-8956

610-997-8800
Fax: 610-997-0485 sales@hovus.com
www.hovus.com
HOVUS Incorporated is a flexible packaging consultation and sales organization that is focused on the needs of wholesale food manufacturer's in the private, public and not-for-profit sectors.
Owner: Alfred Haus
ahaus@hovus.com
Number Employees: 10-19

23887 Howard Fabrication
PO Box 90550
City of Industry, CA 91715-0550

626-961-0114
Fax: 626-961-8533
Custom stainless steel mixing and storage tanks for food, pharmaceutical and dairy products
President: John Gill
Sales Manager: Ron Reed
Estimated Sales: Below $5 Million
Number Employees: 10
Square Footage: 160000

23888 Howard Imprinting Machine Company
4519 Terrace Manor Drive
PO Box 15027
Houston, TX 77041

713-869-4337
Fax: 813-881-1554 800-334-6943
howard.imprinting@gte.net
www.howardimprinting.com
Manufacturer and exporter of hot stamp imprinting machinery
President: James Wrobbel
Estimated Sales: $3-5 Million
Number Employees: 5-9

23889 Howard Overman & Sons
517 N Bradford Street
Baltimore, MD 21205-2403

410-276-8445
Fax: 410-254-6358
Household and commercial brooms
Estimated Sales: Less than $500,000
Number Employees: 4

23890 (HQ)Howard-Mccray
831 E Cayuga St
Philadelphia, PA 19124-3815

215-464-6800
Fax: 215-969-4890 800-344-8222
www.howardmccray.com
Manufacturer and exporter of commercial refrigerators and freezers, open merchandisers; deli, fish, poultry and red meat service cases; bakery display, proofers, retarders; glass door; step in and reach in units. Alsodistribute beer frosters, bottle coolers, beer dispensers, under counter coolers, and prep tables.
President: Annette Ramsey
aramsey@howardmccray.com
CFO: Marie Ginon
Marketing Director: Diane Scott
Plant Manager: Brian Tyndall
Estimated Sales: $1-10 Million
Number Employees: 100-249
Number of Products: 60
Square Footage: 460000
Parent Co: HMC Enterprises,LLC

23891 Howard-Mccray
831 E Cayuga St
Philadelphia, PA 19124-3815

215-464-6800
Fax: 215-969-4890 hmccray850@aol.com
www.howardmccray.com

President: Will Bell
wbell@howardmccray.com
Estimated Sales: $10-20 Million
Number Employees: 100-249

23892 Howden Group
900 W Mount St
Connersville, IN 47331

765-827-9200
www.howden.com
Rotary and centrifugal air and gas blowers, compressors, high vacuum and industrial compressor equipment.
Chief Executive Officer: Ross Shuster
Estimated Sales: Over $1 Billion

23893 Howe Corp
1650 N Elston Ave
Chicago, IL 60642-1585

773-235-0200
Fax: 773-235-1530 webinfo@howecorp.com
www.howecorp.com
Specialty refrigeration equipment including flake ice mannhies, bin transport systems, packaged refrigeration systems, compressors and pressure vessels
President: Mary C Howe
craig@cmvsharperfinish.com
CFO: M Aguilar
Senior VP: Kevin McCool
Research & Development: A Ahuja
Marketing Director: K McCool
VP Sales: A Ortman
Director Sales/Marketing: Chuck Janovsky
IT: Andrew Ortman
Production Manager: Steve Bokor
Plant Manager: John Myrda
Purchasing Manager: Bob Dondzik
Estimated Sales: $20-50 Million
Number Employees: 20-49
Square Footage: 65000
Brands:
　Conditionaire
　Rapid Freeze

23894 Howell Brothers Chemical Laboratories
5007 Overbrook Ave
Philadelphia, PA 19131-1402

215-477-0260
Manufacturer and exporter of glass cleaners and hair products
President: Douglas C Howell
Manager: David Hart
Production Manager: Charles Thomson
Estimated Sales: $2.5-5 Million
Number Employees: 7
Square Footage: 24000
Type of Packaging: Consumer, Private Label

23895 Howell Consulting
1611-A South Melrose Dr
211
Vista, CA 92081

760-536-3456
Fax: 760-536-3457
inquiry@HowellConsultingGroup.com
www.howellconsultinggroup.com
Control systems, design assembly, installation and service. Consultant and systems integrator for process control systems
Owner: Rodney A Howell
Estimated Sales: Below $5 000,000
Number Employees: 10

23896 Howes S Co Inc
25 Howard St
Silver Creek, NY 14136-1097

716-934-2611
Fax: 716-934-2081 888-255-2611
sales@showes.com www.pressureleaffilter.com
Manufacturer and exporter of job engineered processing and materials handling equipment including classifiers, conveyors, crushers, rotary cutters, horizontal/vertical mixers, continuous liquid mixers and feeders, sifters, elevatorsauger packers and scales
President: Wayne Mertz
bryantd@showes.com
Vice President: Frederick Mertz
Sales: Diana Bryant
Estimated Sales: $10-20,000,000
Number Employees: 10-19

23897 Howes S Co Inc
25 Howard St
Silver Creek, NY 14136-1097

716-934-2611
Fax: 716-934-2081 888-255-2611
sales@showes.com www.pressureleaffilter.com
Bins for bulk storage; hoppers, conveyors, bucket elevators
President: Wayne Mertz
bryantd@showes.com
VP: Fred Mertz
Sales: Diana Bryant
Estimated Sales: $10-20 Million
Number Employees: 10-19
Parent Co: MetalWorks

23898 Howlett Farms
1112 East River Rd.
Avon, NY 14414

585-226-8340
www.howlettfarms.com
Offers marketing and risk management services.
President: Bruce Howlett
Operations Manager: David Walthew *Year Founded:* 1880

23899 Hoyer
753 Geneva Pkwy N
Lake Geneva, WI 53147-4579

262-249-7400
Fax: 262-249-7500
Ice cream processing equipment
President: Gustav Korsholm
Estimated Sales: $5-10 Million
Number Employees: 20-49

23900 (HQ)Hoyt Corporation
251 Forge Rd
Westport, MA 2790

508-636-8811
Fax: 508-636-2088 hoytinc@hoytinc.com
www.hoyt-corp.com
Manufacturer and exporter of vapor recovery systems and dry cleaning equipment including commercial washer extracts, laundry dryers and extractors
Chairman: Jean H Olinger
VP Marketing: Pat King
Contact: Gil Abernathy
gil.abernathy@hoyavc.com
Estimated Sales: $10-20 Million
Number Employees: 10-19
Brands:
　Petro-Miser
　Sniff-O-Miser
　Solvo-Miser

23901 Huard Packaging
685 Discovery Bay Boulevard
Discovery Bay, CA 94514-9443

650-857-1501
Fax: 650-852-8138 800-752-0900

23902 Hub City Brush Co
106 Mc Aulay Dr
Petal, MS 39465-4008

601-584-7314
Fax: 601-544-2600 800-278-7452
www.hubcityindustries.net
Commercial brooms, mops and brushes
Owner: Tyler Cedotal
tcedotal@hubcitybrush.com
VP: Cecil Cedotal
Quality Control: Russel Herrin
Estimated Sales: Less Than $500,000
Number Employees: 10-19
Square Footage: 36720

23903 Hub Electric Company
6207 Commercial Rd
Crystal Lake, IL 60014

815-455-4400
Fax: 815-455-1499 richardvaralightinc@juno.com
Manufacturer and exporter of dimming systems and special lighting equipment
President and CFO: Richard Latronica
VP: Kenneth Hansen
Estimated Sales: Below $1 Million
Number Employees: 5-9

23904 Hub Folding Box Co
774 Norfolk St
Mansfield, MA 02048-1826

508-339-0102
Fax: 508-339-0102 www.hubfoldingbox.com

Paper folding boxes
Owner: Fred Di Rico
fdirico@hubfoldingbox.com
Sales Manager: Lucy Gilligan
Estimated Sales: $20-50 Million
Number Employees: 100-249

23905 Hub Labels Inc

18223 Shawley Dr
Hagerstown, MD 21740-2462

301-790-1660
Fax: 301-745-3646 800-433-4532
jdoyle@hublabels.com www.hublabels.com
Adhesive and pressure sensitive labels
President: Mary Dahbura
thomson_natascha@emc.com
CEO: Abbud S Dahbura
Quality Assurance Manager: Mark Stahle
Sales/Marketing: Belinda Smith
Manager: Pam Kunkle
Production Manager: John Potterfield
General Manager: Mary Dahbura
Purchasing Manager: Nick Myers
Estimated Sales: $10 Million
Number Employees: 100-249
Square Footage: 32000

23906 Hub Pen Company

230 Quincy Avenue
Quincy, MA 02169-6741

617-471-9900
Fax: 617-471-2990 www.hubpen.com
Manufacturer and exporter of felt tip markers, pens, pencils, etc
President: Helen Fleming
Quality Control: Howard Ernest
Sales Manager: Robert McGaughey
Contact: Cheryl Brugliera
cbrugliera@hubpen.com
Estimated Sales: $10-20 Million
Number Employees: 65
Square Footage: 20000
Brands:
    Hub Pen

23907 Hubbell Electric HeaterCo

45 Seymour St
PO Box 288
Stratford, CT 06615-6170

203-380-3306
Fax: 203-378-3593 800-647-3165
info@hubbellheaters.com
www.hubbellheaters.com
Manufacturer and exporter of electric hot water booster heaters for sanitizing water
President: William E Newbauler
Head of Quality Control: Clifford Dineson
Sales Director: Sean Clarker
IT: Jessica Delvalle
jessicad@hubbellheaters.com
Estimated Sales: $5-10 Million
Number Employees: 50-99
Brands:
    Hubbell

23908 Hubbell Lenoir City Inc

2911 Industrial Park Dr
Lenoir City, TN 37771-3209

865-986-9726
Fax: 865-986-4186 800-346-3061
www.hubbell.com
Polymer concrete drain systems
General Manager: John Downey
Cio/Cto: Danny Bowden
dbowden@hubbell.com
Finance Executive: David Redman
Estimated Sales: $20-50 Million
Number Employees: 100-249

23909 Hubbell Lighting Inc

701 Millennium Blvd
Greenville, SC 29607-5251

864-678-1000
Fax: 864-678-1065 www.hubbelllighting.com
Manufacturer and exporter of industrial, commercial, emergency, exit, recessed and track lighting
Vice President: Scott H Muse
smuse@prescolite.com
VP: Scott Veil
VP Sales/Marketing: Richard Barrett
VP Sales: James O'Hargan
Number Employees: 500-999
Parent Co: Hubbell

23910 (HQ)Hubber Technology Inc

9735 Northcross Center Ct # A
Huntersville, NC 28078-7331

704-949-1010
Fax: 704-949-1020 huber@hhusa.net
Huber Technology offers different treatment systems to provide clean and healthy drinking water in order to meet the requirements of different surface water qualities and customer preferences. The systems process includes: coarsematerial separation; oxygenation; fine material separation: flocculation and sedimentation; filtration; oxidation and disinfection; absorption; network protection and water storage.
President: Forstner Gerhard
CEO: Mr. Dana Hicks
Marketing: T.R. Gregg
Number Employees: 10-19
Square Footage: 96000
Parent Co: Hans Huber AG

23911 Hubco Inc

215 S Poplar St
PO Box 1286
Hutchinson, KS 67501-7456

620-663-8301
Fax: 620-663-5053 800-563-1867
www.hubcoinc.com
Manufacturer, importer and exporter of bags including drawstring, cotton, flannel, polypropylene and burlap for flour, rice, popcorn, nuts, etc.; also, specialty food packaging available
President: Merlin Prehein
VP: Trey McPherson
VP: Jim Schmidt
Plant Manager: Fred Moore
Estimated Sales: $5-10 Million
Number Employees: 50-99
Square Footage: 284000
Brands:
    Protexo
    Sentry
    Sentry Ii

23912 Huck Store Fixture Company

1100 N 28th St
Quincy, IL 62301-3447

217-222-0713
Fax: 217-222-0751 800-680-4823
Store fixtures
VP: Mark Flegel
Purchase: Cory Phipps Phipps
Sales and Marketing: Romhamann Hamann
Marketing Director: Christopher Peters
VP Production: Ron Hamann
Number Employees: 250-499
Square Footage: 1208000

23913 Hudson Belting & Svc CoInc

85 E Worcester St
Worcester, MA 01604-3649

508-756-0090
Fax: 508-753-6844 www.hudsonbelting.com
Manufacturer and wholesaler/distributor of food grade belting including leather, rubber, conveyor and timing; installation services available
President: Tom Jennette
hudsonbelting@charter.net
Plant Manager: John Whitney
Estimated Sales: Less Than $500,000
Number Employees: 5-9
Square Footage: 15000
Type of Packaging: Consumer, Food Service

23914 Hudson Control Group Inc

10 Stern Ave
Springfield, NJ 07081-2905

973-376-8265
Fax: 973-376-8265 info@hudsoncontrol.com
www.hudsoncontrol.com
Manufacturer and exporter of custom designed and integrated robotic automation systems including case packers/unpackers; also, software
President: Phil Farrelly
CSO: Cliff Olson, Ph.D.
VP Sales/Marketing: Tom Gilman
Contact: John Celecki
jcelecki@hudsoncontrol.com
Estimated Sales: $1-2.5 Million
Number Employees: 5-9
Square Footage: 12000
Brands:
    Hudson's Total Control For Windows
    Packit

23915 Hudson Poly Bag Inc

578 Main St
Hudson, MA 01749-3099

978-562-7566
Fax: 978-568-0797 800-229-7566
sales@hudsonpoly.com www.hudsonpoly.com
Plain and printed polyethylene and poly propylene bags and sheets, film and narrow width tubing.
President: Marilyn Kinder
marilynkinder@staples.com
CEO: Richard Renwick
Marketing/General Manager: Jim Chapman
Estimated Sales: $5-10 Million
Number Employees: 10-19
Square Footage: 35000
Type of Packaging: Consumer, Food Service, Private Label, Bulk

23916 Hudson Valley Hops

PO Box 292
Beacon, NY 12508

845-202-2398
admin@hvhops.com
www.hvhops.com
Harvester, processor and distributor of hops to brewers in the Hudson Valley
Co-Founder: Justin Riccobono
Co-Founder: Shawn McLearen *Year Founded:* 2013
Type of Packaging: Bulk

23917 Hudson-Sharp Machine Co

975 Lombardi Ave
Green Bay, WI 54304-3735

920-494-4571
Fax: 920-496-1322 800-950-4362
Manufacturer and exporter of packaging machinery including bag makers and pouch makers and fillers
President: Don Pansier
VP: Gilas Blaser
Sales Director: Dennis Jimmel
Plant Manager: Jack Hendrickson
Estimated Sales: $20-50 Million
Number Employees: 50-99
Square Footage: 60000
Brands:
    Amplas Converting Equipment
    Totani Pouch M/C

23918 Hudson-Sharp Machine Company

P.O.Box 13397
Green Bay, WI 54307-3397

920-494-4571
Fax: 920-496-1322 sales@hudsonsharp.com
www.hudsonsharp.com
Manufacturer and exporter of converting and pouch and plastic bag making equipment
President: Peter Hatchell
CFO: Gary Reinert
CEO: Rod Drummond
Research & Development: Danford Anderson
Marketing Director: Mark Smith
Sales Director: Paul Staab
Contact: Michele Allamprese
michele.allamprese@hudsonsharp.com
Operations Manager: Scott Romenesko
Estimated Sales: $50-100 Million
Number Employees: 50-99

23919 Hueck Foils LLC

1955 State Route 34
Suite 2
Wall, NJ 07719-9703

732-974-4100
Fax: 732-974-4111 www.hueckfoils.com
Hueck ia a foil converter supplying flexible packaging materials for the food and pharmecutical industries
Quality Control: Rosalyn White
Marketing: Angela Boggenhofer
Sales: Kevin Judd
Plant Manager: Manfred Rauer
Estimated Sales: $3-5 Million
Number Employees: 5-9
Parent Co: Hueck Folien

23920 Huettinger Electronic Inc

4000 Burton Dr
Santa Clara, CA 95054-1509

408-454-1180
Fax: 408-454-1181 800-910-0035
info-us@huettinger.com www.huettinger.com
Induction cap sealing equipment and power supplies

President: Juergen Mertens
VP Sales: Paul Oranges
Contact: David Fostervold
david.fostervold@us.trumpf.com
Estimated Sales: $3-5 000,000
Number Employees: 5-9

23921 Hughes Co
1200 W James St
Columbus, WI 53925-1028

920-623-2000
Fax: 920-623-4098 866-535-9303
hughes@hughesequipment.com
www.hughesequipment.com
Food processing equipment
President/CEO: Ross Lund
rosslund@hughescompany.biz
Sales Manager: Tracey Lange
Sales Manager: Ryan Metzdorf
Director of Engineering: Todd Belz
Plant Manager: Bill Wandersee
Estimated Sales: $10-20 Million
Number Employees: 20-49
Brands:
 Digisort
 Hughes

23922 Hughes Co
1200 W James St
Columbus, WI 53925-1028

920-623-2000
Fax: 920-623-4098
hughes@hughesequipment.com
www.hughesequipment.com
Machinery for the food processing industry includ-
ing air cleaners; bins; rotary blanchers and cookers;
rotary coolers; bulk unloading feeders; fillers; grad-
ers; inspection tables, etc.
President: Ross Lund
rosslund@hughescompany.biz
Sales Manager: Doug Zadra
Manufacturing Manager: Bill Wandersee
rosslund@hughescompany.biz
Director of Engineering: Todd Belz
Sales Coordinator: Lisa Adam
Number Employees: 20-49

23923 Hughes Manufacturing Company
2301 W Highway 290
Giddings, TX 78942

979-542-0333
Fax: 979-542-0335 800-414-0765
www.hughesmanufacturing.com
Manufacturer and exporter of nylon and plastic
flags, pennants and banners
Manager: Lisa Marek
Operations Manager: Larry Conlee
Operations Manager: Larry Conlee
Estimated Sales: Below $5 Million
Number Employees: 10-19
Square Footage: 40000

23924 Huhtamaki Food Service Plastics
100 N Field Drive
Suite 300
Lake Forest, IL 60045-2520

847-295-6100
Fax: 847-295-9862 800-244-6382

23925 Huhtamaki Inc
9201 Packaging Dr
De Soto, KS 66018-8600

913-583-3025
Fax: 913-583-8756 800-255-4243
President: Clay Dunn
clay.dunn@us.huhtamaki.com
Chief Executive Officer: Jukka Moisio
Estimated Sales: $50-100 Million
Number Employees: 500-999

23926 Huls America
220 Davidson Avenue
Somerset, NJ 08873-4149

732-980-6800
Fax: 732-980-6970
Wine industry enzymes
CEO: Joseph Fuhrman
Marketing Manager: Tom Wickett
Number Employees: 1000

23927 Hungerford & Terry
226 Atlantic Ave
PO Box 650
Clayton, NJ 8312

856-881-3200
Fax: 856-881-6859 sales@hungerfordterry.com
www.hungerfordterry.com
Manufacturer and exporter of water treatment sys-
tems including filters, softeners, demineralizers and
reverse osmosis
President: Allen Davis
Executive VP: Vernon Dawson
VP Sales: Kenneth Sayell
Contact: Douglas Bateman
dbateman@hungerfordterry.com
Estimated Sales: $10-20 Million
Number Employees: 50-99
Square Footage: 40000
Brands:
 Ferrofilt
 Ferrosand
 H&T
 Hungerford & Terry
 Invercab

23928 Hunt Midwest
8300 NE Underground Drive
Kansas City, MO 64161

816-455-2500
Fax: 816-455-2890
mediacontact@huntmidwest.com
www.huntmidwest.com
President: Ora Reynolds
Chairman of the Board: Jim Holland
Vice President and CFO: Don Hagan
Assistant General Manager of Sales: Dick Ringer
Number Employees: 50-99

23929 Hunter Fan Co
7130 Goodlett Farms Pkwy # 400
Cordova, TN 38016-4991

901-743-1360
Fax: 901-248-2258 techsupport@hunterfan.com
www.hunterfan.com
Ceiling fans, programmable thermostats, air purifiers
and humidifiers
President: Robert Beasley
CEO: John Alexander
jalexander@hunterfan.com
Director Sales/Special Markets: Rick Neuman
VP Sales: Brennon Byrney
Estimated Sales: $50-100 Million
Number Employees: 500-999

23930 Hunter Graphics
140 N Orlando Avenue
Suite 140
Umatilla, FL 32784

407-644-2060
Fax: 407-644-0957 www.huntergraphics.com
Consultant specializing in the design of packaging
and labels; support services available
President: Brian Hunter
Estimated Sales: Below $500,000
Number Employees: 1
Square Footage: 14000
Parent Co: Optimal Graphics

23931 Hunter Lab
11491 Sunset Hills Rd # 1
Reston, VA 20190-5280

703-471-6870
Fax: 703-471-4237 sales@hunterlab.com
www.hunterlab.com
Manufacturer and exporter of color measurement
systems
Owner: Phil S Hunter
CFO: Teresa Demangos
R & D: Jim Freal
Quality Control: Ambur Daley
Sales Manager: Paul Barnes
hunter@hunterlab.com
Estimated Sales: $10-20 Million
Number Employees: 50-99
Square Footage: 140000
Brands:
 Colortrend Ht

23932 Hunter Packaging Corporation
865 Commerce Drive
South Elgin, IL 60177-2633

847-741-4747
Fax: 847-741-1100 800-428-4747
Corrugated boxes and displays

Vice President: Tom Pabelick
Office Manager: Susan Brown
Estimated Sales: $3-5 Million
Number Employees: 31
Square Footage: 140000

23933 Hunter Woodworks
21038 S Wilmington Ave
Carson, CA 90810

310-835-5671
Fax: 323-775-2540 800-966-4751
info@hunterpallets.com www.hunterpallets.com
Wooden pallets, boxes and crates
General Manager: Bruce Benton
CEO: Bill Hunter
Sales Manager: Frank Gower
Contact: Jeremy Benz
jeremy@hunterpallets.com
General Manager: Bruce Benton
Number Employees: 100-249
Square Footage: 1000000

23934 Huntington Foam Corp
101 N 4th St
Jeannette, PA 15644-3331

724-522-5144
Fax: 814-265-8627 www.huntingtonfoam.com
Construction and packaging foam
President: Gary B. McLaughlin
CFO: Tom Kuehl
Director of Sales & Enginnering: Ed Flynn
Manager: Jeff Jones
Director of Operations: Benjamin Raygoza
Estimated Sales: $5-10 000,000
Number Employees: 5-9

23935 Huntington Park Rbr Stamp Co
2761 E Slauson Ave
PO Box 519
Huntington Park, CA 90255-3048

323-582-6461
Fax: 323-582-8046 800-882-0029
hprubberstamp@pacbell.net
www.hprubberstamp.com
Marking devices including rubber stamps
President: Mary Barlam
hprubberstamp@pacbell.net
Sales Manager: Robert Barlam
Estimated Sales: $1-2.5 Million
Number Employees: 10-19
Square Footage: 12500

23936 Huntsman Packaging
PO Box 97
South Deerfield, MA 01373-0097

413-665-2145
Fax: 413-665-4854 www.pliantcorp.com
Manufacturer and exporter of co-extruded polyethyl-
ene packaging film
VP Finance: Peter Dube
Chairman: Charles Barker
Plant Manager: Clark Sylvester
Estimated Sales: $50-100 Million
Number Employees: 100-249
Square Footage: 100000
Brands:
 Strata

23937 Huntsman Packaging Corporation
PO Box 11085
Birmingham, Bi 35202-1085

205-328-4720
Fax: 205-322-2505
Plastic film
President/CEO: John Huntsman
Controller: John Clark
Production Manager: Pete Lenzer
Plant Manager: Larry Bearden

23938 Hurlingham Company
1158 W 11th Street
Apt F
San Pedro, CA 90731-3479

310-538-0236
Fax: 310-538-4436
Store fixtures
President: Eusebio Espejo
VP Sales: Michele Duston
Estimated Sales: Below $5,000,000
Number Employees: 30
Square Footage: 25000

23939 Hurri-Kleen Corporation
6000 Southern Industrial Dr
Birmingham, AL 35235
205-655-8808
Fax: 205-655-5392 800-455-8265
Manufacturer and dirtributor of intermediate bulk
containers and related parts and accessories
Estimated Sales: $1-5,000,000
Number Employees: 1-4
Square Footage: 100000
Brands:
Hurri-Kleen

23940 Hurst Corp
175 Strafford Ave # 1
Wayne, PA 19087-3340
610-687-2404
Fax: 610-687-7860 sales@hurstcorp.com
www.hurstcorp.com
De-labeling machinery
Owner: Richard Hurst
sales@hurstcorp.com
Estimated Sales: $5-10 Million
Number Employees: 10-19

23941 Hurst Labeling Systems
20747 Dearborn St
PO Box 5169
Chatsworth, CA 91311-5914
818-701-0710
Fax: 818-701-8747 800-969-1705
info@hurstinternational.net
www.hurstinternational.net
Manufacturer and exporter of pressure sensitive la-
bels and label application equipment
Owner: Ari Lichtenberg
CFO: Rita Rebera
Quality Control: Rick Aranbul
Sales Representative: Melody Nichols
Sales Representative: Chaylon Holland
ari@hurstinternational.net
Estimated Sales: $3-5 Million
Number Employees: 10-19
Square Footage: 26000

**23942 Hurt Conveyor
EquipmentCompany**
6615 8th Ave
Los Angeles, CA 90043-4353
323-541-0433
Fax: 323-541-0442
Belt and chain conveyors
President: Ramesh Soni
VP: Saroj Soni
Number Employees: 7
Type of Packaging: Private Label

23943 (HQ)Huskey Specialty Lubricants
1580 Industrial Ave
Norco, CA 92860-2946
951-340-4000
Fax: 951-340-4011 888-448-7539
sales@huskey.com www.huskey.com
Manufacturer and exporter of food grade grease and
lubricating oils for food processing machinery
President: Sheldy Huskey
R&D: Jim Landry
Vice President: Mike Montgomery
Research & Development: Hugh Woodworth
Foreign Sales Manager: Denis Alonso
Contact: Michael Montgomery
mmontgomery@huskey.com
Plant Manager: Chris Kimball
Purchasing Manager: Cathy Merlo
Estimated Sales: $10-20 Million
Number Employees: 5-9
Square Footage: 120000
Type of Packaging: Private Label, Bulk
Other Locations:
Huskey Specialty Lubricants
Twinsburg OH
Brands:
Huskey

23944 Hussmann Corp
12999 Saint Charles Rock Rd.
Bridgeton, MO 63044-2483
314-291-2000
www.hussmann.com
Commercial and display refrigerators and coolers.
President/CEO: Tim Figge
CFO: Cathy Haigh
Senior VP, Retail Services: Jay Welu

Year Founded: 1906
Estimated Sales: Over $1 Billion
Number Employees: 5000-9999
Parent Co: Panasonic Corporation Of North
America
Brands:
Impact
Protocol™
Protochill™

23945 Hutchison-Hayes International
P.O.Box 2965
Houston, TX 77252-2965
713-455-9600
Fax: 713-455-7753 800-984-3397
sales@hutch-hayes.com www.hutchhayes.com
Centrifuges
Owner: Richard Parks
Quality Control and R&D: Lee Hilpert
Chairman: John Joplin
Estimated Sales: $10-20 Million
Number Employees: 50-99

23946 Huther Brothers
1290 University Avenue
Rochester, NY 14607-1674
585-473-9462
Fax: 585-473-9476 800-334-1115
Manufacturer and exporter of industrial food pro-
cessing cutting blades and circular, straight and spe-
cialty knives
President: George W Huther Iii
CFO: James Aldridge
Bookkeeper: Margie Campaigne
Foreman: Eric Nash
Estimated Sales: $3-5 Million
Number Employees: 10-19
Square Footage: 38000

23947 Hutz Sign & Awning
2415 Hubbard Rd
Youngstown, OH 44505
330-743-5168
Fax: 330-743-2319 hutzsigns@worldnet.att.net
Advertising signs
President: Tom Kling
VP: David Hutz
Estimated Sales: $3-5 Million
Number Employees: 10-19

**23948 Hy-Ko
Enviro-MaintenanceProducts**
PO Box 26116
Salt Lake City, UT 84126-0116
801-973-6099
Fax: 801-973-9746 sales@hyko.com
www.hyko.com
Cleaners including hand, dairy, glass, household and
industrial, pipe, toilet bowl and window; also, wash-
ing compounds, disinfectants and floor polishes
President: Ron Starr
CFO: Ron C Starr Sr
Sales Manager: John Hille
Estimated Sales: $10-20 Million
Number Employees: 20-49

23949 Hy-Ten Plastics Inc
38 Powers St
Milford, NH 03055-4982
603-673-1611
Fax: 603-673-0970 sales@hy-ten.com
www.hy-ten.com
Designer of custom injection molded products
President: Rich Staples
rich.staples@hy-ten.com
Sales/Engineer: Peter Fritsch
VP Operations: Mike McGown
Estimated Sales: $10-20 Million
Number Employees: 50-99
Square Footage: 60000

23950 Hy-Trous/Flash Sales
3R-T Green Street
Woburn, MA 1801
781-933-5772
Hand soaps and cleaning compounds
Estimated Sales: $1-5 Million
Number Employees: 5
Square Footage: 30000
Parent Co: Hy-Trous Corporation
Brands:
Flash
Hy-Trous Plant Foods
Skat

23951 Hyatt Industries Limited
1572 West 4th Avenue
Vancouver, BC V6J 1L7
Canada
604-736-7301
Fax: 604-736-7305 800-482-7446
sales@hyatt-ind.com
President: Lindsay Lawrence
Number Employees: 10

23952 Hybrinetics Inc
225 Sutton Pl
Santa Rosa, CA 95407-8199
707-585-0333
Fax: 707-585-7313 800-247-6900
hybrinet@voltagevalet.com www.voltagevalet.com
Manufacturer and exporter of dimmer controls for
incandescent and fluorescent lighting
President: Rick Rosa
hybrinet@voltagevalet.com
Estimated Sales: $20-50 Million
Number Employees: 20-49
Brands:
Aladdin Products
Star Controls

23953 Hycor Corporation
562 E Bunker Court
Vernon Hills, IL 60061-1831
847-473-3700
Fax: 847-473-0477 technology@parkson.com
www.parkson.com
Wine industry wastewater treatment
CEO: Zain Mahmood
Estimated Sales: $10-25 Million
Number Employees: 250-499

23954 Hyde & Hyde Inc
300 El Sobrante Rd
Corona, CA 92879-5757
951-279-5239
Fax: 951-270-3526 www.hydeandhyde.com
Condiments for the fresh-cut produce industry; cus-
tom packaging and co-packaging
President: Tim Hyde
Number Employees: 250-499
Type of Packaging: Consumer, Private Label

23955 Hyder North America
270 Granite Run Dr
Lancaster, PA 17601-6804
717-569-7021
Fax: 717-560-0577 info@thearrogroup.com
www.thearrogroup.com
Water and wastewater treatment, total outsourcing
solutions
President: G Matthew Brown
CFO: Susan L Long
Estimated Sales: $10-20 Million
Number Employees: 50-99

23956 Hydra-Flex Inc
32975 Industrial Rd
Livonia, MI 48150-1617
734-522-9090
Fax: 734-522-9579 800-234-0832
customerservice@hydra-flex.com
www.hydra-flex.com
Manufacturer and wholesaler/distributor of hoses,
valves, fittings, tubing, etc
President: Charley Blank
cblank@hydra-flex.com
R&D: Jim Poole
VP: Bill Berlin
Sales Manager: Bill Berlin
Warehouse Manager: Jason Pinard
Estimated Sales: $10-20 Million
Number Employees: 10-19

**23957 Hydranautics (A Nitto Denko
Company)**
9119 Princeton Rd
Woodbury, MN 55125
651-739-0443
cbuck@hydranautics.com
www.hydranautics.com

Reverse osmosis, nanofiltration, ultrafiltration and microfiltration crossflow membranes and elements for food, dairy, and beverage production as well as water and wastewater applications. Concentration of proteins, amino acids, fishmeat and vegetable extracts, enzymes, sugars, vitamins, flavors, vinegar, coffee, tea, maple sap and colorants. Also remove color from juices, syrups, flavorings and beverages and can adjust alcohol content.
President: Yukio Nagira
Estimated Sales: $33.34 Million
Number Employees: 60

23958 Hydrel Corporation
12881 Bradley Ave
Sylmar, CA 91342-3828

818-362-9465
Fax: 818-362-6548 www.hydrel.com
Manufacturer and exporter of outdoor lighting fixtures including flood, ingrade and underwater; also, custom environment fixtures
President: Craig Jennings
VP: Dwight Hochstein
VP: Mark Blackford
CFO: John Gay
VP Marketing: Hal Madsen
Sales Manager: Dan Roth
Contact: Trilby Jasinski
tjasinski@hrblock.com
Estimated Sales: $20-50 Million
Number Employees: 100-249
Parent Co: GTY Industries
Brands:
 9000 Series
 Hypak
 Sunlite

23959 Hydrite Chemical Co
300 N Patrick Blvd # 2
Brookfield, WI 53045-5816

262-792-1450
Fax: 262-792-8721 sales@hydrite.com
www.hydrite.com
Manufacturer and wholesaler/distributor of industrial cleaning, sanitaring ingredients and water treatment chemicals
CEO: John Honkamp
john.honkamp@hydrite.com
Sales Director: Rob Adams
Sales Director (Special Chemicals): Rich Carmichael
Purchasing Manager: Chuck Krior
Number Employees: 1000-4999

23960 Hydro Life
503 Maple St
Bristol, IN 46507

574-848-1661
Fax: 574-848-1400 800-626-7130
www.hydrolife.com
President: La Von Troyer
Sales: Roger Egli
Estimated Sales: $1-3 Million
Number Employees: 5-9

23961 Hydro Seal Coatings Company
12151 Madera Way
Riverside, CA 92503-4849

760-723-8992
Fax: 760-723-7206
Wine industry coatings
Vice President of Technology: Sergio Franyutti

23962 Hydro-Miser
906 Boardwalk # B
San Marcos, CA 92069-4071

442-744-5083
Fax: 442-744-5031 800-736-5083
Manufacturer and exporter of portable and thermal storage chillers and cooling towers and systems; also, food processing equipment and supplies
President/CEO: Kimberly Howard
Estimated Sales: $1-2.5 Million
Number Employees: 1-4
Parent Co: Applied Thermal Technologies
Brands:
 Copeland
 Gould

23963 Hydro-Tech EnvironmentalSystems
410 Petaluma Blvd S # A
Petaluma, CA 94952-4278

707-769-9247
Fax: 707-769-9140 800-559-3102
info@htes.com www.htes.com
Wastewater treatment, bad reduction, product recovery, product concentration
Manager: Susan Stone
CFO and CTO: Aron Lavner
Estimated Sales: $.5-1 million
Number Employees: 5-9
Square Footage: 6800

23964 Hydro-Thermal Corp
400 Pilot Ct
Waukesha, WI 53188-2439

262-548-8900
Fax: 262-548-8908 800-952-0121
info@hydro-thermal.com www.hydro-thermal.com
Direct contact steam injection heaters and heat exchangers for liquids and slurries for both industrial and 3A applications
President: Jim Zaiser
jzaiser@hydro-thermal.com
VP: John Warne
Marketing: Kristie Anderson
Estimated Sales: $5-10 Million
Number Employees: 50-99
Brands:
 Hydrohelix
 Hydroheater

23965 HydroCal
22732 Granite Way Ste A
Laguna Hills, CA 92653

949-455-0765
Fax: 949-455-0764 800-877-0765
don@hydrocal.com www.hydrocal.com
Wastewater treatment equipment
President: Donald Meylor
VP: Oilie Breen
Director Marketing/Operationss: Jorge Funez
Sales: Ollie Breen
Contact: Oliver Breen
breen@hydrocal.com
Estimated Sales: $500,000-$1 000,000
Number Employees: 5-9
Number of Products: 8

23966 Hydrocal Inc
23011 Moulton Pkwy # G5
Suite G5
Laguna Hills, CA 92653-1228

949-455-0765
Fax: 949-455-0764 800-877-0765
ollieb@hydrocal.com www.hydrocal.com
President: Don Meylor
info@hydrocal.com
Estimated Sales: $1,000,000-$3,000,000
Number Employees: 5-9

23967 Hydromax Inc
4 Creamery Way
Emmitsburg, MD 21727-8803

301-447-3800
Fax: 301-668-3700 800-326-0602
info@hydromax.net www.hydromax.net
Manufacturer and exporter of water filtration and purification equipment including reverse osmosis, ultraviolet, ozone and filtration technologies
President: Frederick N Reidenbach
Estimated Sales: $1-2.5 Million
Number Employees: 5-9

23968 Hydron
14550 E Easter Avenue
Centennial, CO 80112-4263

303-792-9988
Fax: 303-792-5772
Water and waste water clean uo in processing plants

23969 Hydropure Water Treatment Co
5727 NW 46th Dr
Coral Springs, FL 33067-4005

954-340-3331
Fax: 954-971-0801 800-753-1547
Exporter of rotary vane pumps and water filtration, purification and reverse osmosis systems.
President: Vittorio Sordi
VP: Susan Shasser
Estimated Sales: $1.6 Million
Number Employees: 5-9

Number of Brands: 4
Number of Products: 78
Type of Packaging: Consumer, Food Service
Brands:
 Carbonetor Pumps
 Hydropure Pumps

23970 Hyer Industries
91 Schoosett St
Pembroke, MA 02359-1839

781-826-8101
Fax: 781-826-7944 mail@thayerscale.com
www.thayerscale.com
Manufacturer and exporter of continuous scale weighing systems, flow aid devices, volumetric feeders and pre-blending and continuous compound feeder networks for extrusion processes
Owner: Frank Hyer
sales@thayerscales.com
CFO: Bruce Edward
R & D: Rick Tolles
VP Sales/Marketing: Charles Wesley
Purchasing Agent: Lou Sawyer
Estimated Sales: $10-20 Million
Number Employees: 50-99
Square Footage: 164000
Parent Co: Hyer Industries

23971 Hygiena LLC
941 Avenida Acaso
Camarillo, CA 93012-8755

805-388-8007
Fax: 805-388-5531 www.hygiena.com
All-in-one bacterial testing products for the food and beverage industries
Director of Sales/Business Development: Steve Nason
Contact: Edgar Abarca
eabarca@hygiena.com
Manager: Fred Nason
Estimated Sales: $400 Thousand
Number Employees: 1-4
Brands:
 Ensure Quality Check System
 Systemsure Plus Atp Hygiene
 Ultrasnap Atp Test Devices
 Supersnap High Sensitivity Atp Test
 Snapshot Universal Atp Sample Test
 Aquasnap Water Atp Sample Testing
 Spotcheck Hygiene Surface Test
 Spotcheck Plus Hygiene Surface Test
 Pro-Clean Hygiene Surface Test
 Aller-Snap Protein Residue Test
 Q-Swab Environmental Collection
 Qd-Loop Rapid Dilution Devices

23972 Hygiene-Technik
4743 Christie Drive
Beamsville, ON L0R 1B4
Canada

905-563-4987
Fax: 905-563-6266 info@gotoHTI.com
www.gotoHTI.com
Specializing in the design, development and manufacturing of proprietary dispensing systems.
President: Heiner Ophardt
VP/General Manager: Tony Kortleve-Snider
Business Development Manager: Marina Nava
Number Employees: 50
Square Footage: 180000
Brands:
 Ingo-Man
 Ingo-Top

23973 Hygienic Fabrics Inc
118 S Broad St
P.O.Box 34
Lanark, IL 61046-1204

815-493-2502
Fax: 815-493-1098 sales@hyfab.com
www.hyfab.com
Cheese equipment, firesavers, bandages, fillers, milk
Manager: Shirley Gothard
Vice President: Thomas Laiken
Manager: Rachel Moll
rmoll@hyfab.com
Production Supervisor: Kelly Leicht
Plant Manager: Shirley Gothard
Estimated Sales: Less Than $500,000
Number Employees: 1-4

23974 Hygrade Gloves
30 Warsoff Pl
Brooklyn, NY 11205

718-488-9000
Fax: 718-694-9500 800-233-8100
Manufacturer, importer and exporter of protective
and disposable clothing including gloves, aprons,
goggles, hair nets, uniforms, boots and dust masks
President: Lazar Follman
Contact: Ryan Bowling
r.bowling@hygradesafety.com
Estimated Sales: $1-5 Million
Number Employees: 20-49
Square Footage: 440000
Parent Co: LDF Industries
Brands:
    American Optical
    Comfiwear

23975 Hypro
375 5th Ave NW
St Paul, MN 55112-3288

651-766-6300
Fax: 651-766-6600 800-424-9776
mattc@hypropumps.com
Wine industry pumps, fluid handling products for
the agricultural, pressure cleaning, fire services, in-
dustrial, semiconductor equipment and marine
markets
President: Donald Jorgensen
CFO: Steve Dickhaus
CEO: Paul Meschke
R&D: Bruce Maki
Contact: Tony Engebretson
imtech@pentair.com
Executive Assistant: Myrna Press
Estimated Sales: $75-100 Million
Number Employees: 5-9

23976 Hyster Company
7227 Carroll Rd
San Diego, CA 92121

858-566-4181
Fax: 858-578-6165 800-437-8371
www.hyster.com
CFO: Kevin Kelley
Vice President/GM: David Ohm
General Sales Manager: Bob Pilon
Manager: Scott Stearne
General manager: Steve Smith
Number Employees: 10-19
Parent Co: Hyster-Yale Materials Handling

23977 Hyster Company
7227 Carroll Rd
San Diego, CA 92121

855-804-2118
Fax: 858-578-6165 www.johnson-lift.com
Manufacturer and exporter of automatic storage and
handling systems and industrial trucks; also, service
and rental available
Manager: Scott Stearne
Service Manager: Steve Lacroix
Estimated Sales: $5-10 Million
Number Employees: 10-19
Parent Co: Johnson Machinery
Brands:
    Hyster

23978 Hytrol Conveyor Co Inc
2020 Hytrol St
Jonesboro, AR 72401-6712

870-935-3700
Fax: 800-852-3233 info@hytrol.com
www.hytrol.com
President: Gregg Goodner
ggoodner@hytrol.com
VP of Business Operations: Bob West
VP of Manufactoring Operations: Don Wilson
Estimated Sales: $80 Million
Number Employees: 500-999

23979 I C Technologies
613 W Manlius, St # 1
East Syracuse, NY 13057-2168

315-423-5051
Fax: 315-423-0086 800-554-2832
sra@blistertech.com www.pinholedetector.com
President: Steve Antonacci
sra@blistertech.com
Estimated Sales: $1,000,000-$5,000,000
Number Employees: 5-9

23980 I J White Corp
20 Executive Blvd
Farmingdale, NY 11735-4710

631-293-2211
Fax: 631-293-3788 info@ijwhite.com
www.ijwhite.com
Spiral systems for both the food processing and bakery industries: blast freezing, refrigerated cooling,
proofing, elevating, accumulating, drying, and
pasteurizing
President: Peter J. White
pwhite@ijwhite.com
Estimated Sales: $5-10 Million
Number Employees: 50-99

23981 I M A North America
7 New Lancaster Rd
Leominster, MA 01453-5224

978-537-8534
Fax: 215-826-0400 toddima@aol.com
Bag formers/fillers/sealers, carton machines (fold-
ing, lining, filling, closing), pouch machines, shrink
wrap machine, teabag machinery, wrapping ma-
chines, blister machines
President: Warren Roman
CEO: Krouchiek
CFO: Jerry Krouchick
Estimated Sales: $20-50 Million
Number Employees: 20-49
Parent Co: IMA North America

23982 I. Fm Usa Inc.
9490 Franklin Ave
Franklin Park, IL 60131

847-288-9500
Fax: 847-288-9501 866-643-6872
info@ifmusa.com www.sirman.com
Slicers, panini grills, meat & food processors and
bar equipment.

23983 I.W. Tremont Company
79 4th Ave
Hawthorne, NJ 07506

973-427-3800
Fax: 973-427-3778 www.iwtremont.com
Manufacturer and exporter of filter media including
inspection, analysis, sampling and testing systems
President: Sal Averso
CFO: Andrew Averso
Contact: Salvatore Averso
jimaverso@iwtremont.com
Production Manager: Andrew Averso
Production Manager: James Averso
Estimated Sales: $20-50 Million
Number Employees: 10-19
Square Footage: 10000

**23984 IAFIS Dairy Products Evaluation
Contest**
1451 Dolley Madison Boulevard Suite 10
Mc Lean, VA 22101-3847

703-761-2600
Fax: 703-761-4334 www.fpsa.org
President, Chief Executive Officer: David Seckman
Vice President of Development: Andy Drennan
Director of Sales: Grace Yee
Number Employees: 20-49

23985 IASE Co Inc
161 Industrial Pkwy # 6
Branchburg, NJ 08876-6023

908-218-1104
Fax: 908-218-1337 info@iase.net
www.iase.net
Robotic packaging equipment
President: Michael Degidio
miked@iase.net
Estimated Sales: $2.5-5 Million
Number Employees: 20-49

23986 IB Concepts
657 Dowd Avenue
Elizabeth, NJ 07201-2116

215-739-9960
Fax: 215-739-9963 888-671-0800
www.celwa.com
Manufacturer and exporter of printed, embossed and
molded crepe wadding inserts and liners; also, ab-
sorbent cellulose doilies, pulpboard coasters, die cut
polyester discs, and die cut foam
General Manager: Robert Pettus
Operations Manager: Michael Hersh
Number Employees: 25
Square Footage: 80000

23987 IBA
P.O.Box 37
Florham Park, NJ 07932-0037

973-660-9334
Fax: 908-647-6560 pastoretec@aol.com
Estimated Sales: $1-5 Million
Number Employees: 1-4

23988 IBA Food Safety
6000 Poplar Avenue
Suite 426
Memphis, TN 38119-3981

901-681-9006
Fax: 901-681-9007 800-777-9012
Sterilization, gamma irradiation, electron beam radi-
ation and microorganism reduction systems; materi-
als processing services and installation available
President: Rick Doscher
VP Perishable Foods: Chip Colonna
Number Employees: 1300
Parent Co: IBA Chemin Du Cyclotron
Brands:
    Sterigenics

23989 IBC Shell Packaging
1981 Marcus Ave
New Hyde Park, NY 11042

516-352-5138
rsamaroo@ibcshell.com
ibcshell.com
Custom packaging, display boxes and point of pur-
chase displays for specialty foods.
Chief Executive Officer: Norman Kay
Managing Director & Partner: Phillip Schoonmaker
Logistics Manager: Mike Walker
mikew@ibcshell.com
Estimated Sales: $20-50 Million
Number Employees: 250-499

23990 ICB Greenline
5808 Long Creek Park Dr # Q
Suite Q
Charlotte, NC 28269-3748

704-333-3377
Fax: 704-334-6146 800-331-5312
info@icb-usa.com
Manufacturer and exporter of overhead conveyors
for poultry and meat processing
President: Heinz Dremel
Manager: Iris Chasteen
Estimated Sales: $5.6 Million
Number Employees: 10-19
Square Footage: 200000
Brands:
    Dura-Plate
    Greenline

23991 ICI Surfactants
Strawinskylaan 2555
Amsterdam, ZZ 1077

302-762-0555
Fax: 302-762-4750 800-424-3696
www.ici.com
Food surfactants for bakery, edible oil, dairy, confec-
tionery, and miscellaneous food processors
Manager: Amber Prichett
CFO: Alan Brown
Technical Manager: Wei Shi
Estimated Sales: $.5-1 million
Number Employees: 1-4

23992 ICM Controls
7313 William Barry Blvd
North Syracuse, NY 13212

315-233-5266
800-365-5525
www.icmcontrols.com
HVAC controls.
President: Ronald Kadah
Treasurer: Laurie Kadah
Manager: Scott Dixon
Estimated Sales: $100-500 Million
Number Employees: 200-500

23993 ICOA Inc
111 Airport Rd # 1
Warwick, RI 02889-1049

401-648-0690
Fax: 401-648-0699 888-408-0600
Wireless internet services (design, deployment man-
agement)

Chairman/CEO: George Strouthopoulos
gstrouthop@icoacorp.com
Director/CFO: Erwin Vahlsing
Sales Director: Joe Farrugla
Operations Manager: Chris Browne
Estimated Sales: $4 Million
Number Employees: 20-49
Number of Brands: 7
Brands:
    Airport Network Solutions
    Authdirect
    Cafe.Com
    Linkspot
    Toll Booth
    Webcenter
    Wisezone
    Idockusa

23994 ID Images
2991 Interstate Pkwy
Brunswick, OH 44212
330-220-7300
Fax: 330-220-3838 866-516-7300
customerservice@idimages.com
www.idimages.com
Baggers and printers
Marketing Director: Lisa Stang
Contact: Megan Bailey
mbailey@idimages.com
Estimated Sales: $500,000-$1,000,000
Number Employees: 5
Brands:
    Pack Star
    Park Star Plus
    Versa Color

23995 IDC Food Division
1879 Capital Cir NE
Tallahassee, FL 32308-4598
850-656-5600
Fax: 850-656-3032 800-831-6340
Estimated Sales: $1-5 Million

23996 IDEX Corp
1925 W Field Ct # 200
Suite 200
Lake Forest, IL 60045-4862
847-498-7070
Fax: 847-498-3940 800-843-8210
www.idexcorp.com
Chairman and Chief Executive Officer: Andrew
Silvernail
asilvernail@idexcorp.com
Senior Vice President-Chief Financial Of: Heath
Mitts
Vice President, Tax and International Fi: Gerald
Carter
Senior Vice President, Fluid & Metering: Brett
Finley
Senior Vice President-Health, Science &: Eric
Ashleman
Senior Vice President-Chief Human Resour: Jeffrey
Bucklew
COO: James W Patterson
Estimated Sales: Over $1 Billion
Number Employees: 5000-9999

23997 IDL
4250 Old William Penn Hwy
Monroeville, PA 15146-1626
724-733-2234
Fax: 724-327-6420
Advertising decals including pressure sensitive and
reflective
Sales Manager: Jim Krentz
Estimated Sales: $20-50 Million
Number Employees: 100-249

23998 IEW
49 W Federal Street
Niles, OH 44446
330-652-0113
Manufacturer and exporter of industrial electronic
weighing devices and scales for mobile material
handling equipment
Estimated Sales: $1-5 Million
Brands:
    Criterion
    Sos

23999 IFC Disposables Inc
250 Kleer Vu Dr
Brownsville, TN 38012-2199
731-779-0959
Fax: 731-772-2282 800-432-9473
info@cascades.com www.cascades.com
Nonwoven wiping towels and tissue products
President and CFO: Robert E Briggs
Cmo: Laura Brooks
lbrooks@ifcdisposables.com
Marketing: Laura Brooks
Purchasing Agent: Sherry Elliot
Estimated Sales: $10-20 Million
Number Employees: 50-99
Parent Co: Wyant Corporation
Brands:
    Busboy
    Dusterz

24000 IFS North America
5451 E Williams Blvd Ste 181
Tucson, AZ 85711
520-512-2000
Fax: 520-512-2001 info@ifsna.com
www.ifsna.com
President: Theresa Sheridan
CFO: Mitch Dwight
R&D: William Grant
Contact: Mike Collins
mike.collins@ifsworld.com
Estimated Sales: $20-50 Million
Number Employees: 100-249

24001 IGEN
16020 Industrial Dr
Gaithersburg, MD 20877
301-208-3784
Fax: 301-947-6990
Laboratory testing equipment and kits; safety equipment

24002 IGEN International
16020 Industrial Dr
Gaithersburg, MD 20877-1414
301-208-3784
Fax: 301-947-6990 800-336-4436
m-series@igen.com
Provides biotechnical services to the food and bev-
erage industry
President: Samuel Wohlstadter
Number Employees: 100-249

24003 IGS Store Fixtures
58 Pulaski St
Peabody, MA 01961-3767
978-532-0010
Fax: 617-569-0201
Store fixtures and counters
CFO: Harvey Gordon
Estimated Sales: $10-20 Million
Number Employees: 100-249
Square Footage: 96000
Brands:
    Jahbo Showcases
    Lozier

24004 IHS Heath Information
15 Inverness Way E
Englewood, CO 80112-5710
800-716-3447
Fax: 800-716-6447 800-525-5539
info@ihs.com
Meat industry services (computer systems and software, importing-exporting, publications and information, nutrition labeling, quality control
instruments, sanitation programs); seasonings and
ingredients; meat products
Contact: Clark Pollard
clark.pollard@ihs.com

24005 IMAS Corporation
2905 Brittany Court
St. Charles, IL 60175
630-584-7011
847-274-9383
sphelps@IMASLtd.com www.xspec.com
Software for specification management; also, infor-
mation management consulting available
Vice President: Steven Meier
Estimated Sales: $2.5-5 Million
Number Employees: 20-49
Brands:
    Winspex
    Xspec

24006 IMC Instruments
N60w 14434 Kaul Avenue
Menomonee Falls, WI 53051
262-252-4620
Fax: 262-252-4623 sales@imcinstruments.com
www.imcinstruments.com
Instrumentation for temperature, pressure, humidity,
vacuum and air flow measurement
President: Louis Frias
VP: Ronald Frias
Estimated Sales: $2.5-5 Million
Number Employees: 10
Square Footage: 32000

24007 IMC Teddy Food Service Equipment
50 Ranick Drive East
PO Box 338
Amityville, NY 11701
631-842-2200
Fax: 631-842-2203 800-221-5644
www.imcteddy.com
Stainless steel shelving, floor troughs and gratings,
sinks, can washers, counter tops, floor drains, tables
and cabinets
Partner and President: Asit Majundar
Marketing Manager: Suzane Girrsoli
General Sales Manager: Joe Campbell
Contact: Madelin Fernandez
madelin@imcteddy.com
Purchasing Manager: Madelin Fernandez
Estimated Sales: $5-10 Million
Number Employees: 50-99
Square Footage: 20000

24008 IMECO Inc
3820 S IL Route 26
Polo, IL 61064-9006
815-946-2351
Fax: 815-946-3409 www.imeco.com
Manufacturer and exporter of refrigeration equip-
ment including prime surface evaporative condens-
ers and sub-zero blast freezers
President: Mark Stencel
Controller: Kevin Tribley
kevin.tribley@york.com
General Manager: Ian McGavisk
Quality Controller: Mark Smith
Director Operations: Colin McDonough
Estimated Sales: $50-100 Million
Number Employees: 100-249
Square Footage: 135000
Parent Co: York International

24009 IMI Cornelius
2401 N Palmer Dr
Schaumburg, IL 60196-0001
847-397-4600
Fax: 847-539-6960 800-323-4789
www.cornelius.com
Manufacturer and exporter of ice making and dis-
pensing equipment including beverage, ice, juice
and beer
President: Tim Hubbard
t.hubbard@imi-cornelius.com
Executive VP Sales/Marketing: Joseph Asfoud
President (Wilshire Canada): David Noble
Estimated Sales: $1-5 Million
Number Employees: 250-499
Parent Co: IMI Cornelius

24010 IMI Precision Engineering
325 Carr Dr
Brookville, OH 45309-1921
937-833-4033
Fax: 937-833-4205 www.imi-precision.com
Pneumatic components for the packaging industry
including aluminum and steel NFPA interchangeable
cylinders, rodless cylinders, small bore cylinders and
directional control valves
President: Peter Wallace
Quality Control: John Campbell
Senior VP: Patty Lynch
plynch@usa.norgren.com
Technical Marketing Manager (Actuators): Douglas
Kelly
Estimated Sales: $20-50 Million
Number Employees: 100-249
Square Footage: 47000
Parent Co: IMI Norgren
Brands:
    Airserv
    Airswitch
    Decel-Air

Fast/Bak
Pak-Lap
Tiny Tim

24011 IMI Precision Engineering
72 Spring Ln
Farmington, CT 06032-3140

860-677-0272
Fax: 860-677-4999 800-722-5547
www.imi-precision.com
Solenoid valves, liquid level controls, pressure
switches
Executive Director: Gary Fett
Cmo: Joshua Denison
jdenison@norgren.com
Quality Control: Ned Lanfranco
Marketing: Karen Markie
Operations: Gary Fett
Purchasing: Dave Simons
Estimated Sales: $10-20 Million
Number Employees: 100-249
Parent Co: IMI Norgren

24012 IMO Foods
P.O.Box 236
Yarmouth, NS B5A 4B2
Canada

902-742-3519
Fax: 902-742-0908 imofoods@ns.sympatico.ca
www.imofoods.com
Canned fish
President: Sidney Hughes
Executive VP/General Manager: Phillip Le Blanc
Director Marketing: David Jollimore
Number Employees: 100-249
Parent Co: IMO Foods
Type of Packaging: Consumer, Food Service, Pri-
vate Label
Other Locations:
Brands:
Golden Treasure
Kersen
West Island

24013 IMS Food Service™
1-2 Corporate Dr #136
Shelton, CT 06484-6208

203-929-2254
Fax: 203-926-0916 800-235-7072
Web based foodservice management software
President/Owner: Arnold D'Angelo
VP: Thomas O'Hara
Sales Executive: Scott Ricci
Estimated Sales: $5-10 Million
Number Employees: 33
Parent Co: International Marketing Systems
Type of Packaging: Consumer, Food Service

24014 INA Co
837 Industrial Rd # G
San Carlos, CA 94070-3333

650-631-7066
Fax: 650-873-4729 www.sovaleather.com
Importer of china and plastic bags and garbage bags
Owner: Philip Wong
Estimated Sales: Less than $500,000
Number Employees: 1-4
Brands:
Ina

24015 (HQ)INDEECO
425 Hanley Industrial Ct
St Louis, MO 63144-1511

314-644-4300
Fax: 314-644-5332 800-243-8162
sales@indeeco.com www.indeeco.com
Electric heating elements and systems including heat
transfer systems, circulation and pipeline imped-
ance; exporter of electric heaters and controls
President: Fred Epstein
CEO: John Eulich
Research & Development: Steve Links
Quality Control: Jana Jensen
Marketing Director: Kevin Healy
Operations Manager: Ron Kohlman
Production Manager: Cathy Luster
Purchasing Manager: John ie Harrington
Estimated Sales: $50-100 Million
Number Employees: 100-249
Square Footage: 200000
Other Locations:
INDEECO
Saint Louis MO
Brands:
Hynes

24016 IPEC
185 Northgate Circle
New Castle, PA 16105

800-377-4732
Fax: 724-658-3054
Plastic closures and capping equipment
President: Charles Long
CEO: Joseph Giordano
CFO/Secretary/Treasurer: Shawn Fabry
VP Operations: Jay Martin
Number Employees: 75
Square Footage: 12922

24017 IPG International Packaging Group
5611 Foxwood Drive
Apt B
Agoura Hills, CA 91377-3982

818-865-1428
Fax: 818-889-9691
Consultant specializing in product marketing and
packaging design including structural and graphic
for the consumer market; importer of finished
printed packages
Design: Debbiz Zakrzeudski
Design: Tyson Marquardt
Estimated Sales: Less than $500,000
Number Employees: 4
Type of Packaging: Consumer

24018 (HQ)IPL Inc
140 Commerciale
Saint-Damien, QC G0R-2Y0
Canada

418-789-2880
Fax: 418-789-3153 800-463-4755
info-ipl@ipl-plastics.com www.ipl-plastics.com
Producer of molded plastic products through injec-
tion and extrusion for various industrial sectors, spe-
cially food
President: Julien M,Tivier
CEO: Serge Bragdon
Estimated Sales: $10-$20 Million
Number Employees: 10-19
Type of Packaging: Consumer, Food Service, Pri-
vate Label

24019 IPL Plastics
20 Boyd St
Edmundston, NB E3V 4H4
Canada

506-739-9559
Fax: 506-739-1028 800-739-9595
Manufacturer and exporter of thin wall plastic food
containers; also, molding and printing services
available
Sales Manager: Pierre Boilard
Administrative Services: Claude Nadeau
Operations Manager: Mario Gaudieauit
Number Employees: 100
Square Footage: 180000
Parent Co: IPL

24020 IPM Coffee Innovations LLC
1130 Springtown Road
Suite A
Alpha, NJ 08865

610-865-1900
Fax: 888-762-2173 ipmcoffee@gmail.com
www.ipmcoffee.com
Cappuccino machines
Owner & President: George Strysky
Owner & Office Manager: Lela Evans Strysky

24021 IPS International
20124 Broadway Ave
Snohomish, WA 98296

360-668-5050
Fax: 360-415-9056 info@ipsintl.com
www.independentpetsupply.com
Manufacturer and exporter of thermal and insulated
handling and shipping containers
Estimated Sales: less than $500,000
Number Employees: 1
Brands:
Pal Pac
Sof-Pak
Speedwall

24022 IQ Scientific Instruments
PO Box 389
Loveland, CO 80539-0289

Fax: 970-669-2972 800-227-4224
www.phmeters.com
Manufacturer and exporter of pH meters
President: Malcolm Mitchell
Marketing Director: Kate Roberts
Sales Director: Rod Stark
Estimated Sales: $10-20 Million
Number Employees: 10-19
Brands:
Iq120 Minilab
Iq125 Minilab
Iq150
Iq240
Minilab

24023 IR Systems
725 N Highway A1a
Jupiter, FL 33477-4571

561-743-7171
Fax: 561-743-2121 800-893-7540
info@infrared-systems.com
www.infrared-systems.com
Infrared and conveyorized oven systems
Owner: J J Cunningham
Estimated Sales: less than $500,000
Number Employees: 1-4
Square Footage: 8800

24024 ISM Carton
PO Box 629
Butler, PA 16003-0629

800-378-3430
Fax: 800-827-4762 800-378-3430
Quality products for construction, industrial and
packaging applications
CEO: Mark Kania
CEO: Steve Macefe
Director Operations: Luciano Aldeghi
Estimated Sales: $50-100 Million
Number Employees: 100-249
Type of Packaging: Private Label, Bulk

24025 ISS/GEBA/AFOS
23 Water St
PO Box 480
Ashburnham, MA 01430-1258

978-827-3160
Fax: 978-827-3162 800-269-2367
sales@intlsmokingsystems.com
www.intlsmokingsystems.com
Vacuum packaging equipment, slicers, smokehouses
President: Mark Carlisle
Estimated Sales: $5-10 Million
Number Employees: 1-4

24026 ISi North America
175 Route 46 West
Fairfield, NJ 07004-7316

973-227-2426
Fax: 973-227-4520 800-447-2426
customerservice@isinorthamerica.com
Hand held whippers and soda siphons.
President: Richard W Agresta
Estimated Sales: $5-10 Million
Number Employees: 10-19
Brands:
Espuma

24027 (HQ)ITC Systems
49 Railside Road
Unit 63
Toronto, ON M1H 2X1
Canada

416-289-2344
Fax: 416-289-4790 877-482-8326
sales@itcsystems.com www.itcsystems.com
Manufacturer, importer and exporter of cash card
systems hardware and software for prepaid services
at vending machines and manual food operations;
manufacturer of photo identification cards with
on-line debit/credit balances
Chief Executive Officer, President: Cam Richardson
Vice President of Business Development: Dan
Bodolai
Director Sales: David Hulbert
Purchasing Manager: Janet Exconde
Number Employees: 10
Square Footage: 44000
Other Locations:
ITC Systems
Longwood FL

24028 ITC Systems
49 Railside Road
Toronto, ON M3A 1B3
Canada
416-289-2344
Fax: 416-289-4790 877-482-8326
service@itcsystems.com www.itcsystems.com
Manufacturer, importer and exporter of cash card
systems hardware and software for prepaid services
at vending machines and manual food operations;
manufacturer of photo identification cards with
on-line debit/credit balances
Chief Executive Officer, President: Cam Richardson
R&D: Igor Irlin
Director of Sales: Dave Hulbert
Director Sales: David Hulbert
Plant Manager: Bryan Bull
Purchasing Manager: Janet Exconde
Number Employees: 25
Square Footage: 22000
Parent Co: ITC Systems

24029 ITS/ETL Testing Laboratories
27611 La Paz Rd # C
Laguna Niguel, CA 92677-3938
949-448-4100
Fax: 949-448-4111
Laboratory specializing in microbiological and
chemical testing; also, sanitation and electrical
inspection
Manager: Bill Bocchini
Estimated Sales: $5-10 Million
Number Employees: 1-4

24030 ITT Inc
33 Centerville Rd
Lancaster, PA 17603-4068
717-509-6496
Fax: 717-509-2336 800-366-1111
engvalvescustserve@fluids.ittind.com
www.engvalves.com
Valves: Cam-Line, Cam-Tite, Dia-Flo, Pure-Flo,
Fabri-Valve, Skotch, Richter products
Cmo: Heather Sandoe
heather.sandoe@itt.com
Estimated Sales: $2.5-5 Million
Number Employees: 10-19

24031 ITT Jabsco
1485 Dale Way
Foothill Ranch, CA 92610
949-609-5106
Fax: 949-853-1254 www.jabsco.com
Manufactures food and dairy products pumps
President: Russ David
VP: Oliver Dupre
R&D: Scott Shimer
Quality Control: John Ebeling
Sales Manager: David Farrer
Estimated Sales: $20-50 Million
Number Employees: 250

24032 ITW Angleboard
113 Censors Road
Villa Rica, GA 30180-2120
770-459-5747
Fax: 770-459-1305 www.itw.com
Manufacturer and exporter of protective packaging
profiles for shipping, unitizing and palletization
CEO: David Speer
CFO: James Wooten Jr.
Investor Relations: John Brooklier
Estimated Sales: $1-5 Million
Brands:
Edgeboard

24033 ITW Auto-Sleeve
2003 Case Pkwy S
Suite 3
Twinsburg, OH 44087
330-487-2200
Fax: 330-487-3700 800-852-4571
CFO: Roy Marschke
Estimated Sales: Below $5 Million
Number Employees: 10-19

24034 ITW Diagraph
1 Research Park Dr
St Charles, MO 63304-5685
636-300-2000
Fax: 636-300-2003 800-722-1125
www.diagraph.com
Automated coding and labeling systems for product
identification, case marking, shipment addressing
and barcoding
Manager: Cathie Windle
Marketing Director: Quentin Griesenauer
VP Slaes: John Campbell
Estimated Sales: $50-100 Million
Number Employees: 100-249

24035 ITW Dymon
805 E Old 56 Highway
Olathe, KS 66061
913-829-6296
Fax: 913-397-8707 800-443-9536
cservice@dymon.com
Cleaning supplies including disinfectants, hand
sanitizer wipes and polishing clothes
R&D: Jason McCauley
Quality Control: David Madsen
General Manager: Paul Taylor
Marketing Manager: Andrew Bolin
National Sales Manager: Alan Smith
Contact: Charles Manz
manzcharlesj@itwprobrands.com
General Manager: Paull Taylor
Estimated Sales: Below $5,000,000
Number Employees: 50-99
Parent Co: Illinois Tool Works
Brands:
Antimicrobial Sanitizer Scrubs
Lemon Glo
Metal Polish Scrubs
Scrubs In-A-Bucket

24036 ITW Dynatec
31 Volunteer Dr
Hendersonville, TN 37075-3156
615-824-3634
Fax: 615-264-5248 info@itwdynatec.com
www.itwdynatec.com
Hot melt glue systems
President: Zent Myer
CFO: Doug Betew
CFO: Doug Detew
R & D: Marie McLain
Number Employees: 100-249

24037 ITW Engineered Polymers
2425 N Lapeer Rd
Oxford, MI 48371-2425
248-628-2587
Fax: 248-628-7136 info@ironout.com
Manufacturer and exporter of polyurea elastomeric
coatings, urethane foam systems, application equip-
ment and set-up processing stations. ITW Foamseal
is currently supplying a wide range of urethane
products for many uses in theautomotive, manufac-
tured housing, fenestration, furniture, sports equip-
ment, recreational vehicle, medical, tolling and
infrastructure markets
Manager: Gary Maxson
General Manager: Ted Stolz
Business Manager: Tim Walsh
Estimated Sales: $20-50 Million
Number Employees: 5-9
Square Footage: 50000
Parent Co: Illinois Tool Works
Type of Packaging: Private Label
Brands:
Infraseal

24038 ITW Food Equipment Group
702 S Ridge Ave
Troy, OH 45374
888-978-8381
www.itwfoodequipment.com
Cooking and baking, refrigeration, food preparation,
clean up, holding, weighing and wrapping, ventila-
tion and service.
Chairman/CEO: E. Scott Santi
Vice Chairman: Christopher O'Herlihy
SVP/CFO: Michael Larsen
SVP/General Counsel: Norman Finch
SVP/Chief Human Resources Officer: Mary Lawler
Estimated Sales: $14.1 Billion
Number Employees: 45,000
Parent Co: Illinois Tool Works Inc
Brands:
Hobart
Baxter
Traulsen
Kairak
Vulcan
Wolf
Berkel
Gaylord
Stero
Somat
Master
Red Goat
Peerless Food Equipment
Avery Berkel
Foster
Bonnet
Elro
Gamko
Perfecta
Vesta
Wittco Foodservice Equipment

24039 ITW Hi-Cone
1140 W Bryn Mawr Ave
Itasca, IL 60143-1599
630-438-5300
Fax: 630-438-5315 www.hicone.com
Multi-pack plastic ring carriers for cans and bottles
of beverages,vegetables,fruits, pasta and soup.
President: Tim Gardner
Cmo: Jeff Meitzel
jmeitzel@hi-cone.com
VP Sales: Steve Henn
Estimated Sales: $5-10 Million
Number Employees: 100-249
Parent Co: Illinois Tool Works
Brands:
Hi-Cone

24040 ITW Plastic Packaging
4950 Colorado Blvd
Denver, CO 80216
303-316-6816
Plastic transport packaging products: slip sheets, tier
sheets, EZ Grab LoadLoc, pallets, top frams,
DuraSheets and Replastec Separators, pallets
Contact: Roberta Andersen
roberta.andersen@chilis.com

24041 ITW United Silicone
4471 Walden Ave
Lancaster, NY 14086-9778
716-681-8222
Fax: 716-681-8789 info@unitedsilicone.com
www.unitedsilicone.com
Designer and manufacturer of product decorating
and packaging equipment, supplies, tooling and heat
seal solutions.
President: Kim Jackson
kjackson@unitedsilicone.com
Marketing Manager: Laura Baumann
Sales Director: Eric Steinwachs
Estimated Sales: $20-50 Million
Number Employees: 100-249
Square Footage: 18000
Parent Co: Illinois Toolworks
Type of Packaging: Consumer, Food Service

24042 IVEK Corp
10 Fairbanks Rd
N Springfield, VT 05150-9743
802-886-2238
Fax: 802-886-8274 800-356-4746
ivek@ivek.com www.ivek.com
Precision liquid metering and dispensing systems.
President, CEO & R&D: Mark Tanny
mtanny@ivek.com
CFO: Dennis Crowley
VP, Sales: Frank Dimaggio
Quality Control: Ed Lawrence
Marketing: Tracey Tanny
Public Relations: Pauline Asselin
Operations: Gary Blake
Production: Brad Doody
Plant Manager: Gary Blake
Purchasing: Wade McAllister
Estimated Sales: $3-5 Million
Number Employees: 50-99
Square Footage: 68000
Brands:
Digispense 2000
Digispense 700
Digispense 800
Microspense Ap
Multiplex
Multispense
Ox/Digifeeder
Sanitary Split Case Pump
Syncrospense

24043 IVEK Corp
10 Fairbanks Rd
N Springfield, VT 05150-9743
802-886-2238
Fax: 802-886-8274 800-356-4746
ivek@ivek.com www.ivek.com
Precision small volume liquid dispensing and metering systems
President: Mark Tanny
mtanny@ivek.com
CFO: Dennis Crowley
Vice President: Frank DiMaggio
Research & Development: Mark Tanny
Quality Control: Ken Neal
Marketing Director: Tracey Tanny
Sales Director: Frank DiMaggio
Public Relations: Pauline Asselin
Operations Manager: Gary Blake
Production Manager: Tara Curtis
Plant Manager: Brad Deedy
Purchasing Manager: Wade McAllister
Estimated Sales: Below $5 Million
Number Employees: 50-99

24044 IVEX Packaging Corporation
610 Beriault Rd.
Longueuil, QC J4G 1D8
Canada
450-651-8887
Fax: 450-651-0093 www.ivexpackaging.com
Manufacturer and exporter of packaging materials including corrugated paper and trays.
President: Paul Gaulin
Year Founded: 2008
Estimated Sales: $710 Million
Parent Co: Induspac Inc.
Brands:
Grand Stands
Ivex
M&R
Prime Time
Reflections
Selectware
Sho-Bowls
Ultra Pac

24045 IWS Scales
9885 Mesa Rim Road
Suite 128
San Diego, CA 92191
Fax: 858-784-0542 800-881-9755
iwsscales.com
Manufacturer, importer and exporter of mechanical and electronic scales including platform, receiving, portion, racking, computing, etc
Estimated Sales: $1-3 Million
Number Employees: 50
Square Footage: 40000
Parent Co: Western Scale
Brands:
Airway
West Weigh

24046 Ice-Cap
P.O.Box 292
Piermont, NY 10968-292
718-729-7000
Fax: 718-392-4193 888-423-2270
Manufacturer and exporter of air conditioners
CEO: Mo Siegel
CFO: Mo Siegel
Estimated Sales: $20-50 Million
Number Employees: 10

24047 Icee-USA Corporation
4701 E Airport Dr
Ontario, CA 91761-7817
909-390-4233
Fax: 909-390-4260 800-426-4233
www.icee.com
Manufacturer and exporter of frozen carbonated beverage dispensers; also, point of sale signs and displays available
President: Dan Fachner
CFO: Kent Galloway
VP: Rod Sexton
Contact: Michael Acosta
macosta@icee.com
Estimated Sales: $5-10 Million
Number Employees: 100-249
Square Footage: 88000
Parent Co: J&J Snack Foods Company

24048 Iceomatic
11100 E 45th Ave
Denver, CO 80239-3006
303-371-3737
Fax: 303-371-6296 800-423-3367
customer.service@iceomatic.com
www.iceomatic.com
Ice making equipment since 1952 including cubers, flakers, dispensers, bins and accessories. Provides equipment for restaurants, bars, hotels/motels, hospitals, etc
President: Kevin Fink
kevin.fink@iceomatic.com
CFO: Dave Weller
Quality Control: David Spiciarich
Marketing Director: Keith Kelly
Public Relations: Linda Gleeson
Plant Manager: Randy Karas
Number Employees: 250-499
Brands:
Ice-O-Matic Ice Machines

24049 Ickler Co Inc
2832 1st St S
St Cloud, MN 56301-3894
320-251-8282
Fax: 320-251-8389 800-243-8382
ickler@ickler.com www.ickler.com
Machine shop services, custom fabrication, and retail bearing sales
Owner: Todd Mc Gonagle
ickler@ickler.com
Estimated Sales: $600,000-$700,000
Number Employees: 10-19

24050 Iconics Inc
100 Foxboro Blvd # 130
Foxboro, MA 02035-2883
508-543-8600
Fax: 508-543-1503 800-946-9679
us@iconics.com www.iconics.com
ICONICS is the lead supplier of HMI SCADA, Energy Management, and Productivity Analytics software solutions to the Food and Beverage Industry. ICONICS GENISIS64 HMI/SCADA and Analytix software improves operational performance andproductivity by providing 360 degrees of visibility and real time control for business and production systems.
CEO: Russell Agrusa
russ@iconics.com
VP Finance/Administration, CFO: Paula Agrusa
VP Worldwide Sales: Chris Volpe
Business Development Manager for Buildin: Oliver Gruner
VP Product Marketing: Gary F. Kohrt
VP, Worldwide Sales: Mark Hepburn
Number Employees: 20-49
Square Footage: 96000
Brands:
Alarmwork Multimedia
Genesis32 Enterprise Edition
Genesis For Windows
Pocket Genesis
Winworx
Winworx Open Series

24051 Id Technology
2051 Franklin Dr
Fort Worth, TX 76106-2204
817-626-7779
Fax: 817-626-0553 888-438-3242
marketing@idtechnology.com
www.idtechnologytx.net
Labels, label printer/applicators, label applicators, laser marking, inkjet coding, thermal transfer overprinting
President: Robert Zuilhof
robert.zuilhof@idtechnology.com
CFO: Tina Millwood
VP: Alan Shipman
Marketing: Hilary Taylor
Estimated Sales: $75 Million
Number Employees: 100-249
Other Locations:
Pewaukee WI
Fresno CA

24052 Id Technology
2051 Franklin Dr
Fort Worth, TX 76106-2204
817-626-7779
Fax: 817-626-0553 888-438-3242
marketing@idtechnology.com
www.idtechnologytx.net
Labeling, coding and marking equipment
President: Robert Zuilhof
robert.zuilhof@idtechnology.com
CEO/CFO: Tina Millwood
VP: Alan Shipman
R&D: Mark Snedecor
Marketing: Hillary Taylor
Sales: Alan Shipman
Public Relations: Hillary Taylor
Plant Manager: Kim Pulliam
Purchasing: Kim Pulliam
Estimated Sales: $50 Million
Number Employees: 100-249
Parent Co: Pro Mach Inc

24053 Idaho Beverages Inc
2108 1st Ave N
Lewiston, ID 83501-1604
208-743-6535
Fax: 208-746-2273 dprasil@lewistonpepsi.com
www.lewistonpepsi.com
Distributer of beverages to the food service industry. Brands distributed include Pepsi, Mountain Dew, 7 Up, Cheerwine Soft Drink, Gatorade, Aquafina, Starbucks Coffee and more.
Owner: Dan Prasil
Estimated Sales: $5-10 000,000
Number Employees: 51-200
Type of Packaging: Food Service

24054 Idaho Steel Products Inc
255 E Anderson St
Idaho Falls, ID 83401-2016
208-522-1275
Fax: 208-522-6041 sales@idahosteel.com
www.idahosteel.com
Manufacturer and exporter of food processing equipment including blanchers, cookers, coolers, drum dryers and complete processing lines
President: Delynn Bradshaw
delynn@idahosteel.com
CFO: Craig Parker
Engineering Manager: Alan Bradshaw
Marketing/Public Relations: Davis Christiansen
Sales Director: Bruce Ball
Operations Manager: D Bradshaw
Purchasing Manager: Adam French
Estimated Sales: $10-20 Million
Number Employees: 100-249
Square Footage: 100000

24055 Ideal Office Supply & Rubber Stamp Company
222 E Center Street
Kingsport, TN 37662-0935
423-246-7371
Fax: 423-246-3535
Office supplies including rubber stamps and plastic signs
President: Cynthia Culberton
Number Employees: 12

24056 Ideal Packaging Systems
1662 Broughton Court
Atlanta, GA 30338-4633
770-352-0210
Fax: 770-352-0106 ioealvr@yahoo.com
Pallet stretch wrapping and bundle shrink wrapping equipment
Estimated Sales: $10-20 Million
Number Employees: 5

24057 Ideal Pak Inc
4607 Dovetail Dr
Madison, WI 53704-6302
608-241-1118
Fax: 608-241-4448 800-383-1128
sales@ideal-pak.com www.idealstorage.biz
Industrial liquid filling and closing equipment

Owner: Steve Bethke
steve@ideal-pak.com
Sales & Marketing Director: Russell Schlager
Vice President: Bruce Bierman
Marketing Manager: Steven Meyer
National Sales Manager: Robert D. Whetstone
steve@ideal-pak.com
Operations Manager: Bruce Bierman
Purchasing Manager: Aric Riley
Estimated Sales: $1 Million +
Number Employees: 20-49
Number of Brands: 3
Square Footage: 30000
Type of Packaging: Food Service, Private Label, Bulk

24058 Ideal Sleeves
182 Courtright St
Wilkes Barre, PA 18702-1802

570-823-8456
Fax: 570-823-8458
Tamper evident shrink seals, multipak, sleeves, shrink labels, preforms, seamed and seamless materials including PVC and Pet-G
Manager: Dave Frable
Chief Executive Officer, President: James Dwyer
G.M.: Arlene Warnuck
Manager: Henry Shuffler
henrys@idealsleeves.com
Estimated Sales: $5-10 Million
Number Employees: 20-49

24059 Ideal Stencil Machine &Tape Company
5307 Meadowland Parkway
Marion, IL 62959-5893

618-233-0162
Fax: 618-233-5091 800-388-0162
Manufacturer and exporter of ink including meat branding, hog tattoo, coding and jet printer; also, fountain brushes, conveyor line coders, ink applicators, metal markers and electronic stencil and embossing machines
Sales Manager: Jim Boyd
Executive VP Operations: Marco Ziniti
Estimated Sales: $2.5-5 Million
Number Employees: 20-49
Square Footage: 240000
Brands:
Handy A&C
Ht80
Ideal Mark
Ideco
M074
Meat Marking
Roll-Eze
Speedry

24060 Ideal Wire Works
820 S Date Ave
Alhambra, CA 91803-1414

626-282-0886
Fax: 626-282-2674
Manufacturer and exporter of custom wire display racks, rings and parts in steel or stainless steel
Vice President: Liz Maro
lizmaro@idealwireworks.com
VP: Jim Freitag
Estimated Sales: $2.5-5 Million
Number Employees: 20-49
Square Footage: 40000

24061 Ideal Wrapping Machine Company
81 Sprague Avenue
Middletown, NY 10940-5223

845-343-7700
Fax: 845-344-4248
Manufacturer and exporter of forming, cutting and wrapping machinery for caramel, nougat and toffee candies
President: Lee Quality Tire
General Manager: Jim Horton
Number Employees: 5-9

24062 Ideal of America
205 Regency Executive Park Drive
Suite 309
Charlotte, NC 28217-3989

704-523-1604
Fax: 704-523-1635
Packaging equipment including bundlers, shrink wrappers and automatic baggers

VP: David Katz
Sales Manager: Lana Taylor
Estimated Sales: $1-5 Million
Number Employees: 100-250
Square Footage: 80000

24063 Ideal of America/ValleyRio Enterprise
1662 Broughton Court
Atlanta, GA 30338-4633

770-352-0210
Fax: 770-352-0106 idealvr@yahoo.com
Manufacturer and exporter of stainless steel packaging equipment including fully automated shrink and stretch wrappers
Vice President: Alan Pullock
Estimated Sales: $10 Million
Number Employees: 100-250
Square Footage: 210000
Parent Co: Ideal of America
Brands:
Ideal

24064 Ideas Etc Inc
8305 Dawson Hill Rd
Louisville, KY 40299-5317

502-231-4303
Fax: 502-239-0555 800-733-0337
ideasetc@msn.com www.ideas-etc.com
Manufacturer and exporter of shot and martini glasses, beverage containers and 4-necker T-shirts; importer of martini glasses. Designers and printers of food service calendars and planners
President: Tiffany Gaskin
tiffanygaskin@hotmail.com
Estimated Sales: $500,000+
Number Employees: 1-4
Brands:
Palm Tree Cooler
Splitshot
Yardski

24065 Ideas Well Done LLC
276 E Allen St # 5
Winooski, VT 05404-1570

802-654-8603
Fax: 802-654-8618 877-877-1224
www.ideaswelldone.com
Manufacturer, boilerless atmospheric steamers in 4 and 6 pan sizes, stackable up to 12 pan configuration. convection fan and automatic waterfill makes steam convection and simple
President: Michael G Colburn
mcolburn@ideaswelldone.com
CFO: Bob McLaughlin
VP: Mary Treat
Quality Control: Stephen Bogner
Marketing: Mary Treat
Sales/Public Relations: Mary Esthertrout
Purchasing: Steve Bogner
Estimated Sales: Below $5 Million
Number Employees: 5-9
Number of Brands: 1
Number of Products: 3
Square Footage: 20000
Brands:
Steller Steam

24066 Ideas in Motion
P.O.Box 8504
New Castle, PA 16107-8504

724-924-9680
Fax: 724-924-9665 800-367-3535
Owner: Brian Crisci
Estimated Sales: $1-2.5 Million
Number Employees: 20-49

24067 Idec Corp
1175 Elko Dr
Sunnyvale, CA 94089-2209

408-747-0550
Fax: 408-744-9055 800-262-IDEC
Control components, switches, pushbuttons, sensors and relays
Chairman of the Board: Toshiyuki Funaki
VP: Sada O'Hara
Manager: Jc Aguirre
aguirre.jc@idec.com
Estimated Sales: $50-100 Million
Number Employees: 100-249
Number of Products: 5500

24068 IdentaBadge
3219 Johnston St
Lafayette, LA 70503

337-984-8888
Fax: 337-984-1666 800-325-8247
Name badges, directional signs and advertising specialties and awards
Owner: D A Savoie
CEO: Dale Savoie
VP: Sidney Savoie
Sales: Dottie Blanchard
Public Relations: Dottie Blanchard
Estimated Sales: $5-10 Million
Number Employees: 5-9
Number of Brands: 1
Number of Products: 25
Square Footage: 11000
Parent Co: Trophyland
Type of Packaging: Bulk

24069 Idesco Corp
37 W 26th St # 10
New York, NY 10010-1097

212-784-1800
Fax: 212-889-7033 800-336-1383
info@idesco.com www.idesco.com
Manufacturer and exporter of integrated security systems
President: Andrew Schonzeit
andrew@idesco.com
CFO: Ray O' Connor
VP of Sales: Michael Perlow
VP Sales: Andy Goldstone
Operations Manager: Brian Simpson
Estimated Sales: $10-20 Million
Number Employees: 20-49
Square Footage: 20000
Brands:
Vita

24070 Idexx Laboratories Inc
1 Idexx Dr
Westbrook, ME 04092-2041

207-556-0300
Fax: 207-556-4346 800-548-6733
www.idexx.com
Manufacturer and exporter of cleaning and validation systems including testing kits for salmonella, coliforms/E coli in water, residues in milk and microbiological; also, dehydrated culture media.
President/CEO: Jay Mazelsky
EVP/Chief Financial Officer/Treasurer: Brian McKeon
Corp VP/Software & Engineering Officer: Jeff Dixon
Corp VP/General Counsel/Secretary: Sharon Underberg
Corp VP/Worldwide Operations: John Hart
Corp VP/Chief Information Officer: Ken Grady
Corp VP/Chief Technology Officer: Jeffrey Thomas
Year Founded: 1983
Estimated Sales: $2.4 Billion
Number Employees: 7,000
Brands:
Acumedia
Bind
Colilert
Lightning
Simplate
Snap

24071 Ifm Efector
782 Springdale Dr
Exton, PA 19341-2850

610-524-2000
Fax: 610-524-2020 800-441-8246
customer_service@ifmefector.com
www.ifmefector.com
Industrial sensors including capacitive, inductive and plug-connector type proximity switches, photo-electric controls, flow monitor switches, pressure switches, and temperature sensors
Contact: Deven Ott
deveno@fedex.com
Estimated Sales: $70 Million
Number Employees: 100-249

24072 Igloo Products Corp
777 Igloo Rd
Katy, TX 77494

866-509-3503
www.igloocoolers.com
Ice chest coolers, insulated catering chests, softside catering carriers and beverage and cup dispensers.

Year Founded: 1947
Estimated Sales: $108.90 Million
Number Employees: 1,200
Number of Products: 500+
Square Footage: 10000000
Parent Co: ACON
Type of Packaging: Food Service
Brands:
Igloo
Igloo 2go
Igloo Stralth

24073 Igus Inc
50 N Broadway # 1
Rumford, RI 02916-2600

401-438-2200
Fax: 401-438-7270 800-521-2747
sales@igus.com www.igus.com
Packaging machinery components, cable carriers,
high flex cables, bearings and linear guides
Vice President: Carsten Blase
cblase@igus.com
VP: Carsten Blase
Number Employees: 100-249
Square Footage: 352000
Parent Co: Igus GmbH

24074 Ika-Works Inc
2635 Northchase Pkwy SE
Wilmington, NC 28405-7419

910-452-7059
Fax: 910-452-7693 800-733-3037
process@ikausa.com www.ikausa.com
Laboratory, pilot plant and processing equipment in-
cluding particle size reducers, dispersers and ho-
mogenizers; also, continuous and vertical kneaders,
overhead stirring motors and magnetic stirrers; sani-
tary design servicesavailable
Owner: Rene Steigelman
Vice President: Robert Hardin
Marketing/Sales: Linn Wilson
Sales Director: Michael Janssen
Number Employees: 100-249
Square Footage: 60000
Parent Co: IKA Werke
Brands:
Conterna
Dispax Reactor
Eurostar
Ikamag
Planetron
Ultra-Turrax

24075 Il Valley Container Inc
2 Terminal Rd
Peru, IL 61354-3700

815-223-7200
www.ivcontainer.com
Corrugated containers
President: Timothy Alter
timothyalter@ivcontainer.com
General Manager: Jim Ewert
Estimated Sales: $5-10 Million
Number Employees: 20-49

24076 Ilapak Inc
105 Pheasant Run
Newtown, PA 18940-1820

215-579-2900
Fax: 215-579-9959 marketing@ilapak.com
www.ilapak.com
Flexible horizontal and vertical packaging machin-
ery including fin seal and shrink wrappers, vertical
form/fill/seal, four-side seal pouch, horizontal modi-
fied atmosphere, etc
President: Andrew G Axberg
CEO: Edward Young
eyoung@ilapak.com
CFO: Frank Zellucci
VP Sales: Randy Rice
Estimated Sales: $10-20 Million
Number Employees: 20-49
Square Footage: 36000
Parent Co: Ilapak Holding
Brands:
Alfa
Carrera 1000 M
Carrera 1000 Pc
Carrera 2000 Pc
Carrera 500 M
Cougar
Delta
Delta 3000 D-Cam
Delta 3000 Ld

Delta 3000 Sb
Indy
Rose Forgrove
Sandiacre
Vegatronic 3000
Vegatronic 1000
Vegatronic 2000
Vegatronic 3000

24077 Ilapak Inc
105 Pheasant Run
Newtown, PA 18940-1820

215-579-2900
Fax: 215-579-9959 cpaczkowski@ilapakusa.com
www.ilapak.com
Supplier of industrial wrapping machinery for food
industry
CEO: Edward Young
eyoung@ilapak.com
CEO: Andrew Axberg
Office Manager: Claire Paczkowski
Number Employees: 20-49

24078 Ilc Dover
1 Moonwalker Rd
Frederica, DE 19946-2080

302-335-3911
Fax: 302-335-0762 800-631-9567
customer_service@ilcdover.com
www.ilcdover.com
Pharmaceutical packaging material.
President: Fran DiNuzzo
Year Founded: 1947
Estimated Sales: $100-500 Million
Square Footage: 225000
Brands:
Keg Wrap

24079 Illinois Lock Co
301 W Hintz Rd
Wheeling, IL 60090-5700

847-537-1800
Fax: 847-537-1881 800-733-3907
sales@illinoislock.com www.illinoislock.com
Producers of custom engineered key locks, keyless
locks, electric switch locks, high-security locks, and
wire harness lock assemblies
Sales Exec: Paul Sletzer
Manager: Len Samela
Estimated Sales: $10-20 Million
Number Employees: 50-99
Parent Co: Eastern Company

24080 Illinois Range Company
9555 Ainslie St
Schiller Park, IL 60176-1115

847-928-2490
Fax: 847-928-2782 800-535-7041
Custom stainless steel kitchen equipment including
counters, hoods, ranges, ovens, smallwares, etc
President: John Domdek
Estimated Sales: Below $5 Million
Number Employees: 1-4
Square Footage: 504000

24081 Illinois Restaurant Association
33 W. Monroe
Suite 250
Chicago, IL 60603

312-787-4000
Fax: 312-787-4792 800-572-1086
info@illinoisrestaurants.org
www.illinoisrestaurants.org
To serve the needs of the foodservice industry and
support its future.
President: Sam Toia
Project Manager: Ashley Brandon
Assistant Director of Finance & Administ: Maria
Bello
Contact: Rick Brands
rbrands@mcmaster.com
VP, Operations: Mary Kay Bonoma
Number Employees: 20-49

24082 Illinois Tool Works
155 Harlem Ave
Glenview, IL 60025

224-661-8870
www.itw.com
Dishwashing, cooking, refrigeration and food processing equipment

Chairman/CEO: E. Scott Santi
Vice Chairman: Christopher O'Herlihy
Senior VP/General Counsel/Secretary: Norman
Finch
Senior VP/CFO: Michael Larsen
Estimated Sales: $13.6 Billion
Number Employees: 50,000

24083 Illinois Wholesale CashRgstr
2790 Pinnacle Dr
Elgin, IL 60124-7943

847-310-4200
Fax: 847-310-8490 800-544-5493
www.illinoiswholesale.com
Refurbished point of sale equipment
President: Al Moorhouse
amoorhouse@illinoiswholesale.com
Vice President of Accounting: Bob Tracy
Chief Operating Officer, Vice President: Darin
Moorhouse
Operations Manager: Jeff Burton
Estimated Sales: $10-20 Million
Number Employees: 100-249

24084 Illuma Display
P.O.Box 1531
Brookfield, WI 53008-1531

262-446-9220
Fax: 262-446-9260 800-501-0128
Manufacturer and exporter of curved light boxes,
graphic stands and backlit displays
President: Joe Galati
VP: Tony Galati
Estimated Sales: Less than $500,000
Number Employees: 1-4

24085 Illumination Products Inc
175 Calle Federico Costa
Tres Monjitas Park
San Juan, PR 00918-1307

787-754-7193
Fax: 787-250-7813
Fluorescent light fixtures and lamps
President: Robert Santiago
Quality Control: Raul Millan
Estimated Sales: Below $5 Million
Number Employees: 5-9

24086 Ilsemann Corp
398 Circle Of Progress Dr # 10
Suite 102
Pottstown, PA 19464-3814

610-323-4143
Fax: 610-323-4709 sales@ilsemannusa.com
www.ilsemann.com/index.php?id=company&L=1
Estimated Sales: $1,000,000-$3,000,000
Number Employees: 5-9
Parent Co: Heino Ilsemann GmbH

24087 Image Development
PO Box 218
Plymouth, CA 95669-0218

209-267-1850
Fax: 209-267-1850 id@bauerengraving.com
Chocolate coin imprinting, dies, candy
President: William Bratt
Number Employees: 2

24088 Image Experts Uniforms
1623 Eastern Pkwy
Schenectady, NY 12309-6011

518-377-4523
Fax: 518-374-1236 800-789-2433
www.imageexpertsuniforms.com
Manufacturer and exporter of uniforms
Owner: Tom Salamone
tom@imageexperts.com
CEO: Thomas J Salamone
Estimated Sales: $1-2.5 Million
Number Employees: 10-19
Square Footage: 8000
Parent Co: Image Experts Uniforms
Brands:
Chef Direct
Really Cookin' Chef Gear

24089 Image Fillers
735 Fox Chase # 111
Suite 111
Coatesville, PA 19320-1897

610-466-1440
Fax: 610-466-0116 www.imagefillers.com
Owner: Mike Kelly Sr
Number Employees: 5-9

24090 Image National Inc
16265 Star Rd
Nampa, ID 83687-8415
208-345-4020
Fax: 208-336-9886 jcarico@imagenational.com
Manufacturer and exporter of electric signs, store
fronts and interior graphics
President: Doug Bender
doug.bender@imagenational.com
CEO/CFO: Chuck White
Service Install Manager: Jeff Carico
Sales Manager: Tony Adams
General Manager: Doug Bender
Estimated Sales: $5-10 Million
Number Employees: 100-249
Parent Co: Futura Corporation

24091 Image Plastics
5919 Jessamine Street
Houston, TX 77081-6506
713-772-2811
Fax: 713-772-6445 800-289-2811
Insulated and noninsulated plastic drinkware
VP: Jim Houseal
Director Marketing: Gary Opperman
Director Sales: Mike Barrow
Estimated Sales: $20-50 Million
Number Employees: 100-249
Brands:
Automug
Sportsmate

24092 Imaging Technologies
445 Universal Drive
Cookeville, TN 38506-4603
931-432-4191
Fax: 931-432-4199 800-488-2804
www.icglink.com
Manufacturer and exporter of high resolution ink jet
printing systems for printing bar codes, alphanumer-
ics and graphics on porous surfaces
President: Loyd Tarver
Controller: Ted Bonnay
Vice President of Marketing: Chris Jones
Marketing Manager: Steve Shoup
Contact: Mark Doyle
sales@itiworldwide.com
Number Employees: 30
Square Footage: 24000
Brands:
Iti
Kd Jet Streamer
Marksman
Porelon

24093 Imaje
1650 Airport Rd NW # 101
Kennesaw, GA 30144-7017
678-594-7153
Fax: 770-421-7702 www.markem-imaje.us
Coding, dating and marking equipment, barcoding
systems and inks for food packaging; importer of ink
jet coders; exporter of ink jet coders, inks and
additives
Manager: Linda Kaimesher
CFO: Steve Wakeford
Marketing Director: Alisha Curd
Sales Director: Tim Sines
Contact: Luis Davila
ldavila@markem-imaje.com
Purchasing Manager: Norm Coon
Estimated Sales: G
Number Employees: 1-4
Parent Co: Dover Technologies
Brands:
Crayon
Crayon Z-Tra
Imaje 7s
Lightjet
Lightjet Vector
McP
McP Barcode
McP Series
Prima
Pulsar
S8 1p65
S8 Classic
S8 Contrast
S8 Master

24094 Iman Pack
5762 E Executive Dr
Westland, MI 48185-9125
734-467-9016
Fax: 734-467-8642 800-810-4626
sales@imanpack.com www.imanpack.com
Manufacturer and importer of automatic packaging
equipment including horizontal and vertical
form/fill/seal machinery, shrink wrappers, counting
and weighing scales, case packers, palletizers, etc
President: Antonio Bonotto
Sales/Marketing: Lori Scheinman
National Sales Director: Fred Barbarotto
Contact: Mauro Ferrari
m.ferrari@imanpack.it
Estimated Sales: $1-3 Million
Number Employees: 5-9
Parent Co: Iman Pack SRL
Brands:
Gianopac
Ultravert

24095 Iman Pack
5762 E Executive Dr
Westland, MI 48185-9125
734-467-9016
Fax: 734-467-8642 www.imanpack.it
Packaging equipment including vertical form, fill
and seal baggers
President: Antonio Bonotto
VP: Giovanni Bonotto
Contact: Mauro Ferrari
m.ferrari@imanpack.it
Estimated Sales: $1-3 Million
Number Employees: 5-9
Parent Co: Imanpak

24096 Iman Pack Sigma System
5762 E Executive Dr
Westland, MI 48185
734-467-9016
Fax: 734-467-8642 www.imanpack.com
President: Antonio Bonotto
VP Sales: Massimo Denipoti
Contact: Mauro Ferrari
m.ferrari@imanpack.it
Estimated Sales: $1-5 Million
Number Employees: 5-9

24097 Imar
2301 Collins Avenue
Miami Beach, FL 33139-1639
305-531-5757
Fax: 305-538-2957
Manufacturer, importer and exporter of packaging
machinery for pouches
CEO: Thomas Tennant
Parent Co: Imar
Brands:
Imar

24098 Imdec
2061 Freeway Dr
Suite E
Woodland, CA 95776
530-661-9091
Fax: 530-661-9206
Tomato and fruit processing equipment
President: Glen Langstaff
Contact: David Matthews
trgshop@yahoo.com
Estimated Sales: $1-2.5 Million
Number Employees: 9

24099 Imex Vinyl Packaging
2559 Plantation Center Drive
Matthews, NC 28105
704-815-4600
Fax: 704-815-4601 800-938-4639
sales@imexvp.com www.imexpackaging.com
Clear vinyl bags and packaging.
President & Owner: Steve Jefferey
Operations Manager: Danny Love
Number Employees: 10
Type of Packaging: Consumer, Private Label, Bulk

24100 Impact Awards & Promotions
748 Us Highway 27 N
Avon Park, FL 33825-2639
561-394-8002
Fax: 561-394-9002 888-203-4225
www.impactpromotions.com
Signs, trophies, awards, nameplates and name tags

Owner: Doug Singletary
Marketing: Doug Singletary
Contact: San Woodlee
swoodlee@impactpromotions.com
Estimated Sales: Less than $500,000
Number Employees: 1-4
Square Footage: 6000

24101 Impact Nutrition
1155 S Havana Street
Suite 11-392
Aurora, CO 80012-4019
720-374-7111
www.impactnutrition.net.au
Contract packager of vitamins, minerals, herbal and
nutritional supplements, sports nutrition products,
capsules, tablets and powders
President: Patrick Frazier
General Manager: Julene Frazier
Estimated Sales: $10-20 Million
Number Employees: 20-49
Square Footage: 30000

24102 Impact Products LLC
2840 Centennial Rd
Toledo, OH 43617-1898
419-841-2891
Fax: 419-841-7861 800-333-1541
custserv@impact-products.com
www.impact-products.com
Wholesaler/distributor of toilet bowl mops, soap dis-
pensers, dust pans, plastic pumps, disposable plastic
gloves and washroom accessories
President/Chairman: John Harbal
Founder: James Findlay
Vice President: Cesar Bejar
cbejar69@gmail.com
Quality Assurance Manager: Carolyn Helminiak
Vice President, Marketing: Jeannie McCarthy
Sales & Marketing Executive: Kaiko Laser
Vice President, Operations: Brian Paul
Procurement Manager: James Knechtges
Estimated Sales: $29 Million
Number Employees: 100-249
Square Footage: 155000

24103 Impaxx Machines
550 Burning Tree Rd
Fullerton, CA 92833-1400
714-449-5155
Fax: 714-526-0300 info@label-aire.com
www.label-aire.com
Provides advanced and reliable pressure-sensitive
labeling machinery to blue-chips firms world over
V P: Stuart Moss
CEO: Ken Phillips
Contact: Isaac Zukerman
izukerman@label-aire.com
Estimated Sales: $20-50 Million
Number Employees: 100-249

24104 Imperial
303 Paterson Plank Rd
Carlstadt, NJ 07072-2307
201-288-9199
Fax: 201-288-8990 800-526-6261
imperial@imperialusa.com www.imperialusa.com
Bar stools
Contact: Zachary Dimotta
zdimotta@imperialusa.com
Estimated Sales: $1-5 Million
Number Employees: 15

24105 Imperial
6300 W Howard St
Niles, IL 60714
847-581-3300
Fax: 847-647-3105 800-967-4442
Wholesale bakery
President: Betty Dworkin
Estimated Sales: $2.5-5 000,000
Number Employees: 20-49

24106 Imperial Broom Company
PO Box 8018
Richmond, VA 23223-0018
804-648-7840
Fax: 804-648-0113 888-353-7840
Brooms
Owner: Matthew J Robinson Jr
General Manager: Carlton Robinson
Estimated Sales: less than $500,000
Number Employees: 1-4
Square Footage: 20800

24107 Imperial Containers
13400 Nelson Ave
City of Industry, CA 91746

626-333-6363
Fax: 714-630-2737
Corrugated containers and inner packing
Estimated Sales: $10-20 Million
Number Employees: 20-49
Parent Co: Orange County Container

24108 Imperial Industries Inc
505 W Industrial Park Ave
Rothschild, WI 54474-7917

715-359-0200
Fax: 715-355-5349 800-558-2945
indsales@imperialind.com www.imperialind.com
Bulk storage silos and tanks, liquid waste tanks both
self-contained and truck mounted, portable toilets,
wash sinks and barricades. Also Asme certified
tanks and DOT 407/412 truck mounted tanks.
President: Russ Putnam
HR Executive: Doug Hagen
doug@iimperialind.com
Reaersch/Development: Rial Potter
Quality Control: Doug Hagen
Marketing/Sales Manager: T Aerts
Plant Manager: K Mannel
Purchasing Director: Lisa Schultz
Number Employees: 100-249
Square Footage: 75000
Parent Co: Wausau Tile
Type of Packaging: Bulk

24109 Imperial Manufacturing Co
1128 Sherborn St
Corona, CA 92879-2089

951-281-1830
Fax: 951-281-1879 800-343-7790
imperialsales@imperialrange.com
www.imperialrange.com
Ranges, convection ovens, fryers and filter systems,
char-broilers, hot plates, griddles, roasters,
cheesemelters and griddles/broilers
Sales Manager (Eastern): Daniel Monfort
Manager: Matt Wise
mwise@imperialrange.com
Number Employees: 100-249
Brands:
    Elite

24110 Imperial Packaging Corporation
1 Campbell Street
PO Box 2383
Pawtucket, RI 2861

401-753-7778
Fax: 401-765-5537 info@imperialpkg.com
www.imperialpkg.com
Paper folding boxes
VP: Steven Felici
Owner: Ronald Felici
VP Sales/Marketing: Stevem Felici
Contact: Patrick Gilmartin
pgilmartin@imperialpkg.com
General Manager: Robert Gilmore
Estimated Sales: $10-20 Million
Number Employees: 20-49

24111 Imperial Plastics Inc
21320 Hamburg Ave
PO Box 907
Lakeville, MN 55044-9032

952-469-4951
Fax: 952-469-4724 www.imperialplastics.com
Plastic signs, trays and boxes
President: Dennis Erler
erler.dennis@yahoo.com
Number Employees: 100-249

24112 Imperial Plastics Inc
21320 Hamburg Ave
PO Box 907
Lakeville, MN 55044-9032

952-469-4951
Fax: 952-469-4724 www.imperialplastics.com
Manufacturer and exporter of plastic stoppers and
advertising novelties
President: Dennis Erler
erler.dennis@yahoo.com
Number Employees: 100-249
Type of Packaging: Private Label

24113 Imperial Schrade Corporation
7 Schrade Ct
Ellenville, NY 12428

212-210-8600
Fax: 845-210-8671 www.schradeknives.com
Knive sharpeners, forks, spoons, fish splitting and
stainless knives, shears, etc
Marketing Manager: Rick Marchlik
VP Sales: Jim Strathis
Estimated Sales: $75 Million
Number Employees: 500

24114 Imperial Signs & Manufacturing
924 Eglin St
Rapid City, SD 57701-9525

605-348-2511
Fax: 605-399-2705
Signs including neon, plastic and painted
Estimated Sales: $1-2.5 Million
Number Employees: 10-19

24115 Importers Service Corp
65 Brunswick Ave
Edison, NJ 08817-2512

732-248-1946
Fax: 201-332-4152
Manufacturers of gum arabic, gum acacia, gum
karaya, gum tragacanth and gum ghatti
President: Eric Berliner
Plant Engineer: Chris Berliner
cberliner@importersservice.com
Quality Control: David Hulmes
Product Manager: David Hulmes
Director Sales: Robert Vilim
Office Manager: Nancy Meurer
Plant Manager: Henry Schleckser
Estimated Sales: $20-50 Million
Number Employees: 50-99
Square Footage: 70000
Type of Packaging: Private Label, Bulk

24116 Impress Industries
PO Box 477
Emmaus, PA 18049-0477

610-967-6027
Fax: 610-844-9521
Corrugated boxes for cakes, candy, etc
President: Thomas Galiardo
Controller: Debbie White
Sales Manager: Peter Tisi
Estimated Sales: $20-50 Million
Number Employees: 100-249
Square Footage: 81000

24117 Impress USA Inc
936 Barracuda St
San Pedro, CA 90731

310-519-2400
Fax: 310-519-2281 www.ardaghgroup.com
Manufacturer of metal packaging for the food indus-
try
Quality Control: Rudy Shufeldt
Sales: Linda Zottola
Number Employees: 1-10
Parent Co: Ardagh Group

24118 Imprinting Systems Specialty
803 Pressley Rd # 104
Charlotte, NC 28217-0971

704-527-4545
Fax: 704-527-4546 800-497-1403
www.imprintinginc.com
Pressure-sensitive labels
President: Glenn E Randolph
issilbl@bellsouth.net
Marketing Manager: Mark Kessler
Estimated Sales: $500,000-$1 Million
Number Employees: 5-9

24119 Improved Blow Molding
27 Hillside Dr
Hollis, NH 03049-6158

603-465-6190
Fax: 603-465-6190 800-256-1766
Manufacturer and exporter of plastic blow molding
machinery for food packaging
Owner: Ron Beaulieu
VP Marketing: H Lance Goldberg
VP Engineering: Ronald Beaulieu
Estimated Sales: $500,000-$1 Million
Number Employees: 1-4
Square Footage: 140000
Parent Co: Goodman Equipment Company

Brands:
    Automa
    Impco

24120 Impulse Signs
25 Advance Road
Toronto, ON M8Z 2S6
Canada

416-231-3391
Fax: 416-236-2116 866-636-8273
mgisborne@impulsesigns.com
Manufacturer and exporter of menu boards and table
signs
President/General Manager: Alex Cachia
Director, Marketing: Ron Wynne
VP, Sales: Carole Lynch
Estimated Sales: $1-5 Million
Number Employees: 20-50
Square Footage: 96000
Brands:
    Impulse

24121 Imsco Technology
40 Bayfield Drive
North Andover, MA 01845-6016

978-689-2080
Fax: 978-689-2585
Filtration equipment
Chairman/CEO: Timothy Keating
Estimated Sales: $500,000-$1 Million
Number Employees: 5-9

24122 Imtec Acculine Inc
49036 Milmont Dr
Fremont, CA 94538-7301

510-770-1800
Fax: 802-463-4334 800-854-6832
www.imtecacculine.com
High preformance automated identification systems
President: Paul Mendes
pmendes@imtecacculine.com
CEO: Tim Thompson
Number Employees: 20-49

24123 In Harvest Inc
1012 Paul Bunyan Dr SE
PO Box 428
Bemidji, MN 56601-3447

218-751-8500
Fax: 218-751-8519 800-346-7032
www.indianharvest.com
Beans, grains, pastas and specialty rice blends
CIO/CTO: Mary Dickey
m.dickey@inharvest.com
CFO: Jeffrey Buelow
Director, Sales: Jeff Lande
Director, Culinary Development: Michael Holleman
Estimated Sales: $20-50 Million
Number Employees: 10-19
Number of Brands: 2
Type of Packaging: Consumer, Food Service, Pri-
vate Label, Bulk
Brands:
    InHarvest
    KAMUT®

24124 In Sink Erator
4700 21st St
Racine, WI 53406-5093

262-554-5432
Fax: 262-554-3639 800-558-5700
www.insinkerator.com
Garbage disposal units and hot water dispensers
President: Tim Ferry
tim.ferry@insinkerator.com
CFO: William Ivy
Secretary and Marketing: Cathy Davis
Number Employees: 1000-4999
Parent Co: Emerson Electric Company
Brands:
    In-Sink-Erator

24125 In-Line Corporation
11121 Excelsior Blvd
Hopkins, MN 55343-3434

952-938-0046
Fax: 952-938-0046
Wrappers and skin packaging and premium and pro-
motional packaging
Sales Manager: Chris Thornby
Operations Manager: Don Steen
Estimated Sales: $5-10 Million
Number Employees: 50-99
Square Footage: 340000

Type of Packaging: Bulk

24126 In-Line Labeling Equipment
7282 Spa Road
North Charleston, SC 29418-8437

843-569-2530
Fax: 843-569-2531 800-465-4630
info@labeling.net www.labeling.net
Pressure sensitive labellers and cold glue labellers
President: Greg L Brandon
CFO: Greg L Brandon
Contact: Mark Cowart
mcowart@labeling.net
Estimated Sales: $2.5-5 Million
Number Employees: 10-19
Square Footage: 80000

24127 In-Touch Products
555 W 1100 N
North Salt Lake, UT 84054

801-298-4466
Fax: 801-298-1955 www.intouchhealth.com
Custom thermoformed trays, blisters, clam shells
and other packaging supplies
President: Tim Keniewfki
CEO: Yulun Wang, Ph.D.
CFO: Stephen L. Wilson
EVP, Research & Development: Steve Jordan
EVP, Marketing: Michael Chan
Sales Representative: Douglas Johnson
Operations: Curtis Reeves
Estimated Sales: $5-10 Million
Number Employees: 10

24128 InFood Corporation
1575 Oak Avenue
Evanston, IL 60201-4274

773-338-8485
Software for food processors including inventory,
nutritional analysis/labeling, formulations/BOM,
costing, lot tracking, production planning/schedul-
ing, work orders, yield analysis, QC/statistical
sampling, etc
Estimated Sales: $1-5 Million
Number Employees: 4

24129 InHarvest
1012 Paul Bunyan Dr SE
Bemidji, MN 56601
Fax: 218-751-8519 800-346-7032
www.inharvest.com
Wild rice and specialty grain importer and distribu-
tor
CFO: Jeffrey Buelow
VP, Foodservice Sales: Pete Linder
Type of Packaging: Food Service, Bulk

24130 Incinerator International Inc
2702 N Main St
Houston, TX 77009-6838

713-227-1466
Fax: 713-227-0884 sales@incinerators.com
www.incinerators.com
Manufacturer and importer of material handling
equipment including incinerators, balers, compac-
tors, containers, crushers, trucks, hoppers and envi-
ronmental; exporter of incinerators
Owner: Tom Leervig
sales@incinerators.com
Estimated Sales: $2.5-5 Million
Number Employees: 5-9
Square Footage: 10000
Parent Co: International Environmental Equipment
Company
Brands:
  Iii

24131 Incinerator Specialty Company
6018 Golden Forest Dr
Houston, TX 77092-2360

713-681-4207
Manufacturer and exporter of destructors, afterburn-
ers and incinerators including pathological, garbage,
waste, burners and parts
President: Mick Kromer
Estimated Sales: $1-2.5 Million
Number Employees: 4

24132 Incomec-Cerex Industries
1515 Black Rope Type
Fairfield, CT 06432

203-335-1050
Fax: 203-366-7305 cerexpro@aol.com

Manufacturer and exporter of grain processing
equipment, flavoring spray booths, puffing guns,
drying and infrared toasting ovens and continuous
popcorn popping and caramelizing coating systems
President: Stephan Vandenberghe
Executive Vice Presient: Dennis Norberg
Market Development: Jeff Norberg
Estimated Sales: $25 Million
Number Employees: 60
Number of Brands: 5
Number of Products: 34
Square Footage: 300000

24133 Incredible Logistics Sol
112 W Boca Raton Road
Phoenix, AZ 85023-6249

602-548-1295
Fax: 602-548-0322

24134 Indco
PO Box 589
New Albany, IN 47151-0589

812-945-4383
Fax: 812-944-9742 800-942-4383
info@indco.com www.indco.com
Industrial mixers
President: Mark Hennis
CFO: J T Sims
Vice President: Kris Wilberding
Contact: Linda Potts
linda@indco.com
Estimated Sales: $5-10 Million
Number Employees: 30

24135 Indeco Products Inc
140 Ridge Dr
San Marcos, TX 78666-2052

512-396-5814
Fax: 512-396-5890 888-246-3326
info@indecoproducts.com
www.indecoproducts.com
Plastic strapping and packaging systems and polyes-
ter meat slings
President: Daniel R Springs
R & D: Jesse Hinojosa
General Manager: David Behal
Estimated Sales: $2-5 Million
Number Employees: 10-19
Square Footage: 34000
Brands:
  Linear
  Net-Rap
  Polychem

24136 Indemax Inc
1 Industrial Dr
Vernon, NJ 07462-3466

973-209-2424
Fax: 973-209-2644 800-345-7185
sales@indemax.com www.indemax.com
Manufacturer and exporter of parts for hot melt
equipment
President: A Infurna
Vice President: P Infurna
Quality Control: P Infurna
Sales Director: R Infurna
Plant Manager: C Peterson
Purchasing Manager: J Tapscnyi
Estimated Sales: $5-10 Million
Number Employees: 5-9

24137 (HQ)Independent Can Co
1300 Brass Mill Rd
Po Box 370
Belcamp, MD 21017-1236

410-272-0090
Fax: 410-272-7500
salesdept@independentcan.com
www.independentcan.com
Manufacturer, importer and exporter of decorative
tin containers for coffee, peanuts, cookies, cakes,
popcorn, candies, ice cream, etc
Manager: Cathy Mc Clelland
CEO: Richard D Huether
Marketing: Neil Defrancisco
Sales: Frank Shriver
Public Relations: George R McClelland
Opertaions: G William Goodwin
Plant Manager: Frank Currens
Purchasing: Page Edwards
Estimated Sales: $20-50 Million
Number Employees: 100-249
Square Footage: 360000
Type of Packaging: Consumer, Private Label

Other Locations:
Independent Can Co.
Ontario CA

24138 Independent Can Company: Western Specialty Division
2040 S Lynx Ave
Ontario, CA 91761-8010

909-923-6150
Fax: 909-923-6052 johnt@westernspecialty.com
www.independentcan.com
Owner: John Thompson
VP: John Thompson
Contact: Omar Becerra
omar@independentcan.com
Estimated Sales: $3-5 Million
Number Employees: 5-9

24139 Independent Dealers Advantage
780 Buford Highway Bldg
C-100
Suwanee, GA 30024

678-720-0555
Fax: 678-720-0650 www.idallc.com
Packaging inspection, robotic positioning, 2D
datamatrix code reading
President: Larry Pierson
CEO: Dr. Robert Shillman
CFO: Richard Morin
Senior Vice President: Richard Morin
Estimated Sales: $5-10 000,000
Number Employees: 50-99

24140 Independent Energy
42 Ladd Street
Suite 6
E Greenwich, RI 02818-4358

401-884-6990
Fax: 401-885-1500 800-343-0826
info@IndependentEnergyLLC.com
www.independentenergyllc.com
Wine industry temperature controls
Estimated Sales: $2.5-5 Million
Number Employees: 20-49

24141 Independent Ink
13700 Gramercy Pl
Gardena, CA 90249-2455

310-523-4657
Fax: 310-329-0943 800-446-5538
www.independentink.com
Marking machines and coding and ink jet inks; ex-
porter of inks and solutions
Owner: Barry Brucker
bbrucker@independentink.com
Executive VP/COO: Randa Nathan
International Sales: Nora Valdez
Estimated Sales: $5-10 Million
Number Employees: 20-49
Square Footage: 50000
Type of Packaging: Consumer, Private Label

24142 Independent Packers Corporation
2001 W Garfield St
C102
Seattle, WA 98119

206-285-6000
Fax: 206-285-9236
Fresh and frozen seafood including crab, cod, hali-
but, salmon and tuna
President: Jeffery Buske
Contact: Tammy Findlay
tammy@bbaybrewery.com
Estimated Sales: $3-5 Million
Number Employees: 100-249
Square Footage: 60000
Type of Packaging: Food Service, Private Label

24143 Independent Stave Co
1078 S Jefferson Ave
PO Box 104
Lebanon, MO 65536-3601

417-588-4151
Fax: 417-588-3344
info@independentstavecompany.com
www.independentstavecompany.com
Barrels for wine and whisky producers
Founder: T W Boswell
President: Brad Boswell
Number Employees: 500-999

24144 Index Instruments Us Inc
3305 Commerce Blvd
Kissimmee, FL 34741-4655

407-932-0232
Fax: 407-932-3686 IndexUS@aol.com
www.indexinstrumentsus.com
Refractometers used to measure jams, jellies, candies, crude oil, sugars, edible oils, plastics, beers, adhesives, fruit juices, and many more.
President: Linnell Oakes
Vice President: Jennifer Horn
Estimated Sales: $400 Thousand
Number Employees: 1-4

24145 Indian Valley Industries
PO Box 810
Johnson City, NY 13790-0810

607-729-5111
Fax: 607-729-5158 800-659-5111
www.iviindustries.com
Manufacturer and exporter of burlap and textile bags; also manufacturers and supplies products relating to environmental protection, erosion control, and the containment of both air and waterborn pollutants.
President: Wayne Rozen
CEO: Nilton Rozen
VP Marketing: Phil March
Contact: John Brauer
brauer@iviindustries.com
Estimated Sales: $10-20 Million
Number Employees: 10-19

24146 Indiana Bottle Co
300 W Lovers Ln
Scottsburg, IN 47170-6729

812-752-8700
Fax: 812-752-8702 800-752-8702
mccarty@indianabottle.com
www.indianabottle.com
Custom blow molded, high and low density polyethylene and polypropylene bottles; also, screen printing services available
President: David Keener
mccarty@hsonline.net
Sales Exec: Mike Mc Carty
General Manager: David Baker
mccarty@hsonline.net
Estimated Sales: $3.9 Million
Number Employees: 20-49
Square Footage: 50000

24147 Indiana Carton Co Inc
1721 W Bike St
PO Box 68
Bremen, IN 46506-2123

574-546-3848
Fax: 574-546-5953 800-348-2390
salesservice@indianacarton.com
www.indianacarton.com
Manufacturer and exporter of boxes and cartons
President: David Petty
davidpetty@indianacarton.com
Chairman of the Board: Kenneth Petty
Estimated Sales: $10-20 Million
Number Employees: 50-99

24148 Indiana Glass Company
37 West Broad Street
Columbus, OH 43215

614-224-7141
Fax: 513-563-9639 800-543-0357
www.lancastercolony.com
Manufacturer and exporter of housewares including candleholders, glasses and other beverage containers
Human Resources: Cathy Durham
VP/Marketing: Jerry Vanden Eynden
National Sales Manager: Mark Cunningham
International Sales Manager: Alex Morroni
Estimated Sales: $1-5 Million
Number Employees: 500-999
Parent Co: Lancaster Colony Corporation
Type of Packaging: Bulk

24149 Indiana Michigan Power
110 Wayne St
Fort Wayne, IN 46802

800-311-4634
www.indianamichiganpower.com
Electric utility systems.
President & COO: Toby Thomas
VP, Finance & Customer Experience: David Lucas
VP, Regulatory & External Affairs: Marc Lewis

Estimated Sales: K
Number Employees: 2,400
Parent Co: American Electric Power

24150 Indiana Vac Form Inc
2030 N Boeing Rd
Warsaw, IN 46582-7860

574-269-1725
Fax: 574-269-2723 bret@invacform.com
www.invacform.com
Manufacturer and exporter of custom plastic vacuum and thermoformed products including containers and refrigerator liners
Owner: Donald Robinson
ins@invacform.com
Operations Manager: Roy Szymanski
Production Manager: Bob Stevents
Estimated Sales: $2.5-5 Million
Number Employees: 20-49
Square Footage: 90000
Type of Packaging: Food Service

24151 Indiana Wiping Cloth
2340 Schumacher Dr
Mishawaka, IN 46545

574-255-9666
Fax: 574-255-9676 800-446-9645
Wiping cloths and absorbent products
Manager: Darren Sauer
Estimated Sales: $5-10 Million
Number Employees: 10-19

24152 Indiana Wire Company
803 S Reed Rd
PO Box 947
Fremont, IN 46737

260-495-1231
Fax: 260-495-0087 877-786-6883
sales@indianawireco.com
www.indianawireco.com
Wire mesh decking, shelving, baking equipment and wire products
Sales Manager: Jackie Masternik
Sales Manager: Greg Bosk
Plant Manager: Jeremy Breen
Estimated Sales: $5-10,000,000
Number Employees: 50-99
Parent Co: Indiana Wire Company
Brands:
Indiana Wire

24153 Indianapolis Container Company
PO Box 40006
Indianapolis, IN 46240

317-580-5000
Fax: 800-760-3319 800-760-3318
sales@containerworks.com
www.containerworks.com
Plastic and glass bottles and jars; also, pails
Manager: Stephen Roco
sroco@containerworks.com
CFO: Nancy Heidt
VP: Nancy Lilly
Owner: Tom Asher
Estimated Sales: Below $5 Million
Number Employees: 10-19
Square Footage: 112000

24154 Industrial Air Conditioning Systems
1883 W Fullerton Avenue
Chicago, IL 60614-1923

773-486-4236
Fax: 773-486-4238
Proof boxes, dough rooms, bread and cake coolers and stainless steel sanitary pan trucks
VP: Albert Wentzel
Estimated Sales: $2.5-5 Million
Number Employees: 5-9
Square Footage: 30000

24155 Industrial Automation Specs
17 Research Dr
Hampton, VA 23666-1324

757-766-7520
Fax: 757-766-7505 800-916-4272
sales@iascorp.net www.iascorp.net
Manufacturer and exporter of analog chart recorder
CEO: Kathy Burton
preston@iascorp.net
Owner: Kathy Burton
Marketing Supervisor: Don Crawford
Estimated Sales: $1-2.5 Million
Number Employees: 10-19

Brands:
Pricorder

24156 Industrial Automation Systems
28440 Redwood Canyon Place
Santa Clarita, CA 91390-5724

661-257-3482
Fax: 661-257-7627 888-484-4427
Bag making and closing, food processing, labeling and packaging machinery; also, material handling equipment and conveyor systems
Manager: Peter Adams
Manager: Guido Pydde
Estimated Sales: Less than $500,000
Number Employees: 1-4

24157 Industrial Brush Corporation
P.O.Box 2608
Pomona, CA 91769-2608

909-591-9341
Fax: 909-627-8916 800-228-6146
ibcsales@industrial-brush.com
www.industrialbrush.com
Brushes for industry and food processing
President: John Cottam
Vice Presient: Greg Tripp
Estimated Sales: $10-25 Million
Number Employees: 50-99
Square Footage: 360000

24158 Industrial Ceramic Products
14401 Suntra Way
Marysville, OH 43040

937-642-3897
Fax: 937-644-2646 800-427-2278
sales@industrialceramic.com
www.industrialceramic.com
Manufacturer and exporter of ceramic pizza stones
President: R C Oberst
Contact: Clay Foreman
cforeman@industrialceramic.com
Estimated Sales: $5-10 Million
Number Employees: 20-49
Square Footage: 100000

24159 Industrial Chemical
136 Long Ridge Rd
Bedford, NY 10506

914-234-9303
Fax: 914-234-9305 800-431-1075
sales@industrialchemicaldiv.com
Natural fast deodorization and organic waste digestion
Director of Sales: Andy Sinclair
Estimated Sales: $1-2.5 Million
Number Employees: 10-19

24160 Industrial Chemicals Inc
2042 Montreat Dr # A
Vestavia, AL 35216-4040

205-823-7330
Fax: 205-978-0485 800-476-2042
www.industrialchem.com
Ingredients to water and wastewater treatment chemistry
President: Bill Welsch
CEO: Bill Welch
wlwelsch@industrialchem.com
Sales Manager: L Pickens
Estimated Sales: $20-50 Million
Number Employees: 100-249

24161 Industrial Consortium
110 Gilmer St
Sulphur Springs, TX 75482-2703

903-885-6610
Fax: 903-885-6701 www.icthruput.com
Consultant providing engineering services for packaging companies
President: Dale Stephens
Estimated Sales: $10 Million
Number Employees: 5-9

24162 Industrial ConstructionSvc
215 15th St S
St James, MN 56081-2438

507-375-4633
Fax: 507-375-7513 800-795-8315
cbrown@icsmn.com www.icsmn.com

Design and construction of contamination controlled environments, services of which include biocontainment laboratories, clean rooms, antimicrobial atmospheres for pharmaceutical, bio-medical, and nutraceutical development, and sanitaryenvironments for food and beverage processing and manufacturing.
President: Clint Brown
cbrown@icsmn.com
Sales Representative: Josh Brown
Number Employees: 20-49

24163 Industrial Container Corp
107 Motsinger St
High Point, NC 27260-8836
    336-886-7031
 Fax: 336-886-2044 www.iccpackage.com
Plain, printed and wax corrugated boxes
President: Bernard Rosinsky
CEO: Randy Chambers
randy@iccpkg.com
General Manager: Ron Horney
Number Employees: 10-19

24164 Industrial Contracting & Rggng
41 Ramapo Valley Rd
Mahwah, NJ 07430-1118
    201-444-7504
 Fax: 201-529-3754 888-427-7444
 info@icrnj.com www.industrialcontracting.com
Trucking, rigging, crating & storage machinery
Owner: Joseph Sensale
icrnj@aol.com
Engineer: James Certaro
VP Marketing: Joseph Sensale
Estimated Sales: $1-2.5 Million
Number Employees: 10-19

24165 (HQ)Industrial Crating & Packing
15450 Nelson Pl
Tukwila, WA 98188-5504
    425-226-9205
 Fax: 425-226-9205 800-942-0499
Corrugated boxes and wooden shipping crates
President: Tom Kalil
sales@indcrate.com
Estimated Sales: $1-2.5 Million
Number Employees: 10-19

24166 Industrial Custom Products
2801 37th Ave NE
Minneapolis, MN 55421-4217
    612-782-9048
 Fax: 612-781-1144 877-784-2415
 icp@industrialcustom.com
 www.industrialcustom.com
Specialists in forming heavy-gauge plastics for OEM and material-handling applications. The company specializes in custom applications and is experienced in die-cutting and fabricating a broad range of
President: Herb Houndt
Estimated Sales: $10-20 Million
Number Employees: 20-49

24167 Industrial Design Corporation
2020 SW 4th Ave
Portland, OR 97201-4953
    503-224-6040
 Fax: 503-223-1494 800-224-0707
Facility services including planning, site selection, environmental/permitting, facility design and engineering, industrial engineering, system integration, waste treatment, construction management, commissioning/startup andoperations/maintenance
President: George Lemmon
Corporate Management: Sue King
Vice President: Jim Hall
Marketing Director: Jeff Cross
Contact: Patti Glaze
3635@idc-ibg.com
Purchasing Manager: Mark Varon
Number Employees: 250-499

24168 Industrial Design Fab
2501 Murray St # A
Suite A
Sioux City, IA 51111-1141
    712-224-5600
 Fax: 712-873-5859 877-873-5858
 info@idfi.com www.idfi.com
Designer and manufacturer of conveyor systems for the food industry.

President: Todd Jager
tjager@idfi.com
Number Employees: 20-49

24169 Industrial Devices Corporation
3925 Cypress Drive
Petaluma, CA 94954-5695
    707-789-1000
 Fax: 707-789-0175 sales@idcmotion.com
Electric linear actuators, servo controls and positioning systems for packaging equipment
VP Sales/Marketing: Al Statz
Customer Service Manager: Joe Ording
Estimated Sales: $10-20 Million
Number Employees: 50-99

24170 Industrial EnvironmentalPollution Control
127 Bruckner Boulevard
Bronx, NY 10454-4698
    718-585-2410
 Fax: 718-292-8353
Air pollution control, bacteria control equipment, cleaning and washing equipment and accessories, detergent dipensing systems, drain and sewer cleaning compounds, floor scrubbers and sweepers, odor control equipment, pan, vat and moldwashing, pressure
Manager: James Albanese
Vice President: Mike Mouracade
Food Safety Specialist: Alex Mouracade
Estimated Sales: $1-5 Million
Number Employees: 10-19
Brands:
 Foamatic

24171 Industrial Equipment Company
35 Maple St
Suite 2
Derry, NH 3038
    603-432-2037
 Fax: 603-437-7539
Hand and electric power trucks and fork-lifts
President/CFO: Robert Shaver
Manager: Bob Shaver
Estimated Sales: $2-3 Million
Number Employees: 1-4

24172 Industrial Grinding Inc
2306 Ontario Ave
Dayton, OH 45414-5692
    937-277-6579
 Fax: 937-277-4536 888-322-6579
 sales@industrialgrinding.com
 www.industrialgrinding.com
President: Marcus Wendling
mwendling@industrialgrinding.com
CFO: Sabrina Welch
Estimated Sales: $1-2.5 Million
Number Employees: 10-19

24173 (HQ)Industrial Hardwood
521 F St
Perrysburg, OH 43551
    419-666-2503
Wooden boxes, pallets and skids
Owner: Ashvin Shah
ashvins@hardwoodind.com
General Manager: William Eckel
Estimated Sales: $2.5-5 Million
Number Employees: 1-4
Square Footage: 15000
Other Locations:
 Industrial Hardwood
 Oak Harbor OH

24174 Industrial Hoist Service
21525 N Highway 288b
Angleton, TX 77515-4888
    979-798-7077
 Fax: 979-798-1963 800-766-7077
 www.industrialhoist.com
Air chain hoists
Manager: James Kowalk
Chief Executive Officer: Kevin Rodgers
Senior Vice President, General Manager o: James Kowalik
Vice President of Sales, Division I: Anthony Piwonka
Vice President of Sales: Kurt Charpentier
President, Chief Operating Officer: Mitch Hausman
Vice President of Purchasing: Tony DAmico
Estimated Sales: $20-50 Million
Number Employees: 50-99

Number of Brands: 3
Square Footage: 130000

24175 Industrial Information Systems
393 Cumberland St
Memphis, TN 38112-2712
    901-324-5535
 Fax: 901-324-0104 800-494-7916
Developer of training software for ammonia refrigeration operating engineers
President: Hanns Wittjen
Estimated Sales: $500,000-$1 Million
Number Employees: 5-9

24176 (HQ)Industrial Kinetics
2535 Curtiss St
Downers Grove, IL 60515
    630-655-0300
 Fax: 630-655-1720 800-655-0306
 ikiinfo@iki.com www.iki.com
Manufacturer and exporter of material handling and conveyor systems
Owner: George Huber
Marketing/Sales: Dwight Pentzien
Operations Manager: Dennis Harsnbarger
Production Manager: John Zienda
Plant Manager: John Zienda
Estimated Sales: $10-20 Million
Number Employees: 50-99
Square Footage: 180000
Other Locations:
 Industrial Kinetics
 Atlanta GA
Brands:
 Olson Conveyors
 Pallet-Pro

24177 Industrial LaboratoriesCo
4046 Youngfield St
Wheat Ridge, CO 80033-3862
    303-287-9691
 Fax: 303-287-0964 800-456-5288
 www.industriallabs.net
Full service analytical support to the food industry, dietary and sports supplements, veterinary regulatory and therapeutic monitoring. Analytical support includes food chemistry, food safety monitoring, nutritional analyses, andtesting for other potential contaminants. Provides BAX analyses fo E. coli 0157:H7, Salmonella and Listeria, food safety monitoring
President: Seth Wong
swong@industriallabs.net
Controller: Lisle Goeldner
Supervisor: Geoff Henderson
Manager: Joanne Compton
Business Development Manager: Larisa Moore
Customer Services: Kathie Inman
Lab Manager: Mike Gross
Estimated Sales: $2.5-5 Million
Number Employees: 20-49
Square Footage: 24000

24178 Industrial Laboratory Eqpt Co
3210 Piper Ln
PO Box 220245
Charlotte, NC 28208-6442
    704-357-3930
 Fax: 704-357-3940 ile@ile-textiles.com
 www.ile-textiles.com
Manufacturer and exporter of industrial testing equipment including custom, food and portion scales for analytical, counting and inventory use
President: Harry Simmons
ile@ile-textiles.com
VP: Harry Simmons
Estimated Sales: $1-2.5 Million
Number Employees: 5-9
Square Footage: 20000
Brands:
 Ile
 Multi-Scale
 Ohaus

24179 Industrial Labsales
PO Box 30628
Portland, OR 97294-3628
    800-524-8224
 Fax: 503-255-8367

24180 Industrial Lumber & Packaging
925 W Savidge St
Spring Lake, MI 49409
    616-842-1457
 Fax: 616-842-9352

645

Pallets, skids and wooden boxes and shipping crates
Owner: Jim Walsh
Number Employees: 7
Square Footage: 29600

24181 Industrial Machine Manufacturing
8140 Virginia Pine Ct
Richmond, VA 23237

804-271-6979
Fax: 804-275-0813 sales@uniflow1.com
www.uniflow1.com
Customized hot melt dispensing machinery
President: Marvin Garrett
R & D: Leo Moore
VP Marketing: Leo Moore
Estimated Sales: $1-2.5 Million
Number Employees: 10-19

24182 Industrial Magnetics
1385 S M 75
Boyne City, MI 49712-9689

231-582-3100
Fax: 231-582-0622 800-662-4638
imi@magnetics.com www.magnetics.com
Manufacturer and exporter of magnetic separation
devices for the removal of ferrous and metals.
CEO: Walter Shear
doleary@magnetics.com
Chief Financial Officer: Robin Wottowa
Engineering Manager: Dan Allore
Business Development, Marketing Manager: Dennis
O'Leary
Plant Manager, Purchasing: Casey House
Estimated Sales: $25-30 Million
Number Employees: 51-200
Number of Products: 2000
Square Footage: 76000
Brands:
  Bullet

24183 Industrial Marking Equipment
4152 Lazy Hammock Road
Palm Beach Gardens, FL 33410-6114

561-845-2828
Fax: 561-848-8930
Custom printing systems, printing attatchments for
converting and packaging applications
Estimated Sales: $1-2.5 Million
Number Employees: 5-9

24184 Industrial Nameplate Inc
29 Indian Dr
Warminster, PA 18974-1487

215-322-1111
Fax: 215-953-1161 800-878-6263
www.industrialnameplate.com
Labels, tapes, tags, folding paper boxes, point of
purchase displays, shelf talkers, styrene cards, etc
President: Chuck Mascaro
info@industrialnameplate.com
Manager Marketing: Fred Knup
Estimated Sales: $2.5-5 Million
Number Employees: 20-49
Square Footage: 28000

24185 Industrial Neon Sign Corp
6223 Saint Augustine St
Houston, TX 77021-2612

713-748-6600
Fax: 713-748-6621
Architectural, electrical, magnetic, metal, neon,
painted, plastic, silk screen, vinyl lettering &
wooden signs
Owner: Sarah Jones
Estimated Sales: $470,000
Number Employees: 10-19

24186 Industrial Netting Inc
7681 Setzler Pkwy N
Minneapolis, MN 55445-1883

763-496-6355
Fax: 763-971-0872 800-328-8456
info@industrialnetting.net
www.industrialnetting.com
Plastic netting for meat racks, separators, bird net-
ting and fencing
Owner: Greg Frandsen
gfrandsen@industrialnetting.com
Vice President: David Brentz
Sales: Karen Slater
Estimated Sales: $72,000
Number Employees: 20-49

24187 (HQ)Industrial Piping Inc
800 Culp Rd
PO Box 518
Pineville, NC 28134-9469

704-588-1100
Fax: 704-588-5614 800-951-0988
Manufacturers and exporter of custom fabricated
process equipment including coils, columns, con-
densers, exchangers, mix tanks, piping systems,
pressure vessels, reactors and towers
President: Robert Jones
CEO: Mike Jones
mjones@goipi.com
VP: Michael Roberts
Quality Control: Ron Miller
Business Development: Earl Dowdy
Estimated Sales: $10-20 Million
Number Employees: 20-49
Square Footage: 136000

24188 Industrial Plastics Company
8307 Ball Rd
Fort Smith, AR 72908-8435

479-646-8293
Fax: 479-646-6020 800-850-0916
VP: Jim Rahn
Manager: Kyle Dejaeger
Estimated Sales: $20-50 Million
Number Employees: 100-249
Parent Co: Jarden Corporation

24189 Industrial Product Corp
1 Hollywood Ave # 30
Suite 30
Ho Ho Kus, NJ 07423-1438

201-652-5913
Fax: 201-652-2494 800-472-5913
Manufacturer and exporter of standard and custom
industrial blades for food processing machinery for
pasta, pretzel and baked goods
Owner: Ken Dohner
kendohner@ipdco.com
Estimated Sales: Less Than $500,000
Number Employees: 1-4
Square Footage: 16200

24190 Industrial Pump Sales &Svc
37 William S Canning Blvd
Tiverton, RI 02878-3003

401-624-2977
Fax: 401-624-3373 sales@ipspump.com
www.ipspump.com
Pumps and mixers
President: Bruce Levesque
Estimated Sales: $3-5 Million
Number Employees: 20-49

24191 Industrial Razorblade
575 Nassau St
Orange, NJ 07050-1262

973-673-4286
Fax: 973-673-7165 sales@industrialrazor.com
www.industrialrazor.com
Knives and blades specializing in strip ground
blades; custom manufacturing available
Owner: Frank Florey
frank@industrialrazor.com
VP: Francis Florey
Estimated Sales: Less Than $500,000
Number Employees: 1-4
Square Footage: 10000

24192 Industrial Refrigeration Services
403 Dividend Drive
Hampton, GA 30228

770-946-9235
Fax: 770-946-3115 800-334-0273
C.E.O: Terry Childers

24193 Industrial Screw Conveyors Inc
4133 Conveyor Dr
Burleson, TX 76028-1819

817-641-0691
Fax: 817-556-0224 800-426-4669
sales@screwconveyors.com
www.screwconveyors.com
Dedicated to the design, engineering, and fabrication
of helical flighting, helical screw assemblies, and
helical screw conveyors using helical flighting.
President: Ralph Jones
indscrew@aol.com
Estimated Sales: $5,000,000
Number Employees: 50-99
Square Footage: 480000

24194 Industrial Sign Company
9635 Klingerman Street
South El Monte, CA 91733-1726

562-602-2420
Fax: 562-602-2599 800-596-3720
Point of purchase displays, flags, pennants, banners
and electric signs
Owner: Maria Saavetra
Estimated Sales: $1-2,500,000
Number Employees: 20-49

24195 Industrial Signs
1109 N. AL Davis Rd.
Suite B
Elmwood, LA 70123

504-736-0600
Fax: 504-736-9285 sales@industrialsigns.net
www.industrialsigns.net
Signs including electrical, neon, industrial, etc
President: William F Hunter
Estimated Sales: $2.5-5 Million
Number Employees: 20-49

24196 Industrial Systems Group
5140 Moundview Drive
Red Wing, MN 55066-1100

651-388-2267
Fax: 651-385-2279 800-ROB-OTIC
Estimated Sales: $1-5 Million

24197 Industrial Test SystemsInc
1875 Langston St
Rock Hill, SC 29730-7314

803-329-2999
Fax: 803-329-9743 800-861-9712
its@sensafe.com www.sensafe.com
Tests for water quality parameters.
Owner: Ivars Jaunakais
ivars@sensafe.com
VP: Lea Jaunakais
Marketing: Mike McBride
Sales: George Bailey
Plant Manager: Angelo Perry
Estimated Sales: $5-10 Million
Number Employees: 20-49

24198 Industrial Washing Machine Corporation
PO Box 1509
Jackson, NJ 08527-0266

732-304-9203
Fax: 732-286-0862 inwamacorp@yahoo.com
Pot and pan washers.
President: Joseph Gangi
Number Employees: 10-19
Square Footage: 40000
Brands:
  Industrial

24199 Industrial Washing Machine Corporation
PO Box 506
Matawan, NJ 07747-0506

732-566-4660
Fax: 732-566-2201
Pot and pan washers
President: Joseph Gangi
Estimated Sales: $1-3 Million
Number Employees: 19
Square Footage: 20000
Brands:
  Industrial

24200 Industrial Woodfab & Packaging
18620 Fort St
Riverview, MI 48193-7443

734-284-4808
Fax: 734-284-5308 www.industrialwoodfab.com
Wooden crates, boxes and pallets
President: Richard E Ott
rott@industrialwoodfab.com
Engineer: Tom DeFeyten
Manager: Frank Nicnski
Estimated Sales: $1-2.5 Million
Number Employees: 10-19
Square Footage: 130000

24201 Industries For The Blind
445 S Curtis Rd
Milwaukee, WI 53214-1016

414-778-3040
Fax: 414-933-4316 800-642-8778
info@ibmilw.com www.ibmilwaukee.com

Manufacturer and exporter of household cleaning supplies including plastic window brushes and brooms
President: Charles Lange
VP, Manufacturing: Helen Ritter
National Federal Sales Director: Dan Bailey
IT: Cindy Pinkley
cindy.pinkley@ibmilw.com
Estimated Sales: $10-20 Million
Number Employees: 50-99
Parent Co: Industries For The Blind
Type of Packaging: Consumer, Food Service, Bulk

24202 Industries Inc Kiefer
400 Industrial Dr
Random Lake, WI 53075-1653
920-994-2332
Fax: 920-994-4005
Food service equipment including stainless steel tables
Owner: James Eischen
kieferindustries@yahoo.com
Estimated Sales: $1-2.5 Million
Number Employees: 10-19

24203 Industries of the Blind
920 West Lee Street
Greensboro, NC 27403
336-274-1591
Fax: 336-544-3739 info@iob-gso.com
www.industriesoftheblind.com
Mops including cotton, rayon, wet and dry; also, brooms, wooden mop handles, clipboards and pens
Executive Director: Mike Burge
Contact: Donald Bassett
dbassett@iob-gso.com
General Manager: Derek Davis
Plant Manager: Jack Permer
Purchasing Manager: Bob Gwyn
Estimated Sales: $10-20 Million
Number Employees: 100-249
Square Footage: 260000
Type of Packaging: Consumer

24204 Industrious Software Solutions
500 W Florence Ave
Inglewood, CA 90301-1011
310-672-8700
Fax: 310-419-6000 800-351-4225
www.1st-accounting.com
Developer of operations management software for wholesalers/distributors, manufacturers, exporters and importers
President: David Goguen
david.goguen@iss.com
Quality Control: Gary Zenun
Estimated Sales: $10-20 Million
Number Employees: 20-49

24205 Industronics Service Co
489 Sullivan Ave
PO Box 649
South Windsor, CT 06074-1942
860-289-1551
Fax: 860-289-3526 800-878-1551
service@industronics.com www.industronics.com
Incinerators and commercial furnaces and ovens
President: James Wyse
jwyse@industronics.com
VP: Dean Hills
Estimated Sales: Below $5 Million
Number Employees: 20-49
Brands:
  Consertherm

24206 Indy Lighting
12001 Exit 5 Pkwy
Fishers, IN 46037
317-849-1233
Fax: 317-576-8006
Incandescent, compact fluorescent, recessed, surface and track lighting fixtures
VP Sales: Steve Fetter
VP Marketing: Barry Hindman
Contact: Roger Michel
rmichel@indyltg.com
Manager: Kevin Fagan
Estimated Sales: $10-20 Million
Number Employees: 50-99
Square Footage: 250000
Parent Co: Juno Lighting

24207 Infanti International
3075 Richmond Terrace
Staten Island, NY 10303-1300
718-447-5632
Fax: 718-447-5667 800-874-8590
www.infanti.com
Manufacturer and exporter of serving carts and chairs
Estimated Sales: $3-5 Million
Number Employees: 20-49
Type of Packaging: Food Service

24208 Inficon
2 Technology Pl
East Syracuse, NY 13057
315-434-1100
Fax: 315-437-3803 reachus@inficon.com
www.inficon.com
Instruments for gas leak detection
CEO: Lukas Winkler
Estimated Sales: $373 Million
Number Employees: 1,000

24209 Infinity Tapes LLC
300 Canal St # 7
Lawrence, MA 01840-1420
978-686-0632
Fax: 978-683-5202
Adhesives
Owner: Craig Allard
callard@shepcompany.com
Quality Control: Craig Aalard
Estimated Sales: $20-50 Million
Number Employees: 50-99

24210 Infitec Inc
6500 Badgley Rd
East Syracuse, NY 13057-9667
315-433-1150
Fax: 315-433-1521 800-334-0837
sales@infitec.com www.infitec.com
Timing controls (industrial/time delay), speed controls, flashers, and custom controls.
CEO/CFO/President: George Ehegartner, Sr
HR Executive: Kim Bremerman
kb@infitec.com
Quality Control/Marketing: George Ehegartner, Jr
kb@infitec.com
VP Sales: David Lawrie
Estimated Sales: $10-20 Million
Number Employees: 50-99
Square Footage: 50000
Type of Packaging: Bulk
Brands:
  Inc
  Infitec

24211 Inflatable Packaging
75 Glen Rd # 103
Sandy Hook, CT 06482-1176
203-426-2900
Fax: 203-426-6976 800-520-3383
sales@inflatablepackaging.com
www.inflatablepackaging.com
Air bag dunnage system for internal packaging designed to replace peanuts, compressed paper, expansion foam and air bubble materials. Manufacture Void-Fill Bags, En-Cap Sleeves, and Waffle-Paks in various sizes to meet your shipping requirements
President: Michell Tschantz
mich@inflatablepackaging.com
Estimated Sales: $1-3 Million
Number Employees: 5-9

24212 Infometrix
11807 N Creek Pkwy S # 111
Suite B-111
Bothell, WA 98011-8804
425-402-1450
Fax: 425-402-1040 info@infometrix.com
www.infometrix.com
Analyses for quality control, online monitoring of processes, sensory evaluation and research in the food and beverage industries
President: Brian Rohrback
CEO: Marlana Blackburn
marlana_blackburn@infometrix.com
Sales/Marketing Manager: Paul Bailey
Estimated Sales: Below $5 Million
Number Employees: 10-19
Brands:
  Biocount
  Ein Sight
  Pirouette

24213 Infopro Inc
2920 Norwalk Ct
Aurora, IL 60502-1310
630-978-9231
Fax: 734-638-6139 info@sysmaker.com
www.corrflow.com
Menuing and application development systems
CEO: Sue Graham
Vice President And CFO: Eileen Anderson
Executive Vice President And COO: Greg Capella
Administrative Manager: Susan Boarden
Estimated Sales: $500,000-$1 Million
Number Employees: 5-9
Brands:
  Guidemaker
  Systemaker

24214 Infor
641 Avenue of the Americas
New York, NY 10011
646-336-1700
866-244-5479
www.infor.com
Software for process industries: ERP and EAM software for meat, poultry and beverage processing; software for safety, cost containment, inventory
General Manager, Americas: Rod Johnson
CEO: Kevin Samuelson
CFO: Jay Hopkins
CTO/President, Products: Soma Somasundaram
EVP/Global Chief Customer Officer: Nancy Mattenberger
Estimated Sales: $2.8 Billion
Number Employees: 17,000

24215 Information Access
8801 E Pleasant Valley Rd
Cleveland, OH 44131-5599
216-328-0100
Fax: 216-328-0913 info@infoaccess.net
www.infoaccess.net
Software for food brokers
CEO: Edward Schnell
National Sales Manager: James Garskie
Estimated Sales: $10-20 Million
Number Employees: 1-4

24216 Information Resources
150 N Clinton St
Chicago, IL 60661
312-726-0005
888-262-5973
Supplier of market content, analytic services, and business performance management solutions.
Chairman: Romesh Wadwani
CEO: John Freeland
CFO: Michael Duffy
CEO: John Freeland
Contact: Christine Aceron
christine.aceron@infores.com
Grp President/International Operations: Mark Tims
CTO/CIO: Marshall Gibbs
Estimated Sales: $554 Million
Number Employees: 1,000-4,999
Other Locations:
  Information Resources
  LK, Bel
  Information Resources-UK
  Berkshire, GBR
  IRI Hellas
  New Ionia, Athens
  IRI France
  Chambourcy, France
  IRI USA
  Waltham MA

24217 Informed Beverage Management
420 Minuet Ln
Charlotte, NC 28217
704-527-1709
Fax: 704-527-8509 800-438-5058
www.highjump.com
Computer software and hardware
Manager: Pel Dael
Manager: Jerry Morrow
Manager: Ed Browning
Estimated Sales: $5-10 Million
Number Employees: 10-19

24218 Infra Corp
5454 Dixie Hwy
P.O. Box 300997
Waterford, MI 48329-1615
248-623-0400
Fax: 248-623-1766 888-434-6372
sales@infracorporation.com
www.infracorporation.com
Bar and restaurant equipment, stainless and brass
small wares
President: Bryan A Mc Graw
bryan@infracorporation.com
Estimated Sales: $1-3 Million
Number Employees: 5-9
Square Footage: 48000

24219 InfraTech Corporation
939 N Vernon Avenue
Azusa, CA 91702-2202
626-331-9400
Fax: 626-858-1951 800-955-2476
joe@infratech-usa.com
Comfort heat for patios
President/CEO: Sam Longo
Research & Development: Joe Petro
Marketing Director: Joe Petro
Sales Manager: Joseph Petro
Estimated Sales: $.5-1 million
Number Employees: 90
Square Footage: 150000

24220 Ingersoll Rand Inc
N58 W14686 Shawn Cir
Menomonee Falls, WI 53051
262-232-7275
www.ingersollrand.com
Rotary screw, reciprocating and sliding vane com-
pressors, multistage and positive displacement, cen-
trifugal and side-channel blowers, vacuum
technology and mobile transport products.
CEO: Vicente Reynal
SVP, Industrial Technologies: Todd Wyman
SVP & Chief Financial Officer: Emily Weaver
SVP, General Counsel & CCO: Andrew Schisel
VP, Global Sourcing & Logistics: Chris Neubauer
Year Founded: 1859
Estimated Sales: $2.3 Billion
Parent Co: Kohlberg Kravis Roberts
Brands:
Club Car
ARO
Ingersoll Rand

24221 Ingles Markets
2913 US Highway 70 W
Black Mountain, NC 28711-9103
828-669-2941
Fax: 828-669-3678
customerservice@ingles-markets.com
www.ingles-markets.com
Cakes, cookies, and deli products
President & CEO: James Lanning
CFO/Director/VP Media Relations: Ronald Freeman
Estimated Sales: $31.7 Million
Number Employees: 16,000
Other Locations:
Dairy Manufacturing
Asheville NC
Brands:
Milko
Sealtest

24222 Inglett & Company
151 Walker Road
Statesville, NC 28625-2535
706-738-1488
Fax: 706-736-5416 tFspitzer@hotmail.com
Automatic packaging machinery
Estimated Sales: $5-10 Million
Number Employees: 20-50

24223 Ingman Laboratories
2945 34th Avenue S
Minneapolis, MN 55406-1707
612-724-0121
Fax: 612-724-0603 http://inglabs.pconline.com
Consultant specializing in product development,
food labeling and laboratory services including
chemical and microbiological analysis for the food
and agricultural industries
President: Pete Meland
Public Relations: Kipp Barksdale
Office Manager: Dick Davidson
Chief Chemist: Glenn Kyle

Number Employees: 24
Square Footage: 40000

24224 Ingredient Masters
1080 Nimitzview Dr
Suite 302
Cincinnati, OH 45230
513-231-7432
Fax: 513-231-3104 sales@ingredientmasters.com
www.ingredientmasters.com
Custom-designing bulk dry ingredient and dispens-
ing systems
President: Scott Culshaw
Contact: Ben Culshaw
culshaw@ingredientmasters.com
Estimated Sales: Below $5 Million
Number Employees: 1-4

24225 (HQ)Ingredients Solutions Inc
631 Moosehead Trl
Waldo, ME 04915-3402
207-722-4172
Fax: 207-722-4271 800-628-3166
info@ingredientssolutions.com www.isi.us.com
Independent supplier of Carrageenan. Offers a full
range of Natural and Organic allowed products in-
cluding Xanthan Gums, Sodium Alginates and
Carrageenans for use in dairy, meat & poultry,
sauces & dressings, bakery, confections, petfood,
pharmaceuticals and personal-care applications.
Owner: Donna Ravin
info@ingredientssolutions.com
CEO: Scott Rangus
CFO: Janine Mehuren
Lab Manager: Kevin Johndro
Purchasing: Kristin Grover
Number Employees: 10-19
Type of Packaging: Bulk

24226 Ingredion Inc.
5 Westbrook Corporate Ctr.
Westchester, IL 60154
708-551-2600
Fax: 708-551-2700 800-713-0208
www.ingredion.com
Sweeteners, starches, corn syrups, glucose, and oils
used in food and beverage products.
CEO: James Zallie
Executive VP/CFO: James Gray
Senior VP/General Counsel/CCO: Janet Bawcom
Senior VP/Chief Innovation Officer: Anthony Delio
COO: Robert Stefansic
Year Founded: 1906
Estimated Sales: $5.8 Billion
Number Employees: 11,000
Type of Packaging: Bulk
Brands:
Abc Carrier
Brewer's Crystals
Buffalo
Cerelose
Enzose
Fiberbond
Globe
Globe Plus
Invertose Hfcs
Proferm
Royal
Royal-T
Stablebond
Surebond
Ultrabond
Unidex

24227 Inject Star Of The America's
355 Industrial Dr
Mountain View, AR 72560-8872
870-269-7778
Fax: 203-740-8331 800-253-6475
info@injectstar.com www.injectstar.com
Meat processing equipment and food packaging
equipment
Owner: John Engle
Estimated Sales: Below $5 Million
Number Employees: 5-9

24228 Inksolv 30, LLC.
2495 N Ave
PO Box 66
Emerson, NE 68733
515-537-5344
info@inksolv30.com
www.inksolv30.com
Manufacturer and exporter of powdered hand soap

President: Kevin Wilson
Contact: Allison Franklin
allison.franklin@inksolv30.com
Estimated Sales: $2.5-5 Million
Number Employees: 1-4

24229 Inland Consumer Packaging
17507 S Dupont Hwy
Harrington, DE 19952-2370
302-398-4211
Fax: 302-398-1422 www.gp.com
Folding paper boxes
President: Brent Paugh
Executive Vice President: Christian Fischer
Executive Vice President of Operations: Wesley
Jones
Estimated Sales: $20-50 Million
Number Employees: 100-249

24230 Inland Label & Marketing Svc
2009 West Ave S
La Crosse, WI 54601-6207
608-783-4700
Fax: 608-787-5870 800-657-4413
info@inlandlabel.com www.inlandlabel.net
Labels
Owner: Steve Winterfield
CEO: Mark Glenndenning
mglenndenning@inlandlabel.com
Director of Sales: Don Iverson
Number Employees: 100-249
Square Footage: 41138

24231 Inland Paper Company
1826 S Taylor Pl
Ontario, CA 91761
909-923-4505
Fax: 909-923-9808 www.inlandpaper.com
Stock boxes, poly bags, anti-static bags, packaging
material such as bubble wrap and foam, shipping
supplies such as carton sealing tapes, stretch film,
strammping, and wrapping papers. Janitorial and
safety supples also available.
Vice President: Al Fertal
Year Founded: 1980
Estimated Sales: Less Than $500,000
Number Employees: 11-50

24232 Inland Paperboard & Packaging
210 Mount Phillips Street
Rock Hill, SC 29730-3340
803-366-4103
Fax: 803-366-1648
Corrugated containers, boxes and sheets
CEO: Dale Stahl
Sales Manager: Mannonum Heller
General Manager: George Hare
Estimated Sales: $20-50 Million
Number Employees: 100-249
Parent Co: Temple Inland Company

**24233 Inland Showcase & Fixture
Company**
1473 N Thesta St
Fresno, CA 93703-3791
559-237-4158
Fax: 559-237-7238
Restaurant and store fixtures including plastic coun-
ters
Purchasing Manager: Richard Bertad
Estimated Sales: $10-20 Million
Number Employees: 50-99
Square Footage: 60000

24234 Inline Automation
14758 Bluebird St NW
Anoka, MN 55304
763-434-2828
Fax: 763-755-5757 websales@intelligentline.com
President: Gerald Jilts
Number Employees: 10

24235 Inline Filling Systems
216 Seaboard Ave
Venice, FL 34285-4618
941-486-8800
Fax: 941-486-0077 sales101@fillers.com
www.fillers.com
Manufacturer and exporter of liquid filling equipment, capping machinery, conveyors and unscramblers

President: Sam Lubus
slubus@inlinefillingsysteminc.com
R&D: Jay Carlson
VP Sales: Joe Schemenauer
Estimated Sales: $10,000,000
Number Employees: 20-49
Square Footage: 20000
Brands:
Levelhead 2

24236 Inline Plastic Corp
100 Constitution Dr
McDonough, GA 30253
678-466-3467
Fax: 770-957-4492 www.inlineplastics.com
Clear plastic containers for cakes and desserts, fresh
baked goods, salads, and cut veggies and fruit.
President: Thomas Orkisz

24237 (HQ)Inline Plastic Corp
42 Canal St
Shelton, CT 06484
Fax: 203-924-0370 800-826-5567
www.inlineplastics.com
Clear plastic containers for cakes and desserts, fresh
baked goods, salads, and cut veggies and fruit.
President: Thomas Orkisz
VP of Sales: Augie Lanzetta
Year Founded: 1968
Estimated Sales: $100-500 Million
Number Employees: 200-499

24238 Inline Services
27731 Commercial Park Rd
Tomball, TX 77375-6532
713-973-0079
Fax: 713-973-6614 888-973-0079
www.inlineservices.com
Pigging systems for product displacement and
batching pipe cleaning
President: Gary Smith
glsmith@inlineplc.com
Financial Director: Deanne Schillaci
Vice President: Harvey Diehl
Sales: Jessica Nichols
General Manager: Rick Meade
Warehouse: Russell Williams
Accounts Payable: Susan Thomas
Estimated Sales: $1.5 Million
Number Employees: 20-49

24239 Inman Foodservices Group LLC
3807 Charlotte Ave
Nashville, TN 37209-3736
615-321-5591
Fax: 615-321-5689
foodservicedesign@inman-inc.com
www.inman-inc.com
Consultant specializing in food service facility plan-
ning and design
Owner: John Feilmeier
john.feilmeier@inman-inc.com
Vice President: Brandi Hale
Estimated Sales: $5-10 Million
Number Employees: 5-9

24240 Inmark, Inc
675 Hartman Road
Suite 100
Austell, GA 30168
770-373-3300
Fax: 770-373-3301 800-646-6275
service@inmarkinc.com www.inmarkinc.com
Packaging supplies, plastic food containers
President: Brian Murphy
Vice President: James Curlee
Contact: Chuck Albert
chucka@inmarkpackaging.com
Estimated Sales: $20-50 Million
Number Employees: 50-99

24241 Inmotion Technologies
211 Overlook Dr
Sewickley, PA 15143-2459
412-749-0710
Fax: 412-749-0705
Multi-axis motion control systems for advanced
packaging and printing featuring accurate coordina-
tion and synchronization functions
President, Chief Executive Officer: Lawrence Culp
Contact: David Birarda
david.birarda@inmotiontechnology.com
Estimated Sales: $1-5 Million
Number Employees: 5-9

**24242 Innavision Global Marketing
Consultants**
1615 Count Turf Ln.
Racine, WI 53402
262-633-1000
Equipment manufacturers, distributors and represen-
tatives.
Managing Member: Charles Allison
Estimated Sales: $190,000
Number Employees: 2

24243 Innerspace Design Concepts
16015 Van Aken Boulevard
Apt 104
Shaker Heights, OH 44120-5345
216-295-1589
Fax: 216-295-1593 innerspace@stratos.net
Complete design services for restaurants and stores
CEO: Steven Goldschel
Number Employees: 12
Square Footage: 3500

24244 Innio
1101 W St Paul Ave
Waukesha, WI 53188
contact.en@innio.com
www.innio.com
Jenbacher and Waukesha gas engines.
CEO: Carlos Lange
President, INNIO Waukesha: Bud Hittie
Parent Co: INNIO Jenbacher GmbH & Co OG

24245 Innophos Holdings Inc.
259 Prospect Plains Rd.
Cranbury, NJ 08512
609-495-2495
Fax: 609-860-0138 www.innophos.com
Specialty ingredient solutions for food, health, and
industrial markets, including phosphates, minerals,
botanicals, protiens and other nutrition ingredients.
Chairman/President/CEO: Kim Ann Mink
Senior VP/CFO: Mark Feuerbach
Senior VP/CMO/CTO: Sherry Duff
Year Founded: 2004
Estimated Sales: $785 Million
Number Employees: 1,400

24246 Innoseal Systems Inc
10900 S Commerce Blvd # B
Charlotte, NC 28273-7133
704-521-6068
Fax: 704-521-6038 sales@innoseal.com
President: Jeff Rebh
jeff.rebh@innovativetape.com
Number Employees: 5-9
Parent Co: Twinseal Systems B.V.

24247 Innova Envelopes
7213 Rue Cordner
La Salle, QC H8N 2J7
Canada
514-595-0555
Fax: 514-595-1112 www.supremex.com
Manufacturer and exporter of envelopes
President: Gilles Cyrcs
CFO: Stephan Lavigne
VP/General Manager: Gilles Cyr
R&D: Alain Tremblay
Estimated Sales: $30-50 Million
Number Employees: 200
Parent Co: Supremex

24248 Innova-Tech
1500 E Lancaster Ave # 100
Paoli, PA 19301-1500
610-640-9350
Fax: 610-640-2670 800-523-7299
www.innovatechnologies.in
Wastewater treatment equipment and dissolved air
flotation units
President: John Murphy
Chief Engineer: Greg Laurent
Number Employees: 1-4
Square Footage: 109200

24249 Innovation Moving Systems
310 S 10th St
P.O. Box 700169
Oostburg, WI 53070-1301
920-564-6272
Fax: 920-564-2322 800-619-0625
president@lectrotruck.com www.lectrotruck.com

USA manufacturer of the ORIGINAL battery oper-
ated stail climbing hand truck for over 40 years.
Safely move heavy loads from 600lbs/272kg to
1500lbs/680kg in less time. All models include free
battery, battery charger, strap bar(s), 2year motor
warranty and a 1year entire unit warranty.
President: Kevin Peters
president@lectrotruck.com
Sales/Marketing Executive: Jason Tagel
Estimated Sales: Below $5 Million
Number Employees: 1-4
Square Footage: 34000
Brands:
Lectro Truck

24250 Innovations Expressed LLC
Po Box 1823
Sparta, NJ 07871-3850
201-452-0557
Specialty food packaging i.e. gift wrap/la-
bels/boxes/containers.
Marketing: Jody Shampton-Moore

24251 Innovations by Design
19 Foothill Path
Chadds Ford, PA 19317-9146
610-558-0160
Fax: 610-558-1960
Consultant specializing in food service design, cad
layouts and project administration for cafeterias,
prisons, schools, hospitals, sports arenas, etc
President & CEO: Jon Shaw
VP Of Operations: John Fogleman
Director Of Marketing: Scott Huggins
Director Of Sales: Allen Wells

24252 Innovative Ceramic Corp
432 Walnut St
East Liverpool, OH 43920-3130
330-385-6515
Fax: 330-385-6510 info@innovativeceramic.com
www.innovativeceramic.com
Rubber stamps and high temperature inks
President: Orville Steininger
Estimated Sales: Below $5 Million
Number Employees: 1-4
Square Footage: 20000

24253 Innovative Components
P.O.Box 294
Southington, CT 06489-0294
860-621-7220
Fax: 860-620-0288 800-789-2851
info@liquidlevel.com www.liquidlevel.com
Manufacturer and exporter of sanitary liquid level
instrumentation for level indication, alarms and
controls
Owner: Pete Meade
Sales: Pete Meade
Production: Joe Kubisek
Estimated Sales: $1-2.5 Million
Number Employees: 5-9
Square Footage: 10000

24254 Innovative Controls Corp
1354 E Broadway St
Toledo, OH 43605
419-691-6684
Fax: 419-691-0170
www.innovativecontrolscorp.com
Provides the following services to the food & beverage industry: packaging integration; packaging machine rebuilds and retrofits; automated process
control panels; conveyor systems; bar coding;
verticle form fill seal bagging machines;cup feed-
ers-auger and filling; rebuilds and retrofits of processing equipment; transfer feeds; materials
handling distribution; mills-sugar, flour & meal;
process controls for weighing, blending, & batching;
PLC controlled robotics. Individualconsulting.
President & CEO: Louis Soltis
Marketing Director: Angela Hitchens
Sales Director: Michael Hitchens
Contact: Mark Benton
mbenton@innovativecontrolscorp.com
Director of Operations: Robert Simon
Estimated Sales: $5-7 Million
Number Employees: 20-49
Square Footage: 70000

24255 Innovative Energy
10653 W 181st Ave
Lowell, IN 46356-9451

219-696-3639
Fax: 219-696-5220 info@insul.net
www.insul.net
Specialty food packaging i.e. gift wrap/labels/boxes/containers.
President: Robert Wadsworth
info@insul.net
Marketing: Tammy Snyder
Number Employees: 20-49

24256 Innovative Folding Carton Company
901 Durham Ave
South Plainfield, NJ 07080

908-757-0205
Fax: 908-757-6464
Folding cartons and pressure sensitive labels
President: Shawn Smith
CFO: Bob Sgaitierri
CFO: Robert S Pierre
Quality Control: Will Suton
VP Sales: Shawn Smith
VP Operations: Ray Karst
Estimated Sales: $20-50 Million
Number Employees: 100-249
Square Footage: 100000
Parent Co: Impaxx

24257 Innovative Food Processors Inc
2125 Airport Dr
Faribault, MN 55021-7798

507-334-2730
Fax: 507-334-7969 800-997-4437
sales@ifpinc.biz www.ifpinc.biz
Custom manufacturing services including agglomeration, encapsulation, and packaging for food and beverage powders
CEO: Ephi Eyal
eeyal@ifpinc.biz
Marketing Director: Anna Batsakes
Sales Director: Scott Sijan
Estimated Sales: $23.4 Million
Number Employees: 250-499

24258 Innovative Food Solutions LLC
4516 Kenny Road
Suite 320
Columbus, OH 43220-3711

614-326-1421
Fax: 614-326-1443 800-884-3314
jliebrec@columbus.rr.com
Consulting firm ready to assist you to quickly launch new food products and manufacturing processes, new food industry ingredients, perform technical troubleshooting and produce prototype samples for trade shows and market researchstudies. Areas of experience include organic, natural and nutraceutical/functional food products, including aseptic and retort liquids, and spray dried powders.
President: Jeff Liebrecht
R&D: Jeff Liebrecht

24259 Innovative Foods, Inc.
338 N Canal
Suite 20
South San Francisco, CA 94080

650-871-8912
Fax: 650-871-0837 ed@innovativefoods.org
Infused foods, including using product forming, flavoring, coloring and value added to underutilized raw materials.
Owner: Gilbert Lee
VP/Secretary & Treasurer: Fay Hirschberg
Research & Development: Edward Hirschberg
Contact: David Terry
dterry@innovfoods.com
Estimated Sales: $190 Thousand
Square Footage: 74000

24260 Innovative Marketing
11801 Pierce St.
2nd Floor
Riverside, CA 92505

951-710-3135
Fax: 952-949-8865 800-438-4627
innovativemarketingca.com
Manufacturer and exporter of lid openers for plastic containers
President: Brad Pappas
Operations Manager: Amy Vinar

Estimated Sales: 150000
Number Employees: 1-4
Square Footage: 40000
Brands:
Pco
The Lid Cutter

24261 Innovative Molding
6775 McKinley Ave
Sebastopol, CA 95472

707-829-2666
Fax: 707-829-5212
whunt@innovativemolding.com
www.innovativemolding.com
Manufacturer and exporter of threaded plastic caps and lids for jars and bottles.
Administrator: Alan Williams
awilliams@innovativemold.com
Vice President: Ron Cook
Operations Manager: Warren Hunt
Estimated Sales: $5-10 Million
Number Employees: 50-99
Square Footage: 56000

24262 Innovative Packaging Solution
1692 12th Street
Martin, MI 49070-8745

616-656-2100
Fax: 616-656-2101
Litho cut and stack labels, seals, stickers, label application equipment and computerized artwork
CEO: James Rand
Sr VP: Jim English
Communications Director: Kate Hunter
Estimated Sales: $20-50 Million
Number Employees: 100-249
Square Footage: 30000
Parent Co: Excellence Group

24263 Innovative Plastech
1260 Kingsland Dr
Batavia, IL 60510

630-232-1808
Fax: 630-232-1978 ghernandez@inplas.com
www.inplas.com
Custom thermoforming, tool and package designing, plastic trays
President: Jim Gustafson
CFO: Jake Clever
VP: Edward Gustafson
R&D: Denny Bahl
Quality Control: Girish Raval
Sales: Dave Lyons
Contact: Dennis Bahl
d.bahl@inplas.com
Production: Martine Del Toro
Plant Manager: John Martinez
Purchasing: Larry Rosales
Estimated Sales: $15 Million
Number Employees: 64
Square Footage: 90000
Type of Packaging: Consumer, Private Label

24264 Innovative Plastics Corp
400 Route 303
Orangeburg, NY 10962-1340

845-359-7500
Fax: 845-359-0237
service@innovative-plastics.com
www.innovative-plastics.com
Thermoformed plastics packaging and contract packaging services
President: Don D'Antonio
don@inoplas.com
VP: Bud Macfarlane
Estimated Sales: $35-40 Million
Number Employees: 100-249
Square Footage: 60000
Type of Packaging: Consumer
Other Locations:
Innovative Plastics Corporation
Nashville TN

24265 Innovative Rotational Molding
2300 W Pecan Ave
Madera, CA 93637-5056

559-673-4764
Fax: 559-673-4716 CustServe@IRM-CORP.Com
www.irm-corp.com
Sales and marketing information systems to food and beverage manufacturers, distributors and brokers.

President: Shelly Humphries
shumphries@irm-corp.com
CEO: Art Harding
Sales: Tim Shine
Number Employees: 10-19
Other Locations:
IRM Corporation
Dallas TX
Brands:
Compass Forecast System
Discovery System
Promo Assist

24266 Innovative Space Management
2645 Brooklyn Queens Expressway
Woodside, NY 11377-7826

718-278-4300
Fax: 718-274-0973 contact@ny.diam-int.com
Manufacturer, exporter and designer of shelf management systems and point of purchase displays
VP/General Manager (ISM Division): Bryan Yablans
VP Sales: Winn Esterline
VP Operations: Valerie Vignola
Number Employees: 850
Square Footage: 300000
Parent Co: POP Displays

24267 Inovar Packaging Group
611 Magic Mile St # 205
Arlington, TX 76011-5109

817-277-6666
Fax: 817-275-2770 800-285-2235
info@inovarpkg.com www.inovarpkg.com
Custom printed labels, tags and decals. Also, distribute label applicators and packaging equipment.
President: Gary Cooper
CEO: Dave Young
dyoung@inovarpkg.com
CFO: Kyle Dailey
Research & Development: Alton Berry
Quality Control: Sonya Ayers
Marketing/Sales: Steve Nevil
Operations Manager: Darryl Parham
Purchasing Manager: Mark Ingus
Estimated Sales: $15,000,000
Number Employees: 20-49
Square Footage: 106000
Parent Co: Conti Industries
Type of Packaging: Consumer, Food Service, Private Label, Bulk
Brands:
Kraftmark

24268 Inovatech
3911 Mount Lehman Road
Abbotsford, BC V4X 2N1
Canada

604-857-9080
Fax: 604-857-0843 www.inovatech.com
Number Employees: 10

24269 Inovpack Vector
40 Vreeland Avenue
Suite 107
Providence, RI

888-227-4647
Fax: 203-852-0136
Casings

24270 Inpaco Corporation
PO Box 286
Nazareth, PA 18064-0286

610-759-8544
Fax: 610-759-9021
Wine industry bags

24271 Inpak Systems Inc
540 Tasman St
Madison, WI 53714-3162

608-221-8180
Fax: 608-221-4473 sales@inpaksystems.com
www.inpaksystems.com
Distributor of industrial packaging equipment
President: Gerald Hoague
info@inpaksystems.com
VP: Ronn Ferrell
Marketing: Tom McDonnell
Sales: Dennis Murphy
Operations: Mike Kennedy
Estimated Sales: $3-4 Million
Number Employees: 1-4
Square Footage: 8000
Type of Packaging: Bulk

24272 Inscale
1607 Maple Ave
Terre Haute, IN 47804-3234
812-232-0893
Fax: 812-232-6876 855-839-9147
incell@inscale-incell.com
Checkweighing devices, weight control systems, scales
Owner: Fred Herrmann
General Manager: Paul Herrmann
Estimated Sales: $5-10 Million
Number Employees: 20-49
Square Footage: 140000
Type of Packaging: Bulk

24273 Insect-O-Cutor Inc
1641 Lewis Way
Stone Mountain, GA 30083-1107
770-939-2835
Fax: 770-621-0100 800-966-8480
sales@insect-o-cutor.com www.insect-o-cutor.com
Industrial commercial grade insect light traps; 110 volt, 220 volt, stainless steel, scatterproof, energy-efficient
President: W A Harris
Number Employees: 10-19
Type of Packaging: Private Label
Brands:
Germ-O-Ray
Guardian
Insect-O-Cutor

24274 Insects Limited Inc
16950 Westfield Park Rd
Westfield, IN 46074-9374
317-896-9300
Fax: 317-867-5757 800-992-1991
insectsltd@aol.com www.fumigationzone.com
Manufacturer, exporter and wholesaler/distributor of pest control systems including traps, lures, insect monitoring and detection devices, fumigation products, etc.; importer of cigarette beetle pheromone traps; also, pest controlaudits and seminars available
President: David Mueller
d.mueller@insectslimited.com
CFO: Barbara Bass
VP: John Mueller
General Manager: Patrick Kelley
Estimated Sales: $1 Million
Number Employees: 10-19
Square Footage: 6000
Brands:
Bullet Lure
Lasio
No Survivor
Serrico
Storgard

24275 Insight Distribution Systems
222 Schilling Cir
Suite 275
Hunt Valley, MD 21031-8638
410-403-1100
Fax: 410-329-1114 800-310-3548
Beverage distribution software, specilizing in mobile computers, route accounting, inventory, financials, account management software
President: Bob Jenkin
Estimated Sales: $10-20 Million
Number Employees: 10

24276 Insight Packaging
1000 Muirfield Drive
Hanover Park, IL 60133-5468
630-980-4314
Fax: 630-980-4316 info@insightpack.com
www.insightpack.com
Package food items for other companies
President: Gregory Batton
Estimated Sales: $10-20 Million
Number Employees: 10

24277 Insignia Systems Inc
8799 Brooklyn Blvd
Minneapolis, MN 55445-2398
763-392-6200
Fax: 763-392-6222 800-874-4648
info@insigniasystems.com
www.insigniasystems.com
Manufacturer and exporter of promotional items including signage and software for bar coding and large format printing

President/CEO: Glen P. Dall
VP, Finance: John C. Gonsior
CFO: John C. Gonsior
Quality Control: Bob Norman
VP Marketing: Scott Simcox
Number Employees: 50-99
Brands:
Insignia Pops
Stylus

24278 (HQ)Insinger Co
6245 State Rd
Philadelphia, PA 19135-2996
215-624-4800
Fax: 215-624-6966 800-344-4802
sales@insingermachine.com
www.insingermachine.com
Manufacturer and exporter of commercial dishwashers potato peelers, garbage disposal units, french fry cutters, tray washers and driers and dish, glass, pot and pan washers
President: John Stern
CEO: Robert Cantor
acantor@insingermachine.com
VP Sales/Marketing: Ari Cantor
Chief Engineer: Jim Bittner
Quality Control: Kris Hogan
Marketing Director: Annemarie Fisher
Regional Sales Manager: Don Gazzillo
Vice President of Operations: Kristine Hogan
Purchasing Manager: Kristine Hogan
Estimated Sales: $10-20 Million
Number Employees: 50-99
Square Footage: 130000

24279 Inspired Automation Inc
5321 Derry Ave # D
Agoura Hills, CA 91301-5064
818-991-4598
Fax: 818-597-4820 www.inspiredautomation.com
Automatic net weighing, counting, in-line batching and filling machinery; exporter of automatic net weighing, in-line batching and counting machinery
President: Robert Homes
bob@inspiredautomation.com
Sales: Buzz Holmes
Plant Manager: Joesph Gonzales
Estimated Sales: $3-5 Million
Number Employees: 5-9
Number of Brands: 1
Number of Products: 22
Square Footage: 4000
Type of Packaging: Consumer, Food Service, Private Label, Bulk

24280 Insta-Pro International
10104 Douglas Ave
Urbandale, IA 50322-2007
515-254-1260
Fax: 515-276-5749 800-383-4524
www.insta-pro.com
Manufacturer and exporter of processing equipment for textured soy products
Vice President: Ray Goodwin
rgoodwin@insta-pro.com
President, Chief Executive Officer: Kevin Kacere
R&D: Wilmot Wijeratne
VP: Karl Arnold
Chairman: Wayne Fox
VP International Marketing: Tom Welby
Vice President of Operations: Hennie Pieterse
Estimated Sales: $5-10 Million
Number Employees: 10-19
Parent Co: Triple F
Brands:
Express
Insta-Pro

24281 Instabox
1139 40th Avenue North East
Calgary, AB T2E 6M9
Canada
403-250-9217
Fax: 403-250-8075 800-482-6173
www.instabox.com
Corrugated cardboard boxes and shipping supplies
President: Jim Mace
CFO: Greg Mace
CEO: Greg Mace
Office Manager: Linda Burgher
Manager: Richard Bain
Order Desk: Dale Beck
Number Employees: 40

24282 (HQ)Instacomm Canada
Unit 1, Suite 376
Oakville, ON L6M 2Y1
Canada
905-465-1266
Fax: 905-465-0644 877-426-2783
info@instacomm.com www.instacomm.com
Distributor of guest and server oaging systems
Estimated Sales: $1-5 Million
Number Employees: 1-4
Other Locations:
Instacomm Canada
Creedmoor NC

24283 Institute of Packaging Professionals
1833 Centre Point Circle
Suite 123
Naperville, IL 60563
630-544-5050
Fax: 630-544-5055 info@iopp.org
www.iopp.org
Association for packaging professionals
Religious Leader: Paul Kim
Contact: Eric Berkley
eberkley@iopp.org
Number Employees: 10-19

24284 Institutional & Supermarket
7362 NW 5th St
PO Box 17440
Plantation, FL 33317-1605
954-584-3100
Fax: 954-584-5591 info@iseinc.org
www.iseinc.org
Industrial food serving equipment
Executive Director: Philip Polunsky
phil@iseinc.org
Estimated Sales: $1-2.5 Million
Number Employees: 10-19

24285 Institutional EquipmentInc
704 Veterans Pkwy # B
Bolingbrook, IL 60440-5094
630-771-0990
Fax: 630-771-0994 www.ieiusa.net
Stainless steel counters, shelving and tables including steam
President: Frank Fiene
ffiene@ieiusa.net
VP Manufacturing: Don Wasielweski
Estimated Sales: $5-10 Million
Number Employees: 50-99
Square Footage: 160000

24286 Instrumented Sensor Technology
4704 Moore St
Okemos, MI 48864-1722
517-349-8487
Fax: 517-349-8469 info@isthq.com
www.isthq.com
Owner: Greg Hoshal
hoshal@isthq.com
Estimated Sales: $1-3 Million
Number Employees: 5-9

24287 Insulair
35275 S Welty Rd
Vernalis, CA 95385-9733
209-839-0911
Fax: 209-839-1353 800-343-3402
Manufacturer and exporter of insulated triple-wall paper cups and plastic lids
President: Claus Sadlier
CFO: Larry Nally
Quality Control: Dale Houglant
Sales Director: Frank Gavin
Estimated Sales: $5-10 Million
Number Employees: 5-9
Brands:
Insulair

24288 Intec Video Systems
23301 Vista Grande Dr
Laguna Hills, CA 92653-1497
949-859-3800
Fax: 949-859-3178 800-468-3254
info@intecvideo.com www.intecvideo.com
Rear vision cameras systems
President: Don Nama
Marketing Director: Manuel Mendez
Sales Director: Roy Barbatti
Manager: John Hoover
jhoover@avanquest.com

Estimated Sales: $12 000,000
Number Employees: 20-49

24289 Intech
3825 Grant St
Washougal, WA 98671-2810

360-835-8785
Fax: 360-835-5144 www.intechenterprises.com
President: Tom Cunning
tomc@intechenterprises.com
Estimated Sales: Below $5 Million
Number Employees: 10-19

24290 Intedge Manufacturing
1875 Chumley Rd
Woodruff, SC 29388-8561

864-969-9601
Fax: 864-969-9604 866-969-9605
customer.service@intedge.com www.intedge.com
Food service equipment including textiles,
smallware, baking supplies, timers, thermometers,
utensils, and much more.
Plant Manager: Debi Collier
Number Employees: 20-49
Type of Packaging: Food Service, Private Label
Brands:
    Intedge
    Metalwash

24291 Integrated Barcode Solutions
856 3rd St NW
Valley City, ND 58072

Fax: 530-273-4725
Portable terminal or fixed station data capture appli-
cations that employ bar code technology
Estimated Sales: less than $500,000
Number Employees: 1

24292 Integrated Distribution
2110 S 169th Plz # 200
Omaha, NE 68130-4650

937-445-1936
Fax: 402-397-8451
Computer software for food distribution
President/ CEO/ Chairman: Wiliam Nuti
SVP/ CFO/ Chief Accounting Officer: Bob Fishman
Vice President of Information Technology: Bob
Mawyer
EVP, Services, Hardware Solutions & EQ: Rick
Marquardt
Head of Marketing: Oren Betzaleli
Executive Vice President of Retail Sales: Mike Todd
SVP/ Corp. Services/ Chief HR Officer: Andrea
Ledford
Estimated Sales: $10-20 Million
Number Employees: 50-99

24293 Integrated Packaging Systems
3 Luger Rd # 5
Suite 5
Denville, NJ 07834-2638

973-664-0020
Fax: 973-263-2992 www.ipsnj.com
Tablet counting and liquid filling
President: Michael Fuzia
mfuzia@ipsnj.com
Vice President: Michael McNeila
Technical Manager: Michael Frusteri
Sales Director: Marianne Mooney
General Manager: Phil DePalma
Estimated Sales: $4-5 Million
Number Employees: 5-9
Brands:
    Procount Salt Counter
    Versaflow Liquid Filler

**24294 Integrated Restaurant
Software/RMS Touch**
9 West Ridgely Road
Timonium, MD 21093

201-461-9096
Fax: 410-902-5468
Manufacturer and exporter of P.O.S. touch screen
software for restaurants, bars, cafeterias, etc
President: Richard Adler
VP Sales: Peter Polizanno
Estimated Sales: $2.5-5 Million
Number Employees: 10-19
Square Footage: 12000

24295 Integrated Systems
1904 SE Ochoco Street
Portland, OR 97222-7315

503-654-7886
Fax: 503-654-7868 800-705-6401
Palletizers and depalletizers available in high or low
level infeed with rates up to five layers a minute, options include depalletizing, pallet dispensers, tie
sheets and fully automated multi-palletizer cells
Estimated Sales: $1-5 Million

24296 Intelligent Controls
PO Box 638
Saco, ME 4072

207-283-0156
Fax: 207-283-0158 800-872-3455
webadmin@incon.com www.incon.com
Manufacturer and exporter of microprocessor and
programmable controls including liquid level mea-
surement and process multiplexing systems, supervi-
sory control and data acquisition systems
CEO: Scott Tremble
Director Marketing: John Eastman
VP: Dean Richards
Contact: Vitaliy Demin
vdemin@franklinfueling.com
Estimated Sales: F
Number Employees: 1,000-4,999
Square Footage: 28000
Parent Co: Franklin Fueling Systems

24297 Intelplex Designers
9607 Dielman Rock Island Indus
St Louis, MO 63132-2149

314-983-9996
Fax: 314-983-9989 intouch@intelplex.com
Consultant specializing in the design of restaurant
equipment
Owner: Alan Sherman
intouch@intelplex.com
Estimated Sales: $1-2.5 Million
Number Employees: 1-4

24298 Intentia Americas
1700 E Golf Rd # 9
Schaumburg, IL 60173-5816

847-762-0900
Fax: 847-762-0901 800-796-6839
www.lawson.com
Managing Director, Intentia Australia/Ne: Linus
Parker
Chief Executive Officer, President: Harry Debes
Vice President of Sales: Mikael Anden
Contact: Christine Roe
christine.roe@lawson.com
Estimated Sales: $10-20 Million
Number Employees: 20-49

**24299 (HQ)Inteplast Bags & Films
Corporation**
7503 Vantage Pl.
Delta, BC V4G 1A5
Canada

604-946-5431
Fax: 604-946-5343 www.inteplast.com
Polyethylene produce bags, film, trash can liners and
corrugated sheets
President: John Young
Estimated Sales: $12.4 Million
Number Employees: 90

24300 Inteplast Group LTD
9 Peach Tree Hill Rd
Livingston, NJ 07039-5702

973-994-8000
Fax: 973-994-8028 info@inteplast.com
www.inteplast.com
BOPP films, stretch wrap, and plastic concentrates
and compounds.
President: John D Young
jyoung@inteplast.com
Number Employees: 1000-4999

24301 Inter-Access
100 Carrier Drive
Etobicoke, ON M9W 5R1
Canada

514-744-6262
Fax: 514-744-3176
Executive search firm; also, consultant providing
company re-engineering, manufacturing automation,
ISO quality implementation, business planning and
market surveys

President: Mohamed Geledi-Nami
VP: Edith Chandonnet
Senior Consultant: Tom Schopflocher
Number Employees: 5-9
Square Footage: 2000
Parent Co: Le Groupe Consortium Canada

**24302 Inter-City Welding &
Manufacturing**
10058 E Wilson Rd
Independence, MO 64053-1541

816-252-1770
Fax: 816-252-8321
Industrial belt conveyors
Manager: Mary Robinett
Estimated Sales: $500,000-$1 Million
Number Employees: 1-4

24303 (HQ)Inter-Pack Corporation
PO Box 691
Monroe, MI 48161-0691

734-242-7755
Fax: 734-242-7756
Manufacturer and exporter of corrugated paper and
foam plastic; contract packaging services available
Manager: Frank Calandra
Estimated Sales: $20-50 Million
Number Employees: 20-49

24304 InterMetro Industries
Wilkes-Barre, PA 18705

570-825-2741
Manufacturer of space and productivity solutions
Year Founded: 1929
Number Employees: 400
Number of Products: 30K
Brands:
    Metromax
    Super Adjustable
    Super Erecta

24305 InterSect Business Systems Inc
1921 Kent Road
Kelowna, BC V1Y 7S6
Canada

250-860-0829
Fax: 250-860-0876 sales@distrib-u-tec.com
www.distrib-u-tec.com
Distrib-u-tec Software is a fully integrated operations and cost accounting information management
system designed specifically for food distributors,
processors and packers.
Sales/Marketing: Corrina Cross

24306 InterXchange Market Network
32 Laurens Street
Charleston, SC 29401-1565

803-577-4794
Fax: 803-577-4794 800-577-4794
rrabago@halcyon.com
Brokers and commondity exchanges, computer sys-
tems and software
Number Employees: 45

24307 Interactive Sales Solutions
616 Shadowcrest Ln
Coppell, TX 75019-3401

214-352-9575
Fax: 214-352-5729 800-352-9575
www.issi-ivr.info
Sales force automation software utilizing touch-tone
phones for consumer sales, food service and retail
food broker operations
President: William Godbey
bgodbey@issi-ivr.com
VP: Dean Schenkel
Operations Manager: John Williamson
bgodbey@issi-ivr.com
Estimated Sales: $500,000-$1 Million
Number Employees: 5-9
Square Footage: 8000
Type of Packaging: Bulk
Brands:
    Interactive Sales Manager

24308 Interactive Services Group
600 Delran Pkwy # C
Delran, NJ 08075-1268

856-824-9401
Fax: 856-824-9415 800-566-3310
jbdickinson@isg-service.com

Hand-held computer system maintenance and support. Specialize in supporting Intermec and Symbols systems. Company also has priority software applications for route accounting industry
Owner: Igor Lukov
i.lukov@isg-service.com
CEO: J Dickinson
Director Human Resources: Michele Galan
Estimated Sales: $4 Million
Number Employees: 20-49
Square Footage: 36000

24309 Interamerican Coffee
19500 State Hwy 249 # 255
Houston, TX 77070
713-462-2671
Fax: 713-912-7072 800-346-2810
traders@iaccoffee.com
Green coffee importer and distributer
President: Guy Burdett
Controller: Samantha Marino
Vice President of Operations: John Mason
Estimated Sales: $5-10 Million
Number Employees: 20-49

24310 Interbrand Corporation
555 Market Street
Suite 900
San Francisco, CA 94105
347-334-3502
Fax: 415-593-2250 877-692-7263
inquiries@interbrand.com www.interbrand.com
Consultant for brand logos, packaging, identification and naming
Global CEO: Jez Frampton
Global Chief Creative Officer: Andy Payne
Global CFO & COO: Kelly Gall
Global Chief Strategy Officer: Leslie Butterfield
Contact: Paulette Fox
fox.paulette@interbrand.com
Director of Operations: Michael Levtchenko
Estimated Sales: $5-10 Million
Number Employees: 20-49
Parent Co: Omnicom
Other Locations:
Interbrand Corp.
Chicago IL

24311 Intercard Inc
1884 Lackland Hill Pkwy # 1
St Louis, MO 63146-3569
314-275-8066
Fax: 314-275-4998 info@intercardinc.com
Manufacturer and exporter of credit and debit card systems
CEO: Ray Sherrod
CFO: Gerry Schmidt
Quality Control: Lynn Soreden
Estimated Sales: $10-20 Million
Number Employees: 20-49

24312 Intercomp
3839 County Road 116
Hamel, MN 55340-9342
763-476-2531
Fax: 763-476-2613 800-328-3336
info@intercompcompany.com
www.intercompco.com
Manufacturer and exporter of electronic scales including crane, platform, pallet and portable truck, floor, bench and hanging
Owner: Robert Kroll
Quality Control: Mark Browne
Plant Manager: Jeff Weyandt
Estimated Sales: $20 Million
Number Employees: 50-99
Square Footage: 90000
Brands:
Cs 750
Cw 250
Cw 500
Pw 800
Pw 850

24313 Interfood Ingredients
777 Brickell Ave
Suite 210
Miami, FL 33131
786-953-8320
info@interfood.com
www.interfood.com
Dairy ingredients and products
Managing Director & VP: Reniers Geoffrey
Year Founded: 1970
Estimated Sales: $235 Million

Number Employees: 200
Parent Co: Interfood Holding

24314 Intergraph Corp
7840 N Sam Houston Pkwy W # 20
Suite 100
Houston, TX 77064-3503
281-671-1013
Fax: 281-890-3301 800-899-8787
sales@coade.com www.intergraph.com
Provides software for multiple plant design and engineering disciplines.
Senior VP: Rick Allen
rick.allen@intergraph.com
Estimated Sales: $5-10 000,000
Number Employees: 50-99

24315 Interior Systems Inc
241 N Broadway # 600
Suite 600
Milwaukee, WI 53202-5860
414-224-0957
Fax: 414-224-0972 800-837-8373
info@isiamerica.com www.isiamerica.com
Food service fixtures, furniture, play equipment, artwork and signage
President/CEO: Tony Lutz
tlutz@isiamerica.com
Chairman: Lindsey Bovinet
CFO: Bill Stoll
Vice President-Fulfillment: Mark Huck
IT Manager: Robert Graf
Director Of Sales: Jason Fredrickson
Director-Human Resources: Jim Carlson
Director of Operations: Darin Grobe
Creative Director: Tony Pagliuca
Controller: Zach Schaefer
Estimated Sales: $5-10 Million
Number Employees: 50-99

24316 Interlab
4200 Research Forest Dr # 150
The Woodlands, TX 77381-3237
281-298-9410
Fax: 281-298-9411 888-876-2844
www.polyseed.org
Manufacturer and exporter of microbial products for drain maintenance, odor control, septic systems, etc.; also, in-house and field technical support available
President: Peter Perez
Estimated Sales: $3-5 Million
Number Employees: 5-9
Square Footage: 28400
Brands:
Bio Free Trap Clear
Biofree Septic Clear

24317 Interlake Mecalux
1600 N. 25th Ave.
Melrose Park
Chicago, IL 60160
708-344-9999
Fax: 708-343-9788 www.interlakemecalux.com
Steel racking, warehouse automation, warehouse management software and other storage solutions.
Founder/President: Jose Luis Carrillo Rodriguez
Estimated Sales: $100-$500 Million
Number Employees: 500-999
Brands:
Esmena
Interlake

24318 Interliance
200 E Sandpointe Ave 510
Santa Ana, CA 92707
714-540-8889
Fax: 714-540-6113 800-540-7917
info@interliance.com www.interliance.com
Consultant providing performance improvement, process improvement, quality strategies, policies and procedures, regulatory compliance programs, site specific training, etc
President: Brad Kemp
CFO: Brad Kamth
Quality Control: Brad Kamth
Contact: Linda Apple
lapple@interliance.com
Estimated Sales: $5-10,000,000
Number Employees: 1-4

24319 Intermec Technologies Corporation
6001 36th Ave W
Everett, WA 98203-1264
425-348-2600
Fax: 425-267-2983 info@intermec.com
Labels and tags
President: Tom Miller
CEO: Patrick J Byrne
Chief Technical Officer: Arvin Danielson
Chairman: Larry D Brady
Senior Vice President of Sales and Marke: James McDonnell
Contact: Skip Allen
skipa@foxinternet.com
Senior Vice President of Operations: Dennis Faerber
Estimated Sales: $50-100 Million
Number Employees: 1,000-4,999
Parent Co: Intermec

24320 Intermec/Norand Mobile Systems
6001 36th Avenue West
Everett, WA 98203-12
425-348-2600
Fax: 425-355-9551 800-755-5505
info@intermec.com www.intermec.com
President: Tom Miller
Interim President, Chief Executive Offic: Allen Lauer
Senior Vice President of Solutions: Earl Thompson
Chief Technical Officer: Arvin Danielson
Senior Vice President of Sales and Marke: James McDonnell
Contact: Aaron Fu
afu@radiax.com
Senior Vice President of Operations: Dennis Faerber
Estimated Sales: $1-5 Million
Number Employees: 250-499

24321 Intermex Products USA
1375 Ave S.
Suite 300
Grand Prairie, TX 75050
972-988-1333
Fax: 972-660-5941 800-508-8475
ravera@cydsa.com www.intermexproducts.com
Cydsa, cellophane, bi-oriented polypropylene, coextrusions, printed and laminated plastic films
Contact: Juan Carlos
jcarlos@intermexproducts.com
Estimated Sales: $5-10 Million
Number Employees: 5-9
Parent Co: La Torre

24322 Intermold Corporation
30 Old Mill Rd
Greenville, SC 29607
864-627-0300
Fax: 864-627-0005 sales@intermoldcorp.com
www.intermoldcorp.com
Manufacturer and exporter of plastic injection molding products including bakery proofer cups; custom molding for the baking industry available
President: Alan Butcher
sales@intermoldcorp.com
VP: Jane Butcher
Estimated Sales: $1-2.5 Million
Number Employees: 10-19
Square Footage: 32000

24323 International Adhesive Coating
6 Industrial Dr
PO Box 240
Windham, NH 03087-2020
603-893-1894
Fax: 603-898-9025 800-253-4450
sales@itctapes.com
Manifactures a complete line of double coated, single-coated, transfer tapes, bag sealing, foam and high tack/low tack products along with a wide range of coating and converting capabilities.
Manager: Dennis Salois
dsalois@itctapes.com
Estimated Sales: $5-10 Million
Number Employees: 20-49

24324 International Approval Services
8501 East Pleasant Valley Road
Cleveland, OH 44131-5516
216-524-4990
Fax: 216-642-3463 877-235-9791
Testing service for gas powered cooking equipment

President & CEO: Ash Sahi
EVP, Finance & Administration: Esteban De Bernardis
Regional Vice President, U.S. & Mexico: Rich Weiser
EVP, Science & Engineering: Helene Vaillancourt
Chief Operating Officer: Magali Depras
Estimated Sales: $1-5 Million
Number Employees: 100-249
Parent Co: CSA

24325 International Automation
332 Ramapo Valley Road
Oakland, NJ 7004
     201-651-0500
  Fax: 201-760-9960 www.iaiusa.com
Checkweighers
President: Mark Schultz
Estimated Sales: $.5-1 million
Number Employees: 5-9

24326 International Carbonic
P.O.Box 578
Adelanto, CA 92301
     760-246-3900
  Fax: 760-246-4044 www.ici.us
Carbonated beverage dispensing equipment, including carbonators, valves, fittings and systems; complete sheet metal facility
President: Joe Suarez
Estimated Sales: $20-50 Million
Number Employees: 20-49

24327 International Coatings
2925 Lucy Ln
Franklin Park, IL 60131
     847-451-0279
  Fax: 847-451-0379 800-624-8919
Flooring, coatings
President: Mike Kramer
Marketing Director: Raymond Hurley
Contact: Eileen Henquinet
ehenq@icocoat.com
Estimated Sales: $10-20 Million
Number Employees: 10-19

24328 International Cold Storage
215 E 13th St
Andover, KS 67002-9329
     316-218-4100
  Fax: 316-733-2434 800-835-0001
     www.icsco.com
Walk-in coolers and freezers; exporter of walk-in coolers
President: Matt Madeksza
CFO: Carlos Tlusty
carlos.tlusty@carrier.utc.com
VP, Sales, West: Jim Cook
VP, Sales, Midwest: Mark Norvold
Plant Manager: Jay Risley
Estimated Sales: $10-20 Million
Number Employees: 100-249
Square Footage: 160000
Parent Co: Tyler Refrigeration Company

24329 International ContainerSystems
5401 W Kennedy Boulevard
Suite 711
Tampa, FL 33609-2447
     813-287-8940
  Fax: 813-286-2070 800-444-4274
Carton and container systems
Estimated Sales: $1-2.5 Million
Number Employees: 5-9

24330 International Cooling Systems
300 Granton Drive
Richmond Hill, ON L4B 1H7
Canada
     416-213-5566
  Fax: 416-213-9666 888-213-5566
Manufacturer, importer and exporter of turnkey process cooling systems, cooling towers, chillers, flake and pumpable flow ice machines and water/fluid recirculation stations
President: Victor Gardiman
VP: Otto Novak
Plant Manager: Steve Novak
Number Employees: 10-19
Square Footage: 96000

24331 International Envelope Company
2 Tabas Ln
Exton, PA 19341
     610-363-0900
     Fax: 610-363-2999
Specialty mailing envelopes and filing products
CEO: Sandy Moyer
VP Marketing: Sandy Moyer
Contact: Jennifer Dyer
jdyer@goiec.com
Estimated Sales: $1-5 Million
Number Employees: 250-499
Square Footage: 300000
Parent Co: American Business Products

24332 International Environmental Solutions
6860 Gulfport Blvd S.
Suite 131
South Pasadena, FL 33707-2108
     727-573-1676
  Fax: 727-573-0747 800-972-8348
davidleeti@aol.com www.drycamping.com
Automatic faucet controls
President: Steve Gordon
Estimated Sales: Less than $500,000
Number Employees: 20-49
Square Footage: 16000
Brands:
 Ez Flo
 Med Flo
 Quik Flo
 Sani-Flow

24333 International EquipmentTrading
960 Woodlands Parkway
Vernon Hills, IL 60061-3103
     847-913-0777
  Fax: 847-913-0785 800-438-4522
  info@ietltd.com www.ietltd.com
Buy, lease, rent, trade, sell refurbished analytical isntruments
President: Turgay Kaya
Contact: Ceylan Bilgin
ck@ietltd.com
Estimated Sales: $3-5 Million
Number Employees: 5-9

24334 International Flavors &Fragrances Inc.
521 W. 57th St.
New York, NY 10019
     212-765-5500
  Fax: 212-708-7132 www.iff.com
Scents and flavors.
Chairman/CEO: Andreas Fibig
Executive VP/Integration Officer: Richard O'Leary
Divisional CEO, Scent: Nicolas Mirzayantz
Divisional CEO, Taste: Matthias Haeni
Executive VP, Operations: Francisco Fortanet
Year Founded: 1889
Estimated Sales: $5.1 Billion
Number Employees: 13,600
Number of Products: 38K
Type of Packaging: Bulk

24335 International Food Information Service
The Granary, Bridge Farm
Reading Road, Arborfield
Reading, Berkshire, RG2 9HT
UK
Organization provides high quality food science information products and services to food industry professionals worldwide which includes FSTA/Food Science and Technolcogy Abstracts and Food Science Central. Telephone number is +44118 988 3895 and Fax is +44 118 988 5056.
Marketing Director: Danielle Woolley
Other Locations:
 International Food Information Srvc
 Shinfield/Reading UK

24336 International Food Products
150 Larkin Williams Industrial Ct
Fenton, MO 63026
     800-227-8427
  info@ifpc.com www.ifpc.com
Food ingredients and additives

Chairman: Fred Brown, Sr.
CEO: Clayton Brown
VP, Finance: Kathy Langan
VP, Sales & Marketing: Jamie Moritz
VP, Quality & Regulatory: Mary Ellen Rowland
VP, Manufacturing: Mark Warren
VP, Supply Chain: Jennifer Hoerchler
Year Founded: 1974
Estimated Sales: $150 Million
Number Employees: 50-200
Square Footage: 68000
Type of Packaging: Consumer, Food Service
Other Locations:
 St. Louis MO
 Joplin MO
 Kansas City MO
 Houston TX
 Dallas TX
 Laredo TX
 San Antonio TX
 Indianapolis IN
 Cleveland OH
 Denver CO
 Atlanta GA
 Spokane WA
 Plant City FL
Brands:
 Dairy House Chocolate Dairy Powder©
 Dairy House© Milk Flavors
 Dairy House© Stabalizers
 Dairy House© Vitamins
 Ingredion©

24337 International Foodservice Manufacturers' Association
180 N Stetson Ave
Suite 850
Chicago, IL 60601-6766
     312-540-4400
  Fax: 312-540-4401 ifma@ifmaworld.com
     www.ifmaworld.com
President & CEO: Larry Oberkfell
Chief Financial Officer: Jennifer Tarulis
VP, Member Value: Mike Schwartz
Marketing Director: Cassie Kupfer Norris
VP, Sales & Member Services: Anthony R DePaolo
VP, Communications: Janet Rustigan
Estimated Sales: $20-50 Million
Number Employees: 10-19

24338 International Fresh-CutProduce Association
1600 Duke Street
Suite 440
Alexandria, VA 22314-3400
     703-299-6282
     Fax: 703-299-6288
www.creativew.com/sites/ifpa/index_main.html
Represents leaders in the fresh-cut produce industry who specialize in today's growing fresh food category.
President: Edith Garrett
VP, Technical and Regulatory Affairs: James Roman Gorny, PhD.
Director, Communications: Ken Hodge
Director, Marketing: Loren Queen
Director Membership: Reta Jones
Administrator: Seneta Burns
Number Employees: 5-9

24339 International Fruit Marketing
1201 S Orlando Ave # 340
Winter Park, FL 32789-7107
     407-628-1121
  Fax: 407-628-1829 intlfruit@aol.com
Fruit drinks, pure concentrates and citrus purees
President/CEO: Gene Hays
CFO: Robert Keyes
Vice President: Leland Anderson
Estimated Sales: $13 Million+
Number Employees: 1-4
Parent Co: SECO & Golden 100

24340 International Group Inc
2875 N Main St
Oshkosh, WI 54901-1517
     920-233-5500
     Fax: 920-233-4345
Petroleum wax and wax blends, hot melt coatings and cheese wax
Manager: Gary Fraaza
gfraaza@igtwax.com
General Manager: Gary Fraaza
Production Manager: Tom Brunner

Number Employees: 20-49
Square Footage: 120000

24341 International Inflight Food Service Association
455 S 4th St # 650
Louisville, KY 40202-2554
502-583-3783
Fax: 502-589-3602 ifsa@hqtrs.com
End to end direct marketing provider.
President: David Cawood
Director Administration: Aimee Spigner
Executive of Administration: Phillip Cooke
Estimated Sales: $5-10 Million
Number Employees: 50-99

24342 International Ingredients Corporation
4240 Utah Street
Saint Louis, MO 63116-1820
314-776-2700
Fax: 314-776-3395 iicag@iicag.com
www.iicag.com
Processing of food plant waste
President: Bill Holtgrieve
Chairman: Fred E Brown Jr
Contact: Lisa Filkins
lfilkins@ifpc.com
Estimated Sales: $30-50 Million
Number Employees: 130

24343 International Knife & Saw
1435 N Cashua Dr
Florence, SC 29501-6950
843-662-6345
Fax: 843-664-1103 800-354-9872
iks@iksinc.com www.iksinc.com
Manufacturer and exporter of fruit and vegetable
slicing machinery; also, machine knives
President: Don Weeks
Vice President of Division: Terry Isaacs
Vice President, Metal & Printing Divisio: Jim
Ranson
Sales: Warren Balderson
Manager: Robb Kirkpatrick
rkirkpatrick@iksinc.com
Vice President, Finance & Manufacturing: Mike
Gray
Purchasing Manager of Materials: Sarah Strother
Estimated Sales: $60 Million
Number Employees: 50-99

24344 International Kosher Supervision
351 Keller E Price Street
Suite 200
Keller, TX 76248
817-337-4700
Fax: 817-337-4901 www.ikckosher.com
Kosher food certification agency with rabbinical
staff
Rabbinical Administration: Rabbi Dovid Jenkins
General Manager: Jerry Dillig
Parent Co: Texas K International

24345 International MachineryXchnge
214 N Main St
Deerfield, WI 53531-9644
608-764-5481
Fax: 608-764-8240 800-279-0191
sales@imexchange.com www.imexchange.com
Manufacturer and exporter of re-manufactured ma-
chinery including refrigeration, cheese making, cen-
trifuges, compressors and heat exchangers; also,
tanks and custom control systems
President: Greg Mergen
sales@imexchange.com
Sales Director: George Bamman
Estimated Sales: $5-10 Million
Number Employees: 10-19
Square Footage: 80000

24346 International Meat Inspection Consultants
P.O.Box 264
Germantown, MD 20875-0264
301-570-1058
Fax: 240-821-5939 imic@thefoodtrainer.com
www.thefoodtrainer.com
Consultants, importing/exporting, label expediting
President: Barbara Bennett
CFO: John Cucl
Estimated Sales: $.5-1 million
Number Employees: 1-4

24347 International Media & Cultures
1250 South Parker Road Ste. 203
Denver, CO 80231
303-337-4028
Fax: 303-337-5140 mantha@earthnet.net
www.askimac.com
Cheese anti-caking agent and starter media
President: Malireddy Reddy
Plant Manager: Ed Price
Estimated Sales: $5-10 Million
Number Employees: 10-19

24348 International Molded Packaging Corporation
206 Central Main Street
Central City, SD 57754-2070
605-578-2500
Fax: 605-578-3933 800-307-2194
www.impakcorp.com
President and CEO: Rod Galland
Estimated Sales: Below $5,000,000
Number Employees: 10

24349 International Omni-Pac Corporation
2079 Wright Ave
La Verne, CA 91.750-5822
909-593-2833
Fax: 909-593-2829 bobdavis@omni-pac.com
www.omni-pac.com
Manufacturer and exporter of packaging systems
and juice and soft drink bottle carriers
President: Richard Erickson
Sales Manager: Bob Davis
Contact: Bill Johnston
bjohnston@omni-pac.com
Estimated Sales: Below $5 Million
Number Employees: 5-9
Square Footage: 40000

24350 International PackagingMachinery
PO Box 8597
Naples, FL 34101-8597
941-643-2020
Fax: 941-643-2708 800-237-6496
Manufacturer and exporter of stretch wrapping ma-
chinery including film tensioners and stretch film
delivery systems
Estimated Sales: $5-10 Million
Number Employees: 20-49
Square Footage: 42000
Brands:
Ipm
Roller-Brake
Uni-Tension

24351 International PackagingNetwork
409 N Jefferson Street
Kearney, MO 64060-8379
816-628-3002
Fax: 800-247-4904 800-932-3597
High performance and flexibility polyolefin film
Estimated Sales: $500,000-$1 Million
Number Employees: 1-4

24352 (HQ)International Paper BoxMachine Company
PO Box 787
Nashua, NH 03061-0787
603-889-6651
Fax: 603-882-2865
Manufacturer, exporter and importer of carton fold-
ing and gluing machinery; also, corrugated convert-
ers including liquid-tight packaging
President: Hugh McAdam
Marketing Manager: Larry Macko
Marketing Communications Manager: Michael
Sutcliffe
Estimated Sales: $20-50 Million
Number Employees: 100-249
Square Footage: 165000

24353 International Paper Co.
6400 Poplar Avenue
Memphis, TN 38197
www.internationalpaper.com
Fiber-based packaging, pulp and paper. Products include coated paperboard, containerboard, corrugated
packaging, and other foodservice packaging
material.

Chairman/Chief Executive Officer: Mark Sutton
SVP, Paper the Americas: W. Michael Amick, Jr.
SVP, Corporate Development: John Sims
SVP/Chief Financial Officer: Tim Nicholls
SVP, Industrial Packaging the Americas:
Jean-Michel Ribieras
SVP/Human Resources/Global Citizenship: Thomas
Plath
SVP/General Counsel/Corporate Secretary: Sharon
Ryan
SVP/Global Cellulose Fibers: Catherine Slater
SVP/North American Container: Gegory Wanta
Year Founded: 1898
Estimated Sales: $21.7 Billion
Number Employees: 56,000

24354 International Patterns,Inc.
50 Inez Dr
Bay Shore, NY 11706-2238
631-952-2000
Fax: 516-938-1215
Manufacturer and exporter of illuminated and
nonilluminated menu, changeable letter and write-on
boards, nonneon signs, banners, point of purchase
displays, tray stands, ice-free wine coolers and youth
chairs
President: Shelley Beckwith
shelleyb@u.washington.edu
CFO: Shelly Beckwi
Vice President: Shellay Beckwith
R & D: Paul Kaplan
VP Marketing: Murray Gottieb
VP Sales: Andrew Replan
Production Manager: Ran Alvaeri
Purchasing Manager: Nancy St. Nicholas
Estimated Sales: $5-10 Million
Number Employees: 50-99
Number of Brands: 1
Number of Products: 50
Square Footage: 140000
Type of Packaging: Food Service
Brands:
City Lites
Comet
Grandstand
Lite Writer
Magnetic Menumaster
Menu Master
Menu Master

24355 International Polymers Corp
426 S Aubrey St
Allentown, PA 18109-2769
610-437-5463
Fax: 610-437-1799 800-526-0953
ipc@fast.net www.ipc.org.nz
Reprocessed polyethylene, polypropylene and poly-
styrene
President: David Bates
CEO: Brian Taschler
btaschler@ipc.org
CFO: Frank Pope
Marketing: Bob Barette
VP Production: Blair Manning
Estimated Sales: $20-50 Million
Number Employees: 50-99

24356 International Process Plants-IPP
17 Marlen Drive
Hamilton, NJ 08691-1634
609-586-8004
Fax: 609-586-0002 michaelj@ippe.com
www.ippe.com
Buyers and sellers of new, rebuilt and used process
equipment and plants worldwide. Has an inventory
of over 20,000 items that allow them to offer
on-time and on-budget process solutions
President: Ronald Gale
Executive VP: Jan Gale
VP Sales: Michael Joachim
Number Employees: 500-999

24357 International Reserve Equipment Corporation
46 Chestnut Avenue
Clarendon Hills, IL 60514-1238
708-531-0680
Fax: 630-325-7045
Manufacturer, importer and exporter of food processing equipment including centrifuges, separators,
dryers, screeners, mills, filters, mixers and blenders;
also, pollution control, wastewater treatment and
sludge de-wateringequipment

Owner: Robert Mertz
Marketing Manager: Thomas Mertz
Estimated Sales: $1-5 Million
Number Employees: 2
Brands:
  Centrifuges
  Dewater Equipment
  Filtration Equipment
  Screeners
  Separators

24358 International Roasting Systems
3450 N State St
Ukiah, CA 95482-3055

707-462-6164
Fax: 707-462-5258
Cleaners, blending and mixing equipment (coffee), afterburners, automatic controls, grinders, bin silo systems and storage, bin vibrators, bulk silo services, roasters, smoke control equipment and afterburners, quality controlinstruments and conveying equipment
Owner: Steve Pardini
Management Consultant: Jane Pfeiffer
Estimated Sales: Less Than $500,000
Number Employees: 5-9

24359 International Smoking Systems
23 Water St
PO Box 480
Ashburnham, MA 01430

978-827-3160
Fax: 978-827-3162 800-269-2367
www.intlsmokingsystems.com
Provides smoking and defrosting kilns for salmon and fish processing needs
President: Mark Carlisle
Estimated Sales: Under $500,000
Number Employees: 2

24360 International Tank & Pipe Co
PO Box 590
Clackamas, OR 97015-0590

503-288-0011
Fax: 503-493-0372 888-988-0011
Info@WoodTankandPipe.com
woodtankandpipe.com
Manufacture wood stove tanks and pipe. Install new wood stove tanks and pipe and repair existing tanks and pipe.
President/CEO: Michael Bye
CFO: Jacqueline Bye
R&D/Purchasing Director: Kent Huschka
Quality Control: Matthew Bye
Marketing/Sales/Production: Michael Bye
Estimated Sales: $2-4 Million
Number Employees: 12
Number of Brands: 2
Square Footage: 40000
Type of Packaging: Consumer
Other Locations:
  Portland OR
Brands:
  International Tank & Pipe
  National Tank & Pipe

24361 International Thermal Dispensers
67 Batterymarch St # 600
Boston, MA 02110-3211

617-239-3600
Fax: 617-239-3650 www.atlanticretail.com
Espresso, hot and cold food vending carts and concession equipment
Managing Partner: Bryan W. Anderson
Partner: Brian Mc Donald
Partner: Ben Starr
Broker: James C. Bagley
Broker: Adam Cirel
Broker: Tom Sibley
Broker: Brian Roache
Sales Manager: Anne McCormick
Estimated Sales: $300,000-500,000
Number Employees: 5-9

24362 International Tray Pads
3299 NC Highway 5
P.O. Box 307
Aberdeen, NC 28315-8619

910-944-1800
Fax: 910-944-7356 www.pactiv.com
Manufacturer and supplier of tray pads for meats and case liners for produce and dairy products.
Contact: Larry Norpoth
lrnorpoth@traypads.com
Number Employees: 20-49

24363 International Wax Refining Company
3 Mountain Blvd
Warren, NJ 07059-5613

908-561-2500
Fax: 908-561-7411 www.villagetravel.com
Bee's wax
President: J D Panella
Executive VP: L Powell
Number Employees: 10-19

24364 International Wood Industries
12027 Three Lakes Rd
Snohomish, WA 98290

360-568-3185
Fax: 509-965-6141 800-922-6141
www.nepapallet.com
Manufacturer and exporter of skids, wooden pallets and bins, couch boxes, baggage boxes, household goods
President: Denton Sherry
General Manager: Joe Carlos
Estimated Sales: $10-20 Million
Number Employees: 100-249
Parent Co: International Wood Industries

24365 (HQ)Interplast
1400 Lytle Road
Troy, OH 45373-9401

937-332-1110
Fax: 937-332-0672
Manufacturer and exporter of plastic custom-injection moldings
Sales Manager: Bob Garton
Contact: Jared Langman
jlangman@interplastinc.com
Estimated Sales: $5-10 Million
Number Employees: 50-99

24366 Interroll Corp
3000 Corporate Dr
Wilmington, NC 28405-7422

910-799-1100
Fax: 910-392-3822 800-830-9680
usa-sales@interroll.com www.interroll.us
Manufacturer and exporter of conveyor components and flow storage systems
President: Tim Mcgill
t.mcgill@interroll.com
VP: Richard Keely
VP Sales/Marketing: Steve Vineis
Estimated Sales: $20-50 Million
Number Employees: 100-249
Square Footage: 250
Parent Co: Interroll Holding AG
Brands:
  Driveroll
  Joki
  Logix
  Taperhex Gold

24367 Interroll Corp
3000 Corporate Dr
Wilmington, NC 28405-7422

910-799-1100
Fax: 910-392-3822 800-830-9680
www.interroll.us
President: Tim Mcgill
t.mcgill@interroll.com
VP: Richard Keely
Estimated Sales: $20 Million
Number Employees: 100-249

24368 Interstate Monroe Machinery
2230 1st Avenue S
Seattle, WA 98134-1408

206-682-4870
Fax: 313-891-5449
Manufacturer and exporter of controls and instrumentation equipment
General Manager: Larry Gruendike
Estimated Sales: $1-2.5 Million
Number Employees: 9
Square Footage: 30000
Parent Co: Statco Engineering & Fabrication

24369 Interstate Packaging
2285 Highway 47 N
White Bluff, TN 37187-4126

615-797-9000
Fax: 615-797-9411 800-251-1072
ldoochin@interstatepkg.com
www.interstatepkg.com

Manufacturer and exporter of pressure sensitive labels and poly bags; manufacturer of printed flexible films
President: Michael Doochin
mdoochin@interstatepkg.com
Sales Manager: Lawrence Doochin
Customer Service Representative: Robert Garlock
Purchasing Manager: Liz Gilliam
Estimated Sales: $20-50 Million
Number Employees: 250-499
Square Footage: 100000
Type of Packaging: Consumer

24370 Interstate Showcase & Fixture Company
PO Box 402
West Orange, NJ 07052-0402

973-483-5555
Fax: 973-669-0200
Store fixtures, showcases, wallcases and refrigerated candy cases
CEO: L Miller
Estimated Sales: Less than $500,000
Number Employees: 1-4
Square Footage: 50000

24371 Intertape Polymer Group
741 4th St
Menasha, WI 54952-2801

920-725-4335
Fax: 920-729-4217 800-558-5006
www.itape.com
Manufacturer and exporter of printed and plain pressure sensitive and gummed tapes: kraft paper and reinforced carton sealing; pressure sensitive carton sealing machine systems
President: Dale McSween
Manager: Bob Mc Donald
rmcdonal@itape.com
Product Manager: Steve Pistro
Product Manager: Tom Zettler
Plant Manager: John Cullen
Estimated Sales: $2.5-5 Million
Number Employees: 100-249
Parent Co: Intertape Polymer Group

24372 Intertape Polymer Group
100 Paramount Dr
Suite 300
Sarasota, FL 34232

888-898-7834
www.itape.com
Manufacturer of paper- and film-based, pressure-sensitive and water-activated tapes
President & CEO: Gregory Yull
CFO: Jeffrey Crystal
SVP, Sales: Shawn Nelson
SVP, Operations: Douglas Nalette
Year Founded: 1981
Number Employees: 2,200

24373 (HQ)Intertech Corp
3240 N Ohenry Blvd
Greensboro, NC 27405-3808

336-621-1891
Fax: 336-621-1893 800-364-2255
www.ezgowalker-ball.com
Plastic bottles
President: Jack Worsham
VP: Leon Worsham
VP: Jim Sitton
Estimated Sales: $5-10 Million
Number Employees: 50-99
Square Footage: 232000

24374 (HQ)Intertek USA
70 Codman Hill Rd
Boxborough, MA 01719-1737

978-263-7086
Fax: 978-264-9403 800-967-5352
icenter@intertek.com www.intertek.com
Laboratory specializing in the testing of food service equipment
President: Greegg Tiemann
Chief Executive Officer: Wolfhart Hauser
Division Executive Vice President: Andrew Swift
Marketing Director: Erik Holladay
Business Development Manager: Carlos Velasco
Estimated Sales: $30-50 Million
Number Employees: 50-99
Square Footage: 150000
Other Locations:
  Intertak Testing Services
  Cortland NY

24375 Intralox LLC
301 Plantation Rd
Harahan, LA 70123-5326
504-733-0463
Fax: 504-734-0063 800-535-8848
www.intralox.com
Manufacturer and exporter of USDA accepted and
FDA compliant modular plastic screw conveyors
and conveyor belting
President: James Lapeyre Jr
Marketing Manager: Michelle Waite
National Sales Manager: Da Waters
Number Employees: 500-999
Parent Co: Laitram Corporation
Brands:
Intralox, Inc.

24376 Intralox LLC
301 Plantation Rd
Harahan, LA 70123-5326
504-733-0463
Fax: 504-734-0063 www.intralox.com
Designers and manufacturers of conveyor belt sys-
tems for the meat, poultry, seafood and beverage in-
dustries.
President: James M Lapeyre Jr
Number Employees: 500-999

24377 Intralytix
701 E Pratt St # 400
Rm 4036
Baltimore, MD 21202-3190
410-625-1224
Fax: 410-625-2506 877-489-7424
info@intralytix.com www.intralytix.com
Produces bacteriophage-based products to control
bacterial pathogens in food processing
Number Employees: 10-19

24378 Intrex
149 Grassy Plain St
Bethel, CT 06801-2851
203-792-7400
Fax: 203-778-3991
Waste receptacles, smoking urns and planters; cus-
tom design available
President: Steven Decker
CEO: Mary Edgerton
Quality Control: Jim Patnaude
Chairman: Philip Feinman
Estimated Sales: Below $5 Million
Number Employees: 20-49

24379 Introdel Products
1339 Industrial Drive
PO Box 723
Itasca, IL 60143-1847
630-773-4250
Fax: 907-562-8517 800-323-4772
Water conditioning and filtration products including
nonchemical cartridges for use in steamers, combi
ovens, warewashing equipment, ice machines, water
wash hoods, coffee and tea equipment, post mix
applications, etc
Estimated Sales: $500,000-$1,000,000
Number Employees: 19

24380 Invensys APV Products
10900 Equity Drive
Houston, TX 77041
713-329-1600
Fax: 920-648-1441 apvproducts.us@apv.com
Supplier of a wide range of pumps, valves, heat
exchangers and homogenisers designed for use in
the food, dairy and brewing industries
Executive Director: Jim Keene
Marketing Communications Manager: Antonella
Crimi
Contact: Frank Alphonsoo
frank.alphonsoo@invensys.com
Parent Co: Invensys Limited
Type of Packaging: Food Service, Bulk

24381 Invensys Process Systems
5100 River Road
3rd Floor
Schiller Park, IL 60176-1058
847-678-4300
Fax: 847-678-4300 888-278-9087
answers@apv.com www.apv.com
Project Sales Manager: Enrique Hinojosa
Contact: Anna Butorac
anna.butorac@invensys.com

24382 Invictus Systems Corporation
5505 Seminary Rd Apt 2210n
Suite 202
Falls Church, VA 22041-3544
Fax: 703-503-8064
www.govcon.com/storefronts/invictus
Manufacturer and exporter of custom computer soft-
ware for the food industry including facts panel cre-
ation, nutrition calculators, formula costing, time to
market analysis and operations planning. Our ser-
vices include custom websoftware for both internal
and external use
President: Anthony Latta
CFO: Kim Witney
Chief Scientist: Kenneth Latta
Quality Control: Benson Wetta
Business Developer: Scott Weaver
Estimated Sales: Below $5 Million
Number Employees: 20-49
Number of Products: 3
Square Footage: 30000
Type of Packaging: Bulk

24383 Iowa Rotocast Plastics Inc
1712 Moellers Dr
Decorah, IA 52101-7304
563-382-9636
Fax: 563-382-3016 800-553-0050
irp@irpinc.com
Portable bars, special event carts and super coolers
President: Floyd Mount
VP Sales: Steve Rolfs
Estimated Sales: $10 Million
Number Employees: 100-249

24384 (HQ)Ipec
185 Northgate Circle
New Castle, PA 16105
800-377-4732
Fax: 724-658-3054 www.ipec.biz
Supplier of plastic closures and capping equipment
President: Joseph Giordano Jr
Sales Manager: Robert Harding
Estimated Sales: $22 Million
Number Employees: 75

24385 Irby
2913 S Church St
Rocky Mount, NC 27803
252-442-0154
Fax: 252-442-4909 www.irby.com
Custom fabricated metal food service equipment in-
cluding conveyors, racks, stampers, welders, parts,
etc
President: Mike Wigton
Chief Financial Officer: John Honigfort
Vice President of Supply Chain: Dave Armstrong
Vice President of Sales: Chad Cravens
Chief Operating Officer: Andy Waring
Plant Manager: Tony Whitley
Estimated Sales: $.5-1 million
Number Employees: 1-4
Square Footage: 112000

24386 Iron Out
7201 Engle Rd
Fort Wayne, IN 46804-2228
260-483-2519
Fax: 260-483-2277 888-476-6688
info@summitbrands.com
Cleaning products
Owner: Joel Harter
Executive VP: Stan Stuart
Contact: Mike Brown
mbrown@summitbrands.com
Estimated Sales: $5-10 Million
Number Employees: 5-9
Brands:
All Out
Drain Out
Super Iron Out
Super Iron Out Dignio
Yellow Out

24387 Ironwood Displays
PO Box 632
Niles, MI 49120-0632
231-683-8500
Fax: 231-683-6803
Store fixtures and wooden and plexiglass display
racks
Director Marketing: Judy Truesdell
Number Employees: 25

24388 Irresistible Cookie Jar
PO Box 3230
Hayden Lake, ID 83835-3230
208-664-1261
Fax: 208-667-1347
service@irresistiblecookiejar.com
Cookie and muffin mixes, cookie cutters and decora-
tions
President: Wanda Hall
Estimated Sales: $300,000-500,000
Number Employees: 10
Brands:
Boyds' Kissa Bearhugs
Mimi's Muffins
Susan Winget

24389 Irvine Analytical Labs
10 Vanderbilt
Irvine, CA 92618
949-951-4425
Fax: 949-951-4909 877-445-6554
info@ialab.com www.irvinepharma.com
Laboratory offering chemical and microbiological
analysis for food and food supplements
President: Iassad Kazeminy
CEO: Assad J. Kazeminy
Lab Director: Assad Kazeminy
Regional Sales Representative: JoAnne Nordel
Contact: Tandis Kazeminy
tandis.kazeminy@irvinepharma.com
Business Development Manager: Rambod Omid
Estimated Sales: Less than $500,000
Number Employees: 50-99
Square Footage: 50000
Parent Co: Irvine Analytical Labs

24390 Irvine Pharmaceutical Services
10 Vanderbilt
Irvine, CA 92618
949-951-4425
Fax: 949-951-4909 877-445-6554
custserv@irvinepharma.com
www.irvinepharma.com
Contract laboratory, chemical and microbiological
testing services
President: Iassad Kazeminy
Laboratory Director: Abbass Kamalizad
Contact: Ayla Acosta
ayla.acosta@irvinepharma.com
Business Development Manager: Gregory
McLaughlin
Estimated Sales: $10-20 Million
Number Employees: 50-99

24391 Irwin Research & Development
2601 W J St
Yakima, WA 98902-5291
509-248-0494
Fax: 509-248-3503
crichardson@irwinresearch.com
www.irwinresearch.com
Thermoforming equipment, tooling and granulators.
President: Jere Irwin
Sales and Marketing Representative: Craig
Richardson
Estimated Sales: $10-20 Million
Number Employees: 100-249

24392 Isbre Holding Corporation
225 Glen Rd
Woodcliff Lake, NJ 07677
201-802-0005
Fax: 201-802-0006 info@isbre.com
Bottled spring drinking water.
President: Stevan A Sandberg
Regional Director of Sales: Rene Skanning

24393 Island Delights, Inc.
5104 Greenwich Road
Seville, OH 44273
330-769-2800
Fax: 330-769-3935 866-877-4100
acrall@islanddelights.com
www.islanddelights.com
Coconut candies
Sales: Ann Crall
Sales: Greg Miller
Estimated Sales: $5-10 Million
Number Employees: 15

24394 Island Oasis Frozen Cocktail
3400 Millington Rd.
Beloit, WI 53511
508-660-1177
Fax: 508-660-1435 800-777-4752
www.kerryfoodservice.com
Non-alcoholic beverage mixes; ice shavers and blenders
President & CEO: Gerry Behan
Marketing Director: Abhishek Trivedi
VP of Global & Strategic Accounts: Michael Walsh
Estimated Sales: $20-50 Million
Number Employees: 100-249
Number of Products: 16
Square Footage: 25000
Parent Co: Kerry Food Services
Brands:
    Sb-3x

24395 Island Poly
514 Grand Blvd
Westbury, NY 11590-4712
516-338-4433
Fax: 516-338-4405 800-338-4433
Gloves including vinyl, natural latex, poly and cut resistant; also, natural rubber nitrile, neoprene and poly aprons, bouffant head caps and beard covers
President: Dan Grinberg
Controller: Denise Ramo
Director Marketing: Jane Donnelly
Estimated Sales: $2.5-5 Million
Number Employees: 20-49
Brands:
    Foodhandler
    Jobhandler

24396 Island Scallops
5552 Island Highway W
Qualicum Beach, BC V9K 2C8
Canada
250-757-9811
Fax: 250-757-8370 www.islandscallops.com
Fresh and frozen scallops; marine research hatchery
President/CEO: Robert Saunders
R&D: Barb Bunting
Processing Manager: Lorraine Hopps
Estimated Sales: $1 Million
Number Employees: 10
Type of Packaging: Consumer, Food Service

24397 Isotherm Inc
7401 Commercial Blvd E
Arlington, TX 76001-7142
817-472-9922
Fax: 817-472-5878 info@iso-therm.com
www.iso-therm.com
President: Zahid Ayub
info@iso-therm.com
Engineering Manager: Adnan Ayub
Production Manager: Al Faisal
Estimated Sales: $5-10 Million
Number Employees: 10-19

24398 It's A Corker
P.O.Box 11549
Chattanooga, TN 37401-2549
423-756-1200
Fax: 423-266-5913
Wine industry closures
President: Robert P Corker
Executive Assistant, Chief Executive Off: Carolyn Stringer
Controller: Beth Robertson
CEO: Kim Hudson White
Estimated Sales: $.5-1 million
Number Employees: 5-9

24399 Itac Label & Tag Corp
179 Lexington Ave
Brooklyn, NY 11216-1114
718-625-2148
Fax: 718-625-3806
Manufacturer and exporter of labels including pressure sensitive, magnetic, shipping, bar code and file folder; also, tags and decals
President: Sidney Alder
CEO: James H C Tao
Estimated Sales: $5-10 Million
Number Employees: 10-19
Square Footage: 28000
Brands:
    Ul

24400 Italgi USA
2 Titan Drive
Chestnut Ridge, NY 10977-6727
800-706-9338
Fax: 845-371-6145
Manufacturer of professional pasta machines

24401 Italtech
3425 NW 112 STREET
Miami, FL 33167
305-256-9651
Fax: 305-685-0990 800-547-5075
Pasta and noodle equipment, extruders, dryers, mixers, dies, pasteurizers, noodle cutters, sheeters, Italian equipment for confectionary industry
Engineering Director: Romolo Battistini
Estimated Sales: $2.5-5 Million
Number Employees: 1-4

24402 Item Products
16111 Park Entry Drive
Suite 100
Houston, TX 77041-4077
281-893-0100
Fax: 281-893-4836 800-333-4932
Manufacturer and exporter of carts and storage racks; also, consultant specializing in the design of custom machinery
Marketing Coordinator: Claudia Sears
National Marketing Manager: Jim Boyd
Estimated Sales: $10-20,000,000
Number Employees: 20-49
Square Footage: 60000

24403 Ito Packing Company
707 W South Ave
Reedley, CA 93654
559-638-2531
Fax: 559-638-2282 craigi@itopack.com
Packs and ships fruit
President: Craig Ito
Contact: James Ito
stephi93654@yahoo.com
Estimated Sales: $45 Million
Number Employees: 1,000-4,999
Brands:
    Red Jim
    Ufo

24404 Iug Business Solutions
132 Nassau Street
Room 1402
New York, NY 10038-2424
212-404-6168
Fax: 212-404-6180 dphelps@iug.net
Accessories/supplies i.e. picnic baskets, display fixtures.
Marketing: Edward Ip
Contact: Edward Ip
sales@iug.net
Chief Operating Officer: Michael Lazarus

24405 Ivarson Inc
3100 W Green Tree Rd
Milwaukee, WI 53209-2535
414-351-0700
Fax: 414-351-4551 sales@ivarsoninc.com
www.ivarsoninc.com
Manufacturer and exporter of process and packaging equipment and parts for butter, cheese and margarine industries; also, set-up boxes
President: Glenn Ivarson
givarson@ivarsoninc.com
Engineering Manager: Chuck Ellingson
Manager Technical Services: Jim Wycklendt
Sales Director: Mark Mullinix
Estimated Sales: $10-20 Million
Number Employees: 50-99
Square Footage: 100200

24406 Ivarson Inc
3100 W Green Tree Rd
Milwaukee, WI 53209-2535
414-351-0700
Fax: 414-351-4551 cellingson@ivarsoninc.com
www.ivarsoninc.com
Brining systems, butter processing equipment, cheese equipment, custom fabrication, cutting equipment, heat exchangers, scraped surface, margarine processing equipment, piping, fittings and tubing
President and R&D: Glenn Ivarson
givarson@ivarsoninc.com
CFO: Lennie Ivarson

Estimated Sales: $20-50 Million
Number Employees: 50-99

24407 Ives-Way Products
2030 N Nicole Ln
Round Lake Beach, IL 60073-2288
847-740-0658
Manufacturer and exporter of automatic can sealers for food, giftware or other sealed shipping containers
VP: Laura Ours
Estimated Sales: Less Than $500,000
Number Employees: 1-4
Square Footage: 4000

24408 Iwatani International Corporation of America
2200 Post oak Blvd.
Suite 1150
Houston, TX 77056
713-965-9970
Fax: 713-963-8497 800-775-5506
christopher@iwatani.com www.iwatani.com
Manufacturer and importer of portable butane stoves and induction cookers.
Regional Sales Manager: Karen Buquicchio
National Sales Manager: Gary Rodgers
Estimated Sales: $5-10 Million
Number Employees: 5-9
Parent Co: Iwatani International
Brands:
    Cassette Feu

24409 Izabel Lam International
204 Van Dyke Street
Brooklyn, NY 11231-1038
718-797-3983
Fax: 718-797-0030 info@izabellam.com
www.izabellam.com
Manufacturer and exporter of tabletop products including cutlery, dinnerware and drinkware
Estimated Sales: $500,000-$1 Million
Number Employees: 1-4
Square Footage: 112000
Type of Packaging: Consumer, Food Service
Brands:
    Glacier
    Golden Wind
    Morning Tide
    Mt. Rainbow Series
    Pale Wind
    Rushing Tide
    Sphere
    Splash
    Wind Over Water

24410 J & J Industries Inc
107 Gateway Rd
Bensenville, IL 60106-1950
630-595-8878
Fax: 630-595-9010
Nonmetallic die cut parts including gaskets and noise control materials
Owner: Jerry Haug
jgasket@hotmail.com
General Manager: Grant Cramer
Estimated Sales: $1-2.5 Million
Number Employees: 1-4

24411 J & J Window Sales Inc
600 Cepi Dr
Chesterfield, MO 63005-1244
636-532-3320
Fax: 636-532-3864
www.jandjsidingandwindows.com
Commercial awnings
President: Sue Gittemeier
sue@jandjwindows.com
Estimated Sales: $500,000-$1 Million
Number Employees: 10-19

24412 J & L Honing
4150 S Nevada St
St Francis, WI 53235-4515
414-744-9500
Fax: 414-744-9515 800-747-9501
contact@jlhoning.com www.jlhoning.com
Sanitary finishing for stainless steel tubing; also, ID polishing and honing of tubing and piping available
President: David Putney
VP: David Putney
Operations Manager: Dana Felske

Estimated Sales: Below $5 Million
Number Employees: 5-9
Square Footage: 60000

24413 J & M Industries Inc
300 Ponchatoula Pkwy
Ponchatoula, LA 70454-8311

985-386-6000
Fax: 985-386-9066 800-989-1002
www.jm-ind.com

Packaging supplies
President & CFO: Maurice Gaudet IV
marnold@jm-ind.com
Quality Control: Tim Sanders
Marketing Director: Ricky Brossard
Sales Exec: Mark Arnold
Plant Manager: Lance Powers
Plant Manager: Lance Powers
Purchasing: Ruth Sweeney
Estimated Sales: $20-50 Million
Number Employees: 100-249

24414 J & R Mfg Inc
820 W Kearney St # B
Mesquite, TX 75149-8804

972-289-0801
Fax: 972-288-9488 800-527-4831
sales@jrmanufacturing.com
www.jrmanufacturing.com

Manufacturer and exporter of barbecue pits, broilers,
grills, rotisseries and combo broiler/rotisseries
Vice President: Trent Hamrick
trent.hamrick@jrmanufacturing.net
VP: Larry Bellows
Estimated Sales: $5-10 Million
Number Employees: 20-49
Square Footage: 60000
Brands:
    Combo
    Fabuloso
    Little Red Smokehouse
    Oyler
    Smoke-Master
    Spinnin' Spits
    Wood Show

24415 J A Emilius Sons
537 Woodland Ave
Cheltenham, PA 19012-2195

215-379-6162
Fax: 215-663-8985 800-224-6162
sales@emilius.com www.emilius.com

Machine shop, conveyors, conveyor belt, confec-
tionery equipment confectionery, bakery, food pro-
cess equipment
Owner: Carl A Emilius Iii
CFO: Beth Emilius
Sales: Vince McCabe
Estimated Sales: $1-2.5 Million
Number Employees: 10-19
Number of Brands: 4

24416 J A Heilferty & Co
133 Cedar Ln # 104
Teaneck, NJ 07666-4416

201-836-5060
Fax: 201-836-3275 info@primepak.com
www.primepakcompany.com

Manufacturer, importer and exporter of HDPE and
LLDPE poly bags, sheeting, box and trash can lin-
ers, T-sacks and plain and printed bags
Owner: William Poppe
Chief Financial Officer: Mike Heilferty
VP Sales: William Heilferty
VP Operations: Chris Poppe
Estimated Sales: $20-50 Million
Number Employees: 20-49
Square Footage: 120000
Brands:
    Prime Liner
    Primeliner Sacks
    Primeliners

24417 J C Ford Co
901 S Leslie St
La Habra, CA 90631-6841

714-871-7361
Fax: 714-773-5827 www.jcford.com

Manufacturer and exporter of cooling conveyors,
corn masa feeders, tamale steamers and extruders,
tortilla and chip ovens, tortilla sheeter and corn
cookers and grinders

Sales: Robert Meyer
Customer Service: Desi Sanchez
Engineer: Thomas Dosch
Estimated Sales: $5-10 Million
Number Employees: 5-9
Square Footage: 40000
Brands:
    J.C. Ford Co.

24418 J C Industries Inc
89 Eads St
West Babylon, NY 11704-1186

631-420-1920
Fax: 631-420-0467 800-322-1189

Refuse handling equipment
President: Joseph Celano
jcelano@jcindustriesinc.com
Sales Exec: James Celano
Estimated Sales: $3-5 Million
Number Employees: 20-49

24419 (HQ)J C Whitlam Mfg Co
200 W Walnut St
Wadsworth, OH 44281-1379

330-334-2524
Fax: 330-334-3005 800-321-8358
www.whitlampaint.com

Manufacturer and exporter of refrigeration chemi-
cals, waterless hand cleaners and other cleaning
chemicals
President: Jack Whitlam
sales@jcwhitlam.com
CFO: Doug Whitlam
Senior VP: Doug Whitlam
VP Operations: Steve Carey
Estimated Sales: $5-10 Million
Number Employees: 20-49
Square Footage: 280000

24420 J E M Mfg LLC
1901 Parrish Dr SE
Rome, GA 30161-9576

706-232-1709
Fax: 706-802-1175 www.jemmfg.com

Water pollution treatment and monitoring, analytical
laboratory services
Owner: Chris Mauer
cmauer@jemsalesinc.com
Estimated Sales: $2.5-5 Million
Number Employees: 10-19

24421 J L Becker Co
41150 Joy Rd
Plymouth, MI 48170-4634

734-656-2000
Fax: 734-656-2009 800-837-4328
www.jlbecker.com

Manufacturer and exporter of heat treating furnaces
and conveyor belts including wire mesh and flat
wire
President: John Becker
CEO: Wayne Webbe
CFO: Ellen Beckor
Vice President: John Beckor
Sales Manager: David Peterson
Estimated Sales: $10-20 Million
Number Employees: 20-49
Type of Packaging: Bulk

24422 J L Clark Corp
923 23rd Ave
Rockford, IL 61104-7173

815-962-8861
Fax: 815-966-5862 www.jlclark.com

Manufacturer and exporter of decorative tin cans
and injection molded plastic dispensing closures
President: Philip Baerenwald
pbaerenwald@jlclark.com
CFO: Bill Holiday
Vice President/General Manager: Walt Pietruch
R&D: Ron Axon
Sales: Mike Tolluer
Public Relations: Luanna Grimes
Purchasing: George Mastromatteo
Estimated Sales: H
Number Employees: 250-499
Parent Co: Clarcor Consumer Products
Type of Packaging: Consumer, Food Service, Pri-
    vate Label

24423 J Leek Assoc Inc
145 Peanut Dr
Edenton, NC 27932-9604

252-482-4456
Fax: 252-482-5370

Laboratory providing aflatoxin, microbiological,
pesticide residue and chemical/physical analyses of
food and feed products; services also include prod-
uct development, packaging, shelf life and sensory
studies, etc
Manager Analytical Services: Mike Jackson
Manager: Mike Jackson
Estimated Sales: $1-2.5 Million
Number Employees: 10-19
Square Footage: 21600
Parent Co: Seabrook Enterprises

24424 (HQ)J M Canty Inc E1200 Engineers
6100 Donner Rd
Lockport, NY 14094-9227

716-625-4227
Fax: 716-625-4228 sales@jmcanty.com
www.cantylight.com

Manufacturer and exporter of fiber optic lighting,
image processing and inspection and color analysis
President: Thomas Canty
Quality Control: Dan Raby
VP: Tod Canty
Manager: Chris Miller
chrism@jmcanty.com
Estimated Sales: $5-10 Million
Number Employees: 20-49
Square Footage: 152000
Other Locations:
    Canty
    Dublin, Ireland
Brands:
    Canty

24425 J M Packaging Co
26300 Bunert Rd
Warren, MI 48089-3639

586-771-7800
Fax: 586-771-5440 www.jmindustries.com

Manufacturer and exporter of printed tapes and la-
bels; contract packaging available
Owner: Corey Bunch
cbunch@jmindustries.com
VP: Michael Jones
Estimated Sales: $5-10 Million
Number Employees: 50-99
Type of Packaging: Bulk

24426 J M Swank Co
395 Herky St
North Liberty, IA 52317-8523

319-626-3683
Fax: 319-626-3662 800-593-6375
www.jmswank.com

Food ingredients for the dairy, beverage, meat, bak-
ery, snack, confection, ethnic and prepared foods in-
dustries
CEO: Shawn Meaney
Chief Financial Officer: Philip Garton
Senior Vice President: Paul Hillen
Vice President, Sales & Customer Service: Linda
Loucks
Vice President, Operations: Reggie Hastings
Estimated Sales: $6 Million
Number Employees: 100-249
Parent Co: Conagra Brands
Other Locations:
    Swank Great Lakes
    Carol Stream IL
    Swank South
    Dallas TX
    Swank West
    Denver CO
    Tolleson AZ
    Buena Park CA
    Modesto CA
    Atlanta CA
    Cedar Rapids IA
    Iowa IA
    Kansas KS
    Wichita KS
    Louisville KY
    Mansfield MA

24427 J R Short Milling Co
1580 Grinnell Rd
Kankakee, IL 60901-8246

815-523-9987
Fax: 815-937-3981 800-544-8734
www.shortmill.com
A bakery ingredient supplier company that trans-
forms natural grains into functional foods.
Founder: J.R. Short
COO: Sonny Beckman
sbeckman@shortmill.com
Year Founded: 1910
Estimated Sales: $10-20 Million
Number Employees: 100-249

24428 J Rettenmaier USA LP
16369 US Highway 131 S
Schoolcraft, MI 49087-9150

269-679-2340
Fax: 269-679-2364 877-895-4099
info@jrsusa.com www.jrs.de
Researcher, developer and processor of organic fi-
bers derived from vegetable raw materials that are
used as functional additives and pulps.
Director of Administration & Controlling: Gerhard
Goss
CEO: Thorsten Willmann
Director of Business Development: Curtis Rath
Director of Sales, Food Division: Dia Panzer-Biddle
Manager: Katie Bush
eyeluvme1991@yahoo.com
Estimated Sales: $12 Million
Number Employees: 50-99
Parent Co: J. Rettenmaier & Sohne GmbH & Co
KG

24429 J W Hulme Co
678 7th St W
St Paul, MN 55102-3198

651-222-7359
Fax: 651-228-1181 800-442-8212
sales@jwhulmeco.com
Sport bags, gun cases, duffles, breifcases and lug-
gage.
Owner: Chuck Bidwell
cbidwell@jwhulmeco.com
Estimated Sales: $500,000-1,000,000
Number Employees: 20-49

24430 J&J Corrugated Box Corporation
210 Grove St
Franklin, MA 02038-3119

508-528-6200
Fax: 508-528-2316
Corrugated boxes
Manager: Dan McKinney
General Manager: Richard Koestner
Estimated Sales: $20-50 Million
Number Employees: 100-249
Parent Co: Georgia-Pacific

24431 J&J Mid-South ContainerCorporation
1745 Doug Barnard Pkwy
Augusta, GA 30906-9277

706-798-7420
Fax: 706-793-6947 800-395-1025
www.georgiapacific.com
Corrugated shipping containers
President: Brent Paugh
Chief Executive Officer, President: James Hannan
Executive Vice President: Christian Fischer
Executive Vice President of Operations: Wesley
Jones
Estimated Sales: $20-50 Million
Number Employees: 100-249
Parent Co: Georgia-Pacific Corporation

24432 J&M Laboratories
12 Nordson Dr
Dawsonville, GA 30534

706-216-1520
Fax: 706-216-1517 www.nordson.com
Tea and coffee industry filters
VP: George Porter
Contact: Justin Clark
jclark@nordson.com
Estimated Sales: $30-50 Million
Number Employees: 100-249

24433 J. James
723 Lorimer Street
Brooklyn, NY 11211-1311

718-384-6144
Fax: 718-384-6112 www.jjames.com
Place mats and tray covers
Estimated Sales: less than $500,000
Number Employees: 1-4

24434 (HQ)J. R. Simplot Co.
PO Box 27
Boise, ID 83707-0027

208-336-2110
jrs_info@simplot.com
www.simplot.com
Food manufacturing, seed production, farming, fer-
tilizer manufacturing and frozen-food processing.
Chairman: Scott Simplot
President/CEO: Garrett Lofto
CFO/Treasurer: Brent Moylan
VP, Manufacturing & Supply Chain: Michael
Johnston
Estimated Sales: K
Number Employees: 11,000+
Number of Products: 1000
Type of Packaging: Consumer, Food Service, Pri-
vate Label
Other Locations:
J.R. Simplot Potato Processing
Aberdeen ID
J.R. Simplot Potato Processing
Caldwell ID
J.R. Simplot Potato Processing
Grand Forks ND
J.R. Simplot Potato Processing
Moses Lake WA
J.R. Simplot Potato Processing
Nampa ID
J.R. Simplot Potato Processing
Othello WA
J.R. Simplot Vegetable Processing
West Memphis AR
Brands:
Bent Arm Ale®
Conquest®
Simplot Harvest Fresh Avocados™
RoastWorks®
Simplot Simple Goodness™
Simplot Classic®
Simplot Good Grains™
Farmhouse Originals®
Freezefridge®
Infinity®
Kitchen Craft™
Megacrunch®
NaturalCrisp®
Old Fashioned Way®
SeasonedCrisp®
Select Recipe®
SIDEWINDERS™
Simplot Sweets®
Simplot Thunder Crunch®
Simply Gold®
Skincredibles®
Spudsters®
Tater Pals®
Traditional
True Recipe®
Simplot Daily Pick™
Batter Bites®
JR Buffalos®
Krunchie Wedges®

24435 J. Scott Company
175 Barneveld Ave
San Francisco, CA 94124

415-824-1743
Fax: 415-824-5849 888-OIL-LUBE
jscottco@aol.com
Oils and lubricants
Contact: John Scott
jscottco@msn.com
Manager: John Scott
Estimated Sales: Below $5 Million
Number Employees: 5-9

24436 J.A. Thurston Company
Route 2
Rumford, ME 04276

207-364-7921
Fax: 207-369-9903
Manufacturer and exporter of chairs and stools
VP: John Thurston
Sales: Cindy Giroux

Estimated Sales: $5-10 Million
Number Employees: 5-9

24437 J.C. Products Inc.
66 Ranger Rd
Haddam, CT 6438

860-267-5516
Fax: 860-267-5519
Wire products including displays, racks and bread,
roll and rotisserie baskets
Owner: Charles Helenek
Estimated Sales: $2.5-5 Million
Number Employees: 10-19

24438 J.E. Roy
60 Boulevard Begin
St Claire, QC G0R 2V0
Canada

418-883-2711
Fax: 418-838-8008
Manufacturer, importer and exporter of plastic bot-
tles and bottle nasal plugs
President: Ronald Leclair
Quality Control: Nicoles Mertileau
VP Sales: Sylvie Lefevbre
Number Employees: 55
Square Footage: 18000
Type of Packaging: Consumer, Food Service, Pri-
vate Label
Brands:
Roy
Ropak

24439 J.G. Machine Works
2182 Route 35 South
Holmdel, NJ 07733

732-203-2077
Fax: 732-203-2078 sales@jgmachine.com
www.jgmachine.com
Rotary fillers
Manager: Don Nelson
dnelson@jgmachine.com
National Sales Manager: John McArdle
Number Employees: 20-49

24440 J.H. Carr & Sons
37 S Hudson Street
Seattle, WA 98134-2416

206-763-1937
Fax: 206-763-7033 800-523-8842
jerryacarr@msn.com www.jhcarr.com
Bars, tables and bases, chairs, booths, barstools and
service cabinets
VP Marketing/General Manager: Jerry Carr
Sales Manager: Wayne Muliner
Contact: James Carr
jim.carr@jhcarr.com
Estimated Sales: $5 Million
Number Employees: 25-49
Square Footage: 200000

24441 J.H. Thornton Company
879 N Jan Mar Ct
Olathe, KS 66061

913-764-6550
Fax: 913-764-1314
Manufacturer, exporter and wholesaler/distributor of
conveyor systems; installation services available
President: Douglas Metcalf
Estimated Sales: $3-5 Million
Number Employees: 10

24442 J.I. Holcomb Manufacturing
6400 Rockside Road
Independence, OH 44131-2309

800-458-3222
Fax: 216-524-4381
Cleaners including hand, toilet and bowl,
dishwashing and washing compounds, mops,
brooms, floor polish, soap, insecticides, etc
President: David Stanic
CEO: Shawn Dunmire
Estimated Sales: $52 Million
Number Employees: 500
Number of Products: 1600
Parent Co: Premier Industrial Corporation

24443 J.K. Harman, Inc.
1139 Dixwell Ave
Hamden, CT 06514

203-777-9726
Fax: 203-782-6575 800-248-1627
Custom store fixtures
President: D Harman

Estimated Sales: $5-10 Million
Number Employees: 10-19

24444 J.M. Rogers & Sons
PO Box 8725
Moss Point, MS 39562-0011

228-475-7584

Pallets, drag line mats, skids, lumber, etc.; exporter of pallets
Owner: Louis Rogers
Number Employees: 50

24445 J.M. Swank Company
520 W Penn St
North Liberty, IA 52317-9775

319-626-3683
Fax: 319-626-3662 800-567-9265
www.jmswank.com
Ingredient blending, label and special palletizing, inventory management, quality control and freight consolidation
President: Taylor Strubell
VP: Ron Pardekooper
Contact: George Nulty
george.nulty@conagrafoods.com
Estimated Sales: $29.5 Million
Number Employees: 175
Parent Co: Conagra Brands

24446 J.R. Ralph Marketing Company
4317 E Genesee Street
Suite 210
Syracuse, NY 13214-2114

315-445-0255
Fax: 315-445-0245

Consultant specializing in the introduction and expansion of products to the food industry
Partner: Chris Ralph
Estimated Sales: $1-2.5 Million
Number Employees: 1-4

24447 J.S. Ferraro
130 Adelaide St. W
Ste. 810
Toronto, ON M5H 3P5
Canada

416-306-0018
Fax: 416-583-2456 800-278-0018
info@jsferraro.com jsferraro.com
Offers market intelligence, risk management, and supply chain solutions.
CEO: Alexander Cave
Executive Chairman: John Ferraro
CFO: Eric Nie
EVP, Research & Analysis: Dr. Rob Murphy
SVP, Sales & Merchandising: Roger Despres *Year Founded:* 1988

24448 J.V. Reed & Company
1939 Goldsmith Ln
Suite 121
Louisville, KY 40218-3175

502-454-4455
Fax: 502-587-6025 877-258-7333
Manufacturer and exporter of dust pans, metal waste baskets, signs, tabs, labels, burner covers, hot pads, stove and counter mats, canister sets, etc
Owner: Jean Reid
Chairman Board: Marc Ray
Estimated Sales: $10-20 Million
Number Employees: 1-4
Square Footage: 160000

24449 J/W Design Associates
401 Terry Francois St
Suite 212
San Francisco, CA 94158

415-546-7707
Fax: 415-546-4004 info@webbdesign.com
www.webbdesign.com
Design consultant for restaurants, hotels and resorts
Owner: Kim Webb
Designer: Jack Donald Webb
Estimated Sales: $1-3 Million
Number Employees: 10-19

24450 JAS Manufacturing Company
3228 Skylane Dr
PO Box 702041
Carrollton, TX 75370-2041

972-380-1150
Fax: 972-931-6218
Dust and mist collectors and bakery equipment
Director Production: Jim Singleton

Estimated Sales: $2.5-5 Million
Number Employees: 20-49

24451 JBA International
3701 Algonquin Road
Rolling Meadows, IL 60008-3127

847-590-0299
Fax: 847-590-0394 800-522-4685
Wine industry computer software

24452 JBC Plastics
2239 Gravois Ave
St Louis, MO 63104-2852

314-771-2279
Fax: 314-771-0910 877-834-5526
mail@jbcplastic.com www.jbcplastic.com
Displays, napkin holders and signs
Owner: Cheryl Mc Grath
Customer Service: Jennifer Ward
Estimated Sales: $.5-1 million
Number Employees: 1-4

24453 (HQ)JBT Food Tech
400 Fairway Ave
Lakeland, FL 33801

863-683-5411
Fax: 863-680-3677 hello@jbtc.com
www.jbtc.com
Food processing machinery including fruit and vegetable juice extractors, blanchers, freezers, can closers, corers, pitters, choppers, etc
Chairman/President/CEO: Thomas Giacomini
EVP/Chief Financial Officer/Treasurer: Brian Deck
EVP/President, Liquid Foods: Carlos Fernandez
EVP/General Counsel/Secretary: James Marvin
EVP/President, Protein: Paul Sternlieb
Year Founded: 1884
Estimated Sales: $1,350 Million
Number Employees: 5,000
Parent Co: FMC Corporation

24454 JBT Wolf-Tec Inc
20 Kieffer Ln
Kingston, NY 12401-2209

845-340-9727
Fax: 845-340-9732 www.wolf-tec.com
Massagers and tumblers, pickle injectors, sausage linkers
CEO: Ralf Ludwig
ralf@wolf-tec.com
Estimated Sales: $20-50 Million
Number Employees: 50-99

24455 JC Food
PO Box 5121
Ridgewood, NJ 07451

201-444-4172
Fax: 201-444-3622 info@jc-food.com
www.jc-food.com
School foodservice services from menu planning to providing fresh foods
Owner/President: Joseph Civita
jcivita@jc-food.com
Estimated Sales: $700,000
Number Employees: 5

24456 JCH International
978 E Hermitage Rd NE
Rome, GA 30161-9641

706-295-4111
Fax: 706-295-4114 800-328-9203
info@jchinternational.com
Manufacturer and exporter of industrial and commercial mats and matting for entrance, meat cutting and produce areas; also, specialty flooring available; importer of heavy duty carpets
President: John Hoglund
jchoglund@yahoo.com
Number Employees: 5-9
Type of Packaging: Food Service
Brands:
Champions Sports Tile
Drainthru
Floorsaver
Locktile

24457 JCS Controls, Inc.
460 Buffalo Road
Suite 200
Rochester, NY 14611-1020

585-227-5910
Fax: 585-723-3213 sales@jcs.com
www.jcs.com

JCS has strong core competence in product development (R&D), Aseptic Processing, Mass Balanced Digital In-Line Blending Application, S88 Compliant Batching Systems, and many advanced technology processing systems such as EvaporationSpray Drying, Cheese VAT control, Membrane Processes, and more.
Founder: Philip Frechette
VP: Don Frechette
Operations: Rob Frechette
Estimated Sales: $3.7 Million
Number Employees: 20
Other Locations:

24458 JDG Consulting
2-8 Brookhollow Avenue
Suite 407
Baulkham Hills, NS 2153

312-621-8900
Fax: 312-621-0162 800-243-7037
info@jdgconsulting.com.au
www.greenfuture.com.au
Consultant providing market research and communications
VP: Alan Levitt
Administrative Assistant: Ann Marie Alanes
Number Employees: 3

24459 JDO/LNR Lighting
7980 Pat Booker Road
Suite A1
Live Oak, TX 78233-2603

210-637-6244
Fax: 210-637-6910 800-597-1570
Electric lighting fixtures
VP Marketing: Bob Windro
Manager: Leonard Almendarez
Number Employees: 30

24460 JEM Wire Products
2303 South Main Street
PO Box 2606
Middletown, CT 6457

860-347-0447
Fax: 860-347-9743
Wire products for baskets, displays, racks and shelves; also, custom wire forming and spot welding services available
President: Edward Muzik
Vice President: Tom Muzik
Marketing/Sales: Yale Gordon
Estimated Sales: $2.5-5 Million
Number Employees: 10-19

24461 JGB Enterprises Inc
115 Metropolitan Park Dr
Liverpool, NY 13088-5389

315-451-2770
Fax: 315-451-8503 www.jgbhose.com
Hose assemblies
President: Bob Zywicki
bzywicki@jgbhose.com
Quality Control: Glenn Beede
CFO: Bod Zywicki
Estimated Sales: $50-100 Million
Number Employees: 250-499

24462 JH Display & Fixture
P.O.Box 432
Greenwood, IN 46142

317-888-0631
Fax: 317-888-0671
Manufacturer, importer and exporter of wood, acrylic, metal and glass fixtures. Also custom shelving and tables available. Antique and vintage decorative props for all types of settings
Owner: John Holbrook
VP/Owner: Trudy Holbrook
Estimated Sales: $1-2.5 Million
Number Employees: 5-9

24463 JIT Manufacturing & Technology
4101 Stuart Andrew Boulevard
Suite D
Charlotte, NC 28217-1580

800-804-3910
Fax: 704-522-1603
Art patented print and apply equipment, bar coding systems, distribution programming, labeling and inventory control

24464 JJI Lighting Group, Inc.
11500 Melrose Ave.
Franklin Park, IL 60131-1334

847-451-0700

Manufacturer, importer and exporter of lighting fixtures and systems
CEO: Robert Haidinger
Contact: Claude Sarti
claude.sarti@philips.com
Estimated Sales: $55 Million
Number Employees: 650
Number of Products: 15
Type of Packaging: Private Label, Bulk

24465 JL Industries Inc
4450 W 78th Street Cir
Bloomington, MN 55435-5416

952-835-6850
Fax: 952-835-2218 800-554-6077
www.activarcpg.com
Manufacturer, exporter and importer of fire extinguishers and cabinets, other fire and emergency AED cabinets, metal access panels and roof hatches, dirt control floor mats and gratings, and detention specialties.
President: Carl Coleman
cecoleman@jlindustries.com
Marketing: Nona Peterson
Estimated Sales: $10-20 Million
Number Employees: 50-99
Square Footage: 116000
Parent Co: Activar

24466 JM Huber Chemical Corporation
907 Revolution St
Havre De Grace, MD 21078-3723

410-939-3500
Fax: 410-939-7302 hubermaterials@huber.com
www.huber.com
Industrial inorganic chemicals
President: Tom Lamb
President, Chief Executive Officer: Michael Marberry
R&D: John Clrnelius
Vice President of Environmental: Andrew Miles
Quality Control: Matt Hall
Contact: Chris Bible
etceb@huber.com
Plant Manager: Pat Jackson
Estimated Sales: $20-30 Million
Number Employees: 100-249

24467 JMA
658 Blue Point Road
Holtsville, NY 11742-1848

631-475-0023
Fax: 631-475-0549 800-428-8377
info@crazyhatter.com www.crazyhatter.com
Wine industry bottles
Owner: Jeffery Leibowitz
Estimated Sales: $1-3 Million
Number Employees: 10-19

24468 JMC Packaging Equipment
3470 Mainway Drive
Burlington, ON L7M 1A8
Canada

905-335-4196
Fax: 905-335-4201 800-263-5252
davidk@jmcpackaging.com
www.jmcpackaging.com
Manufacturer and exporter of bagging and bag sealing machinery
Sales Manager: David Kay
Office Manager: Linda Campbell
Number Employees: 10-19
Type of Packaging: Consumer, Food Service, Private Label, Bulk

24469 JP Plastics, Inc.
67 Green Street
Foxboro, MA 02035

508-203-2420
Fax: 508-203-2401 sales@jp-plastics.com
www.jp-plastics.com
Custom vacuum formed packaging products
President: John P Cheever
Contact: Mike Graves
mgraves@clarkeus.com
Estimated Sales: Below 1 Million
Number Employees: 7
Square Footage: 64000

24470 JPS Packaging Company
1972 Akron Peninsula Rd
Akron, OH 44313-4810

330-923-5281
Fax: 330-923-9637

Manufacturer and converter of flexible packaging and label products for use by customers in the food and beverage industry and other niche markets
Plant Manager: Anthony Oakes
Estimated Sales: $1-5 Million
Number Employees: 100-249

24471 JS Giles Inc
8810 Emmott Street
Suite 400
Houston, TX 77040-3592

713-690-3333
Fax: 713-690-3353 800-254-0709
sales@jfgilesinc.com www.jfgilesinc.com
Medium intensity horizontal and vertical mixers
President: John Giles
R & D: Peter Foxon
Estimated Sales: Below $5 Million
Number Employees: 5-9

24472 JUMO Process Control Inc
6733 Myers Rd
East Syracuse, NY 13057-9787

315-437-5866
Fax: 315-697-5860 800-554-5866
www.jumo.net
Meat thermometers, temperature control probes and refrigeration controllers.
President: Carsten Juchheim
CEO: Bernhard Juchheim
Manager: Katherine Blume
katherine.blume@jumo.net
Number Employees: 20-49

24473 JVC Rubber Stamp Company
PO Box 2338
Elkhart, IN 46515

574-293-0113
Fax: 574-293-0113
Rubber stamps
Owner: Ron Cataldo
Estimated Sales: Less than $500,000
Number Employees: 1-4

24474 JVM Sales Corp.
3401 A Tremley Point Rd
Linden, NJ 07036

908-862-4866
Fax: 908-862-4867 anthony@jvmsalescorp.com
jvmsales.com
Italian grated cheeses; custom blends
President & CEO: Mary Beth Tomasino
VP of Sales & Marketing: Anthony Caliendo
Estimated Sales: $2-4 Million
Square Footage: 150000
Type of Packaging: Consumer, Food Service, Private Label, Bulk
Other Locations:
  JVM Sales South
  Delray Beach FL

24475 JVNW
390 S Redwood St
Canby, OR 97013

503-263-2858
Fax: 503-263-2868 800-331-5869
www.jvnw.com
Brewing vessels
President: Donald Jones
CFO: Donald Jones
Contact: Nicole Souter
nicole.s@jvnw.com
Estimated Sales: $5-10 Million
Number Employees: 100-249

24476 JVR/Sipromac
100 W Drullard Ave
Lancaster, NY 14086-1670

716-206-2500
Fax: 716-897-4731 www.jvrinc.com
Vacuum packaging, processing equipment
President: John Radziwon
Parts & Service Manager: Kevin Monk
Contact: Marta Guerra
guerram@hss.edu
Estimated Sales: $2.5 Million
Number Employees: 5-9

24477 JW Aluminum
435 Old Mt Holly Rd
Mt Holly, SC 29445

843-572-1100
Fax: 843-572-1049 800-568-1100
www.jwaluminum.com
Aluminum foil

Chief Executive Officer: Lee McCarter
Chief Financial Officer: Philip Cavatoni
Chief Commercial Officer: Ryan Roush
Chief Operating Officer: Stan Brant
Estimated Sales: $1-5 Million
Number Employees: 10-19
Type of Packaging: Food Service

24478 JW Aluminum Co
2475 Trenton Ave # 5
Williamsport, PA 17701-7904

570-323-4430
Fax: 570-323-6866 www.jwaluminum.com
Aluminum
CEO: Craig Eddy
Estimated Sales: $50-100 Million
Number Employees: 100-249

24479 JW Leser Company
4408 W Jefferson Blvd
Los Angeles, CA 90016-4090

323-731-4173
Fax: 323-731-4175
Sell and manufacture fillers, pumps, homogenizers, tanks, mixers, and filters
President: Ray Leser
Number Employees: 1-4
Brands:
  Alesco
  In-Shear

24480 Jack Langston Manufacturing Company
3700 Elm Street
Dallas, TX 75226-1214

214-821-9844
Fax: 214-824-5777
Commercial refrigerators and walk-in coolers and freezers
President: Olden Phil Paul
Chairman Board: J Langston, Jr.
Plant Manager: David Cormican
Number Employees: 25
Parent Co: Camp Langston

24481 Jack Stack
221 Sheridan Blvd
Inwood, NY 11096-1226

516-371-5214
Fax: 516-371-6880 800-999-9840
info@jackstack.com www.interfreight.net
Manufacturer and importer of mobile plate racks
Manager: Tom Staub
tom@interfreight.net
Managing Director: Tom Staub
Sales Manager: John Falzarano
Sales Manager: Pascale Steingueldoir
Estimated Sales: Less than $500,000
Number Employees: 5-9
Parent Co: Jackstack International

24482 Jack Stone Lighting & Electrical
3131 Pennsy Dr
Landover, MD 20785

301-322-3323
Fax: 301-322-8407 service@jackstone.net
www.jackstone.net
Electrical signs
President: Trevor Stone
Contact: Spencer Stone
sstone@jackstone.net
Operations Manager: Spencer Stone
Estimated Sales: $5-10 Million
Number Employees: 50-99

24483 Jack the Ripper Table Skirting
4003 Greenbriar Drive
Suite A
Stafford, TX 77477

281-240-1024
Fax: 281-240-0343 800-331-7831
www.tableskirting.com
Manufacturer and exporter of table skirting, table cloths, napkins, place mats and tray stand covers
Director Sales: Erik Dean
Customer Service: Jessie Carpenter
Estimated Sales: $1 Million
Number Employees: 20-50

24484 Jacks Manufacturing Company
PO Box 50695
Mendota, MN 55150-0695

651-452-1474
Fax: 651-452-1477 800-821-2089

Manufacturer and exporter of boiler compounds and
carpet and upholstery cleaners
Chairman Board: C Nimis
Director: S Nimis
Office Manager: Sharon Bruesile
Estimated Sales: $2.5-5 Million
Number Employees: 1-4

24485 Jackson Corrugated Container
225 River Rd
Middletown, CT 6457

860-346-9671
Fax: 860-346-9320
Supplier of corrugated packaging.
President: William P Herlihy
info@jacksonbox.com
Estimated Sales: $5.2 Million
Number Employees: 20-49

24486 Jackson Msc LLC
6209 N US Highway 25e
Gray, KY 40734-6583

606-523-1438
Fax: 606-523-9196 888-800-5672
www.jacksonwws.com
Commercial dishwashers and ovens
President: David Crane
david.crane@jacksonmsc.com
VP Sales/Marketing: Mark Whalen
Production/Inventory Control Manager: Teresa
Doan
Purchasing Manager: Sheila Reeder
Estimated Sales: $5-10 Million
Number Employees: 100-249
Square Footage: 436000
Parent Co: ENODIS

24487 Jackson Restaurant Supply
1119 Highway 45 Byp
Jackson, TN 38301-3277

731-664-5100
Fax: 731-664-0978 800-424-8943
usamfg@usamanufacturing.com
Automatic barbecue cookers
President: James Griffith
Estimated Sales: $5-10 Million
Number Employees: 1-4
Square Footage: 64000
Brands:
Hickory Creek Bar-B-Q Cooker

24488 Jacksonville Box & Woodwork Co
5011 Buffalo Ave
Jacksonville, FL 32206-1573

904-354-1441
Fax: 904-354-6088 800-683-2699
info@jaxbox.com www.jaxbox.com
Packaging products including wooden bins for juice,
fruit, egg and vegetable boxes, collapsible pallet
mats for melons and wooden shipping crates
President: Jennings B King
Vice President: J King, Jr.
Sales: Tom More
Manager: Steve Farford
Estimated Sales: $5-10 Million
Number Employees: 10-19

24489 Jaco Equipment Corporation
3166 Main Street
Buffalo, NY 14214-1311

716-836-3755
Fax: 716-836-3756
Forming case packing, cleaning air bottling, clean-
ing washing bottling
President: Maurice Osterman
Number Employees: 5-9

24490 Jacob Holtz Co.
10 Industrial HWY MS-6 Airport Business
Lester, PA 19029

215-423-2800
Fax: 215-634-7454 800-445-4337
info@jacobholtz.com
Supplier and exporter of self-adjusting table glides
Estimated Sales: Below $5 Million
Number Employees: 3
Square Footage: 9600
Brands:
Superlevel

24491 Jacob Tubing LP
3948 Willow Lake Blvd
Memphis, TN 38118-7040

901-566-1110
Fax: 901-566-1910 info@jacob-tubing.com
www.jacob-tubing.com
Primary supplier of modular tubing systems with
pull ring connections to major industries worldwide.
CEO: Birte Mathis
Manager: Volker Eynck
Number Employees: 20-49
Parent Co: Jacob Soehne

24492 Jacob White Packaging
12720 Pennridge Drive
Bridgeton, MO 63044-1235

314-791-6448
Fax: 314-291-6913 800-248-6448
www.jacobwhite.com
Fully automatic horizontal end load cartoner
Estimated Sales: $1-3 Million
Number Employees: 10

24493 Jacobi Lewis Co
622 S Front St
PO Box 1289
Wilmington, NC 28401-5034

910-763-6201
Fax: 910-763-5610 800-763-2433
jl@jacobi-lewis.com www.jacobi-lewis.com
Wholesaler/distributor of equipment, supplies, furni-
ture, etc.; serving the food service market
President: Greg Lewis
Chairman: French Lewis
Vice President: Gloria Ludewic
Marketing/Sales: Chris Gannon
Purchasing Manager: Wilson Horton
Estimated Sales: $7 Million
Number Employees: 10-19
Number of Brands: 700
Square Footage: 45000

24494 Jacobs Engineering Group
1999 Bryan St
Suite 1200
Dallas, TX 75201

214-638-0145
Fax: 214-638-0447 www.jacobs.com
Global, full-service engineering, procurement, con-
struction management and operations firm
Chairman & CEO: Steve Demetriou
President & CFO: Kevin Berryman
Year Founded: 1947
Estimated Sales: $14.98 Billion
Number Employees: 52,000
Other Locations:
Lockwood Greene
Atlanta GA
Lockwood Greene-Enterprise Mill
Augusta GA
Lockwood Greene
Cincinnati OH
Lockwood Greene
Dallas TX
Lockwood Greene
Hampton VA
Lockwood Greene
Knoxville TN
Lockwood Greene
Long Beach CA
Lockwood Greene
Nashville TN
Lockwood Greene
New York NY
Lockwood Greene
Moon Township PA
Lockwood Greene
Saint Louis MO
Lockwood Greene
Pooler GA
Lockwood Greene
Somerset NJ

24495 Jade Products Co
2650 Orbiter St
Brea, CA 92821-6265

714-528-4486
800-884-5233
dpack@maytag.com www.jaderange.com
OEM equipment including commercial cooking
ranges and refrigerators
President: Ray Williams
VP Sales: Lex Poulos
Customer Service Manager: Susan Hopkins
Production Engineering Manager: Peng Wang
Estimated Sales: $2.5-5 Million
Number Employees: 100-249
Parent Co: Maytag Corporation
Brands:
Dynasty
Jade Range
Jade Refrigeration
Utility Refrigeration

24496 Jagenberg
PO Box 1229
Enfield, CT 06083-1229

860-741-2501
Fax: 860-741-2508 www.jagenberg.com
Automatic folding carton gluers and packers
VP: C Himmelsbach
VP Converting Gruop: A Groat
Estimated Sales: $20-50 Million
Number Employees: 100-249
Parent Co: Jagenberg-Werke AG
Brands:
Jagenberg Diana

24497 Jagla Machinery Company
26 Woodland Ave
San Rafael, CA 94901

415-457-7672
Fax: 415-457-1143
Wine industry equipment fabricators
President: Lee Jagla
Estimated Sales: Below $5 Million
Number Employees: 5-9
Square Footage: 5000

24498 Jagulana Herbal Products
PO Box 45
Badger, CA 93603

559-337-2200
Fax: 559-337-2354 888-465-3686
www.immortalityherb.com
Dedicated to researching, developing and marketing
jiaogulan and jiaogulan-based herbal products of the
highest quality
President: Chris Gleen
Research: Michael Blumert
Estimated Sales: $1-3 Million
Number Employees: 1-4

24499 James Austin Co
115 Downieville Rd
P.O. Box 827
Mars, PA 16046

724-625-1535
Fax: 724-625-3288 www.jamesaustin.com
Household chlorine bleaches, laundry and
dishwashing detergents, disinfectants, ammonia,
pines oil cleaners, windshield washer fluid, fabric
softeners and glass cleaners.
President: Harry Austin III
hgaustin@jamesaustin.com
Board Member: John Austin
Board Member: Doug Austin
Board Member: Jack Rea
Year Founded: 1889
Estimated Sales: $52 Million
Number Employees: 100-249
Number of Brands: 10
Number of Products: 30
Square Footage: 180000
Type of Packaging: Consumer, Food Service, Pri-
vate Label
Other Locations:
Ludlow MA
Statesville CA
DeLand FL
Brands:
101
A-1
Austin
Snoee
Wipe Away

24500 James River Canada
137 Bentworth Avenue
North York, ON M6A 1T6
Canada

416-789-5151
Fax: 416-789-3590
Disposable cups, plates and cutlery
Estimated Sales: $1-5,000,000
Number Employees: 250
Parent Co: James River Corporation

24501 (HQ)James Thompson
381 Park Ave S
Rm 718
New York, NY 10016-8806
212-686-5306
Fax: 212-686-9528 inquiry@jamesthompson.com
www.jamesthompson.com
Manufacturer and exporter of buckrams, netting,
cotton goods, burlap, cheesecloth, etc
President: Robert B Judell
Treasurer: Barry Garr
Vice President, Sales/Marketing: Marc Bieler
Site Manager: Steve Luchansky
Vice President, Manufacturing: Steve Luchansky
Merchandise Manager: Gail Boyle
Estimated Sales: $300,000-500,000
Number Employees: 5-9

24502 James V. Hurson Associates
200 N. Glebe Road
Suite 321
Arlington, VA 22203-3755
703-524-8200
Fax: 703-525-8451 800-642-6564
info@hurson.com www.hurson.com
Consultant specializing in food labeling, trademarks
and patents
President: James Hurson
Manager: J Hurson
Estimated Sales: $2.5-5 Million
Number Employees: 20-49

24503 James Varley & Sons
1200 Switzer Ave
Saint Louis, MO 63147
314-383-4372
Fax: 314-383-4379 800-325-8891
General purpose and meat room cleaners, degreas-
ers, sanitizers, housekeeping chemicals, floor polish
and hand soap
President: John Daley
CEO: Jack Daley
Estimated Sales: $5-10 Million
Number Employees: 20-49
Parent Co: Daley International, Ltd
Brands:
   Everwear
   Med-I-San

24504 Jamestown Awning
289 Steele St
Jamestown, NY 14701
716-483-1435
Fax: 716-483-3995
service@jamestownawning.com
www.jamestownawning.com
Commercial awnings
President: Mark Saxton
mark@jamestownawning.com
Estimated Sales: $1-2,500,000
Number Employees: 10-19

**24505 Jamestown Container
Corporation**
2775 Broadway St
Suite 250
Buffalo, NY 14227
216-831-3700
Fax: 216-831-3709 855-234-4054
www.jamestowncontainer.com
Corrugated cartons
President: Larry Hudson
Sales Manager: Jeffrey Davidson
Estimated Sales: $10-20 Million
Number Employees: 50-99
Parent Co: Willamette Industries

24506 Jamieson Laboratories
4025 Rhodes Drive
Windsor, ON N8W 5B5
Canada
519-974-8482
Fax: 519-974-4742 800-265-5088
www.jamiesonvitamins.com
Kefir, yogurt, cod liver oil, vitamins, mineral supple-
ments; water purifying systems and filters.
President/CEO: Mark Hornick
Year Founded: 1922
Estimated Sales: $42 Million
Number Employees: 400
Number of Brands: 22
Square Footage: 40000
Parent Co: CCMP Capital Advisors LLC
Type of Packaging: Consumer

Other Locations:
   Toronto ON
Brands:
   Arthrimin GS™
   Baby-D™
   BodyGUARD™
   Digestive Care™
   Effervescent
   Exxtra-C™
   FluShield™
   Healthy SLEEP™
   Mega Cal™
   NEM®
   Neurosome™
   Nutrisentials™
   Omega Complete™
   Omega-3 Brain™
   Omega-3 Calm™
   Omega-3 Select™
   Prostease™
   ProVitamina™
   Red Dragon™
   Relax & Sleep™
   Slimdown®
   Stressease™

24507 Jamison Door Co
55 Jv Jamison Dr
Hagerstown, MD 21740
301-733-3100
Fax: 240-329-5155 800-532-3667
www.jamisondoor.com
Cold storage refrigerator and freezer doors.
CEO: John T Williams
jw@jamisondoor.com
Purchasing: Don Wilson
Number Employees: 100-249
Number of Brands: 3

24508 Jamison Plastic Corporation
5001 Crackersport Rd
Allentown, PA 18104
610-391-1400
Fax: 610-391-1414
Manufacturer and designer of custom and plastic in-
jection molded products
President: Marc Solda
Contact: Dan Gawer
dan.gawer@npiplastic.com
Estimated Sales: $10-20 Million
Number Employees: 50-99
Square Footage: 210000

24509 Janedy Sign Company
27 Carter St
Everett, MA 2149
617-776-5700
Fax: 617-387-5822
Signs
Owner: William Penney
Estimated Sales: $500,000-$1 Million
Number Employees: 5-9

24510 Janows Design Associates
5323 W Pratt Avenue
Lincolnwood, IL 60712-3121
847-763-0620
Fax: 847-763-0621
Consultant specializing in engineering and design of
commercial food service equipment
President: Quintilla Janows
Principal: Sherwin Janows
Estimated Sales: $500,000-$1 Million
Number Employees: 5-9

24511 Jantec
1777 Northern Star Dr
Traverse City, MI 49696-9244
231-941-4339
Fax: 231-941-1460 800-992-3303
accounting@jantec.com www.jantec.com
Manufacturer and exporter of belt, angle-edge and
spiral conveyors; also, power turns and specialty
stainless steel conveying equipment for food and
washdown applications
Owner: Ronald Sommerfield
ronalds@jantec.com
Number Employees: 20-49

24512 January & Wood Company
PO Box 308
Maysville, KY 41056-0308
606-564-3301
Fax: 606-564-8425
Cotton and cotton/polyester twine

Estimated Sales: $5-10 Million
Number Employees: 50-99

**24513 Japan External Trade
Organization (JETRO) New York**
1221 Avenue Of The Americas
42nd Floor
New York, NY 10020-1079
212-997-0400
Fax: 212-944-8808
Tea
Marketing: Yumika Tanaka

24514 Jarboe Equipment
411 N Bedford St
Georgetown, DE 19947-2197
302-856-7988
Fax: 302-856-7408 800-699-7988
Dealer of new and used food processing equipment
Owner: Ronald Snyder
Estimated Sales: $1-5 Million
Number Employees: 1-4

24515 Jarchem Industries
414 Wilson Ave
Newark, NJ 07105
973-578-4560
Fax: 973-344-5743 info@jarchem.com
www.jarchem.com
Acetates and chlorides
VP: Arthur Hein
CEO: Arnold Stern
Sales Manager: Steve Yonder
Contact: Hein Arthur
hein.arthur@jarchem.com
Estimated Sales: $20-50 Million
Number Employees: 1-4

24516 Jarden Home Brands
1800 Cloquet Ave
Cloquet, MN 55720-2141
218-879-6700
Fax: 218-879-6369 www.jardenhomebrands.com
Matches, toothpicks, plastic cutlery, ice cream
sticks, candles, etc
Estimated Sales: $20-50 Million
Number Employees: 250-499

24517 Jarden Home Brands
14611 W. Commerce Road
P.O Box 529
Daleville, IN 47334
800-392-2575
Fax: 765-557-3250 info@jardenhomebrands.com
www.diamondbrands.com
Cocktail forks, toothpicks, corn-on-the-cob holders,
skewers, candy sticks, spoons, etc; exporter of
woodware and cutlery; importer of toothpicks and
candy apple sticks
Sales Manager: Phil Dvorak
Contact: Jared Anderson
janderson@jardencs.com
Brands:
   Diamond
   Forster
   Permaware
   Universal

24518 Jarisch Paper Box Company
1560 Curran Highway
North Adams, MA 01247-3900
413-663-5396
Fax: 413-664-4889
Boxes including set-up paper and plastic; also, parti-
tions
General Manager: Gary Mallows
Number Employees: 45

24519 Jarke Corporation
750 Pinecrest Dr
Prospect Hts, IL 60070
847-520-4774
Fax: 847-541-0858 800-722-5255
www.gillisindustries.com
Steel pallets and skids; also, racks including portable
stacking, pallet storage and cantilever; nonpowered
trucks and carts for warehouse coolers and freezers
available
President: Harvey Baker
Marketing Director: Liz Cheevers
Sales: George Luft
Estimated Sales: $10-20 Million
Number Employees: 20-49
Square Footage: 240000

Brands:
Airector
Button-On
Cupl-Up
Hi-Drum
Mini-Module
Minitree
Quiktree
Steeltree
Tri-Drum
Utilitier

24520 Jarlan Manufacturing
8701 Avalon Blvd
Los Angeles, CA 90003-3512

323-752-1211
Fax: 323-752-2037

Bar tops and ice bins
President: Craig Malburg
jarlan55@yahoo.com
Estimated Sales: $500,000-$1 Million
Number Employees: 5-9

24521 Jarvis Caster Company
881 Lower Brownsville Rd
Jackson, TN 38301-9667

731-554-2138
800-995-9876

inof@jarviscaster.com www.jarviscaster.com
Manufacturer and exporter of industrial casters and
wheels
President: Rodney Brooks
CFO: Ronnie Fondrun
Vice President: Scott Lackey
Research & Development: Harry Green
Marketing Director: Cary Gillespie
Sales Director: Scott Lackey
Contact: Zachary Minner
zminner@emdeon.com
Operations Manager: Harold Clark
Purchasing Manager: Tracy Hall
Number Employees: 100-249
Square Footage: 800000
Parent Co: Standex International Corporation
Type of Packaging: Bulk
Other Locations:
Jarvis East
Mississauga ON

24522 (HQ)Jarvis Products Corp
33 Anderson Rd
Middletown, CT 06457-4926

860-347-7271
Fax: 860-347-9905 sales@jarvisproducts.com
Meat and poultry processing equipment.
President: Peter Brown
peterdouglas@hotmail.com
Estimated Sales: $14.8 Million
Number Employees: 100-249
Square Footage: 24000
Brands:
Jarvis

24523 Jarvis-Cutter Company
184 Bremen Street
Boston, MA 02128-1738

617-567-7532
Fax: 617-567-5644

General, infectious and pathological waste incinera-
tors and heat recovery boilers
Estimated Sales: $.5-1 million
Number Employees: 6
Parent Co: Jarvis-Cutter

24524 Jasper Seating Company
P.O.Box 231
Jasper, IN 47547-0231

812-481-9259
Fax: 812-482-1548 www.jasperseating.com
Technical Services Manager: Amilcar Ubiera
Sales Territory Manager: Jimi Barreiro
Estimated Sales: $10-20 Million
Number Employees: 100-249

24525 Java Jacket
910 NE 57th Ave # 300
Portland, OR 97213-3615

503-281-6240
Fax: 503-281-6462 800-208-4128
info@javajacket.com www.javajacket.com
Manufacturer and exporter of hot and cold paper cup
coffee sleeves, joe to go boxes and custom sized
sleeves.

President: Jay Sorensen
jay@javajacket.com
CEO: Colleen Sorensen
Estimated Sales: $500,000-$1 Million
Number Employees: 5-9
Brands:
Java Jacket

24526 Jax Inc
W134n5373 Campbell Dr
Menomonee Falls, WI 53051-7023

262-781-3906
Fax: 262-781-3906 800-782-8850
info@jax.com
Jax INC is a manufacturer of high technology, indus-
trial, synthetic and food grade lubricants. Founded in
1955, JAX produces conventional and extreme per-
formance synthetic lubricants for food processing
and numerous other industrysegments. JAX lubrica-
tion products are distributed worldwide.
President/CEO: Eric Peter
CFO: Steve Matiacci
Vice President: Carter Anderson
Marketing Director: Tracey Huebner
Manager: Keely Marlowe
keely@jax.com
Estimated Sales: $10-20 Million
Number Employees: 50-99
Parent Co: Pressure-Lube
Type of Packaging: Private Label, Bulk
Other Locations:
Benhkle Lubricants/Western Regional
Sacramento CA
Brands:
Jax Lubricants

24527 Jax Inc
W134n5373 Campbell Dr
Menomonee Falls, WI 53051-7023

262-781-3906
Fax: 262-781-3906 800-782-8850
Food grade lubricants including antiwear food grade
greases, hydraulic oils and gear oils, food grade air-
line oils, chain and conveyor lubricants and extreme
temperature lubricants
President: Eric J Peter
Manager: Keely Marlowe
keely@jax.com
Estimated Sales: $10-20 Million
Number Employees: 50-99

24528 Jay Packaging Group Inc
100 Warwick Industrial Dr
Warwick, RI 02886-2486

401-244-1300
Fax: 401-738-0137 siteadmin@jaypack.com
www.jaypack.com
Manufacturer and exporter of displays, blister cards,
skin sheets and thermoformed trays and blisters
President: Richard E Kelly
CFO: Fernando Lemos
flemos@jaypack.com
VP Sales: Jim Nattiucci
Estimated Sales: $20-50 Million
Number Employees: 100-249

24529 Jay R Smith Mfg Co
2781 Gunter Park Dr E
Montgomery, AL 36109-1405

334-277-8520
Fax: 334-272-7396 sales@jrsmith.com
www.jrsmith.com
Grease remediation systems and grease intercepters
CFO: Dale Evans
CEO: Jay Smith
Marketing: Charles White
Vice President of Domestic Sales: John Roberts
Plant Manager: Jeff Cannon
Purchasing Director: Bruce Tomlinson
Estimated Sales: $40 Million
Number Employees: 250-499
Number of Products: 200
Square Footage: 250000
Parent Co: Smith Industries

24530 Jay-Bee Manufacturing Inc
522 N Beverly Ave
Tyler, TX 75702-5932

903-597-9343
Fax: 903-593-8725 800-445-0610
jaybeemfg@suddenlinkmail.com
www.jaybeehammermills.com
Manufacturer and exporter of stainless steel hammer
mills for particle reduction of fruits, rice cakes and
spices

President: Edwina Granberry
Estimated Sales: $1-2.5 Million
Number Employees: 10-19
Square Footage: 280000
Brands:
Jay Bee

24531 Jayhawk Boxes
1150 S Union St
Fremont, NE 68025-6137

402-721-6101
Fax: 402-721-7958 800-642-8363
jaystevr@lpco.net www.lpco.co
Corrugated shipping boxes
Manager: Tom Stover
tstover@jaywolfe.com
Estimated Sales: $20 Million
Number Employees: 50-99
Parent Co: Lawrence Paper Company

24532 Jayhawk Manufacturing Co Inc
1426 N Grand Street
Hutchinson, KS 67501-2135

620-669-8269
Fax: 620-669-9815 866-886-8269
www.jayhawkmills.com
Manufacturer and exporter of wet process, stone
grinding and colloid mills used primarily in the pro-
duction of condiments
President: Merle Starr
Estimated Sales: $500,000-$1 Million
Number Employees: 1-4
Brands:
Jayhawk Mills

24533 Jeb Plastics
3519 Silverside Rd Ste 106
Wilmington, DE 19810

302-479-9223
Fax: 302-479-9227 800-556-2247
www.jebplastics.com
Wholesaler/distributor/broker of poly bags, vinyl
bags, heat sealers and packaging supplies
Owner: Sherri Lindner
Estimated Sales: Below $500,000
Number Employees: 1-4
Square Footage: 4000

24534 Jeco Plastic Products LLC
885 Andico Rd
Plainfield, IN 46168-9659

317-839-4943
Fax: 317-839-1209 800-593-5326
www.jecoplastics.com
FDA approved plastic pallet and containers
President/CEO: Craig Carson
craigc@jecoplastics.com
CFO: Sherry Arndt
R & D: Roger Streling
Sales: Paul Koehl
Sales/Customer support: Ann Carson
Plant Manager: Don Andrews
Estimated Sales: Below $5 Million
Number Employees: 20-49
Square Footage: 74000
Type of Packaging: Bulk
Brands:
Perfect Pallet

24535 Jedwards International Inc
141 Campanelli Dr
Braintree, MA 02184-5206

781-848-1473
Fax: 617-472-9359 sales@bulknaturaloils.com
www.bulknaturaloils.com
Organic specialty oils, essential oils, butters, waxes
and botanicals
Contact: Jeremy Bamsch
jeremy@bulknaturaloils.com

24536 Jeffcoat Signs
1611 S Main St
Gainesville, FL 32601-8608

352-377-2322
Fax: 352-377-4249 877-377-4248
info@jeffcoatsigns.com www.jeffcoatsigns.com
Signs including plastic, neon and painted; installa-
tion services available
President: Kevin Jeffers
kevin@jeffcoatsigns.com
Estimated Sales: Less Than $500,000
Number Employees: 5-9
Square Footage: 90000

24537 Jefferson Packing Company
765 Marlene Drive
Gretna, LA 70056-7639

504-366-4451
Fax: 504-366-9382

Packaging solutions
President: William Marciante

24538 Jefferson Smurfit Corporation
1228 Tower Rd
Schaumburg, IL 60173-4308

847-884-1200
Fax: 847-884-7206 supplierzone@smurfit.com
Flexible packaging
President: Gary Mc Daniel
VP: Mark A Polivka
Estimated Sales: $20-50 Million
Number Employees: 100-249

24539 Jemolo Enterprises
100 S Westwood Street
Spc 126
Porterville, CA 93257-7708

559-784-5566
Fax: 209-823-2506 jemoloente@aol.com
www.jemolo.en.ec21.com
Manufacturer and exporter of environmental techno-
logical building systems including water purification
and waste water and sanitation treatment; also, reverse osmosis water treatment systems
President: Fred Niswonger

24540 Jen-Coat, Inc.
132 North Elm Street
PO Box 274
Westfield, MA 01086

877-536-2628
Fax: 413-562-8771 info@jencoat.com
Manufacturer and exporter of plastic coated paper
President: James Kauffman
Contact: Michelle Cotham
michellec@workplacestaff.com
Estimated Sales: $1-5 Million
Number Employees: 250-499
Parent Co: Ana Business Products

24541 Jenco Fan
6393 Powers Ave
Jacksonville, FL 32217-2217

904-731-4711
Fax: 904-737-8322 www.breidert.com
Owner: Patrick M Williams Sr
Contact: Josh Cosgrove
jcosgrove@solerpalau-usa.com
Estimated Sales: $20-50 Million
Number Employees: 100-249
Parent Co: Breidert Air Products

24542 (HQ)Jenike & Johanson Inc
400 Business Park Dr
Tyngsboro, MA 01879-1077

978-649-3300
Fax: 978-392-9980 www.bulk-solids-flow.com
Manufacturer, design engineer and consultant for
bulk solid handling equipment including portable
and stationary containers, hoppers, bins and silos
President: Orlando Andrs
aorlando@jenike.com
V.P. of Technology: T Anthony Royal
Marketing Director: Rod Hossefeld
Sales Director: Brian Pittenger
Estimated Sales: $2.5-5 Million
Number Employees: 20-49
Type of Packaging: Bulk
Other Locations:
    Jenike & Johanson
    Westford MA
Brands:
    Binsert

24543 Jenkins Sign Co
1400 Mahoning Ave
Youngstown, OH 44509-2503

330-799-3205
Fax: 330-799-3024 jenkinsadmin@neo.rr.com
www.jenkinsign.com
Plastic, metal and neon signs
President: J Jenkins
jenkinssales@neo.rr.com
Administrative Assistant: Sue Kaden
Estimated Sales: $3-5 Million
Number Employees: 20-49

24544 Jensen Fittings Corporation
107 Goundry Street
111
North Tonawanda, NY 14120-5998

800-255-4111
Fax: 800-523-4165 800-255-4111
Sanitary stainless steel valves, pumps, and fittings
Estimated Sales: $10-20 Million
Number Employees: 19

24545 Jentek
PO Box 809
North Branford, CT 06471-0809

203-488-5334
Fax: 203-481-9006
Dry coating equipment for ice cream sticks
President: Susanna Jensen
Plant Manager: Christian Jensen
Estimated Sales: $500,000-$1 Million
Number Employees: 1-4

24546 Jergens Inc
15700 S Waterloo Rd
Cleveland, OH 44110-3898

216-486-2100
Fax: 216-481-6193 800-537-4367
info@jergensinc.com www.jergensinc.com
Knobs and handles, cranks, threaded inserts, quick
change devices and hardware, automated tape dis-
pensing equipment, toggle clamps, grippers, slides,
vacuum generators, rotary actuators, pick-n-place,
and remote IO transmissiondevices
President: Jack Schron
jschron@jergensinc.com
CFO: W Howard
Quality Control: J Klindenerg
Estimated Sales: $20-50 Million
Number Employees: 100-249

24547 Jersey Shore Steel Co
70 Maryland Ave
Jersey Shore, PA 17740-7113

570-753-3000
Fax: 570-753-3782 800-833-0277
sales@jssteel.com www.jssteel.com
Wine industry metal grape stakes
Owner: Lorraine Barone
lbarone@jssteel.com
Estimated Sales: $63.40 Million
Number Employees: 250-499

24548 Jervis B WEBB Co
30100 Cabot Dr
Novi, MI 48377

248-553-1000
www.daifuku.com/us
Manufacturer and exporter of conveyor and inte-
grated material handling systems.
President & CEO: Aki Nishimura
Year Founded: 1919
Estimated Sales: $100-250 Million
Number Employees: 1,000
Parent Co: Daifuku Co.
Other Locations:
    Webb, Jervis B., Co.
    Chardon OH

24549 Jesco Industries
950 Anderson Rd
Litchfield, MI 49252

517-542-2353
Fax: 517-542-2501 800-455-0019
www.jescoonline.com
Manufacturer, importer and exporter of hoppers,
dumpers, security trucks, carts, dollies, baskets, wire
mesh partitions, security cages, window guards and
enclosures, etc
Vice President: Tom Sebastian
toms@jescolion.com
VP: B Desjardin
Marketing Director: Bonny DesJardin
Sales Engineer: Phil Risedorph
Estimated Sales: $8 Million
Number Employees: 100-249
Square Footage: 360000
Brands:
    Jesco
    Wipco

24550 (HQ)Jescorp
300 E Touhy Avenue
Suite C
Des Plaines, IL 60018-2669

847-299-7800
Fax: 847-299-7822

Manufacturer and exporter of thermoformed and
laminated containers and films, integrated gas flush-
ing systems, gas flush tray sealers and vacuum
seamers
VP Direct Sales: Jim Sanfilippo
Number Employees: 64
Square Footage: 280000
Brands:
    Belt-Vac
    Map-Fresh
    Map-Seal
    Ms-1400
    Ms-25
    Ms-55
    Ms-700
    Nitro-Flush
    Vbt-1100
    Vbt-250
    Vbt-550

24551 Jess Jones Vineyard
6496 Jones Ln
Dixon, CA 95620-9601

707-678-3839
Fax: 707-678-3898 www.jessjonesvineyard.com
Wines
President: Jess Jones
CEO: Mary Ellen Jones
Estimated Sales: $700,000
Number Employees: 1-4
Square Footage: 20000
Type of Packaging: Consumer, Bulk
Brands:
    California Golden Pop
    Customer's Bags
    Jess Jones Farms

24552 Jesse Jones Box Corporation
499 E Erie Avenue
Philadelphia, PA 19134-1104

215-425-6600
Fax: 215-425-4705
Set-up and folding boxes, specialty containers and
point of purchase displays
Director Sales: Harvey Brenner
Contact: William Fenkel
jjibill@aol.com
Production Manager: Joseph Pomray
Estimated Sales: $3-5 Million
Number Employees: 50-75
Square Footage: 90000
Parent Co: Jesse Jones Industries
Type of Packaging: Bulk

24553 Jessup Paper Box
211 S Railroad St
Brookston, IN 47923

765-490-9043
Fax: 765-563-3424 www.jessuppaperbox.com
Paper boxes and novelties
President: Butch Huber
CFO: Butch Huber
General Manager: Donald Winship
Plant Manager: Donald Cross
Purchasing Manager: Peggy Ruckdeschel
Estimated Sales: Below $5 Million
Number Employees: 20-49

24554 Jet Box Co
1822 Thunderbird
Troy, MI 48084-5479

248-362-1260
Fax: 248-362-2736
Corrugated boxes
Chairman of the Board: Lynda K Zardus
Estimated Sales: Below $5 Million
Number Employees: 20-49

24555 Jet Lite Products
PO Box 279
Highland, IL 62249

618-654-2217
Fax: 618-654-2217
Lighting fixtures and neon signs
President: John D Kutz Jr
Vice President: Roger Huber
Plant Manager: Joe Kutz
Estimated Sales: Below $5 Million
Number Employees: 10-19
Square Footage: 24000

24556 Jet Plastica Industries
1100 Schwab Rd
Hatfield, PA 19440
www.dwfinepack.com
Manufacturer and exporter of molded plastics including packaging kits, tumblers, cutlery and straws
Contact: Donna Alexander
dalexander2@kaplanco.com
Estimated Sales: $43 Million
Number Employees: 600
Square Footage: 300000
Parent Co: D&W Fine Pack

24557 Jetnet Corp
505 North Dr
79 North Industrial Park
Sewickley, PA 15143-2339
412-741-0100
Fax: 412-741-0140 800-245-1036
info@jetnetcorp.com www.jetnetcorp.com
Cutting and boning devices, general packinghouse equipment, uniforms, aprons and clothing; processing equipment, netting and tying machines
President: Donald Sartore
CEO: Bill Attiya
billa@jetnetcorp.com
Estimated Sales: $5-10 Million
Number Employees: 50-99

24558 Jetstream Systems
400 South Emporia St.
Wichita, KN 67202
316-462-9784
Fax: 303-371-9012 855-861-6916
jetstreamsys.com
Manufacturer and exporter of mechanical and air conveyors, palletizers and depalletizers, bottle and can fillers and rinsers
Director Sales: Neal McConnellogue
Director Applications: Vince Jones
Number Employees: 153
Square Footage: 264000
Parent Co: Barry-Wehmiller Company

24559 Jewel Case Corp
110 Dupont Dr
Cranston, RI 02907-3181
401-943-1400
Fax: 401-943-1426 800-441-4447
contact@jewelcase.com www.jewelcase.com
Manufacturer and exporter of gift and promotional packaging for candy, confections, gourmet foods and cutlery/tableware
President: Terri Eisen
teisen@jewelcase.com
Controller: Terry Eisen
Marketing Manager: Lynn Johnson
Sales: Richard Dobuski
Estimated Sales: $10-20 Million
Number Employees: 100-249
Square Footage: 200000
Type of Packaging: Consumer, Private Label, Bulk

24560 Jewell Bag Company
228 Yorktown St
Suite B
Dallas, TX 75208-2045
214-749-1223
Fax: 214-749-1226
FDA approved polyethylene bags
President: Michael Smith
Estimated Sales: $1-2.5 Million
Number Employees: 1-4

24561 Jhrg LLC
303 S Pine St
Spring Hope, NC 27882-9551
252-478-4997
Fax: 252-478-4998 800-849-4997
info@hsarmor.com www.hsarmor.com
Owner: John Holland
jholland@hsarmor.com
Partner: John Holland
jholland@hsarmor.com
Estimated Sales: $1-5 Million
Number Employees: 50-99

24562 (HQ)Jif-Pak Manufacturing
1451 Engineer St # A
Vista, CA 92081-8841
760-597-2665
Fax: 760-597-2667 800-777-6613
info@jifpak.com www.jifpak.com
Manufacturer and exporter of elastic and nonelastic nettings, stockinettes, stuffing horns, semi and automatic netting machines and elastic trussing loops
President: Gary Cleppe
garycleppe@kalleusa.com
Marketing Executive: John Connelly
Operations Ex: Lee Jared
Estimated Sales: $1-5 Million
Number Employees: 5-9
Brands:
Casing-Net
Jif-Pak

24563 Jiffy Mixer Co Inc
1691 California Ave
Corona, CA 92881-3375
951-272-0838
Fax: 951-279-7651 800-560-2903
www.jiffymixer.com
Nonelectric mixers including portable and heavy duty
President: Jeff Johnson
jeff@jiffymixer.com
Production Manager: Douglas Kaus
Office Manager: Al Measham
Estimated Sales: Below $5 Million
Number Employees: 5-9
Square Footage: 12000

24564 Jilson Group
20 Industrial Rd
Lodi, NJ 7644
973-471-2400
Fax: 973-471-3993 800-969-5400
heretohelp@jilson.com www.jilson.com
Manufacturer and importer of casters, wheels, noncorrosive bearings and bearing housings as well as plastic packaging ties.
Chief Financial Officer: Pete Rennard
VP: David Baughn
Products Manager: Steven Becher
Vice President Sales: David Baughn
Contact: Tony Alfano
talfano@jilson.com
Purchasing Manager: Tony Alfano
Estimated Sales: $2.5-5 Million
Number Employees: 10-19
Square Footage: 40000
Brands:
Steinco Casters

24565 Jim Did It Sign Company
PO Box 17
Allston, MA 2134
617-782-2410
Fax: 781-782-5433
Manufacturer and exporter of commercial signs for supermarkets and other businesses
Owner: Robert Thompson
Estimated Sales: $500,000-$1 Million
Number Employees: 5-9

24566 Jim Lake Companies
1350 Manufacturing St # 101
Dallas, TX 75207
214-741-5018
Fax: 214-741-5020 info@jimlakeco.com
www.jimlakeco.com
Rubber stamps and seals
Founder: Jim Lake
Marketing Coordinator: Monica Diodati
Estimated Sales: $500,000-$1 Million
Number Employees: 10-19

24567 Jim Scharf Holdings
PO Box 305 Ave K & 9th St
Perdue, SK S0K 3C0
Canada
306-237-4365
Fax: 306-237-4362 800-667-9727
sales@ezeewrap.com www.ezeewrap.com
Manufacturer and exporter of plastic wrap dispensers, process refrigerator/freezer odor absorbers, shopping bag handles, bagel cutters and lettuce knives; processor of instant lentils
President: Bruna Scharf
Marketing: Leanna Carr
Plant Manager: Mary Ann Cotterill
Estimated Sales: Below $5,000,000
Number Employees: 10
Square Footage: 24000
Brands:
Bagel Buddy
Bakeware Buddy
E-Zee Wrap
Grocery Grip
Heavenly Fresh
Kitchen Buddy
The Lettuce Knife

24568 Jimbo's Jumbos Inc
185 Peanut Dr
Edenton, NC 27932-9604
252-482-2193
Fax: 252-482-7857 800-334-4771
Snacks and peanuts; custom formulation
Manager: Hal Burns
Manager: Debbie Miller
dmiller@jimbosjumbos.com
Number Employees: 100-249
Type of Packaging: Private Label

24569 Jl Analytical Svc Inc
217 Primo Way
Modesto, CA 95358-5749
209-538-8111
Fax: 209-538-3966
Laboratory specializing in food analysis and water testing
President: Mary Jacobs
CEO: Richard Jacobs, Ph.D.
VP: Mark Jacobs
Estimated Sales: $5-10 Million
Number Employees: 50-99

24570 Jms Packaging Consultants Inc
10 Lenbar Cir
New City, NY 10956-4908
845-708-0701
Fax: 845-708-0702 jstrassman@jmspackaging.com
www.jmspackaging.com
Custom gift packaging, plastic set-up and folding boxes
Owner: Joel Strassman
jmspkg@aol.com
CEO: Joel Strassnan
Estimated Sales: Less Than $500,000
Number Employees: 1-4

24571 Jo Mar Laboratories
583 Division St # B
Campbell, CA 95008-6915
408-374-5920
Fax: 408-374-5922 800-538-4545
info@jomarlabs.com www.jomarlabs.com
Health products; contract packaging
President: Joanne Brown
joanne@jomarlabs.com
Estimated Sales: $1-3 Million
Number Employees: 10-19
Square Footage: 14000
Parent Co: Jo Mar Labs
Type of Packaging: Consumer, Private Label

24572 Jogue
14731 Helm Court
Plymouth, MI 48170
734-207-0100
Fax: 734-207-0200 800-521-3888
www.jogue.com
Flavor development
President: Dattu Sastry
Estimated Sales: $5 Million
Number Employees: 20-49
Type of Packaging: Food Service, Private Label

24573 Johanson TransportationSvc
5583 E Olive Ave
Fresno, CA 93727-2559
559-458-2200
Fax: 559-458-2234 800-742-2053
LJohanson@johansontrans.com
www.johansontrans.com
Transporters of dry and temperature controlled freight.
President: Larry Johanson
ljohanson@johansontrans.com
CFO: Janice Spicer
Vice President: Craig Johanson
Chief Operations Officer: Jerry Beckstead
Corporate Accounting & Administration Ma: Becky Martin
Number Employees: 20-49

24574 John Bean Technologies Corp

400 Highpoint Dr
Chalfont, PA 18914-3924

215-822-4600
Fax: 215-822-4553 888-362-3622
sgv.sales@fmcti.com www.jbtc-agv.com
Automated guided vehicles
Manager: Barry Douglas
barry.douglas@jbtc.com
Advertising Manager: Amy Porter
Estimated Sales: $50-100 Million
Number Employees: 100-249

24575 (HQ)John Boos & Co

3601 S Banker St
PO Box 609
Effingham, IL 62401-2899

217-347-7701
Fax: 217-347-7705 888-431-2667
www.johnboos.com
Manufacturer and exporter of cutting boards, butchers' blocks, dining room tables and chairs and stainless steel work tables and sinks
President: Edward Surowiec
gerencia@cibersam.es
Executive Chef: Dustin Muroski
VP Sales: Eric Johnson
Estimated Sales: $10-20 Million
Number Employees: 20-49
Square Footage: 260000
Other Locations:
  John Boos & Co.
  Philipsburg PA
Brands:
  Cucina Americana
  Pro Bowl
  Pro Chef
  Stallion
  The Table Tailors

24576 John Burton Machine Corporation

3251 John Muir Pkwy
Rodeo, CA 94572

510-799-5000
Fax: 510-799-5003 800-664-4178
Packaging machines and case conveyor, case conveyors for cardboard boxes and tote boxes
President: Burton Rice
Sales Director: Burton Rice
Estimated Sales: Below $5 Million
Number Employees: 1-4
Brands:
  Chain-In-Channel

24577 John Crane Mechanical Sealing Devices

227 W Monroe St
Suite 1800
Chicago, IL 60606

www.johncrane.com
Manufacturer and exporter of mechanical seals, bearing isolators, couplings, lubrication systems, heat exchangers and pressure reservoirs.
President & CEO: Jean Vernet
Chief Financial Officer: Celine Boland
Vice President & General Counsel: Jay Angelo
VP & Chief Technology Officer: Joe Haas
Vice President, Global Quality: Rich Steffens
Executive Vice President, Marketing: Patrick Thompson
Year Founded: 1910
Estimated Sales: $900 Million
Number Employees: 6,550
Square Footage: 9000
Parent Co: TI Group

24578 John E. Ruggles & Company

PO Box 8179
New Bedford, MA 02742-8179

508-992-9766
Fax: 508-992-9734
Manufacturer, importer and exporter of varietal fiber regular and dyed rope, twine and braid
President: John Ruggles
Estimated Sales: $5-10 Million
Number Employees: 50-99
Square Footage: 100000

24579 John Henry Packaging

10005 Main St
Penngrove, CA 94951

707-664-8018
Fax: 707-762-1253 800-327-5997

Producer of digital, flexo, embossed, screened labels and cartons
Owner: John Herpeck
Digital Print Manager/Marketing Director: Dan Welty
Number Employees: 5-9
Number of Brands: 30
Square Footage: 8000
Parent Co: John Henry Company
Type of Packaging: Consumer, Food Service, Private Label, Bulk

24580 John J. Adams Die Corporation

10 Nebraska St
Worcester, MA 01604-3628

508-757-3894
Fax: 508-753-8016 jadamsdie@aol.com
Knives; exporter of cutting dies
President and CFO: Richard Adams
General Manager: John J Adams II
Marketing: John Adams
Estimated Sales: $2.5-5 Million
Number Employees: 1-4
Square Footage: 40000

24581 John L. Denning & Company

330 N Washington St
Wichita, KS 67202

316-264-2357
Fax: 316-264-3521
Brooms
President: Ed Collins
Number Employees: 4

24582 John Larkin & Co Inc

96 Ford Rd # 15
Denville, NJ 07834-1359

973-627-7779
Fax: 973-627-7809 john.larkin@verizon.net
www.johnlarkinandcompany.com
Tea and coffee industry repair service
President: John Larkin
john.larkin@verizon.net
Estimated Sales: $1-2.5 Million
Number Employees: 1-4

24583 John Morrell Food Group

PO Box 405020
Cincinnati, OH 45240

800-722-1127
www.johnmorrell.com
Meat products including; ham and turkey, bacon, hot dogs, smoked sausage, lunchmeat, and special reserve hams.
President/CEO, Smithfield Foods: Kenneth Sullivan
Year Founded: 1827
Estimated Sales: Over $1 Billion
Number Employees: 5000-9999
Parent Co: Smithfield Foods
Type of Packaging: Consumer, Food Service, Private Label, Bulk
Brands:
  John Morrell

24584 John Plant Co

112 Greenhill Rd
Ramseur, NC 27316-8749

336-824-2366
Fax: 336-824-3177 800-334-2711
gloves@johnplant.com www.johnplant.com
Manufacturer and importer of gloves and safety supplies
Owner: Robert Jarman
jarman@johnplant.com
CEO: Ron Tesh
Estimated Sales: $2.5-5 Million
Number Employees: 10-19
Square Footage: 48000
Parent Co: John Plant Company

24585 John R Nalbach Engineering Co

621 E Plainfield Rd
Countryside, IL 60525-6913

708-579-9100
Fax: 708-579-0122 neco@nalbach.com
www.nalbach.com
Manufacturer and exporter of high speed powder fillers for instant coffee, ground coffee and drink mixes; also, plastic bottle unscrambles, container orientors and aerosol filling lines.

Owner: Matt Nalbach
CEO: John Nalbach
VP Engineering: David Nowaczyk
VP Marketing: Edward Atwell
VP Sales: Gary Lange
mnalbach@nalbach.com
VP Manufacturing: Phil Testa
Estimated Sales: $5-10 Million
Number Employees: 20-49
Square Footage: 280000

24586 John Rock Inc

500 Independence Way
Coatesville, PA 19320-1689

610-857-4809
Fax: 610-857-4809 www.johnrock.com
Recycled wooden pallets
President: Bill Mac Cauley
bill@johnrock.com
Finance: Steve Hedrick
Lumber: Penn Cooper
Sales: Mike Veneziale
Customer Service: Jeanne Ryan
Operations: Ed Healy
Administration: Robyn Stoltzfus
Facilities/Fleet: Steve Marrs
Estimated Sales: $5-10 Million
Number Employees: 50-99
Square Footage: 200000

24587 John Rohrer ContractingCo

2820 Roe Ln # S
Kansas City, KS 66103-1560

913-236-5005
Fax: 913-236-7291
www.johnrohrercontracting.com
Manufacturer and exporter of concrete floors
Owner: Kirt Courkamp
kirtcourkamp@jrcccolorado.net
EVP: Brandon McMullen
Estimated Sales: $1-2.5 Million
Number Employees: 10-19

24588 John W Keplinger & Sons

2789 Egypt Rd
Norristown, PA 19403-2254

610-666-6191
Fax: 610-666-6215
Flags, banners and flagpoles
Owner: John W Keplinger
Estimated Sales: Less Than $500,000
Number Employees: 1-4

24589 John W. Spaulding Brokerage

2035 W McDowell Rd
Phoenix, AZ 85009-3012

602-254-4777
Fax: 602-258-5623
Wholesaler/distributor of salt products including food grade, water softener, agricultural, etc.; serving the food service market
Owner: John W Spalding Iii
CEO: John Spaulding
Estimated Sales: $500,000-$1 Million
Number Employees: 7
Type of Packaging: Food Service, Private Label, Bulk

24590 Johnson & Sons Manufacturing

534-D West 2nd St.
Elgin, TX 78261

512-285-2462
Fax: 512-285-2464
info@johnsonbaggingequipment.com
www.johnsonbaggingequipment.com
Contact: Brent Johnson
brent@johnsonbaggingequipment.com
Estimated Sales: $300,000-$500,000
Number Employees: 1-4

24591 Johnson & Wales University

8 Abbott Park Pl
Providence, RI 02903-3775

401-598-1000
Fax: 401-598-2880 800-342-5598
President: John J Bowen
Executive VP: Richard J Kosh
rkosh@jwu.edu
Number Employees: 1000-4999

24592 Johnson Associates
600 W Roosevelt Rd
Unit B-2
Wheaton, IL 60187
630-690-9200
Fax: 630-690-9910 sjohnson@jasearch.com
www.jasearch.com
Executive search firm specializing in the food,
non-food and beverage industries
President: Scott Johnson
VP: Mary Johnson
Contact: Don Huston
dhuston@jasearch.com
Estimated Sales: Below $5 Million
Number Employees: 1-4

24593 Johnson Brothers Manufacturing Company
412 W 3rd Street
Elgin, TX 78621-2117
512-285-2462
Fax: 512-285-2464
Bagging scales
Estimated Sales: $1-5 Million
Number Employees: 1-4

24594 Johnson Brothers Sign Co Inc
307 S State St
PO Box 345
South Whitley, IN 46787-1409
260-723-5161
Fax: 260-723-6778 800-477-7516
info@johnsonbros-sign.com
www.johnsonbros-sign.com
Electric, neon and plastic signs
President: Les Cripe
les@johnsonbros-sign.com
Estimated Sales: $1-2.5 Million
Number Employees: 10-19
Square Footage: 37600

24595 Johnson Controls Inc
5757 N Green Bay Ave
P.O. Box 591
Milwaukee, WI 53209-4408
414-524-1200
Fax: 414-524-2077 www.johnsoncontrols.com
Gas and electronic and electromechanical refrigera-
tion controls, HVAC/refrigeration/lighting store
management systems
President: David Myers
CEO: Alex A Molinaroli
alex.a.molinaroli@jci.com
Estimated Sales: Over $1 Billion
Number Employees: 10000+

24596 Johnson Corrugated Products Corporation
PO Box 246
Thompson, CT 06277
860-923-9563
Fax: 860-923-2531
Corrugated packaging materials inlcuding corru-
gated and paper boxes; also, cake and pizza circles
Manager: Andrew Baumont
General Manager: Dick Clark
Estimated Sales: $20-50 Million
Number Employees: 10-19

24597 Johnson Diversified Products
1408 Northland Dr
Suite 406
Mendota Heights, MN 55120-1013
651-688-0014
Fax: 952-686-7670 800-676-8488
info@jdpinc.com www.jdpinc.com
Wholesaler/distributor of food service equipment,
and HACCP related instruments, tools and systems;
serving the food service market
CEO: Thomas Johnson
Vice President: Paul Johnson
Estimated Sales: $5-10 Million
Number Employees: 5-9

24598 (HQ)Johnson Food Equipment Inc
2955 Fairfax Trfy
Kansas City, KS 66115-1317
913-621-3366
Fax: 913-621-1729 800-288-3434
www.baader-johnson.com
Poultry processing equipment

President: Andy Miller
CEO: Oliver Hahn
oliver.hahn@baaderna.com
CFO: Shawn Nicholas
Sr VP: David Crawford
General Sales Manager: Steve Abram
Sales Manager (Food Systems): Bruce Sterling
Estimated Sales: $20-50 Million
Number Employees: 10-19
Square Footage: 70000
Other Locations:
Johnson Food Equipment
Kitchener ON

24599 Johnson Industries Intl
6391 Lake Rd
Windsor, WI 53598-9708
608-846-4499
Fax: 608-846-7195 info@johnsonindint.com
www.johnsonindint.com
Manufacturer and exporter of mozzarella cheese
making machinery
President: Gary Nesheim
gnesheim@johnsonindint.com
Estimated Sales: $5-10 Million
Number Employees: 50-99
Square Footage: 77408
Brands:
Supreme

24600 Johnson Industries Intl
6391 Lake Rd
Windsor, WI 53598-9708
608-846-4499
Fax: 608-846-7195 info@johnsonindint.com
www.johnsonindint.com
Manufacturer cheese processing equipment
President: Gary Nesheim
gnesheim@johnsonindint.com
Owner and Cheese Industry Expert: Peter Nelles
Sales Director: Todd Martin
Plant Manager: Eric Severson
Director Purchasing: Scott Peterson
Number Employees: 50-99
Number of Brands: 4
Square Footage: 200000

24601 Johnson International Materials
2908 Boca Chica Blvd
Brownsville, TX 78521-3506
956-541-6364
Fax: 956-541-1446
Manufacturer and exporter of wiping rags
President: Jim Johnson
VP Marketing: Bob Ewing
Estimated Sales: $20-50 Million
Number Employees: 100-249

24602 Johnson Pump Of America
1625 Hunter Rd
Hanover Park, IL 60133-6767
847-671-7867
Fax: 847-671-7909 www.johnson-pump.com
Positive displacement rotary lobe pumps
CEO: Jerry Assessor
VP Sales: Mitch Pixley
Contact: Gregg Pardus
johnson-pump.americas.marine@spx.com
Production Manager: Tony Wuethrich
Estimated Sales: $20-50 Million
Number Employees: 50-99
Parent Co: Johnson Pumps of America
Brands:
Albin

24603 (HQ)Johnson Refrigerated Truck
215 E Allen St
Rice Lake, WI 54868-2203
715-234-7071
Fax: 715-234-4628 800-922-8360
jtbsales@johnsontruckbodies.com
Manufacturer and exporter of fiberglass composite
plastic refrigerated truck bodies and trailers, and
all-electric truck refrigeration systems.
President: Ron Ricci
rricci@johnsontruckbodies.com
VP Sales/Marketing: Mayo Rude
Public Relations: Nicole King
VP Operations: Chris Olson
Number Employees: 250-499
Square Footage: 268000
Type of Packaging: Food Service

24604 Johnson Starch Molding
13549 W Greenview Drive
Wadsworth, IL 60083-9309
847-872-1989
Fax: 847-872-1988
Boards, starch, conveyors, cooling equipment, cool-
ing tunnels, elevators, bucket, feeder belts
Estimated Sales: $1-5 Million
Number Employees: 4

24605 Johnson-Rose Corporation
5303 Crown Dr
Lockport, NY 14094
716-434-2711
Fax: 716-434-2762 800-456-2055
info@johnsonrose.com www.johnsonrose.com
Aluminum cookware and bakeware; importer and
exporter of commercial kitchen utensils including
ladles, spoons, tongs, mixing bowls, collanders,
steam pans, etc
President: Ernie Berman
ernieberman@johnsonrose.net
CFO: Viola Wilson
Director of Marketing: Mark Kuligowski
Operations Manager: D Kuligowski
Inventory Control: Darrell Szyprygada
Estimated Sales: $2.5-5 Million
Number Employees: 20-49
Square Footage: 82000
Parent Co: Johnson-Rose

24606 Johnston Boiler Co Inc
300 Pine St
Ferrysburg, MI 49409-5131
616-842-5050
Fax: 616-842-1854 info@johnstonboiler.com
www.johnstonboiler.com
Boilers, generators, heat recovery systems, burners,
energy savings, JBC engineering, emission data,
JBC specifications, driving directions
President: R Kim Black
COO: Rick Ewing
rewing@johnstonboiler.com
Director: Pat Baker
Estimated Sales: $5-10 Million
Number Employees: 1-4

24607 Johnston Equipment
#105-581 Chester Road
Annacis Island
Delta, BC V3M 6G7
Canada
604-524-0361
Fax: 604-524-8961 800-237-5159
couttsd@johnstonequipment.com
www.johnstonequipment.com
Manufacturer, wholesaler/distributor and exporter of
material handling equipment including electric fork-
lifts and pallet racking/shelving systems
President & CEO: Michael Marcotte
Regional Sales Manager: John Binns
Sales Manager: Curt Snigol
Estimated Sales: $1-5 Million
Number Employees: 50-99
Square Footage: 66000
Brands:
Pacific Westeel
Serco

24608 Johnstown Manufacturing
1055 S Hamilton Rd
Columbus, OH 43227-1309
614-236-8853
Fax: 614-876-6797
Plastic straws and stirrers
Manager: John Scott
Number Employees: 50-99

24609 Jokamsco Group
22 Lea Ave
Waterford,, NY 12118-1927
518-237-6416
Fax: 518-233-7203 Jokamsco@aol.com
www.hudsonrivergrinding.com
Gears and machine replacement parts for the food
and beverage industry; also, industrial knife grind-
ing available
President: Colleen Swedish
Estimated Sales: $300,000-500,000
Number Employees: 1-4
Square Footage: 10000

24610 Jomac Products
7525 N Oak Park Avenue
Niles, IL 60714-3819
215-343-0800
Fax: 215-343-0912 800-566-2289
Manufacturer and exporter of terrycloth, cut-resistant and nomex gloves, mitts, aprons, pads and sleeves
Marketing Manager: Charlie Lake
Sales Manager: Jim Podall
Number Employees: 499
Type of Packaging: Food Service, Bulk
Brands:
  Cool Blues
  Pott Holdr
  The Shield

24611 Jomar Corp
115 E Parkway Dr
Egg Harbor Twp, NJ 08234-5112
609-646-8000
Fax: 609-645-9166 www.jomarcorp.com
Manufacturer and exporter of plastic injection blow molding machinery and plastic molds and dies
President: William Petrino
Founder: Joseph Johnson
Senior VP: Walter Priest
Contact: Ed Burns
eburns@jomarcorp.com
Estimated Sales: $10-20 Million
Number Employees: 20-49
Square Footage: 90000
Parent Co: Inductotherm Industries
Brands:
  Aquatral
  Jomar

24612 Jomar Plastics Industry
1304 Shoemaker St
Nanty Glo, PA 15943-1255
814-749-9131
Fax: 814-749-8079 800-681-4039
info@floodcity.net
Plastic bags for bakery, meat and poultry
President: Pam Harkcom
VP: Susan Ott
Estimated Sales: $500,000-$1 Million
Number Employees: 1-4
Square Footage: 10000

24613 Joneca Corp
4332 E LA Palma Ave
Anaheim, CA 92807-1806
714-993-5997
Fax: 714-993-2126 info@joneca.com
www.joneca.com
Manufacturer and exporter of dehydrators and waste reduction and water purification systems
President: Edward E Chavez
contactus@joneca.com
Estimated Sales: Below $5 Million
Number Employees: 10-19
Parent Co: Anaheim Marketing International
Brands:
  Aquacare
  Commodore
  Compacta
  Mr. Scrapy

24614 Jones Automation Company
11838 W Carroll Rd
Beloit, WI 53511
608-879-9307
Fax: 608-879-2266
Forming, filling and sealing equipment, stacking and interleaving equipment, vacuum packaging equipment, wrapping and overwrap machines, slicers and weigh-convey systems
Estimated Sales: $1-5 Million
Number Employees: 10

24615 Jones Environmental
2404 Rutland Dr Ste 200
P.O. Box 5387
Fullerton, CA 92838
714-449-9937
Fax: 714-449-9685 www.jonesenv.com
Waste treatment plants capable of anaerobic and aerobic processes for the food and beverage industries; custom design services available

President: Jim Porteous
CEO: Dick Johnson
CFO: Nelda Tallman
Chairman: Richard Johnson
Marketing Assistant: Ann Perry
Production: Arthur Shaffer
Estimated Sales: Less than $500,000
Number Employees: 20-49

24616 Jones Packaging Machinery
8005 Wolftever Dr
Ooltewah, TN 37363
423-238-4558
Fax: 423-238-6018
Packaging machinery
President: Charles Abernathy
CFO: Charles Abernathy
Quality Control: Jeff Smith
Plant Manager: James Dillard
Estimated Sales: Below $5 Million
Number Employees: 10
Square Footage: 24000

24617 Jones-Hamilton Co
30354 Tracy Rd
Walbridge, OH 43465-9792
419-666-9838
Fax: 419-666-1817 888-858-4425
info@jones-hamilton.com
www.jones-hamilton.com
Producer of natural acidulants and pHase.
CFO: Brian Brooks
EVP: Bernard Murphy
Director Research & Development: Carl Knueven
IT: Daniel Dias
dad@jones-hamilton.com
Plant Manager: Chuck Almroth
Estimated Sales: $64 Million
Number Employees: 50-99

24618 Jones-Zylon Co
305 N Center St
West Lafayette, OH 43845-1001
740-545-6341
Fax: 740-545-6671 800-848-8160
miker@joneszylon.com www.joneszylon.com
Institutional tableware, compartments and serving trays, tumblers, cups, bowls, plates and reusable plastic flatware; exporter of dinnerware and flatware
President: Todd Kohl
toddk@joneszylon.net
CEO: Tracey Jackrich
Quality Control: Chuck Laney
Sales (Mid Atlantic): Mike Robertson
Sales (West): Myron Vile
Chairperson: Marion Mulligan-Sutton
Estimated Sales: $5-10 Million
Number Employees: 10-19
Square Footage: 81600
Parent Co: Jones Metal Products Company
Brands:
  Jones Zylon

24619 Jonessco Enterprises
2801 Regal Road
Suite 103
Plano, TX 75075-6315
972-985-7961
Fax: 972-612-1741 www.whereorg.com
Consultant specializing in food technology, marketing and promotion for the supermarket and food service industries
President: Buck Jones
CFO: Buck Jones
R&D: Bill Jacob
Estimated Sales: Below $5 Million
Number Employees: 5
Type of Packaging: Bulk

24620 Jordan Box Co
140 Dickerson St
PO Box 1054
Syracuse, NY 13202-2309
315-422-3419
Fax: 315-422-0318 sales@JordanBoxCo.com
www.jordanboxco.com
Paper boxes
President: Richard M Casper
rick@jordanboxco.com
Estimated Sales: $1-2.5 Million
Number Employees: 10-19

24621 Jordan Paper Box Co
5045 W Lake St
Chicago, IL 60644-2596
773-287-5362
Fax: 773-287-5362
Manufacturer, importer and exporter of paper boxes
President: John M Jordan
jordanpaperbox@att.net
President: Jam Jordan
Estimated Sales: $1-2.5 Million
Number Employees: 5-9
Square Footage: 60000
Type of Packaging: Bulk

24622 Jordan Specialty Company
1245 Route 1 South
Brooklyn, NY 11215-4603
Fax: 718-238-3221 877-567-3265
Transparent card cases, covers, holders and menu covers
Manager: Joshua Handler
Manager: Soul Handler
Estimated Sales: $1-2.5 Million
Number Employees: 20-49
Square Footage: 50000
Brands:
  Bondstar

24623 Jordon Commercial Refrigerator
2200 Kennedy Street
Philadelphia, PA 19137-1820
215-535-8300
Fax: 215-289-1597 800-523-0171
Manufacturer, importer and exporter of refrigerators and freezers
President: Gene Sterner
VP, Sales: Jim Duff
Purchasing Manager: Jerry Joyce
Number Employees: 100-249
Square Footage: 296000
Parent Co: Jordon/Fleetwood/Fogel, LLC
Other Locations:
  Jordon Commercial Refrigerato
  Fleetwood PA
Brands:
  Fleetwood
  Fogel
  Jordon

24624 Jordon-Fleetwood Commercial Refrigerator Company
2200 Kennedy Street
Philadelphia, PA 19137-1820
215-535-8300
Fax: 215-289-1597 www.keepitcool.com

24625 (HQ)Josam Co
525 W US Highway 20
Michigan City, IN 46360-6835
219-872-5531
Fax: 219-874-9539 800-365-6726
www.josam.com
Drains, interceptors, backwater valves, carriers, hydrants and water hammer arrestors
President: Barry Hodgkins
President, Chief Executive Officer: Scott Holloway
CFO: David Szerencse
Vice President of Sales and Marketing: Paula Bowe
Chief Operating Officer: Barry Hodgekins
Estimated Sales: $20-50 Million
Number Employees: 100-249

24626 Josef Kihlberg of America
2400 Galvin Dr
Elgin, IL 60124
Fax: 315-452-9597 800-437-9818
Stapling and strapping tools and fasteners
Estimated Sales: $1-3 Million
Number Employees: 10-19

24627 Joseph Manufacturing Company
5011 Antioch Road
Overland Park, KS 66203-1314
913-677-1660
Fax: 913-677-1658 800-373-6671
Automated and manual label dispensing and applying equipment
V.P.: Shawn Hornung
Estimated Sales: $5-10 Million
Number Employees: 19

24628 Joseph Struhl Co Inc
195 Atlantic Ave
PO Box N
New Hyde Park, NY 11040-5027
516-741-3660
Fax: 516-742-3617 800-552-0023
info@magicmaster.com www.magicmaster.com
Manufacturer and exporter of signs including
open/closed self-adhesive reusable and removable
static vinyl and stock and custom using static cling
vinyl
Managing Director: Cliff Stevens
cliff@magicmaster.com
Sales Manager: H Green
Manager: Cliff Stevens
Estimated Sales: $1-2.5 Million
Number Employees: 10-19
Brands:
    Design Master
    Magic Master
    Ready Made
    Super Moderna

24629 Joseph Titone & Sons
1006 Jacksonville Rd
Burlington, NJ 08016-3802
Fax: 609-386-8978 800-220-4102
www.metrolace.com
Nets and hair nets for food handlers
President: Alfred Titone
CFO/Attorney: John Titone
V.P.: Edward Dormand
Number Employees: 20-49
Square Footage: 110000

24630 Joul, Engineering StaffiSolutions
1245 Route 1 South
Raritan Plaza 1
Edison, NJ 8837
732-548-1069
Fax: 732-632-9795 800-341-0341
Consultant of custom design plant modernization
and automation equipment
Senior VP: Howard Moseman
Estimated Sales: $1-5 Million
Number Employees: 50-99
Parent Co: Joule

24631 Jowat Corp.
PO Box 1368
High Point, NC 27261
336-434-9000
Fax: 336-434-9019 800-322-4583
info@jowat.com www.jowat.com
Packaging hot melts, anti-slip hot melts, casein
glues, pressure sensitives, dextrins, water-based dis-
persions
President/Owner: Rainhard Kramme
Estimated Sales: F
Number Employees: 1,100

24632 Joyce Dayton Corp
3300 S Dixie Dr # 101
Moraine, OH 45439-2318
937-294-6261
Fax: 937-297-7173 800-523-5204
sales@joycedayton.com www.joycedayton.com
Lifts including hydraulic and mechanical powered
President: Patty Deppen
jgoodman@mcdonald-partners.com
CFO: Kim Gockal
Director Sales: Warren Webster
Estimated Sales: $10-20,000,000
Number Employees: 50-99

24633 Joyce Engraving Co Inc
1262 Round Table Dr
Dallas, TX 75247-3504
214-638-1262
Fax: 214-638-5432 sales@joyceengraving.com
www.joyce-engraving.com
Steel stamps, stencils and branding equipment in-
cluding burning, meat and tire
VP: Rick Joyce
ricky@joyceengraving.com
VP: R Joyce
Estimated Sales: Less Than $500,000
Number Employees: 1-4
Square Footage: 40000

24634 Joylin Food Equipment Corporation
51 Chestnut Ln
Woodbury, NY 11797-1918
Fax: 516-742-2123 800-456-9546
joylin1961@aol.com
Manufacturers' representative for food service
equipment
President: Rich Kirsner
Marketing Director: Tom Pitts
Sales Director: M Kohn
Operations Manager: Tom DiRusso
Purchasing Manager: Yvette Western
Estimated Sales: $20-50 Million
Number Employees: 21
Number of Brands: 16
Square Footage: 12000

24635 Jr Mats
1519 Mcdaniel Dr
West Chester, PA 19380-7037
610-344-7225
Fax: 610-696-6760 800-526-7763
justrightmats@aol.com
Manufacturer and distributor of quality entry mat-
ting, kitchen matting and antifatigue matting. Cus-
tom logo mats
Owner: Jay Mc Grath
Sales/Marketing: Jay McGrath
jrmats@comcast.net
General Manager: Jeri Delahanty
Estimated Sales: $1 Million
Number Employees: 1-4
Number of Brands: 10
Number of Products: 25
Square Footage: 116000
Type of Packaging: Consumer, Food Service, Pri-
vate Label, Bulk
Brands:
    Silver Streak

24636 Judel Products
45 Knollwood Road
Suite 24
Elmsford, NY 10523-2822
914-592-6200
Fax: 914-592-1216 800-583-3526
Manufacturer, importer and exporter of glassware
President: Mel Schulweis
VP: John Rufus
Sales Director: Stven Fox
Office Manager: Dorothy See
Estimated Sales: $500,000-$1 Million
Number Employees: 1-4
Parent Co: Tiffany & Company
Type of Packaging: Food Service
Brands:
    Durobor
    Judel
    Opticrystal
    Vintner's Ii
    Vintner's Selection

24637 Judge
300 Conshohocken State Rd #300
W Conshohocken, PA 19428-3820
610-667-7700
Fax: 610-667-1058 888-228-7162
wgladstone@judge.com www.judgeinc.com
Executive search agency specializing in operations
and distribution management
President: Michael F Ferreri
CEO: Martin Judge, Jr.
Estimated Sales: $1-5 Million
Number Employees: 20-49
Parent Co: Judge Group

24638 Juice Merchandising Corp
9237 Ward Pkwy # 104
Suite 104
Kansas City, MO 64114-3382
816-361-5343
Fax: 816-361-2033 800-950-1998
Plastic juice bottles as well as wholesaler/distributor
of juice processing equipment
Owner: Bob Bushman
juice@micro.com
CEO: Helen Bushman
Manager, Operations: Bill Young
Estimated Sales: Below $5 Million
Number Employees: 1-4
Square Footage: 4000
Type of Packaging: Private Label

24639 Juice Tree
10861 Mill Valley Road
Omaha, NE 68154-3975
714-891-4425
Fax: 714-892-3699
Manufacturer and exporter of citrus juice extractors,
pineapple peelers, mobile ice display tables for fresh
fruit products and capped plastic containers for juice
President: James Beck
Plant Administrator: B Copeland
Estimated Sales: $1-2.5 Million
Number Employees: 19
Brands:
    Juice Tree

24640 Juicy Whip Inc
1668 Curtiss Ct
La Verne, CA 91750-5848
909-392-7500
Fax: 626-814-8016 www.juicywhip.com
Hispanic beverage concentrates
President/CEO: Gus Stratton
Purchasing: Craig Allen
Estimated Sales: $4 Million
Number Employees: 5-9
Square Footage: 88000
Brands:
    Juicy Whip

24641 Junction Solutions
9785 Maroon Cir
Suite 410
Englewood, CO 80112
877-502-6355
Fax: 303-327-8804
webinfo@junctionsolutions.com
www.junctionsolutions.com
Advanced enterprise software that allows food and
beverage processors to improve control over opera-
tions, quality, and compliance
CEO/President: Jeff Grell
CFO: Jeff Allen
Product Marketing: George Casey
VP Sales: Michael Frauenhoffer
Contact: Hillary Mccrea
hillary.mccrea@airtalk.com
COO: Jeff Grell
VP Product Development: Greg Penn

24642 Jupiter Mills Corporation
20 Walnut Dr
Roslyn, NY 11576
516-484-1166
Fax: 516-484-1242 800-853-5121
info@jupitermillscorp.com
Manufacturer and exporter of bags, barrels, drums,
bottles, boxes, cans, cartons, cases, containers, foam,
packaging materials, paper, partitions, tapes and
tubes
President: Fred Fisher
Customer Service: Harvey Chestman
Office Manager: Pat Fisher
Estimated Sales: $5,000,000
Number Employees: 20-49
Square Footage: 2000

24643 Jus-Made
9761 Clifford Dr Ste 100
Dallas, TX 75220
972-241-5544
Fax: 972-241-3399 800-969-3746
info@jus-made.com
Beverages and beverage mixes; beverage equipment
President: Gene Barfield
VP Sales: Jim Tanner
Contact: Matt Cook
mcook@jus-made.com
Operations Manager: Mike Sayre
Estimated Sales: $1-3 Million
Number Employees: 50-99
Square Footage: 14000
Type of Packaging: Consumer, Food Service, Pri-
vate Label, Bulk
Other Locations:
    Jus-Made
    Houston TX
Brands:
    Floria Julep
    Orogold

24644 Just Plastics Inc
250 Dyckman St
New York, NY 10034-5354
212-569-8500
Fax: 212-569-6970 info@justplastics.com
www.justplastics.us
Manufacturer and exporter of custom acrylic point
of purchase displays, signs, sneeze guards, menu
holders, tent card holders and containers
President: Robert Vermann
info@justplastics.com
VP: Lois Vermann
Sales Associate: Tommy de Los Angeles
VP: Robert Vermann
Estimated Sales: $20-50 Million
Number Employees: 10-19
Square Footage: 15000

24645 Justman Brush Co
828 Crown Point Ave
Omaha, NE 68110-2828
402-451-4420
Fax: 402-451-1473 800-800-6940
www.justmanbrush.com
Manufacturer and exporter of twisted-in-wire
brushes including bottle, toilet bowl, hospital and
laboratory
Owner: Justman Company
justmanbrush@aol.com
Estimated Sales: $1-2.5 Million
Number Employees: 20-49
Square Footage: 24000

24646 Justrite Rubber Stamp &Seal
1701 Locust St
Kansas City, MO 64108-1401
816-421-5010
Fax: 816-421-1939 800-229-5010
sales@justriterubberstamp.com
www.justriterubberstamp.com
Rubber stamps, daters, self-inking and pre-inked,
custom logos and kits.
Owner: Paul Thomas
justrite01@aol.com
CFO/R&D: Paul Thomas
Estimated Sales: $1-2.5 Million
Number Employees: 1-4
Square Footage: 20000

24647 Jutras Signs & Flags
711 Mast Rd
Manchester, NH 03102-1425
603-622-2344
Fax: 603-623-3562 800-924-3524
graphics@jutrassigns.com
Signs including interior and exterior illuminated,
billboards and neon and electronic message centers;
also, flagpoles and accessories available
President: Cathy Champagne
Contact: Susan Gelinas
sgelinas@jutrassigns.com
General Manager: Joe Champagne
Estimated Sales: Less Than $500,000
Number Employees: 1-4
Square Footage: 40000

24648 Juvenal Direct
PO Box 5449
Napa, CA 94581-0449
707-254-2000
Fax: 707-642-2288 888-254-2060
Grape presses, membrane presses and wine corks
CEO: Manuel Santiago
Number Employees: 8

24649 Jwc Environmental
290 Paularino Ave
Costa Mesa, CA 92626-3314
949-833-3888
Fax: 949-833-8858 800-331-2277
jwce@jwce.com www.jwce.com
Heavy duty solids reduction grinders, screening, and
dewatering equipment
President: Ron Duecker
CFO: John Harrison
Marketing Director: Fritz Egger
Sales Director: Pete Garcia
Contact: Scot Anderson
scota@jwce.com
Estimated Sales: $20-30 Million
Number Employees: 1-4
Square Footage: 55000
Parent Co: JWC International

Brands:
Auger Monster
Channel Monster
Muffin Monster

24650 K & H Corrugated Corp
330 Lake Osiris Rd
Walden, NY 12586-2605
845-778-3555
Fax: 845-778-7417 www.unicorr.com
Corrugated boxes
Manager: Mark Andrews
m.andrews@unicorr.com
Estimated Sales: $20-50 Million
Number Employees: 20-49
Parent Co: K&H Corrugated Case Corporation

24651 K & I Creative Plastics& Wood
582 Nixon St
Jacksonville, FL 32204-3010
904-387-0438
Fax: 904-387-0430 www.kicreativeplastics.net
Displays, sneeze guards, engraved signs, food bins
and condiment trays; also, metal engraved signs,
custom plastic fabricating available, and point of
purchase displays
Owner: Bonnie Osterman
Manager: Bob Korda
sales@kicreativeplastics.net
Estimated Sales: $1-3 Million
Number Employees: 5-9
Square Footage: 24000

24652 K & L Intl
1929 S Campus Ave
Ontario, CA 91761-5410
909-923-9258
Fax: 909-923-9228 888-598-5588
info@knl-international.com
www.knl-international.com
Manufacturer, Importer and Exporter of chopsticks,
toothpicks, guest checks, napkins, plastic T-Shirt
bags, bamboo skewers, matches, sushi containers,
wood sushi plates, wood sushi boats (bridge), swirl
bowls, dried seaweed, eel(unagi), wasabi powder
and soybean (edamame).
President: David Kao
VP: Susan Lin
Marketing Director: Richard Yeang
Manager: May Lin
Estimated Sales: $5-10 Million
Number Employees: 10-19
Number of Products: 20
Square Footage: 100000
Type of Packaging: Food Service, Private Label

24653 K & M Intl Inc
1955 Midway Dr # A
Twinsburg, OH 44087-1961
330-425-2550
Fax: 330-425-3777 www.wildrepublicretail.com
LED signs for display
Owner: G B Pillai
CFO: G Pillai
Sales Manager: Marianne Zmyslinski
gpillai@kmtoys.com
Estimated Sales: $20-50 Million
Number Employees: 20-49

24654 K B Systems Inc
90 Jacktown Rd
Bangor, PA 18013-9504
610-588-7788
Fax: 610-588-7785 www.geminibe.com
Material hadling systems flour/sugar; roll, pita bread
and tortilla equipment
President: Karl Brunner
kbrunner@kbsystemsinc.com
Estimated Sales: $5-10 Million
Number Employees: 20-49

24655 K C Booth Co
1760 Burlington St
N Kansas City, MO 64116-3892
816-471-1921
Fax: 816-471-2461 800-866-5226
info@kcbooth.com www.kcbooth.com
Manufacturer and exporter of benches, front-end
booths, tables and chairs
President: Scott Neuman
scott@kcbooth.com
VP: Scott Neuman
Operations Manager: Jack Buddemeyer

Estimated Sales: $5-10 Million
Number Employees: 20-49
Type of Packaging: Food Service

24656 (HQ)K Katen & Company
65 E Cherry Street
Rahway, NJ 07065-4011
732-381-0220
Manufacturer and importer of linen goods including
tablecloths, napkins, pillowcases and kitchen towels
VP: Pauline Katen
Manager: Benny Yabut
Manager: Steven Richards
Number Employees: 3
Square Footage: 4000
Type of Packaging: Consumer
Brands:
Keepsake Table Fashions

24657 K Trader Inc.
1452 W. 9th Street
Suite D
Upland, CA 91786
909-949-0327
Fax: 909-992-3471 sales@ktraderinc.com
www.ktraderinc.com
Exporter of fresh fruits, vegetables and meats to
overseas markets.
President: Robert Amakasu
Manager: Kay Shimivu
Estimated Sales: $1 Million
Number Employees: 10

24658 K&H Container
126 S Turnpike Road
Wallingford, CT 06492-4371
203-265-1547
Fax: 203-269-6837
Corrugated shipping containers
VP/General Manager: Steve Wasko
Customer Service Manager: Lou Carigliano
Plant Manager: Mark Andres
Estimated Sales: $5-10 Million
Number Employees: 20-49
Square Footage: 70000
Parent Co: K&H Corrugated Case Company

24659 K&R Equipment
2033 Gateway Place
Suite 500
San Jose, CA 95110
408-573-6427
Fax: 408-573-6471 sales@kandrequip.com
Case forming, poly bag insertion, decuffing, case
sealing
President: Owen Kellep
CFO: Adam Kwiek
VP: Richard Lee
Marketing/Sales: Dennis Alexander
Plant Manager: Fred Kruger
Estimated Sales: Below $5 Million
Number Employees: 20-49
Number of Products: 15
Square Footage: 30000

24660 K-C Products Company
16780 Stagg Street
Van Nuys, CA 91406-1635
818-267-1600
Fax: 323-261-5882
Plastic bags and covers; also, vinyl and fabric table
cloths, chair pads, place mats, appliance covers, etc
VP: Ingrid Albrechtson
Operations Manager: George Chamberlain
Estimated Sales: $1-5 Million
Number Employees: 1-4

24661 K-Coe Isom
6125 Sky Pond Dr.
Ste. 200
Loveland, CO 80538
970-685-3500
800-461-4702
www.kcoe.com
Accounting and financial advisement for the agricultural industry.
Year Founded: 1932
Number Employees: 300-500

24662 K-Patents
1804 Centre Point Cir # 106
Naperville, IL 60563-4849
630-955-1545
Fax: 630-955-1585 info@kpatents-usa.com
www.kpatents.com
Process refractometer for in-line liquid concentration measurement
Vice President: Eric Gronowski
eric.gronowski@kpatents-usa.com
Estimated Sales: $1-3 Million
Number Employees: 1-4
Parent Co: K-Patents OY

24663 K-Tron
PO Box
Salina, KS 67402-0017
785-825-1611
Fax: 785-825-8759 info@ktron.com
www.ktron.com
Manufacturer and exporter of pneumatic conveying and feeding systems
General Manager: Todd Smith
Estimated Sales: $20-50 Million
Number Employees: 100-249
Square Footage: 115000
Parent Co: K-Tron America

24664 K-Tron International
Routes 55 and 553
P.O. Box 888
Pitman, NJ 08071-0888
856-589-0500
Fax: 856-256-3281 800-203-4130
www.ktron.com
Maqnufacture feeders for low to high feed rate applications, precision feeding and material control with complete PLC-DCS system integration, vacuum loaders and receivers. Offer volumetric screw feeders, weighbelt feeders, vibratingfeeders, etc
President: Kevin Bowen
Estimated Sales: $77.50 Million
Number Employees: 727
Square Footage: 92000
Parent Co: K-Tron International
Brands:
 Digi-Drive
 K-Commander
 K-Link
 K-Modular
 K-Tron Soder
 K10s
 K2-Modular
 Smart Flow Meter
 Smart Force Transducer

24665 K-Way Products
759 W Commercial St
Mount Carroll, IL 61053-9762
815-244-2800
Fax: 815-244-2799 800-622-9163
Manufacturer and exporter of soda, juice, beer and coffee dispensing equipment including pre and post-mix ice chests, carbonator/chiller dry refrigerated systems and soda and liquor guns
VP Marketing: Gene Deleeuw
VP Sales: John Hiney
Estimated Sales: $5-10 Million
Number Employees: 20-49
Square Footage: 76000
Type of Packaging: Food Service
Brands:
 Bar-O-Matic
 K-Way

24666 K.F. Logistics
10045 International Boulevard
Cincinnati, OH 45246-4845
513-874-0788
Fax: 513-881-5383 800-347-9100
www.buschman.com
Manufacturer and exporter of case conveyors and sortation products
CFO and Sr VP Finance: Robert Duplain
Sr VP Sales/Marketing: Lawrence Frey
Number Employees: 10
Square Footage: 1200000

24667 KANE Bag Supply Co
1200 S East Ave
Baltimore, MD 21224-5099
410-732-5800
Fax: 410-675-0079
Plastic bags

Owner: Karen Kane
kaneandtarp@aol.com
VP: Karen Kane
Estimated Sales: $1-2.5 Million
Number Employees: 10-19
Square Footage: 40000

24668 KAPCO
1000 Cherry Street
PO Box 626
Kent, OH 44240
330-678-1626
Fax: 330-678-3922 800-843-5368
converting@kapco.com www.kapco.com
Manufacturer and exporter of coated and converted pressure sensitive flexible materials, labels, tapes and paper
President: Edward Small
Contact: Dan Barlett
dbarlett@kapco.com
Operations Manager: Phil Zavracky
Estimated Sales: $10-20 Million
Number Employees: 50-99
Square Footage: 180000

24669 KAPS All Packaging
200 Mill Rd.
Riverhead, NY 11901-3125
631-727-0300
Fax: 631-369-5939 www.kapsall.com
Packaging machinery including fluid filling, bottle capping, bottle orienting and bottle cleaning; also, unscramblers, torque meters cap sealers and conveyor systems.
President: Kenneth Herzog
Packaging Solutions: Michael Herzog
mherzog@kapsall.com
Year Founded: 1941
Estimated Sales: Less Than $500,000
Number Employees: 1-4
Square Footage: 65000
Brands:
 Filz-All
 Kaps-All
 Orientainer
 Torq-All

24670 KASCO Sharp Tech Corp
1569 Tower Grove Ave
St Louis, MO 63110-2287
314-771-1550
Fax: 314-771-5162 800-325-8940
service@kascocorp.com www.kascocorp.com
Seasonings and ingredients, knives, chopper plates, grinder plates and other meat processing equipment
President: Brian Turner
bturner@kascocorp.com
CEO: Tom Orelup
Manufacturing Director: Bill McGuire
R & D: Jerry Peterson
Sales: Mark Dobson
Public Relations: David Neu
Production: Larry Jones
Plant Manager: Bill McGuire
Purchasing: Jerry Brooks
Estimated Sales: $10-25 Million
Number Employees: 50-99

24671 KASE Equipment
7400 Hub Pkwy
Cleveland, OH 44125-5735
216-642-9040
Fax: 216-986-0678 info@plastechnic.com
www.kaseequip.com
Manufacturer and exporter of printers for cups, pails, lids and closures
President: Patrick Hawkins
patrick.hawkins@kaseequip.com
CEO: Edward Thomas
Estimated Sales: $50-100 Million
Number Employees: 50-99
Type of Packaging: Consumer, Food Service, Private Label

24672 KATZ Marketing Solutions
295 S Dawson Ave
Columbus, OH 43209-1736
614-252-7824
Fax: 614-252-6113
info@katzmarketingsolutions.com
www.katzmarketingsolutions.com
A marketing and brand management consulting firm specializing in consumer products and food beverage marketing

CEO: Carl Riis
carl.riis@katz-solutions.com
CEO: Tammy Katz
Estimated Sales: Less Than $500,000
Number Employees: 1-4
Type of Packaging: Consumer
Brands:
 Boost
 Borden
 Dearfoams
 Enfamil
 Frito Lay
 Miller Lite
 Mount Vernon Mantel Company
 Pathlire
 Rice Select
 Scotts
 Sopakco
 Titebond

24673 KBR Building Group
5605 Carnegie Boulevard
Suite 200
Charlotte, NC 28209
704-551-2700
Fax: 919-859-9011 www.bekbuildinggroup.com
Products and services for the food and beverage industry includes: processing facilities; pilot plants/test kitchens; distribution and storage facilities (low temperature/food service); research and development facilities;laboratories; offices; and commissaries.
President: Philip Southerland
Chairman/Chief Executive Officer: Luther Cochrane
CFO and CAO: Trilby Carriker
VP: Frank Holley
Vice President Business Development: John McLauglin
Contact: Chris Gentry
cgentry@humana.com
Senior Vice President, Texas Operations: Matt Daniel
Number Employees: 43
Square Footage: 24194

24674 KCL Corporation
PO Box 629
Shelbyville, IN 46176-0629
317-392-2521
Fax: 317-392-4772
Reclosable poly zipper packaging
Estimated Sales: $20-50 Million
Number Employees: 100-249

24675 KD Kanopy
3755 W 69th Pl
Westminster, CO 80030
303-650-1310
Fax: 303-650-5093 800-432-4435
askme@kdkanopy.com www.kdkanopy.com
Manufacturer and exporter of instant set-up canopies, tents and banners; also, customized graphics available
President: John T Matthews
CFO: John T Matthews
Director Marketing: Helene Schmid
Sales: Scott Rudin
Contact: Shelly Bangs
shelly@kdkanopy.com
Sales: Matt Lehman
Estimated Sales: $1-2.5 Million
Number Employees: 20-49
Square Footage: 40000
Brands:
 Kd Bannerpole
 Kd Majestic
 Kd Party Shade
 Kd Starshade
 Kd Starstage

24676 (HQ)KEMCO
8 Thatcher Lane
Wareham, MA 02571-1076
508-295-5959
Fax: 508-291-2364 800-231-5955
www.kemco.or.kr/eng
New and used stainless steel fabrications including sinks, tables, push and tow along carts, exhaust hoods, walk-in coolers and freezers and food service equipment
President & CEO: Byun Jong-Rip
Purchasing/AR/AP: Beverly Limpus
Number Employees: 17
Square Footage: 80000

24677 KES Science & Technology Inc
3625 Kennesaw N Industrial Pkw
Kennesaw, GA 30144-1234
678-290-8619
Fax: 770-425-0837 800-627-4913
info@kesair.com
Food safety air sanitation system for maximum
shelf/storage life, optimum product integrity and re-
duced food spoilage
President: John Hayman
Marketing Manager: Kristi George
National Sales Manager: Jimmy Lee
Billing Contact: Scott Hayman
Estimated Sales: $8 Million
Number Employees: 20-49

24678 KETCH
1006 E Waterman St
Wichita, KS 67211-1525
316-383-8700
Fax: 316-383-8715 800-766-3777
rpasmore@ketch.org www.ketch.org
Electrical extension cords, wooden pallets, shipping
boxes and air filters; contract packaging services
available
President/CEO: Ron Pasmore
rpasmore@ketch.org
Chairman: Fred Badders
CFO: Coral Houdyshell
Vice President of Finance: Sheila Brown
R&D: Pattie Knauff
Vice President of Quality Assurance: Sallie Jensen
Vice President of Human Resources: Pattie Knauff
Estimated Sales: Less than $500,000
Number Employees: 250-499
Square Footage: 120000

24679 KHL Engineered Packaging
1640 S Greenwood Ave
Montebello, CA 90640
323-721-5300
Fax: 323-725-0312
Manufacturer and wholesaler/distributor of flexible
packaging equipment and materials including shrink
and stretch film, tape, poly and corrugated boxes,
chipboard, skin film and poly bags
VP: Jed Wockensuss
General Sales Manager: Bill Browne
Contact: Peter Szymanski
peter.szymanski@khlengpkg.com
Estimated Sales: $5-10 Million
Number Employees: 1,000-4,999
Square Footage: 100000

24680 KHM Plastics Inc
4090 Ryan Rd # B
Gurnee, IL 60031-1201
847-249-4910
Fax: 847-249-4976 dankay@khmplastics.com
www.khmplastics.com
Custom bulk acrylic food bins; importer of acrylic
sign holders. Custom displays for food service
President: Daniel Kay
dankay@khmplastics.com
Marketing Director: Dan Kay
Sales Director: Glenn Murphy
Operations Manager: Dan Bunting
Estimated Sales: $2.5-5 Million
Number Employees: 20-49
Square Footage: 200000
Brands:
    Photo-Mates

24681 (HQ)KHS Co
25 Fox Den Road
West Simsbury, CT 06092
860-658-9454
Prints tags and labels.
Director: Pete Payne
CEO: Kevin Keane
Vice President: Russell Jackson
Marketing Executive: Kesha Briley
Sales Executive: Kerwin Spangler
Estimated Sales: 500,000
Number Employees: 20-49

24682 KIK Custom Products
3900 Joliet St
Denver, CO 80239
303-728-0871
Fax: 303-728-0880 www.kikcorp.com
Contract packager of aerosols, liquids and sticks.

Year Founded: 1993
Estimated Sales: $50-100 Million
Number Employees: 500-999
Type of Packaging: Bulk

24683 KIK Custom Products
24 Mill Ln
P.O. Box 660
Salem, VA 24153
540-389-5401
Fax: 540-904-0113 www.kikcorp.com
Contract packager of aerosols, liquids and sticks.
Number Employees: 50-99
Brands:
    Blue Ridge

24684 (HQ)KIK Custom Products
101 MacIntosh Blvd
Concord, ON L4K 4R5
Canada
905-660-0444
Fax: 905-660-9310 800-276-8260
www.kikcorp.com
Contract packager of aerosols, liquids and sticks.
President & CEO: Jeffrey Nodland
EVP & Chief Administrative Officer: Ben Kaak
EVP, Finance & CFO: Alay Shah
Year Founded: 1993
Estimated Sales: $50-100 Million
Number Employees: 500-999

24685 KION North America
2450 W 5th North St
Summerville, SC 29483-9621
843-875-8000
Fax: 843-875-8329 trucksales.na@kiongroup.com
www.kion-na.com
Dealer of forklifts and similar vehicles made by
Linde and Baoli.
President, CEO & CFO: Max Heller
VP, Operations: Daniel Schlegel
VP, Sales: Michael Gore
VP, Product Development: Christian Loew
Estimated Sales: H
Number Employees: 100-249
Parent Co: Linde Material Handing

24686 KISS Packaging Systems
1399 Specialty Drive
Vista, CA 92081-8521
760-714-4177
Fax: 760-714-4188 888-522-3538
sales@kisspkg.com www.kisspkg.com
Manufacturer and exporter of liquid fillers, cappers,
conveyors, turntables, feeders/orienters, labelers and
integrated packaging systems
Estimated Sales: $2.5-5 Million
Number Employees: 19
Square Footage: 34000

24687 KISS Packaging Systems
1399 Specialty Drive
Vista, CA 92081-8521
760-714-4177
Fax: 760-714-4188 sales@kisspkg.com
Packaging machinery
Estimated Sales: $2.5-5 Million
Number Employees: 19

24688 KL Products, Ltd.
234 Exeter Road
London, ON N6L 1A3
Canada
519-652-1070
Fax: 519-652-1071 800-388-5744
kadmin@klproducts.com www.klproducts.com
Automated food processing equipment. Poultry and
hatchery equipment and washing systems.
President: Patrick Poulin
Vice President, Sales & Marketing: Rick Bennett

24689 KLEEN Line Corp
7 Opportunity Way
Newburyport, MA 01950-4044
978-463-0827
Fax: 978-463-0847 800-259-5973
info@kleenline.com www.kleenline.com
Stainless steel conveyors, wash-down duty, custom
conveyors, single units, complete systems. Manufacturer and system integrator of custom stainless steel
sanitary conveyors and equipment, including controls and automation. Engineeringand consulting
services available for material handling
requirements.

President: James Laverdiere
Vice President: Dave Larcenaire
dave@kleenline.co.za
Sales: Stuart Olsen
Plant Manager: Scott Fallovollita
Estimated Sales: $1-5 Million
Number Employees: 20-49

24690 KLLM Transport Svc LLC
135 Riverview Dr
Richland, MS 39218-4401
601-939-2545
Fax: 601-936-7151 800-925-1000
lpurvis@kllm.com www.kllm.com
President/CEO: James M. Richards, Jr.
Chairman of the Board: William J. Liles III
CFO: Terry Thornton
Vice President-Strategic Partnerships: Milton
Tallant, Jr
V.P. of Sales and Marketing: Moe Shroter
Vice President of Human Resources: Steve SzaboVP
of Operations: Greg Carpenter
Estimated Sales: $1-5 Million
Number Employees: 1000-4999

24691 KM International Corp
320 N Main St
Kenton, TN 38233-1130
731-749-8700
Fax: 256-539-9799 www.kminternational.com
Manufacturer, importer and exporter of plastic bags
and film
President: Kourosh Vakili
CEO: Kevin Vakili
kevinb@kmigroup.com
Estimated Sales: $20-50 Million
Number Employees: 10-19

24692 KMT Aqua-Dyne Inc
635 W 12th St
Baxter Springs, KS 66713-1940
620-856-6222
Fax: 713-864-0313 800-826-9274
sales@aqua-dyne.com www.aqua-dyne.com
Manufacturer and exporter of water blasting and
tank cleaning equipment; also pumps
Manager: Deiter Tischler
VP: Jennifer Rankin
Regional Sales Manager: Jorge Elarba
Marketing: Dennis Williams
Sales/Marketing: Paul Bako
Public Relations: Dennis Williams
Purchasing: Jennifer Rankin
Estimated Sales: $5-10,000,000
Number Employees: 20-49
Square Footage: 170000
Brands:
    Aqua-Dyne

24693 KNF Flexpak Corporation
Rr 3 Box 6b
Tamaqua, PA 18252
570-386-3550
Fax: 570-386-3703 800-823-7786
pfloro@knfcorporation.com
www.knfcorporation.com
Nylon, polyethylene, pan liners, co-extrusion, oven
bags, cook chill, cashings and vacuum bags
Sales Director: David Dunphy
Estimated Sales: $12 Million
Number Employees: 50-99
Number of Brands: 4
Number of Products: 250
Square Footage: 28000
Type of Packaging: Consumer, Food Service, Pri-
vate Label, Bulk

24694 KNOX Stove Works Inc
PO Box 751
Knoxville, TN 37901-0751
865-524-4113
Fax: 865-637-2461 knoxstove@gmail.com
www.knoxstove.com
Coal and wood cooking ranges
President: Joe Anderson
Acct.: David Oglesby
Estimated Sales: $10-20 Million
Number Employees: 5-9
Square Footage: 42000

24695 KOF-K Kosher Supervision
201 The Plaza
Teaneck, NJ 7666

201-837-0500
Fax: 201-837-0126 ceo@kof-k.org
www.kof-k.org
Consultant specializing in kosher certification
CEO: Rabbi Dr. H. Zecharia Senter
Contact: Francine Adler
fadler@kof-k.org
Number Employees: 100-249
Square Footage: 15000

24696 KOFLO Corp
309 Cary Point Dr # A
Cary, IL 60013-2901

847-516-3700
Fax: 847-516-3724 800-782-8427
info@koflo.com www.koflo.com
Static mixers, calibration columns and injection quills.
President: James Federighi
jf@koflo.com
VP: Anthony Federighi
Estimated Sales: $5-10 Million
Number Employees: 10-19
Brands:
    Calibration Columns
    Injection Quills
    Static Mixers

24697 KP Aerofill
P.O.Box 3848
Davenport, IA 52808-3848

563-391-1100
Fax: 563-391-4951 800-257-5622
CEO: Barry Shoulders

24698 KROHNE Inc
4100 N Sam Houston Pky W # 220
Building C-Suite 220
Houston, TX 77086-1466

281-598-0050
Fax: 281-598-0051 866-689-1250
oilandgas@krohne.com us.krohne.com
Flow meters
Marketing: Joe Incontri
Manager: Ron Garcia
Number Employees: 5-9

24699 KSW Corp
1731 Guthrie Ave
PO Box 3224
Des Moines, IA 50316-2197

515-265-5269
Fax: 515-265-9072 kswborp@aol.com
www.kswcorporation.com
Manufacturer and exporter of mechanical blades and knives
President: Paul Naylor
kswcorpdsm@aol.com
National Sales Manager: Michelle Struble
Estimated Sales: $3-5 Million
Number Employees: 10-19
Type of Packaging: Consumer, Food Service

24700 KTG
11353 Reed Hartman Hwy
Cincinnati, OH 45241-2443

513-793-5366
Fax: 866-533-6950 888-533-6900
Wireless temperature tracking computer software
CEO: Jim Flood
VP: Jack Kennamer
VP Sales: Jeff Carletti
VP Operations: Susan Payne
Estimated Sales: $10-20 Million
Number Employees: 5-9
Square Footage: 200000
Brands:
    Bladerunner
    Board-Mate
    Code Red Kit
    Cook-Eze
    Disposer Saver
    Fridgekare
    K-Mars
    Katchall
    Kleen-Cup
    Kleen-Pail
    Kolor Cut
    Kool-Tek
    Kwik-Flo
    Linen-Saver
    Magnetic Scrap Board
    N'Ice Ties
    Poly-Roll
    Poly-Slice
    Polyliner
    Rapi-Kool
    Safetywrap
    Sat-T-Ice
    Sat-T-Mop
    Side Swipe Spatula
    Tableware Retrievers
    Traysaver
    Tuff-Cut
    Whizard Gloves

24701 KTR Corp
122 Anchor Rd
Michigan City, IN 46360-2802

219-879-2792
Fax: 219-872-9150 ktr-us@ktr.com
www.ktrcorp.com
Shaft couplings
President: Bill Ketchum
w.ketcham@ktr.com
CFO: Tedd Slesinsky
Marketing Director: Marshall Marcos
Estimated Sales: $5-10 Million
Number Employees: 20-49

24702 KTech by Muckler
1190 Meramac Road
Suite 207
Manchester, MO 63021

314-631-7616
Fax: 314-631-7409 800-952-0241
ktechinfo@mucklerktech.com
www.mucklertech.com

24703 KUKA Robotics Corp
51870 Shelby Parkway
Shelby Township, MI 48315-1787

800-459-6691
www.kuka.com
Manufacturer and importer of automated robotic material handling and palletizing systems and system integrators
President, KUKA Robotics Corp US: Joseph Gemma

Estimated Sales: Over $1 Billion
Number Employees: 14,256
Parent Co: KUKA Robotics Corporation

24704 KWIK Lok Corp
2712 S 16th Ave
Yakima, WA 98903-9530

509-248-4770
Fax: 509-457-6531 800-688-5945
sales@kwiklok.com www.kwiklok.com
Manufacturer and exporter of bag closures and bag closing machinery using plastic clips and labels
Vice President: Hal Miller
halm@kwiklok.com
VP: Hal Miller
Quality Control: Jim Paxton
Sales: Rich Zaremba
Public Relations: Bill Klancke
Purchasing Director: Kohen Kelly
Estimated Sales: $10-20 Million
Number Employees: 50-99
Brands:
    Kwik Lok
    Striplok

24705 KWIK Lok Corp
2712 S 16th Ave
Yakima, WA 98903-9530

509-248-4770
Fax: 509-457-6531 800-688-5945
www.kwiklok.com
Vice President: Hal Miller
halm@kwiklok.com
VP: Hal Miller
VP Sales: James Forsthe
Estimated Sales: $20-50 Million
Number Employees: 50-99

24706 KWS Manufacturing Co LTD
3041 Conveyor Dr
Burleson, TX 76028-1857

817-295-2247
Fax: 817-447-8528 800-543-6558
sales@kwsmfg.com www.kwsmfg.com

Manufacturer and exporter of bulk elevators and conveyors including belt and screw; also, spare parts and repair services available. Installation and field service available
Owner: Claressa Moore
cmoore@drivetime.com
CEO: Tim Harris
CFO: Olin Miller
Marketing Director: Bill Porterfield
Plant Manager: Joe Radloff
Purchasing Manager: Eddie Maxwell
Estimated Sales: $10-20 Million
Number Employees: 100-249
Square Footage: 250000
Parent Co: J.B. Poindexter & Co., Inc.
Type of Packaging: Bulk

24707 Kadon Corporation
55 W Techne Center Drive
Milford, OH 45150-8901

937-299-0088
Fax: 513-831-5474
Manufacturer and exporter of plastic pallets, tote boxes, storage containers and wash baskets; OEM services available
Sales Manager: Chuck Acton
Administrative Assistant: Linda Brandeburg
Type of Packaging: Bulk

24708 Kady International
30 Parkway Dr
Scarborough, ME 04074-7155

207-883-4141
Fax: 207-883-8241 800-367-5239
kady@kadyinternational.com
www.kadyinternational.com
Manufacturer and exporter of high speed dispersion mills for mixing, blending, dispersing, emulsifying and cooking
President: Robert Kritzer
VP: Todd Kritzer
Sales: Todd Kritler
Estimated Sales: $5-10 Million
Number Employees: 10-19
Square Footage: 200000
Brands:
    Kady
    Kadyzolvers

24709 Kaeser Compressors Inc
511 Sigma Dr
Fredericksburg, VA 22408-7330

540-898-2207
Fax: 540-898-5520 info.usa@kaeser.com
www.oilfreeair.com
Rotary screw compressors, SmartPipe, Rotary screw vacuum packages, Rotary lobe blowers, portable compressors.
President: Reiner Mueller
reiner.mueller@kaeser.com
Number Employees: 100-249

24710 Kafko International LTD
3555 Howard St
Skokie, IL 60076-4052

847-763-0333
Fax: 847-763-0334 800-528-0334
sales@oileater.com www.kafkointl.com
Manufacturer and supplier of cleaning products
President: Ena Dora
edora@kafkointl.com
Number Employees: 100-249

24711 Kagetec
309 Elm Avenue SW
Montgomery, MN 56069

612-435-7640
Fax: 612-435-7641 kagetecusa@gmail.com
www.kagetec.com
Industrial flooring for the dairy, food and brewery industries.

24712 KaiRak
1158 N. Gilbert St
Anaheim, CA 92801

714-870-8661
Fax: 866-210-7542 literature@kairak.com
www.kairak.com
Manufacturer and exporter of remote refrigeration systems, pan chillers and sandwich and pizza prep tables

President/General Manager: Mark Curran
VP Sales & Marketing: Steve Asay
National Sales Manager: Steve Asay
Contact: Brian Casserilla
bcasserilla@kairak.com
Administrative Assistant: Susie Parodi
Estimated Sales: $15 Million
Number Employees: 20-49
Square Footage: 160000
Parent Co: Hobart Corporation
Type of Packaging: Consumer, Food Service
Other Locations:
  KaiRak
  Gardena CA
Brands:
  Advantage Rak
  Pan Chillers

24713 Kaines West Michigan Co
211 E Dowland St
Ludington, MI 49431-2308
                          231-845-1281
  Fax: 231-843-2259 kwmco@aol.com
              www.kwmco.com
Custom welded wire products including racks, trays,
refrigerator/freezer shelving, etc
President: John Kaines
mikefelty@kwmco.com
CEO: Les Kaines
Engineering: Mike Felty
Human Resources: Jody Stewart
Materials Management: Jim Negele
Shipping Manager: Kevin Marcoux
Ordering Department: Nancy Van Liere
Estimated Sales: $5-10 Million
Number Employees: 50-99
Square Footage: 96000

24714 Kal Pac Corp
10 Factory St
Montgomery, NY 12549-1202
                          845-457-7013
  Fax: 845-457-7009 800-852-5722
  info@kalpac.com www.kalpac.com
Manufacturer, importer and exporter of plastic take
out bags
CEO: Mike Nozawa
Sales Representative: Henry Meola
Estimated Sales: $10-20 Million
Number Employees: 10-19
Square Footage: 60000
Type of Packaging: Food Service

24715 Kalco Enterprises
443 Park Avenue South
New York, NY 10016-7322
                          212-627-5311
  Fax: 212-627-3323 800-396-6600
              kalconet@aol.com
Handmade food packaging products.
President: Ariel Kalaty
Sales Manager: Silverio Baranda
Type of Packaging: Consumer, Private Label, Bulk

24716 Kalix DT Industries
36 4th Street
Somerville, NJ 08876-3206
                          514-694-2390
              Fax: 514-694-6552
Filling machines, conveyors, cappers

24717 Kalle USA Inc
5750 Centerpoint Ct
Suite B
Gurnee, IL 60031-5279
                          847-775-0781
  Fax: 847-775-0782 www.kalle.de
Sausage casings and other meat processing supplies.
Sales Manager: John Lample
Number Employees: 10-19
Brands:
  Pullulan
  Sunmalt
  Trehalose

24718 Kalman Floor Co Inc
1202 Bergen Pkwy # 110
Suite 110
Evergreen, CO 80439-9559
                          303-674-2290
  Fax: 303-674-1238 866-266-7146
  Karl.Johnson@kalmanfloor.com
              www.kalmanfloor.com
Seamless industrial concrete floors suitable for the
food and beverage industries.

President: Donald Ytterberg
CEO: Robin Balliet
robin.balliet@kalmanfloor.com
Sales Engineer: Karl Johnson
Sales Engineer: Jeffrey Brown
Number Employees: 5-9

24719 (HQ)Kalsec
3713 W Main St
Kalamazoo, MI 49006
                          269-349-9711
                          800-323-9320
              www.kalsec.com
Natural flavors, colors, extracts; spice oleoresins and
essential oils.
Executive Chairman: George Todd
Research & Development: Don Berdahl
Plant Manager: Harry Todd
Estimated Sales: $3-5 Million
Number Employees: 100-249
Parent Co: Kalamazoo Holdings
Type of Packaging: Food Service, Bulk
Brands:
  Kalsec

24720 Kamflex Corp
1321 W 119th St
Chicago, IL 60643-5109
                          630-682-1555
  Fax: 630-682-9312 800-323-2440
              kamflex@kamflex.com
Manufacturer and exporter of FDA and USDA ap-
proved stainless steel conveyors and systems with
fabric, plastic or steel belts, rotary turntables, air op-
erations, etc
President: Kirit Kamdar
Vice President: Jose Ceja
jceja@kamflex.com
Marketing Director: John Tomaka
Operations Manager: Dave Matan
Estimated Sales: $5-10 Million
Number Employees: 5-9
Square Footage: 70000
Brands:
  Elevair

24721 Kammann Machine
235 Heritage Ave
Portsmouth, NH 03801
                          978-463-0050
              Fax: 630-377-7759
Printing machinery for packaging.
Vice President of Sales and Marketing: Steve
Gilbertson
Sales Manager: Barney Hanrahan
bhanrahan@kammann.com
Estimated Sales: $2.5-5 Million
Number Employees: 5-9
Square Footage: 400000
Brands:
  K-14

24722 Kamran & Co
411 E Montecito St
Santa Barbara, CA 93101-1718
                          805-957-1551
  Fax: 805-962-5915 800-480-9418
              www.kamranco.com
Preparation tables
President: Firouzeh Amiri
firouzeh@kamranco.com
Estimated Sales: $5-10 Million
Number Employees: 20-49
Square Footage: 55200
Type of Packaging: Private Label, Bulk

24723 Kapak Corporation
5305 Parkdale Dr
Minneapolis, MN 55416
                          952-541-0730
  Fax: 952-541-0735 info@kapak.com
Flexible high barrier packaging and sealing equip-
ment; also, rollstock retort films, preformed
pouches, die cuts, handles and closures
CEO: Gary Bell
Sales: Craig Rutman
National Sales Manager: Brian Bell
Director Manufacturing: Kathy Cyracks
Estimated Sales: $20-50 Million
Number Employees: 50-99
Brands:
  Coffee-Pak
  Kap-Pak
  Stan-Pak

24724 Karl Schnell
903 North St
New London, WI 54961-1000
                          920-982-9974
  Fax: 920-982-0580 sales@karlschnell.com
              www.karlschnell.com
Food pumps, emulsifiers, mixers/blenders, cookers,
etc
Manager: John Mauthe
john@karlschnell.com
Estimated Sales: $2.5-5,000,000
Number Employees: 1-4
Square Footage: 10000
Parent Co: Karl Schnell Gmbh
Brands:
  Karl Schnell

24725 Karma
500 Milford Street
Watertown, WI 53094
                          920-262-8688
  Fax: 920-261-3302 800-558-9565
Manufacturer and exporter of hot and cold beverage
and mashed potato dispensers; also, warmers includ-
ing hot fudge
President: Chris Gorski
Vice President: Jerry Scheiber
Marketing VP: Elizabeth Brennecke
VP Sales: Jeremy Scheiber
Contact: Brittany Brantley
brantleyb@karma-inc.com
Estimated Sales: $10-20 Million
Number Employees: 20-49
Square Footage: 120000
Brands:
  Cafe-Matic
  Choco-Matic
  Drink-Master
  Insti-Mash
  Juice-Master
  Tea-Master
  Whip-Master

24726 Karolina Polymers
1508 S Center Street
Hickory, NC 28602-5220
                          828-328-2247
              Fax: 828-322-3674
Plastic film
President: Paul Kolis
VP: Jim Koshinski
Contact: Beth Lail
markf@agri-fab.com
Estimated Sales: $5-10 Million
Number Employees: 20-49
Type of Packaging: Bulk

24727 Karyall Telday Inc
8221 Clinton Rd
Cleveland, OH 44144-1095
                          216-281-4063
  Fax: 216-281-5428 karyall@core.com
              www.karyalltelday.com
Shop pans and tote boxes including aluminum, steel
and stainless steel
President: James Mindek
karyall@core.com
Estimated Sales: $10-20,000,000
Number Employees: 20-49

24728 Kasel Engineering
5911 Wolf Creek Pike
Dayton, OH 45426-2439
                          937-854-8875
  Fax: 937-854-8875 www.kaselengineering.com
Bacon equipment, slicing machines and scales.
Owner: Don Kasel
dkasel@kaselengineering.com
Estimated Sales: A
Number Employees: 5-9

24729 Kasel Industries Inc
3315 Walnut St
Denver, CO 80205-2429
                          303-296-4417
  Fax: 303-293-9825 800-218-4417
              www.kasel.net
Manufacturer and exporter of meat slicers, convey-
ors and automatic loaders
Owner: Ray Kasel
ray@kasel.net
Sls./Mktg. Mgr.: Jon Toby
Quality Control: Galana Kasel

Estimated Sales: $32 Million
Number Employees: 10-19

24730 Kasel Industries Inc
3315 Walnut St
Denver, CO 80205-2429

303-296-4417
Fax: 303-293-9825 800-218-4417
sales@kasel.net www.kasel.net
Slicers
Owner: Ray Kasel
ray@kasel.net
CFO: Oigita Jrausau
Quality Control: Galinajasto Kasel
Estimated Sales: $2.5-5 Million
Number Employees: 10-19

24731 Kashrus Technical Consultants
PO Box 172
Lakewood, NJ 08701-0172

732-364-8046
Fax: 732-363-5451 kashrusy@aol.com
www.kosherconsumer.org
Consultant specializing in the kosher food industry
Owner: Yehuda Shan
Number Employees: 10
Type of Packaging: Consumer, Food Service

24732 Kason
8889 Whitney Dr
Lewis Center, OH 43035-7106

740-549-2100
Fax: 740-549-0701 Central@kasonind.com
www.kasonind.com
Food bins, bumper systems for walls and strip doors;
wholesaler/distributor of commercial refrigeration
hardware and bulk food merchandisers
Manager: Rich Kaiser
central@kasonind.com
Estimated Sales: $1-5 Million
Number Employees: 5-9

24733 Kason Central
7099 Huntley Road
Columbus, OH 43229-1073

614-885-1992
Fax: 614-888-1771
Manufacturer, exporter and wholesaler/distributor of
refrigerator latches and hinges, strip curtains, hood
lights, grease filters, gaskets, stainless steel food ser-
vice hardware, thermometers for ovens and refriger-
ators and plumbingfixtures
Manager: David Katz
Sales Representative: Rich Kaiser
Office Manager: Greg Murray
General Manager: David Katz
Estimated Sales: $1-2.5 Million
Number Employees: 5-9
Square Footage: 8000
Parent Co: Kason Industries
Type of Packaging: Consumer, Food Service, Pri-
vate Label

24734 Kason Industries
140 Herring Road
Newnan, GA 30265

770-254-0553
Fax: 770-253-3370 vinyl@kasonind.com
www.kasonind.com
Commercial food service equipment hardware and
accessories including hinges, latches, feet, legs, door
closers, panel fasteners, sliding door ware, vinyl
strip doors, heated vents, grease extracting filters,
etc
Contact: Debbie Gazaway
drgazawa@kasonind.com
Estimated Sales: $50-100 Million
Number Employees: 8
Number of Products: 400
Square Footage: 6572
Parent Co: Kason Industries
Other Locations:
    Kason Industries
    Forest Hills NY
Brands:
    Doorware
    Easimount
    Panelock
    Safeguard
    Thermal Flex
    Trapper

24735 Kason Vinyl Products
57 Amlajack Blvd
Newnan, GA 30265-1093

770-254-0553
Fax: 770-253-3370 800-472-7450
www.kasonind.com
Vinyl strip curtains and swing doors for refrigeration
and storage
President: Peter Katz
National Sales Manager: Larry Crabtree
Estimated Sales: $50-100 Million
Number Employees: 100-249
Parent Co: Kason Industries
Brands:
    Easimount
    Maximount
    Thermal Flex

24736 Kastalon, Inc.
4100 West 124th Place
Alsip, IL 60803-1876

708-389-2210
Fax: 708-389-0432 800-527-8566
sales@kastalon.com www.kastalon.com
Polyurethane parts and products
President & CEO: Bruce DeMent
Year Founded: 1963
Estimated Sales: $100+ Million
Number Employees: 68

24737 Kathabardehum Idification
1 Executive Dr
Suite 410
Somerset, NJ 08873-4002

732-560-0565
Fax: 732-356-0643 888-952-8422
sales@kathabar.com www.kathabar.com
Dehumidification for all food processing, baking
candy, enrobing, freeze drying, coating, drying,
spraying, dehydration, packaging, etc.
President: Pedro Correa
Global Sales Director: Nick Honko
Vice President: Bill Szabo
Sales Director: Stephen Constant
Contact: Skip Koski
skoski@kathabar.com
Product Manager: Michael Harvey
Estimated Sales: $5-10 Million
Number Employees: 30
Number of Brands: 1
Number of Products: 24

24738 Kaufman Engineered Systems
1260 Waterville Monclova Rd
Waterville, OH 43566-1016

419-878-9727
Fax: 419-878-9726 info@kaufmanengsys.com
www.kaufmanengsys.com
Industrial stretch wrappers, conveyor systems, pick
and place machinery, palletizers and stackers
President: Charlie Kaufman
charlie.kaufman@kaufmanengsys.com
VP: Bob Kaufman
Estimated Sales: $20-50 Million
Number Employees: 50-99

24739 Kaufman Paper Box Company
187 N Main St
Providence, RI 02903-1220

401-272-7508
Fax: 401-272-9738
Set-up boxes for candy and other related products
Owner: Arnold Kaufman
Estimated Sales: $1-2.5 Million
Number Employees: 5-9
Square Footage: 24000
Type of Packaging: Private Label, Bulk

24740 Kauling Wood Products Company
15735 Old Us Hwy 50
Beckemeyer, IL 62219

618-594-2901
Fax: 618-594-4218
www.woodfibre.com/trade/aa009934.html
Material handling equipment including hardwood
pallets and skids; also, pallet mattes/tops
General Manager: Jim Kauling
Estimated Sales: $1-5 Million
Number Employees: 1-4

24741 Kawneer Co Inc
555 Guthridge Ct
Norcross, GA 30092

770-449-5555
Fax: 770-734-1560 www.kawneer.com
Engineering products and solutions.
Chief Executive Officer: Charles "Chip"
Blankenship
Chief E&C Officer: Cynthia Durkin
EVP, Chief Financial Officer: Ken Giacobbe
VP, Treasurer: Peter Hong
EVP, Technology: Raymond Kilmer
EVP, Strategy & Development: Mark Krakowiak
VP, General Counsel: Max Laun
VP, Controller: Paul Myron
EVP, Legal: Kate Ramundo
Year Founded: 1906
Estimated Sales: $50-100 Million
Number Employees: 500-999

24742 Kay Home Products Inc
90 Mcmillen Rd
Antioch, IL 60002-1845

847-395-4940
Fax: 847-395-3305 800-600-7009
www.kayhomeproducts.com
Manufacturer and exporter of patio and tray tables,
lap trays, barbecue grills, etc
Chairman: Edward Crawford
CEO: Jack Murray
Estimated Sales: $1-5 Million
Number Employees: 50-99
Square Footage: 600000
Parent Co: Park-Ohio Industries
Brands:
    Marshallan
    Quaker

24743 Kaye Instruments
101 Billerica Avenue
Suite 7
N Billerica, MA 01862-1256

978-262-0273
Fax: 978-439-8181 800-343-4624
kaye@ge.com www.kayeinstruments.com
Manufacturer and exporter of data acquisition sys-
tems for process monitoring, controlling, archiving
and reporting
President: Kenneth B Hurley
CEO: Ken Hurley
CFO: Al Parenteau
VP Sales/Marketing: Karen Huffman
Number Employees: 120
Square Footage: 240000
Brands:
    Autograph
    Dialog
    Digi-Link
    Digistrip
    Fix Dmacs
    Netpac

24744 Keating Of Chicago Inc
8901 W 50th St
Mc Cook, IL 60525-6001

708-246-3000
Fax: 708-246-3100 800-532-8464
keating@keatingofchicago.com
www.keatingofchicago.com
Manufacturer and exporter of fryers, frying baskets,
serving equipment, griddles, griddle brushes, pasta
cookers, food warmers, hot plates, salting/bagging
stations and grease/oil filtration systems.
President: Eliza Keating
IT: Eliza Moravec
elizaann@keatingofchicago.com
Estimated Sales: $2.5-5 Million
Number Employees: 5-9
Brands:
    Instant Recovery Fryer
    Keating's Incredible Frying Machine
    Miraclean Griddle
    Pasta Plus System

24745 Kedco Wine Storage Systems
564 Smith St
Farmingdale, NY 11735-1111

631-454-7800
Fax: 631-454-4876 800-654-9988
www.kedcowinestoragesystems.com
Manufacturer and importer of store fixtures, glass
doors, temperature-controlled wine storage equipment, display cabinets and refrigeration and wine
racks

VP: David Windt
VP: Ken Windt
Contact: Helene Windt
helene.windt@kedco.com
Estimated Sales: Less Than $500,000
Number Employees: 5-9
Square Footage: 50000

24746 Keen Kutter
20608 Earl St
Torrance, CA 90503
310-370-6941
Fax: 310-370-3851 rshaver814@aol.com
www.keenkutter.shaverspecialty.com
Manufacturer and exporter of vegetable cutters
President: George W Shaver
Manager: Scott Shaver
Estimated Sales: $2.5-5 Million
Number Employees: 20-49
Brands:
Keen' Kutter

24747 Keena Corporation
25 Lenglen Road
Suite 4
Newton, MA 02458-1420
617-244-9800
Fax: 617-527-0056
Reinforced gummed paper, fiberglass, gummed tape
President: Harvey Epstein
Business Manager: Leslie Kent
Estimated Sales: $5 Million
Number Employees: 1-4
Square Footage: 80000

24748 Keene Technology Inc
14357 Commercial Pkwy
South Beloit, IL 61080-2621
815-624-8989
Fax: 815-624-4223 info@ktiusa.com
www.ktiusa.com
Automatic zero speed splicers, rewinders, web tension controls, infeeds, unwind/rewind stands and related web handling equipment.
President: Danny Pearse
dpearse@keenetech.com
Sales Manager: Darrel Spors
Plant Manager: Bill Carpenter
Estimated Sales: $5-10 Million
Number Employees: 50-99
Square Footage: 260000

24749 Keenline Conveyor Systems
1936 Chase Dr
Omro, WI 54963-1788
920-685-0365
Fax: 920-235-0825 mail@keenline.com
www.keenline.com
Manufacturer and exporter of conveying equipment including tabletop chain, belt and case conveyors, accumulators, indexers, pushers, counters, clamps, mergers, dividers, combiners and gripper elevators/de-elevators
President: David Kersztyn
davidk@keenline.com
Vice President: Ed Gamoke
Estimated Sales: $5-10 Million
Number Employees: 20-49
Square Footage: 30000
Brands:
Keenline

24750 Keeper Thermal Bag Co
1006 Poplar Ln
Bartlett, IL 60103-5649
630-213-0125
Fax: 630-213-0134 800-765-9244
keepertb@sbcglobal.net
www.keeperthermalbags.com
Manufacturer and exporter of insulated bags including food, pizza and catering; also, beverage carriers
Owner: Mike Leel
Manager: Mike Leel
Estimated Sales: $1-3 Million
Number Employees: 5-9
Brands:
Kee-Per

24751 (HQ)Kehr-Buffalo Wire FrameCo Inc
127 Kehr St
Buffalo, NY 14211-1522
716-893-4276
Fax: 716-897-2389 800-875-4212
sales@kbwf.net www.kbwf.net
Manufacturer and exporter of custom fabricated store fixtures and point of purchase displays for baked goods, produce and beverage products
Owner: James A Rogers Jr
jrogers@rogersindustrialspgs.com
CFO: James Rogers
Research & Development: James Rogers
Quality Control: James Rogers
Sales Director: George Rogers
Estimated Sales: $3-5 Million
Number Employees: 10-19
Square Footage: 50000
Type of Packaging: Bulk

24752 Keith Machinery Corp
34 Gear Ave
Lindenhurst, NY 11757-1078
631-957-1200
Fax: 631-957-9264 sales@keithmachinery.com
www.keithmachinery.com
Agitators, attritors, autoclaves, bag filling and sealing machines, bag labeling equipment, blenders, bundling machines, carton machines: closing, filling, sealing, checkweighers
VP: John Hatz
Estimated Sales: $10-20 Million
Number Employees: 50-99

24753 Keller-Charles Of Philadelphia
2413 Federal St
Philadelphia, PA 19146-2431
215-732-2614
Fax: 215-732-4327
Tea and coffee industry cans
Owner: Peggy Fields
kcpfields@aol.com
Estimated Sales: $20-50 Million
Number Employees: 20-49

24754 Kelley Advisory Services
PO Box 2193
Northbrook, IL 60065-2193
847-412-9234
Fax: 847-412-9235
Consultant specializing in industrial ingredients, finished products, marketing, sales and distribution
President: H Kelley
VP: M Kelley
Customer Service: Karen Bass
Number Employees: 5
Square Footage: 30000

24755 Kelley Company
1612 Hutton Dr
Suite 140
Carrollton, TX 75006
972-466-0707
800-558-6960
kelley@entrematic.com kelleyentrematic.com
Hydraulic, mechanical and air-powered dock levelers, restraints, controls and seals for loading dock shelters.
Year Founded: 1953
Estimated Sales: $100-500 Million

24756 Kelley Supply Inc
704 Industrial Dr
Colby, WI 54421-9778
715-223-3614
Fax: 715-223-6383 800-782-8573
info@kelleysupply.com www.kelleysupply.com
Cheese equipment, defoamers, dispensers, lubricant
Owner: Bernie Alberts
balberts@kelleysupply.com
Estimated Sales: $5-10 Million
Number Employees: 20-49

24757 Kelley Wood Products
85 River St
Fitchburg, MA 01420-3093
978-345-7531
Fax: 978-343-3070 kwpmainoffice@cc.com
www.kelleywoodpro.com
Wooden skids, boxes, shooks and pallets
Owner: Stephen Kelley
info@kelleywoodpro.com
VP: John Kelley

Estimated Sales: $1-2.5 Million
Number Employees: 10-19

24758 Kelly Box & Packaging Corp
2801 Covington Rd
Fort Wayne, IN 46802-6969
260-432-4570
Fax: 260-432-2042 dcope@kellybox.com
www.kellybox.com
Corrugated cartons and corrugated and wooden boxes
CEO: Thomas J Kelly Jr
Sales Manager: Doug Cope
Customer Service Manager / Estimator: Chris Dowty
Estimated Sales: $5-10 Million
Number Employees: 100-249

24759 Kelly Dock Systems
6720 N Teutonia Avenue
Milwaukee, WI 53209-3119
414-352-1000
Fax: 414-352-2093
Manufacturer and exporter of dock equipment including levers and restraints
Sales/Marketing Manager: Steve Sprunger
Estimated Sales: $20-50 Million
Number Employees: 100-249

24760 Kelman Bottles LLC
1101 William Flynn Hwy
Glenshaw, PA 15116-2637
412-486-9100
Fax: 412-486-6087
Formerly Glenshaw Galss Company, producers of glass containers for the food and beverage industry in the US, Canada and Mexico
President: William Kelman
tromig@kelmanbottles.com
Sales Exec: Tracy Romig
Operations Manager: John Lilley
Plant Manager: Dawn Dietz
Estimated Sales: $660 Thousand
Number Employees: 250-499
Square Footage: 3829

24761 Kelmin Products
P. O. Box 1108
Plymouth, FL 32768
407-886-6079
Fax: 407-886-6579 kelminwik@aol.com
www.kelminproductsinc.com
Chafing fuel, chafing heaters, wick, chafin dish fuel, diethylenol glycol
President: Robert Jankun
CEO: Betty J Jankun
Estimated Sales: $1-3 Million
Number Employees: 10-19
Number of Brands: 1
Number of Products: 3
Square Footage: 28000
Type of Packaging: Food Service, Private Label, Bulk
Brands:
Ultra Pumps
Witte Pumps

24762 Kem A Trix Inc
PO Box 580
Champlain, NY 12919-0580
206-764-4668
Fax: 206-764-7213 888-215-8237
mpenton@kematrix.com www.kematrix.com
Specialty lubricants manufacturer as well as sealants for pumps and valves
President: Norman Katz
Marketing: Jeffrey Katz
Contact: Mable Benton
info@kematrix.com
Estimated Sales: Less Than $500,000
Number Employees: 1-4
Number of Products: 34
Type of Packaging: Consumer, Food Service, Private Label, Bulk

24763 Kemco Systems Inc
11500 47th St N
Clearwater, FL 33762-4955
727-573-2323
Fax: 727-573-2346 800-633-7055
sales@kemcosystems.com
www.kemcosystems.com

System equipment for meat and poultry industry, heaters-water, heat reclaiming systems, water pollution treatment and monitoring, total plant sanitation and waste water treatment systems
President: Carol Gorrel
carolgorrel@kemcosystems.com
CEO: Lee Kesbering
VP: Gerald Van Gils
R & D: Gerald Van Gils
Marketing: Bernie Weintraub
VP Sales: Al Jenneman
Plant Manager: David Gregg
Purchasing: Rod Kummer
Estimated Sales: $10-25 Million
Number Employees: 50-99
Number of Brands: 18
Square Footage: 60000

24764 Kemex Meat Brands
2400 T Street NE
Washington, DC 20002-1919

301-277-2444
Fax: 301-277-0235

Manufacturer and exporter of USDA inspection leg-end insert labels
Owner: Mary Ellen Campbell
Estimated Sales: Less than $500,000
Number Employees: 4

24765 Kemin Industries Inc
2100 Maury St
P.O. Box 70
Des Moines, IA 50317-1100

515-559-5100
Fax: 515-559-5232   800-777-8307
kftcs.am@kemin.com www.kemin.com

Liquid products which help to enhance the shelf life of food items.
Co- Founder: Mary Nelson
CEO: Jennifer Brown
jennifer-l-brown@uiowa.edu
Number Employees: 100-249

24766 Kemper Bakery Systems
300 Forge Way
Rockaway, NJ 07866-2032

973-625-1566
Fax: 973-586-2091

24767 Kemutec Group Inc
130 Wharton Rd # A
Keystone Industrial Park
Bristol, PA 19007-1685

215-788-8013
Fax: 215-788-5113 sales@kemutecusa.com
www.kemutecusa.com

Manufacturer, importer and exporter of blenders, mixers, centrifugal sifters, grinding mills and valves
President: Karin Galloway
klg@kemutecusa.com
Director of Marketing: Kathy Moncur
Estimated Sales: $5-10 Million
Number Employees: 5-9
Square Footage: 40000
Brands:
   Kek
   Mucon

24768 Kemwall Distributors LTD
250 Avenue W
Brooklyn, NY 11223-4610

718-372-0486
Fax: 718-372-3421 fldwr@msn.com

Manager: Charles Feldman
c.feldman@feldware.com
Estimated Sales: $1-3 Million
Number Employees: 5-9

24769 Ken Coat
P.O.Box 575
Bardstown, KY 40004-575

Fax: 270-259-9858   888-536-2628

Manufacturer and exporter of plastisol-coated, metal outdoor furniture including tables, benches, chairs, etc.; also, trash receptacles
President: J R Davis
Sls.: Philip Clemens
Estimated Sales: $5-10 Million
Number Employees: 10-19
Square Footage: 75000

24770 Ken's Beverage Inc
10015 S Mandel St
Plainfield, IL 60585

800-285-2292
orders@kbiparts.com www.kbiparts.com

Beverage dispensing services and equipment for the food service market.
Owner/President/CEO: Ken Reimer
Year Founded: 1985
Estimated Sales: $50-100 Million
Number Employees: 100-249

24771 Kendall Frozen Fruits, Inc.
9777 Wilshire Blvd
Suite 818
Beverly Hills, CA 90212-1908

310-288-9920
Fax: 310-288-9913 susan@kendallfruit.com
www.kendallfruit.com

Frozen fruits including dried, juice concentrates, purees, freeze dried fruit, fruit powders, vegetable products, chocolate covered dried fruit, and yogurt covered dried fruit
President: Susan Kendall
Manager/Berkeley: Deborah Kendall
Manager/Littleton: Larry Kendall
VP Finance: Debra Olk
VP: Mike Daems
VP: Frank Abarca
VP: Kelly Marks
Estimated Sales: $3.6 Million
Number Employees: 14

24772 Kendall Packaging Corporation
633 W Wisconsin Ave
Milwaukee, WI 53203-1918

414-276-4770
Fax: 414-276-5668   800-237-0951
www.kendallpkg.com

Flexible, food, and industrial packaging
President and COO: Eric Erickson
VP Marketing/Sales: Stuart Zeisse
Manager: Randy Mjelde
Contact: Rebecca Kuehl
rebecca@kendallpkg.com
Estimated Sales: $10-20 Million
Number Employees: 20-49

24773 Kendel
5320 Dansher Rd
Countryside, IL 60525-3124

708-813-1520
Fax: 708-813-1539   800-323-1100
www.welchpkg.com

Folding paper boxes; flexo printing and structural and graphic designing services available
Manager: Ian Mercer
VP: Gary Davidson
Manager Account Services: Rick Berg
Estimated Sales: $10-20 Million
Number Employees: 50-99
Square Footage: 280000

24774 Kendon Candies Inc
460 Perrymont Avenue
San Jose, CA 95125

408-297-6133
Fax: 408-297-4008   800-332-2639

Lollipops
President: Kate Glass
Contact: Holly Anderson
h.anderson@kendoncandies.com

24775 Kendrick Johnson & Assoc Inc
9609 Girard Ave S
Minneapolis, MN 55431-2619

952-888-2847
Fax: 952-888-8336   800-826-1271
sales@kendrick-johnson.com
www.kendrick-johnson.com

Plastic dish covers, trays, plates, tumblers, cups and soup and cereal bowls
President: Byron C Hamilton
bhamilton@kendrick-johnson.com
Vice President: Nancy Hamilton
Sales Director: Lori Green
Estimated Sales: Less than $500,000
Number Employees: 1-4

24776 Kennedy Enterprises
4910 Rent Worth Dr
Lincoln, NE 68516-2507

402-423-3210
Fax: 402-423-5129   800-228-0072
shanekei@windstream.net
www.kennedyenterprisesinc.com

Greases and oils, accessory equipment, forming, filling and sealing equipment, vacuum packaging equipment
President: Rick Kennedy
rickkei@windstream.net
Chairman: Maxine Kennedy
Estimated Sales: $1-2.5 Million
Number Employees: 5-9

24777 Kennedy Group
38601 Kennedy Pkwy
Willoughby, OH 44094-7395

440-951-7660
Fax: 440-951-3253
kennedygroup1@kennedygrp.com
www.kennedygrp.com

Developer and manufacturer of labeling, packaging, promotional labels, and identification systems. Manufactures prime labels, clear labels, booklets, coupons, blister cards, instant digital labels, case pack labels, versa-cards, tab-onads, shrink labels, etc
Owner: Patrick Kennedy
kennedypatrick@kennedygrp.com
Marketing/Sales: Patrick Kennedy
Operations Manager: Todd Kennedy
Estimated Sales: $10-20 Million
Number Employees: 50-99
Square Footage: 160000
Type of Packaging: Consumer, Food Service, Private Label, Bulk

24778 Kennedy's Specialty Sewing
Box 250
Erin, ON N0B 1T0
Canada

519-833-9306
Fax: 519-833-2357

Flags, canvas goods, coffee filters and aprons
President: Brenda Broughton
Number Employees: 10-19

24779 Kenray Associates
11576 Highway 150
Greenville, IN 47124-9213

812-923-9884
Fax: 812-923-2820 sales@kenray.com
www.kenray.com

Data processing systems for brokers, distributors and manufacturers including multi-office capability, hardware/software training, integrated e-commerce, EDI and support
President: Kenneth Mcgee Sr
Contact: Sandy Yoshida
syoshida@kenray.biz
Estimated Sales: $1-2.5 Million
Number Employees: 5-9

24780 Kenro
200 Industrial Dr
Fredonia, WI 53021

262-692-2411
Fax: 262-692-9141

Plasticware including trays, dishes and dinnerware
Contact: Sharon Fay
sharon.fay@kenro.com
Estimated Sales: $20-50 Million
Number Employees: 100-249
Parent Co: Carlisle Company

24781 Kensington Lighting Corp
593 Rugh St
Greensburg, PA 15601-5637

724-850-2433
Fax: 724-837-8087   800-434-5005
info@kensingtonUS.com www.kensingtonus.com

Manufacturer and exporter of energy efficient lighting fixtures and flourescent lighting
Owner: Gary Whiteknight
gary@kensingtonus.com
Estimated Sales: $500,000-$1 Million
Number Employees: 5-9
Parent Co: Adience Equities
Type of Packaging: Consumer, Food Service

24782 Kent Co
13301 Biscayne Blvd
North Miami, FL 33181-2039
305-944-4041
Fax: 305-944-1106 800-521-4886
kentcomp@aol.com and www.kent-company.com
Rubber de-feathering fingers for use in chicken or
turkey processing machines.
Sales: Dolly Tomlinson
Manager: Dolly Tomlinson
kentcomp@aol.com
Technical: Edd Woike
Number Employees: 1-4

24783 Kent Corp
4446 Pinson Valley Pkwy
Birmingham, AL 35215-2940
205-856-3621
Fax: 205-856-3622 800-252-5368
sales@kentcorp.com www.kentcorp.com
Manufacturer and exporter of store fixtures includ-
ing modular steel display shelving
President: Mera Craws
crawsm@asme.org
CEO: V Albano
CFO: Sharron Harbison
Sales Director: Allan Solomon
Estimated Sales: $20-50 Million
Number Employees: 100-249
Square Footage: 250000

24784 Kent District Library System
814 W River Center Dr NE
Comstock Park, MI 49321-8955
616-784-2007
Fax: 616-647-3828 lwerner@kdl.org
www.kdl.org
Material handling equipment including skids and
factory trucks
Chairman: Charles R. Myers
Treasurer: Scott Petersen
Technology Director: Mike Carpenter
IT: Shane Hinds
shinds@kdl.org
Plant Supervisor: John McKay
Number Employees: 20-49
Square Footage: 40000
Brands:
  Globe
  Wheel-Ezy

24785 Kent Precision Foods Group Inc
2905 US-61
Muscatine, IA 52761
800-442-5242
www.precisionfoods.com
Pickle and tomato mixes, pectins, jams, jellies, fruit
preservatives, blended spices and seasonings, des-
sert mixes; exporter of dry soft serve and dessert
mixes.
Manager of Business Development: Kirk Kuiper
Vice President of Sales & Marketing: Connie Huck
Year Founded: 1992
Estimated Sales: $69.4 Million
Number Employees: 20-49
Number of Brands: 8
Square Footage: 200000
Parent Co: Kent Corporation
Type of Packaging: Consumer, Food Service, Pri-
  vate Label, Bulk
Other Locations:
  Manufacturing Location
  Bolingbrook IL
Brands:
  Foothill Farms®
  Frostline® Frozen Treats
  DOLE® Soft Serve
  LAND O'LAKES™
  Mrs. Dash® Foodservice
  Sugar Twin®
  Baker's Joy®
  Sqwincher®

24786 Kent R Hedman & Assoc
3312 Woodford Dr # 200
Arlington, TX 76013-1139
817-277-0888
Executive search firm
President: Kent Hedman
Principal: K Dunbar
Estimated Sales: Less Than $500,000
Number Employees: 1-4

24787 Kentfield's
180 Nadina Way
Greenbrae, CA 94904
415-461-7454
Fax: 415-461-5553 888-461-7454
21tchen towels, canvas aprons, canvas totes, cock-
tails napkins
Owner: Donna Vanmalder
CFO: Donna Vanmalder
Estimated Sales: Below $5 Million
Number Employees: 4

24788 Kentmaster Manufacturing Co
1801 S Mountain Ave
Monrovia, CA 91016-4270
626-359-8888
Fax: 626-303-5151 800-421-1477
sales@kentmaster.com
Manufacturer and exporter of portable power beef
and hog slaughtering equipment
Owner: Ralph Karubian
rk@kentmaster.com
Sls./Svce. Mgr.: Joe Leamen
Estimated Sales: $5-10 Million
Number Employees: 20-49

24789 Kentucky Grocers Assn Inc
512 Capital Ave
Frankfort, KY 40601-2839
502-696-9153
Fax: 502-875-1595 info@kgaonline.org
www.kgaonline.org
Committed to being a positive change in the grocery
and convenience store industries.
Executive Director: Ted Mason
ted@kgaonline.org
Estimated Sales: $300,000-500,000
Number Employees: 1-4

24790 Kentucky Power
855 Central Ave
Suite 200
Ashland, KY 41101
800-572-1113
www.kentuckypower.com
Electric utility systems.
President & COO: Brett Mattison
VP, Regulatory & Finance: Ranie Wohnhas
VP, External Affairs & Customer Service: Cynthia
Wiseman
Estimated Sales: K
Parent Co: American Electric Power

24791 Kentwood Spring Water Company
100 Stable Drive
Patterson, LA 70392-0743
985-395-9313
Fax: 985-395-2148 www.kentwoodsprings.com
Coffee service filtration systems; also, bottled and
distilled spring water
Branch Mgr.: Scott Coy
Branch Manager: Dwayne Duplantis
Estimated Sales: $500,000-$1 Million
Number Employees: 9
Parent Co: Syntori
Type of Packaging: Consumer

24792 Kenyon Press
2850 Walnut Ave
Signal Hill, CA 90755-1834
562-424-6600
Fax: 562-424-7599 800-752-9395
sales@kenyonpress.com www.kenyonpress.com
Menus; custom designing available
President: Paul Demarco
pauld@kenyonpress.net
Sls.: Dan Reed
Estimated Sales: Below $5,000,000
Number Employees: 20-49

24793 Kepes
9016 58th Pl
Suite 600
Kenosha, WI 53144
262-652-7889
Fax: 262-652-7787 800-345-3653
inquire@kepes.com www.kepes.com
Carton glue erectors, semiautomatic carton gluing
machines, hot melt glue application equipment, unit
rate and totalizing counters, rubber and urethane
covered machine components and permalube lubrication system

President: Wayne Pagel Jr
w.pagel@kepes.com
Estimated Sales: $10-20 Million
Number Employees: 20-49

24794 Kerian Machines Inc
1709 Highway 81 S
Grafton, ND 58237
701-352-0480
Fax: 701-352-3776 sales@Kerian.com
www.kerianmachines.com
Manufacturer and exporter of fruit and vegetable
graders and sizers
President: John Kerian
CEO: James Kerian
Estimated Sales: $1-2.5 Million
Number Employees: 10-19
Brands:
  Kerian Sizer

24795 Kerrigan Paper ProductsInc
293 Neck Rd
Haverhill, MA 1835
978-374-4797
Fax: 978-521-4067
Corrugated boxes
President: William Law
Estimated Sales: $1-2.5 Million
Number Employees: 5-9

24796 Kerry, Inc
Global Technology & Innovation Center
3400 Millington Rd
Beloit, WI 53511
608-363-1200
www.kerry.com
Food ingredients, encapsulation, ingredient sour-
cing, in-house testing and spray drying services.
CEO/Executive Director: Edmond Scanlon
President/CEO, Kerry Taste & Nutrition: Gerry
Behan
CFO: Marguerite Larkin
President/CEO, North America: Michael O'Neill
Global COO: Alan Barrett
Year Founded: 1972
Estimated Sales: Over $1 Billion
Number Employees: 25,255
Parent Co: Kerry Group Plc
Type of Packaging: Food Service

24797 Kesry Corporation
16133 W 45th Dr
Golden, CO 80403-1791
303-271-9300
Fax: 303-271-3645 www.kevey.com
President: Tom Kissinger
Estimated Sales: $5-10 Million
Number Employees: 5-9

24798 Kess Industries Inc
130 37th St NE
Auburn, WA 98002
253-735-5700
Fax: 253-735-2851 800-578-5564
Manufacturer of an array of standard and custom
equipment for accumulating, chilling, coating, de-
positing, distributing, drying, dumping, metering,
pasteurizing, transferring, washing and weighing
products.
President: K Jell Fogelgren
Sales and Estimating: Ray Cassingham
Estimated Sales: Below $5 Million
Number Employees: 10-19
Square Footage: 48000

24799 Kessenich's Limited
131 S Fair Oaks Ave
Madison, WI 53704-5897
608-249-5391
Fax: 608-249-1628 800-248-0555
www.kessenichs.com
Restaurant equipment
President: Robert Kessenich
CEO: Cheri Martin
Estimated Sales: $2.5-5 Million
Number Employees: 20-49

24800 Kessler Sign Co
2669 National Rd
Zanesville, OH 43701-8257
740-453-0668
Fax: 740-453-5301 800-686-1870
www.kesslersignco.com
Signs and awnings

President: Bob Kessler
bob@kesslersignco.com
Service Director: Mike Taylor
VP: Rodger Kessler
Vice President-Operations: David Kessler
Account Executive: Doug Gabriel
Estimated Sales: $5-10 Million
Number Employees: 20-49

24801 Kett
9581 Featherhill Dr
Villa Park, CA 92861-2633

714-779-8400
Fax: 714-693-2923 800-438-5388
sales@kett.com www.kett.com
Our focus is moisture and organic composition analysis, coating thickness measurement, friction, wear, peel, adhesion and other surface property analyses, rice quality instrumentation and other agricultural test instruments for thegrain and seed marketplace.
Owner: Bob Clark
Number Employees: 1-4

24802 Keurig Dr Pepper
5301 Legacy Dr.
Plano, TX 75024

800-696-5891
www.keurigdrpepper.com
Coffee, hot and cold beverage maker systems, flavored soft drinks, teas, waters, juices, juice drinks, and more.
CEO: Robert Gamgort
CFO: Ozan Dokmecioglu
Chief Legal Officer/General Counsel: Jim Baldwin
Chief Research & Development Officer: David Thomas
Chief Marketing Officer: Andrew Springate
Year Founded: 2018
Estimated Sales: $11 Billion
Number Employees: 25,000
Number of Brands: 81
Number of Products: 530+
Type of Packaging: Consumer, Food Service, Bulk
Other Locations:
  Production
  Castroville CA
  R&D, Professional Services
  Burlington MA
  Production
  Knoxville TN
  Production
  Windsor VA
  Production
  Sumner WA
  Keurig Canada
  Montreal, QC, Canada
Brands:
  Green Mountain Coffee®
  Caribou Coffee®
  Laughing Man®
  Peet's Coffee®
  The Original Donut Shop®
  Van Houtte®
  Revv®
  Tully's Coffe®
  Krispy Kreme®
  Newmann's Own Organics®
  Barista Bros®
  Barista Prima Coffeehouse®
  Br–lerie Mont Royal®
  Br–lerie St. Denis®
  Caf, Escapes®
  Caf, Punta del Cielo®
  Cinnabon®
  Coffee People®
  Diedrich Coffee®
  Donut House Collection®
  Emeril®
  Gloria Jean's Coffees®
  Hollys Coffee®
  Kahl£a®
  Laura Secord®
  Orient Express®
  Timothy's®
  Panera Bread®
  High Brew Coffee®
  Gila Caf,®
  Forto®
  Adagio®
  Dr. Pepper®
  7UP®
  A&W Root Beer®
  Canada Dry®
  Schweppes®
  Sunkist®

Crush®
Sun Drop®
IBC®
Diet Rite®
Squirt®
Vernors®
Royal Crown Cola®
Hires®
Stewart's®
Big Red®
Cplus®
Cactus Cooler®
Nehi Cola®
Tahitian Treat®
Bai®
Deja Blue®
Penafiel®
Snapple®
Straight Up Tea®
Evian®
Neuro®
Vita Coco®
Cora®
Clamato®
Hawaiian Punch®
Margritaville®
Mott's®
Nantucker Nectars®
Orangina®
Mott's®
Nantucker Nectars®
Orangina®
ReaLemon®
Rose's®
SunnyD®

24803 Kew Cleaning Systems
1500 N Belcher Road
Clearwater, FL 33765-1301

800-942-1690
High pressure washers and waste water treatment systems
G.M.: Ed Hilfretz
Number Employees: 12
Brands:
  Kew

24804 Kewanee Washer Corporaton
3209 Saint Andrews Court
Findlay, OH 45840-2948

419-435-8269
Fax: 419-425-0512
Commercial pot and pan washing units
Owner: Judith White
GM: C Paul White
Estimated Sales: Less than $500,000
Number Employees: 1-4
Square Footage: 16
Brands:
  Kewanee K99

24805 Key Automation
1301 Corporate Center Drive
Suite 113
Eagan, MN 55121-1259

651-455-0547
Fax: 651-686-5232 tgriffith@keyauto.com
Standard and custom designed packaging machinery including cartoners and case packers for pouches and bags; also, product handling, orienting and feeding systems
Sls.: David Olson
Estimated Sales: $1-5 Million
Number Employees: 8
Square Footage: 8000
Brands:
  Ccl

24806 Key Container Company
PO Box 71
South Gate, CA 90280

323-564-4211
Fax: 323-564-5127 custsvc@keycontainer.com
www.keycontainer.com
Shipping containers
President: Robert J Watts
Contact: Wanda East
east@keycontainer.com
Estimated Sales: $20-50 Million
Number Employees: 100-249

24807 Key Industrial
997 Enterprise Way
Napa, CA 94558-6209

707-252-1205
Fax: 707-252-9054 800-812-5258
Wine industry equipment
Owner: John Boyanich
jboyanich@keyindustrial.com
Estimated Sales: $5-10 Million
Number Employees: 10-19

24808 (HQ)Key Industries Inc
400 Marble Rd
Fort Scott, KS 66701-8639

620-223-2000
Fax: 620-223-5822 800-835-0365
customerservice@keyapparel.com
Manufacturer and exporter of clothing and uniforms
President/Chief Executive Officer: Chris Barnes
cbarnes@keyapparel.com
Chairman: William Pollock
Controller: Julian McPharson
Senior Vice President: Mike Johnson
Information Technology Manager: Jeff Sweetser
Director, Marketing: Mike Hughey
Estimated Sales: $9 Million
Number Employees: 50-99
Square Footage: 130000

24809 Key International Cranbury
4 Corporate Dr # A
Suite A
Cranbury, NJ 08512-3613

609-235-9693
Fax: 732-972-2630 kevin@keyinternational.com
www.keyinternational.com
Packaging and processing equipment
President: Kevin Beenders
CEO: Valerie Ianieri
CEO: Primo Ianieri
VP Sales: Kevin Beenders
Contact: Jocelyn Aguilu
aguilu.jocelyn@keyinternational.com
Purchasing: Bill Howard
Estimated Sales: Less Than $500,000
Number Employees: 1-4

24810 Key Material Handling Inc
4790 Alamo St
Simi Valley, CA 93063-1837

805-520-6007
Fax: 805-520-3007 800-539-7225
sales@keymaterial.com www.keyrack.com
Stainless steel and aluminum material handling equipment, racks, containers, conveyors, lifts, scales, shelving, tables and trucks; custom fabrication available
Owner: Rick Galbraith
rick@keymaterial.com
Sls.: John Galbraith
Estimated Sales: Less Than $500,000
Number Employees: 1-4
Square Footage: 40000
Brands:
  Interlake
  Keyrack
  Rapid Rack

24811 Key Packaging Co
15th St E
Sarasota, FL 34243

941-355-2728
Fax: 941-351-8708 webinfo@keypackaging.com
www.keypackaging.com
Manufacturer and exporter of thermoformed plastic packaging, containers, food trays and blister packs
President: Earl Smith
earl@keypackaging.com
Quality Control: Gifford Quast
Sales Coordinator: Gene Donohue
Sales Director: Karlson Strouse
Manager: Karlson Strouse
Purchasing Manager: Chris Rathbun
Estimated Sales: $10-20 Million
Number Employees: 50-99
Square Footage: 104000
Type of Packaging: Consumer, Food Service, Bulk

24812 (HQ)Key Technology Inc.
150 Avery St.
Walla Walla, WA 99362

509-529-2161
Fax: 509-394-3538 www.key.net

Design, manufacture and market process automation systems for food and other industries. This technology integrates automated optical inspection systems, specialized conveyor systems, and processing/preparation systems, as well asresearch, development, and world-class engineering.
President: John Ehren
Vice President, Finance: Carson Brennan
Vice President, Global Operations: Shawn Prendiville
Year Founded: 1948
Estimated Sales: $116.33 Million
Number Employees: 500-999
Square Footage: 173000
Other Locations:
Redmond OR
Brands:
Veo™
Manta®
Tegra®
Optyx®
Iso-Flo®
Horizon™
Impulse™
Spiral-Flo™
Symetix®
Remotemd™
Adr®
Smart Shaker®
Tobacco Sorter™ 3
Oncore®
Veg-Mix™
Turbo-Flo®

24813 (HQ)Key-Pak Machines
1221 Us Highway 22
Suite 1
Lebanon, NJ 8833
908-236-2111
Fax: 908-236-7013 www.key-pak.com
An extension of the specialized packaging equipment manufactured by Research & Development Packaging Corp. Specializing in vertical form/fill/seal machines, Key-Pak has consistently expanded its machinery portfolio over the years byadding combinational net-weigh scales, cup indexing system, piston liquid fillers and even conveyors.
CEO: Donald Bogut
Vice President: Chris Wanthouse
Research & Development: Don Bogut
Marketing Director: Christopher Wanthouse
Sales Director: Christopher Wanthouse
Operations Manager: Stan Florey
Estimated Sales: $1-3 Million
Number Employees: 5-9
Number of Brands: 1
Square Footage: 17000
Brands:
Key-Pak

24814 Key-Pak Machines
1221 Us Highway 22
Suite 1
Lebanon, NJ 08833
908-236-2111
Fax: 908-236-7013 www.key-pak.com
Vertical form fill seal machines, net weight scale systems
President: Donald Bogut
Principal: Arthur Bogut
Estimated Sales: $1-3 Million
Number Employees: 5-9

24815 Keystone Adjustable CapCo Inc
1591 Hylton Rd # B
Pennsauken, NJ 08110-1381
856-317-9879
Fax: 856-663-6075 800-663-5439
info@keystonecap.com www.keystonecap.com
Disposable sanitary headwear including paper and cloth chef hats, overseas caps and bouffants, beard covers, hair nets, etc.; also, aprons, shoe covers, nonwoven coveralls and sleeves; exporter of overseas caps, chef hats and hairnets
CEO: Andrew Feinstein
afeinstein@keystonecap.com
Estimated Sales: $50-100 Million
Number Employees: 100-249
Number of Brands: 1
Number of Products: 400
Square Footage: 95000
Type of Packaging: Consumer, Food Service, Private Label, Bulk

Brands:
Classy Caps
Cordon Bleu Chef Hats

24816 Keystone Adjustable CapCo Inc
1591 Hylton Rd # B
Pennsauken, NJ 08110-1381
856-317-9879
Fax: 856-663-6075 800-663-5439
info@keystonecap.com www.keystonecap.com
Tin and aluminum continuous thread caps for glass and plastic containers
President: Dorothy Lynch
CEO: Andrew Feinstein
afeinstein@keystonecap.com
Secy.: Marie Forman
Plant Manager: Rodger Rohebach
Estimated Sales: $2.5-5 Million
Number Employees: 100-249
Square Footage: 18000

24817 Keystone Manufacturing Inc
668 Cleveland St
Rochester, PA 15074
724-775-2227
Fax: 724-775-2739 800-446-7205
sales@keystonemfg.com www.keystonemfg.com
Metal conveyor belting
Owner: Dick Elste
sales@keystonemfg.com
CFO: Richard Elste
Quality Control: Drew Elste
Estimated Sales: $2.5-5 Million
Number Employees: 20-49
Number of Products: 7-10

24818 Keystone Packaging Svc Inc
555 Warren St
Phillipsburg, NJ 08865-3230
908-454-8567
Fax: 908-454-7173 800-473-8567
Polyethylene plastic for packaging, printed and unprinted rolls, sheets and bags
President: John R Schoeneck
jschj@earthlink.net
Estimated Sales: $2.5-5 Million
Number Employees: 10-19
Square Footage: 148000

24819 Keystone Process Equipment
PO Box 446
Philipsburg, PA 16866-446
814-684-5500
Fax: 814-684-7475 sales@keystoneprocess.com
www.keystoneprocess.com
Agitation systems, curd, tank, aseptic processing system, custom fabrication, processing and packaging
Manager: Greg Kearney
Estimated Sales: $1-3 Million
Number Employees: 1-4

24820 Keystone Rubber Corporation
PO Box 9
Greenbackville, VA 23356
717-235-6863
Fax: 717-235-9681 800-394-5661
Manufacturer and exporter of conveyor belting, rubber sheeting hoses, rubber gaskets and fittings; FDA approved materials
President: Gloria Lawson
Sales: Mary Baley
Estimated Sales: $5-10 Million
Number Employees: 10-19
Parent Co: Maryland Rubber Corporation

24821 Keystone Universal Corp
18400 Rialto St
Melvindale, MI 48122-1946
313-388-0063
Fax: 313-388-6495 ebonex@flash.net
www.ebonex.com
Ammonium carbonate lump, chip powder
President: Michelle Toenniges
ebonex@flash.net
Estimated Sales: $1-5 Million
Number Employees: 5-9

24822 Keystone Valve
9100 W Gulf Bank Road
Houston, TX 77240
713-937-5375
Fax: 713-937-5478
Wine industry valves

24823 Khs USA Inc
5501 N Washington Blvd
Sarasota, FL 34243-2249
941-359-4000
Fax: 941-359-4043 877-227-8358
Packaging and special machinery including bag and carton filling and shrink-banding
President: Reno Cruz
Cio/Cto: Terry Kerns
terry.kerns@khs.com
Executive: Paul Rosile
Estimated Sales: $5-10 Million
Number Employees: 100-249
Brands:
Bartelt
Weco

24824 Khs USA Inc
880 Bahcall Ct
Waukesha, WI 53186-1801
262-797-7200
Fax: 262-797-0025 info@khs.com
www.khs.com
Provide filling and packaging services for the beverages and food industries: stainless steel commercial food processing and beverage bottling machinery, processing, continual mixing and blending, rinsing, filling, capping, net weightfillers, aseptic fillers, and labels.
President: Mike Brancato
Cio/Cto: Paul Turinske
paul.turinske@khs.com
Chief Financial Officer: Jim Elliott
Purchasing Manager: Jeff Camargo
Estimated Sales: $106 Million
Number Employees: 250-499
Parent Co: KHS GmbH
Other Locations:
KHS Manufacturing Facility
Sarasota FL

24825 Khs USA Inc
5501 N Washington Blvd
Sarasota, FL 34243-2249
941-359-4000
Fax: 941-359-4043 info@khs.com
Provide filling and packaging services for the beverage and food industries.
Cio/Cto: Terry Kerns
terry.kerns@khs.com
Director of Operations: John Turner
Estimated Sales: $20-50 Million
Number Employees: 100-249
Parent Co: KHS GmbH

24826 Kidde Residential & Commercial
1016 Corporate Park Dr
Mebane, NC 27302-8368
919-563-5911
Fax: 919-563-3954 www.kidde.com
Manufacturer and exporter of portable and hand-held fire extinguishers
Vice President: Bob Amrine
amrine.robert@kiddeus.com
Vice President: Bob Amrine
amrine.robert@kiddeus.com
Number Employees: 250-499
Parent Co: William Holdings
Type of Packaging: Consumer, Food Service, Private Label, Bulk

24827 Kidde-Fenwal Inc
400 Main St
Ashland, MA 01721-2100
508-881-2000
Fax: 508-881-6134 www.kidde-fenwal.com
Fire protection products including clean agent suppression systems, pre-engineered systems, high sensitivity smoke detection devices, alarm and suppression control units, conventional/intelligent fire sensors, alarm devices and specialhazard fire and overheat detection
President: John Sullivan
CFO: Michael Cousindau
Quality Control: Robert Lovell
Number Employees: 250-499

24828 Kiefel Technologies
5 Merrill Industrial Dr # -B
Hampton, NH 03842-1963
603-929-3900
Fax: 603-926-1387
Thermoforming and heat sealing equipment
President: Alfred Rak

Estimated Sales: $10-20 Million
Number Employees: 20-49

24829 Kiefer Brushes, Inc
15 Park Dr
Franklin, NJ 07416
　　　　　　　Fax: 888-239-1986 800-526-2905
Manufacturer, exporter and importer of brushes including oven, floor, window and counter; also, broom and wax applicators, squeegee mop handles, paint rollers and brushes
President and CFO: Edward F Boscia
CEO: Gregory Kiefer
Number Employees: 20-49
Square Footage: 100000
Brands:
　Dispose a Scrub
　Easy Sweep
　Lil Wunder-Miniature Scrub
　Lok-Tight Handle
　Rid-A-Gum

24830 Kikkoman Sales USA Inc.
50 California St
Suite 3600
San Francisco, CA 94111
　　　　　　　415-956-7750
　　　　　www.kikkomanusa.com
Contact: Donna Allison
dallison@kikkomanusa.com
Estimated Sales: I
Number Employees: 100-249

24831 Kilcher Company
1308 Pasadena Avenue S
Apt 11
South Pasadena, FL 33707-3754
　　　　　　　727-367-5839
　　　　　　　Fax: 727-363-1959
Consultant specializing in sales and marketing for the barbecue industry
Pres.: James Kilcher
Number Employees: 16

24832 Kildon Manufacturing
192 Thomas Street
Ingersoll, ON N5C 267
Canada
　　　　　　　519-485-1593
　　　　Fax: 519-485-1084 800-485-4930
Hand cleaners including waterless, lotion and liquid soap
President: Paul White
Secy./Treas.: Nelda Rumble
Quality Control: Donald Parker
Estimated Sales: Below $5 Million
Number Employees: 3

24833 Kilgore Chemical Corporation
880 Heritage Park Boulevard
Suite 200
Layton, UT 84041-5680
　　　　　　　801-546-9909
　　　　　　　Fax: 801-775-9468
Environmentally-safe cleaning chemicals
Estimated Sales: $5-10,000,000
Number Employees: 5-9
Brands:
　Natural Solutions

24834 Killington Wood ProductsCompany
PO Box 696
Rutland, VT 05702-0696
　　　　　　　802-773-9111
　　　　　　　Fax: 802-770-3551
Wooden pallets and boxes
President: William H Carris
Opers. Mgr.: Boris Serkalow
Estimated Sales: $1-2.5 Million
Number Employees: 250-499
Parent Co: Carris Reels

24835 Killion Industries Inc
1380 Poinsettia Ave
Vista, CA 92081-8504
　　　　　　　760-727-5107
　　　Fax: 760-599-1612 800-421-5352
　　　　　sales@killionindustries.com
　　　　　www.killionindustries.com
Manufacturer and exporter of checkstands, and refrigerated fixtures
President: Richard W Killion
richard@killionindustries.com

Estimated Sales: $20-50 Million
Number Employees: 100-249
Square Footage: 200000

24836 Kim Lighting
PO Box 60080
City of Industry, CA 91716-0080
　　　　　　　626-968-5666
　　　Fax: 626-369-2695 sales@kimlighting.com
　　　　　　　www.kimlighting.com
Manufacturer and exporter of lighting fixtures
President: Bill Foley
Regional Sales Manager: Debbie Bell
Estimated Sales: $20-50 Million
Number Employees: 250-499
Parent Co: US Industries

24837 Kimball Companies
75 N Main St
East Longmeadow, MA 01028-2358
　　　　　　　413-525-1881
　　　　　　　Fax: 413-525-2668
Wood, corrugated and plastic boxes, bulk containers, foam pads, plastic skids and collapsible storage bins
VP: David Kimball
VP: D Michael Killoran
Manager: Jeanne Matty
Estimated Sales: Below $5 Million
Number Employees: 5-9
Square Footage: 400000
Type of Packaging: Bulk

24838 (HQ)Kimberly-Clark Corporation
351 Phelps Drive
Irving, TX 75038
　　　　　　　972-281-1200
　　　　　　　www.kimberly-clark.com
Manufacturer and exporter of toilet paper, paper towels, diapers, feminie products, tissues.
Pres., North America Consumer Business: Kim Underhill
Chairman & CEO: Michael Hsu
CFO: Maria Henry
President & Chief Operating Officer: Michael Hsu
Chief Growth Officer: Alison Lewis
Year Founded: 1872
Estimated Sales: $18.5 Billion
Number Employees: 42,000
Number of Brands: 31
Type of Packaging: Consumer, Food Service, Private Label, Bulk
Brands:
　DEPEND
　PLENTITUD
　POISE
　PULL-UPS
　GooDNites
　DRYNITES
　LITTLE SWIMMERS
　SNUGGLERS
　KLEEN BEBE
　GREEN FINGERS
　COTTONELLE
　SCOTTEX
　VIVA
　KOTEX
　KLEENEX
　HUGGIES

24839 Kimberly-Clark Professional
1400 Holcomb Bridge Rd
Roswell, GA 30076
　　　　　　　800-241-3146
　　　kcpinfo@kcc.com www.kcprofessional.com
Paper and nonwoven products including facial and bath tissues, hand towels, disposable wipers and protective garments; also, hand towel dispensers and bath tissue systems
President: Russ Torres
Estimated Sales: $500,000-$1 Million
Number Employees: 1,000-4,999
Parent Co: Kimberly-Clark Corporation
Brands:
　SCOTT
　KLEENEX
　COTTONELLE
　WYPALL
　KIMTECH
　KLEENGUARD
　SMITH & WESSON

24840 Kincaid Enterprises
PO Box 549
Nitro, WV 25143
　　　　　　　304-755-3377
　　　Fax: 304-755-4547 800-951-3377
Manufacturer and exporter of insecticides and other agricultural chemicals
President: R E Kincaid
VP Production: Brian Kincaid
Estimated Sales: $5-10 Million
Number Employees: 5-9
Brands:
　Chloroneb
　Marlate
　Terraneb

24841 Kinder Morgan Inc
6100 Cunningham Rd
Houston, TX 77041-4708
　　　　　　　713-466-0496
　　　Fax: 713-896-8830 www.kindermorgan.com
Conveyor systems including overland, radial, stackers and portable screening plants
Manager: Ron Smith
ronald_smith@kindermorgan.com
VP: Ronald Smith
manager: Ronlad Smith
Estimated Sales: $20-30 Million
Number Employees: 50-99
Square Footage: 54000

24842 Kinematics & Controls Corporation
15151 Technology Dr.
Brooksville, FL 34604-0690
　　　　　　　352-796-0300
　　　Fax: 352-796-4477 800-833-8103
　　　sales@kcontrols.com www.kcontrols.com
Manufacturer and exporter of liquid level sensors and liquid/powder filling machines
President: John Rakucewicz
Contact: Ricky Clotter
ricky@kcontrols.com
Number Employees: 10
Square Footage: 8000

24843 Kinergy Corp
7310 Grade Ln
Louisville, KY 40219-3437
　　　　　　　502-366-5685
　　　Fax: 502-366-3701 kinergy@kinergy.com
　　　　　　　www.kinergy.com
Manufacturer, designer, importer and exporter of bulk solid material handling equipment including bin and container activators, storage pile and rail car dischargers, rail car shakers, feeders, conveyors, deliquefying and deslimingscreens and fluid bed coolers
President: George Dumbaugh
CEO: Scott Greenwell
CFO: Charles Hays
Manager: Lim Adeline
adeline@kinergy.com.sg
Estimated Sales: $10-20 Million
Number Employees: 20-49
Square Footage: 50000

24844 Kinetic Co
6775 W Loomis Rd
Greendale, WI 53129-2700
　　　　　　　414-425-8221
　　　　　　　Fax: 414-425-7927
　　　joseph.masters@knifemaker.com
　　　　　　　www.knifemaker.com
Manufacturer and exporter of perforating blades, machine and packaging knives and slitters
President: Kyle Peerenboom
kylepeerenboom@nestlepurinacareers.com
VP: Cash Masters
VP of Sales: Tina Lawton
General Manager: Ian Finkill
Estimated Sales: $10-20 Million
Number Employees: 50-99
Type of Packaging: Food Service

24845 Kinetic Equipment Company
2146 W Pershing Street
Appleton, WI 54914-6074
　　　　　　　806-293-4471
　　　　　　　Fax: 806-293-1103
Cooling, food processing and material handling equipment and machinery including pump feeders, blenders, dumpers, mixers, conveyors; also, replacement parts

Owner: Joe Offield
V.P.: Susan Stevenson
Purch. Agt.: Herb Chaney
Estimated Sales: $10-20 Million
Number Employees: 5
Brands:
  Cryojet
  Kec I

24846 Kinetico
11015 Kinsman Rd
Newbury, OH 44065-9787

440-564-9111
Fax: 440-564-7641 custserv@kinetico.com
www.kinetico.com
Manufacturer and exporter of water conditioners,
purifiers and filters. Systems are utilized in a wide
variety of residential and commercial applications
that include restaurants, hotels, carwashes, hospitals
and others
President: Toby Thomas
tthomas@kinetico.com
Commercial Sls. Mgr.: George Hohman
CFO: Trevor Wilson
CEO: Shamus Hurley
R&D: Keith Brown
VP Industrial: Chris Hanson
Estimated Sales: $20-50 Million
Number Employees: 250-499
Type of Packaging: Bulk
Brands:
  Kinetico

24847 King 888 Company
PO BOX 51360
Sparks, NV 89436

775-530-5718
Fax: 800-785-3674 800-785-3674
www.king888.com
Energy drinks
Sales Representative: Gary Larson
Type of Packaging: Food Service

24848 King Arthur
646 Shelton Ave
Statesville, NC 28677-6104

704-873-0300
Fax: 704-872-4194 800-257-7244
karthur@i-america.net
Manufacturer and exporter of room service carts,
furniture, sternos, chafers and serving equipment
V.P. Sls./Mktg.: Greg Holroyd
Estimated Sales: $10-20,000,000
Number Employees: 1-4
Parent Co: Falcon Products
Brands:
  Sterno

24849 King Badge & Button Company
17792 Metzler Ln
Suite A
Huntingtn Bch, CA 92647

714-847-3060
Fax: 714-841-3380
Promotional products including badges and buttons.
Available with graphic arts engraving
CEO: Dick Dusterhoft
Manager: Mike Kuskie
Estimated Sales: $300,000+
Number Employees: 1-4
Square Footage: 4400

24850 King Bag & Mfg Co
1500 Spring Lawn Ave
Cincinnati, OH 45223-1699

513-541-5440
Fax: 513-541-6555 800-444-5464
mike@kingbag.com www.kingbag.com
Manufacturer, importer and exporter of bulk han-
dling bags, filters bags and curtains, crumb belts
President: Annie Bunn
annie@kingbag.com
VP: Ron Kirsch Jr
Sales Manager: Mike Jennings
Production Manager: Chris Miller
Estimated Sales: $2.5-5 Million
Number Employees: 20-49
Square Footage: 80000

24851 King Company
4830 Transport Drive
Dallas, TX 75247-6310

507-451-3770
Fax: 507-455-7400 king@kingcompany.com

Manufacturer and exporter of air curtains, process
air conditioning, filtration systems and finned coils
Sls. Mgr.: Thomas Heisler
Marketing Manager: Mike Kaler
Sales Manager: Bruce Glover
Estimated Sales: $1-5 Million
Number Employees: 100-249
Square Footage: 240000
Parent Co: United Dominion Industries
Brands:
  National

24852 King Electric Sign Co
PO Box 1884
Nampa, ID 83653-1884

208-466-2000
Fax: 208-468-0546
kingelectricsigns@hotmail.com
www.king-electric.com
Neon and plastic signs
President: Ron Harrold
Estimated Sales: Less than $500,000
Number Employees: 10

24853 King Engineering-King-Gage
8019 Ohio River Boulevard
Newell, WV 26050

800-242-8871
www.King-Gage.com
Level measurement systems and compressed air fil-
ters
President: Steve Lefevre
Estimated Sales: Below $5 Million
Number Employees: 20-49
Square Footage: 28000
Type of Packaging: Bulk
Brands:
  King Filters
  King-Gage Systems

24854 King Packaging Co
708 Kings Rd
Schenectady, NY 12304-3665

518-370-5464
Fax: 518-393-5464
Contract packaging of cat litter, ice melt products
and decorative landscape stone.
Owner: Bill Venezio
bvenezio@kingpackagingcorp.com
Plant Manager: Anthony Farone
Estimated Sales: Less Than $500,000
Number Employees: 5-9
Number of Brands: 6
Number of Products: 24
Square Footage: 240000
Type of Packaging: Consumer, Private Label

24855 King Plastic Corp
1100 N Toledo Blade Blvd
North Port, FL 34288-8694

941-493-5502
Fax: 941-497-3274 800-780-5502
llathrum@kingplastics.com www.kingplastic.com
Manufacturer and exporter of tamper-resistant plas-
tic containers including cups
President: Debra Cunningham
cunningham@kingplastic.com
VP: Robert King
Marketing Manager: Marjorie Williamson
Sales Manager: Larry Lathrum
Estimated Sales: $10-20 Million
Number Employees: 100-249
Square Footage: 200000
Type of Packaging: Bulk
Brands:
  Seal-Top
  Tamp-R-Saf

24856 King Products
1435 Bonhill Road
Unit 25
Mississauga, ON L5T 1V2
Canada

866-454-6757
Fax: 416-850-9828 sales@mzero.com
www.kingproducts.com
Manufacturer and exporter of outdoor plastic signs,
point of purchase displays and furniture
President: Philippe Moulin
CFO: Roger Whitzel
Number Employees: 90
Parent Co: Meridian Kiosks

24857 King Research Laboratory
PO Box 700
Maywood, IL 60153-0700

708-344-7877
Alarm systems including early warning sonic bug
that detects shoplifting, gun shots and break-ins
through any solid material
President/Inventor: John King
Estimated Sales: Less than $500,000
Number Employees: 4

24858 King Sales & EngineeringCompany
2965 Gatlin Road
Placerville, CA 95667-5116

888-546-4725
Fax: 530-644-8279 888-546-4725
Wine industry labelers, label gluers, parts and repair
Estimated Sales: $1-2.5 Million
Number Employees: 10-19

24859 King Sign Company
355 W Thornton St
Akron, OH 44307

330-762-7421
Fax: 330-762-7422
Plastic, wood, metal and cast aluminum signs
President: Wayne V King
Estimated Sales: $500,000-$1 Million
Number Employees: 1-4

24860 (HQ)King of All Manufacturing
PO Box 178
Clio, MI 48420-0178

810-564-0139
Fax: 810-232-6698
Drain/sewer and septic tank cleaners, dishwashing
machine detergents and restaurant cleaners
Estimated Sales: $1-2.5 Million
Number Employees: 5-9
Square Footage: 32000
Brands:
  King of All

24861 Kingery & Assoc
1347 IL Highway 1
Carmi, IL 62821-4929

618-382-3347
Fax: 618-382-3611 888-844-1665
www.grocerytraders.com
Grocery, meat, produce and HBC
President: Ron Kingery
VP: Woodie Pontey
President: Ron Kingery
Public Relations: Bob Estes
Operations: Steve Kemer
IT: Tammy Sisco
tsisco@yourclearwave.com
Estimated Sales: $10-20 Million
Number Employees: 5-9
Square Footage: 33300
Type of Packaging: Consumer, Food Service, Pri-
  vate Label, Bulk

24862 Kings River Casting
1350 North Ave
Sanger, CA 93657-3742

559-875-8250
Fax: 559-875-1491 888-545-5157
Sales@KingsRiverCasting.Com
Manufacturer and exporter of tables, chairs and
barstools
President/CEO: Pat Henry
henry@kingsrivercasting.com
Vice President: Dale Monteleone
Estimated Sales: Below $5 Million
Number Employees: 10-19
Square Footage: 54000
Parent Co: Kings River Casting
Type of Packaging: Food Service

24863 Kingspan Insulated Panels, Ltd.
Langley Office
5202-272nd Street
Langley, BC
Canada

604-607-1101
877-638-3266
Cold storage and blast freezer doors, as well as controlled environment and low temperature doors for
the food and beverage industry. Also a manufacturer
of paneling and roof panels for industrial buildings.

24864 Kingston McKnight
419 Avenue Del Ora
Redwood City, CA 94062
650-462-4900
Fax: 650-268-3733 800-900-0463
Manufacturer, importer and exporter of slip-resistant safety shoes serving the hospitality industry
Owner: Jeff Mc Knight
VP: Terry Kingston
Contact: Terry Kingston
tphilipk@yahoo.com
Estimated Sales: $1,000,000
Number Employees: 1-4
Square Footage: 10000
Other Locations:
  Kingston McKnight
  Las Vegas NV
Brands:
  Kingston McKnight

24865 Kinsa Group Inc
9779 S Franklin Dr # 200
Franklin, WI 53132-9566
414-421-2000
Fax: 414-421-6000 www.ihobnob.com
Full-service recruiting firm in the food and beverage industry
Vice President: Laurie Hyllberg
laurieh@kinsa.com
Vice President: Michelle Nolan
Estimated Sales: $1-2.5 000,000
Number Employees: 10-19

24866 Kinsley Inc
901 Crosskeys Dr
Doylestown, PA 18902-1025
215-348-7723
Fax: 215-348-7724 800-414-6664
info@kinsleyinc.com www.kinsleyinc.com
Manufacturer and exporter of bottle sorters and un-scramblers, capping and filling machinery, bottle conveyors and timing screws.
President: T Mc Carthy
info@kinsleyinc.com
R&D: James Malloy
Quality Control: James Malloy
Sales: Brandon Concannon
Engineering Manager: David Hansen
Plant Manager: Dan Froehlich
Estimated Sales: Below $5 Million
Number Employees: 5-9
Brands:
  Kinsley Timing Screw
  Roll-Tite

24867 Kinsley Inc
901 Crosskeys Dr
Doylestown, PA 18902-1025
215-348-7723
Fax: 215-348-7724 800-414-6664
www.kinsleyinc.com
Container feed machinery, line combiners, dividers, cap elevator feeders, screw cap tighteners, custom changing parts
President: T Mc Carthy
info@kinsleyinc.com
Senior Engineer: Dave Hanson
Plant Manager: Dan Froehlich
Estimated Sales: $2.5-5 Million
Number Employees: 5-9

24868 Kirkco Corp
2213 Stafford Street Ext
Monroe, NC 28110-9651
704-289-7090
Fax: 704-289-7091 sales@kirkcocorp.com
www.kirkcocorp.com
Food processing, packaging, code dating and case sealing machinery
President: T W Kirkpatrick
sales@kentkcorp.com
Estimated Sales: $1-2,500,000
Number Employees: 5-9

24869 Kisco Manufacturing
5155 Argyle Street
Port Alberni, BC V9Y 1V3
Canada
604-823-7456
Fax: 250-724-5155 www.kiscomanufacturing.com
Manufacturer and exporter of flour silos and scales, conveyor systems and water meters
Pres.: Svend Kuhr
Svce. Mgr.: Peter Kuhr

Number Employees: 5
Square Footage: 14000
Parent Co: Kisco Foods
Brands:
  Kimac
  Kisco
  Mix Master

24870 Kiss International/Di-tech Systems
965 Park Center Drive
Vista, CA 92081-8312
800-527-5477
Fax: 760-599-0207 800-527-5477
Manufacturer and exporter of reverse osmosis water purification systems; also, components and filter cartridges
VP/General Manager: Theresa Hawks
Sales/Customer Service: Becky Rivera
Sales/Customer Service: Kerri Rivera
Number Employees: 22
Square Footage: 80000
Parent Co: Aqua Care Corporation
Brands:
  Di-Tech

24871 Kisters Kayat
5501 N Washington Boulevard
Sarasota, FL 34243-2249
386-424-0101
Fax: 386-424-0266 parts@kkiusa.com
Manufacturer, importer and exporter of high speed tray and wraparound packers, shrink wrappers, tray stackers and turners and case sealers
VP Finance: Peter Welen
VP Engineering: Gary Hunt
Number Employees: 90
Square Footage: 144000
Parent Co: Kisters Maschinenbau GmbH

24872 Kitchen Equipment Fabricating
7007 Stearns St
Houston, TX 77021-4622
713-747-3611
Fax: 713-747-1892
Stainless steel sinks, tables and counters
President: Lloyd Hartsfield
lloyd@kitchenequipfab.com
Estimated Sales: $5-10 Million
Number Employees: 50-99

24873 KitchenRus
1006 S. Milpitas Blvd
Milpitas, CA 95035
408-262-1898
Fax: 408-262-1890 800-796-7797
service@kitchenrus.com www.kitchenrus.com
Cutlery; spreader, salad server set, pepper mill, kitchen utensils, flatware
Estimated Sales: $500,000-$1 Million
Number Employees: 9

24874 Kitchener Plastics
962 Guelph Street
Kitchener, ON N2H 5Z6
Canada
519-742-0752
Fax: 519-742-9247 800-429-5633
Manufacturer and exporter of plastic signs
President: Gabrielle Wolf
Estimated Sales: Below $5 Million
Number Employees: 4

24875 Kitcor Corp
9959 Glenoaks Blvd
Sun Valley, CA 91352-1085
818-767-4800
Fax: 818-767-4658 www.kitcor.com
Custom made stainless steel food processing equipment for hotels, schools, restaurants and hospitals
President: Kent Kitchen
kentkitchen@kitcor.com
Vice President: James Kitchen
Purchasing: Kathleen Anderson
Estimated Sales: $5 Million
Number Employees: 20-49
Type of Packaging: Food Service

24876 Kiva Designs
1350 Hayes St
Suite C-16
Benicia, CA 94510-2945
707-748-1614
Fax: 707-748-1621

24877 Kiwi Coders Corp
265 Messner Dr
Wheeling, IL 60090-6495
847-541-4511
Fax: 847-541-6332 info@kiwicoders.com
www.kiwicoders.com
Marking and coding equipment
Owner: Brent Mc Kay
john.glas@kiwicoders.com
Estimated Sales: $2.5-5 Million
Number Employees: 10-19

24878 Kleen Products Inc
8136 SW 8th St
Oklahoma City, OK 73128-4210
405-495-1168
Fax: 405-495-1175 800-392-1792
ken@joeshandcleaner.com
www.joeskleenproducts.com
Manufacturer and exporter of hand, glass and floor cleaners
CEO: Kenneth Newman
CFO: Kenneth Newman
Vice President: Michael Newman
R&D: Kenneth Newman
Quality Control: Joe Brantley
Estimated Sales: $1.5 Million
Number Employees: 5-9
Type of Packaging: Private Label

24879 Kleer Pak
320 S LA Londe Ave
Addison, IL 60101-3309
630-543-0208
Fax: 630-543-0811 888-550-2247
sales@kleerpak.com
Custom bags/pouches for the packaging industry.
President: Gordhan Patel
g.patel@kleerpak.com
Vice President: Kenneth Johnson
Estimated Sales: $3 Million
Number Employees: 10-19

24880 Klever Kuvers
2889 San Pasqual Street
Pasadena, CA 91107-5364
626-355-8441
Fax: 626-355-1331
Indoor and outdoor vinyl table cloths and vinyl aprons
Owner: Mary Ann Froede
CEO: Ruth Breslow
Estimated Sales: $100,000
Number of Brands: 1
Number of Products: 3-5
Type of Packaging: Consumer, Food Service, Private Label, Bulk
Brands:
  Klever Kuvers

24881 Kliklok-Woodman
5224 Snapfinger Woods Dr
Decatur, GA 30035-4023
770-981-5200
Fax: 770-987-7160 sales@kliklok-woodman.com
www.kliklokwoodman.com
Manufacturer and exporter of flexible packaging machinery for the snack food, confectionery, nut and baking industries including fillers, sealers, weighers, loaders, closers, etc
President: Peter Black
pblack@klikwood.com
CEO: William Crist
Sales Director: T Long
Public Relations: C Kuhr
Estimated Sales: $45 Million
Number Employees: 100-249
Number of Brands: 5
Number of Products: 50
Square Footage: 220000
Parent Co: Kliklok Corporation
Brands:
  Captain
  Certipack
  Clipper
  Concorde
  Cyclone
  Gemini
  Pacer
  Polaris
  Woodman

24882 Kline Process Systems Inc
625 Spring St # 200
Suite 200
Reading, PA 19610-1771

610-371-0300
Fax: 610-371-0300 www.kpsnet.com
Batch control systems, custom fabrication and process control systems for the food and dairy industry
Owner/President: Robert Kline
rob@kpsnet.com
Number Employees: 50-99

24883 Klinger Constructors LLC
8701 Washington St NE
Albuquerque, NM 87113-1680

505-822-9990
Fax: 505-821-0439 www.klingerllc.com
Offers extensive construction and design-build services in commercial, industrial and institutional markets
President: John Gleeson
CEO: Tom Novak
tomn@klingerllc.com
CEO: Tom Novak
Business Development Manager: Shirley Anderson
Estimated Sales: $30 Million
Number Employees: 20-49
Parent Co: Klinger Company

24884 Klippenstein Corp
5399 S Villa Ave
Fresno, CA 93725-8903

559-834-4258
Fax: 559-834-4263 888-834-4258
sales@klippenstein.com www.klippenstein.com
Case sealers, formers and material handling, packaging and conveyor systems
President: Ken Klippenstein
ken@klippenstein.com
President: Richard Klippenstein
General Manager: Ken Klippenstein
Estimated Sales: $1-3,000,000
Number Employees: 10-19
Square Footage: 10000

24885 Klockner Filter Products
8314 Tiogawoods Dr
Sacramento, CA 95828-5048

916-689-2328
Fax: 916-689-1035
Wine industry filtration systems, laboratory instruments and supplies
President: Paris Rivera
Estimated Sales: $1-5 Million
Number Employees: 20-49

24886 Klockner Packaging Machinery
6767 Forest Hill Avenue
Suite 305
Richmond, VA 23225

804-560-7767
Fax: 804-560-7752

24887 Klockner Pentaplast of America
P.O.Box 500
Gordonsville, VA 22942

540-832-3600
Fax: 540-832-5656 kpainfo@kpfilms.com
www.kpfilms.com
Manufacturer and exporter of rigid vinyl, polyester and barex films for form/fill/seal, hot fill, trays, cups, portion packs, rounds, clamshells and modified atmospheric packaging of food and full body shrink sleeves for beverages
Chairman: Bruno Deschamps
CFO: Markus Holzl
Vice President: Michael Tubridy
Research & Development: Dean Inman
Marketing Director: Michael Ryan
Sales Director: Bobby Nolan
Communications Manager: Nancy Ryan
Chief Operating Officer: Stefan Brandt
Number Employees: 500-999
Number of Brands: 17
Type of Packaging: Consumer, Food Service
Brands:
Pentafood

24888 Kloppenberg & Co
2627 W Oxford Ave
Englewood, CO 80110-4391

303-761-1615
Fax: 303-789-1741 800-346-3246
klopco@kloppenberg.com www.kloppenberg.com

Ice storage, handling, carting, dispensing and bagging equipment
President: Joseph R Kloppenberg
CEO: Joe Kloppenberg
joklo@kloppenberg.com
Estimated Sales: Below $5 Million
Number Employees: 50-99
Square Footage: 240000

24889 Kloss Manufacturing Co Inc
7566 Morris Ct
Suite 310
Allentown, PA 18106-9247

610-391-3820
Fax: 610-391-3830 800-445-7100
Processor and exporter of flavoring extracts for Italian ices and slushes; also, concession equipment and supplies, fountain syrups, popcorn, cotton candy, nachos and waffles
Owner: Stephen Lloss
skloss@klossfunfood.com
Estimated Sales: $3-5 Million
Number Employees: 10-19
Square Footage: 120000
Type of Packaging: Food Service, Private Label, Bulk
Brands:
Kloss

24890 Klr Machines Inc
350 Morris St # E
Suite E
Sebastopol, CA 95472-3871

707-823-2883
Fax: 707-823-6954 www.buchervaslin.com
Winery equipment, fruit and vegetable juice processing
Vice President: Scott Wallace
scott.wallace@klrmachines.com
VP: Mike Haswell
Estimated Sales: $5-10 Million
Number Employees: 5-9

24891 (HQ)Kluber Lubrication N America
32 Industrial Dr
Londonderry, NH 03053-2008

603-434-7704
Fax: 603-647-4106 800-447-2238
kevin.wylie@us.kluber.com
www.klubersolutions.com
Specialty lubricants designed for extreme conditions and environments in canning, baking, beverage, confectionery and pasta plants. Kluber offers a full range of products conforming to USDA H1 and H2 requirements. The stringent qualityassurance in components and production makes Kluber the food and beverage industry's partner for healthier and safer world
President: Daniel Alarcon
danielalarcon@klubersolutions.com
CEO: Wolfgang Christandl
North America Marketing Manager: James Sellect, Jr.
Estimated Sales: $20 Million
Number Employees: 50-99

24892 Kluber Lubrication N America
32 Industrial Dr
Londonderry, NH 03053-2008

603-434-7704
Fax: 603-647-4106 kevin.wylie@us.kluber.com
www.klubersolutions.com
President: Daniel Alarcon
danielalarcon@klubersolutions.com
CEO: Wolfgang Christandl
Estimated Sales: $20 Million
Number Employees: 50-99

24893 Knapp Container
17 Old Turnpike Rd
Beacon Falls, CT 6403

203-888-0511
Fax: 203-881-1817
Corrugated boxes and containers
Owner: George A Meder
Estimated Sales: $10-20 Million
Number Employees: 10-19

24894 Knapp Logistics Automation Inc
2124 Barrett Park Dr NW # 100
Suite 100
Kennesaw, GA 30144-3602

770-426-0067
Fax: 678-388-2893 sales.us@knapp.com
www.knapp.com
Owner: Ingomar Penz
Number Employees: 50-99

24895 Knapp Manufacturing
5227 E Pine Ave
Fresno, CA 93727

559-251-8254
Fax: 559-251-8224 sriley@knappmfg.com
Household and industrial cleaners, laundry detergents, disinfectants, germicides and floor polish
President: Mike Knapp
Technical Director: Doug Banta
Contact: Doug Banta
doug@knappmfg.com
G.M.: Sandra Christino
Estimated Sales: $2.5-5 Million
Number Employees: 5-9
Square Footage: 58000
Parent Co: BouMatic, LLC

24896 Knapp Shoes
2469 State Route 54a
Penn Yan, NY 14527

Fax: 315-536-6909
Slip-resistant and steel toe footwear
Pres./COO: Willie Taaffe
Number Employees: 25
Parent Co: Iron Age Corporation

24897 Knechtel Laboratories Inc
7341 Hamlin Ave
Skokie, IL 60076-3902

847-673-4477
Fax: 847-673-4487 info@knechtel.com
www.knechtel.com
Confectionery, pharmaceutical and foods development, troubleshooting and pilot plant operations support
President: Robert Boutin
rboutin@knechtel.com
CFO: Robert Boutin
Estimated Sales: $1-2.5 Million
Number Employees: 10-19
Square Footage: 108000
Type of Packaging: Consumer, Food Service, Private Label, Bulk

24898 Knight Equipment Canada
Unit 6
Mississauga, ON L5N 7X8
Canada

949-595-4800
Fax: 905-542-1536 800-854-3764
cs.knight@idexcorp.com www.knightequip.com
Chemical dispensing equipment and dishwashing machines
Number Employees: 7
Parent Co: Knight Equipment

24899 Knight Equipment International
20531 Crescent Bay Dr
Lake Forest, CA 92630-8825

949-595-4800
Fax: 949-595-4801 800-854-3764
www.knightequip.com
Manufacturer and exporter of low energy dish washing machines; also, pumps, controls and dispensers
President: George Noa
Pres.: Paul Beldham
Sales/Mktg: George Noa
Contact: Joah Bridwell
jbridwell@kofc9487.com
Estimated Sales: $20-50 Million
Number Employees: 1,000-4,999
Brands:
Ultra Wash

24900 Knight Ind
1140 Centre Rd
Auburn Hills, MI 48326-2602

248-377-4950
Fax: 248-377-2135 literature@knight-ind.com
www.knight-ind.com
Air powered positioning equipment and ergonomic lifting equipment

CEO: James Zaguroli Jr
Contact: Greg Akey
gakey@knight-ind.com
Estimated Sales: $20-50 Million
Number Employees: 1-4

24901 Knight Paper Box Company
4651 W 72nd St
Chicago, IL 60629-5882

773-585-2035
Fax: 773-585-3824

Paper folding boxes
Contact: Ginnie Glowicki
gglowicki@knightpack.com
Estimated Sales: $10-20 Million
Number Employees: 50-99
Square Footage: 170000

24902 Knight's Electric Inc
11410 Old Redwood Hwy
Windsor, CA 95492-9523

707-433-6931
Fax: 707-431-2342 info@knightselectric.com
www.knightselectric.com
Wine industry service and repair
President: Barbara Ragsdale
barbara@knightselectric.com
CFO: Barbara Ragstale
Administrator: Barbara Ragsdale
Estimated Sales: $5-10 Million
Number Employees: 20-49

24903 Knobs Unlimited
13350 Bishop Rd
Bowling Green, OH 43402

419-353-8215
Fax: 419-353-8325
Manufacturer and exporter of plastic replacement
knobs for appliances
Owner/Plt. Mgr.: John Cardenas
R & D: William Anderson
R & D: John Cardinas
Estimated Sales: Below $5 Million
Number Employees: 5-9
Square Footage: 17000

24904 Knott Slicers
290 Pine Street
Canton, MA 02021-3353

781-821-0925
Fax: 781-821-0768
Manufacturer and exporter of slicing machinery for
potato chips, yams, plantains, yuccas, bananas, taro
roots, beets, potatoes, tomatoes and bagel sticks
President: Alan Burgess
VP: Steve Burgess
Quality Control: Doug Merrill
Marketing/Sales: Alan Burgess
Operations: Jim Stratis
Estimated Sales: $10-15 Million
Number Employees: 50-99
Number of Products: 5
Square Footage: 120000
Parent Co: Burgess Brothers
Type of Packaging: Food Service

24905 Koch Container
797 Old Dutch Rd
Victor, NY 14564-8972

585-924-1600
Fax: 585-924-7040 koch1@frontiernet.net
www.kochcontainer.com
Corrugated boxes and displays; wholesaler/distributor of corner boards, edge protectors, plastic bags
and fiber tubes
President: Tom Baumgartner
tomb@kochcontainer.com
Mgr. Cust. Svce.: Cheryl Wessells
Estimated Sales: $20-50 Million
Number Employees: 50-99
Parent Co: Buckeye Corrugated

24906 (HQ)Koch Equipment LLC
1414 W 29th St
Kansas City, MO 64108-3604

816-931-4557
Fax: 816-753-4976 info@kochequipment.com
www.ultrasourceusa.com
Manufacturer and distributor of processing, packaging and labeling equipment to the meat, poultry, seafood and general food manufacturing markets
CEO: John Starr
Estimated Sales: $38 Million
Number Employees: 100-249

Number of Brands: 10
Number of Products: 30
Square Footage: 180000
Type of Packaging: Consumer, Food Service, Private Label, Bulk
Brands:
　Cook Master
　Crossweb
　Grand Prize
　Injectamatic
　Intact
　Kats
　Koch
　Market Master
　Portion Master
　Ultravac

24907 Koch Equipment LLC
1414 W 29th St
Kansas City, MO 64108-3604

816-931-4557
Fax: 816-753-4976 800-456-5624
info@kochequipment.com
www.ultrasourceusa.com
Owner: Kyle Huff
kyle.huff@kochsupplies.com
CEO and Chairman of the Board: John D. Starr
Estimated Sales: $50-100 Million
Number Employees: 100-249

24908 Koch Membrane Systems Inc
850 Main St
Wilmington, MA 01887-3388

978-694-7000
Fax: 978-657-5208 888-677-5624
info@kochmembrane.com
www.kochmembrane.com
Developer and manufacturer of innovative membrane filtration systems.
President: Bill Barber
barberb@kochind.com
Number Employees: 250-499

24909 Kochman Consultants LTD
5545 Lincoln Ave
Morton Grove, IL 60053-3430

847-470-1195
Fax: 847-470-1189 info@kclcad.com
www.kclcad.com
Designer and exporter computer software for the
food service industry
President: Ronald Kochman
ron@kclcad.com
R & D: Kevin Kochman
Vice President: Kevin Kochman
Estimated Sales: Below $5 Million
Number Employees: 5-9
Square Footage: 8000
Type of Packaging: Food Service
Brands:
　Kcl Cad Foodservice
　The Kcl Cadalog

24910 Kodex Inc
160 Park Ave # 7
Nutley, NJ 07110-2808

973-235-0606
Fax: 973-235-0132 800-325-6339
sales@kodexray.com www.kodexray.com
Manufacturer, importer and exporter of x-ray inspection systems for detection of contaminants in packaged and fresh food products
President: Gary Korkala
kodex@kodexray.com
General Manager: Don Airey
VP: Gary Korkala
Quality Control: Garrett Sollitto
Sales: Richard Zieminski
Estimated Sales: $3-4 Million
Number Employees: 5-9
Square Footage: 17600
Brands:
　Imagex
　Rapiscan
　Scanvision

24911 Koehler Instrument Co Inc
1595 Sycamore Ave
Bohemia, NY 11716-1732

631-589-3800
Fax: 631-589-3815 800-878-9070
sales@koehlerinstrument.com
www.koehlerinstrument.com

Manufacturer and exporter of lubricant, grease and
viscosity testing equipment
President: Roy Westerhaus
rwesterhaus@koehlerinstrument.com
CFO: Peter Brey
R&D: Dr Raj Shah
Marketing: Dr Wayne Goldenberg
Sales: Atul Gautama
Production: Joseph Russo
Estimated Sales: $10-20,000,000
Number Employees: 50-99
Number of Brands: 2
Number of Products: 200
Square Footage: 35000
Brands:
　Okzdata
　Ruler

24912 Koehler-Gibson Marking
875 Englewood Ave
Buffalo, NY 14223-2334

716-838-5960
Fax: 716-838-6859 800-875-1562
sales@kgco.com www.kgco.com
Manufacturer and exporter of marking devices, steel
stamps, embossing dies, stencils, etc.; also, printing
plates and cutting dies for plastic and corrugated
packaging
Owner: David Koehler
ddk@kgco.com
Estimated Sales: $2.5-5 Million
Number Employees: 20-49
Square Footage: 28000

24913 Kofab
300 Kofab Dr
Algona, IA 50511-7317

515-295-7265
Fax: 515-295-7268 sales@kofab.com
www.kofab.com
Custom food processing equipment and stainless
steel conveyor belt pulleys
Owner: Brian Schiltz
Vice President: Bill Schiltz
Manager: Bill Schiltz
wjschiltz@kofab.com
Plant Manager: Gray Schiltz
Estimated Sales: $1-3 Million
Number Employees: 20-49
Square Footage: 84000

24914 Kohlenberger Associates Consulting Engineering
611 S Euclid St
Fullerton, CA 92838

714-738-7733
Fax: 714-738-3905 kohlenberger@kaceenergy.com
www.kaceenergy.com
Design and engineering consultant specializing in
food processing plants and systems, refrigeration
and freezing systems and cold storage warehouses
President: M Kohlenberger
CFO: Karl Kohlenberger
Vice President: Ted Kohlenberger
Contact: Karl Kohlenberger
karl@kaceenergy.com
Estimated Sales: $500,000-$1 Million
Number Employees: 1-4
Square Footage: 8800

24915 Kohler Awning Inc
2600 Walden Ave
Buffalo, NY 14225-4736

716-685-3333
Fax: 716-685-0126 800-875-9091
sales@kohlerawning.com www.kohlerawning.com
Commercial awnings
President: John Martin Kohler Sr
HR Executive: Pat Kuz
pat@kohlerawning.com
Estimated Sales: $10-20,000,000
Number Employees: 50-99

24916 Kohler Industries Inc
4925 N 56th St # C
Lincoln, NE 68504-1771

402-465-8845
Fax: 402-465-8841 800-365-6708
info@kohlerequip.com www.kohlerequip.com
Food processing and packaging equipment
President/Owner: Jim Kohler
jim@kohlerequip.com
Marketing: Luke Bundy
Sales: Kirt Borer

Estimated Sales: $3-5 Million
Number Employees: 10-19
Square Footage: 54000
Parent Co: Kohler Industries

24917 Kohler Industries Inc
4925 N 56th St # C
PO Box 29496
Lincoln, NE 68504-1771
402-465-8845
Fax: 402-465-8841 800-365-6708
info@kohlerequip.com www.kohlerequip.com
Manufacturer and distributor of freezers, conveyors,
bagging equipment and mixers.
President/Owner: Jim Kohler
jim@kohlerequip.com
IT: Scott Jaquez
Sales: Norm Pavlish
Office Mgr./ Inventory Control: Dave Bonczynski
Number Employees: 10-19

24918 Koke Inc
582 Queensbury Ave
Queensbury, NY 12804-7612
518-793-6767
Fax: 518-793-9747 800-535-5303
info@kokeinc.com www.kokeinc.com
Material handling equipment including pallet jacks,
dock boards and levelers and fork lifts
Pres.: John Koke
CEO: John Koke
Estimated Sales: Below $5,000,000
Number Employees: 20-49
Square Footage: 60000

24919 Kold Pack
5014 Page Ave
Jackson, MI 49201
517-764-1550
Fax: 517-764-1195 800-824-2661
sales@koldpack.com
Coolers and freezers
President: Glen Stuard
Marketing Manager: Ed Sayles
Contact: Kim Laserra
klaserra@koldpack.com
Purchasing Manager: Kim LaSerra
Estimated Sales: $5-10 Million
Number Employees: 10-19
Brands:
Copeland
Heatcraft
Russell
Tecumseh

24920 Kold-Draft
1525 E Lake Rd
Erie, PA 16511-1088
814-453-6761
Fax: 814-455-6336 tomm@kold-draft.com
www.kolddraft.com
CEO: John Brigham
Contact: Shawn Heifner
sheifner@eriemg.com
Estimated Sales: $5-10 Million
Number Employees: 20-49
Parent Co: Uniflow Manufacturing

24921 Kold-Hold
P.O.Box 570
Edgefield, SC 29824-0570
803-637-3166
Fax: 803-637-3046
Manufacturer and exporter of cold plates for refrig-
eration trucks; used in short delivery
President: Paul Cooper
G.M.: Dave Stasktlunas
Number Employees: 100-249
Square Footage: 440000
Parent Co: Tranter
Brands:
Kold-Hold

24922 Kole Industries
PO Box 20152
Miami, FL 33102
305-633-2556
Fax: 305-638-5821
Manufacturer and exporter of corrugated parts, bins
and mailing and shipping room supplies
President: Arthur Kaplan
Contact: Donald Spraque
donald.spraque@koleindustries.com

Estimated Sales: $5-10 Million
Number Employees: 15
Parent Co: National Lithographers

24923 Kolinahr Systems
6840 Ashfield Dr
Blue Ash, OH 45242
513-745-9401
Fax: 513-794-3240 sales@geneng.com
www.geneng.cc
Pallet labeling and pallet load stacking equipment
President: Gary Jenkins
Marketing Director: Bill Walker
Contact: Doug Barnhold
dougbarnhold@kolinahrsystems.com
Estimated Sales: $2 Million
Number Employees: 10-19
Number of Products: 9

24924 Kolpak
2915 Tennessee Ave N
Parsons, TN 38363
731-847-6361
Fax: 731-847-5387 800-826-7036
www.kolpak.com
Manufacturer and exporter of walk-in coolers and
freezers
General Manager: Gerry Senion
VP: Jack Antell
Contact: Jack Antell
j.antell@kolpak.com
Estimated Sales: $50-100 Million
Number Employees: 100-249
Type of Packaging: Food Service

24925 Kolpak Walk-ins
P.O.Box 550
Parsons, TN 38363-0550
731-847-6361
Fax: 731-847-5387 800-826-7036
www.kolpak.com
Manufacturer and exporter of walk-in coolers, freez-
ers and refrigeration systems
Quality Control: Barry Autry
CFO: Tonny Jordan
VP: Jack Antell
Research & Development: Richard Fahey
Marketing Director: Stephanie Ferrell
Plant Manager: Steve Clayton
Estimated Sales: $50-75 Million
Number Employees: 20-49
Parent Co: Manitowoc Foodservice Group
Brands:
Expresso
Kolpake
Polar-Chill
Polar-Pak

24926 Kom International
Place Du Parc, Box 1113
Montreal, QC H2V 4P2
Canada
514-849-4000
Fax: 514-849-8888 www.komintl.com
Managment consulting services in supply chain,
warehouse, distribution
President and CEO: Allan Kohl
COO: Keith Swiednicki

24927 Komatsu Forklift USA
1701 Golf Rd # 100
PO Box 5049
Rolling Meadows, IL 60008-4227
847-437-5800
Fax: 770-784-0700
forkliftmarketing@komatsuna.com
www.komatsuforkliftusa.com
Fork lift trucks
President: Motohisa Kai
CFO: David Adea
Contact: Bill Fruland
bfruland@ktmusa.com
Estimated Sales: $5-10 Million
Number Employees: 20-49
Square Footage: 250000

24928 Komax Systems Inc
15301 Graham St
Huntington Beach, CA 92649-1110
310-830-4320
Fax: 310-830-4320 800-826-0760
www.komax.com
President: Robert Smith
info@komax.com

Estimated Sales: $3,000,000-$5,000,000
Number Employees: 10-19

24929 Kombucha Brooklyn
906 State Route 28
Kingston, NY 12401-7264
917-261-3010
Fax: 888-397-6817
Manufacturer of equipment used to brew kombucha.
Founder and CEO: Eric Childs
info@kombuchabrooklyn.com
Co-Founder: Jessica Childs
Number Employees: 1-4

24930 Komline-Sanderson Engineering
12 Holland Ave
Peapack, NJ 7977
908-234-1000
Fax: 908-234-9487 800-225-5457
info@komline.com www.komline.com
Paddle Dryer/Processor for drying, crystallizing, cal-
cining, tooling, heating, reacting, sterilization. Liquid solid separation filters, filtration with cake
washing and clarification, vacuum filtration products. Pumps, wastewatertreatment sludge by-product
dewatering and drying.
CEO: Russell Komline
rkomline@komline.com
Vice President: Christopher Komline
Purchasing Manager: W Tiger
Estimated Sales: $35-40 Million
Number Employees: 100-249
Square Footage: 85000

24931 Konica Minolta Corp
101 Williams Dr
Ramsey, NJ 07446-1293
201-825-4000
Fax: 201-825-7567 888-473-3637
www.konicaminolta.com
Manufacturer and exporter of color measuring instrumentation including spectrophotometers,
colorimeters, light meters, etc.; also, computer software for color formulation and quality control
CEO: Scott Cohen
scohen@mi.konicaminolta.us
CEO: Jun Haraguchi
Marketing Director: Maria Repici
Number Employees: 500-999

24932 Konica Minolta SensingAmericas
101 Williams Drive
Ramsey, NY 07446
201-785-2413
Fax: 201-785-2482 888-473-2656
Sensory machines
President: Hal Yamazaki
Vice President: Grant Hume
Number Employees: 35

24933 Kontane
1000 Charleston Regional Pkwy
Charleston, SC 29492
843-352-0011
Fax: 828-397-3683 info@kontanelogistics.com
www.kontane.com
Manufacturer and exporter of containers: heavy duty
wooden, household storage and custom built; also,
pallet and export boxes and cleated plywood
President: Ed Byrd
VP: Jason Essenberg
COO: Rusty Byrd
Estimated Sales: $2.5-5 Million
Number Employees: 100-249

24934 Konz Wood Products Co
616 N Perkins St
Appleton, WI 54914-3133
920-734-7770
Fax: 920-734-4811 877-610-5145
info@konzwoodproducts.com
www.konzwoodproducts.com
Pallets, skids and wooden shipping crates
Owner: Lawrence Konz Jr
HR Executive: Bob Beckstrom
info@konzwoodproducts.com
Quality Control: Lawrence A Konz
Estimated Sales: $2.5-5 Million
Number Employees: 50-99
Parent Co: Appleton Lumber Company

24935 Koolant Koolers
2625 Emerald Dr
Kalamazoo, MI 49001

269-349-6800
Fax: 269-349-8951 800-968-5665
www.dimplexthermal.com
Custom and standard liquid coolers and water chillers for the removal of heat from industrial and continuous processes
CEO: Mark Rostagno
VP: Spencer Malcolm
Sales Manager: Kristen Ulsh
Vice President Of Operations: Spencer Malcom
Estimated Sales: $20-50 Million
Number Employees: 50-99
Square Footage: 60000
Brands:
   Koolant Koolers

24936 Kopykake
3699 W 240th St
Torrance, CA 90505-6002

310-373-8906
Fax: 310-375-5275 800-999-5253
sales@kopykake.com www.kopykake.com
Manufacturer and exporter of computerized cake photo printing, edible frosting sheets and edible ink. kartriges, cake decorating equipment and supplies, including drawing projectors, airbrushes and compressors, food colors, disposabledecorating bags, etc
President: Gerry Mayer
gerry@kopykake.com
Vice President: Greg Mayer
Sales Director: Rudy Arce
Estimated Sales: $1-2.5 Million
Number Employees: 20-49
Square Footage: 80000
Type of Packaging: Food Service
Brands:
   Airmaster
   Kobra
   Kopykake
   Kopyrite
   Kroma Jet
   Kroma Kolor

24937 Korab Engineering Company
7727 Beland Avenue
Los Angeles, CA 90045-1128

310-670-7710
Fax: 310-670-7710
Manufacturer, exporter and importer of packaging machinery including liquid fillers, monoblock machinery, automation systems, vertical form fillers, seal machinery, horizontal thermoforming equipment, tray makers, pick and placeequipment, etc
Pres./G.M.: Jacek Zdzienicki
Shop Mgr.: Eric Zuber
Cust. Rel.: Janine Luciano
Number Employees: 5-9
Square Footage: 16000

24938 Korber Medipak Inc
14501 58th St N
Clearwater, FL 33760-2808

727-538-4644
Fax: 727-532-6521 www.kmedipak.com
Specialty molds, dies and packaging machinery
President: Michael DE Collibus
decollibus@kmedipak.com
Estimated Sales: $10-25 Million
Number Employees: 20-49

24939 Kord Products Inc.
325B West Street #200
PO Box 265
Brantford, ON N3T 5M8
Canada

Fax: 519-753-2667 800-452-9070
www.kord.ca
Manufacturer and exporter of plastic injection molded products including blisters, clamshells and fiber protective packaging, custom molded products
President: Don Gayford
CEO: Gerry Docksteader
Research & Development: David Penkmann
Marketing Director: Jon Hensen
Plant Manager: Brock Howes
Purchasing Manager: Rachel St. Laurent
Number Employees: 200

24940 Kornylak Corp
400 Heaton St
Hamilton, OH 45011-1894

513-863-1277
Fax: 513-863-7644 800-837-5676
kornylak@kornylak.com www.kornylak.com
Manufacturer and exporter of material handling equipment including conveyors, multi-directional and plastic skate wheels and gravity controlled live storage systems
President: Thomas Kornylak
Staff, Engineering Department: Richard Kornylak
Marketing/Sales Manager: Anne McAdams
IT: Walter Stortz
walter@kornylak.com
Purchasing Director: Ginger Vizedom
Estimated Sales: $5 Million
Number Employees: 20-49
Square Footage: 400000
Brands:
   Ags 100
   Armorbelt
   Mini-Wheel
   Palletflo
   Superwheel
   Transwheel
   Ts Conveyor
   Zipflo

24941 Kosempel Manufacturing Company
3760 M Street
Philadelphia, PA 19124-5538

215-533-7110
Fax: 215-744-5220 800-733-7122
Custom metal products including bowls, funnels, hoppers and coating pans
Sls.: Rob Borst
Estimated Sales: $5-10 Million
Number Employees: 50-99
Square Footage: 120000

24942 (HQ)Koser Iron Works
PO Box 133
Barron, WI 54812

715-537-5654
bill@poweram.com
Storage racks; also, custom stainless steel fabrication available
President: Willian E Koser
Production Manager: David Fall
Purchasing Manager: David Fall
Estimated Sales: Below $5 Million
Number Employees: 20-49
Square Footage: 60800

24943 Kotoff & Company
324 N San Dimas Ave
San Dimas, CA 91773-2601

626-443-7115
Fax: 626-443-7110
Standard and custom plated wire shelving
President: James Kotoff
VP: Mary Ann Kotoff
Manager: Dean Miller
Estimated Sales: $1-2.5 Million
Number Employees: 5-9
Square Footage: 25000

24944 Koza's Inc
2910 S Main St
Pearland, TX 77581-4710

281-485-1462
Fax: 281-485-8000 800-594-5555
sales@kozas.com www.kozas.com
Manufacturer and exporter of advertising novelties including caps and hats; also, custom cresting available
Owner: Joseph Koza
jek@kozas.com
Estimated Sales: $6 Million
Number Employees: 50-99
Square Footage: 40000

24945 Kraissl Co Inc
299 Williams Ave
Hackensack, NJ 07601-5289

201-342-0008
Fax: 201-342-0025 800-572-4775
kraissl@aol.com www.strainers.com
Strainers, filters, valves for pipelink service

President/CEO: Richard Michel
richard@moviesunlimited.com
Foreman: Winston Philips
Chairman of the Board: Richard Michel
Tech Sales: Bill Henderson
Office Supervisor: Barbara Punthsecca
Estimated Sales: Below $5,000,000
Number Employees: 50-99
Square Footage: 14000
Type of Packaging: Bulk
Brands:
   Kraissl
   Sea-View

24946 Kramer
125 Clairemont Ave
Suite 330
Decatur, GA 30030-2551

404-371-1835
Fax: 404-892-8881
Owner: Myron N Kramer
Estimated Sales: $.5-1 million
Number Employees: 5-9

24947 Kraus & Sons
215 W 35th St
Suite 300
New York, NY 10001

212-620-0408
Fax: 212-924-4081
Manufacturer and exporter of badges, buttons, flags, banners and awnings
Owner: Paul Schneider
Estimated Sales: Below 1 Million
Number Employees: 5-9
Type of Packaging: Food Service

24948 Kreative Koncepts
154 W Washington Street
Marquette, MI 49855-4320

906-228-9354
Fax: 906-228-8918 800-638-2019
Microwave accessories
President: Robert Green
Brands:
   Rib Chef
   Souper 1 Step

24949 Kreissle Forge Ornamental
7947 N Tamiami Trl
Sarasota, FL 34243-1999

941-355-6795
Fax: 941-351-3213
Ornamental iron fixtures
President: Martin Haas
VP: Joey Kreissle
Estimated Sales: Less Than $500,000
Number Employees: 1-4

24950 Krepe-Kraft
1801 Elmwood Ave
Buffalo, NY 14207-2463

716-826-5813
Fax: 716-447-9201 800-637-2536
sales@modpac.com
Specialty paperboard folding cartons, grease-proof cookie boxes, large takeout tote, upscale valentines' day designs and gift basket box
President/CEO: Daniel C. Keane
sales@krepekraft.com
CFO: David B. Lupp
VP & Finance: Daniel Geary
Marketing Manager: Chuck Littlecom
Sales Exec: Katie Niedermeier
Estimated Sales: $10-25 Million
Number Employees: 100-249
Number of Products: 500
Square Footage: 300000
Type of Packaging: Consumer, Food Service, Private Label
Brands:
   Fashionglo

24951 Krewson Enterprises
855 Canterbury Rd
Cleveland, OH 44145-1420

440-871-8780
Fax: 440-871-5127 800-521-2282
airtools@superiorpneumatic.com
www.superiorpneumatic.com
Manufacturer and exporter of adjustable freezer and cooler alarms

President: Bradley Krewson
Contact: Walter Krewson
pshko1@aol.com
Estimated Sales: $5-10 Million
Number Employees: 5-9
Square Footage: 20000
Parent Co: Superior Pneumatic & Manufacturing
Brands:
   Protecto-Freeze
   Protecto-Temp

24952 Krimstock Enterprises
1426 Union Ave
Pennsauken, NJ 08110
        856-665-3676
   Fax: 856-662-8083 krim@bellatlantic.net
Advertising specialties, signs, displays and exhibits;
cutting and engraving services available
Owner: Joseph Crew
Estimated Sales: $1-5,000,000
Number Employees: 5-9
Square Footage: 7000

24953 Krispy Kist Company
120 S Halsted Street
Department R8
Chicago, IL 60661-3508
        312-733-0900
   Fax: 312-733-3508
Manufacturer and exporter of snack food processing
machinery including extruders, fryers, kettles, coat-
ing tumblers, mixers, ovens and peanut roasters
Sales/Operations: J Geiersbach
Office Mgr.: Kevin Coster
Estimated Sales: $1-5 Million
Number Employees: 8
Square Footage: 20000
Type of Packaging: Food Service
Brands:
   Krispy
   Krispy Kist

24954 Krogh Pump Co
251 W Channel Rd
Benicia, CA 94510-1129
        707-747-7585
   Fax: 707-747-7599 800-225-7644
Manufacturer and exporter of horizontal and vertical
centrifugal pumps for abrasive, corrosive, food and
sewage services
Owner: Charles O' Brian
Estimated Sales: $2.5-5 Million
Number Employees: 20-49
Square Footage: 30000
Type of Packaging: Food Service, Private Label

24955 Krones
PO Box 321801
9600 S. 58th St.
Franklin, WI 53132-6241
        414-409-4000
   Fax: 414-409-4100 800-752-3787
   www.kronesusa.com
Food processing and packaging machinery including
blenders, fillers, labelers, bottle washers and rinsers,
palletizers, depalletizers, pasteurizers, etc.
CEO: Christoph Klenk
CFO: Norbert Broger
Chief Sales Officer: Thomas Ricker
Year Founded: 1951
Estimated Sales: $4.1 Billion
Number Employees: 15,299
Square Footage: 232000
Parent Co: Krones AG

24956 Krowne Metal Corp
100 Haul Rd
Wayne, NJ 07470-6616
        973-305-3300
   Fax: 973-872-1129 800-631-0442
customerservice@krowne.com www.krowne.com
Manufacturer and exporter of bar equipment, hand
sinks and faucets
Vice President: James Angood
james.angood@krowne.com
Exec. V.P.: Roger Forman
Vice President: James Angood
james.angood@krowne.com
Estimated Sales: $5-10,000,000
Number Employees: 10-19
Square Footage: 160000

24957 Krueger Food Laboratories
21 Alpha Rd # D
Suite D
Chelmsford, MA 01824-4172
        978-256-1220
   Fax: 978-256-1222 dkrueger@kfl.com
   www.kfl.com
Analytical testing service for pesticide residues and
nutritional labeling; also, microbiology, consultation
and sampling
President: Dana Krueger
Lab Mgr.: Jeanne Maciel
Office Mgr.: Sherida George
Contact: Joe Golemme
jgolemme@kfl.com
Estimated Sales: $5-10 Million
Number Employees: 20-49
Square Footage: 16000

24958 Krueger International Holding
1330 Bellevue St.
Green Bay, WI 54302
        800-424-2432
        info@ki.com
Tables, stools and chairs.
Chairman/CEO: Richard Resch
President: Brian Krenke
Year Founded: 1941
Estimated Sales: $650 Million
Number Employees: 3,000+
Square Footage: 250000

24959 Krusoe Sign Co
5365 Canal Rd
Cleveland, OH 44125-4808
        216-447-1177
   Fax: 216-447-1516
Signs including advertising and plastic
President: Dale Krusoe
krusoesigns@aol.com
Estimated Sales: Less Than $500,000
Number Employees: 1-4

24960 Krystal Holographics
555 W 57th St
New York, NY 10019-2925
        212-261-0400
   Fax: 212-262-0414 800-998-5775
Suppliers of semi-conductors, electro mechanical
components
Owner: Azi Lezi
CEO: Dan Toben
Estimated Sales: $5-10 Million
Number Employees: 50-99

24961 Krystatite Films
PO Box 89
Mar Lin, PA 17951-0089
        570-621-6097
   Fax: 570-622-1037
Flat, centerfolded and tube PVC shrink film for
overwrapping and bundling
Estimated Sales: $1-5 Million

24962 Kuecker Equipment Company
801 W Markey Rd
Belton, MO 64012
        816-331-7070
   Fax: 816-331-7888 info@kuecker.com
   www.kuecker.com
President: Stanley Kuecker
CEO: Mike Langdom
CFO: Alice Kuecker
VP Sales: Jim Kuecker
System Sales: Dan Bingaman
Contact: Bev Rhoades
bev.rhoades@kuecker.com
Estimated Sales: Below $5 Million
Number Employees: 10-19

24963 Kuehne Chemical
86 N Hackensack Ave
Kearny, NJ 07032-4673
        973-589-0700
   Fax: 973-589-4866 info@kuehnecompany.com
   www.kuehnecompany.com
Industrial strength bleach including sodium
hypochlorite; wholesaler/distributor of caustic soda,
caustic potash, chlorine and sulfur
Manager: Emmanuel Cunha
ecunha@kuehnecompany.com
Estimated Sales: $61 Million
Number Employees: 50-99
Square Footage: 10000

24964 Kuepper Favor Company, Celebrate Line
P.O.Box 428
Peru, IN 46970-0428
        765-473-5586
   Fax: 765-472-7247 800-321-5823
   www.partydirect.com
Manufacturer and importer of paper party favors, fa-
vor goodie bags, custom imprinted lite-up favors
and novelties.
President: Mike Kuepper
VP: Douglas Kuepper
Head Of Marketing Department: Jane Grund
Contact: Michael Keeper
mike@partydirect.com
Number Employees: 50-99
Type of Packaging: Consumer, Private Label, Bulk
Brands:
   Celebrate Line
   K Line
   Party Direct

24965 Kuest Enterprise
PO Box 110
Filer, ID 83328-0110
        208-326-4084
   Fax: 208-326-6604
   goldengraingrinder@hotmail.com
Manufacturer and exporter of grain grinders
Founder: Johnnie Kuest
Estimated Sales: $500,000-$1 Million
Number Employees: 1-4

24966 Kuhl Corporation
39 Kuhl Rd
PO Box 26
Flemington, NJ 8822
        908-782-5696
   Fax: 908-782-2751 khk@kuhlcorp.com
   www.kuhlcorp.com
Industrial washing machines for the food industry
President: Henry Kuhl
CEO: Kevin Kuhl
CFO: Rick Kuhl
Marketing/Public Relations: Michael Vella
Contact: Paul Chou
pchou@kuhlcorp.com
Operations Manager: John Pichell
Plant Manager: Al Fisher
Estimated Sales: $12 Million
Number Employees: 70
Square Footage: 40000

24967 Kuriyama Of America Inc
360 E State Pkwy
Schaumburg, IL 60173-5335
        847-755-0360
   Fax: 847-885-0996 800-800-0320
   www.kuriyama.com
Thermoplastic, rubber and metal hose products and
accessories including couplings and fittings for use
in industrial and commerical applications
Marketing: Gary Kammes
Contact: Lauren Allen
lauren.j.allen@moody.edu
Estimated Sales: $70+ Million
Number Employees: 20-49
Type of Packaging: Private Label, Bulk
Other Locations:
   Houston TX
   Santa Fe Springs CA
   Kennesaw GA
   New Egypt NJ
   Mexico

24968 Kurtz Food Brokers
1028 Peach Street
San Luis Obispo, CA 93401
        805-543-3727
   Fax: 866-633-2140 800-696-7423
kevin@kurtzinc.net www.kurtzfoodbrokers.com
Broker of confectionery products, industrial ingredi-
ents, rice, rice crackers, raisins, nuts, etc.
President: Ed Kurtz
Diretor Sales/Marketing: Kevin Magon
Sales Coordinator: Vicki Crawford
Contact: Nicole Ansbro
nicole@kurtzinc.net
Estimated Sales: A
Number Employees: 3
Square Footage: 1500

24969 Kurtz Oil Company
3305 Healy Dr
Winston Salem, NC 27103-1406
336-768-1515
Fax: 336-722-4634
Industrial lubricants
President: Anne Kiger
Estimated Sales: $1-2.5 Million
Number Employees: 1-4
Brands:
Pilot

24970 Kurz Transfer Products LP
3200 Woodpark Blvd
Charlotte, NC 28206-4211
704-927-3700
Fax: 704-927-3701 800-333-2306
sales@kurzusa.com www.kurzusa.com
Metalized and coated films, hot stamping foils and
plastic printing machinery
Cmo: John Keane
john.keane@kurzusa.com
Estimated Sales: $28 Million
Number Employees: 1000-4999
Square Footage: 60000

24971 Kusel Equipment Company
PO Box 87
Watertown, WI 53094-0087
920-261-4112
Fax: 920-261-3151 sales@kuselequipment.com
www.kuselequipment.com
Manufactures stainless steel drainage systems and
cheese equipment.
President: Dave Smith
Contact: Clark Derleth
cderleth@kuselequipment.com
Estimated Sales: $10 Million
Number Employees: 1-4

24972 Kwikprint ManufacturingInc
4868 Victor St
Jacksonville, FL 32207-1702
904-737-3755
Fax: 904-730-0349 800-940-5945
www.kwik-print.com
Manufacturer and exporter of foil, gold and hot
stamping equipment; also, custom stamping dies and
foils; wholesaler/distributor of advertising special-
ties and promotional items
Owner: Mike Bulger
mbulger@kwik-print.com
V.P.: Lynn Cann
Estimated Sales: Below $5 Million
Number Employees: 5-9
Square Footage: 48000
Type of Packaging: Food Service, Private Label,
Bulk
Brands:
Kwikprint

24973 Kysor Panel Systems
4201 N Beach St
Fort Worth, TX 76137
817-230-8703
Fax: 817-281-5521 800-633-3426
jburke@kysorpanel.com
Manufacturer and exporter of refrigerated walk-in
coolers
President: David Frase
Quotations: Gary Holloway
Contact: Shannon Barnes
sbarnes@fidelitylifeandhealth.com
Estimated Sales: $20-50 Million
Number Employees: 100-249
Square Footage: 300000
Parent Co: Scotsman Industries
Other Locations:
Kysor Panel Systems
Goodyear AZ

24974 Kysor/Kalt
7320 NE 55th Ave
Portland, OR 97214-2138
503-235-0776
Fax: 503-249-8452
Walk-in coolers and freezers
Owner: Kevin Kayser
Estimated Sales: $1-3 Million
Number Employees: 1-4
Parent Co: Kysor Industrial Corporation

24975 Kyung Il Industrial Company
10771 El Caballo Avenue
San Diego, CA 92127-3311
858-673-1211
Fax: 858-673-5311
Rotogravure printing, laminated rolls on pouches,
flat standup zipper
President: Lee Sung Ho
CEO: Kyo Sun Kim
Quality Control: Sunyu Kim
Partner: Kyosun Kim
Estimated Sales: Below $5 Million
Number Employees: 4

24976 L & C Plastic Bags
500 Dick Minnich Dr
Covington, OH 45318-1263
937-473-2968
Fax: 937-473-5334 sales@LCPlastics.com
www.lcplastics.com
Plastic and polyethylene bags
President: Rodd Sprenkel
rsprenkel@lcplastics.com
Estimated Sales: Below $5 Million
Number Employees: 10-19

24977 (HQ)L & L Packing Co
527 W 41st St
Chicago, IL 60609-2708
773-285-5400
Fax: 773-285-0366 800-628-6328
www.worldsbeststeak.com
Established in 1955. Supplier of prime and choice
aged beef, pork, veal and lamb.
President: Joel Lezak
Sales Manager: Phil Lombardi
Estimated Sales: $24000000
Number Employees: 20-49
Type of Packaging: Consumer, Private Label

24978 L & M Food Svc Inc
885 Airpark Dr
Bullhead City, AZ 86429-5886
928-754-3241
Fax: 928-754-2241 info@lmfoodservice.com
www.lmfoodservice.com
Wholesaler/distributor of equipment and fixtures
and general merchandise including paper, janitorial
and bar supplies; serving the food service market
President: Ron Laughlin
laughlinrc@lmfoodservice.com
CEO: Andy Roesch
Vice President: Judy Laughlin
Plant Manager: Tom Watkins
Purchasing Manager: Dick Motsinger
Estimated Sales: $14 Million
Number Employees: 20-49
Square Footage: 100000

24979 L & N Label Co
2051 Sunnydale Blvd
Clearwater, FL 33765-1202
727-442-5400
Fax: 727-442-8915 800-944-5401
customerservice@lnlabel.com www.lnlabel.com
Manufacturer and exporter of die cut pressure sensi-
tive labels; blank and printed types and roll, sheet,
long and short runs available. Four color process la-
bels, up to 8 colors.
President: Steve Sabadosh
artdepartment@lnlabel.com
Vice President: Julee Sabadosh
Sales Director: Reyna Martin
IT Executive: John Brand
Production Manager: Curtis Booth
Plant Manager: Dave Gioia
Estimated Sales: $4-5 Million
Number Employees: 20-49
Square Footage: 80000
Type of Packaging: Private Label

24980 L A Cabinet & FinishingCo
810 E Jefferson Blvd
Los Angeles, CA 90011-2593
323-233-7245
Fax: 323-233-7248
Store fixtures
President: Mark Klein
VP: Mark Klein
Estimated Sales: $1-2.5 Million
Number Employees: 10-19

24981 L ChemCo Distribution
3230 Commerce Center Place
Louisville, KY 40211-1900
502-775-8387
Fax: 502-775-5981 800-292-1977
Wholesale distributor of commercial and industrial
janitorial cleaning supplies and equipment; also in-
cluding sell of pesticides, weedicides and herbicides
Estimated Sales: $1.5 Million
Number Employees: 9
Square Footage: 28000

24982 L Cubed Corp
871 Range End Rd
Dillsburg, PA 17019-9463
717-432-9738
Fax: 717-432-8389 800-826-2775
www.tamsystems.com
Bagging machines
Owner: Lin Lobaugh
llobaugh@tamsystemsonline.com
Estimated Sales: $1 Million
Number Employees: 20-49

24983 L G I Intl Inc
6700 SW Bradbury Ct
Portland, OR 97224-7734
503-620-0528
Fax: 503-620-3296 800-345-0534
sales.usa@lgintl.com www.lgitechnology.com
Manufacturer and exporter of pressure sensitive,
front panel, bar code and clean room labels
President: Tim Hartka
tim.hartka@lionbrothers.com
International Sales: Greg Jarmin
Sales Manager: Dale Gremaux
Estimated Sales: $1-5 Million
Number Employees: 20-49
Square Footage: 172000

24984 L T Hampel Corp
W194n11551 Mccormick Dr
Germantown, WI 53022-3000
262-255-4540
Fax: 262-255-9731 800-681-6979
sales@hampelcorp.com www.hampelcorp.com
Manufacturer and exporter of plastic pallets includ-
ing rugged light weight, steel reinforced,
thermoformed, nestable, standard and custom inter-
locking sleeve pack and double decker
President: Lance Hampel
CEO: Dave Brudvig
dbrudvig@thermoformpallets.com
Estimated Sales: $10-20 Million
Number Employees: 100-249
Brands:
Calf-Tel
Intrustor
Pallid

24985 L&A Engineering and Equipment
PO Box 2997
Turlock, CA 95381-2997
209-668-8107
Fax: 209-668-0636
Wine industry processing equipment
Estimated Sales: $1-5 Million
Number Employees: 3

24986 L&A Process Systems
1704 Reliance St
Modesto, CA 95358
209-581-0205
Fax: 209-581-0194
Manufacturer and exporter of evaporators, distiller-
ies, rotary coil vessels for jam and jelly production,
ceramic cross flow micro-filtration and es-
sence/aroma recovery systems
CEO: Don Carter
Estimated Sales: $1-2.5 Million
Number Employees: 5-9

24987 L&H Wood Manufacturing Company
PO Box 441
Farmington, MI 48332-0441
248-474-9000
Fax: 248-474-0269 www.michigancorporates.com
New and used pallets, skids, wood and wirebound
boxes, stretch film and machines, steel and synthetic
strapping and strapping machines
Sales Manager: Bill Lindbert
Controller: Kris Lindbert

Estimated Sales: $5-10 Million
Number Employees: 1-4
Square Footage: 60000

24988 L&L Associates
S87w27765 Lakeview Lane
Mukwonago, WI 53149-9665

281-221-4994

Fax: 262-363-3940 landrew@landassociates.com
L&L Associates are experienced, professional, independent Packaging Consultants offering experience in a full complement of packaging disciplines since 1990. All recommendations for packaging equipment, systems, materials and servicesare objective and selected from the entire packaging industry, both domestically and internationally, as required

24989 L&L Engraving Company
40 Old Lake Shore Road
Gilford, NH 03249-6522

603-524-3032

Fax: 603-524-6106 888-524-3032
Manufacture of stamps, rubber stamps, dating and numbering, coding, dating and marking equipment, advertising signs, plastic signs, plastic and metal fabricators
CEO: Melanie Burgess
Estimated Sales: less than $500,000
Number Employees: 1-4

24990 L&L Reps
4630 200th Street SW
Lynnwood, WA 98036-6608

425-778-9536

Fax: 425-778-6071
Brewing devices (urns, cleaners, coffeemakers), coffee filters, dispensing equipment, filtration equipment
President: Tracy Tayne
Estimated Sales: $5-10 Million
Number Employees: 3

24991 L&M Chemicals
5018 Trenton Street
Tampa, FL 33619-6832

813-247-6007

Fax: 813-247-6473 800-362-3331
lmccbill@gmail.com www.lmcc.com
Industrial chemicals including disinfectants, detergents and hand cleaners
Owner: Robert Pasciuta
Estimated Sales: Less than $500,000
Number Employees: 4
Parent Co: Gator Supply

24992 L&S Pallet Company
15150 Middlebrook Drive
Houston, TX 77058-1210

281-443-6537

Wooden pallets
Secretary/Treasurer: Allan Findley
Estimated Sales: $1-2.5 Million
Number Employees: 5-9

24993 L&S Products
422 Jay St
Coldwater, MI 49036-2112

517-279-9526

Fax: 517-278-8648 info@lsproducts.com
Store fixtures including garment and display racks and steel tubing products
CEO: Mark Neesley
CFO: Shanayne Neesley
R&D: Shanayne Neesley
Estimated Sales: Below $5 Million
Number Employees: 1-4
Square Footage: 120000

24994 L.A. Darling Co., LLC
1401 U.S. Highway 49B
Paragould, AR 72450-3139

800-682-5730

www.ladarling.com
Modular merchandising systems, store fixtures, gondolas and shelving systems, gourmet racks, checkouts, service desks and P.O.P. displays, gondolas, specialty wood and metal fixtures.
CEO: Evarts English
Year Founded: 1897
Estimated Sales: $110.8 Million
Number Employees: 1000-4999
Square Footage: 3000
Parent Co: Marmon Retail Store Equipment LLC

24995 L.C. Thompson Company
1303 43rd St.
Kenosha, WI 53140

262-652-3662

Fax: 262-652-3526 800-558-4018
www.lcthomsen.com
Manufacturer, importer and exporter of dairy processing machinery including control systems, filters, gaskets, hoses, pumps, strainers, thermometers, tubing and valves
President: Wayne Borne
Sls. Mgr.: Mike Dyutka
Service Manager: Mike Dyutka
Sales: Joyce Saftig
Contact: Hose Hooks
hhooks@lcthomsen.com
Number Employees: 20-49
Square Footage: 48000

24996 LA Graphics
15 Ellwood Court
Greenville, SC 29607-5340

864-297-1111
Fax: 864-987-9920

Commercial awnings
Corporate Manager: Nancy Keller
Quality Control: Larry Boeller
Estimated Sales: Below $5,000,000
Number Employees: 50

24997 LA Marche Mfg Co
106 Bradrock Dr
Des Plaines, IL 60018-1967

847-299-1193

Fax: 847-299-3061 www.lamarchemfg.com
Manufacturer and exporter of battery chargers for forklift trucks and vehicles
President: Stan Burg
agalvan@conversantmedia.com
EVP: Raj Dhiman
CFO: Rick Rutkowski
Vice President: J. Vargas
Research & Development: Vance Pearson
Quality Control Manager: Bob Brewer
Marketing Director: S. Burg
Sales Director: John Pawula
Customer Service Manager: Lacy Zyrkowski
agalvan@conversantmedia.com
Director Purchasing: Bob Lewinski
Estimated Sales: $10-20 Million
Number Employees: 100-249
Square Footage: 170000

24998 LA Monica Fine Foods
PO Box 309
Millville, NJ 08332

info@lamonicafinefoods.com
www.lamonicafinefoods.com
Surf clams and ocean clams from US certified waters, serving the fresh, canned and frozen markets.
Founder: Peter LaMonica
Number Employees: 20-49
Square Footage: 360000
Type of Packaging: Consumer, Food Service, Private Label, Bulk
Brands:
  Cape May
  Lamonica

24999 LA Motte Co
802 Washington Ave
Chestertown, MD 21620-1015

410-778-3100

Fax: 410-778-6394 800-344-3100
mkt@lamotte.com
Kits, test strips and meters for water analysis, monitoring sanitizer and caustic or acid cleaner concentrations, process or waste waters and boiler and cooling tower waters
President: David Lamotte
dlamotte@lamotte.com
CFO: Roland Willis
Quality Control: Susan Franklin
Marketing Director: Sue Byerly
VP Sales: Richard Lamotte
Estimated Sales: $50-100 Million
Number Employees: 100-249

25000 LA Rosa Refrigeration &Equip
19191 Filer St
Detroit, MI 48234-2883

313-368-6620

Fax: 313-368-1317 800-527-6723
www.larosaequip.com

Commercial refrigeration equipment including freezers; also, liquid and portable bars, holding cabinets, holding and warming equipment and steam tables
Owner, President: Sebastiano Grillo
sgrillo@larosaequip.com
Vice President: Jerry Grillo
Marketing, Administrations: Chelsea Van Hazenbrouck
Sales and Design Manager: Dan Gudenau
Estimated Sales: $2.5-5 Million
Number Employees: 20-49

25001 LAB Equipment
1326 New Seneca Tpke
Skaneateles, NY 13152

315-685-5781

Fax: 315-685-8106 800-522-5781
service@labequipment.com
www.labequipment.com
Shock, vibration, compression and incline impact test systems, as well as test data acquisition systems
President: Robert Noonan
Sales Director: Thomas Dunne
Estimated Sales: $1-5 Million
Number Employees: 20

25002 LANTECH.COM
11000 Bluegrass Pkwy
Jeffersontown, KY 40299-2399

502-267-4200

Fax: 502-266-5031 800-866-0322
jerryt@lantech.com www.lantech.com
Stretch wrappers, palletizers, conveyor systems
President: Jim Lancaster
jim.l@lantech.com
Estimated Sales: $50-75 Million
Number Employees: 250-499

25003 LANXESS Corp.
111 RIDC Park West Dr
Pittsburgh, PA 15275-1112

800-526-9377

lanxess.us
Specialty chemicals
President & CEO: Antonis Papadourakis

25004 LB Furniture Industries
99 S 3rd St
Hudson, NY 12534

518-828-1501

Fax: 518-828-3219 800-221-8752
sales@lbfurnitureind.com
Manufacturer and exporter of tables, chairs and booths
President: Les Lak
Contact: Penny Abell
penny@lbfurnitureind.com
Estimated Sales: $1-2.5 Million
Number Employees: 10-19
Square Footage: 650000

25005 LBP Manufacturing LLC
1325 S Cicero Ave
Cicero, IL 60804-1404

708-652-5600

Fax: 708-652-5537 sales@lbpmfg.com
www.lbpmfg.com
Manufacturer and exporter of hot cup sleeves, take-out containers and acrylic displays and dispensers
President: Barry Silverstein
Pricing Manager: Mary Lou Medina
CFO: Mike Schaechter
VP: Matthew Cook
R&D and QC: Barry M
Estimated Sales: $10-20 Million
Number Employees: 500-999
Parent Co: Terrace Paper Company
Brands:
  Coffee Clutch
  Coffee on the Move
  Safepak

25006 LCI Corporation
4433 Chesapeake Dr
Charlotte, NC 28216

704-398-7728

Fax: 704-398-7728 info@lcicorp.com
lcicorp.com
Thin-film evaporation systems, agglomeration systems, pelleting presses and feeder equipment manufactures

Manager: Scott Meyers
President: Lacey Hayes
Estimated Sales: $15-30 Million
Number Employees: 100-249
Parent Co: Bacon Industrial Manufacturing

25007 LDC Analytical
28271 Leticia
Mission Viejo, CA 92692-2329
949-586-5340
Fax: 949-586-9373
Wine industry probers and meters

25008 LDI Manufacturing Co
417 North St # 104
Logansport, IN 46947-2775
574-722-3124
Fax: 574-722-7213 800-366-2001
www.ldi-industries.com/LDI.htm
Manufacturer and exporter of exhaust ventilation equipment including commercial exhaust hoods and fans. Distribution of complete, pre-engineered heating and air conditioningequipment system. Custom stainless steel and metalfabrication. Indoor environment air quality equipment systems
Manager: Susan Begley
susan@ldimfg.com
VP Finance: Camille Hall
Marketing Director: Susan Erny
VP Customer Services: Susan Erny
Estimated Sales: $5-10 Million
Number Employees: 5-9
Square Footage: 100000
Type of Packaging: Food Service
Brands:
Greese Gobler
Magic Wash
Smart Hood
Sup-Ex
Top Sergent

25009 LDJ Electronics
1280 E Big Beaver
PO Box 219
Troy, MI 48083-0219
248-528-2202
Fax: 248-689-2525 info@ldj-electronics.com
Process control, monitoring and line monitoring systems; also, computer software systems and services
Public Relations: Derrick Peterman
Estimated Sales: $5-10,000,000
Number Employees: 20-49

25010 LDS Corporation
7900 E Union Ave
Suite 1007
Denver, CO 80237
303-928-1124
Fax: 303-217-7050 866-25 -ARDE
President/CEO: Joe Caston
VP of Finance/CFO: John C. Frank
Estimated Sales: $10-20 Million
Number Employees: 20-49

25011 LECO Corp
3000 Lakeview Ave
St Joseph, MI 49085-2319
269-983-5531
Fax: 269-982-8977 800-292-6141
info@leco.com www.leco.com
Analytical instrumentation
President: Robert J Warren
robert_warren@leco.com
Number Employees: 1000-4999

25012 LECO Corp
3000 Lakeview Ave
St Joseph, MI 49085-2319
269-983-5531
Fax: 269-982-8977 800-292-6141
info@leco.com www.leco.com
Analytical instrumentation for primary and secondary analyses of food, ingredients and flavors
President: Robert J Warren
robert_warren@leco.com
Number Employees: 1000-4999

25013 LEESON Electric Corp
1051 Cheyenne Ave
Grafton, WI 53024-9541
262-377-8810
Fax: 262-377-9025 www.leeson.com
Manufacturer and exporter of electric motors, gears and drives for food processing machinery.

CEO: Henry Knueppel
CFO: Dave Barta
VP: Bud Pritchard
Marketing: Philippe De Gail
Sales: Steve Weber
COO: Mark Gliebe
Number Employees: 500-999
Brands:
Leeson
Speedmaster
Washguard

25014 LEWA Inc
PO Box 6820
Holliston, MA 01746-6820
508-429-7403
Fax: 508-429-8615 888-539-2123
www.lewa-inc.com
Manufacturer and exporter of precision metering and mixing pumps and systems for blending and proportioning all liquids; also, seal-less controlled volume pumps for process services and moderate high pressures
President/Owner: Lee Bollow
lbollow@lewa-inc.com
Marketing: Marlis Morse
Estimated Sales: $10-20 Million
Parent Co: LEWA GmbH

25015 LIS Warehouse Systems
9201 Southern Pine Boulevard
Suite E
Charlotte, NC 28273-5537
704-926-1700
Fax: 704-926-1799 888-547-9670
Software for warehousing, inventory management, material handling and control
Chairman of the Board: Alok Singh
Senior Vice President, Director of Accou: Andrew Kirkwood
VP Sales/Marketing: Bob Carver
Number Employees: 25
Parent Co: LIS

25016 LIST
42 Nagog Park
Acton, MA 01720-3445
978-635-9521
Fax: 978-263-0570
Food processing machinery for viscous, sticky and crust forming materials including mixers, kneaders, dryers, heaters, melters, coolers, etc
CEO: Klaus List
VP Sales: Hefunt Schildknecht
Estimated Sales: $1-5 Million
Number Employees: 20
Square Footage: 18000
Parent Co: LIST AG

25017 LMC International
893 N Industrial Dr
Elmhurst, IL 60126
630-834-7789
Fax: 630-834-4322 info@Latiniusa.com
www.lmcinternational.com
Equipment for the confectionery and bakery industries
Sales/Marketing: Pat Kiel
Sales Director: Roger Hohberger
Sales: Daniel Herman
Estimated Sales: $15 000,000
Number Employees: 50
Number of Brands: 2
Number of Products: 50
Square Footage: 30000
Brands:
Hohberger Products
Latini Products

25018 LMCO
4705 Highway 36 S
Suite 1
Rosenberg, TX 77471-9254
281-342-8888
Fax: 832-595-5000
Brooms, mops and handles
President: Leslie Moore
Estimated Sales: $500,000-$1 Million
Number Employees: 5-9
Square Footage: 18000

25019 LMH
1714 Colfax St
Suite E
Concord, CA 94520
925-686-6400
Fax: 925-686-3836 800-531-6782
Wine industry pumps, mixers, tanks and process equipment; local service, fabrication and equipment repair
Estimated Sales: $5-10 Million
Number Employees: 10-19

25020 LMK Containers
PO Box 1001
Centerville, UT 84014-5001
626-821-9984
Manufacturer, importer and exporter of glass and plastic bottles, jars, caps and containers
Purchasing Director: Robert Frome
Type of Packaging: Consumer, Food Service, Private Label, Bulk
Brands:
Aastro

25021 LPA Software
400 Linden Oaks
Suite 140
Rochester, NY 14625
866-783-9900
www.lpa.com
Prepackaged software, software development and consulting for a variety of business applications including supply chain, semiconductor, internet and client server systems
President: Donald Soule
Vice President: Katrina Adams
Estimated Sales: $300,000-500,000
Number Employees: 120

25022 LPACK-Loersch Corporation
1530 E Race Sreet
Allentown, PA 18109
610-264-5641
Fax: 610-266-0330 www.lpack.com
Manager: Robert Kreger
Estimated Sales: $1,000,000-$3,000,000
Number Employees: 5-9

25023 LPI Imports
901 N Kilpatrick Avenue
Chicago, IL 60651-3326
877-389-6563
Fax: 773-379-5616
Shelving, shelf ledges, shelf dividers, posts and casters; also, labels
General Manager: Alan Kaplan
Parent Co: Leggett & Platt
Brands:
Snake Shelving

25024 LPI Information Systems
10020 Fontana Ln
Overland Park, KS 66207-3640
913-381-9118
Fax: 913-381-9118 888-729-2020
www.datasmithpayroll.com
Manufacturer and exporter of payroll software and tax forms
President: David Land
landlines@datasmithpayroll.com
Number Employees: 20-49
Brands:
Datacheck
Datasmith

25025 LPS Industries
10 Caesar Pl
Moonachie, NJ 07074-1701
201-438-3515
Fax: 201-438-1326 800-275-4577
www.lpsind.com
Custom manufaturer of flexible packaging such as stand up pouches, bags and roll stock. They offer eight color printing, micro hook and loop recloseable options, in-house QA and QR departments with testing lab and a solventlesslamination process.
President & CEO: Madeleine Robinson
Chief Financial Officer: Mary Elmer
Vice President, Marketing: Charles Ardman
Vice President, Sales: Domenick Pasqualone
Vice President, Operations: Phil Pasqualone

Estimated Sales: $50-100 Million
Number Employees: 100-249
Square Footage: 250000
Type of Packaging: Consumer, Food Service, Private Label, Bulk
Other Locations:
   Cerritos CA
   Indianapolis IN
   Marietta GA
   Moonachie NJ

25026 LPS Technology
1009 McAlpin Court
Grafton, OH 44044-1322

440-355-6992
Fax: 440-355-6998 800-586-1410
Manufacturer and exporter of washers, ovens, compressed air systems, conveyors and air vacuums
President: Dean Burke
General Manager: Dave Bobak
Estimated Sales: $1-2,500,000
Number Employees: 10-19
Parent Co: Eton Fab Company

25027 LRM Packaging
41 James St
South Hackensack, NJ 07606-1438

201-342-2530
Fax: 201-342-4351 info@lrmpackaging.com
www.lrmpackaging.com
Contract packager of snack and dry foods, etc
President: Erika Castro
erikacastro@lrmpackaging.com
Director Sales: John Natali, Jr.
Production Manager: Mike Hoskins
Estimated Sales: Below $5,000,000
Number Employees: 20-49
Square Footage: 20000

25028 LSI Industries Inc
10000 Alliance Rd
Blue Ash, OH 45242-4738

513-793-3200
Fax: 513-984-1335 www.lsi-industries.com
Visual merchandising displays and pressure sensitive signs
President: David McCauley
CEO: Dennis W Wells
dennis.wells@lsi-industries.com
Quality Control: Bruce Soleinger
VP Sales/Marketing: Robert Lux
National Sales Manager: Todd Blandford
Estimated Sales: $1-3 Million
Number Employees: 1000-4999

25029 LTI Boyd Corp
600 S Mcclure Rd
Modesto, CA 95357-0520

209-491-4700
Fax: 209-236-0154 888-244-6931
customerservice@boydcorp.com
www.boydcorp.com
Conveyor belting, gaskets, sheet goods, sponge, rubber and cork
Manager: Gregg Mynhier
CEO: Mitch Aiello
mitch.aiello@boydcorp.com
Sales: Jim Hemingway
General Manager: Lyle Hemingway
Estimated Sales: $5-10 Million
Number Employees: 50-99
Square Footage: 160000
Brands:
   Goodyear
   Klinger

25030 LTI Printing Inc
518 N Centerville Rd
Sturgis, MI 49091-9601

269-651-7574
Fax: 269-651-3262 www.ltiprinting.com
Manufacturer and exporter of labels and offset cartons
President: Don Frost
dfrost@ltiprinting.com
Estimated Sales: $20-50 Million
Number Employees: 50-99
Type of Packaging: Consumer, Food Service, Bulk

25031 LVO Manufacturing Inc
808 N 2nd Ave E
Rock Rapids, IA 51246-1759

712-472-3734
Fax: 712-472-2203 marilyn_lvo@yahoo.com
www.lvomfg.com

Bakery equipment
President: Marilyn Mammenga
marilyn_lvo@yahoo.com
CFO: Lambert Benno
Estimated Sales: $5-10 Million
Number Employees: 20-49

25032 LXE
P.O.Box 926000
Norcross, GA 30010-6000

770-447-4224
Fax: 770-447-4405 info@lxe.com
RF computer network systems, logistics, transportation, health care
President: Jim Childress
CEO: Alfred Hansen
CEO: Paul B Domorski
VP Sales: B Johnson
Contact: Philippe Bechet
bechet.p@ems-t.com
Estimated Sales: $50-100 Million
Number Employees: 250-499
Parent Co: EMS technologies

25033 La Creme Coffee & Tea
438 W Mockingbird Lane
Dallas, TX 75247

214-352-8190
Fax: 214-352-8173 877-493-2326
info@lacremecoffeeandtea.com
www.lacremecoffeeandtea.com
Tea and coffee brewers
Estimated Sales: $500,000-$1 Million
Number Employees: 9

25034 La Crosse
W6636 L B White Rd
Onalaska, WI 54650

608-783-2800
Fax: 608-783-6115 800-345-0018
mail@lacrossecooler.com
www.hospitalityinternational.com
Manufacturer and exporter of underbar items including sinks, drain boards, ice chests, cocktail stations and storage units; also, portable bars
CEO: Tony Wilson
CFO: Jack Lauer
Vice President of Development: Ron Provus
Marketing Director: Bridget Crave
Sales Director: Della Indahl
Estimated Sales: $50-100 Million
Number Employees: 100-249
Parent Co: Hospitality International
Brands:
   La Crosse
   Stowaway

25035 La Crosse Milling Company
105 Hwy 35
P.O. Box 86
Cochrane, WI 54622

608-248-2222
Fax: 608-248-2221 800-441-5411
ghartzell@lacrossemilling.com
Whole grain, organic and Kosher grain ingredients including oats, barley and wheat, products include conventional and organic oat flakes, oat flour, oat bran, oat fiber, pearled barley, barley flakes, barley flour, rolled wheat andother specialty milled grains.
President: Dan Ward
Controller/Assistant Treasurer: Teresa Waters
Safety Manager: Bryan Hoch
Quality Control Manager: Lori Dahl
Food Sales Assistant: Michelle Kosidowski
VP Sales: Glen Hartzell
Maintenance Manager: Dale Peterson
Feed Coordinator: Cara Lee Wiersgalla
Estimated Sales: $48.56 Million
Number Employees: 95
Type of Packaging: Bulk

25036 La Crosse Sign Co.
2502 Melby St
Eau Claire, WI 54703

715-835-6189
Fax: 715-835-6868 www.lacrossesign.com
Indoor and outdoor signs including electric, painted, vinyl lettering and neon
VP: Gregory Mitchell
Estimated Sales: $1-2.5 Million
Number Employees: 5-9

25037 La Menuiserie East Angus
25 Rue Willard
East Angus, QC J0B 1R0
Canada

819-832-2746
Fax: 819-832-3474
Wooden pallets
President/CFO: Robert La Pointe
Quality Control/R&D: Robert Lapointe
Estimated Sales: Below $5 Million
Number Employees: 40

25038 La Poblana Food Machines
5952 East Nance Street
Mesa, AZ 85215

480-258-2091
Fax: 480-452-0538
La Poblana Food Machines LLC offers sales and service of commercial-grade tortilla-making equipment. Manufacture their lines as well as custom machinery.
President: Sherrie Soria

25039 La Rinascente Macaroni Company
41 James St
South Hackensack, NJ 07606

201-342-2530
info@lrmpackaging.com
www.lrmpackaging.com
Macaroni, flour and packaged food products.
Consultant: John Natali
Estimated Sales: $20-50 Million
Square Footage: 600000
Type of Packaging: Consumer, Food Service, Private Label, Bulk
Brands:
   La Rinascente Pasta Products

25040 LaCrosse Safety and Industrial
18550 NE Riverside Parkway
Portland, OR 97230-4975

503-766-1010
Fax: 800-558-0188 800-557-7246
Manufacturer and importer of waterproof protective clothing and footwear including vulcanized double coated rubber aprons
President: John McGinnis
Manager: Tammy Woolrage
Sales Director: Ken Furtech
Contact: John Mcginnis
jmcginnis@lacrossefootwear.com
Number Employees: 100-249
Number of Products: 600
Parent Co: Standalone

25041 Labconco Corp
8811 Prospect Ave
Kansas City, MO 64132-2696

816-333-8811
Fax: 816-363-0130 800-821-5525
labconco@labconco.com www.labconco.com
Manufacturer and exporter of scientific laboratory equipment and apparatus with chloride instruments, Kjeldahl nitrogen determination apparatus and fat and fiber apparatus
President: Stephen Gound
stephengound@labconco.com
Executive VP: Mark Weber
VP Marketing: Debbie Kenny
National Sales Manager: Tom Schwaller
Estimated Sales: $30 Million
Number Employees: 100-249
Brands:
   Centrivap
   Flaskscrubber
   Freezone
   Paramount
   Protector
   Purifier
   Rapidvap
   Steamscrubber
   Waterpro

25042 Label Art
2278 Brockett Rd
Tucker, GA 30084

770-939-6960
Fax: 770-939-6960 800-652-1072
Manufacturer and exporter of grocery shelf marking products, warehouse picking labels and continuous and sheet fed laser printer products
National Sales Manager: Deborah Goss
Sales Representative: Lisa Wood

Estimated Sales: $20-50 Million
Number Employees: 100-249
Square Footage: 30000

25043 Label Express
1305 S 630 E
American Fork, UT 84003-3375

801-772-0677
Fax: 801-642-3510 877-639-8600
Labels, shrink bands and folding cartons
CFO: Jeff Sinclair
R&D: Carlene West
General Manager: Mike Kekeegan
Marketing Manager: Derick Sims
Estimated Sales: $20-50 Million
Number Employees: 50-99
Parent Co: Impaxx

25044 Label House
503 S Raymond Ave
Fullerton, CA 92831-5026

714-449-0632
Fax: 714-441-0698 800-499-5858
sales@labelhouse.com www.labelhouse.net
Pressure sensitive labels and tags; wholesaler/distributor of label dispensers and applicators, thermal transfer ribbons, case coders, bar code printers and software
Owner: Al Jiacomin
owner: Karen Freeman
VP Sales: Leone Grant
Estimated Sales: $1-2.5 Million
Number Employees: 10-19

25045 Label Impressions
1831 W Sequoia Ave
Orange, CA 92868-1017

714-634-3466
Fax: 714-634-3468 info@labelimpressions.com
www.labelimpressions.com
High quality customer labels, tags and flexible packaging. Recognized as a quality, green technology manufacturer.
President: Jeff Salisbury
jeff@labelimpressions.com
CEO: Ted Salisbury
CFO: Carolyn Deyse
VP Sales & Sustainability: Jeff Morrow
R&D: Marie Graham
Quality Assurance: Steve Smith
Operations: Rick Ybarra
Estimated Sales: $8 Million
Number Employees: 20-49
Number of Products: 1000
Square Footage: 40000
Type of Packaging: Consumer, Food Service, Private Label, Bulk

25046 Label Makers
8911 102nd St
Pleasant Prairie, WI 53158-2212

262-947-3300
Fax: 262-947-3301 800-208-3331
www.lmipackaging.com
Manufacturer and exporter of heat seal lidding, flexible packaging solutions, daisychain, rollstock & die cut lidding
Owner: Virginia Moran
CEO: Jean Moran
Vice President of Business Development: Randall Troutman
VP Research & Development: Mike Gorzynski
Director of Marketing: Lea Connelly
National Accounts Manager: Gary Morrison
VP Operations: Vince Incandela
Number Employees: 20-49

25047 Label Mill
2416 Jackson Street
Savanna, IL 61074-2836

815-273-4707
Fax: 815-273-7074 800-273-4707
pmills@labelmill.com www.labelmill.com
Standard and custom label applicators
Owner: Andy Mills
Contact: Jill Holtman
jholtman@labelmill.com
Estimated Sales: $1-3 Million
Number Employees: 5-9

25048 Label Products Inc
12571 Oliver Ave S # 700
Suite 700
Burnsville, MN 55337-6664

952-996-0909
Fax: 952-996-0202 877-370-0688
sales@labelproducts.com www.labelproducts.com
Labels including pressure sensitive, UPC and bar code; also, embossed, holographic and computer designed available
President and CFO: Ed Christenson
edc@labelproducts.com
Product Manager: Stu Knilons
Sales Manager: Kevin Peterson
Operations Manager: Kevin Peterson
Production Manager: Stu Knilons
Plant Manager: Kevin Peterson
Estimated Sales: $10-20 Million
Number Employees: 20-49
Square Footage: 29000

25049 Label Solutions
151 W Passaic St # 2
2nd Floor
Rochelle Park, NJ 07662-3105

201-599-0909
Fax: 201-599-9888 ilana@labelsolutions.net
www.labelsolutions.net
Wine industry pressure sensitive labels
President: Ilana Weiss
ilana@labelsolutions.net
Estimated Sales: Below $5 Million
Number Employees: 1-4

25050 Label Specialties Inc
704 Dunn Way
Placentia, CA 92870-6805

714-961-8074
Fax: 714-961-8276 800-635-2386
www.labelspec.com
Labels including scale printer, ingredient printer, bar code, plain, pressure sensitive, stock and custom; also, transfer ribbons
Owner: Micheal Gyure
VP: Thomas Wetterhus
Manager: Maria Arellano
marellano@labelspec.com
Estimated Sales: $1-2.5 Million
Number Employees: 10-19
Square Footage: 18000

25051 Label Supply Company
3013 Sherwood Ln
Colleyville, TX 76034

785-256-2488
Fax: 785-256-2582 800-444-8186
Labeling equipment
Estimated Sales: $.5-1 million
Number Employees: 5-9

25052 Label Systems
56 Cherry St
Bridgeport, CT 06605-2370

203-333-5503
Fax: 203-336-8570 www.labelsystemsinc.com
Labels including pressure sensitive, imprintable and holographic for shelf marking applications
President: Michael Zubretsky
mzubretsky@labelsysinc.com
Quality Control: Howard Sands
R&D: George Houston
VP: Rich Zucker
Estimated Sales: $10-20 Million
Number Employees: 50-99
Parent Co: Bridgestone Company

25053 Label Systems
1150 Kerrisdale Blvd.
Unit 2
Newmarket, ON L3Y 8Z9
Canada

905-836-7844
Fax: 905-853-9357 m.kirby@label-systems.com
www.label-systems.com
Manufacturer and exporter of pressure sensitive label machinery and equipment.
Sales Director: Matthew Kirby
Number Employees: 5
Square Footage: 44000

25054 Label Systems & Solutions
1430 Church St
Bohemia, NY 11716-5028

631-563-4549
Fax: 631-567-4338 800-811-2560
Badges, printers, advertising specialties, labels, tags and tapes; also, art production services available
Sales Manager: Stacy Moller
Estimated Sales: $500,000-$1 Million
Number Employees: 5-9

25055 Label Systems Inc
4111 Lindbergh Dr
Addison, TX 75001-4345

972-387-4512
Fax: 972-387-4935 800-220-9552
sales@labelsystemsinc.com
www.labelsystemsinc.com
Labels including custom designed, pressure sensitive, plain, printed, die cut on rolls and sheeted; also, decals and metal name plates
Owner: Amy Van Brunt
VP: Amy Van Brunt
Quality Control: Marcia Macias
Sales: Rick Brown
amy@labelsystemsinc.com
Public Relations: Sue Van Brunt
Operations/Production: Bruno Contreaus
Purchasing: Yivan Chenn
Estimated Sales: $2.5-5 Million
Number Employees: 20-49
Number of Products: 150

25056 Label Technology Inc
2050 Wardrobe Ave
Merced, CA 95341-6409

209-384-1000
Fax: 209-384-0322 800-388-1990
info@labeltech.com www.labeltech.com
Pressure sensitive labels, tags and flexible packaging; also, label imprinters and applicators
President: Quincy Adams
quincy.adams@labeltech.com
VP Product Development: Dennis Deisenroth
VP Sales: Phil Henderson
Estimated Sales: $2.5-5,000,000
Number Employees: 100-249
Square Footage: 126000

25057 Label World
29 Jet View Dr
Rochester, NY 14624

585-235-0200
Fax: 585-235-0398 800-836-8186
Prime labels
President/CEO: John McDermott
CEO: Janet Allardice
allardice@labelworldusa.com
VP Sales & Marketing: Skylar Rote
Estimated Sales: $10-20 Million
Number Employees: 50-99

25058 Label-Aire Inc
550 Burning Tree Rd
Fullerton, CA 92833-1449

714-441-0700
Fax: 714-526-0300 info@label-aire.com
www.label-aire.com
Manufacturer and exporter of pressure-sensitive label applicators and rotary and incline systems
President: George Allen
gallen@label-aire.com
Marketing Manager: William Claproth
Sales: Steve Winders
Operations: Gene Bukovi
Estimated Sales: $20-50 Million
Number Employees: 100-249
Square Footage: 60000
Parent Co: Impaxx
Type of Packaging: Consumer, Food Service, Private Label, Bulk

25059 Labelette Company
1237 Circle Avenue
Forest Park, IL 60130-2416

708-366-2010
Fax: 708-366-0226 sales@labelette.com
www.labelette.com
Manufacturer and exporter of semi-automatic and automatic labeling machinery
Estimated Sales: $5-10 Million
Number Employees: 20-49
Square Footage: 40000

Brands:
Labelette

25060 Labeling Systems
32 Spruce St
Oakland, NJ 07436

201-405-0767
Fax: 201-405-1179 888-405-4574
lsi@labelingsystems.com
www.labelingsystems.com
Labeling machinery
President: Theodore Zaccheo
Contact: Brian Baker
brian.baker@lsi.com
Estimated Sales: $5-10 Million
Number Employees: 20-49

25061 Labeling Systems Clearwater
PO Box 1955
Largo, FL 33779-1955

727-539-7784
Fax: 727-538-5626 800-749-1057
Supplies for DSD route sales, handheld labelers for
price marking, promotional labeling, date coding
Estimated Sales: $1-2.5 Million
Number Employees: 5-9

25062 Labelmart
11733 95th Ave N
Maple Grove, MN 55369-5551

763-493-0099
Fax: 763-493-0093 888-577-0141
info@cmsitechnologies.com
Pressure sensitive labels and tags including die cut
blank and printed; also, thermal transfer ribbons and
printers
Owner: Steve Nelson
steven@labelmart.com
Estimated Sales: $5-10 Million
Number Employees: 20-49
Parent Co: Computerized Machinery Systems

25063 Labelmax Inc
1209 San Dario Ave
Laredo, TX 78040-4505

956-722-6493
Pressure sensitive labels and thermal transfer and la-
ser sheet; consultant specializing in bar coding
services
CEO: Jorge Martinez
Finance Manager: Edgar Martinez
Estimated Sales: $3-5,000,000
Number Employees: 5-9

25064 Labelprint America
8 Opportunity Way
Newburyport, MA 01950-4043

978-463-4004
Fax: 978-463-9748
accounting@labelprintamerica.com
www.labelprintamerica.com
Labels, decals, tags, pressure sensitive labeling
equipment and thermal imprinters
Owner: Tony Yemma
tony@labelprintamerica.com
President Marketing: Tony Yemma
VP Operations: Bob Haley
Estimated Sales: $2.5-5 Million
Number Employees: 20-49
Square Footage: 84000

25065 Labelquest Inc
493 W Fullerton Ave
Elmhurst, IL 60126-1404

630-833-9400
Fax: 630-833-9421 800-999-5301
gary@labelquest.net www.labelquest.com
Manufacturer and exporter of labels, decals and heat
transfers
President: Pat Vandenberg
Sales Manager: Neil Vandenberg
Estimated Sales: $2.5-5 Million
Number Employees: 50-99
Square Footage: 10000

25066 Labels & Decals International
300 Frontier Way
Bensenville, IL 60106

630-227-0500
Fax: 630-227-1016 info@labels-decals.com
www.labels-decals.com
Pressure sensitive labels and decals

Owner: Cliff Bode
Contact: Steve Bartscher
steve@labels-decals.com
Estimated Sales: $2.5-5 Million
Number Employees: 10-19

25067 Labels By Pulizzi Inc
3325 Wahoo Dr
Williamsport, PA 17701-9243

570-326-1244
Fax: 570-326-3453 www.labelsbypulizzi.com
Customized pressure sensitive labels for food prod-
ucts
President: Charline Pulizzi
cpulizzi@labelsbypulizzi.com
R&D: Joseph Pulizzi
VP: Joseph Pulizzi, Jr.
Manager: Mark Porter
Purchasing Executive: Dalbys Kreisher
Estimated Sales: $10-20 Million
Number Employees: 50-99
Square Footage: 400000

25068 Labels Plus
2407 106th St SW
Everett, WA 98204-3628

425-745-4592
Fax: 425-523-1973 800-275-7587
sales@labelsplus.com www.labelsplus.com
Custom printed pressure sensitive labels
President: Eric C Phillips
Accountant: James Peterson
Contact: John Bitow
johnb@labelsplus.com
Estimated Sales: $10-20 Million
Number Employees: 20-49

25069 Lablynx Inc
1770 The Exchange SE # 240
Atlanta, GA 30339-2038

770-859-1992
Fax: 678-391-6982 800-585-5969
sales@lablynx.com
President: John H Jones
Number Employees: 5-9

25070 Laboratory Devices
PO Box 6402
Holliston, MA 01746-6402

508-429-1716
Fax: 508-429-6583
Manufacturer and exporter of laboratory instruments
Estimated Sales: $1-5 Million
Number Employees: 5

25071 Labpride Chemicals
2281 Light St
Bronx, NY 10466-6136

718-547-5757
Fax: 718-994-0494 800-467-1255
Heavy duty degreasers, disinfectants, sanitizers, de-
tergents, brooms, mops, sponges, squeegees, brushes
and cleaners including glass, oven, walls, bath-
rooms, etc
Owner: Ralph Derose
VP: Domenick DeRose
Operations Manager: James Lanfear
Estimated Sales: $5-10 Million
Number Employees: 20-49
Square Footage: 8000

25072 Labtech Industries
7707 Lyndon St
Detroit, MI 48238-2465

313-862-1737
Fax: 313-862-1131 800-525-8667
www.brycegroup.com
Industrial cleaners and specialty chemicals
President/Co-Owner: Corey Bryce
Co-Owner: Dennis Bryce
cbryce@labtechcorp.com
Estimated Sales: Less than $500,000
Number Employees: 10-19

25073 Labvantage Solutions
200 Broadway
Troy, NY 12180-3289

518-274-1990
Fax: 518-274-7824 www.labvantage.com
Laboratory Information Management Systems
(LIMS), chromatography and a broad spectrum of
other applications

Chief Executive Officer: Jeff Ferguson
Vice President of Professional Services: Anuj Uppal
Vice President of Quality: Fernando Casanova
Business Director: Anneli Friberg
Estimated Sales: $1-5 Million

25074 Labvantage Solutions Inc
265 Davidson Ave # 200
Suite 220
Somerset, NJ 08873-4120

908-231-6703
Fax: 732-560-0121 888-346-5467
nasales@labvantage.com www.labvantage.com
Developer of laboratory information management
systems for sample forecasting, scheduling and
login, data calculations, product specification
checks, quality control and reporting
Manager: Deborah Washington
Marketing Manager: Heather Maguire
VP Sales/Marketing: Don Seitz
Estimated Sales: $10-15 Million
Number Employees: 50-99
Brands:
Labmaestro
Labmaestro Chrom Perfect
Labmaestro Ensemble
Labvantage
Pro-Lims
Seedpak
Trace

25075 Laciny Brothers Inc
6622 Vernon Ave
St Louis, MO 63130-2650

314-862-8330
Fax: 314-862-8332 www.lacinybros.com
Custom fabricated food processing equipment.
President: Timothy Laciny
tlaciny@lacinybros.com
Marketing/Sales/Public Relations: John Ulz
Operations/Production: Rick Gratza
Plant Manager: Don Fitzgerald
Purchasing Manager: Terry Brown
Estimated Sales: $2.5-5 Million
Number Employees: 20-49
Square Footage: 124000

25076 Lacroix Packaging
77 De l'Eglise Street
St-Placide, Quebec, QC J0V 2B0
Canada

450-258-2262
Fax: 450-258-3345
cbouveret@emballagelacroix.com
www.emballagelacroix.com
Customized packaging and labels.

25077 Lacrosse-Rainfair SafetyProducts
3600 S Memorial Dr
Racine, WI 53403-3822

262-554-7000
Fax: 414-554-6619 800-558-5990
info@lacrossesafety.com
Manufactures protective outerware, footwear, aprons
and insulated clothing
CEO: Joe Schneider
CFO: Bruce Bartelt
Vice President: Gregg Liederbach
Public Relations: Anna Gardner
Plant Manager: John Schleicher
Purchasing Manager: Cindy Krause
Estimated Sales: $44 Million
Number Employees: 100-249

25078 Ladder Works
1125 E Saint Charles Rd
Lombard, IL 60148-2085

630-629-7154
Fax: 630-268-9655 800-419-5880
Manufacturer and exporter of flag poles and flags
Owner: Ed Reeder
Inside Sales Manager: Lisa Simpson
Estimated Sales: $10-20,000,000
Number Employees: 20-49
Parent Co: Uncommon USA

25079 (HQ)Lady Mary
126 Lady Mary Lane
PO Box 157
Rockingham, NC 28379-4965

910-997-7321
Fax: 910-997-7324
Round, rectangular, round/square, moisture/grease
proof and recyclable disposable cake boards

President: Mary Stanley
Estimated Sales: $2.5-5 Million
Number Employees: 10-19
Square Footage: 160000
Other Locations:
Lady Mary
Rockingham NC
Brands:
Dainty Boards
Party Plates
Tuftboard

25080 Lafayette Sign Company
47 Sindle Ave
Little Falls, NJ 07424-1650

973-812-5000
Fax: 973-812-8222 800-343-5366
www.lafayettesign.com

Plastic and neon signs
President: John Scott
Permit Coordinator: Gerald Koczot
Estimated Sales: $1-2.5 Million
Number Employees: 10-19

25081 Lafayette Tent & AwningCo
125 S 5th St
Lafayette, IN 47901-1618

765-742-4277
Fax: 765-742-4462 800-458-2955
www.lafayettetent.com

Commercial awnings and rental tents/full line special event rental firm.
President: Henry Ebershoff
CEO: Craig Ebershoff
lta@lafayettetent.com
CFO: Craig Ebershoff
Vice President: Craig Ebershoff
Research & Development: Craig Ebershoff
Quality Control: Craig Ebershoff
Marketing Director: Craig Ebershoff
Sales Director: Craig Ebershoff
Public Relations: Craig Ebershoff
Operations Manager: Craig Ebershoff
Production Manager: Craig Ebershoff
Plant Manager: Craig Ebershoff
Purchasing Manager: Craig Ebershoff
Estimated Sales: $5-10,000,000
Number Employees: 20-49

25082 Lafitte Cork & Capsule Inc
45 Executive Ct
Napa, CA 94558-6267

707-258-2675
Fax: 707-258-0558 800-343-2675
info@lafitte-usa.com www.lafitte-usa.com

Wine industry corks and capsules
President: Angie Allen
aallen@lafitte-usa.com
VP: Barry Rucker
Estimated Sales: $1-2.5 Million
Number Employees: 10-19

25083 Laggren's LLC
100 Whittingham Dr
Monroe Twp, NJ 08831-2610

609-235-9883
Fax: 908-756-7560 dlasser@comcast.net

Commercial awnings, window treatments, canopies, custom draperies, flags, flagpoles, banners, and radiator covers and enclosures.
President: David Lasser
Estimated Sales: $1-2,500,000
Number Employees: 10-19
Square Footage: 14000

25084 Laidig Inc
14535 Dragoon Trl
Mishawaka, IN 46544-6896

574-256-0204
Fax: 574-256-5575 sales@laidig.com
www.laidig.com

Manufacturer and exporter of bulk material steel storage structures and handling systems including conveyors
President: Wyn Laidig
sales@laidig.com
SVP: Tom J Lindenman
Vice President Marketing/Information: Daniel Laidig
Vice President Sales: Mike Laidig
VP, Manufacturing: Dan Collins
Estimated Sales: $5-10 Million
Number Employees: 50-99
Parent Co: LIS Corporation

25085 Lail Design Group
1505 Main St
Saint Helena, CA 94574

707-963-1565
Fax: 707-963-4509 www.laildesign.com

Facility planning and design
Principal Architect: S Doug Osborn
Principal Architect: Paul Kelley
Marketing Director: Tim Martin
Contact: Maria Reyes
mreyes@cordblood.com
Manager: Doug Osborn
Estimated Sales: $1.6 Million
Number Employees: 10-19

25086 Laitram LLC
200 Laitram Ln
Harahan, LA 70123-5308

504-733-6000
Fax: 504-733-5257 800-533-8253
www.laitram.com

Manufactures high-quality, stainless steel equipment for the seafood processing industry. Product line includes shrimp peeling systems, shrimp grading systems, shrimp deveiners, and seafood steam cookers and chillers
President: Paul Gariepy
CEO: James M Lapeyre Jr
Marketing Director: Albert Esparza
Operations Manager: Albert Wilson
Estimated Sales: $8.7 Million
Number Employees: 1000-4999
Parent Co: Laitram Corporation

25087 Lake City Signs
604 Avenue C
Boulder City, NV 89005-2738

702-293-5805
Fax: 705-293-0624

Electric signs, pennants and banners; also, lettering service available
Co-Owner: Denise Henderson

25088 Lake Eyelet Manufacturing Company
123 Old Canal Way
Weatogue, CT 06089-9688

860-628-5543
Fax: 860-628-4899

Eyelet machinery products including bottle capping, ferrules, shells and stampings
Sales Manager: Joseph Ciriello
Estimated Sales: $2.5-5 Million
Number Employees: 50-100

25089 Lake Michigan Hardwood Company
PO Box 265
Leland, MI 49654-0265

231-256-9811

Wooden pallets
Estimated Sales: $2.5-5 Million
Number Employees: 19

25090 Lake Process Systems Inc
27930 W Commercial Ave
Lake Barrington, IL 60010-2442

847-381-7663
Fax: 847-381-7688 800-331-9260
paul@lakeprocess.com www.lakeprocess.com

Cleaning and sanitizing systems, fittings, CIP and COP units, skid systems and sanitary heat exchangers; also, design and installation of process and CIP systems available
President: Paul Harris
Secretary/Treasurer: Rebecca Harris
Estimated Sales: $1-2.5 Million
Number Employees: 10-19

25091 Lake Shore Industries Inc
1817 Poplar St
Erie, PA 16502-1624

814-456-4277
Fax: 814-453-4293 800-458-0463
info@lsisigns.com www.lsisigns.com

Interior and exterior signage; exporter of signs and markers
President: Leo Bruno
info@lsisigns.com
Estimated Sales: $2.5-5 Million
Number Employees: 10-19
Square Footage: 38480

Brands:
Lashimar
Letter-Lites

25092 Lakeland Rubber Stamp Company
PO Box 372
Lakeland, FL 33802-0372

863-682-5111
Fax: 888-465-6373 www.holmesstamp.com

Rubber stamps
President: James Bronson
Quality Control: Hood Thom
VP Marketing: Thomas Hood
Estimated Sales: $10-20 Million
Number Employees: 5-9

25093 Lakeside Container Corp
299 Arizona Ave
Plattsburgh, NY 12903-4429

518-561-6150
Fax: 518-561-4449 www.lakesidecontainer.com

Corrugated boxes and pads
President: George Bouyea
CFO: Paige Raville
Sales: Miki Worden
Plant Manager: Tom Vaughan
Estimated Sales: $1-2.5 Million
Number Employees: 20-49

25094 (HQ)Lakeside Manufacturing Inc
4900 W Electric Ave
Milwaukee, WI 53219-1629

414-645-0630
Fax: 414-902-6545 888-558-8565
info@elakeside.com www.elakeside.com

Manufacturer and exporter of mobile material handling and food service equipment including carts, racks, containers, dispensers, portable beverage bars, etc
President: Joe Carlson
jcarlson@elakeside.com
Chairman/CEO: Lawrence Moon
Chairman of the Board: Lawrence Moon
VP Sales: Alex Carayannopoulos
Estimated Sales: $10-20 Million
Number Employees: 100-249
Brands:
Adjust-A-Fit
Aris
Condi Express
Creation Station
Ergo-One
Extreme Duty
Lakeside
Party Pleaser
Serv 'n Express

25095 Lakeside-Aris Manufacturing
1977 S Allis Street
Milwaukee, WI 53207-1248

414-481-3900
Fax: 414-481-9313 800-558-8565

Manufacturer and exporter of serving carts and culinary display trays
VP: Jon Carlson
VP Sales: Alex Carayannopoulos
Estimated Sales: $10-20 Million
Number Employees: 100-249
Parent Co: Lakeside Manufacturing
Type of Packaging: Consumer, Food Service

25096 Lakeview Rubber Stamp Co
4316 N Lincoln Ave
Chicago, IL 60618-1712

773-539-1525
Fax: 773-539-2718

Rubber stamps
Owner: Terry Lange
lakeviewstamp@aol.com
Estimated Sales: Less Than $500,000
Number Employees: 1-4
Square Footage: 2200

25097 Lakewood Engineering & Manufacturing Company
501 N Sacramento Blvd
Chicago, IL 60612-1099

773-722-4300
Fax: 773-722-1541 800-621-4277
www.lakewoodeng.com

Industrial and portable electric fans and heaters; also, heavy-duty and ball-bearing swivels, plastic and metal christmas tree stands

President: David Hirschfield
VP Marketing: Charles Herndon
Sales/Marketing Executive: Chip Herndon
National Sales Manager: Dennis McCarthy
Purchasing Agent: Lou Petrica
Purchasing Agent: John Sharkey
Estimated Sales: $80 Million
Number Employees: 500-999
Square Footage: 750000

25098 Lakewood Processing Machinery
875 Brooks Ave
Holland, MI 49423-5338
    Fax: 616-392-8977 800-366-6705
info@lakewoodpm.com www.lakewoodpm.com
Sizers, netweight fillers, checkweighers, washers, volumetric fillers, color sorters
President: Mike Miedema
VP Sales & Marketing: Denny Schepel
R & D: Dale Miedima
Contact: Scott Avink
scott.avink@lakewoodfabtech.com
Estimated Sales: $5-10 Million
Number Employees: 10-19

25099 Lako Tool & Mfg Inc
7400 Ponderosa Rd
P.O.Box 425
Perrysburg, OH 43551-4857
    419-662-5256
    Fax: 419-662-8225 800-228-2982
lsmith@lakotool.com www.lakotool.com
Sealing, cutting and punching devices
President: Larry Smith
Sales Manager: Jo Montano
Manager: Lou Montano
lsmith@lakotool.com
Estimated Sales: $2.5-5 Million
Number Employees: 10-19

25100 Lakos Separators & Filtration
1365 N Clovis Ave
Fresno, CA 93727-2282
    559-255-1601
    Fax: 559-255-8093 800-344-7205
info@lakos.com www.lakos.com
Fluid handling systems
Owner: Claude Laval
Contact: Betty Ava
bettya@lakos.com
Estimated Sales: $10-20 000,000
Number Employees: 50-99

25101 Lamar Advertising Co
5321 Corporate Blvd
Baton Rouge, LA 70808-2506
    225-926-1000
    Fax: 225-926-1005 www.lamar.com
Advertising signs including outdoor, painted and poster panel
CEO: Sean E Reilly
sreilly@lamarhq.com
CEO: Kevin Reilly
CFO: Keith Istre
Executive Vice President: Brent McCoy
Chief Marketing Officer: Thomas Teepell
Vice President, Director of National Sal: John Miller
Vice President of Operations: Robert Switzer
Estimated Sales: Over $1 Billion
Number Employees: 1000-4999

25102 Lamar Advertising Co
405 Country Place Pkwy
Pearl, MS 39208-6774
    601-948-3443
    Fax: 601-355-6255 800-893-2560
twall@lamar.com www.lamar.com
Outdoor advertising signs
Manager: Marty Elrod
CEO: Kevin Reilly Jr.
CFO: Keith Istre
Executive Vice Prsident: Brent McCoy
Chief Marketing Officer: Thomas Teepell
Vice President, Director of National Sal: John Miller
Manager: Daryl Ainsworth
dainsworth@lamarhq.com
Vice President of Operations: Robert Switzer
Estimated Sales: $5-10 Million
Number Employees: 20-49

25103 Lamb Sign
11979 Falling Creek Dr
Manassas, VA 20112
    703-791-7960
    Fax: 703-263-1761
Building identification and marking devices including metal letters, directory and bulletin boards and signs
President: Robert W Schneider
VP: R Wiesheier
Estimated Sales: Below $5 Million
Number Employees: 1-4
Square Footage: 61200

25104 Lamb Weston Holdings Inc.
599 S. Rivershore Ln.
Eagle, ID 83616
    208-938-1047
    800-766-7783
    www.lambweston.com
Frozen potato products.
President/CEO: Tom Werner
Senior VP/CFO: Robert McNutt
Senior VP/General Counsel: Eryk Spytek
Year Founded: 1950
Estimated Sales: $3.4 Billion
Number Employees: 7,200
Number of Brands: 8
Type of Packaging: Consumer, Food Service
Other Locations:
    Lamb Weston Manufacturing Plant
    Weston OR
    Lamb Weston Manufacturing Plant
    Kennewick WA
    Lamb Weston Manufacturing Plant
    Prosser WA
    Lamb Weston Manufacturing Plant
    Boise ID
    Lamb Weston Manufacturing Plant
    Alberta, Canada
Brands:
    Sweet Things®
    Colossal Crisp®
    CrispyCoat Fries
    Lamb Weston®
    Lamb's Seasoned®
    Lamb's Supreme®
    LW Private Reserve®
    Stealth Fries®
    Tavern Traditions®

25105 Lambert Company
PO Box 740
Chillicothe, MO 64601-0740
    660-646-2150
    Fax: 660-646-2152 800-821-7667
Manufacturer and exporter of work gloves and headwear
President: James Lambert
CFO: James Lambert
Estimated Sales: $5-10 Million
Number Employees: 6
Type of Packaging: Consumer, Food Service, Private Label

25106 (HQ)Lambert Material Handling
6581 Townline Rd
Syracuse, NY 13206-1175
    315-471-5103
    Fax: 315-478-2804 800-253-5103
Palletizers and conveyor systems
Purchasing: Wendy Lewke
Number Employees: 10-19
Type of Packaging: Consumer
Other Locations:
    Lambert Material Handling
    Baldwinsville NY

25107 Lambertson Industries Inc
1335 Alexandria Ct
Sparks, NV 89434-9597
    775-857-1100
    Fax: 775-857-3289 800-548-3324
sales@lamberston.com
Stainless steel manufacturing
Owner: Jason Weiss
Marketing Director: Justin Pecot
Sales Manager: Ken Hewson
jasonweiss@lamberston.com
Operations Manager: Joseph McCaslin
Production Manager: Oswaldo Garcia
Estimated Sales: $1.5-3,500,000
Number Employees: 20-49
Square Footage: 60000

Brands:
    L.I. Industries

25108 Lambeth Band Corporation
PO Box 50490
New Bedford, MA 02745-0017
    508-984-4700
    Fax: 508-984-4780
Manufacturer and exporter of belting including nylon and urethane elastic bands.
President: Braley Gray
CEO: Lisa Larsen
Estimated Sales: $3-5 Million
Number Employees: 5-9
Square Footage: 14000
Brands:
    Lambeth Band

25109 Lamco Chemical Co Inc
212 Arlington St
Chelsea, MA 02150-2305
    617-884-8470
    Fax: 617-889-4207
Floor wax and cleaner
President: Jim Lam
bonnetto@aol.com
Estimated Sales: $1-3 Million
Number Employees: 1-4

25110 Lamcor
8025 South Willow Street
Unit 109
Minneapolis, NH 3103
    603-647-6386
    Fax: 603-647-6388 info@Lamcor.com
    www.lamcor.com
Tea and coffee industry packaging materials
Estimated Sales: $5-10 Million
Number Employees: 45

25111 Lamcraft Inc
4131 NE Port Dr
Lees Summit, MO 64064-1671
    816-795-5505
    Fax: 816-795-8310 800-821-1333
customer-service@lamcraft.com
    www.lamcraft.com
Laminating equipment and supplies including plastic laminates; also, plastic and paper laminating services for menus, price lists, recipe cards, table tents, etc
Owner: Bob Sabin
rsabin@lamcraft.com
Finance Executive: Darlene Rose
Estimated Sales: $10-20 Million
Number Employees: 10-19

25112 Laminated Paper Products
14491 Wyrick Ave
San Jose, CA 95124-3533
    408-888-0880
Folding cartons
Owner: P Drake
pdrake@laminatedpaperproducts.com
Estimated Sales: less than $500,000
Number Employees: 1-4

25113 Laminated Papers
PO Box 351
Holyoke, MA 01041-0351
    413-533-3906
    Fax: 413-533-2709
Laminated waterproof paper
President: Bernard Adams
Estimated Sales: $20-50 Million
Number Employees: 50-99

25114 Laminating TechnologiesInc
291 N Industrial Way
Canton, GA 30115-8218
    770-345-7144
    Fax: 770-345-7133 866-704-9992
pstoker@bakenship.com www.bakenship.com
Containers for hot and cold food products
Owner: Pat Haddon
phaddon@pkgatl.com
Estimated Sales: $1-5 Million
Number Employees: 20-49

25115 Laminations
3010 E Venture Dr
Appleton, WI 54911-8309

920-831-0596
Fax: 920-831-0612 800-925-2626
webgnc@greatnortherncorp.com
www.laminationsonline.com
Uboard edge protectors
President: Jeff Strenger
Estimated Sales: $10-20 Million
Number Employees: 50-99

25116 Lamitech West
115 Post Street
Santa Cruz, CA 95060

831-425-6625
Fax: 831-425-6627 TPocock@lamitech.com
www.lamitech.com
Manufacturer of paperboard products for food packaging, printing products, custom laminating and other converting services.
Vice President, General Manager: Adam Reiser
Senior Sales Representative: Tim Pocok
Number Employees: 1-4

25117 Lamports Filter Media
777 E 82nd St
Cleveland, OH 44103-1817

216-881-2050
Fax: 216-881-8957 info@lamports.com
www.lamports.com
Manufacturer and exporter of fabricated textiles for air and liquid filtration
President: Walter Senney
Contact: Jennifer Geraci
jennifer.geraci@lamports.com
Estimated Sales: $5-10 Million
Number Employees: 20-49
Square Footage: 120000

25118 Lampson Tractor Equipment
P.O.Box 85
Geyserville, CA 95441-0085

707-967-3554
Fax: 707-967-3575 jmarcust@sbcglobal.net
Power equipment
Manager: Mark Terrell
Estimated Sales: $5-10 Million
Number Employees: 10-19

25119 Lamson & Goodnow
45 Conway St
Shelburne Falls, MA 01370-1420

413-625-6331
Fax: 413-625-9816 800-872-6564
info@lamsonsharp.com
www.lamsonandgoodnow.com
Manufacturer and exporter of culinary knives including butchers' cleavers, bread, cheese and steak
President: Jim Pelletier
jpelletier@lamsonsharp.com
CFO: David Dunn
Marketing: Kurt Saunders
Sales Manager: Kurt Zanner
Plant Manager: Fran Gipe
Estimated Sales: $10-20 Million
Number Employees: 20-49
Type of Packaging: Consumer, Food Service, Private Label, Bulk
Brands:
  Lamson
  Lamson Sharp

25120 Lancaster Colony Corporation
380 Polaris Parkway
Suite 400
Westerville, OH 43082

614-224-7141
www.lancastercolony.com
Amenities including glassware, ice and food molds, iced tea dispensers, wood grain serving trays, ice buckets, aluminum cookware and commercial coffee urns, candles and matting. Foodservice products include frozen appetizers, dips, andsalad dressings.
Executive Chairman: John Gerlach
President & CEO: David Ciesinki
Vice President/CFO: Thomas Pigott
General Counsel/Chief Ethics Officer: Matthew Shurte
Vice President, Investor Relations: Dale Ganobsik
Year Founded: 1969
Estimated Sales: $1.13 Billion
Number Employees: 500-1000
Type of Packaging: Consumer, Food Service, Bulk

Brands:
  Marzetti
  Sister Schubert's
  New York Bakery
  Flatout

25121 Lancaster Laboratories
PO Box 12425
Lancaster, PA 17605

717-656-2300
Fax: 717-656-2681 env@lancasterlabs.com
www.lancasterlabs.com
Analytical laboratory providing comprehensive sanitation and pollution testing, microbiology, method development and validation/quality control services
President: J Wilson Hershey
Manager: Art Pezzica
Directory Contact: Anne Osborn
Contact: Kathy Agosto
kagosto@lancasterlabs.com
Estimated Sales: $20-50 Million
Number Employees: 500-999
Square Footage: 175000

25122 Lancer Corp
100 N Gary Ave
Cuite C
Roselle, IL 60172

847-524-1707
Fax: 847-524-1710 877-814-2271
www.lancercorp.com
Beverage dispensing equipment.
Type of Packaging: Food Service
Other Locations:
  Lancer Corp.
  Beverley

25123 (HQ)Lancer Corp
6655 Lancer Blvd
San Antonio, TX 78219

Fax: 210-310-7250 888-676-5196
generalinfo@lancercorp.com www.lancercorp.com
Beverage dispensing equipment.
President: Wayne Degon
Buyer/Planner: Gerry Law, Jr.
Estimated Sales: $113 Million
Number Employees: 1,500

25124 Landau Uniforms Inc
8410 W Sandidge Rd
Olive Branch, MS 38654-3412

662-895-7200
Fax: 662-895-5099 800-238-7513
Manufacturer, importer and exporter of aprons, shirts and fast-food uniforms
President: Nat Landau
CEO: Bruce Landau
CFO: Nancy Russell
nrussell@landau.com
Vice President: Gregg Landau
Quality Control: Dale Scott
Estimated Sales: $20-50 Million
Number Employees: 250-499
Type of Packaging: Food Service
Brands:
  Landau

25125 Landen Strapping
5050 Prince George Dr
Prince George, VA 23875-2623

804-452-2005
Fax: 804-722-1652 landenservice@gmail.com
plasticstrappingmachines.com
Owner: Margaret Spencer
margaret.spencer@strapmc.com
Number Employees: 20-49

25126 Landis Plastics
5750 W 118th St
Alsip, IL 60803-6012

708-396-1470
Fax: 708-824-3722
Manufacturer and exporter of injected molded plastic packaging supplies including can lids, jar caps, containers, scoops and pails; exporter of containers and lids
Manager: H R Landis
Vice President: Jennifer Bjerga
Purchasing: Tim Brenner
Estimated Sales: $50-100 Million
Number Employees: 300
Square Footage: 102063
Parent Co: Berry Plastics Group, Inc.

25127 Landmark Kitchen Design
1900 W Chandler Blvd # 15-373
Chandler, AZ 85224-6217

602-443-0344
Fax: 623-846-6877 866-621-3192
sean@landmarkphx.com www.landmarkphx.com
Principal: Sean Kellenbarger
Vice President: Sean Kellenbarger
VP R&D: John Andrews
Project Coordinator: Sean P Kellenbarger
Estimated Sales: Below $5 Million
Number Employees: 1-4

25128 Landoll Corp
1900 North St
Marysville, KS 66508-1271

785-562-5381
Fax: 785-562-4891 mhpsales@landoll.com
Manufacturer and exporter of articulated front-wheel steered forklifts and electric forklift trucks for narrow aisle storage applications
Owner: Don Landoll
CEO: Ron Otten
CFO: Dan Caffrry
R&D: Dave Kongs
Quality Control: Henk Crucker
Sales Director: Alan Laney
don.landoll@landoll.com
Estimated Sales: $30-50 Million
Number Employees: 500-999
Number of Brands: 2
Number of Products: 1
Square Footage: 350000
Type of Packaging: Bulk
Brands:
  Bendi
  Pivotmast

25129 Landoo Corporation
331 Maple Avenue
Horsham, PA 19044-2139

785-562-5381
Fax: 785-562-4853 kfox@drexeltrucks.com
Manufacturer and exporter of lift trucks
President: Jon Landoo
CFO: Dan Caffrey
Quality Control: Hank Burker
R & D: Dave Kongs
Marketing Supporting Manager: Jennifer Reynolds
VP Sales Manager: Kim Wanamaker
Export Sales Manager: Dave Pederson
Estimated Sales: $20-50 Million
Number Employees: 10
Square Footage: 65000

25130 Landsman Foodservice Net
2403 Logan Road
Owing Mills, MD 21117

410-363-7038
Fax: 301-330-4299
Employment agency/executive search firm specializing in selection and placement of food service industry personnel
President: Jeffrey Landsman
Estimated Sales: Less than $500,000
Number Employees: 4
Parent Co: Winston Franchise Corporation

25131 Lane Award Manufacturing
1118 S Central Ave
Phoenix, AZ 85004-2734

602-258-8505
Fax: 602-254-5489 800-843-2581
info@laneaward.com www.laneaward.com
Corporate and personal awards, business gifts, advertising and promotional items
President: John Luvisi
National Sales Manager: David Norgord
Contact: Victor Burnau
v.burnau@cox.net
General Manager: Mack Gleekel
Purchasing Manager: Mike Abril
Estimated Sales: Below $5 Million
Number Employees: 20-49
Square Footage: 80000

25132 Lang Manufacturing Co
6500 Merrill Creek Pkwy
Everett, WA 98203-5860

425-349-2400
Fax: 425-349-2733 800-882-6368
info@langworld.com www.langworld.com

Offer a quality line of innovative gas and electric commercial cooking equipment to the commercial, retail, marine, correctional, and government foodservice inductries
President: Dave Ek
CEO: Tracy Olson
Executive VP: Steve Hegge
Manager of Marketing: Annette Steinbach
Vice President of Sales and Marketing: Jim Baxter
Purchasing Manager: Mark Johnston
Estimated Sales: $20-50 Million
Number Employees: 5-9
Square Footage: 90000
Type of Packaging: Food Service
Brands:
   Pane Bella

25133 (HQ)Langen Packaging
6154 Kestrel Road
Mississauga, ON L5T 1Z2
Canada
905-670-7200
Fax: 905-670-5291 sales@langeninc.com
Manufacturer and exporter of packaging machinery and carton and case packers
President: Stuart Cooper
CFO: Alan Makhan
VP Marketing/Sales: Kevin Walsh
VP Engineering: Peter Guttinger
Purchasing Manager: Elinor Workman
Estimated Sales: $20-30 Million
Number Employees: 100
Square Footage: 80000

25134 (HQ)Langer Manufacturing Company
1025 7th Street SW
Cedar Rapids, IA 52404-1918
319-362-1481
Fax: 319-364-7131 800-728-6445
langermfg@aol.com
Manufacturer and exporter of wire products including milk bottle crates, bakery racks, partitioned cases, custom baskets and display racks
President: John R Langer
CEO: James M Langer
Sales: John Langer
Operations: James Langer
Estimated Sales: $2.5 Million
Number Employees: 20-49
Number of Products: 150
Square Footage: 80000

25135 Langer Manufacturing Company
1025 7th Street SW
Cedar Rapids, IA 52404-1918
319-362-1481
Fax: 319-364-7131 800-728-6445
Carriers, racks, P.O.P. displays
President: John R Langer
Estimated Sales: $2 Million
Number Employees: 55

25136 Langsenkamp Manufacturing
1699 South 8th St
Indianapolis, IN 46060
317-773-2100
Fax: 317-585-1715 877-585-1950
rogerm@warnerbodies.com
www.warnerbodies.com
Manufacturer and exporter of canning and food processing machinery including pumps, finishers, tanks, can openers and crushers, etc
President: Rick Manasek
Sales: Roger McNew
Controller: Bryan Lindsay
Estimated Sales: $2.5-5 Million
Number Employees: 18-25
Number of Brands: 1
Number of Products: 10
Square Footage: 62000

25137 (HQ)Langston Co Inc
1760 S 3rd St
Memphis, TN 38109-7712
901-774-4440
Fax: 901-942-5402 lango@bellsouth.net
www.langstonbag.com
Manufacturer and exporter of bags including burlap, produce and multi-wall paper
CEO: Robert Langston
CEO: Robert Langston
Production Manager: Steve Winston

Estimated Sales: $20-50 Million
Number Employees: 50-99

25138 Lanly Co
26201 Tungsten Rd
Cleveland, OH 44132-2997
216-731-1115
Fax: 216-731-7900 sales@lanly.com
www.lanly.com
Designs and builds custom heat processing equipment for an extensive range of industries.
President: Dennis Hill
mmarincic@lanly.com
Sales Exec: Martin F Marincic
Plant Manager: Tim Brooks
Estimated Sales: $5-10 Million
Number Employees: 20-49
Square Footage: 136000

25139 Lanly Co
26201 Tungsten Rd
Cleveland, OH 44132-2997
216-731-1115
Fax: 216-731-7900 lanly@lanly.com
www.lanly.com
Custom heat process equipment: dryers, ovens, material handling equipment and controls
VP: Dennis Hill
Sales Exec: Martin F Marincic
Plant Manager: Tim Brooks
Estimated Sales: $5-10 Million
Number Employees: 20-49

25140 Lanmar Inc
3160 Doolittle Dr
Northbrook, IL 60062-2409
847-564-5520
Fax: 847-564-4682 800-233-5520
ptfe@lanmarinc.com www.lanmarinc.com
PTFE tapes, PTFE fabrics, custom PTFE belts.
President: Martin Jacobs
ttfe@lanmarinc.com
Sales Director: Paul Siegal
Production: Logan Jacobs
Estimated Sales: $1-2.5 Million
Number Employees: 1-4
Type of Packaging: Food Service, Private Label

25141 Lansing Corrugated Products
16248 S Lowell Rd
Lansing, MI 48906-9324
517-323-2752
Fax: 517-323-9322
Corrugated and fiber boxes

25142 Lansmont Corp
17 Mandeville Ct
Monterey, CA 93940-5745
831-655-6600
Fax: 831-655-6606 sales@lansmont.com
www.lansmont.com
Shock, drop, field data recorders, vibration, compression, data acquisition systems.
President: Joe Driscoll
CFO: Patti Monahan
VP: Peter Brown
Vice President Marketing/Business Dvlpmt: Eric Joneson
Customer Support Manager: Eric Whitfield
Customer Support Specialist: Aaron Brown
Estimated Sales: $5-10 Million
Number Employees: 50-99

25143 Larco
210 10th Ave NE
Brainerd, MN 56401-2802
218-829-9797
Fax: 218-829-0139 800-523-6996
sales@larcomfg.com www.larco.com
Manufacturer and exporter of switch mats and controls for machine guarding safety
President: B Wilder
bwilder@mulberrymc.com
Sales Manager: Joe Schultz
Estimated Sales: $2.5-5 Million
Number Employees: 50-99
Parent Co: Acrometal Companies

25144 Larien Products
351 Pleasant St
PMB 224
Northampton, MA 01060
413-586-4000
Fax: 413-585-0101 800-462-9237
lsmith@larien.com www.larien.com
Larien is noted for a patented bagel slicing design that safely isolates the user from the slicing action. We manufacture a consumer model and a commercial model
President: Rick Ricard
CEO: Lois Smith
National Sales Manager: Jim Dodge
Operations: Elizabeth DiVito
Estimated Sales: $1 Million
Number Employees: 1-4
Number of Brands: 4
Number of Products: 4
Type of Packaging: Consumer, Food Service
Brands:
   Bagel Biter
   Bagel Butler
   Commerical Bagel Biter
   Original Bagel Guillotine
   Original Bigfoot Bottle Inversion

25145 Larkin Industries
114 David Green Rd
Birmingham, AL 35244-1648
205-987-1535
Fax: 205-987-0583 800-322-4036
www.larkinhoods.com
Ventilation systems including exhaust hoods and fans, supply fans, heated make-up air units, duct work and roof curbs
Owner: Larkin Strong
larkin.strong@larkinindustries.com
VP: Stephen Ridlespurge
Sales: Thomas Renfroe
Estimated Sales: $2.5-5 Million
Number Employees: 20-49
Square Footage: 80000

25146 Laros Equipment Co Inc
8278 Shaver Rd
Portage, MI 49024-5440
269-323-1441
Fax: 269-323-0456 laros@globalcrossing.net
www.laros.com
Manufacturer and exporter of conveyor systems
President: Tim Vanness
Estimated Sales: $10-20 Million
Number Employees: 20-49
Parent Co: George R. Laure Enterprises

25147 Larose & Fils Lte
2255 Industrial Boulevard
Laval, QC H7S 1P8
Canada
514-382-7000
Fax: 450-667-8515 877-382-7001
info@larose.ca www.larose.ca
Cleaning equipment and supplies including sweepers, pressure washers, germicides, disinfectants, drain openers, etc.; industrial floor polishers and waxstrippers; importer of vacuum cleaners
President: Jean Larose
CEO: Manon Larose
CFO: Richard Colerette
VP: Pierre Larose
Research & Development: Andr^ Foisy
Quality Control: Yves Lafrances
Marketing Director: France Morin
Sales Director: Andr^ Foisy
Public Relations: France Morin
Operations Manager: Manon Larose
Purchasing Manager: Anick Murray
Number Employees: 40
Square Footage: 120000
Parent Co: Labchem
Type of Packaging: Consumer, Food Service, Private Label
Brands:
   Indo
   Rare
   Sensas
   Sublime

25148 Larry B Newman Printing
2010 Middlebrook Pike
Knoxville, TN 37921-5842
865-524-1338
Fax: 865-524-1377 888-835-4566
info@larrynewmanprinting.com
larrynewmanprinting.com
Mounted and unmounted rubber stamps; also, engraved stationery
Owner: Larry Newman
larry@larrynewmanprinting.com
Manager: Brian McMillan
Estimated Sales: Less Than $500,000
Number Employees: 1-4
Square Footage: 21600
Type of Packaging: Consumer, Private Label, Bulk

25149 Larson Pallet Company
W4995 Bjorklund Rd
Ogema, WI 54459
715-767-5131
Fax: 715-767-5888
Pallets
President: Gerald Larson
Secretary: Gerald Larson
Estimated Sales: $1-2.5 Million
Number Employees: 20-49

25150 Laschober & Sovich Inc
20301 Ventura Blvd # 338
Suite 338
Woodland Hills, CA 91364-0949
818-713-9011
Fax: 818-713-1104 llanier@laschobersovich.com
www.laschobersovich.com
Consultant specializing in commercial kitchen design for quick serve restaurants, hotels and casinos, institutional facilities, prisons, hospitals, schools, etc
President: Larry Lanier
llanier@laschobersovich.com
VP, Global Ideation: Klaus Mager
Project Manager: Jonathan Turnbull
VP, Global Ideation: Joy Shelter
Business Development: Carolyn Nott
Estimated Sales: $1-3 Million
Number Employees: 5-9

25151 Lasco Composites
8015 Dixon Dr
Florence, KY 41042-2992
859-371-7720
Fax: 859-371-8466 kemlitesales@kemlite.com
www.kemlite.com
Composite fiberglass reinforced wall/ceiling panels
Executive VP, Business Development: Jim Simmons
Vice President Of Sales: Jack Stambaugh
Plant Manager: Jeff Rasmussen
Estimated Sales: $15-20 Million
Number Employees: 100-249

25152 Lasermation Inc
2629 N 15th St
Philadelphia, PA 19132-3904
215-228-7900
Fax: 215-225-1593 800-523-2759
www.lasermation.com
Manufacturer and exporter of brass and mylar stencils, awards, wine holders, pepper grinding mills and wooden back bar displays. Signs, executive gifts and awards
President: Joseph Molines
jmolines@lasermation.com
Estimated Sales: $1-3 Million
Number Employees: 10-19
Square Footage: 50000
Type of Packaging: Private Label

25153 Lasertechnics
80 Colonnade Rd
Nepean, OC K2E 7L2
613-749-4895
Fax: 613-749-8179
webinquiry@lightmachinery.com
CEO: Martin Janiak

25154 Lasertechnics Marking Corporation
80 Colonnade Road
Nepean, ON K2E 7L2
Canada
613-749-4895
Fax: 613-749-8179
webinquiry@lightmachinery.com

Manufacturer and exporter of laser code markers and date/code marking equipment
CEO: Martin Janiak
Sales/Marketing: Bob Michael
Director Sales Administration: Bob Baker
Estimated Sales: $2.5-5 Million
Number Employees: 20-49
Square Footage: 96000
Parent Co: Quantrad Sensor
Brands:
Blazer

25155 Lask Seating Company
3700 S Iron Street
Chicago, IL 60609-2118
773-254-3448
Fax; 773-254-1373 888-573-2846
stoolsandchairs@aol.com
Wooden and metal chairs, stools, tabletops and bases
CEO: David Prawer
CFO: Judith Friedman
R&D: Howia Prawer
Estimated Sales: $3-5 Million
Number Employees: 25
Square Footage: 168000

25156 Latendorf Corporation
PO Box 205
Brielle, NJ 08730-0205
732-528-0180
Fax: 732-528-6804 800-526-4057
Manufacturer, importer and exporter of bakery machinery
Owner: Malcolm Latendorf
Estimated Sales: $1-5 Million
Number Employees: 50-99
Square Footage: 120000

25157 Latendorf Corporation
PO Box 205
Brielle, NJ 08730-0205
732-528-0180
Fax: 732-528-6804
Conveyor systems
Estimated Sales: $10-25 Million
Number Employees: 73

25158 Laticrete International
91 Amity Rd
Bethany, CT 06524
203-393-0010
Fax: 203-393-1684 800-243-4788
support@laticrete.com www.laticrete.com
President: David Rothbert
CFO: Jim Walker
CEO: David Rothberg
R&D: Clodio Nicolini
Quality Control: Dilsa Hawkins
Contact: Steve Aflague
snaflague@laticrete.com
Estimated Sales: $50-100 Million
Number Employees: 100-249

25159 Latini Products Company
893 Industrial Drive
Elmhurst, IL 60126-1117
630-834-7789
Fax: 630-834-4322 www.latini-hohberger.com
Flat and ball lollipop machines, formers and wrapers
Director: Roger Hohberger
Estimated Sales: $3-5 Million
Number Employees: 10-19

25160 Latter Packaging Equipment
3206 W Jefferson Blvd
Los Angeles, CA 90018
323-737-0440
Fax: 323-737-4867 800-582-7711
info@latter.com www.latter.com
Modular shrink packaging systems including mini L-sealer shrink tunnel systems, one arm bar sealer systems, shrink band tunnels and conveyors and easy open shrink film tab system
President: Melvin Latter
CFO: Melvin Latter
R&D: Melvin Latter
Estimated Sales: $5-10 Million
Number Employees: 10-19

25161 Laub-Hunt Packaging Systems
13547 Excelsior Dr
Norwalk, CA 90650-5236
562-802-9591
Fax: 562-802-8183 888-671-9338
info@laubhunt.com www.laubhunt.com
Manufacturer and exporter of liquid fillers
Vice President: Jeff Hunt
info@laubhunt.com
Quality Control: E J Daniel
Vice President: Jeff Hunt
Marketing Director: Jean Pei
Estimated Sales: Below $5 Million
Number Employees: 5-9
Square Footage: 20000

25162 Laucks' Testing Laboratories
940 S Harney St
Seattle, WA 98108
206-767-5060
Fax: 206-767-5063
Laboratory providing nutrient labeling and chemical and microbiological analyses.and mainly testing labs
President: Mike Owens
Technical Director: Mike Nelson
CFO: Jeff Owens
Chairman: James Owens
Lab Director: Kathy Kreps
Marketing/Sales: Mike Owens
Sr. Project Manager: Hugh Prentice
Estimated Sales: $5-10 Million
Number Employees: 55
Square Footage: 75000

25163 Laughlin Sales Corp
3618 N Grove St
Fort Worth, TX 76106-4466
817-625-7756
Fax: 817-625-0687 www.laughlinconveyor.com
Manufacturer and exporter of conveyor systems including metal belt, chain, vibrating, magnetic, roller, etc.; also, custom designing available
President: Matt Laughlin Jr
VP Engineering/Manufacturing: David Laughlin
Sales Manager: Gene Fields
Estimated Sales: $1-2.5 Million
Number Employees: 1-4
Square Footage: 200000

25164 Lauhoff Corporation
241 Chene St
Detroit, MI 48207
313-259-0027
Fax: 313-259-2652 lauhoff@concentric.net
Cereal flaking mills and cookers, lab equipment and special process machinery
CEO: George H Lauhoff
President: Charles Lauhoff
VP: Greg Brecht
Estimated Sales: $20-30 Million
Number Employees: 10-19
Square Footage: 20000

25165 Laundry Aids
602 Washington Ave # A
Carlstadt, NJ 07072-2902
201-933-3500
Fax: 201-933-5193
Cleaning supplies including ammonia, fabric softener and laundry and dish detergent; contract packager of liquids in plastic bottles
President: R A Yaffa
VP Sales: Ved Sing
Purchasing Agent: Lou Gagliano
Estimated Sales: $40-60 Million
Number Employees: 250-499
Square Footage: 200000
Brands:
Fast'n Easy
Sea Mist

25166 Laundrylux
461 Doughty Blvd
Inwood, NY 11096-1344
516-371-4400
Fax: 516-371-4029 800-645-2205
info@laundrylux.com www.laundrylux.com
Commercial front load washers, dryers and dry cleaning equipment
Owner: Neil Milch
nmilch@laundrylux.com
Estimated Sales: $9 Million
Number Employees: 50-99
Square Footage: 80000

25167 Laurel Awning Co
1573 Hancock Ave
Apollo, PA 15613-8404
724-567-5689
Fax: 724-568-3152 888-567-5689
sales@laurelawnings.com www.laurelawnings.com
Commercial awnings
President: Greg Schmieler
sales@laurelawnings.com
Co-Ownr.: Bonnie Schuster
Estimated Sales: $2.5-5 Million
Number Employees: 10-19

25168 Lauritzen Makin Inc
101 W Felix St
Fort Worth, TX 76115
817-921-0218
Fax: 817-921-3963 www.lmakin.com
www.lmakin.com
Custom restaurant fixtures, bars, hostess stands,
serving lines, benches, stations, cabinets and table
tops
President: J Hatcher James Iii
VP: Bruce Barker
Marketing/Sales Director: Georgia Clarke
General Manager: Robin Irvine
Estimated Sales: $1-2.5 Million
Number Employees: 10-19
Parent Co: Liberty Company

25169 Laval Paper Box
118 Hymus
Pointe Claire, QC H9R 1E8
Canada
450-669-3551
Fax: 514-694-5636
Manufacturer and exporter of cardboard boxes
President: Frank Carbone
Number Employees: 200
Type of Packaging: Bulk

25170 Lavazza Premium Coffees
3 Park Ave # 35
New York, NY 10016-5902
212-725-9196
Fax: 212-725-9475 info@lavazza.it
www.lavazza.com
Manufacturer and importer of Italian coffee and
espresso machines
VP: Ennio Ranaboldo
Contact: Bidya Alie
balie@sovrana.com
Estimated Sales: $10-20 Million
Number Employees: 20-49
Parent Co: LaVazza Premium Coffee
Type of Packaging: Consumer, Food Service

25171 Lavi Industries
27810 Avenue Hopkins
Valencia, CA 91355-3409
661-257-7809
Fax: 661-257-4938 800-624-6225
sales@lavi.com www.lavi.com
Manufacturers of Architectural Metals, Public Guid-
ance Systems,Hospitality Fixtures, Traditional Porta-
ble Post for Hospitality, Rope Ends & Snaps, Beltrac
Series in many lengths, colors and widths, Sign
Frames, Graphics, Sneeze GuardsStemware Racks,
Bellman Carts, Trucks, Specialty Hardware Products
and much more
President: Gavriel Lavi
gavriel@lavi.com
Director Sales: Edward Bradford
Estimated Sales: $20-50 Million
Number Employees: 100-249
Square Footage: 75000
Type of Packaging: Food Service
Brands:
 Beltrac

25172 Lavo Company
4829 W Mill Rd
Milwaukee, WI 53218-1407
414-353-2140
Fax: 414-353-4917
Distributor of liquid soap; also, liquid and paste
floor polish
Manager: Wendy Maus
Estimated Sales: $1-2.5 Million
Number Employees: 1-4
Parent Co: Palmer

25173 Lawless Link
7215 Westboro Pl # 100
San Antonio, TX 78229-4178
210-342-8899
Fax: 210-342-8844 lawlessgrp@aol.com
Recruiter specializing in nationwide placement of
mid-level and executive personnel for the food
industry
President: Kathleen Lawless
CEO: John Lawless
CFO: J P Lawless
Manager: J Lawless
lawlessgrp@aol.com
Estimated Sales: Less Than $500,000
Number Employees: 5-9

25174 Lawrence Equipment Inc
2034 Peck Rd
South El Monte, CA 91733-3727
626-442-2894
Fax: 626-350-5181 800-423-4500
www.lawrenceequipment.com
Manufacturer and exporter of food processing ma-
chinery including corn and flour tortilla systems,
corn based snack lines and pizza forming lines; im-
porter of dough processing equipment
President: John Lawrence
johnlawrence@lawrenceequipment.com
Vice President: Glenn Shelton
International Sales: Dan Woodward
Estimated Sales: $10-20 Million
Number Employees: 100-249
Square Footage: 172000

25175 Lawrence Fabric Structures
3509 Tree Court Industrial Blv
St Louis, MO 63122-6619
636-861-0100
Fax: 636-861-0100 800-527-3840
sales@lawrencefabric.com
www.lawrencefabric.com
Commercial awnings and canopies
President: Mike Bowman
Vice President: Jerry Grimand
Plant Manager: John Hinckley
Purchasing Manager: Matt Roslawski
Estimated Sales: Less Than $500,000
Number Employees: 50-99

25176 Lawrence Glaser Associates
505 S Lenola Rd Ste 202
Moorestown, NJ 8057
856-778-9500
Fax: 856-778-4390
Executive search firm specializing in the selection of
sales and marketing managers
President: Lawrence Glaser
Estimated Sales: Less than $500,000
Number Employees: 5-9
Square Footage: 2000

25177 Lawrence Metal ProductsInc
260 Spur Dr S
Bay Shore, NY 11706-3900
631-666-0300
Fax: 631-666-0336 800-441-0019
info@lawrencemetal.com www.tensatorgroup.com
Manufacturer and exporter of brass, chrome and
stainless steel bar railings; also, glass racks, food
shields and crowd control
President: David Lawrence
CEO: Jeremy Williman
Marketing: Suzanne De Angelo
Director Sales/Marketing: Betty Castro
Estimated Sales: $10-20 Million
Number Employees: 100-249
Square Footage: 160000
Brands:
 Lawrence
 Tensabarrier

25178 (HQ)Lawrence Paper Co
2801 Lakeview Rd
Lawrence, KS 66049-8950
785-843-8111
Fax: 785-749-3904 sales@lpco.net
www.lpco.co
Corrugated boxes
President: Ann Gardner
agardner@ljworld.com
Sales Manager: Mike Sullivan
Estimated Sales: $20-50 Million
Number Employees: 100-249
Square Footage: 230000

25179 Lawrence Schiff Silk Mills
31 W. 34th Street
Suite 7002
New York, NY 10001
212-679-2185
Fax: 212-696-4565 800-272-4433
Manufacturer and exporter of ribbons, tapes, bind-
ings, webbings and trims
President/CEO: Richard J. Schiff
CFO: Bruce Ershler
VP Sales/Marketing: Nancy Sherman
Estimated Sales: $5-10 Million
Number Employees: 10-19

25180 Lawrence Sign
945 Pierce Butler Rte
St Paul, MN 55104-1595
651-488-6711
Fax: 651-488-6715 800-998-8901
info@lawrencesign.com
Signs and advertising displays
CEO: Rob Walker
rwalker@lawrencesign.com
CFO: Susan Joos
Sr. Vice President of Sales: Steve Hirtz
General Manager: Shannon King
Vice President of Sales & Marketing: Chuck Hesse
Office Manager: Brenda Aschoff
Production Manager: Joe Longtin
Estimated Sales: $2.5-5 Million
Number Employees: 20-49

25181 Lawrence-Allen Group
2031 Fairmont Drive
San Mateo, CA 94402-3925
650-345-2909
800-609-2909
info@nutrilabel.com
Consultant specializing in food product nutrition
analysis and services for food processors and the
food service market
Food Technologist: Karen Stiles
Estimated Sales: Below $500,000
Number Employees: 1

25182 Lawson Industries
1320 NW US Highway 50
Holden, MO 64040-9497
816-732-4347
www.lawsonindustries.com
Crates and pallets
Owner: Sergio Gonzalez
sergio.gonzalez@lawsonindustries.com
Estimated Sales: Less Than $500,000
Number Employees: 1-4

25183 Laydon Company
PO Box 69
Brown City, MI 48416-0069
810-346-2952
Fax: 810-346-2900 laydonco@greatlakes.net
Manufacturer and exporter of precision custom plas-
tic injection molding including long and short run
VP: Sandy Fuller
Sales Manager: Connie Dixon
Estimated Sales: $10-20 Million
Number Employees: 50-99
Square Footage: 70000

25184 Layflat Products
901 Tatum St
Shreveport, LA 71107
318-222-6141
Fax: 318-424-2949 800-551-8515
Manufacturer and exporter of screw-type wet mops,
mop heads and handles
Owner: James Beadles
National Sales Manager: Bill Hill
Director Operations: Steve Williams
Estimated Sales: $3-5 Million
Number Employees: 20-49
Square Footage: 50000
Type of Packaging: Consumer, Food Service, Pri-
vate Label
Brands:
 Layflat

25185 Lazer Images Instant Signs
33664 5 Mile Rd
Livonia, MI 48154-2866
734-427-4141
Fax: 734-427-4497 800-875-7446
www.lazerimages.com

P.O.P. sign making equipment including custom signage onto blank or pre-printed stock banners
Owner: Chris Crews
chris@lazerimages.com
Sales/Marketing: Chris Crews
Estimated Sales: Less Than $500,000
Number Employees: 1-4

25186 Lazy Man Inc
560 Independence St # 100
Belvidere, NJ 07823-2028
908-475-5315
Fax: 908-475-3165 800-475-1950
www.lazyman.com
Commercial and domestic gas-fired barbecue equipment and cast iron burners for urns, steam tables, water heaters, hot dog carts, etc
President: G D Mc Glaughlin
CEO: D Nawrocki
Sales Manager: G Williams
Marketing Director: Garland Williams
Sales Director: Garland Williams
Contact: Brian Haun
brian@lazyman.com
Estimated Sales: Below $5 Million
Number Employees: 10-19
Square Footage: 40000
Brands:
  Ccc Burners
  Lazy-Man
  Minute Glow

25187 Lazzari Fuel Co LLC
11 Industrial Way
Brisbane, CA 94005-1001
415-467-2970
Fax: 415-468-2298 800-242-7265
info@Lazzari.com www.lazzari.com
Mesquite lump charcoal and wood chips; importer and exporter of mesquite lump charcoal
Owner: Robert Colbert
CEO: Richard Morgan
Estimated Sales: $1-3 Million
Number Employees: 10-19
Square Footage: 74000
Type of Packaging: Consumer, Food Service, Private Label, Bulk
Brands:
  Lazzari

25188 Le Fiell Co
5601 Echo Ave
Reno, NV 89506-3207
402-592-9993
Fax: 402-592-7776 meatsys@lefiellco.com
www.lefiellco.com
Manufacturer and exporter of conveyors, meat packing and slaughter house machinery, trolley and trucks, meat house, engineering and overhead track switches, hide pullers and dehairers and restrainers for custom installation
Owner: Joe Gonzales
j.gonzales@lefiellco.com
CEO: Brandon Camp
COO: Joe Gonzales
Plant Manager: Dave Gomes
Estimated Sales: $2.5 Million
Number Employees: 20-49
Square Footage: 100000
Brands:
  Le Fiell

25189 Le Fiell Co
5601 Echo Ave
Reno, NV 89506-3207
402-592-9993
Fax: 402-592-7776 meatsys@lefiellco.com
www.lefiellco.com
Owner: Brandon Camp
bcamp@lefiellco.com
Senior Vice President/Co-Owner: Kathlene M. Schmidt
Estimated Sales: $5-10 Million
Number Employees: 20-49

25190 (HQ)Le Jo Enterprises
765 Pike Springs Rd
Phoenixville, PA 19460-4743
484-924-9187
Fax: 484-921-9009 www.lejo.com
Manual food preparation machines, grill maintenance tools, safety table lamps and chafing fuel

President: Deirdre D'Ambro
deirdre@lejo.com
CFO: Lauras Hasan
Quality Control: Rudy Sciubba
VP Sales: Jack Kelly
Estimated Sales: $20-50 Million
Number Employees: 20-49
Other Locations:
  Le-Jo Enterprises
  Malvern PA
Brands:
  Diablo
  Dine Aglow

25191 Le Smoker
321 Park Avenue
Salisbury, MD 21801-4208
410-677-3233
Fax: 410-677-3234
Stainless steel smokers, fire place, grills, wood chips, chunks and charcoal; exporter of smokers
President: Richard Isaacs
VP: Dominique Isaacs
Number of Brands: 3
Square Footage: 12000
Type of Packaging: Food Service
Brands:
  Le Smoker

25192 (HQ)Le Sueur Cheese Co
719 N Main St
Le Sueur, MN 56058-1404
507-665-3353
Fax: 507-665-2820 800-757-7611
info@daviscofoods.com www.daviscofoods.com
Variety of cheese including low-fat, no-fat, enzyme-modified cheeses and other customer specified varieties
President: Mark Davis
Vice President: Jim Ward
Manager: Mitch Davis
mitch.davis@daviscofoods.com
Production Manager: Roger Schroder
Purchasing Manager: Gregory Bush
Estimated Sales: $14.90
Number Employees: 100-249
Square Footage: 12000
Parent Co: Davisco Foods International, Inc.
Other Locations:
  Le Sueur Cheese Plant
  Jerome ID

25193 Leader Corporation
3205 Bishop Dr 105
Arlington, TX 76010
817-640-4610
Fax: 817-649-4182
Estimated Sales: $3-5 Million
Number Employees: 10-19

25194 Leader Engineering-Fab Inc
695 Independence Dr
PO Box 670
Napoleon, OH 43545-9191
419-592-0008
Fax: 419-592-0340 leadengr@bright.net
www.lefusa.com
Filling systems, peelers, peel eliminators and can unscramblers; also, custom design and fabrication available
President: Charles B Leader Jr
CFO: Charles B Leader Jr
Vice President: John Cichocki
jcichocki@lefusa.com
R&D: Charles B Leader Jr
Quality Control: Charles B Leader Jr
Plant Manager: John Hill
Estimated Sales: $5-10 Million
Number Employees: 20-49
Square Footage: 48000
Brands:
  Leader/Fox

25195 Leal True Form Corporation
248 Buffalo Ave
Freeport, NY 11520
516-379-2008
Fax: 516-623-8011 franklintoribio@aol.com
Vacuum formed blisters and trays
Owner: Arnulfo Toribio
Estimated Sales: $1-2.5 Million
Number Employees: 10-19

25196 Leaman Container
5701 E Rosedale St # A
Fort Worth, TX 76112-7732
817-429-2660
Fax: 817-429-2839
customerservice@leamancontainer.com
www.leamancontainer.com
Corrugated boxes
Owner: Steve Leaman
sleaman@leamancontainer.com
VP Marketing: Perry Haynes
Estimated Sales: $20-50 Million
Number Employees: 20-49

25197 Lear Romec
PO Box 4014
Elyria, OH 44036
440-323-3211
Fax: 440-322-3378 chapman@craneaerospace.com
www.learromec.com
Pumps and fluid handling systems
President: Brendan Curran
Director Marketing: Seamus O'Brien
Number Employees: 100-249
Parent Co: Crane Company

25198 Least Cost FormulationsLTD
824 Timberlake Dr
Virginia Beach, VA 23464-3239
757-467-0954
Fax: 757-467-2947 sales@lcfltd.com
www.lcfltd.com
Manufacturer and exporter of material requirement planning and technical software for the blending industry
Owner: Robert Labudde
ral@lcfltd.com
VP Marketing: Joy LaBudde
Estimated Sales: $1 Million
Number Employees: 1-4
Brands:
  Least Cost Formulator
  Market Forecaster
  Qc Assistant
  Qc Database Manager

25199 (HQ)Leathertone
2040 Industrial Dr.
Findlay, OH 45840
419-429-0188
Fax: 419-425-2927 sales@leathertone.com
www.leathertone.com
Plastic labels and signs
President: James Rubenstein
VP: Howard Rubenstein
Estimated Sales: $2.5-5 Million
Number Employees: 10-19

25200 Leaves Pure Teas
1392 Lowrie Avenue
South San Francisco, CA 94080-6402
650-583-1157
Fax: 650-583-1163
Retail and wholesale premium teas in teabags and loose for grocery, food service and specialty retailers
Estimated Sales: $1-5 Million

25201 Leavitt & Parris Inc
256 Read St
Portland, ME 04103-3446
207-797-0100
Fax: 207-797-4194 800-833-6679
contact@leavittandparris.com
www.leavittandparris.com
Awnings; rental company of tents, chairs, tables, etc
President: John Hutchins
Estimated Sales: Below $5,000,000
Number Employees: 10-19

25202 Lebensmittel Consulting
10760 West County Road 18
Fostoria, OH 44830-9623
419-435-2774
Fax: 419-435-9139
Consultant offering laboratory, product development, process development, food testing and genetic engineering services
Owner: Richard Basel
basel1@bright.net
VP: Margaret Basel
Research & Development: Richard Basel
basel1@bright.net
Quality Control: Richard Basel
basel1@bright.net

Number Employees: 10
Square Footage: 20000

25203 Lechler Inc
445 Kautz Rd
St Charles, IL 60174-5301

630-377-6611
Fax: 630-377-6657 800-777-2926
karenberker@lechlerusa.com www.lechlerusa.com
We are one of the largest manufacturers of spray
nozzles, accessories and headers. We produce these
products in various alloys and plastics to serve a
wide variety of fluid applications. From tank wash-
ing nozzles and machines which canclean tanks of
all sizes to air atomizing nozzles which can coat
food or lubricate equipment to standard flat fan and
full cone nozzles which can wash food or mix fluids.
We have the spraying application products for the
food processing industry
President/CEO: Ralph Fish
CEO: Terry Hayden
terry@lechlerusa.com
Marketing/Sales: Karen Berker
Estimated Sales: $10-20,000,000
Number Employees: 50-99
Square Footage: 45000
Parent Co: Lechler GMBH
Brands:
   Lechler
   Spraco
   Tank Cleaning Systems

25204 Leclaire Packaging Corp
W1351 Elmwood Ave
Ixonia, WI 53036-9437

920-206-9902
Fax: 920-206-9904 stucl@aol.com
Corrugated containers and packaging materials
CEO: Daniel Steuber, Jr.
Vice President: James Steuber
Estimated Sales: Below $5 Million
Number Employees: 10-19
Number of Products: 3
Square Footage: 36000
Type of Packaging: Bulk

25205 Leclerc Foods USA
44 Park Drive
Montgomery, PA 17752-8534

570-547-6295
Fax: 570-547-6719 www.leclerc.com
Cookies, snack bars, crackers, cereals and chocolate
Contact: Tina Baier
tbaier@leclercfoods.com
Estimated Sales: $8.2 Million
Number Employees: 74

25206 Leco Plastic Inc
130 Gamewell St
Hackensack, NJ 07601-4230

201-343-3330
Fax: 201-343-0558 info@lecoplastics.com
www.lecosolar.com
Bag and bundle tie, pack handles, die cutting, plastic
ties
Owner: Barry Schwartz
barry.schwartz@lecoplastics.com
Production: Burton Schwartz
Estimated Sales: $1-2.5 Million
Number Employees: 10-19
Square Footage: 28000
Type of Packaging: Bulk

25207 Lee Engineering Company
505 Narragansett Park Drive
Pawtucket, RI 02861-1970

401-725-6100
Fax: 401-728-7840 sales@lee-presto.com
Material handling equipment including pallet stack-
ers and scissor and dock lifts
CEO/President: Bill Sample
Estimated Sales: $10,000,000-$25,000,000
Number Employees: 100-249
Parent Co: Long Reach Holdings

25208 Lee Financial Corporation
8350 N. Central Expressway
Suite 1800
Dallas, TX 75206

972-960-1001
Fax: 972-404-1123 Info@Leefin.com
www.leefin.com
Manufacturer and exporter of corn cutters, pea
shellers and electric nutcrackers

President: Dana Pingenot
CEO & Founder: Richard Lee
CFO: Blake Decker
VP: Teresa Quinn
Contact: Rebecca Anderson
randerson@leefin.com
COO & Director of Human Resources: Jeff Ramsey
Estimated Sales: Below $5 Million
Number Employees: 20-49
Square Footage: 14000

25209 Lee Industries
50 W Pine St
Philipsburg, PA 16866

814-342-0461
Fax: 814-342-5660 www.leeind.com
Custom sanitary process equipment.
President/CFO/COO: Joshua Montler
Chairman & CEO: Robert Montler
rmontler@leeind.com
Vice President, Sales: Gregory Wharton
Year Founded: 1924
Estimated Sales: $100-500 Million
Number Employees: 100-249

25210 Lee Products Co
800 E 80th St
Minneapolis, MN 55420-1396

952-300-2908
Fax: 952-854-7177 info@leeproducts.com
www.leeproducts.com
Hand cleaning pads
President: John Houle
info@leeproducts.com
CFO: Rey Lee
Sales Exec: Faye Roy
Estimated Sales: $5-10 Million
Number Employees: 20-49

25211 Lee Soap Company
6620 E 49th Ave
Commerce City, CO 80022

303-289-9041
Fax: 303-289-9042 800-888-1896
orders@leesoap.com www.leesoap.com
Janitorial supplies including compounders, laundry
detergent and soap
Owner: Carl Kelley
Sales Manager: Jim Sumner
Contact: Dave Himmelberg
daveh@leesoap.com
Estimated Sales: $5-10 Million
Number Employees: 10-19

25212 Leedal Inc
3453 Commercial Ave
Northbrook, IL 60062-1818

847-498-0111
Fax: 847-498-0198 sink@leedal.com
www.consolidateddoorintl.com
Manufacturer, importer and exporter of pot and pan
washers, disposers, power scrubbers, wire shelfing,
hot dog cookers, and steam tables
President: Aj Levin
ajlevin@hotmail.com
CFO: Sheldon Levin
Vice President: A Levin
Quality Control: Levin
Sales Director: Josie Negron
Estimated Sales: $5-10 Million
Number Employees: 20-49
Square Footage: 28000
Type of Packaging: Consumer, Food Service, Pri-
vate Label, Bulk

25213 Leedal Inc
3453 Commercial Ave
Northbrook, IL 60062-1818

847-498-0111
Fax: 847-498-0198 www.consolidateddoorintl.com
Stainless steel equipment, custom fabrication, steam
tables, sinks, and tanks
President: Aj Levin
ajlevin@hotmail.com
Vice President: A Levin
Sales Director: Josie Negron
Estimated Sales: $10-20 Million
Number Employees: 20-49
Square Footage: 14000
Type of Packaging: Consumer, Food Service, Pri-
vate Label, Bulk

25214 Leeds Conveyor Manufacturer Company
PO Box 383
Guilford, CT 06437

203-453-5277
Fax: 203-453-6329 800-724-1088
www.leedsconveyor.com
Conveyor systems including chain and roller in mild
and stainless steel, belt conveyors and mesh chain in
metal and plastic; also, accumulators and unscram-
blers
President: Paul Nangle
CFO: Debbie Nancy Nangle
Manufacturing Manager: Sean LeTarte
Number Employees: 10
Square Footage: 64000

25215 Leeman Labs Inc
110 Lowell Rd
Hudson, NH 03051-4806

603-886-8400
Fax: 603-886-4322 800-634-9942
www.leemanlabs.com
Analytical instrumentation including coupled
plasma spectrometers, metal alloy, cyanide and mer-
cury analyzers and prep systems
CEO: John Leeman
Director Sales Marketing: Bill Driscoll
Contact: Ed Rau
leemanlabsinfo@teledyne.com
Director International Operations: Paul Maaskant
Estimated Sales: $10-20 Million
Number Employees: 5-9
Square Footage: 100000
Brands:
   A30
   Ap/Ps 1214
   Ap/Ps200 Ii
   Dre (Direct Reading Echelle Icp)
   Plasma-Pure

25216 Leer Inc
206 Leer St
New Lisbon, WI 53950-1163

608-562-3161
Fax: 608-562-6022 800-237-8350
info@leerlp.com www.leerinc.com
Manufacturer and exporter of self-service ice mer-
chandising equipment and block ice-makers
VP: Charlotte Maginnis
CEO and Owner and President: Steve Dolenzel
IT: Kevin Kracht
kkracht@leerlp.com
Estimated Sales: $500,000-$1 Million
Number Employees: 100-249
Square Footage: 320000
Parent Co: Leer Manufacturing Partner
Type of Packaging: Bulk
Other Locations:
   Star/Starrett
   Dumas AZ
Brands:
   Leer
   Star
   Starrett

25217 Legacy Plastics
1116 5th St
Henderson, KY 42420-2804

270-827-1318
Fax: 270-831-6510
SCourtney@LegacyPlastics.com
www.legacyplastics.com
A custom thermoplastic Profile extrusion company
offering products such as signage, price channels,
dividers, extrusions and plastic components made
from materials such as: styrene, acrylic, ABS, PVC,
polycarbonate, etc; as well asflexible tubing
products.
President: Roger Courtney
CEO: Doug Bray
CFO: John Brooks
Sales Director: Tom Simmering
Production Manager: Sharon Courtney
Purchasing Manager: Barb Claridge
Estimated Sales: $1.5 Million
Number Employees: 10-19
Number of Products: 100+
Square Footage: 40000
Parent Co: Display Specialties

25218 Legal Sea Foods
1 Seafood Way
Boston, MA 02210-2700
617-530-9000
Fax: 617-782-4479 www.legalseafoods.com
Restaurant chain and gourmet seafood gifts
President: Jason Ananda
jason.a.josephson@williams.edu
CFO: Mark Synott
Quality Control: Steve Martinello
Estimated Sales: $10-100 Million
Number Employees: 100-249

25219 Legge & Associates
PO Box 599
Rockwood, ON N0B 2K0
Canada
519-856-0444
Fax: 519-856-0555
Consultant specializing in the design of food service
and hospitality facilities
Principal: Scott Legge

25220 Leggett & Platt Inc
1 Leggett Road
Carthage, MO 64836-9649
417-358-8131
Fax: 417-358-5840 www.leggett.com
Manufacturer and exporter of store fixtures includ-
ing bakery showcases, cash register stands and
checkouts, bulk shelving and storage units and cus-
tom wood display equipment
President/Director/CEO: David Haffner
Chairman: Richard Fisher
Senior VP/Chief Financial Officer: Matthew
Flanigan
EVP/Chief Operating Officer: Karl Glassman
Director, Quality Assurance: Brad Richards
Marketing Manager: John Patrick
Director, Sales: Diane Holman
Operations Manager: Hal Gimmer
Plant Manager: Jim Winters
Director, Procurement: Jeff Mitchell
Estimated Sales: Over $1 Billion
Number Employees: 10000+
Square Footage: 15491
Parent Co: Reflector Hardware Corporation
Type of Packaging: Consumer, Food Service, Bulk
Other Locations:
Goer Manufacturing Co.
Union MO

25221 Leggett & Platt Storage
11230 Harland Drive
Vernon Hills, IL 60061-1547
847-816-6246
Fax: 847-968-3899 www.focuspg.com
Manufacturer and exporter of cabinets, racks, mobile
storage equipment, shelving, carts, servingware,
buffetware, utensils, utility trucks, dollies and
tote/bus boxes
President: Keith Jaffee
Number Employees: 10-19
Square Footage: 2000000
Parent Co: SPG International, LLC
Other Locations:
Leggett & Platt
Charlotte NC

25222 Legible Signs
2221 Nimtz Road
Loves Park, IL 61111-3928
815-654-7323
Fax: 815-654-9679 800-435-4177
Polyethylene safety signs, aluminum name plates,
custom decals and menu covers
Customer Service: Trina Bentley
Estimated Sales: $1-2.5 Million
Number Employees: 10-19

25223 Legion Industries Inc
370 Mills Rd
Waynesboro, GA 30830-5360
706-554-4411
Fax: 706-554-2035 800-887-1988
www.legionindustries.com
Food service equipment including steam equipment,
kettles, ovens and braising pans
Manager: Susan Riggs
CEO: Chuck Brown
cbrown@legionindustries.com
Estimated Sales: Below $5,000,000
Number Employees: 20-49
Square Footage: 5000

25224 Legion Lighting Co Inc
221 Glenmore Ave
Brooklyn, NY 11207-3307
718-498-1770
Fax: 718-498-0128 800-453-4466
sales@legionlighting.com
www.legionlighting.com
Manufacturer and exporter of architecturally engi-
neered fluorescent lighting equipment
President: Michael Bellovin
VP Sales: Michael Bellovin
Engineering: Wayne Cowell
Sales: Evan Bellovin
Accountant: Gia Carla Rodriguez
Estimated Sales: $5-10 Million
Number Employees: 50-99
Square Footage: 12000
Brands:
Circledome
Comfort-Lume
Compact Cube
Contempo
Corritempo
Drum-Plex
Excelon
Gemini
Legion-Aire
Lytegress
Mod-Plex
Mod-U-Beam
My-T-Lite
Panelume
Paralume
Prismalier
Securlume
Skylume
Teg-U-Lume
Trimlume
Vandalex
Vaportron

25225 Legumex Walker, Inc.
1345 Kenaston Blvd
Winnipeg, MB R6W 4B3
Canada
204-808-0448
Grains
Investor & Media Relations: Marin Landis

25226 Lehi Mills
833 E Main St
Lehi, UT 84043-2286
801-768-4401
Fax: 801-768-4557 877-311-3566
customerservice@lehirollermills.com
lehirollermills.com
Processor of flour, feed and meal; also, pancake
mixes, cookie mixes, brownie mixes, bread mixes
and preserves.
President: Sherman Robinson
COO: Brock Knight
Sales Exec: Steve DE John
sdejohn@lehirollermills.com
Year Founded: 1906
Estimated Sales: $20-50 Million
Number Employees: 20-49
Number of Brands: 3
Type of Packaging: Food Service, Private Label
Brands:
Lehi Roller Mills
Peacock
Turkey

25227 Lehigh Safety Shoe Co LLC
39 E Canal St
Nelsonville, OH 45764-1247
740-753-1951
Fax: 740-753-7240 866-442-5429
clientservices@lehighoutfitters.com
www.lehighsafetyshoes.com
Shoes including steel toe, nonsteel toe and nonslip
CEO: David Sharp
david.sharp@rockybrands.com
Number Employees: 50-99
Brands:
Lehigh

25228 Lehman Sales Associates
3025 Saddle Brook Trl
Sun Prairie, WI 53590
608-575-7712
Fax: 608-837-8421 bob@lehmanequip.com
Manufacturer and exporter of used and rebuilt food
processing and packaging equipment

President: Richard Lehman
Estimated Sales: $1-2.5 Million
Number Employees: 1-4

25229 Lehmann Mills Inc
11000 Youngstown Salem Rd
PO Box 1083
Salem, OH 44460-9654
330-332-9951
Fax: 330-332-2208 888-919-9494
info@lehmannmills.com www.lehmannmills.com
Three-roll horizontal mills, Three-roll vertical mills,
Technical field service Installation start-up and su-
pervision, Operator training and maintenance,Con-
sultation services,In-house CAD engineering,
Custom-designed upgrades, Problemsolving
capabilities
Owner: David Hrovatic
info@lehmannmills.com
Estimated Sales: $5-10 Million
Number Employees: 20-49

25230 Leibinger-USA
2702-B Buell Drive
East Troy, WI 53120
262-642-4030
Fax: 262-642-4033 info@leibinger-group.com
www.leibingerusa.com
A family owned business since 1948 and a premier
manufacturer of security, industrial and commerical
printing solutions, introduces the Jet2 Printer-the
only low maintenance continuous in jet (CIJ) printer
on the market today. The Jet2features a retractable
gutter which creates an air tight seal over the nozzle
eliminating ink from drying in the nozzle. This revolutionary design is far superior to traditional flush
nozzle systems.
President: Gunter Leibinger
Vice President: Steve Talbot
Sales Director: Alexander Deuchert
Number of Products: 3
Type of Packaging: Consumer, Food Service, Private Label, Bulk

25231 Leica Microsystems
3362 Walden Ave
Depew, NY 14043
716-686-3000
Fax: 716-686-3085 800-346-4560
analytical@leica-microsystems.com
Refractometers, microscopes and colony counters
Marketing Director: Thomas Ryan
Sales Director: Terry Grant
Contact: Ludger Althoff
ludger@leica-microsystems.com
Estimated Sales: $2.5-5 Million
Number Employees: 20-49
Parent Co: Leica AG
Brands:
Ar200
Ar600
Arias500
Auto Abbe
Brix 15hp
Brix 30
Brix 35hp
Brix 50
Brix 65hp
Brix 90
Brix 90hp
Leica
Mark Ii
Mark Ii Plus
Oe200

25232 Leichtman Ice Cream Company
175 N Vine St Apt 3b
Hazleton, PA 18201
570-454-2428
Fax: 570-454-2540 800-735-4379
Ice Cream Distributors
Estimated Sales: $5-10 000,000
Number Employees: 15

25233 Leidos Engineering
221 3rd St # A
Newport, RI 02840-1087
401-847-4210
Fax: 401-849-1585 800-729-4210
www.saic.com
Inventory and measurement services, package reduction consulting and customized data managment
software. Global environmental packaging services

President: Anthony Moraco
President, Chief Executive Officer: John Jumper
Executive Vice President of Human Resour: Brian Keenan
Chief Technical Officer: Amy Alving
Marketing: Janie Harris
Chief Operating Officer: Stuart Shea
IT: Roger Wells
roger.k.wells@saic.com
Estimated Sales: $10-20 Million
Number Employees: 50-99

25234 Leister/Heely-Brown Company

1139 Goodwin Rd NE
Atlanta, GA 30324-2715
404-846-0401
Fax: 404-350-2696 800-241-4628
info@heely-brown.com www.heely-brown.com
Hot air tools provide solutions for customers' packaging, shrinking, drying, heating, forming, staking,curing, plastic welding, prototyping, soldering and de-soldering and activating applications
Manager: Nancy Chambers
CFO: Michael Spencer
Estimated Sales: $20-50 Million
Number Employees: 1-4

25235 Leister/Malcom Company

207 High Point Avenue
Unit 7B
Portsmouth, RI 2871
401-683-3199
Fax: 401-683-3177 800-289-7505
www.malcom.com
Hot air equipment for various packaging applications including hand-held heat guns and pallet shrink guns to large process heaters
Chairman: George Bixby
President: Jonathan Bixby
Sales/Marketing Administrator: Sheila Carpenter
President: Jonathan Bixby
Sales/Technical Support: Mary Bass
Application Engineer: Steve Robertson
Chairman: George Bixby
Estimated Sales: $1-3 Million
Number Employees: 1-4

25236 Leister/Uneco Systems

8412 Autumn Drive
Woodridge, IL 60517
630-972-0500
Fax: 630-910-0558 800-700-6894
junewitz@att.net
Plastic weld, packaging, roofing, process heat, drying SMT electronics, Leister hot air tools and blowers
President: John A Unewitz
CFO: John A Unewitz
Sales Director: John Unewitz
Estimated Sales: $1-3 Million
Number Employees: 1-4
Brands:
  Leister Heat Guns

25237 Leland Limited Inc

2614 S Clinton Ave
South Plainfield, NJ 07080-1427
908-561-2000
Fax: 908-668-7716 sales@lelandltd.com
www.lelandgas.com
Manufacturer and exporter of food mixing equipment
Owner: Lee Stanford
lee@lelandgas.com
Engineer: P Bowlin
Customer Service: R Callaway
Estimated Sales: $5-10 Million
Number Employees: 10-19
Brands:
  Leland Southwest

25238 Leland Limited Inc

2614 S Clinton Ave
South Plainfield, NJ 07080-1427
908-561-2000
Fax: 908-668-7716 800-984-9793
sales@lelandltd.com www.lelandgas.com
Manufacturer, importer and exporter of whipped cream machinery and soda syphons
Owner: Lee Stanford
lee@lelandgas.com
Estimated Sales: $5,000,000
Number Employees: 10-19
Square Footage: 30000

Type of Packaging: Food Service
Brands:
  Leland
  Mr. Fizz

25239 Lematic Inc

2410 W Main St
Jackson, MI 49203-1099
517-787-3301
Fax: 517-782-1033 sales@lematic.com
www.auto-op.com
Manufacturer and exporter of bulk packaging, bagging machinery and dry pan cleaners; also, bakery equipment including garlic and French bread makers and slicers for buns, bagels, croissants, etc
Owner: Dale Lecrone
dlecrone@lematic.com
CEO: Dale LeCrone
Director Sales: George Arnold
dlecrone@lematic.com
Estimated Sales: $5-10 Million
Number Employees: 50-99
Square Footage: 60000

25240 Lengsfield Brothers

PO Box 50020
New Orleans, LA 70150-0020
504-529-2235
Fax: 504-524-9281
Manufacturer and exporter of candy boxes

25241 Lenkay Sani Products Corporation

473 Wortman Ave
Brooklyn, NY 11208
718-927-9260
Fax: 718-257-0461
Custom packaging
President: Frank Drayer
Estimated Sales: Below $5 Million
Number Employees: 5-9
Square Footage: 24000

25242 Lenox Corp

1414 Radcliffe St # 1
Bristol, PA 19007-5496
267-525-7800
Fax: 267-525-5618 800-223-4311
lenox@lenox.com www.lenox.com
Manufacturer and exporter of chinaware, stemware, silverplated holloware, crystal gifts and flatware including stainless and sterling
Owner: Walter S Lenox
walter.lenox@lenox.com
CFO: James Burwitt
Quality Control: Dave Summers
Number Employees: 1000-4999
Parent Co: Brown-Foreman
Type of Packaging: Food Service

25243 Lenox Locker Company

PO Box 317
Dunmore, PA 18512-0317
740-375-0730
Fax: 717-222-4141
Sanitation supplies and equipment

25244 Lenser Filtration

1750 Oak St
Lakewood, NJ 8701
732-370-1600
Fax: 732-370-8411 www.lenserusa.com
Polypropylene and other thermoplastic filter elements for use in solids and liquid seperation
Sales: Robert Iovino
Production: Tom Van Leet
tomvanleet@lenserusa.com
Estimated Sales: $5-10 Million
Number Employees: 20-49

25245 Lentia Enterprises Ltd.

17733-66th Ave
Surrey, BC V3S 7X1
Canada
604-576-8838
Fax: 604-576-1064 888-768-7368
Naturally fermented, dehydrated sourdoughs from both wheat and rye flours, specialty malted products such as whole malted rye kernels, aroma malts, colouring malts and clean label bread mixes.
President/Board Member: Karl Eibensteiner
Director: Gertrude Eibensteiner
Estimated Sales: $4.08 Million
Number Employees: 23

25246 Lentz Milling Co

2045 N 11th St
Reading, PA 19604-1201
610-921-0666
Fax: 610-929-3682 800-523-8132
www.lentzmilling.com
Owner: Ted Lentz
Sales/Accounts Supervisor: Jane Adams
tlentz@lentzmilling.com
Estimated Sales: $50-100 Million
Number Employees: 100-249

25247 Lenweaver Advertising

108 W Jefferson St Ste 300
Syracuse, NY 13202
315-422-8729

25248 Lenze Americas

630 Douglas St
Uxbridge, MA 01569
508-278-9100
Fax: 508-278-7873 800-217-9100
info.us@lenze.com www.lenze.com/en-us
Manufacturer of electrical and mechanical drives
President, Lenze Americas: Chuck Edwards
Estimated Sales: I
Number Employees: 1,000-4,999

25249 Leon Bush Manufacturer

1870 Elmdale Avenue
Glenview, IL 60026-1356
847-657-8888
Fax: 847-657-9710
Plastic injection molding for wedding cake plates and ornaments; also, industrial baking utensils and deli trays
Sales Manager: David Drew
Estimated Sales: $500,000-$1 Million
Number Employees: 5-9

25250 Leon C. Osborn Company

1020 Bay Area Blvd
Suite 120
Houston, TX 77289-0014
281-488-0755
Fax: 281-480-9739 dave@leoncosborn.com
www.leoncosborn.com
Washers for fresh pack pickles, brine stock, beets, potatoes, carrots, squash, and other vegetables
President: David S Osborn
Contact: Jim Degreif
jim@leoncosborn.com
Estimated Sales: $.5-1 million
Number Employees: 1-4

25251 Leotta Designers

800 Brickell Ave
Ste 602
Miami, FL 33131
305-371-4949
Fax: 305-371-2844 www.leottadesigners.com
Interior designer; services include space planning, corporate interior design, site selection and lease negotiation
President: Marc J Leotta
VP: J Kalbach
Estimated Sales: $500,000-$1 Million
Number Employees: 5-9

25252 Lepel Corp

W227n937 Westmound Dr # 2
Waukesha, WI 53186-1747
262-782-0450
Fax: 262-782-3299 800-231-6008
www.lepel.com
Process control systems features motion, linear, alignment and cap height detectors, along with idle control and Windows-compatible software for process control, induction cap sealing
Vice President: Al Peters
Sales Coordinator: Bonnie Leivenger
Manager: Bonnie Leitinger
bleitinger@lepel.com
Manager: Bonnie Leitinger
Estimated Sales: $2.5-5 Million
Number Employees: 1-4
Square Footage: 2500
Parent Co: Lepel Corporation
Brands:
  Cspiust Capsealing System
  Lepakjr Capsealing System

25253 Leprino Foods Co.
1830 W. 38th Ave.
Denver, CO 80211

303-480-2600
Fax: 303-480-2605 800-537-7466
www.leprinofoods.com
Mozzarella cheese, cheese blends, and pizza cheese
made especially for pizzeria and foodservice opera-
tors, frozen food manufacturers and private label
cheese packagers.
Chairman/CEO: James Leprino
CFO/SVP, Operations: Lance FitzSimmons
Year Founded: 1950
Estimated Sales: Over $1 Billion
Number Employees: 4,000+
Square Footage: 60000
Type of Packaging: Food Service, Bulk
Other Locations:
Leprino Foods
Allendale MI
Leprino Foods
Fort Morgan CO
Leprino Foods
Ravenna NE
Leprino Foods
Remus MI
Leprino Foods
Roswell NM
Leprino Foods
Waverly NY

25254 Lermer Packaging
202 Washington Avenue
Carlstadt, NJ 07072-3001

908-789-0900
Fax: 908-789-0235

Wine industry packaging
Estimated Sales: $10-20 Million
Number Employees: 20-49

25255 Leroy Signs, Inc.
6325 Welcome Ave N
Brooklyn Park, MN 55429

763-535-0080
Fax: 763-533-2593 info@leroysigns.com
www.leroysigns.com
Plastic and neon signs
Owner: Leroy Reiter
Contact: Andria Reiter
andria.reiter@leroysigns.com
Estimated Sales: $2.5-5 Million
Number Employees: 20-49

25256 Leroy's Restaurant Supply
1306 S Grant Ave
Odessa, TX 79761-6844

432-333-2621
Fax: 915-333-2621 reedbbq@aol.com
Wholesaler/distributor of new and used food service
equipment; serving the food service market
Owner: Audrianna Hinojosa
audrianna@wix.com
Estimated Sales: Less than $500,000
Number Employees: 5-9

25257 (HQ)Les Industries Touch Inc
4025 Lesage
Sherbrooke, QC J1L 2Z9
Canada

819-822-4140
Fax: 819-822-2904 800-267-4140
info@industriestouch.com
www.industriestouch.com
Manufacturer and exporter of toothpicks, skewers,
plastic cutlery, straws etc.
President: Gervais Morier
Sales Director: Gerald Bouchard
Operations Manager: Jean-Yves Blouin
Estimated Sales: $10-20 Million
Number Employees: 50-99
Number of Products: 300+
Square Footage: 90000
Type of Packaging: Consumer, Food Service, Pri-
vate Label, Bulk
Brands:
Touch

25258 Lesco Design & Mfg Co
1120 Fort Pickens Rd
La Grange, KY 40031-9396

502-222-7101
Fax: 502-222-5508 sales@lesco-design.com
www.lescodesign.com
Conveyor belts

President: Lance Kaufman
dkaufman@lescodesign.com
CFO: Steve Herald
VP: Lance Kaufman
VP Sales: Dick Wilder
Estimated Sales: $20-50 Million
Number Employees: 50-99
Square Footage: 115000

25259 Lester Box & Mfg Div
1470 Seabright Ave
Long Beach, CA 90813-1152

562-437-5123
Fax: 562-436-1437 sales@lesterbox.com
www.lesterbox.com
Manufacturer and exporter of wooden boxes and
crates, pallets, skids and foam inserts
Manager: Steve Amato
steve@lesterbox.com
Estimated Sales: $1-2.5 Million
Number Employees: 10-19
Square Footage: 60000

25260 Letica Corp
52585 Dequindre Rd
Rochester Hills, MI 48307-2321

248-652-0557
Fax: 248-608-2153 800-538-4221
www.letica.com
Manufacturer and exporter of plastic shipping con-
tainers, paper and plastic cups and containers for
cultured dairy products and freight lines
CEO: Ilija Letica
iletica@letica.com
CEO: Ilija Letica
Sales Director: David Bradwell
Public Relations: David Schueler
Estimated Sales: $5-10 Million
Number Employees: 1000-4999
Brands:
Letica
Maui Cup

25261 Letrah International Corp
W7603 Koshkonong Mounds Rd
Fort Atkinson, WI 53538-8709

920-563-6597
Fax: 920-563-7515 doughartel@gmail.com
www.hartelinternational.com
Manufacturer, importer and exporter of process con-
trol systems including blending, processing,
clean-in-place, refrigeration, level, load cell, meter-
ing, proportioning and packaging.
President: Douglas Hartel
doughartel@gmail.com
Estimated Sales: Less Than $500,000
Number Employees: 1-4
Square Footage: 5332

25262 Letraw Manufacturing Company
200 Quaker Rd
Box 2
Rockford, IL 61104

815-987-9670
Fax: 815-987-9830 rwartell@letraw.com
www.letraw.com
Cleaning supplies including metal scrubbers and
scouring cloths; importer of Mexican vanilla extract
Partner: Ralph Wartell
Estimated Sales: less than $500,000
Number Employees: 5
Square Footage: 8000
Type of Packaging: Consumer, Food Service

25263 Leuze-Lumiflex
55395 Lyon Industrial Drive
New Hudson, MI 48165-8545

973-586-0100
Fax: 973-586-1590 www.leuze-lumiflex.com
Opto-sensors and work safety products including bar
code readers, clear media detection sensors, clear
and opaque label detection sensors, cap orientation
detection sensors, fork sensors, luminescence sen-
sors, laser distance sensingdevices and safety li
President: Vincent Orrico
Contact: Ben Fifield
bfifield@leuzeusa.com
Estimated Sales: $20-50 Million
Number Employees: 300

25264 Levelmatic
1135 NW 159th Dr
Miami, FL 33169-5882

305-625-2451
Fax: 305-623-0475 800-762-7565
sales@atlasfoodserv.com www.atlasfoodserv.com
Self leveling dispensers for plates, bowls, racks,
trays, etc
President: David Meade
VP Sales: Howard Bolnar
VP Manufacturing: Mark Siegfriedt
Estimated Sales: $10-20 Million
Number Employees: 100-249
Parent Co: Atlas Metal Industries

25265 Levin Brothers Paper
1325 S Cicero Ave
Cicero, IL 60804

708-652-5600
Fax: 708-780-6975 800-545-6200
clutch@idt.net www.lbpmfg.com
Corrugated boxes, tape and packaging materials;
wholesaler/distributor of paper products and restau-
rant supplies
President: Barry Silverstein
CFO: Mike Schaechter
VP: Matthew Cook
Quality Control: Larry Rosenberg
Contact: Suliman Abdallah
abdallah@lbpmfg.com
Estimated Sales: $10-20 Million
Number Employees: 10-19
Square Footage: 250000
Brands:
Safe-Pack

25266 Lewco Inc
706 Lane St
Sandusky, OH 44870-3846

419-625-4014
Fax: 419-625-1247 sales@lewcoinc.com
www.lewcoinc.com
Conveyor systems including belt, bottle and chain,
stainless steel, gravity and powered roller. Also in-
dustrial ovens for drum heating and general thermal
processing applications
President: Pete Gay
peteg@gardeners.com
CFO: Jim Chapman
VP Oven Products: Ron Guerra
Quality Control: Andrews Smith
VP Conveyor Products: Jerry Guerra
Estimated Sales: $10-20 Million
Number Employees: 100-249
Square Footage: 270000
Brands:
Heat-Pro

25267 Lewis & Clark Company
111 Main Street
Suite 130
Lewiston, ID 83501

208-799-9083
Fax: 208-799-9082 vvision@lewiston.com
A consulting engineering firm
President: Jim Luper
Vice President: Eddy Chapman
Contact: Cheryl Teed
cteed@valleyvision.org
Estimated Sales: $500,000-$1,000,000
Number Employees: 1-4

25268 Lewis Label Products Corporation
2300 Race St
Fort Worth, TX 76111

817-834-7334
Fax: 817-834-2210 800-772-7728
cmorvan@lewislabel.com www.lewislabel.com
Pressure sensitive labels
Owner: Gibson Lewis
CFO: Gibson Lewis
VP Sales: George Noah
Contact: Carlos Aguirre
caguirre@lewislabel.com
Manager: Cole Morvan
Estimated Sales: $10-20 Million
Number Employees: 20-49

25269 Lewis M Carter Mfg Co Inc
Highway 84 W
Donalsonville, GA 39845

229-524-2197
Fax: 229-524-2531 800-332-8232
lmc@lmcarter.com www.lmcarter.com

707

Manufacturer and exporter of peanut shellers, cleaners, vibratory conveyors, elevators, sizing shakers, reclaimers, stoners, gravity separators, belt sizers, bean polishers, blanchers and bean ladders. Also air pollution controlequipment
President: Lewis Carter Jr
CFO: Gordon Carpenter
gordon.caarpenter@lmcarter.com
Sales Representative: David Sandlin
Sales Manager: Jack Williams, Jr.
Estimated Sales: $10-20 Million
Number Employees: 100-249
Square Footage: 600000
Brands:
 Lmc

25270 Lewis Packing Company
17480 Shelley Ave
Sandy, OR 97055-8055

503-668-8122

Packaging
Owner: Kris Jones
Estimated Sales: Under $500,000
Number Employees: 1-4

25271 Lewis Steel Works Inc
613 S Main St
Wrens, GA 30833-4534

706-547-6561
Fax: 706-547-3020 800-521-5239
lewisteel@bellsouth.net www.lewissteelworks.com
Refuse containers
Owner/President: Brian Lewis
Chairman of the Board: R A Lewis
IT: Sharlene Garner
lewisteel@bellsouth.net
Estimated Sales: $10-20 Million
Number Employees: 50-99

25272 Lewisburg Container Co
275 W Clay St
P.O. Box 39
Lewisburg, OH 45338-8107

937-962-0101
Fax: 937-962-4504

Corrugated containers
President: Randy Love
Controller: Walter Locker
Vice President: David McKinney
Director, Quality Control: Robert Long
mary.blankenship@ergogenesis.com
Chief Marketing Officer: Tami Meeks
Vice President, Sales & Marketing: David Dennis
Manager: Mary Blankenship
mary.blankenship@ergogenesis.com
Plant Manager: Michael Day
Procurement Manager: Dave McClellan
Estimated Sales: $39 Million
Number Employees: 250-499
Square Footage: 384000
Parent Co: Pratt Properties, Inc.

25273 Lewisburg Printing
170 Woodside Ave
Lewisburg, TN 37091-2866

931-359-1526
Fax: 931-270-3112 800-559-1526
info@lpcink.com www.lpcink.com
Manufacturer and exporter of litho sheet labels, point of purchase advertising brochures, posters and manuals
President: Seawell Brandau
CEO: Thomas Hale Hawkins, IV
CEO: Hale Hawkins
VP Sales: Kirk Kelso
Director Of Operations: Brian Tankersley
Estimated Sales: $5-10 Million
Number Employees: 50-99

25274 (HQ)Lewtan Industries Corporation
PO Box 2049
Hartford, CT 06145-2049

860-278-9800
Fax: 860-278-9019 lewtan@snet.net
Manufacturer and exporter of advertising specialties and promotional products including coasters, mighty grips, skimmers, clips, emblems, tape measures, mouse pads, calendars, etc
President: Douglas Lewtan
Estimated Sales: $10 Million
Number Employees: 20-49
Square Footage: 74000

25275 Lexel
2901 Shamrock Avenue
Fort Worth, TX 76107-1314

817-332-4061
lexel@flash.net
Wooden containers for shipping and storage
President: Pat Alexander
VP/Manager: Lee Ray Davis
Estimated Sales: $500,000-$1 Million
Number Employees: 4

25276 Lexidyne of Pennsylvania
PO Box 5372
Pittsburgh, PA 15206-0372

412-661-4526
Fax: 858-815-7346 800-543-2233
General Manager: Rick Simoni
Number Employees: 10-19

25277 Lexington Logistics LLC
N7660 Industrial Rd
Portage, WI 53901-9451

608-742-5303
Fax: 608-742-9153 800-356-8150
hbreezer@trienda.com www.trienda.com
Plastic thermoformed pallets, self-palletizing shipping systems and material handling devices
President: Curtis Zamec
curtis.zamec@trienda.com
VP Sales/Marketing: Rob Klinko
Number Employees: 250-499
Square Footage: 1000000
Brands:
 Dc Distribution Center
 Enviropal/Recy
 Load Locker
 Weight Lifter
 Wolf Pak

25278 Lexington Logistics LLC
N7660 Industrial Rd
Portage, WI 53901-9451

608-742-5303
Fax: 608-742-9153 800-356-8150
hbreezer@trienda.com www.trienda.com
Plastic, material handling products
President: Curtis Zamec
curtis.zamec@trienda.com
CFO: Jim Masterangelo
VP Marketing: Bob Shimmel
Plant Mgr: David Fiddes
Number Employees: 250-499

25279 Lexington Logistics LLC
N7660 Industrial Rd
Portage, WI 53901-9451

608-742-5303
Fax: 608-742-9153 800-356-8150
bklimko@wilbertinc.com www.trienda.com
President: Curtis Zamec
curtis.zamec@trienda.com
Marketing Manager: Paul Schoeder
Sales Director: Rick Sasse
Estimated Sales: $1-5 Million
Number Employees: 250-499
Square Footage: 1200000
Parent Co: Wilbert

25280 Leyman Manufacturing Corporation
10900 Kenwood Rd
Cincinnati, OH 45242

513-891-6210
Fax: 513-891-4901 866-539-6261
www.leymanlift.com
Manufacturer, importer and exporter of trailer and truck loading and unloading equipment, hydraulic lifts, elevators, tailgates, platforms, carts, dollies and van bodies
President: John McHenry
Marketing: Joann Russo
VP Sales: Chip Drews
Contact: Larry Disque
ldisque@leymanlift.com
Estimated Sales: $20-50 Million
Number Employees: 50-99
Type of Packaging: Food Service
Other Locations:
 Leyman Manufacturing Corp.
 Cincinnati OH

25281 Libbey Inc.
300 Madison Ave.
Toledo, OH 43604

419-325-2100
Fax: 419-325-2749 info@libbey.com
www.libbey.com
Table glassware.
Chairman/CEO: William Foley
william.foley@libbey.com
Senior VP/CFO: Jim Burmeister
Vice President/Chief Information Officer: Dave Anderson
Year Founded: 1818
Estimated Sales: $797.9 Million
Number Employees: 6,230
Number of Brands: 8
Brands:
 Libbey®
 Crisa®
 Lunita®
 Santa Elenita®
 Pyrorey®
 Royal Leerdam®
 Syracuse China®
 World Tableware®

25282 Libby Canada
Unit 26
Mississauga, ON L5L 4M1
Canada

905-607-8280
Fax: 905-607-8130 www.libbey.com
China, glassware, flatware and holloware
CEO: John Mayer
National Accounts Manager: Giulio Accardi
Number Employees: 10
Square Footage: 10400
Parent Co: Libby
Brands:
 Syracuse

25283 Liberty Carton Co.
870 Louisiana Ave. S.
Golden Valley, MN 55426

763-540-9600
800-328-1784
www.libertycarton.com
Specialty packaging, displays, promotional items, and gifts.
CEO: Mike Fiterman
mfiterman@protecta-packsystems.com
CFO: David Lenzen
Year Founded: 1918
Estimated Sales: $100 Million
Number Employees: 100-249
Parent Co: Liberty Diversified International

25284 Liberty Distributing Inc
909 Valley Ave NW
Puyallup, WA 98371-2517

253-922-8506
Fax: 253-922-5107 888-882-8506
www.libertydistributing.com
Distributor of dairy for wholesalers including; milk, cottage cheese, butter, sour cream, ice cream, non-dairy sour cream, cheese, margarine, eggs, yogurt, creamers, chocolate milk & syrups, apple, orange & grape juices, organic milkssoft serve, flavored milk powders, ice cream topper sauces, buttermilk, tea, bread & buns, ice
Owner: Ed Interbitzen
ed@libertydistributing.com
Estimated Sales: $430,000
Number Employees: 20-49
Type of Packaging: Consumer, Food Service, Private Label, Bulk

25285 Liberty Engineering Co
10567 Main St
Roscoe, IL 61073-8830

815-623-7677
Fax: 815-623-7050 877-623-9065
info@libertyengineering.com
www.libertyengineering.com
Manufacturer and exporter of rotary dies, candy molds, starch molding processing equipment and depositing pumps
President: Brian Belardi
bbelardi@libertyengineering.com
Engineering Manager: John Micinski
Quality Control: Rob Klein
Plant Manager: John Akelaitis
Estimated Sales: Below $5 Million
Number Employees: 10-19

Square Footage: 40000
Parent Co: Libco Industries

25286 Liberty Food Svc
1410 Michigan St
Storm Lake, IA 50588-1961

712-732-6379
Fax: 713-732-3325 800-425-1088
www.libertyfoodservice.com
Owner: Tom Agan
Corporate Finance Manager: Liza Gunnerson
Sales/Customer Service Manager: Cindi Daufeldt
tom@libertyfoodservice.com
Estimated Sales: Less Than $500,000
Number Employees: 5-9

25287 Liberty Label
101 W Shrader St
Liberty, MO 64068-2464

816-781-6717
Fax: 620-223-2201 800-783-5285
www.libertylabelsinc.com
Pressure sensitive labels
Estimated Sales: $500,000-$1 Million
Number Employees: 5-9

25288 Liberty Machine Company
125 Derry Court
York, PA 17406-8405

717-848-1493
Fax: 800-745-8150 800-745-8152
Manufacturer and exporter of wire racks and grilles
for refrigerators, ovens, etc.; also, wire material handling equipment
President: Brad Stump
Secretary/Treasurer: Patti Miller
Estimated Sales: $3-5 Million
Number Employees: 20
Square Footage: 36000
Type of Packaging: Food Service

25289 Liberty Ware LLC
PO Box 160450
Clearfield, UT 84016-0450

801-825-5885
Fax: 801-825-5875 888-500-5885
bbbrisko@aol.com
Manufacturer, importer and exporter of frying and
stock pans, flatware, thermometers, disposable
gloves and aprons, tongs, ladles, salt and pepper
shakers and portion control equipment
Owner: Robert Brisko
rbrisko@libertywareusa.com
Estimated Sales: $1-2,500,000
Number Employees: 10-19
Brands:
 Libertyware

25290 Libman Co
220 N Sheldon St
Arcola, IL 61910-1616

217-268-4200
Fax: 217-268-3422 877-818-3380
info@libman.com www.libman.com
Cleaning supplies including brushes, brooms, mops,
scrubbers, etc
President: Derek Arndt
darndt@libman.com
CFO: William Libman
VP Sales/Marketing: Kim Spafford
Treasurer: William Libman
Estimated Sales: $1-2.5 Million
Number Employees: 250-499
Brands:
 Libman

25291 (HQ)Libra Technical Center
101 Liberty St
Metuchen, NJ 08840-1215

732-321-5200
Fax: 32 -21 -203 asktkt@libralabs.com
Manufacturer and marketer of propietary, patented
tests for estimation and measurement of chemical
characteristics of fats and oils, especially with regard to degradation during deep-fat frying. Kits are
correlated with OfficialMethods and are available
for measurement fo Total Polar Materials, Free Fatty
Acids, and ppm alkaline surfactants/soaps (Water
Emulsion Titratables)
President: Michael Blumenthal PhD
Executive VP: Trean Blumenthal
Marketing/Sales: Ken Salzinger

Estimated Sales: $.5-1 million
Number Employees: 1-4
Number of Brands: 1
Type of Packaging: Food Service
Other Locations:
 Libra Technologies
 Metuchen NJ
Brands:
 Veri-Fry
 Veri-Fry Pro

25292 Liburdi Group of Companies
2599 Charlotte Highway
Mooresville, NC 28117

704-230-2510
Fax: 704-230-2555 800-533-9353
info@liburdidimetrics.com www.liburdi.com
Orbital welding equipment for tubes and pipes
President: Joe Liburdi
Estimated Sales: $3 Million
Number Employees: 20-49

25293 License Ad Plate Co
13110 Enterprise Ave
Cleveland, OH 44135-5102

216-265-4200
Fax: 216-265-4203 lapco@stratos.net
www.laline.net
Metal and plastic signs, pressure sensitive and thermal die cut decals, vinyls, mylars, scotchlite, frames,
etc
President: Richard Russell
Estimated Sales: Below $5 Million
Number Employees: 5-9
Square Footage: 12000

25294 Licker Candy Company
1600 E Second Street
Winslow, AZ 86047-4456

520-289-4815
Fax: 520-289-9415

25295 Lido Roasters
3215 Brooklawn Ter
Chevy Chase, MD 20815-3936

301-718-9719
Fax: 301-718-9735
Tea and coffee roasters

25296 Life Extension Foundation
3600 West Commercial Blvd
Fort Lauderdale, FL 33309

954-766-8144
Fax: 954-761-9199 888-895-4771
customerservice@lifeextension.com
www.lifeextension.com
Health and nutritional supplements
President: Bill Faloon
Founder: Saul Kent
Chief Financial Officer: James Murray
Vice President, Sales & Marketing: Rey Searles
Vice President of Purchasing: Connie Richter
Estimated Sales: $25-50 Million
Number Employees: 200+
Type of Packaging: Consumer

25297 Life Spice & Ingredients LLC
216 W Chicago Ave # 2
Chicago, IL 60654-3100

312-274-9992
Fax: 312-274-2381 www.lifespiceingredients.com
Spices
President: Peter Garvy
pgarvy@lifespiceingredients.com
Vice President of Sales & Marketing: Lisa Stern
Vice President of Operations: Holland Schlutz
Estimated Sales: $25 Million
Number Employees: 5-9

25298 Lifeline Technology Inc
116 The American Rd
Morris Plains, NJ 07950-2443

973-984-0525
Fax: 973-984-1520 info@temptimecorp.com
Self-adhesive time/temperature indicator labels that
monitor the cummulative effect of heat over time
Chairman: Jean-Paul Martin
VP: Ted Prusik
Estimated Sales: $2.5-5 Million
Number Employees: 20-49
Number of Brands: 2
Number of Products: 2
Square Footage: 80000
Type of Packaging: Consumer, Food Service, Private Label, Bulk

Brands:
 Fresh-Check
 Fresh-Scan
 Heatmaker Uvm

25299 (HQ)Lifetime Brands Inc
1000 Stewart Ave
Garden City, NY 11530-4814

516-683-6000
Fax: 516-555-0101 questions@lifetimebrands.com
www.lifetimebrands.com
Exporter, importer and manufacturer of cutlery and
gadgets
President: Steven Lizak
Chairman of the Board: Jeffrey Siegel
CFO: Rob Roknznally
VP: Bruce Cohen
VP: Larry Sklute
Number Employees: 1000-4999
Square Footage: 800
Brands:
 Armstrong Forge
 Avanti
 Barclay Geneve
 Carver Aid
 Color Brights
 Color Charms
 Colorgems
 Cordon Bleu
 Country Christmas
 Golden Barclay Geneve
 Heartland
 Jet Cut
 L C Germain
 Marmalade
 Old Homestead
 Paris Splendor
 Pierre Santini
 Pro/Star
 Rack-The-Knife
 Santa Fe
 Southwest
 Sugar Plum
 Tristar
 Welcome Home
 Windy

25300 Lifoam Industries LLC
2 5th St
Peabody, MA 01960-4916

978-278-0008
Fax: 978-278-0015 800-832-4725
Packaging; insulated foam boxes and refrigerated
jello packs
President: Bruce Trusdale
Manager: Randy Caraway
rcar@lifoam.com
Estimated Sales: $10-20 Million
Number Employees: 50-99

25301 Lift Rite
5975 Falbourne Street-Unit 3
Mississauga, ON L5R 3L8
Canada

905-456-2603
Fax: 905-456-1383 www.liftrite.com
Manufacturer and exporter of stackers, pallet trucks,
easy lifts and hi-lifters
President: Mel Griffin
Number Employees: 90

25302 Liftomatic Material Handling
700 Dartmouth Ln
Buffalo Grove, IL 60089-6902

847-325-2930
Fax: 847-325-2959 800-837-6540
sales@liftomatic.com www.liftomatic.com
Manufacturer and exporter of drum handlers, lift
truck attachments and lifting equipment
President: Todd Berg
tpberg@liftomatic.com
Sales Manager: E Darren Berg
Inside Sales: Angela Foster
Estimated Sales: $3-5,000,000
Number Employees: 10-19
Square Footage: 34000
Brands:
 Ergo-Matic
 Parrot-Beak

25303 Light Technology Ind
811 Russell Ave # 302
Suite 302
Gaithersburg, MD 20879-3518

301-990-4050
Fax: 301-990-7525 sales@ltindustries.com
www.ltindustries.com
Manufacturer and exporter of control systems and
instrumentation for quality control measurements in
labs and on line, including, liquid, solid, powders,
pellets, etc.
President: Aviva Landa
Marketing Director: Aviva Landa
Estimated Sales: $1-5 Million
Number Employees: 10-19

25304 Light Waves Concept
The Esquire Building 41st St
4100 1st Ave 3rd Floor North
Brooklyn, NY 11232

212-677-5230
Fax: 347-416-6201 800-670-8137
customerservice@lightwavesconcept.com
www.lightwavesconcept.com
Manufacturer, importer and exporter of lighting fix-
tures and low voltage track lighting
President: Joel Slavis
Estimated Sales: Below $5 Million
Number Employees: 10-19
Square Footage: 12000
Brands:
    Lightwaves

25305 Lighthouse for the Blindin New Orleans
123 State St
New Orleans, LA 70118

504-899-4501
Fax: 504-895-4162 clee@lhb.org
www.lhb.org
Brooms, brushes, cotton and rayon mops, scrubbers
and household textile items; also, remanufactured la-
ser printer cartridges
President: Bill Crist
CEO: Bill Price
Contact: Mary Anderson
manderson@lhb.org
Controller: Ron Wattigny
Estimated Sales: $10-20 Million
Number Employees: 50-99
Square Footage: 800000
Brands:
    Lighthouse
    Skilcraft

25306 Lightolier
631 Airport Rd.
Fall River, MA 02720

508-679-8131
Fax: 508-674-4710 www.lightolier.com
Lighting fixtures.
Year Founded: 1904
Estimated Sales: $100-500 Million
Number Employees: 250-499
Parent Co: Genlyte Group

25307 Lights On
1960 Central Park Ave
Yonkers, NY 10710

914-961-0588
Fax: 914-961-0589
Manufacturer, importer and exporter of lighting fix-
tures
Manager: Glenn Aroni
Estimated Sales: Less than $500,000
Number Employees: 10-19
Square Footage: 6000

25308 Lignetics Inc
31756 Highway 200 E
Sandpoint, ID 83864

208-263-0564
Fax: 208-263-9292 800-544-3834
www.lignetics.com
Barbecue pellets for pellet grills and flavor
enhancers for charcoal
President: Ken Tucker
kent@lignetics.com
General Manager: Lyle Wiese
Regional Manager: Kevin Schaper
VP Sales/Marketing: Bob Wilson
Sales/Traffic Coordinator: Lindsay Turner

Estimated Sales: $2 Million
Number Employees: 20-49
Parent Co: Lignetics
Brands:
    Bbq Pellets
    Grill Master

25309 Lil' Orbits
2850 Vicksburg Ln N
Minneapolis, MN 55447

763-559-7505
Fax: 763-559-7545 800-228-8305
contact@lilorbits.com www.lilorbits.com
Manufacturer and exporter of vending carts, displays
and automatic doughnut and crepe/pancake ma-
chines and accessories
Founder: Ed Anderson
e.anderon@lilorbits.com
President: Charlie Anderson
Vice President: Brian OGara
Marketing: Mike Foster
Sales: Brian O'Gara
Office Manager: Sue Larson
Service Production Manager: Terry OGara
Purchasing: Terry O'Gara
Estimated Sales: $3-5 Million
Number Employees: 10-19
Number of Brands: 2
Number of Products: 10
Square Footage: 100000
Brands:
    Lil' Orbits
    Orbie
    Uni-Matic

25310 Lillsun Manufacturing Co
1350 Harris St
PO Box 767
Huntington, IN 46750-4302

260-356-6514
Fax: 260-356-8337 mail@lillsun.com
www.lillsun.com
Manufacturer and exporter of bakers' woodenware
including pizza and oven peels, paddles and proof-
ing boards
President: Bill Sundermann
mail@lillsun.com
VP: W Sunderman
Estimated Sales: $1-2.5 Million
Number Employees: 5-9

25311 Lillsun Manufacturing Co
1350 Harris St
PO Box 767
Huntington, IN 46750-4302

260-356-6514
Fax: 260-356-8337 mail@lillsun.com
www.lillsun.com
Baker's woodenware; pizza and oven peels
President: Bill Sundermann
mail@lillsun.com
CEO: Gregory Williams
VP: Carrie Williams
Estimated Sales: $1-2.5 Million
Number Employees: 5-9

25312 Lima Barrel & Drum Company
1140 Franklin St
Lima, OH 45804

419-224-8916
Fax: 419-227-3424
New and reconditioned steel drums, barrels and con-
tainers
President: Randy Hersh
Estimated Sales: $5-10 Million
Number Employees: 10-19

25313 Lima Sheet Metal
1001 Bowman Rd
Lima, OH 45804-3409

419-229-1161
Fax: 419-229-8538 www.limasheetmetal.com
Food processing and canning equipment; also, safety
guards, ladders and platforms; repair service avail-
able
President: Bo Emerick
emerick_steve@yahoo.com
Vice President and Senior Fabricator: Tom Emerick
Office Manager: Anne Emerick
Estimated Sales: $1-2.5 Million
Number Employees: 10-19
Square Footage: 44000

25314 Limoneira Co
1141 Cummings Rd
Santa Paula, CA 93060-9783

805-525-5541
Fax: 805-525-8761 info@limoneira.com
www.limoneira.com
Packing house for Sunkist Growers, Inc. citrus fruit.
President/CEO: Harold Edwards
VP/Finance & Administration: Don Delmatoff
Senior VP: Alex M Teague
amteague@limoneira.com
Business Development Manager: David McCoy
Marketing Director: John Chamberlain
Director Packing & Sales: Tomas Gonzales
Director Information Systems: Eric Tovias
Agritourism Operations Manager: Ryan Nasalroad
Estimated Sales: $20 Million
Number Employees: 250-499
Type of Packaging: Food Service

25315 Lin Engineering Inc
16245 Vineyard Blvd
Morgan Hill, CA 95037-7123

408-919-0200
Fax: 408-919-0201 sales@linengineering.com
www.linengineering.com
Supplier of stepping moulder
President: Ted Lin
tlin@linengineering.com
Accounting: Emma Lin
Quality Control: Rob Carl
Estimated Sales: $1-2.5 Million
Number Employees: 5-9

25316 (HQ)Lin Pac Plastics
200 Windrift Court
3
Roswell, GA 30076-3727

770-751-6006
Fax: 770-751-7154
Manufacturer and exporter of plastic egg cartons and
food service packaging containers; also, processing
and packaging trays
Sales/Marketing Manager: James Gullo
Other Locations:
    Lin Pac Plastics
    Sebring FL

25317 LinPac
6842 Templin Ct
San Angelo, TX 76904-4112

325-651-7378
Fax: 325-651-7482 800-453-7393
Manufacturer and exporter of corrugated boxes and
other packaging materials
President: Robert Hanton
Quality Control: Alvin Kennedy
R&D: Sal Flores
President: Nigel Roe
Plant Manager: Danny Lopez
Estimated Sales: $10-20 Million
Number Employees: 20-49
Square Footage: 100000
Parent Co: LinPac

25318 Lincoln
One Lincoln Way
St Louis, MO 63120

314-679-4200
Fax: 314-679-4359 www.lincolnindustrial.com
World leader in the manufacturer and sale of lubrica-
tion systems and industrial pumping equipment for
industry
President: Bart Aitke
Contact: Wayne Chew
wchew@lincare.com
Number Employees: 500-999

25319 Lincoln Coders Corp
2815 Independence Dr
PO Box 8009
Fort Wayne, IN 46808-1326

260-482-8493
Fax: 260-483-2407 800-248-4452
sales@lincolncoders.com www.lincolncoders.com
Carton coders and rubber type and ink rolls
President: Robert Beaver
Estimated Sales: $1-2.5 Million
Number Employees: 10-19

25320 Lincoln Foodservice
1333 East 179th Street
Cleveland, OH 44110

260-459-8200
Fax: 800-285-9511 800-374-3004
www.lincolnfp.com
Designs, manufactures, and markets commercial and institutional foodservice cooking equipment, serving systems, and utensils. The company also manufactures and markets a line of electric Fresh-O-Matic food steamers.
President: Charlie Kingdon
Plant Manager: Jim Muston
Purchasing Manager: Tom Hengy
Number Employees: 250-499
Brands:
  Centurion
  Fresh-O-Matic
  Impinger
  Impinger a La Carte
  Redco
  Traditionalware
  Wear-Ever

25321 Lincoln Suppliers
1225 County Road 45 North
Owatonna, MN 55060

507-451-7410
Fax: 507-451-2968 800-622-8425
www.lincolnsuppliers.com
Agitation systems, milk, silo, tank, aseptic processing equipment, batch control systems, cheese equipment, washer and drier chillers, fillers, milk, steam, heat exchangers, plate, scraped surface, homogenizers, margarine processing equipment, piping, fi
President: Michael Grunwald
Estimated Sales: $5-10 Million
Number Employees: 20-49

25322 Lincoln Tent Inc
3900 Cornhusker Hwy # 1
Suite 1
Lincoln, NE 68504-1581

402-464-1900
Fax: 402-467-4907 800-567-4559
inquiries@lincolntent.com www.lincolntent.com
Commercial awnings
Owner: Tom Miller
inquiries@lincolntent.com
Estimated Sales: $2.5-5 Million
Number Employees: 20-49

25323 Linde Material Handling
1056 Drop Off Dr
Summerville, SC 29486-7224

843-871-0312
Fax: 843-871-5389 www.lmh-na.com
Supplier of industrial lift trucks; which include both electric and internal combustion (IC) forklifts, sideloaders or container handlers, order pickers, tow tractors, high-level stackers, and reach trucks.
President: Brian Butler
Marketing Communications Manager: Meg Merritt
Manager: Don Hanst
Estimated Sales: $50-100 Million
Number Employees: 10-19
Square Footage: 250000
Parent Co: Linde Material Handling
Brands:
  Linde

25324 Linde North America
575 Mountain Ave
Murray Hill, NJ 07974

908-464-8100
Fax: 908-417-5699
Gases and whole industrial welding equipment
President/CEO: Patrick Murphy
Applications Engineer: Michael Abshire
Contact: Jacqueline Cohen
jacqueline.cohen@linde.com
Estimated Sales: $250 Million
Number Employees: 100-249

25325 Line of Snacks Consultants
13220 Castleton Dr
Dallas, TX 75234-5113

972-484-1155
Fax: 972-243-3974
Consultant providing services to the snack industry worldwide for processing, technology, management, marketing, distribution and new product development
President: Donald Petty

Estimated Sales: Below $5 Million
Number Employees: 1-4
Square Footage: 2800

25326 Line-Master Products
PO Box 407
Cocolalla, ID 83813-0407

208-265-4743
Fax: 208-265-9393
Manufacturer and exporter of work benches, push carts and fixed and mobile material handling racks
President: Jackie Warren
Estimated Sales: $1-2.5 Million
Number Employees: 5-9
Parent Co: Sandefur Engineering Company

25327 LineSource
600 Berkshire Avenue
Springfield, MA 01109-1052

413-747-9488
Fax: 413-746-4498
Food processing equipment; custom design services available
President: William Stotler
Vice President: Ken Bonardi
Sales/Marketing: Les Parkos
Estimated Sales: $1-3,000,000
Number Employees: 5-9
Type of Packaging: Consumer, Food Service, Private Label

25328 (HQ)Linear Lighting Corp
3130 Hunters Point Ave
Long Island City, NY 11101-3132

718-361-7552
Fax: 718-937-2747 mike@linearltg.com
Manufacturer and exporter of lighting fixtures
President: Larry Deutsch
larry@linearltg.com
CFO: Lois Shorr
R&D: Kewin Ehrhardt
Estimated Sales: $20-50 Million
Number Employees: 100-249

25329 Linett Company
390 Fountain St
Blawnox, PA 15238

412-826-8531
Fax: 800-530-8329 800-565-2165
Strapping dispensers, castered stocking ladders, oily waste cans, special access ladders, crossovers and carts
President: Fred Schwartz
Vice President: Melvin Solomon
Marketing Director: Ronald Schwartz
Contact: Lynn Waxler
lynn@tri-arc.com
Manager Operations: Nick Valore
Purchasing Manager: Chris Gianfrancesco
Estimated Sales: $10-20 Million
Number Employees: 130
Square Footage: 650000
Brands:
  Castered Safety
  Conveyor Crossovers
  Ladder Crossovers
  Tri-Arc Manufacturing

25330 Linette
PO Box 212
Womelsdorf, PA 19567-0212

610-589-4526
Fax: 610-589-2706
VP: James P Linette
Number Employees: 100-249

25331 Linker Equipment Corporation
5 Evans Terminal
Hillside, NJ 07205

908-353-0700
Fax: 908-353-1621 www.linkercorp.com
Owner, President: David Linker
Regional Manager: Rungkun Roeksangsri
Contact: Barry Brothers
linkercorp@aol.com
Estimated Sales: $10,000,000-$25,000,000
Number Employees: 100-250

25332 Linker Machines
20 Pine St
Rockaway, NJ 07866-3131

973-983-0001
Fax: 973-983-0011 sales@linkermachines.com
www.linkermachines.com

Manufacturer and exporter of automatic sausage linking and peeling machinery; also, general purpose grease
Owner: Jean Hebrank
sales@linkermachines.com
VP: R Hebrank
General Manager: Rob Hebrank, Jr.
Estimated Sales: $2.5-5 Million
Number Employees: 1-4
Square Footage: 8000
Brands:
  Linkerlube
  Ty-Linker
  Ty-Peeler

25333 Linnea's Cake & Candy Supplies
975 Oak St
San Bernardino, CA 92410-2424

909-885-1446
Fax: 909-383-7201 sales@linneasinc.com
www.linneasinc.com
Candy, cake supplies, candy boxes, molds and all ingredients needed for cake and candy manufacturing
Manager: Mike Peterson
CFO: Polly Holman
Manager: Mike Peterson
Quality Control: Frank Romocean
Manager: Christopher Romocean
cromocean@linneasinc.com
Estimated Sales: Below $5 Million
Number Employees: 5-9
Parent Co: Linnea's Candy & Cake Supplies

25334 Linnea's Candy & Cake Supplies
4149 Karg Industrial Pkwy
Kent, OH 44240-6425

330-678-7112
Fax: 330-678-7133 www.linneasinc.com
Candy and cake supplies ,
Owner: Linnea Romocean
linnea@linneasinc.com
Estimated Sales: $5-10 Million
Number Employees: 10-19

25335 Linpac Materials Handling
3626 N Hall Street
Suite 729
Dallas, TX 75219-5127

214-599-9023
Fax: 214-599-9024 www.linpac.com
Supplier of reusable food containers to the supermarket industry

25336 Linpac Plastics
600 Corporate Drive
Suite 450
Fort Lauderdale, FL 33334-3606

954-492-5481
Fax: 954-489-0512 darin_gregg@linpac.com
www.linpac.com
Vice President of Marketing: Adam Barnett
Number Employees: 9

25337 Linvar
237 Hamilton St
Suite 202
Hartford, CT 6106

860-951-3818
Fax: 860-951-3547 800-282-5288
Manufacturer and exporter of metal shelving systems and plastic containers
Vice President: John Ramondetta
General Manager: John Ahern
Estimated Sales: $5-10 Million
Number Employees: 10-19
Square Footage: 50000
Brands:
  Linbin's
  Linshelf

25338 Linx Xymark
16 Lakeside Drive
Marlton, NJ 08053-2705

856-988-7125
Fax: 856-988-7126
Estimated Sales: $1-5 Million

25339 (HQ)Linzer Products Corp
248 Wyandanch Ave
West Babylon, NY 11704-1506

631-253-3333
Fax: 631-253-9750 800-423-3254
info@linzerproducts.com www.linzerproducts.com

Manufacturer and exporter of confectioners' and bakers' brushes and rollers
President: Alan Benson
CEO: Mark Aaronson
elliottw@linzerproducts.com
VP Sales: Brent Swenson
VP Production: Sidney Zichvin
Number Employees: 100-249
Type of Packaging: Consumer

25340 Lion Apparel Inc
7200 Poe Ave # 400
Suite 400
Dayton, OH 45414-2798

937-898-1949
Fax: 937-898-2848 800-548-6614
www.lionprotects.com
Uniforms including work clothing, shirts, trousers, outerwear, cashiers' aprons and smocks
Executive Director: Bill Claire
CEO/Chief Marketing Officer: Stephen Schwartz
sschwartz@lionprotects.com
Chief Financial Officer: Jim Disanto
Senior Vice President: Terry Smith
Research & Development: Donald Aldridge
Director, Marketing: Hayley Fudge
Sales Manager: Jerry Loran
Director, Operations: Gary Lee
Estimated Sales: $66 Million
Number Employees: 100-249
Square Footage: 37000
Parent Co: Lion Apparel

25341 Lion Labels Inc
15 Hampden Dr
South Easton, MA 02375-1159

508-230-8211
Fax: 508-230-8116 800-875-5300
epage@lionlabels.com www.lionlabels.com
Manufacturer and exporter of signage, pressure sensitive labels and decals
President: Jerome Berke
jberke@lionlabels.com
CEO: Michael Berke
CFO: Nina Berke
Sales Director: Moe Decelles
Operations Manager: Ed Page
Production Manager: Bruce Boteliao
Estimated Sales: $4.7 Million
Number Employees: 20-49
Square Footage: 58000
Type of Packaging: Consumer, Food Service, Private Label, Bulk

25342 Lion Laboratories
139 Mill Rock Road E
Old Saybrook, CT 06475-4217

860-388-6911
Fax: 860-388-6216
Non-invasive authenticity testing

25343 Lion/Circle Corp
4600 W 72nd St # 1
Chicago, IL 60629-5881

773-284-3666
Fax: 773-284-3654 info@lioncircle.com
Advertising novelties and specialties including buttons, balloons, key tags, etc.
President: Phillip Carollo
pcarollo@lioncircle.com
Sales/Marketing Executive: Rich Carollo
Purchasing Agent: Mike Webber
Estimated Sales: $1-5 Million
Number Employees: 20-49
Square Footage: 180000

25344 (HQ)Liqui-Box
901 E. Byrd St.
Suite 1105
Richmond, VA 23219

804-325-1400
www.liquibox.com
Food and industrial plastic packaging and packaging systems.
President/CEO: Ken Swanson
Chief Financial Officer: Leanne Parker
Chief Operating Officer: Andrew McLeland
Senior VP, Research & Development: Greg Gard
Senior VP, Sales & Marketing: Paul Kase
Year Founded: 1961
Estimated Sales: $128.6 Million
Number Employees: 684

25345 Liqui-Box Corp
901 E Byrd St # 1105
Richmond, VA 23219-4068

804-325-1400
Fax: 614-888-0982 804-325-1400
liquibox@liquibox.com www.liquibox.com
Manufacturer and exporter of form, fill and seal pouch packaging machinery; also, bag-in-box, retort and dispenser systems
CEO: Terry Barfield
tbarfield@hillcresttransportation.com
Plant Manager: Barry Pritchard
Estimated Sales: $5-10 Million
Number Employees: 500-999
Parent Co: Liqui-Box Corporation

25346 Liquid Assets
1421 Grove Street
Healdsburg, CA 95448-4711

707-527-9308
Fax: 707-527-9306 800-730-1030
Wine industry stainless steel tanks

25347 Liquid Controls LLC
105 Albrecht Dr
Lake Bluff, IL 60044-2242

847-295-1050
Fax: 847-295-8252 800-458-5262
lc-info.lcmeter@idexcorp.com www.lcmeter.com
Blending and batching equipment, flow meters and process control instrumentation
President: Matt Stillings
General Manager: Fred Niemeier
Global VP Sales & Marketing: John Thompson
VP Sales: Royal Wollberg
Number Employees: 250-499
Parent Co: IDEX Corporation

25348 Liquid Sampling Systems
416 Jacolyn Dr NW
Cedar Rapids, IA 52405-3407

319-365-2259
Fax: 319-365-2259 rob@pro-rata.com
www.pro-rata.com
Fluid sampling instrument sales and manufacturing
Owner: Robert Johnson
Estimated Sales: Below $5 Million
Number Employees: 1-4

25349 Liquid Scale
2033 Old Highway 8 NW
New Brighton, MN 55112

651-633-2969
Fax: 651-633-2969 888-633-2969
Manufacturer and exporter of milk silo air agitators, liquid level gauges and controls and needlepoint dividers
Estimated Sales: Under$300,000
Number Employees: 1-4
Square Footage: 6000
Brands:
Liquid Scale
Shimp

25350 Liquid Scale
2033 Old Highway 8 NW
New Brighton, MN 55112

651-633-2969
Fax: 651-633-2969 888-633-2969
Liquid level gauges
President: Dale J Tilden
Estimated Sales: Less than $500,000
Number Employees: 1-4

25351 (HQ)Liquid Solids Control Inc
10 Farm St
Upton, MA 01568-1665

508-529-3377
Fax: 508-529-6591 paulb@liquidsolidscontrol.com
www.liquidsolidscontrol.com
Manufacturer and exporter of in-line process control refractomers for continuous measurement and production; also, quality assurance of dissolved food solids available
President: Paul R Bonneau
usa@liquidsolidscontrol.com
CFO: Paul R Bonneau
VP: Gordon Vandenburg
Estimated Sales: $10-20 Million
Number Employees: 10-19
Square Footage: 50000
Other Locations:
Liquid Solids Control
Victoria BC

Brands:
Lsc Model 614
Lsc Model 725

25352 Liquitane
910 7th Ave
Berwick, PA 18603-1127

570-759-6200
Fax: 570-759-6254 www.cccllc.com
Plastic bottles and containers
Plant Manager: Bryan Statskey
Estimated Sales: $20-50 Million
Number Employees: 100-249
Parent Co: Liquitane

25353 Lista International Corp
106 Lowland St
Holliston, MA 01746-2094

508-429-1350
Fax: 508-626-0353 800-722-3020
sales@listaintl.com www.listaintl.com
Storage and workbench products.
President: Peter Lariviere
CFO: David Gavlik
Vice President: John Alfieri
Marketing: Anne Swagoriusky
Sales: John Alfieri
Estimated Sales: $50-100 Million
Number Employees: 100-249
Number of Brands: 2
Square Footage: 225000
Parent Co: Stanley Black & Decker
Brands:
Storage Wall

25354 Listo Pencil Corp
1925 Union St
Alameda, CA 94501-1345

510-522-2910
Fax: 510-522-3798 800-547-8648
sales@listo.com www.listo.com
Manufacturer and exporter of mechanical marking pencils, carton openers and industrial razor blades
President: Rick Stuart
rick@listo.com
VP: Rick Stuart
Estimated Sales: Less Than $500,000
Number Employees: 1-4
Square Footage: 34000
Brands:
Listo

25355 Litchfield Packaging Machinery
71 Benedict Rd
Morris, CT 06763-1117

860-567-2011
Fax: 860-567-2012 www.litchfieldpackaging.com
Beverage packaging equipment
President: Ric Edwards
Contact: Rick Edwards
lpm@litchfieldpackaging.com
Estimated Sales: Below $5 Million
Number Employees: 5-9
Type of Packaging: Bulk

25356 Litco International Inc
1 Litco Dr
Vienna, OH 44473-9600

330-539-5433
Fax: 330-539-5388 800-236-1903
info@litco.com www.litco.com
Supplier of export pallets, seperator sheets and air bags for the food industry also a supplier of export and domestic pallet solutions and load securement products.
President: Gary Trebilcock
gary@litco.com
CEO: Lionel Trebilcock
VP Sales: Gary Sharon
Estimated Sales: $5 Million
Number Employees: 10-19

25357 Lite-Weight Tool & Mfg Co
8621 San Fernando Rd
Sun Valley, CA 91352-3104

818-767-7901
Fax: 818-767-0010 800-859-3529
info@liteweighttool.com www.liteweighttool.com
Manufacturer and exporter of squeegees including emulsion spreading, handheld and floor
President: C R Brunson
VP: Andy Brunson

Estimated Sales: $500,000
Number Employees: 1-4
Square Footage: 10000

25358 Litecontrol
65 Spring St
Plympton, MA 02367-1701

781-294-0164
Fax: 781-293-2849 www.litecontrol.com
Manufacturer and exporter of lighting fixtures
President/CEO: Brian Golden
brian.golden@litecontrol.com
Senior Accountant: Kristen Woods
VP/Sales: Vince Santini
R&D: Paul Duane
Quality Control: James Pierce
Marketing Manager: Cory Passerello
Sales: Vince Santini
Project Manager: Barbara Goodwin
Estimated Sales: $5-10 Million
Number Employees: 100-249

25359 Lithibar Matik
13521 Quality Drive
Holland, MI 49424-8465

616-399-5215
Fax: 616-399-4026 800-626-0415
sales@besser.com
Bag and case pallets
Estimated Sales: $10-15 Million
Number Employees: 50-100

25360 Lithonia Lighting
1400 Lester Rd NW
Conyers, GA 30012-3908

770-922-9000
Fax: 770-483-2635 comments@lithonia.com
www.lithonia.com
Manufacturer and exporter of electric and fluorescent lighting fixtures
President: Vern Nagel
CFO: Wesley Wittich
wes.wittich@acuitybrands.com
Number Employees: 20-49

25361 Little Giant Pump Company
9255 Covedale Rd.
Fort Wayne, IN 46809

260-824-2900
Fax: 260-824-2909 www.littlegiant.com
Decorative and outdoor lighting fixtures, and water removal and transfer pumps.
Chairman/CEO, Franklin Electric: Gregg Sengstack
Estimated Sales: $100-500 Million
Number Employees: 500-999
Square Footage: 270000
Parent Co: Franklin Electric

25362 Little Rock Broom Works
7710 Jamison Rd
Little Rock, AR 72209-5541

501-562-0311
Fax: 501-562-3887
House and whisk brooms; also, mop heads and sticks
Owner: Evert Hatcher
Estimated Sales: $2.5-5 Million
Number Employees: 20-49

25363 Little Rock Crate & Basket Co
1623 E 14th St
Little Rock, AR 72202-4296

501-376-6961
Fax: 501-372-6252 800-223-7823
Fruit and vegetable shipping containers, wire bound crates for shrimp, fish and vegetables and veneer and novelty fruit baskets
President: William Swann
dbasketman@aol.com
Estimated Sales: $10-20 Million
Number Employees: 50-99
Parent Co: Little Rock Crate & Basket Company

25364 Little Rock Sign
1117 Highway 365 S
Conway, AR 72032-9288

501-372-7403
Fax: 501-327-4337
www.littlerockconwaysign.homestead.com
Advertising, electric and plastic signs
Owner: Bob Whitehouse
bob@littlerockconwaysign.com
General Manager: Laverne Anderson

Estimated Sales: $1-2.5 Million
Number Employees: 10-19

25365 Little Squirt
10 Compass Court
Toronto, ON M1S 5R3
Canada

416-665-6605
Fax: 416-665-5631
Portion controlled and refrigerated cream/milk dispensers
President: Garnet Rich
R&D: Bryan Symonds
Number Employees: 40
Brands:
 Little Squirt

25366 Littleford Day
PO Box 128
Florence, KY 41022-0128

859-525-7600
Fax: 859-525-1446 800-365-8555
sales@littleford.com www.littleford.com
Food processing equipment including mixers, granulators, sterilizers, agglomerators, vacuum dryers, liquid dispensers and pressure cookers; importer and exporter of mixers, dryers and sterilizers
President & CEO: Charles Kroeger
Research & Development: Glen Vice
Marketing & Sales: William R Barker
Contact: Steve Grall
sgrall@littleford.com
Estimated Sales: $50-100 Million
Number Employees: 100-249
Number of Brands: 10
Number of Products: 10
Type of Packaging: Food Service, Private Label

25367 Live Floor Systems
1076 Harrisburg Pike
Carlisle, PA 17013-1615

717-243-6644
Fax: 717-243-9926
Manufacturers of automated loading and unloading systems
Director Sales: Norm Fortney
Number Employees: 20

25368 Livingston-Wilbor Corporation
PO Box 496
Edison, NJ 08818-496

908-322-8403
Fax: 908-322-9230
Manufacturer and exporter of labeler change parts
Purchasing Agent: Chris Haigh
Estimated Sales: $1-2.5 Million
Number Employees: 10-19
Square Footage: 24000
Type of Packaging: Consumer, Food Service, Private Label

25369 Lixi Inc
120 S Lincoln Ave
Carpentersville, IL 60110-1703

847-961-6666
Fax: 847-961-6667 lixi@lixi.com
www.lixi.com
Manufacturer and exporter of inspection systems specializing in automatic detection of defects and rejection from conveyors
President: Brent Burns
bburns@lixi.com
Sales Manager: Joseph Plevak
Production: Ken Belzey
Estimated Sales: $2.5-5 Million
Number Employees: 10-19
Square Footage: 20000

25370 Lixi, Inc.
11980 Oak Creek Pkwy
Huntley, IL 60142

847-961-6666
Fax: 847-961-6667 lixi@lixi.com
www.lixi.com
Small x-ray imaging systems used for monitoring quality assurance, product malfunctions and fault analysis, security inspection and product tampering.
Contact: Brent Burns
bburns@lixi.com

25371 Lloyd Disher Company
5 Powers Lane Place
Decatur, IL 62522-3287

217-429-0593
Fax: 217-423-2611 www.manta.com
Manufacturer and exporter of aluminum alloy Teflon coated ice cream scoops
President: Gordan R Lloyd
Sales Manager: Lucy Murphy
Estimated Sales: $1-5 Million
Number Employees: 4
Square Footage: 10000
Brands:
 Lloyd

25372 Lloyd's Register Quality Assurance
1330 Enclave Pkwy
Suite 200
Houston, TX 77077

281-578-7995
Fax: 281-398-7337 888-877-8001
info-usa@lrqa.com www.lrqausa.com
Company providing quality system certification; serving the food and dairy industries
President: Paul Huber
CFO: Beverly Simmons
Quality Control: Atul Puri
Contact: Micheal Hatcher
mhatcher@mail.montcopa.org
Estimated Sales: $5-10 Million
Number Employees: 1-4

25373 Lloyd's of Millville
102 S 8th St # B
Millville, NJ 08332-3415

856-825-0345
Fax: 856-825-7666 www.lloydsofmillville.com
Commercial awnings
President: Benjamin Lloyd Jr
VP: Rick Lloyd
Estimated Sales: Below $5,000,000
Number Employees: 1-4

25374 Lmi Packaging
8911 102nd St
Pleasant Prairie, WI 53158-2212

262-947-3300
Fax: 262-947-3301 800-208-3331
www.lmipackaging.com
Manufacturer and exporter of heat sealing lidding, flexible packaging solutions, daisychain, rollstock & die cut lidding
Owner: Virginia Moran
CEO: Jean Moran
Vice President of Business Development: Randall Troutman
Vp R&D: Mike Gorzynski
Director of Marketing: Lea Connelly
National Accounts Manager: Gary Morrison
Vp Operations: Vince Incandela
Estimated Sales: $5-10 Million
Number Employees: 20-49

25375 LoTech Industries
12136 W Bayaud Ave Ste 120
Lakewood, CO 80228

303-202-6337
Fax: 303-202-9252 800-295-0199
Manufacturer and exporter of catering and food service custom imprinted utensils including plastic spoons, tongs, cake servers, pizza cutters, ladles, spatulas, and pasta forks
Vice President: Bev Whiteside
Estimated Sales: $2 Million
Number Employees: 3
Type of Packaging: Consumer, Food Service, Private Label, Bulk
Brands:
 Lotech

25376 Load King Mfg
1357 W Beaver St
Jacksonville, FL 32209-7694

904-354-8882
Fax: 904-353-1984 800-531-4975
www.loadking.com
Manufacturer and exporter of garbage and waste compactors, cardboard recycling balers, stainless steel tables, sinks, wire racks, carts, salad bars, checkout counters, etc. Manufactures fixtures and equipment worldwide to the supermarket, restaurant and retail industries

CEO: Charlie Chupp Jr
VP Sales: Charles Chupp
Estimated Sales: $10-20 Million
Number Employees: 100-249
Square Footage: 600000
Type of Packaging: Consumer, Food Service

25377 LoadBank International
4654 35th St
Orlando, FL 32811-6521

407-957-4000
Fax: 407-957-4175 800-458-9010
Manufacturer and exporter of material handling and
distribution equipment including dock staging and
cross-docking systems
President: Doug Hughes
Vice President: Mike Willett
Sales Director: Mike Willett
Operations Manager: John Veitch
Estimated Sales: $1-2.5 Million
Number Employees: 20-49
Number of Brands: 12
Number of Products: 12
Brands:
    Air-Trax
    Dock Xpress
    Loadbank
    Xpresslane

25378 Lobsters Alive Company
1447 Five Islands Rd
Georgetown, ME 4548

207-371-2990
Fax: 815-344-4479 keith@fiveislandslobster.com
fiveislandslobster.com
Wholesaler/distributor of lobster tank supplies and
parts; also, sales and service of new and recondi-
tioned lobster tanks available; design consultant spe-
cializing in large holding systems
General Manager: Joann Baureis
Equipment Specialist: Dennis Baureis
Estimated Sales: $500,000-$1 Million
Number Employees: 1-4
Square Footage: 4000

25379 Lobue's Rubber Stamp Co
1228 Mcgowen St
Houston, TX 77004-1108

713-652-0031
Fax: 713-652-0511
www.lobuesrubberstampco.com
Rubber stamps
President: Grant Gaumer
lobuestamp@earthlink.net
Estimated Sales: $1-2.5 Million
Number Employees: 5-9

25380 Location Georgia
245 Peachtree Center Avenue NE
Atlanta, GA 30303-1222

800-946-4642
Fax: 404-302-8333
locationgeorgia@meagpower.org
President, Chief Executive Officer: Robert Johnston
Sr. Vice President, Chief Administrative: Scott
Jones
Sr. Vice President, Chief Operating Offi: Steven
Jackson

25381 Lock Inspection Systems
207 Authoring Dr
Fitchburg, MA 01420-6094

978-343-3716
Fax: 978-343-6278 800-227-5539
sales@lockinspection.com
www.lockinspection.com

Contact: Walter Army
warmy@lockwoodint.com

25382 Lock Inspection Systems
207 Authority Drive
Fitchburg, MA 01420-6094

978-343-3716
Fax: 978-343-6278 800-227-5539
sales@lockinspection.com
www.lockinspection.com
Manufacturer, importer and exporter of advanced
quality control detection systems including metal detectors, checkweighers and conveyors for the packaging and processing industries

President: Mark D'Onofrio
Marketing Director: Michelle Contois
VP of Sales & Marketing: David Arseneault
Contact: Walter Army
warmy@lockwoodint.com
Production Manager: Brian Clough
Purchasing Manager: John Parker
Estimated Sales: $5-10 Million
Number Employees: 20-49
Square Footage: 120000
Parent Co: Transfer Technology Group PLC

25383 Lockhee Martin Postal Tech Inc
6201 E 43rd St
Tulsa, OK 74135-6562

918-622-2697
Fax: 918-622-2697
Manual, advanced and multiline bar coding and mail
sorting machines
President: Bill Dobbs
Estimated Sales: $10-20 Million
Number Employees: 5-9
Parent Co: Lockheed Martin

25384 Locknane
720 132nd St SW
Suite 207
Everett, WA 98204-9359

425-742-5187
Fax: 425-745-0277 800-848-9854
Manufacturer and exporter of nylon apparel and vi-
nyl aprons; also, jackets
President: Duane Locknane
duane.locknane@locnane.com
Marketing Director: Brent Locknane
Purchasing Manager: Tami Matuizek
Estimated Sales: $3-5 Million
Number Employees: 25
Square Footage: 14000
Type of Packaging: Food Service
Brands:
    Jo-Lock

25385 Locknetics
11819 N Pennsylvania St
Carmel, IN 46032-4555

Fax: 860-584-2136
Manufacturer and exporter of electro-magnetic lock-
ing systems
Finance Executive: Robert Zdanowski
Sales Manager: George Nortonen
Estimated Sales: $20-50 Million
Number Employees: 100-249
Parent Co: Ingersoll-Rand.

25386 Lockwood Greene Engineers
303 Perimeter Ctr N Ste 800
Atlanta, GA 30346

770-829-6500
Fax: 770-818-8100 lockwood@lg.com
www.lg.com
Consultant and designer providing plant and produc-
tion line layout, process and packaging engineering,
automation and control systems and environmental
services
Manager: Angela Davis
Manager: Barry Hall
Sr. VP: Bill Leslie
VP: Fizool Israel
Estimated Sales: $50-100 Million
Number Employees: 250-499
Parent Co: Lockwood Greene Engineers

25387 Lockwood Greene Engineers
1450 Greene St Ste 200
Augusta, GA 30901

706-724-8225
Fax: 706-724-8422
Consultant and designer providing plant and produc-
tion line layout, process and packaging engineering,
automation and control systems and environmental
services
Manager: Tom Sickling
Project Manager: Bob Grahl
Director: Lauren Watters
Estimated Sales: $10-20 Million
Number Employees: 50-99
Square Footage: 12000
Parent Co: Lockwood Greene Engineers

25388 Lockwood Greene Engineers
270 Davidson Ave # 4
Somerset, NJ 08873-4140

732-560-5700
Fax: 732-868-2300 www.lg.com
Consultant and designer providing plant and produc-
tion line layout, process and packaging engineering,
automation and control systems and environmental
services
Manager: Sherman Schwartz
Project Director: Tom Geffert
Senior Vice President, Chief Human Resou:
Don-Hyung Kang
President, Chief Operating Officer: Jong-Sik Kim
Estimated Sales: $20-50 Million
Number Employees: 100-249
Parent Co: Lockwood Greene Engineers

25389 Lockwood Greene Engineers
4201 Spring Valley Road
Suite 1500
Dallas, TX 75244-3669

972-991-5505
Fax: 972-960-2070 www.lg.com
Consultant and designer providing plant and produc-
tion line layout, process and packaging engineering,
automation and control systems and environmental
services
President/COO: Lee McInitre
CEO: Ralph Peterson
Chief Financial Officer: Samuel Iapalucci
Senior Vice President, Chief Human Resou:
Don-Hyung Kang
President, Chief Operating Officer: Jong-Sik Kim
Estimated Sales: $20-50 Million
Number Employees: 60
Parent Co: Lockwood Greene Engineers

25390 Lockwood Greene Engineers
2035 Lakeside Center Way
Suite 200
Knoxville, TN 37922-6595

256-533-9907
Fax: 256-533-7476
Consultant and designer providing plant and produc-
tion line layout, process and packaging engineering,
automation and control systems, environmental ser-
vices and architectural engineering support
Office Manager: Tom Glazener
Estimated Sales: $1-2.5 Million
Number Employees: 19
Parent Co: Lockwood Greene Engineers

25391 Lockwood Greene Engineers
130 Concord Rd
Knoxville, TN 37934-2901

865-218-5377
Fax: 865-777-3834 www.lg.com
Consultant and designer providing plant and produc-
tion line layout, process and packaging engineering,
automation and control systems and environmental
services
President: Cathy Neubert
CEO: Ralph Peterson
Senior Vice President, Chief Human Resou:
Don-Hyung Kang
President, Chief Operating Officer: Jong-Sik Kim
Estimated Sales: $10-20 Million
Number Employees: 10-19
Parent Co: Lockwood Greene Engineers

25392 Lockwood Greene Engineers
2035 Lakeside Center Way
Suite 200
Knoxville, TN 37922-6595

251-476-2400
Fax: 251-344-7400
Consultant and designer providing plant and produc-
tion line layout, process and packaging engineering,
automation and control systems and environmental
services
Office Manager: David Holland
Estimated Sales: $.5-1 million
Number Employees: 5-9
Parent Co: Lockwood Greene Engineers

25393 Lockwood Greene Engineers
7101 Executive Center Drive
Suite 297
Brentwood, TN 37027-3239

615-221-5031
Fax: 615-221-5078 www.lg.com

Consultant and designer providing plant and production line layout, process and packaging engineering, materials handling, automation and control systems and environmental services
President: Lee McIntire
CEO: Ralph Peterson
Senior Vice President, Chief Human Resou:
Don-Hyung Kang
President, Chief Operating Officer: Jong-Sik Kim
Estimated Sales: $1-2.5 Million
Number Employees: 19
Parent Co: Lockwood Greene Engineers

25394 Lockwood Greene Engineers
270 Davidson Ave # 4
Somerset, NJ 08873-4140

732-560-5700
Fax: 732-868-2300 www.lg.com
Consultant and designer providing plant and production line layout, process and packaging engineering, automation and control systems and environmental services
Manager: Sherman Schwartz
Senior Vice President, Chief Human Resou:
Don-Hyung Kang
President, Chief Operating Officer: Jong-Sik Kim
Estimated Sales: $20-50 Million
Number Employees: 100-249
Parent Co: Lockwood Greene Engineers

25395 Lockwood Greene Engineers
165 Road Km 10 Pueblo Viejo
Guaynabo, PR 00968

787-781-9050
Fax: 787-781-0177 www.lg.com
Consultant and designer providing plant and production line layout, process, packaging, engineering, automation and control systems, construction management, environmental services and validation services.
Office Manager: Gene Scott
Director Projects: Jorge Alvarez
Senior Vice President, Chief Human Resou:
Don-Hyung Kang
Marketing Director: Mayra Rodriguez
Validations Manager: Victor Batista
Estimated Sales: $64 Million
Number Employees: 178
Square Footage: 13000
Parent Co: Lockwood Greene Engineers

25396 Lockwood Greene Technologies
1450 Greene St Ste 200
Augusta, GA 30901

505-889-3831
Fax: 505-889-3842
Consultant and designer providing plant and production line layout, process and packaging engineering, automation and control systems and environmental services
Estimated Sales: $2.5-5 Million
Number Employees: 19
Parent Co: Lockwood Greene Engineers

25397 Lockwood Manufacturing
31251 Industrial Rd
Livonia, MI 48150-2035

734-425-5330
Fax: 734-427-5650 800-521-0238
customerservice@lockwoodusa.com
www.lockwoodusa.com
Wine racks, wine storage coolers, and food service equipment.
President: David Lamson
dwlamson@lockwoodusa.com
TBA Sales: David Lawrence
TBA Sales: Chad Buckles
Number Employees: 20-49

25398 Lockwood Packaging
271 Salem Street
Unit G
Woburn, MA 01801-2004

781-938-1500
Fax: 781-938-7536 800-641-3100
Manufacturer and exporter of automatic weighing and bagging equipment and supplies; also, repair and operating services available
President: Richard Gold
VP: Thomas Gold
VP: Hans Van Der Sande
Estimated Sales: $.5-1 million
Number Employees: 20-49

25399 Lodal Inc
620 N Hooper St
Kingsford, MI 49802-5400

906-779-1700
Fax: 906-779-1160 800-435-3500
sales@lodal.com www.lodal.com
Manufacturer and exporter of refuse removal systems
President: Bernie Leger
CFO: Bernard Leger
Director Marketing: Darren Tavonatti
Estimated Sales: $10-20 Million
Number Employees: 100-249

25400 Lodge Manufacturing Company
503 S Cedar Ave
South Pittsburg, TN 37380

423-837-5919
Fax: 423-837-8279 www.lodgemfg.com
Manufacturer, importer and exporter of cast iron cookware, bakeware and servingware
President: Henry Lodge
CEO: Bob Kellermann
CEO: Robert F Kellermann
R&D: Jeanne Scholze
Quality Control: Lou Zarzaur
VP Sales: Gray Bekurs
Contact: Richard Lodge
rlodge@lodgemfg.com
VP Production: Mike Whitfield
Estimated Sales: $20-50 Million
Number Employees: 100-249
Type of Packaging: Consumer, Food Service

25401 Lodging By Charter
206 E Frazier Ave
Liberty, NC 27298-8289

336-622-2201
Fax: 336-622-5000 800-327-2548
info@loewensteininc.com
www.charterfurniture.com
Chairs, stools, tables and table bases
President: Bruce Albertson
CFO: Winson Tortorici
Quality Control: Beata Kaminiski
Manager: Debbie Thompson
dthompson@brownjordan.com
VP Operations: David Biancofiore
Number Employees: 100-249
Square Footage: 330000

25402 Lodi Metal Tech
P.O.Box 967
Lodi, CA 95241-0967

209-334-2500
Fax: 209-334-1259 800-359-5999
Manufacturer and exporter of racks
Manager: Dean Bender
Estimated Sales: $10-20,000,000
Number Employees: 50-99
Square Footage: 310000

25403 Loeb Equipment
4131 S State St
Chicago, IL 60609-2942

773-496-5720
Fax: 773-548-2608 Sales@loebequipment.com
www.loebequipment.com
Wholesaler/distributor of used packaging and processing equipment.
President/CEO: Howard Newman
howardn@loebequipment.com
Marketing Director: Sara Bogin
howardn@loebequipment.com
Sales Manager: Tom Larson
Number Employees: 20-49
Square Footage: 600000

25404 Loeb Equipment
4131 S State St
Chicago, IL 60609-2942

773-496-5720
Fax: 773-548-2608 800-560-5632
www.loebequipment.com
Buy and sell packaging and processing equipment to food industry. Also specialize in certified appraisels, asset managment and liquidators
President: Howard Newman
howardn@loebequipment.com
Vice President: John Hagist
Marketing Director: Sara Bogin
Sales Manager: Tom Larson
Number Employees: 20-49
Type of Packaging: Food Service, Private Label

25405 Logemann Brothers Co
3150 W Burleigh St
Milwaukee, WI 53210-1999

414-445-3005
Fax: 414-445-1460 logemannbalers@aol.com
Manufacturer and exporter of scrap-metal, liber and refuse bales, also; alligator shears, briquettes and guillotines
Owner: Carl Dieterle
carl@milwpc.com
General Sales Manager: Robert Pichta
Estimated Sales: $2.5 Million
Number Employees: 20-49

25406 Logility
470 E Paces Ferry Rd NE
Atlanta, GA 30305

404-261-9777
Fax: 404-264-5206 800-762-5207
ask@logility.com www.logility.com
President and CEO: J. Michael Edenfield
CFO: Vincent Klinges
VP of Research and Development: Mark A. Balte
Vice President of Marketing: Karin L. Bursa
Estimated Sales: $20-25 Million
Number Employees: 100-249

25407 Logility TransportationGroup
1011 East Touhy Avenue
Suite 315
Des Plaines, IL 60018

847-699-6620
Fax: 847-699-6671 www.logility.com
Software for routing, carrier selection, freight audit, order consolidation, freight accounting and transportation management; also, integrated and proven solutions
President, CEO: J. Michael Edenfield
CFO: Vincent Klinges
EVP Sales and Marketing: H. Allan Dow
Vice President of Research and Developme: Mark A. Balte
VP Marketing: Karin L. Bursa
Vice President of Customer Service: Donald L. Thomas
Estimated Sales: $2.5-5 Million
Number Employees: 20-49
Square Footage: 36800
Parent Co: Logility
Brands:
Base Rate
Carrier Select
Dsi Escort
Match Pay
Preshipment Planning
Ship Wise

25408 Logix
10518 NE 68th St # 103
Suite 103
Kirkland, WA 98033-7003

425-828-4149
Fax: 425-828-9682 800-275-8112
www.logix-controls.com
Industrial refrigeration control system for the food, beverage and cold storage industries providing management and facility wide system tracking and reporting. Special fermentation controls available for wineries and alliedindustries
President: Jim Conant
contact@logix-controls.com
CFO: Jim Conant
VP: Micheal Ghan
Sales: Stephen Bowers
Operations: Scott Gillette
Production: Thomas Kulin
Estimated Sales: $2.5-5 Million
Number Employees: 10-19
Number of Brands: 2
Number of Products: 6
Square Footage: 1000
Brands:
Logix

25409 Logo Specialty Advertising Tems
PO Box 270544
Tampa, FL 33688-0544

561-429-4725
800-704-0094
roz@everythinglogo.com
www.logospecialtyadvertisingitems.com
Specialty advertising items
Co-Owner: Roz Kodish

Estimated Sales: less than $500,000
Number Employees: 1-4

25410 Logotech Inc
18 Madison Rd
Fairfield, NJ 07004-2309

973-882-9595
Fax: 973-882-0902 800-988-5646
Pressure sensitive label manufacturer
President: Leslie Gurland
labels@logotech-inc.com
CFO: Rodney Schundler
Research & Development: Jamie Fedor
Quality Control: Bruce Wade
Sales: Halley Mechanic
Estimated Sales: $5,000,000 -$15,000,000
Number Employees: 20-49
Square Footage: 56000

25411 Lohall Enterprises
6755 N Range Line Road
Milwaukee, WI 53209-3209

414-351-1270
Fax: 414-351-4531 lohall@execpc.com
Wrapping paper, wet waxed paper roll and sheet
Vice President: Arnold Garber
Purchasing Manager: Mary Anne Garber
Estimated Sales: $1 Million+
Number Employees: 3

25412 Loma International
283 E Lies Rd
Carol Stream, IL 60188-9421

630-588-0900
Fax: 630-588-1394 800-872-5662
www.loma.com
Manufacturer, exporter and importer of metal detectors and weighing equipment
President: Gary Wilson
CFO: Hary Pommier
Technical Director: Mike Nevin
Manager of IT: Brooke Kruger
Marketing Manager: James Chrismas
Sales Manager: Andrey Ivanov
Contact: Carlos Aillon
carlos.aillon@loma.com
Estimated Sales: $20-50 Million
Number Employees: 50-99
Square Footage: 21000

25413 Loma Systems
283 E Lies Rd
Carol Stream, IL 60188

630-588-0900
800-872-5662
www.loma.com
Inspection systems-metal detectors, check weighess, x-ray inspection systems.
President: Martin Lymn
CFO: Harold Pommier
Sales: Sandy Stillmaker
Contact: Carlos Aillon
caillon@loma.com
Operations: Craig Scachitti
Estimated Sales: $20-$50 Million
Number Employees: 80

25414 Lomont IMT
1516 E. Mapleleaf Drive
Mt. Pleasant, IA 52641

319-385-1528
Fax: 319-385-1533 800-776-0380
info@lomont.com www.lomontimt.com
Industrial safety signs, equipment tags and labels.
Number Employees: 150
Square Footage: 200000

25415 Lone Peak Labeling Systems
1272 W 2240 S # B
Suite B
West Valley City, UT 84119-1444

801-975-1818
Fax: 801-975-1865 800-658-8599
chrisa@lonepeaklabeling.com
www.lonepeaklabeling.com
Labels
President/Owner: Chris Appelbaum
chrisa@lonepeaklabeling.com
Operations: Jason Halling
Estimated Sales: $3.5 Million
Number Employees: 20-49

25416 Lone Star Container Corp
700 N Wildwood Dr
Irving, TX 75061-8832

972-579-1551
Fax: 972-554-6081 800-552-6937
jphipps@lonestarbox.com
www.lonestarcontainer.com
Manufacturer and exporter of corrugated boxes
President: Jerry C Hardison
jhardison@lonestarbox.com
CEO: John McLeod
Manager: Joe Phipps
Estimated Sales: $500,000-$1 Million
Number Employees: 100-249

25417 Lonestar Banners & Flags
212 S Main St
Fort Worth, TX 76104-1223

817-335-2548
Fax: 817-877-1610 800-288-9625
www.fortworthflag.com
Flags, banners, outdoor advertising displays and pennants; exporter of flags
President: James Eggleston
Vice President: Mark Buechelle
info@abcflag.com
VP Marketing: Pam Engelhardt
Estimated Sales: $5-10 Million
Number Employees: 20-49
Square Footage: 80000

25418 Long Company
20 N. Wacker Drive
Suite 1010
Chicago, IL 60606-2901

312-726-4606
Fax: 312-726-4625 800-400-8615
info@thelongco.com
President: Bill Zimmerman
CEO: Roger Masa
V.P. Operations-Consulting Services: Gary Swymeler
Director of Quality, R & D: Albert Bachman
Contact: Jo Rustik
jrustik@thelongco.com
Director of Manufacturing Services: Duane Bull
Purchasing Director: Larry Devereux

25419 Long Food Industries
709 Rock Beauty Road
Fripp Island, SC 29920-7344

843-838-3205
Fax: 843-838-3918 www.longfoodindustries.com
Shrimp, cooked/diced chicken, clam (meat and broth), beef (diced/cooked), lobster, fish and pork
President: Leon Long
Estimated Sales: $10-20 Million
Number Employees: 1
Type of Packaging: Food Service

25420 Long Island Stamp Corporation
5431 Myrtle Ave
Flushing, NY 11385

718-628-8550
Fax: 718-628-8560 800-547-8267
Rubber stamps, signs, labels, daters and seals
Owner: Harriet Pollak
VP: Harry Pollak
Estimated Sales: $1-2.5 Million
Number Employees: 10-19
Square Footage: 9000

25421 Long Range Systems
4550 Excel Pkwy # 200
Suite 200
Addison, TX 75001-5713

214-553-5308
Fax: 214-221-0160 800-577-8101
info@pager.net www.pager.net
A leading innovator of guest and staff paging and management systems for 14 years. We invented the popular coaster pager and now offer more pagers than anyone else. We have over 35 products designed to help you streamline operationsimprove service and increase sales every day. We provide the highest quality, most durable products on the market, plus we offer exclusive products and services no other company can.
Owner: Ken Lovgren
CEO: John Weber
jweber@lrsus.com
Marketing Director: Kevin Hosey
Sales Director: Jim Livingston
Number Employees: 50-99

Brands:
Adverteaser
Coaster Call
Cool Blue
Keycall
Lobster Call
Star Pager
The Butler
The Informant
Total Control

25422 Long Reach ManufacturingCompany
136 Main Street
Suite 4
Westport, CT 06880-3304

713-434-3400
Fax: 713-433-9710 800-285-7000
www.longreach.com
Manufacturer and exporter of lift truck attachments and pallet trucks
Chief Executive Officer: William Masson
Chief Financial Officer: William Masson
Vice President: Pat Poyton
Estimated Sales: $33 Million
Number Employees: 142
Brands:
Rol-Lift

25423 Longaberger Basket Company
701 Chestnut St
Dresden, OH 43821

740-518-8018
Picnic baskets.
Chief Executive Officer: Tami Longaberger
Chief Administrative Officer: Lisa Hittle
lisa.hittle@longaberger.com
Year Founded: 1896
Estimated Sales: $50-100 Million
Number Employees: 6,390
Square Footage: 180000

25424 Longford Equipment International
41 Lamont Avenue
Toronto, ON M1S 1A8
Canada

416-298-6622
Fax: 416-298-6627 888-298-2900
longford@longfordint.com www.longfordint.com
Estimated Sales: $15 Million
Number Employees: 100

25425 Longford Equipment US
938 Manchester Rd
Glastonbury, CT 06033-2629

416-298-6622
Fax: 860-633-8207 feederpro@aol.com
www.longfordint.com
Coupon and leaflet feeding machinery. Also turnkeys attaching to packaging lines available
Owner: Guy Sanderson
Manager: Guy Sanderson
Estimated Sales: $1-2.5 Million
Number Employees: 1-4

25426 Longhorn Imports Inc
2202 E Union Bower Rd
Irving, TX 75061-8814

972-721-9102
Fax: 972-579-4890 800-641-8348
info@longhornimports.com
www.longhornimports.com
Baskets, gift boxes, specialty containers, glassware, seasonal items and packaging products
Owner: Bruce Mc Adoo
longhornim@aol.com
VP/VP Finance: Carol Adoo
Marketing: Wendy Mawhee
Estimated Sales: $3.1 Million
Number Employees: 10-19

25427 Longhorn Packaging Inc
110 Pierce Ave
San Antonio, TX 78208-1928

210-222-9686
Fax: 210-226-7511 800-433-7974
www.longhornpackaging.com
Manufacturer and exporter of converted flexible packaging film and vertical form/fill/seal packaging machinery; also, contract packaging available

President: Holly Ferguson
hferguson@prosper-isd.net
VP: Bill Green
VP Production: Harold Smith
Estimated Sales: $20-50 Million
Number Employees: 50-99
Square Footage: 40000

25428 Longview Fibre Co
300 Fibre Way
Longview, WA 98632-1199

360-575-5290
Fax: 360-575-5934 800-929-8111
www.longviewfibre.com
Paper, corrugated and fibre containers, cushioning
materials and corrugated pallets
Chairman of the Board: Richard Wollenberg
CEO: Frank V McShane
Sales Manager: Fran Goetz
Contact: John Harris
jmharris@longfibre.com
Plant Manager: Harry Johnson
Estimated Sales: $20-50 Million
Number Employees: 1,000-4,999
Square Footage: 400000

25429 Longview Fibre Company
8705 SW Nimbus Ave
Beaverton, OR 97008-4000

503-350-1600
Fax: 323-725-6341 www.longviewfibre.com
Manufacturer and exporter of disposable liquid bulk
bins
Sales Manager: Dennis Dorgan
Vice President of Sales and Marketing: Lou
Loosbrock
Sales Bulk Liquid Packaging: Paul Hansen
Estimated Sales: $1-3 Million
Number Employees: 5-9
Type of Packaging: Bulk
Brands:
  Drumplex
  Liquiplex

25430 Longview Fibre Company
P.O.Box 106
Oakland, CA 94604

510-569-2616
Fax: 510-569-4141 www.longviewfibre.com
Wine industry packaging and design
Vice President of Sales and Marketing: Lou
Loosbrock
Plant Manager: Nathan Dyke
Estimated Sales: $10-20 Million
Number Employees: 50-99
Parent Co: Longview Fibre

25431 Lonza Inc
412 Mount Kemble Ave
Suite 200C
Morristown, NJ 07960

www.lonza.com
BioResearch, pharma and biotech research, water
treatment, agriculture ingredients, and coatings &
composites.
Chief Executive Officer: Richard Ridinger
Chief Financial Officer: Rodolfo Savitzky
Chief Human Resources Officer: Fridtjof Helemann
Chief Operating Officer: Sven Abend
Chief Operating Officer: Marc Funk
Year Founded: 1897
Estimated Sales: $350 Million
Number Employees: 69
Number of Products: 100

25432 Loos Machine
205 W Washington St
Colby, WI 54421-9458

715-223-2844
Fax: 715-223-6140 www.loosmachine.com
Custom designed automated food processing equip-
ment for the dairy, meat and poultry industries.
Owner: Dennis Baumgartner
info@loosmachine.com
Number Employees: 20-49

25433 Loprest Co
2825 Franklin Canyon Rd
Rodeo, CA 94572-2116

510-799-3101
Fax: 510-799-7433 888-228-5982
sales@loprest.com www.loprest.com
Water treatment equipment, ion exchange equipment
and resin

President: Randy Richey
CFO: Randy Richey
Contact: Amy Velazquez
avelazquez@buttecounty.net
Estimated Sales: $1-2.5 Million
Number Employees: 1-4

25434 Lorac Union Tool Co
97 Johnson St
Providence, RI 02905-4518

401-781-3330
Fax: 401-941-7717 888-680-3236
lorac@loracunion.com www.loracunion.com
Manufacturer and exporter of point of purchase dis-
plays and sign holders
President: Richard Carroll
Estimated Sales: $5-10 Million
Number Employees: 10-19
Square Footage: 204000
Parent Co: Lorac Company
Brands:
  Sava-Klip

25435 Lord Label Group
2980 Planters Place
Charlotte, NC 28216-4149

704-394-9171
Fax: 704-394-0641 800-341-5225
Manufacturer and exporter of labels and labeling
equipment
Director Marketing: George McCrary
VP Sales Eastern Region: Jim Prendergast
Sales Manager Western Region: Tom Deegan
Number Employees: 250
Parent Co: Mail-Well
Other Locations:
  Lord Label Group
  Arlington TX

25436 Lord Label Machine Systems
10350A Nations Food Road
Charlotte, NC 28273

704-644-1650
Fax: 704-664-1662 www.satoamerica.com
Manufacturer and exporter of label applicators
General Manager: Les Roisum
Number Employees: 20-49
Square Footage: 72000
Parent Co: Mail Well
Brands:
  Label Robotix
  Predator 1500-3000
  Tr 1000-2000

25437 (HQ)Loren Cook Co
2015 E Dale St
Springfield, MO 65803-4637

417-869-6474
Fax: 417-862-3820 800-289-3267
info@lorencook.com www.lorencook.com
Manufacturer and exporter of fans, blowers and ven-
tilators
President: Gerald Cook
Cmo: Victor Colwell
vcolwell@lorencook.com
Estimated Sales: $77 Million
Number Employees: 1000-4999
Other Locations:
  Loren Cook Co.
  Ashville NC

25438 Lorenz Couplings
PO Box 1002
Cobourg, ON K9A 4K2
Canada

905-372-2240
Fax: 905-372-4456 800-263-7782
www.lorenz.ca
Manufacturer and exporter of stainless steel gasket
couplings for connection of pipe and tube in bulk
handling conveying and vacuum systems
President: Peter Lorenz
CEO: Stacy Warner
Estimated Sales: Below $5 Million
Number Employees: 30
Square Footage: 80000

25439 Lorenzen's Cookie Cutters
2080 Maple Street
Wantagh, NY 11793-4108

516-781-7116
Fax: 516-781-1110 fclorenzen@aol.com
Custom stainless steel cookie cutters
CEO: Margaret Lorenzen

Estimated Sales: $1-5 Million
Number Employees: 2
Square Footage: 1750

25440 Loria Awards
1876 Central Park Ave
Yonkers, NY 10710-2998

914-779-3377
Fax: 914-779-3587 800-540-2927
customerservice@loriaawards.com
www.loriaawards.com
Awards, stemware and name plates; also, imprinting
available
Owner: Roger Loria Sr
VP: Roger Loria Jr
Production Manager: David DiPietro
Estimated Sales: $1-2.5 Million
Number Employees: 10-19
Square Footage: 120000

25441 Lorrich & Associates
11310 Ganesta Road
San Diego, CA 92126-1643

858-586-0823
Fax: 858-586-6210 lorrichusa@aol.com
Consultant specializing in design, marketing and
promotion for the restaurant industry
President: Richard Bartole
VP: Lorraine Bartole
Estimated Sales: Less than $500,000
Number Employees: 1-4

25442 Los Angeles Label Company
6141 Sheila St
Commerce, CA 90040-2406

323-720-1200
Fax: 323-724-1024 800-606-5223
www.lalabel.com
Prime labels, tickets, coupons, variable printing on
tag stock and pressure sensitive materials
Manager: Bruce Frost
President, Chief Executive Officer: Thomas
Waechter
Vice President: John Redgrave
Estimated Sales: $10-20 Million
Number Employees: 50-99
Square Footage: 60000

25443 Los Angeles Paper Box &Board Mills
PO Box 60830
Los Angeles, CA 90060-0830

323-685-8900
Fax: 323-724-2181 bill@lapb.com
Chip board and boxes including rigid, folding, set
up, etc
President: William H Kewell Iii
CFO: Knita Chau
VP Sales: Robert Appoloney
Estimated Sales: $20-50 Million
Number Employees: 20-49

25444 Louie's Finer Meats
Highway 63 North
2025 Superior Avenue
Cumberland, WI 54829

715-822-4728
Fax: 715-822-3150 800-270-4297
lfm@louiesfinermeats.net
www.louiesfinermeats.com
Smoked sausages
Owner/President: Louie Muench Sr
VP: Louie Muench Jr
Number Employees: 4

25445 Louis A Roser Company
608 W 700 S
Salt Lake City, UT 84104

801-363-8849
Fax: 801-328-9670 800-324-6864
roserinfo@laroser.com www.laroser.com
President: Roy Iversen
Estimated Sales: $5-10 Million
Number Employees: 10-19

25446 (HQ)Louis Baldinger & Sons
875 3rd Ave Fl 9
New York, NY 10022-0123

718-204-5700
Fax: 718-721-4986
Manufacturer and exporter of decorative and custom
lighting fixtures

President: Howard Baldinger
Chairman of the board: Daniel Baldinger
Quality Control: Shankar Balmick
VP Sales/Marketing: Linda Senter
Contact: Edison Alulema
ealulema@baldinger.com
Estimated Sales: $10-20 Million
Number Employees: 120
Type of Packaging: Consumer

25447 Louis Jacobs & Son
161 N 4th St
Brooklyn, NY 11211-3279
718-782-3500
Fax: 718-384-1167
Paper table covers, plain, embossed and creped,
sheets and rolls
CEO: Abram Cohen
Estimated Sales: $10-20 Million
Number Employees: 5-9
Square Footage: 36000
Type of Packaging: Food Service, Private Label,
   Bulk
Brands:
   Clothsaver Paper Tabl-Mats
   Duo-Stress Place Mats

25448 Louis Roesch Company
289 Foster City Blvd
Suite B
Foster City, CA 94404-1100
415-621-4700
Fax: 415-621-1152
Paper labels; also, label printing services available
President: Michael A Davos
CFO: Mike Davos
Sales Manager: Bob Davos
Pur Mgr: Jason Hong
Estimated Sales: $10-20 Million
Number Employees: 10

25449 Louisville Bedding Co Inc.
10400 Bunsen Way
Louisville, KY 40299
502-813-8059
loubed.com
Chair pads, table cloths and place mats.
President/CEO: Steve Elias
Vice President, Operations: Steve Thompson
Year Founded: 1889
Estimated Sales: $100-$500 Million
Number Employees: 500-999

25450 Louisville Container Company
4401 W 62nd Street
Indianapolis, IN 46268-4829
502-361-5300
Fax: 317-297-5019 888-539-7225
Plastic and glass bottles and jars; also pails
President: Steve Heidt
Marketing Director: Nancy Heidt
Estimated Sales: $1 Million
Number Employees: 3
Square Footage: 7400

25451 Louisville Dryer Company
1100 Industrial Boulevrd
Louisville, KY 40219
502-969-3535
Fax: 502-962-9028 800-735-3613
mail@louisvilledryer.com
www.louisvilledryer.com
Manufacturer and exporter of rotary drying and
cooling equipment, distillation columns, heat
exchangers, pressure vessels and conveyors
VP Sales: Robin Henry
Process Engineer: John Robertson
Plant Manager: Gary Billion
Estimated Sales: $5-10 Million
Number Employees: 20-49

25452 Louisville Lamp Co
3316 Gilmore Industrial Blvd
Louisville, KY 40213-2173
502-964-4094
Fax: 502-964-1349
customerservice@louisvillelamp.com
www.louisvillelamp.com
Custom fluorescent lighting fixtures
President: Rick Buehner
National Accounts: Mike Davidson
Estimated Sales: $1-2.5 Million
Number Employees: 50-99

25453 Love Controls Division
P.O.Box 373
Michigan City, IN 46361-0373
219-879-8000
Fax: 219-872-9057 800-828-4588
love@love-controls.com www.dwyer-inst.com
Manufacturer, distributor and exporter of tempera-
ture and process control instrumentation and associ-
ated products
President: Stephen Clark
Contact: David Lange
dlange@love-controls.com
Estimated Sales: $75 Million-1 Billion
Number Employees: 100-249
Square Footage: 50000
Parent Co: Dwyer Instruments

25454 Loveshaw Corp
2206 Easton Tpke
PO Box 83
South Canaan, PA 18459
570-937-4921
Fax: 570-937-3229 800-572-3434
info@loveshaw.com www.loveshaw.com
Manufacturer and exporter of packaging machinery
including case sealers and formers; also, ink jet
printers, labeling equipment
President: Doug Henry-Om
Cmo: Wes Carpenter
wcarpenter@loveshaw.com
VP: Mark Craddick
Marketing Manager: Valerie Burke
Sales: Chet Metcalf
Estimated Sales: $10-24 Million
Number Employees: 100-249
Parent Co: ITW
Brands:
   Little David

25455 Low Humidity Systems
8425 Hazelbrand Road NE
Covington, GA 30014
770-788-6744
Fax: 770-788-6745 Info@dehumidifiers.com
www.dehumidifiers.com
Manufacturer and exporter of desiccant
dehumidifiers
Sales Manager: Debra Adams
Estimated Sales: $2.5-5 Million
Number Employees: 10-19
Square Footage: 60000

25456 (HQ)Low Temp Industries Inc
9192 Tara Blvd
Jonesboro, GA 30236-4913
678-674-1317
Fax: 770-471-3715 lt@lowtempind.com
www.lowtempind.com
Manufacturer and exporter of stainless steel, fiber-
glass and wood-free standing and hot food counters.
Custom stainless steel kitchen equipment, serving
lines, buffets and salad bars, portable hot and cold
carts and custom millwork
CEO: William Casey
Executive VP: David W Pearson
dpearson@lowtempind.com
VP Sales: Steve Ballard
Director Purchasing: Dan Casey
Estimated Sales: $10-20 Million
Number Employees: 100-249
Square Footage: 500000
Type of Packaging: Food Service
Brands:
   Cara
   Colorpoint
   Low Temp

25457 Lowe Refrigeration Inc
105 Cecil Ct
Fayetteville, GA 30214-7906
770-461-9001
Fax: 770-461-8020 www.lowerental.com
Vice President: Richard Epton
richard@loweusa.com
VP: Richard Epton
Estimated Sales: $1-3 Million
Number Employees: 10-19

25458 Lowell Paper Box Company
23 Dumaine Ave
Nashua, NH 03063-4070
603-595-0700
Fax: 603-595-6337
Paper folding cartons

President: Paul Connolly
CEO: Mark Dirico
Estimated Sales: $10-20 Million
Number Employees: 100-249

25459 Lowen Color Graphics
1111 Airport Rd
Hutchinson, KS 67501-1983
620-663-2161
Fax: 620-663-1429 800-545-5505
elainem@lowen.com www.buildersigns.com
Point of sale vinyl graphics for floors and fleet and
interior store graphics
Vice President of Sales & Marketing: Darren Keller
Contact: Sergio Desoto
s.desoto@lowen.com
Estimated Sales: Less Than $500,000
Number Employees: 1-4

25460 Lowery's Premium Roast Gourmet Coffee
P.O.Box 1858
Snohomish, WA 98291
360-668-4545
Fax: 360-863-9742 800-767-1783
www.loweryscoffee.com
Coffee and wholesale and custom roasters, espresso
machines, espresso accessories
President: Donald Lowery
CFO: Jeanette Zimmerman
Marketing: Mike Lowery
Contact: Don Lowery
dlowery@loweryscoffee.com
Roast/Operations Manager: Jerry Lowery
Estimated Sales: Below $5 Million
Number Employees: 20-49
Number of Brands: 2
Number of Products: 100
Square Footage: 20000
Type of Packaging: Private Label
Brands:
   Lowery's Coffee
   Pasano's Syrups

25461 Lowry Computer ProductsInc
1607 9th St
St Paul, MN 55110-6717
651-429-7722
Fax: 651-429-6006 800-429-7722
Manager: Karla Bridgeman
Manager: Jim Bergman
jamesb@lowrycomputer.com
Estimated Sales: $20-50 Million
Number Employees: 20-49

25462 (HQ)Loy Lange Box Co
222 Russell Blvd
St Louis, MO 63104-4608
314-776-4712
Fax: 314-776-2810 800-886-4712
info@loylangebox.com www.loylangebox.com
Corrugated shipping containers and point of pur-
chase displays
Owner: Larry Mcmahon
Chairman: C McMahon
VP: J Cochran
Estimated Sales: $2.5-5 Million
Number Employees: 50-99
Square Footage: 192000
Other Locations:
   Loy-Lange Box Co.
   Belle MO

25463 Loyal Manufacturing
1121 S Shortridge Rd
Indianapolis, IN 46239-1081
317-359-3185
Fax: 317-353-9284 www.loyalmfg.com
Custom fabricated metal products including storage
cabinets, shelving racks, etc.; also, cash drawers,
point of sale components and security items
President: Ronald Lambert
CEO: Todd Fox
tfox@loyalmfg.com
Estimated Sales: $2.5-5 Million
Number Employees: 10-19
Square Footage: 26000
Brands:
   Loyal

25464 Lozier Corp
6336 John J Pershing Dr
Omaha, NE 68110-1122
402-457-8000
Fax: 402-457-8478 800-228-9882
www.lozier.com
Manufacturer and exporter of store fixtures
CEO: Sheri Andrews
sandrews@lozier.biz
CEO: Allan G Lozier
Estimated Sales: $500,000-$1 Million
Number Employees: 1000-4999
Parent Co: Lozier Corporation

25465 Ltg Inc
105 Corporate Dr
Spartanburg, SC 29303-5045
864-599-6340
Fax: 414-672-8800 sales@itsllcusa.com
www.ltg.de
Manufacturer and exporter of controlled heat processing systems for the metal container industry
President: Gerhard Seyffer
gerhard.seyffer@ltg-inc.net
General Manager: Bill Lawrence
VP: Brian Schofield
Estimated Sales: $20-50 Million
Number Employees: 1-4
Square Footage: 180000

25466 Lubar Chemical
1208 Iron Street
Kansas City, MO 64116-4009
816-471-2560
Fax: 816-421-2426
Institutional and industrial chemicals including cleaners, degreasers, detergents, floor care products, disinfectants and deodorants; custom blending and private labeling available
Estimated Sales: $5-10 Million
Number Employees: 20-49

25467 Lubriplate Lubricants
129 Lockwood St
Newark, NJ 07105-4720
419-691-2491
Fax: 973-589-4432 800-733-4755
richardm@lubriplate.com www.lubriplate.com
Manufacturer and exporter of food grade lubricating oils and grease
President: Richard Mc Cluskey
Vice President, General Manager, Chief M: Jim Girard
Contact: Michael Barto
mbarto@lubriplate.com
Number Employees: 100-249
Parent Co: Fisk Brothers

25468 Lubriquip
P.O.Box 1441
Minneapolis, MN 55440-1441
612-623-6000
Fax: 612-378-3590 www.lubriquip.com
Automatic lubrication systems for food processing machinery and equipment, stainless steel injectors and feeder assemblies, single point centralized lubrication systems and conveyor systems
President: Rick Morgan
Quality Control: Jack Gacka
Vice President, General Counsel, Secreta: Karen Gallivan
Plant Manager: Ryan Eidenschink
Estimated Sales: G
Number Employees: 1,000-4,999

25469 Lucas Industrial
1445 American Way
PO Box 293
Cedar Hill, TX 75104-8409
972-291-6400
Fax: 972-291-6447 800-877-1720
sales@lucasindustrial.com
www.lucasindustrial.com
Manufacturer, importer and wholesaler/distributor of power transmission products including steel and stainless steel shaft and split collars, linear bearing and shaftings, roller chains and mounted bearing
Owner: Mike Lucas
Sales Manager: Bobby Swann
lucasindustrial@aol.com
Estimated Sales: Below $5 Million
Number Employees: 5-9

25470 Luce Corp
336 Putnam Ave
Hamden, CT 06517-2744
203-787-0281
Fax: 203-230-2753 800-344-6966
Kitchen canisters with moisture absorbing knobs
President: Timothy Pagnam
Estimated Sales: $1-3 Million
Number Employees: 5-9
Brands:
  Blue Magic
  Krispy Kan

25471 Luciano Packaging Technologies
29 County Line Rd
Branchburg, NJ 08876-3417
908-722-3222
Fax: 908-722-5005 lpt@lucianopackaging.com
www.lucianopackaging.com
President: Lawrence W. Luciano
lluciano@lucianopackaging.com
Estimated Sales: $3-5 Million
Number Employees: 10-19

25472 Lucie Sable Imports
3349 Howard St
Skokie, IL 60076-4010
847-677-2867
Fax: 847-677-2018 800-582-4326
luciesable@aol.com
Owner: Lucie Sable
CFO: Mike Kacyn
R & D: Madelaine Brown
Estimated Sales: $2.5-5 Million
Number Employees: 5-9

25473 Lucille Farms
PO Box 517
Montville, NJ 07045-0517
973-334-6030
Fax: 973-402-6361 800-654-6844
Cheeses
President: Al Falivene
CEO: Jay Rosengarten
Number Employees: 90

25474 Luckner Steel Shelving
5454 43rd St
Flushing, NY 11378-1028
718-363-0500
Fax: 718-784-9169 800-888-4212
info@karpinc.com www.karpinc.com
Manufacturer and exporter of wire shelving
President: Burt Gold
bgold@karpinc.com
CFO: Ron Peterson
Marketing: Claudia Holtz
Sales: Chantale Laraque
Estimated Sales: $5-10,000,000
Number Employees: 50-99
Square Footage: 45000
Parent Co: Karp Associates
Brands:
  Penco

25475 Lucks Food Equipment Company
21112 72nd Avenue S
Kent, WA 98032-1339
253-872-2180
Fax: 253-872-2013 811-824-0696
info@lucks.com www.lucks.com
Rack ovens, proof boxes, dividers and rounders, revolving tray ovens, spiral mixers, sheeters and moulders
President: Rick Ellison
Chief Financial Officer: Carl Lucks
Senior Vice President Of Operations: Dan Elliott
VP Marketing: Kurt Lucks
Contact: Tom Scherer
tscherer@lucks.com
Estimated Sales: $20-50 Million
Number Employees: 100-250

25476 (HQ)Luco Mop Co
3345 Morganford Rd
St Louis, MO 63116-1805
314-772-5656
Fax: 314-772-5826 800-522-5826
www.lucomop.com
Mops, brooms and accessories
Owner: John Shalhoub
john@lucomop.com
Estimated Sales: $1-2.5 Million
Number Employees: 10-19

25477 Ludeca Inc
1425 NW 88th Ave
Doral, FL 33172-3017
305-591-8935
Fax: 305-591-1537 info@ludeca.com
Laser tools for machinery alignment and instruments for machine condition monitoring
Manager: Frank Heilemann
CFO: Danny Cermelli
danny.cermelli@ludeca.com
Estimated Sales: $2.5-5 Million
Number Employees: 20-49

25478 Ludell Manufacturing Co
5200 W State St
Milwaukee, WI 53208-2688
414-476-9934
Fax: 414-476-9864 800-558-0800
sales@ludellmfg.com
www.ludellmanufacturing.com
Manufacturer and exporter of ASME certified heat exchangers, custom engineered wastewater heat recovery systems, direct contact water heaters, and boiler feedwater systems, replacement storage tanks and boiler stack economizers
Owner: Robert Fesmire
george.simpson@gcmk.org
Chief Executive Officer: Bob Fesmire
CFO: David Arthur
Quality Control: Richard Ogren
Vice President: Robert Fesmire
george.simpson@gcmk.org
Sales Director: Greg Thorn
george.simpson@gcmk.org
Plant Manager: Gary Nance
Purchasing Manager: Mark Grosskreutz
Estimated Sales: $8.5 Million
Number Employees: 20-49
Number of Brands: 6
Number of Products: 2
Square Footage: 200000

25479 Luetzow Industries
1105 Davis Ave
South Milwaukee, WI 53172-1195
414-762-0410
Fax: 414-762-0943 800-558-6055
www.luetzow.cc
Manufacturer and exporter of polyethylene bags and film, and sheating
President: Albert Luetzow
VP: Brent Luetzow
Estimated Sales: $10-20 Million
Number Employees: 20-49
Square Footage: 160000
Type of Packaging: Consumer, Private Label, Bulk
Brands:
  Luetzow
  Sir Flip Flop

25480 Luhr Jensen & Sons Inc
400 Portway Ave
Hood River, OR 97031-1192
541-386-3811
Fax: 541-386-4917 info@luhrjensen.com
www.luhrjensen.com
Sausage and brine mixes and seasonings and spices; also, sausage making kits, electric smokers and wood flavor fuels
President: Philip Jensen
philipjensen@luhrjensen.com
Customer Service: Linda Gordon
Estimated Sales: $10-20 Million
Number Employees: 250-499
Square Footage: 100000

25481 Luke's Almond Acres
11281 S Lac Jac Ave
Reedley, CA 93654
559-638-3483
Fax: 559-637-7788
Wooden crates and gift boxes; packer of dried fruit and nuts
Owner: Ed Esajin
Owner: Lucas Nersesian
lnersesian@gmail.com
Estimated Sales: less than $500,000
Number Employees: 1-4
Square Footage: 10000
Brands:
  Luke's Almond Acres

25482 Luma Sense TechnologiesInc
3301 Leonard Ct
Santa Clara, CA 95054-2054
408-727-1600
Fax: 408-727-1677 800-631-0176
info@lumasenseinc.com www.lumasenseinc.com
Temperature monitoring sensors used in microwave
food processing development and gas monitoring
systems.
CEO: Michael Chavez
mchavez@clp.com
CEO: Vivek Joshi
Marketing Director: Mark Reis
Public Relations: Judi Seavers
Estimated Sales: $10-20 Million
Number Employees: 50-99
Square Footage: 74000

25483 Lumaco Inc
9-11 E Broadway
Hackensack, NJ 07601-6821
201-342-5119
Fax: 201-342-8898 800-735-8258
valvinfo@lumaco.com www.lumaco.com
Stainless steel manual and pneumatic valves
Owner: Anita Buxbaum
Sales Manager: Don Kiefer
Estimated Sales: $2.5-5 Million
Number Employees: 5-9
Square Footage: 10000

25484 Lumaco Inc
9-11 E Broadway
Hackensack, NJ 07601-6821
201-342-5119
Fax: 201-342-8898 800-735-8258
valvinfo@lumaco.com www.lumaco.com
Sanitary stainless steel valves
Owner: Anita Buxbaum
Estimated Sales: $2.5-5 Million
Number Employees: 5-9
Square Footage: 10000
Brands:
Lumaco

25485 Lumacurve Airfield Signs
9115 Freeway Dr
Macedonia, OH 44056
330-467-2030
Fax: 330-467-2076 800-258-1997
www.lumacurve.com
Manufacturer and exporter of porcelain top tables
President: John A Messner
Quality Control: Craig Fussner
R&D: Dane Scholz
Sales: Neil Messner
Contact: Melanie Rostankowski
melanie@lumacurve.com
Estimated Sales: Below $5,000,000
Number Employees: 20-49
Parent Co: Standard Signs Inc.
Type of Packaging: Food Service
Brands:
Logotop

25486 Lumax Industries
301 Chestnut Ave
Altoona, PA 16601
814-944-2537
Fax: 814-944-6413 sales@lumaxlighting.com
www.lumaxlighting.com
Manufacturer and exporter of lighting fixtures and
H.I.D. luminares including commercial, industrial
and custom
CEO: Vineet Sahni
vineetsahni@lumaxmail.com
CEO: Donald E Snyder
National Sales Manager: Randy Solliday
VP Operations: Ken Merritts
Estimated Sales: $10-20 Million
Number Employees: 100-249
Square Footage: 320000
Type of Packaging: Consumer, Food Service, Pri-
vate Label
Brands:
Light Forms

25487 Lumber & Things
PO Box 386
Keyser, WV 26726
304-788-5600
Fax: 304-788-7823 800-296-5656
www.lumberandthings.com

We have been in business for over 30 years. Our
customers depend on the standards that we build on:
Honesty-Quality-Service. We produce: Recondi-
tioned, Remanufacture and New pallets; Recondi-
tioned, Remanufactured and Recycled
tier/slipsheets; Reconditioned, Remanufactured and
New top frames; Reconditioned and New can and
glass bulk pallets. With an attendant standing by our
24 hour hotline we can provide your company with
delivery within 24 hours of your phone call.
President: Jack Amoruso
National Accounts Manager: Victor Knight
Customer Service Specialist: Patricia Davis
Plant Manager: Jack Amoruso
Purchasing Director: Ken Winter
Number Employees: 100-249
Square Footage: 150000
Type of Packaging: Consumer, Food Service, Pri-
vate Label, Bulk

25488 Lumenite Control Tech Inc
2331 17th St
Franklin Park, IL 60131-3432
847-455-1450
Fax: 847-455-0127 800-323-8510
customerservice@lumenite.com
www.lumenite.com
Manufacturer, importer and exporter of blending and
batching equipment, flow meters, level detectors and
temperature indicators and controllers
Owner: Ron Calabrese
roncalabrese@lumenite.com
Office Manager: Craig Meixner
V.P. Engineering: Ronald Calabrese
Sales manager: David Calabrese
Advertising Manager: Carol Calabrese
Service Representative: Rosa Furio
Estimated Sales: $2.5-5 Million
Number Employees: 10-19
Square Footage: 40000
Brands:
Industrialeveline
Paneleveline

25489 Luminiere Corporation
4269 Park Ave
Bronx, NY 10457-4207
718-295-5450
Fax: 718-295-5451
Manufacturer, importer and exporter of crystal and
bronze chandeliers, electric lamps, lighting fixtures
and display lighting
Owner: Herbert Leggan
VP: A Langsam
VP: N Gussack
Estimated Sales: $3-5 Million
Number Employees: 5-9
Square Footage: 100000

25490 Lumsden Corporation
PO Box 4647
Lancaster, PA 17604
717-394-6871
Fax: 717-394-1640 800-367-3664
sales@lumsdencorp.com www.lumsdencorp.com
CEO: Glenn Farrell
Contact: Kim Le
kle@lumsdencorp.com
Estimated Sales: $10-20 Million
Number Employees: 20-49

25491 Lumsden Flexx Flow
PO Box 4647
Lancaster, PA 17604
717-394-6871
Fax: 717-394-1640 800-367-3664
sales@lumsdenbelting.com
www.lumsdencorp.com
Wire and mesh conveyor belting, chain driven belts,
positive drive pin rolls, furnace curtains and wire
straightening devices; exporter of conveyor belting
President: Glenn Farrell
Quality Control: Glenn Farrell
Sales Manager: Pete Moore
Contact: Clayton Farrell
cfarrell@lumsdencorp.com
Estimated Sales: Below $15 Million
Number Employees: 20-49
Brands:
Flexx Flow

25492 Lunn Industries
1 Garvies Point Road
Glen Cove, NY 11542-2821
516-671-9000
Fax: 516-671-9005
Fiberglass and reinforced plastic containers
President: Bob Robinson
Sales Manager: Don Trachta Reda
Number Employees: 10

25493 Luseaux Labs Inc
16816 Gramercy Pl
Gardena, CA 90247-5282
323-321-0562
Fax: 310-538-3889 800-266-1555
detergents@luseaux.com www.luseaux.com
Manufacturer, importer and exporter of cleaners,
sanitizers and detergents including liquid and
powder
Vice President: Kathy Kalohi
kathy@luseaux.com
Chief Information Officer: Charles Edwards
Office Manager: Kathleen Kalohi
Estimated Sales: $810,000
Number Employees: 5-9
Square Footage: 180000
Type of Packaging: Food Service, Private Label,
Bulk
Other Locations:
Kingman AZ
Brands:
Luseaux

25494 Lustrecal
715 S Guild Ave
Lodi, CA 95240-3153
209-370-1600
Fax: 209-370-1690 800-234-6264
rbeckler@lustrecal.com www.lustrecal.com
Manufacturer and exporter of color anodized and
etched aluminum nameplates and labels
CEO: Clydene Hohenrieder
chohenrieder@lustrecal.com
Estimated Sales: $20-50 Million
Number Employees: 50-99

25495 Luthi Machinery Company, Inc.
1 Magnuson Avenue
Pueblo, CO 81001
719-948-1110
Fax: 719-948-9540 sales@atlaspacific.com
www.luthi.com
Manufacturer and exporter of can filling and dicing
machinery for tuna, salmon, chicken, turkey, pork
and beef
President: Erik Teranchi
CFO/VP: Don Freeman
V.P. & General Manager: Craig Furlo
Marketing/Sales: Robb Morris
Sales: Gini Fisher
Contact: Juan Monroy
jmonroy@luthi.com
Production: Vern Brown
Number Employees: 50
Square Footage: 136000

25496 Luxfer Gas Cylinders
3016 Kansas Ave # 1
Riverside, CA 92507-3445
951-684-5110
Fax: 951-328-1117 www.luxfercylinders.com
President: Andy Butcher
CFO: Micheal Edwards
R&D: Hendy Holrowd
Quality Control: Rick Willson
Estimated Sales: $20-50 Million
Number Employees: 250-499

25497 Luxo Corporation
Ste 105
5 Westchester Plz
Elmsford, NY 10523-1645
914-937-4433
Fax: 914-937-7016 800-222-5896
www.luxous.com
Manufacturer and importer of magnification, ambi-
ent and task lighting fixtures
Regional Sales Manager: Doug Benway
Estimated Sales: $10-20 Million
Number Employees: 50-99
Square Footage: 120000
Parent Co: Luxo ASA
Type of Packaging: Food Service

25498 Lyco Manufacturing
PO Box 2022
Wausau, WI 54402-2022

715-845-7867
Fax: 715-842-8228 info@lycowausau.com
www.lycowausau.com
Stainless steel liquid ring vacuum pumps for food, pharmaceutical, chemical, medical, laboratory and general industrial applications where corrosion resistance is beneficial.
President: Thomas Frane
Number Employees: 50-99

25499 Lyco Manufacturing Inc
115 Commercial Dr
Columbus, WI 53925-1008

920-623-4152
Fax: 920-623-3780 sales@lycomfg.com
www.lycomfg.com
Commercial food processing equipment manufacturer specializing in the areas of heating/cooling, liquid/solid separation, root crop preparation and snap bean processing equipment
CEO: Steve Hughes
steve.hughes@lycomfg.com
Estimated Sales: $4.5 Million
Number Employees: 50-99

25500 Lyco Wausau
P.O.Box 2022
Wausau, WI 54402-2022

715-845-7867
Fax: 715-842-8228 www.lycowausau.com
Manufacturer and exporter of stainless steel liquid ring vacuum pumps and systems for filling, deaerating, cooking, dewatering, conveying, evaporating and packaging
President: Thomas Frane
Estimated Sales: $3-5 Million
Brands:
Lyco
Vaqmer

25501 Lydall
PO Box 2002
Doswell, VA 23047-2002

804-266-9611
www.lydall.com
Packaging products and wooden pallet replacements
President, CEO: Dale G. Barnhart
EVP, CFO: Robert K. Julian
Vice President, Chief Accounting Officer: James V. Laughlan
VP Sales: P Mullins
Vice President, Human Resources: William M. Lachenmeyer
Plant Manager: E Smith
Estimated Sales: $1-5 Million
Number Employees: 100
Parent Co: Lydall

25502 Lyman-Morse Fabrication
19 Elltee Cir
Thomaston, ME 04861-3218

207-594-7655
Fax: 207-594-7790 www.lymanmorse.com
Manager: Johnathan Egan
jegan@lymanmorse.com
General Manager: Mike Young
Manager: Dave Wyllie
Estimated Sales: $3-5 Million
Number Employees: 10-19

25503 (HQ)Lynch Corp
140 Greenwich Ave # 4
Suite 4
Greenwich, CT 06830-6560

203-340-2590
Fax: 401-453-2009
Manufacturer and exporter of glass forming and packaging machines
President: Richard E McGrail
CEO: Ralph R Papitto
ralphp@gemini-cap.com
CFO: Raymond Keller
Estimated Sales: $20-30 Million
Number Employees: 1-4

25504 Lynch-Jamentz Company
5150 Candlewood Street
Lakewood, CA 90712-1925

562-630-6798
Fax: 562-630-5901 800-828-6217

Skewers, hot pan grips, spoons and racks including roasting, baking and broiling
CEO: Ron Trepte, Sr.
Marketing Director: Ron Trepte, Sr.
Secretary: E Trepte
Purchasing Manager: Ron Trepte, Sr.
Estimated Sales: $1-2.5 Million
Number Employees: 10
Square Footage: 48000
Parent Co: Trepte's Wire & Metal Works

25505 Lynden Meat Co
1936 Front St
Lynden, WA 98264-1708

360-354-2449
Fax: 360-354-7687
Livestock slaughtering services, herd managemnt, livestock breeding and grooming, livestock management, livestock selection, ice cube makers, ice block makers, industrial freezers.
Owner: Rick Biesheuvel
Estimated Sales: $3-5 Million
Number Employees: 5-9
Type of Packaging: Consumer

25506 (HQ)Lynn Sign Inc
8 Gleason St
Andover, MA 01810-3324

978-470-1194
Fax: 978-346-8197 800-225-5764
lynnsign@aol.com
Manufacturer and exporter of changeable plastic letters and signs, menu boards, building directories, bulletin boards, display cases, engraving stock and sign holders
Owner: R Rand Richmond
Public Relations: Darlene Reiss
Manager: Lynn Sullivan
Estimated Sales: Less Than $500,000
Number Employees: 1-4
Number of Brands: 1
Square Footage: 34000
Type of Packaging: Bulk
Brands:
Lynnply

25507 Lyon LLC
420 N Main St
Montgomery, IL 60538-1367

630-892-8941
Fax: 630-264-4542 www.lyonworkspace.com
Manufacturer and exporter of metal storage equipment including shelving, cabinets, etc
CEO: R Peter Washington
CEO: R Peter Washington
Marketing Director: Robert Bell
Estimated Sales: $50-100 Million
Number Employees: 1000-4999

25508 Lyons Falls Pulp & Paper
77 E Crystal Lake Avenue
Crystal Lake, IL 60014-6171

815-455-0981
Fax: 815-455-0997
Tea and coffee industry pouch materials (cellophane, paper, films)
Estimated Sales: $1-2.5 Million
Number Employees: 1-4

25509 M & D Specialties Inc
17301 NW Oak Ridge Rd
Yamhill, OR 97148-8119

503-662-4516
Fax: 503-662-3629
Wine industry labelers, pumps
Manager: Kathy Aplin
mdspec@msn.com
Estimated Sales: Less Than $500,000
Number Employees: 1-4

25510 M & E Mfg Co Inc
19 Progress St
Kingston, NY 12401-3611

845-331-2110
Fax: 845-331-4143
customerservice@zframerack.com
Manufacturer and exporter of shelving, racks, tables, cutting boards, trucks, platters, dollies and carts
President: Conor Curley
conor.curley@digicelgroup.com
Executive VP: Don Hall
Estimated Sales: $20-50 Million
Number Employees: 50-99
Square Footage: 40000

Brands:
Butcher Buddy
Deli Buddy

25511 M & G Packaging Corp
22610 Jamaica Ave
Floral Park, NY 11001-3812

718-343-0343
Fax: 516-488-3181 800-240-5288
charles@mgpackaging.com
www.mgpackaging.com
Boxes, cartons, foam, packaging material and plastic bags
President: Charles Rick
VP: Charles Rick
Estimated Sales: $20-50 Million
Number Employees: 5-9
Brands:
Avi

25512 M & H Crate Inc
4022 Fm 347 N
Jacksonville, TX 75766-6696

903-683-5351
Fax: 903-683-9593
Wooden pallets and shipping crates
CEO: Davy Sanders
dfsanders@mhcrates.com
Supervisor: Andy McCown
Estimated Sales: $10-20 Million
Number Employees: 100-249
Square Footage: 40000

25513 M & M Display
7700 Brewster Ave
Philadelphia, PA 19153-3299

215-492-1963
Fax: 215-365-5610 800-874-7171
bobdigiorgio@mmdisplays.com
www.mmdisplays.com
Screen printing, digital printing, p.o.p. displays, metal sign frames, banners, decals, interior graphics, and several patented items including nozzle talkers brand
CEO: Michael Sell
Sales Exec: Robert Digiorgio
Production Manager: Chris Mace
Purchasing Manager: William Gonzacez
Estimated Sales: $11 Million
Number Employees: 50-99
Square Footage: 160000

25514 M & M Equipment Corp
7355 Monticello Ave
Skokie, IL 60076-4024

847-673-0350
Fax: 847-673-0350 sales@mmequip.com
www.mmequip.com
Cutting and boning devices, slaughtering equipment
Owner: Marc Newman
sales@mmequip.com
Estimated Sales: $1-2.5 Million
Number Employees: 10-19

25515 M & M Industries Inc
316 Corporate Pl
Chattanooga, TN 37419-2339

423-821-3302
Fax: 423-821-9017 800-331-5305
cstone@mmcontainer.com www.ultimatepail.com
Life Latch plastic pails suitable for a variety of purposes including the food industry. Uses include livestock feed and grains; pet food storage; seeds; vitamin supplements, etc.
VP: Glenn H Morris Jr
gmorris@m-m-industries.com
Regional Accounts Manager: Rae Green
Regional Accounts Manager: Cindy Stone
Regional Accounts Manager: Tiffany King
Regional Accounts Manager: Janet Rogers
Estimated Sales: $10-25 Million
Number Employees: 100-249

25516 M & M Poultry EquipmentInc
296 Carlton Rd
Hollister, MO 65672-5156

417-334-6641
Fax: 417-332-2881 800-872-9687
drew.horst@mandmpoultry.com
www.mandmpoultry.com
Poultry processing equipment, overhead conveyor chain, picking fingers, misc, spare parts, and feather picker.

President: Rob L Middleton
middletonr@middletongroup.com
Marketing: Larry McGriff
Sales: Sloan Houston
Production: Jason Burkett
Number Employees: 50-99

25517 M & O Perry Industries
412 N Smith Ave
Corona, CA 92880-6903

951-273-1534
Fax: 951-734-2454 sales@moperry.com
www.moperry.com

Filling equipment for the animal health, biotech, diagnostic, medical device, ophthalmic and pharmaceutical markets. liquid and powder filling technologies
President: Phillip Osterhaus
posterhaus@moperry.com
Estimated Sales: $5-10 Million
Number Employees: 20-49

25518 M & O Perry Industries
412 N Smith Ave
Corona, CA 92880-6903

951-273-1534
Fax: 951-734-2454 sales@moperry.com
www.moperry.com

Powder fillers, liquid fillers
President: Phillip Osterhaus
posterhaus@moperry.com
Estimated Sales: $5-10 Million
Number Employees: 20-49

25519 M & Q Packaging Corp
1120 Welsh Rd
North Wales, PA 19454-3794

267-498-4000
Fax: 267-498-0030 www.mqplastics.com
High quality plastic products.
President: David Carlin
Contact: Chris Duplisea
chris@mqplastics.com
Estimated Sales: $26 Million
Number Employees: 10-19
Parent Co: M&Q Plastics Products
Type of Packaging: Food Service

25520 M & R Sales & Svc Inc
1n372 Main St
Glen Ellyn, IL 60137-3576

630-858-6101
Fax: 630-858-6134 800-736-6431
www.mrprint.com
Manufacturer and exporter of belting, switches, etc
CEO: Richard Hoffman
Estimated Sales: $1-2.5 Million
Number Employees: 20-49
Parent Co: M&R Printing Equipment

25521 M & S Automated FeedingSysts
1194 Cliff Rd E
Burnsville, MN 55337-1577

952-894-3263
Fax: 952-895-9910 masafs@msautomated.com
www.msautomated.com

President: Mark Grinager
mark@msautomated.com
Estimated Sales: $3,000,000-$5,000,000
Number Employees: 10-19

25522 M & W Protective Coating LLC
2239 16 3/4 Ave
Rice Lake, WI 54868-8786

715-234-2251

Protective coating
Manager: Douglas Winkel
Manager: Douglas Winkel
Estimated Sales: Less Than $500,000
Number Employees: 1-4

25523 (HQ)M D Stetson Co
92 York Ave
Randolph, MA 02368-1892

781-986-6161
Fax: 781-961-1764 800-255-8651
service@mdstetson.com www.mdstetson.com
Cleaning, degreasing and sanitizing chemicals, liquid hand soap and furniture and floor polish; wholesaler/distributor of maintenance equipment and supplies, industrial sweepers and scrubbers

President: Michael Glass
michael.glass@mdstetson.com
Treasurer and R&D and Quality Control: Andrea
Adams
Estimated Sales: $15-20 Million
Number Employees: 20-49
Square Footage: 104000

25524 M F & B Restaurant Systems Inc
133 Icmi Rd
Dunbar, PA 15431-2309

724-628-3050
Fax: 724-626-0247
Remanufacture conveyor pizza ovens, sell new and used parts
Owner: Mike French
mfrench@edgeoven.com
Vice President: Michael French
Estimated Sales: $400,000
Number Employees: 5-9
Number of Brands: 5
Square Footage: 24000
Brands:
    Lincoln Ovens
    Middleby Marshall Ovens

25525 M F G Inc
5620 19th Ave
Kenosha, WI 53140-3935

262-652-3336
Fax: 262-652-3322 mfgincorp@aol.com
www.mfginc.info
Packaging machinery
President: George Roders
mfgincorp@aol.com
Estimated Sales: $1-5 Million
Number Employees: 5-9

25526 M G America Inc
31 Kulick Rd
Fairfield, NJ 07004-3307

973-575-2509
Fax: 973-808-8421 cradossi@mgamerica.com
www.mgamerica.com
Capsule fillers, liquid and powder fillers, tube fillers, capsule checkweighers, cartoners, case packers and palletizers
President: Fabio Trippodo
Estimated Sales: $2.5-5 Million
Number Employees: 10-19

25527 M G Newell Corp
301 Citation Ct
Greensboro, NC 27409-9027

336-393-0100
Fax: 336-393-0140 800-334-0231
sales@mgnewell.com www.mgnewell.com
We provide equipment and engineered solutions in automation and control, CIP and custom washing systems, field service, calibration, maintenance, repair, fluid handling, heat exchange, installation, material handling, mixing andblending, process design, skidded system fabrication
President: John Sherrill
john.sherrill@mgnewell.com
CFO: Julie Hart
Vice President: Julie Hart
VP Engineering: Tony Saenz
Marketing Director: Gray Sherrill
Human Resources: Deb Gaither
VP/Chief Operating Officer: Michael Sherrill
Estimated Sales: $10-20 Million
Number Employees: 20-49

25528 M J D Trucking
2055 Demarco Dr
Vineland, NJ 08360-1554

856-205-9490
Fax: 856-205-9491 800-458-0439
www.mjdtrucking.net
Owner: John Davey
john@mjdtrucking.net
Estimated Sales: $3-5 Million
Number Employees: 20-49

25529 M M Industries Inc
36135 Salem Grange Rd
P.O. Box 720
Salem, OH 44460-9442

330-332-4958
Fax: 330-332-1543 800-227-7487
info@vorti-siv.com www.vorti-siv.com

Serving and filtration equipment. Manufacturer of sieving, straining and self-cleaning in-line filtration systems. Commonly used for ingredient sifting; particle separation and classification; liquid/solid separation and liquidfiltration
President: Barbara Maroscher
info@vorti-siv.com
VP: Vic Maroscher
Public Relations: Dennis Ulrich
Estimated Sales: $2.5-5 Million
Number Employees: 10-19
Square Footage: 160000

25530 M O Industries Inc
9 Whippany Rd # B1-2
Unit B1-2
Whippany, NJ 07981-1530

973-386-9228
Fax: 973-428-0221 sales@moindustries.com
www.moindustries.com
Manufacturer importer and exporter of movable and stationary drum lifters/positioners; also, dust control blending, crushing and milling size reducers, pallets, stainless steel funnels, quick-release valves, viscous materialdischargers, and stainless steel drums
President: German Leiva
gleiva@moindustries.com
Estimated Sales: $4 Million
Number Employees: 5-9
Brands:
    M.O.-Lift
    Robusto
    Vispro

25531 M S Plastics & Packaging Inc
10 Park Pl # 11
Building 2-1A2
Butler, NJ 07405-1370

973-492-2400
Fax: 973-492-7801 800-593-1802
web@msplastics.com
Polyethylene bags, liners, sheets, stretch wrap, printed bags, tubing, stretch and shrink film and bands; importer of plastic shrink films and bands
Owner: Ellen Saraisky
info@msplastics.com
CFO: Al Saraisky
Estimated Sales: $3-5 Million
Number Employees: 20-49
Brands:
    Banderwrapper
    Disposawrapper
    Freightwrap
    Polybander

25532 M S Willett Inc
220 Cockeysville Rd
Cockeysville, MD 21030-4367

410-771-0460
Fax: 410-771-6972 info@mswillett.com
www.mswillett.com
Manufacturer and exporter of precision equipment to produce stamped and formed metal food, shallow drawn and specialty containers and easy open can ends
President: Gabriel Gauzon
pgauzon@worldbank.org
R&D: Gary Ruby
Quality Control: Robert Burns
Sales Director: Gary Ruby
Public Relations: Linda Ambrose
Plant Manager: Larry Felty
Purchasing Director: Jack Kersch
Estimated Sales: $5 Million
Number Employees: 50-99
Square Footage: 240000

25533 M S Willett Inc
220 Cockeysville Rd
Cockeysville, MD 21030-4367

410-771-0460
Fax: 410-771-6972 info@mswillett.com
www.mswillett.com
Turnkey systems and tooling for the production of light metal packaging components, easy open ends, shallow drawn cans and food tray, hinge cover boxes, and small deep drawn parts
President: Gabriel Gauzon
pgauzon@worldbank.org
Engineering, Development & Sales: Gary Ruby
Quality & Safety: Robert Burns
Public Relations: Linda Ambrose
Manager Manufacturing Serv.: Jack Kersch
T&D Manager: Larry Felty

Estimated Sales: $5-10 Million
Number Employees: 50-99
Square Footage: 292000

25534 M&C Sweeteners
650 Industrial Road
Blair, NE 68008-2649
402-533-1843
Fax: 402-433-1831

25535 M&L Plastics
150 Pleasant St
Easthampton, MA 01027-1887
413-527-1330
Fax: 413-527-8621
Manufacturer and exporter of plastic display containers
Number Employees: 10-19
Parent Co: Paragon Rubber Corporation

25536 M&Q Plastic Products
1120 Welsh Rd
Suite 170
North Wales, PA 19454
267-498-4000
Fax: 267-498-0030 877-726-7287
High Temperture flexible, packaging products ideal for use in oven, microwave, and steamtable applications
Director Sales/Marketing: Tim Blucher
Contact: Ernie Bachert
ebachert@pansaver.com
Product Manager: George Schmidt
Estimated Sales: $2.5-5 Million
Number Employees: 75
Square Footage: 80000
Brands:
Monolyn
Pansaver

25537 M&R Flexible Packaging
PO Box 907
Springboro, OH 45066-0907
937-298-7272
Fax: 937-298-7388 800-543-3380
Manufacturer, importer and exporter of plastic bags, industrial packaging materials, plastics and shipping room supplies
President/Owner: Ronald Morris
Estimated Sales: $2.5-5,000,000
Number Employees: 10-19

25538 M&S Manufacturing
3728 Telegraph Rd
Arnold, MO 63010
636-464-2739
Fax: 636-464-5923
Hot food wells, refrigerated bases, hoods, walk-in coolers and tables including steam, salad, dish and soil
Owner: Darlene Spink
VP Secretary: Darline Spink
Estimated Sales: $500,000-$1 Million
Number Employees: 5-9
Square Footage: 5600

25539 M&S Miltenberg & Samton
2 Hollyhock Road
Wilton, CT 06897-4438
203-834-0002
Fax: 203-834-1002 www.miltsam.com
Carton machines: closing, filling, handling, sealing; coaters, cooling equipment: cooling tunnels, tables; cut and wrap equipment, extruders: chewing gum, coconut candy, confectionery; feeder belts, automatic, batch, rope, screw;feeding and placement system; flow-pack machines, glazing machines, gum sanders, kettles, licorice machines
Contact: Frank Franze
ffranze@miltsam.com
Estimated Sales: $2.5-5 Million
Number Employees: 5-9

25540 M-E-C Co
1400 Main St
Neodesha, KS 66757-1679
620-325-2673
Fax: 620-325-2678
Manufacturer and exporter of dryer systems for nonedible biological materials and foodwastes including convection, total, rotary, and flash tube

President: John Quick
jquick@m-e-c.com
CFO: Jerry Creekmore
R&D: Mike Hudson
Quality Control: Kent Shields
Sales Manager: Gary Follmer
Purchasing: John George
Estimated Sales: $20-50 Million
Number Employees: 100-249
Square Footage: 170000

25541 M-One Specialties
974 W 100 S
Salt Lake City, UT 84104-1198
801-596-2500
Fax: 801-521-6502 800-525-9223
mone@moneplumbing.com
www.m-oneplumbing.com
Faucet and plumbing repair and replacement parts-bathroom hardware and ada parts
President/Owner: George Mattena
mone@moneplumbing.com
Estimated Sales: $5-10,000,000
Number Employees: 10-19
Number of Brands: 164
Number of Products: 2800
Type of Packaging: Bulk

25542 M-TEK Inc
1675 Todd Farm Dr
Elgin, IL 60123
847-741-3500
Fax: 847-741-3569 847-741-3500
mtek@mtekcorp.com www.mtekcorp.com
Vacuum packaging machinery
President: Richard Maskell
VP Marketing/Sales: Rick Tkaczyk
Contact: Norm Buggele
nbuggele@mtekcorp.com
Operations Manager: Alan Wojak
Production Manager: Mark Evans
Purchasing Manager: Jason Aleo
Estimated Sales: $5-10 Million
Number Employees: 20-49
Number of Brands: 2
Type of Packaging: Consumer, Food Service, Private Label, Bulk

25543 M-Tech & Associates
4323 Stonewall Avenue
Downers Grove, IL 60515-2654
630-810-9714
Fax: 630-810-9712
Consultant specializing in implementing MRP scheduling, training, production and process monitoring
Number Employees: 5
Square Footage: 2000

25544 M-Vac Systems Inc
14621 S 800 W # 100
Suite 100
Bluffdale, UT 84065-4863
801-523-3962
www.m-vac.com
The m-vac is a dry or wet vacuuming collection/containment device used to detect and recover surface pathogens.
Owner: Dr. Bruce Bradley
Parent Co: MSI

25545 (HQ)M.E. Heuck Company
1111 Western Row Road
Mason, OH 45040-2649
513-681-1774
Fax: 513-681-2329 800-359-3200
Manufacturer, importer, exporter of kitchen utensils including barbecue tools, nut crackers, shellfish crackers, etc
President: Ramesh Malhotra
CFO: Tim Omelia
VP: Bill Dickmann
R&D: Tim Omelia
Manager: Linda Brandt
Contact: Chris Carthy
c.carthy@heuck.com
Estimated Sales: $20-50 Million
Number Employees: 30
Square Footage: 90000
Brands:
Burpee
H.M. Quackenbush
Mr. Food

25546 M.H. Rhodes Cramer
105 Nutmeg Rd S
South Windsor, CT 6074
860-291-8402
Fax: 860-610-0120 877-684-6464
customer-service@mhrhodes.com
www.mhrhodes.com
Manufacturer, importer and exporter of timers including audible signal and electronic as well as mechanical timers/time switches for OEM's
President: Ken Mac Cormac
Founder: Mark Rhodes, Sr.
Manager Sales: Jim Kline
Customer Service: Bernie Rodrigues
Purchasing Manager: Jeff Carlson
Estimated Sales: $10-20 Million
Number Employees: 100-249
Square Footage: 170000
Type of Packaging: Consumer, Food Service, Private Label, Bulk
Brands:
Mark-Time

25547 MAC Equipment
7901 NW 107th Ter
Kansas City, MO 64153-1910
816-891-9300
Fax: 816-891-8336 sales@macequipment.com
www.macequipment.com
President: Jay Brown
Contact: Mike Althouse
althousem@macequipment.com
Estimated Sales: Below $5 Million
Number Employees: 250-499

25548 MAC Equipment
7901 NW 107th Ter
Kansas City, MO 64153-1910
816-891-9300
Fax: 816-891-8336 800-821-2476
sales@macequipment.com
www.macequipment.com
Equipment: pneumatic conveying and dust collection
President: Jay Brown
Food Group Manager: Stuart Carrico
Contact: Mike Althouse
althousem@macequipment.com
Estimated Sales: $10-20 Million

25549 MAC Tac LLC
4560 Darrow Rd
Stow, OH 44224-1898
330-688-1111
Fax: 330-688-2540 866-262-2822
mactac.americas@mactac.com www.mactac.com
Manufacturer and exporter of pressure sensitive paper, film and foil products
President: Jim Peruzzi
Cmo: Jennifer Bowman
jmbowman@bemis.com
Executive VP: Robert Hawthorne
Purchasing Agent: Hank Cardarelli
Number Employees: 500-999
Parent Co: Bemls Company
Brands:
Copyback
Durascan
Eze-Gloss
Eze-Therm
Mac-Copy
Mac-Gloss
Mac-Jet
Optichrome
Opticlear
Optiscan
Pharmaclear
Pharmalite
Pharmasoft
Polyfilm
Trans Label
Ultrascan

25550 MAF Industries Inc
36470 Highway 99
PO Box 218
Traver, CA 93673
559-897-2905
Fax: 559-897-3422 mafusa@aol.com
www.mafindustries.com
Manufacturer, importer and exporter of packaging equipment including sizers, color sorters, box fillers, robotic bin dumpers, washers, waxers, etc

CEO: Jack Kraemer
CFO/Controller: Raul Mejia
Sales Manager: Leendert Van Der Tas
Manager: Raul Mejia
rmejia@mafindustries.com
Estimated Sales: $10-20 Million
Number Employees: 50-99
Square Footage: 100000
Parent Co: SMCM
Brands:
  Agrobotic Technology

25551 MAK Wood Inc
1235 Dakota Dr # E
Unit E
Grafton, WI 53024-9477

262-387-1200
Fax: 262-387-1400 info@makwood.com
www.makwood.com
Novelty sugars, cranberry, probiotics, lactobacillus and bifidobacterium. Supplier of L-arabinose, L-fucose, L-rhamnose, lactates, and of other probiotics.
Owner: Mark Brudnak
Secretary/Treasurer: Joseph Brudnak
Sr Executive VP: Mark Brudnak
Manager, Technical Sales Services: Eric Baer
mark@makwood.com
Estimated Sales: $380,000
Number Employees: 5-9
Type of Packaging: Private Label, Bulk

25552 MAP Systems International
300 E Touhy Avenue
Des Plaines, IL 60018-2669

847-299-7800
Fax: 847-299-8330
Modified atmospheric packaging, vacuum packaging equipment, blenders, choppers, smokehouses, stuffers, slicers and plant supplies. Products and services for" industrial food processing equipment; industrial food packaging equipment;grocery and restauran equipment; and also butcher supplies and food processing supplies.
Number Employees: 30

25553 MAP Tech Packaging Inc
145 Dillon Rd
Hilton Head Isle, SC 29926-3705

843-342-5900
Fax: 843-342-5924
gfoulke@maptechpackaging.com
www.maptechpackaging.com
Gas sensors that monitors the intake of ammonia, carbon monoxide, chlorine, chlorine dioxide, hydrogen sulfide, hydrogen, oxygen, etc.
President & CEO: Gary Bert
gbert@maptechpackaging.com
Estimated Sales: $1-3 Million
Number Employees: 10-19

25554 MAP Tech Packaging Inc
145 Dillon Rd
Hilton Head Isle, SC 29926-3705

843-342-5900
Fax: 843-342-5924
gfoulke@maptechpackaging.com
www.maptechpackaging.com
President & CEO: Gary Bert
gbert@maptechpackaging.com
Estimated Sales: $1-3 Million
Number Employees: 10-19

25555 MAPS Software
P.O.Box 821
Columbus, MS 39703-0821

662-328-6110
Fax: 662-329-9799
Computer software including point of sale, free and reduced application, purchasing and financial
President: Victor Fuqua
CFO: Sandy David
Representative: Jenny Taylor
Office Manager: Sandy Robinson
Estimated Sales: Below $5 Million
Number Employees: 4

25556 MBC Food Machinery Corp
78 Mckinley St
Hackensack, NJ 07601-4009

201-489-7000
Fax: 201-489-0614
jbattaglia@mbcfoodmachinery.com
www.mbcfoodmachinery.com

Manufacturer and exporter of filling pumps and automatic frozen pasta processing machinery including ravioli, manicotti and cavatelli
President and CFO: John Battaglia
Estimated Sales: Less than $500,000
Number Employees: 5-9

25557 MBX Packaging Specialists
207 N 1st Ave
Wausau, WI 54401-4403

715-845-1171
Fax: 715-848-1054 randy@mbxpkg.com
www.mbxpkg.com
Recycled plastic pallets in custom sizes and styles
President: Gary Yonke
gary@mbxpkg.com
CEO: Harvey H Scholfield Jr
VP Sales: Randy Haupt
Estimated Sales: $10-20 Million
Number Employees: 100-249
Square Footage: 200000
Parent Co: MBX Packaging
Other Locations:
  MBX Packaging
  Beloit WI
Brands:
  Enviro-Board

25558 MC Creation
1550 Bryant Street
Suite 760
San Francisco, CA 94103-4877

415-775-1135
Consultant specializing in home meal replacement concepts and food culture development promoting sushi
Estimated Sales: $300,000-500,000
Number Employees: 1-4

25559 MCD Technologies
2515 South Tacoma Way
Tacoma, WA 98409-7527

253-476-0968
Fax: 253-476-0974 www.mcdtechnologiesinc.com
Manufacturer and exporter of food dryers and evaporators; also, contract toll drying
President: Karin Bolland
info@mcdtechnologiesinc.com
VP: Richard Magoon
Marketing: Leo Schultz
Estimated Sales: $1-2.5 Million
Number Employees: 10-19
Square Footage: 36000
Brands:
  Refractance Window

25560 MCM Fixture Co
21306 John R Rd
Hazel Park, MI 48030-2211

248-547-9280
Fax: 248-547-9270 tawny@mcmstainless.com
Stainless steel food service equipment including cafeteria counters, sinks, tables, hoods and refrigerators; custom fabrication available, custom wall panels, both smooth and quilted, as well as corner guards in all sizes to order.
President: Gary Brown
gary@mcmstainless.com
Vice President: Eric Brown
Estimated Sales: $1-2.5 Million
Number Employees: 10-19

25561 MCNAB Inc
383 E 29th St # 2
Suite 2
Buena Vista, VA 24416-1293

540-261-1045
Fax: 540-261-1268 info@themcnab.com
Owner: Garnette Teass
sales@themcnab.com
Quality Control: Brad Witt
Estimated Sales: $3-5 Million
Number Employees: 10-19

25562 MCR Technologies Group Inc
13420 Galt Rd
PO Box 1016
Sterling, IL 61081-8913

815-622-3181
Fax: 815-622-0819 877-622-3181
sales@weighshark.com
www.mcrtechnologiesgroup.com
Metal detectors
President: Mark Humphreys
mhumphreys@weighshark.com

Estimated Sales: $1.5 Million+
Number Employees: 5-9
Number of Brands: 4
Number of Products: 9
Square Footage: 4000
Type of Packaging: Food Service

25563 MDE Corp
11965 Brookfield St
Livonia, MI 48150-1736

734-744-5480
Fax: 313-931-2015 800-482-3393
mielsen@mdecorp.com www.mdecorp.com
Fillers, air, milk, filtration equipment, heat exchangers, plate, scraped surface, homogenizers, ice and ice cream equipment, ingredient feeders, meters, flow, milk, solids, aseptic processing equipment, batch control systems, andcentrifuges
President: Veronica Burnett
vburnett@mdecorp.com
VP: Robert Nielson Jr
Estimated Sales: $5-10 Million
Number Employees: 20-49

25564 MDH Packaging Corporation
101 Miller Drive
Crittenden, KY 41030-7560

859-746-0993
Fax: 859-746-0933 www.ripnzip.com
Contact: Rainer Garger
rgarger@ripnzip.com
Estimated Sales: $3,000,000-$5,000,000
Number Employees: 10-19

25565 MDI Worldwide
38271 W 12 Mile Rd
Farmington Hills, MI 48331-3041

248-553-1900
Fax: 248-488-5700 800-228-8925
sales@mdiworldwide.com
www.mdiworldwide.com
Designs and manufactures marketing displays, retail displays, commercial sign holders, POP displays and merchandising displays
President: Lisa Sarkisian
lsarkisian@mdiworldwide.com
Number Employees: 100-249
Type of Packaging: Food Service
Brands:
  Postergrip
  Storeworks

25566 MDR International
14861 NE 20th Ave
North Miami, FL 33181

305-944-5019
Fax: 305-949-4136 mdrinc@bellsouth.com
www.mdrinternational.com
Glassware, hurricane glasses, plastic beer mugs, tumblers and mason jar mugs
Owner: Bernard Ghelbendorf
VP Marketing: Gary Fein
Estimated Sales: $2.5-5,000,000
Number Employees: 10-19

25567 MDS Nordion
447 March Road
Ottawa, ON K2K 1X8
Canada

613-592-2790
Fax: 613-592-6937 800-465-3666
Supplies patented food irradiation solutions for the meat, poultry and produce industry. Our equipment and process eliminates food-borne pathogens such as E. coli, Salmonella and Listeria from food, prolongs shelf life and treatsproduct for quarantine and bio-security after harvest
President: Steve West
CFO: Micheal Thomas
Senior Vice President, General Counsel,: Andrew Foti
Product Manager Food and Radiation: Joseph Borsa Ph D
R&D and Director: Pierre Lahaie
Marketing Director: Carolin Vandenberg
Senior Vice President of Sales and Marke: Kevin Brooks
Number Employees: 800
Parent Co: MDS
Brands:
  Centurion

25568 MDS-Vet Inc
3429 Stearns Rd
Valrico, FL 33596-6450

813-653-1180
Fax: 813-684-5953 tbattle@mdsincorporated.com
www.mdsvet.com
Manufacturer and exporter of scopes used to check
bacteria in pipes and tubes
Owner: Jayson Fitzgerald
jfitzgerald@seminolecountyfl.gov
Director Marketing: Trudi Battle
Estimated Sales: Less than $500,000
Number Employees: 5-9

25569 MDT
971 Dogwood Trl
Tyrone, GA 30290-2708

770-631-9074
Fax: 770-486-9903 info.us@mdt-tex.com
Shades,structures and umbrellas for commercial pur-
poses
Manager: Enlai Hooi
enlai.hooi@mdt-tex.com
Estimated Sales: $1-2.5 Million
Number Employees: 1-4

25570 MEPSCO
1888 E Fabyan Pkwy
Batavia, IL 60510-1498
Fax: 630-231-9372 800-323-8535
www.mepsco.com
Estimated Sales: $9 Million
Number Employees: 20-49

25571 MERRICK Industries Inc
10 Arthur Dr
Lynn Haven, FL 32444-1685

850-522-4300
Fax: 850-265-9768 800-271-7834
info@merrick-inc.com www.merrick-inc.com
Manufacturer and exporter of process weighing and
control equipment, belt feeders and loss-in-weight
feeders
CEO: Larry Adams
ladams@acistudios.com
CEO: Joe K Tannehill Sr
Purchasing Manager: Steve Rhinehart
Estimated Sales: $10-20,000,000
Number Employees: 100-249
Square Footage: 55000
Brands:
   Gravimerik
   Mc2
   Mc3
   Superbridge

25572 MGF.com
2700 Cumberland Parkway
Suite 500
Atlanta, GA 30339
Canada

770-444-9686
Cleaning compounds, detergents and disinfectants
Founder, CEO: Mitch Free
Number Employees: 20
Square Footage: 60000

25573 MGM Instruments
925 Sherman Ave
Hamden, CT 06514-1150

203-248-4008
Fax: 203-288-2621 800-551-1415
sales@mgminstruments.com
www.mgminstruments.com
Analyzes and tests plant operations, wastewater
President: Patrick Harewood
Chairman and CEO: George Mismas
georgem@mgminstruments.com
Number Employees: 20-49

25574 MGP Ingredients Inc
100 Commercial St
Atchison, KS 66002-2514

913-367-1480
Fax: 913-367-0192 800-255-0302
selmak@mgpingredients.com
www.mgpingredients.com
CEO: Augustus C Griffin
augustus.griffin@mgpingredients.com
Number Employees: 250-499

25575 MGS Machine Corp
9900 85th Ave N
Maple Grove, MN 55369-6801

763-425-8808
Fax: 763-493-8818 800-790-0627
info@mgsmachine.com www.mgsmachine.com
Packaging machinery manufacturing; feeding and
cartoning
President: Richard Bahr
richard.bahr@mgsmachine.com
Estimated Sales: $10-20 Million
Number Employees: 100-249

25576 MGS Machine Corp
9900 85th Ave N
Maple Grove, MN 55369-6801

763-425-8808
Fax: 763-493-8818 800-790-0627
info@mgsmachine.com www.mgsmachine.com
Vibratory feeders, centrifugal feed systems
President: Richard Bahr
richard.bahr@mgsmachine.com
Estimated Sales: $1-5 Million
Number Employees: 100-249

25577 MIFAB Inc
1321 W 119th St
Chicago, IL 60643-5109

773-341-3030
Fax: 773-341-3047 800-465-2736
sales@mifab.com www.mifab.com
Manufacturer, importer and exporter of grease traps,
oil, sediment and lint interceptors, floor drains, ac-
cess doors, etc
President: Michael Whiteside
mwhiteside@mifab.com
Accounting Manager: Daniel ODekirk
Vice President of Division: Paul Lacourciere
Engineering Manager: Jason Gremchuk
Quality Control Manager: John Murphy
National Sales Manager: Andrew Haines
Purchasing Manager: Alice OConnor
Number Employees: 50-99
Square Footage: 180000
Brands:
   Mifab

25578 MILLIPORE Sigma
290 Concord Rd
Billerica, MA 01821-3405

978-715-4321
Fax: 978-715-1393 www.emdmillipore.com
Wine and food industry filtration equipment.
Multiscreen filter plates, Montage Plasmid Miniprep
kit, Opticap Gamma sterilizable capsules, Ezpak
membranes and membrane dispenser
Chairman: Fran Lunger
CFO: Anthony L Mattacchione
anthony_mattacchione@millipore.com
Number Employees: 500-999

25579 MISCO Refractometer
3401 Virginia Road
Cleveland, OH 44122

216-831-1000
Fax: 216-831-1195 866-831-1999
www.misco.com
Manufacturer and exporter of digital hand-held
abbe/labprator, inline/process refractometers. Estab-
lished in 1949 in Cleveland, Ohio and is recognized
as a world leader in the refractometer industry.
CEO: Michael Rainer
Contact: Tosha Hudson
thudson@misco.com
Number Employees: 10-19
Type of Packaging: Food Service, Bulk
Brands:
   Abbe

25580 MIT Poly-Cart Corp
211 Central Park W # 14j
New York, NY 10024-6020

212-724-7290
Fax: 212-721-9022 800-234-7659
info@mitpolycart.com www.mitpolycart.com
Industrial polyethylene hand carts and trucks
President: Daniel Moss
danielmoss@aol.com
Vice President: Isaac Rinkewick
Research & Development: Isaac Rinkewick
Marketing Director: Sandy Divack
Sales Director: Marty Winnick
Customer Service: Marty Winnick

Estimated Sales: $1-2.5 Million
Number Employees: 10-19
Number of Brands: 1
Number of Products: 50
Type of Packaging: Bulk

25581 MIWE USA
54 Jamestown Road
Belle Mead, NJ 08502-5222

908-904-0221
Fax: 908-904-0241 miweusa@aol.com
www.miwe.de
President: Hary Jacoby
CFO: Hary Jacoby
Quality Control: Hary Jacoby
R&D: Hary Jacoby
Estimated Sales: $5-10 Million
Number Employees: 4

25582 MJ Puehse & Company
P.O. Box 2043
Carefree, AZ 85377

530-677-8863
Fax: 530-683-4011 mjpuehse@mjpuehse.com
www.mjpuehse.com
Sales and Marketing Agency selling ingredients to
food and beverage companies.
President: Michael Puehse

25583 MLS Signs Inc
25733 Dhondt Ct
Chesterfield, MI 48051-2601

586-948-0200
Fax: 586-948-0300 www.phillipssign.com
Neon, acrylic, metal and vinyl letters, illuminated
signs and cake stands; also, crane truck service and
installation available
President: William Siewert
mlssigns@ameritech.net
Estimated Sales: $1-2.5 Million
Number Employees: 10-19
Square Footage: 8000

25584 MMLC
12403 Wellington Park
Houston, TX 77072-3954

281-983-0315
Fax: 713-868-8041 800-727-5700
info@mmldesign.com www.mmldesign.com
President: Jerry Lecontte
Quality Control: Ray Nevill
Estimated Sales: $300,000-500,000
Number Employees: 1-4

25585 MMR Technologies
1400 N Shoreline Blvd Ste A5
Mountain View, CA 94043-1346

650-962-9620
Fax: 650-962-9647 855-962-9620
sales@mmr-tech.com www.mmr-tech.com
Manufacturer and exporter of microminiature refrig-
eration equipment for materials research
CEO: William Little
Sales VP: Robert Paugh
Contact: Lee Asplund
leea@mmr.com
Estimated Sales: $2.5-5 Million
Number Employees: 10-19
Square Footage: 36000

25586 MOCAP Inc
409 Parkway Dr
Park Hills, MO 63601-4435

573-431-4610
Fax: 314-543-4111 800-633-6775
sales@mocap.com www.mocap.com
Transparent tubing
President: Joseph Miller
jmiller@mocap.com
Estimated Sales: $10-20 Million
Number Employees: 50-99

25587 MOCON Inc
7500 Mendelsohn Ave N
Minneapolis, MN 55428-4045

763-493-6370
Fax: 763-493-6358 www.mocon.com
Scientific testing and equipment, permeation, leak
detection, headspace, weighing,testing
President/CEO: Robert Demorest
rdemorest@mocon.com
Estimated Sales: $37 Million
Number Employees: 250-499

25588 MODAGRAPHICS
5300 Newport Dr
Rolling Meadows, IL 60008-3797
847-392-3980
Fax: 847-392-3989 marketing@modagrafics.com
www.modagrafics.com
Manufacturer and exporter of graphics for food
stores and truck fleets
President/Chief Executive Officer: Carlson Lennard
CEO: Paul Pirkle
paul.pirkle@modagrafics.com
Vice President/Chief Financial Officer: Jack Masters
Executive Vice President: Robert Jurgens
Chief Information Officer/IT Director: Betsy
Carlson
Marketing Department: Kate Kummer
Vice President, Operations: Howard Baden
Production Manager: Marty Dorner
Plant Engineering Manager: Salvatore Geraci
Director, Purchasing: Marty Anderson
Estimated Sales: $12 Million
Number Employees: 100-249
Square Footage: 80000

25589 MPBS Industries
2820 E Washington Blvd
Los Angeles, CA 90023-4217
323-268-8514
Fax: 323-268-6305 800-421-6265
www.mpbs.com
Modified atmospheric packaging, vacuum packaging equipment, blenders, choppers, smokehouses,
stuffers, slicers and plant supplies. Products and services for: industrial food processing equipment; industrial food packaging equipment;grocery and
restaurant equipment; and also butcher supplies and
food processing supplies.
President: Michael Dernburg
Manager: Bob Maxwell
bob@mpbs.com
Estimated Sales: $2.5-5 Million
Number Employees: 10-19

25590 MPE Group
6981 N Park Drive
Pennsauken, NJ 08109-4205
856-317-9960
Fax: 856-317-9963 www.mpe.nl
Scraped surface heat exchangers, unique bottom
driven processing veessels, crystallization tanks,
complete processing systems, aseptic processing
systems, vacuum gas packaging systems, vacuum
drying
Estimated Sales: $55 Million
Number Employees: 275

25591 MPI Label Systems
450 Courtney Rd
P.O.Box 70
Sebring, OH 44672-1339
330-938-2134
Fax: 330-938-9878 800-837-2134
info@mpilabels.com www.mpilabels.com
labels and equipment. Some of their products in-
clude flexible packaging, pressure-sensitive labels,
automatic labeling equipment, RFID labels/tags,
roll-fed wrap labels, shrink products, thermal print-
ers, barcode scanners, labelingsoftware and more.
President: Randy Kocher
Marketing Manager: Linda Buttermore
Account Manager Sales: Michele Beckett-Carver
Estimated Sales: $20-50 Million
Number Employees: 500+
Square Footage: 110000
Parent Co: Miller Products
Other Locations:
   Alliance OH
   Baltimore MD
   Charlotte CT
   Danielson CT
   Grand Prairie TX
   Norwich NY
   Stockton CA
   University Park IL
   Wadsworth OH
   Whites Creek TN
Brands:
   Anchorseal
   Mpi 90
   Mpi-L
   Prime Label
   Prime Plus Irc
   Scannable Bar Code Hologram

25592 MPI Simgraph
210 Meijer Dr
Suite B
Lafayette, IN 47905-4694
765-449-4100
Fax: 765-449-1703
Visual packaging software products including Leap-
frog graphic database manager, Imagepak for creat-
ing visual packaging instruction sheets and
Iconworker for creating visual assembly and process
instruction sheets
Estimated Sales: $1-5 Million

25593 MPS North America, Inc.
8236 Nieman Road
Lenexa, KS 66214
913-310-0055
Fax: 913-310-0088 www.mps-group.nl
Food products machinery
President: Serge Cramer
VP: Jerry Frizzell
Operations Manager: John Estrada
Estimated Sales: $2 Million
Number Employees: 1-4
Parent Co: MPS meat processing systems

25594 MRC Bearing Services
1510 Gehman Rd
Harleysville, PA 19438
215-513-4400
Fax: 215-513-4736 800-672-7000
Bearings for the food industry
President: Don Poland
Sales Director: Jay Carlson
Public Relations: Wendy Garle
Estimated Sales: $1-5 Million

25595 MRC Bearing Services
1510 Gehman Road
Kulpsville, PA 19443
215-513-4726
Fax: 888-322-4672 800-672-7000
Bearings
President: Tom Johnstone
Number Employees: 10

25596 MRI Upper Westchester
118 N Bedford Road
Suite 103
Mount Kisco, NY 10549-2554
914-241-2788

25597 MSK Covertech
4170 Jvl Industrial Park Dr
Marietta, GA 30066
770-928-1099
Fax: 770-928-3849 info@msk.us
www.mskcovertech.com
Packaging machinery
Marketing: Marcela Leano
General Manager: Braden Camp
Estimated Sales: $1-5 Million
Number Employees: 8
Parent Co: MSK Covertech Group
Brands:
   Econotech
   Powertech
   Recotech

25598 MSSH
901 N Carver St
Greensburg, IN 47240-1014
812-663-2180
Fax: 812-663-5405 ashleymachine@yahoo.com
Manufacturer and exporter of eviscerating tables,
poultry pickers and scalders
Manager: Jim Israel
CFO: Jim Israel
Estimated Sales: $30-50 Million
Number Employees: 5-9
Square Footage: 8000

25599 MTL Etching Industries
861 Fiske St
Woodmere, NY 11598-2429
516-295-9733
Fax: 516-295-9733
Manufacturer and exporter of advertising specialties,
nameplates, dials, scales, rulers, etc
CEO: Alan Stern
Estimated Sales: $1-3 Million
Number Employees: 10-19

25600 MTP Custom Machinery Corporation
3857 Hyde Park Boulevard
Niagara Falls, NY 14305-1701
716-282-5705
Fax: 716-282-5741 mtpcorp@aol.com
Accumulating conveyors
Estimated Sales: $1-5 Million
Number Employees: 29

25601 Mac Papers Inc
8370 Philips Hwy
Jacksonville, FL 32256-8204
904-733-9660
Fax: 904-733-9622 800-334-7026
www.macpapers.com
Envelopes and die cut paper
Manager: Bob Tees
Vice President: Darnell Babbit
dbabbit@macpapers.com
Plant Manager: Ted Towner
Estimated Sales: $20-50 Million
Number Employees: 100-249
Parent Co: MAC Paper

25602 MacDonald Steel Ltd
200 Avenue Road
Cambridge, ON N1R 8H5
Canada
519-620-0400
Fax: 519-621-4995 800-563-8247
Sales@HDPCANADA.COM www.hdpcanada.com
Number Employees: 10
Parent Co: HDP

25603 MacMillan Bloedel Packaging
4001 Carmichael Rd
Montgomery, AL 36106-3613
334-244-0562
Fax: 334-213-6199 800-239-4464
Manufacturer and exporter of corrugated shipping
containers
VP: J Tignor
Director Marketing: Stewart Williams

25604 Macdonald Signs & Advertising
6364 E State Highway 107
Edinburg, TX 78542-7295
956-787-0016
Fax: 956-787-8466
Magnetic signs
Owner: Lupette Mac Donald
macdonald_printing@yahoo.com
Estimated Sales: Less Than $500,000
Number Employees: 1-4

25605 Machanix Fabrication Inc
13929 Magnolia Ave
Chino, CA 91710-7032
909-590-9700
Fax: 909-590-3932 800-700-9701
www.machanixfab.com
Food processing equipment and supplies including
blenders, mixers, slicers, toasters, etc
CEO: Craig Broswell
machanixfab@gmail.com
Estimated Sales: Less Than $500,000
Number Employees: 1-4
Square Footage: 12000

25606 (HQ)Machem Industries
1607 Derwent Way
Delta, BC V3M 6K8
Canada
604-526-5655
Fax: 604-526-1618
Manufacturer and exporter of alkaline, acid and spe-
cialty cleaners, sanitizers, chain lubes, defoamers,
descalers and chlorine dioxide
General Manager: Paul Grehen
Other Locations:
   Machem Industries
   Regina SK
Brands:
   Dairi-San
   Kloriclean
   Optimum
   Orbit
   Progress
   Rinsol
   Topsan
   Tuff Stuff

25607 Machine Applications Corp
3410 Tiffin Ave
Sandusky, OH 44870-9752
419-621-2322
Fax: 419-621-2321 info@macinstruments.com
www.macinstruments.com
Steam flow meters and high temperature humidity
analyzers
President: James Weit
info@macinstruments.com
Sales Manager: Janet Jarrett
Estimated Sales: Below $5 Million
Number Employees: 5-9
Square Footage: 16000

25608 Machine Builders & Design Inc
806 N Post Rd
Shelby, NC 28150-4247
704-482-3456
Fax: 704-482-3000 www.machinebuilders.com
Manufacturer and exporter of cookie packaging ma-
chinery
President/Owner: Darryl Mims
Finance Manager: Steve Hyde
Vice President: Brad Hogan
Service Manager: Phillip Cannon
Sales Manager: Rick MaDaniel
Engineering Manager: Eric Grayson
Estimated Sales: $5-10,000,000
Number Employees: 20-49

25609 Machine Builders & Design Inc
806 N Post Rd
Shelby, NC 28150-4247
704-482-3456
Fax: 704-482-3000 mbdusa@machinebuilders.com
www.machinebuilders.com
Bakery equipment
President: Darryl Mims
Finance Manager: Steve Hyde
Vice President: Brad Hogan
Sales Manager: Rick McDaniel
Service Manager: Phillip Cannon
Estimated Sales: $5-10 Million
Number Employees: 20-49
Type of Packaging: Bulk

25610 Machine Electronics Company
9 Devoe St
Brooklyn, NY 11211
718-384-3211
Manufacturer and exporter of packaging, wrapping
and bag filling machinery
Manager: Tom Costello
Number Employees: 44

25611 Machine Ice Co
8915 Sweetwater Ln
Houston, TX 77037-2706
281-448-7823
Fax: 713-868-4424 800-423-8822
www.machineice.com
Wholesaler/distributor and exporter of mobile ice
centers, ice plants, ice machines and refrigeration
equipment; also, walk-in and reach-in coolers, cold
storage facilities, ice cream makers, etc.; serving the
food service market
President: Dan Celli
Sales Manager: Walter Felix
Estimated Sales: Less Than $500,000
Number Employees: 1-4
Square Footage: 88000

25612 Machine Ice Co
8915 Sweetwater Ln
Houston, TX 77037-2706
281-448-7823
Fax: 713-868-4424 800-423-8822
www.machineice.com
Manufacturer and exporter of ice equipment includ-
ing automatic ice cube makers, dispensers, crushers
and storage bins; also, air conditioning units
President: Dan Celli
Sales Manager: Walter Felix
Estimated Sales: Less Than $500,000
Number Employees: 1-4
Square Footage: 200000

25613 Machinery & Equipment Corp
3401 Bayshore Blvd
Brisbane, CA 94005-1498
415-467-7010
Fax: 415-467-2639 800-227-4544
info@machineryandequipment.com
www.machineryandequipment.com
Buy and sell used processing and packaging equip-
ment. Manufacture sanitary ribbon mixes and sell
new dicers
President: Mike Ebert
CFO: Bryant Caston
Food Division Manager: Don Riochet
Estimated Sales: $4 Million
Number Employees: 10-19

25614 Machinery & Equipment Company, Inc.
PO Box 7632
San Francisco, CA 94120
415-467-3400
Fax: 415-467-2639 800-227-4544
info@machineryandequipment.com
www.machineryandequipment.com
President: Mike Ebert
CFO: Bryan Caston
Number Employees: 20

25615 Machinery Corporation ofAmerica
4401 Capitola Road
Suite 3
Capitola, CA 95010-3572
831-479-9901
Fax: 831-479-4443
Supplier of rebuilt food processing equipment
Contact: Rick Bakanoff
rick.bakanoff@mca-america.com
Estimated Sales: $1 Million
Number Employees: 5

25616 Machinery Engineering Technology
2629 E County Road O
Janesville, WI 53546
608-758-0506
Fax: 608-758-1343 877-758-0506
met-llc@execpc.com
Stainless steel equipment for food filling, sealing
and lidding
Estimated Sales: $3 Million
Number Employees: 5-9

25617 Mack-Chicago Corporation
2555 S Leavitt St
Chicago, IL 60608-5202
773-376-8100
Fax: 773-376-0883 800-992-6225
Point-of-purchase displays, gift boxes and corru-
gated shipping containers; also, fire retardant and
corrugated disposable chafing dishes available
President: Alwin J Kolb
CFO: Alwin J Kolb
Quality Control: Jerry Santeford
Sales Manager: Dale Arnold
Contact: George Pluta
george@mackltd.com
General Manager: Ron Praun
Plant Manager: Ken Kruger
Estimated Sales: $20-50 Million
Number Employees: 100-249
Square Footage: 425000
Parent Co: Mack Packaging Group

25618 Mackenzie Creamery
6722 Pioneer Trl
Hiram, OH 44234-9714
330-569-3368
Fax: 330-569-3387 info@mackenziecreamery.com
www.mackenziecreamery.com
Organic Artisan goat cheeses
Founder/President: Jean Mackenzie
jeanniegoat@yahoo.com
Estimated Sales: Less Than $500,000
Number Employees: 10-19

25619 Mackie International. Inc.
719 Palmyrita Avenue
Riverside, CA 92507
951-346-0530
Fax: 951-346-0541
carmel@mackieinternational.net
www.mackieinternational.net

Stabilizers
President: Ernesto U Dacay
Contact: Amando Briones
a.briones@mackieinternational.net
Estimated Sales: $1 Million
Number Employees: 50-99

25620 Maco Bag Corp
412 Van Buren St
Newark, NY 14513-9205
315-226-1000
Fax: 315-226-1050 www.macopkg.com
Plastic bags and barrier packaging
President: Craig Miller
craig.miller@macobag.com
CEO: J Scott Miller
Number Employees: 100-249
Square Footage: 100000
Type of Packaging: Consumer, Food Service, Pri-
vate Label, Bulk

25621 Macon Awning & Canvas Prod
230 South St
Macon, GA 31206-1066
478-743-2684
Commercial awnings
President: David B Redding Jr
dr@maconcanvas.com
Estimated Sales: $1-2.5 Million
Number Employees: 10-19

25622 Macrie Brothers
750 S 1st Rd
Hammonton, NJ 08037-8407
609-561-6822
Fax: 609-561-6296 bluebuck@bellatlantic.net
Blueberries
Owner/CEO: Paul Macrie III
Superviser: Al Macrie
Operations: Nicholas Macrie
Production: Michael Macrie
Estimated Sales: Below $5 Million
Number Employees: 5
Square Footage: 120000
Type of Packaging: Consumer, Food Service, Pri-
vate Label, Bulk
Brands:
Blue Buck

25623 Macro Plastics Inc
2250 Huntington Dr
Fairfield, CA 94533-9732
707-437-1200
Fax: 707-437-1201 800-845-6555
www.macroplastics.com
Manufacturer high pressure injection molded prod-
ucts for food and agriculture
CEO: Warren Macdonald
wmacdonald@macroplastics.com
CEO: Pat Brandt
Estimated Sales: $10-20 Million
Number Employees: 20-49

25624 Maddox/Adams International
1421 SW 107th Ave
Suite 213
Miami, FL 33174
305-592-3337
Fax: 305-591-2591 alina@maddoxadams.com
www.maddoxmetalworks.com
Food processing equipment for snack foods includ-
ing tortillas, corn chips and popcorn; also, bake and
fry extrusion equipment and nut roasters
Sales: Alina Del Rivero
Estimated Sales: $300,000-500,000
Number Employees: 1-4
Parent Co: Beatrice Companies

25625 MadgeTech, Inc.
879 Maple Street
Contoocook, NH 03229
603-456-2011
Fax: 603-456-2012 info@madgetech.com
www.madgetech.com
Data logging instrumentation used for reading and
monitoring temperatures both during and after the
cooking process.
Contact: Ann Battles
ann@madgetech.com

25626 Madison County Wood Products
3311 Chouteau Ave
St Louis, MO 63103-2911
314-772-1722
Fax: 314-772-1733 www.mcwp.com
New and used hard and soft wood pallets
President: Jim Kesting
Controller: William Brynda
Vice President: Douglas Gaines
Estimated Sales: $12 Million
Number Employees: 100-249
Square Footage: 50000

25627 Madix
1537 S Main St
Goodwater, AL 35072-6620
256-839-6354
Fax: 256-839-5608 www.madixinc.com
Supermarket fixtures and food service showcases
CFO/Senior VP/Chief Information Officer: David
Satterfield
Vice President, Sales: Marcy Stephens
Operations Manager: Jay Dowdle
Plant Manager: Phillip Whitley
Purchasing Director: Kim Wright
Estimated Sales: $50-100 Million
Number Employees: 250-499
Square Footage: 91730

25628 Madix Inc
500 Airport Rd
Terrell, TX 75160-5200
214-515-5400
Fax: 972-563-0792 800-776-2349
www.madixinc.com
Manufacturer and exporter of retail display shelving,
storage, wire and wood display systems
Owner: Thomas A Satterfield
tsatterfield@madixinc.com
Estimated Sales: $56 Million
Number Employees: 500-999
Square Footage: 1070000
Brands:
  Maximum Merchandiser
  Multiple Media Fixture
  Omega

25629 Madsen Wire Products Inc
101 Madsen St
Orland, IN 46776-5417
260-829-6561
Fax: 260-829-6652 bsnyder@madsenwire.com
www.madsenwire.com
Manufacturer and designer of wire baskets, bases,
containers, carts, displays, grids, stands, trays, fan
and clamp guards, shelving, cages, etc. Constructed
out of cold roll steel or stainless steel
President: Steve Cochran
scochran@generalcage.com
Estimator/Customer Service: Gwen Wheaton
Account Manager: Kim Straley
Estimated Sales: $10-20 Million
Number Employees: 20-49
Square Footage: 84000
Type of Packaging: Food Service, Private Label,
  Bulk

25630 Magi Kitch'n
10 Ferry St
Concord, NH 03301-5022
603-225-6684
Fax: 603-230-5548 800-441-1492
sales@pitco.com www.magikitchn.com
Manufacturer and exporter of commercial cooking
equipment including mobile outdoor units and gas,
electric and charcoal broilers; also, broiler-griddles
including mesquite and charcoal
President: Robert Bosa
bosa@magikitchn.com
CFO: Bob Granger
Vice President, General Manager: Greg Moyer
VP: George McMahon
Quality Control: Ray Amitrano
Senior Manager of Sales: Bonnie Bolster
Public Relations: Thomas Cassin
VP Operations: Robert Granger
Vice President of Operations: Steve Reale
Purchasing Manager: Terri Miller
Estimated Sales: $30-50 Million
Number Employees: 20-49
Parent Co: Middleby Corporation
Type of Packaging: Food Service

Brands:
  Magicater
  Magikitch'n

25631 Magic American Corporation
23700 Mercantile Road
Cleveland, OH 44122-5900
216-464-2353
Fax: 216-464-5895 800-321-6330
www.magicamerican.com
Manufacturer and exporter of household cleaning
products including stain removers and floor polish
President: Ross Chawson
VP: Scott Zeilinger
Sales Manager: Bob Beebe
Contact: James Zeilinger
jimmyze@aol.com
Estimated Sales: $10-20 Million
Number Employees: 50
Square Footage: 110000
Brands:
  Goo Gone
  Magic

25632 Magic Seasoning Blends
720 Distributors Row
Po Box 23342
New Orleans, LA 70123-3208
504-731-3590
Fax: 504-731-3576 800-457-2857
www.magicseasoningblends.com
Dry spices, rubs, bottled sauces and marinades.
Owner: Paul Prudhomme
pprudhomme@chefpaul.com
President/CEO: Shawn McBride
CFO: Paula LaCour
R&D Director: Sean O'Meara
VP Sales/Marketing: John McBride
Director of Sales and Marketing: Anna Zuniga
pprudhomme@chefpaul.com
Human Resources Director: Naomi Roundtree
Director of Operations: Joey Duplechain
Vice President of Manufacturing: David Hickey
Purchasing Director: Patricia Cantrelle
Estimated Sales: $9.6 Million
Number Employees: 50-99
Number of Brands: 3
Number of Products: 29
Square Footage: 260000
Type of Packaging: Consumer, Food Service, Pri-
  vate Label, Bulk
Brands:
  Barbecue Magic
  Blackened Redfish Magic
  Blackened Steak Magic
  Breading Magic
  Gravy & Gumbo Magic
  Magic Pepper Sauce
  Magic Sauce & Marinades
  Meat Magic
  Pizza & Pasta Magic
  Pork & Veal Magic
  Poultry Magic
  Salmon Magic
  Seafood Magic
  Shrimp Magic
  Sweetfree Magic
  Vegetable Magic

25633 Magline Inc
1205 W Cedar St
Standish, MI 48658-9563
989-512-1000
Fax: 989-879-5399 800-624-5463
customerservice@magliner.com
www.magliner.com
Aluminum material handling equipment including 2
and 4 wheel hand trucks and delivery ramps; also,
dock equipment
CEO: D Brian Law
Marketing: Carol Sundeck
Sales Manager: Joe Howeth
Number Employees: 50-99
Brands:
  Brake
  Equalizer
  Gemini

25634 Magna Industries Inc
1825 Swarthmore Ave # 1
Suite 1
Lakewood, NJ 08701-4570
732-905-0957
Fax: 732-367-2989 800-510-9856
sales@magnaindustries.com
Racks and carts for bakery and food industries
Owner: Jerry Crominski
sales@magnaindustries.com
Estimated Sales: $10-20 Million
Number Employees: 20-49

25635 Magna Machine Co
11180 Southland Rd
Cincinnati, OH 45240-3295
513-851-6900
Fax: 513-851-6904 800-448-3475
sales@magna-machine.com
www.magna-machine.com
Bakery machinery including horizontal mixers and
depositors
President: Paul Kramer
pkramer@magna-machine.com
VP: Rob Baur
Estimated Sales: $2.5-5 Million
Number Employees: 50-99

25636 Magna Machine Co
11180 Southland Rd
Cincinnati, OH 45240-3295
513-851-6900
Fax: 513-851-6904 800-448-3475
sales@magna-machine.com
www.magna-machine.com
Horizontal, batch, dough, bakery, adhesives, high
viscosity, paint color dye, vacuum and pharmaceuti-
cal chemical mixers
President: Paul Kramer
pkramer@magna-machine.com
VP: Baur
CFO: Windy Willey
Estimated Sales: $2.5-5 Million
Number Employees: 50-99

25637 Magna Power Controls
P.O.Box 13615
Milwaukee, WI 53213-0615
262-783-3500
Fax: 262-783-3510 800-288-8178
lbostrom@magnetek.com www.magnetek.com
Manufacturer and exporter of material handling
equipment including control, electrification and
automation
President: Andy Glass
CFO: Ryan Gyle
CEO: Peter M McCormick
Quality Control: Mark Logic
R & D: Ban Beilfuss
Marketing/Sales: Perry Pabich
Estimated Sales: $20-50 Million
Number Employees: 250-499
Type of Packaging: Bulk

25638 Magnaform Corp
2685 S 4th St
Van Buren, AR 72956-6024
479-474-7569
Fax: 479-474-2641 www.magnaform.com
Owner: Edward Boyd
ed@magnaform.com
Estimated Sales: $1-3 Million
Number Employees: 5-9

25639 Magnatech Corp
6 Kripes Rd
East Granby, CT 06026-9645
860-653-2573
Fax: 860-653-0486 888-393-3602
info@magnatechllc.com www.magnatechllc.com
Sanitary processing tubes and fittings for food processing and dairy industries.
Executive VP: Garry Mccabe
gmccabe@magnatech-lp.com
Number Employees: 20-49

25640 MagneTek
16555 W Ryerson Rd
New Berlin, WI 53151-3633
262-782-0200
Fax: 262-782-1283 www.yaskawa.com
Fractional and integral horsepower AC/DC motors
and speed controls

President & COO, Drives & Motion Divisio: Mike Knapek
President & COO, Drives & Motion Divisio: Mike Knapek
Contact: Shankar Rao
shrao@magnetek.com
Estimated Sales: $50-100 Million
Number Employees: 100-249

25641 Magnetic Products Inc
683 Town Center Dr
Highland, MI 48356-2965

248-887-5600
Fax: 248-887-6100 800-544-5930
info@mpimagnet.com www.mpimagnet.com
Magnetic separators, metal detectors and check weighers
President: Keith Rhodes
keith.rhodes@mpimagnet.com
R&D: Ron Kwaz
Marketing: Ellen Kominars
Sales: Del Butler
Estimated Sales: $6 Million
Number Employees: 20-49
Square Footage: 160000

25642 Magnetic Technologies LTD
43 Town Forest Rd
P.O. Box 257
Oxford, MA 01540-2845

508-987-3303
Fax: 508-987-2875 sales@magnetictech.com
www.magnetictech.com
Magnetic clutches for bottle capping
President: John Deluca
VP: Greg Podstanka
Sales: Howard Schwerdlin
Estimated Sales: $1,000,000-$5,000,000
Number Employees: 10-19

25643 Magnetool Inc
505 Elmwood Dr
Troy, MI 48083-2755

248-588-5400
Fax: 248-588-5710 sales@magnetoolinc.com
www.magnetoolinc.com
Manufacturer and exporter of magnetic separation equipment
President: A T Churchill
atchurchill@magnetoolinc.com
Engineer: Mike Wright
VP: C Sulisz
Estimated Sales: $20-50 Million
Number Employees: 20-49
Square Footage: 40000

25644 Magnum Coffee Packaging
16800 Java Boulevard
Nunica, MI 49448

616-837-0333
Fax: 616-837-0777 www.magnumcoffee.com
Tea and coffee industry packaging materials and machines
Owner: Kevin Kihnke
Estimated Sales: $2.5-5 Million
Number Employees: 20-49

25645 Magnum Custom Trailer &BBQ Pits
10806 Hwy 620 N
Austin, TX 78726

512-258-4101
Fax: 512-258-2701 800-662-4686
sales2@magnumtrailers.com
www.magnumtrailers.com
Manufacturer and exporter of barbecue and catering trailers, custom kitchens and mobile concession stands
President: Charles Mc Lemore
Sales: Todd McLemore
Sales: Richard Westlund
Plat Manager: Jeff Israel
Estimated Sales: $15 Million
Number Employees: 50-99
Square Footage: 200000
Brands:
Magnum

25646 Magnum Systems Inc
1250 Seminary St
Kansas City, KS 66103-2515

913-362-1710
Fax: 913-362-7863 800-748-7000
sales@smootco.com www.magnumsystems.com

Automated packaging machinery
President: Brian Klughardt
Contact: Shannon Beal
sbeal@magnumsystems.com
Estimated Sales: $500,000-$1 Million
Number Employees: 50-99
Parent Co: Taylor Products

25647 Magnuson
1 Magnuson Ave
Pueblo, CO 81001-4889

719-948-9500
Fax: 719-948-9540 sales@magnusoncorp.com
www.magnusoncorp.com
Manufacturer and exporter of processing and packaging machinery including vegetable cutters and peelers, washers and feeders; also, full can palletizers
Owner: Bob Smith
bsmith@magnusoncorp.com
VP/General Manager: Craig Furlo
Estimated Sales: $2.5-5 Million
Number Employees: 20-49
Parent Co: Atlas Pacific Engineering

25648 Magnuson Industries
3005 Kishwaukee St
Rockford, IL 61109-2061

815-229-2970
Fax: 815-229-2978 800-435-2816
www.posi-pour.com
Manufacturer, importer and exporter of portion control liquor pourers and bar supplies
Vice President: Stewart Magnuson
smagnuson@posi-pour.com
VP: Stewart Magnuson
Director Sales: Robert Gough
Estimated Sales: $5-10 Million
Number Employees: 10-19
Square Footage: 80000
Brands:
Posi-Pour

25649 Magnuson Products
66 Brighton Rd
Clifton, NJ 07012-1600

973-472-9292
Fax: 973-472-5686
Industrial cleaning compounds for bottles, dairy, glass, pipes, dishwashers, etc
President: Al Reisch
info@sergeantthem.com
Estimated Sales: $10-20 Million
Number Employees: 1-4

25650 Magpowr
1626 Manufacturers Dr
Fenton, MO 63026-2839

636-343-5550
Fax: 636-326-0608 800-624-7697
magpowr@magpowr.com www.magpowr.com
Equipment components, tension and torque control and capping clutches
Owner: Benson Portnoy
VP: Jeff Hutchings
CEO: Bruce Ryen
Estimated Sales: $10-20 Million
Number Employees: 50-99
Brands:
Magpowr

25651 Magsys Inc
4144 S 112th St
Milwaukee, WI 53228-1914

414-543-2177
Fax: 414-541-9203
Manufacturer and exporter of stainless steel magnetic conveyor equipment for transport of ferrous crowns, caps and closures
President: Rudy Zwiebel
Estimated Sales: Below $5 Million
Number Employees: 1-4
Square Footage: 10000
Brands:
Magsys

25652 Mahaffy & Harder Engineering Company
140 Clinton Road
Fairfield, NJ 07004-0002

973-227-4004
Fax: 973-227-3634

President: A Mahaffy-Berman
Vice President of Engineering: Henry Nixon
Vice President of Sales/Marketing: Russ Garofalo
Vice President of Operations: Mike Summersett
Estimated Sales: $5-10 Million
Number Employees: 50-99

25653 (HQ)Mahoney Environmental
712 Essington Rd
Joliet, IL 60435-4912

815-725-2056
Fax: 815-730-2087 800-892-9392
info@mahoneyenvironmental.com
Grease handling equipment; also, grease collection, recycling and rendering services available
President: Rick Sabol
ricksabol@mahoneyenvironmental.com
Partner: John Mahoney
VP Marketing: Brad Schofield
Equipment Sales Manager: Kyle Taylor
Estimated Sales: $2.5-5,000,000
Number Employees: 50-99
Other Locations:
Mahoney Environmental
Mendota IL
Brands:
The Recycler

25654 Maier Sign Systems
515 Victor Street
Saddle Brook, NJ 07663-6118

201-845-7555
Fax: 201-845-3336
Manufacturer and exporter of bulletin and menu boards, directories, awnings and signs including plastic, metal and neon
President/CEO: Stuart Brown
Estimated Sales: Less than $500,000
Number Employees: 4
Square Footage: 32000
Parent Co: Elms Industries

25655 Mail-Well Label
295 Lillard Dr
Sparks, NV 89434-8902

775-359-1703
Fax: 775-359-1736
Glue-applied paper and metallized and foil labels for wine, beer, beverage products, canned vegetables, fruit and seafood
Site Manager: John Brandoff
VP: Cameron Beddome
Estimated Sales: $50-100 Million
Number Employees: 100-249
Parent Co: Lawson Mardon Group

25656 Mail-Well Label
6901 Rolling Mill Road
Baltimore, MD 21224-2030

410-282-4500
Fax: 410-288-3509 800-637-4879
Paper labels including litho-printed, square or die cut, high gloss and product resistant; also, aqueous coated laminates for corrugated containers
Community Manager: Richard Dix
General Manager: Russell Hoffman
Operations Manager: John Rixham
Estimated Sales: $20-50 Million
Number Employees: 250-499
Square Footage: 85000
Parent Co: Lawson Mardon Packaging

25657 Main Course Consultants
8629 Avers Avenue
Skokie, IL 60076-2201

847-869-7633
Fax: 847-866-0898
Consultant specializing in concept and menu development for restaurants; also, cost analysis, business plans and mystery shopping services available
President: Lee Michaels
Number Employees: 27

25658 Main Lamp Corp
1073 39th St
Brooklyn, NY 11219-1017

718-436-8500
Fax: 718-438-6836 price@nationwidelighting.com
www.mainlampwarehouse.com
Lighting fixtures, table lamps and ceiling fans
President: William Ain
price@nationwidelighting.com
CFO: Misses Ains
Salesperson: J Piccozino
Manager Operations: R Dabideen

Estimated Sales: $2.5-5 Million
Number Employees: 1-4
Square Footage: 200000
Brands:
  Casablanca
  Stiffel
  Weinstock

25659 Mainca USA Inc
411 Eichelberger St
St Louis, MO 63111-1914
> 314-351-4677
> Fax: 314-353-6655 877-677-7761
maincausa@maincausa.com www.maincausa.com
Meat processing equipment; including: mixers, choppers, saws, grinders, moulders and sausage stuffers
President: Dale Schmidt
maincausa@aol.com
Estimated Sales: Under $500,000
Number Employees: 10-19

25660 Maine Industrial Plastics & Rubber Corporation
21 Teague Street
P.O.Box 381
Newcastle, ME 04553
> 207-563-5532
> Fax: 207-563-8457 800-540-1846
> www.miprcorp.com
Conveyor belting, rubber and plastic sheet
President: Henry Lee
Vice President: Whitney Lee
Estimated Sales: $1-3 Million
Number Employees: 9
Square Footage: 48000
Parent Co: Maine Industrial Corp.

25661 Maine Poly Aquisition
PO Box 1385
Windham, ME 04062-1385
> 207-946-7440
> Fax: 207-946-5102
Plastic bags
President: Kimball H Dunton
CFO: Jackie Cooutier
Public Relations: Steve Spencer
Estimated Sales: $10-20 Million
Number Employees: 10

25662 Mainline Industries Inc
1 Allen St # 1
Suite 1
Springfield, MA 01108-1953
> 413-733-5771
> Fax: 413-733-5929 800-527-7917
customerservice@mainlineind.com
> www.mainlineind.com
Manufacturer and exporter of disposable wipers, cleaning towels and scuff pads
President: Paul Motter
paumotter@mainlineind.com
VP: Carlo Rovelli
Quality Control: Angie Smith
Marketing Support: Lee Albert
Estimated Sales: $2.5-5 Million
Number Employees: 5-9
Brands:
  Aquawipes
  Hydroscrubs
  Hydrowype

25663 Mainstreet Menu Systems
1375 N Barker Rd
Brookfield, WI 53045-5215
> 262-782-6000
> Fax: 262-782-6515 800-782-6222
> info@mainstreetmenus.com
Manufacturer and exporter of point of purchase displays, menu boards and order racks. Design, engineer, produce & install menu boards, graphics & displays.
President: Doug Watson
CFO: Bill Hintz
Research & Development: Paul Steinbrenner
Marketing: Angie Herrmann
Estimated Sales: $10-20 Million
Number Employees: 20-49
Parent Co: Howard Company
Type of Packaging: Food Service
Brands:
  Mainstreet

25664 Maja Equipment Company
6005 N 9th Street
Omaha, NE 68110-1121
> 402-346-6252
> Fax: 402-346-6953
Skinning and derinding machinery for fish, poultry, pork and beef; also, rotating evaporators
Product Manager: Steven Lemke
Sales: Kent Rounds
Sales: Aaron Borns
Estimated Sales: $1-5 Million
Number Employees: 20-50

25665 Majestic
60 Cherry Street
Bridgeport, CT 06605-2395
> 203-367-7900
> Fax: 203-335-6973
Manufacturer, importer and exporter of plastic serving and tabletop accessories including beverage glasses, pitchers, bowls, mugs, stemware, ice buckets, plates, trays and coasters; manufacturer of electric lamps and plastic kitchentools and gadgets
Contact: Elliott Zivin
ezivin@majesticgifts.com
Estimated Sales: $2.5-5 Million
Number Employees: 10-19
Parent Co: Zivco
Brands:
  Basket Weave
  Chroma Lamps
  Diner Mug
  Facets
  Ice-Stir-Cools
  Koziol
  Seaglass
  Transitions

25666 Majestic Coffee & Tea
3870 Charter Park Dr
San Jose, CA 95136-1388
> 408-448-6370
> Fax: 408-448-8537
Brewing devices, roasting machines
Estimated Sales: less than $500,000
Number Employees: 1-4

25667 Majestic Flex Pac
3337 Grapevine Street
Mira Loma, CA 91752
> 951-361-0247
> Fax: 951-361-0260
Majestic Flex PAC is a manufacturer and supplier of shrink sleeves, pouches, laminations, and custom bags to numerous industries including that of food and beverage, dairy, bakery and snack, candy and confection.
President: Leonardo Gutierrez
Type of Packaging: Consumer

25668 Majestic Industries Inc
15378 Hallmark Ct
Macomb, MI 48042-4017
> 586-786-9100
> Fax: 586-786-9105 www.majesticind.net
Manufacturer and exporter of treated dusting cloths and wet and dust mops
President: Gavonna Agnew
gagnew@majesticind.com
CEO: Gary Potashnick
Estimated Sales: $1-3 Million
Number Employees: 50-99
Number of Brands: 10
Number of Products: 250
Square Footage: 128000
Type of Packaging: Consumer, Food Service, Private Label, Bulk
Brands:
  Monarch
  Sir Dust-A-Lot
  Sweeping Beauty
  Velva-Sheen

25669 Makat
500 Tillessen Boulevard
Ridgeway, SC 29130-8543
> 803-337-4700
> Fax: 803-337-4701 makatusa@infoave.net
Extruding and depositing machines for confectionery and baking industries, starch and starchless moulded goods as well as center-in-shell, nougat, fondant, fudge, truffles, chocolate, hard candy, and caramel products

Estimated Sales: $2.5-5 Million
Number Employees: 5-9

25670 Mako Services
4297 Buford Dr
Suite 2A
Buford, GA 30518-3400
> 770-932-3292
> Fax: 770-932-3290
Full line seafood, meats
Owner: Joe Connor
Estimated Sales: $10-20 Million
Number Employees: 10-19

25671 Malaysian Palm Oil Board
3516 International Court N.W.
Washington, DC 20008-3022
> 202-572-9719
> Fax: 202-572-9783 mpobtas@aol.com
> www.mpob.gov.my
Offers customer support and technical advisory services to users and potential users of Malaysian palm and palm kernel oil products in the US, Canada, and Latin America
Regional Manager: Rosidah Radzian
Director General: Datuk Dr. Choo Yuen May
Deputy Director General: Dr. Hj. Ahmad Kushairi Din
Estimated Sales: $1-2.5 Million
Number Employees: 1-4

25672 Malco Manufacturing Co
13917 S Main St
Los Angeles, CA 90061-2151
> 310-366-7696
> Fax: 310-366-7694 866-477-7267
info@malcomfg.com www.malcomfg.com
Bun and pie pans, foil containers and aluminum bakery racks
VP: Steve Goodman
Manager: Patricia Hansen
patricia@malcomfg.com
Estimated Sales: $5 Million
Number Employees: 5-9

25673 Malcolm Stogo Associates
41 Tudor Lane
Scarsdale, NY 10583-4909
> 914-472-7255
> Fax: 914-472-8861
International dairy and food consultant specializing in ice cream product development and marketing concept strategies
President: Malcolm Stogo
VP/Treasurer: Barbara Stogo
Number Employees: 7
Square Footage: 6000

25674 Mali's All Natural Barbecue Supply Company
161 Bramblewood Ln
East Amherst, NY 14051-1417
> 716-688-2210
> Fax: 716-688-2795 800-289-6254
> buymali@localnet.com
Manufacturer, importer and exporter of lump charcoal, briquettes and wood for smoking and cooking; also, grilling woods
President: James Maliszewski
CEO: Frances Maliszewski
Estimated Sales: $1-3 Million
Number Employees: 1-4
Number of Brands: 1
Brands:
  Mali's

25675 Mall City Containers Inc
2710 N Pitcher St
Kalamazoo, MI 49004-3490
> 269-381-2706
> Fax: 269-381-7878 800-643-6721
> info@mallcitycontainers.com
> www.mallcitycontainers.com
Corrugated boxes and point of purchase displays
Owner: Ben Boeresma
CEO: Ben Boersma
Sales Manager: Tom Vandenberg
Estimated Sales: $10-15 Million
Number Employees: 50-99

25676 (HQ)Malnove Of Nebraska
13434 F St
Omaha, NE 68137-1181
402-330-1100
Fax: 402-330-2941 800-228-9877
packaging.systems@malnove.com
www.malnove.com
Manufacturer and exporter of folding paperboard cartons
President, CEO: Paul Malnove
CFO: Jim Belcher
VP: Dick Lawson
VP Sales: Michael Querry
Operations: Steve Maynar
Plant Manager: Craig Beaber
Estimated Sales: B
Number Employees: 500-999
Square Footage: 800000
Type of Packaging: Consumer, Food Service, Private Label

25677 Malo Inc
12111 E 51st St # 106
Tulsa, OK 74146-6005
918-583-2743
Fax: 918-583-6208 sales@maloinc.com
www.maloinc.com
Manufacturer and exporter of crateless and overpressure retort systems for low-acid foods in metal and flexible containers
President: Chuck Clugston
cclugston@maloinc.com
VP: Allen Stucky
Marketing/Sales: Rick Holsted
Estimated Sales: $2.5-5 Million
Number Employees: 10-19
Square Footage: 80000
Brands:
Malo

25678 Malo Inc
12111 E 51st St # 106
Suite 106
Tulsa, OK 74146-6005
918-583-2743
Fax: 918-583-6208 sales@maloinc.com
www.maloinc.com
President: Chuck Clugston
cclugston@maloinc.com
Estimated Sales: $3-5 Million
Number Employees: 10-19

25679 Malpack Polybag
120 Fuller Rd
Ajax, ON L1S3R2
Canada
905-428-3751
Fax: 416-297-9874
Low and high density polyethylene t-shut carry-out sacks and bread and bagel bags
President: Guy DiPietro
General Manager: Jim Leo
Secretary: Joe Galea
Number Employees: 210
Square Footage: 240000
Parent Co: Malkpack
Other Locations:
Malpack Polybag
Ajax ON

25680 Maltese Signs
5550 Peachtree Industrial Blvd
Norcross, GA 30071-1450
770-368-0911
Fax: 770-454-7383
Signs
President: Eloi Duguay
CFO: Rejean Pelletiar
VP: Michael Maltese
Estimated Sales: $10 Million
Number Employees: 100-249
Square Footage: 130000

25681 Malteurop North America
3830 W Grant St
Milwaukee, WI 53215
414-671-1166
www.malteurop.com
Processor and exporter of malt, also offers several modes of commercial collaboration, as well as consulting, engineering, and training services.

CEO: Olivier Parent
President, North America: Kevin Eikerman
Chief Commercial & Innovation Officer: Alain Caekaert
Year Founded: 1984
Estimated Sales: $31.5 Million
Number Employees: 100-249
Parent Co: Malteurop
Type of Packaging: Food Service, Bulk

25682 Malthus Diagnostics
35888 Centre Ridge Road
North Ridgeville, OH 44039
440-327-2585
Fax: 440-327-7286 800-346-7202
Automated microbiological analyzers; manufacturer, importer and exporter of incubators and growth media
Director Marketing/Sales: Joseph Carney
Director US Operations: Joseph Carney
Estimated Sales: $1-2.5 Million
Number Employees: 25
Square Footage: 2000
Parent Co: IDG
Brands:
Lab M Media
Malthus System V

25683 Man-O Products
811 Ridgeway Ave
Cincinnati, OH 45229
513-281-5959
Fax: 513-936-6555 888-210-6266
Manufacturer and exporter of protective hand creams and soap products
President: Steve Seltzer
Quality Control: Andy Joseph
Sales Manager: Tom Joseph
Estimated Sales: $5-10 Million
Number Employees: 5-9

25684 Man-Tech Associates
600 Main St
Tonawanda, NY 14150-3723
716-743-1320
Fax: 519-763-2205 800-206-8116
literature@mantech.ca
Laboratory and analytical equipment including PC controlled automated ion analysis and titration systems
President: Edward Godman
Marketing Supervisor: Richard Veilans
Contact: Robert Middleton
rmenegotto@mantech-inc.com
Estimated Sales: Less than $500,000
Number Employees: 1-4

25685 Manabo
501 Main Street
Platte City, MO 64079-8460
816-431-3948
Fax: 816-431-3951
Cutting and boning equipment, sharpening machines and services; safety apparel; sanitation supplies and equipment

25686 (HQ)Management Insight
33 Boston Post Road West
Suite 220
Malborough, MA 1752
508-485-2100
Fax: 508-485-1388 www.mgtinsight.com
Restaurant and food service consultant providing stratigic planning, facility programming, pre-opening planning, market and financial feasibilty studies, audits, menu development, and restaurant revitalization
President/CEO: Jack Mandelbaum
Vice President: Elizabeth Michalski
Director of Operations: Lisa Stone
Estimated Sales: $.5-1 million
Number Employees: 3
Square Footage: 3150

25687 Management Recruiters
1801 Market St, 13th Floor
Philadelphia, PA 19103
941-756-3001
Fax: 215-751-1757 800-875-4000
admin@mriflorida.com www.mrinetwork.com
Consultant specializing in employment search and recruitment

President: R Rush Oster
Contact: Edward Billigmeier
edward.billigmeier@mrinetwork.com
General Manager: Robert Boal
Estimated Sales: less than $500,000
Number Employees: 1-4
Parent Co: Management Recruiters International

25688 Management Tech of America
4742 N 24th Street
Suite 410
Phoenix, AZ 85016-4862
602-381-5800
Fax: 602-251-0903
Manufacturer and exporter of software for the control of material handling systems
Estimated Sales: $10-20 Million
Number Employees: 50-99

25689 Manchester Tool & Die Inc
601 S Wabash Rd
North Manchester, IN 46962-8148
260-982-8524
Fax: 260-982-4575
www.manchestertoolanddie.com
Manufacturer and exporter of packaging equipment and machinery; also, prototype development available
President: Barry Blocher
bablocher@manchestertoolanddie.com
Sales/Supervisor: Robin Brubaker
Production Manager: Steve Music
Plant Manager: Josh Berry
Estimated Sales: $2.5-5 Million
Number Employees: 50-99
Square Footage: 34000

25690 Mancini Packing Co
3500 Mancini Pl
Zolfo Springs, FL 33890-4710
863-735-2000
Fax: 863-735-1172 800-741-1778
rmancini@mancinifoods.com
www.mancinifoods.com
Peppers and olive oil
Chairman/President: Frank Mancini
fmancini@mancinifoods.com
VP: Alan Mancini
Estimated Sales: $11 Million
Number Employees: 50-99
Type of Packaging: Consumer, Food Service, Private Label, Bulk
Brands:
Mancini

25691 Mandarin Soy Sauce Inc
4 Sands Station Rd
Middletown, NY 10940-4415
845-343-1505
Fax: 845-343-0731 info@wanjashan.com
www.wanjashan.com
Soy sauce, asian sauce, rice and vinegar
President: Alvin Lam
alvin.c.lam@chase.com
VP: Mike Shapiro
Estimated Sales: $165 Million
Number Employees: 20-49
Square Footage: 170000
Brands:
Wan Ja Shan

25692 Mandeville Company
2800 Washington Ave N
Minneapolis, MN 55411-1683
612-521-3671
Fax: 612-521-3673 800-328-8490
Manufacturer and wholesaler/distributor of equipment for meat processors, delis and restaurants including saws, grinders, mixers, tumblers, marinators, knives, scales, juicers and slicers; also, reconditioned equipment; serving thefood service market
President: Julie Lane
Secretary: Phyllis Stellmaker
Estimated Sales: $2.5-5 Million
Number Employees: 10-19
Square Footage: 40000

25693 Mane Inc.
2501 Henkle Dr.
Lebanon, OH 45036
513-248-9876
Fax: 513-248-8808 requests@mane.com
www.mane.com
Flavors and seasoning blends

President/CEO: Jean Mane
President: Michell Mane
Executive Vice President: Kent Hunter
Contact: James Abel
james.abel@mane.com
Year Founded: 1871
Estimated Sales: 20-50 Million
Number Employees: 50-99
Square Footage: 65000

25694 Manhattan Truck Lines
91 Michigan Ave
Paterson, NJ 07503-1807

973-278-0190
Fax: 973-278-0582 800-370-7627
info@pariserchem.com www.pariserchem.com
Manufacturer and exporter of warewashing deter-
gents, water-treatment chemicals and institutional
maintenance products. Products include laundry
chemicals, soaps and detergents
Owner: Bill Moakley
bmoakley@pariserchem.com
VP: Andrew Pariser
VP: Scott Pariser
Estimated Sales: $10-20 Million
Number Employees: 10-19
Type of Packaging: Consumer, Food Service, Pri-
vate Label, Bulk

25695 Manitowoc Foodservice
2100 Future Drive
Sellersburg, IN 47172

818-637-7200
Fax: 818-637-7222 800-367-4233
www.manitowocbeverage.com
Manufacturer, importer and exporter of automatic
ice transportation systems, beverage and ice dispens-
ers, faucets, fluid control devices, pumps, timers, bar
guns and carbonators
Manager: Andrew Nelson
CEO: G McCann
Contact: Paul Hanniffy
hanniffypaul@gmail.com
Estimated Sales: $3-5 Million
Number Employees: 5-9
Square Footage: 480000

25696 Manitowoc Ice Machine
2110 S 26th St
Manitowoc, WI 54220-6321

920-682-0161
Fax: 920-683-7589 800-545-5720
www.manitowocice.com
Manufacturer and exporter of ice machines, ice stor-
age bins and reach-in refrigerators and freezers
Vice President: Lee Wichlacz
lee.wichlacz@manitowoc.com
Executive Vice President: Larry Bryce
Vice President of Sales: Kevin Clark
VP International Operations: Mark Kreple
Estimated Sales: $1-5 Million
Number Employees: 250-499
Square Footage: 365000
Parent Co: Manitowoc Foodservice Group

25697 Mankato Tent & Awning Co
1021 Range St
North Mankato, MN 56003-2238

507-625-5115
Fax: 507-625-5111 866-747-3524
www.mankatotent.com
Industrial curtains
President: Charles D Gasswint
Sales/Marketing Executive: Devin Gasswint
Purchasing Manager: Jesse Spiess
Estimated Sales: $1-2,500,000
Number Employees: 5-9
Square Footage: 20000
Type of Packaging: Consumer, Food Service

25698 Mankuta Bros Rubber Stamp Co
1395 Lakeland Ave # 16
PO Box 240
Bohemia, NY 11716-3319

631-589-6880
Fax: 516-694-6063 800-223-4481
info@mankuta.com www.mankuta.com
Rubber stamps and engraved signs; wholesaler/dis-
tributor of marking devices and pre-inked stamps;
embossers; seals; time stamps; etc
Co-Owner: Fred Mankuta
Estimated Sales: Less than $500,000
Number Employees: 20-49
Square Footage: 6000

Brands:
Justrite

25699 Mannhardt Inc
3209 S. 32nd Street
Sheboygan Falls, WI 53082

920-467-1027
Fax: 773-625-5639 800-423-2327
mannhardt1@aol.com mannhardtice.com
Ice storage dispensers and bagging equipment
President: John Williams
Sales: Lori Justinger
Number Employees: 10-19

25700 Mannhart
4401 Blue Mound Rd
Fort Worth, TX 76106

817-421-0100
Fax: 817-421-0246 cm@mannhart.com
Commercial vegetable cutters and salad dryers.
President: Edwin Mannhart
Marketing: Christa Mannhart
Sales: Christa Mannhart
Purchasing: Pat Mannhart
Estimated Sales: $3-5 Million
Number Employees: 10-19
Number of Brands: 1
Number of Products: 1
Square Footage: 30000
Brands:
Mannhart

25701 (HQ)Manning Lighting Inc
1810 North Ave
Sheboygan, WI 53083-4619

920-458-2184
Fax: 920-458-2491 info@manningltg.com
www.digitalspeck.com
Manufacturer and exporter of lighting equipment in-
cluding institutional decorative chandeliers
Owner: Andy Manning
Controller: Mary Kuhfuss
Sales: Liz Manning
amanning@manningltg.com
Estimated Sales: $10-20 Million
Number Employees: 20-49
Type of Packaging: Food Service

25702 Manning Systems
405 Barclay Blvd
Lincolnshire, IL 60069

913-712-5576
Fax: 913-712-5580 800-444-9935
manning@honeywell.com
Portion control trays, polysheets, poly bags
National Sales Manager: Chuck Linn
Estimated Sales: $1-$3 Million
Number Employees: 5-9
Parent Co: Honeywell

25703 Mannkraft Corporation
100 Frontage Rd
Newark, NJ 07114

973-589-7400
Fax: 973-465-6851
Corrugated boxes and point of purchase displays
President: Dennis Mehiel
Marketing Executive: John Prentiss
Sales Manager: Mark Taylor
Contact: Terence Mcnealy
tbmcnealy@yahoo.com
Estimated Sales: $20-50 Million
Number Employees: 100-249

25704 Mansfield Rubber Stamp
174 S Mulberry St
Mansfield, OH 44902-7423

419-524-1442
Fax: 419-524-7083 stamp174@aol.com
www.mansfieldrubberstamp.com
Rubber and pre-inked stamps, engraved plastic and
wood signs and magnetic signs
Owner: Jerry Parrella
stamp174@aol.com
Estimated Sales: Less Than $500,000
Number Employees: 1-4

25705 Manta Ray
N60w14551 Kaul Avenue
Menomonee Falls, WI 53051-5907

888-931-2207
Fax: 262-252-4382
Carton taping, randon carton sealers

25706 Manufacturers Agents forthe Foodservice Industry
1199 Euclid Ave
Atlanta, GA 30307

404-214-9474
Fax: 770-433-2450 info@mafsi.org
www.mafsi.org
Represents the professionalism of our outsourced
sales reps to the industry by providing business information for manufacturers and foodservice
industries.
VP: M Jeffrey Hessel
Contact: Ambrus Amanda
aambrus@mafsi.org
Number Employees: 1-4

25707 Manufacturers CorrugateBox
5830 57th St
Flushing, NY 11378-3110

718-894-7200
Fax: 718-894-2567
Corrugated boxes
Manager: Sheldon Baim
mcc@maspethchamberofcommerce.org
Manager: Steven Etra
Plant Manager: Curatola
Estimated Sales: $20-50 Million
Number Employees: 10-19

25708 Manufacturers Railway Company
One Arsenal Street
Saint Louis, MO 63118

314-577-1775
Fax: 314-577-1810
amund.whittley@anheuser-busch.com
www.trainweb.org
Provides terminal rail-switching services to industries in St. Louis over 42 miles of track and repairs
and rebuilds locomotives for the railroad industry.
Insulated beverage and hopper railcars. Its two
trucking subsidaries, with afleet of 170 specialty designed trailers, furnish cartage and warehousing services at four locations to serve Anheuser-Busch and
other beverage container customers
President: Kurt Andrew
Number Employees: 100-249
Parent Co: Anheuser-Busch Companies

25709 (HQ)Manufacturers Wood Supply Company
1936 Scranton Road
Cleveland, OH 44113-2429

216-771-7848
Fax: 216-771-7848
Manufacturer, importer and exporter of specialty and
industrial wood products including plywood and
masonite boxes, packaging inserts and basket bases;
custom sizing available
Plant Manager: Joseph Rielinger
Estimated Sales: $1-2.5 Million
Number Employees: 6
Square Footage: 40000

25710 Manufacturing Business Systems
100 N Brand Blvd Ste 600
Glendale, CA 91203

818-551-1758
Fax: 253-399-6201 info@formulas.com
www.formulas.com
Wholesaler/distributor of process manufacturing
software
President: Herbert Molano
Estimated Sales: $500,000-$1,000,000
Number Employees: 5-9

25711 Manufacturing Warehouse
110 NW 24th Avenue
Miami, FL 33125-5260

305-635-8886
Fax: 305-633-2266
Manufacturer and exporter of freezers including
walk-in, ice cream and quick freezing; also, walk-in
coolers and doors: strip, supermarket and cold
storage
Estimated Sales: $1-5 Million
Number Employees: 4
Square Footage: 20000

25712 MapFresh
20 Palmetto Pkwy
Suite F
Hilton Head Isle, SC 29926-2459

843-681-5900
Fax: 843-681-5924

Modified atmospheric packaging, trays, conveyor merge units and accessories, gas packaging equipment, vacuum packaging equipment
Estimated Sales: $1-5 Million

25713 Maple Hill Farms
12 Burr Rd
PO Box 767
Bloomfield, CT 06002-2204
860-242-9689
Fax: 860-243-2490 800-842-7304
www.mhfct.com
Milk and ice cream vending machines
President: William Miller
info@maplehillfarm.com
General Manager: Edward Jones
Estimated Sales: $5-10 Million
Number Employees: 10-19

25714 Maple Leaf Awning & Canvas Co
8100 Warden Rd
Sherwood, AR 72120-4214
501-834-8891
Fax: 501-834-5397 800-947-4233
awnings@mapleleafcanvas.com
Commercial awnings
Owner: Jim Wilson
awnings@mapleleafcanvas.com
Estimated Sales: $1-2,500,000
Number Employees: 5-9
Parent Co: Custom Canvas Products
Brands:
Maple Leaf

25715 Mar-Boro Printing & Advertising Specialties
1219 Gravesend Neck Rd
Brooklyn, NY 11229-4209
718-336-4051
Fax: 718-336-7996
Advertising specialties, labels, boxes and bags; also, business cards, commercial printing and typesetting services available
VP: James Bruno
Estimated Sales: $500,000-$1,000,000
Number Employees: 5-9

25716 Mar-Con Wire Belt
2431 Vauxhall Place
Richmond, BC V6V 1Z5
Canada
604-278-8922
Fax: 604-278-8938 877-962-7266
www.metalbelt.com
Manufacturer and exporter of wire mesh conveyor belting, food processing equipment, conveyors and sheet metal fabrications including stamping
President: Michael Chiu
CFO: Michael Chiu
R&D: Michael Chiu
Sales Director: Krey Miller
Production/Purchasing: Nathan Chiu
Estimated Sales: $5 Million
Number Employees: 25
Square Footage: 10000
Brands:
Mar-Con

25717 Mar-Khem Industries
PO Box 2266
Cinnaminson, NJ 8077
Fax: 856-829-9203
Supplier, exporter of closeouts; also, investment recovery and used equipment available
President: Anthony Corradetti
a_corradetti@mar-khem.com
Number Employees: 5-9
Number of Brands: 200
Number of Products: 800
Square Footage: 500000
Type of Packaging: Consumer, Food Service, Private Label, Bulk

25718 Mar-Len Supply Inc
23159 Kidder St
Hayward, CA 94545-1630
510-782-3555
Fax: 510-782-2032 mark@marlensupply.com
www.marlensupply.com
Manufacturer and exporter of biodegradable oil and grease dispersing and removing compounds

Owner/President/office Manager: Shirley Winter
marlensupply@aol.com
Technical Director: Frank Winter
Production/Sales Manager: Mark Wieland
Production Engineer: Curt Winter
Estimated Sales: $500,000-$1 Million
Number Employees: 1-4

25719 Marathon Equipment Co
P.O. Box 1798
Highway 9 S
Vernon, AL 35592-1798
205-695-9105
Fax: 205-695-8813 800-269-7237
www.marathonequipment.com
Commercial waste and recycling equipment including balers and self-contained and stationary compactors.
President/General Manager: Vic Ujihara
Estimated Sales: $47 Million
Number Employees: 250-499
Parent Co: Dover Corporation
Brands:
Bale Tech
Eliminator
Jobmaster
Ram-Jet
Rampro

25720 Marathon Products Inc
627 Mccormick St
San Leandro, CA 94577-1109
510-562-6450
Fax: 510-562-5408 800-858-6872
marathon@marathonproducts.com
www.marathonproducts.com
Environmental monitors
CEO: Jon Nakagawa
jnakagawa@marathonproducts.com
Executive Vice President: Kevin Flynn
Number Employees: 10-19

25721 Marazzi USA
359 Clay Road E
Sunnyvale, TX 75182
972-232-3801
contact.us@marazzitile.com
www.marazziusa.com
Tile manufacturer
EVP, Sales & Marketing: Hector Narvaez
Estimated Sales: I
Number Employees: 6,000

25722 Marble Manor
37231 SE Louden Rd
Corbett, OR 97019-8810
503-695-5531
Fax: 503-695-5534 www.marblemanor.com
Owner: William Marble
Estimated Sales: Less Than $500,000
Number Employees: 1-4

25723 Marburg Industries Inc
1207 Activity Dr
Vista, CA 92081-8510
760-727-3762
Fax: 760-727-5502 marburgind@aol.com
www.marburgind.com
Manufacturer and exporter of tamper evident packaging machinery
VP Marketing: Barbara Paschal
Manager: Barbara Paschal
Estimated Sales: $1-2.5 Million
Number Employees: 10-19
Square Footage: 20000
Type of Packaging: Food Service, Private Label, Bulk
Brands:
Autocapsealer

25724 Marc Refrigeration Mfg Inc
7453 NW 32nd Ave
Miami, FL 33147-5877
305-691-0500
Fax: 305-691-1212 info@marcrefrigeration.com
www.marcrefrigeration.com
Manufacturer and exporter of commercial refrigerators and ice cream freezers
President: Hy Widel
Vice President: Loretta Widelitz
lwidelitz@marcrefrigerationmfginc.com
Treasurer: Hal Videlitz
Secretary: Robert Gordon

Estimated Sales: $5-10 Million
Number Employees: 20-49
Square Footage: 228000
Type of Packaging: Food Service

25725 (HQ)Marcal Paper Mills
1 Market St
Elmwood Park, NJ 07407
201-796-4000
Fax: 201-796-0470 800-631-8451
Tissues, napkins and towels made from recycled paper
Chief Executive Officer: Tim Spring
Contact: Andrew Bender
ab@anchortex.com
Estimated Sales: $80 Million
Number Employees: 800
Other Locations:
Marcal Paper Mills
Augusta GA
Brands:
Aspen
Bella
Fluff Out
Sst
Sani-Hanks
Snowlily
Sunrise

25726 Marcel S. Garrigues Company
560 3rd St
San Francisco, CA 94107
415-421-0371
Fax: 415-957-2638
Tea and coffee industry reconditioners, samplers and weighers
Manager: Lana Jow
Estimated Sales: $500,000-$1 Million
Number Employees: 5-9

25727 Marchant Schmidt Inc
24 W Larsen Dr
Fond Du Lac, WI 54937-8518
920-921-4760
Fax: 920-921-9640 sales@marchantschmidt.com
www.marchantschmidt.com
Manufacturers stainless steel products and equipment for the food and dairy industry
Vice President: Richard F Schmidt
rschmidt@marchantschmidt.com
CEO: Myleen Schmidt
Vice President: Lyle Schmidt
Sales Director: Jeno Thuecks
Estimated Sales: $11 Million
Number Employees: 100-249
Square Footage: 48000

25728 Marchesini Packaging Machinery
43 Fairfield Pl
West Caldwell, NJ 07006-6206
973-575-7445
Fax: 973-575-4051 info@marchesiniusa.com
www.marchesiniusa.com
Bag filling and sealing machines, bag forming machines, bundling machines, carton machines: closing, filling, handling, sealing, casing equipment: packers
President: Roger Toll
roger.toll@marchesiniusa.com
Controller: Elaine Miller
Estimated Sales: $2.5-5 Million
Number Employees: 20-49

25729 Marco Products
923 S Main St
Adrian, MI 49221-3709
517-265-3333
Fax: 517-265-3650
Plastic containers
Manager: Norman Double
Estimated Sales: $2.5-5 Million
Number Employees: 10-19
Square Footage: 108000

25730 Marcus Carton Company
324 S Service Rd
Melville, NY 11747-3270
631-752-4200
Fax: 631-752-0022
Folding paper boxes
Vice President: Nancy Simon
Director Marketing: Douglas Campbell
Estimated Sales: $1-5 Million
Number Employees: 10-19
Square Footage: 74000

25731 Marden Edwards
1866 Verne Roberts Cir
Antioch, CA 94509
925-777-1403
Fax: 925-777-1406 800-332-1838
usasales@mardenedwards.com
www.mardenedwards.com
Packaging
Contact: David Aimson
d.aimson@mardenedwards.com
Estimated Sales: Below 1 Million
Number Employees: 1-4

25732 Marel Food Systems, Inc.
8145 Flint Street
Lenexa, KS 66214
913-888-9110
Fax: 913-888-9124 www.marel.com
Manufacturer of meat hoppers, checkweighers,
scales and end line scales. Also manufacture batter
mixers, flour and bread applicators, spiral and linear
ovens and steam cookers.
CEO: Theo Hoen
CFO: Eric Kaman
Regional Sales Manager: David Bertelsen
Contact: Debra Bernas
dbernas@marel.com

25733 Marel Stork Poultry Processing
1024 Airport Pkwy
Gainesville, GA 30501-6814
770-532-7041
Fax: 770-532-5672
Manufacturer and exporter of poultry processing
equipment
President: Frank Nicoletti
frank.nicoletti@stork.com
Executive VP: Frank Nicoletti
Manager Domestic Sales: Bryon Lovingood
Estimated Sales: $20-50 Million
Number Employees: 100-249
Square Footage: 145000

25734 Marel Stork Poultry Processing
1024 Airport Pkwy
Gainesville, GA 30501-6814
770-532-7041
Fax: 770-532-5672 800-247-8609
info.us@marel.com www.marel.com/poultry
Poultry processing equipment
President: Frank Nicoletti
frank.nicoletti@stork.com
Director: Bob Conklin
Number Employees: 100-249
Parent Co: Marel

25735 Marel Townsend
2425 Hubbell Ave
Des Moines, IA 50317
515-265-8181
Fax: 515-263-3333 800-247-8609
info.townsendusa@stork.com www.marel.com
Processing equipment for meat processing; including single scales, production lines and turnkey
systems
Contact: Maria Bozaan
maria.bozaan@marel.com
Parent Co: Marel

25736 Marel USA
9745 Widmer Road
Lenexa, KS 66215-1260
913-888-9110
Fax: 913-888-9124 888-888-9107
info@marelusa.com www.marel.com
Complete range of super fast scales, software, moni-
toring equipment intelligent portioning, grading
modules, intergrated systems, flatteners, shish-kebab
machines and service contracts
President: Noel Whitten
CFO: Noel Whitten
VP Service: Petur Petursson
Marketing Director: Heather MacKenzie
VP Sales: Larry Campbell
Contact: Michael Jusseaume
michael.jusseaume@marelusa.com
Estimated Sales: $2.5-5 Million
Number Employees: 35
Square Footage: 41600
Parent Co: Marel Hf.

25737 Maren Engineering Corp
111 W Taft Dr
South Holland, IL 60473-2049
708-333-6250
Fax: 708-333-7507 800-875-1038
sales@marenengineering.com
www.marenengineering.com
Manufacturer and exporter of vertical and horizontal
balers for corrugated paper and other applications;
also, shredders, drum crushers and packers
CFO: Lee Norbeck
Vice President: Charles Brown
R & D: David Rudofski
Manager: Greg Hermdon
Estimated Sales: $5-10 Million
Number Employees: 20-49
Parent Co: Kine Corporation

25738 (HQ)Marfred Industries
12708 Bradford St
Sun Valley, CA 91353
818-896-3449
Fax: 818-889-4239 800-529-5156
Corrugated boxes and folding cartons
President: Marvin Fenster
CFO: Marc Fenster
Quality Control: John Ramirez
Marketing: Brian Mallay
Sales/Marketing Manager: Chris Gaff
Operations: Marc Fenster
Plant Manager: Randy Phares
Estimated Sales: $500,000-$1 Million
Number Employees: 100-249
Number of Brands: 50
Number of Products: 5000
Square Footage: 930000
Type of Packaging: Consumer, Food Service, Pri-
vate Label, Bulk

25739 Margia Floors
270 Bellevue Ave.
Newport, RI 2840
401-489-7805
Fax: 228-822-0096 info@margiafloors.com
www.margiafloors.com
Floor and wall coating materials, flooring, floor
grating, building and construction consultants
Estimated Sales: $1-5 Million
Number Employees: 2

25740 Marin Cleaning Systems
3239 Monier Cir
Suite 1
Rancho Cordova, CA 95742-6833
916-635-6861
Wine industry tank cleaners
Owner: Nathan Bari
Estimated Sales: $300,000-500,000
Number Employees: 1-4

**25741 Marineland Commercial
Aquariums**
3001 Commerce St.
Blacksburg, VA 24060-6671
805-529-0083
Fax: 805-529-0852 800-322-1266
consumersupport@unitedpetgroup.com
www.marineland.com
Manufacturer and exporter of display tanks for lob-
sters and fish
President: Gary Smith
CFO: John McGreevy
Vice President: Bill Sheweloff
Quality Control: Fred Bohmour
Sales Manager (West Coast): Jay Dersahagian
Contact: Keri Barton
barton@marineland.com
Estimated Sales: $5-10 Million
Number Employees: 250-499

25742 Marion Body Works Inc
211 W Ramsdell St
Marion, WI 54950-9683
715-754-5261
Fax: 715-754-5776 contactus@marionbody.com
www.marionbody.com
Dry, refrigerated and curtainside vans; also, struc-
tural platforms and glasshaulers
President: James Simpson
jsimpson@marionbody.com
Sales Manager: Mike Foley
Production Manager: Kent Cournoyer

Estimated Sales: $10-20 Million
Number Employees: 100-249
Square Footage: 240000
Brands:
  Marion

25743 Marion Pallet Company
281 Copeland Ave
Marion, OH 43302
740-382-5063
Fax: 740-387-9478 800-432-4117
New and rebuilt wooden pallets
Owner: Devin Needles
Contact: Ashley Karg
akarg@marionstar.com
Estimated Sales: $10-20 Million
Number Employees: 10-19
Square Footage: 20000

25744 Marion Paper Box Co
600 E 18th St
Marion, IN 46953-3304
765-664-6435
Fax: 765-664-6440 sales@marionbox.com
www.marionpaperboxco.com
Manufacturer and exporter of folding and set-up pa-
per boxes; also, die cutting and partitions available.
Also manufactures pads
Owner: Joe Mc Coy
Sales: Jason Priest
marionpaperbox2004@yahoo.com
Manager Operations: David Wilson
Estimated Sales: $2.5-5 Million
Number Employees: 5-9
Square Footage: 30000

25745 Mark Container Corporation
1899 Marina Blvd
San Leandro, CA 94577-4225
510-483-4440
Fax: 510-352-1524 www.wellsfargo.com
Manufacturer and exporter of corrugated boxes
Manager: Shuzair Malik
Estimated Sales: $10-20 Million
Number Employees: 10-19

25746 Mark Products Company
46 Rainbow Trl
Denville, NJ 7834
973-983-8818
Fax: 973-627-6273
Manufacturer and exporter of packaging equipment
and materials including shrink and pallet wrappers
and wrapping films; importer of shrink PVC films
President: Doug Mark
VP: Charles Scweizer
Number Employees: 1-4
Number of Brands: 1
Number of Products: 10
Square Footage: 4000
Type of Packaging: Food Service, Bulk

**25747 Mark Slade
ManufacturingCompany**
PO Box 325
Seymour, WI 54165-0325
920-833-6557
Fax: 920-833-7456 drhandles@new.rr.com
Wood dowels, core plugs, cant hooks, pallets and
displays
Estimated Sales: less than $300,000
Number Employees: 2
Square Footage: 20100

**25748 Mark-It Rubber Stamp & Label
Company**
912 Hope St
Stamford, CT 06907-0031
203-348-3204
Fax: 203-323-7846
Manufacturer and converter of self-stick labels, rub-
ber stamps and marking devices
President: Archie Dean
Executive VP: Archie Dean
Quality Control: Archie Dean
Sales Manager: Jack O'Neil
Estimated Sales: Below $5 Million
Number Employees: 5-9

25749 MarkeTeam
Corporate Office
PO Box 850
Vancouver, WA 98666
360-696-3984
Fax: 360-693-0192 info@marketeamnw.com
www.marketeamnw.com
Manufacturers' representative for food service
equipment including supplies and furniture
President: Daniel Miles
CEO: Jim Mincks
CFO: David Mincks
VP: William Kelly
Estimated Sales: Below $5 Million
Number Employees: 10-19

25750 Market Forge IndustriesInc
35 Garvey St
Everett, MA 02149-4403
406-209-1300
Fax: 617-387-4456 866-698-3188
custserv@mfii.com www.mfii.com
Comerical food service equipment
President: Jeffrey Leckel
Chief Financial Officer: Dave Zappala
Vice President: Robert Stefka
Chief Information Officer: Nancy Murphy
Vice President, Sales & Marketing: Peter Kelley
Sales Manager: Kelly Powers
Vice President, Operations: William McGourty
Production Manager: Hal Hamilton
Facilities Manager: Fred Bartlett
Estimated Sales: $13 Million
Number Employees: 10-19
Square Footage: 14859
Type of Packaging: Food Service

25751 Market Sales Company
PO Box 590639
Newton, MA 02459-0639
617-232-0239
Fax: 617-232-0239
marketsalescompany@comcast.net
Vacuum packaging equipment, vaccum bags and
films.
Vice President: Linda Pollino
Sales Manager: Edward Pollino

25752 Market Sign Systems
75 W Commercial St
Portland, ME 04101-4797
207-773-7585
Fax: 207-773-3151 800-421-1799
info@nimlok-maine.com
Point of purchase aluminum sign holders
Owner: Ken Janson
VP: Marc Breton
Number Employees: 1-4
Square Footage: 2400
Brands:
　Casemate

25753 Marketing & Technology Group
1415 N Dayton St # 115
Chicago, IL 60642-7033
312-274-2200
Fax: 312-266-3363 info@meatingplace.com
www.meatingplace.com
Computer systems and software, meat industry pub-
lications and information
Owner: Mark Lefens
jfranklin@meetingplace.com
Chairman: Jim Franklin
Vice President of Information Systems: Annica
Burns
Director of Marketing: Laurie Hachmeister
Account Executive: Dave Lurie
jfranklin@meetingplace.com
Production Manager: Shirleen Kajiwara
Estimated Sales: $5-10 Million
Number Employees: 20-49

25754 Marketing & Technology Group
1415 N Dayton St
Suite 115
Chicago, IL 60642
312-266-3311
Fax: 312-266-3363 amcguire@meatingplace.com
www.meatingplace.com
Computer systems and software, meat industry publications and information, sales and advertising promotions and materials

Owner: Mark Lefens
VP Editorial: Bill McDowell
Circulation/Marketing Manager: Steve Gardberg
Sales Manager: Mary Lea
Contact: Delorian Allen
dallen@meatingplace.com
Chairman Operations: Jim Franklin
Production Manager: Bernie Schlameuss
Estimated Sales: $5-10 Million
Number Employees: 20-49
Parent Co: Marketing & Technology Group

25755 Marketing Concepts
34 Hinda Blvd
Riverhead, NY 11901-4804
631-727-8886
Fax: 631-369-3903 www.auto-matetech.com
Tea and coffee industry conveying equipment (ele-
vators, machiners and buckets), cappers, cleaners
and closers (for coffee jars)
Owner: Kenneth Herzog
Estimated Sales: $10-20 Million
Number Employees: 20-49

25756 Marketing Management Inc
4717 Fletcher Ave
Fort Worth, TX 76107-6826
817-731-4176
Fax: 817-732-5610 800-433-2004
sales@mmibrands.com www.mmibrands.com
Retail & merchadising marketing, brand develop-
ment, quality assurance, consumer research, con-
sumer response, procurement, inventory
management, category development, package de-
sign, information technology, networking and
e-commercemulti media and more
President: Randy Hurr
CEO: Herb Pease Jr
VP, CFO: Donna Smith
Vice President: Ed Mieskoski
R&D: Bill Bradshaw
VP, Market Solutions: Steve Thomas
Sales: Bill Bradshaw
Public Relations: Joni Grulke
Operations: H Pease Jr
Estimated Sales: $10-20 Million
Number Employees: 50-99
Square Footage: 130000

25757 Marking Devices Inc
3110 Payne Ave
Cleveland, OH 44114-4504
216-861-4498
Fax: 216-241-1479 mdinc@en.com
www.realtyappreciation.com
Manufacturer and exporter of rubber and polymer
printing plates and rubber and steel stamps
Owner: John Enci
VP: John Wacker
Sales Manager: Dave Tully
johne@royalacme.com
Estimated Sales: $2.5-5 Million
Number Employees: 20-49
Square Footage: 22000

25758 Marking Methods Inc
301 S Raymond Ave
Alhambra, CA 91803-1531
626-308-5800
Fax: 626-576-7564 experts@markingmethods.com
www.markingmethods.com
Permanent stress-free marking equipment including
electro-chemical hot stamping for plastics, laser, dot
peen for metal parts and equipment; exporter of
electro-chemical marking equipment, etc
President: Nataly Baltazar
natalyb@markingmethods.com
CEO: A Bennett
CFO: Susan Chu
Sales Director: Victor Amorim
Estimated Sales: Below $5 Million
Number Employees: 20-49
Square Footage: 40000
Brands:
　Mark-300a
　Marking Methods, Inc.

25759 Marklite Line
34 Davis Dr
Bellwood, IL 60104-1047
708-668-4900
Fax: 630-668-4906
Advertising and pressure sensitive tapes and labels;
also, custom printing available

Customer Service: Agnes Vincenzo
Advertising: Maryann Mueller
Estimated Sales: $3-5 Million
Number Employees: 10-19

25760 Marko Inc
1310 Southport Rd
Spartanburg, SC 29306-6199
864-585-2259
866-466-2726
rmeehan@markoinc.com www.markoinc.com
Janitorial cleaners, disinfectants and waxes; whole-
saler/distributor of paper supplies and janitorial
equipment including aerosols and mops
Owner: Anne Meehan
ameehan@markoinc.com
CEO: Ann Meehan
VP Marketing: Richard Meehan, Jr.
Purchasing Manager: Melanie Meehan
Estimated Sales: 800000
Number Employees: 5-9
Number of Brands: 10
Number of Products: 450
Square Footage: 24000
Type of Packaging: Private Label
Brands:
　Marko

25761 Marko Inc
1310 Southport Rd
Spartanburg, SC 29306-6199
864-585-2259
Fax: 864-585-0750 866-466-2756
help@markoinc.com www.markoinc.com
Manufacturer and exporter of table cloths and skirt-
ing; also, napkins, aprons and place mats
Owner: Anne Meehan
ameehan@markoinc.com
VP Sales/Marketing: Tony La Porte
VP Manufacturing: Rob James
Estimated Sales: $10-20 Million
Number Employees: 5-9
Type of Packaging: Food Service
Brands:
　Marko Intl.
　Markoated
　Midwest Marko

**25762 Markwell Manufacturing
Company**
692 Pleasant St
Norwood, MA 2062
781-769-6610
Fax: 781-769-7060 800-666-1123
info@mrkwll.com www.mrkwll.com
Manufacturer, importer and exporter of plier, box
and hand, foot and air operated staplers, tackers and
carton sealers; also, staples, collated nails, marking
crayons, tapes, strech-wrap, and spray ashesives
President: Sam Opland
Contact: Jeff Cobb
markwellusa@gmail.com
Estimated Sales: $1-2.5 Million
Number Employees: 5-9
Square Footage: 27000
Brands:
　Markwell
　Sta-Plyer
　Tackmaster

25763 Marland Clutch Products
PO Box 308
La Grange, IL 60525-0308
708-352-3330
Fax: 877-216-3001 800-216-3515
info@marland.com www.marland.com
Heavy duty, industrial free wheeling clutches and
conveyor back stops
President: Charlie Nins
CFO: John Young
Estimated Sales: $5-10 Million
Number Employees: 3

25764 Marlen
4780 NW 41st Street
Ste 100
Riverside, MO 64150
913-888-3333
Fax: 913-888-5471 www.marlen.com
Portioning and forming equipment, in-line grinders,
pumping equipment and material handling products.

President: Richard Schneider
CEO: Jim Anderson
Regional Sales Manager: Fernando Casado
Contact: Jeff Blansit
jeff.blansit@marlen.com

25765 Marlen International
9202 Barton St
Overland Park, KS 66214

913-888-3333
Fax: 913-888-6440 800-862-7536

Food processing equipment, including: pumps,
portioners, formers and in-line grinders
Vice President: Bill Faivre
Sales Manager: Jarrod McCarroll
Contact: Grant Beck
grant.beck@marlen.com
Estimated Sales: $35 Million
Number Employees: 85
Parent Co: Pfingsten Partners

25766 Marlen International
441 30th St
Astoria, OR 97103-2807

503-861-2273
Fax: 913-888-6440 800-862-7536
www.marlen.com

Continuous flow slicers, dicers, strip cutters, shred-
ders, volumetric rotary/piston fillers, pak-shapers,
specialty conveyors, etc
Manager: Pete Johnson
CFO: Irene Codonau
Vice President: Jarrod McCarroll
Research & Development: Robert Zschoche
Quality Control: David Bogih
Marketing/Sales: Pete Johnson
Regional Sales Manager: Mike Leiker
Public Relations: Jack Walls
Inside Sales: Jack Walls
Production Manager: David Bogh
Plant Manager: Rusty Price
Purchasing Manager: Mark Ross
Estimated Sales: $10-20 Million
Number Employees: 20-49
Square Footage: 120000
Brands:
    Auto-Logger
    Auto-Shredder
    Auto-Slicer
    Automated Boxing Line
    Home-Style
    Mega-Slicer
    Nu-Pak Performance F-Series
    Nu-Pak Portion
    Pak-Shaper
    Pathfinder
    Performance
    Q-Ber
    Table Top

25767 Marlen International
441 30th St
Astoria, OR 97103-2807

800-862-7536
Fax: 913-888-5471 sales@marlen.com
www.marlen.com

Manufactures dicing, filling, slicers and shredding
machinery
Vice President: Jarrod McCarroll
Estimated Sales: $10-20 000,000
Number Employees: 20-49

25768 Marlen Research
P.O.Box 457
Hutchinson, KS 67504-457

316-683-6542
Fax: 316-665-6793 www.marlen.com

Elevators, loaders, lifters, dumpers, tubs, drums,
tanks, vats and buckets for materials handling, processing equipment includes ham presses, molds and
accessories, temperature controls, contact plate and
belt freezers
Estimated Sales: $10-20 Million
Number Employees: 50-99
Parent Co: Marlen Research Corporation

25769 Marlen Research Corporation
9202 Barton St
Shawnee Mission, KS 66214

913-888-3333
Fax: 913-888-6440 sales@marlen.com
www.marlen.com

Designer and manufacturer of food processing
equipment such as pump/vacuumizer, sizers, grind-
ers, exact weight portioners, product racks, dumpers,
vats, continous mold systems, thermal processing
equipment and custom designed tanks andhoppers
President: Adam Anderson
VP: Bill Faivre
Marketing/Sales: Teresa Kem
Sales Manager: Fernando Casado
Contact: James Andrson
sales@marlen.com
Estimated Sales: $6-$7 Million
Number Employees: 50-99
Square Footage: 40000
Brands:
    Gbc
    Marlen
    Reno

25770 Marlen Research Corporation
9202 Barton St
Shawnee Mission, KS 66214

913-888-3333
Fax: 913-888-5471 800-862-7536
sales@marlen.com www.marlen.com

President: Adam Anderson
CFO: Larry Dearnond
Contact: James Andrson
sales@marlen.com
Estimated Sales: $20-50 Million
Number Employees: 50-99

25771 Marley Engineered Products LLC
470 Beauty Spot Rd E
Bennettsville, SC 29512-2770

843-479-4006
Fax: 843-479-5205 800-327-4328
www.marleymep.com

Blowers and fans
President: Tom Blashill
tom.blashill@spx.com
Estimated Sales: $5-10 Million
Number Employees: 500-999

25772 Marlin Steel Wire Products
2640 Merchant Dr
Baltimore, MD 21230-3307

410-644-7456
Fax: 410-644-7457 877-762-7546
sales@marlinwire.com www.marlinwire.com

Steel wire shelving and racks
President: Chris Elwood
chris.elwood@marlinsteel.com
CFO: Susan Fuller
Estimated Sales: $20-50 Million
Number Employees: 20-49
Number of Products: 450
Square Footage: 25000

25773 Marlite
1 Marlite Dr
Dover, OH 44622

330-343-6621
Fax: 330-343-7296 800-377-1221
info@marlite.com www.marlite.com

Manufacturer and exporter of sanitary wall and ceil-
ing panel systems, decorative wall panel systems,
doors/frames, restroom partitions, korelock panels,
retail merchandising display systems, etc
CFO: Kimberly McBride
VP, Sales & Marketing: Greg Triplett
Contact: Nini Abreu
nabreu@marlite.com
Estimated Sales: $21 Million
Number Employees: 251-500
Square Footage: 450000
Brands:
    Accents Frp
    Borders
    Displawall
    Firetest
    Korelock
    Marlite
    Marlite Brand Frp
    Marlite Modules
    Plank
    Surface Systems
    Symmetrix Frp

25774 Marlo Manufacturing
301 Division St
Boonton, NJ 07005-1826

973-423-0226
Fax: 973-423-1638 800-222-0450

Manufacturer, importer and exporter of stainless
steel food service equipment
Founder: Sal Pirruccio
Partner: Larry Dubov
larry@marlomfg.com
VP, Manufacturing: Paul Pirruccio
VP, Sales & Marketing: Larry Dubov
VP, Operations: Paul Tommasi
Plant Manager: Paul Pirruccio
Estimated Sales: $4-6 Million
Number Employees: 1-4
Square Footage: 60000
Type of Packaging: Food Service

25775 Marlow Watson Inc
37 Upton Dr # 1
Wilmington, MA 01887-4452

978-658-0041
Fax: 978-658-0041 800-282-8823
www.watson-marlow.com

Peristaltic hose pumps for metering, transferring and
dispensing
CEO and CFO: James Whalen
Contact: Joakim Cederqvist
jcederqvist@wmbpumps.com
Estimated Sales: $20-50 Million
Number Employees: 5-9
Parent Co: Spirax Sarco Engineering Group
Brands:
    Bioprene
    Marprene
    Watson-Marlow

25776 Maro Paper Products Company
333 31st Ave
Bellwood, IL 60104-1527

708-649-9982
Fax: 708-649-9986 www.marocarton.com

Folding cartons and blister cards
Owner: Joseph Maro
VP: J Maro
Estimated Sales: $5-10 Million
Number Employees: 100-249

25777 (HQ)Marpac Industries
PO Box 784
Philmont, NY 12565-0784

845-336-8100
Fax: 845-336-5006 888-462-7722

Plastic bottles and containers
VP Sales: B Williams
Operations: Gen Gendrow
Estimated Sales: $10-20 Million
Number Employees: 50-99
Square Footage: 68000
Type of Packaging: Consumer, Food Service
Other Locations:
    Marpac Industries
    Kingston NY
Brands:
    E-Z Access

25778 (HQ)Marq Packaging Systems Inc
3801 W Washington Ave
Yakima, WA 98903-1181

509-966-4300
Fax: 509-452-3307 800-998-4301
info@marq.net

Case sealers, product settling & sealing, tray formers
and case erector bottom sealers.
President: Rocky Marquis
CFO: Diahann Curtis
dcurtis@marq.net
VP: Kelli Barton
Sales Co-coordinator: Jim Hansen
Operations: G W Walker
Estimated Sales: $5-10 Million
Number Employees: 20-49
Square Footage: 135000
Type of Packaging: Food Service, Bulk

25779 Marq Packaging Systems Inc
3801 W Washington Ave
Yakima, WA 98903-1181

509-966-4300
Fax: 509-452-3307 800-998-4301
info@marq.net

Wine industry Bag in Box, case sealing
President: Rocky Marquis
CEO: Ted Marquis Sr
CFO: Diahann Curtis
dcurtis@marq.net
Chairman of the Board: Theodore Marquis Sr
Number Employees: 20-49

25780 Marquip Ward United
1300 N Airport Rd
Phillips, WI 54555-1527
715-339-2191
www.marquipwardunited.com
Machinery for corrugated containers
Estimated Sales: $1-5 Million
Number Employees: 500-999
Parent Co: Barry-Wehmiller

25781 Marquip Ward United
1300 N Airport Rd
Phillips, WI 54555
715-339-2191
www.marquipwardunited.com
Manufacturer and exporter of packaging and stacking machinery.
Year Founded: 1898
Estimated Sales: $100-500 Million
Number Employees: 500-999
Parent Co: Barry Wehmiller Companies

25782 Marquis Products
91 Pipin Road
Concord, ON L4K 4J9
Canada
905-738-2082
Fax: 905-738-2417 800-268-1282
Refrigeration equipment including walk-in, reach-in coolers, sliding and glass doors and freezers
President: Vincent Melfi
Number Employees: 30

25783 Marriott Walker Corporation
925 E Maple Rd
Bingham Farms, MI 48009
248-644-6868
Fax: 248-642-1213 mwc@marriottwalker.com
www.marriottwalker.com
Manufacturer and exporter of evaporators, spray dryers, etc
President: Winthrop Walker
VP Engineering: Mark Price
Contact: Mary Ayotte
mayotte@marriottwalker.com
Estimated Sales: $1-2.5 Million
Number Employees: 5-9
Square Footage: 13200
Brands:
  Marriott Walker

25784 Marron Foods
327 Woodlands Rd
Box 15
Harrison, NY 10528
914-967-2442
Fax: 914-967-2220 info@marronfoods.com
www.marronfoods.com
Agglomeration/instantizing ,spray drying, blending, industrial, food serice, consumer pouch/canister packaging
President: Matt Pearson
Number Employees: 100
Brands:
  SlimMilk
  SlimMilk LF
  80WheyUSA
  MaltoPure
  Milkman

25785 (HQ)Mars Air Products
14716 S Broadway
Gardena, CA 90248-1814
310-532-1555
Fax: 310-324-3030 800-421-1266
info@marsair.com www.marsair.com
Manufacturer and exporter of air purifiers and heated and unheated air curtains in electric, gas, steam and hot water for insect control and environmental separation; also, packaged make-up air, cooling, heating and ventilatingsystems
Owner: Jimmy Johnson
johnson@skycatch.com
Vice President: Steve Rosol
Quality Control: Michael Goldman
Marketing Director: Dana Agens
Plant Manager/Purchasing Director: Frank Cuaderno
Estimated Sales: Below $5 Million
Number Employees: 50-99
Square Footage: 392000
Brands:
  Ares
  Combi
  Mars

Whispurr Air
Windguard

25786 Mars Systems
1140 Empire Central Dr
Dallas, TX 75247-4322
214-634-7441
Fax: 972-252-9566
Restaurant entertainment systems
Owner: Robert Morris
Account Executive: Sheila Bellucci
Estimated Sales: $500,000-$1 Million
Number Employees: 5-9

25787 Marsch Pacific Cork & Foil
2427 Pratt Avenue
Hayward, CA 94544-7829
510-429-3200
Fax: 510-429-3200
Wine industry cork and capsule supplies
Estimated Sales: $5-10 Million
Number Employees: 10-19

25788 (HQ)Marsh Company
PO Box 388
Belleville, IL 62222-0388
618-234-1122
Fax: 618-234-1529 800-527-6275
marshco@marshco.com www.marshco.com
Manufacturer, exporter and importer of large and small character ink jet coding systems, marking and sealing machines and supplies
President: Robret Willett
CEO/Chairman: John Marsh
CFO: Mark Kuhn
Quality Control: Mark Wilmsen
R&D: Jerry Robortson
VP Sales/Marketing: P Wagner
Estimated Sales: $20-50 Million
Number Employees: 500
Other Locations:
  Marsh Co.
  S.A. Geneva
Brands:
  Contact Marking
  Dial Taper
  Lcp/Dl
  Lcp/Ml8
  Mini-Mark
  Symbol Jet
  Touch Taper
  Twin Taper
  Ultra Taper
  Unicorn

25789 Marshakk Smoked Fish Company
6980 75th St
Flushing, NY 11379-2531
718-326-2170
Fax: 718-384-6661
Specialty foods
President: Marie Cook
Vice President: Gary Cook
Sales Director: Sean Cook
Estimated Sales: $10-24.9 000,000
Number Employees: 50-99
Type of Packaging: Private Label
Brands:
  Almondina
  Aunt Jenny's
  Babcock
  Boone Maman
  Bovril
  Breadshop
  Brianna's
  Carapelli
  Carr's
  Celestial
  Coco Pazzo
  Colavita
  Consorzio
  Dececco
  Del Verde
  Dell Amore's
  Delouis
  Dessvilie
  Dickinson
  Droste
  Dutch Gold
  Eden
  El Paso
  Finncrisp
  French Market
  Green Mountain
  Grielle

Guiltless Gourmet
Hero
Highland Sugar Vermont
Holgrain
Illy
Knorr
Konriko
La Marne Champ
La Posada
La Preferida
Langnese
Lindt
Maille
Marmite
McCann's
Melba
Melitta
Monnini
New York Flatbread
Old Monk
Poell
Pommery
Pritikin
Qugg
Rao's
Romanoff
Spice Hunter
Spice Island
St. Dalfour
Sunbrand
Texmati
Timpone's
Tip Tree
Tropical Bee
Twinings

25790 Marshall Air Systems Inc
419 Peachtree Dr S
Charlotte, NC 28217-2098
704-525-6230
Fax: 704-525-6229 800-722-3474
customerservice@marshallair.com
www.marshallair.com
Manufacturer and exporter of food warming and conveyorized cooking systems including broilers; also, ventilation systems including hoods and fans
Chairman: Robert Stuck
Chairman: Marina Flick
mflick@marshallair.com
Estimated Sales: $20-50 Million
Number Employees: 50-99
Type of Packaging: Food Service
Brands:
  Autobake
  Autobroil
  Autobroil Omni
  Autogrill
  Automelt
  Autoroast
  Thermoglo

25791 (HQ)Marshall Boxes Inc
715 Lexington Ave
Rochester, NY 14613-1807
585-458-7432
Fax: 585-458-6302 info@marshallboxes.com
www.marshallboxes.com
Wooden boxes, pallets and plywood parts
President: John Skuse
jskuse@marshallboxes.com
Estimated Sales: $2.5-5 Million
Number Employees: 10-19
Square Footage: 44000
Other Locations:
  Marshall Boxes
  Rancho Cucomonga CA

25792 Marshall Ingredients
5740 Limekiln Rd
Wolcott, NY 14590
800-796-9353
cbones@marshallingredients.com
Fruits and vegetables in different forms such as fiber, pellet, whole, diced, sliced, powder, seeds, pomace
National Sales Manager: Casey Koehnlein
Contact: Scott Edwards
sedwards@marshallingredients.com
Type of Packaging: Bulk

25793 Marshall Instruments Inc
2930 E LA Cresta Ave
Anaheim, CA 92806-1833
714-632-8565
Fax: 714-666-2326   800-222-8476
info@marshallinstruments.com
www.marshallinstruments.com
Bi-metallic dial thermometers, distributor of high
performance shock proof pressure gauges
President: Nancy Lynch
info@marshallinstruments.com
VP: Nancy Lynch
Product Manager: Tim Bowers
Estimated Sales: $2.5-5 Million
Number Employees: 20-49
Square Footage: 24000

25794 (HQ)Marshall Paper Products
PO Box 267
East Norwich, NY 11732
Fax: 718-821-5779
Corrugated paper
VP: Brian Sadowsky
Estimated Sales: $1-2.5 Million
Number Employees: 5

25795 Marshall Plastic Film Inc
904 E Allegan St
Martin, MI 49070-9797
269-672-5511
Fax: 269-672-5035   www.marshallplastic.com
Manufacturer and exporter of form, fill, seal and
shrink plastic films and bags
President: Rich Bowman
rbowman@marshallplastic.com
VP: Casey McCarthy
Customer Service: William Rackley
Customer Service: Sylvia Davis
Estimated Sales: $20-50 Million
Number Employees: 20-49
Square Footage: 45500
Brands:
   Marshall Blue
   Marshall Pink Under the Sink

25796 Marshfield Food Safety
1100 N. Oak Avenue
Marshfield, WI 54449
888-780-9897
www.marshfieldfoodsafetyllc.com
Food safety testing facility.
Quality Manager: Debbie Chilson
Marketing: Marsha Barwick
Chief Scientific Officer: Roy Radcliff

25797 (HQ)Marston Manufacturing
13700 Broadway Ave
Cleveland, OH 44125-1945
216-587-3400
Fax: 216-587-0733   www.tomlinsonind.com
Wooden tray stands and oak chairs including high
and booster; also, condiment holders, cast iron cook-
ware, bread boards, sandwich tartans and
underliners
President: H Meyer
CEO: Mike Figas
CFO: Don Calkins
Sales: John DiNapoli
Estimated Sales: $2.5-5 Million
Number Employees: 100-249
Square Footage: 160000
Other Locations:
   Marston Manufacturing
   Richmond VA

25798 Mart CART-Smt
112 E Linden St
Rogers, AR 72756-6035
479-636-5776
Fax: 479-246-6473   800-548-3373
apc@assembledproducts.com
www.assembledproducts.com
Manufacturer and exporter of pressure washers
President: George Panter
Vice President: Bob Sage
Marketing Director: Steve Scroggins
Sales Director: Kent Langum
Plant Manager: R Smith
Purchasing Manager: Don McKenzie
Estimated Sales: $20-30 Million
Number Employees: 100-249
Square Footage: 123000
Parent Co: Assembled Pro Corporation

Brands:
   Spraymaster

25799 Mart CART-Smt
112 E Linden St
Rogers, AR 72756-6035
479-636-5776
Fax: 479-246-6473   800-548-3373
www.assembledproducts.com
President: George Panter
Estimated Sales: $1-5 Million
Number Employees: 100-249

25800 Martco Engravers
792 Main Street
Fremont, NH 03044-3506
603-895-3561
Fax: 603-895-3717
Badges, ribbons, plaques, awards, trophies and rub-
ber stamps
Partner: Arthur Courteau
Estimated Sales: Less than $500,000
Number Employees: 4

25801 Martech Research
15 Myrtle Dr
Bishopville, SC 29010-1764
803-428-2000
Fax: 803-428-1598
bmaresca@martechresearch.com
www.martechenvironmental.com
Custom manufacturing, formulation, private labeling
and toll blending. Shelf life extension products for
fruits, vegetables, oils and beverages.
Founder & President: Amie Maresca
Manager: Benny Maresca
bmaresca@martechresearch.com
Estimated Sales: $3.7 Million
Number Employees: 1-4
Square Footage: 84000
Type of Packaging: Consumer, Private Label, Bulk

25802 Martin Brothers Inc
3057 Cajun Dr
Winnsboro, LA 71295-6849
318-435-4581
Fax: 318-435-4581   800-652-2532
kmartin@teammartinbrothers.com
www.teammartinbrothers.com
Heat exchangers, ice cream equipment, ingredient
feeders, piping, fittings and tubing, sanitary
President: W K Martin
wmartin@teammartinbrothers.com
VP Sales & Marketing: Conrad L. Gaither
Sales: Lamar Johnson
Sales: Kelly Martin
Sales: Dwayne Long
Estimated Sales: $5-10 Million
Number Employees: 10-19

25803 Martin Cab Div
7108 Madison Ave
Cleveland, OH 44102-4093
216-377-8200
Fax: 216-651-2079   www.martincab.com
Manufacturer and exporter of cab enclosures, in-
cluding freezer cabs
President: James Martin
CFO: Jim Markin
Chairman: Pauline Martin
VP Sales/Marketing: James Girard
Estimated Sales: $20-50 Million
Number Employees: 5-9
Parent Co: Martin Sheet Metal

25804 Martin Control Systems Inc
5955 Wilcox Pl
Suite B
Dublin, OH 43016
614-761-5600
Fax: 614-761-5601   SalesEng@MartinCSI.com
www.martincsi.com
Designs, executes and completes industrial control
system and data collection projects to automate man-
ufacturing and process facilities.
President/Owner: Joe Martin
Principal Project Engineer: Rick Derthick
Marketing & Sales Manager: James Sellitto
Contact: Karen Martin
kmmartin@martincsi.com

25805 Martin Electric Plants
280 Pleasant Valley Rd
Ephrata, PA 17522-8620
717-733-7968
Fax: 717-733-1981   800-713-7968
office@martinsice.com   www.martinsice.com
Ice
Owner: Isaac Martin
james@martinselectricplants.com
Sales Manager: Randy Martin
Site Manager: James Martin
james@martinselectricplants.com
Manager: Jerry Martin
Estimated Sales: $500,000-$1 Million
Number Employees: 5-9
Square Footage: 16800

25806 (HQ)Martin Engineering
1 Martin Pl
Neponset, IL 61345-9766
309-852-2384
Fax: 309-594-2432   800-766-2786
info@martin-eng.com   www.martin-eng.com
Manufacturer and exporter of belt conveyors and
cleaners, transfer point skirting systems and electric,
hydraulic and pneumatic vibrators; importer of elec-
tric vibrators
Owner: E H Peterson
CEO: Scott Hutter
CFO: Ron Vick
CTO: R Todd Swinderman
VP: Jim Turner
Public Relations: AD Marti
Estimated Sales: $20-50 Million
Number Employees: 100-249
Square Footage: 130000
Other Locations:
   Martin Engineering
   Walluf
Brands:
   Durt Howg
   Durt Tracker
   Martin

25807 Martin Engineering
1 Martin Pl
Neponset, IL 61345-9766
309-852-2384
Fax: 800-814-1553   800-544-2947
info@martin-eng.com   www.martin-eng.com
Vibration systems and solutions to boost material
flow, linear and rotary vibrators keep material moving while reducing noise and air consumption, includes vibratory feeders, conveyors and compaction
tables for metering transportingand compacting
powder.vibrators in pneumatic, electric and
hydraulic power
President: Scott Hutter
Chief Executive Officer: R Todd Swinderman
Vice President of Sales and Marketing: James
Turner
Vice President of Operations: Robert Nogaj
Number Employees: 100-249

25808 Martin Laboratories
PO Box 1873
Owensboro, KY 42302-1873
270-685-4441
Fax: 270-684-7859   800-345-9352
Manufacturer and exporter of hand cleaners and
soaps including liquid and waterless
President: Harold C Martin
National Sales Manager: Art Wilbert
Contact: Clifford Martin
rwatson@tqsinc.com
Customer Service: Stacia Jarvis
Estimated Sales: $10-20 Million
Number Employees: 5-9
Square Footage: 60000
Brands:
   M30

25809 Martin Sprocket & Gear Inc
3100 Sprocket Dr
Arlington, TX 76015-2898
817-258-3000
Fax: 817-258-3333   mail@martinsprocket.com
www.martinsprocket.com
Wine industry conveyors and screws, power transmission and bulk material handling products,
sprockets, sheaves, gears, couplings, timing pulleys,
interchangeable bushings, screw conveyers (steel
and plastic), bucket elevators, verticalscrew
elevators

President/Owner: Reid Martin
rmartin@martinsprocket.com
CFO: Chuck Reynolds
Estimated Sales: $50-100 Million
Number Employees: 1000-4999

25810 Martin Vibration Systems
990 Degurse Ave
Marine City, MI 48039

810-765-7460
Fax: 810-765-7461 800-474-4538
felcom@pobox.com www.shake-it.com
Feeders, vibrators, dry bulk material handling equipment
President: Mike Lindbeck
Contact: Jay Valuet
valuetj@shake-it.com
Type of Packaging: Bulk

25811 Martin/Baron
5454 2nd St
Irwindale, CA 91706-2000

626-960-5153
Fax: 626-962-1280 www.mbicryo.com
Manufacturer and exporter of food processing equipment, stainless steel conveying systems, cryogenic and mechanical coolers and freezers, steam and radiant heat cookers, spirals, tunnels, cabinets for heat transfer and vertical pizzaovens
President: Jonathan Martin
VP: David Baron
Sales: Allan Weiner
Operations: Carl Gumber
Estimated Sales: $3-5 Million
Number Employees: 10-19
Square Footage: 48000
Brands:
  Mbi
  Martin/Baron

25812 Martingale Paper Company
3022 N 16th St
Philadelphia, PA 19132

215-225-7070
Fax: 215-660-0822
Paperboard boxes and paper stationery products
Owner: Martin Grossman
Estimated Sales: $5-10 Million
Number Employees: 5-9

25813 Martini SRL
20 Industrial Street W
Clifton, NJ 07012-1712

973-778-4927
Fax: 973-778-9820 sales@frazierandson.com
Estimated Sales: Below 1 Million
Number Employees: 10

25814 Marv Holland Industries
10939-120 Street
Edmonton, AB T5H 3R3
Canada

780-453-5044
Fax: 800-361-0263 800-661-7269
custserv@marvholland.com
Manufacturer and distributor of apparel such as business uniforms and flame resistant safety wear for industry and casual clothing.
President: Gene Fyzenky
Number Employees: 100-249

25815 Marvell Packaging Company
490 Us Highway 46
Fairfield, NJ 07004-1906

973-822-9339
Fax: 973-575-6637 800-445-8947
Contract packaging service
Vice President: Barry Berman
Estimated Sales: $10 Million
Number Employees: 50-99
Number of Products: 20
Square Footage: 65000
Type of Packaging: Private Label

25816 Marygrove Awnings-Toledo
3217 Genoa Rd
Perrysburg, OH 43551-9703

419-241-9181
Fax: 419-837-2814 www.marygrove.com
Commercial awnings
President: Don Reinbolt
Manager: Ken Cruzel
kcruzel@marygrove.com

Estimated Sales: Less Than $500,000
Number Employees: 5-9
Parent Co: Toledo Tarp Service

25817 Maryland Packaging Corporation
7030 Troy Hill Dr
Elkridge, MD 21075

410-540-9700
Fax: 410-540-9789 www.marylandpackaging.com
Manufacturer and exporter of shrink wrapping, sleeve bundling, horizontal form/fill/seal, overwrapping and horizontal bagging machinery, also have a contract packaging division
President: John Voneiff II
CEO: Marwan Moheyeldien Sr.
Quality Control Manager: Drexel Nelson
Sales Director: Jay Gibson
HR: Mari Cruz Abarca
Estimated Sales: $5-10,000,000
Number Employees: 60
Square Footage: 50000
Type of Packaging: Consumer, Food Service, Private Label, Bulk
Brands:
  Tpa

25818 Maryland Plastics Inc
251 E Central Ave
Federalsburg, MD 21632-1313

410-754-5566
Fax: 410-754-8882 800-544-5582
sales@marylandplastics.com
www.marylandplastics.com
Accessories/supplies i.e. picnic baskets, cooking implements/housewares.
President: John Soper
jsoper@marylandplastics.com
Marketing: John Bucchioni
Manager: Jerry Dickerson
Number Employees: 50-99

25819 Maryland Wire Belts
8000 Hub Parkway
Cleveland, OH 44125

216-642-9100
Fax: 216-642-9573 800-677-2358
salessupport@bdi-usa.com www.bdi-usa.com
Manufacturer and Exporter of conveyor belting, conveyors and conveyor services
President: William Weber
CEO: Duane Marshall
CEO: Bill Colson
Number Employees: 100-249
Square Footage: 400000
Brands:
  Bfs
  Curve Flex
  Curve Mesh
  Elevayor
  Flat Seat
  Obfs
  Pactite
  Pos-A-Trak
  Precision Belt Series
  Shove-It Rods
  Spun Head

25820 (HQ)Maselli Measurements Inc
7746 Lorraine Ave # 201
Stockton, CA 95210-4234

209-474-9178
Fax: 209-474-9241 800-964-9600
daveodum@maselli.com www.maselli.com/en
Process & laboratory refractometers
President: Mario Maselli
mariomaselli@maselli.com
Quality Control: Mario Maselli
Sales: Dave Odum
Estimated Sales: $2.5-5 Million
Number Employees: 5-9
Number of Brands: 1
Number of Products: 10
Other Locations:
  Maselli Measurements
  Leon, GTO
Brands:
  Lr01 Laboratory Refractometer
  Ur20 Process Refractometer

25821 Maselli Measurements Inc
7746 Lorraine Ave # 201
Stockton, CA 95210-4234

209-474-9178
Fax: 209-474-9241 800-964-9600
daveodum@maselli.com www.maselli.com/en

Liquid analysis machines such as carbonated beverage analysis systems, automatic and in-line refractometers.
President: Mario Maselli
mariomaselli@maselli.com
Sales Manager: Dave Odum
Number Employees: 5-9

25822 Mason Candlelight Company
PO Box 59
New Albany, MS 38652-0059

310-338-6987
Fax: 310-348-0135 800-556-2766
Manufacturer and exporter of tabletop lighting including lamps and candles
VP/General Manager: Robert Gasbarro
Plant Supervisor: Robert Bacher
Estimated Sales: $2.5-5 Million
Number Employees: 9
Square Footage: 180000
Parent Co: Standex International Corporation

25823 Mason City Tent & Awning Co
408 S Federal Ave
Mason City, IA 50401-3837

641-423-0044
Fax: 641-423-8566 customercare@ripflag.com
www.ripflag.com
Commercial awnings and industrial curtains
Manager: Russalyn Davis
customercare@ripflag.com
Estimated Sales: Less Than $500,000
Number Employees: 1-4
Square Footage: 20000
Parent Co: ITF Industries

25824 (HQ)Mason Transparent Package Company
PO Box 852
Armonk, NY 10504-0852

718-792-6000
Fax: 718-823-7279
Printed and converted films and bags including polyethylene, clysar, polypropylene, linear low density, co-extruded, etc.; importer of film
President: Richard Cole
VP: Kevin O'Connell
Estimated Sales: $2.5-5 Million
Number Employees: 10-19
Square Footage: 100000

25825 Mason Ways Indestructible
580 Village Blvd # 330
West Palm Beach, FL 33409-1953

561-478-8838
Fax: 800-693-7745 800-837-2881
www.masonways.com
Materials handling equipment; pallets and accessories, tubs, drums, tanks, vats, buckets
Owner: Judd Ettinger
judd.ettinger@masonways.com
CEO: Allen Mason
Marketing Director: Ira Brichta
Operations Manager: Debbie Shrake
Estimated Sales: $1-5 Million
Number Employees: 1-4
Number of Brands: 6
Number of Products: 60
Type of Packaging: Food Service, Private Label, Bulk

25826 Massachusetts ContainerCorporation
455 Sackett Point Road
North Haven, CT 6473

203-248-2161
Fax: 203-248-0241 www.unicorr.com
Corrugated boxes
VP: Jack Aundre
Contact: Larry Caron
lcaron@unicorr.com
Estimated Sales: $10-20 Million
Number Employees: 100-249
Parent Co: Connecticut Container Corporation
Other Locations:
  Massachusetts ContainerCorp.
  Sharon VT

25827 Massillon Container Co
49 Ohio St SW
Navarre, OH 44662-1183

330-879-5653
Fax: 330-879-2772 benv@vailpkg.com
www.vailpkg.com

Corrugated shipping containers
President: Jodi Frkuska
jodif@vailpkg.com
Quality Control: Cliff Robertson
Accounting: Donna Winter
Estimated Sales: $9 Million
Number Employees: 50-99
Parent Co: Vail Industries

25828 Master Air
415 S Grant St
Lebanon, IN 46052-3605
 317-375-7600
 Fax: 317-375-7607 800-248-8368
Manufacturer and exporter of commercial kitchen
ventilation equipment including hood systems and
fan controls
President: Loren Gard
Sales Engineer: Jim Rader
Office Manager: Sharon Amack
Engineer: Kevin Blandford
Estimated Sales: $2.5-5 Million
Number Employees: 20-49
Square Footage: 118000
Brands:
 Mastertech
 Mastertech Direct Fired

25829 Master Containers
209 SW Phosphate Blvd
Mulberry, FL 33860
 863-425-5571
 Fax: 978-964-1552 800-881-6847
Foam cups and containers
President: Thomas Lyons
VP: Richard Lyone
Marketing Manager: Rachael Pantely
Sales Manager: Elaine Karau
Estimated Sales: $10-20 Million
Number Employees: 50-99

25830 Master Disposers
PO Box 27186
Cincinnati, OH 45227-0186
 513-271-1861
 Fax: 513-271-1867 www.masterdisposers.com
President: Mary Grogan
R&D: Rich Grogan
Estimated Sales: $3-5 Million
Number Employees: 10

25831 Master Magnetics
747 South Gilbert Street
Castle Rock, CO 80104
 303-688-3966
 Fax: 303-688-5303 800-525-3536
 magnet@magnetsource.com
 www.magnetsource.com
Magnetic products for food purification systems in-
cluding ceramic plate, permanent pulleys and hopper
grates; also, shelf marking systems
President: John E Nellessen
Marketing Manager: Jennifer Brown
Contact: Lora Allen
loraa@magnetsource.com
General Manager: Pat Orcutt
Estimated Sales: $3-5 Million
Number Employees: 7
Square Footage: 88700

25832 Master Package Corporation
142 Indianhead Drive
Menomonie, WI 54751
 715-229-2156
 Fax: 715-229-2689 800-347-4144
 mpabich@masterpackage.com
 www.masterpackage.com
Fiber board, cylindrical and metal bound containers
President: Mark Pabich
Office Manager: Carole Buss
Estimated Sales: $5-10 Million
Number Employees: 20-49

25833 Master Paper Box Co
3641 S Iron St
Chicago, IL 60609-1322
 773-927-0252
 Fax: 773-927-8086 877-927-0252
 musser@masterpaperbox.com
 www.masterpaperbox.com
Set-up and heart paper boxes

Owner: Bill Farago
bfarago@masterpaperbox.com
VP/ Sales: Michael Musser
Operations Manager: Bill Farago Jr.
Secretary/Treasurer: Angela Sears
Estimated Sales: $2.5-5 Million
Number Employees: 20-49
Square Footage: 220000

25834 Master Printers
308 Main St
Canon City, CO 81212-3732
 719-275-8608
 Fax: 719-275-8106
Advertising signs
Owner: Susie Smith
masterprinters@brefman.net
VP: Susie Pacheco
Estimated Sales: Less Than $500,000
Number Employees: 1-4

25835 Master Signs-Div Of Masterco
5545 Parkdale Dr
Dallas, TX 75227-3205
 214-381-6207
 Fax: 214-381-1090
Plastic, electric, fluorescent and neon signs; also, il-
luminated awnings and interior graphics
President: Robert Green
masterco@aol.com
CFO: Brenda Green
Estimated Sales: $1-2.5 Million
Number Employees: 20-49
Parent Co: Masterco

25836 Master Tape & Label Printers
4517 N Elston Ave
Chicago, IL 60630-4420
 773-685-4100
 Fax: 773-685-1555 800-621-5801
 www.mastertapeprinters.com
Adhesive, gummed, marking and pressure sensitive
tapes and labels
Owner: Malcolm Grant
malcolm.grant@shaffstall.com
CEO: Melcon Grant
CFO: Malcolm Grant
VP: Andy Casey
Quality Control: Robert Wren
Marketing Director: Bob Wern
Estimated Sales: Below $5 Million
Number Employees: 20-49

25837 Master-Bilt
908 State Highway 15 N
New Albany, MS 38652-9507
 662-534-9061
 Fax: 662-534-6049 800-647-1284
 sales@master-bilt.com www.master-bilt.com
Manufacturer and exporter of commercial refrigera-
tion products including refrigeration and freezer
units, walk-in and reach-in units, etc; also, mer-
chandising units for dairy items and deli cabinets
President: David Parks
Chief Financial Officer: Edward Jacobs
Vice President, Sales & Marketing: Bill Huffman
Vice President, Operations: Eddie Carr
Purchasing: Larry Fry
Estimated Sales: $50-100 Million
Number Employees: 500-999
Square Footage: 64006
Parent Co: Standex International Corporation

25838 (HQ)Masterbuilt Manufacturing Inc
1 Masterbuilt Ct
Columbus, GA 31907-1313
 706-327-5622
 Fax: 706-327-5632
 customerservice@masterbuilt.com
 www.masterbuilt.com
Grills, smokers, fryers, spices, marinades, wheel free
cargo carriers, and bike carriers
Owner: John Mclemore
VP Sales/Marketing: Ben Garnto
jmclemore@masterbuilt.com
Estimated Sales: $10-20,000,000
Number Employees: 50-99
Number of Brands: 4
Type of Packaging: Consumer, Food Service, Pri-
vate Label

25839 Mastercraft
234 W Northland Ave
Appleton, WI 54911
 920-739-7682
 Fax: 920-739-3208 800-242-6602
Paper products including menus, place mats, menu
covers and presentation folders
General Manager: Rick Kerr
Estimated Sales: $1-2.5 Million
Number Employees: 10-19
Square Footage: 25600

25840 Mastercraft Industries Inc
777 South St
Newburgh, NY 12550-4159
 845-565-8850
 Fax: 845-565-9392 800-835-7812
 www.mastercraftusa.com
Manufacturer, importer and exporter of industrial
vacuum cleaners, parts, floor machines, carpet ex-
tractors, automatic scrubbers, steamers, marble/stone
maintenance equipment and chemicals
President: Howard Goldberg
Community Director: Jay Goldberg
Executive VP: Carol Andreasian
Quality Control: Jay Goldberg
Estimated Sales: $10-20 Million
Number Employees: 50-99
Square Footage: 200000
Brands:
 Dynavac
 Quarrymaster
 Sootmaster

25841 Mastercraft International
PO Box 668407
Charlotte, NC 28266-8407
 704-392-7436
 Fax: 704-395-1600
Manufacturer and exporter of packaging machinery
including vertical and horizontal cartoners
President: Dan Rothwell
Engineer: A Christopher
Estimated Sales: $1-2.5 Million
Number Employees: 9
Square Footage: 40000
Brands:
 Mastercraft International
 Memco

25842 Mastercraft Manufacturing Co
3715 11th St # B1
Long Island City, NY 11101-6006
 718-729-5620
 Fax: 718-729-5620
Awards, badges, medals, incentives, premiums and
plaques; exporter of badges; importer of pins and
patches
Owner: Murray Wiener
mwiener@mastercraft-boats.net
General Manager: Peter Borsits
General Manager: Peter Borsits
Estimated Sales: $500,000-$1,000,000
Number Employees: 5-9
Square Footage: 2000

25843 Mastermark
19017 62nd Ave S
Kent, WA 98032
 206-762-9610
 Fax: 206-763-8492
 customerservice@mastermark.net
 www.mastermark.net
Food packaging, rubber pre-ink and self-inking
stampss, interior and exterior architecural signage,
printing coder dies and stencils products
President: Cindy Hutter
CFO: C G
Marketing/Sales: Brian Carter
Contact: David Alldredge
dave@mastermark.net
Operations: CG Gambling
Production: CG Gambling
Estimated Sales: Below $5 Million
Number Employees: 1-4
Square Footage: 100000
Type of Packaging: Consumer, Private Label, Bulk
Brands:
 Mastermark

25844 Masternet, Ltd
690 Gana Court
Mississauga, ON L5S 1P2
Canada
905-295-0005
Fax: 905-795-9293 800-216-2536
www.masternetltd.com
Plastic net, nettingon rolls, net bags, mesh liners, packaging products, wattle nets, protection packaging.
VP: Linda Hartman
Number Employees: 40
Square Footage: 240000

25845 Masterpiece Crystal
96 Trolley St
Jane Lew, WV 26378
304-884-7841
Fax: 304-884-7842 deba@access.mountain.net
Hand blown table and glassware
Owner: Bill Hogan
deba@wvdsl.net
Marketing Director: William Hogan
Sales Manager/Customer Service: Debbie Bailey
Estimated Sales: $5-10 Million
Number Employees: 20-49

25846 Mastex Industries
2035 Factory Ln
Petersburg, VA 23803
804-732-8300
Fax: 804-732-8395
Manufacturer and exporter of electric and thermostatically controlled dish warmers and cooking utensils
President: Frank Mast
National Sales Manager: Paul Christian
Estimated Sales: $1-5 Million
Number Employees: 10-19
Square Footage: 100000
Type of Packaging: Consumer

25847 Mastio & Co
2921 N Belt Hwy # M14
Suite M-14
St Joseph, MO 64506-2070
816-364-6200
Fax: 816-364-3606 info@mastio.com
www.mastio.com
Consultant for the packaging industry providing market research and information, customer satisfaction benchmarking, databases and re-engineering solutions
Owner: Bart Thedinger
Executive VP: Kristina Hidy
khidy@mastio.com
Sales/Marketing Executive: Bart Thedinger
Sales: Kevin Huntsman
MIS Manager: Steve Nash
Estimated Sales: Below $5 Million
Number Employees: 10-19
Square Footage: 34000

25848 Matcon Americas
832 N Industrial Dr
Elmhurst, IL 60126-1132
856-256-1330
Fax: 856-256-1329 druble@idexcorp.com
www.matconibc.com
Matcon is a supplier of processing equipment for dry materials. They use portable containers (Intermediate Bulk Containers or IBSs) in their production. Matcon specializes in recipe batching, powder blender and packaging operations.
Vice President: Dan Ruble
Service Account Manager: Dan Veilleux
Senior Applications Specialist: Phil Spuler
Estimated Sales: $5-10 Million
Number Employees: 5
Square Footage: 11000
Parent Co: Matcon Ltd.

25849 Mateer Burt
700 Pennsylvania Drive
Exton, PA 19341-1129
610-321-1100
Fax: 610-321-1199 800-345-1308
www.mateerburt.com
Manufacturer and exporter of filling and labeling machinery and parts; installation available
Marketing Manager: April Koss
Estimated Sales: $1-5 Million
Number Employees: 50-99
Number of Brands: 7

Number of Products: 4
Square Footage: 320000

25850 (HQ)Material Control
P.O.Box 308
North Aurora, IL 60542
630-892-4274
Fax: 630-892-4931 800-926-0376
www.materialcontrolinc.com
Conveyor safety stop switches, belt cleaners and hood covers, bin aerators; distributor of plastic bins and totes, shelving, cabinets, mats, matting, fans, measurement and gas monitoring instruments and ventilation equipment
Manager: Jack Pierce
Sales Director: Bob Hutchins
Plant Manager: Jim Pierce
Estimated Sales: $3-5,000,000
Number Employees: 5-9
Other Locations:
Material Control
Aurora IL

25851 Material Handling Technology, Inc
113 International Drive
Morrisville, NC 27560
919-388-0050
Fax: 919-388-0051 800-779-2475
mht@mht1.com materialhandlingtech.com
Conveyors, material handling equipment, sortation equipment

25852 Material Storage Systems
8827 Will Clayton Pkwy
Humble, TX 77338-5821
281-446-7144
Fax: 281-446-7391 800-881-6750
info@msshouston.com www.msshouston.com
Manufacturer and exporter of storage and material handling equipment
Owner: Mike Gonzales
Plant Manager: Paul Eye
Estimated Sales: $1-2.5 Million
Number Employees: 20-49
Brands:
Webblock

25853 Material Storage Systems
PO Box 1010
Gadsden, AL 35902
256-543-2467
Fax: 256-547-6725 877-543-2467
Exclusive rights to the Lemanco product line. Major products are modular bolted storage bins, welded silos and refuse containers. Many accessory items are also available
President: Barney Leach
CFO: Cindi Graves
Vice President: Craig Graves
R&D: Randall Wright
Quality Control: Robert Bellow
Marketing Director: Dawn Howell
VP Sales: Craig Graves
Operations Manager: Paul Allen
Production Manager: Paul Allen
Plant Manager: Randal Wright
Purchasing Manager: Robert Bellew
Estimated Sales: $1 Million
Number Employees: 30
Number of Brands: 1
Number of Products: 3
Square Footage: 90000
Brands:
Lamanco

25854 Material Systems Engineering
P O Box 115
Stilesville, IN 46180
317-745-7263
Fax: 317-203-0748 800-634-0904
Bulk conveying systems including pneumatic dust collecting and drag chain; also, designing, engineering and fabrication services available
Owner: George Mc Comb
Purchasing/Office Manager: Rona Campbell
Estimated Sales: $1-2.5 Million
Number Employees: 5-9
Square Footage: 23200

25855 Materials Handling Equipment Company
3800 Quentin St
Denver, CO 80239
303-573-5333
Fax: 303-893-3854
Wholesaler/distributor of material handling equipment
Manager: Jenett Garcia
CFO: Ron Conrad
Estimated Sales: $50-100 Million
Number Employees: 100-249
Square Footage: 60000

25856 Materials Handling Systems
20763 Bollman Place
Savage, MD 20763
410-379-0070
Fax: 410-379-0037 MHSUSA@aol.com
Conveyors, hand trucks, casters and materials handling equipment
Estimated Sales: $10-20 Million
Number Employees: 50-99

25857 Materials Storage Systems
PO Box 1010
Gadsden, AL 35902-1010
256-543-2467
Fax: 256-547-6725 877-543-2467
Bolted nuts
Estimated Sales: $2.5-5 Million
Number Employees: 20-49

25858 Materials Transportation Co
1408 Commerce Dr
PO Box 1358
Temple, TX 76504-5134
254-298-2900
Fax: 254-771-0287 800-433-3110
info@mtcworldwide.com
Manufacturer and exporter of food processing equipment, cookers, dumpers, blenders and screw and belt conveyors
President & CEO: Jim Granfor
CEO: Reg Ackerman
r.ackerman@mtcworldwide.com
VP Sales: Stephen Hicks
Estimated Sales: $23.4 Million
Number Employees: 100-249
Number of Brands: 6
Number of Products: 6

25859 Matfer Inc
16150 Lindbergh St
Van Nuys, CA 91406-1707
818-782-0792
Fax: 818-782-0799 800-766-0333
contact@matferinc.com
www.matferbourgeatusa.com
Manufacturer, importer and exporter of kitchen and bakery utensils including molds, nonstick baking sheets, pastry bags, thermometers, food mills, juicers, casserole dishes, commercial mixers, mandolines, saute pans, etc
Manager: Jean Paul Riou
CEO: Jean Paul Rio
VP: Pierre Perisot
National Sales Manager: Dominique Besson
Manager: Sergey Perevalov
sperevalov@matferinc.com
Estimated Sales: $8 Million
Number Employees: 10-19
Square Footage: 30000
Parent Co: Matfer France

25860 Mathason Industries
6659 Sanzon Rd
Baltimore, MD 21209
410-484-5935
Fax: 410-484-0334 imathason@hotmail.com
Supplier of bakery equipment
President: Susan Mathason
Comptroller: I Mathason
Sales Director: I Mathason
Contact: Irwin Mathason
imathason@hotmail.com
Estimated Sales: $250000
Number Employees: 1-4

25861 Mathews Conveyor
1524 Lebanon Rd
Danville, KY 40422-9601
859-236-9400
Fax: 859-238-7443 800-628-4397
crodgers@mathewsconveyor.com
Conveyor systems and palletizers
President: Chuck Waddle
Chief Executive Officer: Chris Cole
CFO: Bob Duplain
Vice President of Project Management: Alfred Rebello
Chief Technical Officer: Ray Neiser
Marketing Coordinator: Beverly Cooper
Senior Vice President of Sales and Marke: Jim McKnight
Contact: Dave Gooch
dave@mathewsconveyor.com
Vice President of Operations: Chris Arnold
Purchasing Agent: Anna McClellan
Estimated Sales: $85 Million
Number Employees: 250-499
Square Footage: 300000
Parent Co: FKI Logistex

25862 Matik North America
33 Brook St
West Hartford, CT 06110-2350
860-232-2323
Fax: 860-233-0162 sales@matik.com
www.matik.com
President: Jarrett Chouinard
jchouinard@matik.com
Estimated Sales: $3-5 Million
Number Employees: 10-19

25863 Matiss
8800 25th Avenue
St Georges, QC G6A 1K5
Canada
418-227-9141
Fax: 418-227-9144 888-562-8477
doris.boily@matiss.com www.matiss.com
Manufacturer and exporter of bakery processing equipment including greasers, depositors, fillers, cutting and batching systems; also, snack food and pizza processing and packaging equipment; laboratory testing available
President: Jacques Martel
CFO: Pierre Martel
Sales Manager: Francois Henault
Sales Engineer: Patrice Painchaud
General Manager: Jacques Martel
Estimated Sales: Below $5 Million
Number Employees: 90
Square Footage: 80000

25864 Matot-Commercial GradeLift Solutions
2501 Van Buren
Bellwood, IL 60104-2459
708-547-1888
Fax: 708-547-1608 800-369-1070
sales@matot.com www.matot.com
Manufacturer and exporter of electric dumbwaiters
Co-President/ Owner: Anne B. Matot
Co-President: Cathryn Matot
Executive Vice President: Jim Piper
Senior Vice President, Sales: Jim Peskuski
Estimated Sales: $1-2.5 Million
Number Employees: 5-9
Square Footage: 32000

25865 Matrix Engineering
P.O.Box 650728
Vero Beach, FL 32965-0728
772-461-2156
Fax: 772-461-7185 800-926-0528
www.griprock.com
Manufacturer and exporter of safety and slip resistant floor mats and flooring
President: Thomas Hayes
CEO: Edward Saylor
Vice President: Thomas Hayes
Operations Manager: Randi McManus
Number Employees: 19
Number of Brands: 4
Number of Products: 4
Square Footage: 40000
Brands:
 Grip Rock
 Matrix
 Super G

25866 Matrix Group Inc.
16 Yantecaw Ave
Bloomfield, NJ 07003
973-338-5638
Fax: 973-338-0164 info@m8trix.com
www.m8trix.com
Consulting to natural foods maraketplace; master broker
President: Ray Wolfson
rwolfson@m8trix.com
VP: Irene Sherman
Sales: Ray Wolfson
rwolfson@m8trix.com
Estimated Sales: $2.5-5 Million
Number Employees: 5
Number of Brands: 3-6
Type of Packaging: Consumer

25867 Matrix Packaging Machinery
650 N Dekora Woods Blvd
Saukville, WI 53080-1674
262-268-8300
Fax: 262-268-8301 888-628-7491
sales@matrixpm.com www.matrixpm.com
Manufacturer and exporter of vertical form/fill/seal machinery
Gen Mgr/R&D/Quality Control: Marc Willden
Marketing: Lori Stein
Sales Exec: Matt Lanfrankie
Public Relations: John LaBouve
sales@matrixpm.com
Operations: Jane Barnett
Production/Plant Manager: Tim Marchant
Purchasing: Lori Klandrud
Estimated Sales: $15-20 Million
Number Employees: 50-99
Square Footage: 80000
Parent Co: Pro Mach Inc
Brands:
 Matrix 916
 Matrix1000

25868 Matson LLC
45620 SE North Bend Way
North Bend, WA 98045
425-888-6212
Fax: 425-888-6216 800-308-3723
www.corrys.com
Manufacturer and exporter of insecticides
President: Ken Matson
matson@corrys.com
Sales Representative: Dave Grasmann
Estimated Sales: $5-10 Million
Number Employees: 5-9

25869 Mattec Corp
1301 Mattec Dr
Loveland, OH 45140-7300
513-683-1802
Fax: 513-683-1619 800-966-1301
www.epicor.com
Control systems. manufacturers of blow molding, extrusion, blown film applications and related plastic processes. Printing, metal stamping, packaging, assembly and secondary operations
President: Mick Thiel
VP Sales/Marketing: David Monroe
Contact: Lysa Whitt
l.whitt@mattec.com
Estimated Sales: $10-20 Million
Number Employees: 50-99

25870 Matthews Marking Systems Div
6515 Penn Ave
Pittsburgh, PA 15206-4407
412-665-2500
Fax: 412-665-2550 info@matw.com
www.matthewsmarking.com
Manufacturer and exporter of marking equipment for identification of products and packaging; also, turnkey systems available
President: Annette Aranda
aaranda@matthewsinternational.com
Vice President: Peter Hart
Marketing Director: Michelle Staulding
Estimated Sales: $10-20 Million
Number Employees: 100-249
Parent Co: Matthew International Corporation
Other Locations:
 Matthews International Corp.
 10156 Torino
Brands:
 Indent-A-Mark
 Jet-A-Mark

Jet-A-Mark/Linx
Print-A-Mark

25871 Matthiesen Equipment
566 N Ww White Rd
San Antonio, TX 78219-2816
210-333-1510
Fax: 210-333-1563 800-624-8635
ctorres@matthiesenequipment.com
www.matthiesenequipment.com
Manufacturer and exporter of material handling processing machinery for ice including bins, baggers, belt and screw conveyors, crushers, bag closers, drying belts, etc.; exporter and wholesaler/distributor of ice machinery
Office Manager: Claudia Torres
Research & Development: Stephen Niestroy
National Sales Manager: Diane Hardekopf
Sales Engineer: Jerry Bosma
Production Manager: Pete Ruiz
Purchasing: John Barratachea
Estimated Sales: $2.5-5 Million
Number Employees: 5-9
Square Footage: 80000
Parent Co: Tour Ice National
Brands:
 Arrow
 Clinebell
 Hamer
 Kasten/Kamco
 Mgr
 Mannhardt
 Matthiesen
 Turbo
 Vogt

25872 Maui Wowi Fresh HawaiinBlends
5445 DTC Parkway
Suite 1050
Greenwood Village, CO 80111-3142
303-781-7800
Fax: 303-781-2438 877-849-6992
hula@mauiwowi.com www.mauiwowi.com
A Entrepreneur 500 ranked gourmet smoothie and espresso cart franchise.
President: Mark Challis
CEO: Michael Haith
CEO: Michael Haith
Contact: Wei Frank
wei.frank@mauiwowi.com
Estimated Sales: $1-3 Million
Number Employees: 20-49
Number of Brands: 1
Number of Products: 3
Square Footage: 20000
Type of Packaging: Food Service

25873 Maull-Baker Box Company
16685 Lower Valley Ridge Drive
Brookfield, WI 53005-5557
414-463-1290
Fax: 414-463-5975
Manufacturer and exporter of wooden boxes, crates, pallets and skids
President: Jerry Maull
Estimated Sales: $2.5-5 Million
Number Employees: 9

25874 Maurer North America
6324 N Chatham Avenue
Kansas City, MO 64151-2473
816-914-3518
Fax: 816-746-5011
Manufacturer and importer of food processing equipment
President: Rolf Hammann
Parent Co: A.G. Maurer
Brands:
 Atmos
 Maurer

25875 (HQ)Mauser Packaging Solutions
1515 W 22nd St
Suite 1100
Oak Brook, IL 60523
800-527-2267
www.mauserpackaging.com
Recyclable bulk packaging, bulk handling and shipping, and warehouse storage of both liquids and solids.

President & CEO: Kenneth Roessler
Chief Financial Officer: Tom De Weerdt
EVP, Procurement & Logistics: Leslie Bradshaw
Chief Information Officer: Ed DePrimo
EVP/General Counsel/CCO: Patrick Sheller
Year Founded: 2018
Estimated Sales: Over $1 Billion
Number Employees: 11,000
Type of Packaging: Bulk

25876 Mauser, Schindler & Wagner
3102 Wilderness Boulevard E
Parrish, FL 34219-8419

941-776-2230
Fax: 941-776-2239 ken@mauserinc.com
www.schiwa.de/en/international
Weight control systems, slicers
President: Kem Mauser
CFO: Linda Mauser
VP: Linda Mauser
Number Employees: 4
Square Footage: 4800

25877 Maverick Enterprises Inc
751 E Gobbi St
Ukiah, CA 95482-6205

707-463-5591
Fax: 707-463-0188 maverick@saber.net
www.maverickcaps.com
Wine closures and caps
President: Steve Otterbeck
CEO: Charles Sawyer
csawyer@maverickcaps.com
Executive Vice President of Business Dev: Jon Henderson
Vice President of Operations: Fred Koeppel
Estimated Sales: $5-10 Million
Number Employees: 50-99

25878 Maves International Software Corp.
100 York Boulevard
Suite 404
Richond Hill, ON L4B 1J8
Canada

905-882-8300
Fax: 905-882-1550 www.maves.com
President: Aaron Laird
CFO: Audrey Badb
Estimated Sales: C
Number Employees: 60

25879 Max Packaging
109 6th Ave NW
Attalla, AL 35954-2049

256-538-2233
Fax: 256-538-1929 800-543-5369
info@maxpackaging.com
www.maxpackaging.com
Manufacturer and contract packager of disposable plastic cutlery
Owner: Gary Mcfarland
gary@maxpackaging.com
General Manager: D McFarland
Plant Manager: Jay Bailey
Estimated Sales: $5-10 Million
Number Employees: 100-249
Square Footage: 40000
Parent Co: Gadsen Coffee Company

25880 Maxco Supply
605 S Zediker Ave
Parlier, CA 93648

559-646-6700
Fax: 559-646-6710 markf@mx2co.com
www.maxcopackaging.com
Case erectors and tray and bliss box formers for corrugated boxes
President: Max Flaming
CFO: David Bryant
Sales Manager: Paul Flaming
Contact: Louise Arroyo
louise@maxco.com
Estimated Sales: $20-50 Million
Number Employees: 250-499

25881 Maxi-Vac Inc.
PO Box 688
Dundee, IL 60118

855-629-4538
sales@maxi-vac.com
www.maxi-vac.com
Manufacturer and exporter of pressure washers and steam cleaning equipment

President: Jim Nolan
Secretary and Treasurer: Janice Nolan
Estimated Sales: $1-2.5 Million
Number Employees: 1-4
Brands:
    Jet Streamer

25882 Maximicer
4175 Country Road 268
Georgetown, TX 78628

512-259-0500
Fax: 512-258-8804 800-289-9098
info@Maximicer.com
Manufacturer and exporter of optimizers for ice making machinery
President: J L Love
VP Manufacturing & Product Dev: Daniel L Welch
Contact: J Love
j.love@maximicer.com
Estimated Sales: $1-3,000,000
Number Employees: 1-4
Type of Packaging: Food Service, Private Label
Brands:
    Maximicer

25883 Maximus Systems
1250, rue Marie-Victorin
St-Bruno-de-Montarville, QC J3V 6B8
Canada

877-445-6556
info@maximus-systems.com
www.maximus-solution.com
Offers solutions for manufacturing poultry, hog, and dairy.
Business Development: Nizar Barrou
VP, International Sales: Marc Boivin
Year Founded: 2010
Number Employees: 35-50

25884 Maxitrol Company
P.O.Box 2230
Southfield, MI 48037-2230

248-356-1401
Fax: 248-356-0829 info@maxitrol.com
www.maxitrol.com
Owner: Bonnie Kern-Koskela
CFO: Christopher Kelly
Estimated Sales: $20-50 Million
Number Employees: 50-99

25885 Maxwell House & Post
800 Westchester Ave
Rye Brook, NY 10573-1354

914-335-2500
Fax: 914-335-2706
Coffee and breakfast foods
President: Ann Fudge
Estimated Sales: Under $500,000
Number Employees: 1-4
Parent Co: Kraft Foods

25886 May-Wes Manufacturing Inc
120 Eastgate Dr SE
Hutchinson, MN 55350-1929

320-587-2322
Fax: 320-587-6112 800-788-6483
techsupport@maywes.com www.maywes.com
Grain hoppers and crop dividers; also, plastic combine skids
VP: Mark Bruns
Sales Exec: Daryl Peterson
Manager: Connie Lindbeck
Estimated Sales: $2.5-5 Million
Number Employees: 20-49

25887 Maya Overseas Food Inc
4885 Maspeth Ave
Flushing, NY 11378-2109

718-894-5145
Fax: 718-894-5178 888-289-6292
maya.foods@verizon.net
Supplier of South East Asian groceries to retail stores, restaurants and distributors throughout America.
President/Owner: Umesh Mody
maya.foods@verizon.net
Estimated Sales: $17.4 Million
Number Employees: 10-19

25888 Mayco Inc
2811 Mican Dr
Dallas, TX 75212-4602

214-638-4848
Fax: 214-638-4850 david@maycopallet.com
www.maycopallet.com
Wooden pallets
President: David Gwinn
david@maycopallet.com
Office Manager: Melba Gwinn
Corporate Controller: Ricky Thomason
Estimated Sales: Below $5 Million
Number Employees: 10-19
Square Footage: 120000

25889 Mayekawa USA, Inc.
8750 West Bryn Mawr Avenue
Suite 190
Chicago, IL 60631

773-516-5070
sales@mayekawausa.com
www.mayekawausa.com
Freezing, thawing and heating units.
Contact: Bryan Arevalo
barevalo@mayekawausa.com

25890 Maypak Inc
5 Mansard Ct
Wayne, NJ 07470-6040

973-696-0780
Fax: 973-633-8621 info@maypakinc.com
www.maypakinc.com
Fabricated polyethylene, expanded polystyrene and polyurethane foam; also, wooden boxes and fiberboard cartons, cooler packs, die cutting, insulated containers, custom designed cases and inserts.
President: Paul Palombi
paul@maypakinc.com
Number Employees: 10-19

25891 Mayr Corporation
4 North St
Suite 300
Waldwick, NJ 07463

201-445-7210
Fax: 201-445-8019 800-465-6297
info@mayrcorp.com www.mayrcorp.com
Real-time production and process monitoring systems, plant scheduling systems, full bar coding and product traceability and genealogy systems
President: Augie Mustardo
CFO: August Mustardo
Contact: Ken Meli
meli@mayrcorp.com
Estimated Sales: Below $5 Million
Number Employees: 10-19

25892 Mays Chemical Co
5611 E 71st St
Indianapolis, IN 46220-3920

317-842-8722
Fax: 317-576-9630 info@mayschem.com
www.mayschem.com
Chemical ingredients and related products
President: William Mays
williamm@mayschem.com
CFO: Deric Gillispie
Quality Control: Phill Poehler
Marketing Representative: Gloria Yuan
Estimated Sales: $.5-1 million
Number Employees: 50-99

25893 Maytag Corporation
553 Benson Rd.
Benton Harbor, MI 49022

800-344-1274
www.maytag.com
Ranges and stoves.
Chairman/CEO: Marc Bitzer
Executive VP/CFO: Jim Peters
Senior VP/General Counsel: Kirsten Hewitt
Year Founded: 1893
Estimated Sales: $4.7 Billion
Number Employees: 2,500
Square Footage: 116393
Parent Co: Whirlpool Corporation
Brands:
    Admiral
    Hardwick
    Jennair
    Magic Chef
    Maytag

25894 Maywood Furniture Corp
23 W Howcroft Rd
Maywood, NJ 07607-1022

201-845-6517
Fax: 201-845-4586 800-238-6797
sales@maywood.com www.maywood.com
President: Tom McMullen
CEO: Bill DeSaussure
CFO: Barbara Jenkins
Operations Manager: Jack DeSaussure
Plant Engineer: Toni Ljekocevic
Estimated Sales: $10-20 Million
Number Employees: 50-99

25895 Mayworth Showcase WorksInc
1711 W State St
Tampa, FL 33606-1043

813-251-1558
Fax: 813-251-1558
Display cases
Owner: Jack Mayworth
Estimated Sales: $1-3 Million
Number Employees: 5-9

25896 Mba Suppliers Inc.
1000 Fort Crook Rd N
Suite 100
Bellevue, NE 68005-4573

402-597-5777
Fax: 402-597-2444 800-467-1201
www.mbasuppliers.com
New, reconditioned, used and pre-owned food processing and meat equipment and supplies.
Contact: Kevin Hammerle
khammerle@mbasuppliers.com

25897 Mc Call Co
4013 Tennessee Ave
PO Box 2033
Chattanooga, TN 37409-1322

423-821-4583
Fax: 423-821-5950 sales@mccallcompany.com
Wholesaler/distributor of packaging materials
Owner: P Henze
Office Manager: Helen Lemacks
Purchasing: Mike Henze
Estimated Sales: $1-2.5 Million
Number Employees: 1-4

25898 Mc Court Label Co
20 Egbert Ln
Lewis Run, PA 16738-3802

814-362-3851
Fax: 814-362-9764 800-458-2390
mccourt@mccourtlabel.com
Pressure sensitive labels for thermal and laser imprinting
President: David G Ferguson
dferguson@mccourtlabel.com
Quality Control: June Wegner
Operations Manager: Bert Clark
Estimated Sales: $10-20 Million
Number Employees: 50-99
Square Footage: 86000

25899 Mc Lean Packaging
1504 Glen Ave
Moorestown, NJ 08057-1104

856-359-2600
Fax: 856-359-2910 800-923-7801
dave@mcleanpackaging.com
www.mcleanpackaging.com
Manufacturers of Corrugated displays,containers, mini flute single face laminated boxes, vinyl and set-up rigid paper boxes, plastic folding boxes, transperent boxes and cylinders, vacuum forming
President Of Corrugated Division: Stuart Fenkel
Contact: Gary Buchert
gary.buchert@mcleanpackaging.com
Estimated Sales: $30-50 Million
Number Employees: 50-99
Square Footage: 400000

25900 McBrady Engineering Inc
1251 S Larkin Ave
PO Box 2549
Violet, IL 60434

815-744-8900
Fax: 815-744-8901 mcbrady@sbcglobal.net
www.mcbradyengineering.com
Bottle cleaning machinery
President: Garrett McBrady
Sales: David Anderson
Purchasing: Gina Wharrie

Number Employees: 18
Type of Packaging: Consumer, Food Service
Brands:
Duster
Gripper
Model #10
Orbit
Unscrambler
Vial Washer

25901 McCain Produce Inc.
8734 Main Street
Florenceville-Bristol, NB E7L 3G6
Canada

506-392-3036
www.mccainpotatoes.ca
Potato grower and processor
Parent Co: McCain Foods Ltd.
Type of Packaging: Consumer, Food Service

25902 McCarter Corporation
PO Box 351
Norristown, PA 19404-0351

610-272-3203
Fax: 610-275-5120
Manufacturer and exporter of paste and confectionery mixing equipment
President: H Craig McCarter
Number Employees: 17
Square Footage: 150000

25903 McClier
401 E Illinois St # 2
Chicago, IL 60611-4319

312-321-8900
Fax: 312-755-2750
Architects and engineers, building and construction consultants
President: Kenneth Terpin
CFO: Nino Conti
CEO: Daniel McLean
Estimated Sales: $20-50 Million
Number Employees: 250-499

25904 McCormack ManufacturingCompany
PO Box 1727
Lake Oswego, OR 97035

503-639-2137
Fax: 503-639-1800 800-395-1593
Manufacturer and exporter of industrial refrigeration equipment including quick freezing and sub-zero freezers
CEO: Gary Montgomery
VP Engineering: Tom Resseler
Estimated Sales: $10-20 Million
Number Employees: 1-4
Square Footage: 50000

25905 (HQ)McCormick Enterprises
729 S Grove St
Post Office Box 577
Arlington Heights, IL 60006

847-398-8680
Fax: 847-398-8625 800-323-5201
sales@mccormicksnet.com
www.mccormicksnet.com
Processing and conveying equipment; installation services available
Owner: Bill Mc Cormick
CEO: B McCormick
CFO: C Palanca
Estimated Sales: $10-20 Million
Number Employees: 50-99
Other Locations:
McCormick Enterprises
Delton MI

25906 McDowell Industries
PO Box 2087
Memphis, TN 38101-2087

901-527-6596
Fax: 901-525-6596 800-622-3695
Manufacturer and importer of textile bags for vegetables and grain
Manager Customer Service: Scott Feuer
Plant Superintendent: Rod Johnston
Number Employees: 100-249
Square Footage: 500000
Type of Packaging: Consumer, Food Service, Private Label, Bulk
Brands:
McKnit
Softweve McKnit

25907 McGlaughlin Oil Co
3750 E Livingston Ave
Columbus, OH 43227-2282

614-231-2518
Fax: 614-231-7431 800-839-6589
teresa@mcglaughlinoil.com www.faslube.com
Lubricants food grade
CEO: Steve Theodor
steve@faslube.com
Vice President: Dick Green
Sales Director: Dick Green
Estimated Sales: $5-10 Million
Number Employees: 10-19
Type of Packaging: Consumer, Food Service, Private Label, Bulk

25908 McGraw Box Company
PO Box 652
Mc Graw, NY 13101-0652

607-836-6465
Fax: 607-836-6413
Silverware chests and wooden boxes
Owner: Harold J Ousby Iii
Number Employees: 100-249

25909 McGraw Hill/London House
1030 Higgins Rd
Suite 205
Park Ridge, IL 60068-5760

847-292-1900
Fax: 847-292-1906 800-221-8378
Personnel service providing human resource testing and evaluation programs
President: Sam Maurice
Parent Co: MacMillan/McGraw Hill Educational Publishing Company

25910 McGunn Safe Company
29 S La Salle St # 425
Chicago, IL 60603-1599

312-782-3668
Fax: 312-782-4502 800-621-2816
Manufacturer and exporter of safes and other security devices
Partner: Maureen J Mc Gann
Sales/Marketing: Pat McGunn
Estimated Sales: $.5-1 million
Number Employees: 1-4
Square Footage: 100000
Brands:
Cash Handler
Quick Drop
Smart Lock
Smart Safe 2000

25911 McKearnan Packaging
PO Box 7281
Reno, NV 89510-7281

775-356-6111
Fax: 775-356-2181 800-787-7857
surplus@mckernan.com www.mckernan.com
Surplus packaging components
General Manager: Maurice Oschlog
Chief Operating Officer: Frank Maggio

25912 McMillin Manufacturing Corporation
2835 E Washington Blvd
Los Angeles, CA 90023

323-268-1900
Fax: 323-262-5144 www.mcmillinwire.com
Wire products including display and bakery racks and shelving
President: Bruce Goodman
bruceg@mcmillin-mfg.com
Quality Control: Bell Harmon
Estimated Sales: Below $5 Million
Number Employees: 20-49
Square Footage: 120000
Brands:
McMillin Wire

25913 McNeil Food Machinery
1881 E Market Street
Stockton, CA 95205-5673

209-463-4343
Fax: 785-874-4241
Dealer and autioner of used food processing and packaging equipment
Estimated Sales: $10-20 Million
Number Employees: 50-99

25914 McNeil Nutritionals
7050 Camp Hill Rd
Fort Washington, PA 19034
215-273-7000
Fax: 908-874-1120 www.splenda.com
Artificial sweetners
President: Peter Luther
Vice President: Sheila Bergey
Contact: Joan Anton
janton@mcnus.jnj.com
Estimated Sales: $10-20 Million
Parent Co: Johnson & Johnson

25915 McNeil Specialty Products Company
PO Box 2400
501 George St.
New Brunswick, NJ 08903-2400
732-524-3799
Fax: 732-524-3303
artifical sweetners.such as sucralose.
President: Stephen Fanning
Director Sales (North America): Jim Thornton
Director International Sales: Joseph Zannoni
Contact: Donna Fernandez
donna@sucralose.com
Estimated Sales: $10-25million
Number Employees: 20-49
Parent Co: Johnson & Johnson

25916 McNew & Associates, William B.
225 San Marino Drive
San Rafael, CA 94901-1583
415-457-3940
Fax: 415-457-3142 mcnew@netiz.net
Wine industry tank vents
Owner: William McMill
Sales Engineer: Kevin McMill
Estimated Sales: $1-2.5 Million
Number Employees: 1-4
Square Footage: 2000
Type of Packaging: Private Label

25917 McNichols Company
251 Wille Rd # C
Des Plaines, IL 60018-1861
847-376-5848
Fax: 847-635-1115 800-237-3820
www.mcnichols.com
Grip strut safety grating, grate lock grating, fiber-glass grating, safety flooring, bar grating, perforated metal and screens, decorative perforated patterns, wire cloth and screens, filter cloth, testing sieves, hardware cloth andsecurity screens
Manager: Kevin Shrout
Contact: Janet Aleksiak
jaleksiak@mcnichols.com
Estimated Sales: Below $5 Million
Number Employees: 20-49

25918 McNichols Conveyor Company
21411 Civic Center Drive
Suite 204
Southfield, MI 48076
248-357-6077
Fax: 248-357-6078 800-331-1926
sales@mcnicholsconveyor.com
www.mcnicholsconveyor.com
Manufacturer, exporter and designer of conveyors including power roller, gravity roller and belt
President: Robert Iwrey
General Manager: Vince Giannone
Estimated Sales: $2.5-5 Million
Number Employees: 5-9
Brands:
  F.E.I., Inc.
  Gregory-Adams
  New London Engineering
  Omni-Metalcraft
  Rapid Flex
  Roach

25919 McQueen Sign & Lighting
1017 12th Street NE
Canton, OH 44704-1398
330-452-5769
Fax: 330-452-5792 68262mcqsign@cannet.com
Signs including neon, plastic, interchangeable and illuminated letters; also, interior graphics available
Estimated Sales: $500,000-$1 Million
Number Employees: 5-9

25920 (HQ)Mcbrady Engineering Co
1251 S Larkin Ave
Rockdale, IL 60436-9326
815-744-8900
Fax: 815-744-8901 www.mcbradyengineering.com
Manufacturer and exporter of container cleaning equipment
Owner: Garrett Mc Brady
Vice President: Garrett McBrady
Sales: David Anderson
Estimated Sales: $2 Million
Number Employees: 10-19
Number of Brands: 7
Number of Products: 3
Square Footage: 60000
Brands:
  Bottle Air
  Bottle Duster
  Orbit
  Vial Washer-Dryer

25921 Mcbride Sign Co
5493 S Amherst Hwy
Madison Heights, VA 24572
434-847-4151
Fax: 434-845-6980 info@mcbridesigns.com
www.mcbridesigns.com
Signs including advertising, changeable letter, electric, interchangeable, luminous tube, plastic and point of purchase; also, installation and service available
Owner: Tony Mc Bride
tg@mcbridesigns.com
General Manager: Lawrence Bryant
Vice President: Tony McBride
Estimated Sales: $1.25 Million
Number Employees: 10-19
Square Footage: 89000
Type of Packaging: Private Label

25922 Mcclancy Seasonings Co
1 Spice Rd
Fort Mill, SC 29707-9501
803-548-2366
Fax: 803-548-6273 800-843-1968
info@mcclancy.com www.mcclancy.com
Processor and exporter of spices, seasonings and dry food mixes including salad dressing, dips, breadings, batters, gravies, soups, sauces and meat marinades, snack food seasonings, nut and pretzel coatings, whole and ground spices;custom blending available.
President: Reid Wilkerson
Estimated Sales: G
Number Employees: 100-249
Type of Packaging: Consumer, Food Service, Private Label, Bulk
Brands:
  Southern Sweetener©
  Continental Chef©
  Spice Trader©

25923 Mccrone Microscopes & Acces
850 Pasquinelli Dr
Westmont, IL 60559-5594
630-288-7087
Fax: 630-887-7764 www.mccrone.com
Consultant providing microscopy and ultramicro-analytical services including materials analysis, characterization and identification; wholesaler/distributor of microscopes and microscopy supplies
CEO/President: Donald Brooks
VP: Richard Bisbing
Manager: David Wiley
mccrone@mccrone.com
VP/Director Operations: Bonnie Betty
Estimated Sales: $5-10 Million
Number Employees: 50-99
Square Footage: 75000
Parent Co: McCrone Group

25924 Mccullough Industries Inc
13047 County Road 175
P.O.Box 222
Kenton, OH 43326-9022
419-673-0767
Fax: 419-673-8176 800-245-9490
sales@mcculloughind.com
www.mcculloughind.com
Manufacturer and exporter of self dumping hoppers
Owner: Steve Mc Cullough
smm@mcculloughind.com
Owner: W McCullough

Number Employees: 20-49

25925 Mcguckin & Pyle Inc
227 Brandywine Ave
Downingtown, PA 19335
610-269-9770
Fax: 610-873-8970 DConnolly@mcg-pyle.com
www.mcg-pyle.com
Packaging and process equipment
President: Keith Connolly
Chief Executive Officer: Dennis Connolly
Research: Brian Sproul
Operations: Tom Blam
Estimated Sales: $5-10 Million
Number Employees: 20-49

25926 Mcintosh Box & Pallet Co
5864 Pyle Dr
East Syracuse, NY 13057-9459
315-446-9350
Fax: 315-446-5427 800-219-9552
info@mcintoshbox.com www.mcintoshbox.com
Wooden boxes, pallets and skids
President: Rich Huftalen
Accounts Manager/Sales: Brian Hotchkin
Estimated Sales: $2.5-5 Million
Number Employees: 20-49
Square Footage: 200000

25927 Mcintyre Metals Inc
310 Kendall Mill Rd
Thomasville, NC 27360-5524
336-476-3646
Fax: 336-476-3622 800-334-0807
www.mcmetals.com
Manufacturer and exporter of point-of-purchase displays including stock and special designs, powder coated and wire formed
President: Jeff Mc Intyre
jeff@mcmetals.com
VP: Gilbert Luck
Sales Manager: Jim Plumb
VP, Operations: Mike Smith
Estimated Sales: $2.5-5 Million
Number Employees: 20-49

25928 Mckey Perforating Co Inc
3033 S 166th St
New Berlin, WI 53151-3555
262-786-2700
Fax: 262-786-7673 800-345-7373
jmckey@mckey.com
www.mckeyperforatingco-inc.com
Manufacturer and exporter of component parts for food handling equipment and perforated metals and plastics
President/CEO: Jean Mc Key
General Manager: Don Pirlot
dpirlot@mckey.com
Product Development Manager: Tony Elsinger
VP Marketing: Jim Thurman
VP, Sales: Jim Thurman
Director of Operations: James Kuehn
Purchasing Manager: Wayne Schowalter
Estimated Sales: $4700000
Number Employees: 50-99
Square Footage: 280000

25929 (HQ)Mclaughlin Gormley KingCo
8810 10th Ave N
Minneapolis, MN 55427-4372
763-544-0341
Fax: 763-544-6437 800-645-6466
www.mgk.com
Manufacturer and exporter of insecticide concentrates and repellents
President: William D Gullickson Jr
CEO: Steve Gullickson
steve.gullickson@mgk.com
CFO: Tom Majpor
Quality Control: Michael Lunch
Director Marketing: Dan Untiedt
Production Manager: Don Sundquist
Estimated Sales: $20-50 Million
Number Employees: 50-99
Square Footage: 100000
Other Locations:
  McLaughlin Gormley KingCo.
  Baltimore MD

25930 Mclaughlin Paper Co Inc
61 Progress Ave
West Springfield, MA 01089-3323
413-736-6066
Fax: 413-730-6604 800-842-6656
sales@mclaughlinpaper.com
www.mclaughlinpaper.com
Paper, paper board, specialty grades: tissue, foils, metallized paper, release papers, foil board, holographic, heat seal, laminates, velours, papefilm, imports, folding cartons, rigid boxes, corrugated laminates, gift wrap, retail orprivate label, pict
Owner: Daniel Mc Laughlin
Contact: Dan Mclaughlin
dan.mclaughlin@mclaughlinpaper.com
Estimated Sales: $1-2.5 Million
Number Employees: 10-19

25931 Mcmahon's Farm
305 Jackson Rd
Hopewell Jct, NY 12533-8615
845-227-0120
Fax: 845-227-9282 orders@mcmahonsfarm.com
www.mcmahonsfarm.com
Wholesale distributor of organic, natural and specialty foods as well as eggs, dairy and other food products
Owner: Tom Mc Mahon
colette@mcmahonsfarm.com
Owner: Colette McMahon
Number Employees: 20-49

25932 Mcnairn Packaging
6 Elise St
Westfield, MA 01085-1414
413-568-1989
Fax: 413-562-1903 800-867-1898
sales@mcnairnpackaging.com
Packaging paper for the food industry
President: Ken Miller
CFO: Dennis Czosnek
Manager: Roger Pietras
rpietras@mcnairnpackaging.com
COO: Bart Gogarty
Estimated Sales: $19 Million
Number Employees: 50-99

25933 Mcneill Signs Inc
555 S Dixie Hwy E
Pompano Beach, FL 33060-6985
954-946-3474
Fax: 954-946-8051 sales@mcneillsigns.com
www.mcneillsigns.com
Signs including plastic, neon and metal
President: J R Mc Neill
jmcneillsigns@mcneillsigns.com
CFO: Jay R McNeill
R&D: Jay R McNeill
Quality Control: Jay R McNeill
Estimated Sales: $1-2.5 Million
Number Employees: 20-49

25934 Mcneilly Wood Products Inc
120 Neelytown Rd
Campbell Hall, NY 10916-2807
845-457-9651
Fax: 845-457-4220
dan@mcneillywoodproducts.com
www.mcneillywoodproducts.com
Wooden and used pallets and skids
Owner: Dan Mc Neilly
dan@mcneillywoodproducts.com
Vice President: Dan McNeilly
President: Tim McNeilly
Estimated Sales: $5-10 Million
Number Employees: 20-49
Square Footage: 40000

25935 Mcroyal Industries Inc
1421 Lilac St
Youngstown, OH 44502-1339
330-747-8655
Fax: 330-747-3331 800-785-2556
www.mcroyal.com
Manufacturer and exporter of laminated restaurant fixtures including counters, booths, tables, kiosks, etc.; also, point of purchase displays
CEO: John N Lallo
jklallo@mcroyal.com
Purchasing Agent: Don Ceo
Estimated Sales: $2.5-5 Million
Number Employees: 5-9
Square Footage: 56000

Brands:
Formica
Nevamar
Pionite
Wilson Art

25936 MeGa Industries
5109 Harvester Road, Unit 3A
Burlington, ON L7L 5Y9
Canada
905-631-6342
Fax: 905-631-6341 800-665-6342
sales@megaindustries.com
www.megaindustries.com
Manufacturer, importer and wholesaler/distributor of material and bulk handling equipment including vibrating tables, conveyors, bins, feeders, vibrators and bin level controls and indicators
President: Mel Gallagher
Sales: Steve Atkinson
Number Employees: 5-9
Square Footage: 12000
Brands:
Dynapac

25937 Mead & Hunt Inc
6501 Watts Rd # 101
Madison, WI 53719-1397
608-273-6380
Fax: 608-273-6391 888-364-7272
madison@meadhunt.com www.meadhunt.com
Consultant specializing in the design of plant layouts, processing, refrigeration, wastewater treatment and environmental systems; also, cold storage and warehouse and office/labs facilities
President: Rajan Sheth
rajan.sheth@meadhunt.com
Quality Control: Carry Rossa
Vice President: Doug Green
Marketing Director: Mike Pankratz
Food/Dairy Facilities Manager: Scott Freye
Estimated Sales: $20-50 Million
Number Employees: 100-249
Parent Co: Mead & Hunt
Other Locations:
Mead & Hunt
Modesto CA

25938 (HQ)Meadows Mills Inc
1352 W D St
PO Box 1288
North Wilkesboro, NC 28659-3506
336-838-2282
Fax: 336-667-6501 800-626-2282
sales@meadowsmills.com
www.meadowsmills.com
Manufacturer and exporter of stone burr and hammer mills, grits separators, bolters, eccentric sifters, elevating fans, collectors, elbows, piping, self rising corn meal mixer, and hand boggers; christmas tree palletizers
Vice President: Corey Sheets
csheets@meadowsmillscoinc.com
CFO: June Hege
Senior VP: Corey Sheets
VP Sales/Marketing: Brian Hege
VP Product Engineering: Robert Miller
Purchasing: Corey Sheets
Estimated Sales: $5 Million
Number Employees: 20-49
Number of Brands: 4
Square Footage: 210000
Type of Packaging: Consumer, Food Service, Private Label, Bulk
Other Locations:
Meadows Mills
Tynda, Amur
Brands:
Meadows
Stone Burr Mills

25939 Meadwestvaco Corp
501 S 5th St
Richmond, VA 23219-0501
804-444-7939
Fax: 843-745-3028 804-444-1000
Manufacturer and exporter of kraft paper
Chairman and Chief Executive Officer: John A. Luke, Jr.
SVP and Chief Financial Officer: E. Mark Rajkowski
Chief Marketing & Innovation Officer: Diane Teer
Contact: Suzanne Abbot
suzanne.abbot@mwv.com
EVP, Global Operations: Robert A. Feeser

Estimated Sales: $5-10 Million
Number Employees: 1-4
Type of Packaging: Consumer, Food Service, Private Label, Bulk

25940 Measurement Systems Intl
14240 Interurban Ave S # 200
Tukwila, WA 98168-4661
206-433-0199
Fax: 206-244-8470 800-874-4320
info@msiscales.com www.msiscales.com
Manufactures and markets integrated systems solutions for industrial wieghing and process control
President: Ron Wenzel
rwenzel@msiscales.com
CFO: Ronald Wenzel
Quality Control: Rodney Rodems
Product Marketing Manager: Jeff Brandt
Sales Director: Tim Carroll
Purchasing Manager: David Bannister
Estimated Sales: $5-10 Million
Number Employees: 20-49
Brands:
Cellscale
Check-Weigh
Dyna-Link
Msi-6000
Msi-9000
Port-A-Weigh
Porta-Weigh-Plus

25941 Measurex/S&L Plastics
2860 Bath Pike
Nazareth, PA 18064-8898
610-759-0280
Fax: 610-759-0650 800-752-0650
Plastic measuring scoops, plastic apothecary jars and clear plastic cubes
President: John Bungert
Marketing/Sales: Denise Yonney
Purchasing Manager: Ron Timura
Estimated Sales: $10-20 Million
Number Employees: 100-249
Square Footage: 380000
Brands:
Dynagro
Measurex

25942 Meat & Livestock Australia
1401 K Street NW, Ste 602
Washington DC, DC 20005
202-521-2555
Fax: 202-521-2699 www.australian-meat.com
Beef, lamb and goatmeat
Regional Manager: Stephen Edwards
Marketing: Elise Garling
Retail Development: Linden Cowper
Contact: Peter Barnard
pbarnard@mla.com.au
Estimated Sales: $4 Million
Number Employees: 5

25943 Meat Marketing & Technology
1415 N Dayton St
Chicago, IL 60642-2643
312-266-3311
Fax: 312-266-3363 www.meatingplace.com
Computer systems and software, meat industry publications and information, sales and advertising promotions and materials
President: Mark Lefens
Chairman: Jim Franklin
Vice President of Information Systems: Annica Burns
Director of Marketing: Laurie Hachmeister
Account Executive: Dave Lurie
Production Manager: Shirleen Kajiwara
Estimated Sales: $5-10 Million
Number Employees: 20-49

25944 Meat Quality
713 W Prospect Avenue
Springfield, IL 62704-5026
217-744-0150
Fax: 217-744-0630 agmed@msn.com
Quality control instruments, analyzing fat testing
Estimated Sales: $1-5 Million

25945 Meatlonn
2035 Lemoine Avenue
2nd Floor
Fort Lee, NJ 07024-5704
201-944-6814
Fax: 888-510-2350 800-965-5144
info@meatlonn.com www.taikoh-usa.com
Casings
President: Masaki Nomura
Estimated Sales: $5-10 Million
Number Employees: 1-4

25946 Mecco Marking & Traceability
290 Executive Drive
PO Box 307
Cranberry Township, PA 16066
724-779-9555
Fax: 724-779-9556 888-369-9190
info@mecco.com www.mecco.com
For over 100 years MECCO Marking Systems has
partnered with a variety of industries for permanent
marking solutions. Products range from high quality
hand-held marking devices, portable marking tools,
and computer-controlledmarking systems. The lates
technology of bumpy barcode marking systems en-
hance MECCO's position as an industry leader and
innovator for marking solutions
CEO: Dean Frenz
CFO: Christine Grabowski
R&D: Eric McElnoy
Marketing: Todd Hockenberry
VP Sales: Todd Hockenberry
Purchasing: Frank Zowojski
Estimated Sales: $3-5 Million
Number Employees: 20-49
Brands:
Code-A-Can
Code-A-Plas
Code-A-Top

25947 Mechtronics International
705 Old Westtown Rd
Suite E
West Chester, PA 19382-4988
610-431-3655
Fax: 610-431-3774
Waxed paper-single ply and 2-ply rollstock and cut
sheets, bacon layout paper, bakery and cheese inter-
leaf papers, polypropylene film, high density poly-
ethylene film and pasta interleaf.
President: Jonathan Kent
VP: Karen Kent
Contact: Donna Kasznel
donna.kasznel@mechtronicsinternational.com
Estimated Sales: Below $5 Million
Number Employees: 10-19
Type of Packaging: Consumer, Food Service, Pri-
vate Label, Bulk

25948 Mechtronics Paper Corp
1504 Mcdaniel Dr
West Chester, PA 19380-6670
610-429-9860
Fax: 610-429-9864 ericrich1@aol.com
Interleaf paper and film waxed papers, grease proof,
grease-resistant, patty paper, film, no-zorb moisture
and grease resistant paper, 2 ply waxed paper
President/Owner: Eric Osner
ericrich@aol.com
Vice President: Karen Kent
Sales/Marketing Director: Karen Kent
Purchasing: Eric Osner
Estimated Sales: $1-2.5 Million
Number Employees: 1-4
Type of Packaging: Consumer, Food Service, Pri-
vate Label, Bulk

25949 Mectra USA
P.O.Box 350
Bloomfield, IN 47424-0350
812-384-3521
Fax: 812-384-8518 mectralabs@mectralabs.com
www.mectralabs.com
Fully automatic, floor level, bulk palletizer for round
and nonround containers, intelligent bottle stacker,
automatic layer pad, top frame and empty pallet
inserters
President: Tom Clement
Estimated Sales: $1-3 Million
Number Employees: 10-19

25950 Medallion Laboratories
9000 Plymouth Ave N
Minneapolis, MN 55427-3870
763-764-4453
Fax: 763-764-4010 800-245-5615
info@medallionlabs.com www.medallionlabs.com
Testing laboratory providing analytical and microbi-
ological services to the food industry including nu-
trition labeling support, physical testing, shelf life
studies, pesticides and special projects
President: Mike Baim
General Manager: Lisa Povolny
Quality Manager: Sandy Zinn
Marketing Director: Dereen Rief
Sales Director: Ann Diesen
Business Development Manager: Sarah Klaus-Ryan
Operations Manager: Todd Jensen
Technical Manager: David Plank
Estimated Sales: Less than $500,000
Number Employees: 5-9
Parent Co: General Mills

25951 Medallion Laboratories
9000 Plymouth Ave N
Minneapolis, MN 55427-3870
763-764-4453
Fax: 763-764-4010 800-245-5615
info@medlabs.com www.medlabs.com
Chemical, physical and microbiological testing
General Manager: Petros Levis
Technical Manager: David Plank
Business Development Manager: Lisa Povolny
Manager: Lisa Povolny
lisa.povolny@medslab.com
Operations Manager: Kelly Schwenn
Number Employees: 5-9

25952 Medical Packaging Corporation
941 Avenida Acaso
Camarillo, CA 93012-8755
805-388-2383
Fax: 805-388-5531 info@medicalpackaging.com
www.medicalpackaging.com
Industrial and medical device manufacturer special-
izing in specimen collection, custom reagent pack-
aging, and test device design.
CEO: Fred Nason
Director of Operations: Darren Davidson
Estimated Sales: $10-20 Million
Number Employees: 50-99
Type of Packaging: Private Label

25953 (HQ)Mednik Wiping MaterialsCo
6740 Romiss Ct
St Louis, MO 63134-1037
314-524-2200
Fax: 314-524-2221 800-325-7193
isales@riverbendtextiles.com
www.riverbendtextiles.com
Cheesecloths, dish and dusting cloths and paper
towels; also, disposable nonwoven and paper wipers
Owner: Jim Mednik
jmednik@riverbendtextiles.com
Secretary: Nancy Mednik
VP: Richard Wolf
Estimated Sales: $10-20 Million
Number Employees: 20-49

25954 Mee Industries
204 W Pomona Ave
Monrovia, CA 91016
626-359-4550
Fax: 626-359-4660 www.meefog.com
Wine industry fog humidifers
CEO: Eric Adamson
eric.adamson@meefog.com
CEO: Thomas Mee Iii
Estimated Sales: $20-50 Million
Number Employees: 5-9

25955 Meech Static Eliminators USA
2915 Newpark Dr
Barberton, OH 44203-1049
330-564-2000
Fax: 330-564-2005 800-232-4210
info@meech.com www.meech.com
Static control equipment for the packaging industry
Vice President: Matt Fyffe
matt.fyffe@meechusa.com
VP: Matt Fyffe
Estimated Sales: $2.5-5 Million
Number Employees: 10-19

25956 Meguiar's Inc
17991 Mitchell S
Irvine, CA 92614-6015
949-752-8000
Fax: 949-752-5784 jlakkis@meguiars.com
www.meguiars.com
Manufacturer and exporter of furniture and floor
cleaning products including polish
CEO: Barry Meguiar
barry.meguiar@meguiars.com
CEO: Barry Meguiar
Estimated Sales: $20-50 Million
Number Employees: 100-249
Brands:
Meguiar's
Meguiar's Mirror Glaze

25957 Meheen Manufacturing Inc
325 N Oregon Ave
Pasco, WA 99301-4236
509-547-7029
Fax: 509-547-0939 www.meheen-mfg.com
Computer automated carbonated beverage bottling
machines
Owner: Stephanie Cartagena
scartagena@meheen.com
CFO: Dave Meheen
Quality Control: Dave Meheen
R&D: Dave Meheen
Estimated Sales: Less Than $500,000
Number Employees: 1-4
Square Footage: 10000

**25958 Meil Electric Fixture
Manufacturing Company**
1045 W Glenwood Ave
Philadelphia, PA 19133
215-228-8528
Fax: 215-228-3898
Fluorescent lighting fixtures
President: Stephen Dinerman
CFO: Stanley Neil
Estimated Sales: $1-2.5 Million
Number Employees: 5-9

25959 Meilahn Manufacturing Co
5900 W 65th St
Chicago, IL 60638-5499
773-581-5204
Fax: 773-581-5404 www.meilahnmfg.com
Furniture, custom cabinetry and point of purchase
displays
President: Gary Clarin
g.clarin@meilahnmfg.com
VP: Dave Sawyer
Estimated Sales: $5-10 Million
Number Employees: 10-19
Square Footage: 44000

25960 Melcher Manufacturing Co
6017 E Mission Ave
Spokane Valley, WA 99212-1264
509-535-7626
Fax: 509-536-3931 800-541-4227
sales@melcher-ramps.com
www.melcher-ramps.com
Manufacturer and exporter of fiberglass truck-load-
ing ramps
President: Wayne Hardan
Sales Manager: Wendell Anglesey
Plant Manager: Dick Colby
Estimated Sales: Below $5 Million
Number Employees: 10-19

25961 Melco Steel Inc
1100 W Foothill Blvd
Azusa, CA 91702-2818
626-334-7875
Fax: 626-334-6799 info@melcosteel.com
www.melcosteel.com
Canned food sterilizing and cooking equipment in-
cluding pressure vessels, retorts, quick opening
doors, reaction chambers; manufacturer and exporter
of autoclaves
President: Michel Kashou
michelkashou@melcosteel.com
VP: Joe Varela
Chief Engineer: Jeff Cowan
Estimated Sales: $2.5-5 Million
Number Employees: 20-49
Square Footage: 50000
Brands:
Harris

25962 Melitta Canada
10-6201 Highway #7
Vaughan, ON L4H 0K7
Canada
416-243-8979
Fax: 416-243-1808 800-565-4882
mjohnston@melitta.ca www.melitta.ca
Coffee filters; processor of coffee
Estimated Sales: $1-5 Million
Number Employees: 10-20
Parent Co: Melitta North America
Type of Packaging: Consumer

25963 Melitta USA Inc
13925 58th St N
Clearwater, FL 33760-3721
727-535-2111
Fax: 727-535-7376 888-635-4880
consumerrelations@melitta.com www.melitta.com
Processor, importer and exporter of coffee; also, coffee machines and filters
President & CEO: Martin Miller
CEO: Marty Miller
mmiller@melitta.com
Senior Product Manager: Kerrie Tobin
Quality Assurance Manager: Mark Kiczalis
Marketing Director: Chris Hillman
VP Sales: Edward Mitchell
National Sales Manager: Thomas Best
Plant Manager: Matthias Bloedorn
Estimated Sales: $27 Million
Number Employees: 100-249
Square Footage: 104000
Type of Packaging: Consumer, Food Service
Brands:
Melitta

25964 Mell & Co
6700 W Touhy Ave
Niles, IL 60714-4518
Canada
847-647-0100
Fax: 847-470-0581 800-262-6355
customerservice@restaurantdiscountwarehouse.com
Sherbrooke OEM Ltd is an innovative company specializing in the design, fabrication and installation of bulk handling equipment for various industries
Owner: Douglas Warshauer
douglas@mellandengineering.com
Owner: Doug Warshauer
Marketing: Doug McCreight
Estimated Sales: $6.5 Million
Number Employees: 10-19
Brands:
Sherbrooke Oem

25965 Mello Smello LLC
6010 Earle Brown Dr # 100
Minneapolis, MN 55430-4516
763-504-5400
Fax: 763-504-5493 888-574-2964
Mealbags, trayliners and kids premiums, stickers, tattoo's, static cling
President: Joe Morris
jmorris@mellosmello.com
Estimated Sales: $24.4 Million
Number Employees: 50-99
Square Footage: 70000
Parent Co: Miner Group International
Type of Packaging: Food Service, Private Label
Brands:
Pizza Pozze

25966 Melmat Inc
5333 Industrial Dr
Huntington Beach, CA 92649-1516
714-379-4555
Fax: 714-379-4554 800-635-6289
info@melmat.com
Manufacturer and wholesaler/distributor of plastic, bulk and custom molded containers, tote boxes, tubs, tanks and insulated and single-wall bins
Owner: John Melmat
john@mailmat.com
CEO: Laura Kreisberg
CFO: Vera Moeder
Vice President: David Kriegt
Estimated Sales: $1-2.5 Million
Number Employees: 10-19
Square Footage: 44000
Brands:
Kudl-Pak
Space Case

25967 Melrose Displays
2 Brighton Avenue
Passaic, NJ 07055-2002
973-471-7700
Fax: 973-471-6885
Custom point-of-purchase displays and store fixtures in wire, wood, metal, tubing and plastic; also, front end check out fixtures
President: Richard Cohen
CEO: Melvin Cohen
Sr. VP: Gerry Turk
Estimated Sales: $10-20 Million
Number Employees: 150
Square Footage: 450000
Brands:
Quick Step...The Produce Manager

25968 Melsur Corporation
7752 Us Route 5
Westminster, VT 05158-9683
802-463-3969
Fax: 802-463-1353

25969 Melton Hot Melt Applications
745 West Winder Industrial Pkwy
Winder, GA 30680
770-307-0942
Fax: 770-307-0955 888-357-9317
Owner: Tony Laniewicz
Estimated Sales: Below $5 Million
Number Employees: 5-9

25970 Meltric Corporation
4640 W Ironwood Dr
Franklin, WI 53132
414-817-6160
Fax: 414-817-6161 800-824-4031
www.meltric.com
Switch related plugs and receptacles that ensures electrical safety
CEO: Paul Barnhill
Contact: John Baranowski
jbarnowski@meltric.com
Manager: Mark Rasmussen

25971 Melville Plastics
943 Trollingwood Rd
Haw River, NC 27258-8757
336-578-5800
Fax: 336-578-5402 www.ckspackaging.com
Plastic containers for dairy products
Operations Manager: Ken Pierceson
Plant Manager: Dave Sebastian
Estimated Sales: $20-50 Million
Number Employees: 100-249

25972 Melvina Can Machinery Company
30 Casey Rd
Hudson Falls, NY 12839
518-743-0606
Fax: 631-391-9039
Manufacturer, importer and exporter of compound liners, can machinery and oil filter equipment, including can seamers and closers
President: Thomas Cahill
Estimated Sales: $5-10 Million
Number Employees: 10-19
Parent Co: Can Industries

25973 Membrane Process & Controls
922 N 3rd Ave
Edgar, WI 54426-9013
715-352-3206
Fax: 715-352-2194 jstencil@membranepc.com
www.membranepc.com
Membrane filtration, instrumentation and control engineering for the food and dairy industry
President: Joel Stencil
jstencil@membranepc.com
Process/Control Engineer: Joel Stencil
Estimated Sales: $500,000-$1 Million
Number Employees: 10-19

25974 Membrane System Specialist Inc
1430 2nd St N
PO Box 998
Wisconsin Rapids, WI 54494-2914
715-421-2333
Fax: 715-423-6181
membrane@mssincorporated.com
www.mssincorporated.com
Manufacturer and exporter of brine and control systems, evaporators, condensers, filtration and membrane processing equipment, separators, clarifiers, waste water treatment systems and whey processing equipment for dairy industry
Owner: Greg Pesko
membrane@mssincorporated.com
Regional Sales Manager: Marian Oehme
Production Manager: Derek Hibbard
Estimated Sales: Below $5 Million
Number Employees: 5-9
Square Footage: 20840

25975 Memor/Memtec America Corporation
2118 Greenspring Dr
Timonium, MD 21093-3112
410-252-0800
Fax: 410-560-2857 www.pall.com
Wine industry filtration equipment
President, Life Sciences: Yves Baratelli
Chairman & Chief Executive Officer: Lawrence D. Kingsley
Chief Financial Officer: Akhil Johri
Senior Vice President, Operations: Richard Jackson
Chief Technology Officer: Michael Egholm, Ph.D.
Estimated Sales: $1-5 Million
Number Employees: 250-499

25976 Memphis Delta Tent & Awning
296 East St
Memphis, TN 38126-2414
901-522-1238
Fax: 901-522-1241 www.mdtna.com
Aluminum and canvas awnings, tarpaulins and tents; also, bags including canvas, cotton duck, vinyl, nonwoven and filter
Owner: Chuck Cross
memphisdelta@aol.com
Owner & Sales Manager: Paul Gatti
Estimated Sales: $500,000-$1 Million
Number Employees: 10-19
Brands:
Delta

25977 Menasha Corp
1645 Bergstrom Rd
Neenah, WI 54956-9766
920-751-1000
Fax: 920-751-1236 800-558-5073
info@menasha.com www.menashacorporation.com
Corrugated containers
President/CEO: James Kotek
james.kotek@menasha.com
SVP/Chief Financial Officer: Thomas Rettler
VP/General Counsel/Corporate Secretary: Mark Fogarty
Vice President, Human Resources: Rick Fantini
Vice President, Corporate Development: Evan Pritz
Vice President/Corporate Controller: Shannon Van Dyke
Purchasing Manager: Don Feldman
Estimated Sales: Over $1 Billion
Number Employees: 5000-9999
Square Footage: 12523

25978 Menasha Packaging Co LLC
1645 Bergstrom Rd
Neenah, WI 54956-9701
920-751-1000
Fax: 920-751-1236 877-818-2016
info@menasha.com www.menasha.com
Food packaging, packaging for in-store supermarket bakeries
CEO: Michael K Waite
michael.waite@menasha.com
Sales Director: Scott Sanders
Estimated Sales: $10-25 Million
Number Employees: 1000-4999
Parent Co: Menasha Corporation
Type of Packaging: Consumer, Food Service, Private Label, Bulk
Brands:
The Sunrite Line

25979 Mengibar Automation
103 Steam Whistle Dr
Warminster, PA 18974
215-396-2200
Fax: 215-396-6774 info@penntech-corp.com
www.penntech-corp.com
Manufacturers of packaging machinery for the pharmceutical industry

President: Ger Smit
gersmit@mai-jp.net
General Manager: David Mohl
Estimated Sales: $10-20 Million
Number Employees: 1-4
Square Footage: 20000

25980 Menke Marking Devices
13253 Alondra Blvd
Santa Fe Springs, CA 90670-5574
562-921-1380
Fax: 562-921-1184 800-231-6023
sales@menkemarking.com
www.menkemarking.com
Manufacturer and exporter of large and small character ink jet printers, roller coders and rubber and steel codes
President: Stephen Menke
VP: Rocco Falatico
Sales Manager: Paul Carrocino
Estimated Sales: $1-2.5 Million
Number Employees: 10-19
Square Footage: 21000

25981 Mennekes Electrical Products
277 Fairfield Rd # 6
Fairfield, NJ 07004-1931
973-882-0224
Fax: 973-882-5585 800-882-7584
info@mennekes.com www.mennekes.com
20A-100A power plugs, cord drop connectors for portable equipment applications, HP rated NEMA 4X motor disconnects and receptacles with interlocking for OSHA lockout, tagout requirements
President: Tom Bodner
tbodner@mennekes.com
VP: Thomas Bodnar
Vice President of Sales and Marketing: Paul DiAntonio
Vice President of Operations: AnnaMarie Fusaro
Estimated Sales: $20-50 Million
Number Employees: 20-49

25982 Mennel Milling Company
319 S Vine Street
Fostoria, OH 44830
419-435-8151
Fax: 419-436-5150 800-688-8151
info@mennel.com www.mennel.com
Processor of flour used in cake mixes, cookies, snack crackers, breadings, batters, gravies, soups, ice cream cones, pretzels and oriental noodles.
President: D. Ford Mennel
Controller: Lori Kitchen
Senior Technical Advisor: C J Lin
Vice President of Operations: David Marty
Corp Milling Engineer: Joel Hoffa
Year Founded: 1886
Estimated Sales: Below $5 Million
Number Employees: 100-249
Type of Packaging: Bulk

25983 Menu Graphics
PO Box 38397
Olmsted Falls, OH 44138-0397
216-696-1460
Fax: 216-696-1463
Manufacturer and designer of menus and menu accessories
Director: Felicia West
Estimated Sales: $1-2.5 Million
Number Employees: 10-19
Parent Co: AD Art Litho

25984 Menu Men
PO Box 1172
Palm Harbor, FL 34682-1172
727-934-7191
Fax: 727-937-0267
Menus and menu boards, covers, holders and displays
Number Employees: 5-9
Parent Co: Menu Men

25985 Menu Promotions
4510 White Plains Rd
Bronx, NY 10470-1609
718-324-3800
Fax: 718-324-5598
Menu covers
President: Andrea Bongiovanni
andrea@menucovers.biz

Estimated Sales: Less than $500,000
Number Employees: 5-9
Parent Co: Mona Slide Fasteners

25986 Menu Solution Inc
4510 White Plains Rd
Bronx, NY 10470-1609
718-994-9049
Fax: 718-994-6913 800-567-6368
sales@menucovers.biz www.menucovers.biz
Owner: Joel Varrocas
Contact: Jaclyn Barrocas
jaclyn@menucovers.biz
Estimated Sales: $5-10 Million
Number Employees: 20-49

25987 MenuMark Systems
5700 W Bender Court
Milwaukee, WI 53218-1608
414-228-4350
Fax: 414-228-4373

25988 Menulink
7777 Center Ave # 600
Huntington Beach, CA 92647-3099
714-934-6368
Fax: 714-895-2332
Computer software including food cost, inventory, human resources, accounting and labor scheduling
Manager: Bob Thomas
CFO: Ronald Whitaker
Estimated Sales: $5-10 Million
Number Employees: 20-49
Brands:
    Back Office Assistant
    Menulink

25989 Mepsco
1888 E Fabyan Pkwy
Batavia, IL 60510-1498
630-231-4130
Fax: 630-231-9372 800-323-8535
www.mepsco.com
Manufacturer and exporter of mechanical tenderizers and pickle injector machinery for the curing of pork and beef, marinating of chicken and the basting of turkey
President: Robert Benton
Estimated Sales: $9,000,000
Number Employees: 20-49
Square Footage: 32000
Brands:
    Mepsco

25990 Merchandising FrontiersInc
1300 E Buchanan St
Winterset, IA 50273-9589
515-462-4965
Fax: 515-462-4962 800-421-2278
sales@mfi4u.com www.mfi4u.com
Manufacturer and exporter of indoor/outdoor carts, displays and kiosks
Owner: Jerry Mayer
jmayer@merchandisingfrontiers.com
Co-Owner And CEO: Janet Mayer
Estimated Sales: $2.5-5,000,000
Number Employees: 20-49
Square Footage: 62000

25991 Merchandising Inventives
1665 S Waukegan Rd
Waukegan, IL 60085
847-688-0591
Fax: 847-688-0748 800-367-5653
www.merchinv.com
Manufacturer and exporter of point of purchase advertising display hardware components including mobile kits, ceiling fixtures, pole displays, banner hangers, shelf fixtures, display fasteners, etc
CEO: Ethan Berger
CFO: Diane Johnson
Vice President: Dan Jezierny
Quality Control: Aier Torres
Public Relations: Kay Berger
Operations Manager: Dan Jezierny
Production Manager: Jose Gayton
Plant Manager: Sue Kradwitz
Purchasing Manager: Sue Kradwitz
Estimated Sales: $12 Million
Number Employees: 20-49
Number of Products: 2000
Square Footage: 90000
Parent Co: DisplaWerks

25992 Merchandising Systems Manufacturing
2951 Whipple Rd
Union City, CA 94587-1207
650-324-8324
Fax: 650-324-4584 800-523-1468
Manufacturer and exporter of store displays and fixtures
President/Owner: Kyle Robinson
National Account Manager: Carol Sauceda
Contact: Kumar Gaurav
kumar@wireline.net
Estimated Sales: $5-10 Million
Number Employees: 20-49
Square Footage: 176000

25993 Merchants Publishing Company
20 Mills St
Kalamazoo, MI 49048
269-345-1175
Fax: 269-345-6999
Labels, tags and folding cartons
President: M Jack Fleming
CFO: Dick Nagle
VP Sales / Marketing: Ben Behrman
National Sales Manager (Label Division): Frank Brady
Estimated Sales: $10-20 Million
Number Employees: 50-99

25994 Merco/Savory
980 South Isabella R
Mt. Pleasant, MI 48858
989-773-7981
Fax: 800-669-0619 800-733-8821
Manufacturer and exporter of rotisseries, broilers, toasters, hot dog grilling systems, convection, pizza and cookie ovens, heated display cases and food warmers
President: Stephen Whiteley
COO: Marion Antonini
Director Marketing: Barbara Wolf
Director Sales: Alan Oates
Number Employees: 250-499
Square Footage: 30000
Parent Co: ENODIS
Type of Packaging: Food Service

25995 Mercury Equipment Company
15023 Sierra Bonita Lane
Chino, CA 91710-8902
909-606-8884
Fax: 909-606-8885 800-273-6688
Manufacturer and exporter of doughnut making equipment and bakery display cases and fixtures
President: Mike Campbell
Vice President: Joe Campbell
Estimated Sales: $1-3 Million
Number Employees: 6
Square Footage: 20000
Brands:
    Belshaw
    Dca
    Mercury

25996 Mercury Floor Machines Inc
110 S Van Brunt St
Englewood, NJ 07631-3494
201-568-4606
Fax: 201-568-7962 888-568-4606
mrbill@mercuryfloormachines.com
www.mercuryfloormachines.com
Floor scrubbers, vacuums and carpet extractors
President/CEO: William Allen
Quality Control: William Parker
General Manager: Bill Bacich
Estimated Sales: $2.5-5 Million
Number Employees: 10-19
Square Footage: 16000

25997 Mercury Plastic Bag Company
168 7th St
Passaic, NJ 7055
973-778-7200
Fax: 973-778-0549
Polyethylene and polypropylene packaging bags
President: Marvin Rosen
VP Sales: Stuart Rosen
Estimated Sales: $5-10 Million
Number Employees: 20-49

25998 Meriden Box Company
321 Blue Hills Drive
Southington, CT 06489-4605
860-621-7141
Fax: 860-621-7141
Hard and soft wood boxes and pallets

25999 Merieux Nutrisciences
2057 Builders Pl
Columbus, OH 43204-4886
614-486-0150
Fax: 614-486-0151 silliker@silliker.com
www.merieuxnutrisciences.com
Consultant offering analytical services for food processors
Manager: Amitha Miele
Estimated Sales: $5-10 Million
Number Employees: 20-49
Parent Co: Silliker Laboratories

26000 Meritech
600 Corporate Circle
Suite H
Golden, CO 80401-5643
303-790-4670
Fax: 303-790-4859 800-932-7707
www.meritech.com
No-touch automated hygiene equipment to the food processing, food service, medical, cleanroom, daycare, school and prison industries.
President/CEO: Jim Glenn
Sales: Michele Colbert
Contact: Samantha Dill
samanthadill@wiradcom.com
Estimated Sales: $5-10 Million
Number Employees: 10-19
Square Footage: 40000
Type of Packaging: Food Service
Brands:
Chg 2%
Chg 4%
Machine Mochers
Quat E-2
Quat F-5
Shelf Clean A-1

26001 Meriwether Industries
12 Prospect St
Bloomfield, NJ 7003
973-743-0463
Fax: 973-743-0614 800-332-2358
Power transmission and conveyor belts
President: Samuel Wolosin
CFO: Samuel Wolosin
Estimated Sales: $1-2.5 Million
Number Employees: 3
Square Footage: 6000
Brands:
Extremultus
Transilon

26002 Merix Chemical Company
230 W Superior St
Chicago, IL 60654-3595
312-573-1400
Fax: 773-221-3047 www.marxsaunders.com
Manufacturer and exporter of anti-static coatings for polyethylene films; also, anti-fog coatings to prevent moisture and condensation on food display cases
Owner: Bonnie Marx
Manager: Z Blowert
Estimated Sales: $1-5 Million
Number Employees: 5-9
Square Footage: 6000
Brands:
Merix

26003 Merlin Development Inc
181 Cheshire Ln N # 500
Minneapolis, MN 55441-8715
763-475-0224
Fax: 763-475-1626 merlin@merlindev.com
www.merlindevelopment.com
Consultant providing contract research and product development services to the food industry
President: Paul Thompson
General Manager: Paul Thompson
Manager: Kellie Fischer
kfischer@merlindev.com
Estimated Sales: $3-5 Million
Number Employees: 5-9
Square Footage: 17880

26004 Merlin Process Equipment
700 Louisiana St
Houston, TX 77002-2700
713-221-1651
Fax: 713-690-3353
Manufacturer and exporter of mixers
Estimated Sales: $300,000-500,000
Number Employees: 1-4

26005 Merric
4742 Earth City Expy
Bridgeton, MO 63044
314-770-9944
Fax: 314-770-1440 www.merric.com
Tabletops, booths, cabinets and point of sale counters
Owner: Dan Claypool
Administration: Tricia Weiss
Accounts Manager: Karrie Dyas
AutoCAD Engineer: Greg Koets
Engineer/IT: Aaron Pattillo
Sr. Project Manager: Amy DeVries
VP Operations: Tom Boylan
Project Manager: Chris Robertson
Estimated Sales: $2.5-5,000,000
Number Employees: 20-49

26006 Merrill Distributing Inc
1301 N Memorial Dr
Merrill, WI 54452-3188
715-536-4551
Fax: 715-536-5757 800-677-6320
www.merrilldistributing.com
Food service distributor
President: John Schewe
jschewe@merrilldistributing.com
Estimated Sales: Below $5 Million
Number Employees: 50-99

26007 Merrillville Awning Co
1420 E 91st Dr
Merrillville, IN 46410-7174
219-736-9800
Fax: 219-736-9100 800-781-6100
www.awningguy.com
Commercial awnings
Owner: Mike Blessing
mike@awningguy.com
Estimated Sales: $2.5-5,000,000
Number Employees: 10-19

26008 Merryweather Foam Inc
1212 Wynette Rd
Sylacauga, AL 35151-4601
256-249-8546
Fax: 256-249-8548 sales@merryweather.com
www.merryweather.com
Plastic foam parts and pressure-sensitive tapes
General manager: Bellaire Riley
IT: Ed Spraley
ed@merryweather.com
Plant Manager: Cliff Shelnut
Estimated Sales: $5-10 Million
Number Employees: 20-49
Parent Co: Merryweather Foam

26009 (HQ)Merryweather Foam Inc
1212 Wynette Rd
Sylacauga, AL 35151-4601
256-249-8546
Fax: 256-249-8548 www.merryweather.com
Plastic foam parts; fabricator/convertor of polyurethane and polyethylene foams with and without pressure sensitive adhesives and coatings
Director Sales/Marketing: Don Sweigert
Sales Administrator: Tina Rockhold
Customer Service Manager: Theresa Karabinus
IT: Ed Spraley
General manager: Bellaire Riley
Estimated Sales: $10-20 Million
Number Employees: 20-49
Square Footage: 200000
Other Locations:
Merryweather Foam
Sylacauga AL

26010 Mertz L. Carlton Company
6147 W 65th Street
Bedford Park, IL 60638-5303
708-594-1050
Fax: 716-626-1616
Cleaning compounds
Estimated Sales: $2.5-5 Million
Number Employees: 10-19

26011 Mesa Laboratories Inc
12100 W 6th Ave
Lakewood, CO 80228-1252
303-987-8000
Fax: 303-987-8989 800-525-1215
www.mesalabs.com
Manufacturer, importer and exporter of temperature, pressure and humidity monitoring products for processing, distribution and transportation; also, ultrasonic composition analyzers and flow meters
President: Luke Schmieder
CEO: John J Sullivan
john@mesalabs.com
CFO: Steven Peterson
Research And Development: Preston Graves
Quality Control: Jeff Zepp
Marketing: David Price
Sales: Owen Israelsen
Operations: Clint Englehart
Production: Rex Trout
Estimated Sales: $9 Million
Number Employees: 250-499
Number of Brands: 7
Square Footage: 79232
Parent Co: Mesa Laboratories
Brands:
Datatrace

26012 Mesler Group
3725 Okemos Road
Okemos, MI 48864-3929
517-349-7066
Fax: 517-349-7069 mgi@voyager.net
Consulting for the food ingredient industry
President: Fred Mesler

26013 Messina Brothers Manufacturing Company
1065 Shepherd Avenue
Brooklyn, NY 11208-5713
718-345-9800
Fax: 718-345-2441 800-924-6454
Manufacturer, importer and wholesaler/distributor of mops, brooms and brushes
Sales Representative: Robert Messina
General Manager: Lawrence Mirro
Number Employees: 15
Square Footage: 90000
Parent Co: Howard Berger Company

26014 Met-Pro Corp
1550 Industrial Dr
Owosso, MI 48867-9775
989-725-8185
Fax: 989-725-8188 800-392-7621
info@mpeas.com www.mpeas.com
Pumps including fiber glass reinforced, vinyl ester, epoxy and chemical process
Controller: Dave Mogg
COO: Greg Kimmer
greg.kimmer@dualldiv.com
VP/General Manager: R De Hont
Sales/Marketing Manager: E Murphy
Engineering Manager: R Petersen
Estimated Sales: $5 Million
Number Employees: 20-49
Square Footage: 200000

26015 Met-Pro Corp
1550 Industrial Dr
Owosso, MI 48867-9775
989-725-8185
Fax: 989-725-8188 info@dualldiv.com
www.dualldiv.com
Air pollution controls for food processing plants
Controller: Dave Mogg
COO: Greg Kimmer
greg.kimmer@dualldiv.com
Sales Manager: Rob Teich
Estimated Sales: $5-10 Million
Number Employees: 20-49
Square Footage: 240000
Parent Co: Met-Pro Corporation

26016 Metal
141 Metal Park Dr
Columbia, SC 29209-5072
803-776-9252
Fax: 803-776-9610
Restaurant equipment including metal sinks and tables
President: Frances Smoak
fsmoak@mef-inc.com

Estimated Sales: Below $5 Million
Number Employees: 5-9
Square Footage: 120000

26017 Metal Container Corporation
3636 S Geyer Rd # 400
St Louis, MO 63127-1218
314-957-9500
Fax: 314-957-9515 www.budlight.com
More than 20 billion cans and 20 billion lids annuually at its 11 can and lid manufacturing facilities. Supplies about 60% of Anheuser-Bussch's container and lid requirements and is a signifcant supplier to the US soft-drink containermarket
President/Owner: Tony Bhalla
CEO: Joe Sellinger
Contact: Mike Balassi
mike.balassi@anheuser-busch.com
Number Employees: 100-249
Parent Co: Anheuser-Busch Companies

26018 Metal Equipment Company
600 Dover Center Rd
Cleveland, OH 44140-3310
440-835-3100
Fax: 440-835-1780 800-700-6326
Manufacturer, importer and exporter of custom metal industrial carts, storage racks, industrial bottle washers, waste management tanks, guards, platform trucks and pallet carriers
Manager: Bill Reilly
General Manager: Paul Drda
VP: Robert Walzer
Estimated Sales: Below $5 Million
Number Employees: 5-9
Square Footage: 110000

26019 Metal Kitchen Fabricators Inc
5121 April Ln
Houston, TX 77092-3499
713-683-8375
Fax: 713-683-8378
Custom manufacturer of food service equipment including stainless steel shelves, countertops and sinks
Owner: Glen Propes
mks@metalkitchens.net
Estimated Sales: Below $5 Million
Number Employees: 10-19

26020 Metal Master Sales Corp
1159 N Main St
Glendale Heights, IL 60139-3509
630-858-4750
Fax: 630-858-4735 800-488-8729
sales@metalmaster.com www.metalmaster.com
Manufacturer and exporter of food processing equipment and parts, cabinets, hoods, trays, tables, sinks, carts, tableware, canopies, fixtures, art metal, serving lines, bartops and countertops, etc
Owner: Jim Jensen
jjensen@metalmaster.com
VP: Bob Lonrod
Estimated Sales: $2.5-5 Million
Number Employees: 10-19
Square Footage: 104000
Parent Co: Richards Manufacturing & Services Corporation
Brands:
Biltrite
Caterware

26021 Metal Masters Northwest
20926 63rd Ave W
Suite A
Lynnwood, WA 98036-7402
425-775-4481
Fax: 425-775-2618 www.metalmastersnw.com
Custom fabricated stainless steel restaurant products including cooking, heating and serving equipment
Owner: Craig Jeppesen
craig.jeppesen@metalmastersnw.com
VP: Timothy Eaves
Estimated Sales: $1-2.5 Million
Number Employees: 10-19
Square Footage: 20000

26022 Metalcretye Manufacturing Company
4133 Payne Ave
Cleveland, OH 44103-2324
440-526-5600
Fax: 440-526-5601 800-526-5602
sales@metalcreteindustries.com
www.metalcreteindustries.com

Owner: Ron Stankie
Estimated Sales: $3-5 Million
Number Employees: 10-19

26023 Metaline Products Co Inc
101 N Feltus St ,
South Amboy, NJ 08879-1529
732-721-1373
Fax: 732-727-0272 sales@metalineproducts.com
www.metalineproducts.com
Manufacturer and exporter of wood, wire, plastic and corrugated display racks, shelving and point of purchase displays
President: Natalie Papailiou
natalie@mstudio.com
VP: August Zilincar
Estimated Sales: $2.5-5 Million
Number Employees: 20-49
Square Footage: 50000

26024 Metalloid Corp
504 Jackson St
Huntington, IN 46750
260-358-4610
Fax: 260-356-3201 800-686-3201
sales@metalloidcorp.com www.metalloidcorp.com
Manufacturer and exporter of cutting fluids, tapping compounds and hand cleaners
President: Gary Russ
gruss@metalloidcorp.com
VP Marketing: William Fair
Estimated Sales: $2.5-5 Million
Number Employees: 10-19

26025 Metcalf & Eddy
701 Edgewater Dr Ste 200
Wakefield, MA 1880
781-246-5200
Fax: 781-245-6293
Consultant providing water and wastewater treatment services; also, engineering, design, construction, operations and maintenance available
President: Micheal S Burke
Chairman/CEO: John M Dionisio
Contact: Robert Adams
robert.adams@m-e.aecom.com
Number Employees: 20-49
Parent Co: Air & Water Technology

26026 Metcraft
13910 Kessler Drive
Grandview, MO 64030-5312
816-761-3250
Fax: 816-761-0544 800-444-9624
info@powersoak.com
Stainless steel custom fabricated food processing equipment, plumbing fixtures and power soak pot washing systems
President: John Cantrell
President: John Cantrell
Vice President of Distribution: Barry Bergstein
Marketing Director: Virginia Black
President: John Cantrell
Vice President of Operations: John McCreight
Manufacturing Manager: Monty Patton
Estimated Sales: $5-10 Million
Number Employees: 60
Square Footage: 60000
Parent Co: Emco
Brands:
Power Soak

26027 Metko Inc
1301 Milwaukee Dr
New Holstein, WI 53061-1443
920-898-4221
Fax: 920-898-1389 sales@metko.com
www.metko.com
Full-service precision custom metal fabricator offering engineering support, parts, subassemblies and complete assembled parts in a large range of metals and custom finishes.
President: Michael Mc Carthy
CEO/Founder: David McCarthy
Marketing: Jim Kreger
Sales: Jim Kreger
Public Relations: Jim Kreger
Human Resources: Diane McCarthy
Production: Mike Lider
Plant Manager: Mike Lider
Purchasing: Scott Lynch
Estimated Sales: $5-10 Million
Number Employees: 50-99
Square Footage: 42000

Brands:
Custom Metal Fabricator

26028 Metl-Span I Ltd
1720 Lakepointe Drive
Suite #101
Lewisville, TX 75057-2650
972-221-6656
Fax: 972-420-9382 877-585-9969
www.metalspan.com
CEO: Karl F Hielscher
Estimated Sales: $5-10 Million
Number Employees: 100-249

26029 Metlar Us
2248 Roanoke Ave
Riverhead, NY 11901-1822
631-252-5574
Fax: 828-253-7773 www.metlar-us.com
Manufacturer, importer and exporter of fine pore filters
Office Manager: Anne Ogg
Contact: Doreen Kula
dkula@metlar-us.com
Estimated Sales: $1-5 Million
Number Employees: 1-4
Parent Co: US Filter/Schumacher

26030 Meto
P.O.Box 518
Morris Plains, NJ 07950-0518
973-606-5660
Fax: 973-606-5661 800-645-3290
www.meto.com
Barcode printers, applicators, labels
Manager: William E Staehle
Estimated Sales: $5-10 Million
Number Employees: 20-49

26031 Metro Corporation
P.O. Box A
Wilkes Barre, PA 18705
570-825-2741
800-992-1776
www.intermetro.com
Supplier of food service storage, warehandling and transport solutions. The complete range of Metro products puts space to work in virtually avery area-cooler, freezer, dry storage, food preparation, catering and front of thehouse.
President & CEO: John Nackley
Vice President, Sales: Bill O'Donoghue
Year Founded: 1929
Estimated Sales: $100-500 Million
Number Employees: 1000-5000
Type of Packaging: Food Service
Brands:
Flavor Lock
Metromax
Metromax Q
Sani-Stack
Smart Single
Smart Track
Smart Wall
Super Adjustable Super Erecta
Super Erecta
Top Truck

26032 Metro Signs
4224 Losee Road
Suite J
N Las Vegas, NV 89030
702-649-9333
Fax: 702-649-9336 www.sbn.com
Signs; lettering service available
President: Frank Gaskill
Estimated Sales: Less than $500,000
Number Employees: 4

26033 Metron Instruments, Inc
Dock 3 or 4
23103 Miles Road
Cleveland, OH 44128
216-332-0592
Fax: 216-274-9262
sanderson@metroninstruments.com
www.metroninstruments.com
Heat exchangers, plate, centrifuges, milk tester, milk standardizer
Owner: Robert P Carter
Estimated Sales: $1-2.5 Million
Number Employees: 5-9

26034 Metroplex Corporation
PO Box 681987
Houston, TX 77268

281-257-8570
Fax: 281-257-8572
Consultant for corporate and private outplacement
including professional services
President: Willard Jackson
Principal: Reid Matthews
CFO: Bob Stevens
CEO: Zia Qureshi
R & D: Howard Davis
Estimated Sales: $10-20 Million
Number Employees: 50-99

26035 Metropolitan Flag & Banner Co
3237 Amber St # 5
Philadelphia, PA 19134-3227

215-426-2775
Fax: 215-426-5106 Sales@metflag.com
www.metflag.com
Flags and banners
President: Robert Snyder
rob@metflag.com
CFO: Robert Snyder
Quality Control: Robert Snyder
R&D: Robert Snyder
Estimated Sales: Below $5 Million
Number Employees: 10-19

26036 Metrovock Snacks
6116 Walker Avenue
Maywood, CA 90270-3447

323-771-3221
Fax: 323-771-2429 800-428-0522
www.giftbasketsupplies.com
Themed gift baskets
President and QC: Paul Popcorn
Contact: Carol Gregory
csnacks1@aol.com
Estimated Sales: $500,000-$1 Million
Number Employees: 20

26037 Metspeed Labels
6300 Mcpherson St
PO Box 850
Levittown, PA 19057-4728

215-956-9101
Fax: 215-946-7201 888-886-0638
info@metspeedlabel.com www.metspeedlabel.com
Pressure sensitive tags and labels
President: Joe Felix
joe@metspeedlabel.com
VP: Joe Felix
Marketing: Bob Reeder
Estimated Sales: Less Than $500,000
Number Employees: 1-4

26038 Metsys Engineering
9855 W 78th Street
Suite 10
Eden Prairie, MN 55344-8003

952-944-1081
Fax: 952-944-1431
Solutions to consumer product manufacturers
through system engineering, development of operat-
ing documentation and technical training
Sales/Marketing Administrator: Mary Sandler
Estimated Sales: $2.5-5 Million
Number Employees: 20-49

26039 Mettler-Toledo Hi-Speed
1571 Northpointe Pkwy
Lutz, FL 33558

800-447-4439
hispeed@mt.com www.mt.com
Checkweighers, weighing and material handling.
Head of Product Inspection Division: Jonas Greutert
Regional Sales Director: John Fletcher
Estimated Sales: $20-50 Million
Number Employees: 100-249
Type of Packaging: Food Service, Bulk

26040 Mettler-Toledo Process Analytics, Inc
900 Middlesex Turnpike
Building 8
Billerica, MA 01821

800-352-8763
mtprous@mt.com www.mt.com/pro
Manufacturer, importer and exporter of process measurement equipment including pH and dissolved oxygen probes, transmitters and head space analyzers.
Head of Process Analytics Division: Gerry Keller

Estimated Sales: $10-20 Million
Number Employees: 50-99
Square Footage: 20000
Brands:
Infit
Ingold
Inpro
Intrac
Xerolyt

26041 Mettler-Toledo SafelineInc
1571 Northpointe Pkwy
Lutz, FL 33558

800-638-8537
www.mt.com
Metal detectors and x-ray equipment for food prod-
ucts (including bulk, pakced, liquid, slurry and pow-
der) and for pharmaceutical products.
National Sales Manager: Oscar Jeter
Market Communications Specialist: Sarrina Crowley
Estimated Sales: $5 Million
Number Employees: 100-249
Square Footage: 276000
Brands:
Safeline

26042 (HQ)Mettler-Toledo, LLC
1900 Polaris Pkwy
Columbus, OH 43240

800-638-8537
www.mt.com
Manufacturer and exporter of stainless steel scales
and printing devices for processing applications in-
cluding portion control, sorting, box weighing, ship-
ping/receiving and in-motion weighing.
Chief Executive Officer: Olivier Filliol
olivier.filliol@mt.com
Chief Financial Officer: Shawn Vadala
Head of Supply Chain & IT: Oliver Wittorf
Head of Divisions & Operations: Peter Aggersbjerg
Head of Process Analytics Division: Gerry Keller
Head of Industrial Division: Elena Markwalder
Head of Product Inspection Division: Jonas Greutert
Head of Human Resources: Christian Magloth
Year Founded: 1946
Estimated Sales: Over $2 Billion
Number Employees: 10,000

26043 Metz Premiums
250 W 57th St # 25
New York, NY 10107-0001

212-315-4660
Fax: 212-541-4559 metzpremiums@yahoo.com
Manufacturer and importer of uniforms; also adver-
tising specialties including metal pins and key rings,
tote bags, picture frames and ceramic products
VP Sales: Laurie Zelen
Purchasing Manager: Gerry Kroll
Estimated Sales: less than $500,000
Number Employees: 1-4

26044 Metzgar Conveyors
901 Metzgar Dr NW
Comstock Park, MI 49321-9758

616-784-0930
Fax: 616-784-4100 888-266-8390
sales@metzgarconveyors.com
Manufacturer and exporter of conveyors and pack-
age and pallet handling systems
President: D R Metzgar
dr.metzgar@metzgarconveyor.com
VP: Roger Scholten
R & D: Tom Dewey
Marketing: Roger Schotten
Production: Jon Goeman
Purchasing Manager: David Stevens
Estimated Sales: $10 Million
Number Employees: 50-99
Square Footage: 100000

26045 Mex-Char
1119 E 10th St
Douglas, AZ 85607-2301

520-364-2138
Fax: 520-364-2138
Mesquite, horticultural, avicultural, industrial and
granulated charcoal
Owner: Oscar Teran
Estimated Sales: $1-5 Million
Number Employees: 1-4
Square Footage: 80000
Type of Packaging: Bulk

26046 Meyer & Garroutte Systems
P.O Box 5460
San Antonio, TX 78201-0460

210-736-1811
Fax: 210-736-9452 www.meyer-industries.com
CEO: Eugene W Teeter
Estimated Sales: $10-20 Million
Number Employees: 50-99

26047 Meyer Industries
3528 Fredericksburg Rd
San Antonio, TX 78201-3849

210-736-1811
Fax: 210-736-9452 sales@meyer-industries.com
www.meyer-industries.com
Food processing equipment
CEO: Eugene Teeter
eteeter@meyer-industries.com
CFO: Larry Marek
Number Employees: 50-99

26048 Meyer Label Company
15143 Winkler Rd
Fort Myers, FL 33919

239-489-0342
Fax: 201-894-8867
Manufacturer and exporter of pressure sensitive and
roll labels
Owner: Kurt Meyer
VP Sales: Bob Reineke
Estimated Sales: $2.5-5 Million
Number Employees: 1-4
Square Footage: 50000

26049 Meyer Machine & Garroutte Products
3528 Fredericksburg Rd.
P.O.Box 5460
San Antonio, TX 78201-0460

210-736-1811
Fax: 210-736-4662 Sales@meyer-industries.com
www.meyer-industries.com
Manufacturer and exporter of belt and vibratory con-
veyors and feeders, pivoting bucket elevators, spiral
lowerators, fryers, broilers, ovens, live bottom and
bin storage and food seasoning equipment.
President: Eugene Teeter
Quality Control and CFO: Larry Marek
North & South Central Regional Sales Mgr: Roland
Metivier
Northeast/Southeast Regional Sales Mgr: Scott
Carter
Western Regional Sales Mgr: Jim Lassiter
VP Manufacturing: Carroll Fries
Estimated Sales: $10-20 Million
Number Employees: 50-99
Square Footage: 200000
Parent Co: Meyer Industries
Other Locations:
Meyer Machine Co.
West Midlands
Brands:
Dynaflex
Magneflex
Simplex
Vibraflex

26050 Meyer Packaging
PO Box 232
Palmyra, PA 17078-0232

717-838-6300
Set-up paper boxes
VP: Stephen Meyer
Estimated Sales: $10-15 Million
Number Employees: 50-100
Square Footage: 200000

26051 (HQ)Meyers Printing Co
7277 Boone Ave N
Minneapolis, MN 55428-1539

763-533-9730
Fax: 763-531-5771 info@meyers.com
www.meyers.com
Pressure sensitive and roll labels; lithographic, large
format printing and printing on plastics available
CEO: David Dillon
david_dillon@meyers.com
Estimated Sales: $50-100 Million
Number Employees: 250-499

26052 Meyhen International
556 Industrial Way West
Eatontown, NJ 07724
732-363-2333
Fax: 732-905-7696 www.meyhenfingers.com
Food Processing equipment; rubber products
Owner: Meir Toshav
CEO: Henry Stern
Number Employees: 30

26053 Meyn America LLC
1000 Evenflo Dr
Ball Ground, GA 30107-4544
770-967-0532
Fax: 770-967-1318 800-881-6396
sales.usa@meyn.net www.meyn.com
Meat industry processing equipment
President: Heath Jarrett
heath.jarrett@meyn.net
Principal: David McNeal
Sales Director: Rick Boze
Number Employees: 100-249
Parent Co: Cooperatieve Meyn

26054 Mezza
222 E Wisconsin Avenue
Suite 300
Lake Forest, IL 60045-1723
847-735-2516
Fax: 415-727-4471 888-206-6054
Suppliers to the finest kitchens in America with a
worldwide selection of gourmet pantry items
Type of Packaging: Food Service, Private Label

26055 Mia Rose Products
177 Riverside Ave Ste F
Newport Beach, CA 92663
714-662-5465
Fax: 714-662-5891 800-615-2767
www.miarose.com
Manufacturer and exporter of natural, biodegradable
air fresheners, deodorizing mists and home cleaners
made with real citrus
President/CEO: Mia Rose
Marketing/Sales: Carolena Hidalgo
Contact: Carmen Arzate
c.arzate@morrisrose.com
Estimated Sales: $2 Million
Number Employees: 10-19
Square Footage: 8000
Type of Packaging: Consumer, Private Label
Brands:
Air Therapy
Citri-Glow
Pet Air

26056 Miami Awning
3905 NW 31st Ave
Miami, FL 33142-5122
786-615-6503
Fax: 305-576-0514 800-576-0222
sales@miamiawning.com www.miamiawning.com
Commercial awnings
Manager: Joan Garvey
Vice President: Rick Lassiter
rlassiter@dolphins.nfl.com
Estimated Sales: $5-10,000,000
Number Employees: 50-99

26057 Miami Metal
255 NW 25th Street
Miami, FL 33127-4329
305-576-3600
Fax: 305-576-2339
Manufacturer and exporter of chairs, cushions, pads,
table legs and bases and booths
Sales Manager: Carol Sieger
Estimated Sales: $20-50 Million
Number Employees: 100-249
Type of Packaging: Food Service
Brands:
Pompeii Furniture

26058 Miami Systems Corporation
10001 Alliance Rd
Blue Ash, OH 45242
513-793-0110
Fax: 513-793-1140 800-543-4540
info@miamisystems.com
Business forms, salesbooks, cut sheets, unitsets,
continuous register forms, mailers, cardsets, ATM
forms, envelopes, checks, guest checks, gift certificates, labels, etc

President: Samuel Peters
CFO: Jim Enright
Executive VP: Henry Peters
VP Sales/Marketing: Tim Scully
Contact: Kathye Buyok
kathye_buyok@trihealth.com
Estimated Sales: $18 Million
Number Employees: 1,000-4,999

26059 (HQ)Mic-Ellen Associates
1173 Collegeville Rd
Collegeville, PA 19426
610-454-1582
Fax: 610-454-1583 800-872-1252
Consultant specializing in marketing natural prod-
ucts to the health food industry
President: Michael Molyneaux
Number Employees: 5-9
Square Footage: 12000

26060 Micelli Chocolate Mold Company
135 Dale St
West Babylon, NY 11704
631-752-2888
Fax: 631-752-2885 micelliusa@aol.com
www.micelli.com
Manufacturer and exporter of plastic and metal
molds for chocolate products
President: Joseph Micelli
Vice President: John Micelli
Sales Director: John Micelli
Contact: Mike Daly
mike_daly@micelli.com
Plant Manager: John Micelli
Estimated Sales: $3-5 Million
Number Employees: 10-19
Square Footage: 20000

26061 Michael Blackman & Assoc
1106 Broadway
Santa Monica, CA 90401-3008
310-656-1010
Fax: 310-393-9397 800-889-4925
www.michaelblackmanandassociates.com
Consultant providing design services
President: Micheal Blackman
Contact: Adrienne Blackman
adrienne@mbaassoc.com
Estimated Sales: $12,000,000-$15,000,000
Number Employees: 10-19
Square Footage: 8000

26062 Michael Distributor Inc
PO Box 8681
Fountain Valley, CA 92728-8681
Fax: 714-966-1361
Food distributor and related products provider-gro-
cery, cooking oil, meat, sugar, canned foods, pro-
duce, dairy, candy & paper goods. Services to Food
service and retail industries.
President: Miguel Ortega
Estimated Sales: $8 Million
Type of Packaging: Food Service, Private Label

26063 Michael G. Brown & Associates
311 Society Pl
Newtown, PA 18940
215-860-4540
Fax: 215-579-7355
Texture analyzers
Contact: Michael Brown
mgba@voicenet.com
Estimated Sales: $1-5 Million

26064 Michael Leson Dinnerware
P.O.Box 5368
Youngstown, OH 44514
330-726-4788
Fax: 330-726-2274 800-821-3541
www.americanrails.com
Manufacturer, exporter and importer of dinnerware,
flatware, glassware, mugs, plate covers, platters, pre-
miums, incentives, salt and pepper shakers, etc
CEO: Michael Leson
Estimated Sales: $500,000-$1,000,000
Number Employees: 1-4
Parent Co: MLD Group

26065 Michaelo Espresso
309 S Cloverdale St # D22
Ste D22
Seattle, WA 98108-4572
206-695-4950
Fax: 206-695-4951 800-545-2883
info@michaelo.com
Kiosks, carts and vending equipment; importer and
wholesaler/distributor of espresso and granita ma-
chinery and panini grills; serving the food service
market
President: Michael Myers
info@michaelo.com
General Manager: Russ Myers
National Sales Manager: Douglas Pratt
Estimated Sales: $5-10 Million
Number Employees: 10-19
Square Footage: 40000
Type of Packaging: Food Service

26066 Michelman Inc
9080 Shell Rd
Blue Ash, OH 45236-1232
513-793-7766
Fax: 513-793-2504 800-333-1723
general@michem.com www.michelman.com
Water-based performance coatings and coating ap-
plication equipment for the corrugated and pa-
per-converting industries,including floor
polishes,inks,fibre glass,snack food packing
President: Steven Shifman
CFO: Jeff Rodgers
jeff.rodgers@michemprime.com
Vice President: Bob Poletti
Estimated Sales: $20-50 Million
Number Employees: 100-249
Parent Co: Michelman World
Type of Packaging: Bulk

26067 Michelson Laboratories Inc
6280 Chalet Dr
Commerce, CA 90040-3761
562-928-0553
Fax: 562-927-6625 888-941-5050
info@michelsonlab.com www.michelsonlab.com
Testing and analysis including microbiological anal-
ysis, pesticide residues, nutritionals, herbal analysis,
vitamins, FDA import alert analysis, drinking water,
wastewater and HACCP audits,meat processing, sea-
food, poultry, dairyproduce, bakery, spices and sea-
sonings, wastewater and effluent
President: Grant Michealson
grant@michelsonlab.com
Laboratory Director: Stephen Roesch
Instrumentation Manager: Maria Lopez
Chemistry Operations Manager: Roy Lung
Microbiology Asst Manager: Nolberto Colon-Droz
Estimated Sales: $5-10 Million
Number Employees: 50-99
Square Footage: 80000

26068 (HQ)Michiana Box & Crate
2193 Industrial Dr
Niles, MI 49120-1254
269-683-6372
Fax: 269-684-7860 800-677-6372
www.kampsinc.com
GMA and can pallets, bulk bins, export boxes, crates
and skids; exporter of bulk bins
President: Gary Cehovic
CEO: Thomas Kiehl
CFO: Dan Searfoss
Production Manager: Bog Modlin
Estimated Sales: $27 Million
Number Employees: 100-249
Number of Products: 205
Square Footage: 76000
Type of Packaging: Bulk

26069 Michiana Corrugate Products
110 N Franks Ave
Sturgis, MI 49091-1582
269-651-5225
Fax: 269-651-5799 www.michianacorrugated.com
Corrugated and die cut boxes; also, pads, partitions
and chipboard
President: Eric Jones
mcpcust@michianacorrugated.com
Sales Service: Patricia Vanzile
Estimated Sales: $20-50 Million
Number Employees: 20-49
Square Footage: 40000

26070 Michigan Agricultural Cooperative Marketing Association
P.O.Box 30960
Lansing, MI 48909-8460
 517-323-7000
Fax: 517-323-6793 800-824-3779
www.michiganfarmbureau.com
Consultant for apple, cherry, asparagus and plum processors
President: Wayne Wood
Div. Manager: Jerry Campbell
CFO: John Vancermolen
Vice President: Mike Fusilier
Number Employees: 100-249
Parent Co: Michigan Farm Bureau Family of Companies

26071 Michigan Apple Res Committee
13750 S Sedona Pkwy # 3
Suite 3
Lansing, MI 48906-8101
 517-669-8353
Fax: 517-669-9506 800-456-2753
Staff@MichiganApples.com
www.michiganapples.com
Offers marketing, communications, consumer education and research on behalf of Michigan apple growers.
Executive Director: Diane Smith
Account Manager: Mike Bardon
Account Manager: Cam Harrington
Communications and Marketing Manager: Gretchen Mensing, APR
Office/Marketing Coordinator: Esther Haviland
Estimated Sales: $1-2.5 Million
Number Employees: 1-4

26072 (HQ)Michigan Box Co
1910 Trombly St
Detroit, MI 48211-2130
 313-873-8084
Fax: 313-873-8084 888-642-4269
info@michiganbox.com www.michiganbox.com
Manufacturer and exporter of corrugated and pizza boxes, point of purchase displays, crates and pallets; also, custom printed and corrugated carry-out food containers available
President: Elaine Fontana
efontana@michiganbox.com
Sales Manager: Scott Keech
Operations: Ralph Betzler
Estimated Sales: $10-20 Million
Number Employees: 50-99
Square Footage: 400000
Other Locations:
 Michigan Box Co.
 Detroit MI

26073 Michigan Brush Mfg Co
7446 Central St
Detroit, MI 48210-1037
 313-834-1070
Fax: 313-834-1178 800-642-7874
sales@mi-brush.com www.michiganbrush.com
Manufacturer and exporter of brushes, brooms, mops, and paint rollers, also squeegees for food processing and food services.
President: Bruce Gale
mmfgcoinc@aol.com
CFO: Bruse Gale
Estimated Sales: $1-3 Million
Number Employees: 10-19
Number of Brands: 4
Number of Products: 1001
Square Footage: 220000
Type of Packaging: Private Label, Bulk
Brands:
 Dorden
 Mibco
 Mibrush
 Rol-Brush

26074 Michigan Desserts
10750 Capital St
Oak Park, MI 48237-3134
 248-544-4574
Fax: 248-544-4384 800-328-8632
sales@midasfoods.com www.midasfoods.com
Sweet dry mix items
President: Richard Elias
relias@midasfoods.com
Sr VP Sales/Marketing: Gary Freeman

Estimated Sales: $7 Million
Number Employees: 20-49
Square Footage: 180000
Parent Co: Midas Foods India
Type of Packaging: Consumer, Food Service, Private Label, Bulk
Brands:
 American Savory
 Michigan Dessert
 Sin Fill

26075 Michigan Food Equipment
8155 Fieldcrest Dr
Brighton, MI 48116-8316
 810-231-5132
Fax: 810-231-5132
Shrink tunnels, bacon processing equipment and accessories, blenders, frozen meat slicers, flakers and breakers, grinders, stuffers and accessories
Owner: Gary Radtke
Estimated Sales: $1-2.5 Million
Number Employees: 1-4

26076 Michigan Industrial Belting
31617 Glendale St
Livonia, MI 48150-1828
 734-427-7700
Fax: 734-427-0788 800-778-1650
marty@mibelting.com www.mibelting.com
Conveyor belts and power transmission conveyor systems; wholesaler/distributor of conveyor belts, bearings, motors and controls
Owner: Bill Kohler
bill@mibelting.com
Estimated Sales: Below $5 Million
Number Employees: 10-19
Square Footage: 240000

26077 Michigan Maple Block Co
1420 Standish Ave
Petoskey, MI 49770-3049
 231-347-4170
Fax: 231-347-7975 800-447-7975
mmb@mapleblock.com www.butcherblock.com
Manufacturer, importer and exporter of cutting boards, tabletops, carving boards and preparation and bakery tables
President: James Reichart
VP Sales & Marketing: Pat Stanley
VP Sales/Marketing: Russell Foth
Estimated Sales: $5-10 Million
Number Employees: 50-99
Parent Co: Bally Block Company
Type of Packaging: Food Service
Brands:
 Wood Welded

26078 Michigan Pallet Inc
1225 N Saginaw St
St Charles, MI 48655-1024
 989-865-9915
Fax: 989-865-9037
Wooden skids, pallets and boxes
President: Rick Lorentzen
Sales: Duane Schneider
Sales: Dan McGee
Estimated Sales: $5-10 Million
Number Employees: 50-99

26079 Micor Co Inc
3232 N 31st St
Milwaukee, WI 53216-3828
 414-873-2071
Fax: 414-873-3904 800-284-4308
micorox@execpc.com www.micorco.com
Floors, floor sealers, protective coatings, epoxy floors, floor resurfacers
President: Barbara Greenberg
patricknap@aol.com
Sales Exec: Patrick Cox
Estimated Sales: $1-2.5 Million
Number Employees: 5-9

26080 Micro Affiliates
3986 Ballynahown Cirle
Fairfax, VA 22030-2497
 301-881-4115
Fax: 301-881-0340 800-430-1099
www.joesdata.com
Four-way security door viewers
Estimated Sales: $2.5-5 Million
Brands:
 Door Spy

26081 Micro Filtration Systems
PO Box 367
Elon College, NC 27244-0367
 336-570-1933
Fax: 336-570-1933
Wine industry laboratory equipment

26082 Micro Matic
19761 Bahama St
Northridge, CA 91324
 818-701-9765
Fax: 818-341-9501 sac@micro-matic.com
www.micro-matics.com
Manufactures liquid transfer valves and related equipment
President: Peter Muzzonigro
CFO: Jim Motush
Sales Manager: Barry Broughton
Contact: Allen Cossairt
allen@micro-matics.com
Estimated Sales: $20-50 Million
Number Employees: 50-99
Parent Co: Micro Matic AIS
Type of Packaging: Bulk

26083 Micro Qwik
1017 Park St
Cross Plains, WI 53528-9631
 608-798-3071
Fax: 608-798-4452
webmaster@plasticingenuity.com
www.plasticingenuity.com
Dual-ovenable plastic containers
President: Thomas Kuehn
Sales Manager: Denny McGuigan
Sales: Janet Erdman
Estimated Sales: $20-50 Million
Number Employees: 250-499
Parent Co: Plastic Ingenuity

26084 Micro Solutions Ent Tech & Dev
8201 Woodley Ave
Van Nuys, CA 91406-1231
 818-718-0911
Fax: 818-407-7575 800-673-4968
info@mse.com www.mse.com
Packaging equipment including specialties, metal parts, cartoners, conveyors, collators and assembly equipment
President: Martha Sherman
CEO: John Sherman
VP: Scott Sherman
Marketing Manager: Scott Sherman
Contact: Oscar Aguilar
oaguilar@mse.com
Estimated Sales: $1-2.5 Million
Number Employees: 5-9
Square Footage: 100000

26085 Micro Wire Products Inc
120 N Main St
Brockton, MA 02301-3911
 508-584-0200
Fax: 508-584-1188 jwmwp@aol.com
www.microwire-products.com
Manufacturer and importer of welded wire baskets, store diplays and fixtures and dishwasher and tray racks
Owner: Jeff Weafer
jwmwp@aol.com
Controller: Linda Weaver
Treasurer: Arnold Wilson
Estimated Sales: $5-10 Million
Number Employees: 20-49
Square Footage: 280000

26086 Micro-Blend
2550 4th Street
Ingleside, TX 78362-5911
 361-776-0179
Fax: 361-776-3787 microblend@aol.com
Number Employees: 80

26087 Micro-Brush Pro Soap
1830 E Interstate 30
Rockwall, TX 75087-6241
 972-722-1161
Fax: 972-722-1584 800-776-7627
www.prosoap.com
Manufacturer and exporter of hand cleaning scrubs and pastes for removing inks, food coloring and food odors; also, soap dispensers
President: Scott L Self
VP Operations: James Wilkins, III

Estimated Sales: $10-20 Million
Number Employees: 5-9
Square Footage: 36000
Parent Co: Texas Nova-Chem Corporation
Type of Packaging: Food Service
Brands:
　Micro-Brush
　Pro Soap

26088 Micro-Chem Laboratory
Building A, Unit 16
Mississauga, ON L5T 2L5
Canada

905-795-0490
Fax: 905-795-0491 info@micro-chem.com
Consulting laboratory providing microbiological,
nutritional and product development services
President: Ash Mathur
Lab Manager: Nancy Reynolds
Number Employees: 10
Square Footage: 20000

26089 Micro-Strain
291 Stony Run Rd
Spring City, PA 19475

610-948-4550
Manufacturer and exporter of digital and analog
electronic measuring systems and devices including
scales and weighing systems
President: Rolf Jespersen
Estimated Sales: Less than $500,000
Number Employees: 1-4
Square Footage: 10000

26090 MicroAnalytics
4500 140th Avenue
Ste. 101
Clearwater, FL 33762

727-483-5562
Fax: 727-538-4237 info@mapmechanics.com
www.bestroutes.com
Computer software, routing and scheduling software
distribution planning and translation Of distribution
logistics
President: J Michael Hooban
Director Sales: Ted Hooban
Estimated Sales: Below $5 Million
Number Employees: 10-19
Brands:
　Bustops
　Truckstop

26091 MicroFlo Company
530 Oak Court Dr # 100
Memphis, TN 38117-3722

901-432-5000
Fax: 901-432-5100 www.arysta-na.com
Wine industry pheromones
VP: John Reid
Estimated Sales: $20-50 Million
Number Employees: 20-49

26092 MicroThermics, Inc.
3216-B Wellington Ct
Raleigh, NC 27615

919-878-8045
Fax: 919-878-8032 info@microthermics.com
www.microthermics.com
Manufacturer and exporter of laboratory and food
processing equipment for pasteurization and aseptic
purposes.
President: John Miles
Executive Vice President: David Miles
VP Sales, Marketing, Business Operations: David
Miles
Estimated Sales: $5-10 Million
Other Locations:

26093 Microbac Laboratories
101 Bellevue Rd # 301
Suite 301
Pittsburgh, PA 15229-2132

412-459-1060
Fax: 866-515-4668 866-515-4668
microbac_info@microbac.com
www.microbac.com
Consultant/laboratory firm providing environmental
air, water and waste testing for EPA and OSHA com-
pliance; also, food testing for nutritional value, bac-
teria, quality control, etc
President/CEO: J Trevor Boyce
Chairman: A Warne Boyce
Executive Vice President: Warne Boyce
Technical Director: Bryan Hauger
Chief Operating Officer: Sean Hyde

Estimated Sales: $10-20 Million
Number Employees: 10
Square Footage: 30000
Parent Co: Microbac Laboratories

26094 Microbac Laboratories
2000 Corporate Drive
Wexford, PA 15090-7611

724-934-5030
Fax: 724-934-5088 cearle@microbac.com
www.microbac.com
Analytical services and consulting
Executive Vice President: Warne Boyce
Technical Director: Bryan Hauger
Technical Service/Market Development: Thomas
Zierenberg
Contact: Wade Delong
wade.delong@microbac.com
Chief Operating Officer: Sean Hyde
Estimated Sales: $10-20 Million
Number Employees: 250-499

26095 Microbac Laboratories Inc
101 Bellevue Rd # 301
Suite 301
Pittsburgh, PA 15229-2132

412-459-1060
Fax: 866-515-4668 microbac_info@microbac.com
www.microbac.com
Laboratory consultant providing nutritional labeling,
sanitation inspections, plastic container/wrap analy-
sis, shelf-life studies and pathogen testing services
Chairman, President & CEO: J. Trevor Boyce
Senior Vice President: Robert S. Crookston
Technical Director: Bryan Hauger
Chief Operating Officer: Sean Hyde
IT: Lynette Bauer
lbauer@microbac.com
Estimated Sales: $500,000-$1 Million
Number Employees: 250-499
Parent Co: Microbac Laboratories

26096 Microbac-Wilson Devision
3809 Airport Dr NW
Wilson, NC 27896-8649

252-237-4175
Fax: 252-237-9341 www.microbac.com
Analytical laboratory specializing in chemical and
microbiological analysis of food samples. Nutri-
tional label analysis, nutaceutical analysis, and
camera ready nutirtional labels
Executive Director: Robert Dermer
CAO: Jeff Taylor
jeff.taylor@microbac.com
Marketing/Sales: Walter Nogg
Department Manager: Martin Donenco
Estimated Sales: $10-20 Million
Number Employees: 50-99
Square Footage: 42000
Parent Co: Microbac Laboratories

26097 Microbest Inc
670 Captain Neville Dr # 1
Waterbury, CT 06705-3855

203-597-0355
Fax: 203-597-0655 800-426-4246
www.microbest.com
Manufacturer and exporter of cleaning supplies and
equipment including microbial floor cleaners, de-
greasers, treatment products, etc
President: Ed Mc Nerney
emcnerney@microbest.com
CEO: Michael Troup
VP Sales/Marketing: Gary Garavaglin
Estimated Sales: $1-5 Million
Number Employees: 50-99
Brands:
　Bio Cleansing Systems
　Microbest, Inc.

26098 Microbiologics Inc
200 Cooper Ave N
St Cloud, MN 56303-4440

320-253-7400
Fax: 320-253-6250 800-599-2847
info@microbiologics.com
www.microbiologics.com
CEO: Bradley D Goskowicz
bgoskowicz@mbl2000.com
CEO: Robert Corborn
National Sales Manager: Julie Sundgaard
Estimated Sales: $1-5 Million
Number Employees: 50-99

26099 Microbiology International
5111 Pegasus Ct
Suite H
Frederick, MD 21704-8318

301-662-6835
Fax: 301-662-8096 800-396-4276
info@800ezmicro.com www.800ezmicro.com
Supply systems that automate sample preparation,
bacterial enumeration and media preparation/plate
and tube filling; provides complete media prepara-
tion services
Owner: Kevin Klink
Contact: Lauren Axline
lauren.axline@800ezmicro.com
Product Manager: Bill Richman
Estimated Sales: Below $5 Million
Number Employees: 10-19

26100 Microcheck Solutions
9777 West Gulf Bank Ste C-5
PO Box 984
Humble, TX 77347

713-856-9801
Fax: 713-460-0240 800-647-4524
www.microchecksolutions.com
Point of sale equipment
Marketing Manager: Barbara Collins
Sales Manager: Barbara Collins
Estimated Sales: $1-3 Million
Number Employees: 1-4
Square Footage: 20000

26101 Microcool
30670 Hill St
Thousand Palms, CA 92276-2618

760-322-1111
Fax: 760-343-1820 800-322-4364
info@microcool.com www.microcool.com
Wine industry temperature and humidity control sys-
tems, patio misting and cooling
Owner: Mike Lemche
mlemche@microcool.com
Marketing: Mark Stanley
Sales: Jim Murphy
Estimated Sales: $3-5 Million
Number Employees: 10-19

26102 Microdry
5901 W Highway 22
Crestwood, KY 40014-7217

502-241-8933
Fax: 502-241-5907 engineering@microdry.com
www.nemeth-engineering.com
Manufacturer and exporter of industrial microwaves
Owner: Peter Nemeth
info@nemethengineering.com
Systems Specialist: Mark Isgryg
Plant Manager: Herb Bullis
Estimated Sales: $2.5-5 Million
Number Employees: 20-49
Square Footage: 100000

26103 Microflex Corp
2301 Robb Dr
Reno, NV 89523-1901

775-746-6600
Fax: 775-746-6577 800-876-6866
jfarris@microflex.com
Food handling gloves
President: Mike Mattos
CEO: Lloyd Rogers
Director Sales: Chris Verhulst
Contact: Brian Sublett
brians@microflex.com
Manager West Coast Food Service: Karen Baum
Manager Industrial Division: Mike Williamson
Estimated Sales: $20-50 Million
Number Employees: 1-4
Brands:
　Micro Flex

26104 Microfluidics International
90 Glacier Dr # 1000
Suite 1000
Westwood, MA 02090-1818

617-969-5452
Fax: 617-965-1213 800-370-5452
www.microfluidicscorp.com
Manufacturer and exporter of high pressure mixing
equipment for processing emulsions, dispersions,
liposomes, particle size reduction, deagglomeration,
high end food, flavorings and colorants

President: Robert Bruno
CEO: Irwin Gruverman
Controller: Dennis Riordan
Marketing Communications Manager: Wendy Rogalinski
Number Employees: 20-49
Square Footage: 60000
Brands:
Microfluidizer Pro.Equipment

26105 Micromeritics
4356 Communications Dr
Norcross, GA 30093-2901

770-638-7569
Fax: 770-662-3696 www.micromeritics.com
Manufacturer and exporter of analytical instruments for production and process control application
President: Preston Hendrix
Estimated Sales: $20-50 Million
Number Employees: 100-249
Type of Packaging: Bulk

26106 Micron Automation
4516 W North a St
Tampa, FL 33609-2039

813-637-8810
Fax: 813-637-8819 www.morrisautomation.com
President: Peter Buczynsky
Vice President Technical Operations: Ingo Federle
Vice President Sales And Service: Ben Brower

26107 Micron Separations
135 Flanders Rd
Westborough, MA 01581-1031

508-366-8212
Fax: 508-366-5840 800-444-8212
Wine industry filtration equipment
Estimated Sales: $5-10 Million
Number Employees: 50-99

26108 Microplas Industries
2364 Brookhurst Dr
Dunwoody, GA 30338

770-234-0600
Fax: 770-234-0601 800-952-4528
Manufacturer and importer of polyethylene shrink film and black conductive and antistat LDPE and HDPE bags
President: John J Cawley
Estimated Sales: Below $500,000
Number Employees: 1-4
Square Footage: 10000
Brands:
Hi Shrink
Micorduct
Microstat

26109 Micropoint
1077 Independence Ave # B
Mountain View, CA 94043-1601

650-969-3097
Fax: 650-969-2067 www.microfit.com
Manufacturer, importer and exporter of writing and marking pens
President: Paul Vodak
Estimated Sales: less than $500,000
Number Employees: 1-4
Brands:
Art-Stik
Color Brush
Color-Craft
Facts Finder
Fine-Stik
Fits All
Gripper
Ink Stik
Ink-Stik 'n' Holder
Micro-Mini
Mustang
Perma-Mark
Phone Pen
Pinto
Premier
Super Marker
Unimark
White Board Marker
Wik Stik
Win Pen

26110 Micropub Systems International
10 Milford Rd
Rochester, NY 14625

585-385-3990
Fax: 585-385-4387 www.micropub.com

Manufacturer and exporter of beer brewing systems; processor of brewing ingredients
Manager: Barb Smith
Estimated Sales: Below $500,000
Number Employees: 10-19
Square Footage: 80000
Brands:
Micropub

26111 Micropure Filtration Inc
1100 Game Farm Cir
Mound, MN 55364-7900

952-472-2323
Fax: 952-472-0105 800-654-7873
tsenney@micropure.com www.micropure.com
Manufacturer, importer and exporter of food and beverage filtration and regulating devices including segmented stainless steel, cartridge, air, processing, sampler, trap filter removers and air filters, culinary steam.
President: Trey Senney
Estimated Sales: Less Than $500,000
Number Employees: 1-4
Square Footage: 4000
Brands:
Glas-Flo
Mem-Pure
Micro-Pure
Pro-Flo
Segma-Flo
Segma-Pure

26112 Microscan Systems Inc
700 SW 39th St # 100
Renton, WA 98057-2316

425-226-5700
Fax: 425-226-8250 800-762-1149
info@microscan.com www.microscan.com
Bar code scanning equipment
President: Steve Holahan
sholahan@microscan.com
CFO: Mark Milburn
Marketing Director: Laura Hoffman
Sales Director: Bill Westgate
Public Relations: Susan Snyder
Operations Manager: Jerry Naumcheff
Production Manager: Jim Murray
Purchasing Manager: Mike Moritz
Estimated Sales: $10-20,000,000
Number Employees: 100-249
Number of Brands: 1
Number of Products: 9
Type of Packaging: Private Label
Brands:
Microscan

26113 Microtechnologies
123 Whiting St. Ste 1A
Plainville, CT 6062

860-829-2710
Fax: 860-516-1549 888-248-7103
support@temperatureguard.com
www.temperatureguard.com
Manufacturer and exporter of HVAC controls
President: Frank Geissler
Estimated Sales: Below $5,000,000
Number Employees: 5-9
Square Footage: 8000

26114 Microthermics
3216 Wellington Ct # 102
Raleigh, NC 27615-4122

919-878-8045
Fax: 919-878-8032 info@microthermics.com
www.microthermics.com
Specializes in the simulation, scale up, and scale down of UHT, HTST, Aseptic, continuos cooking and hot-fill process
President: John Miles
Vice President: David Miles
Regional Technical Sales Manager: Edgardo Vega
Manager: Mike Gregory
Estimated Sales: $1-3 Million
Number Employees: 20-49

26115 Microtouch Systems Inc
501 Griffin Brook Dr
Methuen, MA 01844-1870

978-659-9000
Fax: 978-659-9100 touch@mmm.com
Point of sale touch screen systems
Contact: Ricardo Alcantara
ralcantara@mmm.com
Number Employees: 500-999

Brands:
Microtouch

26116 Microtron Abrasives
10424 Rodney St
Pineville, NC 28134

704-889-7256
Fax: 704-889-5102 800-476-7237
www.glit-microtron.com
Abrasive and nonabrasive handpads, metal sponges, cellulose sponge products, griddle screens, soap impregnated abrasive pads, nonwoven floor maintenance pads and related accessories
Manager: Jeff Dean
VP/COO: Robert Quigley
Contact: David Blackington
fmcclure@u.washington.edu
Estimated Sales: $20-50 Million
Number Employees: 5-9
Square Footage: 100000
Parent Co: Katy Industries
Brands:
Hef-T-Clean
Jif-Y-Clean
Pot-N-Pan Handler
Soap-N-Scrub

26117 Microwave Research Center
3856 Princeton Cir
Eagan, MN 55123-1520

651-456-9190
Fax: 651-454-6480
Consultants specializing in microwave technology, products and strategies; also, development of single and 2-mode applicators and related switch-mode power supplies
Project Director: Jan Claesson
VP: Per Risman
Estimated Sales: $.5-1 million
Number Employees: 1-4
Square Footage: 10000
Parent Co: Rubbright Group
Brands:
Microduction
Thermalizer

26118 Microworks Pos Solutions Inc
2112 Empire Blvd # 2a
Suite 2A
Webster, NY 14580-1935

585-787-2058
Fax: 585-787-2289 800-787-2068
www.microworks.com
Point of sale hardware and software for dine-in, carry out and delivery restaurants,prism for windows,prism classictouch,prism classiclite
Manager: Tim Freida
timf@microworks.com
Estimated Sales: Less than $500,000
Number Employees: 10-19

26119 Mid Atlantic Packaging Co
14 Starlifter Ave
Dover, DE 19901-9200

302-734-8833
Fax: 302-734-8698 800-284-1332
sales@midatlanticpackaging.com
www.midatlanticpackaging.com
Bags, boxes, fill material, labels, ribbons and bows
Owner: Herb Glanden
Marketing: Don Glanden
Sales Director: Donald Glanden
hgmap@dmv.com
Estimated Sales: $3-7 Million
Number Employees: 20-49
Number of Brands: 50
Number of Products: 25
Square Footage: 60000

26120 Mid Cities Paper Box Company
7661 Fostoria Street
Downey, CA 90241-3240

562-927-1431
Fax: 562-927-3271 877-277-6272
Paper boxes, folding cartons, laminate, foil stamp, window in-house and displays
President/CEO: Ken Sipple
Owner: Norm Sipple
Marketing Director: Angie Saavedra
Sales Director: Mike Sipple
Purchasing Manager: Letha Lands
Estimated Sales: $12 Million
Number Employees: 85
Square Footage: 220000

Type of Packaging: Consumer, Food Service, Private Label

26121 Mid South Graphics
PO Box 110889
Nashville, TN 37222-0889

615-331-4210
Fax: 615-331-4367
Pressure sensitive labels and tags
Customer Service Manager: Patricia Davenport
Estimated Sales: $4 Million
Number Employees: 20-50
Square Footage: 60000

26122 Mid West Quality GlovesInc
835 Industrial Rd
Chillicothe, MO 64601-3218

660-646-2165
Fax: 660-646-6933 800-821-3028
www.midwestglove.com
Manufacturer and exporter of work, garden and sports protective gloves
Chairman of the Board: Stephen Franke
sfranke@midwestglove.com
Marketing Manager: Shirley Fisher
Sales Manager: Clark Carlton
Estimated Sales: $20-50 Million
Number Employees: 100-249
Brands:
  Smart Hands
  Wolverine

26123 Mid-Lands Chemical Company
1202 S 11th St
Omaha, NE 68108-3611

402-346-8352
Fax: 402-346-7694 800-642-5263
orders@midlandsci.com www.midlandsci.com
Manufacturer and exporter of ice packs
Account Manager: Brian Plautz
Operations Manager: Matt Sutej
Estimated Sales: $1-2,500,000
Number Employees: 10-19
Type of Packaging: Food Service, Private Label
Brands:
  Polar Pack

26124 Mid-Southwest Marketing
3900 S Broadway
Edmond, OK 73013-4115

405-341-3962
Fax: 405-359-9043
Bubble gum dispensers; also, maintenance available
Manager: Teresa Brown
Estimated Sales: Less than $500,000
Number Employees: 1-4

26125 Mid-State Awning & Patio Co
113 Musser Ln
Bellefonte, PA 16823-9163

814-355-8979
Fax: 814-355-1405 tepawning@aol.com
www.midstateawning.com
Commercial awnings
President: Terry Phillips
tepawning@aol.com
Estimated Sales: $400,000
Number Employees: 5-9

26126 Mid-State Metal Casting& Mfg
2689 S 10th St
Fresno, CA 93725-2041

559-445-1974
Fax: 559-445-1320
Aluminum casters
President: Dave Pittman
Estimated Sales: Less Than $500,000
Number Employees: 1-4

26127 Mid-States Mfg & Engr Co Inc
509 E Maple St
PO Box 100
Milton, IA 52570-9636

641-656-4271
Fax: 641-656-4225 800-346-1792
www.mid-states1.com
Manufacturer and exporter of steel shipping containers, hand and platform trucks and nonpowered material handling equipment
Cio/Cto: Kevin Early
kevinearly@mid-states1.com
COO: Kevin Early
Purchasing Director: Suzie Lister

Estimated Sales: $5 Million
Number Employees: 20-49
Square Footage: 280000
Type of Packaging: Bulk

26128 Mid-West Wire Products
800 Woodward Hts
Ferndale, MI 48220-1488

248-548-3200
Fax: 248-542-7104 800-989-9881
schargo@midwestwire.com
Manufacturer and exporter of wire baskets and specialties including display, transporter and merchandising trays
President: Richard Geralds
VP: Steven Chargo
Vice President: Christopher Wozniacki
cwozniacki@midwestwires.com
VP Sales: Steven Chargo
VP Manufacturing: William Klein
Estimated Sales: $5-10 Million
Number Employees: 20-49

26129 Midbrook Inc
1300 Falahee Rd # 51
Jackson, MI 49203-4700

517-787-3481
Fax: 517-787-2349 800-966-9274
sales@midbrook.com www.midbrookmetalfab.com
Manufacturer and exporter of washing, drying and wastewater treatment equipment
CEO: Mick Lutz
mlutz@midbrook.com
CEO: Mick Lutz
Manufacturing Manager: E Houghton
Estimated Sales: $20-50 Million
Number Employees: 100-249
Brands:
  Hurricane Systems

26130 Midco Plastics
800 S Bluff St
Enterprise, KS 67441-9112

785-263-8999
Fax: 785-263-8231 800-235-2729
jjahn@midcoplastics.com www.midcoplastics.com
Plastic bags, covers and linings including printed or plain
President: Mike Carney
General Manager/VP: Michael Carney
Treasurer: Jeff Jahn
Estimated Sales: $10-20 Million
Number Employees: 20-49
Square Footage: 54000

26131 Middleby Corp
1400 Toastmaster Dr
Elgin, IL 60120-9272

847-741-3300
sales@middleby.com
www.middleby.com
Manufacturer, importer and exporter of conveyor and convection ovens, ranges, fryers, toasters and steamers.
Chief Executive Officer: Timothy Fitzgerald
Chief Operating Officer: Devid Brewer
Corporate Treasurer: Martin Lindsay
Estimated Sales: #2.72 Billion
Number Employees: 5000-9999
Other Locations:
  Middleby Corp.
  Miramar FL
Brands:
  Middlebe Marshal
  Rofry
  South Bend
  Toast Master

26132 Middleby Marshall Inc
1400 Toastmaster Dr
Elgin, IL 60120-9272

847-741-3300
www.middmarshall.com
Manufacturer and exporter of high speed conveyor ovens for pizza, bagels, pretzels and full service restaurants; also, ranges, broilers, combi ovens, toasters, hot food warmers and steam equipment
President: John Kania
Year Founded: 1888
Estimated Sales: $50-75 Million
Number Employees: 100-249
Square Footage: 285000
Parent Co: Middleby Corporation
Type of Packaging: Food Service

Other Locations:
  Middleby Marshall, CTX
  Elgin IL
Brands:
  Ctx
  Middleby Marshall
  Southbend
  Toastmaster

26133 Middleton Printing & Label Co
200 32nd St SE # A
Grand Rapids, MI 49548-2269

616-247-8742
Fax: 616-247-1352 800-952-0076
www.gomiddleton.com
Pressure sensitive roll and sheet labels, tags, name plates, commerical printing, booklets, forms, custom laser labels, etc.
President: Blake Middleton
blake@gomiddleton.com
Estimated Sales: $1-3 Million
Number Employees: 5-9
Square Footage: 40000

26134 Middough Inc
1901 E 13th St # 300
Suite 400
Cleveland, OH 44114-3542

216-367-6000
Fax: 216-367-6020 contactus@middough.com
www.middough.com
Middough's full service, single-source organization, provides food processors and distributors with professionals versed in HACCP, FDA, GMP, AIB, BISSIC, USDA, 3A Dairy and cGMP, as well as state-of-the-art technology, sanitary andsafety design practices for civil, structural, mechanical, electrical and controls. Applicable products in the food industry includes that of commodities/ingredients; processed foods and beverages.
President/CEO: Ronald Ledin
VP: Paul W. Jahn
Business Development Director: James Bingham
Number Employees: 250-499

26135 Midland Manufacturing Co
101 E County Line Rd
Monroe, IA 50170-7950

641-259-2625
Fax: 641-259-3216 800-394-2625
marianne@midlandmfgco.com
www.midlandmfgco.com
Blow molded plastic containers
President: Terry Vriezelaar
terry@midlandmfgco.com
Vice President: Jeff Vriezelaar
Estimated Sales: $5 Million
Number Employees: 20-49
Square Footage: 100000

26136 Midland Research Labratories
851 N Martway Drive
Olathe, KS 66061-7053

913-888-0560
Fax: 913-492-7860
Boiler water and cooling water treatment, food process chemicals for prevention of can corrosion and spotting plus chlorine dioxide
President: John Opelka
R & D: James Rauh
Quality Control: Fred Hopkins
Estimated Sales: $5-10 Million
Number Employees: 10

26137 Midlands Packaging Corp
4641 N 56th St
Lincoln, NE 68504-1795

402-464-9124
Fax: 402-464-6720
midlandspkg@midlandspkg.com
www.midlandspkg.com
Folding cartons, corrugated containers, and thermoformed plastics.
President: Steven Warman
warmans@midlandspkg.com
Quality Assurance Manager: Pat Moser
Production Services Manager: Doug Smith
Plant Manager: Gary Riecke
Estimated Sales: $20-25 Million
Number Employees: 100-249
Square Footage: 235000

26138 Midmac Systems
590 Hale Ave N
Saint Paul, MN 55128
651-739-1700
Fax: 651-739-1777
Custom machinery, robotics, systems integration, automatic assembly
Contact: Larry Kopacek
midmac@midmac.net
Estimated Sales: $10-20 Million
Number Employees: 50-99

26139 Midvale Paper Box
19 Bailey St
Wilkes Barre, PA 18705-1907
570-824-3577
Fax: 570-824-4639 midvalebox@hotmail.com
www.midvalebox.com
Set-up and folding boxes including pizza boxes, bakery boxes, frozen food boxes, beer 6-packs and 4-packs. stadium trays and meat boxes
President: David Frank
dfrank@midvalebox.com
Estimated Sales: Below $5 Million
Number Employees: 20-49
Number of Products: 150
Square Footage: 200000

26140 Midwest Aircraft Products Co
125 S Mill St
Lexington, OH 44904-9571
419-884-2164
Fax: 419-884-2331 www.midwestaircraft.com
Manufacturer and exporter of food handling equipment including liquid containers, ice drawers, oven racks and beverage drawers and carts for airline food services
Owner: Jerry Miller
j.miller@midwestaircraft.com
CFO: Gayle Gorman Freeman
Engineering Manager: Matt Marles
CEO: Gayle Gorman Freeman
Sales: Richard Baker
Manufacturing: Lee Craii
Production: Gene Wheitner
Purchasing Manager: Chuck Kumisarek
Estimated Sales: $10-20 Million
Number Employees: 10-19
Square Footage: 26000

26141 Midwest Badge & NoveltyCo
3337 Republic Ave
Minneapolis, MN 55426-4108
952-927-9901
Fax: 952-927-9903
Manufacturer, importer and wholesaler/distributor of name badges, buttons and advertising specialties
President: Kevin Saba
kevin.saba@mgincentives.com
Estimated Sales: Less than $500,000
Number Employees: 1-4
Square Footage: 16000
Type of Packaging: Consumer, Private Label, Bulk

26142 Midwest Box Co
9801 Walford Ave # C
Suite C
Cleveland, OH 44102-4788
216-281-3980
Fax: 216-281-5707 www.midwestboxco.com
Corrugated containers
Owner: Suzy Remer
Manager: Susie Remer
susie@midwestboxco.com
Estimated Sales: $10-20 Million
Number Employees: 20-49

26143 Midwest Fibre Products Inc
2819 95th Ave
Viola, IL 61486-9527
309-596-2955
Fax: 309-596-2901
Boxes including corrugated and folding
Owner: Domenico Dulio
Estimated Sales: $5-10 Million
Number Employees: 20-49

26144 Midwest Folding Products
1414 S Western Ave
Chicago, IL 60608
312-666-3366
Fax: 312-666-2606 800-344-2864
sales@midwestfolding.com
www.midwestfolding.com
Banquet and meeting room tables in lighweight plastic, steel edge plywood and high-pressure plastic laminate with plywood core tops. Comfort Leg meeting room tables afford your guests unobstructed knee space and increase seatingcapacity, dual-height cocktail tables, table storage and handling systems are also available
CEO: Darryl Rossen
CFO: Len Farrell
Vice President: Chuck Pineau
Marketing Director: Ken Hufstater
Sales Director: Bob Bishop
Plant Manager: Sam Thomas
Purchasing Manager: Oscar Ortiz
Estimated Sales: $35 Million
Number Employees: 100-249
Number of Brands: 1
Square Footage: 200000
Type of Packaging: Bulk
Brands:
   Midwest

26145 Midwest Foodservice News
2736 Sawbury Boulevard
Columbus, OH 43235-4579
614-336-0710
Fax: 614-336-0713
A regional food service publication with more than 28,000 readers in Ohio, Michigan, Indiana, Kentucky, Pennsylvania, and West Virginia

26146 Midwest Industrial Packaging
PO Box 1927
Spartanburg, SC 29304-1927
864-503-2200
Fax: 864-503-2430 800-910-5592
millichem@milliken.com
www.millikenchemical.com
Packaging tools
President: Thomas J Malone
Estimated Sales: $5-10 Million
Number Employees: 50

26147 Midwest Juice
3993 Roger B Chaffee Mem SE #F
Suite F
Grand Rapids, MI 49548-3404
616-774-6832
Fax: 616-774-0373 877-265-8243
info@midwestjuice.com www.midwestjuice.com
Beverages, coffee dispensers, aseptic portion cups
President: Mike Luhn
Owner: Noel Luhn
Number Employees: 5-9
Type of Packaging: Food Service, Private Label, Bulk
Brands:
   Triarc Beverages
   Veryfine

26148 Midwest Laboratories
13611 B St
Omaha, NE 68144-3693
402-334-7770
Fax: 402-334-9121 info@midwestlabs.com
www.midwestlabs.com
Consultant specializing in sanitation, analysis and testing services
President: Ken Pohlman
Estimated Sales: $500,000-$1 Million
Number Employees: 100-249

26149 Midwest Laboratories
13611 B St
Omaha, NE 68144-3693
402-334-7770
Fax: 402-334-9121 getinfo@midwestlabs.com
www.midwestlabs.com
Laboratory specializing in the testing of food and agricultural products; also complete nutritional labeling, environmental and microbiological services available
CEO: Ken Pohlman
Finance Ex: Laura Honeycutt
Quality Control: Jerry King
Marketing: Brent Pohlman
Estimated Sales: $5-10 Million
Number Employees: 100-249
Square Footage: 130000

26150 Midwest Metalcraft & Equipment
200 Industrial Dr
Windsor, MO 65360
660-647-3167
Fax: 660-647-5580 800-647-3167
sales@4mmc.com.www.4mmc.com
Stainless steel food processing equipment including vats, hoppers, screw conveyors, dumpers, mixers, blenders, liquid chilling systems, bel conveyors, spiral ham slicers an multi-blade band saw.
President: Dennis Brown
Contact: Ed Barnhart
ebarnhart@4mmc.com
General Manager: Jay Warren
Production Manager: Alan Cooper
Estimated Sales: $5-10 Million
Number Employees: 20-49
Number of Brands: 1
Number of Products: 10
Square Footage: 56000

26151 Midwest Paper Products Company
1237 S 11th St
Louisville, KY 40210
502-636-2741
Corrugated boxes
Sales Manager: Woody Heckenkomp
Estimated Sales: $20-50 Million
Number Employees: 20-49
Square Footage: 50000

26152 Midwest Paper Tube & CanCorporation
2800 S 163rd St
New Berlin, WI 53151
262-782-7300
Fax: 262-782-7330
Paper cans and tubes
Owner: Ron Karani
CFO/QC: Sharon Mahoney
Estimated Sales: $5-10 Million
Number Employees: 10-19

26153 Midwest Promotional Group
2011 S Frontage Rd
Summit, IL 60527
708-563-0600
Fax: 708-563-0603 800-305-3388
sales@midwestgrp.com www.midwestgrp.com
Manufacturer and wholesaler/distributor of advertising calendars, embroidered aprons, uniforms, shirts, etc.; also, silk screening available
President: David Lewandowski
CEO: Don Lewandowski
VP: Keith Vacey
Chairman: Don Lewandowski
Sales Director: Rick Dignault
Operations Manager: Roger Wilson
Accounting Executive: Jeff Feichtinger
Estimated Sales: $5-10 Million
Number Employees: 50-99
Square Footage: 33000

26154 (HQ)Midwest Rubber Svc & Supply
14307 28th Pl N
Minneapolis, MN 55447-4867
763-559-2551
Fax: 763-559-4429 800-537-7457
Standard conveyor belts, cleated flexible vanner edges, center guides and die cut rubber collapsible containers; also, custom fabrication, design and field vulcanizing available
Owner: Kathy Kroah
Cio/Cto: John Briesch
jbriesch@midwestrubber.com
Inside Sales Manager: Dave Newell
Purchasing Agent: Todd Winn
Estimated Sales: $300,000-500,000
Number Employees: 20-49
Square Footage: 120000

26155 Midwest Stainless
408 3M Drive NE Suite B
Menomonie, WI 54751
715-235-5472
Fax: 715-235-5484
Manufacturer and exporter of dairy tanks, CIP systems, heat exchangers, cheese presses, pumps, valves, fittings and complete turn-key process systems for the food, dairy and biotechnical industries

President : Joe Maxfield
VP & General Manager: Josh Hoover
Sales Engineer: Tim Jenneman
Operations Manager : Rob Hesse
Estimated Sales: $10-20 Million
Number Employees: 20-49
Square Footage: 38000

26156 Midwest Wire Products LLC
649 S Lansing Ave
Sturgeon Bay, WI 54235-2853

920-743-6591
Fax: 920-743-3777   800-445-0225
mwp@wireforming.com www.wireforming.com
Wire forms, grills, racks, shelves, baskets, etc.; contact services available
President: Eric Vollrath
CFO: Judy Weber
HR Executive: Sally Beisner
mwp@wireforming.com
Engineering: John Buhk
Quality Control: Wendy Woodgate
Marketing/Sales: Dirk Huenink
Production Manager: Mike Noble
Plant Manager: Steve Culver
Purchasing Manager: Judy Weber
Estimated Sales: $7 Million
Number Employees: 50-99
Square Footage: 170000

26157 Midwest Wire Specialties
4545 W Cortland St
Chicago, IL 60639-5104

773-292-6300
Fax: 773-292-6304   800-238-0228
info@midwestwirechicago.com
www.midwestwirechicago.com
Custom point of purchase displays, material handling and filter baskets, guards, wire forms, oven racks and smoke sticks
CEO: Marion K Sitkiewicz
marios@midwestwirechicago.com
Estimated Sales: $50-100 Million
Number Employees: 20-49
Square Footage: 55000

26158 Midwestern Bulk Bag
3230 Monroe St
Toledo, OH 43606-4519

419-241-3112
Fax: 419-241-0080   800-448-6494
New and reconditioned bulk bags, standard and custom made containment racks , polyethylene bags
CEO: Tony O'Neal
VP: Paula Lalor
Production Manager: T King
Estimated Sales: $2.5-5 Million
Number Employees: 5-9
Square Footage: 45000

26159 Midwestern Industries Inc
915 Oberlin Ave SW
Massillon, OH 44647-7661

330-837-4203
Fax: 330-837-4210 info@midwesternind.com
www.midwesternind.com
Round and rectangular vibrating screening equipment, replacements parts and screens, electric screen heating products for rectangular vibrating machines
President: Barb Sylvester
info@midwesternind.com
Estimated Sales: $10-20 Million
Number Employees: 50-99

26160 Mies Products
505 Commerce St
West Bend, WI 53090-1698

262-338-0676
Fax: 262-338-1244   800-480-6437
info@miesproducts.com www.miesproducts.com
Processor and exporter of breading for chicken, fish, meats and vegetables; also, holding and display warmers and electric pressure fryers and filter machines for fats and oils
President: Mike Mies
VP: Mike Mies
Sales: Mark Mey
Purchasing Director: Ed Casey
Estimated Sales: $3-5 Million
Number Employees: 10-19
Number of Brands: 1
Number of Products: 10
Square Footage: 135040
Type of Packaging: Food Service, Private Label

Brands:
　Karbonaid Xx
　Mies

26161 Migali Industries
516 Lansdowne Ave
Camden, NJ 08104-1198

856-963-3600
Fax: 856-963-3604   800-852-5292
contact@migali.com www.migali.com
Manufactures a complete line of G3 reach-in refrigerators and freezers, glass door merchandisers, sandwich tables, pizza preparation tables, and beer equipment. Also distributes Brema Ice Cream Makers, high quality machines inclusingundercounter and modular cubes and flakers.
President: Ernest Migali
Estimated Sales: $5-10 Million
Number Employees: 20-49

26162 Migatron Corp
935 Dieckman St # A
Suite A
Woodstock, IL 60098-9203

815-338-5800
Fax: 815-338-5803   888-644-2876
info@migatron.com www.migatron.com
Manufacturer, exporter and importer of ultrasonic sensors
President: Frank Wroga
info@migatron.com
Estimated Sales: $2.5-5 Million
Number Employees: 10-19
Brands:
　Tubular Sonics

26163 Mikasa Hotelware
1 Mikasa Drive
Secaucus, NJ 07094-2581

201-867-9210
Fax: 201-867-2385   866-645-2721
gwen_opfell@mikasa.com www.mikasa.com
Manufacturer, exporter and importer of china, dinnerware and crystal
VP: Neil Orzeck
Contact: John Beaupre
jbeaupre@mikasa.com
Number Employees: 100-249

26164 Miken Cosmpanies
PO Box 178
Buffalo, NY 14231-0178

716-668-6311
Fax: 716-668-7630
Packaging machinery including pressure sensitive label, adhesive coating, die cutting and foil stamping
President: Michael Bolas
President: M Bolas
Estimated Sales: $20-50 Million
Number Employees: 100-249
Other Locations:
　Miken Cos.
　Buffalo NY

26165 Mil-Du-Gas Company/StarBrite
4041 SW 47th Ave
Fort Lauderdale, FL 33314-4031

954-587-6280
Fax: 954-587-2813   800-327-8583
peter@starbrite.com www.starbrite.com
Manufacturer and exporter of mildew preventers with air fresheners and maintenance and cleaning chemicals
CEO: Peter Dornau
CFO: Jeff Barocas
Executive Vice President: Gregor Dornau
Vice President, Technology: Justin Gould
VP of Marketing / Art Dept & Literature: Bill Lindsey
Senior Vice President, Sales: Marc Emmi
Vice President, Sales: Dennis Torok
Vice President, Operations/Manufacturing: Will Dudman
Number Employees: 20-49
Square Footage: 560000
Parent Co: Ocean Bio-Chem
Other Locations:
　Mil-Du-Gas Co./Star Brite
　Montgomery AL
Brands:
　Extend-A-Brush
　M-D-G Formula-2
　Star Brite

26166 Milan Box Corporation
2090 West Van Hook Street
P.O. Box 30
Milan, TN 38358

731-686-3338
Fax: 731-686-3330 800-225-8057
andrew@milanbox.com www.milanbox.com
Plywood pallet boxes, crates and wirebound and wooden boxes; exporter of wirebound boxes
President: Franklin Dedmon
franklin@milanbox.com
Finance Manager: Donna Hardy
VP: Andrew Dedmon
President/Head Sales/Marketing: Franklin Dedmon
Head of Operations: Freddy McCartney
Head of Production: Rudy Graves
Estimated Sales: $10-20 Million
Number Employees: 50-99
Brands:
　Mylanbox Ibc

26167 Milburn Company
520 Bellevue Street
Detroit, MI 48207-3733

313-259-3410
Fax: 313-259-3415
Manufacturer and exporter of soap and soap dispensers, manufacturing, skincreams and lotions
VP/Marketing: Frank Newman
Estimated Sales: Less than $500,000
Number Employees: 1-4
Square Footage: 20000
Brands:
　Ply Skin Cream

26168 Mile Hi Express
1335 40th St
Denver, CO 80205-3310

303-296-8465
Fax: 303-296-8468 800-332-2064
www.milehiexpress.com
President: Brit Schabacker
dispatch@milehiexpress.com
Comptroller/Operations: Diana Troute
Estimated Sales: $3-5 Million
Number Employees: 10-19

26169 Miles Willard Technologies
655 W Sunnyside Rd
Idaho Falls, ID 83402-4707

208-523-4741
Fax: 208-529-8236 mwt@snackteam.com
www.snackteam.com
Research and development consultant for snack foods and potato processing
Managing Partner: Randy Kern
Research Manager: Veldon Hix
Estimated Sales: $10-20 Million
Number Employees: 10-19
Square Footage: 60000

26170 Military Club & Hospitality
825 Old Country Rd
Westbury, NY 11590-5501

516-334-3030
Fax: 516-334-3059 ebm-mail@ebmpubs.com
www.ebmpubs.com
President: Murry Greenwald
Estimated Sales: $10-20 Million
Number Employees: 1-4

26171 Miljoco Corp
200 Elizabeth St
Mt Clemens, MI 48043-1643

586-777-4280
Fax: 586-777-7891 888-888-1498
info@mijoco.com www.miljoco.com
Manufacturers standard and custom thermometers.
President: Howard M Trerice
htrerice@miljoco.com
Reaserch Development: Heath Trerice
Quality Control: Bruce Trerice
Marketing: Mike Mroz
Sales: Tom Adams
Public Relations: Mike Mroz
Plant Manager: Alex Jakob
Purchasing: Kimberly Trerice
Estimated Sales: $10-20 Million
Number Employees: 20-49
Square Footage: 94000
Brands:
　Miljoco

26172 Mill Engineering & Machinery Company
727 66th Avenue
Oakland, CA 94621-3713
510-562-1832
Barley grain roller mills
Estimated Sales: $500,000-$1 Million
Number Employees: 4

26173 Mill Equipment Co Inc
124 S Dodge St # 3
Burlington, WI 53105-1900
262-763-9101
Fax: 262-763-9102 800-551-9101
skippercad@aol.com www.milleqp.com
Bins: bulk storage, hoppers; bulk handling systems:
conveying, conveyor accessories, conveyor
componenets, conveyors, feeder belts
Estimated Sales: $500,000-$1 Million
Number Employees: 1-4

26174 Mill Wiping Rags Inc
1656 E 233rd St
Bronx, NY 10466-3306
718-994-7100
Fax: 718-994-1973 ragmaster67@optonline.net
www.millwipingrags.com
Manufacturer and exporter of wiping rags, cheese-
cloth and paper wipes, bar towels
President: F Scifo
millrags@optimaline.net
Quality Control: A Pimento
Marketing Director: Eric Saltzman
Sales Director: Eric Saltzman
Plant Manager: F Scifo
Purchasing Manager: Eric Saltzman
Estimated Sales: $2 Million
Number Employees: 50-99
Number of Brands: 3
Number of Products: 100
Parent Co: D. Benedetto
Type of Packaging: Private Label, Bulk

26175 Mill-Rose Co
7995 Tyler Blvd
Mentor, OH 44060-4896
440-946-5727
Fax: 440-255-5039 800-321-3598
www.millrose.com
Manufacturer and exporter of grill and basting
brushes
President: Paul Miller
millrose@en.com
CFO: Vincent Pona
Sales Manager: Gregory Miller
Purchasing Manager: Susan Stallknict
Estimated Sales: $20 Million
Number Employees: 100-249
Brands:
Clean Fit

26176 Millard Manufacturing Corp
10602 Olive St
La Vista, NE 68128-2993
402-331-8010
Fax: 402-331-0909 800-662-4263
sales@millardmfg.com www.millardmfg.com
Conveyors and food processing equipment for can-
ners, poultry and frozen food processors; also, walk
surfaces available
Vice President: Mike Price
mprice@millardmfg.com
VP: Mike Price
VP Administration: Mike Price
VP Sales: Harold Ellis
Purchasing Agent: Lynn Hedell
Estimated Sales: $5-10 Million
Number Employees: 50-99
Square Footage: 130000
Brands:
Optigrip

26177 Millenia Industries Corp
PO Box 953909
Lake Mary, FL 32795-3909
407-804-1193
Fax: 407-804-1934
Manager: Frank Benevento
beneventofrank@milleniahope.com
Estimated Sales: Less Than $500,000
Number Employees: 1-4

26178 Miller Group Multiplex
1610 Design Way
Dupo, IL 62239-1826
636-343-5700
Fax: 618-286-6202 800-325-3350
info@miller-group.com www.otpracks.com
Manufacturer and exporter of store fixtures and dis-
play systems including point of purchase
President: Randy Castle
CFO: Roger Lovejoy
Director Marketing: Tony Evans
Marketing: Catherine Lafarth
Marketing Services: Cathy Berding
Estimated Sales: $10-20 Million
Number Employees: 20-49
Square Footage: 80000
Parent Co: Miller Multiplex
Brands:
Multiplex

26179 Miller Hofft Brands
PO Box 1323
Indianapolis, IN 46206-1323
317-638-6576
Fax: 317-638-9438
Conveying systems, bulk material bins, hoppers and
screw conveyors
President: James Kuester
Estimated Sales: $1-5,000,000

26180 Miller Manufacturing Co
2032 Divanian Dr
Turlock, CA 95382-9501
209-632-3846
Fax: 209-632-1369 miller@thevision.net
www.miller-mfg.com
Recycling machines
President: Richard Veeck
R&D: George Lazich
Estimated Sales: Below $5 Million
Number Employees: 5-9

26181 Miller Metal Fabrication
16356 Sussex Hwy # 2
Bridgeville, DE 19933-3056
302-337-2291
Fax: 302-337-2290 www.millermetal.com
U.S.D.A. approved conveyors, poultry chill tanks
and hand carts; also, parts available
Owner: Marty Miller
marty@millermetal.com
VP: H Thompson
Estimated Sales: $5 Million
Number Employees: 20-49

26182 (HQ)Miller Studio
734 Fair Ave NW
PO Box 997
New Philadelphia, OH 44663-1589
330-339-1100
Fax: 330-339-4379 800-332-0050
www.miller-studio.com
Manufacturer and exporter of pressure sensitive
double-coated tape for decorative trim, mounting,
fastening, etc.; also, adhesive systems
President: John Basiletti
Purchasing Manager: Tina Schlemmer
Sales: Mark Gazdik
Estimated Sales: $5-10 Million
Number Employees: 50-99
Type of Packaging: Consumer
Brands:
Magic-Mounts

26183 Miller Technical Svc
47801 W Anchor Ct
Plymouth, MI 48170-6018
734-414-1769
Fax: 734-738-1975 millerstec@cs.com
www.nextmobilitynow.com
Manufacturer and exporter of rebuilt and used pack-
aging and food processing equipment; also, machin-
ery parts; repair and rebuilding services available
President: James Miller
CEO: Patrick Miller
pmiller@mtsmedicalmfg.com
Estimated Sales: $.5-1 million
Number Employees: 20-49
Square Footage: 6000
Type of Packaging: Food Service

26184 Millerbernd Systems
330 6th St S
P.O. Box 37
Winsted, MN 55395-1102
320-485-2685
Fax: 320-485-3900
Design, manufacture and install processing equip-
ment for the dairy and cheese industries such as pas-
teurization and heat transfer units, controls and
automation systems, agitating tanks, batching/blend-
ing and barrel handlingsystems.
President: Brad Millerbernd
bmillerbernd@millerbernd.com
VP: Terry Voight
National Sales Manager: Lisa Stanger
Product Manager: Frank Bruggman
Purchasing: Sam Zimmerman
Number Employees: 100-249

26185 Millhiser
1125 Commerce Road
Richmond, VA 23224-7505
804-233-9886
Fax: 804-233-1931 800-446-2247
Plastic and cloth bags
President: Willard Foster
VP Sales/Marketing: James Bledsoe
Estimated Sales: $10-20,000,000
Number Employees: 100-249

26186 Milligan & Higgins
PO Box 506
Johnstown, NY 12095
518-762-4638
Fax: 518-762-7039 info@milligan1868.com
www.milligan1868.com
Manufacturer, importer and exporter of kosher ed-
ible and technical gelatins.
Year Founded: 1868
Parent Co: Hudson Industries Corporation
Type of Packaging: Bulk

26187 Milliken & Co
P.O. Box 1926
Spartanburg, SC 29304
864-503-2020
brand@milliken.com
www.milliken.com
Aprons, table cloths and skirting and place mats.
Chief Executive Officer: J. Harold Chandler
Year Founded: 1865
Number Employees: 7,000
Brands:
Ambassador
Embassy
Visa

26188 Milltronics
734 W North Carrier Pkwy
Grand Prairie, TX 75050-1001
817-277-3543
Fax: 817-277-3894 www.milltronics.com
Wine industry measuring devices
Estimated Sales: $10-20 Million
Number Employees: 50-99

26189 Millwood Inc
3708 International Blvd
Vienna, OH 44473-9796
330-393-4400
Fax: 330-393-4401 lwilliamson@citynet.net
www.millwoodinc.com
Pallets and industrial blockings
President: Keith Ainsley
kainsley@millwoodinc.com
CEO: Larry Supple
CPA/Controller: Mark Price
Estimated Sales: $5-10 Million
Number Employees: 20-49

26190 Milprint
PO Box 2968
Oshkosh, WI 54903-2968
920-303-8600
Fax: 920-303-8610 milprint@bemis.com
Printed flexible packaging materials for the confectionery industry, including coatings, laminations,
films and adhesives for foil, cellophane, glassine and
paper

President: Robert Hawthorne
Alliance Manager: Karen Cverko
CFO: Stephanie Rucinski
Quality Control: Dennis Howard
Marketing Manager: Mike Miller
Contact: Dan Kearny
d.kearny@milprint.com
Estimated Sales: $10-20 Million
Number Employees: 10
Parent Co: Bemis Company

26191 Milsek Furniture PolishInc.
5525 E Pine Lake Rd
North Lima, OH 44452

330-542-2700
Fax: 330-542-1059 www.milsek.com
Manufacturer, exporter and wholesaler/distributor of furniture polish and cleaner
President: Jean Hamilton
VP: Susan Bender
Estimated Sales: Under $1 Million
Number Employees: 5-9
Number of Brands: 1
Number of Products: 2
Square Footage: 108000
Brands:
  Milsek

26192 Miltenberg & Samton
4 High Street
Suite 7
Stamford, CT 06902-4923

203-834-0002
Fax: 203-321-1348
High speed flow wrapper, confectionery wrapping machinery, extruders and cooling tunnels for cut and wrap products, complete infeed and discharge systems, flexible packaging films
President: Ronald Kehle
Estimated Sales: $3-5 Million
Number Employees: 8
Square Footage: 200

26193 Milton A. Klein Company
PO Box 363
New York, NY 10021-0006

516-829-3400
Fax: 516-829-3427 800-221-0248
President: Irene Klein
VP: Allen Klein
Number Employees: 15
Square Footage: 6800

26194 Milton Can Company
PO Box 1100
Elizabeth, NJ 07207-1100

908-289-8100
Fax: 908-355-2397
Tea and coffee cans, papers (electrolytic)
Estimated Sales: $25-50 Million
Number Employees: 70

26195 Milvan Food Equipment Manufacturing
Units #1-3
Rexdale, ON M9W 5S5
Canada

416-674-3456
Fax: 416-674-2386
Commerical kitchen equipment including tables, exhaust canopies and back bars
President: Rocco Mazziotta
Number Employees: 10

26196 Milwaukee Dustless Brush Co
1632 Hobbs Dr
Delavan, WI 53115-2029

323-724-7777
Fax: 323-724-1111 sales@milwaukeedustless.com
www.milwaukeedustless.com
Manufacturer, importer and exporter of floor brushes, squeegees, sponge mops, utility brushes and related janitorial maintenance tools
National Sales Manager: Jeff Feder
Estimated Sales: $5-10 Million
Number Employees: 50-99
Brands:
  Speed Squeegy
  Speed Sweep
  Speedy Mop

26197 Milwaukee Sign Company
2076 1st Ave
Grafton, WI 53024

262-375-5740
Fax: 262-376-1686
Manufacturer and exporter of internally illuminated signs and menu systems
President: Kevin Sutherby
R&D: Rick Richards
Contact: Nancy Stansy
rcarlson@kdhe.state.ks.us
Estimated Sales: $20-30 Million
Number Employees: 100-249
Type of Packaging: Food Service, Bulk

26198 Milwaukee Tool & MachineCompany
PO Box 94
Okauchee, WI 53069-0094

262-821-0160
Fax: 262-821-0162 mtmco@execpc.com
Manufacturer and exporter of packaging machinery
President: Richard Mumper
VP: Ralph Mumper
Estimated Sales: $5-10 Million
Number Employees: 10

26199 Mimi et Cie
P.O.Box 80157
Seattle, WA 98108-0157

206-545-1850
Fax: 800-284-3834 www.mimietcie.com
Manufacturer, importer and exporter of decorative packaging including shrink and printed basket wrap and food bags for cookies, candy, etc. Also waxed tissue paper, food containers and custom products including bags, totes andribbons
President: Mark Revere
Estimated Sales: $1-2.5 Million
Number Employees: 50-99
Square Footage: 80000
Type of Packaging: Consumer, Food Service, Private Label, Bulk
Brands:
  Bagskets
  Blooming Bags
  Goodie Bags
  Shimmer

26200 Minarik Corporation
905 East Thompson Avenue
Glendale, CA 91201

800-646-2745
Fax: 800-394-6334 888-646-2745
Contact: Adam Abrahamson
adam.abrahamson@minarik.com
Parent Co: Kaman Corporation

26201 Mince Master
6530 W Dakin St
Chicago, IL 60634-2412

773-282-0722
Fax: 773-282-9744 888-646-2362
tech@mincemaster.com www.mincemaster.com
Emulsifiers, accessories, grinder plates and knives
Owner: Mike Mihailovic
Estimated Sales: $1-3 Million
Number Employees: 10-19

26202 Minges Printing & Advg Specs
323 S Chestnut St
Gastonia, NC 28054-4542

704-867-6791
Fax: 704-867-3596 mingesco@belsouth.net
www.mingesprinting.com
Advertising specialties
President: Gene Minges Sr
sedcbfox@aol.com
Estimated Sales: $500,000-$1 Million
Number Employees: 5-9
Square Footage: 12000

26203 Mini-Bag Company
83 Rome Street
Farmingdale, NY 11735-6699

631-694-3325
FDA approved polyethylene and plastic bags
Estimated Sales: $1-2.5 Million
Number Employees: 4

26204 Minipack
1832 N Glassell Sreet
Orange, CA 92865

714-283-4200
Fax: 714-283-4268 minipack@spm.it
www.minipack-america.com
Owner: Joe Sielski
Member: Joseph Sielski
Estimated Sales: $1-3 Million
Number Employees: 5-9

26205 Minners DesignsInc.
7 W 34th St
Suite 929
New York, NY 10001

212-688-7441
Fax: 212-980-6309 www.minners.com
Glassware and chinaware for the food service market
President: Maureen K Cole
Director Sales: Bernard Durkin
Director Purchasing: Maureen Cole
Estimated Sales: $1-2.5 Million
Number Employees: 5-9

26206 Minnesota Automation
975 3rd St SW
Crosby, MN 56441

218-546-2222
Fax: 218-546-2104 888-800-6861
Packaging machinery, pick and place machines
Manager: Greg Mangan
Marketing/Sales: Ken Campbell
Contact: Stephen Humphrey
sales@graphicpkg.com
Plant Manager: Greg Maegan
Estimated Sales: $25-50 Million
Number Employees: 100-249
Parent Co: Riverwood International Corporation
Brands:
  Minnesota Automation

26207 Minnesota Valley Testing Lab
1126 N Front St
New Ulm, MN 56073-1176

507-354-8517
Fax: 507-359-2890 800-782-3557
crc@mvtl.com www.mvtl.com
Turnkey liquid nitrogen systems
Owner/CEO/President: Thomas R Berg
CEO: Tom Berg
tberg@mvtl.com
Marketing: Rob TRUE
Sales: John Gray
Estimated Sales: $10-20 Million
Number Employees: 100-249
Square Footage: 78000

26208 Minnesuing Acres
8084 South Minnesuing Acres Drive
Lake Nebagamon, WI 54849

715-374-2262
Fax: 715-374-2118 jpolinsky@radisson.com
www.minnesuingacres.com
Consultant providing loyalty reward programs including electronic card and data based marketing, trading stamps, controlled markdowns, sweepstakes and related services
General Manager: Jim Polinsky
CFO: Tim Hennessy
VP/General Manager: Steve Aase
Director Marketing: Curt Lund
National Sales Manager: Brent Christiansen
Contact: Gregg Basset
gbasset@minnesuingacres.com
Estimated Sales: $3-5 Million
Number Employees: 20-49

26209 Minsa Southwest Corp
Hwy 84 E
Muleshoe, TX 79347

806-272-5545
Fax: 806-272-5135
Products for preparation of hot rack table tortillas, fresh or refrigerated, frozen tortilla or enchilada, hand feed tacos, in-line tacos and tortilla chips, extruded corn chips, tamales, and taquitos and/or enchiladas

President: Raul Ayala
raul.ayala@minsa.com
President: Jorge Arturo
CFO: Teresa Sitz
R&D: Jim Barne
Quality Control: Veronica Arroyo
Customer Service Head: Gina Smith
Estimated Sales: $5-10 Million
Number Employees: 50-99

26210 Minuteman Power Boss
175 Anderson St
Aberdeen, NC 28315
    314-283-7304
Fax: 910-944-7409 800-323-9420
info@minutemanintl.com www.powerboss.com
Manufacturer and exporter of power sweepers and scrubbers
President: Greg Rau
VP: Gregory Rau
Advertising Manager: Krista Harris
Estimated Sales: $5-10 Million
Number Employees: 100-249
Square Footage: 200000
Parent Co: Minuteman International
Other Locations:
  Minuteman PowerBoss
  Villa Park IL
Brands:
  Armadillo
  Badger
  Otter
  Prowler

26211 Minuteman Power Box Inc
175 Anderson Street
Aberdeen, NC 800-323-94
    910-944-2105
Fax: 910-944-7409 info@minutemanintl.com
www.powerboss.com
CEO: Greg Rau
Number Employees: 100-249

26212 Mione Manufacturing Company
51 Democrat Rd
Mickleton, NJ 8056
    856-423-1374
Fax: 856-423-6522 800-257-0497
Industrial and consumer use hand soap and laundry detergent
Manager: Benny Sorbello
Estimated Sales: $500,000-$1 Million
Number Employees: 1-4
Square Footage: 24000
Brands:
  Mione W P-1

26213 Miracle Exclusives
PO Box 2508
Danbury, CT 06813-2508
    203-796-5493
Fax: 203-648-4871 info@miracleexclusives.com
www.miracleexclusives.com
Home appliance pressure cooker
Vice President: Burn Wick
Estimated Sales: $500,000-$1 Million
Number Employees: 5

26214 Miroil
602 Tacoma St
Allentown, PA 18109-8103
    610-437-4618
Fax: 610-437-3377 800-523-9844
hgos1946@gmail.com www.miroil.com
Manufacturer and exporter of frying oil stabilizer, filter aids and clean and reusable filters for fryers; also, testing for polar and alkaline contaminants
President: Bernard Friedman
Manager: J Wessner
Contact: Bernard Firedman
bfiredman@miroil.com
Estimated Sales: $5-10 Million
Number Employees: 1-4
Square Footage: 140000
Brands:
  Ez Flow
  Frypowder
  Miroil

26215 Miron Construction Co.
1471 McMahon Dr.
Neenah, WI 54956
    920-969-7000
Fax: 920-969-7393
business.development@miron-construction.com
www.miron-construction.com
Pre-construction, construction management, design-build, general construction and industrial services to numerous markets, including the food processing industry.
President/CEO: David Voss
Vice President/COO: Tim Kippenhan
Secretary/Treasurer/CFO: Dean Basten
Year Founded: 1918
Estimated Sales: $500 Million
Number Employees: 1,500+
Square Footage: 112000

26216 Mirro Company
1115 W 5th Ave
Lancaster, OH 43130
    800-848-7200
Fax: 920-684-1929
Cookware, bakeware, tools and gadgets
Owner: Dave Moore
Estimated Sales: $1-5 Million
Number Employees: 1-4
Parent Co: Newell Companies
Type of Packaging: Food Service
Brands:
  Mirro Foley
  Rema
  Wearever

26217 Mirro Products Company
PO Box 2243
High Point, NC 27261
    336-885-4166
Fax: 336-885-1066
Plastic displays, vacuum-formed snack racks, plastic and electric signs
President: David Horney
Estimated Sales: $5-10 Million
Number Employees: 10-19

26218 Mirror Tech Mfg Co Inc
286 Nepperhan Ave
Yonkers, NY 10701-3403
    914-423-1600
Fax: 914-423-1667 mirrortech@verizon.net
www.mirror-tech.com
Glass, metal and acrylic observation convex mirrors
President: Richard Cleary
mirrortech@verizon.net
Treasurer and CFO: D Barnett
Quality Control: Frank Serine
Estimated Sales: Below $5 Million
Number Employees: 20-49
Square Footage: 28000

26219 Mission Laboratories
2433 Birkdale St
Los Angeles, CA 90031
    323-223-1405
Fax: 323-223-9968 888-201-8866
srose@missionlabs.net www.missionlabs.net
Commercial and household cleaning and sanitary supplies including floor finish and strippers, carpet cleaners, disinfectants, hand soaps, heavy duty cleaners/degreasers, sweeping compounds, etc. Supplier to the food industry andsuppliers to food service
President: Robert Rosenbaum
CFO: Robert Rosenbaum
Quality Control: David Schultz
Executive VP Sales/Marketing: Jim Ryan
Contact: Margarita Arzate
m.arzate@missionlabs.net
Estimated Sales: $20-50 Million
Number Employees: 20-49
Square Footage: 75000
Type of Packaging: Consumer, Food Service, Private Label, Bulk

26220 Missouri Equipment
2222 N 9th St
St Louis, MO 63102-1412
    314-621-0144
Fax: 314-621-4170 800-727-6326
meco2222@sbcglobal.net
Sink tops, counters and tables
President: Gregory Klapp
VP: C Klapp

Estimated Sales: $5 Million
Number Employees: 20-49
Square Footage: 120000

26221 Missouri Grocers Assn
315 N Ken Ave
Springfield, MO 65802-6213
    417-831-6662
Fax: 417-831-3907 www.missourigrocers.com
A non-profit, state-wide organization representing retailers, wholesalers, distributors, brokers, suppliers, vendors and manufacturters that formulate the grocery industry in the State of Missouri.
State Director: Dan Shaul
Estimated Sales: $5-10 Million
Number Employees: 5-9

26222 Mister Label, Inc
PO Box 326
Bluffton, SC 29910
    843-815-2222
Fax: 843-815-5488 800-732-0439
misterlabel@msn.com www.misterlabel.com
Manufacturer and exporter of labels including pressure sensitive, heat seal, gummed, tyvek and tag-stock
President: Todd Elliot
Chief Operating Officer: Kelly Elliot
Estimated Sales: $5-10 Million
Number Employees: 11
Square Footage: 30000
Type of Packaging: Food Service, Private Label, Bulk

26223 Mitec
2445 Meadowbrook Pkwy
Duluth, GA 30096-4636
    770-813-5959
Fax: 770-813-1818 888-854-1851
www.mitec.com
Manufacturers of insulated metal panels for commercial, industrial and cold storage buildings.
President: Bryan A. Shaver
bshaver@mitecnet.com
Estimated Sales: $1-5 Million
Number Employees: 100-249

26224 Mitsubishi Caterpillar Mcfa
2121 W Sam Houston Pkwy N
Houston, TX 77043-2316
    713-365-1000
Fax: 713-365-1441 800-228-5438
www.mcfa.com
Lift trucks and tires
CEO: Shigeru Tanemura
Mktg Head: Jennifer Evans
Estimated Sales: $3-5 Million
Number Employees: 500-999

26225 Mitsubishi Fuso Truck Of America
2015 Center Square Rd
Swedesboro, NJ 08085-1683
    856-467-4500
Fax: 856-467-4695 877-829-3876
R&D: Jim Peary
CEO: Jecka Glasman
jglasman@mitfuso.com
CEO: Bob Mc Dowell
Estimated Sales: $10-20 Million
Number Employees: 50-99

26226 Mitsubishi Gas ChemicalAmerica
655 Third Avenue
24th Floor
New York, NY 10017
    212-687-9030
Fax: 212-687-2812 888-330-6422
contact@mgc-a.com www.mgc-a.com
Contact: Satoshi Hayashi
satoshi.hayashi@mitsubishicorp.com
Estimated Sales: C
Number Employees: 250-499

26227 (HQ)Mitsubishi Intl. Corp.
520 Madison Avenue
Floor 18
New York, NY 10022-4327
    212-759-5605
Fax: 212-605-1810 800-442-6266
Food commodities: coffee, cocoa, dairy products, fruits, vegetables and frozen juice concentrates. Food ingredients, enzymes, emulsifiers, baking agents.

President: James Brumm
CFO: Yasuyuki Sugiura
Executive VP/COO: Yoshihiko Kawamura
Sales/Purchasing Representative: Patrick Welch
Contact: Keigo Ando
keigo.ando@mitsubishicorp.com
Number Employees: 250-499
Other Locations:
Seattle WA

26228 Mitsubishi Polyester Film, Inc.
2001 Hood Rd.
PO Box 1400
Greer, SC 29652

864-879-5000
Fax: 864-879-5006 contact@m-petfilm.com
www.m-petfilm.com
Biaxially oriented polyester films, and copolyester
shrink sleeve film.
President/CEO: Dennis Trice
Year Founded: 1991
Estimated Sales: $61 Million
Number Employees: 600
Number of Brands: 1
Number of Products: 100
Square Footage: 24239
Parent Co: Mitsubishi Chemical Corporation
Brands:
Hostaphan®

26229 Mity Lite Inc
1301 W 400 N
Orem, UT 84057-4442

801-224-0589
Fax: 801-224-6191 800-909-8034
info@mitylite.com www.mitylite.com
Lightweight and durable folding tables, folding
chairs, stacking chairs, carts, lecterns, portable parti-
tions and portable dance floors.
CEO: John Dudash
johnd@mitylite.com
Marketing Manager: Michael Peterson
Sales/Marketing Director: Kevin Stoker
Number Employees: 10-19
Square Footage: 108850
Brands:
Myti Host Chair
Myti Lite Tables
Myti Taff Chair
Summit Lectern
Swift Set Folding Chairs

26230 (HQ)Miura Boilers
1900 The Exchange SE # 330
Suite 330
Atlanta, GA 30339-2050
Canada

770-916-1695
Fax: 770-916-1858 atlanta@miuraz.com
Steam and hot water boilers for the food processing
plant.
President: Masashi Hirose
President: Mark Utzinger
Sales: Mike Mazzei
Manager: Yo Nakagawa
Estimated Sales: $1-2.5 Million
Number Employees: 5-9

26231 Mlp Seating
950 Pratt Blvd
Elk Grove Vlg, IL 60007-5119

847-956-1700
Fax: 847-956-1776 800-723-3030
www.mlpseating.com
Manufacturer and exporter of chairs, tables and bar
stools
President: Ralph D Samuel
rdsamuel@mlpseating.com
R&D: Ralph D Samuel
Quality Control: Goerge Stembridge
Sales: Steven Seres
Estimated Sales: $5-10 Million
Number Employees: 20-49

26232 Mmi Engineered Soultions Inc
1715 Woodland Dr
Saline, MI 48176-1614

734-429-4664
Fax: 734-429-4664 800-825-2566
info@moldedmaterials.com www.mmi-es.com
Manufacturer and exporter of custom molded totes
and trays for processing and shipping
Manager: Mike Wolf
COO: R Campbell
VP Engineering: T Elkington

Estimated Sales: Below $5 Million
Number Employees: 50-99
Square Footage: 160000

26233 Mobern Electric Corporation
8200 Stayton Dr.
Suite 500
Jessup, MD 20794

301-725-3030
Fax: 301-953-9310 800-444-9288
sales@mobern.com www.mobern.com
Lighting fixtures
Estimated Sales: $5-10 Million
Number Employees: 50-99

26234 Mobil Composite Products
PO Box 5445
Norwalk, CT 06856-5445

203-831-4200
Fax: 203-831-4222 800-BUY-TREX

26235 Mocon Inc
7500 Boone Ave N # 110
Minneapolis, MN 55428-1026

763-493-7229
Fax: 763-493-6358 info@mocon.com
www.mocon.com
Manufacturer and exporter of instrumentation, con-
sulting, and laboratory services to medical, pharma-
ceutical, food and other industries worldwide.
Develops and manufactures high technology instru-
mentation and provides consulting andanalytical ser-
vice to research laboratories, manufacturers and
quality control departments in the life sciences,
food/beverage, polymer/adhesives, electronic and
other industries
CEO: Robert Demorest
CFO: Darrell Lee
VP: Doug Lindemann
Research And Development: Dan Mayer
Marketing: Guy Wray
Sales: Betty Kauffman
Public Relations: Sophia Dilberakis
Production: Tim Ascheman
Estimated Sales: $25 Million
Number Employees: 120
Square Footage: 50000
Brands:
Gsa
Oxtran
Pac Check
Pac Guard
Permatran
Profiler
Skye

26236 Modar
1394 E. Empire Ave.
Benton Harbor, MI 49022

269-925-0671
Fax: 269-925-0020 800-253-6186
modar@qtm.net
Manufacturer and exporter of ready-to-assemble
store fixtures, shelving, point-of-purchase displays,
furniture and storage cabinets; also, particle board
laminating services available
President: Dennis Rousseau
Sales Manager: Gary Cichon
Inside Sales Manager: Jim Hendrix
Estimated Sales: $12.7 Million
Number Employees: 90
Square Footage: 300000
Other Locations:
Warehousing
Bridgman MI
Sales, Marketing, Design
Middletown CT

26237 Modern Baking Magazine
Ste 2300
330 N Wabash Ave
Chicago, IL 60611-7619

847-299-4430
Fax: 847-296-1968
Baking Inustry information
Estimated Sales: $1-3 Million
Number Employees: 10-19

26238 Modern Brewing & Design
3171 Guerneville Road
Santa Rosa, CA 95401-4028

707-542-6620
Fax: 707-542-3147

Manufacturer and exporter of barrel microbrewing
and brewpub equipment; also, support tanks and
stainless steel wine storage vessels
President: Daniel Shulte
Secretary: Russell Kargell
VP: Robert Kral
Number Employees: 32

26239 Modern Electronics Inc
280 Independence Ave
Grand Cane, LA 71032-5171

318-872-4764
Fax: 318-872-4768 www.me-equip.com
Pecan processing equipment
President: Richard M Oliver
Quality Control: Richard Oliver
Estimated Sales: $1-2.5 Million
Number Employees: 5-9

26240 Modern Metalcraft
1257 East Wackerly Rd.
Midland, MI 48642

989-835-3291
Fax: 989-835-8431 800-948-3182
www.modernmetalcraft.com
Metal products including displays
President/CEO: John D. Moore
Product Group Manager: Frank Robison
Estimated Sales: Below $5 Million
Number Employees: 10-19
Square Footage: 60000

26241 Modern Metals Industries
128 Sierra St
El Segundo, CA 90245

310-516-0851
Fax: 310-322-8617 800-437-6633
Metal cabinets, industrial carts and material han-
dling equipment
VP: Robert Lee Sherrill
Estimated Sales: $1-2,500,000
Number Employees: 19

26242 Modern Packaging
3245 N Berkeley Lake Rd NW
Duluth, GA 30096

770-622-1500
Fax: 770-814-0046
www.modernpackaginginc.com
Contract packager of condiments and liquid food
items; warehouse providing dry, cooler and humid-
ity-controlled storage of foodstuffs, liquid packaging
products and seasonal sales items; also, pick and
pack and rail siding available
President: Herb Sodel
VP: Nancy Sodel
Estimated Sales: $3.6 Million
Number Employees: 50-99
Square Footage: 400000

26243 Modern Packaging Inc
505 Acorn St
Deer Park, NY 11729-3601

631-595-2437
Fax: 631-595-2742
info@modernpackaginginc.com
www.modernpackaginginc.com
Designs and manufactures precision packaging sys-
tems for the food, dairy, cosmetic and drug indus-
tries
President: Golam Alam
purchasing@modernpackaginginc.com
Estimated Sales: Less Than $500,000
Number Employees: 1-4
Square Footage: 120000

26244 Modern Paper Box Company
166 Valley Street
Bldg 3
Providence, RI 02909-2458

401-861-7357
Fax: 401-272-2040
Paper boxes
Contact: Krista Olson
kolson@polygon.net
Number Employees: 10

26245 Modern Plastics
88 Long Hill Cross Rd # 4
Shelton, CT 06484-4783

203-333-3128
Fax: 203-333-4625 800-243-9696
customerservice@modernplastics.com
www.modernplastics.com

Plastic films.distributors of plastic sheets, tubes and films,provide custom fabrication. brands-ABS, Acetal, Ardel, Arlon, Acetron, Acculum, Acrylic, Benelex, ceanese, celazole PBI, Ensitep, hyzod sheets, isoplat, kel-F, Kydexkynar, lexan, MD nylon, Macrolux, Merlon, nylon, PAS, Peek, PCTFE, Phenolics, PET, PVDF, Radel, PVC, Rexolite, Rulon, Sanalite, Sintra, Sintimid, Surlyn, Teflon, Torlon, TPX, Valox, Victrex, Vespel, Warps, Xenoy, Zelux, Zytel
President: Bing Carbone
bcarbone@modernplastics.com
CEO: James Carborne
CFO: Patrick Roderick
Corporate VP: Robert Carbone
Quality Control: Daryl Guberman
Distribution Plastic Sales: Raymond Aneiro
VP Operations: Patrick Roderick
Fabrication/Production: Mark Moriarty
Corporate Purchasing Manager: John Fucci
Estimated Sales: $2.5-5 Million
Number Employees: 20-49

26246 Modern Process Equipment Inc
3125 S Kolin Ave
Chicago, IL 60623-4890
773-254-3929
Fax: 773-254-3935 solutions@mpechicago.com
www.mpechicago.com
Manufacture and market size reduction equipment for the coffee, food, chemical, mineral and pharmaceutical industry
President: Daniel Ephraim
daniel@mpechicago.com
Vice President: Phil Ephraim
Sales Director: Scott Will
Estimated Sales: $5-10 Million
Number Employees: 20-49

26247 Modern Stamp Company
1305 Saint Paul St
Baltimore, MD 21201
410-685-0505
Fax: 410-727-2146 800-727-3029
baumstamps@aol.com
Stamps, checks, seals, stencils, signs, trophies, awards, badges, labels, inks, printing dies, date and lot coding equipment and ink jet coders
Sales Manager: Dennis Burns
Manager: George Pagels
Estimated Sales: $1-2.5 Million
Number Employees: 5-9
Square Footage: 20000

26248 Modern Store Fixtures Company
1359 Medical District Drive
Dallas, TX 75207
214-634-2505
Fax: 214-634-2543 800-634-7777
customerservice@modernstore.com
www.modernstore.com
Glass display cases and store fixtures
VP: Lillian Knopf
General Manager: Bruce Meltzer
Estimated Sales: $5-10 Million
Number Employees: 10-19
Square Footage: 62000

26249 Modesto Tent & Awning
4448 Sisk Rd
Modesto, CA 95356-8729
209-545-6150
Fax: 209-545-6152
signs1@modestotentandawning.com
www.midvalleytarp.com
Awnings, canopies, tarps and tents
Owner: Suzanne Caragan
suzanne.caragan@kp.org
Secretary and Treasurer: Leonard Rigg
VP: Barney Valk
Estimated Sales: $1-2,500,000
Number Employees: 10-19
Square Footage: 36000

26250 Modular Packaging
6 Aspen Dr
Randolph, NJ 07869-1103
973-970-9393
Fax: 973-970-9388
customer.services@modularpackaging.com
www.modularpackaging.com

Packaging machinery including unscrambler desiccant feeders, shrink bundlers, cottoners, blister and case packers, cappers, etc.; importer of cartoners, case and blister packers, counters, etc.; exporter of liquid fillers, tube fillersand cottoners
President: Clifford Smith
cliffs@modularpackaging.com
Vice President: Bradford Smith
Estimated Sales: $3-5,000,000
Number Employees: 10-19
Square Footage: 36000
Brands:
  Eclipse
  Modular Kt
  Omega

26251 Modular Packaging
6 Aspen Dr
Randolph, NJ 07869-1103
973-970-9393
Fax: 973-970-9388
customer.service@modularpackaging.com
www.modularpackaging.com
Packaging line design, integration and service support, liquid filling lines, filling, blister packaging, closing and labeling machines
President: Clifford Smith
cliffs@modularpackaging.com
Estimated Sales: $3-5 Million
Number Employees: 10-19

26252 Modular Panel Company
63 David Street
New Bedford, MA 02744-2320
508-993-9955
Fax: 508-993-9957
Manufacturer and exporter of insulated panels for freezers and coolers
President: James Chadwick
Drafting Engineer: Pasquale Sbardella
Estimated Sales: Below $5 Million
Number Employees: 10

26253 Modularm Corporation
61 Mall Dr
Commack, NY 11725
631-864-3860
Fax: 631-864-3863
A temperature and refrigeration monitoring systems manufacturer with innovative products designed to protect perishables, save energy and increase operator safety.
President: Donald Olsen
Marketing Director: Bryan Barash
Sales Director: Marci Norwood

26254 Modulightor Inc
246 E 58th St
New York, NY 10022-2011
212-371-0336
Fax: 212-371-0335 www.modulightor.com
Manufacturer, importer and wholesaler/distributor of lighting fixtures
Owner: Ernst Wagner
ernst@modulightor.com
Estimated Sales: $1-2.5 Million
Number Employees: 10-19
Square Footage: 26000
Brands:
  Modulator

26255 Modutank Inc
4104 35th Ave
Long Island City, NY 11101-1410
718-392-1112
Fax: 718-786-1008 800-245-6964
info@modutank.com www.modutank.com
Above-ground, modular bolted steel tanks, liquid storage tanks, settling tanks, containment for earthen materials and slurries as well as a wide range of secondary containment systems for sanitary applications, tanker trucks andwheeled vehicles.
President: Reed Margulis
info@modutank.com
Estimated Sales: $1-5 Million
Number Employees: 10-19
Number of Products: 10

26256 Moeller Electric
4140 World Houstn Pkwy Ste 100
Houston, TX 77032
832-613-6250
Fax: 832-613-6225 800-394-5687
www.moellerusa.net

Motor controls, miniature and standard circuit breakers and custom control panels; also, switches including cam, PLC, pushbutton and safety limit
President: John Hamm
VP Marketing: Tom Thornton
Estimated Sales: $20-50 Million
Number Employees: 5-9

26257 Moen Industries
10330 Pioneer Blvd
Suite 230
Santa Fe Springs, CA 90670
562-946-6381
Fax: 562-946-3200 800-732-7766
rstorms@moenindustries.com
Manufacturer and exporter of corrugated box forming and sealing equipment
Owner: Carl Moen
Sales Co-coordinator: Iris Walker
Contact: Noreen Boos
boos@moenindustries.com
Purchasing Manager: Lori Maxey
Estimated Sales: $5-10 Million
Number Employees: 50-99
Square Footage: 76000
Brands:
  Blissmaster
  Lamo-Bliss
  Lamo-Tray

26258 Moffat
12000 Crownpoint Drive
Suite 100
San Antonio, TX 78233-5315
210-590-9381
Fax: 210-590-9479 866-589-0664
start.cortera.com
Half and full size electric and gas infrared convection ovens; also, proofers
Estimated Sales: $.5-1 Million
Number Employees: 5-10
Parent Co: Moffat
Brands:
  Bakbar
  Turbofan

26259 Mohawk Northern Plastics
PO Box 583
Auburn, WA 98071
253-939-8206
Fax: 253-939-4015 800-426-1100
Extruded and printed flexible polyethylene packaging including bags and film
President: Dan Mc Farland
CFO: Dan McFarlan
Sales Manager: Tom Couples
Estimated Sales: $20-50 Million
Number Employees: 100-249

26260 Mohawk Paper Mills
1400 Crescent Vischer Ferry Road
Clifton Park, NY 12065
518-371-6700
www.mohawkterrace.com
Coated and uncoated printing paper
Estimated Sales: $50-100 Million
Number Employees: 250-499

26261 Mohawk Western PlasticsInc
1496 Arrow Hwy
P.O. Box 463
La Verne, CA 91750-5297
909-593-7547
Fax: 909-596-8691
jhenderson@mohawkwestern.com
www.mohawkwestern.com
Polyethylene bags
President: Chris Mordoff
CEO: John Mordoff
cmordoff@mohawkwestern.com
Estimated Sales: $5-10 Million
Number Employees: 20-49

26262 Moisture Register Products
9567 Arrow Route
Suite E
Rancho Cucamonga, CA 91730
909-941-7776
Fax: 909-941-1830 800-966-4788
sales@aquameasure.com
www.moistureregisterproducts.com
Manufacturer and exporter of computers for measuring moisture content in solids for the food processing industry

Owner: John Lundstrom
Sales: Gabriel Cote
craig.mitchell@bankofamerica.com
Contact: Craig Mitchell
craig.mitchell@bankofamerica.com
Estimated Sales: $3-5 Million
Number Employees: 10-19
Parent Co: Aqua Measure Instrument Company
Brands:
Bsp901
Smart Ii

26263 Mol Belting Co
2532 Waldorf Ct NW
Grand Rapids, MI 49544-1478
616-453-2484
Fax: 616-453-2008 800-729-2358
sales@molbelting.com www.molbelting.com
Materials handling equipment, conveyors and accessories
President: Rick Mol
rmol@molbelting.com
Estimated Sales: $10-20 Million
Number Employees: 50-99

26264 Mold-Rite Plastics LLC
2222 Highland Rd
Twinsburg, OH 44087-2231
330-425-4206
Fax: 330-425-4586 marketing@weatherchem.com
www.weatherchem.net
A packaging company that designs, develops, and
delivers innovative dispensing closures.
CEO: Jennifer Altstadt
CFO: Bill Wolf
Research & Development: Barry Daggett
VP Marketing: Anna Fedova-Levi
Director of Sales: Jack Hotz
VP Operations: Carol Rinder
Estimated Sales: $10-20 Million
Number Employees: 100-249
Square Footage: 80000
Parent Co: Weatherhead Industries
Type of Packaging: Consumer, Food Service, Private Label
Brands:
Agricap
Flapper
Tec-Loc
Top-Squeeze

26265 Molded Container Corporation
1622 N Lombard St
Portland, OR 97217-5534
503-233-8601
Fax: 503-233-0621
Plastic containers and lids
Manager: Rick Copes
Estimated Sales: $16 Million
Number Employees: 100-249
Square Footage: 160000

26266 Molded Fiber Glass TrayCompany
6175 Highway 6
Lihesville, PA 16424
814-683-4500
Fax: 814-683-4504 800-458-6050
info@mfgtray.com www.mfgtray.com
Manufactures reinforced composite trays, containers, and flats used in the confectionery, bakery, food
service, pharmaceutical, and electronics industries as
well as many other markets for in-process handling
of goods.
Manager: Ron Orr
Contact: Eric Bennett
ebennett@moldedfiberglass.com
Estimated Sales: $20-50 Million
Number Employees: 100-249

26267 Molded Pulp Products
1780 Dreman Avenue
Cincinnati, OH 45223-2456
513-681-3016
Fax: 513-681-5121
Custom molded products
Estimated Sales: $20-50 Million
Number Employees: 50-99

26268 Molding Automation Concepts
1760 Kilkenny Ct
Woodstock, IL 60098
815-337-3000
Fax: 815-337-3020 800-435-6979
sales@macautomation.com
www.macautomation.com
Manufacturer and exporter of horizontal, incline and
elevator belt conveyors for automatic box, tote bag
and tray filling systems
President: Frank Altvedt
R&D: Frank Altvedt
Sales Manager: Randy Artheid
Contact: April Booze
april@centerforenrichedliving.org
Estimated Sales: $10-20,000,000
Number Employees: 50-99
Type of Packaging: Bulk

26269 Moli-International
1150 W Virginia Ave
Denver, CO 80223-2026
303-777-0364
Fax: 303-777-0658 800-525-8468
sales@moliinternational.com
www.moliinternational.com
Manufacturer and exporter of displays, sampling and
merchandising covers, pans, trays, clear plexiglass,
service carts, ice bins, water stations, sinks and
sneeze guards
Owner: Larry Larson
llarson@moliinternational.com
Secretary/Treasurer: Larry Larson
Estimated Sales: $500,000-$1 Million
Number Employees: 5-9
Square Footage: 25000
Type of Packaging: Food Service
Brands:
Merchant & Moli-Shields

26270 Moline Machinery LLC
114 S Central Ave
PO Box 16308
Duluth, MN 55807-2302
218-624-5734
Fax: 218-628-3853 800-767-5734
sales@moline.com www.moline.com
Manufacturer and exporter of proofing, frying and
dough processing systems for doughnuts, specialty
breads, snack foods and yeast raised products
President: Gary Moline
gmoline@moline.com
Sales Manager: Terry King
Engineering Director: Larry Meyer
Estimated Sales: $10-20 Million
Number Employees: 50-99
Square Footage: 190000
Brands:
Moline

26271 Molins/Sandiacre Richmond
8191 Brook Rd # G
Richmond, VA 23227-1334
804-421-8795
Fax: 804-421-8798 864-486-4000
sandiacre.usa@molins.com
Manufacturer, importer and exporter of packaging
machinery
Founder: Herman Hayssen
Vice President of Sales and Marketing: Dan Minor
Estimated Sales: $10-20 Million
Number Employees: 1-4

26272 Moll-Tron
1457 Ammons St
Lakewood, CO 80214-6108
303-969-8888
Fax: 303-969-8110 800-525-9494
www.molitron.com
Manufactures complete line of commercial kitchen
exhaust equipment including restaurant wet scrubbers, water scrubbing ventilators and restaurant odor
control systems for restaurants and other commercial
kitchens.
President: Scott Airhart
scott@molitron.com
Estimated Sales: Less Than $500,000
Number Employees: 1-4
Brands:
Moli-Tron

26273 Mollenberg-Betz Inc
300 Scott St
Buffalo, NY 14204-2293
716-614-7473
Fax: 716-614-7465 vmollen@mollenbergbetz.com
www.mollenbergbetz.com
Cold storage facilities, freezers, refrigeration equipment and parts; also, design and installation services
available. Design and installation of refrigeration
systems, suppliers of refrigeration equipment and
parts-service
Owner: Knut Lerdal
klerdal@hotmail.com
Quality Control: John Paytash
Executive VP: Joe Kilijanski
Purchasing: Gene Kaderbeck
Estimated Sales: $30 Million
Number Employees: 50-99
Square Footage: 30000

26274 Mollers North America Inc
5215 52nd St SE
Grand Rapids, MI 49512-9702
616-942-6504
Fax: 616-942-8825 www.mollersna.com
Designers and manufacturers of valve packing
equipment, bag handling conveyors, automatic bag
palletizers, pallet handling conveyors,
stretch-hooders and shrinkwrapping systems
Executive VP: Tom Wagner
Executive VP: Carlos Saenz
Contact: Brandi Ackerman
b.ackerman@mollersna.com
Estimated Sales: $10 Million
Number Employees: 50-99
Square Footage: 100000
Parent Co: Maschinenfabrik Mollers GmbHu Company

26275 Moly-XL Company
Ih 295 Business Ctr
Westville, NJ 8093
856-848-2880
Fax: 856-848-2799
Industrial greases, oils and lubricants
President: Frank Iacovone
VP: Kenneth Kunz
Number Employees: 5-9
Square Footage: 20000
Parent Co: Master Lubricants Company
Brands:
Moly-Xl

26276 Momar
1830 Ellsworth Industrial Drive NW
Atlanta, GA 30318-3746
800-556-3967
info@momar.com www.momar.com
Manufacturer and exporter of industrial maintenance
chemicals, water treatment products, lubricants and
cleaning chemicals for the food processing industry
Estimated Sales: $34 Million
Number Employees: 300
Square Footage: 50000
Brands:
Aquatrol
Lubest
Mochem
Momarket

26277 Momence Pallet Corp
11414 E State Route 114
Momence, IL 60954-3882
815-472-6451
Fax: 815-472-6453 www.momencepallet.com
Wooden pallets
President: Andrew Cryer
Secretary/Treasurer: Norm Cryer
Estimated Sales: $2.5-5 Million
Number Employees: 20-49
Square Footage: 100000

26278 Monadnock Paper Mills Inc
117 Antrim Rd
Bennington, NH 03442-4205
603-588-3311
Fax: 603-588-3158
Manufacturer and exporter of paper including uncoated cover, text, technical specialty and converting, nonwovens

President/Chairman/CEO: Richard Verney
rverney@mpm.com
Managing Director: Keith Hayward
Vice President/CFO/Treasurer: Andrew Manns
Vice President: Julie Hughes
Director, Information Technology: Joseph Gleason
Quality Control Manager: Richard Beahm
Vice President, Sales: James Clemente
Plant Manager: Dave Burnham
Purchasing Manager: Denise Long
Estimated Sales: $68 Million
Number Employees: 100-249
Square Footage: 300000

26279 Monarc Group
2928 41st Avenue
Suite 910b
Long Island City, NY 11101-3303
866-848-4283
Fax: 866-873-8625

26280 Monarch-McLaren
329 Deerhide Crescent
Weston, ON M9M 2Z2
Canada
416-741-9675
Fax: 416-741-2873
Manufacturer, importer and wholesaler/distributor of conveyor and transmission belting, V-belts, timing belts, variable speed belts, hoses, pulleys, chains, sprockets, bearings, speed reducers, casters, motors, couplings, belt lacingleather packings, etc
President: Terence Whitfield
Sales Manager: Brian Flint
Estimated Sales: Below $5 Million
Number Employees: 10
Square Footage: 72400
Brands:
  Monarch-Mclaren
  Polyplast
  Yorkcord
  Yorkedge
  Yorkflex
  Yorkgrip
  Yorklink
  Yorklon
  Yorkmate
  Yorkpack
  Yorktex
  Yorktex Leather

26281 Monastary Mustard
840 South Main Street
Angel, OR 97362
503-949-6321
Info@MonasteryMustard.com
monasterymustard.com
Mustard
Mustard Flavor Creator: Sister Terry Hall

26282 Monitor Company
P.O.Box 4411
Modesto, CA 95352-4411
209-523-0500
Fax: 209-523-4267 800-537-3201
Manufacturer and exporter of temperature recorders
Estimated Sales: $1-5 Million
Number Employees: 15
Brands:
  Temprecord

26283 Monitor Technologies LLC
44W320 Keslinger Rd
Elburn, IL 60119
630-365-9403
Fax: 630-365-5646 800-601-6204
monitor@monitortech.com www.monitortech.com
Level and flow monitoring products for powder and bulk solids
President/Owner: Craig Russell
Estimated Sales: $5+ Million
Number Employees: 20-49
Type of Packaging: Private Label
Brands:
  Bulksonics
  Dustalarm

26284 MonoSol
707 E 80th Pl
Merrillville, IN 46410
219-762-3165
Fax: 219-755-4062 www.monosol.com
Manufacturer of water-soluble films that can be used in the food manufacturing process.

Senior Manager, New Business Development:
Dorota Bartosik
Marketing & Sales Administrator: Kate Triemstra
Contact: Chris Addis
caddis@monosol.com
Parent Co: Kuraray
Other Locations:
  Production Facility
  Portage IN
  Production Facility
  La Porte IN
  Production Facility DuneLand
  Portage IN
  UK Production Facility
  Hartlebury, UK
  Production Facility
  Saijo, Japan

26285 Monoflo International Inc
882 Baker Ln
Winchester, VA 22603-5722
540-665-1691
Fax: 540-665-9785 800-446-6693
sales@miworldwide.com
Collapsible plastic containers
Owner: Gus Nusu
monoflo@miworldwide.com
Estimated Sales: $10-20 Million
Number Employees: 100-249

26286 Monon Process EquipmentCo
6289 N 150 E
Monon, IN 47959-8010
219-253-7777
Fax: 219-253-8580 www.mononprocess.com
President and CEO: Troy Paluchniak
sales@mononprocess.com
Estimated Sales: Below $5 Million
Number Employees: 1-4

26287 Monroe Environmental Corp
810 W Front St
Monroe, MI 48161-1627
734-242-7654
Fax: 734-242-5275 800-992-7707
sales@mon-env.com www.mon-env.com
Manufacturer oil mist, smoke and vapor collectors, venturi scrubbers, dust collectors, water & wastewater clarifiers.
Owner: Gary Pashaian
gpashaian@monroeenvironmental.com
Sales Manager: Adam Pashaian
Operations Manager: Rob Cardella
Estimated Sales: $15 Million
Number Employees: 50-99
Square Footage: 70000

26288 (HQ)Monroe Extinguisher Co Inc
105 Dodge St
Rochester, NY 14606-1503
585-235-3310
Fax: 585-235-7312 tcurtain@monroekitchen.com
www.monroeextinguisher.com
Custom stainless steel kitchen equipment: sinks, tables and hoods
President: Thomas Curtin
tcurtin@monroeextinguisher.com
Sales: Anthony Salemme
Plant Manager: Craig Mackey
Purchasing: Adam Curtain
Estimated Sales: Below $5 Million
Number Employees: 10-19
Square Footage: 50000
Other Locations:
  Monroe Kitchen Equipment
  Rochester NY

26289 Monsol
1701 County Line Road
Portage, IN 46368-1234
219-762-3165
Fax: 219-763-4477 800-237-9552
info@monosol.com www.monosol.com
Packaging water soluble film
General Manager: P Scott Bening
Product Development Manager: Jonathan Gallagher
Contact: Marianne Austin
marianneaustin@monosol.com
Clerk: Darlene Taylor
Estimated Sales: $1-5 Million
Number Employees: 50-99

26290 Montague Co
1830 Stearman Ave
Hayward, CA 94545-1018
510-785-8822
Fax: 510-785-3342 800-345-1830
www.montaguecompany.com
Manufacturer and exporter of commercial gas and electric cooking equipment. Products include convection ovens, deluxe griddles, heavy duty & medium duty ranges, counter equipment, fryers, over-fired and under-fired broilers, deckovens, chinese ranges, induction cooking equipment, under-counter refrigeration, and custom island suites.
President: Thomas Whalen
twhalen@montague-inc.com
VP Finance: R Erickson
VP Sales/Marketing: Gary Rupp
Purchasing: Lisa Catanzano
Estimated Sales: $30-30 Million
Number Employees: 100-249
Type of Packaging: Food Service
Brands:
  Grizzly
  Hearthbake
  Legend
  Vectaire

26291 Montalbano Development Inc
3275 Veterans Meml Hwy # B15
Ronkonkoma, NY 11779-7665
631-737-2236
Fax: 631-467-1035 800-739-9152
www.montalbanoinc.com
Provider of computer services for the food industry including
Owner: Chris Montalbano
chrism@montalbanoinc.com
VP: Chris Montalbano
Manager: Steghen Naroney
Estimated Sales: $2.5-5,000,000
Number Employees: 20-49

26292 Monte Glove Company
1208 Industrial Park Road
Wilkesboro, NC 28697-8490
662-263-5353
Fax: 662-263-5771
Work gloves, oven mitts, hand pads, sleeves
President: Glenn Clarke
Sales Manager: Theresa Lewis
Production: John Hall
Estimated Sales: $10-20 Million
Number Employees: 50-99
Parent Co: Golden Needles Knitting
Type of Packaging: Food Service, Private Label

26293 Monte Package Co
3752 Riverside Rd
Riverside, MI 49084-5101
269-849-1722
Fax: 269-849-0185 800-653-2807
www.montepkg.com
Packaging materials including boxes
President: Tony Monte
tonym@montepkg.com
Owner: Sam Monte
Estimated Sales: $10-20 Million
Number Employees: 10-19

26294 Montebello Container Corp
14333 Macaw St
La Mirada, CA 90638-5208
714-994-2351
Fax: 714-994-3875 sales@montcc.com
www.montcc.com
Corrugated containers
President: R. Anthony Salcido
Vice President: John Salcido
Production Superintendent: Roger Esquer
Estimated Sales: $5-10 Million
Number Employees: 100-249

26295 Montebello Packaging
1036 Aberdeen St
Hawkesbury, ON K6A 1K5
Canada
613-632-7096
Fax: 613-632-9638 bpilon@montebellopkg.com
www.montebellopkg.com
Aluminum aerosol cans & aluminum/laminate tubes

President: Betty Pilon
Chief Financial Officer: Greg Labuschagne
Vice President, Sales: Tom Zopf
Director of Information Technology: Jean-Francois Leclerc
Director of Quality Operations: Fred Long
Director of Sales: John Iorii
Estimated Sales: $20-50 Million
Number Employees: 240
Parent Co: The Jim Pattison Group
Brands:
    M-Bond
    M-Purity Ring
    M-Purity Seal

26296 Montello Inc
6106 E 32nd Pl # 100
Suite 100
Tulsa, OK 74135-5495

    918-665-1170
Fax: 918-665-1480 800-331-4628
www.montelloinc.com
Specialty industrial chemicals
President: Allen Johnson
allenj@montelloinc.com
Estimated Sales: $2.5 Million
Number Employees: 5-9

26297 Monterey Bay Food Group
661 Meadow Rd
Aptos, CA 95003-9786

    831-685-8600
Fax: 831-685-8656
Consultant providing strategic planning, marketing and product management; also, assessment of products and business opportunities
Market Research Manager: Amy Seibert
Contact: Charles Dyer
charley@mbfoodgroup.com
Operations Manager: Lora Keyte
Estimated Sales: $1-2.5 Million
Number Employees: 5-9

26298 Monument Industries Inc
159 Phyllis Ln
Bennington, VT 05201-1663

    802-442-8187
Fax: 802-442-8188
Manufacturer and exporter of polyethylene bags
Vice President: Jay L Whitten
VP: Jay L Whitten
Estimated Sales: $5-10 Million
Number Employees: 20-49

26299 Moog Components Group
1501 N Main St
Blacksburg, VA 24060-2523

    540-552-0382
Fax: 540-951-3832 800-382-5366
sales@electro-tec.com www.moog.com
Sliprings
Manager: Michelle Layne
mlayne@moog.com
Estimated Sales: $50-100 Million
Number Employees: 250-499

26300 Moog Inc
400 Jamison Rd # 26
East Aurora, NY 14052

    716-652-2000
Fax: 716-687-4457 800-272-6664
www.moog.com
Brushless servo motors and drives
President/COO/CEO: John Scannell
Chairman: Robert T. Brady
CFO: Donald Fishback
Manager: Kelly Lalley
Estimated Sales: Over $1 Billion
Number Employees: 10000+

26301 Moon Valley Circuits
12350 Maple Glen Rd
Glen Ellen, CA 95442

    707-996-4157
jill@moonvalleycircuits.com
www.moonvalleycircuits.com
Wine industry temperature controls
Owner: Mike Miller
mike@moonvalleycircuits.com
Quality Control: Michael Miller
CFO: Michael Miller
R&D: Michael Miller
Estimated Sales: Less Than $500,000
Number Employees: 1-4

26302 Moore Efficient Communication Aids
PO Box 11023
Denver, CO 80211

    303-433-8456
Fax: 303-433-8450
Marking devices, rubber stamps and sign systems
Owner: Ed Moore
Executive Secretary: Pam Craig
Production Manager: Leroy Eddy
Estimated Sales: $1-2.5 Million
Number Employees: 5-9
Square Footage: 30000
Type of Packaging: Private Label, Bulk
Brands:
    Lifetime
    Trodat
    X Stamper

26303 Moore Paper Boxes Inc
2916 Boulder Ave
Dayton, OH 45414-4834

    937-278-7327
Fax: 937-278-5932
Manufacturer and exporter of paper boxes
President: Charles Moore
Estimated Sales: $10-20 Million
Number Employees: 5-9

26304 Moore Production Tool Spec Inc
37531 Grand River Ave
Farmington Hills, MI 48335-2879

    248-476-1200
Fax: 248-476-6887
Manufacturer and exporter of sealing jaws, knives, anvils and packaging tooling
President: Durk Moore
CEO: Richard Moore
President: Richard Moore
Sales: Brian Carfango
Estimated Sales: $2.5-5 Million
Number Employees: 20-49
Square Footage: 56000

26305 Moore Push-Pin Co
1300 E Mermaid Ln
Glenside, PA 19038-7696

    215-233-5700
Fax: 215-233-0660 www.push-pin.com
Converting and batching equipment, specialty fasteners
President: Alice Cataldi
alicecataldi@push-pin.com
Estimated Sales: $5-10 Million
Number Employees: 50-99

26306 Moorecraft Box & Crate
101 Royster Street
PO Box 1528
Tarboro, NC 27886-1528

    252-823-2510
Fax: 252-823-2228 steve@moorecraft.com
www.moorecraft.com
Wood and plywood shipping boxes and crates and custom pallets
Owner: Stephen Redhage
VP: Sharon Redhage
Contact: Steve Redhage
steve@moorecraft.com
Estimated Sales: $1-2.5 Million
Number Employees: 50-99
Square Footage: 9000

26307 Moran Canvas Products Inc
8135 Center St
La Mesa, CA 91942-2907

    619-462-7778
Fax: 619-462-7776 800-515-1130
morancanvas@sbcglobal.net
www.morancanvas.com
Commercial awnings
Owner: Don Bell
CFO: Paulette Moran
Sales Manager: Roger Smith
don@myshadydesigns.net
Estimated Sales: Below $5,000,000
Number Employees: 10-19

26308 (HQ)Morgan Brothers Bag Company
PO Box 25577
Richmond, VA 23260-5577

    804-355-9107
Fax: 804-355-9100

Textile bags for hams, peanuts, citrus fruits, scallops and crops
Owner: Jim Edge
VP: Annabel Lewis
Estimated Sales: $20-50 Million
Number Employees: 50-99
Square Footage: 37800

26309 Morgan Corp
111 Morgan Way
PO Box 588
Morgantown, PA 19543-7714

    610-286-5025
Fax: 610-286-0581 800-666-7426
info@morgancorp.com www.morgancorp.com
President: James Youse
james.youse@morgancorp.com
Estimated Sales: $1-5 Million
Number Employees: 1000-4999
Parent Co: J.B. Poindexter & Co

26310 Morning Star Coffee, Inc.
207 Carter Dr Ste E
West Chester, PA 19382-4506

    610-701-7022
Fax: 610-701-7032 888-854-2233
Specialty coffee roasters
President: Thomas Gaspar
Contact: Charles Streitwieser
cmarks@citymission.org
VP, Operations: Antonio Sordi
Estimated Sales: $75-100 Million
Number Employees: 5-9

26311 Morning Star Foods
8 Joanna Court
East Brunswick, NJ 08816-2108

    800-237-5320
Fax: 732-432-3928
Manufacturer and marketer of consumer packaged goods
President/CEO: Herman Graffinder
CFO: Craig Miller
Sr. VP Marketing: Toby Purdy
Sr. VP Operations: Samuel Hillin
Parent Co: Dean Foods Company
Type of Packaging: Private Label, Bulk

26312 Morphy Container Company
17 Woodyatt Drive
Brantford, ON N3R 7K3
Canada

    519-752-5428
Fax: 519-752-2260
Packaging containers including corrugated boxes
Office Manager: Barbara Shaw
Production Manager: Peter Hird
Square Footage: 12000

26313 Morris & Associates
803 Morris Dr
Garner, NC 27529

    919-582-9200
Fax: 919-582-9100 info@morris-associates.com
www.morris-associates.com
Custom refrigeration equipment for the foodprocessing industry. Specializing in industrial ice makers and storage and delivery systems.
CEO: Bill Morris III
Research & Development: John Shell
Marketing Director: Virginia Arello
Sales Director: Bobby Cathey
Operations Manager: David Maw
Production Manager: Ron Correia
Purchasing Manager: Tomc Patterson
Estimated Sales: $5-10 Million
Number Employees: 10-19
Number of Products: 20+
Square Footage: 100000
Brands:
    Chill Master
    Ice Master

26314 Morris Industries
8130 Cryden Way
Forestville, MD 20747

    301-568-5005
Fax: 301-420-4140 www.morris-industries.com
Pressure sensitive labels
President: Dave Morris
CEO: Dave Shotland
Estimated Sales: $3-5 Million
Number Employees: 10-19
Square Footage: 18000

26315 Morris Transparent Box Co
945 Warren Ave
East Providence, RI 02914-1423
401-438-6116
Fax: 401-434-9779 MorrisBox@aol.com
www.morristransparentbox.com
Plastic wedding cake boxes and covers
President: Alfred T Morris Jr
VP: Jean Morris
Estimated Sales: $2.5-5 Million
Number Employees: 20-49

26316 Morrison Timing Screw Co
335 W 194th St
Glenwood, IL 60425-1501
708-331-6600
Fax: 708-756-6620 info@morrison-chs.com
www.morrison-chs.com
Manufacturer and exporter of timing screws and automatic can opening systems
President: Nick Wilson
CEO: Nancy Wilson
Vice President: Lois Hayworth
Vice President of Operations: Chris Wilson
IT: Tim Dupin
tim.dupin@morrison-chs.com
Estimated Sales: $10-20 Million
Number Employees: 20-49

26317 Morrison Weighing Systems Inc
7605 50th St
Milan, IL 61264-3272
309-799-7311
Fax: 309-799-7313 www.morrisonweighing.com
Checkweighing devices, weight control systems, scales, weigh-convey systems
President: Donald G Morrison
don-morrison@mchsi.com
Estimated Sales: $1-2.5 Million
Number Employees: 5-9

26318 Morrissey Displays & Models
20 Beverly Rd
Port Washington, NY 11050
516-883-6944
Fax: 516-767-2379
Manufacturer and exporter of display booths
Owner: Stuart Morrissey
Estimated Sales: $500,000-$1 Million
Number Employees: 1-4

26319 Morrow Technologies Corporation
12000 28th Streett North
St Petersburg, FL 33716
727-531-4000
Fax: 727-531-3531 877-526-8711
sales@janusdisplays.com www.janusdisplays.com
Manufacturer and exporter of interior electronic signs including Leo, LCD and Plasma
Owner: Sharon Morrow
CEO: John Morrow
Controller: Kathy Naranjo
Marketing: Rhonda Candreva
Sales Manager: Steve Asbrand
Number Employees: 20-49
Brands:
  Janus

26320 Morse Manufacturing Co Inc
727 W Manlius St
East Syracuse, NY 13057-2145
315-437-8475
Fax: 315-437-1029 inquiry@morsedrum.com
www.morsemfgco.com
Drum handling equipment, fork attachments for drum moving and drum mixers; exporter of drum handling equipment including rotators, handlers and tumblers
President: Nate Andrews
Chairman Of the Board: Robert Andrews
randrews@morsedrum.com
Marketing: Ralph Phillips
Sales Manager: Phil Mulpagano
Number Employees: 20-49
Number of Brands: 1
Number of Products: 100

26321 Mortec Industries Inc
29240 County Road R
P.O. Box 977
Brush, CO 80723-9444
970-842-5063
Fax: 970-842-5061 800-541-9983
joe@mortecscales.com www.mortecscales.com
Manufacturer and exporter of electronic weighing scales; wholesaler/distributor of computer hardware and software; serving the food service market
Owner: Joe Kral
mortecscales@gmail.com
Estimated Sales: $1-2.5 Million
Number Employees: 1-4
Type of Packaging: Consumer, Food Service

26322 (HQ)Moseley Realty LLC
31 Hayward St # A2
Franklin, MA 02038-2166
508-520-6915
Fax: 508-520-6915 800-667-3539
info@moseleycorp.com www.moseleycorp.com
Modular merchandising systems including carts, kiosks, point of purchase displays and store systems; also, design and architectural consulting services available
President: Thomas C Moseley Jr
tmoseley@moseleycorp.com
COO: Richard Kerley
Sr. VP: Christine Milloff
Estimated Sales: $10-20 Million
Number Employees: 10-19
Square Footage: 100000
Other Locations:
  Moseley Corp.
  Dallas TX

26323 Moser Bag & Paper Company
32485 Creekside Drive
Cleveland, OH 44124-5221
216-341-4111
Fax: 216-341-6507 800-433-6638
Specialty bags including paper, glassine and kraft
President: Ted Welles
Estimated Sales: $5-10 Million
Number Employees: 20-49
Type of Packaging: Food Service
Brands:
  Stubby Clear-Vue
  Stubby Less Crush

26324 Moss Inc
2600 Elmhurst Rd
Elk Grove Vlg, IL 60007-6312
847-238-4200
Fax: 847-238-4604 800-341-1557
www.mossinc.com
Custom labels including pressure sensitive, multi-panel and on-pack for recipes, coupons, product information, etc
President and CEO: Dan Patterson
CEO: Meagan Alwert
malwert@mossinc.com
EVP and CFO: Mark Ollinger
Executive Vice President of Research and: Bob Frey
Executive Vice President of Operations: Vince Marler
VP Production Logistics: Joe Donley
Number Employees: 100-249
Brands:
  Fix-A-Form

26325 Mosshaim Innovations
13901 Sutton Park Drive S
Suite 120
Jacksonville, FL 32224-0229
614-985-3000
Fax: 614-985-0703 888-995-7775
Portable, 120 volt, vitro ceramic glass stovetops. Also produces 120 volt drop-in stovetops. Patented technology will replace gas and induction portables
President: James Sarvadi
Quality Control: Tom Dorothy
R & D: James Sarvadi
VP Marketing: Donald Lewis
VP Operations: James Sarvadi
Estimated Sales: Below $5 Million
Number Employees: 10
Number of Brands: 2
Square Footage: 40000
Parent Co: Mosshaim Innovations
Brands:
  Le Gourmates
  Series S

26326 Mosuki
105 Bridge Road
Islandia, NY 11749-5207
631-234-4111
Fax: 631-234-2940 varduino@aol.com
Espresso machines/accessories

26327 Motion Industries Inc
1605 Alton Rd
Birmingham, AL 35210-3770
205-956-1122
Fax: 205-951-1172 877-609-7975
www.motionindustries.com
Equipment parts and supplies.
CEO: Timothy P Breen
timothy.breen@motion-ind.com
Manager: Matt McComb
Estimated Sales: Over $1 Billion
Number Employees: 5000-9999

26328 Motion Technologies
10 Forbes Rd
Northborough, MA 01532-2501
508-460-9800
Fax: 508-460-5090 800-468-2976
www.autofry.com
Ventless, enclosed, automated deep fryers
President: William Mc Mahon
wmcmahon@motiontechnology.com
Sales: Jamie Fisher
National Sales Manager: James Hall
Estimated Sales: $2.5-5 Million
Number Employees: 20-49
Square Footage: 17000
Brands:
  Autofry

26329 Motom Corporation
631 Il Route 83
Suite 180
Bensenville, IL 60106-1342
630-787-1995
Fax: 630-787-1795
Manufacturer and exporter of drying and baking ovens, cleaning and automated material handling equipment
President: T Teshigawara
VP: W Kojima
Number Employees: 16
Parent Co: Tsukamoto Industrial Trading Company

26330 Motoman
805 Liberty Ln
West Carrollton, OH 45449
937-847-6200
Fax: 937-847-6277
customerservice@motoman.com
www.motoman.com
Robotic automation including packaging and palletizing
President: Steve Barhorst
Contact: Chris Anderson
chris.anderson@motoman.com
Estimated Sales: $45 Million
Number Employees: 250-499
Square Footage: 182000
Parent Co: Yaskawa Company
Type of Packaging: Consumer, Food Service
Brands:
  Motoman

26331 Mouli Manufacturing Corporation
1 Montgomery Street
Belleville, NJ 07109-1305
201-751-6900
Fax: 201-751-0345 800-789-8285
moulimfg@aol.com
Manufacturer, importer and exporter of stainless steel food service equipment including cheese shredders, choppers, cutter, peelers, pots, pans and vegetable processors, etc
VP: P Varkala
Sales: Chris Varkala
Estimated Sales: $1-5 Million
Number Employees: 5-9
Square Footage: 60000
Brands:
  Mouli

26332 Mound Tool Co
9301 Watson Industrial Park
St Louis, MO 63126-1578
314-968-3991
Fax: 314-968-1240 info@moundtool.com
President: R Osborne
Manager: Edward Simo
info@moundtool.com
Estimated Sales: Below $5 Million
Number Employees: 10-19

26333 Mount Hope Machinery Company
1 Technology Dr
Westborough, MA 01581-1786
508-616-9458
Fax: 508-616-9479
Web control equipment for textiles, paper, plastics,
film and foil
President: Bertram Staudenmaier
President: Doug Milner
Director Applications: Carl Wertz
Sales Director: Kevin Frank
Customer Service Support Manager: Ed Gaudette
Estimated Sales: $10-20 Million
Number Employees: 50-99
Parent Co: BTR Paper Group

26334 Mount Vernon Plastics
460 Ogden Avene
Mamaroneck, NY 10543
914-698-1122
Fax: 914-698-1707 info@mtvernonplastics.com
www.mtvernonplastics.com
Plastic bags
Manager: Michael Dino
Estimated Sales: $2.5-5 Million
Number Employees: 10-19

26335 Mountain Pacific Machinery
515 S 9th St
Boise, ID 83702-7006
208-345-9033
Fax: 208-345-9037 877-466-9031
parts@mountpac.com www.mountpac.com
Dealers of food processing, packaging and material
handling equipment
Sales: Josh Wiechman
Manager: Jeff Wiechman
jwiechman@mountpac.com
Manager: Jeff Wiechman
Estimated Sales: $10-20 Million
Number Employees: 1-4

26336 Mountain Pride
421 Bell Dr
PO Box 6077
Ketchum, ID 83340
208-725-5600
Fax: 208-725-5601
President: Stuart Siderman
Estimated Sales: $.5-1 million
Number Employees: 1-4

26337 Mountain Safety Research
4000 1st Avenue South
Seattle, WA 98134
206-505-9500
Fax: 206-682-4184 800-877-9677
info@msrgear.com www.cascadedesigns.com
Manufacturer, importer, and exporter of camp
stoves, fuel bottles, water filtration products and
cook sets
President: Joe Mc Sweeney
Research & Development: Kevin Gallagher
Manager Marketing/Sales: Michael Glavin
Director, Government Sales: Tim Davis
Contact: Dave Bartholomew
dbartholomew@msrgear.com
VP Operations/Engineering: R Michael Ligrano
Manager Product: Gail Snyder
Estimated Sales: $10-20 Million
Number Employees: 1-4
Number of Brands: 1
Number of Products: 250
Square Footage: 160000
Parent Co: Recreational Equipment
Type of Packaging: Consumer
Brands:
Alpine/Xpd
Cloudliner
Denali
Msr
Msr Carabiners
Miniworks

Rapid Fire
Superfly
Water Works
Whisperlite
X-Gk

26338 Mountain Secure Systems
1350 Kansas Ave
Longmont, CO 80501-6546
303-678-9898
Fax: 303-651-7171 800-MSI-PEAK
www.mountainsecuresystems.com
Software MES, specification
Manager: Ken Dickson
ken.dickson@mountainsecuresystems.com
Estimated Sales: $5-10 Million
Number Employees: 20-49

26339 Mountain States Processing
1293 Denver Ave
Fort Lupton, CO 80621-2649
303-857-0380
mtnstatespr@aol.com
Industrial equipment and machinery
President: David Morgan
Estimated Sales: $1 Million
Number Employees: 1-4
Square Footage: 12000

26340 Mountain-Pacific Machinery
11705 SW 68th Ave # 200
Portland, OR 97223-8694
503-639-7635
Fax: 503-639-7707 877-466-9031
parts@mountpac.com www.mountpac.com
Dealers of food processing, packaging and material
handling equipment
President: Dean Smith
jchilson@mountpac.com
Sales: Josh Wiechman
Estimated Sales: $3-5 Million
Number Employees: 5-9

26341 Mountaingate Engineering
540 Division Street
Campbell, CA 95008-6906
408-866-5100
Fax: 408-866-8896
Can and end drying, curing and sterilizing systems
Estimated Sales: $1-5 Million
Parent Co: Nordson Corporation Container Systems

26342 (HQ)Mouron & Co Inc
1025 Western Dr
Indianapolis, IN 46241-1436
317-243-7955
Fax: 317-243-2514 info@mouronandco.com
www.mouronstainless.com
Stainless steel tables and counters
President: T H Mouron
tom@mouronandco.com
VP: G Mouron
Engineer: P Skrojane
General Manager: Phil Skorjanc
Accounting: Mark Bryant
Estimated Sales: $2.5-5 Million
Number Employees: 10-19

26343 MovinCool/DENSO Products and Services Americas
3900 Via Oro Ave
Long Beach, CA 90810-1868
310-513-7319 800-264-9573
info2@movincool.com movincool.com
Supplier of portable spot air conditioning.
Marketing Communications Manager: Eddie
Stevenson
Estimated Sales: $50-75 Million
Number Employees: 100-249
Brands:
Movincool

26344 Moyer Diebel
3765 Champion Blvd
Winston Salem, NC 27105-2667
336-661-1992
Fax: 336-661-1979 info@moyerdiebel.com
www.moyerdiebel.com
Manufacturer and exporter of commercial dishwashers
President: Lin Senseing
lsenseing@championindustries.com
Sales Associate: Robert Croker

Estimated Sales: $20-50 Million
Number Employees: 100-249

26345 Moyer Packing Co.
741 Souder Rd.
Elroy, PA 18964
Fax: 970-346-4611 800-967-8325
www.mopac.com
Boxed and ground beef, and fresh and frozen boxed
beef.
Year Founded: 1877
Estimated Sales: Less Than $500,000
Parent Co: JBS USA
Type of Packaging: Consumer, Private Label, Bulk
Brands:
Mopac

26346 Moyno
PO Box 960
Springfield, OH 45501
937-327-3111
Fax: 937-327-3177 www.moyno.com
Manufacturer and exporter of progressing cavity
pumps and pinch valves
VP Operations: Norman Shearer
Product Manager: Andy Kosiak
VP Sales: Bob Lepera
Contact: Paul Reiss
paul.reiss@nov.com
Engineering Manager: Dale Parrett
Plant Manager: Todd Brown
Estimated Sales: $20-30 Million
Number Employees: 250-499
Square Footage: 240000
Parent Co: National Oilwell Varco
Brands:
Moyno
R&M

26347 Mp Equip. Co.
4305 Hamilton Mill Rd
Suite 400
Buford, GA 30518
770-614-5355
Fax: 770-614-5303 www.mpequipment.com
Designer and manufacturer of new equipment for the
poultry, meat and seafood industries. Also sell
pre-owned equipment such as batter mixers and applicators, frying systems, breaders, ovens, formers
and reject conveyors.
President: Jerrill Sprinkle
General Manager: Jeff Sprinkle

26348 Mpp Inc
346 Huntingdon Ave
Waterbury, CT 06708-1430
203-574-5400
Fax: 203-597-9448 chromerolls@mpp.net
www.mpp.net
Chromium roll fabricating and surface finishing
company that provides rebuilding, grinding, plating
and finishing services for all web processing applications used in the manufacturing of plastic sheet &
film, paper, non-woven fabricsand food processing
industries.
President: Gary Nalband
gnalband@mpp.net
Vice President Sales & Marketing: Rimas Kozica
Operations Manager: Carlos Pacheco
Plant Manager: Richard Hall
Number Employees: 50-99

26349 (HQ)Mr Ice Bucket
345 Sandford St
New Brunswick, NJ 08901-2320
732-545-0420
Fax: 732-846-3383 www.mricebucket.com
Manufacturer and exporter of vinyl ice buckets and
plastic trays and tumblers
President/CEO: Fred Haleluk
fhaleluk@mistericebucket.com
Information Systems Manager: Elaine Herman
Sales Manager: Sudesh Rajpal
Estimated Sales: $1-2.5 Million
Number Employees: 5-9
Square Footage: 40000
Brands:
Mr. Ice Bucket

26350 Mr. Bar-B-Q
5650 University Parkway
Suite 400
Winston-Salem, NC 27105
516-752-0670
Fax: 516-752-0683 800-333-2124
mzemel@mrbarbq.com www.mrbarbq.com
Manufacturer and importer of portable butane
stoves, lighters, cookers and buffet and omelet
stations
President/CEO: Marc Zemel
Senior VP: Adam Schillen
Director-Sales & Marketing: Wendy Sender
Senior VP -Sales: Jeff Lynch
VP operations: Michael Guadagno
Estimated Sales: $10-20 Million
Number Employees: 20-49
Square Footage: 68000
Brands:
Chef Master

26351 (HQ)Mrs Clark's Foods
740 SE Dalbey Dr
Ankeny, IA 50021-3908
515-964-8036
Fax: 515-964-8397 800-736-5674
info@mrsclarks.com www.mrsclarks.com
Shelf-stable beverages, sauces and dressings
President: Ron Kahrer
QC: Ned Williams
Sales: Julie Southwick
Plant Manager: John Weber
Purchasing: Ron Mathis
Estimated Sales: $450,000
Number Employees: 100-249
Number of Brands: 12
Number of Products: 50
Square Footage: 240000
Parent Co: AGRI Industries
Type of Packaging: Consumer, Food Service, Private Label
Brands:
Alljuice
Nature's Choice

26352 Mrs. Smith's Bakeries
7001 Asheville Hwy
Spartanburg, SC 29303-1875
864-503-9101
Fax: 864-503-9129
Pies and cobblers
Founder: Amanda Smith
Parent Co: Schwan's Consumer Brands
Brands:
MRS. SMITH'S

26353 Mt Valley Farms & Lumber Prods
1240 Nawakwa Rd
Biglerville, PA 17307-9728
717-677-6166
Fax: 717-677-9283 admin@mtvalleyfarms.com
www.mtvalleyfarms.com
Hardwood bins, skids and pallets; also, sawdust
President: Henry L Taylor
CFO: Patrick McCreary
VP/Operations: H Michael Taylor
R & D: Jemay Lua
Estimated Sales: Below $5 Million
Number Employees: 50-99
Square Footage: 208000
Other Locations:
Mountain Valley Farms &Lumbe
Biglerville PA
Brands:
Enviro-Logs

26354 Mt Vernon Neon Inc
1 Neon Dr
Mt Vernon, IL 62864-6723
618-242-0645
Fax: 618-244-6926 www.everbrite.com
Neon signs
Founder: Charles Wamser
Plant Manager: Steve Porter
Estimated Sales: $10-20 Million
Number Employees: 100-249
Parent Co: Everbright Electric Signs

26355 Mt Vernon Packaging Inc
135 Progress Dr
Mt Vernon, OH 43050-4772
740-397-3221
Fax: 740-393-2002 888-397-3221
Tommy@mountvernonpackaging.com
mountvernonpackaging.com
Paper boxes
President: Donald Nuce
dnuce@mountvernonpackaging.com
Estimated Sales: $5-10 Million
Number Employees: 5-9

26356 Mt. Lebanon Awning & Tent Company
P.O.Box 27
Presto, PA 15142
412-221-2233
Fax: 412-221-0204 info@mtlebanonawning.com
www.mtlebanonawning.com
Commercial awnings
President: Robert Campbell
Estimated Sales: $1-2,500,000
Number Employees: 10-19

26357 Mtc Food Equipment
17708 Widme Rd NE
Unit D
Poulsbo, WA 98370
360-697-6319
Fax: 360-697-6738 mtc@mtcfoodequipment.com
www.mtcfoodequipment.com
De-boning machines, bowl choppers, vacuum packers, slicers, grinders, meat saws, ice machines, stuffing machines, freezing equipment, smokehouses, filleting machines, skinning machines, and many other types of food processmachinery.
Owner: Todd Comstock
Estimated Sales: $500,000
Number Employees: 1-4
Square Footage: 2367

26358 Mts Seating
7100 Industrial Dr
Temperance, MI 48182-9105
734-847-3875
Fax: 734-847-0993 info@mtsseating.com
www.mtsseating.com
Manufacturer and exporter of metal stack chairs, bar stools, pedestal tables and bases and a complete line of hospitality and food service seating
President: Bart Kulish
Marketing Manager: Eric Foster
Sales VP: Greg Piper
Estimated Sales: $20-50 Million
Number Employees: 250-499
Square Footage: 200000
Parent Co: Michigan Tube Swagers Fabricators
Type of Packaging: Food Service

26359 Muckler Industries, Inc
355 Leesmeadow Rd.
Suite 207
Saint Louis, MO 63125
314-631-7616
Fax: 314-631-7409 800-444-0283
ktechinfo@mucklertech.com
Manufacturer and exporter of commercial kitchen hoods, baffle filters, waterwash and grease extractors, engineered commercial ventilation and utility distribution systems
National Sales Manager: Douglas Muckler
Sales: Sean Wood
Estimated Sales: $2.5-5 Million
Number Employees: 10
Square Footage: 60000
Type of Packaging: Food Service
Brands:
Challenger
Contender
Edc
Finalist
Performer

26360 (HQ)Muellermist Irrigation Company
2612 S. 9th Ave.
P.O. Box 6307
Broadview, IL 60155
708-450-9595
Fax: 708-450-1403 info@muellermist.com
www.muellermist.com
Manufacturer and exporter of underground lawn sprinkling and solar roof cooling systems

President: Tammy Boralli
Contact: Tammy Buralli
tburalli@muellermist.com
Estimated Sales: $10-20 Million
Number Employees: 50-99
Square Footage: 36000
Type of Packaging: Bulk
Brands:
Fanjet

26361 Mugnaini Imports
11 Hangar Way
Watsonville, CA 95076
831-761-1767
Fax: 831-728-5570 888-887-7206
mugnaini@mugnaini.com www.mugnaini.com
Supplier and importer of wood burning ovens and gas fire
Owner: Andrea Smith
Contact: Curt Corcoran
curt@mugnaini.com
Manager: Ken Belardi
Estimated Sales: Less than $500,000
Number Employees: 1-4

26362 Mulholland Co
1332 N Main St
Fort Worth, TX 76164-9117
817-624-1153
Fax: 817-624-1445 www.mulhollands.com
Plastic signs and nameplates
Manager: Dean Brown
Cmo: Nick Griffin
ngriffin@mulhollands.com
Marketing Manager: Sonny Muholland
Estimated Sales: $10-20 Million
Number Employees: 50-99

26363 Mulholland-Harper Company
PO Box C
Denton, MD 21629-0298
410-479-1300
Fax: 410-479-0207 800-882-3052
Manufacturer and exporter of electric fixtures and signs including electric, plastic, metal and outdoor and exterior identification
President: Patrick Hanrahan
Manufacturing Manager: Michael Conner
Estimated Sales: $5-10 Million
Number Employees: 50-99
Square Footage: 200000

26364 Mulligan Associates
286 Barbados Dr
Mequon, WI 53092
414-305-0840
Fax: 262-242-3944 800-627-2886
gene@mulliganassociates.com
Manufacturer, importer and exporter of high and low volume citric and noncitric juicers, fruit and vegetable peelers, water vending machines and sugar cane and wheat grass extractors
President: Gene Mulligan
CFO: Gene Mulligan
Quality Control: Gene Mulligan
Marketing: Gene Mulligan
Sales Director: Gene Mulligan
General Manager: Bonnie Mulligan
Estimated Sales: $2 Million
Number Employees: 50-99
Square Footage: 30000
Parent Co: AOJ Manufacturing
Type of Packaging: Food Service

26365 Mulligan Sales
P.O.Box 90008
City of Industry, CA 91715-0008
626-968-9621
Fax: 626-369-8452
Dairy, preservatives, acids, bakery, gums, stabilizers, dehydrated fruits and vegetables
President: Jeff Mulligan
Sales Manager: Dean Lenz
Estimated Sales: $20-50 Million
Number Employees: 10-19
Square Footage: 30000

26366 Mullnix Packages Inc
3511 Engle Rd
Fort Wayne, IN 46809-1117
260-747-3149
Fax: 260-747-1598
bschmitz@mullinixpackages.com

Plastic containers for frozen foods, prepared salads and fresh, refrigerated and controlled atmosphere products
President: Luke Gross
President, Chief Executive Officer: Gene Gentili
VP Sales/Marketing: Tim Love
Regional Sales Manager, Central US: Brian Schmitz
Operations Manager: Carey Edwards
Estimated Sales: $20-50 Million
Number Employees: 500-999
Square Footage: 118000

26367 Multi-Color Corp
1836 Sal St
Green Bay, WI 54302-2114
920-468-1269
Fax: 920-468-6793 800-236-8208
www.multicolorcorp.com
Labels including flexo, pressure sensitive and glue applied; also, pressure sensitive films and tags
President: Andrew Walker
Controller: Jim Gombar
CFO: James Gombar
Operations: Gary Karnopp
Quality Control: Greg Liplante
Estimated Sales: $10-20 Million
Number Employees: 50-99
Square Footage: 80000
Parent Co: NorthStar Print Group

26368 Multi-Fill Inc
4343 W 7800 S Ste B
West Jordan, UT 84088
801-280-1570
Fax: 801-280-4341 info@multi-fill.com
www.multi-fill.com
Volumetric filling equipment for the food processor. Line configurations for cooked rice, short/long pasta, vegetables, fruits, ready-to-eat salads (cut, sliced, IQF, blanched, or raw). New technology for the MPF fillers allows forfaster changeover, tighter accuracy's, increased cleanliness of fill, and results in less down time.
President: Richard Price
rt72@netzero.net
Sales Director: Bill Allred
Estimated Sales: Below $5 Million
Number Employees: 10-19
Square Footage: 22000

26369 Multi-Pak
180 Atlantic St
Hackensack, NJ 07601-3301
201-342-7474
Fax: 201-342-6525 www.multipakcorp.com
Manufacturer and exporter of refuse compactors for multi-dwelling units, hotels, hospitals and restaurants; also, attaching containers, odor control equipment and other collection systems. Hopper door repairs, chute cleaning, recyclingsystem
President: Niel Cavanaugh
ncavanaugh@multipak.com
Chairman of the Board/CFO/R&D: Niel Cavanaugh
Estimated Sales: $2.5-5 Million
Number Employees: 20-49
Square Footage: 24000

26370 Multi-Panel Display Corporation
107 Georgia Ave
Brooklyn, NY 11207-2401
718-495-3800
Fax: 718-346-0871 800-439-0879
Display racks and swing type display boards and panels; exporter of display units
President: Tommy Weber
VP: Zipora Weber
Contact: Daniel Weber
multipanel@aol.com
Estimated Sales: Less than $500,000
Number Employees: 5-9
Square Footage: 40000

26371 Multi-Plastics Extrusions Inc
600 Dietrich Ave
Hazleton, PA 18201-7754
570-455-2021
Fax: 570-455-0178 www.multi-plastics.com
Manufacturer and exporter of transparent biaxially oriented polystyrene sheets used for pressure and vacuum forming
Cmo: Paul Hinspeter
paul.hinspeter@alcoa.com
VP/General Manager: Eugene Whitacre
Plant Manager: Juan Escobar

Estimated Sales: $20-50 Million
Number Employees: 100-249

26372 MultiFab Plastics
60B Tenean Street
Boston, MA 02122-2738
617-287-1411
Fax: 617-287-0299 888-293-5754
info@multifab.com
Bagel and bulk food bins, acrylic displays, cases, table tents and sign holders
President: Stan Lisowski
Vice President: David Lisowski
Estimated Sales: $1-2.5 Million
Number Employees: 10-19

26373 MultiMedia Electronic Displays
11370 Sunrise Park Dr
Rancho Cordova, CA 95742-6542
916-852-4220
Fax: 916-852-8325 800-888-3007
info@multimedialed.com www.multimedialed.com
Manufacturer and exporter of programmable electronic signs
President: William Y Hall
CEO: Rex Williams
Marketing Director: Karen Klueh
Contact: Steven Craig
scraig@multimedialed.com
Operations Manager: Paul Selems
Plant Manager: George Pappas
Estimated Sales: $5-10 Million
Number Employees: 20-49
Number of Brands: 5
Number of Products: 200
Parent Co: SignUp
Type of Packaging: Food Service

26374 Multibulk Systems International
6 W 3rd Street
Wendell, NC 27591-8086
919-366-2100
Fax: 919-676-7716
Manufacturer and exporter of bulk bag flexible containers
Sales Manager: John Watson
Estimated Sales: $500,000-$1,000,000
Number Employees: 5-9
Type of Packaging: Private Label
Brands:
Multibulk

26375 Multifeeder Technology Inc
4821 White Bear Pkwy
St Paul, MN 55110-3325
651-407-3100
Fax: 651-407-3199 info@multifeeder.com
www.multifeeder.com
Friction Feeders
President: Neal Nordling
Estimated Sales: Less Than $500,000
Number Employees: 1-4

26376 Multifilm Packaging Corp
1040 N Mclean Blvd
Elgin, IL 60123-1709
847-695-7600
Fax: 847-695-7645 800-837-9727
info@multifilm.com
Constantia Multifilm is an integrated manufacturer of flexible packaging solutions for the food, beverage, and confectionery industries.
President: Chris Rogers
chris.rogers@constantia-multifilm.com
Vice President Finance: Robert Tate
Graphics Manager: Terry Piatkowski
New Business Development Manager: Marcus Magnusson
Vice President Sales and Marketing: Chris Rogers
Customer Service: Nancy Jung
Production Manager: Mike Huey
Plant Manager: Dave Rohrschneider
Estimated Sales: Below $5 Million
Number Employees: 50-99
Type of Packaging: Consumer

26377 Multigrains Bread Co
117 Water St
Lawrence, MA 01841-4720
978-691-6100
Fax: 978-373-4801 www.multigrainsbakeries.com
Multigrain breads

President: Joseph Faro
joseph@multigrainsbakeries.com
EVP/Director R&D: Chuck Brandano
Director of Quality: Adam Gabour
Director of Purchasing: Darren Gaiero
Number Employees: 100-249

26378 Multikem Corp
700 Grand Ave
Ridgefield, NJ 07657-1524
201-941-4520
Fax: 201-941-5239 800-462-4425
multikem@mindspring.com www.multikem.com
President: Larry Muhlberg
multikem@mindspring.com
Estimated Sales: $5-10 Million
Number Employees: 5-9

26379 Multiplex Co Inc
2100 Future Dr
Sellersburg, IN 47172-1874
812-256-7777
Fax: 636-527-4313 800-787-8880
www.google.com
High capacity dispensing systems for beverages including beer; also, water filtration systems
President & Chief Operating Officer: J. Kisling
Chief Executive Officer: Terry Growcock
Contact: John Bell
jbell@manitowocfsg.com
Estimated Sales: $34.6 Million
Number Employees: 1-4
Square Footage: 10000000
Parent Co: Manitowoc Foodservice Group
Brands:
Beermaster
Computap
Intercept
Pr/O-Rox
Re-Fresh

26380 Multipond America Inc
2301 Hutson Rd
Green Bay, WI 54303-4712
920-490-8249
Fax: 920-490-8482 sales-us@multipond.com
Multipond America Inc, is a wholly owned subsidiary of Multipond, Germany which is the sales and service division of the German based manufacturing company ATOMA. Mutlipond Weighing Technology and mutlihead weigher systems for thepackaging industry stands for the maximum accuaracy, performance, and reliability. We work closely with our customers on continuous improvement in all aspects of our design. We develop and produce customized multihead weigher systems for ourcustomers.
Vice President: Fred Horn
fwd@multipondamerica.com
Controller: Paul Plutz
Project Manager: Keven Diederich
Research/Development: John Tuchscherer
VP Sales/Marketing: Frederick Horn
Technical Sales Engineer: Jerry Van Lannen
Estimated Sales: $10 Million
Number Employees: 5-9

26381 (HQ)Multisorb Technologies Inc
325 Harlem Rd
Buffalo, NY 14224-1893
716-824-8900
Fax: 716-824-4128 800-445-9890
info@multisorb.com www.multisorb.com
Manufacturer and exporter of active packaging technologies for food packaging, including odor absorbers, desiccants, and moisture regulators, and odor and other volatile absorbers.
President: James Renda
jrenda@multisorb.com
Marketing: Tom Powers
Marketing Communications Coordinator: Kay Krause
Number Employees: 500-999
Square Footage: 340000
Other Locations:
Multisorb Technologies
Orchard Park NY
Brands:
Freshmax
Freshpax
Minipax
Natrasorb
Sorbicap

26382 Multisorb Technologies Inc
325 Harlem Rd
Buffalo, NY 14224-1893
716-824-8900
Fax: 716-824-4128 info@multisorb.com
www.multisorb.com
President: James Renda
jrenda@multisorb.com
Estimated Sales: $1-3 Million
Number Employees: 500-999

26383 Multivac
21209 Durand Ave
Union Grove, WI 53182-9711
262-878-0366
Fax: 262-878-4019 800-640-4213
www.multivacinc.com
Stainless steel material handling equipment; also, industrial vacuum equipment and dust collectors
Owner: Wally Haag
multivac@wi.net
V.P.: Margaret Haag
Plant Manager: Dwane Hartlage
Estimated Sales: Below $5 Million
Number Employees: 20-49
Square Footage: 60000
Parent Co: M&W Shops

26384 Multivac Inc
11021 N Pomona Ave
Kansas City, MO 64153-1146
816-891-0555
Fax: 816-891-0622 800-800-8552
muinc@multivac.com
Wholesaler/distributor, importer and exporter of thermoform, fill and seal packaging equipment; also, tray sealers, chamber vacuum packaging and labeling equipment; sales support services available
President: Michel Defenbau
CEO: Werner Britz
werner.britz@multivacsa.com
CEO: Jan Erik Kuhlmann
CFO: Danny Liker
Sales Director: Norm Winkel
Estimated Sales: $50-60Million
Number Employees: 100-249
Square Footage: 60000
Parent Co: Multivac Export AG

26385 Mumper Machine Corporation
5081 N 124th St
Butler, WI 53007
262-781-8908
Fax: 262-781-1253
Manufacturer and exporter of vegetable topping and conveying equipment
President: Jordy Mumper
Estimated Sales: $500,000-$1 Million
Number Employees: 5-9

26386 Mundial
63 Broadway # 1
Norwood, MA 02062-3558
781-762-0053
Fax: 781-762-0364 800-487-2224
info@mundial-usa.com www.mundialusa.com
Manufacturer, importer and exporter of knives, scissors and shears
President: Adilson Delatorre
CFO: John Keese
Sales VP: Rich Zirpolo
Estimated Sales: $1-2.5 Million
Number Employees: 1-4
Square Footage: 200000
Parent Co: Zivi-Hercules
Type of Packaging: Consumer, Food Service, Bulk

26387 Munson Machinery Co
210 Seward Ave
PO Box 855
Utica, NY 13502-5750
315-797-0090
Fax: 315-797-5582 800-944-6644
info@munsonmachinery.com
www.munsonmachinery.com
Mixers, blenders and size reduction equipment for bulk solid materials.
Partner/VP/COO: Thomas Dalton III
Marketing Manager: Charles Divine
Regional Sales Manager: Darren Woods
Estimated Sales: $5-10 Million
Number Employees: 20-49
Square Footage: 90000

26388 Munters Corp
79 Monroe St
Amesbury, MA 01913-3204
978-388-0600
Fax: 978-241-1219 800-843-5360
www.munters.com
Manufacturer and exporter of continuous desiccant dehumidification systems
President: Mike Mc Donald
Cmo: Scott Haynes
shaynes@munters.com
Estimated Sales: $20-50 Million
Number Employees: 250-499
Square Footage: 175000
Parent Co: Munters Corporation

26389 Murata Automated Systems
PO Box 667609
2120 Queen City Drive
Charlotte, NC 28266
704-573-2250
Fax: 704-394-2001 800-428-8469
info@muratec-usa.com www.muratec-usa.com
Automated material handling and control systems including storage and retrieval, guided vehicles, conveyors, monorails, etc.; also, software
President: Masaharu Nishio
Manager Projects: Masato Ohzawa
CFO: Dale Mitchell
Quality Control: Gary Reynoles
Estimated Sales: $.5-1 million
Number Employees: 100
Parent Co: Murato Machinery

26390 Murk Brush Company
P.O.Box 726
New Britain, CT 06050-0726
860-249-2550
Fax: 860-249-2550
Brushes for the food and beverage industry, FDA approved brush construction; specialist in OEM Brush Design
Sales: Dave Hames
Estimated Sales: 500000
Number Employees: 1-4
Number of Products: 2600
Square Footage: 28000
Type of Packaging: Bulk

26391 Murnane Co
607 Northwest Ave
Northlake, IL 60164-1398
708-449-1200
Fax: 708-449-1231 www.murnanecompanies.com
Packaging materials and paperboard boxes
President: Frank J Murnane Jr
Vice President: Patrick J Murnane
pjmurnane@murnanecompanies.com
Estimated Sales: $20-50 Million
Number Employees: 50-99

26392 Murnell Wax Company
237 Memorial Drive
Springfield, MA 01104-3228
781-395-1323
Fax: 781-395-8160
Floor polish and cleaners
Estimated Sales: $1-2.5 Million
Number Employees: 6

26393 Murotech
550 Mckinley Rd
St Marys, OH 45885-1803
419-394-6529
Fax: 419-394-6820 800-565-6876
muropeeler@aol.com www.murotech.com
Manufacturer, exporter and importer of semi-automatic peeling machines for fruits and vegetables including oranges, apples, mangos, cantaloupes and rutabegas
President: Naonobu Kenmoku
Quality Manager: Rick Wiley
Sales Manager: S. Sugimoto
Production Manager: Koichi Uchida
Estimated Sales: $500,000-$1 Million
Number Employees: 100-249
Square Footage: 4000
Parent Co: Muro Corporation
Brands:
Muro

26394 (HQ)Murray Envelope Corporation
1500 N Main St
Suite C
Hattiesburg, MS 39401-1911
601-583-8292
Fax: 800-423-7589 murray@netdoor.com
Manufacturer and exporter of filing folders and envelopes
Owner: Marvin Murry
CFO: Joae Comprtallo
R & D: Lenda Wisa
Estimated Sales: Below $5 Million
Number Employees: 1-4

26395 Murray Runin
531 Cascade Court
Mahwah, NJ 07430-2750
201-512-3885
Fax: 201-512-3850 consultrun@aol.com
Management consultant specializing in operational and distribution problem solving
Owner: Murray Runin

26396 Murtech Manufacturing
835 Fairfield Avenue
Kenilworth, NJ 07033-2059
908-245-1556
Fax: 908-245-8707
Grids for bottle tanking
Owner: Mike Blazinsky
Estimated Sales: Less than $500,000
Number Employees: 4

26397 (HQ)Murzan Inc
2909 Langford Rd # A700
Rd. 1-700
Peachtree Cor, GA 30071-1512
770-448-0583
Fax: 770-448-0967 murzan@murzan.com
www.murzan.com
Manufacturer and exporter of food processing pumps and drum unloading, turnkey and bag-in-box blending/batching systems
Owner: Alberto Bazan
murzan@aol.com
CEO: Alberto Bazan
Estimated Sales: $2,600,000
Number Employees: 50-99

26398 Music City Metals Inc
2633 Grandview Ave
Nashville, TN 37211-2202
615-255-4481
Fax: 615-255-4482 800-251-2674
musiccitymetals@musiccitymetals.net
www.musiccitymetals.net
Cast iron hot plates, gas burners, cooking grids, cast iron and stainless steel burners, grids and grates for gas grills.
President: Bo Richardson
musiccitymetals@musiccitymetals.net
Estimated Sales: $1-2.5 Million
Number Employees: 10-19
Brands:
Kings Kooker

26399 Muskegon Awning & Fabrication
2333 Henry St
Muskegon, MI 49441-3097
231-759-0911
Fax: 231-759-3200 800-968-3686
mailman@muskegonawning.com
www.muskegonawning.com
Awnings and canvas related products
President: David Bayne
dbayne@muskegonawning.com
CEO: Gordon Moen
President: Lora Davis
Sr. Sales Representative: Peter Yonkavit
Estimated Sales: Below $5 Million
Number Employees: 5-9
Square Footage: 57200

26400 Muskogee Rubber Stamp &Seal Company
23549 S 450 Rd
Fort Gibson, OK 74434
918-478-3046
Seals, daters, magnetic signs, price marking inks and rubber stamps
Owner: Sarah Turner
Owner: Paul Owen

Estimated Sales: Less than $500,000
Number Employees: 1-4

26401 Muth Associates
53 Progress Ave
Springfield, MA 01104-3266

413-734-2107
Fax: 413-734-2107 800-388-0157
info@muthassociates.com muthassociates.com
Wholesaler/distributor of adsorbent materials
President: Cis Lafond
cislafond@muthassociates.com
CEO: Doug Muth
CFO: Sandra Peterson
Estimated Sales: $5-10 Million
Number Employees: 10-19
Number of Products: 300
Square Footage: 52000
Type of Packaging: Private Label, Bulk
Brands:
Desi-Pak
Sorb-It
Tri-Wall

26402 Mutual Stamping & Mfg Co
655 Plains Rd
P.O.Box 5060
Milford, CT 06461-1736

203-877-3933
Fax: 203-877-1822 800-735-3933
Wine industry stainless steel barrels
Owner: Jay Fox
info@drumsofsteel.com
Estimated Sales: $500,000-$1 Million
Number Employees: 5-9

26403 My Serenity Pond
15009 Held Cir
Cold Spring, MN 56320

320-363-0411
Fax: 320-363-0339 www.myserenitypond.com
Identification products including nameplates, and
stamp business forms
President: Marlin Boeckmann
Estimated Sales: $300,000-500,000
Number Employees: 1-4
Square Footage: 40000

26404 My Style
614 NW Street
Raleigh, NC 27603

919-832-2526
Fax: 919-832-1546 800-524-8269
Wholesaler/distributor, importer and exporter of
teak, cast aluminum, stainless steel and hardwood
outdoor furniture; also, wooden and market
umbrellas
Director: Ward Usmar
Owner: Klaus Weihe
Owner: Eik Niemann
Marketing Administrator: Ceri Usmar
Number Employees: 1-4
Square Footage: 13500
Brands:
Caribbean Shade Market Umbrellas
Lingot Stainless & Hardwood Floors
Siesta Shade Market Umbrellas
Teake Furniture

26405 Mycom Group
110-6620 McMillan Way
Richmond, BC V6W 1J7
Canada

604-270-1544
Fax: 604-270-9870
Refrigeration equipment and supplies
President: Yasushi Sasaki

26406 Mycom Sales
210 Summit Ave
Suite C12
Montvale, NJ 07645

201-307-9199
Fax: 201-307-1566
Estimated Sales: $1-3 Million
Number Employees: 1-4

26407 Mycom/Mayekawa Manfacturing
16825 Ih 35 N
Selma, TX 78154-1223

210-599-4536
Fax: 210-599-4538
Manager: Pete Valdez

Estimated Sales: $1-3 Million
Number Employees: 1-4

26408 Myers Container
21301 Cloud Way
Hayward, CA 94545-1216

510-785-8235
Fax: 510-271-6215 jcutt@myerscontainer.com
www.myerscontainer.com
Manufacturer, exporter and reconditioner of steel
drums including aseptic, hot pack food, conical and
vegetable oil
President: John Cutt
Chief Executive Officer: Kyle Stavig
CFO: Thomas Holmes
Quality Control: Dana Zanone
Manager Food Sales: Roger Thornton
Manager: Benjamin Rivera
brivera@myerscontainer.com
Estimated Sales: $50-100 Million
Number Employees: 10-19
Square Footage: 500000
Parent Co: IMACC Corporation
Brands:
Pureliner
Purestack
Purevac

26409 Myers Ice Company
102 N 9th St
Garden City, KS 67846-5350

620-275-5751
Fax: 620-275-8574 800-767-5751
Ice
Co-Owner: Craig Myers
c.myers@myersice.com
Co-Owner: Carl Myers
Estimated Sales: $1-2.5 Million
Number Employees: 10-19
Brands:
Myers Ice Co.

26410 Myers Restaurant SupplyInc
1599 Cleveland Ave
Santa Rosa, CA 95401-4280

707-570-1200
Fax: 707-542-0350 800-219-9426
brett@myersrestaurantsupply.com
www.myersrestaurantsupply.com
Wholesaler/distributor of restaurant and bar equip-
ment and supplies; serving the food service market
Owner: Rob Myers
CEO: Jon Myers
CFO: Brett Livingstone
Estimated Sales: $2.5-5 Million
Number Employees: 20-49
Square Footage: 44000

26411 N & A Mfg
203 Inman St
Mallard, IA 50562-7509

712-425-3512
Fax: 712-425-3308 spraymatic@iowatelecom.net
www.pressuresprayers.net
Agricultural high pressure hot and cold washers,
power scrapers and accessories for high pressure
washer systems
President: Virgil Auten
Sales Manager: Troy Auten
Estimated Sales: $1-2.5 Million
Number Employees: 1-4
Square Footage: 13400
Brands:
Spraymatic
Vibramatic

26412 N A P Engineering
10965 Harborside Dr
Largo, FL 33773-4428

727-544-3118
www.napengineering.com
Manufacturer of Rotary Fillers and Sealers, Inline
Tray Fillers and Sealersand Specialty Parts.
President: Paul Desocio
glouli@tampabay.rr.com
Estimated Sales: Less Than $500,000
Number Employees: 1-4

26413 N.A. Krups
7 Reuten Dr
Closter, NJ 07624-2120

201-767-5500
Fax: 201-784-3710 www.krupsusa.com
Brewing devices

President: Mark Navarre
Estimated Sales: $10-20 Million
Number Employees: 50-99

26414 N.G. Slater Corporation
42 W 38th St Rm 200
Suite 1002
New York, NY 10018

212-768-9434
Fax: 212-869-7368 800-848-4621
info@ngslater.com www.ngslater.com
Manufacturer and distributors of custom imprinted
and specialties, badges, buttons and emblems
Owner: Robert Slater
VP: Alan Slater
Estimated Sales: $1-3,000,000
Number Employees: 5-9

26415 NACCO Materials HandlingGroup
4000 NE Blue Lake Road
Fairview, OR 97024-8710

503-721-6205
Fax: 503-721-1364 www.hysterusa.com
Manufacturer and exporter of forklift trucks
Engineering Manager: Darrel Libby
Contact: Bob Downey
bob.downey@nmhg.com
Estimated Sales: $50-100 Million
Number Employees: 141
Square Footage: 68384
Parent Co: NACCO Industries

26416 NAP Industries
667 Kent Ave
Brooklyn, NY 11249-7500

718-625-4948
Fax: 718-596-4342 877-635-4948
info@napind.com www.napind.com
Manufacturer and exporter of bags including heat
sealed, meat, plastic, polyethylene and shopping;
also, pressure sensitive tapes
President: Leo Lowy
morris@napind.com
Sales Exec: Morris Lowy
Estimated Sales: $5-10 Million
Number Employees: 20-49

26417 NB Corporation of America
46750 Lakerville Blvd.
Fremont, CA 94538

510-490-1420
Fax: 510-490-1733 888-562-4175
info@nbcorporation.com www.nbcorporation.com
President: Toru Yamazaki
Estimated Sales: $3-5 Million
Number Employees: 10-19

26418 NCC
21005 Obrien Rd
Groveland, FL 34736-9590

352-429-9036
Fax: 352-429-9039 800-429-9037
novelty@aol.com www.partyplasticsplus.com
Hotel and restaurant supplies including catering and
buffet trays, plastic drinkware, pitchers, bowls and
serving utensils
President: Sara Michaeli
sara@global-nation.com
CEO: Asher Michaeli
CFO: Joe Michaeli
VP: Sara Coslett
R&D: Joe Michaeli
Marketing: Ed Coslett
Sales Manager: Ed Coslett
Public Relations: Sara Coslett
Manager: Sara Michaeli
Plant Manager: Paul Patin
Estimated Sales: $1-2.5 Million
Number Employees: 20-49
Square Footage: 125000
Parent Co: Novelty Crystal Corporation
Type of Packaging: Food Service

26419 NCR Corp
Atlanta, GA 30308

937-445-1936
800-225-5627
www.ncr.com
Point-of-sale systems including self-ordering kiosks,
guest and table management, kitchen production and
payment processing.

Executive Chairman: Frank Martire
President & CEO: Michael Hayford
EVP/CFO: Andre Fernandez
EVP/General Counsel: Jim Bedore
EVP, NCR Hospitality: Dirk Izzo
SVP & GM, NCR Retail: David Wilkinson
SVP/Chief Information Officer: William (Bill) Vancuren
EVP, NCR Global Sales: Dan Campbell
EVP, Global Customer Services: J. Robert Ciminera
Chief Operating Officer: Owen Sullivan
Year Founded: 1884
Estimated Sales: $6.4 Billion
Number Employees: 34,000

26420 NCR Counterpoint
4325 Alexander Dr
Alpharetta, GA 30022

800-852-5852
www.counterpointpos.com
Consultant providing point of sale, back office and headquarter solutions for quick and full service establishments.
President & CEO: Michael Hayford
Chief Operating Officer: Paul Laungenbahn
EVP, CFO & Chief Accounting Officer: Bob Fishman
EVP, CAO & Chief Human Resources Officer: Andrea Ledford
SVP & Chief Information Officer: William Vancuren
SVP, General Counsel & Secretary: Edward Gallagher

26421 NDC Infrared EngineeringInc
5314 Irwindale Ave
Irwindale, CA 91706

626-960-3300
Fax: 626-939-3870 info@ndcinfrared.com
www.ndcinfrared.com
Manufacturer and exporter of on-line instrumentation for measurement of moisture, fat/oil, protein and caffeine including testers and analyzers
President: Bromley Beadle
Marketing Manager: Raymond Shead
Sales/Marketing Executive: Bill Diltz
Contact: Drew Cheshire
jhazlett@verrents.com
Estimated Sales: $20-50 Million
Number Employees: 50-99
Square Footage: 50000
Parent Co: Fairey Group
Brands:
Mm710
Tm710

26422 NECO/Nebraska Engineering
9364 N 45th St
Omaha, NE 68152-1328

402-453-6912
Fax: 402-453-0471 800-367-6208
www.necousa.com
Manufacturer and exporter of grain processing and handling equipment including cleaners, augers, spreaders, conveyors, dryers and aeration fans
President: Steve Campbell
VP: Bryan Hayes
Marketing Director: Steve Campbell
Sales Manager: Pat McCarthy
Manager: William Hiltgen
Plant Manager: Rick Wulf
Purchase Head: Rick Wuls
Estimated Sales: Below $5 Million
Number Employees: 50-99
Square Footage: 300000
Parent Co: GLOBAL Industries

26423 NEPA Pallet & ContainerCo
12027 3 Lakes Rd
Snohomish, WA 98290-5502

360-568-3185
Fax: 360-568-9135 www.nepapallet.com
Manufacturer and exporter of pallets and bins
President: Denton Sherry
dsherry@nepapallet.com
Estimated Sales: $5-10 Million
Number Employees: 100-249

26424 NIMCO Corp
1000 Nimco Dr
Crystal Lake, IL 60014-1704

815-459-4200
Fax: 815-459-8119 info@nimco.com
www.nimco.com

Form, fill seal for gable-top cartons
President: Jerry Bachner
nimco@nimco.com
Estimated Sales: $5-10 Million
Number Employees: 20-49

26425 NJM Packaging
56 Etna Rd
Lebanon, NH 03766-1419

603-448-0300
Fax: 603-448-4810 800-432-2990
info@njmpackaging.com www.njmpackaging.com
Packaging equipment and labeling equipment
President/CEO: Michel Lapierre
Director International Sales: Marc Lapierre
CFO: Jim Moretti
moretti@njmpackaging.com
Vice President Operations Finances: Andre Caumartin
Vice President: Daniel Lapierre
Marketing Director: Marla Stallmann
VP Sales: Mark LaRoche
Human Resources: Todd Savage
Number Employees: 10-19

26426 NJM Packaging
56 Etna Rd
Lebanon, NH 03766-1419

603-448-0300
Fax: 603-448-4810 800-432-2990
info@njmpackaging.com www.njmpackaging.com
Wine industry labeling equipment
President & CEO: Michel Lapierre
CFO: Jim Moretti
moretti@njmpackaging.com
VP: Daniel Lapierre
Marketing: Marla Stallman
Director International Sales: Marc Lapierre
Estimated Sales: $5-10 Million
Number Employees: 10-19

26427 NJM/CLI
8 Plateau Street
Pointe Claire, QC H9R 5W2
Canada

514-630-6990
Fax: 514-695-0801
Manufacturer, exporter and importer of packaging machinery including fillers, cappers, labelers, tablet and capsule counters, etc
President: Michel LaPierre
Director: Charles Lapierre
VP: Dan Lapierre
Marketing: Louise Lafleur
VP Sales: Mark Laroche
Number Employees: 150
Square Footage: 80000
Parent Co: NJM/CLI Packaging Systems International
Brands:
Blipack
Cli
Cremer
New Jersey Machine

26428 (HQ)NOVOLEX
5160 W Missouri Ave
Glendale, AZ 85301-6002

623-842-2236
Fax: 623-930-9406 800-243-0306
www.novolex.com
Polyethylene food and utility bags, printed bags, trash can liners, sleeves, tubing, interfold and sheeting
Manager: Ron Shaw
rshaw@fortuneplastics.com
VP Sales/Marketing: Ed Gillespie
Estimated Sales: $20-50 Million
Number Employees: 20-49
Other Locations:
Fortune Plastics
Phoenix AZ
Brands:
Duraliner
Dynaplas
Enviroplas
Hid-Tuff

26429 NPC Display Group
105 Avenue L
Newark, NJ 7105

973-589-2155
Fax: 973-589-2414
Containers including paper, corrugated and solid fiber

President: Dennis Mehiel
CFO: Allen Edelman
Contact: Donna Wiggs
donna.wiggs@usdisplaygroup.com
Number Employees: 100-249

26430 NS International
800 Kirts Blvd # 300
Troy, MI 48084-4880

248-362-8570
Fax: 248-352-9125 george@nsusa.com
www.ns-international.net
High speed, vertical 3 or 4 sided fill and seal machine for liquids and paste with multi-task programmable control
President: Arthur McMillen
Contact: Yoshi Ida
yoshi@nsusa.com
Estimated Sales: $20-50 Million
Number Employees: 1,000-4,999

26431 NSF International
789 N Dixboro Rd
Ann Arbor, MI 48105

734-769-8010
Fax: 734-769-0109 800-673-6275
info@nsf.org www.nsf.org
Organization sets public health standards and tests and certifies products and systems
CEO: Kevan Lawlor
lawlor@nsf.org
Number Employees: 2800

26432 NST Metals
721-723 East Main Street
Louisville, KY 40202

502-584-5846
Fax: 502-584-3481
Manufacturer and exporter of food processing equipment, pressure vessels, hoppers, bins and silos
President: Joe Harvey
VP: Kenneth Harvey
VP: Brian Harvey
Estimated Sales: $1-2.5 Million
Number Employees: 5-9
Square Footage: 28000
Type of Packaging: Consumer, Bulk

26433 NTN Wireless
6080 Northbelt Dr.
Norcross, GA 30071

770-277-2760
Fax: 770-277-2765 800-637-8639
james.frakes@ntn.com
Manufacturer and exporter of wireless server call systems and in-house server, guest and table ready paging systems
President: Mark Degortor
Number Employees: 20-49
Square Footage: 16000
Parent Co: Hysen Technologies
Brands:
Beck 'n Call
Economy Pager
Perfect Pager
Serv 'r Call
Table Turner

26434 NTS
126 Peach State Court
Suite A-C
Tyrone, GA 30290-2744

770-631-0203
Fax: 770-631-0718
CFO: Philippe Jafflin
Estimated Sales: $10-20 Million
Number Employees: 20-49

26435 NYP
10 Site Rd
Leola, PA 17540-1849

717-656-0299
Fax: 717-656-0350 800-541-0961
padiv@nyp-corp.com www.nyp-corp.com
Plain and printed bags including multi-wall, paper, polyethylene, woven polypropylene, burlap, cotton and mesh; importer of woven polypropylene bags
VP: Christopher LaBelle
VP Sales: Gerald LaBelle
Sales/Customer Service: Don Ament
dament@nyp-corp.com
Manager: Beverley Campbell
Division Manager: Robert Ellis
Purchasing Manager: Katie Gorsuch

Estimated Sales: less than $500,000
Number Employees: 1-4
Square Footage: 30000
Parent Co: NYP Corporation
Type of Packaging: Private Label, Bulk

26436 Nagel Paper & Box Company
3286 Industrial Drive
Saginaw, MI 48601

989-753-4405
Fax: 989-753-2493 800-292-3654
info@nagelpaper.com www.nagelpaper.com
Fiber tubes, caps and plugs
Contact: James Baker
james@nagelpaper.com
Estimated Sales: $1-3 Million
Number Employees: 18
Square Footage: 80000
Type of Packaging: Food Service

26437 Nalco Water
1601 W Diehl Rd
Naperville, IL 60563-1198

Fax: 800-288-0878 800-288-0879
customerservice.us@nalco.com www.ecolab.com
Process chemicals, water treatment, waste water
treatment.
EVP & President, Global Industrial: Darrell Brown
EVP & GM, Global Food & Beverage: Nicholas
Alfano
Year Founded: 1928
Estimated Sales: $4.2 Billion
Number Employees: 11,500
Parent Co: Ecolab Inc

26438 Nalge Process Technologies Group
75 Panorama Creek Dr
Rochester, NY 14625-2385

585-586-8800
Fax: 585-586-8431 nnitech@nalgenunc.com
www.nalgenunc.com
Manufacturer and exporter of blowers, fans, fittings,
hoses, liquid mixers, pipe tube and hose clamps,
safety equipment and tanks
Marketing: Karen Dally
Sales Manager: John Cooling
Contact: Charlie Amico
camico@nalgenunc.com
Product Manager: Greg Felosky
Number Employees: 500-999
Parent Co: Sybron Corporation

26439 Nalge Process Technologies Group
29 Brookfield Drive
Lafayette, NJ 07848-2006

973-579-1313
Fax: 973-579-3908 800-988-4876
Bins
Estimated Sales: $5-10 Million
Number Employees: 38

26440 Naltex
220 E Saint Elmo Rd
Austin, TX 78745

512-447-7000
Fax: 512-447-7444 800-531-5112
sales@naltex.com www.delstarinc.com
Manufacturer and exporter of plastic mesh, heat
sealing and header bags; also, case liners
Marketing: Marjorie Wilcox
Product Manager: Susan Emory
semory@delstarinc.com
Plant Manager: Scott Mc Henry
Estimated Sales: $20-50 Million
Number Employees: 100-249
Square Footage: 110000
Brands:
  Flex Net
  Mari-Net
  Naltex
  Shur-Grip
  Softliner
  Texliner

26441 Naman Marketing
9870 Pineview Avenue
Theodore, AL 36582-7403

251-438-2617
Fax: 251-433-5032
President: George Naman

26442 Namco Controls Corporation
760 Beta Dr # F
Cleveland, OH 44143-2334

440-460-1360
Fax: 440-460-3800 800-626-8324
www.namcocontrols.com
Manufacturer and exporter of packaging and mate-
rial handling presence and position sensors includ-
ing photoelectric, laser scanner, rotary cam switch
and proximity
President: Alex Joseph
Marketing Manager: Chuck Juda
VP Sales/Marketing: Bob Joyce
Plant Manager: Jamy Robins
Number Employees: 1-4
Parent Co: Danaher Corporation
Other Locations:
  Namco Controls Corp.
  Herzhorn
Brands:
  Cylindicator
  Lasernet
  Namco
  Snap-Lock

26443 Namco Machinery
5421 73rd Pl
Maspeth, NY 11378

Fax: 718-803-0165
Manufacturer and exporter of bottle washing ma-
chinery for laboratory glassware
President: Manning E Cole
jackjackson54@aol.com
Sales Manager: R Jackson
Estimated Sales: $3-5 Million
Number Employees: 5-9

26444 Nameplate
87 Empire Dr
St Paul, MN 55103-1856

651-228-1522
Fax: 651-228-1314 www.nameplatesdiv.com
Badges, medals, name plates, signs, stamps, tags and
labels
President: G Mellgren
g.mellgren@dmpolystamps.com
Estimated Sales: $2.5-5 Million
Number Employees: 50-99
Parent Co: St. Paul Stamp Works

26445 Napa Fermentation Supplies
575 Third St # A
Napa, CA 94559-2701

707-255-6372
Fax: 707-255-6462 napafermentation@aol.com
www.northnaparotary.org
Wine industry fermentation supplies
Owner: Pat Watkins
Manager: Megan Furth
Estimated Sales: less than $500,000
Number Employees: 5-9

26446 Napa Valley Bung Works
151 Camino Dorado
Napa, CA 94558-6213

707-963-0241
Fax: 707-963-0241
Bung hole stoppers
Estimated Sales: $1-5 Million
Number Employees: 5-9

26447 Napa Wooden Box Co
369 S Kelly Rd
American Canyon, CA 94503-9647

707-224-6447
Fax: 707-224-1613 www.napawoodenbox.com
Wooden gift boxes, wooden specialty packaging,
wooden displays
President: Greg Chase
greg@napawoodenbox.com
Estimated Sales: $5-10 Million
Number Employees: 20-49

26448 Napco Graphics Corporation
200 Covington Drive
Bloomingdale, IL 60108-3105

630-529-2900
Fax: 630-529-4395 www.napco.com
Flexographic printing, four-color process labels,
thermal labels, thermal ribbons, custom pres-
sure-sensitive labels
President: Geno Napolitano
Estimated Sales: $10-20 Million
Number Employees: 50-99

26449 Napco Security Systems Inc
333 Bayview Ave
Amityville, NY 11701-2800

631-842-0253
Fax: 631-789-9292 salesinfo@napcosecurity.com
www.napcosecurity.com
Manufacturer and exporter of electronic security
systems and accessories including control panels
President/Chairman/Secretary: Richard Soloway
SVP, Operations & Finance/Director: Kevin Buchel
SVP, Engineering Development: Michael Carrieri
SVP Corporate Sales & Marketing: Jorge Hevia
Vice President, Sales: Scott Schramme
Contact: John Banks
jbanks@napcosecurity.com
Purchasing: Edward Daber
Estimated Sales: $71 Million
Number Employees: 5-9
Square Footage: 90000
Brands:
  Magnum Alert

26450 Napoleon Appliance Corporation
214 Bayview Drive
Barrie, ON L4N 4Y8
Canada

705-726-4278
Fax: 705-725-2564 866-820-8686
wecare@napoleonproducts.com
www.napoleongrills.com
Manufacturer and exporter of gas grills
President: Wolfgang Schroeter
VP: Ingrid Schroeter
Research & Development: Steve Schwartz
Quality Control: Steve Taylor
Marketing/Sales: David Blain
Plant Manager: Michael Pulfer
Purchasing Manager: Lynda Allen
Number Employees: 100
Number of Brands: 11
Square Footage: 600000
Parent Co: Wolf Steel
Brands:
  Elegance
  Emerald
  Horizon
  Lifestyle
  Napoleon
  Premiere
  Prestige
  Signature
  Ultrachef

26451 NaraKom
PO Box 368
Peapack, NJ 07977-0368

908-234-1776
Fax: 908-234-0964
Distributor of Nara milling, sizing, coating, and
powder surface modification technology in the
Americas
President: C Komline
Number Employees: 20-49
Parent Co: Komline-Sanderson Engineering Corpo-
ration

26452 Nashua Corporation
250 S. Northwest Highway
Suite 203
Park Ridge, IL 60068

402-397-3600
Fax: 402-392-6080 800-323-4265
www.nashua.com
Manufacturer and exporter of computer and pressure
sensitive labels
President: Andrew Albert
CFO: John Patenaude
VP: Michael Jarrett
VP: Mike Jarrutt
Contact: Charles Bonnier
cbonnier@nashua.com
Number Employees: 100-249

26453 Nashua Corporation
44 Franklin Street
Nashua, NH 03064-2665

603-661-2004
Fax: 603-880-5671 info@amstock.com
www.nashua.com
Manufacturer and exporter of industrial tape and la-
bels
President: Andrew Albert
CFO: John Petenaude

26454 Nashville Display Manufacturing Company

306 Hartmann Drive
Lebanon, TN 37087

615-743-2900
Fax: 615-743-2901 888-743-2572
dissales@nashvilledisplay.com
www.nashvilledisplay.com
Manufacturer and exporter of displays and merchandisers for retail products
President: David L Rollins
CFO: Jeff McCeann
VP: E White
Quality Control: Charles Brittain
R & D: Juris Leikartt
Sales Manager: Richard Hornsay
Office Manager: Jere Lane
Estimated Sales: $10-20 Million
Number Employees: 20-49
Square Footage: 1600000

26455 Nashville Wire Products

295 Driftwood St
Nashville, TN 37210

615-743-2480
Fax: 615-255-8349 www.nashvillewire.com
Wire oven and warming racks and barbecue grids
President: David L Rollins
Shipping Manager: Levon Mathis
Division Manager: Steven Rollins
Plant Manager: Roy Binkley
Estimated Sales: $20-50 Million
Number Employees: 10-19
Square Footage: 140000
Parent Co: Nashville Wire Products Manufacturing Company

26456 Nashville Wraps LLC

242 Molly Walton Dr
Hendersonville, TN 37075-2154

615-431-5000
Fax: 800-646-0046 800-547-9727
info@nashvillewraps.com
www.nashvillewraps.com
Bags and bows, gift wrap, tissue paper, ribbon, candy boxes, food packaging, custom printing and eco-friendly retail packaging
Marketing Director: James Meadows
Estimated Sales: Less Than $500,000
Number Employees: 1-4

26457 Natale Machine & Tool Co Inc

339 13th St
Carlstadt, NJ 07072-1917

201-933-5500
Fax: 201-933-8146 800-883-8382
www.circle-d.com
Manufacturer and exporter of emergency lighting including flash, flood and spot lights; also, HID, quartz and commercial lighting available
CEO: Dominick Natale
VP: Lynn Natale
Sales: John Cocozzo
Production/Plant Manager/Purchasing: John Cocozzo
Estimated Sales: $3-5 Million
Number Employees: 10-19
Square Footage: 30000
Brands:
Circle D Lights
Streamlight

26458 Nation/Ruskin

206 Progress Dr
Montgomeryville, PA 18936

267-654-4000
Fax: 267-654-4010 800-523-2489
Natural and synthetic sponges; also, cloths and brushes
President: Raymond Adolf
VP Sales: John Holcombe
VP Sales: Stan Ruskin
Contact: Sandy Adolf
sadolf@nationalhardwareshow.com
Estimated Sales: $1-3 Million
Number Employees: 10-19
Brands:
Ez-One

26459 National Ammonia Co

735 Davisville Rd # 3
Southampton, PA 18966-3277

215-322-1238
Fax: 215-322-7791 800-643-6226
sales@tannerind.com www.tannerind.com
Anhydrous ammonia and aqua ammonia for uses including refrigeration applications, metal treating, chemical, pharmaceutical and petroleum industries, agriculture, reprographincs, resins, polymers, acid neutralization, water treatmentand explosives
CEO: Raymond Tanner
VP: Greg Tanner
Estimated Sales: $30-50 Million
Number Employees: 100-249

26460 National Band Saw Co

25322 Avenue Stanford
Santa Clarita, CA 91355-1214

661-294-9552
Fax: 661-294-9554 800-851-5050
harley@nbsparts.com www.nbsparts.com
Manufacturer, exporter and wholesaler/distributor of replacement parts for meat slicing and cutting machinery; importer of slicing knives, tenderizers and bread slicing and patty-making machines; wholesaler/distributor of office andshipping supplies
Owner: Enrique Barbosa
enriqueb@nbarizona.com
VP: Chris Tuttle
R & D: Ron Voytek
Director of IT Computer Services: Jason Jasperson
Production: Ron Voytek
Estimated Sales: Below $5 Million
Number Employees: 10-19
Square Footage: 12200
Type of Packaging: Consumer, Food Service, Private Label, Bulk

26461 National Bar Systems

16571 Burke Lane
Huntington Beach, CA 92647-4537

714-848-1688
Fax: 714-848-2788 www.nbsmfg.com
Manufacturer and exporter of stainless steel under-bar equipment including sinks, work tables and ice storage equipment
President: Johnny Lee
VP: John Ashkarian
CFO: Joe Kim
Contact: Joe Kim
joek@nbsmfg.com
Estimated Sales: $5-10 Million
Number Employees: 5-9

26462 National Cart Co

3125 Boschertown Rd
St Charles, MO 63301-3263

636-947-3800
Fax: 636-723-4477 sales@nationalcart.com
www.nationalcart.com
Manufacturer and exporter of oven racks, bun pans and pan tray carts
CEO: Brian Gillis
zroach@kumc.edu
CEO: Robert Unnerstall
Estimated Sales: $20-50 Million
Number Employees: 100-249
Square Footage: 100000

26463 National Chemicals Inc

105 Liberty St
PO Box 32
Winona, MN 55987-3706

507-494-8848
Fax: 507-454-5641 800-533-0027
Detergents, sanitizers and cleaners for food service use
Chairman of the Board: Louis Landman
clandman@natlchem.com
Estimated Sales: $10-20 Million
Number Employees: 10-19
Number of Brands: 21
Number of Products: 46

26464 National Computer Corporation

211 Century Drive
Suite 100-B
Greenville, SC 29607

866-944-5164
Fax: 864-235-7688 www.nccusa.com
Manufacturer, importer and exporter of point of sale systems

President: Douglas Harris Jr
Contact: Mary Harris
mharris@nccusa.com
Estimated Sales: $5-10,000,000
Number Employees: 10-19

26465 National Construction Services

PO Box 820
Frazer, PA 19355

610-647-8050
Fax: 610-647-8540 800-557-8050
President: Lee Krow
krow@krbassociates.com
CFO: Lee Krow
R&D: Lee Krow
Quality Control: Lee Krow
Estimated Sales: $5-10 Million
Number Employees: 10-19

26466 National Construction Technologies Group

4967 Kensington Gate
Excelsior, MN 55331-9345

952-474-7126
Fax: 952-474-7370
Specialized concrete surfaces including surface preparation, surface coatings, concrete construction
Estimated Sales: $1-5 Million

26467 (HQ)National Conveyor Corp

2250 Yates Ave
Commerce, CA 90040-1914

323-725-0355
Fax: 323-725-1440 info@natconcorp.com
Manufacturer and exporter of utensil washers, conveyor equipment, dish handling systems and waste reduction systems
Owner: Frank Bargas
Customer Service Manager: Luis Vargas
fra_cie@netzero.com
Engineer Manager: Joseph Marin
Estimated Sales: $2.5-5 Million
Number Employees: 10-19
Square Footage: 60000
Type of Packaging: Food Service
Brands:
Power Dishtable
Roto-Stak
Uni-Band

26468 National Datacomputer

900 Middlesex Tpke
Suite 5-1
Billerica, MA 01821

978-663-7677
Fax: 978-667-1869
Computer systems: handheld systems, route accounting, sales automation
CEO: William B Berens
Contact: Carla Bacucci
carla.bacucci@ndcomputer.com
Estimated Sales: $10-25 Million
Number Employees: 5-9

26469 National Discount Textile

2210 Defoor Hills Rd NW
Atlanta, GA 30318-2200

404-351-1630
Fax: 404-351-1631
www.national-discount-textiles.com
Owner: Murray Shelton
nina@buccaneerinc.com
Number Employees: 10-19

26470 National Distributor Services

3033 S Parker Road
Suite 400
Aurora, CO 80014-2921

303-755-4411
Fax: 303-755-4545
Manufacturer and exporter of forklifts
President: B Anthony Reed
CEO: Tony Reed
Number Employees: 50

26471 National Drying Machry Co Inc

2190 Hornig Rd
Philadelphia, PA 19116-4202

215-464-6070
Fax: 215-464-4096 info@nationaldrying.com
www.nationaldrying.com

Manufacturer and exporter of thermal processing equipment including dehydrators, dryers, ovens, roasters, blanchers, coolers and multi-tier and multi-pass conveyor systems and feeders
President: Richard Parkes
Director Marketing/Sales: Paul Branson
Director: Richard Eckard
Estimated Sales: $20-50 Million
Number Employees: 5-9
Square Footage: 80000
Parent Co: Apollo Sheet Metal

26472 National Emblem
PO Box 5325
Carson, CA 90749-5325

310-515-5055
Fax: 310-515-5966 800-877-5325
www.nationalemblem.com
Embroidered and screen printed emblems, caps, keyrings and woven labels
President: Milton Lubin Sr
CFO: Alicia Bsiez-Sounds
National Sales Manager: Marvin Grimm
Sales Director: Milton Lobin, Jr.
Estimated Sales: $20-50 Million
Number Employees: 250-499

26473 National Embroidery SvcInc
3390 E Main Rd # 1
Portsmouth, RI 02871-4240

401-683-4724
Fax: 401-683-0012 800-227-1451
sales@nationalembroidery.com
www.nationalembroidery.com
Custom embroidered uniforms, hats, shirts, vests, chef coats and aprons
President and R&D: Dale Wood
Quality Control: Eileen Wood
CEO and CFO: Dale B Wood
Estimated Sales: Less than $500,000
Number Employees: 5-9
Square Footage: 10000

26474 National Energy Consultants
PO Box 562
Cedar Falls, IA 50613-0027

319-231-0857
Fax: 877-553-0187 888-841-6987
info@nationalenergyconsultants.com
www.nationalenergyconsultants.com
Energy consulting, procurement, management and consolidated billing capabilities
Number Employees: 10-19

26475 (HQ)National Equipment Corporation
801 E 141st St
Bronx, NY 10454

718-585-0200
Fax: 718-993-2650 800-237-8873
sales@unionmachinery.com
www.unionmachinery.com
Manufacturer, importer and exporter of used and reconditioned food processing and packaging equipment
VP: Arthur Greenberg
VP: Richard Greenberg
VP: Charles Greenberg
Contact: David Feinne
dfeinne@unionmachinery.com
Number Employees: 20-49
Square Footage: 1800000
Other Locations:
National Equipment Corp.
Naucalpan

26476 National FABCO Manufacturing
12927 Gravois Rd
St Louis, MO 63127-1714

314-842-4571
Fax: 314-842-8088
Custom designed food serving equipment including counters, sinks, refrigerated carts, hoods, countertops and tables
President: John Gates
john.gates@sefa.com
VP: Frank Ruggeri
Estimated Sales: $10-20 Million
Number Employees: 20-49
Square Footage: 11000
Type of Packaging: Food Service, Private Label
Brands:
Cleveland
Groen

Hatc
Hubort
Southbend
Thermobend
Traulsen
Victory

26477 National Foam
180 Sheree Blvd # 3900
Exton, PA 19341-1272

610-363-1400
Fax: 610-524-9073 webmaster@kidde-fire.com
www.kidde-fire.com
Manufacturer and exporter of foam fire extinguishing chemicals and equipment
Manager: Bobby Nelson
CFO: Larry Mansfield
Contact: Herbert Cooper
herbert.cooper@nationalfoam.com
Estimated Sales: $20-50 Million
Number Employees: 100-249
Parent Co: Racal-Chubb

26478 National Food Laboratories Inc
365 N Canyons Pkwy # 101
Suite 201
Livermore, CA 94551-7703

925-828-1440
Fax: 925-243-0117 www.covance.com
Consulting laboratory specializing in market research, sensory analysis, process and product development, analytical services and pilot plant services
President: Kevin Buck
buckk@thenfl.com
VP, Finance & Administration: Mindy Hungerman
Quality Assurance and Safety Manager: Bob Takens
Division Manager: Rupinder Jaura
VP, Business Development: Angie McKenzie
Estimated Sales: $10-20 Million
Number Employees: 50-99
Square Footage: 120000
Parent Co: National Food Processors Association

26479 National Food Product Research Corporation
318 Main Street
P.O.Box 419
West Newbury, MA 01985-0519

978-363-2144
Fax: 978-363-2073 800-363-2144
Consultant providing marketing research for food, products, equipment and services
Owner: John Sibley
nfpsib@greennet.net
Executive VP: John Sibley
Estimated Sales: Below $5 Million
Number Employees: 10-19

26480 National Honey Board
11409 Business Park Cir # 210
Suite # 210
Firestone, CO 80504-9203

303-776-2337
Fax: 303-776-1177 800-553-7162
honey@nhb.org
Educates consumers about the benefits and uses for honey and honey products.
Chairperson, Board Member: Brent Barkman
CEO, Board Member: Bruce Boynton
Vice Chairperson, Board Member: Mark Mammen
Director Scientific Affairs: Marcia Cardetti
Marketing Director: Tami Yanosk
IT Administrator and Webmaster: Darren Brown
Number Employees: 5-9

26481 National Hotpack
3538 Main Street
Stone Ridge, NY 12484

845-255-5000
Fax: 845-687-7481 800-431-8232
hotpack@spindustries.com www.hotpack.com
Hotpack manufactures and sells enviromental rooms and chambers, stability rooms and chambers, humidity rooms and chambers, glassware washers and dryers, vacuum ovens, sterilizers and autoclaves, C-O2 incubators, general purposeincubators, ovens, refrigerators, freezers
President/CEO: Bill Downs
CFO: Michael Bonner
Marketing: Shireen Scott
Sales: James Shiever
Estimated Sales: $65 Million
Number Employees: 100-249

Square Footage: 70000
Parent Co: SP Industries
Brands:
Heinicke
Hotpack
National Labortory Products
Oem Products

26482 National Instruments
4119 Fordleigh Rd
Baltimore, MD 21215-2292

410-764-0900
Fax: 410-951-2093 866-258-1914
jrosen@filamatic.com www.filamatic.com
Manufacturer and exporter of liquid filling, capping and turnkey packaging equipment
CEO: Robert Rosen
VP Marketing/Sales: Jim Striese
Manager: Mark Evans
mark.evans@filamatic.com
Estimated Sales: $10-20 Million
Number Employees: 50-99
Brands:
Capamatic
Dial-A-Fill
Econofil
Filamatic
Synchromat

26483 National Interchem Corporation
13750 Chatham Street
Blue Island, IL 60406-3218

773-638-5100
Fax: 773-638-8769 800-638-6688
www.nichemical.com
Manufacturer and exporter of industrial cleaning and maintenance chemicals
Director Sales: Greg Fishman
Estimated Sales: $2.5-5 Million
Number Employees: 10-19

26484 National Label Co
2025 Joshua Rd
Lafayette Hill, PA 19444-2426

610-825-3250
Fax: 610-834-8854 www.nationallabel.com
Manufacturer and exporter of pressure sensitive labeling equipment and labels
Exec VP: James Shacklett IV
Estimated Sales: $50-100 Million
Number Employees: 250-499
Type of Packaging: Bulk

26485 National Marker Co Inc
100 Providence Pike
North Smithfield, RI 02896-8046

401-762-9700
Fax: 401-762-1010 800-453-2727
sales@nationalmarker.com
www.nationalmarker.com
Plastic safety signs
President: Michael Black
mblack@nationalmarker.com
Marketing Director: Patricia O'Hara
Estimated Sales: $5-10 Million
Number Employees: 50-99

26486 National Marking Products Inc
5606 Greendale Rd
Henrico, VA 23228-5816

804-266-7691
Fax: 804-266-6110 800-482-1553
www.nationalmarking.com
Promotional items including rubber stamps, plastic signs, shipping supplies, bronze tablets, labels, tags and awards
President/Owner: Richard Reinhard
ric@nationalmarkingproducts.com
Manager: Brenda Puryear
Estimated Sales: Below $5 Million
Number Employees: 10-19
Square Footage: 30000

26487 National Menuboard
4302 B St NW # D
Auburn, WA 98001

253-859-6068
Fax: 253-859-8412 800-800-5237
Menu boards including illuminated, nonilluminated, indoor and outdoor
President: Dave Medzegian
dave@nationalmenuboard.com
Sales Representative: Wendi Adsley

Estimated Sales: Below $5 Million
Number Employees: 5-9
Square Footage: 40000

26488 National Metal Industries
203 Circuit Avenue
West Springfield, MA 01089-4016

413-785-5861
Fax: 413-737-2309 800-628-8850
www.national-metal.com

Manufacturer and exporter of metal stamps and parts for food processing equipment
Sales Manager: Bryan Costello
Estimated Sales: $10-20 Million
Number Employees: 50-99
Parent Co: Standex International Corporation

26489 (HQ)National Novelty Brush Co
505 E Fulton St
Lancaster, PA 17602-3022

717-299-5681
Fax: 717-397-0991 www.nnbc-pa.com

Manufacturer and exporter of brushes, applicators and metal screw caps
President: Richard Seavey
rseavey@nnbc-pa.com
CFO: Bryan Howett
Quality Control: Sandy Donley
Sales Manager: Ronald Vellucci
Customer Service: Marianne Walsh
Estimated Sales: $20-50 Million
Number Employees: 100-249

26490 National Oilwell Varco
125 Flagship Dr
North Andover, MA 01845-6119

978-687-0101
Fax: 978-687-8500 800-643-0641
inquiry@kenics.com www.chemineer.com

Processing equipment: static and high shear mixers and heat exchangers
Manager: Mark Raymond
Quality Control: John Cercone
Marketing Director: Dave Ryan
Manager: George Hanna
ghanna@kenics.com
Purchasing Manager: Laura Parker
Estimated Sales: $20-50 Million
Number Employees: 20-49
Parent Co: Robbins & Meyers
Brands:
Greerco
Kenics

26491 National Package SealingCompany
10791 SE Skyline Drive
Santa Ana, CA 92705-7413

714-630-1505
Fax: 714-632-3217

Manufacturer and exporter of electric and manual dispensers for gummed carton sealing tapes and labels
President: William Amneus
Marketing Director: Fay Amneus
Estimated Sales: $2.5-5 Million
Number Employees: 19
Square Footage: 80000

26492 National Packaging
PO Box 4798
Rumford, RI 02916-0798

401-434-1070
Fax: 401-438-5203 www.multiwall.com

Manufacturer and exporter of cloth winding reels and single faced corrugated paper
President: Charles M Dunn
Estimated Sales: $20-50 Million
Number Employees: 10-19
Parent Co: Real Reel Corporation

26493 (HQ)National Pen Co
12121 Scripps Summit Dr # 200
San Diego, CA 92131-4609

858-675-3000
Fax: 858-675-3030 info@nationalpen.com
www.nationalpen.com

Ink pens
President: Thomas Liguorii
Chief Executive Officer: Dave Thompson
Chief Financial Officer: Rich Obrigawitch
SVP, North America Direct: Ron Childs
Number Employees: 100-249

26494 National Plastics Co
15505 Cornet St
Santa Fe Springs, CA 90670-5511

562-926-4511
Fax: 562-926-0222 800-221-9149
mra@natcos.com www.menucovers.com

Menu covers, loose leaf binders, wine lists, check presenters, transparent price card holders and pad holders; exporter of menu covers
President: Gregory Mitchell
gregm@natcos.com
Marketing Director: Mark Anderson
Sales Director: Brian Bromm
Office Manager: Bryan Carr
Plant Manager: Benjamin Jimenez
Estimated Sales: $5-10 Million
Number Employees: 50-99
Square Footage: 36000
Parent Co: National Plastic Company of California

26495 National Poly Bag Manufacturing Corporation
220 West Street
Brooklyn, NY 11222-1350

718-629-9800
Fax: 718-629-0265

Plastic bags and film
Estimated Sales: $1-5 Million
Number Employees: 12

26496 National Polymers
7920 215th St W
Lakeville, MN 55044-9015

952-469-4977
Fax: 952-469-2051 800-328-4577
scoops@nationalmeasures.com

Plastic measures for powdered and liquid products
President: Dennis Anderson
CFO: Mac Moore
Sales Manager: Mac Moore
Manager: Paul Kinney
Production/Advertising: Wes Anderson
Estimated Sales: Less Than $500,000
Number Employees: 1-4
Type of Packaging: Bulk

26497 National Printing Converters
4310 Bonavita Dr
Encino, CA 91436

818-906-7936

Manufacturer and exporter of data processing printed, pressure sensitive, laser, on-line pattern adhesive and vinyl shelf marking labels and shelf talkers
President: Brain Buckley
Chairman: Robert Buckley
Operations Manager: Richard Atkins
Estimated Sales: $.5-1 million
Number Employees: 1-4
Square Footage: 110000
Brands:
Label Data-Set

26498 National Provisioner
7300 N. Linder Ave.
Skokie, IL 60077-3217

847-763-9534
Fax: 847-763-9538 NP@halldata.com
www.provisioneronline.com

26499 National Purity LLC
6840 Shingle Creek Pkwy # 23
Brooklyn Center, MN 55430-1459

612-672-0022
Fax: 612-672-0027 www.nationalpurity.com

Soaps, detergents, cleaning agents and soap based industrial lubricants
President: Sean Spillane
sspillane@nationalpurity.com
National Account Manager: Bill Stark
Field Account Manager: Sean Spillane
Estimated Sales: $20-50 Million
Number Employees: 5-9
Square Footage: 52000

26500 National Restaurant Supply Company
2513 Comanche Rd NE
Albuquerque, NM 87107

877-654-6554
sales@nrsupply.com www.nrsupply.com

Wholesaler/distributor of equipment, supplies, china, silverware, tabletop items, furniture and stainless steel fabrication; serving the food service market.

26501 National Scoop & Equipment Company
PO Box 325
Spring House, PA 19477-0325

215-646-2040

Manufacturer, wholesaler/distributor and importer of pails, buckets, scales, scoops, skimmers, dippers, disposable paper clothing, sinks and trucks
Manager: Ken Johnson

26502 National Sign Corporation
1255 Westlake Ave N
Seattle, WA 98109-3531

206-282-0700
Fax: 206-285-3091 info@nationalsigncorp.com
www.nationalsigncorp.com

Manufacturing, installation and servicing of interior and exterior signage, including ADA signs.
President: Timothy Zamberlin
Estimated Sales: $5-10 Million
Number Employees: 35
Square Footage: 60000

26503 National Sign Systems
4200 Lyman Ct
Hilliard, OH 43026-1213

614-529-6628
Fax: 614-850-2552 800-544-6726
sales@natsignsys.com www.natsignsys.com

Signs, menu systems, copy strips and HVAC equipment screens
President: James Cullinan
jcullinan@natsignsys.com
CFO: Paul Saokendach
VP Sales/Marketing: Paul Falkenbach
Estimated Sales: $10-20,000,000
Number Employees: 100-249
Square Footage: 310920

26504 National Stabilizers
1846 Business Center Dr
Duarte, CA 91010-2997

626-359-4584
Fax: 626-359-4586

Stabilizers
President: Robert Burger
Quality Control: Raivo Partma
VP Sales: Robert Burger
Sales/Purchasing: Tomas Martinez
Estimated Sales: $2.5-5 Million
Number Employees: 5 to 9
Brands:
Stabak
Stacol

26505 National Steel Corporation
100 Quality Drive
Ecorse, MI 48229-1850

734-953-3603
Fax: 734-953-3601

Tin plate and chromium coated steel for production of containers, ends, closures and crowns

26506 National Stock Sign Co
1040 El Dorado Ave
Santa Cruz, CA 95062-2825

831-476-2020
Fax: 831-476-1734 800-462-7726
nationalstock@sbcglobal.net

Safety, parking and no smoking signs
President: Henrietta Cooper
Marketing Manager: Lorraine Kirkpatrick
General Manager: Joel Kirkpatrick
Estimated Sales: $1-3 Million
Number Employees: 10-19
Square Footage: 30000
Brands:
Nassco

26507 National Sunflower Assn
2401 46th Ave SE # 206
Suite 206
Mandan, ND 58554-4829

701-328-5100
Fax: 701-328-5101 888-718-7033
johns@sunflowernsa.com www.sunflowernsa.com

Non-profit corporation designed to advance the sunflower industry.

Executive Director: John Sandbakken
Meeting Planner & Advertising Sales: Lerrene Kroh
BusinessOffice Manager: Tina Mittelsteadt
Number Employees: 5-9

26508 National Tape Corporation
5128 Storey Street
New Orleans, LA 70123-5320

504-733-8020
Fax: 504-734-8751 800-535-8846
Manufacturer and exporter of pressure sensitive labels and tapes including masking, duct, electrical, pressure sensitive and marking
VP Sales: Joel Teachworth
VP: Robert Wiswall
Number Employees: 100
Square Footage: 520000

26509 National Time RecordingEqpt
64 Reade St # 2
New York, NY 10007-1870

212-227-3310
Fax: 212-227-5353 info@nationaltime.net
www.nationaltime.net
Manufacturer and exporter of time clocks, time stamps and thermometers
VP: K Kelly
Estimated Sales: $5-10 Million
Number Employees: 10-19

26510 National Towelette
1726 Woodhaven Dr
Bensalem, PA 19020-7108

215-245-7300
Fax: 215-245-7390 info@towelettes.com
www.flexwipes.com
Individually wrapped moist towelettes
President: Tim Brock
brock@towelettes.com
CFO: Tim Bro
Number Employees: 50-99
Square Footage: 50000

26511 National Velour Corp
36 Bellair Ave
Warwick, RI 02886-2206

401-737-8300
Fax: 401-738-7418 800-556-6523
service@nationalvelour.com
www.nationalvelour.com
Manufacturer and exporter of flock for packaging and displays; also, custom flocking and stock lines available
President: Oscar Der Manouelian
Estimated Sales: $5-10 Million
Number Employees: 10-19

26512 National Wooden Pallet & Container Association
1421 Prince Street
Suite 340
Alexandria, VA 22314-2805

703-519-6104
Fax: 703-519-4720 palletcomm@aol.com
www.palletcentral.com
Manufacture, repair and distribute pallets and wood packaging in unit-load solutions.
President/CEO: Brent J. McClendon, CAE
Vice President of Operations and Events: Isabel Sullivan
Sales Director: Joni Leonardo
Contact: Patrick Atagi
patrick@palletcentral.com
Number Employees: 10-19

26513 Nationwide Boiler Inc
42400 Christy St
Fremont, CA 94538-3141

510-490-7100
Fax: 510-490-0571 800-227-1966
info@nationwideboiler.com www.catastak.com
President/Owner: Jeff Shallcross
jeff@nationwideboiler.com
Chairman Of The Board: Richard Bliss
Estimated Sales: $5-10 Million
Number Employees: 20-49

26514 Nationwide Pennant & Flag Mfg
7325 Reindeer Trl
San Antonio, TX 78238-1214

210-684-3524
Fax: 210-680-2329 800-383-3524
sales@napmfg.com www.napmfg.com

Manufacturer and exporter of pennants, flags, flagpoles, banners and decals
President: Donald W Engelhardt
CEO: Rick Sutton
Sales: Joe Pyland
Estimated Sales: $10-20 Million
Number Employees: 50-99
Square Footage: 120000

26515 Nationwide Wire & BrushManufacturing
411 Evergreen Drive
Lodi, CA 95242-4629

209-334-9660
Fax: 209-334-9432
Power brooms and brushes for the food industry
President: Richard Savage
Sales Manager: Jim Olvera
Estimated Sales: Below $5 Million
Number Employees: 35

26516 Native Lumber Company
8 N Branford Road
Wallingford, CT 06492-2712

203-269-2625
Wooden pallets
Co-Owner: Dick Smith
Estimated Sales: $2.5-5 Million
Number Employees: 9

26517 Natural Marketing Institute
272 Ruth Rd # 1
Harleysville, PA 19438-1927

215-513-7300
Fax: 215-513-1713 www.nmisolutions.com
Consultant to food industry specializing in consumer research, market analysis and brand and product development.
Owner: Sandra Carrow
sandra.carrow@nmisolutions.com
Managing Partner: Steve French
Public Relations: Dana Marinari
Number Employees: 1-4
Square Footage: 20000
Parent Co: Mic-Ellen Associates

26518 Nature Most Laboratories
Trigo Business Park
60 Trigo Drive
Middletown, CT 06457-6157

860-346-8991
Fax: 860-347-3312 800-234-2112
sales@naturemost.com
Manufacturer, importer and exporter of products, vitamins, oils, minerals, herbal supplements
President: Robert Trigo
Marketing: Sam Schwartz
Sales: Donna Platnum
Operations: Fred Wuschner
Estimated Sales: $5-10 Million
Number Employees: 20-49
Number of Brands: 3
Number of Products: 300
Square Footage: 80000
Type of Packaging: Consumer, Private Label
Brands:
    Naturemost Labs
    Trigo Labs

26519 Nature Soy Inc
713 N 10th St
Philadelphia, PA 19123-1902

215-765-3289
Fax: 215-765-3266 support@naturesoy.com
Manufacturer/supplier of healthy soy and vegetarian products to the ethnic market
President: Yat Wen
CEO: Gene He
he@naturesoy.com
EVP: Fenjin He
Estimated Sales: $2.4 Million
Number Employees: 20-49
Square Footage: 35000

26520 Nature's Own
11 Fred Roddy Avenue
Attleboro, MA 2703

508-399-8690
Fax: 508-399-8693 www.naturesown.com.au
Natural hardwood charcoal and grilling/smoking woods; importer of herbwoods; exporter of hardwood charcoal

President/Owner: Don Hysko
VP: Holly Hysko
Sales Manager: Dana Bracket
Estimated Sales: $2.5-5 Million
Number Employees: 5-9
Square Footage: 50000
Brands:
    Loon
    Nature's Own
    Pfb (Produits Forresters Baasques)
    Treestock

26521 Naughton Equipment Sales
1203 Madison St
Fort Calhoun, NE 68023-3524

402-468-4682
Fax: 402-468-4683 866-858-4682
sales@naughtonequipment.com
www.naughtonequipment.com
Foof processing equipment for the meat, poultry, and fisch industries
President: Daniel Naughton
VP: Kathy Naughton
R & D: Ed Kermeen
Marketing: Jerry Naughton
Estimated Sales: $1-3 Million
Number Employees: 1-4
Square Footage: 60000
Brands:
    Carcos Splutting Saw
    Ez Splitter Ii

26522 Navco
11929 Brittmoore Park Dr
Houston, TX 77041-7226

832-467-3636
Fax: 832-467-3800 800-231-0164
sales@navco.us www.navco.us
Manufacturer and exporter of material handling equipment including pneumatic and electric vibrators
President: Mark Neundorfer
Marketing Manager: Ben Snider
Number Employees: 10-19

26523 Navy Brand
3670 Scarlet Oak Blvd
St Louis, MO 63122-6606

636-861-5500
Fax: 636-861-5509 800-325-3312
navybrand@navybrand.com www.navybrand.com
Manufacturer and wholesaler/distributor of industrial degreasers, cleaners and water treatment systems for boilers and cooling towers
President: Ed Schooling
CEO: Edwin Schooling
Director Sales: Jack Julier
IT: Edwin Schooling
eschooling@navybrand.com
Estimated Sales: $1.5 Million
Number Employees: 10-19
Square Footage: 200000

26524 Naylor Association Solutions
5950 NW 1st Pl
Gainesville, FL 32607-6060

352-332-1252
Fax: 352-331-3525 www.naylor.com
Publications
Manager: Jason Dolder
jdolder@naylor.com
Number Employees: 250-499

26525 Neal Walters Poster Corporation
PO Box 480
Bentonville, AR 72712-0480

501-273-2489
Fax: 501-271-2132
Manufacturer and exporter of billboard and point of purchase posters, product markings, decals, bar code and pressure sensitive labels, business and computer forms, etc
President: James Walters
Secy./Treas.: Thomas Walters
V.P.: John Walters
Estimated Sales: $500,000-$1 Million
Number Employees: 9
Square Footage: 60000

26526 Nebraska Bean
85824 519th Ave
Clearwater, NE 68726-5239
402-887-5335
Fax: 402-887-4709 800-253-6502
brett@nebraskabean.com www.nebraskabean.com
Experienced grower, processor and packager of
quality popcorn. The fully integrated operation of-
fers microwave, bulk, private label and poly bags of
popcorn
President: Brett Morrison
brett@nebraskabean.com
VP: Brett Morrison
Sales: Michelle Steskal
Estimated Sales: $10-20 Million
Number Employees: 20-49
Number of Brands: 1
Square Footage: 10000
Type of Packaging: Consumer, Food Service, Pri-
vate Label, Bulk
Brands:
Morrison Farms

26527 Nebraska Neon Sign Co
1140 N 21st St
Lincoln, NE 68503-1698
402-476-6563
Fax: 402-476-3461 nesignco@gmail.com
www.nebraskaneonsign.com
Signs including neon, wooden, illuminated, etc
President: Robert Norris
bnorris@nebraskasign.com
Estimated Sales: $2.5-5 Million
Number Employees: 20-49

26528 Necedah Pallet Co Inc
703 N Harvey St
Necedah, WI 54646-8179
608-565-2619
Fax: 608-565-2979 800-672-5538
necedahpallet@tds.net
Wooden pallets and skids
Sales/Marketing: Steve Schultz
General Manager: Terry Hess
Estimated Sales: $2.5-5 Million
Number Employees: 20-49
Square Footage: 40000
Parent Co: Northern Pallet & Supply
Type of Packaging: Bulk

26529 Nederman
102 Transit Ave
Thomasville, NC 27360-8927
336-821-0800
Fax: 336-821-0890 800-533-5286
www.nederman.com
Manufacturer and importer of dust collection filters,
cyclones, grinders, pipe clamps and ducts
President: Tom Ballus
tom.ballus@nederman.com
Marketing Director: Tarey Cullen
VP Sales: Steve McDaniel
Estimated Sales: $20-50 Million
Number Employees: 100-249
Brands:
Clean-Sweep
Quick-Fit
Vortex

26530 Nederman
102 Transit Ave
Thomasville, NC 27360-8927
336-821-0800
Fax: 336-821-0890 800-533-5286
www.nederman.com
Nederman LLC is a leading manufacturer of state of
the art Dust, Fume, and Mist Collection Systems for
the paper industry and recycling processes. Our
products deliver consistent reliability, low energy
consumption and compliance withOSHA and NFPA
combustible dust requirements. Our experience and
proven techniques have allowed us to save customers up to 80 percent on their energy costs.
President: Tom Ballus
tom.ballus@nederman.com
Sales: Rob Williamson
Estimated Sales: $3-5 Million
Number Employees: 100-249

26531 Nefab
204 Airline Drive
Suite 600
Coppell, TX 75019
469-444-5320
Fax: 847-985-3200 800-536-7261
www.nefab.com
No-nail, lightweight, collapsible export containers
made from plywood and steel
President: Lars-ake Rydh
President, Chief Executive Officer: David MArk
Executive Vice President: Anders M"rk
Contact: Brad Ackerman
brad.ackerman@nefab.com
Estimated Sales: $2.5-5 Million
Number Employees: 5-9

26532 Nefab Packaging Inc
850 Mark St
Elk Grove Vlg, IL 60007-6704
847-787-0340
Fax: 630-595-7230 lori.brownstein@nefab.com
www.nefab.us
Plywood, no-nail, foldable and reusable packaging
systems for transport, storage and internal distribu-
tion
President, Chief Executive Officer: David MArk
Executive Vice President: Anders M"rk
Estimated Sales: $2.5-5 Million
Number Employees: 100-249
Parent Co: Nefab A.B.
Brands:
Repak

26533 Nefab Packaging Inc
850 Mark St
Elk Grove Vlg, IL 60007-6704
847-787-0340
Fax: 630-595-7230 800-536-7261
www.nefab.com
No-nail, collapsible, export and reusable containers,
easy to assemble and available in custom and stock
sizes-made from a combination of plywood and
steelContainers are delivered flat and designed to
customer's specification.providing packaging solu-
tions.cost effective transport containers
President, Chief Executive Officer: David MArk
Executive Vice President: Anders M"rk
Sales Director: Lori Brownstein
Estimated Sales: $2.5-5 Million
Number Employees: 100-249
Type of Packaging: Consumer

26534 (HQ)Nefab Packaging Inc.
204 Airline Dr
Suite 100
Coppell, TX 75019
Fax: 469-444-5308 800-322-4425
www.nefab.com
Industrial crates material handling products includ-
ing pallets
Contact: Stephanie Carreon
scarreon@nefab.us
Estimated Sales: $5-10 Million
Number Employees: 10
Square Footage: 92000

26535 Nefab Packaging, Inc.
204 Airline Drive
Suite 100
Coppell, TX 75019
469-444-5308
Fax: 603-367-4329 800-322-4425
www.nefab.us
Manufacturer and exporter of wooden industrial
packaging and distribution equipment including pal-
lets, skids, crates and boxes; also, milling services
available
Director of Global Business Development: Ken
Wilson
Chief Executive Officer: Brian Bulatao
VP: Andi Wilson
Executive Vice President: Eric Howe
Contact: Stephanie Carreon
scarreon@nefab.us
Number Employees: 400

26536 Neff Packaging
10 Kingbrook Pkwy
Simpsonville, KY 40067-5625
502-722-5020
Fax: 502-722-5070 800-445-4383
rdneff@neffpackaging.com
www.neffpackaging.com

Folding paper boxes and cartons
Owner: Robert D Neff
CEO: R Neff
rdneff@neffpackaging.com
Marketing Director: R Neff
Estimated Sales: $1-2.5 Million
Number Employees: 50-99
Parent Co: Neff Courier Group

26537 Neilson Canvas Company
715 W Washington St
Sandusky, OH 44870-2334
419-625-0581
Fax: 419-625-4315
Commercial awnings
President: Robert Nielsen
VP: Darcy Neilson
Estimated Sales: $1-2,500,000
Number Employees: 10-19

26538 (HQ)Nelipak
3720 W Washington St
Phoenix, AZ 85009-4765
602-269-7648
Fax: 602-269-7640 drichardson@flexpakcorp.com
www.nelipak.com
Thermoformed products including shelf organizers,
freezer trays, point of purchase displays and ship-
ping and handling trays; also, contract packaging in-
cluding club packs, assembly, shrink packaging,
display packout, bagging andlabeling
President: Donald Bond
qstein@flexpak.net
CFO: Steve Merray
Quality Control: Carlos Pineda
Marketing Director: Don Richardson
Operations Manager: Rick Colton
Purchasing Manager: Jim Boley
Estimated Sales: $20-50 Million
Number Employees: 100-249
Square Footage: 82000
Type of Packaging: Consumer, Food Service, Pri-
vate Label, Bulk

26539 Nelles Automation
7000 Hollister St
Houston, TX 77040-5617
713-939-9399
Fax: 713-939-0393
tom.christopher@telvent.abengoa.com
www.telvent.com
Manufacturer and exporter of automated control sys-
tems and circuit boards for electric utility
President: Dave Jardine
CFO: Manuel Fanchez
VP: Tom Christopher
Estimated Sales: $1-3 Million
Number Employees: 5-9
Parent Co: Valmet

26540 Nelson & Associates Recruiting
PO Box 2686
Kirkland, WA 98083
425-823-0956
Fax: 425-820-4541 nelson@foodrecruiter.com
www.foodrecruiter.com
Personnel recruiter specializing in executive, mana-
gerial and technical food industry positions
President: Kenneth Nelson
Estimated Sales: Below $5 Million
Number Employees: 1-4

26541 Nelson Co
4517 North Point Blvd
Sparrows Point, MD 21219-1798
410-477-3000
Fax: 410-388-0246 info@nelsoncompany.com
www.nelsoncompany.com
Wooden pallets and skids; wholesaler/distributor of
plastic and metal pallets, shrink and stretch wraps,
angleboards and void fillers
President: Arthur Caltrider
IT Executive: John Williams
jack.williams@nelsoncompany.com
Estimated Sales: $5-10 Million
Number Employees: 50-99
Parent Co: Nelson Company

26542 Nelson Container Corp
W180n11921 River Ln
Germantown, WI 53022-6308
262-250-5000
Fax: 262-250-5015 contact@nelsoncontainer.com
www.nelsoncontainer.com

Containers and corrugated boxes
President: Thomas Nelson
President: Tom Nelson
Estimated Sales: $20-50 Million
Number Employees: 20-49

26543 Nelson Custom Signs
1199 S Sheldon Rd
Plymouth, MI 48170-2192

734-455-0500
Fax: 734-455-0800

Signs including neon, painted, wooden, etc
Manager: Pete Nelson
Estimated Sales: Less than $500,000
Number Employees: 1-4

26544 Nelson, Gene
12786 Old Redwood Hwy
Healdsburg, CA 95448-9512

707-433-5138
Fax: 707-433-9214

Wine industry wood bungs
Owner: Gene Nelson
Contact: Mike Parker
mike@abwoodtech.com
Estimated Sales: less than $500,000
Number Employees: 5-9

26545 Nelson-Jameson Inc
2400 E 5th St
Marshfield, WI 54449-4661

715-387-1151
Fax: 715-387-8746 800-826-8302
sales@nelsonjameson.com
www.nelsonjameson.com

Wholesale distributor serving food and beverage
processors. Wide-line distributor of sanitation, main-
tenance, laboratory, processing and flow control,
personnel and safety supplies
President: Jerry Lippert
j.lippert@nelsonjameson.com
CEO: John Nelson
CEO: Bruce Lautenschlager
Estimated Sales: $50-75 Million
Number Employees: 50-99
Number of Brands: 750+
Other Locations:
Nelson-Jameson
Twin Falls ID
Nelson-Jameson
Turlock CA

26546 Nemco Electric Company
207 S Horton St
Seattle, WA 98134-1929

206-622-1551
Fax: 206-622-4449

Lighting equipment including custom chandeliers
for hotel lobbies and banquet rooms and portable
fluorescent work lights; also, custom lighting fix-
tures available
President: Arnold Larson
VP: Judy Larson
Estimated Sales: $1-2.5 Million
Number Employees: 1-4
Square Footage: 80000

26547 Nemco Food Equipment
301 Meuse Argonne St
PO Box 305
Hicksville, OH 43526-1143

419-542-7751
Fax: 419-542-6690 800-782-6761
mwibel@nemcofoodequip.com

Manufacturer and exporter of vegetable slicers and
cutters
President: Jarod Martenies
vanney75@yahoo.com
Estimated Sales: $10-20 Million
Number Employees: 50-99
Type of Packaging: Food Service

26548 Nemeth Engineering Assoc
5901 W Highway 22
Crestwood, KY 40014-7217

502-241-1502
Fax: 502-241-5907 info@nemeth-engineering.com
www.nemeth-engineering.com

Manufacturer and exporter of radio frequency heating systems for drying, baking, moisture leveling,
proofing, thawing, tempering and deinfestation
President: Peter Nemeth
pnemeth@nemeth-engineering.com
Sales Manager: Ned Snow
Sales Associate: Bobbie Gardner

Estimated Sales: $5-10 Million
Number Employees: 20-49
Square Footage: 150000

26549 Neo-Image Candle Light
1331 Blundell Road
Mississauga, ON L4Y 1M6
Canada

905-273-3020
Fax: 905-273-6905 800-375-8023
info@candlesjustonline.com www.neo-image.com

Candles and accessories
Sales Manager: Ric Jones
General Manager: Steve Stratakos
Estimated Sales: $15 Million
Number Employees: 25-49
Parent Co: North America Candle
Brands:
Neo-Image

26550 Neo-Ray Products
537 Johnson Avenue
Brooklyn, NY 11237-1304

718-456-7400
Fax: 718-456-5492 800-221-0946

Manufacturer and exporter of architectural grade
fluorescent lighting systems
National Sales Manager: Andrew Gross
Estimated Sales: $20-50 Million
Number Employees: 100-249

26551 Neogen Corp
620 Lesher Pl
Lansing, MI 48912-1509

517-372-9200
Fax: 517-372-2006 800-234-5333
foodsafety@neogen.com www.neogen.com

Manufacturer, importer and exporter of food patho-
gen testing kits
CEO: John Adent
Marketing Manager: Margaret Cyr
General Manager: Mark Mozola
Estimated Sales: $2.5-5 Million
Number Employees: 1000-4999
Parent Co: Vysis
Brands:
Gene-Trak

26552 (HQ)Neokraft Signs Inc
686 Main St
Lewiston, ME 04240-5800

207-782-9654
Fax: 207-782-0009 800-339-2258
www.neokraft.com

Aluminum, neon and plastic signs; also wide format
digital thermal printing
President: Peter Murphy
Partner: Peter Murphy
VP: Phil Bolduc
Marketing Director: Paul Lessard
Estimated Sales: Below $5 Million
Number Employees: 20-49
Square Footage: 20000

26553 (HQ)Neon Design-a-Sign
26022 Cape Dr Bldg H
Laguna Niguel, CA 92677

949-348-9223
Fax: 949-348-1736 888-636-6327

Manufacturer and exporter of signs including
changeable, fiber-optic neon and programmable
LED message displays. Also have a full line of LED
lighting.
President: Timothy Piper
CEO: Christine Busnardo
Contact: Tim Piper
piper@neon-das.com
Estimated Sales: $600,000
Number Employees: 1-4
Square Footage: 8000
Brands:
Logo River
Neon Design-A-Sign
Neon Light Pegs

26554 Neonetics Inc
900 S Main St
Hampstead, MD 21074-2202

410-374-8057
Fax: 410-374-8056 AlanObligin@yahoo.com

Manufacturer, importer and exporter of neon signs

Owner: Allen Obligen
neonman@neonetics.com
CFO: Brad Sogollss
VP: Brad Sotoloff
Estimated Sales: Less Than $500,000
Number Employees: 1-4
Brands:
Ne-On the Wall
Neonetics

26555 Neos
12797 Meadowvale Road NW
Suite B
Elk River, MN 55330-1171

763-441-0705
Fax: 763-441-0706 888-441-6367
neosinc@att.net www.neos-server.org

Manufacturer and exporter of packaging machinery
for rigid plastic containers; also, burrito and sliced
bread dispensers, conveyors with filler depositers,
folding tables for assembly and fillers
President: Jack T Mowry
CFO: Greg Erlandson
National Sales Manager: Joe Gibbs
Estimated Sales: $1-2.5 Million
Number Employees: 5-9
Square Footage: 48000

26556 (HQ)Nercon Engineering & Manufacturing
PO Box 2288
Oshkosh, WI 54903-2288

920-233-3268
Fax: 920-233-3159

Manufacturer and exporter of table top, belt and case
conveyors, bi-directional tables, vertical accumula-
tors, label removers, twist rinsers, bottle emptiers,
can coolers, etc
President: Jim Nerenhausen
CEO: Jay Nerenhausen
Marketing: Jim Streblow
Estimated Sales: $10-20 Million
Number Employees: 100-249
Square Footage: 166500
Other Locations:
Nercon Engineering & Manufact
Oconto WI
Brands:
Easy-Rol

26557 Net Material Handling
1300 W Fond Du Lac Ave
Milwaukee, WI 53205

414-263-1300
Fax: 414-263-7544 800-558-7260

Two and four-wheel hand trucks, two-wheel electric
trucks, dollies, carts, ramps, etc
President: Wendy Alzell
VP: Wayne Kappel
Contact: Mike Kappel
victor@runningrebels.org
Estimated Sales: $1-2.5 Million
Number Employees: 1-4
Square Footage: 28000
Brands:
Escalera
Magline
Yeats

26558 Net Pack Systems
36 Oak Street
Oakland, ME 04963-5019

207-465-4531
Fax: 207-465-9662

Bags including netting, open mesh, heat sealed,
plastic and polyethylene for cooking, fruits, vegeta-
bles, poultry, meat and refrigeration
President: Edward Johnson
Operations Manager: Douglas Johnson
General Manager: Edward Johnson
Estimated Sales: $1-2.5 Million
Number Employees: 5-9

26559 Netzsch Pumps North America
119 Pickering Way
Exton, PA 19341-1311

610-363-8010
Fax: 610-363-0971 netzsch@netzschusa.com
www.pumps.netzsch.com

Manufacturer and exporter of pumps, filter presses
and grinding mills

CEO: Dr Tilo Stahl
CFO: Mark Vitcov
VP: John Maguire
R&D: Harry Way
Quality Control: Bill Pye
Marketing: Kelly Rismiller
Public Relations: Kelly Rismiller
Production: Bob Hopple
Plant Manager: Bob Maxwell
Purchasing: Bob Hoffman
Estimated Sales: $30 Million
Number Employees: 50-99
Square Footage: 85000
Parent Co: Netzsch

26560 Neugart
3047 Industrial Blvd # 12
Bethel Park, PA 15102-2537
412-835-4154
Fax: 412-835-4194 sales@neugartusa.com
www.neugartusa.com
Planetary gearboxes, angle gearboxes, custom made
gears, honing, motor mounting
President: Gerhard Antony
VP sales: Tim Francis
Estimated Sales: $1-3 Million
Number Employees: 5-9

26561 Neupak
4607 Dovetail Drive
Madison, WI 53704
608-241-1118
Fax: 608-241-4448 800-383-1128
sales@ideal-pak.com www.neupak.com
Manufacture liquid filling machines
President, Chief Executive Officer: Steve Bethke
Vice President: Bruce Bierman
Marketing Manager: Steven Meyer
National Sales Manager: Robert Whetstone
Estimated Sales: $1-5 Million
Number Employees: 17

26562 Neupak
4607 Dovetail Drive
Madison, WI 53704-6302
608-241-1118
Fax: 608-241-4448 800-383-1128
sales@ideal-pak.com www.neupak.com
New weight and volumetric filling systems, auto-
matic and semi-automatic machines for filling
drums, totes, pails, can and jugs with foaming and
nonfoaming products
President, Chief Executive Officer: Steve Bethke
Vice President: Bruce Bierman
Sales & Marketing Director: Russell Schlager
National Sales Manager: Robert D. Whetstone
Estimated Sales: $1-5 Million
Number Employees: 17

26563 Neutec Group
1 Lenox Ave
Farmingdale, NY 11735
516-870-0877
Fax: 516-977-3774 888-810-5179
info@neutecgroup.com www.neutecgroup.com
Manufacturer of technologies for the quality control
and research and development laboratory.
Founder & CEO: Ronen Neutra
VP: Orna Zohar-Neutra

26564 Nevlen Co. 2, Inc.
96 Audubon Road
Wakefield, MA 01880-1200
978-462-7777
Fax: 978-462-7774 800-562-7225
nevlen@nevlen.com
Manufacturer and exporter of van equipment includ-
ing roof racks, shelving, drawer units and partitions
VP: James Capomaccio
VP: M Nickerson
Executive VP/Treasurer: J Capomaccio
Estimated Sales: $2.5-5 Million
Number Employees: 20-49
Square Footage: 208000
Brands:
Nevlen

26565 (HQ)Nevo Corporation
50 Hayney Ct
PO Box 601
Ronkonkoma, NY 11779-7220
631-585-8787
Fax: 631-585-9285

Manufacturer and exporter of roll-in and rotating
rack convection ovens
President: Richard Gehnrich
Treasurer: Leon Pedigo
VP: Wayne Pedigo
Estimated Sales: $1-3 Million
Number Employees: 20-49
Square Footage: 46000

26566 New Age Industrial
16788 US Highway 36
PO Box 520
Norton, KS 67654-5488
785-877-5121
Fax: 785-877-2616 800-255-0104
janet@newageindustrial.com
www.newageindustrial.com
Manufacturer and exporter of aluminum backroom
equipment including mobile platters, lug carts,
racks, shelving, dollies and tables
President: Dakota Criqui
dcriqui@newagefoodserviceequipment.com
VP: Tom Sharp
Sales Director: Allen Hasken
Estimated Sales: $10-20 Million
Number Employees: 100-249
Type of Packaging: Food Service

26567 New Attitude Beverage Corporation
PO Box 117385
Burlingame, CA 94011-7385
310-414-6501
Fax: 310-414-6547 newattbev@aol.com
Unique package designs and products beverages for
the industry
Estimated Sales: $2 Million
Number Employees: 22
Type of Packaging: Consumer, Food Service

26568 New Brunswick Intl Inc
76 Veronica Ave
Somerset, NJ 08873-3417
732-828-3633
Fax: 732-828-4884 marketing@nbidigi.com
www.nbidigi.net
Scales, labels, wrapping and overwrap machines
President: John Baumann
john.baumann@nbi-digi.com
CFO: Victor Liras
R & D: Ed Hearon
Estimated Sales: $5-10 Million
Number Employees: 20-49

26569 New Brunswick Scientific Co
175 Freshwater Blvd
Enfield, CT 06082-4444
860-253-6700
800-645-3050
info@eppendorf.com www.nbsc.com
Laboratory equipment including biological shakers,
media preparation equipment and fermentors
CEO: Abdul Abdellah
aabdul-qawi@eppendorf.com
Estimated Sales: $47 Million
Number Employees: 250-499
Square Footage: 243000
Parent Co: Eppendorf, Inc.

26570 New Carbon Company
PO Box 71
Buchanan, MI 49107-0071
574-247-2270
Fax: 574-247-2280 newcarbon@qtm.net
www.goldenmalted.com
This company has 4 separate entries all of which are
duplicates. Three of the entries are to be deleted and
only one kept.

26571 New Castle Industries Inc
1399 County Line Rd
New Castle, PA 16101-2955
724-654-2603
Fax: 724-656-5620 800-897-2830
info@nordsonxaloy.com
CEO: Walter Cox
Contact: Walter Cox
wcoxjr@xaloy.com
Estimated Sales: $1-5 Million
Number Employees: 10-19
Parent Co: Nordson XALOY Incorporated

26572 New Centennial
P.O.Box 708
Columbus, GA 31902-0708
706-323-6446
Fax: 706-327-9921 800-241-7541
Non-refrigerated and refrigerated side and rear- ac-
cess truck bodies and trailers for the beverage and
food distribution industry
Manager: Bob Hudak
Marketing Director: Wes Hauglie
Sales Director: Dan Burt
Plant Manager: Bob Hudak
Purchasing Manager: Tim Fitzpatrick
Estimated Sales: $10-20 Million
Number Employees: 50-99

26573 New Chief Fashion
3223 E 46th St
Vernon, CA 90058-2407
323-582-5322
Fax: 323-581-0077 800-639-2433
www.newchef.com
Manufacturer and exporter of aprons, uniforms and
chef hats
Owner: Lucien Salama
lucien@newchef.com
Estimated Sales: Less Than $500,000
Number Employees: 1-4
Type of Packaging: Food Service

26574 New Court
3200 Court St
Texarkana, TX 75501-6619
903-838-0521
Fax: 903-838-9452
Laminated sanitary insulated and noninsulated wall
and ceiling panels including fiberglass, painted alu-
minum and stainless steel
President: Calvin Court
ctcourt@msn.com
VP Marketing: Melvin Court
Sales Director: Jodi Shewmaker
Estimated Sales: $20-50 Million
Number Employees: 100-249
Brands:
New-Glass
Poly-Liner

26575 New Data Systems Inc
19 Claremont Ln
Suffern, NY 10901-7011
845-357-7744
Fax: 845-357-7933
Accounting and trading position software for im-
porters, exporters and commodity traders
Owner: Peter Bellin
peter@catstoday.com
Estimated Sales: $1-2.5 Million
Number Employees: 1-4

26576 New England Cheese Making Supply Company
54 Whately Rd
Suite B
South Deerfield, MA 01373
413-397-2012
Fax: 413-397-2014 info@cheesemaking.com
www.cheesemaking.com
Ingredients and supplies for cheesemaking and home
dairy needs
Owner: Ricki Carroll
ricki@cheesemaking.com
Estimated Sales: Below $5 Million
Number Employees: 1-4

26577 New England Label
1213 US Route 302
Barre, VT 5641
802-476-6393
Fax: 802-476-7159 800-368-3932
salesoffice@wnpinc.com www.wnpinc.com
Pressure sensitive labels
Sales Representative: Vicki Adams
Contact: Randy Ensminger
rensminger@newenglandlabel.com
General Manager: Jim Veness
Production Manager: Chris Rivers
Estimated Sales: $500,000-$1 Million
Number Employees: 5-9
Square Footage: 7626
Parent Co: Willington Company

26578 New England Machinery Inc
2820 62nd Ave E
Bradenton, FL 34203-5305
941-755-5550
Fax: 941-751-6281 info@neminc.com
Manufacturer and exporter of hopper/elevators and bottling machinery including unscramblers, orienters, cappers, lidders, puckers, de-puckers, gap transfers and more
Owner: Pat Charles
pat.charles@jacksonhealth.org
Director Sales/Marketing: Marge Bonura
VP Manufacturing: Geza Bankuty
Number Employees: 100-249
Square Footage: 160000
Brands:
   N.E.M.

26579 New England Overshoe Company
1193 S Brownell Rd
Williston, VT 05495-7416
802-846-8880
Fax: 802-863-6888 888-289-6367
Neos@overshoe.com
Footwear for the food and pharmaceutical industry, soles that keep particles from being spread, a Poly Urethane Upper that does not harbor bacteria and can be cleaned both inside and out reducing biohazard contamination
President: Scott Hardy
Marketing Coordinator: Robyn Terranova
Estimated Sales: $2.4 Million
Number Employees: 5-9
Parent Co: Linckia Development

26580 New England Pallets & Skids
250 West St
Ludlow, MA 01056-1248
413-583-6628
Fax: 413-583-5187 info@nepallets.com
www.nepallets.com
Wooden pallets
President: Cynthia Kawie
Estimated Sales: $1-2.5 Million
Number Employees: 10-19
Square Footage: 200000
Type of Packaging: Consumer, Food Service

26581 (HQ)New England Wooden Ware
205 School St # 201
Suite 201
Gardner, MA 01440-2781
978-630-3600
Fax: 978-630-1513 800-252-9214
www.newoodenware.com
Manufacturer, importer and exporter of corrugated paper boxes
President: David Urquhart
VP Sales: R Goguen
Quality Control Manager: Don Broderick
Sales Manager: Mark Salisbury
Contact: Judith Berman
judithb@mediatemanagement.com
VP Production: D Urquhart
Estimated Sales: Less Than $500,000
Number Employees: 1-4
Square Footage: 386000
Other Locations:
   New England Wooden WareCorp.
   Fitchburg MA

26582 New Era Label Corporation
51 Valley St
Belleville, NJ 07109-3011
973-759-2444
Fax: 973-759-2993
Seals, stickers and labels including paper, pressure sensitive, spot carbon, carbon interleaved and consecutively numbered
Sales: Fred Iannone
Manager: Tom Savano
Estimated Sales: $1-5 Million
Number Employees: 10-19

26583 New Generation SoftwareInc
3835 N Freeway Blvd # 200
Suite 200
Sacramento, CA 95834-1954
916-920-2200
Fax: 916-920-1380 800-824-1220
admin@ngsi.com www.ngsi.com
Financial, distribution and business intelligence software solutions

President: Bernard B Gough
bgo@ngsi.com
Estimated Sales: $10-20 Million
Number Employees: 50-99

26584 New Hatchwear Company
Bay 104, 4711
13th Street N.E.
Calgary, AB T2E 6M3
Canada
403-291-2525
Fax: 403-291-2521 800-661-9249
Uniform apparel including skirts, blouses, dresses, aprons, tunics, slacks, smocks, vests, jackets, tailored blazers, formals, kitchen whites, service coats, industrial clothing and outerwear, security, law enforcement and military.
Purchasing Manager: Sandra Dimitrijevic
Number Employees: 50-99
Type of Packaging: Consumer, Food Service, Private Label

26585 New Haven Awnings
178 Chapel St
New Haven, CT 06513-4209
203-562-7232
Fax: 203-624-4124 800-560-5650
info@nhawning.com www.nhawning.com
Commercial awnings
President: Dan Barnick
Partner: Tom Gumkowski
Estimated Sales: $5-10,000,000
Number Employees: 10-19

26586 New High Glass
12713 SW 125th Ave
Miami, FL 33186-5404
305-232-0840
Fax: 305-251-7622 800-GLA-SSUS
sales@newhigh.com www.newhighglass.com
Wine industry bottles and closures
President: Enrico Raccah
len@newhigh.com
Estimated Sales: $10-20 Million
Number Employees: 20-49

26587 New Hope Natural Media
1401 Pearl Street
Suite 200
Boulder, CO 80302
303-939-8440
Fax: 303-998-9020 info@newhope.com
Supplements and ingredients
Executive Director: Len Monheit
Sr Marketing Manager: Brad Mastrine
Sales: Kim Merselis
Contact: Nicole Aulik
naulik@newhope.com
Estimated Sales: $25 Million
Number Employees: 45
Square Footage: 60000

26588 New Horizon Foods
33440 Western Ave
Union City, CA 94587-3202
510-489-8600
Fax: 510-489-9797
Dough conditioners, bread bases, natural mixes, beverage, cake, muffin, pudding, meat spices, spice blends, snack and chip seasonings, custard, ice cream, waffle cone and sauce mixes and bases; exporter of dough conditioners and cakeand muffin mixes
Owner: Ken Crawford
kenc@newhorizonfoodsinc.com
Senior Vice President: Yael Melzer
Number Employees: 10-19
Parent Co: Tova Industries
Type of Packaging: Consumer, Food Service, Private Label, Bulk

26589 New Horizon Technologies
3100 Geo Washntn Way
Richland, WA 99354
509-372-4868
Fax: 509-372-4869 www.feandc.com
Food irradiation processing facility specializing in fresh fruits and vegetable, poultry, meat and seafood for R&D applications

President/ CEO: Richard T French
EVP/ CEO: DeVerne Dunnum
CFO: Bassel Younes
VP Market Development: Carl Holder
EVP, Business Development: Richard French Jr.
VP Operations: Dave Eakin
Estimated Sales: $500,000-$1,000,000
Number Employees: 1-4

26590 New Jersey Department OfAgriculture
Po Box 330
Trenton, NJ 08625
609-292-8856
logan.brown@ag.state.nj.us
www.state.nj.us
Agriculture
Secretary Of Agriculture: Douglas Fisher
Contact: Patricia Gray
patricia.gray@dhs.state.nj.us

26591 New Jersey Wire Stitching Machine Company
1841 Old Cuthbert Road
Cherry Hill, NJ 08034
856-428-2572
Fax: 856-428-3069 sales@newjerseywire.com
www.newjerseywire.com
Manual and auto bag closers for poly, mesh and drawstring bags at high speeds; also, wire stitchers for fiber and corrugated containers, trays, metals, display boxes and plastics
Manager: Mike Menaquala
CEO: Fred Rexon
Contact: Mike Menquale
info@newjerseywire.com
General Manager: Michael Menaquale
Estimated Sales: $500,000-$1 Million
Number Employees: 1-4
Square Footage: 40000
Parent Co: Precision Automation Company

26592 New Klix Corporation
551 Railroad Avenue
South San Francisco, CA 94080-3450
650-761-0622
Fax: 650-589-6735 800-522-5544
Manufacturer and exporter of warewash, laundry detergents and cleaning compounds
President: Rodrigo Ortiz
VP: Lautaro Ortiz
Estimated Sales: $2.5-5 Million
Number Employees: 19
Square Footage: 110000
Type of Packaging: Food Service, Private Label
Brands:
   Klix

26593 New Lisbon Wood ProductsManufacturing Company
1127 S Adams St
New Lisbon, WI 53950
608-562-3122
Fax: 608-562-3221 acewoodproducts@excite.com
www.acewoodproducts.com
Custom wooden pallets, skids and crates
Owner: David Brinkman
Marketing: Linda Brinkman
Sales: Sonya Brach
Plant Manager: Dan Batten
Estimated Sales: $1-2.5 Million
Number Employees: 10-19
Square Footage: 40000
Parent Co: Ace Wood

26594 New London Engineering
1700 Division St
New London, WI 54961-9137
920-982-4030
Fax: 920-982-6800 800-437-1994
nlesales@nleco.com www.nleco.com
Conveyors including line and table top chain
President: Martin Bonneson
CEO: Frank Ferdon
Quality Control: Dale Turdell
Director Sales/Marketing: Dale Trudell
Estimated Sales: $10-20 Million
Number Employees: 50-99
Square Footage: 100000
Parent Co: Bonntech International

26595 New Mexico Products Inc

503 Vineyard Rd NE
Albuquerque, NM 87113-1020

505-345-7864
Fax: 505-344-2581 877-345-7864

Wooden boxes, crates and custom pallets including softwood only
President: David St John
nmpoffice@flash.net
Sales Director: Matt Walker
Office Manager: Stella Torres
Estimated Sales: Less Than $500,000
Number Employees: 1-4
Square Footage: 12000

26596 New Pig Corp

1 Pork Ave
PO Box 304
Tipton, PA 16684-9001

814-684-0101
Fax: 814-684-0961 800-468-4647
salesdept@newpig.com www.newpig.com

Industrial leak, spill, safety, maintenance, storage, handling and repair products
President: Nino Vella
CEO: Charlie Craig
charlie.craig@transedgetruck.com
CFO: Jim Crlin
Executive VP: Doug Hershey
Quality Control: Steve Klling
R & D: Mark Woytowich
Director of Public Relations: Carl DeCaspers
Purchasing Manager: Bill Lidwell
Estimated Sales: Below $5 Million
Number Employees: 250-499

26597 New Resina Corporation

27455 Bostik Court
Temecula, CA 92590

951-296-6585
Fax: 951-296-5018 800-207-4804
sales@resina.com www.resina.com

President: Michael Tom
CEO: Andy Lask
Number Employees: 10-19

26598 New South Co Inc

3700 Claypond Rd # 6
Myrtle Beach, SC 29579-7330

843-236-9399
Fax: 843-236-9454

Wooden pallets
President/Chief Executive Officer: Don Kayne
SVP, Corporate & Legal Affairs: David Calabrigo
SVP, Finance/Chief Financial Officer: Alan Nicholl
Vice President/Treasurer: Patrick Elliott
SVP, Sales & Marketing: Wayne Guthrie
Vice President, Human Resources: Onkar Athwal
Estimated Sales: $50-100 Million
Number Employees: 5-9
Square Footage: 49705
Parent Co: Canfor Corporation

26599 New Tiger International

117 State Street,
Westbury, NY 11590

516-942-9312
Fax: 516-942-9306 newtiger6688@yahoo.com
www.greatporcini.com

Dried, frozen, fresh and canned mushrooms
Marketing: Richard Lin
Contact: Shari Baldwin
sbaldwin@greatporcini.com

26600 New Way Packaging Machinery

PO Box 467
Hanover, PA 17331

717-637-2133
Fax: 717-637-2966 800-522-3537
sales@labeler.com

Manufacturer and exporter of labeling machinery
President: Edward Abendschein
Contact: Merle Mcmaster
merle@labeler.com
Estimated Sales: $10-20 Million
Number Employees: 5-9

26601 New York Corugated Box Co

239 Lindbergh Pl # 1
Paterson, NJ 07503-2821

973-742-5000
Fax: 973-742-7666 www.nycorrugatedbox.net

Corrugated cartons and inserts

President: Robert Rosner
General Manager: Robert Rosner
Estimated Sales: $2.5-5 Million
Number Employees: 5-9
Square Footage: 28000

26602 New York Folding Box CoInc

20 Continental Dr
Stanhope, NJ 07874-2658

973-347-6932
Fax: 973-347-2303 ken@nyfoldingbox.com
www.nyfoldingbox.com

Folding boxes
President: Harry Kaplan
Chairman of the Board: Jerome Joseph Kaplan
VP: Robert Kaplan
Sales Manager: Sal Vassallo
Estimated Sales: $5-10 Million
Number Employees: 5-9

26603 New York State Electric& Gas

1 Corporate Dr
Binghamton, NY 13902

607-762-7200
Fax: 607-762-8614 800-572-1111
custserv@nyseg.com www.nyseg.com

President: Jim Laurito
Senior VP: Jeffrey K Smith
gsmith@nyseg.com
Estimated Sales: $1-5 Million
Number Employees: 1000-4999

26604 New-Ma Co. Llc

4618 44th St SE
Grand Rapids, MI 49512

616-942-5500
Fax: 616-942-5511 www.newma.it

Horizontal and vertical packaging machines, counting and weighing systems.
Contact: Nico Nicoletti
n.nicoletti@newmapackaging.com

26605 Newark Wire Cloth Co

160 Fornelius Ave
Clifton, NJ 07013-1844

973-778-4478
Fax: 973-778-4481 800-221-0392
info@newarkwire.com www.newarkwire.com

Manufacturer, exporter and importer of wire cloth, filters, strainers, testing sieves, etc. Manufacturers of the Sani Cloan Strainer product line. Consisting of: inline, side inlet, and hi-capacity basket strainers. Custom fabricationsare a specialty.
President/Owner: Richard Campbell
rcampbell@newarkwire.com
Estimated Sales: $5-10 Million
Number Employees: 20-49
Square Footage: 120000
Type of Packaging: Food Service

26606 Newcastle Co Inc

3812 Wilmington Rd
New Castle, PA 16105-6134

724-658-4516
Fax: 724-658-5100 ncco@newcastleco.com
www.newcastleco.com

Manufacturer and integrator of load transfer systems, palletizers, pallet dispensers, sheet dispensers, and conveyors.
Owner: Dennis Alduk
ncco@losch.net
Number Employees: 5-9
Brands:
  Floor Level
  Palavator

26607 Newco Enterprises Inc

3650 New Town Blvd
St Charles, MO 63301-4357

636-946-1330
Fax: 314-925-0029 800-325-7867
www.newcocoffee.com

Coffee and tea brewing equipment and water treatment systems; exporter of commercial coffee brewers
Owner: Karen Enke
CFO: Mcenke Karen
VP Marketing: Anthony Westcott
VP, Sales: Jason College
s.murthy@trafinfo.com
Estimated Sales: $10-20 Million
Number Employees: 100-249
Square Footage: 160000

26608 Newco Inc

1 Hicks Ave # A
Newton, NJ 07860-2629

973-383-7777
Fax: 973-383-0506 www.newco.com

Decorative facing for paneling and wall coverings
President: James Berezny
Estimated Sales: $20-50 Million
Number Employees: 20-49

26609 Newcourt, Inc.

PO Box 182
Madison, IN 47250-0182

800-933-0006
Fax: 812-265-6455

Composite laminated floorings for mezzanines
Sales Director: John Gramke
Number Employees: 2

26610 Newell Brands

6655 Peachtree Dunwoody Rd
Atlanta, GA 30328

consumer.inquiries@newellco.com
www.newellbrands.com

Manufacturer and exporter of food service, sanitary maintenance and material handling products.
President & CEO: Ravi Saligram
Unit CEO, Appliances & Cookware: David Hammer
Unit CEO, Food: Kris Malkoski
CFO & President, Business Operations: Christopher Peterson
Chief Legal & Administrative Officer: Bradford Turner
Chief Human Resources Officer: Steve Parsons
Chief Customer Officer: Mike Hayes
Chief Procurement Officer: Steve Nikolopoulos
Year Founded: 1903
Estimated Sales: $14.7 Billion
Number Employees: 49,000
Type of Packaging: Consumer, Food Service

26611 Newlands Systems

602-30731 Simpson Road
Abbotsford, BC V2T 6Y7
Canada

604-855-4890
Fax: 604-855-8826 mail@nsibrew.com

Manufacturer and exporter of brewing equipment and machinery
President: Brad McQuhae
Director Marketing: Loch McJannett
Number Employees: 10
Square Footage: 80000
Type of Packaging: Food Service

26612 (HQ)Newly Weds Foods Inc

2501 N Keeler Ave
Chicago, IL 60639-2131

773-489-6224
Fax: 773-489-2799 800-621-7521
nwfnorthamerica@newlywedsfoods.com
www.newlywedsfoods.com

Processor and exporter of breadings, batters, seasoning blends, marinades, glazes and capsicum products
President: Charles T. Angell
CFO: Brian Johnson
SVP Sales & Marketing: Bruce Leshinski
R&D: Jim Klein
Sales Director: Jim Chin
Contact: Mary Adderhold
madderhold@newlywedsfoods.com
VP Manufacturing: Mike Hopp
Plant Manager: Leo Vogler
Director of Purchasing: Tom Lisack
Estimated Sales: $959 Million
Number Employees: 1-4
Square Footage: 1500000
Other Locations:
  Newly Weds Foods
  Bethleham PA
  Newly Weds Foods
  Chicago IL
  Newly Weds Foods
  Cleveland TN
  Newly Weds Foods
  Watertown MA
  Newly Weds Foods
  Yorkville IL
  Newly Weds Foods
  Horn Lake MS
  Newly Weds Foods
  Edmonton AB
  Newly Weds Foods
  Montreal QC
  Newly Weds Foods
  Toronto ON

Brands:
Batter Blends
Blended Breaders
Newly Weds

26613 Newman Labeling Systems
4400 Route 9 South
Suite 1000
Freehold, NJ 07728
609-597-8722
Fax: 609-597-8755 newmanmps@aol.com
www.newmanlabeling.com
President: John W Clayton
Vice President Operations: Michael Semiraro
Estimated Sales: $1-5 Million
Number Employees: 10-19

26614 Newman Sanitary Gasket Co
964 W Main St
P.O.Box 222
Lebanon, OH 45036-9173
513-932-7379
Fax: 513-932-4493 customer@newmangasket.com
www.newmangasket.com
Manufacturer and exporter of foodgrade sanitary
process piping gaskets, seals and F.D.A. O-rings.
Also custom molded rubber parts
President: David W Newman
davidn@newmangasket.com
CEO: Tom Moore
VP: Betsy Newman
Marketing Director: Larry Hensel
Customer Service Manager: Cindy Swagler
Plant Manager: Matt Agricola
Estimated Sales: $1-5,000,000
Number Employees: 50-99
Square Footage: 65000
Type of Packaging: Private Label, Bulk
Brands:
Newman

26615 Newmarket Corp
135 Commerce Way
Portsmouth, NH 03801-3243
804-788-5555
Fax: 603-436-1826 888-829-8871
www.newmarket.com
Windows based sales, marketing and catering software
CEO: Sean O Neill
CFO: Ken Smaha
Contact: Kristen Acheson
kacheson@newmarketinc.com
Estimated Sales: $33.4 Million
Number Employees: 380
Square Footage: 27000
Brands:
Breeze
Ccbreeze
Cvbreeze
Delphi
Delphi 7.0
Global Sfa
Regional Delphi

26616 Newport Electronics Inc
2229 S Yale St
Santa Ana, CA 92704-4401
714-540-4914
Fax: 714-968-7311 800-639-7678
info@newportus.com www.microinfinity.com
NEWPORT® is known for designing and manufac-
turing the world's most accurate industrial
intrumention. Prestotek brand of products in-
cludes: pH, ORP, conductivity, Resistivity, salt, and
much more. Offered as panel mount of handheld
instruments.
President: Milton Hollander
Manager: Dick Hollander
Estimated Sales: $1-3 Million
Number Employees: 50-99
Parent Co: Newport Electronics
Type of Packaging: Private Label
Brands:
Pocket Pal
Presto-Tek

26617 Newstamp Lighting Factory
227 Bay Rd
P.O. Box 189
North Easton, MA 02356-2673
508-238-7073
Fax: 508-230-8312 www.newstamplighting.com
Wall and ceiling lights

Owner: Robert Zeitsiff
bob@newstamplighting.com
VP Marketing: Charles Edwards
Estimated Sales: $1-2.5 Million
Number Employees: 20-49

26618 Newstamp Lighting Factory
227 Bay Rd
PO Box 189
North Easton, MA 02356-2673
508-238-7073
Fax: 508-230-8312 info@newstamplighting.com
www.newstamplighting.com
Electric lighting fixtures, metal stamping equipment,
plumbing products and security windows; exporter
of electric lighting fixtures
President: Robert Zeitsiff
bob@newstamplighting.com
VP: Sandra Zeitstiff
Clerk: Charlotte Zeitsiff
Estimated Sales: $2.5-5 Million
Number Employees: 20-49
Square Footage: 68000

26619 Newtech Inc
11 Hedding Dr
Randolph, VT 05060-1032
802-728-9170
Fax: 802-728-9163 800-210-2361
dewater91@msn.com
www.newtechdewatering.com
Manufactures dewatering systems for wastewater
President: Robert Dimmick
robert@dimmickservices.com
Estimated Sales: $3 Million
Number Employees: 10-19

26620 Newton Broom Co
1508 W Jourdan St
PO Box 358
Newton, IL 62448-2006
618-783-4424
Fax: 618-783-2442 sales@newtonbroom.com
www.newtonbroom.com
Brooms, mops and staple brushes
Manager: Don Leventhal
don@newtonbroom.com
Manager: Becky Shamhart
Estimated Sales: Below $5 Million
Number Employees: 20-49

26621 Newton OA & Son Co
16356 Sussex Hwy
Bridgeville, DE 19933-3056
302-337-3782
Fax: 302-337-3780 800-726-5745
solutions@oanewton.com www.oanewton.com
Manufacturer and exporter of weighing equipment
and pneumatic and mechanical material handling
systems including dust collection
President: Rob Rider
Number Employees: 20-49

26622 Newwaveenviro
6595 S Dayton St # 3100
Greenwood Vlg, CO 80111-6189
303-221-3232
Fax: 303-221-3233 800-592-8371
customerservice@newwaveenviro.com
Water filtration systems and accessories
President: Virgil Archer
Manager: Sheri Archer
sheri.archer@newwaveenviro.com
Estimated Sales: $1-3 Million
Number Employees: 20-49

26623 Nexel Industries Inc
11 Harbor Park Dr
Port Washington, NY 11050-4656
516-484-5225
Fax: 516-625-0084 800-245-6682
nexelinfo@nexelwire.com www.nexelwire.com
Manufacturer, importer and exporter of material
handling and storage systems including solid steel
and wire shelving, trucks and carts
Vice President: Dibuseng Moloi
dmoloi@businessmonitor.com
VP: John Svitek
Inside Sales Manager: Howard Ziporkin
National Sales Manager: Jerry Mark
Number Employees: 100-249
Square Footage: 2400000
Type of Packaging: Food Service, Private Label

Brands:
Loadmaster
Nexel
Nexelite
Nexelon
Poly-Z-Brite
Space-Trac

26624 Nexen Group
560 Oak Grove Pkwy
St Paul, MN 55127-8500
651-484-5900
Fax: 651-286-1099 800-843-7445
info@nexengroup.com www.nexengroup.com
Producer of precision motion control equipment.
Products include industrial clutches, brakes, web
guides, tension and automated assembly tools.
CEO: Hutch Schilling
VP, Sales & Marketing: Tim Dillon
Estimated Sales: $20-50 Million
Number Employees: 200-500
Other Locations:
Webster WI

26625 Nexeo Solutions
5200 Blazer Pkwy
Dublin, OH 43017-3309
614-790-3333
Fax: 614-790-4427 877-343-3278
csr@ashchem.com www.nexeosolutions.com
President: Charlie Brown
crbrown@ashland.com
Chairman, Chief Executive Officer: Jim OBrien
Vice President: Blair Boggs
Senior Vice President of Research and De: Fran
Lockwood
Director of Marketing: John Stotz
Director of Corporate Communications: Gary
Rhodes
Estimated Sales: Over $1 Billion
Number Employees: 1000-4999

26626 Nexira
15 Somerset St
Somerville, NJ 08876-2828
908-707-9400
Fax: 908-707-9405 800-872-1850
info-usa@nexira.com www.nexira.com
Nexira is a global leader in natural ingredients and
botanical extracts for food nutrition and dietary supplements. Nexira built its reputation as the world
leader in acacia gum and now manufactures a wide
range of functional and nutritional ingredients, anti-
oxidants, and active botanicals for weight manage-
ment, sports nutrition, digestive and cardiovascular
health. It manufactures the following ingredients for
the food and health industry: acacia gun, botanical
extracts and powders.
President: Stephane Dondain
heese@cnius.com
VP: Teresa Yazbek
Marketing/Logistics Specialist: Nina Segura
Sales: Bob Bremer
Estimated Sales: $14 Million
Number Employees: 10-19
Number of Brands: 25
Number of Products: 100
Type of Packaging: Bulk
Brands:
FIBREGUM
VINITROX
EXOCYAN
CACTi-NEA
NEOPUNTIA
ID-ALG
INSTANTGUM
SPRAYGUM
EFICACIA
EQUACIA
THIXOGUM

26627 Nexthermal
1045 Harts Lake Rd
Battle Creek, MI 49037-7357
269-964-0271
Fax: 269-964-4526 800-937-4681
sales@hotset.com
Cartridge, coil, band, strip and tubular heaters, tem-
perature controls, thermocouples, connectors
President: Srekumar Bandyopadhyay
kumar@nexthermal.com
Estimated Sales: $5-10 000,000
Number Employees: 100-249

26628 Nhs Labs Inc
11665 W State St
Star, ID 83669-5223
208-939-5100
Fax: 208-939-5100 888-546-8694
info@nutritionmanufacturer.com
www.nutritionmanufacturer.com
Private label sports drinks, supplements, and energy drinks
CEO: Larry Leach
Number Employees: 50-99
Square Footage: 74000

26629 Ni Source Inc
801 E 86th Ave
Merrillville, IN 46410-6272
219-647-5990
Fax: 219-853-5161 www.nisource.com
Air pollution control, chilling units, heating systems, recording and monitoring devices and controls
Chairman of the Board: Gary L Neale
CEO: Joseph Hamrock
hamrock@nisource.com
CEO: Eileen O Odum
Estimated Sales: Over $1 Billion
Number Employees: 5000-9999

26630 Niagara Blower Company
673 Ontario St
Buffalo, NY 14207
716-875-2000
Fax: 716-875-1077 800-426-5169
sales@niagarablower.com
www.niagarablower.com
Manufacturer and exporter of custom refrigeration systems including bacteria-free, frost-free moisture management, evaporators, condensers and dehumidification
President: Peter Demakos
Marketing Assistant: Jen Dorman
Sales Manager: Phil Rowland
Contact: David Anderson
danderson@niagarablower.com
COO: Peter Demakos
Estimated Sales: $10-20 Million
Number Employees: 50-99
Square Footage: 200000
Brands:
Aero Heat Exchanger
Hygrol
No Frost

26631 Niantic Awning Company
PO Box 864
Windham, NH 3087
978-225-0108
Fax: 860-739-0168 info@necpa.org
www.necpa.org
Commercial awnings
President: Scott Massey
Vice President: Cheryl Yennaco
Vice President: Mike Cornell
Estimated Sales: Less than $500,000
Number Employees: 5-9

26632 (HQ)Nice-Pak Products Inc
2 Nice-Pak Park
Orangeburg, NY 10962-1376
845-365-1700
800-444-6725
www.nicepak.com
Manufacturer and exporter of cleaning and sanitizing supplies including moist towelettes, disposable wash cloths, surface disinfectants and hand sanitizers.
Chief Executive Officer: Robert Julius
Chief Operating Officer: Ron Gordon
Analytic Chemist: Elmira Abdelnasser
eabdelnasser@nicepak.com
Year Founded: 1955
Estimated Sales: $165.5 Million
Number Employees: 2,500
Square Footage: 28000
Type of Packaging: Consumer, Food Service, Private Label
Brands:
Alcohol Prep Pads 100's
Nice-N-Clean
Pdi
Rub a Dubs
Sani-Cloth
Sani-Hands
Sani-Wipe
Wet-Nap 1000-Pak

26633 Nicholas Machine and Grinding
7500 San Felipe St
Suite 600
Houston, TX 77063-1790
713-914-8077
Fax: 713-972-1164 800-747-1256
Owner: James Nail

26634 Nicholas Marketing Associates
179 Larch Ave
Bogota, NJ 07603-1222
201-343-9414
Fax: 201-343-3256
Consultant specializing in marketing and promotion
Director: Gary Fermature
Managing Director: Nicholas Zampetti, Jr.
Estimated Sales: $1-2.5 Million
Number Employees: 2

26635 Nichols Specialty Products
10 Parker Street
Southborough, MA 01772-1949
508-481-4367
Fax: 508-481-7806
Manufacturer and exporter of bottle and can capping machinery
President: Larry Quinlan
CEO: Janet Wellman
CFO: Shannon Quinlan
Number Employees: 10
Brands:
Kinex

26636 Nichols Wire
1547 Helton Dr
Florence, AL 35630
256-764-4271
Fax: 256-767-5152
Teabag wire
President: Earl D Thomason
Contact: Francesca Cohen
fcohen@nicholswire.com
Estimated Sales: $25-50 Million
Number Employees: 100-249

26637 Nicol Scales & Measurement LP
7239 Envoy Ct
Dallas, TX 75247-5103
214-428-8181
Fax: 214-428-8127 800-225-8181
sales@nicolscales.com www.nicolscales.com
Manufacturer and exporter of industrial scales and force measuring equipment; also, leasing available
President, CEO: Ted Tabolka
ted@nicolscales.com
Director of Finance: Oliver Jackson
Vice President, Service: Steve Ford
Director of Sales and Marketing: Jim Budke
Estimated Sales: $5-10 Million
Number Employees: 20-49

26638 Nicomac Inc
80 Oak St # 201
Norwood, NJ 07648-1342
201-768-9501
Fax: 201-768-9504 800-628-0006
sales@nicosgroup.com www.nicomac.com
Autoclaves, coaters, ceiling grid systems, ceiling panels, coatings, tabletaquous, design services, doors, automatic and manual, floor finishes, modular rooms, ovens, steam generators, sterilizers, autoclave, stopper sterilizing tablet hoppers
President: Francesco Nigris
Manager: Rosanne Cangialosi
rosannec@nicomac.com
Manager: Rosanne Cangialosi
Estimated Sales: $5 Million
Number Employees: 1-4

26639 (HQ)Nicosia Creative Expresso
355 W 52nd St Fl 8
New York, NY 10019
212-515-6600
Fax: 212-265-5422 info@niceltd.com
www.niceltd.com
Consultant to the food industry; packaging design services available
President: Davide Nicosia
Contact: David Balch
balch@niceltd.com
Estimated Sales: Below $5,000,000
Number Employees: 20-49
Square Footage: 8000

Type of Packaging: Consumer, Food Service, Private Label, Bulk
Other Locations:
Nicosia Creative Expresso
Madrid

26640 Nidec Minster Corp.
240 West Fifth Street
Minster, OH 45865
www.minster.com
Presses for production of food and beverage cans, ends, and easy open ends
President: John Winch
Estimated Sales: $118 Million
Number Employees: 500

26641 Nieco Corporation
7950 Cameron Drive
Windsor, CA 95492
707-284-7100
Fax: 707-284-7430 800-643-2656
sales@nieco.com www.nieco.com
Manufacturer and exporter of automatic bun grilling and meat broiling machines for hamburgers, steaks, chicken and fish
President: Ed Baker
Executive VP: John Brown
Contact: Steve Alcocer
salcocer@nieco.com
Estimated Sales: $10-20 Million
Number Employees: 50-99
Square Footage: 150000
Type of Packaging: Food Service

26642 Nifty Packaging
4 Jocama Blvd
Old Bridge, NJ 08857-3513
732-591-1140
Fax: 732-591-8477 800-631-2172
contactus@niftypack.com www.niftypack.com
Shipping room products, tape, tape and label dispensers, stretch film, strapping and tools and envelopes
President: Norman Ferber
Estimated Sales: $10-20 Million
Number Employees: 5-9

26643 Nigrelli Systems Purchasing
16024 County Road X
Kiel, WI 53042-9741
920-693-3165
Fax: 920-693-3634 800-693-3144
www.aquamasterfountains.com
Manufacturer and exporter of continuous motion case and tray packing systems, tray formers, plastic tray denesting systems, bulk container and bottled water packers, wrap around packers and shrinkwrapping equipment
President: Nicholas Nigrelli
VP Sales: David O'Keefe
Estimated Sales: Less Than $500,000
Number Employees: 1-4

26644 Nijal USA
1920 S 1st St
Minneapolis, MN 55454-1055
651-353-6702
Fax: 612-395-5257
Meat and bakery processing equipment
President: Michael Halbaut

26645 Nijhuis Water Technology
560 W Washington Blvd
Unit 320
Chicago, IL 60661-2693
Canada
312-466-9900
Fax: 312-300-4105 info@nijhuis-water.com
www.nijhuis-water.nl
Provides complete wastewater treatment systems and installation services
Vice President: Adriaan Van Der Beck
Parent Co: Nijhuis Water Technology B.V.

26646 Nikka Densok
610 Garrison St # D
Lakewood, CO 80215-5882
303-202-6190
Fax: 303-202-6195 800-806-4587
sales@nikkadensok.com www.nikkadensok.com
Leak detection systems for food product packaging
President: Brian Ball
Estimated Sales: $5-10 Million
Number Employees: 5-9
Parent Co: Nikka Densok

26647 Nilfisk, Inc.
740 Hemlock Rd
Suite 100
Morgantown, PA 19543
Fax: 610-286-7350   800-645-3475
www.nilfiskcfm.com
Powered cleaning equipment
Exec. VP, Americas: Andrew Ray

26648 Nimbus Water Systems
41840 McAlby Ct # A
Murrieta, CA 92562-7080
951-894-2800
Fax: 760-591-0106   800-451-9343
www.nimbuswater.com
Manufacturer and exporter of water treatment equipment; also, consultant providing water and water recycle systems design services
Founder: Donald Bray
CEO: Mike Faulkner
VP Marketing/Sales: Tony Pagliano
Contact: Sid Brandhuber
sid@nimbuswater.com
Purchasing Manager: Bree Ann Plange
Estimated Sales: $2.5-5 Million
Number Employees: 1-4
Number of Products: 50
Square Footage: 140000
Brands:
   Nimbus Cs
   Nimbus Fs
   Nimbus N
   Nimbus Sierra
   Nimbus Watermaker

26649 Nina Mauritz Design Service
603 W Park Avenue
Libertyville, IL 60048-2664
847-968-4438
Fax: 847-816-8618
Consultant specializing in space allocation, traffic flow, design and specification of food service equipment and interior finishes for commercial kitchens, cafeterias and dining areas
Principal: Nina Mauritz

26650 Niro
1600 Okeefe Rd
Hudson, WI 54016
715-386-9371
Fax: 715-386-9376   www.niroinc.com
Custom fabrication, filtration equipment, aseptic processing equipment, heat recovery systems, deaerators, dryers, fluid bed, spray, pilot plants, process control, high pressure pumps and homogenizers
President: Steve Kaplan
VP: Eric Bryars
VP: Christian Svensgaard
Marketing Coordinator: Heather Szymanski
Contact: Tim Huntley
thuntley@nilpeter.net
Manager Food/Dairy Evaporators: Bo Bjarekull
Estimated Sales: $20-50 Million
Number Employees: 100-249
Parent Co: GEA Group
Other Locations:
   Niro
   Columbia MD

26651 Niro Inc
1600 Okeefe Rd
Hudson, WI 54016
715-386-9371
Fax: 715-386-9376   www.niroinc.com
Powder handling and packing systems
VP: Eric Bryars
Contact: Tim Huntley
thuntley@nilpeter.net
Estimated Sales: $20-50 Million
Number Employees: 100-249

26652 Niroflex, USA
PO Box 90
Deerfield, IL 60015
847-400-2638
Fax: 847-919-3809   metalmesh@niroflex.com
www.niroflex.com
Maker of stainless steel mesh gloves and apparel that is designed to protect workers in the meat and poultry food processing industry.
Vice President: Loren Rivkin

26653 Nita Crisp Crackers LLC
454 S. Link Lane
Fort Collins, CO 80524
970-482-9090
Fax: 970-482-1043   866-493-4609
www.nitacrisp.com
Artisan flatbreads in small batches or in bulk to natural grocers, specialty food stores, and restaurants from coast to coast
Managing Partner: Steve Landry
CEO: Paul Pellegrino
Customer Service / Sales: Michele Hattman
Estimated Sales: $170,000
Number of Products: 1
Square Footage: 5614
Type of Packaging: Consumer, Food Service, Bulk
Brands:
   Nita Crisp

26654 Nitech
911 E 23rd St
Columbus, NE 68601-3736
402-563-3188
Fax: 402-563-2792   800-237-6496
info@nitechIPM.com   www.nitechipm.com
Turntables and stretch wrapping equipment
Owner: Roger Bettenhousen
rogerb@nitechindustries.com
Sales Director: Chris Bettenhausen
Estimated Sales: $2.5-5,000,000
Number Employees: 20-49
Type of Packaging: Bulk

26655 Nitsch Tool Co Inc
1715 Grant Blvd
Syracuse, NY 13208-3017
315-472-4044
Fax: 315-472-4051
Manufacturer and exporter of machine knives for baking
Owner: Leonard Nitsch
Estimated Sales: Less than $500,000
Number Employees: 1-4

26656 Nitta Corp Of America
7605 Nitta Dr
Suwanee, GA 30024-6666
770-497-0212
Fax: 770-623-1398   800-221-3689
www.nitta.com
Urethane and PVC conveyor belts, rubber covered, leather power transmission belts
Vice President: Tracy Mc Soley
tmcsoley@nitta.com
VP: Tracy Mc Soley
Marketing/Sales: Bruce Cooper
VP Operations: Kim Millsaps
Estimated Sales: $5-10 Million
Number Employees: 50-99

26657 Nolon Industries
PO Box T
Mantua, OH 44255
330-274-2283
Fax: 330-274-2283
Manufacturer and exporter of fiberglass reinforced plastic boxes
President: Nick Nicolanti
Type of Packaging: Bulk

26658 Nolu Plastics
30152 Aventura
Rancho Santa Margarita, CA 92688-2019
866-765-8744
Fax: 866-447-6587   800-346-7822
solusteam@solusii.com   www.solusii.com
Plastic conveyor components, guide rails, chain supports, PVC conveyor rollers
Inside Sales: Kathy Yakas
District Manager: Kevin Dahill
Number Employees: 35
Number of Products: 15

26659 Nomaco
501 Nmc Dr
Zebulon, NC 27597-2762
919-655-0801
Fax: 919-269-7936   info@nomaco.com
www.nomaco.com
Plastic foam extrusions
President: Julian Young
jyoung@nomaco.com
CEO: Mick Dannin

Estimated Sales: $10-20 Million
Number Employees: 1-4

26660 Nomafa
975 Old Norcross Rd # A
Lawrenceville, GA 30045-4321
770-338-5000
Fax: 770-338-5024   sales.ads.us@albint.com
www.albanydoorsystems.com
Plant Manager: Dan Garrau
Estimated Sales: $20-50 Million
Number Employees: 100-249
Parent Co: Albany International

26661 Nook Industries
4950 E 49th St
Cleveland, OH 44125-1016
216-271-7900
Fax: 216-271-7020   800-321-7800
www.nookindustries.com
Ball bearing screws, thread screw products, worm gear actuators, splines and mechanical power jacks
President & CEO: Joseph Nook III
Estimated Sales: $10-25 Million
Number Employees: 100-249

26662 (HQ)Nor-Lake
11 Keewaydin Drive
Salem, NH 03079
603-893-9701
Fax: 603-893-7324   www.norlake.com
Refrigeration systems including walk-in coolers, walk0in freezers, milk coolers, ice cream freezers, environmental rooms, plasma refrigerators and chromatography refrigerators.
Chairman of the Board: Roger Fix
President/Chief Executive Officer: David Dunbar
VP/Chief Legal Officer/Secretary: Deborah Rosen
Chief Financial Officer: Thomas DeByle
Chief Accounting Officer: Sean Valashinas
Group VP, Food Service Group: John Abbott
Warehouse Supervisor: Cory Schlosser
Procurement Manager: Terry Clay
Estimated Sales: $26 Million
Number Employees: 300
Square Footage: 20000
Parent Co: Standex International Corporation
Type of Packaging: Food Service
Brands:
   Barrier
   Classic
   Fineline
   Foodbank
   Kold Locker
   Nova Ii
   Thermo Flow

26663 NorCrest Consulting
2044 County Road 512
Divide, CO 80814
719-687-7635
Consultant specializing in business management and technical information on fermentation, yeast products and genetic engineering for the food ingredient and biotechnology industries
President: John Norell
VP: Beverly Norell
Number Employees: 14
Square Footage: 8000

26664 (HQ)Noral
88 Pleasant Street S.,
Natick, MA 01760-563
508-653-5574
Fax: 508-653-1828   800-348-2345
Manufacturer and exporter of portable digital thermometers and probes including temperature measurement griddle probes, insertion, handheld and compact
President: Albert Ladanyi
CEO: Dr Deszo Ladanyi
VP Sales: Vincent Passiatore
Contact: Harry Erickson
harrye@noral.com
Operations: Dave Gilgenback
Purchasing Director: Mark O'Malley
Estimated Sales: $1-2.5 Million
Number Employees: 20
Square Footage: 80000

26665 Norandal
801 Crescent Centre Drive
Suite 600
Franklin, TX 37067
615-771-5700
Fax: 615-771-5701 investrel@noralinc.com
www.norandaaluminum.com
Manufacturer and exporter of laminated foil and aluminum foil pie plates
VP, Communication & Investor Relations: John Parker
Contact: David Hamling
david.hamling@noralinc.com
Estimated Sales: $97 Million
Number Employees: 820
Parent Co: Noranda
Type of Packaging: Private Label, Bulk

26666 Norback Ley & Assoc
3022 Woodland Trl
Middleton, WI 53562-1900
608-233-3814
Fax: 608-233-3895 www.norbackley.com
Manufacturer and exporter of food safety, HACCP and thermal processing software in English, Spanish, French, and Japanese
Owner: Kathleen A Ley
Chief Executive Officer: Sebastian Norback
CFO: Kathryn Olszewski
Estimated Sales: Less Than $500,000
Number Employees: 1-4
Number of Brands: 9
Number of Products: 14
Brands:
    Aprenda Haccp
    Do Haccp
    Do Sop
    Learn Haccp
    Record Haccp
    Tform
    Tpro

26667 Norback Ley & Assoc
3022 Woodland Trl
Middleton, WI 53562-1900
608-233-3814
Fax: 608-233-3895 www.norbackley.com
Provider of software tools for the food safety industry
President: Kathleen Ley
CFO: John Norback
R&D: John Norback
Quality Control: Kathleen Ley
Estimated Sales: Less Than $500,000
Number Employees: 1-4

26668 Norcal Beverage Co
2150 Stone Blvd
West Sacramento, CA 95691
916-372-0600
Fax: 916-374-2605 www.ncbev.com
Producer and wholesaler/distributor of beers, hard ciders, and nonalcoholic beverages. Also contract manufacturing and equipment solutions.
President & CEO: Shannon Deary-Bell
Chairman: Donald Deary
EVP, Marketing & External Affairs: Roy Grant Deary III
EVP, Transportation & Logistics: Timothy Deary
Year Founded: 1937
Estimated Sales: $36.7 Million
Number Employees: 500-999
Square Footage: 152000
Type of Packaging: Consumer, Food Service, Bulk
Brands:
    Anheuser-Busch Inbev®
    Activate Drinks
    Alaskan® Brewing Company
    Arizona Iced Tea
    Arrowhead Spring Water
    Black Diamond Brewing Company®
    Calistoga Water
    Crispin® Cider
    Crown Imports®
    Firestone Walker Brewery™
    Fox Barrell Hard Cider®
    Go Girl Energy Drink
    Icelandic Spring Water
    Illy Chilled Coffee
    Nestle Nesquick
    Rogue® Brewery
    Sierra Nevada®
    Speed Energy Drink
    Wyders® Cider

Budweiser®
Busch®
Natural Light®
O'Doul's®
Michelob Light®
Hurricane®
King Cobra®
Rolling Rock®
Shock Top Belgian White™
Jack's Pumpkin Spice™
Beach Bum Blonde Ale™
Dominion
Fordham
Goose Island Honker's Ale
Kona Pale Ale
Redhook Esb
Starr Hill Amber Ale
Widmer Hefeweizen
Ziegenbock®
Land Shark Lager™
Redbridge®
Wild Blue™
Stella Artois
Bass
Beck's
Boddingtons Pub Ale
Hoegaarden
Leffe Blonde
Czechvar Lager
Kokanee®
Kirin Ichiban
Margaritaville Paradise Key Teas
Lost Energy®
Monster Energy®
Rumba™ Energy Juice
Unbound Energy
Icelandic Glacial Water
Bacardi Silver™
Tilt®

26669 Norden Inc
230 Industrial Pkwy # A
Branchburg, NJ 08876-3580
908-252-9483
Fax: 908-707-0073 sales@norden-pac.se
www.nordenmachinery.com
Tube filling and cartoning machinery; also, automatic tube feeders
President: Geron Adolffon
Sales Director: Fredrik Nusson
Estimated Sales: $5-10 Million
Number Employees: 5-9
Parent Co: Norden Pac International AB

26670 Nordic Doors
PO Box 20
Dumas, AR 71639-0020
800-827-0326
Fax: 870-382-6140

26671 Nordic Printing & Packaging
5017 Boone Ave N
New Hope, MN 55428
763-535-6440
Fax: 763-535-1821 moneta.lv
Lithopraphic printed and folding cartons
Owner: Dee Dee Foster
CFO: Dee Dee Faster
Quality Control: Mary Rubink
Sales Director: Rick Parkin
Contact: Dee Foster
dee.foster@marcomnordic.com
Office Manager: Lee Thomson
Purchasing Manager: Jeff Vander Plaats
Estimated Sales: $10-20 Million
Number Employees: 50-99
Type of Packaging: Consumer, Food Service, Private Label, Bulk

26672 Nordson Corp
11475 Lakefield Dr
Duluth, GA 30097-1557
770-497-8971
Fax: 866-667-3329 800-683-2314
pkgwebcontacts@nordson.com www.nordson.com
Manufacturer and exporter of adhesive dispensers and applicators, adhesives, coatings, heat sealers and coating, gluing, labeling and packaging machinery
President: John Raven
VP: John Keane
Manager Marketing Communication: Dave Grgetic
Business Developmental Specialist: Salieta Stone
Estimated Sales: $20-50 Million
Number Employees: 250-499

26673 Nordson Sealant Equipment
45677 Helm St
PO Box 701460
Plymouth, MI 48170-6025
734-459-8600
Fax: 734-459-8686 sales@sealantequipment.com
www.sealantequipment.com
Manufacturer and exporter of adhesive and food dispensing machinery
President/Chairman: Carl Schultz
Sales/Marketing/Public Relations: James Schultz
Contact: Randy Cochran
r.cochran@sealantequipment.com
Estimated Sales: $10-20 Million
Number Employees: 50-99

26674 Noren Products Inc
1010 Obrien Dr
Menlo Park, CA 94025-1409
650-322-9500
Fax: 650-324-1348 866-936-6736
sales@norenproducts.com
www.norenproducts.com
Manufacturer and exporter of heat pipes, compact cabinet coolers, thermal pins, AcoustiLock, and HyTec Coolers.
Owner: Kimberely Dawn
Estimated Sales: $10-20,000,000
Number Employees: 50-99
Brands:
    Compact

26675 Norgren Inc.
5400 S Delaware St
Littleton, CO 80120
800-514-0129
www.imi-precision.com
Pneumatic and fluid control products such as filters, regulators, lubricators, fittings and valves
President, Americas Region: Ryan Schroeder
Estimated Sales: $100-200 Million
Number Employees: 5,000-9,999

26676 Norgus Silk Screen Co Inc
58 Sylvan Ave
Clifton, NJ 07011-2736
973-365-0600
Fax: 973-365-2749 www.gasolineadvertising.com
Shelf tackers, dividers, point of purchase signs, window banners and signage
President: Sanjay Thakker
s.thakker@gasolineadvertising.com
Estimated Sales: $30-50 Million
Number Employees: 5-9
Square Footage: 8000

26677 Norland International
PO Box 67189
Lincoln, NE 68506
402-441-3737
Fax: 402-441-3735 bk@norlandintl.com
www.norland-intl.com
Bottled water plants, water distillation systems, small bottle filler options, ozone generating systems, pre-treatment systems, blow molding equipment
Owner: Mike Mc Farland
Estimated Sales: $1-2.5 Million
Number Employees: 20-49

26678 Norman International
4501 S Santa Fe Ave
Vernon, CA 90058-2129
323-582-7132
Fax: 323-582-3464 800-289-8644
un4g@yahoo.com www.normaninternational.com
Manufactures vinyl radio frequency heat seald bags, is also an importer of vinyl zipper bags for retail packaging.
President: Norman Levine
Vice President: Chris Werner
chris@normaninternational.com
Estimated Sales: $20-50 Million
Number Employees: 20-49

26679 Normandie Metal Fabricators
55 Channel Drive
Port Washington, NY 11050-2216
516-944-9141
Fax: 516-944-3670 800-221-2398
Cabinets, carts, dollies, racks, tables, pizza ovens and transport equipment
VP Sales: Jordan Klein
VP Operations: Bill Koines
Number Employees: 20-49

26680 Norpak Corp
70 Blanchard St
Newark, NJ 07105-4702
973-589-4200
Fax: 973-578-8845 800-631-6970
sales@norpak.net www.norpak.net
Manufacturer, importer and exporter of plain and printed food wrap including foil laminated, waxed and freezer paper; also, baking pan liners and interfolded deli sheets
President: Anthony Coraci
CFO: Lidia Gelasmagas
VP/General Manager: Robert Godown
Sales Manager: Michael Pacyna
Manager: Pedro Oliveira
poliveira@norpak.com
Estimated Sales: $20-30 Million
Number Employees: 20-49
Square Footage: 100000
Brands:
    Delwrap
    Lightning Wrap
    Meat Pak
    Mica Wax
    Nuparch
    War Wrap

26681 Norris Products Corporation
675 Cincinnati Batavia Pike
Cincinnati, OH 45245
513-688-7300
Fax: 513-688-0042 877-543-2278
service@norriscorp.com www.norriscorp.com
Two-wheel portable hand carts
Owner: Paul Wilhelm
CFO: Rose Mappin
Marketing Director: Mark Glassmeyer
Estimated Sales: $10-20 Million
Number Employees: 20-49
Brands:
    Caddy-All
    Jet Set
    Super Cart

26682 Norristown Box Company
PO Box 377
Norristown, PA 19404-0377
610-275-5540
Fax: 610-275-6585
Set-up and folding paper boxes for pharmaceutical, glass, confectionery and industrial instruments
President: John P Eliff
Office Manager: S Fryer
Estimated Sales: $2.5-5 Million
Number Employees: 5-9
Brands:
    Norrbox

26683 Norristown Box Company
PO Box 377
Norristown, PA 19404-0377
610-275-5540
Fax: 610-275-6585
Posters, paperboard, folding and set-up boxes
President: John P Eliff
Estimated Sales: $2.5-5 Million
Number Employees: 5-9

26684 Norse Dairy Systems
1740 Joyce Ave
Columbus, OH 43219-1026
614-294-4931
Fax: 614-299-0538 800-338-7465
kmcgrath@norse.com www.norse.com
Filling equipment for the ice cream industry; also, ice cream cones and push-up tubes
President: Scott Fullbright
CEO: Scot Fulbright
sfulbr@norse.com
CFO: Randy Harvey
R & D: Gunther Brinkman
Director Operations: John Deininger
Estimated Sales: $1 million
Number Employees: 250-499
Parent Co: George Weston Ltd.

26685 North American Container Corp
1811 W Oak Pkwy # D
Suite D
Marietta, GA 30062-2279
770-431-4858
Fax: 770-431-6957 800-929-0610
www.nacontainer.com
Custom manufactured bulk boxes and fibercore wood replacement material
President: Michael Grigsby
mgrigsby@nacontainer.com
Estimated Sales: $10-20,000,000
Number Employees: 10-19
Type of Packaging: Bulk

26686 North American DeerFarmers Association
9301 Annapolis Road
Suite 206
Lanham, MD 20706-3132
301-459-7708
Fax: 301-459-7864 info@nadefa.org
www.nadefa.org
Committed to promoting deer farming and ranching.
President: Jill Bryar Wood
Executive Director: Barbara Fox
Number Employees: 1-4

26687 North American Packaging Corp
140 E 30th St
New York, NY 10016-7319
212-213-4141
Fax: 212-213-4145 800-499-3521
info@packagingonline.com
www.packagingonline.com
Manufacturer and importer of shopping, paper and plastic bags, gift boxes and stationery including letterhead, business cards, gift certificates, roll and sheet labels, press kits, catalogs, fliers, etc
Manager: John Destefano
Manager: John DeStefano
Estimated Sales: Below $5,000,000
Number Employees: 1-4

26688 North American Plastic Manufacturing Company
8 Park Lawn Dr
Bethel, CT 6801
203-794-1310
Fax: 203-598-0068 800-934-7752
perl@napcomfg.com www.napcomfg.com
Self-adhesive plastic hangers, hang tabs and point of purchase hangstrip systems for display packaging
Owner: Robert Laperriere
Sales Manager: Dean Kyburz
Estimated Sales: $1-5 Million
Number Employees: 1-4
Square Footage: 18000
Brands:
    Pop Strip

26689 North American Roller Prod Inc
PO Box 2142
Glen Ellyn, IL 60137-6342
630-858-9161
Fax: 630-858-9103 info@narp-trapo.com
www.narp-trapo.com
Conveyor rollers and specialty conveyors
President: Jerry Miller
info@narp-trapo.com
General Manager: Jerry Miller
Year Founded: 1981
Estimated Sales: Less than $500,000
Number Employees: 5-9

26690 North American Signs
3601 Lathrop St
South Bend, IN 46628-6108
574-234-5252
Fax: 574-289-8118 800-348-5000
POBox30@northamericansigns.com
www.northamericansigns.com
Electric and neon signs
President: John Yarger
jmy1@northamericansigns.com
CEO: Noel Yarger
CFO: Tom Yarger
Production Manager: Doug McCoigge
Estimated Sales: $10-20 Million
Number Employees: 50-99

26691 North Atlantic Equipment Sales
Route 376
Hopewell Jct, NY 12533
845-221-2201
Fax: 845-227-7795
Analyzes and tests plant operations, infrared, total solids, fat, protein, process control

President: Varick Stringham
CFO: Varick Stringham
R&D: Varick Stringham
Quality Control: Varick Stringham
Estimated Sales: $500,000-$1 Million
Number Employees: 5-9

26692 North Carolina's Southeast
707 West Broad Street
P.O.Box 2556
Elizabethtown, NC 28337
800-787-1333
Fax: 910-862-1482 locate@ncse.org
www.ncse.org
President: Steve Yost
Finance and Office Manager: Tammy Etheridge
Director: Paul G Butler Jr
Director of Business Development: Joe Melvin
Plant Manager: Derek Pringle
Estimated Sales: $1-3 Million
Number Employees: 5-9

26693 North Company
E1683 Larson Road
Waupaca, WI 54981-8734
715-258-6104
Fax: 715-258-4986 foodjobs@execpc.com
Executive search firm specializing in research and development
Executive Recruiter: Henry Warmbier, Ph.D.
Recruiter: Lori Warmbier
Number Employees: 2

26694 North Fork Weld & SteelSupl
68230 Main Rd
Greenport, NY 11944
631-477-0671
Fax: 631-477-0702 sales@nfwss.com
www.nfwelding.com
Wine industry netting reels
President: Joseph Schoenstein
sales@nfwss.com
VP: Fred Shonestein
Estimated Sales: $1-2.5 Million
Number Employees: 10-19

26695 North Side Packing Co
2200 Rivers Edge Dr
New Kensington, PA 15068-4542
724-335-4666
Fax: 724-335-2249
customerservice@northsidefoods.com
www.northsidefoods.com
Processing
President: Robert G Hofmann Ii
CFO: Robert Muhl
R&D: Paula McDaniel
Quality Control: John Stavencon John
Contact: Deborah Rihs
deborah.rihs@northsidefoods.com
Estimated Sales: Less Than $500,000
Number Employees: 1-4

26696 North Star
2120 Hewitt Avenue
Everett, WA 98201-3616
425-252-9600
Fax: 425-252-7598 www.northstarinc.com
Espresso carts, coffee grinders
President: Craig Bunney
craigbunney@gmail.com
Estimated Sales: $1-2.5 Million
Number Employees: 5-9

26697 North Star Engineered Products
28905 Glenwood Rd
Perrysburg, OH 43551-3020
419-726-2645
Fax: 419-666-1549
Manufactures equipment to process fresh cut vegetables and fruit, including fruit processing centrifuges
Owner: Tom Ziems
tsz@glassline.com
CFO: John K Clement
Sales Manager: Joe Moroni
Technical Services: Buddy Santus
Estimated Sales: $2.5-5 Million
Number Employees: 10-19
Type of Packaging: Bulk
Brands:
    Helical
    Mini Brute
    Six Shooter
    Tornado

26698 North Star Ice EquipmentCorporation
8151 Occidental Ave S
P.O.Box 80227
Seattle, WA 98108-4210
206-763-7300
Fax: 206-763-7323 800-321-1381
info@northstarice.com www.northstarice.com
Manufacturer and exporter of industrial ice makers and related handling equipment. Products include Flake Ice Makers, Liquid Ice Generators, Ice Storage Systems, Ice Delivery Systems and more.
President: Logan Shepardson
Vice President Sales & Marketing: Tom Crawford
Sales & Marketing Administrator: Jennifer Ward
Director of Operations & Finance: Rachel Camarillo
Estimated Sales: $10-20 Million
Number Employees: 11-50
Square Footage: 60000
Brands:
 Cold Spell
 Coldisc

26699 NorthStar Print Group
1222 Perry Way
Watertown, WI 53094
920-206-8626
Fax: 920-262-8582 www.multicolorcorp.com
Label production
CEO: Richard Gasper
CFO: Jim Gombar
R&D: Jerry Fowler
Quality Control: Grieg Petere
Marketing: Terry Fowler
Sr. VP Manufacturing: Andy Walker
Plant Manager: Greg Petre
Estimated Sales: $60 Million
Number Employees: 100-249
Parent Co: Journal Communications

26700 Northbrook Laboratories
1818 Skokie Boulevard
Northbrook, IL 60062-4106
847-272-8700
Fax: 847-272-2348 877-366-3522
djalw@northlandlabs.com www.northlandlabs.com
Laboratory analysis for food, feed and environmental applications
President: Jamal Alwattar
Contact: Zeek Agosto
zagosto@northlandlabs.com
Estimated Sales: $5-10 Million
Number Employees: 50-99

26701 Northcoast Woodworks
381 Buffalo Street
Conneaut, OH 44030-2451
440-593-6249
Fax: 440-593-6249
Wine industry wooden gift boxes

26702 Northeast Box Co
1726 Griswold Ave
Ashtabula, OH 44004-9213
440-992-5500
Fax: 440-992-7820 800-362-8100
www.northeastbox.com
Corrugated boxes, shipping containers and point of purchase displays; consultant specializing in J.I.T. warehousing manufactured to specifications
Owner: Ron Marchewka
ron@northeastbox.com
CFO: Peter Adano
VP/Secretary/Treasurer: Paul Seibert
General Manager: Billy Powers
Estimated Sales: $20-50 Million
Number Employees: 50-99
Square Footage: 60000

26703 Northeast Container Corporation
125 Washington Ave
Dumont, NJ 07628-3066
201-385-6200
Fax: 201-385-7356
Corrugated shipping containers
President: John Payne
Estimated Sales: $8-9 Million
Number Employees: 50-99
Square Footage: 130000

26704 Northeast Distributors Inc
210 Essex St # 3
Suite 3
Whitman, MA 02382-1514
781-447-0073
Fax: 781-447-6337 sales@nedinc.com
www.nedinc.com
Ice equipment, piping, fittings and tubing
CEO: Kenneth G Peterson
Quality Control: Linda Mahoney
Sales Exec: Philip Mohan
Estimated Sales: Below $5 Million
Number Employees: 20-49

26705 Northeast Fresh Foods Alliance
20 Scanlon Drive
2nd Floor
Randolph, MA 02368-1745
781-963-9726
Fax: 781-963-9728 neffa1@aol.com
Executive Director: Andrea Walker
Director Sales/Show Manager: John Scolponeti
Number Employees: 1-4

26706 Northeast Laboratory Svc
289 China Rd
Winslow, ME 4901
207-873-7711
Fax: 207-873-7022 866-591-7120
bmears@binax.com www.binax.com
Food technology laboratory service specializing in USDA certified listeria-salmonella and KAB/nutritional analysis and food-born illness investigations; also, product development and shelf life determination
President: Roger Piasio
Production Planning Manager: Eva Chase
Administration Manager: Vicki Massey
Lab Manager: Pam Doughty
Estimated Sales: $6-8 Million
Number Employees: 50-99
Square Footage: 108000
Parent Co: BINAX
Type of Packaging: Consumer, Food Service, Private Label, Bulk

26707 Northeast Packaging Co
875 Skyway St
Presque Isle, ME 04769-2063
207-764-6271
Fax: 207-496-3171 www.nepcobags.com
Paper and poly bags
President: Robert Umphrey
rumphrey@mfx.net
Sales Representative: Ken Joy
General Manager: Chris Burtchell
Production Manager: Jesse Harris
Number Employees: 50-99
Type of Packaging: Consumer, Private Label

26708 Northeast Packaging Materials
20 Robert Pitt Dr # 202
Monsey, NY 10952-3340
845-426-2900
Fax: 845-426-3700 sbraun@nepack.com
www.nepack.com
Manufacturer and exporter of barrier films; available in roll stock and pouches
President and QC: Stewart Braun
Estimated Sales: Below $5,000,000
Number Employees: 1-4

26709 Northeastern Products Corp
115 Sweet Rd
PO Box 98
Warrensburg, NY 12885-4754
518-623-3161
Fax: 518-623-3803 800-873-8233
info@nep-co.com www.nep-co.com
Manufacturer and exporter of meat smoking sawdust including hickory, maple, cherry and alder
President: Gary Shiavi
CEO: Paul Schiavi
Marketing Director: Richard Morgan
Estimated Sales: Below $5 Million
Number Employees: 50-99
Square Footage: 80000

26710 Northern Berkshire Tourist
121 Union St
North Adams, MA 01247-3533
413-663-9204
Marking devices, rubber stamps, pads, ink, decals, engraved nameplates,architectural signs,etc

President: John Luczynsky
Estimated Sales: $300,000-500,000
Number Employees: 1-4
Parent Co: JPDS

26711 Northern Box Co Inc
1328 Mishawaka St
Elkhart, IN 46514-1809
574-264-2161
Fax: 574-262-8943
Corrugated shipping boxes
President: Heidi Linder
VP: Tina Linder
Manager: Dick Scheve
northernboxco@aol.com
Estimated Sales: $5-10 Million
Number Employees: 20-49

26712 Northern Metal Products
6601 Ridgewood Road
St Cloud, MN 56303
320-252-3442
Fax: 320-252-2832 800-458-5549
sales@northmet.com
www.northernmetalproducts.com
Wire and tubing point of purchase merchandising displays and fixtures
President: Larry Leutt
CEO and President: Larry Lautt
Sr. Sales Engineering: Chuck Lauer
Contact: Kenneth Arceneau
k.arceneau@norwire.com
General Manager: Marc Illies
Estimated Sales: $10-20 Million
Number Employees: 100-249
Square Footage: 300000
Parent Co: St. Cloud Industry

26713 Northern Metals & Supply
2100 Llano Rd # N3
Santa Rosa, CA 95407-6430
707-575-0555
Fax: 707-575-4088
Wine and food industry stainless sanitary fittings, butterfly valve, ball valves, stainless pipe and tubing, pipe fittings, and stainless and aluminum raw material
President: Thomas F Obuchowski
Estimated Sales: $5-10 Million
Number Employees: 1-4

26714 Northern Package Corporation
201 W 86th Street
Minneapolis, MN 55420-2784
952-881-5861
Fax: 952-881-6758
Corrugated paper boxes
General Manager: Joe Gerow
Number Employees: 55
Parent Co: Liberty Diversified Industries

26715 Northern Stainless Fabricating
P.O.Box 6715
Traverse City, MI 49696-6715
231-947-4580
Fax: 231-947-9074
Manufacturer and exporter of custom made stainless steel kitchen equipment for food service and institutional use including salad bars, dish tables and prep tables
President: Mike Fisher
Chief Estimator: Harry Muse
CFO: Michael J Fisher
VP Production: Bruce Muzzarelli
Estimated Sales: $10-20 Million
Number Employees: 50-99
Square Footage: 60000

26716 Northfield Freezing Systems
PO Box 98
Northfield, MN 55057-0098
507-645-9546
Fax: 507-645-6148 800-426-1283
Manufacturer and exporter of freezers, coolers, chillers, hardeners and spiral conveying freezing systems
President: Tim Colies
Sales/Marketing Executive: Larry Deboer
Purchasing Agent: Bill Westby
Estimated Sales: $20-50 Million
Number Employees: 120
Parent Co: Frigo Schndia

26717 Northland Consultants
3741 Highway 556
RR2
Sault Ste. Marie, ON P6A 5K7
Canada
705-541-8490
www.northlandconsultants.ca
Marketing consultant specializing in brand development for food products
Managing Partner: Marko Koskenoja
Estimated Sales: Less than $500,000
Number Employees: 1-4

26718 Northland Corp
1260 E Van Deinse St
Greenville, MI 48838-1400
616-754-5601
Fax: 616-754-0970 800-223-3900
sales@northlandnka.net
www.documentofconformity.com
Custom refrigeration, commercial and residential
President: Mike Bufton
CFO: Karen Braund
Vice President: Brad Stauffer
Research & Development: Jim Holland
Quality Control: Rick Waldorf
Marketing Director: Gerry Reda
Public Relations: Sindy Angi
Operations/Plant Manager: Kent Coon
Plant Manager: Kent Coon
Purchasing Manager: Richard Burns
Estimated Sales: $10-20 Million
Number Employees: 100-249
Square Footage: 440000
Parent Co: AGA Food Service Group
Brands:
Imperial

26719 Northland Corp
1260 E Van Deinse St
Greenville, MI 48838-1400
616-754-5601
Fax: 616-754-0970 800-223-3900
customerservice@northlandnka.net
www.documentofconformity.com
President: Gordon Stauffer
CFO: Brad Stauffer
R & D: Jim Holland
Quality Control: Jim Nielsen
Plant Manager: Kent Coon
Estimated Sales: Below $5 Million
Number Employees: 100-249
Parent Co: Aga Rangemaster Group

26720 Northland Labs
1818 Skokie Blvd
Northbrook, IL 60062-4106
847-272-8700
Fax: 847-272-2348 800-366-3522
djalw@northlandlabs.com www.northlandlabs.com
Consultant specializing in food testing and analysis services for microbiological contamination, chemical analysis/composition and nutritional labeling
President: Jamal Alwattar
Contact: Ezequiel Agosto
zagosto@northlandlabs.com
General Manager: D Alwatter
Estimated Sales: $1-5 Million
Number Employees: 5-9
Square Footage: 28000

26721 Northland Process Piping
1662 320th Ave
Isle, MN 56342-4303
320-679-2119
Fax: 320-679-2785 mnoffice@nppmn.com
www.nppmn.com
Brine and clean-in place systems, floor plates and drains, platforms, walkways and stairs, pumps, tanks, tubing and valves
Owner: Jennifer Hawk
CFO: Kathy Tramm
Project Sales/Customer Service: Dan Tramm
jennifer.hawk@kellogg.com
Human Resources: Natalie Geist
Foreman: Eirik Andersen
Purchasing/Customer Service: Bruce Richards
Number Employees: 100-249
Other Locations:
Roswell GA
Lemoore CA
Horseheads NY

26722 Northview Laboratories
616 Heathrow Dr
Lincolnshire, IL 60069
847-564-8181
Fax: 847-564-8269
Independent testing laboratory offering microbiological, sterility assurance, chemistry & toxicology services. Specialized services including water system validation and monitoring, environmental chamber storage and feeding studies
Manager: Martin Spalding
Quality Control: Leonart Wojtowicz
CEO: Martin J Spalding Sr
Marketing Director: Laura Ritter
Sales Director: Trisha Daugherty
Contact: Meredith Puljung
meredith.puljung@sgs.com
Plant Manager: Richard Harrington
Estimated Sales: $20-50 Million
Number Employees: 100-249
Square Footage: 23000

26723 Northview Laboratories
106 Venture Boulevard
Spartanburg, SC 29306-3805
864-574-7728
Fax: 864-574-7873
Independent testing laboratory offering microbiological, sterility assurance, chemistry and toxicology services
President: Delores Bruce
CFO: Ed Kelley
Vice President of Leasing: David Happ
Chief Operating Officer: Rolland Baribeau
Estimated Sales: $1-2.5 Million
Number Employees: 15
Square Footage: 92000
Other Locations:
Northview Laboratories
Spartanburg SC
Northview Laboratories
Hercules CA

26724 (HQ)Northview Pacific Laboratories
1880 Holste Rd
Northbrook, IL 60062
847-564-8181
Fax: 510-964-0551 www.ndt.org
Consultant offering food testing services
Manager: Mario Sotelo
Quality Control: Sarah Khan
VP: Thomas Spalding
R & D: Lonny Barish
Estimated Sales: $10-20 Million
Number Employees: 50-99
Parent Co: Northview Labs
Other Locations:

26725 Northville LaboratoriesInc
100 Rural Hill St
Northville, MI 48167-1538
248-349-1500
Fax: 248-349-1505 sales@jogue.com
www.jogue.com
Flavors
President: Dattu Sastry
chamber@northville.org
Estimated Sales: $10-20 Million
Number Employees: 20-49

26726 Northwest Analytical Inc
111 SW 5th Ave # 800
Portland, OR 97204-3606
503-224-7727
Fax: 503-224-5236 888-692-7638
nwa@nwasoft.com www.nwasoft.com
Manufacturer and exporter of SPC charting workstation and statistical quality control (SQC) software for control charting, process capability analysis and plant floor data collection
Chairman: Clifford S L Yee
CEO: Bob Ward
bward@nwasoft.com
CFO: T Olin Nichols
VP: Jeff Cawley
R&D: Louis Halvorsen
VP Marketing: Peter Guilfoyle
VP Sales: Jim Petrusich
Estimated Sales: $10-20,000,000
Number Employees: 20-49

26727 Northwest Art Glass
9003 151st Ave NE
Redmond, WA 98052-3513
425-861-9600
Fax: 425-861-9300 800-888-9444
www.nwartglass.com
Manufacturer and importer of etched glass separators and screens, brass posts, traffic control systems, liscourts and sneeze guards
Owner: Richard Mesmer
richard@cascadegac.com
Metal Sales/Operations: Steve Bolens
richard@cascadegac.com
Estimated Sales: $1-2.5 Million
Number Employees: 10-19
Square Footage: 17000
Type of Packaging: Bulk

26728 Northwest Cherry Growers
105 S.18th Street
Suite 205
Yakima, WA 98901-2176
509-453-4837
Fax: 509-453-4880 info@nwcherries.com
www.nwcherries.com
Provides educational information of the health benefits of cherries.
President: B.J. Thurlby
Promotion Director: James W. Michael
International Marketing Director: Keith Hu
International Program Coordinator: Teresa Baggarley
VP International Marketing: Eric Melton
Contact: Teresa Baggarley
teresa@nwcherries.com
Office Manager/Controller: Joanne Daniels
Estimated Sales: $1-3 Million
Number Employees: 5-9

26729 Northwest Food Processors Assn
8338 NE Alderwood Rd # 160
Portland, OR 97220-6811
503-327-2200
Fax: 503-327-2201 www.nwfpa.org
Promotes the food processing industry by including events, membership application, advocacy and issues.
President: David Mcgiverin
dmcgiverin@nwfpa.org
Executive VP: David Klick
Events & Marketing Mgr.: Karen Waggoner
Sales Coordinator: Sarah Emerson
Accounting & Operations Dir.: Patty Pepin
Number Employees: 10-19

26730 Northwest Laboratories
241 S Holden St
Seattle, WA 98108-4359
206-763-6252
Fax: 206-763-3949 postmaster@nwlabs1896.com
www.nwlabs1896.com
Consultant offering analysis, testing and food research services
CEO: Richard Schefsky
Estimated Sales: $1-3 Million
Number Employees: 5-9
Square Footage: 63000

26731 Northwest Molded Products Classic Line
4915 21st Street
Racine, WI 53406-5028
262-554-4412
Fax: 262-554-8370
Small, rigid molded plastic boxes, hot stamp decorating, foam inserts and custom molding
Estimated Sales: $5-10 Million
Number Employees: 20-49

26732 Northwest Products
600 Oak St
Archbold, OH 43502-1579
419-445-1950
Fax: 419-446-2984 www.quadcorehab.org
Wooden pallets
COO: Philip Zuver
COO: Philip Zuver
Executive Director: Bruce Abell
Sales Representative: John Miller
Executive Director: Phillip Zuver
Estimated Sales: $20-50 Million
Number Employees: 50-99
Parent Co: Quadco Rehabilitation Center

26733 Northwestern
15054 Oxnard St
Van Nuys, CA 91411
818-786-1581
Fax: 818-786-5063 russbrown@northwestern.com
Display cases and store fixtures
President: C Wayne Noecker
CFO: Rughann Etz
VP: Douglas Noecker
Contact: Audrie Chun
audrie@northwestern.com
Estimated Sales: $10-20 Million
Number Employees: 50-99

26734 Northwestern Corp
922 Armstrong St
PO Box 490
Morris, IL 60450-1921
815-942-1300
Fax: 815-942-4417 800-942-1316
sales@nwcorp.com
Manufacturer and exporter of vending machinery
President: Richard Bolen
nwsales@nwcorp.com
CFO: Angie Stropel
R&D: Angie Stropel
Quality Control: Angie Stropel
Sales Director: Diane Olson
Estimated Sales: $10-20 Million
Number Employees: 20-49
Square Footage: 100000

26735 Northwind Inc
13300 Maple Hill Rd
Alpena, AR 72611-3008
870-437-5360
Fax: 870-437-2595 877-937-2585
www.northwindinc.com www.northwindinc.com
Sanitary conveyors, wash stations, meat hoppers,
tanks, catwalks and support equipment
President: Mark Ogier
nw@northwindinc.com
Quality Control: Tim Ogier
Secretary: Tim Ogier
Estimated Sales: Below $5,000,000
Number Employees: 10-19

26736 Norvell Co Inc
4002 Liberty Bell Rd
Fort Scott, KS 66701-8638
620-223-3110
Fax: 620-223-3115 800-653-3147
www.norvellco.com
Manufacturer and exporter of flour mill sifters for
the processing of flour, spices, cereals, etc.; also, ag-
itators for blending
Office Manager: Barbara Fitts
General Manager: Mark Shank
Manager: Mark Shank
Estimated Sales: $5-10 Million
Number Employees: 20-49
Square Footage: 80000
Type of Packaging: Food Service
Brands:
Jet Sifter
Santare
Super Drive Sifter

26737 Norwalt Design Inc
961 State Route 10 # 2a
Randolph, NJ 07869-1921
973-927-3200
Fax: 973-927-2841 norwalt@norwalt.com
www.norwalt.com
Bottle capping and plugging equipment, rotary disc
and parts feeders, unscramblers, elevator hoppers
and assembly machines
President: Walter McDonald
Director Marketing: Anthony Conte
Manager: Michael Seitel
mike@norwalt.com
Estimated Sales: $2.5-5 Million
Number Employees: 20-49
Square Footage: 60000

26738 Norwood Marking Systems
2538 Wisconsin Ave
Downers Grove, IL 60515
630-968-0646
Fax: 630-968-7672 800-626-3464
Manufacturer and exporter of coding systems and
accessories including hot stamp imprinters, thermal
transfer printers, embossers, hot stamp and thermal
transfer ribbon supplies and steel type

General Manager: Larry Kulik
Sales Director: Cliff Vanwey
Estimated Sales: $20-50 Million
Number Employees: 50-99
Parent Co: Illinois Tool Works

26739 Norwood Paper Inc
7001 W 60th St
Chicago, IL 60638-3101
773-788-1528
Fax: 708-656-5310 www.norwoodpaper.com
Paper boards, box fillers and layering sheets
Owner: Mike Bayne
mike@norwoodpaper.com
Sales Manager: Darin Rakowsky
Sales Manager: Matt Zeman
mike@norwoodpaper.com
Estimated Sales: $10-20,000,000
Number Employees: 5-9

26740 Nosaj Disposables
PO Box 1290
Paterson, NJ 7509
973-279-4190
Fax: 973-279-6929 800-631-3809
Trash liners, hand cleaners, disposable industrial pa-
per towels and cloth wipers
President: Stanley Slosberg
Sales Director: Harold Gelvan
Estimated Sales: $5-10 Million
Number Employees: 10-19
Square Footage: 80000

26741 Nosco
651 S Martin Luther King Jr
Waukegan, IL 60085-7500
847-360-4806
Fax: 847-360-4924 rxquality@nosco.com
www.nosco.com
Folding cartons and labels including roll and cut;
also, instructional enclosures and printing of promo-
tional literature available
President: Russell Haraf
CFO: Michael Biesboar
Estimated Sales: $20-50 Million
Number Employees: 250-499
Square Footage: 200000

26742 Noteworthy Company
100 Church St
Amsterdam, NY 12010
800-696-7849
Fax: 518-842-8317
Bags including polyethylene, take home, patch, soft
loop and molded handle, etc.; also, holiday
Owner: Carol Constigino
CFO: John Cloanglo
Contact: Debi Crisalli
dcrisalli@noteworthyinc.com
Estimated Sales: $10-20 Million
Number Employees: 250-499

26743 Nothum Food Processing Systems
631 S Kansas Ave
Springfield, MO 65802
417-831-2816
Fax: 417-866-4781 800-435-1297
nothum@nothum.com www.nothum.com
Manufacturer and exporter of batter applicators,
breaders, pre-dusters, fryers, shuttle conveyors, char
markers, coaters, blanchers, filters, ovens, polar
therm and stack freezers, etc.
President/Chief Executive Officer: Robert Nothum
nothum@nothum.com
Sales & Marketing: Robert Nothum
Number Employees: 30

26744 Nottingham Spirk
2200 Overlook Rd
Cleveland, OH 44106-2326
216-231-7830
Fax: 216-231-6275 www.nottinghamspirk.com
Custom designed packaging and displays
President: John Nottingham
phil_stewart1224@yahoo.com
Manager: Jeff Kalman
Facilities: Phil Stewart
Estimated Sales: $5-10 Million
Number Employees: 50-99

26745 Nova Hand Dryers
12801 Worldgate Drive
Suite 500
Herndon, VA 20170
Canada
703-615-3636
Fax: 877-385-1291
Manufacturer and exporter of warm air hand dryers
Sales Manager: Maurine Cohen
Number Employees: 45
Parent Co: Avmor
Brands:
Nova

26746 Nova Industries
999 Montague St
San Leandro, CA 94577
510-357-0171
Fax: 510-357-3832 www.bordenlighting.com
Manufacturer and exporter of glare control devices
and lighting fixtures including custom made and in-
candescent
President: James Borden
VP: Floyd Shreeve
Contact: Bobby Aquino
baquino@bordenlighting.com
Estimated Sales: $2.5-5 Million
Number Employees: 20-49
Square Footage: 28000

26747 Novacart Inc
512 W Ohio Ave
Richmond, CA 94804-2040
510-215-8999
Fax: 510-215-9175 877-896-6682
info@novacartusa.com www.novacartusa.com
President: Giorgio Anghileri
Manager: Joe Miglia
joe@novacartusa.com
Estimated Sales: $3-5 Million
Number Employees: 10-19
Parent Co: Novacart Italy

26748 Novamex
500 W Overland Ave
Suite 300
El Paso, TX 79901
www.novamex.com
Markets and exports a variety of foods and bever-
ages from Mexico.
Logistics Coordinator: Susana Barreda
susana.barreda@novamex.com
Executive Vice President: Sanford Gross
International Market Development: Raymundo
Gomez
Year Founded: 1986
Estimated Sales: $150 Million
Number Employees: 250-499
Type of Packaging: Food Service
Brands:
Cholula Hot Sauce
D'Gari Gelatin

26749 Novar
6060 Rockside Woods Bl N # 400
Suite 400
Cleveland, OH 44131-2378
216-682-1600
Fax: 216-682-1614 800-348-1235
customerservice@novar.com www.novar.com
Computerized control systems for rack and case re-
frigeration, store heating and cooling
President: Paul J Orzeske
VP: Dean Lindstorm
Executive VP: David Weber
Number Employees: 10-19
Square Footage: 280000
Brands:
Spectrum

26750 Novax Group/Point of Sales
42 Broadway
New York, NY 10004-1617
212-684-1244
Fax: 212-684-2337
Point of sale systems and software
Manager: Reggie Menof
Manager: Charles Chen
Estimated Sales: $1-2.5 Million
Number Employees: 5-9
Parent Co: POS Technology

26751 Novelis Foil Products
3560 Lenox Road
Atlanta, GA 30326

404-760-4000
Fax: 706-812-2039 800-776-8701
www.novelis.com
Aluminum foil, rolls, sheets and disposable containers
Manager: Charlie Aheran
Marketing Director: Beverly Duncan
Sales Director: Charlie Ahern
Contact: Christina Abdelnour
christina.abdelnour@novelis.com
Controller: Ed McGee
Number Employees: 10-19
Type of Packaging: Consumer, Food Service, Private Label, Bulk
Brands:
　Alcan

26752 (HQ)Novelty Advertising
1148 Walnut St
Coshocton, OH 43812-1769

740-622-3113
Fax: 740-622-5286 800-848-9163
Manufacturer and exporter of calendars and advertising specialties
President: Gregory Coffman
gcoffman@noveltyadv.com
Owner: Greg Coffman
Owner: Thad Coffman
VP: Jim McConnell
Estimated Sales: $5-10 Million
Number Employees: 20-49
Type of Packaging: Consumer, Food Service, Bulk

26753 Novelty Baskets
PO Box 1481
Hurst, TX 76053-1481

817-268-5426
Fax: 817-423-6693
A manufacturer of wire basket displays for use in ice cream convenience stores
Owner: Ken Miller
Operations Manager: Ken Miller
Number Employees: 10

26754 Novelty Crystal
3015 48th Ave
Long Island City, NY 11101-3419

718-458-6700
Fax: 718-458-9408 800-622-0250
joe@noveltycrystal.com www.noveltycrystal.com
Plastic caterware which includes; plastic serving trays, plastic bowls, plastic bowls, plastic tumblers, plastic pitchers, plastic stemware and plastic serving accessories.
Owner: Ed Coslett
e.coslett@noveltycrystal.com
VP: Asher Michaeli
VP: Joseph Michaeli
CFO: Ashur Michaeli
Estimated Sales: $2.5-5 Million
Number Employees: 20-49
Square Footage: 240000
Type of Packaging: Consumer, Food Service

26755 Noveon Inc
9911 Brecksville Rd
Cleveland, OH 44141-3247

216-447-5000
Fax: 216-447-5740
Piping components for touch industrial fluid applications and a superior balance of properties that provide longer service in hot corrosive environments
President: Stephen Kirk
CEO: Kan Kim
kan.kim@noveon.com
Estimated Sales: Over $1 Billion
Number Employees: 500-999

26756 Novolex
101 E Carolina Ave
Hartsville, SC 29500

843-857-4800
800-845-6051
supplier.hotline@novolex.com www.novolex.com
Tea and coffee industry bags (flexible); bags for grocery stores; carryout bags; tortilla steam bags.
Chairman & CEO: Stanley Bikulege
CFO: Paul Palmisano
VP & Corporate Treasurer: Janet Gibbons
SVP, Innovation: Adrianne Tipton

Year Founded: 2003
Estimated Sales: $2.3 Billion
Number Employees: 7,000
Brands:
　HILEX POLY
　DURO BAG
　BAGCRAFT PACKAGING
　DE LUXE PACKAGING
　GENERAL PACKAGING PRODUCTS
　INTERNATIONAL CONVERTER
　SHIELDS
　HERITAGE BAG
　BURROWS PACKAGING

26757 Novus
650 Pelham Blvd
Suite 100
St. Paul, MN 55114

952-944-8000
Fax: 952-944-2542 800-328-1117
www.novusglass.com
Manufacturer and exporter of plastic polish and scratch remover and auto glass replacement products
President: Keith Beverige
Contact: Allan Dmore
dmore.allan@novuspolish.com
Number Employees: 1,000-4,999
Square Footage: 40000
Parent Co: TCG International
Type of Packaging: Consumer
Brands:
　Novus Plastic

26758 Now Plastics Inc
136 Denslow Rd
East Longmeadow, MA 01028-3188

413-525-1010
Fax: 413-525-8951 info@nowplastics.com
www.nowplastics.com
NOW Plastics offers an extensive line of high performance film sustracts including but not limited to; PET, BOPP, CPP, PVC, MOPP, FOPP, OPS, Nylon, Non Woven, Synthetic Paper, Skin Film, Retort films and Co-extrusions. AdditionallyNOW Plastics supplies various types of micro-perforated, laser perforated or high clarity bags and films for bakery and produce packaging.
President: Oded Edan
CEO: Larry Silverstein
ls@nowplastics.com
CEO: Larry Silverstein
Estimated Sales: $10-20,000,000
Number Employees: 10-19
Square Footage: 40000
Type of Packaging: Bulk

26759 Nowakowski
9909 S 57th St
Franklin, WI 53132-8685

414-423-9900
Fax: 414-423-6300 800-394-5866
Stainless steel fabricated food processing equipment and other metal products
President: Jeff Nowakowski
Vice President: James Nowakowski, Sr.
Sales Director: Bill Redmond
Plant Manager: James Nowakowski, Jr.
Estimated Sales: $2-5 Million
Number Employees: 20-49
Square Footage: 74600

26760 Nozzle Nolen Inc
3975 Coconut Rd
Palm Springs, FL 33461-4003

561-964-6200
Fax: 561-272-2623 800-226-6536
www.nozzlenolen.com
Pest control systems
Manager: Mike Antropoli
mikea@nozzlenolen.com
Estimated Sales: $1-2,5,000,000
Number Employees: 20-49
Parent Co: Nozzle Nolen

26761 Nrd LLC
2937 Alt Blvd
P.O.Box 310
Grand Island, NY 14072-1292

716-773-7634
Fax: 716-773-7744 800-525-8076
sales@nrdinc.com www.nrdinc.com
Manufacturer and exporter of static control products to increase safety, productivity and product quality including ionizers.

President: Doug Fiegel
dfiegel@nrdinc.com
Chairman: Sal Alfiero
Director Sales & Marketing: Greg Gumkowski
Production Manager: Kathleen Kowalik
Purchasing Manager: Jim Zoldowski
Number Employees: 20-49
Type of Packaging: Bulk

26762 Nrd LLC
2937 Alt Blvd
PO Box 310
Grand Island, NY 14072-1292

716-773-7634
Fax: 716-773-7744 800-525-8076
sales@nrdinc.com www.nrdinc.com
Self-powered static control equipment for labeling, printing, coating and converting
President: Doug Fiegel
dfiegel@nrdinc.com
Marketing Manager: Colleen Coancy-O'Donnell
Sales Manager: Mike Grimaldi
Number Employees: 20-49

26763 Nrd LLC
2937 Alt Blvd
P.O.Box 310
Grand Island, NY 14072-1292

716-773-7634
Fax: 716-773-7744 800-525-8076
sales@nrdinc.com www.nrdinc.com
President: Doug Fiegel
dfiegel@nrdinc.com
Number Employees: 20-49

26764 Nu CO2 LLC
2800 SE Market Pl
Stuart, FL 34997

772-221-1754
Fax: 772-781-3500 800-472-2855
www.nuco2.com
CO2 systems for fountains; also, service available.
President: Gerald Miller
VP, Finance: Felicia Gallagher
VP, Business: John Templin
General Counsel: David Markatos
VP, Sales: Randy Gold
VP, Human Resources: Jeff Gilheney
VP, Field Operations: Derek Burton
Year Founded: 1995
Estimated Sales: $100-500 Million
Number Employees: 1,100
Brands:
　Nuco2

26765 Nu-Con Equipment
1610 Lake Dr W
Chanhassen, MN 55317

952-279-5205
Fax: 952-279-5206 877-939-0510
Turnkey sanitary process, conveying, and packaging solutions from raw material handling to consumer packaged goods. Sanitary and USDA approved process equipment and systems with easy to clean features
President: Marv Deam
Vice President: Mike Salvador
Marketing/Sales Executive: Marvin Deam
Contact: Bob Mortenson
bmortenson@nucon.com
Purchasing Manager: Tom Haider
Estimated Sales: $20-50 Million
Number Employees: 20-49
Square Footage: 30000
Parent Co: Nu-Con

26766 Nu-Dell Manufacturing
2250 E Devon Ave # 349
Des Plaines, IL 60018-4507

847-803-4500
Fax: 847-803-4584 sales@nudell.com
www.posterframescentral.com
Electric blackboards and signs, point of purchase displays, easels, rope lights, changeable message and marker boards and other indoor signage
Owner: David Block
Sales Director: Mari Carmona
Customer Service: Janis Vazquez
Estimated Sales: $10-20 Million
Number Employees: 5-9
Parent Co: Nu-Dell Manufacturing Company
Type of Packaging: Food Service
Brands:
　Ad-Lite

Glo-Glaze
Glo-Ons
Glolite

26767 Nu-Meat Technology
PO Box 599
Scotch Plains, NJ 07076-0599

908-232-7342
Fax: 908-232-5534
Choppers, chub separators, massagers and tumblers,
meat tenderizers, mechanical, pickle injectors,
slicers
Estimated Sales: $20-50 Million
Number Employees: 20-49

26768 Nu-Star Inc
1425 Stagecoach Rd
Shakopee, MN 55379-2798

952-445-8295
Fax: 952-445-0231 800-800-9274
jadams@nustarinc.com
Manufacturer and exporter of carts for lifting, push-
ing and pulling
President: Scott Lorch
slorch@nustarinc.com
CFO: James Coan
VP Power Pusher Division: Scott Lorch
VP Sales & Marketing: John D Adams
Estimated Sales: $5-10,000,000
Number Employees: 20-49
Type of Packaging: Bulk

26769 Nu-Tex Styles, Inc.
285 Davidson Ave # 104
Somerset, NJ 08873

732-485-5456
Fax: 732-873-0854 info@nu-tex.com
www.nu-tex.com
Manufacturer, importer and exporter of industrial
fabrics and wiping rags including cheesecloth and
dusting cloth
President: Howard Bromwich
howard@nu-tex.com
Estimated Sales: $1-2.5 Million
Number Employees: 1-4
Number of Brands: 3
Number of Products: 57
Square Footage: 360000

26770 Nu-Towel Co
208 Bennington Ave
Kansas City, MO 64123-1914

816-842-2909
Fax: 816-842-8679 800-800-7247
Disposable wipers, towels and rags
Owner: Dennis Wacknov
CEO: Paul Wacknov
Quality Control: Jason Wacknov
Director Operations: Pat Isbell
Estimated Sales: $1-2.5 Million
Number Employees: 10-19
Square Footage: 140000
Parent Co: American Textile Mills
Brands:
Alabama Rag
Arkansas Rag
California Rag
Carolina Rag
Colorado Rag
Georgia Rag
Illinois Rag
Indiana Rag
Iowa Rag
Kansas City Rag
Kansas Rag
Kentucky Rag
Louisiana Rag
Michigan Rag
Minnesota Rag
Mississippi Rag
Missouri Rag
Nebraska Rag
New Mexico Rag
Ohio Rag
Oklahoma Rag
Pennsylvania Rag
Tennessee Rag

**26771 (HQ)Nu-Trend Plastics
Thermoformer**
119 Sewald St
Jacksonville, FL 32204-1731

904-353-5936
Fax: 904-353-2035

Manufacturer and exporter of thermoformed plastic
containers, trays and inserts
CEO: Michael Corrigan
CFO: Mike Corrigan
Estimated Sales: $2-2.5 Million
Number Employees: 5-9
Square Footage: 30000
Type of Packaging: Consumer, Food Service, Pri-
vate Label

26772 Nu-Vu Food Service Systems
5600 13th Street
Menominee, MI 49858

906-863-4401
Fax: 906-863-5889 800-338-9886
sales@nu-vu.com www.nu-vu.com
Ovens,proofers, oven/proofers, carts,racks,and
roll-in rack ovens.
President: Najib Maalouf
Research & Development: Matt Deming
Sales Director: Reza McDaniel
Contact: Matt Deming
mdeming@nu-vu.com
Director Of Purchasing: Wendy Swanson
Estimated Sales: $1-5 Million
Number Employees: 100-249

26773 NuTone
9825 Kenwood Rd
Suite 301
Cincinnati, OH 45242

513-527-5100
Fax: 513-527-5177 888-336-3948
www.nutone.com
Manufacturer and exporter of range hoods, exhaust
fans, heaters, central cleaning systems, etc.
CEO: David Pringle
CFO: Bill Kissell
Quality Control: Gloria Wrenn
Contact: Jimmie Cheek
jcheek@nutone.com
Manager: Fabio Fronda
Number Employees: 500-999
Parent Co: Nortek

26774 Nuance Solutions Inc
1140 E 103rd St
Chicago, IL 60628-3010

773-785-2300
Fax: 800-621-1276 800-621-8553
cjh@nuancesol.com www.nuancesolutions.com
Manufacturer and exporter of liquid and jelly hand
soap, degreasers, disinfectants, pine oil germicide,
sanitizers and hard surface cleaners
Owner: James Flanagan
jflana1@nuancesol.com
VP Marketing: Neil Houtsma
Estimated Sales: $20-50 Million
Number Employees: 50-99
Square Footage: 150000
Parent Co: Bullen Metawest
Type of Packaging: Bulk

26775 Nucon Corporation
111 S Pfingsten Ste 100
Deerfield, IL 60015

847-564-3505
Fax: 847-509-0011 877-545-0070
customersupport@brightsparktravel.com
www.brightsparktravel.com
Manufacturer and exporter of plastic pallets
Owner: Mitchell Slotnick
VP Sales/Marketing: Allan Wasserman
Estimated Sales: $2.5-5,000,000
Number Employees: 20-49

26776 Nulco Lighting
123 Dyer St
Suite 2
Providence, RI 2903

401-728-5200
Fax: 401-728-8210
Decorative electric lighting fixtures
President: Kent Nulman
CEO: Robert Delogo
CFO: Robert Geloge
R & D: Richard Ruggeri
Quality Control: Joe Lenk
National Sales Manager: Stephen Rice
Estimated Sales: $5-10 Million
Number Employees: 100-249

26777 Numatics Inc
46280 Dylan Dr # 100
Novi, MI 48377-4910

248-596-3200
Fax: 248-596-3201 insidesales@numatics.com
www.numatics.com
Cmo: David K Dodds
david.dodds@numatics.com
VP: David K Dodds
Estimated Sales: $1-5 Million
Number Employees: 500-999

26778 Numeric Computer Systems Inc
275 Oser Ave
Hauppauge, NY 11788-3609

631-486-9000
Fax: 631-486-9032 800-321-7822
www.numericcomputersystems.com
President / CEO: Robert Hochberg
robert.hochberg@ncssuite.com
Managing Director: Pedro Toro
CFO: Wayne Hochberg
Executive VP-Strategy and Business Devel: Allen
Dickason
COO: Mark Hochberg
Estimated Sales: $5-10 Million
Number Employees: 1-4

26779 Nuova Distribution Centre
6940 Salashan Pkwy
Bldg-A
Ferndale, WA 98248-8314

360-366-2226
Fax: 360-366-4015 info@nuovadistribution.com
www.nuovadistribution.com
Manufacturer and importer of coffee and espresso
grinders, sandwich grills and espresso, cappuccino
and Italian slush/granita machines
President: Roberto Bresciani
roberto@nuovadistribution.com
Coordinator: Vic Bialas
Estimated Sales: $1-3 Million
Number Employees: 10-19
Brands:
Nuova Simonelli

26780 Nuova Simonelli USA
1915 1st Ave S
Seattle, WA 98134-1405

206-223-5533
Fax: 206-223-5525 info@nuovadistribution.com
www.nuovadistribution.com
Espresso machines and accessories, grinders
Member: Robert Bresciani
Estimated Sales: $1-3 Million
Number Employees: 1-4

26781 Nutec Manufacturing Inc
908 Garnet Ct
New Lenox, IL 60451-3569

815-722-2800
Fax: 815-722-2831 815-722-5348
sales@nutecmfg.com www.nutecmfg.com
Manufacturer, importer and exporter of food form-
ing equipment including patties formers, cubers and
conveyors
President: Ken Sandberg
CEO: Zibe Gibson
bids@nutecmfg.com
Vice President: Mike Barnett
Research & Development: Bob Nard
Marketing Director: Mike Barnett
Sales Director: Mike Barnett
IT: Jeff Regan
Production Manager: John Goetzinger
Plant Manager: Ken Galloy
Purchasing: John Goetzinger
Estimated Sales: $2.5-5 Million
Number Employees: 10-19
Square Footage: 20000
Brands:
Nutec
Provatec

26782 Nutec Manufacturing Inc
908 Garnet Ct
New Lenox, IL 60451-3569

815-722-2800
Fax: 815-722-2831 suggestions@nutecmfg.com
www.nutecmfg.com
Food forming and depositing equipment
President: Ken Sandberg
IT: Jeff Regan
bids@nutecmfg.com

Estimated Sales: $10-20 Million
Number Employees: 10-19

26783 Nutec Manufacturing Inc
908 Garnet Ct
New Lenox, IL 60451-3569

815-722-2800
Fax: 815-722-2831 sales@nutecmfg.com
www.nutecmfg.com
Food processing equipment
President: Ken Sandberg
IT: Jeff Regan
bids@nutecmfg.com
Estimated Sales: $5-10 Million
Number Employees: 10-19

26784 Nutra Food Ingredients, LLC
4683 50th Street SE
Kentwood, MI 49512

616-656-9928
Fax: 419-730-3685
sales@nutrafoodingredients.com
www.nutrafoodingredients.com
Functional and nutritional ingredients supplier to the
food, beverage, nutraceutical and cosmetics indus-
tries
President: Bryon Yang
Director of Business Development: Tim Wolffis
Quality Control: Monica Mylet
monica.mylet@nutrafoodingredients.com
Director of Sales and Marketing: Clarence Harvey
Year Founded: 2004
Estimated Sales: Under $500,000
Number Employees: 1-4
Other Locations:
  Distribution Center
  Edison NJ
  Distribution Center
  Carson CA

26785 Nutraceutical International
1777 Sun Peak Dr.
Park City, UT 84098

435-655-6000
800-669-8877
info@nutraceutical.com www.nutraceutical.com
Supplements.
CEO: Chad Clawson
Vice President/CFO: Cory McQueen
Chief Marketing Officer: John D'Alessandro
Senior VP, Sales: David Bunch
COO: Camilla Shumaker
Year Founded: 1993
Estimated Sales: $188.07 Million
Number Employees: 810
Square Footage: 6103
Type of Packaging: Consumer, Food Service, Bulk
Brands:
  Solaray®
  KAL®
  Food Source®
  Sunny Green®
  VegLife®
  Veglife®
  Allvia®
  Complimed®
  bioAllers®
  Herbs for Kids®
  NatraBio®
  Homeopathy for Kids®
  NaturalCare®
  Nutra BioGenesis®
  Oakmont Labs®
  Pioneer®
  VAXA®
  Zand®
  Nature's Herbs®
  Natural Balance®
  Natural Sport®
  BuckPower™
  FunFresh Foods®
  Dowd & Rogers™
  Miztique™
  Paleo Planet™
  Refrigerator Fresh™
  Sweet Moose™
  Taste Waves™
  World Berries™
  The Real Food Trading Co.™
  Zylicious™
  Spring Drops®
  Honey Gardens™
  Montana Big Sky™
  Premier One®

26786 Nutri-Bake Inc
1208 Rue Bergar
Laval, QC H7L 5A2
Canada

450-933-5936
Fax: 888-263-3208 info@nutri-bake.com
www.organic-baked-goods.com
Manufacturer and wholesaler of baked goods
President: Peter Tsatoumas

26787 Nutrifaster Inc
209 S Bennett St
Seattle, WA 98108-2226

206-767-5054
Fax: 206-762-2209 800-800-2641
Sales@Nutrifaster.com www.nutrifaster.com
Manufacturer and exporter of centrifugal juice ex-
tractors
President: Bert Robins
Sales/Service: Fred Davies
Manager: Rocco Robins
sales@nutrifaster.com
Estimated Sales: Less than $500,000
Number Employees: 5-9
Type of Packaging: Food Service
Brands:
  Nutrifaster N-350

26788 Nutrin Distribution Company
1627 Connecticut Ave NW
Suite 3
Washington, DC 20009

Fax: 815-301-9184 888-718-3235
adam@nutrin.com www.nutrin.com
Supplier of peanut products, importer with
just-in-time deliver in the US and Canada. Products
include peanut flour, butter, oil, extract, and essence
as well as roasted and chopped peanuts.
President: Adam Benado

26789 Nutrinfo Corporation
108 Water Street
Watertown, MA 02472-4696

617-923-2377
Fax: 617-926-6360 800-676-6686
Consultant to the U.S. food and dietary supplement
industries providing services including design, food
technology, marketing, promotion, sanitation, test-
ing, nutritional analysis and international food
labeling
President: Richard Litner
VP: Sanjeev Mohanti
Director Science: Thomas Hansen
Number Employees: 11
Square Footage: 6000

26790 Nutrinova
1601 Lbj Fwy
Dallas, TX 75234-6034

972-443-4000
Fax: 972-443-4994 800-786-3883
www.nutrinova.com
A global technology and specialty materials com-
pany that engineers and manufacturers a wide vari-
ety of products essential to everyday living.
President: Graham Hall
cheryl.colline@nutrinova.com
Chairman, Chief Executive Officer: Mark Rohr
Vice President: Jiro Okada
Marketing Manager North America: Patricia Hanley
Contact: Colline Cheryl
cheryl.colline@nutrinova.com
Chief Operating Officer: Doug Madden
Number Employees: 5-9
Parent Co: Nutrinova Nutrition Specialists & Food
Ingredients GmbH

26791 Nutrisciences Labs
70 Carolyn Boulevard
Farmingdale, NY 11735

631-247-0600
855-492-7388
info@nutricaplabs.com www.nutrasciencelabs.com
Nutritional supplements including vitamins, miner-
als, and sports supplements
President/Founder: Jason Provenzano
Chief Executive Officer: Jonathan Greenhut
VP Digital Marketing: Andrew Goldman
VP Sales: Blayney McEneaney
Operations Manager: Dana Roveto
Estimated Sales: $45 Million
Number Employees: 40
Parent Co: Twinlab Consolidation Corporation

26792 Nutrition & Food Associates
PO Box 47007
Plymouth, MN 55447

763-550-9475
Fax: 763-559-3675 info@nutriform.com
www.nutriform.com
Manufacturer and exporter of computer software for
product development, nutrition labeling, recipe and
menu analysis
President: Patricia Godfrey
Estimated Sales: Below $5 Million
Number Employees: 1-4
Type of Packaging: Food Service
Brands:
  Nutriform

26793 Nutrition Network
4199 Campus Drive
Suite 550
Irvine, CA 92612-4694

949-753-7998
Fax: 949-497-8991
Nutrition support consultant providing services to
food producers, dietitians and consumers
CEO: Charlene Rainey
Director Technical Services: Leslie Nyquist
Estimated Sales: $500,000-$1 Million
Number Employees: 5-9
Square Footage: 6000

26794 Nutrition Research
504 S 13th St
Livingston, MT 59047

406-222-3541
Fax: 406-823-6499 www.livingstonhealthcare.org
Research and development firm offering turnkey as-
sistance in the design and processing of natural
foods, vitamin, mineral and herbal supplements, etc
President: Lee Dreyer
CEO: Bren Lowe
Human Resources Director: Connie Dunn

26795 Nutsco Inc
1115 S 2nd St
Camden, NJ 08103-3232

856-966-6400
Fax: 856-966-6544 www.nutsco.com
Supply chain management for high quality raw ca-
shews
President: Fransisco A Neto
VP: Patricio Assis
Marketing: Sueli Vieira
Sales: Sueli Vieira
Plant Manager: Steve McCall
Estimated Sales: $5-10 Million
Number Employees: 10-19
Square Footage: 50800
Parent Co: Usibras (Brazil)

26796 Nutty Bavarian
305 Hickman Dr
Sanford, FL 32771-6905

407-444-6322
Fax: 407-444-6335 800-382-4788
bruno@nuttyb.com www.nuttyb.com
Cinnamon nut glaze syrup and fresh roasted gourmet
nuts; Manufacturer of nut roasting carts and
warmers as well as paper and plastic cones and gift
tins for nuts
Owner: David Brent
bruno@nuttyb.com
Customer Service Manager: Amber Stefanisko
Controller: Keya Morgan
Vice President of Sales: David Zangenberg
bruno@nuttyb.com
Production Manager: Ed Conrado
Estimated Sales: $500,000-$1 Million
Number Employees: 10-19
Square Footage: 28800
Type of Packaging: Consumer, Bulk
Brands:
  Nbr 2000
  Nutty Bavarian

26797 Nyco Products Co
5332 Dansher Rd
Countryside, IL 60525-3124

708-579-8100
Fax: 708-579-9898 800-752-4754
bstahurski@nycoproducts.com
www.nycoproducts.com
Cleaning and sanitation supplies including deodorants, detergents, emulsifying agents, metal polish
and glass, pipe, toilet bowl and drain cleaners

President: Robert Stahurski
jwunderlich@nycoproducts.com
VP Sales: John Wunderlich
Sales Exec: John Wunderlich
VP Operations: Robert Houston
Estimated Sales: $5-10 Million
Number Employees: 50-99
Square Footage: 150000
Parent Co: NYCO Products Company

26798 Nydree Flooring
1115 Vista Park Dr # C
Ste D
Forest, VA 24551-4686
        434-525-5252
Fax: 434-525-7437 800-682-5698
www.nydreeflooring.com
Commercial flooring
Owner: Barry Brubaker
VP Radiation: James Myron
Estimated Sales: $500,000-$1 Million
Number Employees: 50-99
Square Footage: 72000
Parent Co: Appliant Radian Energy Corporation
Brands:
    Packing House

26799 Nyman Manufacturing Company
275 Ferris Ave
Rumford, RI 02916-1033
        401-438-3410
Fax: 401-438-5975
Manufacturer and exporter of plastic cups, dinner-
ware, lids, caps and covers; also, paper cups
Marketing Director: Laura Coupal
General Manager (Paper): Walter Bennett
General Manager (Plastic): Al Domenici
Type of Packaging: Food Service
Brands:
    First Choice
    Natural Choice
    Popular Choice

26800 O A Newton & Son Co
16356 Sussex Hwy # 1
PO Box 397
Bridgeville, DE 19933-3056
        302-337-8211
Fax: 302-337-3780 800-726-5745
solutions@oanewton.com www.oanewton.com
Materials handling and control, feed and grain han-
dling, irrigation
President: Rob F Rider Jr
Chairman of the Board: Robert Rider
Estimated Sales: $10-20 Million
Number Employees: 20-49

26801 O K Mfg
2340 S 900 W # A
South Salt Lake, UT 84119-1553
        801-974-9116
Fax: 801-974-5458 800-748-5480
okmfgsales@gmail.com www.gumball-depot.com
Bubble gum and novelty vending equipment and
plush cranes
President: Jeff Ostler
k_ausler@okmfg.net
Sales Exec: Kurt Ausler
Owner/Production: Jeff Ostler
Estimated Sales: $5-10 Million
Number Employees: 5-9
Square Footage: 208000
Brands:
    Ok

26802 O'Brian Tarping SystemsInc
2330 Womble Brooks Rd E
Wilson, NC 27893-7947
        252-291-2141
Fax: 252-291-1416 800-334-8277
sales@obriantarping.com www.obriantarping.com
Commercial awnings, unautomatic tarting systems
President: Woody O'Brian
woody@obriantarping.com
Estimated Sales: $3-5 Million
Number Employees: 20-49

26803 O'Brien Bros Inc
51 Doty Cir
West Springfield, MA 01089-1307
        413-734-7121
Fax: 413-737-1642 800-343-0949
joeobrien@obrienbrothersinc.com
www.obrienbrothersinc.com

Locks and locksmith supplies
Owner: Joe O'Brien
joeobrien@obrienbrothersinc.com
Estimated Sales: $.5-1 million
Number Employees: 1-4

26804 O'Brien Installations
4435 Corporate Drive
Burlington
Ontario, CA L7L 5T9
Canada
        905-336-8245
Fax: 905-331-6494 info@obrieninstall.com
www.obrieninstall.com
Manufacturer and exporter of cranes
President: George O'Brien
Marketing Coordinator: John Marchetti
Sales Director: Wayne Davis
Production Manager: Randy Mullin
Purchasing Manager: Krys Klain
Estimated Sales: $1-10 Million
Number Employees: 50-99
Square Footage: 80000
Parent Co: O'Brien Material Handling
Other Locations:
    O'Brien Material Handling
    Memramock, NB

26805 O'Dell Corp
13833 Indian Mound Rd
Ware Shoals, SC 29692-3533
        864-861-2222
Fax: 864-861-3171 800-342-2843
www.odellcorp.com
Manufacturer, importer and exporter of household
and janitorial mops, brooms, brushes and handles
CEO: Wh O'Dell
who@odellcorp.com
VP: Paul O'Dell
Customer Service: Gayle O'Dell
Estimated Sales: $10-20 Million
Number Employees: 100-249
Square Footage: 170000
Brands:
    Kitchen Queen

26806 O-Cedar
2188 Diehl Road
Aurora, IL 60502
        217-379-2377
Fax: 217-379-9901 800-543-8105
www.ocedar.com
Brooms including corn, rattan, bamboo, etc
President: Stanley Koschnick
General Manager: Stanley Kochnick
Estimated Sales: $1-5 Million
Number Employees: 50-99
Parent Co: Freudenberg Household Products LP

26807 O-Cedar
2188 Diehl Road
Aurora, IL 60502
        219-726-8128
800-543-8105
www.ocedar.com
Manufacturer and exporter of industrial brooms and
brushes
Plant Manager: Mike White
Parent Co: O'Cedar Vining

26808 O.B.S. Trading
2370 N High
Suite 3
Jackson, MO 63755
        573-243-6999
Fax: 573-243-8723 www.obstrading.com
Planning and designing to finding the best machines
for meat processing
President: Henning Bollerslev

26809 (HQ)O.C. Adhesives Corporation
PO Box 3058
Ridgefield, NJ 07657-3058
        973-279-8134
Fax: 973-279-0338 800-662-1595
Industrial water based adhesives for plastic film
laminating, bottle labeling and difficult to stick sur-
faces and UV coated stock
President: Stanley Meyers Phd
Technology Director: Leonard Gross
Director Marketing: Sy Eckstein
Estimated Sales: $2.5-5 Million
Number Employees: 10-19
Square Footage: 50000

26810 O.D. Kurtz Associates
242 Hurst Road NE
Palm Bay, FL 32907-1566
        321-723-0135
Fax: 321-723-0151 www.odk.com
Laboratory specializing in extraneous analysis, sani-
tation appraisals and AOAC food testing
Estimated Sales: $500,000-$1 Million
Number Employees: 5-9

26811 O.K. Marking Devices
1358 Cornwall Street
Regina, SK S4R 2H5
Canada
        306-522-2856
Fax: 306-569-3566
Stencils, engraved signs, tags, corporation seals and
rubber and photopolymer stamps
President: Fl Clark
Estimated Sales: Below $5 Million
Number Employees: 7
Square Footage: 4000

26812 O/K International Corporation
73 Bartlett Street
Marlborough, MA 01752-3071
        508-303-8286
Fax: 508-303-8207 800-521-2908
sales@okcorp.com www.okcorp.com
Hot-air sealers, case erectors, case liners and con-
veyor systems, strech wrappers
Marketing Director: Ann Marie Kellett
Contact: Marcela Barragan
mbarragan@okcorp.com
Plant Manager: Hans Mentink
Estimated Sales: $5-10 Million
Number Employees: 25-49
Type of Packaging: Consumer, Bulk

26813 OCS Checkweighers Inc
2350 Hewatt Road
Snellville, GA 30039
        678-344-8300
Fax: 678-344-8030 info.usa@ocs-cw.com
www.ocs-cw.com
Packaging machinery
President: Ingolf Latz
CEO/CFO: Theo Dueppre
Sales Manager: Rachel Edwards
Contact: Jeff Borrelli
jeff.borrelli@ocs-cw.com
Estimated Sales: $1.5 Million
Number Employees: 13

26814 OI Analytical
151 Graham Rd
College Station, TX 77845-9654
        979-690-1711
Fax: 979-690-0440 oimail@oico.com
www.oianalytical.com
Cmo: Gary Englehart
genglehart@oico.com
CEO: J Bruce Lancaster
Estimated Sales: G
Number Employees: 50-99

26815 OK Stamp & Seal Company
1608 Linwood Blvd
Oklahoma City, OK 73106-5052
        405-235-7853
Fax: 405-232-4139
Rubber stamps
President: Steve Fagundes
Estimated Sales: Less than $500,000
Number Employees: 1-4

26816 OMNOVA Solutions
175 Ghent Road
Fairlawn, OH 44333
        330-869-4200
www.omnova.com
Plastic, calendered, plain and printed vinyl film
Chairman/President/CEO: Kevin McMullen
Senior Vice President/CFO: Michael Hicks
Senior VP/Chief Information Officer: Douglas
Wenger
Director, Marketing Paper Products: Robin McCann
Director, National Sales: Dan Fox
Contact: Patricia Abdulla
patricia.abdulla@omnova.com
Chief Administrative Officer: Michael Curran
Plant Manager: Lee Szwast
Purchasing Director: Robert Culp

Estimated Sales: $1.13 Billion
Number Employees: 2,390
Square Footage: 10124
Parent Co: GenCorp

26817 OMRON Systems LLC
55 Commerce Dr
Schaumburg, IL 60173-5302
224-520-7650
Fax: 847-843-7686 www.omron.com
Electronic cash registers with software for fast food, fine dining and cafeteria markets; also, touch screen systems for restaurants and hospitality
President, CEO: Yoshihito Yamada
jcornet@omronost.com
CFO: Yoshinori Suzuki
Director, EVP: Akio Sakumiya
Sales Exec: Jac Cornet
Estimated Sales: $15-20 Million
Number Employees: 1-4

26818 OMRON Systems LLC
55 Commerce Dr
Schaumburg, IL 60173-5302
224-520-7650
Fax: 847-843-7686 800-556-6766
omroninfo@omron.com www.omron.com
Instrumentation and control products including PLCs, sensors and temperature controllers
President: Craig Bauer
jcornet@omronost.com
CEO: Tastu Goto
Sales Exec: Jac Cornet
Estimated Sales: $4.6 Million
Number Employees: 1-4
Square Footage: 30000
Parent Co: Omron Corporation
Brands:
Smart Factory

26819 OMYA, Inc.
9987 Carver Rd
Suite 300
Cincinnatti, OH 45242
513-387-4600
800-749-6692
www.omya.com
Fillers and pigments from calcium carbonate and dolomite, and distributor of chemical products.
President: Anthony Colak
CFO: Michael Phillips
Secretary: Leonard Eisenberg
Asst Sec: Patricia Kirkendall
Manager Technology Services: Michael Roussel
Sales Manager: Maria Burt
Contact: Hilary Allard
hilary.allard@omya.com
Manager: Scott McCalla
Manager Projects Engineering: Scott Schaffner
Director of Engineering: Rob Tikoft
Director Purchasing: Derrell Riley
Estimated Sales: $4.3 Million
Other Locations:
Proctor VT
Cincinnati OH
Woodland WA
Kingsport TN
Lucerne Valley CA
Johnsonburg PA
Florence VT
Hawesville KY
Sylacauga AL
Superior AZ
Long Beach CA

26820 ORB Weaver Farm
3406 Lime Kiln Road
New Haven, VT 05472
802-877-3755
marjorie@orbweaverfarm.com
www.orbweaverfarm.com
Fresh fruits and vegetables, and fine cheeses
President: Marjorie Susman
marjorie@orbweaverfarm.com

26821 ORBIS
1055 Corporate Center Dr
Oconomowoc, WI 53066-4829
262-560-5000
Fax: 262-560-5841 800-890-7292
info@orbiscorporation.com
www.orbiscorporation.com
Plastic containers, hand-held and bulk and pallets

CEO: Jim Kotek
Marketing Director: Pete Budney
Public Relations: Samantha Goetz
Purchasing Manager: Robert Kroening
Number Employees: 100-249
Parent Co: Menasha Corporation
Type of Packaging: Food Service, Bulk

26822 ORBIS
1055 Corporate Center Dr
Oconomowoc, WI 53066-4829
262-560-5000
Fax: 262-560-5841 info@orbiscorporation.com
www.orbiscorporation.com
Plastic pallets and containers
President: William F Ash
Sales Manager: Jo Ann Bahling
Sales Manager: Sherri Brigowatz
Sales Manager: Sally Meyers
Estimated Sales: $20-50 Million
Number Employees: 100-249
Parent Co: Menasha Corporation Convoy Plastic Pallets

26823 ORBIS
1055 Corporate Center Dr
Oconomowoc, WI 53066-4829
262-560-5000
Fax: 262-560-5841 800-999-8683
info@orbiscorporation.com
www.orbiscorporation.com
Total returnable packaging systems, containers, pallets, interiors
President: Linda Balwinski
linda.balwinski@orbiscorporation.com
CEO: Dave Schopp
Estimated Sales: $20-50 million
Number Employees: 100-249

26824 ORBIS
1055 Corporate Center Dr
PO Box 389
Oconomowoc, WI 53066-4829
262-560-5000
Fax: 262-560-5841 800-890-7292
info@orbiscorporation.com
www.orbiscorporation.com
Provides reusable packaging for the bakery, dairy, beverage, red meat/poultry and general food processing industry.
President: William F Ash
VP Finance: Mark Gorzek
VP Marketing/Sales: James Solum
VP Sales: Tim Henkel
VP Human Resources: Tom Bissell
VP Operations: Mike McKay
Number Employees: 100-249
Square Footage: 15011
Parent Co: Menasha Corporation

26825 ORBIS RPM
5250 E Terrace Drive
Suite 106
Madison, WI 53718
608-852-8840
Fax: 608-237-8162 www.corbiplastics.com
Packaging materials including plastic reusable pallets, divider sheets/layer pads and top frames.
President: Jack Graham
General Manager: Chad Feehan
Parent Co: Menasha Corporation
Type of Packaging: Food Service

26826 (HQ)OSF
650 Barmac Drive
Toronto, ON M9L 2X8
Canada
416-749-7700
Fax: 416-740-6365 800-465-4000
Manufacturer and exporter of store fixtures, showcases and displays; also, steel shelving
CEO: Harry Shier
Co-Chairman: Milton Shier
Number Employees: 2100
Square Footage: 8800000
Other Locations:
OSF
Blackstone VA
Brands:
Century Line
Tufkote
Vista Classic Line

26827 OSRAM SYLVANIA
100 Endicott Street
Danvers, MA 01923
978-777-1900
Fax: 978-750-2152 800-544-4828
www.sylvania.com
President: Charles Jerabeck
President, Chief Executive Officer: Rick Leaman
Contact: Michael Abbott
michael.abbott@sylvania.com
Number Employees: 10,000

26828 OTD Corporation
P.O.Box 510
Hinsdale, IL 60522-0510
630-321-9232
Fax: 574-254-5092
Manufacturer and exporter of aluminum containers, racks and pallets
President: James Ogle
Controller: Jean Chatman
Estimated Sales: $20-30 Million
Number Employees: 1-4

26829 OTP Industrial Solutions
3601 N Fruitridge Ave
Terre Haute, IN 47804-1756
812-466-2734
Fax: 812-466-2831 860-953-7632
www.otpnet.com
Manufacturer and exporter of overhead bridge cranes, wire rope winches, conveyors and reciprocating feeders
Manager: Walt Tompkins
CEO/Engineer: Steve White
CFO: Jim Bennett
Vice President: Joe Goda
Marketing Director: Dave Parks
Sales Director: Tom Bland
Public Relations: Tom Bland
Plant Manager: Steve Rowe
Purchasing Manager: Jerry Taylor
Estimated Sales: $16.5 Million
Number Employees: 10-19
Square Footage: 40000

26830 (HQ)OWD
PO Box 1260
Tupper Lake, NY 12986-0260
518-359-2944
Fax: 518-359-2994 800-836-1693
www.jarden.com/phoenix.zhtml?c=72395&p=irol..
.ID.
Manufacturer and exporter of plastic spoons, forks, knives, straws, cups and plates
CEO: James E. Lillie
CFO: John Breshahan
Vice President: Rachel Wilson
R & D: Allison Malkin
VP Sales: Al Huggins
Estimated Sales: Less than $500,000
Number Employees: 100-249
Square Footage: 260000
Parent Co: Jarden Corporation
Other Locations:
O.W.D.
La Fayette GA
Brands:
Lady Dianne

26831 OXO International
601 West 26th St
Suite 1050
New York, NY 10001
212-242-3333
Fax: 717-709-5350 www.oxo.com
Manufacturer of kitchen utensils and appliances
President: Edward Ahn
eahn@oxo.com
VP, Sales: Michael Cleary
Estimated Sales: $2.5-5 Million
Number Employees: 50-99
Number of Products: 1000
Type of Packaging: Consumer
Brands:
Oxo Goodgrips

26832 Oak Barrel Winecraft
1443 San Pablo Ave
Berkeley, CA 94702-1045
510-849-0400
Fax: 510-528-6543 info@oakbarrel.com
www.oakbarrel.com

Oak barrels for wine and beer making, bottles and stoppers for wine, vinegar starter culture and bottling and brewery machinery; importer of wine presses, crushers and barrels; also, wholesaler/distributor of vinegar starter cultureand barrels
President and CFO: Bernard Rooney
info@oakbarrel.com
Vice President: Homer Smith
Estimated Sales: $5-10 Million
Number Employees: 1-4
Square Footage: 12000

26833 Oak Creek Pallet Company
5059 N 119th Street
Milwaukee, WI 53225-3607
414-762-7170
Fax: 414-762-3070
Wooden pallets, boxes and crates
President: Gary LaMaster
Number Employees: 90

26834 Oak International
1160 White St
Sturgis, MI 49091
269-651-9790
Fax: 269-651-7849 www.cimcool.com
Manufacturer and exporter of FDA approved cutting, stamping and drawing oils; also, grinding coolants and cleaners
Sr. VP Sales/Operations: F Edwards
Contact: Michelle Dressler
michelle_dressler@milacron.com
Plant Manager: Jim Phillips
Estimated Sales: $5-10 Million
Number Employees: 10-19
Square Footage: 52000
Brands:
Oak Draw
Oak Kleen
Oak Kool
Oak Kote
Oak Protect
Oil Rids

26835 Oak Street Manufacturing
255 Welter Dr
Monticello, IA 52310
319-465-4042
Fax: 877-465-4042 877-465-4344
www.oakstreetmfg.com
Manufacturer and distributor of restaurant furnishings
President/Owner: Cindy Bagge *Year Founded:* 1995

26836 Oakes & Burger
PO Box 665
Niles, OH 44446-0665
800-321-0106
Fax: 330-652-2617
Aseptic processing equipment, batch control systems, chillers, clean rooms and equipment, custom fabrication, deaerators, homogenizers, ice equipment, ingredient feeders, meters, expert systems, filters

26837 Oakes Carton Co
5575 Collingwood Ave
Kalamazoo, MI 49004-1525
269-381-6022
Fax: 269-381-2948 www.oakescarton.com
Paper folding cartons
Owner: Judy Day
VP Sales Manager: James Savage
judyd@oakescarton.com
Customer Service: Oakes Carton
Office Manager / Accounting / Human Reso: Judee Buckhout
Estimated Sales: $2.5-5 Million
Number Employees: 20-49

26838 Oakite Products
P.O.Box 7
New Providence, NJ 07974-0007
908-464-6900
Fax: 908-464-5354 800-526-4473
ceasternbranch@chemetall.com
Developer. manufacturer and supplier of state-of-the-art specialty chemical products.
President: Don LeBart
CEO: Ron Felber
Estimated Sales: $75-$80 Million
Number Employees: 50-99

26839 Oaklee International
125 Raynor Ave
Ronkonkoma, NY 11779-6666
631-436-7900
Fax: 631-436-7985 800-333-7250
service@oaklee.com www.oaklee.com
Shrink film, sleeve labels, promotional packaging, protective packaging
Executive Director: Alice Zebrowski
alice@oaklee.com
Sales Exec: Alice Zebrowski
Number Employees: 100-249

26840 Oaklee International
125 Raynor Ave
Ronkonkoma, NY 11779-6666
631-436-7900
Fax: 631-436-7985 800-333-7250
service@oaklee.com www.oaklee.com
Executive Director: Alice Zebrowski
alice@oaklee.com
Sales Exec: Alice Zebrowski
Estimated Sales: $5-10 Million
Number Employees: 100-249

26841 Oakton Instruments
PO Box 5136
Vernon Hills, IL 60061-5136
888-462-5866
Fax: 847-247-2984 888-462-5866
info@4oakton.com www.4oakton.com
Provides pH, ORP, conductivity/TDS, dissolved oxygen, relative humity, time, temperature, and barometric pressure instrumentation, baths, ovens, vacuum pumps, desiccators, clamps and magnifiers
Marketing Director: Bob Langie
Estimated Sales: $1-5 Million
Brands:
Oakton

26842 Oates Flag Co Inc
10951 Electron Dr
Louisville, KY 40299-6410
502-267-8200
Fax: 502-267-8246 sales@oatesflag.com
www.oatesflag.com
Flags and pennants; silk screening, athletic lettering and embroidery available
Owner: C R Oates
randy@oatesflag.com
Marketing Director: Reggie Oates
Estimated Sales: Below $5 Million
Number Employees: 10-19

26843 Obergurg Engineering
1814 Empire Industrial Court
Suite G
Santa Rosa, CA 95403-1946
707-542-4153
Fax: 707-542-4152
Wine industry label design
Manager: Joan Murphy
Number Employees: 7

26844 Oc Lugo Co Inc
15 Third St # 2
New City, NY 10956-4946
845-480-5121
Fax: 845-480-5122 info@oclugo.com
www.oclugo.com
Supplier of chemicals, vitamins, minerals, gelatins and food ingredients. OC Lugo's other division is Critical Filtration supplies
President: Richard Lugo
rlugo@oclugo.com
Estimated Sales: $830,000
Number Employees: 5-9

26845 Occidental Chemical Corporation
5 Greenway Plaza
P.O. Box 27570
Houston, TX 77046-0506
713-215-7000
Fax: 716-278-7880 www.oxy.com
Chemicals including bottle cleaning compounds; processor of soda for carbonated soft drinks
President and CEO: Stephen I. Chazen
Contact: Alison Frey
alison_frey@oxy.com
Plant Manager: Candace Jaunzemis
Director Purchasing: Tony Orbegoso
Estimated Sales: $.5-1 million
Number Employees: 1-4
Parent Co: Occidental Petroleum

26846 Occidental Chemical Corporation
5005 L B J Fwy
Suite 2200
Dallas, TX 75244
972-404-3800
Fax: 972-448-6631 800-733-3665
www.oxychem.com
Basic chemicals concentrated in the chloro-vinyls including chlorine, caustic soda, ethylene dichloride and polyvinylchloride
President: James Lienert
CFO: Dennis Blake
Site Manager: Rick Zelley
Number Employees: 3000
Parent Co: Occidental Petroleum Corporation

26847 Oceanpower America
222 Meadows Lane NE
Leesburg, VA 20176
305-721-7823
info@email.oceanpower.com
www.oceanpoweramerica.com
Manufacturer of ice cream machines *Year Founded:* 1996

26848 (HQ)Ockerlund Industries
1555 Wrightwood Court
Addison, IL 60101
708-771-7707
Fax: 708-620-1630 guyo@ockerlund.com
Corrugated, plastic and wooden boxes
President: Stan Joray
jjoray@oxbox.biz
CEO: Guy Ockerlund
Estimated Sales: $10-20 Million
Number Employees: 100-249

26849 Ocme America Corporation
2200 N Susquehanna Trail
York, PA 17404-1652
717-843-6263
Fax: 717-843-6748 tsnelbaker@ocmeusa.com
www.ocme.it
Packaging machinery including fillers, depalletizers, wrap-around case packers, shrink wrap machines and palletizers
President: Emmanuel Gattescht
egattescht@ocme.it
President: Tony Intriona
R&D: Anthony Trona
Sales Coordinator: Thelma Snelbaker
Estimated Sales: $5-10 Million
Number Employees: 10
Square Footage: 16000
Parent Co: Ocme SRL

26850 Ocs Checkweighers, Inc.
2350 Hewatt Rd
Snellville, GA 30039
678-344-8030
Fax: 678-344-8030 info.usa@ocs-cw.com
www.ocs-cw.com
High-speed weighing systems.
Contact: Jeff Borrelli
jeff.borrelli@ocs-cw.com

26851 Odell's
Reno, NV
800-635-0436
odellscustomerservice@venturafoods.com
www.popntop.com
Popping oils and popcorn toppings.
Co-owner: Arthur Anderson
Co-owner: Vikki Anderson

26852 Oden Machinery
199 Fire Tower Dr
Tonawanda, NY 14150-5813
716-874-3000
Fax: 716-874-1589 800-658-3622
sales@odencorp.com www.odencorp.com
Manufacturer and exporter of volumetric and net weight filling machinery for liquid and semi-l;iquid products.
President: Gary Gellerson
ggellerson@odenmachinery.com
Marketing Director: Phyllis Phallen
Sales Director: Gary Laidman
Number Employees: 20-49
Brands:
Grav/Tronic
Mega/Fill
Net/Mass
Pro/Fill

Pro/Matic
Servo/Fill

26853 Odenberg Engineering
4038 Seaport Blvd
West Sacramento, CA 95691
916-371-0700
Fax: 916-371-5471 800-688-8396
sales@odenberg.com
Manufacturer and exporter of batch steam peelers, chillers/freezers and sorters
President: Maurice Moynihan
VP: Ashley Hunter
Contact: Noel Basquel
noel.basquel@odenberg.com
Production Sales Manager: Diamond Meagher
Estimated Sales: $10-20,000,000
Number Employees: 20-49
Parent Co: Odenberg Engineering

26854 Odessa Packaging Services
202 N Bassett St
Clayton, DE 19938
302-653-8474
Fax: 302-653-8612 800-633-7726

26855 Odor Management
1 Corporate Dr # 100
Suite 100
Long Grove, IL 60047-8887
847-304-9111
Fax: 847-304-0989 800-662-6367
www.odormanagement.com
President: Phil Coffey
coffey@omiindustries.com
Lead Scientist, Research and Development: Laura Haupert
Director of Marketing and Brand Developm: Melinda Adamec
National Sales Director: Tom Minett
Chief Operating Officer and Director of: Charles Timcik
Director of Operations: Stephen Lattis
Estimated Sales: Less Than $500,000
Number Employees: 1-4

26856 Oenophilia
1713 Legion Road
Chapel Hill, NC 27517-2359
919-942-1250
Fax: 919-942-5718
Wine and bar accessories

26857 Oerlikon Balzers Coating USA
1181 Jansen Farm Ct
Rogers Business Park
Elgin, IL 60123-2595
847-695-5200
Fax: 847-695-4051 info.balzers.us@oerlikon.com
www.oerlikon.com/balzers/us
President: Kristen Kunz
CEO: Hans Br,,ndle
CFO: Volker Dostmann
Manager: Gary Cunningham
gary.cunningham@oerlikon.com
Number Employees: 20-49

26858 Oerlikon Leybold Vacuum
5700 Mellon Rd
Export, PA 15632-8900
724-327-5700
Fax: 724-325-3577 www.oerlikon.com
Manufacturer, importer and exporter of vacuum pumps and systems
Chief Executive Officer: Andreas Widl
Vice President: P Albert
Manager of Technical Services: Joachim GstAhl
Marketing Director: M Vitale
Head of Sales: Werner SchAdler
Manager: Jim Hupp
Chief Operating Officer, Chief Operating: Wolfgang Ehrk
Plant Manager: Dennis Pellegrino
Number Employees: 1-4
Square Footage: 596000
Parent Co: Leybold AG
Brands:
Sogevac

26859 Oerlikon Leybold Vacuum
5700 Mellon Rd
Export, PA 15632-8900
724-327-5700
Fax: 800-215-7782 www.oerlikon.com

Packaging machinery
Owner: Lori Arola
VP: Maura Powers
Marketing Director: Mario Vitale
Human Resources Manager: Valerie Mooney
Estimated Sales: $60 Million
Number Employees: 1-4
Square Footage: 62000

26860 Oetiker Inc
6317 Euclid St
Marlette, MI 48453-1426
989-635-3621
Fax: 989-635-2157 800-959-0398
info@us.oetiker.com www.oetiker.com
Supplier of hose clamps and rings
CEO: Chris Parker
Quality Control: Dan Roche
Marketing Coordinator: Christine Lowe
Sales Director: Brian Milek
Account Manager: Brent Christenen
Production Manager: Bruce Christensen
Purchasing Manager: Shelly Davies
Estimated Sales: $10-20 Million
Number Employees: 100-249
Parent Co: Hans Oetiker AG

26861 Ogden Manufacturing Company
103 Gamma Drive
Pittsburgh, PA 15238
412-967-3906
Fax: 412-967-3930 cs@ogdenmfg.com
www.ogdenmfg.com
Manufacturer and exporter of electric heating elements and microprocessor-based temperature controls
VP: Randy Lee
Marketing Manager: Gordon Hollander
Contact: Barbara Lee
cs@ogdenmfg.com
Estimated Sales: $5-10 Million
Number Employees: 150-250
Square Footage: 260000
Brands:
Etr
Mighty Blade

26862 Ohaus Corp
7 Campus Dr # 300
Parsippany, NJ 07054-4413
973-377-9000
Fax: 973-593-0359 800-672-7722
marla.bormann@ohaus.com
Manufacturer and exporter of electronic, analytical, precision top loading and moisture balances; also, portable and bench scales
President: Ted Xia
ted.xia@ohaus.com
CFO: Peter Minder
Estimated Sales: $25-50 Million
Number Employees: 250-499
Brands:
Ohaus

26863 Ohio Conveyor & Supply Inc
1310 N Main St
Findlay, OH 45840-3703
419-422-3825
Fax: 419-422-4490
Conveyors and wholesaler/distributor of conveyor belts
President: John R Snyder
jrsnyder@ohioconveyorsupply.com
Estimated Sales: $1-2.5 Million
Number Employees: 5-9

26864 Ohio Magnetics Inc
5400 Dunham Rd
Maple Heights, OH 44137-3653
216-662-8484
Fax: 216-662-2911 800-486-6446
sales@ohiomagnetics.com
www.ohiomagnetics.com
Manufacturer and exporter of magnetic separators, metal detectors and conveyors
Manager: John Wohlgemuph
Sales Manager: Ken Richendollar
General Manager: John Wohlgemuth
Plant Manager: Tim Essick
Purchasing: Bob Zajc
Estimated Sales: $10-20 Million
Number Employees: 20-49
Square Footage: 288000
Parent Co: Ohio Magnetics

Brands:
Stearns

26865 Ohio Medical Corp
1111 Lakeside Dr
Gurnee, IL 60031-2489
847-855-0500
Fax: 847-855-6300 800-448-0770
www.ohiomedical.com
Filters, air
President: James Koppa
CEO: Halden Zimmermann
halden.zimmermann@ohiomedical.com
Chairman of the Board: Craig R Schifter
Sales: Martin Jindra
Estimated Sales: $20-50 Million
Number Employees: 100-249

26866 Ohio Rack Inc
1405 S Liberty Ave
PO Box 3517
Alliance, OH 44601-4231
330-823-8200
Fax: 330-823-8136 800-344-4164
ohiorack@cannet.com www.ohiorack.com
Wholesaler/distributor of used portable stack racks and pallet rack systems; manufacturer of new portable stack racks
President: George Pilla
ohiorack@cannet.com
Estimated Sales: Below $5,000,000
Number Employees: 5-9

26867 Ohio Soap Products Company
1340 E 289th St
Wickliffe, OH 44092
440-585-1100
Fax: 216-341-9900 www.diamondshine.com
Industrial soap
VP Sales: Scott Soble
Estimated Sales: $10-20 Million
Number Employees: 19
Brands:
Ohio

26868 Ohlson Packaging
490 Constitution Dr
Taunton, MA 02780-7389
508-977-0004
Fax: 508-977-0007 sales@ohlsonpack.com
www.ohlsonpack.com
Manufacturer and exporter of automatic stainless steel weighing machinery for bagging or boxing pasta, frozen foods, candy, produce, etc
Owner: John Ohlson Jr
Vice President: John Ohlson
Estimated Sales: $7 Million
Number Employees: 10-19

26869 Ohly Americas
35 Adams St NE
Hutchinson, MN 55350
320-587-2481
Fax: 320-587-8617 800-321-2689
info@ohly.us www.ohly.com
Yeast, dry condiments such as sweeteners and sauce powders.
Chief Executive Officer: Ralf Fink
Global Chief Financial Officer: Christian Hoika
Global Marketing & Supply Chain Director: Jan Bebber
Global Sales Director: Rainer Huttermann
Global HR Director: Lene Kruse
Global Operations Director: Marc Gerigk
Estimated Sales: $100-500 Million
Parent Co: ABF Ingredients-Division of Associated British Foods

26870 Oil Skimmers Inc
12800 York Rd # G
Cleveland, OH 44133-3682
440-237-4600
Fax: 440-582-2759 800-200-4603
info@oilskim.com www.oilskim.com
Waste oil removal
President: Jeff Mann
jeff@oilskim.com
President/CEO: William Townsend
VP: Jim Petrucci
Marketing Director: Mary Petit
CIO/Sales Manager: Rob Fiorilli
Estimated Sales: $2.7 Million
Number Employees: 20-49
Square Footage: 100000

26871 Oil-Dri Corporation of America
410 N Michigan Ave
Suite 400
Chicago, IL 60611

800-233-9802

info@oildri.com www.oildri.com
Developer of products for consumer, industrial and automotive, agricultural, sports fields and fluids purification markets.
VP & Chief Financial Officer: Dan Smith
Chief Operating Officer: Mark Lewry
Year Founded: 1941
Estimated Sales: $262 Million
Number Employees: 500-999
Brands:
   Oil-Dri

26872 Ojeda USA
460 Southport Commerce Blvd
Spartanburg, SC 29306

864-574-6004

Fax: 864-574-6005 www.ojedausa.com
Commercial refrigeration equipment, specializing in novelty freezers and open air display cases
VP: Mark Thompson *Year Founded:* 2005

26873 Ok Kosher Certification
391 Troy Ave
Brooklyn, NY 11213-5322

718-756-7500

Fax: 718-756-7503 info@ok.org
www.ok.org
Consultant specializing in kosher certification services
Owner: Don Levy
rdylevy@ok.org
Chief Customer Relations Officer: Eli Lando
CFO: Thelma Lezy
Manager: Levi Marmulsteyn
R&D: Rikal Fogelman
Director: Chaim Fogelman
Operations Manager: Rikal Fogelman
Estimated Sales: $2.5-5 Million
Number Employees: 20-49

26874 Ok Kosher Certification
391 Troy Ave
Brooklyn, NY 11213-5322

718-756-7500

Fax: 718-756-7503 info@ok.org
www.ok.org
Manufacturers and suppliers of Kosher food, wine and utensils
Owner: Don Levy
rdylevy@ok.org
Estimated Sales: $2.5-5 Million
Number Employees: 20-49

26875 Ok Uniform Co Inc
253 Church St # B
New York, NY 10013-3438

212-791-9789

Fax: 212-791-9795 866-700-5765
www.okuniform.com
Manufacturer and exporter of uniforms including restaurant wear, formal wear and work/industrial wear; a complete line of anywhere shoes/clogs; full line of tuxedos and formal wear for men and women. We also carry disposable uniformscoveralls, etc
CEO: Ellie Cohen
CFO: Ezra Cohen
Sales Manager: Ivan Cohen
Public Relations: Taimara K
Manager: George Gross
Estimated Sales: $1-2.5 Million
Number Employees: 5-9
Number of Brands: 4
Brands:
   Big Ben
   Car Hartt
   Dickies
   Red Kap

26876 Oklabs
921 NW 72nd Street
Oklahoma City, OK 73116-7107

405-843-6832

Fax: 405-843-6832
Laboratory providing microbiological, protein, fat, moisture and salt analysis; consultant specializing in product and process development
President: Walter Seideman
Estimated Sales: $500,000-$1 Million
Number Employees: 5-9

26877 Oklahoma Neon
6550 E Independence Street
Tulsa, OK 74115-7861

918-835-1548

Fax: 918-835-0528 888-707-6366
Awnings, channel letters and architectural, plastic, neon and electric signs; also, service and installation
President: Randy Olmstead
Vice President: Gene Russell
Estimated Sales: $5-10 Million
Number Employees: 50-99

26878 Okura USA Inc
9970 Lakeview Ave
Lenexa, KS 66219-2502

913-599-1111

Fax: 913-599-0096 800-772-1187
www.vanguardshrinkfilms.com
Manufacturer and importer of polyolefin heat shrinkable packaging films
President: John Campbell
john.campbell@okura-usa.com
Sales Manager: Mike Coyle
Sales Manager: Bill Filer
Estimated Sales: $1-2.5 Million
Number Employees: 5-9
Square Footage: 50000
Parent Co: Okura Industrial Company

26879 Olam Spices
205 East River Park Pl
Suite 310
Fresno, CA 93720

559-447-1390

USA@olamnet.com
www.olamgroup.com
Edible nuts, cocoa, coffee, cotton and spices and vegetable ingredients
Co-Founder/Group CEO: Sunny Verghese
Year Founded: 2002
Estimated Sales: $13.9 Billion
Number Employees: 5,000+
Number of Products: 47
Parent Co: Olam International
Type of Packaging: Bulk
Other Locations:
   USA Head Office
   Fresno CA

26880 Olcott Plastics
95 N 17th St
St Charles, IL 60174-1636

630-584-0555

Fax: 630-584-5655 888-313-5277
sales@olcottplastics.com www.olcottplastics.com
Manufacturer, importer and exporter of plastic containers, jars and jar closures.
President: Joe Brodner
joe.brodner@olcottplastics.com
CFO: Mark Herzog
Quality Manager: Perry Norsworthy
Sales Manager: Troy Rusch
Human Resources Director: Sandy Allen
Purchasing: Teresa Casey
Estimated Sales: $12.6 Million
Number Employees: 50-99
Square Footage: 120000
Type of Packaging: Consumer, Private Label, Bulk

26881 Old Dominion Box
190 Norman Court
Des Plaines, IL 60016-2437

847-342-8760

Fax: 847-870-8179
Boxes

26882 (HQ)Old Dominion Box Co Inc
186 Dillard Rd
Madison Heights, VA 24572-2530

434-929-6701

Fax: 434-929-6354 www.olddominionbox.com
Boxes, cartons and containers
Owner: Malcolm Sydnor
VP Marketing/Sales: Amy Buhler-Scott
Contact: Rick Blankenship
rblankenship@olddominionfootwear.com
General Manager: William Hutter
Estimated Sales: $50-100 Million
Number Employees: 1-4

26883 Old Dominion Box Company
PO Box 77
Burlington, NC 27216-0077

336-226-4491

Fax: 336-570-1217

Manufacturer and exporter of small paper and set-up boxes
Estimated Sales: $500,000-$1 Million
Number Employees: 4
Parent Co: Mark IV Industries

26884 Old Dominion Wood Products
800 Craddock St
PO Box 11226
Lynchburg, VA 24501-1700

434-846-3019

Fax: 434-846-1213 800-245-6382
csodwp@att.net www.olddominionwood.net
Manufacturer, importer and exporter of chairs, tray stands, laminated trash receptacles, booths, tabletops and table bases
Owner: George R Harris
Customer Service: Sherri Stilwell
Sales Director: Dennis Hunt
IT: Cindi Rice
crice@olddominionwoodproducts.com
Estimated Sales: $3-5 Million
Number Employees: 10-19
Number of Products: 1000
Square Footage: 120000

26885 Old English Printing & Label Company
13661 Sandy Malibu Pt
Delray Beach, FL 33446

561-997-9990

Fax: 610-668-7920
Labels and forms; also, printing services available
President: H Brooks
Estimated Sales: $1-2.5 Million
Number Employees: 1-4

26886 Old Mansion Inc
3811 Corporate Rd
PO Box 1839
Petersburg, VA 23805

804-862-9889
800-476-1877

www.oldmansion.com
Quality spices, seasonings, coffee and teas
Sales: Tom Mullen
Number Employees: 20-49
Type of Packaging: Consumer, Food Service, Private Label, Bulk

26887 Olde Country Reproductions Inc
145 N Hartley St
York, PA 17401-3334

717-848-1859

Fax: 717-845-7129 800-358-3997
pewtarex@epix.net
Manufacturer and exporter of pewter plates, mugs, goblets, trays, skillets, platters, bowls, servers, candle sticks, ice coolers, ladles, pans and kettles
President: W Swartz
VP Sales: Chris Kiehl
Manager: Chris Kiehl
ckiehl@pewtarex.com
Estimated Sales: $20-50 Million
Number Employees: 20-49
Number of Brands: 2
Number of Products: 2000
Square Footage: 50000
Type of Packaging: Bulk
Brands:
   Pewtarex
   York Pewter

26888 Olde Thompson Inc
3250 Camino Del Sol
Oxnard, CA 93030-8998

805-983-0388

Fax: 805-983-1849 800-827-1565
jshumway@oldethompson.com
www.oldethompson.com
Wood, metal and plastic kitchenware; also, aluminum platters and peppermills
VP: Jeff Shumway
Contact: Anne Kerwien
Estimated Sales: $5-10 Million
Number Employees: 100-249
Brands:
   Olde Thompson

26889 Ole Hickory Pits
333 N Main St
Cape Girardeau, MO 63701-7205

573-334-3377
Fax: 573-334-3377 800-223-9667
main@olehickorypits.com
www.olehickorypits.com
Manufacturer and exporter of commercial barbecue pits
President: David Knight
main@olehickorypits.com
CFO: David Scherer
Sales Coordinator: Margaret Wiggins
Estimated Sales: Below $5 Million
Number Employees: 20-49
Square Footage: 40000
Type of Packaging: Consumer, Food Service, Private Label, Bulk
Brands:
  Ole Hickory Pits

26890 Oles De Puerto Rico Inc
350 Calle D
Bayamon, PR 00959-1927

787-786-1700
Fax: 787-740-3222 oles@poque.com
Envelopes and continous forms
President: John R Young
CFO: Moreno
Quality Control: Megiul Medina
General Manager: Raphael Moreno
Director Manufacturing: Roberto Soltero
Plant Manager: Miguel Medina
Estimated Sales: $5-10 Million
Number Employees: 1-4
Parent Co: Oles Envelope Corporation

26891 Olive Can Company
1111 Bowes Rd
Elgin, IL 60123

847-468-7474
Fax: 847-468-7695
Manufacturer and exporter of decorative custom tins and trays
Executive VP/General Manager: Virginia Price
National Sales Manager: Tom Doyle
Trade Show Manager: Carolyn Wisniewski
Number Employees: 125
Square Footage: 288000

26892 Oliver Bentleys
13 W York St
Savannah, GA 31401-3703

912-201-1688
Fax: 877-395-7335 ollieb@oliverbentleys.com
www.oliverbentleys.com
Maker of dog treats.
Contact: Eric Zimmerman
ezimmerman@eastdilsecured.com
Number Employees: 5-9

26893 Oliver Manufacturing Company
17777 Us Highway 50
Rocky Ford, CO 81067

719-254-7813
Fax: 719-254-6371 888-254-7813
contactus@olivermanufacturing.com
www.olivermanufacturing.com
Cleaners (green coffee), graders (automatic and pneumatic), reclaiming machinery
President/CEO: Brian Burney
Chief Engineer: Shane Pritchard
Director of Sales/ Marketing: Jon Moreland
Sales Director: Thomas Helman
Contact: Scott Blakley
scott.blakley@olivermanufacturing.com
Chief Operating Officer: Joe Pentlicki
Material Control Manager: Jeffrey Fawcett
Estimated Sales: $5-10 Million
Number Employees: 20-49
Square Footage: 60000
Brands:
  Fluid Dryer
  Hi-Cap
  Linear Separator
  Maxi-Cap

26894 Oliver Packaging & Equipment Co.
3236 Wilson Dr NW
Walker, MI 49534

616-356-2950
Fax: 616-233-1132 800-253-3893
oliver-info@oliverquality.com
www.oliverquality.com
Bakery and meal packaging equipment
President/Owner: Chadd Floria

26895 Oliver Products Company
511 6th St NW
Grand Rapids, MI 49504

616-456-5290
Fax: 616-456-5820 www.oliverproducts.com
President: John R Green
CFO: Jim Johnson
R&D: Jack Knodlauch
Quality Control: Loura Keena
Contact: Lisa Miller
lmiller@oliverquality.com
Estimated Sales: $50-100 Million
Number Employees: 100-249

26896 Olivina. LLC
4555 Arroyo Road
Livermore, CA 94550

925-455-8710
charles@theolivina.com
www.theolivina.com
Olive oils
President/Owner/CEO: Charles Crohare
charles@theolivina.com
General Manager: Alice Crohare
Estimated Sales: $25 Million
Number Employees: 20

26897 Olmarc Packaging Company
Ste 1100
350 N La Salle Dr
Chicago, IL 60654-5131

708-562-2000
Fax: 708-562-9044
Packaging service
President: Cain Olmarc
VP: Mark Olmarc
CEO: Kenneth Marchetti
Estimated Sales: $20-50 Million
Number Employees: 900

26898 Olney Machinery
9057 Dopp Hill Road
PO Box 280
Westernville, NY 13486

315-827-4208
Fax: 315-827-4249 info@olneymachinery.com
www.olneymachinery.com
Manufacturer, importer and exporter of canning and food packing machinery
President: W Floyd Olney
Secretary and Treasurer: J Olney
Estimated Sales: $2.5-5 Million
Number Employees: 20-49

26899 Olson Wire Products Co
4100 Benson Ave
Baltimore, MD 21227-1487

410-242-7900
Fax: 410-247-4206 randy@olsonwireproducts.com
Racks including bakery, bottle, display, refrigerator and wire. Also refrigerator shelves and trays
President: Randy Olson
randy@olsonwireproducts.com
Estimated Sales: $20-50 Million
Number Employees: 50-99

26900 Olympia International
4203 Pan American Blvd
P.O. Box 6836
Laredo, TX 78045-7954

956-725-8558
Fax: 956-723-6968 www.olympiaintl.com
Tea and coffee samplers and weighers
President: Sergio Velasquez
sergio@olympiaintl.com
Vice President: Patsy Gonzalez
Estimated Sales: $1-2.5 Million
Number Employees: 10-19

26901 Olympus America Inc
3500 Corporate Pkwy
Center Valley, PA 18034-8229

484-896-5000
Fax: 631-844-5620 800-446-5260
www.olympusamerica.com
Testing and inspection equipment: industrial videoscopes, fiberscopes and rigid boroscopes, video cameras, packaging and assembly line equipment
President: Mark Gumz
CFO: Harryirnob Kawamata
Quality Control: Timothy Sullivan
Contact: Chris Abbott
chris.abbott@olympus.com
Estimated Sales: C
Number Employees: 50-99

26902 Omaha Fixture Mfg
10320 J St
Omaha, NE 68127-1018

402-331-8692
Fax: 402-593-5716 800-637-2257
Service@OmahaFixture.com
www.omahafixture.com
Store fixtures
Sales Manager: Dan Gould
Catalog Sales Manager: Roger King
Contact: Joel Alperson
alperson.joel@omahafixture.com
Number Employees: 10-19

26903 Omaha Neon Sign Co
1120 N 18th St
Omaha, NE 68102-4192

402-341-6077
Fax: 402-341-7654 800-786-6366
sales@omahaneon.com
Signs including changeable letter, electric, luminous tube, neon and plastic
President: Samuel J Marchese
Cio/Cto: Sean Cornett
seancornett@omahaneon.com
Estimated Sales: $5-10 Million
Number Employees: 50-99

26904 Omar Awnings & Signs
202 Wesley St
Johnson City, TN 37601-1720

423-282-9180
Fax: 423-282-3970 800-274-6627
info@omarawning.com www.omarawning.org
Commercial awnings
Owner: Susan Snowden
Production Manager: Bobenn Ette
Estimated Sales: $1-2,500,000
Number Employees: 20-49

26905 Omcan Inc.
3115 Pepper Mill Court
Mississauga, ON L5L 4X5
Canada

800-465-0234
Fax: 905-607-0234 sales@omcan.com
www.omcan.com
Manufacturer and importer of food processing machinery
Estimated Sales: $500,000-$1 Million
Number Employees: 1-4
Square Footage: 600000

26906 Omcan Manufacturing & Distributing Company
3115 Pepper Mill Court
Mississauga, ON L5L 4X5
Canada

905-607-0234
Fax: 905-828-0897 800-465-0234
sales@omcan.com www.omcan.com
Manufacturer and exporter of butcher knives; personalized knives available; wholesaler/distributor of food service equipment and supplies including cutters, slicers, choppers, bowls, vegetable processors, mixers, etc.; serving the foodservice market
Owner: Tar Nella
General Manager: Tarcisio Nella
Number Employees: 30
Square Footage: 600000

26907 Omega Company
P.O.Box 4047
Stamford, CT 06907-0047
203-359-1660
Fax: 203-359-7700 800-848-4286
www.omega.com
Consultant providing food process, architectural design and engineering services
Contact: Edward Maahoney
vanzetti@msn.com
Estimated Sales: $1-2.5 Million
Number Employees: 2
Type of Packaging: Bulk

26908 Omega Design Corp
211 Philips Rd
Exton, PA 19341-1336
610-363-6555
Fax: 610-524-7398 800-346-0191
sales1@omegadesign.com www.omegadesign.com
Manufacturer and exporter of secondary orienters, desiccant feeders, plastic bottle unscramblers, wrap around case packers and shrink bundling, tray loading and wrapping equipment; importer of wrap around case packers and tray loading and wrapping equipment
President: Glenn Siegele
gsiegele@omegadesign.com
VP Sales/Marketing Manager: Randy Caspersen
International Sales Manager: Niall McDermott
Food/Beverage Manager: Paul Sherman
Estimated Sales: $10-20 Million
Number Employees: 50-99
Square Footage: 90000

26909 Omega Industrial Products Inc
795 N Progress Dr
Saukville, WI 53080-1613
262-284-4184
Fax: 262-284-4199 800-279-6634
omega@omegaindl.com www.omegaindl.com
Manufacturer and exporter of conveyor and wall guards, handrails and steel safety barriers stairs
President: John Weber
omega@omegaindl.com
CFO: John Weber
Operations Manager: James Pautmann
Number Employees: 10-19
Square Footage: 27000
Brands:
Omega Protective Systems
Quick-Step Stair Systems
Trak-Shield

26910 Omega Industries
1011 Hanley Industrial Ct
St Louis, MO 63144-1907
314-961-1668
Fax: 314-961-8172 omegaiijtm@msn.com
www.omegaindinc.com
Acrylic food bins, oak and plastic bakery racks, floor and counter bakery bins, vacuum formed trays and wood, wire and plastic point of purchase displays
President: Joseph T Mort
Vice President: Linda Mort
Quality Control: Adam Mort
Sales Director: Jackie Williams
Production Manager: Joseph Howard
Plant Manager: Danny Astroth
Estimated Sales: $1-2 Million
Number Employees: 5-9
Square Footage: 50000
Type of Packaging: Consumer, Bulk

26911 Omega Products Inc
6291 Lyters Ln
Harrisburg, PA 17111-4622
717-561-1105
Fax: 717-561-1298 800-633-3401
omega@omegajuicers.com
www.omegajuicers.com
Manufacturer and exporter of fruit and vegetable juice extractors
President: Rob Boyd
rboyd@omegajuicers.com
VP Sales: James Pascotti
Estimated Sales: $1600000
Number Employees: 10-19
Square Footage: 80000
Brands:
Omega

26912 Omega Thermo Products
205 S Wisconsin Ave
Stratford, WI 54484
715-687-8102
Fax: 715-687-8053 800-470-1126
omega@laser-plate.com
www.omegathermoproducts.com
President: Phillip Kraft
Vice President: Martin Reuter
mreuter@laser-plate.com
Insider Sales Manager: Chuck Knetter
Engineering Manager: Don Hessefort
Plant Manager: Patrick Jenkins
Purchasing Agent: Matt Mackie
Estimated Sales: Below $5 Million
Number Employees: 20-49

26913 Omicron Steel Products Company
11701 Park Lane S
Jamaica, NY 11418-1014
718-805-3400
Fax: 718-805-3401
Manufacturer, importer and exporter of shelving, worktables, benches, counters, racks, storage cabinets, carts, hand trucks, conveyors, store fixtures, chairs and stools
Sales Manager: Jerry Czajowski
Estimated Sales: $1-5 Million
Number Employees: 6
Parent Co: Omicron Group

26914 Omni Apparel
113 Kingsbridge Dr
Carrollton, GA 30117-5246
770-838-1008
Fax: 770-838-1038 oapparel@bellsouth.com
www.omniapparel.com
Butcher frocks, aprons, sweatshirts, t-shirts, golf shirts and hats which can be custom embroidered with your company logo.
Owner: Brenda Horsley
brendahorsley@omniapparel.com
Number Employees: 10-19

26915 Omni Controls Inc
5309 Technology Dr
Tampa, FL 33647-3523
813-971-5001
Fax: 813-960-4779 800-783-6664
sales@omnicontrols.com www.omnicontrols.com
Manufacturer and exporter of pressure, flow, temperature and sanitary transmitters
President: Bryan Nye
zacharyillare@aforesearch.com
Accountant: Dianne Delarenzo
Sales Director: Frank Most
Estimated Sales: $2.5-5 Million
Number Employees: 1-4
Square Footage: 2000
Brands:
Omni Controls

26916 Omni Craft Inc
5640 Feltl Rd
Hopkins, MN 55343-7911
952-988-9944
Fax: 952-938-2035
Manufacturer, exporter and designer of exhibits and displays
Owner: Mike Rendahl
mrendahl@omnicraft.com
Estimated Sales: Less Than $500,000
Number Employees: 1-4
Square Footage: 120000
Type of Packaging: Consumer, Food Service

26917 Omni Facility Resources
2105 W Belmont Avenue
Chicago, IL 60618-6413
800-905-5061
Fax: 773-248-9791
Plant sanitation services

26918 Omni International
935 Cobb Place Blvd NW # 110
Kennesaw, GA 30144-6802
770-421-0058
Fax: 770-421-0206 800-776-4431
omni@omni-inc.com www.omni-inc.com
Manufacturer and exporter of mechanical shear homogenizers and dispersers suited for R/D, QA/QC, content analysis, fat replacement, beverages, dairy, etc

President: Karl Jahn
omni@omni-inc.com
Vice President: James Partridge
Quality Control: Eric Ruwe
Manufacturing Manager: Pete Tortorelli
Estimated Sales: Below $5 Million
Number Employees: 20-49
Square Footage: 40000
Type of Packaging: Food Service, Private Label
Brands:
Omni-Glh
Omni-Macro
Omni-Mixer
Omni-Th
Omni-Uh
Shear Flow

26919 Omni Lift Inc
1485 S 300 W
Salt Lake City, UT 84115-5137
801-486-3776
Fax: 801-486-3780 omnibelt@aol.com
www.omni-lift.com
Conveyor belts and belt cleaners
Manager: Jim Gillett
omnibelt@aol.com
VP Operations: Jim Gilett
Estimated Sales: $500,000-$1,000,000
Number Employees: 1-4

26920 Omni Metalcraft Corporation
4040 Us Highway 23 N
Alpena, MI 49707
989-358-7000
Fax: 989-358-7020 info@omni.com
www.omni.com
Manufacturer and exporter of skatewheel, belt, roller, vertical and chain conveyors
Chairman of the Board: Ronald W Winter
VP Sales/Marketing: Paul Diamond
Contact: Leeck Austin
austinl@omni.com
Estimated Sales: $20-50 Million
Number Employees: 50-99
Square Footage: 130000

26921 Omni Technologies Inc
779 Rudolph Way
Greendale, IN 47025-8378
812-539-4144
Fax: 812-539-4437 info@omnitechnologies.com
www.omnitechnologies.com
Packaging machinery, custom compression molded polyurethane parts and small quantities, runs of injection molded parts
President: Steve Geiser
sgeiser@omnitechnologies.com
Estimated Sales: $4 Million
Number Employees: 50-99

26922 Omnimark Instrument Corporation
1320 S Priest Dr # 4
Tempe, AZ 85281-6959
480-784-2200
Fax: 480-784-4738 800-835-3211
info@omniwww.com
Moisture analyzers
President: Brian Taylor
Contact: Charlene Byers
chbyers@yahoo.com
Estimated Sales: $2.5-5 Million
Number Employees: 10-19

26923 Omnion
185 Plain St Rockland
Rockland, MA 02370-0614
781-878-7200
Fax: 781-878-7465 omnion@world.std.com
Manufacturer and exporter of oxidative stability analytical instrumentation for the food industry
President: Frank Mcgovern McGovern
Technical Specialist: Cheryl Porter
Estimated Sales: $1-3,000,000
Number Employees: 5-9
Type of Packaging: Bulk

26924 Omnipak Import Enterprises Inc
2916 120th St
Flushing, NY 11354-2506
718-353-3741
Fax: 718-353-3741 800-348-6664
info@omnipakimport.com
www.omnipakimport.com

Coffee, espresso coffee, espresso equipment, spring
water, espresso bar furniture, espresso machine parts
Owner: Gregory Di Mattino
gregory@omnipak.com
CEO: Kathy Tuschetpa
Estimated Sales: $10-20 Million
Number Employees: 10-19

26925 Omnitech International

2715 Ashman Street
Midland, MI 48640

989-631-3377
Fax: 989-631-0812 info@omnitechintl.com
www.omnitechintl.com
Manufacturer and exporter of turnkey can and can
end systems for domestic and international installa-
tion
CEO: Lee Rouse
Vice President/Business Manager, Plastic: Phil
Sarnacke
Operations Manager/Controller: Carolyn Owen
Estimated Sales: $5-10 Million
Number Employees: 10-19
Square Footage: 24000

26926 Omnitemp Refrigeration

9300 Hall Road
Downey, CA 90241-5309

562-923-9660
Fax: 562-862-7466 800-423-9660
www.omniteaminc.com
Manufacturer and exporter of display cases and heat
recovery and refrigeration equipment
Owner: Don Hyatt
CEO, President: Mr. Haasis
Plant Manager: Jess McKeoun
Estimated Sales: $1-5 Million
Number Employees: 50-99
Type of Packaging: Food Service

26927 On Assignment Inc

6230 Jonestown Rd # A
Suite A
Harrisburg, PA 17112-6257

717-545-6530
Fax: 717-652-8914 800-998-3411
harrisburg@labsupport.com
www.onassignment.com
Consulting services
Account Executive: Chris Quevedo
Manager: Craig Miller
craig.miller@onassignment.com
Estimated Sales: Less Than $500,000
Number Employees: 5-9
Parent Co: On Assignment

26928 On Site Gas Systems Inc

35 Budney Rd
Newington, CT 06111-5133

860-667-8888
Fax: 860-667-2222 888-748-3429
info@onsitegas.com www.onsitegas.com
On Site Gas designs and manufacturers PSA, mem-
brane and combustion based oxygen and nitrogen
gas generation systems. Applications within the food
industry utilizing food and beverage nitrogen in-
clude that of: beveragemixing/dispensing; coffee
producers/packers; fruit orchards/storage; perishable
transportation; winemakers; and kiln/grain drying.
Snack food packaging.
President/Founder: Frank Hursey
CEO: Guy Hatch
Chief Engineer: Sanh Phan
Vice President Sales: Bob Wolff
PR: Maylin O Conner
Vice President Manufacturing: Sean Haggerty
Number Employees: 20-49

26929 On-Campus Hospitality

P.O.Box 1500
Westbury, NY 11590-0812

516-334-3030
Fax: 516-334-3059 ebm-mail@ebmpubs.com
www.ebmpubs.com
President: Murry Greenwald
Estimated Sales: $10-20 Million
Number Employees: 20-49

26930 On-Hand Adhesives

940 Telser Rd
Lake Zurich, IL 60047-6714

847-437-7773
Fax: 847-437-8006 800-323-5158
gluguru@on-hand.com www.gluguru.com

Hot melt equipment and adhesives for case sealing
and palletizing rebuilding machinery
Owner, President & Secretary: Mike Cooper
Chairman, Treasurer: George Cooper
Vice President: Lin Sliwa
Vice President: Margaret Cooper
Estimated Sales: $2.5-5 Million
Number Employees: 10-19
Square Footage: 27600

26931 OnTrack Automation Inc

592 Colby Drive
Waterloo, ON N2V 1A2
Canada

519-886-9090
Fax: 519-886-9306 ontrack@psangelus.com
www.ontrack-inc.com
Manufacturer and exporter of bottling machinery in-
cluding orienters line conveyors, labeling change
parts, feedscrews
President: Ward Flannery
Plant Manager: Ed Gardiner
Purchasing Manager: Daren Ste. Marie
Number Employees: 20-49
Parent Co: Joseph E. Seagram & Sons

26932 Oneida Food Service

200 S Civic Center Dr
Columbus, OH 43215

Fax: 315-361-3745 800-828-7033
FSCustomerService@oneida.com
www.oneida.com
Manufacturer, importer and exporter of stainless
steel and silver plated hollowware and flatware;
also, dinnerware, glassware, crystal and china.
Chief Executive Officer: James Joseph
Year Founded: 1848
Estimated Sales: I
Number Employees: 1,000-4,999
Number of Brands: 9
Parent Co: Oneida
Brands:
Buffalo
Calp
D.J.
Noritake
Oneida
Rego
Sant' Andrea
Schonwald
Schott

26933 Oneida LTD Silversmiths

163 Kenwood Ave # 181
Oneida, NY 13421-2829
Canada

315-361-3000
Fax: 315-361-3700 888-263-7195
sales@oneida.com www.oneida.com
Distrubutor of tabletop supplies including flatware,
china, glassware and hollowware
Senior VP: Paul E Gebhardt
paul.gebhardt@oneida.com
Sales Manager: Frank Fan
Number Employees: 5-9
Number of Brands: 15
Number of Products: 8000
Square Footage: 400000
Parent Co: Oneida
Type of Packaging: Food Service
Brands:
D.J.
Delco Buffalo
Oneida
Rego
Sant Andrea
Schonwald
Schott Zwiesel

26934 (HQ)Onevision Corp

5805 Chandler Ct # A
Westerville, OH 43082-9076

614-794-1144
Fax: 614-794-3366 neil@onevisioncorp.com
www.craftbrewquality.com
Can inspection systems
President: Neil Morris
neil@onevisioncorp.com
Quality Control: Matt Allaire
Director Sales: Mike Raczynski
Estimated Sales: Below $5 Million
Number Employees: 5-9
Square Footage: 9000

Other Locations:
OneVision Corp.
Riverside CA

26935 Onguard Industries LLC

1850 Clark Rd
Havre De Grace, MD 21078-4000

410-272-2000
Fax: 410-272-3346 800-365-2282
sales@onguardindustries.com
www.onguardindustries.com
CEO/Chairman: Douglas Ramer
CEO: Chris Maistros
cmaistros@onguardindustries.com
Chief Financial Officer: Dennis Wessel
CEO: Chris Maistros
Quality Coordinator: Jim Gorham
VP Operations: Chris Maistros
Number Employees: 100-249

26936 Onguard Industries LLC

1850 Clark Rd
Havre De Grace, MD 21078-4000

410-272-2000
Fax: 410-272-3346 800-304-2282
sales@onguardindustries.com
www.onguardindustries.com
Protective clothing and non-slip boots.
CEO: Chris Maistros
cmaistros@onguardindustries.com
Number Employees: 100-249

26937 Onset Computer Corp

470 Macarthur Blvd
Bourne, MA 02532-3838

508-743-3100
Fax: 508-759-9100 800-564-4377
sales@onsetcomp.com www.onsetcomp.com
Design and manufacturing of miniature, bat-
tery-powered data loggers
President: Justin Testa
justin_testa@onsetcomp.com
Product Application Specialist: Herman Gustafson
Estimated Sales: $13 Million
Number Employees: 100-249
Square Footage: 40000

26938 Onsite Sycom Energy Corporation

1010 Wisconsin Avenue NW
Suite 340
Washington, DC 20007-3680

202-625-4126
Fax: 202-625-1067

26939 Ontario Glove and Safety Products

5 Washburn Drive
Kitchener, ON N2R 1S1
Canada

519-886-3590
Fax: 519-886-3597 800-265-4554
sales@ontarioglove.com www.ontarioglove.com
Manufacturer and importer of gloves including
PVC, cotton, latex and neoprene; wholesaler/distrib-
utor and exporter of leather and synthetic aprons
President: John McCarthy
CFO: Randell Moore
Quality Control: Truedy Henric
Number Employees: 10

26940 Op Sec Security

2 Applegate Dr
Trenton, NJ 08691-2342

609-632-0800
Fax: 609-632-0850 www.jdsu.com
Holograms
President: Kenneth Traub
Number Employees: 50-99
Parent Co: JDS Uniphase Corporation

26941 (HQ)Opal Manufacturing Ltd

10 Compass Court
Toronto, ON M1S 5R3
Canada

416-646-5232
Fax: 416-646-5242 rosa@nrttech.com
www.customvendingmachines.com
Manufacturer and exporter of custom vending ma-
chines and refrigerated liquid portion control cream
dispensers
Sales: Brian Simon
Number Employees: 10

Brands:
Little Squirt
Opal

26942 Open Date Systems
Georges Mill Rd
Sunapee, NH 3782

603-763-3444
Fax: 603-763-4222 877-673-6328
sales@opendate.com www.opendate.com
Coding systems including hot stamp, thermal transfer and fully and semi-automatic carton; feeding systems
President/CEO: Thierry Brousse
CFO: Nikki MacLennan
Vice President: Rick Berquist
Marketing/Sales: Don Morong
Contact: James Poitras
james@opendate.com
Production Manager: Terry Bartlett
Purchasing: Marcia Crawford
Estimated Sales: $3,000,000
Number Employees: 5-9
Square Footage: 6000
Parent Co: Open Date Equipment
Brands:
Eurocode
Printmaster
Sprint
Thermocode

26943 Opie Brush Company
16400 E Truman Rd
Independence, MO 64050-4161

816-246-6767
Fax: 816-833-8955 800-877-6743
Manufacturer and exporter of custom made and industrial brushes including flour milling
Marketing: Connie Dulin
General Manager: Connie Dulin
Plant Manager: James Dulin
Estimated Sales: $500,000-$1 Million
Number Employees: 5-9
Number of Brands: 1
Square Footage: 24000

26944 Optek Inc
5229 Cheshire Rd
Galena, OH 43021-9407

740-548-4700
Fax: 740-548-4999 800-533-8400
wtkavage@optek-inc.com www.optek-inc.com
Manufacturer and exporter of volume flow measurement systems for belt conveyors, tablet counting systems and control systems including moisture, temperature and fill level
President/CFO: Dr. Marvin E. Monroe
VP: William Kavage
Estimated Sales: Below $5 Million
Number Employees: 1-4
Square Footage: 30000
Brands:
Check Fill

26945 Optek-Danulat
N118w18748 Bunsen Dr
Germantown, WI 53022-6322

262-437-3600
Fax: 262-437-3699 888-551-4288
info@optek.com www.optek.com
High performance inline photometric analyzers for industrial liquid and gas processing applications, and photemetric measuring systems for the food, beverage and dairy industries.
CEO: Juergen Danulat
Vice President: Rik Meyer
rmeyer@optek.com
Marketing & Sales Communications Manager: Aleah Schmitz
Number of Products: 50
Square Footage: 27000

26946 Optel Vision
2680 Boul Du Parc Technologique
Quebec, QC G1P 4S6
Canada

418-688-0334
Fax: 418-688-9397 866-688-0334
info@optelvision.com www.optelvision.com
Packaging line inspection systems. Label inspector, barcode inspector, date code inspector, blister pack inspector

President: Louis Roy
CFO: Nancy Houley
Vice President: Jean Lafortune
R&D: Mathew Kowalcyk
Marketing/Public Relations: Jenny Normandeau
Sales Director: Pierre Turcotte
Estimated Sales: Below $5 Million
Number Employees: 40
Square Footage: 12000

26947 Optex
13661 Benson Ave
Chino, CA 91710

909-993-5770
Fax: 310-533-5910 800-966-7839
www.optexamerica.com
Manufacturer and exporter of alarm systems and sensors
President: Robert Blair
VP Marketing/Sales: Jay Kessel
Contact: Norma Armstrong
narmstrong@optexamerica.com
Estimated Sales: $20-50 Million
Number Employees: 25-30
Parent Co: Optex
Brands:
Morse
Optex

26948 Optical Security Group
1932 Valley View Lane
Dallas, TX 75234

972-247-1288
Fax: 303-534-1010 osllc@sbcglobal.net
Manufactures lenticular products
President: Mark Turange
CEO: Mark Turnage
Contact: Koko Katanjian
kkatanjian@opticalsecurityllc.com
Estimated Sales: $1-5 Million
Number Employees: 50-99

26949 Optima Corp
1330 Contract Dr
Green Bay, WI 54304-5681

920-339-2222
Fax: 920-339-2233 info@optima-usa.com
www.optima-packaging.com
Filling and packaging machines
President: Tom Seifert
thomas.seifert@optima-usa.com
Marketing Director: Cathy Hendricks
Estimated Sales: $5-10 Million
Number Employees: 50-99
Parent Co: Optima Packaging Group

26950 Optima International
10601 Jefferson Chemical Rd
Conroe, TX 77301

936-441-1333
Fax: 936-760-1141
info@optima-international.co.uk
www.optima-international.com
President: Simon Spiller
Quality Control: Christie Coites
Number Employees: 10

26951 Optimal Automatics
120 Stanley St
Elk Grove Village, IL 60007

847-439-9110
Fax: 847-439-9115 www.autodoner.com
Vertical broiler manufacturer
President/Owner: John Georgis

26952 Optipure
2605 Technology Drive
Bldg 300
Plano, TX 75074

972-422-1212
Fax: 972-422-6262 kaldstadt@filterxpress.com
www.procamcontrols.com
Water filters and water filtration equipment; full line of filtration products for foodservice applications (ice machines, steam equipment, coffee./tea, espresso, balers, fountain, beverages).
Owner: Roy Sebert
Director Sales/Marketing: Keefe Aldstadt
Contact: Keese Aldstadt
keefe@filterxpress.com
Estimated Sales: $2.5-5 Million
Number Employees: 10-19
Number of Brands: 1

Number of Products: 50+
Parent Co: Procam Controls Inc
Type of Packaging: Consumer, Food Service, Private Label, Bulk
Brands:
Opti Pure

26953 Oracle Hospitality
500 Oracle Pkw
Redwood, CA 94065

650-506-7000
800-392-2999
www.oracle.com/industries/hospitality
Manufacturer and exporter of management system software for hospitality, food and beverage, table seating for hotels, motels, casinos and other leisure and entertainment businesses.
Chairman & Chief Technology Officer: Lawrence Ellison
Vice Chairman: Jeffrey Henley
Chief Executive Officer: Safra Catz
Chief Corporate Architect: Edward Screven
Year Founded: 1977
Estimated Sales: $39.50 Billion
Number Employees: 136,000
Parent Co: Oracle Corporation
Type of Packaging: Food Service
Other Locations:
Micros Systems/Fidelio Softwa
Elk Grove Village IL
Brands:
Fidelio
Micros

26954 Oracle Packaging
220 Polo Rd
Winston Salem, NC 27105-3441

336-777-5000
Fax: 336-777-5440 800-952-9536
Folding cartons for the dairy industry
President: Ted McLaren
CEO: Scott Dickman
scottdickman@oraclepkg.com
Plant Manager: Berkley Cooke
VP: Lou Carozza
Estimated Sales: $10-20 Million
Number Employees: 250-499
Square Footage: 110000

26955 Orange Plastics
1825 S Acacia Ave
Compton, CA 90220

310-609-2121
Stretch film, pallet wrap and produce and grocery bags
National Sales Manager: Michael Kopulsky
Estimated Sales: $20-50 Million
Number Employees: 100-249

26956 Orangex
104 E 40th Street
New York, NY 10016-1801

212-986-9353
Fax: 212-986-9357 sales@orangex.com
www.orangex.net

26957 Oration Rubber Stamp Company
RR 94
Columbus, NJ 8022

908-496-4161
Fax: 908-496-4989
Rubber stamps for food packaging
Customer Representative: Carole Vorhis
Manager: Chris Baier
Parent Co: Cosco

26958 Orber Manufacturing Co
1655 Elmwood Ave # 30
Cranston, RI 02910-4933

401-781-0050
Fax: 401-781-7720 800-761-4059
Metal specialties including badges, medals, emblems and key chains
Vice President: Larry Shwartz
Estimated Sales: $1-3 Million
Number Employees: 10-19

26959 Orbis Corp.
39 Westmore Drive
Rexdale, ON M9V 4Y6
Canada

416-745-6980
Fax: 416-745-1874 800-890-7292
info@orbiscorporation.com
www.orbiscorporation.com

Injection moulding
President: Howard Walton
Sales: Relph Kert
Number Employees: 250-499
Brands:
 Norseman

26960 Orbisphere Laboratories
3 W Main St
Buford, GA 30518

770-932-1400
Fax: 770-932-1230 gthomas@hachultra.com
Gas analyzers for in-lines process and laboratory use
Contact: John Franklin
fjohn@orbisphere.com
Estimated Sales: $500,000-$1 Million
Number Employees: 1-4

26961 Orca Inc
199 Whiting St
New Britain, CT 06051-3146

860-223-4180
Fax: 860-826-1729 www.orca-mfg.com
Manufacturer and exporter of custom caps including
can, glass and screw neck ends
Owner: Brian Melanson
bmelanson@orca-mfg.com
Estimated Sales: $5-10 Million
Number Employees: 50-99
Square Footage: 60000

26962 Orchard Gold
1762 Hester Avenue
PO Box 28481
San Jose, CA 95159

408-279-8822
Fax: 209-835-2044
President: Ron Ruscigno
Brands:
 Corral Hollow Ranch
 Orchard

26963 Orchem Corporation
4293 Mulhauser Rd
Fairfield, OH 45014

513-874-9700
Fax: 513-874-3624 craig.feltner@orchemcorp.com
www.orchem.com
Food and beverage cleaning and sanitation.
President: Oscar Robertson
General Manager: Craig Feltner
craig.feltner@orchemcorp.com
Estimated Sales: $5-10 Million
Number Employees: 20-49

26964 Order-Matic Corporation
PO Box 25463
Oklahoma City, OK 73125-0463

405-672-1487
Fax: 405-672-5349 800-767-6733
www.ordermatic.com
Electronic restaurant equipment including communi-
cation systems and POS systems for fast food and
drive-thru restaurants
President: William B Cunningham
CFO: Dan Webb
Vice President: Greg Cunningham
National Sales Manager: Paul Barron
Contact: Stanley Chandy
chandy@ordermatic.com
Estimated Sales: $20-50 Million
Number Employees: 100-249

26965 (HQ)Ore-Cal Corp
634 Crocker St
Los Angeles, CA 90021-1002

213-623-8493
Fax: 213-228-6557 800-827-7474
CustomerService@ore-cal.com www.ore-cal.com
Shrimp, pangasius, mahi mahi, swordfish, calamari,
breaded shrimp, and ready mixed entree dishes such
as; shrimp scampi, seafood gumbo, cioppino, shrimp
pad thai, and shrimp torn kha soup.
President: William Shinbane
Human Resources: Josephine Davif
Controller/Vice President Finance: Mark Feldstein
Vice President: Mark Shinbane
Lab Director: Avito Moniz
Human Resources Compliance & Regulatory:
Wendy Gomez
Manager of National Sales: Shelley Gee
Manufacturing Supervisor: Rick Kanase
Estimated Sales: $10.9 Million
Number Employees: 50-99

Number of Brands: 1
Number of Products: 11+
Square Footage: 240000
Type of Packaging: Consumer, Food Service, Pri-
vate Label, Bulk
Brands:
 Harvest of the Sea®

26966 Oreck Manufacturing Co
1400 Salem Rd
Cookeville, TN 38506-6221

504-733-8761
Fax: 504-733-6709 800-989-3535
ddesporte@oreck.com www.oreck.com
Industrial vacuum cleaners
President: Thomas A Oreck
CEO: David Oreck
CFO: San Eilers
Quality Control: Scott Dessen
Marketing Director: Nancy Willy
Estimated Sales: Less Than $500,000
Number Employees: 1-4
Brands:
 Oreck

26967 Oregon Pacific Bottling
93487 Sixes River Road
Sixes, OR 97476-9713

541-332-7307
Fax: 541-332-1603
Bottling, labeling
Number Employees: 10

26968 Orelube Corp
20 Sawgrass Dr
Bellport, NY 11713-1549

631-205-9700
Fax: 631-205-9797 800-645-9124
info@orelube.com www.orelube.com
Manufacturer and exporter of lubricants including
aluminum complex EP grease, chain oil and syn-
thetic grease
Owner: Robert Silverstin
robert@orelube.com
Purchasing Agent: Donna Klempka
Estimated Sales: $5-10 Million
Number Employees: 10-19
Square Footage: 132000
Brands:
 Bakesafe 500
 Boelube Aerospace
 Et-2a
 Et-2s
 Ht-1001
 Ht-500
 Ocean 7
 Orelube Industrial

26969 Organic Products Co
1963 E Irving Blvd
Irving, TX 75060-4555

972-438-7321
Fax: 972-438-7321 ink@opcompany.com
www.opcompany.com
Marking inks
General Manager: Arthur Botvin
ink@opcompany.com
Estimated Sales: Less Than $500,000
Number Employees: 1-4
Brands:
 Opco
 Organic Products
 Sentry Seal
 Torgue Seal

26970 Orics Industries
240 Smith St
Farmingdale, NY 11735

718-461-8613
Fax: 718-461-4719 info@orics.com
www.orics.com
Manufacturer and exporter of tray sealers for vac-
uum gas flush map packaging
Owner: Ori Cohen
Contact: Staci Banta
staci_banta@orics.com
Number Employees: 20-49

26971 Oriental Motor USA Corporation
2580 W 237th Street
Torrance, CA 90505-5217

310-325-0040
Fax: 310-257-0297 800-816-6867
techsupport@orientalmotor.com
www.orientalmotor.com
President: Manatoshi Yamauchi
Contact: Gulay Yildirim
gulayyildirim@moeller.com
Estimated Sales: $20-50 Million
Number Employees: 80

26972 Original Lincoln Logs
5 Riverside Dr
PO Box 135
Chestertown, NY 12817

518-494-5500
Fax: 518-494-7495 800-833-2461
info@lincolnlogs.com www.lincolnlogs.com
Wooden pallets, boxes, crates and skids; also, used
and reconditioned pallets and crates
Owner: Andrea Demetriou
andreademetriou@lincolnlogs.com
Plant Manager: Robert Rust
Estimated Sales: $500,000-$1 Million
Number Employees: 50-99
Square Footage: 24000

26973 Original Packaging & Display Company
4161 Beck Avenue
Saint Louis, MO 63116-2632

314-772-7797
Fax: 314-772-7271
Solid and set-up paper boxes
Member: Herbert J Strather
Sales Director: Ken Monschein
General Manager: Ed Taylor
Plant Manager: Mark Nehhans
Purchasing Manager: Todd Brock
Estimated Sales: $300,000-500,000
Number Employees: 20
Type of Packaging: Consumer, Food Service

26974 Original Wood Seating
PO Box 48393
Atlanta, GA 30362

678-966-0406
Fax: 678-894-3886 www.owseating.com
Custom restaurant seating

26975 Orion Packaging SystemsInc
4750 County Road 13 NE
Alexandria, MN 56308-8022

901-888-4170
Fax: 901-365-1071 800-333-6556
sales@orionpackaging.com
www.orionpackaging.com
Manufacturers a wide range of high-quality stretch
wrapping machines for virtually any pallet load of
product unitizing application. Machines ore avail-
able in rotary tower, turntable or orbital ring styles.
Orion equipment features allstructural steel con-
struction, high-efficiency powered prestretch film
delivery with easy threading, and the best warrenty
in the industry
Manager: Glenn Greene
CFO: Marsha Greene
Advertising Manager: Peter Vilardi
Contact: Dennis Alexander
dalexander@orionpackaging.com
Operations Manager: Glenn Greene
Plant Manager: Andre LaVigne
Estimated Sales: Less Than $500,000
Number Employees: 1-4
Number of Brands: 10
Number of Products: 34
Square Footage: 200000
Parent Co: Pro Mach
Other Locations:
 Orion
 Laval Quebec, Canada

26976 Orion Research
100 Cummings Ctr
Beverly, MA 01915

978-232-6000
www.scientificcomputing.com
Manufacturer and exporter of analytical instruments
for the measurement of sodium, pH chemical species
in solutions and moisture in foods.
Estimated Sales: $100-500 Million
Parent Co: Scientific Computing

Brands:
Orion
Perphect
Ross

26977 Orkin LLC
2170 Piedmont Rd NE
Atlanta, GA 30324-4135

844-512-4777
www.orkin.com
Pest control, fly control, rodent control, bird control, odor control.
President: Eugene Iarocci
Director of Quality Systems: Zia Siddiqi
Year Founded: 1901
Estimated Sales: $100-500 Million
Number Employees: 8,000

26978 Orr's Farm Market
Po Box 906
Martinsburg, WV 25402-0906

304-263-1027
Fax: 304-263-1153 dondove@orrsfarmmarket.com
www.orrsfarmmarket.com
Farm market

26979 Ortemp
11889 Creek Hollow Rd
Healdsburg, CA 95448

707-433-4459
Fax: 707-433-4450
Wine industry temperature warning devices

26980 Orthodox Union
11 Broadway # 13
New York, NY 10004-1587

212-563-4000
Fax: 212-564-9058 koegelp@ou.org
World's largest and most respected kosher certification, over 400,000 products.
President: Martin Nachimson
nachimsonm@ou.org
CEO: Eli Edelman
Marketing: Phyllis Koegel
Number Employees: 100-249

26981 (HQ)Ortmayer Materials Handling
926 Bedford Ave
Corner Willoughby
Brooklyn, NY 11205-3913

718-875-7995
Fax: 718-875-6385 goldy@ortmayer.com
www.ortmayer.com
Material handling equipment including hand carts, semi line skids, stock trucks, lockers and shelving, also distributors of Magline and B&P alum hand trucks
President: Mendel Gross
mendel@ortmayer.com
Vice President: Noson Schelhter
Estimated Sales: $4 Million
Number Employees: 5-9
Square Footage: 20000

26982 Orwak
10820 Normandale Boulevard
Minneapolis, MN 55437-3112

612-881-9200
Fax: 612-881-8578 800-747-0449
www.orwak.us
Manufacturer and exporter of trash compactors and recycling balers
Estimated Sales: $500,000-$1 Million
Number Employees: 4
Brands:
Orwak

26983 Osage Food Products Inc
120 W Main St # 200
Washington, MO 63090-2121

636-390-9477
Fax: 636-390-9485 sales@osagefood.com
www.osagefood.com
Osage is a multi-dimensional company supplying ingredients and food products. Our ingredients for manufacturing. Our packaged goods division supplies national brands and private label products for food service and retail. Our specialtyproducts division works with manufacturers, marketing residual ingredients and finished goods that are needed to sell
President: William Dickinson

Estimated Sales: $2.5-5,000,000
Number Employees: 5-9
Type of Packaging: Consumer, Food Service, Private Label, Bulk
Brands:
Central Volky
Oven Gem

26984 Oscartek
361-367 Beach Rd
Burlingame, CA 94010

650-342-2400
Fax: 650-342-7400 855-885-2400
www.oscartek.com
Display cases
CEO: Rabih Ballout

26985 Oscartielle Equipment Company
855 Mahler Road
Burlingame, CA 94010-1603

650-827-3510
Fax: 650-827-3511 800-672-2784
Gelato and ice cream displays
President: Rabih S Ballout
rballout@otl-usa.com
Number Employees: 10

26986 Osgood Industries
601 Burbank Rd
Oldsmar, FL 34677-4903

813-855-7337
Fax: 813-855-3068 sales@osgoodinc.com
Fillers and heat sealers for containers
President: Martin Mueller
mmueller@osgoodinc.com
Executive VP: Richard Mueller
Estimated Sales: $20-50 Million
Number Employees: 100-249
Type of Packaging: Food Service, Private Label, Bulk

26987 Osgood Industries
601 Burbank Rd
Oldsmar, FL 34677-4903

813-855-7337
Fax: 813-855-3068
Manufactureer of trays, containers and packaging for the dairy and food industries.
President: Martin J Mueller
mmueller@osgoodinc.com
Number Employees: 100-249

26988 Oshikiri Corp Of America
10425 Drummond Rd
Philadelphia, PA 19154-3898

215-637-8112
Fax: 215-637-6041 www.oshikiri.com
Bakery mixers, molders and proofers
Estimated Sales: $2.5-5 Million
Number Employees: 20-49

26989 Osram Sylvania
129 Portsmouth Ave
Exeter, NH 03833-2105

603-772-4331
Fax: 603-772-1072 www.sylvania.com
Quartz tubing, sockets, infrared heaters
President: Charles Jerabek
President, Chief Executive Officer: Rick Leaman
Quality Control: Lake Patterson
Manager of Corporate Communications: Anne Guertin
Plant Manager: Michael Huelsemann
Estimated Sales: $25-50 Million
Number Employees: 250-499

26990 Osram Sylvania
100 Endicott St # 1
Danvers, MA 01923

978-777-1900
Fax: 978-750-2152 800-544-4828
communications@sylvania.com
www.sylvania.com
Lamps and ballasts
President: Charles Jerabeck
President, Chief Executive Officer: Rick Leaman
CFO: Martin Goetzeler
Quality Control: Russell Liddle
R&D and Executive Director: John Gustafson
Manager Sales/Marketing: Bob Nigrello
Contact: Debra Barshinger
debra.barshinger@sylvania.com
Number Employees: 10,000

Brands:
Capsylite
Dulux
Lumalux
Metalarc
Octron

26991 Oss Food Plant Sanitation Services
1050 Tower Lane
Bensenville, IL 60106

Fax: 630-521-0092 800-905-5061
www.ossfoodplantsanitation.com
Sanitation cleaning, environmental cleaning, staffing for maintenance and operation

26992 Ossid Corp
4000 College Rd
PO Drawer 1968
Battleboro, NC 27809-8500

252-446-6177
Fax: 252-442-7694 800-334-8369
sales@ossid.com www.ossid.com
Food packaging equipment.
Owner/President: Bud Lane
Principal/VP Finance: Kim Brewer
VP/General Manager: Ernie Newell
Sales Director: Jason Angel
Number Employees: 50-99
Square Footage: 80000

26993 (HQ)Osterneck Company
Highway 72 E
Lumberton, NC 28358

910-738-2416
Fax: 910-739-2881 800-682-2416
Manufacturer and exporter of plastic bags and woven polypropylene products
Vice President: Leroy Freeman
Estimated Sales: $1-5 Million
Number Employees: 50-99
Square Footage: 400000
Brands:
O-Tex

26994 Ostrem Chemical Co. Ltd
2310-80 Avenue
Edmonton, AB T6P 1N2
Canada

780-440-1911
Fax: 780-440-1241 inquiries@ostrem.com
www.ostrem.com
Industrial cleaning compounds
President: Roar Tungland
CFO: Ben Tungland
Marketing Director: Ken Sagan
Number Employees: 40
Square Footage: 160000
Type of Packaging: Private Label

26995 Ott Packagings
719 Route 522
Selinsgrove, PA 17870-1298

570-374-2811
Fax: 570-374-2891
Set-up boxes
Chairman of the Board: Robert McNeil
Quality Control Manager: Bob Vanhorn
Sales Manager: Steve Stancaco
Contact: Doug Marshall
dmarshall@ottpkg.com
Operations Manager: Wes Craig
Purchasing Mgr: John Clark
Estimated Sales: $5-10 Million
Number Employees: 50-99

26996 Ottenheimer Equipment Company
PO Box 4395
Lutherville Timonium, MD 21094-4395

410-597-9700
Fax: 410-252-7775
Wholesaler/distributor of food service equipment; serving the food service market; also, consultant for the design of food facilities
Estimated Sales: $.5-1 million
Number Employees: 1-4

26997 Otterbine Barebo Inc
3840 Main Rd E
Emmaus, PA 18049-9598

610-965-6018
Fax: 610-965-6050 800-237-8837
info@otterbine.com www.otterbine.com
Water aeration systems

Owner: Charles Barebo
charliebarebo@otterbine.com
Sales Manager: Charlie Barebo
Estimated Sales: $1-3 Million
Number Employees: 20-49
Brands:
    Concep2

26998 Otto Braun Bakery Equipment
115 Dingens Street
Buffalo, NY 14206-2304

716-824-1252
Fax: 716-824-6076

Bakery racks, proofers, coaters, frying screens,
doughnut fryers and hand trucks
President: Rudolph Hug
Secretary/Treasurer: Arthur Karneth
Estimated Sales: $1-2.5 Million
Number Employees: 4

26999 Otto Material Handling
14609 Sorrel Ct
Charlotte, NC 28278-8322

704-587-1055
Fax: 704-587-9368   800-942-2758
info@otto-usa.com

Plastic waste containers
President: R Otto
Sales/Marketing Coordinator: Meredith Burris
Estimated Sales: $10-20 Million
Number Employees: 10-19

27000 Ottumwa Tent & Awning Co
635 W 2nd St
P.O.Box 494
Ottumwa, IA 52501-2312

641-682-2257
Fax: 641-682-4357
www.ottumwatentandawning.com

Commercial awnings
President: Jim Cagwin
j.cagwin@kyoutv.com
Estimated Sales: Less Than $500,000
Number Employees: 1-4

27001 Ouachita Machine Works
120 N Hilton St
West Monroe, LA 71291-7499

318-396-1468
Fax: 318-396-1668

Manufacturer and exporter of packaging machinery
including automatic and stretch balers
President: Jimmy Dulaney
jdulaney@omwinc.com
CFO: Jimmy Dulaney
R&D: Don Hudson
Quality Control: Jimmy Dulaney
Estimated Sales: Below $5 Million
Number Employees: 20-49
Parent Co: Ouachita Machine Works

27002 Ouellette Machinery Systems
1761 Chase Dr
Fenton, MO 63026-2037

636-343-7200
Fax: 636-326-0249   800-545-7619
sales@omsinc.net   www.omsinc.net

Bulk palletizers and depalletizers; case, drum, pail
palletizers; pallet and container conveyors, pallet
stackers and unstackers, sheet stackers and
unstackers .
President: Joseph Ouellette
sales@omsinc.net
VP Design: Richard Ouellette
Purchasing: Robert Del Pietro
Estimated Sales: $10-20 Million
Number Employees: 20-49
Square Footage: 146460

27003 Our Name is Mud
224 W 29th St
New York, NY 10001-5204

212-244-4711
Fax: 800-972-9982   877-683-7867
www.ournameismud.com

Emphasizing engineering for bulk material handling,
process, bag opening and disposal systems
Owner: Lorrie Veasey
CEO: Kip Veasey
CFO: John Nelsen
Marketing: Victoria Compton-Jorasch
Sales: Jill Bukzin
Public Relations: Victoria Compton-Jorasch
Estimated Sales: $3-5 Million

Type of Packaging: Bulk

27004 Outlook Packaging
PO Box 775
Neenah, WI 54957-0775

920-722-1666
Fax: 920-722-0008

Manufacturer, importer and exporter of flexible
packaging materials for meat, cheese, candy, frozen
food, fish, poultry and other various industrial
applications
President: Joe Baksha
Contact: Dennis Grabski
Estimated Sales: G
Number Employees: 250-499
Square Footage: 83000
Parent Co: Flexible Technology
Type of Packaging: Bulk

27005 Outotec USA Inc
8280 Stayton Dr # M
Suite M
Jessup, MD 20794-9609

301-543-1200
Fax: 301-543-0002 www.outotec.com

Manufacturer and exporter of energy recovery sys-
tems including waste incinerators and waste disposal
equipment; also, fluidized bed systems and fabrica-
tion services available
CEO: Paul Abbott
paul.abbott@outotec.com
Plant Manager: Mark Castle
Purchasing Manager: Joe Malloy
Estimated Sales: $50 Million
Number Employees: 10-19
Number of Brands: 1
Square Footage: 30000
Parent Co: Idaho Energy Partnership

27006 Outside the Lines, Inc
640 Michael Drive
Sonoma, CA 95476

707-933-0687

Consulting for the Wine & Hospitality Industry: executive search, onine sexual harassment prevention
training, customer satisfaction surveys, employee
satisfaction surveys, training progrm development.
President: Margie Tosch

27007 Outterson, LLC
7747 Woodstone Drive
Cincinnati, OH 45244-2855

513-474-3521

Specializes- brew pubs, wineries and
microdistilleries
Estimated Sales: $1.5 Million
Number Employees: 1

27008 Ovalstrapping Inc
120 55th St NE
Fort Payne, AL 35967-8140

256-845-1914
Fax: 256-845-1493 info@ovalstrapping.com

Strapping and strapping machines
Marketing Assistant: Jolie Martin
Sales Exec: Ronnie Berry
Plant Manager: Howard G Owen
Estimated Sales: $5-10 Million
Number Employees: 20-49

27009 Oven Deck Shop
11560 184th Pl
Orland Park, IL 60467-4904

708-478-6032
Fax: 708-849-3186

Baking stones for deck pizza ovens and revolving
pizza and bagel ovens
Sales Director: Mike Casey
Manager: Mark Otoole
Estimated Sales: Below $5 Million
Number Employees: 1-4
Number of Brands: 2
Number of Products: 1
Square Footage: 8000
Type of Packaging: Private Label

27010 Ovention
635 South 28th Street
Milwaukee, WI 53215

855-298-6836
connect@oventionovens.com oventionovens.com

Commercial oven manufacturer

Marketing: Jordan Robinson-Delaney
General Manager: Steve Everett

27011 Ovenworks
8300 Austin Avenue
Morton Grove, IL 60053-3209

847-965-3700
Fax: 847-965-8585 800-899-OVEN
www.ovenworkspizza.com

Revolving tray ovens, rotating rack ovens, small
specialty oven proofers
Estimated Sales: $10-20 Million
Number Employees: 50-99

27012 (HQ)Overhead Conveyor Co
1330 Hilton Rd
Ferndale, MI 48220-2898

248-547-3800
Fax: 248-547-8344 800-396-2554
www.occ-conveyor.com

Supplier/mfg of material handling (conveyor) sys-
tems and (spurgeon) stacking machines for non-fer-
rous metals
President: Thomas Woodbeck
CEO: M Woodbeck Jr
Marketing & Sales Manager: Catherine Nall
Estimated Sales: $10-30 Million
Number Employees: 50-99
Square Footage: 200000
Parent Co: Spurgeon Company

27013 Overnight Labels Inc
151 W Industry Ct # 15
Deer Park, NY 11729-4600

631-242-4240
Fax: 631-242-4385 800-472-5753
custservice@overnightlabels.com
www.overnightlabels.com

US-based manufacturer specializing in labels, shrink
sleeves, and flexible packaging. Multiple award
winner, including awards for print and environmental excellence
Co-Owner: Don Earl
Co-Owner: Diane Pannizzo
Number Employees: 50-99
Type of Packaging: Consumer, Food Service, Private Label, Bulk

27014 Owens-Illinois Inc
1 Michael Owens Way
Perrysburg, OH 43551-2999

567-336-5000
glass@o-i.com
www.o-i.com

Manufacturer and exporter of plastic bottles, con-
tainers, closures and carriers including HDPE, PVC,
PET, LDPE, multilayer and barex
Chairman and Chief Executive Officer: Al
Stroucken
CEO: Andres A Lopez
andres.lopez@o-i.com
SVP and CFO: Steve Bramlage
SVP and General Counsel: Jim Baehren
SVP and Chief Administrative Officer: Paul Jarrell
Estimated Sales: Over $1 Billion
Number Employees: 10000+

27015 Oxbo International Corp
100 Bean St
Clear Lake, WI 54005-8400

715-263-2112
Fax: 715-263-3324 800-628-6196
atalbott@oxbocorp.com www.oxbocorp.com

Manufacturer and exporter of pea, bean and sweet
and seed corn harvesting machinery and vibratory
sorting tables
President: Andy Tallobt
Cmo: Doug Aherns
daherns@oxbocorp.com
VP Sales: Andrew Talbott
Inside Sales: Doug Ahrens
Human Resources: Deborah Arcand
Estimated Sales: $10-20 Million
Number Employees: 100-249
Square Footage: 220000
Brands:
    One Row Trac-Pix
    Pixall Big Jack Mark Ii
    Pixall Corn Puller
    Pixall Cornstalker Db18
    Pixall Cornstalker El20
    Pixall One-Row Pull-Pix

Pixall Super Jack
Pixall Vst

27016 Oxidyn
3712 Summer Pl
Raleigh, NC 27604-4252

919-790-6767
Fax: 919-790-6768

Custom contract assembling
Owner: Melvin Rogers
Estimated Sales: $500,000-$1 Million
Number Employees: 5-9

27017 Oxoid
Suite 100
Nepean, ON K2G 1E8
Canada

613-226-1318
Fax: 613-226-3728 800-567-8378
webinfo.ca@oxoid.com

A manufacturer and distributor of diagnostic test and
control in microbiology
Marketing Director: Brian Kemp
Sales Director: Jeff Crawford
Estimated Sales: $15 Million
Number Employees: 50-100
Parent Co: Oxoid

27018 Oystar North America
523 Raritan Center Parkway
Raritan Center
Edison, NJ 08837

732-343-7600
Fax: 732-343-7601 www.oystar-group.com

Solutions for packaging machines.
President/CEO: Barry Shoulders
VP Finance: Suzanne Zeitler
VP Sales/Marketing: Tom Riggins
VP Manufacturing Operations: Frederick Priester
VP Purchasing: Linda Petersen
Number Employees: 235
Square Footage: 10228

27019 Oyster Bay Pump Works Inc
78 Midland Ave # 1
PO Box 725
Hicksville, NY 11801-1537

516-933-4500
Fax: 516-933-4501 info@obpw.com
www.obpw.com

Manufacturer and exporter of dispensers including
single channel, multi-channel and conveyor systems
for metering fluids
President: Eyal Angel
eangel@obpw.com
Sales/Marketing: Michael Dedora
Estimated Sales: $5-10 Million
Number Employees: 20-49
Square Footage: 40000
Type of Packaging: Consumer, Food Service, Private Label, Bulk

27020 Ozark Tape & Label Co
2061 E Mcdaniel St
Springfield, MO 65802-2926

417-831-1444
Fax: 417-831-1424

Printed pressure sensitive tapes, tags and labels
R&D: Steve Lane
Manager: Steve Lane
Manager: Steve Lane
Production Manager: Steve Lane
Estimated Sales: $1-2.5 Million
Number Employees: 10-19
Square Footage: 10000

27021 Ozarka Drinking Water
4718 Mountain Creek Pkwy
Dallas, TX 75236

817-354-9526
www.ozarkawater.com

Drinking water
Manager: Randy Payne
Estimated Sales: $20-50 Million
Number Employees: 100-249
Parent Co: Ozarka Houston Water Company

27022 Ozotech Inc
2401 E Oberlin Rd
Yreka, CA 96097-9577

530-842-4189
Fax: 530-842-3238 ozotech@ozotech.com
www.ozotech.biz

Manufactures ozone generators, air preparation and
water treatment systems for commercial, industrial
and home uses
President: Ken Mouw
km@ozotech.com
Administration Director: Nancy Mouw
Marketing Director: Kat Hoag
Sales Manager: Steve Christopher
Purchasing Manager: Cari Burke
Number Employees: 20-49
Type of Packaging: Consumer, Private Label

27023 P & A Food Ind Recruiters
188 Liberty Way
Woodbury, NJ 08096-6822

856-384-4774
Fax: 856-384-8074 foodrecruit@comcast.net
www.pandafoodrecruit.com

Executive search firm specializing in permanent se-
lection and placement of executive, managerial and
technical personnel in the food industry only
President: Paul Sundstrom
foodrecruit@comcast.net
VP and Partner: Andrew Sundstrom
Operations Manager: Dieter Sievers
Estimated Sales: Less Than $500,000
Number Employees: 1-4
Parent Co: Winston Franchise Corporation

27024 P & F Machine
301 S Broadway
Turlock, CA 95380-5414

209-667-2515
Fax: 209-667-4945 eparker@pfmetals.com
www.pfmetals.com

Manufacturer and exporter of custom engineered
and fabricated food, poultry and wine processing
equipment
Contact: Brian Alves
balves@pfmetals.com
Purchasing Agent: Jim Wells
Estimated Sales: less than $500,000
Number Employees: 50-99

27025 P & L Specialties
1650 Almar Pkwy
Santa Rosa, CA 95403-8253

707-573-3141
Fax: 707-573-3140 888-313-7947
sales@pnlspecialties.com www.pnlspecialties.com

Winery equipment
President: Edwin L Barr
ebarr@pnlspecialties.com
Estimated Sales: $10-20 Million
Number Employees: 20-49

27026 P & L System
819 Pickens Industrial Drive
Suite 5
Marietta, GA 30062-3159

678-355-9809
Fax: 678-354-7253 nstyrin@hotmail.com
www.pandl.co.uk

CEO: Chris Lee
Estimated Sales: Below $5 Million
Number Employees: 6

27027 P M Plastics
627 Capitol Dr
Pewaukee, WI 53072-2514

262-691-1700
Fax: 262-691-4405 jkildow@pmplastic.com
www.pmplastic.com

Molded plastic signs, diplays and packaging prod-
ucts
HR Executive: Rhonda Schmitt
rschmitt@pmplastic.com
Engineering: John Matejcik
Quality Control: Ryan Ford
Sales: Jeff Kildow
Manager: William E Ford Jr
Plant Manager: William Ford, Jr.
Estimated Sales: $10-20 Million
Number Employees: 100-249

27028 P R Farms Inc
2917 E Shepherd Ave
Clovis, CA 93619-9152

559-299-0201
Fax: 559-299-7292 pat@prfarms.com
www.prfarms.com

President: Pat V Ricchiuti
pat@prfarms.com
CEO: Pat V Ricchiuti

Estimated Sales: $10-20 Million
Number Employees: 100-249

27029 P&E
108 Marcia Dr
Altamonte Spgs, FL 32714-2913

407-857-3888
Fax: 407-857-0900 800-438-0674

Packaging equipment including bag-in-box and
cases
Office Manager: Beverly Smith
Estimated Sales: $5-10,000,000
Number Employees: 50-99

27030 P&H Milling Group
1060 Fountain Street North
Cambridge, ON N3E 0A1
Canada

519-650-6400
Fax: 519-650-6429 info@dovergrp.com

Baking ingredients and flours
President: Sheila LaLang

27031 P.F. Harris Manufacturing Company
PO Box 1122
Alpharetta, GA 30009

904-389-5686
Fax: 904-384-0979 800-637-0317
info@pfharris.com www.pfharris.com

Manufacturer, importer and exporter of insecticides
and pest control devices including roach tablets
General Manager: Franklin Goodman
Contact: Beth Cline
beth@pfharris.com
Estimated Sales: $300,000-500,000
Number Employees: 4
Square Footage: 24000
Brands:
Harris Bug Free
Harris Famous

27032 P.L. Thomas & Company
119 Headquarters Plaza
Morristown, NJ 07960

973-984-0900
Fax: 973-984-5666 www.plthomas.com

Supplier of extracts, natural color and flavorings,
herbs and probiotics.
President: Paul Flowerman

27033 PAC Equipment Company
PO Box 8
Garfield, NJ 07026-0008

973-478-1008
Fax: 973-478-1008

Solid waste equipment, compactors and roll offs
President: Walter Johns
Number Employees: 10

27034 PAL Marking Products
10 Princess Street
Sausalito, CA 94965-2210

415-332-2596
Fax: 415-332-2598

Wine industry labelers
Estimated Sales: less than $500,000
Number Employees: 1-4

27035 PAM Fastening Technology Inc
1108 Continental Blvd # A
Charlotte, NC 28273-6485

704-583-2425
Fax: 704-394-9339 800-699-2674

Hot-melt adhesives and hot-melt applicators,
autofeed system
Owner: Ted Minchew
VP: Edward Minchew
Estimated Sales: $5-10 Million
Number Employees: 5-9

27036 PAR Tech Inc
8383 Seneca Tpke
New Hartford, NY 13413

800-448-6505
www.partech.com

Manufacturer and exporter of computerized cash
registers.
President & CEO: Dr. Donald Foley
Chief of Staff & Strategy: Karen Sammon
Chief Financial Officer: Bryan Menar
VP/General Counsel/Corporate Secretary: Cathy
King
VP, Business & Financial Relations: Chris Byrnes

Year Founded: 1978
Estimated Sales: $118 Million
Number Employees: 500-999
Type of Packaging: Food Service

27037 PAR Visions Systems Corporation
8375 Seneca Tpke
New Hartford, NY 13413-4957

703-433-6300
Fax: 315-768-3838 800-448-6505
www.parlms.com

X-ray inspection systems
VP: John W Sammon Iii
Estimated Sales: $1-5 Million
Number Employees: 10-19

27038 PAR-Kan
2915 W 900 S
Silver Lake, IN 46982-9300

260-352-2141
Fax: 260-352-0701 800-291-5487
info@par-kan.com www.par-kan.com

Manufacturer and exporter of recycled grease containers, lids, screens and caster frames
President: David Caldwell
CFO: Richard Burton
rburton@par-kan.com
Marketing: Todd Sheets
Sales: Carolyn Montel
Estimated Sales: $10-20 Million
Number Employees: 50-99
Brands:
  Par-Kan

27039 PASCO
2600 S Hanley Rd # 450
St Louis, MO 63144-2593

314-781-2212
Fax: 314-781-9986 800-489-3300
pasco@pascosystems.com www.pascosystems.com

Manufacturer and exporter of packaging machinery including slipsheet and pallet dispensers and bag, drum, pail and case palletizers
President: Dominic Spitalieri
spitalierid@pasco-group.com
CFO: Teresa Ovelgoenner
Executive VP: Sandy Elfrink
Sales Manager: Darin Everett
Estimated Sales: $10-20,000,000
Number Employees: 20-49
Square Footage: 50000

27040 PBC
185 Route 17 North
Mahwah, NJ 07430

201-512-0387
Fax: 201-512-1459 800-514-2739
brewing@pubbrewing.com www.pubbrewing.com

Stainless steel tanks; importer of beer and wine filters; exporter of microbrew systems
President: Erwin Eibert
CFO: David Generso
VP: Ralph Eibert
Design Engineer: Dino Benvenuto
Estimated Sales: $3.5 Million
Number Employees: 10-19

27041 PBC Manufacturing
185 Route 17 North
Mahwah, NJ 07430-1212

201-512-0387
Fax: 201-512-1459 800-514-2739
www.pubbrewing.com

Wine industry SS vessels, packaging, filtration
Owner: Erwin Eibert
Manager: Mat Swanson
Production Manager: Ralph Eivert
Estimated Sales: $1-5 Million
Number Employees: 10-19

27042 PBI Dansensor America
139 Harristown Rd # 102
Glen Rock, NJ 07452-3326

201-251-6490
Fax: 201-251-6491 jm@pbi-dansensor.com
www.pbi-dansensor.com

President: Jim Margiotta
Chief Executive Officer, Managing Direct: Jesper Bilde
Marketing Director: Karsten Kejlhof
Estimated Sales: Below $5 Million
Number Employees: 10-19

27043 PBM Inc
1070 Sandy Hill Rd
Irwin, PA 15642-4747

724-863-0550
Fax: 724-863-3283 800-967-4PBM
info@pbmvalve.com www.pbmvalve.com

Valve manufacturing
CEO: Stuart Zarembo
Controller: Nancy Mayer
Engineering/Manufacturing Manager: Jeff Kerr
Quality Control: Ed Docherty
Marketing/Sales Manager: Jay Giffen
COO: Mark Nahorski
Plant Manager: Mark Nahorski
Purchasing Manager: Phil Kochasic
Estimated Sales: $15 Million
Number Employees: 50-99

27044 PC/Poll Systems
3162 Cedar Crest Rdg
Suite B
Dubuque, IA 52003

563-556-3556
Fax: 563-556-0405 800-670-1736
www.pcpoll.com

Manufacturer and exporter of software providing the ability to connect a PC to a cash register; compatible with all Casio ECR's NCR 2170, 2113, CRS 2000 and 3000 and Samsung 6500; also, provides collection, display, printing, export ofreports, etc
Support: Gary Bishop
Estimated Sales: $2.5-5 Million
Number Employees: 5-9
Square Footage: 2400

27045 PCI Inc
10800 Baur Blvd
St Louis, MO 63132-1629

314-872-9333
Fax: 314-872-9104 800-752-7657
sales@pcistl.com www.pcistl.com

Toilet bowl cleaners and drain openers
President: Stephen Mclaughlin
smclaughlin@pcistl.com
Technology: Scott Kretzer
Estimated Sales: $5-10 Million
Number Employees: 20-49
Square Footage: 84000
Brands:
  Acid Free
  Brite Bowl
  Chief 90
  Drain Power
  Jet White
  Scout 20

27046 PCM Delasco Inc
11940 Brittmoore Park Dr
Houston, TX 77041-7225

713-896-4888
Fax: 713-896-4806 www.pcmusainc.com

Designer and manufacturer in Progressive Cavity, Peristaltic and hose pump and offers solutions for a wide range of applications
President: Bruno Lafont
Estimated Sales: Less than $500,000
Number Employees: 1-4

27047 (HQ)PDC International
1106 Clayton Ln # 521w
Austin, TX 78723-2489

512-302-0194
Fax: 512-302-0476 sales@pdc-corp.com
www.pdceurope.com/

Manufacturer and exporter of heat shrinkable tamper-evident seal and sleeve label machinery.
President: Neal Konstantin
Chief Executive Officer: Anatole Konstantin
VP: Alcyr Coelho
Marketing & Sales Director North America: Alcyr Coelho
Sales Representative: Reid Vail
Purchasing: Paul Strauss
Estimated Sales: $20-50 Million
Number Employees: 50-99
Square Footage: 17000
Other Locations:
  PDC International Corporation
  Austin TX

27048 PDMP
105 Loudoun St SW
Leesburg, VA 20175-2910

703-777-8400
Fax: 703-777-8430 wmt@pdmpinc.com
www.pdmpantiqueprints.com

Contract manufacturer of packaging materials including foam extrusions and molding
President: William Teringo
Estimated Sales: Less Than $500,000
Number Employees: 5-9

27049 PDQ Plastics Inc
7 Hook Rd # T
Bayonne, NJ 07002-5006

201-823-0270
Fax: 201-823-0345 800-447-7141
hartson@pdqplastics.com www.pdqplastics.com

Plastic pallets
President: Barry Nathans
VP/General Manager: Harston Poland
Estimated Sales: $1-2.5 Million
Number Employees: 10-19
Square Footage: 200000

27050 PEAK Technologies, Inc.
10330 Old Columbia Rd
Columbia, MD 21046

410-312-6000
Fax: 410-309-6219 800-926-9212
www.peaktech.com

Systems integrator of automatic identification and data collection equipment and systmes
Contact: Steve Arcidiacono
steve.arcidiacono@peak-ryzex.com
Estimated Sales: $52 Million
Number Employees: 777
Square Footage: 7350
Parent Co: Moore Corporation
Other Locations:
  PEAK Technologies-North East
  Hasbrouck Heights NJ
  PEAK Technologies
  Dover NH
  PEAK Technologies NYC
  New York NY
  PEAK Technologies-North Central
  Itasca IL
  PEAK Technologies-New England
  Nashua NH
  PEAK Technologies Canada Limited
  Mississauga, ON, Canada

27051 PFI Displays Inc
40 Industrial St
PO Box 508
Rittman, OH 44270-1525

330-925-9015
Fax: 330-925-8520 800-925-9075
jtricomi@pfidisplays.com www.pfidisplays.com

Manufacturer and exporter of point of purchase displays, exhibits and store fixtures
President: Anthony R Tricomi
Chairman of the Board: Vincent Tricomi
Vice President of Sales: Jim Tricomi
Estimated Sales: $5-10 Million
Number Employees: 20-49
Square Footage: 140000

27052 PFM Packaging MachineryCorporation
1271 Ringwell Drive
Newmarket, ON L3Y 8T9
Canada

905-836-6709
Fax: 905-836-7763 info@pfmnorthamerica.com
www.pfmnorthamerica.com

PFM has over 40 years of experience in manufacturing over 35 different models of flow wrappers-both vertical and horizontal.
President: Elizabeth Fioravanti
Engineering Manager: Mike Borza
Marketing Director: Jackie Pineau
Sales Director: Lana Pratt
Estimated Sales: $4.5 Million
Number Employees: 40
Square Footage: 200000

27053 PHD Inc
9009 Clubridge Dr
Fort Wayne, IN 46809-3000

260-747-6151
Fax: 260-479-2312 800-324-8511
phdinfo@phdinc.com www.phdinc.com

Grippers, cylinders, escapements, slides, rotary actuators, sheet metal clamps
CEO: Harry Neff
CEO: Harry Neff
Estimated Sales: $40 Million+
Number Employees: 100-249

27054 PHF Specialists
P.O.Box 7697
San Jose, CA 95150-7697
408-275-0161
Fax: 408-280-0979 phfspec@pacbell.net
www.phfspec.com
HACCP programs for vegetables, meats, seafood and food service, thermal process design and validation and third party audits
Owner: Pamela Hardt-English
Estimated Sales: Below 1 Million
Number Employees: 1-4

27055 PHI Enterprises
12832 Garden Grove Boulevard
Suite E
Garden Grove, CA 92843-2014
714-537-7858
Fax: 714-537-8228 800-971-9955
phienterprises@aol.com www.phienterprises.com

27056 PIAB Vacuum Conveyors
65 Sharp Street
Hingham, MA 02043-4311
781-792-0003
Fax: 781-337-6864 800-321-7422
info@piab.com www.piab.com
Material handling/processing systems: pneumatic vacuum conveyor
Vice President of Business Development: Ed McGovern
CEO: Donald Spradlin
Contact: Linda Bearce
lbearce@piab.com
Estimated Sales: $10-20 Million
Number Employees: 45

27057 PLM Trailer Leasing
5722 S Naylor Rd
Livermore, CA 94551-8300
925-245-0056
Fax: 925-245-0185 877-736-8756
www.plmtrailer.com
President, Chief Executive Officer: Keith Shipp
acapone@plmtrailer.com
CEO: Hugh Fehrenbach
Vice President of Sales: Mark Domzalski
Site Manager: Anthony Capone
acapone@plmtrailer.com
Estimated Sales: $3-5 Million
Number Employees: 1-4

27058 PM Chemical Company
5319 Grant Street
San Diego, CA 92110-4010
619-296-0191
Manufacturer and exporter of detergents, soaps and food processing cleaners
President: John Mehren
soapies@pacbell.net
CEO: Bernard Mehren
Estimated Sales: $1-2.5 Million
Number Employees: 5-9
Square Footage: 40000
Brands:
  Astro
  Pure Chem
  Red X
  Sofwite

27059 PM Plastics
3970 Parsons Rd
Howell, MI 48855-9617
517-546-9900
Fax: 517-546-7097 800-854-2920
www.pmpnet.com
President: Don Verna
Estimated Sales: $10-20 Million
Number Employees: 50-99

27060 PMC Global Inc.
12243 Branford St.
Sun Valley, CA 91352
818-896-1101
Fax: 818-897-0180 info@pmcglobalinc.com
www.pmcglobalinc.com

Custom cutlery, chemical intermediates and packing services.
Founder/CEO/President: Philip Kamins
pkamins@pmcglobal.com
EVP/Chief Financial Officer: Thian Cheong
Year Founded: 1974
Estimated Sales: $1.3 Billion
Number Employees: 5000-9999
Type of Packaging: Consumer, Food Service

27061 PME Equipment
230 Route 206
Suite 405
Flanders, NJ 07836
973-927-2700
Fax: 973-927-4411 www.pmeequipment.com
Representatives
Estimated Sales: $1-2.5 Million
Number Employees: 5-9
Square Footage: 1200

27062 PMI Cartoning Inc
850 Pratt Blvd
Elk Grove Vlg, IL 60007-5117
847-593-0876
Fax: 847-437-1627 btisma@pmicartoning.com
www.pmicartoning.com
Custom designed carton packaging machinery and systems
President: Branko Tisma
btisma@pmicartoning.com
Vice President of Sales: Tony BLESS
Vice President of Sales: Tony Bless
Estimated Sales: $2.5-5 Million
Number Employees: 50-99

27063 PMI Food Equipment Group
701 S Ridge Ave
Troy, OH 45374-0001
937-332-3000
Fax: 937-332-2852 www.hobartcorp.com
Equipment and systems including ovens, salad bars, electronic weighing, wrapping and labeling systems, etc
President: John McDonough
VP: Ken Kessler
Vice President: Jack Gridley
Research Director of Research: David Sprinkle
Business Development Manager: John Davis
Contact: Jennifer Monnin
jennifer.monnin@hobartcorp.com
Number Employees: 1,000-4,999
Parent Co: Premark International
Brands:
  Adamatic
  Foster
  Hobart
  Stero
  Tasselli
  Vulcan
  Wolf

27064 PMMI Bookstore
11911 Freedom Drive
Suite 600
Reston, VA 20190
571-612-3200
Fax: 703-243-8556 888-275-7664
pmmiwebhelp@PMMI.org www.pmmi.org
Packaging and processing
President and CEO: Charles D. Yuska
Executive Assistant: Corinne G Mulligan
CAE, Vice President, Finance: Craig Silverio
Director, Technical Services: Fred Hayes
Vice President, Market Development: Jorge Izquierdo
Contact: Monjur Alum
monjur@pmmi.org
Director, Operations: Caroline Abromavage
Number Employees: 20-49

27065 (HQ)POS Pilot Plant Corporation
118 Veterinary Road
Saskatoon, SK S7N 2R4
Canada
306-978-2800
Fax: 306-975-3766 800-230-2751
pos@pos.ca www.pos.ca

Wide variety of industries served, including food and ingredients, fats and oils, nutraceutical and functional food, cosmetics, cosmeceuticals and fragrances, feeds and biotechnology. Total capability under one roof, including fullsolvent extraction, algae and yeast based biomass extraction,analytical services and custom processing. services supported by in-house analytical,methods, development, logistics, and information research.
President & CEO: D.A. Kelly
VP: Paul Fedec
Manager of Quality: Grace Varga
VP, Operations and Corporate Affairs: Heather Ryan
Public Relations: Marilyn Huber
VP, Operations: Grace Varga
Purchasing: Sandra Bodnar
Number Employees: 87

27066 POSitively Unique
591 Boxford Lane
Columbus, OH 43213-2603
614-755-2469
Fax: 614-575-2578
Windows based POS Systems for the hospitality industry
President: Gary Zomonski
Number Employees: 6

27067 PPC Perfect Packaging Co
26974 Eckel Rd
PO Box 286
Perrysburg, OH 43551-1214
419-874-3167
Fax: 419-874-8044
Manufacturer and exporter of custom wooden boxes for machinery and related equipment and domestic, export and military packaging; also, heated warehousing available
Owner: Anil Sharma
Estimated Sales: Less Than $500,000
Number Employees: 1-4
Square Footage: 28000

27068 PPG Industries Inc
500 Techne Center Dr
Milford, OH 45150-2763
513-576-0360
Fax: 513-576-3053 www.ppg.com/packaging
Pretreatment chemicals, interior and exterior coatings for the metal packaging industry
President: Michael Horton
Human Resources: Casandra Tembo
Vice President of Research and Developme: Charles Kahle
Vice President of Operations: John Richter
Vice President of Purchasing: Stephen Lampe
Estimated Sales: $20-50 Million
Number Employees: 50-99

27069 PPI
11800 Industriplex Blvd
#9
Baton Rouge, LA 70809-5187
225-330-4602
Fax: 225-752-1163 sales@podpack.com
www.podpack.com
Co-packer for single serve coffee and tea products, includes espresso pods, Cups, Cold Brew One™ pods, quick serve restaurant pods, OCS coffee and tea pods, and hotel in-room pods. Also offer custom packaging services.
CEO: William Powell
Quality Control: Gary Kennington
Executive VP/Chief Operating Officer: Tom Martin
Customer Service Supervisor: Priscilla Short
Supply Chain Manager: Drew Brown
Estimated Sales: Less Than $500,000
Number Employees: 1-4
Type of Packaging: Food Service, Private Label

27070 PPI Printing Press
3008 Main St
Union Gap, WA 98903-1758
509-453-6130
Fax: 509-453-4159
Manufactures thermoform packaging— blisters, blisterboard and skinboard, clamshells, food trays and printed inserts
Manager: Jim Burde
Estimated Sales: $5-10 Million
Number Employees: 50-99

27071 PPI Technologies Group

1610 Northgate Blvd
Sarasota, FL 34234

941-359-6678
Fax: 941-359-6804 rcmpp@aol.com
www.ppitechnologies.com
Manufacturer and supplier of stand up pouch machinery
President: Stuart Murray
CEO: R Charles Murray
CFO: Karena Thomas
Vice President: Sandra Christensen
Research & Development: Rudi Kleer
Quality Control: Gary Bush
Marketing: Richard Murray
Marketing/Sales: Robert Libera
Contact: Andre Beukes
abeukes@redi2drinqgroup.com
Operations Manager: Peter Aeberhard
Production Manager: Pete Ceconci
Plant Manager: Sean Reed
Purchasing Manager: Tom Richard
Estimated Sales: $20 Million
Number Employees: 40
Number of Brands: 7
Number of Products: 10
Square Footage: 60000
Parent Co: Profile Packaging Inc-Paksource Group LLC
Type of Packaging: Food Service
Brands:
Laudenberg
Nishibe
Psgjme
Psglee

27072 PQ Corp

300 Lindenwood Dr
Malvern, PA 19355-1740

610-651-4200
Fax: 610-651-4504 ed.myszak@pqcorp.com
www.pqcorp.com
President: Stanley W Silverman
CEO: George J Biltz
george.biltz@pqcorp.com
CEO: Michael R Boyce
Number Employees: 1000-4999

27073 PROCON Products

869 Seven Oaks Blvd # 120
Suite 120
Smyrna, TN 37167-6482

615-355-8000
Fax: 615-355-8001 mail@proconpump.com
www.proconpumps.com
Manufacturer and exporter of positive displacement rotary vane pumps
President: Paul Roberts
proberts@proconpump.com
VP, Sales & Business Development: Jim Kelly
Product Manager: Jeff Kulikowski
Purchasing Agent: Tracy Harris
Estimated Sales: $10-25 Million
Number Employees: 20-49
Parent Co: Standex International
Type of Packaging: Food Service

27074 PROMA Technologies

24 Forge Pkwy
Franklin, MA 02038

508-541-7700
Fax: 508-541-7777 800-343-6977
Holographic metallized paper
President: Frank Sereno
CFO: Robert Kynoch
Marketing Director: Harry Mann
Estimated Sales: $20-50 Million
Number Employees: 1-4
Square Footage: 140000

27075 PSI

1901 S Meyers Rd # 400
Suite 400
Oakbrook Terrace, IL 60181-5260

630-705-9290
Fax: 800-548-7901 www.psiusa.com
Consultant specializing in nutritional labeling testing, sanitation audits and microbiological and chemical food testing

Cmo: David Albee
dalbee@periph.net
Executive Vice President: Tom Boogher
Manager: Rodney Ortega
Sales Manager: Sharon Winders
District Manager: John Southerland
Number Employees: 60
Square Footage: 40000
Parent Co: PSI

27076 PSI Preferred Solutions

7819 Broadview Road
Cleveland, OH 44131-6146

216-642-1200
Fax: 216-642-1166 800-522-4522
www.stayflex.com
Fiberglass wall and ceiling paneling, floor and wall coating materials, paints, enamels and coating, insulated building panels, insulation-floors, ceilings, refrigerated structures and corrosion control
President: John Stahl
Contact: Connie Thompson
cthompson@blueskysolution.co.uk
Estimated Sales: $500,000-$1 Million
Number Employees: 5-9

27077 PTI Packaging

1055 Saddle Rdg
Portage, WI 53901

920-623-3566
Fax: 920-623-5659 800-501-4077
protech@powerweb.net
Manufacturer and exporter of palletizers, conveyors, sheet dispensers, pallet dispensers/conveyors and package accumulators
President: John Wildner
jwildner@ptipackaging.com
Estimated Sales: $2.5-5,000,000
Number Employees: 1-4

27078 PTR Baler & Compactor Co

2207 E Ontario St
Philadelphia, PA 19134-2615

267-345-0490
Fax: 215-533-8907 800-523-3654
sales@ptrco.com www.ptrco.com
Manufacturer and exporter of vertical recycling balers and waste compaction systems
President/CEO: Michael Savage
IT: Joseph Bennett
jbennett@tramrail.com
Estimated Sales: $30 Million
Number Employees: 100-249
Number of Brands: 3
Square Footage: 135000
Parent Co: RJR Enterprises
Brands:
Trampak

27079 PURA

9848 Glenoaks Boulevard
Sun Valley, CA 91352-1045

818-768-0451
Fax: 661-257-6385 800-292-7872
Manufacturer and exporter of ultraviolet and filtration water treatment products
Vice President: Edwin Roberts
Regional Sales Manager: Brad Hess
Estimated Sales: $1-2.5 Million
Number Employees: 10-19
Square Footage: 320000
Parent Co: Hydrotech
Brands:
Pura

27080 PURAC America

111 Barclay Blvd
Lincolnshire, IL 60069

608-752-0449
Fax: 847-634-1992 pam@purac.com
www.purac.com
President: Gerrit Vreeman
Contact: Lisette Nanning
l.nanning@puracaps.com
Estimated Sales: $20-50 Million
Number Employees: 20-49

27081 PVI Industries LLC

3209 Galvez Ave
Fort Worth, TX 76111-4509

817-335-9531
Fax: 817-332-6742 800-784-8326
pbothner@pvi.com www.pvi.com
Hot water generation for sanitation and process

President: Craig Adams
CEO: Chris Bollas
cbollas@pbi.com
CFO: Lynn Meadows
R & D: Frank Myers
Quality Control: John Calland
Sales: Chris Bollas
Number Employees: 20-49

27082 Pa R Systems Inc

707 County Road E W
St Paul, MN 55126-7007

651-528-5200
Fax: 651-483-2689 800-464-1320
info@par.com
Manufacturer and exporter of cranes, hoists and crane controls
General Manager: Joe Hoff
CEO: Mark Wrightsman
mwrightsman@par.com
VP: Neil Skogland
Director Sales/Marketing: Jaems Nelson
Estimated Sales: $10-20 Million
Number Employees: 100-249
Type of Packaging: Bulk

27083 Pa R Systems Inc

707 County Road E W
St Paul, MN 55126-7007

651-528-5200
Fax: 651-483-2689 800-464-1320
info@par.com www.par.com
A leader in the design, construction, installation and support of large-scale, as well as small and precise, high-precision robotic and matieral handling equipment and systems.
President: Mark A Wrightsman
CEO: Mark Wrightsman
mwrightsman@par.com
CFO: Brad Yopp
Research & Development: Albert Sturm
Quality Control: Jenny Conlin
Marketing Director: Karen Knoblock
Sales Director: Brian Behm
Production Manager: Wayne Skiba
Purchasing Manager: Kallie Swartz
Estimated Sales: $80 Million
Number Employees: 100-249
Square Footage: 60000
Brands:
Cimroc
Ederer
Jered
Mec
M"Zak
Nr
Pr
Ssi Robotics
Tr
Vector
Xr

27084 Pac Strapping Products

307 National Rd
Exton, PA 19341-2647

610-363-8805
Fax: 610-363-7349 800-523-7752
info@strapsolutions.com www.strapsolutions.com
Plastic strapping and accessories for strapping
President: Edwin A Brownley Jr
CFO: Pete Sylvester
ps@strapsolutions.com
Estimated Sales: $20-50 Million
Number Employees: 20-49

27085 PacTech Engineering

4444 Carver Woods Drive
Cincinnati, OH 45242-5532

513-792-1090
Fax: 513-891-4232 www.pactech.com
Engineering consultant specializing in packing systems including feasibility, conceptual, design, installation, etc
CEO: Sam Pantano
Business Development Manager: Tina Eckert
Contact: Richard Mckee
mckee@pactech.com
Estimated Sales: $1-5 Million
Number Employees: 20-49
Square Footage: 20000

27086 Pace Labels Inc
104 Twenty Nine Ct
Williamston, SC 29697-9497
864-840-9511
Fax: 864-855-3637 800-789-1592
Pressure sensitive labels
Owner: Stuart Pace
pacepres@aol.com
CEO: W Stuart Pace
Estimated Sales: $1-2.5 Million
Number Employees: 5-9
Square Footage: 40000
Type of Packaging: Consumer, Food Service, Private Label, Bulk

27087 Pace Packaging Corp
3 Sperry Rd
Fairfield, NJ 07004-2004
973-227-1040
Fax: 973-227-7393 800-867-2726
sales@pacepackaging.com
www.pacepackaging.com
Manufacturer and exporter of high speed plastic bottle unscramblers
President/CFO: Kenneth F Regula
Vice President-Sales: Glenn G. Kelley
Quality Control: Mike Regula
Sales Manager: Glenn Kelley
Manager: Sam Jarkas
jarkas@pacepkg.com
VP Manufacturing: Ken Regula
Estimated Sales: $5-10 Million
Number Employees: 20-49
Square Footage: 60
Brands:
Omni-Line

27088 Pace Products
2764 N.Green Valley Pkwy
Henderson, NV 89014
702-272-0048
Fax: 702-272-0668 800-796-2675
pacecork@msn.com
Special packaging
Owner: Michael Piluso
Estimated Sales: $1-5 Million
Number Employees: 1-4

27089 Pacemaker Packaging Corp
7200 51st Rd
Woodside, NY 11377-7631
718-458-1188
Fax: 718-429-2907
info@pacemakerpackaging.com
Bag closers and fillers
President: Emil Romotzki
mmromotzki@aol.com
Sales Coordinator: Gene Cignoli
Estimated Sales: $1-2.5 Million
Number Employees: 5-9
Brands:
Pacemaker
Unibagger

27090 Pacer Pumps
41 Industrial Cir
Lancaster, PA 17601-5927
717-656-2161
Fax: 717-656-0477 800-233-3861
sales@pacerpumps.com www.pacerpumps.com
Manufacturer and exporter of pumps including self-priming centrifugal nonmetallic, hand operated and powered drum
Manager: Glenn Geist
sales@pacerpumps.com
General Manager: Denzel Stoops
Marketing: Art Foster
Sales: Ron Hock
Manager: Glenn Geist
sales@pacerpumps.com
Purchasing Manager: Ernie Stoltzfus
Estimated Sales: $5-10 Million
Number Employees: 20-49
Square Footage: 144000
Parent Co: Serfilco
Brands:
Camelot
Pacer

27091 Pacific Bag
15300 Woodinville Redmond Road NE
Suite A
Woodinville, WA 98072
425-455-1128
Fax: 425-455-1886 800-562-2247
bags@pacificbag.com www.pacificbag.com
Flexible packaging and packaging equipment
CEO: Mark Howley
Estimated Sales: $5-10 Million
Number Employees: 20-49

27092 Pacific Bearing Company
P.O.Box 6980
Rockford, IL 61125-1980
815-389-5600
Fax: 815-389-5790 800-962-8979
marketing@pacific-bearing.com
CEO: Robert Schroeder
President: Glen Michalske
Quality Control: Paul Bertolasi
Contact: Shawn Anderson
shawn.anderson@pacific-bearing.com
Estimated Sales: $10-20 Million
Number Employees: 100-249

27093 Pacific Coast Container
11010 NE 37th Cir
Suite 110
Vancouver, WA 98682
360-892-3451
Fax: 360-892-4955 www.saxco.com
Wine industry glass containers
Manager: Mark Petays
Estimated Sales: $2.5-5 Million
Number Employees: 10-19

27094 Pacific Expresso
716 Frederick St
Santa Cruz, CA 95062-2205
831-429-1920
Fax: 831-459-0798 888-429-1920
info@pacificespresso.com
Artisan Coffees Roasted to Order. Pacific Espresso has a long standing tradition of excellent customer service to supplement their high quality coffees, teas and espresso machines.
President: Tim O'Connor
tim@pacificespresso.com
Operations: Paula Berman
Estimated Sales: $500,000-$1 Million
Number Employees: 5-9

27095 Pacific Handy Cutter Inc
2968 Randolph Ave
Costa Mesa, CA 92626-4312
714-662-1033
Fax: 714-662-7595 800-229-2233
info@pacifichandycutter.com www.go-phc.com
Tool and blade manufacturer: safety carton cutters, point blades, and specialized hook knives
President/CEO: Mark Marinovich
Sales: Dave Puglisi
Contact: Joe Garavaglia
joe@pacifichandycutter.com
Estimated Sales: $10-20 Million
Number Employees: 1-4

27096 Pacific Harvest Products
13405 SE 30th Street
Bellevue, WA 98005-4454
425-401-7990
Dry blends, sauces, dressings, bases
Contact: Nicholas Ade
n.ade@pnb.org
Number Employees: 20-49
Type of Packaging: Consumer, Food Service, Private Label, Bulk
Brands:
Firmenich

27097 Pacific Isles Trading
465 Monroe Avenue
Township of Washington, NJ 07676-4928
201-666-8849
Fax: 201-666-6053 jzberkman@aol.com
Gift containers and specialty packaging made of abaca

27098 Pacific Merchants
149 S Burlington Avenue #507
Los Angeles, CA 90049
818-988-8999
Fax: 818-988-6999 888-207-8999
info@pacificmerchants.com
www.pacificmerchants.com
Hard wood kitchen utensils
Marketing: Bruce Mannis

27099 Pacific Northwest Canned Pear
105 S 18th St # 205
Yakima, WA 98901-2176
815-263-6259
Fax: 509-453-4880
mmiller@pnw-cannedpears.com
www.eatcannedpears.com
Provides information to retail and foodservice customers about canned pears.
President: B J Thurlby
Business Manager: Ken Severn
Estimated Sales: $1-2.5 Million
Number Employees: 20-49

27100 Pacific Northwest Wire Works
3250 International Pl
Dupont, WA 98327-7707
Fax: 425-656-9090 800-222-7699
Wire shelving for refrigerators, stoves, etc
Manager: James Bennett
Estimated Sales: Below $5 Million
Number Employees: 10-19

27101 Pacific Oasis Enterprise Inc
8413 Secura Way # B
Santa Fe Springs, CA 90670-2297
562-698-9146
Fax: 562-698-9147 800-424-1475
POEUS@PacificOasis.com
Manufacturer, importer and exporter of stainless steel scouring pads for the cleaning of pans, grills, ovens, etc.; also, disposables including aprons and gloves
President: S C Chen
scchen@pacificoasis.com
Quality Control: Nick Sumgsun
General Manager: Daisy Reyes
Manager: Nely Go
Estimated Sales: $2.5-5 Million
Number Employees: 1-4

27102 Pacific Ozone Technology
6160 Egret Ct
Benicia, CA 94510-1269
707-747-9600
Fax: 707-747-9209 info@pacificozone.com
www.pacificozone.com
Pacific Ozone is the leading manufacturer of advanced disinfection air-cooled ozone generators and packaged ozone systems for industrial applications including precision dissolved ozone control, instruments and UL control panelsresponse now service and over 9,000 installations worldwide.
Director: Brian Johnson
Sales Administration Manager: Michelle McHale
Estimated Sales: $500,000-$1 Million
Number Employees: 25

27103 Pacific Packaging Machinery
1284 Puerta Del Sol
San Clemente, CA 92673
949-369-2425
Fax: 949-369-2429 sales@pacificpak.com
www.pacificpak.com
Packaging machinery liquid fillers for all industries
Contact: Pete Carpino
information@pacificpak.com
Estimated Sales: $5-10 Million
Number Employees: 20-49

27104 Pacific Packaging Systems
2125 Williams St
San Leandro, CA 94577-3224
510-352-1070
Fax: 510-352-8535 800-272-7774
Wine industry shrink wrap equipment
Estimated Sales: $5-10 Million
Number Employees: 5-9

27105 Pacific Paper Box Co
4916 Cecilia St
Cudahy, CA 90201-5994
323-771-7733
Fax: 323-562-0934

Rigid paper and plastic boxes
President: Joseph Erhardt
VP: Craig Harrison
Estimated Sales: $5-10 Million
Number Employees: 20-49
Square Footage: 140000
Parent Co: Pacific Paper Box Company

27106 Pacific Pneumatics
8576 Red Oak Avenue
Rancho Cucamonga, CA 91730-4822
909-481-8300
Fax: 909-481-8308 800-221-0961
sales@pacpneu.com www.pacpneu.com
Chillers, pneumatic and portable conveyors, vacuum
pumps, dryers and material handling equipment
Estimated Sales: $1-5 Million
Number Employees: 6

27107 Pacific Press Company
1215 Fee Ana St.
Anaheim, CA 92807
714-525-0630
Fax: 714-525-2664 800-878-8029
sales@pacpress.com www.pacpress.com
Wine industry frame filters
Owner: Sean Duby
Contact: Steve Bender
stevebender@pacpress.com
Estimated Sales: $2.5-5 Million
Number Employees: 20-49

27108 Pacific Process Machinery
2062 Stonefield Lane
Santa Rosa, CA 95403-0951
707-523-4122
Fax: 707-523-4418
Dealer of rebuilt and used centrifuges dryers, evapo-
rators, presses, and other processing equipment
Estimated Sales: $1-5 Million

27109 Pacific Process Technology
7370 Cabrillo Avenue
La Jolla, CA 92037-5201
858-551-3298
Fax: 858-459-2362
Filtration and pasteurization systems, separators,
clarifiers, pump feeders/stuffers and cheese process-
ing equipment including grinders and mixers
President: Bill Loy
VP Engineering: John Perlman
VP Marketing: Jeff Campbell

27110 Pacific Refrigerator Company
328 S Mountain View Avenue
San Bernardino, CA 92408-1415
909-381-5669
Fax: 909-888-1203
Manufacturer and exporter of walk-in cooler and
freezers
President: John Gomez
Estimated Sales: Below $5 Million
Number Employees: 10

27111 Pacific Scale Company
16002 SE 106th Ave
P.O. Box 1606
Clackamas, OR 97015
503-657-7500
Fax: 503-657-5561 800-537-1886
psco@pacifier.com www.pacificscale.com
Steel, stainless steel and aluminum platform floor,
livestock and lift truck scales; also, tank mounts and
batching meters
President: Harry Baughn
VP: Joel Offield
Secretary: Lee Offield
Estimated Sales: $2.5-5 Million
Number Employees: 5-9
Square Footage: 14600
Brands:
Lift-N-Weigh
Tuf-N-Low

27112 Pacific Scientific
201 W Rock Rd
Radford, VA 24141-4026
815-226-3100
Fax: 815-226-3080
Generator motors

President: David Burnworth
Quality Manager: Shaz Bashir
Vice President of Sales: Ross Hamilton
Contact: Jeffrey Cassaro
cassarojeff@danahermotion.com
Director of Operations: Arnold Pinto
Estimated Sales: $50-100 Million
Number Employees: 250-499

27113 Pacific Scientific Instrument
481 California St
Grants Pass, OR 97526
541-479-1248
Fax: 541-479-3057 800-866-7889
infogp@hachultra.com
Manufacturer and exporter of instruments for detect-
ing and measuring minute particles
President: Simon Appleby
Contact: Carroll Davis
carroll.davis@particle.com
Production Manager: Brian Bosch
Production Manager: Joe Gecsey
Estimated Sales: $50-100 Million
Number Employees: 100-249
Square Footage: 10000
Brands:
Hiac Royco

27114 Pacific Sign Construction
12339 Oak Knoll Rd
Poway, CA 92064-5319
858-486-8006
Fax: 858-486-8124 pacsign@pacificsign.com
Manufacturer and exporter of luminous signs
President: Roy Flahive
flahive@pacificsign.com
Estimated Sales: $500,000-$1 Million
Number Employees: 5-9

27115 Pacific Southwest Container
P.O.Box 3351
Modesto, CA 95353-3351
209-526-0444
Fax: 209-522-8746 800-772-0444
bsmith@teampsc.com www.teampsc.com
Wine industry point of purchase packaging
President/Owner: John Mayol
Executive Vice President of Sales and Ma: Bryan
Smith
Contact: Marc Crandall
mcrandall@teampsc.com
Estimated Sales: $20-50 Million
Number Employees: 250-499

27116 Pacific Spice Co
6430 E Slauson Ave
Commerce, CA 90040-3108
323-890-0895
Fax: 323-726-9442 www.pacspice.com
Spices and herbs
President: Akiba Schlussel
akiba@pacspice.com
Estimated Sales: G
Number Employees: 100-249
Square Footage: 150000
Type of Packaging: Consumer, Food Service, Pri-
vate Label, Bulk
Brands:
Pacific Natural Spices

27117 Pacific Steam Equipment, Inc.
10648 Painter Ave
Santa Fe Springs, CA 90670
562-906-9292
Fax: 562-906-9223 800-321-4114
sales@pacificsteam.com
Manufacturer and exporter of boilers; distributor of
food processing machinery
Owner: David Ken
President: William Shanahan
Vice President: Shin King
Marketing Manager: Simon Lee
Sales Manager: Santiago Kuan
Contact: Dave Kang
res@pacificsteam.com
Estimated Sales: $2.9 Million
Number Employees: 25
Square Footage: 90000

27118 Pacific Store Designs Inc
11781 Cardinal Cir
Garden Grove, CA 92843-3815
714-636-4440
Fax: 714-636-4442 800-772-5661
psd4cmiller@sbcglobal.net
www.pacificstoredesigns.com
Manufacturer and exporter of retail store fixtures in-
cluding shelving, general contractor, architecturer
and desgin services trade show exhibits and custom
woodworking items specializing in small to medium
sized convenience, gourmetand health food stores;
also, installation services available
President: Chris Miller
Sr. Vice President: James Raynor
Research & Development: Sonia Quintana
Quality Control: Erv Miller
Plant Manager: Ken Kasper
Estimated Sales: Less Than $500,000
Number Employees: 1-4
Square Footage: 13200
Type of Packaging: Private Label

27119 Pacific Tank
17177 Muskrat Ave
Adelanto, CA 92301
760-246-6136
Fax: 760-246-6062 800-449-5838
pactankltd@aol.com
Double wall, fiberglass and storage tanks, food pro-
cessing equipment and material handling equipment
President: Norvald Farestveit
CFO: Robert Clanton
Estimated Sales: Below $5,000,000
Number Employees: 10-19
Square Footage: 10000

27120 Pack & Process
309 136th Ct E
Bradenton, FL 34212
Fax: 302-658-6928 877-777-8425
Contract packaging for food, ingredients. Horizontal
and vertical form-fill, standup pouching, sachet
President: Steven A Ames
Estimated Sales: Less than $500,000
Number Employees: 10

27121 Pack Air Inc
449 S Green Bay Rd
Neenah, WI 54956-2374
920-727-3000
Fax: 920-727-3010 salesis@packairinc.com
www.packairinc.com
Accumulating conveyors
President: Rob Mc Carry
rob_m@packairinc.com
CEO: Pete Clater
Sales Manager: Rob McCarry
Manager: Ron Mc Carry
Estimated Sales: $10 Million
Number Employees: 50-99

27122 Pack All
3003 W Hirsch St
Melrose Park, IL 60160-1738
708-410-1140
Fax: 708-410-1137 888-806-9800
laurac@pack-all.com www.pack-all.com
Packaging equipment: shrink packaging machinery
and tamper evident neck banding
President: Dennis Favale
dennis@pack-all.com
Office Administrator: Laura Cannata
Estimated Sales: $1-3 Million
Number Employees: 5-9

27123 Pack Line Corporation
3026 Phillips Ave
Racine, WI 53403
262-635-6966
Fax: 262-634-0512 800-248-6868
packrite@packrite.com www.packrite.com
Manufacturer, importer and exporter of semi-auto-
matic and automatic fillers and capping, and sealing
machinery
Manager: Dave Bornhuepter
CFO: Michael Beilinson
Vice President: Nick Maslovets
Marketing Director: Erica Kosinski
Estimated Sales: $1 Million
Number Employees: 5-9
Square Footage: 8000
Parent Co: Pack Line

27124 Pack Process Equipment
17025 N Scottsdale Rd # 100
Scottsdale, AZ 85255-5887

480-513-7676
Fax: 480-513-7677
Agitators, bag forming machines, bar formers, batch kneaders, blanchers, blenders, brushes, wrapping, foiling, carton machines: closing, filling, forming, handling, sealing, chocolate equipment
Manager: Lisa Smoke
Estimated Sales: $3-5 Million
Number Employees: 10-19

27125 Pack Rite Machine Mettler
3026 Phillips Ave
Mt Pleasant, WI 53403-3585

262-635-6966
Fax: 262-634-0521 800-248-6868
packrite@packrite.com www.packrite.com
Manufacturer and exporter of bag closing, and packaging machinery
Manager: Dave Bornhuepter
dave.bornhuepter@mt.com
General Manager: Dave Bornhuetter
Estimated Sales: $3-5 Million
Number Employees: 5-9
Square Footage: 24000
Parent Co: Mettler-Toledo
Brands:
    Pack Rite

27126 Pack Rite Machine Mettler
3026 Phillips Ave
Mt Pleasant, WI 53403-3585

262-635-6966
Fax: 262-634-0521 800-248-6868
packrite@packrite.com www.packrite.com
Manufactures and distributes sealing and handling products including poly sealers, thermo sealers, band sealers, conveyors & accumulating tables.
Marketing Executive/General Manager: Dave Bornhuetter
Manager: Dave Bornhuepter
dave.bornhuepter@mt.com
Manufacturing Supervisor: Dale Klinkhammer
Number Employees: 5-9
Square Footage: 10410
Parent Co: Mettler-Toledo, Inc

27127 Pack Star
220 S. 5th Ave
City of Industry, CA 91746

626-922-0537
Fax: 626-330-8658
Packaging Machinery and Materials
Estimated Sales: $3-5 Million
Number Employees: 5-9

27128 Pack West Machinery
5316 Irwindale Ave # B
Baldwin Park, CA 91706-2034

626-814-4766
Fax: 626-814-1615 www.ratioflo.com
Manufacturer and exporter of packaging machinery including top driven and in-line cappers
Owner: Bill Ellison
Marketing/General Manager: Loren Lauxen
Estimated Sales: $2.5-5,000,000
Number Employees: 20-49

27129 Pack'R North America
1921 W Wilson Street
Suite A171
Batavia, IL 60510-1680

630-761-3104
Fax: 630-761-3105 www.filling-equipment.com
Net weight liquid fillers and software
General Manager: Pierre Guillon
Estimated Sales: $1-5 Million
Number Employees: 1-4

27130 Pack-A-Drum
862 Hawksbill Island Dr
Satellite Beach, FL 32937-3850

321-773-1551
Fax: 321-779-3816 800-694-6163
profits@packadrum.com www.pack-a-drum.com
Manufacturer and exporter of manually operated trash compactors/deflators, waste containers and platform carts with free waste management consulting for customers.

President: William E Wagner
pack-a-drum@cfl.rr.com
CFO: Kelli Wagner
VP Marketing: Erik Wagner
VP Sales: Mark Wagner
Director Customer Service: Kirk Wagner
Estimated Sales: $2 Million
Number Employees: 5-9
Number of Brands: 1
Number of Products: 10
Square Footage: 200000
Brands:
    Pack-A-Drum

27131 Pack-Rite
95 Day Street
Newington, CT 06111-1299

860-953-0120
Fax: 860-953-3354
Wooden boxes; also, packaging services available
Sales Manager: Oleg Ouchakof
Estimated Sales: $1-2.5 Million
Number Employees: 10-19

27132 Package Automation Corporation
53016 Highway 60, Acheson Industrial
Spruce Grove, AB T7X 3L3
Canada

780-962-6265
Fax: 780-962-6215 sales@pacauto.com
www.packageautomation.com

27133 Package Concepts & Materials Inc
1023 Thousand Oaks Blvd
Greenville, SC 29607-5642

864-458-7291
Fax: 864-458-7295 800-424-7264
sales@packageconcepts.com
www.packageconcepts.com
Cook-in casings for meat and poultry processing
President: Peter Bylenga
Estimated Sales: $10-20 Million
Number Employees: 50-99
Square Footage: 100000
Type of Packaging: Food Service

27134 Package Containers Inc
777 NE 4th Ave
Canby, OR 97013-2398

503-266-2721
Fax: 503-266-8650 800-266-5806
sales@packagecontainers.com
www.packagecontainers.com
Specialty paper converting. Produce merchandising paper totes and wire ties. Importer/distributor of poly products.
President/CEO: Robert Degnan
Director of Operations: John Stupfel
CFO/Controller: Rolland Royce
MW Regional Sales: Mary Pytko
NE Regional Sales: P R Morris
Director of Sales & Marketing: Scott Koppang
Estimated Sales: F
Number Employees: 50-99
Number of Brands: 6
Number of Products: 5
Square Footage: 80000
Type of Packaging: Food Service, Private Label
Brands:
    Adver-Tie
    Home Toter
    Insta-Tie
    Skirt Tie

27135 Package Converting Corp
380 Dwight St
Holyoke, MA 01040-5891

413-533-2992
Fax: 413-533-5201
Flexible packages, vacuum packaging materials, vacuum packaging equipment, beef, lamb, meat
Estimated Sales: $1-2.5 Million
Number Employees: 50-99

27136 Package Conveyor Co
123 S Main St
Fort Worth, TX 76104-1222

817-332-7195
Fax: 817-334-0855 800-792-1243
wapowers@flash.net
Manufacturer and exporter of conveying equipment including flat, inclined and floor-to-floor belts

Owner: Jack Powers
pcco@flash.net
President: Doyle Powers
Estimated Sales: $2.5-5 Million
Number Employees: 10-19
Parent Co: W.A. Powers Industries

27137 (HQ)Package Machinery Co Inc
80 Commercial St
Holyoke, MA 01040-4704

413-315-3801
Fax: 413-732-1163
customerservice@packagemachinery.com
www.packagemachinery.com
Manufacturer and exporter of rebuilt packaging and injection molding equipment; also, parts
President: Katherine E Putnam
kputnam@packagemachinery.com
Marketing Manager: Meg Cook
General Manager: Paul Stiebel
Estimated Sales: $2.5-5 Million
Number Employees: 20-49
Square Footage: 44000
Brands:
    Package

27138 Package Nakazawa
16233 Hartsook Street
Encino, CA 91436-1304

818-708-3771
Fax: 818-907-9756
yokuaki@americanaccessusa.com
www.packagenakazawa.com
President: Yokoaki Nazakwa
Sales Contact: Yoko Okuaki
Estimated Sales: $300,000-500,000
Number Employees: 3

27139 Package Products
3126 Preble Avenue
Pittsburgh, PA 15233-1084

412-766-1234
Fax: 412-766-6335
Estimated Sales: $10-20 Million
Number Employees: 50-99

27140 Package Service Company of Colorado
1800 NW Vivion Rd
Northmoor, MO 64150-9611

816-891-8300
Fax: 816-891-9032 800-748-7799
Pressure sensitive labels, printed packaging and promotional coupons
Chairman: Jeff Nedblake
Quality Control: Bill Krumrei
R & D: Larry Johnson
Marketing Director: Mike Steczak
VP Sales: Dennis Shannon
Estimated Sales: $20-50 Million
Number Employees: 100-249
Square Footage: 57000

27141 Package Supply Equipment
P.O.Box 19021
Greenville, SC 29602

404-344-8551
Fax: 864-277-0957
Wine industry corks and closures
President: Gary Daniels
CEO: Gary Daniels Sr
Estimated Sales: $50-75 Million
Number Employees: 5-9

27142 Package Systems Corporation
109 Connecticut Mills Avenue
Danielson, CT 06239-1653

860-774-0363
Fax: 860-774-5326 800-522-3548
Pressure sensitive rolls and sheets, labels, label machinery and grease proof polystyrene inserts for meats, poultry, etc.; importer of cellophane; exporter of labels
Sales/Marketing Executive: Charles Pingeton
VP Sales: Randall Duhaime
Estimated Sales: $2.5-5 Million
Number Employees: 20-49
Square Footage: 132000

27143 Packagemasters
52 Sindle Avenue
Little Falls, NJ 07424-1619

973-890-7511
Fax: 973-890-0470

Tea and coffee bags and packaging film supplies, pouch materials

27144 (HQ)Packaging & Processing Equipment
121 Earl Thompson Road
Ayr, ON N0B 1E0
Canada

519-622-6666
Fax: 519-622-6669
Manufacturer and exporter of new, used, rebuilt and custom built blister packagers, bottle sorters, cappers, cartoners, case packers and sealers, cleaners, conveyors, fillers, heat sealers, kettles, labelers, mixers, palletizerstanks, etc
President: P Wiese
CEO: Peter Weise
Other Locations:
Packaging & Processing Equipm
Windhagen

27145 Packaging Aids Corporation
P.O.Box 9144
San Rafael, CA 94912-9144

415-454-4868
Fax: 415-454-6853 sales@paçaids.com
www.paçaids.com
Manufacturer, importer and exporter of sealing machinery for meat, produce, poultry and seafood; also, vacuum chambers and form/fill machinery
President: Serge Berguig
Quality Control: Dana McDaniel
National Sales/Marketing Manager: R Perrone
Sales Manager (Eastern Region): Jerry Henry
Estimated Sales: $5-10 Million
Number Employees: 20-49
Brands:
Audion

27146 Packaging Associates
4 Middlebury Boulevard
Randolph, NJ 07869-1121

973-252-8890
Fax: 973-252-8894 cliffbridge@msn.com
Tamper-evident and CT plastic closures and bottles including PET, PP and HDPE; also, contract packaging of powders and liquids available
President: Stu Weinshanker
Business Development Manager: Paul Ludgate
Sales Manager: Jim Lawson
Estimated Sales: $3-5 Million
Number Employees: 15
Square Footage: 20000
Type of Packaging: Consumer, Food Service, Private Label, Bulk

27147 Packaging By Design Of Il
1460 Bowes Rd
Elgin, IL 60123-5539

847-741-5600
Fax: 847-741-5666
mike@packaging-by-design.com
www.packaging-by-design.com
Flexographic packaging for the food industry product line of which includes roll-stock surface printed films; roll-stock custom laminations; roll-stock reverse printed and laminated, and preformed bags
VP: Charles Graziano
Sales Manager: Michael Graziano
Manager: Steve Madeck
smadeck1207a@aol.com
General Manager: Ira Krakow
Number Employees: 20-49
Type of Packaging: Consumer

27148 Packaging Concept Company
1801 N Kentucky Avenue
Evansville, IN 47711-3853

812-464-2525
Fax: 812-464-8080
Design and development of plastic bottle closure
President: Bruno Zumbuhl
Estimated Sales: Below $5 Million
Number Employees: 10

27149 Packaging Consultants Associated Inc
7820 Airport Hwy
Pennsauken, NJ 08109

856-488-0277
Fax: 856-488-0957 info@thenewpca.com
Packaging equipment, heat seal
President: Joseph R Morgan
CFO: Vincent Giannetti

Estimated Sales: $2.5-5 Million
Number Employees: 5-9

27150 (HQ)Packaging Corporation of America
1 N Field Court
Lake Forest, IL 60045

800-456-4725
www.packagingcorp.com
Boxes of all sizes.
Chairman & CEO: Mark Kowlzan
mkowlzan@packagingcorp.com
SVP & Chief Financial Officer: Robert Mundy
EVP, Corrugated Products: Thomas Hassfurther
SVP, Mill Operations: Charles Carter
SVP/General Counsel/Secretary: Kent Pflederer
SVP, Sales & Marketing, Corrugated Prod.: Thomas W.H. Walton
Estimated Sales: Over $1 Billion
Number Employees: 14,600
Parent Co: Packaging Corporation of America

27151 Packaging Design Corp
101 Shore Dr
Burr Ridge, IL 60527-5887

630-323-1354
Fax: 630-323-2802 info@pack-design.com
www.pack-design.com
Corrugated boxes
President: Scott Jones
sjones@pack-design.com
Vice President: Scott Jones
Sales Director: Benjamin Gercone
Production Manager: Don Hlavac
Estimated Sales: $6 Million
Number Employees: 20-49
Square Footage: 70000

27152 Packaging Distribution Svc
2308 Sunset Rd
Des Moines, IA 50321-1141

515-243-3156
Fax: 515-243-1741 mail@pdspack.com
www.pdspack.com
Wiping cloths
Owner: Bruce Sherman
bsherman@pdspack.com
Number Employees: 20-49

27153 (HQ)Packaging Dynamics
PO Box 5332
Walnut Creek, CA 94596-1332

925-938-2711
Fax: 925-938-2713 dlehm19148@aol.com
Manufacturer, importer and exporter of packaging machinery including horizontal and vertical form/fill/seal machinery, liquid fillers and bottling lines, cartoners, wrappers, bundlers and tea baggers
President: Richard Novak
Engineering Manager: Mike Sanchez
Marketing: Banchez
Sales Manager: Fred Wermuth
Estimated Sales: $2.5-5 Million
Number Employees: 5-9
Square Footage: 20000

27154 Packaging Dynamics
35B Carlough Rd
Bohemia, NY 11716

631-563-4499
Fax: 631-563-4893 dlehm19148@aol.com
www.packagingdynamics.com
Liquid filling and packaging equipment
Owner: Eric Lehmann
Estimated Sales: $2.5-5 Million
Number Employees: 10-19

27155 (HQ)Packaging Dynamics Corp
3900 W 43rd St
Chicago, IL 60632-3421

773-843-8000
Fax: 773-254-8136
Manufacturer and exporter of packaging machinery including liquid filling
CEO: Patrick T Chambliss
pchambliss@pkdy.com
Vice President of Human Resources: Paul Christensen
Estimated Sales: $2.5-5 Million
Number Employees: 1000-4999
Square Footage: 40000
Other Locations:
Packaging Dynamics Ltd.
Hartwell GA

27156 Packaging Dynamics International
17153 Industrial Hwy
Caldwell, OH 43724-9779

740-732-5665
Fax: 740-732-7515
laminations@ici-laminating.com
Manufacturer and exporter of aluminum beverage and can liners, containers for biscuits and sandwich wrap; also, laminated paper
President: Darin Barton
VP: Gerry Medlin
Estimated Sales: $15-20 Million
Number Employees: 50-99
Parent Co: Alupac
Brands:
I-Rap

27157 Packaging Enterprises
12 N. Penn Ave
Rockledge, PA 19046

215-379-1234
Fax: 215-379-1166 800-453-6213
fillers@packagingenterprises.com
www.packagingenterprises.com
Manufacturer and exporter of plastic bags and pouches
President: Lee Sanford
Contact: Terry Geyer
terry@packagingenterprises.com
Estimated Sales: $1-2.5 Million
Number Employees: 1-4
Square Footage: 72000
Type of Packaging: Private Label, Bulk
Brands:
Sobo

27158 Packaging Enterprises
12 N. Penn ave.
Rockledge, PA 19046

215-379-1234
Fax: 215-379-1166 800-453-6213
fillers@packagingenterprises.com
www.packagingenterprises.com
Manufacturer and exporter of filling machinery for liquids and viscous food products
President: Terrence Geyer
VP: Timothy Geyer
Contact: Terry Geyer
terry@packagingenterprises.com
Estimated Sales: $2.5-5 Million
Number Employees: 10-19
Number of Products: 15
Square Footage: 13600
Type of Packaging: Private Label
Brands:
Geyer

27159 Packaging Equipment & Conveyors, Inc
52853 County Road 7
Elkhart, IN 46514-9522

574-266-6995
Fax: 574-264-6210
Manufacturer and exporter of liquid and aerosol filling line equipment; also, modular conveying systems, bi-directional accumulation tables, flight-bar sorters, tube taping machines, orienting systems, de-palletizers, can de-elevatorsand product hoppers
Manager: Dennis Kline
Vice President: Brenda Arbogast
Research & Development: Brad Wegner
Sales Director: Chuck Reed
Operations Manager: Dennis Kline
Estimated Sales: $3 Million
Number Employees: 5-9
Number of Products: 16
Square Footage: 40000
Type of Packaging: Private Label
Brands:
Connect-A-Veyor

27160 Packaging Graphics LLC
60 Delta Dr
Pawtucket, RI 02860-4556

401-725-7700
Fax: 401-727-2700
Blister cards
Manager: Gary Stiffler
Estimated Sales: $20-50 Million
Number Employees: 100-249
Square Footage: 250000

27161 Packaging Group
360 Spinnaker Way
Concord, ON L4K 4W1
Canada

905-761-7040
Fax: 905-761-7266

Supplier of flexible packaging materials. Cello-Foil Holdings has acquired the company as of September 2005
President: Ted Hue
CFO: Frank Petti
Parent Co: Cello-Foil Holdings, Corp

27162 Packaging Machine Service Company
2260 Lithonia Industrial Boulevard
Suite C
Lithonia, GA 30058-4668

770-482-4808
Fax: 770-482-9371 800-871-4764
pmscom@aol.com

Glueformer, in-line tri-seal closer, autoload end load cartoner
Estimated Sales: $1-2.5 Million
Number Employees: 10-19

27163 Packaging Machinery
2303 W Fairview Ave
Montgomery, AL 36108-4158

334-265-9211
Fax: 334-265-9218

Manufacturer and exporter of material handling equipment, designer packaging machinery, conveyors, etc
Finance/Treasurer: Bruce Murchison
Estimated Sales: $1-2.5 Million
Number Employees: 5-9
Type of Packaging: Bulk

27164 Packaging Machinery & Equipment
179-181 Watson Ave
West Orange, NJ 7052

973-325-2418
Fax: 973-325-6937 packmach@aol.com
www.packagingmachineryandequipment.com

Manufacturer and exporter of cartoners and machinery including marking, printing, dating and coding; also, rebuilding of packaging equipment available
President: James Lyle Clark
Secretary: Mary Cameron
Quality Control: Dennis McDermott
Estimated Sales: Below $5 Million
Number Employees: 1-4

27165 Packaging Machinery International
1260 Lunt Avenue
Elk Grove Village, IL 60007-5618

847-640-1512
Fax: 847-640-8732 800-871-4764
www.pmi-intl.com

Manufacturer and exporter of packaging machinery and equipment including shrink wrappers and bundlers
President: Branko Vukotic
CFO: Branko Vukotic
VP: Randy Spahr
Estimated Sales: $5-10 Million
Number Employees: 20-49
Square Footage: 56000

27166 Packaging Machinery Svc
4217 E Jefferson Ave
Fresno, CA 93725-9707

559-834-4400
Fax: 559-834-4835 877-402-1404
pmsc@bellsouth.net
www.packagingmachineryservices.com

Owner: Doug Bridger
tbri591434@aol.com
Estimated Sales: $1-5 Million
Number Employees: 1-4

27167 Packaging Machines International
9511 River St
Schiller Park, IL 60176-1019

847-640-1512
Fax: 847-640-8732 800-871-4764

President: Branko Vukotic
CFO: Randy Swpahr
Estimated Sales: $5-10 Million
Number Employees: 10

27168 Packaging Materials Co
6995 Industrial Ave
El Paso, TX 79915-1116

915-772-9012
Fax: 915-779-8751 800-325-4195
dbarron@writeme.com
www.packagingmaterials.com

Pressure sensitive labels including heat seal, dry gum and bar code
President: Armando Barron
abarron@packagingmaterials.com
VP: Larry Muther
Estimated Sales: Less Than $500,000
Number Employees: 1-4
Square Footage: 64000

27169 Packaging Materials Inc
62805 Bennett Ave
Cambridge, OH 43725-9490

740-432-6337
Fax: 740-439-4718 800-565-8550

Polyethylene film and bags including shrink, bundle wrap, form-fill-seal, on rolls, etc.; also, six color printing available
President: Ron Funk
CFO: Amanda Johnson
VP Manufacturing: Ron Funk
VP Sales: Bill Funk
VP Production: Ron Funk
Estimated Sales: $5-10 Million
Number Employees: 20-49
Type of Packaging: Food Service, Private Label, Bulk

27170 Packaging Partners, Ltd.
951 Thorndale Avenue
Bensenville, IL 60106-1139

630-238-1964
Fax: 630-238-2801

Founder: Grover L. Foote
Sales Representative: Hoyt Diehl
Type of Packaging: Consumer

27171 Packaging Parts & Systems
22831 Avenida Empresa
Rcho Sta Marg, CA 92688

949-888-7221
Fax: 949-888-7112 www.extremepkg.com

Owner: Ray Uttaro
Estimated Sales: $1-3 Million
Number Employees: 1-4

27172 (HQ)Packaging Products Corp
6820 Squibb Rd
Mission, KS 66202-3224

913-262-3033
Fax: 913-789-8698

Manufacturer and exporter of printed and converted flexible packaging materials including sheet and roll
President: Jack Joslin
CEO: Laird Dowgray
dlaird@packagingcorp.com
Sales/Marketing: Laird Dowgray
Sales Manager: Tom Zammit
COO: Jack Joslyn
Billing & Accounts Receivable: Cindy Hansen
Number Employees: 50-99
Square Footage: 74000
Other Locations:
   Packaging Products Corp.
   Rome GA

27173 Packaging Progressions
102 G P Clement Dr
Collegeville, PA 19426-2044

610-489-9096
Fax: 610-489-8394 sales@pacproinc.com
www.pacproinc.com

A full line of stainless steel packaging/processing equipment for the food industry; alignment, centralizer, interleaver, counter stacker
President: Larry Ward
lward@pacproinc.com
Sales Director: Drew Ward
Estimated Sales: $2.5-5,000,000
Number Employees: 20-49
Type of Packaging: Food Service, Private Label, Bulk

27174 Packaging Service Co Inc
1904 Mykawa Rd
Pearland, TX 77581-3210

281-485-4320
Fax: 281-485-3242 800-826-2949
sales@packserv.com www.packserv.com

Contract packager and exporter of charcoal starter, all-purpose cleaners, lamp oil and household chemicals; private labeling available
President: Gean-Pierre Baizan
websales@packserv.com
Quality Control: Carl Caldwell
VP/General Manager: Jean-Pierre Baizan
Manager Grocery/Sales: Larry Lubs
Export Manager: George Foster
Plant Manager: Luis Dela Cruz
Estimated Sales: $20-25 Million
Number Employees: 100-249
Square Footage: 150000

27175 Packaging Solutions
11600 Magdalena Avenue
Los Altos Hills, CA 94024-5150

650-917-1022
Fax: 510-791-7606

Trays, cartons, labels, inserts and cold temperature shippers
President: Clayton Bussey
Co-Owner: Jerry Chaine
Estimated Sales: $1-2.5 Million
Number Employees: 5-9

27176 Packaging Specialties Inc
1663 S Armstrong Ave
Fayetteville, AR 72701-7232

479-521-2580
Fax: 479-521-2748 800-247-3446
gmathews@psi-ark.com

Flexographic printing
President: Kaaren Biggs
CEO: Robert Farrell
rfarrell@psi-ark.com
Estimated Sales: $20-50 Million
Number Employees: 100-249

27177 Packaging Store
1255 Howard St
San Francisco, CA 94103

415-558-8100
Fax: 415-558-0625 www.the-packaging-store.com

Wine industry foam carriers
President: Richard Neill
Contact: Arlen Jenkins
arlen.jenkins@thepackagingstore.com
Estimated Sales: $1-2.5 Million
Number Employees: 20-49

27178 Packaging Systems Automation
2200 Niagara Ln N
Plymouth, MN 55447

763-473-1032
Fax: 763-473-1204

Continuous motion cartoner, pouch flattener
Owner: Steven Swanlund
Estimated Sales: $20-50 Million
Number Employees: 20-49

27179 (HQ)Packaging Systems Intl
4990 Acoma St
Denver, CO 80216-2030

303-244-9000
Fax: 303-298-1016 www.pkgsys.com

Manufacturer and exporter of bag filling and weighing machinery, portable flexible conveyors, bag openers, stackers, palletizers and material handling machinery
President: Michael Lott
mlott@pkgsys.com
Chairman of the Board: H Lott
Quality Control: Jenee Jenee
Sr. VP Sales/Marketing: A Guyton
Estimated Sales: $5-10 Million
Number Employees: 20-49
Square Footage: 150000
Parent Co: St. Regis Paper Company

27180 Packaging Technologies
145 Main St
Tuckahoe, NY 10707-2906

914-337-2005
Fax: 914-337-8519 800-532-1501
info@ptiusa.com www.ptiusa.com

Food packaging, filling, sealing equipment and inspection systems, both visual and package integrity systems. Also, leak testing equipment for filled and empty packages, off-line/SPC and 100% on-line systems, vision inspectionequipment for packages and air-borne ultrasonic systems for seal integrity

President and CEO: Tony Stauffer
R & D: Mike Noller
Vice President: Oliver Stauffer
Marketing Director: Sylvia Stauffer
Sales Manager: Jesse Sklar
Manager: Oliver Stauffer
ostauffer@pti.com
Operations Manager: Heinz Wof
Estimated Sales: $5-10 Million
Number Employees: 20-49

27181 Packaging Technologies
P.O.Box 3848
Davenport, IA 52808-3848

563-391-1100
Fax: 563-391-4951 800-257-5622
sales@packt.com www.ptipacktech.com
Manufacturer and exporter of packaging, food pro-
cessing and analyzing machinery
President: Barry Shoulders
Marketing: Julie Doty
Sales: Tom Riggins
Contact: Mary Baltzell
mary.baltzell@packt.com
Estimated Sales: $37 Million
Number Employees: 100-249
Square Footage: 200000
Parent Co: WKA

27182 Packaging Technologies
145 Main St
Tuckahoe, NY 10707-2906

914-337-2005
Fax: 914-337-8519 info@ptiusa.com
www.ptiusa.com
President: Tony Stauffer
Vice President: Oliver Stauffer
Sales Manager: Jesse Sklar
Manager: Oliver Stauffer
ostauffer@pti.com
Estimated Sales: $10-20 Million
Number Employees: 20-49

27183 Packaging and Converting Hotline
809 Central Ave Suite 200
PO Box 1052
Fort Dodge, IA 50501-1052

515-955-1600
Fax: 515-955-1668 800-247-2000
www.packaginghotline.com
Packing supplies
CEO: Gale W McKinney Ii
Estimated Sales: $50-100 Million
Number Employees: 100-249

27184 Packexpo.Com
11911 Freedom Drive
Suite 600
Reston, VA 20190

703-243-8555
Fax: 703-243-8556 expo@pmmi.org
www.pmmi.org
President: Charles Yuska
Executive Assistant: Corinne Mulligan
CFO: Marry N Japour
Director, Tradeshow Marketing: Jeannine Gibson
Director, Business Intelligence: Paula Feldman
Senior Director, PR/Communications: Julie
Ackerman
Director, Operations: Caroline Abromavage
Vice President, Administration: Katie Bergmann
Number Employees: 20

27185 Packing Material Company
PO Box 252
Southfield, MI 48037

248-489-7000
Fax: 248-489-7009
Manufacurer of boxes, cases, skids, wooden pallets,
packaging films and foams used for temperature sen-
sitivity. Also corrugated products, forest products,
strapping, plastic fabrication and thermal pak
President: James Foster
VP: Gary Turnbull
VP: Gary Turnbull
General Manager: Jack Smylie
Controller: James Gross
Estimated Sales: $1-2.5 Million
Number Employees: 10-19
Number of Products: 11
Type of Packaging: Private Label, Bulk
Brands:
Thermalpak

27186 Packing Specialities
11350 Kaltz Ave
Warren, MI 48089

586-758-5240
Fax: 586-758-3557 sales@packspec.net
www.packspec.net
Corrugated containers
President: Kurt Tabor
Contact: Brian Bazick
bbazick@packspec.net
Manager: Joe Zehel
Estimated Sales: $5-10 Million
Number Employees: 20-49
Parent Co: Ecorse Packaging Specialties

27187 PacknWood
213 W 35th Street
14th Floor
New York, NY 10001

201-604-3840
Fax: 201-604-3863 contact@packnwood.com
www.packnwood.com
Eco-friendly food service products
CEO: Adam Merran
Number Employees: 11-50

27188 Packotronics
1813 Elmdale Avenue
Glenview, IL 60026-1355

947-487-1281
Ovens, makeup lines, depositors, packaging
President: Roger Hollando

27189 Packrite Packaging
3900 Comanche Drive
Archdale, NC 27263

336-431-1111
Folding boxes
General Manager: Hollis Kelley, Sr.
Estimated Sales: $5-10 Million
Number Employees: 50-99
Square Footage: 150000
Parent Co: Caraustar Industries

27190 Packworld USA
539 S Main St
Nazareth, PA 18064-2728

610-746-2765
Fax: 610-759-1766 sales@packworldusa.com
www.packworldusa.com
Sealing machinery including heatseal presses for
tray lidding and irregular shapes, bag/pouch, rotary
belt, etc
President: Charles H Trillich
kfeyti@packworldusa.com
CFO: Kathy Feyti
VP: Helma Young
Quality Control and R&D: Gabe Munoz
General Manager: Frank Welles
Estimated Sales: Below $5 Million
Number Employees: 10-19
Number of Products: 10

27191 Packworld USA
539 S Main St
Nazareth, PA 18064-2728

610-746-2765
Fax: 610-759-1766 sales@packworldusa.com
www.packworldusa.com
Precision validatable heat sealers for accurate tem-
perature control
President: Charles Trillich
kfeyti@packworldusa.com
Estimated Sales: $5-10 Million
Number Employees: 10-19

27192 Pacmac Inc
1501 S Armstrong Ave
Fayetteville, AR 72701-7230

479-521-0525
Fax: 479-521-2448 800-834-1544
fterminella@pacmac.com www.pacmac.com
Manufacturer and exporter of vertical form/fill/seal
machinery
Administrator: Joe Terminella
Manager: Frank Terminella
terminella@pacmac.com
Estimated Sales: $2.5-5,000,000
Number Employees: 20-49
Square Footage: 200000
Brands:
Ter-A-Zip

27193 Pacmaster by Schleicher
130 Wicker St
Sanford, NC 27330-4265

919-775-7318
Fax: 919-774-8731 800-775-7570
soa@interpath.com www.intimus.com
President: Jack Costelloe
Sales: Kathy Ainsworth
Estimated Sales: $10-20 Million
Number Employees: 50-99

27194 Pacmatic Corporation
8325 Green Meadows Drive N
Lewis Center, OH 43035-9451

740-657-8283
Fax: 740-657-8483 800-468-0440
uspacmatic@aol.com
Automatic horizontal bagger from film roll, pallet
stretch wrapper, flowpack wrapping machine
Estimated Sales: $5-10 Million
Number Employees: 10-19

27195 Pacmoore Products
1844 Summer St
Hammond, IN 46320-2236

219-932-2666
Fax: 219-932-3344 866-610-2666
solutions@pacmoore.com www.pacmoore.com
Ingredient processing services
President: Brittany Lewis
britt_cheese@hotmail.com
Corporate Controller: Lee Randall
VP Quality Assurance: Giri Veeramuthu
VP Sales & Marketing: Chris Bekermeier
National Sales Director: Tony Weber
VP Human Resources: Susan Bondy
VP Operations: Scott Reid
VP Engineering: Brent Ness
Estimated Sales: $3.4 Million
Number Employees: 100-249
Type of Packaging: Consumer, Food Service, Pri-
vate Label, Bulk

27196 Paco Label Systems Inc
1 Hombre Dr
Tyler, TX 75707

903-561-2125
Fax: 903-561-3455 800-346-4185
www.pacolabel.com
Labels
Owner: Rowe Anderson
randerson@pacolabel.com
General Manager: Rowe Anderson
Office Manager: Mary June Goodson
Estimated Sales: Below $5 Million
Number Employees: 10-19
Type of Packaging: Bulk

27197 Paco Manufacturing
2120 Addmore Ln
Clarksville, IN 47129-9151

812-283-7963
Fax: 812-283-7992 www.pacomanufacturing.com
Stretch wrap
General Manager/VP: G Morris
Contact: Sue Foulks
mmikes@multisy.com
Estimated Sales: $10-20 Million
Number Employees: 20-49
Square Footage: 70000
Parent Co: Precision Automation Company

27198 Pacosy
8480 Darnley
Mount Royal, QC H4T 1M4
Canada

514-738-4894
Fax: 514-738-8633 contact@pacosy.com
www.pacosy.com
Hand dryers

27199 Pacquet Oneida
1600 Westinghouse Boulevard
Charlotte, NC 28273-6327

973-777-5600
Fax: 973-777-2155 800-631-8388
Laminations for snack food, confectionery, pasta,
bakery and coffee markets
President: Pet Matthais
Number Employees: 200
Parent Co: Butler & Smith
Brands:
Ful-Lok

817

27200 Pactiv
2023 Encino Vista Street
San Antonio, TX 78259-2431
210-481-3280
Fax: 210-481-3281
Territory Manager: Lawrence Treger
Type of Packaging: Consumer

27201 Pactiv LLC
1900 W Field Ct
Lake Forest, IL 60045
800-476-4300
www.pactiv.com
Manufacturer and exporter of bags, cartons, containers, film, trays, etc.
Chief Executive Officer: John McGrath
Year Founded: 1965
Estimated Sales: $7.3 Billion
Number Employees: 11,000
Parent Co: Reynolds Group Holdings, LLC

27202 Pacur
3555 Moser St
Oshkosh, WI 54901-1270
920-236-2888
Fax: 920-236-2882
Manufacturer and exporter of packaging materials; extruder of PET, PP, PETG, CPET, APET, RPET and recycled materials
President: Ron Johnson
rjohnson@pacur.com
R&D: Tim Wiycha
Director Sales/Marketing: Richard Knapp
Estimated Sales: $20-50 Million
Number Employees: 100-249
Square Footage: 80000
Parent Co: Rexham

27203 Paddington Corporation
400 Kelby St
Suite 8
Fort Lee, NJ 07024-2938
201-461-7800
Fax: 201-461-2677 www.paigecompany.com
Storage boxes
Owner: Allan Levine
VP National Accounts: Larry McGinn
VP Sales: Gary Ruvo
Group Brand Manager: Scott Green
Sales Director: Richard Ambler
Brand Manager: John Shavlen
Group Brand Manager: Jaime Friedman
Purchasing Manager: Elaine Griffith
Estimated Sales: $20-50 Million
Number Employees: 1-4
Parent Co: Diageo United Distillers and Vinters

27204 Padinox
489 Brackley Point Road
P.O. Box 20106
Winsloe, PE C1A 9E3
Canada
902-629-1500
Fax: 902-629-1502 800-263-9768
paderno@padinox.ca www.paderno.com
Manufacturer and exporter of stainless steel cookware including pots, pans, gadgets, utensils and bakeware
President: Jim Casey
VP: Tim Casey
Marketing: Scott Chandler
Production: Ernie Bremman
Number Employees: Oover 200
Brands:
  Chaudier
  Paderno

27205 Pafra/Veritec
260 Us Highway 46
Fairfield, NJ 07004-2324
973-575-2752
Fax: 973-575-2649 800-357-2372
Hot and cold adhesive equipment, noncontact gun assemblies, glue detection, bar code verification
Estimated Sales: $1-5 Million
Number Employees: 20-49

27206 Page Slotting Saw Co Inc
3820 Lagrange St
Toledo, OH 43612-1425
419-476-7475
Circular blade machine knives, perforators and slitters for paper, leather and plastic food packaging

President: James Bouldin
General Manager: Bill Gibbons
Estimated Sales: $5-10 Million
Number Employees: 20-49
Square Footage: 16000

27207 Paget Equipment Co
417 E 29th St
Marshfield, WI 54449-5312
715-384-3158
Fax: 715-387-0720 paget@northsidecomp.com
www.pagetequipment.com
Manufacturer and exporter of process control systems, spray dryers, evaporators, tanks, heat exchangers, wet separators, blenders and conveyors
President: James Reigel
jimr@pagetequipment.com
CFO: James Reigel
Quality Control: Steve Desmet
Sales: Richard Wermersen
Project Engineer: Brian Johnson
Estimated Sales: $5-10 Million
Number Employees: 50-99
Square Footage: 88000
Parent Co: JBL International

27208 Pagoda Industries Inc
777 Commerce St
Reading, PA 19608-1308
610-678-8096
Fax: 610-678-8036
Industrial detergents and degreasers including floor cleaners and equipment cleaners
Owner: Dave Weaver
VP Sales: Blair Weaver
ppidave@dejazzd.com
Estimated Sales: Below $5 Million
Number Employees: 1-4
Number of Products: 50
Square Footage: 8000

27209 Pak 2000 Inc
189 Governor Wentworth Hwy
Mirror Lake, NH 3853
603-569-3700
Fax: 603-569-5478
World's leading producer of high quality shopping bags and tamper evidence security bags targeting major brands in sectors such as luxury, cosmetics, fashion & retail, fine food and beverage worldwide. We are equipped to provide acomplete service from concept development through to production, logistics and customer support worldwide
Vice President: William B Gram
CEO: Nina Virga
Vice President: William B Gram
Marketing Director: Veronique Aboohe
VP Sales/Marketing: Mary Sieninmer
Estimated Sales: $20-50 Million
Number Employees: 50-99
Number of Products: 56
Parent Co: Asia Pulp and Paper
Brands:
  Cartier
  Chanel
  Estee Lauder
  Guerlain
  Nordstrom
  Tiffany

27210 Pak Technologies
7025 W Marcia Rd
Milwaukee, WI 53223
414-438-8600
Fax: 414-977-1458
Packager and distributer
Owner: Kevin Scheule
Contact: Jim Barringer
jbarringer@paktech.com

27211 Pak-Rapid
1050 Colwell Ln Bldg 4
Conshohocken, PA 19428
610-828-3511
Fax: 610-828-4290 www.pakrapid.com
Vertical and horizontal packaging machinery for vitamins, liquids and powders
Sales: Jim Wallace
Sales: Lisa Crawford
Estimated Sales: $1-2.5 Million
Number Employees: 10-19
Square Footage: 20000

27212 Pak-Sak Industries I
122 S Aspen St
Sparta, MI 49345-1442
616-887-8837
Fax: 616-887-7411 800-748-0431
www.packagingpersonified.com
Plain and printed polyethylene film and plastic bags
Marketing: Dave Rimer
Marketing Manager: Tom Wright
Business Manager: Doug Dolder
IT Executive: Mark Christensen
paksakacct@voyager.net
Estimated Sales: $20-50 Million
Number Employees: 100-249
Square Footage: 80000
Parent Co: Maxco

27213 Pak-Sher
2500 N Longview St
Kilgore, TX 75662-6840
903-984-8596
Fax: 903-984-1524 www.paksher.com
Carry out, deli, bakery, seafood and hot food bags, interfolded sheets, drink carriers and sine wave bags; also, custom packaging available
President: John Decker
jdecker@att.eu
VP Sales/Marketing: Tom Croninn
Estimated Sales: $20-50 Million
Number Employees: 100-249

27214 Paket Corporation
9165 S Lake Shore Dr
Chicago, IL 60617
773-221-7300
Fax: 773-221-7316 info@paketcorp.com
www.paketcorp.com
Contract packager of private label items.
President: Mark O'Malley
Vice President Sales: Carvel Massengale
Estimated Sales: $8-10 Million
Square Footage: 210000
Type of Packaging: Private Label

27215 Paket Corporation/UniquePack
9165 S. Harbor Avenue
Chicago, IL 60617-4436
773-221-7300
Fax: 773-221-7316 www.paketcorp.com
Packaging service
President: Mark O'Malley
Controller: Stella Diaz
Vice President of Manufacturing: Mike Hintz
Estimated Sales: $3-5 Million
Number Employees: 20-49

27216 Pakmark
PO Box 228
Chesterfield, MO 63006-0228
636-532-7877
Fax: 636-532-9634 800-423-1379
pakmark@pakmark.com
Manufacturer and exporter of decorative pressure sensitive labels and tapes; also, hot-stamped and embossed foil
Estimated Sales: $1-2.5 Million
Number Employees: 10-19
Brands:
  Signette

27217 Paktronics Controls
23555 Telegraph Road
Southfield, MI 48033-4129
248-356-1400
Fax: 248-356-0829 info@maxitrol.com
www.maxitrol.com
Manufacturer, importer and exporter of temperature controls
President: David Sundberg
Inside Sales: Toni Thompson
Purchasing Manager: Linda McCleskey
Estimated Sales: $2.5-5 Million
Number Employees: 10
Square Footage: 21600
Parent Co: Maxitrol Company
Brands:
  Beta Series
  Pakstat
  Paktronics
  Trakstat

27218 Palace Packaging Machines Inc
4102 Edges Mill Rd
Downingtown, PA 19335-1954
610-873-7252
Fax: 610-873-7384 palace@unscramblers.com
www.unscramblers.com
Plastic bottle handling and cap/lid feeding systems.
Component feeding and counting systems also available for food, beverage, and medical applications
President: Stephen Taraschi
cserve@unscramblers.com
Marketing: Stephen Taraschi
Estimated Sales: $5-10 Million
Number Employees: 20-49
Square Footage: 70000

27219 Paley-Lloyd-Donohue
125 Bayway Ave
Elizabeth, NJ 07202-3006
908-352-5835
Fax: 908-352-8042
Janitorial supplies including cheesecloth and germicidal multi-purpose cleaners
President: Bill Paley
CFO: Bill Paley
VP: Rick Paley
Estimated Sales: $5-10 Million
Number Employees: 5-9
Square Footage: 40000
Brands:
   Lemon Kleen 32

27220 Palintest USA
1455 Jamike Ave # 100
Suite 100
Erlanger, KY 41018-3147
859-341-7423
Fax: 859-341-2106 info@palintestusa.com
www.palintest.com
Water testing equipment
Vice President: Ken Kershner
ken.kershner@palintestusa.com
VP: David Miller
VP: David Miller
Estimated Sales: $1-2.5 Million
Number Employees: 10-19
Parent Co: The Halma Group

27221 Pall Corp
25 Harbor Park Dr
Port Washington, NY 11050-4664
516-484-5400
Fax: 516-484-5228 866-905-7255
foodandbeverage@pall.com www.pall.com
The largest and most diverse filtration, separations and purifications company in the world. For the food and beverage industries, Pall has developed filtration and advanced filtration systems that meet market needs for reliability andcost effectiveness.
President/CEO/CFO: Lawrence D. Kingsley
President, Life Sciences: Yves Baratelli
President, Industrial: Ruby Chandy
Vice President, Finance & Treasurer: R. Brent Jones
Chief Technology Officer: Michael Egholm, Ph.D
Senior Vice President, Business Developm: H. Alex Kim
Chief Human Resources Officer: Linda Villa
Senior Vice President, Global Operations: Kenneth V. Camarco
Estimated Sales: Over $1 Billion
Number Employees: 10000+

27222 Pall Corp
25 Harbor Park Dr
Port Washington, NY 11050-4664
516-484-5400
Fax: 516-484-5228 866-905-7255
foodandbeverage@pall.com www.pall.com
Researching and developing filtration and advanced separation systems that will help improve the quality of products for the food and beverage processor.
Chairman & Chief Executive Officer: Lawrence Kingsley
CEO: Rainer Blair
rainer_blair@pall.com
Chief Financial Officer: Akhil Johri
CEO: Eric Krasnoff
Chief Technology Officer: Michael Egholm
SVP, Corporate Strategy: H. Alex Kim
Market Sales Manager: Kathleen Berry
Senior Vice President, Operations: Richard Jackson
Estimated Sales: Over $1 Billion
Number Employees: 10000+

27223 Pall Corp
25 Harbor Park Dr
Port Washington, NY 11050-4664
516-484-3600
Fax: 516-801-9754 foodandbeverage@pall.com
www.pall.com
Filtration, seperations, and purification products.
President: Jennifer Honeycutt
SVP, Finance General & Administrator: Jeffrey Figg
SVP & General Counsel: Cathleen Colvin
Chief Technology Officer: Martin Smith
SVP, Global Operations: Wayne Hewitt
VP, Business Development & Strategy: Martin Wirtz
President, Pall Industrial: Naresh Narasimhan
Year Founded: 1946
Estimated Sales: $2.7 Billion
Number Employees: 10,000+

27224 Pall Filtron
50 Bearfoot Rd # 1
Northborough, MA 01532-1551
508-393-1800
Fax: 508-393-1874 800-345-8766
piannucci@pall.com www.pall.com
Filtration and separation systems for food and beverage applications
Sr. VP: Jamie Monat
VP Sales: Piers O'Donnell
Contact: Engin Ayturk
engin_ayturk@pall.com
Estimated Sales: $20-50 Million
Number Employees: 50-99
Parent Co: Pall Group
Other Locations:
   Pall Filtron
   Shinagawa-Ku
Brands:
   Emflon
   Fluorodyne
   Hdc Ii
   Pallcell
   Pallsep
   Profile Ii Plus
   Ultipleat
   Ultipor Gf/Gf Plus
   Ultipor N66

27225 Pallet Management Systems
PO Box 339
Lawrenceville, VA 23868-0339
804-848-2164
Fax: 804-848-4888 800-446-1804
New and used wooden, metal and plastic pallets; also, pallet repair, management, distribution and recovery services available
Chairman/CEO: Johnary Lucy
Director: Donald Norwood
Estimated Sales: $20-50 Million
Number Employees: 100-249
Square Footage: 63000

27226 Pallet Masters
655 E Florence Ave
Los Angeles, CA 90001-2319
323-758-1713
Fax: 323-758-9600 800-675-2579
Pallets
Owner: Steve Anderson
Inside Sales Manager: Bridgette Lathem
sanderson@palletmasters.com
General Manager/Controller: Tim Hwang
Estimated Sales: Below $5 Million
Number Employees: 20-49
Parent Co: Trojan Transportation

27227 Pallet One Inc
1470 US Highway 17 S
Bartow, FL 33830-6627
863-533-1147
Fax: 863-533-3065 800-771-1148
sales@PalletOne.com www.palletone.com
Pallets
Chairman, President, CEO: Howe Wallace
CFO: Casey A Fletcher
cfletcher@palletone.com
VP and CFO: Casey Fletcher
Vice President of Sales: Keith Reinstetle
Chief Operating Officer: Al Holland
Estimated Sales: Less than $500,000
Number Employees: 1000-4999
Square Footage: 160000

27228 Pallet One Inc
1470 US Highway 17 S
Bartow, FL 33830-6627
863-533-1147
Fax: 863-533-3065 800-771-1148
www.palletone.com
Manufacturer and exporter of wooden pallets and harvesting bins
CEO/President/Chairman: Howe Q. Wallace
CFO: Casey A Fletcher
cfletcher@palletone.com
Vice President: Donnie Isaacson
Vice President of Sales: Keith M. Reinstetle
COO: Matt B. Sheffield
Estimated Sales: $10-20 Million
Number Employees: 1000-4999
Parent Co: IFCO

27229 Pallet One Inc
165 Turkey Foot Rd
Mocksville, NC 27028-5930
336-492-5565
Fax: 336-492-5682
Wooden pallets and skids
Cmo: Ed Cartner
ecartner@palletone.com
Estimated Sales: $1-5 Million
Number Employees: 100-249
Parent Co: Palex Company

27230 Pallet Pro
9980 Clay County Hwy
Moss, TN 38575-6333
931-258-3661
Fax: 931-258-3280 800-489-3661
barkybeaver@info-ed.com
Pallets
Manager: Mary Strong
CEO: J Smith
Quality Control: Jackie Trent
VP Manufacturing: J Wix
VP Marketing: K Donaldson
Estimated Sales: $10-20 Million
Number Employees: 20-49
Square Footage: 30000

27231 Pallet Reefer International LLC
4000 Highway 56
Houma, LA 70363-7817
731-616-2219
Fax: 985-868-3715 800-259-3693
lsaia@palletreefer.com
Member of the Board: Louis P Salia III
Number Employees: 10,000+

27232 Pallet Service Corp
11201 90th Ave N
Maple Grove, MN 55369-4048
763-391-8020
Fax: 763-391-8026 888-391-8020
sales@palletservice.com www.palletservice.com
Pallets; also, recycling of cardboard available
President: Robert Wenner
palletserv@aol.com
Sales: Tom Saari
Manager: Scott Wicklund
Estimated Sales: $5-10 Million
Number Employees: 50-99

27233 Pallets Inc
99 1/2 East St
PO Box 326
Fort Edward, NY 12828-1813
518-747-4177
Fax: 518-747-3757 sales@pltsinc.com
www.palletsincorporated.com
Wooden pallets, skids and crates
President: Clint Binley
cbinley@palletsincorporated.com
Sales Manager: Clinton Binley
Estimated Sales: $2.5-5 Million
Number Employees: 20-49

27234 Pallister Pallet
14035 70th Street
Wapello, IA 52653-9596
319-523-8161
Fax: 319-523-5429
Wooden pallets
Secretary/Treasurer: Heather Pallister
VP: Ted Pallister
Estimated Sales: $3 Million
Number Employees: 20-49
Square Footage: 90000

27235 Pallox Incorporated
7221 Hickory Ln
Onsted, MI 49265
517-456-4101
Fax: 517-456-7821
Manufacturer and exporter of wooden pallets, skids and boxes; also, pallet repair and design available; also heat treat pallets for ISPM-15 standard
President: R J Moore
Estimated Sales: $2.5 Million
Number Employees: 20-49
Number of Products: 100
Square Footage: 36000

27236 Palm Bay Imports
301 Yamato Road
Suite 1150
Boca Raton, FL 33487-4917
561-362-9642
Fax: 561-362-7296 800-872-5622
Wines
Logistics: Frank Vella
Marketing Director: Dana Friedman
Sales Manager: Patty Becker
Human Resources Manager: Rosemary Olenick
Estimated Sales: $38 Million
Number Employees: 100-249
Type of Packaging: Consumer, Bulk
Brands:
 Alexander Grappa
 Aneri
 Anselmi
 Bauchant
 Bertani
 Blue Fish
 Bodegas Campillo
 Boissiere
 Bottega Vinaia
 Boulard
 Brown Brothers
 Candido
 Cavit
 Circus
 Citra
 Col Dorcia
 Ey
 Firstland
 Frapin
 Frotious
 Santana
 Sella & Mosca

27237 (HQ)Palmer Distributors
23001 W Industrial Dr
St Clair Shores, MI 48080-1187
586-498-2900
Fax: 586-772-4627 800-444-1912
sales@palmerpromos.com
www.palmerpromos.com
Manufacturer and exporter of display cases, card holders, bowls, tray covers, light boxes and syrup bottles
President: Jim Palmer
jpalmer@palmerpromos.com
VP: Mark Armstrong
Food Service Sales Manager: Michael Lacoursiere
Estimated Sales: $10-20 Million
Number Employees: 50-99
Square Footage: 100000
Type of Packaging: Food Service
Brands:
 Pdi
 Ppp

27238 Palmer Fixture Company
1255 Winford Ave
Green Bay, WI 54303-3707
950-884-8698
Fax: 920-884-8699 800-558-8678
info@palmerfixture.com www.palmerfixture.com
Manufacturer, importer and exporter of paper towel, tissue, and napkin dispensers including a universal hands-free towel dispenser
Owner: Bill Palmer
Vice President: Greg Kampschroer
Contact: Siggi Witt
siggi@palmerfixture.com
Purchasing Manager: Chris Worth
Estimated Sales: $820,000
Number Employees: 7
Square Footage: 44000
Brands:
 Economy

Holdit
Natures Plumber

27239 Palmer Snyder
400 N Executive Drive
Brookfield, WI 53005-6068
262-780-8780
Fax: 262-780-8790 800-762-0415
lpage@palmersnyder.com www.palmersnyder.com
Manufacturer and exporter of plywood and plastic folding tables, wooden folding chairs maintenence free, galerie series chairs and transport cars for tables and chairs
CEO: Richard Bibler
VP Sales: Craig Clarke
Sales Representative: Chelsea Stecker
Estimated Sales: $1-2.5 Million
Number Employees: 100-250
Square Footage: 600000
Parent Co: Palmer Snyder
Other Locations:
 Palmer Snyder
 Elkhorn WI
Brands:
 Palmer Snyder

27240 Palmer Wahl
234 Old Weaverville Rd
Asheville, NC 28804-1260
828-658-3131
Fax: 828-658-0728 800-421-2853
info@palmerwahl.com
Manufactures temperature and pressure instrumentation. Process Industrial and RTD thermometers, Bimetal, Dial and Sanitary thermometers, infrared thermal imagers, Temperature Recording Labels and Chart Recorders, Pressure gauges andThermowells.
Owner: Stephen Santangelo
Vice President: Schuyler Tilly
Quality Control: Paul Lankford
VP Sales: Gary Lux
Brands:
 All Star
 Cleanliners
 Digi-Stem
 Heat Prober
 Heat Spy
 Temp-Plate

27241 Palmetto Canning
3601 US Highway 41 N
Palmetto, FL 34221
941-722-1100
pcrbaggs@tampabay.rr.com
palmettocanning.com
Canning and packaging sauces and beverage
Estimated Sales: $5-10 Million
Number Employees: 1-4
Square Footage: 128000
Type of Packaging: Consumer, Private Label
Brands:
 Palmalito

27242 Palmetto Packaging
1131 Edwards Cir
Florence, SC 29501-2838
843-662-5800
Fax: 843-662-5668
CustomerService@palmettopackaging.com
Corrugated and fiber boxes
President: David Searcy
HR Executive: John Taylor
jtaylor@palmettopackaging.com
Estimated Sales: $5-10 Million
Number Employees: 50-99

27243 Palmland Paper Company
708 NE 2nd Ave
Fort Lauderdale, FL 33304
954-764-6910
Fax: 954-779-3849 800-266-9067
Paper place mats, dinner and cocktail napkins, etc
Chairman of the Board: Bernard Beauregard
Secretary: Linda Dunn
Estimated Sales: $2.5-5 Million
Number Employees: 5-9
Square Footage: 16000

27244 Palo Alto Awning
750 W San Carlos
San Jose, CA 95126
650-968-4270
Fax: 650-968-3676 800-400-4270
info@PaloAltoAwning.com
www.paloaltoawning.com

Commercial awnings
President: John Ashman
Estimated Sales: $1-2.5 Million
Number Employees: 10-19

27245 Paltier
1701 Kentucky St
Michigan City, IN 46360
219-872-7238
Fax: 219-872-9480 800-348-3201
Manufacturer and exporter of engineered storage rack systems including cantilever and drive-in/drive-thru
VP/General Manager: James Washington
Plant Manager: Glenn Clark
Estimated Sales: $20-50 Million
Number Employees: 100-249
Square Footage: 110000
Parent Co: Lyon Metal Products
Type of Packaging: Food Service
Brands:
 Interchange
 Pal Dek
 Pal Gard
 Paltier

27246 Pamco Label Co Inc
2200 S Wolf Rd
Des Plaines, IL 60018-1934
847-803-2200
Fax: 847-803-2209 info@pamcolabel.com
www.resourcelabel.com
Pressure sensitive tape and labels
Cmo: Danny Fishbein
dfishbein@pamcolabel.com
Controller: Maureen Brandes
CEO: Alan M Berkowitz
Vice President of Operations: Dave Heaster
Estimated Sales: $10 Million
Number Employees: 100-249
Square Footage: 52000

27247 Pan American Papers Inc
5101 NW 37th Ave
Miami, FL 33142-3232
305-635-2534
Fax: 305-635-2538 jvl@panampap.com
www.panampap.com
Distributors of paper
Sr. VP: Jesus Roca
panampap@bellsouth.net
Executive VP: Francisco Valdes
Estimated Sales: $20-50 Million
Number Employees: 10-19
Square Footage: 80000

27248 Pan Pacific Plastics Inc
26551 Danti Ct
Hayward, CA 94545-3917
510-785-6888
Fax: 510-785-6886 888-475-6888
panpacplastics@aol.com
Manufacturer, exporter and importer of plastic bags
President: Ying Wang
mtan@pppmi.com
Marketing/Sales: Mike Tan
Sales Exec: Mike Tan
Estimated Sales: $20-50 Million
Number Employees: 20-49
Square Footage: 40000
Parent Co: Pan Pacific Group Companies
Type of Packaging: Consumer, Food Service, Private Label, Bulk

27249 Panamerican Logistics
1270 Woolman Pl
Atlanta, GA 30354-1392
404-767-1700
Fax: 404-559-4380
Handling facitility
Owner: Camilo Bundia
operations@panamlogistics.com
Estimated Sales: $3-5 Million
Number Employees: 10-19

27250 Panasonic Commercial Food Service
2 Riverfront Plaza
Newark, NJ 07102
na.panasonic.com/us/industries/food-service-technology
Commercial microwave ovens, vacuum cleaners, compact fluorescent light bulbs and ventilating fans; importer of rice cookers.

CEO, US Company: Mototsugu Sato
Year Founded: 1918
Estimated Sales: $79 Billion
Number Employees: 257,533
Brands:
Panasonic

27251 Panhandler, Inc.

PO Box 1329
Cordova, TN 38088-1329

800-654-7237
Fax: 901-336-6377 panhandlerpads@yahoo.com
www.panhandlerinc.com
Manufacturer and exporter of pot holders, bakers'
gloves and bakery oven pads
Owner: Don White
CEO: Sherrie Nischwitz
Vice President: Christy Graves
Number Employees: 8
Square Footage: 24000
Type of Packaging: Food Service
Brands:
Panhandler Safety-Wall
Panhandler Twin-Terry

27252 Panoramic Inc

1500 N Parker Dr
Janesville, WI 53545-0732

608-754-8850
Fax: 608-754-5703 800-333-1394
packages@panoramicinc.com
www.panoramicinc.com
Food, Retail and Industrial Packaging, Stock PET
Food Tubs/Containers. Thermoformed Plastic Clam-
shells, Blisters, Trays, Containers, Custom Packag-
ing Designs, Rigid Set-Up Boxes (Box/Tray
Combinations). Contract Packaging/Fulfill-
ment.In-House Design, Tooling, Prototypes
Cio/Cto: Charlie Miller
charlie.miller@panoramic.com
CEO: Rick Holznecht
Estimated Sales: $20-50 Million
Number Employees: 100-249

27253 Panther Industries Inc

8990 Barrons Blvd # 101
Highlands Ranch, CO 80129-2347

303-703-9876
Fax: 720-283-9462 800-530-6018
sales@print-n-apply.com www.print-n-apply.com
Supplies labeling equipment for the food industry
President: James Thompson
jthompson@print-n-apply.com
CFO: James Thompson
R&D: James Thompson
Quality Control: Jim Thompson
Estimated Sales: $1 Million
Number Employees: 5-9

27254 Paoli Properties

2531 11th St
Rockford, IL 61104-7219

815-965-0621
Fax: 815-965-5393
Manufacturer and exporter of one-step deboners and
desinewers for meat, poultry and seafood
President: Louis Paoli
info@stephenpaoli.com
CFO: Louis Paoli
Sales: Neal Ryan
General Manager: Shawn Lee
Estimated Sales: $5-10 Million
Number Employees: 10-19
Square Footage: 760000
Brands:
Paoli One Step

27255 Papelera Puertorriquena

PO Box 119
Utuado, PR 00641-0119

787-894-2098
Fax: 787-894-0517
Paper and plastic bags
President: Jose A Rios Montalvo
Manager: Jose Rios
Number Employees: 80
Parent Co: All Plastic Products

27256 Paper Box & Specialty Co

1505 Sibley Ct
Sheboygan, WI 53081-2456

920-459-2440
Fax: 920-459-2463 888-240-3756
Linda.quast@paperboxandspecialty.com
www.paperboxandspecialty.com
Manufacturer and exporter of set-up and folding car-
tons, poly-coated cheese liners and gift boxes
President: David Van Der Puy
Contact: Nicole Spielvogel
tgesch@pathconit.com
Estimated Sales: $2.5-5 Million
Number Employees: 20-49
Square Footage: 150000

27257 (HQ)Paper Converting MachineCompany

2300 S Ashland Ave
Green Bay, WI 54304

920-494-5601
Fax: 920-494-8865 www.pcmc.com
Printing presses print narrow to wide flexographic
printing on film, paper, labels, non-woven board
stock.
President: Tim Sullivan
Vice President of Sales: Mark Zastrow
Sales Engineer: Mike Callahan
mikecallahan@pcmc.com
Year Founded: 1919
Estimated Sales: $237 Million
Number Employees: 1,000
Parent Co: Barry-Wehmiller Companies, Inc.

27258 Paper Converting Machine Company

1163 Glory Rd
Green Bay, WI 54304

920-494-5601
Fax: 920-494-8865 www.pcmc.com
Printing presses print narrow to wide flexographic
printing on film, paper, labels, non-woven board
stock.
Square Footage: 880000
Parent Co: Barry-Wehmiller Companies Inc
Other Locations:
Aquaflex
Boucherville, PQ Canada
Brands:
Aquaflex
Chromas
Els
Fpc
Instaprep

27259 Paper Machinery Corp

8900 W Bradley Rd
Milwaukee, WI 53224-2822

414-354-8050
Fax: 414-354-8614 info@papermc.com
www.papermc.com
Paperboard cup and package forming machines
Owner: Donald W Baumgartner
donaldbaumgartner@papermc.com
CFO: Scott Koehler
CEO: Donald W Baumgartner
Estimated Sales: $20-50 Million
Number Employees: 100-249

27260 Paper Pak Industries

1941 N White Ave
La Verne, CA 91750-5663

909-392-1750
Fax: 909-392-1732 www.paperpakindustries.com
Meat and poultry absorbent pads
COO: Dennis Murphy
VP Packing Products: Jim Gillispie
Manager: Bob Schindel
bschindel@paperpakindustries.com
Estimated Sales: $20-50 Million
Number Employees: 50-99
Brands:
Dri-Sheet
Securely Yours
Zap Soakers

27261 (HQ)Paper Pak Industries

1941 N White Ave
La Verne, CA 91750-5663

909-392-1750
Fax: 909-392-1760
salesinfo@paperpakindustries.com

Supplier of absorbent product packaging to the lead-
ing food processors, supermarket chains, and pack-
aging manufacturers and distributors
President/CEO: Ron Jensen
VP/General Counsel: Marty Michael
Director of Technology: Sayandro Versteylen
VP Sales/Marketing: John Terrien
Manager: Bob Schindel
bschindel@paperpakindustries.com
Estimated Sales: $15-$18 Million
Number Employees: 50-99
Type of Packaging: Food Service, Bulk

27262 Paper Product Specialties

PO Box 363
Waukesha, WI 53187-0363

262-549-1730
Fax: 262-549-3614 www.lauterbachgroup.com
Pressure sensitive labels and tags; also, heat seal pa-
per and flexible packaging
President: Shane Lauterbach
Marketing/Sales: Dean Dimitriou
Estimated Sales: $20-50 Million
Number Employees: 50-99
Square Footage: 50000

27263 Paper Products Company

1543 Queen City Ave
Cincinnati, OH 45214

513-921-4717
Fax: 513-251-5553
info@paperproductscompany.com
www.paperproductscompany.com
Folding cartons and foil laminated, poly coated
nested bakers' trays
President: Dennis Smith
Sales Manager: Jim Davis
Contact: Karen Campbell
karen@paperproductscompany.com
Estimated Sales: $5-10 Million
Number Employees: 20-49
Brands:
Bakers' Gold

27264 Paper Service

PO Box 45
Hinsdale, NH 03451-0045

603-239-6344
Fax: 603-239-8861 www.paperservice.com
Manufacturer and exporter of paper napkins, wrap-
ping and tissue paper
CEO: G O'Neal
Operations Manager: R O'Neal
Estimated Sales: $10-20 Million
Number Employees: 20-49
Square Footage: 400000
Type of Packaging: Food Service, Private Label

27265 Paper Systems Inc

6127 Willowmere Dr
Des Moines, IA 50321-1230

515-280-1111
Fax: 515-280-9219 800-342-2855
nate@paper-systems.com
Manufacturer and exporter of pallets and disposable
and returnable bulk containers for food grade liquids
and powders
Owner: William Chase
psi@paper-systems.com
Estimated Sales: Below $5 Million
Number Employees: 10-19
Type of Packaging: Bulk
Brands:
Ez-Bulk
Ez-Flow
Ez-Pak
Ez-Pallet
Stack-Sack

27266 Paper Tubes Inc

15900 Industrial Pkwy
PO Box 35140
Cleveland, OH 44135-3322

216-362-2964
Fax: 216-362-2980 800-343-8823
sales@custompapertubes.com
www.custompapertubes.com
Produce custom containers for the food industry.
Samples available upon request

President: Jodi Lombardo
jlombardo@custompapertubes.com
Founder: Luther Stevens
Sales Director: Phil VanDuyn
Vice President of Sales & Marketing: Kevin Kline
Marketing Manager: Emily Miller
Assistant Sales Manager: David Esper
Manufacturing Director: Paula Murad
Estimated Sales: Below $5 Million
Number Employees: 20-49
Square Footage: 30000
Type of Packaging: Consumer, Private Label

27267 Paper Tubes Inc
15900 Industrial Pkwy
PO Box 35140
Cleveland, OH 44135-3322

216-362-2964
Fax: 216-362-2980 800-343-8823
sales@custompapertubes.com
www.custompapertubes.com
Cosmetic pakaging, food grade packaging and see
through packaging
President: Jodi Lombardo
jlombardo@custompapertubes.com
Founder: Luther Stevens
Vice President of Sales/Marketing: Kevin Kline
Marketing Manager: Emily Miller
Assistant Sales Manager: David Esper
Manufacturing Director: Paula Murad
Number Employees: 20-49

27268 Paper Works Industries Inc
8800 Sixty Rd
Baldwinsville, NY 13027-1235

315-638-4355
Fax: 315-638-8421 800-847-5677
www.paperworksindustries.com
High barrier rotogravure printed folding cartons
made from recycled boxboard; also, can and bottle
carriers
CEO: Carlton Highsmith
Logistics: Leo Basciano
Manufacturing: Robert Derby
Plant Manager: Leo Basciano
Estimated Sales: $50-100 Million
Number Employees: 100-249
Parent Co: Lawson Mardon Group

27269 Paper-Pak Products
9740 Canterbury Street
Leawood, KS 66206-2106

913-341-7524
Fax: 913-341-7553 rcrossland@paperpak.com
Regional Sales Manager: Robin Crossland

27270 Paperbag Manufacturers Inc
4131 NW 132nd St
Opa Locka, FL 33054-4510

305-685-1100
Fax: 305-685-2200 888-678-2247
baglady@paperbag.com www.paperbag.com
Bags for packaging tea, coffee and more
Vice President: Susan Hernandez
baglady@paperbag.com
Owner: Adam Cohen
VP: Susan Hernandez
Estimated Sales: $1 Million
Number Employees: 10-19

27271 Papertech
108-245 Iell Avenue
North Vancouver, BC V7P 2K1
Canada

604-990-1600
Fax: 604-990-1606 877-787-2737
info@papertech.ca www.papertech.ca
Manufacturer and exporter of dairy processing
equipment including clean-in-place systems, milk
processors and process control instruments
President: Kari Hilden
Marketing Coordinator: Tanja Kannisto
Number Employees: 30
Brands:
    Optec

27272 Paperweights Plus
3661 Horseblock Road
Suite Q
Medford, NY 11763-2232

631-924-3222
Fax: 631-345-0752

Manufacturer, importer and exporter of advertising
specialties including emblems, ID badges, name
plates, lapel pins, key rings and paperweights
President: Darlene Reynolds
Estimated Sales: Less than $500,000
Number Employees: 1-4
Square Footage: 1700

27273 Papillon Ribbon & Bow
35 Monhegan Street
Clifton, NJ 07013

973-928-6128
Fax: 973-246-1065 800-229-2998
sales@papillonusa.com www.papillonusa.com
Packaging ribbons and bows
President: Wong Vinci
Vice President Finance: Jimmy Cheung
Marketing: Dan Schwatzbach
Contact: Jimmy Cheung
j.cheung@papillonusa.com
Estimated Sales: $7.6 Million
Number Employees: 40

27274 Pappas Inc.
575 E Milwaukee St
Detroit, MI 48202

313-873-1800
Fax: 313-875-7805 800-521-0888
info@pappasinc.com www.pappasinc.com
Makers of fine cutlery, emulsifying equipment,
blades, parts and supplies.
Contact: John Pappas
john@pappasinc.com

27275 Paques ADI
182 Main St
Unit 6
Salem, NH 03079

603-890-5434
Fax: 603-898-3991
Supplier of wastewater treatment systems:, anaero-
bic, UASB, aerobic, hybrid
VP: Al Cocci
Estimated Sales: $1-5 Million
Number Employees: 5-9

27276 Par-Pak
3450 Lang Rd
Houston, TX 77092

713-686-6700
Fax: 713-686-5553 www.parpak.com
Rigid plastic containers
Owner: Mohammed Ebrahim
VP Sales: David Goralski
Contact: Courtney Adkinson
courtneyadkinson@gmail.com
Operations Manager: Ali Virani
Estimated Sales: $5-10 Million
Number Employees: 20-49
Square Footage: 96000
Parent Co: Par-Pak

27277 (HQ)Par-Pak
14345 Northwest Freeway
Houston, TX 77040

713-686-6700
Fax: 713-686-5553 888-727-7252
www.parpak.com
Manufacturer and exporter of clear plastic contain-
ers for food packaging; also, catering trays
President: Sajjad Ebrahim
VP Technical: Dominic DiDomizio
VP Sales: David Goralski
Estimated Sales: $5-10 Million
Number Employees: 20-49
Square Footage: 210000
Brands:
    Cake-Mix
    Ebony
    Invisi-Bowl
    Invisible Packaging
    Quartz Collection

27278 Parachem Corporation
2733 6th Ave
Des Moines, IA 50313

515-280-9445
Fax: 515-280-7600
Manufacturer and exporter of hand soap, hand soap
dispensers, anti-bacterial soap systems in leaf form,
etc

President: Beryl Halterman
Marketing Manager: Carla Stephens
Office Manager: Dean Blum
Purchasing Manager: Dean Blum
Estimated Sales: Below $5 Million
Number Employees: 1-4
Square Footage: 48000
Parent Co: Flightags
Brands:
    Cleaf
    Jardin Savon

27279 Paraclipse
2271 E 29th Ave
Columbus, NE 68601-3166

402-563-3625
Fax: 402-564-2109 800-854-6379
ljochen@paraclipse.com www.paraclipse.com
Manufacturer and exporter of decorative indoor
lighted fly traps and industrial fly traps for public
dining areas, kitchen and food preparation areas.
Outdoor lighted mosquito trap for restaurant outside
serving areas and patios.
CFO: Cheryl Ditter
Sales Manager: Len Jochens
Manager: Abby Cremers
acremer@paraclipse.com
Estimated Sales: $3-6 Million
Number Employees: 10-19
Square Footage: 216000
Brands:
    Insect Inn Iv

27280 Parade Packaging
333 Washington Blvd
Mundelein, IL 60060

847-566-6264
Fax: 847-566-2017
Plastic bags and films
General Manager: Jerry Alexander
Manager: Scott Silverstein
s.silverstein@fortuneplastics.com
Estimated Sales: $10-20 Million
Number Employees: 50-99
Parent Co: Parade Packaging Materials

27281 (HQ)Paradigm Packaging Inc
1252 E Seventh Ave
Upland, CA 90786

909-985-2750
Fax: 909-985-8463
Injection blow-molded plastic containers and injec-
tion molded closures
President: Robert Donnahoo
VP: Mike Mc Allister
Customer Service: Sophia Ibara
Estimated Sales: $10-20 Million
Number Employees: 1-4
Other Locations:
    Trans Container Corp.
    West Valley City UT
Brands:
    Trc

27282 Paradigm Technologies
PO Box 25540
Eugene, OR 97402-0457

541-345-5543
Fax: 541-345-5549 paratech@presys.com
Food and dairy processing equipment and material
handling equipment
Owner: Charles Nutter
Brands:
    Alan Bradley
    Ge

27283 Paradise Inc
1200 W Dr. Martin Luther King Jr. blvd.
Plant City, FL 33563-5155

813-752-1155
Fax: 941-754-3168 paradisefruitco@hotmail.com
www.paradisefruitco.com
Candied fruits
Chairman/CEO: Melvin Gordon
President/Director: Randy Gordon
rgordon@paradisefruitco.com
Senior Vice President, Sales: Tracy Schulis
Executive Vice President: Mark Gordon
VP/Corporate Sales: Ron Peterson
Estimated Sales: $21 Million
Number Employees: 100-249
Number of Brands: 6
Square Footage: 275000
Type of Packaging: Consumer, Food Service, Pri-
vate Label, Bulk

Brands:
PARADISE
PENNANT
SUNRIPE
MOR-FRUIT
DIXIE BRAND
WHITE SWAN

27284 Paradise Plastics
116 39th St
Brooklyn, NY 11232-2712

718-788-3733
Fax: 718-965-4030
www.f.t.domdex.com/fc14kparadisepictures
Plastic garbage bags
President: Kathy Cooper
kcooper@paradiseplastics.com
Estimated Sales: $20-50 Million
Number Employees: 20-49

27285 Paradise Products
PO Box 568
El Cerrito, CA 94530-0568

510-524-8300
Fax: 510-524-8165 800-227-1092
100 page catalog of theme decorations and party
supplies for special events and sales promotions
cateterias and clubs
Controller: Alice Rickey
Sales: Shirley Imai
Number Employees: 14
Number of Products: 3000
Square Footage: 80000
Brands:
Fling Decorating Kits

27286 Paragon Electric Company
PO Box 28
Two Rivers, WI 54241-0028

920-793-1161
Fax: 920-793-3736
Refrigeration defrost controls for walk-in and
reach-in coolers and refrigerated display cases
VP/General Manager: Bob Stalder
Sales Manager: Mike Simino
Estimated Sales: $20-50 Million
Number Employees: 500

27287 Paragon Films Inc
3500 W Tacoma St
Broken Arrow, OK 74012-1164

918-250-3456
Fax: 918-355-3456 800-274-9727
jpt@paragon-films.com www.paragonfilms.com
Manufacturer and exporter of packaging materials
including stretch and specialty films and hand ap-
plied and pallet stretch wrap
President: Mike Baab
mbaab@paragon-films.com
Estimated Sales: $20-50 Million
Number Employees: 100-249

27288 Paragon Group USA
3433 Tyrone Boulevard N
St Petersburg, FL 33710-1136

727-341-0547
Fax: 727-302-9816 800-835-6962
Manufacturer and exporter of ozone generators de-
signed to electronically eliminate odors without the
use of chemicals; also, food preservation equipment
President: David Kocksten
R & D: Phillip Rod
VP Sales: Susan Duffy
Purchasing Manager: Chuch Pacino
Estimated Sales: $1-2.5 Million
Number Employees: 10
Square Footage: 20800
Brands:
Zontec

27289 Paragon International
731 W 18th St
Nevada, IA 50201-7847

515-382-8000
Fax: 515-382-8001 800-433-0333
www.manufacturedfun.com
Manufacturer and exporter of popcorn machines and
carts
Owner: Dave Swegle
Quality Control: Bill Tierce
VP Sales/Marketing: Tom Berger
Manager Customer Service: Sandra Holubar

Estimated Sales: $3-5,000,000
Number Employees: 20-49
Square Footage: 25000
Brands:
1911 Originals
Thrifty Pop

27290 Paragon Labeling
1607 9th St
St Paul, MN 55110-6717

651-429-7722
Fax: 651-429-6006 800-429-7722
info@paragonlabeling.com
www.paragonlabeling.com
Manufacturer and exporter of printing machines and
supplies and custom labeling systems
Director of Label Manufacturing Operatio: Karla
Bridgeman
CFO: Ed Clarke
Vice President: Craig Blonigen
VP: Craig Blonigen
Sales/Marketing: Craig Blonigen
Contact: Randy Black
randyb@lowrycomputer.com
Operations Manager: Ken Koehler
Production Manager: Matt Thoreson
Plant Manager: Ken Koehler
Estimated Sales: $5 Million
Number Employees: 5-9
Square Footage: 160000
Parent Co: Lowry Computer Products Company
Brands:
Paragon

27291 Paragon Labeling
1607 9th St
St Paul, MN 55110-6717

651-429-7722
Fax: 651-429-6006 800-429-7722
info@paragonlabeling.com
www.paragonlabeling.com
Labels, labeling machines, print and apply labelers,
ribbons, printers, and scanners
Director of Label Manufacturing Operatio: Karla
Bridgeman
Sr. VP: David Heiff
VP: Craig Boligen
Contact: Randy Black
randyb@lowrycomputer.com
Estimated Sales: $12 Million
Number Employees: 5-9

27292 (HQ)Paragon Packaging
7700 Centerville Rd
Ferndale, CA 95536

707-786-4004
Fax: 707-786-4014 888-615-0065
Rfcohn@gmail.com
Gift packaging including boxes and plastic contain-
ers
Owner: Ron Cohn
Production Manager: Ed Davis
Estimated Sales: $1-2.5 Million
Number Employees: 1-4
Square Footage: 3000

27293 Parallel Products Inc
401 Industry Rd
Louisville, KY 40208-1692

502-471-2444
Fax: 813-289-4283 800-883-9100
CustomerServices@parallelproducts.com
www.parallelproducts.com
Processing technologies for food wastes
President: Gene Keisel
genek@parallelproducts.com
Controller: David Kenney
Vice President of Business Development: Tim
Cusson
Vice President Sales and Marketing: Ken Reese
National Sales Manager: Ed Stewart
Corporate HR Manager, Director of Corpor: Hal
Park
Vice President of Operations: Bob Pasma
National Customer Service Manager: Denise Gibson
Plant Manager: Russ Hohn
Number Employees: 10-19

27294 Paramount Industries
304 N Howard Ave
PO Box 259
Croswell, MI 48422

810-679-2551
Fax: 810-679-4045 800-521-5405
piisales@paramountlighting.com
www.paramountlighting.com
High performance lighting for specialized environ-
ments
President: Craig Bailey
piiadv@paramountlighting.com
VP Sales: Derryl Fewins
Sales: Angie Smiley
Plant Manager: Jim Jarchow
Estimated Sales: Below $5 Million
Number Employees: 50-99
Square Footage: 90000
Brands:
Aerolux
Cleanroom
Craft Lite
Guardcraft
Techniseal
Vandalume

27295 (HQ)Paramount ManufacturingCompany
353 Middlesex Ave
Wilmington, MA 1887

978-657-4300
Fax: 978-658-5215
Store fixtures, cafeteria counters and table and wall
units
Owner: Louis Tarantino
Contact: Joseph Chinnis
joseph.chinnis@paramountmfg.com
Estimated Sales: $2.5-5 Million
Number Employees: 10-19

27296 Paramount Packaging Corp
1221 Walt Whitman Rd
Melville, NY 11747-3010

516-333-8100
Fax: 516-333-9720 ppc735@aol.com
www.paramountcontainer.com
Designer and builder of custom food equipment and
machinery that include sanitary conveyor system, reciprocating nose conveyor/feeder system, high speed
bread product slicing and separating, and band saw
bread products slicing andseparating
Owner: Shawn Murphy
dave@nyli.com
Number Employees: 10-19

27297 Paramount Packing & Rubber Inc
4012 Belle Grove Rd
Baltimore, MD 21225-2699

410-789-2233
Fax: 410-789-2238 866-727-7225
info@paramountpacking.com
www.paramountpacking.com
Gaskets
President: Jay Huber
info@paramountpacking.com
CEO: James Huber
Vice President: Byron Huber
Quality Control: Joe Kammerzel
Sales Director: Joel Hayer
Estimated Sales: $500,000-$1 Million
Number Employees: 5-9
Number of Brands: 100
Number of Products: 85
Square Footage: 15000
Type of Packaging: Consumer

27298 Parasol Awnings
4834 Hickory Hill Rd
Memphis, TN 38141

901-368-4477
Fax: 901-368-1798 sales@parasolawnings.com
Commercial awnings
Manager: Michael Folk
Contact: Marie Anthony
manthony@parasolawnings.com
Chief Manager: Michael Fold
Estimated Sales: $2.5-5 Million
Number Employees: 10-19

27299 Paratherm Corporation
31 Portland Rd
Conshohocken, PA 19428
610-941-4900
Fax: 610-941-9191 800-222-3611
info@paratherm.com www.paratherm.com
Manufacturer and exporter of food-grade heat transfer fluids for precise and uniform temperature control in food processing applications
President: John Fuhr
Research & Development: Jim Oetinger
Marketing Director: Andy Andrews
Sales Director: Jim Oetinger
Contact: Andy Andrews
aandrews@paratherm.com
Purchasing Manager: Anne Grabowski
Estimated Sales: $2.5-5 Million
Number Employees: 1-4
Number of Brands: 1
Number of Products: 9
Square Footage: 20000
Brands:
Paratherm Nf
Paratherm Or

27300 Parish Manufacturing Inc
7430 New Augusta Rd
Indianapolis, IN 46268-2291
317-872-0172
Fax: 317-872-1242 800-592-2268
www.parishmfg.com
Manufacturer and exporter of bag-in-box liquid packaging systems
President: Richard Smith
rsmith@parishmfg.com
Estimated Sales: $10-20 Million
Number Employees: 20-49
Square Footage: 56000
Type of Packaging: Consumer, Food Service, Bulk

27301 Parisi Inc
305 Pheasant Run
Newtown, PA 18940-3423
215-968-6677
Fax: 215-968-3580
Manufacturer and exporter of bars, booths, counters, tabletops and buffet equipment; also, bakery, confectionery and deli display cases
President: Ron Germain
rgermain@parisi-royal.com
CFO: Gary Graf
Marketing Director: Eleanor Parisi
Sales Director: Dave Moore
Sales: Bill Matnias
Operations Manager: Steve Dickier
Estimated Sales: $10-20 Million
Number Employees: 50-99
Square Footage: 180000

27302 (HQ)Parisian Novelty Company
17859 Tipton Ave
Homewood, IL 60430
773-847-1212
Fax: 773-847-2608
Printed plastic signs and labels
General Manager: Norman Weinberg
Estimated Sales: less than $500,000
Number Employees: 50-100

27303 Parity Corp
11812 N Creek Pkwy N # 204
Bothell, WA 98011-8202
425-487-0997
Fax: 425-487-2317 www.paritylink.com
Manufacturer and exporter of accounting, systems integration and inventory control software
Owner: Arvid Tellevik
atellevik@paritycorp.com
R & D: John Ratliff
VP: George Fletcher
Office Administrator: Cindy Kouremetis
Estimated Sales: $5-10,000,000
Number Employees: 20-49
Square Footage: 4000

27304 Parity Corp
11812 N Creek Pkwy N # 204
Suite 204
Bothell, WA 98011-8202
425-487-0997
Fax: 425-487-2317 Info@ParityCorp.com
Develops specialized software and related services for the food industry; industry specific business management tools

Owner: Arvid Tellevik
atellevik@paritycorp.com
Estimated Sales: $5-10 Million
Number Employees: 20-49

27305 Park Custom Molding
940 S Park Avenue
Linden, NJ 07036-1646
908-486-8882
Fax: 908-486-1376
Plastic packaging products
VP Sales: Edward Joffe
Estimated Sales: $2.5-5 Million
Number Employees: 20-49

27306 Parker Sales & Svc
69 Parker Ln
Sparta, NC 28675-8341
336-372-2812
Fax: 336-372-4119 filtersrus@skybest.com
www.psasinc.com
Dust collection filters
Owner: Charles Moyer
chuckm@psasinc.com
Estimated Sales: $5-10 Million
Number Employees: 20-49
Square Footage: 40000

27307 (HQ)Parker-Hannifin Corp
6035 Parkland Blvd
Cleveland, OH 44124
216-896-3000
Fax: 216-896-4000 800-272-7537
c-parker@parker.com www.parker.com
Motion control technologies and systems, providing precision-engineered solutions.
President & Chief Operating Officer: Lee Banks
Chairman & Chief Executive Officer: Thomas Williams
twilliams@parker.com
Executive VP Finance/Admin. & CFO: Catherine Suever
VP/General Counsel/Secretary: Joseph Leonti
Year Founded: 1917
Estimated Sales: $14.3 Billion
Number Employees: 57,170

27308 Parker-Hannifin Corp
HVAC Filtration Division
100 River Ridge Circle
Jeffersonville, IN 47130
Fax: 866-601-1809 866-247-4827
www.parker.com
Filtration products including filter bags, cartridges and systems.
President & Chief Operating Officer: Lee Banks
Chairman & Chief Executive Officer: Thomas Williams
Brands:
Fulflo

27309 Parker-Hannifin Corp
Electromechanical & Drives Division
1140 Sandy Hill Rd
Irwin, PA 15642
Fax: 707-584-8015 800-358-9070
www.parker.com
PC-based control, HMI software, industrial PCs, OI workstations.
President & Chief Operating Officer: Lee Banks
Chairman & Chief Executive Officer: Thomas Williams

27310 Parker-Hannifin Corp
Gas Separation & Filtration Division
4087 Walden Ave
Lancaster, NY 14086
978-858-0505
Fax: 978-478-2501 800-343-4048
www.balstonfilters.com
Parker Balston filters, compressed air dryers, and nitrogen generators.
President & Chief Operating Officer: Lee Banks
Chairman & Chief Executive Officer: Thomas Williams

27311 Parker-Hannifin Corp
Hose Products Division
30242 Lakeland Dr
Wickliffe, OH 44092
440-943-5700
Fax: 440-943-3129 ihporders@parker.com
www.parker.com

Food and beverage hoses with internally expanded couplings; internal expansion crimpers available.
President & Chief Operating Officer: Lee Banks
Chairman & Chief Executive Officer: Thomas Williams

27312 Parkland
PO Box 266342
Houston, TX 77207-6342
713-926-5055
Fax: 713-926-7358
Manufacturer and exporter of air conditioners, refrigerators and heating and ventilation equipment
President: J P Landers
Office Manager: John Rosales
Number Employees: 10
Type of Packaging: Food Service

27313 (HQ)Parkson Corp
1401 W Cypress Creek Rd # 100
Fort Lauderdale, FL 33309-1969
908-464-0700
Fax: 954-974-6182 www.parkson.com
Manufacturer and exporter of bulk material conveyors, bucket elevators and slide and diverter gates; importer of shaftless spirals
Owner: Steven Lombardi
CEO: Zain Mahmood
Director Marketing: Charlene Low
Estimated Sales: $1-2.5 Million
Number Employees: 250-499
Square Footage: 120000
Parent Co: Conelco
Brands:
Corra-Trough

27314 Parkson Corp
562 Bunker Ct
Vernon Hills, IL 60061-1831
847-816-3700
Fax: 847-816-3707 technology@parkson.com
www.parkson.com
Provider of equipment and systems for water/process water and wastewater treatment including screens, sand filters, dewatering presses, inclined plate clarifiers, conveyors, filter presses, sludge thickeners and thermodryers andaeration
President: Axel Johnson, Inc
CEO: William Acton
Marketing Director: Charlene Low
Sales Director: Michael Miller
Number Employees: 10-19
Parent Co: Parkson Corporation
Brands:
American Bulk Conveyors
Hycor Screening & Dewatering Equip.
Parkson Dynasand Gravity Filters
Parkson Lamella Plate Settlers

27315 Parkson Corporation
PO Box 408399
Fort Lauderdale, FL 33340-8399
954-974-6610
Fax: 954-974-6182 www.parkson.com
Supplier of innovative, cost effective solutions for potable water, process water, and industrial and municipal wastewater problems.
President/CEO: Zain Mahmood
Estimated Sales: G
Number Employees: 250-499
Parent Co: Axel Johnson Company

27316 Parkway Plastic Inc
561 Stelton Rd
Piscataway, NJ 08854-3868
732-752-3636
Fax: 732-752-2192 800-881-4996
sales@parkwayjars.com
www.store.parkwayjars.com
Manufacturer and exporter of polystyrene, linear polyethylene and polypropylene jars, bottles, boxes and caps
President: Debbie Coyle
dcoyle@parkwayproducts.com
Estimated Sales: $10-20 Million
Number Employees: 50-99

27317 Parlor City Paper Box Co Inc
2 Eldredge St
Binghamton, NY 13901-2600
607-772-0600
Fax: 607-772-0806 parcitybox@aol.com
Manufacturer and exporter of trays and printed folding boxes

President: David Culver
Sales/Marketing: Jeffrey Culver
Office Manager: Juanita Mendez
Estimated Sales: $5-10 Million
Number Employees: 20-49
Square Footage: 204000

27318 Parrish's Cake Decorating

225 W 146th St
Gardena, CA 90248-1803
310-324-2253
Fax: 310-324-8277 800-736-8443
Aluminum cake pans, cookie cutters, artificial icing, candy molds, plates and pillars, pastry bags, food colors and flavorings
President: Bob Parrish
customerservice@parrishsmagicline.com
VP: Norma Parrish
Estimated Sales: $1-3 Million
Number Employees: 10-19
Number of Products: 4000
Square Footage: 180000
Type of Packaging: Consumer, Food Service, Private Label, Bulk
Brands:
  Magic Line
  Magic Mist
  Magic Mold
  Perma-Ice

27319 Parsons Manufacturing Corp.

1055 Obrien Dr
Menlo Park, CA 94025
650-324-4726
Fax: 650-324-3051
Manufacturer and exporter of sample cases, tote boxes, travel cases and shipping cases
Owner: Alan Parsons
VP Sales/Marketing: Steve Wurzer
Contact: Alan Hall
alan.hall@parsons.com
Estimated Sales: $20-50 Million
Number Employees: 20-49

27320 Parta

2000 Summit Rd
Kent, OH 44240-7140
330-678-7745
Fax: 330-676-6310 800-543-5781
www.partaonline.org
Set-up paper boxes, vacuum formed parts, plastic lids and folding cartons
Secretary, Treasurer, General Manager, P: John Drew
jdrew@partaonline.org
Estimated Sales: $5-10 Million
Number Employees: 100-249
Square Footage: 200000

27321 Partex Corporation

G-4415 Richfield Road
Flint, MI 48506
810-736-5656
Fax: 810-736-5100
Parts for ice cream dispensing equipment
Number Employees: 5

27322 Particle Sizing Systems

8203 Kristel Circle
Port Richey, FL 34668
727-846-0866
Fax: 727-846-0865 sales@pssnicomp.com
www.pssnicomp.com
Particle sizers
President: David Nicoli
Finance Manager: Carrey Hasapidis
Bookkeeper: Inge Griffith
Head Marketing: Patrick Ohagen
Contact: Heather Belfi
belfi@pssnicomp.com
Head Production: Chris Rowan
Purchasing Manager: Ray Ruttan
Estimated Sales: $2.5-5 Million
Number Employees: 20-49
Square Footage: 12000

27323 Partner Pak

5322 Oceanus Dr # 101
Huntington Beach, CA 92649-1031
714-799-7879
Fax: 714-799-2858 info@partnerpak.com
www.partnerpak.com
Owner: Gary Eddington
gary@partnerpak.com

Estimated Sales: $1-3 Million
Number Employees: 5-9

27324 Partners International

PO Box 27
Hanover, NH 03755-0027
603-643-8574
Fax: 603-643-3835
Consultant specializing in international acquisitions and export development
VP: Joan Drape
Estimated Sales: $1-5 Million

27325 Partnership Resources

1069 10th Ave SE
Minneapolis, MN 55414-1388
612-331-2075
Fax: 612-331-2887 www.partnershipresources.org
Manufacturer and exporter of electric infrared heating systems and based power controllers
Manager: Dan Mc Calister
danmccalister@partnershipresources.org
Chief Executive Officer: Norm Munk
Marketing Manager: James Lee
Manager: Dan Mc Calister
danmccalister@partnershipresources.org
Chief Operating Officer: Julie Zbaracki
Number Employees: 50-99
Square Footage: 360000
Brands:
  Chambir
  Controlir
  Hi-Tempir
  Lineir
  Paneir
  Spotir
  Stripir

27326 Party Linens

7780 S Dante Ave
Chicago, IL 60619
773-731-9281
Fax: 773-731-7669 800-281-0003
www.partylinens.com
Manufacturer and importer of specialty linens and table skirting for various table shapes
Owner: Ed Denormandie
Estimated Sales: $2.5-5 Million
Number Employees: 10-19
Square Footage: 20000
Parent Co: DeNormandie Towel & Linen

27327 Party Perfect Catering

3030 Audley Street
Houston, TX 77098-1926
713-522-3932
Fax: 713-522-1746 800-522-5440
Catering, event and kitchen production software
Owner: Ruth Meric
Sales Manager: Kelly Folk

27328 Party Yards

950 S Winter Park Drive
Suite 101
Casselberry, FL 32707-5451
407-696-9440
Fax: 407-696-6963 877-501-4400
partyyards@aol.com www.partyyards.com
Manufacturer, importer and exporter of plastic cups
VP: Andrew Baron
Sales Contact: Peter Dorney
Estimated Sales: $2.5-5 Million
Number Employees: 5-9
Square Footage: 48000
Parent Co: Party Yards
Brands:
  Glow
  Glow Shots
  Party Yards

27329 Parvin Manufacturing Company

6033 W Century Blvd # 1180
Los Angeles, CA 90045-6424
310-645-4411
Fax: 323-585-0427 800-648-0770
Manufacturer, importer and exporter of protective clothing and supplies including oven/barbecue mitts, aprons, skillet handle covers and insulated pizza delivery bags
Owner: Michael Provan
VP: Rick Resnick
Estimated Sales: $10-20 Million
Number Employees: 5-9
Square Footage: 68000

Brands:
  Flameguard
  Footguard
  Pro-Cut

27330 Pasco Poly Inc

407 River Dock Rd
Weiser, ID 83672-5819
208-549-1861
Fax: 208-549-0530 www.pascopoly.com
Wine industry tanks
Chairman of the Board: David D Rule
Estimated Sales: Less Than $500,000
Number Employees: 1-4

27331 Pasquini Espresso Co

1501 W Olympic Blvd
Los Angeles, CA 90015-3803
213-739-8826
Fax: 213-385-8774 800-724-6225
pasquini@pasquini.com www.pasquini.biz
Manufacturer and exporter of commercial espresso equipment
President: Ambrose Pasquini
pasquini@pasquini.com
VP: Guy Pasquini
National Sales Manager: Sergio Laganiere
Estimated Sales: Below $5 Million
Number Employees: 20-49
Square Footage: 24000
Type of Packaging: Food Service

27332 Pasta Filata International

154 Pine Street
Montclair, NJ 07042-4910
973-744-6640
Fax: 973-744-1488
Estimated Sales: $1-5 Million
Number Employees: 2

27333 Pastabiz Pasta Machines

2129 Harrison St
San Francisco, CA 94110-1321
415-431-5049
Fax: 415-621-4613 www.brickovens.biz
Pasta machines
Owner: Emilio Mitidieri
info@pastabiz.com
Estimated Sales: $300,000-500,000
Number Employees: 5-9

27334 Pastry Art & Design

12 W 37th St # 9
New York, NY 10018-7480
212-239-0855
Fax: 212-967-4184
Magazine
President: Michael Schneider
Estimated Sales: $3-5 Million
Number Employees: 10-19

27335 Patchogue-Medford Library

54-60 East Main Street
Patchogue, NY 11772
631-654-4700
Fax: 631-289-3999 www.pmlib.org
Information source
Manager: Dina M Chrils
Contact: John Marcozzi
jmarcozzi@seds.org
Number Employees: 100-249

27336 Pate International

2350 Taylor St # 1
Suite 1
San Francisco, CA 94133-1818
415-928-4400
Fax: 415-928-0690 info@pateinternational.com
www.pateinternational.com
Wine industry packaging
President: Susan Pate
susan@pateinternational.com
Estimated Sales: Less Than $500,000
Number Employees: 1-4

27337 Pater & Associates

P.O.Box 54884
Cincinnati, OH 45254
Fax: 513-474-4829 payday11@aol.com
Printed and plain flexible packaging films, pouches, and bags; folding paperboard cartons; bag closing equipment and loks

Owner: James Pater Jr
CFO: James Pater Jr
Sales: James Pater Jr
Purchasing Director: James Pater Jr

27338 Patio Center Inc
1507 Eraste Landry Rd
Lafayette, LA 70506-1996
337-233-9896
Fax: 337-232-7178 patiocenter@patiocenter.com
Commercial awnings
President: Herman D Richard
VP: Ryan Richard
Estimated Sales: Below $5 Million
Number Employees: 20-49

27339 Patio King
10744 SW 190th St
Cutler Bay, FL 33157-7616
305-316-7508
www.patioking.com
Gas and charcoal outside and commercial barbecues
for restaurants
Contact: King Patio
Secretary: Edith Garcia
Estimated Sales: $1-2.5 Million
Number Employees: 1-4
Square Footage: 6000

27340 Patlite Corp
20130 S Western Ave
Torrance, CA 90501-1307
310-328-3222
Fax: 310-328-2676 888-214-2580
sales@patlite.com www.patlite.com
Visual and audible warning devices
President: Fumio Sawamura
Sales: Sandra Rodriguez
Number Employees: 10-19

27341 Patrick & Co
2100 N Stemmons Fwy # Tm2927
Suite 2927
Dallas, TX 75207-3001
214-761-0900
Fax: 214-761-1985 info@patrickandcompany.com
Metal signs, name plates, badges, office supplies,
stationery and furniture
Owner: Patrick Ongena
Sales Manager: Mark Rodby
Estimated Sales: $500,000-$1 Million
Number Employees: 1-4

27342 Patrick E. Panzarello Consulting Services
8001 Grove Street
Sunland, CA 91040-2111
818-353-0431
Fax: 818-951-6638
Consultant specializing in architectural design ser-
vices, health department permits
President: Patrick Panzarello
CEO: Mike Hess
CFO: Ed Navarrette
Estimated Sales: 200000

27343 Patrick Signs
5411 Randolph Rd
Rockville, MD 20852
301-770-6200
Fax: 301-770-0083 jpn123@prodigy.net
Signs; also, installation services available
Owner: Constance Nusbaum
Estimated Sales: $1-5 Million
Number Employees: 20-49

27344 Patterson Fan Co Inc
1120 Northpoint Blvd
Blythewood, SC 29016-8873
803-691-4750
Fax: 803-691-4751 800-768-3985
info@pattersonfan.com www.pattersonfan.com
Industrial fans, air movement equipment
President: Vance Patterson
Regional Manager: Albert Howell
Vice President, Chief Operating Officer: Thomas
Salisbury
Estimated Sales: $10-20 Million
Number Employees: 50-99

27345 Patterson Industries
250 Danforth Road
Scarborough, ON M1L 3X4
Canada
416-694-3381
Fax: 416-691-2768 800-336-1110
process@pattersonindustries.com
www.pattersonindustries.com
Designers, engineers and manufacturers of quality
time proven equipment for the food industries; Rib-
bon and Paddle mikers, ThoroBlender Double Cone
Blenders, Conaform Double Cone Vacuum Dryers,
Ribbon and Paddle type round bodydryers, pressure
vessels and heat exchangers and general mixing and
agitation equipment
President: H Haischt
CFO: Seth Mendonza
Research & Development: Mike Lindsey
Sales Director: M Lindsey
Estimated Sales: $2,500,000
Number Employees: 10-20
Square Footage: 120000
Brands:
 Conaform
 Thoroblender

27346 (HQ)Patterson Laboratories
11930 Pleasant Street
Detroit, MI 48217-1620
313-843-4500
Fax: 313-843-9416
Industrial chemicals and cleaners including bottled
ammonia, bleaches, window cleaners and detergents
VP Produce: Darrell Cardwell
Administration: Richard Hodgkinson
Estimated Sales: $1-5 Million
Number Employees: 50-99
Square Footage: 180000
Brands:
 Blue Ribbon
 Ful-Value
 Steer Clear

27347 (HQ)Patterson-KelleyHars Company
PO Box 458
East Stroudsburg, PA 18301-0458
570-421-7500
Fax: 570-421-8735 www.patkelco.com
Batch and continuous blenders, dryers, compact wa-
ter heaterand gas fired boilers for commercial, insti-
tutional and industrial applications
Manager: Mark Lasewicz
Marketing Director: Ruth Ann Rocchio
Sales Manager: Jef Potters
Contact: Christine Bushta
c.bushta@patkelco.com
Estimated Sales: $35 Million
Number Employees: 100-249
Square Footage: 200000
Brands:
 Cross-Flow
 Twin-Shell
 Zig-Zag

27348 Patty O Matic Machinery
185 Squankum Rd
Farmingdale, NJ 07727-3753
732-938-2757
Fax: 732-938-5809 877-938-5244
info@pattyomatic.com www.pattyomatic.com
Molding equipment for meat, seafood, vegetables,
etc.; also, meat preparation machinery, portion con-
trol equipment and weight control equipment
Owner: Daniel Miles
Sales Director: Daniel Miles
daniel.miles@wtwinter.com
Estimated Sales: $1-2.5 Million
Number Employees: 5-9
Brands:
 Patty-O-Matic

27349 Patty Paper Inc
1955 N Oak Dr
Plymouth, IN 46563-3412
574-935-8439
Fax: 574-936-6053 800-782-1703
www.pattypaper.com
Manufacturer and supplier of specialty papers for
wrapping meat, cheese and deli items, bakery style
picking paper and waxed paper.
Manager: Sherry Simmons
Number Employees: 1-4

27350 Paul G. Gallin Company
222 Saint Johns Avenue
Yonkers, NY 10704-2717
914-964-5800
Fax: 914-964-5293
Manufacturer and exporter of uniforms and accesso-
ries
Estimated Sales: $25-50 Million
Number Employees: 18
Square Footage: 12000
Type of Packaging: Bulk

27351 Paul Hawkins Lumber Company
RT 2 Box 387A
Mannington, WV 26582
304-986-2230
Wooden lift truck pallets
Owner: Paul Hawkins
Estimated Sales: $2.5-5 Million
Number Employees: 1-4

27352 Paul Mueller Co Inc
1600 W Phelps St
Springfield, MO 65802
417-575-9000
800-683-5537
contact@paulmueller.com www.paulmueller.com
Stainless steel processing systems and equipment for
the food, dairy, beverage, chemical, pharaceutical,
biotechnology, and pure water industries. Also the
erection of vessels in the field, expanded scope,
transportation and electricalcontrols.
President & CEO: David Moore
Chief Financial Officer: Ken Jeffries
General Manager, Business Development: Gregg
Shirey
Markting Manager: Jay Holden
Human Resources Manager: Denise Silvey
Financial & Operations Manager: Michael Payne
Year Founded: 1940
Estimated Sales: $200 Million
Number Employees: 1000-4999
Square Footage: 975000
Other Locations:
 Osceola IA
Brands:
 Accu-Therm
 Avalanche
 Maximice
 Pyropure
 Sentry Ii
 Temp Plate
 Vapure

27353 Paul N. Gardner Company
316 NE 1st St
Pompano Beach, FL 33060-6608
954-946-9454
Fax: 954-946-9309 800-762-2478
gardner@gardco.com www.gardco.com
Producer of physical testing instruments. Their
brands include Gardco and EZ Zahn Viscosity Cup.
President: Paul Gardner
tjohns@gardco.com
Vice President, International Sales: Sandra Bride
Marketing: Sherri Thompson
Sales Manager: Bill Bride
Manager, Customer Service: Cheryl Wilson
Manager & Director: Lisa Richards
Estimated Sales: $7 Million
Number Employees: 33

27354 Paul O. Abbe
P.O.Box 80
Bensenville, IL 60106-0080
630-350-2200
Fax: 630-350-9047 sales@pauloabbe.com
www.aaronequipment.com
Manufacturer and exporter of tumble and agitated
mixers and blenders for powders and solids; also,
batch vacuum and fluidized dryers and ball and peb-
ble mills
VP: Alan Cohen
Vice President of Business Development: Bruce
Baird
Estimated Sales: $5-10 Million
Number Employees: 20-49
Square Footage: 140000
Brands:
 Fluidized
 Forberg Ii
 Rota-Blade
 Rota-Cone

27355 Paul O. Abbe
139 Center Avenue
Little Falls, NJ 07424-2220
973-256-4242
Fax: 973-256-0041 sales@pauloabbe.com
www.pauloabbe.com
Chemical processing equipment: ball and pebble
mills, vacuum dryers, blenders and mixers
VP: Allen Cohen
Estimated Sales: $10-20 Million
Number Employees: 4

27356 Paul T. Freund Corporation
P.O.Box 130
Palmyra, NY 14522
315-597-4873
Fax: 315-597-4188 800-333-0091
Set-up, paper covered and candy boxes
CEO: Paul Freund Jr
VP Marketing: Thomas Farnham
Estimated Sales: $10-20 Million
Number Employees: 100-249

27357 Pavailler Distribution Company
232 Pegasus Avenue
Northvale, NJ 07647-1904
201-767-0766
Fax: 201-767-1723
Bakery equipment
Estimated Sales: $2.5-5 Million
Number Employees: 9
Square Footage: 22400

27358 Pavan USA Inc
Connelly Rd
Emigsville, PA 17318
717-767-4889
Fax: 717-767-4656 www.pavan.com
Design and engineering of technologies and
intergrated product lines for cereal base food.
President: Dave C Parent
VP/General Manager: David Parent
Estimated Sales: $1-3 Million
Number Employees: 1-4
Square Footage: 20000
Parent Co: Pavan SrL
Brands:
  Mapimpianti
  Pavan
  Toresani

27359 Paxall
7300 Monticello Ave
Skokie, IL 60076-4025
847-677-7800
Fax: 847-677-7139
Tea and coffee industry packaging machines
Estimated Sales: $1-5 Million
Number Employees: 1-4

27360 Paxar
500 E 35th Street
Paterson, NJ 07504-1720
973-684-6564
Fax: 973-684-0235
Woven labels
Estimated Sales: $20-50 Million
Number Employees: 20-49

27361 Paxon Polymer Company
Baton Rouge
Baton Rouge, LA 70892
225-775-4330
Fax: 225-774-6632
Estimated Sales: $1-5 Million

27362 Paxton Corp
86 Tupelo St # 5
Unit 5
Bristol, RI 02809-2837
401-396-9062
Fax: 203-925-8722 paxton@paxtoncorp.com
Food processing machines such as cutters, slicers,
shredders, dicers, graters, and strip cutters, for vege-
tables, fruits, cheeses, and nuts
President: Leif Jensen
paxton@paxtoncorp.com
CFO: Monica Wingard
Sales Director: Steven King
Estimated Sales: $3-5 Million
Number Employees: 1-4
Square Footage: 30000
Brands:
  Alexanderwerk

Hallde
Paxton

27363 Paxton North America
5300 Port Royal Road
Springfield, VA 22151
703-321-7600
Fax: 703-321-9426 800-336-4536
info@paxton.com www.paxton.com
Plastic tote containers and bulk boxes
Estimated Sales: Below $500,000
Number Employees: 7

27364 Paxton Products Inc
10125 Carver Rd
Blue Ash, OH 45242-4798
513-891-7474
Fax: 513-891-4092 800-441-7475
sales@paxtonproducts.com
www.paxtonproducts.com
A leader in energy saving, application-specific air
systems. Designs and manufactures compact, en-
ergy-efficient compressors, blowers, air knives and
drying systems.
General Manager: Barbara Stefl
Engineering Manager: Steve Pucciani
Quality Control: Charlie Hertel
International Sales Manager: Rick Immell
Customer Service: Anne Tomsic
Operations Manager: Stan Coley
Buyer: Sherry Driskell
Number Employees: 20-49

27365 Payne Controls Co
Rocky Step Rd
Scott Depot, WV 25560
304-757-7353
Fax: 304-757-7305 800-331-1345
info@PaynEng.com www.payneng.com
Manufacturer and exporter of material handling equipment and SCR controls for ma-
terial handling equipment and SCR controls for ov-
ens and process temperature controls
President: Roger Westfall
roger@payneng.com
Manager Marketing Services: Jean Miller
Estimated Sales: $5-10 Million
Number Employees: 10-19
Square Footage: 72000
Brands:
  Sentrol 3l
  Sentrol Em3

27366 Pci Membrane Systems Inc
1615 State Route 131
Milford, OH 45150-2667
513-575-3500
Fax: 513-575-7393
Membrane filtration
CEO: Sandy Maxwell
Vice President: David Pearson
Estimated Sales: $500,000-$1 Million
Number Employees: 5-9

27367 Peace Industries
1100 Hicks Rd
Rolling Meadows, IL 60008-1016
847-259-1620
Fax: 847-259-9236 800-873-2239
pchartier@spotnails.com www.spotnails.com
Manufactures a wide range of industrial fastening
products including nails, staples, pins, brads and
tools for use in packaging, furniture/woodworking,
construction, factory-built housing and many other
industries.
President: Mark R Wilson
CFO: Rex Janderman
Vice President: Win Waterman
Marketing Director: Candi Mortenson
Sales Director: Win Waterman
Contact: Leon Larosa
llarosa@spotnails.com
Plant Manager: Sy Akbari
Purchasing Manager: Alice Mortenson
Estimated Sales: $10-20 Million
Number Employees: 50-99
Type of Packaging: Bulk

27368 (HQ)Peacock Crate Factory
225 Cash St
PO Box 1110
Jacksonville, TX 75766
903-586-0988
Fax: 903-586-7476 800-657-2200

Manufacturer and exporter of wood veneer gift, fruit
and vegetable baskets; also, store fixtures and
displays
President: Richard S Peacock
CFO: Claudia Vastal
Vice President: Speedy Peacock
Estimated Sales: Below $5 Million
Number Employees: 20-49
Other Locations:
  Peacock Crate Factory
  Jacksonville TX

27369 Pearson Packaging Systems
8120 W Sunset Hwy
Spokane, WA 99224-9048
509-838-6226
Fax: 509-747-8532 800-732-7766
info@pearsonpkg.com www.pearsonpkg.com
Manufacturer and exporter of case forming, case
packing, tray forming, bottom, top or end sealing,
carrier erecting, multipacking, partition and bag in-
serting machinery, and magazine feeding machinery
CEO: Michael Senske
psenske@pearsonpkg.com
CFO: Randy Bell
Vice President of Engineering: Leo Robertson
Marketing/Sales: Mark Ewing
Vice President of Sales and Marketing: Randy
Denny
Estimated Sales: $10-20 Million
Number Employees: 100-249
Square Footage: 220000
Type of Packaging: Food Service, Private Label,
Bulk

27370 Pearson Packaging Systems
8120 W Sunset Hwy
Spokane, WA 99224-9048
509-838-6226
Fax: 509-747-8532 800-732-7766
sales@goodmanpkg.com www.pearsonpkg.com
Case/tray packaging equipment
CEO: James A Goodman
President, Chief Executive Officer: Michael Senske
psenske@pearsonpkg.com
Vice President of Engineering: Leo Robertson
President: Billy Goodman
Vice President of Sales and Marketing: Randy
Denny
Number Employees: 100-249

27371 Pearson Research Assoc
PO Box 1778
Santa Cruz, CA 95061-1778
831-429-9797
Fax: 831-426-7010 info@pearsonresearch.com
www.pearsonresearch.com
Consultant specializing in market research, survey
design, consumer tests, sensory evaluation, focus
groups, etc
Owner: Adrian Pearson
adrian@pearsonresearch.com
Number Employees: 1-4

27372 Pearson Signs Service
2031 Hanover Pike
Hampstead, MD 21074-1336
410-239-3838
Fax: 410-239-3848
Signs including metal, wood, paper, plastic and neon
Owner: Herb Shaffer
Estimated Sales: $1-5 Million
Number Employees: 5-9
Square Footage: 6000

27373 Pease Awning & Sunroom Co
21 Massasoit Ave
East Providence, RI 02914-4439
401-438-2850
Fax: 401-434-6520 president@necpa.org
www.peasecompany.com
Commercial awnings; also, installation services
available
President: Ted Franklin
sales@peasecompany.com
VP: Donald Franklin
Purchasing Manager: Edwin Franklin
Estimated Sales: $1-5 Million
Number Employees: 10-19
Square Footage: 84000

27374 Pecan Deluxe Candy Co
2570 Lone Star Dr
Dallas, TX 75212-6308

214-631-3669
Fax: 214-631-5833 800-733-3589
pdcc_info@pecandeluxe.com
www.pecandeluxe.com
Dessert and baked goods ingredients: toffees, nuts,
chocolate coated items, flavor bases, sauces
President: Jay Brigham
Chairman of the Board: Bennie Brigham
bennie_brigham@pecandeluxe.com
Chief Financial Officer: Keith Hurd
Chief Operating Officer: Tim Markowicz
VP Quality Assurance: Rick Hintermeier
VP Operations: Mike Cavin
Inventory/Production Coordinator: Wayne Miller
Purchasing Manager: James Mitchell
Estimated Sales: $20-50 Million
Number Employees: 250-499
Number of Products: 2000
Square Footage: 63000
Type of Packaging: Bulk

27375 Pechiney Plastic Packaging
716 Tanager Lane
West Chicago, IL 60185-5949

630-293-8050
Fax: 630-293-8064
Food Sales/Marketing: David Quinn
Estimated Sales: $1-5 Million
Type of Packaging: Consumer

27376 Pechiney Plastic Packaging
8770 W Bryn Mawr Ave
Chicago, IL 60631

773-399-0255
Fax: 773-399-8549
Flexible packaging and plastic bottles
President: Ilene Gordon
CFO: Robert Mosesian
Quality Control: Rey Brunelle
Contact: Eileen Lerum
eileen.lerum@alcan.com
Estimated Sales: $20-50 Million
Number Employees: 250-499

27377 (HQ)Peco Controls Corporation
1439 Emerald Ave
Modesto, CA 95351

510-226-6686
Fax: 510-226-6687 800-732-6285
info@pecocontrols.com www.pecocontrols.com
Manufacturer and exporter of monitors for inspect-
ing fill and vacuum/pressure levels, contents and la-
bels of packages; also, automatic container sampling
systems and two-piece can metrology systems
President: F Allan Anderson
Vice President: Aslam Khan
Quality Control: Cheong Chan
Contact: Allan Anderson
a.anderson@pecocontrols.com
Estimated Sales: $3-5 Million
Number Employees: 35
Square Footage: 64000
Type of Packaging: Consumer, Private Label
Other Locations:
Peco Controls Corp.
Pershore, Wozos
Brands:
Criterion
Gamma 101p
Sample Trac
Vac Trac
Valv-Chek

27378 Peekskill Hair Net
201 S Division Street
Peekskill, NY 10566-3611

914-737-1524
Fax: 914-788-3890
Acetate, nylon and rayon protective hair nets and
caps
President: John Kotowski
Secretary/Bookkeeper: Gertrude DeFazio
Treasurer: John Kotowski
Number Employees: 10
Square Footage: 12000

27379 Peerless Cartons
1073 Martingale Drive
Bartlett, IL 60103-5676

312-226-7952
Fax: 312-226-6861

Folding cartons
President: Larry Mitchell
Estimated Sales: $2.5-5 Million
Number Employees: 19

27380 Peerless Conveyor & MfgCorp
201 E Quindaro Blvd
Kansas City, KS 66115-1424

913-342-2240
Fax: 913-342-2237 www.peerlessconveyor.com
Conveyors and conveying equipment for bulk mate-
rials including grain sugar
President: William S Walker
wwalker@peerlessconveyor.com
Sales Director: Chuck Leonard
Production Manager: Seth Rodriquez
Estimated Sales: $2.5-5 Million
Number Employees: 20-49
Square Footage: 80000

27381 Peerless Dough Mixing and Make-Up
P.O.Box 769
Sidney, OH 45365-0769

937-492-4158
Fax: 937-492-3688 800-999-3327
www.thepeerlessgroup.us
Dough machinery
President: Dane Belden
Chairman/CEO: Robert Zielsdorf
Estimated Sales: $20-50 Million
Number Employees: 100-249

27382 Peerless Food Equipment
500 S Vandemark Rd
Sidney, OH 45365-8991

937-492-4158
Fax: 937-492-3688 www.peerlessfood.com
Manufacturer and exporter of snack food and bakery
processing equipment including conveyors, coolers,
depositors, icers, mixers, pumps, topping applicators
and bagel machinery
General Manager: George Hoff
Director of Marketing: Sherri Swabb
Director of Sales: Richard Taylor
Estimated Sales: 5-10 Million
Number Employees: 100-249
Square Footage: 208000

27383 Peerless Food Equipment
500 S Vandemark Rd
Sidney, OH 45365-8991

937-492-4158
Fax: 937-492-3688 info@petersmachinery.com
www.peerlessfood.com
Manufacturer and exporter of food processing ma-
chinery including stackers and cookie sandwiching
and wrapping equipment
General Manager: George Hoff
Controller: David Alexander
Director, Marketing And Customer Support: Sherri
Swabb
Sales Director: Richard Taylor
Human Resource Manager: Kathy Weldy
Plant And Materials Manager: Mike Gniazdowski
Estimated Sales: $7 Million
Number Employees: 100-249
Parent Co: Peerless Group

27384 Peerless Gouet LLC
2039 Clipper Drive
Lafayette, CO 80026-3160

720-890-7306
Fax: 720-890-1286 jwp@indra.com
President: John Parr

27385 Peerless Lighting Corporation
PO Box 2556
Berkeley, CA 94702-0556

510-845-2760
Fax: 510-845-2776 www.peerless-lighting.com
Manufacturer and exporter of institutional and com-
mercial fluorescent lighting fixtures
President: Douglas Herst
VP: Jim Young
Manager Marketing Services: Margaret Einhorn
Contact: Michael Brunasso
michael.brunasso@peerless-lighting.com
Estimated Sales: $10-20 Million
Number Employees: 50-99

27386 Peerless Machine & ToolCorp
1804 W 2nd St
Marion, IN 46952-3362

765-662-2586
Fax: 765-662-6067
peerlessmt@peerlessmachine.com
www.peerlessmachine.com
Paper converting machinery, paper plates and trays
Owner: Jeff Carson
jeffreycarson@peerlessmachine.com
Estimated Sales: $2.5-5 Million
Number Employees: 20-49

27387 (HQ)Peerless Machinery Corporation
PO Box 769
Sidney, OH 45365

937-492-4158
Fax: 937-492-3688 800-999-3327
www.thepeerlessgroup.us
Manufacturer and exporter of bakery mixers, divid-
ers, blenders and rounders
President: Dane Belden
Director Marketing: Terry Bartsch
VP Sales: Michael Booth
Contact: David Alexander
dalexander@thepeerlessgroup.us
Estimated Sales: $20-50 Million
Number Employees: 100-249
Square Footage: 75000
Other Locations:
Peerless Machinery Corp.
Odessa FL
Brands:
Hallmark
Peerless
Royal
Supergrain

27388 Peerless Ovens
334 Harrison St
Sandusky, OH 44870

419-625-4514
Fax: 419-625-4597 800-548-4514
www.peerlessovens.com
Manufacturer and exporter of bakery and pizza ov-
ens, griddles and ranges
President: Bryan Huntley
peerless@lrbcg.com
Estimated Sales: $1-2.5 Million
Number Employees: 10-19
Square Footage: 200000
Type of Packaging: Food Service

27389 Peerless Packages
23600 Mercantile Rd # A
Cleveland, OH 44122-5971

216-464-3620
Fax: 216-464-3440
Plastic and paper bags and boxes
Sales: Lynn Harmon
Sales Manager: Lynn Harmon
Estimated Sales: $1-2.5 Million
Number Employees: 5-9

27390 Peerless of America
109 Schelter Rd
Lincolnshire, IL 60069-3603

847-634-7500
Fax: 847-634-7506
Manufacturer and exporter of refrigeration and air
conditioning equipment including evaporators,
finned coils, heat transfer products and unit and
flash coolers
Owner: Igor Gordon
VP Sales/Marketing: Michael Schopf
Estimated Sales: $20-50 Million
Number Employees: 100-249
Square Footage: 395000

27391 Peerless-Premier Appliance Co
119 S 14th St
Belleville, IL 62220-1715

618-233-0475
Fax: 618-235-1771 info@premierrange.com
www.premierrange.com
Manufacturer and exporter of gas and electric ranges
President: Joseph Geary
CEO: Robert Burggraf
burggraf@premierrange.com
CEO: Alex Volansky
Chairman of the Board: William T Sprague
VP Marketing: Allan Gramlich
National Sales Manager: Robert Volkmann

Estimated Sales: $20-50 Million
Number Employees: 100-249
Square Footage: 300000
Brands:
    Eagle
    Heritage By Orbon
    Mark Royal
    Modern Chef
    Premier

27392 Peerless-Winsmith Inc
172 Eaton St
Springville, NY 14141

716-592-9310
Fax: 716-592-9546 www.winsmith.com
Manufacturer and exporter of worm gear speed reducers for material handling conveyors and machinery; also, food processing and bottling machinery.
IT Manager: Gary Fraser
fraser@winsmith.com
Quality Assurance Manager: Bruce DeMont
Year Founded: 1901
Estimated Sales: $100-500 Million
Number Employees: 100-249

27393 Pel-Pak Container
1107 Dowzer Ave
Pell City, AL 35125

205-338-2993
Fax: 205-338-6120 800-239-2699
Corrugated boxes
President: Jeanette L Chasteen
Plant Manager: Mike Richerzhagen
Number Employees: 19

27394 Pelco Packaging Corporation
269 Mercer St.
Stirling, NJ 07980

908-647-3500
Fax: 908-647-1868
customerservice@pelcopackaging.com
www.pelcopackaging.com
Plastic material handling equipment and packaging including boxes
President: Arthur J Brinker
Estimated Sales: $1-2.5 Million
Number Employees: 15

27395 Pelican Displays
109 E 1st St
Homer, IL 61849-1101

217-896-2628
Fax: 217-896-2628 800-627-1517
Wood, polyethylene and acrylic bulk food display bins
Owner: David Lucas
Estimated Sales: $1-5 Million
Number Employees: 1-4
Square Footage: 17000

27396 Pelican Marine Supply LLC
2911 Engineers Rd
Belle Chasse, LA 70037-3150

504-392-9062
Fax: 504-394-5528 www.pelicanmarinedist.com
Beef, pork, poultry, fish, seafood and general groceries
President: Peter Bretchel
Manager: James Lutz
jameyl@pelicanmarinedist.com
Estimated Sales: $10-20 Million
Number Employees: 5-9

27397 Pelican Products Inc
1049 Lowell St
Bronx, NY 10459-2608

718-860-3220
Fax: 718-860-4415 800-552-8820
info@pelicanproducts.com www.pelican.com
Manufacturer and exporter of molded plastic advertising specialties, imprinted premiums and promotional give-aways including coasters, stirrers, cocktail forks, corkscrews and ball point pens
Vice President: David Silver
david@pelicanproducts.com
CEO: Harold Silver
Vice President: Dave Silver
Estimated Sales: $2.5-5 Million
Number Employees: 10-19
Square Footage: 40000

27398 Pell Paper Box Company
PO Box 584
Elizabeth City, NC 27907-0584

252-335-4361
Fax: 252-335-9639 murry@series2000.com
Set-up and folding boxes for frozen foods, baked goods and promotional and specialty products
COO: P Murry Pitts
General Manager: Tony Rossi
Estimated Sales: $10-20 Million
Number Employees: 50-99
Square Footage: 170000

27399 Pellenc America
955 S Virginia Street
Suite 116
Reno, NV 89502-0413

702-853-3455
Fax: 702-853-4554
Wine industry pruning equipment

27400 Pellerin Milnor Corporation
700 Jackson St
P.O. Box 400
Kenner, LA 70063-0400

504-467-9591
800-469-8780
milnorinfo@milnor.com www.milnor.com
A leading commercial and industrial laundry equipment manufacturer. Washer-extractors range in size from 25 lb to 700 lb capacity; dryers from 30-550 lb. These models are available with a variety of controls from very simple to quitesophisticated, depending upon your food and beverage linen needs.
Chairman & CEO: James Pellerin
Vice President: Mike Dineen
mdineen@milnor.com
VP, Sales & Marketing: Richard Kelly
Year Founded: 1947
Estimated Sales: $100+ Million
Number Employees: 530
Square Footage: 400000
Brands:
    E-P Plus
    System 7

27401 Pelouze Scale Company
7400 W 100th Place
Bridgeview, IL 60455-2438

708-430-8330
Fax: 800-654-7330 800-323-8363
www.pelouze.com
Manufacturer and exporter of mechanical and electronic timers, food thermometers and food portion, dietetic, electronic digital and shipping and receiving scales
VP: Dan Maeir
VP: Dan Maeir
National Sales Manager: Jack Kramer
Customer Service Manager: Laura Anton
Estimated Sales: $50-100 Million
Number Employees: 140
Parent Co: Sunbeam
Type of Packaging: Consumer, Food Service

27402 Pemberton & Associates
3610 Nashua Drive
Mississauga, ON L4V 1X9
Canada

905-678-8900
Fax: 905-678-8989 800-668-6111
pemco@pemcom.com www.pemcom.com
President: Dennis Hicks
R&D: Keith Tse
Vice President: Bill Froggatt
Number Employees: 20

27403 Pemberton & Associates
152 Remsen Street
Brooklyn, NY 11201
Canada

718-923-1111
Fax: 718-923-6065 800-736-2664
career@pencom.com www.pencom.com
Manufacturers full service representative of meat and poultry processing, and packaging equipment
Founder, President: Wade Saadi
Vice President of Operations: Jim Kenner
Number Employees: 15

27404 Penasack Co Inc
49 Sanford St
PO Box 396
Albion, NY 14411-1117

585-589-5873
Fax: 585-589-0046 penasack@rochester.rr.com
www.penasack.com
Manufacturer and fabricator of stainless steel products
President: Gerard Da More
penasack@rochester.rr.com
Engineering Manager: Jeff Kinser
Operations: Mike Hrycelak
Estimated Sales: $3-5 Million
Number Employees: 20-49
Square Footage: 80000
Parent Co: GDM Enterprises
Type of Packaging: Food Service, Private Label, Bulk

27405 Penco Products
P.O.Box 158
Skippack, PA 19474

610-666-0500
Fax: 610-666-7561 800-562-1000
customerservice@pencoproducts.com
www.pencoproducts.com
Manufacturer and exporter of shelving, work benches, storage cabinets, pallet racks and lockers
President: Greg Grogan
VP Sales/Marketing: Bill Vain
Estimated Sales: $20-50 Million
Number Employees: 250-499
Brands:
    Clipper
    Erectomatic
    Hi-Performance
    Rivit Orite

27406 Penda Form Corp
200 S Friendship Dr
New Concord, OH 43762-9641

740-826-5000
Fax: 740-826-5001 800-837-2574
Material handling equipment including trays, pallets and covers; exporter of electrical components
President: John Knight
jknight@fabri-form.com
VP Sales: Larry Howard
Manager Customer Service: Dennis Hardin
jknight@fabri-form.com
Plant Manager: Jerry Andrech
Number Employees: 50-99

27407 Pengo Attachments Inc
13369 60th St SW
Cokato, MN 55321-4210

320-286-5581
Fax: 320-286-5583 800-599-0211
pengosales@pengoattachments.com
www.pengoattachments.com
Custom fabricated conveyor screws for food applications
Cio/Cto: Dave Bailey
dbailey@paladinbrands.com
VP/ General Manager: Brian Rickards
Engineering Manager: Eric Matthias
Vice President-Sales/Marketing: Dana Scudder
HR Business Partner: Ray Waite
Operations Manager: Jim Groat
Product Manager: Mary Pohlman
Division Controller: John Ricke
Estimated Sales: $10-20 Million
Number Employees: 100-249
Square Footage: 84000
Parent Co: Crown Holdings

27408 Penguin Natural Food Inc
4400 Alcoa Ave
Vernon, CA 90058-2412

323-727-7980
Fax: 323-727-7983 www.penguinfoods.com
Rice, baking mixes, potato mixes, cornbreads, pastas and rice blends.
President: Scott Nairne
Estimated Sales: $20-50 Million
Number Employees: 50-99
Type of Packaging: Consumer, Food Service, Private Label

27409 Peninsula Plastics
2800 Auburn Ct
Auburn Hills, MI 48326-3203
248-852-3731
Fax: 248-852-5482 800-394-8698
www.peninsulaplastics.com
Custom vacuum formed packaging products
President: Richard Jositas
Controller/CFO: Grace McKinney
Vice President: Ryan Victory
ryanvictory@peninsulaplastics.com
General Manager: Roderick Zielinski
Estimated Sales: $10-20 Million
Number Employees: 50-99
Square Footage: 60000

27410 Penley Corporation
PO Box 277
West Paris, ME 04289-0277
207-674-2501
Fax: 207-674-2510 800-368-6449
Manufacturer, importer and exporter of wooden
toothpicks, matches, chopsticks, etc.; also, plastic
cutlery and drinking straws
Owner: Richard Penley
Director Sales/Marketing: Stephen Gilman
Director Manufacturing: Robert Warrington
Estimated Sales: $5-10 Million
Number Employees: 10-19

27411 Penn Barry
605 Shiloh Rd
Plano, TX 75074-7210
972-212-4700
pennbarrysales@pennbarry.com
www.pennvent.com
Fans and ventilation equipment
President: Scott Adamson
sadamson@pennbarry.com
Number Employees: 50-99
Parent Co: Air System Components, Inc.

27412 Penn Barry
605 Shiloh Rd
Plano, TX 75074-7210
972-212-4700
Fax: 972-212-4701
pennbarrysales@pennbarry.com
www.pennbarry.com
Single source for commercial and industrial ventila-
tion product solutions.
President: Scott Adamson
sadamson@pennbarry.com
Number Employees: 50-99
Square Footage: 120000
Parent Co: Air System Components, Inc.
Brands:
　Supreme
　Bayley Fan
　Penn Ventilation
　Barry Blower
　Industrial Air

27413 Penn Bottle & Supply Company
7150 Lindbergh Boulevard
Philadelphia, PA 19153-3008
215-365-5700
Fax: 215-365-2320
Plastic and glass bottles
CEO and President: Richard Probinsky
VP Finance and Administration: Paul Silverman

27414 Penn Products
91 Main Street
Portland, CT 6480
860-342-2500
Fax: 860-342-5563 800-490-7366
service@pennproductsusa.com
www.pennproductsusa.com
Custom injection molded plastic boxes and contain-
ers
VP Operations: Ray Pennoyer
Administrator: Raymond Pennoyer Iii
Estimated Sales: $2.5-5 Million
Number Employees: 20-49
Number of Brands: 1
Square Footage: 40000
Type of Packaging: Private Label, Bulk

27415 Penn Refrigeration Service Corporation
P.O.Box 1261
Wilkes Barre, PA 18703-1261
570-825-5666
Fax: 570-825-5705 800-233-8354
sales@pennrefrig.com
Manufacturer and exporter of refrigeration equip-
ment and systems including walk-in coolers and
freezers
President: Albert Finarelli Jr
afinarelli@pennrefrig.com
Plant Manager: John Gosciewski
Estimated Sales: $5-10 Million
Number Employees: 50-99

27416 Penn Scale ManufacturingCompany
150 W Berks St
Philadelphia, PA 19122
215-739-9644
Fax: 215-739-9640 sales@pennscale.com
www.pennscale.com
Scales and scoops
President: Larry Biren
Owner: Andy Levin
Quality Control: Andy Levin
Contact: Mary Biren
mary.biren@pennscale.com
Estimated Sales: $300,000
Number Employees: 5-9
Square Footage: 24000
Brands:
　Penn Scale

27417 PennPac International
8200 Flourtown Avenue
Suite 6b
Wyndmoor, PA 19038-7969
215-836-1380
Fax: 215-836-7885
Plastic containers
Estimated Sales: less than $500,000
Number Employees: 1

27418 Pennsylvania Food Merchants Association
P.O.Box 870
Camp Hill, PA 17001-0870
717-731-0600
Fax: 717-731-5472 800-543-8207
pfma@aol.com www.pfma.org
Our mission is to improve the profitability of com-
panies in the retail and wholesale food distribution
industry.
President/CEO: David Mc Corkle
CFO: Dwight Cromer
Sr. VP Association Services: Randolph St.John
Vice President, Sales & Marketing: Autumn Thomas
Sales Support Specialist: Michele Weaver
Contact: Steve Halterman
shalterman@memoco.com
Administrative Assistant: Jennifer Hamelin
Number Employees: 50-99

27419 Penny Plate
PO Box 3003
Haddonfield, NJ 08033
856-429-7583
Fax: 856-429-7166 mmiller@pennyplate.com
www.pennyplate.com
Aluminum food service containers
Assistant to CEO: George Buff
CEO: George Buff
Contact: Nancy Arno
narno@pennyplate.com
Estimated Sales: $30-50 Million
Number Employees: 100-249

27420 Pensacola Rope Company
PO Box 1926
Slidell, LA 70459-1926
850-968-9760
Fax: 850-968-1669
Solid braided nylon cord and rope
President: Thomas Fields
Estimated Sales: $500,000-$1 Million
Number Employees: 4

27421 Penske Truck Leasing Corp
2675 Morgantown Rd
Reading, PA 19607-9676
610-775-6000
844-376-4095
www.gopenske.com
Truck leasing service.
President: Brian Hard
brian.hard@penske.com
Year Founded: 1969
Estimated Sales: $8.4 Billion
Number Employees: 36,000
Parent Co: Penske Corp

27422 Pentad Group Inc
7234 Francisco Bend Dr
Delray Beach, FL 33446
561-362-8678
Fax: 561-495-9777 labelsaver@aol.com
www.labeloff.com
Logos on any item, wine related products such as
wine label removers, wine label albums, glassware,
coolers, aprons, posters, etc
CEO: Marvin Pesses
Vice President: Marvin Pesses
Contact: Elaine Pesses
mpesses@yahoo.com
Estimated Sales: $2.5-5 Million
Number Employees: 5
Number of Products: 46
Type of Packaging: Consumer, Private Label
Brands:
　Labeloff Wine Label Removers

27423 Pentair Valves & Controls
3950 Greenbriar Dr
Stafford, TX 77477-3919
281-274-4400
Fax: 281-240-1800 www.pentair.com
Manager: Frank Hoban
frank.hoban@pentair.com
Plant Manager: Andy Masullo
Number Employees: 500-999

27424 Pentwater Wire ProductsInc
474 S Carroll St
Pentwater, MI 49449-8772
231-869-6911
Fax: 231-869-4020 877-869-6911
pwp@pentwaterwire.com www.pentwaterwire.com
Racks, displays, containers, assemblies, shelving
and baskets
President: Ivan Ewing
iewing@pentwaterwire.com
Vice President: Dwight Swanson
Sales Director: Mike Piper
Estimated Sales: $5-10 Million
Number Employees: 50-99
Square Footage: 200000
Brands:
　On Guard

27425 Peoria Meat Packing
1300 W Lake St
Chicago, IL 60607-1512
312-738-1800
Fax: 312-738-1180 www.peoriapacking.com
Packaging
Owner: Harry Katsiavlos
Estimated Sales: $10-20 Million
Number Employees: 1-4

27426 Peoria Tent & Awning
3012 W Farmington Road
Peoria, IL 61604
309-674-1128
Fax: 309-697-9871 info@peoriaawning.com
www.peoriaawning.com
Commercial awnings
Owner: Mark Hutchison
Estimated Sales: $1-2,500,000
Number Employees: 20-49
Parent Co: PAMA Group

27427 Pepetti's Hygrade Egg Product
100 Trumbull Street
Elizabeth, NJ 07206-2105
908-351-9618
Fax: 908-351-7528 www.papetti.com
Estimated Sales: $.5-1 million
Number Employees: 1-4

27428 Pepper Mill
558 S Broad St
Mobile, AL 36603-1124
251-433-7919
Fax: 251-433-3364 800-669-5175
Trivet boards and brushes including wire and bristle
President: Scott Gonzalez
scott@3geroges.com
VP Finance: Siobhan Gonzalez
Estimated Sales: $.5-1 million
Number Employees: 1-4
Square Footage: 2000
Brands:
 Fajita Trivet
 Monster
 Roughneck

27429 (HQ)Pepper Source Inc
2720 Athania Pkwy
Metairie, LA 70002-5904
504-885-3223
Fax: 504-885-3187 www.peppersource.com
Sauces and glazes, dry blends, custome rubs and
packaging services.
President: Joe Morse
Contact: Shannon Glover
sglover@peppersource.com
Vice President of Operations: Paul Liggio
Production Supervisor: Mike Bartels
Estimated Sales: $15 Million
Number Employees: 5-9
Type of Packaging: Food Service, Private Label,
 Bulk
Other Locations:
 Pepper Source
 Van Buren AR
 Pepper Source
 Rogers AR

27430 PepperWorks
303 Industrial Way
Suite 5
Fallbrook, CA 92028
760-723-0202
Fax: 760-723-2227 info@wine-master.com
Wine industry tasting room supplies
Manager: Biby Zeledon

27431 Pepperell Paper Company
9 S Canal Street
Lawrence, MA 01843-1412
978-433-6951
Fax: 978-433-6427
Manufacturer and exporter of specialty papers in-
cluding acid free, beater dyed colors, packaging,
supercalendered, grease, mold and flame resistant,
crepe, flour bag, kraft, etc
Sales Manager: Steve Ulicny
Number Employees: 4
Square Footage: 400000
Parent Co: James River Corporation
Brands:
 Strypel
 Styprint
 Stysorb

27432 Pepperl & Fuchs Inc
1600 Enterprise Pkwy
Twinsburg, OH 44087-2245
330-425-3555
Fax: 330-425-4607 sales@us.pepperl-fuchs.com
www.pepperl-fuchs.us
Industrial controls and sensors
President: Wolfgang Mueller
wmueller@us.pepperl-fuchs.com
R&D: Hurman Witch
CEO: Wolfgang Mueller
Estimated Sales: $20-50 Million
Number Employees: 100-249

27433 PepsiCo.
700 Anderson Hill Rd.
Purchase, NY 10577
914-253-2000
www.pepsico.com
Global brands food, snack and beverage company.
Chairman/CEO: Ramon Laguarta
President, Global Foodservice: Anne Fink
Vice Chairman/CFO: Hugh Johnston
EVP/Chief Scientific Officer: Rene Lammers
Year Founded: 1898
Estimated Sales: $67.1 Billion
Number Employees: 263,000
Number of Brands: 54
Square Footage: 40000

Type of Packaging: Consumer
Brands:
 Pepsi®
 Frito-Lay®
 Quaker®
 Tropicana®
 Gatorade®
 Pure Leaf®
 Mountain Dew®
 Bubly®
 Naked®
 Lipton®
 Starbucks Frappacino®
 Aquafina®
 Brisk®
 Kevita®
 Life WTR®
 Sierra Mist®
 Stubborn Soda®
 IZZE®
 Propel®
 O.N.E®
 AMP ENERGY Organic®
 SOBE®
 Mug Root Beer®
 Doritos®
 Stacy's Pita Chips®
 Bare®
 Sabra®
 Ruffles®
 Smartfood®
 Cheetos®
 Tostitos®
 Fritos®
 Near East®
 Maker®
 Imag!ne®
 Sun Chips®
 Off The Eaten Path®
 Rold Gold®
 Miss Vickies®
 Red Rock Deli®
 Cracker Jack®
 Nut Harvest®
 Life®
 Matador®
 Santitas®
 Funyuns®
 Cap'n Crunch®
 Pasta Roni®
 Rice A Roni®
 Maui Style®
 Sabritones®
 Munchos®
 Grandma's®
 Aunt Jemima®

27434 Per Pak/Orlandi
131 Executive Boulevard
Farmingdale, NY 11735
631-756-0110
Fax: 631-756-0256 Info@orlandi-usa.com
www.orlandi-usa.com
Contract packager offering high-speed over wrap-
ping, form fill and seal for liquids, powders and
cartoning
President: Sven Dobler
COO: Per Dobler
Controller: David Hays
VP Marketing: Dale Beal
Plant Manager: Mike Cheff
Estimated Sales: $5-10 Million
Number Employees: 50-99
Parent Co: Jefferson Smurfit Corporation

27435 Per-Fil Industries Inc
407 Adams St
Riverside, NJ 08075-3098
856-461-5700
Fax: 856-461-0741 www.per-fil.com
Manufacturer and exporter of filling machinery for
liquids, powder, paste, granules and food products
President: Shari Becker
Director/Chairman: Horst Boellmann
per-fil@sales.com
Service Manager: Tobin Wrice
National and International Sales: Shari Becker
Estimated Sales: Below $5 Million
Number Employees: 20-49
Square Footage: 29000
Brands:
 Micro-Recharger
 Rotary Recharger

27436 Perception
3307 S College Avenue
Unit 113
Fort Collins, CO 80525-4196
970-226-1941
Fax: 970-221-4809

27437 Peregrine Inc
5301 N 57th St # 102
Lincoln, NE 68507-3164
402-466-4011
Fax: 402-466-1639 800-777-3433
info@peregrine-inc.com www.peregrine-inc.com
Manufacturer and exporter of material handling
equipment including four-wheel steering trailers
President: Troy Rivers
troy@peregrine-inc.com
Office/Sales Manager: Joyce Schiermann
Estimated Sales: $1-2,500,000
Number Employees: 5-9
Type of Packaging: Bulk
Brands:
 Quad-Steer

27438 Perfecseal
9800 Bustleton Ave
Philadelphia, PA 19115
215-673-4500
Fax: 215-676-1311 800-568-7626
www.perfecseal.com
Heat seal coated materials, coated paper and lamina-
tions, laminated films, tubing, header bag packaging
President: Paul Verbeten
CEO: Alan McClure
R&D: Richard Craig
Quality Control: Gail Turner
CFO: Ben Travey
Contact: Janet Voegele
jvoegele@bemis.com
Plant Manager: Gail Turner
Estimated Sales: $83.8 Million
Number Employees: 100-249

27439 Perfect Equipment Inc
4259 Lee Ave
Gurnee, IL 60031-2175
847-244-7200
Fax: 847-244-7205 800-356-6301
info@perfectequip.com www.perfectequip.com
Manufacturer and exporter of beverage and condi-
ment dispenser systems, custom fabricated stainless
steel bar and restaurant equipment including
underbar and portable and back bar units, glycol
units and water chillers
President: Sanford Hahn
sandy@perfectequip.com
CEO: Kay Hahn
Sales/ Administration: Kathy Pino
Operations Manager/ R&D: Alan Hale
Plant Manager: Alan Hale
Purchasing: Gene Wood
Estimated Sales: $5-10,000,000
Number Employees: 20-49
Square Footage: 28000
Type of Packaging: Food Service

27440 Perfect Fit Glove Company
85 Innsbruck Dr
Cheektowaga, NY 14227
716-668-2000
Fax: 716-668-3224 800-245-6837
perfectfitglove@perfectfitglove.com
Safety equipment and hand protection
Manager: Greg Wall
Estimated Sales: $50-75 Million
Number Employees: 50-99

27441 Perfect Fry Company
615 71st Avenue SE
Calgary, AB T2H 0S7
Canada
403-255-7712
Fax: 403-255-1725 800-265-7711
profits@perfectfry.com www.perfectfry.com
Manufacturers ventless countertop deep fryers des-
ignated for commercial deep-frying without the
instalation of hoods and vents

Vice President of Business Development: Gary Calderwood
CFO: Sharon Hyasdick
Vice President, General Manager: Greg Moyer
Research & Development: Shaun Calderwood
Senior Manager of Sales: Bonnie Bolster
Vice President of Operations: Steve Reale
Plant Manager: Jeff Scott
Estimated Sales: Below $5 Million
Number Employees: 20
Square Footage: 60000
Parent Co: Perfect Fry Corporation
Type of Packaging: Food Service
Brands:
  Perfect Fry

27442 Perfect Plank Co
2850 S 5th Ave
Oroville, CA 95965-5851
530-533-7606
Fax: 530-533-2814 800-327-1961
www.perfectplank.com
Laminated wood countertops, butcher blocks, tabletops and sign blanks
Sales Manager: Terry Horne
Manager: Terry Horne
perfectplank@att.net
General Manager: Jim Horne
Production Manager: Bob Horne
Sales and Accounts Payable: Adam Horne
Estimated Sales: $1-2.5 Million
Number Employees: 10-19
Square Footage: 120000

27443 Perfect Score Company
9326 Garfield Blvd
Cleveland, OH 44125-1313
216-883-8000
Fax: 216-883-8800 sales@theperfectscore.com
www.theperfectscore.com

27444 Perfex Corporation
32 Case St
Poland, NY 13431
315-826-3600
Fax: 315-826-7471 800-848-8483
perfex@perfexonline.com www.perfexonline.com
Manufacturer and exporter of PVC floor and neoprene rubber squeegees, polypropylene, chemical resistant and hygienic brooms and brushes, shovels and stainless steel clean room flat mopping systems
President: Michael Kubick
Marketing Manager: Mike Dougherty
Sales: Irene Gouthier
Customer Service Supervisor: Trudy Pickerd
Estimated Sales: $1-2.5 Million
Number Employees: 10-25

27445 Performance Contracting
11145 Thompson Ave.
Lenexa, KS 66219
913-888-8600
800-255-6886
info@pcg.com www.performancecontracting.com
Construction of specialized facilities for cold storage, food processing and distribution.
President/CEO: William Massey
Vice President/CFO: Alan Clayton
Vice President/General Counsel: Rod Eisenhauer
Chief Operating Officer: Jason Hendricks
Year Founded: 1984
Estimated Sales: $871 Million
Number Employees: 7,000
Square Footage: 36000

27446 Performance Imaging Corp
5392 Leon St
Oceanside, CA 92057-3654
760-721-2925
Fax: 760-721-2925 800-266-5742
info@performanceimaging.com
www.performanceimaging.com
Specializing in machine vision inspection systems offering complete package inspection. Capabilities include label inspection, character recognition and verification, cap inspection and fill level; custom application softwareavailible
Contact: Michael Russe
m.russe@performanceimaging.com
Estimated Sales: $2.5-5 Million
Number Employees: 10-19

27447 Performance Packaging
6430 Medical Center St # 102
Suite 102
Las Vegas, NV 89148-2403
702-240-3457
Fax: 702-240-3453 ppsales@pplv.co
www.pplv.co
President: Robert Reinders
robreinders@performace-packaging.com
CFO: Bruce Moore
Estimated Sales: Below $5 Million
Number Employees: 5-9

27448 Performance Packaging
251 N Roeske Avenue
Trail Creek, IN 46360-5072
219-874-6226
Fax: 219-874-3011
Corrugated boxes and packaging materials
VP Sales/Marketing: Will Childers
Contact: Dotti Kasten
dotti.kasten@plastipak.com
Estimated Sales: $5-10 Million
Number Employees: 2
Square Footage: 200000

27449 Perl Packaging Systems
80 Turnpike Dr # 2
Middlebury, CT 06762-1830
203-598-0066
Fax: 203-598-0068 800-864-2853
Manufacturer and exporter of straight line liquid filling machines, piston fillers, portable cappers, rotary unscramblers, cap and bottle orienter feeders and labelers
President: David Baker
Estimated Sales: $3-5 Million
Number Employees: 5-9
Square Footage: 40000

27450 Perley-Halladay Assoc
1037 Andrew Dr
West Chester, PA 19380-4293
610-840-6300
Fax: 610-647-1711 800-248-5800
sales@perleyhalladay.com
www.perleyhalladay.com
Manufacturer and exporter of refrigerated buildings, walk-in coolers and process freezers
Owner: Boone Flint
bf@perleyhalladay.com
Office Mngr.: Jim Sonvogni
Estimated Sales: $2.5-5 Million
Number Employees: 1-4

27451 Perlick Corp
8300 W Good Hope Rd
Milwaukee, WI 53223-4524
414-353-7060
Fax: 414-353-7069 800-558-5592
perlick@perlick.com www.perlick.com
Manufactuer of bar and beverage dispensing equipment for the foodservice industry.
President, CEO: Paul Peot
pap@perlick.com
CFO: Mike Pitialip
VP of Manufacturing: Tim Carpenter
VP of Marketing & Business Development: Tim Ebner
VP of Commercial Sales: Jim Koelbl
Number Employees: 250-499
Square Footage: 1112000
Type of Packaging: Food Service

27452 Permacold Engineering Inc
3005 NE Argyle St
Portland, OR 97211-1946
503-249-8190
Fax: 503-249-8322 800-455-8585
info@permacold.com www.permacold.com
Refrigeration contractors: parts, service, overhaul and construction
Owner: Steve Jackston
steve.jackson@permacold.com
Vice President: Randy Clelokit
Marketing: Lindsay Jackson
Sales Director: Randy Cieldna
Operations Manager: Steve Jackson
Estimated Sales: $20-50 Million
Number Employees: 50-99

27453 Permaloc Security Devices
PO Box 4699
Silver Spring, MD 20914
301-681-6300
Fax: 301-681-7552
Installation and monitoring of alarm systems
Owner: James Wolfe
Secretary/Treasurer: John Goetz
Vice President: Berthol Harbrant
Estimated Sales: $500,000-$1 Million
Number Employees: 20-49
Square Footage: 7000

27454 Perna USA
2129 Center Park Dr
Charlotte, NC 28217-2904
704-357-0264
Fax: 704-377-3106 800-997-3762
info@permausa.com www.permausa.com
Manager: Kevin Keating
Contact: Joanna Adkins
jadkins@permausa.com
Estimated Sales: $5-10 Million
Number Employees: 5-9
Parent Co: perma-tec GmbH u. Co. KG

27455 Perplas
4073 Shoreside Cir
Tampa, FL 33624-2373
610-268-1620
Fax: 610-268-1621 800-898-0378
sales@perplascorp.com www.perplascorp.com
Estimated Sales: $1-5 Million

27456 Perry Videx LLC
25 Mount Laurel Rd
Hainesport, NJ 08036-2711
609-267-1600
Fax: 609-267-4499 info@perryvidex.com
www.perryvidex.com
Wholesaler/distributor, importer and exporter of used food processing equipment; serving the food service market
President/ CEO: Gregg Epstein
gepstein@perryvidex.com
VP-Finance: Bob Bowdoin
VP- Production: Ron Mueller
Sales: Pete D'Angelo
Estimated Sales: $5-10 Million
Number Employees: 20-49

27457 Perten Instruments
6444 S 6th Street Rd # A
Springfield, IL 62712-6882
217-585-9440
Fax: 217-585-9441 888-773-7836
lblack@perten.com www.perten.com
Manufacturer, importer and exporter of spectrometers, gluten and alpha analysis testing equipment, laboratory sample mill grinders and NIR analyzers
President: Gavin O'Reilly
goreilly@perten.com
Manager Western: Carl Meuser
Manager Eastern: Walter Munday
Sales/Marketing Manager: Wes Shadow
Estimated Sales: $2.5-5 Million
Number Employees: 20-49
Square Footage: 16000
Parent Co: Perten Instruments AB
Brands:
  Da 7000
  Skcs

27458 Perten Instruments
6444 S 6th Street Rd # A
Springfield, IL 62712-6882
217-585-9440
Fax: 217-585-9441 jpowers@perten.com
www.perten.com
Analytical laboratory services, analyzing fat testing
President: Gavin O'Reilly
goreilly@perten.com
CEO: Sven Holmlund
Manager: Gavin O'Reilly
Estimated Sales: $2.5-5 Million
Number Employees: 20-49

27459 Perten Instruments
PO Box 7398
Reno, NV 89510-7398
702-829-8199
Fax: 775-829-8196 info@perten.com
www.perten.com

Tea and coffee industry moisture analyzers, quality control instruments
Chief Executive Officer: Sven Holmlund
Sales/Marketing Manager: Wes Shadow
Number Employees: 110

27460 Peryam & Kroll Research
6323 N Avondale Ave # 211
Suite 211
Chicago, IL 60631-1930

     773-774-3100
Fax: 773-774-7956 800-747-5522
info@pk-research.com www.pcmrewardcenter.com
President/CEO: James M. Ondyak
ondyak@pk-research.com
Chairman of the Board: Beverley J. Kroll
CFO: Eric Maddux
Senior Vice President: Dr. Richard Popper
Estimated Sales: $5-10 Million
Number Employees: 250-499

27461 Peskin Sign Co
3991 Simon Rd
Youngstown, OH 44512-1390

     330-783-2470
Fax: 330-783-9704

Plastic and neon signs
President: Gerry Peskin
VP: Jerry Peskin
Estimated Sales: Less Than $500,000
Number Employees: 5-9

27462 Pestcon Systems Inc
1808 Firestone Pkwy NE
Wilson, NC 27893-7991

     252-237-7923
Fax: 252-243-1832 800-548-2778
info@pestcon.com www.degeschamerica.com
Marketer of stored commodity pesticide protection products
Sales Exec: George Hunt
Estimated Sales: $1-5 Million
Number Employees: 10-19
Other Locations:
  Pestcon Systems
  Wilson NC

27463 Pester-USA
110 Commerce Drive
Allendale, NJ 07401-1656

     201-327-7009
Fax: 201-327-7824 pester-usa@pester.com
www.pester.com/en
End-of-line equipment, overwrapping, stretch/shrink bundling, case packing, palletizing
Vice President: Joachim Eckart
Contact: Walter Berghahn
walter-berghahn@pester.com
Estimated Sales: $5-10 Million
Number Employees: 10-19

27464 Petal
30 W 31st St
New York, NY 10001

     212-947-3662
Fax: 212-279-5107
Consultant specializing in research and development for beverage flavors
Estimated Sales: Below $500,000
Number Employees: 1-4

27465 Peter Drive Components
5148 Kennedy Rd
Suite 600
Fayetteville, GA 30214

     678-904-0853
Fax: 770-371-5063
Solutions for shaft/hub connections
Estimated Sales: $1-3 Million
Number Employees: 1-4

27466 Peter Dudgeon International
740 Kopke St
Honolulu, HI 96819-3315

     808-841-8211
Fax: 808-842-5093
Plastic materials
President: Peter Dudgeon
Treasurer: Shawn D Badham
Vice President: Andrew W Dudgeon
Contact: Jorge Delgado
jdelgado@gourmetfoodsinc.com
Estimated Sales: $5-10 Million
Number Employees: 5-9

27467 Peter Gray Corporation
44 Park St
Andover, MA 01810-3692

     978-470-0990
Fax: 978-475-6663
Stainless steel stampings, deep drawn parts, cylinders, pans, burners, barbecue housings and thermoset molded plastics, etc
Chairman, President, Chief Executive Off: Michael Strianese
Executive Vice President of Corporate St: Curtis Brunson
Director Sales: Mark Marchessault
Senior Vice President of Operations: Richard Cody
Estimated Sales: $1-5 Million
Number Employees: 1-4
Square Footage: 320000
Parent Co: Peter Gray Corporation

27468 Peter Kalustian Associates
239 Reserve Street
Boonton, NJ 07005-1301

     973-334-3008
Fax: 973-334-2757
Consultant specializing in manufacturing management, engineering, construction and marketing for the fat, margarine, shortening, cocoa butter substitute, fatty acid and derivative industries
President: Peter Kalustian
Number Employees: 3
Square Footage: 2700

27469 Peter Pan Sales
PO Box 8658
St. John's, NL A1B 3T1
Canada

     709-747-1990
Fax: 709-747-1482 800-563-9090
peterpan@nfld.com
Paper and plastic distributor
President: D Spurrell
Vice President: Chris Spurrell
Number Employees: 15
Square Footage: 88000

27470 Peter Pepper Products Inc
17929 S Susana Rd
Compton, CA 90221-5597

     310-639-0390
Fax: 310-639-6013
customerservice@peterpepper.com
www.peterpepper.com
Trash receptacles, reusable containers, displays, store fixtures and tables
President: Sigi Pepper
sigipepper@peterpepper.com
CFO: Michael Pepper
Quality Control: Bob Caceres
Marketing/Sales: Kip Pepper
Purchasing Manager: Chuck Martlaro
Estimated Sales: $10-20 Million
Number Employees: 50-99
Brands:
  Minimint
  Peppermint
  Tasque

27471 (HQ)Peterboro Basket Co
130 Grove St
PO Box 120
Peterborough, NH 03458-1756

     603-924-3861
Fax: 603-924-9261 www.peterborobasket.com
Insulated coolers and baskets including fruit, vegetable and shopping
CEO: Russell E Dodds
rdodds@peterborobasket.com
Estimated Sales: $10-20 Million
Number Employees: 50-99
Square Footage: 72000

27472 Peterson Fiberglass Laminates
PO Box 158
Shell Lake, WI 54871-0158

     715-468-2306
Fax: 715-468-7923
Brine tanks, flume and canal brining systems, cheese conveyors and fiberglass tanks for live fish transport
Vice President: Wayne Peterson
Estimated Sales: $500,000-$1 Million
Number Employees: 9
Square Footage: 32000

27473 Peterson Manufacturing Company
24133 W 143rd St
Plainfield, IL 60544

     815-436-9201
Fax: 815-436-2863 800-547-8995
callpmc@peterson-mfg.com
www.peterson-mfg.com
Manufacturer and exporter of metal storage racks
President: Gerry Kusiolek
CFO: Dicks Jenkins
Chairman of the Board: David Peterson
Estimated Sales: $5-10 Million
Number Employees: 50-99

27474 Peterson Sign Co
660 Mapunapuna St
Honolulu, HI 96819-2031

     808-521-6785
Fax: 808-836-1496 petersonsignco@cs.com
www.petersonsign.com
Signs including magnetic, engraved and silk screened
President: Chito Batoon
cbatoon@petersonsign.com
Estimated Sales: $1-2.5 Million
Number Employees: 100-249

27475 Petoskey Plastics
5725 Commerce Blvd
Morristown, TN 37814-1096

     423-586-8917
Fax: 423-587-1524 www.petoskeyplastics.com
Open zipper/recloseable and take-out food bags
President: Paul Keiswetter
General Manager (Morristown): Gary Ramsey
General Manager (Santa Fe Springs): Dennis Waggoner
Vice President of Sales and Marketing: Charles Lee
Director of Operations: Steven Smith
Plant Manager: Gordon Thompson
Number Employees: 100-249

27476 (HQ)Petro Moore Manufacturing Corporation
3641 Vernon Blvd
Long Island City, NY 11106-5123

     718-784-2516
Fax: 718-784-7099
Manufacturer and exporter of steel folding legs and folding and stackable tables
President: Robert Murphy
Secretary: Jan DeRosa
Estimated Sales: Below $5 Million
Number Employees: 5-9
Square Footage: 40000
Type of Packaging: Food Service

27477 Petro-Canada Lubricants
2310 Lakeshore Road
Mississauga, ON L5J 1K2
Canada

     866-335-3369
Fax: 905-822-7450 www.petro-canada.ca
Petro-Canada is a world class producer of more than 350 advanced lubricants, specialty fluids, food grade grease and lubricants
Number Employees: 10
Number of Products: 350
Parent Co: Suncor Energy Inc
Type of Packaging: Consumer, Food Service, Private Label, Bulk

27478 Petrochem Insulation
110 Corporate Pl
Vallejo, CA 94590

     707-644-7455
Fax: 707-644-4908 800-520-2705
www.petrocheminc.com
Petrochem is your premier single source specialty contractor.providing mechanical isulation,heat tracing, removable pad fabrication, fireproofing, scaffolding,floor coatings and abatement services. working nationwide fromsevenregional offices.
President: Art Lewis
Marketing Director: Brian Benson
Sales Director: Brian Benson
Contact: Paul Aceto
paul@silverspoonevents.com
Estimated Sales: $1-5 Million
Number Employees: 250-499

27479 (HQ)Petroleum Analyzer Co LP
8824 Fallbrook Dr
Houston, TX 77064-4855
281-940-1803
Fax: 281-580-0719 800-444-8378
sales@paclp.com www.paclp.com
Manufacturer and exporter of analyzers including
total nitrogen, sulfur and fluoride; also, sulfur-selec-
tive and nitrogen-specific GC and HPLC detectors
President: Jereon Schmits
jereon@paclp.com
CEO: Randy Wreyford
Marketing Director: Cindy Goodman
Sales Manager: Emmanuel Filaudeau
Number Employees: 500-999
Square Footage: 120000
Other Locations:
Antek Instruments
Dusseldorf

27480 Pexco Packaging Corporation
PO Box 6540
Toledo, OH 43612
419-470-5935
Fax: 419-470-5940 800-227-9950
www.pexcopkg.com
Bags including plain and printed polyethylene, poly-
propylene and styrene recloseable; also, roll stock
available
President: William Buri
Controller: Gene Roach
Production Manager: Thomas Jesionowski
Estimated Sales: $5-10 Million
Number Employees: 20-49
Square Footage: 80000

27481 Pez Candy Inc
35 Prindle Hill Rd
Orange, CT 06477-3616
203-795-0531
Fax: 203-799-1679
Candy and dispensers
President: Joseph Vittoria
CEO: Christian Jegen
jegen@pezcandyinc.com
CFO: Brian Fry
VP Marketing: Peter Vandall
VP Sales: Dan Silliman
VP Operations: Mark Morrissey
Estimated Sales: $3,100,000
Number Employees: 100-249
Type of Packaging: Consumer
Other Locations:
PEZ Candy
Orange CT
Brands:
Pez

27482 Pfankuch Machinery Corporation
5885 149th St W Ste 101
Apple Valley, MN 55124
952-891-3311
Fax: 952-891-5168 pfankuchmachine@msn.com
Manufacturer, importer and exporter of packaging
machinery including feeders, collators, counters and
wrappers
CEO: Claus Pfankuch
Estimated Sales: $3-5,000,000
Number Employees: 5-9
Square Footage: 22000
Parent Co: Pfankuch Maschinen

27483 Pfeil & Holding Inc
5815 Northern Blvd
Woodside, NY 11377-2297
718-545-4600
Fax: 718-932-7513 800-247-7955
info@cakedeco.com www.cakedeco.com
Bakers' equipment and utensils, cake decorations,
pastry bags, pans, tubes, tier separators, flavors and
ingredients
President: David Gordils
davidg@cakedeco.com
CEO: Sy Stricker
Sales Director: Jenn Covalluzzi
Estimated Sales: $5-10 Million
Number Employees: 20-49
Number of Products: 7000
Square Footage: 200000
Brands:
PFEIL

27484 PhF Specialist
P.O.Box 7697
San Jose, CA 95150-7697
408-275-0161
Fax: 408-280-0979 www.phfspec.com
Owner: Pamela Hardt-English
Estimated Sales: $300,000-500,000
Number Employees: 1-4

27485 Pharmaceutic Litho & Label Co.
3990 Royal Ave
Simi Valley, CA 93063
805-285-5162
Fax: 805-285-5182 800-882-9743
www.pharmaceuticlitho.com
Label printer
President/Owner: Jason Laurence
CEO: Bill Burch
Sales: Ken Zaves
Operations: Ed Bergmann
Year Founded: 1964
Number Employees: 51-100
Square Footage: 75000

27486 Pharmaceutical & Food Special
P.O.Box 7697
San Jose, CA 95150-7697
408-275-0161
Fax: 408-280-0979 phfspec@pacbell.net
www.phfspec.com
Importer and exporter of temperature sensing equip-
ment; also, consulting services available including
plant and process design, training, seminars and
FDA/USDA regulation compliance packaging
design
President: Pamela Hardt-English
Quality Control: Peter Cocotas
Vice President: Peter Cocotas
Food Tecnologist: Kim Cortes
Estimated Sales: Below $5 Million
Number Employees: 1-4
Square Footage: 10000

27487 Phase Fire Systems
2685 S Melrose Drive
Vista, CA 92081
760-741-2341
Fax: 760-741-2218 888-741-2341
www.phasefiresystems.com
Shrink packaging machinery including sleevers and
banders; also, tunnel ovens
President: Noel Perez
Secretary/Accounts Payable: Nicole Perez
Purchasing Manager: John Edgar
Estimated Sales: $1-2.5 Million
Number Employees: 9

27488 Phase II Pasta Machine Inc
55 Verdi St
Farmingdale, NY 11735-6316
631-293-4259
Fax: 631-293-4572 800-457-5070
pastamachine@aol.com
Manufacturer, exporter and importer of commercial
pasta equipment
President: Michael Wilson
pastamachines@aol.com
Estimated Sales: Less Than $500,000
Number Employees: 1-4
Square Footage: 11000
Brands:
Pastamagic
Pastamatic

27489 Phelps Industries
P.O.Box 190718
Little Rock, AR 72219-0718
501-568-5550
Fax: 501-568-3363 www.phelpsfan.com
Manufacturer and exporter of platform dump trucks
and live floor hoppers for bulk handling
Owner: Donald Phelps
Vice President: John Phelps
Estimated Sales: $10-20 Million
Number Employees: 50-99

27490 Phenix Label Co
11610 S Alden St
Olathe, KS 66062-6923
913-327-7000
Fax: 913-327-7010 800-274-3649
info@phenixlabel.com www.phenixlabel.com
Manufacturer and exporter of custom printed labels

President: Hans Peter
hpeter@phenixlabel.com
CFO: Mark Volz
VP: Mike Darpel
Quality Control: Gina Waltmire
Estimated Sales: $10-20 Million
Number Employees: 100-249
Square Footage: 70000
Parent Co: Phenix Box & Label Company
Type of Packaging: Consumer, Food Service, Pri-
vate Label

27491 Philadelphia Glass Bending Company
2520 Morris Street
Philadelphia, PA 19145-1716
215-726-8468
Fax: 215-336-3002
Lighting fixtures
Estimated Sales: $20-50 Million
Number Employees: 50-99
Parent Co: Seagull Lighting Products

27492 Philipp Lithographing Co
1960 Wisconsin Ave
PO Box 4
Grafton, WI 53024-2623
262-377-1100
Fax: 262-377-6660 800-657-0871
help@philipplitho.com www.philipplitho.com
Manufacturer and exporter of labels and point of
purchase displays
President/CEO: Peter Buening
pbuening@philipplithographing.com
CFO/Treasurer: Dave Kaehny
Vice President/General Counsel: Stacy Buening
Estimated Sales: $5-10 Million
Number Employees: 50-99
Square Footage: 70000
Type of Packaging: Private Label

27493 Philips Lighting Company
PO Box 6800
Somerset, NJ 08875-6800
732-563-3000
Fax: 732-563-3641 www.lighting.philips.com
Manufacturer and exporter of lamps including in-
candescent, fluorescent, HID, specialty, miniature,
etc
CEO: Ed Crawford
Director Channel Marketing: Paul Lienesch
Contact: Koen Joosse
koen.joosse@philips.com
Estimated Sales: $30-50 Million
Number Employees: 10,000

27494 Phillips Gourmet Inc
1011 Kaolin Rd
PO Box 190
Kennett Square, PA 19348-2605
610-925-0520
Fax: 610-925-0527 info@phillipsgourmet.com
www.phillipsmushroomfarms.com
Mushrooms
President: Marshall Phillips
marshall@phillipsgourmet.com
Number Employees: 100-249
Parent Co: Phillips Mushroom Farms
Type of Packaging: Consumer, Food Service
Brands:
Bella

27495 Phillips Plastics and Chemical
3200 Southwest Fwy
suite 3200
Houston, TX 77027-7538
713-552-9595
Fax: 713-552-0231 800-537-3746
www.phillipsakers.com
Food packaging, industrial packaging, clear rigid
and flexible packaging, conventional equipment
Contact: Harris Gregory
harris.clm@phillipsakers.com
Number Employees: 100-249

27496 Phillips Refrigeration Consultants
4014 Balmoral Drive
Champaign, IL 61822-8552
217-355-0319
Fax: 217-355-0324
President: John Phillips
Number Employees: 3

27497 (HQ)Philmont Manufacturing Co.
370 Overpeck Pl
Englewood, NJ 07631
201-816-5867
Fax: 201-569-3426 888-379-6483
Table padding and tablecloths
President: Bruce Strongwater
Quality Control: Jason Strongwater
Executive VP: Michael Rattner
CFO: Catherine Maren
VP Marketing: Adrian Trautman, Jr.
National Sales Manager: Bill Sarna
Estimated Sales: $20-30 Million
Number Employees: 100
Square Footage: 35000

27498 Phoenix & Eclectic Network
172 N York St
Elmhurst, IL 60126-2762
630-530-4373
Fax: 630-530-0651
Consultant providing packaging design services to
food processors
Estimated Sales: $1-5 Million
Number Employees: 5-9

27499 Phoenix Closures Inc
1899 High Grove Ln
Naperville, IL 60540-3996
630-544-3475
Fax: 630-420-4774
greatcaps@phoenixclosures.com
www.phoenixclosures.com
Manufacturer and exporter of caps and seals
President: Bert Miller
CFO: Rich Classen
Quality Control: Jim Twohij
VP Sales/Marketing: Jeff Davis
Sales Director: Tim Ferrel
Estimated Sales: $20-50 Million
Number Employees: 250-499
Number of Products: 1000
Square Footage: 100000
Brands:
    Accugard
    Accuseal
    Sealgard
    Softseal
    Sureseal
    Torkgard
    Tritab

27500 Phoenix Coatings
19893 Berenda Blvd
Madera, CA 93638
559-675-8122
Fax: 559-673-2571 800-464-1958
Decorative wine bottles
President/CEO: Tom Burk
Owner: Bob Pricer
Controller: Gordon Begman
Contact: Gordon Begeman
gman@phoenixcoatings.com
Office Manager: Craig Alton
Safety Officer: Mark Pankratz
Estimated Sales: $500,000-$1 Million
Number Employees: 5-9

27501 Phoenix Contact Inc
586 Fulling Mill Rd
Middletown, PA 17057-2966
717-944-1300
Fax: 717-944-1625 800-586-5525
info@phoenixcon.com www.phoenixcontact.com
President & CEO: Jack Nehlig
jnehlig@phoenixcon.com
Estimated Sales: $50-100 Million
Number Employees: 500-999

27502 Phoenix Engineering
8162 Market St # H
Suite H
Youngstown, OH 44512-6200
330-726-3477
Fax: 608-827-5898 www.phoenixdesigneng.com
Filling and heat sealing equipment
Owner: Christopher Jones
cjones@phoenixdesigneng.com
Number Employees: 5-9

27503 Phoenix Engineering
13208 Arctic Circle
Santa Fe Springs, CA 90670-5510
562-407-0512
Fax: 562-407-0518 800-991-1395
sales@pouchmachines.com
www.pouchmachines.com
Resins for cast and blown films for food packaging
President and CFO: Lynn Worthington
Contact: Brian Dykema
sales@pouchmachines.com
Estimated Sales: $1-2.5 Million
Number Employees: 1-4

27504 Phoenix Industries Corp
114 N Bedford St
Madison, WI 53703-2610
608-251-2533
Fax: 608-256-2604 888-241-7482
www.negusboxbag.com
Manufacturer and exporter of corrugated ice cream
containers; wholesaler/distributor and exporter of
packaging supplies including bags
President: Rod Shaughnessy
contact.nequs@negusboxbag.com
Sales: Greg Koch
Operations: Al Baler
Estimated Sales: $1-5 Million
Number Employees: 5-9
Square Footage: 40000
Parent Co: Phoenix Industries Corporation
Brands:
    Negus Octapak
    Negus Square Pak

27505 Phoenix Process Equipment
2402 Watterson Trl
Louisville, KY 40299-2536
502-499-6198
Fax: 502-499-1079 phoenix@dewater.com
www.dewater.com
President: Gary L Drake
CFO: Stephen Kovaka
Manager: Vlad Zalmanov
vzalmanov@phoenixprocess.com
Estimated Sales: $5-10 Million
Number Employees: 20-49

27506 Phoenix Sign Company
112 Clemons Rd
Aberdeen, WA 98520-0112
360-532-1111
Fax: 360-637-8557
Neon, electric, wooden and plastic signs
Owner: Faron Lash
Estimated Sales: $.5-1 million
Number Employees: 1-4

27507 Phoenix Wholesale Foodservice
16 Forest Pkwy
Building J
Forest Park, GA 30297-2015
404-363-9800
Fax: 404-363-4562 800-613-1998
sales@coboco.net www.phoenixwfs.com
Fruits, vegetables, dairy, eggs, dressings, prepared
meals, oil, tofu and bottled water
Vice President: Carol Peterman
carolp@coboco.net
VP: Richard Monahan
Manager of Sales: David Cowart
Specialty Buyer: Billy Sowers
Estimated Sales: $9.5 Million
Number Employees: 250-499
Square Footage: 320000

27508 Photo Graphics Co
5100 Martha Truman Rd # C
Grandview, MO 64030-1172
816-761-3333
Fax: 816-761-3032 www.nameplates-labels.com
Industrial name plates and labels
Manager: Andy Ortbals
andy@pgnameplates.com
Production Manager: Andrew Ortbals
Estimated Sales: Less Than $500,000
Number Employees: 1-4
Square Footage: 19200
Brands:
    Metalphoto

27509 Phytopia Inc
6947 Forest Glen Dr
Dallas, TX 75230-2358
214-750-7322
Fax: 214-750-7910 888-750-9336
barbara@phytopia.com www.phytopia.com
Culinary trained registered dietitian specializing in
low-fat recipe development and nutritional analysis
Owner: Barbara Gollman, MS, RD
bgollman@phytopia.com
Estimated Sales: Less Than $500,000
Number Employees: 1-4

27510 Phytotherapy Research Laboratory
W Fourth S
PO Box 627
Lobelville, TN 37097-0627
931-593-3780
Fax: 931-593-3782 800-274-3727
Herb extracts
President: Brent Davis
Estimated Sales: $500,000-$1 Million
Number Employees: 1-4
Square Footage: 50000
Type of Packaging: Private Label
Brands:
    Forest Center
    Hahg
    Prl

27511 Piab USA Inc
65 Sharp St
Hingham, MA 02043-4311
781-337-7309
Fax: 781-337-6864 800-321-7422
info@piab.com www.piab.com
Vice President: Greg Anderson
andersong@piab.com
Vice President of Business Development: Ed
McGovern
Estimated Sales: $10-20 Million
Number Employees: 20-49

27512 Piab USA Inc
65 Sharp St
Hingham, MA 02043-4311
781-337-7309
Fax: 781-337-6864 800-321-7422
info-usa@piab.com www.piab.com
N.A. distributor and manufacturer of vacuum con-
veyors and pumps for company based in Sweden
President: Chuck Weilbrenner
Vice President: Greg Anderson
andersong@piab.com
Estimated Sales: $10-20 Million
Number Employees: 20-49

27513 Piab Vacuum Products
65 Sharp St
Hingham, MA 2043
781-792-0003
Fax: 781-337-6864 800-321-7422
info@piab.com www.piabusa.com
Vacuum pumps, suction cups, vacuum filters, pneu-
matic conveyors, etc
President: Chuck Weilbrenner
CEO: Don Spradlin
Marketing Director: Ed McGraven
Sales: Jack Gray
Contact: Jaime Bohorquez
jbohorquez@piab.com
Estimated Sales: $10-20 Million
Number Employees: 50-99

27514 Piacere International
1101 Air Way
Glendale, CA 91201-2403
818-240-7335
Fax: 818-240-0558 800-432-3288
Espresso machines and accessories, pre-brewed
espresso, roasters, powders
Manager: Dick Forque
Estimated Sales: $1.5 Million
Number Employees: 30

27515 Picard Bakery Equipment
1325 E Notre-Dame Estate
Victoriaville, QC G6P 4B8
Canada
819-758-1883
Fax: 819-758-1465

Picard Ovens, Inc is the proud manufacturer of the REVOLUTION HYBRID OVEN, moduler deck oven, LP200 baking stone, SPITFIRE pizza oven, PRG rotisserie ovenm and much more.
President: Gilles Picard
Chief Financial Officer: Isabella Dupua
Vice President: Guy Picard
Research: Phillipe Lamay
Quality Control: Francis Picard
Marketing: Kristina Marchelli
Sales: Eric Ambrosio
Public Relations: Kristina Marchelli
Operations: Francis Picard
Estimated Sales: $5-10 Million
Number Employees: 10

27516 Pick Heaters

P.O.Box 516
West Bend, WI 53095

262-338-1191
Fax: 262-338-8489 800-233-9030
info1@pickheaters.com www.pickheaters.com
Manufacturer and exporter of direct steam injection liquid heating systems including heat exchangers, water heaters, hose stations and clean-in-place; also, cookers including food/starch, fruit and vegetable purees, etc
CEO: Prudence Hway
Executive VP: Michael Campbell
Estimated Sales: $2.5-5 Million
Number Employees: 25
Brands:
  Constant Flow
  Pick
  Sanitary
  Variable Flow

27517 Pickard China

782 Pickard Ave
Antioch, IL 60002-1574

847-395-3800
Fax: 847-395-3827 finest@pickardchina.com
www.pickardchina.com
Manufacturer and exporter of stock and custom fine china
President: Andrew P Morgan
amorgan@pickardchina.com
International Sales VP: Larry Smith
Estimated Sales: $5-10 Million
Number Employees: 20-49
Square Footage: 120000
Brands:
  Pickard

27518 Pickle Packers International Inc.

1101 17th Street NW
Suite 700
Washington, DC 20036

202-331-2456
www.ilovepickles.org
Sponsors research, representing industry before government agencies, educational materials and providing networking opportunities to its members.
Contact: Dennis Beal
dbeal@robgroup.com
Estimated Sales: $.5-1 million
Number Employees: 1-4

27519 Pickney Molded Plastics

3970 Parsons Rd
Howell, MI 48855-9617

517-546-9900
Fax: 517-546-7097 800-854-2920
www.pmpnet.com
Food transport systems
President: Don Verna
Estimated Sales: $10-20 Million
Number Employees: 50-99

27520 Pickwick Manufacturing Svc

4200 Thomas Dr SW
Cedar Rapids, IA 52404-5055

319-393-7443
Fax: 319-393-7456 800-397-9797
wcorey@pickwick.com www.pickwick.com
Manufacturer and exporter of poultry processing equipment including batch scalders, pickers and conveyorized eviscerating lines
President: Walter F Corey
wcorey@pickwick.com
CEO: Walter F Corey
Estimated Sales: $20-50 Million
Number Employees: 100-249
Square Footage: 100000

Brands:
  Dunkmaster
  Econo System
  Hom-Pik
  Pickwick
  Spin-Pik

27521 Picnic Time Inc

5131 Maureen Ln
Moorpark, CA 93021-1783

805-529-4500
Fax: 805-529-7474 888-742-6429
info@picnictime.com www.picnictime.com
Picnic baskets
President: Mario Tagliati
picnictime@picinctime.com
Managing Partners: Paul Cosaro
Managing Partners: Danny Corbucci
Vice President/Founder: Gustavo Cosaro
Marketing: Danny Corbucci
Sales Exec: Scott Mccormick
Estimated Sales: $5.4 Million
Number Employees: 50-99

27522 Pieco

2179 145th Ave
Manchester, IA 52057-8935

563-927-3352
Fax: 563-927-2310 800-334-3929
sales@pieco.com www.pieco.com
Cutting and boning devices, sharpening machines and services, sharpening and overhaul equipment, bone chips and cartilage removal, emulsifiers, accessories
Owner: Jerry York
jerry@pieco.com
Estimated Sales: $1-2.5 Million
Number Employees: 5-9

27523 Pieco

2179 145th Ave
Manchester, IA 52057-8935

563-927-3352
Fax: 563-927-2310 800-334-3929
www.pieco.com
Circular blade sharpeners and rotary surface grinders, grinder parts, wheels, knives and also recondition mechanical deboning equipment.
Owner: Jerry York
jerry@pieco.com
Number Employees: 5-9

27524 Piepenbrock Enterprises

919 State Route 33
Freehold, NJ 07728-8454

732-683-0991
Fax: 732-683-0992 800-942-0052
www.siebler.de
Pouching machine for tablets, caplets and capsules
Estimated Sales: $1-5 Million

27525 Pieper Automation

825 Ontario Rd
Green Bay, WI 54311-8017

920-465-4600
Fax: 920-465-4601 sales@pieper-automation.com
www.pieper-automation.com
Control systems integration, design and build custom automation machinery and control panels
Director of Sales: Paul Wenner
Number Employees: 100-150

27526 Pier 1 Imports

453 Chestnut Ridge Rd
Woodcliff Lake, NJ 07677-7679

201-666-4500
Fax: 201-666-8525 800-448-9993
www.pier1.com
Espresso machines, wood burning ovens and pasta equipment; importer of pasta and espresso equipment
Manager: Lauren Sanders
Estimated Sales: $1-3 Million
Number Employees: 10-19
Type of Packaging: Food Service
Brands:
  Cap-O-Mat

27527 Pierce Laminated Products Inc

2430 N Court St
Rockford, IL 61103-3999

815-968-9651
Fax: 815-968-7601 www.piercelaminated.com
Countertops and store fixtures

President: Eric Lindroth
eric@piercelaminated.com
Vice President: Eric Lindroth
Estimated Sales: $2.5-5 Million
Number Employees: 20-49
Square Footage: 70000

27528 Pierrepont Visual Graphics Inc

15 Elser Ter
Rochester, NY 14611-1607

585-235-5620
Fax: 585-235-8376 info@pvrochester.com
www.pvrochester.com
Signs, directory boards, vinyl letters, pressure sensitive decals, banners, posters and T-shirts
President: Scott Zappia
scott@pierrepont.com
Vice President: Terry Zappia
Estimated Sales: $1-2.5 Million
Number Employees: 10-19
Square Footage: 68000
Type of Packaging: Private Label

27529 Pike Awning Co

7300 SW Landmark Ln
Portland, OR 97224-8029

503-624-5600
Fax: 503-968-5440 800-866-9172
sales@pikeawning.com www.pikeawning.com
Commercial awnings
Owner: Tony Spear
Vice President: Ken Spearing
Estimated Sales: $2.5-5 Million
Number Employees: 20-49

27530 (HQ)Pilant Corp

4100 W Profile Pkwy
Bloomington, IN 47404-2546

812-334-7090
Fax: 317-392-4772 800-366-3525
Manufacturer and exporter of custom and stock recloseable and polyethylene bags
Manager: Peter Lenzen
Executive VP: Ronald Thieman
VP Sales: Dick Zurich
Manager: Curt Howard
howard@pliantcorporation.com
Estimated Sales: $3-5 Million
Number Employees: 5-9
Square Footage: 1400000
Other Locations:
  KCL Corp.
  Dallas TX

27531 Pilgrim Plastics

1200 W Chestnut St
Brockton, MA 02301-5574

508-436-6300
Fax: 508-580-0829 800-343-7810
www.pilgrimplastics.com
Manufacturer and exporter of plastic point of purchase displays, including window displays, door displays, counter change mats, shelf displays, membership cards, change cashing cards, promotional items, rulers, luggage tags, etc
President: Mark Abrams
mabrams@starprintingcorp.com
CFO: Mark Abrams
Quality Control: Jason Abrams
Estimated Sales: Below $5 Million
Number Employees: 50-99
Square Footage: 320000

27532 Pillar Technologies

475 E Industrial Dr
PO Box 110
Hartland, WI 53029-2336

262-912-7200
Fax: 262-912-7272 888-PIL-LAR6
www.pillartech.com
Induction sealers
Sales: Brad Budde
Manager: Tammy Wentlandt
tammyw@tastefullysimple.com
General Manager: Mark Stohl
Number Employees: 20-49
Parent Co: Illinois Tool Works Inc

27533 Pilot Brands

PO Box 10107
Zephyr Cove, NV 89448

775-588-8850
Fax: 775-588-8380 800-621-5262
info@pilotbrands.com www.pilotbrands.com
President: Kitt Barkley

27534 Pilz Automation Safety LP
7150 Commerce Blvd
Canton, MI 48187-4289
734-354-0272
Fax: 734-354-3355 888-650-7450
info@pilzusa.com www.pilzusa.com
CEO: Thomas Pilz
Manager: Michael Beerman
m.beerman@pilzusa.com
Estimated Sales: Below $5 Million
Number Employees: 20-49

27535 Pinckney Molded Plastics
3970 Parsons Rd
Howell, MI 48855
517-546-9900
Fax: 517-546-7097 800-854-2920
Cases, crates, dollies, trays, totes, pallets
President: Don Verna
Chairman of the Board: Leland Blatt
Sales Manager: Dave Heyink
Contact: Rich Kruyer
rkruyer@pmpnet.com
Estimated Sales: $10-20 Million
Number Employees: 50-99

27536 Pine Bluff Crating & Pallet
2600 S Persimmon St
Pine Bluff, AR 71603-3667
870-879-2287
Fax: 870-879-1190 866-415-1075
www.pinebluffcrating.com
Wooden pallets and skids
President: Mark Thicksten
Operations Manager: Zach Thicksten
Pallet Production Manager: Robert Ferguson
Customer Accounts/office operations: Mark Thicksten
Estimated Sales: $2.5-5 Million
Number Employees: 20-49

27537 Pine Point Fisherman's Co-Op
96 King St.
Scarborough, ME 04074
207-883-3588
Fax: 207-883-6772 lobster@maine.rr.com
lobsterco-op.com
Lobsters
Estimated Sales: $1-3 Million
Number Employees: 5-9

27538 Pine Point Wood Products Inc
19380 CO Rd 81
Osseo, MN 55311
763-428-4301
Fax: 763-428-4304 pineptwood@msn.com
Custom cut wooden pallets, skids, crates and containers
Owner: Jay Talbot
Quality Control: Larry Corbin
Sales Manager: Don Lenz
Sales: Larry Corbin
Estimated Sales: $10-20 Million
Number Employees: 10-19

27539 Pinn Pack Packaging LLC
1151 Pacific Ave
Oxnard, CA 93033-2472
805-385-4100
Fax: 805-981-0444 www.pinnpack.com
Custom thermoformed blisters, clamshells and trays; also, cups and cookie containers
President: Samuel Hong
General Manager: Brian Yamaguchi
Vice President: Dale Hong
daleh8567@aol.com
VP Operations: Sam Hong
Estimated Sales: $20-50 Million
Number Employees: 100-249
Square Footage: 43000

27540 Pinnacle Foods Inc.
222 W Merchandise Mart Plaza
Chicago, IL 60654
312-549-5000
877-266-2472
www.pinnaclefoods.com
Packaged and frozen foods.
President & CEO, Conagra: Sean Connolly
Year Founded: 1998
Estimated Sales: $3.14 Billion
Number Employees: 4,900
Parent Co: Conagra Brands
Type of Packaging: Consumer

Brands:
Vlasic®
Birds Eye®
Mrs. Paul's®
Duncan Hines®
Log Cabin®
Mrs. Butterworth's®
Van de Kamp's®
Tim's® Cascade Snacks
Armour®
Open Pit®
Brooks®
Lender's®
Nalley®
Celeste®
Aunt Jemima®
Comstock Wilderness®
Husman's®
Snyder®
Erin's®
Hawaiian®
El Restaurante®
Bernstein's®
Smart Balance®
Earth Balance®
Udi's®
Glutino®
Evol®
Gardein®

27541 Pinnacle Furnishing
10564 Nc Highway 211 E
Aberdeen, NC 28315
910-944-0908
Fax: 910-944-0920 866-229-5704
www.pinnaclefurnishings.com
Manufacturer and exporter of chairs and tables for restaurants, casinos, hotels and banquets
President: Jack Berggren
R&D: Jack Berggren
Vice President: Steve Laufer
Quality Control: Sarah Swanson
Regional Sales Representative: Bunnie Strauh
Estimated Sales: $2.5-5,000,000
Number Employees: 20-49
Square Footage: 80000

27542 Pino's Pasta Veloce
1903 Clove Road
Staten Island, NY 10304-1607
718-273-6660
Fax: 718-720-5906
Pasta sauce, pasta heaters
Manager Marketing: Joe Klaus
VP Operations: Al Cappillo
Estimated Sales: $2.5-5,000,000
Number Employees: 1-4
Parent Co: AEI
Type of Packaging: Consumer, Food Service
Brands:
Pino's Pasta Veloce

27543 Pinquist Tool & Die Company
63 Meserole Avenue
Brooklyn, NY 11222
718-389-3900
Fax: 718-349-3168 800-752-0414
www.pinquisttool.com
Metal stampings, display hardware, banner stands and wire and tubing racks
President: Richard Pinquist
Sales Director: C Oshinsky
Estimated Sales: Below $5 Million
Number Employees: 20-49
Square Footage: 20000

27544 Pioneer Chemical Co
13717 S Normandie Ave
Gardena, CA 90249-2609
310-366-7393
Fax: 310-366-7193
customerservice@pioneerchem.com
www.pioneerchem.com
Janitorial supplies, disinfectants, soaps and cleaning equipment
President: Jose Alvarez
jose@pioneerchem.com
Manager: Mary Alvarez
Estimated Sales: Below $5 Million
Number Employees: 10-19

27545 Pioneer Labels Inc
1195 S Lipan St # C
Suite C
Denver, CO 80223-3094
303-744-1606
Fax: 303-744-2443 877-744-1606
kevin@pioneerlabels.com www.pioneerlabels.com
Labels
President: Kevin Daly
kevin@pioneerlabels.com
Estimated Sales: Less Than $500,000
Number Employees: 1-4

27546 (HQ)Pioneer Manufacturing Co Inc
4529 Industrial Pkwy
Cleveland, OH 44135-4505
216-671-5500
Fax: 216-671-5502 800-877-1500
www.pioneerathletics.com
Aerosol insecticides, dustless chemical floor polishing mops, liquid quick drying floor wax and patching material for freezer and cooler floors
Owner: Doug Schattinger
dschat@aol.com
Estimated Sales: $20-50 Million
Number Employees: 100-249
Square Footage: 68000
Brands:
Advance
Kent

27547 Pioneer Marketing International
188 Westhill Drive
Los Gatos, CA 95032-5032
408-356-4990
Fax: 408-356-2795 www.pioneer.com
Corn, soybeans, alfalfa, canola, wheat, sunflowers; marketing, sales and product promotion
Partner: Russ Tritomo
Director Sales: Ed DeSoto
Estimated Sales: $1-5 Million
Number Employees: 4
Brands:
Pioneer©
Encirca©
Nutrivail

27548 Pioneer Packaging
220 Padgette St
Chicopee, MA 1022
413-378-6930
Fax: 413-378-6963
info@pioneerpackaginginc.com
Vacuum formed folding cartons
Owner: Jeffrey Shinners
Contact: Scott Anschuetz
sanschuetz@pioneerpackaginginc.com
Estimated Sales: $5-10 Million
Number Employees: 50-99

27549 Pioneer Packaging & Printing
1220 Lund Blvd
Anoka, MN 55303-1092
763-323-8308
Fax: 763-323-8207 800-708-1705
Folding paper boxes
President: Greg Polack
President/CEO: Greg Pollack
CFO: Richard Hall
Quality Control: Jon Maguessen
Contact: Sherry Tollefson
stollefson@pioneerpackaginginc.com
Estimated Sales: $10-20 Million
Number Employees: 100-249

27550 Pioneer Packaging Machinery
135 Farrs Bridge Rd
Pickens, SC 29671
864-878-4999
Fax: 864-878-8642
President: Howard Frist
Estimated Sales: $5-10 Million
Number Employees: 10

27551 Pioneer Plastics Inc
1584 US Highway 41a N
Dixon, KY 42409-9328
270-639-9133
Fax: 270-639-5882 800-951-1551
sales@pioneerplastics.com
www.pioneerplastics.com

Manufacturer and exporter of rigid molded clear plastic containers including round, square, oval and rectangular
President: Edward Knapp
CFO: Edward Knapp Jr
Marketing Manager: Wayne Fiester
Customer Service: David Fiester
Estimated Sales: $5-10 Million
Number Employees: 50-99
Type of Packaging: Consumer, Food Service

27552 Pioneer Sign Company
PO Box 583
Lewiston, ID 83501-0583
208-743-1275
Signs; crane installation service available
Owner: Bradley Keller
Estimated Sales: $1-2.5 Million
Number Employees: 19
Parent Co: Pioneer Sign Company

27553 (HQ)Piper Products Inc
300 S 84th Ave
Wausau, WI 54401-8460
715-842-5382
Fax: 715-848-1870 800-544-3057
info@piperonline.net www.piperonline.net
Aluminum racks, transport cabinets, dollies, proofer cabinets, hot boxes, pans and accessories; exporter of aluminum racks and transport cabinets
President: Roger D Sweeney
CEO: Tony Sweeney
National Sales Manager: R Joseph Graf
Customer Service: Evelyn Yakich
Estimated Sales: $10-20 Million
Number Employees: 50-99
Type of Packaging: Food Service
Other Locations:
Piper Products
Wausau WI

27554 Piper Products Inc
300 S 84th Ave
Wausau, WI 54401-8460
715-842-5382
Fax: 715-848-1870 800-544-3057
www.piperonline.net
Manufacturer and exporter of ovens, proofers, combination oven/proofers, transport and heated cabinets and bakery racks, cafeteria, buffet lines, tray delivery carts and support equipment
CEO: Tony Sweeney
CEO: Tony Sweeney
Estimated Sales: $10-20 Million
Number Employees: 50-99
Type of Packaging: Food Service
Brands:
Piper Products
Super Systems

27555 Piqua Paper Box Co
616 Covington Ave
PO Box 814
Piqua, OH 45356-3205
937-773-0313
Fax: 937-773-0142 800-536-2136
www.piquapaperbox.com
Rigid and folding cartons, vinyl and specialty packaging
President: Brian T Gleason
Estimated Sales: $5-10 Million
Number Employees: 50-99
Square Footage: 170000

27556 Pitco Frialator Inc
509 Route 3a
Bow, NH 03304-3102
603-225-6684
Fax: 603-230-5548 800-258-3708
dpacka@maytag.com www.pitco.com
Manufacturer and exporter of commercial cooking equipment including standard, high capacity, doughnut/bakery and high efficiency fryers, pasta cookers, frying filters and baskets
President: Scott Blasingame
sblasingame@pitco.com
Director Materials: Steve Karas
VP/General Manager: Robert Granger
VP Engineer: George McMahon
Estimated Sales: $20-50 Million
Number Employees: 20-49
Parent Co: G.S. Blodgett Corporation
Type of Packaging: Food Service

Brands:
Frialator
Pitco

27557 Pittsburgh Corning Corp
800 Presque Isle Dr
Pittsburgh, PA 15239-2799
724-327-6100
Fax: 724-387-3805
Manufacturer and exporter of moisture resistant glass insulation for floors, walls and roofs of food and beverage buildings, coolers and freezers
CEO: Jim Kane
jim_kane@pghcorning.com
Manager: Erik Elthiele
Chief Financial Officer/VP, Finance: Joseph Kirby
Vice President: Jean Collet
Vice President, Information Technology: Peter Atherton
Sales Manager: Steve Oslica
Director, Global Supply Chain: John Holzwarth
Estimated Sales: $45 Million
Number Employees: 20-49
Brands:
Foamglas

27558 Pittsburgh Tank Corp
1500 Industrial Dr
Monongahela, PA 15063-9753
724-258-0200
Fax: 724-258-7350 800-634-0243
sales@pghtank.com www.pghtank.com
Aluminum, carbon steel and stainless steel storage tanks
President: James Bollman
sales@pghtank.com
Vice President: Phil Duvall
Research & Development: Jeff Farrar
Sales Director: John Thompson
Purchasing Manager: Tracie Doman
Estimated Sales: 5-10 Million
Number Employees: 50-99
Number of Products: 6
Square Footage: 70000
Type of Packaging: Bulk

27559 Pittsfield Weaving Company
PO Box 8
Pittsfield, NH 3263
603-435-8301
Fax: 603-435-6753
Woven labels
President: Gilbert Bleckmann
Controller: Robert Russell
Estimated Sales: $10-20 Million
Number Employees: 50-99

27560 Pizzamatic USA
130 E 168th St
South Holland, IL 60473-2836
708-331-0660
Fax: 708-331-0663 888-749-9279
sandy@pizzamaticusa.com www.pizzamatic.com
Pizza production systems and pizzeria equipment
Co-founder: Clifford E. Fitch Jr
Sales: Sandy Johnson
Estimated Sales: $1-5 Million
Number Employees: 10-19

27561 Placemat Printers
Old Rt. 22 & 863
P.O. Box 699
Fogelsville, PA 18051-0699
610-285-2255
Fax: 610-285-2607 800-628-7746
sales@mastercraftprinting.com
www.mastercraftprinting.com
Full scale commercial print e-design shop
President: Darlene Pinto
Estimated Sales: Below $5 Million
Number Employees: 10-19

27562 Placon Corp
6096 Mckee Rd
Fitchburg, WI 53719-5103
608-271-5634
Fax: 608-271-3162 800-541-1535
betterdesign@placon.com www.placon.com
Thermoformed plastic packages, blister packages, box inserts, medical disposables and food container trays

President: Jan Acker
CEO: Dan Mohs
dmohs@placon.com
CEO: Dan Mohs
CFO: Rick Terrin
Estimated Sales: $50-75 Million
Number Employees: 250-499

27563 Placon Corp
1227 Union Street Ext
PO Box 548
West Springfield, MA 01089-4022
413-785-1553
Fax: 413-731-5952 800-342-2011
info@plasticpkg.com www.placon.com
Injection molded plastic food containers and lids
President: Susan Weiss
sweiss@plasticpkg.com
CFO: Edd Katotlam
Estimated Sales: $10-25 Million
Number Employees: 100-249

27564 (HQ)Plainview Milk Products
130 2nd St SW
Plainview, MN 55964-1394
507-534-3872
Fax: 507-534-3992 800-356-5606
www.plainviewmilk.com
Butter, whey and milk; custom agglomeration and spray drying
General Manager: Dallas Moe
dmoe@plainviewmilk.com
Controller: Janna Van Rooyen
Sales Manager: Darrell Hanson
Plant Manager: Donny Schreiber
Number Employees: 50-99
Square Footage: 18060
Type of Packaging: Consumer, Food Service, Private Label, Bulk
Brands:
Greenwood Prairie

27565 Planet Products Corp
4200 Malsbary Rd
Blue Ash, OH 45242-5598
513-984-5544
Fax: 513-984-5580 info@planet-products.com
www.planet-products.com
Manufacturer and exporter of sausage and frankfurter loading, cheese stick equipment. Manufacturer of turnkey systems in automating sandwich assembly and other ready to eat products
Owner: Kathy Randolph
krandolph@planet-products.com
CEO: Mike F
VP: John Abraham
Marketing: Jennifer Coromel
Estimated Sales: $10-20 Million
Number Employees: 20-49
Brands:
Link N Load
Servo-Pak

27566 Plas-Ties Co
14272 Chambers Rd
Tustin, CA 92780-6994
714-542-4487
Fax: 714-972-2978 800-854-0137
info@plasties.com www.plastictyer.com
Strip and air curtains and food service doors
Owner: Lou Contreras
Sales Manager: Jesse Garcia
Estimated Sales: $5-10 Million
Number Employees: 20-49
Square Footage: 240000

27567 Plascal Corp
361 Eastern Pkwy
PO Box 590
Farmingdale, NY 11735-2713
516-249-2200
Fax: 516-249-2256 800-899-7527
plascal@aol.com www.plascal.com
Manufacturer and exporter of plain, printed, laminated and PVC plastic film and sheeting
CEO: Mark Hurd
President: Fred Hurd
Estimated Sales: $10-20 Million
Number Employees: 100-249

27568 Plaskid Company
PO Box 162841
Austin, TX 78716-2841

512-328-7785
Fax: 714-972-2978 800-854-0137
Coatings to frictionize plastics, application systems
for films and foam

27569 Plassein International
200 S Biscayne Boulevard
Suite 900
Miami, FL 33131-5344

860-429-5070
Fax: 860-429-5071 866-752-7734

27570 Plasseint International
920 Wilshire Drive
Libertyville, IL 60048-1858

847-680-5835
Fax: 847-680-1478 rickk101@aol.com
A packaging firm, manufacture plastic packaging
materials in US and Canada

27571 Plast-O-Matic Valves Inc
1384 Pompton Ave # 1
Suite 1
Cedar Grove, NJ 07009-1095

973-256-9344
Fax: 973-256-4745 info@plastomatic.com
www.plastomatic.com
Thermoplastic valves
VP: Bob Sinclair
Estimated Sales: $10-25 Million
Number Employees: 50-99

27572 Plastech
205 W Duarte Rd
Monrovia, CA 91016-4529

626-358-9306
Fax: 626-303-6288
Manufacturer and exporter of plastic point of pur-
chase displays
Owner: Pat Delaney
CFO: Pat Delaney
Contact: Laurie Castro
jauthier@solarcity.com
Estimated Sales: Below $5 Million
Number Employees: 10-19
Type of Packaging: Consumer, Bulk

27573 Plastech Corp
2080 General Truman St NW
Atlanta, GA 30318-2010

404-355-9682
Fax: 404-355-5410 info@plastech.com
www.plastech.com
Thermoformed plastic products including blister and
clamshell packaging, trays and signs; also, in-house
product design and tool making, computerized trim-
ming, finishing and decorating, assemblies and
prototypes available
President: Larry W Lee
accounting@plastech.com
Quality Control: Darius Lee
Sales/Marketing: David Lee
Estimated Sales: Below $5 Million
Number Employees: 20-49

27574 Plasti Print Inc
1620 Gilbreth Rd
Burlingame, CA 94010-1405

650-652-4950
Fax: 650-652-4954 www.plasti-print.com
Plastic pressure-sensitive labels and shelf strips
President: Michael Magpantay
mom@truecar.com
CEO: Helen Vigil
VP: Rodney Vigil
Estimated Sales: Below $5 Million
Number Employees: 5-9
Square Footage: 9000

27575 Plasti-Clip Corp
38 Perry Rd
Milford, NH 03055-4308

603-672-1166
Fax: 603-672-6637 800-882-2547
sales@plasticlip.com www.plasticlip.com
Manufacturer and exporter of point of purchase clips
and fasteners including displays, price tags, tickets,
etc; also, coupon holders, employee (and visitor) ID
badging software and supplies
President: Daniel Faneuf
sales@plasticlip.com

Estimated Sales: $1-2.5 Million
Number Employees: 5-9
Number of Brands: 50
Number of Products: 1000
Square Footage: 14000
Brands:
  3m
  Anchor
  Arrow Clip
  Crystal View
  Dc Uni-Clip
  E-Z Rak-Clip
  Flex-Holder
  Grip Clip
  Gt Uni-Clip
  Magnaclamp
  Mid-Trak
  Plasti-Rivet
  Premium Trak-Clip
  Presto Galaxy
  Snap'n Clip
  Springrip
  Take-1
  The Messenger
  Thum-Screw
  Trak Clip
  Uni-Badge
  Uni-Strap
  Wobblers

27576 Plasti-Line
445 S Gay Street
Suite 100
Knoxville, TN 37902-1133

865-938-1511
Fax: 865-947-8531 800-444-7446
Manufacturer and exporter of plastic, metal, interior
and exterior illuminated signs including menu
boards and point of purchase displays
VP Marketing: Mickey Davis
Marketing Manager: Mary Ann Herrick
Estimated Sales: $20-50 Million
Number Employees: 500-999

27577 Plasti-Mach Corporation
704 Executive Blvd # G
Valley Cottage, NY 10989-2023

845-267-2985
Fax: 845-267-2825 800-394-1128
plastimach@plastimach.com www.plastimach.com
Manufacturer and exporter of used equipment in-
cluding thermoforming, extrusion and heat sealing
President: Robert Rosen
VP: Jerry Hammerman
Contact: Tammy Sabat
tammysabat@plastimach.com
Estimated Sales: $1-5 Million
Number Employees: 5-9
Square Footage: 40000

27578 Plastic Art Signs
3931 W Navy Blvd
Pensacola, FL 32507-1256

850-455-4114
Fax: 850-455-5033 866-662-7060
www.plasticartssigns.com
Neon and plastic signs
President: Jon Navarro
jon@plasticartssigns.com
Estimated Sales: $500,000-$1 Million
Number Employees: 10-19

27579 Plastic Assembly Corporation
1 Sculley Rd. Unit A
Ayer, MA 01432-632
Fax: 978-772-6096 patrickmagmus@aol.com
Plastic containers
President: Regis M Magnus
R & D: Patric Magnus
Estimated Sales: Below $5 Million
Number Employees: 10
Square Footage: 150000
Brands:
  Blinky

27580 Plastic Container Corp
2508 N Oak St
Urbana, IL 61802-7207

217-352-2722
Fax: 217-352-2822 jgentles@netpcc.com
www.netpcc.com
Plastic bottles

President & CEO: Ron Rhoades
Sales Manager: Jo Ellen Gentles
Sales Representative: John Foote
Number Employees: 50-99
Square Footage: 500000
Type of Packaging: Consumer

27581 Plastic Craft Products Corp
744 W Nyack Rd
PO Box K
West Nyack, NY 10994-1998

845-358-3010
Fax: 845-358-3007 800-627-3010
pc@plastic-craft.com www.plastic-craft.com
Plastic film and acrylic signs
President: Mark Brecher
pc@plastic-craft.com
VP Sales: Mark Brecher
Operations Manager: Yung Nguyen
Estimated Sales: $2.5-5 Million
Number Employees: 20-49
Square Footage: 66000

27582 Plastic Equipment
305 Rock Industrial Park Drive
Bridgeton, MO 63044-1214

800-645-5439
Fax: 314-739-3240 800-270-6225

27583 Plastic Fantastics/BuckSigns
823 Siskiyou Boulevard
Ashland, OR 97520-2168

541-482-2223
Fax: 541-482-2223 800-482-1776
Push-type portion control food dispensers, brochure
holders, picture frames, signs, magazine holders,
grocery displays, medical appliances, bulk food dis-
pensers, display boxes, acrylic wine racks, engraved
and sand blasted woodsigns
Owner: Michael Buckley
CEO: Barbara Buckley
CFO: Issac Reed
Estimated Sales: $2.5-5 Million
Number Employees: 4
Square Footage: 2800

27584 Plastic Ingenuity
1017 Park St
Cross Plains, WI 53528-9631

608-798-3071
Fax: 608-798-4452 www.plasticingenuity.com
Thermoformed packaging, tooling & extrusion ser-
vices for the food packaging industry.
President: Tom Kuehn
tom@plasticingenuity.com
Number Employees: 250-499

27585 Plastic Packaging Technologies
750 S 65th St
Kansas City, KS 66111-2301

913-287-3383
Fax: 913-287-9420 800-468-0029
info@plaspack.com www.plaspack.com
President: David Staker
CFO: Deena Staus
Quality Control: John Seevers
R&D: John Seevers
Number Employees: 100-249

27586 Plastic Printing LLC
320 Clay St
Dayton, KY 41074-1256

859-581-5700
Fax: 859-291-2112 877-581-7748
csr@plasticprintinginc.com
Plastic advertising items
President: Barry Henry
plasticprt@yahoo.com
Manager: Shawn Davis
Estimated Sales: Below $5 Million
Number Employees: 1-4
Square Footage: 12654

27587 Plastic Suppliers Inc
2400 Marilyn Ln
Columbus, OH 43219

614-471-9100
800-722-5577
www.plasticsuppliers.com

Complete line of unsupported film substrates for the label market including Labelflex, a biaxially oreinted polysterne label stock film, polyester film, polypropylene films for labeling, packaging and lamination applications, PVC andsynthetic papers; also new shrink label films. Whether your products call for durability, printability or over all appearance, Plastic suppliers is your total films solution
President & CEO: George Thomas
thomas@plasticsuppliers.com
Managing Director: Bart DeKeyser
Chief Financial Officer: Michael DuFrayne
Chief Technical Officer: Francisco Cavalcanti
Director of R&D/New Product Development: Ed Tweed
VP, Sales & Markting for the Americas: Brad Bastion
VP of Manufacturing: Erich Emhuff
Operations Manager: Denis Vynckier
Year Founded: 1949
Estimated Sales: $100-500 Million
Number Employees: 250-499
Brands:
  Labelflex
  Polyflex
  Tip-On

27588 Plastic Supply Inc
8 Liberty Dr
Londonderry, NH 03053-2251
603-260-6101
Fax: 603-668-1691 800-752-7759
sales@plasticsupply.com www.plasticsupply.com
Lobster tanks
President: John Murphey
sales@plasticsupply.com
General Manager: Bill Johnson
Estimated Sales: $2.5-5 Million
Number Employees: 10-19
Square Footage: 23000
Parent Co: Plastic Supply Inc
Brands:
  Atlantic Lobster

27589 Plastic Systems Inc
465 Cornwall Ave
Buffalo, NY 14215-3125
716-835-7555
Fax: 716-835-7776 800-604-7159
www.plasticsystems.com
Custom molding of vacuum formed parts
President: Daniel E Mcnamara
daniel@plasticsystems.com
Estimated Sales: $1-2.5 Million
Number Employees: 5-9

27590 Plastic Tagtrade Check
1201 Woodside Ave
Essexville, MI 48732-1285
989-892-7913
Fax: 989-892-7988
Plastic badges and tags
President: Earl J Mast
President: Earl J Mast
Office Manager: Alice Brennan
Estimated Sales: $10-20 Million
Number Employees: 10-19

27591 Plastic Turning Company
331 Hamilton Street
Leominster, MA 01453-2313
978-534-8326
Plastic signs and canopies
Proprietor: Ruth Nickel
Estimated Sales: Less than $500,000
Number Employees: 4
Square Footage: 5000

27592 Plastican Corporation
271 Us Highway 46
Suite G110
Fairfield, NJ 07004-2489
973-227-7817
Fax: 973-227-6821
Plastic containers
President: John Carrico
Manager: Kathy Gaiser
Estimated Sales: $5-10 Million
Number Employees: 5-9

27593 Plasticard-Locktech Intl
605 Sweeten Creek Ind Park
Asheville, NC 28803-1774
828-210-4754
Fax: 828-210-4755 800-752-1017
www.plicards.com
Key cards and lock systems
CEO: Mark Goldberg
mgoldberg@plicards.com
Sales Representative: Tom Smith
Estimated Sales: $2.5-5 Million
Number Employees: 250-499

27594 Plastics Color Corp
14201 Paxton Ave
Chicago, IL 60409
800-922-9936
www.plasticscolor.com
Color concentrates for thermoplastic, pre-colored, natural and clear materials.
President: Joseph Byrne
Office Assistant: Clyde Smith, III
Year Founded: 1964
Estimated Sales: $100-500 Million
Number Employees: 100
Square Footage: 250000

27595 Plastics Inc
9249 Highway 14 W
Greensboro, AL 36744
334-624-8801
Fax: 334-624-4889 www.plasticsinc.com
Plastic milk containers
President: W E Burt
Estimated Sales: $10-20 Million
Number Employees: 20-49

27596 Plastics Industries
213 Dennis St
Athens, TN 37303-2995
423-745-6213
Fax: 951-894-0124 800-894-4876
www.pi-inc.com
Blowmolded plastic bottles
President: Nicholas Rende
VP Sales/Marketing: Dennis Niles
Contact: Jones Dean
jdean@plastecproducts.com
Estimated Sales: $10-20 Million
Number Employees: 20-49
Square Footage: 130000

27597 Plastilite Corporation
P.O.Box 12457
Omaha, NE 68112
402-453-7500
Fax: 402-571-6739 800-228-9506
info@plastilite.com www.plastilite.com
Foam coolers designed to keep products frozen during shipping
Sales Representative: Greg Montgomery
Contact: Tom Colligan
tcolligan@plastilite.com
Principal: Tom Colligan
Estimated Sales: $10+ Million
Number Employees: 50-99
Square Footage: 150000
Brands:
  Chubby 7 Day Cooler

27598 Plastimatic Arts Corporation
3622 N Home St
Mishawaka, IN 46545
574-254-9000
Fax: 574-254-9001 800-442-3593
sales@pacbannerworks.com
www.pacbannerworks.com
Coding, dating and marking equipment and plastic signs
Owner: Tim Rink
Contact: Dan Clark
dan@pacbannerworks.com
Estimated Sales: $5-10 Million
Number Employees: 20-49
Parent Co: Rink Riverside Printing

27599 (HQ)Plastipak Industries
30 Taschereau Boulevard
Suite 210
La Prairie, QC J5R 5H7
Canada
800-387-7452
Fax: 450-619-1444 www.plastipak.ca
Rigid plastic packaging

President: Normand Tanguay
CFO: Guy Bellemare
Vice President: Yves Gosselin
Estimated Sales: $80,000,000
Number Employees: 400
Number of Products: 5000
Type of Packaging: Food Service, Private Label

27600 Plastipak Packaging
41605 Ann Arbor Road
Plymouth, MI 48170
734-354-3510
Fax: 734-455-0556 info@plastipak.com
www.plastipak.com
Manufacturer and exporter of PET and HDPE bottles and containers
President/CEO: William C Young
Estimated Sales: $5-10 Million
Number Employees: 100-249

27601 Plastipro
5200 W Century Blvd
Los Angeles, CA 90045
417-325-7182
Fax: 310-693-8620 800-779-0561
www.plastproinc.com
Plastic insulated jacketing systems for pipes, tanks, vessels, walls, etc
General Manager: Bill Bitterman
VP: Christy Gonzales
Estimated Sales: $2.5-5,000,000
Number Employees: 19
Square Footage: 30000
Brands:
  P.I.C. Plastics, Inc.

27602 Plastiques Cascades Group
Suite 400
Montreal, QC H3A 1G1
Canada
514-284-9850
Fax: 514-284-9866 888-703-6515
www.cascadesreplast.com
Manufactures meat trays, pre-padded trays, plates and ProZorb meat pads. Specializes in plastic thermoforming and operates in the retail and industrial markets under the brand names of Plastichange Benpac and Deli-Tray
President: Mario Plourve
General Manager: Mario Lacharite
R & D: Claude Cossette
Marketing Assistant: Barbara Hogg
Sales/Marketing Executive: Sandra Hudon
Estimated Sales: $30-50 Million
Number Employees: 10
Parent Co: Plastiques Cascades
Type of Packaging: Consumer, Food Service, Private Label, Bulk
Brands:
  Frig-O-Seal
  Gourmet
  Maxima
  Plastichange
  Pro-Zorb

27603 Plastocon
1200 W 2nd St
Oconomowoc, WI 53066-3403
262-569-3131
Fax: 262-569-3135 800-966-0103
hottray@plastocon.com www.plastoconinc.com
Manufacturer and exporter of temperature-maintaining meal delivery systems including insulated food trays, mugs, delivery carts, bowls, tray inserts, lids and hot and cold carts; also, rethermalizers and drying and storage racks
President: Joe Camielewski
CEO: Joe Chmielewski
joe.chmielewski@plastoconinc.com
National Sales Manager: Jerry L. Marks
Number Employees: 50-99
Type of Packaging: Food Service, Private Label
Other Locations:
  Hot Tray Division
  Columbia SC
Brands:
  Hot Tray

27604 Plaxall Inc
546 46th Ave
Long Island City, NY 11101-5248
718-784-4800
Fax: 718-784-4611 800-876-5706
info@plaxall.com

Custom thermoformed plastic clamshells, cups and trays; also, experimental model workshop, machine shop and in-plant sheet extrusion of plastic materials
President: James M Pfohl
CEO: Ray Schiffner
rschiffner@plaxall.com
Vice President: Andrew Kirby
Estimated Sales: $10-20 Million
Number Employees: 100-249
Square Footage: 180000
Parent Co: Design Center

27605 Playtex Products, LLC
890 Mountain Ave.
New Providence, NJ 07974
888-310-4290
www.playtexproductsinc.com
Protective neoprene and latex gloves
CEO: Michael Gallagher
Contact: Edward Bleistein
ebleistein@playtex.com
Estimated Sales: $1-5 Million
Number Employees: 1750

27606 Plaze Inc
105 Bolte Ln
St Clair, MO 63077-3219
636-629-3400
800-986-9509
info@plaze.com www.plaze.com
Contract packager of aerosol and liquid pan coating products
President: Shelly Anderson
sanderson@plzaeroscience.com
VP Sales: Hugh Davison
VP Manufacturing: Dennis Bullock
Plant Manager: Bob Thornton
Purchasing Manager: Denise Steen
Number Employees: 100-249
Square Footage: 400000
Type of Packaging: Private Label

27607 PlexPack Corp
1160 Birchmount Road
Unit 2
Toronto, ON M1P Z08
Canada
416-291-8085
Fax: 416-298-4328 855-635-9238
info@emplex.com www.plexpack.com
Bag sealing and automated bagging equipment and the bamark line of shrink and sleeve wrapping equipment
President/CEO: Paul Irvine
Vice President: John Lewitt
Number Employees: 20-49
Type of Packaging: Consumer, Food Service, Private Label

27608 Plicon Corporation
4949 Schatulga Road
Columbus, GA 31907-1945
706-561-9999
Fax: 706-563-0567
Coffee industry pouch materials (cellophane, paper, films)
Estimated Sales: $10-30 Million
Number Employees: 20-50

27609 Plitek LLC
69 Rawls Rd
Des Plaines, IL 60018-1326
847-827-6680
Fax: 847-827-6733 800-966-1250
sales@plitek.com
Tea and coffee industry valve applications
President: Rich Andracki
rich.andracki@plitek.com
Estimated Sales: $10-20 Million
Number Employees: 50-99

27610 Plus Pharma
2460 Coral St
Vista, CA 92081-8430
760-597-0200
Fax: 760-597-0734 info@pluspharm.com
www.pluspharm.com
Herbs, gelatin and vegetarian capsules
President: Bill Roberts
Estimated Sales: Less Than $500,000
Number Employees: 1-4

27611 Pluto Corporation
PO Box 391
French Lick, IN 47432
812-936-9988
Fax: 812-936-2828 alan.friedman@plutocorp.com
www.plutocorp.com
Contract packager and exporter of household cleaners; also blowmold HDPE plastic bottles
President: Alan J Friedman
Plant Manager: Dennis Kaiser
Estimated Sales: $5-10 Million
Number Employees: 100-249
Square Footage: 240000
Parent Co: AHF Industries

27612 Plymold
615 Centennial Dr
Kenyon, MN 55946-1297
507-789-5111
Fax: 507-789-8315 800-759-6653
seating@plymold.com www.foldcraft.com
Manufacturer and exporter of tabletops, booths, indoor/outdoor clusters, millwork, tables, chairs, waste receptacles, salad bars and cabinets
Founder: Harold Nielsen
CEO: Chuck Mayhew
Marketing Coordinator: John Price
Contact: Jodie Anderson
andersonjodie@plymold.com
Estimated Sales: $20-50 Million
Number Employees: 100-249
Square Footage: 275000
Parent Co: Foldcraft
Brands:
Dur-A-Edge
Plymold

27613 (HQ)Plymouth Tube Company
2061 Young St
East Troy, WI 53120
262-642-8201
Fax: 262-642-8486 sales@plymouth.com
www.trent-tube.com
Specialty manufacturer of precision steel tubing, steel and titanium near-net shapes, and steel and titanium cold drawn shapes.
President: Donald Van Pelt
VP Development: Scott Curnel
VP Marketing/Sales: Steve Bohnenkamp
Contact: Mike Kennerson
mkennerson@plymouth.com
Number Employees: 250-499

27614 Pneucon
4802 Industry Dr
Central Point, OR 97502-3286
541-690-1700
Fax: 541-690-1713 800-545-1355
info@pneucon.com www.pneucon.com
Orifices
President: Wayland Gillrspie
Contact: Brian Miner
miner@pneucon.com
Estimated Sales: Less Than $500,000
Number Employees: 1-4

27615 Pneumatic Conveying Inc
960 E Grevillea Ct
Ontario, CA 91761-5612
909-923-2901
Fax: 909-923-4491 800-655-4481
sales@pneu-con.com
www.pneumaticconveyingsolutions.com
Manufacturer and exporter of customized pneumatic conveying equipment
President: Wayland Gillrspie
Sales Engineer: David Gordon
Sales Administrator: Jennifer Edmondson
Estimated Sales: $2.5-5 Million
Number Employees: 20-49
Square Footage: 120000
Parent Co: Pneumatic Conveying
Brands:
Pneu-Con

27616 Pneumatic Scale Angelus
10 Ascot Pkwy
Cuyahoga Falls, OH 44223-3325
330-923-0491
Fax: 330-923-5570 sales@pneumaticscale.com
www.pneumaticscale.com
Manufacturer and exporter of liquid and dry fillers, cappers, and can seamers

President: William Morgan
Marketing Director: Bethany Hilt
Sales Director: Paul Kearney
Contact: Karl Barkhurst
kbarkhurst2@master-lighting.com
Operations Manager: Paul Kelly
Purchasing Manager: Dave Bellet
Estimated Sales: Less Than $500,000
Number Employees: 1-4
Square Footage: 130000
Parent Co: Barry-Wehmiller Company
Type of Packaging: Consumer, Food Service, Private Label, Bulk

27617 Poblocki Sign Co
922 S 70th St
Milwaukee, WI 53214-3163
414-453-4010
Fax: 414-453-3070 www.poblocki.com
Exhibition cases, exterior and interior custom signs and message boards; custom design services available
President: David Drury
CEO: Brian Johnson
bjohnson@poblocki.com
VP: Mark Poblocki
Estimated Sales: $10-20 Million
Number Employees: 100-249
Square Footage: 200000

27618 Pocantico Resources Inc
55 S Broadway # 1
Tarrytown, NY 10591-4004
914-631-1760
Fax: 914-631-7863 info@pocanticoresources.com
www.pocanticoresources.net
Nutritional ingredients supplier.
Owner: Chris Dilorenzo
chris@pocanticoresources.net
Estimated Sales: $10-20 Million
Number Employees: 5-9

27619 Podnar Plastics Inc
1510 Mogadore Rd
Kent, OH 44240-7599
330-673-2255
Fax: 330-673-2273 800-673-5277
www.rez-tech.com
Manufacturer and exporter of injection blow-molded plastic products including bottles and point-of-purchase containers
President: Jack Podnar
Marketing Director: Jack Podnar
Sales Director: C Allen Clarke
Plant Manager: Scott Podnar
Estimated Sales: $5-10 Million
Number Employees: 20-49
Square Footage: 94000
Type of Packaging: Bulk

27620 Pohlig Brothers
8001 Greenpine Rd
N Chesterfield, VA 23237-2259
804-275-9000
Fax: 804-275-9900 info@pohlig.com
www.pohlig.com
Custom folding and rigid set-up paper boxes
President: Susan Gaffney
rpittman@foodlion.com
Estimated Sales: $9 Million
Number Employees: 50-99
Square Footage: 220000

27621 Pointing Color
2526 Baldwin Street
Saint Louis, MO 63106-1949
651-770-7888
Fax: 651-770-7999
Dyes, dispersions for food products

27622 Polanis Plastic of America
820 Freeway Drive N
Suite 208
Columbus, OH 43229-5404
614-848-5560
Fax: 614-848-5570 www.polinas.com
Biaxially oriented polypropylene films, food and confectionery films, antifog films, metallized films, lamination and tape base films

27623 (HQ)Polar Bear
2695 Pine Grove Rd
Cumming, GA 30041

770-292-9222
Fax: 888-776-5598 888-438-7924
polarbear@usa.net www.polarbearcoolers.com
Distributor of commercial refrigeration freezers, ice
cubers, ice dispensers and ice storage bins
Owner: Michael Kennis
General Manager Sales/Distribution: Vic Lemieux
Contact: Geoff Cole
geoff@polarbearcoolers.com
General Manager Production Plant: Dwayne
Whitehill
Estimated Sales: $5-10,000,000
Number Employees: 5-9
Type of Packaging: Private Label

27624 Polar Beer Systems
26035 Palomar Rd
Sun City, CA 92585-9710

951-928-8174
Fax: 619-449-0464
Manufacturer and exporter of food service equip-
ment including beverage dispensers, servers and
preparation equipment; also, carts
Owner: Sandy Blais
admin@polarbeersystems.com
Estimated Sales: $2.5-5 Million
Number Employees: 10-19
Type of Packaging: Food Service

27625 Polar Hospitality Products
2046 Castor Ave
Philadelphia, PA 19134

215-535-6940
Fax: 215-535-6971 800-831-7823
bradk@the-polar.com www.the-polar.com
Manufacturer and exporter of menu covers and wine
list covers, check presenters and coasters
President: Brad Karasik
National Sales Manager: Lisa Dale
Customer Service Manager: Arlinda Candelaria
Estimated Sales: $1 Million
Number Employees: 20-49
Square Footage: 72000
Parent Co: Polar Manufacturing
Brands:
  Polar

27626 Polar Ice
2423 W Industrial Park
Bloomington, IN 47404-2601

812-333-1528
Fax: 812-333-1591 800-733-0423
Packaged ice
President: Don Kinser
Treasurer: Pam Kinser
Number Employees: 10
Square Footage: 20000

27627 Polar King Transportation
4410 New Haven Ave
Fort Wayne, IN 46803-1650

260-428-2575
Fax: 260-428-2533 888-541-8330
www.polarking.com
Constructed and ready to operate walk-in coolers
and freezers for outdoor use
Marketing Director: Kris Markham
Manager: Mike Lovett
mikel@polarking.com
Manager: Mike Lovett
Number Employees: 5-9
Square Footage: 150000
Brands:
  Polar King

27628 Polar Peaks
16845 N 29th Avenue
Suite I-303
Phoenix, AZ 85053-3053

480-949-4787
Fax: 602-547-8939

27629 Polar Plastics
4210 Thimens Blouevard
St Laurent, QC H4R 2B9
Canada

514-331-0207
Fax: 514-331-7604 info@polarplastic.ca
www.polarplastic.ca

Manufacturer and exporter of disposable plastic ta-
bleware including plates, cups, utensils and dish
covers
President: David Stevenson
Plant Manager: Claude Jacques
Estimated Sales: $30-50 Million
Number Employees: 250
Type of Packaging: Consumer, Food Service

27630 Polar Process
PO Box 190
Plattsville, ON N0J 1S0
Canada

519-896-8077
Fax: 519-896-1850 877-896-8077
Manufactures sanitary equipment meeting
3A/USDA standards. Pumps, pump feeders, extrud-
ers, depositors, and on-line blenders for viscous
products. Ultrasonic cutting systems. Conveyors,
rental units available. Free testing.
CEO/President: Roger Venning
Sales: Tim Venning
Operations: Peter Solomon
Plant Manager: Mark Karlsen
Estimated Sales: $1-5 Million
Number Employees: 20-49
Number of Products: 10
Brands:
  P0lar Pump
  Polar Extruder
  Polar Ultrashear

27631 Polar Tech Industries Inc
415 E Railroad Ave
Genoa, IL 60135-1200

815-784-9000
Fax: 815-784-9009 800-423-2749
info@polar-tech.com www.polar-tech.com
At the forefront of temperature controlled and protective packaging innovation since 1984. Polar Tech
industries is the largest manufacturer of temperature
assured packaging materials. Offering over 100 sizes
of insulated containersnew dry ice making equipment, a complete line of ICE-BRIX refrigerants and
cold packs, insulated totes and wine shippers, specialized cakes, candy, sausage and meat shippers,
large insulated transports, pallet covers, packaging
tape, labels andshipping supplies.
General Manager: Autumn Santeler
Account Representative: Leann Schuman
Account Representative: Liz Suobata
Account Representative: Allen Cole
Customer Service Manager: Lora Evans
Inside Sales: Angie Dellinger
IT: Donald Santeler
dons@polar-tech.com
Number Employees: 10-19

27632 Polar Ware Company
2806 N 15th St
Sheboygan, WI 53083-3943

920-458-3561
Fax: 920-458-2205 800-237-3655
customerservice@polarware.com
www.polarware.com
Manufacturer and exporter of deep drawn and stain-
less steel items including steam table pans and cov-
ers, trays, pans, pots, bowls, containers, smallwares,
bar supplies, etc.; importer of smallwares, barware,
chafers, beverage serversaccessories and sinks
CEO: Jerry Baltus
Executive VP: Rick Carr
Marketing Director: Steph Wittmus
National Sales Manager: Dick Ballwahn
Contact: Tom Dinolfo
tom_sharp@sharp-residential.com
Production Manager: Peter Hansen
Purchasing Manager: Tom Kennedy
Estimated Sales: $20-50 Million
Number Employees: 100-249
Square Footage: 250000
Brands:
  Polar Ware
  Yukon

27633 Polibak Plastics America Inc
113 Executive Dr # 116
Suite 116
Sterling, VA 20166-9559

703-964-0339
Fax: 703-709-1012 888-765-4225
info@polibakusa.com www.polibakusa.com
Bioriented polypropylene film, cast polypropylene
film, metalized films, polyethylene.

Vice President: Tolga Baki
tbaki@polybakusa.com
VP: Tolga Baki
Sales Manager: Erdogan Alkan
Estimated Sales: Over $1 Billion
Number Employees: 1000-4999

27634 Poliplastic
415 Rue Saint-Valier
Granby, QC J2G 7Y3
Canada

450-378-8417
Fax: 450-378-0220
Plastic bags including plain, printed and shopping
President: Michael Friedman
Number Employees: 70

27635 Pollard Brothers
5504 N Northwest Hwy
Chicago, IL 60630-1188

773-763-6868
Fax: 773-763-4466 info@pollardbros.com
www.pollardbros.com
Individual lunch tables
President: Jason Hein
info@pollardbros.com
Marketing Director: Will Hein
Estimated Sales: Below $5 Million
Number Employees: 10-19

27636 Pollinger Company
8100 Nathanael Greene Lane
Charlotte, NC 28227-0654

704-535-2177
Fax: 704-535-4572 pollingerd@aol.com
Batching and blending systems
President: Don Pollinger
Contact: Elliot Schnitzer
eschnitzer@polingerco.com
Estimated Sales: $30-50 Million
Number Employees: 10

27637 Poly One Corp
33587 Walker Rd
Avon Lake, OH 44012-1145
Canada

440-930-1000
Fax: 440-930-3799 866-765-9663
www.polyone.com
Buckets, pails and containers
President: Robert Hanlin
CEO: Robert M Patterson
robertmpatterson@polyone.com
VP: Bob Connely
Estimated Sales: Over $1 Billion
Number Employees: 5000-9999
Parent Co: Hamlin

27638 Poly Plastic Products Inc
21 Schultz Dr
PO Box 220
Delano, PA 18220

570-467-3000
Fax: 570-467-3001 www.polyplasticproducts.com
Plastic bags and film
President: Steven Redlich
stevenredlich@polyplasticproducts.com
Chairman of the Board: Alfred Teo
Accounting Manager: Donna Petri
VP Sales: Vince Oberto
Vice President of Operations: Tim McGowan
Production Manager: Brad Smith
Plant Manager: John Boyer
Purchasing Manager: Donna McGowan
Number Employees: 100-249
Square Footage: 312000

27639 Poly Processing Co
8055 Ash St
French Camp, CA 95231-9667

209-982-4904
Fax: 209-982-0455 877-325-3142
sales@polyprocessing.com
www.polyprocessing.com
Manufacturer and exporter of molded plastic tanks
Quality Control: John Bnnlanco
Sales Manager: Del Mann
Manager: John Blanco
Estimated Sales: $2.5-5 Million
Number Employees: 50-99

27640 Poly Shapes Corporation
41740 Schadden Rd
Elyria, OH 44035
Fax: 847-428-8869 800-605-9359
Printed and plain plastic bags including custom shaped
Vice President: Don Harreld
Sales Manager: Tom Drake
Operations Manager: Don Paulson
Estimated Sales: $5-10 Million
Number Employees: 20-49
Square Footage: 90000

27641 Poly-Clip System Corp
1000 Tower Rd
Mundelein, IL 60060-3816
224-778-7533
Fax: 847-949-2815 800-872-2547
gil@polyclip-usa.com www.polyclip.com
Package closure systems
President: Gil Williams
contact@polyclip.us
Senior Executive Assistant: Pat Mangioni
VP Sales/Marketing: Gil Williams
Estimated Sales: $20-50 Million
Number Employees: 50-99

27642 PolyConversions, Inc.
505 E Condit Dr
Rantoul, IL 61866-3604
217-893-3330
Fax: 217-893-3003 888-893-3330
info@polycoUSA.com www.polycousa.com
Supplier of personal protective apparel for industrial safety, food processing, controlled environments, etc.
President: Ronald Smith
Sales Manager: Scott Carlson
Estimated Sales: $10-20 Million
Number of Brands: 2
Number of Products: 15
Square Footage: 47000
Brands:
Diposables
Protecting Wear
Polywear
Vr

27643 PolyMaid Company
PO Box 1466
Largo, FL 33779-1466
727-507-9321
Fax: 727-524-8271 800-806-9188
www.polymaid.com
Manufacturer and exporter of food mixers and coffee flavoring tumble mixers with removable plastic liners
President: Ken Orthner
VP Operations: Susan Orthner
Number Employees: 4
Square Footage: 20000
Brands:
Polymaid

27644 Polyair
330 Humberline Drive
Toronto, ON M9W 1R5
Canada
416-679-6600
Fax: 416-679-6610 888-765-9847
marketing@polyair.com www.polyair.com
Estimated Sales: $1-5 Million

27645 Polyair Packaging
808 E 113th St
Chicago, IL 60628-5150
773-995-1818
Fax: 773-995-7725 888-pol-yair
marketing@polyair.com www.polyair.com
Protective packaging and insulation
President: Alan Castle
CFO: Henry Schriback
Plant Manager: Carl Honaker
Estimated Sales: $20-50 Million
Number Employees: 50-99

27646 Polybottle Group
7464 132nd Street
Surrey, BC V3W 4M7
Canada
604-594-4999
Fax: 604-594-3257 www.polybottle.com
Stock and custom plastic containers including wide and narrow mouth

CEO: Chris Hornsby
Sales Manager: Don Kendall
Human Resources: Maggie Pederson
Number Employees: 205
Square Footage: 160000
Parent Co: ABC Group

27647 Polychem Corp
6277 Heisley Rd
Mentor, OH 44060
440-357-1500
Fax: 440-352-9553 www.polychem.com
Polyester strapping/polypropylene strapping.
President & CEO: Brian Jeckering
Year Founded: 1974
Estimated Sales: $100 Million
Number Employees: 100-249

27648 Polyclutch
457 State Street
North Haven, CT 06473-3094
203-248-6397
Fax: 262-786-3280 800-298-2066
sales@aaman.com www.polyclutch.com
Mechanical and pneumatic slip clutches for overload protection and torque control
President: Gerald H Shaff
CEO: Gerald Shaff
Contact: Ken Kraynak
ken@polyclutch.com
Number Employees: 20-49

27649 Polycon Industries
1001 E 99th Street
Chicago, IL 60628-1693
773-374-5500
Fax: 773-374-9805
Manufacturer and exporter of plastic bottles and containers; also, various types of labeling and silk screening available
VP: Dan Faro
Plant Manager: Fred Palmer
Estimated Sales: $1-5 Million
Number Employees: 100-250
Square Footage: 210000

27650 Polyfoam Corp
2355 Providence Rd
PO Box 906
Northbridge, MA 01534-1085
508-234-6323
Fax: 508-234-2123
Plastic foam products
President: Thomas L Coz
CEO: Tom Coz
tcoz@pollyfoamcorp.com
Estimated Sales: $5-10 Million
Number Employees: 100-249

27651 Polymer Solutions International
15 Newtown Woods Road
PO Box 310
Newtown Square, PA 19073
877-444-7225
info@prostack.com www.prostack.com
Bottled water racks
President: Daniel Kelly
Estimated Sales: $170,000
Number Employees: 1
Square Footage: 1706

27652 Polymercia
609 Fertilla Street
Carrollton, GA 30117-3927
770-830-7434
Fax: 770-830-7377 800-762-1678
info@polymerica.com www.polymerica.com
Estimated Sales: $1-5 Million
Number Employees: 10-19

27653 (HQ)Polypack Inc
3301 Gateway Centre Blvd
Pinellas Park, FL 33782-6108
727-578-5000
Fax: 727-578-1300 info@polypack.com
www.polypack.com
Engineer and manufacturer of shrink packaging equipment including shrink-wrap robotic infeeds and collation, continuous motion form fill seal machines
President/Founder: Alain Cerf
Estimated Sales: $10-20 Million
Number Employees: 50-99

Type of Packaging: Consumer, Food Service, Private Label, Bulk
Other Locations:
Polypack
Shanghai

27654 Polyplastic Forms Inc
49 Gazza Blvd
Farmingdale, NY 11735-1494
631-249-5011
Fax: 631-249-8504 800-428-7659
sales@polyplasticforms.com
www.polyplasticforms.com
Advertising signs and letters including plastic, foam, wood, metal, vinyl, etc
President: Nancy Behrens
n.behrens@polyplasticforms.com
CEO: Diane Garrett
Marketing Director: Richard Garrett
Sales Director: Wayne Maciura
Plant Manager: Jim Dietz
Estimated Sales: $2.5-5 Million
Number Employees: 20-49

27655 Polyplastics
10201 Metropolitan Dr
Austin, TX 78758-4944
512-339-9293
Fax: 512-339-9317 800-753-7659
sales@1polyplastics.com www.polyplastics.com
Manufacturer, exporter and wholesaler/distributor of rigid and flexible foamed plastics
President: Dave McArthur
VP: Tim Buckley
Sales Director: Tim Buckley
Manager: Tito Robledo
trobledo@1polyplastics.com
Manufacturing Manager: Harry Stevens
Estimated Sales: $2.5-5 Million
Number Employees: 5-9
Square Footage: 56000
Parent Co: Buckley Industries
Brands:
Avi
Monarch
Rubatex
Sealed Air
Sentinel
Specialty Composites Ear
Uniroyal Ensolite

27656 Polypro International Inc
7300 Metro Blvd
Suite 570
Edina, MN 55439-2346
952-835-7717
Fax: 952-835-3811 800-765-9776
polypro@polyprointl.com www.polyprointl.com
Guar and cellulose gums
President: Mark Kieper
polypro@polyprointl.com
Controller: Jennifer Jansson
Senior Account Manager, Sales/Technical: Louise Polizzotto
Customer Service/Logistics: Janet Burger
Estimated Sales: $2.5-5 Million
Number Employees: 1-4
Type of Packaging: Bulk
Brands:
Procol
Progum
Viscol

27657 Polyscience
6600 W Touhy Ave
Niles, IL 60714-4516
847-647-0611
Fax: 847-647-1155 800-229-7569
culinary@polyscience.com www.polyscience.com
Producer of constant temperature control equipment
President: Philip Preston
HR Executive: Pat Shamburg
pshamburg@polyscience.com
Marketing: Bob Bausone
Sales: Jason Sayers
Operations: Wayne Walter
Estimated Sales: $10-20 Million
Number Employees: 100-249
Square Footage: 128000
Parent Co: Preston Industries

27658 Polysource Inc
555 E Statler Rd
PO Box 916
Piqua, OH 45356
    937-381-0001
Fax: 937-778-9300 800-290-6323
ewehtje@polysource.com www.polysource.com
Innovative plastic foam solutions for applications
President: Erick Wehtje
CEO: Andrew Palmer
apalmer@polysource.com
Sales/Product Development Manager: Randy Dickerson
Number Employees: 20-49

27659 Polyspec
6614 Gant Rd
Houston, TX 77066
    281-397-0033
Fax: 281-397-6512 888-797-0033
www.polyspec.com
Contact: Monica Bohannon
mbohannon@itw.com
Estimated Sales: $5-10 Million
Number Employees: 20-49

27660 (HQ)Polytainers
197 Norseman Street
Toronto, ON M8Z 2R5
Canada
    416-239-7311
Fax: 416-239-0596 800-268-2424
www.polytainersinc.com
Designer and manufacturer of thinwall rigid plastic containers for the food and dairy industry
President: Robert Barrett
Number Employees: 600
Square Footage: 1000000

27661 Polytarp Products
11 Lepage Court
Toronto, ON M3J 2AE
Canada
    416-633-2231
Fax: 416-633-1685 800-606-2231
www.polytarp.com
Polyethelene film, sheeting, bags and food grade
President: Steve Ghantous
Estimated Sales: $21 Million
Number Employees: 150
Square Footage: 19106

27662 Polytemp Corp
1116 Middle River Rd
Middle River, MD 21220-2412
    410-687-9000
Fax: 410-687-9629 info@polytempcorp.com
www.polytempcorp.com
A leader in the cold storage construction field, specializing in design, furnishing and installation of insulated panels, cold storage doors, floor insulation and vapor barriers
Vice President: Brian Clarke
info@polytempcorp.com
VP: Brian Clarke
Estimated Sales: $.5-1 million
Number Employees: 1-4

27663 Polytop Corporation
P.O.Box 68
Slatersville, RI 02876
    401-767-2400
Fax: 401-765-2694
Dispensing closures
President: Steve B Wilson
CFO: Kevin Rowles
Estimated Sales: $20-50 Million
Number Employees: 250-499

27664 Polytype America Corporation
10 Industrial Ave
Suite 4
Mahwah, NJ 07430-3530
    201-995-1000
Fax: 201-995-1080 www.wifag-polytype.com
Dry offset printing equipment for plastic containers, cups, lids, tubes, jars, vials, metal cans and can ends.
President: Pieter S Vander Griendt
VP Sales Converting North America: Glenn Whitmore
Senior Sales Representative: Rod Brynildsen
VP Sales Wifag USA: Joseph Ondras
Operations Manager: Jim Dominico
Sales Manager Decorating: Felix Gomez
Number Employees: 1000
Parent Co: wifag//polytype

27665 (HQ)Pomona Service & Pkgng Co LA
2733 Central Sta
Yakima, WA 98902
    509-452-7121
Fax: 509-576-3942
Manufacturer and exporter of produce handling and packaging equipment
President: John Muller
pomonasvc@aol.com
Estimated Sales: $1-2.5 Million
Number Employees: 5-9

27666 Ponce Carribian Distributors
PO Box 11946
San Juan, PR 00922-1946
    787-840-0404
Fax: 787-840-9474 info@ablesales.com
www.ablesales.com
Candy
General Manager: Luis Bornes
Estimated Sales: Under $500,000
Number Employees: 20-49

27667 Pop Tops Co Inc
10 Plymouth Dr
South Easton, MA 02375-1192
    508-238-8585
Fax: 508-230-2851 800-647-8677
sales@poptopssportswear.com
www.poptopssportswear.com
Sportswear for employee uniforms and advertising promotions; also, canvas bags; screenprinting and embroidering available
President: James Fine
VP Marketing: Jim Fine
Manager: Jonathan Fine
jonathan@poptopssportswear.com
Estimated Sales: $2.5-5 Million
Number Employees: 20-49

27668 Pop n Go
12429 East Putnam St
Whittier, CA 90602
    562-945-9351
Fax: 562-945-6341 888-476-7646
Popcorn vending machines
CEO: Melvin Wyman
Contact: Pop Go
sportmel@msn.com
Estimated Sales: Below $500,000
Number Employees: 10-19
Brands:
  Pop N Go

27669 Popcorn Connection
7615 Fulton Avenue
North Hollywood, CA 91605-1805
    818-764-3279
Fax: 818-765-0578 800-852-2676
Popcorn and nuts
Owner: Kevin Needle
VP: Ross Wallach
Estimated Sales: $300,000
Number Employees: 3
Number of Products: 20
Square Footage: 14000
Type of Packaging: Consumer, Food Service, Private Label, Bulk
Brands:
  Corn Appetit
  Corn Appetit Ultimate
  Fruit Corn Appetit
  Video Munchies

27670 Porcelain Metals Corporation
400 South 13th Street
PO Box 7069
Louisville, KY 40210
    502-635-7421
Fax: 502-635-1200
Manufacturer and exporter of cooking equipment including barbecue and charcoal grills, domestic cooktops and accessories
Manager: Randy Smitley
OEM Sales Management: Bob Miller
Estimated Sales: $10-20 Million
Number Employees: 20-49
Square Footage: 350000
Type of Packaging: Consumer, Private Label

Brands:
  Barbecue Bucket
  Gourmet Grid
  Kingsford

27671 Port Canaveral Authority
445 Challenger Rd # 301
Suite 301
Cape Canaveral, FL 32920-4100
    321-783-7831
Fax: 321-783-4651 www.portcanaveral.com
Transportation
Chief Executive Officer: John Walsh
jwalsh@portcanaveral.org
Deputy Executive Director, Chief Financi: Roger Rees
CEO: Stanley Payne
Sr. Director, Information Systems: Mark Lorusso
Chief of Police & Public Safety: Joe Hellebrand
Sr. Director of Business Development: Robert Giangrisostomi
Deputy Director, Human Resources: Brenda Morrish
Sr. Director, Cruise and Port Operations: Mike Meekins
Number Employees: 100-249

27672 Port Erie Plastics Inc
909 Troupe Rd
Harborcreek, PA 16421-1018
    814-899-7602
Fax: 814-899-7854 jconnole@porterie.com
www.porterie.com
Lightweight plastic pallets and custom modling
President: John Johnson
CEO: Robert Batcho
rbatcho@athenaswc.com
Quality Control: Mike Malin
CEO: William C Witkowski
Marketing/Sales Manager: John Connole
Estimated Sales: $20-50 Million
Number Employees: 250-499
Parent Co: Port Erie Plastics

27673 Port Of Pasco
1110 Osprey Pointe Blvd
Suite 201
Pasco, WA 99301-5827
    509-547-3378
Fax: 509-547-2547 portofpasco@portofpasco.org
www.portofpasco.org
Director of Finance & Administration: Linda O'Brien
Executive Director: James Toomey
Executive Assistant & Public Information: Vicky Keller
Number Employees: 5-9

27674 Portable Cold Storage
860 Us Route One
Edison, NJ 08540
    609-252-1105
Fax: 609-252-1107 800-535-2445
www.portablecoldstorage.com
Rent refrigerated trailers and containers. All electric three phase equipment. -15°F to +75F indoors or outdoors
Operations Manager: N Kewley
Estimated Sales: $1 Million+

27675 Portco Corporation
3601 SE Columbia Way Ste 260
Vancouver, WA 98661
    360-696-4167
Fax: 360-695-4849 800-426-1794
info@portco.com www.portco.com
Paper and polyethylene bags for fruit, vegetables, grains, pasta products and fish; also, printed film rollstock for form and fill; custom printing available
President: Howard M Wall Jr
CEO: Andy Stewart
Controller: Chip Nipschke
VP: Brian Williamson
Estimated Sales: $20-50 Million
Number Employees: 100-249
Square Footage: 240000

27676 Portec Flowmaster
PO Box 589
Canon City, CO 81215-0589
    719-275-7471
Fax: 719-269-3750 800-777-7471
Curved belt conveyors, curved spiral conveyors, chutes, straight conveyors.Rollers for conveyors motorized pulleys for conveyors

President/CEO: Lawrence Weber
CEO: Kirk Mortin
Marketing: Dick Watkins
Sales: Ken Cline
Contact: Dick Alter
dick.alter@portec.com
Estimated Sales: $20-50 Million
Number Employees: 100-249
Square Footage: 80000
Parent Co: J. Richard Industries
Brands:
    Portec Flowmaster
    Portec Pathfinder

27677 Porter & Porter Lumber
PO Box 157
Fort Gay, WV 25514

    304-648-5133
    Fax: 304-648-7283

Wooden pallets and skids
Owner: H S Porter Iii
Estimated Sales: $1-5 Million
Number Employees: 10-19

27678 (HQ)Porter Bowers Signs
3300 101st Street
Des Moines, IA 50322-3866

    515-253-9622
    Fax: 515-253-9915

Manufacturer and exporter of signs including neon, painted, indoor and outdoor
Estimated Sales: $1-2.5 Million
Number Employees: 5-9

27679 Portion-Pac Chemical Corp.
400 N Ashland Ave
Suite 1
Chicago, IL 60622

    312-226-0400
Fax: 312-226-5400 info@portionpaccorp.com
    www.portionpaccorp.com
Manufacturer/exporter of cleaning products including pre-measured floor cleaners and detergents, bathroom and glass cleaner, air freshener odor counteractant, carpet shampoo, final rinse sanitizers, extraction detergent andstrippers/degreasers
President: Marvin Klein
Vice President: John Miller
SFS Pac Division Manager: Chuck Ainsworth
Estimated Sales: $10-20 Million
Number Employees: 20-49
Type of Packaging: Consumer, Food Service
Brands:
    Base Pac
    Bowlpack
    Depotpac
    Foam Pac
    Germicidal
    Glass Pac
    Mop Pac
    Mop Paclite
    Neutrapac
    Pot & Pan Pac
    Restore Pac
    Sani Pac
    Scrub Pac
    Steam Pac
    Strip Pac

27680 Portland Paper Box Company
226 SE Madison St
Portland, OR 97214-3317

    503-233-6271
Fax: 503-232-4922 800-547-2571
Folding paper boxes
Estimated Sales: $5-10 Million
Number Employees: 20-49

27681 Portola Allied
275 Commerce Ave
New Castle, PA 16101-7625

    724-658-4306
Fax: 724-657-8597 800-521-1368
Molds for blow molding
Manager: John Piezer
R&D: Pat Taylor
CFO: Bill Stoewer
Estimated Sales: $50-100 Million
Number Employees: 50-99

27682 Portugalia Imports
23 Tremont St
Fall River, MA 02720-4821

    508-679-9307
Fax: 508-673-1502 portugaliaimports.com
Seafood, breads, vegetables, and other specialty foods
President/Owner: Fernando Benevides
benevidesf@portugaliaimports.com
Vice President: Michael Benevides *Year Founded:* 1988

27683 Poser Envelope
1999 Harrison St # 100
Oakland, CA 94612-3517

    510-251-6100
Fax: 510-444-5253 800-208-6100
Die cut envelopes; also, printing services available
Manager: Heidi Crouch
Sales/Marketing Manager: Doug Drendel
Production Manager: Rick Pallas
Plant Manager: Brain Stee
Estimated Sales: $3-5 Million
Number Employees: 10-19

27684 Posimat S A
1646 NW 108th Ave
Miami, FL 33172-2007

    305-477-2029
Fax: 305-477-8044 888-767-4628
    miami@posimat.com www.posimat.com
Bottle unscramblers, storage silos and bulk conveyors
President: Jaime Marti
Estimated Sales: Below $5 Million
Number Employees: 5-9
Number of Brands: 10
Number of Products: 5
Square Footage: 1600

27685 Positech Corp
191 N Rush Lake Rd
Laurens, IA 50554-1299

    712-841-4548
Fax: 712-841-4765 800-831-6026
Material handling machinery including manipulators, rotary manifolds and torque arms; exporter of manipulators
President: Peter Hong
CEO: Mike Olson
CFO: Kent Radford
Quality Control: Kent Radford
Sales/Marketing Manager: Brett Stumbo
Purchasing Agent: Kay Anderson
Estimated Sales: $50-75 Million
Number Employees: 50-99
Square Footage: 65000
Parent Co: Columbus McKinnon Corporation
Brands:
    Reaction Arm
    Sam
    Taurus

27686 (HQ)Positive Employment Practice
1 Muller Court
New City, NY 10956-3508

    845-638-6442
Consultant specializing in business coaching and problem solving support including project design, marketing strategies, organization building, financial performance, etc
Business Coach: Steven Caccavo
Contact: Karen Caccavo
steve@constructivebusiness.info
Number Employees: 1-4

27687 Poss USA
6643 Cupecoy Drive
Salt Lake City, UT 84121-3242

    801-453-1996
    Fax: 801-943-1670

27688 Posterloid Corporation
4862 36th St
Long Island City, NY 11101-1918

    718-729-1050
Fax: 718-786-9310 800-651-5000
Manufacturer and exporter of menu boards and displays
President: Robert Sudack
Sales Manager: Allied Collins
Contact: Basil Mcpherson
bmcpherson@posterloid.com

Estimated Sales: $10-20 Million
Number Employees: 100-249

27689 Potdevin Machine Co
26 Fairfield Pl
West Caldwell, NJ 07006-6207

    973-227-8828
Fax: 201-288-3770 sales@potdevin.com
    www.potdevin.com
Wine industry labeling machines
President: Robert S Potdevin
rsp@potdevin.com
Director/Sales: James Barnes
Estimated Sales: $5-10 Million
Number Employees: 20-49

27690 Potlatch Corp
601 W 1st Ave # 1600
Suite 1600
Spokane, WA 99201-3807

    509-835-1500
Fax: 509-835-1555 www.potlatchcorp.com
Manufacturer and exporter of paper products including napkins, toilet paper, paper towels and facial tissues
Executive Director: Mark Ohleyer
CEO: Michael J Covey
michael.covey@potlatchcorp.com
Manager: Mike Lappa
Director Marketing: Cynthia Dickerson
National Sales Manager: Mike Redden
Estimated Sales: $50-100 Million
Number Employees: 500-999
Parent Co: Potlatch Corporation
Brands:
    Potlatch
    Spa
    Velure

27691 Powdersize Inc
20 Pacific Dr
Quakertown, PA 18951-3601

    215-536-5605
Fax: 215-536-6630 thigley@powdersize.com
Contract micronizing, milling and classification and processing of pharmaceutical, food, cosmetic, and industrial dry powders in compliance with current Good Manufacturing Practices, and adherence to the principles of Total QualityManagement
President: Wayne Sigler
wsigler@powdersize.com
Founder: Lowell Histand
Partner: Thomas Moran
Estimated Sales: $1-5 Million
Number Employees: 10-19
Number of Products: 30
Square Footage: 40000
Type of Packaging: Private Label

27692 Powell Systems
162 Churchill Hubbard Rd
Youngstown, OH 44505-1321

    330-759-9220
Fax: 330-759-9434 leah@powell-systems.com
    www.powellsystems.com
Materials handling containers, metal stampings, bulk packaging equipment and scales
President: Bill Powell
bill@powell-systems.com
Founder: Willaim J. Powell
Manager: Bill Powell
bill@powell-systems.com
Estimated Sales: Less Than $500,000
Number Employees: 1-4

27693 Power Brushes
756 S Byrne Rd # 1
Toledo, OH 43609-1062

    419-385-5725
Fax: 419-382-0756 800-968-9600
    president@powerbrushes.com
    www.powerbrushes.com
Manufacturer and exporter of custom designed brushes for harvesting, cleaning, peeling and packing of fruits and vegetables
President: Tom Parseghian
Sales Director: Scott Dunckel
Manager: Paul Sneider
tafttool@aol.com
Estimated Sales: $3 Million
Number Employees: 20-49

27694 Power Electronics Intl Inc
561 Plate Dr # 8
East Dundee, IL 60118-2467
847-836-2071
Fax: 847-428-7744 800-362-7959
www.peinfo.com
Manufacturer and exporter of variable speed and AC powered drives
President: Victor Habisohn
Sales Manager: Michael Habisohn
Service Manager: Adam Jezek
Estimated Sales: $20-50 Million
Number Employees: 50-99

27695 Power Flame Inc
2001 S 21st St
P.O. Box 974
Parsons, KS 67357-4911
620-421-0480
Fax: 620-421-0948 800-862-4256
csd@powerflame.com www.powerflame.com
Small immersion tube gas, drier and oven burners
President: Chris Allen
callen@powerflame.com
Sales/Marketing Executive: Bob Rizza
Customer Service Manager: Mark Dunlap
callen@powerflame.com
Purchasing Agent: Jerry Cruz
Estimated Sales: $10-20 Million
Number Employees: 250-499
Square Footage: 200000

27696 (HQ)Power Group
40w222 Old Lafox Rd
St Charles, IL 60174
630-587-3770
Fax: 630-377-4603
Dedicated and multi-customer manufacturing, packaging and logistics facilities in the food industry. Operates 25 facilities in four countries and has been providing manufacturing outsourcing and integrated supply chain solutions toFortune 100 customers since 1968
CEO: Wayne Sims
Sr. VP: Ken Battista
VP Sales: Jay Toelkes
Estimated Sales: $.5-1 million
Number Employees: 1-4
Square Footage: 14000000
Type of Packaging: Consumer, Food Service, Private Label, Bulk
Other Locations:
   Power Group
   Guildford Surrey

27697 Power Industrial Supply
80 Sebastopol Road
Santa Rosa, CA 95407-6929
707-544-3994
Fax: 707-544-3996
Boiler, control and process piping equipment
Contact: Cheryl Peterson
cpeterson@powerindustries.com
Estimated Sales: $2 Million
Number Employees: 16

27698 Power Industries Inc
520 Barham Ave
Santa Rosa, CA 95404-5934
707-545-7904
Fax: 707-541-2200 sales@powerindustries.com
www.powerindustries.com
Wine industry hoses, pipes, fittings, stainless steel tanks and construction
President: Rick Call
rickc@powerindustries.com
CFO: Kem Thangvall
Estimated Sales: $20-50 Million
Number Employees: 10-19

27699 Power Logistics
1200 Internationale Pkwy
Suite 300
Woodridge, IL 60517-4976
815-936-1800
Fax: 815-936-1970 www.powergroup.com
Warehouse offering cooler, freezer and dry storage for frozen, refrigerated and nonperishable food products
VP Business Development: Ken Battista
Director Operations: Drew Walker
Estimated Sales: $1-2.5 Million
Number Employees: 19
Parent Co: Power Group

27700 Power Machine Company
118 Brookfield Drive
Moraga, CA 94556-1747
510-658-9661
Fax: 510-653-3848
Wine industry pumps and compressors
VP: Christopher Adam
CEO: Elfriede Knight
VP/General Manager: Christopher Adam
Marketing Manager: Henry Zacata
Public Relations Manager: Caral Frawman
Estimated Sales: $5-10 Million
Number Employees: 10-19

27701 (HQ)Power Packaging Inc
525 Dunham Rd
St Charles, IL 60174
630-377-3838
www.powerpackaging.com
Full-service contract manufacturer for dry foods, beverage mixes, bulk blending and filling, hot fill, organic, nutraceuticals, aseptic and commissary. Designs, owns and operates multi-customer and dedicated food manufacturingfacilities nationwide.
President: Gordon Gruszka
Senior Director, Quality Assurance: Keith Schafer
Executive Director, Sales & Marketing: Chuck Woods
Senior Director, Engineering: Gary Gross
Estimated Sales: $50-100 Million
Number Employees: 1000-4999

27702 Power Packaging Inc
401 N Main Hwy 26
Rosendale, WI 54974
920-872-2181
www.powerpackaging.com
Full-service contract manufacturer for dry foods, beverage mixes, bulk blending and filling, hot fill, organic, nutraceuticals, aseptic and commissary. Designs, owns and operates multi-customer and dedicated food manufacturingfacilities nationwide.
Estimated Sales: $50-100 Million
Number Employees: 1,600

27703 Power Soak by Metcraft
13910 Kessler Drive
Grandview, MO 64030-2810
816-761-3250
Fax: 816-761-0544 info@powersoak.com
www.powersoak.com
President: John Cantrell
Vice President of Distribution: Barry Bergstein
Sales Manager: Mary Cunningham
Vice President of Operations: John McCreight
Manufacturing Manager: Monty Patton
Estimated Sales: $10-15 Million
Number Employees: 50-100

27704 Power-Pack Conveyor Co
38363 Airport Pkwy
Willoughby, OH 44094-7562
440-975-9955
Fax: 440-975-0505
ppcc@power-packconveyor.com
www.power-packconveyor.com
Belt conveyors
President: Kevin Ensinger
ppcc@power-packconcp.com
CFO: Jim Ensinger
VP: Jim Ensinger
R&D: Jim Ensinger
Estimated Sales: $5-10 Million
Number Employees: 20-49

27705 Poweramp
W194n11481 Mccormick Dr
Germantown, WI 53022-3035
262-255-1510
Fax: 262-255-4199 800-643-5424
sales@poweramp.com www.docksystemsinc.com
Manufacturer and exporter of dock levelers including pit-style, edge of dock, truck, truck restraining systems, dock seals and shelters, etc
Owner: Ed Mguire
Vice President: Mike Pilgrim
Estimated Sales: $25 Million
Number Employees: 50-99
Square Footage: 100000
Parent Co: Systems

27706 Powertex Inc
1 Lincoln Blvd # 101
Suite 101
Rouses Point, NY 12979-1087
518-297-2634
Fax: 518-297-2634 800-769-3783
seabulk@powertex.com www.powertex.com
Manufacturer and exporter of dry powder and bulk plastic liners for use in ocean containers and truck trailers
President: Stephen Podd
stephen@powertex.com
Chairman/CEO: Victor Podd
Sales Manager: Patricia Olsen
Estimated Sales: $10-20 Million
Number Employees: 50-99
Square Footage: 130000
Brands:
   Powerbulk
   Powerliner
   Powertex Meatstrap
   Seabulk Powerliner

27707 Powertex Inc
1 Lincoln Blvd # 101
Suite 101
Rouses Point, NY 12979-1087
518-297-2634
Fax: 518-297-2634 seabulk@powertex.com
www.powertex.com
Tea and coffee container liners
President: Stephen Podd
stephen@powertex.com
Sales/Marketing: Patricia Olsen
Estimated Sales: $10-20 Million
Number Employees: 50-99

27708 Poynette Distribution Center
W8070 Kent Rd
Poynette, WI 53955-9713
608-635-4396
Fax: 608-635-7308 lakesidefoods.com
Peas, green beans, tomatoes, corn and sauerkraut
Sr. VP Operations: Daniel C Cavanaugh
VP Customer Service: James I Ferguson
General Manager: Ross Moland
Plant Manager: Mike Hull
Estimated Sales: $10-20 Million
Number Employees: 20-49
Parent Co: Stokely USA
Type of Packaging: Consumer, Private Label

27709 Ppm Technologies LLC
500 E Illinois St
Newberg, OR 97132-2307
503-538-3141
Fax: 503-538-8575 800-246-2034
allen.sales@fmcti.com www.ppmtech.com
Vibratory and belt conveyors, bucket elevators, optical sorters, controls and ingredient application and storage systems
Manager: Mark Eaton
CEO: Robert Petersen
robert.petersen@ppmtech.com
VP: Mark Eaton
Marketing: Neil Anderson
Regional Sales Manager: Ellen Hao
Estimated Sales: $1-5 Million
Number Employees: 100-249
Square Footage: 600000
Parent Co: FMC Technologies
Brands:
   Allen
   Fmc

27710 Ppm Technologies LLC
500 E Illinois St
Newberg, OR 97132-2307
503-538-3141
Fax: 503-538-8575 steve.austin@fmcti.com
Manager: Mark Eaton
CEO: Robert Petersen
robert.petersen@ppmtech.com
Regional Sales Manager: Ellen Hao
Estimated Sales: $1-5 Million
Number Employees: 100-249

27711 Prairie Packaging Inc
314 Mooresville Blvd
Mooresville, NC 28115-7909
704-660-6600
Fax: 704-660-7604 info@polarplastic.ca
www.wincup.com

Plastic cutlery, plates, bowls, tumblers, stemware and take-out containers; also, custom molded items for the food service and consumer markets
Director: Don Towne
CEO: Eric Cohen
VP Marketing: Dave Hicks
Plant Manager: Philip Goudreault
Estimated Sales: $31.1 Million
Number Employees: 250-499
Brands:
   Alpha
   Belle
   Gild
   Infinity
   Legend
   Pro
   Perfection
   Polar Pal
   Polaronde
   Prodigy
   Signature
   Xl

27712 Prairie View Industries
2620 Industrial Ave
Fairbury, NE 68352-1355
402-729-4055
Fax: 402-729-4058 800-554-7267
info@pvifs.com www.pvifs.com
Accessories, benches, can racks, carts, dollies, drip catcher, dunnage racks, equipment stands, hotshelves, organizers, pan racks, picnic table, pizza racks, platform trucks, ramps, shelving carts, sinks, tables
Owner: Richard Allen
rallen@pviramps.com
Number Employees: 50-99

27713 (HQ)Prater Industries
2 Sammons Ct
Bolingbrook, IL 60440-4995
630-759-9595
Fax: 630-759-6099 877-247-5625
info@praterindustries.com
www.praterindustries.com
Sizing, separation, particle reduction/enlargement equipment
President/CEO: R Scott Prater
Chairman: Robert Prater
rprater@praterindustries.com
CFO: David Utterback
Marketing: Katie Meyers
Estimated Sales: $5-10 Million
Number Employees: 50-99
Square Footage: 110000
Other Locations:
   Prater Industries
   Sterling IL
Brands:
   Mega-Mill
   Rota-Sieve

27714 Pratt Industries
5620 Departure Dr
Raleigh, NC 27616-1841
919-334-7400
Fax: 919-850-9353 www.prattindustries.com
Corrugated boxes
Manager: Pam Blackwell
Quality Control: Ed Allen
Sales Manager: Rick White
Manager: Tony Dilbeck
Estimated Sales: $20-50 Million
Number Employees: 50-99
Parent Co: Pratt Industries

27715 Pratt Industries
1975 Sarasota Business Pkwy NE
Conyers, GA 30013-5745
678-607-1433
Fax: 678-607-1473 800-428-9269
www.prattindustries.com
Corrugated boxes
Sales: Michael Wilkie
Estimated Sales: $20-50 Million
Number Employees: 50-99

27716 Pratt Industries
220 Plantation Rd
New Orleans, LA 70123-5312
504-733-7292
Fax: 504-734-8920 www.prattindustries.com
Manufacturer and marketer of advanced intermodal equipment

President: Jim Hale
CFO: Gary Byrd
R&D: Mark Nay
Manager: Heidi Lecair
hlecair@mhm-inc.com
Estimated Sales: $10-20 Million
Number Employees: 50-99

27717 (HQ)Pratt Poster Company
3001 E 30th Street
Indianapolis, IN 46218-2850
317-545-0842
Fax: 317-927-0653 800-645-1012
tpratt@prattcorp.com
Point of purchase advertising signs, flags, pennants and banners
CEO: Sarah Pratt
National Sales Manager: Thomas Pratt
Contact: Ron Huckabee
rhuckabee@prattcorp.com
Estimated Sales: $10-20 Million
Number Employees: 100-249
Type of Packaging: Bulk

27718 Prawnto Systems
4770 Interstate 30 W
Caddo Mills, TX 75135-7634
903-527-4149
Fax: 903-527-4951 800-426-7254
sales@prawntomachine.com www.prawnto.net
Manufacturer and exporter of shrimp processing equipment including cutters, processing stations and deveiners
CEO: Don Morris
sales@prawntomachine.com
VP: Derrell Sawyer
Sales: Derrell Sawyer
Estimated Sales: $1,000,000
Number Employees: 1-4
Number of Brands: 2
Number of Products: 7
Square Footage: 7000
Brands:
   Prawnto
   Shrimperfect

27719 Prawnto Systems
4770 Interstate 30 W
Caddo Mills, TX 75135-7634
903-527-4149
Fax: 903-527-4951 800-426-7254
sales@prawntomachine.com
President: Don Morris
sales@prawntomachine.com
Estimated Sales: Below $5 Million
Number Employees: 1-4

27720 Praxair Inc
10 Riverview Dr
Danbury, CT 06810
716-879-4077
Fax: 800-772-9985 800-772-9247
info@praxair.com www.praxair.com
Manufacturer and exporter of nitrogen freezing systems for food packaging.
Chairman & CEO: Steve Angel
SVP & Chief Financial Officer: Matthew White
Executive Vice President: Eduardo Menezes
Executive Vice President: Anne Roby
VP/General Counsel/Corporate Secretary: Guillermo Bichara
Year Founded: 1907
Estimated Sales: $11.44 Billion
Number Employees: 26,000
Parent Co: Linde plc
Brands:
   Linde

27721 Precision
1135 NW 159th Dr
Miami, FL 33169-5882
305-625-2451
Fax: 305-623-0475 800-762-7565
sales@atlasfoodserv.com www.atlasfoodserv.com
Food transport carts, heated and refrigerated conveyors, buffet equipment, milk and ice cream units and modular serving systems
President: David Meade
VP Sales: Howard Bolner
VP Manufacturing: Mark Siegfriedt
Estimated Sales: $10-20 Million
Number Employees: 100-249
Parent Co: Atlas Metal Industries

27722 Precision Automation CoInc
1841 Old Cuthbert Rd
Cherry Hill, NJ 08034-1478
856-428-7400
Fax: 856-428-1270
sales@precisionautomationinc.com
www.precisioncovert.com
Chairman of the Board: G Frederick Rexon Sr
Cio/Cto: Dan Pamonio
dpp@precisionautomationinc.com
Estimated Sales: $10-20 Million
Number Employees: 50-99

27723 Precision Automation Co
2120 Addmore Ln
Clarksville, IN 47129-9166
812-283-7963
Fax: 812-283-7992
in@precisionautomationinc.com
www.precisionautomationinc.com
President: G Mooris
Estimated Sales: $1-3 Million
Number Employees: 20-49

27724 Precision Automation CoInc
1841 Old Cuthbert Rd
Cherry Hill, NJ 08034-1478
856-428-7400
Fax: 856-428-1270
sales@precisionautomationinc.com
President: Glen A Morris
Founder: Fred. Rexon Sr
Chairman: Fred Rexon Sr
Estimated Sales: $3.5 Million
Number Employees: 50-99
Square Footage: 45

27725 Precision Brush
6700 Parkland Blvd
Cleveland, OH 44139-4341
440-498-0140
Fax: 800-252-0834 800-252-4747
info@precisionbrush.com www.brushes.info
Manufacturer and exporter of custom metal channel strip brushes in various shapes and sizes
President: Jim Benjamin
jim@precisionbrush.com
General Manager: Mike Porter
Estimated Sales: $2.5-5 Million
Number Employees: 10-19
Square Footage: 36000

27726 Precision Component Industries
5325 Southway St SW
Canton, OH 44706-1943
330-477-6287
Fax: 330-477-1052
tricia@precision-component.com
www.precision-component.com
Manufacturer and exporter of special production machinery, tools, dies, fixtures, short and long run production machining, stamping services and cans
President: Tricia Gerak
tfino@saralee.com
CEO: Patricia Gerak
President: Tony Gerak
Sales Manager: Lewis Page
Purchase Manager: George Melson
Estimated Sales: Below $5 Million
Number Employees: 20-49
Parent Co: Brennan Industrial Group
Type of Packaging: Bulk

27727 Precision Micro Control
2075 Corte Del Nogal # N
Carlsbad, CA 92011-1415
760-930-0101
Fax: 760-930-0222 info@pmccorp.com
www.pmccorp.com
Four axis packaged controller with motion control features
Head Marketing Team: David Clark
Number Employees: 50-99

27728 Precision Plastics Inc
6405a Ammendale Rd # A
Beltsville, MD 20705-1203
301-937-8001
Fax: 301-937-4184 800-922-1317
www.precisionplastics.com
Plastic food service products including sneeze guards, heat shields, condiment racks, menu/card holders, ice trays, buffet bars, signage, etc. Also a 3M product distributor

Owner: Oliver Hofe
oliver@precisionplastics.com
Administrator Assistant: Vicki Juneau
Marketing Manager: Chris Marshall
Estimated Sales: $2.5-5 Million
Number Employees: 20-49
Square Footage: 30000

27729 Precision Plus
6416 Inducon Dr W
Sanborn, NY 14132-9019
716-297-2039
Fax: 716-297-8210 800-526-2707
info@precisionplus.com www.precisionplus.com
Vacuum pump replacement parts
Manager: Joseph Miller
joseph.miller@precisionplus.com
Estimated Sales: $7 Million
Number Employees: 20-49
Number of Brands: 15
Number of Products: 2000
Square Footage: 80000
Parent Co: BOC Group, Inc.
Type of Packaging: Food Service
Brands:
  Alcatel
  Boc Edwards
  Boce Stokes
  Busch
  Ebara
  Kinney
  Leybold
  Precision Scientific
  Ristschic
  Varian
  Welch

27730 Precision Pours
12837 Industrial Park Blvd
Minneapolis, MN 55441-3910
763-694-9291
Fax: 763-694-9343 800-549-4491
ricksandvik@precisionpours.com
Manufacturer and exporter of pour spouts for liquor,
syrups and cooking oils; wholesaler/distributor of
pour cleaning systems
President: Rick Sandvik
ricksandvik@precisionpours.com
Accounting: Patrick Sandvik
VP Sales: Duane Nording
Estimated Sales: Below $5,000,000
Number Employees: 10-19
Square Footage: 9600
Brands:
  Rack & Pour
  Sure Shot

27731 Precision Printing & Packaging
801 Alfred Thun Rd
Clarksville, TN 37040-5348
931-906-0798
Fax: 931-920-9001 800-500-4526
Metallized and paper glue-applied labels
Chairman of the Board: Joseph Sellinger
National Sales Manager: Reba Meek
Contact: April Sizemore
sizemore.april@anheuser-busch.com
Plant Manager: Rod Stough
Estimated Sales: $50-100 Million
Number Employees: 1-4
Parent Co: Anheuser-Busch Companies

27732 Precision Solutions Inc
2525 Tollgate Rd
Quakertown, PA 18951-5306
215-536-4400
Fax: 215-536-4096
info@precisionsolutionsinc.com
www.precisionsolutionsinc.com
Representative for many manufacturers of scale and
measurement equipment
Owner: Dan Kendra
dan_kendra@precisionsolutionsinc.com
Technical Service Consultant: Trevor Filipowicz
Number Employees: 10-19

27733 Precision Stainless Inc
501 N Belcrest Ave
Springfield, MO 65802-2504
417-865-8724
Fax: 417-865-0906
Wine industry aseptic processing equipment, bins
and blenders and equipment fabrication
Sales Engineer: Bert Adams

Estimated Sales: $25-50 Million
Number Employees: 50-99

27734 Precision Systems Inc
16 Tech Cir # 100
Suite 100
Natick, MA 01760-1038
508-655-7010
Fax: 508-653-6999 precisionsystems@msn.com
www.precisionsystemsinc.com
Milk cryoscopes manufacturing, testing, incoming
inspection and final Q.C oeomerers and chemistry
analyzers
President: Charles Bell
CFO: Ann Rogers
VP: Jennifer Knapp
Quality Control: Bob Atwood
Estimated Sales: $1-5 Million
Number Employees: 20-49
Number of Brands: 20
Number of Products: 100
Square Footage: 45600
Type of Packaging: Private Label
Brands:
  Analette
  Cryoscopes
  Osmette

27735 Precision Temp Inc
11 Sunnybrook Dr
Cincinnati, OH 45237-2103
513-641-4446
Fax: 513-641-0733 800-934-9690
service@precisiontemp.com
www.precisiontemp.com
Manufacturer and exporter of gas booster heaters for
high temperature water
Vice President: Steve Aldrich
aldrich@precisiontemp.com
CEO: Rick Muhlhauser
Vice President: Fred Rohtzeid
Estimated Sales: $2-4,000,000
Number Employees: 10-19
Square Footage: 40000
Type of Packaging: Food Service
Brands:
  Precision Temp

27736 (HQ)Precision Wood Products
PO Box 529
Vancouver, WA 98666-0529
360-694-8322
Fax: 360-696-1530 palletmfg@aol.com
Manufacturer and exporter of wooden pallets and
containers
President: Marley Petersen Jr
Contact: Tim Darrow
info@palletpricing.com
Estimated Sales: $5-10 Million
Number Employees: 50-99

27737 Precision Wood of Hawaii
PO Box 529
Vancouver, WA 98666-0529
808-682-2055
Fax: 808-682-2465
Pallets, wooden boxes and crates; also, rebuilder of
recycled wooden pallets
VP/General Manager: T Ross
Estimated Sales: $1-2.5 Million
Number Employees: 50-100

27738 Precit
710 Tech Park Drive
La Vergne, TN 37086-3622
615-287-8255
Fax: 615-287-8355 800-338-4585
jeff.watson@franke.com
Parent Co: Franke

27739 Preco Inc
500 Laser Dr
Somerset, WI 54025-9774
715-247-3285
Fax: 715-247-5650 800-775-2737
sales@precoinc.com www.precoinc.com
President/CEO: Tim Burns
Manager: Mary Amos
mamos@precoinc.com
Estimated Sales: $1-5 Million
Number Employees: 100-249

27740 Preferred Machining Corporation
3730 S Kalamath Street
Englewood, CO 80110-3493
303-761-1535
Fax: 303-789-9300 sales@pmc1.net
Manufacturer and exporter of fillers, pumps/stuffers,
formers and vacuumizers for poultry, beef, etc. As
well as end liners and accessories for the can making
industry
Vice President: Jim Abbott
Marketing Director: Tom Hoffmann
Estimated Sales: $10-20 Million
Number Employees: 50
Brands:
  Prc Weight Control Filler
  Versaform

27741 Preferred Packaging
PO Box 700
Mount Gilead, NC 27306
336-884-0792
Fax: 336-884-5829
preferredmichael@northstate.net
Folding paper boxes
President: William H Drummond
VP Sales/Marketing: Michael Drummond
Estimated Sales: $5-10 Million
Number Employees: 30
Square Footage: 43000
Type of Packaging: Consumer, Food Service, Pri-
vate Label

27742 Preferred Packaging Systems
440 S Lone Hill Avenue
San Dimas, CA 91773
Fax: 909-592-5640 800-378-4777
www.ghlpackaging.com
Manufactures, engineers and designs packaging
equipment.
Estimated Sales: $10-15 Million
Number Employees: 15
Square Footage: 30000

27743 Premier
5721 Dragon Way
Suite 113
Cincinnati, OH 45227-4518
513-271-0600
Fax: 859-581-5525 800-354-9817
www.excellead.com
Manufacturer and exporter of paper plates, hot dog
holders, food trays and foil laminated ashtrays
Owner: Thomas P Santen
VP/General Manager: J Paul Taylor
Sales: Lori Roberts
VP Operations: Viea Gerwin
Plant Manager: Mike McCann
Estimated Sales: $5-10 Million
Square Footage: 80000
Type of Packaging: Private Label
Brands:
  Teddy Bear

27744 Premier Brass
255 Ottley Dr NE Ste A
Atlanta, GA 30324-3926
404-873-6000
Fax: 404-873-9993 800-251-5800
info@premierbrass.com www.premierbrass.com
Manufacturer, importer and exporter of brass and
chrome components for custom foodguards, display
cases and railing systems
President: Alex Mazingue
Vice President: Pep Matus
General Manager: Fred Boyajian
Estimated Sales: $1-2.5 Million
Number Employees: 10-19
Square Footage: 50000
Parent Co: Great Eastern Distributors
Type of Packaging: Food Service
Brands:
  Premier Brass

27745 Premier Foods
871 Harbour Way S
Richmond, CA 94804-3612
707-554-4623

27746 Premier Glass & Package Company
PO Box 5612
Napa, CA 94581
707-224-1660
Fax: 707-224-1660

Wine bottles and packaging
President: Kent Robert
Owner: Stuart Humpert
Estimated Sales: Less than $500,000
Number Employees: 1-4

27747 (HQ)Premier Packages
9438 Watson Industrial Park
Saint Louis, MO 63126-1523

314-961-6588
Fax: 314-961-6589 800-466-6588
info@premierpackages.com
Bakery boxes, folding cartons and trays; also, die
cutting available
Co-Owner: Jeff Petroski
Estimated Sales: $1-2.5 Million
Number Employees: 5-9
Square Footage: 32000

27748 Premier Plastics Inc
4880 S 134th St
Omaha, NE 68137-1614

402-346-2998
Fax: 402-346-7679 866-446-2998
www.premierplasticsinc.com
Thin gauge packaging for short runs
President: Wayne Alter
walter@premierplasticsinc.com
Sales Manager: Franklin Berry
Customer Service Manager: Elizabeth Laska
walter@premierplasticsinc.com
Estimated Sales: $3-5 Million
Number Employees: 20-49
Square Footage: 30000

27749 Premier Restaurant Equipment
7120 Northland Ter N
Brooklyn Park, MN 55428-1573

763-544-8800
Fax: 763-544-7949 info@premiereq.com
www.boelterpremier.com
Provider of design and production services
Owner: James Hara
info@premiereq.com
Estimated Sales: $5-10,000,000
Number Employees: 20-49

27750 Premier Skirting Products
241 Mill St
Lawrence, NY 11559-1209

516-239-6581
Fax: 516-239-6810 800-544-2516
info@premierskirting.com
www.premierskirting.com
Manufacturer and exporter of table and skirting
cloths, napkins, chair covers and place mats
Owner: Ross Yudin
ross@premeirskirting.com
CEO: C VanDewater
CFO: Linda Ehrlich
Manager: Ross Yudin
ross@premeirskirting.com
Plant Manager: Wayne Rizzo
Estimated Sales: $1-2.5 Million
Number Employees: 10-19
Square Footage: 20000

27751 Premier Southern TicketCo
7911 School Rd
Cincinnati, OH 45249-1596

513-489-6700
Fax: 513-489-6867 800-331-2283
sales@premiersouthern.com
Coupons and numbered pressure sensitive labels
President: Kirk Schulz
kirks@premiersouthern.com
Sales Manager: Bill Reilly
Estimated Sales: $5-10 Million
Number Employees: 20-49
Parent Co: Price Chopper

27752 Premium Air Systems Inc
1051 Naughton Dr
Troy, MI 48083-1911

248-680-8800
Fax: 248-680-8808 877-430-0333
leonardf@premiumair.net www.premiumair.net
Custom stainless steel food service tables, sinks,
hoods, custom ventilation systems, refrigeration and
HV/AC equipment; also, installation available
President: Leonard Framalin
leonardf@premiumair.net
Sales Manager: Gilbert St.Louis
Engineer Manager: Ken Comito

Estimated Sales: $5-10 Million
Number Employees: 50-99

27753 Premium Foil Products Company
PO Box 32309
Louisville, KY 40232

502-459-2820
Fax: 502-454-5488
Manufacturer and exporter of aluminum foil con-
tainers
President: A J Kleier
VP/General Manager: Robert Moses
Contact: Robert Moses
musherone@aol.com
Estimated Sales: $5-10 Million
Number Employees: 20-49
Type of Packaging: Food Service, Bulk

27754 Premium Ingredients International US, LLC
285 E Fullerton Ave
Carol Stream, IL 60188-1886

630-868-0300
Fax: 630-868-0310 info@prinovausa.com
www.prinovausa.com
Food ingredients and aroma chemicals
President: Donald Thorp
CEO: Richard Thorp
CFO: Donald Cepican
VP: Daniel Thorp
Research/Development Director: Suzanne Johnson
VP Sales/Marketing: Richard Calabrese
Contact: Kim Sean
kim.sean@prinovausa.com
Estimated Sales: $30-35 Million
Number Employees: 100
Parent Co: AMC Chemicals
Other Locations:
Premium Ingredients International
Holladay UT
Premium Ingredients International
Ellisville MO
Premium Ingredients International
Cranford NJ
Premium Ingredients Int'l(UK)
London, England

27755 Premium Pallet
5000 Richmond Street
Philadelphia, PA 19137-1815

215-535-2559
Fax: 215-535-2570 800-648-7347
Skids and pallets
President: Erik Bronstein
Number Employees: 40
Square Footage: 1980

27756 Prengler Products
14845 State Highway 56
Sherman, TX 75092-4621

903-892-9791
Fax: 903-893-9536 craig@prenglerproducts.com
www.prenglerproducts.com
Point of purchase displays
President: Craig S Prengler
craig@prenglerproducts.com
Estimated Sales: $500,000-$1 Million
Number Employees: 10-19
Square Footage: 56000

27757 Prent Corp
2225 Kennedy Rd
Janesville, WI 53545-0885

608-754-0276
Fax: 608-754-2410 prent@prent.com
www.prent.com
Custom thermal former
Owner: Joe Pregont
jpregont@prent.com
Marketing Director: Vicki Damron
Estimated Sales: $50-100 Million
Number Employees: 500-999

27758 Prentiss
3600 Mansell Rd Ste 350
Alpharetta, GA 30022

770-552-8072
Fax: 770-552-8076 info@prentiss.com
www.prentiss.com
Manufacturer, importer and exporter of pesticides,
insecticides and rodenticides
President: Richard A Miller
VP/Purchasing: Jeffery Miller
Sales Director: Larry Eichler

Estimated Sales: $10-20 Million
Number Employees: 5-9
Square Footage: 150000
Type of Packaging: Private Label, Bulk
Brands:
Prentox

27759 Prepared Foods Magazine& Food Engineering Magazine
2401 W. Big Beaver Rd
Suite 700
Troy, MI 48084

248-362-3700
Fax: 303-431-0193
Magazine source

27760 Pres-Air-Trol Corporation
704 Bartlett Ave.
Altoona, WI 54720

715-831-6353
Fax: 419-818-0897 800-431-2625
info@senasys.com www.presair.com
Manufacturer and exporter of foot pedals and
switches including pneumatic/electric and shock, ex-
plosion and water-proof; pressure and vacuum
switches, thermometers, thermostats
President: Arthur Blumenthal
Vice President: Doreen Bassin
Sales: Juana Magana
Contact: Ivon Graner
ivong@presair.com
Production/Plant Manager: Chris Felon
Purchasing: Marie Schuartz
Estimated Sales: $10-20 Million
Number Employees: 20-49
Square Footage: 24000
Brands:
Control Safe
Disposertrol
Magictrol
Pres-Air-Trol
Tinytrol

27761 Pres-On Products
21 W Factory Rd
Addison, IL 60101

630-543-9370
Fax: 630-628-8025 800-323-7467
Manufacturer and exporter of liners including induc-
tion seal, PE, styrene and self-sealing
Division VP: Tom Cummins
Contact: John Lesavage
johnl@preson.com
VP Manaufacturing: Frank Edes
Estimated Sales: $20-50 Million
Number Employees: 15

27762 Pres-On Tape & Gasket Corp
2600 E 107th St
Bolingbrook, IL 60440-3196

630-628-2255
Fax: 630-628-8025 800-323-7467
www.pres-on.com
Induction and pressure sealed cap liners, gasketing
tapes of vinyl foam
Founder: Henry L. Gianatasio
Executive VP: Kat Liepins
kliepins@preson.com
Estimated Sales: $10 Million
Number Employees: 20-49

27763 Prescolite
695 Walnut Ave
Vallejo, CA 94592-1134

707-562-3500
Fax: 510-577-5022 www.prescolite.com
Manufacturer and exporter of lighting fixtures in-
cluding electric, incandescent, mercury and outdoor
Marketing Manager: John Taylor
Estimated Sales: $20-50 Million
Number Employees: 250-499
Parent Co: US Industries

27764 Presence From Innovation LLC
2290 Ball Dr
St Louis, MO 63146-8602

314-423-9777
Fax: 314-423-0420 info@pfinnovation.com
www.pfinnovation.com
Manufacturer and exporter of universal gravity feed
systems, ice barrel coolers and display and merchan-
dising equipment
President: Jim Watt
Number Employees: 250-499

Brands:
Iceman
Ultra Glide

27765 Presentations South
4748 Jetty St
Orlando, FL 32817-3183

407-657-2108
Fax: 407-849-0930
Manufacturer, designer and exporter of industrial
displays, attraction exhibits, etc
Estimated Sales: $2.5-5 Million
Number Employees: 1-4
Square Footage: 120000

27766 President Container Inc
200 W Commercial Ave
Moonachie, NJ 07074-1684

212-244-0345
Fax: 201-933-9574
pcsales@presidentcontainer.com
www.presidentcontainer.com
Corrugated boxes
President: Lucia Sannicandro
forzals@aol.com
Vice President: Richard Grossbard
General Manager: Larry Grossbard
Vice President of Production: Joe Restifo
Estimated Sales: $20-50 Million
Number Employees: 50-99
Square Footage: 200000

27767 Presque Isle Wine Cellars
9440 W Main Rd
North East, PA 16428-2699

814-725-1314
Fax: 814-725-2092 800-488-7492
info@piwine.com www.piwine.com
Wines and wine-making supplies
Owner: Doug Moorhead
doug@piwine.com
Co-Owner: Laury Bouttcher
Estimated Sales: Below $5 Million
Number Employees: 10-19
Type of Packaging: Private Label
Brands:
Presque Isle Wine

27768 Pressed Paperboard Technologies LLC
30400 Telegraph Rd
Bingham Farms, MI 48025-4537

248-646-6500
Fax: 248-646-6532 sales@papertrays.com
www.papertrays.com
Press formed, dual-ovenable paperboard trays for
the frozen food, school and institutional feeding and
pizza industries.
Owner: Lawrence Epstein
Vice President Sales: Al Fotheringham
Contact: Michelle Frasure
michellefrasure@papertrays.com

27769 Pressure Pack
PO Box 3007
Williamsburg, VA 23187-3007

757-220-3693
Fax: 757-229-7612
Asceptic, food processing, heat sealing and can fill-
ing machinery
Owner: Robert Fox
VP Technology: Joseph Marcy
Estimated Sales: $1-5,000,000
Number Employees: 1-4

27770 Prestige Label Company
151 Industrial Dr
Burgaw, NC 28425

910-259-3600
Fax: 910-259-6312 800-969-4449
www.prestigelabelsco.com
Labels including thermal, thermal transfer, laser,
computer, styrene inserts, prime, bar code and con-
secutive numbers
Manager: Terie Syme
Estimated Sales: $5-10 Million
Number Employees: 20-49
Square Footage: 36000
Type of Packaging: Private Label

27771 Prestige Metal ProductsInc
885 Anita Ave
PO Box 700
Antioch, IL 60002-2462

847-395-0775
Fax: 847-395-0792 rfq@prestigemetals.com
www.prestigemetals.com
Custom sheet metal fabrication
President: Gordon Miller
info@prestigemetals.com
Estimated Sales: $2.5-5 Million
Number Employees: 20-49
Square Footage: 38000

27772 Prestige Plastics Corporation
8207 Swenson Way
Delta, BC V4G 1J5
Canada

604-930-2931
Fax: 604-930-2936
Manufacturer, importer and exporter of bins, tote
and plastic boxes, cartons, point of purchase dis-
plays and signs; also, die cutting and design services
available
President: Bill Schoenbaum
Sales Manager: James Berry
Estimated Sales: $10-20 Million
Number Employees: 10-19

27773 Prestige Skirting & Tablecloths
60 Dutch Hill Rd # 4a
Orangeburg, NY 10962-1722

845-358-6900
Fax: 845-359-2287 800-635-3313
prestigeskirting@aol.com
Manufacturer and exporter of tablecloths, napkins,
banquet skirting, clips with Velcro, skirt hangers,
chair covers, working racks and custom made linens
President: Marilyn Enison
Office Manager: Emily Valerie Ross
Sales Manager: Paul Tessler
Customer Service: Jane Smithers
Estimated Sales: $5-10 Million
Number Employees: 10-19
Square Footage: 20000
Brands:
Hangars

27774 Prestolabels.Com
31 Industry Park Court
Tipp City, OH 45371

Fax: 937-667-5687 800-201-7120
andy.heinl@prestolabels.com
www.prestolabels.com
Digital labels and tags
President: Tony Heinl
CEO: Rick Heinl
CFO: Gene Harris
R&D/Sales: Andy Heink
QControl/Operations/Plant Manager: Gary Packott
Marketing/Public Relations: Pat Larson
Contact: Andy Heink
andy@repacorp.com
Production: Rob Sloan
Purchasing: Heidi Ponlman
Estimated Sales: $35 Million
Number Employees: 160
Parent Co: Repacorp, Inc
Type of Packaging: Consumer, Food Service, Pri-
vate Label, Bulk

27775 Preston Scientific
1450 N Hundley St
Anaheim, CA 92806-1322

714-632-3700
Fax: 714-632-7355
Manufacturer and exporter of computer systems in-
cluding data acquisition sub-systems
President and CEO: Bernard Spear
Executive VP: Phillip Halverson
President: Bill Boston
Sales Manager: Charles McGuire
Plant Manager: Amber Brideisca
Purchasing Manager: Robert Exley
Estimated Sales: $1-2.5 Million
Number Employees: 1-4
Square Footage: 48000
Parent Co: Halear
Brands:
Presys1000

27776 Pretium Packaging
200 W 20th St
Hermann, MO 65041-1602

573-486-2811
Fax: 573-486-2443 www.pretiumpkg.com
Manufacturer and exporter of custom packaging and
mustard bottles
President: Keith Harbison
Plant Manager: Bob Gillig
Estimated Sales: $20-50 Million
Number Employees: 50-99

27777 Pretium Packaging
512 Forest Rd
Hazle Twp, PA 18202-9389

570-459-1800
Fax: 570-459-6462 petjars@aol.com
www.pretiumpkg.com
Clear polyester food jars and bottles
President: Keith Harbison
Cmo: Tom Marchetto
Human Resources: Jane Mindler
Sales Manager: Bob Plesnicher
VP Manufacturing: Raymond Eble
Estimated Sales: $20-50 Million
Number Employees: 50-99
Square Footage: 63000
Parent Co: Pretium Packaging

27778 Pretium Packaging
15450 South Outer Forty Drive
Suite 120
Chesterfield, MO 63017

812-522-8177
Fax: 314-727-8200 314-727-8673
customerservice@pretiumpkg.com
www.pretiumpkg.com
Blow molded plastic bottles in HDPE, PVC, LPDE
and EPET; also, labeling and decorating available
CFO: Bob Mohrmann
Contact: Daniel Lally
dlally@harbison.com
Manager: John Cannaday
Plant Manager: Joe Wolf
Estimated Sales: $10-20 Million
Number Employees: 50-99

27779 Pretium Packaging, LLC.
15450 S Outer Forty
Suite 120
Chesterfield, MO 63017

314-727-8200
pretiumpkg.com
Manufacturer and exporter of plastic bottles and
containers used for syrup.
SVP, Sales of Marketing: Mark Howell
Year Founded: 1992
Estimated Sales: $232.23 Million
Number Employees: 1200
Square Footage: 300
Parent Co: Harrison
Type of Packaging: Bulk

27780 Pretty Products
1255 Karl Ct
Wauconda, IL 60084-1098

847-526-5505
Fax: 847-526-5271 800-726-4849
sales@purdyproducts.com
www.purdyproducts.com
Chemicals, sanitizers, cleaners and degreasers for
food service equipment
President: Robert D Husemoller
rdh@purdyproducts.com
Estimated Sales: $5-10 Million
Number Employees: 5-9

27781 Pri-Pak Inc
2000 Schenley Pl
Greendale, IN 47025-1593

812-537-7300
Fax: 812-537-7310 www.pripak.com
Wine coolers
CFO: Diane Tidwell
dtidwell@pripak.com
Plant Manager: Gary Dunn
Estimated Sales: $50-75 Million
Number Employees: 100-249

27782 Pride Container Corporation
4545 W Palmer St
Chicago, IL 60639

773-227-6000
Fax: 773-227-2645

Corrugated containers
President: Jeff Sharfstein
CFO: Jeff McReynolds
Chairman of the Board: Richard Sharfstein
VP Sales: Michael Weiss
Estimated Sales: $20-50 Million
Number Employees: 100-249

27783 Pride Neon Inc
3010 W 10th St
Sioux Falls, SD 57104-6204
605-336-3561
Fax: 605-336-6938 signs@prideneon.com
www.prideneon.com
Indoor and outdoor signs including neon and
back-lit; also, awnings
President: George Menke Jr
bret@prideneon.com
Secretary/Treasurer: Dick Menke
Vice President: Bob Menke
R&D: Nike Menke
Service Manager: Mitch Menke
Sales Exec: Bret Menke
Assistant Financial Manager: Dan Menke
Production Manager: Nick Menke
Estimated Sales: $1,800,000
Number Employees: 20-49

27784 Pride Polymers LLC
1111 N 20th Ave
Yakima, WA 98902-1207
509-452-3330
Fax: 509-452-8850 info@pridepolymers.com
www.pridepolymers.com
Owner: Joe O'Malley
joeo@pridepolymers.com
Estimated Sales: Less Than $500,000
Number Employees: 1-4

27785 Prima® Wawona
7108 N Fresno St
Suite 450
Fresno, CA 93720
559-787-8780
prima.com
Tree fruits, including peaches, plums, nectarines and
apricots.
President & CEO: Dan Gerawan
Retail Sales Manager: Ben Vived
Estimated Sales: Over $1 Billion
Number Employees: 500-999
Brands:
Sweet 2 Eat

27786 Primary Liquidation
80 Orville Dr
Bohemia, NY 11716-2534
631-244-1410
Fax: 516-229-2741
Supplier of surplus closeout liquidation inventories
of a food and grocery nature. Over 29 years of expe-
rience
President: Paul Klein
Estimated Sales: Less Than $500,000
Number Employees: 1-4
Type of Packaging: Consumer, Food Service

27787 Prime Equipment
10201 E Buckeye Ln
Spokane Valley, WA 99206-4270
509-928-8947
Fax: 509-928-0690
Packaging machinery
Contact: Bart Triesch
btriesch@primeequipusa.com
Estimated Sales: $1-2.5 Million
Number Employees: 5-9

27788 Prime Inc.
2740 N. Mayfair Ave.
Springfield, MO 65803
417-866-0001
Fax: 417-521-6878 800-321-4552
www.primeinc.com
Refrigerated, flatbed, and tanker carrier services to
an international customer base.
President/Founder: Robert Low
rlow@primeinc.com
Director, Finance: Dean Hoedl
General Counsel: Steve Crawford
Director, Technology: Rodney Rader
Director, Marketing: Keith McCoy
Vice President, Sales & Marketing: Steve Wutke
Director, Operations: Pat Leonard

Year Founded: 1970
Estimated Sales: $500 Million
Number Employees: 500-999

27789 Prime Label ConsultantsInc
536 7th St SE
Washington, DC 20003-2737
202-546-3333
Fax: 202-543-4337 800-766-5225
info@primelabel.com www.primelabel.com
Consulting services to processors affected by Fed-
eral food labeling regulations
President: Joe Bechtold
Owner/CEO: Elizabeth Bechtold
liz@primelabel.com
Director, Software Development: Fred Mosher
Food Technologist: Ames Perry
Office Manager: Pat Yingling
Estimated Sales: $1-2.5 Million
Number Employees: 5-9

27790 Prime ProData
800 N Main St
North Canton, OH 44720
330-497-2578
Fax: 330-497-7206 877-497-2578
www.primepro.com
Accounting systems software with consultants spe-
cializing in computer systems software analysis
President: Susan Caghan
Contact: Sean Buck
sbuck@primepro.com
Estimated Sales: $1-3 Million
Number Employees: 5-9
Brands:
Pcas
Prime Prodata

27791 Prime Tag & Label
1516 F Ave SE
Hickory, NC 28602
828-327-4012
Fax: 828-327-4018 887-710-7771
Manager: Monica Commisso
Estimated Sales: Below 1 Million
Number Employees: 5-9

27792 PrimeSource Equipment
PO Box 2389
Addison, TX 75001-2389
214-273-4900
Fax: 214-273-4999 800-737-8567
sales@primesourcefse.com
A wholesale food service distribution company
CEO: Charles James

27793 Primera Technology
2 Carlson Pkwy N # 375
Plymouth, MN 55447-8800
763-475-6676
Fax: 763-475-6677 800-797-2772
sales@primeralabel.com www.primera.com
Labels
President: Chris Lange
fsouthward@southward.com
Estimated Sales: $13.3 Million
Number Employees: 10-19

27794 Primex Plastics Corp
1235 N F St
Richmond, IN 47374-2448
765-966-7774
Fax: 765-935-1083 800-222-5116
sales@primexplastics.com
www.primexplastics.com
Rolls and sheets of polystyrene
President: Michael Cramer
mcramer@primexplastics.com
VP: John Kittner
Estimated Sales: $75-100 Million
Number Employees: 500-999

27795 Primlite Manufacturing Corporation
407 S Main St
Freeport, NY 11520
516-868-4411
Fax: 516-868-4609 800-327-7583
sales@primelite-mfg.com www.primelite-mfg.com
Manufacturer and exporter of outdoor lighting fixtures, plastic globes and store fixtures including custom designed prismatic glass ceiling and wall
fixtures

President: Benjamin Heit
Quality Control Manager: Joanne Heit
Estimated Sales: $3-5 Million
Number Employees: 10-19
Square Footage: 60000

27796 Primo Roasting Equipment
1309 S Lyon St
Santa Ana, CA 92705-4608
714-556-5259
Fax: 714-556-5690 800-675-0160
dion@primoroasting.com www.primoroasting.com
Coffee roaster manufacturing
CEO: Dion Humpreys
Manager: Dion Humphreys
dion@primoroasting.com
Estimated Sales: $500,000-$1 Million
Number Employees: 5-9

27797 Primo Water Corporation
101 N Cherry St
Suite 501
Winston-Salem, NC 27101
844-237-7466
primowater.com
Water dispensers, purified bottled water, self-service
refill drinking water.
Chief Executive Officer: Jerry Fowden
Chief Financial Officer: Jay Wells
Chief Accounting Officer: Jason Ausher
VP/General Counsel/Secretary: Marni Morgan-Poe
SVP/Global Human Resources: Steve Edman
Estimated Sales: K
Number Employees: 10,000+
Type of Packaging: Consumer, Food Service, Pri-
vate Label, Bulk
Other Locations:
Cliffstar Manufacturing Plant
East Freetown MA
Cliffstar Manufacturing Plant
Fontana CA
Cliffstar Manufacturing Plant
Fredonia NY
Cliffstar Manufacturing Plant
Greer SC
Cliffstar Manufacturing Plant
Joplin MO
Cliffstar Manufacturing Plant
N East PA
Cliffstar Manufacturing Plant
Walla Walla WA
Cliffstar Manufacturing Plant
Warrens WI
Cott Beverage Manufacturing Plant
Calgary, Alberta, Canada
Cott Concentrate Manufacturing
Columbus GA
Brands:
ALHAMBRA
ATHENA
BELMONT SPRINGS
CRYSTAL SPRINGS
DEEP ROCK WATER
HINCKLEY SPRINGS
KENTWOOD SPRINGS
SIERRA SPRINGS
SPARKLETTS
CANADIAN SPRINGS
JAVARAMA
STANDARD COFFEE
TERRAZA
S&D COFFEE & TEA
AIMIA FOODS
RCCI

27798 Primus Laboratories
2810 Industrial Parkway
Santa Maria, CA 93455-1880
805-922-0055
Fax: 805-922-2462 800-779-1156
www.primuslabs.com
Wine industry analytical services
President: Bob Stovicek
Estimated Sales: $5-10 Million
Number Employees: 250-499

27799 Prince Castle Inc
355 Kehoe Blvd
Carol Stream, IL 60188-1833
630-462-8801
Fax: 630-462-1460 800-722-7853
info@princecastle.com www.princecastle.com

Manufacturer and exporter of preparation and holding equipment including warming and toasting equipment, electronic cooking timers and computers, grill tools, high chairs, fry baskets and shortening filters, dispensers, drink mixerscutters and slicers
President: Ted Bethke
ted@aviation-schools.com
Product Marketing Manager: Richard Blauvelt
VP Sales/Marketing: William Kinney
Number Employees: 100-249
Square Footage: 240000
Parent Co: Marmon Group
Type of Packaging: Food Service
Brands:
  Comfortline
  Excalibur
  Fasline
  Frequent Fryer
  Merlin
  Multi Mixer
  Portion-All
  Redi-Grill

27800 Prince Industries Inc
5635 Thompson Bridge Rd
Murrayville, GA 30564-1209
    770-536-3679
Fax: 770-535-2548 800-441-3303
www.princeindustriesinc.com
Manufacturer and exporter of poultry processing equipment including deboners, grinders and meat pumps
President: Jesse Prince
prinind@bellsouth.net
CFO: Jesse Prince
Vice President: Dottie Prince
National Sales Manager: Jesse Prince
General Manager: Kam Singh
Estimated Sales: $2.5-5 Million
Number Employees: 5-9
Square Footage: 24000

27801 Prince Seating Corp
1355 Atlantic Ave
Brooklyn, NY 11216-2810
    718-363-2300
Fax: 718-363-9800 800-577-4623
info@PrinceSeating.com www.princeseating.com
Wood and metal chairs, tables and barstools
Owner: Abe Belsky
abe.belsky@chairfactory.net
VP: Abe Belsky
Contract Sales: Peri Lissauer
Estimated Sales: $5 Million
Number Employees: 50-99
Square Footage: 260000

27802 Princeton Shelving
873 Center Point Road NE
Cedar Rapids, IA 52402-4664
    319-369-0355
Fax: 319-369-0387
Dealer rep. and distributor of pallet racks, wire decking and containers, POP displays, carts (hand, service), racks, steel and wire shelving. Over 500 different companies
Estimated Sales: $1-5,000,000

27803 Prinova
285 Fullerton Ave
Carol Stream, IL 60188-1886
    630-868-0300
Fax: 630-868-0310 info@prinovausa.com
www.prinovausa.com
Ascorbic acid, B vitamins and amino acids
Owner: Donald Thorp
sales@premiumingredients.com
Number Employees: 10-19

27804 Print & Peel
620 12th Ave
New York, NY 10036-1004
    212-226-7007
Fax: 212-226-7174 800-451-0807
Printed and nonprinted pressure sensitive paper labels, film, paper, etc
President: Linda Owen
VP/Sales: Ronald Steinberg
Contact: Steve Owen
steveo@lvadhesive.com
Estimated Sales: $5-10 Million
Number Employees: 20-49

27805 Print Ons/Express Mark
505 Cuthbertson St
Monroe, NC 28110-3809
    704-289-8261
Fax: 704-289-2158
Printed and embroidered shirts
Director Sales Marketing: John Schnader
Estimated Sales: $500,000-$1,000,000
Number Employees: 1-4
Brands:
  Express Mark
  Print Ons

27806 Print-O-Tape Inc
755 Tower Rd
Mundelein, IL 60060-3817
    847-362-1476
Fax: 847-949-7449 800-346-6311
customerservice@printotape.com
www.printotape.com
Pressure sensitive labels and tapes
President: Carl J Walliser
CFO: Marty Justin
R&D: Roger Haase
Quality Control: Ron Quba
Marketing Manager: Eddie Walschner
Estimated Sales: $10-20 Million
Number Employees: 50-99

27807 Print-Tech
330 E Kilbourn Avenue
Suite 1085
Milwaukee, WI 53202-3146
    608-241-5027
Fax: 608-249-7760 800-682-7746
President: Ryan Simons
R&D: Ryan Simons
Quality Control: Randy Agisv
Contact: Randy Heisz
rheisz@bcblaw.net
Estimated Sales: $5-10 Million
Number Employees: 50

27808 Printape Corporation ofAmerica
174 Passaic St
Garfield, NJ 07026-1358
    973-815-1880
Fax: 973-815-1882
Printed, pilfer proof, carton sealing, paper tapes
President: Jerry Bialick
Estimated Sales: $20-50 Million
Number Employees: 50-99

27809 Printcraft Marking Devices Inc
1193 Military Rd
Buffalo, NY 14217-1845
    716-873-8181
Fax: 716-873-2751 pmdinc@banet.net
Engraved and rubber stamps
Owner: Lynn Wuertzer
printcraft@verizon.net
Manager: Ruff Wuertzer
Estimated Sales: Less Than $500,000
Number Employees: 1-4

27810 Printex Packaging
555 Raymond Dr
Islandia, NY 11749-4844
    631-234-4300
Fax: 631-234-4840 info@printexpackaging.com
www.printexpackaging.com
President: Barbara Colangelo
valerie.bernard@ubs.com
R & D: Joe Heller
Estimated Sales: $20-30 Million
Number Employees: 50-99

27811 Printpack Inc
210 Kansas City Ave
Shreveport, LA 71107-6637
    318-226-8661
www.printpack.com
Polyethylene bags for bakeries
Customer Demand Analyst: Vicki Hamaoka
Market Development Manager: Scott Mitchell
Manager: Kay Davis
kdavis@printpack.com
Maintenance Manager: Fred Irle
Estimated Sales: $50-100 Million
Number Employees: 100-249
Parent Co: Printpack

27812 (HQ)Printpack Inc.
2800 Overlook Pkwy. NE
Atlanta, GA 30339
    404-460-7000
info@printpack.com
www.printpack.com
Printed, coated, laminated and flexible film, rolls, sheets and heat sealing paper; also, candy bar and meat wrappers.
Chairman & CEO: Jimmy Love
Senior VP & CFO: Tripp Seitter
Year Founded: 1956
Estimated Sales: Over $1 Billion
Number Employees: 1000-4999

27813 Printpak
14651 Dallas Pkwy
Suite 320
Dallas, TX 75254-1639
    972-392-3101
Fax: 972-392-1129 www.printpakllc.com
President: Dennis Love
Estimated Sales: $1-3 Million
Number Employees: 1-4
Type of Packaging: Consumer

27814 Printpak
14651 Dallas Pkwy
Suite 320
Dallas, TX 75254-1639
    972-392-3101
Fax: 404-691-8143 800-451-9985
www.printpak.com
President: Dennis Love
Estimated Sales: $1-3 Million
Number Employees: 1-4

27815 Printsafe Inc
12125 Kear Pl
Poway, CA 92064-7131
    858-748-8600
Fax: 858-748-8640 info@printsafe.com
www.wireandcablemarking.com
President: Tom Hittle
CEO: Alan Anderson
aanderson@imbee.com
Estimated Sales: $5-10 Million
Number Employees: 20-49

27816 Printsource Group
128 Main St
Wakefield, RI 02879-3567
    401-789-9339
Fax: 401-789-1750 csr@printsource.com
www.printsourceri.com
Decals, labels, name plates and advertising signs including magnetic, vinyl and hot die cut, printing on plastic containers
President, Chief Executive Officer: Donald Shortman
Sr. Account Manager: Deb Saccoccio
Manager: Mary Lungwitz
mary@printsource.com
Production Manager: Bruce Gibbs
Estimated Sales: Less Than $500,000
Number Employees: 5-9
Square Footage: 140000
Type of Packaging: Private Label, Bulk

27817 Priority Food Processing
635 Oakwood Rd
Lake Zurich, IL 60047
    847-438-1338
Fax: 847-438-1599
Contract dry food blending and packaging
President: Andy Burke
Quality Control: Rodney Hart
Contact: Charles Trinchetilla
charles@conagrafoods.com
Estimated Sales: $50-100 Million
Number Employees: 100-249

27818 Priority One America
3255 Medalist Drive
PO Box 2408
Oshkosh, WI 54903
Canada
    920-235-5562
Fax: 866-580-2312
www.priorityonepackaging.com
Manufacturer, exporter and importer of palletizers, conveyors, depalletizers and packaging machinery
President: Colin Cunningham
Controller: Carolyn Schnefer

Estimated Sales: $10-20 Million
Number Employees: 100
Square Footage: 30000
Parent Co: Priority One Packaging

27819 Priority One Packaging
815 Bridge Street
Waterloo, ON N2V 2M7
Canada

519-746-6950
Fax: 519-746-3578 800-387-9102
products@priorityonepackaging.com
www.priorityonepackaging.com
Priority One is a manufacturer of palletizing and
depalletizing equipment. Included in the product
range are both high and low level palletizers, small
footprint palletizers, multi-line (shuttle and rotary)
palletizers, pailpalletizers, bulk palletizers, high and
low depalletizers, table-top and mat-top conveyor
systems, pressured and pressureless single filers,
bottle and case elevators/lowerators, rinsers, magnetic elevators, cable track, full load stackers,
labellersand line integration
Owner/CEO: Colin Cunningham
President: Brian Webster
VP: Drew Cameron
Estimated Sales: $30 Million
Number Employees: 120
Square Footage: 100000
Brands:
  Langguth
  Pro-Pal

27820 Priority One Packaging
Machinery
124 N Columbus Street
Randolph, WI 53956
Canada

800-882-4995
Fax: 920-326-6551 800-387-9102
inquiry@arrowheadsystems.com
www.priorityonepackaging.com

27821 Priority Plastics Inc
704 Pinder Ave
Grinnell, IA 50112-9700

641-236-4798
Fax: 641-236-3478 800-798-3512
www.showme.com
Custom silk screened printed plastic canisters and
plastic bottles; exporter of plastic bottles
President: Lawrence Den Hartog
Plant Manager: Gary Vowels
Estimated Sales: $20-50 Million
Number Employees: 20-49
Square Footage: 28000
Brands:
  Sho-Me

27822 Prism
3180 Presidential Drive
Suite C
Atlanta, GA 30340-3900

770-455-4544
Fax: 770-454-7876

Business solutions

27823 Prism
8300 NW 53rd St
Suite 103
Miami, FL 33166-7710

305-599-9033
Fax: 305-594-9280
Sanitation supplies and services
Manager: Manny Gonzalez
Estimated Sales: Less than $500,000
Number Employees: 1-4

27824 Prism Visual Software Inc
1 Sagamore Hill Dr
Port Washington, NY 11050-2135

516-944-5920
Fax: 516-944-5243 info@prismvs.com
www.prismvs.com
Routing/scheduling software
Owner: David Cullen
CEO: Marc J. Eisenberg
CFO: Robert G. Costantini*VP:* John J Stolte, Jr
VP Marketing: Lynn Keating
Vice President of Sales: Andrew Kuneth
Estimated Sales: $3 Million
Number Employees: 10-19

27825 Prism Visual Software Inc
1 Sagamore Hill Dr
Port Washington, NY 11050-2135

516-944-5920
Fax: 516-944-5243 sales@prismvs.com
www.prismvs.com
Readquest, Prisms route management/palm pilot so-
lution for food and beverage companies
Owner: David Cullen
CEO: Lorraine Keating
lorrainek@prismvs.com
CEO: Lorraine Keating
Marketing: Lynn Keating
Sales Director: Michael Del Colle
Operations: Chris Heinrich
Estimated Sales: $1.5 Million
Number Employees: 10-19

27826 Pro Active Sltns Chaska
12502 Xenwood Ave
Savage, MN 55378-1225

952-890-1820
Fax: 952-890-3844 800-788-7449
www.proactivesolutionsusa.com
Industrial cleaners
President: Sean Teske
CEO: Paul Moe
General Manager: Monica Tucker
Manager: Wade Hustad
wade.hustad@chaskachem.com
Director Production Deptartment: Jeff Gray
Plant Manager: Jeff Gray
Estimated Sales: Below $5 Million
Number Employees: 10-19

27827 Pro Active Solutions USA LLC
301 Bridge St
Green Bay, WI 54303-1511

920-437-8658
Fax: 920-437-4006 800-411-6734
www.prochemicals.com
Rapid method for microbial contamination detection
Owner: Doug Storhoff
doug@prochemicals.com
Estimated Sales: $2.5-5 Million
Number Employees: 20-49

27828 Pro Bake Inc
2057 E Aurora Rd # P
Suite Pq
Twinsburg, OH 44087-1938

330-425-4427
Fax: 330-425-9742 800-837-4427
probake@probake.com www.probake.com
Bakery equipment reconditioning
President: Maureen Jarvis
maureenj@probake.com
Sales Promotion Manager: Jeff Salenger
Estimated Sales: $5-10 Million
Number Employees: 10-19

27829 Pro Controls Inc
1312 Gordon Rd # 1
Yakima, WA 98901-1725

509-457-3386
Fax: 509-457-3491 800-488-3386
Process control systems
Owner: Paula O'Brien
brien@procontrolsinc.com
Estimated Sales: $1-2,500,000
Number Employees: 10-19

27830 Pro Line Co
10 Avco Rd # 1
Haverhill, MA 01835-6997

978-521-2600
Fax: 978-374-4885 bench@1proline.com
www.1proline.com
Manufacturer and exporter of ergonomic
workstations for production and lab areas
Owner: Derek Coughlin
President, Chief Executive Officer: Robert W
Hatfield
bench@1proline.com
Sr. VP: Bob Simmons
Estimated Sales: $3-5 Million
Number Employees: 20-49
Type of Packaging: Bulk

27831 Pro Media Inc
W127n8690 Westbrook Xing
Menomonee Falls, WI 53051-3342

262-532-2600
Fax: 262-532-2627 800-328-0439
sales@promediaus.com
Specializing in manufacturer, distributor, and opera-
tor frequency programs
President: Tom Collier
info@promediaus.com
Executive VP: Rick Stolowski
VP Incentive Sales: Jim Egan
Estimated Sales: $10-20,000,000
Number Employees: 10-19
Square Footage: 18000

27832 Pro Pack Systems Inc
1354 Dayton St # A
Salinas, CA 93901-4426

831-771-1300
Fax: 831-771-1303
Adhesive systems, wax systems for wineries, ink jet
coding, cave/tray packing
Owner: Mike Armento
mikea@propacksystems.com
Estimated Sales: Below $5 Million
Number Employees: 5-9
Square Footage: 8

27833 Pro Refrigeration
326 8th St SW
Auburn, WA 98001-5914

253-735-1189
Fax: 253-735-2631 www.prochiller.com
Refrigeration equipment
VP/CEO/General Manager: Jim Vander Giessen
info@prorefrigeration.com
Chief Financial Officer: Gary Duim
Operations Manager: Matthew Perala
Inventory Control: Kelly Phelps
Purchasing Manager/Technical Support: Rande
Routledge
Number Employees: 20-49

27834 Pro Scientific
PO Box 448
Monroe, CT 06468-0448

203-452-9431
Fax: 780-452-9753 prosci@aol.com
www.proscientific.com/chef.html
Handheld and bench top mechanical homogenizers,
laboratory and custom homogenizers
Estimated Sales: $1-2.5 Million
Number Employees: 10-19

27835 Pro Scientific Inc
99 Willenbrock Rd
Oxford, CT 06478-1032

203-267-4600
Fax: 203-267-4606 800-584-3776
sales@proscientific.com www.proscientific.com
Manufactures laboratory homogenizers from
handheld to larger benchtop programmable models.
North American distributor of Andreas Hettich
Centifuges which range in size from micro to
floor-model. Also distribute a full line ofincubators,
water and oil baths and ovens
Owner: Donald Peronace
don@madisonavecreative.com
Sales/Marketing: Holly Yacko
Estimated Sales: $5-10 Million
Number Employees: 10-19
Number of Brands: 3
Number of Products: 40
Brands:
  Hettich
  Memmert
  Pro
  Riebosam

27836 Pro Sheet Cutter
705 S Electric Avenue
Alhambra, CA 91803-1639

626-576-0785
Fax: 626-576-8895
Extrusion fabrication systems, sawing systems,
low-level radioactive and mixed waste containers,
transloader, grinders, computer controlled slit mask
fabricator and electronically integrated control
system bandsaw

27837 Pro-Ad-Co Inc
655 N Tillamook St
Portland, OR 97227-1886

503-288-5885
Fax: 503-281-8725 800-287-5885
www.proadco.com
Labels, screen printed decals, signs, point of purchase displays, bumper stickers and metal and engraved name plates
Owner: Cliff Overholt
sales@proadco.com
Estimated Sales: $5-10 Million
Number Employees: 10-19

27838 Pro-Com Security Systems
2975 W Executive Parkway
STE 156
Lehi, UT 84043

801-770-7233
Fax: 801-770-7233 877-776-2669
procomsecurity.com
Long range radio security systems
Parent Co: Sonitrol Company

27839 Pro-Dex Inc
2361 Mcgaw Ave
Irvine, CA 92614-5831

949-769-3200
Fax: 949-769-3281 800-562-6204
sales@omsmotion.com www.pro-dex.com
Motion controllers, motors, drives
VP: Phil Brown
Chief Executive Officer, President: Michael Berthelot
Vice President of Regulatory Affairs: Joseph Rotino
Marketing: Julie Kealy
Vice President of Sales and Marketing: Frank Noone
Estimated Sales: $5-10 Million
Number Employees: 50-99

27840 Pro-Flo Products
30 Commerce Rd
PO Box 390
Cedar Grove, NJ 7009

973-239-2400
Fax: 973-239-5817 800-325-1057
Manufacturer, importer and exporter of water treatment and filtration equipment, drinking water coolers, chillers and dispensers
President: Louis Reyes
Quality Control: Nicaolas Iannaccio
Estimated Sales: $657,000
Number Employees: 5-9
Square Footage: 8400

27841 Pro-Gram Plastics Inc
700 Pro Gram Pkwy
Geneva, OH 44041-1168

440-466-8080
Fax: 440-466-8099 sales@programplastics.com
www.programplastics.com
Blow-molded plastic bottles
President: Walter Sargi
sw@programplastics.com
Sales Exec: Robert Sweitzer
Production Manager: Robert Sweitzer
Estimated Sales: $5-10 Million
Number Employees: 20-49
Square Footage: 128000

27842 Pro-Tex-All Co
210 S Morton Ave
Evansville, IN 47713-2448

812-424-8268
Fax: 812-424-8330 800-755-5458
drm@protexall.com www.protexall.com
Facility maintenance chemicals, supplies and equipment for industry and commerce
Owner: Jim Kuhn
jkuhn@protexall.com
President: James Kuhn
Vice President: Mike Kuhn
Customer Service: Carla Richards
Estimated Sales: $5-10 Million
Number Employees: 10-19
Square Footage: 59000

27843 Pro-Western Plastics
30 Riel Drive
PO Box 261
St Albert, AB T8N3Z7
Canada

780-459-4491
Fax: 800-428-4756 800-661-9835
wayne.hunt@pro-westernplastics.com
www.pro-westernplastics.com
President: Wall Lacroix
Quality Control: Trevor Hansen
CFO: Wall Lacroix
R&D: Wall Lacroix
Number Employees: 275

27844 ProAmpac
12025 Tricon Rd.
Cincinnati, OH 45246

513-671-1777
800-543-7030
www.proampac.com
Polythylene and paper bags, and specialty films. Custom plastic and paper shopping bags, polymailers and specialty films. (Blown film with six monolayer lines, two 3-layer lines and on 7-layer line).
Chairman/CEO: Tony Pritzker
Year Founded: 1966
Estimated Sales: $121.7 Million
Number Employees: 1,100
Square Footage: 815000
Parent Co: PPC Partners
Type of Packaging: Consumer, Food Service, Private Label

27845 (HQ)ProBar Systems Inc.
92 Caplan Ave.
Suite 607
Barrie, ON L4N 0Z7
Canada

800-521-7294
info@probarsystems.com www.probarsystems.com
Manufacturer and exporter of beverage dispensing machines including computer controlled bar pouring and inventory systems, juice dispensers and soft drink machines
President: Charles M Stimac Jr
CFO: John Hornbeck
Research & Development: Mike Smith
Quality Control: Greg Gemmell
Marketing: Chris Burden
Sales Director: Kris Croft
Operations Manager: Carlos DeMelo
Production/Plant Manager/Purchasing: Jimmy Neuman
Estimated Sales: $300,000-500,000
Number Employees: 1-4
Number of Brands: 3
Number of Products: 3
Type of Packaging: Private Label
Brands:
  Ultra Bar

27846 ProMach
50 East Rivercenter Blvd
Suite 1800
Covington, KY 41011

513-831-8778
Fax: 513-831-5795 866-776-6224
www.promachbuilt.com
Packaging products and machinery
President & CEO: Mark W. Anderson

27847 ProRestore Products
1016 Greentree Road
Suite 115
Pittsburgh, PA 15220

412-264-8340
Fax: 412-920-2905 800-332-6037
sales@prorestoreproducts.com
www.prorestoreproducts.com
Manufacturer and exporter of deodorants, cleaners and disinfectants
President: Cliff Zlotnik
Contact: Mike Kerner
mikek@prorestoreproducts.com
Estimated Sales: $5-10 Million
Number Employees: 20-49
Parent Co: RPM International Inc.
Type of Packaging: Food Service, Private Label, Bulk
Brands:
  Mediclean
  Microban

  Unikleen
  Unsmoke

27848 ProTeam
12438 W Bridger Street
Boise, ID 83713

208-377-9555
Fax: 208-377-8444 800-541-1456
customerservice.proteam@emerson.com
www.pro-team.com
ProTeam became a global phenomenon in the commercial cleaning world after introducing a game-challenging design innovation, the lightweight backpack vacuum. Today ProTeam offers a full range of innovative vacuums, including the newProGuard wet/dry line.
CEO: Matt Wood
Contact: Richard Coombs
r.coombs@pro-team.com
Estimated Sales: $50-100 Million
Number Employees: 50
Square Footage: 5000

27849 ProVisions Software
36 Thurber Boulevard
Smithfield, RI 02917

401-232-2600
Fax: 401-232-7778 800-422-4782
info@caisoft.com www.caisoft.com/provisions
Software

27850 Proact Inc
3195 Neil Armstrong Blvd
Eagan, MN 55121-2256

651-289-3158
Fax: 651-686-0312 877-245-0405
info@proactinc.org www.proactpackaging.com
Sub-contract packager of food products
President,CEO: Steven Ditschler
sditschler@proactinc.org
Controller: Pat McGuire
Director of Production: David Cavalier
Estimated Sales: $$2.5-5 Million
Number Employees: 100-249
Square Footage: 120000

27851 Probat Inc
601 Corporate Woods Pkwy
Vernon Hills, IL 60061-3111

847-415-5253
Fax: 847-793-8611 877-683-8113
info@probatburns.com www.probatburns.com
Bin silo systems, bin vibrators, blending and mixing equipment, cleaners, afterburners, augers, automatic controls, bag emptier, bulk silo servicees, magnetic separation, moisture analyzers, quality control instruments and cuppingequipment.
President: Karl Schmidt
Vice President of Sales & Marketing: Launtia Taylor
Estimated Sales: $5-10 Million
Number Employees: 20-49

27852 Probiotic Solutions
1331 W Houston Ave
Gilbert, AZ 85233-1816

480-961-1220
Fax: 480-961-3061 800-961-1220
info@probiotic.com www.probiotic.com
President: Lyndon Smith
Sales Director: Diana Burtrum
probiotic@probiotic.com
Estimated Sales: $1-5 Million
Number Employees: 10-19
Parent Co: Bio Huma Netics, Inc.

27853 Procedyne Corp
11 Industrial Dr
New Brunswick, NJ 08901-3657

732-249-8347
Fax: 732-249-7220 mail@procedyne.com
www.procedyne.com
Manufacturer and exporter of fluidized bed systems including dryers, granulators and thermal processors. Engineering and research and development facility with laboratory and pilor plant. Offer process design, process development andscale-up testing
President: H Kenneth Staffin
CEO: Kenneth Staffin
kstaffin@procedynecorp.com
VP Process Technology: Thomas Parr
VP Products: Bob Archibald
Chairman of the Board: Dr H Kenneth Staffin

Estimated Sales: $10-20 Million
Number Employees: 50-99
Square Footage: 120000
Type of Packaging: Bulk
Brands:
Mikrodyne

27854 Procell Polymers
PO Box 33
Baton Rouge, LA 70821-0033

225-978-8069
Fax: 866-860-1269
Cellulose gum, guar gum, xanthan gum and other specialty products.
Manager: David Hatcher
Manager: Harry Steeghs
Type of Packaging: Bulk

27855 Procesamiento De Carne
122 S Wesley Ave
Mt Morris, IL 61054-1451

815-734-4171
Fax: 815-734-4201 www.wattnet.com
Equipment for meat processors
President: Gregory A Watt
Estimated Sales: $15 Million
Number Employees: 50-99

27856 Process Automation
P.O.Box 457
Hurst, TX 76053

817-488-9546
Fax: 817-283-1813 800-460-9546
www.processauto.net
Process controls and stainless steel manufacturing for food and beverage industries
President: Scott Carlson
CFO: Steppnie Duelm
Estimated Sales: $30-50 Million
Number Employees: 20-49

27857 Process Displays
5800 S Moorland Rd
New Berlin, WI 53151

262-782-3600
Fax: 262-782-3857 800-533-1764
Manufacturer and exporter of point of purchase displays, vacuum form trays, case dividers, rail strips, counter mats, menu board and deli signs and decals
President: Bob Zanotti
Vice President: Brendon Rowan
Contact: Lori Gebhard
gebhard@pdisplays.com
Estimated Sales: $2.5-5 Million
Number Employees: 50-99
Square Footage: 200000
Parent Co: Process Retail Group

27858 Process Engineering & Fabrication
20 Hedge Ln
Afton, VA 22920

540-456-8163
Fax: 540-456-8171 800-852-7975
www.processengineeringinc.com
Manufacturer and exporter of custom industrial refrigeration systems, spiral conveyor systems and stainless steel food processing equipment; also, installation services available
President: Bart Shellabarger
CEO: Bob Amacker
CFO: Bruce Neidlinger
Chief Freezing Officer: Charley Marckel
Sales: Jimmy Sokora
Contact: Bruce Neidlinger
bruce@processengineeringinc.com
Estimated Sales: Below $5 Million
Number Employees: 10
Square Footage: 40000

27859 Process Heating Co
2732 3rd Ave S
PO Box 84585
Seattle, WA 98134-1983

206-682-3414
Fax: 206-682-1582 866-682-1582
inquire@processheating.com
www.processheating.com
Manufacturer and exporter of industrial immersion heaters, circulation heating systems and fuel oil preheaters

President: Rick Jay
rick@processheating.com
CEO: Ron Jay
Marketing: Mike Peringer
Sales/Industrial: Eric Olden
Estimated Sales: $3-5 Million
Number Employees: 10-19
Number of Products: 15
Square Footage: 15000
Brands:
Lo-Density

27860 Process Heating Corp
547 Hartford Tpke
Shrewsbury, MA 01545-4002

508-842-5200
Fax: 508-842-9418 proheat@gis.net
www.proheatcorp.com
Manufacturer and exporter of ovens, furnaces, air pollution control incinerators and process heating equipment; also, rebuilding and remodeling available
President: Brad Green
proheat@gis.net
Estimated Sales: Below $5,000,000
Number Employees: 5-9

27861 Process Plus
5320 S 39th Street
Phoenix, AZ 85040

602-470-8051
Fax: 602-470-1654
President: Gerald Schneerer

27862 Process Sensors Corp
113 Cedar St # S1
Milford, MA 01757-1192

508-473-9901
Fax: 508-473-0715 www.processsensors.com
Manufacturer, importer and exporter of moisture measuring instruments
President: Robert Winson
robertwinson@outback.com
Estimated Sales: $5-10,000,000
Number Employees: 20-49

27863 Process Solutions
6701 Garden Rd # 1
Riviera Beach, FL 33404-5900

561-840-0050
Fax: 561-840-0070 sales@processsolutions.net
www.processsolutions.net
Manufacturer and exporter of drum lifters and inverters, stainless steel drums, bins, tanks, control panels and systems, etc.; importer of stainless steel bins and butterfly valves
President: Howard Rosenkranz
Vice President: H Rosenkranz
Estimated Sales: $5-10 Million
Number Employees: 20-49
Brands:
Ergoscoop
Omegalift
Pharmaseal

27864 Process Systems
102 Covington Drive
Barrington, IL 60010-6611

847-842-8618
Fax: 847-842-8619 IlliniPick@aol.com
Sanitary process equipment including modelsam steam jacketed and vacuum/pressure kettles, high and low shear mixers
Estimated Sales: $3-5 Million
Number Employees: 20-50
Square Footage: 30000
Brands:
Model Sam

27865 Processors Co-Op
1110 Powers Pl
Alpharetta, GA 30009-8389

770-664-1516
Fax: 770-636-3006
Seafood, meats, poultry
President, CEO: Alan Brown
alanjr@cutyourfoodcost.com
Director of Marketing: Terrie Bradley
Operations Manager: Robert Bragg
Director of Purchasing: Bill Larsen
Estimated Sales: $10-20 Million
Number Employees: 10-19

27866 Prodo-Pak Corp
77 Commerce St
Garfield, NJ 07026-1811

973-777-7770
Fax: 973-772-0471 sales@prodo-pak.com
Manufacturer, importer and exporter of form/fill/seal packaging machines for pouches and tube fillers; also, conveyor systems and labeling equipment
President: John Mueller
sales@prodo-pak.com
Research & Development: Rudy Degenars
Operations/Plant/Purchasing Manager: Ralph Isler
Estimated Sales: $5-10 Million
Number Employees: 20-49
Number of Brands: 1
Number of Products: 10
Square Footage: 20000

27867 Product Dynamics
10608 163rd Pl
Orland Park, IL 60467-8858

708-364-7060
Fax: 708-349-0488
www.productdynamicsdivision.com
Product Dynamics offers Product design and formulation, consumer and product research, qualitative insight and analytical sensory testing. They collabrate with your marketing business planning and research and development teams toaddress your strategic and tatical product issues.
President: Lawrence Platt
CEO: Jeff Widdowson
j.widdowson@rqa-inc.com
Executive Vice President: Mary Ann Platt
Vice President/General Manager: Judy Lindsey
Estimated Sales: $1-3 Million
Number Employees: 10-19
Parent Co: RQA, Inc

27868 Product Saver
12838 Stainless Drive
Holland, MI 49424

616-399-2220
Fax: 616-399-7365 jswiatlo@nbe-inc.com
www.productsaver.com
Bag openers, fillers and closers, reclaiming machinery and recovery systems
President: Ed Swiatlo
General Manager: Jess Swiatlo
Estimated Sales: $1-5 Million
Number Employees: 10-19

27869 Product Solutions
N Street
220
Wilkes Barre, PA 18701-1706

570-825-0600
Fax: 570-825-0600 888-776-3765
prodsol@aol.com
Consultant providing design and engineering of food service equipment; also, aesthetic and engineering improvements to existing equipment available
President: Robert Cohn
Sales Director: Sandee Cohn
Estimated Sales: $1-2.5 Million
Number Employees: 1-4
Square Footage: 10000

27870 Production Equipment Co
401 Liberty St
Meriden, CT 06450-4500

203-235-5795
Fax: 203-237-5391 800-758-5697
www.productionequipmentcompany.com
Manufacturer and exporter of overhead cranes and hoists; also, steel fabricators
Owner: Bud Davis
VP Sales/Marketing: Rosewell Davis
bdavis@productionequipment.com
Estimated Sales: $5-10 Million
Number Employees: 20-49

27871 Production Packaging & Processing Equipment Company
1713 East Victory Drive
Savannah, GA 31404

912-856-4281
Fax: 912-354-4615 www.kettles.com
Manufacturer, exporter and wholesaler/distributor of new and rebuilt packaging and processing equipment including mixers, fillers, cap tighteners, labeling, cappers, kettles and tanks

President: Louis R Klein
CEO: Jeff Klein
Estimated Sales: $2.5-5 Million
Number Employees: 5-9
Square Footage: 100000
Brands:
  P3

27872 Production Systems
850 Mountain Industrial Dr NW
Marietta, GA 30060
770-424-9784
Fax: 770-424-8392 800-235-9734
Manufacturer and exporter of package and case conveyors and packaging and palletizing systems; also, integrated control systems for production and processing plants
President: Michael Anderson
Manager Marketing Series: Sharon Phillips
Engineer Manager: Wayne Marlow
Estimated Sales: $5-10 Million
Number Employees: 20-49
Square Footage: 100000
Brands:
  Package To Pallet

27873 Production Techniques Limited
18 Echelon Place, East Tamaki
PO Box 58-874 Greenmount
Auckland, NZ 2013
New Zealand
649-274-3514
Fax: 649-274-3515 sales@ptl.co.nz
www.ptl.co.nz
Provides manufacturing and processing equipment for the chocolate, candy, confectionery and bakery industries. Specialized plant manufacturing covers a wide range of plant applications including standard pieces of equipment such asmelters, depositors, enrobers, moulding plants, cooling tunnels, temperers and decorators.
Managing Director: Jim Halliday
Technical Director: Mike Nevines
Director of Sales and Marketing: Nick Halliday

27874 Productos Familia
1511 Calle Loiza
Santurce, PR 00911-1846
787-268-5929
Fax: 787-268-7717 www.nosotrasonline.com
Supplier of soft paper tissues; wholesaler/distributor, importer and exporter of toilet paper, paper towels and napkins; serving the food service market
President: Fabio Posada
VP: Carlos Upegui
Number Employees: 7
Square Footage: 12000
Parent Co: Productos Familia SA
Type of Packaging: Food Service

27875 Products A Curtron Div
5350 Campbells Run Rd
Pittsburgh, PA 15205-9738
412-787-9750
Fax: 412-787-3665 800-888-9750
info@tmi-pvc.com www.curtronproducts.com
Manufacturer and exporter of leading food safety products such as strip doors, air doors, rack covers, swinging doors, hood enclosures, display cooler curtains, milk cooler curtains and eutectic packs
Manager: Joseph Klaynjans
Contact: Steve Battaglia
stevebattaglia@curtronproducts.com
Estimated Sales: Less Than $500,000
Number Employees: 1-4
Square Footage: 100000
Parent Co: TMI
Brands:
  Save-T

27876 Profamo Inc
7506 Albert Tillinghast Dr
Sarasota, FL 34240
941-379-8155
Fax: 941-379-8699 info@profamo.com
www.profamo.com
Provides sales and services for manufacturers of quality assurance and process control equipment for the brewing and beverage industries.
President: Klaus Nimptsch
Technical Information Specialist: Chris Nimptsch
Contact: Chris Nimptsch
chris@profamo.com

Estimated Sales: $300,000-500,000
Number Employees: 1-4

27877 Professional Bakeware Company
11739 N Highway 75
Willis, TX 77378-5740
866-710-1936
Fax: 936-890-8760 800-440-9547
Bakeware, cookware, servingware, displayware and indestructable alumaware
President: David Beauregard
Vice President: Jennifer Beauregard
Marketing/Design: Judy Beck
Public Relations: Stephanie Samudio
Plant Manager: Sterling Samudio
Estimated Sales: $10-20,000,000
Number Employees: 20-49
Number of Brands: 5
Number of Products: 500
Square Footage: 15000
Type of Packaging: Food Service, Bulk

27878 Professional Engineering Assoc
8007 Vine Crest Ave # 5
Suite 5
Louisville, KY 40222-8661
502-429-0432
Fax: 502-429-0552
Automated parts feeding systems, feeders, conveyors, screens and process system dryers/coolers
President: Virgil Plummer
Sales Manager: Neal Plummer
Estimated Sales: $2.5-5 Million
Number Employees: 5-9

27879 Professional Image
12437 E 60th St
Tulsa, OK 74146-6906
918-461-0609
Fax: 918-615-1836 800-722-8550
sales@calvertco.com
www.professionalimagepackaging.com
Printing and packaging
President/Owner: Cynthia Calvert-Copeland
Marketing: Jennifer Giebel
Estimated Sales: $8 Million
Number Employees: 20-49

27880 Professional Marketing Group
912 Rainier Avenue S
Seattle, WA 98144-2840
206-322-7303
Fax: 206-322-4351 800-227-3769
www.vacuumpackers.com
Importer, exporter and wholesaler/distributor of commercial grade flush and nonflush vacuum packing machinery
Owner: Thom Dolder
Estimated Sales: $2.5-5 Million
Number Employees: 5-9

27881 Proffitt Manufacturing Company
404 Mitchell Street
Dalton, GA 30721-2705
706-278-7105
Fax: 706-225-4419 800-241-4682
Manufacturer and exporter of dust control mats
CEO: John R Proffitt Jr
VP: W Masters
Manager: Fred Lester
Estimated Sales: $3-5 Million
Number Employees: 50
Square Footage: 132000
Brands:
  Endurance
  Master Turf
  New Age
  Rib Tred
  Ruff N Tuff

27882 Profire Stainless Steel Barbecue
9621 S Dixie Hwy
Miami, FL 33156
305-665-5313
Fax: 305-666-3315 info@profirebbq.com
Outdoor barbecues, built-in-grills, portable grills and other accessories
President and CFO: David Zisman
Contact: Alex Alonzo
lester.perdomo@profirebbq.com
Estimated Sales: $10-20 Million
Number Employees: 10

27883 Progress Lighting
101 Corporate Dr # L
Spartanburg, SC 29303-5043
864-599-6000
Manufacturer and exporter of commercial, interior and exterior lighting
Contact: Robert Childs
rchilds@progresslighting.com
Warehouse Manager: Grant Barrett
Director, Purchasing: Jeff Pickens
Estimated Sales: $77 Million
Number Employees: 5-9
Square Footage: 35000
Parent Co: Hubbell Incorporated
Type of Packaging: Bulk

27884 Progressive Flexpak
1138 Pond Road
Glencoe, MO 63038-1322
800-565-3407
Bottle label, snack, candy, coffee printing films, process, flexo, roto and bag making

27885 Progressive Packaging Inc
14700 28th Ave N # 35
Suite 35
Minneapolis, MN 55447-4876
763-541-1440
Fax: 763-541-1510 800-844-7889
info@progressivepackaging.com
www.progressivepackaging.com
Packaging materials and equipment.
President: John Mork
jmork@progressivepackaging.com
VP: C J Mork
Estimated Sales: $1.4 Million
Number Employees: 10-19
Square Footage: 12000

27886 Progressive Plastics
14801 Emery Ave
Cleveland, OH 44135
216-252-5595
Fax: 216-252-6327 800-252-0053
marketing@progressive-plastics.com
www.progressive-plastics.com
Manufactures and design plastic containers for the food and beverage industries. PET, HDPE, PP, PVC, FDA, CGMP, 150 9001 compliant
President & CEO: David Spence
Quality Control: Mary Anne Golba
Contact: Robert Bell
robert@progressive-plastics.com
Operations Manager: Jason Castro
Purchasing Manager: Glen Maringer
Estimated Sales: $20-50 Million
Number Employees: 250-499
Square Footage: 300000
Type of Packaging: Bulk

27887 Progressive Software
6836 Morrison Blvd Ste 104
Charlotte, NC 28211
704-295-7000
Fax: 704-849-6401 info@xpient.com
Point of sale and back office software
Marketing Manager: Ryan Willis
VP Global Sales/Marketing: Karen Holick
Contact: Jonathan Kaufman
jonathan.kaufman@xpient.com
Estimated Sales: $1-3,000,000
Number Employees: 50-99
Parent Co: Tridex Corporation
Brands:
  Iris

27888 Progressive Technology International
3826a Branch River Road
Manitowoc, WI 54220-9479
920-683-2000
Fax: 920-683-9276 888-683-2003
Food processing equipment manufacturers
President: Dale Gehrig
Vice President: Mark Kugsh
Sales Director: Julio Rivera
Estimated Sales: $1-2.5 Million
Number Employees: 4

27889 (HQ)Progressive Tractor &Implement Co.
4947 Bridge Street Hwy
PO Box 2869
Parks, LA 70582
337-845-5080
Fax: 337-845-5090 www.ptieq.com
Sugar cane loaders and harvesters
President: V Kenneth Broussard
Purchasing Manager: Trisha Brasseaux
Estimated Sales: $1-3 Million
Number Employees: 5-9
Square Footage: 56000
Brands:
Broussard

27890 Proheatco Manufacturing
3427 Pomona Boulevard
Suite D
Pomona, CA 91768-3260
909-598-7445
Fax: 909-598-3514 800-423-4195
Manufacturer and exporter of ovens, heaters and
steam heated systems; exporter of heaters
President: Ralph J Schaefer
Estimated Sales: $1-2.5 Million
Number Employees: 10-19
Square Footage: 24000

27891 Prolamina
975 Broadway St
Wrightstown, WI 54180-1067
920-996-1900
Fax: 920-996-1905 800-765-9283
tbauer@coating-excellence.com
www.coatingexcellence.com
CEO: Rita Cox
rcox@coating-excellence.com
Estimated Sales: $50-75 Million
Number Employees: 500-999

27892 Prolon
305 Industrial Ave
Port Gibson, MS 39150-2868
601-437-0061
Fax: 601-437-3068 888-480-9828
www.prolon.biz
Melamine dinnerware, tote boxes, food storage con-
tainers, school trays, etc
VP: Steve Gluck
Sales/Marketing: Sylvia Saxon
Estimated Sales: $20-50 Million
Number Employees: 50-99
Square Footage: 116000
Parent Co: Perstorp
Brands:
Prolon Products

27893 Proluxe
PO Box 869
Paramount, CA 90723-0869
562-531-0305
Fax: 562-869-7715 800-594-5528
www.proluxe.com
Manufacturer and exporter of pizza and tortilla
presses, dough and vending carts, pizza slicing
guides, clam shell and tortilla warming grills, pan
racks, conveyor and tray ovens and sauce rings; also,
custom stainless steelfabrication available
President: Eugene Raio
VP/General Manager: Daniel Raio
Director of Marketing: Michael Cole
Vice President of Sales: Mike Cervantes
Number Employees: 50
Square Footage: 180000
Brands:
Doughcart
Doughpro
Hotslot
Personnal
Pizzacart

27894 Promac
PO Box 9818
Fresno, CA 93794-0818
559-271-9222
Fax: 559-271-9312 888-776-6220
Wine, food and beverage industry process machinery
Estimated Sales: $20-50 Million
Number Employees: 20-49

27895 Promarks
1915 E Acacia St
Ontario, CA 91761-7921
909-923-3888
Fax: 909-923-3588 www.promarksvac.com
Vacuum sealing and vacuum packaging machines.
Also manufacture dicer, stuffer, tumbling and brine
injector machines.
Owner: Karen Chiu
karen@promarksvac.com
Number Employees: 10-19

27896 Promega
2800 Woods Hollow Rd
Madison, WI 53711
608-274-4330
Fax: 608-277-2516 800-356-9526
www.promega.com
Manufacturer of a kit for testing genetically modi-
fied organisms in food
Chairman & CEO: Dr. William Linton
VP, Global Sales: Lisa Witte
Estimated Sales: $300 Million
Number Employees: 1200

27897 Promens
100 Industrial Drive
PO Box 2087
St. John, NB E2L 3T5
Canada
506-633-0101
Fax: 506-658-0227 800-295-3725
Trays, cups, jars and plastic packaging for the food
and beverage industry. Also manufacture bins, bin
liners, ingredient bins and dump tubs.

27898 Prominent Fluid Controls Inc
136 Industry Dr
R.I.D.C. Park West
Pittsburgh, PA 15275-1014
412-787-2484
Fax: 412-787-0704 sales@prominent.us
www.prominent.us
Manufacturer disinfection equipment, chlorine diox-
ide and ozone generators
General Manager: Mike Weber
Finance Director: Fran Perfett
VP: Garth Debruyn
Marketing Director: Noel Twyman
National Sales Manager: Mike St Germain
Manager: Mark Botticello
markb@prominent.us
Operations Director: Jim DiNardo
Estimated Sales: $34 Million
Number Employees: 100-249
Number of Products: 25
Square Footage: 32500

27899 Prominent Fluid Controls Inc
136 Industry Dr
Pittsburgh, PA 15275-1014
412-787-2484
Fax: 412-787-0704 www.prominent.us
Manufacture chemical feed equipment, metering
pumps, process controllers, sensors, desinfection
equipment
President: Victor Dulger
President, Chief Executive Officer: Andreas Dulger
Executive Vice President of Manufacturin: Rainer
Dulger
CFO: Fran Persett
Director of Marketing: Noel Twyman
Director of Sales and Marketing: Mike St
Manager: Mark Botticello
markb@prominent.us
Director of Operations: Jim DiNardo
Estimated Sales: $10 Million
Number Employees: 100-249
Number of Products: 75
Parent Co: ProMinent DosierTechnick GmbH

27900 Promo Edge
5029 Industrial Road
Wall Township, NJ 07727-3651
732-938-4242
Fax: 732-938-3301
Pressure sensitive labels
Customer Relations: Joanne Switzer
Plant Manager: Ray Mass

27901 Promotion in Motion Companies
PO Box 558
Closter, NJ 07624-0558
201-784-5800
800-369-7391
mail@promotioninmotion.com
www.promotioninmotion.com
Brand name confections, fruit snacks and other fine
foods
President/CEO: Michael Rosenberg
mrosenberg@promotioninmotion.com
Executive Director: Frank McSorley
COO: Basant Dwivedi
Number Employees: 250-499
Type of Packaging: Private Label

27902 Pronova Biopolymer
135 Commerce Way
Suite 201
Portsmouth, NH 03801-3200
603-433-1231
Fax: 603-433-1348 800-223-9030
bess.mosley@pronova.com www.pronova.com
Processor, importer and exporter of industrial ingre-
dients including alginates, propylene glycol
alginates, chitin and chitosan
General Manager: Sandra Platt
Manager Customer Service: Bess Mosley
Number Employees: 5-9
Parent Co: Pronova Biopolymer
Brands:
Pro Floc
Seacure

27903 Pronova Biopolymer
1735 Market Street
Philadelphia, PA 19103-7501
603-433-1231
Fax: 603-433-1348 800-223-9030
www.pronova.com
Solutions for the world's food and pharmaceutical
markets (Omega-3 fatty acids and ultra pure, high
concentrate alginates); onsite electrolytic hydro-
gen/oxygen gas supply systems and cooling/heating
solutions based on Transcritical C-2technology
Information and Internet and HES: Age Wik
Finance/IT: Richard Clemm
Business Development: Kenneth Bern
Business Development: Carl Christian Bachke
Business Development: Bjorn Poul Ringvold
Finance/Divisional Accounting: Kirsti Botheim
Number Employees: 200

27904 Pronto Products Company
11765 Goldring Rd
Arcadia, CA 91006
626-358-5718
Fax: 626-358-9194 800-377-6680
www.prontoproducts.com
Wire products including chrome and stainless steel
dispensers and frying baskets
President: William Parrott
VP: Martha Wagner
Estimated Sales: $20-50 Million
Number Employees: 20-49

27905 Propac Marketing Inc
4556 Sunbelt Dr
Addison, TX 75001-5131
972-733-3199
Fax: 972-733-3790
karen_johnson@propacmarketing.com
www.marsmilitary.com
Packaging for promotional materials including mar-
keting materials, coupons, literature, table tents, etc.;
also, demonstration kits
President: Charles Daigle
Senior Account Director: Arthur Kaplan
Account Executive: Charles Daigle
Estimated Sales: $1-2.5 Million
Number Employees: 20-49

27906 Propak
5230 Harvester Road
Burlington, ON L7L 4X4
Canada
905-681-2345
Fax: 905-681-1023 800-263-4872
Sheets, cookie liners, displays and containers includ-
ing point of purchase and corrugated shipping
President: H Keith Munt
CFO: Cris Gumbs
Sales Director: John Nadon
Plant Manager: Colin Carr

Number Employees: 100
Square Footage: 314000

27907 Prospero Equipment Corp
123 Castleton St
Pleasantville, NY 10570-3405
914-769-6252
Fax: 914-769-6786 888-732-1222
President: Tony Prospero
prospero@cloud9.net
Estimated Sales: $10-20 Million
Number Employees: 10-19

27908 Prosys Innovative Packaging Equipment
422 E 17th Street
Webb City, MO 64870-2956
417-673-3870
Fax: 417-673-7971 800-231-3455
info@prosysfill.com www.prosysfill.com
Cartridges, squeeze tubes and containers, automatic filling equipment, automatic metal tube filler
Division Manager: Don Sonntag
Estimated Sales: $10-20 Million
Number Employees: 20-49

27909 Protectowire Co Inc
60 Washington St
Pembroke, MA 02359-1833
781-924-5384
Fax: 781-826-2045 pwire@protectowire.com
www.protectowire.com
Manufacturer and exporter of fire detection systems for refrigerated storage
President: Andrew Sullivan
asullivan@protectowire.com
CFO: Steve Loughlin
VP North American Sales: John Whaling
Chairman of the Board: Carol M Sullivan
Quality Assurance Manager: Richard Twigg
Sales Engineer: John Whaling
Sales Engineer: James Roussel
Estimated Sales: $5-10 Million
Number Employees: 20-49
Brands:
Firesystem 2000
Protectowire

27910 Protein Research
1852 Rutan Dr
Livermore, CA 94551-7635
925-243-6300
Fax: 925-243-6308 800-948-1991
info@proteinresearch.com
www.proteinresearch.com
Amino acid, vitamin and mineral supplements
Owner: Robert Matheson
robert@proteinresearch.com
Director: Theodore Aarons
VP Operations: Daniel Aarons
Estimated Sales: $5-10 Million
Number Employees: 50-99
Number of Products: 12
Square Footage: 132000
Type of Packaging: Private Label, Bulk

27911 Protex International Corp.
180 Keyland Ct
Bohemia, NY 11716-2657
631-563-4250
Fax: 631-563-4206 800-835-3580
b.kennedy@protex-intl.com www.protex-intl.com
Camera domes, simulated surveillance and cash boxes, safety and detection mirrors, high security locks and annunciators
President: David Wachsman
CFO: Bill Ciccareli
CEO: Steve Migliorino
VP Sales: Bob Frazier
Contact: Chris Kelsch
c.kelsch@vanguardprotexglobal.com
Estimated Sales: $20-50 Million
Number Employees: 50-99
Square Footage: 34000

27912 Protexall
1025 S. Fourth St
Greenville, IL 62246
618-664-6990
Fax: 877-776-8397 800-334-8939
Manufacturer and exporter of uniforms

President: Wayne Williams
CEO: Lois Williams
Vice President: Wade Williams
Sales Rep Coordinator: Dona Tredge
Operations Head: Randy Woods
Estimated Sales: $5-10 Million
Number Employees: 50-99
Square Footage: 200000
Parent Co: DeMoulin Bros. and Co.

27913 Prototype Equipment Corporation
1081 S Northpoint Blvd
Waukegan, IL 60085-8215
847-596-9000
Fax: 847-596-9001 sales@goodmanpkg.com
Custom packaging machinery, case erectors, case and tray packers and sealers, packaging integration, electronic equipment and supplies
President: James Goodman
President, Chief Executive Officer: Michael Senske
Vice President of Engineering: Leo Robertson
Vice President of Sales and Marketing: Randy Denny
Contact: Becky Kendall
bgkendall@pearsonpkg.com
Estimated Sales: $10-25 Million
Number Employees: 50-99

27914 (HQ)Prototype Equipment Corporation
1601 Northwind Blvd
Libertyville, IL 60048-9613
847-680-4433
Fax: 847-816-6374
Manufacturer, exporter and importer of robotic packaging equipment including flexible bag packers, case formers, pick and place packers, bulk case packers, top sealers and vertical snack food packers
Owner: Matthew Clatch
Director Sales/Marketing: Bruce Larson
VP Production: William Goodman
Estimated Sales: $300,000-500,000
Number Employees: 5-9
Square Footage: 168000
Brands:
Goodman
Pouch Pak
Universal

27915 Providence Packaging
143 Barley Park Ln
Mooresville, NC 28115-7912
704-660-1469
Fax: 704-660-0988 866-779-4945
info@providencepackaging.com
Molded foam containers, reflective foil packaging, refrigerants (ice packs), corrugated shipping containers, paper products, tapes, poly, plastic and supplies
Secretary: Deby King
Marketing: David Vance
Contact: Ryan Corbin
ryan@providencepackaging.com
Estimated Sales: Less Than $500,000
Number Employees: 1-4

27916 Provisioner Data Systems
3467 W Hillsboro Boulevard
Suite 6
Deerfield Beach, FL 33442-9473
800-611-6592
Fax: 954-427-7007 800-611-6592
Computer systems for the food industry. Meat and seafood processing systems
Number Employees: 15

27917 Provisur Technologies
9150 W 191st St
Mokena, IL 60448-8727
708-479-3500
Fax: 708-479-3598 815-485-4400
info@provisur.com
Food processing equipment: forming machines, multi-loaf slicers and automatic transport equipment
Contact: Chris Blodgett
chris@formax.us
Number Employees: 5-9

27918 Provisur Technologies
9150 W 191st St
Mokena, IL 60448-8727
708-479-3500
Fax: 708-479-3598 marketing@formaxinc.com

Advanced forming and slicing systems for the food processing industry. Also provide tooling, filling systems and packaging supplies.
VP N. American Sales/Marketing/Service: Kevin Howard
Contact: Chris Blodgett
chris@formax.us
Number Employees: 5-9

27919 Provisur Technologies
1116 E Main St
Whitewater, WI 53190-2103
262-473-5254
Fax: 262-473-5867 800-558-9507
www.provisur.com
Poultry & meat grinders, mixers and food processing equipment.
President & CEO: Mel Cohen
HR Executive: Nancy Blum
nblum@idcnet.com
Vice President, Sales & Marketing: Kevin Howard
Number Employees: 100-249

27920 Provisur Technologies, Inc.
9150 W 191st St
Mokena, IL 60448-8727
708-479-3500
Fax: 708-479-3598 info@provisur.com
www.provisur.com
Food processing equipment: ground, formed and further processed; freezing; separation; slicing for bacon and ready to eat; material handling systems; paper converting; complete systems
Other Locations:
Mokena IL
Tinley Park IL
Whitewater WI
Badhoevedorp, Netherlands
Cocarneau, France
Indaiatuba, Brazil
Bangkok, Thailand
Shanghai, China

27921 (HQ)Prudential Lighting
1737 E 22nd St
Vernon, CA 90058-1008
213-746-0360
Fax: 213-746-8838 800-421-5483
info@prulite.com www.plpsocal.com
Custom and standard fluorescent lighting fixtures with wet, damp and clean room applications; also, linear systems
Owner: Jeff Ellis
ejeff@prulite.com
Vice President: Jeff Ellis
Quality Control: Albert Pastina
Sales Director: Jon Steele
ejeff@prulite.com
Manager: Alice Elliott
Estimated Sales: $10-20 Million
Number Employees: 500-999
Square Footage: 200000
Brands:
Galv
Pru Lites

27922 Pruitt's Packaging Services
2201 Kalamazoo Avenue SE
Grand Rapids, MI 49507-3783
616-243-0553
Fax: 616-243-4424 800-878-0553
Wooden pallets and boxes, watermelon bins, skids and grocery wraparounds
President: John Pruitt
Secretary/Treasurer: Ruby Gilewski
Sales/Marketing Executive: Brian Hager
Supervisor: James McNitt
Estimated Sales: Below $5 Million
Number Employees: 8
Square Footage: 32000

27923 Prystup Packaging Products
101 Prystup Drive
PO Box 1039
Livingston, AL 35470-1039
205-652-9583
Fax: 205-652-2696 info@prystup.com
www.prystup.com
Folding boxes

President: J Leslie Prystup
CFO: Kathryn Prystrup
VP: James Emroy
R&D: Ronald Harwell
Quality Control: Jason Guin
Marketing: Rick Framer
Sales: Paul Sparkman
Public Relations: Suzanne McGahey
Production: Roy Rainer
Plant Manager: Craig Ray
Purchasing: Rickey Rogers
Estimated Sales: $10-20 Million
Number Employees: 100-249
Number of Brands: 6
Square Footage: 220000
Type of Packaging: Consumer, Private Label

27924 Psc Floturn Inc
1050 Commerce Ave # 1
Union, NJ 07083-5080

908-687-3225
Fax: 908-687-1715 sales@flow-turn.com
www.stainlessbeltcurves.com
Manufacturer, importer and exporter of USDA listed powered belt curve and custom straight conveyors
President: Herman Migdel
Product Manager: J Grabowski
Vice President: Larry Cerpetier
danotsc@aol.com
Operations Manager: Dan Otero
Estimated Sales: $2.5-5 Million
Number Employees: 10-19
Square Footage: 144000
Brands:
    Floturn

27925 Psion Teklogix
1810 Airport Exchange Blvd
Erlanger, KY 41018-3196

859-372-4100
Fax: 859-371-6422 800-322-3437
President: Ron Caines
Chief Executive Officer: John Conoley
Vice President of Human Resources: Maija Michell
Chief Technical Officer: Mike Doyle
Chief Marketing Officer: Nick Eades
Vice President of Operations: Rob Gayson
Estimated Sales: $50-75 Million
Number Employees: 100-249

27926 Psyllium Labs
1701 E Woodfield Road
Suite 636
Schaumburg, IL 60173

888-851-6667
info@psyllium.com www.psylliumlabs.com
Psyllium, chia and quinoa
Operations Executive: Drew West
Other Locations:
    Manufacturing Facility
    North Gujarat, India
    Manufacturing Facility
    Santa Cruz, Bolivia

27927 Public Service Company of Oklahoma
212 E 6th St
Tulsa, OK 74119

888-216-3523
www.psoklahoma.com
Electric utility systems.
President & COO: Peggy Simmons
VP, Regulatory & Finance: Matthew Horeled
VP, External Affairs: Tiffini Jackson
Year Founded: 1913
Estimated Sales: K
Parent Co: American Electric Power

27928 Publix Super Market
PO Box 407
Lakeland, FL 33802-0407

800-242-1227
www.publix.com
Groceries, produce, meat, seafood, deli, floral, beer, wine and dairy.
President/CEO: Todd Jones
Chairman: William Crenshaw
CFO: David Phillips
Year Founded: 1930
Estimated Sales: $38.1 Billion
Number Employees: 197,000
Other Locations:
    Bakery Manufacturing
    Atlanta GA
    Dairy/Fresh Foods Manufacturing

Deerfield Beach FL
Fresh Foods Manufacturing
Jacksonville FL
Bakery/Deli/Dairy Manufacturing
Lakeland FL
Dairy Manufacturing
Lawrenceville GA

27929 Pucel Enterprises Inc
1440 E 36th St
Cleveland, OH 44114-4117

216-881-4604
Fax: 216-881-6731 800-336-4986
www.pucelenterprises.com
Manufacturer and exporter of material handling equipment, stock carts, drum lifters and hand, shop and platform trucks, benches and cabinets
President: M Ann
amleissa@pucelenterprises.com
Vice President: Robert Mlakar
Plant Manager: Ronald Cook
Estimated Sales: $5-10,000,000
Number Employees: 50-99
Square Footage: 105000

27930 Puget Sound Inline
300 Chestnut Ridge Road
Woodcliff Lake, NJ 07677-7731

253-983-9390
Fax: 253-627-2029 800-831-1117
sales@pugetsoundinline.com
www.pugetsoundbmw.com
Manufactures thermoforming blister packaging— trays, computer, clamshell packaging, electrical, retail display and food
President: Bob Shupe
Estimated Sales: $1-2.5 Million
Number Employees: 10-19

27931 Pulse Systems
422 Connie Avenue
Los Alamos, NM 87544

505-662-7599
Fax: 505-662-7748 www.psilasers.com
Manufacturer and exporter of laser marking and coding systems
President: Edward J McLellan
VP: Linda McLellan
Contact: Holly Page
hpage@pulsesystem.com
Chief Operating Officer: Linda Mclellan
Estimated Sales: $1-3 Million
Number Employees: 1-4
Type of Packaging: Consumer, Private Label, Bulk
Brands:
    Pulseprint

27932 Pulsetech Products Corp
1100 S Kimball Ave
Southlake, TX 76092-9009

817-329-6099
Fax: 817-329-5914 800-580-7554
ppc@pulsetech.net www.pulsetech.net
Battery maintenance systems, digital battery analyzers, battery chargers and conditioning systems
President: Pete Smith
petesmith@specialized.net
VP/Sales/Marketing: Scott Schilling
Business Manager: Rick Gregory
Business Development Manager: Rick Gregory
Manager: Shawn Doonan
Public Relations: Kevin Hosey
VP/Military Programs: Mark Witt
Director Military Programs: Mark Abelson
Estimated Sales: $500,000-$1 Million
Number Employees: 100-249

27933 Pulva Corp
105 Industrial Dr W
Valencia, PA 16059-3321

724-898-2555
Fax: 724-898-3192 800-878-5828
sales@pulva.com www.pulva.com
Grinding mills, parts and feeders
Owner: Ed Ferree
R&D: Bruce Dene
Quality Control: Bruce Dene
Sales Director: L Ward
ed@pulva.com
Estimated Sales: $20-50 Million
Number Employees: 20-49

27934 Pump Solutions Group
1815 S. Meyers Road
Oakbrook Terrace, IL 60181

630-487-2240
Fax: 630-487-2250 info@psgdover.com
www.psgdover.com
Pumps used to assist manufacturers and ingredients users to improve production yields while preserving color, aroma, texture, viscosity, purity and safety.
VP of Marketing: Walter Bonnett
Contact: Gajendra Aggarwalregional
gajendra@psgdover.com
Other Locations:
    Grand Rapids MI
    Grand Terrace CA
    North Wales PA

27935 Purac America
111 Barclay Blvd
Lincolnshire, IL 60069

608-752-0449
Fax: 847-634-1992 pam@purac.com
www.purac.com
Producer of lactic acid, lactates and lactitol
President: Gerrit Vreeman
Vice President: Peter Kooijman
Marketing Manager: Casper Ravesteijn
VP Sales: Peter Hooijman
Contact: Lisette Nanning
l.nanning@puracaps.com
Estimated Sales: $20-50 Million
Number Employees: 20-49
Type of Packaging: Bulk

27936 Puratos Corp
1941 Old Cuthbert Rd
Cherry Hill, NJ 08034-1417

856-428-4300
Fax: 856-428-2939 800-654-0036
info@puratos.com www.puratos.com
Baking ingredients
President: Denis Wellington
Cmo: Matt Crumpton
matt.crumpton@puratos.com
Marketing Manager: Sheila Caufield
Estimated Sales: $500,000-$1 Million
Number Employees: 100-249

27937 Pure & Secure LLC-Cust Svc
4120 NW 44th St
Lincoln, NE 68524-1623

402-467-9300
Fax: 402-467-9393 800-875-5915
info@mypurewater.com www.mypurewater.com
Manufacturer and exporter of water treatment equipment; also, bottling and molding equipment
President: A E Meder
ae@pureandsecure.com
Sales Manager: Jason Harrington
Sales Manager: Alan Billups
Estimated Sales: $5-10 Million
Number Employees: 20-49
Square Footage: 90000
Brands:
    Pure Water
    Ultima

27938 Pure Fit Nutrition Bars
216 Technology Dr # E
Irvine, CA 92618-2416

949-679-7997
Fax: 949-679-7998 866-782-3348
info@purefit.com www.purefit.com
Manufacturer and exporter of fittings, hoses and assemblies
Founder/ CEO: Robb Dorf
robbdorf@purefit.com
Vice President: Robert Elbich
Sales Manager: John Cooling
Number Employees: 1-4
Parent Co: Nalge Process Technologies

27939 Pure Life Organic Foods
6625 W Sahara Ave
Suite 1
Las Vegas, NV 89146

708-990-5817
info@purelifeorganicfoods.com
www.purelifeorganicfoods.com
Organic sugars, coconut milk and coconut oil
Managing Director: Pradeep Mathur
Sales and Marketing Head: Sayida Bano
Parent Co: Pure Diets Intl. Ltd.
Type of Packaging: Bulk

27940 Pure Process Systems
5440 Alder Dr
Houston, TX 77081-1704
713-663-1677
Fax: 713-664-6444 800-879-2326
Pure Process Systems is a design-build environmental engineering and technology application company that utilizes current and innovative technologies to treat, reclaim, and reuse water and residuals for a variety of industriesincluding the food and beverage market.
CEO: Dan Curry
dcurry@ceconet.com
Vice President: Jim Revel
Vice President, Information Systems: Bill Zeis
Senior Project Engineer: Hoon Chung
Project Manager: Marc Thomas
Vice President of Sales: Joe Miniot
Vice President of Operations: Dale Thompson
Number Employees: 5-9

27941 Pure-1 Systems
25 Coligni Ave
New Rochelle, NY 10801-2605
914-576-5800
Fax: 914-235-8849 sales@pure1.com
www.pure1.com
Plumbed water colors, point-of-use water color products, hot and cold bottled water colors with patented Everfull self-filling bottle
Owner: Frank Pisano
Estimated Sales: $1-5 Million
Number Employees: 1-4

27942 Pure-Chem Products Company
8371 Monroe Ave
Stanton, CA 90680
714-995-4141
Fax: 714-527-7802
President: Bill King
Contact: Bruce Bereiter
cren@hoaghospital.org
Estimated Sales: $2.5-5 Million
Number Employees: 10-19

27943 PureCircle USA
200 W Jackson Blvd
8th Floor
Chicago, IL 60606
630-361-0374
info.usa@purecircle.com
purecircle.com
Stevia
CEO: Lai Hock Meng
CFO: Lim Kian Thong
Year Founded: 2001
Estimated Sales: $127 Million
Parent Co: PureCircle Limited
Type of Packaging: Bulk

27944 Purico USA
497 Bramson Ct # 202
Suite 202
Mt Pleasant, SC 29464-8325
843-881-6684
Fax: 843-881-6492 sales@puricousa.com
www.purico.com
Complete range of papers for all types of tea and coffee bags
Manager: Joe Szorc
Estimated Sales: $5-10 Million
Number Employees: 5-9

27945 Puritan Manufacturing Inc
1302 Grace St
Omaha, NE 68110-2591
402-341-3793
Fax: 402-341-4508 800-331-0487
purmfg@ixnetcom.com www.purmfg.com
Custom fabricated conveyors, mixers, hoppers, tanks, cereal puffing machinery and catwalks; exporter of cereal puffing machinery
President/Owner: Bill Waters
VP & General Manager: Dave Waters
Estimated Sales: $5-10 Million
Number Employees: 20-49
Square Footage: 350000
Brands:
Puritan

27946 Puritan/Churchill Chemical Company
1341 Capital Circle SE
Suite E
Marietta, GA 30067-8718
404-875-7331
800-275-8914
Manufacturer and exporter of deodorants, warewash systems and chemicals, disinfectants and cleaners including kitchen, industrial laundry and window
President: Richard Bruce
VP Finance: Regina Crothers
Director Marketing: Adam Gould
Number Employees: 240
Parent Co: Gibson Chemical Industries

27947 Purity Foods Inc
417 S Meridian Rd
Hudson, MI 49247-9709
517-448-2050
Fax: 517-448-2070 800-997-7358
info@purityfoods.com
www.natureslegacyforlife.com
Beans, grains, seeds, cereals, cookbooks, flours, granola, pastas, pretzels and sesame sticks.
President: Donald Stinchcomb
Regional Sales Manager: Hezeden Graye
Manager: Gabby Williamson
gabby.williamson@purityfoods.com
Estimated Sales: Less Than $500,000
Number Employees: 1-4
Square Footage: 60000

27948 Purity Laboratories
17387 63rd Ave
Lake Oswego, OR 97035-5205
503-297-3636
Fax: 503-297-3738 800-977-3636
www.puritylabsinc.com
Food analyst consultant that determines cleanliness and nutritional value
VP: Ken Ayers
Manager: Bernd Scholz
bscholz@kirkmangroup.com
Estimated Sales: Below $5 Million
Number Employees: 10-19
Square Footage: 5400

27949 Purity Products
200 Terminal Dr
Plainview, NY 11803-2312
516-767-1967
Fax: 516-767-1722 800-256-6102
customercare@purityproducts.com
www.puritypgoducts.com
Sauces, mayonnaise, vinegar, mustard, salad dressings, vegetable oils, jellies, pickles
President: William Schroeder
President, Chief Executive Officer: Jahn Levin
jahn@purityproducts.com
CFO: Bruce Morecroft
Vice President of Quality Assurance: Richard Conant
Marketing: Al Rodriquez
Operations: Ricky Montejo
Purchasing Director: Charles Menezes
Estimated Sales: Less Than $500,000
Number Employees: 20-49
Square Footage: 400000
Parent Co: Sea Specialties Company
Type of Packaging: Food Service, Private Label, Bulk
Brands:
Chef's Choice
Cheryl Lynn
Ideal
Purity

27950 Purolator Facet Inc
8439 Triad Dr
Greensboro, NC 27409-9018
336-668-4444
Fax: 336-668-4452 800-852-4449
info@purolator-facet.com
www.purolator-facet.com
Manufacturer and exporter of self-cleaning and sterilizable stainless steel filters for viscous fluids, food and steam
President: Russ Stellfox
rstellfox@purolator-facet.com
Program Manager: Mark Willingham
Director Sales/Marketing: Kevin Nelson

Number Employees: 100-249
Square Footage: 360000
Parent Co: Dayco Products
Brands:
Metaledge
Poromesh
Poroplate

27951 Puronics Water Systems Inc
5775 Las Positas Rd
Livermore, CA 94551-7819
925-456-7000
Fax: 925-456-7010
Water treatment systems for the consumer and commercial markets. Puronics solutions include technologies such as water conditioning, filtering, micro-filtration, filtration, carbon filtration, reverse osmosis and ultra violetdisinfection.
Chief Financial Officer: Mark Cosmez
esparzaroyr@puronics.com
Director of Commercial Sales: Roy Esparza
esparzaroyr@puronics.com

27952 Put-Ons USA
7308 Aspen Lane N
Suite 149
Brooklyn Park, MN 55428-1020
763-425-9216
Fax: 763-425-9211 888-425-1215
Uniforms
President: Brian Peterson
Sales Director: Varlerie Peterson
Estimated Sales: Less than $500,000
Number Employees: 4
Square Footage: 6000
Brands:
Put-Ons U.S.A.

27953 Putnam Group
35 Corporate Dr
Trumbull, CT 06611-6319
203-452-7270
Fax: 203-268-8071
Importer and wholesaler/distributor of promotional items; also, marketing consultant services available
VP: Ann Rerat
Estimated Sales: Less than $500,000
Number Employees: 1-4

27954 Putsch & Co Inc
354 Cane Creek Rd
Fletcher, NC 28732
828-684-0671
Fax: 828-684-4894 800-847-8427
info@putschusa.com www.putschusa.com
Beet refinery equipment
CFO/R&D: Dieter Mergner
Engineering: Henning Wedemeyer
Sales: Jon E. DeBuvitz
Customer Service: Jeanne West
Manager: Dieter Mergner
Parts/ Supply Chain: Olav Seimer
Plant Superintendent: Dieter Mergner
Estimated Sales: $2.5-5 Million
Number Employees: 20-49
Parent Co: H. Putsch & Company

27955 Pyramid Flexible Packaging
120 E La Habra Boulevard
La Habra, CA 90631-5475
562-690-2208
Fax: 562-690-7892
Contact: Darryl Shimada
dshimada@pyramidhotelgroup.com
Estimated Sales: $1-3 Million
Number Employees: 30

27956 Pyro-Chem
1 Stanton St
Marinette, WI 54143
715-732-3465
Fax: 715-732-3569 800-526-1079
charding@tycoint.com www.pyrochem.com
Manufacturer and exporter of pre-engineered fire fighting systems
CEO: John Fort
Technical Services Engineer: Curt Harding
Technical Services Engineer: Brian Chernetski
General Manager Sales/Marketing: William Vegso
Contact: Edgar Alvarez
ealvarez@tycoint.com
Product Manager: Katherine Adrian
Estimated Sales: $1-5 Million
Number Employees: 12

Square Footage: 60000
Parent Co: Borg-Warner/Wells Fargo Alarm
Brands:
  Kitchen Knight

27957 Pyromation Inc
5211 Industrial Rd
Fort Wayne, IN 46825-5152
260-484-2580
Fax: 260-482-6805 sales@pyromation.com
www.pyromation.com
Manufacturer and exporter of 3A compliant CIP
thermocouples. RTDs, temperature sensors,
thermowells, transmitters, connection heads, wire
and cable
President: Peter Wilson
kim@pyromation.com
Marketing Manager: Greg Craghead
Sales Manager: Scott Farnham
Estimated Sales: $25-30 Million
Number Employees: 100-249
Square Footage: 40000

27958 Pyrometer Instrument CoInc
92 N Main St # 18
PO Box 479
Windsor, NJ 08561-3209
609-443-5522
Fax: 201-768-2570 800-468-7976
information@pyrometer.com www.pyrometer.com
Manufacturer, importer and exporter of controllers,
sensors, chart recorders, indicators, alarms and por-
table pyrometers; also, pressure transmitters and
temperature measurement systems
Owner: Dave Crozier
sales@pryometer.com
CEO: D Crozier
Marketing: Mickey Otto
Estimated Sales: $2.4 Million
Number Employees: 10-19
Number of Brands: 2
Number of Products: 12
Square Footage: 30000
Brands:
  Philips/Pma
  Pyro

27959 Q & B Foods
Irwindale, CA
626-334-8090
Fax: 626-969-1587 customerservice@qbfoods.com
www.qbfoods.com
Dressings, marinades, sauces and mayonnaise
President/Owner: Jerry Shepherd
Estimated Sales: $20-50 Million
Number Employees: 50-99
Square Footage: 50000
Type of Packaging: Private Label
Brands:
  Kewpie
  The Ojai Cook
  Rice Road

27960 Q A Supplies LLC
1185 Pineridge Rd
Norfolk, VA 23502-2043
757-855-3094
Fax: 757-855-4155 800-472-7205
info@QAsupplies.com www.qasupplies.com
Supplier of insulated refrigiwear insulated clothing,
boots and gloves, hot/cold transport bags & covers,
temperature measurements, thermometers and
alarms.
President: David Cowles
dcowles@qasupplies.com
Sales: Russ Holt
Number Employees: 10-19

27961 Q C Industries
4057 Clough Woods Dr
Batavia, OH 45103-2587
513-753-6000
Fax: 513-753-6001 www.qcconveyors.com
Conveyors, washdowns, timing belts
President: David Dornbach
ddornbach@qcindustries.com
Marketing Supervisor: Chris Thompson
Estimated Sales: $10-20 Million
Number Employees: 20-49

27962 Q Laboratories
1400 Harrison Ave
Cincinnati, OH 45214-1606
513-471-1300
Fax: 513-471-5600 office@qlaboratories.com
www.qlaboratories.com
Consultant providing laboratory testing services in-
cluding microbiology and analytical chemistry sup-
port, QC/release, antimicrobial efficacy and GMP
testing, plant sanitation audits, nutrition labeling and
preservative analysis
President: David Goins
dgoins@qlaboratories.com
Microbiology Group Leader: Meghan McDonough
Vice President of Sales & Marketing: Michelle
Kelly
Director of Business Development: Mark Goins
Estimated Sales: $2.5-5 Million
Number Employees: 100-249
Square Footage: 26000

27963 Q Pak Inc
2145 Mccarter Hwy
Newark, NJ 07104-4407
973-483-4404
Fax: 973-484-7896 qpak@earthlink.net
www.qpakcorp.com
Plastic bottles
President: Michael Formica
Contact: Justin Formica
jformica@qpakcorp.com
Estimated Sales: $2.5-5 Million
Number Employees: 20-49

27964 Q Vac
1973 E. Via Arado
Rancho Dominguez, CA 90220
310-898-3400
Fax: 310-898-3430 888-879-7822
Sales@Newaypkg.com www.qvac.com
Skin packaging machines, roller press die cutting,
automatic conveyor belt blistering sealers, and vac-
uum forming machines
Estimated Sales: $1-2.5 Million
Number Employees: 5-9

27965 Q-Matic Technologies
355 East Kehoe Boulevard
Carol Stream, IL 60188-1817
847-263-7324
Fax: 847-263-7367 800-880-6836
Manufacturer and exporter of conveyor ovens
Sales Manager: David Cook
Production Manager: Frank Agnello
Estimated Sales: $1-2.5 Million
Number Employees: 7
Square Footage: 20000
Type of Packaging: Food Service
Brands:
  Q-Matic

27966 QAD Inc
100 Innovation Pl
Santa Barbara, CA 93108-2268
805-566-6000
Fax: 805-565-4202 www.qad.com
Meat industry computer systems, software, consul-
tants, data processing
CEO: Nolan Adams
nadams@thecenter.nasdaq.org
CEO: Karl F Lopker
Estimated Sales: $20-50 Million
Number Employees: 1000-4999

27967 (HQ)QBD Modular Systems
5255 Steven Creeks Blvd
#187
Santa Clara, CA 95051
408-890-8924
Fax: 905-459-1478 800-663-3005
daryl@qpd.com www.qpd.com
Manufacturer and exporter of merchandising coolers
and modular display cases
President: Jeff Jaffer
CFO: Mohammed Chowdhary
Number Employees: 40
Brands:
  Qbd

27968 QC
P.O.Box 514
Southampton, PA 18966-0514
215-355-3900
Fax: 215-355-7231 ejpcsolar@qclaboratories.com
www.qclaboratories.com
Consultant specializing in the testing of food and
dairy products; also, environmental testing available
President: Thomas Heins
Quality Control: Rich Royer
Contact: Schopbach Allen
schopbach@qclaboratories.com
Estimated Sales: $20-50 Million
Number Employees: 100-249
Square Footage: 30000
Parent Co: Land O'Lakes

27969 QDC Plastic Container Co
111 W Mount Hope Ave
Lansing, MI 48910-9093
517-319-4194
Fax: 517-319-4304 800-652-2330
qdcplastics@acd.net www.qdcplastics.com
Supplier of plastic bottles for beverages
President: Stan Martin
qdcplastics@acd.net
Operations Manager: Ken David
Estimated Sales: $10-20 Million
Number Employees: 50-99
Type of Packaging: Bulk

27970 QMI
426 Hayward Ave N
St Paul, MN 55128-5379
651-501-2337
Fax: 651-501-5797 qmi2@aol.com
Manufacturer and exporter of aseptic sampling and
transfer systems for liquids; also, sampling system
for bioreactors
President: Darrell Bigalke
Manager: Gwen Raddatz
Estimated Sales: Below $5 Million
Number Employees: 1-4
Square Footage: 8000
Parent Co: Quality Management
Brands:
  Qmi
  Qmi Safe Septum

27971 QMS International, Inc.
1833 Folkway Drive
Mississauga, Ontario, ON
Canada
905-820-7225
Fax: 905-820-7021 info@qmsintl.com
www.qmsintl.com
Manufacturer and supplier of new and refurbished
tying machines and supplies for the meat, poultry
and seafood industries.

27972 QNC Inc
12021 Plano Rd # 160
Dallas, TX 75243-5400
972-669-2948
Fax: 972-669-8990 888-668-3687
sales@q-n-c.com www.q-n-c.com
Hot air ovens
President: Paul Artt
paul@q-n-c.com
Estimated Sales: Below $5,000,000
Number Employees: 5-9
Brands:
  Quik 'n Crispy

27973 QSR Industrial Supply
1888 W Point Drive
Cherry Hill, NJ 08003-2850
856-427-4270
Fax: 856-427-6736 800-257-8282
sales@qsrind.com
Industrial lighting with shatter-resistant and protec-
tive coated bulbs including fluorescent, incandescent
and outdoor
President: David Diamondstein
Manager: Dave Drake
Sales Manager: Rick Jackson
Estimated Sales: $5-10 Million
Number Employees: 20-49
Square Footage: 7000
Brands:
  Permalux Shatter-Kote

27974 QUIKSERV Corp
11441 Brittmoore Park Dr
PO Box 40466
Houston, TX 77041-6919

713-849-5882
Fax: 713-849-5708 800-388-8307
sales@quikserv.com www.quikservtest.com
Manufacturer and exporter of food service
drive-thru windows, security transaction drawers,
BR glass, and air curtains; custom fabrications
available
CEO: Jason T. Epps
sales@quikserv.com
Marketing/Sales: Ray Epps
Sales Director: Sophia Navarro
Plant Manager: Jack Weaver
Purchasing Manager: Jason Epps
Number Employees: 20-49
Square Footage: 152000
Brands:
   Quikserv

27975 Qosina Corporation
2002-Q Orville Dr. N.
Ronkonkoma, NY 11779

631-242-3000
Fax: 631-242-3230 info@qosina.com
www.qosina.com
OEM components supplier to the medical, cosmetic,
cleanroom, veterinary and pharmaceutical industries.
President/CEO: Scott Herskovitz
Year Founded: 1980
Estimated Sales: $100+ Million
Number Employees: 50-99

27976 Qst Industries Inc
550 W Adams St # 200
Suite 200
Chicago, IL 60661-3665

312-930-9400
Fax: 312-930-0118 carlevato.jeff@qst.com
www.qst.com
CEO: Terra Bobadilla
niyaz.mulla@nuveen.com
Regional Sales Manager: Sue Wech
Number Employees: 50-99
Type of Packaging: Consumer

27977 (HQ)Qsx Labels
220 Broadway
Everett, MA 2149

617-389-7570
Fax: 617-381-9280 800-225-3496
rkaress@qsxlabels.com www.qsxlabels.com
Manufacturer and exporter of labels including ther-
mal, laser, pin feed, graphic, bar code, etc.; also, la-
bel applicators and dispensers
President and CEO: Mike Karess
CFO: Robert Karess
Vice President: Robert Karess
Marketing: Robert Karess
Plant Manager: Peter Kozowylt
Estimated Sales: $5-10 Million
Number Employees: 20-49
Square Footage: 120000
Type of Packaging: Private Label
Brands:
   Quikstik

27978 Quadra-Tech
864 E Jenkins Avenue
Columbus, OH 43207-1317

614-443-0630
Fax: 614-737-5429 800-443-2766
info@quadra-techinc.com
www.quadra-techinc.com
Work tables, fry baskets and specialty smallwares
Manager: Tim Mc Cormick
General Manager: Tim McCormick
Sales Director: Rob Zigler
Contact: Max Barr
maxbarr@quadra-techinc.com
Estimated Sales: $10-20,000,000
Number Employees: 100-249

27979 Quadrant Epp USA Inc
2710 American Way
PO Box 9086
Fort Wayne, IN 46809-3011

260-479-4100
Fax: 260-478-1074 800-628-7264
americas.epp@qplas.com
www.quadrantplastics.com

Standard and custom food grade components and
wear resistant UHMW-PE conveying equipment
President: Roland Finch
Vice President: Mark Edele
Marketing Communication Manager: Connie Brown
National Sales Manager: Robert Blackwood
Manager: Ron Niebel
ron.niebel@qplas.com
Number Employees: 50-99
Square Footage: 337712
Other Locations:
   Scranton PA
   Delmont PA
   Reading PA
   Wytheville VA
Brands:
   Redirail
   Tivar

27980 Quadrel Labeling Systems
7670 Jenther Dr
Mentor, OH 44060-4872

440-602-4700
Fax: 440-602-4701 800-321-8509
labeling@quadrel.com www.quadrel.com
Manufacturer and exporter of labeling equipment
President: Lon Deckard
VP/General Manager: Charles Wepler
Marketing: Joe Uhlir
Sales: Christine Burrier
Operations: Shirley Chambers
Estimated Sales: $15-20 Million
Number Employees: 50-99
Square Footage: 80000
Type of Packaging: Consumer, Food Service
Brands:
   Moduline
   Premier
   Q31
   Q32
   Rotary
   Table Line
   Versaline

27981 Quadro Engineering
613 Colby Drive
Waterloo, ON N2V-1A1
Canada

519-884-9660
Fax: 519-884-0253 quadrosales@idexcorp.com
www.quadro.com
Manufactures and markets an innovative line of size
reduction mills, emulsifiers, powder dispertion units
and vacuum conveyors for the food industry
President: Keith McIntosh
Marketing Manager: Richard Franzke
Number Employees: 100
Number of Brands: 3
Number of Products: 6
Other Locations:
   Millburn NJ
Brands:
   Quadro

27982 Quaker Chemical Company
PO Box 554
Columbia, SC 29202-0554

803-765-9520
Fax: 803-765-9522 800-849-9520
www.quakerchem.com
Janitorial supplies and equipment including mops
and floor finish-acrylics for high speed buffers and
general use; exporter of cleaning chemicals
President: Josie Hendrix
Contact: Joseph Anderson
anderson@quakerchem.com
Estimated Sales: $5-10 Million
Number Employees: 5-9
Square Footage: 40000
Brands:
   Fibercare 5000
   Panther Power
   Perma Glo
   Sunburst
   Superwear

27983 (HQ)Quaker Oats Company
555 W. Monroe St.
Suite 1
Chicago, IL 60661

312-821-1000
www.quakeroats.com

Cookies, oats, oatmeal, farina, granola bars, puffed
wheat, puffed rice, barley, groats, shredded wheat,
pancake syrups and mixes, flour, corn syrups, baking
mixes, pasta and corn meal.
Senior VP/General Manager: Robbert Rietbroek
IT: Mike Lyons
mike.lyons@pepsi.com
Estimated Sales: Over $1 Billion
Number Employees: 10000+
Number of Products: 195
Parent Co: PepsiCo
Type of Packaging: Consumer, Food Service
Brands:
   Quaker
   Life

27984 Quali-Tech Tape & Label
6695 Grove St
Denver, CO 80221-2126

Fax: 303-431-4405
Grocery store and pressure sensitive labels; also, pa-
per tape
President: Gloria Schlaht
Contact: Tony Pontious
tpontious@qualitechscan.com
Estimated Sales: $500,000-$1 Million
Number Employees: 1-4

27985 Qualicon
PO Box 80357
Wilmington, DE 19880-0357

302-695-5300
Fax: 302-695-5301 800-863-6842
Automated instruments that performs ribotyping to
get genetic fingerprints that can identify an organism
below species level, microbial charecterization, gmo
detection and measurement, food safety and quality
management services
President: Kevin Huttman
Chief Executive Officer: Eldon Roth
CFO: Beth Peck
Senior Vice President, General Counsel: Thomas
Sager
R & D: Lance Bolton
Quality Control: Shawn Anderson
Marketing Manager: Megan DeStefano
Director of Sales: Craig Drinkwater
Number Employees: 10

27986 Qualiform, Inc
689 Weber Drive
Wadsworth, OH 44281

330-336-6777
Fax: 330-336-3668
www.qualiformrubbermolding.com
Manufacturer and exporter of custom molded rubber
stoppers
President: Nick Antonino
CFO: Andy Antonino
Quality Control: Duane Lawrence
Contact: Andy Antonino
aantonino@qualiforminc.com
Estimated Sales: Below $5 Million
Number Employees: 10

27987 Qualita Paper Products
3101 W Macarthur Blvd
Santa Ana, CA 92704-6907

714-540-0994
Fax: 714-540-1077 800-611-4010
www.qualitapaper.com
Paper baking molds, baking cups, carboard trays,
doilies, cake boxes, ice cream containers and cups,
cake boards, panettone molds and boxes, hard-bot-
tom bags
President: Homar Aguirre
Vice President: Fabrice Clement
Estimated Sales: $860,000
Number Employees: 5-9
Parent Co: A.B.M. Inc.

27988 Quality Aluminum & Hm Imprvmt
1514 Gardner Blvd
Columbus, MS 39702-2802

662-329-2525
Fax: 662-329-3725
Commercial awnings
Owner: Sarah Mattison
smattison@cableone.net
Estimated Sales: $1-2,500,000
Number Employees: 5-9

27989 Quality Assured Label Inc
1600 5th St S
Hopkins, MN 55343-7814
952-933-7800
Fax: 952-930-1505 sales@qal.com
www.qal.com
Custom pressure sensitive labels
Chairman: Robert Westmeyer
CEO: Robert Westnever
VP: Joe Farnko
Research & Development: Joe Farnko
Marketing Head: Petero Cattori
Estimated Sales: $20-50 Million
Number Employees: 20-49

27990 Quality Assured Packing
568 S Temperance Avenue
Fresno, CA 93727-6601
209-931-6700
Fax: 209-931-0286
Industrial tomato ingredient processor and supplier
Estimated Sales: $10-25 Million
Number Employees: 60

27991 Quality Bakers of America
1275 Glenlivet Drive
Suite 100
Allentown, PA 18106-3107
973-263-6970
Fax: 973-263-0937 www.qba.com
Wholesale bakers' cooperative providing consulting
services including marketing, sales, product devel-
opment, research and development, nutritional
analysis, etc
Chairman: Sherman Strider
President/Manager: Norman Trapp
VP/Finance: Donald J. Cummings
Director: Judith Moderacki
Research & Development: Andrew Maier
Contact: Don Cummings
dcummings@qba.com
Estimated Sales: $1.6 Million
Number Employees: 20-49
Brands:
Sunbeam

**27992 (HQ)Quality Cabinet & Fixture
Co**
885 Gateway Center Way # 201
San Diego, CA 92102-4538
619-266-1011
Fax: 619-266-0878 quality1@qcfc.com
www.qcfc.com
Manufacturer, exporter and importer of store fixtures
and wood cabinets
President: Tim Paradise
tpa@qcfc.com
Sales/Marketing: Laura Cohen
Estimated Sales: $10-20 Million
Number Employees: 100-249

27993 Quality Chekd Dairies Inc
901 Warrenville Rd
Suite 405
Lisle, IL 60532-4309
630-717-1110
Fax: 630-717-1126 mmurphy@qchekd.com
www.qchekd.com
Services for dairy market: food safety, training, pro-
curement and marketing, lab sampling and consulta-
tion.
Managing Director: Peter Horvath
phorvath@qchekd.com
CFO: Bruce Tom
Marketing Director: Molly Murphy
Estimated Sales: $100-500 Million
Number Employees: 10-19
Brands:
Quality Chekd Dairy Products

27994 Quality Container Company
1236 Watson St
Ypsilanti, MI 48198
734-481-1373
Fax: 734-481-8790 www.qualitycontainer.com
Manufacturer and exporter of high density polyeth-
ylene containers
Manager: Rob Salemi
CFO: Jamie Barche
Quality Control: Robert Johnson
VP Sales/Marketing: Robert Bell
Contact: Jamie Barche
jbarche@alphap.com

Estimated Sales: $20-50 Million
Number Employees: 50-99
Square Footage: 160000
Other Locations:
Quality Container Company
Thomasville GA

27995 Quality Containers
128 Milvan Drive
Weston, ON M9L 1Z9
Canada
416-749-6247
Fax: 416-749-3293
Manufacturer and exporter of tin cans and slip cover,
friction top and open top containers
President: Patrick Henry
Number Employees: 20
Square Footage: 32000

**27996 Quality Containers of New
England**
83 Portland St
Yarmouth, ME 04096
207-846-5420
Fax: 207-846-3755 800-639-1550
Packaging and containerizing products
President: Gregory H Leonard
VP/Treasurer: Kevin Burns
Plant Manager: David Holub
Estimated Sales: $1-2.5 Million
Number Employees: 10-19
Square Footage: 12000

27997 Quality Control Equipment Co
4280 E 14th St
Des Moines, IA 50313-2604
515-266-2268
Fax: 515-266-0243 www.qcec.com
Manufacturer and exporter of automatic wastewater
and dry material samplers, open channel flow meters
and flumes
President: Richard Miller
rmiller@qualitycontrolequipmentco.com
Quality Control: Tim Johnston
Sales Director: Joyce Hanson
Manager: Mike Wright
Purchasing Manager: Tim Johnston
Estimated Sales: $1-3 Million
Number Employees: 20-49
Type of Packaging: Bulk

27998 Quality Controlled Services
11971 Westline Industrial Drive
Suite 200
St. Louis, MO 63146
314-851-3100
Fax: 636-827-6761 800-325-3338
postmaster@delve.com
Data collection firm for marketing and sensory re-
search
President: Laura Livers
CEO: Noel Sitzmann
Controller: Doug Ortwerth
Senior Vice President, Operations: Kim Reale
Account Manager: Jessica Lynch
Senior Vice President of Operations: Kim Reale
Estimated Sales: $1-5 Million

27999 Quality Corporation
2401 S Delaware St
Denver, CO 80223
303-777-6608
Fax: 303-777-6488 800-383-3018
Manufacturer and exporter of truck-carried forklifts
President: Kc Ensor
CFO: Kenton C Ensor Jr
Contact: Daniel Collins
dcollins@qscorp.net
Estimated Sales: $10-20 Million
Number Employees: 50-99
Type of Packaging: Bulk

28000 Quality Croutons
4031 S Racine Ave
Chicago, IL 60609
773-890-2343
Fax: 773-927-8228 800-334-2796
Croutons and packaging services
President: David M Moore
Marketing/Sales: Deadra Ashford
Contact: Brandon Beavers
bbeavers@infomatrix.com
Production Manager: Keith Taylor

Estimated Sales: $1900000
Number Employees: 20-49
Square Footage: 140000
Type of Packaging: Food Service, Private Label,
Bulk

**28001 Quality Cup Packaging
Machinery Corporation**
5408 3M Drive N.E.
Menomonie, WI 54751
800-732-4624
Fax: 715-235-1111 info@qualitycup.com
www.qualitycup.com
President: Jeff James
Estimated Sales: $300,000-500,000
Number Employees: 5

28002 Quality Fabrication & Design
955 Freeport Pkwy # 400
Coppell, TX 75019-4455
972-304-3266
Fax: 972-745-4244
AlexPier@quality-fabrication.com
www.quality-fabrication.com
Manufacturer and exporter of stainless steel food
processing equipment including corn handling, fry-
ers, seasoning systems, corn cooking systems,
conveyors, etc
President: Alex Pier
alexpier@quality-fabrication.com
VP: Vondel Kremeier
Technical Sales: Harvey Norman
Operations Manager: Roger Pier
Estimated Sales: $12-15 Million
Number Employees: 50-99
Square Footage: 170600

28003 Quality Films
19459 Thompson Ln
Three Rivers, MI 49093-9089
269-679-5263
Fax: 616-679-4261
Polyolefin packaging film
President: Blaine Rabbers
Assistant General Manager: Carol Huskey
Marketing/Sales: Bowie Grant
VP Operations: Richard Rabbers
Estimated Sales: $5-10 Million
Number Employees: 10
Square Footage: 132000

28004 Quality Food Equipment
10935 Weaver Ave
South El Monte, CA 91733
626-442-9281
Fax: 626-442-8386 800-423-3744
Blenders, grinders, massagers and tumblers, pickle
injectors and slicers
Sales/Marketing Manager: Mo Fikry
Contact: Mike Anderson
manderson@qualityfoodequipment.com
Manager: Bob Maxwell
Estimated Sales: $1-2.5 Million
Number Employees: 5-9

28005 Quality Food Products Inc
172 N Peoria St
Chicago, IL 60607-2311
312-666-4559
Fax: 312-666-7133
Eggs
President: George Aralis
Owner: Jim Aralis
qfp@earthlink.net
Estimated Sales: $10-20 Million
Number Employees: 10-19

28006 Quality Highchairs
13461 Van Nuys Blvd
Pacoima, CA 91331-3059
818-896-3620
Fax: 818-896-3532 800-969-9635
qualityhigchairs12@sbcglobal.net
Hardwood high/youth chairs, booster seats, and tray
stands
President: Gilbert Raynosa
Estimated Sales: Less than $500,000
Number Employees: 1-4
Square Footage: 20000
Brands:
Classi-Tray Stand
His-470
Saferstep
Versa-Chair

28007 Quality Industries

3716 Clark Ave
Cleveland, OH 44109

216-961-5566
Fax: 216-961-5569 qirolls@stratos.net

Rolls and precision parts for packaging and processing equipment
President: Jerald Kaplan
Vice President: Jim Kaplan
Contact: Christel Cooper
ccooper@mytqg.com
Estimated Sales: $500,000-$1 Million
Number Employees: 5-9
Square Footage: 20000

28008 (HQ)Quality Industries Inc

130 Jones Blvd
La Vergne, TN 37086-3227

615-793-3000
Fax: 615-793-2347 www.qualityindustries.com

Manufacturer and exporter of food service equipment, stainless steal sifter cabinets; also, custom metal fabrication available
President: Fred Apple
CEO: Stanley Bryan
stanley.bryan@qualityindustries.com
CFO: Jeff Mayfield
CEO: Jeff Mayfield
Quality Control: Terry Tidwell
R&D: Micheal Taylor
Estimated Sales: $20-50 Million
Number Employees: 250-499
Square Footage: 190000

28009 Quality Ingredients

14300 Rosemount Dr
Burnsville, MN 55306-6925

952-898-4002
Fax: 952-898-4421 info@qic.us
www.qic.us

Powders: shortening, cream, whip, cheese, lemon.
Services: spray drying, chilling and product development.
Director, Strategy/Marketing: Valorie Klemz
Manager: Stewart Flanery
sflanery@qic.us
Chief of Operations: Robert St.Louis
Estimated Sales: 19 Million
Number Employees: 50-99
Number of Brands: 2
Square Footage: 50000
Type of Packaging: Consumer, Food Service, Private Label, Bulk
Brands:
QuIC-FLAVOR
QuIC-CHEESE

28010 Quality Mop & Brush Manufacturers

341 Great Plain Avenue
Needham, MA 02492-4130

617-884-2999
Fax: 617-884-3999

Mops, brooms, brushes, mop/broom handles and gloves
President: Donald Ferris
Estimated Sales: $1-2.5 Million
Number Employees: 5-9
Brands:
Telescopic

28011 Quality Natural Casing

2431 Wright Blvd
Hebron, KY 41048-8123

859-689-5311
Fax: 859-689-5177 800-328-8701
www.qualitycasing.com

Casings: collagen, fibrous, natural
President: Robert Novachich
Estimated Sales: $5-10 Million
Number Employees: 10-19

28012 Quality Packaging Inc

851 Sullivan Dr
PO Box 1720
Fond Du Lac, WI 54935-9106

920-923-3633
Fax: 920-924-3830 800-923-3633
www.qpack.com

Offers experience in package design, materials and equipment for various types of packaging.
President: Larry Wills
lwills@qpack.com
Plant Manager: Kevin Graham

Estimated Sales: $14.1 Million
Number Employees: 50-99

28013 Quality Plastic Bag Corporation

3430 56th Street
Flushing, NY 11377-2122

718-429-1632
Fax: 718-429-1634 800-532-2247

Plastic bags
Estimated Sales: $2.5-5 Million
Number Employees: 10-19
Square Footage: 30000
Type of Packaging: Bulk

28014 Quality Seating Co

4136 Logan Way
Youngstown, OH 44505-5703

330-747-0181
Fax: 330-747-0183 800-323-2234
www.gasserchair.com

Manufacturer and exporter of furniture including booths, chairs and tables
President: Jay Buttermore
jbuttermore@taylorseating.com
CEO: Roger Gasser
CFO: Frank Joy
Vice President: Marylou Joy
Research & Development: Mel Textoris
Marketing Director: Anthony Johntony
Sales Director: Paula Rapone
Operations Manager: Jim Humparies
Purchasing Manager: Paula Rapone
Estimated Sales: $2.5-5 Million
Number Employees: 20-49
Number of Brands: 1
Number of Products: 100
Square Footage: 200000
Parent Co: Quality Upholstering Company

28015 Quality Transparent BagCo

110 Mcgraw St
Bay City, MI 48708-8276

989-893-3561
Fax: 989-893-3004 bagcentral@aol.com

Polyethylene bags
President: Steve Kessler
bagcentral@aol.com
CEO: Leonard Kessler
Director Corporation Services: Tony Bloenk
Quality Control: Mery Carey
Estimated Sales: $5-10 Million
Number Employees: 10-19
Square Footage: 248000
Other Locations:
Quality Transparent Bag
Lawrenceburg TN
Brands:
Best Buy
Valu Pak

28016 Qualtech

1880, Rue L,on-Harmel
Quebec, QC G1N 4K3
Canada

418-686-3802
Fax: 418-686-3801 888-339-3801
info@qualtech.ca www.qualtech.ca

Specializing in stainless steel components and fabrications equipment
President: Andre Giguere
Customer Service: Andre Turcotte
Other Locations:
Saint-Laurent, QC
Scarborough, ON

28017 Qualtrax Inc

105 Industrial Dr
Christiansburg, VA 24073-2536

540-382-4234
Fax: 540-382-4701 800-277-3077
www.qualtrax.com

Computer software
CEO: Marty Muscatello
VP Sales/Marketing: Gary Overstreet
Manager: Megan Hash
mhash@ccs-inc.com
Estimated Sales: $930,000
Number Employees: 5-9
Square Footage: 8204

28018 Quanex Building Products Corp

1800 West Loop S # 1500
Suite 1500
Houston, TX 77027-3246

713-961-4600
Fax: 713-439-1016 www.quanex.com

Glass doors and display units designed to improve thermal performance for refrigerated products, also glass sealant for same
Vice President: Larry Johnson
ljohnson@homeshield.com
President, Chief Executive Officer: Dave Petratis
Vice President, Controller: Deborah Gadin
Quality Manager: Christoph Rubel
Director of Marketing: Erin Johnson
Sales Manager: Andreas Schultheiss
Executive Vice President, Chief Operatin: Curtis Stevens
Estimated Sales: $5-10 Million
Number Employees: 1000-4999

28019 Quantek Instruments

183 Magill Dr
Grafton, MA 01519-1327

508-839-3940
Fax: 508-393-1877 sales@quantekinstruments.com
www.quantekinstruments.com

Oxygen and carbon dioxide analyzers
Contact: Larry Davis
sales@quantekinstruments.com
Estimated Sales: $3-5 Million
Number Employees: 20-49

28020 Quantem Corp

1457 Lower Ferry Rd # 1
Ewing, NJ 08618-1493

609-883-9191
Fax: 800-800-1531 609-883-9879
info@quantemcorp.com www.quantemcorp.com

Production Manager: S Sunderland
Estimated Sales: $2 Million
Number Employees: 20-49
Square Footage: 15000
Brands:
Analog Thermostats
Data Loggers
Defrost Controllers
Digital (Appliance) Thermometers
Digital Thermostats
Temperature Sensors
Ventilation Controllers

28021 Quantis Secure Systems

7255 Standard Drive
Hanover, MD 21076-1389

410-712-6020
Fax: 410-712-0329 800-325-6124

Security, fire alarm and intercom systems
President: Kevin Robison
Estimated Sales: $2.5-5 Million
Number Employees: 20-49
Parent Co: BET

28022 Quantum Net

PO Box 49
Sewickley, PA 15143

704-376-0509
Fax: 704-551-0941

Netting plastics, netting and tying machines
President: George Seal
Estimated Sales: $500,000-$1 Million
Number Employees: 6

28023 Quantum Performance Films

601 E Lake St
Streamwood, IL 60107-4101

630-289-5237
Fax: 630-213-6209 800-323-6963

Manufacturer and exporter of flexible polypropylene films
CEO: Robert Dea
Director Marketing: Mark Montsinger
Director Sales: Bill Rowe
Number Employees: 100-249
Square Footage: 1800000
Parent Co: Hood Industries
Brands:
Mirage
Qlam
Qpet

28024 Quantum Storage SystemsInc
15800 NW 15th Ave
Miami, FL 33169-5606

305-687-0405
Fax: 305-688-2790 800-685-4665
sales@quantumstorage.com
www.quantumstorage.com
Plastic storage containers, metal shelving and mobile storage cabinets and carts
President: Hose Babani
ed@quantumstorage.com
VP: Dean Cohen
Marketing: Jose Babani
Sales: Elizabeth Faller
Estimated Sales: $3-5,000,000
Number Employees: 10-19
Square Footage: 300000
Parent Co: M&M Plastics
Type of Packaging: Consumer

28025 Quantum Topping SystemsQuantum Technical Services Inc
9524 West Gulfstream Road
Frankfort, IL 60423

815-464-1540
Fax: 815-464-1541 888-464-1540
information@q-t-s.com www.q-t-s.com
Manufacturer and designer of manual and automated portion control, cheese, IQF meat, and IQF vegetable. Topping application equipment and pepperoni slicing equipment
President: David White
CEO: Mark Freudinger
Sales Manager: Jim Machura
Contact: John Bautz
jbautz@q-t-s.com
Estimated Sales: $3-5 Million
Number Employees: 20
Square Footage: 76000

28026 Quasar Industries
1911 Northfield Dr
Rochester Hills, MI 48309-3824

248-852-0300
Fax: 248-852-0442 sales@quasar.com
www.quasar.com
Microwave ovens
President: Shane Majesky
shanemajesky@hotmail.com
CEO: Denise Higgins
VP Sales: Dave Bearden
Number Employees: 50-99

28027 Queen City Awning
7225 E Kemper Rd
Cincinnati, OH 45249-1030

513-530-9660
Fax: 513-530-0662 info@queencityawning.com
Commercial awnings
Owner: Pete Weingartner
qca_pete@fuse.net
Estimated Sales: Below $5,000,000
Number Employees: 20-49

28028 Quest
PO Box 73381
San Clemente, CA 92673-0113

949-643-1333
Fax: 949-362-4937 foods4you@aol.com
Consultant specializing in nutrition analysis and labeling services for dry, frozen and refrigerated products
President: Harry Messersmith

28029 Quest Corp
12900 York Rd
North Royalton, OH 44133-3623

440-230-9400
Fax: 440-582-7765 info@2quest.com
www.2quest.com
Electronic scales, weighing and batching systems and data acquisition/transmission systems; exporter of weighing and batching systems
Owner: David Fischer
dfischer@2quest.com
Sales/Marketing Manager: Daniel Donovan
Operations Manager: Jerome Kelly
Estimated Sales: $2.5-5 Million
Number Employees: 19

28030 Quetzal Foods International Company
3419 Iberville Street
New Orleans, LA 70119-5322

504-486-0830
Fax: 504-486-0830

28031 Quick Judith & Assoc
13944 Roberts Rd
P.O. BOX 188
Hancock, MD 21750-1620

301-678-5737
Fax: 301-678-5730 www.whereorg.net
Consulting firm specializing in regulatory and quality control, labeling, etc
President: Judith Quick
judyquick@hughes.net
Estimated Sales: Less Than $500,000
Number Employees: 1-4
Square Footage: 800

28032 Quick Label Systems
600 E Greenwich Ave
West Warwick, RI 02893-7526

401-828-4000
Fax: 401-822-2430 877-757-7978
info@quicklabel.com www.quicklabel.com
CFO: Joseph Oconnell
CEO: Everett V Pizzuti
epizzuti@astromed.com
CEO: Albert W Ondis
Estimated Sales: G
Number Employees: 250-499

28033 Quick Label Systems
600 E Greenwich Ave
West Warwick, RI 02893-7526

401-828-4000
Fax: 401-822-2430 877-757-7978
info@quicklabel.com www.quicklabel.com
Specialty food packaging i.e. gift wrap/labels/boxes/containers.
Principal: Kevin Pizzuti
CEO: Everett V Pizzuti
epizzuti@astromed.com
Estimated Sales: $45,000
Number Employees: 250-499

28034 Quick Point Inc
1717 Fenpark Dr
Fenton, MO 63026-2939

636-343-9400
Fax: 636-343-3587 800-638-1369
www.quickpoint.com
Manufacturer, supplier and exporter of advertising specialties
CEO: John Goessling
CFO: Doug Bozler
Vice President: Duane Mayer
Marketing Director: Duane Mayer
Sales Director: Joe Keely
Operations Manager: Rick Smith
Production Manager: Bryan Frenzel
Purchasing Manager: Dave Miller
Number Employees: 100-249

28035 Quick Stamp & Sign Mfg
805 General Mouton Ave
P. O. Box 3272
Lafayette, LA 70501-8509

337-232-2171
Fax: 337-232-4561 sales@qrstamp.com
www.qrstamp.com
Manufacturer and wholesaler/distributor of regular and self-inking rubber stamps, grocery marking ink, price markers for deposit stamps, daters and numberers
President: Patrick Gaubert
sales@qrstamp.com
Estimated Sales: Less Than $500,000
Number Employees: 1-4
Square Footage: 7200

28036 QuickLabel
600 E Greenwich Ave
West Warwick, RI 02893-7526

401-828-4000
Fax: 401-822-2430 877-757-7978
info@quicklabelsystems.com www.quicklabel.com
Digital color thermal transfer printers, barcode label printers, labelers, print and apply systems, labels, thermal transfer ribbon
President & CEO: Gregory Woods
CFO: David Smith

Estimated Sales: $50 Million
Number Employees: 250-499
Square Footage: 125000
Parent Co: AstroNova
Type of Packaging: Consumer, Food Service, Private Label, Bulk
Other Locations:
Astro-Med
Longucuil, Quebec
Astro-Med
Slough, United Kingdom
Astro-Med
Trappes, France
Astro-Med
Rodgau, Germany
Astro-Med
Milano, Italy

28037 Quickdraft
1525 Perry Dr SW
Canton, OH 44710-1098

330-477-4574
Fax: 330-477-3314 www.Quickdraft.com
Hot dog/sausage casing removal systems, draft inducer's to vent out the heat produced from ovens & boilers and food conveying systems.
Manager: Joseph Ovnic
joe.ovnic@quickdraft.com
Number Employees: 20-49

28038 Quickie Manufacturing Corp
1150 Taylors Ln # 2
Suite 2
Cinnaminson, NJ 08077-2577

856-829-7900
Fax: 856-786-9318 help@quickie.com
www.quickie.com
Mops, brushes, brooms, sponges and scourers
President: Peter Vosbikian
Sr. VP Sales: David Vosbikian
Executive VP Sales/Marketing: Vince Cella
Estimated Sales: $10-20 Million
Number Employees: 50-99

28039 Quikwater Inc
8939 W 21st St
Sand Springs, OK 74063-8515

918-241-8880
Fax: 918-241-8718 sales@quikwater.com
www.quikwater.com
QuikWater manufactures a 99% thermal efficient direct contact water heater that provides potable hot water on demand. Water heated with a QuikWater can be used for domestic purposes, as a food ingredient and for sterilization andsanitation processes. With tremendous thermal efficiency, QuikWater can create up to 40% fuel savings compared to traditional methods.
President: Dana Weber
Marketing: Kay Weiman
Sales: Tammy Collins
Manager: Melissa Arms Trong
marmstrong@hot-water-heater.com
Number Employees: 10-19
Number of Brands: 3
Number of Products: 1
Brands:
Econowater
Quikwater
Twintower

28040 Quintex Corp
205 25th Ave S
Nampa, ID 83686-7399

208-467-1113
Fax: 509-924-7991 www.qntx.com
Custom and stock plastic bottles; also, printing services available
President: Dorothea Christiansen
Regional Sales Manager: Bruce McElwain
Customer Service: George Ferriola
Estimated Sales: $10-20 Million
Number Employees: 10-19
Square Footage: 144000

28041 Quintex Corp
3808 N Sullivan Rd # 8a
Spokane Valley, WA 99216-1618

509-924-7900
Fax: 509-924-7991 www.qntx.com
Manufactures blow mold plastic containers
President: Dorothea Christiansen
CFO: Bob Pullis
Quality Control: Bill Masscy

Estimated Sales: $10-20 Million
Number Employees: 50-99

28042 Quipco Products Inc
1401 Mississippi Ave
Suite 5
Sauget, IL 62201-1084

314-993-1442
Fax: 618-271-2311
Manufacturer and exporter of custom and standard service food equipment including counters, racks, sinks and tables; also, custom stainless steel fabrication available
President: James Nations
nations@nationsfoodservice.com
VP/Owner: Jerry Chervitz
Office Manager: Tena Holmes
Estimated Sales: $1-3 Million
Number Employees: 5-9
Square Footage: 40000

28043 Qwik Pack Systems
16571 Saddlebrook Ln
Moreno Valley, Mo 92551

951-232-2507
Fax: 909-242-6019
qwikpacksystemsinc@yahoo.com
Automatic and semiautomatic carton sealing and taping machines. Robotics, L-Sealers, automatic stretch wrap machines, strapping machines and adhesive tapes
President: James Mahoney
Estimated Sales: $10-20 Million
Number Employees: 1-4
Number of Brands: 1
Number of Products: 31
Square Footage: 500000
Type of Packaging: Food Service
Brands:
    Qwik Pack Systems

28044 Qyk Syn Industries
8527 NW 66th Street
Miami, FL 33166-2636

305-594-3366
Fax: 305-594-0075 800-354-5640
bobbiebridge@aol.com
Formed plastic and custom neon signs, faces, letters,architectural panels and menu boards
CEO: Ernest Hunt
Estimated Sales: $1-5 Million
Number Employees: 10
Square Footage: 7200

28045 R & D Brass
25 Sprout Creek Ct
Wappingers Falls, NY 12590-6342

845-223-6104
Fax: 845-223-6195 800-447-6050
RDBRASSINC@AOL.COM
Brass sneeze guards, booth dividers, railings, glass racks and crowd control products
Owner: Ed Davis
rdbrassinc@aol.com
Estimated Sales: Less Than $500,000
Number Employees: 1-4
Square Footage: 20000

28046 R A Jones & Co Inc
2701 Crescent Springs Pike
Ft Mitchell, KY 41017-1591

859-341-1807
Fax: 859-341-0519 www.rajones.com
Manufacturer and exporter of automatic carton loading machines, case and tray packers, continuous web form, fill and seal machinery, bottle uncasers, pouch makers, fillers and robotic solutions; also provide complete partial lineintegration services
CEO: Barry Shoulders
shoulders.b@rajones.com
Estimated Sales: $300,000-500,000
Number Employees: 250-499
Parent Co: The Coesia Group

28047 R C Molding Inc
19 Freedom Ct
Greer, SC 29650-4525

864-879-7279
Fax: 864-879-7309
customerservice@rcmolding.com
www.rcmolding.com
Thermoplastic injection molded parts for boxes
President: William Humphrey
whumphrey@rcmoulding.com

Estimated Sales: $1-2.5 Million
Number Employees: 10-19
Square Footage: 80000

28048 R C Musson Rubber Co
1320 E Archwood Ave
PO Box 7038
Akron, OH 44306-2825

330-773-7651
Fax: 330-773-3254 800-321-2381
info@mussonrubber.com www.mussonrubber.com
Floor mats
President: Bennie D Segers
bsegers@mussonrubber.com
Vice President: Robert Segers
Research & Development: Joe Kostko
Estimated Sales: $5-10 Million
Number Employees: 20-49

28049 R C Smith Co
14200 Southcross Dr W
Burnsville, MN 55306-6973

952-854-0711
Fax: 952-854-8160 800-747-7648
info@rcsmith.com www.rcsmith.com
Store fixtures
President: Peter Smith
psmith@rcsmith.com
Marketing Manager: Sarah Dunne
Estimated Sales: $2.5-5 Million
Number Employees: 20-49
Square Footage: 40000

28050 R F Hunter Co Inc
113 Crosby Rd # 9
Dover, NH 03820-4389

603-742-9565
Fax: 603-742-9608 800-332-9565
info@rfhunter.com www.rfhunter.com
Manufacturer and exporter of filtration equipment for edible oils
President: Paul Santoro
sales@rfhunter.com
Estimated Sales: $500,000-$1 Million
Number Employees: 5-9
Brands:
    Ecco One
    Hunter Filtrator Hf Series
    Mini Max Iii

28051 R F Mac Donald Co
10261 Matern Pl
Santa Fe Springs, CA 90670-3249

714-257-0900
Fax: 714-257-1176
jim.macdonald@rfmacdonald.com
www.rfmacdonald.com
Wine industry pumps
Manager: Christopher Sentner
VP Pump Division: Robert Sygiel
VP Boiler Division: Chris Sentner
Co-President: James T McDonald
Estimated Sales: $20-50 Million
Number Employees: 20-49

28052 (HQ)R F Schiffmann Assoc.
149 W 88th St
Suite 1
New York, NY 10024-2424

212-362-7021
microwaves@juno.com
www.microwaveinnovations.com
Consultant specializing in microwave technology applications
President: Robert Schiffmann
microwaves@juno.com
CFO: Ernest Stein
VP: Marilyn Schiffmann
Estimated Sales: Less Than $500,000
Number Employees: 1-4
Square Footage: 8000

28053 R F Technologies Inc
330 Lexington Dr
Buffalo Grove, IL 60089

800-598-2370
info@rftechno.com www.rftechno.com
Drive thru system sales, repairs, POS, Big Dog Surveillance systems, timers, order confirmation, digital signage, customer music entertainment and wired intercom systems.
Director of IT: Steve Combs
Vice President, Marketing: Dan Wenger

Year Founded: 1989
Estimated Sales: $50-100 Million
Number Employees: 50-99

28054 R H Saw Corp
28386 W Main St
Barrington, IL 60010-1830

847-381-8777
Fax: 847-381-9492 rhsaw@aol.com
Manufacturer, importer and exporter of cutlery, blades, grinder plates and knives including metal, wood and plastic
President: Ralph Hirsch
rhsaw@aol.com
CEO: Larry Adler
Estimated Sales: $500,000-$1 Million
Number Employees: 1-4

28055 R J Mc Cullough Co
1980 Old Philadelphia Pike # A
Rte 340
Lancaster, PA 17602-3431

717-735-8772
Fax: 717-735-8774
Commercial awnings
Owner: J R Mc Cullough
Estimated Sales: Less Than $500,000
Number Employees: 5-9

28056 R K Electric Co Inc
7405 Industrial Row Dr
Mason, OH 45040-1301

513-204-6060
Fax: 513-204-6061 800-543-4936
www.rke.com
Manufacturer and exporter of relays and voltage suppressors for HVAC applications
President: John L Keller
jkeller@rke.com
Estimated Sales: $5-10 Million
Number Employees: 10-19

28057 R Murphy Co Inc
13 Groton Harvard Rd
Ayer, MA 01432-1846

978-772-3481
Fax: 978-772-7569 888-772-3481
sales@rmurphyknives.com
www.murphyknives.com
Industrial knives including carving, butchers', fish scaling and slitting
President: Douglas Bethke
dbethke@rmurphyknives.com
Plant Manager: Charles Liebfried
Estimated Sales: $2.5-5 Million
Number Employees: 10-19

28058 R P Adams
225 E Park Dr
Tonawanda, NY 14150-7813

716-877-2608
Fax: 716-877-9385 800-896-8869
info@rpadams.com www.rpadams.com
President: Richard Adams
rba@rpadams.com
VP: Dan Petko
Estimated Sales: $9 Million
Number Employees: 50-99

28059 R R Donnelley
111 E Wacker Dr
Chicago, IL 60601-3713

312-565-2727
Fax: 312-326-8001 800-742-4455
www.rrdonnelley.com
Signs including permanent point of purchase, plastic and neon; also, displays and merchandising systems, pressure sensitive labels, rotary letterpress and screens
President, CEO: Thomas J. Quinlan, III
Contact: Leonard Abel
leonard.abel@rrd.com
Number Employees: 50-99
Square Footage: 800000
Other Locations:
    Banta Specialty Converting
    Sturtevant WI

28060 R R Street & Co
215 Shuman Blvd # 403
Naperville, IL 60563-5100

630-416-4244
Fax: 630-416-4150 www.4streets.com
Manufacturer and exporter of dry cleaning detergents, fabric finishes, spotters and filtration products

President: L R Beard
lbeard@4streets.com
CFO: James Beecher
Estimated Sales: $5-10 Million
Number Employees: 5-9

28061 R T C
2800 Golf Rd
Rolling Meadows, IL 60008-4023
847-640-2400
Fax: 847-640-5175 gcohen@rtc.com
Manufacturer and exporter of merchandising displays, signs, nonmechanical coolers and interactive, electronic, in store point of purchase displays
President: Bruce Vierck
CEO: Richard Nathan
rnathan@rtc.com
Sr VP: Howard Topping
Estimated Sales: $500,000-$1 Million
Number Employees: 250-499
Square Footage: 700000

28062 (HQ)R Wireworks Inc
517 Baldwin St
Elmira, NY 14901-2225
607-733-7169
Fax: 607-734-8859 800-550-4009
sales@rwireworks.com www.shoprwireworks.com
Point of purchase displays and fixtures
President: Ned Rubin
nrubin@rwireworks.com
Quality Control: Terry Cosgelo
Marketing Manager: Deb Eighmey
Estimated Sales: $2.5-5 Million
Number Employees: 20-49

28063 R X Honing Machine Corp
1301 E 5th St
Mishawaka, IN 46544-2899
574-259-1606
Fax: 574-259-9163 800-346-6464
www.rxhoning.com
Manufacturer and exporter of honing and sharpening machines for restaurant knives
President: R J Watson
Estimated Sales: $5-10 Million
Number Employees: 5-9
Square Footage: 11000
Brands:
   Mini Rx Hone

28064 R&C Pro Brands
1655 Sally Road
Wayne, NJ
973-633-7374
Disinfectants, washing compounds, polishes and cleaners including glass, hand, carpet and windows
President: John Culligan
VP Marketing: Karen Messer
National Sales Manager: Michael Tracy
Parent Co: Reckitt & Colman PLC

28065 R&D Glass Products
1808 Harmon Street
Berkeley, CA 94703-2496
510-547-6464
Fax: 510-547-3620 www.angelfire.com
Wine industry labware
President: Doug Dobson
Estimated Sales: Below $5 Million
Number Employees: 10-19

28066 R&G Machinery
7204 Beckwith Road
Morton Grove, IL 60053-1723
847-966-1530
Fax: 773-265-6311
Tanks, kettles
President: Sofi Rahmon
Estimated Sales: $1-2.5 Million
Number Employees: 4
Square Footage: 100000

28067 R&R Corrugated Container
PO Box 399
Terryville, CT 06786-0399
860-584-1194
Fax: 860-582-5051
Corrugated boxes
President: Richard Braverman
CFO: Wayne
Estimated Sales: $10-20 Million
Number Employees: 50-99

28068 R&R Industries
1000 Calle Cordillera
San Clemente, CA 92673
949-361-9238
Fax: 949-361-9360 800-234-1434
rrosen@rrind.com www.rrind.com
Embroidered and printed promotional clothing
President: Richard Rosen
Marketing Manager: Richard Rosin
Production Manager: Robin Grohman
Estimated Sales: $20-50 Million
Number Employees: 50-99

28069 R-Biopharm Inc
870 Vossbrink Dr
Washington, MO 63090-1067
269-789-3033
Fax: 866-922-5856 info@r-biopharm.com
www.r-biopharm.com
Mycotoxin test kits, enzymatic and microbiological test kits for the detection of residues, food constituents and microbiological contaminnts. Screen for hormones, antibiotics, genetically modified materials, specified risk materialsallergens and pathogens in a reliable and cost-effective manner.
President: Kurt Johnson
Vice President: Sean Tinkey
Contact: Carol Donnelly
carol@r-biopharmrhone.com
Estimated Sales: $1.3 Million

28070 R. Markey & Sons
5 Hanover Sq
Rm 1202
New York, NY 10004
212-482-8600
Fax: 212-344-5838
rmarkeycoffee@compuserve.com
Tea and coffee samplers and weighers
President: Michael Steele
Contact: Joseph Aglione
aglione@rmarkey.com
Estimated Sales: $1-2.5 Million
Number Employees: 20-49
Parent Co: R Markey & Sons

28071 (HQ)R.C. Keller & Associates
14 Passage Lane
Suite 110
Barnegat, NJ 08005-3340
973-694-8810
Fax: 973-649-3535
Consultant specializing in packaging, processing and automation systems integration, facilities design, project management, industrial engineering and operations research
Estimated Sales: $1-5 Million
Number Employees: 1

28072 R.G. Stephens Engineering
707 W 16th Street
Long Beach, CA 90813-1410
562-435-6244
Fax: 562-435-1664 800-499-3001
Food processing equipment and supplies, conveyor systems, waste handling equipment and systems and process control systems; also, engineering, design, fabrication and installation services available
General Manager: Ralph Stephens
Manager: Ken Diehl
VP: Diane Stephen
Number Employees: 6

28073 R.H. Chandler Company
1040 Claridge Pl
Saint Louis, MO 63122-2431
314-962-9353
Fax: 314-962-1661
Manufacturer and importer precision machined parts
President: Robert H Chandler
Number Employees: 7
Square Footage: 23200

28074 R.I. Enterprises
PO Box 351
Hernando, MS 38632-0351
662-429-7863
Fax: 662-429-2561
Wire display racks
President: R Gates
Secretary/Treasurer: B Gates
VP: L Gates

Estimated Sales: $500,000-$1 Million
Number Employees: 19
Square Footage: 44000

28075 R.L. Instruments
16009 Arminta Street
Van Nuys, CA 91406
818-780-1800
Fax: 818-780-1978
Refractometer products, spectrophotometers, pH meters and related products, and microwave moisture and solids analyzer
Owner: April Hodges
Estimated Sales: Below $5 Million
Number Employees: 1-4

28076 R.N.C. Industries
3105 Sweetwater Road
Suite 220
Lawrenceville, GA 30044-8547
770-368-8453
Fax: 770-368-8490 888-844-3864
sales@rncind.com www.rncind.com
Packaging supplies: gift wrap, labels, boxes and containers.
President: Lawrence Clark
Cfo: Charlotta Clark
Marketing: Taylor Clark
Contact: Salma Abdullahi
salma@rncind.com
Estimated Sales: $4.9 Million
Number Employees: 46

28077 R.P. Childs Stamp Company
161 Prokop Av
Ludlow, MA 1056
413-733-1211
Fax: 413-737-6865
Marking devices, rubber stamps, parts, pads, numbering machines and time recorders
President: Roland Stebbins
Estimated Sales: Below $5 Million
Number Employees: 2 to 4

28078 R.R. Scheibe Company
29 Westgate Rd
Newton Center, MA 2459
508-584-4900
Fax: 508-580-2644 www.scheibeco.com
Serving trays, snack tables and tray stands
Owner: Alan Hackel
Estimated Sales: Below $5 Million
Number Employees: 30

28079 RA Jones & Company
7800 Cooper Rd # 102
Cincinnati, OH 45242-7733
513-891-7800
Fax: 859-341-0519 www.rajones.com
Cartoners, pouch/sachet machines, multipackers, case packers, robotics, integrated systems
President: Bonsild Gordon
Contact: Tanja Bruner
tbruner@rajones.com
Estimated Sales: $80 Million
Number Employees: 1-4

28080 RAM Center
5140 Moundview Dr
Red Wing, MN 55066
651-385-2271
Fax: 651-385-2180 800-309-5431
info@autoequipllc.com www.autoequipllc.com
Manufacturer and exporter of systems for robotic packaging and material handling; including palletizers for cold room and washdown applications
General Manager: Steve Halverson
R&D: Cory Doln
Executive VP: Dave Muelken
Quality Control: Dave Mulken
Director Sales/Marketing: Steve Valade
Estimated Sales: $10-20 Million
Number Employees: 20-49
Parent Co: RAM Center
Brands:
   Ram Center

28081 RAO Contract Sales Inc
94 Fulton St # 4
Paterson, NJ 07501-1200
201-652-1500
Fax: 973-279-6448 888-324-0020
info@rao.com www.rao.com

Manufacturer and exporter of menu and bulletin boards, pedestal displays, etc
Owner: Brian Bergman
brian@rao.com
Account Executive: George Cross
Account Executive: Marsha Holland
Estimated Sales: $1-5 Million
Number Employees: 5-9
Square Footage: 40000
Brands:
    Tak-Les

28082 RAO Design Intl
9451 Ainslie St
Schiller Park, IL 60176-1139
847-671-6182
Fax: 847-671-9276 raodesign@aol.com
www.blow-fill-sealassociates.com
Turn-key operation setup, PET machines, engineering and consulting, blow mold making, blow-fill seal machines, blow molding
CEO: Kumar Murkurthy
Marketing Director: David Muiukurthy
Manager: M Surya
aptbfs@aol.com
Estimated Sales: $5-10 Million
Number Employees: 20-49

28083 RAPAC Inc
65 Industrial Park
Oakland, TN 38060-4048
Fax: 901-465-1183 800-280-6333
www.ringcompanies.com
Plastic bottles and jars
Contact: Connie East
connie.east@rapac.com
Estimated Sales: $32 Million
Number Employees: 1-4
Square Footage: 50000

28084 RAS Process Equipment Inc
324 Meadowbrook Rd
Trenton, NJ 08691-2503
609-371-1220
Fax: 609-371-1200 www.ras-inc.com
Manufacturer and exporter of process equipment including pressure vessels, heat exchangers, reactors, columns and storage tanks
Owner: John Bonacorda
jbonacorda@ras-inc.com
Director: John Bonacorda
VP: John Bonacorda
Estimated Sales: $5-10 Million
Number Employees: 20-49
Square Footage: 80000

28085 RBA-Retailer's Bakers Association
14239 Park Center Drive
Laurel, MD 20707-5261
301-725-2149
Fax: 301-725-2187 301-725-2187
Communications Director: Dawn Rivera
Estimated Sales: $1-5 Million
Number Employees: 15

28086 RBM Manufacturing Co
1570 W Mission Blvd
Pomona, CA 91766-1247
909-620-1333
Fax: 909-620-6119 info@rbmcsi.com
Art technology for the bulk material handling industry; conveying, surge and distribution systems, vibratory conveyors, belt conveyors, bucket elevators, controlled by the most advanced electronic instrumentation, either withconventional or computerized
President: Roobik Kureghian
info@rbmcsi.com
Estimated Sales: Below $5 Million
Number Employees: 10-19

28087 RBS Fab Inc
230 N Hoernerstown Rd
Hummelstown, PA 17036-9562
717-566-9513
Fax: 717-566-9268 www.rbsfab.com
Custom designed food processing equipment
Owner: Terry Smith
rbssabinc@verizon.net
CEO: Joann Smith
Office Manager: Denise Ajala
Production: Edward Rupp

Estimated Sales: $2.5-5 Million
Number Employees: 5-9
Square Footage: 48000

28088 RCS Limited
1301 Commerce Street
Birmingham, AL 35217-3603
205-841-9955
Fax: 205-841-2106
Designs and builds contractor for cold storage warehouses
Marketing/Sales: Laura Williams

28089 RDA Container Corp
70 Cherry Rd
Gates, NY 14624-2592
585-247-2323
Fax: 585-247-5680 www.rdacontainer.com
Corrugated boxes
President: Alan Brant
alan@yahoo.com
Founder: Peter R. Brant
President: Peter R Brant
Sales Manager: Jack Fennell
Mngr.: Bob Bardeen
Estimated Sales: $10-20 Million
Number Employees: 50-99

28090 RDM International
11643 Otsego Street
North Hollywood, CA 91601-3628
818-985-7654
Fax: 818-760-2376 bobmoore@rdmintl.com
www.rdmintl.com
Processor, importer and exporter of fruits including frozen, dried, powderes, flakes and canned; also, fruit concentrates and purees, oils, nuts, pumpkin, sweet potatoes/yams and coconut
President/Sales: Bob Moore
Operations: Peri Abel
Number of Brands: 135
Number of Products: 280
Square Footage: 276000
Type of Packaging: Food Service, Private Label, Bulk
Brands:
    Beesweet Blueberries
    Berry Fine Raspberries
    Big Banana Perfet
    Big Boy Blazin Berries
    Big Red Rhubarb
    Bubba's Yams
    Fruit To the World
    Gourmet Brand Blackberries
    Mountain Mats' Apples
    Pacific Coconut
    Perfect Peach
    Petes Pumpkin
    Rain Sweet
    Rippin Cherries
    Tru Blue Blueberries

28091 RDM Technologies
4711 East 355 Street
Willoughby, OH 44094
Canada
440-954-3500
Fax: 440-954-3501 sales@bevcorp.com
www.bevcorp.com
Estimated Sales: C
Parent Co: Bevcorp LLC

28092 RDM-Sesco
4711 East 355 Street
Willoughby, OH 44094
440-954-3500
Fax: 440-954-3501 sales@bevcorp.com
www.bevcorp.com
President: David Kemp Sr
CFO: Tim Frantz
Quality Control: Jim Hannah
Number Employees: 60

28093 RDS of Florida
6861 SW 196th Ave
Suite 203-204
Fort Lauderdale, FL 33332
305-994-7756
Fax: 305-772-1090 sales@rdsflorida.com
www.rdsflorida.com
Restaurant point of sale systems including table and quick service, wireless headsets and close circuit t.v

President: Joe Pollock
General Manager: Matt Sutton
Account Manager: David Henderson
Estimated Sales: $5-10 Million
Number Employees: 10-19

28094 REA Elektronik
7307 Young Dr
Suite B
Cleveland, OH 44146-5369
440-460-0552
Fax: 440-232-5335 www.rea-systeme.com
Owner: Ray Turchi
Contact: Gary Carr
gary.carr@goarmy.com
Estimated Sales: $.5-1 million
Number Employees: 1-4

28095 REI Systems Inc
45335 Vintage Park Plz # 100
Sterling, VA 20166-6721
703-256-2245
Fax: 703-256-9372 info@reisystems.com
Custom-designed conveyor equipment and systems
CEO: Shyam Salona
salona@reisys.com
Estimated Sales: $1-5 Million
Number Employees: 500-999

28096 REM Ohio Inc
11530 Century Blvd
Cincinnati, OH 45246-3305
513-381-3700
www.rem-oh.com
Chemical cleaners, sanitizers and detergents
President: Gary Farraria
VP: B Nelson
Controller: Larry Schirmann
Sales Manager: E Newman
Estimated Sales: $2.5-5 Million
Number Employees: 10-19
Square Footage: 200000

28097 RES & Associates
300 N Wolf Rd
Suite B
Wheeling, IL 60090-2900
847-541-0080
Fax: 847-541-0212 800-741-5919
President: Ralph E Squaglia Jr
Contact: Robert Seddon
rseddon@res-associates.com
Estimated Sales: $500,000-$1 Million
Number Employees: 1-4

28098 RETROTECH, Inc
127 John Street
Suite 400
West Henrietta, NY 14586-9120
585-924-6333
Fax: 585-924-6334 866-915-2777
www.retrotech.com
Automated warehousing systems
Vice President: Len DeWeerdt
Tactical Marketing Specialist: Cynthia Hamann
VP Operations: Peter Hartman
Estimated Sales: $10-20 Million
Number Employees: 100-249
Number of Brands: 2
Number of Products: 3

28099 REX Pure Foods
2121 Chartres St
New Orleans, LA 70116
504-525-7305
800-344-8314
info@rexfoods.com www.rexfoods.com
Seafood spices and seasonings, sauces, blends, vinegar and mustard; packaging services
President: J Geldart
CEO: Jenni Ratliff
VP, Chief Marketing Officer: Gene Ratliff
Estimated Sales: $2.5 Million
Number Employees: 1-4
Type of Packaging: Consumer, Food Service, Bulk
Brands:
    Rex

28100 RFC Wire Forms Inc
525 Brooks St
Ontario, CA 91762-3702
909-984-5500
Fax: 909-984-2322 800-334-0937
rfcmark@verizon.net www.rfcwireforms.com

Soft drink backs, displays and display cases, cooler displays, cooler racks, custom design and manufacturing of displays and racks
President: Donald Kemby
rfcdon@aol.com
CFO: Jay Munoz
Vice President: Don Kemby
Research & Development: Greg Lunsmann
Quality Control: Donald Kemby
Sales Director: Mark Arriola
Production Manager: Jesse Dunn
Purchasing Manager: Mike Manning
Estimated Sales: $20-30 Million
Number Employees: 20-49
Square Footage: 30000

28101 RGF Environmental GroupInc
1101 W 13th St
Riviera Beach, FL 33404-6701
561-848-1826
Fax: 561-848-9454 800-842-7771
requests@rgf.com www.rgf.com
CEO: Ronald G Fink
rfink@rgf.com
Estimated Sales: $1-5 Million
Number Employees: 50-99

28102 RGN Developers
44 Gales Dr Apt 4
New Providence, NJ 7974
Fax: 908-665-6901 rgnsoft@aol.com
Design engineer specializing in software development, technology transfers, engineering specifications and start-up in food, dairy and pharmaceutical plants
President: Raja Nori
Estimated Sales: $2.5-5 Million
Number Employees: 4

28103 RH Forschner
P.O.Box 1212
Monroe, CT 06468-8212
203-929-6391
Fax: 203-925-2933 800-243-4032
web.orders@swissarmy.com www.swissarmy.com
Cutlery, knives, scabbards for cutting and deboning, safety apparel professional swiss knives
President: Susanne Recher
CEO: Carl Elsener
CFO: Thomas M Lupinski
CEO: Rick Taggart
Estimated Sales: $1-2.5 Million
Number Employees: 100-249

28104 RHG Products Company
599 Topeka Way
Suite 200
Castle Rock, CO 80109
303-663-1779
Fax: 319-366-7792 800-553-8131
info@tuckerusa.com www.tuckerusa.com
High level window washers, aluminum telescoping handles, brushes, detergent tablets, window and awning cleaning systems, spot free water
President: Irvin Lee Tucker
VP/General Manager: Robin Bradley Tucker
CFO: Robin Tucker
R&D: Robin Tucker
Quality Control: Robin Tucker
Estimated Sales: $5-10,000,000
Number Employees: 10-19
Brands:
Tucker

28105 RJ Jansen Company
10831 1st St
Highway KR
Sturtevant, WI 53177
262-884-0511
Fax: 262-884-0512 richard@rjjansen.com
Chocolate equipment: decorating, enrobing, pumping systems. Cluster machine, coaters, cutting machines: carmel, cream centers; depositors: chocolate, liquid, portable, wire-cut
President: Richard Jansen
Estimated Sales: $3-5 Million
Number Employees: 5-9

28106 RJ Jansen Confectionery
10831 1st Street
Sturtevant, WI 53177-3338
262-884-0511
Fax: 262-884-0512 richard@rjjansen.com
www.rjjansen.com

Enrobers, depositors, coaters and packaging equipment, bag and pouch sealers, bag filling and sealing machines, bag forming machines
President: Richard Jansen
richard@rjjansen.com
Estimated Sales: Below 1 Million
Number Employees: 5-9

28107 RJ Wetrz Products Company
519 Austin Avenue
Pittsburgh, PA 15243-2027
724-926-4566
Manufacturer of kits, accessories

28108 RJO Produce Distr Inc
1177 W Shaw Ave
Fresno, CA 93711-3704
559-222-7200
Fax: 559-222-7277 www.rjoproduce.com
Procurement, inspection and delivery of fruits and berries. Also market analyses reports, marketing, and inventory control
Owner: John O'Rourke
sales@rjoproduce.com
Estimated Sales: $3-5 Million
Number Employees: 5-9

28109 RJR Executive Search
11999 Katy Freeway
Suite 585
Houston, TX 77079
281-368-8550
Fax: 281-368-8560 sschorejs@rjrsearch.com
www.rjrsearch.com
Executive search firm specializing in selection and placement of consumer packaged goods and services personnel
Research Assistant: Sherry Schorejs
VP: Ray Schorejs
VP: Bob O Dell
Industrial Sales / Operations: Vince Lyden
vlyden@rjrsearch.com
Estimated Sales: $1-3 Million
Number Employees: 5-9

28110 RL Instruments
9 Main St # 2e
Douglas, MA 01516
508-476-1935
Fax: 508-476-1927 800-427-4361
www.rlinstruments.com
Refractometers, spectrophotometers, moisture balances, pH meters, and parts and service
Owner: April Hodges
Sales Manager: Todd Hodges
Estimated Sales: Below $5 Million
Number Employees: 5-9

28111 RLS Equipment Company
PO Box 282
Egg Harbor City, NJ 08215-0282
609-965-0074
Fax: 609-965-2509 800-527-0197
www.rlsequipment.com
Winery and fruit processing equipment
President: Robert L Stollenwerk
Estimated Sales: $.5-1 million
Number Employees: 7

28112 RLS Logistics
Rosario Leo Building
2185 Main Road
Newfield, NJ 08344
856-694-2500
800-579-9900
info@rlslogistics.com www.rlslogistics.com
Transportation, warehousing and fulfillment to the frozen and refrigerated food industry.
Chief Executive Officer, President: Anthony Leo
Vice President of Development: John Gaudet
Director of Operations: Greg Deitz

28113 RM Waite Inc
45 6th Street
Clintonville, WI 54929
715-823-4327
Fax: 715-823-7311 rmwaite@frontiernet.net
Replacement parts and rebuiling machinery for meat processors
President: Rick Waite
VP: Marsha Waite
Estimated Sales: $768,000
Number Employees: 6
Square Footage: 400

28114 (HQ)RMF Companies
4417 Martha Truman Rd
Grandview, MO 64030-1119
816-839-9258
info@rmfworks.com
www.rmfworks.com
Manufacturer and exporter of food processing equipment focusing on flow-thru massaging, marinating, deboning and portioning; vacuum packaging equipment; freezers and chilling equipment; and engineering services, including turnkeysystems and plant design. Parent company of RMF Steel, Challenge RMF & RMF Freezers.
President/CEO: Jeff Brauner
Estimated Sales: $50-100 Million
Number Employees: 50-99

28115 RMI-C/Rotonics Manaufacturing
736 Birginal Dr
Bensenville, IL 60106-1213
630-773-9510
Fax: 630-773-4274 chicago@rotonics.com
www.rotonics.com
Manufacturer and exporter of polyethylene containers molded from FDA/USDA approved resin including material handling, shipping and storage; also, barrels, drums, tilt trucks, mobile bins, totes and custom molded parts available
Manager: Jay Rule
Sales Director: Michael Morrison
Estimated Sales: $20-50 Million
Number Employees: 50-99
Square Footage: 38000
Parent Co: Rotonics Manufacturing
Type of Packaging: Bulk
Brands:
Bulkatilt
Bulkitank
Gripper
Tabletote

28116 RMX Global Logistics
35715 U.S.
Highway 40 Building B
Evergreen, CO 80439
888-824-7365
Fax: 303-674-3803 888-824-7365
www.rmxglobal.com
Shelf stable, high barrier food packaging
President: Steve Whaley

28117 ROI Software, LLC
P.O.Box 2747
Knoxville, TN 37901-2747
865-522-2211
Fax: 865-522-7907 www.resourceopt.com
Software; also, consulting services available
President: T Brient Mayfield
Estimated Sales: Below $5 Million
Number Employees: 10-19

28118 RPA Process Technologies
PO Box 1087
Marblehead, MA 01945-5087
781-631-9707
Fax: 781-631-9507 800-631-9707
www.rosedisplays.com
Manufacturer and exporter of displays including 3-D hanging, hanging sign, window and hall; also, price card holders
President: Michael Hoffman
Assistant to President: Carol Jones
Sales Manager: Tracy Hatfield
Number Employees: 15
Square Footage: 12800
Brands:
Biclops Installation Tool
Clearly Invisible Hooks
Gotcha-Sure Snap Sign Holder
One-Up
Perfect Hanging System
Ropole
Smartbox
Supergotcha

28119 RSI ID Technologies
I-94 at McKnight Road
St. Paul, MN 55144-1000
619-656-2515
Fax: 619-872-0662 888-364-3577
solutions.3m.com/wps/portal/3M/en_US/WW3/Co
untry/

President: John Freund
CEO: Wolff Bielas
Chief Technical Officer: Bruce Roesner
Estimated Sales: $1-5 Million
Number Employees: 50-99
Parent Co: 3M

28120 RTG Films

120 New Britain Blvd
Chalfont, PA 18914-1832

215-822-0600
Fax: 215-822-0662 film@rtgpkg.com
www.rtgpkg.com
Flexible Packaging Films consisting of Polypropylene, Polyethylene, Lidding, Forming, Printed, Laminations
Sales: Tom Cheatle
Estimated Sales: Below $5 Million
Number Employees: 10-19
Parent Co: Roberts Technology Group, Inc.

28121 RTI Inc

1325 Williams Dr
Marietta, GA 30066

770-590-4300
Fax: 770-590-4313 800-937-1290
info@internetRTI.com
Point of purchase and inventory software
Owner: James Clutter
Sales/Marketing Executive: Greg Waddell
Contact: Lane Alexander
alexander.lane@internetrti.com
Estimated Sales: $10-20 Million
Number Employees: 20-49

28122 RTI Laboratories

31628 Glendale St
Livonia, MI 48150-1827

734-422-5342
Fax: 734-422-5342 information@rtilab.com
www.rtilab.com
Laboratory facility specializing in environmental, chemical, metallurgical, and industrial hygiene analyses
President: Jerry Singh
CFO: Ralph Davis
VP: Fred Hoitash
Quality Control: Charles O'Bryan
Sales Director: Patricia Jennings
Number Employees: 20-49
Square Footage: 36000

28123 RTI Shelving Systems

40-19 80th Street
Elmhurst, NY 11373

212-279-0435
Fax: 212-465-1795 800-223-6210
info@rtishelving.com www.rtishelving.com
Manufacturer and exporter of steel filing systems, steel and wire shelving, racks, bins and storage systems
Owner: Bhim Motilal
Office Manager: Darryl Buyckes
Estimated Sales: $5-10 Million
Number Employees: 10-19

28124 RTS Packaging

250 N Mannheim Rd
Hillside, IL 60162-1835

708-338-2800
Fax: 708-338-2882 webmaster@rocktenn.com
www.rocktenn.com
Corrugated paper and fiberboard box partitions
Manager: Mary Sachs
CFO: Nancy Garner
Estimated Sales: $20-50 Million
Number Employees: 100-249
Parent Co: Sonoco Products Company

28125 RTS Packaging

869 State Route 12
Frenchtown, NJ 08825-4223

908-782-0505
Fax: 908-782-0583 www.rocktenn.com
Wine industry corrugated partitions
Manager: Jeff Connlain
Manager: Greg Lawrence
glawrence@rocktenn.com
Estimated Sales: $25-50 Million
Number Employees: 100-249

28126 RTS Packaging

250 N Mannheim Rd
Hillside, IL 60162-1835

708-338-2800
Fax: 708-338-2882 800-558-6984
webmaster@rocktenn.com
Wine industry fiber partitions
Manager: Mary Sachs
Manager: Betch Cambell
Estimated Sales: $20-50 Million
Number Employees: 100-249

28127 RTS Packaging

16 Washington Ave
Scarborough, ME 04074-8311

207-883-8921
Fax: 207-883-5189 www.rtspackaging.com
Packaging
General Manager: David Boudreau
Estimated Sales: $20-50 Million
Number Employees: 50-99

28128 RVS

5151 Allendale Lane
Taneytown, MD 21787-2155

410-756-2600
Fax: 410-756-6450 www.evapco.com
Architecture and engineering firm providing facility planning, design and construction services to the food and beverage industries.we ofer architecture planning and design and civil structural mechanical and electrical design formanufacturing warehouse and distribution facilities.
President: Bill Bartley
Number Employees: 5-9

28129 (HQ)RW Products

101 Heartland Blvd
Edgewood, NY 11717-8315

631-349-8400
Fax: 516-349-8407 800-345-1022
www.rwproducts.com
Retail displays, racks and fixtures
General Manager: Jon Scott
VP Sales: Martin Baum
Estimated Sales: $.5-1 million
Number Employees: 1-4

28130 RWH Packaging

PO Box 6335
Oakland, CA 94603-0335

510-535-0700
Fax: 510-535-0702
Wine industry packaging
President: Randy Haight
Estimated Sales: Below $5 Million
Number Employees: 10

28131 RWI Resources

3401 Old Wagon Rd
Marietta, GA 30062-5513

770-977-3950
Fax: 770-973-4299 866-545-4794
Developer and marketer of carbonated beverage
Estimated Sales: Below $500,000
Number Employees: 5-9

28132 RXI Silgan Specialty Plastics

541 Technology Dr
Triadelphia, WV 26059-2711

304-547-9100
Fax: 304-547-9200
silgan_sales@silganplastics.com
www.silganplastics.com
Manufacturer and exporter of plastic caps, jar covers, sifter and plug fitments and bottles; custom injection molding available
VP Engineering: Vice Exner
VP Sales: Tony Marceau
Operations Manager: Phil Sanderson
Estimated Sales: $36 Million
Number Employees: 100-249
Square Footage: 168400
Parent Co: Silgan Plastics
Type of Packaging: Consumer, Food Service, Private Label, Bulk
Other Locations:
  RXI Plastics
  Richmond VA
Brands:
  Cs Assembled

28133 Rabbeco

22900 Miles Rd
Cleveland, OH 44128

212-564-0664
Fax: 973-529-0224 mb@packlinecorp.com
www.packline.com
Automatic and semiautomatic filling, sealing and capping systems, cup filling and sealing, bag forming, filling and sealing, bottle lines, shrink wrapping machines, fillers for liquid and paste products
President: Michael Beilinson
Estimated Sales: $.5-1 million
Number Employees: 1-4

28134 Rabin Worldwide

731 Sansome St
2nd Floor
San Francisco, CA 94111

415-522-5700
Fax: 415-522-5701 info@rabin.com
www.rabin.com
Owner: Irving Rabin
Estimated Sales: $15 Million
Number Employees: 20-49

28135 Raburn

1060 Thorndale Ave
Elk Grove Vlg, IL 60007-6747

847-350-2229
Fax: 847-350-2657 www.ecolab.com
Manager: Mark Swisher
Estimated Sales: $50-100 Million
Number Employees: 50-99
Parent Co: ECOLAB

28136 Racine County Court Cmmssnr

730 Wisconsin Ave
Racine, WI 53403-1238

262-636-3181
Fax: 262-636-3689 800-242-4202
www.wicourts.gov
Labels including litho printed, pressure sensitive, die-cut and gummed; also, commercial printing services available
President: James A. Ladwig
Manager: Anisa Dunn
anisa.dunn@goracine.org
Estimated Sales: Below $5 Million
Number Employees: 10-19

28137 Racine Paper Box Manufacturing

3522 W Potomac Ave
Chicago, IL 60651

773-227-3900
Fax: 773-227-3983
Manufacturer and exporter of boxes including set-up, fancy and folding
President: Navnit Patel
Contact: Atul Patel
atul.patel@ipaksolutions.com
Estimated Sales: $1-2.5 Million
Number Employees: 10-19

28138 Racket Group

713 Walnut St
Kansas City, MO 64106-1615

816-283-0490
Fax: 816-842-8998 mail@racketgroup.com
www.racketgroup.com
Tableware for the airline catering industry
President and CFO: Joseph Hoagland
mail@michadamenities.com
Estimated Sales: $5-10 Million
Number Employees: 10-19

28139 Racks

7684 St. Andrews Avenue
San Diego, CA 92154

619-661-0987
Fax: 619-661-0988 www.racksinc.com
Point of Purchase displays.
President: Doug Wall
CFO: Don Wall
VP: Doug Wall
Sales: William Schiffman
Contact: Rick Kniffin
rkniffin@racksinc.com
Production Manager: Mark Kleffel
Estimated Sales: $20-50 Million
Square Footage: 100000

28140 Raco Mfg & Engineering Co
1400 62nd St
Emeryville, CA 94608-2099
510-658-6713
Fax: 510-658-3153 800-722-6999
sales@racoman.com www.alarmagent.com
Controlled atmosphere monitors, alarms, controls
and probes
President: Constance Brown
cbrown@racoman.com
VP Sales/Marketing: James Brown
Estimated Sales: $20-50 Million
Number Employees: 100-249
Brands:
  Chatterbox
  Verbatim

28141 Radcliffe System
Suite 305
Toronto, ON M2J 4R4
Canada
416-493-3844
Fax: 416-493-1616
Estimated Sales: $1-5 Million
Number Employees: 5-9

28142 Radding Signs
PO Box 4653
Springfield, MA 1101
413-736-5400
Fax: 413-736-1866
Illuminated and nonilluminated signs including cus-
tom made electric, office building, directional, ga-
rage and outdoor advertising
Estimated Sales: $1-2.5 Million
Number Employees: 10-19
Parent Co: Rador

28143 Rademaker USA
5218 Hudson Dr
Hudson, OH 44236-3738
330-650-2345
Fax: 330-656-2802 rademaker@rademakerusa.com
www.rademaker.com
President: Ronald Gates
rgates@rademaker.com
Vice President: William Palumbo
Estimated Sales: $5-10 Million
Number Employees: 10-19

28144 Radiant Industrial Solutions
2121 Brittmoore Rd # 3900
#3900
Houston, TX 77043-2227
713-972-0196
Fax: 713-974-0253 sales@radiantuv.com
www.radiantuv.com
Waste water management throught the use of ultravi-
olet light.
President: Troy Smith
Director Business Strategy: Mike Guettette
Manager: Collin Brack
cbrack@radiantuv.com
Technical Manager: John Shol
Number Employees: 10-19

28145 Radiation Processing Division
P.O.Box 5064
Parsippany, NJ 07054-6064
973-267-5660
Fax: 973-267-5667 800-442-1969
Manufacturer and exporter of radiation sanitation
and pathogen elimination equipment for the removal
of bacteria from raw materials and food ingedients
President: Robert Solotist
President: Bruce Welt PhD
Estimated Sales: $1-5 Million
Number Employees: 20-49
Square Footage: 120000
Parent Co: Alpha Omega Technology

28146 Radio Cap Company
1331 N Pine St
San Antonio, TX 78202-1219
210-472-1649
Fax: 800-766-4812
Advertising promotion caps
VP: Christopher Edelen
VP Sales: Eileen Guina
Estimated Sales: $1-5 Million
Number Employees: 1-4
Parent Co: Norwood Promotional Products

28147 Radio Frequency Co Inc
150 Dover Rd
Millis, MA 02054-1335
508-376-9555
Fax: 508-376-9944 rfc@radiofrequency.com
www.radiofrequency.com
Manufacturer and exporter of radio frequency
post-baking dryers and pasteurization equipment.
President: Tim Clark
tclark@radiofrequency.com
Estimated Sales: $5-10 Million
Number Employees: 20-49
Square Footage: 26
Parent Co: Radio Frequency Company
Brands:
  Macrowave

28148 Radius Display Products
800 Fabric Xpress Way
Dallas, TX 75234-7260
972-406-1221
Fax: 972-406-1321 888-322-7429
info@radiusdp.com www.radiusdp.com
Manufacturer and exporter of table skirting and
clips.
President: Darla Andrews
dandrews@radiusdisplay.com
CEO: Michelle Stacy
VP Sales: Sherry Day
Estimated Sales: $2.5-5 Million
Number Employees: 50-99
Brands:
  Omniclip Ii

28149 Rafael Soler
135 Walworth Avenue
White Plains, NY 10606-2720
914-761-4609
Fax: 914-683-3755 info@deprosa.dk
www.derprosa.es
Laminations, labels, acrylic and PVDC coatings,
bottle labels, food packing
President: Raphael Hernandez Soler

28150 Ragtime
4218 Jessup Rd
Ceres, CA 95307-9604
209-667-5525
Fax: 209-634-2667 ragtimewest@earthlink.net
www.ragtimewest.com
Manufacturer and exporter of coin and floppy disk
operated pianos, monkey organs, animated food dis-
pensers and dioramas and calliopes; importer of dec-
orative plastic pipe
Owner: Ken Caulkins
ken@ragtime.com
Manager: Glenn Kern
Estimated Sales: $1-2.5 Million
Number Employees: 5-9
Square Footage: 40000
Brands:
  Active Magnetics

**28151 Rahmann Belting & Industrial
Rubber Products**
3100 Northwest Blvd
Gastonia, NC 28052-1167
704-864-0308
Fax: 704-868-4651 888-248-8148
Manufacturer and exporter of industrial conveyors
and transmission belting including oriented nylon,
monofilament and food, etc
Owner: Ron Dayton
CEO: Ronald Dayton
Estimated Sales: $2.5-5 Million
Number Employees: 5-9
Square Footage: 60000

28152 Rahr Malting Co
800 1st Ave W
Shakopee, MN 55379-1148
952-445-1431
info@rahr.com
www.rahr.com
Malt and brewing supplies
CEO: Gary Lee
Contact: April Abbott
aabbott@rahr.com
Year Founded: 1847
Estimated Sales: $43.6 Million
Number Employees: 5-9
Type of Packaging: Bulk

28153 Railex Corp
8902 Atlantic Ave
Ozone Park, NY 11416-1497
718-845-5454
Fax: 718-738-1020 800-352-3244
tech@railexcorp.com www.railexcorp.com
Supplier and exporter of electric and stationary coat
and hat check equipment; also, garment racks
President: Abe Rutkovsky
railex@railexcorp.com
VP: Sam Rutkovsky
Sales: Bill Quirke
Estimated Sales: $10-20 Million
Number Employees: 20-49
Square Footage: 70000
Brands:
  Railex

28154 RainSoft Water Treatment System
2080 E. Lunt Ave
Elk Grove Vlg, IL 60007
847-437-9400
Fax: 847-437-1594 comments@rainsoft.com
www.rainsoft.com
Manufacturer and exporter of water treatment equip-
ment including filters, purifiers, reverse osmosis sys-
tems and ultraviolet
President: Robert Ruhstorfer
Commercial Department: Bob Krinner
Estimated Sales: $1-5 Million
Number Employees: 100-249
Square Footage: 280000
Brands:
  Amazon
  Classic Apollo
  P-12 Hydefiner
  Ultrefiner

28155 Rainbow Industrial Products
825 Morgantown Rd
Reading, PA 19607-9533
610-373-1400
Fax: 610-373-7448 800-426-5751
Manufactures modular plastic belt and flat top
chains and markets a full line of stainless/carbon
steel, case conveyor and multi-flex chains, custom
molded rubber inserts
President: Christopher Nigon
Estimated Sales: $5-10 Million
Number Employees: 500-999

28156 Rainbow Neon Sign Company
202 S Lockwood Dr
Houston, TX 77011-3198
713-923-2759
Fax: 713-923-2875
Advertising signs including neon, plastic and flex
face lighted
President: Louis Freund
VP/Secretary: Naida Freund
Estimated Sales: $500,000-$1 Million
Number Employees: 5-9
Square Footage: 18000

28157 Rainbow Sign Co
257 W 3300 S
Salt Lake City, UT 84115-3432
801-466-7856
Fax: 801-466-1144 www.rainbowsign.com
Neon signs
Owner/Sales: Vincent Coley
Owner/ Sales: Vince Coley
Office Manager: Barbara Barnes
Estimated Sales: $1-2.5 Million
Number Employees: 5-9

28158 Rairdon Dodge Chrysler Jeep
12828 NE 124th St
Kirkland, WA 98034-8309
425-821-1777
Fax: 425-814-3180
www.dodgechryslerjeepofkirkland.com
Manufacturer and exporter of checkstands and dis-
play fixtures
Owner: Jack Carroll
Director Sales: Ginny Hansen
Estimated Sales: $5-10 Million
Number Employees: 50-99
Square Footage: 680000

28159 Ralph L. Mason
8344 Patey Woods Rd
Newark, MD 21841
410-632-1766
Fax: 410-632-1142
Wooden pallets
VP: Tom Mason
Plant Manager: Bruce Wood
Estimated Sales: $1-5 Million
Number Employees: 10-19
Square Footage: 120000

28160 Ralph's Grocery Company
1014 Vine Street
Cincinnati, OH 45202-1100
310-884-9000
Fax: 310-884-2601 888-437-3496
www.ralphs.com
General groceries: bakery products, beverages,
meats, deli and seafood.
President: Donna Giordano
Contact: Darian Griffin
darian.griffin@ralphs.com
VP of Sales: Kenny Kimball
VP, Public Relations: Kendra Doyel
Estimated Sales: $100-500 Million
Number Employees: 500-999
Parent Co: The Kroger Company
Brands:
  Ralphs

28161 Ralphs Pugh Conveyor Rollers
3931 Oregon St
Benicia, CA 94510-1101
707-745-6363
Fax: 707-745-3942 800-486-0021
sales@ralphs-pugh.com www.ralphs-pugh.com
Manufacturer and exporter of rollers, idlers and
bearings for conveyors
President: William Pugh
williamg@ralphs-pugh.com
Vice President: Tom Anderson
Estimated Sales: $5-10 Million
Number Employees: 20-49

28162 Ram Equipment Co
W227N913 Westmound Dr
Waukesha, WI 53186-1700
262-513-1114
Fax: 262-513-1115 tiefmach@execpc.com
www.tiefmach.com
Manufacturer and exporter of baking, blending and
batching equipment, bins, control systems, enrobers,
extruders and feeders; manufacturer of custom,
pump feeding systems for pumping high viscosity
products for food and industrialapplications
President: James E Tiefenthaler
jtief@tiefmach.com
VP: Norman Searle
Estimated Sales: Less Than $500,000
Number Employees: 1-4
Number of Brands: 2
Number of Products: 20
Square Footage: 4800

28163 Ram Industries
PO Box 610
Erwin, TN 37650-0610
423-743-6126
Fax: 423-743-6128 800-523-3883
Heat sealed plastic and vinyl products including ad-
vertising novelties, bags, date code label pouches,
3-ring binders, menu covers and ticket, notepad and
guest check holders
VP: Keith Patton
Director Sales: Jack Degatis
Estimated Sales: $1-5 Million
Parent Co: Plasco Products

28164 Ram Machinery Corp
11 Cricket Ln
Burlington, CT 06013-1301
860-673-5511
Fax: 860-675-9419
miller@rammachinerycorp.com
Used packaging and production equipment
President: Richard Miller
Estimated Sales: $1-2.5 Million
Number Employees: 5-9

28165 Ramco Innovations Inc
1207 Maple St
West Des Moines, IA 50265-4497
515-225-6933
Fax: 515-225-6933 800-280-6933
www.ramcoi.com
President: Hank Norem
hnorem@ramcoinnovations.com
Estimated Sales: $10-20 Million
Number Employees: 20-49

28166 (HQ)Ramco Systems Corp
3150 US Highway 1 # 206
Lawrence Twp, NJ 08648-2420
609-620-4800
Fax: 609-620-4860 800-472-6461
www.ramco.com
Computer software services and prepackaged soft-
ware
Vice Chairman/Managing Director/CEO: P R
Venketrama Raja
CFO: K Ramachandran
Senior VP: Bivek Luthra
bivekluthra@rsc.ramco.com
Chief Marketing Officer: Barbara Angius Saxby
COO: Kamesh Ramamoorthly
Estimated Sales: $20.7 Million
Number Employees: 20-49
Other Locations:
  San Jose CA
  Frankfurt, Germany
  Central Milton, UK
  Basel, Switzerland
  New Delhi, India
  Malaysia, Asia
  Singapore, Asia
  Durban, South Africa
  Dubia, Middle East

28167 Ramondin USA Inc
2557 Napa Vly Corporate Dr # G
Suite G
Napa, CA 94558-6295
707-944-2277
Fax: 707-257-1408 www.ramondin.com
Wine industry capsules
Manager: Steve Galvan
Estimated Sales: $1-3 Million
Number Employees: 5-9

28168 Ramoneda Bros Stave Mill
13452 Rixeyville Rd
Culpeper, VA 22701
540-825-9166
Fax: 540-547-3271
Manufacturer and exporter of oak staves
Owner: Vincent Ramoneda
ramonedabros@aol.com
Partner: Vincent Ramoneda
Manager: Vincent Ramoneda
Estimated Sales: $5-10 Million
Number Employees: 5-9

28169 Ramsay Signs Inc
9160 SE 74th Ave
Portland, OR 97206-9345
206-623-3100
Fax: 503-777-0220 www.ramsaysigns.com
Neon and electrical indoor and outdoor advertising
signs
Owner: Darryl Paulsen
General Manager: Joe Gibson
VP: John Olds
Estimated Sales: Less Than $500,000
Number Employees: 1-4

28170 Ramsey Winch Co
4707 N Mingo Rd
Tulsa, OK 74117-5904
918-438-2760
Fax: 918-438-6888 info@ramsey.com
www.ramsey.com
Checkweighers, conveyor accesories including belt
tracking, conveyors and metal detecting
CEO: Bruce Barron
Chairman of the Board: Robert Heffron
Estimated Sales: $25-50 Million
Number Employees: 250-499

28171 Rancolio North America
8102 Lemont Rd # 1200
Woodridge, IL 60517-7773
630-427-1703
Fax: 630-493-4265 www.rancilio.com

VP: Glenn Surlet
Contact: Chris Gittens
cgittens@ranciliogroupna.com
Estimated Sales: $300,000-500,000
Number Employees: 1-4

28172 (HQ)Rand-Whitney Group LLC
1 Agrand St
Worcester, MA 01607-1699
508-791-2301
Fax: 508-792-1578 www.randwhitney.com
Paper, wooden and corrugated boxes and wooden
skids and crates; also, plastic foam fabricating and
molding
President: David Walsh
CEO: Edwin Davis
edavis@randwhitney.com
CEO: Peter Hamilton
Estimated Sales: $10-20 Million
Number Employees: 500-999

28173 (HQ)Rand-Whitney Group LLC
1 Agrand St
Worcester, MA 01607-1699
508-791-2301
Fax: 508-792-1578 joconnor@randwhitney.com
www.randwhitney.com
Corrugated boxes, containers, displays and protec-
tive packaging
President: Robert Kraft
CEO: Edwin Davis
edavis@randwhitney.com
CEO: Edwin Davis
Sales Manager: Jerry O'Connor
Estimated Sales: $20-50 Million
Number Employees: 500-999

28174 Rand-Whitney Group LLC
1 Agrand St
Worcester, MA 01607-1699
508-791-2301
Fax: 508-792-1578 www.randwhitney.com
Folding paper boxes, cartons and containers
CEO: Edwin Davis
edavis@randwhitney.com
Estimated Sales: H
Number Employees: 500-999
Parent Co: Kraft Group LLC

28175 Rand-Whitney Packaging Corp
166 Corporate Dr
Suite 200
Portsmouth, NH 03801-6815
508-791-2301
Fax: 603-822-7396 www.randwhitney.com
Corrugated containers
President/CEO: Edwin Davis
VP (Rand-Whitney): Dwight Hamlin
Contact: Beth Saengsour
beths@randwhitney.com
Operations Manager: Raymond Hey
Estimated Sales: Less Than $500,000
Number Employees: 1-4
Square Footage: 160000
Parent Co: Rand-Whitney Group LLC

28176 Randall Manufacturing Inc
722 N Church Rd
Elmhurst, IL 60126-1402
630-782-0001
Fax: 630-782-0003 800-323-7424
info@randallmfg.com www.randallmfg.com
Manufacturer and exporter of bulkheads for refriger-
ator trailer partitions, plastic strip curtains for cool-
ers and freezers and insulated pallet covers and
curtain walls
President: Fred Jevaney
fjevaney@randallmfg.com
CFO: Philip Pick
VP: Fred Jevaney
Number Employees: 50-99
Square Footage: 80000
Type of Packaging: Food Service, Bulk
Brands:
  Conservador
  Insul-Wall
  Tough One

28177 Randall Printing
707 Centre Street
Brockton, MA 02302-3310
508-588-3830
Fax: 508-588-3830
Labels, forms and booklets

Estimated Sales: Less than $500,000
Number Employees: 1-4

28178 Randell ManufacturingUnified Brands

252 South Coldwater Road
Weidman, MI 48893

Fax: 888-864-7636 888-994-7636
www.unifiedbrands.com

Stainless steel preparation tables, custom equipment, refrigerators, freezers, precise temperature solutions, equipment stands, and hot food tables.
Estimated Sales: $50-100 Million
Number Employees: 250-499
Parent Co: Dover Corporation
Brands:
  Rancraft
  Randell
  Ranserve

28179 Randware Industries

P.O.Box 414
Prospect Heights, IL 60070-0414

847-299-8884
Fax: 847-299-8885 info@randware.com
www.randware.com

Food display items including chafing dishes with logos
Manager: Neal Katz
Estimated Sales: $3-5 Million
Number Employees: 1-4
Brands:
  Chafer Shield

28180 Ranger Blade Manufacturing Company

PO Box 205
1561 South Main
Traer, IA 50675

Fax: 319-478-8298 800-377-7860
info@rangerblade.com

Household and professional metal cutlery including processing and packaging machinery blades
President: Rex Betts
CFO: Louis Rausch
Quality Control: Matt Devick
Sales Manager: Steve Droste
Estimated Sales: $5-10 Million
Number Employees: 20-49
Square Footage: 32000
Parent Co: Clearline Cutlery

28181 Ranger Tool Co Inc

5786 Ferguson Rd
Memphis, TN 38134-4533

901-213-0458
Fax: 901-386-8088 800-737-9999

Manufacturer and exporter of peelers which remove cellulose casing from frankfurters and sausages
President: Eleanor Kiss
Estimated Sales: $2.5-5 Million
Number Employees: 5-9
Brands:
  Apollo Peeler

28182 Rankin Delux

3245 Corridor Dr
Mira Loma, CA 91752-1030

951-685-0081
Fax: 951-685-0084 rankinone@aol.com
www.rankindelux.com

Broilers, griddles, hot plates, cheese melters, stock pot and oriental ranges, etc
President/CEO: Dick Jones
Chairman: William Rankin
VP: Peggy Jones
Manager: Virna Alcantara
rankinone@aol.com
Estimated Sales: $2.5-5 Million
Number Employees: 20-49

28183 Ranpak Corp

7990 Auburn Rd
Painesville, OH 44077-9701

440-354-4445
Fax: 440-639-2198 800-726-7257
inquiries@ranpak.com www.ranpak.com

Packaging, cushioning
President: David Gabrielsen
CEO: Dave Gabrielsen
dgabrielsen@ranpak.com
Estimated Sales: $20-50 Million
Number Employees: 100-249

28184 Ransco Industries

1655 Mesa Verde Avenue
Suite 250
Ventura, CA 93003-6518

805-487-7777
Fax: 805-486-7024

Industrial refrigeration and freezing equipment; also, design and construction services available
VP Product: Robert Briner
Marketing Manager: Taylor Hobson
Sales Manager: Lou Coppo
Production Manager: Jim Topp
Estimated Sales: $10-20 Million
Number Employees: 50-99

28185 Rapa Products (USA)

1 Depot Lane
Seabrook, NH 03874-4492

603-474-5508
Fax: 603-474-3919

Natural casings
Estimated Sales: $1-5 Million
Number Employees: 8

28186 Rapak

1201 Windham Pkwy # D
Suite D
Romeoville, IL 60446-1699

815-372-3670
Fax: 630-296-2195 www.rapak.com

Bag-in-Box liquid packaging systems for dairy, edible oil, fruits/purees, juices, liquid egg, post mix/syrup, sauces, water, wine
President: Kevin Grogan
kevin.gorgan@rapak.com
SVP: Paul Petriekis
Marketing/Sales Director: Pierre Ferrai
VP Sales: Joe Pranckus
Number Employees: 100-249
Square Footage: 121000
Parent Co: DS Smith Group

28187 Rapat Corp

919 Odonnel St
Hawley, MN 56549-4313

218-483-3344
Fax: 218-483-3535 800-325-6377
www.rapat.com

Manufacturer and exporter of material handling equipment including conveyors and conveyor belting
Owner: Thomas Sparrow
Sales Manager: Greg Deal
tsparrow@rapat.com
Estimated Sales: $10-20 Million
Number Employees: 50-99

28188 (HQ)Rapid Displays Inc

4300 W 47th St
Chicago, IL 60632-4404

773-927-5000
Fax: 773-927-6446 800-356-5775
info@rapiddisplays.com www.rapiddisplays.com

Manufacturer and designer of advertising point of purchase displays
President: David Abramson
dabramson@rapiddisplays.com
President: David Abramson
VP: Brian Mc Cormick
Quality Control: Jim Guadgnola
VP/Sales Manager: Pierre Pype
Estimated Sales: $20-50 Million
Number Employees: 100-249
Square Footage: 360000

28189 Rapid Industries Inc

4003 Oaklawn Dr
Louisville, KY 40219-2701

502-968-3645
Fax: 502-968-6331 800-787-4381
info@rapidindustries.com www.rapidi.com

Manufacturer, importer and exporter of conveyors including trolley, enclosed track, power, free and floor
President: Mary Sheets
Controller: Jansen Nally
Marketing Manager: Paul McDonald
Sales Manager: Walt Hiner
Estimated Sales: $20-50 Million
Number Employees: 50-99
Type of Packaging: Bulk

28190 Rapid Pallet

100 Chestnut St
Jermyn, PA 18433-1433

570-876-4000
Fax: 570-876-4002

Manufacturer and exporter of lumber pallets
President: John Conrad
conrad@aacr.org
Estimated Sales: $10-20 Million
Number Employees: 50-99

28191 Rapid Rack Industries

14421 Bonelli St
City of Industry, CA 91746

626-333-7225
Fax: 626-333-5265 800-736-7225
www.rapidrack.com

Racks and mobile aisle and mezzanine systems; importer of wire storage racks; exporter of wire and storage rack
CEO: William Marvin
CEO: Vaughn Sucevich
Marketing Director: Clara Banegas
VP Sales: Steve Painter
Contact: Margaret Andrade
m_andrade@haylorfinancial.com
Operations Manager: Rosemarie Kodarte
Production Manager: Alfredo Calderon Kodarte
Plant Manager: Ed Sledge
Purchasing Manager: Dennis Fachler
Estimated Sales: $30-50 Million
Number Employees: 250-499
Square Footage: 192000
Parent Co: Hampshire Equity Partners
Type of Packaging: Consumer

28192 Raque Food Systems

11002 Decimal Dr
Louisville, KY 40299-2420

502-267-9641
Fax: 502-267-2352 sales@raque.com
www.raque.com

Food processing equipment
President: Glenn Raque
VP: Ed Robinson
Director Marketing: Tim Kent
IT Executive: David Ross
dcross07@yahoo.com
Estimated Sales: $20-50 Million
Number Employees: 50-99

28193 Rasco Industries

730 Tower Drive
Hamel, MN 55340

763-478-5100
Fax: 763-478-5101 800-537-3802
www.rasco.com

Screen sectional loading dock doors used with existing commercial rolling, high, vertical, standard lift and side sliding doors; also, overhead screen door systems and service door screen inserts
VP/Sales Manager: Rick Brown
Inside Sales Manager: Victoria Scully
Estimated Sales: $3-6 Million
Number Employees: 22
Square Footage: 100000
Brands:
  The Bug Blocker

28194 Ratcliff Hoist Company

1655 Old County Rd
San Carlos, CA 94070-5205

650-595-3840
Fax: 650-595-5687

Material handling equipment including hoists
President: Bruce Ratcliff
ratcliffhoist@yahoo.com
Chairman: Ralph A Ratcliff
Estimated Sales: $1-2.5 Million
Number Employees: 10-19

28195 Rath Manufacturing Company

P.O.Box 389
Janesville, WI 53547

608-754-2222
Fax: 608-754-0889 800-367-7284

Manufacturer and exporter of stainless steel pipes and tubing
President: Harley Aplan
CEO: Michael G Schwartz
VP Sales: James Coenen
Estimated Sales: $50-100 Million
Number Employees: 100-249

28196 Rathe Productions
555 W 23rd Street
New York, NY 10011-1011
212-242-9000
Fax: 212-242-5676
Displays and exhibits
Contact: Ryan Peacock
rpeacock@rathe.com
Estimated Sales: $10-20 Million
Number Employees: 50-99

28197 Ratioflo Technologies
1284 Puerta Del Sol
San Clemente, CA 92673
949-369-2425
Fax: 949-369-2429 www.ratioflo.com
Fillers, pail lidders, and denesters
OWNER: Dale Tanner
Estimated Sales: Below $5 Million
Number Employees: 10
Number of Products: 5

28198 Rational Cooking Systems
895 American Lane
Schaumburg, IL 60173-4575
847-755-9583
Fax: 847-755-9584 888-320-7274
info@rationalusa.com
Manufacturer and importer of combination ovens
President: Peter Schon
Marketing Director: Werner Jochem
Sales Director: Robert Bratton
Contact: Gunter Blaschke
g.blaschke@rational-online.com
Estimated Sales: $2.5-5 Million
Number Employees: 20-49
Parent Co: Rational AG
Brands:
Clima Plus Combi
Climaplus Control
Rational Combi-Steamers

28199 Ray C. Sprosty Bag Company
323 E Liberty St
Wooster, OH 44691
330-264-8559
Fax: 330-263-4621
Film and bags including multi-wall, woven polypropylene, burlap, cotton and paper
President: Ray C Sprosty Iii
CFO: Pam Farthing
Quality Control: Tom Catamzarite
General Manager: Tom Catanzarite
Estimated Sales: $10-20 Million
Number Employees: 10-19
Square Footage: 30000

28200 Ray-Craft
2067 W 41st St
Cleveland, OH 44113
216-651-3330
Fax: 216-651-8714
Manufacturer and exporter of advertising novelties and promotional materials
President: Thomas Topp
Office Manager: Agnes Milter
Estimated Sales: $500,000-$1 Million
Number Employees: 9

28201 (HQ)Raymond Corp
22 S Canal St
Greene, NY 13778
607-656-2311
Fax: 607-656-9005 800-235-7200
www.raymondcorp.com
Manufacturer and exporter of electric forklift trucks
President/ Operations: Michael G Field
Chief Financial Officer: Edward J Rompala
VP, General Counsel: Lou Callea
EVP Sales & Marketing: Timothy Combs
VP Sales: Gary Kirchner
EVP, Human Resources: Stephen E VanNostrand
Vice President, Distribution Development: Patrick McManus
Estimated Sales: $130,000
Number Employees: 1000-4999
Square Footage: 1000000

28202 Rayne Sign Co
813 S Adams Ave
Rayne, LA 70578-5626
337-334-4276
Fax: 337-334-4263 www.rayneplasticsigns.com
Plastic signs including illuminated outdoor

President: Hilman Meche
hilman@rayneplasticsigns.com
Secretary: Verline Meche
Manager: Blaine Meche
Estimated Sales: $1-2.5 Million
Number Employees: 5-9

28203 Raypak Inc
2151 Eastman Ave
Oxnard, CA 93030-5194
805-278-5300
Fax: 805-278-5489 www.raypak.com
Manufacturer and exporter of water heating equipment including boosters
Vice President: Michael Sentovich
msentovich@raypak.com
VP: Louis Falzer
Number Employees: 250-499
Square Footage: 235000
Parent Co: Rheem
Other Locations:
Raypak
Victoria

28204 Raypress Corp
380 Riverchase Pkwy E
Hoover, AL 35244-1813
205-989-3731
Fax: 205-989-7203 800-423-3731
sales@raypress.com www.raypress.com
Pressure sensitive labels and tags
President: Thomas Ray
tray@raypress.com
Estimated Sales: $5-10 Million
Number Employees: 20-49

28205 (HQ)Raytek Corporation
P.O.Box 1820
Santa Cruz, CA 95061-1820
831-458-1110
Fax: 831-425-4561 800-866-5478
solutions@raytek.com www.raytek.com
Monitor hot and cold holding, reheating, cooling, and storage temperature instantly in steam tables, warming ovens, freezers, display cases and coolers with the new Raytek Mini Temperature Food Safety infrared thermometer
President: Carl Pickard
VP: Jim Love
Marketing: Fernando Lisboa
Sales: Bob Bader
Public Relations: Kate McGuire
Estimated Sales: $20-50 Million
Number Employees: 100-249
Number of Brands: 1
Type of Packaging: Private Label

28206 Raytheon Co
870 Winter St
Waltham, MA 02451-1449
781-522-3000
Fax: 781-860-2172 www.raytheon.com
Manufacturer and exporter of dehydration equipment for sugar, minerals, chemicals, corn and grain; also, evaporators, vacuum pans, dryers, crystallizers, granulators and coolers; engineering design services available
Chief Executive Officer: Thomas A. Kennedy
tkennedy@raytheon.com
SVP and Chief Financial Officer: David C. Wajsgras
Senior Vice President: Keith J. Peden
Estimated Sales: Over $1 Billion
Number Employees: 10000+
Square Footage: 1200000
Brands:
Stearns-Roger

28207 Razor Edge Systems
303 N 17th Ave E
Ely, MN 55731-1853
218-365-6419
Fax: 218-365-5360 800-541-1458
sales@razoredgesystems.com
www.razoredgesystems.com
Cutting and boning devices, sharpening machines and services, general packinghouse equipment, maintenance, sharpening and overhaul equipment
CEO: Eddie Bravo
eddieb@razoredgesystems.com
Service Technician: Jim Dally
Sales/Service Representative: Robert Sanders
Manager: Joann O'Reilly
Estimated Sales: Less Than $500,000
Number Employees: 1-4

28208 Rea UltraVapor
665 Tradewind Drive
Unit 10
Ancaster, ON L9G 4V5
Canada
905-572-0946
Fax: 905-304-3067 800-323-3865
mail@ultravapor.com www.ultravapor.com
Food equipment sanitation and infection control.

28209 Read Products Inc
3615 15th Ave W
Seattle, WA 98119-1392
206-283-2510
Fax: 206-282-8339 800-445-3416
info@cuttingboards.com
www.sagecuttingsurfaces.com
Manufacturer and exporter of food preparation cutting boards and tools
President: Charles R Read
cread@cuttingboard.com
Marketing Manager: Chuck Read
Inside Sales/Production Manager: Robert Read
Estimated Sales: $5-10 Million
Number Employees: 10-19
Square Footage: 80000
Type of Packaging: Food Service
Brands:
Read Woodfiber Laminate

28210 Readco Kurimoto LLC
460 Grim Ln
York, PA 17406-7949
717-848-2801
Fax: 717-848-2811 800-395-4959
readco@readco.com www.readco.com
Manufacturer and exporter of containerized batch and continuous processing mixers
President: David Sieglitz
Manager: Ce Tyson
gtyson@readco.com
Estimated Sales: $5-10 Million
Number Employees: 20-49
Brands:
Cbm

28211 Reading Bakery Systems Inc
380 Old West Penn Ave
Robesonia, PA 19551-8903
610-693-5816
Fax: 610-693-5512 info@readingbakery.com
www.readingbakery.com
Manufacturer and exporter of extruders, cookers, topical seasoning applicators, multifuel ovens, guillotine dough cutters, dough handling systems and biscuit, cookie and cracker sheeters and laminators
President: Joseph Zaleski
EVP/ CFO: Chip Czulada
Director of Engineering: Tremaine Hartranft
Director, Science & Innovation Center: Ken Zvoncheck
VP, Sales & Marketing: David Kuipers
VP of Sales: Shawn Moye
Human Resources Manager: Roseann Reinhold
Vice President of Operations: Travis Getz
Estimated Sales: $10-20 Million
Number Employees: 50-99
Square Footage: 62000

28212 (HQ)Reading Box Co Inc
250 Blair Ave
Reading, PA 19601-1906
610-372-7411
Fax: 610-372-2143
Wooden boxes
President: Brent Atkins
Estimated Sales: Below $5 Million
Number Employees: 10-19

28213 Reading Plastic Fabricators
94 Dries Rd # A
Reading, PA 19605-9225
610-926-3245
Fax: 610-926-7026 www.readingplastic.com
Custom fabricated plastic wear materials including tanks, hoods, covers and guards; also, clear acrylic and polycarbonate displays and nylon and derlin conveyor parts
President: Tom Funk
Quality Control Manager: Kenny Williams
National Sales Manager: Patty Alagna
HR Controller: Tracie Smith
General Manager: Tim Long
Office Manager: Susan Laird

Estimated Sales: $2.5-5 Million
Number Employees: 10-19
Square Footage: 20000

28214 Reading Technologies Inc
1031 Macarthur Rd
Reading, PA 19605-9402
610-372-9200
Fax: 610-372-1984 800-521-9200
info@driair.com www.rti-pbe.com
President: Paul Flynn
paul@briair.com
Estimated Sales: $3-5 Million
Number Employees: 10-19

28215 Ready Access
1815 Arthur DriveWest
Chicago, IL 60185
630-876-7766
Fax: 630-876-7767 800-621-5045
ready@ready-access.com www.ready-access.com
Manufacturer and exporter of pass-thru windows
and air curtain systems for fast food establishments
President: John Radek
CFO: Robert McKeever
R & D: Scott Hammac
Marketing/Sales/Public Relations: Kristy Rivera
Sales Director: Vince Asta
Operations/Production: Bob McKeever
Estimated Sales: $5-10 Million
Number Employees: 20-49
Square Footage: 70000

28216 Ready White
532 Main St # 4
Holyoke, MA 01040-5647
413-534-4864
Fax: 413-534-4864
Wiping rags
Owner: Leon E Barlow
Estimated Sales: Less than $500,000
Number Employees: 1-4

28217 Rebel Green
1317 Towne Square Rd
Mequon, WI 53092
262-240-9992
Fax: 262-241-5054 ali@rebelgreen.com
www.rebelgreen.com
Food sanitation equipment
Owner: Melina Marcus
Operations Manager: Kristina Nosbisch
Estimated Sales: Under $500,000
Number Employees: 2-10
Brands:
Rebel Green

28218 Rebel Stamp & Sign Co
307 Choctaw Dr
Baton Rouge, LA 70805-7653
225-387-4634
Fax: 225-344-1218 800-860-5120
orders@rebelstamp.com www.rebelstamp.com
Marking devices including stamps, daters, etc.; also,
interior and exterior office signage including name
plates, name badges, etc
President: Lewis Roeling
orders@rebelstamp.com
Estimated Sales: $500,000-$1 Million
Number Employees: 5-9
Square Footage: 12000
Brands:
Royal Mark

28219 Recco International
3940 Platt Springs Rd
West Columbia, SC 29170-1606
803-356-4003
Fax: 803-356-4439 800-334-3008
sales@reccointernational.com
www.reccointernational.com
Manufacturer and exporter of printed labels and
tapes
Owner: John W Etters
john@reccointernational.com
General Manager: Craig Hall
Estimated Sales: $20-50 Million
Number Employees: 20-49

28220 Rechner Electronics Industries
8651 Buffalo Ave # 3
Niagara Falls, NY 14304-4382
716-283-8744
Fax: 716-283-2127 800-644-1756
service@htmsensors.com www.htmsensors.com
Supplier of sensing devices
Owner: Ed Figarski
edf@htmsensors.com
Vice President: Arthur Ramsay
Estimated Sales: Less Than $500,000
Number Employees: 1-4

28221 Red Diamond Coffee & Tea
400 Park Ave
Moody, AL 35004
800-292-4651
qcdept@reddiamond.com www.reddiamond.com
Coffee, tea pods and coffee brewers.
VP, Sales Development: John Padgett
VP, Manufacturing: Joe George
Year Founded: 1906
Estimated Sales: $45.9 Million
Number Employees: 100-249
Square Footage: 195000
Type of Packaging: Consumer, Food Service, Private Label, Bulk
Brands:
Red Diamond Coffee & Tea

28222 Red Kap Industries
P.O.Box 140995
Nashville, TN 37214-0995
615-565-5000
Fax: 615-565-5284 www.vfc.com
Uniforms
Vice President of Corporate Relations: Cindy
Knoebel
Account Executive: Ray Hoff
Director of Corporate Communications: Carole
Crosslin
Estimated Sales: $20-50 Million
Number Employees: 250-499
Brands:
Red Kap

28223 (HQ)Red Lion Controls Inc
20 Willow Springs Cir
York, PA 17406-8473
717-767-6511
Fax: 717-764-0839 www.redlion.net
A range of control devices that include process measurement and control, and digital measurement and
control
President: Sandy Albright
sandya@redlion-controls.com
Development: Vincent Paolizzi
Sales Director: George Simok
Estimated Sales: $20-$50 Million
Number Employees: 100-249
Square Footage: 100000

28224 Red River Lumber Company
2959 Saint Helena Highway N
Saint Helena, CA 94574-9703
707-963-1251
Fax: 707-963-3142
Manufacturer and exporter of redwood boxes
Estimated Sales: $5-10 Million
Number Employees: 20-49

28225 Red Star BioProducts
433 E Michigan Street
Milwaukee, WI 53202-5104
414-347-3936
Fax: 414-347-3912 800-528-3388
Number Employees: 50-99

28226 Red Valve Co Inc
600 N Bell Ave # 200
Carnegie, PA 15106-4315
412-279-0044
Fax: 412-279-7878 valves@redvalve.com
www.redvalve.com
A complete line of pinch valves and control valves
for use in the food industry; aeration and sparging
products, flexible connectors, and instrument protection devices
President: Chris Raftis
craftis@redvalve.com
Chairman: Spiros G Raftis
Marketing Manager: David Schneider
Estimated Sales: $20-50 Million
Number Employees: 100-249

Type of Packaging: Bulk

28227 Red-Ray Manufacturing Co Inc
10 County Line Rd # 22
Suite 22
Branchburg, NJ 08876-6009
908-722-0040
Fax: 908-722-2535 burners@red-ray.com
www.red-ray.com
Gas-fired and infrared process burners
President: Thomas Bannos
toneal@red-ray.com
Chairman of the Board: Robert S Adelson
Vice President, Product & Applications M: Tim
O'Neal
Applications Engineering: Mike Strand
Controller: Jorge Acosta
Estimated Sales: $5-10 Million
Number Employees: 10-19

28228 Reddi-Pac
215 W Church Rd
Suite 112
King of Prussia, PA 19406-3203
610-265-1827
Fax: 610-992-1407 www.naturalfertilitycenter.com
Laminated and formed paperboard
Owner: Meredith L Murphy

28229 Redding Pallet Inc
5323 Eastside Rd
Redding, CA 96001-4534
530-241-6321
Fax: 530-241-3475 www.redding.com
Manufacturer and exporter of hardwood and softwood pallets
President: Don Lincoln
Estimated Sales: $1-5 Million
Number Employees: 10-19

28230 Redex Packaging Corporation
860 E State Pkwy
Schaumburg, IL 60173-4529
847-882-9500
Fax: 847-882-9570

28231 Redi-Call Inc
5655 Riggins Ct # 22
Reno, NV 89502-6554
775-331-0183
Fax: 775-331-2730 800-648-1849
sales@redi-callusa.com www.redi-callusa.com
Manufacturer, importer and exporter of stainless
steel cup and lid dispensers, condiment holders for
bars, circular wheel check holders for restaurant
kitchens, stainless steel pump units, squeeze bottles,
waitress/waiter paging/callstations, etc
President: Melinda James
VP: Eric Seltzer
Purchasing Agent: Dave Schankin
Estimated Sales: Less Than $500,000
Number Employees: 1-4
Square Footage: 80000
Brands:
Redi-Call
Speed-Rak
Top O' Cup

28232 Redi-Print
49 Mahan St
Unit B
West Babylon, NY 11704
631-491-6373
Fax: 631-491-6372 rediprint1@aol.com
Manufacturer and exporter of pre-printed menu paper and menu designing software
President: Tom Vlahakis
Estimated Sales: $300,000-500,000
Number Employees: 10
Square Footage: 5000

28233 Redicon Corporation
2824 Woodlawn Ave NW
Canton, OH 44708-1424
330-477-2100
Fax: 330-477-2101
Systems supplier for beverage and food can manufacturers: complete systems for draw, redraw, cans,
shell (lid) systems for beverage cans, end systems
for CWI cans, die sets for existing systems; both low
and high volume requirements
Owner: Tracee Mc Afee-Gates

28234 Redlake Imaging Corporation
11633 Sorrento Valley Road
San Diego, CA 92121-1039
858-481-8182
Fax: 858-792-3179 800-462-4307
Packaging production, manufacturing, inspection
Estimated Sales: $10.5 Million
Number Employees: 20-49

28235 Redlake MASD
6295 Ferris Sq
Suite A
San Diego, CA 92121-3248
858-481-8182
Fax: 858-350-9390 800-462-4307
President: Stephen Ferrell
Contact: Mary Hardison
mhardison@red-lake.com
Estimated Sales: $15-20 Million
Number Employees: 100-250

28236 Redwood Vintners
12 Harbor Dr
Novato, CA 94945-3507
415-892-6949
Fax: 415-892-7469 www.vinarium-usa.com
Distribution and marketing of wines
Sales Contact: Charles Daniels
Estimated Sales: $20-50 Million
Number Employees: 50-99
Brands:
    Redwood Vintners

28237 Reed & Barton Food Service
144 West Brittania Street
Taunton, MA 02780
508-824-6611
Fax: 508-822-7269 800-797-9675
Flatware and holloware
President/Chief Executive Officer: Timothy Riddle
Manager: Jill Pedro
VP, Finance/CFO/Treasurer/Controller: Stephen Normandine
Vice President, Information Technology: Paul Bartlet
SVP, Sales & Marketing: Joe D'Allessandro
Director, Sales: Angie Miller
Contact: John Alakel
jalakel@reedandbarton.com
Director, Purchasing & Planning: Rocco Davanzo
Estimated Sales: $25 Million
Number Employees: 98
Number of Brands: 5
Square Footage: 500000
Parent Co: Reed & Barton Silversmiths
Type of Packaging: Food Service

28238 Reed Ice
Lincolnton, GA
706-359-3127
Fax: 706-359-5465 800-927-9612
reedice@nu-z.net www.reedice.com
Manufacturer, wholesaler and distributor of ice;
serving the food service market.
Owner: Talmadge Reed
Estimated Sales: $20-50 Million
Number Employees: 10-19
Type of Packaging: Private Label, Bulk

28239 Reed Oven Co
1720 Nicholson Ave
Kansas City, MO 64120-1453
816-842-7446
Fax: 816-421-0422 www.reedovenco.com
Manufacturer and exporter of revolving shelf and
rack ovens, proofers, retarders, fermentation rooms
and steam cabinets
President: Kay Davies
reedoven@mindspring.com
Marketing Director/ IT Supervisor: Chris Davies
Operations: Brad Mitchell
Administrative Assistant: Linda Zeller
Plant Manager/ Engineer: Tim Davies
Purchasing Manager: Linda Zeller
Estimated Sales: $2.5-5 Million
Number Employees: 10-19
Square Footage: 72000
Brands:
    Reed

28240 Reef Industries Inc
9209 Almeda Genoa Rd
Houston, TX 77075-2339
713-507-4200
Fax: 713-507-4295 800-231-6074
ri@reefindustries.com www.reefindustries.com
Reinforced film laminates and plastics.
Owner: Phillip Cameron
Vice President: Tameka Crawford
tamekacrawford@crossmark.com
Sales Manager: Jeff Garza
Number Employees: 100-249
Brands:
    Armorlon
    Banner Guard
    Griffolyn
    Permalon
    Roll-A-Sign
    Terra Tape

28241 Reelcraft Industries Inc
2842 E Business 30
Columbia City, IN 46725-8451
260-248-8188
Fax: 260-248-2605 800-444-3134
reelcraft@reelcraft.com www.reelcraft.com
Manufacturer and exporter of industrial-grade hose,
cord and cable reels, including stainless steel.
President: Walter Sterneman
wsterneman@reelcraft.com
Estimated Sales: Over $50 Million
Number Employees: 100-249
Square Footage: 130000
Type of Packaging: Consumer, Food Service

28242 Reeno Detergent & Soap Company
9421 Midland Boulevard
Saint Louis, MO 63114-3327
314-429-6078
Fax: 314-429-6078
Manufacturer, importer and exporter of powder and
liquid laundry detergents and industrial cleaners
President: Colleen Trotter
VP Sales: Tim Trotter
VP Purchasing: Brad Trotter
Estimated Sales: $1-2.5 Million
Number Employees: 5-9
Brands:
    Borax-Splash
    Borax-Sudz
    Woolmaster

28243 Rees Inc
405 S Reed Rd
Fremont, IN 46737-2129
260-495-9811
Fax: 260-495-2186 sales@reesinc.com
www.reesinc.com
Manufacturer and exporter of industrial control
switches including cable, palmbutton and stop-start
President: Daniel Breeden
db@reesinc.com
Estimated Sales: $1-5 Million
Number Employees: 10-19
Square Footage: 70000

28244 Reese Enterprises Inc
16350 Asher Ave E
Rosemount, MN 55068-6000
651-423-1126
Fax: 651-423-2662 800-328-0953
info@reeseusa.com www.reeseusa.com
Manufacturer, importer and exporter of plastic doors
and door strips, aluminum roll-up mats, aluminum
stair treads, floor mats and grates, weatherstrips and
thresholds
President: Jim Beitzell
beitzell@reeseusa.com
National Sales/Marketing Manager: Edward Green
Estimated Sales: $10-20 Million
Number Employees: 1-4
Number of Products: 4
Square Footage: 160000
Parent Co: Astro Plastics

28245 Reeve Store Equipment Co
9131 Bermudez St
Pico Rivera, CA 90660-4507
562-949-2535
Fax: 562-949-3862 800-927-3383
info@reeveco.com www.reeveco.com
Manufacturer and exporter of point of purchase displays, tags, card holders and fixtures

President: John Frackelton
COO: Jim Thompson
jthompson@reeve.com
Manager Sales/Marketing: Robert Frackelton
Estimated Sales: $20-50 Million
Number Employees: 50-99
Square Footage: 160000

28246 Reeves Enterprises
1350 Palomares St # A
La Verne, CA 91750-5230
909-392-9999
Fax: 909-392-0124 www.californialocker.com
Store fixtures; also, woodworking services available
President and CFO: Dennis Reeves
dennis@dreevesinc.com
Accounting: Michelle Scherer
Vice President: Brad Reeves
Engineering: Al Gonzaga
Sales: Joe Greco
Estimated Sales: Below $5,000,000
Number Employees: 5-9

28247 Refcon
220 Route 70
Medford, NJ 8055
609-714-2330
Fax: 609-714-2331
Manufacturer and exporter of curved display cases
for candy, baked goods, deli meat, fish and poultry
President: Herman Jakubowski
Manager/Manufacturing: Len Pushkantser
Engineer: Rapael Colon
Estimated Sales: $3-5 Million
Number Employees: 20-49
Square Footage: 88000

28248 Refinishing Touch
9350 Industrial Trace
Alpharetta, GA 30004
770-751-7227
Fax: 770-475-4782 800-523-9448
sales@therefinishingtouch.com
www.therefinishingtouch.com
Firm providing refinishing and refurbishing services
for furniture
Founder, President: Mario Insenga
National Sales Manager: Roberta Bernhardt
Contact: Amber Coelho
amberc@therefinishingtouch.com
Estimated Sales: $500,000-$1 Million
Number Employees: 5-9

28249 Reflectronics
3881 Leighton Ln
Lexington, KY 40515
888-415-0441
Fax: 888-415-0442 info@reflectronics.com
www.reflectronics.com
Optical sensors for process monitoring and control
Estimated Sales: A
Number Employees: 2
Number of Products: 2

28250 Reflex International
6624 Jimmy Carter Boulevard
Norcross, GA 30071-1727
770-729-8909
Fax: 770-729-8805 800-642-7640
Point of purchase software, touch screen monitors,
peripheral printers, mag card readers, kiosk cabinets,
scanners and rack mounted open and close chassis
displays
Marketing Director: John Dodrill
Sales Manager: Bryan Graves
Estimated Sales: $5-10 Million
Number Employees: 45
Square Footage: 180000
Parent Co: CTX International

28251 Refractron TechnologiesCorp
5750 Stuart Ave
Newark, NY 14513-9798
315-331-6222
Fax: 315-331-7254 sales@refractron.com
www.refractron.com
Manufacturer, importer and exporter of advanced
porous ceramic filters including water, process, gas,
micro, cross-flow, ceramic membrane, air, etc.; also,
diffusers including liquid and gas

Owner: Bob Stanton
CFO: Darrell Johanneman
Director R & D: Gregg Crume
VP, Sales & Marketing: Adam Osekoski
bstanton@refractron.com
Estimated Sales: $10-20 Million
Number Employees: 50-99
Square Footage: 130000
Type of Packaging: Private Label
Brands:
  Durasieve
  Refractite
  Solidome

28252 Refrigerated Design Tech
1808 Fm 66
Waxahachie, TX 75167-5507
972-938-1100
Fax: 972-937-0970 800-736-9518
randall@rdtonline.com
Custom made refrigeration equipment and systems
President: Randall Dyess
randall@rdtonline.com
Quotations: Brent Dyess
Purchasing: Jim Wright
Estimated Sales: $2.5-5 Million
Number Employees: 10-19
Parent Co: RJS Company

28253 Refrigerated Warehouse Marketing Group
PO Box 530
La Verne, CA 91750-0530
909-625-4512
Fax: 909-625-4612

28254 Refrigerated Warehousing
198 High Trail Vista Cir
Jasper, GA 30143
770-894-4012
Fax: 706-692-3749 800-873-2008
dshine@rwizero.com www.rwizero.com
Designer and constructor of refrigeration warehouses and processing facilities
President: Dennis M. Shine
Estimated Sales: $1-2.5 Million
Number Employees: 1-4

28255 Refrigeration Design & Svc
14 Union Hill Rd
Conshohocken, PA 19428-2727
267-316-0800
Fax: 610-834-0807 www.refrigerationdesign.com
President: Micheal Zion
Estimated Sales: $10-20 Million
Number Employees: 10-19

28256 Refrigeration Engineering
3123 Wilson Dr NW
Grand Rapids, MI 49534-7565
616-453-2441
Fax: 616-453-0750 800-968-3227
www.hussmann.com
Commercial refrigeration equipment including cases and walk-in coolers; also, sales and services available
Manager: John Atsma
Manager: Dave Mulka
dave_mulka@hussmann.com
Parts Manager: Carl Boltz
Estimated Sales: $10-20 Million
Number Employees: 10-19

28257 (HQ)Refrigeration Research
525 N 5th St
PO Box 869
Brighton, MI 48116-1293
810-227-1151
Fax: 810-227-3700 info@refresearch.com
www.refresearch.com
Manufacturer and exporter of component parts for commercial refrigeration systems
Vice President: Michael Ramalia
mramalia@refresearch.com
Vice President: M Ramalia
Estimated Sales: $5-10 Million
Number Employees: 100-249
Type of Packaging: Bulk

28258 Refrigeration Systems Company
1770 Genessee Ave
Columbus, OH 43211
614-263-0913
Fax: 614-263-6660 columbus@rsc-gc.com

President: Robert Appleton
CEO: Tom Leighty
Contact: Keith Agler
k.agler@rsc-gc.com
Estimated Sales: $10-20 Million
Number Employees: 50-99

28259 Refrigeration Technology
595 Portal Street
Cotati, CA 94931-3023
707-792-1934
Fax: 707-792-1417 800-834-2232
Wine industry refrigeration units

28260 Refrigerator Manufacturers LLC
17018 Edwards Rd
Cerritos, CA 90703-2422
562-926-2006
Fax: 562-926-2007 sales@rmi-econocold.com
Manufacturer, importer and exporter of walk-in cold storage rooms and environmental chambers
President: Lawrence Jaffe
VP: Leo Lewis
Contact: Tony Bedy
tbedy@airdyne.com
Estimated Sales: $10-20 Million
Number Employees: 5-9
Square Footage: 80000
Brands:
  Econocold
  Rmi

28261 Refrigiwear Inc
54 Breakstone Dr
Dahlonega, GA 30533-7603
706-973-5000
Fax: 706-864-5898 800-645-3744
keepmewarm@refrigiwear.com
www.refrigiwear.com
Manufacturer and exporter of insulated and protective work clothing, head, hand, and footwear, thermal insulated blankets and carts and pallet covers
President: Ronald Breakstone
rbreakstone@refrigiwear.com
Vice President: Mark Silberman
Quality Control: Kate Bishop
Marketing: Kristy Chrisciaske
VP Sales: Don Byerly
Vice President/Operations: Scotty Depriest
Estimated Sales: $25 Million
Number Employees: 100-249
Square Footage: 80000
Brands:
  Iron Tuff
  Refrigiwear
  Storm Trac
  Weatherguard

28262 Refrigiwear Inc
54 Breakstone Dr
Dahlonega, GA 30533-7603
706-973-5000
Fax: 706-864-5898 800-645-3744
customerservice@refrigiwear.com
www.refrigiwear.com
President/CFO: Ronald Breakstone
rbreakstone@refrigiwear.com
Vice President: Scotty Depriest
Marketing Manager: Kate Bishop
Chief Operating Officer: Mark Silberman
Estimated Sales: $10-20 Million
Number Employees: 100-249

28263 Refrigue USA
3845 Shopton Rd
Suite 350
Charlotte, NC 28217-3030
704-347-1511
Fax: 704-347-1448
Safety equipment and apparel

28264 Regal Box Corp
923 E Garfield Ave
Milwaukee, WI 53212-3494
414-562-5890
Fax: 414-562-0341
Corrugated boxes
President: John Schwartz
Estimated Sales: Below $5 Million
Number Employees: 1-4

28265 Regal Custom Fixture Company
22 Burrs Rd., Bldg. C
PO Box 446
Westampton, NJ 08060-0446
609-261-3323
Fax: 609-261-4929 800-525-3092
Manufacturer and exporter of display cases including bakery, deli and candy
VP: Mike Rainbolt
National Sales Manager: Shawn Adair
Number Employees: 20-49
Type of Packaging: Food Service
Brands:
  Regal

28266 Regal Equipment Inc
4171 State Route 14
Ravenna, OH 44266-8739
330-325-9000
Fax: 330-325-7900 sales@regalequipment.com
www.regalequipment.com
Dealer of used and rebuilt cutters, dicers, blanchers, centrifuges grinders, and other food processing equipment
President: Kenneth Regal
Estimated Sales: $1-3 Million
Number Employees: 5-9

28267 Regal Manufacturing Company
5438 W Roosevelt Road
Chicago, IL 60644-1495
773-921-3071
Fax: 773-921-3076
Metal and wooden bar stools and dining chairs
President: Gerald Saviano
Contact: D Lund
d@regalmfg.com
Estimated Sales: $5-10 Million
Number Employees: 20-49
Square Footage: 70000

28268 Regal Pinnacle Integrations
220 Route 70
Medford, NJ 08055-9522
609-714-2330
Fax: 609-714-2331 www.rpiindustries.com
President: Peter C Palko
pcpalko@rpiindustries.com
Estimated Sales: $5-10 Million
Number Employees: 100-249

28269 Regal Plastic Company
5310 Canterbury Road
Mission, KS 66205-2611
816-483-3040
Fax: 816-483-7948 800-852-1556
Thermoformed FDA approved tote boxes and freezer spacers
President: A Bashor
CFO: J Streeter
VP Sales: L Haber
Plant Manager: Doug Meyer
Estimated Sales: $50-100 Million
Number Employees: 50-99

28270 Regal Plastic Supply Co
1500 Burlington St
Kansas City, MO 64116-3815
816-471-6390
Fax: 816-221-5822 800-444-6390
jnorman@regalplastic.com www.regalplastic.com
Acrylic items including food containers, store fixtures, advertising signs and name plates
President: Harry R Greenwald
CEO: Enzo Castelli
Manager: Shawn Slavik
shawn@regalplastic.com
Estimated Sales: $1-2.5 Million
Number Employees: 20-49
Square Footage: 10000

28271 Regal Power Transmission Solutions
7120 New Buffington Rd
Florence, KY 41042
859-342-7900
www.regalpts.com
Conveying products: motorized and traditional conveyor pulleys, conveyor modules, module plastic belts, conveying chain. Bearing products: beverage bearings, high temperature bearings
CEO: Mark Gliebe

Estimated Sales: $164 Million
Number Employees: 1000-4999
Number of Brands: 16

28272 (HQ)Regal Ware Inc
1675 Reigle Dr
Kewaskum, WI 53040-8923

262-626-2121
Fax: 262-626-8565 www.regalware.com
Manufacturer, importer and exporter of frying and
sauce pans, coffee makers and urns
President/CEO: Jeffery Reigle
Chairman: James Reigle
SVP/Chief Financial Officer: Gerald Koch
SVP/Chief HR Officer: David Lenz
Sales Director: Jim Dorn
SVP Operations: Joe Swanson
Purchasing: John McCormack
Estimated Sales: $36.8 Million
Number Employees: 500-999
Square Footage: 500000
Other Locations:
  Regal Ware
  Jacksonville AR
Brands:
  Kitchen Pro
  La Machine
  Poly Perk
  Regal

28273 Regency Coffee & Vending
2022 E Spruce Cir
Olathe, KS 66062-5404

913-829-1994
Fax: 913-393-0097 Regency@RegencyCoffee.com
www.regencycoffee.com
Coffees, teas and snacks
Owner: Nancy Robinson
regency@regencycoffee.com
Estimated Sales: $205 Million
Number Employees: 10-19
Number of Brands: 8
Number of Products: 80
Type of Packaging: Consumer, Food Service, Pri-
vate Label, Bulk

28274 Regency Label Corporation
217 Berger Street
Wood Ridge, NJ 07075-1802

201-342-2288
Fax: 201-438-3439
Printed labels including pressure sensitive
VP Marketing: Mike Pagano
Estimated Sales: less than $500,000
Number Employees: 1-4

28275 Reggie Balls Cajun Foods
501 Bunker Rd
Lake Charles, LA 70615-3875

337-436-0291
Fax: 337-433-9851 www.ballscajunfoods.com
Cajun seasonings and mixes; Contract packaging
and private labeling
Owner/President: Reginald Ball
Estimated Sales: Less Than $500,000
Number Employees: 1-4
Type of Packaging: Private Label

28276 Regina USA
305 E Mahn Ct
Oak Creek, WI 53154-2101

414-571-0032
Fax: 414-571-0225 sales.us@reginachain.net
Manufacturer, of metal and plastic power transmis-
sion chains, conveying chains and plastic belts
President: Carlo Garbagnati
VP Sales/Marketing: Michael Hager
Sales: Brian Kelley
IT: Sandy Martino
smartino@reginausa.com
Estimated Sales: $20 Million
Number Employees: 10-19
Square Footage: 65000
Parent Co: Regina Industria SPA
Brands:
  Regina

28277 Regina-Emerson
1604 S West Avenue
Waukesha, WI 53189-7434

262-521-1790
Fax: 262-521-1790
Belting

28278 Regional Produce
624 16th Ave W
Birmingham, AL 35204-1421

205-324-4569
Fax: 205-252-4434 800-726-0711
www.regionalproduce.net
Regional foodservice distributor.
Director of Purchasing: Jason Kenwright
Number Employees: 50-99
Square Footage: 30000
Type of Packaging: Consumer, Food Service
Brands:
  Granny's

28279 Rego China Corporation
200 Broadhollow Road
Suite 400
Melville, NY 11747-4806

516-753-3700
Fax: 516-753-3728 800-221-1707
www.oneida.com
Manufacturer, importer and exporter of chinaware
President, CEO: Foster Sullivan
Sales Manager: Frank Fan
Estimated Sales: $300,000-500,000
Number Employees: 40
Parent Co: Oneida
Type of Packaging: Food Service

28280 Reheis Co
235 Snyder Ave
Berkeley Heights, NJ 07922-1150

908-464-1500
Fax: 908-464-7726 rduffy@reheis.com
Chemicals and pharmaceuticals
General Manager: Douglas McF+R2441arlend
Plant Manager: Gerry Kirwan
Estimated Sales: Less Than $500,000
Number Employees: 1-4
Parent Co: General Chemicals

28281 Rehrig Pacific Co
4010 E 26th St
Los Angeles, CA 90058

323-262-5145
Fax: 323-269-8506 800-421-6244
info@rehrigpacific.com www.rehrigpacific.com
Plastic injection molding, returnable plastic crates
and pallets.
President: William Rehrig
wrehrig@rehrigpacific.com
Year Founded: 1913
Estimated Sales: $101.4 Million
Number Employees: 1000-4999

28282 Reichert Analytical Instruments
3362 Walden Avenue
Depew, NY 14043

716-686-4500
Fax: 716-686-4545 www.reichertai.com
Hand held digital refractometers.
Contact: Ashley Agnew
aagnew@reichert.com

28283 Reid Boiler Works
920 10th St
Bellingham, WA 98225

360-714-6157
Fax: 360-734-6660
Canning retorts and pressure vessels
President: Robert Reid
Office Manager: Shirley Maytag
Estimated Sales: Less than $500,000
Number Employees: 1-4

28284 Reid Graphics Inc
7 Connector Rd
Andover, MA 01810-5922

978-474-1930
Fax: 978-474-1931 800-887-7461
pzackular@reidgraphics.com
www.reidgraphics.com
Labels and decals
President: Stephen Dunlevy
reidgrafx@aol.com
General Manager: Robert Stewart
Estimated Sales: $10-20 Million
Number Employees: 20-49

28285 Reidler Decal Corporation
264 Industrial Pk. Road
PO Box 8
Saint Clair, PA 17970

570-429-1528
Fax: 570-429-1528 800-628-7770
marketing@reidlerdecal.com
www.reidlerdecal.com
Manufacturer and exporter of decals, plastic safety
signs, fleet graphics, reflective markings, reflective
striping and roll labels
President: Edward Reidler
Marketing Coordinator: Maralynn Hudock
Estimated Sales: $5-10 Million
Number Employees: 20-49
Square Footage: 100000
Brands:
  Ad Vantage
  Fleet Mark

28286 Reilly Foam Corporation
1101 E Hector St # 1
Conshohocken, PA 19428-2382

610-834-1900
Fax: 610-834-0769 www.reillyfoam.com
Plastic foam sheets including die cut, laminated and
pressure sensitive
Owner: Charles Reilly
VP Marketing: Stephen Phillips
Estimated Sales: $20-50 Million
Number Employees: 100-249
Square Footage: 249000

28287 Reiner Products
196 Mill St
Waterbury, CT 06706-1208

203-574-2666
Fax: 203-755-8178 800-345-6775
info@reinerproducts.com
www.reinerproducts.com
Manufacturer, importer and exporter of salt and pep-
per shakers
Owner: Patrick Bergin
Estimated Sales: $2.5-5 Million
Number Employees: 10-19

28288 Reinhold Sign Svc Inc
2070 Holmgren Way
Green Bay, WI 54304-4593

920-494-7161
Fax: 920-494-8720 sales@reinholdsigns.com
www.vehiclewrapsgreenbay.com
Interior and exterior signage, truck and trailer letter-
ing and vinyl letters
President: John Gage
john@reinholdsign.com
Sales & Service Manager: Robert Ott
Estimated Sales: $1-5 Million
Number Employees: 10-19
Square Footage: 32000

28289 Reinke & Schomann
3745 N Richards St
Milwaukee, WI 53212

414-964-1100
Fax: 414-964-1995
sales@reinkeandschomann.com
www.reinkeandschomann.com
Manufacturer and exporter of steel and stainless
steel screw conveyors and components
President: Frederick Schomann
VP Engineering/Sales: Ken Buchholz
Estimated Sales: Below $5,000,000
Number Employees: 5-9
Square Footage: 30000

28290 Reis Robotics
856 Commerce Pkwy
Carpentersville, IL 60110

847-741-9500
Fax: 847-844-0745 www.kuka.com
Manufacturer and importer of automated robotic ma-
terial handling and palletizing systems and system
integrators
President, KUKA Robotics Corp US: Joseph
Gemma

Year Founded: 1957
Estimated Sales: K
Number Employees: 10-19
Square Footage: 45000
Parent Co: KUKA Robotics Corporation

28291 (HQ)Reiser
725 Dedham St
Canton, MA 02021-1450

734-821-1290
Fax: 781-821-1316 sales@reiser.com
High-quality food processing and packaging equipment that includes tray sealing, vacuum and form/fill/seal packaging equipment as well as processing machines used for stuffing, portioning, grinding, injecting, extruding and slicing.Equipment can be used as stand-alone machines or as complete systems.
President/CEO: Roger Reiser
Engineering/R&D Technician: Dan Flaherty
Contact: Ahmad Adam
mhansen@reiser.com
Estimated Sales: $23 Million
Number Employees: 5-9
Brands:
  Amfec
  Fomaco
  Holac
  Ross
  Seydelmann
  Vemag

28292 Reit-Price ManufacturingCompany
532 W Chestnut St
Union City, IN 47390

765-964-3252
Fax: 765-964-5343 800-521-5343
customerservice@reitprice.com www.reitprice.com
Wet and dust mops, squeegees, push brooms, floor brushes and handles
President: Roger Stewart
Sales Manager: R Stewart
Estimated Sales: $10-20 Million
Number Employees: 20-49
Square Footage: 100000
Brands:
  Black Cat

28293 Relco Unisystems Corp
2281 3rd Ave SW
Willmar, MN 56201-2799

320-231-2210
Fax: 320-231-2282
lorencorle@relcounisystems.com
www.relco.net
Provides dairy and food plants with customized cheese, whey, soy, and processing equipment and systems through design, engineering, fabrication, installation, and commissioning. Relco process and control systems are recognized asindustry leaders because of their application knowledge, understanding of sanitary and regulatory requirements, and focus on consumer needs
President: Loren Corle
lcorle@relco.com
VP: M Douglas Rolland
Estimated Sales: $20-50 Million
Number Employees: 50-99

28294 (HQ)Reliable Container Corporation
12029 Regentview Ave
Downey, CA 90241-5517

562-745-0200
Fax: 562-861-3969 www.reliablecontainer.com
Manufacturer and exporter of corrugated boxes and foil-lined, coated, printed and plain cake circles and pads
President: Dan Brough
VP: Andrew Rosen
VP: Robert Schwartz
Estimated Sales: $20-50 Million
Number Employees: 100-249
Square Footage: 112500
Other Locations:
  Reliable Container Corp.
  Tijuana, Baja CA

28295 Reliable Fire Equipment
12845 S Cicero Ave
Alsip, IL 60803-3083

708-444-7339
Fax: 708-389-1150 fire@reliablefire.com
www.reliablefire.com

Wholesaler/distributor of restaurant fire supression and security systems, alarm monitoring, fire alarms, portable, industrial and special hazard fire extinguishers, emergency lights, smoke detectors and first aid equipment, servingthe food service market.
President: Debra Horvath
Vice President: Barbara Horvath
VP Sales: Robert Marek
Purchasing Manager: Tim Zurek
Estimated Sales: $22 Million
Number Employees: 50-99
Number of Brands: 30
Number of Products: 200
Square Footage: 40000

28296 Reliable Food Service Equipment
Units 5,7,8
Concord, ON L4K 1L3
Canada

416-738-6840
Fax: 416-739-7271
sales@restaurantequipmentdepot.com
www.restaurantequipmentdepot.com
Steam tables, ovens, freezers, sinks, etc
President: Frank Gambino
Number Employees: 8

28297 Reliable Label
1427 Centre Cir
Downers Grove, IL 60515-1045

630-620-8100
Fax: 630-620-8125 800-323-7265
sales@reliablelabel.com www.reliablelabel.com
Labeling services
President: Kevin Callahan
callahan@reliablelabel.com
Estimated Sales: $10-20 Million
Number Employees: 20-49

28298 Reliable Tent & Awning Co
501 N 23rd St
Billings, MT 59101-1341

406-252-4689
Fax: 406-252-6508 800-544-1039
sales@reliabletent.com www.reliabletent.com
Commercial awnings
President: Dave Niemer
dave@reliabletent.com
Estimated Sales: $1-2,500,000
Number Employees: 10-19
Type of Packaging: Private Label

28299 Reliance Product
1093 Sherwin Road
Winnipeg, MB R3H 1A4
Canada

204-633-4403
Fax: 204-633-5193 800-665-0258
www.relianceproducts.com
Shipping containers including HDPE pails and bottles includesCamping lines
President: Charles Schiele
CFO: Arla Ervett
VP General Manager: Linda Lemer
Sales Manager: Peter Harvey
Number Employees: 10
Parent Co: Moll Industries

28300 Reliance-Paragon
2070 Wheatsheaf Lane
Philadelphia, PA 19124-5041

215-743-1231
Fax: 215-742-1584
Packaging products including set-up, paper and folding boxes; also, plastic boxes
VP: Larry Chatzkel
Plant Supervisor: William Scnappor
Estimated Sales: $1-5 Million
Number Employees: 50-99
Square Footage: 120000

28301 (HQ)Remco Industries International
PO Box 480008
Fort Lauderdale, FL 33348-0008

954-462-0000
Fax: 954-564-0000 800-987-3626
remco2mill@aol.com www.remcousa.com

Manufacturer and exporter of cooking equipment including wood burning and infrared rotisseries and pizza ovens; also, spit racks, bagel ovens and warming carts; manufacturer and importer of wood burning, infrared and carousel brickpizza ovens; manufacturer of grease free chicken wing roaster the Wing King and BBQ Boy
President/CEO: Romano Moreth
CFO: Susan Test
Vice President: Rob Moreth
R&D/Plant Manager: Remy Moreth
Quality Control: Wayne Wilkenson
Marketing/Public Relations: Pascal Ledesma
Sales Director: Joe Obrien
Operations: David Finch
Production Manager: Vean George
Plant Manager: Sean Harker
Purchasing Manager: Ed Moreth
Estimated Sales: $7-8 Million
Number Employees: 20-49
Number of Brands: 3
Number of Products: 6
Square Footage: 160000
Type of Packaging: Food Service

28302 Remco Products Corp
4735 W 106th St
PO Box 698
Zionsville, IN 46077-8761

317-876-9856
Fax: 317-876-9858 800-585-8619
www.remcoproducts.com
Ice and beverage dispensing products
Founder: Richard Garrison
President: David Garrison
Accounting: Cristal Garrison
Vice President Sales & Marketing: Steve Hawhee
Sales Representative: Paula Pearson
Operations: Mike Garrison
Customer Service: Amye Kersey
Number Employees: 10-19

28303 Remco Products Corp
4735 W 106th St
Zionsville, IN 46077-8761

317-876-9856
Fax: 317-876-9858 800-585-8619
sales@remcoproducts.com
www.remcoproducts.com
Remco Products sells a high quality line of products to the food processing, sanittation, pharmaceutical, safety, and material handling industries. Our tubs and polyropylene shovels have been used in these areas for over 30 years. TheVikan line of cleaning brooms, brushes, and squeegees is specifically designed to meet the stringent hygienic requirements of these different industries. We can also provide you with other hand tools such as scoops, scrapers, mixing paddles, forkkand rakes.
President: David Garrison
Marketing/Sales Support: Richard L. Williams
Director/Sales and Marketing: Chuck Bush
President of Operations: Richard L. Garrison
Estimated Sales: $2.5-5 Million
Number Employees: 10-19
Number of Brands: 2
Number of Products: 737
Square Footage: 96000
Brands:
  Remco

28304 Remcon Plastics Inc
208 Chestnut St
Reading, PA 19602-1809

610-376-2666
Fax: 610-375-4750 800-360-3636
info@remcon.com www.remcon.com
ISO 9001 certified material handling equipment, including bulk bins, liquid shippers, drums, pallets, tanks, aseptic packaging equipment, lockers, tote boxes, safety barriers, hoppers and candy trays. Structural foam molding androtational molding
President: Antonio Andino
antonio.andino@remcon.com
Marketing/Inside Sales Manager: Sylvie Mackenzie
Regional Sales Manager: Michael Pierotti
Purchasing Manager: Susan Cook
Estimated Sales: $10-20 Million
Number Employees: 100-249
Square Footage: 280000
Type of Packaging: Private Label, Bulk
Brands:
  Remcon

28305 Remcraft Lighting Products
12870 NW 45th Ave
PO Box 54-1487
Miami, FL 33054
305-687-9031
Fax: 305-687-5069 800-327-6585
customerservice@remcraft.com
www.bacimirrors.com
Manufacturer and exporter of electric and fluorescent lighting fixtures
President: Jeffrey Robboy
CEO: Michell Roboy
Estimated Sales: $1-2.5 Million
Number Employees: 20-49
Square Footage: 80000
Type of Packaging: Consumer, Private Label
Brands:
Baci
Remcraft

28306 Remel
12076 Santa Fe Dr
P.O. Box 14428
Lenexa, KS 66215
Fax: 800-621-8251 800-255-6730
www.remel.com
Manufacturer and exporter of microbiology products including culture media, dehydrated culture media identification kits, reagents and stains.
President & CEO, Thermo Scientific: Marc Casper
Year Founded: 1973
Estimated Sales: Over $1 Billion
Parent Co: Thermo Fisher Scientific
Brands:
Chrisope
Ids
Remel

28307 Reminox International Corporation
7207 Bay Drive
Apt 13
Miami, FL 33141-5457
305-865-0925
www.creminox.com
Sales Manager: Roberto Garcia
Estimated Sales: $1-5 Million

28308 Remmele Engineering
677 Transfer Rd
Saint Paul, MN 55114
651-643-3700
Fax: 651-642-5665 800-854-7742
www.aspectautomation.com
Packaging and filling
President: Terry Johnson
Quality Control: Jim Schaefer
Chairman of the Board: William J Saul
Contact: Florinel Ciubotaru
florinel.ciubotaru@remmele.com
Estimated Sales: $75-100 Million
Number Employees: 100-249

28309 Remmey Wood Products
PO Box 1020
Southampton, PA 18966-0720
215-355-3335
Fax: 215-355-3781
Packaging and shipping products including wood pallets, boxes, skids, crates, etc
VP Marketing: Donald Remmey Jr
Estimated Sales: $2.5-5 Million
Number Employees: 20-49

28310 Remote Equipment Systems
11390 Old Roswell Road
Alpharetta, GA 30004-2058
770-777-2627
Fax: 770-777-2662 800-803-9488
Data loggers for material handling systems
VP Sales: Doug Reed
Estimated Sales: $5-10 Million
Number Employees: 20-49

28311 Rempak Industries
2125 Center Avenue #200
Fort Lee, NJ 07024-5810
201-585-9007
Fax: 201-585-0918
Contract packager of portion control powders, liquids and solids
President: Gene Cohen
Estimated Sales: Less than $500,000
Number Employees: 14

Type of Packaging: Consumer, Food Service, Private Label

28312 Remstar International
41 Eisenhower Dr
Westbrook, ME 04092
207-854-1861
Fax: 207-854-1610 800-639-5805
info@remstar.com www.remstar.com
Manufacturer, importer and exporter of automated storage and retrieval systems
President: Gary Gould
Marketing Director: Ed Romaine
Contact: Brian Baker
brian.baker@kardexremstar.com
Estimated Sales: $20-50 Million
Number Employees: 20-49
Parent Co: Kardex A.G.

28313 Renard Machine Company
PO Box 19005
Green Bay, WI 54307-9005
920-432-8412
Fax: 920-432-8430
Manufacturer and exporter of packaging machinery including fillers, sealers, labelers, weighers and wrappers; also, paper converting equipment including fixing, cutting, etc
Division Controller: Gary Rossman
Production Manager: Carl Strebel
Plant Manager: Ken Harvey
Estimated Sales: $5-10 Million
Number Employees: 50-99
Square Footage: 300000
Parent Co: Paper Converting Machine Company

28314 Renato Specialty Product
3612 Dividend Drive
Garland, TX 75042
972-272-4800
Fax: 972-272-4848 866-575-6316
renatos@renatos.com www.renatos.com
Manufacturer and exporter of food service equipment including broilers, ovens, griddles, grills and rotisseries
President, Founder: Renato Riccio
Estimated Sales: $1-2.5 Million
Number Employees: 5-9
Type of Packaging: Consumer, Food Service

28315 Renau Electronic Lab
9309 Deering Ave
Chatsworth, CA 91311-5858
818-341-1994
Fax: 818-341-8063 info@renau.com
www.renau.com
President: Karol Renau
cdomanski@renau.com
Estimated Sales: $10-20 Million
Number Employees: 20-49

28316 Render
1800 Elmwood Avenue
Buffalo, NY 14207-2410
716-447-1010
Fax: 716-447-8918 888-446-1010
Bakery display cases with solid wood construction, rearload options, adjustable shelving and accesory bins, and an internal lighting system specifically to enhance bakery products
President: Robert Nehin
Number Employees: 10

28317 Rennco LLC
300 S Elm St
Homer, MI 49245-1337
517-568-4121
Fax: 517-568-4798 800-409-5225
sales@rennco.com www.rennco.com
Manufacturer and exporter of vertical L-Bar sealers
VP/General Manager: Eric Vorm
Marketing Director: Jeanne George
Contact: Teresa Farmer
teresafarmer@rennco.com
Director of Operations: Terry Draper
Number Employees: 70
Parent Co: Pro Mach
Type of Packaging: Consumer, Food Service, Bulk
Brands:
Renwrap

28318 Reno Technology
3310 E 4th Ave
Hutchinson, KS 67501-1962
620-663-2753
Fax: 620-665-5793 800-562-8065
www.megafab.com
President: Mieke Ellwood
mieke@renocountycddo.org
Estimated Sales: $10-20 Million
Number Employees: 50-99

28319 Renold Ajax
100 Bourne St # 2
Westfield, NY 14787-9706
716-326-3121
Fax: 716-326-6121 800-879-2529
www.renold.com
Custom design vibratory materials handling equipment: dewatering units, conveyors, feeder, screeners, bulk bab and box weigh filling systems, bulk bag unloading stations
President: Adriano Ambos
adriano.ambos@renold.com
Estimated Sales: $20-50 Million
Number Employees: 250-499

28320 Renold Products
P.O.Box A
Westfield, NY 14787-0546
716-326-3121
Fax: 716-326-6121 800-879-2529
ainfo@renoldajax.com www.renold.com
Manufacturer and exporter of material handling equipment including mechanical power transmission products and packer weigh scales and conveyors.
President: Thomas Murrer
Business Development Director: Alan Dean
Estimated Sales: $20-50 Million
Number Employees: 100-249
Square Footage: 120000
Parent Co: Renold PLC
Brands:
Ajax
Renold

28321 Renovator's Supply
PO Box 2515
Conway, NH 3818
800-659-0203
Fax: 603-447-1717
Manufacturer and exporter of hardware, lighting, plumbing and gift accessories; also, solid brass, iron, porcelain and stainless steel sinks and work centers
President: Cindy Harris
Estimated Sales: $10-20 Million
Number Employees: 100-249
Brands:
Renovator's Supply

28322 Reotemp Instrument Corp
10656 Roselle St
San Diego, CA 92121-1524
858-784-0710
Fax: 858-784-0720 800-648-7737
sales@reotemp.com www.reotemp.com
Manufactures temperature and pressure instrumentation. Provide bimetal thermometers, pressure gauges, diaphragm seals, transmitters, RTD's and thermocouples and related accessories.
President: Joanne Lin
joanne.lin@intel.com
VP/General Manager: John Sisti
Quality/Engineering Manager: Cora Marsh
Marketing Manager: Nathan O'Connor
Sales Manager, Global Sales: Mark Leonelli
Purchasing Associate: Stacy Munoz
Estimated Sales: $6 Million
Number Employees: 20-49
Square Footage: 15000

28323 Replacements LTD
1089 Knox Rd
Mc Leansville, NC 27301-9228
336-697-3000
Fax: 336-697-3100 800-737-5223
inquire@replacements.com
www.replacements.com
Manufacturer and exporter of household and institutional cutlery
CEO: Robert L Page
robert.page@replacements.com
Director Marketing: Maron Atkins
General Manager: James Robellard

Estimated Sales: $5-10 Million
Number Employees: 500-999
Square Footage: 140000
Parent Co: Syratech

28324 Republic Foil
55 Triangle St
Danbury, CT 06810
    203-743-2731
    Fax: 203-743-8838 800-722-3645
Manufacturer and exporter of aluminum foil on coils
President: John Jehle
CFO: Fred Wallace
Contact: Joan Garofalo
joan.garofalo@garmcousa.com
Estimated Sales: $20-50 Million
Number Employees: 50-99
Square Footage: 100000
Type of Packaging: Bulk
Brands:
    Republic High Yield

28325 Republic Refrigeration Inc
2890 Gray Fox Rd
Monroe, NC 28110-8422
    704-225-0410
    Fax: 704-283-2180
info@republicrefrigeration.com
www.republicrefrigeration.com
Design, install and maintain industrial refrigereation systems.
Vice President: Annmarie Greene
greene@carlyle.com
CEO: Walter F. Teeter
Founder: Henry Saye
Vice President: Robert G. Belanger
Director of Process Refrigeration: Joe Ramsey
Director of Business Development: Wayne Donaldson
Regional Manager: Banks Thomas
Insulation Project Manager: Jamie R. Foster
Estimated Sales: Less Than $500,000
Number Employees: 1-4

28326 Republic Sales
5131 Cash Rd
Dallas, TX 75247-5805
    469-930-0518
    Fax: 214-631-3673 800-847-0380
info@republicsales.com www.republicsales.com
President: George Goff
Vice President/International: Dan Marlett
Marketing: Nicole Taylor
Sheet Metal Sales: Andrew Servais
Contact: Gerardo Alaniz
gerardoalaniz@republic-mfg.com
Production: Raul Maldonado
Estimated Sales: $1-5 Million
Number Employees: 10-19

28327 Republic Storage Systems LLC
1038 Belden Ave NE
Canton, OH 44705
    330-438-5800
    Fax: 330-454-7772 800-477-1255
sales@republicstorage.com
www.republicstorage.com
Steel storage products including lockers, shelving and storage racks. Also shop furniture
President: Chris Carr
CFO: Eric Cook
CEO: James T Anderson
Marketing Director: Cathy Maxin
Sales Director: Ed Meek
Contact: Erin Allen
eallen@sibcycline.com
Estimated Sales: $20-50 Million
Number Employees: 500-999
Square Footage: 1300000
Brands:
    Mondrian
    Wedge Lock

28328 Rer Services
19431 Business Center Dr # 17
Northridge, CA 91324-6408
    818-993-1826
    Fax: 818-993-0016 rerserv@flash.net
Manufacturer and exporter of packaging machinery
Owner: Rick Ray
Estimated Sales: $2.5-5,000,000
Number Employees: 5-9

28329 Research & Development Packaging Corporation
1221 Us Highway 22
Suite 1
Lebanon, NJ 08833
    908-236-2111
    Fax: 908-236-7013
President: Donald Bogut
donald.bogut@key-pak.com
Estimated Sales: $1-3 Million
Number Employees: 5-9

28330 Research Products Co
1835 E North St
Salina, KS 67401-8567
    785-825-2181
    Fax: 785-825-8908
Insecticides
President: Monte White
montewhite@researchprod.com
Marketing Coordinator (Flour Division): Edna Richard
Estimated Sales: $20-50 Million
Number Employees: 50-99
Parent Co: McShares

28331 Resina
27455 Bostik Court
Temecula, CA 92590
    951-296-6585
    Fax: 951-296-5018 800-207-4804
sales@resina.com www.resina.com
Manufacturer and exporter of container capping machines
CEO: Micheal Tom
Director Sales: Andrew May
Sales Director: Tina Tricome
Estimated Sales: $10-20 Million
Number Employees: 1-4
Square Footage: 70000
Brands:
    Resina

28332 Resource Equipment
1547 Palos Verdes Mall
Walnut Creek, CA 94597-2228
    925-825-5536
    Fax: 925-687-5513 800-324-1030
www.reisite.net
President: Jeff Slamal
Owner: Kenneth Gottfried
Contact: Ken Gottfried
specbuilt@aol.com
Estimated Sales: Below $5 Million
Number Employees: 2

28333 Resource One/Resource Two
6900 Canby Ave # 106
Reseda, CA 91335
    818-343-3451
    Fax: 818-343-3405 info@resourceone.com
www.resourceoneinc.com
Table cloths, napkins and chair covers
Founder/ CEO: Roberta Karsch
Contact: Thomas Patston
tpatston@rocs.com
Estimated Sales: $5-10,000,000
Number Employees: 20-49

28334 Resource Optimization
P.O.Box 2747
Knoxville, TN 37901-2747
    865-522-2211
    Fax: 865-522-7907
Software for quantification of ingredients in multi-level products
President: T Brient Mayfield
R&D: Bill Walter
Estimated Sales: Below $5 Million
Number Employees: 10-19

28335 Resources in Food & FoodTeam
222 S Central Ave # 202
St Louis, MO 63105-3509
    314-727-0002
    Fax: 314-727-5590 800-875-1028
www.rifood.com
Professional placement service for the food industry
President: Bonnie Pollock
VP Sales/Marketing: Mike Bray
Marketing Secretary: Marylynn Hayes
Estimated Sales: $300,000-500,000
Number Employees: 1-4
Parent Co: Resources In Food And Food Team

28336 Respirometry Plus, LLC
PO Box 1236
Fond Du Lac, WI 54937-7527
    Fax: 920-922-1085 800-328-7518
operations@respirometryplus.com
www.respirometryplus.com
Manufacturer and exporter of bench and on-line respirometer
Owner: Louis Sparagarto
CEO: Robert Arthur
Contact: Tim Keuler
tim@respirometryplus.com
Estimated Sales: $1-2,500,000
Number Employees: 10

28337 Restaurant Data
1 Bridge St
Irvington, NY 10533-1560
    732-667-5885
    Fax: 914-591-5494 800-346-9390
info@netsoftsolutions.com restaurantdata.com
Cashew and other nuts; Co-packing services
President: James Santo
R&D: Paul Mlynar
Contact: Jeff Kydd
jeff@foodservicereport.com
Purchasing Director: Joe Di Donato
Estimated Sales: $1-2 Million
Number Employees: 1-4
Number of Brands: 1
Number of Products: 12
Square Footage: 48000
Type of Packaging: Consumer, Private Label, Bulk
Brands:
    Nutsco

28338 Restaurant Development Svc
7404 Helmsdale Rd
Bethesda, MD 20817-4628
    301-263-0400
    Fax: 301-263-0151
info@restaurantdevelopment.com
www.restaurantdevelopment.com
Consultant specializing in business planning for restaurants
Owner: Paul Fields
pfields@restaurantdevelopment.com
Estimated Sales: less than $500,000
Number Employees: 10-19

28339 Restaurant Partners
1030 N Orange Ave # 200
Orlando, FL 32801-1030
    407-839-5070
    Fax: 407-839-3388
contact@restaurantpartnersinc.com
www.restaurantpartnersinc.com
Consultant providing strategic and expansion planning services for restaurants
Owner: Dave Manuchia
dmanuchia@restaurantpartnersinc.com
Sr Consultant: George Cheros
VP, Operations: Eric Sheen
Estimated Sales: $500,000-$1 Million
Number Employees: 10-19

28340 Restaurant TechnologiesInc
2250 Pilot Knob Rd # 100
Suite 100
Mendota Heights, MN 55120-1127
    651-796-1600
    Fax: 651-379-4914 888-796-4997
customercare@rti-inc.com www.rti-inc.com
President: Paul Plooster
CEO: Jeffrey R. Kiesel
CFO: Robert E. Weil
VP: Brad Schoendauer
Vice President, Engineering & Quality As: Bradley J. Schoenbauer
Vice President, Sales/Marketing: Sara Sampson
Vice President, Operations: Leanne E. Branham
Estimated Sales: $1-3 Million
Number Employees: 100-249

28341 Restaurant Workshop
PO Box 122
Franklin, AR 72536-0122
    734-434-7761
    Fax: 734-434-7761 866-434-7761
Restaurant Workshop provides training and educational material to the food service and hospitality industries. Employee and management training
President: Jeff Crawford
VP/Public Relations: Kip Jaros

Type of Packaging: Food Service

28342 Retail Automations Products
45 W 38th Street
New York, NY 10018
Fax: 212-391-0575 800-237-9144
www.alohapos4me.com
Reseller of aloha computer point of sale, inventory tracking, smart card, automated delivery, touch screen and accounting systems; also, catering software, internet security. Also the tri-state area's premiere integrator of foodservice automation technologies. Through Aloha POS software, we serve NYC, Long Island and Southern CT. POS Inventory-tracking, seurity cameras, automated delivery, touch screen and accounting systems.
Contact: Robert Breitenstein
robert.breitenstein@rap-pos.com
Estimated Sales: $500,000-$1 Million
Number Employees: 10
Square Footage: 12000
Brands:
Aloha
Business Works Accounting
Cater Ease

28343 Retail Decor
PO Box 4019
Ironton, OH 45638-4019
740-532-9559
Fax: 740-532-5288 800-726-3402
Decor packages for commercial interiors including aisle directories, end display pricers, check lane signal lights, chalk, menu and bulletin boards, signage, custom wall graphics, etc.; installation services available
Estimated Sales: $500,000-$1,000,000
Number Employees: 6
Square Footage: 20000

28344 Retalix
2490 Technical Dr
Miamisburg, OH 45342
937-445-1936
Fax: 937-384-2280 877-794-7237
www.ncr.com
Manufacturer and exporter of computer software including point of sale backoffice and headquarters systems for supermarkets, grocery stores and convenience stores
President: Ronen Levkovich
CEO: Shuky Sheffer
CFO: Sarit Sagiv
Head Innovation & Portfolio Strategy: Dr,Gill Roth
Marketing: Oren Betzaleli
Sales Director: Rick Cumberland
Contact: Jefferson Alcott
j.alcott@retalix.com
Operations Manager: Eli Spirer
Estimated Sales: $10-20 Million
Number Employees: 50-99
Square Footage: 60000
Parent Co: Retalix, Ltd
Type of Packaging: Consumer
Brands:
Consumer Scan

28345 Retrotec
W197N7577 F and W Ct
Lannon, WI 53046
262-253-9677
Fax: 262-253-9685 info@retrotecinc.com
Full line of still and end over end rotating batch retorts, processes and style of hermetically sealed package in full or partial water immersion
President: Henry Cathers
Estimated Sales: $1-2.5 Million
Number Employees: 5-9

28346 Revent Inc
100 Ethel Rd W
Piscataway, NJ 08854-5967
732-777-9433
Fax: 732-777-1187 info@revent.com
www.revent.com
Manufacturer and exporter of ovens including deck, mini and bake and roast rack; also, proof boxes
President: Torvjorn Alm
t.alm@revent.com
Quality Control: Tom Parker
Estimated Sales: $1-3 Million
Number Employees: 5-9
Square Footage: 200000
Parent Co: Revent International

Brands:
Do-Sys
Revent

28347 Revere Group
9310 4th Ave S
PO Box 80157
Seattle, WA 98108-4601
206-545-1850
Fax: 206-545-3676
www.customzipperpouches.com
Packaging supplies (accessories, bags, boxes, confectionery supplies, equipment, gift asket supplies, wrapping film, box pads and trays, ribbons, tissue, thermal transfer ribbon and gift wrap)
Vice President: Tom DE Angelo
tom@rgroup.com
Vice President: Tom DE Angelo
tom@rgroup.com
Number Employees: 50-99

28348 Revere Group
9310 4th Ave S
Seattle, WA 98108-4601
206-545-1850
Fax: 206-545-3676 info@rgroup.com
www.customzipperpouches.com
Specialty food packaging i.e. gift wrap/boxes/containers.
Vice President: Tom DE Angelo
tom@rgroup.com
Vice President: Tom DE Angelo
tom@rgroup.com
Marketing: Bill Revere
Estimated Sales: $190,000
Number Employees: 50-99

28349 Revere Packaging
39 Pearce Industrial Rd
Shelbyville, KY 40065-8125
502-633-1404
Fax: 502-633-9547 800-626-2668
www.reverepackaging.com
Foil containers and polystyrene plastic items
Estimated Sales: $61 Thousand
Number Employees: 50-99
Square Footage: 2178

28350 Reviss Service
175 E Hawthorn Pkwy # 142
Suite 142
Vernon Hills, IL 60061-1493
847-680-4522
Fax: 847-680-5159
Irradiation
Vice President: John Schrader
john.schrader@reviss.com
Vice President: John Schrader
john.schrader@reviss.com
Number Employees: 1-4

28351 Rex Art Manufacturing Corp.
655 N Queens Avenue
Lindenhurst, NY 11757-3004
631-884-4600
Fax: 631-884-4611
Point of purchase displays including plastic wood and steel; also, metal specialties and aluminum sheet metal and tubing; custom rack fabrications available
President/General Manager: Robert Santangelo
Number Employees: 50
Square Footage: 80000

28352 Rex Carton Co Inc
4528 W 51st St
Chicago, IL 60632-4597
773-581-4115
Fax: 773-581-4120 info@rexcarton.com
www.rexcarton.com
Corrugated boxes
President: Ronald Lemar
ron@rexcarton.com
VP/Plant Manager: Sal Arena
Customer Service: Greg Fleck
Plant Manager: Joe Lara
Controller: Diane Green
Estimated Sales: $5-10 Million
Number Employees: 20-49

28353 Rex Chemical Corporation
2270 NW 23rd St
Miami, FL 33142
305-634-2471
Fax: 305-634-5546 877-634-5539
rexchem@bellsouth.net www.rexchemical.com
Liquid and powder cleaners; wholesaler/distributor of janitorial supplies
President: Beatriz Granja
Contact: Mary Meier
m.meier@sandc.com
Estimated Sales: $10-20 Million
Number Employees: 20-49

28354 Rexam Containers
743 Westgate Road
Deerfield, IL 60015-3136
847-945-2249
Fax: 847-945-4938 carrollpjx@aol.com
Director Sales: Patrick Carroll

28355 Rexcraft Fine Chafers
4139 38th Street
Long Island City, NY 11101-3617
718-361-3052
Fax: 718-361-3054 888-739-2723
rexchafer@aol.com
Manufacturer and exporter of banquetware including chafers, coffee/tea brewers and urns, hollowware, steam table inserts, serving trays and food warmers
President: Ahsan Ullaha
VP: John Berman
Engineer & Designer: David Berman
Number Employees: 40
Square Footage: 36000
Brands:
Rexcraft

28356 Rexford Paper Company
5802 Washington Ave
Suite 102
Racine, WI 53406-4088
262-886-9100
Fax: 262-886-9130
Manufacturer, wholesaler/distributor and exporter of gummed, and reinforced paper and tapes including plain and printed, heat seal coated, lightweight meat packaging, gummed stay and pressure sensitive carton closure
CFO: Muriel Fincle
Sales Service Manager: James Carse
Sales Manager: Rory Wolf
Estimated Sales: $5-10 Million
Number Employees: 10-19
Parent Co: Inland Paperboard & Packaging
Type of Packaging: Consumer, Food Service
Brands:
Lok-A-Box
Redcore
Rexford
Safe-T-Seal

28357 (HQ)Rexnord Corporation
Corporate Headquarters
511 Freshwater Way
Milwaukee, WI 53204
414-643-3000
866-739-6673
www.rexnord.com
Manufacturer, importer and exporter of belt, bottle and chain conveyors.
President & CEO: Todd Adams
SVP/Chief Financial Officer: Mark Peterson
SVP, Business & Corporate Development: Rodney Jackson
Chief Human Resources Officer: George Powers
Chief Information Officer: Mike Troutman
VP/General Counsel/Secretary: Patty Whaley
Year Founded: 1891
Estimated Sales: $1 Billion
Number Employees: 8,000
Brands:
Autogard
Cambridge
Centa
Duralon
Euroflex
Falk
Link-Belt
Rex
Stearns
Thomas
Tollok

Berg
Highfield

28358 Rexnord Corporation
Power Transmission Headquarters
4701 W Greenfield Ave.
Milwaukee, WI 53214

866-739-6673
www.rexnord.com
Bearings, couplings, gear drives, PT drive components, conveying solutions (including FlatTop), and industrial chain.
President & CEO: Todd Adams
President, Process & Motion Control: Kevin Zaba

28359 Rexroth Corporation
5150 Prairie Stone Pkwy
Hoffman Estates, IL 60192-3707

847-645-3600
Fax: 847-645-0804 www.boschrexroth-us.com
Manufacturer and importer of servodrives and controls for motion control of processing and packaging machinery
President, Chief Executive Officer: Berend Bracht
VP Sales/Marketing: Richard Huss
Contact: Quentin Gilbert
quentin.gilbert@boschrexroth-us.com
Estimated Sales: $20-50 Million
Number Employees: 1,000-4,999
Square Footage: 50000
Parent Co: Rexroth Corporation
Brands:
Indramat

28360 Reyco Systems Inc
1704 Industrial Way
Caldwell, ID 83605-6906

208-795-5700
Fax: 208-795-5749 info@reycosys.com
www.reyco.com
Manufacturer and exporter of pneumatic waste conveying, dewatering and fryer oil recovery equipment
General Manager: Rex McArthur
Account Manager: Marilyn McGrew
Design Manager: Jeff Denkers
Sales Director: Kathryn Brown
Manager: Wyland Atkins
awyland@reycosys.com
Plant Manager: Rex McArthur
Purchasing Manager: David Lethcoe
Estimated Sales: $5-10,000,000
Number Employees: 5-9
Brands:
Cornell Pumps and Pumping Systems
Dynavac and Watervac Water Systems
Oil Miser Oil Recovery Systems
Pneumatic Conveying Systems
Ventilation & Process Air Systems

28361 Reynold Water Conditioning
24545 Hathaway St
Farmington Hills, MI 48335-1549

248-620-1433
Fax: 248-888-5005 800-572-9575
info@reynoldswater.com www.reynoldswater.com
Water softeners, filters and purifiers
President: James Reynolds
jamie@reynoldswater.com
VP: James Reynolds Jr
Estimated Sales: Less Than $500,000
Number Employees: 1-4
Square Footage: 22000
Type of Packaging: Consumer
Brands:
Clearstream
Oxy-Catalytic
Soft-Sensor
Softstream
Turbo Sensor
Twin-Stream

28362 Reynolds Foodservice Packaging
6603 W Broad Street
Richmond, VA 23230-1723

804-281-2525
Fax: 804-281-3289 pnquick@rmc.com
Offers more than 1,000 products designed for the food service industry including foil, film, aluminum and plastic containers and lids, food service bags, catering trays, sandwich bags and wraps, baking cups and trays
General Contact: Paula Quick
Estimated Sales: $3-5 Million
Number Employees: 5-9

28363 Rez-Tech Corp
1510 Mogadore Rd
Kent, OH 44240-7531

330-673-4009
Fax: 330-673-2273 800-673-5277
Blow and injection molded clear plastic food containers
Chairman Of Board: Tom Podnar
Co-President/CEO: Jack Podnar
CEO: Scott Podnar
VP: Craig Podnar
CEO: Jack Podnar
Purchasing Manager: Martha Sth
Estimated Sales: $2.5-5 Million
Number Employees: 20-49
Square Footage: 90000
Type of Packaging: Consumer, Food Service, Private Label

28364 Rhee Brothers
7461 Coca Cola Dr
Hanover, MD 21076

410-799-6656
Fax: 410-381-9080 www.rheebros.com
Asian food products
President: Syng Rhee
CFO: Ha Chang
Contact: Phillip Ahn
phillipahn@rheebros.com
Estimated Sales: $20-50 Million
Number Employees: 100-249
Type of Packaging: Private Label

28365 Rheo-Tech
640 Sanders Ct
Gurnee, IL 60031-3135

847-367-1557
USDA certified pumps and extruders for cheese, licorice candy, ground meat, sausage meat, fillings, peanut butter, etc
President: John Mowli
Estimated Sales: $1-2,5,000,000
Number Employees: 1-4

28366 Rheometric Scientific
109 Lukens Drive
New Castle, DE 19720-2765

732-560-8550
Fax: 732-560-7451
Rheometers, viscometers, thermal analyzers and process controllers
VP: Joseph Musanti
Managing Director: Don Becker
Marketing Manager: Joyce Altauia
Director Sales: Sean Kohl
Sales Manager: Michael Goliner
District Manager of Rheology: Howard Eubanks
Number Employees: 100-249

28367 Rheon
445 Holly Street
Laguna Beach, CA 92651-1746

949-497-3150
Fax: 949-497-3951
Manufacturer, importer and exporter of food processing equipment including automated mass production lines and flexible compact tables

28368 Rheon USA
2 Doppler
Irvine, CA 92618-4306

949-768-1900
Fax: 949-855-1991 us.info@rheon.com
www.rheon.com
Manufacturer, importer and exporter of food processing equipment including automated mass production lines and flexible compact tables
General Manager: Kiyo Kamiyama
Sales Coordinator: Terry Smith
Manager Engineering Sales: Kazu Onuki
Manager: Kazu Onuki
us.info@rheon.com
Estimated Sales: $500,000-$1 Million
Number Employees: 20-49
Brands:
Cwc System
Ez Table

28369 Rheon, U.S.A.
9490 Toledo Way
Irvine, CA 92618

949-768-1900
Fax: 949-855-1991 www.rheon.com

Dough sheet & pastry equipment, bread equipment and encrusting machines.
Contact: Hiroshi Kimura
hiroshi.kimura@rheon.com

28370 Rhineland Cutlery
345 Stan Dr
Melbourne, FL 32904-1085

321-725-2101
Fax: 321-253-0737 www.rhinelandcutlery.com
Cooking implements, housewares
Principal: Phillip McMahon
Estimated Sales: Less Than $500,000
Number Employees: 1-4

28371 Rhino Foods Inc
79 Industrial Pkwy
Burlington, VT 05401-5435

802-862-0252
Fax: 802-865-4145 info@rhinofoods.com
www.rhinofoods.com
Ice cream, brownies, cookie dough batter, cakes, truffles, pie squares and baking inclusions.
President/Owner: Ted Castle
tcastle@rhinofoods.com
Director of Finance & Administration: Jayne Magnant
Research & Development Specialist: Rob Douglas
Quality Assurance Manager: Lauren Weber
Director of Marketing: Dan Kiniry
Marketing Manager/Demand Planner: Gillian Bell
Director of Operations: Gene Steinfeld
Year Founded: 1981
Estimated Sales: $25 Million
Number Employees: 100-249
Number of Brands: 2
Square Footage: 29000
Type of Packaging: Consumer, Food Service, Private Label, Bulk
Brands:
Chessters
Vermont Velvet

28372 Rhoades Paper Box Corporation
PO Box 1666
Springfield, OH 45501

937-325-6494
Fax: 937-324-1597 800-441-6494
www.3g-graphics.com
Paper set-up boxes used for fine candies
Owner: Jeanie Lape
Sales Manager: Pat Hays
Estimated Sales: $2.5-5 Million
Number Employees: 20-49
Square Footage: 100000
Parent Co: Graphic Paper Products Corporation

28373 Rhode Island Label WorkInc
14 Clyde St
West Warwick, RI 02893-3504

401-828-6400
Fax: 401-828-8884
Seals and labels including UPC/bar code, pressure sensitive, gum, ungummed and transfer
President: William H Cole
rilabel@aol.com
Estimated Sales: Less Than $500,000
Number Employees: 1-4
Square Footage: 10000

28374 Rhodes Bakery Equipment
14330 SW McFarland Boulevard
Portland, OR 97224-2906

503-232-9101
Fax: 503-232-9206 800-426-3813
sales@kook-e-king.com www.kook-e-king.com
Manufacturer and exporter of cookie depositors and cutters
Marketing/Sales: Jan Duncan
Number Employees: 10-19
Square Footage: 120000
Brands:
Kook-E-King

28375 Rhodes Machinery International
1350 S 15th St
Louisville, KY 40210

502-213-3865
Fax: 502-213-0096 www.rsisystemsinc.net
Manufacturer and exporter of tow line conveyors
President: William Rhodes
Plant Manager: Mark Wolford

Estimated Sales: $1-3 Million
Number Employees: 5-9
Parent Co: Rhodes Systems Worldwide
Type of Packaging: Bulk

28376 Ribble Production
1601 Mearns Road
Warminster, PA 18974-1115
215-674-1706
Fax: 215-674-0123
Decorative toppings, nonpareils, jimmies and mixes;
custom manufacturing and packaging
VP: Joseph Van Houten
Number Employees: 20-49
Type of Packaging: Consumer, Food Service, Private Label, Bulk

28377 Ricca Chemical Co
1490 Lammers Pike
Batesville, IN 47006-8631
812-932-1160
Fax: 812-932-1254 888-467-4222
www.riccachemical.com
Laboratory chemicals used for quality control
President: Peter J Ricca
Manager: Paul Brandon
pbrandon@riccachemical.com
Estimated Sales: $5-10 Million
Number Employees: 10-19

28378 (HQ)Rice Lake Weighing Systems
230 W Coleman St
Rice Lake, WI 54868-2422
715-234-9171
Fax: 715-234-6967 800-472-6703
prodinfo@ricelake.com www.ricelake.com
Manufacturer and exporter of heavy capacity scales
and computer interface equipment; also, full metal
services available
Cmo: Pat Ranfranz
pranfranz@ricelake.com
VP: Rick Tyree
Regional Sales Director: Matt Crawford
Estimated Sales: $2.5-5 Million
Number Employees: 250-499
Square Footage: 100000

28379 Rice Packaging Inc
356 Somers Rd
Ellington, CT 06029-2628
860-872-8341
Fax: 860-872-0880 800-367-6725
info@ricepackaging.com www.ricepackaging.com
Custom printed folding cartons, stock boxes, point
of purchase displays and pressure sensitive and embossed foil labels
President: Clifford Rice
cliff@ricepackaging.com
Sales Manager: Angelo Salvatore
Estimated Sales: $10-20 Million
Number Employees: 50-99

28380 Rice Paper Box Company
PO Box 62096
1187 East 68th Avenue
Colorado Springs, CO 80962-2096
303-733-1000
Fax: 303-733-6789
Rigid set up, folding and transparent paper boxes
President: Douglas E Miller
CFO: David Rice
VP: Eugene Rice
Sales/Marketing: Michael Porter
Director of Operations: Matt Juhasz
Estimated Sales: Below $5 Million
Number Employees: 45

28381 Rich Xiberta USA Inc
450 Aaron St
Cotati, CA 94931-3068
707-795-1800
Fax: 707-795-1667 www.xiberta.com
Natural, high-end quality cork manufacturers
President: Ferran Botifoll
Contact: Rich Xiberta
r.xiberta@xiberta.com
Estimated Sales: Below $5 Million
Number Employees: 5-9

28382 Richard Read Construction Company
302 North First Avenue Suite #2
Arcadia, CA 91006
626-445-3002
Fax: 626-445-1027 888-450-7343
RRCCO@Pacbell.net
Plastic containers and bottles
Owner: Richard Read
rrcco@pacbell.net
Estimated Sales: $1-5 Million
Number Employees: 1-4

28383 Richards Industries Systems
4 Fairfield Cres
West Caldwell, NJ 07006-6296
973-575-7480
Fax: 973-575-6783 www.rifab.com
Bucket Z-type conveyors, dumpers, skip hoists and
material lifts; also, steel fabricators for all shapes
and forms of industrial equipment
Owner: Chuck Wampler
pspina@richardsind.com
VP: Chuck Wampler
Sales: Patricia Spina
Estimated Sales: $5-10 Million
Number Employees: 10-19
Square Footage: 50000

28384 Richards Packaging
4721 Burbank Rd
Memphis, TN 38118-6302
901-360-1121
Fax: 901-360-0050 800-583-0327
memphissales@richardspackaging.com
www.richardsmemphis.com
Manufacturer, exporter and importer of glass and
plastic bottles and jars; also, droppers, sprayers and
closures
CEO: Robert Boord
Estimated Sales: $10 Million
Number Employees: 10-19
Number of Brands: 100
Number of Products: 1000
Square Footage: 60000

28385 Richardson International
2800 One Lombard Pl.
Winnipeg, MB R3B 0X8
Canada
204-934-5961
866-217-6211
communications@richardson.ca
www.richardson.ca
Grains and oilseed.
President/CEO: Curt Vossen
Year Founded: 1857
Estimated Sales: $28.6 Billion
Number Employees: 2,500
Type of Packaging: Consumer, Food Service, Private Label, Bulk

28386 Richardson Researches
480 Grandview Drive
South San Francisco, CA 94080
510-653-4385
Fax: 510-785-6857 info@richres.com
www.richres.com
Consultant for new products and process development; also, courses available in chocolate and confectionery technology
President: Terence Richardson
CEO: Rose Marie Richardson
VP: RM Richardson
Estimated Sales: $1-2.5 Million
Number Employees: 5-9

28387 Richardson Seating Corp
2545 W Arthington St
Chicago, IL 60612-4107
312-829-4040
Fax: 312-829-8337 800-522-1883
sales@richardsonseating.com
www.richardsonseating.com
Bar and counter stools, logo seating and stack, dining, upholstered and club chairs and consumer furniture
Owner/CEO: Earl Lichtenstein
National Sales Manager: Jim Spatzek
Manager: Mike Liren
mike@richardsonseating.com
Estimated Sales: $10-20 Million
Number Employees: 20-49
Square Footage: 150000

28388 Richardson's Stamp Works
8566 Katy Fwy # 127
Suite 124
Houston, TX 77024-1811
713-973-0314
Fax: 713-973-0314
Stamp pad ink, name plates and badges, signs and
rubber and plastic stamps
President: Marjorie Waltman
Estimated Sales: $300,000-500,000
Number Employees: 5-9

28389 (HQ)Richmond Corrugated BoxCompany
PO Box 7715
Richmond, VA 23231
804-222-1300
Fax: 804-222-4897 www.richbox.com
Corrugated boxes and die cut products
President: Mark Williams
Vice President/General Manager: Chuck White
Structural Design: Wayne Johnson
Quality Control: Walters Spence
Sales: George Bayer
Contact: Brooke Hatcher
brookeh@richbox.com
Sales Manager: Mike Kelly
Production Manager: Mark Lawrence
Estimated Sales: $2.5-5 Million
Number Employees: 20-49
Square Footage: 96000
Other Locations:
Richmond Corrugated BoxCo.
Wilmington NC

28390 Richmond Printed Tape &Label
1901 N Penn Road
Hatfield, PA 19440-1961
804-798-4753
Fax: 804-798-0632 800-522-3525
Pressure sensitive tapes and labels
President: Scott Moeller
Quality Control: Kevin Moller
Manager Sales/Marketing: Mark Moeller
Estimated Sales: Below $5 Million
Number Employees: 15

28391 Richway Industries
504 N Maple St
PO Box 508
Janesville, IA 50647-7704
319-987-2976
Fax: 319-987-2251 800-553-2404
info@richwayind.com
Chemicals and equipment
President: R Borglum
rborglum@richwayind.com
Estimated Sales: $5-10 Million
Number Employees: 20-49

28392 Rico Packaging Company
3617 S Ashland Avenue
Chicago, IL 60609-1320
773-523-9190
Fax: 773-523-7965
Manufacturer and exporter of printed flexible packaging
President: William Wrigeyjr
CFO: Carol Riley
Manager: Don Bicking
R & D: William Wrigeyjr
Estimated Sales: $10-20 Million
Number Employees: 10
Parent Co: Wrigley

28393 Ricoh Technologies
1022 Santerre St
Grand Prairie, TX 75050-1937
972-602-0210
Fax: 972-602-3126 800-585-9367
Commercial fryers
President: Mac Shinagawa
Sales Representative: David Coronado
Estimated Sales: $2.5-5,000,000
Number Employees: 20-49
Parent Co: Sivex Corporation
Brands:
Aqua Pro

28394 Ridg-U-Rak
120 S Lake St
North East, PA 16428
866-479-7225
www.ridgurak.com

Racks including storage, flow, pushback, structural and cold-formed; custom designing available.
VP, Manufacturing: John Pellegrino
National Sales & Marketing Manager: Dave Olson
Estimated Sales: $27 Million
Number Employees: 250-499
Square Footage: 160000

28395 RidgeView Products LLC
2527 East Avenue S
La Crosse, WI 54601-6759
608-781-5946
Fax: 608-781-4408 888-782-1221
www.ridgeproducts.com
Manufacurer of brush and broom products
President: Keith Martin
Marketing/Sales: Roshelle Easterday
Number Employees: 4

28396 Rieke Packaging Systems
500 W 7th St
Auburn, IN 46706-2006
260-925-3700
Fax: 260-925-2493 sales@riekecorp.com
www.riekepackaging.com
Manufacturer and exporter of dispensing equipment including pumps, pourspouts and faucets
CEO: David M Pritchett
dpritchett@riekecorp.com
CEO: Lynn Brooks
CFO: Chris Baron
VP: Don Laipple
Marketing Director: Wayne Schmidt
Director Of Sales: William Heimach
Purchasing Manager: Jim Szink
Estimated Sales: $1-5,000,000
Number Employees: 250-499
Type of Packaging: Consumer, Food Service
Brands:
Englass
Flexspout
Flo-King
Flo-Rite
Fnd-30
Hybrid
Maxi
Multi-Meter
R-30

28397 Rietschle
1800 Gardner Expy
Quincy, IL 62305
Fax: 410-712-4148 800-247-2158
Vacuum pumps and compressors
President: Stephen J Lovell
Marketing Manager: Ron Heller
Estimated Sales: $10-20 Million
Number Employees: 60

28398 Rig-A-Lite Inc
8500 Hansen Rd
PO Box 12942
Houston, TX 77075-1096
713-378-7800
Fax: 713-943-8354 www.rigalite.com
Innovative and energy efficient lighting solutions for food processing environments, where rugged lighting products are required. Offer a complete line of high pressure hose down and corrosion resistant lighting products for severeenvironments suitable for almost any applications using florescent, HID, incandescent and LED lamping.
R&D: Syed Hasan
Marketing: Ross Blanford
Sales: Paul Markee
Contact: Maxine Hernandez
lovey1986@gmail.com
Operations: Walter Despain
Purchasing: Gordon Logan
Estimated Sales: $10-25 Million
Number Employees: 100
Parent Co: AZZ incorporated

28399 Rigid Plastics Packaging Institute
1667 K St
NW Suite 1000
Washington, DC 20006
202-974-5200
Fax: 202-296-7005 www.plasticsindustry.org
Plastics
President: William Cartuaex
Number Employees: 100-249

28400 Rigidized Metal Corp
658 Ohio St
Buffalo, NY 14203-3185
716-849-4760
Fax: 716-849-0401 800-836-2580
hr@rigidized.com www.rigidized.com
Manufacturer, importer and exporter of embossed metal parts for conveyors, packaging machinery and food processing equipment
Manager: Os Putman
osputman@rigidized.com
VP Sales: Louis Martin
Estimated Sales: $2.5-5,000,000
Number Employees: 50-99
Brands:
Rigid-Tex
Rigidized

28401 Riley & Geehr
2205 Lee Street
Evanston, IL 60202-1559
847-869-8100
Fax: 847-869-4765
Flexible pouches, stand-up pouches, shaped pouches, zipper pouches
CEO: Tom Riley
Sales Director: Diane Riley
Estimated Sales: $5-10 Million
Number Employees: 80
Type of Packaging: Consumer, Food Service, Private Label, Bulk

28402 Riley Cole ProfessionalRecruitment
4110 Redwood Road
Suite 201
Oakland, CA 94619-2370
510-336-2333
Fax: 510-428-2072
Executive search firm
Co-Partner: Donald Cole
Co-Partner: James Riley
Partner: James Riley
Estimated Sales: Below $5 Million
Number Employees: 2

28403 Rimex Metals Inc
2850 Woodbridge Ave
Edison, NJ 08837-3616
732-549-3800
Fax: 732-549-6435 sales@rimexusa.com
www.rimexmetals.com
President: Barbara Brandt
barbara.brandt@rimexmetals.com
Estimated Sales: $10-20 Million
Number Employees: 20-49

28404 Rio Syrup Co
2311 Chestnut St
St Louis, MO 63103-2298
314-436-7700
Fax: 314-436-7707 800-325-7666
flavors@riosyrup.com www.riosyrup.com
Syrups, extracts and concentrates, slush flavors and bases, fountain syrups and liquid food colors
President: Phillip Tomber
phil@riosyrup.com
Estimated Sales: $500,000-$1 Million
Number Employees: 5-9
Number of Products: 1200
Square Footage: 92000
Type of Packaging: Consumer, Food Service, Bulk
Brands:
Rio

28405 Rios, J J
4890 E Acampo Rd
Acampo, CA 95220-9601
209-333-7167
Fax: 209-333-3715
Wine industry vineyard services
Owner: Jose Rios
rios.jose.j@gmail.com
Estimated Sales: Less Than $500,000
Number Employees: 5-9

28406 Ripon Manufacturing Co Inc
652 S Stockton Ave
Ripon, CA 95366-2798
209-599-2148
Fax: 209-599-3114 800-800-1232
sales@riponmfgco.com www.riponmfgco.com
Manufacturer and exporter of edible nut processing equipment and conveyance systems

President: Glenn Navarro
sales@riponmfgco.com
VP: Ernst Boesch
Sales: Bruce Boyd
Purchasing: Denise Judd
Estimated Sales: $6 Million
Number Employees: 20-49
Square Footage: 126000

28407 Risco USA Corp
60 Bristol Dr
PO Box 198
South Easton, MA 02375-1193
508-230-3336
Fax: 508-230-5345 888-474-7267
info@riscousa.com www.riscousa.com
Equipment manufacturer to the meat and poultry industry which includes; stuffers, vacuum stuffers and systems
President: Alan Miller
amiller@riscousa.com
VP: P Kean
Technician: Victor Silva
Estimated Sales: $2.5-$5 Million
Number Employees: 10-19

28408 Ritchie's Foods
527 S West St
Piketon, OH 45661-8042
740-289-4393
Fax: 740-289-4375 800-628-1290
ritchiefoods.com
Foodservice distributor
CEO: James Ritchie
jritchie@ritchiefoods.com
Estimated Sales: $17.4 Million
Number Employees: 20-49
Square Footage: 30000
Type of Packaging: Consumer, Food Service

28409 Rite-Hite
8900 N Arbon Dr
Milwaukee, WI 53223
414-355-2600
Fax: 414-355-9248 800-841-4283
www.ritehite.com
Loading dock equipment, industrial doors, safety barriers, HVLS fans, industrial curtain walls, and more.
President & CEO: Steve Masters
Non-Executive Chairman: Michael White
Year Founded: 1965
Estimated Sales: $100-500 Million
Number Employees: 1000-4999

28410 Ritt-Ritt & Associates
5105 Tollview Drive
Suite 110
Rolling Meadows, IL 60008-3724
847-827-7771
Fax: 847-827-9776
Executive search firm specializing in job placement for the food and hospitality industries
Chairman: Art Ritt
President: William Morris
Estimated Sales: Less than $500,000
Number Employees: 1-4
Square Footage: 4400

28411 Ritz Packaging Company
54 Knickerbocker Avenue
Brooklyn, NY 11237-1636
718-366-2300
Fax: 631-476-4358
Paper boxes for ravioli, pasta, doughnuts, breadsticks and candy
Estimated Sales: less than $500,000
Number Employees: 1-4

28412 (HQ)Rival Manufacturing Company
800 E 101st Terrace
Suite 100
Kansas City, MO 64131-5308
816-943-4100
Fax: 816-943-4123 www.rivco.com
Manufacturer and exporter of can openers, vegetable and fruit shredders/slicers, mini choppers, slow cookers and ice cream freezers
Number Employees: 100-249
Other Locations:
Rival Manufacturing Co.
Kansas City MO

Brands:
Chop 'n Shake
Crock Pot
Dolly Madison

28413 River City Sales & Marketing
11700 Congo Ferndale Rd
Alexander, AR 72002-7007
501-316-3663
Fax: 501-794-0605
Owner: Vick Pannell
vickpannell@vickpannell.com
Estimated Sales: $1-5 Million
Number Employees: 1-4

28414 Riverside Industries
PO Box D
St Helens, OR 97051-0280
503-397-1922
Fax: 503-397-1527
Contract packager of liquids, powders, creams and solids
Executive Director: Cindy Stockton
Director Marketing: John Briggs
Number Employees: 50-99
Square Footage: 16000

28415 (HQ)Riverside ManufacturingCompany
301 Riverside Drive
P.O. Box 460
Moultrie, GA 31776-0460
800-841-8677
Manufacturer and exporter of industrial uniforms and clothing for bottlers, bakers, dairy workers, security officers and distillers
President/Chief Executive Officer: Lisa Vereen Zeanah
Contact: Norman Bergman
nbergman@riversideuniforms.com
Estimated Sales: $104 Million
Number Employees: 2,000
Square Footage: 1000000
Brands:
Riverside

28416 Riverside ManufacturingCompany
3405 N Arlington Heights Rd
Arlington Hts, IL 60004-1581
847-577-9300
Fax: 847-577-9318 800-877-3349
info@flagmaster.org www.riversidemedicalsc.com
Manufacturer and exporter of custom made plastic and fluorescent display pennants, flags and banners
VP Marketing: Andy Krupp
Estimated Sales: $1-5 Million
Number Employees: 20-49
Square Footage: 80000
Type of Packaging: Food Service
Brands:
Flagmaster

28417 Riverside Wire & Metal Co.
PO Box 122
Ionia, MI 48846-0122
616-527-3500
Fax: 616-527-8550
Wire racks and baskets
Owner: Don Shephard
Estimated Sales: $500,000-$1 Million
Number Employees: 5-9
Parent Co: Col-Mell
Type of Packaging: Consumer, Food Service

28418 Riverview Foods
1360 Bethleham Road
PO Box 765
Warsaw, KY 41095
859-567-5211
Fax: 859-567-5213
Smoked meats, barbecue and tomato sauces; research and development services
President: Bob Weldon
VP Sales/Marketing: Robert Schroeder
General Manager: Mike Benton
Number Employees: 50-99
Square Footage: 100000
Type of Packaging: Consumer, Food Service, Private Label, Bulk
Brands:
Riverview Foods Authentic

28419 Riverwood International
814 Livingston Ct SE
Marietta, GA 30067-8940
770-644-3000
Fax: 770-644-2962
investor.relations@graphicpkg.com
Paperboard and paperboard packaging machinery company
President: Thomas H Johnson
CEO: David W Scheible
Marketing Manager: Hous King
Contact: Sylvia Gillenwaters
sylvia.gillenwaters@riverwood.com
Estimated Sales: $50-100 Million
Number Employees: 10,000

28420 Riverwood International
3350 Riverwood Pkwy SE
Atlanta, GA 30339-6401
770-984-5477
Fax: 770-644-2620 www.riverwood.com
Packaging systems and machinery for beverages, produce, etc
CEO: Stephen Humphrey
CFO: Don Baldwin
Estimated Sales: $50-100 Million
Number Employees: 100-249

28421 Riviana Foods Inc.
PO Box 2636
Houston, TX 77252
713-529-3251
sales@riviana.com
www.riviana.com
Rice and pasta.
President/CEO: Bastiaan de Zeeuw
bdezeeuw@riviana.com
Senior VP/CFO: Michael Slavin
Senior VP, Operations: Brett Beckfield
Senior VP, Marketing: Sandra Kim
Senior VP, Human Resources: Gerard Ferguson
Year Founded: 1965
Estimated Sales: $500 Million
Number Employees: 1,000-4,999
Number of Brands: 28
Parent Co: Ebro Foods, S.A.
Type of Packaging: Consumer, Food Service, Private Label, Bulk
Other Locations:
Corporate Office
Houston TX
Plant
Brinkley AR
Plant
Carlisle AR
Plant
Clearbrook MN
Plant
Hazen AR
Plant
Memphis TN
Brands:
Mahatma®
Carolina®
Minute®
Success®
AA Brand®
Adolphus®
Blue Ribbon Rice®
Colusa Rose®
Comet Rice®
Gourmet House®
Pear Blossom®
Rice Select®
River Rice®
Sello Rojo®
Water Maid®
Wonder®
Ronzoni™
American Beauty™
No Yolks®
Skinner®
Creamette®
Light 'n Fluffy®
Mrs. Weiss'®
New Mill®
Prince®
San Giorgio®
Wacky Mac®

28422 Rixie Paper Products Inc
10 Quinter St
Pottstown, PA 19464-6514
610-323-9220
Fax: 610-323-6146 800-377-2692
www.sonoco.com
Manufacturer and exporter of disposable paper products including coasters: cellulose, pulpboard, budgetboard, nonwoven, etc.; also, placemats and sanitary caps for drinking glasses
President: Tom Johnson
Chairman: Roger Schrum
roger.schrum@sonoco.com
VP Sales/Marketing: Smitty Thomas
VP Operations: Kent Adicks
Plant Manager: Lee Burg
Estimated Sales: $5-10 Million
Number Employees: 10-19
Parent Co: Engraph
Type of Packaging: Food Service
Brands:
Cupkin
Rixcaps
Sof-Ette

28423 Rjo Associates
3645 Cortez Rd W Ste 140
Bradenton, FL 34210
941-756-3001
Fax: 941-756-0027 admin@mriflorida.com
Search consultants for technical product development and marketing in food and food ingredient manufacturing
President: R Rush Oster
Estimated Sales: Less than $500,000
Number Employees: 1-4
Parent Co: Management Recruiters

28424 Rjr Technologies
7875 Edgewater Dr
Oakland, CA 94621-2001
510-638-5901
Fax: 510-638-5958 Service@rjrpolymers.com
www.rjrtechnologies.com
Manufacturer and exporter of flexible packaging products including folding foil cartons, barrier films and aluminum foil; also, printing and lamination available
President & CEO: Wil Salhuana
CFO: Tony Bregante
Estimated Sales: $1-5 Million
Number Employees: 100-249

28425 Rjs Carter Co Inc
251 5th St NW # D
New Brighton, MN 55112-6864
651-636-8818
Manufacturer and exporter of synthetic rubber balls for sifter and screener cleaning
President: John Galt
Estimated Sales: Less Than $500,000
Number Employees: 1-4
Brands:
Screwballs

28426 Ro-An Industries Corporation
6420 Admiral Ave
Flushing, NY 11379
718-366-8971
Fax: 718-821-3838 800-255-7626
Plastic bag machinery
President: Angelo Cervera
Contact: Eric Schwarz
schwarz@roan.com
Estimated Sales: $10-20 Million
Number Employees: 100-249

28427 Roaring Brook Dairy
Po Box 753
Chappaqua, NY 10514
646-559-9330
Fax: 866-733-6736 roaringbrookdairy@gmail.com
Cheesemaking kits
Marketing: Leslie Kozupsky
Estimated Sales: $88,000
Number Employees: 2

28428 Robar International Inc
3013 N 114th St
Milwaukee, WI 53222-4289
414-259-1104
Fax: 414-259-0842 800-279-7750
rhoelzl@robarinternational.com
Dispoza-Pak trash compactors.

President: Robert Hoelzl
rhoelzl@robarinternational.com
VP: Daniel Hoelzl
Estimated Sales: Below $5 Million
Number Employees: 5-9
Brands:
　Dispoza-Pak

28429 Robatech USA Inc
1005 Alderman Dr # 108
Suite 108
Alpharetta, GA 30005-3825
　　　　　　　770-663-8380
　　Fax: 770-663-8381 info@robatechusa.com
　　　　　　　www.robatech.com
Hot melt and cold adhesive application equipment,
patten controls
CEO: Deon Strauss
Contact: Steve Green
sgreen@robatechusa.com
Estimated Sales: $500,000-$1 Million
Number Employees: 1-4
Parent Co: Robatech Group

28430 Robatech USA Inc
1005 Alderman Dr # 108
Suite 108
Alpharetta, GA 30005-3825
　　　　　　　770-663-8380
　　Fax: 770-663-8381 info@robatechusa.com
　　　　　　　www.robatech.com
CEO: Deon Strauss
Contact: Steve Green
sgreen@robatechusa.com
Estimated Sales: $1-3 Million
Number Employees: 1-4

28431 Robbie Manufacturing Inc
10810 Mid America Dr
Lenexa, KS 66219-1295
　　　　　　　913-492-3400
　　Fax: 913-492-1543 800-255-6328
Packaging equipment and materials
President/CEO: Irv Robinson
COO: Pepper Stokes
Executive VP Sales/Marketing: Doug Larson
Product Development Director: Jeff Linton
Estimated Sales: $20-50 Million
Number Employees: 100-249
Square Footage: 94596
Type of Packaging: Food Service, Private Label

28432 Robby Vapor Systems
10224 NW 47th Street
Sunrise, FL 33351-7970
　　　　　　　954-746-3080
　　Fax: 954-746-0036 800-888-8711
　　　　　robbyvapor@aol.com
Manufacturer, importer and exporter of stainless
steel vapor cleaning systems and carts
President: Fran Vogt-Strauss
Office Manager: Lisa Skewes
Estimated Sales: $500,000-$1 Million
Number Employees: 9
Square Footage: 22240
Brands:
　Robby Vapor Systems
　Vapor Dragon

28433 Robecco
99 Park Ave # 7
New York, NY 10016-1506
　　　　　　　212-286-8585
　　Fax: 212-490-8966 sales@robecoinc.com
　　　　　　　www.robecoinc.com
Supplier of vinyl sheeting
President: Maurice Rosenthal
Estimated Sales: $10-20 Million
Number Employees: 20-49

28434 Robelan Displays Inc
395 Westbury Blvd
Hempstead, NY 11550-1900
　　　　　　　516-564-8600
　　Fax: 516-564-8077 865-564-8600
　　main@robelan.net www.robelan.net
Merchandising fixture and food display units; im-
porter of theme props
President: Andrew Abatemarco
CFO: John Didiovanni
HR Executive: Rob Abatemarco
main@robelan.net
VP Sales: Rob Abutemarco
Customer Service: Carol Kirk

Estimated Sales: $5-10 Million
Number Employees: 50-99
Type of Packaging: Food Service

28435 Robert Bosch LLC
38000 Hills Tech Dr
Farmington, MI 48331
　　　　　　　917-421-7209
　　　　　　　www.bosch.us
Filling and sealing equipment
President, North America: Mike Mansuetti
CFO: Maximiliane Straub
Estimated Sales: $80 Billion
Number Employees: 400,100
Parent Co: Robert Bosch GmbH
Brands:
　Svk
　Trans-Zip

28436 Robert C Vncek Design Assoc
30 Eric Trl
Sussex, NJ 07461-4110
　　　　　　　973-702-8553
　　Fax: 973-702-8553 www.rcvdes.com
Consulting firm providing packaging design, development, engineering, graphics, validation, source reduction, troubleshooting and project management
services
Contact: Robert Vincek
rcvdes@warwick.net
Estimated Sales: Below $500,000
Number Employees: 5

28437 Robert-James Sales
699 Hertel Ave
Buffalo, NY 14207-2341
　　　　　　　716-871-0091
　　Fax: 716-871-0923 800-777-1325
　　RJSales@RJSales.com www.RJSales.com
Manufacturer and exporter of fittings, pipes, tubing,
hose clamps and sanitary stainless steel valves
Sales Manager: Thomas Callahan
Estimated Sales: $50-100 Million
Number Employees: 100-249

28438 Robertet Flavors
10 Colonial Dr.
Piscataway, NJ 08854
　　　　　　　732-981-8300
　　　　Fax: 732-981-1717
　　robertetFlavors@robertetUSA.com
　　　　　　www.robertet.com
Flavorings.
Chairman/CEO: Philippe Maubert
Head of the Flavourings Division: Olivier Maubert
CFO: Gilles Audoli
Managing Director, Flavourings Division: Antoine
Kastler
Director, Industrial Operations: Herve Bellon
Year Founded: 1850
Estimated Sales: $524.9 Million
Number Employees: 1,800
Number of Brands: 5+
Square Footage: 16805
Parent Co: Robertet SA
Type of Packaging: Food Service
Other Locations:
　Robertet Culinary
　Schoten, Belgium
Brands:
　Citra-Next®
　Natur-Cell®
　Flavour Sensations
　Smart® Flavours
　Accord® Flavours

28439 Roberts Packaging Equipment
424 Howard Ave
Des Plaines, IL 60018-1910
　　　　　　　847-390-9410
　　Fax: 847-390-6170 888-221-0700
Contract packager and manufacturer of high speed
pouch packaging equipment
President: Robert G Koppe
Director Sales/Marketing: Michael Boyd
Manager: Alex Waterman
axwaterman@cloudps.com
Estimated Sales: $2.5-5 Million
Number Employees: 50-99
Square Footage: 80000

28440 Roberts Pallet Co
607 County Road 500
Ellington, MO 63638-7759
　　　　　　　573-663-7877
　　　　Fax: 573-663-7873
Wooden pallets
Owner: Phillip Roberts
palletgal6@aol.com
VP: Wes Roberts
Estimated Sales: Less than $500,000
Number Employees: 20-49
Square Footage: 18000

28441 Roberts Poly Pro Inc
5416 Wyoming Ave
Charlotte, NC 28273-8861
　　　　　　　704-588-1794
　　Fax: 704-588-1821 800-269-7409
　　info@robertspolypro.com
　　　　www.robertspolypro.com
Manufacturer and exporter of converting equipment
and systems including folder/gluers, case packers,
prefeeders, turntables, stack turners, etc.; also, plastic packaging components and machinery including
label and pour spoutapplicators, etc
President: Vipul Deshani
vipul.deshani@vvfltd.com
VP Engineering: Claude Monsees
Estimated Sales: $5-10 Million
Number Employees: 50-99
Square Footage: 140000
Parent Co: Pro Mach

28442 Roberts Systems
8506 S Tryon St # A
Charlotte, NC 28273-3549
　　　　　　　704-588-5210
　　Fax: 704-588-8199 800-269-7409
　　　　sales@robertssystems.com
Motion cartoner and automatic inserter
Estimated Sales: $.5-1 million
Number Employees: 1-4

28443 Roberts Technology Group
120 New Britain Blvd
Chalfont, 18 18936-9637
　　　　　　　215-822-0600
　　Fax: 215-822-0662 info@rtgpkg.com
　　　　　　　www.rtgpkg.com
Bandages bundling, shrink

28444 Roberts-Gordon LLC
1250 William St
Buffalo, NY 14206-1885
　　　　　　　716-852-4400
　　Fax: 716-852-0854 800-828-7450
　　　　　www.robertsgordon.com
Gas-fired infrared heaters and energy management
systems
President: Meredith Christman
christman@rg-inc.com
R & D: Mak Murdlch
Marketing Director: Madonna Courtney
Sales Director: Kevin Mahoney
Plant Manager: Roy Wyzykowski
Purchasing Manager: Judith Cloon
Estimated Sales: $20-50 Million
Number Employees: 100-249

28445 Robertson Furniture Co Inc
890 Elberton St
Toccoa, GA 30577-3479
　　　　　　　706-886-1494
　　Fax: 706-886-8998 800-241-0713
　　tzirkle@robertson-furniture.com
　　　　www.robertson-furniture.com
Manufacturer and importer of chairs, tables, booths,
steel frame seating and casegoods
President: Scott Hodges
tzirkle@robertson-furniture.com
Director Sales/Marketing: Tim Zirkle
Sales Exec: Tim Zirkle
Estimated Sales: $10-20 Million
Number Employees: 50-99
Square Footage: 400000
Type of Packaging: Food Service, Private Label

28446 Robin Shepherd Group
1301 Riverplace Blvd.
Suite 1100
Jacksonville, FL 32207
　　　　　　　904-359-0981
　　Fax: 904-359-0808 877-896-8774
　trsginfo@shepheragency.com www.trsg.net

Consultant providing food product development, point of purchase display design, public relations and marketing services; importer, exporter and packager of specialty foods including condiments and sauces
President: Robin Shepherd
VP Marketing: Tom Nuijens
Contact: Marina Martin
mmartin@shepherdagency.com
Estimated Sales: $5-10 Million
Number Employees: 20-49
Square Footage: 20000
Type of Packaging: Consumer, Food Service, Private Label

28447 Robinett & Assoc
2011 N Collins Blvd # 701
Suite 701
Richardson, TX 75080-2689
972-234-1945
Consultant providing designing and engineering of heating, ventilation, air conditioning, plumbing, electrical, security, fire, smoke detection and alarm and energy management facilities
President: Robert Robinett
Estimated Sales: Less Than $500,000
Number Employees: 1-4
Square Footage: 3200

28448 (HQ)Robinette Co
250 Blackley Rd
Bristol, TN 37620-5028
423-968-7800
Fax: 423-968-7982 www.therobinetteco.com
Printed paper for flour, cornmeal, sugar, construction industry, and food industry
President: Joseph Robinette
CEO: Bill Bouton
bbouton@therobinetteco.com
CFO: Gary Hunt
Vice President: Gary Hunt
Quality Control: Payne Greg
Customer Service: Laura Mann
Estimated Sales: $20-50 Million
Number Employees: 100-249
Square Footage: 200000
Type of Packaging: Consumer, Food Service, Private Label
Other Locations:
  Robinette Co.
  Bristol TN
Brands:
  Shinglgard
  Shinglwrap

28449 Robinson Cold Storage
24415 NE 10th Ave
Ridgefield, WA 98642
360-887-3501
Frozen foods storage
President/CEO: Allen Nirenstein
Chairman: Thomas Klein
Estimated Sales: Less than $500,000
Number Employees: 1-4

28450 Robinson Industries Inc
3051 W Curtis Rd
Coleman, MI 48618-8549
989-465-6111
Fax: 989-465-1217 info@robinsonind.com
www.robinsonind.com
Manufacturer and exporter of thermoformed and injection molded plastic pallets, trays and totes. Also, consumer items. Custom designed.
President: Bin Robinson
CEO: Inez Kaleto
CFO: Kurt Schefka
Research & Development: Jeff Sankler
Quality Control: Rod Crites
Marketing: Ronda Robinson
VP Sales/Sales Manager: Mark Weidner
Production: Tom Roberts
Plant Manager: Melissa Jellum
Purchasing: Jason Pahl
Estimated Sales: $40 Million
Number Employees: 100-249
Square Footage: 152005

28451 Robinson Tape & Label
32 Park Drive East
Branford, CT 6405
203-481-5581
Fax: 203-481-6076 800-433-7102
www.robinsontapeandlabel.com

Pressure sensitive tapes and labels; wholesaler/distributor of tape machines and shipping supplies
President: Edward Pepe
Marketing: Sarah Yale
Sales: Mike Dellavalle
Contact: Timothy Grahm
timothygrahm@robinsontapeandlabel.com
Production: Anthony Martone
Purchasing: Dennis Smith
Estimated Sales: $5-10 Million
Number Employees: 10-19
Square Footage: 22000
Type of Packaging: Consumer, Food Service, Private Label, Bulk

28452 Robinson/Kirshbaum Industries
261 E 157th St
Gardena, CA 90248
310-354-9948
Fax: 310-354-9921 800-929-3812
contact@rki-inc.com www.rki-inc.com
Beverage equipment including dispensers, water filtration, etc
VP: Bruce Kirshbaum
Contact: Jon Robinson
jrobinson@rki-inc.com
Estimated Sales: $1-2,500,000
Number Employees: 5-9

28453 Robinson/Kirshbaum Industries
261 E 157th St
Gardena, CA 90248
310-354-9948
Fax: 310-354-9921 support@rki-inc.com
www.rki-inc.com
Beverage equipment including dispensers, water filtration, etc
President: Jon Robinson
jrobinson@rki-inc.com
Executive VP: Bruce Kirshbaum
R&D: Bruce Kirshbaum
Estimated Sales: Below $5 Million
Number Employees: 1-4

28454 Robocom Systems Intl
1111 Broadhollow Rd # 100
#100
Farmingdale, NY 11735-4819
631-753-2180
Fax: 843-881-4893 info@robocom.com
www.robocom.com
Computer software for order processing, inventory control, purchasing and warehouse management
President/Owner: Fred Radcliffe
fradcliffe@robocom.com
VP: Rick Register
VP, Customer Services: Richard Adamo
Number Employees: 1-4
Brands:
  Csw
  Control Ii

28455 Robocom Systems Intl
1111 Broadhollow Rd # 100
Suite 100
Farmingdale, NY 11735-4819
631-753-2180
Fax: 516-795-6933 800-795-5100
info@robocom.com www.robocom.com
Develops and implements logistic warehouse solutions designed to maximize productivity and streamline warehouse operations. Services provide inlcude software development and installation, and support
President/Owner: Fred Radcliffe
fradcliffe@robocom.com
VP, Customer Services: Richard Adamo
Estimated Sales: Below $5 Million
Number Employees: 1-4

28456 Robot Coupe
280 S Perkins St
Ridgeland, MS 39157-2719
601-898-8411
Fax: 601-898-9134 800-824-1646
info@robotcoupeusa.com
Manufactures commercial food processors, vegetable preparation units, and combination processing units.
President: Jay Williams
VP: David Mouck
VP/Controller: C Redding
VP Marketing: David Mouck
National Accounts Manager: David Mouck

Estimated Sales: $10-20 Million
Number Employees: 50-99
Square Footage: 60000
Type of Packaging: Food Service
Brands:
  Robot Coupe

28457 (HQ)Robotic Vision Systems
486 Amherst Street
Nashua, NH 03063-1224
781-821-0830
Fax: 781-828-8942 800-646-6664
Bar code scanners, data collection systems, decoders, machine vision, and scanners
Senior VP: John Agapakis
Estimated Sales: $1-5 Million
Number Employees: 100-249

28458 Rocheleau Blow Molding Systems
117 Industrial Road
Fitchburg, MA 01420-4697
978-345-1723
Fax: 978-345-5972 sales@rocheleautool.com
www.rocheleautool.com
Extrusion blow molding and plastic blow molding machinery
President: Steven Rocheleau
Number Employees: 10-19

28459 (HQ)Rochester Midland Corp
155 Paragon Dr
Rochester, NY 14624-1167
585-336-2200
Fax: 585-266-8919 800-535-5053
webmaster@rochestermidland.com
www.rochestermidland.com
Cleaning/sanitary equipment and supplies including dish washing compounds, detergents, disinfectants, floor polish, chemicals, etc.; also, insecticides and insect control systems
CEO: Harlan D Calkins
Estimated Sales: $2.5-5 Million
Number Employees: 500-999

28460 Rochester Midland Corp
155 Paragon Dr
Rochester, NY 14624-1167
585-336-2200
Fax: 585-266-8919 800-387-7174
www.rochestermidland.com
Deli and butcher paper and latex and poly gloves
Chairman/ CEO: H.D. Calkins
key person: Brenda Barr
National Sales Manager: Bob Guberman
Manager: Brenda Barr
National Account Manager: Matt Willoughby
Estimated Sales: $10-20 Million
Number Employees: 500-999

28461 Rochester Midland Corp
155 Paragon Dr
Rochester, NY 14624-1167
585-336-2200
Fax: 585-266-8919 800-836-1627
www.rochestermidland.com
Manufacturer and exporter of production cleaning and sanitizing chemicals for food and beverage processing facilities; also, water and wastewater treatment chemicals
President/Chief Operating Officer: Michael Coyner
CEO: Kathy Lindahl
klindahl@rochestermidland.com
Chief Financial Officer: Lisa Steel
Senior Vice President: Al Swierzewski
Senior Vice President, Marketing: Owen Foster
Vice President, Sales: Mike Burroughs
Senior Vice President, Operations: Howard Shames
Purchasing Manager: Richard Roy
Estimated Sales: $83 Million
Number Employees: 500-999
Square Footage: 190000
Brands:
  Brandguard

28462 Rock Valley Oil & Chemical Co
1911 Windsor Rd
Loves Park, IL 61111-4293
815-654-2401
Fax: 815-654-2428 www.rockvalleyoil.com

'Today, Rock Valley has grown to be recognized as an international manufacturer and supplier of superior quality industrial lubricants, metalworking and hydraulic fluids, as well as reference oils and calibrating fluids tailored to theautomotive and heavy truck industry'. www.rockvalleyoil.com
President: Roger Schramm
sales@rockvalleyoil.com
Estimated Sales: $12.5 Million
Number Employees: 50-99
Brands:
   Sun Oil
   Viscor
   Viscosity

28463 Rock-Tenn Company
504 Tasman St
Norcross, GA 30071

608-223-6272
Fax: 608-246-1145 www.rocktenn.com
Manufacturer and exporter of folding paper cartons, boxes and displays
Owner: Bill Rock
General Manager: Gary Adrian
Estimated Sales: $5-10 Million
Number Employees: 1-4

28464 Rockaway Baking
PO Box 392
Rockaway, NJ 07866-0392

973-625-3003
Fax: 973-625-4271 877-762-5225
rockbake@aol.com
Automatic equipment for baking industry; specializing in English muffin systems, materials handling conveyors, spiral conveyors for freezing, proofing and cooling
Estimated Sales: $1 Million
Number Employees: 2

28465 Rocket Man
2501 Maple St
Louisville, KY 40211-1163

502-775-7502
Fax: 502-775-7519 800-365-6661
sales@rocketman.com www.rocketman.com
Manufacturer, importer and exporter of backpack drink dispensers and portable beverage dispensing equipment
Owner: Mike Hinson
Contact: Mazen Masri
mazenm@rocketman.com
Estimated Sales: $1-3 Million
Number Employees: 10-19
Square Footage: 20000
Brands:
   Rocket Man

28466 Rockford Chemical Co
915 W Perry St
Belvidere, IL 61008-3498

815-544-3476
Fax: 815-544-0532
Boiler compounds
President: Vann W Rossmiller
Estimated Sales: $1-2.5 Million
Number Employees: 1-4

28467 Rockford Sanitary Systems
5159 28th Ave
Rockford, IL 61109-1720

815-229-5077
Fax: 815-229-5108 800-747-5077
www.rkfdseparators.com
Grease, oil, sand and lint separators; also, trench drains
President: Merritt Mott
mjmott@aol.com
CEO: James Griffin
VP Engineering: Bryce Russell
Quality Control: Jim Griffin
Estimated Sales: $5-10 Million
Number Employees: 20-49
Square Footage: 68000

28468 Rockford-Midland Corporation
1715 Northrock Ct
Rockford, IL 61103

815-877-0212
Fax: 815-877-0419 800-327-7908
Manufacturer and exporter of fully and semi-automatic case packers and sealers including hot melt, cold glue and tape

President: Adrienne Murphy
Sales Director: Donna Bonetti
Production Manager: Tim Vronch
Purchasing Manager: Karen Steiner
Estimated Sales: $5-10 Million
Number Employees: 20-49
Square Footage: 80000
Brands:
   Casestar
   Sealstar

28469 Rockland Foods
300 Corporate Drive
Suite14
Blauvelt, NY 10913-1162

845-358-8600
Fax: 845-358-9003 800-962-7663
rfi@rfiingredients.com www.rfiingredients.com
Owner: Jeff Wuagneux
Quality Control: Pi-Yu Hsu
Contact: Jennifer Diliddo
jennifer.diliddo@rfiingredients.com
Estimated Sales: $1-5 Million
Number Employees: 10-19

28470 Rockland Technology
817 S Mill Street
Suite 104
Lewisville, TX 75057-4637

972-221-6190
Fax: 972-420-0055
President: Thomas Bronson
tbronson@diamondtouchpos.com
Estimated Sales: Below $5 Million
Number Employees: 20

28471 Rockline Industries
4343 S Taylor Dr
Sheboygan, WI 53081

920-453-2769
800-558-7790
customercareteam@racklineind.com
www.racklineind.com
Private label consumer products; including coffee filters and baby wipes.
President: Randy Rudolph
Year Founded: 1976
Estimated Sales: $100-500 Million
Brands:
   Bake Fresh
   Brew Rite
   Fresh'n Up
   Natural Brew
   Star

28472 Rockwell Automation Inc
1201 S 2nd St
Milwaukee, WI 53204

414-382-2000
www.rockwellautomation.com
Industrial automation equipment, machinery and components.
Chairman & CEO: Blake Moret
blmoret@ra.rockwell.com
SVP/Chief Technology Officer: Sujeet Chand
SVP, Control Products & Solutions: Ted Crandall
SVP, Corporate Development: Elik Fooks
SVP/Chief Financial Officer: Patrick Goris
SVP/General Counsel/Secretary: Rebecca House
SVP/Global Sales & Marketing: Thomas Donato
SVP, Connected Enterprise Consulting: Bob Murphy
Year Founded: 1903
Estimated Sales: $6.3 Billion
Number Employees: 22,000
Brands:
   Rockwell Automation
   Allen-Bradley
   FactoryTalk

28473 Rocky Shoes & Boots Inc
39 E Canal St
Nelsonville, OH 45764

740-753-3130
866-442-4908
www.rockyboots.com
Nonslip service shoes and boots.
Chairman: Mike Brooks
Chief Executive Officer: Jason Brooks
Chief Financial Officer: Tom Robertson
President, Operations: Richard Simms
President, Manufacturing/Operations: Dave Dixon

Year Founded: 1932
Estimated Sales: $100-500 Million
Number Employees: 1000-4999
Brands:
   4 Way Step

28474 Roddy Products Pkgng CoInc
1 Merion Ter
Aldan, PA 19018-3000

610-623-7040
Fax: 610-623-0521 joearoddy@aol.com
Manufacturer and exporter of wooden shipping crates
President: Joseph Masticola Sr
CFO: Joseph Masticola Sr
IT: Tina Moore
marieroddy@aol.com
Estimated Sales: $1-2.5 Million
Number Employees: 10-19

28475 Rodem Inc
5095 Crookshank Rd
Cincinnati, OH 45238-3366

513-922-0096
Fax: 513-922-1680 sales@rodem.com
www.rodem.com
Agitation systems, curd, milk, silo, tank, analyzers/tests, plant operations,chlorine, total solids, chillers, clean rooms and equipment, custom fabrication, deaerators, dispensers, milk, ice equipment, ingredient feeders, laddersvat, margarine process
President: Chris Diener
cdiener@rodem.com
R&D: Stan Pritchart
Chairman of the Board: Robert Diener
Estimated Sales: $30-50 Million
Number Employees: 50-99

28476 Rodes Professional Apparel
4938 Brownsboro Road
Louisville, KY 40222

502-584-3112
Fax: 502-584-8840 info@rodes.com
www.rodes.com
Uniforms, aprons and shoes
President: Lawrence Smith
Number Employees: 80
Parent Co: Lithgow Industries

28477 Rodo Industries
44 Meg Drive
London, ON N6E 3R4
Canada

519-668-3711
Fax: 519-668-3257 sales@rodoinc.com
www.rodoinc.com
Stacking and regular chairs, fast food seating, cushions, pads, bar/counter stools, tables including legs, bases and booths
President: Randy Snow
CFO: Gary Forgrade
R&D: Gary Forgrade
Quality Control: Gary Forgrade
Sales: Hugh Crosby
Estimated Sales: $3.5 Million
Number Employees: 45

28478 Roechling Engineered Plastics
PO Box 2729
Gastonia, NC 28053-2729

704-922-7814
Fax: 704-922-7651 800-541-4419
Manufacturer and exporter of conveyor components, industrial plastics, HDPE, PP, UHMW and PVDF; also, sheets, tubes and profiles
President: Lewis Carter
Quality Control: Brychan Griffiths
Marketing: Tim Brown
Sales: Paul Krawczyk
Contact: Kathy Millen
millen@roechling.com
Number Employees: 50-99
Square Footage: 560000
Brands:
   Polystone Cut-Rite
   Sustamid
   Sustarin
   Sustatec

28479 Roechling Machined Plastics
1551 Woodward Drive Ext
Greensburg, PA 15601

724-834-1340
Fax: 724-834-5822 www.roechling-plastics.us

Fiberglass plastic machining
Estimated Sales: $20-50 Million
Number Employees: 20-49

28480 Roesch Inc
100 N 24th St
Belleville, IL 62226-6659

618-233-2760
Fax: 618-233-1186   800-423-6243
sales@roeschinc.com www.roeschinc.com
Enameling of steel and cast iron, stoves, refrigerators and specialty parts, including high temperature ceramic coatings and metal fabricatiors of sheet metal parts
President: Jason Baughman
j.baughman@roeschinc.com
Executive Vice President: Debbie Voges-Schneider
Sales Manager: Debbie Thomas
Estimated Sales: $10-20 Million
Number Employees: 50-99

28481 Roeslein & Assoc Inc
9200 Watson Rd # 200
Suite 200
St Louis, MO 63126-1528

314-729-0055
Fax: 314-729-0070 sales@roeslein.com
www.roesleinae.com
Owner: Dave May
dmay@roeslein.com
CFO: Fritz Dickmann
Estimated Sales: $5-10 Million
Number Employees: 100-249

28482 Rofin-Baasel Inc
68 Barnum Rd
Devens, MA 01434-3508

978-635-9100
Fax: 978-635-9199 www.rofin.com
President: Walter Volkmar
Contact: Derrick Brewster
brewster@rofin.com
Number Employees: 1000-4999

28483 Roflan Associates
5314 S Yale Avenue
Suite 1100
Tulsa, OK 74135-6251

978-475-0100
Fax: 978-475-4144
Lighting fixtures
VP/Manager: Mike Lacharite
Number Employees: 22

28484 Roha USA LTD
5015 Manchester Ave
St Louis, MO 63110-2011

314-289-8300
Fax: 314-531-0461   888-533-7642
roha.usa@rohagroup.com www.roha.com
Distributors of synthetic colors, lake pigments and dye blends. Custom blends. Patent pending, dust free colors
CEO: Rohit Tibrewala
Research & Development: Mike Chin
Estimated Sales: $2.5-5 Million
Number Employees: 50-99
Number of Brands: 3
Parent Co: Roha Dyechem
Brands:
    Dust Free Form of Fd&C Colors

28485 Rohm America Inc.
2 Turner Place
Piscataway, NJ 08855

732-981-5250
Fax: 732-981-5382
Contact: Gerald Bagenski
gerald.bagenski@evonik.com
Estimated Sales: $1-5 Million

28486 Rohrer Corp.
717 Seville Rd
PO Box 1009
Wadsworth, OH 44282

800-243-6640
info@rohrer.com www.rohrer.com
Manufacturer and exporter of skin packaging, blister cards and stretch pack cards
National Sales Director: Jim Price
Year Founded: 1973
Estimated Sales: $50-100 Million
Number Employees: 100-249
Type of Packaging: Bulk

28487 Rolfs @ Boone
1773 219th Ln
P.O. Box 369
Boone, IA 50036

515-432-2010
Fax: 515-432-5262   800-265-2010
info@boonegroup.com www.boonegroup.com
Manufacturer and exporter of dust systems, high and low bag filters, cyclones, ducting, fittings, bearing and belt alignment instrumentation and hazard and motion monitoring controls
President: Kevin Miles
Sales: Greg Knoxx
Dust Control: Delmar Mains
Production Manager: Brian Huffman
Estimated Sales: $5-10 Million
Number Employees: 10-19
Square Footage: 112000

28488 Roll Rite Corp
3480 Investment Blvd
Hayward, CA 94545-3811

510-293-1444
Fax: 510-293-1450   800-345-9305
info@rollrite.com www.roll-rite.net
Material handling equipment including factory hand trucks, wheels, casters, skewing racks and nonpowered equipment; exporter of wheels and casters
CEO/President: Mario Sequeira
ms@roll-rite.net
Estimated Sales: $1-2.5 Million
Number Employees: 5-9
Square Footage: 17800
Brands:
    Alumiflex
    Areo
    Bassick
    Colson
    Dutro
    Hamilton
    Magliner
    Roll Rite Super Caster
    Roll-Rite Corp.
    Wesco

28489 Roll-O-Sheets Canada
130 Big Bay Point Road
Barrie, ON L4N 9B4
Canada

705-722-5223
Fax: 705-722-7120   888-767-3456
info@roll-o-sheets.com
Manufacturer, importer and exporter of converted PVC film; wholesaler/distributor of vacuum pouches, table covers, Cellophane and plastic sandwich and ovenable containers
General Manager: Bryce Atkinson
Number Employees: 20
Square Footage: 88000
Brands:
    Row L
    Row S
    Wrap It

28490 Rolland Machining & Fabricating
43 Ventnor Avenue
Moneta, VA 24121-5350

973-827-6911
Fax: 973-827-5699
Custom fabricated plastic materials including ducts, fittings, tanks, trays, etc.; also, general machining in soft metals and plastic
President: Mary Rolland
Number Employees: 10
Square Footage: 8000

28491 Rollhaus Seating Products Inc
2109 Borden Ave # 4
Long Island City, NY 11101-4531

718-729-9111
Fax: 718-729-9117   800-822-6684
www.seatingproducts.com
Booths, chairs and folding tables
President: Michael Rollhaus
33mrbb@gmail.com
Estimated Sales: $2.5-5,000,000
Number Employees: 20-49

28492 Rollon Corp
30 Wilson Dr # A
Sparta, NJ 07871-4408

973-300-5492
Fax: 973-300-9030   877-976-5566
infocom.usa@rollon.com www.rolloncorp.com
Contact: A Lou
l.woloszyn@rolloncorp.com
Estimated Sales: $5 Million
Number Employees: 1-4

28493 Rollprint Packaging Prods Inc
320 S Stewart Ave
Addison, IL 60101-3310

630-628-1700
Fax: 630-628-8510   800-276-7629
mail@rollprint.com www.rollprint.com
Manufacturer and exporter of flexible food packaging materials including lidding, pouches, peelable and non-peelable composites. FlexForm and ClearForm line of forming webs provide tough, puncture resistant substrates that provideuniform film draw without snapback for frozen food applications including: poultry, meat, seafood, bakery, pizza, vegetables, fruits, and bakery goods.
President: Dhuanne Dodrill
ddodrill@rollprint.com
CFO: David Reed
Marketing Manager: Edward Verkuilen
Estimated Sales: $20-50 Million
Number Employees: 100-249
Square Footage: 198000
Type of Packaging: Consumer, Food Service, Private Label, Bulk
Brands:
    Allegro
    Clearfoil
    Flexform
    Forte
    Multimix
    Propapeel
    Propaseal

28494 Rollstock Inc
5720 Brighton Ave
Kansas City, MO 64130-4532

816-444-1789
Fax: 616-570-0430   800-295-2949
rollstockkc@aol.com www.rollstock.com
Horizontal form, fill and seal machine, vacuum, map, cap
Sales: Tom Foley
Plant Manager: Gary Filippone
Estimated Sales: $1-5 Million
Number Employees: 5-9

28495 Rollstock Inc
5720 Brighton Ave
Kansas City, MO 64130-4532

816-444-1789
Fax: 616-570-0430   800-954-6020
rollstockkc@aol.com www.rollstock.com
Vacuum packaging machines for the meat industry.
Sales: Tom Foley
Number Employees: 5-9
Parent Co: Azzar Group

28496 Romaco Inc
6 Frassetto Way # D
Unit D
Lincoln Park, NJ 07035-2055

973-709-0691
Fax: 973-605-1360
Printing and labeling systems for bottles
Estimated Sales: $5-10 Million
Number Employees: 1-4

28497 Romanow Container
346 University Ave
Westwood, MA 02090-2309

781-320-9200
Fax: 781-461-5900 www.romanowcontainer.com
Manufacturer and exporter of corrugated and wooden boxes, foam converters and fabricators; also, contract packaging available
Owner: Theodore Romanow
info@romanowcontainer.com
Estimated Sales: $5-10 Million
Number Employees: 100-249

28498 Romanow Container
346 University Ave
Westwood, MA 02090-2309
781-320-9200
Fax: 781-461-5900 www.romanowcontainer.com
Corrugated fiber boxes
President: Theodore Romanow
info@romanowcontainer.com
Executive VP: Richard Romanow
Estimated Sales: $20-50 Million
Number Employees: 100-249
Square Footage: 145000

28499 Romatic Manufacturing Co
1200 Main St S
Southbury, CT 06488-2159
203-264-3442
Fax: 203-264-3442
Metal caps for bottles, cans and jars
President: Roger Hebert
CEO: Rob Pecci
rpecci@romaticmanufacturing.com
CEO: Rob Pecci
Estimated Sales: $20-50 Million
Number Employees: 100-249

28500 Rome LTD
1427 Western Ave
Sheldon, IA 51201
712-324-5391
Fax: 712-324-5394 800-443-0557
www.romegrindingsolutions.com
Processing equipment
President: Craig Jongerius
craigjongerius@rome-ltd.com
Quality Control: Tim McDonald
Sales Director: Jim Justi
Estimated Sales: $10-20 Million
Number Employees: 20-49

28501 Rome Machine & Foundry Co
906 Walnut Ave SW
PO Box 5383
Rome, GA 30161-6166
706-234-6763
Fax: 706-232-0337 800-538-7663
Manufacturer and exporter of custom fabricated conveyors and food processing machinery
President: Albert Berry
aberry@romemachine.com
Sales/Marketing Manager: Willis Rogers
Chief Engineer: Jay Burnett
Purchasing Manager: Ted Porterfield
Estimated Sales: $1-2.5 Million
Number Employees: 10-19
Square Footage: 129600

28502 Romicon
1300 W Lodi Avenue
Suite 19a
Lodi, CA 95242-3000
209-333-8100
Fax: 209-333-2947
Wine industry filtration equipment
Estimated Sales: $500,000-$1 Million
Number Employees: 5-9

28503 Romme Lag USA Inc
27905 Meadow Dr # 9
Evergreen, CO 80439-2110
303-674-8333
Fax: 303-670-2666 mail@rommelag.com
www.rommelag-engineering.com
Supplier of packaging machinery specializing in blow/fill/seal machines for the aseptic filling of liquids in plastic
Manager: Tim Kram
tim.kram@rommelag.com
President and General Manager: Anke Henke
Estimated Sales: Less Than $500,000
Number Employees: 1-4

28504 Ron Teed & Assoc
26W325 Menomini Dr
Wheaton, IL 60189-5987
630-462-7662
Fax: 630-462-7669 ronteed@aol.com
Owner: Ronald Teed
ronteed@aol.com
Estimated Sales: $.5-1 million
Number Employees: 1-4

28505 Ron Ungar Engineering Inc
1595 Walter St # 4
Suite 4
Ventura, CA 93003-5613
805-642-3555
Fax: 805-642-0326 800-235-5644
Owner: Ron Ungar
Estimated Sales: $1-3 Million
Number Employees: 5-9

28506 Ron Vallort & Associates
502 Forest Mews Dr
Oak Brook, IL 60523
630-734-3821
Fax: 630-734-3822 ronvallort@aol.com
Engineering and building consultants specializing in site planning, facility design, construction management and operational analysis for the food industry including processing, freezing, storage and distribution
President: Ron Vallort

28507 Ron Vallort and Associates, Ltd
2 S. Atrium Way
606
Elmhurst, IL 60126
630-334-3821
Fax: 630-734-3822 ronvallort@aol.com
Engineering and building consultants specializing in site planning, process design, facility design, construction management, expert investigation and building analysis for the food industry including processing, freezingstorage/distribution, sanitation and refrigeration.
President: Ron Vallot
Estimated Sales: Below $5 Million
Number Employees: 10

28508 RonI
8001 Tower Point Dr
Charlotte, NC 28227
704-847-2464
Fax: 866-543-9532 866-543-8635
info@roni.com www.roni.com
Material handling applications including rollhandling, clean room, product pouring and weighing
President: John Hebert
CFO: Lena Melton
Contact: Don Bedel
don.bedel@roni.com
Estimated Sales: $1-2.5 Million
Number Employees: 30
Brands:
LIFT-O-Flex
Voyager
MOBI-Crane
Movomech

28509 Ronchi America
63 Duncan Cir
Hiram, GA 30141-3237
678-398-7413
Fax: 770-694-6071 info@ronchiamerica.com
www.ronchipackaging.com
Plastic bottle unscramblers, bottle fillers, advanced flowmeter filling technology, pump cappers, case packaging, and integrated lines
VP: Frank Chitg
Contact: Michele Falsini
m.falsini@ronchiamerica.com
Estimated Sales: $2.5-5 Million
Number Employees: 10-19
Square Footage: 60000
Parent Co: Ronchi Mario

28510 Rondo Inc
51 Joseph St
Moonachie, NJ 07074-1027
201-229-9700
Fax: 201-229-0018 800-882-0633
info@us.rondo-online.com
Manufacturer, importer and wholesaler/distributor of high volume bakery equipment including mixers and sheeters
President: Jerry Murphy
jerry.murphy@rondo-online.com
VP Sales: Andrea Henderson
Estimated Sales: $2.5-5 Million
Number Employees: 20-49

28511 Rondo of America
209 Great Hill Rd
Naugatuck, CT 6770
203-723-7474
Fax: 203-723-5831 custserv@rondopackaging.com
www.rondopackaging.com
Manufacturer and exporter of protective packaging, automatic packaging machinery and paper boxes
Owner: James Sinkins
Contact: Donna Pendleton
donna@rondopackaging.com
Estimated Sales: $5-10 Million
Number Employees: 20-49
Parent Co: Interrondo

28512 Ronell Industries
298 Cox St
Roselle, NJ 07203-1798
908-245-5255
Fax: 908-241-4244
Environmental services including cleaning and sanitation
President: Ronald Globerman
VP: John Carroll
Contact: Jim Daley
jimdaley@ronellmanagedservices.com
Estimated Sales: $5-10 Million
Number Employees: 10-19

28513 Roni LLC
8026 Tower Point Dr
Charlotte, NC 28227-7726
704-847-2464
Fax: 704-714-5317 866-543-8635
www.liftoflex.com
Automated ergonomic material handling systems and equipment.
Owner: Gunner Lofgren
Number Employees: 5-9

28514 Ronnie Dowdy
1839 Batesville Blvd
Batesville, AR 72501
870-251-3222
Fax: 870-251-3763 800-743-5611
Transportation firm providing refrigerated trucking services including local, long and short haul
Owner: Ronnie Dowdy
Owner: Sandra Dowdy
Contact: David Bergan
dbergan@ronniedowdy.com
Number Employees: 250-499

28515 Ronnie's Ceramic Company
5999 3rd St
San Francisco, CA 94124
415-822-8068
Fax: 415-822-8966 800-888-8218
Manufacturer and exporter of tableware, platters, coffee mugs and water pitchers
President: Risly Cheung
Vice President: Risly Chin
Estimated Sales: $3-5,000,000
Number Employees: 15
Square Footage: 8500
Brands:
Ronnie's Ocean
Terramoto

28516 Roofian
8605 Kewen Ave
Sun Valley, CA 91352-3123
818-768-9945
Fax: 818-768-9285 800-431-3886
roofian@juno.com www.roofian.com
Gift and floral baskets
Owner: Shelia Missaghi
roofian@juno.com
VP: Shahla Roofian
Estimated Sales: $1.1 Million
Number Employees: 10-19

28517 (HQ)Rooto Corp
3505 W Grand River Ave
Howell, MI 48855-9610
517-546-8330
Fax: 517-548-5162
Manufacturer and exporter of ammonia, liquid soap and chemical cleaners for drains, toilets and septic tanks

Manager: Penny Rulason
National Sales Manager: Roger Sheets
Manager: Roger Sheets
roger.sheets@rootocorp.com
Plant Manager: Ken Wood
Purchasing Manager: Dennis West
Estimated Sales: $2.5-5 Million
Number Employees: 20-49
Square Footage: 1000000
Type of Packaging: Consumer, Food Service, Private Label
Brands:
  Blue Ribbon
  Rooto

28518 Ropak
1515 W.22nd Street
Suite 550
Oak Brook, IL 60523
Canada

800-527-2267
sales@bwaycorp.com www.ropakcorp.com
Manufacturer and exporter of polyethylene containers
President: Greg Toft
Sales Representative: Ricahrd Harrison
Operations Manager: Nevin McKay
Number Employees: 110
Parent Co: Bway Corporation
Type of Packaging: Food Service, Bulk

28519 Ropak Manufacturing Co Inc
1019 Cedar Lake Rd SE
Decatur, AL 35603-1730

256-350-4241
Fax: 256-350-1611 sales@ropak.com
www.ropak.com
Manufacturer and exporter of form/fill/seal, liquid/dry and vertical/horizontal packagers, stik-pak packager
President/CEO: Ernest Matthews
VP, Electrical Engineer: Richard Matthews
Business Development: Chuck Garrett
VP Operations: Ernest Matthrews
Purchasing Manager: Ken Ray
Estimated Sales: $5-10,000,000
Number Employees: 20-49
Brands:
  Expresspak

28520 Roplast Industries Inc
3155 S 5th Ave
Oroville, CA 95965-5858

530-532-9500
Fax: 530-532-9576 800-767-5278
sales@roplast.com www.roplast.com
Integrated domestic manufacturer of plastic
(LDPE/LLDPE) film and bags.
President: Robert Bateman
r.bateman@leeassociates-temeculavalley.ccsend.com
COO: Chris Mann
Director of Sales: Roxanne Vaughan
Sales Manager: Erik Johansen
r.bateman@leeassociates-temeculavalley.ccsend.com
Estimated Sales: $20-30 Million
Number Employees: 100-249
Square Footage: 130000
Type of Packaging: Food Service, Private Label

28521 (HQ)Rosco Inc
14431 91st Ave
Jamaica, NY 11435-4302

718-526-2652
Fax: 718-297-0323 800-227-2095
www.roscomirrors.com
Manufacturer and exporter of acrylic and glass convex safety mirrors
President: Sol Englander
Quality Control: George Lewandowski
VP and Finance: Danny Englander
VP Engineering and Ops: Ben Englander
National Sales Manager: Dave Mostel
Sales Manager: Joe Liberman
Contact: Amy Ahn
aahn@roscomirrors.com
Estimated Sales: $5-10 Million
Number Employees: 5-9
Square Footage: 140000

28522 Rose City Awning Co
2728 NW Nela St
Portland, OR 97210-1714

503-226-2761
Fax: 503-222-5060 800-446-4104
sales@rosecityawning.com
www.rosecityawning.com
Canvas products, vinyl door strips, moving pads, solar screen transparent shades, tarpaulin, awnings, cloth and polythylene taper, polyethylene film and rope including nylon, sisal, manilas, poly, twine, etc
Owner: Pam Butcher
sales@rosecityawning.com
Sales Department: Ida Pfenning
Factory Manager: Mike Pedersen
Estimated Sales: Below $5 Million
Number Employees: 10-19
Square Footage: 4000

28523 Rose City Label
7235 SE Label Ln
Portland, OR 97206-9339

503-777-4711
Fax: 503-777-4799 800-547-9920
info@rclabel.com
Labels including pressure sensitive, flexo, hot stamped, embossed, sheet fed and custom printed
President/ Co-Owner: Scott Pillsbury
scott@tlmi.com
CFO: Whitney Pillsbury
Marketing: Scott Pillsbury
Sales Manager: Walt Ostergard
Estimated Sales: $5-10 Million
Number Employees: 10-19

28524 Rose City Printing & Packaging
900 SE Tech Center Dr
Suite 100
Vancouver, WA 98683

503-241-6486
Fax: 503-241-3604 800-704-8693
info@rcpp.com
Folding cartons, blister cards and beverage carriers
President: Richard L Safranski
CEO: Chuck Parsons
CFO: Chris Farm
Quality Control: Steve Rautenbach
Marketing Director: Kathryn Rautenbach
Sales Director: Dave Wehrman
Contact: Armando Herrera
aherrera@rcpp.com
Operations Manager: Ken Karallis
General Manager: Steve Lobis
Estimated Sales: $5-10 Million
Number Employees: 100-249
Square Footage: 124000

28525 Rose Forgrove
1 Illinois St Ste 300
Suite 400
Saint Charles, IL 60174

630-443-1317
Fax: 630-377-3069 www.hayssen.com
Manufacturer and exporter of flow wrappers for food and candy
VP Sales: Liam Buckley
Number Employees: 3
Square Footage: 5000
Parent Co: Howven
Brands:
  Flowpak

28526 Rose Forgrove
1 Illinois St
Suite 300
Saint Charles, IL 60174

630-443-1317
Fax: 630-377-3069
Hermatic seals and other high quality wrapping applications

28527 Rose Plastic
525 Technology Dr
Coal Center, PA 15423-1053

724-938-0511
Fax: 724-938-8532 www.rose-plastic.us
President: Ken Donahue
info.us@rose-plastic.us
Executive Vice President Technical and M: Peter Hess
Western Sales Director: Lisa Montgomery
Director of Human Resources: Jen Capozza
Estimated Sales: $300,000-500,000
Number Employees: 50-99

28528 Rosemount Analytical Inc
2400 Barranca Pkwy
Irvine, CA 92606-5018

949-757-8500
Fax: 949-757-3001 800-543-8257
www.emersonprocess.com
Liquid analyzers including pH, conductivity, ORP, residual chlorine, dissolved ozone and oxygen refractometers, water activity measurement systems and gas analyzers and systems
President: Ken Biele
ken.biele@emersonprocess.com
President: Ken Biele
Marketing Manager: John Wright
Sales Manager: Ken Partridge
Estimated Sales: $50-100 Million
Number Employees: 100-249
Parent Co: Fisher-Rosemont

28529 Rosenthal ManufacturingCo Inc
1840 Janke Dr
Northbrook, IL 60062-6704

847-714-0404
Fax: 847-714-0440 800-621-1266
411@rosenthalmfg.com www.rosenthalmfg.com
Sheeting machines
Owner: Lorelei Rosenthal
info@rosenthalmfg.com
Estimated Sales: $10-20 Million
Number Employees: 20-49

28530 Rosenwach Tank Co LLC
4025 Crescent St
Long Island City, NY 11101-3897

212-972-4411
Fax: 718-482-0661 info@rosenwachgroup.com
www.rosenwachgroup.com
Manufacturers of wooden and steel water towers, wooden cheese vats, tanks, planters and benches
Owner: Andrew Rosenwach
amr@rosenwachgroup.com
Chairman of the Board: Wallace Rosenwach
Estimated Sales: $5-10 Million
Number Employees: 50-99
Parent Co: Rosenwach Group

28531 Roseville Charcoal & Mfg Co
500 Monroe St
Zanesville, OH 43701-3875

740-452-5473
Fax: 740-452-5474
Manufacturer and exporter of industrial and commercial charcoal briquettes including hardwood, granular and lump
President: Tim R Longstreth
Estimated Sales: $1-2.5 Million
Number Employees: 1-4

28532 Ross & Wallace Inc
204 Old Covington Hwy
Hammond, LA 70403-5121

985-345-1321
Fax: 985-345-1370 800-854-2300
customerservice@rossandwallace.com
www.rossandwallace.com
Manufacturer and exporter of paper and plastic bags and wrappings
President: Ken Ross
Chairman: Albert Ross
Estimated Sales: $10-20 Million
Number Employees: 50-99
Square Footage: 350000
Type of Packaging: Consumer, Bulk

28533 Ross Computer Systems
19 W 44th St
Suite 715
New York, NY 10036

212-221-7677
Fax: 212-221-0362
Software for route accounting and manufacturing, handheld sales tracking-ordering-route settlement systems and host systems including Bakers Dozen and PrepMaster
Owner: Seymour Weiss
Contact: Arlene Davis
arlened@rossusa.com
Estimated Sales: $1-2.5 Million
Number Employees: 10-19

28534 Ross Computer Systems
214 S Peters Rd Ste 208
Knoxville, TN 37923
865-690-3008
Fax: 865-690-1089 www.afsi.com
Manufacturer and exporter of computer hardware
and software; also, consulting services available
President: Louis Schumacher
CEO: Jesse Hermann
CFO: Mark Schonau
Executive VP: Louis Schumacher
Chief Technology Officer: Suhas Gudihal
VP Sales: Greg Roberts
Chief Customer Officer: Lisa Whinney
Estimated Sales: Below $5 Million
Number Employees: 10-19

28535 Ross Cook
8630 Fenton Street
Suite 824
Silver Spring, MD 20910
301-565-4035
Fax: 408-929-9944 800-233-7339
lookingforanswers@cookross.com
www.cookross.com
Centrifugal blowers and exhausters and industrial
vacuum systems
President: Mike Fisher
Contact: Dwight Anderson
dwighta@cookross.com
VP Operations: Bill Splinder
Estimated Sales: $10-20 Million
Number Employees: 20-49
Square Footage: 88000

28536 Ross Engineering Inc
32 Westgate Blvd
Savannah, GA 31405-1400
912-238-3300
Fax: 912-238-5983 800-524-7677
www.mixers.com
Manufacturer and exporter of food processing
equipment including mixing, blending and disper-
sion machinery
President: Richard Ross
COO: D Hathaway
d_hathaway@rossengineering.net
Vice President: David Hathaway
Estimated Sales: $10-20,000,000
Number Employees: 20-49
Square Footage: 60000
Parent Co: Charles Ross & Son Company

28537 Ross Industries Inc
5321 Midland Rd
Midland, VA 22728
540-439-3271
Fax: 540-439-2740 sales@rossindinc.com
www.rossindinc.com
Food processing and packaging equipment including
pre-formed tray seal machines, tunnel freezers, mechanical tenderizers and meat presses.
Estimated Sales: $20-50 Million
Number Employees: 100-249

28538 Ross Industries Inc
5321 Midland Rd
Midland, VA 22728-2135
540-439-3271
Fax: 540-439-2740 800-336-6010
sales@rossindinc.com www.rossindinc.com
President: Michel Defenbac
mdefencac@rossindinc.com
Estimated Sales: $20-50 Million
Number Employees: 100-249

28539 Ross Systems
2 Concourse Pkwy NE # 800
Atlanta, GA 30328-5588
770-351-9600
Fax: 770-351-0036 info@rossinc.com
www.keops.com
Computer software design and programming service
President: J Patrick Tinley
CEO: Peter Yip
Contact: Jay Jordan
jjordan@cdcsoftware.com
Estimated Sales: $30-50 Million
Number Employees: 50-99

28540 Ross Systems & ControlsInc
34 Westgate Blvd
Savannah, GA 31405-1400
912-238-5800
Fax: 912-238-1905 866-797-2660
mail@rosssyscon.com www.rosssyscon.com
Owner: Paul Rose
Account Executive: Mike Ellis
Manager: Gary Barber
gbarber@rosssyscon.com
Estimated Sales: $1-5 Million
Number Employees: 5-9

28541 Ross Technology Corp
104 N Maple Ave
Leola, PA 17540-9799
717-656-5600
Fax: 717-656-3281 800-345-8170
www.rosstechnology.com
Manufacturer and exporter of storage rack systems
including pallet rack, drive-in, thru-flow and push
back
Owner: Don Spicher
Vice President: Jay Otto
jotto@rosstechnology.com
Sales Manager: Tom Crippen
Estimated Sales: $20-50 Million
Number Employees: 100-249
Square Footage: 54000
Type of Packaging: Bulk

28542 Rosson Sign Co
3071 Broadway
Macon, GA 31206-1551
478-788-3905
Fax: 478-788-8020 jrosson@rossonsign.com
www.rossonsign.com
Electric, neon, painted and plastic signs
President: Jack T Rosson
jrosson@rossonsign.com
Estimated Sales: $1-2.5 Million
Number Employees: 10-19

28543 Roth & Associates PC
554 E Maple Rd # 100
Troy, MI 48083-2805
248-583-1221
Fax: 248-583-3221
President: Robet Roth Jr
Estimated Sales: $5-10 Million

28544 Roth Sign Systems
606 Lakeville Street
Petaluma, CA 94952-3324
707-778-0200
Fax: 707-765-6079 800-585-7446
Manufacturer and exporter of menu, black and chalk
boards; also, signs including changeable letter, ad-
vertising, luminous tube, plastic, etc
Owner: Lary Mathews
Estimated Sales: $500,000-$1 Million
Number Employees: 10
Square Footage: 80000
Parent Co: Rothcoast Company

28545 Roth Young Bellevue
PO Box 3306
Bellevue, WA 98009-3306
425-454-0677
Fax: 425-453-4552
Executive search firm
Owner: B K Lee
Division Manager: Robert Richardson
CFO: David Salzberg
VP: C Salzberg
R&D: Bob Richardson
Estimated Sales: Below $5 Million
Number Employees: 5-9

28546 Roth Young Chicago
1100 W Northwest Highway
Suite 106
Mount Prospect, IL 60056
847-797-9211
Fax: 847-797-9303
Employment agency/executive search firm specializ-
ing in permanent selection and placement of food in-
dustry personnel
Number Employees: 10
Square Footage: 3600
Parent Co: Winston Franchise Corporation

28547 Roth Young Farmington Hills
31275 Northwestern Hwy
Farmington Hills, MI 48334-2558
248-539-9242
Fax: 248-626-7079 rydetroit@worldnet.att.net
Executive search firm specializing in the selection
and placement of food industry personnel
President: Samuel Skeegan
Number Employees: 5-9
Square Footage: 6000
Parent Co: Winston Franchise Corporation

28548 Roth Young Hicksville
P.O.Box 7365
Hicksville, NY 11802-7261
516-822-6000
Fax: 516-822-6018
Executive search firm specializing in selection and
placement of food industry personnel
Owner: George Jung
Estimated Sales: Below $500,000
Number Employees: 1-4
Square Footage: 2960
Parent Co: Winston Franchise Corporation

28549 Roth Young Minneapolis
6212 Vernon Court S
Minneapolis, MN 55436-1669
952-932-0769
Fax: 952-831-7413 800-356-6655
Executive search firm specializing in selection and
placement of professional and managerial personnel
in the retail and grocery industries
Estimated Sales: $500,000
Number Employees: 6
Square Footage: 6400
Parent Co: Winston Franchise Corporation

28550 Roth Young Murrysville
3087 Carson Ave
Murrysville, PA 15668-1814
724-733-5900
Fax: 724-733-0183 rothyoungpit@cs.com
Employment agency/executive search firm specializ-
ing in selection and placement of food industry
personnel
President: Leonard Di Naples
Director (Health Care): Ann Marie Panzek
VP: Len DiNaples Jr
Estimated Sales: Below $5 Million
Number Employees: 1-4
Parent Co: Winston Franchise Corporation

28551 Roth Young New York
122 E 42nd Street Room 320
New York, NY 10168-0300
212-557-8181
Employment agency/executive search firm specializ-
ing in selection and placement of food industry per-
sonnel; See our ad on the spine of the print product
VP: David Silver
VP: Eric Kugler
Number Employees: 2
Parent Co: Winston Franchise Corporation

28552 Roth Young Washougal
24 S A Street
Suite A
Washougal, WA 98671-2101
360-835-3136
Fax: 360-835-9383 info@ruthyoung.com
Employment agency/executive search firm specializ-
ing in selection and placement of food industry
personnel
President: David Salzberg
Estimated Sales: Less than $500,000
Number Employees: 4
Parent Co: Winston Franchise Corporation

28553 Roth Young of Tampa Bay
14914 Winding Creek Ct
Tampa, FL 33613-1603
813-269-9889
Fax: 813-269-9919 800-646-1513
Employment agency/executive search firm specializ-
ing in selection and placement of food industry
personnel
President: Barry Cushing
Estimated Sales: $400,000
Number Employees: 1-4
Square Footage: 2000
Parent Co: Winston Franchise Corporation

28554 (HQ)Rothchild Printing Company

7920 Barnwell Ave
Flushing, NY 11373-3727

718-899-6000
Fax: 718-397-1921 800-238-0015

Coupons, tags and labels including multiple page, paper, foil, flat, rolls and die-cut
VP: Paul Rothchild
Estimated Sales: $10-20 Million
Number Employees: 50-99
Square Footage: 80000

28555 Rotisol France Inc

341 N Oak St
Inglewood, CA 90302-3312

310-671-7254
Fax: 310-671-8171 800-651-5969
info@rotisolusa.com www.rotisolusa.com

Manufacturer, importer and exporter pizza and rotisserie ovens; also, grills
Owner: Jim Doar
Head Accounts: Milene Berry
Business Development Manager: Orlane Parsons
Director Sales: Alain Lebret
Sales Coordinator: Cedric Dauphin
Office/Customer Service Manager: Kate Gramcko
jim@rotisolusa.com
Estimated Sales: $2.5-5 Million
Number Employees: 5-9
Parent Co: Rotisol S.A.

28556 Roto-Flex Oven Co

135 E Cevallos
San Antonio, TX 78204-1795

210-222-2278
Fax: 210-222-9007 877-859-1463
doug@rotoflexoven.com www.rotoflexoven.com

Manufacturer and exporter of food service equipment and pizza ovens
CEO: Richard Dunfield
service@rotoflexoven.com
CFO: Ed Dunfield
Vice President: Doug Dunfield
Marketing Director: Marijke Carey
Plant Manager: Jose Briano
Estimated Sales: $2 Million
Number Employees: 5-9
Number of Brands: 2
Number of Products: 10
Square Footage: 50000
Type of Packaging: Consumer, Food Service
Brands:
Dual-Flex
Js-1
Roto-Flex Oven
Roto-Smoker

28557 Roto-Jet Pump

P.O.Box 209
Salt Lake City, UT 84110-0209

801-359-8731
Fax: 801-355-9303 www.rotojet.com

Specialty pumps including high pressure washing, centrifugal screw impeller and abrasive/corrosive resistant
CEO: Joseph W Roark
Director Marketing: Steven Osborn
Sales Manager: Sebastien Dumas
Estimated Sales: $1-5 Million
Number Employees: 500-999
Brands:
Ash
Galigher
Roto Jet
Wemco

28558 (HQ)Rotonics Manufacturing

17038 S Figueroa St
Gardena, CA 90248

310-327-5401
Fax: 310-538-5579 corporate@rotonics.com
www.rotonics.com

Manufactures FDA approved containers, bins, totes, hoppers, pallets for the food industry
Chairman/CEO: Sherman McKinniss
CFO: Doug Russell
VP: Dawn Whitney
Number Employees: 50-99
Other Locations:
Rotonics Manufacturing
Bensenville IL
Rotonics Manufacturing
Commerce City CO
Rotonics Manufacturing
Bartow FL

Rotonics Manufacturing
Gardena CA
Rotonics Manufacturing
Caldwell ID
Rotonics Manufacturing
Gainesville TX
Rotonics Manufacturing
N Las Vegas NV
Rotonics Manufacturing
Brownwood TX
Rotonics Manufacturing
Knoxville TN
Rotonics Manufacturing
Miami FL

28559 Rotronic Instrument Corp Inc

135 Engineers Rd # 150
Suite 150
Hauppauge, NY 11788-4018

631-348-6844
Fax: 631-427-3902 800-628-7101
sales@rotronic-usa.com www.rotronic-usa.com

Water activity measuring instrumentation
Manager: David P Love
david@rotronic-usa.com
Vice President: David Love
Marketing Director: Rose Mannarino
Estimated Sales: $2.5-5 Million
Number Employees: 10-19

28560 Rotronics Manufacturing

736 Birginal Dr
Bensenville, IL 60106-1213

630-773-9510
Fax: 630-773-4274 chicago@rotonics.com
www.rotonics.com

Storage containers and systems, tanks, drums
Manager: Jay Rule
Estimated Sales: $20-50 Million
Number Employees: 50-99

28561 Round Noon Software

14785 Preston Road
Suite 550
Dallas, TX 75254-7899

972-789-5191
info@roundnoon.com

Restaurant management software
Estimated Sales: $1-5 Million

28562 Round Paper Packages Inc

511 Enterprise Dr # 2
Erlanger, KY 41017-1516

859-331-7200
Fax: 859-331-7285 www.roundpaperpackages.com

Fiber and paper cans, tubes and cores
President: James Meier
rppinc@insightbb.com
VP: Linda Meier
Marketing: David Meier
Sales Exec: Linda J Meier
Estimated Sales: $20-50 Million
Number Employees: 20-49

28563 Roundup Food Equip

180 Kehoe Blvd
Carol Stream, IL 60188-1814

630-784-1000
Fax: 630-784-1650 800-253-2991
www.ajantunes.com

Manufacturer and exporter of toasters, steamers and hot dog grills
President: Glenn Bullock
customerservice@roundupfoodequip.com
Chairman of the Board: Virginia M Antunes
CFO: Bill Nelson
R & D: Tom Goodman
VP Marketing: Thomas Krisch
Estimated Sales: $5-10 Million
Number Employees: 100-249
Parent Co: A.J. Antunes & Company

28564 Rovema

650 Hurricane Shoals Rd NW
Lawrenceville, GA 30045-4460

770-513-9604
Fax: 770-513-0814 jnielsen@rovema.com

Vertical form-fill-seal machines, horizontal form-fill-seal machines, zipper applicators, cartoners, end-packing machines

President: Klaus Kraemer
Research & Development: Donald Harmon
Sales Director: Charlotte Koellner
Contact: Darlene Crawley
darlene@rovema.com
Operations Manager: Ronald Kahlmann
Purchasing Manager: Dave Henninger
Estimated Sales: $10-20 Million
Number Employees: 50-99

28565 Rowe International

2517 Shadowbrook Drive SE
Grand Rapids, MI 49546-7457

616-246-0483
www.roweinternational.com

Manufacturer and exporter of currency changers, bill acceptors, under-the-counter safes, jukeboxes and vending machines including refrigerated food, snack and popcorn
Controller: Scott Van Dam
Senior Vice President, Sales & Marketing: John Margold
Human Resources Executive: Linda Roer
Purchasing: Chris Steffes
Estimated Sales: $160 Thousand
Number Employees: 3
Square Footage: 3096
Brands:
Rowe
Rowe Ami

28566 Rowland Technologies

320 Barnes Rd
Wallingford, CT 06492-1804

203-269-9500
Fax: 203-265-2768 www.rowlandtechnologies.com

Manufacturer and exporter of decorative plastic and polycarbonate packaging film
President: Peter Connerton
pconnerton@rowtec.com
Sales Manager: Carl Heflin
Estimated Sales: $5-10 Million
Number Employees: 20-49
Square Footage: 120000

28567 Rowlands Sales Company

Butler Industrial Park
PO Box 552
Hazleton, PA 18201-0552

570-455-5813
Fax: 570-454-4790 800-582-6388
rowlands@rowlands.com www.rowlands.com

Aseptic processing equipment, batch control systems, cheese equipment, blenders, heat exchangers, plate, scraped surfaces, tubular, homogenizers, ice equipment, ingredient feeders
President: William Rowlands
CEO: David Rowlands
Contact: Linda James
ljames@rowlands.com
Estimated Sales: $10-20 Million
Number Employees: 20-49

28568 Rownd & Son

PO Box 1495
Dillon, SC 29536-1495

803-774-8264

Vegetable shipping containers
CEO: Annie Dollison
VP Sales: Harry Rownd
Estimated Sales: $2.5-5 Million
Number Employees: 20-49

28569 Rox America

PO Box 5561
Spartanburg, SC 29304-5561

864-463-4352
Fax: 864-463-4670 800-458-3194
info@roxenergy.com www.zimmer-usa.com

Flavor and taste assessment and stability for analytical services and instrumentation
President: Roland Zimmer
Vice President of Technology: Juergen Merz
National Sales Director: Bob Patterson
Estimated Sales: $1 Million
Square Footage: 3500

28570 (HQ)Roxanne Signs Inc

23413 Woodfield Rd
Gaithersburg, MD 20882-3015

301-428-4911
Fax: 301-253-5833 rox_signs@yahoo.com
www.roxannesigns.com

Custom designed menu signs, menus and advertising specialty items including logos, banners, neon signs, window lettering, etc
President: Roxanne Riley
roxannsigns@gmail.com
Estimated Sales: Less Than $500,000
Number Employees: 1-4

28571 (HQ)Roxide International
24 Weaver St
Larchmont, NY 10538

914-630-7700
Fax: 914-235-5328 800-431-5500
roxide@aol.com

Manufacturer and importer of insecticides, repellents, swatters, traps, fly paper, baits and muldicides; also, graffiti removers, organic cleaners and lubricants; exporter of fly paper and insecticides
President: James Cowen
Estimated Sales: $2.5-5 Million
Number Employees: 10
Type of Packaging: Food Service
Brands:
Aeroxon
Revenge
Roxo

28572 Roy's Folding Box
5140 Richmond Rd
Cleveland, OH 44146-1331

216-464-1191
Fax: 216-464-1562

Paper folding boxes
Owner: Sue Harky
Controller: Jeff Stuteman
Estimated Sales: $1-3 Million
Number Employees: 5-9

28573 Royal ACME
3110 Payne Ave
Cleveland, OH 44114-4504

216-241-1477
Fax: 216-241-1479 sales@royalacme.com
www.agwstamps.com

Rubber stamps
Owner: John Enci
johne@royalacme.com
Estimated Sales: $1-2.5 Million
Number Employees: 10-19

28574 Royal Broom & Mop Factory Inc
5717 Plauche Ct
New Orleans, LA 70123-4119

504-818-2244
Fax: 504-818-2266 800-537-6925
sales@royalbroom.com www.royalbroom.com

Brooms and mops; wholesaler/distributor of brushes and paint sundries
Owner: William Staehle III
CEO: Donald Staehle
donald@royalbroom.com
CFO: Donald Staehle
Estimated Sales: $5-10 Million
Number Employees: 5-9
Square Footage: 36000
Type of Packaging: Consumer, Private Label

28575 Royal Chemical Co Inc
204 Memory Ln
Albemarle, NC 28001-5402

704-982-5513
Fax: 704-982-3018 800-650-6346

Janitorial and industrial cleaning compounds
President: Joyce Morton
Sales/Marketing Executive: Madilyn Lampley
Purchasing Agent: Boyce Hill
Estimated Sales: Less Than $500,000
Number Employees: 1-4

28576 Royal Cup Coffee
PO Box 170971
Birmingham, AL 35217-0971

800-366-5836
webjava@royalcupcoffee.com
www.royalcupcoffee.com

Coffee, tea, and coffee equipment.
CEO: Bill Smith
Chief Financial Officer: William Wann

Year Founded: 1896
Estimated Sales: $100-$500 Million
Number Employees: 859
Number of Brands: 4
Square Footage: 260000

Type of Packaging: Food Service
Other Locations:
Royal Cup
Birmingham AL
Brands:
Prideland™
Royal Cupe
ROAR™
H.C. Valentine™

28577 Royal Display Corporation
725 Main St
Middletown, CT 6457

860-344-9988
Fax: 860-344-1045 800-569-1295
service@royaldisplay.com

Custom wire display racks, point of purchase displays and signs and shelves
President: Rick Wright
VP: Laurie Ambrose
Contact: Heather Eyres
heather@royaldisplay.com
Estimated Sales: $2.5-5 Million
Number Employees: 20-49
Square Footage: 100000

28578 Royal Ecoproducts
119 Snow Boulevard
Vaughan, ON L4K 4N9
Canada

905-761-6406
Fax: 905-761-6419 800-465-7670

Manufacturer and exporter of plastic pallets
President: Burno Casciato
President: Maircein Tarascandalo
Director Sales/Marketing: Anthony DiNunzio
Sales Coordinator: Vince Franze
Number Employees: 30

28579 Royal Group
1301 S 47th Ave
Cicero, IL 60804-1516

708-656-2020
Fax: 708-656-2108 www.royalbox.com

Corrugated containers, boxes and crates; also, die cuts available
President: Jay King
CEO: Kathleen Allen
kallen@royalbox.com
Marketing Director: Doug Holizllan
Sales Manager: Ken Hirsh
Purchasing Manager: Karen Hutinson
Estimated Sales: $5-10 Million
Number Employees: 100-249
Square Footage: 180000

28580 Royal Industries Inc
4100 W Victoria St
Chicago, IL 60646-6727

773-478-6300
Fax: 773-478-4948 800-782-1200
www.royalindustriesinc.com

Wholesaler/distributor of restaurant supplies; serving the food service market
President: Ervin Naiditch
CFO: Joe Lewis
VP: Jay Johnson
Estimated Sales: $10-20 Million
Number Employees: 20-49
Square Footage: 400000

28581 Royal Label Co
50 Park St
Dorchester, MA 02122-2611

617-825-6050
Fax: 617-825-2678 sales@royallabel.com
www.royallabel.com

Manufacturer and exporter of pressure sensitive labels, price tags, decals, name plates and panels
Owner/President: Paul Clifford Jr.
pdc@royallabel.com
VP: Paul Ryan
Director of QA: Craig DiGiovanni
Business Development: Marychristine Clifford
Operations Manager: Paul Pelletier
Operations & Scheduling: Steve Gefteas
Plant Manager: Paul Pelletier
Controller: Eileen Clifford
Estimated Sales: Below $5 Million
Number Employees: 20-49
Square Footage: 50000

28582 Royal Oak Enterprises
1 Royal Oak Ave
Roswell, GA 30076-7583

678-461-3200
Fax: 678-461-3220 www.royal-oak.com

Manufacturer and exporter of instant light charcoal briquettes and natural lump charcoal
Owner: James Keeter
jkeeter@royaloakenterprises.com
VP Sales/Marketing: Harold Ovington
Sales Manager: Brian Kerrigan
jkeeter@royaloakenterprises.com
Estimated Sales: $1-5 Million
Number Employees: 50-99

28583 Royal Paper Box Co
1105 S Maple Ave
Montebello, CA 90640-6007

323-728-7041
Fax: 323-722-2646 www.royalpaperbox.com

Paper boxes
CEO: James Hodges
james.hodges@royalpaperbox.com
Estimated Sales: $50-100 Million
Number Employees: 100-249

28584 Royal Paper Products
PO Box 151
Coatesville, PA 19320

610-384-3400
Fax: 610-384-5106 800-666-6655
www.royalpaper.com

Manufacturer and importer of place mats, coasters, bibs, napkin bands, chef hats, aprons, gloves, toothpicks, sword picks, arrow picks, skewers, coffee stirrers, griddle blocks/screens, scouring pads and metal sponges
President: David Milberg
CEO/CFO: Vince Mazzei
Executive VP: Fred Leibowitz
Quality Control: Debbie Sumka
Marketing Director: Todd Straves
Sales Director: Mark LaRusso
Contact: Candy Warfel
candyw@royalpaper.com
Plant Manager: Ross Glazer
Estimated Sales: $5-10 Million
Number Employees: 20-49
Number of Brands: 1
Number of Products: 300
Square Footage: 480
Type of Packaging: Food Service, Private Label, Bulk
Brands:
Royal Land

28585 Royal Prestige Health Moguls
1025 Old Country Road
Suite 206
Westbury, NY 11590-5654

516-997-1775
Fax: 516-759-1997 888-802-7433
Servicioalcliente@royalprestige.com.mx
www.royalprestige.com

Cookware, water and air purifcation equipment, china, crystal, tableware and cutlery
President: Steven Pollack
District Manager: Matt Rubin
Estimated Sales: $1-3 Million
Number Employees: 10
Square Footage: 800
Parent Co: Royal Prestige Distribution Center
Type of Packaging: Consumer

28586 Royal Range Industries
1768 W 1st Street
Irwindale, CA 91702-3259

626-812-4434
Fax: 626-812-4437

Estimated Sales: $3-5 Million
Number Employees: 20-49

28587 Royal Silver Mfg Co Inc
3300 Chesapeake Blvd
Norfolk, VA 23513-4099

757-855-6004
Fax: 757-855-0017 contact@royalsilver.com

Stainless steel flatware
President: Lloyd Gilbert Jr
Secretary and Treasurer: Edward Landreth
President: Alan Gilbert Jr
Estimated Sales: $2.5-5 Million
Number Employees: 5-9
Square Footage: 144000

28588 Royal Welding & Fabricating
1000 E Elm Ave
Fullerton, CA 92831-5022
714-680-6669
Fax: 714-680-6646 info@royalwelding.com
www.royalwelding.com
Custom stainless steel process tanks; also, vacuum chambers, mixers and cookers
President: Wallace Cook
CFO: Sekyung Kim
Vice President/Chief Engineer: Brad Card
Quality Control: Merritt Read
Chief Engineer: Collie Janda
General Manager: Wallace Cook
Estimated Sales: $4.0 Million
Number Employees: 20-49
Square Footage: 116000
Parent Co: Cook & Cook
Brands:
Dimple Plate

28589 Royalton Foodservice Equip Co
9981 York Theta Dr
North Royalton, OH 44133-3545
440-237-0806
Fax: 440-237-1694 800-662-8765
sales@RoyaltonFoodService.com
Food service equipment including baking, roasting and holding ovens and cabinets
President: Leonard May
Service Engineer: Fred McKinney
CFO: Pat Tatton
Quality Control: David Kinshaw
IT: Hannelore May
hmay@mayind.com
Estimated Sales: $10-20 Million
Number Employees: 20-49

28590 Royce Corp
PO Box 729
Glendale, AZ 85311-0729
Canada
602-256-0006
Fax: 623-435-2030 info@roycemasonry.com
Manufacturer and exporter of wire and metal shelving, production line trucks, warehouse bins, point of purchase displays and racks; also, custom designed for chip, beverage, soups and biscuits
President: George Knowles
General Manager: Glenn Millar
Customer Service: Dave Haywood
Manager Operations: John Fox
Number Employees: 50
Square Footage: 212000
Parent Co: Royce Corporation
Type of Packaging: Consumer, Food Service, Private Label, Bulk
Brands:
Royce

28591 Royce Rolls Ringer Co
16 Riverview Ter NE
Grand Rapids, MI 49505-6245
616-361-9266
Fax: 616-361-5976 800-253-9638
info@roycerolls.net www.roycerolls.net
Manufacturer and exporter of stainless steel mopping equipment, multi and single roll toilet paper dispensers, restroom fixtures and janitorial cleaning carts
President: Charles Royce Jr
VP: Charles Royce
Marketing Director: William Swartz
IT: Angelica Tant
angel@roycerolls.net
Estimated Sales: $1-3 Million
Number Employees: 20-49
Square Footage: 117200

28592 (HQ)Rqa Product Dynamics
10608 163rd Pl
Orland Park, IL 60467-8858
708-364-7055
Fax: 708-364-7061 info@rqa-inc.com
www.rqa-europe.com
Consultant providing quality assurance evaluations of consumer products and competitive product comparison; also, consumer complaint, domestic and international product retrievals, product recalls, quality consulting services, etc;product development, sensory evaluation and consumer research at new state of the art facility.

President: Lawrence Platt
Executive VP: Mary Ann Platt
Sales: Pamela Vaillancourt
Contact: Cheryl Alesso
c.alesso@rqa-inc.com
Number Employees: 5-9
Other Locations:
RQA
Calabasas CA

28593 Rtech Laboratories
4001 Lexington Ave N
St Paul, MN 55126-2934
651-481-2207
Fax: 651-486-0837 800-328-9687
kkinn@landolakes.com www.rtechlabs.com
Research laboratory offering focus groups, analytical testing, sensory evaluation, nutrition labeling, pilot plant facilities, etc
Business Development Manager: Carle Shanks
Sales: Annette Sass
Sales: Annette Sass
Estimated Sales: $5-10 Million
Number Employees: 100-249
Square Footage: 34000
Parent Co: Land O'Lakes

28594 Rtech Laboratories
4001 Lexington Ave N
St Paul, MN 55126-2934
651-481-2207
Fax: 651-486-0837 800-328-9687
awdotterweich@landolakes.com
www.rtechlabs.com
Microbiology and chemistry testing, sensory, evaluation and custom processing services for the retail, food service and food development markets
General Manager: Alecia Dotterweich
Sales: Annette Sass
Estimated Sales: $5-10 Million
Number Employees: 100-249
Parent Co: Land O'Lakes, Inc.

28595 RubaTex Polymer
PO Box 1050
Middlefield, OH 44062-1050
440-632-1691
Fax: 440-632-5761 www.universalpolymer.com
Manufacturer and exporter of plastic straws, can coolers and stoppers
President: Joe Colebank
VP: Andy Cavanagh
Sales/Marketing Manager: Philip Moses
Estimated Sales: $3-5 Million
Number Employees: 5-9

28596 Rubbair Door
100 Groton Shirley Rd
Ayer, MA 01432-1050
978-772-0480
Fax: 978-772-7114 800-966-7822
info@rubbair.com www.rubbair.com
Vinyl and plastic interior and exterior double impact doors
Manager: Alex Eckel
CEO: Alan Eckel
CFO: Joe Tunneva
Sales Director: Randy Gowld
General Manager: Alex Eckel
Purchasing Manager: John Waldron
Estimated Sales: $1-5 Million
Number Employees: 20-49
Number of Products: 12
Parent Co: Eckel Industries

28597 Rubber Fab Molding & Gasket
26 Brookfield Dr
Sparta, NJ 07871-3212
973-579-2959
Fax: 973-579-7275 866-442-2959
sales@rubberfab.com www.rubberfab.com
Hygienic seals, sanitary gaskets, hose assemblies, valve, pump and filler machine components in a wide range of high purity elastomer materials
President: Patrick Parisi
Chief Executive Officer: Bob DuPont, Sr.
Chief Financial Officer: Daniel Licini, CPA
Quality Assurance: Allison Luke
Marketing Department: Laura Schnitzer
Sales Manager: Gary Johnson
Materials Manager: Kellie Cash
Estimated Sales: $6.5 Million
Number Employees: 20-49

28598 Rubber Stamp Shop
PO Box 610
Accokeek, MD 20607-610
Fax: 301-423-2208 800-835-0839
Rubber stamps; also, letter press printing services available
President: Carl Harlow
VP: Carl Harlow
Estimated Sales: less than $500,000
Number Employees: 1-4
Square Footage: 2500
Parent Co: Rubber Stamp Shop

28599 Rubbermaid
4110 Premier Dr.
High Point, NC 27265
888-895-2110
www.rubbermaid.com
Ice coolers and chests, thermal jugs and containers, re-freezable ice substitutes and lunch kits, and hummingbird feeders and accessories.
President/CEO, Newell Brands: Michael Polk
Year Founded: 1920
Estimated Sales: $114.70 Million
Number Employees: 1,426
Number of Products: 15
Parent Co: Newell Brands Inc.
Type of Packaging: Food Service
Other Locations:
Rubbermaid Specialty Products
Winchester VA
Brands:
Rubbermaid®

28600 Rubbermaid Canada
586 Argus Road
Oakville, ON L6J 3J3
Canada
905-279-1010
Fax: 905-279-5254 chpcanada@rubbermaid.com
www.rubbermaidcommercial.com
Commercial dinnerware
Estimated Sales: $1-5,000,000
Parent Co: Rubbermaid Commercial Products
Brands:
Rubbermaid

28601 (HQ)Rubbermaid Commercial Products
2000 Overhead Bridge Rd NE
Cleveland, TN 37311-4692
423-476-4544
Fax: 423-559-9393
www.rubbermaidcommercial.com
Manufacturer and exporter of mops and cleaning aids
President: Neil Eibeler
Finance Manager: Kevin Rogers
Operations Manager: Frank McNeely
Production Manager: Phillip Carlton
Plant Manager: Steve Jones
Purchasing Senior Specialist: Jack Burke
Estimated Sales: $50-100 Million
Number Employees: 250-499
Parent Co: Newell Rubbermaid Inc.

28602 Rubbermaid Commercial Products
1400 Laurel Blvd
Pottsville, PA 17901-1427
570-622-7715
Fax: 570-622-3817 800-233-0314
united@unitedrecept.com
www.rubbermaidcommercial.com
Manufacturer and exporter of fiberglass, steel aluminum, marble and cement waste receptacles; also, smokers' urns, planters and restroom accessories
President/CEO: Richard Weiss
CFO: Rick Piger
rpiger@unitedrecept.com
Vice President: Layton Dodson
Marketing Director: Tom Palangio
Plant Manager: George Derosa
Purchasing Manager: Margaret Zimmerman
Estimated Sales: $50-100 Million
Number Employees: 100-249
Square Footage: 145000

28603 (HQ)Rubicon Industries
848 E 43rd St
Brooklyn, NY 11210-3500
718-434-4700
Fax: 718-434-6174 800-662-6999
sales@rubiconhx.com www.manninglewis.com

Stainless, carbon and high alloy steel and tube heat transfer equipment; also, pressure vessels, stainless steel tanks, reactors and ribbon blenders
President: Michael Rubinberg
sales@rubiconhx.com
Estimated Sales: $500,000-$1,000,000
Number Employees: 20-49

28604 Ruby Manufacturing & Sales
9853 Alpaca St
South El Monte, CA 91733-3101
626-443-1171
Fax: 626-443-0028 info@rubymfg.com
www.rubymfg.com
Manufacturer and exporter of vegetable juice extractors
Owner: Dan Turner
info@rubymfg.com
Estimated Sales: $500,000-$1 Million
Number Employees: 5-9
Type of Packaging: Food Service

28605 Rudd Container Corp
4600 S Kolin Ave
Chicago, IL 60632-4497
773-847-7600
Fax: 773-847-7930 ruddbox@aol.com
www.ruddcontainer.com
Corrugated cartons and point of purchase displays
President: Darrell J. Rudd
ruddbox@aol.com
Vice President: Ted Bihun
Design Manager: Lynna Cavallo
Sales Manager: Errol Dolin
Customer Service: Ann Rudd
Plant Manager: Ken Coyle
Estimated Sales: $15 Million
Number Employees: 20-49
Square Footage: 100000

28606 Rudolph Industries
1176 Cardiff Boulevard
Mississauga, ON L5S 1P6
Canada
905-564-6160
Fax: 905-564-6155 info@rudolphind.com
www.rudolphind.com
Machine knives and injector needles for food processors
President: Bill Rudolph
Number Employees: 10
Square Footage: 80000
Parent Co: W. Rudolph Investments

28607 Rudy's L&R
432 W 38th St
New York, NY 10018-2816
212-245-4966
Fax: 212-262-4815
Suppliers of expresso and capuccino machines
President: Louis Martinez
Estimated Sales: Less than $500,000
Number Employees: 1-4

28608 Rueff Sign Co Inc
1530 E Washington St
Louisville, KY 40206-1831
502-582-1714
Fax: 502-584-6427 www.rueffsigns.com
Signs including electric, plastic, metal and wooden
President: Robert C Rueff
bob@rueffsigns.com
Estimated Sales: Below $5 Million
Number Employees: 20-49

28609 Ruffino Paper Box Co
63 Green St
Hackensack, NJ 07601-4082
201-487-1260
Fax: 201-487-3926 www.ruffinopackaging.com
Folding paper boxes
Owner: Raymond Ruffino
ruffinopkg@aol.com
VP: Raymond Ruffino
Director Sales/Marketing: Rosanne Baleccny
Estimated Sales: $1-2.5 Million
Number Employees: 10-19

28610 Ruggles Sign Company
101 Kuhlman Blvd.
Versailles, KY 40383
859-879-1199
Fax: 859-873-1697 www.rugglessign.com
Neon and plastic signs

President: Tim Cambron
CFO: Anna Cambron
Design Development: Jason Elmore
National Sales & Marketing: Elizabeth Pitchford
Sales & Special Projects: Tony Shaw
Office Manager: Lisa Smith
Production Manager: John Ratcliff
Account Manager: Elizabeth Pitchford
Purchasing: Brad Turpin, Jr
Estimated Sales: $5-10 Million
Number Employees: 50-99
Square Footage: 110000

28611 (HQ)Ruiz Flour Tortillas
1200 Marlborough Ave
Riverside, CA 92507
909-947-7811
Fax: 909-947-2338 info@ruizflourtortillas.com
www.ruizflourtortillas.com
Traditional and specialty, ethnic and gourmet flour tortillas serving food manufacturers, foodservice industry, restaurant distributors, retail food brokers, and specialty retail outlets
Founder: Edward Ruiz
CFO: Uriel Maciaf
Vice President: Vickie Salgado
R&D: David Rodriguez
Manager: Maria Lopez
Contact: Oscar Figari
oscarfigari@ruizflourtortillas.com
Purchasing: Carmen Sandoval
Type of Packaging: Food Service, Private Label, Bulk

28612 Ruland Manufacturing CoInc
6 Hayes Memorial Dr
Marlborough, MA 01752-1830
508-485-1000
Fax: 508-485-9000 800-225-4234
sales@ruland.com www.ruland.com
Owner: Robert Ruland
bob.ruland@ruland.com
Number Employees: 50-99

28613 Rusken Packaging
PO Box 2100
Cullman, AL 35056-2100
256-775-0014
Fax: 256-734-3008 www.rusken.com
Corrugated containers
President: Greg Rusken
Office Manager: Robin Marty
Sales Manager: Joy Jackson
Estimated Sales: $20-50 Million
Number Employees: 20-49

28614 Russel T. Bundy Associates, Inc.
417 E Water St
P.O. Box 150
Urbana, OH 43078
800-652-2151
info@bundybakingsolutions.com
www.bundybakingsolutions.com
Remanufacturer of baking equipment
President: Tom Bundy
CEO: Gilbert Bundy
Sales Manager: Terry Bauer
tbartsch@shaffermanufacturing.com
Estimated Sales: $10-20 Million
Number Employees: 10-19

28615 Russell
201 Thomas French Dr
Scottsboro, AL 35769-7405
800-288-9488
russell.htpg.com
Commercial refrigeration systems
Director of Sales & Marketing: Paul Westbrook
Parent Co: Rheem

28616 Russell Finex Inc
625 Eagleton Downs Dr
Pineville, NC 28134-7424
704-588-9808
Fax: 704-588-0738 800-849-9808
www.russellfinex.com
Sieving, filtering, separation equipment
President: John Edwards
shuan.edwards@russellfinex.com
Managing Director: Ray Singh
Estimated Sales: $1-2.5 Million
Number Employees: 20-49
Parent Co: Russell Group

28617 Russell-William
1710 Midway Rd
Odenton, MD 21113-1128
410-551-3602
Fax: 410-551-9076
Store fixtures and point of purchase displays
CEO: Robert Williams
CEO: Robert Williams
Sales Manager: Rick Sauer
Contact: Russell Winter
russell@william-russell.com
Estimated Sales: $20-50 Million
Number Employees: 100-249

28618 Rust-Oleum Corp
11 Hawthorn Pkwy
Vernon Hills, IL 60061
847-367-7700
800-367-7700
www.rustoleum.com
Flooring, floor and wall coating materials, paints, enamels and coatings.
President: Ed Voorhees
Human Resources & Administration: Stephen Gillmann
Year Founded: 1921
Estimated Sales: $199.80 Million
Number Employees: 100-249

28619 Rutan Poly Industries Inc
39 Siding Pl
Mahwah, NJ 07430-1896
201-529-1474
Fax: 201-529-4440 800-872-1474
sales@rutanpoly.com www.rutanpoly.com
Polyethylene film, bags, tubing and sheeting
President and CEO: Arnold Tanowitz
bagman@rutanpoly.com
Vice President: Esther Tanowitz
Estimated Sales: $5-10 Million
Number Employees: 20-49
Square Footage: 92800
Type of Packaging: Food Service

28620 Rutherford Engineering
1731 Apaloosa
Rockford, IL 61107
815-623-2141
Fax: 815-623-7170
Manufacturer and exporter of fillers, valves and packaging equipment
President: Ashwin Patel
Estimated Sales: $950,000
Number Employees: 15
Square Footage: 27000
Brands:
Akra-Pak
Rutherford

28621 Rutler Screen Printing
1000 S. 27th Street
Easton, PA 18045
610-829-2999
Fax: 610-829-2994 orders@rutler.com
www.rutler.com
Garments, point of purchase displays, posters, decals, bumperstickers, T-shirts, etc
Owner: John Shubert
Contact: Ian Frey
ian@rutler.com
Estimated Sales: $1-2.5 Million
Number Employees: 10-19

28622 Ryan Technology Inc.
2705 SE 39th Loop # B
Suite B
Hillsboro, OR 97123-8415
503-648-9967
Fax: 503-640-3846 800-277-2290
info@ryanslicer.com www.ryanslicer.com
Rotary table and in-line horizontal slicers
President: John Ryan
ryanslicer@aol.com
Sales: Sandra Ryan
Estimated Sales: Less Than $500,000
Number Employees: 1-4

28623 (HQ)Ryder System, Inc
11690 NW 105th St
Miami, FL 33178
305-500-3726
800-467-9337
www.ryder.com

Transportation firm providing leasing and transportation management services; also, vehicle maintenance and inventory deployment services available
Chairman & CEO: Robert Sanchez
EVP/Chief Legal Officer/Secretary: Robert Fatovic
EVP/Chief Financial Officer: Scott Parker
EVP/Chief Sales Officer: John Gleason
EVP/Chief Marketing Officer: Karen Jones
SVP/Chief Human Resources Officer: Frank Lopez
SVP/Chief Information Officer: Rajeev Ravindran
SVP/Chief Procurement Officer: Tim Fiore
Estimated Sales: $7.3 Billion
Number Employees: 39,600
Square Footage: 440000
Other Locations:
  Ryder Integrated Logistics
  Birmingham AL

28624 Ryowa Company America
555 Bonnie Ln
Elk Grove Village, IL 60007
847-952-8363
.Fax: 847-952-8309 800-700-9692
contact@ryowaamerica.com
www.ryowaamerica.com
Conveyors, conveyor merge units and accessories for packaging and slicers and slicer applicatiors for processing
President: Hiroshi Hayashi
hiroshi.hayashi@ryowaamerica.com
Technical Sales Manager: Bill Linahan
Estimated Sales: Less than $500,000
Number Employees: 1-4

28625 Ryson International
300 Newsome Dr
Yorktown, VA 23692-5006
757-898-1530
Fax: 757-898-1580 sales@ryson.com
www.ryson.com
Materials handling equipment
President: Scott Christensen
schristensen@ryson.com
CFO: Ragnhild Rygh
Estimated Sales: Below $5 Million
Number Employees: 10-19

28626 Rytec Corporation
780 N Water St
Milwaukee, WI 53202-3512
414-273-3500
Fax: 414-273-5198 888-467-9832
info@rytecdoors.com
www.rytecdoors.com
Manufacturer and exporter of high-speed, rolling and folding doors including cold storage
Chairman: Donald Grasso
Regional Manager: Jamie Lilly
Marketing Manager: Scott Blue
Estimated Sales: $20-50 Million
Number Employees: 250-499
Brands:
  Bautam
  Clean-Roll
  Fast-Fold
  Fast-Seal
  Preda

28627 Ryter Corporation
32732 730th Avenue
Saint James, MN 56081-5516
507-642-8529
Fax: 507-642-3692 800-643-2184
Bacteria and enzyme products for waste water treatment, drains, grease traps and odor control
President: Terry Etter
Sales Manager: Barb Nelson
Estimated Sales: $1-2.5 Million
Number Employees: 9
Brands:
  Odormute

28628 Ryther-Purdy
174 Elm St
PO Box 622
Old Saybrook, CT 06475-4105
860-388-4405
Fax: 860-388-9401 tpurdy@rytherpurdy.com
www.rytherpurdy.com
Lighting standards and fixtures
President: Timothy Purdy
tpurdy@rytherpurdy.com
Estimated Sales: $1-2.5 Million
Number Employees: 5-9

28629 S & G Resources Inc
266 Main St # 23
Olde Medfield Square
Medfield, MA 02052-2056
508-359-7771
Fax: 508-359-7775 877-359-7776
sandg@sandgresources.com www.sgresources.net
President: Michael I Goldman
sandg@sandgresources.com
Estimated Sales: Below $5 Million
Number Employees: 1-4

28630 S & H Uniform Corp
1 Aqueduct Rd
White Plains, NY 10606-1003
914-937-6800
Fax: 914-937-0741 800-210-5295
info@sandhuniforms.com
www.sandhuniforms.com
Uniforms, aprons, smocks, caps and visors
President: Glen Ross
info@sandhuniforms.com
Vice President: Kevin Ross
Sales Manager: Pat Kraft
Estimated Sales: $35 Million
Number Employees: 50-99
Square Footage: 50000
Type of Packaging: Private Label
Brands:
  S&H Uniforms

28631 S & J Laboratories Inc
4669 Executive Dr
Portage, MI 49002-9389
269-324-7383
Fax: 269-324-7384 info@sandjlab.com
www.sandjlab.com
Food laboratory service providing chemical, microbiological and physical analysis for food, feed and ingredients
President: Sheree Lin
shereelin@sandjlab.com
Vice President: James Lin
Estimated Sales: $500,000-$1 Million
Number Employees: 5-9
Square Footage: 16000

28632 S & L Store Fixture
3755 NW 115th Ave
Doral, FL 33178-1857
305-599-8906
Fax: 305-599-8906 800-205-4536
info@slstoredisplays.com www.usahanger.com
Manufacturer and exporter of store fixtures including metal shelving
President: Ronald Maier
VP: Ron Maier
Estimated Sales: $2.5-5 Million
Number Employees: 10-19
Square Footage: 128000
Brands:
  Kent Supermatic

28633 S & R Products
765 Oak Rd
Bronson, MI 49028-9353
517-369-2351
Fax: 517-369-2424 800-328-3887
www.sandrproductsllc.com
Manufacturer and wholesaler/distributor of automatic liquor control pourers
Owner: Scot Kubasiak
scott.kubasiak@srproducts.com
Sales Manager: Rick Sandvik
Estimated Sales: Less Than $500,000
Number Employees: 1-4
Square Footage: 14000
Parent Co: Kazico
Brands:
  Cheapshot

28634 S & S Metal & Plastics Inc
3740 Morton St
Jacksonville, FL 32217-2276
904-730-4655
Fax: 904-739-1394 c.strickland@ssmetal.com
www.ssmetal.com
Plastic signs
President: Cindy Strickland
c.strickland@ssmetal.com
VP: Tim Clifton
Estimated Sales: $5-10 Million
Number Employees: 20-49

28635 S & S Soap Co
815 E 135th St
Bronx, NY 10454-3584
718-585-2900
Fax: 718-585-2902
Powdered, liquid and hand soap; also, detergents
President: David Sebrow
david@sssoap.com
Estimated Sales: $10-20 Million
Number Employees: 10-19
Square Footage: 80000
Brands:
  Pink Magic
  White Magic

28636 S & S Svc Parts
409 Saint Croix Ave
New Richmond, WI 54017-2609
715-246-3299
Fax: 715-246-3212 sales@bagcloser.com
www.bagcloser.com
Hand sealers, band sealers, bagging scales, conveyors, palletizers and vertical form fill and seal systems
Owner: Mike Preece
mike@ssserviceparts.com
Sales Director: Tim Tonkson
Estimated Sales: $500,000-$1 Million
Number Employees: 5-9

28637 S & W Pallet Co
2120 Divider And Natchez Trace
Camden, TN 38320-6559
731-584-4540
Fax: 731-584-2664 800-640-0522
sales@swpallet.com www.swpallets.com
Wooden pallets and skids
President: Jackie Wimberly
jackiewimberly@swpallets.com
Manager: Jackie Wimberly
Estimated Sales: $5-10 Million
Number Employees: 50-99

28638 S E & M
2660 Perrowville Rd
Forest, VA 24551-1859
434-525-7707
Fax: 434-525-7739 800-488-6055
info@se-m.com www.se-m.com
President: Jack Balrd
Vice President: Cb Messer
cbmesser@se-m.com
CFO: Jack Balrd
Estimated Sales: Below $5 Million
Number Employees: 20-49

28639 S Hochman Company
PO Box 1204
Danville, CA 94526-8204
925-838-9990
Fax: 925-743-1234 800-999-9511
Food and beverage industry
Owner: Shayel M Hochman Jr

28640 S I Jacobson Mfg Co
1414 Jacobson Dr
Waukegan, IL 60085-7600
847-623-1414
Fax: 847-623-2556 800-621-5492
plzang@sij.com www.sij.com
CEO: Seth Greenwald
sigreenwald@gmail.com
Estimated Sales: $50-100 Million
Number Employees: 100-249

28641 S J Controls Inc
2248 Obispo Ave # 203
Suite 203
Signal Hill, CA 90755-4026
562-494-1400
Fax: 562-494-1066 info@sjcontrols.com
www.sjcontrols.com
Manufacturer and exporter of blending and batching equipment, process control systems, flow meters and level detectors; also, engineering services available
President: Dave Olszewski
CAO: Noel Brown
nbrown@sjcontrols.com
CFO: Cindy Pawn
Engineer: Steve Czaus
Estimated Sales: Below $5 Million
Number Employees: 5-9

28642 S Kamberg & Co LTD
445 Northern Blvd # 25
Great Neck, NY 11021-4804
516-482-4141
Fax: 516-482-4147 www.skamberg.com
Supplier of Corn Meal, Dairy Products, Fats, Flour, Fruits, Honey, Nut Meats, Seeds, Sprinkles/Chocolate and Tomoato Products.
President: Doreen Tiseo
dtiseo@skamberg.com
CEO: Mark Kamberg
Sales Manager: Mark Glickman
Estimated Sales: $5-10 Million
Number Employees: 5-9

28643 S L Doery & Son Inc
299 Rockaway Tpke
Lawrence, NY 11559-1269
516-239-8090
Fax: 516-239-0696
Commerical awnings
President: Tom Peppe
Estimated Sales: Less than $500,000
Number Employees: 5-9

28644 S L Sanderson & Co
173 Sandy Springs Ln
Berry Creek, CA 95916-9759
530-589-3062
Fax: 530-589-3062 800-763-7845
Manufacturer and exporter of handheld capsule fillers and tampers; wholesaler/distributor of gelatin capsules
President: Cydney Sanderson
capsulefillers@gmail.com
Estimated Sales: Less Than $500,000
Number Employees: 1-4
Number of Products: 6
Brands:
Cap. M. Quik

28645 S Walter Packaging Corp
2900 Grant Ave
Philadelphia, PA 19114-2310
215-676-8890
Fax: 215-698-7119 888-429-5673
shop@swalter.com www.swalter.com
Bags, boxes, ribbons, bows, gift wrap, tissue paper and labels for packaging supplies.
President: John Dowers
john@swalter.com
Finance Executive: Maury Jaffe
EVP: James Leddy
SVP Marketing/Sales: Paula Wilmer
Human Resources Manager: Barbara Guido
john@swalter.com
VP Operations: Marc Leventhal
Purhcasing Agent: Beth Lopergola
Estimated Sales: $70 Million
Number Employees: 100-249
Square Footage: 200000

28646 (HQ)S&M Manufacturing Company
PO Box 1637
Cisco, TX 76437-1637
254-442-1380
Fax: 254-442-1643 800-772-8532
Mops and brooms
President: George Owens
Executive VP: Gail Hogan
VP: Sandy Boyett
Estimated Sales: Below $5 Million
Number Employees: 5-9
Brands:
Sheen Master

28647 S&O Corporation
527 Layton Rd
Gallaway, TN 38036
901-867-2223
Fax: 901-867-3760 800-624-7858
Garbage bags
President: Terry Draughon
VP: Tommy White
Contact: Toi Spearmon
tois@sandocorporation.com
Estimated Sales: $5-10 Million
Number Employees: 20 to 49

28648 S&P Marketing, Inc.
11100 86th Ave
Maple Grove, MN 55369
763-559-0436
Fax: 763-557-1318
Fruit ingredients including tropical and temperate fruit juices, purees, dried fruits, powders and more. Niche products include tamarind, coconut cream, alphonso mango puree, prickly pear juice, puree, powder, fiber and oil.
President: Chareonsri Srisangnam
Marketing/R&D: Vinod Padhye
om@snpmarketing.com
Contact: Om Padhye
om@snpmarketing.com
Type of Packaging: Food Service, Bulk

28649 S&P USA Ventilation Systems, LLC
6393 Powers Ave
Jacksonville, FL 32217
904-731-4711
Fax: 904-737-8322 800-961-7370
www.solerpalau-usa.com
Manufacturer and exporter of commercial restaurant exhaust fans and ventilation equipment
Owner: Patrick M Williams Sr
VP Sales: Mike Wanek
Contact: Karen Antonell
karen.antonell@healogics.com
Manufacturing/Product Manager: Jim Webster
Estimated Sales: $10-20 Million
Number Employees: 100-249
Square Footage: 150000
Parent Co: Breidert Air Products
Type of Packaging: Consumer, Food Service, Private Label, Bulk
Brands:
Breidert Air
Jennfan
Stanley

28650 S&R Machinery
943 Underwood Rd
Olyphant, PA 18447-2619
570-489-1212
Fax: 570-489-2572 800-229-4896
Manufacturing automated packaging machinery for your business
President: Brain McCarthy
Sales: Tim McAndrew
Production: Tim Mcandrew
Plant Manager: Tim Mc Andrew
Estimated Sales: $1-2.5 Million
Number Employees: 1-4
Number of Brands: 12
Number of Products: 1
Square Footage: 28000
Type of Packaging: Food Service

28651 S-H-S International of Wilkes
1124 Highway 315 Blvd
Wilkes Barre, PA 18702-6943
570-825-3411
Fax: 570-825-7790
Recruiter of technical and managerial personnel for the food industry
Owner: Christopher Hackett
President: Chris Hackett
Estimated Sales: $1-3 Million
Number Employees: 10-19

28652 S. B. C. Coffee
19529 Vashon Highway SW
Vashon, WA 98070-6029
206-463-5050
Fax: 206-463-5051
Import and retail coffee equipment and supplies
President: J Stewart
Estimated Sales: $500,000-$1 000,000
Number Employees: 5-9
Type of Packaging: Private Label, Bulk

28653 S. Katzman Produce
Hunts Point Market
Row B, Unit 213
Bronx, NY 10474
718-991-4700
Fax: 718-589-3655 info@katzmanproduce.com
katzmanproduce.com
Fruits and vegetables

President: Stephen Katzman
VP, Finance: Gary Allen
Director of Operations: Andrew Roy
Manager: Mario Andreani
Estimated Sales: $50-100 Million
Number Employees: 5-9
Type of Packaging: Food Service

28654 S.L. Canada Packaging Machine
1391 Kebet Way
Port Coquitlam, BC V3C 6G1
Canada
604-941-6538
Fax: 604-941-2924 info@marpak.ca
President: George Davis
Number Employees: 20-40

28655 S.S.I. Schaefer System International Limited
140 Nuggett Court
Brampton, ON L6T 5H4
Canada
905-458-5399
Fax: 905-458-7951 sales@ssi-schaefer.ca
Plastic, steel, stacking and nesting storage containers
General Manager: Otto Fasthuber
Number Employees: 25

28656 S.V. Dice Designers
1836 Valencia Street
Rowland Heights, CA 91748-3050
909-869-7833
Fax: 909-869-0515 888-478-3423
Manufacturer and exporter of packaging machinery including case packers, erectors and sealers
President: Todd Dice
VP: Don Jameson
Engineer: Kent Martins
Estimated Sales: $2.5-5 Million
Number Employees: 1-4
Square Footage: 60000

28657 SA Wald Reconditioners
534 Foothill Road
Bridgewater, NJ 08807-2236
908-218-0627
Fax: 201-433-0098
Tea and coffee industry equipment and machinery reconditioning
Estimated Sales: $1-5 Million
Number Employees: 7

28658 SAF Products
433 E Michigan St
Milwaukee, WI 53202-5104
414-221-6333
Fax: 414-615-4000 800-641-4615
www.safbankproducts.com
CEO: John Riesch
Estimated Sales: $10-20 Million
Number Employees: 50-99

28659 SASA Demarle
8 Corporate Dr
Cranbury, NJ 08512-3630
609-395-0219
Fax: 609-395-1027 sales@demarleusa.com
www.demarleusa.com
President: Hatsuo Takeuchi
Finance & Administration Manager: Andrew Rozek
Vice President: Pierre Bonnet
Marketing & Sales Administrator: Brandon Iacometta
Contact: Pierre Bonnet
pierre.bonnet@sasademarle.com
Estimated Sales: $5-10 Million
Number Employees: 10-19

28660 SASOL North America
900 Threadneedle
Suite 100
Houston, TX 77079
281-588-3000
Fax: 281-588-3144 info@us.sasol.com
www.sasolnorthamerica.com
Medium chain triglycerides, release agents, emulsifiers, fats

President: Charles Putnik
SNA Finance Manager: Patrick Cain
Vice President, Sasol US Operations: Mike Thomas
Research & Development Manager: Holger Ziehe
Marketing: Barbara Pagliocca
Sales: Barbara Pagliocca
Contact: Kevin Dedeaux
kdedeaux@energyxxi.com
Manager O&S US Operations: Paul Hippman
Estimated Sales: $5-10 Million
Number Employees: 500-999

28661 SBA Software
10460 NW 29th Ter
Doral, FL 33172-2527
305-477-7366
Fax: 305-477-7175 800-222-8324
sales@restez.com www.pintodesigns.net
Point of sale hospitality and back office software
Owner: Pelia Pinto
Director Development: Roman Teller
Technical Services Director: Brad Sherman
Estimated Sales: $5-10 Million
Number Employees: 1-4
Brands:
    Rest Ez

28662 SBB & Associates
4708 S Old Pch Rd Ste 100a
Norcross, GA 30071
770-449-7610
Fax: 770-449-1839 www.eventective.com
Executive personnel search firm
President: Mark Barlow
Estimated Sales: Below $5 Million
Number Employees: 1-4

28663 SBN Associates
5702 Larchmont Drive
Erie, PA 16509-2918
814-454-6326
Fax: 814-459-3359
Computer systems and software for the meat industry

28664 SBS of Financial Industries
28 New Hampton Road
Washington, NJ 07882-4002
908-689-5520
Fax: 908-689-5774
Electronic card processing and check vertification services for the food service industry
CEO: Joe Kaplan
Director New Business Development: Linda Booth
VP: Tim Jochner
Parent Co: Superior Bankcard Service (SBS)

28665 SCA Hygiene Paper
PO Box 719
San Ramon, CA 94583-5719
925-830-2970
Fax: 925-830-0628 800-992-8675
Industrial food wipes, toilet tissue, towels, polishing cloths and soaps
EVP: Dan Filippini
Marketing Specialist: Debbie Allyn
Estimated Sales: $1-5 Million
Number Employees: 100-250
Brands:
    Mevon
    Tork

28666 SCA Tissue
Cira Centre, Suite 200
2929 Arch Street
Philadelphia, PA 19104
920-725-7031
Fax: 920-727-8801 866-722-8675
www.torkusa.com
Paper products including napkins, table cloths, place mats, tray covers, towels and toilet and facial tissue
President: Joe Raccuia
Director Marketing: Greg Linnemanstons
Sr. VP Sales/Marketing: Pete Chiericozzi
VP Distribution Sales: Joe Selzer
Estimated Sales: $5-10 Million
Number Employees: 250-499
Parent Co: Chesapeake Corporation
Brands:
    Main Street
    Park Avenue
    Park Avenue Ultra
    Second Nature Plus

28667 SCA Tissue North America
1 River St
S Glens Falls, NY 12803-4768
518-743-0240
Fax: 518-793-2650 www.sca.com
Napkins, paper towels and toilet paper
President: Joe Raccuia
joe.raccuia@sca.com
Director Marketing/National Accounts: Scott Milburn
Sr VP Sales/Marketing: Don Lewis
Estimated Sales: $50-100 Million
Number Employees: 250-499
Brands:
    Ovation

28668 SCK Direct Inc
905 Honeyspot Rd
Stratford, CT 06615-7140
203-377-4414
Fax: 203-377-8187 800-327-8766
sales@fastinc.com www.kitchenbrains.com
Manufacturer and exporter of appliance timers and controls for frying, cooking, roasting, proofing, retarder-proofing, baking, etc.; also, portable shortening filter machines and software systems for appliance diagnostics
Chairman: Bernard G Koether
bkoether@mysck.com
President: George F Koether
CEO: Seth Lukash
Sales Operations Manager: Sherry Kraynak
Estimated Sales: $10-20 Million
Number Employees: 50-99
Brands:
    Fastfilter
    Fastimer
    Fastpak
    Fastron
    Sck

28669 SCK Direct Inc
905 Honeyspot Rd
Stratford, CT 06615-7140
203-377-4414
Fax: 203-377-8187 800-327-8766
sales@fastinc.com www.kitchenbrains.com
Food processing appliance controls
Chairman: Bernard G Koether
bkoether@mysck.com
Sales Operations Manager: Sherry Kraynak
Estimated Sales: $10-20 Million
Number Employees: 50-99

28670 (HQ)SDIX
111 Pencader Dr
Newark, DE 19702-3322
302-456-6789
Fax: 302-456-6770 800-544-8881
sales@sdix.com www.sdix.com
SDIX is a leader in developing accurate, simple, and rapid tests for pathogens. Our Rapidchek Tests for E.coli 0157, Listeria and Salmonella Enteritidis give you confidence in test reslutls, shortened product hold times and loweroverall testing costs. Rapidchek is Simply Accurate.
President/CEO: Fran DiNuzzo
R&D: Klaus Linopaintner
Marketing: Tim Lawink
Contact: Anthony Simonetta
anthony@haydenir.com
Estimated Sales: $30 Million
Number Employees: 5-9
Brands:
    Inquest
    Rapid Assays
    Rapid Prep

28671 SEC
106 N Main St
Plymouth, MI 48170
734-455-4500
Fax: 734-455-1026
Ceiling fan, light fixture and protective wire guards; also, industrial ceiling-suspended fans
President: Donald Keeth
National Sales Manager: Patricia Keeth
Estimated Sales: $1-2.5 Million
Number Employees: 10-19

28672 SEI Consultants
429 South St
Slidell, LA 70460-8834
985-781-1015
Fax: 985-781-1025 800-738-1000
info@seihq.com www.seihq.com
Software for food processing, packing and distribution
President: James Stolt
jim@seihq.com
VP Sales/Marketing: Donald Tyler
Estimated Sales: Less than $500,000
Number Employees: 10-19
Brands:
    Sei

28673 SEMCO
1211 W. Harmony
PO Box 505
Ocala, FL 34478-0505
800-451-3383
Fax: 352-351-3088 800-749-6894
salesatsemco@aol.com
Spinner racks, grid systems, peg hooks, dump bins, pegboard and slatwall fixtures; also, custom display items
VP: Adrian Simonet
Marketing: Tammy Robinson
Sales: Tammy Robinson
Public Relations: Fran Smith
Estimated Sales: $1-5 Million
Number Employees: 100-250
Square Footage: 540000
Parent Co: Leggett & Platt

28674 SEMCO Systems
6355 Kestrel Road
Mississauga, ON L5T 1Z5
Canada
905-670-9301
Fax: 905-670-9367 800-730-5859

28675 SERCO Laboratories
2817 Anthony Lane South
Suite 104
St. Anthony, MN 55418
612-782-9716
Fax: 612-782-9782 800-388-7173
www.sl-ser.com
Environmental testing laboratory
CEO: David Allen
Project Manager: Diane Anderson
Contact: Dave Allen
da@sl-ser.com
Estimated Sales: $500,000-$1 Million
Number Employees: 5-9

28676 SFB Plastics
P.O.Box 533
Wichita, KS 67201-0533
316-262-0409
Fax: 316-712-0112 800-343-8133
sales@sfbplastics.com www.sfbplastics.com
Packaging equipment
President: David Long
CFO: David Long
R&D: David Long
Quality Control: Debbie Stevens
Contact: Cindy Andersen
candersen@sfbplastics.com
Estimated Sales: $10-20 Million
Number Employees: 50-99

28677 (HQ)SFBC, LLC dba Seaboard Folding Box
P.O Box 547
Fitchburg, MA 01420
978-342-8921
Fax: 978-342-1105 800-225-6313
info@seaboardbox.com www.cjfox.com
Boxes, cards, labels and tags
President: Robert Starr
Quality Control: Les Coster
Marketing Manager: Joe Wescott
VP Marketing: Jill Fox-Tabak
Public Relations: Joe Wescott
Estimated Sales: $1-2.5 Million
Number Employees: 100-249
Square Footage: 260000
Type of Packaging: Private Label
Other Locations:
    C.J. Fox Co.
    Providence RI

28678 SFK Danfotech, Inc.
8301 N.W. 101st Terrace #7
Kansas City, MO 64153
816-891-7357
Fax: 816-891-0550
Automated cutting, slaughtering, deboning and processing machines for the meat industry.
Contact: Soren Rasmuessen
sales@sfk.com

28679 SFS intec, Inc
Spring Street & Van Reed Rd
Wyomissing, PA 19610
610-376-5751
Fax: 610-376-8551 610-376-8551
www.sfsintecusa.com
Freezing, material handling, chilling, automated freezing, automated chilling
Managing Director: R John Smith
Contact: Maryann Joyal
jmar@sfsintec.biz
Estimated Sales: $5-10 Million
Number Employees: 10-19

28680 SG Frantz Company
PO Box 1138
Trenton, NJ 08606-1138
215-943-2930
Fax: 215-943-2931 800-227-7642
sales@sgfrantz.com www.sgfrantz.com
Magnetic separation equipment and industrial processing equipment including dry materials, liquids and slurries and laboratory equipment
VP: Steve Fortunate
Estimated Sales: $1-5 Million
Number Employees: 1

28681 SGS International
201 State Rt 17 # 2
Rutherford, NJ 07070-2597
201-935-1500
Fax: 201-508-3193 800-747-9047
Environmental and social accountability management systems registration; ISO 14001 training includes IRCA-accredited lead assessor and internal auditing courses, EMS implementation, environmental laws and regulations
Chairman of the Board: Ernani Perez
VP: Michael J Brigante
Estimated Sales: $2.5-5 Million
Number Employees: 20-49

28682 SHURflo
3545 Harbor Gateway S
Suite 103
Costa Mesa, CA 92626
714-371-1550
Fax: 714-242-1362 800-854-3218
customer_service@shurflo.com www.shurflo.com
Manufacturer and exporter of pumps including gas operated demand, liquid, electric and dual inlet gas systems for beverage syrups and condiments.
Chairman & CEO, Pentair: Randall Hogan
EVP & Chief Financial Officer: John Stauch
SVP/Chief Accounting Officer/Treasurer: Mark Borin
SVP & Chief Marketing Officer: John Jacko
SVP/General Counsel/Secretary: Angela Jilek
Year Founded: 1968
Estimated Sales: $100-500 Million
Number Employees: 250-499
Parent Co: Pentair Inc.
Type of Packaging: Food Service

28683 SI Systems Inc
101 Larry Holmes Dr # 500
Suite 500
Easton, PA 18042-7723
610-252-7321
Fax: 610-252-3102 800-523-9464
www.sihs.com
Material handling equipment including horizontal transport, order fulfillment and sortation systems
President/CEO: John C Molloy
molloy@sihs.com
CFO: Deborah Mertz
Director Business Development: Dean Stavraka
Director Marketing: Mary Denvir
VP Marketing & Sales: Ed Romaine
VP Operations: Victor Egberts
Purchasing: Tony Franco
Estimated Sales: $10-20 Million
Number Employees: 20-49

Brands:
Sps 3000

28684 SICK Inc
6900 W 110th St
Bloomington, MN 55438-2397
952-946-6800
Fax: 952-941-9287 800-325-7425
www.sickusa.com
A global manufacturer of sensors, safety systems, machine vision and automatic identification products for industrial applications. Including: 2D and 2D machine vision cameras, Color Vision Sensors (CVS), and capacitative sensors.
President: Tony Peet
tony.peet@sick.com
Managing Director: Renate Sick-Glaser
Marketing Director: Maria Mueller
Sales Manager: Marion Bentin
Number Employees: 1000-4999
Parent Co: SICK, Inc

28685 SICOM Systems
4434 Summer Meadow Dr
Doylestown, PA 18902
Fax: 215-489-2769 800-547-4266
sales@sicompos.com
The SL18, a Linux-based color touch screen, point of sale ssytem for the quick service restaurant environment.
President: William Doan
Contact: Wendy Kemmerer
wkemmerer@sicompos.com
Estimated Sales: $10-20,000,000
Number Employees: 50-99

28686 SIG Combibloc
5327 Fisher Road
Columbus, OH 43228-9511
614-347-9971
Fax: 614-876-8678 800-843-2562
www.sigcombibloc.com
Aseptic packaging systems, aseptic filling equipment
President: Stphen Walliser
Estimated Sales: $50-100 Million
Number Employees: 25

28687 SIG Combibloc USA, Inc.
2501 Seaport Drive
River Front Suite 100
Chester, PA 19013-9791
610-546-4200
Fax: 610-546-4201 www.sigcombibloc.com
Manufacturer and exporter of aseptic carton filling and packaging systems for liquid foods and beverages
President: Yerry Derrico
Director Marketing: Bob Abamson
VP Sales/Marketing: Geoff Campbell
Contact: Kevin Abrams
kevin.abrams@sig.biz
Estimated Sales: $50-100 Million
Number Employees: 100-249
Parent Co: PKL Verpackungssysteme GmbH

28688 SIG Pack Services
2401 Brentwood Rd
Raleigh, NC 27604-3686
919-872-5561
Fax: 919-877-0887 www.sigpack.com
Tea and coffee industry, bag and pouch sealers, bag filling and sealing machines, brushes, wrapping, foiling, carton machines: closing, filling, forming, sealing, closing equipment: bag closure, heat seal, conveyor accesories
President: Harold Carr
Estimated Sales: Below $5 Million
Number Employees: 20-49

28689 SIG Packaging Technologies
PO Box 5838
Norwalk, CT 06856-5838
203-845-8900
Fax: 203-846-3792
Packaging machinery
Estimated Sales: $1-5 Million
Number Employees: 20-50

28690 SIGHTech Vision Systems
2953 Bunker Hill Lane
Suite 400
Santa Clara, CA 95054
408-282-3770
Fax: 408-413-2600 sales@sightech.com
www.sightech.com
Manufacturer and exporter of quality control and assurance machinery for visual inspection
Chairman, Chief Executive Officer: Art Gaffin
Director Marketing Communications: Jeanette Hazelwood
VP Sales/Marketing: Francis Tapon
Contact: Martha Cogan
mcogan@sightech.com
Estimated Sales: $1-2.5 Million
Number Employees: 4
Brands:
Sightech

28691 SIMBA USA
99 Lake Park Drive
Morehead, KY 40351
606-784-2008
Fax: 606-784-0057 info@simbausa.com
www.somaiagroup.com
Personalized towels
Contact: Hiten Somaia
hiten.somaia@simbatex.com.au

28692 SIMS Manufacturing Co Inc
134 N 1st Ave
Yakima, WA 98902-2617
509-453-7690
Fax: 509-457-8606 dau@simsmfg.com
www.simsmfg.com
Manager: Dustin Kissel
dustinkissel@gmail.com
Estimated Sales: $10-20 Million
Number Employees: 20-49

28693 SIPROMAC Inc.
240 Industriel Boulevard
Saint-Germain-de-Grantha, QC J0C 1K0
Canada
819-395-5151
Fax: 819-395-5343 855-395-5252
www.sipromac.com
President: Dave Couture
Vice President/Mktg & Sales Mgr.: Andre Francoevr
Research & Development: Yoann Frechette
Purchasing Manager: Richard Tremblay
Estimated Sales: $1-5 Million
Number Employees: 27

28694 SIT Indeva Inc
3630 Green Park Cir
Charlotte, NC 28217-2866
704-357-8811
Fax: 704-357-8866 info@sit-indeva.com
www.sit-indeva.com
Manufacturer and importer of material handling equipment including balancers
Vice President: Stefania Zanardi
szanardi@sit-indeva.com
VP: Stefania Zanardi
Estimated Sales: $2.5-5 Million
Number Employees: 10-19
Parent Co: Scaglia America
Type of Packaging: Bulk
Brands:
Liftronic Balancer

28695 SIT Indeva Inc
3630 Green Park Cir
Charlotte, NC 28217-2866
704-357-8811
Fax: 704-357-8866 info@sit-indeva.com
www.sit-indeva.com
Lifting devices for payloads
Vice President: Stefania Zanardi
szanardi@sit-indeva.com
VP: Stefania Zanardi
Estimated Sales: Below $5 Million
Number Employees: 10-19

28696 SJ Industries
7217 Lockport Place
Suite 101
Lorton, VA 22079-1596
703-751-5400
Fax: 703-370-3672
inquiry@arrowheadsystems.com

Accumulating conveyors, bottle rinsers, both twist and positive gripper type, can rinsers using ionized air and water, bidirectional accumulation tables, can and bottle warmer, can and bottle pasteurizer and coolers, plastic casewasher, preheater for ho
Estimated Sales: $5-10 Million
Number Employees: 30

28697 SK Food International
4666 Amber Valley Parkway
Fargo, ND 58104
701-356-4106
Fax: 701-356-4102 skfood@skfood.com
www.skfood.com
Family-owned import/export company and bulk grain supplier.
Type of Packaging: Bulk
Other Locations:
SK Food Specialty Processing
Moorhead MN

28698 SKF Motion Technologies
1530 Valley Center Pkwy # 180
Bethlehem, PA 18017-2266
610-861-3700
Fax: 610-861-4811
Ball and roller screws for linear drive systems
Manager: Jim Brown
Estimated Sales: $20-50 Million
Number Employees: 20-49

28699 SKW Biosystems
2021 Cabot Blvoulevard
Langhorne, PA 19047-1810
215-702-1000
Fax: 215-702-1015
Estimated Sales: $10-20 Million
Number Employees: 50-99

28700 SKW Gelatin & Specialties
PO Box 234
Waukesha, WI 53187-0234
Canada
262-650-8393
Fax: 262-650-8456 800-654-2396
gelatin.usa@rousselot.com www.rousselot.com
Food processing equipment manufacturer specializing in vacuum packaging machines (table top, single/double chamber, automatic and belted chambers) shring tunnels, tray sealers, thermoforming machines, injectors, tumblers, massagers andsmokehouses. Exports internationally to more than 50 countries.
President: Geoge Masson
CFO: Steve Smith
Estimated Sales: C
Number Employees: 10

28701 SKW Industrial Flooring
23700 Chagrin Boulevard
Cleveland, OH 44122-5506
216-831-5500
800-537-4722
Polymer flooring systems with exceptional chemical impact and wear resistance
Estimated Sales: $1-5 Million
Number Employees: 250-499

28702 SLT Group
303 Ridge Rd
Dayton, NJ 08810
732-837-3096
www.sltgroup.com
Basmati rice, lentils, beans, flour & spice
CEO: Sandip Patel
Estimated Sales: $38.9 Million
Number Employees: 9
Brands:
Heritage Select Brand

28703 SLX International
3453 Empresa Drive
Suite A
San Luis Obispo, CA 93401-7328
805-541-8356
Fax: 805-541-8320 800-883-9121
Reusable shipping containers
President and CEO: Edward De Temple
VP Engineering: Thomas DeTemple
Estimated Sales: $5-10 Million
Number Employees: 19

28704 SMC Corp Of America
10100 Smc Blvd
Noblesville, IN 46060-8701
317-899-4440
Fax: 317-899-3102 800-726-7621
mrhode@smcusa.com www.smcusa.com
Low to high speed packing machines including shrink wrappers, multi packers, wrap around case packers, handle applicators and turn key complete lines.
Vice President: Linda Abell
labell@smcusa.com
VP: Steve Lefevre
Sales Representative: Mike Rhode
Estimated Sales: $1-5 Million
Number Employees: 100-249

28705 SMC Corp Of America
10100 Smc Blvd
Noblesville, IN 46060-8701
317-899-4440
Fax: 317-899-3102 800-762-7621
dbrushi@smcusa.com www.smcusa.com
Vice President: Steve Ade
sade@smcusa.com
Vice President: Steve Ade
sade@smcusa.com
Estimated Sales: $1-5 Million
Number Employees: 100-249

28706 SMI USA
5500 South Cobb Dr. Building 400
Suite 5
Smyrna, GA 30080
404-799-9929
Fax: 860-688-5577 sales.us@smigroup.net
www.smigroup.it
General Manager: Walter Gallo
Number Employees: 10-19

28707 SMP Display & Design Group
4215 Cromwell Rd
Chattanooga, TN 37421
423-892-3720
Fax: 423-855-1869 800-251-6308
smp-display@smp-display.com
www.smp-display.com
Contact: George Guthrie
gguthrie@smpinstore.com

28708 SOPAKCO Foods
215 S Mullins St
Mullins, SC 29574-3207
843-464-0121
Fax: 423-639-7270 800-276-9678
www.sopakco.com
Pasta sauces; also, retortable pouch manufacturer, canner and contract packager of poultry, meat, fish, pasta, vegetable, bean, fruit and dessert products, flexible, semi-rigid and glass containers
CEO: Al Reitzer
CFO: Steve Keight
R&D: Jim Dukes
Quality Control: Phyllis Calhoun
General Manager: Wynn Pettibone
Plant Manager: Carl Whitmore
Purchasing Director: Beverly Stacey
Estimated Sales: $5-10 Million
Number Employees: 100
Square Footage: 400000
Parent Co: Unaka Corporation
Type of Packaging: Consumer, Food Service, Private Label

28709 SP Graphics
PO Box 1591
Santa Rosa, CA 95402-1591
707-542-9492
Fax: 707-542-9492
Wine industry label design

28710 (HQ)SP Industries
2982 Jefferson Rd.
Hopkins, MI 49328
269-793-3232
Fax: 269-793-7451 800-592-5959
info@sp-industries.com www.sp-industries.com
Manufacturer and exporter of hydraulic cart/dumpers, vertical balers, recycling equipment and refuse, precrusher and self-contained compactors

Owner/President: Denny Pool
Vice President: Roger Arndt
Marketing Mgr: David Jackiewicz
Sales Manager: Gene Koelsch
Office Manager: Elise Pool
Production Mgr: Julie Tahaney
Estimated Sales: $10-20 Million
Number Employees: 20-49
Square Footage: 100000

28711 SP Industries Inc
935 Mearns Rd
Warminster, PA 18974-2811
215-672-7800
Fax: 215-672-7807 800-523-2327
cs@spindustries.com www.spindustries.com
Manufactures Wilmad-LabGlass NMR & EPR tubes, hotpack incubators, chambers and glassware washers, VirTis Laboratory to production scale freeze dryers, FTS Smart Freeze Dryers Technology anf Precision Thermal Control Equipment, Genevacevaporator systems, and Hull Luophilization Systems.
CEO: Patrick Addvensky
patrick.addvensky@spindustries.com
CEO: Chuck Grant
CEO: Charles Grant
Marketing Director: Jennifer Colaiacomo
Sales: Robert Hoesly
Number Employees: 50-99
Square Footage: 280000

28712 (HQ)SPG International
11230 Harland Dr NE
Covington, GA 30014-6411
770-787-9830
Fax: 770-787-7432 877-503-4774
info@spgusa.com www.spgusa.com
Manufacturer and exporter of aluminum and stainless steel carts, racks and bakery shelving
Owner: Steve Durnell
steve.durnell@leggett.com
President, Chief Executive Officer: Steven DarnelL
VP Mfg.: Jose Lopez
Vice President of Business Development: Dave Mack
Vice President of Operations: Bob Buehler
Number Employees: 100-249
Square Footage: 320000
Parent Co: Keggerr & Platt Storage Products Group
Type of Packaging: Food Service
Other Locations:
Kelmax Equipment Co.
San Luis Potosi

28713 SPI's Film and Bag Federation
1667 K St., NW
Suite 1000
Washington, DC 20006-1620
202-974-5200
Fax: 202-296-7005 www.plasticsindustry.org
President: William Cartuaex
CFO: John Maguire
R&D: Tommy Fouthall
Contact: Bill Carteaux
bill.carteaux@spi.com
Number Employees: 100-249

28714 (HQ)SPX Corporation
13320-A Ballantyne Corporate Place
Charlotte, NC 28277
980-474-3700
www.spx.com
Manufactures a wide range of food process technologies from control valves to integrated food processing equipment.
President & CEO: Gene Lowe
Global Operations: J. Randall Data
VP/General Counsel/Secretary: John Nurkin
VP/Treasurer/Chief Financial Officer: Scott Sproule
VP & Chief Human Resources Officer: Tausha White
Year Founded: 1912
Estimated Sales: $1.6 Billion
Number Employees: 4,500
Square Footage: 10411
Brands:
Anhydro
Apv
Bran+Luebbe
Clydeunion Pumps
Copes-Vulcan
Delair
Deltech
Dollinger

Gd Engineering
Gerstenberg Schroder
Hankison
Jemaco
Johnson Pump
Lightnin
M&J Valve
Plenty
Pneumatic Products
Waukesha Cherry-Burrell

28715 (HQ)SPX Flow Inc
13320 Ballantyne Corporate Pl
Charlotte, NC 28277

704-449-9187
800-252-5200
communications@spxflow.com www.spxflow.com
Manufacturer, importer and exporter of fat crystallization machinery for the processing of mayonnaise, salad dressings, margarine and shortening
President & CEO: Marc Michael
President, Food & Beverage: Dwight Gibson
VP & CFO: Jaime Easley
Chief Strategy Officer: Brian Taylor
Estimated Sales: $1.5 Billion
Number Employees: 5000-9999

28716 SPX Flow Inc
135 Mount Read Blvd
Rochester, NY 14611-1921

585-436-5550
Fax: 585-527-1742 www.spxflow.com
Mixers and impeller systems for industrial water and wastewater treatment.
Number Employees: 250-499
Parent Co: SPX Flow Inc

28717 SQP
602 Potential Pkwy
Schenectady, NY 12302-1041

518-831-6800
Fax: 518-831-6890 800-724-1129
www.specialtyqualitypackaging.com
Tissue, paper food trays, plastic straws and stirrers, napkins, chicken boxes and paper hinged takeouts
Owner: Amar Martin
Plant Manager: Barbara Flaming
National Sales Manager: William Gnatek
Sales Manager: Richard Bonaker
rjssbonaker@msn.com
Plant Manager: Larry Meyers
Estimated Sales: $20-50 Million
Number Employees: 100-249
Type of Packaging: Bulk
Brands:
Valay

28718 SRC Vision
PO Box 1666
Medford, OR 97501

541-776-9800
Fax: 541-779-4104
Computerized optical sorting systems for the detection and automatic removal of defects from food processing lines; specialists in vision automated systems
Estimated Sales: $1-5 Million
Number Employees: 1-4

28719 SRI
203 Frances Ln
Barrington, IL 60010

847-382-3877
Fax: 847-382-3878 abean5452@aol.com
www.srimatch.com
Owner: Alan Bean
CEO: Allen Bean
Contact: Charlie Garza
cgarza@sriservices.com
Estimated Sales: $300,000-500,000
Number Employees: 1-4

28720 SSE Software Corporation
P.O. Box 384
Buckner, KY 40010

502-553-8653
Fax: 888-866-1931 contact@ssestandards.com
www.ssesoftware.com
Sanitary CAD/Design software
President: James Wynn
Number Employees: 12

28721 SSOE Group
1001 Madison Ave
Toledo, OH 43604-5585

419-255-3830
Fax: 419-255-6101 lslusher@ssoe.com
www.ssoe.com
Engineering consultant specializing in the design of food plants and food process design
Senior Project Manager: Joe Badalomenti
CEO: Bob Howell
bhowell@ssoe.com
Executive Vice President: Bob Howell
Senior Vice President: Mike Murphy
Division Manager: Ken Gruenhagen
Estimated Sales: Less Than $500,000
Number Employees: 500-999

28722 SSW Holding Co Inc
1100 W Park Rd
Elizabethtown, KY 42701-3168

270-769-5526
Fax: 270-769-0105 info@sswholding.net
www.sswholding.net
Manufacturer and exporter of wire racks and refrigerator and freezer shelving and baskets
President: Paul Kara
Marketing: Brad Nall
VP Sales/Marketing: Mark Gritton
Marketing Manager: Brad Nall
Contact: Richard Baker
r.baker@sswholding.net
Product Development Manager: Jeff Ambrose
Number Employees: 1-4
Square Footage: 1120000
Parent Co: SSW Holding Company
Other Locations:
SSW Holding Co.
Fort Smith AR

28723 ST Restaurant Supplies
#1-1678 Fosters Way
Delta, BC V3M 6S6
Canada

604-524-0933
Fax: 604-524-0633 888-448-4244
Manufacturer, importer and wholesaler/distributor of chef hats, hairnets, gloves and aprons; also, woodenware and nylon/metal scrubbers
President: Terry Kuehne
CEO: Sandy Lee
Sales: Sabastien Lachat
Purchasing: Sandy Lee
Number Employees: 21
Number of Products: 220
Square Footage: 160000
Type of Packaging: Food Service, Private Label, Bulk
Other Locations:
ST Restaurant Supplies
Dallas TX

28724 STA Packaging Tapes
100 S Puente St
Brea, CA 92821-3813

714-255-7888
Fax: 800-235-8273 800-258-8273
Carton sealing tape, hand dispensers, case sealers
President: Ikusuke Shimizu
CEO: Ernest J Wong
CFO: Matt Minami
VP: Stephen Wilson
R&D: Dinesh Shah
Marketing: Melissa Morris
Contact: Pat Hagglof
phagglof@aptosshoesandapparel.com
Plant Manager: C Fang
Estimated Sales: $20-50 Million
Number Employees: 100-249
Square Footage: 185000

28725 STARMIX srl
Via dell'Artigianato, 5
Marano, VI 36035

044- 57- 659
Fax: 044- 57- 203 info@starmix.it
Food service equipment including meat slicers
Estimated Sales: $300,000-500,000
Number Employees: 1-4
Brands:
Fleetwood

28726 STD Precision Gear
318 Manley St # 4
West Bridgewater, MA 02379-1087

508-580-0035
Fax: 508-580-0071 888-783-4327
sales@stdgear.com
Manufacturer and exporter of corrosion-proof precision gears, sprockets, ratchets, splines, pulleys, etc
President: James Manning
CFO: Doug Grant
Sales Director: Susan Dauwer
Estimated Sales: $1-2 Million
Number Employees: 20-49
Square Footage: 26000
Brands:
Std Precision Gear & Instrument

28727 STERIS Corp
5960 Heisley Rd
Mentor, OH 44060-1834

440-354-2600
www.steris.com
Laboratory equipment including sterilizers, glassware washers and dryers, detergents, and surface disinfection.
President & Chief Executive Officer: Walter Rosebrough, Jr.
VP, Global Marketing: Tamara Struk
VP, Sales & Marketing: Trey Howard
Year Founded: 1987
Estimated Sales: $2.78 Billion
Number Employees: 12,000

28728 STM Mortgage Co
2626 Cole Ave
Dallas, TX 75204-1083

214-665-9544
Fax: 214-634-9219 800-766-7861
Commercial specialty printing: fleet graphics and P.O.P and architectural and digital products
Controller: Terry Thomas
CFO: Robert Schlezier
VP: Tim Allen
Customer Service Manager: Larry Morrow
Plant Manager: Mark Kitzman
Estimated Sales: $5-10 Million
Number Employees: 5-9

28729 STOBER Drives Inc
1781 Downing Dr
Maysville, KY 41056-8683

606-759-5090
Fax: 606-759-5045 800-711-3588
sales@stober.com
President: Peter Feil
pfeil@stober.com
CFO: Peter Fiel
R&D: Shane Art
Quality Control: Mick Michelle
Estimated Sales: $5-10 Million
Number Employees: 100-249

28730 STRAPEX Corporation
2601 Westinghouse Blvd
Charlotte, NC 28273

704-588-2510
Fax: 704-588-6838 800-346-1804
Plastic strapping equipment for the security of loads during transport
General Manager: Bill Drake
Controller: Glenn Boyd
Estimated Sales: $10-20 Million
Number Employees: 20-49

28731 SUEZ Water Technologies & Solutions
4636 Somerton Rd
Trevose, PA 19053

866-439-2837
www.suezwatertechnologies.com
Food and beverage water and wastewater treatment
CEO: Heiner Markhoff
CFO: Mamta Patel
Chief Marketing Officer: Ralph Exton
Other Locations:
BetzDearborn
Horsham PA
Brands:
Aquafloc
Bio Scan
Ferroquest
Polymate
Polyquest
Sterisafe

28732 SV Dice Designers
1836 Valencia Street
Rowland Heights, CA 91748-3050
909-869-7833
Fax: 909-869-0515 888-478-3423
Bag in box system, case packers, high speed case
erectors, case semers
Owner: S Virgil Dice
Estimated Sales: $2.5-5 Million
Number Employees: 1-4

28733 SV Research
7429 Allentown Blvd
Harrisburg, PA 17112-3609
717-540-0370
Fax: 717-540-0380
Optical character recognition and optical character
verification system designed to provide complete in-
spection on labeling and packaging lines and fully
automatic spray nozzle monitoring system for quick
and easy retrofit into mostcoating machines
President: Ron Lawson
Sales Director: Bob Leiby
Contact: Susan Baker
s.baker@seidenader.com
Estimated Sales: Below $5 Million
Number Employees: 20-49

28734 SWF Co
1949 E Manning Ave
Reedley, CA 93654-9462
559-638-8484
Fax: 559-638-7478 800-344-8951
www.swfcompanies.com
Manufacturer and exporter of automatic case and
tray loading machinery
Vice President: Braden Beam
braden.beam@thieletech.com
VP/ General Manager: Ed Suarez
Director Engineering: Dan Nourian
Sales/Marketing Executive: Gregory Cox
Product Manager: Craig Friesen
Special Project Manager: Dennis Decker
Estimated Sales: $10-20 Million
Number Employees: 100-249
Square Footage: 400000
Parent Co: Thiele Technologies
Brands:
Sure Way

28735 SWF Co
1949 E Manning Ave
Reedley, CA 93654-9462
559-638-8484
Fax: 559-638-7478 800-344-8951
info@swfcompanies.com www.swfcompanies.com
Flexible bags, case loaders, horizontal tray formers,
lidding equip
Vice President: Roland Parker
rolandp@swfcompanies.com
VP: Ed Suarez
Number Employees: 100-249

28736 SWF Co
1949 E Manning Ave
Reedley, CA 93654-9462
559-638-8484
Fax: 559-638-7478 800-344-8951
cfriesen@swfcompanies.com
www.swfcompanies.com
Vice President: Marc Atoui
matoui@swfcompanies.com
VP: Ed Suarez
VP Sales/Marketing: Bob Williams
Product Manager: Craig Friesen
Number Employees: 100-249

28737 SWF Co
1949 E Manning Ave
Reedley, CA 93654-9462
559-638-8484
Fax: 559-638-7478 800-344-8951
cfriesen@swfcompanies.com
www.swfcompanies.com
Vice President: Braden Beam
braden.beam@thieletech.com
Vice President, General Manager: Ed Suarez
Product Manager: Craig Friesen
Estimated Sales: $1-5 Million
Number Employees: 100-249

28738 SWF McDowell
5505 Carder Road
Orlando, FL 32810-4738
407-291-2817
Fax: 407-293-7054 800-877-7971
Manufacturer and exporter of carton forming and
packaging systems including case, inverted bottle
and drop packers, top sealers and case erectors
Service Manager: David Robertson
Operations Manager: Dennis Ramey
Estimated Sales: $1-5 Million
Number Employees: 50-99
Square Footage: 72000
Parent Co: SWF Machinery

28739 SYSPRO USA
959 South Coast Drive
Suite 100
Costa Mesa, CA 92626
714-437-1000
800-369-8649
info@us.syspro.com us.syspro.com
Services: analytics software, packaging, food trace-
ability software.
President: Joey Benadretti
CEO: Brian Stein
Chief Financial Officer: Doug Garnhart
Chief Marketing Officer: Dawna Olsen
PR Manager: Stanley Goodrich
Year Founded: 1978
Estimated Sales: $4.8 Million
Number Employees: 51-200
Brands:
SYSPRO

28740 Saatitech
247 Route 100
Somers, NY 10589-3231
914-767-0100
Fax: 914-767-0109 800-719-7130
info.US@saatitech.com
Manager: Todd Burt
Number Employees: 50-99

28741 Sabate USA
902 Enterprise Way # M
Napa, CA 94558-6288
707-256-2830
Fax: 707-256-2831 sabateusa@sabate.com
Wine and spirits corks and closures
President: Eric Mertier
CFO: Olivier Poissonnier
Estimated Sales: Below $5 Million
Number Employees: 5-9

28742 Sabel Engineering Corporation
1010 East Lake Street
Villard, MN 56385
320-554-3611
Fax: 320-554-2650 www.massmanllc.com
Manufacturer and exporter of automatic case pack-
ers and tiering mechanisms for collating multiple
layers
President: Herbert Sabel
Engineering Manager: Stan Lundguist
Sales Director: Gary Ensey
Manager: Dave Rosenburg
General Manager: Noel Barbulesco
Estimated Sales: $5-10 Million
Number Employees: 20-49
Square Footage: 28800
Parent Co: Massman Automation Designs, LLC
Brands:
Carousel Caser
Descender

28743 (HQ)Sabert Corp
2288 Main St
Sayreville, NJ 08872-1476
732-721-5546
Fax: 732-721-0622 800-722-3781
sabert@sabert.com www.sabert.com
Plastic disposable plates, platters, containers and
bowls; exporter of disposable platters and bowls
President: Katya Connor
kconnor2216@msn.com
Marketing Director: Mark Seckinger
Sales Director: Bob Shemming
Estimated Sales: $5-10 Million
Number Employees: 100-249
Square Footage: 200000
Other Locations:
Sabert Corp.
Brussels

Brands:
Freshpack Bowls
Roma Gold
Roma Marble
Roma Silver
Ultima

28744 Sabert Corp
2288 Main St
Sayreville, NJ 08872-1476
732-721-5546
Fax: 732-721-0622 www.sabert.com
Designs, manufactures and distributes quality,
cost-effective solutions for packaging, displaying,
serving and storing fine food.
President: Katya Connor
kconnor2216@msn.com
VP: Gary Westrol
VP Sales/Marketing: Robert Shemming
VP Human Resources: Brian Duffy
VP Operations: Mark Fessler
Assistant Product Manager: Cameron McGettigan
Number Employees: 100-249
Type of Packaging: Consumer, Food Service

28745 Sable Technology Solution
1628 Norwood Dr
St Paul, MN 55122-2754
651-994-8441
Fax: 510-293-8553 800-722-5390
info@sabletechnology.com
Manufacturer and exporter of compact point of sale
systems for table and quick service restaurants
Executive VP: Adrian Bryan
VP Sales: James Files
Estimated Sales: $1-5 Million
Number Employees: 20-50
Square Footage: 16000
Type of Packaging: Food Service

28746 Sackett Systems
1033 Bryn Mawr Ave
Bensenville, IL 60106-1244
630-766-5500
Fax: 630-766-5631 800-323-8332
sales@sackett-systems.com
www.sackettsystems.com
Lift trucks, carriers, racks, etc
President: Leonard Maniscalco
Director of Sales: Chris Lareau
Contact: Mike Borton
mborton@sackett-systems.com
Regional Accounts Manager: Andy Kerrins
Estimated Sales: $5-10 Million
Number Employees: 10-19

28747 (HQ)Sacramento Bag Manufacturing
440 N Pioneer Ave
Suite 300
Woodland, CA 95776-1788
530-662-6130
Fax: 530-662-6381 tiffanyj@sacbag.com
www.sacbag.com
Bags including raschel knit, polyethylene, burlap,
polypropylene and cotton
Sales: Larry Deman
Customer Service Reps: Kathy Anderson
General Manager/Controller: Paresh Shah
Accounts Receivables: Suvo Lahiri
Plant Manager: Dennis Joost
Estimated Sales: $2.5-5 Million
Number Employees: 20-49
Square Footage: 110000
Parent Co: Acme Bag Company
Other Locations:
Sacramento Bag Manufacturing
Vernon CA

28748 (HQ)Sadler Conveyor Systems
1845 William Street
Montreal, QC H3J 1R6
Canada
519-941-4858
Fax: 519-941-7339 888-887-5129
Custom conveying systems for case and pallet han-
dling from horizontal to vertical applications
President: Stephen Sadler
Vice President: Neil Sadler
R & D: Neil Sadler
Marketing Director: Luc Martineau
Sales Director: Chris Morin
Production Manager: Marcel Richard
Engineering: Eric Allard

Estimated Sales: Below $5 Million
Number Employees: 10
Square Footage: 144000
Other Locations:
Sadler Conveyor Systems
Hartford CT
Brands:
Hercules
Ls-Q50
Sadler
Uni-Flo

28749 Saeco
7905 Cochran Rd # 100
Cleveland, OH 44139-5470
440-528-2000
Fax: 440-542-9173 estronic@aol.com
Manufacturer and importer of espresso and cappuccino machines including self-grinding, fully automatic and manual
President: John Mc Cann
Marketing Manager (Commercial Products): Julianna Benedick
Sales Manager (Housewares): Elizabeth Will
Contact: Kevin Lemaster
k.lemaster@saeco-usa.com
Estimated Sales: $2.5-5 Million
Number Employees: 20-49
Square Footage: 80000
Parent Co: Estro/Saeco
Type of Packaging: Consumer, Food Service
Brands:
Estro Da-Line
Saeco Housewares

28750 Saeplast Canada
PO Box 2087
St John, NB E2L 3T5
Canada
506-633-0101
Fax: 506-658-0227 800-567-3966
saeplast@saeplastcanada.com
Manufacturer and exporter of plastic pallets and insulated containers for transporting fruits, vegetables, frozen foods and fresh fish
President: Torfi Gudmundsson
CFO: Dave Burnan
Number Employees: 50-60
Brands:
Dynoplast

28751 Saf-T-Gard International Inc
205 Huehl Rd
Northbrook, IL 60062-1972
847-291-1600
Fax: 847-291-1610 800-548-4273
safety@saftgard.com www.saftgard.com
Disposable gloves, mesh gloves
President: Richard Rivkin
rrivkin@saftgard.com
Quality Control: Tom Rearer
Chairman of the Board: Norman Rivkin
Estimated Sales: $10-20 Million
Number Employees: 50-99

28752 Safe-T-Cut Inc
97 Main St
Monson, MA 01057-1320
413-267-9984
Fax: 413-267-9585 info@safetcut.com
www.safetcut.com
Manufacturer and exporter of safety knives for cutting films, foams and cartons
President: Richard Baer
CEO: Mary Clark
CFO: Debra Baer
Manager: Debbie Baer
info@safetcut.com
Number Employees: 10-19
Number of Products: 10
Brands:
Safe T Cut

28753 Safety Fumigant Co
197 Beal St # 2
Hingham, MA 02043-1599
781-749-1199
Fax: 781-740-4996 800-244-1199
safetyfumigant@aol.com www.safetyfumigant.com
Insecticides
President: John Hall
safetyfumigant@aol.com
Estimated Sales: Less than $500,000
Number Employees: 10-19

28754 Safety Light Corporation
4150 Old Berwick Rd
Suite A
Bloomsburg, PA 17815
570-784-4344
Fax: 570-784-1402
Self-luminous nonelectric exit and safety signs
President: C Richter White
Contact: Greg Beese
gbeese@safetylight.com
Plant Manager: Larry Harmon
Estimated Sales: $2.5-5 Million
Number Employees: 20-49

28755 Safety Seal Industries
447 Main Street
Catskill, NY 12414-1317
518-943-1300
Fax: 518-943-0873
customer-service@tmi-pvc.com

28756 Safeway Solutions
2804 SE Loop 820
Fort Worth, TX 76140-1012
817-237-6373
Fax: 817-237-2613 info@safewaysolutions.com
Chief Executive Officer: Randall Price

28757 Sage Automation Inc
4925 Fannett Rd
Beaumont, TX 77705-4305
409-842-8040
Fax: 409-842-9141 800-731-9111
rbeller@sagerobot.com www.sagerobot.com
Custom material handling and case packing
President: Don W Cawley
doncawley@sagerobot.com
Applications Engineer: Greg White
Marketing/Technology: Jason Blake
Business Development: Randy Beller
Public Relations: Rodney Gonzalez
Estimated Sales: $10-20 Million
Number Employees: 50-99

28758 Sahara Date Company
8456A Tyco Road
Vienna, VA 22182
703-745-7463
info@saharadate.com
www.saharadate.com
Dates
Co-Founder: Maile Ramzi
Co-Founder: Jean Houpert
Estimated Sales: $6.9 Million
Number Employees: 34
Brands:
Sahara Date Company

28759 Sailor Plastics
08 Main Ave.
PO Box 309
Adrian, MN 56110
507-483-2469
Fax: 507-483-2777 800-380-7429
sales@sailorplastics.com www.sailorplastics.com
Plastic bottles
President & Owner: Lorin Krueger
Estimated Sales: $3 Million
Number Employees: 2-10
Brands:
Honey Bears
French Square
Sailor Plastics

28760 Saint-Gobain Corporation
20 Moores Rd
Malvern, PA 19355
610-893-6000
Fax: 855-639-6629
SGNorthAmericaInfo@saint-gobain.com
www.saint-gobain-northamerica.com
Building materials for a variety of industries including commercial construction.
Chairman, Saint-Gobain North America: Tom Kinisky
Senior Manager, Commercial Sales: Heather Whitaker
Commercial Business Development Manager: Brittany Wright
National Accounts Manager: Bernie Shalvey
Year Founded: 1967
Estimated Sales: $6.2 Billion
Number Employees: 15,000
Parent Co: Compagnie de Saint-Gobain S.A.

28761 Saint-Gobain Performance Plastics
31500 Solon Rd
Solon, OH 44139
www.plastics.saint-gobain.com
Products for food and beverage dispensing, food processing, packaging, quick service, and raw milk collection.
Production: Scott Yudkin
Estimated Sales: $10-20 Million
Number Employees: 50-99

28762 (HQ)Salem China Company
1000 S Broadway Avenue
Salem, OH 44460-3773
330-337-8771
Fax: 330-337-8775 salem-urfic@worldnet.att.net
Custom manufacturer and exporter of chinaware, dinner sets, teapots, beer steins, stainless flatware and mugs; importer of dinnerware sets
Secretary: Carolyn Brubaker
Estimated Sales: $500,000-$1 Million
Number Employees: 10-19

28763 Salem-Republic Rubber Co
475 W California Ave
Sebring, OH 44672-1922
330-938-9801
Fax: 330-938-9809 800-425-5079
srr@salem-republic.com www.salem-republic.com
Manufacturer, importer and exporter of FDA approved hoses and hose assemblies, rubber tubing and pipes
President: Drew Ney
dney@salem-republic.com
VP Corporate Development: Anthony Kindler
Sales Manager: Raymond Willis
Estimated Sales: $10-20 Million
Number Employees: 50-99
Brands:
Champion
Flexrite
Vol-U-Flex

28764 Sales Building Systems
9325 Progress Pkwy
Mentor, OH 44060
440-639-9100
Fax: 440-639-9190 800-435-7576
Consultant specializing in restaurant chain database marketing
President: Pat White
CFO: Jack Zaback
Founder: Tim McCarthy
VP Sales: Cindy Venable
Contact: Terry Goins
haleyhaddix@justiceretail.com
Operations Manager: Shelly Furness
Estimated Sales: $5-10,000,000
Number Employees: 50-99
Number of Products: 2

28765 Sales Partner System
789 S Nova Rd
Ormond Beach, FL 32174
386-672-8434
Fax: 386-673-4730 800-777-2924
www.spsi.com
Computer software for sales automation
CEO: Larry Frank
VP/General Manager: Ken Yontz
President: Jal Belix
Number Employees: 10-19

28766 SalesData Software
6340 San Ignacio Avenue
San Jose, CA 95119-1209
408-281-5811
Fax: 408-281-3736 www.act.com
Computer software for the food service industry including point of sale management systems, cash and sale analysis, menu costing, marketing tools, inventory control and purchase ordering; also, installation and training servicesavailable
President: Binh Nguyen
Parent Co: Aureflam Corporation
Brands:
Restaurant Basics
Retail Basics

28767 Salient Corp
203 Colonial Dr # 101
Horseheads, NY 14845-8602

607-739-4511
Fax: 607-739-4045 info@salient.com
www.salient.com
Developer of strategic sales management solutions
for high volume businesses, Windows-based soft-
ware and sales management software tools for sales
data online, service rep productivity and a
high-power work-order tracking system
President: Guy Amisano
gamisano@salient.com
Sales Director: Larry Beuter
Marketing Director: John Shannon
Business Development: Mike Dzikowski
Operations Manager: Sandy Houper
Estimated Sales: $5-10 Million
Number Employees: 100-249

28768 Salinas Valley Wax Paper Co
1111 Abbott St
Salinas, CA 93901-4501

831-424-2747
Fax: 831-424-5883
Manufacturer and importer of printed and plain
packaging paper including kraft, laminated, waxed,
tissue, pads, box liners, etc
President: Chas Nelson
CEO: Charles Nelson
charles@svwpco.com
VP: Bill Zimmerman
Plant Manager: Richard Johnson
Estimated Sales: $10-20 Million
Number Employees: 20-49
Number of Brands: 1
Square Footage: 80000
Type of Packaging: Private Label, Bulk
Brands:
    Ratan
    Salinas Valley Wax Paper Co.

28769 Salonika Imports Inc
3509 Smallman St
Pittsburgh, PA 15201-1936

412-682-2700
800-794-2256
www.salonika.net
Mediterranean culinary products
President/Owner: Chris Balouris
sales@salonika.net
Number Employees: 5-9

28770 Salvajor Co
4530 E 75th Ter
Kansas City, MO 64132-2081

816-363-1030
Fax: 816-363-4914 800-SAL-AJOR
sales@salvajor.com www.salvajor.com
Manufacturer, importer and exporter of commercial
food waste disposal and waste handling systems
President: Timothy Dike
cadman@modelwarships.com
Vice President: Don Misenhelter
Research & Development: Chris Hohl
National Sales Manager: Dennis Easteria
Purchasing Manager: P Cooper
Estimated Sales: $10-20 Million
Number Employees: 50-99
Square Footage: 80000
Brands:
    Scrapmaster
    Troughveyor

28771 Sam Pievac Company
14044 Freeway Dr
Santa Fe Springs, CA 90670

562-404-5590
Fax: 562-404-7566 800-742-8585
mjohnson@spcdisplays.com
www.sampievaccompany.com
Store fixtures and displays
President/COO: Matt Johnson
Chairman/CEO: Scott Pievac
VP: Michael Pievac
VP, Sales: Robin Hess
Contact: Eric Canavan
ecanavan@pievac.net
Estimated Sales: $10-20 Million
Number Employees: 20-49
Square Footage: 29000

28772 Sambonet USA
1180 Mclester St # 8
Elizabeth, NJ 07201-2931

908-351-4800
Fax: 908-351-3351 www.sambonet.it
Wholesaler/distributor and importer of general mer-
chandise including cutlery, trays, coffee and tea ser-
vice equipment, chafing dishes, etc.; serving the
food service market
President: Pierre Luigi Coppo
CFO: Harish Patel
VP: Andrea Viannello
Quality Control: Harish Patel
Estimated Sales: $2.5-5 Million
Number Employees: 5-9
Parent Co: Paderno SpA

28773 Samco Freezerwear
3499 Lexington Ave N # 205
Ste 205
St Paul, MN 55126-7070

651-638-3888
Fax: 651-638-3896 info@polarwear.com
www.freezerwear.com
Insulated industrial clothing including pants, jackets,
full suits, hoods, vests, safety boots and light and
heavy weight
President: Thomas Bramwell Sr
CEO: Tom Bramwell Jr
CFO: Richard Schuster
VP: Dave Bramwell
Quality Control: David Bramwell
Estimated Sales: $12-18 Million
Number Employees: 1-4
Square Footage: 160000

28774 Samsill Corp
5740 Hartman Rd
Fort Worth, TX 76119-6234

817-536-1906
Fax: 817-535-6900 800-255-1100
www.samsill.com
Presentation and storage products including binders,
sheet protectors and menu covers
Executive Director: Michelle McLaughlin
CEO: James Bankes
jbankes@samsill.com
CFO: Dave Paton
Executive VP Marketing/Sales: Bob Schultz
Number Employees: 100-249
Type of Packaging: Food Service

28775 Samson Controls
4111 Cedar Boulevard
Baytown, TX 77523-8588

281-383-3677
Fax: 281-383-3690 www.samson-usa.com
Manufacturer and exporter of controls and control
systems, flow regulators, valves and valve operators
President: Siegfried Hanicke
Contact: Javier Delamora
jdelamora@aerodynamix.com
Estimated Sales: $2.5-5 Million
Number Employees: 20-49
Parent Co: Samson Controls

28776 Samsung Electronics America, Inc.
85 Challenger Rd.
Ridgefield Park, NJ 07660

201-229-4000
800-726-7864
www.samsungusa.com
Consumer electronics and digital products, including
refrigerators, ranges, microwaves and more.
President/Chief Executive Officer: Young Hoon
Eom
CFO: Roh Hee-chan
Year Founded: 1978
Estimated Sales: $9.4 Billion
Number Employees: 1,700
Parent Co: Samsung Electronics Co., Ltd.

28777 Samuel P. Harris
55 Pawtucket Avenue
Rumford, RI 2916

401-438-4020
Fax: 401-438-8980
Vacuum formed plastic packaging materials
President: Kenneth Hatch
Treasurer: David Brower
VP Operations: Suzanne Manzak
Estimated Sales: $5-10 Million
Number Employees: 100-249

28778 Samuel Pressure Vessel Group
2121 Cleveland Ave
PO Box 100
Marinette, WI 54143-3711

715-453-5326
Fax: 888-506-4271 spvg@samuel.com
Fabricator of custom designed screw conveyors,
heat exchangers, sanitary tanks, pressure vessels
from stainless steel and other high alloy metals with
sanitary finish
President: Barry Berquist
Quality Control: Gary Anderson
Sales Director: Robert Eaton
Manager: Paul Anderson
paulanderson@samuelpressurevesselgroup.com
Plant Manager: Lenny Bartz
Purchasing Manager: Ann Kelash
Estimated Sales: $10 Million
Number Employees: 500-999
Square Footage: 130000
Parent Co: The Samuel Pressure Vessel Group

28779 Samuel Strapping Systems Inc
1401 Davey Rd # 300
Woodridge, IL 60517-4991

630-783-8900
Fax: 630-783-8901 800-323-4424
www.samuelstrapping.com
Manufacturer and exporter of steel and plastic
straps; also, carton closing machines
President: Robert Hickey
rhickey@samuelstrapping.com
CFO: Richard Louis
Controller: Dick Louis
Sales/Marketing: Tom Gould
Marketing Manager: Cy Slifka
Purchasing Manager: Joe Capoccio
Estimated Sales: $30-50 Million
Number Employees: 20-49
Parent Co: Samuel Manu-Tech

28780 Samuel Strapping Systems
2000 K Boyer S Drive
Fort Mill, SC 29173

803-802-3203
Fax: 803-802-3209 smt@samuelmanutech.com
www.samuelstrapping.com
Plastic strapping
President: Robert Hickey
Quality Control: Donna Shicely
Estimated Sales: $1-5 Million
Number Employees: 10
Parent Co: Samuel Manu-Tech

28781 Samuel Underberg Food Store
1784 Atlantic Ave
Brooklyn, NY 11213-1208

718-363-0787
Fax: 718-363-0786
Wire butter and cheese cutters, electric graters, meat
hooks, box openers and fish scalers
CEO: David Chalom
Estimated Sales: $1-2.5 Million
Number Employees: 1-4
Number of Brands: 100
Number of Products: 2100

28782 Samuels Products Inc
9851 Redhill Dr
Blue Ash, OH 45242-5694

513-891-4456
Fax: 513-891-4520 800-543-7155
www.samuelsproducts.com
Computer and pressure sensitive labels and printed
bags
Owner: Millard Samuels
mes@samuelsproducts.com
National Sales Manager: Tim Kroger
Purchasing Manager: Rick Helton
Estimated Sales: $5-10 Million
Number Employees: 20-49
Square Footage: 120000

28783 San Aire Industries
101 W Felix St
Fort Worth, TX 76115

817-924-8105
Fax: 817-921-3963 800-757-1912
sales@san-aire.com www.san-aire.com
Manufacturer and exporter of commercial dish,
trayware, pot and pan dryers
President: Hatcher James
hjames@sanaire.com
VP Sales/Marketing: Bruce Barker

Estimated Sales: $1-2.5 Million
Number Employees: 1-4
Brands:
　Powerdry

28784 San Diego Health & Nutrition
PO Box 1318
Bonita, CA 91908-1318
　　　　　　　　　619-470-3345
　Fax: 619-470-3822 www.sdhnsclasses.com
Consultant providing food safety and sanitation
training
Partner: Jack Ezroj
Estimated Sales: $100,000
Number Employees: 1-4

28785 San Diego Paper Box Company
PO Box 1219
Spring Valley, CA 91979-1219
　　　　　　　　　619-660-9566
　Fax: 619-660-9570 www.sdpbc.com
Folding cartons
President: Sidney B Chapman
CFO: Richard Chapman
R&D: Richard Chapman
Vice President of Sales and Marketing: Jeff
Shipman
jeff.shipman@sdpbc.com
Production Manager: Gilbert Bernal
Estimated Sales: $20-50 Million
Number Employees: 50-99

28786 San Fab Conveyor
2000 Superior St
Sandusky, OH 44870-1824
　　　　　　　　　419-626-4465
　　　　　　　　Fax: 419-626-6376
Manufacturer, importer and exporter of package and
bulk conveying components and systems including
stainless, pallet handling and table top conveyors,
carton sealers and stainless case tapers
Owner: Timothy Shenigo
Manager (Packaging Equipment): Don Williams
Engineering Manager: Charles Wheeler
Estimated Sales: $5-10 Million
Number Employees: 10-19
Square Footage: 320000
Brands:
　San Fab

28787 San Jamar
555 Koopman Ln
Elkhorn, WI 53121-2012
　　　　　　　　　262-723-6133
　Fax: 262-723-4204 800-248-9826
　info@sanjamar.com www.sanjamar.com
Manufacturer and exporter of built-in dispensing
units for condiments and disposable paper products
including cups, towels and napkins; also, bar sup-
plies and check management systems
President: Charles Colman
CFO: Andy Skerkowitz
Marketing Manager: Topper Woelfer
Senior Sales Coordinator: Michael Johnson
Estimated Sales: $10-20 Million
Number Employees: 100-249
Number of Brands: 3
Number of Products: 600
Type of Packaging: Consumer, Food Service
Brands:
　Classic
　Gourmet

28788 San Joaquin Pool Svc & Supply
8576 Live Oak Rd
Stockton, CA 95212-9305
　　　　　　　　　209-952-0680
　　　　　　　　Fax: 209-466-1080
Soaps, disinfectants and sterilizers
VP: Mick Albright
Regional Sales Manager: Mike Valasquez
Estimated Sales: Less Than $500,000
Number Employees: 1-4

28789 San Jose Awnings
755 Chestnut St
San Jose, CA 95110-1832
　　　　　　　　　408-350-7000
　Fax: 408-350-7001 800-872-9646
　　　　　sales@sanjoseawning.com
　　　　　www.sanjoseawning.com
Commercial awnings
President: Michael Yaholkovsky
sales@sanjoseawning.com

Estimated Sales: $1-2.5 Million
Number Employees: 10-19

28790 San Juan Signs Inc
736 E Main St
Farmington, NM 87401-2716
　　　　　　　　　505-326-5511
　Fax: 505-326-5513 linda@sanjuansigns.com
　　　　　　　　www.sanjuansigns.com
Advertising displays and signs
President: Clint L Roper
clint@sanjuansigns.com
VP: Teri Roper
Office Manager: Phyllis Davis
Estimated Sales: $1-2.5 Million
Number Employees: 20-49
Square Footage: 11200

28791 San Marco Coffee, Inc.
3120 Latrobe Dr
Suite 280
Charlotte, NC 28211-2186
　　　　　　　　　704-366-0533
　Fax: 704-366-0534 800-715-9298
　　　　　www.sanmarcocoffee.com
American coffee, espresso, cappuccino
Chief Executive Officer: Marc Decaria
marc@sanmarcocoffee.com
Number Employees: 5-9
Type of Packaging: Consumer, Food Service, Pri-
vate Label
Brands:
　San Giorgio

28792 San Miguel Label Manufacturing
PO Box 1401
Ciales, PR 00638-1401
　　　　　　　　　787-871-3120
　　　　　　　　Fax: 787-871-0443
Labels and plastic bags
Estimated Sales: $1-5 Million
Number Employees: 20-50
Square Footage: 40000

28793 San-Rec-Pak
9995 SW Avery St
PO Box 3210
Tualatin, OR 97062-3210
　　　　　　　　　503-692-5552
　　　　　　　　Fax: 503-692-4477
Manufacturer and exporter of maltsters' machinery
Manager: Karla Mc Combs
Estimated Sales: $3-5 Million
Number Employees: 10-19
Parent Co: Kloster Corporation

28794 SanSai North America
Franchising, LLC
1365 E. Gladstone Street
Suite 300
Glendale, CA 91203-2678
　　　　　　　　　909-599-9456
　Fax: 818-244-2470 800-368-5594
　　　　　　　　www.sansaiusa.com
Ingredients for chocolate making
Owner: Peter Han
Estimated Sales: $1-5 Million
Number Employees: 10-19
Parent Co: Nestle USA

28795 Sanchelima International
1783 NW 93rd Ave
Miami, FL 33172
　　　　　　　　　305-591-4343
　Fax: 305-591-3203 sales@sanchelimaint.com
　　　　　　　　www.sanchelimaint.com
Manufacturer and exporter of dairy and cheese mak-
ing equipment, fillers and sealers, homogenizers,
molds, centrifugal separators, bottle unscramblers,
pasteurizers, tanks and valves; processor and
exporter of cultures
President: Juan A Sanchelima
Technical Director: Jesus Gonzalez
CFO: Maximo Questa
Estimated Sales: $5-10 Million
Number Employees: 10-19

28796 Sanco Products Co Inc
330 Harrison Ave
Greenville, OH 45331-1566
　　　　　　　　　937-548-2225
　　　　　　　　Fax: 937-548-0132
Disinfectants, insecticides, etc

President: John Saylor
sanco@embarqmail.com
Quality Control: John Saylor
Estimated Sales: Below $5 Million
Number Employees: 5-9

28797 Sancoa International
92 Ark Rd
Lumberton, NJ 08048
　　　　　　　　　609-953-5050
　　　　　　　　Fax: 856-273-2710
Manufacturer, exporter and importer of pressure sen-
sitive labels and shrink sleeves
President: Joseph Sanski
Controller: Roger Spreen
CFO: Kevin Austin
Quality Assurance Manager: Bob Zimmerman
Contact: Mark Brennan
mbrennan@sancoa.com
Estimated Sales: $20-50 Million
Number Employees: 250-499

28798 Sanden Vendo America Inc
10710 Sanden Dr
Dallas, TX 75238
　　　　　　　　　214-765-9066
　Fax: 800-541-5684 800-344-7216
　　　　　　　　www.vendoco.com
Automatic and manual vending machines for bottles
and cans
President: Bernt Voelkel
CEO: Frank Kabei
Contact: Bryce Batchelor
bbatchelor@vendoco.com
Number Employees: 500-999
Parent Co: Sanden Corporation

28799 Sanders Manufacturing Co
1422 Lebanon Pike
Nashville, TN 37210-3159
　　　　　　　　　615-254-6611
　Fax: 615-242-3732 866-254-6611
Advertising specialties
President: Julie Sanders
jsanders@samcoline.com
Manager: Paul Cowan
Mngr.: Paul Cowan
Estimated Sales: $10-20 Million
Number Employees: 50-99
Square Footage: 92000
Brands:
　Samco

28800 Sanderson Computers
450 W Wilson Bridge Road
Worthington, OH 43085-2237
　　　　　　　　　614-781-2525
　　　　　　　　Fax: 614-781-2755
Software for the process, food and formulations in-
dustries
Owner: Gary Sanderson
Marketing (US): David Lee
President US Operations: Carl Parker
Parent Co: Sanderson Group PLC
Brands:
　Formul8

28801 Sandler Seating
1175 Peachtree Street NE
Suite 1850
Atlanta, GA 30361
　　　　　　　　　404-982-9000
　Fax: 404-321-7882 www.sandlerseating.com
Manufacturer and exporter/importer of tables and
chairs for hotels, restaurants, and food courts
U.S. Director of Sales: Rusty Wolf
Chief Executive Officer: Roy Sandler
Sales Manager: Anita Haslett
Estimated Sales: $5-10 Million
Number Employees: 5-9
Brands:
　Sandler Seating

28802 Sandusky Plastics
400 Broadway Street
Sandusky, OH 44870-2006
　　　　　　　　　419-626-8980
　Fax: 419-616-1803 800-234-7587
　　　　　　　　www.whirley.com
Thermoformed plastic containers
President: Lincoln Sokolski
Administrator: Holly Colvin
Human Resources: DiAnn Savko

Estimated Sales: $50-100 Million
Number Employees: 250-499

28803 Sandvik Process SystemsInc

21 Campus Rd
Totowa, NJ 07512-1211

973-790-1600
Fax: 973-790-9247

Process equipment for drying vegetables, fruits, and rice, roasters for nuts and beans, freezers for seafood and slurries for freeze drying, melt solidification systems, cooling tunnels and dropformers for chocolate and steam cookingtunnels for meat
Marketing Director: Craig Batsbh
Manager: Paula Benish
paula.benish@sandvik.com
Manager: Craig Bartsch
Estimated Sales: $1-5 Million
Number Employees: 50-99

28804 Sandvik Process Systems

30 Stockholm
Box 510, SE-101
Sweden, NJ 7512

973-790-1600
Fax: 973-790-9247 www.sandvik.com

Manufacturer and exporter of food processing equipment including dryers, coolers, freezers, drop-formers and steam cookers
President: Olof Faxander
Chairman: Anders Nyr,n
Marketing Manager: Craig Bartsch
Estimated Sales: $1-5 Million
Number Employees: 55
Parent Co: Sandvik
Brands:
  Roto-Former

28805 Sandy Butler Group

1375 Jackson St
Suite 401
Ft Myers, FL 33901

239-357-6162
Fax: 239-333-0481 jerome@sandybutlergroup.com
www.sandybutlergroup.com

Balsamic, oilve oil, flavored olive oil, pasta, vegetables, wine vinegar and salts

28806 Sanford Redmond

780 E 134th St
Bronx, NY 10454-3527

718-792-7000
Fax: 718-292-0010

Small disposable containers for cream, jams, ect
Estimated Sales: $1-2.5 Million
Number Employees: 10-19

28807 Sanford Redmond Company

65 Harvard Ave
Stamford, CT 06902

203-351-9800
Fax: 718-292-0010

Manufacturer and exporter of wrapping, food processing and packaging machinery
President: S Redmond
Contact: Sanford Redmond
ezpaks@sanred.com
Estimated Sales: $1-2,500,000
Number Employees: 5-9

28808 Sangamon Mills

PO Box 467
Cohoes, NY 12047

518-237-5321
Fax: 518-237-6282

Knit wash and dish cloths
President: Ella Fisher
Estimated Sales: Below $5 Million
Number Employees: 10-19
Brands:
  Sunflower
  White Swan

28809 Sani-Fit

620 S Raymond Avenue
Suite 9
Pasadena, CA 91105-3261

626-395-7895
Fax: 626-395-7899

Manufacturer, importer and exporter of stainless steel sanitary fittings, diaphragm valves and food processing fitting components
Estimated Sales: $1-5,000,000

Brands:
  Bradford Cast Metals
  Garitech
  Sanifit
  Topline

28810 Sani-Matic

P.O.Box 8662
Madison, WI 53708-8662

608-222-1935
Fax: 608-222-5348 800-356-3300
info@sanimatic.com www.sanimatic.com

Cleaning systems for the food and pharmaceutical industries. Product lines include clean-out-of-place parts washers, clean-in-place systems, rinse/foam/sanitize pressure systems, conveyorized wash tunnels, and a variety of cabinetwashers to clean vats, racks, pallets, ibc, bin, totes and other product handling items.
President: Ted Lingard
Marketing: Kelsy Boyd
Sales: Chad Dykstra
Contact: John Leach
johnl@sanimatic.com
Plant Manager: Wayne Huebner
Estimated Sales: $20 Million
Number Employees: 100-249
Number of Products: 10
Square Footage: 40000
Brands:
  Sani-Matic
  Ultra Flow

28811 Sani-Pure Food Laboratories

178-182 Saddle River Road
Saddle Brook, NJ 07663-4619

201-843-2525
Fax: 201-843-4934 sanipure.labs@verizon.net
www.sanipure.com

Quality control lab testing facility specializing in microbiological, extraneous matter, packaging materials, pesticide residue, pharmalogical, water and effluent testing services
Owner: Ronald Snitcher
Estimated Sales: $1-2.5 Million
Number Employees: 10-19
Square Footage: 15000

28812 Sani-Tech Group

PO Box 1010
Andover, NJ 07821-1010

973-579-1313
Fax: 973-579-3908

28813 Sani-Top Products

PO Box 117
De Leon Springs, FL 32130-0117

386-985-4667
Fax: 386-985-6094

Manufacturer and exporter of plastic trays, bowls, servers and food covers; also, acrylic specialty display cases
President: A David Logan
CEO: Joyce Monaco
Purchasing Manager: Walt Houdeshell
Estimated Sales: $1-3 Million
Number Employees: 10-19
Parent Co: Mastercraft Products Corporation

28814 SaniServ

451 E County Line Rd
Mooresville, IN 46158

317-831-7030
Fax: 317-831-7036 800-733-8073
sdowling@saniserv.com www.saniserv.com

Manufacturer and exporter of batch machines, freezers and dispensers for ice cream, shakes, frozen beverages/cocktails, yogurt and custard; processor of cappuccino; importer of visual slush machines
President: Robert Mc Afee
CFO: Allen McCormick
Contact: Robert Mcafee
rmcafee@saniserv.com
Number Employees: 50-99
Square Footage: 300000
Parent Co: MD Holdings
Type of Packaging: Consumer, Food Service, Private Label
Brands:
  Saniserv

28815 Sanicrete

24535 Hallwood Ct
Farmington Hills, MI 48335-1667

248-893-1000
Fax: 248-893-1000

Designer of sanitary floor and lining systems for the food and beverage industries.
Contact: Mike Fortman
mikef@sanicrete.com
Number Employees: 10-19

28816 Sanitary Couplers

275 S Pioneer Boulevard
Springboro, OH 45066-1180

513-743-0144
Fax: 513-743-0146 reseal@compuserve.com

Manufacturer and exporter of high purity sanitary hoses, fittings and hose assemblies
General Manager: Jeffrey Zornow
Manager: Mark Hess
Sales Manager (Western Region): Jason Parks
Customer Service: Tracy Brandenburg
Estimated Sales: $2.5-5 Million
Number Employees: 9
Square Footage: 80000
Parent Co: Norton Performance Plastics
Brands:
  Challenger
  Cleargard
  Gladiator
  Permaseal
  Protector
  Reseal
  Sanigard
  Sentry

28817 (HQ)Sanitech Inc

7207 Lockport Pl # H
Lorton, VA 22079-1534

703-339-7001
Fax: 703-339-6848 800-486-4321
www.sanitechcorp.com

Manufacturing sanitation systems for food processing and food service operations
President/CEO: alan weinstein
sumeersharma@sanitech.com
CFO: Pash Bhalla
VP: Bill Hannigan
Director Marketing: Sumeer Sharma
Sales Exec: Sumeer Sharma
Production: Tom Wines
Plant Manager: J R Bhalla
Purchasing Manager: Mike Sherman
Estimated Sales: $5 Million
Number Employees: 5-9
Square Footage: 20000
Brands:
  Sanitech Mark Series Systems

28818 (HQ)Sanitek Products Inc

3959 Goodwin Ave
Los Angeles, CA 90039-1187

818-242-1071
Fax: 818-242-1071 818-242-1071
info@sanitek.com www.sanitek.com

Manufacturer and exporter of floor finishes, hand cleaners and industrial chemicals; also, liquid soap and specialty chemicals available
President: Robert L Moseley
info@sanitek.com
VP: David Moseley
R&D and QC: Ronald Ostroff
Estimated Sales: $5-10 Million
Number Employees: 10-19
Square Footage: 160000
Type of Packaging: Consumer, Private Label

28819 Sanitor Manufacturing Co

1221 W Centre Ave
Portage, MI 49024-5384

269-327-3001
Fax: 269-327-4562 800-379-5314
customerservice@sanitorusa.com
www.sanitorusa.com

Paper toilet seat covers and dispensers
President: David J Dietrich
dave@sanitorusa.com
Director Sales/Marketing: Mike Fawley
Estimated Sales: $5-10 Million
Number Employees: 10-19
Square Footage: 50000
Brands:
  Neat Seat

28820 Santa Fe Bag Company
4950 E 49th Street
Vernon, CA 90058-2736

323-585-7225
Fax: 323-585-0313
Multi-wall and paper bags
President: David Sugarman
Estimated Sales: $10-20 Million
Number Employees: 20-49

28821 Santa Ynex Trading Company
500 N 8th Street
Suite B
Lompoc, CA 93436-4946

805-737-7967
Fax: 805-737-1844
Wine industry corks and capsules

28822 Santana Products
801 E Corey St
Scranton, PA 18505-3523

570-343-7921
Fax: 570-348-2959 800-368-5002
Storage systems
Contact: Glenn Fischer
glenn.fischer@wachovia.com
Estimated Sales: $20-50 Million
Number Employees: 100

28823 Sapac International
PO Box 2035
Fond Du Lac, WI 54936-2035

920-921-5060
Fax: 920-921-0822 800-257-2722
Palletizers; importer of bag filling and sealing equipment
Project Manager: Henry Brown
President/National Sales Manager: Bruce McMurry
Controls Manager: Jerome Haser
Number Employees: 1-4
Parent Co: Sapac

28824 Sapat Packaging Industry
PO Box 65723
Albuquerque, NM 87193-5723

505-275-9251
Fax: 505-271-8830
Estimated Sales: $.5-1 million
Number Employees: 1-4

28825 Sarasota Restaurant Equipment
2651 Whitfield Ave Ste 101
Sarasota, FL 34243

941-924-1410
Fax: 941-923-1510 800-434-1410
Manufacturer and wholesaler/distributor of restaurant and kitchen equipment
Owner: Marylin Snodell
Project Manager: Thomas Moon
Sales Manager: Joe Todd
Estimated Sales: $2.5-5 Million
Number Employees: 10-19
Square Footage: 20000

28826 Sardee Industries Inc
2211 W Washington St
Orlando, FL 32805-1254

407-297-6362
Fax: 407-297-6362 www.sardee.com
Container and lid conveyor handling systems including air, vacuum, magnetic and mechanical; also, PET bottle palletizers/depalletizers
Manager: Mike Schreiber
mschreiber@sardee.com
Manager: Bill Bryer
Estimated Sales: $1-2.5 Million
Number Employees: 20-49
Square Footage: 200000

28827 Sardee Industries Inc
5100 Academy Dr # 400
Suite 400
Lisle, IL 60532-4208

630-824-4200
Fax: 630-824-4225 sales@sardee.com
www.sardee.com
Manufacturer and exporter of palletizers, depalletizers and pallet, container and end handling equipment
President: Steve Sarovich
ssarovich@sardee.com
Sales Director: Gary Bishop
Estimated Sales: $5-10 Million
Number Employees: 10-19

Square Footage: 100000
Parent Co: Sardee Industries

28828 Sargent & Greenleaf
P.O.Box 930
Nicholasville, KY 40340-0930

859-885-9411
Fax: 859-885-3063 800-826-7652
www.sglocks.com
Security products including money safe locks and exit devices with alarms
President: Bill Demtsey
R&D: Mike Clarke
CEO: Jerry A Morgan
Quality Control: Wayne Landa
Director Marketing: Gary Kepler
Customer Services Manager: Brian Costley
Estimated Sales: $20-50 Million
Number Employees: 100-249
Brands:
  Arm-A-Dor
  Secure Panic Hardware

28829 (HQ)Sargento Foods Inc
1 Persnickety Pl
Plymouth, WI 53073-3544

920-893-8484
Fax: 920-893-8399 800-243-3737
www.sargento.com
Natural and processed cheese manufacturer.
CEO: Louis Gentine
Executive VP: Karri Neils
karri.neils@sargentocheese.com
Estimated Sales: Over $1 Billion
Number Employees: 1000-4999
Type of Packaging: Consumer, Food Service, Private Label, Bulk
Brands:
  Sargento
  Snack Bites™
  Chef Blends®
  Artisan Blends®
  Natural Blends®
  Ultra Thin®
  Balanced Breaks®

28830 Sartorius Corp
131 Heartland Blvd
Edgewood, NY 11717-8315

631-254-4249
Fax: 631-254-4253 800-635-2906
info.investor@sartorius.com
www.sartorius-omnimark.com
Filtration and weighing products including lab and moisture determination balances and industrial scales
President: Silvano Ghirardi
VP: Maurice Knapp
Director Marketing Communications: Arnold Breisblatt
Estimated Sales: $50-100 Million
Number Employees: 100-249
Square Footage: 35000
Parent Co: Sartorius AG
Other Locations:
  Sartorius Corp.
  Mississauga ON

28831 Sartorius Corp
131 Heartland Blvd
Edgewood, NY 11717-8315

631-254-4249
Fax: 631-254-4253 800-635-2906
www.sartorius-omnimark.com
Wine industry filtration and weighing equipment
President: Silvano Ghirardi
VP: Maurice Knapp
Estimated Sales: $50-100 Million
Number Employees: 100-249

28832 Sasib Beverage & Food North America
808 Stewart Drive
Plano, TX 75074-8101

800-558-3814
Manufacturer and exporter of high speed beverage fillers and processing systems, labelers, bottle washers, rinsers, casers, palletizers and turnkey beverage production facilities
President: Claudia Salvi
VP Manufacturing: Robert Prescott
Estimated Sales: $20-50 Million
Number Employees: 186

Square Footage: 300000
Parent Co: Sasib Beverage
Brands:
  Alfa
  Meyer
  Mojonnier
  Pama
  Sarcmi
  Simonazzi

28833 Sasser Signs
750 Craghead St
Danville, VA 24541

434-792-2696
Fax: 434-793-8964 800-752-6091
Electric signs and billboards including neon
Owner: Cindy Sasser-Hill
VP: Diane Sasser
Estimated Sales: $1-2.5 Million
Number Employees: 10-19
Square Footage: 30000

28834 Satake USA
10905 Cash Rd
Stafford, TX 77477

281-276-3600
Fax: 281-494-1427 cvincent@satake-usa.com
www.satake-usa.com
Manufacturer and exporter of sorters including color, nut meat and tomato; also, rice processing and cereal milling equipment available
President: J J Naoki
VP Marketing: Peter Cawthorne
Marketing Specialist: Sandra Langlois
Contact: Mathew Abraham
mabraham@satake-usa.com
Estimated Sales: $20-50 Million
Number Employees: 100-249
Parent Co: Satake Corporation
Other Locations:
  Satake (USA)
  Cheshire, UK
Brands:
  3vision
  Colorwatch
  Scanmaster
  Shell-Ex
  Summa-6

28835 Saticoy Lemon Association
600 E Third Street
Oxnard, CA 93030

805-654-6543
Fax: 805-654-6510 webmaster@saticoylemon.com
www.saticoylemon.com
Agricultural Cooperative that is owned by the lemon grower members of which the marketing of the fruit is handled through their affiliation with Sunkist Growers, Inc.
President: Glenn Miller
Chief Financial Officer: Mike Dillard
Exchange/Business Development Manager: John Eliot
Field Manager: David Coert
Sales Coordinator: Jose Mendez
MIS Director: Lee Raymond
Personnel Director: Michael Dennington
Production Manager: Ron Davis
Plant Superintendent: Albert Rivera
Shipping Supervisor: Albert Palacio
Type of Packaging: Food Service

28836 Sato America
10350 Nations Ford Rd # A
Charlotte, NC 28273-5824

704-644-1662
Fax: 704-644-1662 888-871-8741
www.satoamerica.com
Manufacturer and exporter of bar code printers
President: Robert Linse
robertlinse@satoamerica.com
Marketing Manager: Nikki Aunn
Number Employees: 50-99
Type of Packaging: Consumer, Food Service, Private Label, Bulk
Brands:
  Sato

28837 Satoris America
1403 Heritage Drive
Suite B
Northfield, MN 55057

507-663-6100
Fax: 507-663-6123 877-603-6100

Company's products and services includes auto-claves and retorts, customer service, sales and replacement parts for German technology food safety systems. sales of new retorts, as well as replacement parts for stock retorts used insterilization of commercial food products. Official supplier of OEM parts for retort brnads stock, satori stocktec, satoris.
CEO: Oliver Barth
Sales: Pam Tidona
Estimated Sales: $4,000,000
Brands:
Satori Stocktec
Satoris
Stock

28838 Saturn Overhead Equipment
100 Apgar Dr
Somerset, NJ 08873-1146
732-560-7210
Fax: 973-465-4219 800-631-4473
sgordon@saturnoe.com www.saturnoe.com
Hoists including overhead electric wire and rope
President: Stephen Gordon
CFO: Debbie Swerdlow
VP: Eugenio Moutela
Quality Control: Gert Martens
Estimated Sales: Below $5 Million
Number Employees: 5-9

28839 Sauereisen
160 Gamma Dr
Pittsburgh, PA 15238
412-963-0303
Fax: 412-963-7620 questions@sauereisen.com
www.sauereisen.com
Corrosion-resistant material of construction, corrosion and skid-resistant flooring
CEO: Eric Sauereisen
Quality Control: Craig Maloney
Number Employees: 40

28840 Saunder Brothers
Bacon Street
Bridgton, ME 4009
207-647-3331
Fax: 207-647-2064
Manufacturer and exporter of wooden candy sticks, skewers and plain dowels
Co-Owner/President/General Manag: Read Grover
Co-Owner/VP: Robert Berry
Sales Manager/Treasurer: Terri Grover
Number Employees: 24

28841 Saunders Manufacturing Co.
PO Box 12539
N Kansas City, MO 64116-0539
816-842-0233
Fax: 816-842-1129 800-821-2792
goldenstar@goldenstar.com www.goldenstar.com
Manufacturer and exporter of regular and dust mops including antimicrobial, cotton wet, disposable and rayon; also, mop handles and frames and carpet mats and mattings
President: Gary Gradinger
National Sales Manager: Ssteve Lewis
VP Manufacturing: Mike Julo
Estimated Sales: $20-50 Million
Number Employees: 20-49
Square Footage: 100000
Parent Co: Golden Star
Type of Packaging: Consumer, Food Service, Private Label, Bulk

28842 Saunders West
975 N Todd Ave
Azusa, CA 91702-2226
626-691-1111
Fax: 626-691-0116 888-932-8836
west@saunderscorp.com www.saunderscorp.com
Pressure sensitive and adhesive tapes; also, die cutting of roll stock available
CEO: Robert McCollum
Sales Manager: Mike Hibbard
Contact: Jeff Oyster
joyster@saunderscorp.com
Manager: John Sciacca
Manager: Jon Tarian
General Manager: Wilson Wong
Estimated Sales: $10-20 Million
Number Employees: 1-4
Square Footage: 42000
Parent Co: R.S. Hughes Company

28843 Sauvagnat Inc
12200 Herbert Wayne Court
Suite 180
Huntersville, NC 28078-6396
704-948-0440
Fax: 704-948-0190 800-258-5619
Outdoor furniture including chairs, tables and lounges
President: Bradford Elliot
CEO: John Menas
Marketing Director: Shannon Lowe
Number Employees: 15
Parent Co: Groupe Sauvagnat
Brands:
Allibert
Triconfort

28844 Sauve Company Limited
151 Mill St
Amherst, WI 54406
715-824-2502
Fax: 715-824-2192
Executive recruiters for the food and dairy industry
President: Gordon Sauve
Vice President: Diane Sauve
Estimated Sales: Less than $500,000
Number Employees: 10

28845 Savage Brothers Company
1125 Lunt Ave
Elk Grove Vlg, IL 60007
847-981-3000
Fax: 847-981-3010 800-342-0973
info@savagebros.com www.savagebrothers.com
Supplier of cookers, mixers, stoves, chocolate melting and processing tanks, kettles, mixing bowls and pumps for food depositing, transferring and metering
President: David Floreani
Marketing Manager: Robert Parmley
Contact: John Weeks
john@savagebros.com
Estimated Sales: $2.5-5,000,000
Number Employees: 20-49
Square Footage: 20000
Type of Packaging: Food Service
Brands:
Firemixer
Hi-Speed Cooker
Liftiltruk

28846 Savanna Pallets
805 Tall Pine Ln
Cloquet, MN 55720-3164
218-879-8553
Fax: 218-879-8560 pallets@frontiernet.net
www.savannapallets.com
Pallets
Owner: Al Raushel
chadraushel@savannapallets.com
Manager: Al Raushel
Estimated Sales: $1-2.5 Million
Number Employees: 20-49

28847 Savanna Pallets
106 E 1st Ave
PO Box 308
McGregor, MN 55760
218-768-2077
Fax: 218-768-3112 pallets@frontiernet.net
www.savannapallets.com
Skids and pallets
President: Allen Raushel
VP: Al Raushel
Contact: Craig Joriman
craigjoriman@savannapallets.com
Estimated Sales: $1-5 Million
Number Employees: 50-99
Square Footage: 20000

28848 Savasort Inc
6811 Garden Rd
Riviera Beach, FL 33404-5997
561-848-8744
Fax: 561-840-8515 800-255-8744
info@savasort.com www.agilitymats.com
Document sorting equipment
President: Phillip Elmore
savasort@aol.com
Estimated Sales: Less Than $500,000
Number Employees: 1-4
Square Footage: 36000

28849 Save-A-Tree
1338 Berkeley Way
P.O.Box 862
Berkeley, CA 94701
510-843-5233
Fax: 510-843-4906 lolalone@yahoo.com
Organic cotton bags
Proprietor: Penny Marienthal
Contact: Chris Hawkins
chawkins@saveatreeprinting.com
Estimated Sales: Below $5,000,000
Number Employees: 1

28850 Save-O-Seal Corporation
PO Box 553
Elmsford, NY 10523-0553
914-592-3031
Fax: 914-592-4511 800-831-9720
Manufacturer and exporter of bagging machines and heat sealing equipment; also, coated slitting blades
President: Tullio Muscariello
Sales: Anna DeLuca
Estimated Sales: $2.5-5 Million
Number Employees: 5-9

28851 Saver Glass Inc
841 Latour Ct # B
Suite B
Napa, CA 94558-7546
707-259-2930
Fax: 707-259-2933 www.saverglass.com
Wine and spirits bottles
CEO: Sally Arnold
sjt@saverglass.com
VP Fainance: Michael Graham
Manager: Mike Graham
Estimated Sales: $500,000-$1 Million
Number Employees: 10-19
Parent Co: Saverglass group

28852 Savogran Co
259 Lenox St
Norwood, MA 02062-3463
781-762-2371
Fax: 781-762-1095 800-225-9872
www.savogran.com
Paint remover and cleaning powder
Contact: Mark Conti
mconti@savogran.com
Estimated Sales: $20-50 Million
Number Employees: 20-49
Brands:
Dirtex

28853 Savoye Packaging
645 Edison Way
Reno, NV 89502-4136
775-351-0501
Fax: 775-857-3601
Wine industry polyaluminum capsules
Owner: Hanna Lasilla
Estimated Sales: $10-20 Million
Number Employees: 5-9

28854 Saxco International LLC
200 Gibraltar Rd # 101
Horsham, PA 19044-2385
215-443-8100
Fax: 215-443-8370 800-245-1016
info@saxcointl.com www.saxco.com
Wine industry packaging materials
President: Herb Sachs
CEO: Matthew Malenfant
matthew@saxcointl.com
Estimated Sales: $5-10 Million
Number Employees: 10-19

28855 Saxco International LLC
200 Gibraltar Rd # 101
Horsham, PA 19044-2385
215-443-8100
Fax: 215-443-8370 info@saxcointl.com
www.saxco.com
Wine industry closures
President: Herbert L Sachs
CEO: Matthew Malenfant
matthew@saxcointl.com
Estimated Sales: $5-10 Million
Number Employees: 10-19

28856 Sayco Yo-Yo Molding Company
2 Sunset Ave
Cumberland, RI 2864
401-724-5296

Manufacturer and exporter of advertising promotions and novelties including yo-yos, yo-yo promotions
President: Lawrence Sayegh
Plant Manager: Leroy Sayegh
Purchasing Manager: Larry Sayco
Estimated Sales: Under $300,000
Number Employees: 5
Square Footage: 3000
Parent Co: L.J. Sayegh & Company
Type of Packaging: Consumer, Private Label
Brands:
    Sayco
    Sayco Tournament

28857 Scaltrol Inc
460 Brogdon Rd # 500
P.O. Box 3288
Suwanee, GA 30024-2314
678-541-5138
Fax: 877-769-2751 800-868-0629
rzimmerman@scaltrolinc.com
www.scaltrolinc.com
Manufacturer and exporter of water treatment units for removal of scale and staining
Owner: Austin Hansen
Business Manager: Hilda Epsten
Manager: Rob Zimmerman
rzimmerman@scaltrolinc.com
Operations Manager: Sunday Christopher
Number Employees: 1-4
Square Footage: 10000
Brands:
    Scaltrol

28858 Scan Coin
20145 Ashbrook Pl # 110
Ashburn, VA 20147-3375
703-729-8600
Fax: 703-729-8606 800-336-3311
info@scancoin-usa.com www.scancoin-usa.com
Manufacturer and importer of coin and currency handling equipment including counting, sorting and packing
President/Chief Executive Officer: Per Lundin
Contact: Gaaron Gilham
gilham@scancoin-cds.com
Estimated Sales: Below $5 Million
Number Employees: 5-9
Parent Co: Scan Coin AB
Type of Packaging: Consumer

28859 Scan Corporation
110 Lithia Pinecrest Rd Ste G
Brandon, FL 33511
813-653-2877
Fax: 813-654-3949 800-881-7226
sales@scancorporation.com
www.scancorporation.com
Manufacturer and exporter of point of sale systems including touch screen p.c.'s and terminals, membrane keyboards and scanning equipment
President: Frank Harrison
Estimated Sales: $10-20 Million
Number Employees: 10-19

28860 Scan Group
1820 S Mohawk Dr
Appleton, WI 54914-4732
920-730-9150
Fax: 920-730-8991 www.scangroup.net
Paper tableware including plates, cups and napkins
Manager: Steve Mueller
Estimated Sales: $5-10 Million
Number Employees: 1-4

28861 ScanTech Sciences
4940 Peachtree Industrial Blvd.
Ste. 340
Norcross, GA 30071
470-359-3660
info@scantechsciences.com
www.scantechsciences.com
Designs and manufactures E-beam systems for food treatment. Offers services for growers, wholesalers, retailers, and food safety directors.
Co-Founder & Chairman: Dolan Falconer
CEO: Dwayne House
CFO: H. Martin Rice
Co-Founder & COO: Chip Starns
Year Founded: 2009
Number Employees: 35-50

28862 Scandia Packaging Machinery Co
15 Industrial Rd
Fairfield, NJ 07004-3017
973-473-6100
Fax: 973-473-7226 jbrown@scandiapack.com
www.scandiapack.com
Manufacturer and exporter of automatic packaging equipment for overwrapping, bundling, banding, multipacking, cartoning and collating
President: Bill Bronander
wbb@scandiapack.com
Finance: Cecelia G. Bronander
Engineering: Arthur Goldberg
Sales Representative: Carolyn Placentino
Customer Service: Maria Van Ness
Sales Manager: James J. Brown
Parts Department: Lewis D'Allegro
Estimated Sales: $10-20 Million
Number Employees: 20-49
Square Footage: 61200

28863 Scanning Devices Inc
31 Dunham Rd # 2
Unit 1
Billerica, MA 01821-5701
978-362-1123
Fax: 978-362-8693 mail@scanningdevices.com
www.scanningdevicesinc.com
Photoelectric control and optical activated counters, optical sensors and scanners Force Measurement instrumentation,Display devices
Contact: Dave Chanoux
dave.chanoux@scanningdevices.com
Estimated Sales: $2.5-5 Million
Number Employees: 1-4

28864 Scattaglia Farm LLC
10400 E Avenue U
Littlerock, CA 93543-3121
661-944-3880
Fax: 661-944-5790
President: Louis Scattaglia
louis.scattaglia@scattagliafarms.com
Estimated Sales: $50-100 Million
Number Employees: 50-99

28865 Schaefer Machine Co Inc
200 Commercial Dr
Deep River, CT 06417-1682
860-526-4000
Fax: 860-526-4654 800-243-5143
schaefer@schaeferco.com www.schaeferco.com
Manufacturer and exporter of label gluing and cementing machinery
Owner: Robert Gammons
schaefer01@snet.net
Estimated Sales: $1-3 Million
Number Employees: 5-9
Square Footage: 40000
Brands:
    Schaefer Ms Label

28866 Schaefer Technologies Inc
4901 W Raymond St
Indianapolis, IN 46241-4733
317-546-4081
Fax: 317-546-4095 800-435-7174
www.schaefer-technologies.net
Distributor of quality equipment specialized in the fit the needs of the pharmaceutical, health, food and cosmetic industries
President: Steven Schaefer
CEO: Christina Cadwallader
ccadwallader@schaefertech.us
Estimated Sales: $5-10 Million
Number Employees: 50-99
Number of Products: 19

28867 Schaeff
8657 S. Beloit Ave
Bridgeview, IL 60455
Fax: 708-598-1877 888-436-7867
www.schaafequipment.com
Fork lift trucks, tow tractors and electric rider material transport vehicles
Owner: Bill Schaaf
Sales Manager: Melanie Bohle
Estimated Sales: $10-20 Million
Number Employees: 5-9
Square Footage: 288000

28868 Schaeffler Group USA Inc
308 Springhill Farm Rd
Fort Mill, SC 29715-9784
803-548-8500
Fax: 803-548-8599 info.us@schaeffler.com
www.schaeffler.us
CEO: Bruce Warmbold
bruce@ina.com
Estimated Sales: $1-5 Million
Number Employees: 500-999

28869 Schaerer USA Corp
15501 Red Hill Ave
Suite 200
Tustin, CA 92780
562-989-3004
Fax: 562-989-3075 888-989-3004
info@schaererusa.com www.schaererusa.com
Supra-automatic espresso machines.
Director of Sales: Jim Crowley
jcrowley@schaererusa.com
Year Founded: 1993
Parent Co: M. Schaerer AG
Brands:
    Schaerer

28870 Schaffer Poidometer Company
5421 Claybourne Street
Pittsburgh, PA 15232-1623
412-281-9031
Fax: 412-281-1911
Poidometers for weighing and blending large quantities of raw ingredients
Owner: Joseph Pfenninger
Estimated Sales: Less than $500,000
Number Employees: 4
Square Footage: 20000

28871 Schanno Transportation
837 Apollo Rd
Eagan, MN 55121-2387
651-457-9700
Fax: 651-552-5835 800-544-6172
Estimated Sales: $1-5 Million
Number Employees: 100-249

28872 Scheb International
27 Clarington Way
North Barrington, IL 60010-6932
847-381-2573
Fax: 847-381-2573 schebltd@aol.com
www.schebltd.com
Manufacturer and exporter of tote, storage and material handling boxes; also, bulk carbon dioxide storage and delivery systems for beverage use; importer of carbon dioxide bulk delivery systems
Estimated Sales: $1-5 Million
Number Employees: 3
Parent Co: Carbo Carbonation Company
Type of Packaging: Food Service
Brands:
    Carbo Mizers
    Econ-O-Totes

28873 Schebler Co
5665 Fenno Rd
Bettendorf, IA 52722-5711
563-359-0110
Fax: 563-359-8430 www.schebler.com
Conveying and weighing equipment, vibratory feeders and food eqiupment
CEO: Gerald McClure
CFO: Jim Booe
Quality Control: Ron Wildermuth
Marketing Director: Don Gbeault
Sales Director: John Guinta
Production Manager: Larry Jones
Purchasing Manager: Barbara Welsch
Estimated Sales: $20-30 Million
Number Employees: 100-249
Square Footage: 190000

28874 Scheidegger
345 Kear St Ste 200
Yorktown Heights, NY 10598
914-245-7850
Fax: 914-243-0976
Manufacturer, importer and exporter of tamper evident sealing and full body sleeving machinery
VP Sales/Marketing: Dipak Modi
Number Employees: 2
Parent Co: Sch. S.A.

28875 Schenck Process
746 E Milwaukee St
Whitewater, WI 53190-2125

262-473-2441
Fax: 262-473-2489 888-742-1249
mktg@accuratefeeders.com
www.schenckaccurate.com
Manufacturing and supplying superior volumetric and gravimetric feeders, weighfeeders, solids flow meters, bulk bag discharging systems, and vibratory feeders to a wide variety of markets throughout the world.
President: Dirk Maroske
CEO: Dennis Hummel
d.hummel@schenckprocess.com
CFO: Neal Mueller
Number Employees: 100-249
Parent Co: Schenck AccuRate
Brands:
Mechatron Gravimetric Feeders
Mechatron Volumetric Feeders
Sac Master Bulk Bag Dischargers
Solid Flow Vibratory Feeders
Tuf-Flex Volumetric Series Feeders

28876 Schenck Process
746 E Milwaukee St
P.O.Box 208
Whitewater, WI 53190-2125

262-473-2441
Fax: 262-473-2489 888-742-1249
mktg@accuratefeeders.com
www.schenckaccurate.com
Vibratory feeders with loss-in-weight batch control systems and loss-in-weight continuous flow systems; also, portable universal bin and feeder combination, bulk bag discharger, box dumps, weightbelts, and screw feeders
President: Dirk Maroske
CEO: Jay Brown
Research & Development: Bob Stephenson
Marketing Director: Mike Koras
Sales Director: Chris Isom
Regional Sales Manager: Rick Pruden
Plant Manager: Bill Samborski
Purchasing Manager: Angie Adams
Estimated Sales: $3-4 Million
Number Employees: 100-249
Square Footage: 128000
Parent Co: Schenck Process
Brands:
Accuflow
Solidsflow

28877 Schenck Process
746 E Milwaukee St
Whitewater, WI 53190-2125

262-473-2441
Fax: 262-473-2489 800-558-0184
mktg@accuratefeeders.com
www.schenckaccurate.com
Dry material feeders
President: Dirk Maroske
CEO: Christoper Aberle
c.aberle@schenckprocess.com
Marketing Manager: Gary Kuehneman
Estimated Sales: $20-50 Million
Number Employees: 100-249

28878 Schermerhorn Inc
165 Front St # D12
Chicopee, MA 01013-1270

413-598-8348
Fax: 413-594-8439
Paper set-up boxes
President: Nicholas Dobrilla
nicholas@schermerhorn-realestate.com
Estimated Sales: $20-50 Million
Number Employees: 20-49
Square Footage: 37000

28879 Scherping Systems
PO Box 10
Winsted, MN 55395-0010

320-485-4401
Fax: 320-485-2666
Custom stainless steel tanks, cheese making machinery and clean-in-place systems; also, design installation and control services available

President: Tim High
CFO: Cindy Tellinghuisen
Sales Manager: George Schwinghammer
Contact: Ryan Anderson
ryan.anderson@tetrapak.com
Plant Manager: Harvey Dvorak
Number Employees: 100-249

28880 Schiefer Packaging Corporation
160 Beverly Rd
Syracuse, NY 13207-1302

315-422-0615
Fax: 315-478-4140

Boxes for food products
President: Charles Simek
Estimated Sales: $1-2.5 Million
Number Employees: 1-4

28881 Schiff & Co
1120 Bloomfield Ave # 103
Ste 103
West Caldwell, NJ 07006-7131

973-227-1830
Fax: 973-227-5330 RSchiff13@aol.com
www.schiffandcompany.com
Regulatory services for the food and cosmetic industry.
Owner: Robert Schiff
rschiff13@aol.com
VP: Jack Parker
Business Development: John Round
Estimated Sales: $2.5-5 Million
Number Employees: 1-4
Square Footage: 6000

28882 (HQ)Schiffenhaus Industries
2013 McCarter Hwy
Newark, NJ 07104

973-484-5000
Fax: 973-484-8628
Corrugated paper boxes and P.O.P. displays
President: J Anton Schiffenhaus
CEO: Steven Grossman
Estimated Sales: $28.7 Million
Number Employees: 100-249

28883 Schiffmayer Plastics Corp.
1201 Armstrong St
Algonquin, IL 60102

847-658-8140
Fax: 847-658-0863
Capping and closing supplies
President: Karl F Schiffmayer
Quality Control: Gary Hunt
Estimated Sales: $20-30 Million
Number Employees: 70

28884 Schlagel Inc
491 Emerson St N
Cambridge, MN 55008-1316

763-689-5991
Fax: 763-689-5310 800-328-8002
sales@schlagel.com www.schlagel.com
Manufacturer and exporter of feed and grain equipment
CEO: Chris Schlagel
chris@schlagel.com
Sales Manager: Jeff Schwab
Purchasing Manager: Drew Stoffell
Estimated Sales: $10-20 Million
Number Employees: 50-99

28885 Schleicher & Company ofAmerica
5715 Clyde Rhyne Drive
Sanford, NC 27330

919-775-7318
Fax: 919-774-8731 800-775-7570
soa@interpath.com
Distributor and supplier of compactors and balers, paper shredders
President: Jack Costelloe
VP: John Ulam
Marketing Manager: Libby Nelson
Estimated Sales: $10-20 Million
Number Employees: 20
Square Footage: 100000
Brands:
Intimus
Olympia
Schleicher

28886 Schleicher & Schuell MicroSience
800 Centennial Ave # 1
Piscataway, NJ 08854-3911

973-245-8300
Fax: 973-245-8301 800-645-2302
www.whatman.com
Microbiological media, membranes, monitors, HACCP kits, MI agar & broth, Coliform broth, Listeria swabs, E coli media, paper filtration, glass filtration, sample preparation filtration, ultra filtration for pharmaceutical research andproduction, cell counters
President: Keith Jaythaward
Quality Control: Berni Reedes
Senior VP: Richard Dool
VP Marketing: John Perini
VP Sales: Joseph Murdock
Operations Manager: Louis Gugliotta
Estimated Sales: $9-12 Million
Number Employees: 10-19
Parent Co: Schleicher & Schuell MicroScience, GmbH
Brands:
Biopath

28887 Schloss Engineered Equipment
10555 E Dartmouth Ave
Suite 230
Aurora, CO 80014

303-695-4500
Fax: 303-695-4507
Drum and bar screens, compactors, grit and sludge collectors, flocculators and conveyors
President: Kristy Schloss
Contact: Charles Snyder
charles.snyder@swe.org
Estimated Sales: $5-10 Million
Number Employees: 5-9

28888 (HQ)Schlueter Company
310 N. Main Street
Janesville, WI 53545

608-755-5444
Fax: 608-755-5440 800-359-1700
www.schlueterco.co
Manufacturer and exporter of dairy and food plant equipment including process tanks, conveyors, hoppers, sanitizing systems (CIP-COP-HY pressure-foam), liquid/solid separators, strainers, filters, rotary drums, etc.; also, carts andwork tables
President: Brad Losching
VP: H Losching
Marketing Manager: C Benskin
Estimated Sales: $10-20 Million
Number Employees: 50
Square Footage: 200000
Other Locations:
Schlueter Co.
Fresno CA
Brands:
Safgard

28889 Schlueter Company
310 N Main St
Janesville, WI 53545

608-755-5444
Fax: 608-755-5440 800-359-1700
schlueter@socket.net www.schlueterco.com
Custom plastic blow molding, recreational, medical, toys, industrial and others all under the category if custom moulding. also post moulding and resins under the category of plastic moulding
President: Bradley W Losching
Estimated Sales: $5-10 Million
Number Employees: 50-99

28890 Schlueter Company
310 N. Main Street
PO Box 548
Janesville, WI 53545

608-755-5444
Fax: 608-755-5440 800-359-1700
www.schlueterco.com
Clean rooms and equipment, custom fabrication, flow diversion stations
President: Brad Losching
Marketing: Charles Benskin
Plant Manager: Erik Eide
Estimated Sales: $10-20 Million
Number Employees: 35
Square Footage: 80000
Type of Packaging: Food Service

28891 Schmalz
5200 Atlantic Ave
Raleigh, NC 27616-1870
919-713-0880
Fax: 919-713-0883 schmalz@schmalz.us
www.schmalz.com
Supplier of; vacuum lifting equipment, vacuum
components & gripping systems
President: Volker Schmitz
volker.schmitz@schmalz.us
CFO: Kevin Saylor
Estimated Sales: $10 Million
Number Employees: 10-19
Parent Co: Schmalz

28892 Schmersal
660 White Plains Rd # 160
Suite 160
Tarrytown, NY 10591-5185
914-347-4775
Fax: 914-347-1567 888-496-5143
salesusa@schmersal.com www.schmersal.com
Man and machine safeguarding devices
President: Peter Engstrom
CFO: Mario Tucci
Manager: John Monahan
Estimated Sales: $3-5 Million
Number Employees: 20-49

28893 Schmidt Progressive
360 Harmon Ave
P.O. Box 380
Lebanon, OH 45036-8801
513-934-2600
Fax: 513-932-8768 800-272-3706
steve@schmidtprogressive.com
Design, engineering and manufacturing display fix-
tures for the supermarket, bakery, concession, food
service and floral industries.
Owner/CEO: Julia Rodenbeck
julia@schmidtprogressive.com
VP Sales/Marketing: Stephen Moore
VP Sales/Marketing: Stephen Moore
VP Administration: Joseph Perdy
VP Manufacturing: Don Blades
Plant Manager: Robert Newton
Purchasing Manager: Don Blades
Estimated Sales: $2-5 Million
Number Employees: 20-49
Square Footage: 240000
Brands:
Food Furniture
Schmidt

28894 Schneider Electric
70 Mechanic St
Foxboro, MA 02035
781-534-7535
www.schneider-electric.us
Manufacturer and exporter of programmable logic
controllers and software.
Chairman & CEO: Jean-Pascal Tricoire
Deputy CEO/Finance & Legal Affairs: Emmanuel
Babeau
CFO: Steven Laham
EVP, Supply Chain, North America: Annette
Clayton
Business Analyst: Aric Luck
Global Marketing: Chris Leong
EVP, International Operations: Luc R,mont
Year Founded: 1836
Estimated Sales: $100-500 Million
Number Employees: 500-999
Parent Co: Groupe Schneider
Brands:
Modicom
Square D
Telemechanique

28895 Schneider Packaging Eqpt Co
5370 Guy Young Rd
Brewerton, NY 13029-8706
315-676-3035
Fax: 315-676-2875 sales@schneiderequip.com
www.schneiderequipment.com
Manufacturers case packing and robotic palletizing
equipment and integrates conveyors, case eleva-
tors/lowerators, pallet dispensers, slip sheet dispensers and shuttle transfer cars for full unit loads.
CEO: Alex Naugle
alexnaugle@gmail.com
Estimated Sales: $500,000-$1 Million
Number Employees: 100-249
Square Footage: 400000

28896 Schnuck Markets, Inc.
11420 Lackland Rd.
PO Box 46928
St. Louis, MO 63146
314-994-9900
800-264-4400
nourish.schnucks.com
Grocery, bakery, deli, dairy, seafood, meat, frozen
foods, produce, floral, liquor, and more.
Chairman/CEO: Todd Schnuck
Year Founded: 1939
Estimated Sales: $3.1 Billion
Number Employees: 14,500
Brands:
Valutime
Schnucks
Full Circle
Top Care
Schnucks
Culinaria

28897 Schober USA Inc
4690 Industry Dr
Fairfield, OH 45014-1923
513-489-7393
Fax: 513-489-7485 800-344-8324
solutions@schoberusa.com www.schoberusa.com
Rotary die cutting equipment
President: Jill Sanner
jsanner@osu.edu
CFO: Marion Hixon
Manager: Marion Hixson
Estimated Sales: $1-2.5 Million
Number Employees: 5-9

28898 Schoeneck Containers Inc
2160 S 170th St
New Berlin, WI 53151-2287
262-786-9360
Fax: 262-786-0772 www.schoeneck.com
Plastic bottles
President: Scott Chambers
schambers@schoeneck.com
Chairman: Robert Schoeneck
CFO: Jim Anderson
Estimated Sales: Below $5 Million
Number Employees: 100-249
Square Footage: 240000

28899 Scholle IPN
2500 Cooper Ave
Merced, CA 95348
209-384-3100
Fax: 209-384-3166
NorthAmerica@scholleipn.com
www.scholleipn.com
Supplier of bag-in-box packaging, metallized plas-
tics and paper, flexible shipping containers, industry
leading bag-in-box tap and filling technology, ma-
rine salvage devices and battery electrolyte.
President & CEO: William Scholle
Global Program Director: Robert Kilmer
Year Founded: 1947
Estimated Sales: $227.30 Million
Number Employees: 1900
Square Footage: 35000
Brands:
Rhino

28900 Schoneman Inc
4540 Park Ave
Ashtabula, OH 44004-6967
440-998-2273
Fax: 440-998-2285 800-255-4439
steve@schoneman.com
Software for meat, poultry, seafood and produce
companies
President: Steve Schoneman
steve@schoneman.com
Number Employees: 5-9

28901 School Marketing Partners
32302 Camino Capistrano # 207
San Juan Cpstrno, CA 92675-4506
949-487-1515
Fax: 949-661-7778 800-565-7778
www.schoolmenu.com
Menus for school cafeterias
Manager: Lana Huie
Estimated Sales: Below $5 Million
Number Employees: 5-9
Brands:
B.J. Spot
Tooned-In Menus

28902 Schreck Software
1420 Interlachen Cir
Woodbury, MN 55125-8859
651-731-6822
Food costing, inventory and margin management
software

28903 Schreiber Foods Inc.
400 N. Washington St.
Green Bay, WI 54301
920-437-7601
Fax: 920-437-1617 contact@schreiberfoods.com
www.schreiberfoods.com
Dairy products such as cheese, yogurt, milk, milk
powders and more.
President/CEO: Ron Dunford
SVP/CFO: Matt Mueller
SVP, U.S. Operations: Tony Nowak
SVP, Information Services: Tom Andreoli
SVP, Quality & Innovation: Vinith Poduval
SVP & Chief Commercial Officer: Trevor Farrell
Year Founded: 1945
Estimated Sales: Over $1 Billion
Number Employees: 8,000
Type of Packaging: Consumer, Food Service, Pri-
vate Label, Bulk
Other Locations:
Tempe AZ
Gainesville GA
Carthage MO
Clinton MO
Monett MO
Mt Vernon MO
Ravenna NE
Shippensburg PA
Nashville TN
Stephenville TX
Logan UT
Smithfield UT
Wisconsin Rapids WI
Brands:
American Heritage
Clearfield
Cooper
Laferia
Lov-It
Menu
Raskas
Ready-Cut
School Chioce
Schreiber

28904 Schroeder Machine
165 Balboa St # C2
Ste C-2
San Marcos, CA 92069-1347
760-591-9733
Fax: 760-591-4019 sales@ssmci.com
www.schroedermachinetechnologies.com
Manufacturer and exporter of automatic case pack-
ing and erecting machines
Owner: John Schroeder
CFO: Richard Jones
Chief Mechanical Engineer: Patrick Burton
Marketing: Sandy Delepovitz
Sales Manager: Matt Brown
jschroeder@ssmci.com
Public Relations: Sandy Delepovit
Operations: David Barriello
Estimated Sales: $1 Million
Number Employees: 5-9
Square Footage: 160000
Type of Packaging: Private Label
Brands:
Formnumatic
Quadnumatic

28905 Schroter, USA
508 Clinton Street
Defiance, OH 43512-2635
419-782-2430
Fax: 419-784-9717
Air pollution control and environmental services,
drying rooms, ovens, smokehouses, refrigeration
systems, tempering systems and accessories

28906 Schubert Packaging Systems
4505 Excel Pkwy
Addison, TX 75001-5677
972-233-6665
Fax: 972-233-3422 sales@schubertpackaging.com
www.schubertpackaging.com
Casing equipment, packers

913

Manager: Doug Granowski
Head of Sales: Gerald Grad
Contact: Wolfgang Haas
whaas@schubertpackaging.com
Estimated Sales: $500,000-$1 Million
Number Employees: 10-19

28907 Schurman's Wisconsin Cheese Country

1401 Hwy 23 North
Dodgeville, WI 53533

608-935-5741
Fax: 608-794-2194
dodgeville@schurmanscheese.com
www.schurmanscheese.com
Broker of health foods, natural cheeses, packaging
and private label items
President: Lorraine Schurman
CEO: Jim Morgan
CFO: Jim Morgan
R&D: John Schurman
Quality Control: Jim Morgan
Estimated Sales: $10-20 Million
Number Employees: 20-49
Type of Packaging: Private Label

28908 Schutte Buffalo Hammermill

61 Depot St
Buffalo, NY 14206-2203

716-855-1555
Fax: 716-855-3417 800-447-4634
info@hammermills.com www.hammermills.com
Hammer mills including crushers, pulverizers, and
grinders .
Owner: Tom Warne
warne@hammermills.com
General Manager/Co-Owner: Jim Guarino
Estimated Sales: $5-10 Million
Number Employees: 20-49
Square Footage: 100000

28909 Schwaab, Inc

11415 W. Burleigh Street
Milwaukee, WI 53222
Fax: 800-935-9866 800-935-9877
schwaab@schwaab.com www.schwaab.com
Rubber and steel stamps, corporate and notary seals
and name plates
President, Chief Executive Officer: Doug Lane
Vice President and Controller: Bill Yentz
Vice President and Controller: Bill Yentz
VP Sales: Sara Wagner
Contact: Pamela Bielmeier
bielmeier@schwaab.com
Chief Operating Officer: Jeremiah McNeal
Estimated Sales: Below $5 Million
Number Employees: 100-249

28910 Schwab Paper Products Co

636 Schwab Cir
Romeoville, IL 60446-1144

815-372-2233
Fax: 815-372-1701 800-837-7225
info@schwabpaper.com www.schwabpaper.com
Manufacturer and exporter of layerboards, wax pa-
per and steak paper for bakery, confectionery, frozen
meat, seafood and poultry packaging
President: Kathy Schwab
CEO: Michael Schwab
mike@schwabpaper.com
Estimated Sales: Below $5 Million
Number Employees: 1-4
Square Footage: 120000
Brands:
  Econo-Board
  Frees-It
  Ovenable
  Quilon Bakeable Paper

28911 Schwartz Manufacturing Co

1000 School St
PO Box 328
Two Rivers, WI 54241-3533

920-793-1375
Fax: 920-793-2235 service@schwartzmfg.com
www.schwartzmfg.com
Filters and filter systems for the dairy, food, bever-
age and brewery industries.
Sales Exec: Alessandra Schwartz
Number Employees: 20-49

28912 Schwarz Supply Source

8338 Austin Ave
Morton Grove, IL 60053

800-323-4903
info@schwarz.com www.schwarz.com
Food service packaging including take-out and pizza
boxes.
President: Andy McKenna
Vice President: Kevin Pittner
Vice President, Sales: Dan Arkus
Year Founded: 1907
Estimated Sales: $100-500 Million
Number Employees: 250-499

28913 Schwerdtel Corporation

530 van Buren Street
Ridgewood, NJ 7450

201-485-8160
Fax: 201-485- 815 www.schwerdtel.de
Automatic filling machines for sealants and food
concentrates
President & CFO: Cay Werner
Senior Sales Manager: Florian Mendheim
Estimated Sales: $1-2.5 Million
Number Employees: 1-4

28914 Scienco Systems

3240 N Broadway
Saint Louis, MO 63147-3515

314-621-2536
Fax: 314-621-1952 www.sciencofast.com
Manufacturer and exporter of food and preservative
tablets, oil/water separators, grease traps and waste
water treatment equipment
General Manager: Jim Predeau
Sales Manager: Gary Wotli
Estimated Sales: $2.5-5 Million
Number Employees: 10-19
Parent Co: Smith Loveless

28915 Scientech, Inc

5649 Arapahoe Ave
Boulder, CO 80303-1399

303-444-1361
Fax: 303-444-9229 800-525-0522
inst@scientech-inc.com www.scientech-inc.com
Electronic balances and scales
President: Tom O'Rourke
VP/COO: Tom Campbell
Contact: Mike Brunner
mbrunner@scientech-inc.com
Estimated Sales: $2 Million
Number Employees: 10-19
Number of Brands: 6
Number of Products: 75
Square Footage: 52000
Brands:
  Astral Laser Power
  Mentor Laser Power
  Sa Analytical
  Sg General
  Sl Laboratory
  Sp Precision
  Synergy Laser Power
  Ultra Laser Power
  Vector Laser Power

28916 Scientific Fire Prevention

47-25 34th Street
Suite 203
Long Island City, NY 11101

718-433-3880
Fax: 718-433-0652 sales@scientificfire.com
www.scientificfire.com
Fire prevention and exhaust systems; also, indoor air
quality testing services available
President: Roy Leonard
Marketing Director: Jeffrey Schwartz
Contact: Brian Higgins
brian@scientificfire.com

28917 Scientific Process & Research

P.O.Box 5008
Kendall Park, NJ 08824-5008

732-846-3477
Fax: 732-846-3029 800-868-4777
info@spar.com www.spar.com
Manufacturer and exporter of extruder, timing and
conveyor screws and extruder barrels; exporter of
extruder screws and software
Production Manager: Felicia Cappo
Estimated Sales: $2.5-5 Million
Number Employees: 10-19
Square Footage: 80000

28918 Scope Packaging

PO Box 3768
Orange, CA 92857

714-998-4411
Fax: 714-998-5323
Manufacturer and exporter of corrugated boxes
President: Michael Flinn
VP Marketing: Cindy Baker
Contact: Christine Maple
christinem@scopepackaging.com
Estimated Sales: $20-50 Million
Number Employees: 50-99
Type of Packaging: Bulk

28919 (HQ)Scorpio Apparel

3318 Commercial Avenue
Northbrook, IL 60062-1909

847-559-3100
Fax: 847-559-3103 800-559-3338
Manufacturer and exporter of uniforms
President: Allan L Klein
CEO: Lew Klein
Vice President: Carolyn Philips
Sales Director: Juli Shapiro
Estimated Sales: $2 Million
Number Employees: 34
Square Footage: 14000
Type of Packaging: Private Label
Other Locations:
  Scorpio Products
  Chicago IL
Brands:
  9th Wave
  Scorpio
  Vespron

28920 Scot Young Research LTD

503 Renick St
St Joseph, MO 64501-3660

816-233-4898
Fax: 816-232-3701 www.syrclean.com
Manufacturer and exporter of ergonomic and color
coded mopping systems
General Manager: Myong Stracener
Contact: Jamie Carpentier
jamie.carpentier@syrclean.com
Estimated Sales: Less Than $500,000
Number Employees: 1-4
Brands:
  Syr

28921 Scotsman Beverage System

2007 Royal Lane
Suite 100
Dallas, TX 75229-3279

972-488-1030
Fax: 972-243-8075 800-527-7422
Parent Co: ENODIS

28922 Scotsman Ice Systems

101 Corporate Woods Pkwy.
Vernon Hills, IL 60061

847-215-4500
Fax: 847-913-9844 800-726-8762
customer.relations@scotsman-ice.com
www.scotsman-ice.com
Ice machines including flakers and nugget makers
and hotel dispensing bins, drink dispensers, water
filtration systems, etc.
President: Kevin Clark
CFO: Jo Rendino
Estimated Sales: $92 Million
Number Employees: 800
Square Footage: 36000
Parent Co: Scotsman Industries
Type of Packaging: Consumer, Food Service
Other Locations:
  Scotsman Ice Systems
  La Verne CA
Brands:
  Cm3 Cubers
  Dc33 Luxury
  Fme Flakers
  Nme Nugget
  Scotsman
  Slim Line Cubers
  Tde Dispensers

28923 Scott & Daniells

264 Freestone Ave
Portland, CT 06480-1640

860-342-1932
Fax: 860-342-2436

Folding cartons

VP: Robert Papa
VP Operations: Kevin Robrge
Plant Manager: Robert Papa
Estimated Sales: $10-20 Million
Number Employees: 50-99
Square Footage: 240000

28924 Scott Equipment Co
605 4th Ave NW
New Prague, MN 56071-1121

952-758-2591
Fax: 952-758-4377 800-264-9519
dave.lucas@scottequipment.com
www.scottequipment.com
Mixers, dryers, high speed blenders, size reduction, de-packaging, turbo dominator, and horizontal batch mixers, available in carbon or stainless steel
President: Dave Lucas
CEO: Richard Lucaas
IT: Joshua Lucas
joshua.lucas@gmail.com
Estimated Sales: $20-50 Million
Number Employees: 50-99

28925 Scott Group
10801 Corkscrew Rd # 336
Estero, FL 33928-9451

239-949-2252
Fax: 239-949-0346 www.chicos.com
Services and marketing communication
Managing Partner: Stephen Scott
Estimated Sales: $3-5 Million
Number Employees: 10-19

28926 Scott Laboratories Inc
2220 Pine View Way
Petaluma, CA 94954-5687

707-765-6666
Fax: 707-765-6674 800-797-2688
info@scottlabsltd.com www.scottlab.com
Wine industry equipment and supplies
President/Owner: Bruce Scott
Senior Vice President: Tom Anders
Sales Representative: Peter Anderson
Vice President of Sales: Bob Fithian
Vice President of Operations: Bruce Edwards
Estimated Sales: $5-10 Million
Number Employees: 50-99

28927 Scott Packaging Corporation
340 N 12th St
Philadelphia, PA 19107-1102

215-925-5595
Packaging products including thermoformed trays, blisters and clamshells
Owner: Scott Page
Estimated Sales: $300,000-500,000
Number Employees: 1-4
Square Footage: 24000
Parent Co: Supplies Unlimited

28928 Scott Pallets Inc
8660 Crowder St
Amelia Court Hse, VA 23002

804-561-2514
Fax: 804-561-2664 800-394-2514
www.scottpalletsinc.com
Wooden pallets
President: Joanne Scottwebb
scottpallets@tds.net
Quality Control: Joanne Scott
Manager: Ray Hoerger
Estimated Sales: $2.5-5 Million
Number Employees: 10-19
Square Footage: 40000
Brands:
　Gma
　Gpc

28929 Scott Process Equipment& Controls
15 Southgate Drive
Guelph, ON N1G 3M5
Canada

519-836-6902
Fax: 519-836-3325 888-343-5421
info@scottpec.com www.scottpec.com
Processing equipment and controls.
President: Ladislav Rudik
Estimated Sales: $1.3 Million
Number Employees: 5
Square Footage: 4855

28930 Scott Sign Systems
7525 Pennsylvania Ave # C
PO Box 1047
Sarasota, FL 34243-5065

941-355-5171
Fax: 941-351-1787 800-237-9447
mail@scottsigns.com www.scottsigns.com
Manufactures signs and sign systems including letters, logos, graphics and architectural signs.
President: Steve Evans
Cio/Cto: Maurice Aguinaldo
mauricea@scottsigns.com
Estimated Sales: $1-5 Million
Number Employees: 20-49
Square Footage: 150000
Parent Co: Identity Group
Brands:
　Brailldots
　Braillplaques
　Scotslants
　Scott-A.D.A.'s Brailleters
　Scott-Elites
　Scott-Thins
　Scott-Trax
　Snap-Ins
　Tabbee

28931 Scott Turbon Mixer
9351 Industrial Way
Adelanto, CA 92301-3932

760-246-3430
Fax: 760-246-3505 800-285-8512
sales@scottmixer.com www.haywardgordon.com
Manufacturer and exporter of sanitary mixing equipment for dairy, beverage and meat; also, complete systems including tanks, platforms and piping, lab and pilot plant mixers
Owner: William Scott
bill@scottmixer.com
Sales Director: Tim Moore
Estimated Sales: $1-5 Million
Number Employees: 20-49
Square Footage: 50000
Brands:
　Scott Turbon

28932 Scott Turbon Mixer
9351 Industrial Way
Adelanto, CA 92301-3932

760-246-3430
Fax: 760-246-3505 800-285-8512
sales@scottmixer.com www.haywardgordon.com
Owner: William Scott
bill@scottmixer.com
Estimated Sales: $5-10 Million
Number Employees: 20-49

28933 (HQ)Scott's Liquid Gold-Inc
4880 Havana St # 400
Denver, CO 80239-2432

303-373-4860
Fax: 303-576-6151 800-447-1919
www.scottsliquidgold.com
Household and industrial polishes and air fresheners
Chairman of the Board: Mark Goldstin
CEO: Mark E Goldstein
mgoldstein@slginc.com
R&D and Quality Control: Sharon Moore
CEO: Mark E Goldstein
VP Marketing: Jeff Hinkle
Sales Operations Manager: Linda Melphy
Estimated Sales: $20-30 Million
Number Employees: 50-99
Brands:
　Touch of Scent

28934 Scranton Lace Company
PO Box 121
Forest City, PA 18421

570-344-1124
Fax: 570-344-1125 800-822-1036
slclace@icontech.com
Cotton and lace tablecloths, window curtains, place mats and accessories
President: Robert Hyne
CEO: Jennifer Herman
VP Sales: Carol Rabe
Office Manager/EDI COOrd: Wendy Yannuzzi
Estimated Sales: $10-20 Million
Number Employees: 50-99
Square Footage: 1200000
Parent Co: Jerry's SportCenter

Brands:
　Black Tie Collection
　Classic Home Collection

28935 Screen Print Etc
1081 N Shepard St # E
Anaheim, CA 92806-2819

714-630-1100
Fax: 714-630-3719
Display and exhibit boards, decals, flags, pennants, banners and signs; also, commercial printing, graphic design and plastic printing services available
Owner: Ray Lynch
rlynch@screenprintetc.com
Estimated Sales: $530 Million
Number Employees: 5-9
Square Footage: 4000
Type of Packaging: Private Label, Bulk

28936 (HQ)Screw Conveyor Corp
700 Hoffman St
Hammond, IN 46327-1827

219-931-1450
Fax: 219-931-0209 sales@screwconveyor.com
Screw conveyors and accessories, elevator buckets, industrial and grain bucket elevators, hydraulic truck dumpers, screw lifts, tube screws and belt conveyor idlers
Owner: Garry M Abraham
sales@screwconveyor.com
Manager of Engineering & Procurement: Steve Rauhut
VP Marketing/Sales: Randy Block
Sales Manager: Anita Kozlowski
Customer Service Supervisor/Sales Engine: Robert Belko
Senior Applications Engineer: Barry Stacy
Estimated Sales: $10-20 Million
Number Employees: 20-49
Other Locations:
　SCC Industries
　Guadalajara, Jal.
Brands:
　Enduro-Flo
　Enduro-Roll
　Exacta-Flo
　Kewanee
　Rigid-Flo
　Screw-Lift
　Super-Flo

28937 Scrivner Equipment Co Inc
1811 Hopoca Rd
Carthage, MS 39051-9449

601-267-7614
Industrial equipment and supplies
Owner: Martin Scrivner
pscrivnerequipco@aol.com
Estimated Sales: $200,000
Number Employees: 1-4
Square Footage: 2625

28938 Scroll Compressors LLC
1675 Campbell Rd
Sidney, OH 45365-2479

937-498-3011
Fax: 937-498-3203 www.emersonclimate.com
Manufacturer and exporter of compressors for air conditioning and refrigeration
President: Tom Bettcher
Number Employees: 10-19
Type of Packaging: Food Service
Brands:
　Copeland

28939 Se Kure Controls Inc
3714 Runge St
Franklin Park, IL 60131-1112

847-288-1111
Fax: 847-288-9999 800-250-9260
info@se-kure.com www.se-kure.com
Manufacturer, importer and exporter of safes, vaults, security mirrors and cameras and anti-shoplifting devices
Founder/President/CEO: Roger Leyden
rogerleyden@se-kure.com
Executive VP Administration & Finance: Laura Greenwell
National Sales Manager: John Mangiameli
Estimated Sales: $20-50 Million
Number Employees: 100-249
Number of Products: 500
Square Footage: 200000

28940 Sea Breeze Fruit Flavors
441 Main Road
Towaco, NJ 07082-1201
973-334-7777
Fax: 973-334-2617 800-732-2733
info@seabreezesyrups.com
www.seabreezesyrups.com
Syrups including chocolate, pancake and milkshake;
sundae toppings, bar mixes, juice concentrates, soda,
iced tea, lemonade, fruit juice, flavored water and
beverage dispensing equipment.
President: Steve Sanders
Vice President: Josh Sanders
Technical Director: Frank Maranino
Contact: George Apostolopoulos
george@seabreezesyrups.com
Production Manager: Paul Maranino
Estimated Sales: $25-49.9 Million
Number Employees: 50-99
Number of Brands: 6
Type of Packaging: Consumer, Food Service, Private Label
Brands:
  Bosco
  Joshua Miguel
  New York Bash
  Sea Breeze
  Toshimi
  Tropic Beach

28941 Sea Gull Lighting Products, LLC
306 Elizabeth Lane
Corona, CA 92880-2504
951-273-7380
Fax: 800-877-4855 800-347-5483
Info@SeaGullLighting.com
www.seagulllighting.com
Lighting fixtures
Vice President, Marketing: Ace Rosenstein
Estimated Sales: $1-2.5 Million
Number Employees: 5-9

28942 Seaboard Bag Corporation
3412 Moore St
Richmond, VA 23230-4444
Fax: 804-355-9100
Multi-walled and pasted paper valve bags
Owner: Jim Edge
Estimated Sales: $10-20 Million
Number Employees: 50-99
Parent Co: Morgan Brothers Bag Company

28943 Seaboard Carton Company
1140 31st Street
Downers Grove, IL 60515-1212
708-344-0575
Fax: 708-344-4058
Folding cartons
Estimated Sales: $10-20 Million
Number Employees: 50-99
Square Footage: 180000

28944 Seaboard Folding Box Corp
35 Daniels St
Fitchburg, MA 01420-7606
978-342-8921
Fax: 978-342-1105 800-255-6313
info@seaboardbox.com www.seaboardbox.com
Manufacturer and exporter of paper boxes
President: Alan Rabinow
CEO: Allen Rabinow
allen.rabinow@jordanind.com
Number Employees: 100-249

28945 Seaga Manufacturing Inc
700 Seaga Dr
Freeport, IL 61032-9644
815-297-9500
Fax: 815-297-1700 info@seaga.com
www.seaga.com
Vending equipment for cold beverage merchandisers, soda and beverage vendors, e-cigarette vending equipment, custom vending equipment
President: Steven Chesney
schesney@seagamfg.com
Chairman of the Board and Owner: Steven Chesney
Estimated Sales: $30-50 Million
Number Employees: 100-249
Parent Co: Seaga Manufacturing

28946 Seajoy
6619 S Dixie Hwy
PO Box 344
Miami, FL 33143
305-669-0108
Fax: 302-663-0312 877-537-1717
www.seajoy.com
Shrimp including raw head-on whole shrimp, raw
shell-on tails, raw shell-on E-Z peel meats, raw
peeled & deveined tail on or off, uncut, raw peeled,
butterfly meat, raw breaded shrimp meat, and raw
peeled & deveined meat on skewers
Administrative President: Peder Jacobson
VP Sales & Operations: Brad Price
Estimated Sales: $220 Thousand
Brands:
  Seajoy®
  Cjoy®
  Bluefield®
  Seabrook®

28947 Seal King North America
21720 Hamburg ave
Lakeville, MN 55044
952-469-6639
Fax: 803-364-5008 800-582-4372
info@sealking.com www.sealking.com
Bag sealing tape, double coated foam tapes, tissue
tapes and polyester tape, spooled tapes, fingerlift
tapes for plastic and paper envelopes and siliconised
release liners
President/Founder: Ben Nelson
Contact: Cheryl Alben
cheryl.alben@medtronic.com
Number Employees: 12

28948 Seal Pac USA
5901 School Ave
Richmond, VA 23228-5447
804-261-0580
Fax: 804-261-0581 info@sealpac-us.com
Distributor of tray sealers
Number Employees: 1-4

28949 Seal Science Inc
17131 Daimler St
Irvine, CA 92614-5508
949-251-1832
Fax: 949-253-3141 800-576-7325
westernsales@sealscience.com
www.sealscience.com
Manufactures gaskets, molded rubber products, engineered seal solutions, O-rings, teflon seals, vacuum cups and diaphragms; custom plastic machining
CEO: Rick Tuliper
rickt@sealscience.com
Marketing/Sales: Doug Albin
Purchasing Manager: Christy Seastedt
Estimated Sales: $5-10 Million
Number Employees: 100-249
Square Footage: 25000
Parent Co: Seal Science East

28950 Seal the Seasons
501 W Franklin St
Suite 106
Chapel Hill, NC 27516
919-245-3535
Fax: 919-930-8970 hello@sealtheseasons.com
www.sealtheseasons.com
Frozen produce
Founder & CEO: Patrick Mateer
Controller: Dawn Paffenroth
Chief Sales Officer: Jonathan Mills
COO: Alex Piasecki
Number Employees: 2-10
Brands:
  Seal the Seasons

28951 Seal-A-Tron Corp
3815 SE Naef Rd
Portland, OR 97267-5615
503-652-5200
Fax: 503-652-5205 800-487-3257
drehs@seal-a-tron.com www.seal-a-tron.com
Industrial shrink wrap equipment
Owner: Warner Duemmer
wduemmer@seal-a-tron.com
Technical Assistance: Werner Duemmer
Customer Service Officer: John Borich
Estimated Sales: Below $5 Million
Number Employees: 10-19

28952 Seal-O-Matic Corp
2542 Humbug Creek Rd
Jacksonville, OR 97530-9618
541-846-1000
Fax: 541-846-1004 800-631-2072
info@sealomatic.com www.sealomatic.net
Manufacturer, importer and exporter of shrink wrap
and packaging equipment including gummed tape
dispensers, safety knives, shipping room equipment,
price labeling guns, staplers, staples, etc
President: Mel Ortner
Vice President: Janine Ortner
Marketing Director: Greg Sparre
Contact: Janine Ortner
janine@sealomatic.com
Purchasing Manager: Kim Westmoreland
Estimated Sales: $1-3 Million
Number Employees: 10-19
Square Footage: 10000
Brands:
  Flash
  Labelmaster
  Lewis
  Pricemaster

28953 Seal-Tite Bag Company
4324 Tackawanna St
Philadelphia, PA 19124
717-917-1949
Fax: 215-288-5664
Transparent and flexible packaging, plastic and heat
sealed and plastic bags; also, plastic film and poly
labels
Estimated Sales: $1-2.5 Million
Number Employees: 8
Brands:
  Seal-Tite

28954 Sealed Air Corp
2415 Cascade Pointe Boulevard
Charlotte, NC 28208
980-430-7000
800-391-5645
www.sealedair.com
Flexible plastic packaging materials including film,
food packaging and shrink wrap. The inventors of
Bubble Wrap.
Chairman/Chief Executive Officer: Ted Doheny
SVP/Chief Supply Chain Officer: Emile Chammas
SVP/Chief Financial Officer: Jim Sullivan
VP/Chief Human Resources Officer: Susan Edwards
SVP/Chief Commercial Officer: Karl Deily
VP/General Counsel/Secretary: Angel Willis
VP/Chief Strategy Officer: Sergio Pupkin
Year Founded: 1960
Estimated Sales: $4.7 Billion
Number Employees: 15,500

28955 Sealeze Inc
8000 Whitepine Rd
N Chesterfield, VA 23237-2263
804-743-0982
Fax: 804-271-3428 800-787-7325
www.sealeze.com
Strip brush for sealing out debris, shielding, guiding
on conveyors, positioning products during production and static dissipation.
President: Molly Kent
kentm@jacksonlea.com
Number Employees: 20-49

28956 Sealstrip Corp
103 Industrial Dr
Gilbertsville, PA 19525-8832
610-367-6282
Fax: 610-367-7727 888-658-7997
hhartmann@tearstripsystems.com
www.tearstripsystems.com
Shrinkable teartape, shrink tape applicators,
resealable bags and systems
Owner: Harold Forman
hforman@sealstrip.com
Manufacturing Manager: Jacob Greth
Estimated Sales: $2.5-5 Million
Number Employees: 50-99

28957 Sealstrip Corporation
200 N Washington St
Boyertown, PA 19512-1115
610-367-6282
Fax: 610-367-7727 www.sealstrip.com
Manufacturer and exporter of resealable packaging
equipment and materials

President: Joanne Forman
Owner: Harold Forman
R&D: Ajrlod Forman
Sales: Heather Hartman
Manufacturing Manager: Jacob Greth
Estimated Sales: Below $5 Million
Number Employees: 20-49
Square Footage: 28000
Brands:
  Everfresh
  Fresh Pak
  Sealstrip
  Serv & Seal

28958 SeamTech
24231 Fuhrman Rd
Acampo, CA 95220-9766

209-464-4610
Fax: 209-464-1438 www.seamtechpk.com
Service parts and sales of fillers, seamers and warehouse equipment
President: Pete Saavedra
CFO: Pete Saavedra
Quality Control: Jason Saavedra
Estimated Sales: Below $5 Million
Number Employees: 5

28959 Search West
PO Box 641609
Los Angeles, CA 90064-6609

310-203-9797
Executive search firm recruiting middle to upper level managers, professionals and executives in sales, administrative and technical areas
President: Bob Cowan
Estimated Sales: $500,000-$1 Million
Number Employees: 50-100

28960 Season Harvest Foods
4906 El Camino Real # 206
Suite 206
Los Altos, CA 94022-1444

650-968-2273
Fax: 877-413-3894 sales@seasonharvestfoods.com
www.seasonharvestfoods.com
Organic vegetable and spice supplier.

28961 Seasons 4 Inc
4500 Industrial Access Rd
Douglasville, GA 30134-3949

770-489-5405
Fax: 770-489-2938 jkodobocz@seasons4.net
www.seasons4.net
Manufacturer and exporter of custom engineered HVAC systems for supermarkets
President: Lewis Watford
lwatford@seasons4.net
VP Sales: Todd Smith
Purchasing Manager: Rick Rothschild
Estimated Sales: $50-100 Million
Number Employees: 250-499
Square Footage: 145000

28962 Seatex Ltd
445 TX-36
Rosenberg, TX 77471

713-357-5300
Fax: 713-357-5301 800-829-3020
kaimes@seatexcorp.com www.seatexcorp.com
Providers of turn key chemical compounding, toll manufacturing and private label packaging services. Areas of expertise includ the food service, food processing, automotive, institutional and industrial laundry, janitorialindustrial and oilfield service markets.
President/CEO: Jim Nattier
CFO: John Nowak
VP: Kelly Aimes
R&D: Don Trepel
Director QA/QC: Don Trepel
Sales/Marketing: Tom Austin
Sales/Marketing: Kelly Aimes
Contact: Deneen Case
dcase@seatexcorp.com
Operations/Production: Dan Boone
Warehouse/Logistics: Jim Dockery
VP Purchasing: Larry Brown
Estimated Sales: $26 Million
Number Employees: 85
Number of Products: 400
Square Footage: 220000
Type of Packaging: Consumer, Food Service, Private Label, Bulk

28963 Seating Concepts Inc
125 Connell Ave
Rockdale, IL 60436-2466

815-730-7980
Fax: 815-730-7969 800-421-2036
sales@seating-concepts.com
www.seating-concepts.com
Manufacturer and exporter of chairs, booths, cafeteria counters, tables and waste receptacles; importer of chairs
Owner: Marianne Dieter
Sales Director: Chris Mazzoni
mdieter@travstor.com
Estimated Sales: $3,000,000
Number Employees: 50-99
Type of Packaging: Food Service

28964 Seattle Boiler Works Inc
500 S Myrtle St
Seattle, WA 98108-3495

206-762-0737
Fax: 206-762-3516 www.seattleboiler.com
Manufacturer and exporter of boilers, heat exchangers and pressure vessels; also, stainless steel fabrication, pipe and tube bending services available
Owner: Craig Hopkins
chopkins@seattleboiler.com
VP: Craig Hopkins
Quality Control: Craig Hopkins
Estimated Sales: $5-10 Million
Number Employees: 20-49
Square Footage: 140000
Type of Packaging: Bulk

28965 Seattle Menu Specialists
5844 South 194th Street
Kent, WA 98032

206-784-2340
Fax: 206-782-7778 800-622-2826
customerservice@seattlemenu.com
www.seattlemenu.com
Manufacturer and designer of menu, wine and guest check covers and placemats; exporter of menu covers
President: Dale Phelps
Operations Manager: Lonnie Axtell
Purchasing Manager: George Rought
Estimated Sales: Below $5 Million
Number Employees: 10
Brands:
  Duracrafic

28966 Seattle Plastics
309 S Cloverdale St # E7
#E7
Seattle, WA 98108-4591

206-233-0869
Fax: 206-233-0874 800-441-0679
info@seattleplastics.com www.seattleplastics.com
Display cases, bagel and coffe bins and lid holders; also, custom fabrication available
President: Mike Albanese
info@seattleplastics.com
Estimated Sales: $1-2,500,000
Number Employees: 5-9

28967 Seattle Refrigeration &Manufacturing
1057 S Director St
Seattle, WA 98108

206-762-7740
Fax: 206-762-1730 800-228-8881
Manufacturer and importer of compressors, pressure vessels, belt and spiral freezers, condensers, heat exchangers, ice makers, chillers, freezers, hoses, pumps, etc.; importer of compressors, plate freezers and valves; exporter ofcompressors, and ice makers
President: Tracy Abbott
R&D: Frank Kanpp
Quality Control: Bob Petersen
Service Manager: Don Irons
Estimated Sales: $5-10 Million
Number Employees: 10-19
Square Footage: 30600
Parent Co: Seattle Refrigeration
Brands:
  Alco
  Asme
  C.P.
  Carrier
  Copeland
  Dunham-Bush
  Eagle Signal
  F.E.S.
  Frick
  Fuller
  Grasso
  Henry
  Howden
  Howe
  Johnson (Penn)
  Paragon
  Ranco
  Sabroe
  Shank
  Sporian
  Sullair
  Tecumseh
  Vitter
  Wolf Linde
  York

28968 Seattle's Best Coffee
18870 103rd Avenue
Vashon, WA 98070-5229

206-463-5050
Fax: 206-463-5764
Tea and coffee industry, bags (brick packs, flexible, and valve packs)
Estimated Sales: $1-5 Million
Number Employees: 6

28969 Seattle-Tacoma Box Co
23400 71st Pl S
Kent, WA 98032-2994

253-854-9700
Fax: 253-852-0891 info@seattlebox.com
www.seattlebox.com
Manufacturer and exporter of wooden produce and corrugated boxes
Vice President: Michael Nist
mike@seattlebox.com
Marketing Director: Rob Nist
Estimated Sales: $30-50 Million
Number Employees: 20-49

28970 Seattle-Tacoma Box Co
23400 71st Pl S
Kent, WA 98032-2994

253-854-9700
Fax: 253-852-0891 www.seattlebox.com
Custom designed corrugated boxes and wood boxes. Skids, pallets, wooden containers, plastic bags, styrofoam and other packaging supplies.
Owner: Jacob Nist
Vice President: Michael J Nist
mike@seattlebox.com
Sales: Joseph Nist
Number Employees: 20-49

28971 Sebesta Blomberg & Assoc
2381 Rosegate
Roseville, MN 55113-2625

651-634-0775
877-706-6858
info@sebesta.com www.lionbrand.com
President: James Sebasta
Contact: Rob Costello
rcostello@sebesta.com
Number Employees: 1-4
Square Footage: 160000

28972 Sebring Container Corporation
PO Box 359
Salem, OH 44460

330-332-1533
Fax: 330-332-2205
Flat corrugated containers
President: William Mc Devitt
Sales Manager: John Berlin
Contact: Amy Cannon
a.cannon@sebringcontainer.com
Estimated Sales: $10-20 Million
Number Employees: 20-49

28973 Seco Industries
6858 E Acco St
Commerce, CA 90040-1902

323-726-9721
Fax: 323-726-9776 sales@seco-ind.com
www.gramatech.com
Barrier packaging, heat sealing equipment, and vacuum sealers
CEO: Charles De Heras
randy@seco-ind.com
Vice President: Jerome Druss

Estimated Sales: $5-10 Million
Number Employees: 20-49
Square Footage: 120000

28974 Seco Industries
6858 E Acco St
Commerce, CA 90040-1902

323-726-9721
Fax: 323-726-9776 sales@seco-ind.com
www.gramatech.com
CEO: Charles De Heras
randy@seco-ind.com
Estimated Sales: $1-5 Million
Number Employees: 20-49

28975 Security Link
816 N Gilbert Street
Danville, IL 61832

217-446-4871
Fax: 309-685-7161
Alarm systems
General Manager: Deborah Morris
dmorris@adt.com
Estimated Sales: Less than $500,000
Number Employees: 1-4

28976 Security Packaging
PO Box 892
North Bergen, NJ 07047-0892

201-854-1955
Fax: 201-854-1978
Corrugated boxes
President: Norbert Mester
Estimated Sales: $1-2.5 Million
Number Employees: 5-9
Square Footage: 3000

28977 Sedalia Janitorial & Paper Supplies
4211 S 65 Highway
Sedalia, MO 65301

660-826-9899
Janitorial and paper supplies
Estimated Sales: $1-5 Million
Number Employees: 1

28978 Sedex Kinkos
PO Box 1198
Tualatin, OR 97062-1198

503-692-3550
Fax: 503-692-1860 800-800-6271
www.fineartsgraphics.com
Wine industry label printing
Estimated Sales: $5-10 Million
Number Employees: 10

28979 Sediment Testing Equipment
7366 N Greenview Ave
Chicago, IL 60626-1924

773-465-3634
Fax: 773-465-4309 800-853-7323
info@sedimenttesting.com
www.sedimenttesting.com
Sediment testing equipment and supplies recommended for scorch-particles testing of reconstituted
nonfat dry milk and coffee, determining sediment or
extraneous matter in milk products and batch sample
testing when quality-controlstandards have been est
President: Kathleen S Fox
Estimated Sales: $.5-1 million
Number Employees: 1-4

28980 Seeds of Change
P.O. Box 4908
Rancho Dominguez, CA 90220

888-762-7333
www.seedsofchange.com
Organic, non-GMO seeds of herbs and vegetables
Co-Founder: Alan Kapuler
CEO: Andrew Behar
Year Founded: 1989
Estimated Sales: $58 Million
Number Employees: 120
Parent Co: Mars, Inc.

28981 Seepex Inc
511 Speedway Dr
Enon, OH 45323-1057

937-864-7150
Fax: 937-864-7157 800-695-3659
sales@seepex.net www.seepex.com
Designs, manufactures, and sells Progressive Cavity
Pumps and Pump accessories.

President: Michael Dillon
CEO: Florencio Alvarez
falvarez@seepex.com
VP: Francis Harris
R&D: Mathew Brown
Quality Control: Robert Mentz
Marketing/Public Relations: Daniel Lakovic
Director, Sales: Mark Murphy
Product Manager: Joe Zinck
Purchasing: Robert Mentz
Estimated Sales: $30 Million
Number Employees: 250-499
Number of Brands: 1
Number of Products: 1000
Square Footage: 40000
Parent Co: Seepex
Brands:
Map
Seepex
Tricam

28982 Sefar
111 Calumet St
Depew, NY 14043-3734

716-683-4050
Fax: 716-683-4053 www.sefar.us
President: David Koebcke
david.koebcke@sefar.us
CEO: Art Alex
R & D: Richard Gaiser
Number Employees: 50-99

28983 Sefi Fabricators Inc
50 Ranick Dr E
PO Box 338
Amityville, NY 11701-2822

631-842-2200
Fax: 631-842-2203 info@sefifabricators.com
www.imcteddy.com
Custom stainless steel food service equipment,
countertops, cabinets, floordrains, lab furniture,
shelving, grating sinks and tables
President: Asit Majumdar
imcteddy@aol.com
Sales Manager: Louis Stanley
Sales Engineer: Barry Greene
Customer Service: Maria Fernandez
Estimated Sales: $2.5-5 Million
Number Employees: 20-49
Square Footage: 34000
Type of Packaging: Consumer, Food Service, Pri-
vate Label, Bulk

28984 Seiberling Associates Inc
655 3rd St # 203
Suite 203
Beloit, WI 53511-6269

608-313-1235
Fax: 608-313-1275 craig.guyse@seiberling.com
Consultant providing engineering services and pro-
ject management; also, installation and start-up ser-
vices available
Vice President: Don Huett
don.huett@seiberling.com
CFO: Don Hewitt
VP: Don Huett
Estimated Sales: $2.5-5 Million
Number Employees: 20-49

28985 Seidenader Equipment
25 Hanover Rd # 210
Florham Park, NJ 07932-1424

973-301-9800
Fax: 973-301-9090 800-342-6910
www.seidenader.de
Manufacturers of fully automatic inspection ma-
chines for parental products, semi-automatic inspec-
tion machines, exterior vial washers, and tray
loaders
Manager: Eileen Scanlon
Marketing Manager: Sara Savastano
Contact: Ed Chobanoff
echobanoff@svresearch.com
Estimated Sales: $500,000-$1 Million
Number Employees: 1-4

28986 Seidman Brothers
25 6th St
Chelsea, MA 02150-2422

617-884-8110
Fax: 617-884-4284 800-437-7770
info@seidmanbros.com

Commercial kitchen exhaust systems. custom stain-
less steel, and distributors of food service equip-
ment.
President: Allen Seidman
General Manager: Jack Seidman
Sales: Gina Venezia
Operations Manager: Rick Seidman
Estimated Sales: $5-10 Million
Number Employees: 10-19

28987 Seiler Plastics
9750 Reavis Park Dr
St Louis, MO 63123-5316

314-685-3267
Fax: 314-815-3025 888-673-4537
rjones@seilerpc.com www.seilerpc.com
Plastic products including tubing profiles, sheets,
etc.; die cutting and thermoforming services avail-
able
Owner: John Sieler
VP: Paul Benson
Sales Manager: Paul Dyer
Contact: Paul Meyer
p.meyer@seilerpc.com
Estimated Sales: $5-10 Million
Number Employees: 10-19
Square Footage: 48000

28988 Seitz Memtec America Corporation
635 Shannon Corners Rd
Dundee, NY 14837-9158

607-243-7568
Fax: 607-243-5251
Wine industry equipment
Owner: Joe Gibson

28989 Seitz Schenk Filter Systems
2118 Greenspring Drive
Lutherville, MD 21093-3112

443-322-2494
Fax: 443-322-2496 877-716-8778
info@benelogic.com www.benelogic.com
Filters and filtration equipment
CEO: Matthew T Oros
Estimated Sales: $5-10 Million
Number Employees: 250-499

28990 Seitz Stainless Inc
17578 400th St
Avon, MN 56310-9735

320-746-2781
Fax: 320-746-2782 sales@seitzstainless.com
www.seitzstainless.com
Custom fabrication, dryers, spray, heat recovery sys-
tems, heat exchangers, pasteurizers, tubular
President: Jeff Haviland
sales@seitzstainless.com
Sales Exec: Nicole Hagman
Estimated Sales: $10-20 Million
Number Employees: 20-49

28991 Seiz Sign Co Inc
1231 Central Ave
Hot Spgs Natl Pk, AR 71901-6037

501-623-3181
Fax: 501-623-4594 david@seizsigns.com
www.seizsigns.com
Advertising signs
President: David Hamilton
VP & Billboard Sales: Tammy Hamilton
Office Manager: Shannon McLean
Estimated Sales: $1-2.5 Million
Number Employees: 10-19

28992 Sekisui TA Industries
100 S Puente St
Brea, CA 92821-3813

714-255-7888
Fax: 800-235-8273 800-258-8273
www.sta-tape.com
Manufacturer and exporter of FDA approved
B.O.P.P. pressure sensitive tapes and semi and fully
automatic carton sealing machinery
President: Ikusuke Shimizu
CEO: Ernest J Wong
CFO: Matt Minami
VP: Stephen J Wilson
R&D: Dinesh Shan
Marketing Administrator: Melissa Morris
Contact: Alison Barth
barth@cmu.edu
Plant Manager: C P Fang

Estimated Sales: $20-50 Million
Number Employees: 100-249
Square Footage: 185000
Parent Co: Sekisui Chemical
Brands:
  Sta Series
  Sta-Pack
  Supreme

28993 Selby Sign Co Inc
2138 Bypass Rd
Pocomoke City, MD 21851-2756
                                    410-742-0095
        Fax: 410-957-1074 www.selbysign.com
Exterior and interior illuminated signs including
electronic message centers, time/temperature units,
neon, etc.; also, installation and maintainence
available
Owner: David Selby
davidselby@selbysign.com
VP: Steve Selby
Production Manager: Doug Dryden
Estimated Sales: $1-2.5 Million
Number Employees: 20-49
Square Footage: 12000

28994 Selby/Ucrete IndustrialFlooring
26383 Broadway Ave
Cleveland, OH 44146-6516
                                    440-232-6644
        Fax: 216-839-8822 800-445-6182
Owner: Chuck Slaby
Estimated Sales: $1-5 Million
Number Employees: 1-4

28995 Selco Products Company
605 S East St
Anaheim, CA 92805-4842
                                    714-917-1333
        Fax: 714-917-1355 800-257-3526
sales@selcoproducts.com www.selcoproducts.com
Selco offers mechanical and electronic temperature
controls, control knobs, and digital and analog panel
meters
CEO: Tim Wilkinson
Marketing Manager: Michelle Blakeslee
Sales Manager: Russell Kido
Estimated Sales: $5-10 Million
Number Employees: 50-99

28996 Select Appliance Sales,Inc.
159 West Harris Avenue
San Francisco, CA 94080
                                    650-588-9100
        Fax: 650-588-9108 888-235-0431
                    www.selectappliance.com
President: Russell Zipkin
Marketing Manager: Ming Chu
Estimated Sales: 3MM
Number Employees: 4

28997 Select Stainless
11145 Monroe Rd
PO Box 158
Matthews, NC 28105-6564
                                    704-841-1090
                        Fax: 704-841-1590
        generalinfo@selectstainless.com
        www.selecthealthcareproducts.com
Owner: Benjamin Williams
Vice President: Mike Auten
President: Ben Williams
National Sales Manager: Doug Joyner
bwilliams@selectstainless.com
Estimated Sales: $3-5 Million
Number Employees: 100-249

28998 Select Technologies Inc
8093 Graphic Dr NE
Belmont, MI 49306-9448
                                    616-866-6700
        Fax: 616-866-6770 www.select-technologies.com
Designer, builder and installer of plant facility &
utility systems and production lines for processing
and material handling.
Owner: Eric Staley
ericstaley@select-technologies.com
Number Employees: 5-9

28999 Selective Foods
P.O. Box 446
Carnegie, PA 15106
                                    412-458-1930
    Fax: 412-458-1932 info@selectivefoods.net
                www.selectivefoodmarketing.com
To help food manufacturers, operators and distribu-
tors succeed in the evolving Western Pennsylvania
market.
Partner/Sales: Ken Fisher
Partner/Sales: Susan Battaglia
Customer Service: Paula Sapienza
Square Footage: 3000

29000 Selecto
1400 Market Place Blvd # 109
Cumming, GA 30041-7925
                                    770-205-0800
                        Fax: 770-448-7021
Tea and coffee industry, filtration equipment
Owner: Kirk Sherrill
Number Employees: 5-9

29001 (HQ)Selecto Scientific
3980 Lakefield Ct
Suwanee, GA 30024
                                    678-475-0799
        Fax: 678-475-1595 800-635-4017
        Customer-service@selectoinc.com
                    www.selectoinc.com
Manufacturer and exporter of water filters for scale
reduction, taste and odor and sediment for fountain
dispensing equipment, coffee makers, ice equipment
and steamers
Owner: Terry Libin
Co-founder and CEO: Ehud Levy
Director R&D/QC: Cang Li
VP Sales/Marketing: Terry Libin
Contact: Alisha Kuzma
alisha_kuzma@mckinsey.com
Purchasing Manager: Kenny Powell
Estimated Sales: $1-3 Million
Number Employees: 10-19
Square Footage: 136000
Brands:
  Leadout
  Supraplus
  Uptaste

29002 Selig Chemical Industries
1100 Spring St NW # 550
Atlanta, GA 30309-2848
                                    404-876-5511
        Fax: 404-875-2629 www.seligenterprises.com
Disinfectants, insecticides, household cleaners,
soaps, sanitizers and polishes
President: S Stephen Selig
Chief Financial Officer: Ronald J. Stein, CPA
Co-Owner & Senior Vice President: Cathy Selig
Director Marketing: Tom Graves
Estimated Sales: $5-10 Million
Number Employees: 50-99

29003 Sellers Cleaning Systems
420 3rd St
Piqua, OH 45356-3918
                                    937-778-8947
        Fax: 937-773-2238 seller@internetMCI.com
Wine industry, sanitation processing unit
Manager: Mike Kemp
Estimated Sales: $500,000-$1 Million
Number Employees: 250-499

29004 Sellers Engineering Division
PO Box 48
Danville, KY 40423-0048
                                    859-236-3181
                        Fax: 859-236-3184
Manufacturer and exporter of boiler feed systems,
steam and hot water boilers, water heaters and
deaerators
President & Public Relations: G. Miller
CEO/CFO: S Miller
Controller: J. Sizemore
VP Research & Development: Bill Doughty
Quality Control: L Gambrel
Marketing Director: R Larson
Sales Director: R Larson
Production/Plant Manager: R Woolum
Plant Manager: R Woolum
Purchasing Manager: P Coffman
Estimated Sales: $20-50 Million
Number Employees: 78
Square Footage: 64000

Type of Packaging: Food Service
Other Locations:
  Sellers
  Dallas TX
  Weestern Engineering
  Danville KY
Brands:
  Sellers

29005 Selma Wire Products Company
County Road 700 E
Selma, IN 47383
                                    765-282-3532
                        Fax: 765-282-4428
Wire store display racks
Estimated Sales: $1-2.5 Million
Number Employees: 20-49
Parent Co: Mid-West Metal Products Company

29006 Selo
196 120th Ave # A
Holland, MI 49424-3309
                                    616-392-7849
                        Fax: 616-392-2262
Equipment for materials handling, processing,
slaughtering and temperature control
Owner: Paul Sale
Estimated Sales: $1-5 Million
Number Employees: 5-9

29007 Seltzer Chemicals
5927 Geiger Ct
Carlsbad, CA 92008
                                    760-438-0089
        Fax: 760-438-0336 800-735-8137
Wholesaler/distributor of custom blended bulk fine
chemicals, vitamin pre-mixes and colors
Executive VP: Trent Seltzer
Estimated Sales: $50-100 Million
Number Employees: 50-99
Square Footage: 60000
Type of Packaging: Bulk

29008 Semanco International
500 Clanton Road
Suite H
Charlotte, NC 28217-1310
                                    704-527-9010
                        Fax: 704-527-8290
Electronic process evaluation systems for soft drink
bottlers, bottling lines, all blended products, wine
processing, packaging lines and fruit and juices
Number Employees: 20-49

29009 Semco Manufacturing Company
705 E Us Highway 83
PO Box 1686
Pharr, TX 78577
                                    956-787-4203
        Fax: 956-781-0620 semcoice.com
Manufacturer and exporter of mobile/portable ice
plants, slush ice makers, hydro coolers, freezers and
vegetable harvesting and packing equipment
President: James Hatton
Sales Director: Jason Hatton
Contact: Raul Mora
raul@semcomfgco.com
Purchasing Manager: Rod Bradley
Estimated Sales: Below $5 Million
Number Employees: 20-49
Square Footage: 60000
Brands:
  Semco

29010 Semco Plastic Co
5301 Old Baumgartner Rd
St Louis, MO 63129-2944
                                    314-487-4557
                    www.semcoplastics.com
Manufacturer and exporter of plastic products in-
cluding drinking straws, boxes and advertising
novelties.
President: Chuck Voelkel
cvoelkel@semcoplastic.com
Year Founded: 1944
Estimated Sales: $100-500 Million
Number Employees: 100-249
Square Footage: 450000

29011 Semi-Bulk Systems Inc
159 Cassens Ct
Fenton, MO 63026-2543
                                    636-343-4500
        Fax: 636-343-2822 800-732-8769
        info@semi-bulk.com www.semi-bulk.com

Manufacturer and exporter of mixers including batch and continuous; also, dry ingredient handling interface systems
President: Jeff Doherty
CEO: Charles Attack
Chief Financial Officer: Al Moresi
Vice President: Ron Bentley
Research/Development: Iris Freidel
Controller: All Moresi
Sales/Marketing: Ronald Bentley
Public Relations: Diana McMahon
Operations/Production/Purchasing: Bernie Klipsch
Estimated Sales: $10 Million
Number Employees: 20-49
Square Footage: 220000
Brands:
　Vacucam

29012 Sencon Inc
6385 W 74th St
Chicago, IL 60638-6128
　　　　　　　　　　　　　708-496-3100
　　Fax: 708-496-3105 sales@senconinc.com
　　　　　　　　　　　www.sencon.com
Specialized control devices, sensors, and quiality instruments to the metal packaging industry; tooling protective systems, line control devices and a range of manual and automatic quality gauges
Owner: Winston Shields
Technical Manager: Ian Blackledge
Estimated Sales: $10-20 Million
Number Employees: 50-99

29013 Sencorp White
400 Kidds Hill Rd
Hyannis, MA 02601-1850
　　　　　　　　　　　　　508-771-9400
　　Fax: 508-790-0002 info@sencorpwhite.com
　　　　　　　　　　　www.sencorpwhite.com
Storage and retrieval systems, vertical and horizontal carousels, transporters, robots and power columns
CEO: Brian Urban
brian.urban@dtindustries.com
VP Operations: John Molloy
VP Marketing: Richard Frye
Estimated Sales: Less than $500,000
Number Employees: 100-249

29014 Seneca Environmental Products
Airport Industrial Park 1685 S. County
PO Box 429
Tiffin, OH 44883
　　　　　　　　　　　　　419-447-1282
　　　　　　　　　　　Fax: 419-448-4048
Manufacturer and exporter of sanitary type dust collectors including stainless steel, carbon steel, reverse jet, cartridge, cyclone, shaker and cylindrical; also, noise pollution control equipment, miscellaneous sanitary and steelfabrication
President: C Harple
Sales Manager: Don Harple
Estimated Sales: $1-3 Million
Number Employees: 20-49
Square Footage: 100000

29015 Seneca Tape & Label
13821 Progress Pkwy
Cleveland, OH 44133-4398
　　　　　　　　　　　　　440-237-1600
　　Fax: 440-237-0427 800-251-0514
　　sales@senecalabel.com www.senecalabel.com
Pressure sensitive labels
Vice President: Paul Macmorob
pmacmurdo@senecalabel.com
VP Finance: John Hoopingarner
Estimated Sales: $2.5-5 Million
Number Employees: 50-99

29016 Senior Flexonics
300 E Devon Ave
Bartlett, IL 60103-4608
　　　　　　　　　　　　　630-837-1811
　　Fax: 630-837-2672 800-473-0474
　　　　　　　　　　　www.seniorflexonics.com
Deep fryer hoses and filters
President: John Divine
Sales Manager: Gerry Blanchet
Contact: Robert Chambers
robertc@flexonics.com
Estimated Sales: $5-10,000,000
Number Employees: 10-19
Parent Co: Senior Flexonics

Brands:
　Filter-Master
　Fryer Pro

29017 (HQ)Senior Housing Options Inc
1510 17th St
Denver, CO 80202-1202
　　　　　　　　　　　　　303-595-4464
　　Fax: 303-595-9225 800-659-2656
　　　info@seniorhousingoptions.org
　　　www.seniorhousingoptions.org
Plain and printed plastic bags; also, plastic film
President: James A. Roberts
Controller: Vicky Campbell
Vice-President: Teri Romero
Quality Assurance Director: Jennifer Marcols
Estimated Sales: Less Than $500,000
Number Employees: 5-9

29018 Senomyx Inc
4767 Nexus Center Dr
San Diego, CA 92121-3051
　　　　　　　　　　　　　858-646-8300
　　　　　　　　　　　Fax: 858-404-0752
Flavor ingredients.
President/CEO: John Poyhonen
john.poyhonen@senomyx.com
CFO/SVP: Tony Rogers
VP/General Counsel/Corporate Secretary: Catherine Lee
SVP/Chief Commercial Development Officer: Sharon Wicker
VP, Information Technology: Lorenzo Pena
Estimated Sales: $28 Million
Number Employees: 50-99
Number of Brands: 3
Brands:
　Bittermyx®
　Savorymyx®
　Sweetmyx®

29019 Sensaphone
901 Tryens Rd
Aston, PA 19014-1522
　　　　　　　　　　　　　610-558-2700
　　Fax: 610-558-0222 877-373-2700
　　sales@sensaphone.com www.sensaphone.com
Wine industry security systems
President: Kenneth E Blanchard
VP Marketing/Sales: Mary Ellen Gomeau
Vice President of Sales and Marketing: Bob Douglass
Manager: Brook Abboud
babboud@sensaphone.com
Estimated Sales: $5-10 Million
Number Employees: 1-4
Square Footage: 60000

29020 Sensidyne
1000 112th Circle North
Suite 100
St. Petersburg, FL 33716
　　　　　　　　　　　　　727-530-3602
　　Fax: 727-539-0550 800-451-9444
　　info@sensidyne.com www.sensidyne.com
Manufacturer and exporter of gas detection and air sampling systems
President: Howie Mills
VP: Glenn Warr
Quality Control: George Mason
Marketing: Mary Slattery
National Sales Manager: Gary Queensberry
Contact: Mabie Eggleston
meggleston@sensidyne.com
Estimated Sales: $10-20 Million
Number Employees: 50-99

29021 Sensient Colors Inc
2515 N Jefferson Ave
St Louis, MO 63106-1939
　　　　　　　　　　　　　314-889-7600
　　Fax: 314-658-7318 800-325-8110
　　　foodcolors.stl@sensient.com
　　　www.sensientfoodcolors.com
Global food and beverage color manufacturer.
President, Color Group: Michael Geraghty
Parent Co: Sensient Technologies Corporation
Type of Packaging: Consumer, Food Service, Private Label, Bulk

29022 Sensient Flavors and Fragrances
2800 W Higgins Road
Suite 900
Hoffman Estates, IL 60169
　　　　　　　　　　　　　847-755-5300
　　　　　　　　　　　Fax: 847-755-5350
　　corporate.communications@sensient.com
　　　www.sensientflavorsandfragrances.com
Flavoring extracts and syrups.
President, Flavors & Fragrances Group: E. Craig Mitchell
Estimated Sales: $100-200 Million
Number Employees: 1,000-4,999
Parent Co: Sensient Technologies Corporation

29023 Sensitech
P.O.Box 599
Redmond, WA 98073-0599
　　　　　　　　　　　　　425-883-7926
　　Fax: 425-883-3766 800-999-7926
　　info@sensitech.com www.sensitech.com
Temperature and humidity measurement in food and beverages
Manager: Mike Hanson
Contact: Andy Englehardt
a.englehardt@sensitech.com
Estimated Sales: $10-25 Million
Number Employees: 50-99
Parent Co: Sensitech

29024 Sensitech Inc
8801 148th Ave NE
P.O.Box 599
Redmond, WA 98052-3492
　　　　　　　　　　　　　425-883-7926
　　Fax: 425-883-3766 800-999-7926
　　　　　　　　　　　www.sensitech.com
Manufacturer and exporter of time/temperature and humidity monitors for perishable commodities in transit, storage or processing
Manager: Mike Hanson
CFO: Mike Hurton
Senior Director of Quality Assurance: Dave Ray
Director Marketing: Susan Milant
VP Sales: Dan Vache
Estimated Sales: $10-20 Million
Number Employees: 50-99

29025 Sensitech Inc
800 Cummings Ctr
Suite 258X
Beverly, MA 01915
　　　　　　　　　　　　　978-927-7033
　　　　　　　　　　　　　800-843-8367
　　info@sensitech.com www.sensitech.com
Temperature monitoring systems and electronic temperature monitors and recorders for perishable products; also, hand-held HACCP compliance systems.
President: Mike Hurton
mike.hurton@sensitech.com
Director of Quality: Dave Ray
VP, Global Marketing & Communications: Elizabeth Darragh
VP, Product Development & Operations: Scott Hubley
Estimated Sales: $100 Million
Number Employees: 1000-4999
Square Footage: 6000
Brands:
　Quickcheck
　Temptale
　Temptale 2
　Temptale 3
　Temptale 4

29026 Sensor Systems
8929 Fullbright Ave
Chatsworth, CA 91311-6179
　　　　　　　　　　　　　818-341-5366
　　Fax: 818-341-9059 info@sensorantennas.com
　　　　　　　　　　　www.sensorantennas.com
Moisture measurement and control instrumentation
President: Mayra Alatorre
mayra_alatorre@med3000.com
Director of Sales and Marketing: Mike Crow
Estimated Sales: $1-2.5 Million
Number Employees: 100-249

29027 Sensors Quality Management
156 Duncan Mill Road
Suite 19
Toronto, ON M3B 3N2
Canada

416-444-4491
Fax: 416-444-2422 800-866-2624
sqm@sqm.ca www.sqm.ca

Consultant specializing in the evaluation of company operations including quality assurance, competition analysis, integrity inspections, training programs, research and surveys, marketing, promotions, etc
President: David Lipton
VP: Craig Henry
VP: Craig Henry
Number Employees: 10

29028 Sensory Computer Systems
144 Summit Avenue
Berkeley Heights, NJ 7922

908-665-6464
Fax: 908-665-6493 800-579-7654
johnream@sensorysims.com
www.sensorysims.com

Sensory testing and market research software used for laboratory, central location and point-of-sale testing of consumer survey data
Director: John Ream
Contact: Francois Abiven
f.abiven@reperes.net
Account Manager of Logistics, Chief Oper: Elena Keegan
Estimated Sales: $500,000-$1 Million
Number Employees: 5-9

29029 Sensory Spectrum
554 Central Ave
New Providence, NJ 07974-1555

908-376-7000
Fax: 908-376-7040
spectrum@sensoryspectrum.com
www.sensoryspectrum.com

Consultant specializing in sensory evaluation techniques applied to the understanding of consumer products through descriptive analysis, advanced sensory methodology, qualitative and quantitative consumer research, experimentaldesign, etc
President: Gail Vance-Civille
gvciville@sensoryspectrum.com
Marketing Executive: Emily Engler
Sales Executive: Marie Rudolph
Estimated Sales: $5-10 Million
Number Employees: 20-49

29030 Sentinel Lubricants Inc
15755 NW 15th Ave
PO Box 694240
Miami, FL 33169-5651

305-625-6400
Fax: 305-625-6565 800-842-6400
info@sentinelsynthetic.com
www.sentinelsynthetic.com

Manufacturer and exporter of food grade synthetic lubricants including nontoxic oil and grease
CEO: R Chaban
VP: J C Barroso
Research & Development: Charles Clay
Quality Control: Phil Sauder
Marketing Director: Emile Freidman
Sales: Raul Oquendo
Public Relations: Marta Garcia
Operations Manager: Randye Chaban
Production Manager: Juanillo Barroso
Plant Manager: Philip Sauder
Purchasing Manager: Martha Garcia
Estimated Sales: $18 Million
Number Employees: 10-19
Number of Brands: 200
Number of Products: 400
Square Footage: 50000
Type of Packaging: Consumer, Private Label
Brands:
  Biosyn
  Sentinel
  Sentishield
  Sl Nt

29031 Sentinel Polyolefins
P.O.Box 355
West Hyannisport, MA 02672-0355

508-775-5220
Fax: 508-771-1554 800-457-3234

Crosslinked polyethylene foam and specialty elastomers for packaging applications including multi-density lamination for end-caps packaging
Estimated Sales: $1-3 Million
Number Employees: 1-4

29032 Sentron
7117 Stinson Ave # C
Gig Harbor, WA 98335-4902

253-851-7881
Fax: 253-851-7899 800-472-4361
www.sentron.ca

Nonglass, ion sensitive field effect transistor(ISFET) and pH measurement equipment
Marketing: Eric Amundson
Technical Sales Manager: Eric Amundson
Number Employees: 5-9
Square Footage: 24000
Other Locations:
  Sentron
  9300 AC Roden
Brands:
  Sentron

29033 Sentry Equipment Corp
966 Blue Ribbon Cir N
Oconomowoc, WI 53066-8666

262-567-7256
Fax: 262-567-4523 sales@sentry-equip.com
www.sentry-equip.com

Manufacturer and exporter of sanitary samplers for milk, cream, whey, orange juice, viscous food products, wastewater liquids and slurries
President: Michael Farrell
CEO: John Hazlehurst
john_h@sentryequipment.com
Marketing Director: Lynn Castrodale
Sales Director: Doris Hoeft
Number Employees: 100-249
Brands:
  Isolok

29034 Sentry Equipment/Erectors Inc
13150 E Lynchburg Salem Tpke
Forest, VA 24551-4328

434-525-0769
Fax: 434-525-1701 sales@sentryequipment.com
www.sentryequipment.com

Conveyor belts and equipment
President: Adam Vinoskey
Estimated Sales: $50-100 Million
Number Employees: 250-499

29035 Sentry/Bevcon North America
16630 Koala Road
PO Box 578
Adelanto, CA 92301-0578

800-854-1177
Fax: 760-246-4044 800-661-3003
sales@ici.us www.ici.us

Manufacturer and exporter of portable bars and dispensers including soda, juice, coffee, liquor and beer
President: Joe Suarez
Quality Control: Jerry Wheeler
R & D: Jerry Wheeler
Marketing: Ken Wogberg
Sales: Amber Micham
Public Relations: Ken Wogberg
Technical Support: Jerry Wheeler
President: Joe Suarez
Number Employees: 35
Square Footage: 224000
Parent Co: International Carbonic
Type of Packaging: Consumer, Food Service, Private Label
Brands:
  Bevcon
  Ici

29036 Separators Inc
5707 W Minnesota St
Indianapolis, IN 46241-3825

317-484-3745
Fax: 317-484-3755 800-233-9022
separate@sepinc.com www.separatorsinc.com

Leader in the sale and repair of reconditioned centrifuges.
President/CEO: Joe Campbell
COO/CFO: Joe Mansfield
Director of Manufacturing: Dan Goss
Estimated Sales: $10-20 Million
Number Employees: 20-49
Square Footage: 60000

29037 Sepragen Corp
1205 San Luis Obispo St
Hayward, CA 94544-7915

510-475-0650
Fax: 510-475-0625 info@sepragen.com
www.sepragen.com

Manufacturer and exporter of process control systems and instruments and separation machinery for the dairy industry
CEO/ CTO: Vinit Saxena
CFO: Henry Edmunds
Director Quality & Tech Support: Salah Ahmed
Number Employees: 20-49

29038 Septimatech Group
106 Randall Drive
Waterloo, ON N2V 1K5
Canada

519-746-7463
Fax: 519-746-3464 888-777-6775
sales@septimatech.com www.septimatech.com

Septimatech is the total solution provider in line changeover products, innovation, services, research and development. Specializing in Quick Change Tooling solutions, Customer Container Handling solutions and enhancements, andproviding RXNT®, Unison® Guide Rails, and OEM parts.
President & CEO: Sharron Gilbert
VP Engineering/Innovation: Glenn Bell
VP Marketing/Sales/Service: Gord Beaton
VP Manufacturing/Quality: Quinn Martin
Number Employees: 50-99
Number of Brands: 2

29039 Septipack
2313 Benson Mill Rd
Sparks Glencoe, MD 21152-9420

410-472-2575
Fax: 410-771-1528

Aseptic packaging systems
President: Herve Franceschi
Estimated Sales: $300,000-500,000
Number Employees: 1-4

29040 Sequa Can Machinery
6949 S Potomac St
Englewood, CO 80112

Fax: 201-933-9029

Machinery for the 2-piece can industry: cuppers, rutherford decorators and base coaters, can industry products tooled, cuppers, shell presses and DRD systems and FM&S replacement parts
President: Gus Reall
CFO: Bob Mayone
Quality Control: John Agar
Number Employees: 175

29041 Sequoia Pacific
20940 Avenue 296
Exeter, CA 93221-9713

559-562-3726
Fax: 415-442-0563

Wine industry, label printing
Chairman: James Matthews
CEO: Michael Marino
CFO: Ruth Damsker
Estimated Sales: $20-50 Million
Number Employees: 1-4

29042 SerVend International
2100 Future Drive
Sellersburg, IN 47172-1868

812-246-7000
Fax: 812-246-9922 800-367-4233
www.servend.com

Manufacturer and exporter of ice makers, beverage, cup and ice dispensers, ice storage bins and beverage dispensing valves
CEO: Terry Growcock
VP Sales/Marketing: Lonnie Shafer
Director Marketing: Elaine Momson
Contact: Greg Gummere
greg.gummere@manitowoc.com
Estimated Sales: $20-30 Million
Number Employees: 250
Square Footage: 155000
Parent Co: Manitowoc Foodservice Group
Other Locations:
  SerVend International
  Clackamas OR
Brands:
  Flomatic
  Servend

29043 Serac Inc
300 S Westgate Dr
Carol Stream, IL 60188-2243

630-510-9343
Fax: 630-510-9357 serac@serac-usa.com
www.serac-inc.com
Filling and packaging machinery
President: Christopher Lebraun
Manager: Ron Ercolani
rone@serac-usa.com
Number Employees: 20-49

29044 (HQ)Serfilco
2900 Macarthur Blvd
Northbrook, IL 60062-2007

847-509-2900
Fax: 847-559-1995 800-323-5431
sales@serfilco.com www.serfilco.com
Designs, manufactures and markets a broad line of
corrosion resistant high performance pumps, agita-
tors, filtration systems and instruments.
President: James Berg
jamesb@serfilco.com
Marketing: Chuck Schultz
Operations: Mike Berg
Production Manager: Jerry Swooda
Estimated Sales: $10-20 Million
Number Employees: 20-49
Other Locations:
Serfilco Ltd.
Lancaster PA
Brands:
Guardian
Space'saver
Titan '90

29045 Sergeant E M Pulp & Chem Co
66 Brighton Rd
Clifton, NJ 07012-1600

973-472-9111
Fax: 973-472-5686 www.sergeantchem.com
President: A Reisch
Estimated Sales: $10-20 Million
Number Employees: 5-9

29046 Sermatech ISPA
12505 Reed Rd., #100
Sugar Land, TX 77478-2876

410-644-4500
Fax: 410-644-1766 800-882-4772
Applicator of nonstick coatings for food processing
and handling equipment including mixers, enrobers,
chutes, dryers, etc
Owner: Ron Kaufmann
VP: Scott Vogt
Sales Director: Paul Kellogg
Sales: Rob Aldave
Purchasing Manager: Wes Prince
Estimated Sales: $10-20 Million
Number Employees: 20-49
Square Footage: 140000
Parent Co: Sermatech International
Brands:
Fluoroshield-Magna
Teflon

29047 Sermia International
100-742 Boulevard Industrial
Blainville, QC J7C 3V4
Canada

450-433-7483
Fax: 450-433-7484 800-567-7483
info@sermia.com www.sermia.com
Manufacturer and exporter of filters for liquids
Number Employees: 10
Brands:
Sermia

29048 Serpa Packaging Solutions
7020 W Sunnyview Ave
Visalia, CA 93291-9639

559-651-2339
Fax: 559-651-2345 800-348-5453
sales@serpapackaging.com www.serpapkg.com
Manufacturer and exporter of cartoners and case
packers and erectors; also, custom designs and turn-
key applications available
President/CEO: Fernando M Serpa
fsepra@serpapackaging.com
Director Of Marketing: Rich James
Estimated Sales: $10,000,000
Number Employees: 50-99
Square Footage: 92000

29049 Serr-Edge Machine Company
4471 W 160th St
Cleveland, Cl 44135-2625

216-267-6333
Fax: 216-267-2929 800-443-8097
Manufacturer and exporter of industrial and com-
mercial sharpening machines for scissors, knives
and shears
President: Linda Ribar Oakley
Owner: Matthew Oakley
Estimated Sales: Below $5 Million
Number Employees: 5-9
Brands:
Easisharp
Keenedge
Tru-Hone

29050 Sertapak Packaging Corporation
PO Box 1500
Woodstock, ON N4S 8R2
Canada

519-539-3330
Fax: 519-539-4499 800-265-1162
Manufacturer and exporter of returnable and ex-
pandable packaging systems, containers, pallets and
sealed edge plastic corrugated slip sheets
President: C J David Nettleton
CEO: Alison Clarke
CFO: Bruce Orr
Number Employees: 10
Brands:
Rak Pak
Sertote

29051 Serti Information Solution
7555, Beclard Street
Montreal, QC H1J 2S5
Canada

514-493-1909
Fax: 514-493-3575 800-361-6615
info@serti.com www.serti.com
Consulting services providing software and solu-
tions for a solid foundation on completing-achieving
all your information technology projects
President: LOUIS LAPORTE
Vice-President, finance & operations: MAURICE
LANTHIER
Vice-President, IT Consulting Services: ODILE
PATRY
Vice-President, Business Development: FRANCIS
GINGRAS

29052 (HQ)Servco Equipment Co
3189 Jamieson Ave
St Louis, MO 63139-2519

314-781-3189
Fax: 314-645-7003 www.servco-stl.com
Manufacturer and exporter of conveyors and under
and back bar refrigerators
President: Earl Gates Jr
Sales Exec: Helen Gage
Estimated Sales: $5-10 Million
Number Employees: 20-49
Square Footage: 112000
Brands:
Gates
Servco

29053 Server Products Inc
3601 Pleasant Hill Rd
PO Box 98
Richfield, WI 53076-9417

262-628-5100
Fax: 262-628-5110 800-558-8722
spsales@server-products.com
www.server-products.com
Manufacturer and exporter of small pumps, food dis-
pensers and warmers, bars and accessories, rails and
pizza ovens
President: Chris Falkner
spsales@server-products.com
VP Sales: Ron Ripple
VP Production: Carol Miller
Estimated Sales: $10-20 Million
Number Employees: 50-99
Square Footage: 250000

29054 Service Brass & AluminumFittings
190 N Wiget Lane
Suite 202
Walnut Creek, CA 94598-2440

925-977-8320
Fax: 925-256-0318

Wine industry, hose fittings
Estimated Sales: Under$500,000
Number Employees: 25-49

29055 Service Ideas
2354 Ventura Dr
Woodbury, MN 55125-4403

651-730-8800
Fax: 651-730-8880 800-328-4493
sales@serviceideas.com www.serviceideas.com
Manufacturer, importer and exporter of insulated
serving plates, beverage servers, dispensers, pitchers
and buffet bowls
President: Christina Brandt
laura@serviceideas.com
VP & HR Manager: Megan Blohowiak
Foodservice Sales Director: Andy Krawczyk
Site Manager: Laura Bjorkman
laura@serviceideas.com
Operations Director: Mark Bolowiak
Estimated Sales: $10-20 Million
Number Employees: 20-49
Square Footage: 80000
Brands:
Aero-Serv
Brew'n'pour Lid
Eco-Serv
Magnetag
Metallic Luster
New Generation
Sculptured Ice
Thermo-Plate
Thermo-Serv
Thermo-Serv Sculptured Ice

29056 Service Manufacturing
1601 Mountain St
Aurora, IL 60505-2402

630-898-1394
Fax: 630-898-7800 888-325-2788
tvickers@theramp.net www.rocktenn.com
Manufacturer, importer and exporter of custom
packaging products including insulated coolers,
cases and bags
President: Camerina Torres
Vice President: David Goodman
Marketing/Sales: Matthew Sheridan
Plant Manager: Octavio Serrano
Purchasing Manager: Clarence Eisernman
Estimated Sales: $10-20 Million
Number Employees: 10-19
Square Footage: 376000
Type of Packaging: Bulk
Brands:
Service Manufacturing
Sun Valley

29057 Service Master Co LLC
150 Peabody Place
Memphis, TN 38103

888-937-3783
www.servicemaster.com
Facilities management, plant operations and mainte-
nance, ground and landscaping management, custo-
dial services, energy management.
Interim CEO & Chair: Naren Gursahaney
SVP & Chief Financial Officer: Anthony DiLucente
SVP & Chief Transformation Officer: Pratip
Dastidar
SVP, Business Development: Dion Persson
Chief Human Resources Officer: David Dart
Year Founded: 1929
Estimated Sales: $2.59 Billion
Number Employees: 13,000

29058 Service Neon Signs
6611 Iron Pl
Springfield, VA 22151

703-354-3000
Fax: 703-354-5810 info@snsigns.org
www.snsigns.org
Neon, plastic and aluminum on-site identification
signs
CEO: Mark Luxenburg
VP/General Manager: Robert Gray
Sales: George Marino, Jr.
Plant Manager: Jack Evans
Purchasing Manager: Mike Volpe
Estimated Sales: $5-10 Million
Number Employees: 50-99
Square Footage: 150000

29059 Service Sales Corporation
390 Richmond St E
South St Paul, MN 55075-5939
651-451-2206
Fax: 651-451-2710 800-225-6128
Wholesaler/distributor of labels, price marking equipment, bar code printers and thermal supplies
President: Rob Iten
Estimated Sales: $5-10 Million
Number Employees: 10-19
Square Footage: 56000

29060 Service Stamp Works
1227 W Jackson Boulevard
Chicago, IL 60607-2895
312-666-8839
Fax: 312-666-4167 marionk@hsonline.net
Rubber stamps, printing plates and food inks
Operations Manager: Peter Haack
Estimated Sales: $500,000-$1 Million
Number Employees: 5-9

29061 Service Tool International
39 S La Salle St
Suite 1410
Chicago, IL 60603
847-439-7000
Fax: 847-439-7009
Easy-open conversion systems, shell manufacturing systems, and integrated manufacturing lines for ends, shells, or EOE; partial product list: carbide scroll dies, tab dies, lane dies, single, double and multi-dies, beader tooling, andcurler tooling
President: Loren Scheel
CEO: John Tensland
R & D: Just Klingel
Quality Control: Mike Fries
Estimated Sales: $10-20 Million
Number Employees: 20-49

29062 Servin Company
51518 Industrial Dr
Suite E
New Baltimore, MI 48047
586-725-5571
Fax: 586-725-5573 800-824-0962
www.information.com
Reusable coated nylon bags
VP: Charles Clandinen
Sales Manager: Charles Clendinen
Estimated Sales: $.5-1 million
Number Employees: 5-9

29063 Servomex
525 Julie Rivers Dr # 185
Sugar Land, TX 77478-2845
281-295-5800
Fax: 281-295-5899 800-862-0200
www.servomex.com
Servomex food pack analyzers offer simple, fast and accurate analysis of oxygen and carbon dioxide in soft packages or rigid containers
VP: Claire Lucarino
Marketing: Jane Hammond
Sales: Susan Harris
Contact: Brian Anderson
banderson@servomex.com
Plant Manager: Ed Arestie
Purchasing Director: Jon Pryer
Estimated Sales: $10-20 Million
Number Employees: 20-49
Brands:
  1450 Food Pack Analyzer
  574 Portable Oxygen Analyzer

29064 Servomex Inc
4 Constitution Way # I
Woburn, MA 01801-1042
281-295-5800
Fax: 781-938-0531 800-433-2552
americas_sales@servomex.com
www.servomex.com
Oxygen and carbondioxide CAP/MAP analyzers
Estimated Sales: $10-20 Million
Number Employees: 20-49

29065 Servpak Corp
5844 Dawson St
Hollywood, FL 33023-1910
954-962-4262
Fax: 954-962-5776 800-782-0840
www.serv-pak.com

Manufacturer and exporter table-topheat seal packaging machinery forrigid and semi rigid trays covered by pre-cut lids or lid film on a roll
Owner: Joel Mahler
Estimated Sales: Less than $500,000
Number Employees: 10-19
Square Footage: 4000

29066 Sesame Label System
1501 Third Ave
New York, NY 10028
212-989-3020
Fax: 212-989-3021 800-551-3020
Labels, decals and name plates; also, custom printing available
Purchasing: Tony Jackson
Estimated Sales: $2.5-5 Million
Number Employees: 10
Square Footage: 4000

29067 Sessions Co Inc
801 N Main St
Enterprise, AL 36330-9108
334-393-0200
Fax: 334-393-0240
CEO: H Moultrie Sessions Jr
CFO: Jeff Outlaw
sesscom@frost.snowhill.com
Estimated Sales: $2.5-5 Million
Number Employees: 50-99

29068 Set Point Paper Company
31 Oxford Rd
Mansfield, MA 02048-1126
508-339-0700
Fax: 508-339-9929 800-225-0501
Food containers, cups, specialty bags and folding cartons
Manager: Elizabeth Dudley
VP: Michael Keneally
VP: Richard Madigan Jr
Estimated Sales: $300,000-500,000
Number Employees: 1-4
Square Footage: 250000
Brands:
  Smart Cup
  Smart Seal

29069 Setaram/SFIM
210 Lakeview St
Grand Prairie, TX 75051-4998
972-262-4900
Fax: 972-641-3711
sales@stormlawnandgarden.com
www.stormlawnandgarden.com
Thermal analysis instrumentation for fats, liquids, etc
Owner: R L Storm
Estimated Sales: $2.5-5 Million
Number Employees: 5-9

29070 Setco
34 Engelhard Dr
Monroe Twp, NJ 08831
609-655-4600
Fax: 609-655-0225 www.setco.com
Manufacturer and exporter of plastic bottles
Contact: Bob Loftus
bobl@setcousa.com
Plant Manager: Ray Agondo
Estimated Sales: $50-100 Million
Number Employees: 250-500
Parent Co: APL Company

29071 Setco
P.O.Box 68008
Anaheim, CA 92817-0808
714-777-5200
Fax: 714-777-5355
Stock and custom plastic bottles
President: Don Parodi
VP Sales/Marketing: Thomas Dunn
Estimated Sales: $1-5 Million
Number Employees: 250-499
Parent Co: McCormick & Company
Other Locations:
  Setco
  Monroe Township NJ

29072 Seton Indentification Products
20 Thompson Rd
PO Box 819
Branford, CT 06405-2842
203-488-8059
Fax: 203-488-5973 800-571-2596
seton_mailroom@seton.com www.seton.com
Signs, tags, labels, identification and safety products
Cmo: Dave Giroux
dave_giroux@seton.com
Manager: Pascal Deman
Estimated Sales: Less than $500,000
Number Employees: 250-499
Brands:
  Set Mark

29073 Setter, Leach & Lindstrom
730 2nd Ave S # 1100
Minneapolis, MN 55402-2455
612-338-8741
Fax: 612-338-4840 www.leoadaly.com
Consultant specializing in design and project management of food distribution centers
President: Bob Egge
Chairman: Leo Daly
Vice President: Charles Dalluge
Estimated Sales: $20-50 Million
Number Employees: 100-249

29074 Setterstix Corp
261 S Main St
Cattaraugus, NY 14719-1312
716-257-3451
Fax: 716-257-9818 nan@setterstix.com
Manufacturer and exporter of rolled paper sticks for the confectionery industry
President: Paul Elly
pelly@setterstix.com
CFO: Ron Wasmund
Sales: Nan Mikowicz
Plant Manager: Eric Pritchard
Estimated Sales: $10-15 Million
Number Employees: 50-99
Square Footage: 60000
Parent Co: Knox Industries
Brands:
  Setterstix

29075 Seven B Plus
46161 SE Wildcat Mountain Dr
Sandy, OR 97055
503-668-5079
Fax: 503-668-6347
Smokers

29076 Seven Mile Creek Corp
315 S Beech St
Eaton, OH 45320-2311
937-456-3320
Fax: 937-456-3320 800-497-6324
sevenmile@voyager.net www.sevenmilecreek.com
Industrial and promotional aprons; also, silk screening available
President: William Cressell
sevenmile@voyager.net
Estimated Sales: Less Than $500,000
Number Employees: 5-9
Square Footage: 80000

29077 Severn Newtrent
2660 Columbia St
Torrance, CA 90503-3802
310-618-9700
Fax: 310-618-1384 800-777-6939
www.severntrentservices.com
Manufactures machines and equipment for use in service industries, water purification systems
President, Chief Executive Officer: Martin Kane
VP: Marwan Nesicolaci
Contact: Chad Dannemann
cdannemann@severntrentservices.com
Estimated Sales: $10-20 Million
Number Employees: 100-249

29078 Severn Trent Svc
3000 Advance Ln
Colmar, PA 18915-9432
215-822-2901
Fax: 215-997-4062
marketing@capitalcontrols.com
www.severntrentservices.com

Manufacturer and exporter of water treatment systems including chlorinators, ultraviolet sterilization systems, pH/orp monitors and chlorine, ammonia and fluoride residue analyzers
President, Chief Executive Officer: Martin Kane
Marketing Manager: Anne Penkal
Plant Manager: Jeff Dohnam
Estimated Sales: $20-50 Million
Number Employees: 100-249

29079 (HQ)Severn Trent Svc
580 Virginia Dr # 300
Suite 300
Fort Washington, PA 19034-2723
    215-646-9201
    Fax: 215-283-3487 www.severntrentservices.com
Supplier of water and wastewater treatment solutions
President/CEO: Martin Kane
Senior VP/CFO: Stephane Bouvier
VP Marketing/Business Development: Thomas Mills
Contact: Rick Bacon
rbacon@severntrentservices.com
Operations Director: Alex Lloyd
Estimated Sales: Less Than $500,000
Number Employees: 1-4

29080 Seville Display Door
27495 Diaz Road
Temecula, CA 92590-3414
    951-676-6161
    Fax: 951-676-7728 800-634-0412
Glass refrigerator and PVC sliding doors
Owner: Randy Fitzpatrick
Estimated Sales: $2.5-5 Million
Number Employees: 10-19
Square Footage: 120000

29081 (HQ)Seville Flexpack Corp
9905 S Ridgeview Dr
Oak Creek, WI 53154-5556
    414-761-2751
Fax: 414-761-3140 kskempk@sevilleflexpack.com
    www.sevilleflexpack.com
Manufacturer and exporter of flexible packaging materials, stand-up pouches and cold seal coatings
President: Jan Drzewiecki
Director Sales: Jay Yakich
VP Manufacturing: James Yakich
Estimated Sales: $20-50 million
Number Employees: 50-99
Square Footage: 12000000
Other Locations:
   Seville Flexpack Corp.
   Waco TX
Brands:
   Fastseal
   Flexfilm
   Hide-A-Winner
   Up-Right

29082 Seville Flexpack Corp
9905 S Ridgeview Dr
Oak Creek, WI 53154-5556
    414-761-2751
    Fax: 414-761-3140
    kskempka@sevilleflexpack.com
Flexible packages, packaging materials
President: Jan Drzewiecki
CFO: Cris Mercener
VP: Jim Yakich
VP Marketing and Sales: Jay Yakich
Marketing Manager: Mark Hoffman
Sales Manager: J Yakich
Operations Manager: Jim Yakich
Production Manager: Dave Gras
Purchasing Manager: Roger Kline
Estimated Sales: $20-50 Million
Number Employees: 50-99
Parent Co: Seville Flexpack Corporation

29083 Sew-Eurodrive Inc
1295 Old Spartanburg Hwy
P.O. Box 518
Lyman, SC 29365
    864-439-8792
    Fax: 864-949-3039 www.seweurodrive.com
Manufacturer and exporter of drives, motors and accessories.
Chief Executive Officer: Juegon Blickle
Marketing Communications/Tradeshow Mgr.:
JoAnn Greenup
Year Founded: 1931
Estimated Sales: $100-500 Million

Number Employees: 250-499
Square Footage: 250000
Brands:
   Movidrive
   Movidyn
   Movimot
   Movitrac
   Snuggler

29084 Sexton Sign
PO Box 5555
Anderson, SC 29623-5555
    864-226-6071
    Fax: 864-226-4074
Commercial electric signs
Estimated Sales: $1-5 Million

29085 Seymour Housewares
885 N Chestnut St
Seymour, IN 47274
    812-522-5130
    Fax: 812-522-5294 800-457-9881
Shopping carts, ironing tables, pad and cover sets and laundry products
President: Norman Proulx
Director Marketing: Kurt Tyler
VP Sales: Tony Taggart
Estimated Sales: $20-50 Million
Number Employees: 100-249

29086 Seymour Woodenware Company
522 Seymour St
Seymour, WI 54165
    920-833-6551
    Fax: 920-833-7698 qadamski@new.rr.com
Wooden boxes and baskets including cheese, wine, coffee, gift, veneer, etc
President: Quintin J Adamski
qadamski@new.rr.com
General Manager: Steven Adamski
Estimated Sales: $1-2.5 Million
Number Employees: 10-19
Square Footage: 50000

29087 Sfb Plastics Inc
1819 W Harry St
P.O.Box 533
Wichita, KS 67213-3243
    316-262-0400
    Fax: 316-712-0112 800-343-8133
sales@sfbplastics.com www.sfbplastics.com
Manufacturer and exporter of polyethylene air flow separators, pallets, pallet equipment and industrial blow molded plastic containers
President: David Long
dlong@sfbplastics.com
Quality Control: Debbie Speven
Marketing: John Fosse
Sales: John Fosse
Estimated Sales: $10-20 Million
Number Employees: 50-99
Square Footage: 168000

29088 Shadetree Canopies
6317 Busch Blvd
Columbus, OH 43229-1864
    614-844-5990
    Fax: 614-844-5991 800-894-3801
    www.shadetreecanopies.com
Manufacturer and exporter of retractable awnings
Owner: Colin Leveque
CFO: Richard O Keith
Quality Control: Ken Wagner
VP Marketing: Dwayne Williams
Sales: Don Preston
Estimated Sales: $2.5-5 Million
Number Employees: 10-19
Parent Co: Certain Teed
Brands:
   Shade Tree

29089 Shae Industries
PO Box 1268
Healdsburg, CA 95448-1268
    707-431-2337
    Fax: 707-431-8060
Manufacuring quality stainless steel products for the winery, microbrewery and dairy industries
Owner: Darrell Beer
Estimated Sales: Less Than $500,000
Number Employees: 1-4

29090 Shafer Commercial Seating
4101 East 48th Ave
Denver, CO 80216
    303-322-7792
    Fax: 303-393-1836
Manufacturer and exporter of booths, chairs, cushions, pads, stools and tables including legs and bases
President: Randall Shafer
CFO: Dick Gish
CEO: Richard Gish
R & D: Dennis Trutcman
Marketing Director: Richard Howard
Contact: Darren Lingle
dalin@shafer.com
Purchasing Manager: Carla Rembolt
Estimated Sales: $18 Million
Number Employees: 100-249
Type of Packaging: Food Service

29091 Shaffer Sports & Events
601 W 6th Street
Houston, TX 77007
    713-699-0088
    Fax: 713-426-1672 shaffers@coshocton.com
    www.shaffersports.com
Commercial awnings
Manager: Robert Hamilton
Contact: Dion Baccus
baccusd@shaffersports.com
Estimated Sales: $1-5 Million
Number Employees: 20-49

29092 Shah Trading Company
3451 McNicoll Avenue
Scarborough, ON M1V 2V3
Canada
    416-292-6927
    Fax: 416-292-7932 info@shahtrading.com
    www.shahtrading.com
Rice, spices, beans, peas, and lentils, specialty flours and nuts and dried fruits.
Other Locations:
   Pulse and Canning Plant
   Scarborough ON
   Rice Plant
   Scarborough ON
Brands:
   Dunya Harvest

29093 Shambaugh & Son
7614 Opportunity Dr
Fort Wayne, IN 46825
    260-487-7777
    Fax: 260-487-7701 www.shambaugh.com
Construction/engineering services for industrial, commercial and institutional industries.
Chief Executive Officer: Paul Meyers, Jr.
Chief Financial Officer: Mark Veerkamp
Vice President & Controller: Thomas Scare
Senior Vice President & General Counsel: William Meyer
Corporate Safety Director: Thomas O'Connor, Jr.
Senior Vice President: Jeffrey Johns
Chief Operating Officer: Robert Vincent
Year Founded: 1926
Estimated Sales: $100-250 Million
Number Employees: 1000-4999
Square Footage: 100000
Parent Co: EMCOR Group, Inc.

29094 Shammi Industries
390 Meyer Cir # A
Corona, CA 92879-6617
    951-340-3419
    Fax: 951-340-2716 800-417-9260
    info@sammonsequipment.com
    www.sammonsequipment.com
Manufacturer, importer and exporter of banquet and transport equipment including carts, heated cabinets, racks, tables, dollies and shelving
President: Dani Pollard
traci@curryelectric.com
Estimated Sales: $1-2.5 Million
Number Employees: 10-19
Square Footage: 42000
Brands:
   Queen Mary's
   Samco

29095 (HQ)Shamrock Foods Co
3900 E. Camelback Rd.
Suite 300
Phoenix, AZ 85018

602-233-6400
800-289-3663
www.shamrockfoodservice.com
General line items, groceries, meats, produce, dairy products, frozen foods, baked goods, equipment and fixtures, general merchandise and seafood; serving the food service market.
President: Kent McClelland
CFO: Stephen Down
Year Founded: 1922
Estimated Sales: Over $1 Billion
Number Employees: 1000-4999
Number of Brands: 45
Type of Packaging: Food Service
Other Locations:
    Phoenix AZ
    Commerce City CO
    Albuquerque NM
    Eastvale CA
Brands:
    Fair Meadow
    Bountiful Harvest™
    Brickfire Bakery®
    Intros®
    Cobblestreet Market®
    Katy's Kitchen®
    Pier Port®
    Prarie Creek®
    ProClean®
    ProPak™
    ProSystem®
    ProWare™
    Rejuv®
    Trescerro®
    Villa Frizzoni®
    Vista Verde™
    Shamrock Farms®
    Gold Canyon Meat Co.™
    Markon®
    Jensen Foods®
    Coffee Roasters Ridgeline®
    Azar®
    B&G Foods, Inc.®
    Brown Paper Goods®
    Bueno®
    Cheese Merchants®
    Custom Culinary™
    Ecolab®
    Florida's Natural®
    Hormel Foods®
    Kellogg's®
    Kraft Heinz®
    Lamb Weston®
    Michael Foods Inc.®
    Mission Foodservice®
    NCCO®
    Nestl, Professional®
    Perdue®
    Rema Foods Imports®
    Rich's®
    Roland®
    Schreiber®
    Smithfield Farmland®
    Sugar Foods Corporation®
    Tysom™

29096 Shamrock Foods Co
Boise Foods Branch
1495 N Hickory Ave
Meridian, ID 83642

208-884-8400
www.shamrockfoodservice.com
Serves Idaho, Oregon and Utah.
Parent Co: Shamrock Foods Co

29097 Shamrock Foods Co
Colorado Foods Branch
5199 Ivy St
Commerce City, CO 80022

800-289-3595
coinfo@shamrockfoods.com
www.shamrockfoods.com
Serves Colorado, Western Kansas, Western Nebraska and Wyoming.
Senior VP: Kent Mullison
kent_mullison@shamrockfoods.com
Number Employees: 500-999
Parent Co: Shamrock Foods Company

29098 Shamrock Foods Co
Arizona Foods Branch
2540 N 29th Ave
Phoenix, AZ 85009-1682

602-233-6400
Fax: 928-537-3428 800-289-3663
azinfo@shamrockfoods.com
www.shamrockfoodservice.com
Estimated Sales: $100+ Million
Number Employees: 10-19
Parent Co: Shamrock Foods Company

29099 Shamrock Foods Co
Southern California Foods Branch
12400 Riverside Dr
Eastvale, CA 91752

855-664-5166
cainfo@shamrockfoods.com
www.shamrockfoodservice.com
Parent Co: Shamrock Foods Company

29100 Shamrock Foods Co
New Mexico Foods Branch
2 Shamrock Way NW
Albuquerque, NM 87120

877-577-1155
nminfo@shamrockfoods.com
www.shamrockfoodservice.com
Serves New Mexico and West Texas.
Parent Co: Shamrock Foods Company

29101 Shamrock Paper Company
1 Convent Street
Saint Louis, MO 63104

314-241-2370
Fax: 314-241-9230 info@shamrockpaper.com
www.shamrockpaper.com
Butcher, locker and kraft wrapping paper
President: William Firestone
Vice President: Rick Bliss
VP Sales: Sally Lippmann
Estimated Sales: $5-10Million
Number Employees: 10-19
Square Footage: 100000
Type of Packaging: Consumer, Food Service, Private Label, Bulk
Brands:
    Somethin' Special
    Sun Bright

29102 Shamrock Plastics
633 Howard St
Mt Vernon, OH 43050-3709

740-392-5555
Fax: 740-392-3555 800-765-1611
jay.ruffner@shamrockplastics.com
www.shamrockplastics.com
Plastic packaging and containerizing products including wicketed and bakery bags
Owner: Tom Ruffner
tom.ruffner@shamrockplastics.com
Account Representative: Susan Orlando
Sales Exec: Tom Ruffner
Estimated Sales: $3-5 Million
Number Employees: 10-19
Square Footage: 170000

29103 Shamrock Technologies Newark
255 Pacific St
Newark, NJ 07114-2824

973-242-3859
Fax: 732-242-8074
marketing@shamrocktechnologies.com
www.shamrocktechnologies.com
Manufacturer and exporter of powdered waxes and PTFE (polytetrafluoroethylene); also, dispersions and emulsions including carnauba, PE, PP, paraffin, microcrystalline and blends
Owner: William B Neuberg
President: Bill Neueerg
Marketing Manager: Melanie McCarroll
Estimated Sales: $20-50 Million
Number Employees: 5-9

29104 Shanghai Freemen
2035 Route 27
Suite 08817
Edison, NJ 08817

732-981-1288
info@shanghaifreemen.com
shanghaifreemen.com

Dietary supplements and food and beverage ingredients, such as vitamins, stevia, natural beta carotene, energy beverage ingredients, amino acids and joint health products; their collection includes glucosamine, chondroitin, hyaluronicacid, fish gelatin, collagen, ascorbic acid, natural vitamin E, green tea extract, L-Glutamine, L-Valine, melatonin, probiotics, bromelain, vanillin, Sopure Stevia and many more.
President: Hanks Li
Director, Business Development Eastern: Paul Niemann
Director, Business Development Western: Lottie Siann
VP, Sales & Marketing: Christine Balediata
Year Founded: 1995
Estimated Sales: $100 Million
Number Employees: 51-200
Parent Co: Zhucheng Haotian Pharm Co.
Type of Packaging: Bulk
Other Locations:
    Shanghai Freemen Europe B.V.
    The Hague

29105 Shanker Industries
301 Suburban Avenue
Deer Park, NY 11729

631-940-9889
Fax: 631-940-9895 877-742-6561
sales@shanko.com www.shanko.com
Manufacturer and exporter of decorative wall and ceiling tiles for hotels and restaurants
President: John Shanker
VP Advertising and Finance: Francine Shanker
VP Sales: David Shanker
Contact: Grace Chai
grace@shanko.com
Estimated Sales: $500,000-$1 Million
Number Employees: 5-9
Square Footage: 120000
Type of Packaging: Food Service

29106 Shanzer Grain Dryer
PO Box 2371
Sioux Falls, SD 57101-2371

605-336-0439
Fax: 605-336-9569 800-843-9887
sales@dwindustries.us
Manufacturer and exporter of grain dryers
Owner: Marian Leuning
Secretary/Treasurer: Dave Leuning
VP: Marian Leuning
Estimated Sales: $3-5 Million
Number Employees: 20-49
Parent Co: D&W Industries

29107 Shaped Wire
900 Douglas Road
Batavia, IL 60510-2294

630-406-0800
Fax: 630-406-0003 www.shapedwire.com
Packaging materials
President: William Wolford
Contact: Teri Grandt
tgrandt@leggett.com
Estimated Sales: $20-50 Million
Number Employees: 50-99

29108 Shared Data Systems
P.O.Box 7787
Charlotte, NC 28241-7787

704-588-2233
Fax: 704-588-7154 800-622-2140
Custom-made software for material handling systems
President: Larry Jones
CFO: Doug Yoder
Estimated Sales: $5-10 Million
Number Employees: 20-49

29109 Sharon Manufacturing Inc
540 Brook Ave
Deer Park, NY 11729-6802

631-242-8870
Fax: 631-586-6822 800-424-6455
info@sharonmfg.com www.sharonmfg.com
Manufacturer and exporter of replacement parts for gable top and reconditioned fillers for dairy and juice products
President: Robert Stamm
rob@sharonmfg.com
Number Employees: 5-9

29110 Sharp Brothers
201 Orient St
Bayonne, NJ 7002
201-339-0404
Manufacturer and exporter of yeast extruders and cutters
Owner: Basem Abdelnour
Estimated Sales: $500,000-$1 Million
Number Employees: 1-4
Square Footage: 8750

29111 (HQ)Sharp Electronics Corporation
Sharp Plaza
Mahwah, NJ 7495
201-529-8200
Fax: 201-529-8425 800-237-4277
www.sharpusa.com
Manufacturer and importer of commercial microwave ovens
President: Joel Biterman
CEO: Raymond Philippon
Chairman: Toshiaki Urushisako
Senior VP: Robert Scaglione
Number Employees: 1,000-4,999
Square Footage: 600000
Type of Packaging: Consumer, Food Service, Private Label
Other Locations:
Sharp Electronics Corp.
Romeoville IL

29112 Sharp Packaging Systems Inc
N62W22632 Village Dr
Sussex, WI 53089-3972
262-246-8815
Fax: 262-246-8885 800-634-6359
info@sharppackaging.com
www.sharppackaging.com
Pre-opened plastic bags on a roll, specialty films, and automatic bagging machines
President: Mike Menz
mikem@sharppackaging.com
CEO: Jim Kornfeld
Estimated Sales: $20-50 Million
Number Employees: 250-499

29113 Sharpe Measurement Technology
97 West Avenue
Stratford, CT 06615-6112
203-380-1776
Fax: 203-386-0087 info@smt-usa.com
www.smt-usa.com
Continuous thickness gauges and rolling mill control systems
Estimated Sales: $2.5-5 Million
Number Employees: 9

29114 Sharpsville Container Corp
600 W Main St
Sharpsville, PA 16150-2058
724-962-1100
Fax: 724-962-1226 800-645-1248
sales@scacon.com www.sharpsvillecontainer.com
Stainless steel and plastic tanks, stock pots, drums, hoppers, mixing and steaming kettles, etc.; also, plastic boxes and stainless steel hand carts; custom fabrication available
President: Thom Rigsby
Cio/Cto: Beverly Hunkus
bhunkus@scacon.com
Controller: Joe Higgins
Sales/Customer Service: Laura Puskar
Plant Manager: Michel Altenor
Estimated Sales: $10-20 Million
Number Employees: 50-99
Square Footage: 200000
Parent Co: Spartanburg Stainless Products

29115 Sharpsville Container Corp
600 W Main St
Sharpsville, PA 16150-2058
724-962-1100
Fax: 724-962-1226 800-645-1248
sales@scacon.com www.sharpsvillecontainer.com
Stainless steel and rotationally molded plastic vessels
President: Rick Mallat
Cio/Cto: Beverly Hunkus
bhunkus@scacon.com
Controller: Joe Higgins
Plant Manager: Michel Altenor
Estimated Sales: $10-20 Million
Number Employees: 50-99

29116 Shashi Foods
55 Esandar Dr
Toronto, ON M4G 4H2
Canada
416-645-0611
Fax: 416-645-0612 866-748-7441
Spices, herbs, seasoning blends and specialty flours, also, custom grinding, blending, bottling, and bagging.
President: Sujay Shah
VP: Ajay Shah
Estimated Sales: $7.37 Million
Number Employees: 30
Brands:
Elephant Brand
Shashi
King of Spice
Patak's

29117 Shat R Shield Inc
116 Ryan Patrick Dr
Salisbury, NC 28147-5624
704-633-2100
Fax: 704-633-3420 800-223-0853
ayost@shatrshield.com www.shatrshield.com
Manufacturer and exporter of plastic-coated and shatter-proof fluorescent lamps and Teflon-coated 125 and 250 watt infrared heat lamps
Owner: Bob Nolan
bnolan@shatrshield.com
Marketing Coordinator: Anita Yost
VP Sales/Marketing: Marty Pint
Marketing/Communications Manager: Bill Hahn
Estimated Sales: Below $5 Million
Number Employees: 50-99
Square Footage: 84000
Type of Packaging: Food Service
Brands:
Shat-R-Shield

29118 (HQ)Shaw & Slavsky Inc
13821 Elmira St
Detroit, MI 48227-3099
313-834-3990
Fax: 313-834-2680 800-521-7527
www.shawppcdesign.com
POP signs for grocery retailers. Also manufacture a wide variety of metal sign holders, poster floor stands, large-format graphics and signage, checkout lights, custom light boxes and custom fixtures.
President: Tom Smith
Estimated Sales: $10-20 Million
Number Employees: 50-99
Square Footage: 200000
Other Locations:
Shaw & Slavsky
Detroit MI
Brands:
Tube-Lok

29119 Shaw-Clayton Corporation
90 Montecito Road
San Rafael, CA 94901-2378
415-472-1522
Fax: 415-472-1599 800-537-6712
www.shaw-clayton.com
Manufacturer and exporter of small hinged lid containers
President: H Shaw
Sales: L Smith
Public Relations: S Hanson
Estimated Sales: Less than $500,000
Square Footage: 8000
Type of Packaging: Consumer
Brands:
Flex-A-Top

29120 Shawano Specialty Papers
W7575 Poplar Rd
Shawano, WI 54166-6082
715-526-2181
800-543-5554
paper@littlerapids.com www.littlerapids.com
Manufacturer and exporter of paper including glazed, wet crepe, dry crepe tissue and serim reinforced tissue
Vice President: Ron Thiry
rthiry@littlerapids.com
Estimated Sales: $50-100 Million
Number Employees: 100-249
Parent Co: Little Rapids Corporation
Type of Packaging: Consumer, Bulk

29121 Sheahan Sanitation Consulting
424 Hazelnut Drive
Oakley, CA 94561-2404
925-625-9683
Fax: 925-625-2310 800-554-4243
Sanitation and food safety consultant providing training, surface hygiene testing and chemical and hygiene audits and inspections
Estimated Sales: $500,000-$1 Million
Number Employees: 1

29122 Shear/Kershman Laboratories
701 Crown Industrial Ct # F
Suite F
Chesterfield, MO 63005-1135
636-519-8900
Fax: 636-519-0959 www.shearkershman.com
Research and development consultant for the food and confectionery industries; also, sourcing for material and co-packing available
Vice President: Alvin Kershman
akershman@shearkershman.com
Executive Vice President & Co-Founder: Al Kershman
VP Pharmaceuticals Division: Arthur B. Hermelin
Research & Development: Harold Cole
Office Manager: Sue Wagoner
Estimated Sales: $570,000
Number Employees: 5-9
Square Footage: 12000

29123 Sheboygan Paper Box Co
716 Clara Ave
PO BOX 326
Sheboygan, WI 53081-5349
920-458-8373
Fax: 920-458-2901 800-458-8373
www.spbox.com
Folding cartons, displays, blister cards. Specializing in polycoated and microflute packaging
President: Tom Liebl
Branch Manager: Tom Van De Kreeke
Executive VP: Larry Schneider
Director Sales/Marketing: David Moga
Estimated Sales: $10-20 Million
Number Employees: 100-249
Square Footage: 412000
Type of Packaging: Consumer, Food Service, Private Label, Bulk

29124 Sheffield Platers Inc
9850 Waples St
San Diego, CA 92121-2921
858-546-8484
Fax: 858-546-7653 800-227-9242
mwatkins@sheffieldplaters.com
www.sheffieldplaters.com
Coffee urns; wholesaler/distributor of punch bowls, chaffing sets, trays, etc.; serving the food service market; repair and replating services available
President: Dale L. Watkins Jr
dwatkins@sheffieldplaters.com
VP: Mark E. Watkins
Director, Business Development: Vincent Noonan
VP, Marketing: Mark Watkins
VP, Sales: Mark Watkins
Estimated Sales: $2.5-5 Million
Number Employees: 20-49
Square Footage: 68000

29125 (HQ)Shelby Co
865 Canterbury Rd
Westlake, OH 44145-1496
440-871-9901
Fax: 440-871-0326 800-842-1650
www.shelbycompany.com
Printed folding cartons and point of purchase advertising signs
President: Richard Rapacz
Controller: Wayne McGan
Executive VP: Sue Hintze
Manager: Kevin Smith
ksmith@shelbycothe.com
Plant Manager: Brian Charlton
Estimated Sales: $5-10 Million
Number Employees: 50-99
Square Footage: 200000
Type of Packaging: Consumer

29126 Shelby Pallet & Box Company
PO Box 27
Shelby, MI 49455-0027
231-861-4214
Fax: 231-861-0054

Pallets and skids
President: Brad Smith
Number Employees: 9

29127 (HQ)Shelby Williams Industries Inc
810 W Highway 25 70
Newport, TN 37821-8044
423-623-0031
Fax: 866-319-9371 800-873-3252
www.shelbywilliams.com
Manufacturer and exporter of seating; importer of wicker chairs
President: David Morley
Chairman and CEO: Franklin Jacobs
VP Operations: Marty Blaylock
Plant Manager: Bob Drey
Number Employees: 1000-4999
Parent Co: Falcon Industries
Other Locations:
Williams, Shelby, Industries
Statesville NC

29128 Shelby Williams Industries Inc
810 W Highway 25 70
Newport, TN 37821-8044
423-623-0031
Fax: 866-319-9371 800-873-3252
www.shelbywilliams.com
President: David Morley
CFO: Jean Fleetwood
R & D: Terry Roche
Quality Control: Marriane Carter
Plant Manager: Bob Drey
Number Employees: 1000-4999
Parent Co: Falcon Products

29129 Shelcon Inc
2081 S Hellman Ave # J
Suite J
Ontario, CA 91761-8024
909-947-4877
Fax: 909-947-1083 www.shelconconveyors.com
Soiled tray, tray assembly and plating conveyors; also, display rotisseries
President: Jon Clark
CEO: John Silvas
shelconconveyors@verizon.net
Estimated Sales: $1-2.5 Million
Number Employees: 5-9
Square Footage: 14800

29130 (HQ)Shelden, Dickson, & Steven Company
6114 Country Club Road
Omaha, NE 68152-2020
402-571-4848
Manufacturer and exporter of vending machines, fluorescent light fixtures, wall safes, etc
President: Richard Lebron
Estimated Sales: $.5-1 million
Number Employees: 16
Square Footage: 200000

29131 Sheldon Wood Products
PO Box 339
Toano, VA 23168-0339
757-566-8880
Fax: 757-566-2230
Wooden pallets and skids
President: S Sheldon
Number Employees: 25

29132 Shell Oil Company
3333 Hwy 6 S
Houston, TX 77082-3101
281-544-9900
855-697-4355
HOU-OSP-Chemicals-CRC-Americas@shell.com
www.shell.us
Oil & chemical manufacturer
Chief Executive Officer: Ben van Beurden
Year Founded: 1890
Estimated Sales: $305 Billion
Number Employees: 92,000
Parent Co: Royal Dutch Shell PLC

29133 Shelley Cabinet Company
1407 N 630 E
Shelley, ID 83274
208-357-3700
Fax: 208-357-7447
Custom cabinets and counter tops

President: Dan Tschikof
Purchasing Manager: Greg Wilklund
Estimated Sales: $500,000-$1 Million
Number Employees: 10-19
Square Footage: 20000

29134 Sheman Toy Corporation
150 Oakwood Ave
Orange, NJ 07050-3912
973-673-2350
President: Lee Saal
Estimated Sales: Below $5 Million
Number Employees: 1-4

29135 (HQ)Shen Manufacturing Co Inc
40 Portland Rd
Conshohocken, PA 19428-2717
610-825-2790
Fax: 610-834-8617
Manufacturer, importer and exporter of placemats, chair pads, pot holders, oven mitts, aprons, bar mops, dish towels and cloths inclduing table, dish, scrub, dusting and polishing
President: Elissa Vogt
e.vogt@johnritz.net
CFO: Robert Steidle
VP Sales/Marketing: Howard Steidle Jr
Estimated Sales: $5-10 Million
Number Employees: 20-49

29136 Shepard Brothers Co
503 S Cypress St
La Habra, CA 90631-6126
562-697-1366
Fax: 562-697-5786 800-645-3594
info@shepardbros.com www.shepardbros.com
Manufacturer and exporter of cleaners, sanitizers and water treatment and waste treatment systems; also, consultant specializing in sanitation
President: Georgia Anglin
georgia@njcost.com
CEO: Ron Shepard
VP Sales: Tony Terranova
Estimated Sales: $15-20 Million
Number Employees: 50-99

29137 Shepard Niles Parts
220 N Genesee St
Montour Falls, NY 14865-9646
607-535-7111
Fax: 607-535-7323 800-727-8774
mike.baker@konecranes.com
www.shepard-niles.com
Hoists and genuine Shepard Niles replacement parts
Manager: Michael Baker
Number Employees: 10-19
Type of Packaging: Bulk
Brands:
Cleveland Tramrail
Enduro
Liftabout
Safpowrbar

29138 Sheridan Sign Company
124 Wilson St
Salisbury, MD 21801-4100
410-749-7441
Fax: 410-749-4179
Signs including painted, electric and neon
President: Eugene F Trapkin
Manager: Marlynn R Schaeffer
Estimated Sales: Below $5 Million
Number Employees: 10-19

29139 Sherwood Tool
10100 Reisterstown Road
Owings Mills, MD 21117-3815
860-828-4161
Fax: 860-828-5387
Manufacturer and exporter of packaging machinery
President: Paul R Corazzo Sr
Parent Co: Sherwood Industries
Type of Packaging: Food Service, Private Label
Brands:
Shercan

29140 Shibuya International
1070 Reno Avenue
Modesto, CA 95351-1176
209-529-6466
Fax: 209-529-1834
www.shibuya-international.com

Importer of food processing and packaging machinery including aseptic filling systems, cappers, cartoners, unscramblers, casers, uncasers, washers, cleaners, pasteurizers, warmers, coolers, conveyors and labelers
President: Ken Saisho
CEO: Ian Greenland
Estimated Sales: $1-3 Million
Number Employees: 4
Square Footage: 66800
Parent Co: Shibuya Kogyo Company

29141 Shick Esteve
4346 Clary Blvd
Kansas City, MO 64130-2329
816-861-7224
Fax: 816-921-1901 877-744-2587
info@shickesteve.com www.shickesteve.com
Ingredient automation systems provider
President & CEO: Tim Cook
Executive VP & CFO: Blake Day
Director, Sales & Marketing: Jason Stricker
Estimated Sales: $40 Million
Number Employees: 100-249

29142 Shields Bag & Printing Co
1009 Rock Ave
Yakima, WA 98902-4629
509-248-7500
Fax: 509-248-6304 800-541-8630
www.shieldsbag.com
Manufacturer and exporter of plain and printed mono and co-extrusion polyethylene, nylon and polypropylene film and bags; also, commercial printing services available.
President: Bill Shields
bshields@shieldsbag.com
Estimated Sales: $50-100 Million
Number Employees: 500-999
Square Footage: 300000

29143 Shields Products Inc
530 Exeter Ave
West Pittston, PA 18643-1755
570-655-4596
Fax: 570-655-0262
Packaging materials including shredded cellophane, tissue, waxed paper and parchment
Owner: Warren Hemmelwright
Estimated Sales: Less Than $500,000
Number Employees: 1-4

29144 Shiffer Industries
41 Moana Ave
Kihei, HI 96753-7170
216-524-6546
800-642-1774
Manufacturer and exporter of assemblers, handlers, formers, feeders, index transferers, sorters, orienters, fillers, meters, markers, cutters, counters, loaders, unloaders, dispatchers, dedimplers, deburrers, labelers, etc.; customdesigning available
Office Manager: L Mangal
President: Stuart Shiffer
Estimated Sales: $2.5-5 Million
Number Employees: 20-49

29145 Shild Company
9 Lispenard St
New York, NY 10013-2290
212-431-7489
Fax: 212-941-1702 866-435-2949
shild1@aol.com www.shieldpress.com
Advertising specialties, wine list covers, manufacturers Of corporate executive leather goods
Owner: Steven Shield
VP: Abe Horawitzch
Marketing: Abe Horowitz
Sales: Abe Horowitz
Purchasing: Abe Horowitz
Estimated Sales: $500,000-$1,000,000
Number Employees: 05to10
Number of Products: 75
Type of Packaging: Consumer, Food Service

29146 Shillington Box Co LLC
3501 Tree Court Ind Blvd
St Louis, MO 63122-6683
636-825-6471
Fax: 636-225-5306 info@shillingtonbox.com
www.shillingtonbox.com
Corrugated boxes

Estimated Sales: $18 Million
Number Employees: 50-99
Square Footage: 112000

29147 Shimadzu Scientific Instrs
7102 Riverwood Dr
Columbia, MD 21046-2502

410-381-1227
Fax: 410-381-1222 800-477-1227
www.shimadzu.com
Provides instruments for the food testing industry.
President: Alex Bready
alex.bready@gmail.com
Manager: Will Bankert
Estimated Sales: $1-2.5 Million
Number Employees: 250-499
Parent Co: Shimadzu Corporation

29148 Shingle Belting
420 Drew Ct # A
King Of Prussia, PA 19406-2681

610-239-6667
Fax: 610-239-6668 800-345-6294
belting@shinglebelting.com
www.shinglebelting.com
Manufacturer and exporter of flat sheet and profile
thermoplastic conveyor belting including PU, PVC
and polyester and bakery belts
President/ Owner: Rennie Keating
CFO: Frank Manley
fmanley@shinglebelting.com
Marketing Coordinator: Monica Berry
Sales VP: Bob Frasetto
Operations: Frank Manley
Plant Manager: Bob Bolan
Estimated Sales: $5-10 Million
Number Employees: 20-49
Square Footage: 60000
Brands:
   European Monofilements
   Polyflex
   Rounthane
   Veethane

29149 Ship Rite Packaging
161 Woodbine Street
Bergenfield, NJ 07621-2839

201-385-4747
Fax: 201-385-2448 800-721-7447
www.shipritebags.com
Flexible polyethylene film; also, bags including
flexible polyethylene, ziplock, rollstock and
wicketted; custom printing available
President: Mayer Schlisser
Estimated Sales: $1-2.5 Million
Number Employees: 1-4

29150 Shipley Basket Mfg Co
191 Shipley Ln
Dayton, TN 37321-5589

423-775-2051
Fax: 423-775-2145 800-251-0806
shipleybasket@aol.com www.shipleybasket.com
Manufacturer and exporter of fruit and vegetable
baskets
President: Diane Shipley
arthell3@aol.com
Estimated Sales: $5-10 Million
Number Employees: 20-49

29151 Shipmaster Containers Ltd.
380 Esna Park Drive
Markham, ON L3R 1G5
Canada

416-493-9193
Fax: 416-493-6223 info@shipmaster.com
www.shipmaster.com
Corrugated paper containers
Estimated Sales: $10-15 Million
Number Employees: 50-99

29152 Shippers Paper ProductsCo
808 Blake Rd
Sheridan, AR 72150-8476

870-942-4043
Fax: 870-942-5933 800-468-1230
inquiry@itwshippers.com
www.shippersproducts.com
Manufacturer and exporter of paper and plastic
dunnage bags
Contact: Jacqueline Garcia
jackie.garcia@shippersproducts.com
Plant Manager: Jeff Maness
Number Employees: 10-19

29153 Shippers Supply
2815A Cleveland Avenue
Saskatoon, SK S7K 8G1
Canada

306-242-6266
Fax: 306-933-4333 800-661-5639
saskatoon@shipperssupply.com
www.shipperssupply.com
Manufacturer and wholesaler/distributor of printed
labels, pressure sensitive tapes, corrugated boxes,
material handling equipment, stretch and shrink film
and shipping supplies
President: Ron Brown
CFO: Miles Jern
Branch Manager: Neil Nutter
Number Employees: Oover 200
Square Footage: 400000

29154 Shippers Supply
2815A Cleveland Avenue
Saskatoon, SK S7K 8G1
Canada

306-242-6266
Fax: 306-933-4333 800-661-5639
saskatoon@shipperssupply.com
www.shipperssupply.com
Manufacturer, wholesaler/distributor and importer of
printed labels, pressure sensitive tapes, corrugated
boxes, material handling equipment, stretch film and
shipping supplies; exporter of labels and printed
tape
President: Ron Brown
Branch Manager: Ken Nordyke
Number Employees: Oover 200
Square Footage: 400000
Brands:
   Labelgraphics
   Redeman

29155 Shippers Supply
102 King Edward Street E
Winnipeg, NB R3H 0N8
Canada

204-772-9800
Fax: 204-772-9834 800-661-5639
winnipeg@shipperssupply.com
www.shipperssupply.com
Printed labels, pressure sensitive tapes, corrugated
boxes, material handling equipment, stretch film and
shipping supplies
President: Ron Brown
Branch Manager: Bob Letchford
Number Employees: 10
Square Footage: 400000

29156 Shippers Supply, Labelgraphic
8-3401 19 Street NE
Calgary, AB T2E 6S8
Canada

403-291-0450
Fax: 403-291-3641 800-661-5639
airways@shipperssupply.com
www.shipperssupply.com
Manufacturer and wholesaler/distributor of printed
labels, pressure sensitive tapes, corrugated boxes,
material handling equipment, stretch film and ship-
ping supplies
President: Ron Brown
General Manager: Dennis Rhind
Branch Manager: Jerry Pierce
Number Employees: Oover 200
Square Footage: 400000
Parent Co: Shippers Supply

29157 Shivvers
613 W English St
Corydon, IA 50060-1015

641-872-1007
Fax: 641-872-1593 www.shivvers.com
Manufacturer and exporter of continuous flow dry-
ing equipment and computer controls for dryers
President: Carl Shivvers
CFO: Ron Raasch
shivvers@shivvers.com
VP: Carl Shivvers
Assistant Sales Manager: Jim Ratliff
Estimated Sales: $20-50 Million
Number Employees: 100-249
Square Footage: 120000
Parent Co: Shivvers Manufacturing

29158 ShockWatch
5501 Lyndon B Johnson Fwy
Suite 350
Dallas, TX 75240

214-630-9625
Fax: 214-638-4512 800-393-7920
info@shockwatch.com www.shockwatch.com
Damage prevention products for shipping and hand-
ing of fragile and environmentally sensitive goods.
President/CEO: Tony Fonk
Vice President, Chief Financial Officer: Robert
Hutson
VP, Global Marketing & NA Sales: Tyson Stuelpe
Vice President, Operations: Jim Edwards
Estimated Sales: $9 Million
Number Employees: 70
Other Locations:
   ShockWatch Manufacturing
   Graham TX
   Shockwatch Europe, BV
   The Netherlands
   ShockWatch China
   ShangHai
   Shockwatch Latin America
   Mexico
Brands:
   Shock Switch
   Shock Watch

29159 Shoes for Crews/Mighty Mat
1400 Centrepark Blvd # 31
West Palm Beach, FL 33401-7402

561-683-5090
Fax: 561-683-3080 800-667-5477
scotts@shoesforcrews.com
www.shoesforcrews.com
Shoes for Crews Slip-Resistant Footwear will
prevent your slips and falls with over 38 styles to
choose from at prices starting at $24.98. We offer
the exclusive $5000 Slip & Fall Warranty: If any
employee slips and falls wearing SHOESFOR
CREWS, we will reimburse your company up to
$5000 on the paid workers comp claim. Call us at
1-877-667-5477 for details
Chairman of the Board: Stanley Smith
Contact: Stan Smith
s.smith@shoesforcrews.com
Estimated Sales: $5-10 Million
Number Employees: 1-4
Type of Packaging: Private Label
Brands:
   Shoes For Crews

29160 Shook Kelley Design Group
2151 Hawkins St
Suite 400
Charlotte, NC 28203

704-377-0661
www.shookkelley.com
Brand strategy, architecture and design consultancy,
specializing in food retailing and consumption.
Founding Partner & Principal: Terry Shook
Founding Partner & Principal: Kevin Kelley
Chief Financial Officer: Brenda Lally
Founding Principal: Frank Quattrocci
Founding Principal: Stan Rostas
Year Founded: 1992
Estimated Sales: $350 Million

29161 Shoppers Plaza USA
PO Box 450
Dewitt, MI 48820-0450

517-327-9949
Fax: 517-886-9633
Retailer of industrial food equipment
Estimated Sales: Below 1 Million
Number Employees: 5

29162 Shore Distribution Resources
18 Manitoba Way
Marlboro, NJ 07746-1219

732-972-1297
Fax: 732-972-7669 800-876-9727
shordist@aol.com
Wholesaler/distributor of packaging materials and
equipment including plastic containers, polyester
film, cellophane and polypropylene; also, carry out
platters, bowls, disposable thermometers and food
safety products
President: Elaine Shore
CEO: Harvey Shore
shordist@aol.com
Sales: Harvey Shore
Operations: Scott Shore

Estimated Sales: $1-2.5 Million
Number Employees: 5-9
Square Footage: 12000
Type of Packaging: Food Service

29163 Shore Paper Box Co
9821 Riverton Rd
PO BOX 149
Mardela Springs, MD 21837-2164

410-749-7125
Fax: 410-860-2188 office@shorepaperbox.com
www.shorepaperbox.com
Set-up paper boxes; also, die cutting and hot stamping available. made to order only
President: Sharon Steckman
ssteckman@shorepaperbox.com
Chairman: Vernon Taylor
CFO: Vernon Taylor
Vice President: Mary Thompson
Quality Control: Mary Thompson
Estimated Sales: Below $5 Million
Number Employees: 10-19

29164 Shorewood Engineering Inc
865 Industrial Blvd
Waconia, MN 55387-1045

952-442-2526
Fax: 952-442-4036
sales@shorewoodengineering.com
www.shorewoodengineering.com
Packaging machinery
Owner: Matt Donahoe
matt@shorewoodengineering.com
Estimated Sales: $1-2.5 Million
Number Employees: 5-9

29165 Shorewood Packaging
1 Kero Rd
Carlstadt, NJ 07072-2604

201-933-3203
Fax: 203-754-6020
shorewoodmarketing@ipaper.com
Set-up fancy boxes
President: Mark Shore
Chairman: John Faraci
Senior Vice President of Corporate Devel: Cato Ealy
Contact: Steve Emergen
steve.emergen@ipaper.com
Estimated Sales: $20-50 Million
Number Employees: 100-249

29166 Shouldice Brothers SheetMetal
400 W Dickman Rd
Battle Creek, MI 49037

269-962-5579
Fax: 269-962-8114
shobro@shouldicebrothers.com
www.shouldicebrothers.com
Bins, ovens and material handling equipment including conveyors, hoppers and carts
President: Dave Shouldice
Secretary and Treasurer: Dave Shouldice
VP: Dave Middlesworth
Contact: Davi Vanmiddleswort
vanmiddleswort@shouldicebrothers.com
Estimated Sales: $2.5-5 Million
Number Employees: 20-49

29167 Showa-Best Glove
579 Edison St
P.O. Box 8
Menlo, GA 30731-6335

706-862-2302
Fax: 706-862-6000 800-241-0323
usa@showabestglove.com
Manufacturer and exporter of protective gloves
CEO: Bill Alico
Cmo: Tom Eggleston
teggleston@showabestglove.com
CFO: Andrew Akins
R&D: Bill Williams
Customer Service Rep: Deborah Ellenburg
Estimated Sales: $50-100 Million
Number Employees: 500-999
Brands:
  Black Knight
  D Flex
  Ndex
  Ndex Free
  Nitri Pro
  Nitty Gritty

29168 Showeray Corporation
2028 E 7th St
Brooklyn, NY 11223

718-965-3633
Fax: 718-965-3647
Manufacturer, importer and exporter of tablecloths
Estimated Sales: $1-5 Million
Number Employees: 50-99
Square Footage: 120000

29169 Shrinkfast Marketing
460 Sunapee St
Newport, NH 03773-1488

603-863-7719
Fax: 603-863-6225 800-867-4746
info@shrinkfast-998.com
www.shrinkfast-998.com
Manufacturer and exporter of portable propane operated heat guns for shrinkwrap and palletizing applications
CFO: Chuck Milliken
cmilliken@ameriforge.com
Manager Sales/Marketing: Douglas Barton Jr
Estimated Sales: $5-10 Million
Number Employees: 5-9

29170 Shure-Glue Systems
600 Vine Street
Suite 1004
Cincinnati, OH 45202

513-333-0014
Fax: 513-874-3612 sales@shure-glue.com
www.suhrelaw.com
Owner: Joe B Suhre Iv
Estimated Sales: Below $5 Million
Number Employees: 1-4

29171 Shurtape Technologies LLC
1712 8th St Dr sE
Hickory, NC 28602

828-322-2700
Fax: 828-322-4029 888-442-8273
custservice@shurtape.com www.shurtape.com
Commodity, industrial grade and specialty adhesive tapes.
Chief Executive Officer: Jim Shuford
Executive Vice President: Stephen Shuford
Vice President, Marketing: Jeff Pierce
Year Founded: 1996
Estimated Sales: $650 Million
Number Employees: 1,500
Parent Co: STM Industries
Brands:
  Duck® Brand
  Frogtape®
  Kip®
  Painter's Mate
  Shurtape® Brand
  T-Rex®

29172 Shuster Corporation
4 Wright St
New Bedford, MA 02740

508-999-3261
Fax: 508-991-8585 info@shustercorp.com
www.shustercorp.com
Specialty ball and roller bearings including ceramic anticorrosive bearings for harsh applications;
President: Steven Shuster
Quality Control: John Sinlk
Contact: Stephen Anderson
sanderson@shustercorp.com
Estimated Sales: $5-10 Million
Number Employees: 20-49
Parent Co: Genuine Parts Company

29173 Shuster Laboratories
85 John Rd
Canton, MA 02021-2826

781-821-2200
Fax: 781-821-2200 800-444-8705
Consultant and contract research and development firm providing research and development for product development, sensory testing, nutrition analysis/labeling, HACCP, GMP, audits, regulatory liaison, shelf-life studies andmicrobiological and analytical testing
President: Philip Katz
CEO: Roy Lamothe
Director Marketing: Patricia Baressi
Contact: Tina Astore
bettina.astore@strquality.com
Estimated Sales: $10-20 Million
Number Employees: 100-249

Square Footage: 126000
Parent Co: Hauser Chemical Research Company
Other Locations:
  Shuster Laboratories
  Smyrna GA

29174 Shuster Laboratories
85 John Rd
Canton, MA 02021-2826

781-821-2200
Fax: 781-821-2200 800-444-8705
Product development, product formulation, sensory evaluation, market research, quality assurance, analytical and microbiological testing
President: Thil Katz
Manager: Ed Sarcione
CEO: Roy Lamothe
National Sales Manager: Eric Wieland
Contact: Tina Astore
bettina.astore@strquality.com
Estimated Sales: $10-20 Million
Number Employees: 100-249
Square Footage: 42000

29175 (HQ)Shuttleworth North America
10 Commercial Rd
Huntington, IN 46750-8805

260-356-8500
Fax: 260-359-7810 800-444-7412
inc@shuttleworth.com
www.collaborativeconveyor.com
Custom engineered solutions, conveyors, devices and material handling systems
President: Carol Shuttleworth
CEO: Steve Bucher
smbucher@gmail.com
Estimated Sales: $10-20 Million
Number Employees: 50-99
Number of Brands: 4
Square Footage: 9200
Parent Co: Shuttleworth
Other Locations:
  Shuttleworth
  Petaling Jaya
Brands:
  Clean Glide
  Slip-Torque
  Slip-Trak
  Zone Control

29176 Si-Lodec
4611 S 134th Place
Tukwila, WA 98168-3202

206-244-6188
Fax: 714-731-2019 800-255-8274
Manufacturer and exporter of scales including mobile, portable axle and force measurement
President: Rick Beets
Director International Sales: Arthur Tyson
Number Employees: 80
Square Footage: 60000

29177 Sicht-Pack Hagner
Musbacher Str. 21-23
Dornstetten/ Hallwangen, QC D-72280
Canada

004- 7-43 2
Fax: 004- 74-3 31 800-454-5269
info@sicht-pack-hagner.de
www.sicht-pack-hagner.de
President: Heirich Hagner
Number Employees: 10

29178 (HQ)Sico Inc
7525 Cahill Rd
Minneapolis, MN 55439-2745

952-941-1700
Fax: 952-941-6688 800-328-6138
sales@sicoinc.com www.sico-wallbeds.com
Manufacturer and exporter of room service carts and mobile folding banquet and buffet tables; also, fuel-powered and electric food warmers. Also manufacture portable dance floors, and portable stages, and bellmans carts and trucks
President: Jerry Danielson
jdanielson@sicoinc.com
President: Ken Steinbauer
CFO: Keith Dahlen
Vice President, Global Sales: Jerry Danielson
Marketing: Joel Mondshane
National Sales Manager: Heidi Niesen
Vice President, Operations: James Kline
Plant Manager: Pam Heller
Estimated Sales: $20-50 Million
Number Employees: 100-249

Type of Packaging: Food Service
Other Locations:
  SICO America
  Singapore
Brands:
  Sico

29179 Sidel Inc
5600 Sun Ct
Norcross, GA 30092-2892
678-221-3000
Fax: 770-447-0084 800-453-7439
www.sidel.com
Sidel is the leading global provider of PET solutions for liquid packaging. We are committed to being an innovative, responsive, and reliable partner, providing sustainable solutions for the beverage industry.
Zone VP: Sebastien Geffrault
CFO: Richard Edwards
richard.edwards@sidel.com
Estimated Sales: $19.60 Million
Number Employees: 100-249

29180 Sidney Manufacturing Co
405 N Main Ave
PO Box 380
Sidney, OH 45365-2345
937-492-4154
Fax: 937-492-0919 800-482-3535
www.sidneymanufacturing.com
Equipment used in handling wet and dry bulk materials with a customer base in industries such as grain, wood byproducts, cellulose fibers, animal feeds, flour, pellets, powders, food products and the line. ALso manufacture aline of industrial personnel elevators from 300lbs to 1000lbs capacity four passengers.
President: Steve Baker
sbaker@sidneymfg.com
Executive Vice President: Paul Borders
Engineering Manager: Tom Gross
Design Engineer: Josh Hicks
Sales Engineer/Customer Service: Joe Swartz
Purchasing Agent: Ward Cartwright
Estimated Sales: Below $5 Million
Number Employees: 20-49
Square Footage: 100000
Brands:
  Smc
  Sidney

29181 Sieberts Engineers
4951 Indiana Ave # 100
Lisle, IL 60532-3818
630-824-1515
Fax: 630-824-1535
john.joanis@siebertengineers.com
www.siebertengineers.com
Consulting engineers for food manufacturers
President: John Joanis
Contact: Jim Delapena
jim.delapena@sei-eng.com
Estimated Sales: $5-10 Million
Number Employees: 20-49

29182 Sielt Stone
6965 Union Park Center
Midvale, UT 84047-6008
801-268-9100
Fax: 801-268-9114 800-688-9781
Number Employees: 10

29183 Siemens Dematic
507 Plymouth Ave NE
Grand Rapids, MI 49505
616-913-7700
Fax: 616-913-7701 877-725-7500
usinfo@dematic.com www.dematic.com
Chief Executive Officer: Alan Bradley
CEO: John K Baysore
Contact: James Lindstrom
james.lindstrom@dematic.com
Estimated Sales: $3-5 Million
Parent Co: Siemens AG

29184 Siemens Industry Inc
3333 Old Milton Pkwy
Alpharetta, GA 30005-4437
770-751-2000
Fax: 770-751-4333 800-743-6367
AC/DC drives, programmable controllers and industrial systems
CEO: Denis Sadlowski
CFO: Harry Volande
Contact Person in USA: Andreas Klenke

Estimated Sales: Less than $500,000
Number Employees: 250-499
Parent Co: Siemens

29185 Siemens Measurement Systems
1000 Pittsford Victor Rd
Pittsford, NY 14534-3822
585-248-3050
800-568-7721
verax_info@moore-solutions.com
Data collection and analysis systems and software for statistical process control applications for food and beverage processors
President: Aubert Martin
Senior Vice President, Chief Information: Craig Berry
Executive Vice President of Global Sales: Paul Vogel
Number Employees: 20-49
Square Footage: 24000
Brands:
  Focus Plus
  Sentinel
  Sentry/Sentry Plus

29186 Sierra Converting Corporation
1400 Kleppe Ln
Sparks, NV 89431
775-331-8221
Fax: 775-331-8385 800-332-8221
www.sierraconverting.com
Manufactures, prints and laminates packaging for the food and snack industries; zippered pouches and pouch bags
President: Robert Yarhi
VP: Daniel Yarhi
Quality Control: Victor Seballes
Sales: Jim Harmon
Contact: Chris Back
chrisb@washington.k12.ga.us
Operations: Bill Anglos
Productions: Ron Vurwip
Plant Manager: Otis Wilson
Purchasing: Chris Back
Estimated Sales: $20-30 Million
Number Employees: 75
Type of Packaging: Consumer, Food Service, Private Label

29187 Sierra Dawn Products
1814 Empire Industrial Ct # D
Santa Rosa, CA 95403-1946
707-535-0172
Fax: 707-588-0757 www.sierradawn.com
Manufacturer and exporter of liquid soaps, recycled packaging and household cleaning products with vegetable-based ingredients
President: Chris Maurer
chris@sierradawn.com
VP: Janet Jenkins
Estimated Sales: $1-2.5 Million
Number Employees: 1-4
Brands:
  Lifetree

29188 Sifter Parts & Svc
29807 State Road 54
Wesley Chapel, FL 33543-4507
813-991-9400
Fax: 813-991-9700 800-367-3591
Info@SifterParts.com
Filters and sifters
Owner: Bob Williams
bob@ourtroopsonline.com
CFO: Tim Robinson
CEO: Bob Williams
Quality Control: Derek Williams
Estimated Sales: $5-10 Million
Number Employees: 10-19

29189 Sig Pack
2107 Livingston St
Oakland, CA 94606-5218
510-533-3000
Fax: 510-534-3000 800-824-3245
butlerp@parsons-eagle.com
www.sigpacksystems.com
Manufacturer and exporter of vertical form/fill/seal machinery, linear scales and combination weighers
Regional Sales Manager: Pete Butler
Production Manager: Gary Barlettano
Estimated Sales: $1-5 Million
Number Employees: 50-100

Square Footage: 160000
Parent Co: SIG Pack International
Brands:
  Golden Eagle
  Infinity
  Phasor

29190 Sigma Engineering Corporation
39 Westmoreland Ave
White Plains, NY 10606
914-682-1820
Fax: 914-682-0599 info@sigmaus.com
www.sigmaus.com
Manufacturer and exporter of drum pumps and forming extruders
President: Edward Derrico
Estimated Sales: $5-10 Million
Number Employees: 5-9
Square Footage: 40000

29191 Sigma Industrial Automation
5450 Fm 1103
Schertz, TX 78108-2110
210-659-5000
Fax: 210-659-3443 800-578-5060
dean@sigma-usa.com
Data collection in washdown environments, washdown computers, food processing-SPC, high speed and manual box labeling
Owner: Kathleen Chinni
kathi@sigma-usa.com
Director-SPC/QA: Dr. Guy Gibson
VP-Systems Engineering: Jeff Chinni
Engineering Manager: Rick Curcio
GM-Sales Director: Dean Chinni
kathi@sigma-usa.com
Applications Development Manager: Doug Lansdowne
Accounts Receivable: Anita Torres
Estimated Sales: $1-2.5 Million
Number Employees: 10-19

29192 Sigma Industries
4905 Hoffman Street
Suite B
Elkhart, IN 46516
574-295-9660
Fax: 574-293-8552 cs@sigma-wire.com
Manufacturer and exporter of material handling equipment including pallets, pallet racks, decking and steel wire mesh containers
President: Stanley Jurasek
CFO: Stanley Jurasek
Sales Director: Jan Richardson
Estimated Sales: $2.5-5 Million
Number Employees: 10-19
Brands:
  Junior
  Palletainer
  Rigitainer

29193 Sign Art
6225 Old Concord Rd
Charlotte, NC 28213-6311
704-597-9801
Fax: 704-597-9808 800-929-3521
randy.souther@signartsign.com
www.signartsign.com
Electric signs; installation services available
Owner: Randy Souther
rsouther@signartsign.com
Director Project Management: Sue Prince
CFO: Randy Souther
Sales Leader: Earl Floyd
rsouther@signartsign.com
General Manager: Bill Sundberg
Estimated Sales: $2.5-5 Million
Number Employees: 20-49

29194 Sign Classics
1014 Timothy Dr
San Jose, CA 95133-1042
408-298-1600
Fax: 408-298-3177
Manufacturer and exporter of custom signs and designs including restaurant
President: Kenneth Fisher
Sales Manager: Clare Wild
Estimated Sales: $1-2.5 Million
Number Employees: 10-19

29195 Sign Expert
2044 Rose Ln
Pacific, MO 63069-1161
314-968-3565
Fax: 636-257-3566 800-874-9942
www.signexperts.com
Manufacturer and exporter of advertising signs
President: Paul Stojeba
paul@signexperts.com
CFO: Deb Stojeba
Estimated Sales: Less than $500,000
Number Employees: 5-9

29196 Sign Factory
13905 Artesia Blvd
Cerritos, CA 90703-9001
562-809-1443
Fax: 562-809-1435 www.cerritossigns.com
Flags, pennants, banners and signs; lettering service
available
Owner: Ernst Dinkel
Manager: Ernie Dinkel
signfactorycerritos@gmail.com
Estimated Sales: Less Than $500,000
Number Employees: 1-4
Square Footage: 8000

29197 Sign Graphics
2317 E Florida St
Evansville, IN 47711
812-476-9151
Fax: 812-479-5147
Signs and custom directory systems; also, vehicle
and window lettering engraving and decals
President: Brad Nash
Plant Manager: Kerry Dubuque
Estimated Sales: $500,000-$1 Million
Number Employees: 5-9
Square Footage: 8000

29198 Sign Products
1664 Terra Ave # 1
Sheridan, WY 82801-6135
307-672-3145
Fax: 307-672-9829 800-532-4753
54663signprod@aol.com
www.signproductsinc.com
Restaurant signage including neon and road boards
Manager: Terry Reimers
sales@signproductsinc.com
Sales: Paul Cox
Estimated Sales: Less Than $500,000
Number Employees: 1-4
Parent Co: Billings Neon

29199 Sign Systems, Inc.
23253 Hoover Road
Warren, MI 48089
586-758-1600
www.signsystemsofmichigan.com
Manufacturer and exporter of metal and plastic advertising signs
Manager: Barbara Warren
Contact: Dave Sedlarz
d.sedlarz@signsystemsofmichigan.com
Type of Packaging: Consumer, Food Service, Bulk

29200 Sign Warehouse
2614 Texoma Dr
Denison, TX 75020-1053
903-462-7700
Fax: 800-966-6834 800-699-5512
www.signwarehouse.com
Signs
Owner: Chris Grip
Sales/Design: Gary Gale
chris.grip@signwarehouse.com
Manager: Rhonda Cummings
Estimated Sales: $1-2.5 Million
Number Employees: 100-249

29201 SignArt Advertising
PO Box 2
Van Buren, AR 72957-0002
479-474-8581
Fax: 479-474-4708
Interior and exterior signs
President: Charles Jannen
VP: Gene Jennen
In-House Sales Manager: Linda Jennen
Contact: Chuck Jennen
signart@aol.com

29202 Signal Equipment
3616 E Marginal Way S
Seattle, WA 98134-1130
206-324-8400
Fax: 206-623-0510 800-542-0884
Fire and security systems and emergency generator
systems
President: Tony Hastings
Estimated Sales: $5-10 Million
Number Employees: 5-9
Square Footage: 16000
Brands:
  Edwards
  Energy Dynamics
  F.G. Wilson
  Generac

29203 Signature Foods
73-D Enterprise Drive
Pendergrass, DR 30587
706-693-0098
Co-packer and support manufacturer for food com-
panies
President: Oran B Talkington
Estimated Sales: $3.3 Million
Number Employees: 23

29204 Signature Packaging
18 Dockery Dr
West Orange, NJ 7052
973-324-1838
Fax: 973-884-1909 800-376-2299
Plain and printed polyethylene bags for chicken, potatoes, fruits, etc.; also, paper and turkey tags, closures, packaging machinery, paper wrap, etc.;
wholesaler/distributor of produce and specialty
foods
Estimated Sales: less than $500,000
Number Employees: 1-4
Square Footage: 5000

29205 Signco Inc
3113 Merriam Ln
Kansas City, KS 66106-4615
913-722-1377
Fax: 913-722-3614 signs@signcokc.com
www.signcokc.com
Signs and decals; also, screen printing, vinyl
graphics available
President: Mike Sailer
signs@signcokc.com
Estimated Sales: Less Than $500,000
Number Employees: 5-9

29206 Signco Stylecraft
2611 Crescentville Rd
Cincinnati, OH 45241-1588
513-771-9090
Fax: 513-326-3090 800-733-0045
info@signcoscreenprinting.com
www.inky-tees.com
Printed T-shirts for food service vendors
President/Owner: Craig Howell
craig@signco.net
Vice President: Scott Howell
Head of the Art Department: Steve Diedling
Sales: Mary Beth
Estimated Sales: $1-2.5 Million
Number Employees: 10-19

29207 Signet Graphic Products
9037 Saint Charles Rock Rd
St Louis, MO 63114-4253
314-426-0200
Fax: 314-426-3535
Signs, banners and decals; fleet graphics available
Corporate Secretary: Ilene Leichtle
Manager: Bill Jones
Estimated Sales: $10-20 Million
Number Employees: 10-19
Square Footage: 140000

29208 Signet Marking Devices
3121 Red Hill Ave
Costa Mesa, CA 92626-4567
714-549-0341
Fax: 714-549-0972 800-421-5150
sales@signetmarking.com
www.signetmarking.com
Manufacturer and exporter of steel type marking
equipment
Owner: Melba Andrews
m.andrews@signetmarking.com
Operations Manager: Brian McGiffin
Estimated Sales: Below $5,000,000
Number Employees: 10-19

29209 Signets/Menu-Quik
7280 Industrial Park Boulevard
Mentor, OH 44060-5383
440-946-8676
Fax: 440-946-4646 800-775-6368
menuboardsales@signets.com
Menu boards
President: Robert Ledenican
Vice President: Terence Zuik
Marketing/Sales: Brenda Rolf
Number Employees: 25

29210 Signmasters
18421 Gothard St # 300
Huntington Beach, CA 92648-1236
949-364-9128
Fax: 949-364-6743
Banners, signs, flags and pennants
Owner: Mike Suzanski
Estimated Sales: Less than $500,000
Number Employees: 1-4

29211 Signode Industrial Group LLC
3650 W Lake Ave
Glenview, IL 60026-1215
847-724-6100
Fax: 847-657-5323 800-323-2464
www.signodegroup.com
Manufacturer and exporter of protective packaging
systems, equipment and consumables for steel and
plastic strapping, stretch film and tape
CEO: Mark Burgess
mburgess@signodecorp.com
Director National Sales: Jeff Osisek
Manager: George Heller
Estimated Sales: $3-5 Million
Number Employees: 5000-9999
Parent Co: Illinois Tool Works
Brands:
  Apex
  Contrax
  Gemini
  High Strength Tenex
  Magnus
  Octopus
  Spiral Grip
  Tenax

29212 Signode Industrial Group LLC
3650 W Lake Ave
Glenview, IL 60026-1215
847-724-6100
Fax: 847-657-5323 800-323-2464
ccunningham@signode.com
www.signodegroup.com
President: Russell Flaum
CEO: Mark Burgess
mburgess@signodecorp.com
CFO: John Mayfield
Number Employees: 5000-9999

29213 Signs & Designs
620 E Rancho Vista Blvd
Palmdale, CA 93550-4753
661-947-4473
Fax: 661-947-3559 888-480-7446
sales@signsanddesigns.tv www.signsanddesigns.tv
Wood, metal, plastic, electrical and neon signs
Owner: Craig Mc Nabb
Estimated Sales: $1-2.5 Million
Number Employees: 10-19

29214 Signs & Shapes Intl
2320 Paul St
Omaha, NE 68102-4030
402-331-3181
Fax: 402-331-2729 800-806-6069
www.walkaroundmascots.com
Manufacturer and exporter of standard and custom
cold air-inflated walk-around costumes; also, signs
and character shapes; grand opening packages
available
President: Lee Bowen
lee@walkaround.com

Estimated Sales: Below $5 Million
Number Employees: 20-49
Square Footage: 26000
Type of Packaging: Food Service

29215 Signs O' Life
45 Bodwell St
Avon, MA 2322

800-750-1475
Fax: 508-583-9780
Illuminating and nonilluminating signs and graphics
Owner: Alvin Barber
VP: Steven Supinski
Estimated Sales: $1-2.5 Million
Number Employees: 10-19

29216 Signtech Electrical Advg Inc
4444 Federal Blvd
San Diego, CA 92102-2505

619-527-6100
Fax: 619-527-6111 sales@signtechusa.com
www.signtechus.com
Commercial awnings
President: David Schauer
CEO: Harold Schauer Jr.
hs@signtechusa.com
CFO: Kimra Schauer
VP Sales: Art Navarro
Estimated Sales: Less than $500,000
Number Employees: 50-99

29217 Siko Products Inc
2155 Bishop Cir E
Dexter, MI 48130-1565

734-426-3476
Fax: 734-426-3453 800-447-7456
sales@sikoproducts.com www.siko-global.com
Position, feedback devices
President: Maurizio Masullo
IT / Web Admin: Peter Crist
Sales Engineer: Cary Mulvany
Customer Service/Sales: Jim Schnebelt
Office Manager/Returns: Terry Miller
Shipping: Lisa LaRoe
Estimated Sales: $1-2.5 Million
Number Employees: 5-9

29218 Silent Watchman Security Services LLC
P.O. BOX 3017
Danbury, CT 06813

203-743-1876
Fax: 203-743-9814 800-932-3822
info@silentwatchman.net
Manufacturer and exporter of smoke and infrared intrusion detectors, recording door locks, CCTV and multiplex security systems
President: Vincent Dascano
General Manager: Gary Sherman

29219 Silesia Grill Machines Inc
4770 County Road 16
St Petersburg, FL 33709-3130

727-544-1340
Fax: 727-544-2821 800-237-4766
sales@veloxgrills.us www.veloxgrills.com
Manufacturer and exporter of high speed contact grills, crepe makers, panini grills and bucket openers
Owner: Silesia Grill
veloxgrills@aol.com
Estimated Sales: Less Than $500,000
Number Employees: 1-4
Type of Packaging: Food Service
Brands:
    Silesia

29220 Silesia Grill Machines Inc
4770 County Road 16
St Petersburg, FL 33709-3130

727-544-1340
Fax: 727-544-2821 800-267-4766
silesia@tampabay.rr.com www.veloxgrills.com
Manufacturer and exporter of high speed contact grills, crepe machines and bucket openers
Owner: Silesia Grill
veloxgrills@aol.com
Estimated Sales: Less Than $500,000
Number Employees: 1-4
Type of Packaging: Food Service

29221 Silgan Containers LLC
21800 Oxnard St # 600
Suite 600
Woodland Hills, CA 91367-3609

818-710-3700
Fax: 818-593-2255 www.silgancontainers.com
Plastic and aluminum closures for bottles and aluminum containers, capping machinery and feed systems
President: Thomas J Synder
tsynder@silgancontainers.com
Estimated Sales: Over $1 Billion
Number Employees: 1000-4999
Type of Packaging: Bulk
Brands:
    Drop-Lok
    Jetflow
    Magna Torq
    Pharma-Lok
    Plasti-Lug
    Ro
    Wing-Lok

29222 Silgan Plastic Closure Sltns
1140 31st St
Downers Grove, IL 60515-1212

630-515-8383
Fax: 724-657-8597 800-727-8652
www.silganpcs.com
Manufacturer and exporter of tamper evident plastic bottle closures and related capping machinery
President: Tom Blaskow
CEO: Jack Watts
R&D: Borilla
Quality Control: Jee Book
Director: Bill Lauderbaugh
Sales/Marketing Manager: Don Kirk
General Manager: Alex Williams
Estimated Sales: $10-20 Million
Number Employees: 1000-4999
Parent Co: Partola Packaging
Other Locations:
    Partola Packaging
    Chino CA

29223 (HQ)Silgan Plastic Closure Sltns
1140 31st St
Downers Grove, IL 60515-1212

630-515-8383
Fax: 630-369-4583 800-767-8652
Manufacturer and exporter of capping equipment and closures
President: James Taylor
CEO: Kevin Kwilinski
kevin@portpack.com
CFO: Deniss Berk
CEO: Brian Bauerbach
Quality Control: Jo Beni Kisto
VP Sales/Services: Ross Markely
Number Employees: 1000-4999
Other Locations:
    Portola Packaging
    Guadalajara
Brands:
    Cap Snap
    Nepco
    Portola Packaging

29224 (HQ)Silgan Plastic Closure Sltns
185 Northgate Cir
New Castle, PA 16105-5537

724-658-3004
Fax: 724-658-5138 www.ipec.biz
Manufacturer and supplier of plastic closures and capping equipment
President: Joseph Giordano
jgiordano@ipec.biz
Sales Manager: Robert Harding
Estimated Sales: $8-10 Million
Number Employees: 50-99
Square Footage: 340000
Other Locations:
    Brewton AL

29225 Silgan Plastics Canada
14515 North Outer Forty
Suite 210
Chesterfield, MO 63017
Canada

416-293-8233
Fax: 314-469-5387 800-274-5426
www.silganplastics.com
Manufacturer and exporter of plastic jars, bottles and closures including standard screw cap, child resistant and dispensing

National Sales Manager: David Meharg
Contact: Britt Babiarz
britt.babiarz@silganplastics.com
Estimated Sales: $1-5 Million
Number Employees: 100
Square Footage: 460000
Parent Co: Silgan Plastics Corporation

29226 Silgan Plastics LLC
14515 North Outer 40 Rd # 210
Suite 210
Chesterfield, MO 63017-5746

314-542-9223
Fax: 314-469-5387 800-274-5426
www.silganplastics.com
HDPE bottles and stock/private containers, closures and fitments
President: Sarah T Macdonald
sarah.macdonald@silganplastics.com
CEO: Derek Schmidt
Estimated Sales: $61.5 Million
Number Employees: 1000-4999
Square Footage: 265000
Other Locations:
    Silgan Plastics
    Ottawa OH

29227 Silgan White Cap LLC
1140 31st St
Downers Grove, IL 60515-1212

630-515-8383
Fax: 630-515-5326 800-515-1565
www.americas.silganwhitecap.com
Manufacturer and exporter of metal and plastic vacuum closures and related sealing equipment including cappers
CEO: Anthony J Allott
VP Sales: George Sullivan
Estimated Sales: $10-20 Million
Number Employees: 50-99
Square Footage: 20000
Parent Co: Schmalbach Lubecca
Type of Packaging: Bulk
Brands:
    Plast-Twist
    Twist-Off

29228 (HQ)Sillcocks Plastics International
PO Box 421
Hudson, MA 01749-0421

978-568-9000
Fax: 978-562-7128 800-526-4919
www.428main.com
Manufacturer and exporter of advertising novelties including plastic credit, debit and photo/ID cards; also, mag stripe signature panels, holography and security printing available
CEO and President: John Herslow
VP Sales/Marketing: Michele Logan
Estimated Sales: $3-5 Million
Number Employees: 10-19
Square Footage: 244000
Brands:
    Silcard

29229 Silliker Canada Company
90 Gough Road
Markham, ON L3R 5V5
Canada

905-479-5255
Fax: 519-822-0132
customercare@sillikercanada.com
Technical Sales Manager: Greg Forster
Number Employees: 90
Parent Co: M□RIEUX NUTRISCIENCES CORPORATION

29230 Silliker Laboratories Of Ga
2169 W Park Ct # G
Stone Mountain, GA 30087-3553

770-469-2701
Fax: 770-469-2883
kurt.westmoreland@silliker.com
www.merieuxnutrisciences.com
Consultant for sanitation, testing, analysis, etc
Manager: Robert Yemm
Regional Manager: Kurt Westmoreland
Manager: Robert Yemm
Estimated Sales: $2.5-5 Million
Number Employees: 20-49
Parent Co: Silliker Laboratories

29231 Silliker Laboratories-Pa Inc
6390 Hedgewood Dr
Allentown, PA 18106-9588
610-366-0264
Fax: 610-366-9357 silliker@silliker.com
www.silliker.com
Food consultant providing plant sanitation, microbiological research and analysis of foods and infestation
Vice President: Bob Colvin
Microbiology Manager: Kathy Jost-Keating
VP: Bob Colvin
Estimated Sales: $5-10 Million
Number Employees: 50-99
Parent Co: Silliker Laboratories Group

29232 Silliker, Inc
111 E Wacker Dr
Suite 2300
Chicago, IL 60601
312-938-5151
www.silliker.com
Laboratory providing food testing, microbiological and chemical analysis, technical consulting and audits for HACCP/GMPs employee training services and custom research
President: James Ondyak
VP: Jim Hayes
Marketing Communications Manager: Jessica Sawyer-Lueck
Contact: Kristin Carlson
kristyn.j.carlson@rrd.com
Number Employees: 50-99
Parent Co: BioMerieux Alliance

29233 Silver King Refrigeration Inc
1600 Xenium Ln N
Minneapolis, MN 55441-3706
763-923-2441
Fax: 763-553-1209 800-328-3329
info@silverking.com www.silverkingrefrig.com
Refrigerated bulk milk dispensers
President: Corey Kohl
Executive VP: Benjuman Rubin
Marketing Head: Benjuman Rubin
Estimated Sales: $15-20 Million
Number Employees: 100-249
Parent Co: Prince Castle
Brands:
Norris
Silver King

29234 Silver King Refrigeration Inc
1600 Xenium Ln N
Minneapolis, MN 55441-3706
763-923-2441
Fax: 763-553-1209 800-328-3329
info@silverking.com www.silverkingrefrig.com
Manufacturer and exporter of refrigerators, freezers, prep tables, ice cream cabinets, bulk milk and salad dispensers, display cases and fountainettes
President: Corey Kohl
Executive VP: Benjamin Rubin
Estimated Sales: $15-20 Million
Number Employees: 100-249
Parent Co: Prince Castle
Type of Packaging: Food Service
Brands:
Silver King

29235 Silver Mountain Vineyards
PO Box 3636
Santa Cruz, CA 95063-3636
408-353-2278
Fax: 408-353-1898 info@silvermtn.com
www.silvermtn.com
Wine
President: Jerold O'Brien
info@silvermtn.com
Estimated Sales: Less Than $500,000
Number Employees: 1-4
Type of Packaging: Private Label
Brands:
Silver Mtn Vineyards

29236 (HQ)Silver Spur Corp
16010 Shoemaker Ave
Cerritos, CA 90703-2239
562-921-6880
Fax: 562-921-7916 vivian@silverspurcorp.com
www.silverspurcorp.com
Manufactures glass bottles, glass containers, HDPE (High Density Polyethlene) Packers, PET (polyethylene terephthalare) containers and closures. 1

President: James Hao
Vice President: Vivian Chu
vivian@silverspurcorp.com
Marketing: Alvin Hao
Operations Manager: Vivian Chu
Plant Manager: James Wilder
Estimated Sales: $9 Million
Number Employees: 100-249
Square Footage: 200000

29237 Silver State Plastics Inc
2626 8th Ave
Greeley, CO 80631-8412
970-346-8667
Fax: 970-346-9191
silverstateplastics@comcast.net
Plain and printed polyethylene bags
Owner: James Cornforth
james.cornforth@silverstateplastics.com
Sales: Vickie Walker
Plant Manager: Richard Dailey
Estimated Sales: $5-10 Million
Number Employees: 10-19
Square Footage: 80000
Type of Packaging: Private Label

29238 Silver Weibull
14800 E Moncrieff Place
Aurora, CO 80011-1211
303-373-2311
Fax: 303-373-2319
Manufacturer and exporter of sugar centrifugals, reheaters and crystallizers
Manager Technical Process: Tommy Persson
Business Unit Manager (Worldwide): Derrald Houston
Manager: Randy Copsey
Estimated Sales: Below $5 Million
Number Employees: 3
Square Footage: 200000
Parent Co: Consolidated Process Machinery
Brands:
Silver-Weibull

29239 Silverson Machines Inc
355 Chestnut St
PO Box 589
East Longmeadow, MA 01028-2702
413-525-4825
Fax: 413-525-5804 800-204-6400
fran@silverson.com www.silverson.com
Manufacturer, supplier and exporter of food processing equipment including blending and batching equipment, high shear mixers, colloid mills and homogenizers; also, laboratory equipment and supplies
President: Harold Rothman
Clerk/VP: David Rothman
VP: Anne Rothman
Sales Manager: Brian Martin
IT: Frances Carhart
fran@silverson.com
General Manager: Michael Boyd
Estimated Sales: $2.6 Million
Number Employees: 10-19
Parent Co: Silverson Machines
Brands:
Flashblend
Silverson

29240 Simco
2257 N Penn Rd
Hatfield, PA 19440-1998
215-822-2171
Fax: 215-822-3795 800-203-3419
www.megapathdsl.net
Packaging, static control, electrostatic charging, web cleaning
President: Gary Swink
Sales: Lou Gieleonora
Manager: Michael Oldt
moldt@simcomail.com
Estimated Sales: Less Than $500,000
Number Employees: 1-4

29241 Simco
2257 N Penn Rd
Hatfield, PA 19440-1998
215-822-2171
Fax: 215-822-3795 800-203-3419
www.megapathdsl.net
President: Gary Swink
Manager: Michael Oldt
moldt@simcomail.com

Estimated Sales: Less Than $500,000
Number Employees: 1-4

29242 (HQ)Simkar Corp
700 Ramona Ave
Philadelphia, PA 19120
215-831-7700
Fax: 215-831-7703 www.simkar.com
Manufacturer and exporter of lighting fixtures including fluorescent, vaporproof, H.I.D., parabolic deep cell, waterproof, strip, undershelf display and overhead.
Chief Executive Officer: Glenn Grunewald
Year Founded: 1952
Estimated Sales: $100-$500 Million
Number Employees: 500-999
Square Footage: 275000
Type of Packaging: Consumer, Food Service, Private Label, Bulk
Other Locations:
Simkar Corp.
Philadelpia PA
Brands:
Channelites
Fashion Fluorescent
Para-Spec
Ultratensity
Vangard

29243 Simkins Industries Inc
317 Foxon Rd # 3
East Haven, CT 06513-2038
203-787-7171
Fax: 203-782-6324 www.simkinsindustries.com
Folding boxes; also, glassine and greaseproof paper and paperboard
President: Leon Simkins
Chief Financial Officer: Anthony Battaglia
Contact: Anthony Battaglia
abattaglia@simkinsindustries.com
Estimated Sales: Less Than $500,000
Number Employees: 1-4
Square Footage: 1600

29244 (HQ)Simmons Engineering Corporation
1200 Willis Ave
Wheeling, IL 60090
847-419-9800
Fax: 847-419-1500 800-252-3381
sales@simcut.com www.simcut.com
Manufacturer and exporter of cutting knives and blades for bread, cake, fish, fruit, vegetables and meat products
President/Owner: Bruce Gillian
VP/General Manager: Colin Murphy
Customer Service & Marketing Manager: Erin O'Brien
Contact: Lorenzo Barrios
l.barrios@simcut.com
Estimated Sales: $5-10 Million
Number Employees: 50-99
Square Footage: 60000
Brands:
Tru-Trak

29245 Simolex Rubber Corp
14505 Keel St
Plymouth, MI 48170-6002
734-453-4500
Fax: 734-453-6120 info@simolex.com
www.simolex.com
Manufacturer and exporter of rubber products including beverage hoses, juice tubing, milk hoses, gaskets, seals and bottle stoppers
President: Bob Dungarani
info@simolexrubber.com
Estimated Sales: $10-20 Million
Number Employees: 20-49
Square Footage: 50000
Type of Packaging: Food Service

29246 Simon S. Jackel Plymouth
684 Hidden Lake Drive
Tarpon Springs, FL 34689-2600
727-942-3991
Consultant specializing in product and ingredient development and improvement for companies supplying baking ingredients and products
Director: Simon Jackel PhD

29247 Simonds International
135 Intervale Rd
PO Box 500
Fitchburg, MA 01420-6519
Canada

978-345-7521
Fax: 978-424-2212 nlaflamme@simondsint.com
www.simondsinternational.com
Manufacturer, exporter and importer of knives for
packaging and food processing equipment, cryovac,
etc
President: Roy Erdwins
roy.erdwins@simondsinternational.com
Sales Manager: Fred Adams
Number Employees: 100-249
Square Footage: 60000
Parent Co: IKS International

29248 Simonds International
135 Intervale Rd
P.O. Box 500
Fitchburg, MA 01420-6519

978-345-7521
Fax: 978-424-2212 800-343-1616
www.simondsinternational.com
Manufacturer and exporter of band and hack saws
and saw blades, circular machine knives, files and
investment castings
President: Roy Erdwins
roy.erdwins@simondsinternational.com
Chairman: John Consentino
Chief Financial Officer: Henry Botticello
Vice President: Chip Holm
Engineering & R&D Manager: Rick Brautt
Vice President, Sales & Marketing: David Miles
Sales Manager: Tim House
Operations Supervisor: Dick Vain
Plant Manager: Roy Erdwins
Purchasing Agent: Valerie Johnson
Estimated Sales: $83 Million
Number Employees: 100-249
Square Footage: 400000

29249 Simoniz USA Inc
201 Boston Tpke
Bolton, CT 06043-7203

860-646-0172
Fax: 860-645-6070 800-227-5536
wgorra@simonizusa.com www.simonizusa.com
Manufacturer and exporter of waterless hand clean-
ers, soap and specialty chemicals
President: William Gorra
CEO: Mark Kershaw
mkershaw@simonizusa.com
VP Marketing: Michele O'Neal
Estimated Sales: F
Number Employees: 50-99

29250 Simonson Group
35 Washington Street
Winchester, MA 01890-2927

781-729-8906
Fax: 781-729-5079
Consultant specializing in marketing research and
product development; serving food service manufac-
turers and restaurants
Executive VP: Barbara Simonson
Estimated Sales: $1-5 Million
Number Employees: 1-4

29251 Simplex Filler Co
640 Airpark Rd # A
Napa, CA 94558-7569

707-265-6801
Fax: 707-265-6868 800-796-7539
www.simplexfiller.com
Manufacturer and exporter of piston and pressure
fillers for bottle, can, jar and bag filling; also, con-
veyors, unscramblers, lid droppers, accumulators
and heated hoppers
CEO: G Donald Murray
Estimated Sales: $1-5 Million
Number Employees: 10-19
Square Footage: 30000
Parent Co: Wild Horse Industrial Corporation
Brands:
  Simplex

29252 Simplex Time Recorder Company
1936 E Deere Avenue
Suite 120
Santa Ana, CA 92705-5732

949-724-5000
Fax: 978-630-7856

Manufacturer and exporter of fire alarms and time
recorders
General Manager: Russell Stafford
Area/Branch Manager: Gary Holmes
Estimated Sales: $1-5 Million
Number Employees: 100
Brands:
  Simplex

29253 Simplex Time Recorder Company
1936 E Deere Avenue
Suite 120
Santa Ana, CA 92705-5732

949-724-5000
Fax: 978-630-7856 800-746-7539
Manufacturer and exporter of fire alarm and security
systems
General Manager: Russell Stafford
Estimated Sales: $1-5 Million
Number Employees: 20

29254 Simplimatic Automation
1046 W London Park Dr
Forest, VA 24551

434-385-9181
Fax: 434-385-7813 800-294-2003
sales@simplimatic.com www.simplimatic.com
Manufacturer and exporter of product handling
equipment including tray film packaging systems,
palletizers and de-palletizers, rinsers and conveyor
systems.
Chief Executive Officer: Tom DiNardo
Year Founded: 1965
Estimated Sales: $100+ Million
Number Employees: 51-200
Square Footage: 60000
Brands:
  Simpli-Clean
  Simpli-Flex
  Simpli-Pak
  Simpli-Pal
  Simpli-Snap
  Sure-Grip

29255 Simply Manufacturing
E11259 County Road Pf
Prairie Du Sac, WI 53578

608-643-6656
www.simplymfg.com
Meat processing accessories and replacement parts
such as vats, meat sticks, ham press towers, screens,
and portable racks.
Contact: Mike Disrud
mike.disrud@simplymfg.com

29256 Simply Products
RR 5
Box 5299
Kunkletown, PA 18058-9696

610-681-6894
Fax: 610-681-6885
Software for point of sale and back office systems
President: Dave Rottkamp
VP Operations: Allison Ohl
Number Employees: 6
Square Footage: 8000
Brands:
  Simply Food

29257 Simpson Electric
2916 Kelly Dr
Elgin, IL 60124-4349

847-697-2260
Fax: 847-697-2272 cservice@simpsonelectric.com
www.simpsonelectric.com
Process control systems
Founder: Ray Simpson
Estimated Sales: $20-50 Million
Number Employees: 10-19

29258 Sims Machinery Co Inc
3621 45th St SW
PO Box 446
Lanett, AL 36863-6305

334-576-2101
Fax: 334-576-3116 sales@simsmachinery.com
www.simsmachinery.com
Manufacturer and exporter of stainless steel food
grade tanks; also, custom stainless steel fabrications
available
CEO: Lynn Duncan
Sales Manager: Bryant Hollon

Estimated Sales: $5-10 Million
Number Employees: 10-19
Square Footage: 80000

29259 Sims Superior Seating
6951 Highway 42
Locust Grove, GA 30248-4640

770-957-9667
Fax: 770-954-1935 800-729-9178
simssales@simsseating.com www.simsseating.com
Restaurant hospitality seating, booths, tabletops and
bases, kitchen equipment covers and plantters
Owner: Cathy Sims
CFO: Kathryn Sims
VP: Charles Sims
Sales: T Wonder
csims@simsseating.com
Plant Manager: T Wonder
Estimated Sales: $5-10 Million
Number Employees: 20-49
Square Footage: 56000

29260 Sinco
3965 Pepin Avenue
Red Wing, MN 55066-1837

860-632-0500
Fax: 860-632-1509 800-243-6753
Manufacturer and exporter of safety netting systems
for guarding material handling equipment including
conveyors, pallet racks, etc
President: David Denny
Estimated Sales: $10-20 Million
Number Employees: 40

29261 Sine Pump
14845 W 64th Ave
Arvada, CO 80007-7523

303-425-0800
Fax: 303-425-0896 888-504-8301
pumps@sundyne.com www.sinepump.com
Manufacturer and exporter of sanitary positive dis-
placement pumps for the food and dairy industries
including low-shear, low-pulsation and high-suction.
designs, manufactures and supports industrial pump
and compressor products for theprocess fluid and
gas industries
President: William Taylor
Human Resources: Christine Lopez
Area Sales Manager: Brad Juntunen
After Market Specialist: Chuck Zachrich
Number Employees: 500-999
Parent Co: Sundyne Corporation
Brands:
  Sine Pump

29262 Sinicrope & Sons Inc
1124 Westminster Ave
Alhambra, CA 91803-1294

323-283-5131
Fax: 323-283-3399
Store fixtures
President: Gary Sinicrope
gary@sinicropeandsons.com
VP: Sandra Sinicrope
Estimated Sales: Below $5,000,000
Number Employees: 20-49

29263 Sioux Corp
1 Sioux Plz
Beresford, SD 57004-1500

605-763-3333
Fax: 605-763-3334 888-763-8833
email@sioux.com www.sioux.com
Manufacturer and exporter of hot, cold and combi-
nation pressure washers and steam cleaners; also,
all-electric and explosion-proof units available
President/Owner: Jack Finger
CEO: Amanda Cooper
acooper@sioux.eu
Marketing Manager: Jessica Johnson
Sales Manager: Meg Andersen
Regional Manager-International Sales (: David
Nelson
Estimated Sales: $2.5-5 Million
Number Employees: 20-49
Number of Products: 500+
Brands:
  Dakota
  Sioux
  Steam-Flo

29264 Sioux Falls Rbr Stamp Works
212 S Main Ave
Sioux Falls, SD 57104-6310
605-334-5990
Fax: 605-334-0750 855-334-5990
www.sfrubberstamp.com
Rubber stamps
President: Paul Brue
order.sfrubberstamp@midconetwork.com
Estimated Sales: $1-5 Million
Number Employees: 1-4

29265 Sipco
12610 Galveston Road
Webster (Houston), TX 77598
281-480-8711
Fax: 281-480-8656 info@sipco-mls.com
www.sipco-mls.com
Mechanical linkage solutions
Manager: Tom Jones
Accountant: Marissa Reise
Estimated Sales: $10-20 Million
Number Employees: 20-49
Parent Co: Standalone
Type of Packaging: Private Label, Bulk

29266 Sipco Products
4301 Prospect Road
Peoria Heights, IL 61616-6537
309-682-5400
Fax: 309-637-5120 terry@sipcoproducts.com
www.pnduniforms.com
Ashtray receptacles, smoking urns, safety related items, wire racks and plastic bag holders; exporter of ashtray receptacles
President: Eileen Grawey
Office Manager: Audrey Wylie
Contact: Sharon Brick
sharon@sipcoproducts.com
Estimated Sales: $3-5 Million
Number Employees: 1-4
Square Footage: 40000
Type of Packaging: Food Service
Brands:
  Rack-A-Bag
  Sipco Dunking Station

29267 Sirco Systems
2828 Messer Airport Highway
Birmingham, AL 35203
205-731-7800
Fax: 205-731-7885
Manufacturer and exporter of food storage equipment including steel drums
VP Sales: Jack Matheson
Estimated Sales: $5-10 Million
Number Employees: 50-99
Parent Co: Jemison Investment Company

29268 Sirman Spa/IFM USA
9490 Franklin Ave
Franklin Park, IL 60131-2833
847-288-9500
Fax: 847-288-9501 www.ifmusa.com
CEO: Alessandro Lorengato
Estimated Sales: $1-5 Million
Number Employees: 1-4

29269 Sitka Store Fixtures
PO Box 410247
Kansas City, MO 64141-0247
816-531-8290
Fax: 816-753-5701 800-821-7558
Wooden retail store fixtures including customer service centers and bakery, deli, produce and feature display
President: Patrick Clifford
Sales/Design: Brian Kipper
Project/Production Manager: Dave Sellers
Number Employees: 21
Square Footage: 68000
Parent Co: Cliff-Stan Industries

29270 Sitma USA
Via Vignolese
Spilamberto, MO 41057
390-597-8031
Fax: 390-597-8030 800-728-1254
sitmausa@sitma.com www.sitma.com
Manufacturer and importer of packaging equipment including horizontal form, fill and seal systems and bundle wrappers

President: Aris Ballestrazzi
CEO/Managing Director: Pete Butikis
National Sales Manager: Al Lindsay
Estimated Sales: $2.5-5 Million
Number Employees: 10-19
Square Footage: 66000
Parent Co: Sitma Machinery SPA
Other Locations:
  Sitma USA
  BP 28-77013 Melun Cedex

29271 Sitram/Global Marketing
PO Box 5503
Parsippany, NJ 07054-6503
973-515-0085
Fax: 973-515-3467 800-515-8585
Manufactures stainless steel cookware with new surface technology, cybernox
President: Christopher D Boyhan
Vice President: Allan Wolk
Estimated Sales: $1-2.5 Million
Number Employees: 19
Parent Co: Sitram France
Brands:
  Catering
  Cybernox
  Magnum
  Profiserie

29272 Sivetz Coffee
349 SW 4th St
Corvallis, OR 97333-4622
541-753-9713
Fax: 541-757-7644
Roasted coffee beans, extracts, almond kernels, hazelnut kernels, and coffee roasting machines
President: Mike Sivetz
Number Employees: 1-4
Type of Packaging: Consumer, Bulk
Brands:
  Sivetz Coffee Essence

29273 Six Hardy Brush Manufacturing
1172 East St S
Suffield, CT 06078-2410
860-623-8465
Specialty bakers' and confectioners' brushes
President: Steven Pierz
Estimated Sales: $2.5-5 Million
Number Employees: 5 to 9
Square Footage: 6400

29274 Skalar Inc
5012 Bristol Industrial # 107
Suite 107
Buford, GA 30518-1775
770-945-6008
Fax: 770-416-6718 800-782-4994
info@skalar-us.com www.skalar-us.com
Wine industry lab equipment, flow analyzers, process analyzers, robotic analyzers
President: Lel Seruyzken
CFO: Sjaak Surrer
Quality Control: Jomen Ting
Estimated Sales: Below $5 Million
Number Employees: 10-19

29275 Skc Inc
850 Clark Dr # 2
Budd Lake, NJ 07828-4313
973-347-7000
Fax: 973-347-7775 800-526-2717
jbrown@skcfilms.com www.skcfilms.com
Polyester film
President: Y J Joon
Contact: Chai Chuly
cchai@skcfilms.com
Estimated Sales: Less Than $500,000
Number Employees: 5-9

29276 (HQ)Skd Distribution Corp
13010 180th St
Jamaica, NY 11434-4108
718-525-6000
Fax: 718-276-4595 800-458-8753
rachel@skdparty.com www.biggiftbow.com
Manufacturer and exporter of plastic molders and fabricators, rigid foam fillers, wedges and foam packing inserts for boxes
Manager: Richard Mark
VP: Jack Schnitt
Marketing: Bill Stephan
Contact: Stanley Ast
sast@skdparty.com

Estimated Sales: $5-10 Million
Number Employees: 20-49
Square Footage: 1080000

29277 Skinetta Pac-Systems
55742 Currant Road
Mishawaka, IN 46545-4808
574-254-1950
Fax: 219-254-1955 info@skinetta.com
Packaging machinery: end-of-line machines
Estimated Sales: $2.5-5 Million
Number Employees: 4

29278 Skinner Sheet
3536 Bee Cave Road
Suite 211
West Lake Hills, TX 78746-5474
512-328-7785
Fax: 512-328-7786
Corrugated board products

29279 (HQ)Skrmetta Machinery Corporation
3536 Lowerline Street
New Orleans, LA 70125-1004
504-488-4413
Fax: 504-488-4432
Manufacturer and exporter of shrimp peeling and deveining machinery
President: Eric Skrmetta
VP: Dennis Skrmetta
Estimated Sales: $5,800,000
Number Employees: 55
Square Footage: 40000
Other Locations:
  Skrmetta Machinery Corp.
  New Orleans LA

29280 Slautterback Corporation
11475 Lakefield Drive
Duluth, GA 30097-1511
831-373-3900
Fax: 831-373-0385 800-827-3308
www.slautterback.com
Manufacturer and exporter of hot melt adhesive packaging equipment
President: Fred Erler
President, Chief Executive Officer: Michael Hilton
Marketing Manager: Jim Pagnella
Vice President of Systems: Douglas Bloomfield
Number Employees: 135
Square Footage: 252000
Parent Co: Nordson Corporation

29281 Slicechief Co
3333 Maple St
P.O. Box 80206
Toledo, OH 43608-1147
419-241-7647
Fax: 419-241-3513
Manufacturer and exporter of nonelectric vegetable/fruit slicers and cheese shredders
President: Sue Brown
Estimated Sales: $2.5-5 Million
Number Employees: 1-4
Type of Packaging: Food Service
Brands:
  Chief 900 Series

29282 Slidell
PO Box 39
New Market, MN 55054-0039
507-451-0365
Fax: 507-451-2405 800-328-1769
Packaging equipment for paper or plastic needs
Estimated Sales: $20-50 Million
Number Employees: 100

29283 Slip Not
2545 Beaufait St
Detroit, MI 48207-3467
313-923-0400
Fax: 313-923-4555 800-754-7668
info@slipnot.com www.slipnot.com
SlipNOT manufactures NSF registered stainless steel slip resistant flooring products from floor plates, drain covers, bar grating, ladder rungs/covers, to stair treads/covers, perforated and expanded metal retrofit plates. SlipNOTproducts can withstand the extreme cold of cyrogenics and heat of cookers, as well as caustic cleaning agents.
President: William S Molnar
National Sales Manager: Brian Pelto

Estimated Sales: $.5-1 million
Number Employees: 20-49
Parent Co: WS Monar Comapany
Brands:
  Flex-Grip
  Grid-Grip
  Grip-Grate
  Grip-Plate
  Slipnot

29284 Slip-Not Belting Corporation
PO Box 386
Kingsport, TN 37662

423-246-8141
Fax: 423-246-7728

Manufacturer and exporter of leather, plastic and perlon transmission and conveyor belting
President/CEO: David Shivell
CEO: Phill Shivell
Marketing: David Shivell
Estimated Sales: $3-5 Million
Number Employees: 5-9

29285 Slm Manufacturing Corp
215 Davidson Ave
Somerset, NJ 08873-4190

732-469-7500
Fax: 732-469-5546 800-526-3708
slminfo@slmcorp.com www.slmcorp.com

Semi-rigid plastic cut to size roll form tubing that can be combined with stock end caps to form complete tooling-free packages
Owner: Thomas Vajtay
tvajtay@slmcorp.com
Estimated Sales: $2.5-5 Million
Number Employees: 5-9

29286 Smalley Manufacturing Co Inc
10640 Dutchtown Rd
Knoxville, TN 37932-3205

865-966-5866
Fax: 865-675-1618 droberto@smalleymfg.com
www.smalleymfg.com

Conveyor, feeder and storage systems
President: Dale Roberto
VP Sales: Mike Green
Sales Engineer: Keith Iddins
Sales: Mark Kipfer
Estimated Sales: $10-20 Million
Number Employees: 50-99
Square Footage: 92000

29287 Smalley Package Company
PO Box 231
Berryville, VA 22611

540-955-2550
Fax: 540-955-4590

Wooden, pallets, pallet boxes, baskets; also, recycled/remanufactured pallets
President: Robert W Smalley Jr
Vice President: James Livengood
Sales Director: William Hair
Estimated Sales: $5-10 Million
Number Employees: 1-4

29288 Smartscan, Inc
33083 Eight Mile Road
Livonia, MI 48152

248-477-2900
Fax: 248-477-7453 ussales@smartscan.com
www.smartscaninc.com

Variable beam spacing, link systems, marshaling boxes, and light curtaining
President: Paul Budesheim
paul.budesheim@smartscaninc.com
CFO: Paul Budesheim
Quality Control: Paul Budesheim
General Manager: Paul Budesheim
Estimated Sales: $20-50 Million
Number Employees: 20-49
Number of Products: 4

29289 Smetco
PO Box 560
14633 Ottaway Rd NE
Aurora, OR 97002

503-678-3081
Fax: 503-678-3095 800-253-5400
www.smetco.com

Manufacturer and exporter of pallet handling systems for sorting and repair; also, conveyors, scissor lifts, dispensers, stackers and turn tables

President: John Smet
CFO: Kelly Wick
Vice President: John Smets
Marketing Director: Ken Butler
Contact: Carloyn Herman
carolynh@smetco.com
Estimated Sales: $1-3 Million
Number Employees: 20-49
Square Footage: 116000
Brands:
  Smetco
  Stackers

29290 Smico Manufacturing Co Inc
6101 Camille Ave
Oklahoma City, OK 73149-5036

405-946-1461
Fax: 405-946-1472 800-351-9088
www.smico.com

Manufacturer and exporter of vibrating screens and gyratory sifters
President: Randall Stoner
smico@smico.com
CEO: Erick Held
VP: Tim Douglass
Sales: Holly Lindsey
Operations: Randall Stoner
Purchasing Director: Jane Wenk
Estimated Sales: $5-10 Million
Number Employees: 20-49
Square Footage: 92000

29291 Smith & Loveless Inc
14040 Santa Fe Trail Dr
Lenexa, KS 66215-1284

913-888-5201
Fax: 913-888-2173 800-898-9122
answers@smithandloveless.com
www.smithandloveless.com

Water and wastewater treatment and transfer equipment
President: Frank Rebori
CFO: David Ferbezar
Estimated Sales: $30-50 Million
Number Employees: 250-499

29292 Smith & Taylor
1071 Howell Mill Rd NW
Atlanta, GA 30318-5557

404-872-8135
Fax: 404-872-0471 sunlow1@aol.com

Owner: Danny Graham
Sales Director: Jerry Hernnebaul
Estimated Sales: $3-5 Million
Number Employees: 10-19

29293 Smith Design Associates
205 Thomas St
Bloomfield, NJ 07003

973-429-2177
Fax: 973-429-7119 laraine@smithdesign.com
www.smithdesign.com

Package design and brand identity
President: Laraine Smith
CFO: James C Smith
Contact: Laraine Blauvelt
laraine@smithdesign.com
Estimated Sales: $5 Million
Number Employees: 10-19
Type of Packaging: Consumer, Private Label

29294 Smith Packaging
6045 Kestrel Road
Mississauga, ON L5T 1Y8
Canada

905-564-6640
Fax: 905-564-5681

Manufacturer and exporter of boxes, cartons and containers
President: Mervin Hillier
Operations Manager: Gerard Gregoire
Number Employees: 100
Type of Packaging: Consumer, Bulk

29295 Smith Pallet Co Inc
159 Polk Road 29
PO Box 207
Hatfield, AR 71945-7002

870-389-6184
Fax: 870-389-6194 spallet@windstream.net
www.smithpallet.com

Skids, crating, dunnage, boxes and hooked and soft-wood pallets

President: Jim Wilson
jwilson@smithpallet.com
Sales Manager: Tate Mendoza
Sales: Jim Mabry
General Manager: Lyle Wilson
Controller: Bryan Schoeppey
Plant Manager: Dalton Doughty
Estimated Sales: Below $5 Million
Number Employees: 100-249

29296 Smith, RD, Company
PO Box 186
Eau Claire, WI 54702

715-832-3479
Fax: 715-832-7456 800-826-7336
www.rdsmithco.com

Centrifuges, cheese equipment, flow diversion stations, heat exchangers, ladders, vats
President: Frederick Smith
Controller: Steve Burk
Vice President of Administration: Joan Bliesener
Vice President of Operations: Bob Kutchera
Estimated Sales: $5-10 Million
Number Employees: 10-19

29297 Smith-Berger Marine
7915 10th Ave S
Seattle, WA 98108-4404

206-764-4650
Fax: 206-764-4653 sales@smithberger.com
www.smithberger.com

Processing machinery for pacific salmon prior to canning; leasing available
President: Bonnie Warrick
CFO: Bonnie Warrick
Sales Exec: Tom Phipps
Estimated Sales: $1-2.5 Million
Number Employees: 20-49
Square Footage: 30000
Brands:
  Berger
  Smith Berger

29298 Smith-Emery Co
781 E Washington Blvd
Los Angeles, CA 90021-3091

213-745-5333
Fax: 213-741-8620 mktla@smithemery.com
www.smithemery.com

Consultant specializing in air pollution analysis
President: James E Partridge
VP Marketing: Fred Partridge
Estimated Sales: $10-20 Million
Number Employees: 100-249

29299 Smith-Lee Company
2920 N Main St.
PO Box 2038
Oshkosh, WI 54901

315-363-2500
Fax: 315-363-9573 800-327-9774
marketing@hoffmaster.com www.hoffmaster.com

Manufacturer and exporter of paper plates, place mats, napkins, bottle caps and packaged lace and linen doilies
President: Jonathan M Groat
VP Sales: Thomas Hennessey
VP Manufacturing: Alan Mattei
Estimated Sales: $10-20 Million
Number Employees: 50-99
Parent Co: Hoffmaster Group, Inc
Brands:
  Serv-Ease

29300 Smith-Lustig Paper Box Manufacturing
2165 E 31st St
Cleveland, OH 44115

216-621-0454
Fax: 216-621-0483

Manufacturer and exporter of paper boxes
President: Richard Ames
Contact: Jim Di Francesco
jdifrancesco@smithlustigbox.com
Estimated Sales: $5-10 Million
Number Employees: 20-49

29301 Smokaroma
62 Bar-B-Que Avenue
P.O.Box 25
Boley, OK 74829-0025

918-667-3341
Fax: 918-667-3935 800-331-5565
www.smokaroma.com

Manufacturer and exporter of barbecuing, smoking and cooking equipment for hamburgers, hot dogs, sausage patties, chicken fillets, etc.; also, spices for meat and barbecue sauce mix
Owner: Maurice W Lee Iii
CEO: Maurice Lee Jr
Marketing Director: Tonia Guess
Estimated Sales: $5-10 Million
Number Employees: 10-19
Square Footage: 160000
Brands:
  Bar B O Boss Sauce Mix
  Bar Bq Boss
  Instant Burger
  One Step Prep Mix
  Red Rub

29302 Smoke Right
4602 S Pulaski Rd
Chicago, IL 60632-4038
647-933-0623
Fax: 312-425-0020 888-375-8885
Smoke-free ashtrays
Owner: Anna Greengurg
Circulation Coordinator: Envija Svanberga
Marketing Director: Roseanna Mazzei
Production Manager: Lynne Campbell
Estimated Sales: $300,000-500,000
Number Employees: 1-4
Brands:
  Smoke Right

29303 Smokehouse Limited
4867 NC Highway 22 N
Franklinville, NC 27248
336-824-1424
Fax: 336-824-1026 800-554-8385
info@smokehouselimited.com
www.smokehouselimited.com
Supplies pneumatic seals and foam over door gaskets for smokehouses, brine chillers and other processing equipment.

29304 Smoot Co
1250 Seminary St
Kansas City, KS 66103-2599
913-362-1710
Fax: 913-362-7863 800-748-7000
smootco@aol.com www.magnumsystems.com
President: Gary Saunders
gsaunders@magnumsystems.com
Estimated Sales: $10-20 Million
Number Employees: 50-99

29305 Smurfit Kappa
1161 E Walnut St
Carson, CA 90746-1317
310-537-8190
Fax: 310-604-4880
Designer and manufacturer of corrugated packaging displays, industrial containers, cardboard counter displays, bulk boxes, cardboard sheets, marketing displays, pallet display, point of purchase displays, shipping containers, shippingboxes and custom consumer packaging.
President: Lewis Eagle
CEO: Brenda Beltran
brenda@empirepackaginganddisplays.com
VP: Norman Eagle
Estimated Sales: $10-20 Million
Number Employees: 50-99
Type of Packaging: Consumer, Food Service, Private Label, Bulk

29306 Smurfit Stone
504 Thrasher St
Norcross, GA 30071-1967
314-656-5300
Fax: 716-694-9262 www.smurfit.com
Packaging materials including corrugated boxes
Contact: Rod Castor
rcastor@smurfit.com
General Manager: Andrew Giambroni
Estimated Sales: Below $5 Million
Number Employees: 50-99
Parent Co: Jefferson Smurfit

29307 Smurfit Stone
504 Thrasher St
Norcross, GA 30071-1967
314-656-5300
Fax: 408-293-1022 www.smurfit.com

Containerboard and corrugated containers, point-of-purchase displays, specialty boxes, consumer packaging, recycled materials packaging and containers and packaging
Executive Secretary: Karen Korienek
Executive Secretary (Carol Stream): Janelle Lenza
VP Sales/Marketing (Carol Stream): James Duncan
Manager E-Commerce: Greg St Laurent
Executive Secretary (Procurement): Ronald Daniels
Contact: Rod Castor
rcastor@smurfit.com
Manager: Chad Wilson
VP (Procurement): Mark O'Bryan
Estimated Sales: $10-20 Million
Number Employees: 20-49
Square Footage: 220000
Parent Co: Jefferson Smurfit Group
Type of Packaging: Consumer, Private Label, Bulk

29308 Smurfit Stone Container
8182 Maryland Ave
Suite 1100
St Louis, MO 63105-3915
314-679-2300
Fax: 314-679-2300
Folding cartons, corrugated containers and labels including printed paper, foil and heat transfer; exporter of linerboard
VP Corporate Sales/Marketing: Jack Straw
Marketing: James P Duncan
Contact: Mary Duda
mduda@smurfit.com
Estimated Sales: $1-5 Million
Number Employees: 20-49
Parent Co: Jefferson Smurfit Group

29309 Smurfit Stone Container
1980 S 7th St
San Jose, CA 95112
408-925-9391
Fax: 408-293-1022 888-801-2579
bags@smurfit.com www.smurfit-stone.com
Valve bag filling systems, force air packers, jet flow impeller packers, easiflow screw packers, gravity fill bags, bulk bag fillers, bag sealer
Manager: Chad Wilson
Estimated Sales: $10-20 Million
Number Employees: 20-49

29310 Smurfit-Stone ContainerCorp
13833 Freeway Dr
Santa Fe Springs, CA 90670-5701
714-523-3550
Fax: 562-921-0620 www.westrock.com
Corrugated boxes and displays
CFO: Paul Hailey
Cmo: Tom Vogan
tvogan@smurfit.com
President: Dale McClurgh
Quality Control: Debra Heyeen
Sales Manager: Morgan Welch
Production Manager: Paul Smith
Estimated Sales: $30-50 Million
Number Employees: 100-249
Square Footage: 250000
Parent Co: Stone Container Corporation

29311 Smurfit-Stone ContainerCorporation
4364 SW 34th St
Orlando, FL 32811
407-843-1300
Fax: 407-843-8459 888-254-6696
pkequipment@smurfit.com
www.smurfit-stone.com
President: Tom Graham
Contact: Amer Aganovic
aganovica@transitair.com
Estimated Sales: $20-50 Million
Number Employees: 20-49

29312 Smyrna Container Co
4676 S Atlanta Rd SE
Atlanta, GA 30339-1503
404-794-4305
Fax: 404-799-7209 800-868-4305
Paper folding boxes for bakeries, pizza and carry-out
President: Blair Harrell
bharrell@smyrnacontainer.com
Estimated Sales: $1-2.5 Million
Number Employees: 10-19
Square Footage: 50000

29313 Smyth Co
311 W Depot St
Bedford, VA 24523-1937
540-586-2311
Fax: 540-586-0549 800-950-7011
www.smythco.com
Pressure sensitive, sheeted, in-mold and PET labels; also, graphic design services available
Manager: Ben Witt
bwitt@smytheco.com
Marketing Communications Manager: Bill Orme
VP Sales/Marketing: Bill Bumgarner
Estimated Sales: $20-50 Million
Number Employees: 100-249
Square Footage: 125000

29314 (HQ)Smyth Co LLC
1085 Snelling Ave N
St Paul, MN 55108-2705
651-646-4544
Fax: 651-646-2385 800-473-3464
info@smythco.com www.smythco.com
Manufacturer of sheet-fed and pressure sensitive labels, coupons, and high speed labelers for consumer goods packaging.
President: Jim Lundquist
Chief Executive Officer: John Hickey
Chief Financial Officer: David Baumgardner
Executive Vice President: Daniel Hickey
Quality Control Manager: Donna Niedenfuer
Purchasing Manager: Tom Schoolmeesters
Estimated Sales: $41 Million
Number Employees: 10-19
Square Footage: 110000
Parent Co: G.G. McGuiggan Corporation
Other Locations:
  Smyth Companies
  Bedford PA

29315 Snack Food Assn
1600 Wilson Blvd # 650
Arlington, VA 22209-2510
703-836-4500
Fax: 703-836-8262 800-628-1334
www.snacintl.org
International trade association reprsenting snack manaufacturers and suppliers.
President: James Mccarthy
cmelchert@sfa.org
CEO: Tom Dempsey
Director of Finance and Administration: Paul Downey
Vice President, Meetings & Events: Liz Wells
Manager, Marketing and Member Services: David Walsh
Manager, Meetings & Events: Meegan Smith
Number Employees: 20-49

29316 Snap Drape Inc
2045 Westgate Dr # 100
Carrollton, TX 75006-9478
972-466-1030
Fax: 972-466-1049 800-527-5147
info@snapdrape.com www.snapdrape.com
Manufacturer and exporter of table skirting and drapes
President: Timothy Nealon
tmengel@msmandf.com
Contact: Daielon Sasser
Sales Manager: Kevin Burns
Estimated Sales: $10-20 Million
Number Employees: 50-99
Type of Packaging: Food Service

29317 Snap Drape International
2045 Westgate Dr
Suite 100
Carrollton, TX 75006
972-466-1030
Fax: 972-466-1049 800-527-5147
info@snapdrape.com www.snapdrape.com
President: Darrin Garlish
CEO: Felton Norris
CFO: John Phillips
Vice President: Ray Belknap
Marketing Manager: Tammy Brazeal
Sales Manager: Kevin Burns
Contact: Tim Nealon
t.nealon@msmandf.com
Operations Manager: Jose Aguado
Estimated Sales: $10-20 Million
Number Employees: 50-99

29318 Snapware
4101 Bonita Place
Fullerton, CA 92835-1007

714-446-9212
Fax: 714-446-9217 800-334-3062
www.snapware.com
Manufacture of Food Service containers, caps, and closures
President: John Lown
VP: Jim Spillane
Marketing: Heidi Slocumb
Sales: George Ghesquiere
Estimated Sales: $20-46 Million
Number Employees: 50-100
Number of Brands: 6
Number of Products: 15
Square Footage: 90000
Brands:
   Living Hinge
   Make a Gift Products
   Sandcap
   Snap'n Stack
   Snap-N-Serve
   Snapware

29319 Snee Chemical Co
5565 Pepsi St
New Orleans, LA 70123-3221

504-734-7633
Fax: 504-734-5221 800-489-7633
www.sneechemical.com
Janitorial supplies including detergents and soaps
President: Mitchell Mark
mmark@sneechemical.com
Estimated Sales: $5-10 Million
Number Employees: 20-49

29320 Sneezeguard Solutions
2508 Paris Rd
Columbia, MO 65202-2514

573-443-5756
Fax: 573-449-7126 800-569-2056
www.sneezeguardsolutions.com
Manufacturer and exporter of sneeze guards
President: Sydney Baumgartner
sneezeguard@centurytel.net
CFO: Susan Baumgaltner
Marketing: Bill Pfeiffer
Plant Manager: John Bazzell
Estimated Sales: $1-3 Million
Number Employees: 5-9
Number of Brands: 14
Number of Products: 14
Square Footage: 40000
Brands:
   Magic Buss
   Next Generation Magic Buss
   Plexus
   Sampler
   Sneezeguard

29321 Snowden Enterprises Inc
3257 E Central Ave
Fresno, CA 93725-2506

559-237-5546
Fax: 559-237-6383
SO2 dispensers
President: Kirk Snowden Shermer
Contact: Heather Pemble
heather.pemble@wellsfargo.com
Estimated Sales: $10-20 Million
Number Employees: 10-19

29322 Snyder Crown
602 Industrial St
Marked Tree, AR 72365-1909

870-358-3400
Fax: 870-358-3140
Manufacturer and exporter of custom, rotational-molded plastic transport tanks, storage bins and containers
Director Marketing: David Kelley
Director Operations: Dale Givens
Plant Manager: Ronnie Stone
Estimated Sales: $10-20 Million
Number Employees: 20 to 49

29323 Snyder Industries Inc
736 Birginal Dr
Bensenville, IL 60106-1213

630-773-9510
Fax: 630-773-4274 877-768-6642
www.snydernet.com
Manager: Jay Rule

Estimated Sales: $30-50 Million
Number Employees: 50-99

29324 Snyder Industries Inc.
4700 Fremont Street
P.O. Box 4583
Lincoln, NE 68504

Fax: 402-465-1220 800-351-1363
www.snyderplasticsolutions.com
Custom rotational molded plastic containers
President: David Fair
Contact: Marjorie Badousek
mbadousek@snydernet.com
Production Manager: Claretta Jo Segura
Number Employees: 20-49

29325 SoOPAK
2280 Drew Road
Mississauga, ON L5S 1B8
Canada

855-766-7225
905-677-9666
soopak.com
Cartons and boxes
President: Jiang Yajun
Sales Manager: Tony Li
Year Founded: 2014
Number Employees: 11-50
Type of Packaging: Consumer

29326 Sobel Corrugated Containers
18612 Miles Rd
Cleveland, OH 44128

216-475-2100
Fax: 216-475-2107
Corrugated containers
President: Arthur Sobel
Executive VP: Terry Sobel
Estimated Sales: $20-50 Million
Number Employees: 20-49

29327 Soco System USA
1931 Mac Arthur Rd
Waukesha, WI 53188-5702

262-547-0777
Fax: 262-547-4707 800-535-SOCO
info@socosysteminc.com
www.johnmayecompany.com
End-of-line packing and handling systems, case sealers and palleters
Owner: John Maye
Service Manager: Tage Peterson
Sales Director: Hans Sondersted
Contact: Paul Bangs
pb@socosystem.com
Estimated Sales: $5-10 Million
Number Employees: 10-19

29328 Soco System USA
1931 Mac Arthur Rd
Waukesha, WI 53188-5702

262-547-0777
Fax: 262-547-4707 800-441-6293
www.johnmayecompany.com
Owner: John Maye
Accounts: Don Mertins
Sales: Jeff Devorse
Contact: Paul Bangs
pb@socosystem.com
Operations: John Maye
Estimated Sales: $5-10 Million
Number Employees: 10-19
Type of Packaging: Consumer

29329 Sodexo Inc
9801 Washingtonian Blvd
Gaithersburg, MD 20878

301-987-4000
888-763-3967
NorAmSodexoInsights@sodexo.com
www.sodexousa.com
Food Service management business.
CEO, Government: Brett Ladd
SVP & CFO: Ramesh Mahal
Year Founded: 1966
Estimated Sales: $9.5 Billion
Number Employees: 133,000
Parent Co: Sodexo

29330 Sohn Manufacturing
PO Box X
Elkhart Lake, WI 53020-0427

920-876-3361
Fax: 920-876-2952

Label printing and die-cutting machines, automatic label dispensers and paper converters; also, inks, printing plates, label stocks and printed labels
President: Wallace Beaudry
Estimated Sales: $20-50 Million
Number Employees: 100-249
Square Footage: 100000

29331 Solapak
8219 Saint James Avenue
Elmhurst, NY 11373-3720

718-457-9589
Fax: 718-396-2875
Automatic wrapping machines
President: Wang
Number Employees: 10-19

29332 Solarflo Corp
22901 Aurora Rd
Bedford, OH 44146-1701

440-439-1680
Fax: 440-439-8612 www.solarflo.com
President: Jeff Briggs
jeffb@solarflo.com
Production & Chief Technician: Dave Frederick
Purchasing: Mike Kane
Estimated Sales: $3-5 Million
Number Employees: 10-19

29333 Solazyme Inc
225 Gateway Blvd
S San Francisco, CA 94080-7019

650-589-5883
Fax: 650-989-6700
Microalgae-based healthy food ingredients and oils. Microalgae-derived lipid, protein and fiber-based products for nutrition, taste, texture and functionality.
CEO: Jonathan Wolfson
CFO & COO: Tyler Painter
Contact: Annie Chang
achang@solazyme.com
Estimated Sales: Less Than $500,000
Number Employees: 1-4
Type of Packaging: Bulk
Other Locations:
   Global Headquarters
   San Francisco CA
   Midwestern Operations
   Peoria IL
   South American Operations
   Sao Paulo, Brazil

29334 Solbern Corp
8 Kulick Rd
Fairfield, NJ 07004-3385

973-227-3030
Fax: 973-227-3069 sales@solbern.com
www.solbern.com
Manufacturer and exporter of container filling and dough folding equipment
President: Gil Foulon
VP: Jorge Espino
VP: Tom Berger
Marketing Director: Jorge Espino
Sales: Jorge Espino
Operations: Tom Berger
Estimated Sales: $5-10,000,000
Number Employees: 20-49
Square Footage: 24000

29335 Solganik & Associates
116 N Jefferson St
Dayton, OH 45402-1385

937-438-1666
Fax: 937-433-2354 800-253-8512
Consultant specializing in retail food service and product development
VP: Carin Solganik
Estimated Sales: $500,000-$1 Million
Number Employees: 50-99
Square Footage: 20000

29336 Solid Surface Acrylics
800 Walck Rd # 14
North Tonawanda, NY 14120-3500

716-743-1870
Fax: 716-743-0475 888-595-4114
info@ssacrylics.com
www.solid-surface-acrylics.com
Acrylic solid surface tabletops, cutting boards, serving trays, planters, logo tops

President: Jack Tillotson
jtillotson@ssacrylics.com
CEO: Robert Barenthaler
Designer: Melissa Aldrich
VP Sales: Allen Vaillancourt
Shipping Manager: Barb Smith
Plant Manager: Mark Lawrence
Estimated Sales: $2.5-5 Million
Number Employees: 20-49
Square Footage: 120000
Brands:
    Dinelle

29337 Solka-Floc
1 Park 80 Plaza W
Saddle Brook, NJ 07663-5808

201-712-1188
Fax: 201-712-1250

29338 Sollas Films & PackagingSystems
146 Keystone Drive
Montgomeryville, PA 18936-9637

215-283-3250
Fax: 215-283-3254 film@rtgpkg.com
www.rtgpkg.com
Acrylic coated, shrinkable, and co-ex polypropylene,
polyethylene films, polyolefin films, and printed,
pearlescent, mettalized, barrier, laminations, cellophane, mylar and tear-tape specialty films, wrapping
equipment, bandingequipment and cartostretch

29339 Solo Cup Company
150 Spouth Saunders Rd.
Lake Forest, IL 60045

info@solocup.com
www.solocup.com
Single-use cups, plates, cutlery, take-out contaiers.
CEO, Dart Container Corporation: Jim Lammers
Year Founded: 1936
Estimated Sales: $1.6 Billion
Number Employees: 6,400
Parent Co: Dart Container Corporation
Type of Packaging: Consumer, Food Service, Pri-
    vate Label, Bulk

29340 Solo Foods
5315 Dansher Road
Countryside, IL 60525

800-328-7656
info@solofoods.com www.solofoods.com
Cake and pastry fillings, almond paste and marzipan,
pie and dessery fillings, marshmallow and toasted
marshmallow creme, fruit butters, Asian dipping
sauces and marinades, seasoning mixes.
President: John Sokol Novak
COO: Ralph Pirritano
Contact: Sami Abdel-Malek
sabdel-malek@solofoods.com
Estimated Sales: $20-50 Million
Parent Co: Sokol and Company
Type of Packaging: Consumer, Food Service, Pri-
    vate Label
Brands:
    Baker
    Solo
    Simon Fischer
    Chun's

29341 Solon Manufacturing Company
7 Grasso Ave
North Haven, CT 6473

203-230-5300
Fax: 207-474-7320 800-341-6640
Wooden spoons and sticks for ice cream novelties
President: Steve Clark
CEO/CFO: Larry Feinn
Marketing Director: Jayne Norman
Sales Director: Grover Kilpatrick
Contact: Steve Laack
steve.laack@solon.com
Estimated Sales: $10-20 Million
Number Employees: 100-249
Type of Packaging: Private Label, Bulk

29342 Solus Industrial Innovations
30152 Aventura
Rcho Sta Marg, CA 92688-2019

949-589-3900
Fax: 949-858-0300 solusteam@solusii.com
www.solusii.com
CEO: Garland Jones
Contact: Sandra Leonard
solusteam@solusii.com

Estimated Sales: $50-100 Million
Number Employees: 100-249

29343 Solutions By Design
451 Clovis Ave # 130
Suite #130
Clovis, CA 93612-1338

559-326-7899
Fax: 559-436-5263 800-888-4084
support@solutionsbydesign.com
www.solutionsbydesign.com
Wine industry research
Owner: Rhoads Donald
rhoads.donald@solutionsbydesign.com
Marketing Director: Sherry Netto
Estimated Sales: $2.5-5 Million
Number Employees: 10-19

29344 Solutions Plus
2275 Cassens Drive
Suite 147
Fenton, MO 63026-2574

636-349-4922
Fax: 636-349-8027
Analytical standards and testing reagents
President: Nancy Brinner
Partner: Peter Ricca
Estimated Sales: $1-5 Million
Number Employees: 15
Square Footage: 8500

29345 Solvay Specialty Polymers LLC
4500 Mcginnis Ferry Rd
Alpharetta, GA 30005-2203

770-772-8200
Fax: 770-772-8454 www.solvayplastics.com
Research for industrial carbon fibers and engineer-
ing polymers
Number Employees: 100-249

29346 Solvay Specialty Polymers LLC
4500 Mcginnis Ferry Rd
Alpharetta, GA 30005-2203

770-772-8200
Fax: 770-772-8454 888-765-3378
www.solvayplastics.com
Polyvinylidene choloride extrusion resins,
polyvinylidene chloride soluble resins, and
polyvinylidene chloride aqueous dispensions
President: Roger Kurne
CEO: George Corbin
Number Employees: 100-249
Parent Co: Solvay Group

29347 Solve Needs International
10204 Highland Rd
White Lake, MI 48386

248-698-3200
Fax: 248-698-3070 800-783-2462
sales@solveneeds.com
Manufacturer, importer and exporter of corrugated
bins, boxes, dividers, drawers, shelving, cantilever
and pallet racks, hydraulic and scissor lifts, pallet
jacks, stairways, rolling ladders, casters, wheels,
carts, platform andutility trucks, new equipment and
repair parts, etc
President: Don Burski
Estimated Sales: $3-5 Million
Number Employees: 5-9
Square Footage: 200000
Brands:
    Ecoa
    Equipment Company of America

29348 Solvit
7001 Raywood Rd
Monona, WI 53713-2299

608-222-8624
Fax: 608-222-8733 888-314-1072
www.solvitnow.com
Solvit all-purpose pine cleaner including window,
toilet bowl cleaner, warewashing compounds, de-
greasers and rat and mouse bait stations
President: J H Kelly
solvit1@aol.com
Estimated Sales: $550,000
Number Employees: 1-4
Square Footage: 20000
Type of Packaging: Consumer, Food Service, Pri-
    vate Label
Brands:
    Solvit

29349 Solvox Manufacturing Company
PO Box 26506
Milwaukee, WI 53226

414-774-5664
Fax: 414-774-0888
Food grade defoamers including kosher; manufac-
turer of food grade cleaning compounds, sanitizers,
food ingredients commoditites, processing aids and
waste water tratment
VP: Glen Polzin
Marketing: Bill McCoy
Sales: Kim Ireland
Operations: Shane Ireland
Purchasing: Shane Ireland
Estimated Sales: $20-50 Million
Number Employees: 10
Number of Products: 100
Square Footage: 58000
Parent Co: Hydrite Chemical Company

29350 Somat Company
3200 Lakeville Hwy
Petaluma, CA 94954-5675

707-762-0071
Fax: 707-762-5036 www.stero.com
Director of Operations: Terry Goodfellow
General Manager: Lin Sensening
Parts Department: Wendy Grado
Director of Operations: Terry Goodfellow
Estimated Sales: D
Number Employees: 10,000

29351 Somerset Food Service
910 Highway 461
Somerset, KY 42503-0799

606-274-4858
Fax: 606-274-5141 800-264-2633
www.somersetfoods.com
Food distributor
President/CEO: Tim Williams
Co-Owner: Mac Goodby
Estimated Sales: $20-50 Million
Number Employees: 100-249

29352 Somerset Industries
1 Esquire Rd
Billerica, MA 1862

978-667-3355
Fax: 978-671-9466 800-772-4404
somerset@smrset.com www.smrset.com
Manufacturer and exporter of bakery equipment in-
cluding dough sheeters, rollers, fillers, depositors,
bread molders and croissant machines
CEO: Andrew Voyatzakis
Estimated Sales: $2.5-5 Million
Number Employees: 10
Brands:
    Cdr
    Gpf-1
    Somerset
    Spm-45

29353 Somerville Packaging
7830 Tranmere Drive
Mississauga, ON L5S 1L9
Canada

905-678-8211
Fax: 905-678-7462 info@cascades.com
Aluminum foil and cartons for milk, frozen foods,
juice and cereal
Estimated Sales: $1-5 Million
Number Employees: 1800
Parent Co: Paperboard Industries Corporation

29354 Somerville Packaging
5760 Finch Ave. East
Toronto, ON M1B 5J9
Canada

416-754-7228
Fax: 416-754-9574
Folding cartons and packaging systems
Customer Service Manager: D Hayes
Plant Manager: K Mucha
Estimated Sales: $1-5 Million
Number Employees: 100-250
Parent Co: Paperboard Industries Corporation

29355 Something Different Linen
474 Getty Ave
Clifton, NJ 07011

973-772-8019
Fax: 973-772-6519 800-422-2180
Manufacturer and exporter of tablecloths, skirting
and napkins; custom sizes available

939

President: Mitchell Smith
Quality Control: Micheal Gates
Sales Manager: Wally Rachmaciej
Contact: Aricelis Baiz
abaez@somethingdifferentlinen.com
Estimated Sales: $20-50 Million
Number Employees: 50-99
Parent Co: Something Different Linen

29356 Sommer Awning Company
1160 W 16th Street
Indianapolis, IN 46202

317-257-4300
Fax: 317-257-1973 855-257-4301
www.sommerawning.com
Commercial awnings
President/ Sales: Steve Sommer
CFO/ COO: Moises Lopez
Contact: Kent King
kent@apsigngroup.com
Estimated Sales: $300,000-500,000
Number Employees: 1-4

29357 Sommers Plastic ProductCo Inc
31 Styertowne Rd
Clifton, NJ 07012-1713

973-777-7888
Fax: 973-777-7890 800-225-7677
sales@sommers.com www.sommers.com
Manufacturer and exporter of plastic packaging
products including sheeting, fabrics, cloths and film
President: Ed Schecter
eschecter@aol.com
VP: Fred Schecter
R&D: Fred Schecter
Estimated Sales: $5-10 Million
Number Employees: 20-49

29358 Sonderen Packaging
2906 N Crestline St
PO Box 7369
Spokane, WA 99207-4809

509-487-1632
Fax: 509-483-2964 800-727-9139
www.sonderen.com
Paper folding boxes
President: Andrea Anger
andrea.anger@sonderen.com
Sales Manager: Steve Agen
Estimated Sales: $5-10 Million
Number Employees: 100-249
Square Footage: 170000

29359 Sonic Air Systems Inc
1050 Beacon St
Brea, CA 92821-2938

714-255-0124
Fax: 714-255-8366 800-827-6642
asksonic@sonicairsystems.com
www.sonicairsystems.com
Drying systems, air knives, blowers
Owner: Mary Hsu
yanina@pacificclinics.org
Estimated Sales: $5-10 Million
Number Employees: 20-49

29360 Sonic Corp
1 Research Dr
Stratford, CT 06615-7184

203-375-0063
Fax: 203-378-4079 866-493-1378
kurt.limbacher@sonicmixing.com
www.sonicmixing.com
Manufacturer and exporter of food processing ma-
chinery including propeller mixers, agitators, contin-
uous inline multiple-feed liquid blending systems,
colloid mills and homogenizing systems.
President: Robert Brakeman
rob.brakeman@sonicmixing.com
Sales Manager: Kurt Limbacher
Estimated Sales: $2.5-5 Million
Number Employees: 10-19
Square Footage: 26000
Brands:
 Sonolator
 Tri-Homo
 Typhoon
 Wizard

29361 Sonicor
82 Otis St
West Babylon, NY 11704-1406

631-920-6555
Fax: 631-920-6080 800-864-5022
customerservice@sonicor.com
Ultrasonic and nonultrasonic cleaning equipment for
processing machinery
President: Mike Parker
Marketing Manager: Gary Levanti
VP Sales: Ed Parker
Contact: Augusto D'Agostino
augusto@sonicor.com
Estimated Sales: $2.5-5 Million
Number Employees: 10-19

29362 Sonics & Materials Inc
53 Church Hill Rd # 2
Newtown, CT 06470-1699

203-270-4600
Fax: 203-270-4610 800-745-1105
info@sonics.com www.sonicsandmaterials.com
Manufacturer and exporter of liquid processing sys-
tems, food processing equipment, and food cutting
equipment.
President/CEO: Robert Soloff
CEO: Thomas Bennetti
tbennetti@sonics.com
Quality Control: Dan Grise
Sales Manager: Lois Baiad
Biotechnology Manager: Mike Donaty
North Am. Sales Mngr., Welding Products: Brian
Gourley
Estimated Sales: $10-20 Million
Number Employees: 50-99
Square Footage: 90000
Brands:
 Vibra-Cell

29363 Sonoco Alloyd
1500 Paramount Pkwy
Batavia, IL 60510-1468

630-879-0121
www.alloyd.com
Blister card packaging and insert cards
Vice President: Jim Lassiter
Estimated Sales: $10-20 000,000
Number Employees: 50-99
Parent Co: Sonoco Products Co

29364 Sonoco Paperboard Specialties
3150 Clinton Ct
Norcross, GA 30071

770-476-9088
Fax: 770-476-0765 800-264-7494
www.sonocospecialties.com
Manufacturer and exporter of biodegradable and re-
cyclable paperboard glassware caps used in the
lodging, food and hospital industries for sanitary
purposes
General Manager: Jeff Burgner
Division Controller: Gus Copeletti
gus.copeletti@sonoco.com
Plant Manager: Kelly Mowen
Plant Manager: Bill Janda
Estimated Sales: $5-10 Million
Number Employees: 20-49
Square Footage: 132000
Parent Co: Sonoco Products Co
Type of Packaging: Consumer, Food Service, Pri-
vate Label, Bulk

29365 Sonoco Products Co
1 N 2nd St
Hartsville, SC 29550-3305

843-383-7000
800-377-2692
corporate.communications@sonoco.com
www.sonoco.com
Global manufacturer of consumer and industrial
packing products and provider of packaging
services.
President & CEO: R. Howard Coker
VP & CFO: Julie Albrecht
EVP: Rodger Fuller
Corporate VP & CIO: Rick Johnson
VP, Marketing & Innovation: Marcy Thompson
Year Founded: 1899
Estimated Sales: $5 Billion
Number Employees: 21,000

29366 Sonoco ThermoSafe
3930 N Ventura Dr
Suite 450
Arlington Heights, IL 60004

800-323-7442
www.thermosafe.com
Insulated containers
Estimated Sales: $5-10 Million
Number Employees: 50-99
Square Footage: 92000
Parent Co: Sonoco Products Co

29367 Sonofresco
1365 Pacific Dr
Burlington, WA 98233

360-757-2800
Fax: 360-757-8172 office@sonofresco.com
sonofresco.com
Coffee roasting equipment.
Chief Operating Officer: Robert Penrose
Year Founded: 2000
Number Employees: 5-9
Parent Co: Coffee Holding Company, Inc.
Type of Packaging: Food Service

29368 Sonoma Pacific Company
1540 S Greenwood Avenue
Montebello, CA 90640-6536

323-838-4374
Fax: 323-838-4381
Manufacturer and recycler of pallets and skids in-
cluding hardwood, softwood and plywood
Regional Manager: Tony Serge
District Manager: Len Spitzer
Number Employees: 60
Square Footage: 500000
Parent Co: Palex

29369 Sonoma Signatures
4381 17th Street
San Francisco, CA 94114-1804

415-864-2582
Fax: 415-864-2582
Tea and coffee industry jars (glass)

29370 Soodhalter Plastics
PO Box 21276
Los Angeles, CA 90021

213-747-0231
Fax: 213-746-8125 soodhalterplastics@yahoo.com
Manufacturer, importer and exporter of party and bar
accessories including plastic cocktail forks, stirrers
and picks
President: Jackie Wolfson
CFO: Jackie Wolfson
Estimated Sales: $5-10 Million
Number Employees: 10-19

29371 Sooner Scientific
1501 Riverbluff Rd
PO Box 180
Idabel, OK 74745

405-237-0302
Fax: 580-286-4268 800-991-1974
DNA electrophoresis products
Estimated Sales: $1-2.5 Million
Number Employees: 1-4

29372 Sophia Foods
480 Wortman Ave
Brooklyn, NY 11208

718-272-1110
Fax: 718-272-1230 www.sophiafoods.com
Oil, vinegar, salt, vegetables, rice and grains, sauces
and spreads, pasta, crackers, grissini, cakes and
cookies, preserves and juices.
CEO: Candace Abitbul
candace@sophiafoods.com
Director of Sales & Business Development: Paul
Berger
Year Founded: 1991
Estimated Sales: $2.4 Million
Number Employees: 11-50
Type of Packaging: Consumer, Food Service
Brands:
 Sophia

29373 Sopralco
6991 W Broward Blvd
Plantation, FL 33317-2907

954-584-2225
Fax: 954-584-3271 sopralco@aol.com
Ready-to-drink espresso

Owner: Peter Marciante
VP: Arcelia De Battisti
Marketing: Ana Ordaz
Estimated Sales: $1,500,000
Number Employees: 1-4
Square Footage: 1250
Parent Co: Sopralco
Type of Packaging: Consumer, Food Service
Brands:
    Espre
    Espre-Cart
    Espre-Matic

29374 Sorensen Associates
999 NW Frontage Rd
Suite 190
Troutdale, OR 97060
                         503-665-0123
        Fax: 503-666-5113 800-542-4321
                         www.tns.com
Market research consultant specializing in in-store
shopper surveys and new product development for
the packaged goods industry
President: Herb Sorensen
CFO: Jack Birnbach
Sr. VP: James Sorensen
VP Marketing: Bill Hruby
Contact: Don Sorensen
d.sorensen@sorensenvance.com
Estimated Sales: $2.5-5 Million
Number Employees: 20-49
Square Footage: 10000

29375 Sorenson
632 NW California Street
Chehalis, WA 98532
                         360-748-8877
        Fax: 360-748-1288 800-332-3213
        dsorenseon@sorensontransport.com
                www.sorensontransport.com
Owner: Darrell E Sorensen
Estimated Sales: $5-10 Million
Number Employees: 10-19

29376 Sorg Paper Company
901 Manchester Avenue
Middletown, OH 45042
                         513-420-5300
                    Fax: 513-420-5324
Paper products: abrasive coating, bactericides, cot-
ton furnish, deeptone colors, fiberglass pulp matrix,
flame retardant, latex, moisture barrier, recycled/post
consumer, wet strength resin, specialty pulps, u.v.
coatings and watermarking
VP Sales/Marketing: Joe Piela
Production Manager (Tissue): Carl Eisenmenger
Production Manager (Decorative): Bill Huggins
Number Employees: 200

29377 Sortex
39161 Farwell Dr
Fremont, CA 94538-1050
                         510-797-5000
        Fax: 510-797-0555 sales@sortex.com
                         www.sortex.com
Manufacturer and exporter of color sorters and vi-
sion systems
VP Sales: Mike Evans
Sales Director of Product: Christoph Naef
Head of Corporate Communications: Corina Atzli
Number Employees: 20-49
Square Footage: 80000
Parent Co: Buhler
Brands:
    Sortex

29378 Sortie/Kohlhaas
PO Box 534
Monee, IL 60449-0534
                         708-534-3940
                    Fax: 708-534-8013
Sorting devices

29379 Sossner Steel Stamps
180 Judge Don Lewis Blvd
Elizabethton, TN 37643-6006
                         423-543-4001
        Fax: 423-543-8546 800-828-9515
info@sossnerstamps.com www.sossnerstamps.com
Manufacturer and exporter of marking stamps
President: Neil Friedman
International Sales: Vianney Cabrera
General Manager: Russel Lacy

Estimated Sales: $5-10 Million
Number Employees: 20-49
Square Footage: 94000
Parent Co: Sossner Steel Stamps
Brands:
    2-In-1 Time-Saver
    Roll-A-Matic
    Shal-O-Groove
    True-Sharp

29380 Soten
21572 Surveyor Cir
Huntington Beach, CA 92646-7067
                         714-969-9510
                    Fax: 714-969-9520

29381 Soudal Accumetric
350 Ring Rd
Elizabethtown, KY 42701-6777
                         270-769-3386
        Fax: 270-765-2412 800-928-2677
                    www.accumetricinc.com
USDA approved silicone sealant used for packaging
CEO: James V Hartlage Jr
CFO: Charlie Casper
ccasper@accumetricinc.com
VP: Alan Hartlage
VP Domestic Sales/Marketing: Ed Linz
Operations: Joe Fowler
Purchasing: Tim Patterson
Estimated Sales: $50-100 Million
Number Employees: 100-249
Square Footage: 75000
Brands:
    Boss

29382 Sould Manufacturing
PO Box 21064
Winnepeg, NB R3R 3R2
Canada
                         204-339-3499
                    Fax: 204-334-6844
Concession carts
Number Employees: 9

29383 Source Distribution Logistics
2s700 Horseshoe Dr
Batavia, IL 60510
                         630-761-1231
                    Fax: 630-761-2974
Sales and marketing consultant for the warehousing
industry
President: Thomas Peters
Estimated Sales: $300,000-500,000
Number Employees: 1-4

29384 Source Marketing
761 Main Ave # 2
Norwalk, CT 06851-1080
                         203-291-4000
        Fax: 203-291-4010 800-536-1235
info@source-marketing.com www.sourcecxm.com
Textile screen printing
President: Janie Goldberg
CEO: Paul Antonevich
antonevich@source-marketing.com
Estimated Sales: $1-5 Million
Number Employees: 50-99
Type of Packaging: Bulk

29385 Source Packaging Inc
215 Island Rd
Mahwah, NJ 07430-2130
                         201-831-0005
        Fax: 201-831-0009 888-665-9768
                    www.casesbysource.biz
Manufacturer of custom and stock carrying cases
and transport care.
President: Alan Alder
Sales Director: Veronica Knipping
veronica@sourcepac.com
Estimated Sales: $5-10 Million
Number Employees: 10-19
Square Footage: 80000

29386 Source for Packaging
227 E 45th Street
New York, NY 10017-3306
                         212-687-4700
        Fax: 212-687-4725 800-223-2527
Manufacturer and exporter of shopping bags, promotional items, labels, foil, pressure sensitive tapes;
also, packaging design services available

President: Jay Raskin
VP Sales/Operations: Louis Cruz
Estimated Sales: $50-100 Million
Number Employees: 250-499

29387 South Akron Awning Co
763 Kenmore Blvd
Akron, OH 44314-2196
                         330-848-7611
Fax: 330-753-4224 info@southakronawning.com
                www.southakronawning.com
Commercial awnings and renter of tents and party
supplies.
President: Ranell Minear
jack@southakronawning.com
Vice President: Mike Halgaga
Sales: Jack Carroll
Estimated Sales: $1-2.5 Million
Number Employees: 10-19

29388 South Jersey Awning
101 Oak Avenue
Egg Harbor Township, NJ 08234-2211
                         609-646-2002
                    Fax: 609-646-2656
Commercial awnings
President: Steve Alberts
Estimated Sales: $500,000-$1,000,000
Number Employees: 5-9

29389 South Jersey Store Fixtures Co
773 Kaighn Ave
Camden, NJ 08103-2405
                         856-365-6664
        Fax: 856-365-9010 www.infoaroundphilly.com
Wholesaler/distributor of food service equipment in-
cluding broilers, bar equipment, barbecues, chairs,
beverage coolers, dishwashers, freezers, shelving,
slicers, stools, toasters, kitchen ventilating systems,
etc.; serving the foodservice market
President: George Fatlowitz
CEO: Edward Fatlowitz
Manager: Ismel Eema
Estimated Sales: Below $5 Million
Number Employees: 1-4
Square Footage: 200000

29390 South River Machine
115 S River Street
Hackensack, NJ 07601-6909
                         201-487-1736
                    Fax: 201-487-1508
Mixing/kneading mixers and pasta machinery for
ravioli, cavatelli, manicotti, noodles, etc
Estimated Sales: $500,000-$1 Million
Number Employees: 4

29391 South Shore Controls Inc
4485 N Ridge Rd
Perry, OH 44081-9760
                         440-259-2500
        Fax: 440-259-5015 mail@southshorecontrols.com
                    www.southshorecontrols.com
Manufacturer and exporter of controls and control
panels for food processing equipment, material han-
dling equipment, freezers, etc
President: Rick Stark
rjs@southshorecontrols.com
Sales Director: John Sauto, Jr.
Estimated Sales: $6 Million
Number Employees: 20-49
Square Footage: 58000

29392 South Valley Citrus Packers
9600 Road 256
Terra Bella, CA 93270
                         559-906-1033
        Fax: 559-525-4206 vcpg@vcpg.com
Packinghouse and licensed shipper of Sunkist Grow-
ers Inc. citrus products.
Manager: Cliff Martin
Grower Service Representative: Maribel Nenna
General Manager Visalia Citrus Packing: Bob
Walters
Parent Co: Visalia Citrus Packing Group
Type of Packaging: Food Service

29393 South Valley Mfg Inc
9665 New Ave
Gilroy, CA 95020-9135
                         408-842-5457
                    Fax: 408-842-1097

Food processing equipment including brine tanks, kettles, steam blanchers, atmospheric can cookers, coolers, deaerators, sterilizers, tubular heat exchangers
President: Paul L Jennings
Estimated Sales: Below $5 Million
Number Employees: 5-9
Square Footage: 18000
Brands:
South Valley Manufacturing

29394 South Well Co
928 N Alamo St
San Antonio, TX 78215-1576
210-223-1831
Fax: 210-223-8517 sales@southwellco.com
www.southwellco.com
Pre-inked rubber stamps for check endorsement
Owner: Wilson P Southwell Jr
scott@southwellco.com
CEO: Wilson P Southwell Jr
Sales Exec: Scott Southwell
Estimated Sales: $2.5-5 Million
Number Employees: 10-19
Brands:
Super-Stamp

29395 Southbend
1100 Old Honeycutt Rd
Fuquay Varina, NC 27526-8971
919-762-1000
Fax: 919-552-9798 800-348-2558
sbgeneral@southbendnc.com
www.buildmybattery.com
Manufacturer and exporter of commercial cooking equipment including broilers, fryer systems, restaurant ranges, convection, steamers, kettles, braising pans and cabinets
President: Nestor Ibrahim
COO: Selim Bassaul
CFO: Dave Baker
VP: Rob August
Research & Development: Ray Wi
VP Sales: Jonette Wylie
National Sales Manager: Mitch Cohen
Estimated Sales: $50 Million
Number Employees: 100-249
Square Footage: 135000
Parent Co: Middleby Corporation
Brands:
Southbend

29396 Southeast Asia Market
52 15th St
Brooklyn, NY 11215
718-965-6500
info@seamarketny.com
www.seamarketny.com
Asian foods and produce
Operations Manager: Cathy Chow
General Manager: Kevin Liang
Bilingual Purchasing Agent: Dan Josephson
Estimated Sales: $6.6 Million
Number Employees: 11-50
Brands:
Eton Dumplings

29397 Southeastern FiltrationSysts
158 Railroad St
Canton, GA 30114-3060
770-720-2800
Fax: 770-720-2900 800-935-8500
gerhard@sfes.com www.sfes.com
Water treatment systems for high and low temperature applications
Owner: John Brandreth Iii
j.brandreth@sfes.com
VP Marketing: Gerhard Zamorano
Estimated Sales: $1-2,500,000
Number Employees: 10-19
Square Footage: 22000
Brands:
Hydroblend
Microlene
Scalestick

29398 Southeastern Fisheries Assn
1118 Thomasville Rd # B
Tallahassee, FL 32303-6238
850-224-0612
Fax: 850-222-3663 bobfish@aol.com
www.sfaonline.org
Hot sauces, fisheries

Executive Director: Robert P Jones
Chairman: Dennis Henderson
Executive Director: Robert Jones
Number Employees: 1-4

29399 Southend Janitorial Supply
11422 S Broadway
Los Angeles, CA 90061-1898
323-754-2842
Fax: 323-779-5457 leday@aol.com
www.triple-s.com
Janitorial supplies and equipment
President: John Leday
leday@aol.com
Estimated Sales: $5-10 Million
Number Employees: 5-9

29400 Southern Ag Co Inc
942 N Main St
PO Drawer 546
Blakely, GA 39823-2029
229-723-4262
Fax: 229-723-3223 souagcom@windstream.net
Manufacturer and exporter of conveyors, elevators, sizers and separators for peanuts; also, grain bins
Owner: Harold Still
Estimated Sales: $2.5-5 Million
Number Employees: 10-19

29401 Southern Atlantic LabelCo
1300 Cavalier Blvd
Chesapeake, VA 23323-1528
757-485-0508
Fax: 757-487-9712 800-456-5999
info@salinc.com www.multicolorcorp.com
Pressure sensitive roll labels, coupons, tags, polystyrene inserts, 4 color process, 9 color in line printing, 16-inch web capacity, static cling and screen printed point of purchase, foil stamping and bar codes
CEO: Chil Daper
CEO: Phillip W Draper
President: James Cumming
CEO: Phillip W Draper
Sales Manager: Kurt Webber
Estimated Sales: $20-50 Million
Number Employees: 100-249
Square Footage: 33000

29402 Southern Automatics
2845 Brooks Street
Lakeland, FL 33803-7379
863-665-1633
Fax: 863-665-2500 800-441-4604
Manufacturer, importer and exporter of high-volume fruit and vegetable packing machinery; also, compact optic sorters and sizers
President: Hugh Oglesby
VP: Scott Oglesby
Estimated Sales: $1-3 Million
Number Employees: 20
Square Footage: 40000
Parent Co: Future Alloys

29403 Southern Awning & Sign Company
532 Industrial Drive
Woodstock, GA 30189-7214
770-516-8652
Fax: 770-516-3940
Commercial awnings
President: Ron Dinsmore
Number Employees: 5

29404 Southern California Packaging
4102 Valley Blvd
Walnut, CA 91789-1404
909-598-3198
Fax: 909-598-1363 info@scpe.com
www.scpe.com
Packaging supplies
CEO: David Byrne
dbyrne@scpe.com
Estimated Sales: $3-5 Million
Number Employees: 10-19
Brands:
Ruby Kist

29405 (HQ)Southern Champion Tray LP
220 Compress St
PO Box 4066
Chattanooga, TN 37405-3724
423-756-5121
Fax: 423-756-0223 800-468-2222
cchapellin@sctray.com

Manufacturer and exporter of paperboard folding cartons
President & CEO: John Zeiser
CEO: Mark Lonqnecker
Vice President: Bruce Zeiser
National Sales Manager: Paul Powell
Operations Manager: Jim Skidmore
Number Employees: 250-499
Square Footage: 650000
Type of Packaging: Consumer, Food Service, Private Label, Bulk
Other Locations:
Southern Champion Tray L.P.
Chattanooga TN

29406 Southern Container Corporation
140 W Industry Ct
Deer Park, NY 11729
631-586-6006
Fax: 631-586-6068
Corrugated packaging including die cut, pre-print and hi-graphic; also, point-of-purchase displays
CEO: Steven M Grossman
Sales Manager: Barry Kolevzon
Contact: Noelle Pastore
noelle.pastore@southerncontainer.com
Estimated Sales: $20-50 Million
Number Employees: 100-249

29407 Southern Express
2305 N Broadway
Saint Louis, MO 63102-1405
770-662-0220
800-444-9157
Manufacturer and designer of restaurant kiosks, mobile merchandisers and mobile carts
Manager: Michael Samborn
Number Employees: 20
Parent Co: Duke Manufacturing Company

29408 Southern Film Extruders
2327 English Road
High Point, NC 27262
336-885-8091
Fax: 336-885-1221 800-334-6101
sales@southernfilm.com www.southernfilm.com
FDA polyethylene packaging films
Owner: Joseph Martinez
Chief Financial Officer: John Barnes
Quality Control Manager: Tom Vanpelt
Vice President, Sales: Lanny Rampley
Warehouse Manager: Austin Fisher
Estimated Sales: $24 Million
Number Employees: 145
Square Footage: 115000
Type of Packaging: Private Label

29409 Southern Gardens Citrus
1820 County Road 833
Clewiston, FL 33440-9222
863-983-3030
Fax: 863-983-3060 800-339-6025
www.ussugar.com
Citrus juices, not-from-concentrate and concentrated citrus by-products
Finance Executive: Ginny Pena
Contact: Dan Casper
dcasper@southerngardens.com
Estimated Sales: $25-50 Million
Number Employees: 100-249

29410 Southern Imperial Inc
1400 Eddy Ave
Rockford, IL 61103-3198
815-310-9120
Fax: 815-877-7454 800-747-4665
grothmeyer@southernimperial.com
www.southernimperial.com
Manufacturer and exporter of scanning hooks, display hooks, wire racks and baskets, clip strips, J-hooks, paper and adhesive labels and merchandising accessories
President: Stan C Valiulis
ekuehl@southernimperial.com
CFO: Dean Zanseil
Quality Control: Denise Bermingham
R&D: Tom Zeliulis
Marketing Manager: Tom Valiulis
Estimated Sales: $20-30 Million
Number Employees: 100-249
Square Footage: 320000

29411 Southern Metal Fabricators Inc
1215 Frazier Rd
Albertville, AL 35950-0719
256-891-4343
Fax: 256-891-0922 800-989-1330
sales@southernmetalfab.com
www.southernmetalfab.com
Manufacturer and exporter of ventilating systems, ducts, hoods, blowpipes, fittings, tanks, hoppers, railings, funnels, racks, boxes, vats and conveyors
President/CEO: Charles Bailey
charles.bailey@southernmetalfab.com
CFO: Teresa Hammett
Vice President: Regenia Bailey
Quality Control: Donnie Buchanan
Sales Manager: Bud Weed
Operations Manager: Danny Murray
Estimated Sales: $5 Million
Number Employees: 20-49
Square Footage: 189000

29412 (HQ)Southern Missouri Containers
900 N Belcrest Ave
Springfield, MO 65802-2513
417-831-2685
Fax: 417-831-7912 800-999-7666
Corrugated boxes
President: Rich Bachus
rich.bachus@smcpackaging.com
Chairman/CEO/Secretary: Kevin Ausburn
Finance Manager: Ron Thomas
Vice President: Benjamine Jones
Quality Control Director: Galen Perry
Chief Operating Officer: John Pojunos
Estimated Sales: $63 Million
Number Employees: 100-249
Square Footage: 153000
Other Locations:
    Southern Missouri Containers
    Kansas City MO

29413 Southern Packaging Machinery
PO Box 112
Athens, GA 30603-0112
706-208-0814
Fax: 706-208-0815 sales@southernpackaging.com
www.benchmarkautomation.net
Corrugated paper containers
CEO: Don Evans
Director of Sales: Vince Tamborello
Estimated Sales: $2.5-5 Million
Number Employees: 5-9

29414 Southern Packaging Machinery
PO Box 112
Athens, GA 30603-0112
706-208-0814
Fax: 706-208-0815 sales@southernpackaging.com
www.benchmarkautomation.net
Horizontal form/fill/seal pouch packaging machinery
Owner: Roy Miller
Engineering Manager: Mike Rupert
Director, Sales: Vince Tamborello
Estimated Sales: $5-10 Million
Number Employees: 5-9
Type of Packaging: Food Service

29415 Southern Packaging Machinery
PO Box 112
Athens, GA 30603-0112
706-208-0814
Fax: 706-208-0815 800-922-8030
sales@southernpackaging.com
www.benchmarkautomation.net
Owner: Roy Miller
Engineering Manager: Mike Rupert
Regional Sales Manager: Jay Cavanaugh
Contact: Billy Barrick
billy@benchmarkautomation.net
Number Employees: 5-9

29416 Southern Pallet
24 Produce Place
P O Box 11075,
Christchurch, NZ 38101
901-942-4603
Fax: 901-942-4613
enquiries@southernpallet.co.nz
southernpallet.co.nz
Wooden shipping crates and pallets
Manager: Verna Frye
Production Manager: Louis Ratchford

Estimated Sales: $500,000-$1 Million
Number Employees: 5-9

29417 Southern Perfection Fab
232 GA Highway 49 S
Byron, GA 31008-6937
478-956-5441
Fax: 478-956-4001 800-237-4726
www.southernperfection.com
President/CFO: Gordon Hale
ghale@southernperfection.com
Estimated Sales: Below $5 Million
Number Employees: 20-49

29418 Southern Pride Distributing
401 S Mill St
Alamo, TN 38001-1913
731-696-3175
Fax: 731-696-3180 800-851-8180
parts@sopride.com www.southernpride.com
Manufacturer and exporter of ovens including mobile, revolving and warming; also, commercial barbecue equipment, smokers and rotisseries
President/CEO: Mike Robertson
VP: Jared Robertson
Quality Control: Bret Robertson
Marketing Director: Jack Griggs
Operations Manager: Jerry Cadle
Plant Manager: Marty Degrini
Purchasing: Rich Rowell
Estimated Sales: $10 Millions
Number Employees: 5-9
Square Footage: 130000
Type of Packaging: Food Service
Brands:
    Southern Pride

29419 Southern Rubber Stamp
2637 E Marshall St
Tulsa, OK 74110-4757
918-587-3818
Fax: 918-587-3819 888-826-4304
sales@southernmark.com www.southernmark.com
Manufacturer and exporter of rubber stamps, seals, numbering machines, embossers, special inks, etc
President: Mike Forehand
mike@perfectseal.net
VP: David Parnell
Estimated Sales: Less Than $500,000
Number Employees: 5-9
Type of Packaging: Consumer, Food Service, Bulk
Brands:
    Perfect Seal

29420 (HQ)Southern Store FixturesInc
275 Drexel Rd SE
Bessemer, AL 35022-6416
205-428-4800
Fax: 205-428-2552 800-552-6283
chughes@southerncasearts.com
Manufacturer, exporter and designer of mobile and modular refrigerated cases for deli, bakery, salads, produce and floral; store and fixture design and installation services available
President: Gene Cary
Cmo: Dan Mcmurray
dmcmurray@southernstorefixtures.com
National Sales Manager: Joe Moore
Estimated Sales: $10-20 Million
Number Employees: 250-499
Square Footage: 216000

29421 Southern Tailors Flag &Banner
1862 Marietta Blvd NW
Atlanta, GA 30318-2803
404-367-8660
Fax: 404-367-8654 877-655-2321
www.southerntailors.com
Custom flags, banners, ribbons, buttons and other advertising specialties; also, engraving available
Owner: Neal Zucker
nzucker@southerntailors.com
Estimated Sales: $1-2.5 Million
Number Employees: 10-19
Square Footage: 14000
Parent Co: Southern Tailors

29422 Southern Tool
738 Well Road
West Monroe, LA 71292-0138
786-866-9865
Fax: 318-387-5372 800-458-3687
www.southern-tool.com
Manufacturer and exporter of packaging equipment

President: Dale Doty
Plant Manager: Buck Carlisle
Number Employees: 65
Square Footage: 200000
Parent Co: Southern Tool

29423 Southern United States Trade Association
701 Poydras Street
Suite 3845
New Orleans, LA 70139
504-568-5986
Fax: 504-568-6010 susta@susta.org
www.susta.org
Marketing services
Executive Director: Bernadette Wiltz
Deputy & Financial Director: Troy Rosamond
Director, Marketing & Communications: Danielle Viguerie
Office Manager: Sondleta B. Johnson
Year Founded: 1973
Number Employees: 11-50

29424 Southland Packaging
303 E Alondra Boulevard
Gardena, CA 90248-2809
213-532-3720
Estimated Sales: $2.5-5 Million
Number Employees: 10-19

29425 Southline Equipment Company
P.O.Box 8867
Houston, TX 77249
713-869-6801
Fax: 713-869-2875 800-444-1173
www.eqdepot.com
Wholesaler/distributor of material handling equipment including new and used forklift trucks, parts, service and rental in addition to industrial sweepers/scrubbers.
Manager: Jeff Jones
Finance: F Rigell
Marketing Director: Bob McClelland
Sales Manager: M Zinda
Operations Manager: M Gunter
Estimated Sales: $20 Million
Number Employees: 50-99
Square Footage: 60000

29426 Southpack LLC
1 Hartford Sq # 19
New Britain, CT 06052-1174
860-224-2242
Fax: 860-224-2445 spc@southpack.com
www.southpack.com
Custom thermoforming and contract packaging
Owner: Lynn Mogielnicki
lynn@southpack.com
VP: Kurt Mogielnicks
Number Employees: 20-49
Square Footage: 60000
Type of Packaging: Food Service, Private Label, Bulk

29427 Southwest Endseals
4323 South Drive
Houston, TX 77053-4820
832-399-3900
Fax: 832-399-3903 866-832-1454
info@swformseal.com www.swformseal.com
Ceiling jaws for packaging machines
President: John Deterling
Number Employees: 10-19

29428 Southwest Fixture
8909 Chancellor Row
Dallas, TX 75247-5324
214-634-2800
Fax: 214-634-2847
Store fixtures
Owner: Dan Thor
danthor@comcast.net
VP: A Winkler
Estimated Sales: $2.5-5 Million
Number Employees: 5-9

29429 Southwest Indiana and American Cold Storage
P.O.Box 875
Newburgh, IN 47629-0875
812-858-3555
Fax: 812-858-3558
Manager: Larry Taylor
Number Employees: 1-4

943

29430 Southwest Neon Signs
7208 South W.W. White Rd
San Antonio, TX 78222-5204

210-648-3221
Fax: 210-648-4709 800-927-3221
www.southwestsigns.com
Indoor and outdoor advertising and electric signs
President: Chad Jones
Sales Manager: Greg Burkette
Estimated Sales: $10-20 Million
Number Employees: 50-99
Square Footage: 100000

29431 Southwest Vault Builders
596 Bennett Ln
Lewisville, TX 75057-4806

469-671-5800
Fax: 469-671-5812 800-749-1431
Specializes in cold storage construction
President: Larry Nolan
lnolan@southwestvault.com
Number Employees: 50-99

29432 Southwestern Electric Power Company
428 Travis St
Shreveport, LA 71101

888-216-3523
www.swepco.com
Electric utility systems.
President & COO: Albert Smoak
VP, Regulatory & Finance: Thomas Brice, Jr
VP, External Affairs: Brian Bond
Estimated Sales: K
Parent Co: American Electric Power

29433 (HQ)Southwestern Porcelain Steel
201 E Morrow Road
Sand Springs, OK 74063-6531

918-245-1375
Fax: 918-241-7339
Porcelain enamel tops for steel tables, counters and
signs; importer of cast iron stove top grates; also,
silk screen porcelain graphics available
Vice President: Jim Bigelow
Plant Superintendent: Don Bushnell
Estimated Sales: $5-10 Million
Number Employees: 20-50
Square Footage: 512000

29434 Southworth Products Corp
11 Gray Rd
Falmouth, ME 04105-2027

207-878-0700
Fax: 207-797-4734 800-743-1000
www.southworthproducts.com
Material handling equipment including lift tables,
dock lifts, container tilters, vertical conveyors, man-
ual palletizers, elevating transporters, rotators,
upenders and adjustable workstations
Owner: Lewis P Cabot
lcabot@southworthproducts.com
CFO: Mike Nordman
Marketing Program Manager: Meredith Herzog
Sales Manager: Randy Moore
Director Product Support: James Galante
Estimated Sales: $5-10 Million
Number Employees: 50-99
Parent Co: Southworth International Group

29435 Soyatech Inc
1369 State Highway 102
Bar Harbor, ME 04609-7019

207-288-4969
Fax: 207-288-5264 800-424-7692
www.soyatech.com
Consultant specializing in soybean processing and
product development services
President: Peter Golbitz
Chief Executive Officer: Chris Erickson
cerickson@highquestpartners.com
Publisher & Operations Director: Keri Hayes
Marketing/Sales: Susan Bradley
Regional Sales Manager: Mark Phillips
Publisher & Operations Director: Keri Hayes
Estimated Sales: Less Than $500,000
Number Employees: 5-9

29436 Soynut Butter Co
4220 Commercial Way
Glenview, IL 60025-3597

847-635-9960
Fax: 847-635-6801 800-288-1012
www.soynutbutter.com

Peanut free peanut butter, made from roasted soy.
President: Steve Grubb
s.grubb@soynutbutter.com
Estimated Sales: Below $5 Million
Number Employees: 5-9

29437 Spaceguard Products
711 S Commerce Dr
Seymour, IN 47274-4023

812-523-3044
Fax: 812-523-3362 800-841-0680
www.spaceguardproducts.com
Woven wire partitions
President: Eddie Murphy
eddie@fedsource.com
VP Sales: Gary Myers
Estimated Sales: $5-10 Million
Number Employees: 20-49
Brands:
   Ford Logan Wire
   Space Guard 2000

29438 Spacekraft Packaging
1811 W Oak Pkwy
Marietta, GA 30062-2216

770-429-3500
Fax: 770-429-3535 800-483-1168
www.spacekraft.com
Manufacture of laminated panels.
Estimated Sales: $1-5 Million
Number Employees: 10-19
Square Footage: 20000

29439 Spacekraft Packaging
4901 W. 79th Street
Indianapolis, IN 46268

317-871-6999
Fax: 317-871-6993 800-599-8943
www.spacekraft.com
Packaging containers for liquid, semi-bulk products
Contact: Jeffery Alexander
jeffery@weyerhaeuser.com
Estimated Sales: $5-10 Million
Number Employees: 20-50

29440 Spacesaver Corp
1450 Janesville Ave
Fort Atkinson, WI 53538-2798

920-563-6362
Fax: 920-563-2702 800-492-3434
ssc@spacesaver.com www.spacesaver.com
Manufacturer and exporter of mobile high-density
storage systems
President: Paul Olsen
R&D: David Klumb
Vice President: Bill Wettstein
CFO: Ryan Bittner
Marketing Director: Christopher Batterman
Sales Director: Kevin Carmody
Public Relations: Karen King
Operations Manager: Jim Muth
Purchasing Manager: Patricia Cropp
Estimated Sales: $75-100 Million
Number Employees: 250-499
Parent Co: KI
Type of Packaging: Bulk

29441 Span Tech LLC
1115 Cleveland Ave
Glasgow, KY 42141-1011

270-651-9166
Fax: 270-651-7533 billy_miller@spantechllc.com
www.spantechllc.com
USDA and BISSC approved modular side flexing
conveyor systems with plastic belting
CEO: James Layne
james_layne@spantechllc.com
Engineering Director: Lavon Riegel
Quality Control: Paul Chambers
Marketing/Sales: Genia Johnson
Operations: Jimmy Wiley
Production/Plant Manager: Phillip Coleman
Purchasing: Alf McDougal
Estimated Sales: $20-50 Million
Number Employees: 50-99
Square Footage: 50000
Brands:
   Designer System
   Minispan
   Maxispan
   Monospan
   Multispan

29442 Spanco Crane & Monorail Systems
604 Hemlock Rd
Morgantown, PA 19543-9710

610-286-7781
Fax: 610-286-0085 800-869-2080
www.spanco.com
Manufacturer and exporter of stainless steel material
handling equipment including cranes and conveyor
systems and components
Vice President: George Nolan
gnolan@spanco.com
VP: George Nolan
Sales Manager: George Nolan
Estimated Sales: $20-50 Million
Number Employees: 50-99

29443 Spann Sign Company
PO Box 546
Kenosha, WI 53141-0546

262-658-1288
Fax: 262-658-1878
Electric, neon and plastic signs
President: Duane Laska
Number Employees: 6
Brands:
   Spann Signs

29444 Sparkler Filters Inc
101 N Loop 336 E
Conroe, TX 77301-1446

936-756-4471
Fax: 936-756-4519 sales@sparklerfilters.com
www.sparklerfilters.com
Manufacturer and exporter of filter systems includ-
ing fryer oil and liquid; also, manual and automatic
President: J T Reneau
jim@sparklerfilters.com
CFO: Robert Thompson
VP: Jose Sentmanat
Quality Control: James Dunklin
Marketing: Jose Sentmanat
Sales: Tom Buttera
Public Relations: Norm Hofer
Operations/General Manager: Link Reneau
Plant Manager: Alan Powell
Purchasing: Phil Lawson
Estimated Sales: $5-5.5 Million
Number Employees: 20-49
Number of Brands: 2
Square Footage: 140000
Type of Packaging: Food Service
Brands:
   Sparklaid
   Sparkler

29445 Sparks Belting Co
3800 Stahl Dr SE
Grand Rapids, MI 49546-6148

616-949-2750
Fax: 616-949-8518 800-451-4537
sbcinfo@sparksbelting.com
www.sparksbelting.com
Wholesaler/distributor of food-approved and pack-
age handling conveyor belting; manufacturer of mo-
torized pulleys; importer of thermoplastic belting,
motorized pulleys and rollers
President: Steven Swanson
CFO: Martha Vrias
VP: Steven Bayus
Quality Control: Dave Vanderwood
Marketing: Frank Kennedy
Contact: Andy Balog
ajbalog@sparksbelting.com
Operations: Bruce Dielema
Production: Joe Graver
Plant Manager: John Grasmeyer
Purchasing Director: Mark White
Estimated Sales: $20-50 Million
Number Employees: 100-249
Square Footage: 52000
Brands:
   Dura-Drive Plus
   Microrollers

29446 Sparks Companies
P.O.Box 17339
Memphis, TN 38187

901-766-4600
Fax: 901-766-4462 info@informaecon.com
Agriculture research and consulting company
Chairman of the Board: Willard Sparks
Estimated Sales: $10-15 Million
Number Employees: 100-249

29447 Spartan Flag Co
323 S Shabwasung St
Northport, MI 49670

231-386-5150
Fax: 231-386-5904

Flags, pennants and banners
President: Cheryl Feipke
VP: Milt Seipke
Estimated Sales: Below $5 Million
Number Employees: 10-19

29448 Spartan Showcase
702 Spartan Showcase Drive
P.O. Box 470
Union, MO 63084

636-583-4050
Fax: 636-583-4067 800-325-0775

Manufacturer and exporter of bakery and deli
wallcases, merchandising and self-serve display
cases and dry and refrigerated showcases; also, cus-
tom glass and wood fixtures
CEO: Mike Lause
VP Marketing: Steve Lause
Sales Director: Royce Buehrlen
Manager: Greg Hall
Estimated Sales: $14 Million
Number Employees: 120
Square Footage: 400000
Parent Co: Leggett & Platt Inc

29449 Spartan Tool LLC
1506 Division St
Mendota, IL 61342-2426

815-539-7411
Fax: 815-539-9786 800-435-3866
customerservice@spartantool.com
www.spartantool.com

Drain and sewer cleaning equipment
Member of the Board: Tom Pranka
tpranka@spartantool.com
Advertising Manager: Nancy Dessing
Sales Manager: Bill Madden
Estimated Sales: $10-20 Million
Number Employees: 10-19

29450 Spartanburg Steel Products Inc
121 Broadcast Dr
Spartanburg, SC 29303-4711

864-699-3200
Fax: 864-699-3250 800-974-7500
www.ssprod.com

Pressurizable stainless steel beverage, beer, and
chemical containers
President: Richard Dye
CEO: Dick Dye
CFO: Barry Whipple
Quality Control: Daniel Ahein
VP Sales/Marketing: Del Strandburg
Operations: Buck Wiggins
Production: Chuck Manahan
Purchasing: Tyler Evans
Estimated Sales: $3-5 Million
Number Employees: 100-249
Square Footage: 800000
Parent Co: Reserve Group

29451 Spartanics
3605 Edison Pl
Rolling Meadows, IL 60008-1077

847-394-5700
Fax: 847-394-0409 sales@spartanics.com
www.spartanics.com

Blanking and die-cutting systems, optical and me-
chanical counters, laser cutting machines, digital
printing equipment, converting systems, finishing
equipment, material handling machinery, screen
printing systems.
President: Thomas Ohara
tohara@spartanics.com
Vice President of Sales & Marketing/Inte: Mike
Bacon
Marketing Coordinator: Jeanette DesJardins
National Sales Manager-US: Rick Roberts
Number Employees: 20-49
Type of Packaging: Food Service

29452 Spartec Plastics
PO Box 620
Conneaut, OH 44030-0620

440-599-8175
Fax: 440-593-2003 800-325-5176

Manufacturer and exporter of extruded low and high
density polyethylene and polypropylene products in-
cluding thermoplastic and rolled sheets, rods, tex-
tured cutting boards and sanitary paneling systems
with antibacterial additives
Operations Manager: Ernie Szydlowski
Estimated Sales: $2.5-5 Million
Number Employees: 19
Square Footage: 190000
Brands:
 Arp
 Permaclean
 Resinol

29453 Spartech Plastics
1444 S Tyler Rd
Wichita, KS 67209

316-722-8621
Fax: 316-722-4875 www.spartech.com

Sheet and roll plastics and plastic film
Contact: Patricia Asher
patricia.asher@spartech.com
Plant Manager: Steve Zubke
Estimated Sales: $20-50 Million
Number Employees: 100-249
Square Footage: 60000
Parent Co: Atlas Alchem
Type of Packaging: Bulk

29454 Spartech Plastics
1325 Adams St
Portage, WI 53901

608-742-7123
Fax: 608-745-1703 800-998-7123
www.spartech.com

Extruder of plastic sheet and rollstock
VP: Steven J Ploeger
Quality Control: Tim Hofp
Marketing: Kurt Kassner
Sales: Scott Eaton
Contact: Jay Eggleston
eggleston@spartech.com
Operations: Don Asch
Plant Manager: Don Asch
Purchasing: Jay Eggleston
Estimated Sales: $20-50 Million
Number Employees: 100-249
Square Footage: 170000
Parent Co: Spartech Plastics

29455 Spartech Poly Com
120 South Central Avenue
Suite 1700
Clayton, MI 63105-1705

314-721-4242
Fax: 314-721-1447 888-721-4242
mark.garretson@spartech.com www.spartech.com

Compounder of PVC for tubing & other applications
Manager: Nate Sofer
CEO: Natehen Sofer
Marketing/Sales: Mark Garretson
Contact: Matt Sweeney
matt.sweeney@spartech.com
Estimated Sales: $10-20 Million
Number Employees: 20-49
Number of Products: 250
Parent Co: Spartech Corporation

29456 Spear Packing
25 Home News Row
New Brunswick, NJ 08901-3645

732-247-4212

Beverages
President: John Ciullo
Estimated Sales: $50-100 Million
Number Employees: 50

29457 Special Events Supply Company
P.O. Box 12415
Hauppauge, NY 11788

Fax: 631-436-7715 specialevt@aol.com

Promotional goods including display equipment,
banners and pennants
Estimated Sales: $300,000-500,000
Number Employees: 1-4

29458 Special Products
1526 South Enterprise
Springfield, MO 65804

417-881-6114
Fax: 417-881-7314 cs@fhfoodequipment.com
www.fhfoodequipment.com

Brushes, centrifuge parts and fittings, flow meters,
homogenizers, pumps, thermometers and valves

Owner: Wilbur Feagan
Manager: Dennis Wiggins
Inside Sales Manager: Stacy Toal
Purchasing Manager: Bob Collins
Estimated Sales: Below $5 Million
Number Employees: 1-4
Parent Co: Mid-America Dairymen

29459 Specialities Importers & Distributers
85 Division Avenue
PO Box 409
Millington, NJ 07946

908-647-6485
Fax: 908-647-8305 800-899-6689
www.specialitiesinc.com

Deli: cheeses, cured meats and hams.
President: Ron Schinbeckler
r.schinbeckler@specialitiesinc.com
Vice President, Sales & Marketing: Richard Kessler
Year Founded: 1991
Type of Packaging: Food Service
Brands:
 Bellentani
 Carpuela
 Bayonne Ham
 Ermitage
 leBistro
 Solera©

29460 Specialized Packaging London
5 Cuddy Boulevard
London, ON N5W 5R6
Canada

519-659-7011
Fax: 519-452-3197 www.spgroup.com

Litho-printed cutter boxes and folding cartons for
food, beverage, paper and personal care products
President: Carlton Highsmith
Site Manager: Don Gray
CFO: Lamaemig Rosekrans
Quality Control: Scott Laking
Director Operations: Robert Gariepy
Number Employees: 200
Parent Co: Lawson Mardon Group
Brands:
 Pakastrip

29461 Specialty Blades
9 Technology Drive
PO Box 3166
Staunton, VA 24402-3166

540-248-2200
Fax: 540-248-4400

Manufacturer and exporter of custom made indus-
trial-duty food blades including stainless, high-speed
and tool steel or carbide; also, prototyping available
President & CEO: Peter Harris
Contact: Dan Andrew
dan@specialtyblades.com
Estimated Sales: $8.5 Million
Number Employees: 50-99
Square Footage: 160000
Type of Packaging: Consumer, Food Service, Pri-
vate Label, Bulk

29462 Specialty Box & Packaging
1040 Broadway
Menands, NY 12204-2590

518-465-7344
Fax: 518-465-7347 800-283-2247
wrapit@acmenet.net

Packaging
President: Eric Fialkoff
efialkoff@specialtybox.com
Vice President: Jason Fialkoff
Graphic Design/Print Media: Jessica L. Jones
Business Office Manager: Daphne Playotes
Estimated Sales: $5-10 Million
Number Employees: 5-9

29463 Specialty Cheese Group Limited
24 King Street
Apt 4
New York, NY 10014-4937

212-243-7274
Fax: 212-243-0807 cheesenyc@aol.com

Consultant specializing in new product development
for cheese; also, retail buying, training and merchandising services for supermarkets, wholesalers and
manufacturers available
President: Lynne Edelson
Number Employees: 1

29464 Specialty Commodities Inc
1530 47th St N
Fargo, ND 58102-2858

701-282-8222
Fax: 701-264-5744
www.specialtycommodities.com
Manufacturer and importer of specialty ingredients for snack food, dairy, bakery, cereal, energy bar and confectionery. Products include dehydrated, dried fruit, legumes, nuts, seeds, spices and grains.
President: Ken Campbell
Vice President: Kevin Anderson
Number Employees: 10-19
Parent Co: Archer Daniels Midland Company
Type of Packaging: Private Label, Bulk
Other Locations:
Corporate Office
Fargo ND
Processing Plant
Lodi CA
Processing Plant
Stockton CA
Processing Plant
Modesto CA

29465 Specialty Equipment Company
1415 Mendota Heights Rd
Mendota Heights, MN 55120

651-452-7909
Fax: 651-452-0681 sales@specialtyequip.com
Manufacturer, importer and exporter of high pressure washing equipment
CEO: Sheldon Russell
President: Bryan Russell
Estimated Sales: $20-50 Million
Number Employees: 20-49
Square Footage: 70000
Type of Packaging: Consumer, Bulk

29466 Specialty Equipment Company
1221 Adkins Rd
Houston, TX 77055

713-467-1818
Fax: 713-467-9130 www.specialtyequipment.com
Manufacturer of packaging machinery and material handling systems, including liquid fillers, custom dry solids fillers, drum and pallet conveyors, and palletizers.
Year Founded: 1969
Estimated Sales: $257 Million
Type of Packaging: Food Service
Other Locations:
Specialty Equipment Cos.
Etten-leur
Brands:
Beverage Air
Bloomfield Industries
Carter Hoffmann
Gamko
Nova
Taylor Company
Wells Manufacturing
World Dryer

29467 Specialty Films & Associates
2000 Arbor Tech Dr
Hebron, KY 41048

859-647-4100
Fax: 859-647-4105 800-984-3346
Plastic flexible packaging products including vacuum, zipper and stand-up pouches; also, forming and nonforming film including vertical form/fill/seal
President: Jane Dirr-Cherot
CEO: Tony Cherot
Estimated Sales: $20-50 Million
Number Employees: 50
Square Footage: 40000
Brands:
Spec-Bar
Spec-Flex
Spec-Plus
Spec-Up
Spec-Vac
Spec-Zip

29468 Specialty Food America Inc
5055 Huffman Mill Rd
Hopkinsville, KY 42240-9162

270-889-0017
888-881-1633
www.specialtyfoodamerica.com
Herbs and spices; cooking related supplies and contract packaging
Owner: Thomas L Marshall
specialtyfoodtom@gmail.com

Estimated Sales: Less Than $500,000
Number Employees: 1-4
Square Footage: 4800
Type of Packaging: Consumer, Private Label
Brands:
Lucini Honestete
Sonoma Syrups

29469 Specialty Lubricants
8300 Corporate Park Dr
Macedonia, OH 44056-2300

330-425-2567
Fax: 330-425-9637 800-238-5823
steve@speclubes.com www.speclubes.com
Food grade lubricants; contract packaging for private labeling
Manager: Kathy Turner
COO: Sherry Bugenske
R&D: Stve Bugenske
Quality Control: Keith Lahrmer
Marketing Director: Steve Bugenske
Sales Director: Rick Beichner
Plant Manager: Chuck Turner
Purchasing Manager: Marge Bugenske
Estimated Sales: $10-20 Million
Number Employees: 20-49
Number of Brands: 1
Number of Products: 8
Square Footage: 69040
Type of Packaging: Private Label
Brands:
Huskey Specialty Lubricants

29470 Specialty Packaging Inc
3250 W Seminary Dr # A
Fort Worth, TX 76133-1145

817-922-9727
Fax: 817-922-8262 800-284-7722
Food service paper bags and wrap
President: H Dorris
spac@earthlink.net
R&D: Herman Chenezert
Estimated Sales: $10-20 Million
Number Employees: 50-99

29471 Specialty Paper Bag Company
17625 East Railroad St.
PO Box 8445
City of Industry, CA 91748-0445

718-893-8888
Fax: 718-893-5662 800-962-2247
Plain and printed bags including bread, food, kraft paper and plastic
Foreman: Brian Birchall
Number Employees: 18
Square Footage: 95000

29472 Specialty Saw Inc
30 Wolcott Rd
Simsbury, CT 06070-1445

860-658-4419
Fax: 860-651-5358 800-225-0772
info@specialtysaw.com www.specialtysaw.com
Band saws, carbide-tipped saw and high speed steel blades, saw machinery and coolants
Owner: Anthony Scearce
anthony@scearcelaser.com
Estimated Sales: $3 Million
Number Employees: 10-19

29473 (HQ)Specialty Wood Products
900 Lumac Rd
Clanton, AL 35045-9610

205-755-6016
Fax: 205-755-3678 800-322-5343
info@specwood.com www.specwood.com
Store fixtures and gift baskets
President: Bonny Smith
info@specwood.com
Sales Exec: K Smith
Estimated Sales: Below $5 Million
Number Employees: 20-49
Type of Packaging: Food Service

29474 Specific Mechanical Systems
6848 Kirkpatrick Crescent
Victoria, BC V8M 1Z9
Canada

250-652-2111
Fax: 250-652-6010 info@specific.net
www.specificmechanical.com
Manufacturer and exporter of stainless steel process and storage tanks, pressure vessels and mixers

President and CEO: Phil Zacharias
CFO: Bill Cumming
Engineering Manager: Tom Goldbach
Quality Control: Darren Combs
Sales Director: Blaine Clouston
Plant Manager: Bill Cummings
Estimated Sales: Below $5 Million
Number Employees: 40
Square Footage: 72000

29475 Spectape Inc
2771 Circleport Dr
Erlanger, KY 41018-1083

859-283-2044
Fax: 859-283-2068 www.spectape.com
Pressure sensitive tape
President: Maurice J Halpin Iv
mohalpin@spectape.com
Quality Control: Maury Halpin Jr
Production Manager: Leo Henrichs
Estimated Sales: Below $5 Million
Number Employees: 10-19
Square Footage: 120000

29476 Spectratek TechnologiesInc
5405 Jandy Pl
Los Angeles, CA 90066-7005

310-822-2400
Fax: 310-822-2660 888-442-6567
mkelem@spectratek.net www.spectratek.net
Holographic film and glitter
President: Michael Wanlass
CEO: Michael Dedonato
mjdcgb@hotmail.com
CFO: Michael Dedonaco
Estimated Sales: $10-20 Million
Number Employees: 20-49

29477 Spectro
1515 Us Highway 281
Marble Falls, TX 78654-4507

830-798-8786
Fax: 830-798-8467 800-580-6608
www.spectro.com
Manufacturer and exporter of X-ray fluorescent elemental analyzers
Manager: Robert Bartek
Marketing Communications Manager: Gisela Becker
VP Sales/Marketing: Phil Almquist
Contact: Andreas Eerden
aeerden@spectro.com
Estimated Sales: $3-5 Million
Number Employees: 5-9
Square Footage: 120000

29478 Spectronics Corp
956 Brush Hollow Rd
Westbury, NY 11590-1714

516-333-4840
Fax: 516-333-4859 800-274-8888
www.spectroline.com
Manufactures a variety of ultraviolet lamps useful to the foodand beverage industry
President: Jonathan Cooper
jcooper@spectroline.com
Estimated Sales: $30 Million
Number Employees: 100-249

29479 Spectrum Ascona
1305 Fraser St
Suite D2
Bellingham, WA 98229-5800

360-647-0877
Fax: 360-734-8106 800-356-1473
Bags, boxes, ribbons, cups, gift basket supplies, shrink wrapping equiment, and films
Owner: Bruce Maynard
Estimated Sales: $1-2.5 Million
Number Employees: 1-4

29480 Spectrum Enterprises
3220 Kratzville Road
Evansville, IN 47710-3357

812-425-1771
Fax: 812-425-1637
Rubber stamps and pads
General Manager: Thomas Evans
Estimated Sales: Less than $500,000
Number Employees: 4

29481 Spectrum Plastics
3311 S Jones Boulevard
Suite 209
Las Vegas, NV 89146-6775
702-876-8650
Fax: 702-876-8260
Custom and standard plastic bags

29482 Spee-Dee Packaging Machinery
P.O.Box 656
1360 Grandview Parkway
Sturtevant, WI 53177
262-886-4402
Fax: 262-886-5502 877-375-2121
info@spee-dee.com www.spee-dee.com
Manufacturer and exporter of volumetric cup-type
and auger filling equipment for powders, granulars
and pastes
President: James P Navin
Vice President: Timm Johnson
Operations Manager: Paul Navin
Estimated Sales: Below $5 Million
Number Employees: 20-49
Square Footage: 20000
Brands:
    Digitronic
    Spee-Dee

29483 Speedrack Products Group LTD
7903 Venture Ave NW
Sparta, MI 49345-9427
616-887-0002
Fax: 616-887-2693 www.speedrack.net
Storage racks including adjustable tubular and structural steel
Owner: Ron Ducharme
sales@speedrack.net
CFO: H W Baird
CEO: Ron Ducharme
Marketing Director: Butch Newland
Estimated Sales: $30-50 Million
Number Employees: 20-49
Square Footage: 280000

29484 Speedways Conveyors
PO Box 9
Lancaster, NY 14086-0009
716-893-2222
Fax: 716-893-3067 800-800-1022
Aluminum conveyors including gravity, powered,
pallet flow and line shaft; exporter of pallet flow
systems
Executive VP: John Jacobowitz
VP Sales: Daniel Buckley
Estimated Sales: $5-10 Million
Number Employees: 50-99
Square Footage: 440000
Type of Packaging: Consumer, Food Service
Brands:
    C-Square
    Clean Wheel
    Q-50

29485 Spencer Business Form Company
PO Box 229
Spencer, WV 25276
304-372-8877
Fax: 304-372-8902
Rubber stamps and office supplies
President: Milton S Griffith
Estimated Sales: $300,000-500,000
Number Employees: 5

29486 Spencer Packing Company
PO Box 753
Washington, NC 27889-0753
252-946-4161
Fax: 252-946-4162
Processor and packer of pork
President: Harold Spencer
Estimated Sales: $1,250,000
Number Employees: 10-19

29487 Spencer Research Inc
1290 Grandview Ave
Columbus, OH 43212-3439
614-488-3123
Fax: 614-421-1154 800-488-3242
www.spencer-research.com
Consultant specializing in consumer testing for technical product development providing sensory testing, statistical experimental design and analysis

Owner: George Maynard
spencerresearch1@aol.com
President: Betty Spencer
Estimated Sales: $5-10 Million
Number Employees: 20-49
Square Footage: 30000

29488 Spencer Strainer Systems
6205 Gheens Mill Rd
Jeffersonville, IN 47130
812-282-6300
Fax: 812-282-7272 800-801-4977
spencer@spencerstrainer.com
www.spencerstrainer.com
MIG and TIG welding, general machining, drilling,
boring, cutting, surface grinding, mill and lathe
work; stainless steel filtration systems; Spencer
strainer system
President: Glenn Spencer
Contact: Paul Deaver
pdeaver@spencerstrainer.com
Number Employees: 5-9

29489 Spencer Turbine Co
600 Day Hill Rd
Windsor, CT 06095-4706
860-688-8361
Fax: 860-688-0098 800-232-4321
marketing@spencer-air.com
www.spencerturbine.com
Manufacturer and exporter of central vacuum systems, tubing, fittings and centrifugal blowers; also,
air and gas handling equipment, air knives and
pressure fans
President/CEO: Mike Walther
mwalther@spencer-air.com
VP: Paul Burdick
Marketing Manager: Janis Cayne
Sales: Jim Yablonski
Estimated Sales: $20-50 Million
Number Employees: 100-249
Square Footage: 200000
Brands:
    Dirt Eraser
    Fume Eraser
    Industravac
    Jet-Clean
    Power Mizer
    Sump-Vac
    Top Hat
    Vortex

29490 Sperling Boss
51 Station Street
Box 100
Sperling, MB R0G 2M0
Canada
204-626-3401
Fax: 204-626-3252 877-626-3401
sperling@sperlingind.com www.sperlingind.com
Designs, manufactures, and installs equipment and
building for the beef and hog processing industry.
Manager: Jeff Nicolajsen

29491 (HQ)Sperling Industries
2420 Z St
Omaha, NE 68107-4430
402-556-4070
Fax: 402-556-2927 sperlingboss@aol.com
Manufacturer and exporter of meat processing
equipment including sausage makers, cookers, renderers, cutters, presses and grinders, as well as food
processing machinery. Also material handlers and
conveyors
President: Craig Ellett
Executive VP: C Schmidt
Manager: Allen Tegtmneier
Estimated Sales: $3-5 Million
Number Employees: 10-19
Square Footage: 400000
Other Locations:
    Cincinnati Boss Co.
    Bellevue NE
Brands:
    Boss
    Chop Cut
    Excoriator
    Permeator

29492 Sperling Industries
2420 Z St
Omaha, NE 68107-4430
402-556-4070
Fax: 402-556-2927 800-647-5062
sperling@sperlingind.com

Meat and food processing equipment; exporter of
meat packing house equipment
President: Craig Ellett
Manager: Jim Adrian
adrian@sperlingind.com
Manager: Jeff Nicolajsen
Estimated Sales: $3-5 Million
Number Employees: 10-19
Square Footage: 7000
Parent Co: Cincinnati-Boss Company

29493 Sperling Industries
2420 Z St
Omaha, NE 68107-4430
402-556-4070
Fax: 402-556-2927 800-647-5062
ronb@sperlingomaha.com
Meat rail equipment and accessories, conveyor systems and accessories, architects and engineers, consultants, on-rail kill systems and accessories
President: Craig Ellett
CFO: Craig Ellett
R & D: Russel Nicolajsen
Manager: Brock Pappas
pappas@sperlingind.com
Estimated Sales: $3-5 Million
Number Employees: 10-19

29494 Spicetec Flavors & Seasonings
11 Conagra Drive
Omaha, NE 68102
402-240-4005
800-921-7502
jaime.emanuel@conagrafoods.com
President/Consumer Foods: Andr, Hawaux
CEO: Gary Rodkin
EVP/CFO: John Gehring
EVP: Colleen Batcheler
EVP, Research, Quality & Innovation: Al Bolles
President/Commercial Foods: Paul Maass
EVP/Chief Marketing Officer: Joan Chow
President/ConAgra Foods Sales: Doug Knudsen
SVP/Human Resources: Nicole Theophilus
Plant Manager: Liam Doherty
Number Employees: 10-19
Parent Co: ConAgra Foods

29495 Spin-Tech Corporation
1024 Adams St
Suite A
Hoboken, NJ 7030
201-659-6110
Fax: 201-963-7674 800-977-4692
Beverage fountains, candelabra, serving trays and
liquid fuel candles; exporter of beverage fountains,
table candles and floral holders
Owner: Frank Pasquale
Estimated Sales: $1-2.5 Million
Number Employees: 5-9
Square Footage: 50000

29496 Spinco Metal Products Inc
1 Country Club Dr
Newark, NY 14513-1250
315-331-6285
Fax: 315-331-9535 cthayer@spincometal.com
www.spincometal.com
Manufacturer and exporter of copper refrigeration
components, brass flow metering devices and stainless steel beverage lines, welded and brazed assemblies, cut to length tubing
President: Robert C Straubing
crstraubing@spincometal.com
Engineering/Quality Manager: David Gardner
Quality Assurance Coordinator: Craig Thayer
Inside Sales: Connie Rios
Estimated Sales: $10-20 Million
Number Employees: 50-99
Square Footage: 120000

29497 Spinzer
799 Roosevelt Road
Bldg 6
Glen Ellyn, IL 60137-5908
630-469-7184
Fax: 630-469-7185 www.spinzer.us/
Stirrers for hot and cold beverages, drinking straws
Estimated Sales: 100000
Number of Brands: 1
Number of Products: 2
Parent Co: SPINZER OFFICE SUPPLIES
Type of Packaging: Consumer, Bulk

29498 Spir-It/Zoo Piks
200 Brickstone Sq # G05
Andover, MA 01810-1439
978-964-1551
Fax: 978-964-1552 800-343-0996
Manufacturer and exporter of plastic cutlery, picks, sticks, stirrers, straws and other food service accessories; importer of wooden stirrers and toothpicks
President: Donald McCann
CFO: Peter Maki
VP Sales/Marketing: Joe Pierro
Sales/Marketing Manager: Marva White
Number Employees: 100-249
Square Footage: 320000
Type of Packaging: Food Service
Other Locations:
Spir-It/Zoo Piks
Dallas TX
Brands:
Glassips
Hob Nob
Oakhill
Spir-It

29499 Spiral Biotech Inc
2 Technology Way
Norwood, MA 02062-2680
781-320-9000
Fax: 781-320-8181 800-554-1620
mail@aicompanies.com
Manufacturer and exporter of laboratory equipment including fast sample dilutors, spiral platers, automated plate counters and colony counting systems; importer of microbial air samplers and filter bags; wholesaler/distributor of microbial air samplers
President: John Coughlin
VP Operations: P Emond
Estimated Sales: $10-20 Million
Number Employees: 50-99
Square Footage: 6000
Parent Co: Advanced Instruments
Brands:
Autoplate 4000
Casba Ii
Casba Iv
Labpro Gravimetric

29500 Spiral Manufacturing CoInc
11419 Yellow Pine St NW
Minneapolis, MN 55448-3158
763-392-2336
Fax: 763-755-6184 800-426-3643
info@spiralmfg.com www.spiralmfg.com
Manufacturer and exporter of commercial and industrial HVAC, ventilation, air conditioning and pneumatic conveying, dust and fume collection distribution systems
President: Tom Menth
Contact: Jesiah Durene
jdurene@spiralmfg.com
Estimated Sales: $5-10 Million
Number Employees: 1-4

29501 Spiral Slices Ham Market
1930 Division St
Detroit, MI 48207-2153
313-259-6262
Fax: 313-259-4219
Manufacturer and distributor of vertical ham slicing machines
Owner: Don Bonanno
Estimated Sales: Below $5 Million
Number Employees: 1-4

29502 Spiral Systems
8630 Farley Way
Fair Oaks, CA 95668
916-852-0177
Fax: 916-966-7771 800-998-6111
info@spiralsystems.com www.spiralsystems.com

29503 Spiral-Matic Corp
7772 Park Pl
Brighton, MI 48116-8387
248-486-5080
Fax: 248-486-5081 contact@spiralmatic.com
www.spiralmatic.com
Slicing blades, slicers
President: Dan Mcphail
dan@spiralmatic.com
Manager: Bill Mc Phail
Estimated Sales: $1-2.5 Million
Number Employees: 10-19
Square Footage: 20

29504 Spirax Sarco Inc
1150 Northpoint Blvd
Blythewood, SC 29016-8873
803-714-2000
Fax: 803-714-2222 800-575-0394
insidesalesleads@spirax.com
www.spiraxsarco.com/us
Air eliminators
President: Lorraine Wiseman
lwiseman@spirax.com
Regional Manager: Ed Beedle
Branch Manager: Steve Williams
Estimated Sales: Below $5 Million
Number Employees: 1000-4999
Number of Products: 12
Square Footage: 103000
Type of Packaging: Private Label

29505 Spirit Foodservice, Inc.
200 Brickstone Square
Suite G-05
Andover, MA 01810
978-964-1551
Fax: 978-964-1552 800-343-0996
www.spiritfoodservice.com
Manufacturer and exporter of plastic swizzle sticks, picks, napkin holders, tip trays, napkins, drinking straws and disposable drinkware; also, custom imprinting available
Contact: Peter Maki
maki@spir-it.com
Estimated Sales: $5-10 Million
Number Employees: 100-249
Brands:
Zoo

29506 Spiro-Cut Equipment Co
3005 Bledsoe St
Fort Worth, TX 76107-2905
817-877-3266
Fax: 817-877-3742 888-887-4267
info@spirocut.com www.spirocut.com
Meat slicers
President: Tom Misfeldt
info@spirocut.com
Estimated Sales: $1 Million
Number Employees: 5-9
Square Footage: 2200

29507 Spiroflow Systems Inc
1609 Airport Rd
Monroe, NC 28110-7393
704-291-9595
Fax: 704-291-9594 info@spiroflowsystems.com
www.spiroflow.com
CEO: Jeff Dudas
jeffdudas@spiroflowsystems.com
Manager: Marline Carlisle
Estimated Sales: Below $5 Million
Number Employees: 100-249

29508 Spokane House of Hose Inc
5520 E Sprague Ave
Spokane Valley, WA 99212-0880
509-535-3638
Fax: 509-535-3670 800-541-6351
sales@spokanehose.com www.spokanehose.com
Full color menu cards
Owner: Larry Hayden
sales@spokanehose.com
Estimated Sales: $1-2.5 Million
Number Employees: 20-49

29509 Spontex
100 Spontex Dr
Columbia, TN 38401
931-388-5632
Fax: 931-490-2105 800-251-4222
sales@mapaglove.com
Cellulose sponges, scrubbers, and rubber gloves
President: Peter Moeller
CFO: Greg Grmez
Quality Control: Dewitt Loexton
R&D: Rick Mallernebb
VP Sales: T Gladfelter
Contact: Patrick Spear
patrick.spear@mapaglove.com
VP Manufacturing: R Schmidt
Purchasing Manager: Cindy Brindley
Estimated Sales: $50-75 Million
Number Employees: 100-249
Square Footage: 193000
Parent Co: Hutchinson SA

Brands:
Spontex

29510 Sportsmen's Cannery & Smokehouse
182 Bayfront Loop
Winchester Bay, OR 97467
541-271-3293
Fax: 541-271-9381 800-457-8048
karch@presys.com www.sportsmenscannery.com
Processor and canner of salmon, albacore tuna, sturgeon and shellfish
Manager: Brandy Roelle
Owner: Mikayle Karcher
Number Employees: 1-4
Type of Packaging: Consumer, Private Label
Brands:
Winchester

29511 Spot Wire Works Company
413 Green St
Philadelphia, PA 19123
215-627-6124
Fax: 215-627-0950
Stainless steel and wire shelves, trays and display racks; also, wire parts and guards
President: Eli Brownstein
Estimated Sales: $10-20 Million
Number Employees: 10-19
Square Footage: 20000

29512 Spray Drying
5320 Enterprise St # J
Sykesville, MD 21784-9354
410-549-8090
Fax: 410-549-8091 sales@spraydrysys.com
www.spraydrysys.com
Manufacturer and exporter of spray dryers
President: Jeff Bayliss
bayliss@spraydrysys.com
Quality Control: Jess Bayliss
Vice President: Jeff Bayliss
Estimated Sales: Below $5 Million
Number Employees: 5-9
Square Footage: 7000

29513 Spray Dynamics LTD
108 Bolte Ln
St Clair, MO 63077-3218
636-629-7366
Fax: 636-629-7455 800-260-7366
spraydynamics@heatandcontrol.com
www.spraydynamics.com
Manufacturer and exporter of liquid and dry ingredient applicators and dispensers for food processing machinery.
Owner: Dave Holmeyer
Accounts Payable: Melanie Booher
Marketing Coordinator: Stephanie Butenhoff
Sales Representative: George Wipperfurth
Service Manager: Craig Booher
Estimated Sales: $2.5-5 Million
Number Employees: 20-49
Brands:
Clog-Free Slurry Spray Encoater
Delta Dry
Delta Liquid
Econoflo
Enhancer
Master Series
Meter Master
Micro-Meter Airless
Powder Xpress
Soft Flight
Unispense

29514 Spray Tek Inc
344 Cedar Ave
Middlesex, NJ 08846-2433
732-469-0050
Fax: 732-302-0866 www.spray-tek.com
Spray drying
Vice President: David Brand
david.brand@spray-tek.net
VP: David Brand
Estimated Sales: $20-50 Million
Number Employees: 50-99

29515 Spraying Systems Company
North Avenueand Schmale Road
PO Box 7900
Wheaton, IL 60187
630-655-5000
Fax: 630-260-0842 info@spray.com
www.spray.com
Manufacturer and exporter of nozzles, spray guns,
portable spray systems and spray nozzle accessories
including connectors, ball fittings, valves, regula-
tors, etc
President/CEO: James Bramsen
VP Manufacturing: Don Fox
VP/COO: Dave Smith
Sr Applications Engineer: Wes Bartell

29516 Spraymation Inc
5320 NW 35th Ave
Fort Lauderdale, FL 33309-7014
954-484-9700
Fax: 954-484-9778 800-327-4985
sales@spraymation.com www.spraymation.com
Standard and Custom designed hot melt, cold
adesive and fluid dispensing equipment, featuring
Electromatic Applicator Heads for the application of
beads, dots, spray patterns and slot coating; DC Pat-
tern Controllers, Pumping Systemsand Temperature
Control Units
President: Eric J Cocks Sr
R&D: David Kerzel
Quality Control: Ken Jones
Estimated Sales: Below $5 Million
Number Employees: 20-49

29517 Sprayway Inc
1005 S Westgate St
Addison, IL 60101-5021
630-628-3000
Fax: 630-543-7797 800-332-9000
info@spraywayinc.com
Manufacturer and exporter of aerosol products in-
cluding all purpose and glass cleaners, dust control
sprays and insecticides
President: Michael Rohl
CFO: Roger Hayes
rhayes@spraywayinc.com
VP Sales/Marketing: Bob Potvin
Estimated Sales: $10-20 Million
Number Employees: 100-249
Number of Brands: 1
Square Footage: 160000
Type of Packaging: Private Label
Brands:
Crazy Clean
Dust Up
Sprayway
Tru-Nox

29518 Spring Air Systems
1464 Cornwall Road
Unit 9
Oakville, ON L6J 7W5
Canada
905-338-2999
Fax: 905-338-0179 866-874-4505
www.springairsystems.com
Specializes in kitchen ventilation systems
Number Employees: 10

29519 Spring Cove Container Div
301 Cove Lane Rd
Roaring Spring, PA 16673-1619
814-224-5141
Fax: 814-224-5783 scc@roaringspring.com
www.springcove.com
Corrugated cartons
President: Daniel B Hoover
dhoover@roaringsprint.com
Sales: P Adams
Plant Manager: Johnathen Sneed
Estimated Sales: $20-50 Million
Number Employees: 20-49
Parent Co: Roaring Spring Blank Book Company

29520 Spring USA Corp
127 Ambassador Dr # 147
Naperville, IL 60540-4079
630-527-8600
Fax: 630-527-8677 800-535-8974
springusa@springusa.com
Products range from chafing dishes to professional
cookware, from induction ranges to coffee urns.

President: Tom Brija
springusa@springusa.com
Sales/Marketing Supervisor: Kelly Boyle
Estimated Sales: $2.5-5,000,000
Number Employees: 5-9
Parent Co: Spring Switzerland
Brands:
Blackline
Brigade
Brigade +
Endurance
Flix
Mr. Induction
Vulcano

29521 Spring Wood Products
4267 Austin Rd
Geneva, OH 44041
440-466-1135
Fax: 440-466-1138
Wooden pallets and shipping containers
CEO: Jacob Castrilla
VP: Gregory Castrilla
VP: Thomas Castrilla
Estimated Sales: $2.5-5 Million
Number Employees: 20-49

29522 (HQ)Springer-Penguin
PO Box 199
Mount Vernon, NY 10552-0199
914-699-3200
Fax: 914-699-3231 800-835-8500
Manufacturer and exporter of refrigerators, file cabi-
nets and wood office furniture including conference
tables, bookcases, etc.; importer of wooden
bookcases
Number Employees: 10
Square Footage: 80000
Brands:
Penguin

29523 Springfield Metal Products Co
8 Commerce St
Springfield, NJ 07081-2903
973-379-4600
Fax: 973-379-7314
jd.sommer@springfieldmetalproducts.com
www.springfieldmetalproducts.com
Sheet metal and structural fabrications in stainless
steel and aluminum
President: John Sommer
jd.sommer@verizon.net
VP/Secretary: Irene Powell
Estimated Sales: Below $5 Million
Number Employees: 10-19
Square Footage: 12000

29524 Springport Steel Wire Products
4906 Hoffman Street
Suite B
Elkhart, IN 46516
574-295-9660
Fax: 574-293-8552 cs@sigma-wire.com
www.sigmawire.com
Manufacturer and exporter of handling equipment
including containers, pallets, wire and mesh shelv-
ing and conveyor guards
Estimated Sales: $2.5-5 Million
Number Employees: 20-50
Brands:
Wire Dek
Wiretainer

29525 Springprint Medallion
1431 Marvin Griffin Road
Augusta, GA 30906-3852
800-543-5990
Fax: 800-982-6434
Custom printed place mats, napkins, coasters and
tray covers
VP Sales/Marketing: Layne Allen
VP Converting Operations: Eric Simmons
Number Employees: 2
Parent Co: Marcal Paper Mills

29526 Sprinkman Corporation
PO Box 390
Franksville, WI 53126-0390
262-835-2390
Fax: 262-835-4325 800-816-1610
www.sprinkman.com

Wholesaler/distributor of dairy and food processing
equipment and supplies; consultant specializing in
the design processing systems; also, installation and
reconditioning services available
Chief Operating Officer: Robert Sprinkman
CFO: Dale Metcoff
President: Brian Sprinkman
Vice President: Merlin Winchell
Contact: Jimmi Sukys
j.sukys@sprinkman.com
Estimated Sales: $30 Million
Number Employees: 100
Square Footage: 35000
Parent Co: W.M. Sprinkman Corporation

29527 Sprinter Marking Inc
1805 Chandlersville Rd
Zanesville, OH 43701-4644
740-453-1000
Fax: 740-453-6750 sales@sprintermarking.com
www.sprintermarking.com
Automatic ink code dating and marking machinery
for cups
CEO: Bob Bishop
Estimated Sales: $1-5 Million
Number Employees: 10-19
Square Footage: 12000
Brands:
Sprinter

29528 Sprouts Farmers Market Inc.
5455 E. High St.
Suite 111
Phoenix, AZ 85054
www.sprouts.com
National grocery store chain specializing in fresh
foods and health foods.
Chief Executive Officer: Jack Sinclair
Chief Financial Officer: Denise Paulonis
Chief Operating Officer: Dan Sanders
Year Founded: 2002
Estimated Sales: $5.2 Billion
Number Employees: 30,000
Brands:
Country Kitchen Meals
Henry's Heritage Bread
Sprouts
Sunflower

29529 Spudnik Equipment Co
584 W 100 N
PO Box 1045
Blackfoot, ID 83221-5518
208-684-4120
Fax: 208-785-1497 www.spudnik.com
Manufacturer and exporter of potato handling equip-
ment and parts including pliers, scoopers, convey-
ors, sorters, bins, bulk beds, van unloaders,
semi-trailers, etc
CEO: Rolf Geier
Sales Manager: Dennis Schumacker
Engineering Manager: Andrew Blight
Estimated Sales: $10-20 Million
Number Employees: 100-249
Square Footage: 200000

29530 Spurgeon Co
1330 Hilton Rd
Ferndale, MI 48220-2837
248-547-3805
Fax: 248-547-8344 800-396-2554
Manufacturer and exporter of conveyors, unscram-
blers, alumninum casting and stacking equipment;
importer of aluminum casting and stacking
equipment
CEO: Andy Willermet
awillermet@yoplait.fr
VP: Thomas Woodbeck
VP: Bernie Makie
Estimated Sales: $10-20 Million
Number Employees: 50-99
Square Footage: 200000
Parent Co: Overhead Conveyor Company

29531 (HQ)Spurrier Chemical Companies
PO BOX 16297
Atlanta, GA 30321
770-968-9222
Fax: 770-968-7281 800-795-9222
www.spurrierchemical.com
Cleaning products including institutional and indus-
trial chemicals and detergents

CEO: Robin Spurrier
CFO: Tony DiStefano
Vice President: Donald Ryel
Research & Development: Bruce Lavery
Quality Control: Karen Rowe
VP Distribution Sales & Kansas/Missouri: Marshall Ryel
Sales Director: Kurt Luhmann
Operations Manager: Marcia Ryel
Production Manager: Marcia Ryel
Plant Manager: Todd Hardesty
Purchasing Manager: Jeff Alfaro
Estimated Sales: $10-20 Million
Number Employees: 50-99
Square Footage: 120000
Type of Packaging: Food Service, Private Label
Other Locations:
Spurrier Chemical Companies
Clwyd, North Wales

29532 Squar-Buff
1000 45th Street
Oakland, CA 94608-3314
510-655-2470
Fax: 510-652-0969 800-525-6955
Manufacturer and exporter of floor and rug cleaning machinery
Number Employees: 5

29533 Squid Ink Mfg Inc
7041 Boone Ave N
Minneapolis, MN 55428-1504
763-795-8856
Fax: 763-795-8867 800-877-5658
info@squidink.com www.squidink.com
Ink jet coding and inks, coding and marking equipment, and date codes batch numbers product identification
Owner: Kevin Blair
kblair@engagetechnologies.net
Vice President: Loyd Tarver
Engineering: Chris Miller
Marketing Manager: Chad Carney
Estimated Sales: $5-10 Million
Number Employees: 20-49

29534 (HQ)Squire Corrugated Container Company
PO Box 405
South Plainfield, NJ 7080
908-561-8550
Fax: 908-561-2791 info@squirebox.com
Corrugated packaging
President: James Beneroff
Sales Manager: James Benneroth
Contact: Seymour Beneroff
beneroff@squirebox.com
Estimated Sales: $10-20 Million
Number Employees: 100-249

29535 Squirrel Systems
3157 Grandview Highway
Vancouver, BC V5M 2E9
Canada
604-412-3300
Fax: 604-434-9888 800-388-6824
squirrel@squirrelsystems.com
www.squirrelsystems.com
Manufacturer and exporter of electronic point of sale terminals
Vice President of Research and Developme: Joe Cortese
Vice President of Corporate Sales: David Atkinson
Estimated Sales: $20-30 Million
Number Employees: 100-250
Brands:
Squirrel

29536 St Joseph Packaging Inc
PO Box 579
St Joseph, MO 64502-0579
816-233-3181
Fax: 816-233-2475 800-383-3000
Custom industrial packaging offset/flexo printing, diecut/cello windowing, laminating and direct print on mini-flute corrigated
President: C Hamilton Jr
CFO: Patty Waitkoss
CEO: Brad Keller
Quality Control: Don Kragel
Marketing: Pam Hurley
Plant Manager: Josh Hamilton
Purchasing: Kenny Hayter

Estimated Sales: $15 Million
Square Footage: 220000
Type of Packaging: Consumer, Food Service, Private Label

29537 St Onge Ruff & Associates
2400 Pershing Road
Ste 400
Kansas City, MO 64108
816-329-8700
Fax: 816-329-8701 800-800-5261
marketing@transystems.com
Engineering firm specializing in the planning, design and construction of processing and distribution facilities
Number Employees: 5-9

29538 St. Clair Pakwell
120 25th Ave
Bellwood, IL 60104-1201
708-547-7500
Fax: 708-547-9052 800-323-1922
Manufacturer and exporter of decorative packaging including wrapping paper
Estimated Sales: $20-50 Million
Number Employees: 100-249
Parent Co: Field Container Corporation
Type of Packaging: Food Service, Bulk

29539 St. Elizabeth Street Display Corporation
21 Main Street
West Wing, Suite 349
Hackensack, NJ 07601
201-883-0333
Fax: 201-883-1333 bill@stelizdisp.com
www.stelizdisp.com
Point of sale displays
President: William Talaia
Estimated Sales: Below $5 Million
Number Employees: 20-49

29540 St. George Crystal
1101 William Flynn Hwy
Glenshaw, PA 15116-2637
724-523-6501
Fax: 724-523-0707 800-677-0261
Wine industry glassware
President: Richard Rifenburgh
Estimated Sales: $50-100 Million
Number Employees: 275

29541 St. Louis Carton Company
1620 N Jefferson Ave
Saint Louis, MO 63106
314-241-0990
Fax: 314-241-0991 www.stlcarton.com
Folding paper boxes
President: Bonnie Green
Estimated Sales: $1-2.5 Million
Number Employees: 1-4

29542 St. Louis Stainless Service
2305 N Broadway
St Louis, MO 63102
636-343-3000
Fax: 314-231-5074 800-735-3853
www.dukemfg.com
Tables, cabinets, counters, sinks and floor troughs
President: Don Durham
Estimated Sales: $5-10,000,000
Number Employees: 5-9

29543 St. Pierre Box & LumberCompany
66 Lovely St
Canton, CT 6019
860-693-2089
Fax: 860-693-6155
Wooden boxes, pallets and steel skids
President: John St Pierre
Estimated Sales: $500,000-$1 Million
Number Employees: 5-9

29544 St. Simons Trading
PO Box 5511
Hilton Head Island, SC 29938
843-757-9889
800-621-9935
Estimated Sales: $.5-1 million
Number Employees: 1-4

29545 Sta-Rite Ginnie Lou Inc
245 E South 1st St
PO Box 435
Shelbyville, IL 62565-2332
217-774-3921
Fax: 217-774-5234 800-782-7483
www.sta-riteginnielou.com
Manufacturer, importer and exporter of nylon hair nets, hairpins, bobbypins and haircare accessories.
Chairman: Robert Bolinger
CEO: Noel Bolinger
noelbolinger@consulated.net
Sales Director: Linda Stewardson
Estimated Sales: $1 Million
Number Employees: 5-9
Number of Brands: 10
Number of Products: 1300
Square Footage: 32000
Type of Packaging: Consumer, Food Service, Private Label, Bulk
Brands:
Ginnie Lou
Sta-Rite

29546 Staban Engineering Corp
65 N Plains Industrial Rd # 5
PO Box 8
Wallingford, CT 06492-5832
203-294-1997
Fax: 203-294-0583 888-782-2261
sales@staban.com www.staban.com
Packaging machinery
President: Dennis Bandecchi
Estimated Sales: $2.5-5 Million
Number Employees: 10-19

29547 Stablized Products
1832 W Square Drive
High Ridge, MO 63049-1968
636-677-5764
Fax: 636-376-5811 800-546-7349

29548 Stackbin Corp
29 Powder Hill Rd
Lincoln, RI 02865-4424
401-333-1600
Fax: 401-333-1952 800-333-1603
www.stackbin.com
Stackable storage systems for small parts
President: William A Shaw
wshaw@stackbin.com
Quality Control and VP: Scott Shaw
Sales Supervisor: Andrew Porter
Estimated Sales: $10-20 Million
Number Employees: 10-19

29549 Stadia Corporation
691 Corporate Cir
Golden, CO 80401-5622
303-273-0336
Fax: 303-273-1414 800-765-6600
sales@cognitive.com www.cogsol.com
Print and apply labeling equipment
President: Patrick Frinat
Marketing Manager: Vic Barczyk
Number Employees: 100-249

29550 (HQ)Stafford-Smith Inc
3414 S Burdick St
Kalamazoo, MI 49001-4888
269-343-1240
Fax: 269-343-2509 800-968-2442
djs@staffordsmith.com www.staffordsmith.com
Freezers, dishwashers, ranges, slicers, fryers, refrigeration equipment, etc
President: David J Stafford Sr
Cio/Cto: Randy Clark
rclark@staffordsmith.com
Estimated Sales: $50-75 Million
Number Employees: 100-249
Other Locations:
Stafford-Smith
Lansing MI

29551 Stage Coach Sauces
3829 Reid St
Palatka, FL 32177-2509
386-328-6330
Fax: 386-328-6330 info@stagecoachsauces.com
www.stagecoachsauces.com
Contract packager and exporter of sauces and condiments including steak, barbecue, pepper, chicken wing and seafood; also, contract packaging of wet and dry products available.

President: Terry Geck
VP Marketing: Lisa Marie Geck
Plant Manager: Terry Geck
Estimated Sales: $3-5 Million
Number Employees: 5-9
Square Footage: 20000
Type of Packaging: Consumer, Food Service, Private Label
Brands:
  Stage Coach Sauces

29552 Stainless
305 Tech Park Drive
Suite 115
La Vergne, TN 37086-3633
954-421-4290
Fax: 954-421-4464 800-877-5177
www.stainless.com
Manufacturer and exporter of stainless steel kitchen and dining room equipment including tables and sinks
VP/General Manager: Edward Umphlette
VP Sales: Tom Kassab
Estimated Sales: Less than $500,000
Number Employees: 4
Square Footage: 920000
Parent Co: Franke USA Holding
Other Locations:
  Stainless
  Holland MI

29553 Stainless Equipment Manufacturing
5950 Cedar Springs Road
Suite 125
Dallas, TX 75235-6816
214-357-9600
Fax: 214-358-4959 800-736-2038
Metal sinks, counters and work tables for hotels and restaurants
Shop Foreman: Rex Riddle
Plant Manager: Bill Cross
Purchasing Agent: Patricia Corder
Estimated Sales: $5-10 Million
Number Employees: 35
Parent Co: White Swan

29554 Stainless Fabricating Company
860 Navajo St
Denver, CO 80204-4317
303-573-1700
Fax: 303-573-3776 800-525-8966
Stainless steel counters, tabletops, dish tables, shelving and sinks
President: Jeff Manion
Estimated Sales: $5-10 Million
Number Employees: 20-49

29555 Stainless Fabrication Inc
4455 W Kearney St
PO Box 1127
Springfield, MO 65803-8705
417-865-5696
Fax: 417-865-7863 800-397-8265
sfi-info@stainlessfab.com www.stainlessfab.com
Design and manufacture high quality, custom, shop and field fabricated stainless steel processing equipment including tanks, dryers, reaactors, columns, sanitary processing tunnels and other vessels
President: Sherry Miller
jeff.harris@trivantis.com
Estimated Sales: $16 Million
Number Employees: 100-249
Square Footage: 90000

29556 Stainless International
2650 Mercantile Dr Ste C
Rancho Cordova, CA 95742
916-638-7370
Fax: 916-638-1172 888-300-6196
www.all-stainless.com
Stainless steel hoods, under counter bar equipment, sinks, dish tables and counters; also, custom fabrication services available
President: Ted Lambertson
CFO: Monica Lambertson
Estimated Sales: $2.5-5 Million
Number Employees: 20-49

29557 Stainless Motors Inc
7601 Nita Pl NE
Rio Rancho, NM 87144-8707
505-867-0224
Fax: 505-867-0225 info@stainlessmotors.com
www.stainlessmotors.com
Stainless steel power transmission equipment
Owner: John Oleson
john@stainlessmotors.com
Engineering: John Oleson
Sales/Customer Service: Gene Filion
john@stainlessmotors.com
Marketing/Human Resources: Lori Costa
Estimated Sales: $1.2 Million
Number Employees: 20-49
Square Footage: 22000

29558 Stainless One DispensingSystem
790 Eubanks Drive
Vacaville, CA 95688-9470
800-722-6738
Fax: 707-448-1521 888-723-3827
autobar@aol.com
Manufacturer and exporter of beer dispensing equipment
VP: Clark Smith
Number Employees: 3
Brands:
  Perfect Pour
  Stainless One

29559 Stainless Products
1649 72nd Ave
P O Box 169
Somers, WC 53171
262-859-2826
Fax: 262-859-2871 800-558-9446
sales@stainless-products.com
www.stainless-products.com
Manufacturer and exporter of stainless steel fabrications including O-rings, pumps, gauges, welding and valves; also, clean-in-place systems
President: Cindy Gross
jerickson@stainless-products.com
President: Cindy Gross
Sales/Purchasing: Mike Shoop
Estimated Sales: $1-5 Million
Number Employees: 20-49
Type of Packaging: Bulk

29560 Stainless Specialists Inc
T7441 Steel Ln
Wausau, WI 54403-8732
715-675-4155
Fax: 715-675-9096 800-236-4155
www.ssi-wis.com
Manufacturer installation and exporter of stainless steel food processing and equipment, conveyors, tanks and work platforms
President: Roger Prochnow
CFO: Paul Kinate
Sr VP Sales: Mike Slattery
R&D: Steve Radant
Quality Control: Brian Stoffel
Marketing/Sales/Public Relations: Roger Prochnow
Operations: Keith Christian
Production: Shannon Herdt
Plant Manager: Keith Christian
Purchasing: Corey Eimmer
Estimated Sales: $20 Million
Number Employees: 100-249
Square Footage: 15000

29561 Stainless Steel
800 Aviation Parkway
Smyrna, TN 37167
888-437-2653
Fax: 954-421-4464 800-877-5177
www.stainless.com
Manufacturer and distributor of french fry dispensers and food service equipment
Parent Co: Franke
Brands:
  Robofry

29562 Stainless Steel Coatings
835 Sterling Road
P.O.Box 1145
South Lancaster, MA 01561-1145
978-365-9828
Fax: 978-365-9874 info@steel-it.com
www.steel-it.com
Manufacturer and exporter of anti-corrosion and stainless steel pigmented paint coatings

President: Michael Faigen
Estimated Sales: $1-2,500,000
Number Employees: 10-19
Number of Brands: 2
Number of Products: 14
Square Footage: 20000
Brands:
  Steel It
  Steel It Lite

29563 Stainless Steel Fabricator Inc
15120 Desman Rd
La Mirada, CA 90638-5737
714-739-9904
Fax: 714-739-0502 info@cookking.net
www.ssfab.net
Ovens, broilers, deep fat fryers, continuous oil filters and conveyor systems
President: Craig Miller
craig@cookking.net
Executive VP: Dick Naess
Marketing Director: Coby Naess
Number Employees: 50-99
Square Footage: 110000

29564 Stainless Steel Fabricators
11967 State Highway 64 W
Tyler, TX 75704-6939
903-595-6625
Fax: 903-592-8819 info@ssftexas.com
www.ssftexas.com
Stainless steel, corrugated, copper and brass vent hood systems, countertops, sinks, tables and shelving
President/ Owner: Greg King
Sales & Marketing: Ryan King
Estimated Sales: $5-10,000,000
Number Employees: 10-19

29565 (HQ)Stainless Steel Fabricator Inc
15120 Desman Rd
La Mirada, CA 90638-5737
714-739-9904
Fax: 714-739-0502 info@ssfab.net
www.ssfab.net
Food processing machinery
President: Phil Benoit
phil@ssfab.net
Sales Representative: Dick Naess
Estimated Sales: $20-50 Million
Number Employees: 50-99

29566 StainlessDrains.com
PO Box 1278
Greenville, TX 75403
888-785-2345
Fax: 877-785-2342
Manufactures a full line of stainless steel drains and drain products, from roof drains to sanitary floor drains.

29567 Stamfag Cutting Dies
2 Braley Point Road
Po Box 1249
Bolton Landing, NY 12814-1249
518-644-2054
Fax: 518-644-2546 www.stamfag-usa.com
Manufacturing and cutting dies for label printers and lithographers
Type of Packaging: Consumer, Food Service, Private Label, Bulk

29568 Stampede Meat, Inc.
7351 S 78th Ave
Bridgeview, IL 60455
Fax: 888-376-9349 800-353-0933
stampedemeat.com
Beef, pork and chicken products
CEO & President: Brock Furlong
CFO: Vito Giustino
COO: Jim Scott
VP, Technical Innovation & Development: Dennis Gruber
VP, Food Safety & Quality Assurance: Adam Miller
Sr. VP, Sales & Marketing: Ray McKiernan
Director, Human Resources: Christina Hackney
VP, Production: Krys Harbut
Estimated Sales: $45.5 Million
Number Employees: 250-499
Square Footage: 140000
Type of Packaging: Consumer, Food Service
Other Locations:
  Cook Processing Facility
  Oak Lawn IL

Brands:
Cro-Magnon
Cro-Man
Cro-Mag
Stampede
Mission Hill Bistro

29569 Stampendous
1122 N Kraemer Pl
Anaheim, CA 92806-1922

714-688-0288
Fax: 714-688-0297 800-869-0474
stamp@markenterprises.com
www.stampendous.com
Manufacturer and exporter of stain and spot removers
Owner: Fran Sieford
stamp@stampendous.com
General Manager: Mark Bruhns
Product Manager: Regina Ashbaugh
Estimated Sales: $5-10 Million
Number Employees: 50-99
Square Footage: 40000
Brands:
Spoto

29570 Stancase Equipment Company
165 Chubb Ave
Suite 3
Lyndhurst, NJ 07071

201-434-6300
Fax: 201-434-1508
Cheese equipment, agitators, cutters, forks, knives
President: Michael Koss
Executive: Joel Koss
Estimated Sales: $5-10 Million
Number Employees: 50-99

29571 Stand Fast Pkgng Prods Inc
350 S Church St
Addison, IL 60101-3750

630-543-6390
Fax: 630-543-6390 scott@standfastpkg.com
www.standfastpkg.com
Corrugated boxes and dispaly packaging
Owner: John Carman Sr
CEO: John Carmen
HR Executive: Tracy Miller
tracy@standfastpkg.com
Research & Development: Keith Carman
Quality Control: John Carman
Sales Manager: Scott Carmen
Plant Manager: Jon Clair
Purchasing Manager: Phil Lynch
Estimated Sales: $20-25 Million
Number Employees: 100-249
Square Footage: 90000
Type of Packaging: Consumer

29572 (HQ)Standard Casing Company
165 Chubb Ave
Lyndhurst, NJ 07071-3503

201-434-6300
Fax: 201-434-1508 800-847-4141
Manufacturer, importer and exporter of sausage processing equipment including stuffers as well as sausage casings
President: Michael Koss
Executive VP: Joel Koss
Manager Sales: Richard Theise
Contact: Patricia Wisniewski
patriciaw@standardcasing.com
Estimated Sales: $10-20 Million
Number Employees: 50-99
Square Footage: 70000
Type of Packaging: Bulk
Brands:
Gold Hog Casings
Platinum Hog Casings
Stancase
Standard

29573 Standard Folding Cartons Inc
7520 Astoria Blvd # 100
Flushing, NY 11370-1645

718-396-4522
Fax: 718-507-6430 stanfold@aol.com
www.thestandardgroup.com
Manufacturer and exporter of folding cartons
President: Louis Cortes
Manager: Tanya Borges
tanyab@thestandardgroup.com
Estimated Sales: $20-50 Million
Number Employees: 20-49

29574 Standard Paper Box MachCo Inc
347 Coster St # 2
Bronx, NY 10474-6813

718-328-3300
Fax: 718-842-7772 800-367-8755
SPBM@prodigy.net www.spbmco.com
Manufacturer and exporter of box making machinery
President: Bruce Adams
Sales: Ronnie Nadel
Estimated Sales: $5-10 Million
Number Employees: 10-19
Square Footage: 200000
Brands:
Standard Econocut Die Cutters
Standard Excalibur Die Cutters
Standard Folder Gluers

29575 Standard Pump
1540 University Dr
Auburn, GA 30011

770-307-1003
Fax: 770-307-1009 866-558-8611
info@standardpump.com www.standardpump.com
Barrel and container pumps and flow control systems are commonly used through out the food processing, cosmetics, pharmaceutical, bio-tech, chemical processing, waste water treatment, plating, medical, semi-conductor, agriculture andpetroleum industries.
President: Don Murphy
Vice President: Christopher Murphy
Contact: Jacob Berg
jacobberg@standardpump.com
Estimated Sales: $2-3 Million
Number Employees: 5-9
Square Footage: 80000

29576 Standard Rate Review
PO Box 23415
San Antonio, TX 78223

210-532-6000
Fax: 210-532-6200 info@standardratereview.com
www.standardratereview.com
President: Alan Ziperstein

29577 Standard Refrigeration Co
321 Foster Ave
Wood Dale, IL 60191-1432

708-345-5400
Fax: 708-345-3513
stanref.customerservice@alfalaval.com
www.alfalaval.us
Manufacturer and exporter of heat exchangers for refrigeration applications
Materials & Logistics Manager: Frank Nimesheim
Senior Vice President, Equipment: Mark Larsen
Research and Development Manager: Gary Kaiser
Quality Control Manager: Kevin Lenihan
Market Unit Manager, Refrigeration: Dan Aiken
Business Development Manager: Yao Jeppsson
Manager: Joseph Shukys
joe@btureps.com
General Manager: Phil Lucas
Product Portfolio Manager: Mark Hetherington
Factory Manager: Therese Huff
Estimated Sales: $50-100 Million
Number Employees: 100-249

29578 Standard Terry Mills
38 Green St
Souderton, PA 18964-1702

215-723-8121
Fax: 215-723-3651
Manufacturer and exporter of knitted and woven dish cloths, kitchen towels, oven mitts, aprons, food covers and pot holders; importer of kitchen towels
President: Kerry Gingrich
VP Production: G Nam
Estimated Sales: $10-20 Million
Number Employees: 1-4
Square Footage: 200000

29579 Standard-Knapp Inc
63 Pickering St
Portland, CT 06480-1987

860-342-1100
Fax: 860-342-1557 800-628-9565
info@standard-knapp.com
www.standard-knapp.com
Automated packaging machinery including vertical case, continuous motion tray, shrink and bottle packers

President: Arthur Tanner
CEO: Michael Weaver
mweaver@standard-knapp.com
CFO: Michael Montano
CEO: Robert Reynolds
R&D: Mike Weaver
Quality Control: David Lou
VP Marketing: Kristofer Kolstad
Estimated Sales: $5-10 Million
Number Employees: 100-249

29580 Standex International Corp.
11 Keewaydin Dr.
Salem, NH 03079

603-893-9701
Fax: 603-893-7324 www.standex.com
Food service equipment, air distribution products, casters, supermarket cart wheels, pumps, point of purchase displays, hydraulic cylinders, etc.
President/Chief Executive Officer: David Dunbar
VP/Chief Financial Officer: Thomas DeByle
VP/Chief Legal Officer/Secretary: Alan Glass
Year Founded: 1955
Estimated Sales: $635 Million
Number Employees: 5,400
Brands:
APW Wyott
Bakers Pride
BKI Worldwide
Federal Industries
Master-Bilt
Nor-Lake
Procon Products
Tri-Star Manufacturing
Ultrafryer

29581 Stanford Chemicals
12640 E Northwest Hwy # 411
Dallas, TX 75228-8091

972-682-5600
Fax: 972-682-9553
Industrial cleaning compounds
President: Ted Egerton
Customer Service: Lynnette Ladd
Chemist: Kenn Gretz PhD
Estimated Sales: $1-3 Million
Number Employees: 5-9
Square Footage: 40000

29582 Stanfos
3908 69th Avenue NW
Edmonton, AB T6B 2V2
Canada

780-468-2165
Fax: 780-465-4890 800-661-5648
info@stanfos.com www.stanfos.com
Manufacturer, exporter and wholesaler/distributor of dairy, food and meat processing equipment including pasteurizers
President: Lang Jameson
Sales Manager: Shawna Bungax
Number Employees: 10-19

29583 Stanley Access Technologies
65 Scott Swamp Rd
Farmington, CT 06032-2803

717-597-6958
Fax: 877-339-7923 800-722-2377
S-SAT-SatInfo@sbdinc.com
www.stanleyaccess.com
Manufacturer and exporter of automatic doors including fireproof, sliding, swinging and electrical; also, access control systems and door operating devices
President: Justin Boswell
International Sales/Marketing: Jennifer Loranger
Customer Service: Susan Martin
Administrative Assistant: Jennifer Almeida House
Estimated Sales: Below $500,000
Number Employees: 5-9
Parent Co: Stanley Works
Brands:
Dura-Glide
Magic-Access
Magic-Swing
Sentrex
Stan-Ray

29584 Stanley Black & Decker Inc
1000 Stanley Dr
New Britain, CT 06053-1675

860-225-5111
CorporateRequest@sbdinc.com
www.stanleyblackanddecker.com

Fastening equipment and hand tools manufacturer.
President & CEO: James Loree
jloree@stanleyworks.com
EVP & Chief Financial Officer: Donald Allan, Jr.
VP, Corporate Tax & Treasurer: Michael Bartone
VP & Chief Accounting Officer: Jocelyn Belisle
VP & Chief Information Officer: Rhonda Gass
VP, Investor Relations: Dennis Lange
Chief Communications Officer: Shannon Lapierre
SVP/General Counsel/Secretary: Janet Link
Chief Technology Officer: Mark Maybury
Chief Human Resources Officer: Joseph Voelker
Year Founded: 1843
Estimated Sales: $12.74 Billion
Number Employees: 60,767
Number of Brands: 22
Type of Packaging: Private Label, Bulk
Brands:
  STANLEY
  DeWALT
  BLACK + DECKER
  CRAFTSMAN
  CRIBMASTER
  IRWIN
  LENOX
  LISTA
  MAC TOOLS
  PORTER-CABLE
  FACOM
  BOSTITCH
  VIDMAR
  SONITROL
  PROTO
  AEROSCOUT
  CAM

29585 Stanley Roberts
501 Hoes Ln Ste 108
Piscataway, NJ 08854
                              973-778-5900
              Fax: 973-778-8542
Flatware
President: Edward Pomeranz
Estimated Sales: $20-50 Million
Number Employees: 20-49

29586 Stanly Fixtures Co Inc
11635 NC 138 Hwy
Norwood, NC 28128-7509
                              704-474-3184
        Fax: 704-474-3011 sandeel@cvnc.net
              www.stanlyfixtures.com
Store fixtures
President: Todd Curlee
ronnyaldridge@stanlyfixtures.com
Quality Control/CFO: Boyce Thompson
Sales Exec: Ronald Aldridge
Manager: Kenny Bowers
Senior Project Manager/Estimator: Harold
Thompson
Estimated Sales: $10-20 Million
Number Employees: 50-99

29587 Stanpac, Inc.
Spring Creek Road
R.R. # 3
Smithville, ON L0R 2AO
Canada
                              905-957-3326
        Fax: 905-957-3616 www.stanpacnet.com
Ice cream packaging, refillable glass milk bottles
and closures, and glass bottles for the beverage and
wine industries.
President: Steve Witt
Vice President, Marketing: Murray Bain
Vice President, Sales: Andrew Witt
Vice President, Operations: Ian Killins
Purchasing: Barry Kirk

29588 (HQ)Staplex Co Inc
777 5th Ave
Brooklyn, NY 11232-1695
                              718-768-3333
        Fax: 718-965-0750 800-221-0822
        info@staplex.com www.staplex.com
Electric staplers for packaging applications. Made in
the U.S.A.
President: Doug Butler
info@staplex.com
CEO: Phil Reed
Estimated Sales: $5-10 Million
Number Employees: 20-49
Brands:
  Accuslitter

Staplex
Tabster

29589 Stapling Machines Co
41 Pine St # 30
Rockaway, NJ 07866-3139
                              973-627-4400
        Fax: 973-627-5355 800-432-5909
        sales@smcllc.com www.package-testing.com
Manufacturer and exporter of packaging machinery
for wirebound containers
President: Norbert Weissburg
n.weissberg@package-testing.com
Estimated Sales: $10-20 Million
Number Employees: 10-19
Parent Co: Stapling Machines Company

29590 Star Container Company
2635 E Magnolia St
Phoenix, AZ 85034
                              480-281-4200
              Fax: 480-281-4201
Biaxillary-oriented PET containers including wide
mouth, narrow neck, custom and stock
VP and General Manager: Paul Ellis
Project Engineer: Phil Blank
Purchasing Agent: Earnest LaFrance
Estimated Sales: $20-50 Million
Number Employees: 1-4
Parent Co: Tech Group

29591 Star Container Corporation
175 Pioneer Dr
Leominster, MA 01453
                              978-537-1676
              Fax: 978-537-9119
Corrugated boxes
President: Nick Campagna
General Manager: Bill Ferzoco
Human Resources: Marlene Nazare
Estimated Sales: $20-50 Million
Number Employees: 100-249
Square Footage: 180000

29592 Star Filters
PO Box 518
Timmonsville, SC 29161-0518
                              843-346-3101
        Fax: 843-346-3736 800-845-5381
        invest@hilliard.com www.hilliard.com
Manufacturer and exporter of disposable filters and
stainless steel plate and frame filter presses for pro-
cess filtration applications; also, polypropylene
dewatering presses for wastewater applications
Regional Sales Manager: Scott Thomas
Regional Sales Manager: Frank Reid
Sales/Marketing Executive: Howard Reed
Estimated Sales: $2.5-5 Million
Number Employees: 20-49
Square Footage: 140000
Parent Co: Hillard Corporation
Brands:
  Carbon Comet
  Easy Earth
  Star

29593 Star Glove Company
106 S Oak St
Odon, IN 47562
                              812-636-7395
        Fax: 812-636-8038 800-832-7101
        starglov@dmrtc.net www.starglove.com
Gloves including industrial knitted, canton flannel,
hot mill, double palm and cut resistant
VP: Eric Moll
Sales: Marc Gebhart
Contact: Akane Suzuki
asuzuki@tri-starglove.com
Estimated Sales: $10-20 Million
Number Employees: 50-99
Parent Co: Star Glove Company

29594 Star Industries, Inc.
P.O. Box 178
La Grange, IL 60525
                              708-240-4862
        Fax: 708-240-4915 bob@starhydrodyne.com
              www.starhydrodyne.com
Manufacturer and exporter of automatic floor scrub-
bing systems
Executive Director: Susan Frassato
Regional Sales Manager: Scott O'Brien

Estimated Sales: $2.5-5 Million
Number Employees: 50-100
Square Footage: 160000
Brands:
  Star Hydrodyne

29595 Star Label Products Inc
42 Newbold Rd
Fairless Hills, PA 19030-4308
                              215-295-3441
        Fax: 215-295-1994 800-394-6900
        info@starlabel.com www.starlabel.com
Owner: Shev Okumus
shev@starlabel.com
CFO: Sevket Okumus
Estimated Sales: $2.5-5 Million
Number Employees: 20-49

29596 Star Manufacturing IntlInc
10 Sunnen Dr
PO Box 430129
St Louis, MO 63143-3800
                              314-678-6303
        Fax: 314-781-4344 800-264-7827
        technical@star-mfg.com www.star-mfg.com
Manufacturer and exporter of food service equip-
ment including gas and electric cooking equipment,
sandwich grills, toasters/waffle bakers, hot dog
equipment, condiment dispensers, popcorn equip-
ment, specialty warmers, dispensing
anddisplay/merchandising equipment
President/CEO: Frank Ricchio
VP Sales/Marketing: Tim Gaskill
VP Engineering: Doug Vogt
VP: Mike Barber
Marketing Director: Cindi Benz
Sales Director: Phil Kister
Contact: Ibrahim Nestor
nibrahim@star-mfg.com
Estimated Sales: $1-3 Million
Number Employees: 50-99
Square Footage: 380000
Type of Packaging: Food Service
Brands:
  Chromemax
  Galaxy
  Jetstar
  Starmax

29597 Star Micronics
1150 King Georges Post Rd
Edison, NJ 08837-3731
                              732-623-5500
        Fax: 732-623-5590 800-782-7636
        sales@starmicronics.com www.starmicronics.com
Miniature electronic buzzers, audio transducers and
dot matrix, thermal and P.O.S. printers utilized in re-
tail and restaurant applications
President: Takayuki Aoki
Marketing Manager: Patty McCarthy
Number Employees: 1,000-4,999
Parent Co: Star Micronics Company

29598 Star Pacific Inc
1205 Atlantic St
Union City, CA 94587-2002
                              510-471-6555
        Fax: 510-471-4339 800-227-0760
        starpac@aol.com
Manufacturer and exporter of cleaning compounds
including household/consumer detergents
Chairman of the Board: Joon Moon
Manager: Ed Kubiak
starpacnew@aol.com
Estimated Sales: $5-10 Million
Number Employees: 10-19
Square Footage: 114000
Type of Packaging: Consumer
Brands:
  Blue Ribbon
  Blue Ribbon Classic

29599 Star Poly Bag Inc
200 Liberty Ave
Brooklyn, NY 11207-2904
                              718-384-7034
        Fax: 718-384-2342 rachel@starpoly.com
              www.starpoly.com
Manufacturer and exporter of plastic bags including
shopping, food, confectioners', heat sealed, etc.;
also, packaging materials including cellulose acetate
film and garbage and ice cream can liners

President: Rachel Posen
Contact: Rivkah Ffe
rivkah@starpoly.com
Production: Hershy Rosenfeld
Estimated Sales: Below $5 Million
Number Employees: 1-4
Square Footage: 100000

29600 Star Restaurant Equipment & Supply Company
18430 Pacific St
Fountain Valley, CA 92708
714-683-2658
Fax: 818-782-8179 www.chefstoys.com
Wholesaler/distributor of food service equipment
and supplies; serving the food service market
President/Owner: Les Birken
Purchasing: Lee Siegel
Estimated Sales: $5 -10 Million
Number Employees: 10-19
Square Footage: 30000

29601 Star-K Kosher Certification
122 Slade Avenue
Suite 300
Baltimore, MD 21208
410-484-4110
Fax: 410-653-9294 star-k@star-k.org
www.star-k.org
International Kosher certification service
President: Dr. Avrom Pollak
Executive Vice President: Patricia (Pesi) Herskovitz
Contact: Patricia Herskovitz
patricia.herskovitz@starkosher.com
Development Director: Steve Sichel
Estimated Sales: $3.5 Million
Number Employees: 250

29602 Starbrook Industries Inc
325 S Hyatt St
Tipp City, OH 45371-1241
937-473-8135
Fax: 937-473-0331 www.starbrookind.com/
Product line includes forming and non-forming food
packaging films designed for Bi-Vac, Dixie Pak and
Multi Vac machines.
Sales Manager: Richard Anderson

29603 Starflex Corporation
204 Turner Rd
Jonesboro, GA 30236
770-471-2111
Fax: 770-478-1304
Poultry packing and processing
Chairman of the Board: Ollie Wilson Jr
VP: Bob Polkinghorne
Estimated Sales: $5-10 Million
Number Employees: 20-49

29604 Starkey Chemical Process Company
PO Box 10
La Grange, IL 60525
708-352-2565
Fax: 708-352-2573 800-323-3040
Rubber cement, duplicating fluids, printing chemi-
cals, hand cleaners, toners and gelled alcohol cook-
ing and heating fuels; exporter of ink marking and
duplicating fluids
President: Linda Yates
Estimated Sales: $1-2.5 Million
Number Employees: 20-49
Square Footage: 54000
Brands:
    Bantam
    Perf
    Starkey
    Super Key

29605 Starlite Food Service Equipment
9200 Conner St
Detroit, MI 48213-1238
313-521-6600
Fax: 313-521-2400 888-521-6603
Stainless steel food service equipment including
work tables, refrigerators, freezers, canopies, hoods,
shelving, storage units, sinks, etc
Owner: Rodney Gullett
VP Operations: Ettore Commisso
Controller: Maria Kraft
Estimated Sales: Below $5 Million
Number Employees: 5-9
Square Footage: 32000

29606 Start International
4270 Airborn Dr
Addison, TX 75001-5182
972-248-1999
Fax: 972-248-1991 800-259-1986
info@startinternational.com
www.startinternational.com
Tape and label dispensers, hand-held label applica-
tors, semi-automatic bottle labeler
President: Dan Sternberg
dan@startinternational.com
Vice President: Todd Sternberg
Marketing Director: Melanie Riddick
Production Manager: Mike Pfattenberger
Estimated Sales: $1-2.5 Million
Number Employees: 5-9
Brands:
    The Label Dispenser
    The Tape Dispenser

29607 Starview Packaging Machinery
1840 St Regis Blvd
Dorval, QC H9P 1H6
Canada
514-920-0100
Fax: 514-920-0092 888-278-5555
info@starview.net www.starview.net
Plastic packaging machinery.
Technical Director: Iwan Heynen
Number Employees: 15
Square Footage: 36216
Type of Packaging: Private Label
Brands:
    Starview

29608 (HQ)Statco Engineering
7595 Reynolds Cir
Huntington Beach, CA 92647-6752
714-375-6300
Fax: 714-375-6314 800-421-0362
www.statco-engineering.com
Distributor and systems integrators for the sanitary
processing marketing in North America. Products
include pumps, valves, heat exchangers, homogeniz-
ers, separators, fillers, conveyor systems, instrumen-
tation/controls and otherpackaging and processing
equipment
Manager: Kathleen Hall
CFO: James Statham
Vice President: David Statham
Marketing Director: Randy Smith
Sales Director: Eric Perkins
Estimated Sales: $50 Million
Number Employees: 20-49

29609 State Container Corp
111 W Commercial Ave
Moonachie, NJ 07074-1704
201-933-5200
Fax: 201-933-0968 dawn@statecontainer.com
Corrugated and fiber boxes
President: John Smith
Cmo: Carmine Barresi
cbgb@statecontainer.com
Director, Administration & Finance: Jane Smith
Estimated Sales: $50-100 Million
Number Employees: 50-99

29610 (HQ)State Industrial Products Corp
5915 Landerbrook Dr # 300
Suite 300
Mayfield Heights, OH 44124-4034
216-861-7114
Fax: 216-861-5213 877-747-6986
www.stateindustrial.com
Disinfectants and soap
President/Chief Executive Officer: Hal Uhrman
CEO: Jeff Pantel
jpantel@stateindustrial.com
Corporate Controller: Scott Moore
Vice President, Research & Development: Tammy
Westerman
Senior Marketing Executive: Watson Boxley
Sales Manager: Jamie Montague
Operations Manager: Chrystal Singer
Director, Warehouse Operations: Keith Clouston
Estimated Sales: $96 Million
Number Employees: 500-999
Square Footage: 240000

29611 State Products
4485 California Avenue
Long Beach, CA 90807-2417
562-495-3688
Fax: 562-495-5788 800-730-5150
Manufacturer and exporter of standard baking pans,
cookie sheets, French bread frames and fiberglass
fabric liners coated with silicon rubber
Chairman: Arthur Haskell
Estimated Sales: $1-2.5 Million appx.
Number Employees: 20
Square Footage: 106000

29612 Statex
3947 Street Hubert
Montreal, QC H2L 4A6
Canada
514-527-6039
Fax: 514-524-0343
Wholesaler/distributor of sensory analysis software;
consultant offering training, technical support and
quality control services
Vice President: Michel Guillet
Estimated Sales: $1-5,000,000

29613 Stavin Inc
358 Blodgett St
Cotati, CA 94931
707-285-2050
Fax: 415-331-0516 info@stavin.com
www.stavin.com
Wine industry oak infusion systems
President: Allan Sullivan
Manager: Michael Bittner
mbittner@stavin.com
General Manager: Jemie Zenk
Estimated Sales: $500,000-$1 Million
Number Employees: 20-49
Type of Packaging: Private Label

29614 Stay Tuned Industries
8 W Main St
Clinton, NJ 08809-1290
908-730-8455
Fax: 908-735-8180
Wholesaler/distributor and exporter of steel and alu-
minum cans and easy-open ends; also, consultant for
can manufacturers
Owner: Ray Slocum
Estimated Sales: $500,000-$1 Million
Number Employees: 1-4
Square Footage: 1800

29615 Steamway Corporation
2128 S Leslie Ln
Scottsburg, IN 47170
812-889-0896
Fax: 812-889-2269 800-259-8171
hopkins@scottsburg.com
Microwavable food containers
President/CEO: Gary Hopkins Sr
CFO: Drusilla Hopkins
VP: Gary Hopkins
R&D: Gary Hopkins Sr
Quality Control: Gary Hopkins
Marketing/Sales: Tim Barrett
Estimated Sales: $50 Million
Number Employees: 5-9
Number of Brands: 1
Number of Products: 15
Square Footage: 100000
Type of Packaging: Food Service, Private Label

29616 Stearns Packaging Corp
4200 Sycamore Ave
Madison, WI 53714-1330
608-246-5150
Fax: 608-246-5149 www.stearnspkg.com
Cleaning supplies including detergents
President: John Everitt
bill.bestman@stearnspkg.com
Controller: Dennis Stuart
Product Manager: Darla Steinborn
Sales Exec: Bill Bestmann
Purchasing Manager: Jeff Hanson
Estimated Sales: $20-50 Million
Number Employees: 20-49
Square Footage: 500000
Brands:
    Stearns
    Vallley View

29617 Stearns Technical Textiles Company
100 Williams Street
Cincinnati, OH 45215-4602
513-948-5292
Fax: 513-948-5281 800-543-7173
Manufacturer and exporter of hot oil filters for deep fryers and medium and heavy duty nonabrasive scrub pads; manufacturer of milk filters
Director Sales: Kevin Finn
Customer Service Manager: Joanne Heidotting
Estimated Sales: $20-50 Million
Number Employees: 100-249
Square Footage: 50000
Brands:
　Ffc
　Scrubbe
　Stearns

29618 Stearnswood Inc
320 3rd Ave NW
PO Box 50
Hutchinson, MN 55350-1625
320-587-2137
Fax: 320-587-7646 800-657-0144
info@stearnswood.com www.stearnswood.com
Manufacturer and exporter of corrugated cartons, wooden boxes, crates, plastic pallets and bulk shipping cartons and bins
Owner: Paul Stearns
Sales Director: Paul Stearns
paul@stearnswood.com
Operational Manager: Mark Stearns
Plant Manager: Corey Stearns
Purchase Agent: Steve Fitzloff
Estimated Sales: 100000
Number Employees: 20-49
Square Footage: 60000
Type of Packaging: Bulk
Brands:
　Flow Max
　Ultra Bin

29619 Steel Art Co
189 Dean St
Norwood, MA 02062-4542
617-566-4079
Fax: 617-566-0618 800-322-2828
info@steelartco.com www.steelartco.com
Manufacturer and exporter of metal signs, letters and plaques
President: John Borell
Director of Sales/Marketing: Charles Blanchard
CFO: Stew Dobson
Vice President: Stewart Dobson
Manager of Design & Engineering: Ciaran Dalton
Vice President of Sales: Charles Blanchard
Customer Service Manager: Kindra Jones
Vice President of Operations: Ashley Borell
Lead Production Manager: Jorge Aguirre
A/R-Credit Manager: Robert Smith
Estimated Sales: $5-10 Million
Number Employees: 100-249

29620 Steel Art Signs
37 Esna Park Drive
Markham, ON L3R 1O9
Canada
905-474-1678
Fax: 905-474-0515 800-771-6971
thrivnak@steelart.com www.steelart.com
Electric signs
President: Tom Hrivnak
Sales Manager: Gene Mordaunt
Operations Manager: Jorge Dasilva
Number Employees: 90
Square Footage: 348000

29621 (HQ)Steel City Corporation
PO Box 1227
Youngstown, OH 44501-1227
330-792-7663
Fax: 330-792-7951 800-321-0350
jsmith@scity.com www.scity.com
Manufacturer, wholesaler/distributor, importer and exporter of plastic bags, plastic and wire racks and coin operated vending machines; manufacturer and importer of rubber bands
President: C Kenneth Fibus
CFO: Mike Janak
Quality Control: Steve Speece
National Sales Manager: Jim Smith
VP Sales: Lee Rouse
Sales Department: Erika Flaherty

Estimated Sales: $30-50 Million
Number Employees: 100-249
Square Footage: 150000

29622 Steel Craft FluorescentCompany
191 Murray St
Newark, NJ 07114-2751
973-349-1614
Fax: 973-824-0825
Manufacturer and exporter of fluorescent lighting fixtures

Estimated Sales: $1-3 Million
Number Employees: 10-19

29623 Steel King Industries
2700 Chamber St
Stevens Point, WI 54481
715-341-3120
Fax: 715-341-8792 800-553-3096
info@steelking.com www.steelking.com
Manufacturer and exporter of racks including pallet, pushback, flow, cantilever and portable. Products also inlcude steel containers and guard railing
President: Jay Anderson
Marketing Director: Don Heemstra
National Sales Manager: Skip Eastman
Contact: Chrissy Christenson
c.christenson@renters-choice-inc.com
Plant Manager: Ralph Gagas
Estimated Sales: $20-50 Million
Number Employees: 100-249
Parent Co: VCI
Brands:
　Sk 2000
　Sk 2500
　Sk 3000
　Sk 3400
　Sk 3600 Rock

29624 Steel Products
750 44th Street
Marion, IA 52302-3841
319-377-1527
Fax: 319-377-4580 800-333-9451
www.marioniron.com
Hot chocolate and cappuccino dispensers; exporter of hot chocolate dispensers and parts
Customer Service: Lori Pickart
Operations Manager: Bryce Sandell
Estimated Sales: $1-2.5 Million
Number Employees: 5-9
Square Footage: 66000
Parent Co: ConAgra Foods

29625 Steel Storage Systems Inc
6301 Dexter St
Commerce City, CO 80022-3128
303-287-0291
Fax: 303-287-0159 800-442-0291
info@steelstorage.com
Manufacturer and exporter of material handling equipment including roller conveyors, sheet racks and drawers
President: Brian Mc Callin
Estimated Sales: $5-10 Million
Number Employees: 20-49
Type of Packaging: Bulk
Brands:
　Spacesaver

29626 Steelite International USA
4041 Hadley Rd
South Plainfield, NJ 07080-1111
908-755-0357
Fax: 908-755-7185 800-367-3493
usa@steelite.com www.steelite.com
Importer of ceramic commercial china
CEO: R J Chadwick
Marketing Director: Karen Gowarty
Contact: Kimberly Faloon
kfaloon@steeliteusa.com
Estimated Sales: $5-10 Million
Number Employees: 10-19
Parent Co: Steelite International
Type of Packaging: Food Service

29627 Steelmaster Material Handling
503 Commerce Park Drive SE
Suite B
Marietta, GA 30060-2745
770-425-7244
Fax: 770-423-7545 800-875-9900

Manufacturer and exporter of new and used warehouse equipment including pallet racks and shelving
President: Mike Miller
CEO: Deborah Molley
Plant Manager: James Young
Estimated Sales: $1-2.5 Million
Number Employees: 5-9
Square Footage: 40000
Brands:
　Bilt

29628 Steep & Brew
855 E Broadway
Monona, WI 53716-4012
608-223-0707
Fax: 608-223-0355 www.steepandbrewcoffee.com
Espresso machines and accessories, grinders,roast coffees, wholesale and resale of coffee
Owner: Mark Ballering
mb@steepnbrew.com
Vice President: Mark Mullee
Estimated Sales: $10-20 Million
Number Employees: 10-19

29629 Stefanich & Company
1933 N Farris Avenue
Fresno, CA 93704-5912
559-237-2295
Fax: 559-237-2299 stefanich@aol.com
Stainless steel fittings
President: Steven Stefanich

29630 (HQ)Stegall Mechanical INC
2800 5th Ave S
Birmingham, AL 35233-2820
205-251-0330
Fax: 205-328-1988 800-633-4373
www.stegallmechanical.com
Manufacturer and exporter of food service ventilation equipment including ventilation/exhaust hoods and fans; also, custom fabrications in stainless steel and wood available
President: Vince Chiarella
vchiarella@stegallmechanical.com
Estimated Sales: $10-15 Million
Number Employees: 20-49
Type of Packaging: Food Service

29631 Stein-DSI
PO Box 98
Northfield, MN 55057-0098
507-645-9546
Fax: 507-645-6148 larrydeboer@fmcti.com
Supplier of food processing solutions
Estimated Sales: $10-20 Million
Number Employees: 50-99

29632 Steiner Company
401 W Taft Drive
Holland, IL 60473-2015
708-333-2003
Fax: 800-578-2507 800-222-4638
Manufacturer and exporter of waterless hand and skin soaps; also, soap dispensers
President: Guy Marchesi
Director OEM Sales: Craig Brown
Marketing Director: Karen Siravo
VP Sales: Greg Fachet
Contact: Brent Stack
bstack@stnr.com
Estimated Sales: $10-20 Million
Number Employees: 50-99
Parent Co: Steiner Company
Type of Packaging: Private Label
Brands:
　Bulkmaster
　Change-O-Matic
　Economaster
　Handmaster
　Papermaster
　Swiss Air
　Wesco

29633 Steiner Industries Inc
5801 N Tripp Ave
Chicago, IL 60646-6013
773-588-3444
Fax: 773-588-3450 800-621-4515
info@steinerindustries.com
www.steinerindustries.com
Manufacturer and exporter of air freshener and soap dispensers; also, garment lockers, soaps, lotions and hand cleaners

President: Raefel Krammer
rk@steinerindustries.com
Marketing: Karen Siravo
Sales Director: Greg Fachet
Estimated Sales: $10-20 Million
Number Employees: 50-99
Parent Co: Steiner Corporation
Type of Packaging: Consumer, Food Service, Bulk
Brands:
    Bulkmaster
    Change-O-Matic
    Economaster
    Handmaster
    Papermaster
    Swiss Air
    Wesco

29634 Steingart Associates Inc
5211 Main St
South Fallsburg, NY 12779-5422

845-434-4321
Fax: 845-436-8609 www.steingartprinting.com
Advertising specialties, envelopes, brochures, letter-
heads, business cards, posters, etc
President: Ira Steingart
isteingart@steingartprinting.com
VP: Cindy Perlmutter
Estimated Sales: $1-2,500,000
Number Employees: 5-9

29635 Steinmetz Machine WorksInc
44 Homestead Ave
Stamford, CT 06902-7213

203-327-0118
Fax: 203-327-4942 smwct@aol.com
Machinery for the baking industry
President: Sharon Walsh
smwct@aol.com
Estimated Sales: $3-5 Million
Number Employees: 5-9

29636 (HQ)Stellar Group
2900 Hartley Rd
Jacksonville, FL 32257

904-260-2900
800-488-2900
info@stellar.net www.stellar.net
Provides design, engineering, construction and me-
chanical services on design/build, general contract-
ing and construction management projects.
President/Owner: Michael Santarone
Chairman & CEO: Ronald Foster
CFO: Clint Pyle
Exec. VP: Brian Kappelle
Estimated Sales: $500 Million
Number Employees: 639

29637 Stellar Steam
276 E Allen St
Suite 5
Winooski, VT 05404

802-654-8603
Fax: 802-654-8618
Boilerless steamers
President: Michael G Colburn
Quality Control: Steven Bogner
Estimated Sales: Below $5 Million
Number Employees: 20-49

29638 Stello Products Inc
840 W Hillside Ave
PO Box 89
Spencer, IN 47460-1117

812-829-2246
Fax: 812-829-6053 800-878-2246
info@stelloproducts.com www.stelloproducts.com
Signs including metal and silk screen
President: Todd Zellers
todd.zellers@stelloproducts.com
Foreman: John Summerlot
Estimated Sales: $500,000-$1 Million
Number Employees: 10-19
Square Footage: 36000

29639 (HQ)Stelray Plastic Products Inc
50 Westfield Ave
Ansonia, CT 06401-1121

203-735-9412
Fax: 203-735-9412 800-735-2331
www.stelray.com
Plastic injection molded products

29640 Step Products
1500 Chisholm Trail
Round Rock, TX 78681

512-255-0888
Fax: 815-646-4896 800-777-7837
www.stepproducts.com
Fluorinated HDPE containers and plastic compo-
nents
General Manager: Jim Niemeyer
Sales: Scott Ellison
Sales: Diane Sherin
Number Employees: 35
Square Footage: 40000

29641 Stephan Machinery GmbH
1385 Armour Blvd.
Mandelein, IL 60060

847-247-0182
Fax: 847-247-0184
Processing lines and machines for the food, dairy,
meat, confectionary and convenience food industries.
Contact: Rolf Heinze
heinze@stephan-machinery.com

29642 Stephan Machinery, Inc.
1385 Armour Blvd
Mundelein, IL 60060

224-360-6206
Fax: 847-247-0184 800-783-7426
weirich@stephan-machinery.com
www.stephan-machinery.com
Designs, engineers and builds the finest food pro-
cessing equipment available.
CEO: Olaf Pehmoller
CFO: Gunter Dahling
Sales Manager: Eric Weirich
Contact: Rolf Heinze
heinze@stephan-machinery.com
Operations Director: Dirk Kuhnel
Estimated Sales: $7 -10 Million
Number Employees: 5-9
Square Footage: 28000
Brands:
    Microcut
    Stephan

29643 Steri Technologies Inc
857 Lincoln Ave
Bohemia, NY 11716-4100

631-563-8300
Fax: 631-563-8378 800-253-7140
steri@steri.com www.steri.com
Manufacturer, importer and exporter of dryers in-
cluding vacuum shelf, lab and band; also, pressure
leaf and vacuum filters
President: Clemens Nigg
steri@steri.com
Estimated Sales: $10-20 Million
Number Employees: 10-19
Square Footage: 30000
Type of Packaging: Private Label
Brands:
    Funda
    Zwag Nutsche

29644 Steri Technologies Inc
857 Lincoln Ave
Bohemia, NY 11716-4100

631-563-8300
Fax: 631-563-8378 800-253-7140
steri@steri.com
Stainless steel motors and worm reducers for sani-
tary applications, continuous vacuum band dryers,
pressure extractors and Aseptomag aseptic valves
President: Clemens Nigg
steri@steri.com
Estimated Sales: $10-20 Million
Number Employees: 10-19

29645 Sterigenics International
2015 Spring Rd
Suite 650
Oak Brook, IL 60523

630-928-1700
800-472-4508
info@sterigenics.com www.sterigenics.com

Irradiator of spices, dried herbs, food packaging,
closures with seals, filaments, bottle closures,
pouches, plastic bottles, and liquid poly-liners.
President: Phil MacNabb
Contact: Amy Edwards
aedwards@sterigenics.com
Number Employees: 20-49
Brands:
    Sterigenics

29646 Steril-Sil Company
PO Box 495
Bowmansville, PA 17507

717-405-2258
Fax: 617-739-5063 800-784-5537
orders@sterilsil.com www.sterilsil.com
Manufacturer and exporter of condiment and silver-
ware dispensers, containers and covers
President: David Stiller
CFO: Laura McEachern
VP: Bernard Chiccariello
Sales: Brian Schilling
brian@sterilsil.com
Estimated Sales: $500,000-$1 Million
Number Employees: 1-4
Parent Co: Stiller Equipment Corporation

29647 Steritech Food Safety &Environmental Hygiene
7600 Little Avenue
Charlotte, NC 28226

704-971-4725
Fax: 704-544-8705 800-868-0089
contact@steritech.com www.steritech.com
Consultant providing food safety audits, pest pre-
vention and food safety training to the food process-
ing and hospitality industries
Executive Chairman, Founder: John Whitley
Chief Executing Officer: Rich Ennis
Chief Financial Officer: Mike Lynch
Vice President of HR: Jennifer Courtney-Trice
Board Member: Mark Jarvis
VP Pesticides (Mid-Atlantic Region): Eric Eicher
Contact: Mitch Anderson
mitch.anderson@steritech.com
Chief Operating Officer: Rich Ennis
Number Employees: 30

29648 Sterling Ball & Jewel
2900 S 160th St
New Berlin, WI 53151-3606

262-641-8610
Fax: 262-641-8653 800-423-3183
dazarello@corpemail.com www.sterlco.com
Manufacturer and exporter of temperature control
units & other heating & cooling equipment
President: Jeff Ackerberg
jeff.ackerberg@kohler.com
VP: Mike Zvolanek
Marketing: Bill Desrosiers
Sales: Wayne Lange
Public Relations: Nichole Saccomonto
Operations Manager: Rich Cramer
Number Employees: 100-249
Parent Co: Sterling
Type of Packaging: Private Label

29649 Sterling China Company
511 12th Street
Wellsville, OH 43968-1303

330-532-1609
Fax: 330-532-4587 800-682-7628
Vitrified china
Vice President: Bruce Hill
National Sales Manager: Brian Lewis
Estimated Sales: $10-20 Million
Number Employees: 250-500
Square Footage: 250000

29650 Sterling Corp
2001 E Gladstone St # B
Glendora, CA 91740-5381

909-305-0968
Fax: 909-981-1441 800-932-9561
www.stercorp.com
Manufacturer and importer of security equipment in-
cluding fire and burglar alarms and systems; also, in-
stallation services available
Manager: Bill Jones
bill@stercorp.com
Estimated Sales: $2.5-5,000,000
Number Employees: 1-4

President: Lawrence D Saffran
General Manager: John Therriaelt
Contact: Les Alderich
lalderich@stelray.com
Estimated Sales: Less Than $500,000
Number Employees: 1-4

29651 (HQ)Sterling Electric Inc
7973 Allison Ave
Indianapolis, IN 46268-1613

317-872-0471
Fax: 800-474-0543 800-654-6220
websales@sterlingelectric.com
www.sterlingelectric.com
Production of customized/standard AC induction
motors along with drive products such as; AC adjustable frequency controls, DC permanent magnet
motors and controls, mechanical adjustable speed
transmissions, shaft mounts and screwconveyors,
and cycloidal reducers and gearmotors
President: Walter Mashburn
walter@sterlingelectric.com
Sales: Roman Wiggins
Manager: Walter Mashburn
Number Employees: 20-49
Other Locations:
Sterling Distribution Center
Indianapolis IN
Sterling Power Systems
Hamilton, ON

29652 Sterling Net & Twine Company
P.O.Box 411
Cedar Knolls, NJ 07927

973-783-9800
Fax: 973-783-9808 800-342-0316
Manufacturer and exporter of nets and netting, conveyors, pallets and custom bags for produce and customer packaging
President: James Van Loon
Sales Manager: Jerry Eick
Estimated Sales: $5-10,000,000
Number Employees: 20-49
Square Footage: 32000

29653 Sterling Novelty Products
1940 Raymond Dr
Northbrook, IL 60062-6715

847-291-0070
Fax: 847-291-0120
Manufacturer and exporter of U.S. flag sets, nylon
mesh scouring cloths and plastic food bags
President: Marvin Glasser
Secretary/Treasurer: Michael Glasser
Estimated Sales: $1-3 Million
Number Employees: 10-19
Square Footage: 10000
Parent Co: Sterling Novelty

29654 Sterling Paper Company
1845 Progress Avenue Columbus
Ohio, PA 19134-2799

215-744-5350
Fax: 215-533-9577 800-282-1124
www.sterling-paper.com
Manufacturer, exporter and importer of paper plates,
Chinese food pails and food trays; also, boxes including cake, pizza, doughnuts, sausage, steak,
pastry, etc
President: Martin Stein
Secretary: John Paul
VP: Suzy Faigen
Estimated Sales: $10-20 Million
Number Employees: 50-99
Square Footage: 650000
Brands:
Aristocrat

29655 Sterling Process Engineering
333 Mccormick Blvd
Columbus, OH 43213-1526

614-868-5151
Fax: 614-868-5152 800-783-7875
sales@sterlingpe.com www.sterlingpe.com
Stainless steel process tanks, pipe/tubing,
clean-in-place systems, stainless steel conveyor,
platforms, skid mounted process equipment, design,
fabrication and installation of food and beverage
process system
President: Jerry Martin
jmartin@sterlingpe.com
Sales Director: Jack Selvages
Operations Manager: Russ Flax
Estimated Sales: $10-20 Million
Number Employees: 20-49
Square Footage: 70000

29656 Sterling Rubber
675 Woodside Street
Fergus, ON N1M 2M4
Canada

519-843-4032
Fax: 519-843-6587
Manufacturer and exporter of rubber gloves
President: Robert Joyce
Manager Quality Assurance: Norma Ford
Number Employees: 30
Square Footage: 54000

29657 (HQ)Sterling Scale Co
20950 Boening Dr
Southfield, MI 48075-5737

248-358-0590
Fax: 248-358-2275 800-331-9931
sales@sterlingscale.com www.sterlingscale.com
Manufacturer, importer, exporter and wholesaler/distributor of industrial scales; manufacturer of engineering software for weighing equipment
President: E Donald Dixon
CFO: J Dixon
Vice President: Tom Ulicny
Research & Development: T Klauinger
Quality Control: Jeff Shultz
Marketing Director: Tom Ulicny
Plant Manager: J Holcomb
Purchasing Manager: S Latucca
Estimated Sales: $2-3 Million
Number Employees: 20-49
Number of Brands: 5
Number of Products: 100
Square Footage: 112000
Brands:
Sterling
Sterling Eliminator

29658 Sterling Systems & Controls
24711 Emerson Rd
Sterling, IL 61081-9171

815-625-0852
Fax: 815-625-3103 800-257-7214
sci@sterlingcontrols.com www.prater-sterling.com
Manufacturer, importer and exporter of batching and
weighing process controls for dry and liquid products; also, weighing systems for poultry and meat
President: Don Goshert
VP/General Manager: Don Goshert
Western Sales: Bob Rogan
South/Southeastern Sales: Dean Considine
Northeastern Sales: Marty Gustafson
Estimated Sales: $2.5-5 Million
Number Employees: 10-19
Square Footage: 21000
Parent Co: Prater Industries

29659 Sterling Truck Corporation
4747 N Channel Ave
Portland, OR 97217-7613
Fax: 440-269-5979 800-785-4357
www.sterlingtrucks.com
Senior VP: John Merrifield
Sales: Richard Saward
Contact: Vaughn Burrell
vburrell@sterlingtrucks.com
Estimated Sales: $20-30 Million
Number Employees: 100-249

29660 Sterner Lighting Systems
701 Millennium Blvd
Greenville, SC 29607-5251

864-678-1000
Fax: 320-485-2881 866-898-0131
www.sternerlighting.com
Manufacturer and exporter of indoor and outdoor
lighting equipment
General Manager: Mike Naylor
Marketing Manager: Sherry Thomson
Plt Mgr: Ken Lehner
Estimated Sales: $10-20 Million
Number Employees: 20-49
Parent Co: Hubbel Lighting
Type of Packaging: Food Service
Brands:
Softform

29661 Sterno
1064 Garfield Street
Lombard, IL 60148

630-792-0080
Fax: 630-792-9914
Manufacturer and exporter of candles, including table, birthday, tapers, and table lamps

President: Richard T Browning
Number Employees: 50-99
Parent Co: Sterno
Type of Packaging: Food Service
Brands:
Chafing Fuels
Handy Fuel Brand
Tabie Lamps & Stereo Brand

29662 Stero Co
3200 Lakeville Hwy
Petaluma, CA 94954-5903

707-762-0071
Fax: 707-762-5036 800-762-7600
www.stero.com
Commercial dish, glass, pot/pan and tray washers
Manager: Terry Goodfellow
VP Sales/Marketing: Lars Noren
Contact: Dan Ancheta
dancheta@stero.com
Estimated Sales: Less Than $500,000
Number Employees: 1-4
Square Footage: 66000
Parent Co: PMI
Brands:
Stero

29663 Stertil Alm Corp
200 Benchmark Industrial Dr
Streator, IL 61364-9400

815-673-5546
Fax: 815-673-2292 800-544-5438
info@stertil-ALM.com www.stertil-alm.com
US manufacturer of bulkbag discharge and fill lifts,
welding and assembly positioner. ALM specializes
in custom heavy duty lifting equipment.
President: Doug Grunnet
grunnet@almcorp.com
Sales Director: Patricia Galick
Estimated Sales: $10-20 Million
Number Employees: 20-49
Square Footage: 110000
Brands:
Ibc

29664 Steven Label Corp
11926 Burke St
Santa Fe Springs, CA 90670-2546

562-698-9971
Fax: 562-698-1507 800-752-4968
slc4you@stevenlabel.com www.stevenlabel.com
Labels including bar code and pressure sensitive;
also, decals
President: Steve Stong
steve.stong@stevenlabel.com
Estimated Sales: $20-50 Million
Number Employees: 100-249

29665 Stevens Linen Association
137 Schofield Ave
Suite 5
Dudley, MA 1571

508-943-0813
Fax: 508-949-1847 800-772-9269
www.co-store.com/stevenslinen
Manufacturer and exporter of linen goods, pot holders and place mats
President: Gregory Kline
VP Sales/Marketing: Nancy Dalrymple
Contact: Timothy Barnardo
timothyb@stevenslinen.com
Estimated Sales: $10-20 Million
Number Employees: 100-249
Square Footage: 150000

29666 Stevens Transport
9757 Military Pkwy
Dallas, TX 75227-4805

972-216-9254
Fax: 972-289-8545 800-823-9369
www.stevenstransport.com
Transportation firm providing refrigerated and dry
rail and long haul TL and LTL services
President: Clay Aaron
Chairman and CEO: Steven Aaron
Executive Vice President: Michael Richey
mrichey@stevenstransport.com
Estimated Sales: Over $1 Billion
Number Employees: 5000-9999

29667 Stevenson-Cooper Inc
1039 W Venango St
PO Box 46345
Philadelphia, PA 19140-4391
215-223-2600
Fax: 215-223-3597 waxcooper@aol.com
Manufacturer and exporter of oils including cotton-seed and palm oils; also, manufacturer of paraffin and sealing wax
President: Dennis Cooper
dcooper@stevensonseeley.com
R&D: Tammy Pullins
Estimated Sales: Below $5 Million
Number Employees: 5-9

29668 (HQ)Stewart Assembly & Machining
7234 Blue Ash Rd
Cincinnati, OH 45236-3660
513-891-9000
Fax: 513-891-0449 sales@stewartam.com
www.stewartam.com
Manufacturer and exporter of packaging machinery
President: Jim Weckenbrock
VP Sales: Ray Meyer
Estimated Sales: $5-10 Million
Number Employees: 10-19
Type of Packaging: Bulk

29669 Stewart Laboratories
21639 Route 322
Strattanville, PA 16258
814-379-3663
Fax: 814-379-3601 800-640-7869
Laboratory glassware detergents
Owner: Stanley Segelbaum
National Sales Manager: Stanley Stewart
Customer Service Manager: Joyce Berk
Estimated Sales: $2.5-5 Million
Number Employees: 1-4
Square Footage: 10000
Brands:
    Labkol
    Labkolax
    Labkolite

29670 Stewart Marketing Services
11122 NE 41st Drive
Apt 31
Kirkland, WA 98033-7725
425-889-2455
Fax: 425-889-8786
Consultant specializing in sales and advertising for the frozen food market in the Pacific Northwest
President: Bill Stewart

29671 Stewart Mechanical Seals
3600 Pegasus Dr # 10
Suite #10
Bakersfield, CA 93308-7090
661-391-9332
Fax: 661-391-9336 bill@stewartseals.com
www.gatorgaskets.com
Supplier of sealing and packing parts for machinery used in the foodservice packing industry
Contact: Bill Stewart
bill@stewartseals.com
Estimated Sales: $450,000
Number Employees: 5-9
Square Footage: 8800
Type of Packaging: Consumer, Private Label, Bulk
Brands:
    Four Aces
    M&R

29672 Stewart Sutherland Inc
5411 E V Ave
Vicksburg, MI 49097-8387
269-649-0530
Fax: 269-649-3961 www.ssbags.com
Sandwich wraps and bags including bakery, french bread, candy, doggie, foil insulated, french fry, sandwich, pizza, etc
President: John Stewart
CEO/VP/Pub Relations & Operations: Tom Farrell
tomf@ssbags.com
Quality Control: Anna Liggett
Research & Devel/Marketing & Sales: Shelley Averill
Quality Control: Irene Carroll
VP Sales: Jack Bailey
VP Production: William Moran
Plant Manager: Dick Vandrestradten
Purchasing: Loretta Johnson

Estimated Sales: $42 Million
Number Employees: 100-249

29673 Stewart Systems Baking LLC
808 Stewart Dr
Plano, TX 75074-8197
972-422-5808
Fax: 972-509-8734 www.stewart-systems.com
Conveyors, ovens and proofers
Vice President: Jim Makins
Sales: Bill Camp
Estimated Sales: $20-50 Million
Number Employees: 100-249
Parent Co: Sasi B. Baking

29674 Stewart Systems Baking LLC
808 Stewart Dr
Plano, TX 75074-8197
972-422-5808
Fax: 972-509-8734 800-558-3814
www.stewart-systems.com
Designs and manufactures a wide variety of packaging and processing equipment for all industries, with a particular emphasis on fruits and vegetables, beer and softdrinks, consumer foodstuffs, household goods, and petroleum products
Sales: Bill Camp
Estimated Sales: $20-30 Million
Number Employees: 100-249

29675 StickerYou
Toronto, ON
Canada
416-532-7373
support@stickeryou.com
www.stickeryou.com
Custom stickers and labels
President: Andrew Witkin
Business Development: Barry Witkin
Director of Marketing: Ana Caracaleanu
Sales Manager: Stephen Fields
Social Content & Community Manager: Cy Svendson
Director of Production: Bret Simpson
Year Founded: 2008
Estimated Sales: Under $500,000
Number Employees: 51-200

29676 Stickney Hill Dairy Inc
15371 County Road 48
Kimball, MN 55353-9771
320-398-5360
Fax: 320-398-5361 sales@stickneydairy.com
www.stickneydairy.com
Goat cheeses
General Manager: Cheryl Willenbring
Quality Assurance Manager: Kathy Ratka
Manager: Frankie Lenzmeier
flenzmeier@stickneydairy.com
Estimated Sales: $2 Million
Number Employees: 10-19

29677 Stiles Enterprises Inc
114 Beach St # 1w
PO Box 92
Rockaway, NJ 07866-3529
973-625-9660
Fax: 973-625-9346 800-325-4232
www.stilesenterprises.com
Packaging machine replacement parts-rubber parts, conveyor belts, drive belts, fabricated belts, resurface rubber rollers, parts for cappers, fillers, labelers, bottle unscramblers, case tapers, form/fill/seal baggers , heattunnels.
Owner: Rich Stiles
CFO: Nancy Stiles
R&D: John Dubowchik
Sales: Ken Stiles
info@stilesenterprises.com
Estimated Sales: $5-10 Million
Number Employees: 10-19

29678 (HQ)Stock America Inc
900 Cheyenne Ave # 700
Suite 700
Grafton, WI 53024-1653
262-375-4100
Fax: 262-375-4101 michaelg@stockamerica.com
www.stockpackaging.com
Wholesaler/distributor of full-water and steam retorts, temperature and pressure monitoring equipment, fillers, packaging containers and sealing equipment.

President: Michael Galvin
Vice President: Victoria Schlegger
CEO: Michael Galvin
Vice President: Tim Schurr
Marketing: Donette Lambert
Sales Manager: Rick Eleew
Contact: Jay Brunner
jayb@stockamerica.com
Estimated Sales: $5-10 Million
Number Employees: 10-19
Number of Brands: 8
Number of Products: 5
Square Footage: 72000
Type of Packaging: Consumer
Other Locations:
    Stock America
    Montreal PQ
    Stock America
    Cary NC

29679 Stocker & Son Inc
34 Suydam Ln
Bayport, NY 11705-2198
631-472-1881
Fax: 631-472-8069 www.stockerandsons.com
German made slicing blades and chopping knives for the food processing industry
Owner: Lee Stocker
Estimated Sales: $1-2.5 Million
Number Employees: 1-4

29680 Stoffel Seals Corp
36 Stoffel Dr
Tallapoosa, GA 30176
770-574-2696
Fax: 770-574-7937 800-422-8247
www.stoffel.com
Stoffel Seals is a key supplier for product identification and branding systems, packaging enhancements, advertising premiums/promotional products, employee identification badges, tamper evident security seals and many other custommanufactured products. Our specialty items for the food and beverage industry include ham bone guards, trussing loops, rotisserie tags, tray pack inserts, pricing/shellfish tags, metal seals, string
Quality Control: Henry Bosshard
Marketing: Valerie Cates
Sales: Mark Swan
Production: Mike Brown
Plant Manager: Norbert Falk
Purchasing: James Westmoreland
Estimated Sales: $40 Million
Number Employees: 250-499
Square Footage: 180000
Parent Co: Stoffel Seals
Type of Packaging: Consumer, Food Service, Private Label, Bulk
Brands:
    Prestige

29681 Stoffel Seals Corp
36 Stoffel Dr
Tallapoosa, GA 30176
770-574-2696
Fax: 770-574-7937 800-422-8247
www.stoffel.com
We are the supplier of choice for product identification and branding systems, packaging enhancements, advertising premiums/promotional products, employee identification badges, tamper evident security seals and many other custommanufactured products. Our specialty include ham bone guards, trussing loops, rotisserie tags, turkey lifters, tray pack inserts, pricing/shellfish tags, metal seals for kosher foods, elastic string tags, bottle neckers and cohes
President and CEO: Charles Fuehrer
Executive VP: Norbert Falk
Vice President: Joe Williams
Marketing Director: Pat Renz
Sales Director: Joe Cusack
Plant Manager: Norbert Falk
Estimated Sales: $50-100 Million
Number Employees: 250-499
Square Footage: 40000
Type of Packaging: Consumer, Private Label, Bulk
Brands:
    Prestige

29682 Stogsdill Tile Co
14604 Harmony Rd
Huntley, IL 60142-9201
847-669-1255
Fax: 847-669-1278 800-323-7504
info@stogsdilltile.com www.stogsdilltile.com
Manufacturer and exporter of stainless steel floor
drains; also, acid brick and monolithic flooring in-
stallation services available
President: Gloria Stogsdill
gstogsdill@stogsdilltile.com
Operations Manager: Ivan Gonzalez
Estimated Sales: $1-5 Million
Number Employees: 1-4
Square Footage: 32000

29683 Stokes
400 Kitts Hillroad
Hyannis, MA 02601
215-788-3500
Fax: 215-781-1122 800-635-0036
www.stokesdti.com
Tablet presses, tabletting dedusters, tooling,
granulators, metal detectors, automated control systems, encapsulation equipment and size reduction
equipment
President: Brayan Urban
Marketing: Barb McPeditt
Number Employees: 100

29684 Stokes Material Handling Systs
1000 Crosskeys Dr
Doylestown, PA 18902-1019
215-340-2200
Fax: 215-230-9280 nwfeigles@stokesmhs.com
www.stokesmhs.com
Conveyor systems; custom designing available-spe-
cializing in USDA/FDA approved systems
Owner: Jonathan Doughty
doughty@stokesmhs.com
Marketing Director: Steve Heinel
VP Operations: Neal Feigles
Estimated Sales: $8,500,000
Number Employees: 10-19
Square Footage: 12000

29685 Stolle Machinery Co LLC
6949 S Potomac St
Centennial, CO 80112-4036
303-708-9044
Fax: 303-708-9045 www.stollemachinery.com
High-speed wide and narrow coil and sheet-fed shell
systems for D-I and D-R-D cans, complete draw-re-
draw can systems and air cup conveyors; other ser-
vices include complete rebuilds, speed-ups and
retolling of shell and cuppingpresses
President: Ralph P Stodd
CEO: Bob Eisaman
robert.eisaman@stollemachinery.com
VP: David Bolek
CFO: Jimm Miceli
Estimated Sales: $2.5-5 Million
Number Employees: 100-249

29686 Stone Container
12112 Greens Ferry Road
Moss Point, MS 39562-8836
502-491-4870
Fax: 502-491-7283
Corrugated boxes
General Manager: Michael Cash
Estimated Sales: $5-10 Million
Number Employees: 20-49

29687 Stone Container
150 N Michigan Ave # 1700
Chicago, IL 60601-7597
312-346-6600
Fax: 312-580-2299 www.smurfit-stone.com
Manufacturer and exporter of envelopes, plastic film
and bags: multi-wall, paper and plastic
President: Pat Moore
Estimated Sales: $10-20 Million
Number Employees: 10,000
Parent Co: Stone Container

29688 Stone Enterprises Inc.
10011 J St
Suite 3
Omaha, NE 68127
402-753-0500
Fax: 402-502-8102 877-653-0500
sales@stoneent.net www.stoneent.net

Designer and manufacturer of custom built machinery, refurbished machines and replacement parts.
Contact: Kim Banat
kbanat@24hourfitness.com

29689 Stone Soap Co Inc
2000 Pontiac Dr
Sylvan Lake, MI 48320-1758
248-706-1000
Fax: 248-706-1001 800-952-7627
sales@stonesoap.com www.stonesoap.com
Manufacturer, importer and exporter of cleaning
products including hand cleaners, detergents and
soaps
President: Ken Stone
stonesoap@stonesoap.com
National Sales Manager: Patty Muskat
Purchasing Agent: Jacqueline ElChemmas
Estimated Sales: $5-10 Million
Number Employees: 10-19
Square Footage: 200000
Brands:
  Sport Mate

29690 Stoner
PO Box 65
Quarryville, PA 17566
717-786-7355
Fax: 717-786-9088 800-227-5538
timesaver@stonersolutions.com
www.stonersolutions.com
FDA approved specialty lubricants
President: Rob Ecklin
Owner: John H Stoner
Sales Manager: Tim Bupp
Contact: Jon Farrel
timesaver@stonersolutions.com
Estimated Sales: $5-10 Million
Number Employees: 1-4
Brands:
  Food Grade

29691 Stoneway Carton Company
3047 78th Ave SE # 203
Mercer Island, WA 98040-2847
206-232-2645
Fax: 206-232-2725 800-498-2185
Manufacturer and exporter of cartons, pads, and
parts. Also graphic and structural design
President: Charles E Farrell
General Manager: Russ Salger
Sr. Account Executive Sales: Art Wical
Purchasing Manager: Troy Giesinger
Estimated Sales: $2.5-5 Million
Number Employees: 1-4
Square Footage: 240000

29692 Stonhard
1000 E Park Ave
Maple Shade, NJ 08052
800-257-7953
info@stonhard.com www.stonhard.com
Manufacturer and installer of polymer floors, high
performance epoxy floors.
Director of Technical Service: Jeff Beam
Year Founded: 1922
Estimated Sales: $260 Million
Number Employees: 1000-4999

29693 Stonhard, Inc.
1000 E Park Ave
Maple Shade, NJ 08052
www.stonhard.com
Floor, wall and lining systems
CEO: David Reif
Contact: John Kurtz
Estimated Sales: $260 Million
Number Employees: 1,001-5,000

29694 Stor-Loc
880 N Washington Ave
Kankakee, IL 60901-2004
815-936-0774
Fax: 815-936-0767 800-786-7562
sales@storloc.com www.stor-loc.com
High density storage equipment, drawer cabinets
and workstations
President: Michael J Ryan
mryan@stor-loc.com
Quality Control: Ed Ryan
Estimated Sales: Below $5 Million
Number Employees: 20-49
Parent Co: Ryan Metal Products

Brands:
  Stor-Frame

29695 Stor-Rite Freezer Storage
215 N Mill Rd
Vineland, NJ 08360-3433
856-696-1451
Fax: 856-696-1451
Manager: Bob Bradway
Estimated Sales: $1-5 Million
Number Employees: 5-9

29696 Storad Tape Company
126 Blaine Ave
Marion, OH 43301-0493
740-382-6440
Fax: 740-383-3241 sales@storadlabel.com
www.storadlabel.com
Pressure sensitive labels
President: Bob Hord
Estimated Sales: $5-10 Million
Number Employees: 10-19

29697 Storage Unlimited
1001 N Kenneth Street
Nixa, MO 65714-8401
417-725-3014
Fax: 417-725-5750 800-478-6642
Manufacturer and exporter of racks including can,
storage, dunnage, pan, tray; also, dish mobiles
President: Glenn Scott
Secretary: Mary Van Noy
Office Manager: Lisa Lewellen
Estimated Sales: 700000
Number Employees: 5-9
Square Footage: 24000
Brands:
  Always Can

29698 Storax
72 Sherwood Road
Bromsgrove, UK B60 3DR
845-130-3090
Fax: 152-757-6144 info@storaxsystems.com
Mobile rack systems
VP Operations: Jim McLain
Number Employees: 10
Parent Co: Barpro Group

29699 Stork Fabricators Inc
525 Vossbrink Dr
Washington, MO 63090-1046
636-239-7424
Fax: 636-239-7322 sales@texwrap.com
www.storkfab.com
Fully automatic shrink wrap machinery including;
horizondal side seals, tunnels, L-sealers, belted and
flighted conveyors and high speed wrappers, our
machines are touchscreen operated for easy set-up
President: Robert Stork
CFO: David Hood
VP & R&D: Brian Stork
Quality Control: Steve Angell
Marketing: Tom Dickman
Estimated Sales: $10-20 Million
Number Employees: 50-99
Square Footage: 72000

29700 Stork Food Dairy Systems
P.O.Box 1258
Gainesville, GA 30503-1258
770-535-1875
Fax: 770-536-0841 jan.kuiper@stork.com
www.sfds.com
Sales and service of various integrated processing
and packaging systems for food, dairy, juice and
beverage industry
CEO: Bath Dowdy
VP: Jan Lucas-Kuiper
Executive VP: Ben Hamer
Quality Control: Robert Terhaar
Contact: Andr Haket
andr.haket@stork.com
Estimated Sales: Below $5 Million
Number Employees: 10-19

29701 Stork Food Machinery
3525 W Peterson Ave
Suite 611
Chicago, IL 60659-3318
773-583-7793
Fax: 773-583-8155 800-81S-TORK
Automatic warehouse systems, aseptic packaging
systems and aseptic processing equipment

Manager: Nicole Stack
Estimated Sales: $.5-1 million
Number Employees: 1-4

29702 Stork Townsend Inc.
PO Box 1433
Des Moines, IA 50306-1433

515-265-8181
Fax: 515-263-3333 800-247-8609
info.townsendusa@stork.com
www.townsendeng.com

Manufacturer and exporter of meat processing machinery including pork, fish and poultry skinners, sausage stuffers, linkers, bacon injectors, sausage coextrusion, sausage loaders and meat harvesting systems.
President: Theo Bruinsma
Regional Sales Manager: David Bertelsen
Contact: Janet Bergeron
janet.bergeron@marel.com
Estimated Sales: $20-50 Million
Number Employees: 100-249
Type of Packaging: Food Service
Brands:
    Townsend

29703 Storm Industrial
PO Box 14666
Shawnee Mission, KS 66285-4666

913-599-3650
Fax: 559-277-9580 800-745-7483

Manufacturer and exporter of plastic and brass valves including pilot mini, automatic drain, speed control exhaust, solenoid, hydraulic nonelectric, slip, pressure regulating, electric and barbed drain; also, wire connectors
Number Employees: 50
Square Footage: 80000
Parent Co: Imperial Valve Company
Brands:
    Imperial

29704 Stormax International
90 Manchester St
Concord, NH 03301-5129

603-223-2333
Fax: 603-223-2330 800-874-7629

Manufacturer, importer and exporter of filling, sealing and lidding machinery for cups, trays, tubs and paper containers
President: Earl Gestewitz
Estimated Sales: Below $5 Million
Number Employees: 1-4
Parent Co: Stormax International A/S

29705 Storopack Packaging Systs USA
12007 Woodruff Ave
Downey, CA 90241-5603

562-803-5582
Fax: 562-803-4462 800-827-7225
www.storopack.com

Manufacturer, converter and recycler of EPS (Expanded Polystyrene) with primary activities that include the conversion of EPS, natural starch, paper and plastic cushioning materials
Manager: John Melat
VP Marketing: Paul Deis
Estimated Sales: $20-50 Million
Number Employees: 50-99
Type of Packaging: Private Label, Bulk

29706 Storsack Inc
7111 Perimeter Park Dr # 300
Houston, TX 77041-4048

713-461-0840
Fax: 713-461-0654 800-841-4982
info@storsack.com

Global manufacturer of flexible intermdiate bulk bags
CEO: Bruce Boyd
Sales Director of Public Relations: Sonja GrAger
Estimated Sales: $10-25 Million
Number Employees: 20-49
Brands:
    Cleanmaster
    Guardmaster
    Safemaster
    Spacemaster
    Tripmaster

29707 Stout Sign Company
6425 W Florissant Ave
Saint Louis, MO 63136-3622

314-385-4600
Fax: 314-385-9412 800-325-8530
www.stoutsign.com

Manufacturer and exporter of point of purchase signs and displays; silk screening available
President: Patrick Conners
Sales Manager: Randall Simonian
Contact: Redmond Egart
regart@stoutsign.com
VP Operations: Lee Witt
Estimated Sales: $15-20 Million
Number Employees: 100-249
Square Footage: 140000
Parent Co: Stout Industries of Delaware

29708 Strahl & Pitsch Inc
230 Great East Neck Rd
West Babylon, NY 11704-7602

631-669-0175
Fax: 631-587-9120 www.strahlpitsch.com

Confectionery waxes, custom blending
President: Brian Ardito
bardito@spwax.com
Marketing Manager: Dan Damico
Estimated Sales: $20-50 Million
Number Employees: 20-49

29709 Strahman Valves Inc
2801 Baglyos Cir
Lehigh Valley Industrial Park VI
Bethlehem, PA 18020-8033

484-893-5080
Fax: 484-893-5099 877-787-2462
strahman@strahman.com

Manufacturer and exporter of cleaning products, hoses and valves
President/CEO: August Percoco
apercoco@strahman.com
CFO: Dan Eckel
VP: Kevin Carroll
Director of IT: Eric Hays
Director Quality Control: Arthur Pultz
Marketing Manager: Vanessa Reagle
VP Sales: Jan Willem Savelkoel
Customer Service Manager: Rosalind Bowens
VP Operations: William Doll
Purchasing & Inventory Control M: Chris Lipinski
Estimated Sales: $10-20 Million
Number Employees: 100-249
Type of Packaging: Bulk

29710 Straight Line Filters
701 Christiana Ave
Wilmington, DE 19801-5842

302-654-8805
Fax: 302-655-5038

Food-processing vacuum belt filters
Manager: Kenneth Seibert
Estimated Sales: $1-2.5 Million
Number Employees: 10-19

29711 Straits Steel & Wire Co
902 N Rowe St # 100
Ludington, MI 49431-1495

231-843-3416
Fax: 231-843-8096 www.sswholding.net

Wire shelves, racks, fruit and vegetable baskets and displays
Vice President: Steve Koss
VP: James Boals
Estimated Sales: $20-50 Million
Number Employees: 100-249

29712 Strand Lighting
10911 Petal St
Dallas, TX 75238-2424

214-647-7880
Fax: 714-899-0042 www.strandlighting.com

Manufacturer and exporter of electric and incandescent lighting fixtures
President: Tim Burnham
peter.rogers@philips.com
VP Marketing: Peter Rogers
Sales Exec: Pete Borchetta
Estimated Sales: $20-30 Million
Number Employees: 20-49
Parent Co: Rank Industries America
Type of Packaging: Food Service

29713 Strapack
30860 San Clemente St
Hayward, CA 94544-7135

510-475-6000
Fax: 510-475-6090 800-475-5006
www.strapack.com

Strapping machines, corrugated converting machine
Owner: Keisho Yamamoto
Contact: Asami Cillo
anc@strapack.com
Estimated Sales: $10-20 Million
Number Employees: 10-19

29714 Strapex Corporation
2601 Westinghouse Blvd
Charlotte, NC 28273

704-588-2510
Fax: 704-588-6838 800-346-1804

Bottle and can containers
Estimated Sales: $10-20 Million
Number Employees: 20-49

29715 Strasburger & Siegel
7249 National Dr Ste 2
Hanover, MD 21076

410-712-7373
Fax: 410-712-7378 888-726-3753
www.eurofinsus.com

Consultant to food technologists for product formulation, evaluation, analysis, etc
President: Rick Gjesdal
Director: Tom Light
Contact: Wendy Bowie
wendybowie@eurofinsus.com
Estimated Sales: $1-2.5 Million
Number Employees: 20-49

29716 Stratecon
5215 Mountain View Road
Winston Salem, NC 27104-5117

336-768-6808
Fax: 336-765-5149 cbeckstc@bellsouth.net
www.stratecon-intl.com

Consultant specializing in strategic planning, start-up feasibility, marketing research, technology assessment, project management, etc. for the food industry
Estimated Sales: Below $500,000
Number Employees: 2
Square Footage: 4000

29717 Stratecon InternationalConsultants
5215 Mountain View Road
Winston Salem, NC 27104-5117

336-768-6808
Fax: 336-765-5149
weck@foodbusinessresource.com
www.stratecon-intl.com

We combine the experience of twelve seasoned food industry professionals who work together to fulfill client needs. Members have skills in processed foods and ingredients. Specialties: business development, coffee manufacturingdietary fibers, due diligence, food safety, fortification, process and equipment development, product introduction, strategic planning, and training. See website for individual consultant locations
Coordinator: Catherine Side
Estimated Sales: Below $500,000
Number Employees: 2

29718 Strategic Equipment & Supply
8360 E Via De Ventura
Scottsdale, AZ 85258-3172

480-905-5530

Food service equipment
Estimated Sales: Less than $500,000
Number Employees: 1-4

29719 Stratis Plastic Pallets
5677 W 73rd St
Indianapolis, IN 46278

317-328-8000
Fax: 317-328-8080 800-725-5387
sales@pallets.com www.pallets.com

Plastic pallets
President: Andrew Elder
Contact: Reed Elder
relder@pallets.com
Estimated Sales: $300,000-500,000
Number Employees: 1-4

29720 (HQ)Stratix Corp
4920 Avalon Ridge Pkwy
Peachtree Cor, GA 30071-1572
770-326-7580
Fax: 770-326-7591 800-883-8300
info@stratixcorp.com www.stratixcorp.com
Bar code generation software, bar code verification
equipment, bar code pressure sensitive labels, verifi-
cation/label printing systems and thermal transfer/di-
rect thermal printers
President & CEO: Gina Gallo
gina.gallo@ipaper.com
CEO: Bonney Shuman
CFO: John Pumpelly
Marketing Director: Kathryn Fraas
SVP, of Sales: Brian Burkett
VP, Operation: Ross Homans
Estimated Sales: $10-20 Million
Number Employees: 100-249
Other Locations:
 Stratix Corporation
 St. Leonards
Brands:
 Bar Code Creator
 Symart Systems
 Xaminer

29721 Straub Designs Co
2238 Florida Ave S # A
Suite A
St Louis Park, MN 55426-2880
952-546-6686
Fax: 763-546-3056 800-959-3708
parts@straubdesign.com www.straubdesign.com
Manufacturer and exporter of packaging and taping
machinery
President: Dennis Schuette
dschuette@straubdesign.com
Sales: Mark Baillie
Sales: Glenn Baillie
Estimated Sales: $2.5-5 Million
Number Employees: 20-49
Square Footage: 40000

29722 Straub Designs Co
2238 Florida Ave S # A
St Louis Park, MN 55426-2880
952-546-6686
Fax: 763-546-3056 parts@straubdesign.com
www.straubdesign.com
Manufacturer and exporter of hand and electric
grinding mills for dry and oily materials including
beans, nuts and herbs and for preparing laboratory
samples for analysis
President: Dennis Schuette
dschuette@straubdesign.com
Office Manager: Judy Haag
Number Employees: 20-49
Parent Co: Clinton Separators, Inc.
Brands:
 Quaker City

29723 Straubel Company
1891 Commerce Drive
De Pere, WI 54115
920-336-1412
Fax: 920-336-1308 888-336-1412
sharil@straubelcompany.com
Disposable plastic and paper products including ta-
ble covers; also, plastic banquet tables, drop cloths,
and laminations
President: Thomas Tess
Vice President: Craig Nothstine
VP Sales: Jay McDowell
Contact: Duane Bashell
duane@straubelcompany.com
VP Operations: Paul Piikila
Production Planning: Brenda Scray
Plant Manager: John Westcott
Supply Chain Management: Shari Linksens
Estimated Sales: Below $5 Million
Number Employees: 10-19
Square Footage: 80000
Brands:
 Breez Proof
 Picnic Time
 Table Mate

29724 Streamfeeder
315 27th Ave NE
Minneapolis, MN 55418
763-502-0000
Fax: 763-502-0100 info@streamfeeder.com
www.streamfeeder.com

Electromechanical products and friction feeders for
inserting, feeding and collating
President: Mitch Speicher
Contact: Emily Lang
emily.lang@streamfeeder.com
Estimated Sales: $10-20 Million
Number Employees: 20-49

29725 Streater Inc
411 S 1st Ave
Albert Lea, MN 56007-1794
507-373-0611
Fax: 507-373-7630 800-527-4197
salesinfo@streater.com www.streater.com
Store fixtures including gondolas and wall cases
President: Thomas Stensrude
Cmo: Peter Nelson
peter@streater.com
Finance Executive: Dan Juntunen
Marketing: Dan Heckmann
Sales: Dave Sprunt
Estimated Sales: $1-3 Million
Number Employees: 100-249
Square Footage: 2240000
Parent Co: Joyce International

29726 Streator Dependable Mfg
1705 N Shabbona St
Streator, IL 61364-2100
815-672-0551
Fax: 815-672-7631 800-798-0551
sales@streatordependable.com
www.streatordependable.com
Manufacturer and importer of material handling
equipment including containers, pallets, stacking
racks, skids and spools
President: Paul A Walker
pwalker@streatordependable.com
Marketing: Bill Bontemps
Sales Manager: Nathan Hovious
Number Employees: 100-249
Square Footage: 200000

29727 Stretch-Vent Packaging System
PO Box 51462
Ontario, CA 91761-1062
909-947-3993
Fax: 909-947-0579 800-822-8368
Manufacturer, importer and exporter of vented pro-
duce wrap
VP Sales/Marketing: T Lasker
Director Sales/Operations: Phil Beach
Estimated Sales: $10-20 Million
Number Employees: 50-99
Type of Packaging: Consumer, Bulk
Brands:
 Stretch-Vent
 Vex-Cap

29728 Stretchtape
18460 Syracuse Ave
Cleveland, OH 44110
216-486-9400
Fax: 216-486-9444 888-486-9400
info@stretchtape.com www.stretchtape.com
President: Sean Mc Donald
Estimated Sales: $1-5 Million
Number Employees: 20-49

29729 Stribbons
2921 W Cypress Creek Rd
Suite 101
Fort Lauderdale, FL 33309
305-628-4000
Fax: 305-621-6109 info@mncstribbons.com
www.stribbons.com
Decorative packaging services: giftwrap, labels,
boxes and containers.
Marketing: Michael Flynn
Contact: Harold Tepper
htepper@mncstribbons.com

29730 Stricker & Co
500 Kent Ave
La Plata, MD 20646
301-934-8346
Fax: 301-870-3112
Signs, printed labels and point of purchase displays
Owner: Susan Stiles
Estimated Sales: Less Than $500,000
Number Employees: 1-4
Square Footage: 10000

29731 Stricklin Co
1901 W Commerce St
Dallas, TX 75208-8104
214-637-1030
Fax: 214-747-7872 tjohnson@baldwinmetals.com
www.stricklincompany.com
Manufacturer and exporter of blenders, cookers and
mixers; also, repair services available
President: Tom Johnson
tom.johnson@baldwinmetals.com
Controller: Don Smith
Engineer: Mitch Withem
Estimated Sales: Below $5 Million
Number Employees: 20-49
Square Footage: 120000
Parent Co: Baldwin Metals
Brands:
 Stricklin
 Strico

29732 Stripper Bags
121 Quail Run Road
Henderson, NV 89014-2129
800-354-2247
Fax: 702-898-9938
Manufacturer and exporter of preprinted poly bags
for food portioning and rotation; also, labels including peel/stick and disposable for food rotation
President: Mark Tenner

29733 Strohmeyer & Arpe Co Inc
106 Allen Rd # 203
Basking Ridge, NJ 07920-3851
908-580-9100
Fax: 908-580-9300 800-628-2374
sales@strohmeyer.com www.strohmeyer.com
Natural waxes including beeswax, carnauba,
candelilla, ouricouri and Japan wax, bulk honey, private label canned fruits, vegetables and seafood
President: Charles Kocot
ckocot@strohmeyer.com
Estimated Sales: $5-10 Million
Number Employees: 5-9

29734 Strong Hold Products
6333 Strawberry Ln
Louisville, KY 40214-2930
502-363-4175
Fax: 502-363-3827 800-880-2625
info@strong-hold.com
www.strongholdindustrial.com
Industrial welded storage cabinets and shelving
President: Thomas Diebold
VP: Tina Gillenwoater
Vice President: Tom Diebold
Sales Director: Peggy Drake
Plant Manager: Dannis Hughbanks
Estimated Sales: $10-20 Million
Number Employees: 100-249
Square Footage: 216000
Parent Co: Fabricated Metals

29735 Strongarm
425 Caredean Drive
Horsham, PA 19044
215-443-3400
Fax: 215-443-3002 sales@strongarm.com
www.strongarm.com
Operator interface mountings and systems
President: Tom Holden
Sales Manager: Bill Flemming

29736 Stronghaven Containers Co
11135 Monroe Rd
Matthews, NC 28105-6564
704-847-7743
Fax: 704-847-5871 800-222-7919
info@stronghaven.com www.stronghaven.com
Manufacturer and exporter of corrugated boxes
Estimated Sales: $1-5 Million
Number Employees: 20-49
Square Footage: 500000

29737 Stroter Inc
PO Box 892
Freeport, IL 61053
815-616-2506
Fax: 815-244-2102 diane@stroter.com
www.stroter.com
Spare parts, electric motors and complete replace-
ment units

29738 Structural Transport
888 E Porter Rd
Norton Shores, MI 49441-5848

231-798-6342
Fax: 231-798-0198
dscripps@structuralconcepts.com
www.structuralconcept.com
President: David P Geerts
Quality Control: Jeff Cimnes
Chairman: James Doss
Manager: John Bell
johnbell@structuralconcept.com
Estimated Sales: $30-50 Million
Number Employees: 5-9

29739 Structure
3000 E 1st Ave Ste 126
Denver, CO 80206

303-329-9560
Fax: 303-329-0833
President: Tom Noto
Vice President: Todd McAtee
Estimated Sales: $2.5-5 Million
Number Employees: 20-49

29740 (HQ)Structure Probe
PO Box 656
West Chester, PA 19381-0656

610-436-5400
Fax: 610-436-5755 800-242-4774
spi3spi@2spi.com www.2spi.com
Independent laboratory offering problem solving
and analysis
President and Chairman of the Board: Violet Garber
Corporate Secretary and Vice President: Kim
Murray
Vice President: Eugene Rodek
Vice President, Technical: Andrew W. Blackwood,
Ph.D.
Quality Officer: Andrew W. Blackwood, Ph. D.
Office Manager: Nancy Blackwood
Estimated Sales: $1-2.5 Million
Number Employees: 10-19
Square Footage: 80000
Other Locations:
   Structure Probe
   Fairfield CT

29741 Stryco Wire Products
1110 Flint Road
North York, ON M3J 2J5
Canada

416-663-7000
Fax: 416-663-7001
Wire baskets and shelving, cooler shelves, slide
guards and barbecue grills
President: Calford Robinson
CFO: Jana Bonder
Quality Control: Ken Duffney
R&D: Ede Zendai
Number Employees: 30-40

29742 Stuart W Johnson & Co
1002 Mobile St
Lake Geneva, WI 53147-2449

262-248-8851
Fax: 262-248-0277 800-558-5904
sales@stuartjohnsonco.com
Aseptic processing equipment, centrifuges, cheese
equipment, filtration equipment, clean rooms and
equipment, cutting equipment, fillers, pin, milk,
steam, flow diversion stations, heat exchangers,
plate, tubular, homogenizersladders, vat, meters,
flow
President: Eric Behling
eric.behling@stuartjohnsonco.com
Estimated Sales: $5-10 Million
Number Employees: 10-19

29743 Studd & Whipple Company
PO Box 17
Conewango Valley, NY 14726-0017

716-287-3791
Fax: 716-287-3309
Wooden pallets and pre-cut pallet materials
Estimated Sales: $10-20 Million
Number Employees: 8
Parent Co: Crawford Manufacturing Company

29744 (HQ)Sturdi-Bilt Restaurant Equipment
7150 Nollar Rd
Whitmore Lake, MI 48189

313-231-4911
Fax: 800-444-2895 800-521-2895
sbrei@juno.com www.sturdibilt.com
Kitchen equipment and ventilation systems
Chairman: Arnold H Robinson
Secretary: Ruth Ann Robinson
Sales Director: Shirley Van Reuter
Estimated Sales: $2.5-5 Million
Number Employees: 5-9

29745 Stutz Products Corp
606 S Walnut St
Hartford City, IN 47348-2627

765-348-2510
Fax: 765-348-1001 info@stutzproducts.com
Food processing machine knives
President: Bill Musselman
bill@stutzproducts.com
Estimated Sales: Less Than $500,000
Number Employees: 5-9
Square Footage: 12000

29746 Stylmark Inc
6536 Main St NE
PO Box 32008
Minneapolis, MN 55432-4314

763-574-7474
Fax: 763-574-1415 800-328-2495
info@stylmark.com www.stylmark.com
Manufacturer and exporter of back-lit, edge-lit and
nonlit graphic display products; also, static graphic
display products, sequential image, programmable
multi-image and scrolling units available.
President: Andy Steinfeldt
CEO: Javier Barral Amil
jbarralamil@stylmark.com
Number Employees: 100-249
Brands:
   A-Frame
   Edgelite
   Graphic Revolutions
   Impact Island
   Litewall
   Luminaire
   Luminaire Ultra
   Luminaire Ultra Ii
   Movingpix
   Neon Plus E
   Print Frame
   Stretchframe
   Triad

29747 Suan Farma
17 Zink Place
Suite 9
Fair Lawn, NJ 07410

201-343-1188
info@suanfarma.com
suanfarmausa.com
Distributor of ingredients for the pharma- and
nutraceutical industries.
Other Locations:
   Fair Lawn NJ
   Tempe AZ
   Bogota, Colombia
   Juarez, Mexico
   Caracas, Venezuela
   Sao Paulo, Brasil
   Madrid, Spain
   Barcelona, Spain
   Fribourg, Switzerland
   Shenyang, China
   Mumbai, India
   Dubai, UAE

29748 Suburban Corrugated BoxCompany
6363 Keokuk Rd
Indianhead Park, IL 60525-4341

630-920-1230
Fax: 630-920-1353 subcorr1@aol.com
Corrugated boxes
VP: Gene Mazurek
Estimated Sales: $2.5-5 Million
Number Employees: 10-19

29749 Suburban Laboratories Inc
1950 S Batavia Ave # 150
Suite 150
Geneva, IL 60134-3330

708-544-3260
Fax: 708-544-8587 800-783-5227
dan@suburbanlabs.com www.suburbanlabs.com
Consultant and analyst for the food and sanitation
industries providing analytical, enviromental and
microbiological testing, nutritional assays and water
and sterility testing
President: Jarrett Thomas
jarrett@suburbanlabs.com
Business Dev. Manager: Shane Clarke
VP, Sales: Dan Galehar
Estimated Sales: $2.5-5 Million
Number Employees: 20-49

29750 Suburban Sign Company
19611 Jasper Street NW
Anoka, MN 55303-9642

763-753-8849
Fax: 763-753-8225
Signs including advertising, plastic, painted and
wooden
Owner: Burt Pfeifer
Number Employees: 2

29751 Suburban Signs
5051 Greenbelt Rd
College Park, MD 20740

301-474-5051
Fax: 301-345-1196 www.suburbansigns.com
Signs
President: Robert Wells
VP: Joel Hurst
Estimated Sales: Below $5 Million
Number Employees: 1-4
Square Footage: 4200

29752 Success Systems
45 Church St P.O. Box 2457
st. 106
Stamford, GA 06906

404-252-6002
Fax: 203-921-1660 800-653-3345
mkt@success-systems.com
www.success-systems.com
Computer systems and software
VP: Howard Spiller
Estimated Sales: $1-5 Million
Number Employees: 20-49
Square Footage: 40000

29753 Sudmo North America, Inc
1330 Anvil Road
Machesney Park, IL 61115

815-639-0322
Fax: 815-639-1135 800-218-3915
www.sudmona.com
Supplier of valves and components to the food,
dairy, beverage and pharmaceutical industries
Director of Sales: Jim Banks
Contact: Deb Baggs
dbaggs@sudmona.com
Estimated Sales: $5-10 Million
Number Employees: 10-19
Parent Co: Pentair

29754 Suffolk Iron Works Inc
418 E Washington St
PO Box 1943
Suffolk, VA 23434-4518

757-539-2353
Fax: 757-539-1520 info@suffolkironworks.com
www.suffolkironworks.com
Manufacturer and exporter of peanut machinery and
bulk material handling systems
Owner: John C Harrell
charrell@suffolkironworks.com
VP: Jenny Winslow
Senior Project Engineer: John Harrell
Estimated Sales: $5-10 Million
Number Employees: 20-49

29755 Sugar Creek
2101 Kenskill Ave
Washington Ct Hs, OH 43160-9404

740-335-7440
Fax: 740-335-7443 800-848-8205
www.sugarcreek.com
Manufacturer of bacon and turkey bacon.

Chairman/CEO: John Richardson
COO: Michael Richardson
CFO: Tom Bollinger
tbollinger@sugar-creek.com
VP of Quality Assurance: Rob Howe
VP of Sales: Jim Coughlin
Plant Manager: Dan Sileo
Estimated Sales: $20 Million
Number Employees: 1000-4999
Number of Brands: 1
Type of Packaging: Consumer, Food Service, Bulk
Other Locations:
    Cincinnati OH
    Hamilton OH
    Frontenac KS
    Cambridge City IN
Brands:
    Sugar Creek

29756 Sugar Plum LLC
5756 W Main St
Houma, LA 70360-1745

985-872-9524
Fax: 985-872-9664
Designer cakes, wedding cakes, holiday cakes, confectionary, and various other desserts
Owner: Cindy Dugas
thesugarplum1@comcast.net
Number Employees: 10-19
Square Footage: 10000

29757 Sugarplum Desserts
20381 62nd Avenue
Building 5
Langley, BC V3A SE6
Canada

604-534-2282
Fax: 604-534-2280 info@sugarplumdesserts.com
www.sugarplumdesserts.com
Thaw and serve cheesecakes and thaw and bake cookies
President: Leslie Goodman
Number Employees: 15
Square Footage: 32000

29758 Suhner Manufacturing
S Suhner Drive
Rome, GA 30162

706-235-8046
Fax: 706-235-8045
Chairman of the Board: Otto Suhner
Estimated Sales: $20-30 Million
Number Employees: 100-250

29759 Sultan Linen Inc
313 5th Ave
New York, NY 10016-6518

212-689-8900
Fax: 212-689-8965
Manufacturer and exporter of decorative linens, towels, table cloths, place mats and aprons
President: Daniel Sultan
daniel@sultanslinens.com
Sales Manager: Daniel Sultan
Estimated Sales: $500,000-$1 Million
Number Employees: 1-4
Parent Co: SLI Home Fashions

29760 Sumitomo Machinery Corp
4200 Holland Blvd
Chesapeake, VA 23323-1529

757-485-3355
Fax: 757-485-0643 800-SMC-YCLO
www.sumitomodrive.com
Mechanical and electrical adjustable speed drives, parallel shaft and right angle reducers, shaft mounted gear motors, and helical, planetary, spiral bevel, gear reducers
President: Ron Smith
Executive VP: James Magee
CFO: Nobuhiao Kawamusa
Estimated Sales: $50-75 Million
Number Employees: 250-499

29761 Summit Commercial
770 Garrison Ave
Bronx, NY 10474-5603

718-893-3900
Fax: 718-842-3093 800-932-4267
info@summitappliance.com
www.summitappliance.com
Equipment
President: Felix Storch
Vice President: Paul Storch

Estimated Sales: $40-50 Million
Number Employees: 100
Number of Brands: 1
Number of Products: 170
Square Footage: 150000
Brands:
    Summit

29762 Summit Industrial Equipment
930 Riverside Pkwy # 30
Broderick, CA 95605-1511

916-372-5890
Fax: 916-372-1973 www.summitindustrial.com
Air compressors
Manager: Mark Kabnick
Communications Director: Chris Fisher
Vice President of Corporate Communicatio: Annika Berglund
Estimated Sales: $5-10 Million
Number Employees: 5-9

29763 Summit Machine Builders Corporation
550 W 53rd Place
Denver, CO 80216-1612

303-294-9949
Fax: 303-294-9622 800-274-6741
Manufacturer and exporter of automation and automated assembly equipment including dry and fibrous product feeding, filling and dispensing systems; also, ingredients dispensing and automatic micro weighing equipment
President: Scott Harris
Director Sales: Mike Schmehl
Estimated Sales: $5-10 Million
Number Employees: 85
Square Footage: 200000
Brands:
    Sro Feeder
    Vibra-Meter Feeder

29764 Summit Premium Tree Nuts
8680 Greenback Lane
Suite 250
Orangevale, CA 95662

916-988-1081
Fax: 916-988-1089 www.summittreenuts.com
Premium tree nuts
President: Dale Darling

29765 Summitville Tiles Inc
15364 State Route 644
Summitville, OH 43962

330-223-1511
Fax: 330-223-1414 info@summitville.com
www.summitville.com
Ceramic tiles
President: David Johnson
dwjohnson@summitville.com
CFO: Rich Finnicun
Estimated Sales: $20-50 Million
Number Employees: 100-249

29766 Sun Industries
16115 S 450 E
Goodland, IN 47948

219-297-3195
Fax: 219-297-3010 www.sunind.com
Packaging machinery and equipment
President: Carl Potsch
cpotsch@aol.com
Estimated Sales: $1-2.5 Million
Number Employees: 10-19

29767 Sun Paints & Coatings
4701 East 7th Avenue
PO Box 75070
Tampa, FL 33605

813-367-4444
Fax: 813-367-0263 800-247-9691
www.suncoatings.com
Manufacturer and exporter of window, tile and mildew cleaners
President: Barton Malina
Contact: Tom Crosier
tcrosier@sunpaintsandcoatings.com
Estimated Sales: $5-10 Million
Number Employees: 20-49
Square Footage: 200000

29768 Sun Plastics
PO Box 37
Clearwater, MN 55320-0037

320-558-6130
Fax: 320-558-6119 800-862-1673
Thermoformed plastic packaging for food
President: Paul Amundson
Plant Manager: Ken Doble
Estimated Sales: $2.5-5 Million
Number Employees: 20-49
Square Footage: 48000

29769 Sun Ray Sign Group Inc
376 Roost Ave
Holland, MI 49424-2032

616-392-2824
Fax: 616-392-5797
Signs
Owner: Scott Tardiff
scott.tardiff@itworld.com
Estimated Sales: Less Than $500,000
Number Employees: 1-4

29770 Sunbeam Products Co LLC
623 Main St
Toledo, OH 43605-1745

419-691-1551
Soap and detergents
Owner: Todd Lincoln
sunbeamtodd@bex.net
Estimated Sales: $1-2.5 Million
Number Employees: 1-4

29771 Sunco & Frenchie
489 Getty Avenue
Clifton, NJ 07011

Fax: 973-478-1063 973-478-1011
www.sunconatural.com
Dried fruits, nuts, granola, raw sugar, quick oats, corn meal, and juice.
Co-Owner: Joel Ammar
Year Founded: 2009
Estimated Sales: $1-5 Million
Number Employees: 15
Brands:
    Frenchie©
    Sunbest©
    Sunco©

29772 Sundance Architectural Prod
4249 L B Mcleod Rd
Orlando, FL 32811-5600

407-297-1337
Fax: 407-296-4330 800-940-1337
info@sdap.com www.sdap.com
Commercial awnings and fabric structures
Owner: Paula Toot
paula.toot@sdap.com
Estimated Sales: $5-10 Million
Number Employees: 50-99

29773 (HQ)Sundyne Corp
14845 W 64th Ave
Arvada, CO 80007-7523

303-425-0800
Fax: 303-425-0896
Air/gas compressor pumps and pumping equipment
President: Jeff Wiemelt
jwiemelt@sundyne.com
CFO: John O'Toole
VP/General Manager: Jeff Wiemelt
Human Resources Director: Marie Weiss-Rich
Estimated Sales: $41.8 Million
Number Employees: 250-499

29774 Sunflower Packaging
8952 NW 24th Ave
Miami, FL 33147

305-591-3388
Fax: 305-591-9356 lungmeng@lung-meng.com
www.lung-meng.com
Packaging machinery
Manager: Allen Tsai
General Manager: Allen Tsai
Estimated Sales: $5-10 Million
Number Employees: 10-19

29775 Sungjae Corporation
Po Box 6525
Irvine, CA 92616

949-757-1727
Fax: 949-757-1723

Printed flexible packaging,packing materials, bags, films, wrap, wrapping zipper bag,stand up bag and shrink film.
President: Kim Eunhee
Marketing Director: Vin Eun Hee
Estimated Sales: $5-10,000,000
Number Employees: 8
Parent Co: Sungjae Corporation

29776 Sungjae Corporation
27 Highpoint
Irvine, CA 92603

949-757-1727
Fax: 949-757-1723
Rotogravure printed flexible packaging, packaging materials, bags, film, wrap, wrapping, printers, printing
Owner: Minhee Kim
Marketing Head: Min Hee
Estimated Sales: Less than $500,000
Number Employees: 1-4

29777 Sunkist Growers
27770 Entertainment Dr.
Valencia, CA 91355

661-290-8900
www.sunkist.com
Fruit juices, fruit drinks, healthy snacks, baking mixes, carbonated beverages, confections, vitamins, frozen novelties, salad toppings, freshly peeled citrus, chilled jellies and nonfood products.
Chief Executive Officer: Jim Phillips
Chief Operating Officer: Christian Harris
Year Founded: 1893
Estimated Sales: $1 Billion
Number Employees: 6,000
Type of Packaging: Food Service, Private Label
Other Locations:
Sunkist Growers
Toronto Canada ON
Sunkist Growers
Cary NC
Sunkist Growers
Pittsburgh PA
Sunkist Growers
Buffalo NY
Sunkist Growers
Stafford TX
Sunkist Growers
Visalia CA
Sunkist Growers
Cherry Hill NJ
Sunkist Growers
West Chester OH
Sunkist Growers
Detroit MI
Sunkist Growers
Long Valley NJ
Sunkist Growers
Phoenix AZ
Sunkist Growers
Clackamas OR
Sunkist Growers
Anjou Canada QC

29778 Sunland Manufacturing Company
1658 93rd Ln NE
Minneapolis, MN 55449

763-785-2247
Fax: 763-785-9667 800-790-1905
www.sunlandmfg.com
Polyethylene bags
Owner: Pat Haley
Estimated Sales: $2.5-5 Million
Number Employees: 10-19
Square Footage: 16000

29779 Sunmark Special Markets
10820 Sunset Office Dr
St Louis, MO 63127-1016

314-822-2800
Fax: 314-984-9433
Hard and soft candy
President: L Delicandro
Sales Director: Charles Dodson
Number Employees: 100-249
Parent Co: Nestle USA

29780 Sunmaster Of Naples Inc
900 Industrial Blvd
Naples, FL 34104-3612

239-261-3581
Fax: 239-261-7499 info@sunmasterinc.com
www.titanscreen.com
Commercial awnings

President: John Wilkinson
john@sunmasterinc.com
Vice President: David Rinker
Estimated Sales: $2.5-5,000,000
Number Employees: 20-49

29781 Sunny Cove Citrus LLC
1315 E Curtis Ave
Reedley, CA 93654-9317

Fax: 559-626-7210
Packinghouse and licensed shipper of citrus products for Sunkist Growers Inc.
President: Tom Clark
Field Manager: Justin Kulikov
Controller: Warren Lee
Office Manager: Vera Fast
Square Footage: 340000
Type of Packaging: Food Service

29782 Sunpoint Products
PO Box 567
Lawrence, MA 01842-1267

978-794-3100
Fax: 978-685-7840
Disinfectants, anti-bacterial soaps, etc
President: Brooks O Kane
Sales Manager: Bob Monroe
Number Employees: 3
Brands:
Red Cross Nurse

29783 (HQ)Sunroc Corporation
PO Box 13150
Columbus, OH 43213-0150

302-678-7800
Fax: 302-678-7809 800-478-6762
literature@sunroc.com www.sunroc.com
Manufacturer and exporter of electric and bottled water coolers,drinking fountains and point-of-use coolers
President: Anthony Salamone
CFO: Mark Whitaker
Director Engineering: Ronald Greenwald
Quality Control: Tom Huber
VP Sales/Marketing: John Ott
Contact: Mel Sloan
msloan@sunroc.com
Estimated Sales: $20-50 Million
Number Employees: 100-249
Square Footage: 250000
Brands:
Softtouch

29784 Sunset Paper Products
3148 Divernon Avenue
Simi Valley, CA 93063-1611

323-587-4488
Fax: 323-587-1313 800-228-7882
Manufactures baking and candy cups
President: Alan Newman
Estimated Sales: $20-50 Million
Number Employees: 50-99

29785 Sunset Sales
PO Box 446
Hurricane, UT 84737-0446

435-635-3199
Fax: 435-635-0205
Commercial food packaging and processing machinery
Estimated Sales: $1-5 Million
Number Employees: 9

29786 Sup Herb Farms
300 Dianne Dr
Turlock, CA 95380-9523

209-633-3600
Fax: 209-633-3644 800-787-4372
www.supherbfarms.com
Processors and marketers of culinary herbs and specialty products the selection of which includes fresh, frozen and freeze-dried varieties.
President: Mike Brem
EVP/Strategic Planning & CFO: Francis Contino
SVP/General Counsel & Secretary: Robert Skelton
VP/Human Relations: Cecile Perich
Number Employees: 100-249
Parent Co: McCormick & Company Inc

29787 Supelco Inc
595 N Harrison Rd
Bellefonte, PA 16823-6217

814-359-3441
Fax: 814-359-5459 800-247-6628
techservice@sial.com
Chromatography products for analysis and purification
President: Ryan Adams
ryan.adams@sial.com
Vice President: Russel Gant
Research & Development: Mark Robillard
Marketing Director: Don Hobbs
Sales Director: Marty McCoy
Public Relations: Diane Lidgett
Operations/Production: Rod Datt
Production Manager: Tom Henderson
Plant Manager: Rod Datt
Purchasing Manager: Jim Heiserl
Estimated Sales: $50-75 Million
Number Employees: 250-499
Parent Co: Sigma-Aldrich Corporation

29788 Super Beta Glucan
5 Holland # 109
Irvine, CA 92618-2570

949-305-2599
Fax: 626-203-0655 service@superbetaglucan.com
www.superbetaglucan.com
Mushroom Beta Glucan (Immulink MBG)
Founder: Dr. S.N. Chen
Vice President: Sherwin Chen
Number Employees: 5-9

29789 Super Cooker
6049 Peterson Rd
Lake Park, GA 31636-4003

229-559-1662
Fax: 229-559-1611 800-841-7452
Manufacturer and exporter of portable barbecue grills and smokers including charcoal, wood and gas
Owner: Ben Futch
ben@supercooker.com
Estimated Sales: $3-5,000,000
Number Employees: 10-19

29790 Super Radiator Coils
451 Southlake Blvd
N Chesterfield, VA 23236-3091

804-794-2887
Fax: 804-379-2118 800-229-2645
vainfo@superradiatorcoils.com www.srcoils.com
Coils and heat exchangers; exporter of coils, evaporators and condensors
Cmo: John Perez
john.perez@superradiatorcoils.com
Estimated Sales: $30+ Million
Number Employees: 100-249
Square Footage: 112000
Parent Co: Super Radiator Coils
Other Locations:
Super Radiator Coils
Phoenix AZ
Brands:
Super

29791 Super Seal ManufacturingLimited
670 Rowntree Dairy Road
Woodbridge, ON L4L 5T8
Canada

905-850-2929
Fax: 905-850-4440 800-337-3239
info@supersealmfg.com www.supersealmfg.com
Manufacturer and exporter of energy saving devices, retail and industrial impact traffic, P.V.C. and bi-folding doors, dock seals, truck shelters and inflatable seals and shelters
President: Renato Torchetti
Director Sales (USA): Paul Ricci
Number Employees: 10
Square Footage: 160000
Brands:
Atmo

29792 (HQ)Super Steel
7900 W Tower Ave
Milwaukee, WI 53223-3253

414-355-4800
Fax: 414-355-0372 www.supersteel.com
Fabricated metal parts

Vice President: Jason Gaare
jason.gaare@supersteel.com
Chief Financial Officer: Brad Nennig
Vice President: Jason Gaare
jason.gaare@supersteel.com
Director, Quality Assurance: Dan Klumpyan
Sales Manager: Dale Wilson
Public Relations Contact: Heather Krugler
General Manager: Greg Gaberino
Director, Project Management: Dan Brook
Plant Manager: Joe Rouse
Director, Engineering & Purchasing: Jason Gaare
Estimated Sales: $50-100 Million
Number Employees: 250-499
Square Footage: 650000
Other Locations:
   Super Steel Products Corp.
   Troy OH

29793 Super Sturdy
200 Rock Fish Drive
Weldon, NC 27890-2106

252-536-4833
Fax: 252-536-2118 800-253-4833
Custom stainless steel mobile carts, sinks, tables and cabinets
VP: Salvatore Pirruccio
Estimated Sales: $2.5-5 Million
Number Employees: 17
Square Footage: 66000
Parent Co: Marlo Manufacturing Company

29794 Super Vision International
9400 Southridge Park Ct # 200
Orlando, FL 32819-8643

407-857-9900
Fax: 407-857-0050
Manufacturer and exporter of signs, lighting and lighting fixtures
President: Mike Bauer
Chairman of the Board: Brett M Kingstone
Sales (USA): Rick Hunter
International Sales: Paula Vega
Number Employees: 50-99
Square Footage: 320000
Brands:
   Endglow
   Sideglow
   Supervision

29795 Super-Chef Manufacturing Company
9235 Bissonnet Street
Houston, TX 77074

713-729-9660
Fax: 713-729-8404 800-231-3478
Manufacturer and exporter of broilers, fryers, griddles, warming units, ovens, hoods, ranges, hot plates, food concession trailers and compact kitchens with recirculating filter hoods
President: Chris Pappas
CEO: Regina Seale
CFO: Isabel Repka
VP: Ed Seale
R&D: Chris Pappas
Quality Control: Ed Seale
Marketing: Regina Seale
Sales: Isabel Repka
Public Relations: Regina Seale
Operations: Chris Pappas
Production: Barry Berg
Plant Manager: Barry Berg
Purchasing: Ed Seale
Number Employees: 20-49
Number of Brands: 2
Square Footage: 160000
Brands:
   Fat Mizer
   Kompact Kitchen
   Super Chef

29796 Superflex Limited
152 44th St
Brooklyn, NY 11232-3310

718-768-1400
Fax: 718-768-5065 800-394-3665
sales@superflex.com www.seal-proof.com
Manufacturer and exporter of P.V.C. flexible suction and discharge reinforced hoses, liquid tight conduit and electrical tubing used for pumps, refrigerators, dairy equipment, beverage dispensers, etc
President: Yigal Elbaz
yelbaz@superflex.com
VP: Y Elbaz

Estimated Sales: Less Than $500,000
Number Employees: 1-4
Brands:
   Rollerflex
   Sealproof
   Superflex

29797 Superfos Packaging Inc
11301 Superfos Dr SE
2630 Taastrup
Cumberland, MD 21502-8772

301-759-3145
Fax: 301-759-4905 800-537-9242
superfos@superfos.com www.superfos.com
Rigid open top plastic containers
President: Mike Bosley
bmichael@rpc-superfos.com
CEO: Rene Valentin
CFO: Lars Hoeyer Tindbaek
Executive VP: Soren Marcussen
Quality Manager: Michal Kaminski
Sales Manager: Stephen Towl
Estimated Sales: $10-$20 Million
Number Employees: 100-249
Parent Co: Superfos Emballagelas
Brands:
   Flex Off
   Ring Lock
   Vapor Lock

29798 Superior Belting
6 Andrews St
PO Box 8678
Greenville, SC 29601-3902

864-605-0076
Fax: 864-269-9754
salesdepartment@superiorbelt.com
www.superiorbelt.com
Conveyor belting for the food processing industry
President: Leonard Sandy Chace
sales@superiorbelting.com
CFO: Allan Thompson
R&D: Sandy Chace
Estimated Sales: Below $5 Million
Number Employees: 10-19

29799 (HQ)Superior Brush Company
3455 W 140th St
Cleveland, OH 44111

216-941-6987
Fax: 216-252-8838
Manufacturer and exporter of metal strip brushes; also, custom design services available
VP Sales/Marketing: Richard Mertes
Estimated Sales: $10-20 Million
Number Employees: 20-49
Square Footage: 22000

29800 Superior Distributing Co
103 N 32nd St
Louisville, KY 40212

502-778-6661
Fax: 502-775-7519 800-365-6661
www.superiordisplayboards.com
Manufacturer and exporter of FDA approved wiping cloths, polyethylene bags, hairnets, beard guards, gloves and butchers' paper
Owner: Michael Hinson
Sales Manager: Susan Thrapp
Manager: Robert Mc Roberts
Estimated Sales: $5-10 Million
Number Employees: 1-4

29801 Superior Food MachineryInc
7635 Serapis Ave
Pico Rivera, CA 90660-4516

562-949-0396
Fax: 562-949-0180 800-944-0396
info@Superiorinc.com www.superiorinc.com
Manufacturer, importer, exporter and designer of tortilla and tortilla chip processing equipment; also, corn feeders, ovens and washers
Owner: Maria Castro
General Sales Manager: Rick Rangel
Customer Service Manager: Mark Reyes
maria@superiorinc.com
Estimated Sales: $5-10 Million
Number Employees: 20-49
Square Footage: 7000

29802 Superior Imaging Group Inc
22710 72nd Ave S
Kent, WA 98032-1926

253-872-7200
Fax: 253-872-7202 888-872-7200
sales@superiorimaging.com
www.superiorimaging.com
Commercial screen printing on nontextiles
Owner: Eric Richards
CFO: Michelle McKenzie
Contact: Jerry Blaha
blaha@superiorimaging.com
Estimated Sales: Less Than $500,000
Number Employees: 1-4

29803 Superior Industries
315 State Highway 28
Morris, MN 56267-4699

320-589-2406
Fax: 320-589-3892 800-321-1558
info@superior-ind.com www.superior-ind.com
Manufacturer and exporter idlers and portable conveying equipment
President: Riley Arndt
rarndt@supind.com
Estimated Sales: $15-20 Million
Number Employees: 500-999

29804 Superior Label Company
625 Gotham Pkwy
Carlstadt, NJ 07072-2403

201-438-4500
Fax: 201-438-8126 800-877-3795
superior95@aol.com
Pressure sensitive label application equipment including primary labeler or bar code printer and applicator

29805 Superior Linen & Work Wear
3001 Cherry St
Kansas City, MO 64108-3124

816-931-4477
Fax: 816-931-0504 800-798-7987
sales@superiorlinen.com www.superiorstyle.com
Table covers, uniforms, aprons,towels, table cloths, table skirts, chef wear, oxford shirts, and polo shirts
Chairman of the Board: William G Kartsonis
wgk@superiorline.net
Estimated Sales: $20-50 Million
Number Employees: 50-99
Type of Packaging: Consumer, Private Label

29806 Superior Menus
PO Box 6
Mankato, MN 56002-8465

800-464-2182
Fax: 800-842-9371
customerservice@superiormenus.com
www.superiormenus.com
Supplier of hospitality mints, various menus covers, laminators and laminating products, table tents, menu inserts, gift certificates, placemats, chef apparel and aprons, napkin bands, name badges, menu display racks, window messageboards, guest checks, server pads
Parent Co: Thayer

29807 Superior Neon Signs Inc
2515 N Oklahoma Ave
Oklahoma City, OK 73105-3094

405-528-5515
Fax: 405-528-5535 www.superiorneon.com
Sign manufacturer
President: Dan Lorant
dan.lorant@superiorneon.com
Estimated Sales: $1-2.5 Million
Number Employees: 20-49

29808 Superior Packaging Equipment Corporation
3 Edison Pl
Suite 4
Fairfield, NJ 7004

973-575-8818
Fax: 973-890-7295 www.superiorpack.com
Manufacturer and exporter of cartoning machinery including forming, gluing, inserting, closing, sealing and opening
President: Glenn Rice
Executive VP: Russell Rice
Estimated Sales: $5-10 Million
Number Employees: 10
Square Footage: 76000

29809 Superior Product PickupServices
5707 W Howard Street
Niles, IL 60714-4012
847-647-4720
Fax: 847-647-4739 www.productpickup.com
Consultant offering market research on consumer products
Estimated Sales: $1-5 Million
Number Employees: 20
Square Footage: 10000

29810 Superior Products Company
P.O.Box 64177
Saint Paul, MN 55164
651-636-1110
800-328-9800
comments@superprod.com
Wholesale Distributor of foodservice equipment and supplies
Contact: Charlette Edwards
charlette_edwards@ndgstp.com
Number Employees: 1-4
Type of Packaging: Food Service
Other Locations:
  Alexandria VA
  Anaheim CA
  Atlanta GA
  Baltimore MD
  Boston MA
  Charlotte NC
  Cleveland OH
  Dallas TX
  Hartford CT
  Orlando FL
  Pennsauken NJ
  Reno NV
  San Diego CA
Brands:
  Next Day Gourmet
  Superior Monogram

29811 Superior Tank
11415 Erie Ave SW
Beach City, OH 44608-9589
330-756-2030
Fax: 330-756-2015 superiortank@yahoo.com
www.superiortankinc.com
Wine industry stainless steel tanks
Owner: Thomas Burkey
superiortank@yahoo.com
VP: Byron Kovalaske
VP Sales: Byron Kovalaske
Estimated Sales: $20-50 Million
Number Employees: 20-49

29812 Superior Uniform Group
10055 Seminole Blvd
Seminole, FL 33772
800-727-8643
info@superioruniformgroup.com
www.superioruniformgroup.com
Manufacturer and exporter of aprons, restaurant smocks, sheeting, knit shirts, hats and cloth bags.
Chief Executive Officer: Michael Benstock
Executive Vice President: Peter Benstock
COO/CFO/Treasurer: Andrew Demott, Jr.
VP/General Counsel/Secretary: Jordan Alpert
Year Founded: 1920
Estimated Sales: $100-$500 Million
Square Footage: 60000

29813 Superior-Studio Specialties
2239 Yates Ave
Commerce, CA 90040-1913
323-278-0100
Fax: 323-278-0111 800-354-3049
jake@superiorstudio.com www.superiorstudio.com
Decorative items, lighting and theme props
Manager: Erin Allen
erin@superiorstudio.com
Estimated Sales: $1-5 Million
Number Employees: 5-9
Parent Co: Superior Specialties LLC

29814 Superklean Washdown Products
1550 Bryant Street
Suite 750
San Francisco, CA 94103-4877
415-252-2861
Fax: 415-255-2032 superkln@aol.com
Spray nozzles, hot and cold water mixer-hose stations, steam and cold water mixer-hose stations, swivel fittings, 3-piece fittings, and accessories

29815 Supermarket Associates
4209 Pin Oak Drive
Durham, NC 27707-5270
919-493-0994
Fax: 919-493-0994
Consultant specializing in advertising, marketing and management services for the food retailing industry
President: Sheldon Sosna
VP: Charles Ebner
Estimated Sales: $500,000-$1 Million
Number Employees: 1-4
Square Footage: 2000

29816 SuppliesForLess
905 G St
Hampton, VA 23661
757-245-7675
Fax: 757-244-4819 800-235-2201
Floating advertising balloons and blimps and flexible neon rope lights
Estimated Sales: $1-3 Million
Number Employees: 10-19
Square Footage: 243000
Brands:
  Bend-A-Lite
  Blimpy
  Giant

29817 Supply Corp
1351 Elkhorn Rd
Lake Geneva, WI 53147-1078
262-248-8837
Fax: 262-248-9530 800-558-2455
supplies@supplycorp.com www.supplycorp.com
Industrial safety, sanitation supplies, lubricants and tools for maintence, food processing supplies, cleaning supplies, brushes, mops, gloves, containers and material handling products
President: Rex Anderson
CEO: Roland Johnson
Sales: Rex Anderson
Number Employees: 5-9
Parent Co: Stand Alone Company

29818 Supply One Inc
12322 E 55th St
Tulsa, OK 74146
www.supplyone.com
Wholesaler/distributor of paper and plastic products, janitorial chemicalsand equipment; serving the food service market.
President & CEO: Bill Leith

29819 Supramatic
3313 Lakeshore Boulevard West
Toronto, ON M8W 1M8
Canada
416-251-3266
Fax: 416-251-1433 877-465-2883
info@supramatic.com www.supramatic.com
Manufacturer and importer of espresso, coffee and cappuccino machines; importer of coffee beans
President: Rene Peterson
Estimated Sales: Below $5 Million
Number Employees: 3

29820 Supreme Corporation
2572 East Kercher Road
Goshen, IN 46528
574-533-0331
Fax: 574-642-4729 800-642-4889
info@supremecorp.com
Manufacturer and exporter of refrigerators, freezers and refrigerated truck cars
CEO: Herbert M Gardner
VP Marketing/Sales: Rick Horn
Contact: David Allen
dallen@supre.com
Estimated Sales: $10-20 Million
Number Employees: 2
Type of Packaging: Bulk

29821 Supreme Corporation
5901 S 226th St
Kent, WA 98032-4861
253-395-8712
Fax: 253-395-8713
Synthetic wine closures, synthetic closures for specialty food bottles
President: Robert Anderson
CEO: Bob De Monte
Contact: Bob Anderson
banderson@supremecorq.com

Estimated Sales: $5-10 Million
Number Employees: 50-99

29822 Supreme Fabricators
19127 Pioneer Blvd Spc 18
Artesia, CA 90701
323-583-8944
Fax: 323-583-8946
Stainless steel tanks and automatic storage and handling systems
President: Dean Graves
Estimated Sales: $500,000-$1,000,000
Number Employees: 1-4

29823 Supreme Metal
3125 Trotters Parkway
Alpharetta, GA 30004-7746
Fax: 770-740-6010 800-645-2526
Manufacturer and exporter of stainless steel hot food tables, sinks, ice storage equipment and wait stations; also, bars, bins and glass racks
President: Rick Schwartz
VP Sales: Lisa Finegan
National Sales Manager: Sandy Hill
Contact: Talisha Hardy
talishahardy@gmail.com
Type of Packaging: Food Service

29824 Supreme Murphy Truck Bodies
4000 Airport Dr NW
Wilson, NC 27896
252-291-2191
Fax: 252-291-9183 800-334-2298
Refrigerated truck, trailer and van bodies
Estimated Sales: $10-25 Million
Number Employees: 100

29825 Supreme Products
PO Box 154308
Waco, TX 76715-4308
254-799-4941
Fax: 254-799-4943 sales@supremeproducts.com
Food and beverage concession trailers and vending carts.
President: Pat Hood
VP: Hugh Hood
Number Employees: 10
Square Footage: 70000
Brands:
  Supreme

29826 (HQ)Surco Products
290 Alpha Dr
RIDC Industrial Park
Pittsburgh, PA 15238
412-252-7000
Fax: 412-252-1005 800-556-0111
www.surcopt.com
Manufacturer and exporter of air fresheners, deodorants and insecticides
President: Arnold Zlotnik
CEO: Bernard Surloff
Estimated Sales: $10-20 Million
Number Employees: 50-99
Square Footage: 114000
Type of Packaging: Consumer, Private Label, Bulk
Brands:
  2-In-One Deodorizer
  24 Hour Odor Absorber
  Air-Savers
  Air-Scent
  Ban-O-Dor
  End Smoke
  Fresh As a Baby
  Garb-O-Flakes
  Odomaster
  Oh No!
  Potty Fresh
  Round the Clock
  Rug Aroma
  Sani-Aire
  Sani-Flakes
  Sani-Scent
  Scatter
  Scent-Flo
  So-Fresh
  Sta-Fresh
  Surco
  Surcota
  Zorb-It-All

29827 Sure Beam Corporation
9276 Scranton Rd Ste 600
San Diego, CA 92121
858-795-6300
Fax: 858-552-9973
Provider of electronic pasteurization systems and services
President: Terrance Bruggeman
Contact: Laura Peschel
lpeschel@surebeam.com
Number Employees: 50-99

29828 Sure Clean Corporation
PO Box 1
Two Rivers, WI 54241-0001
920-793-3838
Fax: 920-793-1555
Detergent, soap, household cleaners, etc
Estimated Sales: $1-5 Million

29829 Sure Kol Refrigerator
490 Flushing Ave
Brooklyn, NY 11205-1615
718-625-0601
Fax: 718-624-1719 surekol@hughes.net
www.surekol.com
Walk-in refrigerators
Owner: Jack Waslin
jwaslin@surekol.com
Estimated Sales: $2.5-5 Million
Number Employees: 10-19
Square Footage: 32000
Brands:
Sure-Kol

29830 Sure Shot Dispensing Systems
100 Dispensing Way
Lower Sackville, NS B4C 4H2
Canada
902-865-9602
Fax: 902-865-9604 888-777-4990
sales@sureshotdispensing.com
www.sureshotdispensing.com
President: Michael Duck
VP: David Macaulay
R&D: Ian Maclean
Quality Control: Peter Black
Marketing: Chad Wiesner
Sales: William Morris
Operations: Garth I
Production: Dennis Dickinson
Plant Manager: Ken Lawrence
Purchasing Director: Tracey S
Number Employees: 90
Square Footage: 260000

29831 Sure Torque
12100 West 6th Avenue
Lakewood, CO 80228
303-987-8000
Fax: 303-987-8989 800-387-6572
spearson@suretorque.com www.suretorque.com
Manufacturer and exporter of container closure torque measurement instruments including near and on-line, automatic and electronic
Owner: Michelle Bergeron
R&D: Steve Pearson
Technical Engineer: Tibor Szenti
Sales/Technical: Gloria LaCroix
Director Operations: Jeff Dubrow
Estimated Sales: Below $5 Million
Number Employees: 1-4
Square Footage: 5000
Brands:
Torque Tester

29832 Sure-Feed Engineering
12050 49th St N
Clearwater, FL 33762
727-571-3330
Fax: 727-571-3443 www.pb.com
Feeders, attaching systems
Sales/Marketing: Abe Mammau
Contact: Ron Kinney
ron.kinney@pb.com
Manager: Joe Springer
Estimated Sales: $1-2.5 Million
Number Employees: 100-249

29833 Surekap Inc
579 Barrow Park Dr
Winder, GA 30680-3417
770-867-5793
Fax: 770-867-5799 support@surekap.com
www.surekap.com
Manufacturer and exporter of liquid filling and bottle and capping equipment including plastic, metal, tamper evident, CRC, etc
President: John Antoine
john@surekap.com
Estimated Sales: $10-20 Million
Number Employees: 5-9

29834 Surface Measurement Systems
2125 28th St SW # 1
Suite 1
Allentown, PA 18103-7380
610-798-8299
Fax: 610-798-0334 sales@smsna.com
www.smsna.com
Automated laboratory systems measuring all materials for food industry
Manager: Joe Domingue
Director Sales/Marketing: Joe Domingue
Manager: Andrea Gimbar
agimbar@smsna.com
Estimated Sales: $1-5 Million
Number Employees: 10-19

29835 Surface Skil Corporation
3270 Homeward Way
Fairfield, OH 45014-4236
724-935-9020
Fax: 724-935-9010 800-228-5400
wjr@sgi.net
We clean concrete, install seamless resinous flooring systems for all types of food facilities
CFO: Phil Buda
Sales Director: Bill Esau

29836 Surfine Central Corporation
PO Box 5698
Pine Bluff, AR 71611-5698
870-247-2387
Fax: 870-247-9830
Paper bags
President: Bob Ratchford
Number Employees: 45

29837 Surtec Inc
1880 N Macarthur Dr
Tracy, CA 95376-2841
209-820-3700
Fax: 209-820-3793 800-877-6330
orderdesk@surtecsystem.com
www.surtecsystem.com
Manufacturer, importer and exporter of floor cleaning systems, chemicals and high-speed buffing machines
Owner: William Fields
CFO: Bill Haag
VP/Director Reaserch/Development: Don Fromm
Manager Sales: Kurt Grannis
william.fields@surtecsystem.com
Estimated Sales: $5-10 Million
Number Employees: 50-99
Square Footage: 140000

29838 Sus-Rap Protective Packaging
4010 Suburban Drive
Danville, VA 24540-6116
434-836-1666
Fax: 434-836-7606 800-558-7078
www.multiwall.com
Supplier of paper products
Manager: Melvin Shumate

29839 Sussman Electric Boilers
4320 34th St
Long Island City, NY 11101
718-937-4500
Fax: 718-937-4676 800-238-3535
seb@sussmancorp.com www.sussmanboilers.com
Manufacturer and exporter of electric boilers including steam, hot water, stainless steel and humidification, also, steam superheaters and steam-to-steam generators

President: Charles Monteverdi
Marketing: Louise Mound
Sales: Louise Mound
Production: Ben Cavanna
bcavanna@sussmancorp.com
Plant Manager: Ben Cavanna
Purchasing Manager: Arthur Perlman
Estimated Sales: $10-20 Million
Number Employees: 50-99
Parent Co: Sussman-Automatic Corporation
Brands:
Sussman

29840 Sutherland Stamp Company
PO Box 151319
San Diego, CA 92175-1319
858-233-7784
Fax: 858-233-0105
Badges, medals, plastic signs and rubber stamps
Owner: Richard Branch
Number Employees: 3

29841 Sutter Process Equipment
P.O.Box 5459
Walnut Creek, CA 94596-1459
925-937-1405
Fax: 707-642-2288 888-254-2060
Wine presses
Owner: Jerry Denham
Number Employees: 10-19
Square Footage: 88000
Parent Co: S.A. Juvenal
Type of Packaging: Private Label

29842 (HQ)Sutton Designs
215 N Cayuga Street
Ithaca, NY 14850-4329
607-277-4301
Fax: 607-277-6983 800-326-8119
Plexiglass counter cards, menu holders and displays
CFO: L Karro
VP Marketing: Dan Steele
Sales Director: Mark Miller
Purchasing Manager: Ned Ficher
Estimated Sales: $7.5 Million
Number Employees: 42
Number of Products: 350
Square Footage: 20000

29843 Suzhou-Chem Inc
396 Washington St
Suite 318
Wellesley, MA 02481
781-433-8618
Fax: 781-433-8619 info@suzhouchem.com
www.suzhouchem.com
Food and beverage ingredients including ascorbic acid, sodium ascorbate, calcium ascorbate, sodium saccharin granular, sodium saccharin dehydrate, sodium saccharin powder, calcium saccharin, insoluble saccharin, acesulfame-kaspartame, caffeine, potassium, sorbic acid, etc.
President: Joan Ni
Estimated Sales: $302 Million
Number Employees: 5-9
Type of Packaging: Bulk

29844 Svedala Industries
621 S Sierra Madre St
Colorado Springs, CO 80903-4016
719-471-3443
Fax: 719-471-4469 denversala@aol.com
www.metso.com
Manufacturer and exporter of thermal heat exchangers
Manager: Kirk Smith
Production Manager (Thermal Equipment): Siegfried Nierenz
Estimated Sales: $20-50 Million
Number Employees: 20-49
Brands:
Holo Flite

29845 Svedala Industries
621 S Sierra Madre St
Colorado Springs, CO 80903-4016
719-471-3443
Fax: 719-471-4469 denversala@aol.com
www.metso.com
Manufacturer and exporter of belt conveyor components for bulk material handling systems
Manager: Kirk Smith
Manager: Rick Pummell
Manager Sales Administration: Jim Danielson

Estimated Sales: $20-50 Million
Number Employees: 20-49
Parent Co: Svedala Industries

29846 Sverdrup Facilities
222 S Riverside Plz # 1400
Chicago, IL 60606-6001
312-416-0990
Fax: 312-416-1700 800-337-3239
Engineers, architects, planners, food technologists, sanitation specialists and construction experts, processing plants and productions systems
Contact: Jacob Prizer
jprizer@devereux.org
Estimated Sales: $5-10 Million
Number Employees: 20-49

29847 Sverdrup Facilities
801 N 11th Blvd
Saint Louis, MO 63102-1815
314-552-8339
Fax: 314-552-8453 800-325-7910
Consultant specializing in architecture, construction and engineering design services for sanitary processing facilities, etc
VP: Bill Vicary

29848 Svresearch
7429 Allentown Blvd
Harrisburg, PA 17112-3609
717-540-0370
Fax: 717-540-0380
President: Ron Lawson
Contact: Susan Baker
s.baker@seidenader.com
Estimated Sales: $3-5 Million
Number Employees: 20-49

29849 Swan Label & Tag Co
929 2nd Ave # A
PO Box 308
Coraopolis, PA 15108-1434
412-264-9000
Fax: 412-264-7259 info@swanlabel.com
Manufacturer and exporter of pressure sensitive labels and tags
President: Jill Clendenning
jill@swanlabel.com
Art/Graphic Department: Justin Kevish
Sales: Jill Clendenning
Customer Service: Gilda Clendenning
General Manager: Mike Chieski
Estimated Sales: $10-20 Million
Number Employees: 5-9

29850 Swancock Designworks
755 Sherri Court
Bosque Farms, NM 87068-9770
603-465-2015
Fax: 603-465-2015
Wine industry label design

29851 Swander Pace & Company
101 Mission Street
Suite 1900
San Francisco, CA 94105-1529
415-477-8500
Fax: 415-477-8510 info@spcap.com
www.spcap.com
Consultant offering strategy development, acquisitions and divestitures, market and competitive assessments, category management, salesforce optimization, etc
President: Bill Tace
Managing Director: Bill Pace
Managing Director: Todd Hooper
VP: Pete Boylan
Contact: Peter Boylan
peter@spcap.com
Estimated Sales: $5-10 Million
Number Employees: 20-49

29852 Swanson Wire Works Industries, Inc.
4229 Forney Rd
Mesquite, TX 75149
972-288-7465
Fax: 972-285-3030 swwind@prodigy.net
Powder coated and regular wire shelves, display racks and barbecue grills
President: David J Burroughs
VP: Ken Brunson

Estimated Sales: $5-10 Million
Number Employees: 20-49
Square Footage: 200000

29853 Sweco Inc
8029 Dixie Hwy
PO Box 1509
Florence, KY 41042-2941
859-371-4360
Fax: 859-283-8469 800-807-9326
info@sweco.com www.sweco.com
Manufacturer and exporter of FDA approved separation/screening equipment
President: David M Sorter
davidsorter@sweco.com
VP Engineering: Brad Jones
Marketing Manager: Jeff Dierig
Number Employees: 250-499
Parent Co: M-I LLC
Brands:
Supertaut Plus Ii
Vibro-Energy

29854 Sweet Manufacturing Co
2000 E Leffel Ln
PO Box 1086
Springfield, OH 45505-4625
937-325-1511
Fax: 937-322-1963 800-334-7254
sales@sweetmfg.com www.sweetmfg.com
Specialize in bulk material handling, conveying and processing equipment.
President/CEO: Alicia Sweet Hupp
Vice President: Julio Contreras
sales@sweetmfg.com
VP Marketing: Mike Gannon
VP Sales: Julio Contreras
Number Employees: 50-99
Square Footage: 140000
Brands:
Calormatic®
Filte-Veyor®
Gollath®
Quick-Key®
Silver-Grip®
Silver-Span®
Silver-Sweet®

29855 Sweetener Supply Corp
9501 Southview Ave
Brookfield, IL 60513-1529
708-588-8400
Fax: 708-588-8460 888-784-2799
sweetenersupply.com
Manufacturer and distributor of sweeteners for the food, beverage and confectionery industries.
Number Employees: 20-49
Number of Brands: 5
Brands:
Delicious™
Ridgeland™
Ambersweet
Sur Sweet™
Ultraclear™

29856 Sweeteners Plus Inc
5768 Sweeteners Blvd
Lakeville, NY 14480-9741
585-346-3193
Fax: 585-346-2310 www.sweetenersplus.com
Manufacturer and distributor of liquid and dry sweeteners including white and brown sugar, organic and kosher products, fructose, maltitol, corn syrup, and invert syrups. Also bottling, custom blending, and liquid fondants. Shippedregionally long haul by rail and short haul by trucks and nationally by distribution products
President & CEO: Carlton Myers
Quality Assurance Manager: Mark Rudolph
VP Sales: Mark Whitford
Operation Manager: Bill Devine
Estimated Sales: $14.7 Million
Number Employees: 1-4
Type of Packaging: Food Service, Bulk

29857 Sweetware
2821 Chapman St # A
Oakland, CA 94601-2133
510-436-8600
Fax: 510-436-8601 800-526-7900
inquiries@sweetware.com www.sweetware.com
Manufacturer and exporter of inventory control, order entry, invoicing, accounts receivable, recipe formula costing and nutrition analysis software

---

Owner: David Dunetz
info@sweetware.com
Estimated Sales: $500,000-$1 Million
Number Employees: 1-4
Brands:
Nutra Coster
Smallpics
Stock Coster

29858 Swift Creek Forest Products
20200 Patrick Henry Hwy
Jetersville, VA 23083-2118
804-561-4498
Fax: 804-561-6137
Pallets and skids
President: Scott Long
swftcreek@aol.com
Estimated Sales: $2.5-5 Million
Number Employees: 20-49

29859 (HQ)Swing-A-Way Manufacturing Company
4100 Beck Ave
St Louis, MO 63116-2694
314-773-1488
Fax: 314-773-5187
Manufacturer, importer and exporter of corkscrews, ice crushers and can and jar openers
President: Dorothy Rhodes
Estimated Sales: $10-20 Million
Number Employees: 50-99
Square Footage: 250000
Type of Packaging: Consumer
Other Locations:
Swing-A-Way Manufacturing Co.
Saint Louis MO
Brands:
Swing-A-Way

29860 Swirl Freeze Corp
1261 S Redwood Rd # H
Salt Lake City, UT 84104-3705
801-886-1196
Fax: 801-973-7620 800-262-4275
sales@swirlfreeze.com www.swirlfreeze.com
Manufacturer and exporter of ice cream and frozen yogurt blending machinery
President: D Heinhold
Vice President: K Heinhold
Marketing Director: D Savage
Estimated Sales: $1 Million
Number Employees: 1-4
Number of Brands: 1
Number of Products: 6
Square Footage: 30000
Type of Packaging: Consumer
Brands:
Swirl Freeze

29861 Swirl Freeze Corp
1261 S Redwood Rd # H
Unit H
Salt Lake City, UT 84104-3705
801-886-1196
Fax: 801-973-7620 800-262-4275
sales@swirlfreeze.com www.swirlfreeze.com
Supplier of ice cream and frozen yogurt blending machinery
President: Duane Heinhold
VP: Ken Heinhold
Estimated Sales: $.5-1 million
Number Employees: 1-4
Square Footage: 30000

29862 Swisher Hygiene
4725 Piedmont Row Drive
Suite 400
Charlotte, NC 28210
908-353-8500
Fax: 908-353-6752 800-444-4138
contact@swsh.com www.swsh.com
Manufacturer and exporter of dishwashing and laundry products
President: Norman Lubin
Vice President: Mark Sherman
Contact: Bill Ainsley
bainsley@swsh.com
Estimated Sales: $10-20 Million
Number Employees: 50-99
Type of Packaging: Food Service
Brands:
Sanolite

29863 Swissh Commercial Equipment
5520 Chabot 203
Montreal, QC H2H 2S7
Canada
514-524-6005
Fax: 514-524-3305 888-794-7749
info@swissh.ca www.swissh.com
Technologically advanced dishwashers.
President: Bruno O Frank
Marketing: Elyse Pastor
Production: Miguel Viche
Number Employees: 7
Number of Brands: 4
Number of Products: 50
Square Footage: 16000
Brands:
Swissh

29864 Swisslog Logistics Inc
161 Enterprise Dr
Newport News, VA 23603-1369
757-887-8080
Fax: 757-887-5588 800-777-6862
www.swisslog.com
Manufacturer and exporter of integrated and auto-
mated material handling software and equipment
President: Karl Puehringer
Chief Executive Officer: Remo Brunschwiler
Sr. VP Marketing: Brad Moore
Estimated Sales: $20-50 Million
Number Employees: 50-99
Square Footage: 50000
Parent Co: Swisslog

29865 Swisslog Logistics Inc
161 Enterprise Dr
Newport News, VA 23603-1369
757-887-8080
Fax: 757-887-5588 800-783-9840
wds.us@swisslog.com www.swisslog.com
President: Karl Puehringer
Chairman: Hans Ziegler
CFO: Christian M,,der
Estimated Sales: $5-10 Million
Number Employees: 50-99

29866 Swivelier Co Inc
600 Bradley Hill Rd # 3
Blauvelt, NY 10913-1171
845-353-1455
Fax: 845-353-1512 info@swivelier.com
www.swivelier.com
Lighting, including track, low-voltage display,
clamp-on, display and accent, lighting fixtures, light
converters and extenders
President: I Schucker
is@swive.com
VP Manufacturing: Gerard Phelan
Estimated Sales: $5-10 Million
Number Employees: 1-4
Square Footage: 480000
Brands:
Convert-A-Lite
Cozy-Lite
Litestrip
Star Track
Swivelier

29867 Sybo Composites LLC
404 Riberia St
St Augustine, FL 32084-5108
904-599-7093
Fax: 937-746-9706 800-874-4088
Manager: Martin South
Sales Director: Pam South
Number Employees: 1-4
Square Footage: 20000

29868 Sycamore Containers
215 Fair St
Sycamore, IL 60178
815-895-2343
Fax: 815-895-5555 www.landsberg.com
President: Lawrence Kendzora
Contact: Craig Bates
cbates@landsberg.com
Manufacturing Executive: Marvin Barnes
Estimated Sales: $10-15 Million
Number Employees: 20-49

29869 (HQ)Syfan USA Corporation
PO Box 203
Everetts, NC 27825-0212
877-792-2547
Fax: 252-792-3185 www.syfanusa.com
Packaging, shrink films, over wrap, bread bags, skin
films
Executive V.P: Ramy Diga
President: Frank Marrowitz
Product Development Manager: Alan Castle
Regional Manager: Bruce Paster
Contact: Alaine Chesson
alaine@syfanmfg.com
Estimated Sales: $1-2.5 Million
Number Employees: 10
Type of Packaging: Consumer, Food Service, Pri-
vate Label

29870 Symmetry Products Group
55 Industrial Cir
Lincoln, RI 02865-2643
401-365-6272
Fax: 401-365-6273 www.symmetryproducts.com
Manufacturer and exporter of signs; also, theme and
architectural designing available
President: Steven Lancia
Marketing Director: Justine Ruizzo
Sales Director: Rich Dowd
Plant Manager: Tony Chernasky
Estimated Sales: $20-50 Million
Number Employees: 100-249
Square Footage: 150000
Parent Co: Lance Industries

29871 Sympak, Inc.
1385 Armour Blvd.
Mundelein, IL 60060
847-247-0182
Fax: 847-247-0184 sympak-usa@sympak.com
www.sympak-usa.com
Processing and packaging equipment for the dairy,
confectionery/baking industries and convenience
stores.
Contact: Erich Weirich
eric.weirich-usa@sympak.com
Number Employees: 600

29872 Symtech,Inc
P.O. Box 2627
Spartanburg, SC 29304-2627
219-477-4554
Fax: 219-464-3352 www.strayfieldfastran.co.uk
Contact: Alberto Beani
abeani@symtech-usa.com

29873 Synchro-Systems Technology
4563 Nance Road
Stanfield, NC 28163-8630
704-888-6407
Fax: 704-888-5080
Indexing, collating, and accumulating machinery,
auto-loaders

29874 Syngenta
P.O. Box 18300
Greensboro, NC 27419
800-334-9481
www.syngenta-us.com
Offers products and services for growers concerning
crop protection, seed treatments, planting, pest solu-
tions, and sustainability.
CEO: J. Erik Fyrwald
Year Founded: 2000
Number Employees: 28,000

29875 Synthron Inc.
420 W Fleming Drive
Suite C
Morganton, NC 28655-3966
828-437-8611
Fax: 828-437-4126
Processor and exporter of detergents and oil and wax
emulsifying agents
President: Raymond Pinard
Estimated Sales: $5-10 Million
Number Employees: 10-19
Type of Packaging: Bulk

29876 Syracuse China Company
2801 Court St
Syracuse, NY 13208-3241
315-455-5671
Fax: 315-455-6763 800-448-5711
www.libbey.com

China
President: Charles S Goodman
Contact: Christopher Novak
chris.novak@libbey.com
Estimated Sales: Below $500,000
Number Employees: 500-999
Parent Co: Libbey

29877 Syracuse Label Co
110 Luther Ave
Liverpool, NY 13088-6726
315-422-1037
Fax: 315-422-6763 www.syrlabel.com
Pressure sensitive labels
President: Kathy Alamio
kathy@syrlabel.com
Estimated Sales: $20-50 Million
Number Employees: 100-249

29878 (HQ)Sysco Corp
1390 Enclave Pkwy
Houston, TX 77077
281-584-1390
Fax: 281-584-1737 800-337-9726
www.sysco.com
Food products, equipment and supplies for the food
service industry
President/CEO: Tom Ben,
Chairman: Jackie Ward
EVP/Chief Financial Officer: Joel Grade
SVP/Chief Accounting Officer: Anita Zielinski
SVP/Merchandising: Brian Todd
SVP/Sysco Labs & Customer Experience: Brian
Beach
EVP/Supply Chain: Scott Charlton
SVP/Sales & Marketing: Bill Goetz
EVP/Administration & Corp. Secretary: Russell
Libby
SVP/US Foodservice Operations: Greg Bertrand
Year Founded: 1969
Estimated Sales: $59 Billion
Number Employees: 67,000
Type of Packaging: Food Service

29879 Sysco Corp
1 Sysco Dr
Lincoln, IL 62656-0620
217-735-6100
Food products, equipment and supplies for the food
service industry
Type of Packaging: Food Service

29880 Sysco Corp
1 Liebich Ln
Halfmoon, NY 12065-1421
518-877-3200
Food products, equipment and supplies for the food
service industry
Type of Packaging: Food Service

29881 Sysco Corp
601 Comanche Rd NE
Albuquerque, NM 87107
505-761-1200
Food products, equipment and supplies for the food
service industry
Type of Packaging: Food Service

29882 Sysco Corp
4500 Corporate Dr NW
Concord, NC 28027
704-786-4500
Food products, equipment and supplies for the food
service industry
Type of Packaging: Food Service

29883 Sysco Corp
4000 W 62nd St
Indianapolis, IN 46268-2518
317-291-2020
Food products, equipment and supplies for the food
service industry
Type of Packaging: Food Service

29884 Sysco Corp
1509 Monad Rd
Billings, MT 59107
406-247-1100
Food products, equipment and supplies for the food
service industry
Type of Packaging: Food Service

29885 Sysco Corp
7705 National Tpke
Louisville, KY 40214
502-364-4300
Food products, equipment and supplies for the food service industry
Type of Packaging: Food Service

29886 Sysco Corp
136 S Mariposa Rd
Modesto, CA 95354
209-527-7700
Food products, equipment and supplies for the food service industry
Type of Packaging: Food Service

29887 Sysco Corp
1951 E Kansas City Rd
Olathe, KS 66061
913-829-5555
Food products, equipment and supplies for the food service industry
Type of Packaging: Food Service

29888 Sysco Corp
600 Packer Ave
Philadelphia, PA 19148
215-463-8200
Food products, equipment and supplies for the food service industry
Type of Packaging: Food Service

29889 Sysco Corp
900 Kingbird Rd
Lincoln, NE 68521
402-423-1031
Food products, equipment and supplies for the food service industry
Type of Packaging: Food Service

29890 Sysco Corp
250 Wieboldt Dr
Des Plaines, IL 60016-3192
847-699-5400
Food products, equipment and supplies for the food service industry
Type of Packaging: Food Service

29891 Sysco Corp
20 Theodore Conrad Dr
Jersey City, NJ 07305
201-433-2000
Food products, equipment and supplies for the food service industry
Type of Packaging: Food Service

29892 Sysco Corp
9494 S Prosperity Rd
West Jordan, UT 84081
801-563-6300
Food products, equipment and supplies for the food service industry
Type of Packaging: Food Service

29893 Sysco Corp
10710 Greens Crossing Blvd
Houston, TX 77038
713-672-8080
Food products, equipment and supplies for the food service industry
Type of Packaging: Food Service

29894 Sysco Corp
10510 Evendale Dr
Cincinnati, OH 45241
513-563-6300
Food products, equipment and supplies for the food service industry
Type of Packaging: Food Service

29895 Sysco Corp
714 2nd Pl
Lubbock, TX 79401
806-747-2678
Food products, equipment and supplies for the food service industry
Type of Packaging: Food Service

29896 Sysco Corp
2400 County Road J
St Paul, MN 55112
763-785-9000
Food products, equipment and supplies for the food service industry
Type of Packaging: Food Service

29897 Sysco Corp
6601 Changepoint Dr
Anchorage, AK 99518
907-565-5567
Food products, equipment and supplies for the food service industry
Type of Packaging: Food Service

29898 Sysco Corp
3700 Sysco Ct SE
Grand Rapids, MI 49512-2083
616-949-3700
Food products, equipment and supplies for the food service industry
Type of Packaging: Food Service

29899 Sysco Corp
5000 Beeler St
Denver, CO 80238
303-585-2000
Food products, equipment and supplies for the food service industry
Type of Packaging: Food Service

29900 Sysco Corp
99 Spring St
Plympton, MA 02367
781-422-2300
Food products, equipment and supplies for the food service industry
Type of Packaging: Food Service

29901 Sysco Corp
1451 River Oaks Rd W
Harahan, LA 70123
504-731-1015
Food products, equipment and supplies for the food service industry
Type of Packaging: Food Service

29902 Sysco Corp
3905 Corey Rd
Harrisburg, PA 17109
717-561-4000
Food products, equipment and supplies for the food service industry
Type of Packaging: Food Service

29903 Sysco Corp
1000 Sysco Dr
Calera, AL 35040
205-668-0001
Food products, equipment and supplies for the food service industry
Type of Packaging: Food Service

29904 Sysco Corp
One Whitney Drive
Harmony, PA 16037
724-452-2100
Food products, equipment and supplies for the food service industry
Type of Packaging: Food Service

29905 Sysco Corp
8000 Dorsey Run Rd
Jessup, MD 20794
410-799-7000
Food products, equipment and supplies for the food service industry
Type of Packaging: Food Service

29906 Sysco Corp
4400 Milwaukee St
Jackson, MS 39209-2636
601-354-1701
Food products, equipment and supplies for the food service industry
Type of Packaging: Food Service

29907 Sysco Corp
4359 B.F. Goodrich Blvd
Memphis, TN 38118-7306
901-795-2300
Food products, equipment and supplies for the food service industry
Type of Packaging: Food Service

29908 Sysco Corp
2225 Riverdale Rd
College Park, GA 30337
404-765-9900
Food products, equipment and supplies for the food service industry
Type of Packaging: Food Service

29909 Sysco Corp
33300 Peach Orchard Rd
Pocomoke, MD 21851
410-677-5555
Food products, equipment and supplies for the food service industry
Type of Packaging: Food Service

29910 Sysco Corp
1350 W Tecumseh Rd
Norman, OK 73069-8200
405-717-2700
Food products, equipment and supplies for the food service industry
Type of Packaging: Food Service

29911 Sysco Corp
5710 Pan Am Ave
Boise, ID 83716
208-345-9500
Food products, equipment and supplies for the food service industry
Type of Packaging: Food Service

29912 Sysco Corp
20701 E Currier Rd
Walnut, CA 91789
909-595-9595
Food products, equipment and supplies for the food service industry
Type of Packaging: Food Service

29913 Sysco Corp
22820 54th Ave S
Kent, WA 98032-4898
206-622-2261
Food products, equipment and supplies for the food service industry
Type of Packaging: Food Service

29914 Sysco Corp
26250 SW Parkway Center Dr
Wilsonville, OR 97070
503-682-8700
Food products, equipment and supplies for the food service industry
Type of Packaging: Food Service

29915 Sysco Corp
611 S 80th Ave
Tolleson, AZ 85353
623-936-9920
Food products, equipment and supplies for the food service industry
Type of Packaging: Food Service

29916 Sysco Corp
131 Sysco Ct
Columbia, SC 29209
803-239-4000
Food products, equipment and supplies for the food service industry
Type of Packaging: Food Service

29917 Sysco Corp
100 Inwood Rd
Rocky Hill, CT 06067-3422
860-571-5600
Food products, equipment and supplies for the food service industry
Type of Packaging: Food Service

29918 Sysco Corp
800 Trinity Drive
Lewisville, TX 75056
769-384-6000
Food products, equipment and supplies for the food service industry
Type of Packaging: Food Service

29919 Sysco Corp
4577 Estes Pkwy
Longview, TX 75603-0900
903-252-6100
Food products, equipment and supplies for the food service industry
Type of Packaging: Food Service

29920 Sysco Corp
1 Sysco Dr
Jackson, WI 53037
262-677-1100
Food products, equipment and supplies for the food service industry
Type of Packaging: Food Service

29921 Sysco Corp
2001 W Magnolia Ave
Geneva, AL 36340
334-684-4000
Food products, equipment and supplies for the food service industry
Type of Packaging: Food Service

29922 Sysco Corp
7000 Harbour View Blvd
Suffolk, VA 23435
757-673-4000
Food products, equipment and supplies for the food service industry
Type of Packaging: Food Service

29923 Sysco Corp
1501 Lewis Industrial Dr
Jacksonville, FL 32254
904-786-2600
Food products, equipment and supplies for the food service industry
Type of Packaging: Food Service

29924 Sysco Corp
900 Tennessee Ave
Knoxville, TN 37921-2630
865-545-5600
Food products, equipment and supplies for the food service industry
Type of Packaging: Food Service

29925 Sysco Corp
1 Hermitage Plz
Nashville, TN 37209
615-350-7100
Food products, equipment and supplies for the food service industry
Type of Packaging: Food Service

29926 Sysco Corp
3225 12th Ave N
Fargo, ND 58102
701-293-8900
Food products, equipment and supplies for the food service industry
Type of Packaging: Food Service

29927 Sysco Corp
1032 Baugh Rd
Selma, NC 27576
919-755-2455
Food products, equipment and supplies for the food service industry
Type of Packaging: Food Service

29928 Sysco Corp
7062 Pacific Ave
Pleasant Grove, CA 95668
916-569-7000
Food products, equipment and supplies for the food service industry
Type of Packaging: Food Service

29929 Sysco Corp
12180 Kirkham Rd
Poway, CA 92064
858-513-7300
Food products, equipment and supplies for the food service industry
Type of Packaging: Food Service

29930 Sysco Corp
1999 Dr Martin Luther King Jr Blvd
Riviera Beach, FL 33404
561-842-1999
Food products, equipment and supplies for the food service industry
Type of Packaging: Food Service

29931 Sysco Corp
300 N Baugh Way
Post Falls, ID 83854
208-777-9511
Food products, equipment and supplies for the food service industry
Type of Packaging: Food Service

29932 Sysco Corp
3100 Sturgis Rd
Oxnard, CA 93030
877-205-9800
Food products, equipment and supplies for the food service industry
Type of Packaging: Food Service

29933 Sysco Corp
5900 Stewart Ave
Fremont, CA 94538
510-226-3000
Food products, equipment and supplies for the food service industry
Type of Packaging: Food Service

29934 Sysco Corp
910 South Blvd
Baraboo, WI 53913-2793
608-356-8711
Food products, equipment and supplies for the food service industry
Type of Packaging: Food Service

29935 Sysco Corp
4747 Grayton Rd
Cleveland, OH 44135
216-201-3000
Food products, equipment and supplies for the food service industry
Type of Packaging: Food Service

29936 Sysco Corp
41600 Van Born Rd
Canton, MI 48188-2797
734-397-7990
Food products, equipment and supplies for the food service industry
Type of Packaging: Food Service

29937 Sysco Corp
5800 Frozen Rd
Little Rock, AR 72209
501-562-4111
Food products, equipment and supplies for the food service industry
Type of Packaging: Food Service

29938 Sysco Corp
1260 Schwab Rd
New Braunfels, TX 78132
830-730-1000
Food products, equipment and supplies for the food service industry
Type of Packaging: Food Service

29939 Sysco Corp
12500 NW 112th Ave
Medley, FL 33178
305-651-5421
Food products, equipment and supplies for the food service industry
Type of Packaging: Food Service

29940 Sysco Corp
1 Sysco Pl
Ankeny, IA 50021
515-289-5300
Food products, equipment and supplies for the food service industry
Type of Packaging: Food Service

29941 Sysco Corp
200 Story Rd
Ocoee, FL 34761
407-877-8500
Food products, equipment and supplies for the food service industry
Type of Packaging: Food Service

29942 Sysco Corp
2508 Warners Rd
Warners, NY 13164
315-672-7000
800-736-6000
Food products, equipment and supplies for the food service industry
Type of Packaging: Food Service

29943 Sysco Corp
5081 S Valley Pike
Harrisonburg, VA 22801
540-434-0761
Food products, equipment and supplies for the food service industry
Type of Packaging: Food Service

29944 Sysco Corp
36 Thomas Dr
Westbrook, ME 04092
207-871-0700
Food products, equipment and supplies for the food service industry

Type of Packaging: Food Service

29945 Sysco Corp
3850 Mueller Rd
St Charles, MO 63301
636-940-9230
Food products, equipment and supplies for the food service industry
Type of Packaging: Food Service

29946 Sysco Corp
15750 Meridian Pkwy
Riverside, CA 92518
951-601-5300
Food products, equipment and supplies for the food service industry
Type of Packaging: Food Service

29947 Sysco Corp
199 Lowell Ave
Central Islip, NY 11722
631-342-7400
Food products, equipment and supplies for the food service industry
Type of Packaging: Food Service

29948 Sysco Corp
900 Hwy 10 S
St Cloud, MN 56304
320-251-3200
Food products, equipment and supplies for the food service industry
Type of Packaging: Food Service

29949 Sysco Corp
3000 69th St E
Palmetto, FL 34221
941-721-1450
Food products, equipment and supplies for the food service industry
Type of Packaging: Food Service

29950 Sysco Corp
6201 E Centennial Pkwy
Las Vegas, NV 89115
702-632-1800
Food products, equipment and supplies for the food service industry
Type of Packaging: Food Service

29951 Systech Illinois
2401 Hiller Rdg
Suite A
Johnsburg, IL 60051
815-344-6212
Fax: 815-344-6332
illinstr@illinoisinstruments.com
www.systechillinois.com
President: Brian Cummings
Contact: Donna Palmer
d.palmer@systechillinois.com
Estimated Sales: $5-10 Million
Number Employees: 20-49

29952 Systech International
2540 US Highway 130
Suit 128
Cranbury, NJ 08512-3519
609-235-0004
Fax: 609-395-0064 800-847-7123
www.systech-tips.com
President: Robert Dejean
CFO: Kenith Kirktatrick
Director of Sales: Paulo Machado
Contact: Joseph Costa
joseph@systech.com
Number Employees: 1-4

29953 System Concepts Inc
15900 N 78th St # 201
Scottsdale, AZ 85260-1215
480-951-8011
Fax: 480-951-2807 800-553-2438
ftsales@foodtrak.com www.foodtrak.com
SCI's FOOD-TRAK® System is a food & beverage management system that enables foodservice operations to increase purchasing and accounting efficiencies; reduce cost of goods and increase asset security.
President/Founder: William Schwartz
CEO: Bill Schwartz
bills@foodtrak.com
Estimated Sales: Below $5 Million
Number Employees: 20-49

Brands:
  Food-Trak

29954 System Graphics Inc
1530 S Kingshighway Blvd
St Louis, MO 63110-2228
     314-773-4151
    Fax: 314-773-3338 800-221-7858
labels@systemsgraphics.com
www.systemsgraphics.com
Pressure sensitive and paper labels for food products
President: Martin Daly
martindaly@systemsgraphics.com
Estimated Sales: $2.5-5 Million
Number Employees: 20-49

29955 System Packaging
28905 Glenwood Rd
PO Box 109
Perrysburg, OH 43551-3020
     419-666-9712
  Fax: 419-666-1549 sales@systempackaging.com
www.systempackaging.com
Owner: Tom Ziems
tsz@glassline.com
Estimated Sales: $1-5 Million
Number Employees: 5-9

29956 System Plast
130 Wicker St
Suite B
Sanford, NC 27330-4265
     919-775-5716
    Fax: 919-775-5720 800-726-2630
info@systemplast.com www.solusii.com
CEO: Garland Jones
Estimated Sales: $1-5 Million
Number Employees: 10-19

29957 System-Plast
2000 Boone Trail Rd
Sanford, NC 27330
     919-775-5716
    Fax: 919-775-5720 info@systemplast.com
www.systemplast.com
Conveyor components
Member: Sergio Marcitti
CEO: Garland Jones
Vice President-Finance: Marco Manzoni
Director of Engineering: Ted Van Der Hoeven
VP Marketing & Sales: Dick Overtoom
Procurement Manager: Stephan Petzold
Estimated Sales: $5-10 Million
Number Employees: 10-19

29958 Systemate Numafa
6390 Hickory Flat Hwy
Canton, GA 30115-9224
     770-345-1055
    Fax: 770-345-5926 800-240-3770
www.carnetts.com
Industrial washing systems, tote washers, pallet
washers, tray washers, rack washers, drum washers,
vat washers
Manager: Michael Warren
National Sales Manager: Scott Hazenbroek
Number Employees: 20-49

29959 Systems Comtrex
101 Foster Rd # B
Moorestown, NJ 08057-1118
     856-778-9322
    Fax: 856-778-9322 800-220-2669
Sales@Comtrex.com www.comtrex.co.uk
Manufacturer and exporter of point of sale terminals,
peripherals and software
CEO: Duane Reed
duane.reed@comtrex.co.uk
CEO: Jefferey C Rice
Estimated Sales: $1-3,000,000
Number Employees: 10-19
Type of Packaging: Food Service
Brands:
  Comtrex
  Pcs5000 System

29960 Systems IV
6641 W Frye Rd
Chandler, AZ 85226
    Fax: 480-961-1247 800-852-4221
sales@systemsiv.com www.systemsiv.com
Manufacturer and exporter of food service water
treatment systems for ice makers, steamers, coffee
machines, proofers, misters and post mix systems

President: Leroy Terry
Quality Control: Dave Terry
Manager Sales/Marketing: Sean Terry
Contact: David Terry
davecterry@gmail.com
Number Employees: 20-49
Brands:
  System Iv

29961 Systems Modeling Corporation
504 Beaver St
Sewickley, PA 15143
     412-741-3727
    Fax: 412-741-5635 www.rockwell.com
Simulation and scheduling software
President: Keith Bush
Estimated Sales: $20-50 Million
Number Employees: 10

29962 Systems Online
1001 NW 62nd St
Fort Lauderdale, FL 33309-1900
     954-840-3467
    Fax: 954-376-3338 support@sysonline.com
www.sysonline.com
EZ Trade, the ultimate forms based e-trading solu-
tion/distribution management software DiMan for
Windows95/98,2000; e-commerce, inventory, sales,
purchasing, accounting
Estimated Sales: $1-2.5 Million
Number Employees: 1-4

29963 Systems Technology Inc
1351 Riverview Dr
San Bernardino, CA 92408-2945
     909-799-9950
    Fax: 909-796-8297
info@systems-technology-inc.com
www.systems-technology-inc.com
Manufacturer and exporter of packaging machinery
President: John G St John
johnstjohn@systems-technology-inc.com
CFO: Steve Fox
Estimated Sales: $10-20 Million
Number Employees: 20-49
Square Footage: 80000
Parent Co: Baldwin Technology Corporation

29964 Systems Technology Inc
1351 Riverview Dr
San Bernardino, CA 92408-2945
     909-799-9950
    Fax: 909-796-8297
info@systems-technology-inc.com
www.systems-technology-inc.com
STI, Systems Technology has been a worldwide
leader in packing machinery for over 30 years. Our
high-speed wraparound cartoning technology for the
automated packaging of books, CDs, DVD's videos,
and a varitey of other products in arange of protective corrugated carton blanks has made us a preferred supplier in the fulfillment industry
President: John G St John
johnstjohn@systems-technology-inc.com
Controller: Steve Fox
Estimated Sales: $20-50 Million
Number Employees: 20-49

29965 T & A Metal Products Inc
1671 Hurffville Rd
Deptford, NJ 8096
     856-227-1700
    Fax: 856-227-1805
Stainless steel kitchen equipment
Owner: Nicholas Demarco
Estimated Sales: $5-10 Million
Number Employees: 5-9

29966 T & C Stainless
1016 Progress Rd
Mt Vernon, MO 65712-1057
     417-466-4704
    Fax: 417-466-4705 Sales@TC-Stainless.com
www.tcstainless.com
President: Terry L Cook
terryc@tc-stainless.com
Estimated Sales: $5-10 Million
Number Employees: 20-49

29967 T & M Distributing Co
12 Sunset Way
Henderson, NV 89014-2003
     702-458-1962
    Fax: 702-458-1160 www.rallyshirts.com

Flags, pennants and banners
Owner: Mitchell Patton
m.patton@rallyshirts.com
Estimated Sales: Less Than $500,000
Number Employees: 1-4

29968 (HQ)T & S Brass & Bronze Work
2 Saddleback Cv
Travelers Rest, SC 29690-2232
     864-834-4102
    Fax: 864-834-3518 800-476-4103
tsbrass@tsbrass.com www.tsbrass.com
T&S produces a full line of faucets, fittings, and
specialty products for the food service, industrial,
commercial plumbing, and laboratory markets all
across the world.
President: I Claude Theisen
CEO: Claude Theisen
claudetheisen@tsbrass.com
Vice President: Craig Ashton
Research & Development: Jeff Baldwin
Quality Control: Gary Cole
Marketing Director: Eva Fox
Sales Director: Ken Gallagher
Public Relations: Mary Alice Bowers
Operations Manager: Bob Clemment
Assembly Supervisor: David Whitlock
Purchasing Manager: Steve Abercrombie
Estimated Sales: $20-50 Million
Number Employees: 250-499
Type of Packaging: Consumer, Food Service, Pri-
vate Label, Bulk
Brands:
  Sage
  T&S Brass and Bronze

29969 T & S Brass & Bronze Work
2 Saddleback Cv
PO Box 1088
Travelers Rest, SC 29690-2232
     864-834-4102
    Fax: 864-834-3518 800-476-4103
www.tsbrass.com
T&S produces a full line of faucets, fittings and specialty products for the foodservice, industrial, commercial plumbing, and laboratory markets.
President: Claude Theisen
claudetheisen@tsbrass.com
Number Employees: 250-499
Type of Packaging: Consumer, Food Service, Private Label, Bulk

29970 T & S Perfection Chain Prods
301 Goodwin Rd
Cullman, AL 35058-0307
     256-734-6538
    Fax: 256-734-1610 888-856-4864
info@tsperfection.com www.tsperfection.com
Manufacturers welded and weldless chains and
chain accessories. Also, upholstery nails, furniture
glides, escutcheon pins and commercial can openers
President: Tom Pretak
VP Human Resources: Carol Soliani
CFO: Ken Rizzi
Chairman of the Board: Allen M Sperry Sr
VP Sales: Frank Silano
Estimated Sales: $10-20 Million
Number Employees: 50-99
Square Footage: 200000
Type of Packaging: Food Service

29971 T & T Industries Inc
5070 S Highway 95
Fort Mohave, AZ 86426-7200
     928-768-4511
    Fax: 928-768-4766 800-437-6246
tandtinc@pacbell.net www.twistems.com
Manufactures paper, foil & plastic twist ties
President: John Vaughan
COO: John Mayberry
CFO: John Mayberry
R&D: Pat Clemmons
Quality Control: Art Vigil
Director Sales/Marketing: Jim Doherty
Number Employees: 20-49
Brands:
  Twis-Tags
  Twist-Ems

29972 T & T Valve & Instrument Inc
1181 Quarry Ln # 150
Suite 150
Pleasanton, CA 94566-8458
925-484-4898
Fax: 925-484-4727 sales@tt-valve.com
www.tt-valve.com
Wine industry valves
President: Sanford B Wolfe
Engineering Support, Design & Major Proj: Sanford
Wolfe
Sales Manager: Delain Murphy
Office Manager: Terri Stark
tstark@willisseafood.net
Inventory Control, Purchasing: Javier Cendejas
Estimated Sales: $1-5 Million
Number Employees: 5-9

29973 T D Sawvel Co
5775 Highway 12
Maple Plain, MN 55359-9777
763-479-4322
Fax: 763-479-3517 877-488-1816
www.sawvelautomation.com
Manufacturer and exporter of denesters, fillers, sealers and lidders for plastic and paper containers for
dairy and nondairy products; also, blenders,
variegators, inline and rotary machines; custom design services available
President: Troy Sawvel
troy@tdsawvel.com
Estimated Sales: $1-3 Million
Number Employees: 10-19
Square Footage: 32000
Brands:
    Bottomup

29974 T E Ibberson Co
828 5th St S
Hopkins, MN 55343-7785
952-938-7007
Fax: 952-939-0451 tei@ibberson.com
www.ibberson.com
Consultant specializing in design, engineering and
construction services for new or expanding food and
oil seed processing plants
President: Mark Geitzenauer
mark.geitzenauer@ibberson.com
Vice President: Gerry Leukam
Marketing: Glenn Higgins
Estimated Sales: $1-5 Million
Number Employees: 100-249
Square Footage: 90000
Parent Co: The Industrial Company

29975 T E Ibberson Co
828 5th St S
Hopkins, MN 55343-7785
952-938-7007
Fax: 952-939-0451 tei@ibberson.com
www.ibberson.com
Design, engineering and construction services
President: Mark Geitzenauer
mark.geitzenauer@ibberson.com
Estimated Sales: $1-3 Million
Number Employees: 100-249

29976 T J Smith Box Co
515 S I St
PO Box 1643
Fort Smith, AR 72901-4323
479-782-8275
Fax: 479-782-8276 877-540-7933
Folding and set-up paper boxes
Owner: Chris Hahn
tjsmithboxcompany@gmail.com
Estimated Sales: $2.5-5 Million
Number Employees: 20-49
Type of Packaging: Consumer, Food Service, Pri-
vate Label, Bulk

29977 T Q Constructors
911 2nd Ave
Dayton, KY 41074-1203
859-655-6700
Fax: 859-655-6704 888-655-0300
mail@tqconstructors.com www.tqconstructors.com
TQ provides total quality mechanical process system
fabrication and installation for the food, beverage,
cosmetic, and pharmaceutical industries.

Project Director: Kent Fennell
kfennell@tqconstructors.com
National Account Manager: David Cauley
Vice President: John Bardo
Project Engineer: Greg Dennis
Local Account Manager: Larry Schuler
Regional Account Manager: Tom Burkhart
Operations Manager: Bill Sharkey
Number Employees: 50-99

29978 T&G Machinery
Unit 5
Orangeville, ON L9W 4N6
Canada
519-940-3527
Fax: 519-940-4558

29979 T&S Blow Molding
117 Simott Road
Scarborough, ON M1P 4S6
Canada
416-752-8330
Fax: 416-752-1909
Manufacturer and exporter of plastic bottles and jars
President: Donald Seaton
CEO: Peter Barker
CFO: Eric Lakien
Sales: Donna Strong
Plant Manager: Grant Ross
Estimated Sales: $14 Million
Number Employees: 10
Number of Brands: 5
Number of Products: 300
Square Footage: 136000
Type of Packaging: Consumer, Food Service, Pri-
vate Label, Bulk

29980 T-Drill Industries Inc
1740 Corporate Dr # 820
Norcross, GA 30093-2934
770-381-4460
Fax: 770-925-3912 800-554-2730
sales@t-drill.com www.t-drill.fi
Pipe and tube fabricating equipment
President: Kenny Dockins
rperez@aflac.com
Vice President: Mark Sanders
Industrial Sales: John Hodges
Estimated Sales: $2.8 Million
Number Employees: 10-19

29981 T.D. Rowe Company
18890 S Susana Road
Compton, CA 90221-5706
310-639-6710
Fax: 310-604-3227
Vending machines
VP Sales: John Hulick
Estimated Sales: $2.5-5 Million
Number Employees: 20-49

29982 T.J. Topper Company
2734 Spring St
Redwood City, CA 94063
650-365-6962
Fax: 650-368-4547
Institutional and antique coffee makers; also, urns
including coffee, hot chocolate, iced tea, tea and hot
water
President: Willard Dann
Estimated Sales: $2.5-5 Million
Number Employees: 20-49
Parent Co: Tilley Manufacturing Company

29983 T.K. Designs
2551 State Street
Carlsbad, CA 92008
760-434-6225
Fax: 760-434-0058
Indoor-outdoor countertops, wall and easel,
chalk-crayon boards

29984 T.K. Products
1565 N Harmony Cir
Anaheim, CA 92807-6003
714-621-0267
Fax: 714-693-3762
Manufacturer, importer and exporter of high speed
and high shear mixers, dispersers and kneaders
President: Hisashi Furuichi
Marketing Director: Masaki Mori
Estimated Sales: $1-2,500,000
Number Employees: 4
Parent Co: T.K. Japan

29985 T.O. Plastics
1325 American Boulevard E
Suite 6
Minneapolis, MN 55425-1152
952-854-2131
Fax: 952-854-2154 www.toplastics.com
Manufacturer and exporter of plastic sheeting and
thermoformed and foam packaging materials
CFO: Doug Cundell
National Sales Manager: Jeff Smesmo
Contact: Karen Bohn
karen@toplastics.com
Estimated Sales: $20-50 Million
Number Employees: 10
Type of Packaging: Bulk

29986 TA Instruments Inc
159 Lukens Dr
New Castle, DE 19720-2795
302-427-4000
Fax: 302-427-4001 www.tainstruments.com
Thermal analysis and rheology instruments
President: Terrence P Kelly
tkelly@tainstruments.com
CFO: Randy Mercner
Vice President: Terry Kelly
R&D: Jan Wenstrut
Quality Control: John Gaito
Marketing Director: George Dallas
Estimated Sales: $75-100 Million
Number Employees: 100-249
Brands:
    Ar Series Rheometers
    Q Series Thermal Analysis

29987 TAC-PAD
1370 Reynolds Avenue
Irvine, CA 92614
949-851-4337
Fax: 949-252-8079 800-947-1609
Pressure sensitive labels and warehouse and bin tags
Estimated Sales: $1-5 Million
Number Employees: 5-9

29988 TAWI-USA Inc
683 Executive Dr
Willowbrook, IL 60527-5603
630-655-2905
Fax: 630-655-2907 sales@tawiusa.com
www.tawi.com
Vacumove lifting device
Manager: Mike Lee
mlee@tawiusa.com
Estimated Sales: $2 Million
Number Employees: 5-9

29989 TC/American Monorail
12070 43rd St NE
Saint Michael, MN 55376
763-497-7000
Fax: 763-497-7001 www.tcamerican.com
Manufacturer and exporter of cranes and monorail
systems
President: Paul Lague
Sales/Marketing: Beth Keene
Sales Administration Manager: Bill Swanson
Contact: Jami Brown
jbrown@andersencorp.com
Number Employees: 100-249
Square Footage: 180000

29990 TCC Enterprises
16310 Arthur Street
Cerritos, CA 90703-2129
562-802-0998
Fax: 562-802-5069 800-725-8233
Heat sealers, product bag sealers and reclosable bags
Estimated Sales: $10-25 Million
Number Employees: 46

29991 TCG Technologies
1050 Thomas Jefferson Stree
NW-Suite 2300
Washington, DC 20007
972-820-4759
Fax: 703-847-5041 800-226-9999
info@domin-8.com
Rotary cappers, retorquers, torque release chucks
Owner: Tim Flachman
CEO: Bob Franseth
Number Employees: 5-9
Square Footage: 8000

29992 TCT&A Industries
308 E Anthony Drive
Urbana, IL 61802
217-328-5749
Fax: 217-328-5759 800-252-1355
info@awning-tent.com
Commercial awnings
President: Byron Yonce
CEO: Kevin Yonce
Vice President, Chief Financial Officer: Wanda
Yonce
Chairman: Wayne Yonce
Vice President of Sales: Ron Crick
Office Administrator: Mary Crider
Production Manager: Byron Yonce
Director of Installations: Matthew Steinkruger
Estimated Sales: $3-5 Million
Number Employees: 20-49

29993 (HQ)TDF Automation
PO Box 816
Cedar Falls, IA 50613-0040
319-277-3110
Fax: 319-277-7023 800-553-1777
sales@doerfer.com www.doerfercompanies.com
Manufacturer and exporter of display cartoning and
casepacking systems; also, collaters/loaders and
product handling machinery; consultant specializing
in designing automated systems; custom fabricating
services available
President: David Takes
Chairman: Sunder Subbaroyan
Plant Manager: Curt Barfels
Estimated Sales: $1-2.5 Million
Number Employees: 10
Square Footage: 320000
Type of Packaging: Consumer, Food Service
Other Locations:
Doerfer Engineering
Eagan MN

29994 TDH
20520 W Wekiwa Rd
Sand Springs, OK 74063-8192
918-241-8800
Fax: 918-241-8884 888-251-7961
www.tdhmfginc.com
Manufacturer and exporter of mixers, presses,
pumps and automation equipment
Owner: John Owens
tdhmfginc@earthlink.net
VP: J Owens
VP: R Owens
Estimated Sales: Less Than $500,000
Number Employees: 1-4
Square Footage: 16000

29995 TEC
P.O.Box 1086
Gualala, CA 95445-1086
707-884-9655
Fax: 707-884-9656 vickitec@aol.com
www.kirkdenson.com
Winery equipment
Owner: Anthony Agliolo
Partner: Vicki Mastbaum
Estimated Sales: Less than $500,000
Number Employees: 1-4

29996 TEC America
4401 Bankers Cir
Atlanta, GA 30360
770-453-0868
Fax: 770-449-1152
Electronic cash registers, scales, point of sale sys-
tems and scanners for grocery stores, restaurants,
convenience stores, etc.; also, thermal transfer/direct
printers
President: Harry Murata
CFO: K Fujii
Executive VP: Ken Fujii
Quality Control: Jeff Warren
Sales Director: Mike Calderwood
Contact: Steven Bermudez
sbermudez@toshibatecusa.com
Estimated Sales: $50-100 Million
Number Employees: 50-99
Parent Co: Toshiba TEC Corporation

29997 TEI Analytical Svc Inc
7177 N Austin Ave
Niles, IL 60714-4617
847-647-1345
Fax: 847-647-0844 gayle@teianalytical.com
www.teiasi.com
Laboratory offering chemical testing
President: Gayle O'Neill
gayle@teianalytical.com
Estimated Sales: $500,000-$1 Million
Number Employees: 1-4

29998 TEMP-TECH Company
PO Box 2941
Springfield, MA 01101-2941
413-783-2355
Fax: 413-782-7220 800-343-5579
sales@temp-tech.com
Heatstones, thermal bags, tray totes and plastic
smallwares including trays, plates and covers; ex-
porter of trays
President: Jack Anderson
VP: Chuck Attridge
Contact: Greg Schurch
greg@temp-tech.com
Purchasing Agent: Layla O'Shea
Estimated Sales: $2 Million
Number Employees: 5-9
Square Footage: 24000
Type of Packaging: Food Service
Brands:
Temp-Tech

29999 TEQ
11320 Main St
Po Box 68
Huntley, IL 60142-7396
847-669-5291
Fax: 847-669-2720 800-874-7113
info@teqnow.com www.teqnow.com
Plastic containers and blister skin packaging materi-
als
President: Randall Loga
CAO: Paul Sepe
psepe@tekpackaging.com
VP, Finance & Administration: Paul Sepe
Director of Sales & Marketing: Todd McDonald
Director of Operations: Peter Jasinski
Estimated Sales: $10-20 Million
Number Employees: 50-99
Parent Co: ESCO Technologies
Brands:
Combo/Combo

30000 TES-Clean Air Systems
2021 Las Positas Ct Ste 119
Livermore, CA 94551
510-656-5333
Fax: 510-656-5335 sales@paçaids.com
www.tesinc.com
President: James Harris

30001 TESTO
P.O.Box 1030
Sparta, NJ 07871-5030
973-579-3400
Fax: 973-579-3222 800-227-0729
info@testo.com www.ita.cc
Manufacturer and importer of thermometers, probes
and data loggers
Manager: Melissa Curro
VP: Andrew Kuezkuda
Marketing/Sales: John Bickers
Estimated Sales: $3-5 Million
Number Employees: 10-19
Square Footage: 20000
Parent Co: TESTO GMBH
Type of Packaging: Consumer, Food Service
Brands:
Testoterm

30002 TGI Texas
8700 Clay Road
Suite 100
Houston, TX 77080-8104
909-772-6658
Fax: 626-574-8123

30003 TGR Container Sales
2374 Davis Street
San Leandro, CA 94577-2206
510-562-2251
Fax: 510-562-3226 800-273-6887
Storage containers; also, leasing services available

Manager: Nelio Fernandes

30004 TGW International
5 Spiral Dr Ste 3
Florence, KY 41042
859-647-7383
Fax: 859-647-7877 800-407-0173
sales@tgwint.com
Circular and straight machine knives and cutters for
food processing and packaging equipment
President: Jeff Littmer
Vice President: Jeff Litmer
Marketing Director: Debbie Busching
Estimated Sales: Below $5 Million
Number Employees: 5-9
Parent Co: Wolstenholme Machine Knives

30005 (HQ)THARCO
2222 Grant Ave
San Lorenzo, CA 94580-1804
510-276-8600
Fax: 510-317-2728 800-772-2332
sales-slz@tharco.com www.tharco.com
Corrugated boxes, packaging materials and displays;
exporter of corrugated boxes and foam cushion
packaging
President: Oscar Fears
Marketing Manager: Steve Malmquist
Sales Manager: Don Godshall
Estimated Sales: $20-50 Million
Number Employees: 1000-4999
Square Footage: 550000
Other Locations:
THARCO
Algona WA

30006 THARCO
2222 Grant Ave
San Lorenzo, CA 94580-1804
510-276-8600
Fax: 510-317-2728 800-446-6676
sales-slz@tharco.com www.tharco.com
Shipping containers
President: Oscar Fears
Estimated Sales: $20-50 Million
Number Employees: 1000-4999

30007 THE Corporation
PO Box 445
Terre Haute, IN 47808-0445
812-232-2151
Fax: 800-783-2534 800-783-2151
corpies@thecorp.org
Graphic design, prepress, printing plates for packag-
ing primary foods
CEO: Kenneth Williams
Sales Director: Dave Bryan
Estimated Sales: $3 Million
Number Employees: 31
Square Footage: 128000

30008 TKF Inc
726 Mehring Way
Cincinnati, OH 45203-1809
513-241-5910
Fax: 513-651-2792 www.tkf.com
Manufacturer, designer and exporter of custom vertical conveyor systems, including continuous vertical
lift conveyors, reciprocating vertical lift conveyors,
pallet handling conveyors, zero-pressure accumulating conveyors, and overheadmonorail conveyors
Owner: Ronald Eubanks
VP Sales: Jim Walsh
reubanks@tkf.com
Estimated Sales: $20-50 Million
Number Employees: 50-99

30009 TKO Doors
N56w24701 N Crporate Cir Ste A
Sussex, WI 53089
262-820-1217
Fax: 262-820-1273 800-575-3366
www.tkodoors.com
Automatic doors and accessories, loading dock
equipment
Manager: Wayne Strauss
Marketing Manager: Rob Innps
Estimated Sales: $5-10 000,000
Number Employees: 50-99

30010 (HQ)TLB Corporation
150 Willard Avenue
PO Box 6954
Ellicott, MD 21042

410-773-9443
Fax: 203-233-1268 inquiries@respectrisk.com
Manufacturer, importer and exporter of pre-fabricated waste water treatment plants and pumping stations; also, effluent can be sanitized for reuse
President/Chief Engineer: Thomas Bond
Finance: Russell Correll
Production Manager: Thomas Farrell
Number Employees: 20-49
Square Footage: 60000
Brands:
  Hart Boost
  Hart Treat
  Hartlift
  Oxy Tower

30011 TLC & Associates
5600 Bell Street
Suite 105, PMB 167
Amarillo, TX 79109

806-353-1517
Fax: 806-335-4321
Management consulting in the food service industry.
President: Charles King

30012 TMB Baking Equipment
480 Grandview Drive
South San Francisco, CA 94080

650-589-5724
Fax: 650-589-5729 contact@tmbbaking.com
www.tmbbaking.com
President: Michel Suas
Estimated Sales: $3-5 Million
Number Employees: 10-19

30013 TMCo Inc.
10801 Hammerly Blvd.
Suite 232
Houston, TX 77043

713-465-3255
Fax: 713-465-3237 gwyn.childress@tmcousa.com
www.tmco-usa.com
Cereal chemists' laboratory equipment
President/CFO: Roland Temme
Quality Control/R&D: John Alberf
Manager: John Albers
Estimated Sales: $10-20 Million
Number Employees: 50-99
Parent Co: TMCO
Brands:
  Mixograph

30014 TMCo Inc.
10801 Hammerly Blvd.
Suite 232
Houston, TX 77043

713-465-3255
Fax: 713-465-3237 gwyn.childress@tmcousa.com
www.tmco-usa.com
Manufacturer and exporter of displays
President: Roland Temme
VP Manufacturing: Joe Smith
Estimated Sales: $10-20 Million
Number Employees: 50-99

30015 TMF Corporation
850 West Chester Pike
Suite 303
Havertown, PA 19083

610-853-3080
Fax: 610-789-5168 info@tmfcorporation.com
www.tmfcorporation.com
Pallets
Contact: Debbie Bergen
d_bergen@tmfcorporation.com
Number Employees: 4
Square Footage: 3016

30016 TMI-USA
11491 Sunset Hills Rd # 310
Suite 310
Reston, VA 20190-5244

703-668-0114
Fax: 703-668-0118 qi.xiangyu@tmigi.com
www.tmi-orion.com
Manufacturers of data loggers for sterilization processors

President: Guillaume Favre
CEO: Jean-Luc Favre
jeanlucfavre@tmigi.com
VP: Guillaume Favre
Sales Manager: Emmanuel Cisternino
Operations Manager: Myriam Vidal
Estimated Sales: Less Than $500,000
Number Employees: 1-4

30017 TMS
2 Lombard Street
San Francisco, CA 94111-6206

415-665-2565
Fax: 415-362-1756 800-447-7223
Refrigerated and nonrefrigerated cargo and storage containers
President: Robert Skinner
General Manager: Scott Weiser
Estimated Sales: $300,000-500,000
Number Employees: 1-4

30018 TMT Software Company
Eastpoint 1
6085 Parkland Blvd
Mayfield Heights, OH 44124

216-831-6606
Fax: 216-831-3606 800-401-6682
solutions@tmwsystems.com
Manufacturer and developer of fleet and equipment maintenance management software including PM scheduling, fuel, parts, tire, warranty, bar coding, shop planner, mechanics workstation and accounting programs; software operates on LANWAN, PCs and IBM AS/400
President: David Wangler
EVP, Finance: Jeffery Ritter
Vice President: Renaldo Adler
EVP, Marketing: Scott Vanselous
SVP, Sales: Dave Schildmeyer
EVP, Operations: Rod Strata
Estimated Sales: $3-5 Million
Number Employees: 20-49
Number of Products: 3
Square Footage: 14000
Brands:
  Tmt Transman

30019 TMT Vacuum Filters
407 S. College
Danville, IL 61832

217-446-0742
Fax: 217-446-0744
www.modernmachinebaggers.com
Bag filling machinery; also, industrial maintenance and repair available
President: Manny Mechalas
CFO: Manny Mechalas
Estimated Sales: $1-2.5 Million
Number Employees: 10-19

30020 TNA Packaging Solutions
702 S Royal Lane
Suite 100
Coppell, TX 75019-3800

972-462-6500
Fax: 972-462-6599
mark.lozano@tnasolutions.com
www.tnasolutions.com
Manufacturer and exporter of packaging systems including vertical form/fill/seal machinery; importer of multi-head scales and metal detectors
Founder & Director: Nadia Taylor
Founder & CEO: Alf Taylor
Group Finance Manager: Peter Calopedis
VP-Americas: Alfredo Blanco
Group Marketing Manager: Shayne De la Force
Group Sales Manager: Patrick Avelange
Group Operations Manager: Natasha Avelange
Group Manufacturing Manager: Andrew Smith
Estimated Sales: $3.5 Million
Number Employees: 240
Square Footage: 192000
Brands:
  Robag

30021 TNN-Jeros, Inc.
P.O. Box 12
Byron, IL 61010

815-978-2210
Fax: 815-234-5915 www.tnn-jeros.com
Cleaning and washing equipment for the baking and food service industries.

30022 TNT Container Logistics
10751 Deerwood Park Blvd # 200
Jacksonville, FL 32256-4836

904-928-1400
Fax: 904-928-1410 800-272-3129
www.tntlogistics.com
Dairy industry packaging containers
Senior VP: Mark Johnson
Director: Joseph Keller
Number Employees: 100-249

30023 TNT Container Logistics
10751 Deerwood Park Blvd # 200
Jacksonville, FL 32256-4836

904-928-1400
Fax: 904-928-1410 800-272-2129
mal_perry@tnt.com.au
Senior VP: Mark Johnson
Director: Joseph Keller
Number Employees: 100-249

30024 TOPS Software Corporation
275 W Campbell Rd
Suite 600
Richardson, TX 75080

972-739-8677
Fax: 972-739-9478 800-889-2441
info@topseng.com www.topseng.com
Offers packaging software and truck loading software for packaging and distribution professionals.
President: Bill Rehring
Contact: Erika Ledesma
eledesma@topseng.com
Manager: Reet Randhawa
Estimated Sales: $1-2.5 Million
Number Employees: 10-19

30025 TPS International
7650 Binnacle Lane
Owings, MD 20736-3102

301-855-3541
Fax: 301-855-0474
Forming tubes and shoulders for form full seal bagging machines
Founder: Don Wooldridge
Estimated Sales: $2.5-5 Million
Number Employees: 19

30026 (HQ)TRC
15005 Enterprise Way
Middlefield, OH 44062

440-834-0078
Fax: 440-834-0083
Manufacturer and exporter of staple set brushes; also, custom injection molding of thermoplastic materials
Owner: Terry Ross
terry.martinez@apparelnews.net
VP Sales/Marketing: Dan Armstrong
Plant Manager: William O'Donnell
Estimated Sales: $10-20 Million
Number Employees: 100-249
Square Footage: 80000

30027 TRFG Inc
300 E Auburn Ave
Springfield, OH 45505-4703

937-322-2040
Fax: 937-322-2254
Sales and sales management; representing a wide range of packaged goods like confections, salted snacks, natural foods
President: Jeff Kreidenweis
jkreidenweis@aol.com
Estimated Sales: $3-5 Million
Number Employees: 1-4
Type of Packaging: Food Service, Private Label

30028 TRITEN Corporation
3657 Briarpark
Houston, TX 77042

713-690-9050
Fax: 713-690-9080 832-214-5000
info@triten.com www.triten.com
Manufacturer and exporter of plunger pumps, water blasting equipment and accessories

Chairman/President/ CEO: John Scott Arnoldy
President/Chief Executive Officer: Thomas Amonet
Executive Vice President/Chief Financial: Donald O. Bainter
Executive Vice President and Chief Opera: Gary J. Baumgartner
Contact: Jack Adams
j.adams@triten.com
Product Manager: John Matlock
Estimated Sales: $1-2.5 Million
Number Employees: 100-249
Square Footage: 50000
Brands:
  Hydro-Laser

30029 TSA Griddle Systems
395 Penno Road
Suite 100
Kelowna, BC VIX 7W5
Canada
                              250-491-9025
  Fax: 250-491-9045 info@griddlesystems.com
                www.griddlesystems.com
Manufacturer and exporter of food processing equipment including pancake, waffle, french toast, egg patty and baked goods; also, mixers, blenders, depositors and cooling systems
President: Kevin Forrest
Estimated Sales: Below $5 Million
Number Employees: 10
Square Footage: 40000

30030 TSE Industries Inc
4370 112th Ter N
Clearwater, FL 33762-4902
                              727-573-7676
  Fax: 727-572-0487 800-237-7634
  inquire@tse-industries.com www.tse-rubber.com
Custom rubber molding
Owner: Rob Clingle
Vice Chairman/Director: Helen Klingel
Director: Diane Klingel
CEO: Robert R Klingel Sr
VP Rubber Products Division: Louis Mirra
VP Speciality Chemicals Division: William Stephens
VP Plastics/Machine Shop Division: Gary Reese
VP Materials: Mark Neuman
robclingle@tse-industries.com
Estimated Sales: $10-20 Million
Number Employees: 100-249
Square Footage: 150000

30031 TSG Merchandising
410 E Walnut Street
Perkasie, PA 18944-1618
                              215-453-9220
                         Fax: 215-453-7710
Designer of point of purchase displays, store fixtures, etc
President: Paul Schmidt
Number Employees: 10-19

30032 TTS Technologies
160 Farm Hill Cir
Roswell, GA 30075-4263
                              770-640-7808
  Fax: 770-622-9183 admin@ttstechnologies.com

30033 TULSACK
10405b E 55th Pl
Tulsa, OK 74146-6502
                              918-664-0664
  Fax: 918-664-0849 800-228-1936
                www.tulsack.com
Handled paper bags
President: Jarrod Dyess
HR Executive: Tina Schroeder
tina@tulsack.com
Estimated Sales: $10-20 Million
Number Employees: 100-249
Parent Co: Denmar Products

30034 TURBOCHEF Technologies
2801 Trade Center Drive
Carrollton, TX 75007
                              214-379-6000
  Fax: 214-340-6073 800-908-8726
                www.turbochef.com
Designs, develops, manufactures and markets speed cooking solutions

President: James K. Pool III
CEO: James Price
CFO: Al Cochran
COO: Paul Lehr
VP Marketing: David Shave
Sr VP Global Sales/Business Development: Peter Ashcraft
Contact: Max Abbott
max.abbott@turbochef.com
Plant Manager: Jeanean Weaver
Vice President Procurement: Rusty Rose
Estimated Sales: $10-20 Million
Number Employees: 10
Square Footage: 22000
Brands:
  Turbochef

30035 (HQ)TVC Systems
284 Constitution Ave
Portsmouth, NH 03801-5616
                              603-431-5251
  Fax: 603-431-8909 888-431-5251
  info@tvcsystems.com www.tvcsystems.com
Turnkey process control and information systems
President: Jim Fradsham
fradsham@tvcsystems.com
CEO: Nels Tyring
Operations Manager: Linda Tyring
Estimated Sales: $5-10 Million
Number Employees: 10-19
Square Footage: 14000

30036 TVT Trade Brands
18503 Pines Blvd.
Suite 308
Pembroke Pines, FL 33029
                              954-353-9003
  Fax: 954-507-5933 info@tvttrade.com
                www.tvttrade.com
Ethnic foods: Mediterranean, European, Asian, Latin-American, Middle Eastern, African and Australian; spices, superfoods and delicatessen.
Global Business Development Manager: Rubert Velasquez
Estimated Sales: $1-5 Million
Number Employees: 10-20
Type of Packaging: Food Service
Other Locations:
  Warehouse
  Miami FL
Brands:
  Mystik Spices
  Origin Foods
  Powerbite

30037 TW Metals Inc
760 Constitution Dr
Suite 204
Exton, PA 19341
                              610-458-1300
                www.twmetals.com
Steel, nickel alloys, aluminum, copper, brass, carbon alloys in all metal configurations. Processing equipment services for cutting, shearing, leveling, and slitting, distributor of fittings and flanges.
President & CEO: Kirk Moore *Year Founded:* 1907

30038 TWM Manufacturing
1960 Concession 3
Leamington, ON N9Y 2E5
Canada
                              519-326-0014
  Fax: 519-326-7746 888-495-4831
                sales@tugweld.com
Premium quality custom made food processing machinery and automated mechanical systems/specialists in stainless steel
President: John Friesen
VP: Jake Friesen
Estimated Sales: $2-3 Million
Number Employees: 13
Square Footage: 88000
Brands:
  Cluster Buster
  Tugweld
  Twm

30039 TXS
124 Commercial Avenue
B
Rogers, AR 72757
                              501-631-1363
  Fax: 501-631-1294 800-562-6552

30040 Table De France: North America
390 George St
Suite 404-407
New Brunswick, NJ 8901
                              732-565-0820
  Fax: 732-565-0828 888-680-4616
  JFagan390@cs.com www.tabledefrance.net
Silver utensils and tabletop supplies
VP: James Fagan
Parent Co: Christoff Silver
Brands:
  Christoff

30041 Table Talk Pies Inc
120 Washington St # 1
Worcester, MA 01610-2751
                              508-798-8811
                         Fax: 508-798-0848
  customerservice@tabletalkpie.com
                www.tabletalkpie.com
4, 6, 8, 9, and 10 inch pies in a variety of dessert and fruit flavors
Director of Sales/Marketing: Bob Littlefield
Inside Sales: Tara Tula
Sales/Marketing: Louise Lindberg
Logistics: Valdemar Siqueira
Estimated Sales: $40 Million
Number Employees: 50-99
Brands:
  Table Talk

30042 Tablecheck Technologies, Inc
13276 Research Blvd # 103
Austin, TX 78750
                              512-219-9711
  Fax: 512-219-6964 800-522-1347
  info@tablecheck.com www.tablecheck.com
Manufacturer and exporter of electronic seating systems
President: Barbara Horan
Estimated Sales: $1-5 Million
Number Employees: 5-9
Number of Brands: 1
Number of Products: 1
Square Footage: 3200
Brands:
  Tablecheck

30043 Tablecraft Products Co Inc
801 Lakeside Dr
Gurnee, IL 60031-2489
                              847-855-9000
  Fax: 847-855-9012 800-323-8321
                info@tablecraft.com
Manufacturer, importer and exporter of smallwares, salt and pepper shakers, condiment and beverage dispensers, bar supplies, kitchen utensils, coffee equipment, baskets, salad bowls, rangettes, etc
President: Dave Burnside
dburnside@tablecraft.com
CFO: Ron Kostrewa
Vice President: Larry Davis
General Manager: Ted Rutkowski
Marketing Director: Amy Garrard
Sales Director: Dave Burnside
Plant Manager: Ted Rotkowski
Purchasing Manager: Larry Davis
Number Employees: 5-9
Square Footage: 400000
Parent Co: Hunter Manufacturing Company
Brands:
  Kenket
  Seattle Series
  Superlevel
  Tablecraft

30044 Tables Cubed
2305 Manor Ridge Drive
Chesterfield, MO 63017
                              314-843-3001
  Fax: 314-843-2127 800-878-3001
Occasional tables for hospitality environment.
President: Don Depke
Sales: Seth Lieberman
Estimated Sales: C
Number Employees: 5-9

30045 Tablet & Ticket Co
1120 Atlantic Dr
West Chicago, IL 60185-5103
                              630-231-6611
  Fax: 630-231-0211 800-438-4959
                sales@tabletandticket.com
                www.tabletandticket.com

Custom menu display boards including stainless steel, brass, aluminum, illuminated and nonilluminated; also, matching bulletin boards available
President: Brian Blair
brianb@tabletandticket.com
CFO: Tom Evans
Estimated Sales: $5-10 Million
Number Employees: 10-19
Square Footage: 30000

30046 Taconic
P.O.Box 69
Petersburg, NY 12138

518-658-3202
Fax: 518-658-3988 800-833-1805
info@4taconic.com www.4taconic.com
Manufacturer, importer and exporter of PTFE and silicone coated fiberglass fabrics and tapes; also, reusable and nonstick coated cake rings and liners for trays, bagel boards, ovens, roasting and proofing
Executive: Philippe Heffley
Sales: Al Hepp
Contact: Jeffrey Browne
jeffrey.browne@taconic.com
Estimated Sales: $20-50 Million
Number Employees: 100-249
Brands:
   Tefbake

30047 Tafco Inc
PO Box 269
Hyde, PA 16843-0269

814-765-5378
Fax: 814-765-5410 800-233-1954
bridgettwhite@walkins.com www.walkins.com
Walk-in coolers and freezers
President/CEO: William Carr
VP: Gary Brannon
Vice President of Sales: Bridgett White
Contact: Chris Aughenbaugh
caughenbaugh@walkins.com
Estimated Sales: $20-50 Million
Number Employees: 100-249

30048 Tag-Trade Associated Group
1730 W Wrightwood Ave
Chicago, IL 60614-1972

773-871-1300
Fax: 773-871-8432 800-621-8350
www.tagltd.com
Napkins, place mats, tablecloths, wine racks and buckets and candles
National Sales Manager: Nancy Mathyer
Estimated Sales: $20-50 Million
Number Employees: 50-99

30049 Talbert Display
5713 Hart St
Fort Worth, TX 76112-6918

817-429-4504
Fax: 817-457-4066
Store fixtures and cabinets
Owner: Mark Talbert
Estimated Sales: Less than $500,000
Number Employees: 1-4
Square Footage: 24000

30050 (HQ)Talbot Industries
1211 W Harmony St
Neosho, MO 64850-1636

417-451-5900
Fax: 417-451-7830
Point of purchase displays, store displays and steel wire products
President: Jerral Downs
VP (National Accounts): Mike Howley
Quality Control: Greg Harris
Human Resources: Beth Foust
VP Sales: Jeff Talbot
Manager: Laurie Borland
laurie.borland@leggett.com
Number Employees: 250-499
Square Footage: 800000
Other Locations:
   Talbot Industries
   Point TX

30051 Tallygenicom
15345 Barranca Pkwy
Irvine, CA 92618-2216

714-368-2300
800-665-6210
printers@tally.com www.tally.com

Manufacturer and provider of industrial and back-office enterprise printing solutions for office/industrial marketplace and distribution supply chain.
Chief Executive Officer: Randy Eisenbach
Chief Financial Officer: Rhonda Longmore-Grund
VP, Worldwide Engineering/CTO: Bill Matthews
SVP, Global Sales Marketing: Mark Edwards
VP, Sales & Marketing, Asia-Pacific: Albert Ching
Vice President, Global Operations: Sean Irby
Estimated Sales: $50-100 Million
Number Employees: 500-999
Square Footage: 140000
Parent Co: Printronix
Brands:
   Computer Printers
   Tally Printer Corporation

30052 Tamanet (USA) Inc
16541 Gothard St
Suite 112
Huntington Beach, CA 92647

714-698-0990
Fax: 714-842-5600 800-441-8262
jeff@tamanetusa.com www.tamanetusa.com
Knited net for wrapping pallets
President: Nackem Dorou
Contact: Bobbie Smith-Cruz
bobbie@tamanetusa.com
Estimated Sales: $5-10 Million
Number Employees: 1-4
Parent Co: TAMA Plastic Industry

30053 Tamarack Products Inc
1071 N Old Rand Rd
Wauconda, IL 60084-1239

847-526-9333
Fax: 847-526-9353 info@tamarackproducts.com
www.tamarackproducts.com
Manufacturer and exporter of printing, labeling and die cutting equipment
President: David Steidinger
dsteidinger@tamarackproducts.com
Estimated Sales: $2.5-5 Million
Number Employees: 20-49

30054 Tampa Bay Copack
15052 Ronnie Dr # 100
Dade City, FL 33523-6011

352-567-7400
Fax: 352-567-2257
Contract manufacturing beverage bottling, pastuerizer, formulation, private label, product development.
President: Scot Ballantyne
Research & Development: Vince Curetto
Contact: Valerie Hval
vhval@tampabaycopack.com
Number Employees: 5-9
Square Footage: 34000
Type of Packaging: Private Label

30055 Tampa Corrugated CartonCompany
3517 N 40th Street
Tampa, FL 33605-1641

813-623-5115
Fax: 813-626-2153
Manufacturer and exporter of custom and stock boxes including corrugated, paper and paper folding; also, cartons
General Manager: Ron Pollard
Estimated Sales: $10-20 Million
Number Employees: 50-99

30056 Tampa Pallet Co
2402 S 54th St
Tampa, FL 33619-5364

813-626-5700
Fax: 813-623-5180 TAMPAPALLET@AOL.COM
www.tampapallet.com
Manufacturer and exporter of wooden pallets, crates and boxes
Owner, President: Fred Haman
tampapallet@aol.com
Estimated Sales: $5-10 Million
Number Employees: 5-9

30057 Tampa Sheet Metal Co
1402 W Kennedy Blvd
Tampa, FL 33606-1847

813-251-1845
Fax: 813-254-7399 sales@tampasheetmetal.com
www.tampasheetmetal.com

Aluminum, steel and stainless steel cabinets, hoppers, pipes, tanks, etc
President: John L Jiretz
president@tampasheetmetal.com
General Manager: J Jiretz
Estimated Sales: $1-2,500,000
Number Employees: 10-19

30058 Tanaco Products
3465 Bonnie Hill Dr
Los Angeles, CA 90068-1325

360-332-6010
Fax: 360-332-0936
Manufactures conventional Tanaco plastic plug valves and rebuilding of all types of plug valves, also manufacturers tanaco in-line automatic and hand actuated plug valves
Owner: Annelie Hoyer
Estimated Sales: Less than $500,000
Number Employees: 1-4
Other Locations:
   Tanaco Products
   Vancouver, B.C., Canada

30059 Tangent Systems
8030 England Street
B
Charlotte, NC 28273-5978

704-554-0830
Fax: 704-554-0820 800-992-7577
sales@versid.com www.versid.com
Manufacturer and exporter of temperature measurement and data logging instruments
Sales Manager: Mary Lynn Rogers
Estimated Sales: $1-2.5 Million
Number Employees: 10
Brands:
   Tempest
   Versid

30060 Tangerine Promotion
900 Skokie Blvd # 275
Suite 275
Northbrook, IL 60062-4034

847-313-6000
Fax: 847-313-6092
info@tangerinepromotions.com
www.tangerinepromotions.com
Promotional products and marketing agency
President/CEO: Steve Friedman
CFO/COO: Adam Rosenbaum
Sales Director: Michael Gertz
Manager: Jon Lavarre
jlavarre@tangerineme.com
Director of Production: Carolyn Boehm
Estimated Sales: $2.8 Million
Number Employees: 10-19
Square Footage: 28000

30061 Tangible Vision
320 Billingsly Ct # 50
Suite 50
Franklin, TN 37067-4707

615-771-7177
Fax: 630-969-7523 800-763-8634
www.tangiblevision.net
Software for customer service, accounting, manufacturing, etc
Owner: Paul Reeves
paul@tangiblevision.net
VP Marketing: Kathy Harmon
Estimated Sales: $2.5-5 Million
Number Employees: 5-9

30062 Tango Shatterproof Drinkware
P.O.Box 737
Walpole, MA 02081

888-898-2646
Fax: 508-668-0543 Kpicchi@IslandOasis.com
www.tango-shatterproof.com
Shatterproof glasses, tumblers and pitchers
General Manager: Paul Shilo
Sales: Marie Sandre
Parent Co: Island Oasis
Brands:
   Tango Shatterproof

30063 Tank Temp Control
23275 NE Dayton Ave
Newberg, OR 97132-6816

503-538-8267
Fax: 503-538-1837 888-960-9090
www.tanktemp.com
Wine industry temperature monitoring
Owner: Curtis Jungwirth

Estimated Sales: Less than $500,000
Number Employees: 1-4

30064 Tantec
630 Estes Avenue
Schaumburg, IL 60193-4403

847-524-5506

Fax: 847-524-6956 mrtantec@aol.com

Industrial equipment including static control, corona treating and surface measuring
President: Waltraud Legat
Contact: Jeff Gradus
jeff@tantec.com
Estimated Sales: $2.5-5 Million
Number Employees: 20

30065 Tap Packaging Solutions
2160 Superior Ave. E
Cleveland, OH 44114

800-827-5679

Fax: 800-276-2572 contact@tap-usa.com
tap-usa.com

Packaging containers: consumer brand, photography, confections, paperboard
Chairman: David Chilcote
President & CEO: J. Anthony Hyland
Quality Manager: Kamal Haddad
Vice President, Sales & Marketing: Jordana Revella
Manager, Human Resources: Christina Balint
Vice President, Operations: Matthew Moir
Year Founded: 1906
Estimated Sales: $50-70 Million
Number Employees: 51-200
Type of Packaging: Consumer

30066 Tape & Label Converters
8231 Allport Ave
Santa Fe Springs, CA 90670-2105

562-945-3486

Fax: 562-696-8198 888-285-2462
www.stickybiz.com

Printer of high quality short run digital and large run flexographic pressure sensitive lavels. 35+ years of experience with food and beverage labels. Customers are small family owned companies to Fortune 500.
CEO: Robert Varela Sr.
Research & Development: Robert Varela Jr.
Quality Control: Roger Varela
Marketing: Mas Crawford
Sales: Mas Crawford
Public Relations: Mas Crawford
Operations: Robert Varela Sr.
Production: Roger Varela
Plant Manager: Randy Varela
Purchasing: Robert Varela Jr.
Estimated Sales: $1-2.5 Million
Number Employees: 10-19
Square Footage: 24000
Type of Packaging: Consumer, Food Service, Private Label

30067 Tape & Label Engineering
2950 47th Avenue N
St Petersburg, FL 33714-3132

727-527-6686

Fax: 727-526-0163 800-237-8955

Die-cut cloth, foil, mylar, paper and pressure-sensitive labels; wholesaler/distributor of pressure sensitive application equipment
Manager: Bob White
Marketing Director: Chuck Pullich
Sales Director: Charlie Goldson
Production Manager: Tom Bowers
tom.bowers@tle.net
Purchasing Manager: Michael Summers
Estimated Sales: $10-20 Million
Number Employees: 50-100
Square Footage: 168000
Parent Co: Weber Marking Systems
Type of Packaging: Consumer, Private Label

30068 Tapesolutions
1217 Rabas Street
Algoma, WI 54201-1985

847-776-8880

Fax: 847-776-8890 800-323-6026

Manufacturers of security tapes and labels
CEO: Terrence Fulwiler
Estimated Sales: $5-10 Million
Number Employees: 5-9
Square Footage: 10000
Parent Co: W.S Packaging

30069 Taprite-Fassco Mfg Inc
3248 Northwestern
San Antonio, TX 78238-4043

210-523-0800

Fax: 210-520-3035 800-779-8488
sales@taprite.com www.taprite.com

CO2 regulators, BIB packs, portable bars, and asessory items for the beverage industry
President: David Lease
dlease@taprite.com
CFO: Scott Cary
Estimated Sales: $20-50 Million
Number Employees: 50-99

30070 Tar-Hong MELAMINE USA
780 Nogales St
City Of Industry, CA 91748-1306

626-935-1612

Fax: 626-585-1609 cservice@tarhong.com
www.tarhong.com

Plastic dinnerware, stainless steel flatware and tumblers
Owner: Eddie Liu
Manager: Ralph Liu
Manager: Joe Wen
Estimated Sales: $5-10 Million
Number Employees: 5-9

30071 Tara Communications
698 Litchfield Lane
Dunedin, FL 34698-7429

303-417-9602

Fax: 303-413-1869

Consultant specializing in sales and advertising for the natural products industry
Partner: Joel Packman
Partner: Tish Packman
Number Employees: 1-4

30072 Tara Foods LLC
1900 Cowles Ln
Albany, GA 31705-1514

229-431-1330

Fax: 229-439-1458 www.thekrogerco.com

Sauces, peanut butter, food color
Sales Manager: Marilyne Moore
Plant Manager: Jesse Turner
Estimated Sales: $25-49.9 Million
Number Employees: 100-249
Parent Co: Kroger Company

30073 Tara Linens
PO Box 1350
Sanford, NC 27331-1350

919-774-1300

Fax: 919-774-3525 800-476-8272

Manufacturer and exporter of table linens including cloths, napkins, place mats, skirting, runners, aprons and tray and chair covers; importer of table aprons
President: Brooks Pomeranz
Number Employees: 100-249
Square Footage: 480000
Parent Co: Cascade Fibers Company
Brands:
  Checkmate
  Classic
  Nouveau
  Queens Linen
  Windsor

30074 Tara Tape
250 Canal Rd
Fairless Hills, PA 19030

215-736-3644

Fax: 215-428-4510 800-366-8272
sales@taratape.com

Filament tape, strapping tape, tearstrip tape, printed tape, overlaminate, laminated label stocks
President: Tom Dodd
Estimated Sales: $2.5-5 Million
Number Employees: 50-99

30075 Tarason Packaging, LLC.
1101 Keisler Road
Conover, NC 28613

828-464-4743

Fax: 828-465-5517

Pressure sensitive labels, hang tags and cloth printed labels
President: Kevin McKenna
Operations Manager: Ronnie A. Caldwell
Estimated Sales: Below $5 Million
Number Employees: 10-19

30076 Target Industries
95 S River Bend Way
North Salt Lake, UT 84054

866-617-2253

Fax: 801-383-3251 info@targetlabel.com
www.targetlabel.com

Extruded plastic bags, sheetings, discs, liners and tubings; also, converter of polyamide/plastic casings for processed meat, cheese and poultry; importer of plastic casings
President: Tom Fox
CFO: Warren Greenberg
Sales Manager: Guy Eric
Estimated Sales: $10-20 Million
Number Employees: 50-99
Square Footage: 106000

30077 Tartaric Chemicals Corporation
515 Madison Ave Rm 1902
New York, NY 10022

212-752-0727

Fax: 212-207-8037 www.tartarics.com

President: Alessandro Bonecchi
Estimated Sales: $2.5-5 Million
Number Employees: 5-9

30078 Task Footwear
1251 1st Ave
Chippewa Falls, WI 54729-1408

715-723-1871

Fax: 715-720-4260 800-962-0166

Steel toe, nonsteel and slip resistant shoes
Wholesale Manager: Linda Jackson
CEO: Daniel Hunt
VP Marketing: Herb Steinmetz
Estimated Sales: $1-5,000,000
Number Employees: 250-499
Brands:
  Mason

30079 Tasler Inc
1804 Tasler Dr
Webster City, IA 50595-7625

515-832-5200

Fax: 515-832-2721 www.tasler.com

Wooden pallets
President: Greg Tasler
gtasler@tasler.com
Estimated Sales: $20-50 Million
Number Employees: 100-249

30080 Tate Western
36 Aero Camino
Goleta, CA 93117-3105

805-685-5544

Fax: 805-685-3695 800-903-0200

Manufacturer, importer and exporter of automatic chemical dispensers including warewash, laundry and metering pumps
President: Russ Kovacevich
Sales Manager: Glen Kent
Estimated Sales: $5-10 Million
Number Employees: 25
Square Footage: 34000
Parent Co: Shurflo Pump Manufacturing
Brands:
  Gorilla Bowl
  Tate Western
  Versa Pro

30081 Taylor Box Co
293 Child St
PO Box 343
Warren, RI 02885-1907

401-245-5900

Fax: 401-245-0450 800-304-6361
info@taylorbox.com www.taylorbox.com

Manufacturer and exporter of specialty paper and metal boxes for consumer goods and confectionery items
President: Dan Shedd
Design/Engineering: Julie Passey
Sales/Marketing: Daniel Shedd
Administration: Martha Lemoi
Production: Donna Costa
Estimated Sales: $10-20 Million
Number Employees: 20-49

30082 Taylor Made Custom Products
66 Kingsboro Ave
Gloversville, NY 12078-3415
518-725-0681
Fax: 518-725-4335
tmginfo@taylormadegroup.com
www.taylormadecustomproducts.com
Commercial awnings
President/CEO: Andy Jobbins
CFO: Robert Khalife
Secretary: John Taylor
Contact: Emory Lyons
elyons@taylormadesystems.com
Estimated Sales: $1-3,000,000
Number Employees: 5-9
Parent Co: Taylor Made Group

30083 Taylor Manufacturing Co
128 Talmadge Dr
PO Box 625
Moultrie, GA 31768-5049
229-985-5445
Fax: 229-890-9090 www.peasheller.com
Manufacturer and exporter of motor driven shelling
machinery for peas and beans
President/CFO: Terry Taylor Sr
VP: Terry Taylor
Estimated Sales: Below $5 Million
Number Employees: 5-9

30084 Taylor Precision Products
2220 Entrada Del Sol # A
Suite A
Las Cruces, NM 88001-3920
575-526-0945
Fax: 575-526-4626 info@taylorusa.com
www.taylorprecisionproducts.com
Thermometers including digital and mechanical, instant read, pocket and hand-held; for meat, candy, jelly, scales, portion control, receiving and utility
Chief Financial Officer/COO: Donald Robinson
Executive VP: Ajit Shanbhag
ashanbhag@taylorusa.com
Director, Information Technology: Nancy Carson
Quality Assurance Manager: Steve Mowad
Director, Marketing: Liz Wentland
Estimated Sales: $50 Million
Number Employees: 20-49
Square Footage: 85000
Other Locations:
Taylor Precision Products
Juarez, Mexico
Taylor Precision Products
Las Cruces NM
Brands:
Bi-Therm
Taylor
Tru-Temp

30085 Taylor Precision Products
2311 W 22nd St # 200
Oak Brook, IL 60523-5625
630-954-1250
Fax: 630-954-1275 866-843-3905
info@taylorusa.com www.taylorusa.com
Manufactures thermometers, scales and related measurement devices.
CFO: Donald Robinson
VP: Donald Robinson
Director Sales/Marketing: Kent Beaverson
Contact: Elvira Abate
eabate@taylorusa.com
Estimated Sales: $1-2,500,000
Number Employees: 10-19
Type of Packaging: Consumer, Food Service, Private Label, Bulk

30086 (HQ)Taylor Products Co
2205 Jothi Ave
Parsons, KS 67357-8477
620-421-5550
Fax: 620-421-5586 888-882-9567
sales@magnumsystems.com
www.magnumsystems.com
Manufacturer and exporter of bag filling and unloading bagging scales, applicable for open mouth, valve, drum/box and bulk bags
CEO: Gary Saunders
CFO: Debra Weidert
Sales Manager: Brad Schultz
Estimated Sales: $20-50 Million
Number Employees: 20-49
Square Footage: 208000

Other Locations:
Taylor Products Co.
Decatur AL
Brands:
Avatar
Weigh Trac

30087 Taylor-Made Labels Inc
17252 Pilkington Rd # A
Lake Oswego, OR 97035-5393
503-699-5000
Fax: 503-699-0408 800-878-8654
dtaylor@taylormadelabels.com
www.taylormadelabels.com
Manufacture of custom pressure sensitive labels and tags. Distributor of label application equipment.
President: Paul Taylor
ptaylor@taylormadelabels.com
Vice President: Dan Taylor
Plant Manager: Mike Summers
Estimated Sales: $20-50 Million
Number Employees: 50-99

30088 Taymar Industries
4-151 Monterey Ave
Palm Desert, CA 92201-2388
760-775-2424
Fax: 760-775-2420 800-624-1972
Plastic product display cases; also, stock and custom pieces available
VP: Bob Stevens
Marketing: Dave Parkinson
Sales Manager: Bonnie Miller
Estimated Sales: $1-2.5 Million
Number Employees: 30

30089 Teaco
5800 Monroe Rd
Charlotte, NC 28212-6104
704-535-5305
Fax: 704-531-5801 globaoco2K@cs.com
Teabag wire, threads
President: Steven Cropp
Estimated Sales: $1-2.5 Million
Number Employees: 5-9

30090 Teamwork Technology
7700 Riverside Drive
Dublin, OH 43016-9044
419-782-4990
Fax: 419-782-3577 www.fessmann.com
Continuous and batch smokehouses, smoke generators and chill equipment
Number Employees: 2

30091 Tec Art Industries Inc
28059 Center Oaks Court
Wixom, MI 48393
248-624-8880
Fax: 248-624-8066 800-886-6615
www.tecartinc.com
Back lit signs, banners, poster and banner stands, metal tackers, counter stools, custom floor mats and neon. Over 300 in stock-Title Signs available.
CEO: Steve Bolin
COO/CFO: Kimberly Perrigan
VP Sales/Marketing: Michele Wehr
Contact: Jeffrey Dunstan
jdunstan@tecartinc.com
Estimated Sales: $5 Million +
Number Employees: 20-49
Square Footage: 64000
Brands:
Alumtec Elite
Alumtec
Tec Frames
Tecneon
Tectwo

30092 Tec-Era Engineering Corporation
1860 Altamont Dr
Felton, CA 95018
831-438-1930
Fax: 831-438-1939
Water treatment equipment
President: Gerald G Green
Estimated Sales: Less than $500,000
Number Employees: 5-9

30093 Tec5USA
80 Skyline Dr
Plainview, NY 11803
516-653-2000
quality control and food safety equipment.
General Manager: Dan Fields

Number Employees: 11-50

30094 Tech Development
6800 Poe Ave
Dayton, OH 45414
937-898-9600
Fax: 937-898-8431 www.tdi-turbotwin.com
Turbo machinery, propulsion simulators, pumps, industrial air motors and engine air starters
Manager: Tom Jacobs
Field Service Engineer: Mike Briscoe
Marketing Coordinator: Anita Hamilton
Northern Regional Sales Manager: Bob Englet
Customer Service: Deanne Hartman
General Manager: William Nordby
Estimated Sales: $10-20 Million
Number Employees: 100-249

30095 (HQ)Tech Lighting LLC
7400 Linder Ave
Skokie, IL 60077-3219
847-410-4400
Fax: 847-410-4500 800-323-3226
lblcseast@lbllighting.com
Manufacturer, importer and exporter of lighting fixtures
President/Owner: Steve Harriott
Vice President: Dennis Beard
dbeard@lbllighting.com
Sales: Krista Fischer
Plant Manager: Don Clark
Purchasing Director: Cathy Santiago
Number Employees: 100-249
Square Footage: 140000
Parent Co: Encompass Lighting

30096 Tech Pak Solutions
85 Bradley Drive
Westbrook, ME 04092-2013
207-878-6667
Fax: 425-883-9455
Temperature controlled management for food products.
Vice President: Richard Brown

30097 Tech-Roll Inc
PO Box 959
Blaine, WA 98231-0959
360-371-4321
Fax: 360-371-0752 888-946-3929
www.hydraulicdrummotors.com
Hyrdaulic motorized pulleys for the meat, poultry and food processing equipment industries.
Number Employees: 1-4

30098 Techform
PO Box 270
Mount Airy, NC 27030
336-789-2115
Fax: 336-789-2118
www.plasticingenuity.com/techform/
Custom thermoformed plastic products including blisters, clamshells, trays, cups, lids, etc.; also, contract packaging services available
President: Richard Wimbish
Quality Control: Allan Hick
Sales/Administrative: Shannon Branch
Estimated Sales: $5-10 Million
Number Employees: 10-19
Square Footage: 114000
Type of Packaging: Consumer, Food Service, Private Label, Bulk

30099 Technetics Industries
1201 N Birch Lake Boulevard
St. Paul, MN 55110-5246
651-777-4780
Fax: 651-777-5582 800-536-4880
www.tecweigh.com
Weighing systems and equipment
President: Jon Madgett
CFO: Dteven Fiank
Service Manager: Chuck Svoboda
Marketing Director: Andrew Holloway
Regional Manager: Jeff Desjardin
Estimated Sales: $1-5 Million
Number Employees: 20-49
Type of Packaging: Private Label

30100 Techni-Chem
1 N Maple Grove Rd
Boise, ID 83704-8265
800-635-8930
Fax: 208-376-3605 800-635-8930
brian@technichemcorp.com
Liquid and dry cleaning compounds for restaurant
stove hoods
President: Brian Rencher
brian@technichemcorp.com
Estimated Sales: $750,000
Number Employees: 1-4
Number of Brands: 200
Number of Products: 1
Square Footage: 20000
Brands:
Technichem

30101 TechniStar Corporation
7825 Fay Avenue
Suite 200
La Jolla, CA 92037
858-454-1400
Fax: 858-300-5118 info@technistar.com
www.technistar.com
Robotic carton loaders, casing equipment, packers,
conveyor or accessories, belt tracking

30102 Technibilt/Cari-All
700 E P St
Newton, NC 28658
828-464-7388
Fax: 828-464-7603 800-233-3972
custserv@technibilt.com www.technibilt.com
Manufacturer and exporter of wire shelves, carts,
stacking baskets, dunnage and display racks, secu-
rity units, stock trucks, containers, utility/shopping
carts and high density storage sytems
President: Pierre Lafleur
General Manager: Marcel Bourgeoys
Sales Manager: Charles Nicely
Estimated Sales: $20-50 Million
Number Employees: 250-499
Square Footage: 260000
Parent Co: Cari-All Products
Type of Packaging: Food Service
Brands:
Adapta-Flex
Adapta-Plus

30103 Technical Inc
3445 N Causeway Blvd # 1001
Suite 1001
Metairie, LA 70002-3721
504-733-0300
Fax: 504-733-0345 support@tcal.com
Owner: Lee Cabes
lcabes@tcal.com
Founder/CEO: Leon Cabes
Estimated Sales: $.5-1 million
Number Employees: 5-9

**30104 Technical Instrument
SanFrancisco**
7545 Carroll Rd
San Diego, CA 92121-2401
858-578-1860
Fax: 858-578-2344 800-765-1860
www.tsystemsinternational.com
Wine industry laboratory equipment
President: David Everitt
Chairman, Chief Executive Officer: Samuel Allen
Vice President: Aaron Wetzel
Manager of Marketing: Brett Bedard
Vice President of Sales and Marketing: Christoph
Wigger
Vice President of Public Affairs: Charles Stamp
Senior Vice President of Operations: Lawrence
Sidwell
Estimated Sales: $50-100 Million
Number Employees: 100-249

30105 Technical Tool Solutions Inc.
766 Oakwood Ave
Lake Forest, IL 60045
847-235-5551
Fax: 847-574-2506 sales@techtoolsolutions.com
www.techtoolsolutions.com
Portable machining and welding equipment.
Manager: Carl Middelegge
carl@techtoolsolutions.com
Number Employees: 1-4

30106 TechnipFMC
11740 Katy Freeway
Energy Tower 3
Houston, TX 77079
218-591-4000
www.technipfmc.com
Manufacturer and exporter of flow and level control
equipment, environmental analyzers and process
control instrumentations including flow meters,
level controls, valves, oil detectors, etc.
Chairman & CEO: Douglas Pferdehirt
EVP & Chief Financial Officer: Maryann Mannen
EVP & Chief Legal Officer: Dianne Ralston
EVP/Chief Technology Officer: Justin Rounce
EVP, People & Culture: Agnieszka Kmieciak
Estimated Sales: $13 Billion
Number Employees: 37,000
Square Footage: 268000
Brands:
Envirolert
Leveltronic

30107 Technipac
31515 Cambria Ave
Le Sueur, MN 56058-4509
Canada
507-665-6658
Fax: 507-665-2870 www.custompouches.com
Wooden boxes, containers, skids and pallets
President: Mark Steele
VP, Sales & Development: Greg Melchoir
Manager: Bonnie Dahn
Estimated Sales: Below $5 Million
Number Employees: 50-99

30108 Techniquip
530 Boulder Ct # 103
Suite 103
Pleasanton, CA 94566-8318
925-523-3421
Fax: 925-251-0704 888-414-0789
blue@techniquip.com www.techniquip.com
Digital refractometers
Owner: George Grauer
gg@techniquip.com
Estimated Sales: $2.5-5 Million
Number Employees: 10-19

30109 Technistar Corporation
1725 Gaylord Street
100
Denver, CO 80206-1208
303-651-0188
Fax: 303-651-5600 support@ew3.com
www.technistar.com
Manufacturer and exporter of flexible robotic pack-
aging equipment including carton loaders, case
packers, palletizers, kit assembly, vision inspection
and system integration
Chief Engineer: Rick Tallian
Sales Manager: Mike Weinstein
Number Employees: 85
Square Footage: 172000
Brands:
Galileo
Standard Systems

30110 Technium
68 Stacy Haines Road
Medford, NJ 08055
609-702-5910
Fax: 609-702-5915
Manufacturer, exporter and importer of juice ma-
chines
Chief Executive Officer: Ian Bell
Vice President of Product Development: Jeronimo
Barrera
Chief Technical Officer: Dan Gaul
Vice President of Sales: Sean Cullinane
Estimated Sales: $1-3 Million
Number Employees: 10
Square Footage: 32000
Brands:
Power Glide
Technium

30111 Techno-Design
1664 Frogtown Rd #203
Union, KY 41091
844-615-7281
Fax: 859-534-0939 800-641-1822
https://bdtechnodesigns.com

Machinery for frozen pasta products including
manicotti, lasagna, ravioli, stuffed rigatoni, etc.;
also, blanchers
Owner: Ruben Diaz
Estimated Sales: $500,000-$1 Million
Number Employees: 1-4
Square Footage: 16000

30112 Technomic Inc
300 S Riverside Plz # 1200
Suite 1200
Chicago, IL 60606-6637
312-876-0004
Fax: 312-876-1158 foodinfo@technomic.com
www.technomic.com
Research and consulting firm specializing in emerg-
ing channel/segment analyses, new product research,
strategic planning, acquisition studies and local
market planning
President: Ron Paul
VP: Alan Hyatt
IT: Chris Urban
curban@technomic.com
Estimated Sales: $5-10 Million
Number Employees: 50-99

30113 Technoquip Co
19515 Wied Rd # A
Suite A
Spring, TX 77388-4590
281-350-1970
Fax: 281-350-4239 sales@technoquip.com
www.technoquip.com
Filtration systems
President: Angel Santiago
sales@technoquip.com
Number Employees: 5-9

30114 Tecnocap
1701 Wheeling Ave
Glen Dale, WV 26038
304-845-3402
Fax: 304-843-5475 800-999-2567
sales@tecnocapclosures.com
www.tecnocapclosures.com
Metal closures for glass jars and bottles for the food,
beverage and cosmetics industries
President/Owner: Paolo Ghigo
Number Employees: 850+

30115 Tecogen Inc
45 1st Ave
Waltham, MA 02451-1105
781-466-6400
Fax: 781-466-6466 800-678-0550
products@tecogen.com www.tecogen.com
Natural gas engine-driven refrigeration systems
Chairperson: Angelina M. Galiteva
Chief Executive Officer: Dr. John N. Hatsopoulos
Chief Financial Officer: Bonnie Brown
Principal Engineer: Joseph Gehret
Vice President of Sales: Jeffrey Glick
Estimated Sales: $5-10 Million
Number Employees: 50-99

30116 Tectonics
62 Old Route 12 N
Westmoreland, NH 3467
603-352-8894
Fax: 603-352-8897
Plastic sheets and boxes
President: Kenneth Bergmann
Estimated Sales: Less Than $500,000
Number Employees: 1-4
Square Footage: 20000

30117 Tecumseh Products Co.
5683 Hines Dr.
Ann Arbor, MI 48108
734-585-9500
Fax: 734-352-3700 www.tecumseh.com
Refrigeration compressors, condensing units and
gasoline engines, power train components and cen-
trifugal pumps; exporter of ice making, refrigerating
and cooling machinery.
CEO: Douglas Murdock
douglas.murdock@tecumseh.com
Executive VP/CFO: Michael Baursfeld
General Counsel: Carrie Williamson
Year Founded: 1934
Estimated Sales: $854 Million
Number Employees: 5,800
Square Footage: 7176000

Other Locations:
Tecumseh Products Co.
Paris
Brands:
Tecumseh

30118 Tecweigh
1201 N Birch Lake Blvd
St Paul, MN 55110-6709

651-777-4780
Fax: 651-777-5582 800-536-4880
info@tecweigh.com www.tecweigh.com
Manufacturer and exporter of volumetric and
gravimetric feeders, weigh belts, belt scales,
batching systems and bulk bag dischargers
CFO: John Madgett Jr
Quality Control: Steve Frank
President: John P Madgett Sr
Regional Manager: Jeff Desjardin
Estimated Sales: $10-20 Million
Number Employees: 20-49
Square Footage: 60000
Brands:
Flex-Feed
Multi-Weigh
Tec Line
Tecweigh

30119 Tedea-Huntliegh
20630 Plummer street
Chatsworth, CA 91311

818-701-2750
Fax: 818-701-2799 800-423-5483
info@celesco.com www.celesco.com
Load cells and indicators
President: Michael Katz
Quality Control: Tony Roblen
Marketing: Mark Armstrong
Sales: Mark Armstrong
Estimated Sales: $2.5-5 Million
Number Employees: 35

30120 Tee-Jay Corporation
415 Howe Ave
Suite 202
Shelton, CT 6484

203-924-4767
Fax: 203-924-2967
Manufacturer and exporter of industrial sponge rub-
ber products
Owner: Thomas J Mc Queeney Jr
Estimated Sales: Less than $500,000
Number Employees: 1-4

30121 (HQ)Teepak LLC
1011 Warrenville Rd # 255
Lisle, IL 60532-0910

630-493-9080
Fax: 630-719-3805 800-621-0264
www.viscofan.com
Meat casings and plastic films
President/CEO: Paul Murphy
Sales Director: Joseph Wallner
Estimated Sales: $2 Million
Number Employees: 20-49

30122 Teilhaber ManufacturingCorp
2360 Industrial Ln
Broomfield, CO 80020-1612

303-466-2323
Fax: 303-466-2366 800-358-7225
www.teilhaber.com
Manufacturer and exporter of pallet racks, shelving
and storage accessories
President: Norm Ooms
nooms@teilhaber.com
VP Sales: Don Rutkowski
Estimated Sales: $.5-1 million
Number Employees: 50-99
Square Footage: 140000
Brands:
C.U.E.

30123 Tek Visions
40970 Anza Rd
Temecula, CA 92592-9368

951-506-9709
Fax: 951-506-4035 800-466-8005
tekv@primenet.com www.tekvisions.com
Manufacturer, importer and exporter of touch monitors, PCs and POS systems. TechVisions specializes
in fast-loading, quickly-developed and memorable
Web sites that are within any budget!

Owner: Tom Cramer
VP, Sales: Nick Christie
Tech Support Engineer: Fred Meyerhofer
VP, Sales: Tom Cramer
tom@tekvisions.com
Estimated Sales: $5-10 Million
Number Employees: 5-9

30124 Teknor Apex Co
420 S 6th Ave
City Of Industry, CA 91746-3128

626-968-4656
Fax: 626-968-4040 800-556-3864
www.teknorapex.com
PVC film
VP Marketing: Wayne Small
Plant Manager: Bill Boseman
Number Employees: 100-249

30125 Teksem LLC
19 Wayne Street
Jersey City, NJ 07302-3614

646-552-5807
Fax: 503-213-9627
President: Burak Arikan
burak@burakarikan.com
VP Marketing: Burak Arikan
Estimated Sales: $5 Million
Type of Packaging: Private Label, Bulk
Other Locations:
Fruit Acres Farm Market
Coloma MI

30126 Tel-Tru Manufacturing Co
408 Saint Paul St
Rochester, NY 14605-1734

585-232-1440
Fax: 585-232-3857 800-232-5335
info@teltru.com
Manufactures and distributes instrumentation prod-
ucts such as Bimetal Thermometers, Digital Ther-
mometers, Temperature and Pressure Transmitters,
pressure gauges, and accessory products that are de-
signed and manufactured for worldwidedistribution
to sanitary, industrial OEM, HVAC, and food service
markets.
President: Andy Germanow
Cmo: Kati Chenot
kchenot@teltru.com
Marketing Manager: Kati Chenot
Sales Manager: Yvonne O Brien
Estimated Sales: $20-50 Million
Number Employees: 100-249
Square Footage: 100000
Brands:
Check-Temp Ii
Tel-Tru

30127 TeleTech Label Company
113 Commerce Dr
Fort Collins, CO 80524-2764

970-221-2275
Fax: 970-221-2530 888-403-8253
www.teletech.com
Manufacturer and exporter of pressure sensitive and
extended format promotional labels and weather and
ultra-violet resistant tags; also, digital printing on
films and hot stamping available
President: Carol Hargadine
Director Sales/Marketing: Lindsay Woods
Estimated Sales: $3-5 Million
Number Employees: 5-9
Brands:
Polytech

30128 Telechem Corp
6477 Peachtree Industrial # D
Atlanta, GA 30360-2126

770-451-7117
Fax: 770-451-7758 800-637-0495
carson@telechem.com www.telechem.com
Water treatment chemicals, hand cleaners, detergents
and sanitation chemicals; also, project services
available
CEO/Founder: Les Washington
Director: Les Washington
Marketing: Dena Stacks
Sales Exec: Donny Mize
Estimated Sales: $2.5-5 Million
Number Employees: 10-19
Square Footage: 18000
Parent Co: Sun Mar

30129 Teledyne Benthos Inc
49 Edgerton Dr
North Falmouth, MA 02556-2826

508-563-1000
Fax: 508-563-6444 taptone@teledyne.com
www.taptone.com
Manufacturer and exporter of package inspection
equipment and leak detectors
General Manager: Francois Leroy
CFO: Franke Dunne
Director of Research: Bob Melvin
Director of QC/QA: Andrew Bonacker
Marketing Manager: Melissa Rossi
Sales/Marketing Director: Doug McGowen
Director of Production: Rick Martin
Estimated Sales: $5-10 Million
Number Employees: 100-249
Parent Co: Teledyne Technologies
Type of Packaging: Bulk

30130 Teledyne Benthos Inc
49 Edgerton Dr
North Falmouth, MA 02556-2826

508-563-1000
Fax: 508-563-6444 800-423-4044
www.benthos.com
President: Ronald Marsiglio
CMO: Doug Mcgowen
dmcgowen@benthos.com
CFO: Frank Dunne
Vice President: Richard Martin
Estimated Sales: F
Number Employees: 100-249

30131 Teledyne ISCO
4700 Superior St
Lincoln, NE 68504-1328

402-464-0231
Fax: 402-465-3064 800-228-4373
www.isco.com
Instruments for rapid fat/oil analysis, wastewater
monitoring
Cmo: Vikas V Padhye
vpadhye@teledyne.com
VP: Vikas V Padhye
Estimated Sales: $50 Million
Number Employees: 250-499

30132 Teledyne TEKMAR
4736 Socialville Foster Rd
Mason, OH 45040-8265

513-229-7042
Fax: 513-229-7050 800-874-2004
tekmarinfo@teledyne.com
www.teledynetekmar.com
Manufacturer and exporter of equipment used for
flavors and fragrance analysis, bacterial count analy-
sis and food packaging material studies
Manager: Charlie Fulmer
Cio/Cto: Kym Silber
kym_silber@teledyne.com
CFO: Cindy Reed
Chairman of the Board: Robert Mehrabian
Director Operations: Ron Uchtman
Estimated Sales: $20-50 Million
Number Employees: 50-99
Parent Co: Rosemount
Brands:
3100 Sample Concentrator
7000 Ht High Temperature Headspace
Vector Chns/O Analyzer

30133 Telesonic Packaging
805 E 13th St
Wilmington, DE 19802-5000

302-658-6945
Fax: 302-658-6946 telesonics@aol.com
www.telesoniconline.com
Manufacturer and exporter of flexible and shrink
packaging equipment, form/fill/seal and bagging
machinery and horizontal flow wrappers
Owner: Bernard Katz
telesonics@aol.com
Estimated Sales: $1-5,000,000
Number Employees: 5-9
Square Footage: 20000
Brands:
Versapak

30134 (HQ)Televend
111 Croydon Rd
Baltimore, MD 21212

410-532-7818
Fax: 410-532-7818

Manufacturer and exporter of computer terminal systems and custom application software including supermarket incentive gaming; importer of computer software
President: Stephen R Krause
CEO: Nat Miller
CFO: Sam Katz
VP: George Panda
R&D: SR Krause
Quality Control: Earl Davis
Marketing/Sales: Nat Miller
Contact: Sam Katz
sktv@comcast.net
Operations: RM Martin
Production: Charles Caplan
Plant Manager: Earl Davis
Purchasing: Geroge Panda
Estimated Sales: $1-3 Million
Number Employees: 50-99
Number of Brands: 12
Number of Products: 11
Square Footage: 5000
Type of Packaging: Bulk
Brands:
    Chain-Data
    Prize Box

30135 Tema Systems Inc
7806 Redsky Dr
Cincinnati, OH 45249-1632
                    513-792-2840
        Fax: 513-489-4817 www.tema.net
Centrifuge parts, filtration and recycling equipment, separators, clarifiers and whey processing equipment; exporter of centrifuges and separators
President: Mike Mullins
changar.glori@lexisnexis.com
Technical Manager: Mike Vastola
Estimated Sales: $10-20 Million
Number Employees: 20-49
Square Footage: 30000
Parent Co: Siebtechnik
Brands:
    Conidur
    Conturbex

30136 Temco
2100 Dennison St
Oakland, CA 94606
                    707-746-5966
    Fax: 707-746-5965 sales@temcoscales.com
                www.temcoscales.com
Manufacturer and exporter of packaging machinery including weighers, bag openers, fillers, sealers and case and can fillers
President: David Travis
Engineer: Rob Vincent
Equipment Sales: Jeff Reed
Plant Manager: Bob Breitenstein
Estimated Sales: Below $5 Million
Number Employees: 10
Square Footage: 36000

30137 Temkin International
213 Temkin Way
Payson, UT 84651
                    800-235-5263
        info@temkininternational.com
            www.temkininternational.com
Flexible film packaging (zipper pouches, wicketed bags, sandwich bags) and digital printing services
Owner: Danny Temkin
Sales Manager: Eric Hopkins
Production Manager: Marcelo Menjivar
Year Founded: 1980
Number Employees: 200-500
Brands:
    Cello Wrap
    Hyper Clear
    Loft 213
    Party Bags

30138 (HQ)Temp Air Inc
3700 W Preserve Blvd
Burnsville, MN 55337-7746
                    952-894-3000
    Fax: 952-707-5104 800-836-7432
                www.temp-air.com
Chemical-free pest control, environmental air systems and air cleaners

CEO: Jim Korn
jkorn@temp-air.com
Product Manager: Mimoun Abaraw
Technical Field Represative: Warren Barich
Marketing Manager: Jessica Anderson
National Sales Manager: Tom Danley
Estimated Sales: $20-50 Million
Number Employees: 50-99

30139 Temp Air Inc
3700 W Preserve Blvd
Burnsville, MN 55337-7746
                    952-894-3000
    Fax: 952-707-5104 800-836-7432
    info@temp-air.com www.temp-air.com
Provide chemical pest management for milling operations and processors
Chairman of the Board: Ruth E Rupp
CEO: Jim Korn
jkorn@temp-air.com
Sales Director: Mimoum Abarow
Number Employees: 50-99
Square Footage: 140
Parent Co: Rupp Industries

30140 Tempco Electric Heater Corporation
607 N Central Ave
Wood Dale, IL 60191-1452
                    630-350-2252
    Fax: 630-350-0232 888-268-6396
    info@tempco.com www.tempco.com
Manufacturer and exporter of industrial and commercial electric heating elements including air, band, bolt and cartridge heaters; temperature sensors and controls, including thermocouples and RTDs.
President: Fermin Adames
faadames@tempco.com
Quality Control: Tony Ocosta
Estimated Sales: $30 Million
Number Employees: 400
Square Footage: 260000

30141 Tempera/Sol
74 Hightland Cir
Suite 126
Wayland, MA 01778-1731
                    508-358-0090
            Fax: 978-358-0099
Industrial equipment to temper, thaw, chill, crust, freeze, or cook food
President: Ronald Snider

30142 Temple-Inland
6400 Poplar Avenue
Memphis, TN 38197
                    901-419-9000
    internationalpaper.comm@ipaper.com
            www.templeinland.com
Shipping containers
Contact: Omar El-Shishini
omar.el-shishini@ipaper.com
Estimated Sales: $50-100 Million
Number Employees: 100-249
Parent Co: International Paper

30143 Templock Corporation
The Vercal Building 170
Santa Barbara, CA 93130
                    805-962-3100
    Fax: 805-962-3110 800-777-1715
    sales@templock.com www.templock.com
Manufacturer and exporter of PVC heat shrinkable tubing for tamper-evident seal, label and sleeve applications
President: William Spargur
Executive VP: Paul Montgomery
Sales Manager: Kristine Hille
Estimated Sales: $5-10 Million
Number Employees: 20-49
Square Footage: 60000
Brands:
    Templock

30144 Tenchy Machinery Corporation
P.O.Box 284
Eastpointe, MI 48015
                    586-773-8822
    Fax: 586-445-1358 sales@techmachinery.com
Manufacturer and distributor of twistwrapping, pillowpack and overwrap packaging machinery
Brands:
    Tenchi

30145 Tenent Laboratories
6555 Quince Road
Suite 202
Memphis, TN 38119-8214
                    901-272-7511
    Fax: 901-272-2926 800-880-1038
Analytical chemistry services for food industry, nutrition labeling, microbiology, lipid analysis, fatty acid profiles, proximate chemistry, vitamin and mineral
Estimated Sales: $1-5 Million
Number Employees: 100-250

30146 Tenka Flexible Packaging
5418 Schaefer Ave
Chino, CA 91710
                    909-628-2788
    Fax: 909-902-0097 888-836-5255
    info@tenkapack.com www.tenkapack.com
Coffee bags; bags for snack foods, pet foods, gourmet items, specialty foods and various other products; stand up pouches, flat pouches, foil bags and paper bags
Sales Executive: Angie Ramirez
Contact: Dawn Aubry
dawn@tenkapack.com
Regional Manager: Corrine Douglas

30147 Tennant Co.
701 N. Lilac Dr.
P.O. Box 1452
Minneapolis, MN 55422
            Fax: 763-513-2142 800-553-8033
    info@tennantco.com www.tennantco.com
Clean room and sanitation equipment and supplies, power sweeper/scrubbers, floor coatings and flooring.
President/CEO/Director: Chris Killingstad
Managing Director: Junzo Tsuda
Vice President/Chief Financial Officer: Thomas Paulson
Vice President, Global Operations: Don Westman
Vice President, Technology: Thomas Bruce
Director, Public Relations: Michael Buckley
Vice President, Operations: Steven Weeks
Year Founded: 1870
Estimated Sales: $739 Million
Number Employees: 1000-4999
Number of Brands: 4
Type of Packaging: Bulk
Brands:
    Tennant®
    Nobles®
    Alfa
    Orbio® Technologies

30148 Tenneco Inc
500 N Field Dr
Lake Forest, IL 60045-2595
                    847-482-5000
    Fax: 847-482-5940 800-403-3393
                www.tenneco.com
Manufacturer and exporter of dual oven pressed paperboard trays
Chairman: Gregg Sherrill
gsherrill@tenneco.com
CEO: Hari N Nair
CFO/EVP: Kenneth R Trammell
SVP, General Counsel & Corp. Secretary: James Harrington
Marketing Administration: Carly Rhoads
VP Sales North America: William Read
SVP, Global HR & Administration: Gregg A Bolt
Estimated Sales: Over $1 Billion
Number Employees: 10000+
Square Footage: 1172000
Parent Co: Tenneco Packaging
Type of Packaging: Food Service
Brands:
    Pressware

30149 Tenneco Packaging
777 Oakmont Lane
Westmont, IL 60559-5511
                    630-850-7034
            Fax: 303-452-0430
Corrugated boxes and interior cushion packaging
Sales Manager: Michael Farmer
Contact: Karen Mcgill
karen_mcgill@packagingcorp.com
Estimated Sales: $1-5 Million
Parent Co: Tenneco Packaging

30150 Tenneco Specialty Packaging
2907 Log Cabin Drive SE
Smyrna, GA 30080-7013
404-350-1300
Fax: 404-350-1489 800-241-4402
Manufacturer and exporter of foam and barrier modified atmosphere packaging trays, disposable tableware, plastic utensils and foam cups
Manager: Ross Eckerman
Number Employees: 1500
Parent Co: Tenneco
Type of Packaging: Consumer, Food Service

30151 Tennessee Mills
5546 Clay County Highway
Red Boiling Springs, TN 37150-5265
615-699-2253
Fax: 615-699-2033
Wooden pallets
Owner: W White
VP Marketing/Sales: David White
Estimated Sales: $2.5-5 Million
Number Employees: 20-49

30152 Tennessee Packaging
1500 Elizabeth Lee Pkwy
PO Box 418
Loudon, TN 37774-5687
865-458-3567
Fax: 423-337-0881 800-968-6894
swinfield@tnpkg.com
www.buckeyecorrugated.com
Corrugated boxes
Division President: Scott Winfield
Cio/Cto: Terri Wall
twall@tnpkg.com
Sales Manager: Scott Barnett
Administrative Operations Manager: Terri Wall
Production Manager: Don Laurie
Estimated Sales: $10-20 Million
Number Employees: 50-99
Parent Co: BCI Companies

30153 Tennsco Corp
201 Tennsco Dr
Dickson, TN 37055-3014
615-446-8000
Fax: 615-446-7224 800-251-8184
info@tennsco.com www.tennsco.com
Manufacturer and exporter of wire shelving systems, lockers and cabinets
CEO: Lester Speyer
VP Sales: Hal McCalla
Plant Manager: Johnnie Morris
Purchasing Manager: Mickey Self
Estimated Sales: $80 Million
Number Employees: 500-999
Square Footage: 1400000
Type of Packaging: Food Service
Brands:
Logic

30154 Tenor Controls Company
2120 S Calhoun Rd
New Berlin, WI 53151-2218
262-782-3800
Fax: 262-782-3880 800-468-4494
tenor@execpc.com
Timers, relays and controls
Estimated Sales: $1-5 Million
Number Employees: 5-9

30155 Tente Casters Inc
2266 S Park Dr
Hebron, KY 41048-9537
859-586-5558
Fax: 859-586-5859 800-783-2470
info@tente-us.com www.tente.us
NSF listed casters; importer of casters
President: Brad Hood
Vice President: Renne Beltramo
Marketing Director: Sabine Batsche
Sales Director: Aaron Romer
Production Manager: Sue Dinkel
Estimated Sales: $10-20 Million
Number Employees: 100-249
Square Footage: 130000
Parent Co: TENTE-ROLLEN Gmbh

30156 Tente Casters Inc
2266 S Park Dr
Hebron, KY 41048-9537
859-586-5558
Fax: 859-586-5859 800-783-2470
info@tente-us.com www.tente.us
NSF certified casters and wheels.
CEO: Brad Hood
Marketing: Sabine Batsche
Sales: Aaron Romer
Plant Manager: Sue Dinkel
Estimated Sales: $20 Million
Number Employees: 100-249
Square Footage: 65000

30157 Tente Casters Inc
2266 S Park Dr
Hebron, KY 41048-9537
859-586-5558
Fax: 859-586-5859 800-783-2470
info@tente-us.com www.tente.us
Company is a manufacturer of NSF Certified casters and wheels.
CEO: Brad Hood
Marketing/Public Relations: Sabine Batasche
Sales Director: Aaron Romer
Plant Manager: Sue Dinkel
Estimated Sales: $20 Million
Number Employees: 100-249
Square Footage: 65000

30158 Tepromark International
249 5th Avenue SE
Osseo, MN 55369
763-273-8484
Fax: 763-273-8486 800-645-2622
www.tepromark.com
Floor mats, corner guards and railings
VP: Harold Klein
Sales Associate: Diane Mazuelerich
Manager: Alvin Templeton
Estimated Sales: $10-20 Million
Number Employees: 10-19

30159 Terkelsen Machine Company
Airport Road
Hyannis, MA 2601
508-775-6229
Fax: 508-778-4441
Manufacturer and exporter of baling wire for bulk packaging
President: Russell Terkelsen
Number Employees: 4

30160 Terlet USA
520 Sharptown Rd
Swedesboro, NJ 08085
856-241-9970
Fax: 856-241-9975
Aseptic and sterile process equipment and systems.
Founder: J.W. Terlet
CEO: Philip Stibbe
Contact: Bart Brouwer
b.brouwer@jongia.com
Estimated Sales: $1-2 Million
Parent Co: Stibbe Management Group

30161 Terminix
3050 Whitestone Expy # 303
Flushing, NY 11354-1995
516-671-2411
Fax: 718-939-4161 866-319-6528
www.terminix.com
Manufacturer and exporter of waste disposal and pest control systems
Owner: Anthony Tabacco
Chief Operating Officer: Larry Pruitt
VP, Customer Experience: Phil Barber
Chief Marketing Officer: Kevin Kovalski
Vice President of Sales: Steve Good
VP, Communications: Valerie Middleton
Vice President of Operations: Larry Pruitt
Estimated Sales: $2.5-5 Million
Number Employees: 20-49
Parent Co: Terminix Commercial Services
Brands:
Terminix

30162 Terphane Inc
2754 W Park Dr
Bloomfield, NY 14469-9385
585-657-5800
Fax: 585-657-5838 800-724-3456
mail@terphane.com www.terphane.com

Manufacturer, importer and exporter of polyester film
General Manager: Dan Roy
Sales/Marketing Manager: Brian Ochsner
Human Resources Manager: Karen VanDerEems
Plant Manager: Chuck Mac Cary
Estimated Sales: $10-20 Million
Number Employees: 50-99
Square Footage: 320000
Brands:
Terphane

30163 Terracon Corp
1376 W Central St # 130
Suite 130
Franklin, MA 02038-7100
508-429-8737
Fax: 508-429-8737 sales@terracon-solutions.com
www.terracon-solutions.com
Wine industry plastic tanks. These tanks are also used in water/waste treatment, biotech, pharmaceutical, plating/etching, food, medical, ceramics, aquaculture and semiconductor markets
President: Rob Jewett
Technical Sales: Joe Bolandrino
Sales Manager: Bernie Lanaham
Contact: Joe Bolandrina
jbolandrina@tricatgroup.com
Operations Manager: Rob Jewett
Estimated Sales: $5-10 Million
Number Employees: 10-19

30164 Terriss Consolidate
807 Summerfield Ave
Asbury Park, NJ 07712-6970
732-988-2044
Fax: 732-502-0526 800-342-1611
terriss@terriss.com www.terriss.com
Laboratory equipment: testing equipment, stainless steel fabricators, mixing tanks, tables, and sinks
Owner: Judy Bodnobich
Research and Development: Marc Epstein
Sales: Edward DellaZanna
terriss@terriss.com
Estimated Sales: $1.8 Million
Number Employees: 10-19
Square Footage: 25000

30165 Terry Manufacturing Company
PO Box 130041
Birmingham, AL 35213-0041
205-250-0062
Fax: 334-863-8835
Manufacturer and exporter of uniforms
President: Roy Terry
Estimated Sales: $1-2.5 Million
Number Employees: 1-4
Type of Packaging: Food Service

30166 Tesa Tape Inc
5825 Carnegie Blvd
Charlotte, NC 28209-4633
704-554-0707
Fax: 704-553-5677 800-429-8273
customercare@tesatape.com www.tesatape.com
Manufacturer and exporter of pressure sensitive adhesive tape
President: Carston Myer
cmyer@tesatape.com
CEO: Torsten Schermer
Estimated Sales: H
Number Employees: 50-99
Parent Co: tesa AG
Type of Packaging: Consumer, Food Service, Private Label, Bulk
Brands:
Nopi
Tesa
Tuck

30167 Testing Machines Inc
40 Mccullough Dr
New Castle, DE 19720-2066
302-613-5619
Fax: 302-613-5019 800-678-3221
info@testingmachines.com
www.testingmachines.com
Manufacturer and exporter of crush, permeation, humidity, thickness and printability testing machinery
CEO: John Sullivan
Vice President: Richard Young
Marketing Director: Dave Muchorski
Sales Director: Richard Young

Estimated Sales: $10-20,000,000
Number Employees: 100-249
Brands:
  Lab Master

30168 Testo
P.O. Box 1606
Berlin, MA 21811

410-777-8555
Fax: 973-579-3222 800-227-0729
info@testo.com www.ita.cc
Digital thermometers, data loggers, portable instruments for humidity, air velocity and water quality
Manager: Melissa Curro
VP: Andrew Kuczkuda
Quality Control: Cate Mariott
Marketing Manager: Lori Lyonn
Estimated Sales: Below $5 Million
Number Employees: 10-19

30169 (HQ)Tetra Pak
Communications
3300 Airport Rd
Denton, TX 76207

940-380-4630
www.tetrapak.com
Components and systems for processing, packaging and distribution of liquid foods; serving the dairy and beverage industries.
President & CEO: Adolfo Orive
EVP, Supply Chain Operations: Eric Baudier
SVP, Corporate Communications: Nicholas Bloch
SVP, Finance: Bruce Burrows
EVP, Processing Solutions & Equipment: Ola Elmqvist
EVP, Services: Roberto Franchitti
Cluster VP, Americas: Tatiana Liceti
SVP, Legal Affairs & General Counsel: Pal Lunning
SVP, Human Resources: Phil Read
Year Founded: 1943
Estimated Sales: $11.5 Billion
Number Employees: 24,800
Brands:
  Tetra Brik Aseptic
  Tetra Rex

30170 Tetra Pak
600 Bunker Ct
Vernon Hills, IL 60061

847-955-6000
Fax: 847-955-6500 www.tetrapak.com
Components and systems for processing, packaging and distribution of liquid foods; serving the dairy and beverage industries.
Parent Co: Tetra Laval Group

30171 Tetra Pak
12255 Ensign Avenue N
Champlin, MN 55316

763-421-2721
www.tetrapak.com
Components and systems for processing, packaging and distribution of liquid foods; serving the dairy and beverage industries.
Type of Packaging: Consumer, Food Service, Private Label
Brands:
  Tetra Alblend
  Tetra Albrix
  Tetra Alcarb Spark
  Tetra Alcip
  Tetra Alcross
  Tetra Aldose
  Tetra Alvac
  Tetra Alvap
  Tetra Alwin
  Tetra Brik Aseptic
  Tetra Centri
  Tetra Classic
  Tetra Fino
  Tetra Plantcare
  Tetra Plantmaster
  Tetra Plantopt
  Tetra Plex
  Tetra Prisma
  Tetra Rex
  Tetra Spiraflo
  Tetra Tebel
  Tetra Therm
  Tetra Top
  Tetra Wedge
  Treta Alex
  Treta Alfast
  Treta Almix
  Treta Alrox
  Treta Alsafe
  Treta Alscreen

30172 Tetra Pak
423 Arlington Ave
Fond Du Lac, WI 54935

www.tetrapak.com
Components and systems for processing, packaging and distribution of liquid foods; serving the dairy and beverage industries.

30173 Tew Manufacturing Corp
470 Whitney Rd
PO Box 87
Penfield, NY 14526-2326

585-586-6120
Fax: 585-586-6083 800-380-5839
info@tewmfg.com www.tewmfg.com
Manufacturer and exporter of fruit and vegetable cleaning equipment
Owner: William H Tew
tewmfg@aol.com
Estimated Sales: Less Than $500,000
Number Employees: 1-4
Square Footage: 16000

30174 Texas Baket Company
100 Myrtle Drive
Jacksonville, TX 75766-1110

903-586-8014
Fax: 903-586-0988 800-657-2200
sales@texasbasket.com www.texasbasket.com
Wooden baskets, display racks and hand-painted baskets
President: Mardin Swanson
CFO and R&D: Troy Parker
Quality Control: David Habberle
Estimated Sales: Below $5 Million
Number Employees: 100-249

30175 Texas Corn Roasters
3300 X A Meyer Rd
Granbury, TX 76049-2306

817-573-7313
Fax: 817-561-5006 800-772-4345
cornroaster@live.com
Mobile corn roasters and concession trailers
Owner: Ken O'Keefe
Number Employees: 1-4

30176 Texas Hill Country Barbacue
919 State Highway 46 E
Boerne, TX 78006-5758

830-336-2858
Fax: 830-336-2991 866-302-7289
Barbacued foods and smoked meats, product line of which includes smoked beef brisket, smoked sausage, chopped beef BBQ with sauce, pulled pork with sauce, whole smoked chicken, whole smoked turkey, spiral cut ham and smoked BBQsauce.
CEO: Jesse Tindall
Sales & Marketing: Hal McCall
Type of Packaging: Food Service

30177 Texas Neon Advertising Inc
245 W Josephine St
San Antonio, TX 78212-4153

210-734-6694
Fax: 210-734-6697
Indoor and outdoor signs including neon
President: George Ryan
gryan@texasneonadv.com
Estimated Sales: $1-2.5 Million
Number Employees: 10-19

30178 (HQ)Texas Refinery Corp
840 N Main St
Fort Worth, TX 76164-9486

817-332-1161
Fax: 817-332-6110 trc711@texasrefinery.com
www.texasrefinery.com
Food machinery lubricants
President: Jerry Hopkins
CEO: A M Pate III
CFO: Chuck Adamson
VP: Jim Peel
R&D: Seth Davis
Sales: Dennis Parks
Purchasing: Barbara Main
Estimated Sales: $20-50 Million
Number Employees: 50-99

30179 Texas Spice Co
2709 Sam Bass Rd
Round Rock, TX 78681-1811

512-255-8816
Fax: 512-255-4189 800-880-8007
contact@texas-spice.net www.texas-spice.com
Wholesale and retail custom blending, spices, seasoning blends, bases, extracts, flavors, coffee & tea
Owner: Beckie Forsyth
Contact: Jason Spangler
spangler@texas-spice.net
Estimated Sales: Less Than $500,000
Number Employees: 1-4
Type of Packaging: Food Service
Brands:
  Texas Spice

30180 Texican Specialty Products
10900 Brittmoore Park Dr Ste H
Houston, TX 77041

713-896-9924
Fax: 713-896-9925 800-869-5918
www.texicanspecialty.com
Tostada dispensers and warming cabinets
President: Donald J Spilger
Vice President: V Spilger
Contact: Jb Spilger
generalsales@texicanspecialty.com
Estimated Sales: $500,000
Number Employees: 1-4
Number of Brands: 1
Number of Products: 2
Square Footage: 7600

30181 Texpak Inc
892 Route 73 N
Suite 1
Marlton, NJ 08053-1228

856-988-5533
Fax: 856-988-5524 texpak@bellatlantic.net
Roasters (machines), bin silo systems and storage, blending and mixing equipment (coffee), computer systems, grinders
Estimated Sales: $1-5 Million

30182 Textile Buff & Wheel
511 Medford St # 1
Charlestown, MA 02129-1495

617-241-8100
Fax: 617-241-7280 www.textilebuff.com
Manufacturer and exporter of wiping cloths, mill remnants, cheesecloths and cotton gloves
Owner: Jerold Wise
Partner: Andrew Wise
Estimated Sales: $5-10 Million
Number Employees: 20-49
Square Footage: 200000

30183 Textile Products Company
2512-2520 W Woodland Drive
Anaheim, CA 92801-2636

714-761-0401
Fax: 714-761-2928
Manufacturer and exporter of cheesecloth wiping rags and disposable rags
Marketing Director: Pearl Seratelli
Estimated Sales: $1-5 Million
Parent Co: Textile Products

30184 Texture Technologies Corporation
18 Fairview Rd
Scarsdale, NY 10583

914-472-0531
Fax: 914-472-0532
marcj@texturetechnologies.com
www.texturetechnologies.com
Manufacturer, importer and exporter of measurement instrumentation and software for testing food texture; also, bloom gel testers
President: Boine Johnson
CEO: Marc Johnson
CFO: Sue Perko
Quality Control: Joseph Piperis
Contact: James Fabry
jimf@texturetechnologies.com
Estimated Sales: $5 Million
Brands:
  Ta-Xt2
  Texture Expert For Windows

30185 Thamesville Metal Products Ltd
2 London Road
Thamesville, ON N0P 2K0
Canada
519-692-3963
Fax: 519-692-5213 bulldogsteelwool@kent.net
www.bulldogsteelwool.ca
Steel wool scouring pads
President: Robert Schieman
CFO: Greg Schieman
Estimated Sales: Below $5 Million
Number Employees: 10
Square Footage: 240000
Brands:
　Bulldog

30186 Tharo Systems Inc
2866 Nationwide Pkwy
PO Box 798
Brunswick, OH 44212-2362
330-273-4408
Fax: 330-225-0099 800-878-6833
info@easylabel.fr www.tharo.com
Manufacturer and exporter of computer software for
custom designing and printing bar code, RFID, and
food ingredient labels, printers and printer/applica-
tors, ribbons, labels, label rewinds, unwinds, and
dispensers
President: Michelle Lyngoe
m_lyngoe@aimforsafety.com
VP Marketing: Lauren Shaarda
Sales Director: James Danko
Operations: Randy Thatcher
Estimated Sales: $5-10 Million
Number Employees: 10-19
Number of Brands: 1000
Number of Products: 4
Brands:
　Cab Produkttechnik
　Datamax Corporation
　Dispensa-Matic
　Easylabel
　Sony Chemicals
　Tharo

30187 The Canvas Exchange Inc
2324 Dennison Avenue
Cleveland, OH 44109
216-749-2233
Fax: 216-749-0987 ceiawning@sbcglobal.net
www.ceiawning.com
Manufacturer of commercial awnings.
President: Hank Proctor
Contact: Kevin Potoczak
kevin@ceiawning.net
Account Rep.: Kevin Potoczak
Year Founded: 1984
Estimated Sales: $500,000-$1 Million
Number Employees: 5-9

30188 The Carriage Works
1877 Mallard Ln
Klamath Falls, OR 97601-5522
541-882-0700
Fax: 541-882-9661 sales@carriageworks.com
www.carriageworks.com
Manufacturer, importer and exporter of food service
and retail merchandising carts, in-line concepts, ki-
osks and machines including espresso, hot dog, ice
cream and beverage
President & CEO: Brian Dunham
VP, Sales & Marketing: Lori Butler
Estimated Sales: $5-10 Million
Number Employees: 20-49

30189 The Consumer Goods Forum
8455 Colesville Rd # 705
Silver Spring, MD 20910
301-563-3383
Fax: 301-563-3386
washington@theconsumergoodsforum.com
www.theconsumergoodsforum.com/index.aspx
Bringing together consumer goods manufacturers
and retailers for efficiency and postive change.
Co-Chairman: Dick Boer
Co-Chairman: Paul Bulcke
Contact: Thomas Bailey
t.bailey@theconsumergoodsforum.com
Number Employees: 20-49

30190 The Good Food Institute
1380 Monroe St. NW
Ste. 229
Washington, DC 20010
866-849-4457
www.gfi.org
Offers marketing, design, legal, business, and media
consultations.
Co-Founder & Executive Director: Bruce Friedrich
Director of Finance & General Counsel: Sarah
David
Director of Development: Susan Halteman
Director of Communications: Annie Gull *Year
Founded:* 2015

30191 The Lobster Place
75 Ninth Avenue
Chelsea Market
New York, NY 10011
212-255-5672
info@lobsterplace.com
lobsterplace.com
Lobster, seafood
President: Brendan Hayes
CEO: Ian MacGregor
Lead Sales Executive: Joe Cooper
Contact: Renee Alevras
ralevras@lobsterplace.com
Operations Manager: Christian Quintana
Purchasing Manager: Mark Grobman

30192 The National Provisioner
155 N. Pfingsten Rd.
Suite 205
Deerfield, IL 60015
847-763-9534
Fax: 847-763-9538 www.provisioneronline.com
Manufacturer and exporter of material handling
products including conveyors and laser guided auto-
mated vehicle systems
Owner: Elmer Hartford
COO: Kevin Donahue
Engineer Manager: Todd Frandsen
Vice President of Services: Tom Egan
Sales Manager: Diana Rotman
Contact: Andy Hanacek
hanaceka@bnpmedia.com
Number Employees: 100-249
Square Footage: 300000
Brands:
　Pulverlaser

30193 The Procter & Gamble Company
1 P&G Plaza
Cincinnati, OH 45202
513-983-1100
Fax: 513-983-9369 800-692-0132
us.pg.com
Baby diapers, fabric care, feminine products, sham-
poos, paper towels, toilet paper, tissues, condition-
ers, dishwashing detergent, home cleaning products,
razors, shaving gels, supplements, pregnancy tests,
cough syrup, and more.
Chairman, President & CEO: David Taylor
CFO: Jon Moeller
Estimated Sales: $67.6 Billion
Number Employees: 97,000
Number of Brands: 57
Type of Packaging: Consumer
Brands:
　Always
　Ariel
　Luvs
　Pampers
　Tide
　Bounce
　Cheer
　Downy
　Dreft
　Era
　Gain
　Ace
　Rindex 3en1
　Bounty
　Charmin
　Puffs
　Always Discreet
　Tampax
　Head & Shoulders
　Aussie
　Herbal Essences
　Old Spice
　Pantene
　Cascade
　Dawn
　Febreeze
　Joy
　Mr. Clean
　Swiffer
　Salvo
　Ambi Pur
　Comet
　Braun
　Gillette
　Venus
　The Art of Shaving
　Align
　Clearblue
　Meta
　Pepto-Bismol
　Prilosec OTC
　Vicks
　ZzzQuil
　Crest
　Fixodent
　Oral-B
　Scope
　Ivory
　Olay
　Safeguard
　Secret
　Native
　Snowberry
　SK-II

30194 The Pub Brewing Company
EAST COAST
185 Route 17 North
Mahwah, NJ 07430
201-512-0387
Fax: 201-512-1459 www.pubbrewing.com
President: Erwin Eibert
Estimated Sales: $5-10 Million
Number Employees: 10-19

30195 The Pub Brewing Company
WEST COAST
3600 C Standish Avenue
Santa Rosa, CA 95407
Fax: 201-512-1459 www.pubbrewing.com
President: Erwin Eibert
Estimated Sales: $5-10 Million
Number Employees: 10-19

30196 The Rubin Family of Wines
5220 Ross Rd
Sebastopol, CA 95472-2158
707-887-8130
Fax: 707-887-8160 wine@rubinfamilyofwines.com
rubinfamilyofwines.com
Wines
Founder: Ron Rubin
Winemaker: Joe Freeman
Estimated Sales: Under $500,000
Number Employees: 1-4
Type of Packaging: Private Label
Brands:
　River Road Vineyards

30197 The Tombras Group
830 Concord Street
Knoxville, TN 37919
865-524-5376
Fax: 865-524-5667 jwelsch@tombras.com
www.tombras.com
President: Charles P Tombras Jr
Estimated Sales: $5-10 Million
Number Employees: 100+

30198 Theimeg
58 W Shenango St
Sharpsville, PA 16150-1154
724-962-3571
Fax: 724-962-4310 www.cattron.com
Remote control systems for cranes, locomotives and
other industrial machinery
President: John Paul
Estimated Sales: $10-15 Million
Number Employees: 10-19
Parent Co: Theimeg

30199 Theingredienthouse
120 Applecross Rd # 2
2nd Fl
Pinehurst, NC 28374-8520
910-693-0037
Fax: 877-542-4844 info@theingredienthouse.com
www.theingredienthouse.com

Supplier of food ingredients to food manufacturers such as high intensity sweeteners, soluble fibers, hydrocolloids, agave syrup, polyols, insoluble fibers, sugar alcohols, cooling compounds
President, COO: Rudi Van
CEO: Graham Hall
graham.hall@theingredienthouse.com
Vice President Quality Assurance: Jeff Lewis
VP Marketing: Peter Brown
VP Sales: Janet Timko
Customer Service Director: Ann Hall
VP Operations: Kevin Lovett
Estimated Sales: $300 Thousand
Number Employees: 5-9

30200 (HQ)Theochem Laboratories Inc
7373 Rowlett Park Dr
Tampa, FL 33610-1101
813-237-6463
Fax: 813-237-2059 800-237-2591
www.theochem.com
Manufacturer and exporter of chemical cleaners and inorganic cleaning compounds
COO and President: John Theofilos
Director Operations: Lenny Wydotis
Estimated Sales: $20-50 Million
Number Employees: 5-9
Square Footage: 250000
Brands:
 Solutions For a Cleaner World

30201 Theos Foods
119 N Duke St
Hummelstown, PA 17036-1310
717-566-5622
Fax: 717-566-5592 800-755-8436
Cost effective bulk packaged items such as Theo's Stromboli, and pre-baked sandwiches also available
President and CFO: Ted Atanasoff
theosfoods@verizon.net
Manager: Barry Broadwater
Estimated Sales: $5-10 Million
Number Employees: 20-49

30202 Therm L Tec Building Systems
15115 Chestnut St
Basehor, KS 66007-9207
913-728-2662
Fax: 913-724-1446 www.thermltec.com
Insulated commercial cold storage panels, partitions, doors and liners
Sales: Dennis Bixby
Contact: Joshua Cole
jcole@thermltec.com
Estimated Sales: $5-10 Million
Number Employees: 1-4
Square Footage: 300000
Brands:
 Therm-L-Bond

30203 Therm-Tec Inc
20525 SW Cipole Rd
Sherwood, OR 97140-8339
503-625-7575
Fax: 503-625-6161 800-292-9163
www.thermtec.com
Manufacturer and exporter of solid, animal and human crematories, and hospital waste incinerators; also air pollution control equipment
Owner: Dean Robbins
thermtec@earthlink.net
Estimated Sales: Below $5 Million
Number Employees: 10-19
Square Footage: 160000
Brands:
 Therm-Tec

30204 Therma Kleen
10212 S Mandel St # A
Plainfield, IL 60585-5374
630-820-6700
Fax: 630-305-8696 800-999-3120
steamtk@aol.com www.therma-kleen.com
Manufacturer and exporter of steam cleaners and pressure washers
President: Andy Heller
VP: Linda Heller
IT: Linda Hubbell
steamtk@aol.com
Estimated Sales: $500,000-$1 Million
Number Employees: 5-9
Square Footage: 5600
Brands:
 Therma-Kleen

30205 Thermaco Inc
646 Greensboro St
PO Box 2548
Asheboro, NC 27203-4739
336-629-4651
Fax: 336-626-5739 800-633-4204
info@thermaco.com www.thermaco.com
Manufacturer and exporter of pre-treatments and automatic solid and grease/oil removal units for restaurants and food processing plants
President: William Batten
info@thermaco.com
Estimated Sales: $1-2.5 Million
Number Employees: 10-19
Square Footage: 12000
Brands:
 Big Dipper
 Big Flipper
 Superceptor

30206 Thermafreeze
776 Lakeside Drive
Mobile, AL 36693-5114
251-666-2011
Fax: 251-666-5660
Solutions for the safe shipment of temperature-critical media
President: J Murray
Contact: Joseph Murray
joseph.murray@thermafreeze.com

30207 Thermal Bags By Ingrid Inc
131 Sola Dr
Gilberts, IL 60136-9748
847-836-4400
Fax: 847-836-4408 800-622-5560
Mary@ThermalBags.com www.thermalbags.com
Manufacturer and exporter of thermal food bags, racks, thermal hoods, insulated carrying bags, pizza delivery pouches and catering bags. Also lightweight insulated bags for the carry-out market and advertising specialites
Inventor & CEO: Ingrid Kosar
ingrid@thermalbags.com
Marketing Director: Fred Kosar
Estimated Sales: $2.5-5 Million
Number Employees: 5-9
Type of Packaging: Food Service
Brands:
 Food Carriers
 Thermal Bags By Ingrid

30208 Thermal Engineering Corp
2741 The Blvd
Columbia, SC 29209-3527
803-783-0750
Fax: 803-783-0756 800-331-0097
www.tecinfrared.com
Under-fired infrared gas charbroilers and griddles for the consumer and food service industry
President: Bill Best
CEO: W H Best
wh.best@tecinfrared.com
CFO: Tony Stihom
Sales/Marketing Executive: Johnny Johnson
Sales Manager: Jack Whitten
Public Relations: Renee Pecks
Estimated Sales: $20-50 Million
Number Employees: 100-249
Parent Co: Thermal Engineering Corporation
Type of Packaging: Food Service

30209 Thermal Package TestingLaboratory
41 Pine Street
Rockaway, NJ 07866-3139
973-627-4405
Fax: 973-627-5355 800-432-5909
info@package-testing.com
www.package-testing.com
Testing: ASTM, ISTA, Unidot, vibration, drop; inafine impact, compression, environmental chambers, pallet loads, supersacks, drums
President: David Dixon
Estimated Sales: $.5-1 million
Number Employees: 5-9

30210 Thermal Technologies
630 Park Way
Broomall, PA 19008-4209
610-353-8887
Fax: 610-353-8663
Produce repening systems for the fruit industry. Also design, engineering and construction of cold rooms

Estimated Sales: $.5-1 million
Number Employees: 1-4

30211 Thermaline Inc
1531 14th St NW # 1
Auburn, WA 98001-3518
253-833-7118
Fax: 253-833-7168 800-767-6720
info@thermaline.com www.thermaline.com
Plate heat exchangers, tubular heat exchangers, skid mounted pasteurization systems, boiler packages and CIP systems
President: Jerry Sanders
jsanders@thermaline.com
Estimated Sales: $1-2.5 Million
Number Employees: 5-9

30212 Thermalogic Corp
22 Kane Industrial Dr
Hudson, MA 01749-2922
978-562-5974
Fax: 978-562-6753 sales@thlogic.com
www.thermalogic.com
Temperature control systems including analog, digital indicating and microprocessor based
Owner: Lou Grein
CEO: John Dubois
john@thlogic.com
Estimated Sales: $20-50 Million
Number Employees: 20-49

30213 Thermedics Detection
220 Mill Road
Suite 1
Chelmsford, MA 01824-4127
978-251-2002
Fax: 978-251-2010 888-846-7226
Sorting systems, soft rejectors, moisture analysis and inspection equipment including fill level, net content, package integrity, foreign particle and chemical
Chairman, President, Chief Executive Off: James Hambrick
Corporate Vice President of Human Resour: Andrew Panega
Corporate Vice President of Research and: Robert Graf
Director Sales (North America): Ron Pokraka
Corporate Vice President of Operations: Mike Vaughn
Production Manager: George McNeil
Parent Co: Thermedics

30214 Thermex Thermatron
10501 Bunsen Way # 102
Suite 102
Louisville, KY 40299-2563
502-493-1299
Fax: 502-493-4013
sales@thermex-thermatron.com
www.thermex-thermatron.com
Industrial microwave equipment and RF heat sealing equipment.
Owner: Ray Lund
VP Marketing: John Hokanson
Sales Director: Robert Dachert
ray@thermex-thermatron.com
Sales: Mark Isgrigg
Operations Manager: Zoly Bogdan
Estimated Sales: $7 Million
Number Employees: 20-49
Number of Brands: 2
Square Footage: 144000
Brands:
 Thermatron
 Thermex

30215 Thermo BLH
75 Shawmut Rd
Canton, MA 02021-1408
781-821-2000
Fax: 781-828-1451 sales@blh.com
www.blh.com
Weighing system, scales, and web tension measurement systems
President: Robert Murphy
CEO: Bob Murphy
Vice President: Rainer Halmberg
Quality Control: Jay Bailey
Marketing Director: Art Koehler
Estimated Sales: $16 Million
Number Employees: 1-4
Parent Co: Thermo Electron

30216 Thermo Detection
27 Forge Pkwy
Franklin, MA 02038-3135
508-520-0430
Fax: 508-520-1732 866-269-0070
www.thermo.com
Manufacturer and exporter of moisture and other
consistent process analyzers and monitors
Administrator: Michael Nemergut
VP Sales/Marketing: Terry Rose
National Sales Manager: Don Piatt
Inside Sales: Jill Holman
Number Employees: 50-99
Square Footage: 80000
Parent Co: Thermedics Detection
Brands:
Micro Lab
Micro Quad
Quadra Beam 6600

30217 Thermo Fisher Scientific
168 Third Ave
Waltham, MA 02451
781-622-1000
800-678-5599
www.thermofisher.com
Laboratory equipment including quality control sup-
plies/machinery.
President & CEO: Marc Casper
SVP & General Counsel: Michael Boxer
SVP & Chief Financial Officer: Stephen Williamson
EVP & Chief Operating Officer: Mark Stevenson
SVP/President, Customer Channels: Gregory
Herrema
SVP/President, Specialty Diagnostics: Gianluca
Pettiti
SVP/President, Reigions: Syed Jafry
SVP, Integrations: Shiraz Ladiwala
Estimated Sales: $25 Billion
Number Employees: 75,000
Brands:
APPLIED BIOSYSTEMS
THERMO SCIENTIFIC
INVITROGEN
FISHER SCIENTIFIC
UNITY LAB SERVICES

30218 Thermo Instruments
84 Horseblock Rd
Unit D
Yaphank, NY 11980
631-924-0880
Fax: 631-924-0923
Hydrometers and thermometers
President: Michael Charzuk
Estimated Sales: $500,000-$1 Million
Number Employees: 1-4
Brands:
Thermo

30219 Thermo Jarrell Ash Corporation
27 Forge Pkwy
Franklin, MA 02038-3135
508-520-1880
Fax: 508-520-1732 www.thermo.com
Instruments used to analyze water, oil and metal
content
General Manager: Mark Whiteman
Contact: John Bowman
john.bowman@thermo.com
Number Employees: 400

30220 Thermo King Corp
314 W 90th St
Bloomington, MN 55420-3693
952-887-2200
Fax: 952-887-2615 888-887-2202
bridgeton_contact_center@irco.com
www.thermoking.com
Freezers, heaters, refrigeration equipment, temperature indicators and controllers, and refrigeration
trucks
President: Donald Ashton
donald_ashton@thermoking.com
VP: John Cobb
Number Employees: 10000+
Parent Co: Westinghouse

30221 Thermo Pac LLC
1609 Stone Ridge Dr
Stone Mountain, GA 30083-1109
770-934-3200
www.thermopacllc.com

Wide range of thin-to-thick viscosity liquids includ-
ing processed cheese sauces, tomato-based sauces
and other savory or sweet sauces. Also peanut but-
ter, in pouches, single serve cups and dried powder
sticks.
Manager: Dave Barnes
Controller/Director: Leticia Simbach
IS Manager: Glenn Corbin
Administrative Assistant: Jean Williams
Plant Manager: John Stevens
Purchasing Manager: Buddy Wilson
Estimated Sales: $12.4 Million
Number Employees: 100-249
Square Footage: 120000
Parent Co: AmeriQual Group LLC
Type of Packaging: Consumer, Food Service, Pri-
vate Label, Bulk

30222 Thermo Service
3901 Pipestone Rd
Dallas, TX 75212-6017
214-631-0307
Fax: 214-631-0566 800-635-5559
samples@thermoserv.com www.thermoserv.com
Molded plastic servingware and insulated beverage
ware and speciality cups and mugs
President: Joe Betras
CEO: Jay Rigby
Marketing Director: Peggy Hock
National Sales Director: Jon Hock
COO: Tom Morris
Purchasing: Beverly Robbins
Estimated Sales: $40 Million
Number Employees: 100-249
Parent Co: New Thermo Serv, Ltd.

30223 Thermo Wisconsin
PO Box 5030
De Pere, WI 54115-5030
920-766-7200
Fax: 920-766-5211 www.thermo.com
Stainless steel tanks and vessels
Manager Custom Fabrication: Jeff Loker
Designer: Scott Brauer
Estimated Sales: Less than $500,000
Number Employees: 1-4
Square Footage: 560000
Parent Co: Thermo Electron Corporation

30224 Thermo-KOOL/Mid-South Ind Inc
723 E 21st St
Laurel, MS 39440-2457
601-649-4600
Fax: 601-649-0558 sales@thermokool.com
www.thermokool.com
Manufacturer and exporter of self-contained, re-
mote, quick connect and walk-in refrigeration
equipment
President: Randolph McLaughlin
CEO: Patricia McLaughlin
VP: Randplph McLaughlin
Sales Manager: Gary Crocker
Plant Manager: Duane Eldridge
Purchasing: Lee Thames
Estimated Sales: $20-50 Million
Number Employees: 100-249
Square Footage: 123000
Brands:
Thermo-Kool

30225 ThermoWorks
1762 W 20 S
Suite 100
Lindon, UT 84042
801-756-7705
Fax: 801-756-8948 800-393-6434
www.thermoworks.com
President: Randy Owen
Contact: Tricia Buss
tricia.buss@thermoworks.com
Estimated Sales: Below $5 Million
Number Employees: 5-9

30226 Thermodynamics
6780 Brighton Blvd
Commerce City, CO 80022
Fax: 918-251-2826 800-627-9037
www.okpallets.com
Reusable plastic pallets, bins, boxes, containers and
trays including standard and custom; exporter of
plastic pallets

CEO: Sheri Orlowitz
General Manager: Robert Lux
Production Manager: Shawn Harley
Plant Manager: Robert Luxtwood
Purchasing Manager: Ray Carr
Estimated Sales: $5-10 Million
Number Employees: 20-49
Square Footage: 70000
Parent Co: Shan Industries

30227 Thermodyne Foodservice Prods
4418 New Haven Ave
Fort Wayne, IN 46803-1650
260-428-2535
Fax: 260-428-2533 800-526-9182
www.tdyne.com
Manufacturer and exporter of conduction ovens
President: Vincent Tippmann Sr
General Manager: Sue Brown
IT: Dave Schenkel
dave.schenkel@polarking.com
Number Employees: 1-4
Square Footage: 600000
Parent Co: Polar King International

30228 Thermodyne International LTD
1841 S Business Pkwy
Ontario, CA 91761-8537
909-923-9945
Fax: 909-923-7505 sales@thermodyne.com
www.thermodyne.com
Manufacturer and exporter of reusable plastic con-
tainers and instrument shipping and carrying cases;
also, custom vacuum forming services available
President: Gary Ackerman
gackerman@thermodyne-online.com
Sr. VP: Gary Ackerman
Chairman of the Board: Gary S Ackerman
Estimated Sales: $10-20 Million
Number Employees: 50-99
Brands:
Rack-Pack
Shok-Stop

30229 Thermoil Corporation
7 Franklin Avenue
Brooklyn, NY 11211-7801
718-855-0544
Fax: 718-643-6691
Manufacturer and exporter of industrial oils and
greases
Estimated Sales: $10-20 Million
Number Employees: 10-19

30230 Thermolok Packaging Systems
5050 Prince George Drive
Prince George, VA 23875-2623
452-001- 001
Fax: 804-452-2011 thermolok7@aol.com
www.strapmc.com
Manufacturers of plastic strapping equipment,
stretch film machines and tape machines
Estimated Sales: $1-2.5 Million
Number Employees: 1-4

30231 Thermomass
1000 Technology Dr
PO Box 950
Boone, IA 50036-4457
515-433-6088
Fax: 515-433-6088 800-232-1748
www.thermomass.com
Composite sandwich walls used for cold or frozen
storage units, also wineries
President: Tom Stecker
R&D: Rex Donahey
Contact: Rich Brownrigg
rbrownrigg@thermomass.com
Estimated Sales: $5-10 Million
Number Employees: 10-19

30232 Thermoquest
3661 Interstate Park Road N
Suite 100
Riviera Beach, FL 33404-5906
561-383-2000
Fax: 561-383-2043 888-383-2025
www.palmbeachschools.org
Manufacturer and exporter of stainless steel pots and
pans
General Manager: Ralph Kearney
Number Employees: 50
Parent Co: Floaire
Type of Packaging: Food Service

Brands:
Floware

30233 Thermos Company
475 N Martingale Road
Suite 1100
Schaumburg, IL 60173
847-439-7821
Fax: 847-593-5570 800-243-0745
customer@grilllovers.com www.thermos.com
Vacuum insulated bottles and carafes, stainless steel
thermal cookware, ice buckets, coffee presses and
airpot coffee dispensers
Chairman: Shouji Toida
Executive VP: Rick Dias
Director Special Marketing Division: Nedda Glenn
Contact: Praveen Amudala
amudala@thermos.com
Estimated Sales: $1-2,500,000
Number Employees: 500-999
Brands:
Thermos

30234 Thermoseal
1310 Highway 287 S
Suite 105
Mansfield, TX 76063-5705
817-453-0813
Fax: 817-453-0594
Sealers
President: Shawn Kennedy

30235 Theta Sciences
11835 Carmel Mountain Road
Suite 1304
San Diego, CA 92128-4609
760-745-3311
Fax: 760-745-5519
Manufacturer, importer and exporter of electronic
instruments specializing in food process control and
personnel hazard monitoring
President: Hal Buscher
VP: Bob LeClair
VP: Dave Furuno
Estimated Sales: $1-2.5 Million
Number Employees: 9
Square Footage: 19200
Brands:
Theta Sciences

30236 Thiel Cheese & Ingredients
N7630 County Hwy BB
Attn: Kathy Pitzen
Hilbert, WI 54129
920-989-1440
Fax: 920-989-1288 kathyp@thielcheese.com
www.thielcheese.com
Manufacturer and custom formulator of processed
cheeses that are used primarily as ingredients in
other food products
President: Steven Thiel
Sales: Kathy Pitzen
Number Employees: 50-99
Type of Packaging: Consumer, Food Service, Pri-
vate Label, Bulk
Brands:
Thiel

30237 Thiele Engineering Company
810 Industrial Park Boulevard
Fergus Falls, MN 56537
218-739-3321
Fax: 218-739-9370 info@swfcompanies.com
www.thieletech.com
Manufacturer and exporter of cartoners and case
packers
VP Sales: Wayne Slaton
Number Employees: 260
Square Footage: 173900
Parent Co: Barry-Wehmiller Company

30238 Thiele Technologies Inc
315 27th Ave NE
Minneapolis, MN 55418-2715
612-782-1200
Fax: 612-782-1203 www.thieletech.com
Packaging and palletizing equipment
CEO: Laurence P Smith
laurence.smith@thieletech.com
Sales/Marketing Manager: Todd Sandell
Estimated Sales: $20-50 Million
Number Employees: 500-999

30239 Thiele Technologies Inc
315 27th Ave NE
Minneapolis, MN 55418-2715
612-782-1200
Fax: 612-782-1203 800-542-3647
www.thieletech.com
Conveying, insulation converting and bagging
equipment, conveyors
CEO: Laurence P Smith
laurence.smith@thieletech.com
CFO: Keith Skerrett
R&D: Bob Odom
Marketing/Sales Manager: Todd Sandell
Estimated Sales: $20-30 Million
Number Employees: 500-999

30240 Thiele Technologies-Reedley
1949 E Manning Ave
Reedley, CA 93654-9462
559-638-8484
Fax: 559-638-7478 800-344-8951
Sales@ThieleTech.com www.thieletech.com
Manufacturer and exporter of corrugated box form-
ing and sealing machinery, case erectors, automatic
case packers, case openers/positioners, cartoners and
robotics automation.
President: Larry Smith
VP: Ed Suarez
Sales Director: Craig Friesen
Contact: Stephen Akins
stephen.akins@thieletech.com
Number Employees: 250-499
Square Footage: 400000
Parent Co: Barry-Wehmiller
Other Locations:
SWF Machinery
Orlando FL

30241 Thielmann Container Systems
6301 Gravel Ave
Alexandria, VA 22310
703-836-4003
Fax: 703-836-4070
Cylindrical and cubic containers
Estimated Sales: $1-3 Million
Number Employees: 5-9

30242 Thinque Systems Corporation
4130 Cahuenga Boulevard
Suite 128
Toluca Lake, CA 91602-2847
818-752-1350
Fax: 818-752-1355 sales@thinque.com
www.thinque.com
President: George Bayz
VP Business Development: Rich Love
VP Marketing: Ellen Libenson
Estimated Sales: $27 Million
Number Employees: 150

30243 Thirstenders International
11518 Bedford St
Houston, TX 77031-2108
713-664-8050
Fax: 713-559-8449 www.thirstenders.com
Manufacturers proprietary, mobile delivery systems
for food, beverages and consumer products.
President: Fred Ash
info@thirstenders.com
Quality Control: Lee Grover
R&D: Fred Ash
Estimated Sales: Below $5 Million
Number Employees: 1-4

30244 Thirty Two North Corporation
32north Corporation16 Pomerleau Street
Biddeford, ME 04005
800-782-2423
Fax: 207-284-5015 800-782-2423
info@32north.com
Safety shoes, detachable anti-slip soles
Owner: Anne Gould
Estimated Sales: Below $5 Million
Number Employees: 10

30245 Thomas J Payne Market Devmnt
865 Woodside Way
San Mateo, CA 94401-1611
650-340-8311
Fax: 650-340-8568 tpayne@tjpmd.com
www.tjpmd.com
Consultant specializing in marketing development
and food technology

President: Tom Payne
CEO: Thomas J Payne
tpayne@tjpmd.com
Market Development Activities: Edith Nagy
Estimated Sales: $500,000-$1 Million
Number Employees: 1-4

30246 Thomas L. Green & Company
380 Old West Penn Ave
Robenosia, PA 19551
610-693-5816
Fax: 610-693-5512 info@readingbakery.com
www.readingbakery.com
Manufacturer and exporter of bakery machinery in-
cluding automatic band ovens, dough mixers, con-
veyors for crackers and cookies, biscuit cutters,
dough formers and dough sheeters
Chairman: Thomas Lugar
EVP & CFO: Chip Czulada
CEO: Terry Groff
CFO: Charles Czulada
Quality Control: Mike Johnson
VP, Sales and Marketing: David Kuipers
VP of Sales, Americas: Shawn Moye
VP, Operations: Travis Getz
Estimated Sales: $5-10 Million
Number Employees: 10-19

30247 Thomas Lighting Residential
10275 W Higgins Rd, 8th Floor
Rosemont, IL 60018
Fax: 800-288-4329 800-825-5844
info@thomaslighting.com
www.thomaslighting.com
Manufacturer and exporter of outdoor lighting fix-
tures
Sales Manager: Sheryl Fraga
Number Employees: 350

30248 Thomas Precision, Inc.
3278 S Main St
Rice Lake, WI 54868-8793
715-234-8827
Fax: 715-234-6737 800-657-4808
sales@tpm-inc.com www.tpm-inc.com
Manufacturer and exporter of stainless steel and al-
loy replacement parts for food processing equipment
including grinder plates, blades and screens; also,
build and rebuild separating machines and augers
CEO: Roger Norberg
Sales: Jerry Klasen
Plant Manager: Kevin Nyra
Purchasing Agent: Rod Stoyke
Estimated Sales: $10 Million
Number Employees: 60
Square Footage: 48000
Brands:
Tpm

30249 Thomas Pump & Machinery
120 Industrial Dr
Slidell, LA 70460-4650
985-649-4300
Fax: 985-649-4300 www.thomaspump.com
Cleaning and washing equipment, pressure washers,
heaters-water, heat reclaiming systems, automobile
products
President: Jim Thomas
tpump@thomaspump.com
VP of Finances: Rebecca Rhoto
VP of Inside Sales: Craig Robinson
VP of Operations: Joe Galey
Estimated Sales: $1-3 Million
Number Employees: 20-49

30250 Thomas Pump & Machinery
120 Industrial Dr
Slidell, LA 70460-4650
985-649-4300
Fax: 985-649-4300 tpump@thomaspump.com
www.thomaspump.com
Owner: Jim Thomas
tpump@thomaspump.com
Estimated Sales: $2.5-5 Million
Number Employees: 20-49

30251 Thomas Tape & Supply CoInc
1713 Sheridan Ave
Springfield, OH 45505-2263
937-325-6414
Fax: 937-325-2850 www.thomastape.com
Manufacturer and exporter of sealing tape including
paper, cloth, reinforced glass fiber, gummed, and
pressure sensitive tape

President: David Simonton
dave11@thomastape.com
Sales/Marketing Executive: Kevin Amidon
Estimated Sales: $300,000-500,000
Number Employees: 5-9
Square Footage: 120000
Brands:
    Paxrite
    Raycord

30252 Thomas Technical Svc
W4780 US Highway 10
Neillsville, WI 54456-6213

715-743-4666
Fax: 715-743-2062

Ultrafiltration and reverse osmosis systems for the dairy industry; wholesaler/distributor of replacement parts
Owner: Randy L Thomas
CEO: Theresa Thomas
CFO: Randy Thomas
Estimated Sales: Below $5 Million
Number Employees: 1-4
Square Footage: 18000
Brands:
    Thomas Fractioner

30253 Thomas Technical Svc
W4780 US Highway 10
Neillsville, WI 54456-6213

715-743-4666
Fax: 715-743-2062

Ultra filtration, reverse osmosis, membrane systems
Owner: Randy L Thomas
randy@thomastechnical.com
Estimated Sales: less than $500,000
Number Employees: 1-4

30254 Thomasen
1303 43rd St
Kenosha, WI 53140

262-652-3662
Fax: 262-652-3526 sales@lcthomsen.com

Custom fabrication, filters, milk, flow diversion stations
President: Wayne Borne
Sales: Joyce Saftig
Estimated Sales: $1-5 Million
Number Employees: 20-49

30255 Thombert
P.O.Box 1123
316 E. 7th Street N.
Newton, IA 50208-1123

641-792-4449
Fax: 641-792-2390 800-433-3572
thombert@thombert.com www.thombert.com

Polyurethane wheels and tires for forklift trucks
Chairman of the Board: Walter Smith
President: Dick Davidson
Sales Marketing Manager: Reggie Collette
Sales Representative: Brandon Mastin
Contact: Paul Ellis
pellis@thombert.com
VP Manufacturing: Terry Beckham
Estimated Sales: $10-20 Million
Number Employees: 50-99
Brands:
    Dyalon
    Vulkollan

30256 (HQ)Thompson Bagel Machine Mfg
8945 Ellis Ave
Los Angeles, CA 90034-3380

310-836-0900
Fax: 310-836-0156 sales@bagelproducts.com
www.bagelproducts.com

Manufacturer and exporter of one and two bank bagel machines including horizontal and vertical; also, two and four row rotary dividers.
President: Steve Thompson
sales@bagelproducts.com
Research & Development: Dan Thompson
Marketing/Sales: Charles Ducat
Operations Manager: Craig Thompson
Estimated Sales: $1-5 Million
Number Employees: 5-9
Number of Products: 10
Type of Packaging: Private Label
Brands:
    Thompson Bagel Machines

30257 Thompson Scale Co
9000 Jameel Rd # 190
Suite 190
Houston, TX 77040-5061

713-932-9071
Fax: 713-932-9379 info@thompsonscale.com
www.thompsonscale.com

Weighing systems and packaging machinery controls
President: Bobbie Thompson
bobbie.thompson@thompsonscale.com
Estimated Sales: $2 Million
Number Employees: 10-19
Square Footage: 9000

30258 Thomsen Group LLC
1303 43rd St
Kenosha, WI 53140-2738

262-652-3662
Fax: 262-652-3526 800-558-4018
sales@lcthomsen.com www.lcthomsen.com

Wine industry pumps and valves
President: Wayne Borne
Sales: Joyce Saftig
Manager: Jon Huges
j.huges@lcthomsen.com
Number Employees: 10-19

30259 (HQ)Thomson-Leeds Company
450 Park Avenue S
2nd Floor
New York, NY 10016-7320

914-428-7255
Fax: 914-428-7047 800-535-9361

Manufacturer, importer and exporter of displays, fixtures, package designs and point of purchase merchandising materials. Broker of specialty displays
President: Vince Esposito
CEO: Douglas Leeds
Director Marketing: Peter Weiller
Estimated Sales: $2.5-5 Million
Number Employees: 50-99
Square Footage: 80000
Brands:
    Fiberpoptics
    Freelight
    Greenpop
    Security Peg Hook
    Stockpop

30260 Thor Inc
1280 W 2550 S
Ogden, UT 84401-3278

801-393-3312
Fax: 801-621-3298 888-846-7462

Custom formulating and contract packaging for vitamins and supplements in liquids, capsules and powders
Owner: Whittle Allen
whittle.allen@thor.com
Estimated Sales: $10-20 Million
Number Employees: 10-19
Type of Packaging: Private Label

30261 Thorco Industries LLC
1300 E 12th St
Lamar, MO 64759

417-682-3375
Fax: 417-682-1326 800-445-3375

Manufacturer and exporter of point of purchase displays, wire grids, store fixtures, bag holders and baskets
President: John Kuhahl
CFO: Jeff Gardener
Quality Control: Rodney Walters
Contact: Sarah Dorris
sdorris@lauracookseymusic.com
Number Employees: 500-999
Parent Co: Marmon Corporation

30262 Thoreson Mc Cosh Inc
1885 Thunderbird
Troy, MI 48084-5472

248-362-0960
Fax: 248-362-5270 800-959-0805
sales@thoresonmccosh.com
www.thoresonmccosh.com

Manufacturer and exporter of dryers, hoppers, loaders and loading systems, tilters and bulk handling systems
President: David Klatt
sales@thoresonmccosh.com
Sales Exec: Steven Taugher

Estimated Sales: $10-20 Million
Number Employees: 20-49
Type of Packaging: Bulk

30263 Thorn Smith Laboratories
7755 Narrow Gauge Rd
Beulah, MI 49617-9792

231-882-4672
Fax: 231-882-4804 auric@thornsmithlabs.com
www.thornsmithlabs.com

Manufacturer and exporter of temperature specific sterilizer controls for use in quality assurance programs
President: Robert Brown
Plant Manager: Melanie Cederholm
Estimated Sales: Below $5 Million
Number Employees: 1-4
Square Footage: 17200
Brands:
    Diack
    Vac

30264 Thornton Plastics
745 W Pacific Ave
Salt Lake City, UT 84104-1022

801-322-3413
Fax: 801-359-2800 800-248-3434
sales@thorntonplastics.com
www.thorntonplastics.com

Transparent plastic snap-cap vials
President: Briton C Mc Conkie
briton@thorntonplastics.com
VP: Jean Eastham
Estimated Sales: Below $5 Million
Number Employees: 5-9
Square Footage: 34000

30265 Thorpe & Associates
227 N Chatnam Ave
Siler City, NC 27344-3443

919-742-5516
Fax: 919-742-4657

Manufacturer and importer of chairs and tables
President: Bill Thorpe
VP Design: William Thorpe
VP Sales: Van Thorpe
Estimated Sales: Less than $500,000
Number Employees: 500
Square Footage: 400000

30266 Thorpe Rolling Pin Co
336 Putnam Ave
Hamden, CT 06517-2744

203-787-0281
Fax: 203-230-2753 800-344-6966

Rolling and pizza pins
President: Timothy Pagnam
Estimated Sales: $1-2.5 Million
Number Employees: 20-49

30267 Three P
333 Andrew Ave
Salt Lake City, UT 84115-5113

801-486-7407
Fax: 801-571-4896

Manufacturer and exporter of custom printed and pressure sensitive decals, labels, tags, signs, etc
Owner: Edd Lancaster
Quality Control: Ernie Ashcroft
Marketing: Denise Lancaster
Sales: Edd Lancaster
Estimated Sales: $500,000-$1 Million
Number Employees: 5-9
Type of Packaging: Private Label, Bulk

30268 Three-A Sanitary Standards Symbol
6888 Elm Street
Suite 2D
McLean, VA 22101

703-790-0295
Fax: 703-761-6284 3-AINFO@3-A.org
www.3-a.org

To enhance product safety for consumers of food, beverages, and pharmaceutical products.
Executive Director: Timothy Rugh
Contact: Angus Abels
aabels@3-a.org

30269 Threshold Rehabilitation Svc
1000 Lancaster Ave
Reading, PA 19607-1699

610-777-7691
Fax: 610-777-1295 www.trsinc.org

989

Contract packagers
President: Ronald Williams
tdesanto@trsinc.org
Sales/Marketing: Nancy Benjamin
VP Program Operations: Tom McNelis
Year Founded: 1973
Estimated Sales: $20-50 Million
Number Employees: 250-499
Square Footage: 20000

30270 Thunder Pallet Inc
625 Menomonee St
Theresa, WI 53091-9805

920-488-4211
Fax: 920-488-4306 800-354-0643
Wooden pallets, skids, boxes, crates, etc
President: Ben Mahsem
ben@thinderpallet.com
Estimated Sales: Below $5 Million
Number Employees: 50-99

30271 Thunderbird Food Machinery
P.O. BOX 4768
4602 Brass Way
Blaine, WA 98231

214-331-3000
Fax: 214-331-3581 866-875-6868
tbfm@tbfm.com www.thunderbirdfm.com
Importer and wholesaler/distributor of food process-
ing equipment including mixers, dough sheeters,
vegetable and bread slicers, meat grinders, etc
Owner: Ky Lin
Marketing Director: Kara M
Estimated Sales: $1-2.5 Million
Number Employees: 5-9

30272 Thunderbird Label Corportion
70 Clinton Road
Fairfield, NJ 07004-2928

973-575-6677
Fax: 973-575-4970
Pressure sensitive labels including prime, coupon,
tamper-evident and four color process
President: Karl Beierle
VP Sales: George Coughlin
Estimated Sales: $2.5-5 Million
Number Employees: 19
Square Footage: 48000

30273 Thurman Scale
4025 Lakeview Crossing
Groveport, OH 43125

614-221-9077
Fax: 614-221-8879 800-688-9741
thurmanscales@fancor.com
www.thurmanscale.com
Weighing equipment
Contact: Neil Copley
ncopley@thurmanscale.com
Estimated Sales: $.5-1 million
Number Employees: 1-4
Parent Co: Fancor

30274 Thwing-Albert Instrument Co
14 W Collings Ave
West Berlin, NJ 08091-9134

856-767-1000
Fax: 856-767-2615 info@thwingalbert.com
www.thwingalbert.com
Thwing-Albert Instrument Company provides a
complete offering of tensile testers and other materials testing instruments for quality control, research
& development and process control applications
worldwide.
President: Joseph Raab
jraab@thwingalbert.com
VP/Sales/Marketing: Steven Berg
Estimated Sales: $5-10 Million
Number Employees: 50-99

30275 Tiax LLC
35 Hartwell Ave
Lexington, MA 02421-3102

781-879-1200
Fax: 617-498-7200 800-677-3000
lupien.bernard@tiaxllc.com www.tiaxllc.com
Consultant specializing in technology, product and
marketing services, health, safety, product formulation, and research and development.

President: Nadine Andon
andon.n@tiaxllc.com
VP: Arthur Schwope
VP Sales: Bernard Lupien
VP Operations: Boyd Boucher
Purchasing Manager: Jose Bairos
Estimated Sales: $20-50 Million
Number Employees: 1-4
Square Footage: 120000
Other Locations:
   Cupertino CA
   Irvine CA

30276 Tibersoft
2200 W Park Dr # 430
Westborough, MA 01581-3961

508-898-9555
Fax: 508-898-1820 888-888-1969
info@tibersoft.com www.tibersoft.com
Founder: Christopher Martin
CEO: Tom Beninghof
tom.beninghof@tibersoft.com
Vice President, Founder: Mary Wilson
Estimated Sales: $1-5 Million
Number Employees: 20-49

30277 Tidland Corp
2305 SE 8th Ave
Camas, WA 98607-2261

360-834-2345
Fax: 360-834-5865 800-426-1000
Manufactures air expanding shafts, chucks, air
brakes, slitting knife holders and electronic slitting
positioning machines
President: Quino Lorente
Cmo: Stephanie Tuggle
stuggle@tidland.com
Director International Marketing: John Rupp
Estimated Sales: Below $5 Million
Number Employees: 100-249

30278 Tieco-Unadilla Corporation
22 Depot Street
Unadilla, NY 13838

607-369-3236
Fax: 607-369-2011 877-889-6540
tieco@tyups.com www.tyups.com
Manufacturer and exporter of tying devices for se-
curing bundles and pallets
President: Scott McLean
Estimated Sales: Below $500,000
Number Employees: 5-9
Brands:
   Ty-Up

30279 Tiefenthaler Machinery Co, Inc
W227 N913 Westmound Dr
Waukesha, WI 53186

262-513-1111
Fax: 262-513-1113
President: James Tiefenthaler
Estimated Sales: $5-10 Million
Number Employees: 5-9

30280 Tier-Rack Corp
425 Sovereign Ct
Ballwin, MO 63011-4432

636-527-0700
Fax: 636-256-4901 800-325-7869
info@tier-rack.com www.tier-rack.com
Manufacturer and exporter of portable storage racks
Owner: Scott Ten Eyck
steneyck@tier-rack.com
General Manager: George Willis
Controller: Ward Wilson
Estimated Sales: $1-2.5 Million
Number Employees: 10-19
Square Footage: 150000
Brands:
   Tier-Rack

30281 Tifa (CI)
109 Stryker Lane
Building 3, Suite 4&5
Millington, NJ 8844

908-829-3230
Fax: 908-829-3240 go@tifausa.com
www.tifausa.com
Manufacturing of aeorsol fogging equipment for
public health
President: Gamel Osman
Chairman: Vladimir Alexanyan
Vice President: Deirdre Cerciello
Estimated Sales: $1-2.5 Million
Number Employees: 10-19

30282 Tiffin Metal Products Co
450 Wall St
Tiffin, OH 44883-1366

419-447-8414
Fax: 419-447-8512 800-537-0983
www.tiffinmetal.com
Stainless steel lockers and special sheet metal fabri-
cation, ergonomic seating, stainless, plated polyure-
thane seats for washdown areas, adjustable work
tables, packing stands and anti-fatigue matting
President/CEO: Will Heddles
CEO: Willard P Heddles
wheddles@tiffinmetal.com
Chief Financial Officer: Timothy Demith
VP Outdoor/Custom & OEM Products: Ron Myers
VP Security Products & Marketing: Andrew Beebe
Marketing Manager: Mike Wittman
National Sales Manager Custom/OEM: Rodney
Osmena
Estimated Sales: $5-10 Million
Number Employees: 50-99

30283 Tiger-Vac
73 SW 12th Ave # 107
Dania, FL 33004-3523

954-925-3625
Fax: 954-925-3626 800-668-4437
sales@tiger-vac.com
Industrial vacuum cleaners, specializes in systems
for clean manufacturing areas and contamination
controlled environments, foodgrade vacuums, con-
tinuous duty vacuums, vacuums with high efficiency
President: Rocco Mariani
rmariani@tiger-vac.com
Estimated Sales: $1-2.5 Million
Number Employees: 50-99
Number of Products: 15

30284 Tilly Industries
4210 Blvd Poirier
St Laurent, QC H4R 2C5
Canada

514-331-4922
Fax: 514-331-4924 www.tillyindustries.com
Manufacturer and exporter of aluminum foil dies for
pie plates and containers
VP: Dagmar Tilly
Estimated Sales: $1-5 Million
Number Employees: 8
Square Footage: 36000
Parent Co: Maven Engineering Corporation

30285 Timberline Consulting
3333 S Bannock St # 600
Suite 800
Englewood, CO 80110-2450

303-781-3977
Fax: 303-781-4305
Owner: Daniel David
ddaniel@timberlineconsulting.com
Estimated Sales: $810,000
Number Employees: 10-19

30286 Timbertech Company
1055 White Mountain Highway
Milton, NH 03851-4443

603-669-7743
Fax: 603-669-2024 800-572-5538
Pallets including new and rebuilt 48 x 40 grocery;
also, disposal
Owner and President: Rod Van Sciver
Office Manager: Nancy Boudreau
Estimated Sales: $2.5-5 Million
Number Employees: 20-49
Square Footage: 50000

30287 Timco Inc
2 Greentown Rd
Buchanan, NY 10511-1007

914-736-0206
Fax: 914-736-0395 800-792-0030
sales@timco-eng.com www.timco-eng.com
Rigging gear, hardware, jacks and rollers: sheaves,
chain guides
Owner: Marc Walter
Sales: Joe Yaniv
marc@licharzmail.com
Plant Manager: Barry Volaski
Estimated Sales: $6 Million
Number Employees: 20-49
Number of Brands: 3
Number of Products: 30

30288 Time Products
3780 Browns Mill Rd SE
Atlanta, GA 30354
404-767-7526
Fax: 404-767-7010 800-241-6681
tymebill@aol.com
Cleaning compounds
VP and General Manager: Bill Drew
CEO: John Theophilis
Chairman of the Board: Steve Theofilos
Marketing Director: Stan Lanch
Production Manager: Rod Abrahansen
Estimated Sales: $20-50 Million
Number Employees: 20-49
Square Footage: 100000
Parent Co: Theochem Laboratories
Brands:
  Time-Saver

30289 Timely Signs Inc
2135 Linden Blvd
Elmont, NY 11003-3901
516-285-5339
Fax: 516-285-9637 800-457-4467
sales@timelysigns.net
Manufacturer and exporter of labels, marketing
signs and banners; wholesaler/distributor of comput-
erized sign making equipment
President: Gene Goldsmith
signs11003@aol.com
Estimated Sales: $1-2.5 Million
Number Employees: 5-9
Square Footage: 4000
Brands:
  Duracast
  Timely Signs
  Ulta Mag

30290 Timemed Labeling Systems
27770 N Entertainment Drive
Suite 200
Valencia, CA 91355
818-897-1111
Fax: 818-686-9317 intl@pdcorp.com
www.pdchealthcare.com
Manufacturer and exporter of pressure-sensitive la-
bels, embossed seals and printed gummed tapes
President: Jerry Nerad
General Manager: Lee Smith
Contact: Tima Fanning
tima.fanning@phoenix.edu
Plant Manager: Dave Luther
Estimated Sales: $10-20 Million
Number Employees: 20-49
Parent Co: Timemed Labeling Systems

30291 (HQ)Tin Box Co Of America Inc
216 Sherwood Ave
Farmingdale, NY 11735-1718
631-845-1600
Fax: 631-845-1610 800-888-8467
info@tinboxco.com www.tinboxco.com
Decorative metal boxes
Owner: Lloyd Roth
Director of Sales: Andy Siegel
Sales Manager: Richard Spitz
rothl@tinboxco.com
Estimated Sales: $5-10 Million
Number Employees: 20-49
Square Footage: 80000

30292 Tinadre Inc
15310 Amberly Dr # 180
Tampa, FL 33647-1640
813-866-0333
Fax: 813-866-0462 tinadre@gte.net
www.tinadre.net
Turnkey customer frequency pre-paid private label
cards, electronic gift certificates and payment pro-
cessing services for food service operators; also,
POS software and hardware
Owner: Michael Crochet
VP: Mike Crochot
VP: Zachary Tapp
Production: Steven Malcanas
Estimated Sales: $500,000-$1 Million
Number Employees: 5-9

30293 Tindall Packaging
1150 E U Ave
Vicksburg, MI 49097
269-649-1163
Fax: 616-649-1163
Manufacturer and exporter of filling equipment for
dairy, deli and cultured products; also, single and
two-flavor variegators
President: Marianne Tindall
marianne@tindallpackaging.com
VP: Marianne Tindall
Quality Control: Frank Tindall
Number Employees: 5

30294 Tinwerks Packaging Co
1237 W Capitol Dr
Addison, IL 60101-3116
630-628-8600
Fax: 630-628-0330 www.tinwerks.com
Tins
Vice President: Joseph Marlovits
sales@tinwerks.com
VP: Peter Goschi
Sales: Joseph Marlovits
Number Employees: 5-9

30295 Tiny Drumsticks
43-66 11th St.
New York, NY 11101
917-526-3263
info@tinydrumsticks.com
www.tinydrumsticks.com
Supplies kitchens and kitchen designs.
President & CEO: Benjamin Sloan
Year Founded: 2013
Square Footage: 5000
Type of Packaging: Food Service

30296 Tipper Tie Inc
2000 Lufkin Rd
Apex, NC 27539-7068
919-362-8811
Fax: 919-362-4839 www.tippertie.com
Clippers, aluminum clips, aluminum wire products,
electric fence supplies and netting
President: Gernot Foerster
Chief Financial Officer: Roman Steiger
Vice President: Robert Cleveland
Directory, Quality: Tim Downes
Marketing Executive: Emy Mooffitt
Sales Manager: Bryan Wilkins
Officer Manager: Ashley Gideon
Purchasing: Sue Chandler
Estimated Sales: $35 Million
Number Employees: 100-249
Square Footage: 130000
Parent Co: Dover Corporation
Brands:
  Tipper Clippers

30297 (HQ)Tippmann Group
9009 Coldwater Rd # 300
Fort Wayne, IN 46825-2072
260-490-3000
Fax: 260-490-1362 tippsales@tippmanngroup.com
www.tippmanngroup.com
Design and building construction of refrigerated
warehouses/facilities
CEO: John V Tippmann Sr
Contact: Kyle Angelet
kangelet@tippmanngroup.com
Number Employees: 50-99

30298 Tisma Machinery Corporation
1099 Estes Avenue
Elk Grove Village, IL 60007-4907
847-427-9525
Fax: 847-427-9550 bwilliams@swfcompanies.com
Manufacturer and exporter of automatic cartoning
machinery and systems
Estimated Sales: $10-20 Million
Number Employees: 50-99
Square Footage: 176000

30299 Titan Corporation
3033 Science Park Rd
San Diego, CA 92121
858-552-9565
Fax: 858-535-3609
Markets technology for the electronic irradation of
food products
President: Andy Ivers
Contact: Matt Armato
m.armato@titanandco.com
Number Employees: 250-499
Brands:
  Surebean

30300 Titan Industries Inc
735 Industrial Loop Rd
New London, WI 54961-2600
920-982-6600
Fax: 920-982-7750 800-558-3616
www.titanconveyors.com
Manufacturer and exporter of conveyors
President: Dan Baumbach
dbaumbach@titansystems.com
Estimated Sales: $5-10 Million
Number Employees: 20-49
Square Footage: 84000

30301 Titan Plastics
433 Murray Hill Pkwy
East Rutherford, NJ 7073
201-935-7700
Fax: 201-935-1584
Plastic containers
President: Rich Probinsky
Contact: Carol Vail
carolv@pennbottle.com
Estimated Sales: $10-20 Million
Number Employees: 10-19
Square Footage: 200000
Parent Co: Penn Bottle & Supply Company

30302 Titan Ventures International, Inc
170 Millennium Blvd
Moncton, NB E1E 2G8
Canada
506-858-8990
Fax: 506-859-6929 800-565-2253
sales@bakemax.com www.bakemax.com
Wholesaler/distributor of Planetary Mixers, Hot Dog
Roller Grills, Slicers, Spiral Mixers, Water Meters,
Bakery Equipment, Countertop Pizza or Pie Sheeter,
Electric Display Food Warmers, Deli or Meat Equip-
ment, Bread SlicersReversible Sheeters, Bun Divid-
ers and more
Chief Financial Officer: Cathy Flanagan
Sales: Shawn Melanson
Estimated Sales: $3-5 Million
Number Employees: 5
Square Footage: 48000
Type of Packaging: Bulk

30303 Tlf Graphics Inc
235 Metro Park
Rochester, NY 14623-2618
800-356-2701
Fax: 585-272-5525 800-356-2701
www.tlfgraphics.com
Label printing
Owner: Ronald Le Blanc
Contact: Tod Bitter
tod@staples.com
Estimated Sales: $10-20 Million
Number Employees: 5-9

30304 Tnemec Co Inc
123 W 23rd Ave
N Kansas City, MO 64116-3094
952-746-1909
Fax: 816-842-3904 800-TNE-MEC1
www.tnemec.com
High performance paints, coatings and floor top-
pings, industrial steel maintenance paints and prim-
ers, concrete, brick and masonry waterproofing
materials, chemical resistant coatings for steel
President & COO: Chase Bean
Marketing Director: Mark Thomas
Manager: Melanie Watt
Estimated Sales: H
Number Employees: 100-249

30305 Tni Packaging Inc
333 Charles Ct # 101
West Chicago, IL 60185-2604
630-293-3030
Fax: 630-293-5303 800-383-0990
www.tnipackaging.com
Manufacturer and exporter of open mesh netting
bags, pre-tied elastic poultry trusses and mechanical
meat tenderizers
President: Jerry J Marchese
jmarchese@tnipackaging.com
Marketing Director: Ana Tirado
Sales Director: Jane Larsen
Plant Manager: Victor Castijelo
Estimated Sales: $3-5 Million
Number Employees: 5-9
Number of Brands: 7

Number of Products: 4
Square Footage: 48000
Type of Packaging: Consumer, Food Service, Private Label, Bulk
Brands:
Chicken-Tuckers
Mister Tenderizer
Net-All
Tie-Net

30306 Tnn-Jeros Inc
697 N Colfax St
PO Box 12
Byron, IL 61010-1439

312-261-6004
jens_hedegaard@tnn-jeros.com
www.tnn-jeros.com
Supplier of cleaning and washing equipment for food manufacturers
Partner: Jens Hedegaard
jeros@jeros.us
Number Employees: 10-19

30307 Toastmaster
1400 Toastmaster Drive
Elgin, IL 60120-9274

847-741-3300
Fax: 847-741-0015 mww@middleby.com
www.toastmastercorp.com
Manufacturer and exporter of broilers, fryers, griddles, grills, hot plates, ovens, ranges, rotisseries and toasters
President: Mark Sieron
Estimated Sales: $1-5 Million
Number Employees: 5-9
Parent Co: Middleby Corporation

30308 Todd Construction Services
1206 Price Ave
Pomona, CA 91767-5840

909-469-6242
Fax: 909-469-6241
Designers, engineers and planners for the food production and cold storage industry
President: Glenn Todd
Contact: Carrie Todd
carrie@toddconstructionservices.com
Estimated Sales: $5-10 Million
Number Employees: 5-9

30309 Todd Uniform
PO Box 29107
Saint Louis, MO 63126-0107

800-458-3402
Fax: 800-231-8633
Uniforms
Sales: Robin Berry

30310 Todd's
PO Box 4821
Des Moines, IA 50305

515-266-2276
Fax: 515-266-1669 800-247-5363
Variety of food products, wet and dry, kosher and organic certified.
President/CEO: Alan Niedermeier
Quality Control: Diana Burzloff
Public Relations: Alissa Douglas
Operations: Duane Hettkamp
Production: Jeff Sullivan
Plant Manager: John Routh
Purchasing: Danielle Robinson
Estimated Sales: $1-3 Million
Number Employees: 30
Number of Brands: 40
Number of Products: 200
Square Footage: 320000
Type of Packaging: Consumer, Food Service, Private Label, Bulk
Brands:
Butcher's Friend
Papa Joe's Specialty Food

30311 Token Factory
2131 South Ave
La Crosse, WI 54601

608-785-2439
888-486-5367
custserv@tokenfactory.com
www.tokenfactory.com
Manufacturer and exporter of plastic tokens and swizzle sticks
President: Dale Stevens
Sales Manager: Rosie Hundt

Estimated Sales: $1-2.5 Million
Number Employees: 11

30312 Tokheim Co
560 31st St
Marion, IA 52302-3724

319-362-4847
Fax: 319-377-7953 800-747-3442
info@tokheimco.com www.tokheimco.com
Manufacturer and exporter of liquid level gauges for large storage tanks
President: Vicky Barnes
Quality Control: Chris Peyton
VP: Thomas Barnes
Sales: Barb Riffey
Manager: Tom Barnes
tom.barnes@tokheimco.com
Estimated Sales: Less Than $500,000
Number Employees: 1-4
Square Footage: 40000

30313 (HQ)Tolan Machinery Company
PO Box 695
164 Franklin Ave.
Rockaway, NJ 7866

973-983-7212
Fax: 973-983-7217 www.tolanmachinery.com
Manufacturer and exporter of tanks, reactors, hoppers, bins, heat exchangers, storage vessels and fermentors
President: John Tolpa
VP, General Manager: Stephen Tolpa
Chief Engineer: Bill Ebbinghouser
VP Sales/Marketing: Thomas Spencer
Operations Manager: Brian T. Gill
Estimated Sales: $10-20 Million
Number Employees: 20-49
Square Footage: 80000

30314 Tolas Health Care Packaging
905 Pennsylvania Blvd
Feasterville Trevose, PA 19053

215-322-7900
Fax: 215-322-9034 marketing@tolas.com
www.tolas.com
Printed and converted paper, foil and plastics for packaging; exporter of paper, barrier films and foils
President: Carl D Marotta
CFO: Chuck Klink
Quality Control: Skip Peacock
R & D: Chris Perry
Marketing Team Leader: Denise Dilissio
Sales Director: Leslie Love
l.love@ciprianopi.com
Operations Manager: Dave Preikszas
Purchasing Manager: Jim McNally
Estimated Sales: $20 Million
Number Employees: 100-249
Square Footage: 50000

30315 Tolco Corp
1920 Linwood Ave
Toledo, OH 43604-5293

419-241-1113
Fax: 419-241-3035 800-537-4786
tolco@tolcocorp.com www.tolcocorporation.com
Funnels, soap dispensers, spouts, containers, scoops, pumps and trigger spray and plastic bottles
President: Robert Jones
r.jones@tol-co.com
VP Sales/Marketing: George Notarianni
VP Operations: W Spengler
Purchasing Agent: T Denker
Estimated Sales: $5-10 Million
Number Employees: 50-99
Square Footage: 100000
Brands:
Spraymist

30316 Toledo Sign Co Inc
2021 Adams St
Toledo, OH 43604-5431

419-244-4444
Fax: 419-244-6546 tsigns@toledosign.com
www.toledosign.com
Changeable, letter, electric, luminous tube, interchangeable, point of purchase and plastic signs
President: Brad Heil
bradheil@toledosign.com
Estimated Sales: $2.5-5 Million
Number Employees: 20-49

30317 Toledo Ticket Co
3963 Catawba St
PO Box 6876
Toledo, OH 43612-1492

419-476-5424
Fax: 419-476-6801 800-533-6620
www.toledoticket.com
Manufacturer and exporter of labels and coupons
President: Roy Carter
VP Sales and Marketing: Tom Carter
Estimated Sales: $5-10 Million
Number Employees: 20-49

30318 Toledo Wire Products
3601 Expressway Dr S
Toledo, OH 43608

419-729-5446
Fax: 419-729-0241 888-430-7445
Wire display racks
President: Ann Obertacz
anno@toledowire.com
Contact: Ken Obertacz
VP Sales: Rick Breivik
Production Manager: Ken Obertacz
Estimated Sales: $2.5-5 Million
Number Employees: 10-19

30319 Tom Lockerbie
1023 County Highway 20
Edmeston, NY 13335-2524

315-737-5612
Fax: 315-737-5183
Air agitated ice builders
Estimated Sales: $500,000-$1 Million
Number Employees: 3

30320 Tom McCall & Associates
6 Nanticoke Crossing Plaza
Millsboro, DE 19966-9511

410-539-0700
Fax: 212-689-5761
Recruiting and placement agency specializing in sales and management personnel
Manager: Charley Greene
Assistant Manager: Emma Jean Smith
Estimated Sales: $500,000-$1 Million
Number Employees: 10-19
Square Footage: 1400

30321 (HQ)Tomac Packaging
271 Salem Street
Unit G
Woburn, MA 01801-2004

781-938-1500
Fax: 781-938-7536 800-641-3100
Automatic weighing and bagging equipment for the produce industry; also, repairing and operating services available
President: Richard Gold
VP: Thomas Gold
VP: Hans Van Der Sande
Estimated Sales: $.5-1 million
Number Employees: 40
Square Footage: 8000
Other Locations:
Tomac Packaging
Idaho Falls ID

30322 Tomco2 Systems
3340 Rosebud Rd
Loganville, GA 30052-7341

770-979-8000
Fax: 770-978-5861 800-832-4262
tomco@tomcoequipment.com
www.tomcosystems.com
Tomco equipment company has developed products and services to suit all phases of co2 usage with storage. delivery and co2 application-driven equipment.tomco2's full range of products matches your carbon dioxide requirements. EPAcertified professional parts and service technicians are availible 24hrs a day 7 days a week. the company has supplied co2 storage and applications equipment since 1970.
President: John Toepke
CEO: Jack Toepke
jacktoepke@tomcoequipment.com
Cfo: Lynn Brown
Quality Control: Louis Pittaluga
Vice President Sales: Dan Tenpleton
Operations: Ken Mercer
Purchasing: Rayna Hewitt
Estimated Sales: $20-50 Million
Number Employees: 100-249

30323 Tomlinson Industries
13700 Broadway Ave
Cleveland, OH 44125-1945
216-587-3400
Fax: 216-587-0733 800-945-4589
jengle@tomlinsonind.com www.tomlinsonind.com
Manufacturer and exporter of faucets and fittings,
kettles, warmers and dispensers for cups, cones, lids,
straws, napkins and condiments; also, table top orga-
nizers, thermal platters and cook and serve skil-
lets;foodservice glovescutting boards and
anti-fatigue mats.
President: Michael Figas
CEO: H Meyer
CFO: Donald Calkins
VP: Louis Castro
Quality Control: John Silcox
Marketing: Jeanne Engle
Operations: Kenneth Sidoti
Purchasing: Michael Ritley
Estimated Sales: $20-50 Million
Number Employees: 100-249
Square Footage: 120000
Parent Co: Meyer Company
Brands:
  Frontier Kettle
  Glenray
  Melco
  Modular Dispensing Systems
  No-Drip
  Tomlinson

30324 Tomric Systems Inc
85 River Rock Dr # 202
Suite 202
Buffalo, NY 14207-2170
716-854-6050
Fax: 716-854-7363 www.tomric.com
Custom molds, supplies, equipment and packaging
for chocolate
President: Timothy M Thill
tthill@tomric.com
Estimated Sales: $1-5 Million
Number Employees: 50-99

30325 Tomsed Corporation
420 McKinney Pkwy
Lillington, NC 27546
910-814-3800
Fax: 910-814-3899 800-334-5552
Manufacturer and exporter of access control equip-
ment including high security and waist-high turn-
stiles, handicapped gates, portable posts and sign
holders; wholesaler/distributor of portable and fixed
crowd railing
President: Robert Sedivy
CEO: Thomas Sedivy
CFO: Karin Sedivy
Sales: Russell Socles
Estimated Sales: $15 Million
Number Employees: 100-249
Number of Brands: 9
Number of Products: 100
Square Footage: 220000
Brands:
  Entry Gard
  Lawrence Model 88
  Roto Gard
  Round Nose
  Safesec
  Tomsed
  Tut-50e
  Tut-50r

30326 Tonnellerie Mercier
171 Spring Grove Avenue
San Anselmo, CA 94960-2410
415-453-2069
Fax: 650-463-5485 www.tonnellerie-mercier.com
Wine industry cooperage
Partner: Ken Deis

30327 Tonnellerie Montross
139 Jenkins Point Road
Montross, VA 22520-3524
804-493-9186
Fax: 804-493-0435 lilreeht@aol.com
www.tonnellerie-mercier.com
Wine industry cooperage and French oak barrels of
all sizes
President: Jackqus Reche
Number Employees: 10

30328 Tonnellerie Radoux USA Inc
480 Aviation Blvd
Santa Rosa, CA 95403-1069
707-284-2888
Fax: 707-284-2894 800-755-4393
www.tonnellerieradoux.com
Wine industry cooperage
Manager: Norm Leighty
Quality Control: Lee Iller
President, Chief Executive Officer, Pres: Michel
Tapol
Manager: Lee Iller
rx.usa@radoux-usa.com
Estimated Sales: $5-10 Million
Number Employees: 10-19
Square Footage: 100000
Parent Co: Radoux

30329 Tonnellerie Remond
793 Broadway
Sonoma, CA 95476-7010
707-935-2176
Fax: 707-935-4774 remondsonoma@aol.com
Wine industry cooperage
Manager: Todd Stanfield
remondsonoma@aol.com
Manager: Todd Stanfield
Estimated Sales: $1-3 Million
Number Employees: 1-4

30330 Tooterville Trolley Company
5422 Bice Lane
Newburgh, IN 47630-8815
812-858-8585
Fax: 812-858-8580
Manufacturer and exporter of mobile carts including
shaved ice, fruit and salad bar; also, soda vending
machines
Owner: Thomas Rennels
Number Employees: 1
Square Footage: 2400
Brands:
  Jolly Trolley
  Tooterville Express

30331 (HQ)Top Line Process Equipment Company
PO Box 264
Bradford, PA 16701
814-362-4626
Fax: 814-362-4453 800-458-6095
topline@toplineonline.com
www.toplineonline.com
Supplier of hygienic stainless steel process equip-
ment
CEO: Dan McCone
VP: Kevin O'Donnell
Marketing: Debra Fowler
Sales: John Quteri
Contact: Thomas Nicola
tnicola@toplineonline.com
Operations: Tom Wilson
Plant Manager: Tim Fox
Purchasing: Marlene Raszmann
Number Employees: 5-9
Brands:
  Top Flo

30332 Top Source Industries
503 S Westgate St # C
PO Box 1246
Addison, IL 60101-4531
630-543-1886
Fax: 630-543-2076 800-362-9625
Clear acrylic display cases, floor, counter and wall
displays, trade show displays, counters, cabinets and
custom plastic products
President: Viola Wycislak
VP Sales: Gene Wycislak
Estimated Sales: $350,000
Number Employees: 1-4
Square Footage: 20000

30333 Topco Associates LLC
150 Northwest Point Blvd.
Elk Grove Village, IL 60007
847-676-3030
Fax: 847-676-4949 consumerservices@topco.com
www.topco.com
Grocery, frozen, dairy, and bakery, branded meat,
equipment and supplies, business services, world
brands and diverting.

President/CEO: Randall Skoda
rskoda@topco.com
Executive VP/CFO: Thomas Frey
Senior VP & General Counsel: Andy Broccolo
Senior VP, Fresh: Scott Caro
Year Founded: 1944
Estimated Sales: $1 Billion
Number Employees: 250-499
Number of Brands: 21
Type of Packaging: Consumer, Food Service, Pri-
vate Label
Other Locations:
  Visalia CA
  West Palm Beach FL
  Miami FL
  Quincy MA
  Yakima WA
Brands:
  Food Club®
  Shur Fine®
  Tippy Toes®
  Paws®
  Simply Done™
  @ease®
  Sweet P's®
  Buckley Farms™
  Harvest Club®
  Over the Top®
  Cape Covelle®
  Papa Enzo's®
  CharKing®
  Culinary Tours®
  Top Care®
  Full Circle®
  Pure Harmony®
  Wide Awake Coffee Co.®
  Cow Belle Creamery's™
  Valu Time®
  Nostimo®

30334 Topflight Grain Co-Op
400 E Bodman St
Bement, IL 61813-1299
217-678-2261
Fax: 217-678-8113 www.topflightgrain.com
Stores and distributes corn and grains
Manager: Derrick Bruhn
Manager: Yoshi Hatanaka
hatanaka@us.astellas.com
Estimated Sales: $10-20 000,000
Number Employees: 50-99

30335 Topos Mondial Corp
600 Queen St
Pottstown, PA 19464-6031
610-970-2270
Fax: 610-970-1619 Sales@toposmondial.com
www.toposmondial.com
Owner: Louis Doleac
ldoleac@verizon.net
Vice President: Damian Morabito
Estimated Sales: $5-10 Million
Number Employees: 20-49

30336 Tops Business Forms
1001 Rialto Rd
Covington, TN 38019-4242
901-476-4094
Fax: 785-233-4291 800-762-7283
www.tops-products.com
Business forms
President: Rodney Olson
Estimated Sales: Less Than $500,000
Number Employees: 1-4

30337 Tops Manufacturing Co
83 Salisbury Rd
Darien, CT 06820-2225
203-655-9367
Coffee and tea equipment including percolators,
knobs, handles, carafes, coffee makers and filters,
tea infusers, liquid coffee flavors, glass cups, instant
and ground coffee dispensers, measuring spoons, etc
President: Michael Davies
michael@endeavourpartners.net
VP: Pat Himmel
Sales Manager: Ernie Hurlbut
Estimated Sales: Less Than $500,000
Number Employees: 1-4
Square Footage: 31400
Type of Packaging: Consumer, Food Service
Brands:
  Brick-Pack Clip
  Fitz-All
  Flav-A-Brrew

Kaf-Tan
Measure Fresh
Perma-Brew
Rapid Brew
Tops

30338 Tor Rey Refrigeration Inc
3741 Yale St
Houston, TX 77018-6563

713-884-1988
Fax: 281-564-3246 888-265-3462
www.tor-rey-refrigeration.com
Wholesaler/distributor of meat grinders and parts,
saws, slicers, scales and bandsaw blades
Owner: Jesus Iglecis
gmanager@tor-rey.com
Estimated Sales: $10-20 Million
Number Employees: 5-9

30339 Tor Rey USA
3737 Yale St
Houston, TX 77018

713-884-1988
Fax: 713-564-3246
Chopper plates and knives, choppers, grinder plates
and knives, grinders and scales
Owner: Jesus Iglecis
Contact: Patricio Bacco
latinexport@tor-rey.com
Estimated Sales: $10-20 Million
Number Employees: 5-9

30340 Toray Plastics America Inc
50 Belver Ave
North Kingstown, RI 02852

Fax: 401-294-2154 800-453-6866
www.toraytpa.com
Biaxially oriented film, polyprolylene film,
metallized.
President & CEO: Michael Brandmeier
Year Founded: 1926
Estimated Sales: $18 Billion
Number Employees: 46,000
Parent Co: Toray Industries Inc

30341 Torbeck Industries
355 Industrial Dr
Harrison, OH 45030-1483

513-367-0080
Fax: 513-367-0081 800-333-0080
Producer of material handling and safety equipment
used inmanufacturing, distribution and warehousing
facilities throughout North America.
President: R L Torbeck Jr
Estimated Sales: $10,000,000-$49,900,000
Number Employees: 50-99
Square Footage: 80000
Brands:
Astrodeck
Quik-Space
Saf-T-Rail

30342 Toroid Corp
225 Wynn Dr NW
Huntsville, AL 35805-1958

256-837-7510
Fax: 256-837-7512 toroidcorp@hotmail.com
www.toroidcorp.com
Custom weighing equipment, load cells and repair-
ing load cells.
President: Anne Paelian
toroidcorp@hotmail.com
Vice President/Sales Manager: Paul Paelian
Estimated Sales: $1 Million
Number Employees: 10-19
Square Footage: 80000
Brands:
Lowboy
Omniflex

30343 Toromont Process Systems
395 W 1100 N
North Salt Lake, UT 84054-2621

801-292-1747
Fax: 801-292-9908
www.toromontpowersystems.com
Manufacturer and exporter of custom designed in-
dustrial and chemical refrigeration systems
President: Hugo Sorenson
CFO: Jerry Frailec
Manager: Jim Shepherd
Contact: Vladimir Kratser
vkratser@toromontsystems.com

Estimated Sales: $30-50 Million
Number Employees: 10
Square Footage: 70000
Parent Co: Toromont Industries
Other Locations:
Toromont Process Systems
Malden MA

30344 Toronto Fabricating & Manufacturing
1021 Rangeview Road
Mississauga, ON L5E 1H2
Canada

905-891-2516
Fax: 905-891-7446 sales@tfmc.com
www.tfmc.com
Manufacturer and exporter of tables, chairs, table
tops and bases, benches, barstools and decorative
lighting sconces and fixtures
Manager: Allan Farnum

30345 Toronto Kitchen Equipment
1150 Barmac Drive
North York, ON M9L 1X5
Canada

416-745-4944
Fax: 416-745-3217
Stoves, ovens, hoods, mixers, slicers and grills
General Manager: Paul Antolin
Number Employees: 20-49

30346 Torpac Capsules
333 Route 46
Fairfield, NJ 07004

973-244-1125
Fax: 973-244-1365 www.torpac.com
Processor, importer and exporter of gelatin capsules;
manufacturer and exporter of capsule filling
machinery
President: Raj Tahil
Quality Control: Ajay Varma
Estimated Sales: Below $5 Million
Number Employees: 10
Square Footage: 40000
Type of Packaging: Consumer
Brands:
Torpac

30347 Tortilla Industry Associ
8300 Douglas Ave Ste 800
Dallas, TX 75225

214-706-9193
Fax: 214-706-9194
This Association was created to serve the emerging
tortilla industry.
Number Employees: 1-4

30348 Tosca Ltd
1032 Bay Beach Road
Green Bay, WI 54302

920-617-4000
Fax: 920-465-9198 info@toscaltd.com
www.toscaltd.com
Plastic containers for food storage
President: John Frey
Business Development: Robin Last
VP: Michael Fechter
Contact: Sarah Conway
sconway@toscaltd.com
VP Operations: Greg Gorske
Plant Manager: Curt Dhein
Estimated Sales: $40 Million
Number Employees: 180
Square Footage: 21000

30349 Toscarora
2901 W Monroe Street
Sandusky, OH 44870-1810

419-625-7343
Fax: 419-625-1171
Manufacturer and exporter of custom designed plas-
tic thermoformed food trays; also, custom designed
cookie trays
Operations Manager: Joe Knight
Plant Manager: Mike LaFond
Estimated Sales: $10-20 Million
Number Employees: 50-99
Square Footage: 200000

30350 Toska Foodservice Systems
W197n7577 Fw Court
Lannon, WI 53046

262-253-4782
Fax: 262-253-9685

Designer and manufacturer of commercial modular
combination kitchens serveries. Supplier of cus-
tomer operated order and payment system. Supplier
of prepaid card systems
President: Guenter Toska
Sales Manager: Thomas Conlan
Estimated Sales: Below $5 Million
Number Employees: 10

30351 Toss Machine Components
539 S Main St # 1
Nazareth, PA 18064-2795

610-759-8883
Fax: 610-759-1766 info@tossheatseal.com
www.tossheatseal.com
Heatsealing plastic materials, temperature control-
lers, dataloggers, heatseal bands, transformers,
back-up materials, heatseal bars
President: Charles Trillich
ctrillich@packworldusa.com
Vice-President: Helma Young
Sales Manager: Andy Becan
Estimated Sales: $5-10 Million
Number Employees: 10-19
Square Footage: 400000
Type of Packaging: Consumer, Food Service

30352 Total Control Products
2001 Janice Avenue
Melrose Park, IL 60160-1010

708-345-5500
Fax: 708-345-5670
Electronic controls
Estimated Sales: $10-20 Million
Number Employees: 50-99

30353 Total Foods Corporation
6018 W Maple Rd
West Bloomfield, MI 48322-4404

248-851-2611
Fax: 248-737-2035
Manager: Dave Owens
Estimated Sales: $50-100 Million
Number Employees: 5-9

30354 (HQ)Total Identity Group
255 Pinebush Road
Cambridge, ON N1T 1B9
Canada

519-622-4040
Fax: 519-622-4031 877-551-5529
info@pridesigns.com www.pridesigns.com
Custom signs and awnings
Manager: David Kurty
CFO: Dan Cass
Marketing Director: Lara Fedele
Operations Manager: Joel Shenton
Purchasing Manager: Denise Carroll
Number Employees: 100-249

30355 Total Lubricants
5 N Stiles St
Linden, NJ 07036-4208

908-862-9300
Fax: 908-862-1647 IBU-CSR@total-us.com
http://keystonelubricants.com/keystone/index.htm
Product lines includes food machinery lubricants; air
compressor fluids; metalworking lubricants; and
maintenance lubricants.
Human Resources: Steve Daubert
Food Industry Sales Specialist: Jim Cancila
Food Industry Sales Specialist: Bruce Wolfe
Contact: Mark Catano
mark.catano@total-us.com
International Food Industry Specialist: Christine
Richard
Estimated Sales: H
Number Employees: 10,000

30356 Total Quality Corp
320 Soundview Rd
Guilford, CT 06437-2973

203-689-5435
Fax: 203-483-7449 800-453-9729
tqcinfo@totalqualitycorp.com
www.totalqualitycorp.com
Off-line inspection for contamination, container
equipment, inspection and systems division
Marketing Director: Kimberly Seneco
Contact: Stephen Evon
s.evon@totalqualitycorp.com
Estimated Sales: $1-2.5 Million
Number Employees: 1-4

30357 Total Quality Corporation
PO Box 723
Branford, CT 06405-0723
203-483-7447
Fax: 203-483-7449 800-453-9729
tqcinfo@totalqualitycorp.com
www.totalqualitycorp.com
X-ray inspection service for raw and finished products
Office Manager: Kymberly Seneco
Estimated Sales: $1-2.5 Million
Number Employees: 4
Square Footage: 20000

30358 Total Scale Systems
1040 N Dutton Avenue
Santa Rosa, CA 95401-5042
707-526-2221
Fax: 707-526-0644
Wine industry scales
Estimated Sales: $1-5 Million
Number Employees: 6

30359 Toter Inc
841 Meacham Rd
Statesville, NC 28677-2983
704-872-8171
Fax: 704-878-0734 800-772-0071
toter@toter.com www.toter.com
Manufacturer and exporter of carts and lifter systems
President: Jeff Gilliam
jgilliam@wastequip.com
VP Sales: Rick Hoffman
Estimated Sales: $50-100 Million
Number Employees: 50-99
Brands:
Toter Worksaver

30360 Touch Controls
520 Industrial Way
Fallbrook, CA 92028
760-723-7900
Fax: 760-723-7910 800-848-4385
Rugged sized touch screens, industrial computers, industrial enclosures, fiberoptic transmission systems
Estimated Sales: $5-10 Million
Number Employees: 20-49

30361 Touch Menus
1601 116th Ave NE # 111
Bellevue, WA 98004-3010
425-881-3100
Fax: 425-881-2980 800-688-6368
Manufacturer and exporter of touch screen point of sale systems and software; also, credit card services available
VP: Darrin Howell
Marketing Manager: Gill Gilman
Estimated Sales: $5-10 Million
Number Employees: 5-9
Square Footage: 8000
Type of Packaging: Private Label
Brands:
Cats
Editpro
Touch Menus
Trapr

30362 Tourtellot & Co
99 Colorado Ave
Warwick, RI 02888
401-734-4200
Wholesaler/distributor of produce; serving the food service market; also, retail consultation services available.
Vice President: Jamie Manville
Vice President & Part Owner: Steve Sigal
Year Founded: 1898
Estimated Sales: $20-50 Million
Number Employees: 20-49
Square Footage: 65000

30363 Tower Pallet Co Inc
5211 County Road X
PO Box 5006
De Pere, WI 54115-9798
920-336-3495
Fax: 920-336-3025
Pallets and skids
President: William Koltz
tpc@towerpallet.net
VP/Treasurer: Randy Koltz

Estimated Sales: $2.5-5 Million
Number Employees: 20-49

30364 Townfood Equipment Corp
72 Beadel St
Brooklyn, NY 11222-5232
718-388-5650
Fax: 718-388-5860 800-221-5032
customerservice@townfood.com
www.townfood.com
Asian barbecue equipment, cooking utensils, china, soup stoves, ovens, ranges, smokers and electric rice cookers; importer of hand hammered woks and gas rice cookers; exporter of rice cookers, ranges and smokers
President: Charles Suss
Founder: Morris Suss
VP: Sada Nair
R&D/Quality Control: Ken Trosterman
Marketing Executive: Marianne Suss
Sales: Mary Ann Balk
Equipment Specialists: Sincere Chan
Production: Ken Tosterman
Purchasing Director: Sada Nair
Estimated Sales: $5-10 Million
Number Employees: 10-19
Square Footage: 100000
Type of Packaging: Consumer, Private Label
Brands:
Rice Master
York & Masterrange

30365 Townsend Research Laboratories, Inc
1339 Sadlier Circle W Drive
Indianapolis, IN 46239
317-375-0893
Fax: 317-375-1046
Food microbiology and consulting
President: Lou Townsend
Lab Director: Rick Ehrhardt
Quality Manager: Raymond Leiber
Sales Manager: Susan Hughes

30366 Townsend-Piller Packing
719 19 4th Avenue
Cumberland, WI 54829
715-822-4910
Packing supplies and equipment
President: Robert Townsend

30367 Toyo Seikan Kaisha
707 Skokie Blvd # 670
Northbrook, IL 60062-2857
847-509-3080
Fax: 847-509-3088
Total packaging system, from material to processing
Owner: Masa Morotomi
Estimated Sales: $1-5 Million
Number Employees: 1-4

30368 Toyota Tsusho America Inc.
805 3rd Ave.
17th Floor
New York, NY 10022
212-355-3600
www.taiamerica.com
International trading, supply-chain services, and intermediate goods processing. Engages in business opportunities related to industrial and consumer products and services.
President/CEO: Ichiro Kashitani
Chairman: Jun Karube
CFO: Hideyuki Iwamoto
Year Founded: 1960
Estimated Sales: $5.3 Billion
Number Employees: 100-249
Square Footage: 16234
Parent Co: Toyota Tshusho Corporation

30369 Traco Manufacturing Inc
620 S 1325 W
Orem, UT 84058-4987
801-225-8040
Fax: 801-226-1509 866-516-1205
www.tracopackaging.com
Shrink film, tamper-resistant packaging, heat sealer machines

President: John Palica
CFO: John Hiatt
HR Executive: Scott Goodman
sgoodman@traco-mfg.co
Quality Control: Craig Johnson
VP Sales: Ron Moore
Purchasing Manager: Craig Johnson
Estimated Sales: Below $5 Million
Number Employees: 50-99
Square Footage: 40000
Brands:
Impulse Heat Sealer
Shrink Bags
Shrink Bands & Preforms

30370 Trade Fixtures
1501 Westpark Dr # 5
Little Rock, AR 72204-2457
501-664-1318
Fax: 501-664-9253 800-872-3490
cservice@tradefixtures.com www.h2optimized.net
Manufacturer and exporter of molded displays for bulk food items including gravity and scoop bins
Manager: Scott Johnson
sjohnson@tradefixtures.com
Quality Control: Walter Baumgarten
President: Scott Johnson
VP Sales: Clay Odom
VP Sales: Doug Holland
General Manager: Joe Herrmann
Purchasing Manager: Roy Jackson
Estimated Sales: $5-10 Million
Number Employees: 50-99
Square Footage: 112000
Parent Co: Display Technologies

30371 Trade Wings
4929 Wyaconda Rd
Rockville, MD 20852-2443
301-770-8770
Fax: 301-770-8771
Owner: Nader Dibiglari
Estimated Sales: Under$500,000
Number Employees: 5-9

30372 Tradeco International Corp
1107 S Westwood Ave
PO Box 1155
Addison, IL 60101-4920
630-628-1112
Fax: 630-628-6616 800-628-3738
ventura@tradecointl.com www.tradecointl.com
Manufacturer and importer of chinaware including plates, cups, saucers and hollowware
President: Leslie D Plass
lplass@tradecointl.com
Estimated Sales: $1-3,000,000
Number Employees: 10-19
Type of Packaging: Consumer
Brands:
Ventura China

30373 Trademarx Inc
1443 E Washington Blvd.,
Pasadena, CA 94110
626-795-0587
Fax: 626-795-0548 sales@trademarx.net
www.trademarx.net
Manufacture disposable plastic and paper products for the foodservice industry.
President/CEO: Scott James
CFO/Public Relations: Jenny Wang
VP/R&D: Peter Song
Quality Control: Shelly Lu
Marketing/Sales: Scott James
Estimated Sales: $5 Million
Number Employees: 250-499
Number of Brands: 3
Number of Products: 100
Square Footage: 680000
Type of Packaging: Consumer, Food Service, Private Label, Bulk
Brands:
Jay
Purex
Trademarx

30374 Tradepaq Corporation
30 Montgomery Street
Jersey City, NJ 07302
201-716-2665
Fax: 201-435-9916 www.tradepaq.com
Supplier of commodity trading software

CFO: Charles Griffs
Sales: Deborah Laska
Contact: David Janay
djanay@tradepaq.com
Estimated Sales: $5-10 Million
Number Employees: 10-19

30375 Traeger Industries
10450 SW Nimbus Ave
Building R, Suite A
Portland, OR 97223

503-845-9234
Fax: 503-94 -155 800-872-3437
traeger@traegerindustries.com
www.traegergrills.com
Manufacturer and exporter of wood pellet smokers
and cooking appliances
President: Joseph Traeger
VP Sales/Marketing: Randy Traeger
VP Production: Mark Traeger
Estimated Sales: $5-10 Million
Number Employees: 50-99
Square Footage: 108000
Brands:
  Traeger

30376 Traex
101 Traex Dr
Dane, WI 53529

608-849-2500
Fax: 608-849-2580 800-356-8006
www.libbey.com
Manufacturer, importer and exporter of food trays,
straw dispensers, portion control and napkin dis-
pensers, bus boxes, dishracks and tabletop
accessories
Marketing: Lori Barger
Contact: Allen Byers
allen.byers@libbey.com
Plant Manager: Steve Boeder
Purchasing Agent: Rose Ohlert
Estimated Sales: $10-20 Million
Number Employees: 100-249
Square Footage: 30000
Parent Co: Menasha Corporation
Brands:
  Barkeep
  Batter Boss
  Cupro
  Dripcut
  Kondi-Keeper
  Lidpro Lid Dispenser
  Quik-Pik
  Rackmaster
  Sauce Boss
  Self Service System
  Straw Boss
  T-Rex

30377 (HQ)Tragon Corp
350 Bridge Pkwy
Redwood City, CA 94065-1061

650-412-2100
Fax: 650-412-2001 800-841-1177
info@tragon.com www.tragon.com
Consultant specializing in product testing, market
research and management consultation services.
Quantitative and qualitative market research
President/CEO: Douglas Vort
Co-Founder: Herbert Stone
hstone@tragon.com
VP: Rebecca Bleibaum
Marketing: Joseph Salerno
Chief Operating Officer: Brian Adkins
Estimated Sales: $2.5-5 Million
Number Employees: 20-49
Square Footage: 21000
Other Locations:
  Tragon Corporation
  Buffalo Grove IL
Brands:
  Prop
  Prop Plus
  Qda
  Qda Software

30378 Traitech Industries
100 Four Valley Drive
Unit C
Vaughan, ON L4K 4T9
Canada

905-695-2800
Fax: 905-695-0737 877-872-4835
info@traitech.com www.traitech.com

Manufacturer and exporter of ventilated merchandis-
ing trays, baskets and displays custom manufacturer
President: Tom Penton
VP: Ryan Slight
Type of Packaging: Consumer, Food Service, Pri-
vate Label, Bulk
Brands:
  California
  California Trays

30379 Trak-Air/Rair
555 Quivas St
Denver, CO 80204-4915

303-779-9888
Fax: 303-694-3575 800-688-8725
sales@trak-air.com www.trak-air.com
Manufacturer and exporter of hot air and greaseless
countertop fryers; also, pizza ovens
President: Dale Terry
dterry@coloradosalesinc.com
Estimated Sales: $1-2 Million
Number Employees: 20-49
Square Footage: 64000
Type of Packaging: Food Service
Brands:
  Rair 2000
  Rair 7000
  Trak-Air Ii
  Trak-Air V

30380 Traker Systems
43460 Ridge Park Dr # 250
Suite 250
Temecula, CA 92590-3736

951-693-1376
Fax: 951-693-1386 800-314-6863
www.itracker.net
Traker Systems is an inventory management and inventory software application that enables manufacturing and transportation industries the power to
regulate, dominate, or manipulate services and products, purchasing, receivinginvoicing, pricing, product allocation, bar coding, forms and shipping into
one, convenient package.
Owner: Kuba Fandl
kubaf@trakersystems.com
Number Employees: 10-19

30381 Tramontina USA
12955 W Airport Blvd
Sugar Land, TX 77478-6119

281-340-8400
Fax: 281-340-8410 800-221-7809
tusa@tramontina-usa.com
www.tramontina-usa.com
Cutlery, cookware and servingware
President: Antonio Galafassi
Manager Food Service Sales: Steve Kozicki
Sales Assistant (Food Service): Debbie Rademacher
Contact: Rawan Abdeljaber
rabdeljaber@sizzlingplatter.com
Estimated Sales: $10-20,000,000
Number Employees: 250-499

30382 Trane Inc
800-E Beaty St
Davidson, NC 28036

704-655-4000
www.trane.com
Manufacturer and exporter of roof top and self-con-
tained air conditioner; also, heat pumps including
water-source.
President, Commercial HVAC Americas: Donald
Simmons
President, Residential HVAC & Supply: Jason
Bingham
Year Founded: 1913
Estimated Sales: $10 Billion
Number Employees: 29,000
Parent Co: Ingersoll Rand
Brands:
  Aire Systems
  Centravac
  Earthwise Systems
  Integrated Comfort Systems
  Intellipack
  Service First
  Tracer Summit
  Tracker
  Trag
  Trane
  Unit Trane
  Varitrac
  Varitrane

30383 Trans Flex Packagers Inc
34 Burnham Ave
PO Box 127
Unionville, CT 06085-1263

860-673-2531
Fax: 860-673-6238 www.tfpackagers.com
Flexible plastic bags including cellulose, polyethyl-
ene and polypropylene
Owner: Mike Kaplan
mike@tfpackagers.com
Estimated Sales: $5-10 Million
Number Employees: 20-49
Square Footage: 50000

30384 Trans World Services
72 Stone Pl
Melrose, MA 02176-6016

781-665-9200
Fax: 781-665-6649 800-882-2105
twsinc@gis.net
Manufacturer and exporter of thermometers and
sandwich packaging materials including crystal
wrap and cellophane; also, packaging machinery.
Consumer, institution and processor packaging of
T-shirts, USDA/FSIS partner
President: Thomas E Ford
CFO: Thomas Foid
Vice President: Dan Tuono
R&D: Thomas Foid
Quality Control: Thomas Foid
Sales/Marketing: Ira Siegal
Estimated Sales: $10-20 Million
Number Employees: 10-19
Square Footage: 208000
Type of Packaging: Food Service

30385 (HQ)Trans-Chemco Inc
19235 84th St
PO Box 9
Bristol, WI 53104-9184

262-857-2363
Fax: 262-857-9127 800-880-2498
info@trans-chemco.com www.trans-chemco.com
Manufacturer, importer and exporter of chemicals
including defoamers and antifoamers; also, labora-
tory research and development for products and
special needs
President: Susanne Gardiner
CFO: Irene Swan
VP/Director: Merle Gardiner
VP R&D: Merle Gardiner
Operations Manager: Sheila Cleveland
Estimated Sales: $1-3 Million
Number Employees: 10-19
Square Footage: 60000
Brands:
  Trans-10
  Trans-100
  Trans-30

30386 Transbotics Corp
3400 Latrobe Dr
Charlotte, NC 28211-4847

704-362-1115
Fax: 704-364-4039 www.tfransbotics.com
Design, development, support and installation of
Automatic Guided Vehicles, or transportation robots,
with an emphasis on complete customer satisfaction.
Supplier of Automatic Guide Vehicle Systems, AGV
controls technology, engineeringservices, AGV bat-
teries, charges and other related products
CEO: Claude Imbleau
EVP: Neville Croft
Service/ Quality System Manager: Robert Stiteler
Marketing & Aftermarket Sales: Jayesh Mehta
Sales: Chuck Rossell
Public Relations: Ryan Willis
Operations: Mark Ramsey
Purchasing Manager: David Melton
Estimated Sales: $1-5,000,000
Number Employees: 20-49
Parent Co: NDC Automation
Type of Packaging: Bulk

30387 Transition Equipment Company
444 Laguna Vista Road
Santa Rosa, CA 95401

707-537-7787
Fax: 707-537-7174 vickitec@aol.com
www.transitionequipment.com
Used equipment, winery, packaging and beverage
Fiscal Operations Manager: Eileen Paul
Director of Sales: Vicki Mastbaum
vicki@transitionequipment.com

Estimated Sales: Below $500,000
Number Employees: 3

30388 Transnorm System Inc
1906 S Great Southwest Pkwy
Grand Prairie, TX 75051-3580

972-606-0303
Fax: 972-606-0768 800-259-2303
sales@transnorm.com www.transnorm.com
Manufacturer and exporter of belt curve conveyors
including mini edge, power, spiral, straight, etc
President: Kay L Wolfe
VP: Rick Lee
Estimated Sales: $20-50 Million
Number Employees: 10
Square Footage: 80000
Parent Co: Transnorm System GmBH
Brands:
　F.R.P.
　Safeglide

30389 Transparent Container Co
325 S Lombard Rd
Addison, IL 60101-3023

630-458-9031
Fax: 312-666-3163
marketing@transparentcontainer.com
Containers
President: Dan Greiwe
dgreiwe@transparentcontainer.com
CFO: Ron Pranger
VP/Sales: Dan Wyss
General Manager: Steve Fifer
Estimated Sales: $5-10 Million
Number Employees: 50-99

30390 Tranter INC
1900 Old Burk Hwy
Wichita Falls, TX 76306-5904

940-723-7125
Fax: 940-723-5131 sales@tranter.com
www.tranter.com
Surface and plate heat exchangers, cabinet liners for
walk-in refrigerator/freezing rooms, freezing storage
units, cold and hot food displays; exporter of heat
exchangers
President: Charles Monachello
CEO: Roy Mason
CFO: Arnold Downes
VP: Roy Mason
Research & Development: Jeff Mathur
Marketing Director: Ronald Stonecipher
Sales Director: Frank Kierzkowski
Purchasing Manager: Czeech Richardson
Number Employees: 100-249
Square Footage: 480000
Parent Co: Tranter
Brands:
　Colbank
　Freeztand
　Maxchanger
　Platecoil
　Snobanc
　Snopan
　Steempan
　Superchanger

30391 Trap-Zap Environmental
255 Braen Ave
Wyckoff, NJ 07481-2948

201-251-9970
Fax: 201-251-0903 800-282-8727
labelle@trapzap.com
Biological products for greasetraps, drains and sep-
tic systems, septic system additives and floor and
surface cleaners; also, consultant providing
wastewater management, turnkey programs and
greasetrap maintenance
President: Robert Belle
rbelle@trapzap.com
National Accounts Manager: Rick Albano
Estimated Sales: $2.5-5 Million
Number Employees: 10-19
Square Footage: 10000
Brands:
　Bio-Zap
　D-Grade
　Trap-Zap Plus

30392 Traub Container Corporation
22475 Aurora Road
Cleveland, OH 44146-1270

216-475-5100
Fax: 216-475-5015

Corrugated displays, shipping containers and fiber-
board sheets
Sales Manager: Bob Mavity
General Manager: Donald Colombo
Plant Manager: Dale Kiaski
Estimated Sales: $10-20 Million
Number Employees: 135
Square Footage: 250000
Parent Co: MacMillan Bloedel Packaging

30393 Traulsen & Co
4401 Blue Mound Rd
Fort Worth, TX 76106-1928

817-625-1168
Fax: 817-624-4302 800-825-8220
Manufacturer and exporter of commercial refrigera-
tors and freezers including display, stainless steel,
anodized aluminum, vinyl, reach-in, roll-in and
pass-through
Manager: Gary Hoying
Vice President: Pepe Griffo
Marketing Director: Mark Kauffman
Operations: Gary Hoying
Purchasing: John Hebert
Estimated Sales: $20-50 Million
Number Employees: 10-19
Square Footage: 300000
Parent Co: ITW
Other Locations:
　Traulsen & Co.
　New Troy MI
Brands:
　Show-Off
　Traulsen
　Ultima
　Ultra

30394 Travaini Pumps USA
200 Newsome Dr
Yorktown, VA 23692-5002

757-988-3930
Fax: 757-988-3975 800-535-4243
customerservice@travaini.com www.travaini.com
Liquid ring vacuum pumps
President: Dominic Gemmiti
Vice President: Federico Colagrande
Estimated Sales: $10-20 Million
Number Employees: 20-49

30395 Travelon
700 Touhy Ave
Elk Grove Vlg, IL 60007-4916

847-621-7000
Fax: 847-621-7001 800-537-5544
www.travelonbags.com
Manufacturer, importer and exporter of metal dis-
plays and carts
Owner: Don Godshaw
dong@travelonbags.com
VP Marketing: Kathy Novak
Estimated Sales: $1-5 Million
Number Employees: 100-249
Square Footage: 100000
Type of Packaging: Consumer

30396 Travis Manufacturing Corp
13231 Salem Church St NE
Alliance, OH 44601-9441

330-875-1661
Fax: 330-875-4240
Custom fabricated stainless steel tables, shelving
President: Roger W Oberlin
VP: Brian Taranto
Estimated Sales: Less Than $500,000
Number Employees: 1-4
Square Footage: 17000

30397 Tray-Pak Corp
251 Tuckerton Rd
Reading, PA 19605-1154

610-926-5800
Fax: 610-926-9140 info@traypak.com
www.traypak.com
Thermoformed plastic trays
President: John Rusnock
CEO: William Barrick
bbarrick@traypak.com
CEO: Randy Simcox
Marketing: William Mosier
Estimated Sales: $20-50 Million
Number Employees: 250-499

30398 Traycon Manufacturing Co
555 Barell Ave
Carlstadt, NJ 07072-2891

201-939-5555
Fax: 201-939-4180 info@traycon.com
www.traycon.com
Manufacturer and exporter of conveyors and carts
for dish and tray handling systems
CEO: Nicholas Pisto
VP: Candice Pisto
Estimated Sales: $5-10 Million
Number Employees: 20-49
Square Footage: 40000
Brands:
　Dw
　Ra
　Rdb
　Rdl
　Sdb
　Sdl
　Ssw
　Traycon

30399 Tree Saver
2830 S Shoshone Street
Englewood, CO 80110-1204

303-781-2646
Fax: 303-762-8616 800-676-7741
www.savers.com
Reusable bags including cloth grocery, trash liner
and produce
Operations Manager: Carol Sweet
Estimated Sales: $500,000-$1 Million
Number Employees: 19
Brands:
　Tree Saver Bags

30400 TreeHouse Foods, Inc.
2021 Spring Rd.
Suite 600
Oak Brook, IL 60523

708-483-1300
info@treehousefoods.com
www.treehousefoods.com
Cereals, snack foods, condiments, frozen baked
goods and frozen prepared meals.
President/CEO: Steven Oakland
Executive VP/CFO: William Kelley
Senior VP/COO: C. Shay Braun
Estimated Sales: $6.3 Billion
Number Employees: 13,489
Number of Brands: 4
Type of Packaging: Consumer, Private Label
Brands:
　Bay Valley Foods
　TreeHouse Private Brands
　Flagstone Foods
　E.D. Smith

30401 Treen Box & Pallet Inc
1950 Street Rd # 400
Bensalem, PA 19020-3752

215-639-5100
Fax: 215-639-8530 www.treenpallet.com
Wooden boxes, pallets and skids
President: George Geiges
ggeiges@comcast.net
VP: A Geiges
Estimated Sales: $30 Million
Number Employees: 20-49
Square Footage: 30000

30402 Treier Popcorn Farms
16793 County Line Rd
Bloomdale, OH 44817

419-454-2811
Fax: 419-454-3983 ptreier@wcnet.org
Popcorn including bagged, natural, buttered and
microwaveable; wholesaler/distributor of commer-
cial popcorn poppers and other concession supply
equipment; serving the food service market
President: Don Treier
Secretary/Treasurer: Peggy Treier
Estimated Sales: $500,000-$1 Million
Number Employees: 15
Number of Brands: 2
Number of Products: 6
Square Footage: 12000
Parent Co: Treier Family Farms
Type of Packaging: Consumer, Food Service, Bulk
Brands:
　Lake Plains
　Pelton's Hybrid Popcorn

30403 Treif USA
230 Long Hill Cross Rd
Shelton, CT 06484-6160
203-929-9930
Fax: 203-849-8517 treifusa@treif.com
www.treif.com
High speed, high-output slicing and dicing equipment
President: Robert Linke
Contact: Alicia Clayton
aclayton@treif.com
Estimated Sales: $1-2.5 Million
Number Employees: 5-9

30404 Treif USA Inc
50 Waterview Dr # 130
Suite 130
Shelton, CT 06484-4377
203-929-9930
Fax: 203-929-9949 info@treif.com
www.treif.de
High-speed slicing machines, bone in or boneless
high volume dicing machines
President: Terry Albrecht
terry.albrecht@treif.com
Vice President: Bill Render
Marketing Director: Alicia Kidd
terry.albrecht@treif.com
Estimated Sales: $6.0 Million
Number Employees: 5-9
Parent Co: Treif Machinery GmbH

30405 Trent Corp
1384 Yardville Hamilton Squ Rd
Trenton, NJ 08691-3343
609-587-7515
Fax: 609-586-9710 trentboxmfgco@aol.com
www.trentbox.com
Packaging materials including bikini packs, box lids
and corrugated containers
President: Carl A Angelini
Quality Control: Bob Campbell
Sales/Marketing Executive: Charles Baumann
Purchasing Agent: Lynda Saganowski
Estimated Sales: $10-20 Million
Number Employees: 10-19
Brands:
   Kwik-Pak
   Twin-Pak

30406 Trenton Mills Inc
400 Factory St
PO Box 107
Trenton, TN 38382-2012
731-855-1323
Fax: 731-855-9000 sales@trentonmills.com
www.trentonmills.com
Stockinette knit for meat packing and filters
Owner: Bobby Blakely
blakely@trentonmills.com
Operations: Bubby Blakely
Estimated Sales: $3-5 Million
Number Employees: 20-49
Square Footage: 520000
Parent Co: Dyersburg Fabrics

30407 Treofan America LLC
6001 Gun Club Rd
Winston Salem, NC 27103-9727
336-766-9448
Fax: 336-766-8260 800-424-6273
www.treofan.com
Packaging films and labels
Manager: Grant Gustason
grant.gustason@treofan.com
Number Employees: 20-49

30408 (HQ)Trepte's Wire & Metal Works
14822 Lakewood Boulevard
Bellflower, CA 90706-2857
562-630-6798
Fax: 562-630-5901 800-828-6217
rontrepte@hotmail.com
Skewers, hot pan grips, spoons and racks including
roasting, baking and broiling
President and CEO: A Ron Trepte Sr
Secretary: E Trepte
Number Employees: 10
Square Footage: 48000
Brands:
   E-Z-V

30409 Trevor Industries
8698 S Main St
Eden, NY 14057
716-992-4775
Fax: 716-992-4788
Manufacturer, importer and exporter of plastic
drinking straws and cocktail stirrers
Owner: Gary Ballowe
VP Administration: Karen Amico
Plant Manager: Robert Martin
Estimated Sales: $5-10 Million
Number Employees: 20-49
Square Footage: 150000

30410 Trevor Owen Limited
80 Barbados Boulevard
Unit 5
Scarborough, ON M1J 1K9
Canada
416-267-8231
Fax: 416-267-1035 866-487-2224
sales@trevorowenltd.com www.trevorowenltd.com
Manufacturer and exporter of banners and insulated
food delivery bags
President: Pierre Barcik
Sales Executive: Trevor Owen
Number Employees: 10
Square Footage: 40000

30411 Tri County Citrus Packers
12143 Avenue 456
Orange Cove, CA 93646-9504
559-626-5010
Fax: 559-626-7951 vcpg@vcpg.com
Packinghouse and licensed shipper of citrus products for Sunkist Growers, Inc.
Manager: John Kalendar
Assistant Manager: Eric Fultz
Manager: John Clower
jclower@vcpg.com
Number Employees: 50-99
Parent Co: Visalia Citrus Packing Group

30412 Tri Tool Inc
3041 Sunrise Blvd
Rancho Cordova, CA 95742-6502
916-288-6100
Fax: 916-288-6160 800-345-5015
customer.service@tritool.com www.tritool.com
Manufactures pipe cutting and welding preparation
equipment
President: Jennifer Arsenault
jennifer.a.arsenault@wellsfargo.com
CEO: Jerry VanDer Pol
Chairman: George J Wernette
CFO: Tom Meyer
R & D: Dale Flood
Sales: Daryl Anderson
Production: Jim Bergstrand
Purchasing: Barbara Porter
Estimated Sales: $20-50 Million
Number Employees: 100-249
Type of Packaging: Bulk

30413 Tri-Boro Shelving & Partition
300 Dominion Dr
Farmville, VA 23901-2371
434-315-5600
Fax: 434-315-0139 800-633-3070
sales@triboroshelving.com
www.triboroshelving.com
Shelving, bin units, mobile shelf trucks and service
carts
Owner: Fred Demaio
fdemaio@triboroshelving.com
CFO: Tony De Maio
Estimated Sales: $2.5-5 Million
Number Employees: 20-49
Square Footage: 400000
Brands:
   Boxer
   Rivet Rak
   Stor-It
   Sturdi-Frame

30414 Tri-Clover
PO Box 7731
Richmond, VA 23231-0231
804-545-8120
Fax: 804-545-0194 800-558-4060
Pumps, valves, fittings, blenders, filter, batch control
systems, cheese equipment, fillers, gravity, milk,
flow diversion stations

Marketing Director: Chip Bresette
Public Relations: Joyce Bergh
Estimated Sales: $1-5 Million
Number Employees: 250-499

30415 Tri-Connect
111 Frank Lloyd Wright Lane
Oak Park, IL 60302-2644
708-660-8190
Fax: 312-951-6243 triconnect@aol.com
Wholesaler of England Farmhouse Biscuits packaged in gift tins and boxes, d'Orsay Chocolatier featuring imported Belgian chocolate and petit four
desserts. Private labeling available
President: Tony Birbeck
CEO: Linda Murphy
CFO: Anthony Cioffi
Estimated Sales: Below $5 Million
Number Employees: 5
Type of Packaging: Private Label, Bulk
Brands:
   Farmhouse Biscuits

30416 Tri-K Industries Inc
2 Stewart Ct
PO Box 10
Denville, NJ 07834-1028
973-298-8850
Fax: 201-750-9785 rebecca.morton@tri-k.com
www.tri-k.com
Owner: Manoj Agarwal
manoj.agarwal@galaxysurfactants.com
Number Employees: 20-49

30417 Tri-Pak Machinery Inc
1102 N Commerce St
Harlingen, TX 78550-4814
956-423-5140
Fax: 956-423-9362
dfitzgerald@tri-pakmachinery.com
www.tri-pak.com
Manufacturer and exporter of fruit and vegetable
processing machinery including belt and chain conveyors, graders, sizers, cleaners, packers and wax
coaters; also, graders for shrimp
President: David A Fitzgerald
VP: Charles M. Kilbourn
Director of Sales and Marketing: James W.
Fitzgerald
Sales: Robert E. Fitzgerald
Director of Operations: Daniel J. Groves
Purchasing: Chuck Kilbourn
Estimated Sales: $5-10 Million
Number Employees: 20-49
Square Footage: 516000

30418 Tri-Seal
900 Bradley Hill Rd
Blauvelt, NY 10913-1196
845-353-3300
Fax: 845-353-3376
LinersNorthAmer@tekni-plex.com
tri-seal.tekni-plex.com
Manufacturer and exporter of coextruded thermoplastic bottle cap liners and extruded rigid and flexible PVC tubing and profiles
CEO: F Smith
President: Bruce Burus
VP Sales/Marketing: Walter Burgess
Estimated Sales: $5-10 Million
Number Employees: 50-99
Square Footage: 440000
Brands:
   Tri-Foil
   Tri-Gard
   Tri-Lam
   Tri-Seal

30419 (HQ)Tri-State Plastics
PO Box 337
Henderson, KY 42419-0337
270-826-8361
Fax: 270-826-8362
Manufacturer and exporter of injection molded food
containers
Owner: Mike Walden
VP/Secretary/Treasurer: Mike Walden
Estimated Sales: less than $500,000
Number Employees: 1-4
Square Footage: 70000
Type of Packaging: Private Label, Bulk

30420 Tri-State Plastics
PO Box 496
Glenwillard, PA 15046-0496
724-457-6900
Fax: 724-457-6901 www.crightonplastics.com
Manufacturer and exporter of vacuum formed plastic
products including trays, covers, guards, material
handling components, etc.
President/ Sales: Chris Crighton
General Manager: Michael Lopez
Production Manager: Charles Goetz

30421 Tri-Sterling
1050 Miller Dr
Altamonte Spgs, FL 32701-7505
407-260-0330
Fax: 407-260-7096
Manufacturer and exporter of packaging equipment
and shrink wrappers
VP: Ken Schilling
Marketing: Thomas Jimenez
Estimated Sales: $20-50 Million
Number Employees: 100-249
Brands:
Genesis Ii

30422 Tri-Tronics
7705 Cheri Ct
PO Box 25135
Tampa, FL 33634-2419
813-886-4000
Fax: 813-884-8818 800-237-0946
info@ttco.com www.ttco.com
Manufacturer and exporter of material handling and
automation application controls including photoelec-
tric sensors, registration scanners, photoelectric eyes
and flexible plastic/glass fiber optic light guides
President: Scott Seehawer
scotts@ttco.com
VP/Sales Manager: Dennis Henderson
Estimated Sales: $10-20 Million
Number Employees: 50-99
Square Footage: 56000
Brands:
Color Mark
D.C. Eye
Mity-Eye
Smarteye
Tiny-Eye
U.S. Eye
Visioneye

30423 Triad Pallet Co Inc
4910 Bartlett St
Greensboro, NC 27409-2802
336-292-8175
Fax: 336-292-8175
Wooden skids and pallets
President/CFO: B Bare
Manager: B M Bare
Estimated Sales: Less Than $500,000
Number Employees: 1-4
Square Footage: 8000

30424 Triad Products Company
1913 Commerce Circle
Springfield, OH 45504-2011
937-323-9422
Fax: 937-328-6463
Aprons
President: Louis Jung
Number Employees: 20

30425 Triad Scientific
6 Stockton Lake Blvd
Manasquan, NJ 08736-3024
732-292-1994
Fax: 732-292-1961 800-867-6690
triadscientific@gmail.com www.triadsci.com
Manufacturer and exporter of laboratory equipment
including balances, analysis instrumentation, filtra-
tion, incubators, lamps, microscopes, monitoring
systems, ovens, sterilizers, spectrophotometers, etc.;
also, analysis, designservice and repair available
VP: Tom Leskow
Estimated Sales: $3-5 Million
Number Employees: 1-4
Square Footage: 20000
Type of Packaging: Food Service, Bulk

30426 Triad Scientific
6 Stockton Lake Blvd
Manasquan, NJ 08736-3024
732-292-1994
Fax: 732-292-1961 800-867-6690
triadscientific@gmail.com www.triadsci.com
President: Tom Leskow
Vice-President: Bill Aronoff
Number Employees: 1-4

30427 Triangle Package Machinery Co
6655 W Diversey Ave
Chicago, IL 60707-2293
773-889-0201
Fax: 773-889-4221 800-621-4170
wcray@trianglepackage.com
www.trianglepackage.com
Manufacturer and exporter of bag and carton mak-
ing, closing, filling, packing, weighing and sealing
machinery
President: Bryan Muskat
bmuskat@trianglepackage.com
R&D: Jerone Lasky
Quality Control: Roger Gaw
Director Sales: John Michalson
Purchasing Agent: John Musso
Estimated Sales: $20-50 Million
Number Employees: 100-249
Square Footage: 10000000
Brands:
Acceleron Advantage
Proline
Selectacom
Selectech 32 Controls

30428 Triangle Sign & Svc
11 Azar Ct
Halethorpe, MD 21227-1504
410-247-5300
Fax: 410-247-1944 info@trianglesign.com
www.trianglesign.com
Neon and plastic signs
President: Robert Altshuler
robert.altshuler@trianglesign.com
Estimated Sales: $10-20 Million
Number Employees: 100-249

30429 Tribology Tech Lube
35 Old Dock Rd
Yaphank, NY 11980-9702
631-345-3000
Fax: 631-345-3001 800-569-1757
info@tribology.com www.tribology.com
Manufacturer and exporter of synthetic and specialty
lubricants
President: William Krause
Sales: Paul Anderson
Manager: T Tierney
Operations/General Manager: Terence Tierney
Purchasing: Gail Moore
Estimated Sales: $50-100 Million
Number Employees: 10-19
Number of Products: 300
Square Footage: 35000
Type of Packaging: Private Label, Bulk

30430 Trico Converting Inc
1801 Via Burton
Suite A
Fullerton, CA 92831-5319
714-563-0701
Fax: 714-772-7528 www.printaccess.com
Manufacturer and exporter of flexible packaging;
also, printing and laminating available
President: Larry Schow
lschow@goarmy.com
VP: Tim Love
Estimated Sales: $10-20 Million
Number Employees: 5-9
Square Footage: 40000
Type of Packaging: Consumer, Food Service, Pri-
vate Label, Bulk

30431 Tricor Systems Inc
1650 Todd Farm Dr
Elgin, IL 60123-1145
847-742-5542
Fax: 847-742-5574 800-575-0161
info@tricor-systems.com www.tricor-systems.com
Specialized test instruments including gloss, color
and texture analysis systems aand chocolate temper
meters

President: Tim Allen
mail@tricor-systems.com
Sales Director: Thomas Allen
Estimated Sales: $5-10 Million
Number Employees: 20-49
Square Footage: 37000

30432 Tricor Systems Inc
1650 Todd Farm Dr
Elgin, IL 60123-1145
847-742-5542
Fax: 847-742-5574 800-575-0161
info@tricor-systems.com www.tricor-systems.com
TRICOR is ISO 90001-2008 Certified, ISO
13485:2003 Certified, Mil Spec Certified and FDA
registered manufacturer. TRICOR also offers products designed and manufactured by TRICOR which
include: DOT/Haze Meter, gloss meters,
videophotometers, imaging spectrophotometers,
switch testers, life cycle tester and chocolate temper
meters.
President: Tim Allen
mail@tricor-systems.com
VP of Sales: Thomas Allen
Estimated Sales: $5-10 Million
Number Employees: 20-49
Square Footage: 96000

30433 Tricore AEA
6921 Marine Dr
Mt Pleasant, WI 53406-3946
262-880-3630
Fax: 262-886-1676 infoHQ@TriCore.com
www.tricore.com
Software engineering for the food, dairy, beverage
industries
President: David Mc Carthy
President, Chief Executive Officer: David McCarthy
Engineering/Business Development VP: Steve
Reiter
IT: Chris Edwards
cedwardswi@yahoo.com
Number Employees: 20-49

30434 Trident
1114 Federal Rd
Brookfield, CT 06804-1140
203-740-9333
Fax: 203-775-9660 www.trident-itw.com
Print heads and inks for industrial applications
Manager: Juan Lopez
General Manager: Jean-Marie Gutierrez
Marketing/Sales: Robert Donofrio
Manager: Edward Broadhurst
edward.broadhurst@tridentamericas.com
Estimated Sales: $1-5,000,000
Number Employees: 50-99
Parent Co: ITW
Brands:
A 3000
Allwrite
Hi-Def
Jetwrite
Microcoder
Pixeljet
Ultrajet
Versaprint

30435 Trident Plastics
1009 Pulinski Rd
Ivyland, PA 18974
215-672-5225
Fax: 215-672-5582 800-222-2318
sales@tridentplastics.com
www.tridentplastics.com
Manufacturer and exporter of plastic tubes, sheets,
rods, ducts, films, slabs and signs
President: Ronald Cadic
Sales Manager: Michael Peroni
Contact: William Thomas
vasales@tridentplastics.com
Estimated Sales: $1-2.5 Million
Number Employees: 10-19

30436 Tridyne Process Systems
80 Allen Rd
South Burlington, VT 05403-7801
802-863-6873
Fax: 802-860-1591 sales@tridyne.com
www.tridyne.com
Manufacturer and exporter of automatic weighing
and counting systems including net weighers and
weigh counters; also, baggers, cartoners, conveyors,
etc

President: Susith Wijetunga
Estimated Sales: $1-5 Million
Number Employees: 5-9
Square Footage: 44000
Parent Co: Tridyne Process Systems, Inc
Type of Packaging: Consumer, Food Service, Private Label, Bulk
Brands:
　Tridyne

30437 Trilla Steel Drum Corporation
2959 W 47th St
Chicago, IL 60632-1998

773-847-7588
Fax: 773-847-5550
Steel shipping barrels and drums
Owner: Lester Trilla
CFO: Andy Perpetual
Quality Control: Chris Racawski
Sales Manager: Robert Craven
Estimated Sales: $20-50 Million
Number Employees: 5-9

30438 Trilogy Essential Ingredients
1304 Continental Dr
Abingdon, MD 21009-2334

410-612-0691
Fax: 410-612-9401 info@trilogyei.com
www.trilogyei.com
Flavors, seasonings, liquid spice extracts, proprietary delivery systems and functional ingredients.
Contact: Amy Ashcraft
aashcraft@trilogyei.com
Number Employees: 10-19
Number of Brands: 3
Type of Packaging: Bulk
Brands:
　Tril-Clear™
　CitraSense™
　NextWave™

30439 Trimble Agriculture
10368 N Westmoor Dr.
Westminster, CO 80021

agriculture.trimble.com
Provides solutions for a number of agriculture phases, including land preperation, guidance and steering, planting and seeding, water management, harvest, and data management.
President & CEO: Robert Painter
SVP & CFO: David Barnes

30440 Trimen Foodservice Equipment
1240 Ormont Drive
North York, ON M9L 2V4
Canada

416-744-3313
Fax: 416-744-3347 877-437-1422
paul_cesario@trimen.net www.trimen.net
Manufacturer and exporter of ovens, broilers, tables, booths and refrigeration equipment
President: Paul Cesario
Finance Manager: Grace Giulano
Head Operations: Mario Dipiede
Purchasing Manager: Mario Dipiede
Estimated Sales: $50-75 Million
Number Employees: 10
Type of Packaging: Food Service

30441 Trimline Corp
500 Industrial Dr
Elkhart Lake, WI 53020-1972

920-876-3611
Fax: 920-876-3527 800-555-5895
www.plyco.com
Insulated utility doors including food service and plastic
Plant Manager: Blend Luedtk
CEO: Gary Matz
CFO: Tom Matz
Estimated Sales: $10-20 Million
Number Employees: 20-49
Brands:
　Plyco

30442 Trine Rolled Moulding Corp
1421 Ferris Pl
Bronx, NY 10461-3610

718-828-5200
Fax: 718-828-4052 800-223-8075
info@trinecorp.com www.trinecorp.com

OEM manufacturer of factory direct original F-series baffle grease filters, aluminum, galvanized, stainless steel, all sizes-large inventory, UL/MEA/USA
President: Frank Rella
info@trinecorp.com
Plant Manager: James Lange
Estimated Sales: $5-10 Million
Number Employees: 50-99
Square Footage: 264000
Type of Packaging: Private Label
Brands:
　Trine Baffle

30443 Triner Scale & Mfg Co
8411 Hacks Cross Rd
Olive Branch, MS 38654-4010

662-890-2385
Fax: 901-363-3114 800-238-0152
info@trinerscale.com www.trinerscale.com
Manufacturer and exporter of scales including electronic, postage and platform; stainless steel, washdown and USDA approved
Owner: Arthur Wendt
awendt@trinerscale.com
Estimated Sales: $1-2.5 Million
Number Employees: 10-19
Square Footage: 120000
Brands:
　Triner

30444 Trinidad Benham Corporation
3650 S Yosemite, Suite 300
P.O. Box 378007
Denver, CO 80237

303-220-1400
Fax: 303-220-1490 info@trinidadbenham.com
www.trinidadbenham.com
Dry beans, rice, popcorn, and peas
Vice President: Steve Dipasquale
Estimated Sales: $36.3 Million
Number Employees: 500
Square Footage: 35000
Type of Packaging: Consumer, Food Service, Private Label, Bulk
Brands:
　Jack Rabbit
　Siler's
　Green Earth Organics
　Budget Buy
　Everyday Chef
　Wonder Foil
　Peak
　Master Wrap
　Solfresco
　Diamond
　Cookquik Ranch Wagon
　Sabor Del Campo

30445 Trinity Packaging
55 Innsbruck Dr
Cheektowaga, NY 14227-2703

716-668-3111
Fax: 716-668-3816 800-778-3111
Flexible packaging, process printing and film laminations; exporter of printed laminated rollstock; also, slitting and bag making available
President: Richard Gioia
Chairman: Tony Gioia
tgioia@cello-pack.com
VP: Sam Brown
Operations: Compton Plummer
Purchasing Director: Tim Shiley
Estimated Sales: $20-50 Million
Number Employees: 100-249
Square Footage: 100000
Type of Packaging: Consumer, Food Service, Private Label, Bulk

30446 Trinkle Sign & Display
24 5th Ave
Youngstown, OH 44503-1191

330-747-9712
Fax: 330-747-9712
Manufacturer and exporter of signs and displays
Owner: Robert Page
Estimated Sales: Less Than $500,000
Number Employees: 1-4

30447 (HQ)Trio Packaging Corp
90 13th Ave # 11
Ronkonkoma, NY 11779-6819

631-588-0800
Fax: 631-467-4690 800-331-0492
sales@triopackaging.com www.triopackaging.com
Manufacturer, importer and exporter of form/fill/seal packaging equipment and films
President: John Bolla
john@triopackaging.com
Vice President: Frederick Kramer
Sales Director: Anthony Carris
Estimated Sales: $20-50 Million
Number Employees: 20-49
Square Footage: 20000
Other Locations:
　Trio Packaging Corp.
　Ronkonkoma NY

30448 Trio Products
250 Warden Ave
Elyria, OH 44035

440-323-5457
Fax: 440-323-3247
Manufacturer and exporter of plastic food packaging materials including regular and thermoforming sheets and bacon boards
National Sales Representative: C Derringer
Contact: Christine Hood
christineh@trioproducts.com
Engineering/Technical: Mike Linner
Estimated Sales: $10-20 Million
Number Employees: 10-19
Type of Packaging: Consumer, Private Label, Bulk

30449 Triple A Containers
16069 Shoemaker Ave
Buena Park, CA 90621

714-521-2820
Fax: 714-521-8781 bruce@tripla.com
www.tripla.com
Corrugated shipping containers
Owner: Brad McCroskey
Purchasing: Bob Ryan
Estimated Sales: $20-50 Million
Number Employees: 100-249

30450 Triple A Neon Company
12325 Califa Street
Valley Village, CA 91607-1106

323-877-5381
Fax: 818-763-6255
Neon signs
President: Todd Showalter
Estimated Sales: Less than $500,000
Number Employees: 4

30451 Triple Dot Corp
3302 S Susan St
Santa Ana, CA 92704-6841

714-241-0888
Fax: 714-241-9888 info@triple-dot.com
www.triple-dot.com
Plastic containers, dessicant packages and neck bands; importer of glass containers
Owner: Tony Tsai
tytsai@aol.com
VP: Jason Tsai
Estimated Sales: $5-10 Million
Number Employees: 20-49
Square Footage: 140000
Brands:
　Seca-Pax
　Tdc

30452 Triple S Dynamics Inc
2467 E US Highway 180
Breckenridge, TX 76424-4956

254-559-8266
Fax: 254-559-8057 800-527-2116
sales@sssdynamics.com www.sssdynamics.com
Manufacturer and exporter of conveyors, separators and vibrating screens
Marketing: Jim Tatum
Estimated Sales: $10-20,000,000
Number Employees: 10-19
Square Footage: 125000
Brands:
　Slipstick

30453 Triple-A Manufacturing Company
44 Milner Avenue
Toronto, ON M1S 3P8
Canada
416-291-4451
Fax: 416-291-1292 800-786-2238
Manufacturer and exporter of storage systems, shelving, steel work benches, modular storage drawers, plastic and corrugated bins, welded wire partitions and mezzanines; also, racks including bottle, can, cold storage room, palletwine, wire, barrel, drum, etc
President: Joe Harnest
VP Finance: A Lerman
VP Sales: R Gasner
Buyer: T Kelly
Estimated Sales: $10-20 Million
Number Employees: 35
Square Footage: 240000
Other Locations:
　Triple-A Manufacturing Co. Lt
　Exeter NH

30454 Trisep Corporation
95 S La Patera Ln
Goleta, CA 93117
805-964-8003
Fax: 805-964-1235 sales@trisep.com
www.trisep.com
Manufactures membrane filters and separators, spiral wound reverse osmosis elements
President: James Bartlett Jr
Sr. Vice President -Commercial: Jon Goodman
SpiraSep UF Marketing Mgr.: Mike Snodgrass
International Sales Director: John Waring
Contact: Steve Spicer
steves@provisio.net
Estimated Sales: $8 Million
Number Employees: 50-99

30455 Triune Enterprises
13711 S Normandie Ave
Gardena, CA 90249-2609
310-719-1600
Fax: 310-719-1800 www.triuneent.com
Films, polypropylene, polyester, gas packaging materials, shrink packaging materials, vacuum packaging materials
President: Jerry Christman
jerry@triuneent.com
CFO: John Jerry Christman
Estimated Sales: $4 Million
Number Employees: 20-49

30456 (HQ)Trojan Commercial Furniture Inc.
163 Van Horne
Montreal, QC H2T 2J2
Canada
514-271-3878
Fax: 514-271-8960 877-271-3878
Manufacturer and exporter of wooden restaurant furniture including tables, chairs, booths and counters
President: Dennis Petsinis
Co-President: Chris Petsinis
Number Employees: 10
Square Footage: 24000
Type of Packaging: Food Service, Bulk
Brands:
　Trojan Commercial

30457 (HQ)Trojan Inc
198 Trojan St
Mt Sterling, KY 40353-8000
859-498-0526
Fax: 859-498-0528 800-264-0526
sales@trojaninc.com www.trojaninc.com
Manufacturer and exporter of lighting including long life, energy-efficient incandescent, fluorescent, HID, NSF approved, shatter-resistant, lamps, etc.; also, adapters and plate and exit sign retrofit kits
President: Edward Duzyk
CEO: Dennis Duzyk
sales@trojaninc.com
Estimated Sales: $3-5 Million
Number Employees: 10-19
Square Footage: 340000
Type of Packaging: Food Service
Other Locations:
　Trojan
　Meadville PA
Brands:
　Hytron

Hytronics
Powersaver
Saf-T-Cote

30458 Trola Industries Inc
2360 N George St
York, PA 17406-3202
717-848-3700
Fax: 717-848-6993 tbarton@trolaindustries.com
www.trolaindustries.com
Design, build, install control systems and panels (UL508A)
President: Thomas Barton
Vice President: Steve Halweski
Sales Director: Jim Schneider
customer Service: Shiellyn Hutson
General Manager: Mike Miller
Estimated Sales: $10-20 Million
Number Employees: 10-19
Square Footage: 46000

30459 Tronex Industries
1 Tronex Centre
Denville, NJ 07834
800-833-1181
Fax: 973-625-7630 800-833-1181
information@tronexcompany.com
Manufacturer and distributor of disposable gloves and apparel including bouffant cups, aprons, beard and sleeve covers
CFO: John Prail
Executive VP: Poyee Tai
Marketing Director: Carol Fletcher
Sales Director: Robert Larsen
Operations Manager: Mike Rowe
Number Employees: 20
Square Footage: 320000
Parent Co: Tronex International
Brands:
　Choice
　Tronex

30460 Tronics America
1430 E 86th Pl
Merrillville, IN 46410-6342
219-769-0876
Fax: 219-769-0962 sales@TronicsAmerica.com
www.tronicsamerica.com
Pressure sensitive labeling machines and heat transfer decorators
Manager: Richard Dew
rdew@tronicsamerica.com
Estimated Sales: $1-2.5 Million
Number Employees: 5-9

30461 Tropic KOOL
1232 Donegan Rd
Largo, FL 33771-2904
727-581-2824
Fax: 727-587-7973 www.tropickool.com
Metal parts for vents and air conditioning systems
President: Kenneth W. Bray
General Manager: Ken Bray
Estimated Sales: $5-10 Million
Number Employees: 10-19
Square Footage: 72000

30462 Tropical Soap Company
1512 Silverleaf Dr.
PO Box 112220
Carrollton, TX 75011-2220
972-492-7939
Fax: 972-233-1955 800-527-2368
Coconut oil soap including liquid and bar
Brands:
　Sirena

30463 Trout Lake Farm Company
PO Box 181
Trout Lake, WA 98650
509-395-2025
Fax: 509-395-2749 800-655-6988
www.troutlakefarm.com
Quality Control: Angie Brackhahn
Sales Manager: Martha Jane Hylton
Contact: Sharon Frazey
sharon.frazey@troutlakefarm.com
Operations Supervisor: Danielle Hawkins
General Manager: Lloyd Scott
Number Employees: 50

30464 Trowelon
973 Haven Place
Green Bay, WI 54313-5207
920-499-8778
Fax: 920-499-9065 800-975-8778
Floor and wall coating materials
CEO: Lewis Krueger
Estimated Sales: $5-10 Million
Number Employees: 50-99

30465 (HQ)Troxler Electronic Lab Inc
3008 Cornwallis Rd
PO Box 12057
Durham, NC 27709-0129
919-549-8661
Fax: 919-549-0761 877-876-9537
troxsales@troxlerlabs.com www.troxlerlabs.com
Moisture and density testing equipment
President: Stephen Browne
sbrowne@troxlerlabs.com
Director Product Service: Bill Worrell
Estimated Sales: $10-20 Million
Number Employees: 100-249
Square Footage: 250000

30466 (HQ)Troy Lighting
14508 Nelson Ave
City Of Industry, CA 91744-3514
626-336-4511
Fax: 626-330-4266 800-533-8769
Manufacturer, exporter and importer of electric lighting fixtures including decorative interior, track and recessed; also, exterior including wall, hanging, flush and post lanterns
Owner: Carol Coffey
VP Sales/Marketing: Steve Nadell
carolc@troyesl.com
Estimated Sales: $20-50 Million
Number Employees: 5-9
Square Footage: 100000

30467 Tru Form Plastics
17809 S Broadway
Gardena, CA 90248-3541
310-327-9444
Fax: 310-878-1107 800-510-7999
www.tru-formplastics.com
Food processing/service equipment and supplies, air conditioning and vents, lighting fixtures, point of purchase displays, uniform hats and caps, refrigeration equipment, sinks, etc
President: Douglas Sahm
CEO: Mario Guzman
National Sales Manager: Doug Sahm
Customer Service: Yolanda Cardenas
VP Operations: Mario Guzman
Estimated Sales: $1-2,500,000
Number Employees: 20-49

30468 Tru Hone Corp
1721 NE 19th Ave
Ocala, FL 34470-4701
352-622-1213
Fax: 352-622-9180 800-237-4663
www.truhone.com
Manufacturer and exporter of knife sharpeners
President: James Gangelhoff
truhone@truhone.com
CEO: Fred R Gangelhoff
Estimated Sales: $1-2.5 Million
Number Employees: 10-19
Square Footage: 13200
Brands:
　Tru Hone

30469 Tru Hone Corp
1721 NE 19th Ave
Ocala, FL 34470-4701
352-622-1213
Fax: 352-622-9180 800-237-4663
www.truhone.com
Knife sharpeners and accessories for industrial operations, meat, fish, poultry and produce plants.
President: James Gangelhoff
truhone@truhone.com
Number Employees: 10-19

30470 TruHeat Corporation
P.O.Box 190
Allegan, MI 49010-0190
269-673-2145
Fax: 269-673-7219 800-879-6199
www.truheat.com

Manufacturer and exporter of electric heating elements and assemblies for warming, broiling, frying, steaming and defrosting
President: Larry Nameche
Marketing/Sales: Jim Jennings
Estimated Sales: $10-20 Million
Number Employees: 100-249
Square Footage: 104000

30471 True Food Service Equipment, Inc.
2001 E Terra Ln
O Fallon, MO 63366-4434

636-240-2400
Fax: 636-272-2408 800-325-6152
truefood@truemfg.com www.truemfg.com
Manufacturer and exporter of commercial refrigeration equipment including deli cases, refrigerators, freezers and coolers; also, beer dispensers and pizza prep tables
President: Robert J Trulaske
Contact: Randy Bates
rbates@truemfg.com
Estimated Sales: $.5-1 million
Number Employees: 1-4
Brands:
  True

30472 True Manufacturing
2525 Lakeview Rd
Mexico, MO 65265

636-240-2400
Fax: 636-272-2408 truefoodservice@truemfg.com
www.truemfg.com
President: Robert Trulaske
Contact: Charles Hon
chon@truemfg.com
Estimated Sales: $.5-1 million
Number Employees: 1-4

30473 True Pac
420 Churchmans Rd
New Castle, DE 19720-3157

302-326-2222
Fax: 302-326-9330 800-825-7890
info@truepack.com www.truepack.com
Manufacturer and exporter of insulated shipping containers
Owner: Steve Nam
steve@truepack.co.kr
Manager: Joan Carter
Estimated Sales: $1-5 Million
Number Employees: 20-49

30474 Truesdail Laboratories
14201 Franklin Avenue
Tustin, CA 92780-7008

714-730-6239
Fax: 714-730-6462 rgates@truesdail.com
www.truesdail.com
Consultant offering laboratory testing and sanitary analysis
Owner: John Hill
Chief Scientist: Steve Roesch
Quality Assurance: Michael Ngo
Contact: Paymon Abri
paymon@truesdail.com
Chief Operating Officer: Randy Gates
Estimated Sales: $10-20 Million
Number Employees: 50-99
Square Footage: 120000

30475 Truitt Bros Inc
1105 Front St NE
PO Box 309
Salem, OR 97301-1034

503-362-3674
Fax: 503-581-5912 800-547-8712
truittbros@truittbros.com www.truittbros.com
Canned green beans, cherries, pears and plums; also, shelf stable entrees
Founder and CEO: David Truitt
davidt@truittbros.com
Estimated Sales: $20-50 Million
Number Employees: 500-999
Type of Packaging: Consumer, Food Service, Private Label
Brands:
  Truitt Bros.

30476 Truly Nolen Pest Control
3636 E Speedway Blvd
Tucson, AZ 85716-4018

520-327-3447
Fax: 52- 32- 400 877-977-1553
www.trulynolen.com
Pest control systems
President: Truly Nolen
trulynolencaguas@trulynolen.net
Estimated Sales: $1-2.5 Million
Number Employees: 50-99

30477 Trumbull Nameplates
1101 Sugar Mill Dr
New Smyrna Beach, FL 32168

386-423-1105
Signs and pressure sensitive labels
General Manager: Frank Tisler
Number Employees: 1-4
Square Footage: 3600

30478 Try Coffee Group
320 Carlisle Street
Harrisburg, PA 17104-1226

717-238-8381
Fax: 717-238-9173 www.trycoffee.com
Brewers, grinders
Estimated Sales: $5-10 Million
Number Employees: 10

30479 Tryco Coffee Service Annex Warehouse
3146 Corporate Place
Hayward, CA 94545-3916

510-293-9199
Fax: 510-293-0971 annextryco@aol.com
www.annextryco.net
Blending and mixing equipment (coffee), cleaners (green coffee), reconditioners, samplers, weighers, storage, consolidations, and packaging
CEO: Terry Sloat
Number Employees: 40

30480 Tubesales QRT
800 Roosevelt Road
suite 410
Glen Ellyn, IL 60137-5839

800-545-5000
Fax: 800-545-5883
www.plumbingnet.com/listt.html

30481 Tucel Industries, Inc.
2014 Forestdale Rd.
Forestdale, VT 05745-0146

802-247-6824
Fax: 802-247-6826 800-558-8235
Manufacturer and exporter of produce sponges and food preparation brushes including pastry; also, janitorial supplies including brushes, brooms, scours and squeegees
President: John Lewis Jr
CEO: Joanne Raleigh
Estimated Sales: $3-5 Million
Number Employees: 20-49
Square Footage: 180000
Type of Packaging: Consumer, Food Service, Private Label, Bulk
Brands:
  Cycle Line
  Fused
  Hygienic Fusedware
  Sponge 'n Brush
  Tu-Scrub
  Tucel

30482 Tuchenhagen
6716 Alexander Bell Drive
Suite 125
Columbia, MD 21046-2186

410-910-6000
Fax: 410-910-7000
Manufacturer and exporter of compact modular skid-mounted processing units and systems including blending, mixing, yeast pitching, etc.; also, valves, in-line flow measuring instruments and sanitary fittings, etc.; also, consultationservices available
Marketing Coordinator: Mads Michael Skaarenborg
Sales Director: Dave Medlar
Estimated Sales: $2.5-5 Million
Number Employees: 20-49
Parent Co: Tuchenhagen North America

30483 Tuchenhagen North America
90 Evergreen Dr
Portland, ME 04103-1066

207-797-9500
Fax: 207-878-7914 info.TNA@geagroup.com
Process components for the milk processing and beverage industries.
President: David Medlar
COO: Tim Jenneman
tim.jennemen@geagroup.com
Sales Manager: Ulf Thiessen
Number Employees: 10-19

30484 Tuchenhagen-Zajac
90 Evergreen Dr
Portland, ME 04103-1066

207-797-9500
Fax: 207-878-7914
Liquid processing
President: Dave Metler
CFO: Ralf Brockman
COO: David Harding
Estimated Sales: $5-10 Million
Number Employees: 5-9

30485 Tuckahoe Manufacturing Co
327 Tuckahoe Rd
Vineland, NJ 08360-9243

856-696-4100
Fax: 856-691-7312 800-220-3368
Strip doors; wholesaler/distributor of vinyl strip, sheet and panel materials and soft impact doors
President/Owner: John Tombleson
Estimated Sales: Less Than $500,000
Number Employees: 1-4
Square Footage: 3600

30486 Tucker Industries
2835 Janitell Road
Colorado Springs, CO 80906-4104

719-527-4848
Fax: 719-527-1499 800-786-7287
action@burnguard.com www.burnguard.com
Manufacturer and exporter of burn protective garments including oven mitts, aprons and hot pads
President: Vincent A. Tucker
Safety Director: Les Burns
CFO: Hathy Tucker
Quality Control: Hathy Tucker
VP Marketing: Paul Weklinski
Contact: Andrea Mabe
andrea@burnguard.com
Estimated Sales: Below $5 Million
Number Employees: 20-49
Square Footage: 172000
Brands:
  Burnguard
  Safestep
  Vaporguard

30487 (HQ)Tucson Container Corp
6601 S Palo Verde Rd
Tucson, AZ 85756-5044

520-746-3171
Fax: 520-741-0962 www.tucsoncontainer.com
Manufacturer and exporter of fiber and corrugated boxes; also, packaging materials and foam products
President: John Widera
Manager: Daniel Robinson
Controller: Christel Widera
Sales Service Manager: Karina Walters
Manager: Joaquin Rivadeneyra
joaquin.rivadeneyra@tucsoncontainer.com
Production Supervisor: Eladios Cortez
Plant Manager: Joaquin Rivadeneyra
Purchasing Agent: Chris Woolridge
Estimated Sales: $16 Million
Number Employees: 50-99
Square Footage: 160000
Other Locations:
  Tucson Container Corp.
  El Paso TX

30488 Tudor Pulp & Paper Corporation
17 White Oak Dr
Prospect, CT 6712

203-758-4494
Fax: 203-758-4498
Manufacturer and importer of specialty paper for packaging including grease resistant, oil resistant, industrial and electric
VP Sales: Stephen Hansen
Manager: Brad Russell

Estimated Sales: $1-5 Million
Number Employees: 10-19

30489 Tufco International
P.O.Box 456
Gentry, AR 72734-0456

479-736-2201
Fax: 479-736-2947 800-364-0836
info@tufcoflooring.com www.tufcoflooring.com
Flooring
President: Brent Mills
VP Sales: Russell Cox
Estimated Sales: Below $5 Million
Number Employees: 50-99

30490 Tufty Ceramics Inc
47 S Main St
PO Box 785
Andover, NY 14806

607-478-5150
ktufty@infoblvd.net
www.tuftyceramics.com
Manufacturer and exporter of terracotta bakeware
including nonstick, microwaveable and dishwasher
safe
President: Karen Tufty
Estimated Sales: Below $500,000
Number Employees: 1-4
Brands:
Alfred Bakeware

30491 Tulip Molded Plastics Corp
714 E Keefe Ave
Milwaukee, WI 53212-1668

414-963-3120
Fax: 414-962-1825 tulip@tulipcorp.com
www.tulipcorp.com
President: Fred Teshinsky
fteshinsky@phi-tulip.com
Principal: Courtland Hientze
Senior VP: Alan Schmidt
Estimated Sales: $20-50 Million
Number Employees: 20-49

30492 Tully's Coffee
3100 Airport Way S
Seattle, WA 98134

206-233-2070
Fax: 206-233-2077 www.tullys.com
Retailer, wholesaler, and distributor of coffee and
coffee products
President: Carl Pennigton Sr
Contact: Kerry Carlson
kc@tullys.com
Estimated Sales: H
Number Employees: 1,000-4,999
Brands:
Tullys

30493 Tulox Plastics Corporation
P.O.Box 984
Marion, IN 46952

765-664-5155
Fax: 765-664-0257 800-234-1118
sales@tulox.com www.tulox.com
Tubes and toppers that are available in rounds,
squares, rectangulars, triangulars, and custom
shapes, transparent, opaque, colored, or striped
President: John Sciaudone
Vice President: Bill Patuzzi
National Sales Director: Christopher Sciaudone
Contact: Christopher Sciaudone
sales@tulox.com
Type of Packaging: Consumer

30494 Tulsa Plastics Co
6112 E 32nd Pl
Tulsa, OK 74135-5406

918-664-0931
Fax: 918-622-2943 888-273-5303
sales@tulsaplastics.com www.tulsaplastics.com
Store fixtures, sky lights, plastic sheet materials,
plastic signs and displays
President: Raleigh Blakemore
rblakemore@tulsaplastics.com
CFO: Jim Blakemore
Estimated Sales: Below $5 Million
Number Employees: 10-19

30495 Tupperware Brands Corporation
14901 South Orange Blossom Trail
Orlando, FL 32837

800-366-3800
comments@tupperware.com
www.tupperwarebrands.com
Plastic storage containers and cookware.
Interim CEO: Christopher O'Leary
Executive Vice Chairman: Richard Goudis
VP/Controller: Madeline Otero
EVP/CFO: Cassandra Harris
EVP/Chief Legal Officer: Karen Sheeran
EVP/Chief Strategy & Marketing Officer: Asha
Gupta
EVP/Chief Talent & Engagement Officer: Lillian
Garcia
EVP, Product Innovation & Supply Chain: William
Wright
Year Founded: 1946
Estimated Sales: $2.3 Billion
Number Employees: 13,500
Brands:
Tupperware

30496 Turbo Refrigerating Company
P.O.Box 396
Denton, TX 76202-0396

940-387-4301
Fax: 940-382-0364 info@turboice.com
Manufacturer and exporter of ice making, storage
and distribution systems; processor of ice
President: El Beard
CFO: Chris Worghington
VP: Dan Aiken
VP Sales/Marketing: T Baker
Estimated Sales: $20-50 Million
Number Employees: 20-49
Parent Co: Henry Vogt Machine Company
Other Locations:
Turbo Refrigerating Co.
Louisville KY

30497 Turbo Systems
4 Glenberry Ct
Phoenix, MD 21131-1400

410-527-2800
Fax: 954-925-4190 rubosysfl@aol.com
www.turbosystemsusa.com
Aerators, bar formers, bottomers, chocolate equip-
ment, vermicelli machines, coaters, conveyors,
cookers
Vice President: Joost DE Koomen
sales@turbosystemsusa.com
Sr. Vice President: Joost J. de Koomen
Estimated Sales: $.5-1 million
Number Employees: 1-4

30498 Turck
3000 Campus Dr
Minneapolis, MN 55441-2656

763-694-2300
Fax: 763-553-0708 888-546-5880
www.turck.us
Leader in providong bus network products. Provid-
ing smart stations, junctions, connectorized cable
and accessories for unique plug-and-play concept to
distributed process control and automation solutions.
These plug-and-play componentsallow for quick in-
stallation of new plant layouts and easy retrofits to
existing plants
President: Murray Death
CEO: David Lagerstrom
david.lagerstrom@turck.com
Number Employees: 250-499
Brands:
Busstop

30499 Turck
3000 Campus Dr
Minneapolis, MN 55441-2656

763-694-2300
Fax: 763-553-0708 800-544-7769
www.turck.us
Provides sensing solutions and related components
by manufacturing and marketing proximity sensors,
cordsets, connection products and automation devices. The company's products are primaly used in
manufacturing automationapplications

President: William Scheneider
CEO: David Lagerstrom
david.lagerstrom@turck.com
CFO: Bill Chrisianson
CEO: David Lagerstrom
R&D: Boss
Quality Control: Bamian Pike
Marketing Director: Grant Bistram
Production Manager: Hanz Ziesch
Estimated Sales: $50-100 Million
Number Employees: 250-499

30500 Turkana Food
555 N Michgan Avenue
Kenilworth, NJ 07033

908-810-8800
Fax: 908-810-8820 info@turkanafood.com
www.turkanafood.com
Ethnic foods: European, Mediterranean and Middle
Eastern.
Business Development: Furkan Bugra Er
Admisinstrative Service Manager: Tuncay Yalim
Estimated Sales: $9-11 Million
Number Employees: 11-50
Type of Packaging: Food Service

30501 Turtle Wax
PO Box 247
Westmont, IL 60559-0247

905-470-6665
Fax: 708-563-4302 distributorinfo@turtlewax.com
www.turtlewax.com
Manufacturer and exporter household cleaners,
dressings and polishes
CEO: Denis J Healy
Chairman: Sondra A Healy
Contact: Huntington Beach
hbeach@turtlewax.com
Estimated Sales: $5-10 Million
Number Employees: 1,000-4,999

30502 Tuthill Vacuum & BlowerSystems
P.O.Box 2877
Springfield, MO 65801-2877

417-865-8715
Fax: 417-865-2950 800-825-6937
vacuum@tuthill.com www.tuthillvacuum.com
Manufacturer and exporter of positive displacement
rotary lobe blowers mechanical vacuum boosters, ro-
tary piston vacuum pumps, liquid ring vacuum
pumps and complete systems
President: John Ermold
Controller: James Ashcraft
Sales/Marketing Director: Mike Branstetter
Contact: Henry Mateja
hmateja@tuthill.com
Estimated Sales: $10-20 Million
Number Employees: 250-499
Number of Brands: 10
Number of Products: 6
Square Footage: 130000
Parent Co: Tuthill Corporation
Brands:
Acousticair
Competitor Plus
Equalizer
Pd Plus

30503 Tuway American Group
191 E Pearl St
Rockford, OH 45882

419-363-3191
Fax: 419-363-2129 800-537-3750
www.tuwaymops.com
Manufacturer, importer and exporter of dust cloths
and mops, carpet cleaning pads and bonnets, scour-
ing pads, wall washing supplies and handles
President: Trudy Koster
Director Sales: M Healy
National Sales Manager: Steve Grimes
Manager: John Feeney
Plant Manager: John Feeney
Estimated Sales: $20-50 Million
Number Employees: 50-99
Parent Co: Tu-Way Products Company
Brands:
Dustmaster
Dustroyer
Speed Trek
Wide Track

30504 Tuxton China
21011 Commerce Point Drive
Walnut, CA 91789-3052
909-595-2510
Fax: 909-595-5353 info@tuxton.com
www.tuxton.com

30505 Twelve Baskets Sales & Market
5200 Phillip Lee Dr SW
Atlanta, GA 30336
404-696-9922
Fax: 404-696-9099 800-420-8840
Wholesaler/distributer of general line items; also,
packer of edible oils
Owner: Ken Mc Millan
ken@twelvebaskets.net
President: Kirk McMillen
Sales: Bob Quinet
Estimated Sales: $20-50 Million
Number Employees: 20-49
Square Footage: 15000

30506 Twenty First Century Design
1008 Madison Ave
Albany, NY 12208-2600
518-446-0939
www.manta.com
Designer of restaurant interiors, mechanical and
electrical systems; also, architectural and engineer-
ing services available
Owner: Menglin Liu
Estimated Sales: $500,000-$1 Million
Number Employees: 6
Square Footage: 10000

30507 Twenty/Twenty Graphics
7895 Cessna Ave # S
Gaithersburg, MD 20879
240-243-0511
Fax: 240-243-0512
Signs, displays and decals; screen printing available
President: Luclere Lee
Estimated Sales: $2.5-5 Million
Number Employees: 10-19

30508 Twi Laq
1345 Seneca Ave
Bronx, NY 10474-4611
718-638-5860
Fax: 718-789-0993 800-950-7627
customerservice@twi-laq.com www.twi-laq.com
Manufacturer and exporter of cleaning chemicals in-
cluding soaps, degreasers, detergents, marble care
chemicals and floor finishes
Vice President: Shanelle Acabeo
sacabeo@twi-laq.com
VP: Robert Wels
VP Operations: Michael Wels
Estimated Sales: $5-10 Million
Number Employees: 10-19
Brands:
Stone Glo
Sun-Glo
Top-Guard
Welsite

30509 Twin City Bottle
1227 E Hennepin Ave
Minneapolis, MN 55414
612-331-8880
Fax: 612-379-5118 800-697-0607
sales@kaufmancontainer.com
Major supplier of all types of containers
CEO: Roger Seid
Estimated Sales: $20-50 Million
Number Employees: 50-99

30510 Twin City Pricing & Label
744 Kasota Cir SE
Minneapolis, MN 55414-2883
612-378-1055
Fax: 612-379-0112 800-328-5076
www.twincityproduce.com
Custom printed labels
President: John Rotondo
Production Manager: Curtis James
Estimated Sales: $10-20 Million
Number Employees: 20-49
Square Footage: 26000

30511 Twin City Wholesale
519 Walker St
Opelika, AL 36801-5999
334-745-4564
Fax: 334-749-5125 800-344-6935
johanna@tcwholesale.com
Wholesaler and distributor of products and supplies
for convenience stores and grocery chains; offers
business floor plan design services.
Owner: Johanna Bottoms
twincity@mindspring.com
Estimated Sales: $76 Million
Number Employees: 50-99

30512 Twin State Signs
14 Gauthier Dr
Essex Junction, VT 05452-2825
802-872-8949
Fax: 802-878-0200 twinsign@together.net
www.twinstatesigns.com
Signs including neon, electric, indoor, outdoor,
wooden, etc.; also, signage repair and installation
services available
President: Mary Denault
twinsign@together.net
CFO/R&D: Ray Denault
Sales Manager: Suzanne Denault
Estimated Sales: Below $5 Million
Number Employees: 5-9
Brands:
Gerber Edge
Scotch Print

30513 Twinkle Baker Decor USA
285 Westlake Couter
Daly City, CA 94015
707-364-2740
karen@twinkle-bd.com
Baking decorations and decorating tools
Operations Manager: Karen Tang
Brands:
Twinkle Baker Decor

30514 Two Rivers Enterprises
490 River St W
Holdingford, MN 56340-4519
320-746-3156
Fax: 320-746-3158 joeh@stainlesskings.com
www.tworiversstainlesskings.com
Restaurant and food service equipment; also pro-
vides renovations of processing plants and on-site
equipment.
President: Robert Warzecha
bobw@stainlesskings.com
Midwest Regional Sales: Joe Herges
Sales Engineer: Jeff Jones
Midwest Regional Sales: Steve Bairett
Number Employees: 20-49

30515 Tyco Fire Protection Products
1400 Pennbrook Pkwy
Lansdale, PA 19446-3840
215-362-0700
Fax: 215-362-5385 800-558-5236
sales@starsprinkler.com
Manufacturer and exporter of automatic self-adjust-
ing fire sprinkler systems including concealed and
recessed
President: Colleen Repplier
colleen.repplier@tycofp.com
Marketing Manager: John Corcoran
International Sales Manager: Patti Kowalski
Number Employees: 500-999
Parent Co: Tyco Corporation
Brands:
Quasar
Starmist

30516 Tyco Fire Protection Products
1 Stanton St
Marinette, WI 54143-2542
715-732-3465
Fax: 715-732-3471 800-862-6785
www.ansul.com
Manufacturer and exporter of fire protection products includes fire extinguishers and hand line units;
pre-engineered restaurant, vehicle, and industrial
systems; sophisticated fire detection/suppression
systems and a complete line of dry chemical, foam,
and gaseoue extinguishing agents.

President: Colleen Repplier
Cmo: David A Pelton
dpelton@tycoint.com
CFO: Dennis Moraros
Operations: Sally Falkenberg
Director, R&D: Jay Thomas
Director, Global Marketing: David Pelton
VP Sales: William Smith
Number Employees: 10-19
Parent Co: Tyco International
Brands:
Ansul Automan
Ansulex
Foray
K-Guard
Piranha
Plus-50
R-102
Sentry

30517 Tyco Plastics
8235 220th St W
Lakeville, MN 55044-8059
952-469-8771
Fax: 952-469-5337 800-328-4080
Manufacturer and exporter of packaging supplies in-
cluding barrier bags, films and pouches for meats,
cheeses, etc
Sales/Marketing: Mike Baarts
Business Unit Manager (Food): Dennis Leisten
Business Unit Manager (Industrial): Tom Lundborg
Purchasing Manager: Gordon Raway
Estimated Sales: $20-50 Million
Number Employees: 100-249
Brands:
Rexfit
Rextape
Startex
Starvac
Starvac Ii
Starvac Iii

30518 Tyco Retail Solutions
6600 Congress Ave
Boca Raton, FL 33487
561-912-6000
www.tycoretailsolutions.com
Manufacturer and exporter of safety systems includ-
ing closed circuit television, electronic article sur-
veillance and access control.
Year Founded: 1968
Estimated Sales: $300 Million
Number Employees: 1000-4999
Brands:
Sensorvision
Ultramax

30519 Tycodalves & Controls
1010 N Edward Ct
Anaheim, CA 92806-2601
714-575-9201
Fax: 714-575-9206 800-972-8926
Wine industry valves
Manager: Eddie Kim
Contact: Larry Taft
ltaff@tycovalves.com
Estimated Sales: $10-20 Million
Number Employees: 10-19

30520 Typecraft Wood & Jones
2040 E Walnut St
Pasadena, CA 91107-5804
626-795-8093
Fax: 626-795-2423 info@typecraft.com
www.typecraft.com
Labels; also, printing available
Estimated Sales: $1-5 Million
Number Employees: 50-99

30521 U B KLEM Furniture Co Inc
3861 E Schnellville Rd
St Anthony, IN 47575-9633
812-326-2236
Fax: 812-326-2525 800-264-1995
info@ubklem.com www.ubklem.com
Chairs, barstools, booths, tables, pedestals and trash
receptacles
President: Wes Graman
wgraman@ubklem.com
CEO: U Butch Klen
Estimated Sales: $10-20 Million
Number Employees: 100-249
Square Footage: 150000

30522 U L Wholesale Lighting Fixture
3443 10th St
Long Island City, NY 11106-5107
718-726-7500
Fax: 718-626-8812 www.ullighting.net
Manufacturer and importer of lighting fixtures
Owner: Charlie Papastylianou
Estimated Sales: $2.5-5,000,000
Number Employees: 10-19
Square Footage: 10000

30523 U Roast Em Inc
16778 W US Highway 63
Hayward, WI 54843-7214
715-634-6255
Fax: 715-934-3221 info@u-roast-em.com
Supplier of green coffee beans, bulk teas, home
roasting supplies and coffee flavorings
Manager: Terry Wall
info@u-roast-em.com
Number Employees: 1-4
Type of Packaging: Consumer
Brands:
Bodum
Fresh Beans

30524 U-Line Corporation
8900 N 55th St
Milwaukee, WI 53223
414-354-0300
Fax: 414-354-0349 800-779-2547
sales@u-line.com www.u-line.com
Ice making machinery, compact freezers and com-
pact, built-in and under-counter refrigerators
VP: Jennifer Seraszewski
CEO: Jennifer U Straszewski
Quality Control: Dean Bycnski
Sales/Marketing Manager: Henry Uline
Contact: Roland Marciniak
roland.marciniak@u-line.com
Vice President of Operations: Andrew Doberstein
Estimated Sales: $20-50 Million
Number Employees: 250-499

30525 U.S. Range
1177 Kamato Rd
Mississauga, ON L4W IX4
Canada
905-624-0260
800-424-2411
www.garland-group.com
Manufacturer of cooking systems.

30526 UAA
2561 N Greenview Avenue
Chicago, IL 60614-2028
773-755-4545
Fax: 773-755-4555 800-813-1711
Paging and surveillance systems including two-way
radios; consulting services available
President: Joe Grody

30527 UBC Food Distributors
12812 Prospect St
Dearborn, MI 48126-3652
877-846-8117
Fax: 313-846-8118 info@wellmadefood.com
www.wellmadefood.com
Honey, chocolates, cookies, juices, and snacks
Sales Manager: Hassan Houssami
Estimated Sales: $10-12 Million
Number Employees: 10
Other Locations:
East Coast NJ
West Coast CA
Brands:
Wellmade Honey

30528 UCB Inc
1950 Lake Park Dr SE
Smyrna, GA 30080
770-970-8338
www.ucb-usa.com
Cellulose and polypropylene specialty films that are
supplied into packaging, industrial and label
markets.
President & Head of Operations: Duane Barnes
Chief Ethics/Compliance Officer: Anisa Dhalla
Head of Corporate Affairs: Patty Fritz
Year Founded: 1928
Estimated Sales: $100+ Million
Number Employees: 7,500
Parent Co: UCB Worldwide
Type of Packaging: Consumer, Food Service, Pri-
vate Label

Brands:
Cellophane
Celloplus
Cellotherm
Natureflex
Optitwist
Propafilm
Propafiol
Propaream
Ratoface
Startwist

30529 UDEC Corp
271 Salem St # A
Woburn, MA 01801-2004
781-933-7770
Fax: 781-933-5366 800-990-8332
Manufacturer and exporter of solid-state fluorescent
emergency, exit and night lights; also, electronic bal-
lasts for back lighting
President: Eugene P. Brandeis
e.brandeis@udeccorp.com
CFO: Janice Ferro
Purchasing Manager: J Ferro
Estimated Sales: Below $5 Million
Number Employees: 5-9
Square Footage: 9200
Type of Packaging: Food Service, Private Label

30530 UDY Corp
201 Rome Ct
Fort Collins, CO 80524-1427
970-482-2060
Fax: 970-482-2067 www.udyone.com
Manufacturer and distributor of protein analyzers,
shakers, sample mills, hay samplers and other gen-
eral lab equipment. Also custom plastic fabrication
for science and general industries.
President: William Lear
bill@udycorp.com
CFO: William Lear
Estimated Sales: Below $5 Million
Number Employees: 5-9
Number of Brands: 3
Number of Products: 20
Brands:
Colorado Hay Products
Cuclone Sample Mills
Dairy Tester Ii
Plastic Fabrication
Protein Color Meter
React-R-Mill

30531 UFE
520 Industrial Way
Fallbrook, CA 92028-2244
760-723-7900
Fax: 760-723-7910
Ruggedized solutions for harsh conditions, clean
rooms and NEMA4X, power touch displays and
workstations feature enhanced infrared
Marketing Manager: Christopher McDonald
VP Sales: Tony Faint
Manager Information Systems: Michael McGinley
Estimated Sales: $1-5 Million
Number Employees: 100-250

30532 UFE Incorporated
1850 Greeley St S
Stillwater, MN 55082
651-351-4273
Fax: 651-351-4272
Caps and closures specializing in custom thermo-
plastic injection molds and molding
President: Martin N Kellogg
CEO: Greg Willis
Estimated Sales: $20-50 Million
Number Employees: 100-249

30533 UFP Technologies
1521 Windsor Dr
Clinton, IA 52732-6611
563-242-2444
Fax: 563-242-0444 888-638-3456
info@ufpt.com www.ufpt.com
Design, prototyping, tooling, testing and manufac-
turing of protective packaging made from 100% re-
cycled paper
CFO: Ron Latiaille
Manager: Susan Waters
swaters@ufpt.com
Estimated Sales: $500,000-$1 Million
Number Employees: 100-249

30534 UNEX Manufacturing
50 Progress Pl
Jackson, NJ 08527
732-928-2800
Fax: 732-928-2828 800-695-7726
span@unex.com www.unex.com
Carton flow track and carton flow accumulating
conveyors
President: Brian Neuwirth
CEO: Mark Newrith
CEO: Frank Neuwirth
Vice President Sales: Mark Neuwirth
Marketing Manager: Mike Levine
Southern Regional Sales Manager: Bill McKenzie
Contact: Maria Bird
m.bird@unex.com
Product Manager: David Scelfo
Estimated Sales: $10-25 Million
Number Employees: 50-99

30535 UPACO Adhesives
4105 Castlewood Rd
Richmond, VA 23234-2707
804-275-9231
Fax: 804-743-8366 800-446-9984
info@worthenind.com
www.worthenindustries.com
Water-based, solvent-based and hot melt adhesives
and coatings
President/CEO: Robert Worthen
Quality Control: Ralph Roane
Marketing/Sales: Steven Adams
Plant Manager: Dave Smith
Estimated Sales: $20-30 Million
Number Employees: 20-49
Square Footage: 40000
Parent Co: Worthen Industries

30536 UPM Raflatac
400 Broadpointe Dr
Mills River, NC 28759
800-992-3882
www.upmraflatac.com
Supplier of self-adhesive label materials and pro-
ducer of HF and UHF radio frequency identification
(RFID) tags and inlays.
Vice President: Dan O'Connell
Year Founded: 1975
Estimated Sales: $1.4 Billion
Number Employees: 3,000

30537 UPN Pallet Company
305 N Virginia Ave
Penns Grove, NJ 8069
856-299-1192
Fax: 856-299-5824
Wooden pallets
Office Manager: Mano Massari
Estimated Sales: $500,000-$1 Million
Number Employees: 5-9
Square Footage: 16000

30538 UPS Logistics Technologies
849 Fairmount Ave # 400
Towson, MD 21286-2601
410-823-0189
Fax: 410-847-6246 800-762-3638
market@upslogistics.com
Street routing and scheduling software, wireless dis-
patch software
COO: Len Kennedy
Director Customer Services: George Evans
Vice President of Product Management: Cyndi
Brandt
Sales Director: Charlie Virden
Public Relations: Lisa Beck
Purchasing Manager: Donna Blizzard
Estimated Sales: $20-50 Million
Number Employees: 100-249
Number of Products: 5
Parent Co: United Parcel Service

30539 US Apple Assn
8233 Old Courthouse Rd # 200
Vienna, VA 22182-3816
703-442-8850
Fax: 703-790-0845 info@usapple.org
www.usapple.org
Provides consumers with information on the health
benefits of apples and apple products.

1005

CEO: Jim Bair
jbair@usapple.org
Vice President of Public Affairs: Diane Kurrle
Director Consumer Health & PR: Wendy Brannen
Office Manager: Laura Stephens
Number Employees: 5-9

30540 (HQ)US Can Company
1101 Todds Lane
Rosedale, MD 21237-2905

410-686-6363
Fax: 410-391-9323 800-436-8021
Manufacturer and exporter of aluminum and tin cans
VP Sales/Marketing: David West
Sales Director: Jack Finnell
Estimated Sales: $20-50 Million
Number Employees: 20-49
Type of Packaging: Consumer, Food Service, Private Label, Bulk

30541 US Cap Systems Corporation
111 Elm St
Suite 204
Worcester, MA 01609-1967

508-754-7283
Fax: 508-752-5546 800-727-5555
President: Emanuel Wohlgemuta
Estimated Sales: $1-5 Million
Number Employees: 1-4

30542 US Chemical
316 Hart St
Watertown, WI 53094-6631

920-261-3453
Fax: 920-206-3979 800-558-9566
www.uschemical.com
Specialty chemicals including warewashing, laundry, maintenance, carpet and floor care chemicals; exporter of cleaning products and dispensing systems
General Manager: Bill Moody
Technical Manager: Cheryl Maas
QC Lab: Brian Truman
Sales Leader: David Kohnke
Contact: Eric Losey
eric.losey@uschemical.com
Plant Manager: Dennis Bollhurst
Estimated Sales: $30-50 Million
Number Employees: 100-130
Square Footage: 150000
Parent Co: Diversey, Inc

30543 US Coexcell Inc
400 W Dussel Dr # C
Maumee, OH 43537-1636

419-897-9110
Fax: 419-897-9112 info@uscoxl.com
www.uscoxl.com
Owner: Bob Huebner
bhuebner@uscoxl.com
President, Chief Executive Officer: Harley Cramer
VP: Mark Woltell
Estimated Sales: $2.5-5 Million
Number Employees: 20-49

30544 US Cooler Company
401 Delaware St
Quincy, IL 62301

217-228-2421
Fax: 217-228-2424 800-521-2665
www.uscooler.com
Walk-in coolers and freezers
President/Owner: Allen Craig
Marketing Director: Kristin Peters
Contact: Tia Albers
tia@uscooler.com
Number Employees: 50-99
Square Footage: 80000
Parent Co: Craig Industries

30545 US Filter
40004 Cook Street
Palm Desert, CA 92211-3299

760-340-0098
Fax: 760-341-9368 www.usfilter.com
Water and wastewater treatment systems and equipment
President: Richard Heckmann
President, Chief Executive Officer: Eric Spiegel
Vice President: Alison Taylor
Corporate Marketing Manager: Mike Markovsky
Executive Vice President of Global Sales: Paul Vogel

Estimated Sales: $1-5 Million
Number Employees: 50-99
Square Footage: 4000000

30546 US Filter
40004 Cook Street
Palm Desert, CA 92211-3299

760-340-0098
Fax: 760-341-9368 www.usfilter.com
Water purification equipment
President: Richard Heckmann
President, Chief Executive Officer: Eric Spiegel
Vice President: Alison Taylor
Executive Vice President of Global Sales: Paul Vogel
Estimated Sales: $50-100 Million
Number Employees: 100-249

30547 US Filter Corporation
2330 Scenic Highway
P.O. Box is 871329
Snellville, GA 30078

518-758-2179
Fax: 518-758-2182
President, Chief Executive Officer: Eric Spiegel
Vice President: Alison Taylor
Executive Vice President of Global Sales: Paul Vogel
Estimated Sales: $1-5 Million

30548 US Filter Dewatering Systems
2155 112th Ave
Holland, MI 49424-9609

616-772-9011
Fax: 616-772-4516 800-245-3006
Manufacturer and exporter of filter presses and other dewatering equipment for processing and waste treatment
President: Ken Hollidge
President, Chief Executive Officer: Eric Spiegel
CEO: Chuck Gordon
Executive Vice President of Global Sales: Paul Vogel
Estimated Sales: $20-50 Million
Number Employees: 100-249
Square Footage: 140800
Brands:
    J-Press

30549 US Filter/Continental Water
5413 Bandera Road
Suite 405
San Antonio, TX 78238-1955

210-523-8181
Fax: 210-523-8393 800-426-3426
www.usfilter.com
Water purification equipment
President, Chief Executive Officer: Eric Spiegel
Vice President: Alison Taylor
Executive Vice President of Global Sales: Paul Vogel
Estimated Sales: Less than $500,000
Number Employees: 1-4
Parent Co: US Filter/Continental Water

30550 US Industrial Lubricants
3330 Beekman St
Cincinnati, OH 45223-2424

513-541-2225
Fax: 513-541-2293 800-562-5454
www.usindustriallubricants.com
Manufacturer and exporter of vegetable oil and liquid soap, synthetic liquid detergent and lubricants including petroleum and synthetic
Co-Owner: Don Mattcheck
dmattcheck@usindustriallubricants.com
R & D: Ted Korzep
Facilities Engineer: Adam Freeman
Inside Sales: Jenny Anderson
USIL National Sales Manager: Dave Darling
Controller: Shannon Schlichte
Estimated Sales: $5-10 Million
Number Employees: 10-19
Number of Brands: 3
Number of Products: 250
Square Footage: 70000
Brands:
    Nusheen
    Oilkraft
    Usil

30551 (HQ)US Label Corporation
2118 Enterprise Rd
Greensboro, NC 27408-7004

336-332-7000
Fax: 336-275-7674
Manufacturer and exporter of printed cloth, woven and paper labels; also, label tape
CFO: Charlie Davis
VP Marketing: Phil Koch
Sales Manager: James Grant
Contact: Edward Tidaback
edward@uslabelcorp.com
Number Employees: 250-499

30552 US Line Company
16 Union Avenue
Westfield, MA 01085-2497

413-562-3629
Fax: 413-562-7328
Manufacturer and exporter of specialized industrial braided synthetics
President: Brad Gage
CFO: Brad Gage
Quality Control: Brad Gage
R&D: Brad Gage
Marketing Director: Bradley Gage
Estimated Sales: Below $5 Million
Number Employees: 15

30553 US Magnetix
7140 Madison Ave W
Minneapolis, MN 55427-3602

763-540-9497
Fax: 763-540-0142 sales@usmagnetix.com
www.usmagnetix.com
Magnetic products; specializing in promotional magnetic products. The company's core competencies include printing, die cutting, assembly, packaging, promotional marketing and graphic design
President: John Condon
john@usmagnetix.com
Sales Business Development Director: Chris Ryder
Art Director: Dean Vaccaro
Lead Production Operator: Neil Deonarain
Production Manager: Keith Johnson
Estimated Sales: $1-2.5 Million
Number Employees: 10-19

30554 US Plastic Corporation
PO Box 104
Swampscott, MA 01907-0104

781-595-1030
Fax: 781-593-6440
Polyethylene and plastic film bags
Estimated Sales: $20-50 Million
Number Employees: 100-249

30555 US Product
1101 Todds Ln
Baltimore, MD 21237-2905

410-686-6364
Fax: 410-687-6741 www.ball.com
Custom and stock decorated tins, cups and closures
President: Bernie Salles
Estimated Sales: $50-100 Million
Number Employees: 100-249

30556 US Seating Products
707 S W 20th Street
Ocala, FL 34471

Fax: 352-629-2860 800-999-2589
info@admiralfurniture.com
www.admiralfurnitureonline.com
Manufacturer and exporter of aluminum and vinyl benches, chairs, cushions and pads, tray stands, tables and booths including legs and bases
President: Peter Villella
Estimated Sales: $10-20 Million
Number Employees: 10
Type of Packaging: Food Service

30557 US Standard Sign
11400 Addison Ave
Franklin Park, IL 60131-1124

847-455-7446
Fax: 847-455-3330 800-537-4790
sales@usstandardsign.com
www.usstandardsign.com
Aluminum sign blanks
President: Rick Mandel
CFO: Steve Fallon
Estimated Sales: $1-2.5 Million
Number Employees: 50-99
Parent Co: Mandel Metals

30558 US Tag & Label
2208 Aisquith St
Baltimore, MD 21218
410-962-2676
Fax: 410-889-1227 800-638-1018
72723.1042@compuserve.com
Labels
Estimated Sales: $1-5 Million
Number Employees: 50-99

30559 US Tsubaki Holdings Inc
301 E Marquardt Dr
Wheeling, IL 60090
847-459-9500
Fax: 847-459-9515 800-323-7790
sales@ustsubaki.com www.ustsubaki.com
Precision roller chains.
Year Founded: 1917
Estimated Sales: $290 Million
Number Employees: 500-1000

30560 USA Canvas Shoppe
2435 Glenda Lane
Dallas, TX 75229
972-484-7633
Fax: 972-620-0364 877-626-8468
awnings@usacanvas.com www.usacanvas.com
Commercial awnings and back-lit awnings
President: Gary Cozart
Contact: Ellen Cozart
ellen.cozart@usacanvas.com
Estimated Sales: $1-2.5 Million
Number Employees: 10-19
Parent Co: Four Seasons Patio and Awning
Company

30561 USC Consulting Group
3000 Bayport Drive
Suite 1010
Tampa, FL 33607
813-636-4004
Fax: 813-636-5099 800-888-8872
www.usccg.com
Consulting services
President: George Coffey
Chairman/CEO: Ronald Walker
President: James Ostrosky
Marketing Director: Gary Brown
Contact: Michelle Maloni
mmaloni@hklaw.com
VP/Senior Operations Manager: Terence Maher
Estimated Sales: $45 Million
Number Employees: 150
Square Footage: 3000

30562 (HQ)USDA-NASS
1400 Independence Ave SW
Washington, DC 20250-0002
202-690-8122
Fax: 202-720-9013 800-727-9540
nass@nass.usda.gov www.nass.usda.gov
The mission is to research and develop knowledge
and technology needed to solve technical agricultural problems of broad scope in order to ensure ade-
quate production of high quality food and
agricultural products
Administrator: Cynthia Clark
Director of Research and Development: Mark Harris
Contact: Art Fairson
art.fairson@ars.usda.gov
Director of Operations: Kevin Barnes
Number Employees: 250-499

30563 USECO
P.O.Box 20428
Murfreesboro, TN 37129-0428
615-893-4820
Fax: 615-893-8705 info@useco.com
Manufacturer and exporter of stainless steel and alu-
minum food service equipment including hot and
cold food service carts, tray line refrigerators, blast
chillers, tray lifters, pellet heaters, etc
President: John Westbrook
VP (Food Service Systems Tech.): Sara Hurt
VP Sales/Marketing (USECO): Paul Murphy
Estimated Sales: $20-50 Million
Number Employees: 50-99
Square Footage: 100000
Parent Co: Standex International Corporation
Type of Packaging: Food Service
Brands:
  Catr
  Remotaire

Rota-Chill
Unitray
Unitron
Useco

30564 Udi's Food
101 East 70th Ave
Denver, CO 80221
303-657-1600
Fax: 303-657-1615 eheiman@udisfood.com
Prepared foods
Owner: Udi Baron
General Manager & Partner Udis Granola: Eric
Clayman
CFO: Jason Kashman
Vice President: Etai Baron
Director of Foodservice: Jared Josleyn
Manager Quality Assurance: Natasha Phipps
Marketing Communications Manager: Heather
Collins
Sales Executive/Manager: Cynthia Drennan
Contact: Jim Heilman
jheilman@udisfood.com
VP Operations/Production Manager: Yosi Lutwak
Human Resources Director: Rosa Woods
Vice President Foodservice: Dana Spaeth

30565 Uhrden
750 Edelweiss Dr.
PO Box 705
Sugarcreek, OH 44681
330-852-2411
Fax: 330-852-2415 800-852-2411
Bulk dumping equipment and vertical reciprocating
conveyors
Chairman of the Board: Kenneth L Cook
General Manager: Mike Sigma
Sales: Rod Synder
Purchasing Agent: Lois Harig
Estimated Sales: Below $5 Million
Number Employees: 20-49
Square Footage: 130000
Brands:
  Tubar

30566 Uhtamaki Foods Services
242 College Ave
Waterville, ME 04901-6226
207-873-3351
Fax: 207-877-6504 www.chinet.com
Biodegradable disposable tableware; serving the
food service industry
Manager: Steve Bosse
CEO: Mark Staton
Contact: Peter Deane
peter.deane@us.huhtamaki.com
Estimated Sales: $1-5 Million
Number Employees: 500-999
Parent Co: Royal Packaging Industries

30567 Ulcra Dynamics
3000 Advance Lane
Colmar, PA 18915-9432
201-489-0044
Fax: 201-489-9229 800-727-6931
Manufacturer and exporter of water treatment sys-
tems
Estimated Sales: $500,000-$1 Million
Number Employees: 10-19
Parent Co: Severn Trent Services

30568 Ullman, Shapiro & UllmanLLP
425 Park Ave 27th Floor
New York, NY 10022
212-755-0299
www.usulaw.com
Manufacturer and exporter of platters, plates, bowls,
tumblers and pitchers
Partner: Marc Ullman
Chief Executive Officer: Zev Weiss
Executive VP: Marvin Lipkind
Estimated Sales: $10-20 Million
Number Employees: 1-4
Square Footage: 300000

30569 Ulmer Pharmacal
1614 Industrial Ave W
Park Rapids, MN 56470-3510
218-732-2656
Fax: 218-732-5300 800-848-5637
www.lobanaproducts.com
Vitamins, disinfectants, chemical detergents and
soaps

President: Al Trudeau
ulmer@unitelc.com
National Sales Manager: Rick Dressler
Estimated Sales: $1-2.5 Million
Number Employees: 5-9
Parent Co: Ulmer Pharmacal Company
Brands:
  Derm Ade
  Lobana
  Peri Garde

30570 Ultimate Textile
18 Market St
Paterson, NJ 07501-1721
973-523-5866
Fax: 973-523-5460 www.ultimatetextile.com
Tabletop accessories including napkins, table cloths
and skirting
President: Roger Glicman
rglicman@pecata.com
Estimated Sales: $20-50 Million
Number Employees: 100-249

30571 Ultra Cool International
PO Box 57844
Sherman Oaks, CA 91413-2844
818-908-9208
Fax: 818-908-4058

30572 Ultra Industries Inc
2801 Carlisle Ave
Racine, WI 53404-1888
262-633-5102
Fax: 262-633-5102 800-358-5872
info@ultradustcollectors.com
www.ultradustcollectors.com
Dust collection equipment, cartridge collectors and
pneumatic filter receivers
President: Ko Kryger
CFO: Evone Hagerman
General Manager: Dave Cleveland
Sales and Marketing Manager: Tom Meyer
Application/Sales Engineer: Daniel Hahn
Contact: Mike Blair
mblair@ultradustcollectors.com
Product Manager: Norman Pratt
Estimated Sales: $2.5-5 Million
Number Employees: 10-19
Square Footage: 2000

30573 Ultra Lift Corp
475 Stockton Ave # E
San Jose, CA 95126-2435
408-287-9400
Fax: 408-297-1199 800-346-3057
info@ultralift.com www.ultralift.com
Powdered material handling equipment products are
specially designed for food and beverage equipment
movers and installers
President: George Dabb
info@ultralift.com
VP: Charae Hewphill
Estimated Sales: $1-2.5 Million
Number Employees: 5-9
Brands:
  Kegmaster
  Ultra Lift

30574 Ultra Packaging Inc
534 N York Rd
Bensenville, IL 60106-1607
630-595-9820
Fax: 630-595-9710 ultrapkg@aol.com
www.ultrapackaging.com
Cartoning machines
Owner: Bob Stockus
ultrapkg@aol.com
Estimated Sales: $1-2.5 Million
Number Employees: 10-19

30575 Ultra Process Systems
733 Emory Valley Road
Oak Ridge, TN 37830-7017
865-483-2772
Fax: 865-483-2979
High temperature process equipment and services to
the dairy and food processors

30576 Ultrafilter
3560 Engineering Drive
Norcross, GA 30092-2819
770-942-5322
Fax: 770-448-3854 800-543-3634

Worldwide supplier of compressed gas, steam and liquid purification equipment. Process filtration: culinary steam filters, sterile gas filters, process liquid filters, tank vent filters, 3-A approved sanitary filter housings, microfiltration cartridges. Compressed air filters and dryers, on-site compressed air quality testing: ultra-survey programs
President: Keith Hayward
Sales/Marketing: Jeff Touo
Number Employees: 20-49
Square Footage: 132000
Parent Co: Ultrafilter GmBH
Other Locations:
  Ultrafilter
  Scarborough ON
Brands:
  Boreas
  Buran
  Ufmt
  Ultrafilter
  Ultrair
  Ultrapac
  Ultraqua
  Ultrasep
  Ultratoc
  Ultrex

30577 Ultrafryer Systems Inc
302 Spencer Ln
San Antonio, TX 78201-2018
   210-731-5000
Fax: 210-731-5099 800-545-9189
ultrafryersales@ultrafryer.com
www.ultrafryer.com
Manufacturer and exporter of gas and electric fryers, filters, breading tables, warmers, cookers and hoods
President: Ed Odmark
CEO: Edward T Odmark
eodmark@ultrafryer.com
National Manager Sales: Steve Ricketson
General Manager: William Collins
Estimated Sales: $10-20 Million
Number Employees: 50-99
Square Footage: 150000
Type of Packaging: Consumer, Food Service
Brands:
  Ultrafryer

30578 Ultrak
6252 W 91st Avenue
Westminster, CO 80031-2909
   303-428-9480
Fax: 303-429-6609
Closed-circuit surveillance equipment
Managing Director: Tom Verzuh
Marketing Coordinator: Linda Pohl
Sales Manager: Chris Staniforth
Number Employees: 24
Square Footage: 14000

30579 Ultralight Plastic
6700 E Rogers Cir
Boca Raton, FL 33487
   561-988-1676
Fax: 561-988-0928 palletbox@hotmail.com
Plastic pallets, pallet bases
CEO: Geoffrey Bourne
Estimated Sales: $12 Million
Number Employees: 5
Parent Co: Ultralight Plastic

30580 Ultrapak
134 Franklin Ave
Dunkirk, NY 14048-2806
   716-366-3654
Fax: 716-366-0041 800-228-6030
www.ultrapak.us
Decorative labels, tamper evident bands, and unitizing sleeves for multipacks
President: Khalid Khan
khalid@ultrapak.us
CFO: William Cook
Marketing Director: Jackie Patterson
Sales Director: Gracie Bane
Production Manager: Dan Lentz
Estimated Sales: $2.5-5 Million
Number Employees: 20-49
Type of Packaging: Food Service

30581 Ultrapar Inc.
13 Flintlock Dr
Warren, NJ 07059-5014
   908-647-6650
Fax: 908-647-1281 chrisparkinson@ultrapar.com
www.ultrapar.com

Wholesaler/distributor of steam filters, culinary steam filtration systems, air sterilizing filters and liquid sterilizing filtration systems.
President: Chris Parkinson
Vice President: Nancy Siconolfi
Estimated Sales: $1-1.5 Million
Number Employees: 3
Square Footage: 7200

30582 Ultratainer
910 Industrial Boulevard
St Jean-Sur-Richelie, QC J3B 8J4
Canada
   514-359-3651
Fax: 514-359-3653 ultra@ultratainer.com
www.ultratainer.com
Collapsible, reusable, stackable, stainless steel and wire mesh containers
CEO: Bert Gaumond
Plant Manager: Dave Lapierre
Purchasing Manager: Lina Levert
Estimated Sales: $10 Million
Number Employees: 30
Square Footage: 50000
Type of Packaging: Bulk

30583 Umec Solar Inc
548 Claire St
Hayward, CA 94541-6412
   510-537-4744
Fax: 510-537-9564 800-933-8632
www.umec.net
Elevators, loaders, lifters and dumpers, belt conveyors, blenders, chup separators, massagers and tumblers, mixers, screw conveyors
President: Barry Brescia
CEO: Benny Brescia
CEO: Ralph Creech
Sales Director: Dennis Dennings
Manager: Cecilia Hewett
Estimated Sales: $2.5-5 Million
Number Employees: 20-49
Type of Packaging: Food Service, Private Label

30584 Unarco Industries LLC
400 SE 15th St
Wagoner, OK 74467-7900
   918-485-9531
Fax: 918-485-2131 800-654-4100
www.unarco.com
Manufacturer and exporter of shopping carts, retail display fixtures, stainless steel tables and accessories, food service containers and carts and warehousing and stocking carts
President: Randy Garvin
CFO: Misty Allen
misty.allen@unarco.com
Sales: Richard Wilkinson
VP International Sales: David Warneke
VP Sales: Richard Wilkinson
Estimated Sales: $50-100 Million
Number Employees: 250-499
Square Footage: 650000
Type of Packaging: Food Service

30585 Unarco Material Handling Inc
407 E Washington St
Pandora, OH 45877
   419-384-3211
Fax: 419-384-7239 800-448-0784
www.unarcorack.com
Manufacturer and exporter of roll-formed pallet rack systems
National Sales Manager: David Johnstone
Manager: Mike Burris
mikeb@clymer-rack.com
Estimated Sales: $10-20 Million
Number Employees: 50-99
Parent Co: Unarco Material Handling, Inc.
Type of Packaging: Bulk

30586 Underwriters Laboratories Inc
2600 NW Lake Rd
Camas, WA 98607-8542
   360-817-5500
Fax: 360-817-6000 877-854-3577
www.ul.com
Testing and certification service for product, environmental and public safety of appliances and equipment

Vice President: Ralph Parker
ralph.j.parker@us.ul.com
CFO: Michael Saltzmen
CEO: Keith E Williams
VP Sales/Marketing: Stuart Paul
Number Employees: 250-499

30587 Uneco Systems
8412 Autumn Drive
Woodridge, IL 60517
   630-910-0505
Fax: 630-910-0558 800-700-6894
junewitz@att.net
President: John Unewitz
junewitz@att.net
Estimated Sales: $1-2.5 Million
Number Employees: 1-4

30588 Unette Corp
1578 Sussex Tpke # 5
Building #5
Randolph, NJ 07869-1833
   973-328-6800
Fax: 973-537-1010 info@unette.com
www.unette.com
Contract packager of food colors, condiments, groceries, etc
President: Joseph R Hark
Sales Service Coordinator: Dawn Stone
Estimated Sales: $4400000
Number Employees: 50-99
Square Footage: 240000

30589 Unex Manufacturing Inc
691 New Hampshire Ave
Lakewood, NJ 08701-5452
   732-928-2800
Fax: 732-928-2828 800-334-8639
span@unex.com www.unex.com
Carton flow truck and storage products
President: Brian Neuwirth
CEO: Frank Neuwirth
CFO: Eilean Brant
VP Sales: Mark Neuwrith
R&D: Haward McIbaine
Marketing Director: Carolann Neuwirth
Northwest Sales Manager: Bill Link
Contact: Deena Brown
dbrown@unix.com
Estimated Sales: Less Than $500,000
Number Employees: 5-9
Brands:
  Pathline
  Spantrack

30590 Unger Co
12401 Berea Rd
Cleveland, OH 44111-1607
   216-252-1400
Fax: 216-252-1427 800-321-1418
info@ungerco.com www.ungerco.com
Supplier of packaging for bakery and deli products. Importer of polyethylene, polyprop and plastic shopping bags, and boxes. Consulting services available
President/CEO: Gerald Unger
info@ungerco.com
Controller: Scott Smith
VP: Diane Tracy
Estimated Sales: $5-10 Million
Number Employees: 10-19
Type of Packaging: Food Service
Brands:
  Bake'n Show
  Deleez
  Ungermatic

30591 Uni Carriers Americas Corp
240 N Prospect St
Marengo, IL 60152-3235
   815-568-0061
Fax: 815-568-0179 800-871-5438
nfcsales@nfcna.com
Industrial gas, lp and electric forklift, walkie and reach trucks
President: Jan Aten
atenjan@unicarriersamericas.com
Director Marketing: Keith Allmandinger
Manager Media Marketing: Tim Haley
atenjan@unicarriersamericas.com
Number Employees: 500-999
Square Footage: 1400000
Parent Co: Nissan Motor Company

30592 Uni First Corp
68 Jonspin Rd
Wilmington, MA 01887-1086
978-658-8888
Fax: 978-657-5663 800-455-7654
ufirst@unifirst.com www.unifirst.com
Supplier of workwear and textile services. Rent, lease, and sell uniforms, protective clothing, custom corporate workwear, floorcare, and other facility services products to all kinds of businesses.
President/CEO: Roland Croatti
CEO: Ronald D Croatti
ronald_croatti@unifirst.com
Estimated Sales: Over $1 Billion
Number Employees: 10000+

30593 Uni-Chains Manufacturing
Hjulmagervej 21
Vejle, DK 7100
457-572-3100
Fax: 457-572-3348 800-937-2864
admin@unichains.com www.unichains.com
Manufactures a comprehensive programs for internal transport offering chains in both steel and plastic, modular plastic belt and conveyor accessories.
President: Soren Pedersen
Number Employees: 10-19
Parent Co: Uni Chains

30594 UniChem Enterprises
1905 S Lynx Place
Ontario, CA 91761
909-321-1000
Fax: 425-696-3568 sales@unichemsupply.com
Raw materials and ingredients supplier to the food, feed, nutraceutical, supplement and cosmetics industries.
Contact: Tony Hang
thang@unichemsupply.com

30595 UniPro Foodservice, Inc.
2500 Cumberland Pkwy. SE
Suite 600
Atlanta, GA 30339
770-952-0871
Fax: 770-952-0872 info@uniprofoodservice.com
www.uniprofoodservice.com
Coffee, tea, cappucino, sugar packets, non-dairy creamer, and coffee bowls, cutlery, foodservice film, paper goods, dry pastas, frozen filled pastas, Italian cheeses, soups, olive oil, sausage and meatballs, tomato products, pizzacrusts and pizza toppings. Pork, produce, dairy, oils/grains, beef, veal, lamb, seafood, and poultry.
CEO: Bob Stewart
CFO: Tracy Britton
Executive VP of Marketing: Keith Durnell
Executive VP, Sales: Scott Strull
Year Founded: 1997
Estimated Sales: $987 Million
Number Employees: 1000-4999
Square Footage: 9303
Brands:
   Code®
   Comsource®
   Nifda®
   Nugget®
   Companions®
   Cortona®
   Reflections®

30596 (HQ)UniTrak Corporation
299 Ward Street
PO Box 330
Port Hope, ON L1A 3W4
Canada
905-885-8168
Fax: 905-885-2614 866-883-5749
info@unitrak.com www.unitrak.com
Manufacturer and exporter of bucket elevators, packaging machinery and conveyors
President: W Gorsline
Engineering Team Leader: Keith Douglas
Scheduling and Special Project: D Snoddon
Marketing Team Leader: Marie Lytle
Operations Manager: D Snoddon
Plant Manager: Ivan Patton
Number Employees: 10
Square Footage: 40000
Other Locations:
   UniTrak Corp. Ltd.
   Furness Vale, High Peak
Brands:
   Bagstarder

Efficia
Tiptrak

30597 Unibloc-Pump Inc
1701 Ashborough Rd SE
Marietta, GA 30067-8925
770-218-8900
Fax: 770-218-8442 info@uniblocpump.com
www.uniblocpump.com
Aseptic processing equipment
Owner: Harry Soderstrom
harry@flowtechdiv.com
Number Employees: 10-19

30598 Unibloc-Pump Inc
1701 Ashborough Rd SE
Marietta, GA 30067-8925
770-218-8900
Fax: 770-218-8442 info@flowtechdiv.com
www.uniblocpump.com
Sanitary lobe pumps and valves
President/Owner: Harry Soderstrom
harry@flowtechdiv.com
Estimated Sales: $4-8 Million
Number Employees: 10-19
Square Footage: 25000

30599 Unichema North America
4650 S Racine Ave
Chicago, IL 60609-3321
773-650-7600
Fax: 773-376-0095
Industrial chemicals, oleic, stearic and fatty acids, lubricating oils and greases
Estimated Sales: $50-100 Million
Number Employees: 100-249

30600 Unidex
2416 North Main Street
Warsaw, NY 14569
585-786-3170
Fax: 585-786-3223 800-724-1302
sales@unidex-inc.com www.unidex-inc.com
Lifting, positioning and manipulating devices including pallet lifting tables, adjustable height work benches, stainless steel lifts and carts, roll handling
President: Arthur Crater
CFO: Tom Baldwin
Quality Control: Don Cunningham
Sales: Sue Gardner
Estimated Sales: $2.5-5 Million

30601 Unifiller Systems
7621 MacDonald Road
Delta, BC V4G 1N3
Canada
604-940-2233
Fax: 604-940-2195 888-733-8444
worldsales@unifiller.com www.unifiller.com
Manufacturs of stainless steel food grade filling and portioning systems for the baking and food service industries. Extensive line of bakery depositors, pumps/depositors and fully automated cake assembly/finishing lines
President: Kuno Kurschner
CEO: Mark Soares
CFO: Ballard Client
Vice President: Benno Bucher
R&D: Andy Fillers
Quality Control: Chris Moora
VP Marketing: Stewart MacPherson
Sales Director: Nick Frost
Number Employees: 50
Brands:
   Deco-Mate
   Handi-Matic
   Uni-Versal

30602 Unifoil Corp
12 Daniel Rd
Fairfield, NJ 07004-2536
973-244-9990
Fax: 973-244-5555 www.unifoil.com
Manufacturer and exporter of laminated and coated aluminum foil; also, metallized and holographic paper and boards
President: Joseph Funicelli
CEO: Milica Bubalo
mbubalo@unifoil.com
CFO: William Mulooney
Quality Control: Robert Galloino
Sales Director: Robert Rumer
Plant Manager: Dwight Penrell

Estimated Sales: $20-50 Million
Number Employees: 50-99

30603 Uniforms To You
9525 S. Cicero Avenue
Oak Lawn, IL 60453
708-424-4747
800-889-6072
www.uniformstoyou.com
Uniforms, work gear and career apparel.
Estimated Sales: $20-50 Million
Number Employees: 500-999
Parent Co: Cintas Corp
Brands:
   Cintas
   Dickies
   Segal
   Uncommon Threads
   Fabian International

30604 Uniforms To You & Co
5600 W 73rd St
Chicago, IL 60638-6273
708-563-0108
Fax: 708-563-5003 800-864-3676
Uniforms and special clothing
Sr. VP Sales/Marketing: Michael DiMino
Contact: Michael DiMino
michaeldimino@uty.com
General Manager: Keith Nacker
Number Employees: 5-9

30605 Uniloy Milacron
5550 Occidental Hwy
Suite B
Tecumseh, MI 49286
517-424-8900
Fax: 517-423-6827 www.milacron.com
Blowmolding and structural foam machinery. Included are stretch blowmolding systems for PET. Molds, tooling, parts, training and technical support.
Chief Executive Officer: Tom Goeke
Chief Financial Officer: Bruce Chalmers
VP/General Counsel/Secretary: Hugh O'Donnell
Chief Human Resources Officer: Mark Miller
Year Founded: 1860
Estimated Sales: $74.5 Million
Number Employees: 5,368

30606 Unimar Inc
3195 Vickery Rd
Syracuse, NY 13212-4574
315-699-4400
Fax: 315-699-3700 800-739-9169
www.unimar.com
Refrigerators. freezers, beverage dispensers, snack bars, C-stoves, and heaters
Owner: Michael Marley
mike@unimar.com
Estimated Sales: $2.5-5 Million
Number Employees: 10-19

30607 Unimove LLC
1145 Little Gap Rd # C
Palmerton, PA 18071-5027
610-826-7855
Fax: 610-826-8422 unimove@ptd.net
www.unimove.com
Manufacturer and exporter of vacuum tube lifting systems
Director: Robert Shannon
unitech@ptd.net
VP: Vincent Julian Jr
Director Marketing: Ken Kasick
Operations: Alan Zimmermann
Purchasing: Charles Kistler
Estimated Sales: 1,000,000
Number Employees: 5-9
Number of Brands: 1
Square Footage: 140000
Brands:
   Unimove

30608 Union Camp Corporation
5050 Ironton Street
Denver, CO 80239-2412
303-371-0760
Fax: 303-375-0718
Inner packaging materials including fiber corrugated boxes; also, enhanced graphics and pre-print available
Sales Manager: Ron Wise
General Manager: Paul Areson

Number Employees: 130
Square Footage: 260000
Parent Co: Union Camp Corporation

30609 Union Cord Products Company
425 N Martingdale Road
Schaumburg, IL 60173

847-240-1500
Fax: 847-240-1576 info@unionleasing.com
www.unionleasing.com
Manufacturer and exporter of gaskets including braided, knitted, rubber insert and poly-jacketed cellulose
CEO: Warren Benis
Estimated Sales: $1-5,000,000
Parent Co: Sasser Family Holdings Inc.

30610 Union Industries
10 Admiral St
Providence, RI 02908

401-274-7000
Fax: 401-331-1910 800-556-6454
Manufacturer and exporter of flexible packaging
President: Harley Frank
Chairman: H Alan Frank
CFO: John Wilbur
Sales Director: Michael Kauffman
Contact: Anne Delany
adelany@unionpaperco.com
Estimated Sales: $23.5 Million
Number Employees: 125
Square Footage: 125000
Type of Packaging: Food Service, Private Label

30611 Union Plastics Co
132 E Union St
Marshville, NC 28103-1141

704-624-2112
Fax: 704-624-6119
Plastic and vinyl hose and tubing
President: Sandra Osborn
Plant Manager: C Osborn
Estimated Sales: Below $5 Million
Number Employees: 5-9

30612 Union Process
1925 Akron Peninsula Rd
Akron, OH 44313

330-929-3333
Fax: 330-929-3034 eli@unionprocess.com
www.unionprocess.com
Manufacturers a broad line of wet and dry milling attritors and small media mills. Also offer a wide assortment of grinding media and provide toll milling and refurbishing services. Also the meading manufacturer of rubber inks forballoons, swim caps and other rubber products.
President: Arno Szegvari
R & D Lab: Margaret Yang
National Sales Manager: Robert Schilling
Production: Craig McCaulley
Plant Manager: Ron Sloan
Estimated Sales: $5-10 Million
Number Employees: 20-49
Square Footage: 56000
Brands:
Attritor

30613 Unipac Shipping
18216 147th Ave # 2
2nd. Floor
Jamaica, NY 11413-3704

718-995-8168
Fax: 718-995-8169 800-586-2711
info@unipacshippinginc.com
www.unipacshipping.com
Absorbent pads for pre-packaging meats, poultry, fish, sprouts, asparagus, apples, pizza, etc
President: Richard Engel
Number Employees: 20-49
Square Footage: 120000

30614 Unipak Inc
715 E Washington St
West Chester, PA 19380-4595

610-436-6600
Fax: 610-436-6069 info@unipakinc.com
www.unipakinc.com
Paper boxes; also, printing services available

President: Tim Craig
tcraig@unipakinc.com
Structural / Graphic Design: Nicole Dana
Sales/Marketing: Teddy Frain
Customer Service: Angela Marchetti
Operations: Mike Golas
Supply Chain and Operations: Zak Allen
Purchasing/Estimating: Jenn Correa
Estimated Sales: $5-10 Million
Number Employees: 50-99

30615 Uniplast Films
1017 Wilson Street
Palmer, MA 01069-1137

413-283-8365
Fax: 413-283-8278 800-343-1295
Film laminates and plastic and coextended film; exporter of plastic film
VP: Fredy Steng
Customer Service: Diane Fihal
Estimated Sales: $1-5 Million
Number Employees: 100
Square Footage: 160000
Parent Co: Uniplast Industries

30616 Unique Boxes
6548 N Glenwood Ave
Chicago, IL 60626

773-743-6617
Fax: 773-254-1023 800-281-1670
rrchagin@aol.com
Box partitions, set-up paper boxes and folding cartons
President: R Chagin
CFO: Rafael Chagin
Contact: Rafael Chagin
rrchagin@aol.com
Estimated Sales: Below $5 Million
Number Employees: 5

30617 Unique Manufacturing
1920 W Princeton Ave Ste 17
Visalia, CA 93277

559-739-1007
Fax: 559-739-7725 888-737-1007
Manufacturer and importer of silverware sleeves, paper napkin bands, beverage coasters, menu covers, chopsticks, flag food picks and paper parasols
President: Irwin Smith
Marketing: Paul Smith
Sales: Erwin Smith
Number Employees: 5-9
Square Footage: 4000

30618 Unique Manufacturing Company
1050 Corporate Ave
Suite 108
North Port, FL 34289

941-429-6600
Fax: 253-669-7645 sales@uniquemanuf.com
www.uniquemanuf.com
Importers and manufacturing of hospitality items. Custom printed stock flag food picks, beverage stirs, paper/foil parasols, napkins bands, silverware sleeves, chenille and foil decorator picks, plastic food picks, chop stickscoasters, paper glass covers, placemats, tray covers, and menu covers and binders
Owner: Michael Jakubowski
Estimated Sales: Below $5 Million
Number Employees: 1-4
Number of Products: 500
Square Footage: 2000
Type of Packaging: Consumer, Private Label
Brands:
American Ingredients
Dole Packaged Foods
Nakand
Nutrin Corp
Qa Products
Quick Dry Foods
Vita Foods

30619 Unique Plastics
372 Rio Rico Drive
Rio Rico, AZ 85648-3517

520-377-0595
Fax: 520-377-0696 800-658-5946
Round plastic trays
Estimated Sales: $1-5,000,000
Number Employees: 20-50
Square Footage: 28000

30620 Unique Solutions
2836 Corporate Pkwy
Algonquin, IL 60102-2564

847-960-1110
Fax: 847-540-1431 info@unique-solutions.com
www.unique-solutions.com
Product line includes inserting and labeling equipment produced in a continuous, perforated bandolier format in addition to that of two or three-dimensional premiums and labels that are inserted (In-Pakrs) or attached to the outside ofprimary packaging (On-Pakrs).
President: Mark Ulan
Chairman/CEO: Joyce Witt
info@unique-solutions.com
Business Development Manager: Brian Dawson
VP Sales: Walter Peterson
COO: Jason Raasch
Production Manager: Norman Hendle
info@unique-solutions.com
Customer Service Representative: Christie Haack
Estimated Sales: $2.5-5 Million
Number Employees: 5-9
Square Footage: 52000
Parent Co: Unique Coupons

30621 Unirak Storage Systems
7620 Telegraph Rd
Taylor, MI 48180-2237

313-291-7600
Fax: 313-291-7605 800-348-7225
sales@unirak.com www.unirak.com
Manufacturer and exporter of racks including adjustable storage, pallet, galvanized, refrigerated, selective, drive-in/thru, deck, pallet flow, push-back and carton flow
Vice President: Eric Gonda
sales@unarak.com
Sales Director: Eric Gonda
Estimated Sales: $3-5 Million
Number Employees: 10-19
Number of Brands: 4
Number of Products: 110
Square Footage: 400000
Type of Packaging: Bulk
Brands:
Unirack Drive-In Rack
Unirak Pallet Rack

30622 Unisoft Systems Associates
4890 Trailpath Drive
Dublin, OH 43016

614-791-1592
Fax: 614-791-1592 800-448-1574
www.unisoft-systems.com
Food management software including inventory, recipe, invoicing, forecasting, nutrient, diet office management, bid list and daily activity
Technical Support: Robert Davis
Research & Development: Diane Clapp
Contact: Diane Bruce
dianebruce@unisoft-systems.com
Estimated Sales: $2.5-5 Million
Number Employees: 19
Square Footage: 4800
Brands:
Food System 4 Windows

30623 (HQ)Unisource ManufacturingInc
8040 NE 33rd Dr
Portland, OR 97211-2016

503-281-4673
Fax: 503-281-5845 800-234-2566
info@unisource-mfg.com
www.unisource-mfg.com
Manufacturer and engineering of industrial hoses and related products
President: Joseph Thompson
CEO: Joe Thompson
jthompson@unisource-mfg.com
Quality Mgr.: Blu Matsell
National Sales Mgr.: Joseph Thompson
General/Human Resources Mgr: Dan Christiansen
Operations/Purchasing Mgr.: Ron Bateman
Purchasing Manager: Ralph Lorusso
Number Employees: 50-99

30624 Unitech Scientific
12026 Centralia Rd # H
Hawaiian Gardens, CA 90716-1067

562-924-5155
Fax: 562-809-3140 info@unitechscientific.com
www.unitechscientific.com

Glucose, fructose, L-malic acid, acetic acid, primary amino nitrogen and other food testkits
President: Geoffrey Anderson
geoff@unitechscientific.com
CEO: Lee Anderson
R & D: Ted Chou
Quality Control: Jim Sisowth
Estimated Sales: Below $5 Million
Number Employees: 5-9

30625 United Ad Label
3075 Highland Parkway
Suite 400
Downers Grove, IL 60515-5560
714-990-2700
Fax: 800-962-0658   800-423-4643
Manufacturer and exporter of pressure sensitive labels
President: Cal Laird
VP Marketing: Brad Baylies
New Markets Manager: Cheryl Hall
cheryl.hall@rrd.com
Estimated Sales: $1-5 Million
Number Employees: 100-250
Type of Packaging: Consumer, Bulk

30626 (HQ)United Air Specialists Inc
4440 Creek Rd
Blue Ash, OH 45242-2832
513-891-0400
Fax: 513-891-4171   800-992-4422
www.uasinc.com
Manufacturer and exporter of air filtration media including electrostatic precipitators, liquid coating and dust collection systems
President: Rich Larson
riclar@uasinc.com
VP Marketing: Lynne Laake
Estimated Sales: G
Number Employees: 250-499
Square Footage: 152500
Other Locations:
    United Air Specialists
    Cincinnati OH
Brands:
    Crystal-Aire
    Dust-Cat
    Dust-Hog
    Smog-Hog
    Smokeeter
    Total-Stat

30627 United Bags Inc
1355 N Warson Rd
St Louis, MO 63132-1598
314-421-3700
Fax: 314-421-0969   800-550-2247
custserv@unitedbags.com www.unitedbags.com
Manufacturer and importer of bags including bulk, burlap, multi-wall, polypropylene, paper and cotton
President: Todd Greenberg
unitedbags@aol.com
CEO: Herbert Greenberg
CFO: Ruth Allen
VP: Todd Greenberg
Estimated Sales: $2.5-5 Million
Number Employees: 20-49
Square Footage: 600000

30628 United Bakery Equipment
19216 S Laurel Park Rd
Rancho Dominguez, CA 90220-6008
310-635-8121
Fax: 310-635-8171 www.ubeusa.com
VP: Mike Bastasch
Director of Domestic/nternational Sales: Tom Sheffield
Manager: Mike Bastasch
Estimated Sales: $10-20 Million
Number Employees: 20-49

30629 United Bakery EquipmentCompany
15815 W 110th St
Shawnee Mission, KS 66219
913-541-8700
Fax: 913-541-0781 www.ubeusa.com
Manufacturer and exporter of slicers and baggers for breads, buns, tortillas, muffins, bagels, etc
President: Frank Bastasch
Vice President: Paul Bastasch
Sales Director: Bob Plourde
Contact: Levent Gokkaya
lgokkaya@untek.com.tr

Estimated Sales: $20-50 Million
Number Employees: 50-99
Square Footage: 32000
Parent Co: United Bakery Equipment Company
Type of Packaging: Food Service, Private Label

30630 United Barrels
1303 Jefferson Street no. 210a
Napa, CA 94559-2470
707-258-0795
Fax: 707-259-5324
Wine barrels, French oak wine barrels
President: Scott Harrop
Estimated Sales: Below $5 Million
Number Employees: 1-4

30631 United Basket Co Inc
5801 Grand Ave
Maspeth, NY 11378-3216
718-894-5454
Fax: 718-326-3378 ubsales@verizon.net
www.unitedbasketco.com
Baskets and gift basket supplies and packaging supplies
Founder: Max Hanfling
CEO: Phil Hanfling
ubsales@verizon.net
Number Employees: 5-9
Square Footage: 56

30632 United Commercial Corporation
20 Avenue At the Cmn
Shrewsbury, NJ 07702-4801
732-935-0025
Fax: 732-935-0022   800-498-7147
wpearl@verizon.net
We supply plastic fabrication for dispensing hot and cold food merchandising equipment and menu systems
President: Wade Pearlman
Estimated Sales: $2 Million

30633 United Desiccants
985 Damonte Ranch Parkway
Suite #320
Reno, NE 89521
505-864-6691
Fax: 505-864-9296   888-659-1377
insidesale@desiccare.com www.desiccare.com
Manufacturer and exporter of desiccant absorption packs; also, humidity indicators for packaging
President: William Monin
General Manager: George Klett
Business Unit Manager: Richard Greenlaw
Number Employees: 300
Parent Co: United Catalysts
Brands:
    Adsormat
    Container Dri
    Desi Pak
    Desi View
    Sorb Pak
    Sorb-It
    Tri-Sorb

30634 United Electric Controls Co
180 Dexter Ave
Watertown, MA 02472-4200
617-926-1000
Fax: 617-926-4354 support@ueonline.com
www.ueonline.com
Manufacturer and exporter of temperature control and detection devices including thermostats, pressure and temperature switches, transducers and sensors for general purpose and sanitary service.
Chief Executive Officer: Dave Reis
Director of Materials: Cheryl O'Connell
Year Founded: 1931
Estimated Sales: $100+ Million
Number Employees: 100-249
Other Locations:
    United Electric Controls Co.
    Milford CT

30635 United Fabricators
1110 Carnall Avenue
Fort Smith, AR 72901-3756
479-782-9169
Fax: 479-783-5901   800-235-4101
Custom stainless steel food service equipment including chef's counters, canopies, sinks, work tables, etc

EVP: Jerry Bollin Jr
Sales Manager: Greg Donald
Contact: Kathy Griffin
griffinkathya@hotmail.com
Office Manager: Jeanne Emery
Estimated Sales: $3.6 Million
Number Employees: 35
Square Footage: 160000
Type of Packaging: Food Service
Brands:
    Unifab

30636 United Filters Intl
901 S Grant St
Amarillo, TX 79101-3625
806-373-8386
Fax: 806-371-7783 info@unitedfilters.com
www.unitedfilters.com
Manufacturer and exporter of string wound filter cartridges and vessels
Manager: David Otwell
Sales Manager (South): David Otwell
Sales Manager (North): Lynn Love
Estimated Sales: $500,000-$1 Million
Number Employees: 10-19
Square Footage: 100000
Parent Co: Perry Equipment Corporation
Brands:
    United Filters

30637 United Fire & Safety Service
979 Saw Mill River Rd,
PO Box 53
Yonkers, NY 10710-0053
914-968-4459
Fax: 914-747-3983
Safety equipment, exhaust hoods and fans and fire suppression systems
President: Maureen Ulley
Estimated Sales: $1-2.5 Million
Number Employees: 5-9

30638 United Flexible
900 Merchants Concourse
Westbury, NY 11590-5142
516-222-2150
Fax: 516-222-2168 captivepackaging@aol.com
Manufacturer and exporter of plastic bags, printed roll stock and shrink packaging and lamination
President/CEO: Aldel Englander
Marketing Head: Elen Blonett
Estimated Sales: $5-10,000,000
Number Employees: 1-4

30639 United Floor Machine Co
7715 S South Chicago Ave # 1
Chicago, IL 60619-2797
773-734-0874
Fax: 773-734-0874   800-288-0848
unico1946@aol.com
Manufacturer and exporter of burnishers, heavy duty floor polishers and scrubbers, carpet shampooers
President/Owner: Richard Leitelt
unico1946@aol.com
VP: David Leitelt
Estimated Sales: Below $5 Million
Number Employees: 1-4
Square Footage: 6000
Brands:
    Aero
    Floor Magic
    Floorite
    Glo-Pro
    Uni-Vac
    Unico

30640 United Industries GroupInc
11 Rancho Cir # 1100
Lake Forest, CA 92630-8324
949-759-3200
Fax: 949-759-3425 info@unitedind.com
www.unitedind.com
Manufacturer and exporter of storage tanks and wastewater treatment and water purification systems; also, designer of water bottling and water purification package plants
Manager: Jim Mansour
Quality Control: John Mansell
VP: M Mulvaney
IT: James P Mansour
info@unitedind.com
Estimated Sales: $20-30 Million
Number Employees: 20-49

30641 United Industries Inc
1546 Henry Ave
Beloit, WI 53511-3668

608-365-8891
Fax: 608-365-1259 www.unitedindustries.com
Stainless steel sanitary finishing and welding equipment; also, tubing and pipe
President: Greg Sturicz
gregsturicz@unitedindustries.com
Estimated Sales: $50-100 Million
Number Employees: 100-249

30642 United Insulated Structures
5430 Saint Charles Rd
Berkeley, IL 60163-1291

708-544-8200
Fax: 708-544-8274 800-821-5538
office@unitedinsulated.com
www.unitedinsulated.com
Design build firm specializing in architecture, engineering and contruction for the food industry
President: Sally Baldwin
sallyb@unitedinsulated.com
EVP: Frank Maratea
SVP: Rich Maleczka
Marketing Director: Connie Maratea
Public Relations: Frank Maratea
Estimated Sales: $10-20 Million
Number Employees: 20-49
Square Footage: 140000

30643 United Label Corp
65 Chambers St
Newark, NJ 07105-2893

973-589-6500
Fax: 973-589-4465 800-252-0917
info@unitedlabelcorp.com
www.unitedlabelcorp.com
Labels
President: Joe Cic
Vice President: John Connor
joconnor@unitedlabelcorp.com
Sales Manager: Harry Stillman
Estimated Sales: $2.5-5 Million
Number Employees: 5-9

30644 United Mc Gill Corp
1 Mission Park
Groveport, OH 43125-1100

614-829-1200
Fax: 614-829-1291 personnel@unitedmcgill.com
www.unitedmcgill.com
Vacuum drying equipment
Owner: James D Mc Gill
Sales Manager: Don Crockett
james.mcgill@unitedmcgill.com
Number Employees: 500-999

30645 United Olive Oil Import
139 Fulton St
Suite 314
New York, NY 10038-2537

212-346-0942
Fax: 212-504-3297 scott@unitedoliveoil.com
www.unitedoliveoil.com
Italian food: olive oils, pasta and tomatoes, beans and grains, vegetables, condiments, coffee, cookies, fish, cheese and spices.
President & CEO: Tommaso Asaro
Business Development Manager: Cristina Ile
Director of Operations: Zach Casso
Estimated Sales: $5.3 Million
Number Employees: 30
Other Locations:
National Distribution Centers
Edison NJ
Southern Warehousing & Distribution
San Antonio TX

30646 United Pentek
8502 Brookville Road
Indianapolis, IN 46239-9427

317-359-3858
Fax: 317-353-9845 800-357-9299
Conveyor systems
Sales Manager: Jeffrey Smeathers
Estimated Sales: $10,000,000-$25,000,000
Number Employees: 100-249

30647 United Performance Metals
3045 Commercial Ave
Northbrook, IL 60062-1912

847-498-3111
Fax: 847-498-2810 888-922-0040
www.upmet.com

Manufacturer and exporter of titanium caustic food processing equipment and machine parts including scrapper, tubing and pipe coils
President: Richard Leopold
Senior VP: Jerry St Clair
Marketing Director: Joanie Leopold
Sales: Steve Gerzel
Operations: Adelberto Cordova
Estimated Sales: $9000000
Number Employees: 20-49
Parent Co: United Performance Metals

30648 United Products & InstrInc
182 Ridge Rd # E
Dayton, NJ 08810-1594

732-274-1155
Fax: 732-274-1151
Spectrophotometers for food and beverage labs
Owner: Albert Chang
achang@unicosci.com
Estimated Sales: $3-5 Million
Number Employees: 20-49

30649 United Ribtype Co
1319 Production Rd
Fort Wayne, IN 46808-1164

260-424-8973
Fax: 260-426-5502 800-473-4039
sales@ribtype.com www.ribtype.com
Manufacturer and exporter of rubber stamps
Owner: Tom Beaver
sales@ribtype.com
VP Sales: John Peirce
Estimated Sales: $3,000,000
Number Employees: 20-49
Square Footage: 40000
Parent Co: Indiana Stamp Company
Brands:
Ribtype

30650 United Seal & Tag Corporation
1544 Market Cir
Building 8
Port Charlotte, FL 33953

941-625-6799
Fax: 941-625-3644 800-211-9552
www.unitedsealandtag.com
Manufacturer and exporter of pressure sensitive, embossed, hot stamp, acetate and vinyl foil labels; also, foil tags
Owner: Robert Freda
Estimated Sales: $500,000-$1 Million
Number Employees: 10-19
Square Footage: 20000

30651 United Showcase Company
PO Box 145
Wood Ridge, NJ 07075-0145

201-438-4100
Fax: 201-438-2630 800-526-6382
Manufacturer and exporter of stainless steel and brass showcases, nonrefrigerated salad cooler cases, collapsible cutting board brackets, pot and pan racks, sneeze guards, guide rails, tray slides, tray slide brackets and salad barshields
President/CEO: Robert Cline
CFO: Doris Cline
VP: Robert Cline
R&D: Robert Cline
Quality Control: William Stevick
Marketing: Robert Cline
Sales/Public Relations: Robert Cline
Operations/Production/Plant Manager: William Stevick
Plant Manager: Bill Stevick
Estimated Sales: $1-2.5 Million
Number Employees: 20-49
Square Footage: 60000

30652 United Sign Corp
4900 Lister Ave
Kansas City, MO 64130-2838

816-923-9512
Fax: 816-923-9512 unitsignkc@aol.com
www.unitedsign.com
Signs including metal, plastic and neon
President: David Pickett
unitsignkc@att.net
Owner: Dave Pickett
Estimated Sales: $2.5-5 Million
Number Employees: 10-19

30653 United Specialty Flavors
999 Willow Grove Street
Suite 2-12e
Hackettstown, NJ 07840-5001

908-850-1118
Fax: 908-850-6099
Flavors and custom flavor delivery systems
President/CEO: William May
Number Employees: 30

30654 United States Systems Inc
1028 Scott Ave
Kansas City, KS 66105-1222

913-281-1010
Fax: 913-281-2901 888-281-2454
gregahawkins@aol.com
www.unitedstatessystems.com
Manufacturer and exporter of portable and stationary pneumatic conveyor systems for dry bulk goods including railcar unloading systems and in-plant transfers; also, storage silos, dust filters and bulk bag/box filling machines
President: Greg Hawkins
gregahawkins@aol.com
General Manager: Mark Aron
Sales Manager: Greg Hawkins
Estimated Sales: $2.5-5 Million
Number Employees: 5-9
Square Footage: 10000
Brands:
A/F Pot
Fwp-7000
P/D Pot
Uss In-Tank Filter System
Vactank
Venturi 25 Air Conveyor
Venturi 30
Vibracone

30655 United Steel Products Company
P.O.Box 407
East Stroudsburg, PA 18301-0407

570-476-1010
Fax: 570-476-4358 www.usprack.com
Manufacturer and exporter of roll-formed and structural steel storage rack systems
President: Martin A Skulnik
Sales: Mary Petronio
Plant Manager: Bob Micco
Purchasing Manager: Maria Sosa
Estimated Sales: $50-100 Million
Number Employees: 100-249
Square Footage: 390000
Parent Co: United Steel Enterprises
Brands:
Storage Rack-Steel-Clad

30656 United Textile Distribution
350 Shipwash Dr
Garner, NC 27529-6890

919-779-4151
Fax: 919-779-6065 800-262-7624
www.unitedtextiledistribution.com
Manufacturer and exporter of disposable food service wipers including cloth and paper; also, towels and absorbent traffic mats; importer of towels
Owner: Rick EtheridgeGradin
ricketheridge@aol.com
Sales Representatives: Dave Shelton
Estimated Sales: $1-5 Million
Number Employees: 5-9
Number of Brands: 20
Number of Products: 4000
Brands:
Absorbant Rugs & Pads
Envirotex
Industrial Traffic Mats

30657 Unitherm Food System
502 Industrial Rd
Bristow, OK 74010-9763

918-367-0197
Fax: 918-367-5440
unitherm@unithermfoodsystems.com
www.unithermfoodsystems.com
Manufactures a full range of stainless steel cooking, chilling, and pasteurizing systems, including spiral ovens, impingement ovens, continuous water cookers, vertical crusters, branders, and infra-red surface pasteurization, waterpasteurization and combination pasteurization systems, as well as a full range of clean room equipment, including hands-free sinks, automatic bootwashers and drains.

President: David Howard
unitherm@unithermfoodsystems.com
Marketing Director: Tom Van Doorn
Estimated Sales: Below $5 Million
Number Employees: 20-49

30658 Unitherm Food System
502 Industrial Rd
Bristow, OK 74010-9763

918-367-0197
Fax: 918-367-5440
www.unithermfoodsystems.com
Steamers & spiral ovens, roasters, smokehouses and
grilling systems, pasteurizing equipment and
chillers.
President: David Howard
unitherm@unithermfoodsystems.com
Number Employees: 20-49

30659 Unity Brands Group
319 W Town Pl
Suite 28
Saint Augustine, FL 32092-3103

904-940-8975
Fax: 866-878-9306 info@unitybrandsgroup.com
unitybrandsgroup.com
Marketing services
President: Praful Mehta
Marketing Executive: William Edwards
Estimated Sales: $1-2.5 Million
Number Employees: 1-10
Type of Packaging: Food Service

30660 Univar USA
2256 Junction Ave
San Jose, CA 95131-1216

408-435-8700
Fax: 408-435-1735 www.univar.com
Chemical compounding and manufacturing, coat-
ings, inks and adhesives, electronics and precision
cleaning, food and pharmaceutical, forest products,
mining, oil, gas and CPI, professional pest control,
waste management and watertreatment
General Manager: Jamie Hanks
President, Chief Executive Officer: Erik Fyrwald
Branch manager: Bob Crandall
Executive Vice President, General Counsel: Amy
Weaver
Manager: Sara Stewart
sara.stewart@univarusa.com
Number Employees: 50-99

30661 Universal Aqua Technologies
2660 Columbia St
Torrance, CA 90503

310-618-9700
Fax: 310-618-1384 800-777-6939
www.severntrentservices.com
CFO: Howard Halem
VP: Marwan Nesicolaci
Quality Control Manager: Mark Wright
Contact: Fernando Guerrero
fguerrero@severntrentservices.com
Estimated Sales: $10-20 Million
Number Employees: 100-249

30662 Universal Beverage Equipment
100 Leland Ct # B
Bensenville, IL 60106-1603

630-227-0250
Fax: 630-227-0253 800-627-0026
Owner: Ed Moriarty
ubeusa@aol.com
Engineering/Technical: Gino Notardonato
Purchasing Executive: Joy Claffey
Estimated Sales: $5-10 Million
Number Employees: 10-19

30663 Universal Coatings
8511 Tower Dr
Twinsburg, OH 44087-2088

330-963-6776
Fax: 330-963-6743
Manufacturer and applicator of electrostatic powder
paints, fluid bed, plastic dip, corrosion resistant and
F.D.A. approved coatings
Owner: John Palik
VP Sales: Ken Palik
japuniv@aol.com
VP Operations: John Palik
Estimated Sales: $20-50 Million
Number Employees: 10-19
Square Footage: 40000

30664 Universal Container Corporation
11805 State Road 54
Odessa, FL 33556-3469

727-376-0036
Fax: 727-372-1957 800-582-7477
Plastic drink containers
President: Kent Bissell
VP: Chip Williams
Estimated Sales: $2.5-5 Million
Number Employees: 18

30665 (HQ)Universal Die & Stampings
735 15th St
Prairie Du Sac, WI 53578-9618

608-643-2477
Fax: 608-643-2024 breunigb@unidie.com
www.unidie.com
Manufacturer and exporter of stainless steel con-
veyor belts for tab conversion systems: for food,
beer and beverage
Owner: Carol Baier
cbaier@unidie.com
Research & Development: Bryan Jaedike
Quality Control: Steve Heyn
Sales Director: Gene Everson
Plant Manager: Karl Anderson
Estimated Sales: $5-10 Million
Number Employees: 20-49
Square Footage: 80000

30666 Universal Dynamics Technologies
100-13700 International Place
Richmond, BC V6V 2X8
Canada

604-214-3456
Fax: 604-214-3457 888-912-7246
Manufacturer and exporter of software for automa-
tion process control equipment
Sales/Marketing Executive: Steve Crotty
Product Manager: Bill Gough

30667 Universal Folding Box
181 S 18th Street
East Orange, NJ 07018-3902

973-482-4300
Fax: 973-676-3628
Folding paper display boxes
President: Frank Pauza
General Manager: Steve Carretero
Estimated Sales: $20-30 Million
Number Employees: 100-250

30668 Universal Folding Box Company
555 13th Street
Hoboken, NJ 07030-6414

201-659-7373
Fax: 201-798-4126
Folding paperboard cartons
VP Manufacturing: Richard Berkey
Number Employees: 100-249
Square Footage: 520000

30669 Universal Handling Equipment
PO Box 3488, Station C
Hamilton, ON L8H 7L5
Canada

905-547-0161
Fax: 905-549-6922 877-843-1122
www.universalhandling.com
Waste disposal units and refuse compactors
President: David Gerard
CFO: James Hreljac
Director Sales/Marketing: Richard Kool
Estimated Sales: $20-50 Million
Number Employees: 10
Square Footage: 80000
Type of Packaging: Food Service

30670 Universal Impex Corporation
780 Fenmar Drive
Toronto, ON M9L 2T9
Canada

416-743-7778
info@universalimpexcorp.com
www.universalimpexcorp.com
Seasonings and spices, sugars, baking products, fla-
vors, fruit jams, condiments, sauces, marinades and
dips, sweeteners, drinks (sodas, nectars, energy
drink), coconut oil, coconut milk and plantain chips.
Operations Manager: Paul Bridgemohan
Estimated Sales: $5.7 Million
Number Employees: 15
Brands:
British Class

Cool Runnings
Mekong

30671 Universal Industries Inc
5800 Nordie Dr
Cedar Falls, IA 50613-6942

319-277-7501
Fax: 319-277-2318 800-553-4446
sales@universalindustries.com
www.universalindustries.com
Manufacturer and exporter of bucket elevators and
belt conveyors
President: Dean Bierschenk
Marketing: Drew McConnell
Sales: Mike Giaaratmnd
Operations: Carolyn Peterson
Purchasing: Gail Snyder
Estimated Sales: $9 Million
Number Employees: 50-99
Square Footage: 240000

30672 Universal Jet Industries
PO Box 70
Hialeah, FL 33011

305-887-4378
Fax: 305-887-4370
Manufacturer and exporter of air curtains
Chairman: L Bass
General Manager: B Warshaw
Number Employees: 12
Square Footage: 36000
Brands:
Uji

30673 Universal Labeling Systems Inc
3501 8th Ave S
St Petersburg, FL 33711-2201

727-327-2123
Fax: 727-323-4403 877-236-0266
sales@universal1.com www.ulsdistributors.com
A complete line of pressure sensitive labeling equip-
ment
President: L Douglas Hall
Director Business Development: Michael Bieda
deidre@walmart.com
CFO: Ivan Campbell
Estimated Sales: $5-10 Million
Number Employees: 20-49
Square Footage: 80000

30674 Universal Machine Co
645 Old Reading Pike
Pottstown, PA 19464-3733

610-323-1810
Fax: 610-323-9343 800-862-1810
Custom built machinery, general and CNC machin-
ing, drilling, boring, cutting, honing, welding, lathe
and mill work
President: Richard Francis
rfrancis@umc-oscar.com
Estimated Sales: $10-20 Million
Number Employees: 50-99

30675 Universal Marketing
1647 Pilgrim Ave
Bronx, NY 10461-4807

914-576-5383
Fax: 914-576-1711 800-225-3114
Wholesaler/distributor, importer and exporter of
commercial kitchen equipment including freezers,
refrigerators, coolers and fast food cooking equip-
ment; serving the food service market
President: James Deluca
VP: Henry Muench
Estimated Sales: Below $5 Million
Number Employees: 7
Square Footage: 12000

30676 Universal Overall
1060 W Van Buren St
Chicago, IL 60607-2988

312-226-3336
Fax: 312-226-1986 800-621-3344
email@universaloverall.com
www.universaloverall.com
Food handlers' shirts, butchers' frocks and beef lug-
gers
President: Sanford Eckerling
email@universaloverall.com
Estimated Sales: $10-20 Million
Number Employees: 100-249

Brands:
Stone-Cutter
Universal

30677 Universal Packaging Inc
1308 Upland Dr
Houston, TX 77043-4719
713-461-2610
Fax: 713-461-1459 800-324-2610
Manufacturer and exporter of vertical form/fill/seal machinery, conveyors, flexible packaging equipment, augers, coders and indexers
Owner: Patricia Wylie
R & D: Bill Huhn
Sales: Jim Hooper
Estimated Sales: Below $5 Million
Number Employees: 10-19
Brands:
Mark Ii
Mark Iii

30678 Universal Packaging Mchry Corp
965 Shadick Dr
Orange City, FL 32763-8904
386-775-2969
Fax: 386-774-4900 800-351-8263
www.universal-ultraspeed.com
Industrial bottling machinery soft drink filling valves
President: Elisha Bethany
Quality Control: Michael Purvis
Sales: Elihu Rivera
Purchasing/Shipping: Thomas Neff
Estimated Sales: $1-2 Million
Number Employees: 10-19

30679 Universal Paper Box
644 NW 44th St
Seattle, WA 98107-4431
206-782-7105
Fax: 206-782-3817 800-228-1045
www.paperboxco.com
Manufacturer and exporter of boxes including rigid, set-up and die-cut; also, PVC lids and bases
Owner: Greg Donald
paperbox@paperboxco.com
Estimated Sales: Below $5 Million
Number Employees: 10-19
Square Footage: 72000
Type of Packaging: Consumer, Food Service, Private Label

30680 Universal Plastics
75 Whiting Farms Rd
Holyoke, MA 01040-2831
413-592-4791
Fax: 413-592-6876 800-553-0120
info@universalplastics.com
www.universalplastics.com
Plastic bags
President: Jay Kumar
kumarj@universalplastics.com
Estimated Sales: $2.5-5 Million
Number Employees: 100-249

30681 Universal Sanitizers & Supplies
2491 Stock Creek Blvd
Rockford, TN 37853
865-573-7296
Fax: 865-573-7298 888-634-3196
info@universalsanitizers.com
Consulting services including sanitation testing and analysis, employee training and vendor audits; wholesaler/distributor of industrial cleaners and sanitizers, water treatment products and conveyor lubricant/santizer systems
President: Amy Rigo
VP: Emilia Rico
Contact: Emilia Rico
emilia.rico@universalsanitizers.com
Estimated Sales: $5-10 Million
Number Employees: 5-9
Square Footage: 16000

30682 Universal Sign Company and Manufacturing Company
PO Box 62032
Lafayette, LA 70596
337-234-1466
Fax: 337-234-2180 unisign@aol.com
www.unisignco.com
Neon and illuminated plastic signs
Owner: Dewey Boudreaux
Marketing Director: Michael Taylor

Estimated Sales: $1-3 Million
Number Employees: 10-19
Square Footage: 30000

30683 Universal Sign Company and Manufacturing Company
PO Box 62032
Lafayette, LA 70596
337-234-1466
Fax: 337-234-2180 unisign@aol.com
www.unisignco.com
Signs including neon, plastic and electric
Owner: Dewey Boudreaux
Marketing Director: Michael Taylor
Estimated Sales: $1-3 Million
Number Employees: 10-19
Square Footage: 30000

30684 Universal Stainless
14002 E 33rd Pl
Aurora, CO 80011
303-375-1511
Fax: 303-375-1626 800-223-8332
info@lpstorage.com
Stainless steel sinks, utility cabinets, counters, racks, tables and shelving
Manager: Robert Buehler
Contact: Robert Beuhler
robert.beuhler@leggett.com
Number Employees: 50-99
Square Footage: 80000
Parent Co: Leggett & Platt Storage Products Group
Brands:
Universal Stainless

30685 Universal Stainless & Alloy
121 Caldwell St
Titusville, PA 16354-2055
814-827-9723
Fax: 814-827-2766 800-295-1909
info@lpstorage.com www.univstainless.com
Stainless steel sinks, shelving, utility cabinets, counters, tables and racks
Manager: Robert Buehler
Manager: Skip Peak
s.peak@univstainless.com
Number Employees: 50-99
Square Footage: 60000
Parent Co: Leggett & Platt

30686 Universal Strapping
630 Corporate Way
Valley Cottage, NY 10989-2002
845-268-2500
Fax: 845-268-7999 800-872-1680
info@universalstrapping.com
www.universalstrapping.com
Manufacturer and sells a complete line of non-metallic and steel strapping. This includes everything from hand grade, all the way up to machine grade strapping, which runs on the most sophisticated strapping machinery availabletoday.
President: Joe Grodz
joe@universalstrapping.com
Number Employees: 1-4

30687 Universal Tag Inc
36 Hall Rd
PO Box 1518
Dudley, MA 01571-5964
508-949-2411
Fax: 508-943-0185 800-332-8247
www.universaltag.com
Printed labels and tags including pressure sensitive and nonpressure sensitive; also, printed specialties available
President: Armand Mandeville
Sales Director: Robert Meyers
Manager: Carol Poirier
carol@universaltag.com
VP Operations: Paul Mandeville
Estimated Sales: $3-5 Million
Number Employees: 20-49
Square Footage: 80000

30688 (HQ)University Products
517 Main St
Holyoke, MA 01040-5514
413-532-3372
Fax: 413-532-9281 800-628-9281
www.universityproducts.com
Pressure sensitive labels

President: John Magoon
Chairman: D Magoon
dlmagoon@universityproducts.com
CFO: Bruce Riggott
Assistant Marketing Manager: Linda McInerney
Advertising Sales Manager: John Dunphy
President, Chief Operating Officer: Scott Magoon
Estimated Sales: $20-50 Million
Number Employees: 50-99

30689 University-Brink
131 Morse Street
Foxboro, MA 02035-5220
617-926-4400
Fax: 617-924-7965
Electric, neon and plastic signs
Estimated Sales: $1-5 Million
Number Employees: 10

30690 Univex Corp
3 Old Rockingham Rd
Salem, NH 03079-2140
603-893-6191
Fax: 603-893-1249 800-258-6358
info@univexcorp.com www.univexcorp.com
Manufacturer and exporter of food preparation machines including ground beef fat analyzers, vertical, electric bench and floor model mixers, electric bench model vegetable peelers, slicers and shredders and gravity feed electric meatslicers
President: John Tsiakos
john@univexcorp.com
VP Marketing: Richard McIntosh
National Sales Manager: John Tsiakos
Estimated Sales: $10-20 Million
Number Employees: 50-99
Type of Packaging: Food Service
Brands:
Perfect Peeler

30691 Uniweb Inc
222 S Promenade Ave
Corona, CA 92879-1743
951-279-7999
Fax: 951-279-7989 800-486-4932
www.uniwebinc.com
Metal store fixtures and displays
CEO: Karl Weber
CEO: Karl F Weber
kweber@uniwebinc.com
Estimated Sales: $20-50 Million
Number Employees: 100-249
Square Footage: 45000

30692 Update International
5801 S Boyle Ave
Vernon, CA 90058-3926
323-585-0616
Fax: 323-585-4021 800-747-7124
stephen@update-international.com
www.update-international.com
Manufacturer, importer and exporter of stainless steel kitchenware and utensils; also, air pots and steam table pans
President: Alec Chung
alec@update-international.com
Controller: Herman Yu
VP: Andrew Lazar
Marketing: Charles Arjavac
Vice President of Sales and Marketing: Steven Linzy
Operations: Jose Aleman
Estimated Sales: $5-10 Million
Number Employees: 50-99
Square Footage: 320000

30693 Upham & Walsh Lumber
2155 Stonington Ave # 209
Hoffman Estates, IL 60169-2058
847-519-1010
Fax: 847-519-3434
Manufacturer and importer of wooden, steel and plastic pallets; also, skids and watermelon and onion bins
Partner: Chris Hayden
c_hayden@uphamwalshlumber.com
Office Manager: Lauren Kowalski
Sales Manager: Sean Hayden
Estimated Sales: $7 Million
Number Employees: 1-4

30694 Upper Limits EngineeringCompany
5662 La Ribera Street
Suite F
Livermore, CA 94550-2528
510-538-8500
Fax: 510-538-8533 888-700-0717
orenm@aol.com
Net weight filler, bag filler sealer
Estimated Sales: $5-10 Million
Number Employees: 10-19

30695 Upright
10715 Kahlmeyer Dr
St Louis, MO 63132-1621
314-426-4347
Fax: 314-426-0145 800-248-7007
www.wyksorbents.com
Manufacturer and exporter of sorbents, anti-slip compounds and spill response products
President: James Dunn
Sales Manager: James Meador
Production: James Callaham
Estimated Sales: $1-3 Million
Number Employees: 10-19
Square Footage: 80000
Brands:
Upright
Wyk

30696 Urania Engineering Co Inc
198 S Poplar St
Hazleton, PA 18201-7198
570-455-7531
Fax: 570-455-0776 800-533-1985
info@uraniaeng.com
www.medicalheatsealing.com
Pouch handling system, heat sealer
President/CEO: Joe Zoba
CEO: Andrew Postupack
apostupack@uraniaengineer.com
Estimated Sales: $5-10 Million
Number Employees: 20-49

30697 Urnex Brands Inc
700 Executive Blvd
Elmsford, NY 10523-1208
914-345-6080
Fax: 914-963-2145 800-222-2826
info@urnex.com www.urnex.com
Manufacturer and exporter of coffee and tea equipment cleaning compounds, urn brushes, lemon covers, lemon wedge bags and shellfish steamer bags
President: Kofi Amoako
kofi.amoako@urnex.com
R & D: Jason Dick
Quality Control: Bill Colter
Sales Manager: Joshua Dick
General Manager: Jay Lazarin
Assist. Mngr: Frankie Dominiquez
Estimated Sales: Less Than $500,000
Number Employees: 1-4
Square Footage: 30000
Brands:
Urnex

30698 Urschel Laboratories
2503 Calumet Avenue
Valparaiso, IN 46384-2200
219-464-4811
Fax: 219-462-3879 info@urschel.com
www.urschel.com
Manufacturer and supplier of high capacity food cutting equipment
President: Robert Urschel
CFO: Dan Marchetti
VP Sales: Tim O'Brien
Contact: Jen Abatie
jabatie@urschel.com
Regional Manager: Alan Major
Plant Manager: Dave Whitenack
Number Employees: 250-499
Square Footage: 500000
Type of Packaging: Food Service
Brands:
Comitrol
Urschalloy
Urschel

30699 Ursini Plastics
RR 2 High Falls Road
Bracebridge, ON P1L 1W9
Canada
705-646-2701

Swizzle sticks
Owner: John Ursini
Number Employees: 1-4

30700 Us Bottlers Machinery Co Inc
11911 Steele Creek Rd
Charlotte, NC 28273-3773
704-588-4750
Fax: 704-588-3808 sales@usbottlers.com
www.usbottlers.com
Manufacturer and exporter of bottling machinery including liquid filling, bottle rinsing, container cleaning and capping equipment
President: Thomas Risser
julie.kimbrell@usbottlers.com
Sales: Julie Kimbrell
Estimated Sales: $10-20 Million
Number Employees: 50-99

30701 Us Flag & Signal
802 Fifth St
Portsmouth, VA 23704-6762
757-497-8947
Fax: 757-497-1819 flagmaker@flagmaker.com
www.flagmaker.com
Flags, pennants and banners
Owner: Dory Wilgus
Number Employees: 20-49

30702 Us Rubber
238 N 9th St # 1
Brooklyn, NY 11211-2160
718-782-7888
Fax: 718-782-8788
Manufacturer and exporter of food hoses, tubing and conveyor belts
Owner: Ken Auster
kauster@usrubbersupply.com
Estimated Sales: $10-20 Million
Number Employees: 20-49

30703 Useco/Epco Products
P.O.Box 20428
Murfreesboro, TN 37129-0428
615-893-8432
Fax: 615-890-3196 800-251-1429
info@useco.com www.useco.com
Number Employees: 10-19
Parent Co: Standex International

30704 Utah PaperBox Company
920 South 700 West
Salt Lake City, UT 84104
801-363-0093
Fax: 801-363-9212 www.upbslc.com
Folding carton, rigid box and litho lam packaging.
President: Steve Keyser
Vice President: Teri Jensen
Sales Service: Tom Harrison
Human Resource Manager: Ben Misik
Controller: Richard Severson
Estimated Sales: $20-50 Million
Number Employees: 200-500
Type of Packaging: Food Service

30705 (HQ)Utica Cutlery Co
820 Noyes St
PO Box 10527
Utica, NY 13502-5053
315-733-4663
Fax: 315-733-6602 800-879-2526
info@uticacutlery.com www.walcostainless.com
Manufacturers of pocket knives and importers of stainless steel cutlery
President: David Allen
davidallen@uticacutlery.com
CFO: Jess Gouger
VP (Walco): Kathleen Allen
International Sales Manager: Dave Meislin
Estimated Sales: $10-20 Million
Number Employees: 100-249

30706 Utility Refrigerator Company
7355 E Slauson Avenue
Los Angeles, CA 90040-3626
323-267-0700
Fax: 323-728-2318 800-884-5233
www.utilityrefrigerator.com
Manufacturer and exporter of commercial cooking equipment, refrigerators and freezers
Customer Service: Larry Gomez
Customer Service: Mark Parra
Customer Service: Martha Gonzalez
General Manager: Mark Champaigne

Estimated Sales: $.5-1 million
Number Employees: 160
Square Footage: 800000
Parent Co: Stery Manufacturing Company
Brands:
Dynasty
Jade Range
Utility

30707 V C 999 Packaging Systems
419 E 11th Ave
Kansas City, MO 64116-4162
816-472-8999
Fax: 816-472-1999 800-728-2999
Sales.US@VC999.com
www.shrinkbagpackaging.com
Vacuum packaging machines, vacuum chamber machines, shrink systems, dryers, vacuum skin pack machines, automatic rollstock machines, preformed tray sealing machines, packaging accessories, packaging material and equipment related topackaging
Owner: Silvio Weder
silvio.weder@vc999.com
Number Employees: 20-49

30708 V C 999 Packaging Systems
419 E 11th Ave
Kansas City, MO 64116-4162
816-472-8999
Fax: 816-472-1999 800-728-2999
www.shrinkbagpackaging.com
Manufacturer and supplier of packaging equipment, materials and supplies such as trays, bags/pouches, containers and film.
President: Silvio Weder
silvio.weder@vc999.com
Number Employees: 20-49

30709 V R Food Equipment Inc
5801 County Rd 41
P.O. Box 25428
Farmington, NY 14425-9998
315-531-8133
Fax: 315-531-8134 800-929-9367
info@vrfoodequipment.com
www.vrfoodequipment.com
Processing and packaging equipment for packaging equipment; fruit, vegetable, aseptic processes.
President: Steven Von Rhedey
steve@vrfoodequipment.com
Controller: Fran Seager
Marketing & Sales Manager: Matthew Moroz
Sales Manager: Steve Casey
Shipping & Receiving Manager: Peter Von Rhedey
Warehouse & Shipping Specialist: Robert Novakowski
Year Founded: 1986
Estimated Sales: $1-2.5 Million
Number Employees: 5-9

30710 V&R Metal Enterprises
272 39th St
Brooklyn, NY 11232-2820
718-768-8142
Fax: 718-768-0921
Lighting fixtures and metal fabrications including pizza pans
Owner: Hon Ng
Estimated Sales: $1-3,000,000
Number Employees: 1-4
Square Footage: 3000

30711 V-Ram Solids
620 S Broadway Ave
PO Box 289
Albert Lea, MN 56007-4526
507-373-3996
Fax: 507-373-5937 888-373-3996
sales@vram.com
Manufacturer, importer and exporter of solids handling pumps for waste/rendering
President: David A Olson
Sales Director: Jeff Hall
Purchasing Manager: Rose Modderman
Estimated Sales: $3-5 Million
Number Employees: 10-19
Brands:
V-Ram

30712 V-Ram Solids
620 S Broadway Ave
Albert Lea, MN 56007-4526
507-373-3996
Fax: 507-373-5937 888-373-3996
sales@vram.com
Pumps designed for the meat industry.
Number Employees: 10-19
Parent Co: Olson Manufacturing Company

30713 VC Menus
P.O.Box 71
Eastland, TX 76448-0071
254-629-2626
Fax: 254-629-1134 800-826-3687
menusales@vcmenus.com www.vcmenus.com
Manufacturer and exporter of menus and covers
President: Cary Meeks
Secretary and Treasurer: Donald Eaves
Corporate Sales/Marketing: Trent Smith
Estimated Sales: $5-10 Million
Number Employees: 20-49
Brands:
  Euro-Menu
  Poly-Menu

30714 VCF Films Inc
1100 Sutton St
Howell, MI 48843-1799
517-546-2300
Fax: 517-546-2984 800-843-4141
contactus@vcffilm.com www.vcffilms.com
Manufacturer and marketer of plastic flexible packaging materials to industrial manufacturers, packagers, distributors, and retailers in North America and internationally
Owner: Reva Kamins
rkamins@vcffilms.com
Estimated Sales: $5-10 Million
Number Employees: 20-49

30715 VCG Uniform
5050 Weat Irving Park Road
Chicago, IL 60641
773-545-3676
Fax: 773-545-0876 800-447-6502
info@vcguniform.com www.vcguniform.com
In-stock and custom uniforms
CEO: Vince Gerage
Estimated Sales: $1-2.5 Million
Number Employees: 10-19
Parent Co: VCG
Other Locations:
  Carlson-Murray
  Chicago IL

30716 VICAM
34 Maple St
Milford, MA 01757-3604
617-926-7045
Fax: 617-923-8055 800-338-4381
vicam@vicam.com www.vicam.com
Mycotoxin testing equipment
President: Hike Hutchens
eejmike__hutchens@waters.com
Estimated Sales: $2.5-5 Million
Number Employees: 1000-4999
Type of Packaging: Bulk

30717 VIFAN Canada
1 Rue Vifan
Lanoraie, QC J0K 1E0
Canada
514-640-1599
Fax: 514-640-1577 800-557-0192
www.vifan.com
Packaging products for the food industry
VP, Sales: Ezra Bowen
Estimated Sales: $185 Million
Number Employees: 245
Number of Brands: 78
Number of Products: 78
Square Footage: 130000
Parent Co: Vibac S.p.A.
Type of Packaging: Food Service
Brands:
  Vifan Bt
  Vifan Cl/Cls
  Vifan Cz

30718 VINITECH
1611 N Kent St
Suite 903
Arlington, VA 22209
703-522-5000
Fax: 703-522-5005 888-522-5001
usa@promosalons.com
Viticulture, viniculture, bottling equipment
Owner: Philippe Bazin
Number Employees: 1-4

30719 VIP Real Estate LTD
3945 S Archer Ave
Chicago, IL 60632-1157
773-376-5000
Fax: 773-376-5091 www.viprealestateltd.com
Manufacturer and exporter of folding boxes, printed folding cartons, point of purchase displays and polylined, freezer-coated boxes for frozen foods. Items manufactured to order
Owner: Sammy Cruz
sammy@viprealestateltd.com
VP: Ray Maza
Marketing: James Coen
Estimated Sales: $5-10 Million
Number Employees: 10-19
Square Footage: 212000
Type of Packaging: Consumer, Food Service, Private Label

30720 (HQ)VMC Signs
102 E Mockingbird Ln
Victoria, TX 77904-2046
361-575-0548
Fax: 361-575-8464 vmcsigns@txcr.net
www.2vmcsigns.com
Interior and exterior neon signs and menus; also, water filtration and air filtration systems
Owner: Tom Willis
tom@vmcsigns.com
General Manager: Aibie McLeroy
Estimated Sales: $1-2.5 Million
Number Employees: 10-19
Square Footage: 100000
Other Locations:
  VMC Signs
  Victoria TX
Brands:
  Vmc-Nsa

30721 VPC Gordon Sign
2930 W 9th Ave
Denver, CO 80204-3713
303-629-6121
Fax: 303-629-1024 sales@gordonsign.com
www.gordonsign.com
Electrical advertising displays, signs and menu boards
President: James Skagen
CFO: Lee Prevost
lprevost@gordonsign.com
Director Sales/Marketing: Harry Grass
Estimated Sales: $10-20 Million
Number Employees: 50-99
Square Footage: 200000
Parent Co: C.G. Industries

30722 VPI
P.O.Box 138
Sheboygan Falls, WI 53085-0138
920-467-6422
Fax: 920-467-2692 vpi@vpicorp.com
www.spartech.com
Plastic film and sheet
President: P Gregory Mickelson
Senior Vice President-Human Resources: Robert Lorah
Estimated Sales: $10-20 Million
Number Employees: 100-249

30723 VPI Manufacturing
11814 S. Election Rd
Ste 200
Draper, UT 84020
801-495-2310
Fax: 866-307-0033 www.vpimanufacturing.com
Manufacturer and exporter of heat shrinkable polyethylene cook-in bags for meat, poultry, etc
President: Aron Perlman
VP: Hessa Tary
Estimated Sales: $4114713
Number Employees: 20-49

30724 (HQ)VT Industries Inc
1000 Industrial Park
P.O. Box 490
Holstein, IA 51025-7730
712-368-4381
Fax: 712-368-4111 800-827-1615
www.vtindustries.com
Manufacturer and exporter of post-formed laminated and solid surface countertops; also, laminated multi-use components
President/Chief Executive Officer: Douglas Clausen
douglas.clausen@vtindustries.com
Chief Financial Officer: Randy Gerritsen
Vice President: Elizabeth Hansch
Director, Information Technology: Teri Luebeck
Vice President, Marketing: Trisha Schmidt
Vice President, Sales & Marketing: John Bowling
Vice President, Operations: Bruce Campbell
Plant Manager: Gary Henry
Estimated Sales: $32 Million
Number Employees: 250-499
Square Footage: 300000
Brands:
  Casemate
  Curvflo
  Durallure

30725 VT Kidron
911 W 5th St
P.O.Box 880
Washington, NC 27889-4205
252-946-6521
Fax: 330-857-8451 800-763-0700
ksales@kidron.com www.kidron.com
Manufacturer and exporter of refrigerated truck bodies and trailers
President: Mike Tucker
Executive VP: John Sommer
Estimated Sales: $5-10 Million
Number Employees: 5-9
Parent Co: TTI
Type of Packaging: Food Service
Brands:
  Glacieruan
  Hackney Ultimate
  Polauan
  Ultra

30726 VWR Scientific
3745 Bayshore Blvd
Brisbane, CA 94005
415-468-7150
Fax: 415-468-1105 800-932-5000
solutions@vwr.com www.vwr.com
Distributors of scientific equipment, supplies, chemicals and furniture
President: Walter Zywottek
VP: Arne Brandon
Contact: Sandy Antalis
sandy.antalis@vwr.com
Number Employees: 250-499

30727 Vac Air Inc
5254 N 124th St
Milwaukee, WI 53225-2902
414-466-1852
Fax: 414-353-5289 www.vac-airinc.com
Cutting and boning devices, vacuum systems, slaughtering equipment, dehairing machines and equipment, hock cutters
President: Chuck Air
cair@vac-air.com
CFO: Mary Baertlein
Quality Control: Lee Baertlein
Estimated Sales: $1-2.5 Million
Number Employees: 5-9
Brands:
  Vac Airr

30728 Vac-U-Max
69 William St
Belleville, NJ 07109-3040
973-759-4600
Fax: 973-759-6449 800-822-8629
info@vac-u-max.com www.vac-u-max.com
Manufacturer, importer and exporter of pneumatic conveying systems and ingredient storage systems; also, handling and batching systems
President: Stevens Pendelton
CEO: H Kadel
VP: Doan Pendleton
IT: Stevens Pendleton
info@vac-u-max.com

Estimated Sales: $10-20 Million
Number Employees: 50-99
Square Footage: 200000
Brands:
  Vac-U-Max

30729 Vacuform Inc.
500 Courtney Road
PO Box 117
Sebring, OH 44672
330-938-9674
Fax: 330-938-9676 info@vacuforminc.com
www.vacuforminc.com
Manufacturer and importer of interior and exterior
signs, menus and image products including point of
purchase displays
President: Kenneth Galloway
CEO: Dennis Kaufman
Contact: Catherine Hubbs
c_hubbs@vacuforminc.com
Estimated Sales: $10-20 Million
Number Employees: 100-249
Square Footage: 400000
Type of Packaging: Food Service

30730 Vacumet Corp
20 Edison Dr
Wayne, NJ 07470-4713
973-628-1067
Fax: 973-628-0491 bfoley@vacumet.com
Manufacturer and exporter of metallized and holo-
graphic films and papers; also microwave susceptor
and barrier films for flexible packaging, label stock
available.
President: Robert Korowicki
Estimated Sales: G
Number Employees: 10-19
Parent Co: Scholle Corporation
Brands:
  Barrier-Met

30731 Vacumet Corporation
7929 Troon Cir
Austell, GA 30168-7759
404-432-6300
Fax: 404-505-8984 800-776-0865
Plain and metallized flexible packaging films and
microwaveable interactive packaging
President: Raymond Woody
Manager: Steve Eulieno
Executive VP: Andy Terakawa
VP Staff/Marketing: Dave McKae
Contact: Anthony Threat
athreat@gadoe.org
Plant Manager: Steve Euliano
Estimated Sales: $10-20 Million
Number Employees: 20-49
Square Footage: 82000
Parent Co: Marubeni America Corporation
Brands:
  Himac
  Himet

30732 Vacuum Barrier Corp
4 Barten Ln
Woburn, MA 01801-5601
781-933-3570
Fax: 781-932-9428 sales@vacuumbarrier.com
www.vacuumbarrier.com
Manufacturer, importer and exporter of cryogenic
pipe systems including liquid nitrogen injection
equipment for pressurizing hot filled beverages,
food, etc
President: Bart Limpens
bart@vbseurope.com
CFO: Leonard Gardner
Vice President: David Gorham
Quality Control and R&d: David Tucker
VP Sales: Edward Hanlon Jr
Purchasing Manager: Douglas Vanaruem
Estimated Sales: $5-10 Million
Number Employees: 20-49
Square Footage: 84000
Brands:
  Linerter
  Linjector
  Semiflex

30733 Vacuum Depositing Inc
1294 Old Fern Valley Rd
Louisville, KY 40219-1903
502-969-4227
Fax: 502-969-3378 sales@vdi-llc.com
www.vdi-llc.com

Sputter and vapor metallized film for solar control,
microwave and anti-static products
President: David Bryant
dbryant@vdi-llc.com
Sales Manager: Teeny Lee
Estimated Sales: $5-10 Million
Number Employees: 20-49
Square Footage: 140000

30734 Vaisala Inc
10 Gill St # D
Woburn, MA 01801-1721
781-933-4500
Fax: 781-933-8029 888-824-7252
www.vaisala.com
Supplier of humidity measurement instrumentation
for process and environmental monitoring. In addition to relative humidity and dewpoint, offers innovative measurement solutions for carbon dioxide,
ammonia, and barometric pressure.Global organization that is ISO9002 certified and committed to
excellence in all facets of the business
CEO: Steve Chansky
Marketing Director: Elizabeth Mann
Sales Director: Gerry Ducharme
Estimated Sales: $20-30 Million
Number Employees: 50-99

30735 Val-Pak Direct Market Systems
8605 Largo Lakes Dr
Largo, FL 33773-4912
727-393-1270
Fax: 727-399-3061 pat_fridley@coxtarget.com
www.valpak.com
Supplier and exporter of coupons
President: Joe Bourdow
Contact: Juliane Abudi
juliane_abudi@valpak.com
Number Employees: 1,000-4,999
Parent Co: Cox Industries
Type of Packaging: Consumer, Bulk

30736 Valad Electric Heating Corporation
PO Box 577
160 Wildey Street
Tarrytown, NY 10591
914-631-4927
Fax: 914-631-4395 info@valadelectric.com
www.valadelectric.com
Manufacturer and exporter of food warming ovens,
hot plates and food warming cabinets
President: Dante Cecchini
VP: Arthur Cecchini
Sales: Mike Sona
Estimated Sales: Below $5 Million
Number Employees: 10-19
Square Footage: 70000
Type of Packaging: Consumer, Food Service

30737 Valco Melton
411 Circle Freeway Dr
West Chester, OH 45246-1213
513-874-6550
Fax: 513-874-3612 sales@valcocincinnatiinc.com
www.valcomelton.com
Manufacturer and exporter of hot melt and cold glue
dispensers
President: Karla Bridges
karla.bridges@valcomelton.com
CFO: Scott Soutar
CEO: Gregory Amend
Purchase: Jim Epp
Sales Manager: Paul Chambers
Estimated Sales: $5-10 Million
Number Employees: 100-249
Square Footage: 200000

30738 Valeo
555 taxter Road
Suite 210
Elmsford, Ny 10523
800-634-2704
Fax: 800-831-9642 800-634-2704
www.valeoinc.com
Manufacturer and exporter of safety accessories in-
cluding back support belts, wrist supports, knee sup-
ports, elbow support, and material handling gloves
President: Lisa Yewer
Estimated Sales: $5-10 Million
Number Employees: 20-49
Square Footage: 240000

30739 Valesco Trading
1 Terminal Road
Lyndhurst, NJ 07071
201-729-1414
Fax: 201-729-1515 aos@valescofoods.com
www.valescofoods.com
Mediterranean olives, sun dried tomatoes, dried figs
and apricots
President: Ali Sozer
Estimated Sales: $3.6 Million
Number Employees: 12
Type of Packaging: Food Service

30740 Valley City Sign Co
5009 West River Dr NE
Comstock Park, MI 49321-8961
616-784-5711
Fax: 616-784-8280 www.valleycitysign.com
Plastic and illuminated signs
Owner: Kim Finley
CEO: Judsor Kovalak Jr
CFO: Sam Kovalak
Sales Representative: Jack Vos
Sales Representative: Jean Hughes
kim.finley@xerox.com
Sales Representative: Jeff Surman
Estimated Sales: $5-10 Million
Number Employees: 50-99
Square Footage: 150000

30741 Valley Container Corporation
858 Kingsland Avenue
Saint Louis, MO 63130-3112
314-652-8050
Fax: 314-652-2719
Corrugated boxes
General Manager: John Clark Sr
Estimated Sales: $5-10 Million
Number Employees: 20-49

30742 (HQ)Valley Container Inc
850 Union Ave
Bridgeport, CT 06607-1137
203-368-6546
Fax: 203-367-5266 flutedpartition@aol.com
www.valleycontainer.com
Manufacturer and exporter of corrugated shipping
containers
President: Arthur Vietze Jr
CEO: Rudy Niederneier
rudy.niederneier@valleycontainer.com
VP Sales: Richard Jackson
Estimated Sales: $20-50 Million
Number Employees: 50-99

30743 Valley Craft Inc
2001 S Highway 61
Lake City, MN 55041-9557
651-345-3386
Fax: 651-345-3606 800-328-1480
customer@valleycraft.com www.valleycraft.com
Manufacturer and exporter of hand and delivery
trucks, trailers and forklift attachments, and storage
equipment, custom-designed manufacturing and pro-
duction equipment.
Owner: Dennis Campbell
Manager: Roger Goff
R&D: Josh Rodewald
Marketing: Daria Dalager
Sales: Dave Minck
Production: Tom Balow
tombalow@valleycraft.com
Plant Manager: Roger Goff
Estimated Sales: $10-20,000,000
Number Employees: 1-4
Number of Brands: 6
Number of Products: 300+
Square Footage: 332000
Parent Co: Liberty Diversified International
Type of Packaging: Consumer, Private Label, Bulk
Brands:
  Dura-Lite
  Proline
  Viking

30744 Valley Fixtures
171 Coney Island Drive
Sparks, NV 89431-6317
775-331-1050
Manufacturer and exporter of cabinet fixtures for
bars, restaurants, casinos, hotels and stores
Sales Manager: Dillon Moore

Estimated Sales: $10-20 Million
Number Employees: 100-249
Square Footage: 100000

30745 Valley Lea LaboratoriesInc
4609 Grape Rd # D4
D4
Mishawaka, IN 46545-8259

574-272-8484
Fax: 574-273-0370 800-822-1283

Laboratory offering quality assurance and microbiological testing for food, dairy and water
Owner: Bob Coffee
Number Employees: 5-9

30746 Valley Packaging SupplyCo
3181 Commodity Ln
Green Bay, WI 54304-5671

920-336-9012
Fax: 920-336-3935
general@valleypackagingsupply.com
www.valleypackagingsupply.com

Manufacturer and exporter of pouches and bags for food and industry
President: Lance Czachor
lance@valleypackagingsupply.com
Treasurer: Richard Czachor
Sales Director: Lance Czachor
Operations Manager: Ty Parsons
Purchasing Manager: Jean Rottier
Estimated Sales: $5 Million
Number Employees: 100-249
Square Footage: 272000
Type of Packaging: Bulk
Brands:
Valley

30747 Valmont Composite Structures
19845 US Highway 76
Newberry, SC 29108-8407

803-276-5504
Fax: 803-276-8940 800-800-9008
www.skp-cs.com

Fiberglass lighting poles including breakaway, ornamental and transmission
Director Sales/Marketing: Bill Griffin
HR Executive: Alice Moore
amoore@skp-cs.com
Operations-Production: Ray Jeffords
Plant Manager: Scott Burriss
Estimated Sales: $1-5 Million
Number Employees: 250-499
Parent Co: K 2

30748 Valspar Corp
P.O. Box 1461
Minneapolis, MN 55440-1461

612-851-7000
valspar.com

Provides coatings and metal decorating inks for food cans, beverage cans, aerosol, paint cans and paper, film and foil markets.
Chief Executive Officer: Gary Hendrickson
gary.h@valspar.com
Executive Vice President: Steven Erdahl
VP, Global Consumer Sales & Marketing: Steven Person
Year Founded: 1866
Estimated Sales: $4.19 Billion
Number Employees: 11,000
Parent Co: Sherwin-Williams Co.

30749 Valspar Paint
101 Prospect Ave
Cleveland, OH 44115

800-845-9061
877-825-7727
www.valsparpaint.com

Industrial and commercial floor coatings in solvent and water based epoxies and urethanes.
Chief Executive Officer: Gary Hendrickson
Executive Vice President: Steven Erdahl
Product Manager: Suzette Bojarski
sbojarski@valspar.com
Square Footage: 328000
Parent Co: Sherwin-Williams Co.

30750 Valu Guide & Engineering
1a Morgan
Irvine, CA 92618-1917

949-472-7336
Fax: 949-837-3481 800-825-8364
www.firstteam.com

Packaging equipment components

President: Joe Duenas
Number Employees: 100

30751 Valvinox
650 1st Rue
Iberville, QC J2X 3B8
Canada

450-346-1981
Fax: 450-346-1067 www.valvinox.it

Manufacturer and exporter of fittings, pumps, stainless steel valves, tubing and pipe
Administrator: Chantal Allard
Number Employees: 10,000
Parent Co: SQRM
Type of Packaging: Bulk

30752 Van Air Systems
2950 Mechanic St
Lake City, PA 16423-2095

814-774-2631
Fax: 814-774-0778 800-840-9906
www.vanairsystems.com

Manufacturer and exporter of compressed air dryers, condensation drain valves, after coolers, filters, oil/water separators, etc.; importer of filters
President: Mark Sunseri
msunseri@vanairinc.com
CEO: J Currie
CFO: Mark Sunseri
VP: Jeff Mace
Sales: W J Ulrich
Estimated Sales: $20 Million
Number Employees: 20-49
Number of Brands: 8
Square Footage: 65000
Brands:
Dry-O-Lite

30753 Van Blarcom Closures Inc
156 Sandford St
Brooklyn, NY 11205-3985

718-855-3810
Fax: 718-935-9855 www.vbcpkg.com

Manufacturer and exporter of metal and plastic caps
Chairman of the Board: Vincent Scuderi Jr
VP Sales/Marketing: John Scuderi
Estimated Sales: $20-50 Million
Number Employees: 500-999

30754 Van Dam Machine Corp
81b Walsh Dr
Parsippany, NJ 07054-5708

973-257-7050
Fax: 973-257-7398 info@vandammachine.com
www.vandamusa.com

Printer
President: Andy Stobb
CFO: Kim Filippone
kfilippone@vandamusa.com
Estimated Sales: $5-10 Million
Number Employees: 10-19

30755 Van Der Graaf Corporation
1481 Trae Lane
Lithia Springs, GA 30122

770-819-6650
Fax: 770-819-6675 www.vandergraaf.com

Drum motors for conveyor belts.
Contact: Jason Kanaris
jkanaris@vandergraaf.com

30756 Van Dereems Mfg Co
40 Schoon Ave
Hawthorne, NJ 07506-1408

973-427-2355
Fax: 973-427-2356

Wooden store fixtures including skids, boxes and laminated workbenches
President: John Vandereems
Estimated Sales: Below $5 Million
Number Employees: 5-9
Square Footage: 20000

30757 Van Leer Flexibles
9505 Bamboo Rd
Houston, TX 77041

713-462-6111
Fax: 713-690-2746 800-825-3766
info@valeron.com www.valeron.com

High density polyethylene film for packaging
Contact: Kevin Clothier
kevin_clothier@valic.com
Estimated Sales: $25-50 Million
Number Employees: 250-499

30758 Van Lock Co
6834 Center St
Cincinnati, OH 45244-3404

513-561-9692
Fax: 513-561-0314 800-878-1826
vanlock@excite.com www.vanlock.com

Locks, padlocks, cam locks and alarm systems
Owner: James S Padjen
jpadjen@vanlock.com
Owner: Chris Padjen
CFO: John Sali
Estimated Sales: $1-2.5 Million
Number Employees: 20-49

30759 Van Nuys Awning Co
5661 Sepulveda Blvd
Van Nuys, CA 91411-2916

818-345-4926
Fax: 818-782-6837 awnings@vannuysawning.com
www.vannuysawning.com

Commercial awnings
President: James Powell
Manager: Roy Megahan
vna5661@earthlink.net
Estimated Sales: $5-10 Million
Number Employees: 20-49

30760 Van Pak Corporation
1188 Walters Way Lane
Saint Louis, MO 63132-2200

314-432-2224
Fax: 314-432-2227 800-811-7710

All types of conveyors, palletizers/depalletizers
President: Jon Vaninger
Estimated Sales: $5-10 Million
Number Employees: 10

30761 Van der Pol Muller International
4801 Harbor Pointe Dr.
Suite 1305
North Myrtle Beach, SC 29582

803-691-8941
Fax: 803-240-1384
benmuller@mullerinternational.com
www.mullerinternational.com

Engineering and consulting company for the food industry, specializing in the baking industry
President: Ben Muller
Estimated Sales: Below $5 Million
Number Employees: 2

30762 VanSan Corporation
16735 E Johnson Dr
City of Industry, CA 91745-2469

626-961-7211
Fax: 626-369-9510

President: Mark E Vanlandingham
Estimated Sales: $1-5 Million
Number Employees: 10-19

30763 Vance Metal FabricatorsInc
251 Gambee Rd
Geneva, NY 14456-1025

315-789-5626
Fax: 315-789-1848 800-234-6752
sales@vancemetal.com www.vancemetal.com

Stainless, structural and aluminum steel tanks
President: Joseph Hennessy
CEO: Joe Hennessy
jhennessy@vancemetal.com
Vice President of Sales: Chris Jennings
Quality and Safety Manager: Brian Mott
Business Development Specialist-Sales: Wade Woodworth
Operations Manager: Len Visco
Purchasing Associate: Laura Gute
Estimated Sales: $10-25 Million
Number Employees: 50-99
Square Footage: 70000

30764 Vanco Products Company
1269 Massachusetts Avenue
Dorchester, MA 2125

617-265-3400

Bakery supplies
President: Chris Anton
Production Manager: Carl Hogenda
Estimated Sales: $5-10 Million
Number Employees: 10-19
Square Footage: 45000
Parent Co: Johnson's Food Products Corporation
Type of Packaging: Consumer

30765 Vancouver Manufacturing
765 S 32nd Street
Washougal, WA 98671-2519
360-835-8519
Fax: 360-835-8521
Wooden pallets
Owner: Al Ely
General Manager: Rob Burnett
Estimated Sales: $20-50 Million
Number Employees: 20-49

30766 Vande Berg SCALES/Vbs Inc
770 7th St NW
Sioux Center, IA 51250-1918
712-722-1181
Fax: 712-722-0900 info@vbssys.com
www.vbssys.com
Conveyor scales, meat/produce sortation systems
Owner: Dave Vande Berg
vbs@mtcnet.net
Office Manager: Diane Vande Berg
Estimated Sales: $5 Million
Number Employees: 20-49
Brands:
Bicerba
Duran
Gse
Vande Berg Scales
Weigh-Tranix

30767 Vanguard Packaging Film
9970 Lakeview Ave
Shawnee Mission, KS 66219-2502
913-599-1111
Fax: 913-599-0096 800-772-1187
President: John Campbell
Estimated Sales: $1-3 Million
Number Employees: 5-9

30768 Vanguard Technology Inc
29495 Airport Rd
Eugene, OR 97402-9524
541-461-6020
Fax: 541-461-6023 800-624-4809
info@vanguardtechnologyinc.com
www.vanguardtechnologyinc.com
High-efficiency gas fired domestic hot water heaters,
gas fired booster water heaters
President: S Kujawa
vti1999@aol.com
Estimated Sales: $1 Million
Number Employees: 1-4
Square Footage: 20000
Type of Packaging: Food Service
Brands:
Firepower
Powermax
Powerpac

30769 Vanmark Equipment
300 Industrial Pkwy
Creston, IA 50801-8102
641-782-6575
Fax: 641-782-9209 800-523-6261
www.vanmarkequipment.com
Manufacturer of industrial food processing for a
wide range of produce products.
Manager: Tom Mathues
Sales: Tom Jones
Manager: Jason Davis
Operations: Rich Shafar
Estimated Sales: $5-10 Million
Number Employees: 20-49
Square Footage: 120000
Brands:
Vanmark

30770 Vanmark Equipment LLC
4252 S Eagleson Rd
Boise, ID 83705
208-362-5588
Fax: 208-362-3171 800-523-6261
sales@vanmarkequipment.com
www.vanmarkequipment.com
Manufacturer and exporter of food processing
equipment for produce including tension blades and
wedge, square and rectangular tension cutters
Owner: George Mendenhall
Estimated Sales: $2.5-5 Million
Number Employees: 10-19

30771 Vansco Products
2652 Lashbrook Avenue
South El Monte, CA 91733-1598
626-448-7611
Fax: 626-448-0221 www.vansco.com
Manufactures adhesive application systems, cold
glue, hot glue, hand and automatic and carton
sealing
President/CEO: Gregory Amend
CFO: Scott Soutar
Vice President: Fred Van Loben Sels
R & D: Eric Sueyoshi
Sales Manager: Richard Goennier
Contact: Grek Ameg
ameg@vansco.com
Plant Manager: Grek Ameg
Estimated Sales: Below $5 Million
Number Employees: 10-19
Square Footage: 32000

30772 Vantage Pak International
221 South St
New Britain, CT 06051-3650
860-832-8766
Fax: 860-832-8766 800-839-9030
Packaging equipment: high speed, multi-size tray
packer of cans and bottles, wrap around tray/case
packers, integrated tray, shrink wrapping systems
Estimated Sales: $5 Million
Number Employees: 20-49

30773 (HQ)Vantage Performance Materials
3938 Porett Dr
Gurnee, IL 60031-1244
847-244-3410
Fax: 847-249-6790 aronson@ppg.com
www.petroferm.com
Manufacturer and exporter of precipitated silica for
anticaking and carrier applications
President: Michael Horton
Vice President: Anup Jain
Vice President of Research and Developme: Charles
Kahle
Marketing Manager: Paul Brown
Manager: Steve Korzeniewski
steve.korzeniewski@polyonics.com
Vice President of Operations: John Richter
Vice President of Purchasing: Stephen Lampe
Estimated Sales: $20-50 Million
Number Employees: 100-249
Type of Packaging: Food Service, Bulk
Brands:
Flo-Gard

30774 Vantage Performance Materials
3938 Porett Dr
Gurnee, IL 60031-1244
847-244-3410
Fax: 847-249-6790 aronson@ppg.com
www.petroferm.com
Organic surfactants, defoamers, emulsifiers, sili-
cones and silicone emulsions
President: Michael Horton
Vice President: Anup Jain
Vice President of Research and Developme: Charles
Kahle
Manager: Steve Korzeniewski
steve.korzeniewski@polyonics.com
Vice President of Operations: John Richter
Vice President of Purchasing: Stephen Lampe
Estimated Sales: $50-100 Million
Number Employees: 100-249

30775 Vantage USA
4740 S Whipple St
Chicago, IL 60632
773-247-1086
Fax: 708-401-1565 www.VantageUSA.net
Organic/natural & commodity wholesaler consolida-
tor/supplier and logistics provider. Specializing in
natural and private label products planning &
development.
Owner: Dan Gash
dan@vantageusa.net
Type of Packaging: Food Service, Private Label,
Bulk
Brands:
Applegate Farms
Cargill
Colavita
Cucina Viva
Eberly
Excalibur
Excel
Gotham
Great Plains
Honeysuckle
Norbest
Prairie Grove
Reichert
Roma
Smart Choice
Taste It
Turano

30776 Vapor Power Intl LLC
551 S County Line Rd
Franklin Park, IL 60131-1013
630-694-5500
Fax: 630-694-2230 888-874-9020
info@vaporpower.com
Manufacturer and exporter of steam generators and
liquid phase heaters
President: Curt Diedrick
CEO: Bob Forslund
Sales Manager: B Corrigan
Number Employees: 20-49
Parent Co: Westinghouse Air Brake Company

30777 Varco Products
PO Box 915
Chardon, OH 44024-0915
216-481-6895
Fax: 216-481-6897
Fluorescent light fixtures and signs
President: Edward Vlack
VP: Norman Arnos
Number Employees: 8
Square Footage: 28000

30778 (HQ)Variant
7169 Shady Oak Road
Eden Prairie, MN 55344-3516
612-927-8611
Fax: 612-927-4624 info@variantinc.com
Manufacturer, importer and exporter of advertising
products
President: Jerry Gruggen
Operations: Jan Davis
Controller: Tom Fournelle
Plant Manager: Ted Fors
Square Footage: 30000
Other Locations:
Variant
Minneapolis MN

30779 Varick Enterprises
P.O.Box 84
Winchester, MA 01890-0184
781-729-9140
Fax: 781-729-9143 800-882-7425
sales@euromachines.com www.euromachines.com
Bar formers, bar take-off machines, batch kneaders,
batch spinners, belting, cooling tunnel, plastic, steel,
wire mesh, conveying, bars, hard candy, cookers,
cooking equipment, cooling equipment
Contact: Fred Hintlian
varick@euromachines.com
Estimated Sales: Below 1 Million
Number Employees: 3

30780 Variety Glass Inc
201 Foster Ave
Cambridge, OH 43725-1219
740-432-3643
Fax: 740-432-8693 www.mosserglass.com
Manufacturer and exporter of drug and laboratory
glassware
President: Thomas Mosser
VP: Tim Mosser
Estimated Sales: $2.5-5,000,000
Number Employees: 10-19

30781 Varimixer North America
14240 S Lakes Dr
Charlotte, NC 28273-6793
980-333-0032
Fax: 704-583-1703 800-221-1138
mixer@varimixer.com www.varimixer.com
Commercial mixers and food preparation equipment
President: Richard Aversa
Sales Manager: Gerald McGuffin
Operations: Charlie Strate
Plant Manager: Charlie Strate
Number Employees: 5-9
Square Footage: 400000
Parent Co: ENODIS
Type of Packaging: Food Service

30782 Varitronic Systems
6835 Winnetka Cir
Brooklyn Park, MN 55428
763-536-6400
Fax: 763-536-0769
Manufacturer and exporter of electronic lettering systems and labels
Manager: David Grey
President: Cathy Hudson
Estimated Sales: $20-30 Million
Number Employees: 5-9
Parent Co: W.H. Brady

30783 Vasconia Housewares
6391 De Zavala Rd # 301
San Antonio, TX 78249-2159
210-545-4241
Fax: 210-558-9568 800-377-6723
Aluminum cookware including pots, pans and pressure cookers
Manager: Jack Nimmo
President: Olivia Lozano
Estimated Sales: Less than $500,000
Number Employees: 1-4
Brands:
　Vasconia

30784 Vasinee Food Corporation
1247 Grand Street
Brooklyn, NY 11211
718-349-6911
Fax: 718-349-7002 800-878-5996
info@vasinee.com vasineefoodcorp.com
Thai and Asian food: bamboo, juices, coconut milk, fruits and vegetables, curry and paste, noodles, preserves, rice, beans, sauces and spices.
Director of Business Development: Valaya Dipongam
Logistics & Orders Coordinator: Daniel Lee
Year Founded: 1978
Estimated Sales: $14.3 Million
Number Employees: 15
Type of Packaging: Food Service, Private Label, Bulk

30785 Vaughan Co Inc
364 Monte Elma Rd
Montesano, WA 98563-9798
360-249-4042
Fax: 360-249-6155 888-249-2467
info@chopperpumps.com
www.chopperpumps.com
Heavy duty chopper pumps for chopping and pumping solids in wastewater without plugging
President: Kevin Hauser
kevin@hausers.com
President: Dale Vaughan
CFO: Pattcornwell Cornwell
Sales Manager: Bob Simonetti
Chief Engineer: Glenn Dorsch
Estimated Sales: $10-20 Million
Number Employees: 50-99

30786 Vaughan-Chopper Pumps
1989 Peabody Road
Suite 235
Vacaville, CA 95687-6286
707-447-6300
Fax: 707-447-6400
info@rockwellengineering.com
www.rockwellengineering.com
Wine industry chopping pumps

30787 Vaughn Belting Co-Main Acct
200 Northeast Dr
PO Box 5505
Spartanburg, SC 29303-6616
864-574-0234
Fax: 864-574-4258 800-533-9086
sales@vaughnbelting.com
www.vaughnbelting.com
Hoses and belts including conveyor, food grade, timing, nylon core, etc
VP: Brian Schachner
Manager: Amanda Hash
vaughnbe@bellsouth.net
Manager: Amanda Hash
Estimated Sales: $5-10 Million
Number Employees: 10-19

30788 (HQ)Vector Corp
675 44th St
Marion, IA 52302-3800
319-377-8263
Fax: 319-377-5574
vector.sales@vectorcorporation.com
www.freund-vector.com
Designs, manufactures, and markets processing equipment for the processing of solid dosage form materials.
President: Max Kubota
max.kubota@vectorcorporation.com
CFO: Tatsuo Matsugaki
VP Marketing: Greg Smith
Sales: Greg Smith
Production: Mike Douglas
Purchasing Director: Keith Wenndt
Estimated Sales: $25-50 Million
Number Employees: 100-249
Square Footage: 75000
Other Locations:
　Vector Corp.
　Huxley IA

30789 (HQ)Vector Packaging
2021 Midwest Rd # 307
Suite 307
Oak Brook, IL 60523-4349
630-968-9040
Fax: 630-434-9650 800-435-9100
info@vectorpackaging.com
www.vectorpackaging.com
Packaging materials
President/CEO: Brian Samuels
VP Sales/Marketing: Dave McCaffrey
Sales Director: Dave Hugg
Contact: Cyndi Draski
cyndi.draski@vectorpackaging.com
VP Operations: David Fiedler
Operations Director: Cyndi Christel
Number Employees: 20-49

30790 Vector Technologies
6820 N 43rd St
Milwaukee, WI 53209
414-247-7100
Fax: 414-247-7110 800-832-4010
sales@vector-vacuums.com
Manufacturer and exporter of dust collectors and vacuum cleaners and conveying systems
President: Stebe Schonberger
CFO: Chris Koe
Contact: Matthew Benson
mbenson@vector-vacuums.com
Operations Manager: Bruce Kolb
Estimated Sales: $5-10 Million
Number Employees: 20-49
Square Footage: 90000
Parent Co: Vector Technologies
Brands:
　Hepavac
　Invader
　Klean Scrub
　Mdc
　Rapid Response
　Spartan
　Titan
　Vec Loader

30791 Vee Gee Scientific Inc
13600 NE 126th Pl # A
Kirkland, WA 98034-8720
425-823-4518
Fax: 425-820-9826 800-423-8842
sales@veegee.com www.veegee.com
Manufacturer and importer of laboratory products including refractometers, volumetric glassware, porcelain and microscopes
Owner: Guy Mc Farland
gmac@veegee.net
Chairman of the Board: Guy McFarland
Estimated Sales: $5-10,000,000
Number Employees: 10-19

30792 Vega Americas Inc
4241 Allendorf Dr
Cincinnati, OH 45209-1501
513-272-0131
Fax: 513-272-0133 800-367-5383
www.vega-americas.com
Manufacturer and exporter of sensors and gauges

President: Ron Hegyesi
r.hegyesi@vega.com
CFO: Ken Seldmenn
Quality Control: Matt Phomas
Advertising Manager: Patrick Schreiber
r.hegyesi@vega.com
Estimated Sales: $20-50 Million
Number Employees: 100-249
Type of Packaging: Bulk
Brands:
　Densart
　Levelart
　Moistart
　Weighart

30793 Vega Mfg Ltd.
Unit 112-1647 Broadway Street
Port Coquitlam, BC V3C 6P8
Canada
604-941-0761
Fax: 604-941-0781 800-224-8342
sales@vegacases.com www.vegacases.com
Bakery Showcases
President: Walter Kollenberg

30794 Vegware
Pierside Pavilion
300 Pacific Coast Hwy. # 110
Huntington Beach, CA 92648
949-543-0422
844-610-0915
us.info@vegware.com www.vegwareus.com
Compostable packaging: hot and cold drink cups, food containers, takeout boxes
Founder: Bob Bond

30795 Velcro USA
95 Sundial Ave
Manchester, NH 03103
Fax: 603-669-9271 800-225-0180
marketing@velcro.com www.velcro.com
Hook and loop industrial fasteners.
President: Fraser Cameron
Year Founded: 1941
Estimated Sales: $100-500 Million
Number Employees: 2,500

30796 Vendome Copper & Brass Works
729 Franklin St
Louisville, KY 40202-6007
502-587-1930
Fax: 502-589-0639 888-384-5161
office@vendomecopper.com
Manufacturer and exporter of copper and confectioners' kettles, distilling apparatus, vacuum pans, evaporators, coils, etc
President: Patricia Seale
pseale@cleansolutionspro.com
Estimated Sales: $5-10 Million
Number Employees: 50-99
Type of Packaging: Food Service

30797 Vent Master
1021 Brevik Place
Mississauga, ON L4W 3R7
Canada
905-624-0301
Fax: 800-665-2438 800-565-2981
Manufacturer and exporter of exhaust fans, air filters, fire safety equipment, heat recovery units, hoods and utility distribution and ventilating systems
Vice President: Mark Meulenbeck
Sales Director: Dan O'Brien
Operations Manager: Barry Carter
Estimated Sales: $1-5 Million
Parent Co: ENODIS
Type of Packaging: Food Service

30798 (HQ)Vent-A-Hood Co
1000 N Greenville Ave
Richardson, TX 75081-2799
972-235-5201
Fax: 972-231-0663 800-331-2492
www.vahdistributing.com
Manufacturer and exporter of hoods
President: Miles Woodall Iii
CEO: Mileas Woodall
Quality Control: David Stiles
sjacobs@ventahood.com
HR Executive: Stewart Jacobs
sjacobs@ventahood.com
Limited Partner: Miles Woodall III
National Sales Manager: Ed Gober

Estimated Sales: $10-20 Million
Number Employees: 100-249

30799 (HQ)Venture Measurement Co LLC

150 Venture Blvd
Spartanburg, SC 29306-3805
864-574-8960
Fax: 864-574-8063 www.venturemeasurement.com
Manufacturer and exporter of level sensors
President: Mark Earl
CFO: Michael Hallinan
R&D: Roy Zielinski
Sales Manager: Rick Ayers
Contact: Russ Barnett
rbarnett@venturemeas.com
Estimated Sales: $30-50 Million
Number Employees: 50-99
Square Footage: 42000
Brands:
Bin-Dicators
Cap Level Iia
Pulse Point
Roto-Bin-Dicator

30800 Venture Measurement Co LLC

150 Venture Blvd
Spartanburg, SC 29306-3805
864-574-8960
Fax: 864-574-8063 800-426-9010
sales@venturemeas.com
www.venturemeasurement.com
Manufacturer and exporter of level measurement, weight and batching instrumentation for tanks, silos and hoppers; also, PC based bulk inventory monitoring software
President: Mark Earl
Quality Control: Bennett Connvlly
R&D: Joe Dejuzman
CFO: Mick Hallinan
Marketing: Jamie Ives
Contact: Jeff Baker
jeff.baker@kistlermorse.com
Estimated Sales: $5-10 Million
Number Employees: 50-99
Brands:
Ld Blous
Ldbxi
Load Disk Ii
Microcell
Multi-Vessel System
Orb
Ou
Rope
Sonocell
Ultracell
Ultrasonic Sensor
Ultraware

30801 Venture Packaging Inc

311 Monroe St
Monroeville, OH 44847-9406
419-465-2912
Fax: 419-465-2702 www.berryplastics.com
Plastics containers
Manager: Howard Weatherwax
Marketing Manager (Container Division): Brent Beeler
Contact: Wendy Schultz
chawkins@gapageants.com
Estimated Sales: Less Than $500,000
Number Employees: 1-4

30802 Venturetech Corporation

10720 Lexington Dr
Knoxville, TN 37932
865-966-2532
Fax: 865-675-2532 800-826-4095
venturet@aol.com
www.venturetechcorporation.com
Soap, detergents, bleaches, etc.; also, insecticides and insect control systems
President: Richards Wills
VP/GM: Brandon Wills
Graphics Manager/Web Development: Justin Marion
Contact: Brandon Wills
venturetech@tds.net
Estimated Sales: $2.5-5 Million
Number Employees: 10-19

30803 Venus Corp

302 Industrial Dr
Blytheville, AR 72315-6892
870-763-3830
Fax: 870-763-4529
Custom fabricated sheet metal including full CNC punching, forming and laser cutting
CEO: Clifford Carver Sr
ccarver@venus.com
Engineer: Chris Carver
Plant Manager: Clifford Carver Jr
Estimated Sales: $2.5-5 Million
Number Employees: 10-19

30804 (HQ)Verax Chemical Co

20102 Broadway Ave
Snohomish, WA 98296-7937
360-668-2431
Fax: 360-668-5186 800-637-7771
info@veraxproducts.com www.veraxproducts.com
Maintenance chemicals and supplies including hand and toilet bowl cleaners, disinfectants, mops, soap and floor polish; importer of cocoa mats
President: Julie Curkendall
Secretary/Treasurer: Sue Copeland
Contact: Brent Casteel
brent@veraxproducts.com
Estimated Sales: Less Than $500,000
Number Employees: 1-4
Square Footage: 30000

30805 Veri Fone Inc

11700 Great Oaks Way # 210
Alpharetta, GA 30022-2463
770-663-0196
Fax: 770-754-3422 www.verifone.com
Payment processing/transaction automation systems
Manager: Robbie Lopez
Director Marketing: Mike Matthis
Industry Marketing Manager: Kathy LeNoir
Product Marketing Manager: Ida Wu
Estimated Sales: $20-50 Million
Number Employees: 100-249

30806 Verify Brand Inc

7277 Boone Ave N
Brooklyn Park, MN 55428
763-235-1400
Fax: 763-235-1401 888-896-7882
www.verifybrand.com/
Verify Brand, Inc. provides product authentication system based on mass serialization. Verify Brand works with brand owners to design, construct, install and support turnkey product serialization and data formation, supply chainauthentication, unauthorized event management and product tracking, and reporting solutions based on the concept of mass serialization.
President: Kevin Erdman
Director Project Management: Curt Tomhave
Contact: Laurie Aukland
laurie.aukland@verifybrand.com

30807 Verilon Products Co

452 Diens Dr
Wheeling, IL 60090-2641
847-541-1920
Fax: 847-541-4525 800-323-1056
sales@verilonvinyl.com www.verilonvinyl.com
Vinyl strips for freezers and coolers
Vice President: Kim Pullen
VP: Kim Pullen
Marketing Director: Linda Mallon
VP Sales: Dorine Hanson
Estimated Sales: Below $5 Million
Number Employees: 10-19
Brands:
Verilon

30808 Vermillion Flooring

1207 S Scenic Ave
Springfield, MO 65802-5199
417-862-3785
Fax: 417-862-3789 www.vermillion-flooring.com
Manufacturer and exporter of serving trays, pantryware, wood-chopping blocks, cedar accessories and wall decor; also, racks including wine, cookbook and mug trees
President: Art Thomas
VP: Gary Robinson
Special Markets Manager: Steve Baker
Estimated Sales: Less Than $500,000
Number Employees: 1-4
Square Footage: 160000

Brands:
10th St. Bakery
Chef's Select
Classic Images

30809 Vermont Bag & Film

PO Box 135
Bennington, VT 05201-0135
802-442-3166
Fax: 802-442-3167
Plastic bags including sandwich, shopping, etc
Sales Manager: James Comi
Estimated Sales: $1-5 Million
Number Employees: 12

30810 Vermont Container Corp

473 Bowen Rd
Bennington, VT 05201-5020
802-442-5455
Fax: 802-442-6910 www.unicorr.com
Corrugated boxes
VP: Gerald Lambert
Contact: Besen Berry
bbesen@unicorr.com
Estimated Sales: $5-10 Million
Number Employees: 20-49
Parent Co: Unicorr Packaging Group

30811 Vermont Tent Co

14 Berard Dr
South Burlington, VT 05403-5809
802-863-6107
Fax: 802-863-6735 800-696-8368
www.vttent.com
Event rental and manufacturer of commercial gas convection ovens
President: John Crabbe Jr.
jcrabbe@vttent.com
CFO: Lon Finkelstein
VP Marketing & Sales: Michael Lubas
VP Operations: Michael Solomon
Estimated Sales: $5-10,000,000
Number Employees: 50-99

30812 Vermont Tissue Paper Company

RR 67a
North Bennington, VT 5257
802-447-7558
Fax: 802-447-8673
Tissue paper
President: Edward Woodard
Estimated Sales: $5-10 Million
Number Employees: 6

30813 Vern's Cheese

312 W Main St
Chilton, WI 53014-1312
920-849-7717
Fax: 920-849-7883 info@vernscheese.com
www.vernscheese.com
Cheeses
President: Vern Knoespel
info@verncheese.com
Estimated Sales: $20-50 Million
Number Employees: 20-49

30814 Vernon Plastics

25 Shelley Road
Haverhill, MA 01835-8033
978-373-1551
Fax: 978-373-6562
Commercial awnings, plastic materials
President: Blair McIntosh
CFO: Joe Juliano
R&D: Dave Morse
VP: Mark Delaney
Marketing Manager: Steve Giaquinta
Estimated Sales: $50-100 Million
Number Employees: 25
Parent Co: Bordon

30815 Veronica's Treats

31 W Grove St # C
Middleboro, MA 02346-1859
508-946-4438
Fax: 508-946-4460 866-576-1122
info@veronicastreats.com
www.veronicastreats.com
Personalized cookies, brownies, and cupcakes
Owner: Hilary Souza
veronicastreats@gmail.com
Number Employees: 10-19
Square Footage: 24000
Type of Packaging: Private Label

30816 Versa Conveyor
PO Box 899
London, OH 43140-0899

740-852-5609
Fax: 740-869-2839 www.versaconveyor.com
Manufacturer and exporter of gravity and power
conveyor
President: Andrew Petitt
Chief Executive Officer: Chris Cole
Vice President of Project Management: Alfred
Rebello
Chief Technical Officer: Ray Neiser
Senior Vice President of Sales and Marke: Jim
McKnight
Vice President of Operations: Chris Arnold
Estimated Sales: $20-50 Million
Number Employees: 100-249
Parent Co: Tomkins Industries

30817 Versa-Matic Pump Company
800 North Main Street
Mansfield, OH 44902

419-526-7296
Fax: 419-526-7289 800-843-8210
customerservice.versamatic@idexcorp.com
www.versamatic.com
Line of air-operated, double diaphragm pumps and
replacement parts, air decompression pumps, 3A
sanitary pumps, and food processing pumps
Estimated Sales: $5-10 Million
Number Employees: 20-49

30818 (HQ)Versailles Lighting
1305 Poinsettia Dr Ste 6
Delray Beach, FL 33444

561-278-8758
Fax: 561-278-8759 888-564-0240
Manufacturer, importer and exporter of lighting fix-
tures and metal tables
President: Max Guedj
CEO: Maurine Locke
CFO: Tung Nguyen
Quality Control: Rajendrauth James
Sales: Samantha Basdeo
Estimated Sales: $3-5 Million
Number Employees: 10-19
Square Footage: 40000
Other Locations:
Versailles Lighting
Delnay FL

30819 Versatile Mobile Systems
19105 36th Ave W
Lynnwood, WA 98036

425-778-8577
Fax: 425-712-0326 800-262-1633
info@versatilemobile.com versatilemobile.com
Mobile and barcode scanner solutions
EVP, Sales: Oliver Poppenberg
Year Founded: 1993

30820 Vertex China
1793 W 2nd St
Pomona, CA 91766-1253

909-594-4800
Fax: 909-595-1993 800-483-7839
info@vertexchina.com www.vertexchina.com
Manufacturer, importer and exporter of dinnerware,
chinaware and tableware including lead-free, micro-
wave/dishwasher safe, cups, saucers, bowls, dishes,
platters and mugs; custom decoration available
President: Hoi Shum
info@vertexchina.com
Sales: Ken Joyce
Estimated Sales: $10-20 Million
Number Employees: 10-19
Square Footage: 50000
Brands:
Alpine
City Square
Crystal Bay
Kentfield
Market Buffet
Rubicon
Sausalito
Vertex

30821 Vertex Interactive
23 Carol Street
Clifton, NJ 07014-1490

973-777-3500
Fax: 973-472-0814

Manufacturer and exporter of balances, weights, bar
code and magnetic strip card readers, industrial
scales and data collection software
Chairman: James Maloy
CEO/President: Ron Byer
Number Employees: 60
Parent Co: Vertex Industries
Brands:
Torbal

30822 Vertical Systems Intl
2126 Chamber Center Dr
Lakeside Park, KY 41017-1669

859-485-9650
Fax: 859-485-9654 sales@vsilift.com
www.vsilift.com
Manufacturer and exporter of vertical lifts, stackers,
conveyors, dumpers, and autostore units
President: Daniel Quinn
dan.quinn@vsilift.com
Member: Daniel Quinn
VP Sales: Steve Templeton
Estimated Sales: $5-10 Million
Number Employees: 5-9
Square Footage: 88000

30823 Vertique Inc
115 Vista Blvd
Arden, NC 28704-9457

828-654-8900
Fax: 828-654-8908
Vertique specializes in warehouse distribution
equipment (Vertique systems and VPS picking and
loading software) for the beverage and food indus-
try, providing complete product services specifically
designed to meet any manufacturingand distribution
need.
Owner: Jay Stingel
VP: John Stingel
Senior Engineer: James Smith
Vice President Sales: Jeff Stingel
Manager: Tom Algai
toma@vertique.com
Estimated Sales: $20-50 Million
Number Employees: 50-99
Type of Packaging: Bulk

30824 Vescom America
2289 Ross Mill Rd
Henderson, NC 27537-5966

252-436-9067
Fax: 252-436-9069 usacanada@vescom.com
Manufacturer, importer and exporter of recycling
systems for food wastes including feeders, shred-
ders, weight controllers, screeners, conveyors, pack-
ers and dust collection systems
Owner: Robert Vrabel
Contact: Lisa Brooks
l.brooks@vescom.com
Estimated Sales: $300,000-500,000
Number Employees: 1-4
Square Footage: 1000

30825 Vetrerie Bruni
3101 W Mcnab Rd
Pompano Beach, FL 33069

954-590-3990
Fax: 954-590-3991 800-432-4825
Glass containers for wine, champagne and food
Estimated Sales: $10-20 Million
Number Employees: 10-19

30826 Vetter Vineyards Winery
8005 Prospect Station Rd
Westfield, NY 14787-9630

716-326-3100
Fax: 716-326-3100 wine@cecomet.net
Wines
Owner: Mark Lancaster
wine@fairpoint.net
Co-Owner: Barbara Lancaster
Estimated Sales: Less Than $500,000
Number Employees: 1-4
Type of Packaging: Private Label
Brands:
Vetter Vineyards

30827 Viacam
313 Pleasant Street
Watertown, MA 02472-2418

617-926-7045
Fax: 617-923-8055 800-338-4381
viacom@viacom.com www.viacom.com

Rapid myocotoxin testing kits, tests for the detection
of DON, fumonisin, ochratoxin and zearalenone and
tests for the detection of listeria, salmonella and sal-
monella enteritidis
President and Chief Executive Officer: Philippe
Dauman
CFO: Wade Davis
Senior Vice President of Investor Relati: James
Bombassei
CFO: Majoire Radlo
Contact: Jim Cary
jim@radlo.com
Estimated Sales: $2.5-5 Million
Number Employees: 20-49

30828 Viatec
777 Fort Street
Victoria, BC V8W 1G9
Canada

250-483-3214
Fax: 269-945-2357 800-942-4702
sales@viatec.com www.viatec.ca
Manufacturer and exporter of dairy processors,
cookers, coolers, stainless and fiberglass tanks, mix-
ers and valves
CEO: Dan Gunn
Marketing & Communications Coordinator: Robbie
Aylesworth
Sales (Stainless): Bob Johnson
Manager of Operations & Finance: Michelle Gaetz
Estimated Sales: $10-20 Million
Number Employees: 50-99
Square Footage: 104000
Brands:
Chemtek
Duratek
Permasan
Resinfab

30829 Viatec Process Storage System
500 Reed St
PO Box 99
Belding, MI 48809-1532

616-794-1230
Fax: 616-794-2487 klk@viatec.com
Manufacturer and exporter of dairy processors,
cookers, coolers, stainless and fiberglass tanks, mix-
ers and valves
Sales Director: Bob Johnson
Plant Manager: Ron Timmer
Estimated Sales: $5,000,000-$9,900,000
Number Employees: 20-49
Square Footage: 52000
Parent Co: Viatec
Brands:
Chemtek
Duratek
Permasan
Resinfab

30830 Viatran Corporation
3829 Forest Park Way
Suite 500
North Tonawanda, NY 14120

716-773-1700
Fax: 716-773-2488 800-688-0030
solutions@viatran.com www.viatran.com
Sanitary, flush/CIP, solid state pressure, level and
flow transmitters
Contact: Matt Carrara
carrara@viatran.com
Number Employees: 50-99

30831 Vibrac LLC-Fax
19 Columbia Dr
Amherst, NH 03031-2305

603-886-3857
Fax: 603-886-3857 www.vibrac.com
Cap torque testing laboratory and on-line
President: Tom Rogers
CEO: Quentin Searle
Vice President of Engineering: Bob Searle
Contact: Ken Diegel
kdiegel@vibrac.com
VP of Operations: Lisa Rogers
Production Manager: Scott Whipple
Plant Manager: Richard Brams
Estimated Sales: $3 Million
Number Employees: 1-4
Number of Brands: 2
Number of Products: 6
Square Footage: 15000

Brands:
Gold Bottle
Torgo

30832 VibroFloors World
1415 Highway 85 N
Suite 310-361
Fayetteville, GA 30214
770-632-9701
Fax: 770-632-9710 info@vibrofloorswg.com
www.vibrofloorsworldgroup.com
High performance and maintenance free flooring for
commercial and industrial work facilities
President: Jackie Smith Jr
CEO: Dejana Gavrilovic
Project Manager: T Freddy Venos
Parent Co: VibroFloors WorldGroup, LLC

30833 Vicksburg Chemical Company
5100 Poplar Ave Fl 24
Memphis, TN 38137-4000
901-747-0234
Fax: 901-747-4031 800-227-2798
jhreeves@aol.com
Processor, importer and exporter of potassium ni-
trates, potassium carbonates, monammonium phos-
phates and monopotassium phosphates
Sales Manager/Distributor: John Reeves
Estimated Sales: $1-5 Million
Number Employees: 100-250
Type of Packaging: Private Label

30834 Vicmore Manufacturing Company
20 Grand Avenue
Brooklyn, NY 11205-1317
718-855-7758
Fax: 718-852-3768 800-458-8663
Manufacturer and exporter of double polished clear
tablecloths, and vinyl and chemical aprons
President: Morris Steinberg
Estimated Sales: $5-10 Million
Number Employees: 50-99

30835 Victone Manufacturing Company
726 W 19th St
Chicago, IL 60616-1024
312-738-3211
Fax: 312-738-3214
Wire racks and stands
President: Joe Di Monte
Plant Manager: Raymond Di Monte
Estimated Sales: $2.5-5 Million
Number Employees: 10-19

30836 Victor Associates
514 Creekside Ct
Golden, CO 80403-1903
720-379-6850
Fax: 303-526-5069
Food consulting
C.E.O: Michael S Victor
mvictor@fralo.com
Estimated Sales: $1-5 Million
Number Employees: 1

30837 Victoria Porcelain
7790 NW 67th St
Miami, FL 33166-2702
305-593-2353
Fax: 305-593-8363 888-593-2353
sales@victoriaporcelain.com
www.victoriaporcelain.com
Porcelain cups, bowls, plates, gravy boats, saucers,
mugs, ovenware, teapots, etc.; importer and exporter
of flatware and knives
President: Jose Espejo
jespejo@victoriaporcelain.com
VP Sales: David Yablin
Customer Service Manager: Phyllis Halpern
Estimated Sales: $2.5-5 Million
Number Employees: 1-4
Square Footage: 40000

30838 Victory Box Corp
645 W 1st Ave
Roselle, NJ 07203-1049
908-245-5100
Fax: 908-245-5670 www.victoryboxcorp.com
Corrugated boxes
President: Alex Landy
VP Sales: Paul Bell
Estimated Sales: $20-50 Million
Number Employees: 100-249

30839 Victory Packaging, Inc.
3555 Timmons Lane
Suite 144
Houston, TX 77027
713-961-3299
Fax: 800-778-7210 800-486-5606
www.victorypackaging.com
Custom and stock corrugated boxes
President: Bryan Burnett
CFO: Vic Samuels
Contact: Christopher Agostisi
cagostisi@victorypackaging.com
Estimated Sales: $62 Million
Number Employees: 900

30840 Victory Refrigeration
110 Woodcrest Rd
Cherry Hill, NJ 08003
856-428-4200
Fax: 856-428-7299 victory@victory-refrig.com
www.victory-refrig.com
Commercial refrigerators and freezers
President: Mark Whalen
CFO: Eileen Kurskin
R&D and Quality Control: Robert Hettinger
Director Sales Marketing: Jim Hurston
Contact: Jeff Yates
jim@informzone.net
Estimated Sales: $30-50 Million
Number Employees: 1-4
Square Footage: 240000
Parent Co: Middleby Corporation
Brands:
Victory

30841 Videojet Technologies Inc
1500 N Mittel Blvd
Wood Dale, IL 60191-1073
800-843-3610
vti.domesticcs@videojet.com www.videojet.com
Manufacturer and exporter of coding and labeling
equipment, printing inks and printing equipment;
also, material handling equipment.
Chief Technology Officer/VP of R&D: John Folkers
Principal Software Engineer: Eric Amy
Mechanical Engineer Manager: Kevin Kuester
Number Employees: 4,000
Parent Co: Donaher Corporation
Brands:
Cheshire
Excel
Inksource
Maxum
Sigmark
Totalsource
Triumph
Videojet

30842 Videojet Technologies Inc
1500 N Mittel Blvd
Wood Dale, IL 60191-1072
630-860-7300
Fax: 630-616-3623 800-843-3610
www.videojet.com
President: Matt Trerotola
Contact: Jay Buckley
jay.buckley@videojet.com
Estimated Sales: $1-5 Million
Number Employees: 1000-4999

30843 Videx Inc
1105 NE Circle Blvd
Corvallis, OR 97330-4285
541-738-5500
Fax: 541-752-5285 support@videx.com
Manufacture portable bar code scanners and ibutton
readers in addition to access control and security
products, electronic locks
President: Steve Braaten
steveb@videx.com
Marketing Director: Stephanie Ulrich
Sales Director: Tish Phillips
Number Employees: 50-99
Number of Brands: 25
Number of Products: 226
Brands:
Authorizer
Barcode Labeler
Cyber Key
Cyber Lock
Cyber Point
Duratrax
Duraward
Laserlite Mx

Laserlite Pro
Omni Wand
Pulse Star
Time Wand I
Time Wand Ii
Touch Access
Touch Alert
Touchprobe

30844 View-Rite Manufacturing
455 Allan St
Daly City, CA 94014-1627
415-468-3856
Fax: 415-468-4784
Manufacturer and exporter of store fixtures
President: Nha Nguyen
nnguyen@viewrite.com
VP: Nha Nguyen
Number Employees: 20-49
Square Footage: 160000

30845 Vifan USA
1 Vifan Dr
Morristown, TN 37814
423-581-6990
Fax: 423-581-9998 866-843-2668
www.vifan.com
Bi-axially polypropylene films, film for industrial
and flexible packaging applications
President: Pietro Battista
CFO: Thomas Mohr
Executive VP: Vittoriano Di Luzio
Contact: F Massey
f.massey@vibac.com
Estimated Sales: $10-20 Million
Number Employees: 100-249
Number of Products: 4
Square Footage: 280000

30846 Viking Corp
210 Industrial Park Dr
Hastings, MI 49058-9631
269-945-9501
Fax: 269-945-4495 800-968-9501
techsvcs@vikingcorp.com
Manufacturer and exporter of fire protection systems
including wet and dry pipe, deluge and fire cycle;
also, valves, sprinklers, spray nozzles and alarm
devices
CEO: Tomdra Groos
CEO: Kevin Ortyl
Marketing Director: Sandra Wake
Sales Director: Bill Phair
Contact: Will Allgood
wallgood@supplynet.com
Purchasing Manager: Jerry Dinges
Estimated Sales: $20-30 Million
Number Employees: 100-249
Parent Co: Tyden Seal Company

30847 Viking Identification Product
8964 Excelsior Blvd
Hopkins, MN 55343
952-935-5245
Fax: 952-935-3764
Pressure sensitive, foil and silk-screened labels
Owner: Tim Faulson
Estimated Sales: Below $5 Million
Number Employees: 5-9

30848 Viking Industries
489 Tumbull Bay Rd
New Smyma Beach, FL 32168
386-428-9800
Fax: 386-409-0360 888-605-5560
Manfacturer and exporter of hot melt adhesive appli-
cation equipment for carton and case sealings; also,
hot wax dispensing systems for wine bottle seals,
cheese products and hot candy
Owner: Walter Warning Jr
VP Sales/Marketing: Douglas White
Estimated Sales: $2.5-5,000,000
Number Employees: 10-19
Square Footage: 40000
Brands:
Sys-Clean
Titan

30849 Viking Label Inc
5652 Lakers Ln
PO Box 10
Nisswa, MN 56468-4701
218-963-2575
Fax: 218-963-4849 800-247-6573
info@vikinglabel.com www.vikinglabel.com
Labels
Owner: Tammie Barry
Sales Manager: Kim Larson
tbarry@vikinglabel.com
Estimated Sales: $5-10 Million
Number Employees: 20-49

30850 Viking Machine & DesignInc
1408 Viking Ln
De Pere, WI 54115-9265
920-336-1190
Fax: 920-336-2970 888-286-2116
Cheese processing equipment for processing of mozzarella, provolone, and blue cheese
President, Founder: Don Lindgren Sr
Engineer and CFO: Dan Lindgren
Founder: Don Lindgren
Quality Control: Rick Felchlin
Sales Director: Rick Felchlin
Plant Manager: Rick Felchlin
Shop Foreman / Project Coordinator / Pur: Rick Felchlin
Estimated Sales: $1-2.5 Million
Number Employees: 1-4
Square Footage: 128640
Brands:
    Hydra Form
    Hydra Mold

30851 Viking Packaging & Display
620 Quinn Avenue
San Jose, CA 95112-2604
408-998-1000
Fax: 408-293-8162
Corrugated containers, protective foam packaging and point of purchase displays
President: Peter Keady
Production: Ed Hirle
Estimated Sales: $20-50 Million
Number Employees: 20-49
Square Footage: 80000

30852 Viking Pallet Corp
9188 Cottonwood Ln N
PO Box 167
Maple Grove, MN 55369-3902
763-425-6707
Fax: 763-425-4400 sales@vikingpallet.com
www.vikingpallet.com
Wooden pallets
Owner/ General Manager: Tim Logan
sales@vikingpallet.com
Office Manager: Kathy Plocharski
Plant Foreman: Mark Aanenson
Estimated Sales: Below $5 Million
Number Employees: 20-49

30853 Viking Pump Inc
406 State St
Cedar Falls, IA 50613-3343
319-266-1741
Fax: 319-273-8157 www.vikingpump.com
Stainless steel rotary pumps and equipment
President: Paul Schwar
CEO: Jason Struthrs
CFO: Steve Huan
Vice President: Joe Michaels
joemichaels@idexcorp.com
Sales Director: Kevin Rhodes
Number Employees: 500-999
Square Footage: 154
Parent Co: IDEX Corp.
Brands:
    Acculobe
    Classic Rotary Lobe Pumps
    Concept Sq
    Duralobe
    Sterilobe

30854 Vilter Manufacturing Corporation
5555 S Packard Ave
Cudahy, WI 53110
414-744-0111
Fax: 414-744-3483 www.vilter.com
Compressors, condensors, air untis and custom packaged systems

President/CEO/COO: Ron Prebish
VP Business Development: Wayne Wehber
VP Sales/Marketing: Mark Stencel
Contact: Mark Stencel
mark.stencel@emersonclimate.com
VP Operations: John Barry
Estimated Sales: $43 Million
Number Employees: 100-249
Number of Brands: 4
Number of Products: 7
Square Footage: 400000
Brands:
    450xl
    Econ-O-Mizer
    Power Pincher
    Steady-Mount
    Super Separator
    Tri-Micro
    V-Plus
    Vmc
    Vilter

30855 Vimco
300 Hansen Access Rd # A
King Of Prussia, PA 19406-2440
610-768-0500
Fax: 610-768-0586 www.vimcoinc.com
Lighting and lamp fixtures including food heating, industrial task, bench and assembly
President: Vic Maggitti, Jr
vic@vimcoinc.com
Sales Manager: Dave Gyuris
Administration: Brandon O'Brien
Plant Manager: Max DiRado
Estimated Sales: $1-3 Million
Number Employees: 50-99

30856 Vin-Tex
1 Mount Forest Drive
Ontario, CA N0G-2L2
519-323-0300
Fax: 519-323-4777 800-846-8399
sales@vintex.com
Reusable packaging bags
Estimated Sales: $5-10 Million
Number Employees: 20-49

30857 Vincent Commodities Corporation
7182 US Highway 14
Middleton, WI 53562
608-831-4447
Fax: 608-833-0555 800-279-4447
vcc20@msn.com
President: Ronald Vincent
Estimated Sales: $2.5-5 Million
Number Employees: 5-9

30858 Vincent Corp
2810 E 5th Ave
Tampa, FL 33605-5638
813-248-2650
Fax: 813-247-7557 vincent@vincentcorp.com
www.vincentcorp.com
Manufacturer and exporter of screw presses for dewatering; also, pectin peel and citrus by-product machinery for liquids separation/solids concentration
President: Robert Johnston
spj110@msn.com
Project Engineer: Bob Johnston
Estimated Sales: $2.5-5 Million
Number Employees: 50-99
Square Footage: 160000
Brands:
    Vincent

30859 Vine Solutions
200 Tamal Plaza
Suite 100
Corte Madera, CA 94925-1172
415-927-3308
Fax: 415-485-6011 tnikaidoh@vinesolutions.com
Consultant specializing in accounting services, strategic market planning, restructuring and restaurant start-up
Owner: Edward Vine
Chief Executive Officer: Edward Levine
Executive Vice President: John Priest
Contact: Janina Bandi
jbandi@vinesolutions.com
Director, Accounting: Takashi Nikaidoh
Estimated Sales: Below $5 Million
Number Employees: 1-4
Square Footage: 3600

30860 Vineco International Products
27 Scott Street W
St Catharines, ON L2R 1E1
Canada
905-685-9342
Fax: 905-685-9551
Manufacturer and wholesaler/distributor of wine and beer making kits
President: Rob Van Wely
CFO: Jason Hough
R&D: Sandra Sartor
Quality Control: Sandra Sartor
Marketing: Michael Hind
Estimated Sales: $5-10 Million
Number Employees: 45
Parent Co: Andres Wines
Type of Packaging: Consumer
Brands:
    Bin 49
    Brew Canada
    California Connoisseur
    European Select
    Kendall
    Lagacy
    Ridge Classic
    Ridge Showcase
    V.I.P. Series

30861 Vintage
225 Clay Street
P.O.Box 231
Jasper, IN 47547
812-482-3204
Fax: 812-936-9979 800-992-3491
humanresources@jaspergroup.us.com
www.jaspergroup.us.com
Bar stools, tables, chairs and benches
President: Mike Elliott
Technical Services Manager: Amilcar Ubiera
Marketing Director: Lisa Kieffner
Sales Territory Manager: Jimi Barreiro
Operations Manager: Ronald Beck
Plant Manager: Mark Kluemper
Purchasing Manager: Dan Herman
Number Employees: 100-249
Parent Co: Jasper Seating Company

30862 Virgin Cola USA
3600 Wilshire Blvd
Los Angeles, CA 90010-2603
213-380-3433
Fax: 213-487-3631
Owner: Virgil Sy

30863 Virginia Artesian Bottling Company
4300 Spring Run Rd
Mechanicsville, VA 23116-6639
804-779-7500
Fax: 866-291-9504 sales@virginiaartesian.com
virginiaartesian.com
Bottled water
Owner: Steven Brown
Sales Manager: Frank Atwood
Production Manager: Nick Brown
Year Founded: 2003
Estimated Sales: Under $500,000
Number Employees: 1-10
Type of Packaging: Food Service
Brands:
    Virginia Artesian©

30864 Virginia Department of Agriculture & Consumer Services
102 Governor Street
Richmond, VA 23219
804-786-3520
webmaster.vdacs@vdacs.virginia.gov
www.vdacs.virginia.gov
Information services for food industry: food safety, lab services, marketing.
Agribusiness Development: Bill Scruggs
Director, Marketing: Keith Long
Public Relations & Marketing: Marshall Payne
Year Founded: 1877
Number Employees: 200-500
Brands:
    Virginia's Finest
    Virginia Grown

30865 Virginia Industrial Services
P.O.Box 532
Waynesboro, VA 22980-391
Fax: 540-943-7192 800-825-3050

Manufacturer and exporter of food processing equipment; also, repair and modification available
President: William Merrill
Estimated Sales: Below $5,000,000
Number Employees: 10-19
Square Footage: 20000

30866 Virginia Plastics Co
3453 Aerial Way Dr SW
Roanoke, VA 24018-1503

540-981-9700
Fax: 540-375-0135   800-777-8541
sales@vaplastics.com   www.vaplastics.com
Manufacturer and exporter of packaging materials including polyethylene film and tubing
President: Mike Callister
Estimated Sales: $5-10 Million
Number Employees: 20-49

30867 Virtual Packaging
530 S Nolen Dr
Southlake, TX 76092-9165

817-328-3945
Fax: 817-328-3901   888-868-7848
sales@virtualpackaging.com
www.virtualpackaging.com
Mock-ups, full-color bags, boxes, cans, labels, shrink film and wrappers
President: Monty Patterson
Marketing Manager: Paul Ferreris
Manager: Rafael Guerra
rafael@virtualpackaging.com
Estimated Sales: Less than $500,000
Number Employees: 20-49

30868 Visalia Citrus Packing Group
19743 Avenue 344
Woodlake, CA 93286

559-564-3351
Fax: 559-564-3865   vcpg@vcpg.com
Golden State Citrus Packers is a licensed commercial shipper of citrus products for Sunkist Growers, Inc.
President: George Lambeth
Manager: John Kalendar
johnkalendar@vcpg.com
Office Manager: Judith Jenkins
Plant Manager: Raul Gamez
Number Employees: 100-249
Parent Co: Visalia Citrus Packing Group
Type of Packaging: Food Service

30869 Viscofan USA Inc
50 County Ct
Montgomery, AL 36105-5506

334-396-0092
Fax: 334-396-0094   800-521-3577
www.viscofan.com
Manufacturer and distributor of artifical casings for the meat industry
President: Jose Maria Fernandez
CEO: Jose Fernandez
fernandezj@usa2.viscofan.com
Sales VP: David Hambert
Product Manager: Tripp Ferguson
Estimated Sales: $1.2 Million
Number Employees: 100-249
Type of Packaging: Consumer, Food Service, Bulk

30870 Visionary Design
620 Wolfs Hollow Dr
Atglen, PA 19310

610-408-0540
Fax: 610-408-0541   vdi@epix.net
Out of the box innovative creativity for the food industry
President: Eugene Gadlardi
Quality Control: Frank Oas
Estimated Sales: Below $5 Million
Number Employees: 3

30871 Visions Espresso Svc
2737 1st Ave S
Seattle, WA 98134-1823

206-623-6709
Fax: 206-623-6710   800-277-7277
info@visionsespresso.com
www.visionsespresso.com
Espresso machine cleaners, espresso machines/accessories, filtration equipment, service espresso machines
Owner: Dawn Loraas
dawn@visions.com
Manager: Bethanie Fritz

Estimated Sales: $500,000-$1 Million
Number Employees: 20-49

30872 Visipak
209 N Kirkwood Rd
St Louis, MO 63122-4029

314-984-8100
Fax: 314-984-0021   800-949-1171
www.visipak.com
Clear plastic tubing
Manager: Mike Boysen
Estimated Sales: $20-50 Million
Number Employees: 100-249

30873 Viskase Co Inc
8205 Cass Ave # 115
Darien, IL 60561-5319

630-874-0700
Fax: 630-874-0178   800-323-8562
www.viskase.com
Manufacturer and exporter of nonedible, fibrous and cellulosic food casings and film including barrier, polypropylene and cook-in
President/CEO: Robert Weisman
VP/COO: Henry Palacci
VP/CFO/Secretary/Treasurer: Charles Pullin
VP Sales, North America: Maurice Ryan
Contact: Eric Wynveen
eric.wynveen@viskase.com
VP Worldwide Operations: Bernard Lemoine
Estimated Sales: $20 Million
Number Employees: 1,000-4,999
Other Locations:
    Viskase Manufacturing Plant
    Kentland IN
    Viskase Manufacturing Plant
    Loudon TN
    Viskase Manufacturing Plant
    Osceola AR
    Viskase Manufacturing Plant
    Escobedo, Mexico
    Viskase Manufacturing Plant
    Sao Paulo, Brazil

30874 Vista International Packaging
1126 88th Pl
Kenosha, WI 53143-6538

262-697-6520
Fax: 262-694-4824   800-558-4058
www.vistapackaging.com
Custom food packaging for meat, poultry and cheese
President/CEO: David Hagman
CFO: Paul Schulz
VP Sales and Marketing: Ron Ramsey
R & D: Lloyd Wallenslager
Quality Control: Marie McMahon
VP Marketing: David Jaeger
VP Sales: Paul Walter
Contact: Anne Eichstedt
aeichstedt@vistapackaging.com
Operations Manager: Mike Schultz
Plant Manager: Steve Vanzeeland
Estimated Sales: $10-20 Million
Number Employees: 5-9
Type of Packaging: Consumer, Food Service, Private Label, Bulk

30875 Vista International Packaging
1126 88th Pl
Kenosha, WI 53143-6538

262-697-6520
Fax: 262-694-4824   800-558-4058
Forming and non-forming films, shrink bags, and tubular plastics for the poultry, meat and cheese industries.
Contact: Anne Eichstedt
aeichstedt@vistapackaging.com
Number Employees: 5-9

30876 Visual Marketing Assoc
9560 Pathway St # 6
Santee, CA 92071-4181

619-258-0393
Fax: 619-258-0790
Backlit and nonbacklit menu display systems and retro-fit menu systems; also, transparency illuminators
President: Dale R Godfrey
Estimated Sales: Below $5 Million
Number Employees: 1-4
Square Footage: 34000
Brands:
    Broadway Menu
    Light Hawk

30877 Visual Packaging Corp
91 4th Ave
Haskell, NJ 07420-1141

973-835-7055
Fax: 973-835-0445   visualpackaging@optimum.net
www.visualpackagingcorp.com
Transparent plastic candy containers and boxes
President: Don Stackhouse
sales@visualpackaging.com
Estimated Sales: $500,000-$1 Million
Number Employees: 5-9

30878 Visual Planning Corp
1320 Route 9 #3314
Champlain, NY 12919

518-298-8404
Fax: 518-298-2368   800-361-1192
info@visualplanning.com
www.visualplanning.com
Scheduling boards-magnetic, perforated, T-card, boardmaster, fixed, rotating, planner sheets, PC software & accessories, AV equipment & supplies-easels, pads, lecterns, bulletin boards, conference cabinets, electronic boardsprojectors, screens, markers, Graphic Arts materials-templates, portfolios, filing systems, precision knives; Signs-labels, badges, nameplates, directory boards, magnetic, etc; office supplies.
President: Joseph Josephson
Marketing: Boris Polanski
Plant Manager: Stefan Neciorek
Purchasing Manager: Paul Harrison
Estimated Sales: $1-3 Million
Number Employees: 20-49
Type of Packaging: Private Label
Brands:
    All Ways
    Kling
    Lecturers' Marker
    Liquid Chalk
    Magnetically Aligned
    Overlay/Underlay
    Triple Erasability System
    Visitint
    Visutate
    Visutype

30879 Vita Craft Corp
11100 W 58th St
Shawnee, KS 66203-2299

913-631-6265
Fax: 913-631-1143   800-359-3444
info@vitacraft.com
Manufacturer and exporter of stainless steel and multi-ply cooking utensils
President: Gary Martin
garymartin@vitacraft.com
CEO: Mamoru Imura
VP: John Ratigan
Estimated Sales: $10-20 Million
Number Employees: 20-49
Parent Co: Rena-Ware Distributors
Type of Packaging: Consumer, Food Service

30880 Vita Juice Corporation
10725 Sutter Ave
Pacoima, CA 91331-2553

818-899-1195
President: Fred Farago
Estimated Sales: $1-5 Million
Number Employees: 1-4

30881 Vita Key Packaging
6975 Arlington Ave
Riverside, CA 92503

909-355-1023
Fax: 909-355-1070
Full service contract packaging, custom formulation and overflow packaging for the food and nutritional supplement industries
Owner: Douglas Delia
Director Operations: Robert Lockovich
Estimated Sales: $2.5-5,000,000
Number Employees: 20-49
Type of Packaging: Private Label, Bulk

30882 VitaMinder Company
23 Acorn St
Providence, RI 02903-1066

401-273-0444
Fax: 401-273-0630   800-858-8840
sales@vitaminder.com   www.medportllc.com

Manufacturer and exporter of multi-compartment vitamin containers, portable blenders for powdered drink mixes and food scales; importer of scales, tablet splitters/crushers and blenders
President: Larry Wesson
CFO: Larry Weffon
Quality Control: Vanessa Honwybhan
VP Sales: James Shuster
Sales Manager: Ken Michaels
Number Employees: 10-19
Parent Co: Ocean Group
Brands:
  Vitaminder

30883 Vitakem Neutraceutical Inc
811 West Jericho Turnpike
Smithtown, NY 11787

855-837-0430
www.vitakem.com

Vitamins and supplements
President/CEO: Bret Hoyt Sr
Contact: Aaron Berkman
aaron@vitakem.com

30884 Vitamix
8615 Usher Rd
Olmsted Twp, OH 44138-2199

440-235-4840
Fax: 440-235-3726 800-437-4654
foodservice@vitamix.com www.vitamix.com
Manufactures highly engineered, high performance commercial food blenders and drink mixers built for outstanding durability and versatility
President: John Barnard
CEO: Jodi Berg
international@vitamix.com
Marketing Director: D Scott Hinckley
Estimated Sales: $20-50 Million
Number Employees: 250-499
Brands:
  Bar Boss
  Blending Station
  Mix'n Machine
  Rinse-O-Latic
  Touch and Go Blending Station
  Vita-Mix Drink Machine
  Vita-Prep
  Vita-Pro

30885 Vitatech Nutritional Sciences
2802 Dow Ave
Tustin, CA 92780-7212

714-832-9700
Fax: 714-731-8482 info@vit-best.com
www.vit-best.com
Vitamins
CEO: Thomas Mooy
VP Supply Chain: Katie Watts
Director of Technical Services: David Jiang
Estimated Sales: $20-50 Million
Number Employees: 100-249
Type of Packaging: Private Label

30886 Vitex Packaging Group
1137 Progress Rd
Suffolk, VA 23434-2301

757-538-3115
Fax: 757-538-3120
Paper based flexible packaging tea tags and envelopes
President: Sandy Arulf
sarulf@vitexpackaging.com
Estimated Sales: $20 Million
Number Employees: 100-249

30887 Vitro Packaging
5200 Tennyson Pkwy Ste 100
Plano, TX 75024

469-443-1100
Fax: 469-443-1258 800-766-0600
www.vitro.com/vitro_packaging/ingles/
Stock and private design glass containers.
President: John Shaddox
Vice President Finance: Kevin Jackson
Vice President Sales & Marketing: Doug Hesche
Contact: Jose Alonso
jalonso@vitro.com
Estimated Sales: $20-50 Million
Number Employees: 50-99
Parent Co: Vitro S.A.

30888 Vitro Packaging
3700 Preston Rd
Plano, TX 75093-7440

972-596-6483
Fax: 972-960-1076 800-766-0600
www.vto.com
Glass bottles in all shapes, sizes and colors
Estimated Sales: $20-50 Million
Number Employees: 50-99

30889 Vitro Seating Products
201 Madison St
St Louis, MO 63102-1329

314-241-2265
Fax: 314-241-8723 800-325-7093
mail@vitroseating.com www.vitroseating.com
Manufacturer and exporter of hotel, restaurant and bar furniture including fountain and bar stools, booths, chairs and tables
CEO: Rose Crofford
rcrofford@ccstl.org
CEO: Stephen Scott
VP of Administration: Mike Scott
Senior Designer: Kim Luce
National Sales Manager: Matt Schliecher
Accounts Receivable Manager: Lauren Rush
VP of Manufacturing: Steve Scott Jr.
Purchasing Mngr./CSR: Matt Schleicher
Estimated Sales: $5-10 Million
Number Employees: 50-99
Square Footage: 450000
Type of Packaging: Food Service

30890 Vivolac Cultures Corp
6108 W Stoner Dr
Greenfield, IN 46140-7383

317-866-9528
Fax: 317-356-8450 800-848-6522
www.vivolac.com
Laboratory specializing in dairy and food microbiological testing, consultation and sanitation
Owner: David Jaramillo
Chief Marketing Officer: Philip Reinhardt
Technical Sales Manager: Rossana Reyes
djaramillo@vivolac.com
Estimated Sales: $1-2.5 Million
Number Employees: 5-9

30891 Vogel Lubrication Systems
1008 Jefferson Ave
Newport News, VA 23607-6122

757-380-0164
Fax: 757-380-0709
Centralized lubrication systems and liquid pumps for industry
President: Robert Amen
Quality Control: Thomas Steinhoff
Contact: Joe Ahrens
jahrens@vogel-lube.com
Estimated Sales: $10-20 Million
Number Employees: 10-19

30892 Vogt Tube Ice
1000 W Ormsby Ave # 19
Louisville, KY 40210-1549

502-635-3000
Fax: 502-634-0479 800-853-8648
info@vogtice.com www.vogtice.com
Manufacturer and exporter ice machines including cubers and crushers
Chairman/ Managing Member: J.T. Sims
President: Tobi Ferguson
CEO: Mark Barter
VP, Business Development & Engineering: Charles Holwerk
Manager of Quality & Manufacturing: Vince Stewart
Commercial Marketing Manager: Tim Burke
International Sales Manager: Ivan Villalba
Estimated Sales: $5-10 Million
Number Employees: 50-99
Type of Packaging: Food Service
Brands:
  Vogt Tube-Ice

30893 Voigt Lighting Industries Inc.
79 Commerce St
Garfield, NJ 7026

973-928-2252
Fax: 973-478- 015 paul@voightlighting.com
www.voightlighting.com
FDA compliant lighting fixtures for food processing areas and warehouses

President: Paul Goldberg
CFO: Frank Stein
Contact: Benny Benyamini
bbb@voigtlighting.com
Estimated Sales: Below $5 Million
Number Employees: 4
Brands:
  Asym-A-Lyte
  Frugalume
  Korode-Not

30894 Volckening Inc
6700 3rd Ave
Brooklyn, NY 11220-5296

718-836-4000
Fax: 718-748-2811 800-221-0276
info@volckening.com www.volckening.com
Manufacturer and exporter of replacement parts for beverage filling machinery; also, industrial brushes
Chairman: William Schneider
wschneider@volckeninginc.com
CEO: F Schneider
Estimated Sales: $10-20 Million
Number Employees: 20-49
Square Footage: 50000

30895 (HQ)Volk Corp
23936 Industrial Park Dr
Farmington Hills, MI 48335-2861

248-477-6700
Fax: 248-478-6884 800-521-6799
sales@volkcorp.com www.volkcorp.com
Manufacturer and exporter of signs, rubber stamps, markers, name badges, envelopes, tapes, tape dispensers, advertising novelties, printing dies, zinc plates, steel stamps, ink cartridges, etc
President: Bill Woolfall
billw@volkcorp.com
Marketing Director: Todd Cruthfield
Sales Director: Ron Harper
Plant Manager: Donald Schultz
Purchasing Manager: Scott Szumanski
Estimated Sales: $5-10 Million
Number Employees: 50-99
Other Locations:
  Volk Corp.
  Grand Rapids MI

30896 Volk Enterprises Inc
1335 Ridgeland Pkwy # 120
Suite 120
Alpharetta, GA 30004-0728

770-663-5400
Fax: 770-663-5411 sales@volkenterprises.com
www.volkenterprises.com
President: Ken Bragg
k.bragg@volkprotectiveproducts.com
Vice President: Daniel J. Volk (DAN)
Regional Sales Manager: Burt Hewitt
Estimated Sales: $500,000-$1 Million
Number Employees: 50-99

30897 Volk Packaging Corp
11 Morin St
Biddeford, ME 04005

207-282-6151
Fax: 207-283-1165 vpc@volkboxes.com
www.volkboxes.com
Manufacturer and exporter of packaging and containerizing supplies including corrugated, fiber and wooden boxes, cartons and containers.
President/Owner: Derek Volk
Chief Executive Officer: Douglas Volk
Chief Financial Officer: Douglas Hellsfrom
Production Manager: Richard Wills
Purchasing Manager: Glorijane Winslow
Estimated Sales: $25-35 Million
Number Employees: 85
Square Footage: 140000

30898 Vollrath Co LLC
1236 N 18th St
Sheboygan, WI 53081-3201

920-457-4851
800-624-2051
vollrathcompany.com
Frozen treat equipment, contract manufacturing, industrial washers and electronic cleaning equipment, and wholesale/retail consumer cookware and bakeware.

President & CEO: Paul Bartlet
pbartlet@vollrathco.com
VP, Human Resources: Jeff Madson
Marketing & Communications Director: Cathy Fitzgerald
SVP, Operations: Dennis Heaney
Year Founded: 1874
Estimated Sales: $100-500 Million
Number Employees: 1000-4999
Type of Packaging: Food Service
Brands:
Impressions
New York, New York
Super Pan Ii

30899 Volta Belting Technology, Inc.
11 Chapin Road
Pine Brook, NJ 07058

973-276-7905
Fax: 973-276-7908 sales@voltabelting.com
www.voltabelting.com
Food conveyor belts, power transmission & timing belts and belt welding tools.
Contact: Denise Buongiorno
denise@voltabelting.com

30900 Volumetric Technologies
401 Cannon Industrial Blvd #1
Cannon Falls, MN 55009

507-263-0034
www.volumetrictechnologies.com
Filling and packaging equipment including conveyors, cup machines, piston fillers/depositors, complete turn key filling lines, dispensing nozzles and net weight filling lines. Applications include meats, soups, dipstaco/burrito/tamale filling, chili, pizzas, bakery items, dairy products, condiments/sauces, precooked dinners, deli products and creamed meats.
President: Timothy Piper
VP: Keith Piper
VP/Secretary: Bruce Piper
Number Employees: 6
Type of Packaging: Bulk

30901 Vomela/Harbor Graphics
444 Fillmore Avenue East
St Paul, MN 55107

651-228-2200
Fax: 651-228-2295 800-645-1012
sales@vomela.com www.vomela.com
Screen and digital printing of graphics and signage for retail , fleet, P.O.P, vehicle, tradeshow and event marketing
President: Thomas Auth
President: Mark Auth
Marketing/Sales: Jeff Noren
Plant Manager: Mark Gillen
Estimated Sales: $1-3 Million
Number Employees: 5-9

30902 Von Gal Corp
3101 Hayneville Rd
Montgomery, AL 36108-3900

334-261-2700
Fax: 334-261-2801 800-542-6570
www.ptchronos.com
Palletizers for baking, bottling and brewing industries
Manager: Paul Probst
Sales Manager: Jason Bennett
Number Employees: 20-49

30903 Vonco Products LLC
201 Park Ave
Lake Villa, IL 60046-8999

847-356-2323
Fax: 847-356-8630 800-323-9077
sales@vonco.com www.vonarma.com
Poly and laminated bags
President: L Lawrence Laske
Chairman: Les Laske
les@vonco.com
VP Sales: Les Laske
Sales Representative: Gary Link
Estimated Sales: $10-20 Million
Number Employees: 100-249
Square Footage: 76000

30904 Voorhees Rubber Mfg Co
6846 Basket Switch Rd
Newark, MD 21841-2214

410-632-1582
Fax: 410-632-1522 info@voorheesrubber.com
www.voorheesrubber.com

Manufacturer, exporter and wholesaler/distributor of rubber candy molds
President: Richard Jackson
info@voorheesrubber.com
Vice President: Teresa Jackson
Estimated Sales: Below $5 Million
Number Employees: 5-9
Brands:
Voorhees

30905 Vorti-Siv
36165Salem GangaRoad
PO Box 720
Salem, OH 44460-0720

330-332-4958
Fax: 330-332-1543 800-227-7487
info@vorti-siv.com www.vorti-siv.com
Manufacturer and exporter of gyrating sieves and tanks; self-cleaning filters
President: Barbara Maroscher
CFO: Barb Groppe
VP: Vic Maroscher
Sales: Dennis Ulrich
Plant Manager: Kevin Penner
Estimated Sales: $3-5,000,000
Number Employees: 10-19
Square Footage: 35000
Parent Co: MM Industries
Brands:
Vorti-Siv

30906 Vortron Smokehouse/Ovens
120 South Main Street
Iron Ridge, WI 53035

608-362-0862
Fax: 608-362-9012 800-874-1949
sales@vortronsmokehouses.com
www.vortronsmokehouses.com
Manufacturer and exporter of food processing machinery, ovens, smokehouses, drying rooms and smoke generators
VP: Dan Mertes
Plant Manager: Dan Mertes
Estimated Sales: $2.5-5 Million
Number Employees: 10-19
Parent Co: Apache Stainless Equipment
Other Locations:
Vortron Smokehouse/Ovens
Beaver Dam WI

30907 Vorwerk
3255 E. Thousand Oaks Blvd.
Thousand Oaks, CA 91362

888-867-9375
service@thermomix.us thermomix.com
Thermomix cooking equipment.
Managing Partner: Reiner Strecker
Managing Partner: Frank Van Oers
Managing Partner: Rainer Christian Genes
Year Founded: 1883
Estimated Sales: $1-2 Billion
Number Employees: 10,000+
Brands:
Thermomix®

30908 Voss Belting & Specialty Co
6965 N Hamlin Ave # 1
Lincolnwood, IL 60712-2598

847-673-8900
Fax: 847-673-1408 info@vossbelting.com
www.vossbelting.com
Rubber and thermoplastic conveyor belting; neoprene and urethane timing belts; high temperature silicone/teflon conveyor belting
President: Richard A Voss
rvoss@vossbelt.com
Estimated Sales: $5-10 Million
Number Employees: 20-49

30909 Vrymeer Commodities
PO Box 545
St Charles, IL 60174-0545

630-377-2584

30910 Vulcan Electric Co
28 Endfield St
Porter, ME 04068-3502

207-625-3231
Fax: 207-625-8938 800-922-3027
sales@vulcanelectric.com
www.vulcanelectric.com

Manufacturer and exporter of heaters including immersion, strip and fin strip, radiant cartridge, band and flexible; also, tubular elements, thermocouples, programmable/mechanical temperature controls and sensors
President: Michael Quick
General Manager: Stan Haupt
CFO: Jenet Floyd
Quality Control: Bob Doglus
Estimated Sales: $20-30 Million
Number Employees: 50-99
Square Footage: 50000
Brands:
Cal-Stat

30911 Vulcan Food Equipment Group
3600 North Point Blvd
Baltimore, MD 21222-2726

410-284-0662
Fax: 410-288-3662 800-814-2028
www.vulcanequipment.com
Manufacturer and exporter of broilers, steam cookers, ranges, fryers and warmers; also, bakery, food processing, hotel, restaurant and pizza ovens
Vice President: Wally Beal
beal@vulcanequipment.com
VP Sales National Accounts: Tom Cassin
VP: Jim Culinane
Director Sales: Dennis Ball
National Accounts Manager: Jim Thompson
Estimated Sales: $10-20 Million
Number Employees: 250-499
Parent Co: ITW Food Equipment Group LLC
Type of Packaging: Food Service

30912 Vulcan Industries
300 Display Dr
Moody, AL 35004-2100

205-640-2400
Fax: 205-640-2412 888-444-4417
hello@vulcanind.com www.vulcanind.com
Manufacturer and exporter of point of purchase display fixtures and products including tubular, sheet metal, hard board, plastic and wire
VP: J Whitley
Quality Control: Steve Brugge
Manager Sales/Marketing: Douglas Stockham
Accountant: Virgil Wells
Plant Manager: James Raynor
Number Employees: 10-19
Square Footage: 330000
Parent Co: Eosco Industries

30913 Vulcan Materials Co
1200 Urban Center Dr
P.O. Box 385014
Vestavia, AL 35242-2545

205-298-3000
Fax: 205-298-2960 www.vulcanmaterials.com
Foam cleaner sanitizer, hard surface disinfectants, chlorine dioxide water treatment and odor control agents
President: David P Clement
clementd@vmcmail.com
Chairman, Chief Executive Officer: Don James
EVP, Chief Financial Officer: John R. McPherson
VP, Marketing Support Services: Sidney F. Mays
National Sales Director: Richard Higby
EVP, Chief Operating Officer: J. Thomas Hill
Estimated Sales: Over $1 Billion
Number Employees: 5000-9999
Square Footage: 240000
Brands:
Absorb
Akta Klor
Bioslide
Dura Klor
Rio Klor

30914 Vynatex
7 Carey Pl
Suite 2
Port Washington, NY 11050

516-944-6130
Fax: 516-767-7056
Custom menu covers, wine books, check presentation folders, guest service directories and in-room hotel products including ice buckets, promotional items, etc.
President: Angela Lamagna
angie@vynatex.com
Sales Manager: Alexander Juarez

Estimated Sales: $1-2.5 Million
Number Employees: 5-9
Square Footage: 60000
Brands:
  Compu-Check
  Dynahyde
  Sculptathane
  Scultahyde

30915 (HQ)W A Powers Co
125 S Main St
Fort Worth, TX 76104-1293
817-332-7151
Fax: 817-334-0855 800-792-1243
info@wapowers.com www.wapowers.com
Conveyor systems including gravity, wheel and
roller powered
President: Doyle Powers
dpowers@wapowers.com
Estimated Sales: $2.5-5 Million
Number Employees: 10-19
Other Locations:
  Powers, W.A., Co.
  Fort Worth TX

30916 W H Cooke & Co Inc
6868 York Rd
P.O.Box 893
Hanover, PA 17331-6814
717-630-2222
Fax: 717-637-9999 800-772-5151
sales@whcooke.com www.whcooke.com
Temperature and RH sensors, temperature and RH
controls, dough temperature boxes, proofer control
systems
President: Shawn Beck
shawnb@whcooke.com
Estimated Sales: Below $5 Million
Number Employees: 10-19

30917 W H Wildman Company
25956 U.S. Route 33
P.O.Box 42
New Hampshire, OH 45870
419-568-7531
Fax: 419-568-7531 scott@wildmanspice.com
www.wildmanspice.com
Wholesale packager; general groceries
Owner: Scott Gray
Estimated Sales: Less than $300,000
Number Employees: 1-4
Type of Packaging: Consumer, Food Service, Pri-
  vate Label, Bulk
Brands:
  Wildman's

30918 W J Egli & Co
205 E Columbia St
Alliance, OH 44601-2563
330-823-3666
Fax: 330-823-0011 info@wjegli.com
Manufacturer and exporter of wire, wood and tube
display racks
President: Jeff Egli
VP: Mike Egli
Marketing Director: Jeff Egli
Estimated Sales: $2.5-5 Million
Number Employees: 20-49
Square Footage: 200000

30919 W L Jenkins Co
1445 Whipple Ave SW
Canton, OH 44710-1321
330-477-3407
Fax: 330-477-8404 info@wljenkinsco.com
www.wljenkinsco.com
Manufacturer and exporter of mechanically operated
fire alarm systems; also, bells and gongs
Owner: Susan Jenkins
info@wljenkinsco.com
Estimated Sales: $2.5-5 Million
Number Employees: 5-9
Parent Co: W.L. Jenkins Company

30920 W R Grace & Co
7500 Grace Dr
Columbia, MD 21044
410-531-4000
Fax: 410-531-4367 www.grace.com
Processor and exporter of silica gel absorbents; also,
clarifying and anticaking agents.

President & Chief Executive Officer: Hudson La
Force
Senior VP & Chief Financial Officer: William
Dockman
Senior VP, Human Resources: Elizabeth Brown
Year Founded: 1832
Estimated Sales: $1.72 Billion
Number Employees: 3,900
Brands:
  Condensation Gard
  Sycoid
  Trisyl

30921 W&H Systems
120 Asia Pl
Carlstadt, NJ 07072
201-933-9849
Fax: 201-933-2144 www.whsystems.com
Provider of distribution logistics service emphasiz-
ing conveyor and computer system and integration
including visual control, manifesting and paperless
picking
President: Don Betman
Executive VP: Ron Quackenbush
CFO: Frank Artizone
VP: Ken Knapp
Contact: Thomas Annunziato
gary.ciolorito@siemens.com
Estimated Sales: $20-50 Million
Number Employees: 100-249
Square Footage: 31000
Brands:
  Buschman
  Promech

30922 W.A. Golomski & Associates
N9690 County Road U
Algoma, WI 54201-9528
920-487-9864
Fax: 920-487-7249
Consultant specializing in product introductions,
motivation programs and total quality management
programs
President: William Golomski
Estimated Sales: Less than $500,000
Number Employees: 4

30923 W.A. Schmidt Company
99 Brower Ave
Oaks, PA 19456
215-721-8300
Fax: 215-721-5890 800-523-6719
www.pencoproducts.com
Manufacturer and exporter of storage systems and
racks
President: Greg Grogan
Estimated Sales: $20-50 Million
Number Employees: 100-249
Square Footage: 246000
Brands:
  H.F. Cradle System

30924 W.G. Durant Corporation
9825 Painter Ave # A-E
Whittier, CA 90605-2700
562-946-5555
Fax: 562-946-5577
Manufacturer and exporter of palletizers, bag pack-
ers, conveyors and system electrical controls
Owner: Zara Badalian
Sales Manager: Jack Schreyer
Estimated Sales: $3-5 Million
Number Employees: 5-9
Square Footage: 600000
Parent Co: Westmont Industries
Brands:
  Hy-Ac Iv

30925 W.M. Barr & Co Inc.
8000 Centerview Pkwy.
Suite 400
Memphis, TN 38106
901-775-0100
Fax: 901-775-5468
Aerosols and liquid cleaners including glass and
hand cleaners.
CEO: Richard Loomis
Year Founded: 1946
Estimated Sales: $100-500 Million
Number Employees: 250-499
Parent Co: W.M. Barr & Company
Brands:
  Citrus Solvent
  Klean Hand

P&D
Pane Relief

30926 W.M. Sprinkman Corporation
1002 Academy Street
P.O.Box 57
Elroy, WI 53929-0057
608-462-8456
Fax: 608-462-8774 800-816-1610
sales@sprinkman.com www.sprinkman.com
Agitation systems, milk, silo, tank, agitators, cutters,
drainers, fines savers, forks, presses, manual, tanks,
starter, custom fabrication, flow diversion stations,
and ladders
General Manager: Larry Willer
Contact: Dennis Kuchel
kucheld@sprinkman.com
Estimated Sales: $1-2.5 Million
Number Employees: 10-19

30927 W.Y. International
2000 S. Garfield Ave.
Los Angeles, CA 90040
323-726-8733
Fax: 323-726-9409 info@wyintl.com
www.wyintl.com
Asian sauces, canned goods, grains, and snacks; Eu-
ropean and Californian wine and oils; machinery &
tools.
President: David N. Wong
Vice President: Henry P. Wong
Year Founded: 1982
Estimated Sales: $2-5 Million
Number Employees: 2-10

30928 WA Brown & Son
209 Long Meadow Dr
Salisbury, NC 28147
704-636-5131
Fax: 704-637-0919
Manufacturer, importer and exporter of walk-in
coolers, freezers, and structural insulated panels
President: Ed Brown
Vice President: Paul Brown
Sales Director: Dave Morris
Contact: Frank Preolette
kellerrd@appstate.edu
Operations Manager: Deric Skeen
Estimated Sales: $25-50 Million
Number Employees: 100-249
Square Footage: 250000
Type of Packaging: Food Service, Private Label
Brands:
  W.A. Brown

30929 WAKO Chemicals USA Inc
1600 Bellwood Rd
N Chesterfield, VA 23237-1326
804-271-7677
Fax: 804-271-7791 labchem@wakousa.com
www.wakousa.com
Specialty chemicals
Manager: Ed Sata
R&D: Hiramatsu Max
CFO: Ed Sata
Manager: William Chang
chang.william@wako-chem.co.jp
Estimated Sales: $20-50 Million
Number Employees: 20-49

30930 WCB Ice Cream
1108 Frankford Ave
Philadelphia, PA 19125-4118
215-425-4320
Fax: 215-426-2034 www.gram-equipment.com
Manufacturer and exporter of fillers, sealers, fittings,
freezers, homogenizers, pumps, tanks and frozen
novelty equipment
Manager: John Dorety
jdorety@wcbicecream.com
Office Manager: Susie Margolis
Plant Manager: Vince Somers
Estimated Sales: $2.5-5 Million
Number Employees: 10-19

30931 WCB Ice Cream
267 Livingston Street
Northvale, NJ 7647
201-784-1101
Fax: 201-784-1116 800-252-5200
wcbice@wcbicecream.com
Cheese equipment, firesavers, heat exchangers,
scraped surface, ice cream equipment, ingredient
feeders

President: Ken Rodi
CFO: Ken Rodi
Quality Control: Harry Colber
Contact: Mick Arnold
marnold@wcbicecream.com
Number Employees: 10,000

30932 WCB Ice Cream USA
267 Livingston Street
Northvale, NJ 07647

215-425-4320
Fax: 215-426-2034 800-644-4320
www.wcbicecream.dk
Dairy equipment and food processing machinery repair and rebuilding
Manager: John Dorety
Contact: Mick Arnold
marnold@wcbicecream.com
Estimated Sales: $1-5 Million
Number Employees: 20-49
Parent Co: Udi And Spx.

30933 WCR
221 Crane St
Dayton, OH 45403

937-223-0703
Fax: 937-223-2818 800-421-4927
info@wcr-regasketing.com
www.wcr-regasketing.com
Plate heat exchangers
Owner: Brad Stevens
Applications Engineer: Heather Comer
Director of Sales and Technical Support: Jeremy Foley
Contact: Edward Aring
earing@wcr-heatexchangers.com
Production Coordinator: Jenna Grigsby
Estimated Sales: $5-10 Million
Number Employees: 20-49

30934 WCS Corp
2498 American Ave
Hayward, CA 94545-1810

510-782-8727
Fax: 510-783-6843 www.royalchemical.com
Cleaning compounds, liquids and powders
Executive VP: Jeanette Conde
Estimated Sales: $20-50 Million
Number Employees: 10-19
Parent Co: Royal Chemical Company

30935 WE Killam Enterprises
PO Box 741
Waterford, ON N0E 1Y0
Canada

519-443-7421
Fax: 519-443-6922
Manufacturer, importer and exporter of packaging equipment including inkjet printers, case coding, full wrap and spot labelers, case and tray packing and sealing machinery and can ejectors, standard knapp, burt, fmc, ace/kore, ualcosystems.
President: Roger Elliott
Number Employees: 1-4
Square Footage: 5000
Brands:
Ace & Icore
Labellett
Mateer-Burt
Sauven
Standard Knapp
Valco

30936 WE Lyons Contruction
1301 Ygnacio Valley Rd
Walnut Creek, CA 94598

925-658-1600
Fax: 925-658-1604 800-493-5966
info@welyons.com www.welyons.com
Design-build construction; manufacturing, food service, food processing, distribution, and USDA design and construction
President: Greg Lyon
CFO: Debora Allan
Estimated Sales: $10-20 Million
Number Employees: 50-99

30937 (HQ)WEBB-Stiles Co
675 Liverpool Dr
PO Box 464
Valley City, OH 44280-9717

330-273-9222
Fax: 330-225-5532 webb-stiles@webb-stiles.com
www.webb-stiles.com

Manufacturer and exporter of custom designed conveyor systems for custom package and pallet handling
CEO: Donald Stiles Jr
Vice President: Larry Birchler
Sales Director: Matthew Weisman
Estimated Sales: $10-20 Million
Number Employees: 100-249
Square Footage: 600000
Other Locations:
Webb-Stiles Co.
Gadsden AL

30938 WEI Equipment
207 Evergreen Ave
Haddon Township, NJ 08108-3508

856-863-9577
Fax: 856-863-9641
Materials handling equipment, elevators, loaders, lifters and dumpers, used and rebuilt equipment, frozen meat slicers, flakers and breakers, grinders, mixers, screw conveyors
President: John Camp
Estimated Sales: $1-2.5 Million
Number Employees: 9

30939 WEI Equipment
4312 Jade Avenue
Cypress, CA 90630

714-827-9510
Fax: 714-209-0023 800-934-4934
Used food processing equipment for the red meat industry
Estimated Sales: $1-2.5 Million
Number Employees: 9

30940 WEIS Markets Inc.
1000 S. 2nd St.
PO Box 471
Sunbury, PA 17801

570-286-4571
866-999-9347
www.weismarkets.com
Grocery, bakery, deli, produce, floral, seafood, and more.
Chair/President/CEO: Jonathan Weis
jweis@weismarkets.com
Year Founded: 1912
Estimated Sales: $3.4 Billion
Number Employees: 18,000
Other Locations:
Manufacturing Facility-Market St
Sunbury PA
Manufacturing Facility-N 4th St
Sunbury PA
Brands:
Weis Five Star
Weis Quality
Full Circle

30941 WES Plastics
561 Edward Avenue
Richmond Hill, ON L4C 9W6
Canada

905-508-1546
Displays, boxes, stands; also, custom fabrication available for acrylic items
Owner: Wayne Simpson
Number Employees: 1-4

30942 WGN Flag & Decorating Co
7984 S South Chicago Ave
Chicago, IL 60617-1096

773-768-8076
Fax: 773-768-3138 sales@wgnflag.com
www.wgnflag.com
Flags, pennants, banners and signs
President: Carl Gus Porter III
VP: Gus Porter
Estimated Sales: $1-2.5 Million
Number Employees: 10-19

30943 WITT Industries Inc
4600 N Mason Montgomery Rd
Mason, OH 45040-9176

513-923-5821
Fax: 877-891-8200 800-543-7417
sales@witt.com www.witt.com
Manufacturer and exporter of wastebaskets and firesafe steel, outside, torpedo and fiberglass waste receptacles; importer of structural foam lockers
President: Tim Harris
Chairman: Marcy Wydman
Director Sales/Marketing: Chris Adams
Purchasing Manager: Rick Royce

Estimated Sales: $10-20 Million
Number Employees: 20-49
Square Footage: 150000
Type of Packaging: Food Service

30944 WMF/USA
85 Price Parkway
Farmingdale, NY 11735-1305

704-882-3898
Fax: 631-694-0820 800-999-6347
consumer@WMFAmericas.com
Wholesaler/distributor of flatware, holloware, cookware, china and crystal
President: Stefan Nisi
VP Sales and Marketing: Peter Braley
National Sales Manager: Emma Popolow
Contact: Markus Glueck
markus.glueck@wmf-usa.com
Parent Co: WMF/AG

30945 WNA
2155 W Longhorn Dr
Lancaster, TX 75134-2916

Fax: 972-224-3067 800-334-2877
www.wna.biz
Manufacturer and importer of plastic fabrications, containers and cups.
Number Employees: 100-249
Brands:
Celebrity Cups

30946 WNA
5930 Quintus Loop
Chattanooga TN 37421-2216

Fax: 800-762-4753 800-404-9318
www.wna.biz
Manufacturer and exporter of injection molded plastic disposables including platters, bowls, utensils and specialty items.
Number Employees: 100-249

30947 WNA
50 E River Center Blvd
Suite 650
Covington, KY 41011-1656

Fax: 978-256-1614 888-962-2877
Manufacturer and exporter of injection molded plastic disposables including platters, bowls, utensils and specialty items.
Estimated Sales: $50-100 Million
Number Employees: 100-249

30948 WNA Hopple Plastics
7430 Empire Drive
Florence, KY 41042-2924

859-283-1570
Fax: 859-283-0061 800-446-4622
Extruded and thermoformed custom plastic packaging including food trays and containers; also, design consultation services available
VP Sales: Brett York
Contact: Mike Evans
mike@hopple.com
Estimated Sales: $20-50 Million
Number Employees: 250-499
Square Footage: 185000
Parent Co: John Waddington

30949 WORC Slitting & Mfg Co
50 Suffolk St # 1
Worcester, MA 01604-3792

508-754-9112
Fax: 508-754-9117 800-356-2961
info@coverallcovers.com
www.coverallcovers.com
Duty vinyl Rack Covers, Velcro Strip Doors, PVC Display Rack, Quality Controlled Anti-Bacterial Covers for Health Care Industry, Carts, Transport Bins, Racks & Equipment, Food Service Equipment, Covers for Slicers, Utility Carts, DishDollies, Mixers
CEO: George Najemy
najemy@aol.com
Estimated Sales: $1 Million
Number Employees: 10-19
Square Footage: 60000
Type of Packaging: Bulk

30950 WP Bakery Group
3 Enterprise Drive
Suite 108
Shelton, CT 06484

203-929-6530
Fax: 203-929-7089 www.kemperusa.com

Bakery equipment
President: Patricia Kennedy
Controller: Karen Smith
VP Marketing/Mixer Product Manager: Shawna Goldfarb
Vice President of Sales: Bruce Gingrich
Estimated Sales: $5 Million
Number Employees: 5-9

30951 WR Key
4770 Sheppard Avenue E
Scarborough, ON M1S 3V6
Canada

416-291-6246
Fax: 416-291-4882 www.wrkey.com
Manufacturer and exporter of stainless steel serving carts, cash boxes, desk trays and card cabinets
President and CEO: Gw Key
R&D and QC: Lisa Key
Sales Manager: Lisa Key
Estimated Sales: $5-10 Million
Number Employees: 40
Type of Packaging: Consumer, Food Service, Private Label

30952 (HQ)WS Packaging Group Inc
2571 S Hemlock Rd
Green Bay, WI 54229

877-977-5177
info@wspackaging.com
www.wspackaging.com
Manufacturer and exporter of labels, tags, folded cartons, instant redeemable coupons, F.D.A. packaging and tape; also, offset printing available.
President & Chief Financial Officer: Jay Tomcheck
Senior Vice Presient of Sales: Becky Smith
Year Founded: 1966
Estimated Sales: $400 Million
Number Employees: 1000-4999
Square Footage: 110000
Type of Packaging: Private Label
Other Locations:
WL Group-Wisconsin Label
Tulsa OK
Brands:
Xl

30953 WS Packaging Group Inc
950 Breezewood Ln
Neenah, WI 54956

888-532-3334
www.wspackaging.com
Manufacturer and exporter of labels, tags, folded cartons, instant redeemable coupons, F.D.A. packaging and tape; also, offset printing available.

30954 WS Packaging Group Inc
1102 Jefferson St
Algoma, WI 54201

800-236-3424
www.wspackaging.com
Manufacturer and exporter of labels, tags, folded cartons, instant redeemable coupons, F.D.A. packaging and tape; also, offset printing available.

30955 WS Packaging Group Inc
3530 Pipestone Rd
Dallas, TX 75212

214-330-7770
www.wspackaging.com
Manufacturer and exporter of labels, tags, folded cartons, instant redeemable coupons, F.D.A. packaging and tape; also, offset printing available.

30956 WS Packaging Group Inc
303 W Marquette Ave
Oak Creek, WI 53154

800-837-3838
www.wspackaging.com
Manufacturer and exporter of labels, tags, folded cartons, instant redeemable coupons, F.D.A. packaging and tape; also, offset printing available.
Square Footage: 84000

30957 WS Packaging Group Inc
29 Jet View Dr
Rochester, NY 14624

800-836-8186
www.wspackaging.com
Manufacturer and exporter of labels, tags, folded cartons, instant redeemable coupons, F.D.A. packaging and tape; also, offset printing available.
Type of Packaging: Consumer, Food Service, Private Label

Brands:
Accorista
Genisis
Roll Tax 200
Supergard

30958 WS Packaging Group Inc
1217 Rabas St
Algoma, WI 54201

800-323-6026
www.wspackaging.com
Labeling solutions, ranging from prime label and equipment to promotional coupons, screen labels and unsupported film labels for the beverage industry

30959 WS Packaging Group Inc
1642 DeBence Dr
Franklin, PA 16323

800-372-1313
www.wspackaging.com
Manufacturer and exporter of labels, tags, folded cartons, instant redeemable coupons, F.D.A. packaging and tape; also, offset printing available.

30960 WS Packaging Group Inc
7400 Industrial Row Dr
Mason, OH 45040-1302

800-877-9596
www.wspackaging.com
Manufacturer and exporter of labels, tags, folded cartons, instant redeemable coupons, F.D.A. packaging and tape; also, offset printing available.

30961 WS Packaging Group Inc
2222 Beebee St
San Luis Obispo, CA 93401

800-234-3320
www.wspackaging.com
Manufacturer and exporter of labels, tags, folded cartons, instant redeemable coupons, F.D.A. packaging and tape; also, offset printing available.

30962 WS Packaging Group Inc
7500 Industrial Row Dr
Mason, OH 45040-1302

800-877-3795
www.wspackaging.com
Manufacturer and exporter of labels, tags, folded cartons, instant redeemable coupons, F.D.A. packaging and tape; also, offset printing available.

30963 WS Packaging Group Inc
1720 James Pkwy
Heath, OH 43056

740-929-2210
www.wspackaging.com
Manufacturer and exporter of labels, tags, folded cartons, instant redeemable coupons, F.D.A. packaging and tape; also, offset printing available.

30964 WS Packaging Group Inc
202 Galewski Dr
Winona, MN 55987

507-452-2315
www.wspackaging.com
Manufacturer and exporter of labels, tags, folded cartons, instant redeemable coupons, F.D.A. packaging and tape; also, offset printing available.

30965 WS Packaging Group Inc
1 Riverside Way
Wilton, NH 03086

800-258-1050
www.wspackaging.com
Manufacturer and exporter of labels, tags, folded cartons, instant redeemable coupons, F.D.A. packaging and tape; also, offset printing available.

30966 WS Packaging Group Inc
10215 Caneel Dr
Knoxville, TN 37931

865-437-3400
www.wspackaging.com
Manufacturer and exporter of labels, tags, folded cartons, instant redeemable coupons, F.D.A. packaging and tape; also, offset printing available.

30967 WS Packaging Group Inc
531 Airpark Dr
Fullerton, CA 92833

714-992-2574
www.wspackaging.com

Manufacturer and exporter of labels, tags, folded cartons, instant redeemable coupons, F.D.A. packaging and tape; also, offset printing available.

30968 WS Packaging Group Inc
11 Col. La Leona
Garcia, NL
Mexico

www.wspackaging.com
Manufacturer and exporter of labels, tags, folded cartons, instant redeemable coupons, F.D.A. packaging and tape; also, offset printing available.

30969 Wabash Power Equipment Co
444 Carpenter Ave
Wheeling, IL 60090-6081

847-541-5600
Fax: 847-541-1279 800-704-2002
info@wabashpower.com www.wabashpower.com
Deaerators, boilers, power generation equipment and technical energy services
President: Pete Wilberscheid
pete.wilberscheid@ubid.com
Estimated Sales: $10-20 Million
Number Employees: 20-49

30970 Waco Broom & Mop Factory
PO Box 1656
Waco, TX 76703-1656

254-753-3581
Fax: 254-753-3595 800-548-7716
msimon7760@aol.com
Mops, brooms and handles
President: Mark Simon
Number Employees: 15
Square Footage: 36000
Brands:
Crown

30971 Waddington North America
6 Stuart Rd
Chelmsford, MA 01824-4108

978-256-6553
Fax: 978-256-1614 888-962-2877
Manufacturer and exporter of disposable plastic dinnerware, drinkware, servingware, cutlery, cutlery packets, straws and stirrers
President: Mike Evans
CEO: Dave Gordon
CFO: Steve Morehouse
Quality Control: Tom Whitcumb
Marketing Director: Al Madonna
Contact: Russell Allen
rallen@mswalker.com
Operations Manager: Jim Messeder
Estimated Sales: $25-100 Million
Number Employees: 250-499
Square Footage: 12000
Parent Co: Waddington PLC
Brands:
Classic Crystal
Classicware
Comet
Crystal Flex
Designerware
Frost Flex

30972 Wade Manufacturing Company
PO Box 23666
Tigard, OR 97281-3666

503-692-5353
Fax: 503-692-5358 800-222-7246
sales@waderain.com www.waderain.com
Manufacturer and exporter of agricultural irrigation systems including handrove, poweroll and center pivot; also, micro irrigation products and aluminum casters
President: Ed Newbegin
VP: Cliff Warner
Contact: Pierre Lameh
plameh@waderain.com
Estimated Sales: $20-50 Million
Number Employees: 50-99
Parent Co: R.M. Wade & Company
Brands:
Wade Rain

30973 WaffleWaffle
43 River Rd
Nutley, NJ 07110-3411

201-559-1286
info@mywafflewaffle.com
mywafflewaffle.com

Waffles: Belgian-style, cones, doughs, mixes, and waffle irons.
Co-Founder: Justin Samuels
Co-Founder: Samuel Rockwell
Vice President, Business Development: Brian Samuels
Chief Marketing Officer: David Song
Vice President, Sales: Bracken Abrams
Director of Operations: Grant Ramsey
Estimated Sales: $2 Million
Number Employees: 12
Type of Packaging: Consumer, Food Service, Private Label
Brands:
   WaffleWaffle

30974 Wag Industries
4117 Grove Street
Skokie, IL 60076-1713
                              773-638-7007
   Fax: 773-533-6951 800-621-3305
                  blunt232@aol.com
Manufacturer and exporter of mobile catering truck units including bar and hot dog carts
President: Gail Gilbert
CEO: Doris Gilbert
CFO: George Gilbert
Quality Control: Gavin London
Purchasing Manager: Gavin Lendan
Estimated Sales: $5-10 Million
Number Employees: 10

30975 Wagner Brothers Containers
4101 Ashland Ave
Baltimore, MD 21205-2924
                              410-354-0044
                     Fax: 410-354-3125
Corrugated boxes
President: Lawrence K Wagner
VP: Lawrence Wagner Jr
Contact: Bill Hampton
bhampton@commercialwagner.com
Estimated Sales: $10-20 Million
Number Employees: 50-99

30976 Wahlstrom Manufacturing
15235 Boyle Ave
Fontana, CA 92337-7254
                              909-822-4677
                     Fax: 909-822-1675
Wire point-of-purchase display racks
Owner: Zach Fener
Estimated Sales: 700000
Number Employees: 5-9
Square Footage: 16000

30977 Wal-Vac
900 47th St SW # A
Suite A
Wyoming, MI 49509-5142
                              616-241-6717
   Fax: 616-241-1771 info@walvac.com
                  www.walvac.com
Manufacturer and exporter of built-in central vacuum cleaning systems
President: David Mol
walvac@walvac.com
VP Operations: David Mol
Estimated Sales: Less Than $500,000
Number Employees: 1-4
Square Footage: 19200
Brands:
   Wal-Vac

30978 Walco
820 Noyes St
PO Box 10527
Utica, NY 13502-5053
                              315-733-4663
   Fax: 315-733-6602 800-879-2526
                  sales@walcostainless.com
                  www.walcostainless.com
Manufacturer, importer and exporter of stainless steel flatware, steak knives, hollow ware, buffetware, and chafers
President: David S Allen
Sales/Marketing: Philip Benbenek
Contact: Phil Bembenek
phil@walcostainless.com
Estimated Sales: $10-20 Million
Number Employees: 100-249
Square Footage: 225000
Parent Co: Utica Cutlery Company
Type of Packaging: Food Service

Brands:
   Walco

30979 Walco-Linck Company
PO Box 5643
Bellingham, WA 98227-5643
                              845-353-7600
   Fax: 845-353-8056 800-338-2329
Manufacturer and exporter of aerosol insecticides, ant and roach baits and fly paper
President: William Burge
Executive VP: Richard Bozzo
CFO and QC: Richard Bozzo
Estimated Sales: $5-10 Million
Number Employees: 15
Brands:
   Tat

30980 Wald Imports
11200 Kirkland Way
Suite 300
Kirkland, WA 98033
                              425-822-0500
   Fax: 425-828-4201 800-426-2822
alsnel@waldimports.com www.waldimports.com
Decorative containers for gift baskets and floral
President: Lou Wald
Controller: Greg Best
VP: Martin Sippy
Sales Coordinator: Andria Blizzard
Contact: Gregory Best
gregorybest@waldimports.com
Order Entry & Invoicing: Gwen McClellan
Estimated Sales: $3.8 Million
Number Employees: 23

30981 Wald Wire & Mfg Co
846 Witzel Ave
Oshkosh, WI 54902-5796
                              920-231-5590
   Fax: 920-231-2212 800-236-0053
waldwire@waldwire.com www.waldwire.com
Wire racks for refrigerators and displays, wire forms, shelving, guards
President: Bob Mueller
rmueller@waldwire.com
Estimated Sales: Below $10 Million
Number Employees: 20-49

30982 Waldon Manufacturing LLC
201 W Oklahoma Ave
Fairview, OK 73737-9602
                              580-227-3711
   Fax: 580-227-2165 800-486-0023
                  www.waldonequipment.com
Forklift trucks, lift truck attachments and compact wheel loaders
Owner: Greg Wickert
CEO: Don Collins Jr
Sales Director: Tim Carroll
Public Relations: Kent Tyler
Operations Manager: Ricky Heflin
Number Employees: 10-19
Brands:
   Lay-Mor
   Waldon

30983 Walker Bag Mfg Co
11198 Ampere Ct
Louisville, KY 40299-3879
                              502-266-5696
   Fax: 502-266-9823 800-642-4949
bagmann@aol.com www.printex-usa.com
Custom designed burlap, canvas, cotton, jute, paper, tote and polypropylene bags; importer of polypropylene bags
CEO: Steve Dutton
steved@printex-usa.com
VP: Steve Dutton
Estimated Sales: $5-10 Million
Number Employees: 20-49

30984 Walker Brush Inc
82 E Main St # 4
Webster, NY 14580-3243
                              585-545-4748
   Fax: 585-342-2264 pgtaft@frontiernet.net
                  www.brushmfg.com
Brushes
Owner: Tom Erb
Sales Director: Timothy Mura
tom@brushmfg.com
Estimated Sales: $500,000-$1 Million
Number Employees: 5-9

30985 Walker Co
121 NW 6th St
Oklahoma City, OK 73102-6026
                              405-235-5319
   Fax: 405-235-1698 800-522-3015
                  info@walkercompanies.com
                  www.walkercompanies.com
Signs, banners and marking devices including rubber stamps
Manager: Sue Stephens
Quality Control: Sue Steven
VP: Kenny Walker
Manager: Melissa Rust
Estimated Sales: Below $5 Million
Number Employees: 20-49

30986 Walker Engineering Inc
9255 San Fernando Rd
Sun Valley, CA 91352-1416
                              818-252-7788
   Fax 818-252-7785 www.walkerairsep.com
Signs, awnings, canopies, flags, pennants and banners
Owner: Robert Walker
sales@airsep.com
Estimated Sales: Below $5 Million
Number Employees: 20-49
Type of Packaging: Bulk

30987 Walker Magnetics Group Inc
20 Rockdale St
Worcester, MA 01606-1922
                              508-853-3232
   Fax: 508-852-8649 800-962-4638
                  sales@walkermagnet.com
                  www.walkermagnet.com
Designer and manufacturer of magnetic workholding chucks, lifting, material handling, and separation applications.
Owner: Eric Englested
Plant Manager: Dick Isabell
Estimated Sales: Below $5 Million
Number Employees: 100-249

30988 Walker Magnetics Group Inc
20 Rockdale St
Worcester, MA 01606-1922
                              508-853-3232
   Fax: 508-852-8649 800-962-4638
info@walkermagnet.com www.walkermagnet.com
Suppliers of conveying systems tailored to the canmaking and can filling industries, magnetic cable conveyors, elevators, loverators, palletizing heads, magnetic twist conveyors, end handling conveyors, magnetic rails, rollers andcomplete turnkey systems
Owner: Eric Englested
Estimated Sales: $10-20 Million
Number Employees: 100-249

30989 Walker Stainless Equipment Co
625 W State St
New Lisbon, WI 53950
                              608-562-7500
                  www.walkerep.com
Manufacturer and exporter of stainless steel transportation and plant equipment tanks for the dairy industry.
Chief Executive Officer: Richard Giromini
President & Chief Operating Officer: Brent Yeagy
SVP & Chief Financial Officer: Jeffery Taylor
SVP, Human Resources: Bill Pitchford
Year Founded: 1943
Estimated Sales: $250-500 Million
Number Employees: 1000-4999
Square Footage: 200000
Parent Co: Wabash National Corporation
Brands:
   Norman Machinery
   Walker

30990 Wall Conveyor & Manufacturing
PO Box 7664
Huntington, WV 25778-7664
                              304-429-1335
   Fax: 304-429-1337 800-456-1335
Package handling conveyors including rebuilt; also, accessories
Owner: Jim Fankhanel
Office Manager: Liz Rexroad
Estimated Sales: $1-2.5 Million
Number Employees: 1-4
Square Footage: 12000

30991 Wallace & Hinz

100 Taylor Way
P.O.Box 708
Blue Lake, CA 95525

707-668-1825
Fax: 707-826-0224 800-831-8282
info@wallaceandhinz.com
www.wallaceandhinz.com
Manufacturer and exporter of bars including portable and modular
Owner: Tom Tellez
Sales Manager: Richard Cook
Estimated Sales: $10-20 Million
Number Employees: 20-49
Square Footage: 30000

30992 Wallace Computer Services

111 South Wacker Drive
Chicago, IL 60606

312-326-8000
Fax: 312-326-8001 888-925-8324
www.wallace.com
Prime, pressure sensitive and linerless labels, bar code and ingredient labeling software and printers including automatic label applicators and dispensers and bar code
Owner: Tushar Pandya
President, Chief Executive Officer: Thomas Quinlan
VP: David Jones
General Sales Manager: Chuck Wilson
Senior Vice President of Public Affairs: Gian-Carlo Peressutti
Estimated Sales: $10-20 Million
Number Employees: 1-4
Parent Co: Wallace Computer Services
Other Locations:
  Wallace Computer Services
  Hinsdale IL
Brands:
  Label-Aire
  Printware

30993 Wallace Computer Services

2275 Cabot Dr
Lisle, IL 60532

630-588-5000
Fax: 630-588-5115 800-323-8447
www.wallace.com
Printed business forms, packaging labels, automatic applicators and bar coding software, direct mail, point of purchase products and product collateral
President: Mike Duffield
Estimated Sales: $50-100 Million
Number Employees: 250-499

30994 Walle Corp

600 Elmwood Park Blvd
New Orleans, LA 70123-3350

504-734-8000
Fax: 504-733-2513 800-942-6761
www.walle.com
Manufacturer and exporter of labels for cans, bottles, plastics, etc.; also, lithographic and flexographic printing available
Vice President: Allen Dummitt
allen_dummitt@walle.com
Vice Chairman/CEO: Michael Keeney
VP: Colleen Rottmann
Estimated Sales: $20-50 Million
Number Employees: 100-249
Square Footage: 300000

30995 Walnut Packaging Inc

450 Smith St
Farmingdale, NY 11735-1105

631-293-3836
Fax: 631-293-3878 info@wpiplasticbags.com
www.wpiplasticbags.com
Manufacturer and exporter of polyethylene bags; also, print designers
Owner: Jose Alvarado
Estimated Sales: $2.5-5 Million
Number Employees: 10-19

30996 Walong Marketing

6281 Regio Ave.
Buena Park, CA 90620-1040

714-670-8899
Fax: 714-670-6668 www.asianfoodsonline.com
Asian foods: rice, cereal and grains, baking mixes, soups, vegetables, fruits, snacks, confections, condiments, sauces, drinks, deli, seafood, meats, kitchenware and canned foods.

Merchandiser: Tony Chiu
Chief Operating Officer: Coo Chen
Product Manager: Nancy Hsu
Estimated Sales: $73.2 Million
Number Employees: 130
Other Locations:
  Beuena Park CA
  Bolingbrook IL
  Duluth GA
  Jersey City NJ
  Stafford TX

30997 Walsh & Simmons Seating

2511 Iowa Ave
Saint Louis, MO 63104

314-664-1215
Fax: 314-664-0703 800-727-0364
sales@walshsimmons.com
www.walshsimmons.com
Manufacturer and exporter of benches, booths, chairs and cushion pads, stools and tables including legs and bases
President: Bill Simmons
Contact: Tony Pezzo
tonyp@walshsimmons.com
Estimated Sales: $10-20 Million
Number Employees: 100-249
Square Footage: 400000
Type of Packaging: Food Service

30998 Walsroder Packaging

7330 South Madison Street
Willowbrook, IL 60527-5588

Fax: 630-789-8489 800-882-9987
sales@walsroder.com
www.walsroderpackaging.com
Plastic and fibrous food casings for sausages and deli meats.
Contact: Gregg Alex
greggalex@walsroderpackaging.com

30999 Waltco Truck Equipment Company

285 Northeast Ave
Tallmadge, OH 44278

330-633-9191
Fax: 330-633-1418 800-211-3074
sales@waltco.com
Truck and hydraulic cylinder electrohydraulic tailgate lifts
CEO: Rod Robinson
Director Marketing/Sales: Ray Thompson
Contact: Chris Adkins
christopher.adkins@waltco.com
Estimated Sales: $30-50 Million
Number Employees: 100-249

31000 Walter Molzahn & Company

1050 W Fullerton Avenue
Chicago, IL 60614

312-528-0550
Cake ornaments and decorations
Type of Packaging: Private Label

31001 Walters Brothers

10489 W State Road 27 70
Radisson, WI 54867-7084

715-945-2646
Fax: 715-945-2878
Brite stack pallets
President: Tim Walters
tim.walters@waltersbrotherslumber.com
Vice President: Timothy Walters
Estimated Sales: $7 Million
Number Employees: 20-49
Square Footage: 20000

31002 Waltham Fruit Company

105 2nd St
Chelsea, MA 02150-1803

617-354-1994
Fax: 617-354-8423 www.baldor.com
Owner: Pat Pizzuto
Chief Executive Officer: Ronald Tucker
Vice President of Materials: Amy Lakin
Vice President of International Sales: Joe Maloney
Estimated Sales: $10-20 Million
Number Employees: 20-49

31003 Walton's Inc

3639 N Comotara St
Wichita, KS 67226-1304

316-262-0651
Fax: 316-262-5136 800-835-2832
www.waltonsinc.com

Manufacturer and exporter of brine pumps; wholesaler/distributor of meat processing equipment and butchers' supplies including saws, slicers and tenderizers, vacuum machines and bags and smokehouses
Owner: Don Walton
CEO: Brett Walton
brett@waltonsinc.com
Sales Director: Kurt Carter
Sales: Mark Schrag
Operations Manager: Brett Walton
Production Manager: Tim Fox
Purchasing Manager: Brett Walton
Estimated Sales: $1.8 Million
Number Employees: 20-49
Number of Brands: 25
Number of Products: 200
Square Footage: 71000
Type of Packaging: Food Service
Brands:
  Double J

31004 Wang Cheong CorporationUSA

193 6th Street
Brooklyn, NY 11215-3104

718-222-0880
Fax: 718-222-9037
Adhesive, stationary and printed tape

31005 Ward Ironworks

2 Broadway Avenue
Welland, ON L3B 5G4
Canada

905-732-7591
Fax: 905-732-3310 888-441-9273
Manufacturer, importer and exporter of material handling machinery including bucket elevators, regular and vibrating conveyors, empty bag compactors, vibrating feeders and screens
President: Guy Nelson
Estimated Sales: $5-10 Million
Number Employees: 10
Square Footage: 200000
Parent Co: Ward Automation

31006 Wardcraft Conveyor & Quick Die

1 Wardcraft Dr
Spring Arbor, MI 49283-9757

517-750-9100
Fax: 517-750-2244 800-782-2779
info@wardcraft.net www.wardcraftconveyor.com
Manufacturer and exporter of pneumatic conveyors and quick die change systems
President: Pat Sprague
psprague@wardcraft.net
VP: Pat Sprague
National Sales: Paul Miner
Estimated Sales: $5-10 Million
Number Employees: 20-49
Square Footage: 72000

31007 Waring Products

314 Ella Grasso Ave
Torrington, CT 06790-2345

860-496-3100
Fax: 860-496-9008 800-492-7464
waring@conair.com www.waringproducts.com
Manufacturer, exporter and importer of commercial food processors, blenders, juice extractors, bar glass washers, rod mixers, food choppers, slicers, ice crushers and glass and can crushers
Manager: Richard Dombroski
HR Executive: James Mc Closkey
james_mccloskey@conair.com
CFO: James McCooskey
Consultant: Larry Casalino
Estimated Sales: $5-10 Million
Number Employees: 50-99
Parent Co: Dynamics Corporation of America
Type of Packaging: Food Service
Brands:
  Acme
  Qualheim
  Waring

31008 Warner Electric Inc

449 Gardner St
South Beloit, IL 61080-1397

815-389-3771
Fax: 815-389-6425 800-234-3369
info@warnerelectric.com www.warnerelectric.com

The Colfax Power Transmission Group is a leading supplier of mechanical and electrical power transmission products to the food processing and packaging industries. With hundreds of years of industry experience, Colfax PT has developedsome of the premier products, delivery programs and services available today.
Marketing VP: Craig Schuele
Sales Manager: Jan Dixon
Contact: Warner Ab
hakan.persson@tollo.com
Number Employees: 1000-4999
Type of Packaging: Bulk

31009 Warren Analytical Laboratory
650 O St
Greeley, CO 80631

970-475-0252
Fax: 970-475-0280 800-945-6669
info@warrenlab.com www.warrenlab.com
Analytical food testing laboratory offering services for nutritional labeling, microbiological testing, chemistry and residue analysis
President: Rob Yemm
Vice President: Michael Aaronson
Sales Director: Kristen Peter
Contact: Michael Aaronson
amichael@warrenlab.com
Estimated Sales: $2.5-5 Million
Number Employees: 20-49
Square Footage: 24000
Parent Co: ConAgra Foods

31010 Warren E. Conley Corporation
1099 3rd Ave SW
Carmel, IN 46032-2564

317-846-5890
Fax: 317-846-5899 800-367-7875
Manufacturer and wholesaler/distributor of maintenance and cleaning products including brooms, brushes, cleaning polish and concentrates, hand soap, window cleaners, insecticides, kitchen degreasers, lime/rust remover, bowl cleansersdrain openers and squeegees
President: Kevin Conley
Estimated Sales: $1-2.5 Million
Number Employees: 1 to 4
Brands:
  Blue Satin
  Butter Better
  Butter Up
  Cut-Off
  Dapper Actor
  Dapper Duster
  Drain Warden
  Kleenitol
  Kleenzup
  Leplus Ultra
  Lime Lite
  Miss Kriss
  One-For-All
  Pastry Pal
  Power Quota
  Reveal
  Satin Doll
  Satin Fan
  Showtime
  Softasilk
  Sparkle 'n' Glo
  Sqyer
  Star Guard
  Swab 'n' Smile
  Terminator
  Tyle Style
  W C Insect Finish One
  Warcon Out

31011 Warren Packaging
879 East Rialto Avenue
San Bernardino, CA 92408

909-888-7008
Fax: 714-690-2905 phil@warrenpkg.com
Folding cartons, marketing displays and packaging solutions
Estimated Sales: $300,000-500,000
Number Employees: 1-4

31012 Warren Pallet Co Inc
601 County Road 627
Bloomsbury, NJ 08804-3426

908-995-7172
Fax: 908-995-4146
Reconditioned wooden pallets; various sizes available

Owner: Donald Tigar Sr
warrenpalletco@ptd.net
VP Marketing (Special Projects): J Bernard Noll Jr
Estimated Sales: $10-20 Million
Number Employees: 20-49

31013 (HQ)Warren Rupp Inc
800 N Main St
Mansfield, OH 44902-4209

419-524-8388
Fax: 419-522-7867 www.warrenruppinc.com
Air-operated, double-diaphragm pumps and accessories
President: John Carter
Co-Founder: Charles Young Jr
District Manager: Tim Zetzman
Estimated Sales: D
Number Employees: 100-249
Parent Co: IDEX Corporation
Brands:
  Sandpiper

31014 Warrenton Products
1410 E Old Us Highway 40
Warrenton, MO 63383-1316

636-456-3492
Fax: 636-456-3422
Contract packaging
Estimated Sales: $50-100 Million
Number Employees: 100-249

31015 Warsaw Chemical Co Inc
390 Argonne Rd
Warsaw, IN 46580-3884

574-267-3251
Fax: 574-267-3884 800-548-3396
wcc@warsaw-chem.com www.warsaw-chem.com
Manufacturer and exporter of sanitary chemicals and compounds
President: Ken Bucher
ken-bucher@warsaw-chem.com
R & D: Jeff Rufner
Quality Control: Scott Ware
Estimated Sales: $10-20 Million
Number Employees: 50-99

31016 Warther Museum
331 Karl Ave
Dover, OH 44622-2767

330-343-7513
Fax: 330-343-1443 info@warthers.com
www.warthercutlery.com
Cutlery
President: Mark Warther
markw@warthers.com
CFO: Juanne Warther
Quality Control: Dale Warther
Estimated Sales: $1-3 Million
Number Employees: 10-19
Square Footage: 10000
Brands:
  Warther Handcrafted Cutlery

31017 Warwick Manufacturing &Equip
1112 12th St
North Brunswick, NJ 08902-1869

732-729-0400
Fax: 732-729-1235 sales@warwickequipment.com
Manufacturer and exporter of new, used and rebuilt packaging and bakery food processing equipment
Managing Director: Gregory Pantchenko
Estimated Sales: Below $500,000
Number Employees: 1-4
Square Footage: 25000

31018 Warwick Products
5350 Tradex Pkwy
Cleveland, OH 44102-5887

216-334-1200
Fax: 216-334-1201 800-535-4404
info@warwickproducts.com
www.warwickproducts.com
Bulk food and bakery displays, barrels, store fixtures and bins including bagel, bulk and candy
Owner: Matt Beverstock
info@warwickproducts.com
General Manager: John Heim
Sales Manager: Jon Murray
info@warwickproducts.com
Estimated Sales: $1-2.5 Million
Number Employees: 50-99

31019 Washing Systems
167 Commerce Dr
Loveland, OH 45140-7727

513-870-4830
Fax: 513-870-4850 800-272-1974
sales@washingsystems.com
www.washingsystems.com
Pallet and tote washers
Owner: Robert Fisher
rfisher@washingsystems.com
VP: Gary Turnbull
Sales Manager: James Smylie
rfisher@washingsystems.com
Estimated Sales: $1-3 Million
Number Employees: 50-99
Brands:
  The Elimmator

31020 Washington Frontier
PO Box 249
Grandview, WA 98930-0249

509-469-7662
Fax: 509-469-7739
Used process equipment sales and fruit and vegetable juice sales
Manager General Operations: Joe Stoops
Estimated Sales: $10-15 Million
Number Employees: 50-100

31021 Washington Group International
600 Montgomery Street
26th Floor
San Francisco, CA 94111-2728

205-995-7878
Fax: 205-995-7777 800-877-0980
www.urs.com
Design consultant providing engineering, procurement, construction and environmental services
VP: Charles Dietz
Marketing/Sales: Bill Lott
Contact: Scott Wilson
scott.wilson@wgint.com
Estimated Sales: $1-5 Million
Number Employees: 500-999
Square Footage: 2000000
Parent Co: Washington Group International

31022 Washington Group International
1020 31st St # 300
Downers Grove, IL 60515-5578

630-829-3000
Fax: 630-829-3513
Worldwide design and construction of manufacturing plants for processed/packaged foods, beverages, agro-industrial
Manager: Robert Nickel
Marketing: Paul Kervan
Sales Director: Gail Luttinen
Contact: John Lasota
john.lasota@wgint.com
Estimated Sales: $50-100 Million
Number Employees: 250-499

31023 Washington State Juice
10725 Sutter Ave
Pacoima, CA 91331-2553

818-899-1195
Fax: 818-899-6042
Manufactures and processes fruit concentrates, blends and natural flavors. Custom blending is available
President: Fred Farago
Estimated Sales: $.5-1 million
Number Employees: 100-249
Type of Packaging: Food Service, Private Label, Bulk

31024 Wasserman Bag Company
26 Frowein Road
Center Moriches, NY 11934

631-909-8656
Fax: 631-878-1569 kwasserman@imperialbag.com
www.wassermanbag.com
Master distributor of bags including paper, burlap, mesh, polyethylene and polyproylene; also, tapes, wire and waxed and dry boxes as well as packaging equipment
President: Karen Wasserman
Operations Manager: Charlie Greco
Estimated Sales: $2.5-5 Million
Number Employees: 10-19
Type of Packaging: Consumer, Food Service, Bulk

31025 Waste Away Systems
132 S 30th St # B
Newark, OH 43055-1994

740-349-2783
Fax: 813-222-0220 800-223-4741
www.wasteawaysystems.com
Compactors, balers and waste reduction and recy-
cling equipment for hospitals, schools and restau-
rants
President: Dennis Calnan
VP Sales: David Fagan
Office Manager: Glenda O'Hara
Estimated Sales: $1-2.5 Million
Number Employees: 10-19
Square Footage: 80000
Brands:
Advance 2000
Convenience Pac 1000
Custom Pac 2000
Twin Chamber 3002
Twin Pac 2203
Twin Pac 2204
Twin Pac 2205

31026 Waste King Commercial
PO Box 4146
Anaheim, CA 92803-4146

714-524-7770
Fax: 714-996-7073 800-767-6293
www.anaheimmfg.com
President: Thomas P Dugan
Number Employees: 100-249

31027 Waste Minimization/Containment
2140 Scranton Rd
Cleveland, OH 44113-3544

216-696-8797
Fax: 216-696-8794 jbecker@cryogenesis-usa.com
www.cryogenesis-usa.com
Manufacturer and exporter of dry ice blast cleaning
equipment
President: Jim Becker
jbecker@cryogenesis-usa.com
Sales Manager: John Whalen
Estimated Sales: Less Than $500,000
Number Employees: 1-4
Brands:
Cryogenesis

31028 Wastequip Inc
6525 Morrison Blvd # 300
Suite 300
Charlotte, NC 28211-0500

704-366-7140
sales@wastequip.com
www.wastequip.com
Manufacturer and exporter of waste handling equip-
ment including compactors, hoists, balers, etc
Manager: Bram Chappell
CEO: Christine Anastasio
canastasio@wastequip.com
VP Sales/Marketing: Donald Sharp
Owner: Roy Holt
Estimated Sales: $5-10 Million
Number Employees: 1000-4999
Square Footage: 308000
Type of Packaging: Bulk

31029 Wastequip Teem
6526 Morrison Blvd
Suite 300
Charlotte, NC 28211

605-336-1333
Fax: 605-334-8704 877-468-9278
sales@wastequip.com www.wastequip.com
Manufacturer and exporter of rear-end loading re-
fuse containers
Manager: Val Bochenek
Estimated Sales: $2.5-5 Million
Number Employees: 20-49
Parent Co: Wastequip

31030 Water & Oil Technologies Inc
52 Eastfield Rd
Montgomery, IL 60538-2402

630-892-2007
Fax: 630-892-7472 800-841-6580
fuelalternatives@sbcglobal.net
Waste treatment and by-product use equipment including natural florculents, systhetic cationic,
nonionic florculents and equipment and by-product
recovery and marketing assistance
President: Ed Laurent

Estimated Sales: $500,000-$1 Million
Number Employees: 1-4

31031 (HQ)Water & Power Technologies
P.O.Box 27836
Salt Lake City, UT 84127

801-974-5500
Fax: 801-973-9733 888-271-3295
Manufacturer and exporter of custom designed
skid-mounted and mobile water purification systems
including reverse osmosis, demineralization,
electrodeionization, ultrafiltration, manganese,
greensand filters, softners, carbon towersand in-line
filtration,'etc.
General Manager: Jim Laraway
Controller: Tom Kirkland
Sales: Bryan Schillar
Purchase Manager: Chuck Gendre
Sales/Marketing: James Laraway
Contact: Alan Acker
alan.acker@a-wpt.com
Operations: Fred Farmer
Plant/Production Manager: Emma Anderson
Purchasing: Lee Courtney
Estimated Sales: $10-20 Million
Number Employees: 50-99
Square Footage: 84000
Type of Packaging: Consumer
Other Locations:
Water & Power Technologies
Portland OR
Water & Power Technologies
Denver CO
Water & Power Technologies
Dallas TX
Water & Power Technologies
Columbia SC
Water & Power Technologies
Houston TX
Water & Power Technologies
Ontario, Canada
Brands:
Smart-Ro
Superskids
Waterpro

31032 Water Equipment Svc
818 Cattlemen Rd
Sarasota, FL 34232-2811

941-371-4995
Fax: 941-377-2649 www.wesinc.com
Water treatment aeration and degassing equipment;
gravity filters
Owner: Anthony DE Loach
tonyd@wesinc.com
VP: Laurie Deloach
Estimated Sales: $2.5-5 Million
Number Employees: 10-19

31033 Water Furnace RenewableEnergy
9000 Conservation Way
Fort Wayne, IN 46809-9794

260-478-5667
Fax: 260-747-2828 bill_dean@waterfurnace.com
www.waterfurnace.com
Manufacturer and exporter of geothermal heating
and cooling systems
CEO: Tom Huntington
CEO: Bruce Ritchey
Director Sales: Mike Murphy
Estimated Sales: G
Number Employees: 500-999
Type of Packaging: Food Service

31034 Water Management Resources
PO Box 219
Overton, NV 89040-0219

706-743-0870
Fax: 702-397-8450 800-552-5797
www.watermr.com
Providing food safety and water conservation
Design & Engineering: Terry Griffiths
Field Sales: Greg Bilyeu
General Manager: Larry Griffiths
Number Employees: 1-4

31035 Water Savers Worldwide
PO Box 1101
Santa Barbara, CA 93102

916-354-0718
Wine industry water treatment
Owner: Bill Wampler
Owner: Lori Wampler

31036 Water Sciences Services, Inc.
280 Emmans Road
PO Box 5000-364
Jackson, TN 38302

973-584-4131
Fax: 731-660-4115
Manufacturer and exporter of ice cubing/bagging
machinery, bottled water sanitizers, bottled spring
water, descaling equipment and water filters
President: Elizabeth Reed
Vice President: Paul Reed
Estimated Sales: $1-2.5 Million
Number Employees: 15
Square Footage: 36000
Brands:
Crystal Clean

31037 Water System Group
27737 Bouquet Canyon Rd # 126
Santa Clarita, CA 91350-3743

661-297-6294
Fax: 818-597-9923 800-350-9283
Reverse osmosis, carbon filtration and water soften-
ing systems
Owner: Miguel Alvarez
VP: Martin Swanson
Estimated Sales: $1-5,000,000
Number Employees: 1-4

31038 Waterlink Technologies
3610 Quantum Blvd
Boynton Beach, FL 33426-8637

561-684-6300
Fax: 561-697-3342 800-684-4844
www.wetpurewater.com
Water purification systems, filters
General Manager: Audrey Pinkerton
Engineering Manager: Mike Mudrick
Operations Manager: Jason Gallegly
Estimated Sales: $10-25 Million
Number Employees: 50-99

31039 Waterlink/Sanborn Technologies
4100 Holiday Street NW
Canton, OH 44718-2556

330-649-4000
Fax: 330-649-4008 800-343-3381
www.waterlink.com
Manufacturer and exporter of liquid/solid separation
equipment and systems, wastewater pretreatment
and food waste dewatering systems
VP Operations: Steve Friedman
Estimated Sales: Below $500,000
Number Employees: 4
Square Footage: 180000

31040 Waterloo Container
2311 State Route 414
Waterloo, NY 13165-9440

315-539-3922
Fax: 315-539-9380 888-539-3922
wcbottles@flare.net www.fastfromstock.com
Wine industry bottles and packaging
Owner: Ben Ahner
CFO: William Lutz
Sales: Mike Shaffer
ben@waterloocontainer.com
Chief Operating Officer: John Dixon
Estimated Sales: $1-2.5 Million
Number Employees: 10-19

31041 Waters Corp
34 Maple St
Milford, MA 01757-3696

508-478-2000
Fax: 508-872-1990 800-252-4752
customerservice@waters.com www.waters.com
Liquid chromatography, mass spectrometry, and
thermal analysis.
President & CEO: Christopher O'Connell
Chairman: Flemming Ornskov
Year Founded: 1959
Estimated Sales: $2.3 Billion
Number Employees: 7,200
Brands:
TA Instruments
ERA
VICAM
Andrew Alliance
Nonlinear Dynamics

31042 Watershed Foods
202 N Ford St
Gridley, IL 61744-3902
309-747-3000
Fax: 309-747-4647
jill.legner@watershedfoods.com
Contract processor of yogurt, purees, fruits and other
healthy snacks. Services include freeze drying and
pumpable liquids and R&D test drying.
President & COO: Jeremy Zobrist
jeremy.zobrist@watershedfoods.com
CFO: Lynette Schick
Director of Food Quality & Safety: Craig Hammond
VP Sales & Marketing: Brandon Rinkenberger
VP & Director Operations: Marc Johnson
Manager: Jill Legner
Estimated Sales: $4.3 Million
Number Employees: 5-9

31043 (HQ)Watlow Electric
12001 Lackland Rd
St Louis, MO 63146
314-878-4600
Fax: 314-878-6814 info@watlow.com
www.watlow.com
Designer and manufacturer of heaters, sensors, con-
trollers and software.
SVP & Chief Financial Officer: Steve Desloge
Welder: Elias Alanis
Year Founded: 1922
Estimated Sales: $330 Million
Number Employees: 2,000
Type of Packaging: Food Service

31044 Watlow Electric
5710 Kenosha St
Richmond, IL 60071
info@watlow.com
www.watlow.com
Designer and manufacturer of heaters, sensors, con-
trollers and software.
Estimated Sales: $330 Million
Number Employees: 2,000
Parent Co: Watlow
Type of Packaging: Food Service
Other Locations:
Watlow
Columbia MO
Watlow
Winona MN
Brands:
Xactpak

31045 Watlow Electric
6781 Via Del Oro
San Jose, CA 95119
www.watlow.com
Designer and manufacturer of heaters, sensors, con-
trollers and software.
Estimated Sales: $330 Million
Number Employees: 2,000

31046 Watts Premier Inc
8716 W Ludlow Dr # 1
Peoria, AZ 85381-4918
480-675-7995
Fax: 602-866-5666 800-752-5582
mail@premierh2o.com www.premierh2o.com
Manufacturer and exporter of water purification
equipment
Vice President: Shannon Murphy
VP: Shannon Murphy
Estimated Sales: $5-10 Million
Number Employees: 20-49
Parent Co: Watts Water Technologies Co.

31047 Watts Radiant Inc
4500 E Progress Pl
Springfield, MO 65803-8816
417-864-6108
Fax: 417-864-8161 800-255-1996
www.wattsradiant.com
President: Mike Chiles
CEO: John Kolson
kolsonj@watts.com
Estimated Sales: $1-5 Million
Number Employees: 100-249

31048 Watts Regulator Co
815 Chestnut St
North Andover, MA 01845-6098
978-688-1811
Fax: 978-794-1848 www.wattswater.com
Valves, grease interceptors and drains.

President & Chief Executive Officer: Robert
Pagano, Jr.
Treasure/VP, Investor Relations: Tim MacPhee
investorrelations@wattswater.com
Chief Human Resources Officer: Jennifer Congdon
EVP/General Counsel/Secretary: Kenneth Lepage
Year Founded: 1874
Estimated Sales: $224 Million
Number Employees: 100-249
Parent Co: Watts Industries
Type of Packaging: Food Service, Private Label

31049 Waukesha Cherry-Burrell
2025 S Hurstbourne Pkwy
Louisville, KY 40220-1623
502-491-4310
Fax: 502-491-4312 800-252-5200
www.halfpricebooks.com
Fluid handling and process equipment including PD
pumps, centrifugal pumps, valves, heat exchangers,
and ice cream equipment
Manager: Jeff Comara
VFO and VP Finance: Ken Rod
Estimated Sales: $1-3 Million
Number Employees: 10-19
Number of Brands: 10
Number of Products: 50
Parent Co: SPX
Brands:
Heat Exhangers
Positive Displacement Pumps
Universal
Votatr

31050 Waukesha Cherry-Burrell
2025 S Hurstbourne Pkwy
Louisville, KY 40220-1623
502-491-4310
Fax: 502-491-4312 www.gowcb.com
Manufacturer and exporter of aseptic processing
equipment, colloid mills, coopers/kettles, fittings,
freezers, ingredient feeders, pumps and tanks
Manager: Jeff Comara
National Sales Manager: Tony Mazza
Sales Manager (Process Prod.): Paul Duddleson
Estimated Sales: $20-50 Million
Number Employees: 10-19
Parent Co: United Dominion Company

31051 Waukesha Foundry Inc
1300 Lincoln Ave
Waukesha, WI 53186-5389
262-542-0741
Fax: 262-549-8440 800-727-0741
www.waukeshafoundry.com
Anti-galling alloys and stainless steel castings
President: Ken Kurek
kkurek@waukeshafoundry.com
VP Sales/Marketing: Gary Evans
Manager Sales/Advertising: Thomas Kerwin
Estimated Sales: $10-20 Million
Number Employees: 250-499

31052 Waukesha Specialty Company
N3355 Us Highway 14
PO Box 160
Darien, WI 53114-5014
262-724-3700
Fax: 262-724-5120
Manufacturer and exporter of fittings, stainless steel
hinges and sanitary valves
President: Stephen Miller
VP: Malcom Miller
Estimated Sales: $1-2.5 Million
Number Employees: 2

31053 Wausau Paper Corp.
100 Paper Pl.
Mosinee, WI 54455
715-693-4470
866-722-8675
torkusa@essity.com www.wausaupaper.com
Towels, tissue, soap, wipers and dispensing system.
President/CEO, Essity: Magnus Groth
Year Founded: 1899
Estimated Sales: $822 Million
Number Employees: 870
Number of Brands: 12
Parent Co: Essity
Type of Packaging: Food Service
Brands:
Artisan
DublSoft
DublNature

EcoSoft
Alliance®
Wave'n Dry®
Optiserv
Optiserv Hybrid®
Optiserv accent®
Revolution®
DublServe®
OptiSource Convertible®
Silhouette®
Dubl-tough®

31054 Wausau Tile/Textura Designs
9001 Business Hwy 51
Rothschild, WI 54474
715-359-3121
Fax: 715-355-4627 800-388-8728
wtile@wausautile.com www.wausautile.com
Manufacturer of architectural products including
pavers, site furnishings, custom precast concrete,
custom precast terrazzo and terrazzo tile.
Vice President: Rob Geurink
rgeurink@wausautile.com
Year Founded: 1953
Estimated Sales: $50-100 Million
Number Employees: 250-499
Square Footage: 550000

31055 Wave Chemical Company
350 5th Avenue
Suite 1806
New York, NY 10118-1806
973-243-5852
Fax: 973-243-5853
Cleaning chemicals and dishwashing detergents
Assistant Manager: Mark Lim
VP: Charles Lim

31056 Waxine
65 River Rd
Suite A
Bow, NH 3304
603-228-8241
Fax: 603-228-2324 mrsrptng@aol.com
Dustless sweeping compounds
President: Richard Seymour
VP/Treasurer: Richard Seymour
Estimated Sales: less than $500,000
Number Employees: 1-4
Square Footage: 4000

31057 Waymar Industries
14400 Southcross Dr W
Burnsville, MN 55306
952-435-7100
Fax: 952-435-2900 888-474-1112
www.plymold.com
Manufacturer and exporter of restaurant, cafeteria
and industrial seating, table tops and trash containers
President: Dick Koehring
CFO: Greg Klingler
Director Manufacturing: Bill Smith
Marketing/Sales: Bill Ziegler
Contact: Jodie Anderson
j.anderson@waymar.com
Operations Manager: Bob Haugen
Plant Manager: Mike Boegeman
Purchasing Manager: Doug Schultz
Estimated Sales: $10-20 Million
Number Employees: 50-99
Square Footage: 280000
Parent Co: Foldcraft Co
Brands:
Waymar

31058 Wayne Automation Corp
605 General Washington Ave
Eagleville, PA 19403-3695
610-630-8900
Fax: 610-630-6116 www.wayneautomation.com
Automatic packaging equipment including partition
inserters, case erectors, case packers and tray
formers; exporter of partition inserters and case
erectors
President: Jay L Bachman, Jr.
CFO: Dorothy Schlosser
dschlosser@wayneautomation.com
VP & General Manager: Jay L Bachman, III
VP, Sales and Marketing: Harry M. Dudley
Estimated Sales: $5-10 Million
Number Employees: 50-99
Square Footage: 60000
Brands:
Ce-15'22

Cpt-25
Sf-400
Wr-25

31059 Wayne Combustion Systems
801 Glasgow Ave
Fort Wayne, IN 46803-1344
260-425-9200
Fax: 260-424-0904 800-443-4625
clagemann@waynecs.com
Manufacturer and exporter of custom gas and oil burners; also, oven, fryer and griddle design analysis available
Manager: Karen Myrice
R & D: Dan Voorhis
Marketing: Karen Wygant
Sales: Dennis Parda
Manager: Paul Wert
pwert@waynecs.com
Purchasing: Phil Fenker
Estimated Sales: $10-20 Million
Number Employees: 50-99
Square Footage: 560000
Parent Co: Scott Fetzer Company
Brands:
Blue Angel
Premix Technology
Wayne

31060 Wayne Engineering
701 Performance Dr
Cedar Falls, IA 50613-6952
319-266-1721
Fax: 319-266-8207 info@wayneusa.com
Manufacturer and exporter of mobile material handling equipment and refuse equipment
CEO: Jim Marks
jimmarks@wayneusa.com
CEO: Kevin Watje
Sales Manager: Dave Severson
Sales Coordinator: Sherry Berak
Estimated Sales: $20-50 Million
Number Employees: 100-249
Square Footage: 60000
Brands:
Cargomaster

31061 Wayne Group LTD
110 Sutter St
San Francisco, CA 94104-4002
415-421-2010
Fax: 415-421-2060 jjw@waynegroup.com
www.waynegroup.com
Executive search firm
Contact: Dwayne Eason
dde@waynegroup.com
Estimated Sales: less than $500,000
Number Employees: 5-9
Parent Co: Wayne Group

31062 Wayne Industries
1400 8th St N
Clanton, AL 35045
205-755-2365
Fax: 205-755-1516 800-225-3148
Indoor and outdoor signs and displays; also, lighted and nonlighted menu boards
National Sales: Bill Weston
Sales Manager: Monte Easterling
Operations Manager: Mike Cooper
Manager: Steve Hill
Manager: Stevde Hill
Estimated Sales: Below $5 Million
Number Employees: 50-99
Square Footage: 250000
Parent Co: Ebsco Industries

31063 Waypoint Analytical Inc
2790 Whitten Rd
Memphis, TN 38133-4753
901-213-2400
Fax: 901-213-2440 support@allabs.com
www.waypointanalytical.com
Fat testing, water treatment systems
President: Scott Mckee
smckee@allabs.com
Estimated Sales: $1-3 000,000
Number Employees: 50-99

31064 WePackItAll
2745 Huntington Dr.
Duarte, CA 91010
626-301-9214
Fax: 626-301-9216 www.wepackitall.com

Contract packager of food supplement tablets and powders in pakettes and blister cards
President: Jack Bershtel
General Manager: Sharla Hughes
Contact: Daisy Acevedo
daisya@wepackitall.com
Plant Manager: Sharla Hughes
Estimated Sales: $5-10 Million
Number Employees: 20-49
Square Footage: 120000

31065 Wearwell/Tennessee Mat Company
P.O.Box 100186
Nashville, TN 37224-0186
615-254-8381
Fax: 615-255-4428 info@wearwell.com
www.wearwell.com
Safety and ergonomic matting
President: Elliot Greenberg
CEO: Steve Goldsmith
National Sales Manager: Nick Mead
Contact: Michael Franklin
michael.franklin@wearwell.com
Estimated Sales: $20-50 Million
Number Employees: 100-249

31066 Weavewood, Inc.
7520 Wayzata Blvd
Golden Valley, MN 55426-1622
763-544-3136
Fax: 763-544-3137 800-367-6460
Manufacturer and exporter of woodenware including bowls, plates, trays, coasters, tongs, susans, fork, spoon and magnetic server sets, etc.; also, aluminum and stainless steel steak platters
President: Howard Thompson
Quality Control: Tim Zanor
R&D: Tim Zanor
CFO: Howard Thompson Jr
Marketing Director: Peter Meyer
Estimated Sales: Below $5 Million
Number Employees: 20-49
Square Footage: 120000
Type of Packaging: Consumer, Food Service, Private Label, Bulk
Brands:
Weavewood

31067 Web Industries
377 Simarano Drive
Suite 220
Marlborough, MA 01752
508-898-2988
Fax: 508-898-3329 800-932-3212
askus@webindustries.com
www.webindustries.com
Suppliers of precision slitting, rewinding, spooling, sheeting, coating/printing, spooling
President: Don Romine
Chief Financial Officer: Carl Rubin
Executive Vice President: Dennis Latimer
Contact: Jeffrey Allen
jallen@webindustries.com
Chief Operations Officer: Mark Pihl
Number Employees: 10

31068 Web Industries Inc
3925 Ardmore Ave
Fort Wayne, IN 46802-4237
260-432-0027
Fax: 260-436-2195 800-366-4584
www.webindustries.com
Insulating tape and textile converting
Manager: Dan Alt
d.alt@ktindustriesinc.com
CEO: Don Romine
Chief Financial Officer: Carl Rubin
Executive Vice President: Dennis Latimer
Vice President Sales And Marketing: Tom Burns
Manager: Dan Alt
d.alt@ktindustriesinc.com
Estimated Sales: $20-50 Million
Number Employees: 50-99
Square Footage: 110000

31069 Web Label
600 Hoover St NE
Suite 500
Minneapolis, MN 55413
612-588-0737
Fax: 612-706-3757 www.weblabel.com
Manufacturer and exporter of pressure sensitive labels

Owner: John Coldwell
Sales Manager: Dave Olson
Contact: James Bullert
jim.bullert@liesch.com
Estimated Sales: $5-10 Million
Number Employees: 20-49
Type of Packaging: Consumer, Bulk

31070 Webb's Machine Design
2251 Montclair Rd
Clearwater, FL 33763-4325
727-799-1768
Fax: 727-791-1639 www.contrast-design.com
Citrus processing equipment
Owner: John D Webb
john@webbsmachinedesign.com
CFO: Jon Weber
R&D: Jon Weber
Quality Control: Jon Weber
Estimated Sales: Below $5,000,000
Number Employees: 5-9

31071 Webb-Triax Company
34375 W 12 Mile Rd
Farmington Hills, MI 48331
248-553-1000
Fax: 440-285-1878 info@jerviswebb.com
Manufacturer and exporter of automated storage and retrieval systems, including cooler and freezer storage systems and deep lane flow rack systems
Sales Director: Fred Cirino
Estimated Sales: $1-5,000,000
Number Employees: 20-49
Parent Co: Jervis B. Webb Company
Type of Packaging: Bulk
Brands:
Ms/Rv
Retriever

31072 (HQ)Webber Smith Assoc
1857 William Penn Way # 200
Lancaster, PA 17601-6713
717-291-2266
Fax: 717-291-4401 800-231-0392
gsmith@webbersmith.com www.webbersmith.com
Engineering design firm specializing in the design and construction of food processing, storage and distribution facilities throughout the usa.
President: Keith Shollenberger
Chairman: Garry Smith
VP: Joe Shaffer
Marketing & Public Relations Manager: Don Landis
Contact: Ed Bianchi
ed.bianchi@webbersmith.com
Estimated Sales: Less Than $500,000
Number Employees: 1-4

31073 Webber Smith Assoc
1857 William Penn Way # 200
Suite 201
Lancaster, PA 17601-6713
717-291-2266
Fax: 717-291-4401 info@webbersmith.com
www.webbersmith.com
A multi-discipline planning, engineering firm which specializes in bakery, meat, poultry, seafood, beverage, prepared foods, fruits and vegetables, confection, grocery distribution, foodservice distribution and public cold storagefacilities.
Contact: Doettner Alice
doettner.alice@webbersmith.com
Estimated Sales: Less Than $500,000
Number Employees: 1-4

31074 Weber Display & Packaging Inc
3500 Richmond St
Philadelphia, PA 19134-6102
215-426-3500
Fax: 215-634-3073 www.weberdisplay-pkg.com
Corrugated shipping boxes
President: Jim Doherty
jimd@weberdisplay-pkg.com
Estimated Sales: $20-50 Million
Number Employees: 100-249

31075 Weber Inc
10701 N Ambassador Dr
Kansas City, MO 64153-1216
816-891-8397
Fax: 816-891-0074 www.weberslicer.com
Manufacturer and supplier of slicing machines for the meat and cheese industry

President: Scott Scariven
HR Executive: Jason Miera
jmiera@weberslicer.com
Estimated Sales: $2.5-5 Million
Number Employees: 20-49

31076 Weber Inc
10701 N Ambassador Dr
Kansas City, MO 64153-1216

816-891-8397
Fax: 816-891-0074 800-505-9591
usasales@weberslicer.com www.weberslicer.com
Slicers for the meat, pork, poultry and cheese processing industries.
HR Executive: Jason Miera
jmiera@weberslicer.com
Number Employees: 20-49

31077 Weber Packaging Solutions Inc
711 W Algonquin Rd
Arlington Heights, IL 60005-4457

800-843-4242
www.webermarking.com
Manufacturer and exporter of pressure-sensitive labels, labeling systems and continuous ink jet systems.
President & CEO: Doug Weber
Vice President, Finance & CFO: Chris Shealy
Year Founded: 1932
Estimated Sales: $100-500 Million
Number Employees: 200-500
Square Footage: 320000
Type of Packaging: Consumer, Food Service, Private Label, Bulk
Other Locations:
    Tape & Label Engineering
    St. Petersburg FL
Brands:
    Legijet
    Legitronic

31078 Weber Scientific Inc
2732 Kuser Rd
Trenton, NJ 08691-1806

609-584-7677
Fax: 609-584-8388 800-328-8378
info@weberscientific.com
www.weberscientific.com
Products for dairy, food and water testing.
President: Nancy Silvester
nsilvester@weberscientific.com
VP: Joyce Arcarese
Account Manager: MaryBeth Karczynski
National Accounts Manager: Sharon Wilson
Account Manager: Nancy Silvester
Purchasing Manager: John Santillo
Estimated Sales: $1-2.5 Million
Number Employees: 5-9
Square Footage: 100000

31079 Weber-Stephen Products Company
200 E Daniels Rd
Palatine, IL 60067

847-934-5700
Fax: 847-407-8900 800-446-1071
support@weberstephen.com www.weber.com
Gas, charcoal, and electric grills. Useful for smoked products or grilled foods in restaurants or events.
President & CEO: James Stephen
Executive VP & CFO: Leonard Gryn
Quality Control Manager: Steve Butirro
Quality Control Manager: Dave Lohbauer
Marketing Manager: Brooke Jones
Media Contact: Melanie Hill
Executive VP Sales, Americas: Dale Wytiaz
Director of Public Relations: Sherry Bale
Operations Manager: Ken Stephen
Product Manager: Trace Weskamp
Plant Manager: Stan Gucwa
Director of Purchasing: Christoher Stephen
Square Footage: 1200000
Brands:
    Weber

31080 Webster Packaging Corporation
715 S Riverside Ave
Loveland, OH 45140

513-683-5666
Fax: 513-683-0535
Corrugated products including shipping containers and displays
President: Denny Philips
Sales Manager: Susan Terlau

Estimated Sales: $20-50 Million
Number Employees: 50-99

31081 Wedgwood USA
1330 Campus Pkwy
Wall Township, NJ 07753-6811

732-938-5800
Fax: 732-938-7108 800-999-9936
Manufacturer and importer of fine bone china tableware
Sales Manager: Michael Durao
Director Hotel/Restaurant Sales: Kathy Santangelo
Estimated Sales: $20-50 Million
Number Employees: 250-499
Square Footage: 368000
Parent Co: Waterford Wedgwood USA
Brands:
    Johnson Brothers
    Mason's Ironstone
    Waterford Crystal
    Wedgwood

31082 Wedlock Paper ConvertersLtd.
2327 Stanfield Road
Mississauga, ON L4Y 1R6
Canada

905-277-9461
Fax: 905-272-1108 800-388-0447
info@wedlockpaper.com www.wedlockpaper.com
Manufacturer and exporter of paper bags
Customer Service: Scott Wedlock
Number Employees: 100
Type of Packaging: Consumer

31083 Wega USA
524 North York Road
Bensenville, IL 60106-1607

630-350-0066
Fax: 630-350-0005 info@expressoshoppe.com
www.expressoshoppe.com
Manufacturer, exporter and importer of coffee grinders and espresso equipment
President: David Dimbert
Estimated Sales: $500,000-$1 Million
Number Employees: 1-4
Square Footage: 20000
Type of Packaging: Food Service
Brands:
    Bunn
    Carioca
    Jura
    Pavoni
    Ranulio
    Saeco
    Wega

31084 Weigh Right Automatic Scale Co
612 Mills Rd # A
Joliet, IL 60433-2843

815-726-4626
Fax: 815-726-7638 800-571-0249
mikep@weighright.com www.weighright.com
Net weigh scales, volumetric fillers, wiegh/count scales. Industries serviced: fresh cut produce, IQF foods, confectionery, coffee, petfood, meat, spice, pharmaceutica, hardware, snack food, nuts, and more
President: Steve Almberg
Marketing Director: Mike Phillips
Estimated Sales: Below $5 Million
Number Employees: 10-19
Square Footage: 20000

31085 WeighPack Systems/Paxiom Group
2525 Louis Amos
Montreal, QC H8T 1C3
Canada

514-422-0808
Fax: 514-932-8118 888-934-4472
info@weighpack.com www.weighpack.com
Manufacturer and exporter of net-weighing systems; also, micro-processors and bagging systems
National Sales Manager: Anthony Delviscio
Number Employees: 30
Square Footage: 400000
Brands:
    Aef-1
    Aef-25
    Aef-7
    B-1
    Bbf
    Multi-Trix
    Vs Bagger

Weigh Pack Systems
Zippy Bagger

31086 Weighpack Systems
2525 Louis Amos
Montreal, QC H8T 1C3
Canada

514-422-0808
Fax: 514-422-0834 888-934-4472
info@weighpack.com www.weighpack.com
Packaging machinery and conveying systems
President: Louis Taraborelli
Sales/Marketing Coordinator: John Brown
Sales Director: Nicholas Taraborelli

31087 (HQ)Weiler & Company
1116 E Main St
Whitewater WI 53190

262-473-5254
Fax: 262-473-5867 800-558-9507
weiler-info@provisur.com
Manufacturer and exporter of meat, poultry and seafood processing equipment including grinders, mixers, screw and belt conveyors, portioning systems, meat/bone separators and mixers/grinders; also, special equipment and designservices available
CEO: Nick Lesar
Corporate Director Equipment Sales: Jim Schumacher
International Sales Manager: Dave Schumacher
Contact: Walter Jackson
wjackson@idcnet.com
General Manager: John Allred
Estimated Sales: $10-20 Million
Number Employees: 100-249
Square Footage: 144000
Other Locations:
    Weiler & Co.
    Sandy UT
Brands:
    Beehive
    Weiler

31088 Weiler Equipment
1116 E Main Street
Whitewater, WI 53190

262-473-5254
Fax: 262-473-5867 800-558-9507
Premier meat grinders and integrated food processing systems
President/CEO: Mel Cohen
VP Sales/Marketing: Kevin Howard
Contact: Walter Jackson
wjackson@idcnet.com

31089 Weinbrenner Shoe Co
108 S Polk St
Merrill, WI 54452-2348

715-536-5521
Fax: 715-536-1172 800-826-0002
www.weinbrennerusa.com
Manufacturer, importer and exporter of slip resisting safety shoes
President: L Nienow
CFO: David Giffleman
VP Sales/Marketing: Fred Girsky
Manager Sales: Shane Baganz
Manager: John Chezel
jschenzel@weinbrennerusa.com
Estimated Sales: $20-50 Million
Number Employees: 50-99
Parent Co: Weinbrenner Shoe Company
Brands:
    Mainstream
    Thorogard
    Thorogood

31090 Weiss Instruments Inc
905 Waverly Ave
Holtsville, NY 11742-1109

631-207-1200
Fax: 631-207-0900 sales@weissinstruments.com
www.weissinstrument.com
Manufacturer and exporter of thermometers and pressure gauges
President: John Weiss
johnw@weissinstruments.com
OEM Sales Manager: Stephen Weiss
Industrial Sales Manager: Thomas Keefe
Number Employees: 100-249
Square Footage: 200000

1037

31091 Weiss Sheet Metal Inc
105 Bodwell St
Avon, MA 02322-1112

508-583-8300
Fax: 508-588-5690
stainlessfab@weiss-sheetmetal.com
www.weiss-sheetmetal.com
Custom stainless steel work tables, counters, sinks
and wall mounted stacked shelves
President: Wayne G DE Lano
wdelano@weiss-sheetmetal.com
Vice President: Brian De Lano
Shop Foreman: James Warfield
Estimator: Al Quieto
Estimated Sales: $3 Million
Number Employees: 10-19
Square Footage: 52000
Type of Packaging: Food Service

31092 (HQ)Welbilt Corporation
500 Summer St # 4
Stamford, CT 06901-4301

203-325-8300
Fax: 203-323-4550 www.aquent.com
Manufacturer and exporter of ventilators, ice ma-
chines and commercial cooking, warming and refrig-
eration equipment including broilers, fryers, ovens,
toasters, rotisseries, mixers, etc
Manager: Maggie Patterson
Vice President of Services: Deb McCusker
Account Director: Damien Rocherolle
Estimated Sales: $5-10 Million
Number Employees: 1-4
Square Footage: 7200000
Other Locations:
 Welbilt Corp.
 Shreveport LA
Brands:
 Belshaw
 Clark
 Cleveland
 Contempo
 Dean
 Euro
 Frymaster
 Garland
 Ice-O-Matic
 Lincoln
 Merco
 Mercury
 Panorama
 Savory
 Titan
 Us Range
 Varimixer

31093 Welbilt Inc.
2227 Welbilt Blvd.
New Port Richey, FL 34655

727-375-7010
Fax: 727-375-0472 877-375-9300
www.welbilt.com
Food and beverage equipment for commercial
foodservice, including refrigerators, freezers, ovens,
grills, fryers and more.
President/CEO: William Johnson
Executive VP/CFO: Martin Agard
Executive VP/General Counsel: Joel Horn
Executive VP/COO: Josef Matosevic
Year Founded: 1902
Estimated Sales: $138 Million
Number Employees: 5,500
Number of Brands: 13
Square Footage: 14120
Other Locations:
 Manitowoc Ice
 Franklin TN
 Manitowoc Company
 Manitowoc WI
Brands:
 Cleveland®
 Convotherm®
 Crem International®
 Delfield®
 Frymaster®
 Garland®
 Kolpak®
 Lincoln®
 Manitowoc®
 Merco®
 Merrychef®
 Multiplex®
 Welbilt®

31094 (HQ)Welch Brothers
9N325 Rt. 25
Bartlett, IL 60103

847-741-6134
Fax: 847-697-0123 mwelch@welchbrothers.com
www.welchbrothers.com
Packer of steaks and portion-controlled meats; also,
slaughtering and locker services available
President and CEO: Ron Hards
VP: Robert Welch
Sales: Bob Jones
Estimated Sales: $2.5-5 Million
Number Employees: 5-9
Square Footage: 36000
Type of Packaging: Consumer, Food Service

31095 Welch Packaging Group Inc
1020 Herman St
Elkhart, IN 46516-9028

574-295-2460
Fax: 574-295-1527 www.welchpkg.com
Corrugated cartons and pallets
President: Austin Adams
adamsat@welchpkg.com
Estimated Sales: $20-50 Million
Number Employees: 100-249

31096 Welch Stencil Company
7 Lincoln Ave.
Scarborough, ME 04074

207-883-6200
Fax: 207-883-8588 800-635-3506
Rubber stamps and engraved signs
President: Terry Davis
VP: Kathy Davis
Estimated Sales: $3-5 Million
Number Employees: 10-19

31097 WellSet Tableware Manufacturing Company
201 Water Street
Brooklyn, NY 11201-1111

718-624-4490
Fax: 718-596-3959

31098 Welliver Metal Products Corporation
672 Murlark Ave NW
Salem, OR 97304

503-362-1568
Fax: 503-585-3374
Manufacturer and exporter of case packagers, size
graders, steam kettles, tanks, size sorters, etc
President: Glenn Welliver
CEO/General Manager: Del Starr
Engineer Manager: Gray Johnson
Quality Control: John Hell
CEO: Del Starr
Estimated Sales: $3-5 Million
Number Employees: 20-49
Square Footage: 54000

31099 Wells Lamont
6640 W Touhy Ave
Niles, IL 60714-4587

847-647-8200
Fax: 847-647-6943 800-323-2830
cservice@wellslamont.com www.wellslamont.com
Vinyl impregnated gloves
President: Jack Akin
jakin@ccfc.com
CFO: Tom Palzer
VP: William Trainer
VP: R Stoller
Marketing Director: Jace Suttner
Estimated Sales: $5-10 Million
Number Employees: 1000-4999
Parent Co: A Marmon Group / Berkshire Hathaway
Company
Brands:
 Golden Gripper
 Grips
 Handy Andy
 No Sweat
 Nob Nob
 Sure Gard
 Tuff Guys
 Wells Lamont
 White Mule

31100 Wells Lamont
6640 W Touhy Ave
Niles, IL 60714-4587

847-647-8200
Fax: 847-647-6943 800-323-2830
kmeger@wellslamont.com www.wellslamont.com
Hand protection including cut-resistant heat resis-
tant, leather and general purpose. Products include
cut-resistant gloves, bakers pad, terry gloves, leather
gloves, jersey gloves, canvas gloves, cut-resistant
and heat resistantsleeves
President: Jack Akin
jakin@ccfc.com
VP: William Trainer
Marketing Coordinator: Michelle Kurtz
Sales Director: Jim Buckingham
Public Relations: Michelle Kurtz
Operations Manager: Bruce Smith
Estimated Sales: Below $500,000
Number Employees: 1000-4999
Type of Packaging: Private Label, Bulk

31101 Wells Lamont
6640 W Touhy Ave
Niles, IL 60714-4587

847-647-8200
Fax: 847-647-6943 800-247-3295
wligcs@wellslamont.com www.wellslamont.com
Hand protection including cut resistant, heat resis-
tant, general purpose, liquid/chemical resistant,
leather gloves and more.
President: Mark Premarathna
mpremarathna@wellslamontindustrial.com
Marketing Coordinator: Dena Riccio
VP Human Resources: Lawrence Rist
Operations Executive: Heat Mathias
Number Employees: 1000-4999
Square Footage: 82000

31102 Wells Manufacturing Company
P.O.Box 280
Verdi, NV 89439

775-345-0444
Fax: 775-345-8220 www.wellsbloomfield.com
Contact: Jeanine Blue
blue@launchtower.com
Estimated Sales: $30-50 Million
Number Employees: 250-499
Parent Co: Carrier Commercial Refrigeration

31103 Wells Manufacturing Company
10 Sunnen Drive
P.O.Box 280
St. Louis, MO 63143-3800

775-345-0444
Fax: 314-781-5445 888-356-5362
www.wellsbloomfield.com
Manufacturer and exporter of commercial griddles,
fryers, broilers, warmers, coffee and tea brewers,
espresso machines and accessories, dispensers,
decanters, etc
President: Paul Angrick
Quality Control: Terry Mees
Sales Manager: Jeanine Blue
Number Employees: 250-499
Square Footage: 308000
Parent Co: Specialty Equipment Companies
Type of Packaging: Food Service

31104 Welltep International Inc
138 Palm Coast Pkwy NE # 192
Palm Coast, FL 32137-8241

386-437-5545
Fax: 386-437-5546
Broker of grocery related products
President: Luis Lopez
Estimated Sales: $1-3 Million
Number Employees: 1-4

31105 Wemas Metal Products
636 36th Avenue NE
Calgary, AB T2E 2L7
Canada

403-276-4451
Fax: 403-277-0725 sales@wemas.com
Manufacturer and exporter of custom stainless steel,
aluminum and exotic metal food processing
machinery
General Manager: Dave Swedak
Sales: Enno Ziemann
Sales: Joanne McCaughey
Number Employees: 44
Square Footage: 180000

31106 Wemco Pumps
P.O.Box 209
Salt Lake City, UT 84110-0209
801-359-8731
Fax: 801-355-9303 www.wemcopump.com
Wine industry pumps
CEO: Joseph W Roark
Marketing Director: Dave Borrowman
Production Manager: Gary Pearson
Estimated Sales: $50-100 Million
Number Employees: 500-999

31107 Wenda America Inc
1823 High Grove Ln
Suite 103
Naperville, IL 60540
844-999-3632
sales@wendaingredients.com
www.wendaingredients.com
Global meat and poultry ingredients manufacturer
and processor.
President: Chad Boeckman
chadb@wendaingredients.com
Year Founded: 1995
Estimated Sales: $200 Million
Number Employees: 200-500
Number of Brands: 7
Type of Packaging: Bulk
Brands:
   Wendaphos®
   Prosur®
   Novapro®
   NatureBind®
   Senor Paprika®
   Koolgel®
   SoyPura®

31108 Wendell August Forge
1605 South Center Street
PO Box 109
Grove City, PA 16127
724-450-8700
Fax: 724-458-0906 800-923-1390
info@wendell.com www.wendellaugust.com
Hand-hammered aluminum, bronze, pewter and ster-
ling silver advertising specialties, collector's items
and gifts
CEO: F W Knecht Iii
Marketing Director: George Kenyon
Sales Director: Erin Pisano
Sales: Carol Snyder
Estimated Sales: $10-20 Million
Number Employees: 100-249
Number of Brands: 1
Number of Products: 100

31109 Wenglor
2280 Grange Hall Rd
Beavercreek, OH 45431
937-320-0011
Fax: 937-320-0033 877-936-4567
info.us@wenglor.com www.wenglor.com
Analog sensors, laser sensors, color sensors, line and
optical sensors, reflex sensors and proximity sensors
General Manager: Tobiaf Schmitt
Estimated Sales: $500,000-$1 Million
Number Employees: 5

31110 Wepackit
1-16 Tideman Drive
Orangeville, ON L9W 4N6
Canada
519-942-1700
Fax: 519-942-1702
Manufacturer and exporter of case packers, erectors,
sealers, de-casers and tray formers
President: David Wiggins
Number Employees: 55-60
Number of Products: 7
Square Footage: 80000

31111 Werthan Packaging
605 Highway 76
White House, TN 37188-9206
615-672-3336
Fax: 615-581-5414
Multi-wall bags
Chairman of the Board: Anthony Werthan
Vice President, Finance/CFO: Jerry Gregg
Quality Control Manager: Tisha Stokes
Manager: Brenda Malugin
brendam@werthan.com
Paper Mill Manager: Mike Palmer
Procurement Manager: Gary Parker

Estimated Sales: $50 Million
Number Employees: 20-49
Square Footage: 5000

31112 Wes Inc
6389 Tower Ln
Sarasota, FL 34240-8810
941-371-7617
Fax: 941-378-5218 800-881-9374
info@wesinc.com www.wesinc.com
Water treatment equipment
Owner: Anthony DE Loach
tonyd@wesinc.com
Estimated Sales: $10-20 Million
Number Employees: 50-99

31113 Wes Tech Engineering Inc
3625 S West Temple
Salt Lake City, UT 84115
801-265-1000
Fax: 801-265-1080 info@westech-inc.com
www.westech-inc.com
Wastewater and water treatment systems; solid and
liquid separators
President: Rex Plaizier
rplaizier@westech-inc.com
VP: Rex Plaizier
Marketing Manager: Marshall Palm
Sales Director: Jeff Easton
Estimated Sales: $30-50 Million
Number Employees: 250-499
Brands:
   Cop
   Simarotor

31114 Wesco Industrial Products
1250 Welsh Rd
North Wales, PA 19454-1820
215-699-7031
Fax: 215-699-3836 800-445-5681
bmunion@wescomfg.com www.wescomfg.com
Material handling products
President: Allen Apter
President: Jamie Johnson
Vice President: Mike Esris
mesris@ra-industries.com
Director of Sales: Mike Esris
Estimated Sales: $10-25 Million
Number Employees: 1-4

31115 Wescor
370 W 1700 S
Logan, UT 84321-5294
435-752-6011
Fax: 435-752-4127 800-453-2725
biomed@wescor.com
Manufacturer and exporter of osmometers and ther-
mómeters
President: Wayne K Barlow
Estimated Sales: $5-10,000,000
Number Employees: 50-99

31116 Wesley International Corp
3680 Chestnut St
Scottdale, GA 30079-1206
404-792-7441
Fax: 404-292-8469 800-241-8649
sales@wesleyintl.com
Manufacturer and exporter of electric vehicles, bur-
den and personnel carriers and trucks including hand
hydraulic pallets, skids and straddles
Sales/Marketing: Lee Gatins
Manager: Jeremy Driver
jeremy.driver@wesleyintl.com
Manager: Vanessa Holiday
Estimated Sales: $5-10 Million
Number Employees: 50-99
Square Footage: 50000
Brands:
   Pack Mule
   Pallet Mule

31117 Wesley-Kind Associates
200 Old Country Rd
Suite 364
Mineola, NY 11501-4240
516-747-3434
Fax: 516-248-2728
Management consultant specializing in plant and
warehouse layouts and operating systems for the
movement, storage and control of materials and
products

Executive Director: Daniel Kind
Director Engineer: Oliver Wesley
Marketing Director: Daniel Kind
Estimated Sales: Less than $500,000
Number Employees: 1-4

31118 West Agro
11100 N Congress Ave
Kansas City, MO 64153
816-891-7700
Fax: 816-891-1606 www.universaldairy.com
Manufacturer and exporter of cleaning and sanita-
tion supplies including clean-in-place systems; also,
sanitation control system consultant
President: Walt Maharay
VP: Thomas Fahey
Contact: Mark Curtis
dan.brookhart@delaval.com
Number Employees: 100-249
Parent Co: Tetra Laval Group

**31119 (HQ)West Carrollton Parchment
Company**
PO Box 49098
West Carrollton, OH 45449
937-859-3621
Fax: 937-859-7610
Manufacturer and exporter of paper including print-
ing, rewinding, sheeting, die cutting, creping and
coating
President: Cameron Lonergan
CEO: Pierce Lonergan
VP Finance Alan Berens
Quality Control: Brandon Carpenter
Sales/Marketing: Larry Teague
Operations: Bob Scancella
Production: Tom Bray
Purchasing Director: Jerry Lienesch
Estimated Sales: $30 Million
Number Employees: 100-249
Number of Products: 150
Square Footage: 260000
Parent Co: Friend Group
Type of Packaging: Food Service
Brands:
   Gvp-100

31120 (HQ)West Chemical Products
1000 Herrontown Rd Ste 2
Princeton, NJ 08540
609-921-0501
Fax: 609-924-4308
Manufacturer and exporter of sanitizing agents in-
cluding detergents and disinfectants; also, insecti-
cides including liquid and fly killing
President: Elwood Phares
CEO: Elwood W Phares Ii
Contact: Bruce Muretta
bmuretta@westchemicalproducts.com
Estimated Sales: G
Number Employees: 100-249
Other Locations:
   West Chemical Products
   Tenefly NJ

31121 West Coast Industries Inc
750 Battery St # 100
Suite 100
San Francisco, CA 94111-1543
580-259-6267
Fax: 415-552-5368 800-243-3150
info@westcoastindustries.com
www.westcoastindustries.com
Restaurant and contract furniture including counters,
tables, etc
President: Rob Liss
Secretary/Treasurer: Ron Liss
VP: Normar Sobel
Estimated Sales: $5-10 Million
Number Employees: 10-19

31122 West Coast Specialty Coffee
71 Lost Lake Lane
Campbell, CA 95008
650-259-9308
Fax: 650-259-8024 rh@specialtycoffee.com
www.specialtycoffee.com
Coffee and coffee equipment and supplies
President: Robert Hensley
rh@specialtycoffee.com
Estimated Sales: $500,000
Number Employees: 2
Type of Packaging: Consumer, Food Service, Bulk

31123 West Hawk Industries
1717 S State St Frnt
Ann Arbor, MI 48104-4684

734-761-3100
Fax: 734-761-8430 800-678-1286
sales@westhawkpromo.com
www.westhawkind.com
Manufacturer and exporter of advertising novelties, decals, signs, banners, calendars, imprinted matches, bags and custom printed cups; also, imprinted mints and chocolates
President: Jan Hawkins
CEO: Harry Hawkins
Vice President: Sarah Spratt
Sales Director: Harry Hawkins
Estimated Sales: $2.5-5 Million
Number Employees: 5-9
Number of Products: 800
Square Footage: 30000
Type of Packaging: Private Label

31124 West Louisiana Ice Svc
1707 Smart St
Leesville, LA 71446-5061

337-239-4530
Fax: 337-238-5095 www.siceco.com
Owner: James S Shapkoff Jr
IT: Salina Johnson
westlaice@bellsouth.net
Estimated Sales: Less Than $500,000
Number Employees: 1-4

31125 West Metals
463 Nightingale Avenue
London, ON N5W 4C4
Canada

519-457-0603
Fax: 519-457-7960 800-300-6667
sales@westmetals.com www.westmetals.com
Glass display cases, cocktail mix and beverage units, sinks, prep and steam tables, work centers, exhaust hoods and fans
Number Employees: 10

31126 West Oregon Wood Products Inc
2305 2nd St
Columbia City, OR 97018-9504

503-397-6707
Fax: 503-397-6887 mross@wowpellets.com
A manufacturer of premium wood fuel pellet, all 100 percent wood fire logs, animal bedding, firestarter, and BBQ pellets. The quality products combined with a strong value proposition has provided us the platform to build categoryleading products. We continue to lead the industry in innovation, product development, and service.
Owner: Christopher Sharron
csharron@wowpellets.com
General Manager: Mike Knobel
Director Marketing/Sales: Mark Ross
Estimated Sales: $1-2.5 Million
Number Employees: 20-49
Square Footage: 560000
Brands:
Blazers
Lil' Devils

31127 West Penn Oil Co Inc
2305 Market St
Warren, PA 16365

814-723-9000
www.westpenn.com
Contract packager of lubricating oils.
President: Larry Lang
lalang@westpenn.com
Year Founded: 1921
Estimated Sales: $20-50 Million
Number Employees: 50-99
Square Footage: 60000
Brands:
Emblem

31128 West Rock
1000 Abernathy Road NE
Atlanta, GA 30328

770-448-2193
www.westrock.com
Produces containerboard and paperboard packaging for food, hardware, apparel and other consumer goods.

Chief Executive Officer: Steven Voohees
EVP/Chief Financial Officer: Ward Dickson
President, Business Development: Jim Porter
President, Consumer Packaging: Patrick Lindner
President, Corrugated Packaging: Jeff Chalovich
President, Multi Packaging Solutions: Marc Shore
Chief Transformation Officer: Shan Cooper
EVP/General Counsel/Secretary: Bob McIntosh
Chief Human Resources Officer: Vicki Lostetter
Chief Environmental Officer: Nina Butler
Chief Communications Officer: Donna Owens Cox
Year Founded: 2015
Estimated Sales: $14.8 Billion
Number Employees: 45,000
Type of Packaging: Consumer, Food Service, Private Label, Bulk

31129 West Star Industries
4445 E Fremont St
Stockton, CA 95215-4007

209-955-8220
Fax: 209-955-8250 800-326-2288
wsi@weststarindustries.com
www.weststarindustries.com
Stainless steel products including sinks, tables, exhaust hoods and refrigeration equipment
President: Michelle Focke
mfocke@weststarindustries.com
VP: William George
Estimated Sales: $5-10 Million
Number Employees: 20-49
Square Footage: 60000
Brands:
West Star

31130 West-Pak
PO Box 763847
Dallas, TX 75376

214-337-8984
Fax: 214-337-8988
Protective packaging
President: Edwin Monroe
Estimated Sales: $10-20 Million
Number Employees: 20-49

31131 Westec Tank & Equipment
1402 Grove St
Healdsburg, CA 95448-4700

707-431-9342
Fax: 707-431-8809 joe@westectank.com
www.westectank.com
Wine industry valves and fittings
President: Wanda Alary
Vice President: Jim Belli
jim@westectank.com
Estimated Sales: $5-10 Million
Number Employees: 20-49

31132 Westeel
PO Box 1370
Saskatoon, SK S7K 3P5
Canada

306-931-2855
Fax: 306-931-2786 www.westeel.com
Storage bins
President: Robert Skull
CFO: Ray Anderson
Quality Control: Linda Thurston
R & D: Bruce Allen
Operations Manager: Bruce Allen
Number Employees: 10
Parent Co: Jenisys

31133 Westerbeke Fishing GearCo Inc
400 Border St
Boston, MA 02128-2402

617-561-9967
Fax: 617-561-3752 800-536-6387
westerbekecompany@gmail.com wfg1.com
Wholesaler/distributor of boots, clothing, cutlery, shovels, netting, forks, containers, gloves, etc.; serving the seafood industry; liferaft annual inspections and netting & vinyl products.
Owner: Elaine Halligan
Sales Director: Ed Creamer
westerbekecompany@gmail.com
Purchasing Manager: Ed Creamer
Estimated Sales: $1 Million
Number Employees: 5-9
Square Footage: 24000

31134 Western Carriers
2220 91st Street
North Bergen, NJ 07047-4713

800-631-7776
201-869-3300
wine@westerncarriers.com
www.westerncarriers.com
Warehouse providing storage for wines and spirits, and the alcoholic beverage industry.
President: Michael Hodes
Contact: Rick Albee
walter@itoasys.com
Estimated Sales: $5-10 Million
Number Employees: 50-99
Square Footage: 3600000
Other Locations:
Vallejo 1,000,000 Sq Ft CA

31135 Western Combustion Engineering
640 E Realty St
Carson, CA 90745-6016

310-834-9389
Fax: 310-834-4795 info@westerncombustion.com
www.westerncombustion.com
Manufacturer, exporter of ovens, oil fryers and food processing equipment
President: Marcia Paul
mpaul@westerncombustion.com
Vice President: Marcia Paul
Estimated Sales: $1-2,500,000
Number Employees: 10-19
Square Footage: 10000

31136 (HQ)Western Container Company
4323 Clary Blvd
Kansas City, MO 64130

816-924-5700
Fax: 816-924-7032
Manufacturer and exporter of cartons including folding, cellophane window and plastic coated
President: Richard Horton
CFO: Allen Booe
Quality Control: Charlie Palmer
Contact: Kyle Adams
kylea@westerncontainer.com
Estimated Sales: $20-50 Million
Number Employees: 100-249

31137 Western Exterminator Co
1732 Kaiser Ave
Irvine, CA 92614-5706

949-954-8023
Fax: 949-474-7767 mlawton@west-ext.com
www.westernexterminator.com
Pest control systems
Founder: Carl Strom
Vice President of Administration: Debbie Byrne
Vice President of Sales: Michael Britt
Contact: Todd Frantz
tfrantz@west-ext.com
Estimated Sales: $2.5-5 Million
Number Employees: 20-49

31138 Western Laminates
431 S 91st Cir
Omaha, NE 68114

402-556-4600
Fax: 402-556-4601
Laminated doors, cabinets and counter tops
President: Bennett Wagner
bwwesternlam@qwestoffice.net
Estimated Sales: Below $5 Million
Number Employees: 10-19

31139 Western Lighting Inc
2349 17th St
Franklin Park, IL 60131-3432

847-451-7200
Fax: 847-451-7275 westernlighting@sbcglobal.net
www.westernlightinginc.com
Light fixtures and illuminated signs
Owner: Norma Heen
vheen@westernlighting.com
Site Manager: Victor Heen
vheen@westernlighting.com
Number Employees: 10-19

31140 Western Pacific Oils, Inc.
201 S Anderson St
Los Angeles, CA 90033

213-232-5117
Fax: 213-232-5102 www.westpacoils.com
Palm oils and coconut oil.

Manager: Y Neman
Contact: Suraj Bhojwani
suraj@westpacoils.com
Estimated Sales: $900 Thousand
Type of Packaging: Food Service, Bulk
Brands:
 Golden Palm Shortening
 Golden Joma Palm Oil
 Golden Palm Margarine
 Golden Palm Cake & Icing
 Golden Coconut Oil

31141 Western Pacific Stge Solutions
300 E Arrow Hwy
San Dimas, CA 91773-3339
909-305-9526
Fax: 909-451-0311 800-888-5707
trogers@wpss.com
Manufacturer and exporter of steel and boltless
shelving, carton flow racks and mezzanine systems
President: Tom Rogers
trogers@wpss.com
Marketing Manager: Diane Gowgill
Estimated Sales: $5-10,000,000
Number Employees: 100-249
Brands:
 Deluxe
 Industrial Structures
 Pacific
 Quik Pik
 Rivetier

31142 Western Plastics
105 Western Dr
Portland, TN 37148-2018
615-325-7331
Fax: 615-325-4924 sales@wplastic.com
Manufacturer, importer and exporter of aluminum
foil rolls, PVC film cutter-boxes, pallet stretch wrap,
perforated food wrap and shrink film
President: Tommy Mcclean
tommy@westernplastics.ie
VP: Gene Ketter
Sales Manager: David Sullender
Estimated Sales: $5-10 Million
Number Employees: 100-249
Square Footage: 120000
Brands:
 Air Flow
 Ez Bander
 Eco Wrap
 Indenti-Film
 Securi Seal
 Strong Bow
 Wp
 Wp Foodfilm
 Wp Handywrap
 Wrapnet

31143 (HQ)Western Plastics
2399 Highway 41 South SW
Calhoun, GA 30701-3346
706-625-5260
Fax: 706-625-0003 800-752-4106
calhoun@wplastics.com www.wplastics.com
Manufacturer and exporter of packaging materials
including plastic film and aluminum foil
President: Tom Cunningham
tcunningham@wplastics.com
CEO: Frederick Young
CFO: George Schultz
Vice President: Frederick Young
Marketing Director: Paul O'Loghlen
Operations Manager: Bobby Hyde
Purchasing Manager: Jeff Silvers
Estimated Sales: $40 Million
Number Employees: 50-99
Square Footage: 100000
Type of Packaging: Food Service, Private Label,
 Bulk
Other Locations:
Brands:
 Eldorado

31144 Western Plastics
2399 US 41 SW
Calhoun, GA 30701
706-625-5260
Fax: 706-625-0003 800-752-4106
calhoun@wplastics.com www.wplastics.com
Foil, foodfilm, pallet stretch film, meat and produce
film
President: Tom Cunningham

Estimated Sales: $10-20 Million
Number Employees: 1-4

31145 Western Polymer Corp
32 Road R SE
Moses Lake, WA 98837-9303
509-765-1803
Fax: 509-765-0327 800-362-6845
www.westernpolymer.com
Processor, exporter and importer of starch; manufac-
turer of starch recovery systems
CEO: Sheldon Townsend
Marketing: Mike Markillie
Estimated Sales: $20-50 Million
Number Employees: 50-99
Parent Co: Moses Lake
Type of Packaging: Bulk

31146 Western Precooling
43990 Fremont Blvd
Fremont, CA 94538-6057
510-656-2220
Fax: 510-656-1137 www.westernprecooling.com
Wine industry refrigeration
President: Maeve Austin
maeve_austin@toyota.com
CFO: Jerry Nopis
Estimated Sales: Below $5 Million
Number Employees: 20-49

31147 Western Pulp Products Co
5025 SW Hout St
Corvallis, OR 97333-9540
541-757-1151
Fax: 541-757-8613 800-547-3407
sales@westernpulp.com www.westernpulp.com
Wine industry pulp byproducts
President: Mel Kelsey
melk@westernpulp.com
CFO: Brad McIntyre
Estimated Sales: $10-25 Million
Number Employees: 50-99

31148 Western Refrigerated Freight Systems
8238 W Harrison Street
Phoenix, AZ 85043
602-254-9922
www.westernrefrigerated.com
Handles all temperature sensitive shipping and dis-
tribution needs throughout California, Arizona &
Nevada
President: Jeff Boley
Estimated Sales: $6 Million
Number Employees: 50
Other Locations:
 Las Vegas NV

31149 Western Square Industries
1621 N Broadway Ave
Stockton, CA 95205-3046
209-944-0921
Fax: 209-944-0934 800-367-8383
info@westernsquare.com www.westernsquare.com
Racks to hold bottled water
President: Trygve Mikkelsen
tmikkelson@westernsquare.com
Accounts Payable / Receivables: Joan Mikkelsen
Chief Engineer: Larry Bartko
Southern Coast Sales: Bobby Fox
Plant Manager: Robert Craven
Purchasing Agent: Russell Danero
Estimated Sales: $6 Million
Number Employees: 20-49
Square Footage: 44000

31150 Western Stoneware
521 W 6th Ave
Monmouth, IL 61462
309-734-2161
Fax: 309-734-5942 www.westernstoneware.com
Manufacturer and exporter of stoneware bean pots,
cheese crocks, canister sets, cups, mugs, soup bowls
and steins
Owner: Jack Horner
CFO: Jean Wiseman
VP: Gene Wiseman
Estimated Sales: Below $5 Million
Number Employees: 20-49

31151 (HQ)Western Textile & Manufacturing Inc.
1750 Bridgeaway
Suite B207
Sausalito, CA 94965
415-431-1458
Fax: 415-431-5980 800-734-8683
westex@bagmakers.com www.bagmakers.com
Manufacturer and exporter of leather goods includ-
ing menu covers
Owner: Craig Storek
Contact: David Hanson
david@bagmakers.com
Office Manager: Lorraine Storek
Estimated Sales: $2.5-5 Million
Number Employees: 1-4

31152 (HQ)Westervelt Co Inc
1400 Jack Warner Pkwy NE
Tuscaloosa, AL 35404-1002
205-562-5000
Fax: 205-562-5010 www.westervelt.com
Custom printed, die-cut and glued folding cartons,
solid bleached sulphate paperboard for food contact
use and line of dual paperboard packaging
President/Chief Executive Officer: Michael Case
mcase@westervelt.com
Vice President, Natural Resources: Jim King
Vice President, Finance: Gary Dailey
Vice President, Business Development: Alicia
Cramer
Vice President, Lumber: Joe Patton
Vice President/Secretary/General Counsel: Ray
Robbins
Estimated Sales: $67 Million
Number Employees: 1000-4999
Square Footage: 90000
Brands:
 E-Z Serve
 Heritage

31153 Westfalia Separator
100 Fairway Ct
Northvale, NJ 07647
201-767-3900
Fax: 201-784-4313 800-722-6622
Equipment for clarifying suspensions, separating
liquids with removal of solids, separating liquid
mixtures of differing densities of viscosities, extract-
ing of active substances, classifying substances, and
concentrating anddewatering of solids.
President: Michael Vick
COO: Hanno Lehmann
CFO: Norbert Breuer
Lab Director: Pete Malanchuk
Quality Control Director: Bill Taylor
Marketing Manager: Frank Kennedy
Sales: Michael Rohr
Contact: Samuel Barcenas
samuel.barcenas@gea.com
VP Operations: Joseph Pavlosky
Purchasing Manager: John Nayancsik
Estimated Sales: $36.7 Million
Number Employees: 530
Square Footage: 105000
Brands:
 Westfalia

31154 Westfield Sheet Metal Works
North 8th St & Monror Ave
PO Box 128
Kenilworth, NJ 7033
908-276-5500
Fax: 908-276-6808 info@westfieldsheetmetal.com
www.westfieldsheetmetal.com
Stainless steel belt guards, bins, booths, cabinets,
canopies, gloves boxes, consoles, carts, casings,
chutes, conveyors, cooling towers, cornices, damp-
ers, ducts, dust collectors, exhaust systems, flues,
guardrails, hoods, hoppersOSHA machine guards,
pressure vessels, U&R racks, skids, tanks. Also a
consultant for engineering, fabrication, and
installation
President: C Johnstone
CEO: Tom Johnstone
CFO: Gregg Wheatley
VP/Office Manager: Lorraine Carine
Quality Control/R&D: William Nicolson
Marketing: Walter Basilone
Sales Director: Hubert Plungis
Chief Engineer: William Nicolson
VP/Manager Production: Thomas Johnstone
Plant Manager: Mike McElroy
Purchasing Manager: Stanley Guididas

Estimated Sales: $10-20 Million
Number Employees: 50-99
Square Footage: 100000

31155 Weston Emergency Light Co
10 Sibley Rd
Weston, MA 02493-2550

781-894-1585
Fax: 781-894-1590 800-649-3756
sales@westonemergencylights.com
www.westonemergencylights.com
Manufacturer and importer of exit signs, lamps and
lighting fixtures; also, emergency light batteries,
portable rechargeable hand lights and flashlights
President: Michelle Flynn
Manager: Thomas Silveira
Clerk: Paul Amsden
Estimated Sales: $5-10 Million
Number Employees: 1-4
Square Footage: 10000

31156 Weston Solutions Inc
1400 Weston Way
PO Box 2653
West Chester, PA 19380-1492

610-701-3000
Fax: 610-701-3186
contactweston@westonsolutions.com,
www.westonsolutions.com
Infrastructure redevelopment firm providing inte-
grated, sustainable solutions
Manager: Richard H Mehl
CEO: William L Robertson
william.robertson@westonsolutions.com
Estimated Sales: $5-10 Million
Number Employees: 1000-4999

31157 Westra Construction
1263 12th Ave E
Palmetto, FL 34221

941-723-1611
Fax: 920-324-5957 800-388-3545
info@westraconst.com www.westraconst.com
Building and construction contractor, design/builder,
construction management and consultants
President and CEO: Don Thayer Jr
CFO: Patrick Flynn
Vice President: Peter Roehrig
VP Operations: Scott Heaze
Marketing Director: Gena Herwig
Sales Director: Scott Clark
Contact: Donald Anderson
donaldanderson@westraconst.com
Operations Manager: Rick Bickert
Estimated Sales: $1.7 Million
Number Employees: 240

31158 Westrick Paper Co
3011 Mercury Rd S
Jacksonville, FL 32207-7981

904-737-2122
Fax: 904-737-9129 info@westrickpaper.com
www.westrickpaper.com
Envelopes, writing tablets and other paper special-
ties
President: Jack Lamb
jack.lamb@westrickpaper.com
Estimated Sales: $5-10 Million
Number Employees: 1-4

31159 Westvaco Corporation
2000 Ogletown Road
Newark, DE 19711-5439

302-453-7200
Fax: 302-453-7280
Folding cartons and MAP packaging; exporter of
ovenware packaging
Business Development Manager: Rufus Miller
Manager (Frozen Foods): Shelly Dicken
National Account Manager: Richard De Ruiter
Estimated Sales: $1-2.5 Million
Number Employees: 9
Square Footage: 120000

31160 Westvaco Corporation
320 Hull St
Richmond, VA 23224

804-233-9205
Fax: 804-232-3975 www.meadwestvaco.com
Contract packager of microwaveable entrees, baked
goods, etc
Sales Manager: John McInerney
Sales: Bob London

Estimated Sales: $20-50 Million
Number Employees: 250-499
Parent Co: Westvaco Corporation

31161 Wetterau Wood Products
10 Corporate Drive
Burlington, MA 1803

602-267-3600
Fax: 715-623-4399 800-986-0958
wetterauwood@yahoo.com www.homestead.com
Pallets and skids
President: Michael Wetterau
VP: Deborah Wetterau
Number Employees: 10

31162 Wexler Packaging Products
777 Schwab Rd # M
Hatfield, PA 19440-3272

215-631-9700
Fax: 215-631-9705 800-878-3878
sales@wexlerpackaging.com
www.wexlerpackaging.com
Paper/poly banding machines
Owner: Kelley Detweiler
kdetweiler@wexlerpackaging.com
Marketing Manager: Joseph Ambrose
Estimated Sales: $5-10 Million
Number Employees: 10-19

31163 Wexxar Corporation
3851 W Devon Avenue
Chicago, IL 60659-1024

630-983-6666
Fax: 630-983-6948 sales@wexxar.com
www.wexxar.com
Manufacturer and exporter of packaging equipment
including tray and case formers and sealers
Vice President of Sales: Jim Stoddard
Estimated Sales: Less than $500,000
Number Employees: 4
Square Footage: 200000
Parent Co: Wexxar Packaging Machinery
Brands:
   Wexxar

31164 Wexxar Packaging Inc
13471 Vulcan Way
Richmond, BC V6V 1K4
Canada

604-930-9500
Fax: 604-930-9368 888-565-3219
sales@wexxar.com www.wexxar.com
Case forming, case sealing by hot glue, cold glue,
tape. Poly bag insertors stainless steel wash down
corrosion resistant machinery
President: William Chu
Marketing Director: Melissa Montague
Parent Co: ProMach Inc
Type of Packaging: Food Service
Brands:
   Bel Line

31165 Weyauwega Star Dairy
109 N Mill St
P.O. Box 658
Weyauwega, WI 54983

920-867-2870
888-813-9720
www.wegastardairy.com
Cheese manufacturer, specializing in Parmesan,
Asiago and Romanao; sting cheeses and curds; meat
products; spreadable cheeses. Provide private label,
shredding and packing services.
President: James Knaus
Contact: Gerard Knaus
gknaus@wegastardairy.com
Estimated Sales: $12.5 Million
Number Employees: 75
Number of Brands: 7
Type of Packaging: Consumer, Food Service, Pri-
   vate Label, Bulk
Brands:
   Weyauwega
   Star Dairy
   Alacreme
   Scott's
   Lakeside's
   Rose Cottage
   Fontina Cheese

31166 Weyerhaeuser Co
220 Occidental Ave S # 7
Seattle, WA 98104-3120

253-924-3215
800-525-5440
www.weyerhaeuser.com
Corrugated boxes
Chairman: Charles Williamson
President/CEO/Director: Daniel Fulton
EVP/Chief Financial Officer: Patricia Bedient
Vice President, Information Technology: Kevin
Shearer
SVP, Research & Development/CTO: Miles Drake
Director, Quality Assurance: Jason Smitherman
Director, Marketing: Jason McIntosh
Director, Sales: Mike Spath
Contact: Jayafri Guha
jayafri.guha@weyerhaeuser.com
Operations Manager: Walt Shriver
Production Manager: Linor Williams
Plant Manager: William Snyder
Purchasing Manager: Karen Andrus-Hughes
Estimated Sales: Less Than $500,000
Number Employees: 1-4
Square Footage: 14672
Parent Co: Wayerhaeuser Company

31167 Whallon Machinery Inc
205 N Chicago St
PO Box 429
Royal Center, IN 46978-2101

574-643-9561
Fax: 574-643-9218 info@whallon.com
www.whallon.net
Manufacturer and exporter of palletizers and
depalletizers for cans, cases and pails
Owner: Leslie Smith
Engineering Manager: Jeff Tevis
Sales Manager: Bruce Ide
lsmith1@whallon.com
Purchasing Manager: Judy Roudebush
Estimated Sales: $10-20 Million
Number Employees: 50-99
Square Footage: 70000

31168 Whatman
800 Centennial Ave # 1
Piscataway, NJ 08854-3911

973-245-8300
Fax: 973-245-8301 www.whatman.com
Provides separations technology and in known
throughout the scientific community for providing
innovative products and solutions.
CEO: Bob Thein
Senior VP: Richard Dool
Contact: Giles Barton
giles.barton@whatman.com
Product Manager: Tiana Gorham
Estimated Sales: $7 Million
Number Employees: 50-99
Other Locations:
   Sanford ME
Brands:
   Whatman

31169 Whatman
PO Box 8223
Haverhill, MA 01835-0723

978-374-7400
Fax: 978-374-7070
Manufacturer and exporter of filters, analytical in-
struments and laboratory equipment and supplies
VP Sales/Marketing: David Largesse
Estimated Sales: $500,000-$1 Million
Number Employees: 50-99
Type of Packaging: Bulk

31170 Wheaton Plastic Containers
1101 Wheaton Ave
Millville, NJ 08332-2003

856-825-1400
Fax: 856-825-1368 wheaton.com
Plastic and glass containers, plastic bottles, caps and
closures
President, Chief Executive Officer: Stephen
Drozdow
Vice President of Global Marketing: Michael Blazes
Vice President of Quality: Nicholas DeBello
Regional Manager: Al Lancto
Vice President of Operations: Gregory Bianco
Number Employees: 250-499

31171 Wheel Tough Company
1597 E Industrial Drive
Terre Haute, IN 47802-9265
812-298-8606
Fax: 812-298-1166 888-765-8833
Manufacturer and exporter of aluminum bar and restaurant furniture including stools, chairs and tables; also, gas and charcoal grills, deep fryers and steamers
President: Rudolph J Stakeman Jr
Estimated Sales: $1 Million
Number Employees: 5
Square Footage: 272000
Brands:
Driver's Seat, The
Trackside Cookery

31172 Whey Systems
PO Box 1689
Willmar, MN 56201-1689
320-905-4122
Fax: 320-231-2282
Provides edible whey processing equipment and systems to the dairy industry. Each system and component is specifically designed to efficiently process the desired whey fraction. Recognized as the world leader in providing lactosedrying systems, with the lowest capital and operating cost to produce high quality edible powder. Providing systems for whey, WPC, lactose, permeate, demineralization, and ammonium lactate.
President: Loren Corle
Product Manager: Jay Gilbert
Number Employees: 20-49

31173 Whirl Air Flow
20055 177th St NW
Big Lake, MN 55309-8015
763-262-1200
Fax: 763-262-1212 800-373-3461
whirlair@whirlair.com www.whirlair.com
Dense and dilute phase pneumatic conveyors including pressure and vacuum
President: E Mueller
emueller@whirlair.com
Marketing Director: Gregg Hedtke
Sales Director: Gregg Hedtke
Plant Manager: Ken Hanley
Purchasing Manager: Wendy Holland
Estimated Sales: $6-7 Million
Number Employees: 20-49
Number of Brands: 45
Square Footage: 100000

31174 Whirley Industries Inc
140 W Harmar St
Warren, PA 16365-2184
814-723-8696
Fax: 814-723-3245 800-825-5575
klabarbera@whirley.com
www.whirleydrinkworks.com
As the world's leading manufacturer of plastic promotional drink containers, Whirley Industries offers a diverse line of products ranging from 12-128 oz
Owner/CEO: Lincoln Sokolski
CFO: Greg Aross
Marketing: Andrew Solkoski
Sales: William Turner
Manager: Kitty Cerra
kcerra@whirleydrinkworks.com
Estimated Sales: $20-50 Million
Number Employees: 250-499
Type of Packaging: Bulk

31175 (HQ)Whisk Products Inc
130 Enterprise Dr
Wentzville, MO 63385-5544
636-327-6262
Fax: 636-327-6288 800-204-7627
whisk@whiskproducts.com
www.whiskproducts.com
Manufacturer and exporter of hand cleaners, germicidal hand soap and dishwashing detergents; also, soap dispensers
Owner: Raymond Lamantia
Sales: Brad LaMantia
ray@whiskproducts.com
Plant Manager: Scott Berg
Purchasing: Lisa Thess
Estimated Sales: $3-5 Million
Number Employees: 10-19
Number of Brands: 1
Number of Products: 32
Square Footage: 46000

Brands:
Metalife
Sir
Whisk
Xcel

31176 Whit-Log Trailers Inc
PO Box 668
Wilbur, OR 97494
541-673-0651
Fax: 541-673-1166 800-452-1234
brett@whitlogtrailers.com
www.whitlogtrailers.com
Manufacturer and exporter of hydraulic material handling equipment including truck mounted and pedestal electric stationary cranes
Owner: Gene Whitaker
gene@whitlogtrailers.com
Sales Manager: Jim Davidson
Estimated Sales: $300,000-500,000
Number Employees: 1-4

31177 White Mop Wringer Company
P.O.Box 16647
Tampa, FL 33687-6647
813-971-2223
Fax: 813-971-6090 800-237-7582
Manufacturer and exporter of janitorial equipment including burnishers, carts, floor and carpet care products and waste baskets and receptacles
Chief Financial Officer: Thomas Halluska
Estimated Sales: $50-100 Million
Number Employees: 100-249
Type of Packaging: Food Service
Brands:
Gator
Microscrub
Mipro
Propak
Pullman-Holt Gansow
Rugboss
Smartbasket

31178 White Mountain Freezer
800 E 101st Terrace
Kansas City, MO 64131-5322
816-943-4100
Fax: 816-943-4123
Manufacturer and exporter of ice cream and fruit processing machinery including freezers, parers and pitters
VP Marketing: Phil Gyori
Marketing Manager: Lori Baker
Production Manager: Melea Burghart
Parent Co: Rival Company

31179 White Mountain Lumber Co
30 E Milan Rd
PO Box 7
Berlin, NH 03570-3566
603-752-1000
Fax: 603-752-1400 www.whitemtnlumber.com
Wooden pallets
President: Barry J Kelley
barry@whitemtnlumber.com
Treasurer: Mark Kelley
Sales Director: Phil Bedard
General Manager/Wholesale Manager: Barry Kelley
Estimated Sales: $10-20 Million
Number Employees: 50-99
Square Footage: 50000

31180 White Oaks Frozen Foods
2525 Cooper Ave
Merced, CA 95348-4313
209-725-9492
Fax: 209-725-9441
www.whiteoakfrozenfoods.com
Reduced Moisture (RM) vegetable ingredients processor.
President: Jack Sollazzo
CEO: Suvan Sharma
Vice President, Sales: Dan Wilkinson
Number Employees: 1-4
Parent Co: Cascade Specialties, Inc.

31181 White Rabbit Dye Inc
4265 Meramec St
St Louis, MO 63116-2615
314-664-6563
Fax: 314-664-5563 800-466-6588
info@whiterabbitdye.com
www.whiterabbitdye.com

Easter egg dyes, kits and food colors; also, wire dippers; exporter of dry food colors
Co-Owner: Julie Consolino
Co-Owner: Jeff Petroski
Estimated Sales: $5-10 Million
Number Employees: 10-19
Square Footage: 32000
Parent Co: Premier Packaging
Type of Packaging: Consumer
Brands:
White Rabbit

31182 White Stokes International
3615 South Jasper Place
Chicago, IL 60609
773-523-7540
Fax: 773-523-0767 800-978-6537
Quality ingredients for bakery, confectionary, and ice cream. Founded in 1906.
President: Nicholas Tzakis
Vice President: George Tzakis
Number Employees: 26

31183 White Way Sign & Maintenance
451 Kingston Ct
Mt Prospect IL 60056
847-391-0200
Fax: 847-642-0272 800-621-4122
Manufacturer and exporter of electronic message displays
President: Robert B Flannery Jr
VP of Sales: Robert Flannery
kcooper@amfam.net
Contact: Keisha Cooper
kcooper@amfam.net
Plant Mgr: Pete Tomaselli
Estimated Sales: $20-50 Million
Number Employees: 100-249

31184 (HQ)Whitford Corporation
33 Sproul Rd
Frazer, PA 19355
610-296-3200
Fax: 610-647-4849 sales@whitfordww.com
www.whitfordww.com
Manufacturer and exporter of nonstick coatings designed for food contact and food associated applications
President: David Willis Jr
Chief Administrative Officer: Joan Eberhardt
CFO: Brian Kilty
Marketing Director: John Badner
Contact: Daniel Brim
daniel.brim@whitfordww.com
Plant Manager: Scott De Bourke
Purchasing Manager: Jill Schultz
Estimated Sales: $30-50 Million
Number Employees: 100
Square Footage: 60000
Brands:
Excalibur
Quantanium
Quantum
Ultralon
Xylac
Xylan
Xylan Eterna
Xylan Plus

31185 Whiting & Davis
PO Box 1270
Attleboro Falls, MA 02763-0270
508-699-0214
Fax: 508-643-9303 800-876-6374
www.whitinganddavis.com/
Manufacturer, exporter and importer of stainless steel ring mesh safety protective clothing including gloves, aprons, arm and body gear
Director Sales/Marketing: Ron DiMarzio
Contact: David Youngerman
david.youngerman@whitingdavis.com
Estimated Sales: $5-10 Million
Number Employees: 100
Square Footage: 400000
Parent Co: WDC Holdings
Brands:
3-Step
Aegis
Ultra Guard
Whiting & Davis

31186 Whitley Manufacturing Company
PO Box 112
Midland, NC 28107

704-888-2625
Fax: 704-888-3023 www.whitleyhandle.com
Mop, broom and shovel handles; importer of dowels
President: Arlene Whitley
CEO: A Whitley
Quality Control: Arlene Whitley
Estimated Sales: $20-50 Million
Number Employees: 20-49
Square Footage: 35000

31187 (HQ)Whitlock Packaging Corp
1701 S Lee St
Fort Gibson, OK 74434-8419

918-478-4300
Fax: 918-478-7360 mollerd@whitlockpkg.com
www.whitlockpkg.com
Contract packager providing glass, steel, aluminum can, PET and plastic packaging services for noncarbonated beverages
President: David Moller
CEO: Bruce Outland
b.outland@compsourceok.com
Vice President: Keith Bishop
VP Marketing/Sales: Terry Milan
VP Sales & Private Label: Bill Towler
VP Human Resource: Ted Smith
VP Manufacturing: Abraham Jospeh
Plant Manager: Joe Tomaskovic
Purchasing Manager: Tammy Sanders
Number Employees: 100-249
Square Footage: 562

31188 Whitmire Microgen Research Lab
3568 Tree Court Industrial Blv
St Louis, MO 63122-6682

636-825-9775
Fax: 636-225-3739 800-777-8570
www.basf.com
Pest control equipment and chemicals
CEO: Tony Accurso
National Sales Manager: Larry Sharp
Director Manufacturing/Logistics: Chuck Sutton
IT Executive: S Sims
steve.sims@wmmg.com
Estimated Sales: $15 Million
Number Employees: 50-99
Parent Co: S.C. Johnson & Son
Brands:
  Advance
  Allure
  Ascend
  Avert
  Mouse Master
  Vector

31189 Whittle & Mutch Inc
712 Fellowship Rd
Mt Laurel, NJ 08054-1004

856-235-1165
Fax: 856-235-0902 jmutch3d@wamiflavor.com
www.wamiflavor.com
President: John C Mutch Jr
Estimated Sales: $10-20 Million
Number Employees: 10-19

31190 WholesalePortal.com
6135 Seaview Avenue NW
Suite 3a
Seattle, WA 98107-2628

206-782-7040
Fax: 206-782-9641
Wholesaler

31191 Wichita Stamp & Seal Inc
807 N Main St
Wichita, KS 67203-3606

316-263-4223
Fax: 316-263-9738
Notary and corporate seals, rubber stamps, interior signs, etc.; also, ink jet printers, coders and FDA approved inks
Owner: Lynne Bird
CFO: Linne Bird
Marketing Director: Martha Hays
Estimated Sales: Less Than $500,000
Number Employees: 5-9

31192 Wick's Packaging Service
7545 S State Road 75
Cutler, IN 46920

574-967-3104
Fax: 765-268-2729 info@wickspackaging.com
www.wickspackaging.com
Manufacturer and exporter of rebuilt vertical form/fill/seal packaging machinery. Distribute plastic pouch making machinery: T-shirt, standup zip lock pouch, and wicketed bags
Owner: Steven Wickersham
Vice President: Barb Wickersham
Research & Development: Craig Wickersham
Contact: Shawn Wickersham
shawn@wickspackaging.com
Packaging Engineer: Shawn Wickersham
Production Manager: Jerry Reef Jr
Estimated Sales: $2.5-5 Million
Number Employees: 1-4
Square Footage: 28000
Type of Packaging: Consumer, Food Service, Private Label, Bulk

31193 Wick's Packaging Service
7545 South State Road 75
Cutler, IN 46920-9670

574-967-3104
Fax: 765-268-2729 info@wickspackaging.com
www.wickspackaging.com
Vertical form seal bag makers
President: Steve Wickersham
Contact: Shawn Wickersham
shawn@wickspackaging.com
Estimated Sales: Below $5 Million
Number Employees: 1-4

31194 (HQ)Wico Corporation
7847 N Caldwell Avenue
Niles, IL 60714-3375

847-583-1320
Fax: 847-583-1043 800-367-9426
Parts and supplies for coin-operated vending and amusement equipment

31195 Wiegmann & Rose Thermxchanger
9131 San Leandro St # 220
Oakland, CA 94603-1208

510-632-8828
Fax: 510-632-8920 jlogan@wiegmannandrose.com
www.wiegmannandrose.com
Designer and manufacturer of ammonia flooded, spray shell and tube chillers for food and wine processing
CEO: Scott E. Logan
Executive VP: R Trent
VP Quality: Jon E. Hammons
Sales: Scott E. Logan
Sales: K Gardner
Administration, Personnel: Suzette I. Logan
Plant Manager: Gary D. Keeler
Purchasing: Will O' Bryant
Estimated Sales: $2.5-5 Million
Number Employees: 20-49
Square Footage: 212000
Parent Co: Xchanger Manufacturing Corporation
Brands:
  Thermxchanger
  Wiegmann & Rose

31196 Wifag Group Polytype America Corp
10 Industrial Ave
Mahwah, NJ 07430-2205

201-995-1000
Fax: 201-995-1080 info@polytype-usa.com
Dry offset printing on plastic containers
President: Pieter S. van der Griendt
VP Sales: Thomas Stuart
Sales Manager: Felix Gomez
Operations Manager: Jim Dominico
Estimated Sales: $1-5 Million
Number Employees: 25
Parent Co: wifag//polytype

31197 Wiginton Corp
699 Aero Ln
Sanford, FL 32771-6699

407-585-3200
Fax: 407-592-9099 www.wiginton.net
Automatic fire sprinkler systems

President: Pete Aziz
pxa@wiginton.net
Sr. Project Manager: Bob Lyle
Manager of Sales: Kenny Trevino
Estimated Sales: $20-50 Million
Number Employees: 20-49

31198 Wika Instrument LP
1000 Wiegand Blvd
Lawrenceville, GA 30043-5868

770-513-8200
Fax: 770-338-5118 800-645-0606
info@wika.com www.wika.us
Full line of mechanical and electronic pressure instruments, temperature instruments and diaphram seals manufactured to stric ISO 9001 standards
President: Dave Wannamaker
Estimated Sales: $20-50 Million
Number Employees: 500-999
Square Footage: 225000
Parent Co: Wika Instrument Corporation
Brands:
  Trend

31199 Wika Instrument LP
1000 Wiegand Blvd
Lawrenceville, GA 30043-5868

770-513-8200
Fax: 770-338-5118 888-945-2872
info@wika.com www.wika.us
President: Bill Anderson
banderson@wika.com
Chief Financial Officer: Steve McCullough
Chief Revenue Officer: Drew Firestone
Quality Control: Bernett Bigts
Estimated Sales: $5-10 Million
Number Employees: 500-999

31200 Wilbur Curtis Co
6913 W Acco St
Montebello, CA 90640-5403

323-837-2300
Fax: 323-837-2406 800-421-6150
info@wilburcurtis.com www.wilburcurtis.com
Manufacturer and exporter of coffee and tea brewing equipment
CEO: Kevin Curtis
krcurtis@wilburcurtis.com
COO: Joe Laws
Estimated Sales: $30-50 Million
Number Employees: 100-249
Square Footage: 105000
Brands:
  Advanced Digital System
  Alpha
  Curtis
  Gemini
  Mercury
  Polaris
  Primo Cappaccino
  Thermologic

31201 Wilch Manufacturing
1345 SW 42nd Street
Topeka, KS 66609-1267

785-267-2762
Fax: 785-267-6825
Manufacturer and exporter of ice cream blenders, cooking grills, freezers and dispensers including slush, cocktail, yogurt and soft serve
President: Bill Young
Sales: Dave White
Purchasing Manager: Dee Kuhn
Number Employees: 45
Square Footage: 102000
Brands:
  Wilch

31202 Wilco Distributors Inc
1200 W Laurel Ave
Lompoc, CA 93436-5158

805-735-2476
Fax: 805-735-3629 800-769-5040
williewilc@aol.com www.wilcodistributors.com
Manufacture and distributor of rodenticides in ther Western portion of the United States and Canada.
President: Blake Hazen
jbhazen@aol.com
Chief Executive Officer, Founder: Donald Willis
VP: Blake Hazen
Estimated Sales: $3-5 Million
Number Employees: 10-19

31203 Wilco Precision Testers
145 Main St
Tuckahoe, NY 10707-2906
914-337-2005
Fax: 914-337-8519 info@ptiusa.com
www.ptipacktech.com
Specialty packaging and inspection machinery for the pharmaceutical, food, container and automotive industries including total container inspection, package integrity testing, e-z open peelable can ends, and filling and heat sealing
Member of the Board: Anton Stauffer
Estimated Sales: $10-20 Million
Number Employees: 20-49

31204 Wilco, USA
181 Woodland Valley Drive
Woodland Park, CO 80863-9314
719-686-0074
Fax: 719-686-0112 gc-schramm@compuserve.com
Leak inspection equipment for all products

31205 Wilden Pump & Engineering LLC
22069 Van Buren St
Grand Terrace, CA 92313-5651
909-422-1700
Fax: 909-783-3440 wilden@psgdover.com
www.psgdover.com
Air operated double diaphragm pumps.
President: Monique Cisneros
mcisneros@nissanriverside.com
VP Finance: William Barton
VP Sales/Marketing: Martino Valela
Director Business Development: Greg Duncan
Director Operations: Dwane Lamb
VP Engineering: Gary Lent
Estimated Sales: $2.4,000,000
Number Employees: 250-499
Brands:
Pro-Flow

31206 Wilder Manufacturing Company
41 Mechanic St
Port Jervis, NY 12771
845-856-5188
Fax: 845-856-1950 800-832-1319
Manufacturer and exporter of holding, warming and transporting equipment including proofing cabinets, bins, racks, utility tables, etc
VP Sales/Marketing: Ray Addington
Estimated Sales: $1-5 Million
Parent Co: Win-Holt Equipment Group
Type of Packaging: Food Service
Brands:
Wilder

31207 Wildes Printing Co Inc
4321 Charles Crossing Dr
4321 Charles Crossing Drive
White Plains, MD 20695-3027
301-870-4141
Fax: 301-932-7495 info@wildes-spirit.com
www.wildes-spirit.com
General commercial markers and stamps
CEO: Katie Stickel
kstickel@wilde-spirit.com
Owner: Katie Stickel
Estimated Sales: $2.5-5 Million
Number Employees: 20-49
Brands:
Crown Marketing

31208 Wilen Professional Cleaning Products
3760 Southside Industrial Pkwy
Atlanta, GA 30354-3219
404-366-2111
Fax: 404-361-8832 800-241-7371
www.wilen.com
Manufacturer and exporter of cleaning equipment and supplies including brushes, scouring and hand pads and floor/carpet products
President: Vance Perry
Quality Control: Rachael Alexander
VP Marketing/Customer Relations: Rhonda Lassiter
Production Manager: John Akin
Purchasing Manager: Norris Minnis
Estimated Sales: $75-100 Million
Number Employees: 100-249
Square Footage: 150000

31209 Wilevco Inc
10 Fortune Dr
Billerica, MA 01821-3996
978-667-0400
Fax: 978-670-9191 sales@wilevco.com
www.wilevco.com
Manufacturer and exporter of automatic batter control systems, rotary atomization spray applicators and swept surface heat exchangers for process chilling systems
President: Leverett P Flint
Chairman/Founder: Putnam Flint
Vice President: John Whitmore
Estimated Sales: Below $5 Million
Number Employees: 10-19
Square Footage: 32000
Brands:
Cryolator
Wilevco

31210 Wilheit Packaging LLC
1527 May Dr
Gainesville, GA 30507-8464
770-532-4421
Fax: 770-532-8956 www.wilheit.com
Corrugated boxes
President and CFO: Philip Wilheit
pwilheit@wilheit.com
Marketing: Barbara Edwards
Estimated Sales: $20-50 Million
Number Employees: 50-99

31211 Wilhelmsen Consulting
455 Falcato Dr
Milpitas, CA 95035-6113
408-946-4525
Fax: 413-235-0121 ewilhel@klarify.com
Consultant providing analytical and business development services; also, food safety and training available
Owner: Eric Wilhelmsen
ewilhel@klarify.com
Estimated Sales: Less Than $500,000
Number Employees: 1-4

31212 Wilhite Sign Company
201 N Joplin
Joplin, MO 66762
417-623-1411
Fax: 417-623-2223
Signs including neon, plastic and painted
President: Jeplin Hipple
Estimated Sales: $500,000-$1 Million
Number Employees: 5-9

31213 Wilkens-Anderson Co
4525 W Division St
Chicago, IL 60651-1674
773-384-4433
Fax: 773-384-6260 800-847-2222
waco@wacolab.com www.wacolab.com
Laboratory and quality control equipment, supplies instruments and chemicals can testing equipment, can seam evaluation equipment
President/CEO: Bruce Wilkens
info@waco-lab-supply.com
Marketing Director: Peter Thomases
Sales Director: Don Hartman
Operations Manager: Eric Jensen
Production Manager: Don Lamonica
Estimated Sales: $6-8 Million
Number Employees: 20-49
Square Footage: 220000
Brands:
Waco

31214 (HQ)Wilkie Brothers Conveyor Inc
1765 Michigan Ave # 2
PO Box 219
Marysville, MI 48040-2046
810-364-4820
Fax: 810-364-4824 www.wilkiebros.com
Manufacturer and exporter of new and reconditioned overhead conveyor systems and equipment including chains, trolleys, attachments and structural components
Owner: Paul Naz
pnaz@wilkiebros.com
Sales Manager: Robert Wilkie
Sales: John Moews
Estimated Sales: $2.5-5 Million
Number Employees: 20-49
Square Footage: 240000

Type of Packaging: Bulk
Brands:
Bluewater Mfg., Inc.
J.B. Webb Co.
R.W. Zig Zag
Unibuilt

31215 (HQ)Wilkinson ManufacturingCompany
PO Box 490
Fort Calhoun, NE 68023
402-468-5511
Fax: 402-468-5521 info@wilkmfg.com
Manufacturer and exporter of aluminum foil pans
President: Bob Dalziel
R&D: Ray Massey Jr
Quality Control: Claude Weimer
Director Marketing: Ray Salinas
Contact: Joseph Richardson
j.richardson@wilkinsonindustries.com
Estimated Sales: $30-50 Million
Number Employees: 250-499
Type of Packaging: Consumer, Food Service

31216 Wilks Precision Instr Co Inc
4800 Green Valley Rd
Union Bridge, MD 21791-9157
410-775-7917
Fax: 410-775-7919
Custom plastic injection molded boxes, trays and funnels
President: Tom Wilks
tbwilks@verizon.net
Estimated Sales: $1-2.5 Million
Number Employees: 5-9

31217 Will & Baumer
PO Box 2992
Syracuse, NY 13220
315-451-1000
Fax: 315-451-0120 info@willbaumer.com
www.willbaumer.com
Manufacturer, importer and exporter of candles, processed beeswax and candlelamps
President: Marshall Ciccone
Sales Director: John Dowd
Contact: Jeff Field
jefff@willbaumer.com
Estimated Sales: $5-10 Million
Number Employees: 50-99
Square Footage: 400000
Type of Packaging: Food Service
Brands:
Brite-Lite
Mood Lite

31218 Will-Pemco Inc
3333 Crocker Ave
Sheboygan, WI 53081-6425
920-458-2500
Fax: 920-458-1265 wpemco@willpemco.com
www.pemco-solutions.com
Sheeting and packaging
President: Mark Maertz
CFO: Jim Wanalstine
CEO: Lee Sleiter
Estimated Sales: $50-100 Million
Number Employees: 100-249

31219 Willamette Industries
PO Box 666
Beaverton, OR 97075-0666
503-641-1131
Fax: 503-526-8830 www.weyerhaeuser.com
Corrugated shipping containers
President: Michael Miller
General Manager: Richard Knapton
Sales Manager: Larry Brill
Estimated Sales: $20-50 Million
Number Employees: 100-249
Square Footage: 240000
Parent Co: Willamette Industries

31220 Willamette Industries
PO Box 666
Beaverton, OR 97075-0666
503-641-1131
Fax: 503-526-8830 www.weyerhaeuser.com
Manufacturer and exporter of corrugated boxes and folding cartons
Plant Manager: David Dickey
Sales Manager: Brent Wagner

Estimated Sales: $20-50 Million
Number Employees: 100-249
Parent Co: Willamette Industries

31221 Willamette Industries
P.O.Box 666
Beaverton, OR 97075-0666

503-641-1131
Fax: 503-526-8830 www.weyerhaeuser.com
Custom shipping containers and full color
floor/counter displays
Sales Manager: Rick Lantello
Assistant Sales Manager: Jim Weiks
Plant Manager: David Dickey
Estimated Sales: $20-50 Million
Number Employees: 100-249
Square Footage: 300000
Parent Co: Willamette Industries

31222 Willamette Industries
2300 Greene Way
Louisville, KY 40220-4040

502-753-0264
Fax: 502-753-0276 800-465-3065
Manufacturer and exporter of liquid bulk one-way
disposable containers
Manager: Jim Woolums
General Manager: Larry Ogle
Sales Manager (Liquid Systems): H Edwin Cross
Estimated Sales: $50-100 Million
Number Employees: 5-9
Brands:
   Willpak Liquid Systems

31223 Willard Packaging Co
18940 Woodfield Rd
Gaithersburg, MD 20879-4717

301-948-7700
Fax: 301-963-2375 www.willardpackaging.com
Corrugated boxes, foam parts and packaging sup-
plies
President: Dale Salkeld
Chairman of the Board: Raymond W Salkeld Jr
Sales Manager: H Harper
Estimated Sales: $20-50 Million
Number Employees: 50-99
Square Footage: 86000

31224 Willett America
1500 N Mittel Boulevard
Wood Dale, IL 60191-1072

817-222-2233
Fax: 817-222-0466 800-259-2600
Ink jet coding systems
President: Wes Lansford
VP Sales: Wayne Moore
Marketing Manager: Terri Carruth
Contact: Derrick Varnell
derrick_varnell@msn.com

31225 William Brown Co Inc
6429 Hegerman St
Philadelphia, PA 19135-3315

215-331-2776
Fax: 215-333-4231 800-962-7696
www.wmbrownco.com
Cutting systems for food processing
President: William Black
Vice President: Kevin Beck
Sales Director: Benjamin Rickards
Estimated Sales: $2.5-5 Million
Number Employees: 5-9

31226 William Hecht
508 Bainbridge Street
Philadelphia, PA 19147

215-925-6223
Fax: 215-923-6798
Display cases and store fixtures; also, architectural
millwork and casework available
President: Stuart Hecht
Number Employees: 49
Square Footage: 100000

31227 William J. Mills & Company
74100 W Front St
P.O.Box 2126
Greenport, NY 11944

631-477-1500
Fax: 631-477-1504 800-477-1535
www.millscanvas.com
Commercial awnings
Owner: William Willets

Estimated Sales: Below 1 Million
Number Employees: 20-49

31228 William Willis Worldwide
310 W Lyon Farm Drive
PO Box 4444
Greenwich, CT 06831-0408

Fax: 203-532-9292 203-532-1919
Executive search firm
President: William H. Willis
wwwinc@aol.com
Estimated Sales: $1-2.5 Million
Number Employees: 3
Square Footage: 3000

31229 Williams & Mettle Company
14309 Sommermeyer Street
Houston, TX 77041-6204

713-939-1830
Fax: 713-939-1337 800-526-4954
Filters and extruder pack screens
President and COO: Alan Arterbury
Chairman/CEO: Ken Howard
VP Finance: Allan Goertz
Number Employees: 140
Square Footage: 190000
Parent Co: WMW Industries

31230 Williams Pallet
9154 Port Union Rialto Rd
West Chester, OH 45069

513-874-4014
Fax: 513-874-5438
Wooden pallets and skids
Estimated Sales: $10-20 Million
Number Employees: 10

31231 Williams Refrigeration
65 Park Ave
Hillsdale, NJ 07642-2109

201-358-6005
Fax: 201-358-0401 800-445-9979
williamsref@msn.com
www.williams-refrigeration.co.uk
Manufacturer and exporter of commercial refrigera-
tion equipment including blast chillers and reach-in,
roll-in and counter refrigerators
Owner: William Gesner
william@williams-refrigeration.co.uk
VP: Nicholas Williams
Engineering Director: Steve Bernard
Marketing Director: Malcolm Harling
Sales Manager: Andy Ward
Purchasing Manager: Lynette Wixey
Number Employees: 250-499
Square Footage: 1400000
Parent Co: Williams Refrigeration
Type of Packaging: Food Service
Brands:
   Williams

31232 Williams Shade & AwningCompany
4834 Hickory Hill Rd
Memphis, TN 38116-3252

901-368-5055
Fax: 901-396-2327
Commercial awnings
President: R Allen Gray
Number Employees: 20

31233 Williamsburg Metal Spinning
263 Kent Ave
Brooklyn, NY 11249-4189

718-782-7040
Fax: 718-384-7424 888-535-5402
williamsburgmetal@hotmail.com
www.williamsburgmetal.com
Round baking pans, heat lamp reflectors and alumi-
num cooking items
President: Thomas Desanti
Estimated Sales: $1-2.5 Million
Number Employees: 10-19
Square Footage: 20000

31234 Williamsburg Millwork
29155 Richmond Tpke
Ruther Glen, VA 22546

804-994-2151
Fax: 804-994-5371
Wooden pallets
President: M R Piland Iii
VP: M Piland

Estimated Sales: $20-50 Million
Number Employees: 20-49
Square Footage: 40000

31235 Williamson & Co
9 Shelter Dr
Greer, SC 29650-4818

864-848-1011
Fax: 864-848-4310 800-849-3263
www.williamsonandcompany.com
Manufacturer and exporter of automated packaging,
data collection and material handling systems, trans-
port trucks and jacks.
President: Dan Williamson
dwilliamson@williamsonandcompany.com
Chief Financial Officer: Larry Williamson
VP: Lester Collins
Operations: Gene Settles
Estimated Sales: $5-10 Million
Number Employees: 50-99

31236 Willow Specialties
34 Clinton St
Batavia, NY 14020-2899

585-344-2900
Fax: 585-344-0044 800-724-7300
info@willowspecialties.com
www.willowgroupltd.com
Baskets and packaging supplies
Owner: Bernie Skalny
bskalny@willowgroupltd.com
Number Employees: 50-99

31237 Willson Industries
1003 Tuckahoe Road
P.O.Box 8
Marmora, NJ 08223

609-390-0756
Fax: 609-390-0757 800-894-4169
Point-of-purchase displays and custom advertising
specialties
President: Edward Willson
Estimated Sales: $1-2.5 Million
Number Employees: 4
Square Footage: 16000

31238 (HQ)Wilson AL Chemical Co
1050 Harrison Ave
Kearny, NJ 07032-5941

201-997-3300
Fax: 201-997-5122 800-526-1188
help@alwilson.com www.alwilson.com
Manufacturer and exporter of laundry and dry clean-
ing stain removers
President: Bob Edwards
bob@alwilson.com
Estimated Sales: $10-20 Million
Number Employees: 10-19

31239 Wilson Steel Products Company
PO Box 70214
Memphis, TN 38107

901-527-8742
Fax: 901-527-8779
Structural steel bins, chutes, hoppers and bucket ele-
vators
President: Robert Wilson
Estimated Sales: $2.5-5 Million
Number Employees: 10-19

31240 Wiltec
P.O.Box 367
Leominster, MA 01453-0367

978-537-1497
Fax: 978-537-7806
Plastic tabletop, partyware and food service products
including cafeteria bowls, ladles, trays, cups, tum-
blers, utensils, tongs, plates, etc
President: Amy Ullman
Sales/Marketing: Diane Holloway
Estimated Sales: $3-5 Million
Number Employees: 10-19
Number of Brands: 2
Number of Products: 100
Type of Packaging: Consumer, Food Service, Pri-
vate Label, Bulk
Brands:
   Galaware
   Wiltec

31241 Wilton Armetale
903 Square St
Mt Joy, PA 17552-1911
717-653-4444
Fax: 717-653-6573   800-779-4586
kadams@armetale.com www.armetale.com
Manufacturer and exporter of metal tabletop ware
and salad bar accessories
President: Ed Leibensperger
eleibensperger@armetale.com
Estimated Sales: $1-5 Million
Number Employees: 50-99
Brands:
  Armetale

31242 (HQ)Wilton Brands LLC
2240 75th St
Woodridge, IL 60517-2333
630-963-7100
Fax: 630-810-2712 info@wilton.com
www.wilton.com
Manufacturer and exporter of kitchenware including
bakeware, cake decorating supplies, tools and gad-
gets; also, picture frames
President: Danielle Detten
CEO: Sue Buchta
sbuchta@wilton.com
Chief Financial Officer: Tom Kasvin
Chief Operating Officer: Mary Merfeld
Estimated Sales: $50 Million
Number Employees: 500-999
Square Footage: 1000000
Brands:
  Copco
  Rowoco
  Weston Gallery
  Wilton

31243 Wilton Industries CanadaLtd.
98 Carrier Drive
Etobicoke, ON M9W 5R1
Canada
416-679-0790
Fax: 416-679-0798 800-387-3300
canadasales@wilton.ca www.wilton.com
Cake, candy and cookie decorating and making sup-
plies
President: Jeff McLaughlin
General Manager: Steve Curtis
Number Employees: 45
Square Footage: 90000
Parent Co: Towerbrook Capital Partners

31244 Win-Holt Equipment Group
141 Eileen Way
Syosset, NY 11791
516-222-0335
Fax: 516-921-0538 800-444-3595
sales@winholt.com www.winholt.com
Material and food handling equipment, food service
equipment and heating, holding and transporting
equipment
President/ COO: Dominic Scarfogliero
Chairman, Chief Executive Officer: Jonathan J
Holtz
R&D: Nancy Korista
Marketing Director: Bruce Schwartz
Sales Director: Jeff Herbert
Sales: Tim Sullivan
President, Chief Operating Officer: Dominick
Scarfogliero
VP Operations: John Jameson
Purchasing Manager: Glen Stein
Estimated Sales: $10-20 Million
Number Employees: 300-500
Number of Brands: 4
Number of Products: 200

31245 Winchester Carton
P.O.Box 597
Eutaw, AL 35462-0597
205-372-3337
Fax: 205-372-9226 www.rocktenn.com
Boxes including recycled paper
President: Ben Williams
Plant Manager: Willie Carpenter
Estimated Sales: $20-50 Million
Number Employees: 100-249
Parent Co: Rock Tenn Company

31246 Wincup Holdings
4640 Lewis Rd
Stone Mountain, GA 30083
770-771-5861
www.wincup.com
Styrofoam bowls, cups and food containers; also,
custom design and printing available.
Chief Executive Officer: Pat Aubry
President, Foodservices: Michael Winters
Executive VP & Chief Financial Officer: Mike Scott
Senior Vice President, Manufacturing: Brad Laporte
Chief Information Officer: Matthew Marrazza
Vice President & Treasurer: Steve Adams
Year Founded: 1962
Estimated Sales: $101.8 Million
Number Employees: 1,000+
Brands:
  Compac
  Profit Pals
  Simplicity
  Styrocups

31247 (HQ)Wind River Environmental
163 Western Ave
Gloucester, MA 01930-4042
978-281-4443
Fax: 978-281-6321 800-332-6025
custsvc@strong-holster.com
www.wrenvironmental.com
Custom made leather menu covers, wine lists, check
presenters and ID badges
Owner: Don Strong
CEO: Rich Cutter
Marketing Director: Larry Angello
Operations Manager: Steve Kaity
Purchasing Manager: Brian Cutter
Estimated Sales: $5 Million
Number Employees: 1-4
Number of Products: 250
Square Footage: 232000
Type of Packaging: Bulk

31248 Windhorst Blowmold
P.O.Box 696
Euless, TX 76039-0696
817-540-6639
Fax: 817-540-0271
Retrofitter and installer of electrical and mechanical
components for the blowmolding industry
Owner: Michael Windhorst
Vice President: Gerry Trainque
Estimated Sales: $500,000-$1 Million
Number Employees: 20-49

31249 Windmill Electrastatic Sprayers
PO Box 220
Hughson, CA 95326-1490
209-883-4405
Fax: 209-883-9565 800-426-5615
www.vrisimo.com
Wine industry sprayers
President and Owner: Fred Brenda
Estimated Sales: $1-3 Million
Number Employees: 5-9

31250 Windmoeller & HoelscherCorporation
23 New England Way
Lincoln, RI 02865
401-334-0965
Fax: 401-333-6491 800-854-8702
info@whcorp.com www.whcorp.com
A supplier of flexographic and gravure printing
press, blown and cast film extrusion systems,
multiwall equipment, plastic sack and bag making
machines, as well as form-fill-seal machinery for the
converting and packaging industry.
President: Hans Deamer
Corporate Controller: Walter Kaehler
Vice President: Andrew Wheeler
Contact: Tom Apple
t.apple@whcorp.com
Estimated Sales: $50-75 Million
Number Employees: 20-49

31251 Windsor Industries Inc
1351 W Stanford Ave
Englewood, CO 80110-5545
303-781-4833
Fax: 866-271-0520 800-444-7654
Manufacturer and exporter of carpet and floor maintenance equipment including wet/dry vacuums, automatic scrubbers, carpet extractors, pressure washers
and polishers

CEO: Elliot Younessian
elliot.younessian@windsorind.com
Financial Services Manager: Pete Dewlaney
Technical Support Manager: Joel Yourzek
Distribution Manager: Mary Millibrandt
Estimated Sales: $75-100 Million
Number Employees: 250-499
Parent Co: Alfred Karcher GmbH & Co. KG
Type of Packaging: Food Service
Brands:
  Fastraction
  Lightening Polishers
  Mr. Steam
  Powertrec Scrubbers
  Versamatic

31252 (HQ)Windsor Wax Co Inc
510 Carolina Back Rd
Charlestown, RI 02813-3809
401-364-5941
Fax: 401-364-3729 800-243-8929
Manufacturer and exporter of floor care products in-
cluding wax polymer finishes, cleaning compounds,
carpet cleaner and concrete coatings; importer of
natural wax and paraffin
Office Manager: M Wojcik
CEO: D Kahn
CEO: David Kahn
Number Employees: 1-4
Brands:
  Konkrete
  Wincoat
  Windsor
  Woodee

31253 Wine Analyst
23230 Ravensbury Avenue
Los Altos Hills, CA 94024-6429
650-949-5929
Fax: 650-941-1892
Wine industry analyst software
President: Ray Smith
Number Employees: 10

31254 Wine Appreciation Guild
360 Swift Ave # 34
S San Francisco, CA 94080-6220
650-866-3020
Fax: 650-866-3029 info@wineappreciation.com
Wine industry tasting room supplies
Manager: James Mackey
Vice President: Elliott Mackey
info@wineappreciation.com
Estimated Sales: $10 Million
Number Employees: 20-49

31255 Wine Cap Company
PO Box 1784
Santa Rosa, CA 95402-1784
707-535-1950
Fax: 707-939-3934 pstaehle@winecap.com
Wax Cap and B-Cap bottle closure systems
CEO: Dwight Pate
Estimated Sales: $500,000-$1 Million
Number Employees: 4

31256 Wine Chillers of California
1104 E 17th St Ste F
Santa Ana, CA 92701
714-541-5795
Fax: 714-541-3139 800-331-4274
Custom builder and provider of wine chilling equip-
ment.
President: Robert Sizemore
CEO: D Sizemore
Estimated Sales: $.5-1,000,000
Number Employees: 1-4
Square Footage: 4000000
Brands:
  Cruvinet
  Vimo Cave
  Vino Temp
  Vinotheque
  Wine Well
  Winekeeper

31257 Wine Concepts
135 Mason Ci
Suite K
Concord, CA 94520
925-521-9001
Fax: 925-521-9006 800-560-0105
Wine industry tasting room supplies
Owner: Gerry Dodd

1047

Estimated Sales: $1-2.5 Million
Number Employees: 10-19

31258 Wine Country Cases
995 Vintage Ave # 100
St Helena, CA 94574-1409

707-967-4805
Fax: 707-967-4807 info@winecountrycases.com
www.winecountrycases.com
Wine industry wooden wine boxes
President: Dan Pina
dan@winecountrycases.com
Owner: Ignacio Delgadillo
Estimated Sales: $2 Million
Number Employees: 50-99

31259 Wine Things Unlimited
PO Box 1349
Sonoma, CA 95476

707-935-1277
Fax: 707-935-3403 800-447-3983
sales@winethings.com www.winethings.com
Wine industry tasting room supplies
President: David Liberstein
Estimated Sales: $1-5 Million
Number Employees: 5-9

31260 Wine Things
1006 S. Milpitas Blvd.
Milpitas, CA 95035

408-262-1898
Fax: 408-262-1890 800-796-7797
service@winethings.com www.winethings.com
Wine racks
President: David Lieberstein
Estimated Sales: $1-5 Million
Number Employees: 5-9

31261 Wine Well Chiller Co
301 Brewster Rd # 3c
Milford, CT 06460-3700

203-878-2465
Fax: 203-878-2466 winewellchiller@aol.com
www.epichead.com
Manufacturer and exporter of high-speed beverage
chillers including wine
Owner: Tyrone Petr
CEO/President: Anabel Fisher
Sales: Melissa Lawless
winewellchiller@aol.com
Production: Tyrone P
Estimated Sales: $1-3 Million
Number Employees: 5-9
Square Footage: 4000
Brands:
   Microchiller
   Wine Well

31262 WineAndHospitalityJobs.com
640 Michael Drive
Sonoma, CA 95476

707-933-0687
Online job board for the wine and hospitality industry.

31263 Winekeeper
625 E Haley St
Santa Barbara, CA 93103

805-963-3451
Fax: 805-965-5393 www.winekeeper.com
Wome dispensing and wine cellaring equipment
President: Norman Grant
Contact: Connie Grant
connie@winaire.com
Number Employees: 5-9
Parent Co: Winekeeper
Brands:
   Cruvinet
   Winekeeper

31264 Wineracks by Marcus
PO Box 2713
Costa Mesa, CA 92628-2713

714-546-4922
Fax: 714-549-8238
Wineracks By Marcus; a strong, accessible,
space-efficient aluminum racks with a sharp, clean
look for restaurants, serious collectors and retail.
Manufactured to order, custom sizes and layout
drawings available
President: Steve Marcus
Estimated Sales: $300,000-500,000
Number Employees: 1-4

31265 Winkler USA LLC
88 S State St
Hackensack, NJ 07601-3920

201-488-9291
Fax: 201-525-0771 info@winklerusa.com
www.winklerusa.com
Sales Director: Cindy Chananie
Contact: Mattia Fiorilli
mfiorilli@winklerusa.com
Number Employees: 100-249

31266 Winmark Stamp & Sign
2284 S West Temple
Salt Lake City, UT 84115-2659

801-486-2011
Fax: 801-467-6265 800-438-0480
sales@winmarkinc.com www.winmarkinc.com
Signage, badges, name plates, notary seals, marking
devices and rubber stamps including pre-inked and
self-inking
Owner: Traci Szwedko
traci@winmarkinc.com
CFO: Traci Szwedko
Estimated Sales: Less Than $500,000
Number Employees: 5-9
Square Footage: 16000

31267 Winn-Sol Products
PO Box 978
Oshkosh, WI 54903-0978

920-231-2031
Lime, rust, scale and milkstone solvents and remov-
ers used in dishwashers
President: James Driessen Sr
Secretary: Jenece Driessen
VP: Connie Hart
Estimated Sales: $300,000-500,000
Number Employees: 1-4
Brands:
   Dairi-Sol
   Industri-Sol
   Lime-Elim

31268 Winnebago Sign Company
PO Box 662
Fond Du Lac, WI 54936-0662

920-922-5930
Fax: 920-922-5930
Luminous tube and plastic signs; also, servicing of
signs available
Owner: Donald E Gross
Sign Installer: Bob Samp
Office Manager: Laura Leichtfuss
Estimated Sales: Less than $500,000
Number Employees: 1-4
Parent Co: Barber Graphix

31269 Winpak Lane Inc
998 S Sierra Way
San Bernardino, CA 92408-2122

909-885-0715
Fax: 909-381-1934 800-804-4224
info@wli.winpak.com www.winpak.com
Manufatures vertical-form-fill-seal packaging for
flexible pouches and cups through innovative machine building and design. Our expertise in liuid filling (ranges 1.5m-19ml and hot-fill capabilities up to
90 degrees excelsiors)mbinedwith a commitment to
never compromise on quality makes Winpak equipment one of the standards in the industry
President: David Stacey
david.stacey@winpak.com
Marketing/Sales: John Schcfer
Estimated Sales: $10-20 Million
Number Employees: 100-249
Parent Co: Wipak Group

31270 Winpak Portion Packaging
998 South Sierra Way
San Bernardino, CA 92408

909-885-0715
Fax: 909-381-1934 800-804-4224
www.winpak.com
Manufacturer and exporter of pre-formed portion
controlled plastic packaging. Diecut for lidding and
filling equipment
President: Thomas Herlihy
Vice President: Jim McMacken
Marketing Director: Debbie Calvarese
Contact: Kathy Boynton
kathy.boynton@winpak.com
Number Employees: 225
Parent Co: Winpak

Type of Packaging: Consumer, Food Service, Private Label

31271 Winpak Technologies
85 Laird Drive
Toronto, ON M4G 3T8
Canada

416-421-1700
Fax: 416-421-7957
Packaging
Director Sales & Marketing: L de Bellefeuille
Manufacturing: J Millwrad
Estimated Sales: $1-5 Million
Number Employees: 250
Square Footage: 600000
Parent Co: Winpak

31272 Wins Paper Products
321 Murray Road
Springtown, TX 76082-6520

817-281-6550
Fax: 817-281-0560 800-733-2420
Manufacturer and wholesaler/distributor of paper
bags; serving the food service market
President: Douglas Wiley
Chairman: Gordon Wiley
Estimated Sales: Below $5 Million
Number Employees: 10
Square Footage: 156000

31273 Winston Industries
2345 Carton Dr
Louisville, KY 40299-2513

502-495-5500
Fax: 502-495-5458 800-234-5286
information@winstonind.com
www.winstonind.com
Manufacturer and exporter of stainless steel ovens,
pressure cookers and holding cabinets
President/ CEO: Valerie Shelton
vshelton@winstonind.com
Quality Control: Tina Thompson
CFO: Bob Leavitt
VP Global Sales: Shaun Tanner
COO: Paul Haviland
VP Manufacturing: Leo Gutgsell
Estimated Sales: $10-20 Million
Number Employees: 100-249
Type of Packaging: Food Service
Brands:
   C-Vap
   C-Vat
   Collettramatic

31274 Winston Laboratories Inc
100 N Fairway Dr # 134
Suite 134
Vernon Hills, IL 60061-1859

847-362-8200
Fax: 847-362-8394 800-946-5229
info@winstonlabs.com
Consultant specializing in nutritional and laboratory
testing for food additives, pesticide residues, MSG,
sulfites, etc.; also, FDA liaison service, HACCP
plans, food plant inspections and certification of
acidified foods and thermalprocesses available
President: Marvin Winston
CEO: Joel E Bernstein
CFO: Barry Hollingsworth
Senior Scientist: Porus Aria PhD
Contact: Ronald Abrahams
ron@winstonlabs.com
Vice President, Operations: David A Henninger
Estimated Sales: $500,000-$1 Million
Number Employees: 10-19
Square Footage: 19500

31275 Winzen Film
P.O.Box 677
407 West 2nd Street
Taylor, TX 76574

903-885-7595
Fax: 903-885-4702 800-779-7595
www.winzen.com
Manufacturer and exporter of plastic container mate-
rials
Manager: Frank Neidhart
CEO: Robert Williamson
Estimated Sales: $10-20 Million
Number Employees: 20-49
Parent Co: BAG Corporation

31276 Wipe-Tex International Corp
110 E 153rd St # 2
Bronx, NY 10451-5230
718-665-0013
Fax: 718-665-0787 800-643-9607
Washed and sterilized cloths including wiping rags, cotton cleaning remnants, kitchen and new hemmed towels; also, cheesecloth
Owner: Alex Fudder
wiperrags@msn.com
VP Sales Marketing: Richard Chesney
Number Employees: 20-49
Square Footage: 200000

31277 (HQ)Wipeco Inc
250 N Mannheim Rd
Hillside, IL 60162-1835
708-544-7247
Fax: 708-544-7248 info@wipeco.com
www.wipeco.com
Wiping rags and nonwoven wipers
President: Jeff Shanken
Chief Executive Officer: Sandy Woycke
Manager: Justin Woycke
jwoycke@wipeco.com
Estimated Sales: $370,000
Number Employees: 5-9

31278 Wire Belt Co Of America
154 Harvey Rd
Londonderry, NH 03053-7473
603-644-2500
Fax: 603-644-3600 sales@wirebelt.com
Stainless steel open-mesh conveyor belting
President: David Greer
dgreer@wirebelt.com
Marketing Director: Richard Spiak
Sales: Richard Spiak
Operations: Scott Monk
Estimated Sales: $20-50 Million
Number Employees: 100-249
Brands:
  Eye-Flex
  Flat-Flex El
  Flat-Flex
  Flat-Flex Xt
  Flex-Turn

31279 Wire Products Mfg
1000 Mathews St
Merrill, WI 54452-2837
715-536-7884
Fax: 715-536-1476
Manufacturer and exporter of wire racks including display and fryer
President: Roger C Dupke
Manager: Jim Dupke
Estimated Sales: $20-50 Million
Number Employees: 20-49
Type of Packaging: Consumer, Food Service, Bulk

31280 Wirefab Inc
75 Blackstone River Rd
Worcester, MA 01607-1493
508-754-5359
Fax: 508-797-3620 877-877-4445
info@wirefab.com www.wirefab.com
Manufacturer and exporter of wire baskets, shelving and racks including doughnut and bagel baskets and deep-fry crumb screens
Owner: A B Zakarian
wirefab@gis.net
CEO: A Zakarian
VP: M M Zakarian
R & D: Larry Clough
Sales: William Binson
wirefab@gis.net
Public Relations: Michael Murdock
Operations: John Michaels
Production: Christopher Bousbouras
Plant Manager: James Hall
Purchasing: Barbara Vasdagalis
Estimated Sales: $5-10 Million
Number Employees: 50-99
Square Footage: 160000
Type of Packaging: Bulk

31281 Wiremaid Products Div
11711 W Sample Rd
Coral Springs, FL 33065-3155
954-545-9000
Fax: 954-545-9011 800-770-4700
info@vutec.com www.vutec.com

Manufacturer and exporter of wire and metal products including displays, racks, shelves, etc
Manager: Bryan Sciullo
CEO: Howard L Sinkoff
howardsinkoff@vutec.com
CFO: Jeff Chanoff
VP: Allen Axman
R&D: Hai Nguyen
Marketing: John Cavanaugh
Sales: Allen Axman
Production: Raul Passalaqua
Plant Manager: Raul Passalaqua
Purchasing: Robert Ciarletto
Estimated Sales: $20-50 Million
Number Employees: 1-4
Square Footage: 100000
Parent Co: Vutec Corporation
Brands:
  Vutec Usa
  Wiremaid Usa

31282 Wireway Husky Corp
6146 Denver Industrial Park Rd
Denver, NC 28037-7805
704-483-1900
Fax: 704-483-1911 800-438-5629
productinfo@wirewayhusky.com
www.wirewayhusky.com
Material handling equipment including pallet racks and cable reel racks
President: Ron Young
ryoung@wirewayhusky.com
VP: Gregory Young
Estimated Sales: $10-20 Million
Number Employees: 100-249
Parent Co: Husky Systems

31283 Wisco Industries Assembly
955 Market St
Oregon, WI 53575-1009
608-835-3300
Fax: 608-835-7399 800-999-4726
info@wiscoind.com
Counter top ovens and warmers for pizza, pretzels and cookies; exporter of pizza ovens, food warmers, toasters and sandwich grills
CEO: Elving Kjellstrom
Marketing Director: Donald Porkner
Sales Director: Randy Kjellstrom
Estimated Sales: $20-30 Million
Number Employees: 5-9
Square Footage: 200000

31284 Wisconsin Aluminum Foundry Co
838 S 16th St
Manitowoc, WI 54220-5004
920-682-8286
Fax: 920-682-7285 inquiries@wafco.com
www.wafco.com
Manufacturer and exporter of griddles,grills, can sealers, sterilizers, pressure cookers, cookware, etc... importer of cookware.
President: Jim Hatt
jhatt@wafco.com
CEO: Philip Jacobs
Quality Control: Don Noworatsky
Estimated Sales: $5-10 Million
Number Employees: 250-499
Number of Brands: 1
Type of Packaging: Consumer
Brands:
  Chef's Design
  Chef-Way

31285 Wisconsin Bakers Assn Inc
2514 S 102nd St # 100
Milwaukee, WI 53227-2154
414-258-5552
Fax: 414-258-5582 www.wibakers.com
Serves as the catalyst for bringing bakers together through special events such as workshops, conferences, conventions, and member events.
Executive Director: David Schmidt
dave@wibakers.com
Number Employees: 1-4

31286 Wisconsin Bench Mfg
507 E Grant St
Thorp, WI 54771-9662
715-669-5360
Fax: 715-669-5929 800-242-2303
www.wibenchmfg.com
Bench tops

General Manager: Steve Burgess
steve@wibench.com
CEO: Phillip Jeska
Estimated Sales: $5-10 Million
Number Employees: 100-249
Square Footage: 70000

31287 Wisconsin Box Co
929 Townline Rd
PO Box 718
Wausau, WI 54403-6681
715-842-2248
Fax: 715-842-2240 www.wisconsinbox.com
Manufacturer and exporter of wooden shipping containers and crates
Owner: Jeff Davis
CFO: Michael Shipway
Vice President of Sales: Gene Davis
jdavis@wisconsinbox.com
Customer Service: Jim Geise
Plant Manager: Bob Schultz
Plant Manager: Charley Ewell
Estimated Sales: $5-10 Million
Number Employees: 20-49
Type of Packaging: Bulk

31288 Wisconsin Box Co
929 Townline Rd
PO Box 718
Wausau, WI 54403-6681
715-842-2248
Fax: 715-842-2240 800-876-6658
garyl@tcrllc.com www.wisconsinbox.com
Manufacturer and exporter of wirebound and collapsible pallet boxes and crates
Owner: Jeff Davis
jdavis@wisconsinbox.com
CEO: Gary LeMaster
Sales Manager: Dennis Maxson
jdavis@wisconsinbox.com
Controller / Human Resources: Michael Shipway
Estimated Sales: $10-20 Million
Number Employees: 20-49
Square Footage: 150000

31289 Wisconsin Converting Inc
1689 Morrow St
Green Bay, WI 54302-2605
920-437-6400
Fax: 920-436-4964 800-544-1935
sc@wisconsinconverting.com
www.wisconsinconverting.com
Mailers and bags including paper, lined, candy and nut bags and self opening food sacks
President: John Brogan
jbrogan@wisconsinconverting.com
CEO: Charles Johns
Marketing Director: Jill Walschinski
VP Operations: Bob McGee
Estimated Sales: $10-20,000,000
Number Employees: 20-49

31290 Wisconsin Film & Bag Inc
3100 E Richmond St
Shawano, WI 54166-3845
715-524-2565
Fax: 715-524-3527 800-765-9224
greggreene@wifb.com www.wifb.com
Polyethylene sheeting and bundling films and bags
Vice President: Mohammad Bashir
bashir.mohammad@wolterskluwer.com
Director of Sales Operations: Leann Gueths
CFO: Al Johnson
V.P. of Major Accounts: Greg Greene
VP: Ian Anderson
Inside Sales Representative: Kristin Gehm
Regional Sales Manager: Tony Hindley
Estimated Sales: Below $5 Million
Number Employees: 100-249
Square Footage: 118000
Brands:
  Atlas
  Inflation Fighter

31291 Wisconsin Precision Casting
W405 County Road L
East Troy, WI 53120-2406
262-642-7307
Fax: 262-642-4115 866-642-7307
cliff@wisconsinprecision.com
www.wisconsinprecision.com

Owner: Clyde Klemowits
cpk@wisconsinprecision.com
VP-Manufacturing: Cliff Fischer
VP-Engineering: Claude Klemowits
Sales and Marketing Manager: Dean Kirschner
Estimated Sales: $10-20 Million
Number Employees: 50-99
Square Footage: 40

31292 Wisdom Adhesives Worldwide
1575 Executive Drive
Elgin, IL 60123
847-841-7002
Fax: 847-841-7009 info@wisdomadhesives.com
www.wisdomadhesives.com
Water-based adhesives, animal glue, hot melts and
custom adhesives
Chief Executive Officer: Jeff Wisdom
Vice President of Technologies: Tom Rolando
Vice President of Sales: Paul Preston
Contact: Ed Marzano
edmarzano@wisdomadhesives.com
Vice President of Operations: Linda Wisdom
Estimated Sales: $1-5 Million
Number Employees: 12

31293 Wishbone Utensil Tableware Line
15 Paramount Pkwy
Wheat Ridge, CO 80215-6615
303-238-8088
Fax: 253-595-7673 866-266-5928
Forever replaces chopsticks. One piece tong, skewer
& ergonomic utensil. Child safe. Dishwasher
friendly. Assisted living compatible. Solution for the
chopstick challenged. Popular among hotel/resorts,
restaurateur and occupationalhealth. Ten mo-
tif-friendly colors. FDA approved. Stylish, durable,
reusable, fun. Sanitized and individually wrapped.
Gourmet quality Feng Shui tableware
CEO: R Farlan Krieger Sr
Estimated Sales: Under $300,000
Number Employees: 9
Number of Brands: 4
Number of Products: 8
Square Footage: 50000
Parent Co: RF Krieger, LLC
Type of Packaging: Consumer, Food Service, Pri-
vate Label, Bulk
Brands:
  Wishbone Utensil Tableware Line

31294 Witt Plastics
P.O.Box 808
Greenville, OH 45331-0808
937-548-7272
Fax: 937-547-6046 800-227-9181
www.wittplastics.com
Roll and sheet high impact polystyrene and poly-
propylene for container and lid stock thermoforming
President: Bob Kramer
Owner/CEO: John Witt
Purchasing Manager: Bill Simmons
Estimated Sales: $10-20 Million
Number Employees: 50-99
Square Footage: 100000

31295 Wittco Foodservice Equipment
7737 N 81st St
Milwaukee, WI 53223-3839
414-365-4400
Fax: 414-354-2821 800-821-3912
www.wittco.com
Manufacturer and exporter of carts including
hot/cold food delivery and insulated tray; also,
cook/chill equipment
Cmo: Jim Sherman
jsherman@wittco.com
Estimated Sales: $5 Million
Number Employees: 20-49
Square Footage: 180000
Parent Co: Nichols Industries
Type of Packaging: Food Service
Brands:
  Meals-On-Wheels

31296 Wittco Foodservice Equipment
7737 N 81st St
Milwaukee, WI 53223-3839
414-365-4400
Fax: 414-354-2821 800-367-8413
www.wittco.com
Manufacturer and exporter of heated food holding
equipment and cook/hold ovens

General Manager: Steve Jensen
CEO: Tim Murray
VP: Jeff Smith
Marketing: Joe Burns
Operations Manager: Dave Braun
Estimated Sales: $5-10 Million
Number Employees: 20-49

31297 Witte Brothers ExchangeInc
575 Witte Industrial
Troy, MO 63379-3964
636-462-8402
Fax: 636-528-6139 800-325-8151
info@wittebros.com www.wittebros.com
Warehousing, transportation and distribution for refrigerated and frozen products including LTL, TL
(also dry), consolidation, freight pooling, rail service, and full freight management capabilities. Full
inventory management. Temprange to -15ºF
2,000,000 cubic feet warehouse with 34 doors and
20,000 square feet refrigerated cross dock.
President: Brent Witte
Sr. Director of Business Development: Laura Wort
Director Of Operations: Shane Carter
Number Employees: 100-249

31298 Witte Co Inc
507 Route 31 S
Washington, NJ 7882
908-689-6500
Fax: 908-537-6806 info@witte.com
www.witte.com
Manufacturer and exporter of vibrating screens, con-
veyors, fluid bed dryers and coolers
President: Tyson Witte
Sales/Marketing: Jim Schak
Engineering Manager: Larry Stoma
Purchasing Manager: Marilyn March
Estimated Sales: $10-20,000,000
Number Employees: 1-4
Square Footage: 60000
Type of Packaging: Private Label
Brands:
  Witte

31299 Wittemann Company
1 Industry Dr
Palm Coast, FL 32137
386-445-4200
Fax: 386-445-7042 us@union.dk
www.wittemann.com
Manufacturer and exporter of carbon dioxide gener-
ation and recovery systems; also, dryers, cylinder
filling units and dry ice systems
President: William Geiger
General Manager: Bill Gieyer
CFO: Cara Brammer
Sales Manager: Gabreil Dominguez
Regional Sales Manager: Daniel Gruber
Contact: Donna Grabowski
donnag@wittemann.com
Product Manager: Jay Soto
Estimated Sales: $3-5 Million
Number Employees: 10-19
Square Footage: 120000

31300 (HQ)Wittern Group
8040 University Blvd
Clive, IA 50325-1171
515-274-3641
Fax: 515-271-8530 855-712-8729
contact@vending.com www.witternfin.com
Manufacturer and exporter of vending machines for
snacks, canned and hot beverages, refrigerated and
frozen foods, desserts, etc
Chairman of the Board: Francis Wittern
President/CEO/Secretary/Treasurer: John Bruntz
jbruntz@wittern.com
Chief Financial Officer: Craig Mile
Vice President, Data Processing: Dave Twedale
Chief Marketing Officer: Mike McGillis
Vice President, Sales: Mike Frye
Purchasing Manager: Ron Harter
Estimated Sales: $9 Million
Number Employees: 250-499
Square Footage: 420000
Parent Co: 8040 Holdings, Inc.
Brands:
  Servomatic

31301 Wna Comet West Inc
1135 Samuelson St
City Of Industry, CA 91748-1222
626-913-4022
Fax: 626-913-1776 800-225-0939
www.olympuspartners.com
Disposable plastic dinnerware including cutlery,
tumblers, plates, bowls, etc
manager: Kurt Rogstad
Executive VP: R Greer
Sales Manager: Michael Sharpe
Manager: Curt Heverly
curt@wna-inc.com
Estimated Sales: $20-50 Million
Number Employees: 250-499
Square Footage: 200000
Parent Co: WNA-Waddington North America

31302 Wnc Pallet & Forest Pdts Co
1414 Smoky Park Hwy
Candler, NC 28715-8237
828-667-5426
Fax: 828-665-4759
Wooden and recycled pallets, skids and boxes; also,
pallet recycling
President: Tom Orr
torr@wncpallet.com
VP: T Orr
Sales: Cyndi Commozi
Manager: Brent Orr
Estimated Sales: $10-20 Million
Number Employees: 100-249

31303 Woerner Wire Works
3008 Evans St
PO Box 11449
Omaha, NE 68111-3272
402-451-5414
Fax: 402-451-5415
Established in 1892. Structural Steel Manufacturer,
ornamental metal work, wholesale wire, fabricated
wire, manufacturers, metal fabricator
President: Daniel Scanlan
dan@woernerwire.com
VP: Sandor Horvath
Project Manager: Rick Weitkemper
Vice President: Daniel J Scanlan
dan@woernerwire.com
Estimated Sales: Below $5 Million
Number Employees: 10-19
Square Footage: 40000

31304 Wohl Associates Inc
50 Floyds Run
Bohemia, NY 11716-2154
631-244-7979
Fax: 631-244-6987 info@wohlassociates.com
www.wohlassociates.com
Dealer of used and rebuilt scrubbers, blanchers,
steamers, labelers, and other food processing equipment
Owner: Andrew Wohl
info@wohlassociates.com
Estimated Sales: $5-10 Million
Number Employees: 10-19

31305 Wohl Associates Inc
50 Floyds Run
Bohemia, NY 11716-2154
631-244-7979
Fax: 631-244-6987 info@wohlassociates.com
www.wohlassociates.com
Buyer and seller of surplus equipment including
blanchers, dicers, mixers, dryers and coolers
Owner: Andrew Wohl
info@wohlassociates.com
CFO: Anndy Wohl
Estimated Sales: $5-10 Million
Number Employees: 10-19

31306 Wohlt Cheese Corp
1005 Orville Dr
P.O. Box 203
New London, WI 54961-9398
920-982-9000
Fax: 920-982-6288
Manufacturer of processed cheeses (including
American cheese, cheese food, cheese spread and
other cheese products); available in loaves and
blocks, flavoured varities, custom blends and vari-
ous melts. Offer shredding and dicingservices.
President: Marilyn Taylor
Quality Manager: Frederick Ladenburger
Production Manager: Mark Gelhausen

Estimated Sales: $19.6 Million
Number Employees: 50-99
Square Footage: 20000
Type of Packaging: Consumer, Food Service, Private Label, Bulk

31307 Wolens Company
PO Box 560964
Dallas, TX 75356-0964

214-634-0800
Fax: 214-634-0880

Manufacturer and exporter of plastic letters and signs
President: Steve Schwartz
Estimated Sales: $1-2.5 Million
Number Employees: 1-4

31308 Wolf Company
3101 S 2nd St
Louisville, KY 40208-1446

800-814-2028
www.wolfequipment.com

Manufacturer and exporter of commercial gas broilers, fryers, griddles, ranges and ovens; also, household ranges and slide-ins.
Chairman & CEO, ITW: E. Scott Santi
Estimated Sales: $100-500 Million
Parent Co: ITW Food Equipment

31309 Wolf Packaging Machines
9310 SW 100th Avenue Road
Miami, FL 33176-1724

305-274-3641
Fax: 305-274-3685

Packaging machines, such as vertical f/f/s machines
Estimated Sales: $1-5 Million

31310 Wolf Works
167 Vard Loomis Court
Arroyo Grande, CA 93420-2919

805-489-2920
Fax: 805-239-1787   800-549-3806
wolfworkswood@hotmail.com

Wine industry wine gift boxes/crates/tasting room items
President: Mark Wolf
Co-Owner: Christina Wolf
Estimated Sales: less than $500,000
Number Employees: 2
Square Footage: 1200

31311 Wolfkiny
PO Box 30970
Columbus, OH 43230-0970

614-863-3144
Fax: 614-863-3296   800-292-3144

Analyzing fat testing, continuous sausage processing systems, emulsifiers, accessories, grinders, massagers and tumblers, pickle injectors, belt and screw conveyors, handling systems for ground meats, dry sausages, hams, pizzatoppings, patties and poultry
Estimated Sales: $5-10 Million
Number Employees: 50-99

31312 Womack International Inc
451 Azuar Ave
Vallejo, CA 94592-1148

707-647-2370
Fax: 707-562-1010   www.womack.com

Manufacturer and exporter of food processing filters including multiple plate, vertical stack and pressure
President: Thomas H. Womack
CEO: Michael Oakes
oakes@womack.com
VP Engineer: Michael Oakes
VP Sales: Stanley Jennings
Estimated Sales: $3-5 Million
Number Employees: 20-49
Square Footage: 100000
Brands:
 Filter-Max
 Micron One

31313 Wonderware Corp
26561 Rancho Pkwy S
Lake Forest, CA 92630-8301

949-727-3200
Fax: 949-727-3270   press@wonderware.com
www.wonderware.com

Industrial automation software, enterprise asset management and maintenance software and enterprise resource planning (ERP) software

President: Sudipta Bhattacharya
Branch Manager: Roy Slavin
Contact: Deon Aardt
deon.aardt@wonderware.com
Estimated Sales: $43.4 Million
Number Employees: 500-999

31314 Wood & Laminates
102 Route 46 E
Lodi, NJ 7644

973-773-7475
Fax: 973-773-8344   gabriels@wlbars.com
www.wlbars.com

Custom-made bars
Owner: Gabriel Salacar
Estimated Sales: $2.5-5 Million
Number Employees: 10-19

31315 Wood Goods Industries
407 S Duncan St
Luck, WI 54853-9082

715-472-2226
Fax: 715-472-8708   info@woodgoods.com
www.woodgoods.com

Table tops and bases for the contract, hospitality and institutional trades
President: Brad Johnson
brad@woodgoods.com
CFO: Brad Johnson
Quality Control: Brad Johnson
Customer Service/Purchasing: David Corredato
Estimated Sales: $5-10 Million
Number Employees: 100-249
Square Footage: 120000

31316 Wood Stone Corp
1801 W Bakerview Rd
Bellingham, WA 98226-9105

360-650-1111
Fax: 360-650-1166   800-988-8103
info@woodstone.net   www.woodstone-corp.com

Manufacturer and exporter of broilers, stone hearth ovens, pizza equipment and rotisseries; cast ceramic available
President: Kurt Eickmeyer
kurte@woodstone.net
CEO: Keith R. Carpenter
COO: Harry E. Hegarty
VP Sales: K Carpneter
President Manufacturing: Harry Hegarty
Estimated Sales: $5-10 Million
Number Employees: 100-249
Square Footage: 100000

31317 Wood Stone Corp
1801 W Bakerview Rd
Bellingham, WA 98226-9105

360-650-1111
Fax: 360-650-1166   800-988-8103
info@woodstone-corp.com
www.woodstone-corp.com

Stone-health cooking equipment
President: Kurt Eickmeyer
kurte@woodstone.net
CEO: Kurt I. Eickmeyer
VP-Finance: Justin Mitchell
Marketing Director: Tamra Nelson
VP-Sales: Phil Eaton
VP Client Relations: Kurt Eickmeyer
Chief Operating Officer: Harry E. Hegarty
Purchasing Agent: Matt Laninga
Estimated Sales: $10-20 Million
Number Employees: 100-249

31318 Woodard
222 Merchandise Mart Plaza
PO Box 1037
Coppell, TX 75019-1037

989-725-4500
Fax: 989-725-4221   800-877-2290
retail3@woodard-furniture.com
www.woodard-furniture.com

Restaurant furnishings including wrought iron and cast and extruded aluminum
President: Dean Engelage
VP Contract Sales/International Sales: Eric Parsons
Estimated Sales: $10-20 Million
Number Employees: 3
Square Footage: 2000000

31319 Woodfold-Marco Manufacturing
1811 18th Ave
PO Box 345
Forest Grove, OR 97116

503-357-7181
Fax: 503-357-7185   info@woodfold.com
www.woodfold.com

Manufacturer and exporter of wood roll up and accordion doors and custom shutters; also, laminated kitchen and machined hardwood products
President: Mark Lewis
Vice President: Randall Roedl
Estimated Sales: $10-20 Million
Number Employees: 100-249
Square Footage: 320000

31320 Woodhead
3411 Woodhead Drive
Northbrook, IL 60062-1812

847-272-7990
Fax: 847-272-8133   888-456-1990
www.danielwoodhead.com

Wiring devices, portable lighting, portable power, cable reels, cord grips, push buttons, and pendants
President: Terry Spandet
Contact: Joseph Nogal
joseph.nogal@connector.com
Estimated Sales: $2.5-5 Million
Number Employees: 100-249

31321 Woods Fabrication
2759 Old State Highway 113
P.O.Box 167
Taylorsville, GA 30178-1706

770-684-5377
Fax: 770-684-0858   www.woodsfab.com

Cooling tunnels and conveyors
Owner/ President: Rickey Woods
info@woodsfab.com
Engineering Manager: Nevin Harne
Safety Manager: Henry Mathews
Sales Manager: John Dodson
Office Manager: Allen Wilson
Procurement: Tim McGinnis
Number Employees: 20-49

31322 Woodson
7 Wynfield Drive
Lititz, PA 7543-8001

717-627-6990
Fax: 717-627-6920   888-627-6990
www.woodsoninc.com

Automatic storage and retrieval systems (AS/RS) specifically designed for high density, deep lane storage warehouses. The AS/RS accommodate pallet and palletless applications and include a fully functional automated warehousemanagement system. For frozen food, dairy and bakery applications
President: J Thomas Woodson
Vice President: Richard Troy
Sales Director: Mark Linesay
Estimated Sales: $5-10 Million
Number Employees: 10-19
Number of Products: 4
Square Footage: 30000

31323 Woodson Pallet Co
165 Pallet St
Anmoore, WV 26323

304-623-2858
Fax: 304-623-2865

Pallets and corrugated boxes
Owner: John Wilt
CFO: William T Woodson
Estimated Sales: Below $5 Million
Number Employees: 5-9

31324 Woodson-Tenent Laboratories
5659 Bremlinger Dr
Dayton, OH 45414

937-236-5756
Fax: 937-236-5756   www.eurofinsus.com

Laboratory specializing in nutritional analysis with amino acid, dietary fiber, microbiological, proximate and vitamin analyses; pesticide and residue testing and mycotoxin screening
Manager: Michael Muse
michaelmuse@eurofinsus.com
Vice President of Corporate Development: Joseph Dunham
Operations Manager, Director of Client S: Jules Skamarak

Estimated Sales: $1-2.5 Million
Number Employees: 1-4
Parent Co: Woodson-Tenent Laboratories

31325 Woodson-Tenent Laboratories
1331 Union Ave
Ste 1500
Memphis, TN 38104-7512

515-280-8378
Fax: 770-536-6909 www.eurofins.com
Laboratory specializing in nutritional analysis with amino acid, dietary fiber, microbiological, proximate and vitamin analyses; pesticide and residue testing and mycotoxin screening available
Manager: Robert W Brooks
Contact: Lars Reimann
lreimann@warrenlab.com
Estimated Sales: $500,000-$1 Million
Number Employees: 100-250
Parent Co: Woodson-Tenent Laboratories

31326 Woodson-Tenent Laboratories
P.O.Box 1292
Des Moines, IA 50306-1292

515-265-1461
Fax: 515-266-5453 www.eurofinsus.com
Laboratory specializing in nutritional analysis of amino acids, dietary fibers, microbiologicals, proximates and vitamins; also, mycotoxin screening
Manager: Ardin Backous
Branch Manager: Cecil Bogy
Vice President of Corporate Development: Joseph Dunham
Operations Manager, Director of Client S: Jules Skamarak
Estimated Sales: $1-2.5 Million
Number Employees: 50-99
Parent Co: Woodson-Tenent Laboratories

31327 Woodson-Tenent Laboratories
P.O.Box 1292
Des Moines, IA 50306-1292

515-265-1461
Fax: 515-266-5453 www.eurofinsus.com
Laboratory specializing in nutritional analyses including amino acids, dietary fibers, microbiological proximates and vitamins; also, pesticide and residue testing and mycotoxin screening
Manager: Ardin Backous
Vice President of Corporate Development: Joseph Dunham
Operations Manager, Director of Client S: Jules Skamarak
Estimated Sales: $2.5-5 Million
Number Employees: 50-99
Parent Co: Woodson-Tenent Laboratories

31328 Woodstock Line Co
83 Canal St
Putnam, CT 06260-1909

860-928-6557
Fax: 860-928-1096 info@woodstockline.com
www.woodstockline.com
Manufacturer and exporter of braided cordage and twine
Owner: Burney Phaneuf
info@woodstockline.com
Estimated Sales: $2.5-5 Million
Number Employees: 10-19
Square Footage: 50000

31329 Woodstock Plastics Co Inc
22511 W Grant Hwy
Marengo, IL 60152-9660

815-568-5281
Fax: 815-568-5339 sales@woodstockplastics.com
www.woodstockplastics.com
Manufacturer and exporter of fabricated plastic displays, dump bins, containers, clamshell and vinyl pouches including sealed, vacuum formed, molded and blow molded
Owner: Brian Jenkner
brianj@woodstockplastics.com
CFO: Matthew Jenkner
Vice President: John Jenkner
Quality Control: Jude Jons
Estimated Sales: $10-20 Million
Number Employees: 20-49
Square Footage: 90000

31330 Woodward Manufacturing
299 Forest Ave
Suite F
Paramus, NJ 7652

201-262-6700
Fax: 201-262-1322
Packaging machinery
President: Cyril H T Woodward
VP: Joseph Giorgio
National Sales Director: Louis Cannizzaro
Estimated Sales: $1-2.5 Million
Number Employees: 10
Brands:
Vac-U-Pac

31331 Woody Associates Inc
844 E South St
York, PA 17403-2849

717-843-3975
Fax: 717-843-5829 info@woody-decorators.com
www.woody-decorators.com
Manufacturer and exporter of automatic confectionery and bakery decorating machinery
President: Harry Reinke
woody@woody-decorators.com
VP: Kerrie Reinke
Sales: Harry Reinke
Estimated Sales: $1-3 Million
Number Employees: 5-9
Square Footage: 2000
Brands:
Woody Stringer

31332 Wooster Novelty Company
45 Washington Street
Floor 6a
Brooklyn, NY 11201-1029

718-852-8934
Fax: 718-624-6925
Cutting board underliners for hot plates
President: Stephen Winaker
Partner: Scott Kail
Estimated Sales: $500,000-$1 Million
Number Employees: 9

31333 Worcester Envelope Co
22 Millbury St
Auburn, MA 01501-3200

508-832-5397
Fax: 508-832-5870 www.worcesterenvelope.com
Commercial and official envelopes
President: Eldon D Pond Iii
epond@worcester-envelope.com
Estimated Sales: $20-50 Million
Number Employees: 250-499

31334 Worcester Industrial Products
7 Brookfield St
Worcester, MA 01605-3901

508-757-5161
Fax: 508-831-9990 800-533-5711
sales@shortening-shuttle.com
www.howardproducts.info
Waste oil transfer systems used to transport waste shortening from fryers to grease dumpsters
President: Martha Hawley
CEO: David Hawley
sales@shortening-shuttle.com
Marketing: Elaine Liad
Vice President of Sales: Jeremiah Hawley
Estimated Sales: $2.5-5 Million
Number Employees: 10-19
Number of Products: 5
Type of Packaging: Food Service
Brands:
Shortening Shuttle

31335 Work Well Company
861 Taylor Road
Unit C
Gahanna, OH 43230-6275

614-759-8003
Fax: 614-759-8013
Manufacturer and exporter of safety gloves and oven mitts
Contact: Bill Balentine
bbalentine@workwell.com
Estimated Sales: $1-5 Million

31336 Workman Packaging Inc.
345 Montee de Liesse
Saint-Laurent, QC H4T 1P5
Canada

514-344-7227
Fax: 514-737-4288 800-252-5208
info@multisac.com www.multisac.com
Manufacturer and exporter of woven and laminated polyethylene and polypropylene bags, covers and wraps
President: Mark Kraminer
CFO: Luc Dumont
Quality Control: Bryan Morton
Director Marketing: Mark Kraminer
Number Employees: 100
Brands:
Multisac
Plastex
Stretch-Tite
Toss 'n' Tote

31337 Worksafe Industries
130t W 10th Street
Huntington Station, NY 11746-1616

516-427-1802
Fax: 516-427-1840 800-929-9000
Manufacturer and exporter of protective clothing including gloves, respirators, goggles and industrial safety equipment
President: Larry Densen
Number Employees: 300

31338 Worksman 800 Buy Cart
9415 100th St
Ozone Park, NY 11416-1707

718-322-2003
Fax: 718-529-4803 800-289-2278
vending@worksman.com www.worksman.com
Manufacturer and exporter of vending carts, trucks, trailers and kiosks.
President: Wayne Sosin
Mobile Food Equity, VP: Jack Beller
Estimated Sales: $5-10 Million
Number Employees: 50-99
Square Footage: 360000
Type of Packaging: Food Service
Brands:
Admar
Worksman Cycles

31339 World Division
12023 Denton Dr
Dallas, TX 75234

972-241-2612
Fax: 972-247-8807 800-433-9843
info@worlddivision.com www.worlddivision.com
Manufacturer and exporter of banners, pennants, streamers and signs
President: John Adams
Sr. VP: Francois Louis
Operations Director: David Fry
Estimated Sales: $5-10,000,000
Number Employees: 1-4

31340 World Dryer Corp
5700 Mcdermott Dr
Berkeley, IL 60163-1196

708-449-6950
Fax: 708-449-6958 800-323-0701
sales@worlddryer.com www.worlddryer.com
Warm air push button and automatic hand dryers, baby changing tables, automatic soap dispensers, 3-in-1 towel dispenser/hand dryer systems and ADA compliant/handicapped approved hand dryers.
President: Tom Vic
CFO: Tom Bic
Vice President: Chris Berl
Marketing Director: Stacey Hefford
Sales Director: Erin Eddy
Estimated Sales: $10-20 Million
Number Employees: 20-49
Square Footage: 100000
Parent Co: Specialty Equipment Companies
Brands:
Airspeed
Electric Aire
Sensamatic
World

31341 World Finer Foods
1455 Broadacres Dr Ste 100
Bloomfield, NJ 07003

973-338-0300
Fax: 973-338-0382 www.worldfiner.com

Specialty food distributor.
President: Frank Muchel
CFO: Jon Beer
Estimated Sales: Less than $500,000
Number Employees: 1-4

31342 World Food Processing LLC
4301 World Food Ave
Oskaloosa, IA 52577-9313
641-672-9651
Fax: 641-672-9596
www.worldfoodprocessing.com
Soybean and soy-based products supplier.
President: Jerry Lorenzen
jlorenzen@worldfoodp.com
Number Employees: 10-19
Other Locations:
   Headquarters
   Oskaloosa IA
   Processing
   Randolph MN
   Processing
   Turtle Lake WI

31343 World Food Tech Services
153 Cherry St
Malden, MA 02148-1603
781-321-3750
Fax: 781-321-3750
Aids in developing the import/export and product
development of spruce in the US market
President: Daniel Casper
VP: Jane Casper
Sales: Jersy Moytasch

31344 World Kitchen
PO Box 1555
Elmira, NY 14902-1555
607-377-8000
Fax: 607-377-8962 800-999-3436
www.worldkitchen.com
Manufacturer and exporter of glassware including
bottles, jars, cookware, trays, urns, etc
President/ CEO: Carl Warschausky
CFO: Stephen Earhart
SVP, Human Resources & Chief Legal Offic: Ed
Flowers
VP Marketing: Clark Kinlin
Contact: David Livingston
livingstond@worldkitchen.com
SVP/ General Manager, Global Business: Lee Mui
Estimated Sales: $5-10 Million
Number Employees: 10-19
Brands:
   Corningware
   Pyrex
   Visions

31345 World Kitchen
5500 Pearl St Ste 400
Rosemont, IL 60018
847-678-8600
Fax: 847-678-9424
Manufacturer and exporter of plastic containers;
wholesaler/distributor and exporter of bakery racks
and food trays; serving the food service market
President: Jim Sharman
CEO: Joe Mallof
Contact: Michael Cwiertniakm
cwiertniakm@worldkitchen.com
Estimated Sales: $20-50 Million
Number Employees: 100-249
Parent Co: Borden Inc.
Type of Packaging: Food Service
Brands:
   Bakers Secret
   Chicago Cutlery
   Corelle
   Corningware
   Cuisinart
   Ekco
   Farberware
   Grilla Gear
   Oxo
   Olfa
   Pyrex
   Regent Sheffield
   Revere
   Visions

31346 World Pride
PO Box 41463
St Petersburg, FL 33743-1463
727-522-5020
Fax: 727-522-2317 800-533-2433
info@ablebrands.com
Kitchen apparel including aprons, chef coats and
hats; also, ice carvers
President: Douglas S Fyvolent
VP Marketing: Douglas Fyvolent
Estimated Sales: $1-2.5 Million
Number Employees: 4
Brands:
   Kitchen Wise
   Laural
   Noble
   Pro-Icer
   Progold
   Provell
   Sterling

31347 World Tableware Inc
300 Madison Ave
Toledo, OH 43604-1561
419-325-2608
Fax: 419-325-2749 800-678-9849
stock@libbey.com www.libbey.com
Importer, exporter and wholesaler/distributor of tab-
letop supplies including flatware, dinnerware and
holloware; serving the food service market
President: John Myer
CEO: Jay Achenbach
achenbachj@libbey.com
Quality Control: Allwyn Cahoun
CEO: John Meier
R & D: Bill Herp
Number Employees: 5-9
Parent Co: Libbey
Type of Packaging: Food Service

31348 World Technitrade
PO Box 72
Villanova, PA 19085-0072
610-525-1600
Fax: 610-525-1600
Confectionery, bakery, and pressure and vacuum
vessels import and export
President: Erwin Von Allmen
Estimated Sales: $1-5 Million

31349 World Trade Center Harrisburg
1000 North Cameron St
Harrisburg, PA 17103
717-843-1090
Fax: 717-854-0087 info@wtccentralpa.org
wtccentralpa.org
Education, informational services, consulting, networking; connects manufacturers and trade service
providers
Executive Director: Tina Weyant
tina@wtccentralpa.org
Event & Membership Coordinator: Jan Kreidler
Number Employees: 2-10

31350 World Variety Produce
Po Box 514599
Los Angeles, CA 90021
323-588-0151
Fax: 323-588-9774 800-588-0151
www.melissas.com
Importer and distributor of specialty produce
President & CEO: Joe Hernandez
CFO: Lee Zeller
Director of Marketing: Bill Schneider
VP Sales: Peter Steinbrick
Director Public Relations: Robert Schueller
Estimated Sales: $20.4 Million
Number Employees: 325
Type of Packaging: Consumer, Food Service, Bulk
Brands:
   Don Enrique
   Jo San
   Melissas

31351 World Water Works
4000 SW 113th St
Oklahoma City, OK 73173-8322
405-943-9000
Fax: 405-943-9006 800-607-7973
Wastewater treatment.
Contact: Kyle Booth
kyle.booth@worldwaterworks.com
Number Employees: 50-99

31352 World Water Works
4 Vernon Lane
Elmsford, NY
800-607-7873
sales@worldwaterworks.com
www.worldwaterworks.com
Designs, builds and installs a line of wastewater
treatment systems
President: Mark Fosshage
Vice President of Technology: Greg Parks
Director of Sales and Marketing: John Schnecker
Contact: Scott Poe
poe@worldwaterworks.com
Estimated Sales: $10 Million
Number Employees: 4

31353 World Wide Beverage
P.O.Box 191
Glencoe, IL 60022-0191
847-835-3444
Fax: 847-835-3434
Manufacturers of accumulating table conveyors,
bag-in-box filling equipment, bag-in-box dispensers,
bottle, can warmers, bottle rinsers and washers
President: Howard Buckner
Estimated Sales: $1-2.5 Million
Number Employees: 1-4
Type of Packaging: Bulk

31354 World Wide Fitting Corp
600 Corporate Woods Pkwy
Vernon Hills, IL 60061-3113
847-793-8456
Fax: 847-588-2212 800-393-9894
sales@worldwidefittings.com
Pneumatic and hydraulic fittings for food processing
machinery
Chairman of the Board: Joseph D Mc Carthy
sales@worldwidefittings.com
VP Sales: Mike Casey
VP Production: Sean McCarthy
Estimated Sales: $5-10,000,000
Number Employees: 100-249

31355 World Wide Hospitality Furn
7311 Madison St # D
Paramount, CA 90723-4038
562-630-2700
Fax: 562-630-2227 800-728-8262
wrldwideh@aol.com www.wwhfurniture.com
Manufacturer and importer of tables, chairs and
booths
CEO: Isaac Gonshor
wrldwideh@aol.com
Estimated Sales: $1-5,000,000
Number Employees: 10-19
Type of Packaging: Food Service
Brands:
   World Wide

31356 World Wide Safe Brokers
112 Cromwell Court
Woodbury, NJ 08096
856-863-1225
Fax: 856-845-2266 800-593-2893
info@worldwidesafebrokers.com
www.worldwidesafebrokers.com
Fire safes, electronic safes, gun safes, safe deposit
boxes, hotel room safes, insulated files, burglary
safe, vaults, vault doors, in-floor safes, depository
safes, custom designed and manufactured safes.
President: Edward Dornisch
VP: Mildred Dornisch
Estimated Sales: $.5-1 million
Number Employees: 3
Square Footage: 16000

31357 Worldwide Dispensers
1201 Windham Parkway
Suite D
Romeoville, IL 60446
630-296-2000
Fax: 630-296-2195 info@dssplastics.com
www.dssmith.com
Fun, fabulous ceramic products. All are bright and
bold with witty sentiments, all designed by artist
Lorrie Veasey. Lead free ceramic, dishwasher and
microwave safe
Estimated Sales: D
Number Employees: 250-499
Number of Products: 200
Type of Packaging: Consumer

31358 Wornick Company

PO Box 55
McAllen, TX 78505-0055

561-227-0765
Fax: 956-631-0857

Meals Ready to Eat (MRE). Humanitarian Daily Rations (HDR)

31359 (HQ)Worthen Industries Inc

3 E Spit Brook Rd
Nashua, NH 03060-5783

603-888-5443
Fax: 603-888-7945 info@worthenind.com
www.upacofootwear.com

Manufacturer and exporter of labels and adhesive tapes
President: Robert Worthen
CEO: Eileen Morin
emorin@worthenind.com
CEO: Eileen Morin
Estimated Sales: $1-3 Million
Number Employees: 100-249

31360 Wrap Pack

1728 Presson Pl
Yakima, WA 98903-2238

509-248-6774
Fax: 509-453-3653 800-879-9727
www.fruitwrap.com

Fruit wrappers and packing needle holders
President: Lance Braden
CFO: Ted Smith
General Manager: G Lance Braden
Plant Manager: Shane May
Estimated Sales: $2.5-5 Million
Number Employees: 20-49

31361 Wrapade Packaging Systems

27 Law Dr # B
Suite B/C
Fairfield, NJ 07004-3206

973-787-1788
Fax: 973-773-6010 888-815-8564
sales@wrapade.com www.wrapade.com

Manufacturer and exporter of vertical, horizontal and stand-up pouch packaging machinery
President: Bill Beattie
bill.b@wrapade.com
Estimated Sales: $2.5-5 Million
Number Employees: 10-19
Square Footage: 88000

31362 Wraps

810 Springdale Avenue
East Orange, NJ 07017-1298

973-673-7873
Fax: 973-673-2240

Manufacturer and exporter of flexible packaging materials, heat sealers and packaging machinery
President: Ralph Barone
General Manager: Michael Mikulis
Sales Manager: Brian Guidera
Contact: Chad Carpenter
chad.carpenter@wrapsforless.com
Estimated Sales: $2.5-5 Million
Number Employees: 20-49
Square Footage: 192000
Brands:
    Clamco

31363 Wright Brothers Paper Box Company

800 Morris St
Fond Du Lac, WI 54935

920-921-8270
Fax: 920-921-8384 info@wbpaperbox.com
www.wbpaperbox.com

Rigid set-up paper boxes and folding cartons
President: Joan Pennau
President: Victor Pupo
Chairman: Frank Erdman
Sales / Customer Service: Diane Seibel
Contact: Barb Bogart
bbogart@wbpaperbox.com
Operations: Mary Vandermolen
Estimated Sales: $5-10 Million
Number Employees: 50-99

31364 Wright Global Graphic Solutions

5115 Prospect St
Thomasville, NC 27360

800-678-9019
Fax: 336-476-8554 800-678-9019
www.wrightglobalgraphics.com

Labels and labeling materials
President/CEO: Greg Wright
Vice President of Marketing: Vicki Fishman
Vice President of Sales: Carol Phillips
Contact: Jason Collett
jcollett@wrightglobalgraphics.com
Estimated Sales: A
Number Employees: 200

31365 (HQ)Wright Metal Products Crates

100 Ben Hamby Dr
Greenville, SC 29615-5700

864-297-6610
Fax: 864-281-0594 www.wrightmetalproducts.com

Machine parts for food handling equipment
Vice President: Marty Hyatt
mhyatt@wrightmetalsinc.com
VP: Jim Camden
General Manager: Jim Camden
Estimated Sales: $10-20 Million
Number Employees: 20-49
Square Footage: 80000
Other Locations:
    Wright Metal Products
    Greenville SC

31366 Wright Plastics Company

1107 Doster Road
Prattville, AL 36067-4329

334-365-9494
Fax: 334-365-9559 800-874-7659

Polyethylene bags and film
Estimated Sales: $10-20 Million
Number Employees: 19

31367 Wt Nickell Co

4360 Winding Creek Blvd
Batavia, OH 45103-1729

513-752-2191
Fax: 513-752-2354 888-899-1991
labels@wtnickell.com www.wtnickell.com

Custom pressure sensitive labels, printer ribbons and stock labels.
President: Rick Meyer
rlmeyer@wtnickell.com
Vice President: Jaime Kinkade
Estimated Sales: Under $1 Million
Number Employees: 5-9
Type of Packaging: Private Label

31368 Wylie Systems

1190 Fewster Drive
Mississauga, ON L4W 1A1
Canada

905-238-1619
Fax: 905-238-5623 800-525-6609
info@wyliemetals.com www.wyliemetals.com

Manufacturer and exporter of railings and partitions for hotels, restaurants, etc.; also, sneeze guards
President: Michael Wylie
Brands:
    Decorail

31369 Wyssmont Co Inc

1470 Bergen Blvd
Fort Lee, NJ 07024-2197

201-947-4600
Fax: 201-947-0324 www.wyssmont.com

Manufacturer, designer and exporter of food processing equipment including rotating tray dryers, lumpbreakers, fixed and rotating bars and self-cleaning airlock feeders; also, solid handling equipment
President: Edward Weisselberg
ebw@wyssmont.com
VP: Joseph Bevacqua
R&D: J Ulrich
VP Sales: Joseph Henderson
Estimated Sales: $2.5-5 Million
Number Employees: 20-49
Square Footage: 40000
Brands:
    Turbo-Dryer

31370 X-Press Manufacturing

271 Fm 306
New Braunfels, TX 78130-2557

830-629-2651
Fax: 830-620-4727 800-365-9440
sales@x-pressmfg.com www.x-pressmfg.com

Display tortilla cookers, pressers and warmers

Owner: Charles Smith
President/Owner: Rex Wilson
Customer Service: Anne Sowell
Shop Manager: Charlie Smith
Estimated Sales: $.5-1 million
Number Employees: 1-4
Square Footage: 7500
Parent Co: Copprex
Brands:
    X-Press

31371 X-R-I Testing Inc

1961 Thunderbird
Troy, MI 48084-5467

248-362-5050
Fax: 248-362-4422 800-973-4800
foodx@aol.com www.xritesting.com

Manufacturer and exporter of in-line and off-line X-ray inspection equipment; also, X-ray inspection services available
President: Scott Thams
Manager: Kurt Andrews
kurta@xrayindustries.com
Estimated Sales: $30-50 Million
Number Employees: 50-99
Square Footage: 30000
Parent Co: X-Ray Industries

31372 X-Rite Inc

4300 44th St SE
Grand Rapids, MI 49512-4009

616-803-2100
888-800-9580
www.xrite.com

Portable hand-held spectrophotometers and colorimeters with supporting computer software for color control applications and color formulation.
Year Founded: 1958
Estimated Sales: $261.5 Million
Number Employees: 500-999
Parent Co: Danaher Corporation
Brands:
    Qa-Master
    Sp68

31373 XL Corporate & ResearchServices

62 White Street
New York, NY 10013-3593

212-431-5000
Fax: 212-431-5111 800-221-2972

Consultant providing product, company or industry research including trademark research on product names, company names and logos, preparation and filing of trademarks and credit reports
President: Robert Blumerang
Counsel: Marc Moel
General Counsel: Arthur McGuire
Estimated Sales: $20-50 Million
Number Employees: 30
Square Footage: 5000
Parent Co: Julius Blumberg

31374 Xango LLC

2889 W Ashton Blvd # 1
Lehi, UT 84043-4968

801-766-3050
Fax: 801-816-8001 877-469-2646

Markets daily dietary supplemental juice beverage made from the mangosteen fruit.
President/Chief Executive Officer: Aaron Garrity
Chairman: Gary Hollister
President Intnl Distributor Relations: Joe Morton
EVP International Relations: Bryan Davis
Quality Assurance Manufacturing: Wayne Davis
Chief Marketing Officer: Gordon Morton
President Operations: Ken Wood
Number Employees: 500-999

31375 Xcel Tower Controls

1600 W 6th St
PO Box 187
Gilbertsville, NY 13776

574-259-7804
Fax: 574-259-5769 800-288-7362
info@xcel.com www.xcel.com

Manufacturer and exporter of control and process control systems, universal programmers, programmable control systems and industrial computers, tower light controllers and monitoring systems
President: Bruce Shepard
CEO: John Brickley
Sales Director: Bruce Shepard

Estimated Sales: $2.5-5 Million
Number Employees: 10-19
Square Footage: 30000

31376 Xcell International
16400 Est 103rd Street
Lemont, IL 60439
630-323-0107
Fax: 630-323-0217 800-722-7751
info@xcellint.com www.xcellint.com
Spice blends, confectionery dessert toppings, coffee
flavors and creamers, teas and coffee and tea acces-
sories.
CEO: Raymond Henning
Estimated Sales: $20-50 Million
Number Employees: 50-99

31377 Xela Pack Inc
8300 Boettner Rd
Saline, MI 48176-9642
734-944-1300
Fax: 734-429-4714 800-742-7225
info@xelapack.com www.xelapack.com
Single and multi-dose packaging alternative to bot-
tles and tubes
Owner: Al Gentile
algentile@mac.com
Estimated Sales: $2.5-5Million
Number Employees: 50-99

31378 Xiaoping Design
73 Hudson Street
New York, NY 10013-2870
212-962-4080
Fax: 212-962-4071 800-891-9896
Custom furniture including tables and chairs also de-
signs for custom furniture
President: Xiaoping Zao
VP/Marketing/Sales/Operations: David Chang
Estimated Sales: $1 Million
Number Employees: 2
Number of Brands: 1
Number of Products: 45

31379 Xpander Pak
1045 Technology Park Drive
Glen Allen, VA 23059-4500
804-266-5000
Fax: 804-266-4474 800-720-1777
sales@xpander.com www.xpander.com
Projective packaging: Xpander Pak super protective
shippers, Safe-T Shipper, Safe-T Shipper ESD
CEO: Joseph Sullivan
Estimated Sales: $1-2.5 Million
Number Employees: 9

31380 Xtreme Beverages, LLC
32565-B Golden Lantern
#282
Dana Point, CA 92629
Canada
949-495-7929
Fax: 949-495-8015 xtremebeverages@cox.net
Wood and bamboo box; wood and bamboo tea chest;
wine box; baskets; tea and coffee accessories; wine
accessories; MDF box; cardboard box; wooded tea
dispenser; wrought iron tea can rack; wood and
bamboo products, candles; candleholders; gourmet
gift packaging and food and beverage gift packaging
President: William Quinley
VP: James Moffitt
Estimated Sales: $5 Million
Number Employees: 4
Type of Packaging: Consumer, Food Service, Private Label, Bulk

31381 Xylem Inc
1 International Dr
Rye Brook, NY 10573
914-323-5700
www.xylem.com
Field, portable, online and laboratory analytical in-
strumentation.
President & Chief Executive Officer: Patrick Decker
SVP/Chief Innovation/Technology Officer: David
Flinton
SVP & Chief Financial Officer: Mark Rajkowski
SVP/President, Measurement & Control: Colin
Sabol
SVP/Chief Human Resources Officer: Kairus
Tarapore
SVP/General Counsel/Corporate Secretary: Claudia
Toussaint
SVP/Chief Marketing Officer: Joseph Vesey

Year Founded: 2011
Estimated Sales: $5.2 Billion
Number Employees: 17,000
Type of Packaging: Bulk

31382 Y-Pers Inc
5622 Tulip St
PO Box 9559
Philadelphia, PA 19124-1698
215-743-1500
Fax: 215-289-6811 800-421-0242
www.ypers.com
Manufacturer and exporter of cheesecloths and uni-
forms including disposable clothing, hairnets and
gloves
President: David Blum
ypers@aol.com
CFO: David Blum
R&D: David Blum
Estimated Sales: Below $5 Million
Number Employees: 10-19

31383 Y-Z Sponge & Foam Products
811 Cundy Avenue
Annacis Island
Delta, BC V3M 5P6
Canada
604-525-1665
Fax: 604-525-1081 info@a-zfoam.com
www.a-zfoam.com
Polyurethane foam

31384 YAAX International
3111 Tieton Dr # 300
Yakima, WA 98902-3628
509-249-5555
Fax: 509-469-2133 info@yaax.com
www.yaax.com
Wholesaler & distributor of fruit juice concentrates
flavors, purees, dehydrated fruit and dairy products,
glass and plastic packaged juices. Supplier of pro-
cessed vegetable products.
President: Bruce Simpson
Marketing: Jennifer Tilley
Number Employees: 2-10
Type of Packaging: Private Label, Bulk

31385 YCU Air/York International
1519 Highway 13 E
Burnsville, MN 55337-2917
952-707-1286
Fax: 952-707-0914 www.york.com
Clean rooms and equipment
Estimated Sales: $1-5 Million

31386 YESCO
1605 S Gramercy Rd
Salt Lake City, UT 84104-4888
801-487-8481
Fax: 801-762-0036 800-444-3847
info@yesco.com www.yesco.com
Manufacturer and exporter of electric signs
President: Michael Young
Cmo: Wes Van Dyke
wvandyke@yesco.com
CFO: Duane Wardle
Sales Manager: Susan Ward
Estimated Sales: $30-50 Million
Number Employees: 250-499

31387 YSI Inc
1725 Brannum Ln
Yellow Springs, OH 45387-1107
937-767-7241
Fax: 937-767-9353 800-765-4974
support@ysi.com www.ysi.com
Instrumentation for the analysis of carbohydrates,
organic acids, sugars, dissolved oxygen, etc.; also,
conductivity meters and temperature devices
President: Richard Omlor
rfielder@ysi.com
CFO: Lee Erdman
VP: Jim Smith
Quality Control: Marek Jezior
Sales Exec: Rick Fielder
Estimated Sales: $50-75 Million
Number Employees: 250-499

31388 YW Yacht Basin
8341 Black Dog Alley
Easton, MD 21601-6329
410-822-0414
Fax: 410-822-1090

Material handling conveyors; also, custom metal,
structural and steel fabrications of stairs and hand-
rails available
President: Douglas Weinmann
VP Sales: David Weinmann
Number Employees: 6
Square Footage: 50000

31389 Yakima Wire Works
1949 E. Manning Avenue
Reedley, CA 93654
559-638-8484
Fax: 559-638-7478 800-344-8951
info@swfcompanies.com www.swfcompanies.com
Manufacturer and exporter of fully and semi-auto-
matic bagging, weighing and batching, modular net
dispensers, check-weighers, dual-belt conveyors and
blowers
President: Gary Germunson
Chairman/VP: Tim Main
Estimated Sales: $.5-1 million
Number Employees: 1-4

31390 Yamada America
1575 Highpoint Drive
Elgin, IL 60123-9303
847-697-1878
Fax: 847-697-2794 800-990-7867
sales@yamadapump.com www.yamadapump.com
Air-operated, double diaphragm pump
President: Steve Kameyama
Estimated Sales: Below $500,000
Number Employees: 3

31391 Yamato Corporation
1775 S. Murray Blvd.
Colorado Springs, CO 80916-4513
719-591-1500
Fax: 719-591-1045 800-538-1762
www.yamatocorp.com
Manufacturer and exporter of electronic and me-
chanical scales, electronic weight printers and com-
puterized weighing systems
President: Sadao Nakamura
CEO: Sado Nakamura
Marketing Director: Gary Mendenhall
Sales Director: Prague Mehta
Contact: Lula Babb
babb@yamatocorp.com
Estimated Sales: $2.5-5 Million
Number Employees: 20-49
Square Footage: 96000
Brands:
Accuweigh
Yamato

31392 Yardney Water Management Syst
6666 Box Springs Blvd
Riverside, CA 92507-0736
951-656-6716
Fax: 951-656-3867 800-854-4788
www.yardneyfilters.com
Manufacturer and exporter of water quality improve-
ment and filtration systems
President: Kenneth Phillips
kennethphillips@yardneyfilters.com
CFO: Kenneth Phillips
Quality Control: Janie Weissberg
Industrial Field Sales Manager: Ron Gamble
Estimated Sales: $5-10 Million
Number Employees: 20-49
Square Footage: 200000
Brands:
Yardney

31393 Yargus Manufacturing Inc
12285 E Main St
Marshall, IL 62441-4127
217-826-8059
Fax: 217-826-8551 layco@yargus.com
www.laycoproautomation.com
Stainless steel equipment including conveyors, hop-
per scales, blenders and bucket elevators; exporter
of conveyor and blender systems
Owner: Jose Aguayo
Vice President US Sales: Mark Anderson
Sales: Lyle Yargus
jaguayo@bigwsales.com
Estimated Sales: $5-10 Million
Number Employees: 100-249
Square Footage: 102000
Brands:
Layco

31394 Yates Industries Inc
23050 E Industrial Dr
St Clair Shores, MI 48080-1177
586-778-7680
Fax: 586-778-6565 sales@yatesind.com
www.yatesind.com
Pneumatic and hydraulic cylinders including stainless steel, food grade and epoxy paint
President: Jennifer Adams
jadams@yatesind.com
Sales/Marketing Manager: Fred Cormier
Estimated Sales: $10+ Million
Number Employees: 20-49
Square Footage: 120
Parent Co: Yates Cylinder

31395 Yeager Wire Works
620 Broad St
Berwick, PA 18603-1418
570-752-2769
Fax: 570-752-2934
Display racks including wire and sheet-metal
President: David Ungemach
VP: Robert Ungemach
Estimated Sales: Less Than $500,000
Number Employees: 1-4

31396 Yerecic Label Co
701 Hunt Valley Rd
New Kensington, PA 15068-7076
724-334-3300
Fax: 724-335-8872 experts@yereciclabel.com
Pressure sensitive labels; printing services available
President: Arthur Yerecic
yerecica@yereciclabel.com
VP: Arthur Yerecic Jr
Estimated Sales: $2.5-5 Million
Number Employees: 5-9
Square Footage: 15000

31397 Yerger Wood Products
3090 Wentling Schoolhouse Road
East Greenville, PA 18041-2313
215-679-4413
Fax: 215-679-8797
Wooden pallets
President: James Yerger Jr
CEO/Sales: Susan Klolz
Estimated Sales: Below $5 Million
Number Employees: 10

31398 Yeuell Name Plate & Label
8 Adele Rd
Woburn, MA 01801-1911
781-933-2984
Fax: 781-933-3569 tbarry@yeuell.com
www.yeuell.com
Nameplates and labels; also, metal etching services available
President: Andrew F Hall Iii
Estimated Sales: $2.5-5 Million
Number Employees: 20-49

31399 (HQ)Yohay Baking Co
146 Albany Ave
Lindenhurst, NY 11757-3628
631-225-0300
Fax: 631-225-4277
Processor, importer and exporter of wafer rolls, specialty cookies, biscotti, and fudge mix, kosher and all natural products. Retail packaging available
Owner: Michael Soloman
solomanyohay@aol.com
Number Employees: 20-49
Type of Packaging: Consumer, Food Service, Private Label, Bulk
Brands:
  Fudge Gourmet
  Gourmet Cookie Place
  Sweetheart Fudge

31400 York Container Co
138 Mount Zion Rd
York, PA 17402-8985
717-757-7611
Fax: 717-755-8090 www.yorkcontainer.com
Corrugated shipping containers
President: Chuck Wolf
CFO: William C Ludwig
wludwig@yorkcontainer.com
Executive VP: Charles Wolf Jr
Estimated Sales: $20-50 Million
Number Employees: 250-499
Square Footage: 200000

31401 York Refrigeration Marine US
5005 York Drive
Norman, OK 73069
206-285-0904
Fax: 206-285-0965 877-874-7378
www.york.com
Reciprocating and screw compressors and customized LT pump recirculation packages; also, freezers
President: Thomas Berfenfeldt
Director Sales and Marketing: Jack Barney
Sales: Slawonir Tabaczynski
Estimated Sales: $10-20 Million
Number Employees: 20-49
Parent Co: York Refrigeration A/S
Brands:
  Sabroe
  Unisab
  Unisafe

31402 York River Pallet Corporation
PO Box 191
Shacklefords, VA 23156
804-785-5811
Fax: 804-785-3702
Wooden pallets and pallet materials
President/CEO: James Potts
Estimated Sales: Below $5 Million
Number Employees: 5-9

31403 York Saw & Knife
295 Emig Rd
P.O.Box 733
York, PA 17406-9734
717-767-6402
Fax: 717-764-2768 800-233-1969
info@yorksaw.com www.yorksaw.com
Manufacturer and exporter of circular and straight knives for food processing; custom and standard specifications available
President: Mike Pickard
mpickard@yorksaw.com
CFO: Todd Gladfeltzer
Quality Control: Tim Wentz
Estimated Sales: $10 Million
Number Employees: 50-99
Square Footage: 130000

31404 York Tape & Label Company
P.O.Box 1309
York, PA 17405-1309
717-266-9675
Fax: 717-266-9837 yorkwebsite@yorklabel.com
www.yorklabel.com
Labels and tags, nameplates, commercial printing and bar coding
President: Timothy Hare
CFO: Dennis Cole
Sales: Karen S Chavez
Quality Control: Tom Walko
VP Sales: John Attayek
Estimated Sales: $50-100 Million
Number Employees: 250-499

31405 York Tent & Awning
7 E 7th Ave
York, PA 17404-2199
717-230-8837
Fax: 717-843-6555 800-864-3510
sales@yorktentandawning.net
www.yorktentandawning.com
Commercial awnings
President: John Musti
yorktent@aol.com
Estimated Sales: $1-2,500,000
Number Employees: 10-19

31406 Yorkraft
2675a Eastern Boulevard
York, PA 17402-2905
717-845-3666
Fax: 717-846-3213 800-872-2044
Food service equipment including cabinetry products, salad bars, buffet lines and merchandising carts; also, decorative lighting panels available
President: David Imhoff
dimhoff@yorkraft.com
VP Operations: Jack Smith
VP: William Imhoff
Estimated Sales: $5-10 Million
Number Employees: 10
Square Footage: 360000

31407 YottaMark
203 Redwood Shores Parkway
Suite 100
Redwood City, CA 94065
650-264-6200
Fax: 650-264-6220 866-768-7878
info@yottamark.com www.yottamark.com
Product fingerprint solution detects and deters counterfeiting, diversion and fraud and allows manufacturers, brand protection personnel, law enforcement officials-even consumers- to authenticate individual products anytimeanywhere.
President/CEO: J Scott Carr
President, Chief Executive Officer: Scott Carr
Engineering VP: Matthew Self
Founder, Chief Marketing Officer: Elliott Grant
Senior Vice President of Sales: Michael Bromme
Chief Operating Officer: Paul Gifford

31408 Young & Associates
8915 58th Pl
Kenosha, WI 53144-7802
262-657-6394
Fax: 262-657-4306
Manufacturer and supplier of food product machinery
President: William B Young
CEO: Bill Young
Public Relations: Nancy Beck

31409 Young & Swartz Inc
39 Cherry St
Buffalo, NY 14204-1298
716-852-2171
Fax: 716-852-5652 800-466-7682
info@youngandswartz.com
Brushes, brooms and janitorial supplies
President: Paul Winzig
paul@buffalobrushworks.com
Estimated Sales: Less Than $500,000
Number Employees: 1-4
Square Footage: 30000

31410 Young Industries Inc
16 Painter St
Muncy, PA 17756-1423
570-546-1826
Fax: 570-546-1888 www.younginds.com
Tea blending equipment, conveying equipment (elevators, machines and buckets), blending and mixing equipment, portioning equipment, bin silo systems and storage, safety/occupational health/environment, listing of equipment, fieldservice, quality assurance, manufacturing, technical information
Owner: John Young
jmyoung@younginds.com
R&D: John Pfeiffer
Estimated Sales: $10-20 Million
Number Employees: 20-49

31411 Young's Lobster Shore Pound
2 Fairview St
Belfast, ME 04915-7208
207-338-1160
Fax: 207-338-1656
Sea food supplier
Owner: Raymond Young
raymond@youngslobsterpound.com
CEO: Katrina Young
Vice President: Diane Young
Quality Control: Joe Young
Estimated Sales: $500,000-$1 Million
Number Employees: 20-49
Type of Packaging: Consumer, Food Service, Private Label, Bulk

31412 Your Place Menu Systems
2600 Lockheed Way
Carson City, NV 89706-0717
775-882-7834
Fax: 775-882-5210 800-321-8105
Manufacturer and exporter of outdoor and indoor illuminated and nonilluminated menu boards
President, Sales Manager: John O Neil
Operations Manager, Product Design: Matt Stutsman
Number Employees: 20-49
Square Footage: 280000
Parent Co: Impact International

31413 Yuan Fa Can-Making
PO Box 14016
Torrance, CA 90503-8016
310-532-5829
Fax: 310-536-4216
Tea and coffee cans

31414 Z 2000 The Pick of the Millenium
819 S Madison Boulevard
Bartlesville, OK 74006-8534
918-335-2030
Fax: 918-335-1789 800-654-7311
Manufacturer and exporter of 45 degree angled dental cleaners
President: Mack Blevins
VP: Pamela Blevins
Estimated Sales: $1-5 Million
Number Employees: 1-4
Square Footage: 15000
Parent Co: Mack Blevins Enterprises
Type of Packaging: Consumer, Food Service, Private Label, Bulk
Brands:
Angled Pro Picks

31415 Z-Loda Systems Engineering Inc
1010 Summer St # 101
Suite 101
Stamford, CT 06905-5533
203-325-8001
Fax: 203-978-0104 www.hugedomains.com
Manufacturer and exporter of vertical lift systems
President: Clifford Mollo
Estimated Sales: Less Than $500,000
Number Employees: 1-4

31416 Z-Trim Holdings, Inc
1101 Campus Drive
Mundelein, IL 60060
847-549-6002
Fax: 847-549-6028 customerservice@ztrim.com
Ingredients
Sales Director: Rick Harris
VP Sales/Applications: Lynda Carroll
Applications Project Manager: Aili Young
Research Chef: Erin Ryan

31417 Zacmi USA
2391 Zanker Road
Suite 320
San Jose, CA 95131-1145
408-433-0100
Fax: 408-433-0224 zacmiUS@aol.com
Processing machinery sales, fillers for all products
President: Charles Hoffman
Estimated Sales: $500,000-$1 Million
Number Employees: 4

31418 Zahm & Nagel Co
210 Vermont St
PO.Box 400
Holland, NY 14080-9735
716-537-2110
Fax: 716-537-2106 800-216-1542
info@zahmnagel.com www.zahmnagel.com
Quality control equipment: CO2 and air testers, pilot plants, carbonating equipment, batch tester filter
President: Dave Koch
sales@zahmnagel.com
Estimated Sales: $5-10 Million
Number Employees: 5-9

31419 Zaloom Marketing Corp
51 James St
South Hackensack, NJ 07606-1438
201-488-3535
Fax: 201-488-8056 800-878-7609
jzzmc@aol.com www.zaloommarketing.com
Consultant specializing in marketing, promotion and food technology; importer of seafood products including imitation crab meat
President: Roy Zaloom
jzzmc@aol.com
Estimated Sales: $10-20 Million
Number Employees: 10-19

31420 Zanasi USA
8601 73rd Ave No. # 38
Brooklyn Park, MN 55428
763-593-1907
Fax: 763-593-1941 800-627-2633
info@zanasiusa.com www.zanasiusa.com
Coding and marking equipment

President: Gianni Zanasi
CFO: Dana Paige
Marketing Director: Jenny Worre
National Sales Manager: Mark Koethe
Estimated Sales: Below $5 Million
Number Employees: 5-9
Square Footage: 8000
Brands:
Jet 2000
Modul Print
Z Jet

31421 Zander Insurance Group
212 Oceola Ave
Nashville, TN 37209-3116
615-356-1700
Fax: 615-352-2850 info@zanderins.com
www.zanderinsurancetips.com
Compressed air and industrial gas purification products
Owner: Bud Zander
jaz@zanderins.com
Estimated Sales: $2.5-5 Million
Number Employees: 50-99

31422 Zapata Industries
2699 S Bayshore Drive
Miami, FL 33133
305-856-8804
Fax: 305-856-3046
Metal crowns, aluminum closures, plastic closures, lining compounds
President: Claudio Zapata
Estimated Sales: $1-2.5 Million
Number Employees: 1-4

31423 Zealco Industries
PO Box 809
Calvert City, KY 42029-0809
800-759-5531
Fax: 270-395-9522
Manufacturer and exporter of high pressure commercial and industrial washing equipment
Parent Co: Purlanco

31424 Zebra Technologies Corporation
3 Overlook Point
Lincolnshire, IL 60069
847-634-6700
Fax: 847-913-8766 866-230-9494
www.zebra.com
Bar code equipment including printers, supplies and software for point-of-application labeling and performance thermal transferring.
Chief Executive Officer: Anders Gustafsson
Chief Financial Officer: Olivier Leonetti
Senior VP, Corporate Development: Michael Cho
Senior VP/General Counsel/Secretary: Cristen Kogl
Chief Marketing Officer: Jeff Schmitz
Senior VP, Global Sales: Joachim Heel
Year Founded: 1969
Estimated Sales: $3.7 Billion
Number Employees: 7,400
Square Footage: 167600
Brands:
Zebra
Zebra Value-Line
Zebra Xii

31425 Zed Industries
3580 Lightner Rd
PO Box 458
Vandalia, OH 45377-9735
937-667-8407
Fax: 937-667-3340 info@zedindustries.com
www.zedindustries.com
Manufacturer and exporter of vacuum and pressure thermoforming equipment, heat sealers, formers/fillers/sealers, blister packers and custom engineered plastic packaging systems
President: Mark Zelnick
dzelnick@zedindustries.com
CFO: Helen Zelnick
VP: Peter Zelnick
Sales: Leonard Loomis
Estimated Sales: $10-20 Million
Number Employees: 50-99
Type of Packaging: Consumer, Food Service, Bulk

31426 Zeeco Inc
22151 E 91st St S
Broken Arrow, OK 74014-3250
918-258-8551
Fax: 918-251-5519 sales@zeeco.com
www.zeeco.com
Manufacturer and exporter of gas and oil food burners used for heating and drying; also, fume/liquid incinerators used for hazardous waste disposal
President: Jason Abbott
jason.abbott@zeeco.com
Chairman: John Zink
Sales Manager: D Caho
Purchasing Manager: D Updike
Estimated Sales: Less Than $500,000
Number Employees: 1-4
Square Footage: 42000

31427 Zeier Plastic & Mfg Inc
2203 Leo Cir
Madison, WI 53704-2615
608-244-5782
Fax: 608-244-1810 DZ@Zeierplastic.com
Manufacturer and exporter of thermoplastic injection molded trays and funnels; also, custom injection molded parts available
Owner: Dennis Zeier
dz@zeierplastic.com
VP: Dennis Zeier
Estimated Sales: $2.5-5 Million
Number Employees: 10-19

31428 Zelco Industries
110 Haven Ave
Mount Vernon, NY 10553
914-699-6230
Fax: 914-699-7082 800-431-2486
office@zelco.com
Lighting fixtures, cooking and barbecuing utensils, stainless steel cutlery and coffee brewers
Chairman of the Board: Noel E Zeller
CEO: Noel Zeller
CFO: Mike Ronan
Vice President: Nicole Zeller
Marketing Director: Terri Manganelli
Sales Director: Mike Boylan
Operations Manager: Robert Jacobs
Estimated Sales: $2.5-5,000,000
Number Employees: 20-49
Square Footage: 55000
Type of Packaging: Consumer, Private Label

31429 Zeltex
130 Western Maryland Parkway
Hagerstown, MD 21740
301-791-7080
Fax: 301-733-9398 800-732-1950
canders@zeltex.com www.zeltex.com
Manufacturer and exporter of near-infrared analyzers for the food, grain and patrochemical industries
President: Todd Rosenthal
Director of Sales: Chris Anders
Number Employees: 20
Brands:
Zeltex

31430 Zeltex
130 Western Maryland Pkwy
Hagerstown, MD 21740-5116
301-791-7080
Fax: 301-733-9398 800-732-1950
canders@zeltex.com www.zeltex.com
Near infrared instrumentation for moisture and product constituents
President: Todd Rosenthal
Director of Sales: Chris Anders
Estimated Sales: $1-5 Million
Number Employees: 24

31431 Zenar Corp
7301 S 6th St
Oak Creek, WI 53154-2047
414-764-1800
Fax: 414-764-1267 mail@zenarcrane.com
www.zenarcrane.com
Manufacturer and exporter of electric overhead cranes and hoist units
President: John Maiwald
CEO: John A Maiwald
jmaiwald@zenarcrane.com
Estimated Sales: $10-20 Million
Number Employees: 100-249

31432 Zenith Cutter
5200 Zenith Pkwy
Loves Park, IL 61111-2735

     815-282-5200
Fax: 815-282-5232 800-223-5202
toddg@zenithcutter.com www.zenithcutter.com
Manufacturer and exporter of machine knives and
cutters; also, custom manufacturing and duplicating
available
President: Cedric Blazer
cedricb@zenithcutter.com
Personnel: Bob Yocum
VP: Robert Yocum
Quality Control: Tim Greve
Director Sales/Marketing: Tim Schoenecker
Production Manager: Terry Willis
Estimated Sales: $20-50 Million
Number Employees: 100-249
Square Footage: 140000
Type of Packaging: Bulk

31433 Zenith Specialty Bag Co
17625 Railroad St
PO Box 8445
City Of Industry, CA 91748-1195

     626-912-2481
Fax: 626-810-5136 800-962-2247
cust.serv@zenithbag.com www.zbags.com
Manufacturer and exporter of paper products includ-
ing custom print, pan liners, wax paper bags and
grease resistant sheets
President: Marco Alcala
m.alcala@zenithbag.com
CEO: Betty Anderson
CFO: Jack Grave
Vice President: Ron Anderson
VP: Ron Anderson
Marketing Director: Susan Washle
Sales Director: Scott Apperson
Operations Manager: Jeff Behrends
Estimated Sales: $10-20 Million
Number Employees: 100-249
Square Footage: 170000
Brands:
  Sta-Fresh
  The Cubby
  Thermal Gard

31434 Zep Superior Solutions
1310 Seaboard Industrial Dr
Atlanta, GA 30318

     404-352-1680
Fax: 404-350-2742 webmaster@zepmfg.com
     www.zepmfg.com
Owner: Marty Zappa
CFO: John Ehrie
Quality Control: Bruce Dunkley
Estimated Sales: $300,000-500,000
Number Employees: 1-4

31435 Zepf Technologies
5320 140th Ave N
Clearwater, FL 33760-3743

     727-535-4100
Fax: 727-539-8944 sales@zepf.com
     www.pneumaticscale.com
Manufacturer and exporter of shrink wrappers, case
packers, bundlers, tray formers, straw applicators,
rotary uncasers, combiners and laners
President: Michael Mc Laughlin
Contact: Doug Dougherty
doug.dougherty@hayssen.com
Estimated Sales: $20-50 Million
Number Employees: 50-99
Square Footage: 45000
Brands:
  Akron
  Akron Hawk
  Akron Spartan
  Flex-Packer
  Flexwrap
  Iac 2000
  Pilot Divider
  Tampco
  Universal

31436 Zephyr Manufacturing Co
200 Mitchell Rd
Sedalia, MO 65301-2114

     660-827-0352
Fax: 660-827-0713 info@zephyrmfg.com
     www.zephyrmfg.com

Processor and exporter of brushes, floor and carpet
cleaners, wet mops, handles, mopsticks, sponges,
frames, squeegees
President: Charles Close
cclose@zephyrtool.com
Estimated Sales: $20-50 Million
Number Employees: 50-99
Brands:
  Dover Grill Scraper
  Zephyr

31437 Zephyrhills Bottled Water Company
6403 Harney Rd
Tampa, FL 33610-9349

     813-630-5763
Fax: 813-620-6862 800-950-9398
Bottled water
President: Kim Jeffery
Marketing Director: John Bryan
Sales Manager: Monica Kelley
Operations Manager: Eddie Edmunds
Estimated Sales: $.5-1 million
Number Employees: 1-4
Parent Co: Perrier Group of America
Type of Packaging: Private Label

31438 Zerand Corp
15800 W Overland Dr
New Berlin, WI 53151-2882

     262-827-3800
Fax: 262-827-3911 www.zerand.com
Manufacturer and exporter of paper board printing
and packaging machinery
VP: Paul Capper
Director Sales/Marketing/Administration: Bill
Dennis
Estimated Sales: $10-20 Million
Number Employees: 50-99

31439 Zero Manufacturing Inc
500 W 200 N
North Salt Lake, UT 84054-2734

     801-298-5900
Fax: 801-299-7389 800-959-5050
sales@apwi.com www.zerocases.com
Vacuum and thermoformed plastic reusable shipping
containers and closures; also, aluminum and steel
modular electronic cabinets and racks
CEO: Ryan Ramsey
ryan.ramsey@zerocases.com
Estimated Sales: $10-20 Million
Number Employees: 250-499
Parent Co: Zero Corporation

31440 Zero Temp
2510 N Grand Ave # 112
Suite 112
Santa Ana, CA 92705-8753

     714-538-3177
Fax: 714-538-1531 gflassoc@aol.com
     www.zerotempcoldstorage.com
Manufacturer and exporter of turn key refrigerated
warehouses, walk-in freezers, walk-in coolers, con-
trolled environment rooms and clean rooms
Owner: Gary F Lyons
gflassoc@aol.com
CEO: Michael Lyons
CFO: Donna Lyons
R&D: David Pinillos
Operations: Pat McBride
Production: Gary Lyons
Estimated Sales: $6 Million
Number Employees: 10-19
Square Footage: 6000
Parent Co: Garry F Lyons & Associates

31441 Zero-Max Inc
13200 6th Ave N
Minneapolis, MN 55441-5509

     763-546-4300
Fax: 763-546-8260 800-533-1731
     www.zeromax.com
Servoclass couplings, composite disk couplings,
torque limiters
President: Doug Moore
dmoore@zero-max.com
Estimated Sales: $20-50 Million
Number Employees: 50-99

31442 Zeroll Company
PO Box 999
Fort Pierce, FL 34954

     772-461-3811
Fax: 772-461-1061 800-872-5000
sales@zeroll.com www.zeroll.com
Manufacturer and exporter of scoops, dishers and
spades
Plant Manager: Thomas Funka Sr
General Manager/CEO: Lenny Van Valkenburg
Plant Manager: Thomas Funka, Jr.
Estimated Sales: $10 Million
Number Employees: 20-49
Number of Brands: 5
Number of Products: 40
Square Footage: 60000
Type of Packaging: Consumer, Food Service, Pri-
vate Label, Bulk
Brands:
  Nuroll
  Roldip
  Universal
  Zeroll
  Zerolon

31443 Zeroloc
9757 NE Juanita Dr # 119
Kirkland, WA 98034-8966

     425-823-4888
Fax: 425-820-9749 www.zeroloc.com
Insulated panel and door systems
Number Employees: 1-4
Other Locations:
  Zeroloc Manufacturing Plant
  Brantford, ON
  Zeroloc Manufacturing Plant
  Langley, BC

31444 Zesto Food Equipment Manufacturing
6450 Hutchison Street
Montreal, QC H2V 4C8
Canada

     514-278-4621
Fax: 514-278-4622 info@zesto.ca
President: George Moshonas
Number Employees: 20

31445 Zimmer Custom-Made Packaging
1450 E 20th St
Indianapolis, IN 46218

     317-263-3436
Fax: 317-263-3427
A leading supplier in the worldwide flexible packag-
ing industry. ZCMP has focused on frozen novelty,
butter/margarine, candy, confectionary and other
food markets and is currently beginning to supply
die cut cone sleeves and die cutlids.
President: Mark Lastovich
CFO: Chuck Bollard
Quality Assurance Manager: Herbert Henson
VP Marketing/Sales: Mike DoBosh
Contact: Mark Murphy
mmurphy@zcmp.com
VP Operations: David Brown
Estimated Sales: $20-50 Million
Number Employees: 20-49
Square Footage: 60000
Other Locations:
  Zimmer Custom-Made Packaging
  Indianapolis IN

31446 Zimmerman Handling Systems
29555 Stephenson Hwy
Madison Heights, MI 48071-2332

     248-398-6200
Fax: 248-398-1374 800-347-7047
seekinfo@irco.com www.irhoist.com
Manufacturer and exporter of ergonomic lifting sys-
tems
President: Gerard Geraghty
National Accounts Manager: Stephen Klostermeyer
Estimated Sales: $10 Million
Number Employees: 20-49
Parent Co: Ingersol-Rand

31447 Ziniz
3955 E Blue Lick Road
Louisville, KY 40229-6047

     502-955-6573
Fax: 502-955-6960
Manufacturer and exporter of package handling conveyors including chain, gravity belt live roller and
overhead trolley; also, installation available

President: Ronny Grant
Marketing/Sales: Paul McDonald
Estimated Sales: $50-100 Million
Number Employees: 250-499
Square Footage: 50000

31448 Zip-Net Inc
801 William Ln
Reading, PA 19604-1523

610-929-9426
Fax: 610-921-1588 www.zip-net.com
President: Andrew Wicklow
Estimated Sales: $20-50 Million
Number Employees: 50-99

31449 Zip-Pak
1800 W Sycamore Rd
Manteno, IL 60950-9369

815-468-6500
Fax: 815-468-6550 800-488-6973
info@zippak.com www.zippak.com
Reclosable and reusable polyethylene bags with
plastic zippers
Vice President: Dave Atkinson
Finance Executive/Controller: Roger Geckner
Vice President: Dave Atkinson
Boniness Unit Manager: Stephen Schaller
Estimated Sales: $10-20 Million
Number Employees: 250-499
Parent Co: Illinois Tool Works

31450 Zip-Pak
1800 W Sycamore Rd
Manteno, IL 60950-9369

815-468-6500
Fax: 815-468-6550 800-488-6973
info@zippak.com www.zippak.com
Resealable zippered packaging
Vice President: Dave Atkinson
Finance Executive: Roger Geckner
Estimated Sales: $10-20 Million
Number Employees: 250-499

31451 Zip-Pak
1800 W Sycamore Rd
Manteno, IL 60950-9369

815-468-6500
Fax: 815-468-6550 info@zippak.com
www.zippak.com
Recloseable zipper products that can be used for
storing a variety of products within the food indus-
try.
Vice President: Dave Anzini
davea@zippak.com
VP/Investor Relations: John Brooklier
SVP/Chief Financial Officer: Ronald Kropp
Finance Executive: Roger Geckner
VP/Research and Development: Lee Sheridan
Senior Vice President: Allan Sutherland
SVP/General Counsel & Secretary: James Wooten
Senior Vice President Human Resources: Sharon
Brady
Vice President Patents & Technology: Mark Croll
Number Employees: 250-499
Parent Co: Illinois Tool Works
Type of Packaging: Consumer

31452 Zip-Pak
4250 NE Expressway
Atlanta, GA 30340

888-866-8091
Fax: 770-454-7350 800-241-1833
www.zippak.com
Recloseable plastic zipper on the top and short side
of the package in-line with any vertical f/f/s ma-
chine, in-line sealing of webless zipper for
recloseable overwrap operations
Vice President: Howie Johnson
Sales/Marketing Manager: Geoff Griffin
Contact: Buddy Linton
buddyl@zippak.com
Estimated Sales: $5-10 Million
Number Employees: 50-99
Square Footage: 228000

31453 Zipskin
3108 Baker Rd
Dexter, MI 48130-1119

734-426-5559
Fax: 734-426-0899
Sanitary hand coverings

President: Gary Gochanour
Estimated Sales: $1-5,000,000
Number Employees: 1-4
Brands:
    Zipkin

31454 Zitropack Limited
240 S LA Londe Ave
Addison, IL 60101-3307

630-543-1016
Fax: 630-543-7216 info@zitropack.com
Remanufactured and repaired food processing
equipment, fillers, filling equipment and sealers
Vice President: Rafael Ortiz
rafael@zitropack.com
VP: Rafael Ortiz
Number Employees: 20-49

31455 Zmd International
600 W 15th St
Long Beach, CA 90813-1508

562-628-0071
Fax: 562-628-0080 800-222-9674
Temperature controlling and trimming equipment
President: Yosi Cohen
VP Marketing: Jacob Horev
Manager Sales: David Maciel
Estimated Sales: $5-10,000,000
Number Employees: 20-49
Number of Products: 7
Square Footage: 92000

31456 Zoia Banquetier Co
4700 Lorain Ave
Cleveland, OH 44102-3443

216-631-6414
Fax: 216-961-5119
www.artisticmetalspinning.com
Food banquet covers, brushes, dollies and carts; ex-
porter of food banquet covers
Owner: Lorraine Hangauer
artistic1@ameritech.net
Secretary: Donald Hangauer
Estimated Sales: $500,000-$1 Million
Number Employees: 1-4
Square Footage: 50000

31457 Zojirushi America Corporation
1149 W., 190th Street
Suite 1000
Gardena, CA 90248

310-769-1900
Fax: 310-323-5522 800-264-6270
www.zojirushi.com
Zojirushi offers a complete line of quality NSF approved vacuum insulated carafe, serving products
and a wide variety of restaurant equipment including
commerical grade rice cookers and warmers, vacuum insulated carafes, Air Pot®beverage dispensers,
Gravity Pot® beverage dispensers, vacuum insulated
creamers and electric soup warmers.
President: Norio Ichikawa
Contact: Jun Mikuchi
j.mikuchi@zojirushi.com

31458 Zol-Mark Industries
470 Logan Avenue
Winnipeg, NB R3A 0R8
Canada

204-943-7393
Fax: 204-943-9803
Commercial steel furniture including chairs, tables
and bar stools for the hospitality industry
Marketing: Hart Goldman
Sales: Aaron Goldman
Plant Manager: Aaron Goldman
Number Employees: 20-49

31459 Zollman's Dark Canyon Coffee
428 S Main Street
Pendleton, OR 97801-2248

541-276-2242
Fax: 541-276-2242 888-548-8555
Coffee roasting; wholesale/retail
President: Garry Zollman
CEO/Owner: Kathi Zollman
Vice President: Shaina Zollman
Estimated Sales: Under $500,000
Number Employees: 1-4
Type of Packaging: Private Label

Brands:
    Dark Canyon Coffee & Tea
    Leter Buck Coffee Co.

31460 Zumbiel Packaging
2100 Gateway Blvd
Hebron, KY 41048

513-531-3600
Fax: 859-689-0763 sales@zumbiel.com
www.zumbiel.com
Boxes, cartons, beverage carriers, transparent plastic
lids and tubes.
Owner: Thomas Zumbiel
Senior Vice President: Joe Yock
VP, Sales & Marketing: Charles Mace
Vice President, Manufacturing: Mark Barton
mbarton@zumbiel.com
Year Founded: 1843
Estimated Sales: $250-500 Million
Number Employees: 200-499
Square Footage: 500000

31461 Zume
250 Polaris Ave.
Mountain View, CA 94043

zume.com
Offers data analysis services to help businesses man-
age and reduce food waste based on a supply and de-
mand formula.
Chairman & CEO: Alex Garden
COO: Mike McMahon
Year Founded: 2018
Number Employees: 350-500

31462 Zume Manufacturing
250 Polaris Ave.
Mountain View, CA 94043

zume.com
Offers packaging options that are manufactured
from agricultural waste. Packaging is 100%
compostable and provides customizable products.
Chairman & CEO: Alex Garden
EVP, Source Packaging: Annette Groenink
COO: Mike McMahon
Year Founded: 2018
Number Employees: 350-500
Parent Co: Zume

31463 Zumtobel Staff Lighting
3300 US Highway 9w
Highland, NY 12528-2630

845-691-6262
Fax: 973-340-9898 www.zumtobelstaff.com
Manufacturer, importer and exporter of lighting fix-
tures
President: Wolfgang Egger
Sales: Allison Craig
Estimated Sales: $50-100 Million
Number Employees: 5-9

31464 Zurn Industries LLC
1801 Pittsburgh Ave
Erie, PA 16502-1998

814-455-0921
Fax: 814-875-1402 855-663-9876
www.zurn.com
Commercial, institutional and industrial building
products
President: Alex Marini
Vice President: Craig Wehr
Sales/Marketing Manager: Jerry Dill
Number Employees: 1000-4999

31465 iFoodDecisionSciences
P.O. Box 82475
Kenmore, WA 98028-2475

206-219-3703
info@idsfoodsafety.com
www.idsfoodsafety.com
Offers software solutions for the agriculture industry, including growing, harvesting, packing and processing, distribution, and pricing.
CEO: Diane Wetherington
Year Founded: 2013
Number Employees: 25-50

Numeric

101, 24499
10th St. Bakery, 30808
1450 Food Pack Analyzer, 29063
1911 Originals, 27289
2-Flap, 19913
2-In-1 Time-Saver, 29379
2-In-One Deodorizer, 29826
2000 Plus, 21199
2001, 22348
21c, 20121
22 K Gold Finish, 20830
24 Hour Odor Absorber, 29826
2404, 18637
2point, 21657
3-36, 21051
3-Cup Measurer, 19999
3-D Degreaser, 20830
3-Step, 31185
302 Hawk Labelers, 20107
3100 Sample Concentrator, 30132
3m, 18281, 18592, 22208, 23882, 27575
3m Littman, 18003
3vision, 28834
4 Way Step, 28473
409, 20657
450xl, 30854
5-Alive, 20685
574 Portable Oxygen Analyzer, 29063
5th Avenue, 23750
7000 Ht High Temperature Headspace, 30132
7up®, 24802
80wheyusa, 25784
815 Mx, 19910
9000 Series, 23958
9th Wave, 28919

A

A 3000, 30434
A Gage, 19429
A Sign of Good Taste, 18087
A World of Good Fortune, 21059
A&B, 18042
A&W Root Beer®, 24802
A-1, 18058, 24499
A-Frame, 29746
A. Thomas Meats, 22498
A.B. Curry's, 22712
A.L. Cook Technology, 20599
A/F Pot, 30654
A2000, 18893
A30, 25215
Aa Brand®, 28421
Aae Series, 18620
Aaladin, 18244
Aantek, 18066
Aastro, 25020
Ab Sealers, 18877
Abanaki Concentrators, 18251
Abanaki Mighty Minn, 18251
Abanaki Oil Grabber, 18251
Abanaki Petro Extractor, 18251
Abanaki Tote-Its, 18251
Abbe, 25579
Abbey Well, 20685
Abc Carrier, 24226
Abco, 18092, 18262
Abco International, 18261
Abel, 18264
Abell-Howe, 20752
Ablex, 18349
Abm, 18099
Abm's Safemark, 18099
Absorb, 30913
Absorbant Rugs & Pads, 30656
Abundant, 18274
Ac Slit & Trim, 18021
Acca, 20808
Acceleron Advantage, 30427
Accent, 18277
Accents Frp, 25773
Accord® Flavours, 28438
Accorista, 30957
Accu-Clear, 18295
Accu-Flo, 18295
Accu-Poly, 18295
Accu-Spray, 21044
Accu-Therm, 27352
Accucap, 18300
Accucapper, 18300

Accuflow, 28876
Accugard, 27499
Acculobe, 30853
Accupour, 21408
Accurol, 22254
Accuseal, 27499
Accusharp, 22784
Accuslitter, 29588
Accutest, 18054
Accuvac, 18300
Accuvue, 20109
Accuweigh, 31391
Ace, 18003, 18271, 18308, 30193
Ace & Icore, 30935
Ace-Tuf, 23543
Acid Free, 27045
Acme, 31007
Acorto, 18331
Acousticair, 30502
Acr Jr., 18112
Acr Powerwatch, 18112
Acrason, 18336
Acrawatt, 18334
Acri Lok, 18336
Acrison, 18336
Across-The-Line, 22502
Acs Industries, Inc. Scrubble, 18113
Act Ii®, 20821, 20822
Action Ade, 23377
Activate Drinks, 26668
Active Magnetics, 28150
Actron, 18352
Acu-Rite, 20433
Acumedia, 24070
Ad Vantage, 28285
Ad-Lite, 26766
Ad-Touch, 22121
Adagio®, 24802
Adamatic, 27063
Adamation, 18360
Adams McClure®, 22187
Adapta-Flex, 30102
Adapta-Plus, 30102
Adex, 18369
Adi-Anmbr, 18124
Adi-Bvf Digester, 18124
Adi-Hybrid, 18124
Adi-Mbr, 18124
Adi-Sbr, 18124
Adjust-A-Fit, 25094
Admar, 31338
Admatch, 18378
Admiral, 23261, 25893
Admire, 19741
Admixer, 18126
Admore®, 22187
Adnaps, 23160
Adolphus®, 28421
Adr, 22706
Adr®, 24812
Ads Laminaire, 21848
Adsormat, 30633
Advance, 27546, 31188
Advance 2000, 31025
Advance Aroma System, 18197
Advance Tabco, 18395
Advanced, 18411
Advanced Digital System, 31200
Advanced Equipment, 18404
Advanced Polybagger, 18420
Advantage, 18614, 19975
Advantage Rak, 24712
Adventra, 23456
Adver-Tie, 27134
Adverteaser, 25421
Aearo/Peltor, 22208
Aef-1, 31085
Aef-25, 31085
Aef-7, 31085
Aegis, 31185
Aep Institutional Products, 18029
Aero, 21199, 30639
Aero Heat Exchanger, 26630
Aero-Counter, 18515
Aero-Serv, 29055
Aerolator, 18448
Aerolux, 27294
Aeromat, 19677
Aeroscout, 29584
Aerospec, 18441
Aerotec, 19677
Aerowhip™, 19108

Aeroxon, 28571
Aew, 18136
Afc, 22438
Afco, 18553
Afta, 23436
Agricap, 26264
Agricare, 23571
Agrobotic Technology, 25550
Ags 100, 24940
Agtron, 18480
Aie, 21134
Aim, 20561
Aimia Foods, 27797
Air Cush'n, 20651
Air Deck, 21628
Air Flow, 22615, 31142
Air Pro, 18548
Air Repair, 21524
Air Solution, 22015
Air Tech, 21498
Air Therapy, 26055
Air-Lec, 18300
Air-Ply, 18221
Air-Savers, 29826
Air-Scent, 18501, 29826
Air-Trax, 25377
Aire Systems, 30382
Aire-02, 18436
Aire-02 Triton, 18436
Airector, 24519
Airflex, 18548
Airform, 19919
Airlite, 22348
Airmaster, 18512, 24936
Airmatic Lube, 19654
Airomat, 18513
Airport Network Solutions, 23993
Airsan, 18516
Airserv, 24010
Airspeed, 31340
Airswitch, 24010
Airway, 24045
Airx, 20498
Aisle Pro, 19763
Ajax, 20721, 28320
Ajilys®, 18517
Ajipro®-L, 18517
Akra-Pak, 28620
Akro-Bins, 19926
Akro-Mils, 19908, 19927
Akron, 31435
Akron Hawk, 31435
Akron Spartan, 31435
Akta Klor, 30913
Alabama Rag, 26770
Alacreme, 31165
Aladdin Products, 23952
Alan Bradley, 27282
Alar, 18527
Alarmwork Multimedia, 24050
Alaskan® Brewing Company, 26668
Albany, 21199
Albi, 22599
Albin, 24602
Alcan, 26751
Alcatel, 27729
Alco, 28967
Alco Tabs, 18542
Alcohol Prep Pads 100's, 26632
Alcojet, 18542
Alcon Plus, 20625
Alconox, 18542
Aleco, 19908
Alegacy, 18026
Alesco, 24479
Alewel's Country Meats, 18551
Alexander Grappa, 27236
Alexanderwerk, 27362
Alexco, 18554
Alexia®, 20821, 20822
Alfa, 24076, 28832, 30147
Alfa-Kortogleu, 22299
Alfred Bakeware, 30490
Algarve, 20964
Algene, 18560
Alhambra, 27797
Align, 30193
Aline, 18565
Alkaline, 18572
Alkazone, 18572
Alkazone Alkaline Booster Drops, 18572
Alkazone Antioxidant Water Ionizer, 18572

Alkazone Vitamins & Herbs, 18572
Alkota, 18573
All a Cart, 18574
All American, 18578
All Out, 24386
All Packaging Machinery, 18877
All Plastic Belting, 19111
All Sorts, 18585
All Star, 27240
All Ways, 30878
All-Bottle, 19581
Allan, 23750
Allegro, 28493
Allen, 27709
Allen Bradley, 22482
Allen-Bailey™, 22187
Allen-Bradley, 28472
Aller-Snap Protein Residue Test, 23971
Alliance, 18613, 18614, 21218
Alliance®, 31053
Allibert, 28843
Alligator, 22627
Alljuice, 26351
Allstrong, 18642
Alltec, 20752
Allure, 31188
Allvia®, 26785
Allwrite, 30434
Alm, 19908
Almond Breeze, 19742
Almond Joy, 23750
Almond Toppers, 19742
Almondina, 25789
Aloe Jell Water Less, 23532
Aloha, 28342
Alox, 23477
Alpaire, 22899
Alpha, 27711, 31200
Alpha Laval Flo, 19401
Alpha-Media, 22257
Alpine, 19576, 30820
Alpine/Xpd, 26337
Alps Model 7385, 18493
Alps Smart Test Module, 18493
Alps Sx-Flex, 18493
Alps Vision Plus, 18493
Alta Dena, 21421
Alumaworks, 18685
Alumicube, 18788
Alumiflex, 28488
Alumin-Nu, 18687
Alumitec Elite, 30091
Alumtec, 30091
Always, 30193
Always Can, 29697
Always Discreet, 30193
Amana, 18333
Amano Jenbrana, 18691
Amano Ocumare, 18691
Amark/Simionato, 18693
Amazon, 28154
Ambassador, 26187
Ambec 10, 22615
Ambec 10r, 22615
Ambersweet, 29855
Ambi Pur, 30193
Ambrose, 18699
Amcel, 18700
Amco, 18692, 18702
Amcoat, 18702
Amcoll, 18702
Ameri-Kart, 19926
American, 23809
American Beauty™, 28421
American Bulk Conveyors, 27314
American Eagle, 18746
American Extrusion International, 18756
American Greetings, 19611
American Heritage, 18903
American Ingredients, 30618
American Led-Gible, Inc., 18785
American Metal Ware, 23420
American Metalcraft, 18795
American Optical, 23974
American Panel, 18805
American Range, 18814
American Sanders Technology, 20599
American Savory, 18821
American Solving, 18821
American Terrain, 18743
American Time & Signal, 18831
American-Lincoln Technology, 20599

Base Pac, 27679
Base Rate, 25407
Baseball Trivia, 21059
Baselock, 18276
Basis, 18946
Basket Weave, 25665
Baskin-Robbins®, 21805
Bass, 26668
Bassick, 28488
Batch, 19481
Batch Lok, 18336
Batch Pik, 19894
Batch-Con, 22634
Batchmaster, 19482, 19484
Bates, 21113
Batiste Dry Shampoo, 20561
Batter Bites®, 24434
Batter Blends, 26612
Batter Boss, 30376
Bauchant, 27236
Bauer Gear Motor, 18678
Bautam, 28626
Baxter, 24038
Bay Valley Foods, 30400
Bayley Fan, 27412
Bayonne Ham, 29459
Bbf, 31085
Bbq Pellets, 25308
Bbq Sauce, 21336
Bd-Iii, 19798
Bdi, 23850
Bdii, 23850
Bdiii, 23850
Beach Bum Blonde Ale™, 26668
Beam, 19506
Beam-Array, 19429
Beam-Tracker, 19429
Beauty, 23152
Beaverite, 19510
Beck 'n Call, 26433
Beck's, 26668
Beehive, 31087
Beer Clean, 21757
Beermaster, 26379
Beermatic, 19203
Beesweet Blueberries, 28090
Behlen Big Bin, 19527
Beka, 19532
Bel Arbors, 22525
Bel Line, 31164
Belco, 19538
Believe It, 20966
Bell, 20000
Bella, 25725, 27494
Belle, 27711
Bellentani, 24459
Bello Lino®, 23811
Bells, 19837
Belmont Springs, 27797
Belnap, 23160
Belshaw, 25995, 31092
Belt Saver 2000, 18095
Belt-O-Matic, 19339
Belt-Vac, 24550
Beltech, 18873, 18874
Beltrac, 25171
Beltway, 19846
Bematek, 19563
Bemistape, 18705
Bend-A-Lite, 29816
Bendi, 25128
Benecel™, 19108
Benier, 19567, 19568
Bennington, 19574
Bent Arm Ale®, 24434
Bentley, 19575
Berg, 19579, 19581, 28357
Bergenfield Cocoa, 22560
Berger, 29297
Berico Dryers, 19527
Berkel, 24038
Berkeley Farms, 21421
Berkwood Farms, 22498
Berner, 19597
Bernstein's®, 20821, 20822, 27540
Berry Fine Raspberries, 28090
Bertani, 27236
Bertil-Ohlsson, 20868
Bertoli®, 20821, 20822
Bessam-Aire, 19607
Best, 19616
Best & Donovan, 19610

Best Buy, 28015
Best China, 23842
Bestdeck, 19518
Bestpack, 22926
Bestread, 19518
Beta Max, 19501
Beta Series, 27217
Beta-900, 19501
Beta-Kleen, 20966
Betadoor, 19624
Bete Spiral, 19625
Better Health Lab, 18572
Better Pack, 19634
Betterway, 19998
Betterway Pourers, 19999
Bev-Con, 22634
Bev-Flex, 18295
Bev-Seal, 18295
Bevcon, 20904, 29035
Bever Marketeer, 19636
Beverage Air, 29466
Beverageware, 23499
Bevlex, 18295
Bevnaps, 23160
Bfm, 19327
Bfs, 25819
Bhl, 18572
Bi-O-Kleen, 19642
Bi-Tex, 23160
Bi-Therm, 30084
Bibby Turboflex, 18678
Bible Verse, 21059
Bicerba, 30766
Biclops Installation Tool, 28118
Big Banana Perfet, 28090
Big Beam, 19649
Big Ben, 26875
Big Boy Blazin Berries, 28090
Big Chief, 21189
Big Dipper, 30205
Big Flipper, 30205
Big Fork, 22498
Big Green, 21079
Big Inch, 19634
Big Red Rhubarb, 28090
Big Red®, 24802
Bigs®, 20821, 20822
Billow, 23160
Bilsom, 21317
Bilt, 29627
Bilt-Rite, 19659
Biltrite, 26020
Bin 49, 30860
Bin-Dicators, 30799
Bind, 24070
Binks Industries, Inc., 19664
Binsert, 24542
Bio Cleansing Systems, 26097
Bio Free Trap Clear, 24316
Bio Scan, 28731
Bio-Bin® Waste Disposal, 21848
Bio-Pak, 22682
Bio-Zap, 30391
Bioallers®, 26785
Biobed, 19691
Biocount, 24212
Biofree Septic Clear, 24316
Biopac, 19669
Biopath, 28886
Bioprene, 25775
Biopuric, 19691
Bioscan Ii, 20910
Bioslide, 30913
Biosolo, 21363
Biosyn, 29030
Biothane, 19691
Birds Eye C&W, 20821, 20822
Birds Eye Voila, 20821, 20822
Birds Eye®, 20821, 20822, 27540
Biro, 19697
Birthday, 21059
Bishamon, 19698, 19908
Bistro, 20256
Bites, 20541
Bittermyx®, 29018
Bke, 19930
Bki Worldwide, 29580
Black, 19709
Black + Decker, 29584
Black Beauty, 22935
Black Cat, 28292
Black Cherry Royal, 23377

Black Diamond Brewing Company®, 26668
Black Knight, 29167
Black Label Bacon®, 23861
Black Tie Collection, 28934
Blackened Redfish Magic, 25632
Blackened Steak Magic, 25632
Blackline, 29520
Blacknight, 18515
Blackwing, 19716
Blackwing Organics, 19716
Bladerunner, 24700
Blake's®, 20821, 20822
Blakeslee, 19719
Blazer, 25154
Blazers, 31126
Blend Tanks, 20875
Blended Breaders, 26612
Blending Station, 30884
Blimpy, 29816
Blinky, 27579
Blipack, 26427
Blissmaster, 26257
Blizzard Beer Systems, 20633
Blo Apco, 19738
Block Graphics®, 22187
Blodgett, 19733
Blodgett Combi, 19733
Blodis, 19713
Bloomfield Industries, 29466
Blooming Bags, 26199
Blow Out, 23039
Blue Angel, 31059
Blue Bonnet®, 20821, 20822
Blue Buck, 25622
Blue Diamond, 19742
Blue Diamond Almonds, 19742
Blue Diamond Hazelnut, 19742
Blue Diamond Macadamias, 19742
Blue Fish, 27236
Blue Magic, 25470
Blue Poly Trolleys, 22890
Blue Ribbon, 27346, 28517, 29598
Blue Ribbon Classic, 29598
Blue Ribbon Rice®, 28421
Blue Ridge, 24683
Blue Satin, 31010
Blue Too, 19741
Bluebird Products, 19754
Bluefield®, 28946
Bluegiant, 19908
Bluewater Mfg., Inc., 31214
Board-Mate, 24700
Boc Edwards, 27729
Boce Stokes, 27729
Boddingtons Pub Ale, 26668
Bodegas Campillo, 27236
Bodum, 30523
Bodyguard™, 24506
Boelube Aerospace, 26968
Bohn, 23692
Boissiere, 27236
Bola, 22599
Bon Terra, 22525
Bonaqua, 20685
Bonar, 19788
Bondalast, 23543
Bonderite, 23726
Bondstar, 24622
Bonfaire, 18908
Bonn Dye, 19789
Bonn Trace, 19789
Bonnet, 24038
Bonnet Buff, 20966
Boone Maman, 25789
Boost, 24672
Borax-Splash, 28242
Borax-Sudz, 28242
Borden, 24672
Border Springs Farm Lamb, 22498
Borders, 25773
Boreas, 30576
Bosco, 28940
Boss, 29381, 29491
Boss (Boots and Gloves), 19806
Bost-Kleen, 19809
Bostitch, 29584
Boston Beam, 19811
Boston Bumper, 19811
Boston Colorguard, 19811
Boston Gear, 18678, 19809
Boston Shearpump, 18126
Boston Tuffguard, 19811

Bottega Vinaia, 27236
Bottle Air, 25920
Bottle Duster, 25920
Bottle-Buster, 22257
Bottom Line, 20788
Bottomup, 29973
Boulard, 27236
Bounce, 30193
Bountiful Harvest™, 29095
Bounty, 30193
Bovril, 25789
Bowlpack, 27679
Bowtemp, 19821
Box'fin, 20531
Boxer, 30413
Boyd's Coffee, 19825
Boyds' Kissa Bearhugs, 24388
Boyer, 19826
Bpe 2000, 19413
Bpl 10000, 18095
Bpl 12000, 18095
Bpl 24000, 18095
Bpl 6000, 18095
Bpl 8600, 18095
Br-Lerie Mont Royal®, 24802
Br-Lerie St. Denis®, 24802
Bradford Cast Metals, 28809
Bragard, 19839
Brailldots, 28930
Braillplaques, 28930
Brailltac, 21199
Brake, 25633
Bran+Luebbe, 28714
Brandguard, 28461
Brandpac, 19069
Branford, 19844
Brass Master, 19846
Braun, 30193
Bravo, 20256, 23571
Breading Magic, 25632
Breadshop, 25789
Breathsavers, 23750
Breco, 19852
Brecoflex, 19852
Bree, 19636
Breez Proof, 29723
Breeze, 26615
Breidert Air, 28649
Brenton, 19857
Brew Canada, 30860
Brew Rite, 28471
Brew'n'pour Lid, 29055
Brewer's Crystals, 24226
Brewmatic, 19863, 22108
Breyers, 20946
Brianna's, 25789
Brick-Pack Clip, 30337
Brickfire Bakery®, 29095
Brico, 19659
Brigade, 29520
Brigade +, 29520
Brill®, 20096
Brisk®, 27433
Brisker, 19874
Brita, 20657
Brite Bowl, 27045
Brite-Lite, 31217
Britepak, 22548
Britex, 19884
British Class, 30670
Brix, 23391
Brix 15hp, 25231
Brix 30, 25231
Brix 35hp, 25231
Brix 50, 25231
Brix 65hp, 25231
Brix 90, 25231
Brix 90hp, 25231
Bro-Tisserie, 19882
Broadway Menu, 30876
Broaster, 19882
Broaster Chicken, 19882
Broaster Foods, 19882
Broaster Recipe, 19882
Broiler Master, 20258
Brooklace, 19885
Brooklyn, 21199, 21866
Brooks, 19888
Brooks®, 20821, 20822, 27540
Brookshire's®, 19889
Brookside, 23750
Broughton®, 21421

Densart, 30792
Denta Brite, 21952
Depend, 24838
Depotpac, 27679
Derm Ade, 30569
Derma-Pro, 22990
Dermal, 23152
Descender, 28742
Desco, 20530, 21556
Desi Pak, 30633
Desi View, 30633
Desi-Pak, 26401
Design Master, 24628
Design Series Counters, 18304
Designbags, 21564
Designer Displpayer, 20256
Designer System, 29441
Designer's Choice, 18155
Designerware, 30971
Designs By Anthony, 22612
Dessvilie, 25789
Destiny Plastics, 18029
Det-O-Jet, 18542
Det-Tronics, 20290
Detecto, 18327, 21576
Detergent 8, 18542
Dewalt, 29584
Dewater Equipment, 24357
Dewied, 21588
Dexter Russell, 21591
Df 5000, 18095
Dft Series, 21640
Di-Tech, 24870
Diablo, 21593, 25190
Diack, 19042, 30263
Dial Taper, 25788
Dial-A-Fill, 26482
Dialog, 24743
Diamond, 21178, 21600, 21602, 21947, 24517, 30444
Diamond 49 Series, 19032
Diamond 52 Series, 19032
Diamond Brite, 21952
Diamond Clear, 21968
Diamond Grip, 21952
Diamond Wipes, 21608
Dickies, 26875, 30603
Dickinson, 25789
Diedrich Coffee®, 24802
Diet Rite®, 24802
Digestive Care™, 24506
Digi, 20520
Digi-Drive, 24664
Digi-Link, 24743
Digi-Stem, 27240
Digibar, 21713
Digisort, 23921
Digispense 2000, 24042
Digispense 700, 24042
Digispense 800, 24042
Digistrip, 24743
Digital (Appliance) Thermometers, 28020
Digital Dining, 21624
Digital Moisture Balance, 20093
Digital Thermostats, 28020
Digitronic, 29482
Digivolt, 23489
Dilusso Deli Company®, 23861
Dimple Plate, 28588
Dine Aglow, 25190
Dine-A-Wipe, 23160
Dine-A-Wipe Plus, 23160
Dinelle, 29336
Diner Mug, 25665
Dinner Check, 20326
Dinnerware, 23499
Dinty Moore®, 23861
Diosna, 19567, 19568
Dipix Vision Inspection Systems, 21638
Diposables, 27642
Dipwell, 21639
Direct Fire Technical, Inc., 21640
Direct It, 21536
Dirt Eraser, 29489
Dirt Killer, 21642
Dirtex, 28852
Discovery Plastics, 19042
Discovery System, 24265
Dishwasher Glisten, 19837
Disintegrator, 19576
Disney, 20946
Dispax Reactor, 24074

Dispensa-Matic, 30186
Dispense Rite, 21647
Dispense-Rite, 21670
Displawall, 25773
Dispomed, 18369
Dispos-A-Way, 19998
Disposable Products Company, 18029
Disposawrapper, 25531
Dispose a Scrub, 24829
Disposer Saver, 24700
Disposertrol, 27760
Disposo-Treet, 23261
Dispoza-Pak, 28428
Dissolve-A-Way, 21399
Distillata, 21658
Ditrac, 19544
Ditting, 21663
Div-10, 22706
Diversified (Dce), 21665
Dixie, 18592, 21677
Dixie Brand, 27283
Dme, 21668
DoA Mar¡A™, 23861
Do Haccp, 26666
Do Sop, 26666
Do-It, 21689
Do-Sys, 28346
Dock Xpress, 25377
Doctor's, 21059
Doering, 21691
Dogflex, 21763
Dogsters, 20946
Dole Food Products, 20020
Dole Packaged Foods, 30618
Dole® Soft Serve, 24785
Dollarwise, 23809
Dollinger, 28714
Dolly Madison, 28412
Dominion, 26668
Don Enrique, 31350
Don Miguel®, 23861
Doncella Chocolates, 22560
Donut House Collection®, 24802
Door Spy, 26080
Doors, 18793
Doorware, 24734
Dopaco, 18029
Dor-Blend, 21720
Dor-Mixer, 21720
Dor-Opener, 21720
Dorden, 26073
Dorell, 21716
Doritos®, 27433
Dorton, 21720
Dositainer, 18241
Dotmark, 21313
Double Cut System, 19146
Double Density Miniroller, 22615
Double J, 31003
Double Planetary, 20448
Doubletalk, 20593
Doughcart, 27893
Doughpro, 27893
Douglas, 21736
Dove, 20633
Dover Grill Scraper, 31436
Dover Phos Foods, 21740
Dow, 18592
Dowd & Rogers™, 26785
Downy, 30193
Dowsport America, 21747
Dox Expander, 18920
Doyen, 22108
Doyon, 21756
Dp, 20064
Dr. Pepper, 20685
Dr. Pepper®, 24802
Drain Out, 24386
Drain Power, 27045
Drain Warden, 31010
Draino, 21757
Drainthru, 24456
Dratco, 21552
Dre (Direct Reading Echelle Icp), 25215
Dreaco, 21762
Dreft, 30193
Dri-Sheet, 27260
Drink-Master, 24725
Drip Catchers, 19999
Dripcut, 30376
Driver's Seat, The, 31171
Driveroll, 24366

Drize, 23160
Drop-Lok, 29221
Droste, 25789
Drum-Mate, 21776
Drum-Plex, 25224
Drumplex, 25429
Dry-O-Lite, 30752
Drynites, 24838
Ds Special, 20121
Dsi Escort, 25407
Du-Good, 21782
Dual Jet, 23693
Dual-Flex, 28556
Dual-Tex, 19878
Dubl-Fresh, 19371
Dubl-Tough®, 31053
Dubl-View, 19371
Dubl-Wax, 19371
Dublnature, 31053
Dublserve®, 31053
Dublsoft, 31053
Ducane, 18434
Duck® Brand, 29171
Duct Axial, 23643
Duff Norton, 20752
Duke's®, 20821, 20822
Dulux, 26990
Dumor, 20639
Dump Clean, 19212
Dump Trap, 23453
Duncan Hies Wilderness®, 20821, 20822
Duncan Hines Comstock®, 20821, 20822
Duncan Hines®, 20821, 20822, 27540
Dunham-Bush, 28967
Dunhill, 21804
Dunkin' Donuts®, 21805
Dunkmaster, 27520
Dunya Harvest, 29092
Duo Shield®, 21362
Duo-Stress Place Mats, 25447
Duo-Touch, 19429
Duplux, 22039
Dupont, 18592
Dur-A-Edge, 27612
Dura, 21814
Dura Klor, 30913
Dura-Base, 23857
Dura-Drive Plus, 29445
Dura-Glide, 29583
Dura-Kote, 20811
Dura-Lite, 30743
Dura-Max, 18074
Dura-Pak, 18693
Dura-Plate, 23990
Dura-San Belt, 20121
Dura-Tool, 18022
Dura-Ware, 21817
Durabit, 22173
Durabrite, 22272
Duracast, 30289
Duracool, 23608
Duracor, 20359
Duracrafic, 28965
Duraclamp, 23450
Duracor, 20359
Durajet, 19021
Duralast, 23543
Duraliner, 26428
Durallure, 30724
Duralobe, 30853
Duralon, 28357
Duralux, 21566
Duran, 30766
Durascan, 25549
Durasieve, 28251
Durastrap, 21859
Duratech, 30828, 30829
Duratrax, 22510, 30843
Duratuf, 23112
Duraward, 30843
Durelco, 21814
Duro, 18328
Duro Bag, 26756
Durobor, 24636
Durt Howg, 25806
Durt Tracker, 25806
Dus-Trol, 23261
Dust 'n Clean, 23160
Dust Free Form of Fd&C Colors, 28484
Dust Up, 20591, 29517
Dust-Cat, 30626

Dust-Hog, 30626
Dustalarm, 26283
Duster, 25900
Dusterz, 23999
Dustkop, 18147
Dustmaster, 30503
Dustroyer, 30503
Dutch Gold, 25789
Dutchess, 21831
Dutro, 20143, 28488
Dw, 30398
Dyalon, 30255
Dymo, 21201
Dyna-Link, 25940
Dynablast, 21844
Dynac, 23641
Dynaflex, 26049
Dynagro, 25941
Dynahyde, 30914
Dynalyser, 18235
Dynamaster, 18321
Dynapac, 25936
Dynaplas, 26428
Dynarap, 20108
Dynaric, 21859
Dynashear, 18126
Dynastrap, 21859
Dynasty, 24495, 30706
Dynatred, 22480
Dynavac, 25840
Dynavac and Watervac Water Systems, 28360
Dynestene, 18187
Dynoplast, 28750
Dynynstyl, 21864

E

E-Binder, 23659
E-P Plus, 27400
E-Z Access, 25777
E-Z Dip, 21882
E-Z Fit Barbecue, 22996
E-Z Lift, 21885
E-Z Rak-Clip, 27575
E-Z Seal, 19275
E-Z Serve, 31152
E-Z Tec, 22252
E-Z-Rect, 18620
E-Z-V, 30408
E-Zee Wrap, 24567
E.D. Smith, 30400
E.D.G.E., 23832
E2 D2, 18185
Eagle, 19908, 20277, 20639, 20951, 21952, 27391
Eagle Absolute, 21952
Eagle Chair, 21956
Eagle Signal, 28967
Eagle Zephyr, 21199
Eagles-7, 19364
Eagleware, 18026, 18550, 21962, 23616
Earl Grey Superior Mixture, 23295
Earth Balance®, 20821, 20822, 27540
Earth Wise Tree Free®, 23811
Earth Wise®, 23811
Earthstone, 21966
Earthwise Systems, 30382
Ease Out, 22999
Easi-63, 22679
Easimount, 24734, 24735
Easisharp, 29049
East Coast, 21970
Easter, 21059
Easterday, 21974
Eastern, 20646, 21983
Easy Connect, 19419
Easy Earth, 29592
Easy Florals, 23828
Easy Gluer, 21946
Easy Heat, 23828
Easy Hinge, 23860
Easy Paks, 21757
Easy Pour, 19943
Easy Strapper, 21946
Easy Strip, 18387
Easy Sweep, 24829
Easy Swing, 22097
Easy Taper, 21946
Easy Up, 21988
Easy-Lock, 23017
Easy-Rol, 26556
Easybar, 21987

Fastseal, 29081
Fat Mizer, 29795
Faultless, 19908, 20143
Fay-Vo-Rite, 22484
Fc-950, 19213
Fc-Pack, 20710
Fda Steel Container, 20875
Fdc, 20707
Feast of Eden, 20144
Febreeze, 30193
Fec, 19935
Federal Industries, 29580
Feldmeier, 22502
Feline Pine, 20561
Fenton Art Glass, 22512
Fernandes, 20685
Fernqvist Prodigy Max, 22516
Ferrell-Ross, 18035, 22518
Ferrofilt, 23927
Ferroquest, 28731
Ferrosand, 23927
Festival Traus, 20256
Fetzer, 22525
Ffc, 29617
Fiamma, 21213
Fib-R-Dor, 22393
Fiber-Pul, 22535
Fiberbond, 24226
Fibercare 5000, 27982
Fibergrate, 22528
Fiberpoptics, 30259
Fiberpro, 22526
Fibersol 2, 18125
Fibrament Baking Stone, 19265
Fibreen Economy, 22780
Fibregum, 26626
Fibrim, 21785
Fico, 22535
Fiddle Faddle®, 20821, 20822
Fidelio, 26953
Fiebing, 22538
Fiesta, 23842
Filamatic, 26482
Fillit, 22545
Fillkit, 22545
Film-Gard, 20257
Filte-Veyor®, 29854
Filter-Master, 29016
Filter-Max, 31312
Filtration Equipment, 24357
Filtrete, 18003
Filtrine, 22558
Filz-All, 24669
Final, 19544
Final Bite!, 19364
Finalist, 26359
Fine, 21246
Fine Pak, 21228
Fine-Mix Dairy, 20656
Fine-Stik, 26109
Fineline, 26662
Finesse, 19928
Finley, 20685
Finncrisp, 25789
Finney, 21883
Fioriware, 22568
Fire Braised Meats®, 23861
Fireguard, 23116
Firemixer, 28845
Firepower, 30768
Firestone Walker Brewery™, 26668
Firesystem 2000, 27909
Firetest, 25773
Fireye, 20290
Firmenich, 27096
Firmware, 23809
First Choice, 26799
First Line, 20808
First Response, 20561
Firstland, 27236
Fischbein, 22581
Fischbein Bag Closing, 18877
Fisher Scientific, 30217
Fiske, 18411
Fiske Associates, 18411
Fits All, 26109
Fitz-All, 30337
Fitzmill, 22594
Fix Dmacs, 24743
Fix-A-Form, 26324
Fixodent, 30193

Flagmaster, 28416
Flagstone Foods, 30400
Flakice, 22602
Flame Gard, 22604
Flame Gard Iii, 22604
Flameguard, 27329
Flapper, 26264
Flash, 23950, 28952
Flash Link, 21524, 21527
Flashblend, 29239
Flaskscrubber, 25041
Flat Seat, 25819
Flat Top, 23082
Flat Wire, 19111
Flat-Flex, 31278
Flat-Flex El, 31278
Flat-Flex Xt, 31278
Flathead Lake Monster Gourmet Soda, 22028
Flatlite, 21878
Flatout, 25120
Flattop, 22140
Flav-A-Brrew, 30337
Flav-R-Fresh, 23652
Flav-R-Savor, 23652
Flavor, 23188
Flavor Classics, 22612
Flavor Depot, 20269
Flavor King Blue, 20666
Flavor King Red, 20666
Flavor Lock, 26031
Flavor Roux, 20050
Flavor Safari, 22458
Flavor Touch, 22612
Flavor Trim, 22612
Flavor Wear, 22612
Flavor Weave, 22612
Flavour Sensations, 28438
Flaw Finder, 18768
Fleet Mark, 28285
Fleetwood, 24623, 28725
Fleischmann's®, 20821, 20822
Flero Star, 18527
Flex - All, 20256
Flex Bag, 21186
Flex Net, 26440
Flex Off, 29797
Flex-A-Top, 29119
Flex-Feed, 30118
Flex-Flo, 21932
Flex-Grip, 29283
Flex-Holder, 27575
Flex-Hone, 19913
Flex-Packer, 31435
Flex-Turn, 31278
Flexbarrier, 21133
Flexco, 22627
Flexfilm, 29081
Flexform, 28493
Flexi-1850, 22633
Flexi-Cell, 22633
Flexi-Guide, 21857
Flexidoor, 23860
Flexilinear, 22633
Flexiloader, 22633
Flexipan, 21533
Flexitainer, 18241
Flexlink, 19220
Flexodisc, 21092
Flexoleed, 21092
Flexonite, 23543
Flexprint, 19546
Flexrite, 28763
Flexshape, 22621
Flexspout, 28396
Flexsteel Contract, 21561
Flexstrap, 22503
Flexstyle®, 21362
Flexwrap, 31435
Flexx Flow, 25491
Flexzorber, 22624
Fling Decorating Kits, 27285
Flintrol, 22211
Flip & Grip, 23143
Flip-N-Fresh, 23499
Flip-Pod, 20305
Flipper the Robocook, 18288
Flix, 29520
Flo-Cold, 22643
Flo-Fil, 23857
Flo-Gard, 30773
Flo-King, 28396
Flo-Pak, 22845

Flo-Pak Bio 8, 22845
Flo-Rite, 28396
Flo-Thru, 20011
Floclean, 19722
Flodin, 19213
Flofreeze, 22873
Flomatic, 22648, 29042
Floor Level, 26606
Floor Magic, 30639
Floor Suds, 18387
Floorite, 30639
Floorsaver, 24456
Florafree, 21425
Floralpro, 18375
Florentine, 18906
Floria Julep, 24643
Florida's Natural®, 29095
Flosite, 23672
Floturn, 28490
Flow Max, 29618
Flow-Flexer, 22634
Floware, 30232
Flowery Jasmine-Before the Rain, 23295
Flowpak, 28525
Fluff Out, 25725
Fluid, 21908
Fluid Dryer, 26893
Fluidflex, 19654
Fluidized, 27354
Fluidpro, 19262
Fluorodyne, 27224
Fluorophos Test System, 18411
Fluoroshield-Magna, 29046
Flushield™, 24506
Fly Eaters, 19364
Fly Jinx, 20591
Fly Ribbons, 19364
Flystop, 19597
Fmc, 27709
Fme Flakers, 28922
Fmi, 22664
Fnd-30, 18396
Foam Pac, 27679
Foamatic, 24170
Foamglas, 27557
Foaming Coil, 23039
Foamkill, 21123
Focus Plus, 29185
Fogel, 22677, 24623
Fogg-It, 20121
Foiltex, 21564
Fold Flat, 21864
Fold Pak Company, 18029
Folder Express®, 22187
Fomaco, 28291
Fonda, 23809
Fontanini®, 23861
Fontina Cheese, 31165
Food Blends, 26656
Food Care, 23571
Food Carriers, 30207
Food Chute, 19940
Food Club®, 30333
Food Furniture, 28893
Food Grade, 29690
Food Service Management Systems, 20686
Food Source®, 26785
Food System 4 Windows, 30622
Food-Trak, 29953
Foodart By Francesco, 22483
Foodbank, 26662
Foodhandler, 24395
Foodservice Suite, 20028
Footguard, 27329
Foothill Farms®, 24785
For Kid's Only, 21059
Foray, 30516
Forberg Ii, 27354
Ford Logan Wire, 29437
Fordham, 26668
Forest Center, 27510
Forklevator, 23559
Forma, 21213
Formflex, 22766
Formica, 25935
Formnumatic, 28904
Formosa Oolong Champagne of Tea, 23295
Forms Manufacturers™, 22187
Formsprag Clutch, 18678
Formul8, 28800
Formula, 22768

Fornap, 23160
Forster, 24517
Fort Howard, 23160
Forte, 22778, 28493
Forto®, 24802
Fortress Technology, 18291
Foster, 24038, 27063
Foster Farms Always Natural, 22788
Foster Farms Fresh & Natural, 22788
Foster Farms Naturally Seasoned, 22788
Foster Farms Organic, 22788
Foster Farms Saut, Ready, 22788
Foster Farms Simply Raised, 22788
Fosters, 22791
Fountainside, 19791
Four Aces, 29671
Four Seasons, 20186
Fox Barrell Hard Cider®, 26668
Foxjet, 22807
Foxware Dc Label, 21276
Foxware Dc Manager, 21276
Foxware Edi Manager, 21276
Foxware Rf Manager, 21276
Fpc, 27258
Fpec, 22408
Frameworks, 20593
Franklinware, 19928
Franrica, 22833
Frapin, 27236
Fred Silver, 19908
Freedom, 23771
Freelight, 30259
Frees-It, 29081
Freezefridge®, 24434
Freezone, 25041
Freeztand, 30390
Freightainer, 23543
Freightwrap, 25531
French Market, 25789
French Square, 28759
Frenchiec, 29771
Frequent Fryer, 27799
Fresh As a Baby, 29826
Fresh Beans, 30523
Fresh Express, 22858
Fresh Express®, 20541
Fresh Facts, 20593
Fresh Pak, 28957
Fresh Step, 20657
Fresh View, 18908
Fresh'n Up, 28471
Fresh-All, 21325
Fresh-Check, 25298
Fresh-O-Matic, 25320
Fresh-Scan, 25298
Fresher Under Pressure, 22657
Freshmax, 26381
Freshpack Bowls, 28743
Freshpak, 18495
Freshpax, 22873
Freze-Cel, 21695
Frialator, 27556
Frick, 28967
Fridgekare, 24700
Friedr. Dick, 22867
Friendly's®, 21421
Frig-O-Seal, 27602
Frigi-Top, 20982
Frigopak, 22873
Friskem, 22877
Friskem-Af, 22877
Fristam, 22878
Fristch Mills, 23185
Frito Lay, 24672
Frito-Lay®, 27433
Fritos®, 27433
Frogtape®, 29171
Frontera®, 20821, 20822
Frontier Kettle, 30323
Frontrunner, 22473
Frost Flex, 30971
Frostee Snow Cones, 23360
Frostline® Frozen Treats, 24785
Frotious, 27236
Fruehauf, 22894
Frugalume, 30893
Fruit & Nadia, 20685
Fruit a Freeze, 20685
Fruit Corn Appetit, 27669
Fruit Rush™, 21421
Fruit To the World, 28090
Fruitcrown, 22896

Khg-7, 23677
Kia Ora, 20685
Kick-Off, 20593
Kid Cuisine®, 20821, 20822
Kidde, 20290
Kilian, 18678
Kimac, 24869
Kimtech, 24839
Kinetico, 24846
Kinex, 26635
King, 23261
King Cobra®, 26668
King Filters, 24853
King Kan, 20882
King of All, 24860
King of Spice, 29116
King-Gage Systems, 24853
Kings Ford, 20657
Kings Kooker, 26398
Kingsford, 27670
Kingston McKnight, 24864
Kinley, 20685
Kinney, 27729
Kinsley Timing Screw, 24866
Kip®, 29171
Kirin Ichiban, 26668
Kisco, 24869
Kisco Bip, 21082
Kit Kat, 23750
Kitchen Best, 20889
Kitchen Bouquet, 20657
Kitchen Buddy, 24567
Kitchen Craft™, 24434
Kitchen Klenzer, 22593
Kitchen Knight, 27956
Kitchen Pro, 28272
Kitchen Queen, 26805
Kitchen Wise, 31346
Kl Box, 20866
Klampress, 18556
Klean Hand, 30925
Klean Scrub, 30790
Kleen Aire, 20882
Kleen Bebe, 24838
Kleen Mist, 20882
Kleen Mor, 20639
Kleen-Cup, 24700
Kleen-Flo, 20548
Kleen-Pail, 24700
Kleenex, 24838, 24839
Kleenflo, 21617
Kleenguard, 24839
Kleenitol, 31010
Kleenseal, 23450
Kleenzup, 31010
Kleer-Measure, 21932
Klever Kuvers, 24880
Kling, 30878
Klinger, 25029
Klix, 26592
Kloriclean, 25606
Klose, 19314
Kloss, 24889
Klucel™, 19108
Knife & Steel, 20478
Knorr, 21246, 25789
Koak Oddy, 19568
Kobra, 24936
Koch, 24906
Koch Filter, 18497
Koffe King, 19737
Kokanee®, 26668
Kol-Boy Products, 21387
Kolatin, 23203
Kold Locker, 26662
Kold-Hold, 24921
Kollmorgen, 18678
Kolor Cut, 24700
Kolor Fine, 23448
Kolpak®, 31093
Kolpake, 24925
Kompact Kitchen, 29795
Kona Pale Ale, 26668
Kondi-Keeper, 30376
Konkrete, 31252
Konriko, 25789
Kook-E-King, 28374
Kool-Rite, 22248
Kool-Tek, 24700
Koolant Koolers, 24935
Koolgel®, 31107
Koolit, 20707

Kopykake, 24936
Kopyrite, 24936
Korelock, 25773
Korode-Not, 30893
Kotex, 24838
Kover All Dust Cap, 19999
Koziol, 25665
Krackel, 23750
Kraft Heinz®, 29095
Kraftmark, 24267
Kraissl, 24945
Kramer Shear Press, 22729
Kranzle, 21642
Krazy Kloth, 20122
Krazy Koolers, 22917
Krazy Strawston, 22917
Krazy Utensils, 22917
Krispy, 24953
Krispy Kan, 25470
Krispy Kist, 24953
Krispy Kreme®, 24802
Kristalene, 21564
Kroma Jet, 24936
Kroma Kolor, 24936
Krueger, 18497
Krunchie Wedges®, 24434
Krupp (Sig Cantech), 20868
Kryospray, 21126
Krystal, 20685
Kudl-Pak, 25966
Kuli, 20685
Kuner's®, 22464
Kuni-Tec, 18295
Kut-Guard, 19621
Kw-2001, 19213
Kwik Lok, 24704
Kwik Whipper, 20288
Kwik-Flo, 24700
Kwik-Hook, 19082
Kwik-Hub, 19082
Kwik-Koils, 22133
Kwik-Pak, 30405
Kwikprint, 24972
Kydex®, 21848
Kynar®, 21848
Kysor/Warren, 23693

L

L C Germain, 25299
L Gage, 19429
L'Il Critters, 20561
L-Lysine, 18517
L-Threonine, 18517
L-Tryptophan, 18517
L-Valine, 18517
L.I. Industries, 25107
La Choy®, 20821, 20822
La Crosse, 25034
La Fresh, 21608
La Machine, 28272
La Marne Champ, 25789
La Napa, 23518
La Posada, 25789
La Preferida, 25789
La Rinascente Pasta Products, 25039
La Victoria®, 23861
Lab M Media, 25682
Lab Master, 30167
Label Data-Set, 26497
Label Robotix, 25436
Label-Aire, 30992
Label-Lyte, 22358
Labelette, 25059
Labelflex, 27587
Labelgraphics, 29154
Labellett, 30935
Labelmaster, 28952
Labelmaster Applicator, 18269
Labeloff Wine Label Removers, 27422
Labkol, 29669
Labkolax, 29669
Labkolite, 29669
Lablex, 22807
Labmaestro, 25074
Labmaestro Chrom Perfect, 25074
Labmaestro Ensemble, 25074
Laborview, 18354
Labpro Gravimetric, 29499
Labvantage, 25074
Lacey Delite, 20397
Lacprodan®, 19049

Lactalins, 23677
Ladder Crossovers, 25329
Lady Dianne, 26830
Lady Swiss, 23523
Lady's Choice, 20561
Laferia, 28903
Lagacy, 30860
Lake Plains, 30402
Lakeside, 25094
Lakeside's, 31165
Lakewood, 18931
Lamanco, 23677
Lamb Weston®, 25104, 29095
Lamb's Seasoned®, 25104
Lamb's Supreme®, 25104
Lambeth Band, 25108
Lamchem, 19094
Lamiflex Couplings, 18678
Laminations®, 23355
Lamo-Bliss, 26257
Lamo-Tray, 26257
Lamonica, 24998
Lamson, 25119
Lamson Sharp, 25119
Lan Elec, 18169
Lancaster, 23750
Land O Lakes®, 21421
Land O'Lakes™, 24785
Land Shark Lager™, 26668
Landau, 25124
Landscape Series, 22320
Langguth, 27819
Langley, 19908
Langnese, 25789
Langser Camp, 18931
Lanico, 20868
Lanimol, 21425
Lapsang Souchong Smoky #1 Blend, 23295
Larco, 22558
Larkin, 23692
Laser, 19581, 20305
Laser 2000, 20761
Laser Diode, 20305
Laser-Link, 22271
Laserlite Mx, 30843
Laserlite Pro, 30843
Lasernet, 26442
Lashimar, 25091
Lasio, 24274
Last Step, 19364
Lastiglas/Munkadur, 22163
Latini Products, 25017
Laudenberg, 27071
Laughing Man®, 24802
Laundry Detergent Ii, 19197
Laura Secord®, 24802
Laural, 31346
Lavosh Hawaii, 18382
Lawrence, 25177
Lawrence Model 88, 30325
Lay-Mor, 30982
Layco, 31393
Layflat, 25184
Lazy-Man, 25186
Lazzari, 25187
Lcp/Dl, 25788
Lcp/Ml8, 25788
Lcs, 20595
Ld Blous, 30800
Ldbxi, 30800
Le Cavernet, 21125
Le Cellier, 19358
Le Fiell, 25188
Le Gourmates, 26325
Le Grand Cruvinet, 21125
Le Grand Cruvinet Mobile, 21125
Le Grand Cruvinet Premier, 21125
Le Smoker, 25191
Le Sommelier, 21125
Lead Out, 19008
Leader, 23543
Leader/Fox, 25194
Leadout, 29001
Leak-Tec, 18768
Learn Haccp, 26666
Least Cost Formulator, 25198
Leather Care, 19713
Leather Magic, 20966
Lebistro, 29459
Lechler, 25203
Lectro Truck, 24249
Lecturers' Marker, 30878

Leer, 25216
Leeson, 25013
Leffe Blonde, 26668
Legacy, 23499
Legatin, 20561
Legend, 18074, 26290, 27711
Legg's Old Plantation, 18067
Legijet, 31077
Legion-Aire, 25224
Legitronic, 31077
Legrow, 19892
Lehi Roller Mills, 25226
Lehigh, 25227
Lehigh Valley®, 21421
Leica, 25231
Leister Heat Guns, 25236
Leland, 25238
Leland Southwest, 25237
Lemon Glo, 24035
Lemon Kleen 32, 27219
Lemonee-8, 20830
Lender's®, 20821, 20822, 27540
Lenel-S2, 20290
Lenox, 29584
Lepakjr Capsealing System, 25252
Leplus Ultra, 31010
Leter Buck Coffee Co., 31459
Letica, 25260
Letter-Lites, 25091
Level Star Ls Level Sensing Fillers, 23678
Levelair, 21657
Levelart, 30792
Levelhead 2, 24235
Levelmatic, 19166
Leveltronic, 30106
Lewa Ecodos, 18783
Lewa Lab, 18783
Lewa Modular, 18783
Lewa Triplex, 18783
Lewis, 28952
Lewis Iqf, 22873
Lexington, 20256
Lexmark Carpet, 21561
Leybold, 27729
Lfc, 21445
Libbey®, 25281
Libby's®, 20821, 20822
Libertyware, 25289
Libitalia, 22142
Libman, 25290
Lid Placers, 23716
Lid Press, 23716
Lid-Off Pail Opener, 19999
Lidd Off, 19998
Lidpro Lid Dispenser, 30376
Life, 27983
Life Wtr®, 27433
Life®, 27433
Lifemount, 22140
Lifestore, 21951
Lifestyle, 26450
Lifetime, 26302
Lifetree, 29187
Lift, 20685
Lift Products, 18877
Lift-N-Weigh, 27111
Lift-O-Flex, 28508
Lift-Rite, 19908
Liftabout, 29137
Liftiltruk, 28845
Liftronic Balancer, 28694
Light 'n Fluffy®, 28421
Light Forms, 25486
Light Hawk, 30876
Lightening Polishers, 31251
Lighthouse, 25305
Lightjet, 24093
Lightjet Vector, 24093
Lightnin, 19401, 28714
Lightning, 24070
Lightning Wrap, 26680
Lightwaves, 25304
Lil Wunder-Miniature Scrub, 24829
Lil' Devils, 31126
Lil' Orbits, 25309
Lilt, 20685
Lily, 21361
Lime Lite, 31010
Lime-Elim, 31267
Linablue A, 21265
Linbin's, 25337
Linc, 20910

Multipurpose, 22039
Multisac, 31336
Multislicer, 23117
Multispan, 29441
Multispense, 24042
Multitech, 19021
Multivac, 21134
Munchie, 20256
Munchos®, 27433
Muro, 26393
Murphy Oil Soap, 20721
Muscle Milk®, 23861
Mustang, 19798, 26109
Mustang Iv, 19798
Mutual Graphics™, 22187
My-T-Lite, 25224
Myers Ice Co., 26409
Mylanbox Ibc, 26166
Mynap, 23160
Mystik Spices, 30036
Myti Host Chair, 26229
Myti Lite Tables, 26229
Myti Taff Chair, 26229

N

N'Ice Ties, 24700
N.E.M., 26578
N.F. Peeler, 19169
Nair, 20561
Nakand, 30618
Naked®, 27433
Nalley®, 20821, 20822, 27540
Naltex, 26440
Nalu, 20685
Nam Power, 19913
Namco, 26442
Nance's Mustards, 19404
Nantucker Nectars®, 24802
Napkin Deli, 20256
Napoleon, 26450
Nassco, 26506
National, 24851
National Drying Wachinery, 19935
National Importers/Twinnings, 20020
National Imprint Corporation®, 22187
National Labortory Products, 26481
National Poultry Company, 21460
National Tank & Pipe, 24360
Native, 30193
Natrabio®, 26785
Natrasorb, 26381
Natur-Cell®, 28438
Natural Balance®, 26785
Natural Blends®, 28829
Natural Brew, 28471
Natural Choice, 26799
Natural Choice®, 23861
Natural Light®, 26668
Natural Lite, 18843
Natural Pure, 20846
Natural Solutions, 24833
Natural Sport®, 26785
Naturalcare®, 26785
Naturalcrisp®, 24434
Nature Scent, 18501
Nature's Best Liquid Live, 18710
Nature's Candy, 20144
Nature's Choice, 26351
Nature's Herbs®, 26785
Nature's Orange, 20498
Nature's Own, 26520
Naturebind®, 31107
Natureflex, 30528
Naturemost Labs, 26518
Natures Plumber, 27238
Naughty But Nice!, 21059
Nbr 2000, 26796
Nbs Sorter, 22254
Ncc, 18179
Ncco®, 29095
Nci, 19254
Ndex, 29167
Ndex Free, 29167
Ne-On the Wall, 26554
Near East®, 27433
Neat Seat, 28819
Neatgards, 23556
Nebraska Rag, 26770
Negus Octapak, 27504
Negus Square Pak, 27504
Nehi Cola®, 24802

Nelson, 21213
Nem®, 24506
Neo-Image, 26549
Neon Design-A-Sign, 26553
Neon Light Pegs, 26553
Neon Plus E, 29746
Neoneon, 21648
Neonetics, 26554
Neopuntia, 26626
Neosyl, 21094
Nepco, 29223
Nestea, 20685
Nestier, 19926
Nestl, Professional®, 29095
Nestle, 19244
Nestle Ice Cream, 20020
Nestle Nesquick, 26668
Net-All, 30305
Net-Rap, 24135
Net/Mass, 26852
Netpac, 24743
Neuro®, 24802
Neurosome™, 24506
Neutraclean, 20489
Neutrapac, 27679
Nevamar, 25935
Never Scale, 20889
Nevlen, 26564
Nevr-Dull Polish, 23150
New Age, 27881
New Generation, 29055
New Jersey Machine, 26427
New London Eng, 18877
New London Engineering, 25918
New Mexico Rag, 26770
New Mill®, 28421
New York Bakery, 25120
New York Bash, 28940
New York Flatbread, 25789
New York, New York, 30898
New-Glass, 26574
Newly Weds, 26612
Newman, 26614
Newmann's Own Organics®, 24802
Newport Coffee Traders, 22564
Nexcare, 18003
Nexel, 26623
Nexelite, 26623
Nexelon, 26623
Next Day Gourmet, 29810
Next Generation Magic Buss, 29320
Nextwave™, 30438
Nice N Easy, 18687
Nice-N-Clean, 26632
Nifda®, 30595
Nimbus Cs, 26648
Nimbus Fs, 26648
Nimbus N, 26648
Nimbus Sierra, 26648
Nimbus Watermaker, 26648
Nishibe, 27071
Nita Crisp, 26653
Nitri Pro, 29167
Nitro-Flush, 24550
Nitty Gritty, 29167
Nme Nugget, 28922
No Frost, 26630
No Name, 22920
No Pudge, 20946
No Survivor, 24274
No Sweat, 31099
No Yolks®, 28421
No-Drip, 30323
No-Tox, 19535
Nob Nob, 31099
Noble, 31346
Nobles®, 30147
Nonlinear Dynamics, 31041
Nopi, 30166
Nor-Lake, 29580
Norbest, 30775
Nordic, 20685
Nordson, 22482
Nordstrom, 27209
Noresco, 20290
Noritake, 26932
Norman Machinery, 30989
Norman Rockwell, 19611
Nornap Jr., 23160
Norpac, 20020
Norrbox, 26682
Norris, 29233

Norseman, 20682, 26959
Northern Pride, 23522
Northstar®, 22187
Northwest Co, 22920
Noryl®, 21848
Nostimo®, 30333
Not So Sloppy Joe®, 23861
Note Minder, 22320
Nouveau, 30073
Nova, 18512, 21213, 23105, 26745, 29466
Nova Ii, 26662
Novapro®, 31107
Novexx, 18284
Novitool, 22627
Novus Plastic, 26757
Now, 19741
Nr, 27083
Nu-Flex, 23543
Nu-Last, 23543
Nu-Nap, 23160
Nu-Pak Performance F-Series, 25766
Nu-Pak Portion, 25766
Nu-Wipes, 18830
Nuco2, 26764
Nugget®, 30595
Numeri-Tech, 18821
Nuova Simonelli, 26779
Nuparch, 26680
Nuroll, 31442
Nusheen, 30550
Nut Harvest®, 27433
Nut Thins, 19742
Nutec, 26781
Nutra Biogenesis®, 26785
Nutra Coster, 29857
Nutra Naturally Essentials, 18093
Nutri Source, 19361
Nutrifaster N-350, 26787
Nutriform, 26792
Nutrilac®, 19049
Nutrin Corp, 30618
Nutripure, 19152
Nutrisentials™, 24506
Nutrition Service Suite, 20028
Nutritionist Iv, 22577
Nutrivail, 27547
Nutsco, 28337
Nuttall Gear, 18678
Nutty Bavarian, 26796

O

O'Doul's®, 26668
O-Tex, 26993
O.N.E®, 27433
Oak Draw, 26834
Oak Farms Dairy, 21421
Oak Kleen, 26834
Oak Kool, 26834
Oak Kote, 26834
Oak Mor, 23448
Oak Protect, 26834
Oakhill, 29498
Oakmont Labs®, 26785
Oakton, 26841
Oasis, 19669, 20685
Oberdorfer, 19348
Obfs, 25819
Oc Guide Bearing, 18010
Ocean 7, 26968
Ocean Spray, 20685, 22028
Octaview, 21416
Octopus, 29211
Octron, 26990
Oddy, 19567
Odom's Tennessee Pride®, 20821, 20822
Odomaster, 29826
Odorid, 19666
Odormute, 28627
Odyssey, 19570, 22348
Oe200, 25231
Oem Products, 26481
Off the Eaten Path®, 27433
Oh No!, 29826
Ohaus, 18327, 24178, 26862
Ohio, 26867
Ohio Rag, 26770
Ohmega, 19936
Oil Concentrator, 18251
Oil Grabber, 18251
Oil Grabber Multi-Belt, 18251
Oil Miser Oil Recovery Systems, 28360

Oil Rids, 26834
Oil-Dri, 26871
Oilkraft, 30550
Ok, 26801
Oklahoma Rag, 26770
Okzdata, 24911
Olay, 30193
Olcott, 23147
Old Dutch, 22593
Old Fashioned Way®, 24434
Old Hickory, 23763
Old Homestead, 25299
Old Monk, 25789
Old Santa Fe, 23409
Old Smokehouse®, 23861
Old Spice, 30193
Old Tyme, 22900
Olde Farm, 23409
Olde Thompson, 26888
Ole, 22599
Ole Hickory Pits, 26889
Oled Desiccant, 21863
Oleocal, 19094
Olfa, 31345
Olson Conveyors, 24176
Olympia, 28885
Omega, 25628, 26250, 26911
Omega 48 Series, 19032
Omega 52 Series, 19032
Omega Buffet Series, 19032
Omega Complete™, 24506
Omega Protective Systems, 26909
Omega-3 Brain™, 24506
Omega-3 Calm™, 24506
Omega-3 Select™, 24506
Omegalift, 27863
Omni, 20256
Omni Controls, 26915
Omni Grid, 19111
Omni Spaceguard, 19908
Omni Wand, 30843
Omni-Beam, 19429
Omni-Glh, 26918
Omni-Line, 27087
Omni-Macro, 26918
Omni-Metalcraft, 25918
Omni-Mixer, 26918
Omni-Th, 26918
Omni-Uh, 26918
Omniclip Ii, 28148
Omniflex, 19111, 30342
Omnivision 1200, 22366
Omnivision 900, 22366
On Guard, 27424
On-Pak, 20035
Oncore®, 24812
One Drop, 22473
One Row Trac-Pix, 27015
One Spray, 22473
One Step Prep Mix, 29301
One Way Bands, 19146
One-For-All, 31010
One-Up, 28118
One-Wipe, 23436
Oneida, 26932, 26933
Onity, 20290
Opal, 26941
Opco, 26969
Open Pit®, 20821, 20822, 27540
Opmview, 18354
Oprishear, 18126
Optec, 27271
Optex, 26947
Opti Pure, 26952
Optic Florentine, 18906
Optichrome, 25549
Optickles, 22526
Opticlear, 25549
Opticrystal, 24636
Optifeed, 18126
Optigrip, 26176
Optima, 21436
Optimist, 20990
Optimum, 25606
Optiscan, 25549
Optiserv, 31053
Optiserv Accent®, 31053
Optiserv Hybrid®, 31053
Optisource Convertible®, 31053
Optitwist, 30528
Opto Touch, 19429
Optyx®, 24812

Pull-Ups, 24838
Pullman, 18276
Pullman-Holt Gansow, 31177
Pullulan, 24717
Pulsar, 22902, 24093
Pulsarr, 19443
Pulse Point, 30799
Pulse Star, 30843
Pulseprint, 27931
Pulverlaser, 30192
Pumice Jell, 23532
Pumicized Advantage Plus, 21768
Pumpsaver, 22624
Pura, 27079
Pure & Simple, 18843
Pure Assam Irish Breakfast, 23295
Pure Chem, 27058
Pure Harmony®, 30333
Pure Leaf®, 27433
Pure Water, 27937
Pure-Life, 20372
Pure-Pak, 22122
Purecop, 23678
Purefil, 23678
Pureliner, 26408
Purestack, 26408
Purevac, 26408
Purex, 30373
Purifier, 25041
Purifry, 23402
Puritan, 23602, 27945
Puritron, 18832
Purity, 21421, 27949
Purity Pat, 23142
Purity Wrap, 18908
Purogene, 19666
Purswab, 23602
Push-Pac, 20550
Push-Pops, 19056
Pushback, 18394
Pushbak Cart, 22173
Put-Ons U.S.A., 27952
Pw 800, 24312
Pw 850, 24312
Pyrex, 20981, 31344, 31345
Pyrex Plus, 20981
Pyro, 27958
Pyropure, 27352
Pyrorey®, 25281

Q

Q Series Thermal Analysis, 29986
Q-50, 29484
Q-Ber, 25766
Q-Can, 21536
Q-Matic, 27965
Q-Swab Environmental Collection, 23971
Q31, 27980
Q32, 27980
Qa Products, 30618
Qa-Master, 31372
Qbd, 27967
Qc Assistant, 25198
Qc Database Manager, 25198
Qd-Loop Rapid Dilution Devices, 23971
Qda, 30377
Qda Software, 30377
Qic, 23672
Qlam, 28023
Qmi, 27970
Qmi Safe Septum, 27970
Qpet, 28023
Quad-Steer, 27437
Quadnumatic, 28904
Quadra Beam 6600, 30216
Quadro, 27981
Quaker, 24742, 27983
Quaker City, 29722
Quaker®, 27433
Qualheim, 31007
Quality, 23261
Quality Chekd Dairy Products, 27993
Quality Paper Products, 18029
Quantanium, 31184
Quantum, 20244, 22348, 31184
Quarrymaster, 25840
Quartz Collection, 27277
Quartzone, 23698
Quasar, 30515
Quat Clean Sanitizer, 19910
Quat E-2, 26000

Quat F-5, 26000
Queen Anne, 20256
Queen Mary's, 29094
Queen O Mat, 18040
Queens Linen, 30073
Qugg, 25789
Quic-Cheese, 28009
Quic-Flavor, 28009
Quick 'n Easy, 19823
Quick Drop, 25910
Quick Dry Foods, 30618
Quick Shift, 21425
Quick Step...The Produce Manager, 25967
Quick-Fit, 26529
Quick-Key®, 29854
Quick-Step Stair Systems, 26909
Quickcheck, 23489, 29025
Quickchiller, 18677
Quickset®, 23811
Quicksilver, 22320
Quickstop, 18995
Quiet Classic®, 21362
Quiet Thunder, 23222
Quiet' Slide, 20531
Quik, 21199
Quik 'n Crispy, 27972
Quik - Go, 22509
Quik Flo, 24332
Quik Lock Ii, 20986
Quik Lok, 19823
Quik Pik, 31141
Quik-Change, 23261
Quik-Fence, 22684
Quik-Pik, 21047, 30376
Quik-Space, 30341
Quik-Wipes, 18830
Quikmix, 21776
Quikserv, 27974
Quikstik, 27977
Quiktree, 24519
Quikwater, 28039
Quilon Bakeable Paper, 28910
Qwik Pack Systems, 28043
Qwik·Pak, 19823

R

R&M, 26346
R-102, 30516
R-30, 28396
R.W. Zig Zag, 31214
Ra, 30398
Rack & Pour, 27730
Rack & Roll, 20143
Rack-A-Bag, 29266
Rack-Pack, 30228
Rack-The-Knife, 25299
Rackmaster, 30376
Rada, 19059
Radarange, 18333
Radarline, 18333
Radiant Ray, 18020
Radiant Wrap, 21131
Radio Pack, 21977
Raid, 21757
Railex, 28153
Railtite, 23450
Rain Sweet, 28090
Rainbow Agar, 19681
Rainbow Delight, 21782
Rainbow of New Colors, 18271
Rair 2000, 30379
Rair 7000, 30379
Rak Pak, 29050
Ralphs, 28160
Ram Center, 28080
Ram-Jet, 25719
Rama, 23621
Rampro, 25719
Ranch Style Beans®, 20821, 20822
Ranco, 28178
Rancraft, 28178
Randell, 28178
Ranserve, 28178
Ranulio, 31083
Rao's, 25789
Rap-In-Wax, 20628
Rap-Up 90, 20788
Rapi-Kool, 24700
Rapid Assays, 28670
Rapid Brew, 30337
Rapid Fire, 26337

Rapid Flex, 25918
Rapid Freeze, 23893
Rapid Prep, 28670
Rapid Rack, 18990, 24810
Rapid Response, 30790
Rapid Sort, 21536
Rapidvap, 25041
Rapiscan, 24910
Rapistan, 21536
Rapplon, 18873, 18874
Rapptex, 18873, 18874
Rare, 25147
Raskas, 28903
Ratan, 28768
Ratiomatic, 22664
Rational Combi-Steamers, 28198
Ratoface, 30528
Raven, 20065
Ray-O-Matic, 18020
Raycord, 30251
Rcci, 27797
Rcs Air Samplers, 19690
Rdb, 30398
Rdl, 30398
Re-Fresh, 26379
Rea-A-Matic, 23275
React-R-Mill, 30530
Reaction Arm, 27685
Read Woodfiber Laminate, 28209
Ready Cheese, 20397
Ready Leaf, 21421
Ready Made, 24628
Ready Roll®, 21362
Ready-Cut, 28903
Real Bacon Toppings, 23861
Realemon®, 24802
Really Cookin' Chef Gear, 24088
Rebel Green, 28217
Record Haccp, 26666
Recotech, 25597
Red - Go, 22509
Red Cross Nurse, 29782
Red Diamond Coffee & Tea, 28221
Red Dragon™, 24506
Red Goat, 24038
Red Jim, 24403
Red Kap, 26875, 28222
Red Label, 23825
Red Line, 22013
Red Rock Deli®, 27433
Red Rub, 29301
Red X, 27058
Redbridge™, 26668
Redco, 25320
Redcore, 28356
Reddi-Wip®, 20821, 20822
Redeman, 29154
Redhook Esb, 26668
Redi-Call, 28231
Redi-Grill, 27799
Redi-Prime, 20978
Redington, 19985
Redirail, 27979
Redwood Vintners, 28236
Reed, 28239
Reese's, 23750
Refillo, 23434
Reflections, 24044
Reflections®, 30595
Refractance Window, 25559
Refractite, 28251
Refrigerated Entre,S, 23861
Refrigerator Fresh™, 26785
Refrigiwear, 28261
Regal, 20542, 21915, 28265, 28272
Regal™, 21362
Regent, 18413
Regent Sheffield, 31345
Regina, 28276
Regional Delphi, 26615
Rego, 26932, 26933
Reichert, 30775
Reineveld, 21445
Reiter Dairy™, 21421
Rejuv®, 29095
Relax & Sleep™, 24506
Relentless Energy Drink, 20685
Reliance®, 21362
Rema, 26216
Rema Foods Imports®, 29095
Remco, 28303
Remcon, 28304

Remcraft, 28305
Remel, 28306
Remotaire, 30563
Remotecontroller, 20686
Remotemd™, 24812
Remtron, 20348
Rencor, 20975
Renew Life, 20657
Renn, 22939
Reno, 25769
Renold, 28320
Renovator's Supply, 28321
Renwrap, 28317
Repak, 26532
Repellence, 21027
Rephresh, 20561
Replens, 20561
Replikale, 22483
Republic, 19908
Republic High Yield, 28324
Reseal, 28816
Reserve, 22048
Resina, 28331
Resinfab, 30828, 30829
Resinol, 29452
Resistat, 20802
Rest Ez, 28661
Restaurant Basics, 28766
Restaurant Manager, 18227
Restore Pac, 27679
Retail Basics, 28766
Retriever, 31071
Retsch, 23209
Reveal, 31010
Revenge, 28571
Revent, 28346
Revere, 20957, 31345
Revolution®, 31053
Revolver, 23771
Revv®, 24802
Rex, 28099, 28357
Rexcraft, 28355
Rexfit, 30517
Rexford, 28356
Rextape, 30517
Reynolds, 18592
Rheostress Rs1, 23503
Rheostress Rs150, 23503
Rheostress Rs300, 23503
Rheostress Rv1, 23503
Rhino, 28899
Rib Chef, 24948
Rib Tred, 28936
Ribtype, 18276, 30649
Rice a Roni®, 27433
Rice Master, 30364
Rice Road, 27959
Rice Select, 24672
Rice Select®, 28421
Rich's®, 29095
Rid-A-Gum, 24829
Ridge Classic, 30860
Ridge Showcase, 30860
Ridgeland™, 29855
Riebosam, 27835
Rietz, 19576, 23871
Rigid-Flo, 28936
Rigid-Tex, 28400
Rigidized, 28400
Rigirtex0, 22528
Rigitainer, 29192
Rimac, 23305
Rindex 3en1, 30193
Ring Dryer, 21811
Ring Jet, 22615
Ring Lock, 29797
Ringmaster I, 20011
Ringmaster Ii, 20011
Rinse-O-Latic, 30884
Rinsol, 25606
Rio, 28404
Rio Klor, 30913
Rippin Cherries, 28090
Rips Toll, 22756
Riser Rims, 23288
Ristschic, 27729
Ritenap, 23160
River of Cream, 23434
River Rice®, 28421
River Road Vineyards, 30196
River Run, 22458
Riverside, 28415

Riverview Foods Authentic, 28418
Rivet Rak, 30413
Rivetier, 31141
Riviera, 20964, 23349
Rivit Orite, 27405
Rixcaps, 28422
Rmi, 28260
Ro, 20821, 20822, 29221
Roach, 25918
Roach Destroyer, 19364
Roach Prufe, 20956
Road Warrior, 23874
Roar™, 28576
Roastworks®, 24434
Robag, 30020
Robby Vapor Systems, 28432
Robofry, 29561
Robot Coupe, 28456
Robusch, 23032
Robusto, 25530
Roca Beige, 23477
Rocket, 23434
Rocket Man, 28465
Rockwell Automation, 28472
Roe-Lift, 21628
Rofry, 26131
Rogue® Brewery, 26668
Rol-Brush, 26073
Rol-Lift, 25422
Roland®, 29095
Rold Gold®, 27433
Roldip, 31442
Roll Former/Divider, 21701
Roll Models, 23543
Roll Rite Super Caster, 28488
Roll Tax 200, 30957
Roll-A-Bench, 20919
Roll-A-Matic, 29379
Roll-A-Sign, 28240
Roll-Eze, 24059
Roll-N-Stor, 23543
Roll-Rite Corp., 28488
Roll-Tite, 24866
Roll-Up, 22573
Roller Lacer, 20654
Roller-Brake, 24350
Rollerflex, 29796
Rollguard®, 23355
Rolling Rock®, 26668
Rolo, 23750
Roma, 30775
Roma Gold, 28743
Roma Marble, 28743
Roma Silver, 28743
Romanoff, 25789
Romantic, 21059
Romo, 22599
Ronnie's Ocean, 28515
Ronningen-Petter, 21994
Ronzoni™, 28421
Rooto, 28517
Roovers, 21201
Ropak, 24438
Rope, 30800
Ropole, 28118
Rosarita®, 20821, 20822
Rose Cottage, 31165
Rose Forgrove, 24076
Rose's®, 24802
Rosina Food Products, 20020
Roskamp, 20084
Rosport Blue, 20685
Ross, 20448, 26976, 28291
Rosy®, 21460
Rota-Blade, 27354
Rota-Chill, 30563
Rota-Cone, 27354
Rota-Sieve, 27713
Rotaball, 20491
Rotajector, 21091
Rotary, 27980
Rotary Dicer, 23117
Rotary Fill-To-Level Filler, 21033
Rotary Piston Filler, 21033
Rotary Recharger, 27435
Rotisserie Keeper, 22640
Roto Gard, 30325
Roto Jet, 28557
Roto Shaker, 18187
Roto-Bin-Dicator, 30799
Roto-Flex Oven, 28556
Roto-Former, 28804

Roto-Jet, 22662
Roto-Sizer, 22662
Roto-Smoker, 28556
Roto-Stak, 26467
Rotocut, 18878
Rotomixx, 18126
Rotopax, 18637
Rotosolver, 18126
Rotostat, 18126
Rototherm, 19093
Rotulos Ferrer, 22519
Roughneck, 27428
Roun' Top, 20882
Round Nose, 30325
Round the Clock, 29826
Roundup, 18023
Rounthane, 29148
Row L, 28489
Row S, 28489
Rowe, 28565
Rowe Ami, 28565
Rowmark, 21199
Rowoco, 31242
Roxi Rimming Supplies, 19999
Roxi Sugar and Salt Spices/Flavors, 19999
Roxo, 28571
Roy, 24438
Royal, 24226, 27387
Royal Crown Cola®, 24802
Royal Cupe, 28576
Royal Flush, 19741
Royal Icing Decoration, 21439
Royal Land, 28584
Royal Leerdam®, 25281
Royal Mark, 28218
Royal-T, 24226
Royal®, 22187
Royce, 28590
Rse, 22902
Rt, 22480, 23669
Rtr 1000, 20754
Rub a Dubs, 26632
Rubatex, 27655
Rubbermaid, 18592, 28600
Rubbermaid®, 28599
Ruberg, 18241
Rubicon, 30820
Ruby Kist, 29404
Ruff N Tuff, 27881
Ruffies, 20257
Ruffles®, 27433
Rug Aroma, 29826
Rugboss, 31177
Ruler, 24911
Rumba™ Energy Juice, 26668
Rushing Tide, 24409
Russell, 24919
Russell Green River, 21591
Russell International, 21591
Russian Caravan Original China, 23295
Rust Bust'r, 20966
Rust Gun, 22473
Rutherford, 28620

S

S & W Beans®, 22464
S!Mply Baked®, 23811
S&D Coffee & Tea, 27797
S&H Uniforms, 28630
S-Ch, 19798
S-Line, 23266
S.O.S., 20657
S.S., 19401
S.S. Ware, 19401
S/M Flaker, 23117
S8 1p65, 24093
S8 Classic, 24093
S8 Contrast, 24093
S8 Master, 24093
Sa Analytical, 28915
Sa Series, 19625
Sa21, 18243
Sabor Del Campo, 30444
Sabra®, 27433
Sabritones®, 27433
Sabroe, 28967, 31401
Sac Master Bulk Bag Dischargers, 28875
Sadler, 28748
Saeco, 31083
Saeco Housewares, 28749
Saf-T-Cote, 30457

Saf-T-Rail, 30341
Safe Heat, 20187
Safe T Cut, 28752
Safe-Lode, 19051
Safe-Pack, 25265
Safe-T-Seal, 28356
Safe-T-Strip, 21027
Safeglide, 30388
Safeguard, 22320, 24734, 30193
Safehold, 22252
Safeline, 26041
Safemaster, 29706
Safepak, 25005
Saferstep, 28006
Safeseal™, 21362
Safesec, 30325
Safestep, 30486
Safety Pak, 22712
Safetywrap, 24700
Safgard, 28888
Safpowrbar, 29137
Saftex Flame - Retardant Mitts, 20426
Safti Keeper, 22640
Sage, 29968
Sahara Date Company, 28758
Sahara Hot Box, 19569
Sailor Plastics, 28759
Salinas Valley Wax Paper Co., 28768
Salmon Magic, 25632
Salometers, 23391
Salsa Primo, 19106
Salt-Master, 21145
Salvo, 30193
Sam, 27685
Samark, 22018
Samco, 28799, 29094
Sample Trac, 27377
Sampler, 29320
San Fab, 28786
San Giorgio, 28791
San Giorgio®, 28421
Sandcap, 29318
Sandiacre, 24076
Sandler Seating, 28801
Sandpiper, 31013
Sandwhich Bros. of Wisconsin®, 20821,
  20822
Sani - Pail, 20256
Sani Air, 19127
Sani Pac, 27679
Sani-Aire, 29826
Sani-Cloth, 26632
Sani-Flakes, 29826
Sani-Flow, 20522, 24332
Sani-Hands, 26632
Sani-Hanks, 25725
Sani-Link Chain, 22890
Sani-Matic, 28810
Sani-Safe, 21591
Sani-Scent, 29826
Sani-Stack, 26031
Sani-Tech, 19401
Sani-Trolley, 22890
Sani-Wheel, 22890
Sani-Wipe, 26632
Sanifit, 28809
Sanigard, 28816
Saniserv, 28814
Saniset, 19847
Sanitaire, 19152
Sanitary, 27516
Sanitary Split Case Pump, 24042
Sanitech Mark Series Systems, 28817
Sanitron, 19152
Sanogene, 19666
Sanolite, 29862
Sant Andrea, 26933
Sant' Andrea, 26932
Santa Elenita®, 25281
Santa Fe, 25299
Santana, 27236
Santare, 26736
Santitas®, 27433
Sanyu, 20868
Sarcmi, 28832
Sargento, 28829
Sas, 22208
Sas Super 90, 19688
Sat-T-Ice, 24700
Sat-T-Mop, 24700
Sateline, 18931
Satin Doll, 31010

Satin Fan, 31010
Sato, 18284, 28836
Satori Stocktec, 28837
Satoris, 28837
Saturn Series, 18620
Sauce Boss, 30376
Sausalito, 30820
Sauven, 30935
Sava-Klip, 25434
Save - All, 20256
Save-A-Nail, 19998
Save-T, 27875
Savetime, 20910
Savlin, 22258
Savory, 31092
Savorymyx®, 29018
Saxon, 22581
Sayco, 28856
Sayco Tournament, 28856
Sb-3x, 24394
Scalestick, 29397
Scaltrol, 28857
Scan-A-Plate, 19082
Scanmaster, 28834
Scannable Bar Code Hologram, 25591
Scanvision, 24910
Scatter, 29826
Scent Flo, 18501
Scent Sation, 19741
Scent-Flo, 29826
Sceptre, 21425
Schaefer Ms Label, 28865
Schaerer, 28869
Schleicher, 28885
Schmidt, 28893
Schnucks, 28896
Scholar, 20981
Schonwald, 26932, 26933
School Choice, 28903
Schott, 26932
Schott Zwiesel, 26933
Schreiber, 28903
Schreiber®, 29095
Schugi, 19576
Schuss, 20685
Schweppes®, 24802
Schwepps, 20685
Sck, 28668
Scoop Away, 20657
Scoop It, 22712
Scoop-N-Bake, 20096
Scope, 30193
Scorpio, 28919
Scotch, 18003
Scotch Painter's Tape, 18003
Scotch Print, 30512
Scotch-Brite, 18003
Scotslants, 28930
Scotsman, 28922
Scott, 24839
Scott Turbon, 28931
Scott's, 31165
Scott-A.D.A.'s Brailleters, 28930
Scott-Elites, 28930
Scott-Thins, 28930
Scott-Trax, 28930
Scottex, 24838
Scotts, 24672
Scotty Ii, 19798
Scourlite, 19053
Scout 20, 27045
Scrapmaster, 28770
Scratch-Guard, 18548
Screen-Flo, 23857
Screeners, 24357
Screw-Lift, 28936
Screwballs, 28425
Screwloose, 21051
Scrollware, 23499
Scrub 'n Shine, 18387
Scrub Pac, 27679
Scrub-Vactor, 21091
Scrubbe, 29617
Scrubs In-A-Bucket, 24035
Sculptathane, 30914
Sculptured Ice, 29055
Scultahyde, 30914
Sdb, 30398
Sdl, 30398
Sdx, 21495
Sdx Iii, 21495
Sea Bag, 19936

Sea Breeze, 28940
Sea Mist, 25165
Sea Watch International, 20020
Sea-View, 24945
Seabrook®, 28946
Seabulk Powerliner, 27706
Seacure, 27902
Seafood Magic, 25632
Seaglass, 25665
Seagram's, 20685
Seajoy®, 28946
Seal N' Serve, 23379
Seal the Seasons, 28950
Seal Weld, 20750
Seal-Tite, 28953
Seal-Top, 24855
Sealcup, 23142
Sealed Air, 27655
Sealgard, 27499
Sealproof, 29796
Sealstar, 28468
Sealstrip, 28957
Sealtest, 24221
Seasonedcrisp®, 24434
Seasonmaster, 22166
Seattle Series, 30043
Seca-Pax, 30451
Second Nature Plus, 28666
Secret, 30193
Securcode Ii, 20910
Secure Panic Hardware, 28828
Securely Yours, 27260
Securi Seal, 31142
Security, 18622
Security Peg Hook, 30259
Securlume, 25224
Seedpak, 25074
Seepex, 28981
Segal, 30603
Segma-Flo, 26111
Segma-Pure, 26111
Sei, 28672
Select Recipe®, 24434
Select Wax, 23828
Select-A-Horn/Strobe, 18185
Select-A-Strobe, 18185
Selectacom, 30427
Selectech 32 Controls, 30427
Selectrak, 22173
Selectware, 24044
Self Service System, 30376
Selford, 23160
Sell Strip, 22473
Sella & Mosca, 27236
Sellers, 29004
Sello Rojo®, 28421
Semco, 29009
Semiflex, 30732
Senor Paprika®, 31107
Sensamatic, 31340
Sensas, 25147
Sensation, 19741
Sensations, 23809
Sensibly Indulgent™ Cupcakes, 20096
Sensitech, 20290
Sensorvision, 30518
Sentinel, 27655, 29030, 29185
Sentio, 21004
Sentishield, 29030
Sentrex, 29583
Sentrol 3l, 27365
Sentrol Em3, 27365
Sentron, 29032
Sentry, 23911, 28816, 30516
Sentry Ii, 23911, 27352
Sentry Seal, 26969
Sentry/Sentry Plus, 29185
Separators, 24357
Sepr, 23209
Sepro Flow, 19739
Sepro Kleen, 19739
Sepro Pure, 19739
Septic Clean, 19364
Serco, 24607
Sergeant, 19183
Series 9000, 18066
Series S, 26325
Series U, 20047
Series100, 18195
Series4000, 18195
Series6000c, 18195
Sermia, 29047

Serrico, 24274
Sertote, 29050
Serv & Seal, 28957
Serv 'n Express, 25094
Serv 'r Call, 26433
Serv-A-Car, 18419
Serv-Ease, 29299
Servco, 29052
Serve-N-Seal, 21027
Servend, 29042
Servi-Shelf, 20121
Service First, 30382
Service Manufacturing, 29056
Service Solutions Series, 22320
Serving Stone, 23288
Servo Ii, 23669
Servo-Pak, 27565
Servo/Fill, 26852
Servomatic, 31300
Servotronic, 19798
Set Mark, 29072
Set-N-Serve, 19166
Set-O-Swiv, 23261
Setterstix, 29074
Seville, 23842
Sew 400, 18127
Sew 800, 18127
Seydelmann, 28291
Sf-400, 31058
Sg General, 28915
Shade Tree, 29088
Shadow, 18185
Shakers Prepackaged Accessories, 19999
Shal-O-Groove, 29379
Shamrock Farms®, 29095
Shank, 28967
Sharp 'n' Easy, 22784
Sharples, 18557
Sharpshooter, 18221
Shashi, 29116
Shat-R-Shield, 29117
Shaw-Box, 20752
Shear Flow, 26918
Shear Pak, 21069
Shear Sharp, 22784
Sheen Master, 28646
Shelby Williams, 20777
Shelf Clean A-1, 26000
Shelfnet, 21931
Shell Fm Fluids and Greasers, 22231
Shell-Ex, 28834
Shelleyglass, 21498
Shelleymatic, 21498
Shelly Williams Seating, 21561
Shelving By the Inch, 18702
Sherbrooke Oem, 25964
Shercan, 29139
Shields, 26756
Shimmer, 26199
Shimp, 25349
Shine-Off, 18387
Shinglgard, 28448
Shinglwrap, 28448
Shiny Sinks Plus, 19434
Ship 'n Shop, 20192
Ship Wise, 25407
Shire Gate, 22498
Sho-Bowls, 24044
Sho-Me, 27821
Shock Switch, 29158
Shock Top Belgian White™, 26668
Shock Watch, 29158
Shockmaster, 18532
Shoes For Crews, 29159
Shok-Stop, 30228
Shooters Made Easy, 19998
Shop Master, 22920
Short Stop, 23515
Short-Stop, 19082
Shortening Shuttle, 31334
Shotskies Gelatin Mixes, 19999
Shove-It Rods, 25819
Show Patrol, 20498
Show-Off, 30393
Shower Patrol Plus, 20498
Showtime, 31010
Shrimp Magic, 25632
Shrimperfect, 27718
Shrink Bags, 30369
Shrink Bands & Preforms, 30369
Shuckman's Fish Co. & Smokery, Inc., 22498
Shufflo, 19169

Shur Fine®, 30333
Shur-Grip, 26440
Shur-Wipe, 23160
Shurtape® Brand, 29171
Sicli, 20290
Sico, 29178
Side Swipe Spatula, 24700
Sideglow, 29794
Sidewinders™, 24434
Sidney, 29180
Siebler, 22299
Sierra Mist®, 27433
Sierra Nevada®, 26668
Sierra Springs, 27797
Siesta Shade Market Umbrellas, 26404
Sight Line, 22039
Sightech, 28690
Sigma, 20694
Sigma Plates, 18197
Sigmark, 30841
Sigmastar, 18197
Sigmatec, 18197
Sigmatherm, 18197
Signature, 21817, 26450, 27711
Signature Select, 20256
Signature Series, 23482
Signet, 21915
Signette, 27216
Silcard, 29228
Silent Service®, 21362
Siler's, 30444
Silesia, 29219
Silform, 21533
Silhouette, 22272
Silhouette®, 31053
Silpat, 21533
Silver King, 29233, 29234
Silver Mtn Vineyards, 29235
Silver Shield, 20608
Silver Sonic, 23222
Silver Streak, 24635
Silver Sword, 18022
Silver-Grip®, 29854
Silver-Span®, 29854
Silver-Sweet®, 29854
Silver-Weibull, 29238
Silverpak, 18298
Silverson, 29239
Silverstone, 22935
Simarotor, 31113
Similac Toddler's Best, 18257
Simon Fischer, 29340
Simonazzi, 28832
Simor, 22588
Simplate, 24070
Simple Solutions, 19150
Simplex, 19634, 20121, 21541, 26049,
    29251, 29252
Simpli-Clean, 29254
Simpli-Flex, 29254
Simpli-Pak, 29254
Simpli-Pal, 29254
Simpli-Snap, 29254
Simplicity, 31246
Simplot Classic®, 24434
Simplot Daily Pick™, 24434
Simplot Good Grains™, 24434
Simplot Harvest Fresh Avocados™, 24434
Simplot Simple Goodness™, 24434
Simplot Sweets®, 24434
Simplot Thunder Crunch®, 24434
Simplux, 22039
Simply Done™, 30333
Simply Food, 29256
Simply Gold®, 24434
Simply Saline, 20561
Simpson Technology, 20599
Sin Fill, 26074
Sine Pump, 29261
Sinkmaster, 18892
Sintra®, 21848
Sioux, 29263
Sipco Dunking Station, 29266
Siplace, 21536
Sir, 31175
Sir Dust-A-Lot, 25668
Sir Flip Flop, 25479
Sirco, 23357
Sirena, 30462
Sirius Ttr, 21863
Sirnap, 23160
Sister Schubert's, 25120

Sivetz Coffee Essence, 29272
Six Shooter, 26697
Six Star, 20256
Sk 2000, 29623
Sk 2500, 29623
Sk 3000, 29623
Sk 3400, 29623
Sk 3600 Rock, 29623
Sk-Ii, 30193
Skat, 23950
Skcs, 27457
Skee, 22065
Skilcraft, 25305
Skillet Style, 20050
Skin Armor, 21768
Skincredibles®, 24434
Skinner's, 19178
Skinner®, 28421
Skippy®, 23861
Skirt Tie, 27134
Skor, 23750
Sky Master, 18321
Skye, 26235
Skylume, 25224
Sl Laboratory, 28915
Sl Nt, 29030
Sl Test, 20454
Sleep'n Bag, 20256
Slide-Rite, 21027
Slim Jim®, 20821, 20822
Slim Line Cubers, 28922
Slimdown®, 24506
Slimline, 22074
Slimmilk, 25784
Slimmilk Lf, 25784
Slip, 20192
Slip-Torque, 29175
Slip-Trak, 29175
Slipnot, 29283
Slipstick, 30452
Smallpics, 29857
Smart, 23866
Smart 300, 18221
Smart Balance®, 20821, 20822, 27540
Smart Chart, 21582
Smart Choice, 30775
Smart Cup, 29068
Smart Factory, 26818
Smart Flow Meter, 24664
Smart Force Transducer, 24664
Smart Frame, 22121
Smart Hands, 26122
Smart Hood, 25008
Smart Ii, 26262
Smart Lock, 25910
Smart Safe 2000, 25910
Smart Scaling, 19139
Smart Seal, 29068
Smart Shaker®, 24812
Smart Single, 26031
Smart System 5, 20048
Smart Track, 26031
Smart Wall, 26031
Smart-Ro, 31031
Smart® Flavours, 28438
Smartbasket, 31177
Smartblade, 23267
Smartbox, 28118
Smarteye, 30422
Smartfood®, 27433
Smartreader, 18112
Smartreader Plus, 18112
Smartscan, 18995
Smartvision, 18112
Smartware, 23809
Smc, 29180
Smetco, 29289
Smith & Wesson, 24839
Smith Berger, 29297
Smithfield Farmland®, 29095
Smog-Hog, 30626
Smoke Right, 29302
Smoke-Master, 24414
Smokeeter, 30626
Smokehouse, 19742
Smokemaster, 18496
Smoking Gun, 22473
Snack Bites™, 28829
Snack Rite, 20238
Snack Zone, 23600
Snack-Mate, 19882
Snake Shelving, 25023

Snap, 24070
Snap Drape, 19354
Snap'n Clip, 27575
Snap'n Stack, 29318
Snap-Ins, 28930
Snap-Lock, 26442
Snap-N-Serve, 29318
Snapoff, 20882
Snapple, 20946
Snapple®, 24802
Snappy, 18387
Snapshot Universal Atp Sample Test, 23971
Snapware, 29318
Sneezeguard, 29320
Sniff-O-Miser, 23900
Sno Van, 23515
Sno-White, 23261
Snobanc, 30390
Snoee, 24499
Snopan, 30390
Snow Ball Ice Shavers, 20607
Snow Proof, 22538
Snowberry, 30193
Snowlily, 25725
Snuggler, 29083
Snugglers, 24838
Snyder®, 27540
So-Dri, 23160
So-Fresh, 29826
Soap-N-Scrub, 26116
Sobe®, 27433
Sobo, 27157
Sodia Lite, 19008
Sof-Ette, 28422
Sof-Knit, 23160
Sof-Pac, 20651
Sof-Pak, 24021
Sof-Tac, 21440
Sofgrip, 21591
Soft 'n Fresh, 23160
Soft 'n Gentle, 23160
Soft Cookies, 23825
Soft Flight, 29513
Soft Light, 20187
Soft N Clean, 19008
Soft Touch, 21952
Soft-Sensor, 28361
Soft-Serve Ice Cream, 22892
Softasilk, 31010
Softform, 29660
Softliner, 26440
Softread, 20120
Softseal, 27499
Softsoap, 20721
Softstream, 28361
Softtouch, 29783
Softweve McKnit, 25906
Sofwite, 27058
Sogevac, 26858
Soil Sorb, 23261
Sokoff, 20427
Sol-Zol, 21080
Solae, 21785
Solar Infrared Heater, 20330
Solar System, 20498
Solaray®, 26785
Solerac, 29459
Solfresco, 30444
Solid Elastomer, 21352
Solid Flow Vibratory Feeders, 28875
Solidome, 28251
Solidsflow, 28876
Solo, 18592, 29340
Solo®, 21362
Solomon Glatt Kosher, 19716
Soloserve®, 21362
Soluflex, 21763
Solutions For a Cleaner World, 30200
Solvaseal, 23529
Solvex Expander, 18920
Solving, 18821
Solvit, 29348
Solvo-Miser, 23900
Somacount, 19575
Somat, 24038
Somat Classic, 20984
Somat Evergreen, 20984
Somerset, 29352
Somethin' Special, 29101
Sonargage, 21103
Sonarswitch, 21103
Sonic Eye, 21004

Sonisift, 18187
Sonitrol, 29584
Sonocell, 30800
Sonolator, 29360
Sonoma Syrups, 29468
Sony Chemicals, 30186
Soot-A-Matic, 23275
Soot-Vac, 23275
Sootmaster, 25840
Sopakco, 24672
Sophia, 29372
Sorb Pak, 30633
Sorb-It, 26401, 30633
Sorbeteer, 22892
Sorbicap, 26381
Sort Director, 21536
Sortex, 29377
Sos, 23998
Souper 1 Step, 24948
South Bend, 26131
South Valley Manufacturing, 29393
Southbend, 26132, 26476, 29395
Southern Pride, 29418
Southern Sweetenerc, 25922
Southwest, 25299
Soy Products, 20656
Soyfine, 20656
Soymilk, 20656
Soypura®, 31107
Sp Precision, 28915
Sp-250 Flattener, 23117
Sp68, 31372
Spa, 27690
Space Case, 25966
Space Guard 2000, 29437
Space Savers, 22080
Space'saver, 29044
Space-Saver, 23884
Space-Trac, 26623
Spacemaster, 29706
Spacerak, 22283
Spacesaver, 20593, 29625
Spam®, 23861
Spann Signs, 29443
Spantrack, 30589
Sparklaid, 29444
Sparkle, 18024, 19995
Sparkle 'n' Glo, 31010
Sparkle-Lite, 19153
Sparkleen 310, 20489
Sparkler, 29444
Sparkletts, 27797
Sparta, 19401, 20256
Spartan, 30790
Spatter-Cote, 21080
Spec-Bar, 29467
Spec-Flex, 29467
Spec-Plus, 29467
Spec-Up, 29467
Spec-Vac, 29467
Spec-Zip, 29467
Special Service Partners™, 22187
Specialized Printed Forms®, 22187
Specialty Composites Ear, 27655
Speco, 19563, 21883
Specon, 22445
Spectrum, 20256, 20642, 26749
Spee-Dee, 29482
Speed Cover, 23770
Speed Energy Drink, 26668
Speed Squeegy, 26196
Speed Sweep, 26196
Speed Trek, 30503
Speed-Flow, 19659
Speed-Lift, 20121
Speed-Rak, 28231
Speedmaster, 22322, 25013
Speedry, 24059
Speedwall, 24021
Speedy Bag Packager, 18583
Speedy Mop, 26196
Sphere, 24409
Spice Hunter, 25789
Spice Island, 25789
Spice Traderc, 25922
Spin-Pik, 27520
Spinbar, 19534
Spinbrush, 20561
Spinnin' Spits, 24414
Spir-It, 29498
Spira/Flo, 21526
Spiraflow, 21044

Spiral Flow, 18527
Spiral Grip, 29211
Spiral-Flo™, 24812
Spiralfeeder, 19212
Spiro-Freeze, 23075
Spiromatic, 19567
Splash, 24409
Splitshot, 24064
Spm-45, 29352
Sponge 'n Brush, 30481
Spontex, 29509
Spookyware, 22917
Sporian, 28967
Sport Kote, 22272
Sport Mate, 29689
Sport Stick, 19716
Sports Cap, 21069
Sports Trivia, 21059
Sportsmate, 24091
Spotcheck Hygiene Surface Test, 23971
Spotcheck Plus Hygiene Surface Test, 23971
Spotir, 27325
Spotlight, 19910
Spoto, 29569
Spraco, 25203
Spray Ball, 20491
Spray Master Technologies, 19119
Spray-Kill With Nylar, 19364
Spraygum, 26626
Spraymaster, 25798
Spraymatic, 26411
Spraymist, 30315
Sprayway, 29517
Spread, 23160
Spredlite, 22039
Spring Drops®, 26785
Springrip, 27575
Sprint, 26942
Sprinter, 29527
Sprite, 20685
Sprouts, 29528
Sps, 22873
Sps 3000, 28683
Spudsters®, 24434
Spun Head, 25819
Spunbond®, 23811
Square D, 28894
Squeezebox, 23273
Squirrel, 29535
Squirt, 18835
Squirt®, 24802
Sqvalene, 21265
Sqwincher®, 24785
Sqyer, 31010
Sro Feeder, 29763
Ssal, 21817
Ssal 2000, 20256
Ssi Robotics, 27083
Sst, 25725
Ssw, 30398
St. Dalfour, 25789
St. Morirz, 20964
Sta Series, 28992
Sta-Dri, 18130
Sta-Flat, 23261
Sta-Fresh, 29826, 31433
Sta-Hot, 22712
Sta-Pack, 28992
Sta-Plyer, 25762
Sta-Rite, 29545
Stabak, 26504
Stablebond, 24226
Stack-N-Roll, 23543
Stack-Sack, 29545
Stackable, 20256
Stackables, 18906
Stackers, 29289
Stacol, 26504
Stacy's Pita Chips®, 27433
Stage Coach Sauces, 29551
Stagg Chili®, 23861
Staging Director, 21536
Stahl Cranesystems, 20752
Stain Devils, 21509
Stain Gun, 22473
Stain Stop, 21509
Stain Wizard, 21509
Stain Wizard Wipes, 21509
Stainless, 18594
Stainless One, 29558
Stainless Steel Bearings, 22890
Stainless Steel Trolleys, 22890

Stainless Steel X-Chain, 22890
Stakker, 23734
Stallion, 24575
Stampede, 29568
Stan-Pak, 24723
Stan-Ray, 29583
Stancase, 29572
Standard, 29572
Standard Coffee, 27797
Standard Econocut Die Cutters, 29574
Standard Excalibur Die Cutters, 29574
Standard Folder Gluers, 29574
Standard Knapp, 30935
Standard Systems, 30109
Standard-Keil, 20800
Stanislaus Food Products, 20020
Stanley, 28649, 29584
Staplex, 29588
Star, 19803, 25216, 28471, 29592
Star Award Ribbon Co.®, 22187
Star Brite, 26165
Star Controls, 23952
Star Dairy, 31165
Star Guard, 31010
Star Hydrodyne, 29594
Star Pager, 25421
Star Plus, 20256
Star Systems, 20048
Star Track, 29866
Starborne, 23261
Starbucks Frappacino®, 27433
Starkey, 29604
Starline, 20633
Starlite, 23515
Starmax, 29596
Starmist, 30515
Starr, 19902
Starr Hill Amber Ale, 26668
Starrett, 25216
Stars, 18849
Startex, 30517
Startwist, 30528
Starvac, 30517
Starvac Ii, 30517
Starvac Iii, 30517
Starview, 29607
Static Mixers, 24696
Staylock®, 21362
Staynap, 23160
Stb Stahlhammer Bommern, 20752
Std Precision Gear & Instrument, 28726
Steady-Mount, 30854
Steak Sauce, 21336
Steakmarkers, 19999
Stealth Fries®, 25104
Steam 'n' Hold, 18288
Steam Pac, 27679
Steam-Flo, 29263
Steamcraft, 20642
Steamflo, 21617
Steamix, 19059
Steamscrubber, 25041
Stearns, 26864, 28357, 29616, 29617
Stearns-Roger, 28206
Steclite, 20256
Sted Stock Ii, 20256
Steel It, 29562
Steel It Lite, 29562
Steelcraft, 21035
Steeline, 20882
Steeltest, 23543
Steeltite, 23450
Steeltree, 24519
Steeluminum, 20256
Steempan, 30390
Steer Clear, 27346
Steffens, 21883
Stein/Checker, 20474
Steinco Casters, 24564
Stella, 21213
Stella Artois, 26668
Steller Steam, 24065
Stephan, 29642
Steri-Flo, 22558
Sterigenics, 23988, 29645
Sterileware, 19534
Sterilin, 21848
Sterilobe, 30853
Sterisafe, 28731
Sterling, 18614, 23841, 29657, 31346
Sterling Eliminator, 29657
Sterno, 24848

Stero, 24038, 27063, 29662
Stewart Sutherland, 18029
Stewart's®, 24802
Stick 'n Stay, 23784
Stieber, 18678
Stiffel, 25658
Stillpax, 18637
Stirator, 21269
Stock, 28837
Stock Coster, 29857
Stockmaster, 20923
Stockpop, 30259
Stone Burr Mills, 25938
Stone Glo, 30508
Stone-Cutter, 30676
Stor-Frame, 29694
Stor-It, 30413
Storage Rack-Steel-Clad, 30655
Storage Wall, 25353
Store'n Pour, 20256
Storeworks, 25565
Storgard, 24274
Storm Trac, 28261
Stouffers, 19244
Stow Away, 23499
Stowaway, 25034
Strahman, 19401
Straight Up Tea®, 24802
Strainomatic, 23672
Strapping, 20250
Strapslicer System, 18301
Strata, 23936
Stratagraph®, 23355
Straw Boss, 30376
Streamlight, 26457
Stressease™, 24506
Stresstech, 18235
Stretch Frame, 20625
Stretch-Tite, 31336
Stretch-Vent, 29727
Stretchframe, 29746
Stricklin, 29731
Strico, 29731
Strip Pac, 27679
Stripir, 27325
Striplok, 24704
Stromag, 18678
Strong Bow, 31142
Strong Scott, 19576
Strong-Scott, 23871
Structolene, 20882
Strypel, 27431
Stuart, 21848
Stubborn Soda®, 27433
Stubby Clear-Vue, 26323
Stubby Less Crush, 26323
Studio Colors, 23160
Sturdi-Frame, 30413
Sturdystyle™, 23811
Stylene, 23160
Stylus, 24277
Styprint, 27431
Styrocups, 31246
Stysorb, 27431
Sublime, 25147
Success®, 28421
Suds - Pail, 20256
Sugar Creek, 29755
Sugar Foods Corporation®, 29095
Sugar Free Cookies, 23825
Sugar Plum, 25299
Sugar Twin®, 24785
Sugardale, 22859
Sullair, 28967
Summa-6, 28834
Summerripe, 22458
Summit, 22504, 29761
Summit Lectern, 26229
Sump-Vac, 29489
Sun Bright, 29101
Sun Chips®, 27433
Sun Drop®, 24802
Sun Oil, 28462
Sun Valley, 29056
Sun-Glo, 30508
Sunbeam, 27991
Sunbestc, 29771
Sunbrand, 25789
Sunburst, 27982
Suncoc, 29771
Sunflower, 28808, 29528
Sunglo, 18434, 23360

Sunkist®, 24802
Sunlite, 23958
Sunmalt, 24717
Sunny Fresh™, 20246
Sunny Green®, 26785
Sunnyd®, 24802
Sunpak, 18434
Sunripe, 21447, 27283
Sunrise, 25725
Sunvista®, 22464
Sup-Ex, 25008
Super, 21051, 29790
Super Adjustable, 24304
Super Adjustable Super Erecta, 26031
Super Bar, 22780
Super Carrot Cutter, 19169
Super Cart, 26681
Super Chef, 18811, 22996, 29795
Super Cutter, 19169
Super Drive Sifter, 26736
Super Erecta, 24304, 26031
Super G, 25865
Super H, 19798
Super Hook, 19082
Super Hot, 18620
Super Iron Out, 24386
Super Iron Out Dignio, 24386
Super Key, 29604
Super Links, 19763
Super Marker, 26109
Super Moderna, 24628
Super Mustang, 19798
Super Pack-Man, 23013
Super Pan Ii, 30898
Super Pik, 19894
Super Power, 20122
Super Sack, 19307
Super Scald, 19894
Super Separator, 30854
Super Sheath, 20365
Super Slicer, 19999
Super Strip, 21080
Super Systems, 27554
Super-Flex, 23543
Super-Flo, 28936
Super-Stamp, 29394
Super-Trete, 21080
Super-Trol, 19898
Superbag, 20886
Superbag Jr., 20886
Superbase, 22272
Superbridge, 25571
Superceptor, 30205
Superchanger, 30390
Superflex, 29796
Superfly, 26337
Superformer, 18095
Supergard, 30957
Supergotcha, 28118
Supergrain, 27387
Superguard, 18622
Superior Monogram, 29810
Superior Rex, 18497
Superior Systems, 23216
Superior's Brand, 22859
Superlast, 23543
Superlevel, 24490, 30043
Supermix, 18181
Superportable, 20550
Supershield, 18185
Superskids, 31031
Supersnap High Sensitivity Atp Test, 23971
Supersorb, 22554
Superstar Strawberry, 23377
Supertaut Plus Ii, 29853
Supertilt, 18181
Supertower, 20550
Supervision, 29794
Superwear, 27982
Superwheel, 24940
Supr Swivel, 21717
Supr-Safe (Gas), 21717
Supra, 20290
Supraplus, 29001
Suprega, 21425
Supreme, 20256, 20666, 24599, 27412, 28992, 29825
Sur Sweet™, 29855
Surco, 29826
Surcota, 29826
Surcotta, 18501
Sure Chef, 23729

Sure Chef Climaplus Combi, 23729
Sure Gard, 31099
Sure Sak, 20257
Sure Shot, 27730
Sure Way, 28734
Sure-Bake, 21227
Sure-Bake & Glaze, 21227
Sure-Grip, 29254
Sure-Kol, 29829
Sure-Stik, 23131
Surebean, 30299
Surebond, 24226
Suredrain, 23850
Sureseal, 27499
Sureshot, 18101
Surety Pwd Hand Soap, 23532
Surface Systems, 25773
Surge, 22966, 23080
Susan Winget, 24388
Suspentec, 21031
Sussman, 29839
Sustamid, 28478
Sustarin, 28478
Sustatec, 28478
Svendborg Brakes, 18678
Svk, 28435
Swab 'n' Smile, 31010
Sweeping Beauty, 25668
Sweet 2 Eat, 27785
Sweet Moose™, 26785
Sweet P'S®, 30333
Sweet Things®, 25104
Sweetfree Magic, 25632
Sweetheart Fudge, 31399
Sweetmyx®, 29018
Swiffer, 30193
Swift Set Folding Chairs, 26229
Swift Tooth Bands, 19146
Swifty, 19823
Swing Arm Diverter, 22254
Swing Top, 20882
Swing-A-Way, 29859
Swingster, 18778
Swirl, 23499
Swirl Freeze, 29860
Swiss Air, 29632, 29633
Swiss Colony Foods, 20733
Swiss Premium®, 21421
Swissh, 29863
Swivelier, 29866
Sword, 18022
Sycoid, 30920
Symart Systems, 29720
Symbol, 22769
Symbol Jet, 25788
Symetix®, 24812
Symmetrix Frp, 25773
Symphony, 20256, 21817, 23750
Symtec, 23611
Synchromat, 26482
Syncrospense, 24042
Synergy, 23771
Synergy Laser Power, 28915
Syr, 28920
Syracuse, 19354, 25282
Syracuse China®, 25281
Syrelec, 21099
Sys-Clean, 30848
Syspro, 28739
System 7, 27400
System Iv, 29960
System Master, 22807
System Sensor, 23235
Systemaker, 24213
Systemsure Plus Atp Hygiene, 23971

T

T&S Brass and Bronze, 29968
T-Line, 23753
T-Rex, 30376
T-Rex®, 29171
T.G. Lee, 21421
Ta Instruments, 31041
Ta-3, 19262
Ta-Xt2, 30184
Tab X-Tra, 20685
Tabbee, 28930
Tabie Lamps & Stereo Brand, 29661
Table De France, 21497
Table Lev'lr, 19998

Table Line, 27980
Table Mate, 29723
Table Talk, 30041
Table Top, 25766
Table Turner, 26433
Tablecheck, 30042
Tablecraft, 30043
Tablet Press 328, 21282
Tabletote, 28115
Tableware Retrievers, 24700
Tabster, 29588
Tackmaster, 25762
Tad, 19698
Tahitian Treat®, 24802
Tak-A-Number, 23239
Tak-Les, 28081
Take 10, 18702
Take 5, 23750
Take a Number, 22271
Take-1, 27575
Tally Printer Corporation, 30051
Tamp-R-Saf, 24855
Tampax, 30193
Tampco, 31435
Tangle-Trap, 20877
Tanglefoot, 20877
Tango Shatterproof, 30062
Tank Cleaning Systems, 25203
Tank Master, 19152
Tann-X, 20966
Tanners Select, 18328
Tap 1, 19581
Tape Culator, 19634
Tape Shooter, 19634
Tape Squirt, 19634
Taperhex Gold, 24366
Taski, 18281
Tasque, 27470
Tasselli, 27063
Taste It, 30775
Taste Master, 22558
Taste Waves™, 26785
Tasty Bakery, 19889
Tat, 30979
Tate & Lyle, 20020
Tate Western, 30080
Tater Pals®, 24434
Taurus, 27685
Tavern Traditions®, 25104
Taylor, 30084
Taylor Company, 29466
Tb Wood's, 18678
Tdc, 30451
Tde Dispensers, 28922
Te-Flex, 22624
Tea-Master, 24725
Teachers, 21059
Teake Furniture, 26404
Tec Frames, 30091
Tec Line, 30118
Tec-Loc, 26264
Tech, 18671
Techni-Brew, 19825
Technichem, 30100
Technicote, 23882
Techniseal, 27294
Technium, 30110
Technomachine, 22142
Technomelt, 23726
Tecneon, 30091
Tectwo, 30091
Tecumseh, 24919, 28967, 30117
Tecweigh, 30118
Teddy Bear, 28743
Tefbake, 30046
Teflon, 29046
Teg-U-Lume, 25224
Tegra®, 24812
Tel-Tru, 30126
Telemechanique, 28894
Telescoper, 19919
Telescopic, 28010
Tellem, 22877
Tellerette, 20359
Temp Care, 23571
Temp Check, 23571
Temp Dot, 21524
Temp Guard, 23868
Temp Plate, 27352
Temp-Lock, 20121
Temp-Lock Ii, 20121
Temp-Plate, 27240

Screen Print Etc, 28935
Sea Gull Lighting Products, LLC, 28941
Seal Science Inc, 28949
SeamTech, 28958
Search West, 28959
Season Harvest Foods, 28960
Seco Industries, 28973, 28974
Seeds of Change, 28980
Sekisui TA Industries, 28992
Selco Products Company, 28995
Select Appliance Sales, Inc., 28996
Seltzer Chemicals, 29007
Senomyx Inc, 29018
Sensor Systems, 29026
Sentry/Bevcon North America, 29035
Sepragen Corp, 29037
Sequoia Pacific, 29041
Serpa Packaging Solutions, 29048
Service Brass & AluminumFittings, 29054
Setco, 29071
Severn Newtrent, 29077
Seville Display Door, 29080
Shae Industries, 29089
Shammi Industries, 29094
Shamrock Foods Co, 29099
Shaw-Clayton Corporation, 29119
Sheahan Sanitation Consulting, 29121
Sheffield Platers Inc, 29124
Shelcon Inc, 29129
Shepard Brothers Co, 29136
Shibuya International, 29140
SHURflo, 28682
Sierra Dawn Products, 29187
Sig Pack, 29189
SIGHTech Vision Systems, 28690
Sign Classics, 29194
Sign Factory, 29196
Signet Marking Devices, 29208
Signmasters, 29210
Signs & Designs, 29213
Signtech Electrical Advg Inc, 29216
Silgan Containers LLC, 29221
Silver Mountain Vineyards, 29235
Silver Spur Corp, 29236
Simplex Filler Co, 29251
Simplex Time Recorder Company, 29252, 29253
Sinicrope & Sons Inc, 29262
SLX International, 28703
Smith-Emery Co, 29298
Smurfit Kappa, 29305
Smurfit Stone Container, 29309
Smurfit-Stone Container Corp, 29310
Snapware, 29318
Snowden Enterprises Inc, 29321
Solazyme Inc, 29333
Solus Industrial Innovations, 29342
Solutions By Design, 29343
Somat Company, 29350
Sonic Air Systems Inc, 29359
Sonoma Pacific Company, 29368
Sonoma Signatures, 29369
Soodhalter Plastics, 29370
Sortex, 29377
Soten, 29380
South Valley Citrus Packers, 29392
South Valley Mfg Inc, 29393
Southend Janitorial Supply, 29399
Southern California Packaging, 29404
Southland Packaging, 29424
SP Graphics, 28709
Specialty Paper Bag Company, 29471
Spectratek Technologies Inc, 29476
Spiral Systems, 29502
Squar-Buff, 29532
STA Packaging Tapes, 28724
Stainless International, 29556
Stainless One DispensingSystem, 29558
Stainless Steel Fabricator Inc, 29563, 29565
Stampendous, 29569
Star Pacific Inc, 29598
Star Restaurant Equipment & Supply Company, 29600
Statco Engineering, 29608
State Products, 29611
Stavin Inc, 29613
Stefanich & Company, 29629
Sterling Corp, 29650
Stero Co, 29662
Steven Label Corp, 29664
Stewart Mechanical Seals, 29671
Storopack Packaging Systs USA, 29705

Strapack, 29713
Stretch-Vent Packaging System, 29727
Summit Industrial Equipment, 29762
Summit Premium Tree Nuts, 29764
Sungjae Corporation, 29775, 29776
Sunkist Growers, 29777
Sunny Cove Citrus LLC, 29781
Sunset Paper Products, 29784
Sup Herb Farms, 29786
Super Beta Glucan, 29788
Superior Food Machinery Inc, 29801
Superior-Studio Specialties, 29813
Superklean Washdown Products, 29814
Supreme Fabricators, 29822
Sure Beam Corporation, 29827
Surtec Inc, 29837
Sutherland Stamp Company, 29840
Sutter Process Equipment, 29841
SV Dice Designers, 28732
Swander Pace & Company, 29851
Sweetware, 29857
SWF Co, 28734, 28735, 28736, 28737
Sysco Corp, 29886, 29912, 29928, 29929, 29932, 29933, 29946
SYSPRO USA, 28739
Systems Technology Inc, 29963, 29964
T & T Valve & Instrument Inc, 29972
T.D. Rowe Company, 29981
T.J. Topper Company, 29982
T.K. Designs, 29983
T.K. Products, 29984
TAC-PAD, 29987
Tallygenicom, 30051
Tamanet (USA) Inc, 30052
Tanaco Products, 30058
Tape & Label Converters, 30066
Tar-Hong MELAMINE USA, 30070
Tate Western, 30080
Taymar Industries, 30088
TCC Enterprises, 29990
TEC, 29995
Tec-Era Engineering Corporation, 30092
Technical Instrument SanFrancisco, 30104
Techniquip, 30108
TechniStar Corporation, 30101
Tedea-Huntliegh, 30119
Tek Visions, 30123
Teknor Apex Co, 30124
Temco, 30136
Templock Corporation, 30143
Tenka Flexible Packaging, 30146
TES-Clean Air Systems, 30000
Textile Products Company, 30183
TGR Container Sales, 30003
THARCO, 30005, 30006
The Pub Brewing Company, 30195
The Rubin Family of Wines, 30196
Thermodyne International LTD, 30228
Theta Sciences, 30235
Thiele Technologies-Reedley, 30240
Thinque Systems Corporation, 30242
Thomas J Payne Market Devmnt, 30245
Thompson Bagel Machine Mfg, 30256
Timemed Labeling Systems, 30290
Titan Corporation, 30299
TMB Baking Equipment, 30012
TMS, 30017
Todd Construction Services, 30308
Tonnellerie Mercier, 30326
Tonnellerie Radoux USA Inc, 30328
Tonnellerie Remond, 30329
Total Scale Systems, 30358
Touch Controls, 30360
Trademarx Inc, 30373
Tragon Corp, 30377
Traker Systems, 30380
Transition Equipment Company, 30387
Trepte's Wire & Metal Works, 30408
Tri County Citrus Packers, 30411
Tri Tool Inc, 30412
Trico Converting Inc, 30430
Triple A Containers, 30449
Triple A Neon Company, 30450
Triple Dot Company, 30451
Trisep Corporation, 30454
Triune Enterprises, 30455
Troy Lighting, 30466
Tru Form Plastics, 30467
Truesdail Laboratories, 30474
Tryco Coffee Service Annex Warehouse, 30479
Tuxton China, 30504

Twinkle Baker Decor USA, 30513
Tycodalves & Controls, 30519
Typecraft Wood & Jones, 30520
UFE, 30531
Ultra Cool International, 30571
Ultra Lift Corp, 30573
Umec Solar Inc, 30583
UniChem Enterprises, 30594
Unique Manufacturing, 30617
Unitech Scientific, 30624
United Bakery Equipment, 30628
United Barrels, 30630
United Industries Group Inc, 30640
Univar USA, 30660
Universal Aqua Technologies, 30661
Uniweb Inc, 30691
Update International, 30692
Upper Limits EngineeringCompany, 30694
US Filter, 30545, 30546
Utility Refrigerator Company, 30706
Valu Guide & Engineering, 30750
Van Nuys Awning Co, 30759
VanSan Corporation, 30762
Vansco Products, 30771
Vaughan-Chopper Pumps, 30786
Vegware, 30794
Vertex China, 30820
View-Rite Manufacturing, 30844
Viking Packaging & Display, 30851
Vin-Tex, 30856
Vine Solutions, 30859
Virgin Cola USA, 30862
Visalia Citrus Packing Group, 30868
Visual Marketing Assoc, 30876
Vita Juice Corporation, 30880
Vita Key Packaging, 30881
Vitatech Nutritional Sciences, 30885
Vorwerk, 30907
VWR Scientific, 30726
W.G. Durant Corporation, 30924
W.Y. International, 30927
Wahlstrom Manufacturing, 30976
Walker Engineering Inc, 30986
Wallace & Hinz, 30991
Walong Marketing, 30996
Warren Packaging, 31001
Washington Group International, 31021
Washington State Juice, 31023
Waste King Commercial, 31026
Water Savers Worldwide, 31035
Water System Group, 31037
Watlow Electric, 31045
Wayne Group LTD, 31061
WCS Corp, 30934
WE Lyons Contruction, 30936
WEI Equipment, 30939
WePackItAll, 31064
West Coast Industries Inc, 31121
West Coast Specialty Coffee, 31122
West Star Industries, 31129
Westec Tank & Equipment, 31131
Western Combustion Engineering, 31135
Western Exterminator, 31137
Western Pacific Oils, Inc., 31140
Western Pacific Stge Solutions, 31141
Western Precooling, 31146
Western Square Industries, 31149
Western Textile & Manufacturing Inc., 31151
White Oaks Frozen Foods, 31180
Wiegmann & Rose Thermxchanger, 31195
Wilbur Curtis Co, 31200
Wilco Distributors Inc, 31202
Wilden Pump & Engineering LLC, 31205
Wilhelmsen Consulting, 31211
Windmill Electrastatic Sprayers, 31249
Wine Analyst, 31253
Wine Appreciation Guild, 31254
Wine Cap Company, 31255
Wine Chillers of California, 31256
Wine Concepts, 31257
Wine Country Cases, 31258
Wine Things Unlimited, 31259
Wine Thingsÿ, 31260
WineAndHospitalityJobs.com, 31262
Winekeeper, 31263
Wineracks by Marcus, 31264
Winpak Lane Inc, 31269
Winpak Portion Packaging, 31270
Wna Comet West Inc, 31301
Wolf Works, 31310
Womack International Inc, 31312
Wonderware Corp, 31313

World Variety Produce, 31350
World Wide Hospitality Furn, 31355
WS Packaging Group Inc, 30961, 30967
Xtreme Beverages, LLC, 31380
Yakima Wire Works, 31389
Yardney Water Management Syst, 31392
YottaMark, 31407
Yuan Fa Can-Making, 31413
Zacmi USA, 31417
Zenith Specialty Bag Co, 31433
Zero Temp, 31440
Zmd International, 31455
Zojirushi America Corporation, 31457
Zume, 31461
Zume Manufacturing, 31462

Colorado

915 Labs, 18008
A-A1 Aaction Bag, 18059, 18060
About Packaging Robotics, 18269
Accu-Labs Research, 18289
Adstick Custom Labels Inc, 18383, 18384
Agripac, 18476
Agworld, 18481
Alcor PMC, 18544
All American Seasonings, 18578
All Valley Packaging, 18592
American Variseal, 18833
Atlas Case Inc, 19158
Atlas Pacific Engineering, 19169
B S C Signs, 19297
Ball Corp, 19408
Belgian Electronic Sorting Technology USA, 19539
BFD Corp, 19326
Birko Corp, 19693
Black River Caviar, 19711
Brass Smith, 19846
Caljan America, 20150
Canon Potato Company, 20193
Canvas Products, 20202
Carts Of Colorado Inc, 20315
Ccw Products, 20356
Chord Engineering, 20547
Cobitco Inc, 20682
Cognitive, 20702
Colorado Nut Co, 20739
Command Communications, 20768
Computer Controlled Machines, 20809
Conveying Industries, 20920
Copperwood InternationalInc, 20959
Cream of the Valley Plastics, 21052
CSAT America, 20092
Del Monte Fresh Produce Inc., 21475
Deline Box Co, 21502
Denver Mixer Company, 21551
Denver Reel & Pallet Company, 21552
Di Engineering, 21592
DMG Financial Inc, 21270
E-Z Lift Conveyors, 21885
Eaton Sales & Service, 21997
ELP Inc, 21913
Emerson Process Management, 22138
ET International Technologies, 21942
Fresca Foods Inc., 22857
Fulton-Denver Co, 22915
G & C Packing Co, 22931
Gates Corp, 23058
Goldco Industries, 23258
Grafoplast Wiremarkers Inc, 23300, 23301
Graphic Packaging Corporation, 23326
Greeley Tent & Awning Co, 23363
GTI, 22999
Hach Co, 23512, 23513
Hach Co., 23514
Herche Warehouse, 23738
Hotsy Corporation, 23877
Hydron, 23968
Iceomatic, 24048
IHS Heath Information, 24004
Impact Nutrition, 24101
Industrial Laboratories Co, 24177
International Media & Cultures, 24347
IQ Scientific Instruments, 24022
ITW Plastic Packaging, 24040
Junction Solutions, 24641
K-Coe Isom, 24661
Kalman Floor Co Inc, 24718
Kasel Industries Inc, 24729, 24730
KD Kanopy, 24675
Kesry Corporation, 24797

KIK Custom Products, 24682
Kloppenberg & Co, 24888
LDS Corporation, 25010
Lee Soap Company, 25211
Leprino Foods Co., 25253
LoTech Industries, 25375
Luthi Machinery Company, Inc., 25495
Magnuson, 25647
Master Magnetics, 25831
Master Printers, 25834
Materials Handling Equipment Company, 25855
Maui Wowi Fresh Hawaiin Blends, 25872
Meritech, 26000
Mesa Laboratories Inc, 26011
Mile Hi Express, 26168
Moli-International, 26269
Moll-Tron, 26272
Moore Efficient Communication Aids, 26302
Mortec Industries Inc, 26321
Mountain Secure Systems, 26338
Mountain States Processing, 26339
National Distributor Services, 26470
National Honey Board, 26480
New Hope Natural Media, 26587
Newwaveenviro, 26622
Nikka Densok, 26646
Nita Crisp Crackers LLC, 26653
NorCrest Consulting, 26663
Norgren Inc., 26675
Oliver Manufacturing Company, 26893
Packaging Systems Intl, 27179
Panther Industries Inc, 27253
Peerless Gouet LLC, 27384
Perception, 27436
Pioneer Labels Inc, 27545
Portec Flowmaster, 27676
Preferred Machining Corporation, 27740
Quali-Tech Tape & Label, 27984
Quality Corporation, 27999
RHG Products Company, 28104
Rice Paper Box Company, 28380
RMX Global Logistics, 28116
Romme Lag USA Inc, 28503
Schloss Engineered Equipment, 28887
Scientech, Inc, 28915
Scott's Liquid Gold-Inc, 28933
Senior Housing Options Inc, 29017
Sequa Can Machinery, 29040
Shafer Commercial Seating, 29090
Shamrock Foods Co, 29097
Silver State Plastics Inc, 29237
Silver Weibull, 29238
Sine Pump, 29261
Stadia Corporation, 29549
Stainless Fabricating Company, 29554
Steel Storage Systems Inc, 29625
Stolle Machinery Co LLC, 29685
Structure, 29739
Summit Machine Builders Corporation, 29763
Sundyne Corp, 29773
Sure Torque, 29831
Svedala Industries, 29844, 29845
Sysco Corp, 29899
Technistar Corporation, 30109
Teilhaber Manufacturing Corp, 30122
TeleTech Label Company, 30127
Thermodynamics, 30226
Timberline Consulting, 30285
Trak-Air/Rair, 30379
Tree Saver, 30399
Trimble Agriculture, 30439
Trinidad Benham Corporation, 30444
Tucker Industries, 30486
Udi's Food, 30564
UDY Corp, 30530
Ultrak, 30578
Union Camp Corporation, 30608
Universal Stainless, 30684
Victor Associates, 30836
VPC Gordon Sign, 30721
Warren Analytical Laboratory, 31009
Wilco, USA, 31204
Windsor Industries Inc, 31251
Wishbone Utensil Tableware Line, 31293
Yamato Corporation, 31391

Connecticut

A.T. Foote Woodworking Company, 18076
Ace Technical Plastics Inc, 18310

Acme Wire Products Company, 18329
Advanced Micro Controls, 18416
Aercology, 18438
Ahlstrom Nonwovens LLC, 18483
Altech, 18669
Altek Co, 18671
Althor Products, 18674
Amodex Products, 18875
Arthur G Russell Co Inc, 19090
Ashcroft Inc, 19107
B.E. Industries, 19309
Bailey Moore Glazer Schaefer, 19374
Bakers Choice Products, 19384
Baumer Limited, 19487
Baumuller LNI, 19488
Bendow, 19566
Berkshire PPM, 19587
Better Packages, 19634
Bjm Pumps, 19706
Blumer, 19760
Bollore Inc, 19781, 19782
Branson Ultrasonics Corp, 19845
Calzone Case Co, 20154
CANBERRA Industries Inc, 20025
Carpenter-Hayes Paper Box Company, 20286
Carrier Corp, 20290
Carrier Transicold, 20292
Champion America Inc, 20426
Champlin Co, 20431
Chemtura Corp, 20504
Clauss Tools, 20605
Cleveland-Eastern Mixers, 20646
Coastal Mechanical Svc Inc, 20671
Coastal Pallet Corp, 20672
Cober Electronics, Inc., 20681
Comasec Safety, Inc., 20758
Composition Materials Co Inc, 20802
Conn Container Corp, 20841
Connecticut Culinary Institute, 20842
Connecticut Laminating Co Inc, 20843
Consolidated Commercial Controls, 20849
Control Concepts, Inc., 20907
Control Module, 20910
Cooper Instrument Corporation, 20950
Cramer Company, 21038
Creative Mobile Systems Inc, 21067
Croll-Reynolds Engineering Company, 21092
Crompton Corporation, 21093
Crown Manufacturing Corporation, 21112
Curtis Packaging, 21161
Custom Bottle of Connecticut, 21168
Daniel J. Bloch & Company, 21338
Dari Farms Ice Cream Inc, 21355
Delavan-Delta, 21496
Demeyere Na, Llc, 21538
Design Label Manufacturing, 21563
Design Specialties Inc, 21566
Devar Inc, 21582
Diebolt & Co, 21617
Dow Cover Co Inc, 21747
Drs Designs, 21775
Dura-Flex, 21815
Duralite Inc, 21821
Durham Manufacturing Co, 21828
E-Lite Technologies, 21878
Eastern Machine, 21980
Edco Industries, 22030
Elgene, 22096
Emery Winslow Scale Co, 22140
EMI, 21919
Entoleter LLC, 22204
Environmental Products Corp, 22216
ERS International, 21931
Fabrichem Inc, 22431
FASTCORP LLC, 22379
Film X, 22546
Fluted Partition Inc, 22666
Food Tech Structures LLC, 22727
Fortune Plastics, Inc, 22783
Gastro-Gnomes, 23056
Gems Sensors & Controls, 23094, 23095
General Analysis Corporation, 23100
General Electric Company, 23108
GEO Graphics-Spegram, 22978
Gerber Innovations, 23164
Glass Industries America LLC, 23198
Goodway Technologies Corp, 23275
H.L. Diehl Company, 23479
Harbour House Bar Crafting, 23593
Harbour House Furniture, 23594
Hartford Containers, 23637
Hartford Stamp Works, 23639

Hasco Electric Corporation, 23648
Henkel Corp., 23726
Hi-Tech Packaging Inc, 23759
Hubbell Electric Heater Co, 23907
IMI Precision Engineering, 24011
IMS Food Service™, 24013
Incomec-Cerex Industries, 24132
Industronics Service Co, 24205
Inflatable Packaging, 24211
Inline Plastic Corp, 24237
Innovative Components, 24253
Intrex, 24378
J.C. Products Inc., 24437
J.K. Harman, Inc., 24443
Jackson Corrugated Container, 24485
Jagenberg, 24496
Jarvis Products Corp, 24522
JEM Wire Products, 24460
Jentek, 24545
Johnson Corrugated Products Corporation, 24596
K&H Container, 24658
KHS Co, 24681
Knapp Container, 24893
Label Systems, 25052
Lake Eyelet Manufacturing Company, 25088
Laticrete International, 25158
Leeds Conveyor Manufacturer Company, 25214
Lewtan Industries Corporation, 25274
Linvar, 25337
Lion Laboratories, 25342
Litchfield Packaging Machinery, 25355
Long Reach ManufacturingCompany, 25422
Longford Equipment US, 25425
Luce Corp, 25470
Lynch Corp, 25503
M&S Miltenberg & Samton, 25539
M.H. Rhodes Cramer, 25546
Magnatech Corp, 25639
Majestic, 25665
Maple Hill Farms, 25713
Mark-It Rubber Stamp & Label Company, 25748
Massachusetts Container Corporation, 25826
Matik North America, 25862
Meriden Box Company, 25998
MGM Instruments, 25573
Microbest Inc, 26097
Microtechnologies, 26113
Miltenberg & Samton, 26192
Miracle Exclusives, 26213
Mobil Composite Products, 26234
Modern Plastics, 26245
Mpp Inc, 26348
Murk Brush Company, 26390
Mutual Stamping & Mfg Co, 26402
Native Lumber Company, 26516
Nature Most Laboratories, 26518
New Brunswick Scientific Co, 26569
New Haven Awnings, 26585
North American Plastic Manufacturing Company, 26688
Omega Company, 26907
On Site Gas Systems Inc, 26928
Orca Inc, 26961
Pack-Rite, 27131
Package Systems Corporation, 27142
Penn Products, 27414
Perl Packaging Systems, 27449
Pez Candy Inc, 27481
Polyclutch, 27648
Praxair Inc, 27720
Pro Scientific, 27834
Pro Scientific Inc, 27835
Production Equipment Co, 27870
Putnam Group, 27953
R&R Corrugated Container, 28067
Ram Machinery Corp, 28164
Reiner Products, 28287
Republic Foil, 28324
RH Forschner, 28103
Rice Packaging Inc, 28379
Robinson Tape & Label, 28451
Romatic Manufacturing Co, 28499
Rondo of America, 28511
Rowland Technologies, 28566
Royal Display Corporation, 28577
Ryther-Purdy, 28628
Sanford Redmond Company, 28807
Schaefer Machine Co Inc, 28865
SCK Direct Inc, 28668, 28669

Scott & Daniells, 28923
Seton Indentification Products, 29072
Sharpe Measurement Technology, 29113
SIG Packaging Technologies, 28689
Silent Watchman Security Services LLC, 29218
Simkins Industries Inc, 29243
Simoniz USA Inc, 29249
Six Hardy Brush Manufacturing, 29273
Solon Manufacturing Company, 29341
Sonic Corp, 29360
Sonics & Materials Inc, 29362
Source Marketing, 29384
Southpack LLC, 29426
Specialty Saw Inc, 29472
Spencer Turbine Co, 29489
St. Pierre Box & Lumber Company, 29543
Staban Engineering Corp, 29546
Standard-Knapp Inc, 29579
Stanley Access Technologies, 29583
Stanley Black & Decker Inc, 29584
Steinmetz Machine Works Inc, 29635
Stelray Plastic Products Inc, 29639
Sysco Corp, 29917
Tee-Jay Corporation, 30120
Thorpe Rolling Pin Co, 30266
Tops Manufacturing Co, 30337
Total Quality Corp, 30356
Total Quality Corporation, 30357
Trans Flex Packagers Inc, 30383
Treif USA, 30403
Treif USA Inc, 30404
Trident, 30434
Tudor Pulp & Paper Corporation, 30488
Valley Container Inc, 30742
Vantage Pak International, 30772
Waring Products, 31007
Welbilt Corporation, 31092
William Willis Worldwide, 31228
Wine Well Chiller Co, 31261
Woodstock Line Co, 31328
WP Bakery Group, 30950
Z-Loda Systems Engineering Inc, 31415

Delaware

AET Films, 18135
ALL-CON World Systems, 18161
Ames Engineering Corporation, 18861
Ashland, 19108
Atlantis Industries Inc, 19153
Bruce Industrial Co Inc, 19908
BUCHI Corp, 19346, 19347
Castle Bag Co., 20336
DCV BioNutritionals, 21256
Diamond Chemical & Supply Co, 21599
DuPont, 21784
Eagle Foodservice   Equipment, 21950
Eagle Group, 21951
Easy Lift Equipment Co Inc, 21985
Engineered Systems & Designs, 22176
Fabreeka International, 22424
Foxfire Marketing Solutions, 22810
Franklin Rubber Stamp Co, 22829
Friskem Infinetics, 22877
GED, LLC, 22970
Ghibli North American, 23172
Graver Technologies LLC, 23336
Harting Graphics, 23640
Honeywell Sensing & Internet of Things, 23844
Ilc Dover, 24078
Inland Consumer Packaging, 24229
Jarboe Equipment, 24514
Jeb Plastics, 24533
Mid Atlantic Packaging Co, 26119
Miller Metal Fabrication, 26181
Newton OA & Son Co, 26621
O A Newton & Son Co, 26800
Odessa Packaging Services, 26854
Qualicon, 27985
Rheometric Scientific, 28366
SDIX, 28670
Straight Line Filters, 29710
TA Instruments Inc, 29986
Telesonic Packaging, 30133
Testing Machines Inc, 30167
Tom McCall & Associates, 30320
True Pac, 30473
Westvaco Corporation, 31159

District of Columbia

Aidi International Hotels of America, 18486
American Gas Association, 18769
Decernis, 21435
FCN Publishing, 22384
Food Insights, 22704
Food Processors Institute, 22718
Gelberg Signs, 23088
Global USA Inc, 23232
Grocery Manufacturers Assn, 23423
Hazmat Business Ideas, 23674
Kemex Meat Brands, 24764
Malaysian Palm Oil Board, 25671
Meat & Livestock Australia, 25942
Nutrin Distribution Company, 26788
Onsite Sycom Energy Corporation, 26938
Pickle Packers International Inc., 27518
Prime Label Consultants Inc, 27789
Rigid Plastics Packaging Institute, 28399
SPI's Film and Bag Federation, 28713
TCG Technologies, 29991
The Good Food Institute, 30190
USDA-NASS, 30562

Florida

A&F, 18045
A-B-C Packaging Machine Corp, 18061
ABC Research Corp, 18088
Abco Products, 18262
Able Brands Inc, 18267
Accu Place, 18286
Acme Sponge & Chamois Co Inc, 18328
Adapto Storage Products, 18363
ADT Inc, 18128
Advanced Separation Technologies, 18422
Advantus Corp., 18431
AFL Industries, 18141
AgTracker, 18462
Air Pak Products & Services, 18494
Akers Group, 18518
Akicorp, 18519
Alger Creations, 18561
Alipack Americas, 18567
All American Container, 18576
All Southern Fabricators, 18586
All State Fabricators Corporation, 18590
All-Right Enterprises, 18595
Allstate Food & Marketing Inc, 18640
Aloe Hi-Tech, 18647
Altira Inc, 18675
Altrua Marketing & Design, 18680
Aluma Shield, 18683
Alumar, 18684
Alumaworks, 18685, 18686
AMC Industries, 18172
Ameri-Khem, 18710
American Coolair Corp, 18736
American Fabric Filter Co Inc, 18757
American Fire Sprinkler Services, Inc, 18759
American Food Equipment, 18762
American Machinery Corporation, 18789
American Panel Corp, 18805
American Radionic Co Inc, 18813
Amerikooler Inc, 18851
AMETEK Inc, 18177
Anchor Glass Container Corporation, 18905
Anderson American Precision, 18916
Anko Products Inc, 18945
Apex Machine Company, 18970
APM, 18200
Aquathin Corporation, 19008
Architecture Plus Intl Inc, 19021
Arctic Industries, 19029
Arctic Seal & Gasket, 19030
Aromatech USA, 19068
Art-Phyl Creations, 19082
Associated Packaging Enterprises, 19125
Astro Pure Water, 19137
Atkins Jemptec, 19142
Atkins Technical, 19143
Atlantic Foam & Packaging Company, 19148
Atlantis Pak USA Inc, 19154
Atlas Bakery Machinery Company, 19156
Atlas Metal Industries, 19166
Atlas Packaging Inc, 19170
Auto Labe, 19198
Auto Quotes, 19200
Automation Packaging, 19234
B H Bunn Co, 19292
B.C.E. Technologies, 19308

Bag Masters, 19370
Bakery Refrigeration & Services, 19391
Bar Maid Corp, 19435
Barnes Machine Company, 19458
Baublys Control Laser, 19485
Bellsola-Pan Plus, 19553
Beltram Foodservice Group, 19561
Benner China & Glassware Inc, 19570
Bestech Inc, 19623
BFT, 19328
Bill Davis Engineering, 19656
Bio Zapp Laboratories, 19670
Biopath, 19687
Blue Ribbon Packaging Systems, 19749
Bodolay Packaging, 19765
Bonar Engineering & Constr Co, 19786
Brandstedt Controls Corporation, 19843
Brazilian Consulate, 19849
Brevard Restaurant Equipment, 19860
Brinkmann Instruments, Inc., 19873
Brisker Dry Food Crisper, 19874
Brooklyn Boys Pizza & Pasta, 19886
Brown International Corp LLC, 19899, 19900
Burdock Group, 19949
Can Creations, 20177, 20178
Capital Packaging, 20209
Carolina Summit Mountain Spring Water, 20280
Caselites, 20324
Cast Film Technology, 20331
CDI Service & Mfg Inc, 20045
CE International Trading Corporation, 20046
Ceramica De Espana, 20408
Chatillon, 20467
Chemdet Inc, 20491
Chep, 20505
Chicago Stainless Eqpt Inc, 20522
Chinet Company, 20537
Chiquita Brands LLC., 20541
Chlorinators Inc, 20542
Clearwater Packaging Inc, 20627
Clextral USA, 20648
CNL Beverage Property Group, 20076
Coast Controls Inc, 20664
Coconut Code, 20686
Coleman Rubber Stamps, 20719
Collins Technical, 20727
Colmar Storage Co Warehouse, 20729
Colonial Paper Company, 20731
Conimar Corp, 20840
Consolidated Baling Machine Company, 20847
Consolidated Label Company, 20855
Continental Industrial Supply, 20889
Control Instrument Service, 20908
Convergent Label Technology, 20918
Conveyor Equipment Manufacturers Association, 20925
Cool Care, 20943
Cool-Pitch Co, 20945
Copack International, 20952
Cork Specialties, 20970
Corrugated Packaging, 20994
Cosgrove Enterprises Inc, 21005
Costa Broom Works, 21010
Covergent Label Technology, 21026
Creative Canopy Design, 21056
Cunningham LP Gas, 21154
Custom Craft Laminates, 21176
Custom ID Systems, 21183
Custom Metal Design Inc, 21187
Dade Engineering, 21292
Dagher Printing, 21295
Dave's Imports, 21378
David Dobbs Enterprise Inc., 21381
Dayco, 21397
Deibel Laboratories, 21454
Deibel Laboratories Inc, 21456
Del Monte Fresh Produce Inc., 21460, 21464, 21465, 21470, 21483, 21487
Deluxe Equipment Company, 21529
Design Group, 21561
Designers Plastics, 21572
Dividella, 21675
Dixie Neon Company, 21681
Dixie Signs Inc, 21686
Donnick Label Systems, 21708
Dosatron International Inc, 21721
Douglas Machines Corp, 21735
Douglas Machines Corp., 21736
Doyen Medipharm, 21754

Dried Ingredients, LLC., 21772
Duo-Aire, 21809
Durango-Georgia Paper, 21823
Duval Container Co, 21834
Dylog USA Vanens, 21841
Dynamic Storage Systems Inc., 21857
Dynasys Technologies, 21861
Dynynstyl, 21864
Ecklund-Harrison Technologies, 22004
Economy Label Sales Company, 22023
Economy Tent Intl, 22026
Eggboxes Inc, 22049
Eldorado Miranda Manufacturing Company, 22067
Electrodex, 22081
Electron Machine Corp, 22083
Electronic Weighing Systems, 22088
ELISA Technologies, Inc., 21912
Elreha Controls Corporation, 22123
Emery Thompson Machine &Supply Company, 22139
Emjac, 22143
Emmeti USA, 22145
Environmental Products, 22215
ESD Waste2water Inc, 21934
Exaxol Chemical Corp, 22326
Excel Chemical Company, 22330
Excellence Commercial Products, 22334
F&G Packaging, 22371
F.M. Corporation, 22376
Fast Industries, 22473
Fawema Packaging Machinery, 22482
Federated Mills, 22497
Filtration Systems, 22556
Fishmore, 22588
Flamingo Food Service Products, 22605
Flatten-O-Matic: Universal Concepts, 22610
Fleetwood Systems, 22617
Flex Pack USA, 22620
Flex Sol Packaging Corp, 22622, 22623
Florart Flock Process, 22650
Florida Knife Co, 22651
Florida Seating, 22653
Fogel Rubin & Fogel, 22678
Food Equipment BrokerageInc, 22698
Food Industry ConsultingGroup, 22702
Food Service Equipment Corporation, 22726
Foodservice Design Associates, 22744
Franklin Crates, 22826
Freeman Electric Co Inc, 22849
Futura 2000 Corporation, 22923
Gainesville Neon & Signs, 23009
Galaxy Chemical Corp, 23011
Galley, 23015
Gaylord Container Corporation, 23069
GEBO Corporation, 22969
Gebo Corporation, 23082
General Equipment & Machinery Company, 23110
General, Inc, 23134
GP Plastics Corporation, 22991
Grain Machinery Mfg Corp, 23305
Gram Equipment Of America, 23307
Grand Cypress, 23310
Graphic Arts Center, 23323
Grimes Co, 23419
Gulf Coast Plastics, 23439
Gulf Coast Sign Company, 23440
Gulf Packaging Company, 23441
Hallberg Manufacturing Corporation, 23532
Hamersmith, Inc., 23540
Hammerstahl Cutlery, 23549
Hand Made Lollies, 23555
Harmar, 23612
Harris Specialty Chemicals, 23629
Harvey's Indian River Groves, 23646
Hatteras Packaging Systems, 23654
HD Barcode, 23488
Hines III, 23787
Hoffman & Levy Inc Tasseldepot, 23806
Hunter Graphics, 23930
Hydropure Water Treatment Co, 23969
IDC Food Division, 23995
Imar, 24097
Impact Awards & Promotions, 24100
Index Instruments Us Inc, 24144
Industrial Marking Equipment, 24183
Inline Filling Systems, 24235
Institutional & Supermarket, 24284
Interfood Ingredients, 24313
International Container Systems, 24329
International Environmental Solutions, 24332

International Fruit Marketing, 24339
International Packaging Machinery, 24350
Intertape Polymer Group, 24372
IR Systems, 24023
Italtech, 24401
Jacksonville Box & Woodwork Co, 24488
JBT Food Tech, 24453
Jeffcoat Signs, 24536
Jenco Fan, 24541
K & I Creative Plastics & Wood, 24651
Kelmin Products, 24761
Kemco Systems Inc, 24763
Kent Co, 24782
Kew Cleaning Systems, 24803
Key Packaging Co, 24811
Khs USA Inc, 24823, 24825
Kilcher Company, 24831
Kinematics & Controls Corporation, 24842
King Plastic Corp, 24855
Kisters Kayat, 24871
Kole Industries, 24922
Korber Medipak Inc, 24938
Kreissle Forge Ornamental, 24949
Kwikprint Manufacturing Inc, 24972
L & N Label Co, 24979
L&M Chemicals, 24991
Labeling Systems Clearwater, 25061
Lakeland Rubber Stamp Company, 25092
Leotta Designers, 25251
Levelmatic, 25264
Life Extension Foundation, 25296
Linpac Plastics, 25336
Load King Mfg, 25376
LoadBank International, 25377
Logo Specialty Advertising Tems, 25409
Ludeca Inc, 25477
Mac Papers Inc, 25601
Maddox/Adams International, 25624
Mancini Packing Co, 25690
Manufacturing Warehouse, 25711
Marc Refrigeration Mfg Inc, 25724
Mason Ways Indestructible, 25825
Master Containers, 25829
Matrix Engineering, 25865
Mauser, Schindler & Wagner, 25876
Mayworth Showcase Works Inc, 25895
Mcneill Signs Inc, 25933
MDR International, 25566
MDS-Vet Inc, 25568
Melitta USA Inc, 25963
Menu Men, 25984
MERRICK Industries Inc, 25571
Mettler-Toledo Hi-Speed, 26039
Mettler-Toledo Safeline Inc, 26041
Meyer Label Company, 26048
Miami Awning, 26056
Miami Metal, 26057
MicroAnalytics, 26090
Micron Automation, 26106
Mil-Du-Gas Company/Star Brite, 26165
Millenia Industries Corp, 26177
Morrow Technologies Corporation, 26319
Mosshaim Innovations, 26325
N A P Engineering, 26412
Naylor Association Solutions, 26524
NCC, 26418
New England Machinery Inc, 26578
New High Glass, 26586
Nozzle Nolen Inc, 26760
Nu CO2 LLC, 26764
Nu-Trend Plastics Thermoformer, 26771
Nutty Bavarian, 26796
O.D. Kurtz Associates, 26810
Old English Printing & Label Company, 26885
Omni Controls Inc, 26915
Osgood Industries, 26986, 26987
P&E, 27029
Pack & Process, 27120
Pack-A-Drum, 27130
Pallet One Inc, 27227, 27228
Palm Bay Imports, 27236
Palmetto Canning, 27241
Palmland Paper Company, 27243
Pan American Papers Inc, 27247
Paperbag Manufacturers Inc, 27270
Paradise Inc, 27283
Paragon Group USA, 27288
Parkson Corp, 27313
Parkson Corporation, 27315
Particle Sizing Systems, 27322
Party Yards, 27328

Hawaii

Idaho

Illinois

Rudd Container Corp, 28605
Rust-Oleum Corp, 28618
Rutherford Engineering, 28620
Ryowa Company America, 28624
S I Jacobson Mfg Co, 28640
Sackett Systems, 28746
Saf-T-Gard International Inc, 28751
Samuel Strapping Systems Inc, 28779
Sardee Industries Inc, 28827
Savage Brothers Company, 28845
Schaeff, 28867
Scheb International, 28872
Schiffmayer Plastics Corp., 28883
Schwab Paper Products Co, 28910
Schwarz Supply Source, 28912
Scorpio Apparel, 28919
Scotsman Ice Systems, 28922
Se Kure Controls Inc, 28939
Seaboard Carton Company, 28943
Seaga Manufacturing Inc, 28945
Seating Concepts Inc, 28963
Security Link, 28975
Sediment Testing Equipment, 28979
Sencon Inc, 29012
Senior Flexonics, 29016
Sensient Flavors and Fragrances, 29022
Serac Inc, 29043
Serfilco, 29044
Service Manufacturing, 29056
Service Stamp Works, 29060
Service Tool International, 29061
Shaped Wire, 29107
Sieberts Engineers, 29181
Signode Industrial Group LLC, 29211, 29212
Silgan Plastic Closure Sltns, 29222, 29223
Silgan White Cap LLC, 29227
Silliker, Inc, 29232
Simmons Engineering Corporation, 29244
Simpson Electric, 29257
Sipco Products, 29266
Sirman Spa/IFM USA, 29268
Smoke Right, 29302
Snyder Industries Inc, 29323
Solo Cup Company, 29339
Solo Foods, 29340
Sonoco Alloyd, 29363
Sonoco ThermoSafe, 29366
Sortie/Kohlhaas, 29378
Source Distribution Logistics, 29383
Southern Imperial Inc, 29410
Soynut Butter Co, 29436
Spartan Tool LLC, 29449
Spartanics, 29451
Spinzer, 29497
Spraying Systems Company, 29515
Sprayway Inc, 29517
Spring USA Corp, 29520
SRI, 28719
St. Clair Pakwell, 29538
Sta-Rite Ginnie Lou Inc, 29545
Stampede Meat, Inc., 29568
Stand Fast Pkgng Prods Inc, 29571
Standard Refrigeration, Inc, 29577
Star Industries, Inc., 29594
Starkey Chemical Process Company, 29604
Steiner Company, 29632
Steiner Industries Inc, 29633
Stephan Machinery GmbH, 29641
Stephan Machinery, Inc., 29642
Sterigenics International, 29645
Sterling Novelty Products, 29653
Sterling Systems & Controls, 29658
Sterno, 29661
Stertil Alm Corp, 29663
Stogsdill Tile Co, 29682
Stone Container, 29687
Stor-Loc, 29694
Stork Food Machinery, 29701
Streator Dependable Mfg, 29726
Stroter Inc, 29737
Suburban Corrugated Box Company, 29748
Suburban Laboratories Inc, 29749
Sudmo North America, Inc, 29753
Superior Product Pickup Services, 29809
Sverdrup Facilities, 29846
Sweetener Supply Corp, 29855
Sycamore Containers, 29868
Sympak, Inc., 29871
Sysco Corp, 29879, 29890
Systech Illinois, 29951
Tablecraft Products Co Inc, 30043
Tablet & Ticket Co, 30045

Tag-Trade Associated Group, 30048
Tamarack Products Inc, 30053
Tangerine Promotion, 30060
Tantec, 30064
TAWI-USA Inc, 29988
Taylor Precision Products, 30085
TCT&A Industries, 29992
Tech Lighting LLC, 30095
Technical Tool Solutions Inc., 30105
Technomic Inc, 30112
Teepak LLC, 30121
TEI Analytical Svc Inc, 29997
Tempco Electric Heater Corporation, 30140
Tenneco Inc, 30148
Tenneco Packaging, 30149
TEQ, 29999
Tetra Pak, 30170
The National Provisioner, 30192
Therma Kleen, 30204
Thermal Bags By Ingrid Inc, 30207
Thermos Company, 30233
Thomas Lighting Residential, 30247
Tinwerks Packaging Co, 30294
Tisma Machinery Corporation, 30298
TMT Vacuum Filters, 30019
Tni Packaging Inc, 30305
Tnn-Jeros Inc, 30306
TNN-Jeros, Inc., 30021
Toastmaster, 30307
Top Source Industries, 30332
Topco Associates LLC, 30333
Topflight Grain Co-Op, 30334
Total Control Products, 30352
Toyo Seikan Kaisha, 30367
Tradeco International Corp, 30372
Transparent Container Co, 30389
Travelon, 30395
TreeHouse Foods, Inc., 30400
Tri-Connect, 30415
Triangle Package Machinery Co, 30427
Tricor Systems Inc, 30431, 30432
Trilla Steel Drum Corporation, 30437
Tubesales QRT, 30480
Turtle Wax, 30501
UAA, 30526
Ultra Packaging Inc, 30574
Uneco Systems, 30587
Uni Carriers Americas Corp, 30591
Unichema North America, 30599
Uniforms To You, 30603
Uniforms To You & Co, 30604
Union Cord Products Company, 30609
Unique Boxes, 30616
Unique Solutions, 30620
United Ad Label, 30625
United Floor Machine Co, 30639
United Insulated Structures, 30642
United Performance Metals, 30647
Universal Beverage Equipment, 30662
Universal Overall, 30676
Upham & Walsh Lumber, 30693
US Cooler Company, 30544
US Standard Sign, 30557
US Tsubaki Holdings Inc, 30559
Vantage Performance Materials, 30773, 30774
Vantage USA, 30775
Vapor Power Intl LLC, 30776
VCG Uniform, 30715
Vector Packaging, 30789
Verilon Products Co, 30807
Victone Manufacturing Company, 30835
Videojet Technologies Inc, 30841, 30842
VIP Real Estate LTD, 30719
Viskase Co Inc, 30873
Vonco Products LLC, 30903
Voss Belting & Specialty Co, 30908
Vrymeer Commodities, 30909
Wabash Power Equipment Co, 30969
Wag Industries, 30974
Wallace Computer Services, 30992, 30993
Walsroder Packaging, 30998
Walter Molzahn & Company, 31000
Warner Electric Inc, 31008
Washington Group International, 31022
Water & Oil Technologies Inc, 31030
Watershed Foods, 31042
Watlow Electric, 31044
Weber Packaging Solutions Inc, 31077
Weber-Stephen Products Company, 31079
Wega USA, 31083
Weigh Right Automatic Scale Co, 31084

Welch Brothers, 31094
Wells Lamont, 31099, 31100, 31101
Wenda America Inc, 31107
Western Lighting Inc, 31139
Western Stoneware, 31150
Wexxar Corporation, 31163
WGN Flag & Decorating Co, 30942
White Stokes International, 31182
White Way Sign & Maintenance, 31183
Wico Corporation, 31194
Wilkens-Anderson Co, 31213
Willett America, 31224
Wilton Brands LLC, 31242
Winston Laboratories Inc, 31274
Wipeco Inc, 31277
Wisdom Adhesives Worldwide, 31292
Woodhead, 31320
Woodstock Plastics Co Inc, 31329
World Dryer Corp, 31340
World Kitchen, 31345
World Wide Beverage, 31353
World Wide Fitting Corp, 31354
Worldwide Dispensers, 31357
Xcell International, 31376
Yamada America, 31390
Yargus Manufacturing Inc, 31393
Z-Trim Holdings, Inc, 31416
Zebra Technologies Corporation, 31424
Zenith Cutter, 31432
Zip-Pak, 31449, 31450, 31451
Zitropack Limited, 31454

Indiana

A T C Inc, 18033
A T Ferrell Co Inc, 18034, 18035
Abresist Kalenborn Corp, 18270
Accu Temp Products Inc, 18288
Advanced Control Technologies, 18400
Advanced Process Solutions, 18421
Aire-Mate, 18504
Airomat Corp, 18513
Alcoa - Warrick Operations, 18539
American Containers Inc, 18734
American Electronic Components, 18748
American Griddle Corp., 18773
American Metal Door Company, 18793
American Ultraviolet Co, 18832
American-Newlong Inc, 18841
AmeriQual Foods, 18711
Ameristamp/Sign-A-Rama, 18855
Anchor Industries, 18907
Anderson Tool & Engineering Company, 18924
Aqua Blast Corp Mfg, 19001
Archibald Frozen Desserts, 19017
Ardagh Group, 19034
Artistic Carton, 19096
Assmann Corp Of America, 19122
Atlas Restaurant Supply, 19171
Balemaster, 19407
Bar Keepers Friend Cleanser, 19434
Basilod Products Corp, 19479
Bell Packaging Corporation, 19545
Berry Global, 19598
Bluffton Motor Works, 19758
BNW Industries, 19339
Brulin & Company, 19910
Bryan Boilers, 19917
Butler Winery, 19977
Caloritech, 20153
Capitol City Container Corp, 20213
Capitol Hardware, Inc.,, 20214
Cardinal Container Corp, 20237
Cardinal Packaging, 20239
Carico Systems, 20249
Carman Industries Inc, 20265, 20266
Carmel Engineering, 20267, 20268
Central Fine Pack Inc, 20382
Century Chemical Corp, 20395
Century Industries Inc, 20399
Chicago Automated Labeling Inc, 20516
Chore-Boy Corporation, 20548
CK Products, 20574
CLARCOR Air Filtration Prods, 20064
Classico Seating, 20602
Closure Systems Intl Inc, 20658
Color Box, 20735
Command Belt Cleaning Systems, 20767
Cornerstone, 20979
Cosco Home & Office Products, 21003
Crawford Packaging, 21049

Creative Industries Inc, 21065
Cummins Power Generation Inc., 21153
Custom Machining Inc, 21185
Custom Poly Packaging, 21196
CXR Co, 20109, 20013
D M Sales & Engineering Co, 21235
Diamond Chain, 21598
Diskey Architectural Signs, 21645
Dolco Packaging Co, 21694
Dometic Mini Bar, 21697
Doughmakers, LLC, 21730
Dow Agro Sciences LLC, 21746
Driall Inc, 21770
Dwyer Instruments Inc, 21836
E-Pak Machinery, 21879
E-Z Dip, 21882
Eash Industries, 21968
EFP Corp, 21901
Ehrgott Rubber Stamp Company, 22051
Elanco Food Solutions, 22063
Electronic Liquid Fillers, 22086
ELF Machinery, 21911
Elliott-Williams Company, 22112
Endress & Hauser, 22160
Environmental Consultants, 22213
Faultless Caster, 22480
FDL/Flair Designs, 22385
Fibertech Inc, 22532, 22533
Flashfold Carton Inc, 22608
Flavor Burst, 22611
Flexible Foam Products, 22630
Flomatic International, 22648
Flow Aerospace, 22656
Fonda Group, 22689
Formflex, 22766
Fort Wayne Awning, 22777
Foster Forbes Glass, 22789
G W Berkheimer Co, 22943
G.V. Aikman Company, 22950
Galbreath LLC, 23013
Garver Manufacturing Inc, 23043
Gary Sign Co, 23052
General Cage, 23102
Genflex Roofing Systems, 23141
Grasso, 23334
Harsco Industrial IKG, 23634
Helmer, 23721
Hewitt Manufacturing Co, 23754
Hodge Design Assoc PC, 23800
Hot Food Boxes, 23874
Howden Group, 23892
Hydro Life, 23960
Indco, 24134
Indiana Bottle Co, 24146
Indiana Carton Co Inc, 24147
Indiana Michigan Power, 24149
Indiana Vac Form Inc, 24150
Indiana Wiping Cloth, 24151
Indiana Wire Company, 24152
Indianapolis Container Company, 24153
Indy Lighting, 24206
Innovative Energy, 24255
Inscale, 24272
Insects Limited Inc, 24274
Iron Out, 24386
Jarden Home Brands, 24517
Jasper Seating Company, 24524
Jeco Plastic Products LLC, 24534
Jessup Paper Box, 24553
JH Display & Fixture, 24462
Johnson Brothers Sign Co Inc, 24594
Josam Co, 24625
JVC Rubber Stamp Company, 24473
KCL Corporation, 24674
Kelly Box & Packaging Corp, 24758
Kenray Associates, 24779
KTR Corp, 24701
Kuepper Favor Company, Celebrate Line, 24964
Lafayette Tent & Awning Co, 25081
Laidig Inc, 25084
Langsenkamp Manufacturing, 25136
LDI Manufacturing Co, 25008
Lillsun Manufacturing Co, 25310, 25311
Lincoln Coders Corp, 25319
Little Giant Pump Company, 25361
Locknetics, 25385
Louisville Container Company, 25450
Love Controls Division, 25453
Loyal Manufacturing, 25463
Madsen Wire Products Inc, 25629
Manchester Tool & Die Inc, 25689

Advanced Insulation Concepts, 18413
Ahlstrom Filtration LLC, 18482
Alltech Inc, 18643
American Fuji Seal, 18767
American Wire Products, 18839
Anderson Wood Products, 18925
Aquionics Inc, 19009
Aventics Corp, 19250
AWP Butcher Block Inc, 18240
Ayr King Corp, 19280
B & W Awning Co, 19288
Balluff Inc, 19415
BEC International, 19317
Blaze Products Corp, 19725
Blendex Co, 19727
Bluegrass Packaging Industries, 19755
Camco Chemicals, 20161
Caraustar, 20226
Carrier Vibrating Equip Inc, 20293
Catalent Pharma Solutions Inc, 20340
CCL Label Inc, 20035
Cello Bag Company, 20364
Central Pallet Mills Inc, 20387
Clayton & Lambert Manufacturing, 20608
Compact Mold, 20790
Corman & Assoc Inc, 20971
Cusham Enterprises, 21166
D D Williamson & Co Inc, 21232
Daniel Boone Lumber Industries, 21337
Engraph Label Group, 22181
F N Sheppard & Co, 22367
Feed The Party, 22498
Foodservice Consultants Society
  International, 22743
Foodworks, 22749
Freudenberg Nonwovens, 22865
Gch Internatonal, 23075
GCJ Mattei Company, 22956
GE Appliances, 22959
Germantown Milling Company, 23166
Graham Pallet Co Inc, 23304
Greensburg Manufacturing Company, 23388
Grindmaster-Cecilware Corp, 23420
Halton Company, 23537
Hoegger Alpina, 23803
Horton Fruit Co Inc, 23864
Ideas Etc Inc, 24064
International Inflight Food Service
  Association, 24341
J.V. Reed & Company, 24448
Jackson Msc LLC, 24486
January & Wood Company, 24512
Ken Coat, 24769
Kentucky Grocers Assn Inc, 24789
Kentucky Power, 24790
Kinergy Corp, 24843
L ChemCo Distribution, 24981
LANTECH.COM, 25002
Lasco Composites, 25151
Legacy Plastics, 25217
Lesco Design & Mfg Co, 25258
Littleford Day, 25366
Louisville Bedding Co Inc., 25449
Louisville Dryer Company, 25451
Louisville Lamp Co, 25452
Martin Laboratories, 25808
Mathews Conveyor, 25861
MDH Packaging Corporation, 25564
Microdry, 26102
Midwest Paper Products Company, 26151
Neff Packaging, 26536
Nemeth Engineering Assoc, 26548
NST Metals, 26432
Oates Flag Co Inc, 26842
Palintest USA, 27220
Parallel Products Inc, 27293
Phoenix Process Equipment, 27505
Pioneer Plastics Inc, 27551
Plastic Printing LLC, 27586
Porcelain Metals Corporation, 27670
Premium Foil Products Company, 27753
Professional Engineering Assoc, 27878
ProMach, 27846
Psion Teklogix, 27925
Quality Natural Casing, 28011
R A Jones & Co Inc, 28046
Rapid Industries Inc, 28189
Raque Food Systems, 28192
Reflectronics, 28249
Regal Power Transmission Solutions, 28271
Revere Packaging, 28349
Rhodes Machinery International, 28375

Riverview Foods, 28418
Rocket Man, 28465
Rodes Professional Apparel, 28476
Round Paper Packages Inc, 28562
Rueff Sign Co Inc, 28608
Ruggles Sign Company, 28610
Sargent & Greenleaf, 28828
Sellers Engineering Division, 29004
SIMBA USA, 28691
Somerset Food Service, 29351
Soudal Accumetric, 29381
Span Tech LLC, 29441
Specialty Films & Associates, 29467
Specialty Food America Inc, 29468
Spectape Inc, 29475
SSE Software Corporation, 28720
SSW Holding Co Inc, 28722
STOBER Drives Inc, 28729
Strong Hold Products, 29734
Superior Distributing Co, 29800
Sweco Inc, 29853
Sysco Corp, 29885
T Q Constructors, 29977
Techno-Design, 30111
Tente Casters Inc, 30155, 30156, 30157
TGW International, 30004
Thermex Thermatron, 30214
Tri-State Plastics, 30419
Trojan Inc, 30457
Vacuum Depositing Inc, 30733
Vendome Copper & Brass Works, 30796
Vertical Systems Intl, 30822
Vogt Tube Ice, 30892
Walker Bag Mfg Co, 30983
Waukesha Cherry-Burrell, 31049, 31050
Willamette Industries, 31222
Winston Industries, 31273
WNA, 30947
WNA Hopple Plastics, 30948
Wolf Company, 31308
Zealco Industries, 31423
Ziniz, 31447
Zumbiel Packaging, 31460

Louisiana

Alcoa - Lake Charles Carbon Plant, 18537
Allpax Products, 18637
Ameriglobe LLC, 18850
Backwoods Smoker Inc, 19363
Bancroft Bag Inc, 19426
Bell Foods, 19543
Bulk Pack, 19937
Calhoun Bend Mill, 20138
Chill Rite Mfg, 20530
Containment Technology, 20875
Cord Tex, 20965
CTI Celtek Electronics, 20103
Delta Container Corporation, 21511
Delta Machine & Maufacturing, 21517
Dixie Maid Ice Cream Company, 21680
Dupuy Storage & Forwarding LLC, 21812
Dynasty Transportation, 21860
Ed Smith's Stencil Works LTD, 22029
Entech Systems Corp, 22195
Entergy's Teamwork Louisiana, 22196
Frosty Factory Of America Inc, 22892
Frymaster/Dean, 22901
Greig Filters Inc, 23402
H A Sparke Co, 23454
Hart Designs LLC, 23636
Honiron Corp, 23846
IdentaBadge, 24068
Industrial Signs, 24195
Intralox LLC, 24375, 24376
J & M Industries Inc, 24413
Jefferson Packing Company, 24537
Kentwood Spring Water Company, 24791
Laitram LLC, 25086
Lamar Advertising Co, 25101
Layflat Products, 25184
Lengsfield Brothers, 25240
Lighthouse for the Blindin New Orleans,
  25305
Magic Seasoning Blends, 25632
Martin Brothers Inc, 25802
Modern Electronics Inc, 26239
National Tape Corporation, 26508
Ouachita Machine Works, 27001
Pallet Reefer International LLC, 27231
Patio Center Inc, 27338
Paxon Polymer Company, 27361

Pelican Marine Supply LLC, 27396
Pellerin Milnor Corporation, 27400
Pensacola Rope Company, 27420
Pepper Source Inc, 27429
PPI, 27069
Pratt Industries, 27716
Printpack Inc, 27811
Procell Polymers, 27854
Progressive Tractor & Implement Co.,
  27889
Quetzal Foods International Company, 28030
Quick Stamp & Sign Mfg, 28035
Rayne Sign Co, 28202
Rebel Stamp & Sign Co, 28218
Reggie Balls Cajun Foods, 28275
REX Pure Foods, 28099
Ross & Wallace Inc, 28532
Royal Broom & Mop Factory Inc, 28574
SEI Consultants, 28672
Skrmetta Machinery Corporation, 29279
Snee Chemical Co, 29319
Southern Tool, 29422
Southern United States Trade Association,
  29423
Southwestern Electric Power Company,
  29432
Sugar Plum LLC, 29756
Sysco Corp, 29901
Technical Inc, 30103
Thomas Pump & Machinery, 30249, 30250
Universal Sign Company and Manufacturing
  Company, 30682, 30683
Walle Corp, 30994
West Louisiana Ice Svc, 31124

Maine

Belleco Inc, 19549
Coastal Products Company, 20673
Corinth Products, 20969
Diamond Pheonix Corporation, 21604
Display Concepts, 21648
Downeast Chemical, 21752
Eam, 21963
EGW Bradbury Enterprises, 21905
F.E. Wood & Sons, 22375
Fluid Imaging Technologies Inc, 22663
Food Business Associates, 22693
Fox Brush Company, 22802
Gardiner Paperboard, 23031
Geiger Bros, 23087
Gerrity Industries, 23167
Goodman Wiper & Paper Co, 23272
H A Stiles, 23455
Hardwood Products Co LP, 23602
Harold F Haines Manufacturing Inc, 23614
Hauser Packaging, 23657
Haven's Candies, 23660
Idexx Laboratories Inc, 24070
Ingredients Solutions Inc, 24225
Intelligent Controls, 24296
J.A. Thurston Company, 24436
Kady International, 24708
Leavitt & Parris Inc, 25201
Lobsters Alive Company, 25378
Lyman-Morse Fabrication, 25502
Maine Industrial Plastics & Rubber
  Corporation, 25660
Maine Poly Aquisition, 25661
Market Sign Systems, 25752
Neokraft Signs Inc, 26552
Net Pack Systems, 26558
Northeast Laboratory Svc, 26706
Northeast Packaging Co, 26707
Penley Corporation, 27410
Pine Point Fisherman's Co-Op, 27537
Quality Containers of New England, 27996
Remstar International, 28312
RTS Packaging, 28127
Saunder Brothers, 28840
Southworth Products Corp, 29434
Soyatech Inc, 29435
Sysco Corp, 29944
Tech Pak Solutions, 30096
Thirty Two North Corporation, 30244
Tuchenhagen North America, 30483
Tuchenhagen-Zajac, 30484
Uhtamaki Foods Services, 30566
Volk Packaging Corp, 30897
Vulcan Electric Co, 30910
Welch Stencil Company, 31096
Young's Lobster Shore Pound, 31411

Manitoba

Arctic Glacier Premium Ice, 19028
Besco Grain Ltd, 19606
Best Cooking Pulses, Inc., 19613
Legumex Walker, Inc., 25225
Reliance Product, 28299
Richardson International, 28385
Sperling Boss, 29490

Maryland

3Greenmoms LLC, 18002
A O A C Intl, 18030
A.K. Robins, 18071
Abicor Binzel, 18266
AD Products, 18115
AK Robbins, 18156
Alpha MOS America, 18656
American Equipment Co, 18751
American Wood Fibers, 18840
Analyticon Discovery LLC, 18901
Artcraft Badge & Sign Company, 19085
ASI/Restaurant Manager, 18227
Awb Engineers, 19264
Awning Enterprises, 19267
Bakeware Coatings, 19393
Baltimore Aircoil Co, 19419, 19420
Baltimore Sign Company, 19421
Baltimore Spice Inc, 19422
Baltimore Tape Products Inc, 19423
Barcoding Inc, 19445
Batching Systems, 19482
Bertels Can Company, 19602
Bioscience International Inc, 19688
Born Printing Company, 19795
Brimrose Corporation of America, 19871
Brooks Barrel Company, 19887
BYK Gardner Inc, 19352
C R Daniels Inc, 19997
Cambridge Intl. Inc., 20158
Cantwell-Cleary Co Inc, 20200
Charles Engineering & Service, 20443
Charles Tirschman Pallet Co, 20450
Claude Neon Signs, 20604
Clyde Bergemann Eec, 20661
Coddington Lumber Co, 20687
Commercial Corrugated Co Inc, 20773
Compliance Control Inc, 20799
Comus Restaurant Systems, 20819
Control Systems Design, 20913
Creative Cookie, 21059
Creative Signage System,, 21071
Crown-Simplimatic, 21121
Cumberland Box & Mill Co, 21148
Cynter Con Technology Adviser, 21216
Cyntergy Corporation, 21217
Dade Canvas Products Company, 21291
Day Basket Factory, 21392
Daystar, 21401
Del Monte Fresh Produce Inc., 21473
Delta Chemical Corporation, 21510
Dirt Killer Pressure Washer, 21642
Display Craft Mfg Co, 21649
Dixie Printing & Packaging, 21683
DomainMarket, 21696
Dryomatic, 21778
Dsr Enterprises, 21780
Dutter's Food, 21833
Eastern Cap & Closure Company, 21976
Elite Spice Inc, 22099
Ellenco, 22105
EVAPCO Inc, 21944
Exquis Confections, 22354
F & F and A. Jacobs & Sons, Inc., 22361
Felco Packaging Specialist, 22501
Fleet Wood Goldco Wyard, 22615
Food Instrument Corp, 22706
Foss Nirsystems, 22787
Franklin Uniform Corporation, 22830
Frazier Precision Instr Co, 22839
G K & L Inc, 22939
Galvinell Meat Co Inc, 23018
Gamse Lithographing Co Inc, 23022
Gann Manufacturing, 23024
Gardenville Signs, 23030
GEA Evaporation Technologies LLC, 22962
Gea Process Engineering Inc, 23078
Gerstel Inc, 23168
Goodwrappers Inc, 23278
H & M Bay Inc, 23452
H H Franz Co, 23462, 23463

Haas Tailoring Company, 23505
Harford Duracool LLC, 23607
Harford Systems Inc, 23608
Harvey W Hottel Inc, 23645
Hedwin Division, 23708
Hill Brush, Inc., 23775
Howard Overman & Sons, 23889
Hub Labels Inc, 23905
Hydromax Inc, 23967
IGEN, 24001
IGEN International, 24002
Independent Can Co, 24137
Insight Distribution Systems, 24275
Integrated Restaurant Software/RMS Touch, 24294
International Meat Inspection Consultants, 24346
Intralytix, 24377
Jack Stone Lighting & Electrical, 24482
Jamison Door Co, 24507
JM Huber Chemical Corpo ration, 24466
KANE Bag Supply Co, 24667
LA Motte Co, 24999
Landsman Foodservice Net, 25130
Le Smoker, 25191
Lido Roasters, 25295
Light Technology Ind, 25303
M S Willett Inc, 25532, 25533
Mail-Well Label, 25656
Marlin Steel Wire Products, 25772
Maryland Packaging Corporation, 25817
Maryland Plastics Inc, 25818
Materials Handling Systems, 25856
Mathason Industries, 25860
Memor/Memtec America Corporation, 25975
Microbiology International, 26099
Mobern Electric Corporation, 26233
Modern Stamp Company, 26247
Morris Industries, 26314
Mulholland-Harper Company, 26363
National Instruments, 26482
Nelson Co, 26541
Neonetics Inc, 26554
North American Deer   Farmers Association, 26686
Olson Wire Products Co, 26899
Onguard Industries LLC, 26935, 26936
Ottenheimer Equipment Company, 26996
Outotec USA Inc, 27005
Paramount Packing & Rubber Inc, 27297
Patrick Signs, 27343
PEAK Technologies, Inc., 27050
Pearson Signs Service, 27372
Permaloc Security Devices, 27453
Polytemp Corp, 27662
Precision Plastics Inc, 27728
Quantis Secure Systems, 28021
Quick Judith & Assoc, 28031
Ralph L. Mason,, 28159
RBA-Retailer's Bakers A ssociation, 28085
Restaurant Development Svc, 28338
Rhee Brothers, 28364
Ross Cook, 28535
Roxanne Signs Inc, 28570
Rubber Stamp Shop, 28598
Russell-William, 28617
RVS, 28128
Seitz Schenk Filter Systems, 28989
Selby Sign Co Inc, 28993
Septipack, 29039
Sheridan Sign Company, 29138
Sherwood Tool, 29139
Shimadzu Scientific Instrs, 29147
Shore Paper Box Co, 29163
Sodexo Inc, 29329
Spray Drying, 29512
Star-K Kosher Certification, 29601
Strasburger & Siegel, 29715
Stricker & Co, 29730
Suburban Signs, 29751
Superfos Packaging Inc, 29797
Sysco Corp, 29905, 29909
Televend, 30134
The Consumer Goods Forum, 30189
TLB Corporation, 30010
TPS International, 30025
Trade Wings, 30371
Triangle Sign & Svc, 30428
Trilogy Essential Ingredients, 30438
Tuchenhagen, 30482
Turbo Systems, 30497
Twenty/Twenty Graphics, 30507

UPS Logistics Technologies, 30538
US Can Company, 30540
US Product, 30555
US Tag & Label, 30558
Voorhees Rubber Mfg Co, 30904
Vulcan Food Equipment Group, 30911
W R Grace & Co, 30920
Wagner Brothers Containers, 30975
Wildes Printing Co Inc, 31207
Wilks Precision Instr Co Inc, 31216
Willard Packaging Co, 31223
YW Yacht Basin, 31388
Zeltex, 31429, 31430

Massachusetts

Acebright Inc., 18312
ACME Sign Corp, 18108
Acryline, 18341
Acumen Data Systems Inc, 18354
Adhesive Applications, 18371
Advanced Instruments Inc, 18411, 18412
Aeration Technologies Inc, 18437
Aero Company, 18439
AERTEC, 18133
All Star Dairy Foods, 18589
Altra Industrial Motion Corp, 18678
Amcel, 18700
American Apron Inc., 18718
American Bag & Burlap Company, 18724
American Holt Corp, 18775
American Insulated Panel Co, 18780
American LEWA, 18783
AMETEK Brookfield, 18175
Analog Devices Inc, 18894
Analogic Corp., 18896
ANVER Corporation, 18191
Anver Corporation, 18960
Applied Analytics, 18987
Arlin Manufacturing Co, 19050
Arthur D Little Inc., 19089
Artisan Industries, 19093
Atlantic Rubber Products, 19151
Auburn Systems LLC, 19181, 19182
Autofry, 19206
Automatic Specialties Inc, 19226
Avon Tape, 19258
Avtec Industries, 19260
Ayer Sales Inc, 19279
Azonix Corporation, 19283
Baird & Bartlett Company, 19376
Batch, 19481
Belt Technologies Inc, 19559
Bematek Systems Inc, 19563
Bete Fog Nozzle Inc, 19625
Blanche P. Field, LLC, 19723
BLH Electronics, 19335
Bostik Inc, 19808
Boston Gear, 19809
Boston Rack, 19810
Boston Retail, 19811
Boston's Best Coffee Roasters, 19813
Brady Enterprises Inc, 19837
Brown Plastics & Equipment, 19904
Bryant Glass, 19918
C & K Machine Co, 19985
C H Babb Co Inc, 19990
Cab Technology Inc, 20113
Cabot Corp, 20114
Cambridge Viscosity, Inc., 20159
Capone Foods, 20218
Caravan Company, 20228
Carman And Company, 20264
CDF Corp, 20044
Cellier Corporation, 20363
Century Products, 20400
Chapman Manufacturing Co Inc, 20437
Charles H Baldwin & Sons, 20445
Charm Sciences Inc, 20454
Chemex Division/International Housewares Corporation, 20494
Chemi-Graphic, 20496
Chilson's Shops Inc, 20532
CMT, 20075
Cold Chain Technologies, 20707
Coleman Manufacturing Co Inc, 20717
Consolidated Thread Mills, Inc., 20857
Control Technology Corp, 20915
Convectronics, 20917
Cooper Decoration Company, 20949
Corning Life Sciences, 20981
Cotter Brothers Corp, 21012

Cove Woodworking, 21025
Covestro LLC, 21028
Craft Corrugated Box Inc, 21034
Crunch Time Information Systems, 21124
CSPI, 20098
Cumberland Farms, 21150
Custom Metalcraft, Architectural Lighting, 21188
Cyborg Equipment Corporation, 21212
D & S Mfg, 21226
Dalton Electric Heating Co, 21320
Danafilms Inc, 21331
Datapaq, 21373
Day Lumber Company, 21393
Decorated Products Company, 21443
Defreeze Corporation, 21448
Del Monte Fresh Produce Inc., 21474
Delta Engineering Corporation, 21514
Delta F Corporation, 21515
Den Mar Corp, 21541
Dennis Engineering Group, 21546
Dennsi Group, 21547
Design Technology Corporation, 21568, 21569
Design-Mark Industries, 21570
Dexter Russell Inc, 21591
Diamond Machining Technology, 21602
Dietzco, 21621
Dimensional Insight, 21632
Dipwell Co, 21639
Double E Co LLC, 21723, 21724
Dow Industries, 21748
Dresco Belting Co Inc, 21767
DSA Software, 21276
DT Packaging Systems, 21285
Dunkin' Brands Inc., 21805
Durastill Export Inc, 21827
Dusobox Company, 21830
Dynabilt Products, 21843
Eastern Container Corporation, 21977
Econocorp Inc, 22019
Edge Resources, 22033
Energy Sciences Inc, 22164, 22165
Erving Industries, 22258
ESI Qual Intl, 21938
Eurosicma, 22300
Extech Instruments, 22355
Fabreeka International Inc, 22426
Fay Paper Products, 22484
Fibre Leather Manufacturing Company, 22536
Firematic Sprinkler Devices, 22572
First Plastics Co Inc, 22579
FLEXcon Company, 22395
Flow of Solids, 22660
Foam Concepts Inc, 22669
Foilmark Inc, 22680
Food Management Search, 22710
Foodmark, Inc., 22740
Foods Research Laboratories, 22742
Foodservice East, 22745
Formation Systems, 22761
FORT Hill Sign Products Inc, 22404
Forte Technology, 22778
Foster Miller Inc, 22790
Frem Corporation, 22852
Friend Box Co, 22869
Frost Manufacturing Corp, 22891
Fuller Box Co, 22908
Fuller Flag Company, 22909
Fygir Logistic Information Systems, 22929
Gamewell Corporation, 23021
General Electric Company, 23109
GHM Industries Inc, 22982
Giltron Inc, 23186
Ginseng Up Corp, 23188
Global Organics, 23226
Gloucester Engineering, 23242
Good Idea, 23267
Grace Tea Co, 23295
Greenfield Paper Box Co, 23386
Greerco High Shear Mixers, 23392
Grinnell Fire ProtectionSystems Company, 23422
Group One Partners, 23433
Gruenewald ManufacturingCompany, 23434
Halmark Systems Inc, 23535
Hampden Papers Inc, 23550
Hano Business Forms, 23575
Hanson Box & Lumber Company, 23580
Hardi-Tainer, 23598
Harpak-Ulma, 23621

Harpak-ULMA Packaging LLC, 23619
Harvard Folding Box Company, 23644
Hazen Paper Co, 23673
Health Star, 23678
Healthstar Inc, 23681
HH Controls Company, 23491
HI-TECH Filter, 23493
Hillards Chocolate System, 23778
Hodge Manufacturing Company, 23801
Holland Co Inc, 23822
Hot Mama's Foods, 23875
Hoyt Corporation, 23900
Hub Folding Box Co, 23904
Hub Pen Company, 23906
Hudson Belting & Svc Co Inc, 23913
Hudson Poly Bag Inc, 23915
Huntsman Packaging, 23936
Hy-Trous/Flash Sales, 23950
Hyer Industries, 23970
I M A North America, 23981
Iconics Inc, 24050
IGS Store Fixtures, 24003
Imsco Technology, 24121
Infinity Tapes LLC, 24209
International Smoking Systems, 24359
International Thermal Dispensers, 24361
Intertek USA, 24374
ISS/GEBA/AFOS, 24025
J&J Corrugated Box Corporation, 24430
Janedy Sign Company, 24509
Jarisch Paper Box Company, 24518
Jarvis-Cutter Company, 24523
Jedwards International Inc, 24535
Jen-Coat, Inc., 24540
Jenike & Johanson Inc, 24542
Jim Did It Sign Company, 24565
John E. Ruggles & Company, 24578
John J. Adams Die Corporation, 24580
JP Plastics, Inc., 24469
Kaye Instruments, 24743
Keena Corporation, 24747
Kelley Wood Products, 24757
KEMCO, 24676
Kerrigan Paper Products Inc, 24795
Kidde-Fenwal Inc, 24827
Kimball Companies, 24837
KLEEN Line Corp, 24689
Knott Slicers, 24904
Koch Membrane Systems Inc, 24908
Krueger Food Laboratories, 24957
Labelprint America, 25064
Laboratory Devices, 25070
Lambeth Band Corporation, 25108
Lamco Chemical Co Inc, 25109
Laminated Papers, 25113
Lamson & Goodnow, 25119
Larien Products, 25144
Legal Sea Foods, 25218
Lenze Americas, 25248
LEWA Inc, 25014
Lifoam Industries LLC, 25300
Lightolier, 25306
LineSource, 25327
Lion Labels Inc, 25341
Liquid Solids Control Inc, 25351
LIST, 25016
Lista International Corp, 25353
Litecontrol, 25358
Lock Inspection Systems, 25381, 25382
Lockwood Packaging, 25398
Lynn Sign Inc, 25506
M D Stetson Co, 25523
M&L Plastics, 25535
Magnetic Technologies LTD, 25642
Mainline Industries Inc, 25662
Management Insight, 25686
Market Forge Industries Inc, 25750
Market Sales Company, 25751
Markwell Manufacturing Company, 25762
Marlow Watson Inc, 25775
Mclaughlin Paper Co Inc, 25930
Mcnairn Packaging, 25932
Metcalf & Eddy, 26025
Mettler-Toledo Process Analytics, Inc, 26040
Micro Wire Products Inc, 26085
Microfluidics International, 26104
Micron Separations, 26107
Microtouch Systems Inc, 26115
MILLIPORE Sigma, 25578
Modular Panel Company, 26252
Moseley Realty LLC, 26322
Motion Technologies, 26328

Mount Hope Machinery Company, 26333
MultiFab Plastics, 26372
Multigrains Bread Co, 26377
Mundial, 26386
Munters Corp, 26388
Murnell Wax Company, 26392
Muth Associates, 26401
National Datacomputer, 26468
National Food Product Research Corporation, 26479
National Metal Industries, 26488
National Oilwell Varco, 26490
Nature's Own, 26520
Nevlen Co. 2, Inc., 26564
New England Cheese Making Supply Company, 26576
New England Pallets & Skids, 26580
New England Wooden Ware, 26581
Newstamp Lighting Factory, 26617, 26618
Nichols Specialty Products, 26635
Noral, 26664
Northeast Distributors Inc, 26704
Northeast Fresh Foods Alliance, 26705
Northern Berkshire Tourist, 26710
Now Plastics Inc, 26758
Nutrinfo Corporation, 26789
O'Brien Bros Inc, 26803
O/K International Corporation, 26812
Ohlson Packaging, 26868
Omnion, 26923
Onset Computer Corp, 26937
Orion Research, 26976
OSRAM SYLVANIA, 26827
Osram Sylvania, 26990
Package Converting Corp, 27135
Package Machinery Co Inc, 27137
Pall Filtron, 27224
Paramount Manufacturing Company, 27295
Pepperell Paper Company, 27431
Peter Gray Corporation, 27467
Piab USA Inc, 27511, 27512
PIAB Vacuum Conveyors, 27056
Piab Vacuum Products, 27513
Pilgrim Plastics, 27531
Pioneer Packaging, 27548
Placon Corp, 27563
Plastic Assembly Corporation, 27579
Plastic Turning Company, 27591
Polyfoam Corp, 27650
Pop Tops Co Inc, 27667
Portugalia Imports, 27682
Precision Systems Inc, 27734
Pro Line Co, 27830
Process Heating Corp, 27860
Process Sensors Corp, 27862
PROMA Technologies, 27074
Protectowire Co Inc, 27909
Qsx Labels, 27977
Quality Mop & Brush Manufacturers, 28010
Quantek Instruments, 28019
R Murphy Co Inc, 28057
R.P. Childs Stamp Company, 28077
R.R. Scheibe Company, 28078
Radding Signs, 28142
Radio Frequency Co Inc, 28147
Rand-Whitney Group LLC, 28172, 28173, 28174
Randall Printing, 28177
Raytheon Co, 28206
Ready White, 28216
Reed & Barton Food Service, 28237
Reid Graphics Inc, 28284
Reiser, 28291
Risco USA Corp, 28407
RL Instruments, 28110
Rocheleau Blow Molding Systems, 28458
Rofin-Baasel Inc, 28482
Romanow Container, 28497, 28498
Royal Label Co, 28581
RPA Process Technologies, 28118
Rubbair Door, 28596
Ruland Manufacturing Co Inc, 28612
S & G Resources Inc, 28629
Safe-T-Cut Inc, 28752
Safety Fumigant Co, 28753
Savogran Co, 28852
Scanning Devices Inc, 28863
Schermerhorn Inc, 28878
Schneider Electric, 28894
Seaboard Folding Box Corp, 28944
Seidman Brothers, 28986
Sencorp White, 29013

Sensitech Inc, 29025
Sentinel Polyolefins, 29031
Servomex Inc, 29064
Set Point Paper Company, 29068
SFBC, LLC dba Seaboard Folding Box, 28677
Shuster Corporation, 29172
Shuster Laboratories, 29173, 29174
Signs O' Life, 29215
Sillcocks Plastics International, 29228
Silverson Machines Inc, 29239
Simonds International, 29247, 29248
Simonson Group, 29250
Somerset Industries, 29352
Spir-It/Zoo Piks, 29498
Spiral Biotech Inc, 29499
Spirit Foodservice, Inc., 29505
Stainless Steel Coatings, 29562
Star Container Corporation, 29591
STD Precision Gear, 28726
Steel Art Co, 29619
Stevens Linen Association, 29665
Stokes, 29683
Sunpoint Products, 29782
Suzhou-Chem Inc, 29843
Sysco Corp, 29900
Table Talk Pies Inc, 30041
Tango Shatterproof Drinkware, 30062
Tecogen Inc, 30115
Teledyne Benthos Inc, 30129, 30130
TEMP-TECH Company, 29998
Tempera/Sol, 30141
Terkelsen Machine Company, 30159
Terracon Corp, 30163
Testo, 30168
Textile Buff & Wheel, 30182
Thermalogic Corp, 30212
Thermedics Detection, 30213
Thermo BLH, 30215
Thermo Detection, 30216
Thermo Fisher Scientific, 30217
Thermo Jarrell Ash Corporation, 30219
Tiax LLC, 30275
Tibersoft, 30276
Tomac Packaging, 30321
Trans World Services, 30384
UDEC Corp, 30529
Uni First Corp, 30592
Uniplast Inc, 30615
United Electric Controls Co, 30634
Universal Plastics, 30680
Universal Tag Inc, 30687
University Products, 30688
University-Brink, 30689
US Cap Systems Corporation, 30541
US Line Company, 30552
US Plastic Corporation, 30554
Vacuum Barrier Corp, 30732
Vaisala Inc, 30734
Vanco Products Company, 30764
Varick Enterprises, 30779
Vernon Plastics, 30814
Veronica's Treats, 30815
Viacam, 30827
VICAM, 30716
Waddington North America, 30971
Walker Magnetics Group Inc, 30987, 30988
Waltham Fruit Company, 31002
Waters Corp, 31041
Watts Regulator Co, 31048
Web Industries, 31067
Weiss Sheet Metal Inc, 31091
Westerbeke Fishing Gear Co Inc, 31133
Weston Emergency Light Co, 31155
Wetterau Wood Products, 31161
Whatman, 31169
Whiting & Davis, 31185
Wilevco Inc, 31209
Wiltec, 31240
Wind River Environmental, 31247
Wirefab Inc, 31280
WORC Slitting & Mfg Co, 30949
Worcester Envelope Co, 31333
Worcester Industrial Products, 31334
World Food Tech Services, 31343
Yeuell Name Plate & Label, 31398

Michigan

A.D. Johnson Engraving Company, 18069
A.D. Joslin Manufacturing Company, 18070
ACCO Systems, 18103

Acco Systems, 18280
Accro-Seal, 18285
Accuflex Industrial Hose LTD, 18295
Ace-Tex Enterprises, 18311
Acromag Inc., 18339
Advance Automated Systems Inc, 18386
Advance Engineering Co, 18390
AGET Manufacturing Co, 18147
Airflow Sciences Corp, 18508
Airmaster Fan Co, 18512
AIS Container Handling, 18154
AJM Packaging Corporation, 18155
Albion Industries Inc, 18532
Albion Machine & Tool Co, 18533
Alex Delvecchio Enterprises, 18552
All Weather Energy Systems, 18593
Alpha Resources Inc, 18660
Alro Plastics, 18665
American Design & Machinery, 18742
American Flag & Banner Co Inc, 18760
Ammeraal Beltech, 18872
Anchor Conveyor Products, 18903
Andex Industries Inc, 18929
Andy J. Egan Co., 18938
Ann Arbor Computer, 18946
APEC, 18194
Arden Companies, 19037
Arlington Display Industries, 19051
Armaly Brands, 19053
Armstrong Hot Water, 19059
Armstrong International, 19060
Armstrong-Hunt, 19062
Assembly Technology & Test, 19120
Astoria Laminations, 19131
Atlas Copco Tools & Assembly, 19159
Auto Pallets-Boxes, 19199
Automatic Handling Int, 19222
Automation Ideas Inc, 19231
Automation Safety, 19236
B & G Products, 19286
B & P Process Equipment, 19287
B H Awning & Tent Co, 19291
Baker Foodservice Design Inc, 19381
Baker Perkins Inc, 19383
Banner Day, 19428
Bayard Kurth Company, 19492
BEI, 19319
Bekum America Corp, 19533
Belle Isle Awning, 19548
Bernal Technology, 19594
BEX Inc, 19324
Bill Carr Signs, 19655
BioSys, 19674
Black River Pallet Co, 19712
Blackmer Co, 19715
Blissfield Canning Company, 19730
Blue Line Foodservice Distr, 19746
Borroughs Corp, 19796
Bosch Packaging Technology, 19802
Bradford Co, 19830
Brechteen, 19851
Bright Technologies, 19867
Brill Manufacturing Co, 19870
Brothers Manufacturing, 19891
Brown Machine LLC, 19901
Bulldog Factory Svc LLC, 19939
Bulman Products Inc, 19941
BW Controls, 19350
Cadillac Pallets, 20123
Cadillac Plastics, 20124
Cadillac Products Inc, 20125
CapSnap Equipment, 20203
Carhartt, 20247
Carroll Packaging, 20298
Carter Products, 20305
Castrol Industrial, 20337
Centrifuge Solutions, 20391
Cepco, 20405
Change Parts Inc, 20434
Chapman Sign, 20438
Charter House, 20458
Chemco Products Inc, 20490
CHEP Pallecon Solutions, 20055
Choctaw-Kaul Distribution Company, 20544
Christman Screenprint Inc, 20551
Chrysler & Koppin Co, 20558
CII Food Svc Design, 20059
Clawson Container Company, 20606
Clipper Belt Lacer Company, 20654
Cobb & Zimmer, 20679
Coding Products, 20690
Coffee Express Roasting Co, 20696

Command Electronics Inc, 20769
Complete Automation, 20794
Complex Steel & Wire Corp, 20798
Constar International, 20861
Contech Enterprises Inc, 20877
Continental Identification, 20888
Control Pak Intl, 20911
Conveyor Components Co, 20922, 20923
Corrugated Specialties, 20995
Coss Engineering Sales Company, 21009
Coy Laboratory Products Inc, 21029
CPM Century Extrusion, 20083
Creative Foam Corp, 21062
Creative Techniques, 21073
Cretel Food Equipment, 21084
Crippen Manufacturing Co, 21086
CSV Sales, 20101
Cummins Label Co, 21152
Darson Corp, 21360
Dart Container Corp., 21362
Dearborn Mid-West Conveyor Co, 21424
Decade Products, 21430
Delfield Co, 21498
Dell Marking Systems, 21504
Dematic USA, 21536
Denstor Mobile Storage Systems, 21548
Design Systems Inc, 21567
Detroit Forming, 21579
Detroit Marking Products, 21580
Detroit Quality Brush Mfg Co, 21581
Diamond Automation, 21597
Dimension Graphics Inc, 21631
Dimplex Thermal Solutions, 21633
Display Pack Inc, 21652
Do-It Corp, 21689
Dorden & Co, 21715
Dover Metals, 21743
Dow Packaging, 21749
Dunkley International Inc, 21806
Dura-Pack Inc., 21816
Dynamet, 21849
E.L. Nickell Company, 21888
Earthy Delights, 21967
EB Eddy Paper, 21892
Eberbach Corp, 22000
Ederback Corporation, 22032
Eliason Corp, 22097
Elopak Americas, 22122
Energymaster, 22166
Engineered Automation, 22168
Engraving Specialists, 22183
Enterprise Envelope Inc, 22201
Ermanco, 22254
Eugene Welding Company, 22283
F & A Fabricating Inc, 22360
Fabri-Kal Corp, 22427
Fabricon Products Inc, 22432
Fantapak, 22461
Faraday, 22462
Farmer's Co-Op Elevator Co, 22467
Fata Automation, 22476
Fettig Laboratories, 22524
Fibre Converters Inc, 22535
Filler Specialties, 22543
Flint Boxmakers Inc, 22641
Flint Rubber Stamp Works, 22642
Flo-Cold, 22643
Fogg Filler Co, 22679
Foley's Famous Aprons, 22686
Frost ET Inc, 22889
Frost Food Handling Products, 22890
Fruit Growers Package Company, 22895
GA Design Menu Company, 22952
Geerpres Inc, 23084
General Formulations, 23114
General Processing Systems, 23124
General Tape & Supply, 23130
Genesee Corrugated, 23135
Gentile Packaging Machinery, 23146
Georg Fischer Disa Pipe Tools, 23149
Giffin International, 23179
GKI Foods, 22984
Glastender, 23202
Globe Fire Sprinkler Corp, 23235
Gold Star Products, 23257
Goldman Manufacturing Company, 23264
Gourmet COFFEE Roasters, 23287
Grand Rapids Chair Company, 23311
Grand Rapids Label, 23312
Grand Valley Labels, 23314
Great Lakes Foods, 23349
Great Lakes Scientific, 23350

Minnesota

Montana

Nebraska

Nevada

Red-Ray Manufacturing Co Inc, 28227
Refcon, 28247
Regal Custom Fixture Company, 28265
Regal Pinnacle Integrations, 28268
Regency Label Corporation, 28274
Reheis Co, 28280
Rempak Industries, 28311
Research & Development Packaging
 Corporation, 28329
Revent Inc, 28346
RGN Developers, 28102
Richards Industries Systems, 28383
Rimex Metals Inc, 28403
RLS Equipment Company, 28111
RLS Logistics, 28112
Robert C Vncek Design Assoc, 28436
Robertet Flavors, 28438
Rockaway Baking, 28464
Rohm America Inc., 28485
Rollon Corp, 28492
Romaco Inc, 28496
Rondo Inc, 28510
Ronell Industries, 28512
RTS Packaging, 28125
Rubber Fab Molding & Gasket, 28597
Ruffino Paper Box Co, 28609
Rutan Poly Industries Inc, 28619
SA Wald Reconditioners, 28657
Sabert Corp, 28743, 28744
Sambonet USA, 28772
Samsung Electronics America, Inc., 28776
Sancoa International, 28797
Sandvik Process Systems, 28804
Sandvik Process Systems Inc, 28803
Sani-Pure Food Laboratories, 28811
Sani-Tech Group, 28812
SASA Demarle, 28659
Saturn Overhead Equipment, 28838
SBS of Financial Industries, 28664
Scandia Packaging Machinery Co, 28862
Schiff & Co, 28881
Schiffenhaus Industries, 28882
Schleicher & Schuell MicroSience, 28886
Schwerdtel Corporation, 28913
Scientific Process & Research, 28917
Sea Breeze Fruit Flavors, 28940
Security Packaging, 28976
Seidenader Equipment, 28985
Sensory Computer Systems, 29028
Sensory Spectrum, 29029
Sergeant E M Pulp & Chem Co, 29045
Setco, 29070
SG Frantz Company, 28680
SGS International, 28681
Shamrock Technologies Newark, 29103
Shanghai Freemen, 29104
Sharp Brothers, 29110
Sharp Electronics Corporation, 29111
Sheman Tov Corporation, 29134
Ship Rite Packaging, 29149
Shore Distribution Resources, 29162
Shorewood Packaging, 29165
Signature Packaging, 29204
Sitram/Global Marketing, 29271
Skc Inc, 29275
Slm Manufacturing Corp, 29285
SLT Group, 28702
Smith Design Associates, 29293
Solbern Corp, 29334
Solka-Floc, 29337
Something Different Linen, 29355
Sommers Plastic Product Co Inc, 29357
Source Packaging Inc, 29385
South Jersey Machine, 29388
South Jersey Store Fixtures Co, 29389
South River Machine, 29390
Spear Packing, 29456
Specialities Importers & Distributers, 29459
Spin-Tech Corporation, 29495
Spray Tek Inc, 29514
Springfield Metal Products Co, 29523
Squire Corrugated Container Company,
 29534
St. Elizabeth Street Display Corporation,
 29539
Stancase Equipment Company, 29570
Standard Casing Company, 29572
Stanley Roberts, 29585
Stapling Machines Co, 29589
Star Micronics, 29597
State Container Corp, 29609
Stay Tuned Industries, 29614

Steel Craft Fluorescent Company, 29622
Steelite International USA, 29626
Sterling Net & Twine Company, 29652
Stiles Enterprises Inc, 29677
Stonhard, 29692
Stonhard, Inc., 29693
Stor-Rite Freezer Storage, 29695
Strohmeyer & Arpe Co Inc, 29733
Suan Farma, 29747
Sunco & Frenchie, 29771
Superior Label Company, 29804
Superior Packaging Equipment Corporation,
 29808
Sysco Corp, 29891
Systech International, 29952
Systems Comtrex, 29959
T & A Metal Products Inc, 29965
Table De France: North America, 30040
Technium, 30110
Teksem LLC, 30125
Terlet USA, 30160
Terriss Consolidate, 30164
TESTO, 30001
Texpak Inc, 30181
The Pub Brewing Company, 30194
Thermal Package Testing Laboratory, 30209
Thunderbird Label Corportion, 30272
Thwing-Albert Instrument Co, 30274
Tifa (CI), 30281
Titan Plastics, 30301
Tolan Machinery Company, 30313
Torpac Capsules, 30346
Total Lubricants, 30355
Tradepaq Corporation, 30374
Trap-Zap Environmental, 30391
Traycon Manufacturing Co, 30398
Trent Corp, 30405
Tri-K Industries Inc, 30416
Triad Scientific, 30425, 30426
Tronex Industries, 30459
Tuckahoe Manufacturing Co, 30485
Turkana Food, 30500
Ultimate Textile, 30570
Ultrapar Inc., 30581
Unette Corp, 30588
UNEX Manufacturing, 30534
Unex Manufacturing Inc, 30589
Unifoil Corp, 30602
United Commercial Corporation, 30632
United Label Corp, 30643
United Products & Instr Inc, 30648
United Showcase Company, 30651
United Specialty Flavors, 30653
Universal Folding Box, 30667
Universal Folding Box Company, 30668
UPN Pallet Company, 30537
Vac-U-Max, 30728
Vacumet Corp, 30730
Valesco Trading, 30739
Van Dam Machine Corp, 30754
Van Dereems Mfg Co, 30756
Vertex Interactive, 30821
Victory Box Corp, 30838
Victory Refrigeration, 30840
Visual Packaging Corp, 30877
Voigt Lighting Industries Inc., 30893
Volta Belting Technology, Inc., 30899
W&H Systems, 30921
WaffleWaffle, 30973
Warren Pallet Co Inc, 31012
Warwick Manufacturing & Equip, 31017
WCB Ice Cream, 30931
WCB Ice Cream USA, 30932
Weber Scientific Inc, 31078
Wedgwood USA, 31081
WEI Equipment, 30938
West Chemical Products, 31120
Western Carriers, 31134
Westfalia Separator, 31153
Westfield Sheet Metal Works, 31154
Whatman, 31168
Wheaton Plastic Containers, 31170
Whittle & Mutch Inc, 31189
Wifag Group Polytype America Corp, 31196
Williams Refrigeration, 31231
Willson Industries, 31237
Wilson AL Chemical Co, 31238
Winkler USA LLC, 31265
Witte Co Inc, 31298
Wood & Laminates, 31314
Woodward Manufacturing, 31330
World Finer Foods, 31341

World Wide Safe Brokers, 31356
Wrapade Packaging Systems, 31361
Wraps, 31362
Wyssmont Co Inc, 31369
Zaloom Marketing Corp, 31419

New Mexico

Action Signs By Stubblefield, 18348
DHP, 21264
Eunice Locker Plant, 22284
Four Corners Ice, 22796
Klinger Constructors LLC, 24883
National Restaurant Supply Company, 26500
New Mexico Products Inc, 26595
Pulse Systems, 27931
San Juan Signs Inc, 28790
Sapat Packaging Industry, 28824
Shamrock Foods Co, 29100
Stainless Motors Inc, 29557
Swancock Designworks, 29850
Sysco Corp, 29881
Taylor Precision Products, 30084

New York

A Snow Craft Co Inc, 18032
A T Scafati Inc, 18037
A&A Line & Wire Corporation, 18040
AAMD, 18081
Abalon Precision Manufacturing
 Corporation, 18250
Abco International, 18260, 18261
Abell-Howe Crane, 18265
ABG Industries, 18094
Accommodation Program, 18282
Acme Awning Co Inc, 18317
Adcraft, 18365
ADD Testing & Research, 18120
Admatch Corporation, 18378
Advance Energy Technologies, 18389
Advance Tabco, 18395
Adwest Technologies, 18433
AERCO International Inc, 18132
Aero-Power Unitized Fueler, 18444
AFGO Mechanical Svc Inc, 18140
Ag-Pak, 18461
Agriculture Consulting Services, 18475
Aigner Index, 18487
Aladdin Transparent Packaging, 18526
Alard Equipment Corp, 18528
Alarm Controls Corp, 18529
Alcoa - Massena Operations, 18538
Alconox Inc, 18542, 18543
Alfa Chem, 18555
All Packaging Machinery Corp, 18583
All Sorts Premium Packaging, 18585
All Star Carts & Vehicles, 18588
Allenair Corp, 18606
Allendale Cork Company, 18607
Allied Adhesive Corporation, 18617
Allied Metal Spinning, 18623
Allsorts Premium Packaging, 18638
Alouf Plastics, 18648
Alpine Store Equipment Corporation, 18664
Altech Packaging Company, 18670
Altek Industries Corporation, 18672
Alufoil Products Co Inc, 18682
Alusett Precision Manufacturing, 18688
ALY Group of New York, 18166
Amcor Group Limited, 18706
American Casting & Mfg Corp, 18731
American Chocolate Mould Co., 18732
American Coaster Company, 18733
American Conveyor Corporation, 18735
American Dixie Group, 18745
American Felt & Filter Co, 18758
American Housewares, 18776
American Menu Displays, 18792
American Metal Stamping, 18794
American Roland Food Corp, 18817
American Star Cork Company, 18824
American Systems Associates, 18828
American Wax Co, 18836
Ameritech Laboratories, 18856
Amherst Stainless Fabrication, 18870
Amscor Inc, 18883
Amsterdam Printing & Litho Inc, 18887
Analite, 18893
Analytical Technologies Inc, 18900
Andco Environmental Processes, 18911
Anderson Instrument Company, 18919

Anderson-Negele, 18927
Andex Corp, 18928
Andrea Basket, 18933
Andy Printed Products, 18939
ANKOM Technology, 18189, 18190
Apex Packing & Rubber Co, 18971
API Heat Transfer Inc, 18197
Apogee Translite Inc, 18976
Apollo Acme Lighting Fixture, 18977
Appleson Press, 18984
Application Software, 18986
Applied Fabric Technologies, 18989
Applied Robotics Inc, 18995
Apv/Crepaco Inc, 19000
APV Engineered Systems, 18209
Architectural Products, 19018
Archon Industries, 19022
Archon Industries Inc, 19023
Arena Products, 19038
Arrow Tank Co, 19076
Art Craft Lighting, 19078
Art Poly Bag Co, 19079
Art-Tech Restaurant Design, 19083
Artistic Packaging Concepts, 19098
Artkraft Strauss LLC, 19099
At-Your-Svc Software Inc, 19139
Atlantic Ultraviolet Corp, 19152
Attias Oven Corp, 19176
Audrey Signs, 19184
August Thomsen Corp, 19190
Auto-Mate Technologies, 19201
Automatic Electronic Machines Company,
 19219
Avins Fabricating Co, 19256
Avne Packaging Services, 19257
Awning Co Inc, 19266
Awnings by Dee, 19269
Axces Systems, 19270
Axelrod, Norman N, 19271
B&K Coffee, 19305
Babcock Co, 19357
Bakers Pride Oven Company, 19385
Bakery Associates, 19386
BAKERY Innovative Technology, 19311,
 19312
Bakery Machinery Dealers, 19390
Balchem Corp, 19400
Bardo Abrasives, 19447
Barrington Nutritionals, 19466
Barrington Packaging Systems Group, 19467
Basic Adhesives, 19475
Baskets Extraordinaires, 19480
Bayside Motion Group, 19498
Beacon Specialties, 19505
Beaverite Corporation, 19510
Bennett Manufacturing Company, 19572
Best Brands Home Products, 19611
Big Apple Equipment Corporation, 19647
Billie-Ann Plastics Packaging, 19657
BINDER Inc., 19331
Black Bear Farm Winery, 19708
Bogner Industries, 19771
Bormioli Rocco Glass Company, 19794
Boska Holland, 19804
Bragard Professional Uniforms, 19839
Braun Brush Co, 19847, 19848
Brewer-Cantelmo Inc, 19861
Brock Awnings LTD, 19883
Buffalo China, 19929
Buffalo Technologies Corporation, 19930
Buffalo Wire Works Co Inc, 19931
Burrell Cutlery Company, 19964
Burrows Paper Corp, 19965, 19966
Bynoe Printers, 19981
CA Griffith International, 20021
Cacao Prieto, 20117
Calia Technical, 20139
Calico Cottage, 20140
Cameo Metal Products Inc, 20164
Capital Industries, 20208
Capitol Awning Co Inc, 20211
Capitol Vial, 20216
Carleton Technologies Inc, 20254
Carlyle Compressor, 20263
Carpet City Paper Box Company, 20287
Carrageenan Company, 20289
Carry-All Canvas Bag Co., 20300
Carts Food Equipment, 20314
Case Manufacturing Company, 20323
Casso-Solar Corporation, 20330
Castella Imports Inc, 20334

Weiss Instruments Inc, 31090
WellSet Tableware Manufacturing Company, 31097
Wesley-Kind Associates, 31117
Wilco Precision Testers, 31203
Wilder Manufacturing Company, 31206
Will & Baumer, 31217
William J. Mills & Company, 31227
Williamsburg Metal Spinning, 31233
Willow Specialties, 31236
Win-Holt Equipment Group, 31244
Wipe-Tex International Corp, 31276
WMF/USA, 30944
Wohl Associates Inc, 31304, 31305
Wooster Novelty Company, 31332
Worksafe Industries, 31337
Worksman 800 Buy Cart, 31338
World Kitchen, 31344
World Water Works, 31352
WS Packaging Group Inc, 30957
Xcel Tower Controls, 31375
Xiaoping Design, 31378
XL Corporate & Research Services, 31373
Xylem Inc, 31381
Yohay Baking Co, 31399
Young & Swartz Inc, 31409
Zahm & Nagel Co, 31418
Zelco Industries, 31428
Zumtobel Staff Lighting, 31463

Newfoundland and Labrador

Frelco, 22851
Peter Pan Sales, 27469
WS Packaging Group Inc, 30968

North Carolina

A B T Inc, 18018
A Line Corporation, 18027
A&M Thermometer Corporation, 18054
A. Klein & Company, 18064
ABB, 18085
Abco Automation, 18259
Adcapitol, 18364
Aerolator Systems, 18448
Ali Group, 18564
Allen Industries Inc, 18604
Alpha Canvas & Awning Co, 18653
American & Efird, 18713
American Air Filter, 18717
American Creative Solutions, 18738
Amiad Filtration Systems, 18871
Anbroco, 18902
Anco-Eaglin Inc, 18909
Andersen Products Inc, 18914
APV Baker, 18208
APV Heat Transfer, 18211
Arjo Wiggins, 19043
Arjobex, 19044
Arneg LLC, 19063
Asset Design LLC, 19121
Astoria General Espresso, 19130
Atlas-Stord, 19174
Automated Machine Technologies, 19214
Axon Styrotech, 19275, 19276
B&H Foods, 19302
Bahnson Environmental Specs, 19373
Bakery Systems, 19392
Bally Refrigerated Boxes Inc, 19417
Beaufurn, 19508
Bennett Box & Pallet Company, 19571
Berger Lahr Motion Technology, 19583
Bertie County Peanuts, 19604
Beverage Air, 19636
Bijur Lubricating Corporation, 19654
Biomerieux Inc, 19684
Black's Products of HighPoint, 19713
Blue Ridge Converting, 19750
Blue Tech, 19752
BOC Plastics Inc, 19341
Bosch Packaging Svc, 19797
Bosch Rexroth Corp, 19803
Bowman Hollis Mfg Corp, 19820
Buhler Aeroglide Corp, 19934
Caraustar Industries, Inc., 20227
Carolina Container, 20275
Carolina Cracker, 20276
Carolina Glove Co, 20277
Carolina Knife, 20278
Carotek Inc, 20283
Carpigiani Corporation of America, 20288

Cates Mechanical Corp, 20346
Cavert Wire Co, 20352
CBS International, 20030
CEM Corporation, 20048
CH Imports, 20054
Chaircraft, 20420
Chambers Container Company, 20424
Champion Industries Inc, 20428
Charles Craft Inc, 20441
Charlotte Tent & Awning, 20452
Chase-Logeman Corp, 20463
Clear View Bag Company, 20623
Coats North America, 20677
Cobb Sign Co Inc, 20680
Coleman Resources, 20718
Comco Signs, 20764
Computer Aided Marketing, 20806
Computerway Food Systems, 20812
Conbraco Industries Inc, 20826
Contemporary Product Inc, 20878
Cooling Technology Inc, 20948
Corbett Timber Co, 20962
COX Technologies, 20081
CPM Wolverine Proctor LLC, 20085
CRF Technologies, 20089
Crown Controls Inc., 21103
Cryovac, 21129
Custom Molders, 21191
David E. Moley & Associates, 21382
Davis Brothers Produce Boxes, 21386
Day & Zimmermann International, 21391
Del Monte Fresh Produce Inc., 21476
Delavan Spray Technologies, 21495
Delta Cyklop Orga Pac, 21513
Dematic Corp, 21534
Dito Dean Food Prep, 21662
Dize Co, 21688
Douglas Battery Manufacturing Company, 21732
Dudson USA Inc, 21794
ELBA, 21910
Engineered Plastics Inc, 22170
Equipment Design & Fabrication, 22233
Equipment Enterprises, 22235
Exel, 22341
Ez Box Machinery Company, 22359
Fab-X/Metals, 22420
Fairchild Industrial Products, 22445
Fischbein LLC, 22581
Flambeau Inc, 22603
Flanders Corp, 22606
Foamex, 22673
Focke & Co Inc, 22675
FoodLogiQ, 22736
Forbo Siegling LLC, 22755
Fox-Morris Associates, 22806
Friedrich Metal Products, 22868
Frigidaire Co., 22872
Furniturelab, 22922
G.W. Dahl Company, 22951
Garland Truffles, Inc., 23037
Gaston County Dyeing Mach Co, 23055
Gea Intec, Llc, 23077
General Espresso Equipment, 23111
General Industries Inc, 23116
Genpak LLC, 23144
Glen Raven Custom Fabrics LLC, 23210
Gough-Econ Inc, 23286
Grease Master, 23345
Greenfield Disston, 23384
Greitzer, 23403
Hackney Brothers, 23515
Hamilton Beach Brands, 23542
Harlan Laws Corp, 23609
Hayward Industries Inc, 23672
HBD Industries, 23484
Henley Paper Company, 23727
Hibco Plastics, 23761
Hildreth Wood Products Inc, 23773
Hoffer Flow Controls Inc, 23805
Honeywell International, 23843
Horner International, 23863
Hubber Technology Inc, 23910
ICB Greenline, 23990
Ideal of America, 24062
Ika-Works Inc, 24074
Imex Vinyl Packaging, 24099
Imprinting Systems Specialty, 24118
Industrial Container Corp, 24163
Industrial Laboratory Eqpt Co, 24178
Industrial Piping Inc, 24187
Industries of the Blind, 24203

Informed Beverage Management, 24217
Ingles Markets, 24221
Inglett & Company, 24222
Innoseal Systems Inc, 24246
International Tray Pads, 24362
Interroll Corp, 24366, 24367
Intertech Corp, 24373
Irby, 24385
J Leek Assoc Inc, 24423
Jacobi Lewis Co, 24493
Jhrg LLC, 24561
Jimbo's Jumbos Inc, 24568
JIT Manufacturing & Technology, 24463
John Plant Co, 24584
Jowat Corp., 24631
Karolina Polymers, 24726
KBR Building Group, 24673
Kidde Residential & Commercial, 24826
King Arthur, 24848
Kirkco Corp, 24868
Kurtz Oil Company, 24969
Kurz Transfer Products LP, 24970
Lady Mary, 25079
LCI Corporation, 25006
Liburdi Group of Companies, 25292
LIS Warehouse Systems, 25015
Lodging By Charter, 25401
Lord Label Group, 25435
Lord Label Machine Systems, 25436
M G Newell Corp, 25527
Machine Builders & Design Inc, 25608, 25609
Marshall Air Systems Inc, 25790
Mastercraft International, 25841
Material Handling Technology, Inc, 25851
Mcintyre Metals Inc, 25927
Meadows Mills Inc, 25938
Melville Plastics, 25971
Micro Filtration Systems, 26081
Microbac-Wilson Devision, 26096
Microthermics, 26114
MicroThermics, Inc., 26092
Microtron Abrasives, 26116
Minges Printing & Advg Specs, 26202
Minuteman Power Boss, 26210
Minuteman Power Box Inc, 26211
Mirro Products Company, 26217
Monte Glove Company, 26292
Moorecraft Box & Crate, 26306
Morris & Associates, 26313
Moyer Diebel, 26344
Mr. Bar-B-Q, 26350
Multibulk Systems International, 26374
Murata Automated Systems, 26389
My Style, 26404
Nederman, 26529, 26530
Nomaco, 26659
North Carolina's Southeast, 26692
O'Brian Tarping Systems Inc, 26802
Oenophilia, 26856
Old Dominion Box Company, 26883
Oracle Packaging, 26954
Ossid Corp, 26992
Osterneck Company, 26993
Otto Material Handling, 26999
Oxidyn, 27016
Packrite Packaging, 27189
Pacmaster by Schleicher, 27193
Pacquet Oneida, 27199
Pallet One Inc, 27229
Palmer Wahl, 27240
PAM Fastening Technology Inc, 27035
Parker Sales & Svc, 27306
Pell Paper Box Company, 27398
Perna USA, 27454
Pestcon Systems Inc, 27462
Pinnacle Furnishing, 27541
Plasticard-Locktech Intl, 27593
Pollinger Company, 27636
Prairie Packaging Inc, 27711
Pratt Industries, 27714
Preferred Packaging, 27741
Prestige Label Company, 27770
Prime Tag & Label, 27791
Primo Water Corporation, 27797
Print Ons/Express Mark, 27805
Progressive Software, 27887
Providence Industries, 27915
Purolator Facet Inc, 27950
Putsch & Co Inc, 27954
Rahmann Belting & Industrial Rubber Products, 28151

Refrigue USA, 28263
Replacements LTD, 28323
Republic Refrigeration Inc, 28325
Roberts Poly Pro Inc, 28441
Roberts Systems, 28442
Roechling Engineered Plastics, 28478
RonI, 28508
Roni LLC, 28513
Royal Chemical Co Inc, 28575
Rubbermaid, 28599
Russell Finex Inc, 28616
San Marco Coffee, Inc., 28791
Sato America, 28836
Sauvagnat Inc, 28843
Schleicher & Company of America, 28885
Schmalz, 28891
Seal the Seasons, 28950
Sealed Air Corp, 28954
Select Stainless, 28997
Semanco International, 29008
Shared Data Systems, 29108
Shat R Shield Inc, 29117
Shook Kelley Design Group, 29160
Shurtape Technologies LLC, 29171
SIG Pack Services, 28688
Sign Art, 29193
SIT Indeva Inc, 28694, 28695
Smokehouse Limited, 29303
Southbend, 29395
Southern Film Extruders, 29408
Spencer Packing Company, 29486
Spiroflow Systems Inc, 29507
SPX Corporation, 28714
SPX Flow Inc, 28715
Stanly Fixtures Co Inc, 29586
Steritech Food Safety & Environmental Hygiene, 29647
STRAPEX Corporation, 28730
Strapex Corporation, 29714
Stratecon, 29716
Stratecon International Consultants, 29717
Stronghaven Containers Co, 29736
Super Sturdy, 29793
Supermarket Associates, 29815
Supreme Murphy Truck Bodies, 29824
Swisher Hygiene, 29862
Syfan USA Corporation, 29869
Synchro-Systems Technology, 29873
Syngenta, 29874
Synthron Inc., 29875
Sysco Corp, 29882, 29927
System Plast, 29956
System-Plast, 29957
Tangent Systems, 30059
Tara Linens, 30073
Tarason Packaging, LLC., 30075
Teaco, 30089
Techform, 30098
Technibilt/Cari-All, 30102
Tesa Tape Inc, 30166
Theingredienthouse, 30199
Thermaco Inc, 30205
Thorpe & Associates, 30265
Tipper Tie Inc, 30296
Tomsed Corporation, 30325
Toter Inc, 30359
Trane Inc, 30382
Transbotics Corp, 30386
Treofan America LLC, 30407
Triad Pallet Co Inc, 30423
Troxler Electronic Lab Inc, 30465
Union Plastics Co, 30611
United Textile Distribution, 30656
UPM Raflatac, 30558
Us Bottlers Machinery Co Inc, 30700
US Label Corporation, 30551
Varimixer North America, 30781
Vertique Inc, 30823
Vescom America, 30824
VT Kidron, 30725
WA Brown & Son, 30928
Wastequip Inc, 31028
Wastequip Teem, 31029
Whitley Manufacturing Company, 31186
Wireway Husky Corp, 31282
Wnc Pallet & Forest Pdts Co, 31302
Wright Global Graphic Solutions, 31364

North Dakota

Adams Inc, 18361
Century Sign Company, 20403

Conviron, 20930
Fargo Automation, 22463
Firebird Artisan Mills, 22571
Great Plains Software, 23356
Integrated Barcode Solutions, 24291
Kerian Machines Inc, 24794
National Sunflower Assn, 26507
SK Food International, 28697
Specialty Commodities Inc, 29464
Sysco Corp, 29926

Nova Scotia

ABCO Industries Limited, 18092
AC Dispensing Equipment, 18101
Chester Plastics, 20510
Day Nite Neon Signs, 21395
Farnell Packaging, 22468
GN Thermoforming Equipment, 22987
IMO Foods, 24012
JDG Consulting, 24458
Sure Shot Dispensing Systems, 29830

Ohio

Abanaki Corp, 18251
ABC Scales, 18089
Accra Laboratory, 18283
Accu-Pak, 18290
AccuLife, 18293
Ace Manufacturing, 18305
ACO Polymer Products, 18111
Acoustical Systems Inc, 18332
Acro Plastics, 18338
Ad Art Litho., 18355
Adam Electric Signs, 18358
Adpro, 18381
Advance Weight Systems Inc, 18397
Advanced Food Equipment LLC, 18406
Advanced Food Systems, 18408
Advanced Organics, 18417
Advanced Poly-Packaging Inc, 18420
Aerotech Enterprise Inc, 18451
AFCO Manufacturing, 18139
AGA Gas, 18144
Agrana Fruit US Inc, 18465
AgriTech, 18471
AIDCO International, 18151
Aidco International, 18485
Air Locke Dock Seal, 18492
Air Technical Industries, 18498
Air-Knife Systems/PaxtonProducts Corporation, 18499
Airflex, 18505
AK Steel Corp, 18157
Akro-Mils, 18520
Akron Cotton Products, 18521
All A Cart Custom Mfg, 18574
All Foils Inc, 18582
Alliance Knife Inc, 18612
Allstate Manufacturing Company, 18641
Alumin-Nu Corporation, 18687
American Box Corporation, 18727
American Cut Edge Inc, 18740
American Electric Power, 18747
American Glass Research, 18771
American Led-Gible, 18785
American Manufacturing-Engrng, 18790
American Pan Co, 18804
American Solving Inc., 18821
American Ventilation Company, 18834
American Wholesale Equipment, 18838
Americana Art China Company, 18842
Ametco Manufacturing Corp, 18862
Ametek Technical & Industrial Products, 18866
Ampac Packaging, LLC, 18877
Ampak, 18878
Ample Industries, 18880
Amster-Kirtz Co, 18886
Amtekco, 18889
Anchor Hocking Operating Co, 18906
Anderson International Corp, 18920
Apex Welding Inc, 18973
Applied Industrial Tech Inc, 18991
Architectural Sheet Metals LLC, 19019
Armco, 19057
Arnold Equipment Co, 19064
Arthur Corporation, 19088
Arthur Products Co, 19091
Artx Limited, 19100
ASC Industries Inc, 18220

Aspect Engineering, 19114
Audsam Printing, 19185
Austin Brown Co, 19193
Austin Co, 19194
Automated Container Corp, 19209
Automated Packaging Systems, 19215
Avalon Foodservice, 19244
Avure Technologies Svc & Sales, 19261
B&J Machinery, 19304
B.E.S.T., 19310
Babcock & Wilcox Power Generation Group, 19356
Baker Concrete Construction, 19380
Bakery Crafts, 19387
Barrette Outdoor Living, 19465
Beech Engineering, 19521
Bel-Terr China, 19536
Belcan Corp, 19537
Benko Products, 19569
Berghausen E Cheml Co, 19584
Berlekamp Plastics Inc, 19588
Berlin Fruit Box Company, 19590
Bessamaire Sales Inc, 19607
Best, 19609
Best & Donovan, 19610
Best Restaurant Equip & Design, 19619
Bethel Engineering & Equipment Inc, 19626
Bettcher Industries Inc, 19630, 19631
Biro Manufacturing Co, 19697
Bishop Machine Shop, 19699
Blako Industries, 19720
Bluffton Slaw Cutter Company, 19759
Boardman Molded Products Inc, 19763
Bolling Oven & Machine Company, 19780
Bonneau Company, 19789
Bonnot Co, 19790
Brand Castle, 19841
Brechbuhler Scales, 19850
Bril-Tech, 19869
Broadway Companies, 19881
Brown Fired Heater, 19898
Bry-Air Inc, 19916
Buckeye Group, 19924
Buckhorn Inc, 19927
Burns Chemical Systems, 19961
C & R Inc, 19987
C Nelson Mfg Co, 19993, 19994
C S Bell Co, 20000
Canton Sign Co, 20198
Canton Sterilized Wiping Cloth, 20199
Capital Plastics, 20210
Caravan Packaging Inc, 20229
Card Pak Inc, 20235
Carhoff Company, 20248
Carnegie Textile Co, 20273
Caron Products & Svc Inc, 20282
Carton Service Co, 20311
Cast Nylons LTD, 20332
CB Mfg. & Sales Co., 20026
CC Custom Technology Corporation, 20032
CCP Industries, Inc., 20038
Ceilcote Air Pollution Control, 20359
Cell-O-Core Company, 20362
Central Coated Products Inc, 20378
Central Fabricators Inc, 20381
Central Ohio Bag & Burlap, 20385
Charles Mayer Studios, 20447
Chart Industries Inc, 20457
Chase Doors, 20459, 20460
Chase Industries Inc, 20461
Chase-Doors, 20462
Chatelain Plastics, 20465
Chatfield & Woods Sack Company, 20466
Chem Pack Inc, 20484
Chemineer, 20500
Chester Hoist, 20509
Chocolate Concepts, 20543
Christy Machine Co, 20553
Cimino Box & Pallet Co, 20565
Cincinnati Convertors Inc, 20567
Cincinnati Foam Products, 20568
Cincinnati Industrial Machry, 20569, 20570
Cintas Corp, 20572
Clamco Corporation, 20592
Cleveland Canvas Goods Mfg Co, 20636
Cleveland Menu Printing, 20637
Cleveland Metal Stamping Company, 20638
Cleveland Mop Manufacturing Company, 20639
Cleveland Motion Controls, 20640
Cleveland Plastic Films, 20641
Cleveland Range, 20642

Cleveland Specialties Co, 20643
Cleveland Vibrator Co, 20644
Cleveland Wire Cloth & Mfg Co, 20645
Climax Packaging Machinery, 20651
Clippard Instrument Lab Inc, 20653
Coblentz Brothers Inc, 20683
Cold Jet, LLC, 20708
Collins & Aikman, 20725
Columbus Instruments, 20751
Columbus Paperbox Company, 20753
Combi Packaging Systems LLC, 20761
Comstar Printing Solutions, 20815
Congent Technologies, 20838
Consolidated Plastics Co Inc, 20856
Continental-Fremont, 20897
Conveyance Technologies LLC, 20919
Convoy, 20931
Corbox-Meyers Inc, 20963
Cornish Containers, 20982
COW Industries Inc, 20080
Crane Pumps & Systems, 21046
Crayex Corp, 21050
Creegan Animation Company, 21074
Cres Cor, 21077
Cresset Chemical Company, 21080
Crown Battery Mfg, 21100
Crown Closures Machinery, 21102
Crown Equipment Corp., 21106
Crystal Creative Products, 21131
CSC Worldwide, 20094
Culinart Inc, 21141
Custom Quality Products, 21198
Custom Tarpaulin Products Inc, 21205
Cutler-Hammer, 21209
Cutrite Company, 21210
D. Picking & Company, 21245
Dairy Specialties, 21306
Damon Industries, 21323
Darcy Group, 21353
Darfill, 21354
Daymark Safety Systems, 21399, 21400
Dayton Bag & Burlap Co, 21403
Dayton Marking Devices Company, 21404
Dayton Reliable Tool, 21405
Dayton Wire Products, 21406
DCS Sanitation Management, 21255
Decko Products Inc, 21439
Degussa Flavors, 21450
Del Monte Fresh Produce Inc., 21462
Demag Cranes & Components Corp, 21532
Desco Equipment Corporation, 21556
Diamond Electronics, 21601
Diamond Roll-Up Door, 21605
Dicks Packing Plant, 21612
Diehl Food Ingredients, 21618
Dillin Automation Systems Corp, 21628, 21629
Dinovo Produce Company, 21637
Distaview Corp, 21657
Distillata, 21658
Distribution Results, 21661
Diversified Capping Equipment, 21665
Dorpak, 21719
Dover Chemical Corp, 21740
Drackett Professional, 21757
Dreaco Products, 21762
DT Industrials, 21283
Du Bois Chemicals, 21781
Dualite Sales & Svc Inc, 21787
DuBois Chemicals, 21783
Duplex Mill & Mfg Co, 21810
Dupps Co, 21811
Durable Corp, 21818
Durashield USA, 21825
E C Shaw Co, 21869
E F Bavis & Assoc Inc, 21870
Eagle Wire Works, 21958
Eaton Corporation, 21991
Ebel Tape & Label, 21998
Eclipse Innovative Thermal Solutions, 22007
Edgerton Corporation, 22036
Edwards Products, 22047
Electro Alarms, 22073
Embro Manufacturing Company, 22130
Emc Solutions, 22131
EMCO, 21915
En-Hanced Products Inc, 22153
Enerfab Inc., 22163
Enting Water Conditioning Inc, 22203
Erie Container, 22249
Esterle Mold & Machine Co Inc, 22276
Eurofins Scientific Inc., 22296

Evans Adhesive Corp LTD, 22304
Executive Match Inc, 22339
Fabohio Inc, 22423
Fair Publishing House, 22441
Fairborn USA Inc, 22443
Falls Filtration Technologies, 22452
Fasson Employee FCU, 22471
FCI Inc, 22383
FECO/MOCO, 22386
Fedco Systems, 22486
Femc, 22506
Ferro Corporation, 22521
FFR Merchandising Inc, 22392
FIB-R-DOR, 22393
Filmco Inc, 22548
Finn & Son's Metal Spinning Specialists, 22565
Fioriware, 22568
Fishers Investment, 22587
Flavorseal, 22613
Food Equipment Manufacturing Company, 22699
Food Industry Equipment, 22703
Food Plant Engineering, 22715
Forest Manufacturing Co, 22759
France Personalized Signs, 22817
Fred D Pfening Co, 22842
Fredrick Ramond Company, 22844
Freely Display, 22847
Freeman Co, 22848
Fremont Die Cut Products, 22853
French Oil Mill Machinery Co, 22855
Fresh Mark Inc., 22859
Frozen Specialties Inc, 22893
Fuller Weighing Systems, 22913
Funke Filters, 22918
G & S Metal Products Co Inc, 22935
G.F. Frank & Sons, 22948
Gabriella Imports, 23002
Gafco-Worldwide, 23005
Garland Floor Company, 23036
Garvey Products, 23045, 23046
Gasser Chair Co Inc, 23054
Gbs, 23074
GE Lighting, 22961
General Bag Corporation, 23101
General Cutlery Co, 23106
General Data Co Inc, 23107
General Films Inc, 23112
Gilson Co Inc, 23185
Glassline Corp, 23201
Glawe Manufacturing Company, 23206
Glo-Quartz Electric Heater, 23217
Globe Food Equipment Co, 23236
GOJO Industries Inc, 22990
Gold Medal Products Co, 23256
Golden Eagle Extrusions Inc, 23259
Golden Needles Knitting & Glove Company, 23260
Goodyear Tire & Rubber Company, 23279
Goshen Dairy Company, 23284
Gralab Instruments, 23306
Grayline Housewares Inc, 23341
Great Lakes Cold Storage, 23348
Greif Brothers Corporation, 23397
Greif Inc, 23398, 23399, 23400
Gross & Co Licensed Bus Pro, 23430
Grote Co, 23431
H P Mfg Co, 23464
Hall China Co, 23526
Hall Safety Apparel, 23529
Hamilton Caster, 23543
Hamilton Manufacturing Corp, 23545
Hamrick Manufacturing & Svc, 23553
Hapco Inc, 23585, 23586
Hardware Components Inc, 23601
Harold M. Lincoln Company, 23617
Harris & Company, 23627
Hartstone Pottery Inc, 23642
Hartzell Fan Inc, 23643
Hathaway Stamps, 23653
Haynes Manufacturing Co, 23667
HBD Thermoid, Inc., 23485
HDT Manufacturing, 23490
Heat Seal, 23690
Hedstrom Corporation, 23707
Heinlin Packaging Svc, 23713
Henkel Consumer Adhesive, 23725
Henny Penny, Inc., 23729
Heritage Equipment Co, 23744
Hewitt Soap Company, 23755
Hexion Inc, 23757

Spring Air Systems, 29518
Stanpac, Inc., 29587
Steel Art Signs, 29620
Sterling Rubber, 29656
StickerYou, 29675
Stryco Wire Products, 29741
Super Seal ManufacturingLimited, 29791
Supramatic, 29819
T&G Machinery, 29978
T&S Blow Molding, 29979
Thamesville Metal Products Ltd, 30185
Toronto Fabricating & Manufacturing, 30344
Toronto Kitchen Equipment, 30345
Total Identity Group, 30354
Traitech Industries, 30378
Trevor Owen Limited, 30410
Trimen Foodservice Equipment, 30440
Triple-A Manufacturing Company, 30453
TWM Manufacturing, 30038
U.S. Range, 30525
UniTrak Corporation, 30596
Universal Handling Equipment, 30669
Universal Impex Corporation, 30670
Ursini Plastics, 30699
Vent Master, 30797
Vineco International Products, 30860
Ward Ironworks, 31005
WE Killam Enterprises, 30935
Wedlock Paper ConvertersLtd., 31082
Wepackit, 31110
WES Plastics, 30941
West Metals, 31125
Wilton Industries CanadaLtd., 31243
Winpak Technologies, 31271
WR Key, 30951
Wylie Systems, 31368

Oregon

A & K Development Co, 18014
AB McLauchlan Company, 18083
Abundant Earth Corporation, 18274
AGC Engineering Portland, 18146
Amax Nutrasource Inc, 18694
American Brush Company, 18729
Anton Kimball Design, 18956
ATW Manufacturing Company, 18236
Autio Co, 19196
Best Manufacturers, 19616
Bi-O-Kleen Industries, 19642
Blue Feather Products Inc, 19743
Boyd's Coffee Co, 19825
Bridgewell Resources LLC, 19865
Can & Bottle Systems, Inc., 20175
Cascade Earth Sciences, 20319
Cascade Signs & Neon, 20320
Cascade Wood Components, 20321
CIDA, 20058
City Grafx, 20585
Clean Water Systems, 20615
Clock Associates, 20655
Coffee Sock Company, 20699
Commercial Dehydrator Systems, 20775
Confection Art Inc, 20834
Contact Industries, 20865
Container Services Company, 20870
Cornell Pump Company, 20978
Crate Ideas by Wilderness House, 21048
Crossroads Espresso, 21095
CRS Marking Systems, 20090
Curtis Restaurant Equipment, 21162
Custom Stamping & Manufacturing, 21202
Dana Labels, 21329
Datalogic ADC, 21372
De Leone Corp, 21411, 21412, 21413
De Paul Industries, 21414
Del Monte Fresh Produce Inc., 21478
Dewatering Equipment Company, 21586
DH/Sureflow, 21262
Dynic USA Corp, 21863
Easybar Corp, 21987
Engineered Food Systems, 22169
Enviro-Pak, 22207
ERO/Goodrich Forest Products, 21930
Esha Research, 22266
Eutek Systems, 22302
Exhibitron Co, 22343
Faulkenberg Inc, 22479
Food Handling Systems, 22701
Food Products Lab, 22719
Fooddesign Machinery & Systems, 22738,
22739

FOODesign from tna, 22403
Fruition Northwest LLC, 22897
G & D Chillers Inc, 22932
Gage Industries, 23006
Gaylord Industries, 23071
GE Interlogix Industrial, 22960
GEM Equipment Of Oregon Inc, 22975,
22976
Gerber Legendary Blades, 23165
Glass Tech, 23200
Grande Ronde Sign Company, 23316
Great Western Chemical Company, 23359
Grecon, 23362
Griffin Bros Inc, 23408
Grigsby Brothers Paper Box Manufacturers,
23414
Hanset Stainless Inc, 23579
Hewlett-Packard, 23756
Industrial Design Corporation, 24167
Industrial Labsales, 24179
Integrated Systems, 24295
International Tank & Pipe Co, 24360
Java Jacket, 24525
JVNW, 24475
Kysor/Kalt, 24974
L G I Intl Inc, 24983
LaCrosse Safety and Industrial, 25040
Lewis Packing Company, 25270
Longview Fibre Company, 25429
Luhr Jensen & Sons Inc, 25480
M & D Specialties Inc, 25509
Marble Manor, 25722
Marlen International, 25766, 25767
McCormack Manufacturing Company, 25904
Molded Container Corporation, 26265
Monastary Mustard, 26281
Mountain-Pacific Machinery, 26340
NACCO Materials HandlingGroup, 26415
Northwest Analytical Inc, 26726
Northwest Food Processors Assn, 26729
Oregon Pacific Bottling, 26967
Pacific Scale Company, 27111
Pacific Scientific Instrument, 27113
Package Containers Inc, 27134
Paradigm Technologies, 27282
Permacold Engineering Inc, 27452
Pike Awning Co, 27529
Plastic Fantastics/Buck Signs, 27583
Pneucon, 27614
Portland Paper Box Company, 27680
Ppm Technologies LLC, 27709, 27710
Pro-Ad-Co Inc, 27837
Purity Laboratories, 27948
Ramsay Signs Inc, 28169
Rhodes Bakery Equipment, 28374
Riverside Industries, 28414
Rose City Awning Co, 28522
Rose City Label, 28523
Ryan Technology Inc., 28622
San-Rec-Pak, 28793
Seal-A-Tron Corp, 28951
Seal-O-Matic Corp, 28952
Sedex Kinkos, 28978
Seven B Plus, 29075
Sivetz Coffee, 29272
Smetco, 29289
Sorensen Associates, 29374
Sportsmen's Cannery & Smokehouse, 29510
SRC Vision, 28718
Sterling Truck Corporation, 29659
Sysco Corp, 29914
Tank Temp Control, 30063
Taylor-Made Labels Inc, 30087
The Carriage Works, 30188
Therm-Tec Inc, 30203
Traeger Industries, 30375
Truitt Bros Inc, 30475
Unisource Manufacturing Inc, 30623
Vanguard Technology Inc, 30768
Videx Inc, 30843
Wade Manufacturing Company, 30972
Welliver Metal Products Corporation, 31098
West Oregon Wood Products Inc, 31126
Western Pulp Products Co, 31147
Whit-Log Trailers Inc, 31176
Willamette Industries, 31219, 31220, 31221
Woodfold-Marco Manufacturing, 31319
Zollman's Dark Canyon Coffee, 31459

Pennsylvania

A A Label Co, 18016

A M S Filling Systems, 18028
A Tec Technologic, 18038
A.A. Pesce Glass Company, 18065
Abel Pumps, 18264
Accommodation Mollen, 18281
Accu-Sort Systems, 18292
ACLAUSA Inc, 18106
Acme International Limited, 18325
Action Technology, 18349
Adhesives Research, 18376
Adhesives Research Inc, 18377
Advantage Puck Technologies, 18427, 18428
Aerocon, 18446
Aerzen USA Corp, 18456
AFCO, 18138
AgroFresh, 18477
AIM, 18152
Air Products & Chemicals Inc, 18495
Air-Scent International, 18501
Air/Tak Inc, 18502
Alcoa Corp, 18540
Alef Custom Packaging, 18549
Alex E Fergusson Co Inc, 18553
All Fill Inc, 18580, 18581
All-Clad METALCRAFTERS LLC, 18594
ALLCAMS Machine Company, 18162
Allegheny Bradford Corp, 18600
Allegheny Technologies Inc, 18601
Allen Gauge & Tool Co, 18603
Allflex Packaging Products, 18609
Alpha Checkweigher, 18654
Alphabet Signs, 18662
American Association-Meat, 18720
American Auger & Accesories, 18721
American Crane & Equip Corp, 18737
American Glass Research, 18772
American Olean Tile Company, 18798
American Packaging Corporation, 18799
American Pallets, 18803
Ameripak Packaging Equipment, 18852,
18853
Ametek, 18863, 18864
Ametek Drexelbrook, 18865
AMETEK Inc, 18176, 18178
Ametek Us Gauge, 18867
Anderson Products, 18922
Andrew H Lawson Co, 18934
Andrew W Nissly Inc, 18935
ANDRITZ, 18187
Apex Fountain Sales Inc, 18969
Arcobaleno Pasta Machines, 19025
Armstrong Engineering Associates, 19058
Asgco Manufacturing Inc, 19105
Associated Products Inc, 19127
ATD-American Co, 18229
Athena Controls Inc, 19141
ATL-East Tag & Label Inc, 18231
Atlas Minerals & Chemicals Inc, 19167,
19168
Atlas Rubber Stamp & Printing, 19172
ATOFINA Chemicals, 18233
Audubon Sales & Svc, 19186
Auger Fab, 19187, 19188
Auger Manufacturing Spec, 19189
Automated Production Systems Corporation,
19216
Automation Devices Inc, 19228
Ay Machine Company, 19278
B T Engineering Inc, 19298
Bacharach Inc, 19359
Backus USA, 19362
Bal/Foster Glass Container Company, 19399
Bally Block Co, 19416
Ballymore Company, 19418
BAW Plastics Inc, 19313
Beach Filter Products, 19502
Beistle Co, 19531
Bennington Furniture Corporation, 19574
Bermar America, 19593
Berner International Corp, 19597
Best Buy Uniforms, 19612
Betz Entec, 19635
Big John Inc, 19651
Bower's Awning & Shade, 19817
Brad's Raw Foods, 19828
Bradley Lifting, 19834
Brewers Outlet-Chestnut Hill, 19862
Brooks Instrument LLC, 19888
BSI Instruments, 19345
Burns Industries, 19963
C Palmer Mfg Co Inc, 19996

C-P Flexible Packaging, 20007, 20008,
20009
C.B. Dombach & Son, 20012
Calcium Chloride Sales Inc, 20134
Calgon Carbon, 20137
Can Corp Of America Inc, 20176
Capway Conveyor Systems Inc, 20222
Carbon Clean Industries Inc, 20232
Carl Strutz & Company, 20251
Carleton Helical Technologies, 20252, 20253
Carton Closing Company, 20310
Cattron Group International, 20348
CCL Container, 20033
Cellucap Manufacturing Co, 20368
Centi Mark Corp, 20376
Century Crane & Hoist, 20396
Ceramic Color & Chemical Mfg, 20406
Chalmur Bag Company, LLC, 20422
Charles Beck Machine Corporation, 20439
Charles Beseler Company, 20440
Charles Gratz Fire Protection, 20444
Chaucer Press Inc, 20471
Chef Specialties, 20479
Chesmont Engineering Co Inc, 20508
Chester-Jensen Co., Inc., 20511
China Lenox Incorporated, 20536
CHL Systems, 20056
Chop-Rite Two Inc, 20546
Chroma Tone, 20554
Chromalox, 20555
Clarkson Supply, 20600
Clayton L. Hagy & Son, 20611
Collegeville Flag & Manufacturing Company,
20723
Colorcon Inc, 20740
Computer Aid Inc, 20805
Conpac, 20845
Consolidated Container Co, 20850
Constantia Colmar, 20859, 20860
Consumer Cap Corporation, 20863
Consumers Packing Company, 20864
Continental Refrigeration, 20893
Continental Refrigerator, 20894, 20895
Contour Packaging, 20898
Control Chief Holdings Inc, 20905
Copper Clad, 20957
Corp Somat, 20984
Corrections Dept, 20989
Corrugated Inner-Pak Corporation, 20993
CPM Wolverine Proctor LLC, 20086
Crane Environmental, 21044
Crc Industries Inc, 21051
Crisci Food Equipment Company, 21087
Crown Cork & Seal Co Inc, 21104
Crown Holdings, Inc., 21107
CSS International Corp, 20100
Custom Brands Unlimited, 21169
Custom Pack Inc, 21192
Dalare Associates Inc, 21311
Daleco, 21312
Damascus/Bishop Tube Company, 21322
Dansk International Designs, 21346
David's Goodbatter, 21358
Day & Zimmermann Group Inc, 21390
DCL Solutions LLC, 21252
Deacom, 21418
DECI Corporation, 21257
DEFCO, 21258
Del Monte Fresh Produce Inc., 21467
Delta/Ducon, 21526
Diablo Chemical, 21593
DL Enterprises, 21267
Don Lee, 21701
Dormant Manufacturing Co, 21717
Double H Plastics, 21726
Doucette Industries, 21728
DPC, 21273
Draeger Safety Inc, 21758
Drehmann Paving & Flooring Company,
21765
Dreumex USA, 21768
DT Converting Technologies - Stokes, 21282
Duerr Packaging Co Inc, 21795
Dunn Woodworks, 21807
Dyco, 21838, 21839, 21840
E K Lay Co, 21874
Eam-Mosca Corporation, 21964
Eastern Bakery Co, 21975
Eastern Design & Development Corporation,
21978
Eaton Electrical Sector, 21992
Edgecraft Corp, 22034

Ehmke Manufacturing, 22050
Eichler Wood Products, 22052
Electrostatics Inc, 22089
Electrotechnology Applications Center, 22090
Elmark Packaging Inc, 22117
Elwell Parker, 22126
EMD Performance Materials, 21917
Emmeti, 22144
Emtrol, 22151
Encapsulation Systems, 22155
Ensinger Inc, 22193
Enviro-Ware, 22210
EPI Labelers, 21926
EPL Technologies, 21928
Equipment Exchange Co, 22238
Ergonomic Handling Systems, 22247
Erie Cotton Products, 22250
Eriez Magnetics, 22252
Ernst Timing Screw Co, 22256
Esbelt of North America: Divison of ASGCO, 22261
Etube & Wire, 22281
Eureka Paper Box Company, 22288
Everedy Automation, 22310
Exact Equipment Corporation, 22322
Exact Packaging, 22325
Expanko Cork Co, 22346
F C MEYER Packaging LLC, 22364
F.B. Leopold, 22373
Fabricated Components Inc, 22428
Facilities Design Inc, 22436
Famco Automatic Sausage Linkers, 22455
Famco Sausage Linking Machines, 22456
Fast Stuff Packaging, 22474
FEI Co, 22387
Fenner Drives, 22508, 22509
Fenner Dunlop Americas Inc, 22510
Fire Protection Industries, 22570
Fisher Scientific Company, 22585
Fitzpatrick Container Company, 22595
Five-M Plastics Company, 22597
Flat Plate Inc, 22609
FlexBarrier Products, 22626
Flexicon, 22634
Flexlink Systems Inc, 22636
Floaire, 22645
Fluid Energy Processing & Eqpt, 22662
FMC Corporation, 22397
FMI Display, 22399
Fogel Jordon Commercial Refrigeration Company, 22677
Follett Corp, 22687
Food Marketing Servives, 22711
Foreman Group, 22757
Forum Lighting, 22786
Fountainhead, 22795
Four Seasons Produce Inc, 22798
Fox Iv Technologies, 22803
Foxcroft Equipment & Svc Co, 22809
FoxJet, 22807
Franke Americas, 22824
FreesTech, 22850
Fres-Co SYSTEM USA Inc, 22856
Friendly City Box Co Inc, 22870
Fun-Time International, 22917
G.G. Greene Enterprises, 22949
Gamajet Cleaning Systems, 23019
Gateway Packaging Corp, 23063
GEA FES, Inc., 22963
GEA PHE Systems North   America, Inc., 22967
GEA Refrigeration North America, 22968
GEI Autowrappers, 22972
GEI PPM, 22973
GEI Turbo, 22974
Gem Refrigerator Company, 23090
Gemini Bakery Equipment, 23091
General Press Corp, 23123
General Tank, 23129
Genesis Machinery Products, 23136
George Lapgley Enterpri ses, 23154
Gessner Products, 23170
Girton Manufacturing Co, 23192
Giunta Brothers, 23193
Glatfelter P H Co, 23204
Glenroy Inc, 23213
Global Canvas Products, 23218
Globe Ticket & Label Company, 23239
Graff Tank Erection, 23299
Graham Engineering Corp, 23302
Grant Chemicals, 23318

Grasselli SSI, 23333
Graybill Machines Inc, 23338
Greydon Inc, 23404
Grill Greats, 23416
Grosfillex Inc, 23429
Habasit America Plastic Div, 23508
Hall-Woolford Wood Tank Co Inc, 23530
Hamilton Awning Co, 23541
Hanel Storage Systems, 23565
Hankison International, 23569
Hardy-Graham, 23606
Harrington Hoists Inc, 23625
Harrington's Equipment Co, 23626
Harro Hofliger Packaging Systems, 23632
Harry Davis & Co, 23633
Heatrex, 23698
Hefferman Interactive, 23710
Heico Chemicals Inc, 23711
Henry Molded Products Inc, 23734
Hershey Co., 23750
Hess Machine Intl, 23751
Horix Manufacturing Co, 23857
Hormann Flexan Llc, 23860
Hosch Properties, 23865
Hoss-S, 23873
Hovus Inc, 23886
Howard-Mccray, 23890, 23891
Howell Brothers Chemical Laboratories, 23894
HSI Company, 23501
Huntington Foam Corp, 23934
Hurst Corp, 23940
Hyder North America, 23955
Ideal Sleeves, 24058
Ideas in Motion, 24066
IDL, 23997
Ifm Efector, 24071
Ilapak Inc, 24076, 24077
Ilsemann Corp, 24086
Image Fillers, 24089
Impress Industries, 24116
Industrial Nameplate Inc, 24184
Inmotion Technologies, 24241
Innova-Tech, 24248
Innovations by Design, 24251
Inpaco Corporation, 24270
Insinger Co, 24278
InterMetro Industries, 24304
International Envelope Company, 24331
International Polymers Corp, 24355
IPEC, 24016
Ipec, 24384
ISM Carton, 24024
ITT Inc, 24030
J A Emilius Sons, 24415
Jacob Holtz Co., 24490
James Austin Co, 24499
Jamison Plastic Corporation, 24508
Jersey Shore Steel Co, 24547
Jesse Jones Box Corporation, 24552
Jet Plastica Industries, 24556
Jetnet Corp, 24557
John Bean Technologies Corp, 24574
John Rock Inc, 24586
John W Keplinger & Sons, 24588
Jomar Plastics Industry, 24612
Jordon Commercial Refrigerator, 24623
Jordon-Fleetwood Commercial Refrigerator Company, 24624
Jr Mats, 24635
Judge, 24637
JW Aluminum Co, 24478
K B Systems Inc, 24654
Keller-Charles Of Philadelphia, 24753
Kelman Bottles LLC, 24760
Kemutec Group Inc, 24767
Kensington Lighting Corp, 24781
Keystone Manufacturing Inc, 24817
Keystone Process Equipment, 24819
Kinsley Inc, 24866, 24867
Kline Process Systems Inc, 24882
Kloss Manufacturing Co Inc, 24889
KNF Flexpak Corporation, 24693
Kold-Draft, 24920
Kosempel Manufacturing Company, 24941
Krystatite Films, 24961
L Cubed Corp, 24982
Labels By Pulizzi Inc, 25067
Lake Shore Industries Inc, 25091
Lancaster Laboratories, 25121
Landoo Corporation, 25129
LANXESS Corp., 25003

Lasermation Inc, 25152
Laurel Awning Co, 25167
Le Jo Enterprises, 25190
Leclerc Foods USA, 25205
Lee Industries, 25209
Leichtman Ice Cream Company, 25232
Lenox Corp, 25242
Lenox Locker Company, 25243
Lentz Milling Co, 25246
Lexidyne of Pennsylvania, 25276
Liberty Machine Company, 25288
Linett Company, 25329
Linette, 25330
Liquitane, 25352
Live Floor Systems, 25367
Loveshaw Corp, 25454
LPACK - Loersch Corporation, 25022
Lumax Industries, 25486
Lumsden Corporation, 25490
Lumsden Flexx Flow, 25491
M & M Display, 25513
M & Q Packaging Corp, 25519
M F & B Restaurant Systems Inc, 25524
M&Q Plastic Products, 25536
Management Recruiters, 25687
Martin Electric Plants, 25805
Martingale Paper Company, 25812
Mateer Burt, 25849
Matthews Marking Systems Div, 25870
Mc Court Label Co, 25898
McCarter Corporation, 25902
Mcguckin & Pyle Inc, 25925
McNeil Nutritionals, 25914
Measurex/S&L Plastics, 25941
Mecco Marking & Traceability, 25946
Mechtronics International, 25947
Mechtronics Paper Corp, 25948
Meil Electric Fixture Manufacturing Company, 25958
Mengibar Automation, 25979
Metro Corporation, 26031
Metropolitan Flag & Banner Co, 26035
Metspeed Labels, 26037
Meyer Packaging, 26050
Mic-Ellen Associates, 26059
Michael G Brown & Associates, 26063
Micro-Strain, 26089
Microbac Laboratories, 26093, 26094
Microbac Laboratories Inc, 26095
Mid-State Awning & Patio Co, 26125
Midvale Paper Box, 26139
Miroil, 26214
Molded Fiber Glass Tray Company, 26266
Moore Push-Pin Co, 26305
Morgan Corp, 26309
Morning Star Coffee, Inc., 26310
Moyer Packing Co., 26345
MRC Bearing Services, 25594, 25595
Mt Valley Farms & Lumber Prods, 26353
Mt. Lebanon Awning & Tent Company, 26356
Multi-Plastics Extrusions Inc, 26371
Nation/Ruskin, 26458
National Ammonia Co, 26459
National Construction Services, 26465
National Drying Machry Co Inc, 26471
National Foam, 26477
National Label Co, 26484
National Novelty Brush Co, 26489
National Scoop & Equipment Company, 26501
National Towelette, 26510
Natural Marketing Institute, 26517
Nature Soy Inc, 26519
Netzsch Pumps North America, 26559
Neugart, 26560
New Castle Industries Inc, 26571
New Pig Corp, 26596
New Way Packaging Machinery, 26600
Newcastle Co Inc, 26606
Nilfisk, Inc., 26647
Norristown Box Company, 26682, 26683
North Side Packing Co, 26695
NYP, 26435
Ocme America Corporation, 26849
Oerlikon Leybold Vacuum, 26858, 26859
Ogden Manufacturing Company, 26861
Olde Country Reproductions Inc, 26887
Olympus America Inc, 26901
Omega Design Corp, 26908
Omega Products Inc, 26911
On Assignment Inc, 26927

Oshikiri Corp Of America, 26988
Ott Packagings, 26995
Otterbine Barebo Inc, 26997
Pac Strapping Products, 27084
Pacer Pumps, 27090
Package Products, 27139
Packaging Enterprises, 27157, 27158
Packaging Progressions, 27173
Packworld USA, 27190, 27191
Pagoda Industries Inc, 27208
Pak-Rapid, 27211
Palace Packaging Machines Inc, 27218
Paratherm Corporation, 27299
Parisi Inc, 27301
Parker-Hannifin Corp, 27309
Patterson-Kelley   Hars Company, 27347
Pavan USA Inc, 27358
PBM Inc, 27043
Penco Products, 27405
Penn Bottle & Supply Company, 27413
Penn Refrigeration Service Corporation, 27415
Penn Scale ManufacturingCompany, 27416
PennPac International, 27417
Pennsylvania Food Merchants Association, 27418
Penske Truck Leasing Corp, 27421
Perfecseal, 27438
Perley-Halladay Assoc, 27450
Philadelphia Glass Bending Company, 27491
Phillips Gourmet Inc, 27494
Phoenix Contact Inc, 27501
Pittsburgh Corning Corp, 27557
Pittsburgh Tank Corp, 27558
Placemat Printers, 27561
Polar Hospitality Products, 27625
Poly Plastic Products Inc, 27638
Polymer Solutions International, 27651
Port Erie Plastics Inc, 27672
Portola Allied, 27681
Powdersize Inc, 27691
PQ Corp, 27072
Precision Solutions Inc, 27732
Premium Pallet, 27755
Presque Isle Wine Cellars, 27767
Pretium Packaging, 27777
Product Solutions, 27869
Products A Curtron Div, 27875
Prominent Fluid Controls Inc, 27898, 27899
Pronova Biopolymer, 27903
ProRestore Producfs, 27847
PTR Baler & Compactor Co, 27078
Pulva Corp, 27933
QC, 27968
Quality Bakers of America, 27991
Quantum Net, 28022
R J Mc Cullough Co, 28055
Rainbow Industrial Products, 28155
Rapid Pallet, 28190
RBS Fab Inc, 28087
Readco Kurimoto LLC, 28210
Reading Bakery Systems Inc, 28211
Reading Box Co Inc, 28212
Reading Plastic Fabricators, 28213
Reading Technologies Inc, 28214
Red Lion Controls Inc, 28223
Red Valve Co Inc, 28226
Reddi-Pac, 28228
Refrigeration Design & Svc, 28255
Reidler Decal Corporation, 28285
Reilly Foam Corporation, 28286
Reliance-Paragon, 28300
Remcon Plastics Inc, 28304
Remmey Wood Products, 28309
Ribble Production, 28376
Richmond Printed Tape & Label, 28390
Ridg-U-Rak, 28394
Rixie Paper Products Inc, 28422
RJ Wetzr Products Company, 28107
Roddy Products Pkgng Co, 28474
Roechling Machined Plastics, 28479
Rose Plastic, 28527
Ross Technology Corp, 28541
Roth Young Murrysville, 28550
Rowlands Sales Company, 28567
Royal Paper Products, 28584
RTG Films, 28120
Rubbermaid Commercial Products, 28602
Rutler Screen Printing, 28621
S Walter Packaging Corp, 28645
S&R Machinery, 28650
S-H-S International of Wilkes, 28651

Semco Manufacturing Company, 29009
Sermatech ISPA, 29046
Servomex, 29063
Setaram/SFIM, 29069
Shaffer Sports & Events, 29091
Shell Oil Company, 29132
ShockWatch, 29158
Sigma Industrial Automation, 29191
Sign Warehouse, 29200
Sipco, 29265
Skinner Sheet, 29278
Snap Drape Inc, 29316
Snap Drape International, 29317
South Well Co, 29394
Southline Equipment Company, 29425
Southwest Endseals, 29427
Southwest Fixture, 29428
Southwest Neon Signs, 29430
Southwest Vault Builders, 29431
Sparkler Filters Inc, 29444
Specialty Equipment Company, 29466
Specialty Packaging Inc, 29470
Spectro, 29477
Spiro-Cut Equipment Co, 29506
Stainless Equipment Manufacturing, 29553
Stainless Steel Fabricators, 29564
StainlessDrains.com, 29566
Standard Rate Review, 29576
Stanford Chemicals, 29581
Start International, 29606
Step Products, 29640
Stevens Transport, 29666
Stewart Systems Baking LLC, 29673, 29674
STM Mortgage Co, 28728
Storsack Inc, 29706
Strand Lighting, 29712
Stricklin Co, 29731
Super-Chef Manufacturing Company, 29795
Supreme Products, 29825
Swanson Wire Works Industries, Inc., 29852
Sysco Corp, 29878, 29893, 29895, 29918, 29919, 29938
Tablecheck Technologies, Inc, 30042
Talbert Display, 30049
Taprite-Fassco Mfg Inc, 30069
TechnipFMC, 30106
Technoquip Co, 30113
Tetra Pak, 30169
Texas Baket Company, 30174
Texas Corn Roasters, 30175
Texas Hill Country Barbacue, 30176
Texas Neon Advertising Inc, 30177
Texas Refinery Corp, 30178
Texas Spice Co, 30179
Texican Specialty Products, 30180
TGI Texas, 30002
Thermo Service, 30222
Thermoseal, 30234
Thirstenders International, 30243
Thompson Scale Co, 30257
TLC & Associates, 30011
TMCo Inc.ÿ, 30013, 30014
TNA Packaging Solutions, 30020
TOPS Software Corpora tion, 30024
Tor Rey Refrigeration Inc, 30338
Tor Rey USA, 30339
Tortilla Industry Associ, 30347
Tramontina USA, 30381
Transnorm System Inc, 30388
Tranter INC, 30390
Traulsen & Co, 30393
Tri-Pak Machinery Inc, 30417
Triple S Dynamics Inc, 30452
TRITEN Corporation, 30028
Tropical Soap Company, 30462
Turbo Refrigerating Company, 30496
TURBOCHEF Technologies, 30034
Ultrafryer Systems Inc, 30577
United Filters Intl, 30636
Universal Packaging Inc, 30677
US Filter/Continental Water, 30549
USA Canvas Shoppe, 30560
Van Leer Flexibles, 30757
Vasconia Housewares, 30783
VC Menus, 30713
Vent-A-Hood Co, 30798
Victory Packaging, Inc., 30839
Virtual Packaging, 30867
Vitro Packaging, 30887, 30888
VMC Signs, 30720
W A Powers Co, 30915
Waco Broom & Mop Factory, 30970

West-Pak, 31130
Williams & Mettle Company, 31229
Windhorst Blowmold, 31248
Wins Paper Products, 31272
Winzen Film, 31275
WNA, 30945
Wolens Company, 31307
Woodard, 31318
World Division, 31339
Wornick Company, 31358
WS Packaging Group Inc, 30955
X-Press Manufacturing, 31370

Utah

AC Label Company, 18102
Allied Electric Sign & Awning, 18619
Amano Artisan Chocolate, 18691
Associated Industrial Rubber, 19124
Aurora Design Associates, Inc., 19192
Big-D Construction Corp, 19653
Bintz Restaurant Supply Company, 19665
Bloemhof, 19734
C P Industries, 19995
Cambelt International Corporation, 20157
Case Lowe & Hart Architects, 20322
Crestware, 21083
Dutro Co, 21832
England Logistics, 22179
Enterprise Dynamics Corporation, 22200
Ernest F Mariani Co, 22255
ESKAY Corporation, 21939
Fred Beesley's Booth & Upholstery, 22841
Genesis Nutritional Labs, 23137
Glo Germ Company, 23216
Hy-Ko Enviro-MaintenanceProducts, 23948
In-Touch Products, 24127
Kilgore Chemical Corporation, 24833
Label Express, 25043
Lehi Mills, 25226
Liberty Ware LLC, 25289
LMK Containers, 25020
Lone Peak Labeling Systems, 25415
Louis A Roser Company, 25445
M-One Specialties, 25541
M-Vac Systems Inc, 25544
Mity Lite Inc, 26229
Multi-Fill Inc, 26368
Nutraceutical International, 26785
O K Mfg, 26801
Omni Lift Inc, 26919
Poss USA, 27687
Pro-Com Security Systems, 27838
Rainbow Sign Co, 28157
Roto-Jet Pump, 28557
Sielt Stone, 29182
Sunset Sales, 29785
Swirl Freeze Corp, 29860, 29861
Sysco Corp, 29892
Target Industries, 30076
Temkin International, 30137
ThermoWorks, 30225
Thor Inc, 30260
Thornton Plastics, 30264
Three P, 30267
Toromont Process Systems, 30343
Traco Manufacturing Inc, 30369
Utah PaperBox Company, 30704
VPI Manufacturing, 30723
Water & Power Technologies, 31031
Wemco Pumps, 31106
Wes Tech Engineering Inc, 31113
Wescor, 31115
Winmark Stamp & Sign, 31266
Xango LLC, 31374
YESCO, 31386
Zero Manufacturing Inc, 31439

Vermont

Ann Clark, LTD, 18947
Bertek Systems Inc, 19601
Bia Diagnostics, 19644
Biotek Instruments Inc, 19689
Blodgett Corp, 19732
Blodgett Oven Co, 19733
Cheese Outlet Fresh Market, 20476
Coffee Enterprises, 20695
Common Sense Natural Soap & Bodycare Products, 20787
Consolidated Container Co, 20852
Edlund Co, 22041

Granville Manufacturing Co, 23321
Green Mountain Awning Inc, 23373
Highland Sugarworks, 23769
Ideas Well Done LLC, 24065
IVEK Corp, 24042, 24043
Killington Wood ProductsCompany, 24834
Melsur Corporation, 25968
Monument Industries Inc, 26298
New England Label, 26577
New England Overshoe Company, 26579
Newtech Inc, 26619
ORB Weaver Farm, 26820
Rhino Foods Inc, 28371
Stellar Steam, 29637
Tridyne Process Systems, 30436
Tucel Industries, Inc., 30481
Twin State Signs, 30512
Vermont Bag & Film, 30809
Vermont Container Corp, 30810
Vermont Tent Co, 30811
Vermont Tissue Paper Company, 30812

Virginia

A&A International, 18039
Accubar, 18294
ACMA/GD, 18107
Action Instruments Company, 18345
AGC, 18145
Alfa Laval Inc, 18557
Alleghany Highlands Economic Development Authority, 18599
Alliance Industrial Corp, 18611
America's Electric Cooperatives, 18712
American Agribusiness Assistance, 18716
AMF Bakery Systems Corp, 18180
Amherst Milling Co, 18869
Anton Paar USA Inc, 18957
Arol Closure Systems Spa, 19065
Ashworth Bros Inc, 19111
Baker & Co, 19378
Baruch Box Company, 19474
Bc Wood Products, 19500
Belvac Production Machinery, 19562
Beryl's Cake Decorating & Pastry Supplies, 19605
Biovail Technologies, 19692
Bizerba USA, 19704
Black Bear Corp, 19707
Blue Print Automation, 19747, 19748
Borgwaldt KC, 19793
Bowlswitch, 19819
Busch LLC, 19968
Cache Box, 20118
Calmar, 20152
Camtech-AMF, 20173
Cantwell-Cleary Co Inc, 20201
Capitol Recruiting Group, 20215
Cardinal Rubber & Seal Inc, 20242
Chemetrics, 20493
Chemtreat, 20503
ChemTreat, Inc., 20488
Composite Can & Tube Institute, 20801
Contract Chemicals, 20900
Conwed Global Netting Sltns, 20932
Corniani, 20980
Crane Research & Engineering, 21047
CSC Scientific Co Inc, 20093
Custom Packaging Inc, 21193
Dacam Corporation, 21288
Dacam Machinery, 21289
Danville Economic Development, 21347
Data Visible Corporation, 21371
Del Monte Fresh Produce Inc., 21486
Delta Pure Filtration Corp, 21519
Detectamet Inc, 21575
Digital Dining, 21624
Dominion Pallet Inc, 21698
Double Envelope Corp, 21725
Dowling Signs Inc, 21751
DreamPak LLC, 21763
Dynaric Inc, 21859
Eagle Bakery Equipment, 21948
EAS Consulting Group LLC, 21890
Electronic Development Labs, 22084
Enpoco, 22189
ENSCO Inc, 21922
Environmental Systems, 22218
Equipment Specialists Inc, 22242
ESS Technologies, 21940
Essentra Packaging Inc., 22273
Eurotherm, 22301

F R Drake Co, 22370
Fabriko, 22433
First Source LLC, 22580
Flexicell Inc, 22633
Food Allergy & Anaphylaxis Network, 22692
Food Technology Corporation, 22729
Franz Haas Machinery-America, 22835
G&H Enterprises, 22944
Gbn Machine & Engineering, 23073
GD Packaging Machinery, 22957
Giesecke & Devrient America, 23178
Good Pack, 23268
HAABTEC Inc, 23481
Hampton Roads Box Company, 23551
Heart of Virginia, 23685
Hilden Halifax, 23772
Hogshire Industries, 23814
Hoppmann Corporation, 23856
Horn & Todak, 23862
Hunter Lab, 23931
IAFIS Dairy Products Evaluation Contest, 23984
Imperial Broom Company, 24106
Industrial Automation Specs, 24155
Industrial Machine Manufacturing, 24181
International Fresh-Cut Produce Association, 24338
Invictus Systems Corporation, 24382
James V. Hurson Associates, 24502
Kaeser Compressors Inc, 24709
Keystone Rubber Corporation, 24820
KIK Custom Products, 24683
Klockner Packaging Machinery, 24886
Klockner Pentaplast of America, 24887
Lamb Sign, 25103
Landen Strapping, 25125
Least Cost Formulations LTD, 25198
Liqui-Box, 25344
Liqui-Box Corp, 25345
Lydall, 25501
Marineland Commercial Aquariums, 25741
Mastex Industries, 25846
Mcbride Sign Co, 25921
MCNAB Inc, 25561
Meadwestvaco Corp, 25939
Micro Affiliates, 26080
Millhiser, 26185
Molins/Sandiacre Richmond, 26271
Monoflo International Inc, 26285
Moog Components Group, 26299
Morgan Brothers Bag Company, 26308
National Marking Products Inc, 26486
National Wooden Pallet & Container Association, 26512
Nova Hand Dryers, 26745
Nydree Flooring, 26798
Oceanpower America, 26847
Old Dominion Box Co Inc, 26882
Old Dominion Wood Products, 26884
Old Mansion Inc, 26886
Pacific Scientific, 27112
Packexpo.Com, 27184
Pallet Management Systems, 27225
Paxton North America, 27363
PDMP, 27048
PMMI Bookstore, 27064
Pohlig Brothers, 27620
Polibak Plastics America Inc, 27633
Pressure Pack, 27769
Process Engineering & Fabrication, 27858
Q A Supplies LLC, 27960
Qualtrax Inc, 28017
Ramoneda Bros Stave Mill, 28168
REI Systems Inc, 28095
Reynolds Foodservice Packaging, 28362
Richmond Corrugated Box Company, 28389
Rolland Machining & Fabricating, 28490
Ross Industries, 28537, 28538
Royal Silver Mfg Co Inc, 28587
Ryson International, 28625
S E & M, 28638
Sahara Date Company, 28758
Sanitech Inc, 28817
Sasser Signs, 28833
Scan Coin, 28858
Scott Pallets Inc, 28928
Seaboard Bag Corporation, 28942
Seal Pac USA, 28948
Sealeze Inc, 28955
Sentry Equipment/Erectors Inc, 29034
Service Neon Signs, 29058
Sheldon Wood Products, 29131

Simplimatic Automation, 29254
SJ Industries, 28696
Smalley Package Company, 29287
Smyth Co, 29313
Snack Food Assn, 29315
Southern Atlantic Label Co, 29401
Specialty Blades, 29461
Suffolk Iron Works Inc, 29754
Sumitomo Machinery Corp, 29760
Super Radiator Coils, 29790
SuppliesForLess, 29816
Sus-Rap Protective Packaging, 29838
Swift Creek Forest Products, 29858
Swisslog Logistics Inc, 29864, 29865
Sysco Corp, 29922, 29943
Thermolok Packaging Systems, 30230
Thielmann Container Systems, 30241
Three-A Sanitary Standards Symbol, 30268
TMI-USA, 30016
Tonnellerie Montross, 30327
Travaini Pumps USA, 30394
Tri-Boro Shelving & Partition, 30413
Tri-Clover, 30414
UPACO Adhesives, 30535
US Apple Assn, 30539
Us Flag & Signal, 30701
VINITECH, 30718
Virginia Artesian Bottling Company, 30863
Virginia Department of Agriculture &
    Consumer Services, 30864
Virginia Industrial Services, 30865
Virginia Plastics Co, 30866
Vitex Packaging Group, 30886
Vogel Lubrication Systems, 30891
WAKO Chemicals USA Inc, 30929
Westvaco, 31160
Williamsburg Millwork, 31234
Xpander Pak, 31379
York River Pallet Corporation, 31402

Washington

Ace Stamp & Engraving, 18309
Achilles USA, 18314
Acorto, 18331
Adamatic, 18359
Adhesive Products Inc, 18374
Aerofreeze, 18447
Aibmr Life Sciences, 18484
AM Test Laboratories, 18168
Ambrose CM Co, 18699
American Autoclaves Co, 18722
American Plywood, 18809
Andgar Corp, 18931
Andrew's Fixture Co, 18936
Apa, 18963
Apollo Sheet Metal, 18978
Applied Handling NW, 18990
ATAGO USA Inc, 18228
B M T USA LLC, 19294
Bags Go Green, 19372
Bargreen Ellingson, 19448, 19449
Baxter Manufacturing Inc, 19490
Belltown Boxing Company, 19554
Belshaw Adamatic Bakery Group, 19556
Bergschrond, 19585
Biocontrol Systems Inc, 19678
Biomed Comm, 19683
Bonar Plastics, 19788
Broadmoor Baker, 19880
Burgess Enterprises, Inc, 19952
Burke Industrial Coatings, 19955
Care Controls, Inc., 20244
CBI Freezing Equipment, 20027
CBi Freezing Equipment, 20031
City Neon Sign Company, 20586
Clearwater Paper Corporation, 20628
Cloudy & Britton, 20660
CM Ambrose Company, 20066
Coastline Equipment Inc, 20674
Colmac Coil Mfg Inc, 20728
Columbia Labeling Machinery, 20746
Columbia Machine Inc, 20748
Columbia Okura LLC, 20749
Comark Instruments, 20757
Combustion Systems Sales, 20763
Commencement Bay Corrugated, 20772
Commercial Creamery Co, 20774
Country Save Products Corp, 21017
Culinary Collective, 21142
Cyrk, 21221
Decagon Devices Inc, 21431

Del Monte Fresh Produce Inc., 21472
Discovery Products Corporation, 21644
DSI, 21277
Dwinell's Central Neon, 21835
Easy-Care Environs, 21986
Easyup Storage Systems, 21988
Eclipse Espresso Systems, 22006
EDT Corp, 21898
Elliott Bay Espresso, 22110
Emerald City Closets Inc, 22134
Esstech, 22274
Everett Rubber Stamp, 22312
Filtercarb LLC/ Filtercorp, 22552
Flakice Corporation, 22602
Flodin, 22646
Flow International Corp., 22657
Foley Sign Co, 22685
Food Plant Engineering, 22714
Formost Packaging Machines, 22767
Frigoscandia, 22873
Frontier Packaging Company, 22888
Futura Equipment Corporation, 22925
Girard Wood Products Inc, 23191
Globe Machine, 23237
GM Nameplate, 22985
Gourmet Display, 23288
Gray Woodproducts, 23337
Grays Harbor Stamp Works, 23343
Hinds-Bock Corp, 23786
Hop Growers Of Washington, 23851
Hovair Systems Inc, 23885
iFoodDecisionSciences, 31465
Independent Packers Corporation, 24142
Industrial Crating & Packing, 24165
Infometrix, 24212
Intech, 24289
Intermec Technologies Corporation, 24319
Intermec/Norand Mobile Systems, 24320
International Wood Industries, 24364
Interstate Monroe Machinery, 24368
IPS International, 24021
Irwin Research & Development, 24391
J.H. Carr & Sons, 24440
Kess Industries Inc, 24798
Key Technology Inc., 24812
KWIK Lok Corp, 24704, 24705
L&L Reps, 24990
Labels Plus, 25068
Lang Manufacturing Co, 25132
Laucks' Testing Laboratories, 25162
Liberty Distributing Inc, 25284
Locknane, 25384
Logix, 25408
Longview Fibre Co, 25428
Lowery's Premium Roast Gourmet Coffee,
    25460
Lucks Food Equipment Company, 25475
Lynden Meat Co, 25505
MarkeTeam, 25749
Marq Packaging Systems Inc, 25778, 25779
Mastermark, 25843
Matson LLC, 25868
MCD Technologies, 25559
Measurement Systems Intl, 25940
Meheen Manufacturing Inc, 25957
Melcher Manufacturing Co, 25960
Metal Masters Northwest, 26021
Michaelo Espresso, 26065
Microscan Systems Inc, 26112
Mimi et Cie, 26199
Mohawk Northern Plastics, 26259
Mountain Safety Research, 26337
Mtc Food Equipment, 26357
National Menuboard, 26487
National Sign Corporation, 26502
Nelson & Associates Recruiting, 26540
Nemco Electric Company, 26546
NEPA Pallet & Container Co, 26423
New Horizon Technologies, 26589
North Star, 26696
North Star Ice EquipmentCorporation, 26698
Northwest Art Glass, 26727
Northwest Cherry Growers, 26728
Northwest Laboratories, 26730
Nuova Distribution Centre, 26779
Nuova Simonelli USA, 26780
Nutrifaster Inc, 26787
Pacific Bag, 27091
Pacific Coast Container, 27093
Pacific Harvest Products, 27096
Pacific Northwest Canned Pear, 27099
Pacific Northwest Wire Works, 27100

Parity Corp, 27303, 27304
Pearson Packaging Systems, 27369, 27370
Phoenix Sign Company, 27506
Pomona Service & Pkgng Co LA, 27665
Port Of Pasco, 27673
Portco Corporation, 27675
Potlatch Corp, 27690
PPI Printing Press, 27070
Precision Wood Of Hawaii, 27737
Precision Wood Products, 27736
Pride Polymers LLC, 27784
Prime Equipment, 27787
Pro Controls Inc, 27829
Pro Refrigeration, 27833
Process Heating Co, 27859
Professional Marketing Group, 27880
Quintex Corp, 28041
Rairdon Dodge Chrysler Jeep, 28158
Read Products Inc, 28209
Reid Boiler Works, 28283
Revere Group, 28347, 28348
Robinson Cold Storage, 28449
Rose City Printing & Packaging, 28524
Roth Young Bellevue, 28545
Roth Young Washougal, 28552
S. B. C. Coffee, 28962
Seattle Boiler Works Inc, 28964
Seattle Menu Specialists, 28965
Seattle Plastics, 28966
Seattle Refrigeration & Manufacturing,
    28967
Seattle's Best Coffee, 28968
Seattle-Tacoma Box Co, 28969, 28970
Sensitech, 29023
Sensitech Inc, 29024
Sentron, 29032
Shields Bag & Printing Co, 29142
Si-Lodec, 29176
Signal Equipment, 29202
SIMS Manufacturing Co Inc, 28692
Smith-Berger Marine, 29297
Sonderen Packaging, 29358
Sonofresco, 29367
Sorenson, 29375
Spectrum Ascona, 29479
Spokane House of Hose Inc, 29508
Stewart Marketing Services, 29670
Stoneway Carton Company, 29691
Superior Imaging Group Inc, 29802
Supreme Corporation, 29821
Sysco Corp, 29913
Tech-Roll Inc, 30097
Thermaline Inc, 30211
Thunderbird Food Machinery, 30271
Tidland Corp, 30277
Touch Menus, 30361
Trout Lake Farm Company, 30463
Tully's Coffee, 30492
Underwriters Laboratories Inc, 30586
Universal Paper Box, 30679
Vancouver Manufacturing, 30765
Vaughan Co Inc, 30785
Vee Gee Scientific Inc, 30791
Verax Chemical Co, 30804
Versatile Mobile Systems, 30819
Visions Espresso Svc, 30871
Walco-Linck Company, 30979
Wald Imports, 30980
Washington Frontier, 31020
Western Polymer Corp, 31145
Weyerhaeuser Co, 31166
WholesalePortal.com, 31190
Wood Stone Corp, 31316, 31317
Wrap Pak, 31360
YAAX International, 31384
Zeroloc, 31443

West Virginia

American National Rubber, 18797
Appalachian Power, 18980
Automatic Timing & Controls, 19227
Bright of America, 19868
Dover Parkersburg, 21744
Fenton Art Glass Company, 22512
Gatewood Products LLC, 23066
Green Sustainable Solutions, 23378
Hamilton Kettles, 23544
Homer Laughlin China Co, 23842
Kincaid Enterprises, 24840
King Engineering - King-Gage, 24853
Lumber & Things, 25487

Masterpiece Crystal, 25845
Orr's Farm Market, 26978
Paul Hawkins Lumber Company, 27351
Payne Controls Co, 27365
Porter & Porter Lumber, 27677
RXI Silgan Specialty Plastics, 28132
Spencer Business Form Company, 29485
Tecnocap, 30114
Wall Conveyor & Manufacturing, 30990
Woodson Pallet Co, 31323

Wisconsin

3DT, LLC, 18001
A & B Process Systems Corp, 18010
A&A Manufacturing Company, 18041
A.B. Sealer, Inc., 18066
AANTEC, 18082
Abatron Inc, 18253
Abbotsford Farms, 18256
Abel Manufacturing Co, 18263
ABJ/Sanitaire Corporation, 18097
Absolute Custom Extrusions Inc, 18271
Accent Store Fixtures, 18277
Acme Equipment Corporation, 18322
Activon Products, 18351
ACUair/York Refrigeration, 18114
Advance Cleaning Products, 18387
Advance Fittings Corp, 18391
Advanced Detection Systems, 18403
Advanced Separations andProcess Systems,
    18423
Agropur MSI, LLC, 18478
Air Logic Power Systems, 18493
Air-Lec Industries, Inc, 18500
Airsan Corp, 18516
Aladdin Label Inc, 18524
Alkar Rapid Pak, 18568, 18569, 18570,
    18571
Allied Glove Corporation, 18622
Allison Systems Inc, 18628
Alloy Products Corp, 18633
Alluserv, 18644
Alstor America, 18666
Alto-Shaam, 18677
Amcor, 18705
American Municipal Chemical, 18796
American Printpak Inc, 18810
Ampco Pumps Co Inc, 18879
AMSOIL Inc, 18186
Anguil Environmental Systems, 18941
Antrim Manufacturing Inc, 18958
Apache Stainless Equipment, 18965, 18966
Applied Technologies, 18996
Aptar Mukwonago, 18999
APV Americas, 18207
APV Fluid Handling, 18210
APV Mixing & Blending, 18212
APV Tanks & Fabricated Products, 18214
Arco Coffee Co, 19024
ASI Technologies, 18226
Associated Bag Co, 19123
Astro Arc Polysoude, 19133
Athea Laboratories, 19140
Atlas Tag & Label Inc, 19173
ATM Corporation, 18232
Autotron, 19242
Aw Sheepscot Holding Co Inc, 19262
B C Holland Inc, 19289
B J Wood Products Inc, 19293
Babcock & Wilcox MEGTEC, 19355
Back to Basics, 19361
Badger Meter Inc, 19366
Badger Plug Co, 19367
Badger Wood Arts, 19368
Bake Star, 19377
Bardes Plastics Inc, 19446
Barr Refrigeration, 19462
Barr Storage, 19463
Basic Concepts, 19476
Beckart Environmental Inc, 19512
BEERCUP.COM, 19318
Behnke Lubricants/JAX, 19529
Bell Laboratories Inc, 19544
Ben H. Anderson Manufacturers, 19564
Bennett's Auto Inc, 19573
Berenz Packaging Corp, 19578
Berg Co, 19581
Berlon Industries, 19592
BFM Equipment Sales, 19327
Bib Pak, 19645
Bilt-Rite Conveyors, 19659

Plastocon, 27603
Plymouth Tube Company, 27613
Poblocki Sign Co, 27617
Polar Ware Company, 27632
Power Packaging Inc, 27702
Poweramp, 27705
Poynette Distribution Center, 27708
Preco Inc, 27739
Prent Corp, 27757
Pres-Air-Trol Corporation, 27760
Print-Tech, 27807
Priority One America, 27818
Priority One Packaging Machinery, 27820
Pro Active Solutions USA LLC, 27827
Pro Media Inc, 27831
Process Displays, 27857
Progressive Technology International, 27888
Prolamina, 27891
Promega, 27896
Provisur Technologies, 27919
PTI Packaging, 27077
Pyro-Chem, 27956
Quality Cup Packaging Machinery
   Corporation, 28001
Quality Packaging Inc, 28012
Racine County Court Cmmssnr, 28136
Ram Equipment Co, 28162
Rath Manufacturing Company, 28195
Rebel Green, 28217
Red Star BioProducts, 28225
Regal Box Corp, 28264
Regal Ware Inc, 28272
Regina USA, 28276
Regina-Emerson, 28277
Reinhold Sign Svc Inc, 28288
Reinke & Schomann, 28289
Renard Machine Company, 28313
Respirometry Plus, LLC, 28336
Retrotec, 28345
Rexford Paper Company, 28356
Rexnord Corporation, 28357, 28358
Rice Lake Weighing Systems, 28378
RidgeView Products LLC, 28395
Rite-Hite, 28409
RJ Jansen Company, 28105
RJ Jansen Confectionery, 28106
RM Waite Inc, 28113

Robar International Inc, 28428
Rockline Industries, 28471
Rockwell Automation Inc, 28472
Rytec Corporation, 28626
S & S Svc Parts, 28636
SAF Products, 28658
Samuel Pressure Vessel Group, 28778
San Jamar, 28787
Sani-Matic, 28810
Sapac International, 28823
Sargento Foods Inc, 28829
Sauve Company Limited, 28844
Scan Group, 28860
Schenck Process, 28875, 28876, 28877
Schlueter Company, 28888, 28889, 28890
Schoeneck Containers Inc, 28898
Schreiber Foods Inc., 28903
Schurman's Wisconsin Cheese Country,
   28907
Schwaab, Inc, 28909
Schwartz Manufacturing Co, 28911
Seiberling Associates Inc, 28984
Sentry Equipment Corp, 29033
Server Products Inc, 29053
Seville Flexpack Corp, 29081, 29082
Seymour Woodenware Company, 29086
Sharp Packaging Systems Inc, 29112
Shawano Specialty Papers, 29120
Sheboygan Paper Box Co, 29123
Simply Manufacturing, 29255
SKW Gelatin & Specialties, 28700
Smith, RD, Company, 29296
Smith-Lee Company, 29299
Soco System USA, 29327, 29328
Sohn Manufacturing, 29330
Solvit, 29348
Solvox Manufacturing Company, 29349
Spacesaver Corp, 29440
Spann Sign Company, 29443
Spartech Plastics, 29454
Spee-Dee Packaging Machinery, 29482
Sprinkman Corporation, 29526
Stainless Specialists Inc, 29560
Stearns Packaging Corp, 29616
Steel King Industries, 29623
Steep & Brew, 29628
Sterling Ball & Jewel, 29648

Stock America Inc, 29678
Straubel Company, 29723
Stuart W Johnson & Co, 29742
Super Steel, 29792
Supply Corp, 29817
Sure Clean Corporation, 29828
Sysco Corp, 29920, 29934
Tapesolutions, 30068
Task Footwear, 30078
Tenor Controls Company, 30154
Tetra Pak, 30172
Thermo Wisconsin, 30223
Thiel Cheese & Ingredients, 30236
Thomas Precision, Inc., 30248
Thomas Technical Svc, 30252, 30253
Thomasen, 30254
Thomsen Group LLC, 30258
Thunder Pallet Inc, 30270
Tiefenthaler Machinery Co, Inc, 30279
Titan Industries Inc, 30300
TKO Doors, 30009
Token Factory, 30311
Tosca Ltd, 30348
Toska Foodservice Systems, 30350
Tower Pallet Co Inc, 30363
Townsend-Piller Packing, 30366
Traex, 30376
Trans-Chemco Inc, 30385
Tricore AEA, 30433
Trimline Corp, 30441
Trowelon, 30464
Tulip Molded Plastics Corp, 30491
Tyco Fire Protection Products, 30516
U Roast Em Inc, 30523
U-Line Corporation, 30524
Ultra Industries Inc, 30572
United Industries Inc, 30641
Universal Die & Stampings, 30665
US Chemical, 30542
Vac Air Inc, 30727
Valley Packaging Supply Co, 30746
Vector Technologies, 30790
Vern's Cheese, 30813
Viking Machine & Design Inc, 30850
Vilter Manufacturing Corporation, 30854
Vincent Commodities Corporation, 30857
Vista International Packaging, 30874, 30875

Vollrath Co LLC, 30898
Vortron Smokehouse/Ovens, 30906
VPI, 30722
W.A. Golomski & Associates, 30922
W.M. Sprinkman Corporation, 30926
Wald Wire & Mfg Co, 30981
Walker Stainless Equipment Co, 30989
Walters Brothers, 31001
Waukesha Foundry Inc, 31051
Waukesha Specialty Company, 31052
Wausau Paper Corp., 31053
Wausau Tile/Textura Designs, 31054
Weiler & Company, 31087
Weiler Equipment, 31088
Weinbrenner Shoe Co, 31089
Weyauwega Star Dairy, 31165
Will-Pemco Inc, 31218
Winn-Sol Products, 31267
Winnebago Sign Company, 31268
Wire Products Mfg, 31279
Wisco Industries Assembly, 31283
Wisconsin Aluminum Foundry Co, 31284
Wisconsin Bakers Assn Inc, 31285
Wisconsin Bench Mfg, 31286
Wisconsin Box Co, 31287, 31288
Wisconsin Converting Inc, 31289
Wisconsin Film & Bag Inc, 31290
Wisconsin Precision Casting, 31291
Wittco Foodservice Equipment, 31295,
   31296
Wohlt Cheese Corp, 31306
Wood Goods Industries, 31315
Wright Brothers Paper Box Company, 31363
WS Packaging Group Inc, 30952, 30953,
   30954, 30956, 30958
Young & Associates, 31408
Zeier Plastic & Mfg Inc, 31427
Zenar Corp, 31431
Zerand Corp, 31438

Wyoming

APW Wyott Food Service Equipment
   Company, 18215
Sign Products, 29198

2020 Title List

Visit www.GreyHouse.com for Product Information, Table of Contents, and Sample Pages.

Opinions Throughout History

Opinions Throughout History: Drug Use & Abuse
Opinions Throughout History: Gender: Roles & Rights
Opinions Throughout History: Globalization
Opinions Throughout History: Guns in America
Opinions Throughout History: Immigration
Opinions Throughout History: National Security vs. Civil & Privacy Rights
Opinions Throughout History: Presidential Authority
Opinions Throughout History: Robotics & Artificial Intelligence
Opinions Throughout History: Social Media Issues
Opinions Throughout History: The Death Penalty
Opinions Throughout History: The Environment
Opinions Throughout History: Voters' Rights

This is Who We Were

This is Who We Were: Colonial America (1492-1775)
This is Who We Were: 1880-1899
This is Who We Were: In the 1900s
This is Who We Were: In the 1910s
This is Who We Were: In the 1920s
This is Who We Were: A Companion to the 1940 Census
This is Who We Were: In the 1940s (1940-1949)
This is Who We Were: In the 1950s
This is Who We Were: In the 1960s
This is Who We Were: In the 1970s
This is Who We Were: In the 1980s
This is Who We Were: In the 1990s
This is Who We Were: In the 2000s
This is Who We Were: In the 2010s

Working Americans

Working Americans, 1880-2011 - Vol. 1 The Working Class
Working Americans, 1880-1999 - Vol. 2: The Middle Class
Working Americans, 1880-1999 - Vol. 3: The Upper Class
Working Americans, 1880-1999 - Vol. 4: Children
Working Americans, 1880-2015 - Vol. 5: At War
Working Americans, 1880-2015 - Vol. 6: Working Women
Working Americans, 1880-2016 - Vol. 7: Social Movements
Working Americans, 1880-2017 - Vol. 8: Immigrants
Working Americans, 1770-1869 - Vol. 9: From the Revolutionary War to the Civil War
Working Americans, 1880-2009 - Vol. 10: Sports & Recreation
Working Americans, 1880-2009 - Vol. 11: Inventors & Entrepreneurs
Working Americans, 1880-2011 - Vol. 12: Our History Through Music
Working Americans, 1880-2011 - Vol. 13: Education & Educators
Working Americans, 1880-2016 - Vol. 14: African Americans
Working Americans, 1880-2018: Vol. 15: Politics & Politicians
Working Americans, 1880-2020: Vol. 16: Farming & Ranching

Education

Complete Learning Disabilities Resource Guide
Educators Resource Guide
The Comparative Guide to Elem. & Secondary Schools
Charter School Movement
Special Education: A Reference Book for Policy & Curriculum Development

General Reference

African Biographical Dictionary
American Environmental Leaders
America's College Museums
Constitutional Amendments
Encyclopedia of African-American Writing
Encyclopedia of Historical Warrior Peoples & Modern Fighting Groups
Encyclopedia of Invasions & Conquests
Encyclopedia of Prisoners of War & Internment
Encyclopedia of Religion & the Law in America
Encyclopedia of Rural America
Encyclopedia of the Continental Congresses
Encyclopedia of the United States Cabinet
Encyclopedia of War Journalism
The Environmental Debate
The Evolution Wars: A Guide to the Debates
Financial Literacy Starter Kit
From Suffrage to the Senate
The Gun Debate: An Encyclopedia of Gun Rights & Gun Control in the US
History of Canada
Human Rights and the United States
Political Corruption in America
Privacy Rights in the Digital Age
Religious Right and American Politics
Speakers of the House of Representatives
The Value of a Dollar 1600-1865 Colonial to Civil War
The Value of a Dollar 1860-2019
US Land & Natural Resources Policy
World Cultural Leaders of the 20th Century

Business Information

Business Information Resources
The Complete Broadcasting Industry Guide: Television, Radio, Cable & Streaming
Directory of Mail Order Catalogs
Environmental Resource Handbook
Food & Beverage Market Place
The Grey House Homeland Security Resources
The Grey House Performing Arts Industry Guide
Guide to Healthcare Group Purchasing Organizations
Guide to U.S. HMOs and PPOs
Guide to Venture Capital & Private Equity Firms
Hudson's Washington News Media Contacts Guide
New York State Directory
Sports Market Place

Consumer Health

Comparative Guide to American Hospitals
Complete Mental Health Resource Guide
Complete Resource Guide for Pediatric Disorders
Complete Resource Guide for People with Chronic Illness
Complete Resource Guide for People with Disabilities
Dementia Handbook & Resource Guide
Older Americans Information Resource

2020 Title List

Visit www.GreyHouse.com for Product Information, Table of Contents, and Sample Pages.

Statistics & Demographics

America's Top-Rated Cities
America's Top-Rated Smaller Cities
Ancestry & Ethnicity in America
The Comparative Guide to American Suburbs
The Hispanic Databook
Profiles of America
Profiles of California
Profiles of Connecticut & Rhode Island
Profiles of Florida
Profiles of Illinois
Profiles of Indiana
Profiles of Massachusetts
Profiles of Michigan
Profiles of New Jersey
Profiles of New York
Profiles of North Carolina & South Carolina
Profiles of Ohio
Profiles of Pennsylvania
Profiles of Texas
Profiles of Virginia
Profiles of Wisconsin
Weather America

Canadian Resources

Canadian Almanac & Directory
Canadian Environmental Update
Associations Canada
Financial Services Canada
Libraries Canada
Canadian Parliamentary Guide
Canadian Venture Capital & Private Equity Firms
Health Guide Canada
Major Canadian Cities: Compared & Ranked, First Edition
Canadian Who's Who
Cannabis Canada
Financial Post Directory of Directors
FP Survey: Industrials
FP Survey: Mines & Energy
FP Survey: Predecessor & Defunct
FP Bonds: Corporate
FP Bonds: Government
FP Equities: Preferreds & Derivatives
Careers & Employment Canada

Weiss Financial Ratings

Financial Literacy Basics
Financial Literacy: How to Become an Investor
Financial Literacy: Planning for the Future
Weiss Ratings Consumer Guides
Weiss Ratings Guide to Banks
Weiss Ratings Guide to Credit Unions
Weiss Ratings Guide to Health Insurers
Weiss Ratings Guide to Life & Annuity Insurers
Weiss Ratings Guide to Property & Casualty Insurers
Weiss Ratings Investment Research Guide to Bond & Money
    Market Mutual Funds
Weiss Ratings Investment Research Guide to Exchange-Traded
    Funds
Weiss Ratings Investment Research Guide to Stock Mutual
    Funds
Weiss Ratings Investment Research Guide to Stocks

Books in Print Series

American Book Publishing Record® Annual
American Book Publishing Record® Monthly
Books In Print®
Books In Print® Supplement
Books Out Loud™
Bowker's Complete Video Directory™
Children's Books In Print®
El-Hi Textbooks & Serials In Print®
Forthcoming Books®
Law Books & Serials In Print™
Medical & Health Care Books In Print™
Publishers, Distributors & Wholesalers of the US™
Subject Guide to Books In Print®
Subject Guide to Children's Books In Print®

Grey House Publishing | Salem Press | H.W. Wilson | 4919 Route, 22 PO Box 56, Amenia NY 12501-0056

SALEM PRESS

2020 Title List

SALEM PRESS

Visit www.SalemPress.com for Product Information, Table of Contents, and Sample Pages.

Critical Insights

Critical Insights: A Midsummer Night's Dream
Critical Insights: A Portrait of the Artist as a Young Man
Critical Insights: A Streetcar Named Desire
Critical Insights: Abraham Lincoln
Critical Insights: Absalom, Absalom!
Critical Insights: Adventures of Huckleberry Finn
Critical Insights: Aeneid
Critical Insights: Albert Camus
Critical Insights: Alice Munro
Critical Insights: Alice Walker
Critical Insights: All Quiet on the Western Front
Critical Insights: American Creative Non-Fiction
Critical Insights: American Multicultural Identity
Critical Insights: American Road Literature
Critical Insights: American Short Story
Critical Insights: American Sports Fiction
Critical Insights: American Writers in Exile
Critical Insights: Ancient Greek Literature
Critical Insights: Animal Farm
Critical Insights: Arthur Miller
Critical Insights: Barbara Kingsolver
Critical Insights: Beloved
Critical Insights: Benjamin Franklin
Critical Insights: Billy Budd, Sailor
Critical Insights: Brave New World
Critical Insights: Censored & Banned Literature
Critical Insights: Charles Dickens
Critical Insights: Civil Rights Literature, Past & Present
Critical Insights: Coming of Age
Critical Insights: Conspiracies
Critical Insights: Contemporary Canadian Fiction
Critical Insights: Contemporary Immigrant Short Fiction
Critical Insights: Contemporary Latin American Fiction
Critical Insights: Contemporary Speculative Fiction
Critical Insights: Cormac McCarthy
Critical Insights: Crime and Detective Fiction
Critical Insights: Crisis of Faith
Critical Insights: Cultural Encounters
Critical Insights: David Foster Wallace
Critical Insights: Death of a Salesman
Critical Insights: Dracula
Critical Insights: Dystopia
Critical Insights: Edith Wharton

Critical Insights: Emily Dickinson
Critical Insights: Ernest Hemingway
Critical Insights: Eugene O'Neill
Critical Insights: F. Scott Fitzgerald
Critical Insights: Fahrenheit 451
Critical Insights: Family
Critical Insights: Feminism
Critical Insights: Flannery O'Connor
Critical Insights: Flash Fiction
Critical Insights: Frederick Douglass
Critical Insights: Gabriel Garcia Marquez
Critical Insights: Gender, Sex and Sexuality
Critical Insights: Geoffrey Chaucer
Critical Insights: George Eliot
Critical Insights: George Orwell
Critical Insights: Good & Evil
Critical Insights: Great Expectations
Critical Insights: Greed
Critical Insights: Gustave Flaubert
Critical Insights: Gwendolyn Brooks
Critical Insights: Hamlet
Critical Insights: Harlan Ellison
Critical Insights: Harlem Renaissance
Critical Insights: Harry Potter Series
Critical Insights: Heart of Darkness
Critical Insights: Henry James
Critical Insights: Herman Melville
Critical Insights: Historical Fiction
Critical Insights: Holocaust Literature
Critical Insights: Horton Foote
Critical Insights: I Know Why the Caged Bird Sings
Critical Insights: In Cold Blood
Critical Insights: Inequality
Critical Insights: Invisible Man
Critical Insights: Isaac Asimov
Critical Insights: Isabel Allende
Critical Insights: Jack London
Critical Insights: James Baldwin
Critical Insights: James Joyce
Critical Insights: James McBride
Critical Insights: Jane Austen
Critical Insights: Jane Eyre
Critical Insights: John Cheever
Critical Insights: John Steinbeck
Critical Insights: John Updike
Critical Insights: Joseph Conrad
Critical Insights: King Lear
Critical Insights: Kurt Vonnegut
Critical Insights: Langston Hughes
Critical Insights: Leo Tolstoy
Critical Insights: LGBTQ Literature
Critical Insights: Life of Pi
Critical Insights: Lillian Hellman
Critical Insights: Literature of Protest
Critical Insights: Little Women
Critical Insights: Lolita
Critical Insights: Lord of the Flies
Critical Insights: Louisa May Alcott
Critical Insights: Louise Erdrich

Critical Insights: Macbeth
Critical Insights: Magical Realism
Critical Insights: Malcolm X
Critical Insights: Margaret Atwood
Critical Insights: Mario Vargas Llosa
Critical Insights: Mark Twain
Critical Insights: Martin Luther King, Jr.
Critical Insights: Mary Shelley
Critical Insights: Maya Angelou
Critical Insights: Midnight's Children
Critical Insights: Midwestern Literature
Critical Insights: Moby-Dick
Critical Insights: Modern Japanese Literature
Critical Insights: Mrs. Dalloway
Critical Insights: Nathaniel Hawthorne
Critical Insights: Nature & the Environment
Critical Insights: Neil Gaiman
Critical Insights: Nineteen Eighty-Four
Critical Insights: Of Mice and Men
Critical Insights: One Flew Over the Cuckoo's Nest
Critical Insights: One Hundred Years of Solitude
Critical Insights: Oscar Wilde
Critical Insights: Paradise Lost
Critical Insights: Paranoia, Fear & Alienation
Critical Insights: Philip Roth
Critical Insights: Political Fiction
Critical Insights: Post-Colonial Literature
Critical Insights: Pride and Prejudice
Critical Insights: Pulp Fiction of the '20s and '30s
Critical Insights: Ray Bradbury
Critical Insights: Raymond Carver
Critical Insights: Rebellion
Critical Insights: Richard Wright
Critical Insights: Robert A. Heinlein
Critical Insights: Robert Frost
Critical Insights: Roberto Bolano
Critical Insights: Romeo and Juliet
Critical Insights: Russia's Golden Age
Critical Insights: Salman Rushdie
Critical Insights: Satire
Critical Insights: Saul Bellow
Critical Insights: Sherman Alexie
Critical Insights: Short Fiction of Flannery O'Connor
Critical Insights: Slaughterhouse-Five
Critical Insights: Social Justice and American Literature
Critical Insights: Southern Gothic Literature
Critical Insights: Southwestern Literature
Critical Insights: Stephen King
Critical Insights: Survival
Critical Insights: Sylvia Plath
Critical Insights: T. S. Eliot

SALEM PRESS

2020 Title List

SALEM PRESS

Visit www.SalemPress.com for Product Information, Table of Contents, and Sample Pages.

Critical Insights (continued)

Critical Insights: Technology & Humanity
Critical Insights: Tennessee Williams
Critical Insights: The American Comic Book
Critical Insights: The American Dream
Critical Insights: The American Thriller
Critical Insights: The Awakening
Critical Insights: The Bell Jar
Critical Insights: The Canterbury Tales
Critical Insights: The Catcher in the Rye
Critical Insights: The Crucible
Critical Insights: The Diary of a Young Girl
Critical Insights: The Fantastic
Critical Insights: The Grapes of Wrath
Critical Insights: The Graphic Novel
Critical Insights: The Great Gatsby
Critical Insights: The Handmaid's Tale
Critical Insights: The Hero's Quest
Critical Insights: The Hobbit
Critical Insights: The House on Mango Street
Critical Insights: The Hunger Games Trilogy
Critical Insights: The Immigrant Experience
Critical Insights: The Inferno
Critical Insights: The Joy Luck Club
Critical Insights: The Kite Runner
Critical Insights: The Metamorphosis
Critical insights: The Odyssey
Critical insights: The Outsiders
Critical Insights: The Pearl
Critical Insights: The Poetry of Baudelaire
Critical Insights: The Poetry of Edgar Allan Poe
Critical Insights: The Red Badge of Courage
Critical Insights: The Scarlet Letter
Critical Insights: The Slave Narrative
Critical Insights: The Sound and the Fury
Critical Insights: The Sun Also Rises
Critical Insights: The Tales of Edgar Allan Poe
Critical Insights: The Woman Warrior
Critical Insights: Things Fall Apart
Critical Insights: Thomas Jefferson
Critical Insights: Tim O'Brien
Critical Insights: To Kill a Mockingbird
Critical Insights: Toni Morrison
Critical Insights: Violence in Literature
Critical Insights: Virginia Woolf & 20th Century Women Writers
Critical Insights: Walt Whitman
Critical Insights: War
Critical Insights: War and Peace
Critical Insights: Willa Cather
Critical Insights: William Faulkner
Critical Insights: Zora Neale Hurston
Critical Insights: Film – Alfred Hitchcock
Critical Insights: Film – Bonnie & Clyde
Critical Insights: Film – Casablanca
Critical Insights: Film – Stanley Kubrick

Literature

Critical Approaches to Literature: Feminist
Critical Approaches to Literature: Moral
Critical Approaches to Literature: Multicultural
Critical Approaches to Literature: Psychological
Critical Survey of American Literature
Critical Survey of Drama
Critical Survey of Graphic Novels: Heroes & Superheroes
Critical Survey of Graphic Novels: History, Theme, and Technique
Critical Survey of Graphic Novels: Independents and Underground Classics
Critical Survey of Graphic Novels: Manga
Critical Survey of Long Fiction
Critical Survey of Mystery and Detective Fiction
Critical Survey of Mythology & Folklore: Gods & Goddesses
Critical Survey of Mythology & Folklore: Heroes and Heroines
Critical Survey of Mythology & Folklore: Love, Sexuality, and Desire
Critical Survey of Mythology & Folklore: World Mythology
Critical Survey of Poetry
Critical Survey of Science Fiction & Fantasy Literature
Critical Survey of Shakespeare's Plays
Critical Survey of Shakespeare's Sonnets
Critical Survey of Short Fiction
Critical Survey of World Literature
Critical Survey of Young Adult Literature
Cyclopedia of Literary Characters
Cyclopedia of Literary Places
Introduction to Literary Context: American Poetry of the 20th Century
Introduction to Literary Context: American Post-Modernist Novels
Introduction to Literary Context: American Short Fiction
Introduction to Literary Context: English Literature
Introduction to Literary Context: Plays
Introduction to Literary Context: World Literature
Magill's Literary Annual
Masterplots
Masterplots, 2010–2018 Supplement
Notable African American Writers
Notable American Women Writers
Novels into Film: Adaptations & Interpretation
Recommended Reading: 600 Classics Reviewed

The Decades

The Sixties in America
The Fifties in America
The Seventies in America
The Eighties in America
The Nineties in America
The Forties in America
The Thirties in America
The Twenties in America
The 2000s in America
The 1910s in America

Grey House Publishing | Salem Press | H.W. Wilson | 4919 Route, 22 PO Box 56, Amenia NY 12501-0056

SALEM PRESS

2020 Title List

SALEM PRESS

Visit www.SalemPress.com for Product Information, Table of Contents, and Sample Pages.

Defining Documents in American History

Defining Documents: American West
Defining Documents: Business Ethics
Defining Documents: Capital Punishment
Defining Documents: Civil Rights
Defining Documents: Civil War
Defining Documents: Dissent & Protest
Defining Documents: Drug Policy
Defining Documents: Environment & Conservation
Defining Documents: Espionage & Intrigue
Defining Documents: Exploration and Colonial America
Defining Documents: Immigration & Immigrant Communities
Defining Documents: LGBTQ+
Defining Documents: Manifest Destiny and the New Nation
Defining Documents: Mental Health
Defining Documents: Native Americans
Defining Documents: Political Campaigns, Candidates & Discourse
Defining Documents: Postwar 1940s
Defining Documents: Prison Reform
Defining Documents: Secrets, Leaks & Scandals
Defining Documents: Slavery
Defining Documents: Supreme Court Decisions
Defining Documents: The 1900s
Defining Documents: The 1910s
Defining Documents: The 1920s
Defining Documents: The 1930s
Defining Documents: The 1950s
Defining Documents: The 1960s
Defining Documents: The 1970s
Defining Documents: The American Revolution
Defining Documents: The Cold War
Defining Documents: The Emergence of Modern America
Defining Documents: The Free Press
Defining Documents: The Gun Debate
Defining Documents: The Legacy of 9/11
Defining Documents: Reconstruction Era
Defining Documents: Vietnam War
Defining Documents: U.S. Involvement in the Middle East
Defining Documents: World War I
Defining Documents: World War II

Defining Documents in World History

Defining Documents: Asia
Defining Documents: Nationalism & Populism
Defining Documents: Renaissance & Early Modern Era
Defining Documents: The 17th Century
Defining Documents: The 18th Century
Defining Documents: The 19th Century
Defining Documents: The 20th Century (1900-1950)
Defining Documents: The Ancient World
Defining Documents: The Middle Ages
Defining Documents: The Middle East
Defining Documents: Women's Rights

Great Events from History

Great Events from History: The Ancient World
Great Events from History: The Middle Ages
Great Events from History: The Renaissance & Early Modern Era
Great Events from History: The 17th Century
Great Events from History: The 18th Century
Great Events from History: The 19th Century
Great Events from History: The 20th Century, 1901-1940
Great Events from History: The 20th Century, 1941-1970
Great Events from History: The 20th Century, 1971-2000
Great Events from History: Modern Scandals
Great Events from History: African American History
Great Events from History: The 21st Century, 2000-2016
Great Events from History: LGBTQ Events
Great Events from History: Human Rights

Great Lives from History

Computer Technology Innovators
Fashion Innovators
Great Athletes
Great Athletes of the Twenty-First Century
Great Lives from History: African Americans
Great Lives from History: American Heroes
Great Lives from History: American Women
Great Lives from History: Asian and Pacific Islander Americans
Great Lives from History: Inventors & Inventions
Great Lives from History: Jewish Americans
Great Lives from History: Latinos
Great Lives from History: Scientists and Science
Great Lives from History: The 17th Century
Great Lives from History: The 18th Century
Great Lives from History: The 19th Century
Great Lives from History: The 20th Century
Great Lives from History: The 21st Century, 2000-2017
Great Lives from History: The Ancient World
Great Lives from History: The Incredibly Wealthy
Great Lives from History: The Middle Ages
Great Lives from History: The Renaissance & Early Modern Era
Human Rights Innovators
Internet Innovators
Music Innovators
Musicians and Composers of the 20th Century
World Political Innovators

History & Government

American First Ladies
American Presidents
Civil Rights Movements: Past & Present
The 50 States
The Ancient World: Extraordinary People in Extraordinary Societies
The Bill of Rights
The Criminal Justice System
The U.S. Supreme Court

SALEM PRESS

2020 Title List

SALEM PRESS

Visit www.SalemPress.com for Product Information, Table of Contents, and Sample Pages.

Social Sciences

Countries, Peoples and Cultures
Countries: Their Wars & Conflicts: A World Survey
Education Today: Issues, Policies & Practices
Encyclopedia of American Immigration
Ethics: Questions & Morality of Human Actions
Issues in U.S. Immigration
Principles of Sociology: Group Relationships & Behavior
Principles of Sociology: Personal Relationships & Behavior
Principles of Sociology: Societal Issues & Behavior
Racial & Ethnic Relations in America
World Geography

Science

Ancient Creatures
Applied Science
Applied Science: Engineering & Mathematics
Applied Science: Science & Medicine
Applied Science: Technology
Biomes and Ecosystems
Earth Science: Earth Materials and Resources
Earth Science: Earth's Surface and History
Earth Science: Earth's Weather, Water and Atmosphere
Earth Science: Physics and Chemistry of the Earth
Encyclopedia of Climate Change
Encyclopedia of Energy
Encyclopedia of Environmental Issues
Encyclopedia of Global Resources
Encyclopedia of Mathematics and Society
Forensic Science
Notable Natural Disasters
The Solar System
USA in Space

Principles of Science

Principles of Anatomy
Principles of Astronomy
Principles of Biology
Principles of Biotechnology
Principles of Botany
Principles of Chemistry
Principles of Climatology
Principles of Communications Technology
Principles of Computer Science
Principles of Ecology
Principles of Mathematics
Principles of Modern Agriculture
Principles of Pharmacology
Principles of Physical Science
Principles of Physics
Principles of Programming & Coding
Principles of Robotics & Artificial Intelligence
Principles of Scientific Research
Principles of Sustainability
Principles of Zoology

Health

Addictions, Substance Abuse & Alcoholism
Adolescent Health & Wellness
Aging
Cancer
Community & Family Health Issues
Complementary & Alternative Medicine
Genetics and Inherited Conditions
Infectious Diseases and Conditions
Magill's Medical Guide
Nutrition
Principles of Health: Anxiety & Stress
Principles of Health: Diabetes
Principles of Health: Obesity
Principles of Health: Pain Management
Psychology & Behavioral Health
Women's Health

Careers

Careers in Building Construction
Careers in Business
Careers in Chemistry
Careers in Communications & Media
Careers in Education & Training
Careers in Environment & Conservation
Careers in Financial Services
Careers in Gaming
Careers in Green Energy
Careers in Healthcare
Careers in Hospitality & Tourism
Careers in Human Services
Careers in Information Technology
Careers in Law, Criminal Justice & Emergency Services
Careers in Manufacturing & Production
Careers in Nursing
Careers in Physics
Careers in Protective Services
Careers in Psychology & Behavioral Health
Careers in Public Administration
Careers in Sales, Insurance & Real Estate
Careers in Science & Engineering
Careers in Social Media
Careers in Sports & Fitness
Careers in Sports Medicine & Training
Careers in Technical Services & Equipment Repair
Careers in the Arts: Fine, Performing & Visual
Careers in Transportation
Careers in Writing & Editing
Careers Outdoors
Careers Overseas
Careers Working with Infants & Children

Business

Principles of Business: Accounting
Principles of Business: Economics
Principles of Business: Entrepreneurship
Principles of Business: Finance
Principles of Business: Globalization
Principles of Business: Leadership
Principles of Business: Management
Principles of Business: Marketing

2020 Title List

Visit www.HWWilsonInPrint.com for Product Information, Table of Contents, and Sample Pages.

The Reference Shelf

Affordable Housing
Aging in America
Alternative Facts, Post-Truth and the Information War
American Military Presence Overseas
Arab Spring
Artificial Intelligence
Business of Food, The
Campaign Trends & Election Law
Conspiracy Theories
Democracy Evolving
Dinosaurs
Embracing New Paradigms in Education
Faith & Science
Families – Traditional & New Structures
Future of U.S. Economic Relations: Mexico, Cuba, & Venezuela
Global Climate Change
Graphic Novels and Comic Books
Guns in America
Hate Crimes
Immigration
Immigration in the United States
Internet Abuses & Privacy Rights
Internet Law
Internet Safety
LGBTQ in the 21st Century
Marijuana Reform
National Debate Topic 2014/2015: The Ocean
National Debate Topic 2015/2016: Surveillance
National Debate Topic 2016/2017: US/China Relations
National Debate Topic 2017/2018: Education Reform
National Debate Topic 2018/2019: Immigration
National Debate Topic 2019/2020: Arms Sales
National Debate Topic 2020/2021: Criminal Justice Reform
New Frontiers in Space
The News and its Future
Paranormal, The
Politics of the Oceans
Pollution
Prescription Drug Abuse
Propaganda and Misinformation
Racial Tension in a Postracial Age
Reality Television
Representative American Speeches, Annual Edition
Rethinking Work
Revisiting Gender
Robotics
Russia
Social Networking
Social Services for the Poor
Space Exploration and Development
Sports in America
The American Dream
The Brain
The Digital Age
The South China Sea Conflict
The Supreme Court
The Transformation of American Cities
The Two Koreas
U.S. Infrastructure
Whistleblowers

Core Collections

Children's Core Collection
Fiction Core Collection
Graphic Novels Core Collection
Middle & Junior High School Core
Public Library Core Collection: Nonfiction
Senior High Core Collection
Young Adult Fiction Core Collection

Current Biography

Current Biography Cumulative Index 1946-2017
Current Biography Monthly Magazine
Current Biography Yearbook

Readers' Guide to Periodical Literature

Abridged Readers' Guide to Periodical Literature
Readers' Guide to Periodical Literature

Indexes

Index to Legal Periodicals & Books
Short Story Index
Book Review Digest

Sears List

Sears List of Subject Headings
Sears: Lista de Encabezamientos de Materia

History

Speeches of the American Presidents
American Reformers
American Game Changers: Invention, Innovation & Transformation

Facts About Series

Facts About American Immigration
Facts About China
Facts About the 20th Century
Facts About the Presidents
Facts About the World's Languages

Nobel Prize Winners

Nobel Prize Winners: 1901-1986
Nobel Prize Winners: 1987-1991
Nobel Prize Winners: 1992-1996
Nobel Prize Winners: 1997-2001
Nobel Prize Winners: 2002-2018

Famous First Facts

Famous First Facts
Famous First Facts About American Politics
Famous First Facts About Sports
Famous First Facts About the Environment
Famous First Facts: International Edition

American Book of Days

The American Book of Days
The International Book of Days

Grey House Publishing | Salem Press | H.W. Wilson | 4919 Route, 22 PO Box 56, Amenia NY 12501-0056